Educators Resource Guide

2022
FOURTEENTH
EDITION

Educators Resource Guide

GREY HOUSE PUBLISHING

PUBLISHER: Leslie Mackenzie
EDITORIAL DIRECTOR: Laura Mars
PRODUCTION MANAGER & COMPOSITION: Kristen Hayes
STATISTICS: David Garoogian
MARKETING DIRECTOR: Jessica Moody

Grey House Publishing, Inc.
4919 Route 22
Amenia, NY 12501
518.789.8700
Fax: 518.789.0545
www.greyhouse.com | books@greyhouse.com

First edition published 1994
Fourteenth edition published 2021
Printed in Canada

Names: Grey House Publishing, Inc., publisher.

Title: Educators resource guide.

Description: Amenia, NY : Grey House Publishing, 2018- | "A Sedgewick Press Book." | Some volumes have incorrect ISSN (1549-7224, Directory of business information resources).

Identifiers: ISSN 2639-7382

Subjects: LCSH: Education—United States—Directories. | Teachers—Employment—United States—Directories. | Education—United States—Information services—Directories. | Associations, institutions, etc.—United States—Directories. | Scholarships—United States—Directories. | Education—United States—Bibliography—Periodicals.

Classification: LCC L901 .E443 | DDC 370—dc23 ISBN: 978-1-64265-840-8

Table of Contents

Introduction

This fourteenth edition of *Educators Resource Guide* is a comprehensive resource designed to provide educators, administrators, and other education professionals access to a unique combination of educational resources and educational statistics and rankings.

Following this introduction are several articles that offer a comprehensive overview of important issues facing education in America today:

Report on the Condition of Education 2021—from the National Center for Education Statistics, this 32-page report, complete with tables and graphs, starts with the Impact of the Coronavirus on Education, and goes on to discuss Family Characteristics; Preprimary, Elementary, and Secondary Education; Postsecondary Education; Population Characteristics and Economic Outcomes, and International Comparisons.

School Choice in the United States: 2019—this report from the National Center for Education Statistics discusses eight leading indicators: School Enrollment Over Time; Public Schools and Enrollment; Private Schools and Enrollment; Household Characteristics of Students in Public and Private Schools; Homeschooling; Reading and Math Performance; School Crime and Safety; and Parental Choice and Satisfaction. This 42-page report includes dozens of charts, graphs, and maps.

Report on Indicators of School Crime and Safety: 2020—this 23-page study from the Institute of Education Sciences discusses the following topics, and is full of supportive graphs and charts: Violent Deaths and School Shootings; Criminal Victimization; Bully Victimization; Incidents and Discipline Problems; Gangs and Hate-Related Speech; Fights, Weapons, and Illegal Substances; Student Perceptions of School Safety; Teacher Reports of Victimization and School Order; Discipline, Safety, and Security Practices; and Postsecondary Campus Safety and Security,

Following these informative reports, listings in *Educators Resource Guide* include associations, publications, trade shows, workshops and training programs designed not only to help educators advance professionally, but also to give them the resources they need to help their students, their schools, and their state meet educational standards. It provides tools for classroom and career management, and resources that truly make a difference in job, school, and student performance.

Listings are thoughtfully organized in 13 chapters and nearly 100 subchapters, making information significantly easier to access than the unfocused data available online or scattered in dozens of different sources. Updated statistics and rankings are designed to help states, school districts, and individual educators better understand their educational environment, crucial to making informed decisions on careers, curriculum and funding.

Praise for previous edition:

> ". . . an important reference source overflowing with information educators may use for their own improvement or as an aid for winning a . . . Race to the Top grant. . . . The glossary is handy and the indexes are accurate. All school, public and academic libraries need an up to date education directory . . . and this is a worthy choice."
>
> ***American Reference Books Annual***

> ". . . This handy tool, appropriate for larger public and academic libraries as well as school districts, will be highly valuable to those writing education grants. . . "
>
> ***Library Journal***

SECTION ONE: RESOURCES

Educators Resource Guide includes nearly 6,300 listings in Section One. Hundreds of records have been updated and dozens of new records added. This section includes 7,873 key contact names, 3,806 fax numbers, 2,983 e-mail addresses, and 4,588 web sites, and is categorized as follows, for easy research:

Associations & Organizations disseminate information, host seminars, provide educational literature and promote study councils. This chapter organizes associations into 16 distinct categories from *Administration* to *Technology*.

The chapter on **Conferences & Trade Shows** lists everything from large conventions of classroom resources and equipment suppliers to small, specialized conferences that target rural education and specific teaching challenges. Events are listed regionally.

Consultants give information on educational consulting services, including curriculum-building guidance, school district organizations, and facility format.

Teaching Opportunities Abroad include not only U.S. government schools, but also American schools overseas. The chapter is organized geographically by region, and provides contact information, grade level and enrollment numbers.

Details on 630 grants, foundations and scholarships can be found in **Financial Resources**. Learn how to obtain funds for individual professional advancement, schools, programs, students, and education districts and communities.

The **Professional Development** listings include *Associations, Awards, Conferences* and *Training Materials.*

Publications list directories and periodicals, each divided into 16 subjects. Find where to publish research findings, which testing materials best suit your needs, how to incorporate technology into your classroom, and where to find innovative classroom supplies.

Publishers include educational publishers of textbooks, testing resources and specific curriculums.

Research results on general learning and training issues, and data on specific subjects, like *Gifted & Talented, Educational Media* and *Scientific Learning*, is easy to find from the **Research Centers** profiled in this edition.

The chapter on **School Supplies** focuses on the latest in *Classroom Technology, Scientific Equipment, Furniture* and *Sports & Playground Equipment.*

Software, Hardware & Internet Resources include 16 subchapters from *Administration* to *Technology in Education* that provide easy access to everything from educational computer programs to web sites with information on classroom resources for every level and subject.

Testing Resources include resources for written materials and web sites in six categories: *Elementary Education, Language Arts, Mathematics, Music & Art, Reading,* and *Secondary Education.*

SECTION TWO: NATIONAL & STATE STATISTICS

Section Two includes six major sections: All Levels of Education; Elementary and Secondary Education; Postsecondary Education; Outcomes of Education; Canadian Education Statistics; and Glossary.

All together, this section includes 467 tables and charts of statistics and rankings not only on the American educational system, but also on Canadian and international education as well.

Within the major sections, specific topics include degrees, enrollment, completions, dropouts, faculty, revenues, expenditures, and student behavior. Many tables offer state-by-state rankings.

Using the most current data available, this section helps to complete the picture for educators making career development decisions, for school administrators interested in comparing fiscal health and educational scores, and for anyone doing educational research.

Following the statistics and rankings is a **Glossary** with over 100 education terms from Accountability to Vocational.

SECTION THREE: INDEXES

Entry & Publisher Name Index–alphabetical list of both entry names and the companies that publish the listed material. Publishers and parent organizations are boldfaced.

Geographic Index–state-by-state listing of all entries.

Subject Index–organized by core subjects plus Special Education and Technology.

Educators Resource Guide 2022 is also available for subscription via Grey House OnLine Database. Subscribers can do customized searches that instantly locate needed information. Visit https://gold.greyhouse.com or call 800-562-2139 to set up a free trial.

Report on the Condition of Education 2021

NCES 2021-144
U.S. DEPARTMENT OF EDUCATION

A Publication of the National Center for Education Statistics at IES

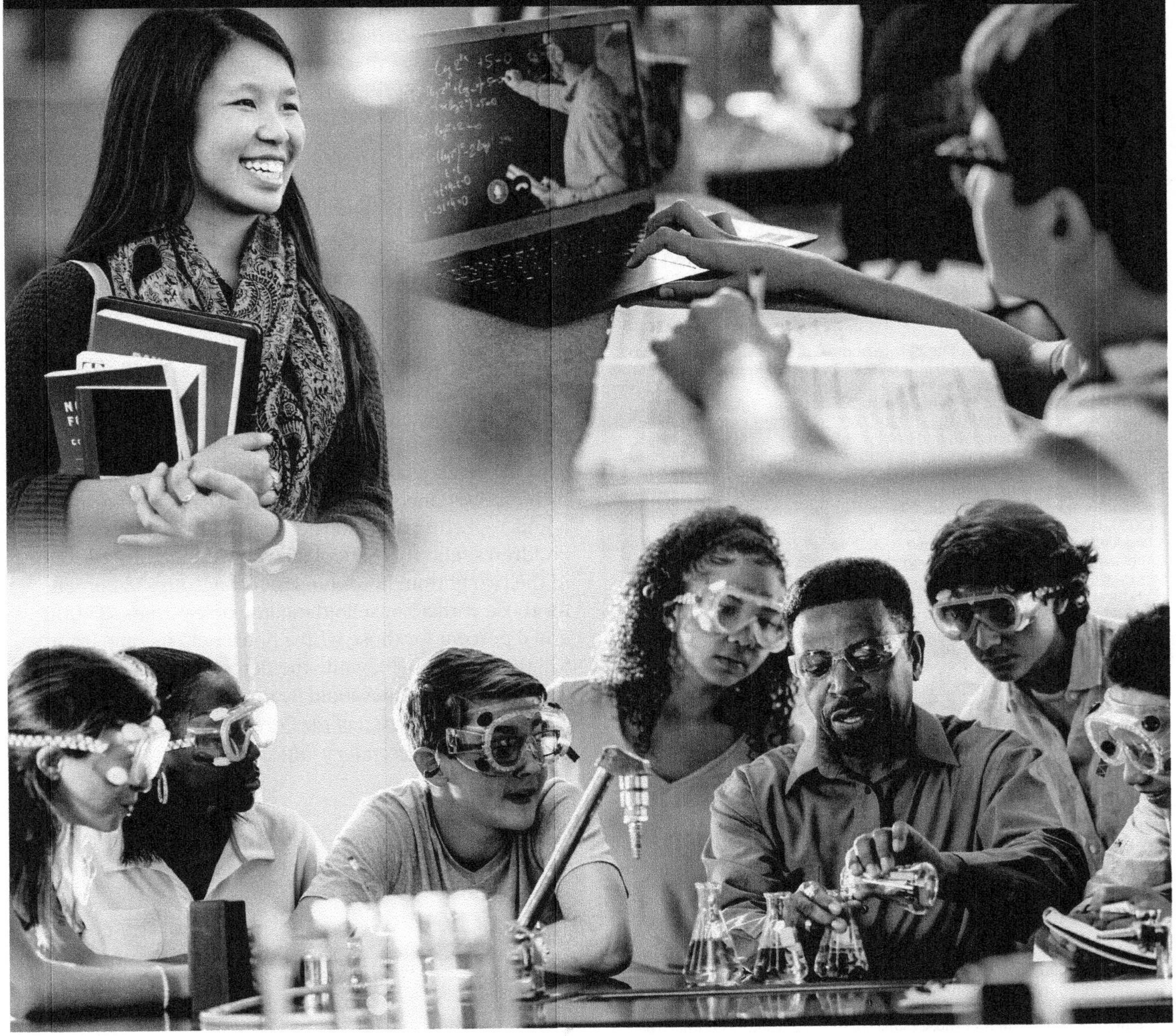

Impact of the Coronavirus Pandemic on Education

The emergence of the coronavirus pandemic brought major disruptions to American society. Health systems were stressed,[3] millions of jobs were lost,[4] businesses were shuttered, and many schools were closed.[5]

Impact of the Coronavirus Pandemic on the Elementary and Secondary Education System

The traditional elementary and secondary education structure, which typically emphasizes an interactive classroom environment, quickly transitioned to online education programs in the spring of 2020 to mitigate the spread of the coronavirus pandemic. Although online programs have enabled education activities to continue while schools have been physically closed, concerns have been raised about whether inequities in access to these online programs could further exacerbate gaps in student performance that existed prior to the pandemic.[6,7]

At the beginning of the 2020-21 school year (September 2 to September 14), among the adults who had children under age 18 enrolled in a public or private school, some 67 percent reported that school classes were moved to a distance learning format using online resources.[8] In order to participate in these remote learning settings, students must have access to computers and the internet. At the beginning of the 2020-21 school year, 91 percent reported that computers were always or usually available to children for educational purposes, and 93 percent reported that internet access was always or usually available to children for educational purposes.

The percentage of adults reporting that computers and internet access were always or usually available to children for educational purposes varied by household income. In general, the percentages were higher for those in the top three household income groups than for those in the bottom three income groups. For example, at the beginning of the 2020-21 school year, the percentages of adults reporting that internet access was always or usually available to children for educational purposes were highest for the top three household income groups (ranging from 96 to 97 percent), and lower for each of the three groups with household income below $75,000 (ranging from 83 to 93 percent) (figure S1).

To mitigate inequities in access to these online programs, some schools and school districts provide computers and interact access to students. Among the adults who had children under age 18 in the home enrolled in a public or private school at the beginning of the 2020-21 school year, 59 percent reported that computers were provided by the children's school or school district, and 4 percent reported that internet access was paid for by the children's school or school district. This also differed by household income. For example, the percentages of adults reporting that internet access was paid for by the children's school or school district were highest for those in the two bottom household income groups (8 percent for those with a household income of less than $25,000 and 6 percent for those with a household income from $25,000 to $49,999), while the percentage was lowest for the group with a household income of $150,000 and more (1 percent) (The Impact of the Coronavirus Pandemic on the Elementary and Secondary Education System).

[3] Melvin, S.C., Wiggins, C., Burse, N., Thompson, E., and Monger, M. (2020, July). *The Role of Public Health in COVID-19 Emergency Response Efforts From a Rural Health Perspective* (Preventing Chronic Disease, Vol. 17, E70), Centers for Disease Control and Prevention. Retrieved February 9, 2021, from https://www.cdc.gov/pcd/issues/2020/20_0256.htm#T2_down. Blumenthal, D., Fowler, E.J., Abrams, M., and Collins, S.R. (2020, July). COVID-19—Implications for the Health Care System, *New England Journal of Medicine, 383*, 1438-1488. Retrieved February 9, 2021, from https://www.nejm.org/doi/full/10.1056/nejmsb2021088.

[4] Handwerker, E.W., Meyer, P.B., Piacentini, J., Schultz, M., and Sveikauskas, L. (2020, December). *Employment Recovery in the Wake of the COVID-19 Pandemic* (Monthly Labor Review), U.S. Bureau of Labor Statistics. Retrieved February 9, 2021, from https://www.bls.gov/opub/mlr/2020/article/employment-recovery.htm.

[5] Education Week. (2020, March 6). *Map: Coronavirus and School Closures in 2019-2020.* Retrieved February 9, 2021, from https://www.edweek.org/leadership/map-coronavirus-and-school-closures-in-2019-2020/2020/03.

[6] U.S. Department of Education, National Center for Education Statistics, *The Condition of Education 2020*, Reading Performance. Retrieved February 9, 2021, from https://nces.ed.gov/programs/coe/indicator/cnb; and Mathematics Performance. Retrieved February 9, 2021, from https://nces.ed.gov/programs/coe/indicator/cnc.

[7] U.S. Department of Education, National Center for Education Statistics, National Assessment of Educational Progress. *Results From the 2019 Mathematics and Reading Assessments at Grade 12.* Retrieved February 9, 2021, from https://www.nationsreportcard.gov/mathematics/supportive_files/2019_infographic_G12_math_reading.pdf.

[8] Data from the 2020 Household Pulse Survey (HPS). The HPS is conducted by the Census Bureau with seven other federal statistical agency partners, including the National Center for Education Statistics (NCES). The HPS has provided weekly or biweekly national and state estimates since April 23, 2020, when data collection began. The survey gathers information from adults about their employment status, spending patterns, food security, housing, mental health, access to health care, transportation, and household educational activities. It also collects information from adults about how children in their households access technology at home for educational purposes. Beginning with the phase 2 data collection on August 19, the HPS includes new questions on household postsecondary attendance plans, whether those plans shifted as a result of coronavirus pandemic, and specific reasons why the postsecondary plans changed.

Figure S1. Among adults 18 years old and over who had children under age 18 in the home enrolled in school, percentage reporting that computers and internet access were always or usually available to children for educational purposes, by income level: September 2 to 14, 2020

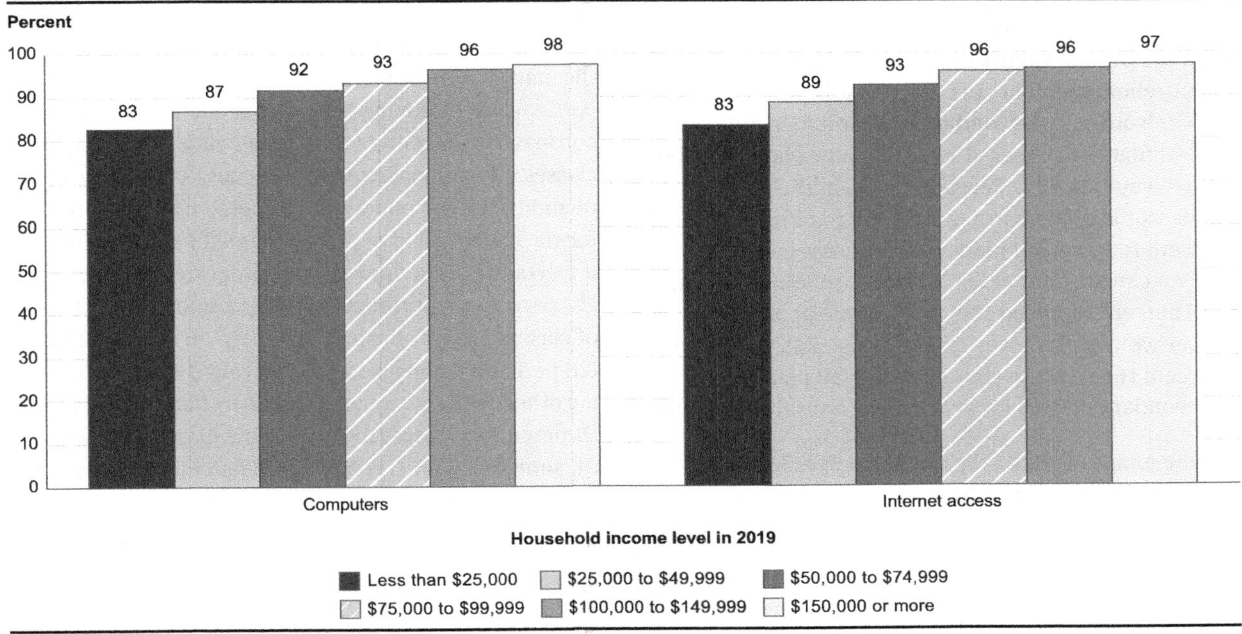

NOTE: Although rounded numbers are displayed, the figures are based on unrounded data. Data in this figure are considered experimental and do not meet NCES standards for response rates. The survey question refers to enrollment at any time during the 2020–21 school year.
SOURCE: U.S. Department of Commerce, Bureau of the Census, Household Pulse Survey, collection period of September 2 to 14, 2020. See *Digest of Education Statistics 2020*, table 218.85.

Impact of the Coronavirus Pandemic on Fall Plans for Postsecondary Education

As with elementary and secondary education, postsecondary education was also heavily impacted by the pandemic. During spring 2020, many postsecondary institutions shifted from in-person classes to online only classes. College practices and programs also changed in other ways ranging from new policies on campus visits and admissions to financial challenges due to loss of tuition and room and board revenue, as well as cancellations of athletic programs.[9] About half (51 percent) of postsecondary students in fall 2020 reported that the coronavirus pandemic was "likely" or "very likely" to negatively affect their ability to complete their degree.[10]

Among adults 18 years old and over who were surveyed during the period August 19 to August 31, 2020 and who had household members planning to take classes in fall 2020 from a postsecondary institution, 45 percent reported that the classes at least one household member planned would be in different formats in the fall (e.g., formats would change from in-person to online), 31 percent reported all plans to take classes in the fall had been canceled for at least one household member, and 12 percent reported that at least one household member would take fewer classes in the fall.[11] In addition, 28 percent reported no change in the fall plans to take postsecondary classes for at least one household member.

The percentage of adults reporting changes in fall 2020 plans for postsecondary education varied by type of programs planned. For instance, the percentage of adults reporting that classes planned would be in different formats for at least one household member was highest for adults who reported that their household members planned to take classes in a bachelor's degree program (61 percent). The percentage of adults reporting no change in plans to take postsecondary classes for at least one household member was highest for those who reported that their household members planned to take classes in a graduate degree program (36 percent). The percentage of adults reporting all plans to take classes in fall 2020 had been canceled for at least one household member was highest for those planning to take classes in certificate or diploma program (47 percent) (figure S2).

For those adults who reported all plans to take classes in fall 2020 had been canceled for at least one household member, the two most frequently cited reasons for the cancellation of plans were already having the coronavirus or having concerns about getting the coronavirus (46 percent) and not being able to pay for classes/educational expenses because of changes to income from the pandemic (42 percent).[12] Other reasons for the cancellation of plans included the following: uncertainty about how classes/programs might change (30 percent), institution changing content or format of classes (e.g., from an in-person to an online format) (26 percent), changes to financial aid (15 percent), caring for others whose care arrangements had been disrupted[13] (11 percent), changes to campus life (9 percent), and caring for someone with coronavirus (2 percent) (*Impact of the Coronavirus Pandemic on Postsecondary Plans of Students*).

[9] National Conference of State Legislatures. *Higher Education Responses to Coronavirus (COVID-19)*. Retrieved February 9, 2021, from https://www.ncsl.org/research/education/higher-education-responses-to-coronavirus-covid-19.aspx.

[10] Gallup. (2020). *State of the Student Experience: Fall 2020*. Retrieved February 9, 2021, from https://www.gallup.com/education/327485/state-of-the-student-experience-fall-2020.aspx.

[11] Because this survey is designed to represent adults 18 years old and over, the estimates indicate the percentages of adults in households with prospective postsecondary students who reported a given change, rather than the percentages of students themselves. Respondents could choose more than one response to reflect the fact that different prospective students within the household may have had distinct changes in postsecondary plans or that an individual prospective student within the household may have had multiple changes in postsecondary plans.

[12] Respondents could select multiple planned postsecondary education levels. Those who selected multiple levels are included in the overall totals but are omitted from individual education levels (see *Digest of Education Statistics* table 302.80 for information on adults selecting multiple education levels). Overall, 20 percent of respondents indicated postsecondary plans at multiple levels in their household.

[13] Examples include loss of day care or adult care programs.

Figure S2. Among adults 18 years old and over who reported that household members planned to take classes in fall 2020 from a postsecondary institution, percentage reporting changes in postsecondary plans for fall 2020 for at least one household member, by type of changes and level of postsecondary education planned: August 19 to August 31, 2020

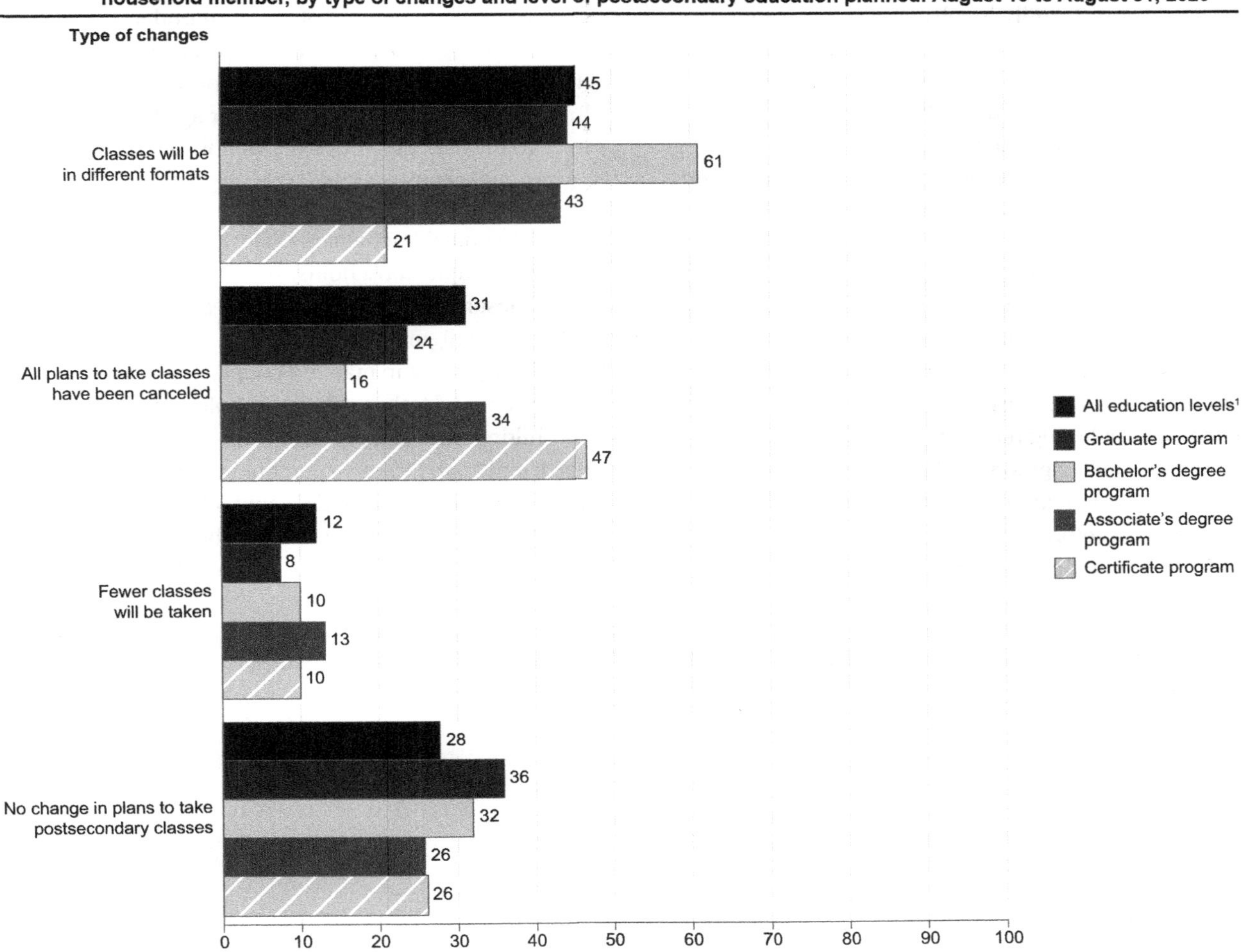

[1] Includes education levels not separately shown.
NOTE: Because this survey is designed to represent adults 18 years old and over, the estimates indicate the percentages of adults in households with prospective postsecondary students who reported a given change, rather than the percentages of students themselves. Respondents could choose more than one response to reflect the fact that different prospective students within the household may have had distinct changes in postsecondary plans or that an individual prospective student within the household may have had multiple changes in postsecondary plans. Respondents could select multiple planned postsecondary education levels. Those who selected multiple levels are included in the overall totals, but are omitted from individual education levels (see Digest table 302.80 for information on adults selecting multiple education levels). Overall, 20 percent of respondents indicated postsecondary plans at multiple levels in their household. Data in this table are considered experimental and do not meet NCES standards for response rates. Although rounded numbers are displayed, the figures are based on unrounded data.
SOURCE: U.S. Department of Commerce, Census Bureau, Household Pulse Survey, August 19 to August 31, 2020. See *Digest of Education Statistics 2020*, table 302.80.

Family Characteristics

This section of the Condition of Education Indicator System presents indicators on family characteristics of children, and family involvement in education. Families provide educational tools and opportunities to children in a variety of ways, including exposure to enrichment activities and technology, access to schools, and familiarity with educational processes. Providing these resources requires social and economic capital. As such, children's educational experiences and their academic achievement are closely associated with their families' socioeconomic characteristics. For example, prior research has found that the risk factors of living in poverty, living in a household without a parent who has completed high school, and living in a single-parent household are associated with poor educational outcomes–including receiving low achievement scores, having to repeat a grade, and dropping out of high school.[14,15] Understanding the distribution of these resources therefore provides important context for understanding the condition of education in the United States.

Characteristics of Children's Families

In 2019, some 16 percent of children under age 18 were in families living in poverty. The poverty rate for children in 2019 was lower than in 2010 (21 percent). Similarly, a lower percentage of children under age 18 in 2019 than in 2010 (9 vs. 12 percent) lived in households where no parent had completed high school.

In 2019, some 63 percent of children under age 18 lived in married-couple households, 26 percent lived in mother-only households, and 8 percent lived in father-only households (figure 1). This pattern–of a higher percentage of children living in married-couple households than in mother- and father-only households–was observed for children across all racial/ethnic groups, except for Black children. Fifty-five percent of Black children lived in mother-only households, compared with 34 percent who lived in married-couple households and 9 percent who lived in father-only households (*Characteristics of Children's Families*).

[14] Pungello, E.P., Kainz, K., Burchinal, M., Wasik, B.H., Sparling, J.J., Ramey, C.T., and Campbell, F.A. (2010, February). Early Educational Intervention, Early Cumulative Risk, and the Early Home Environment as Predictors of Young Adult Outcomes Within a High-Risk Sample. *Child Development, 81*(1): 410–426. Retrieved January 8, 2021, from http://onlinelibrary.wiley.com/doi/10.1111/j.1467-8624.2009.01403.x/full.

[15] Ross, T., Kena, G., Rathbun, A., KewalRamani, A., Zhang, J., Kristapovich, P., and Manning, E. (2012). *Higher Education: Gaps in Access and Persistence Study* (NCES 2012-046). U.S. Department of Education. Washington, DC: National Center for Education Statistics. Retrieved January 8, 2021, from https://nces.ed.gov/pubsearch/pubsinfo.asp?pubid=2012046.

Figure 1. Percentage of children under age 18, by child's race/ethnicity and family structure: 2019

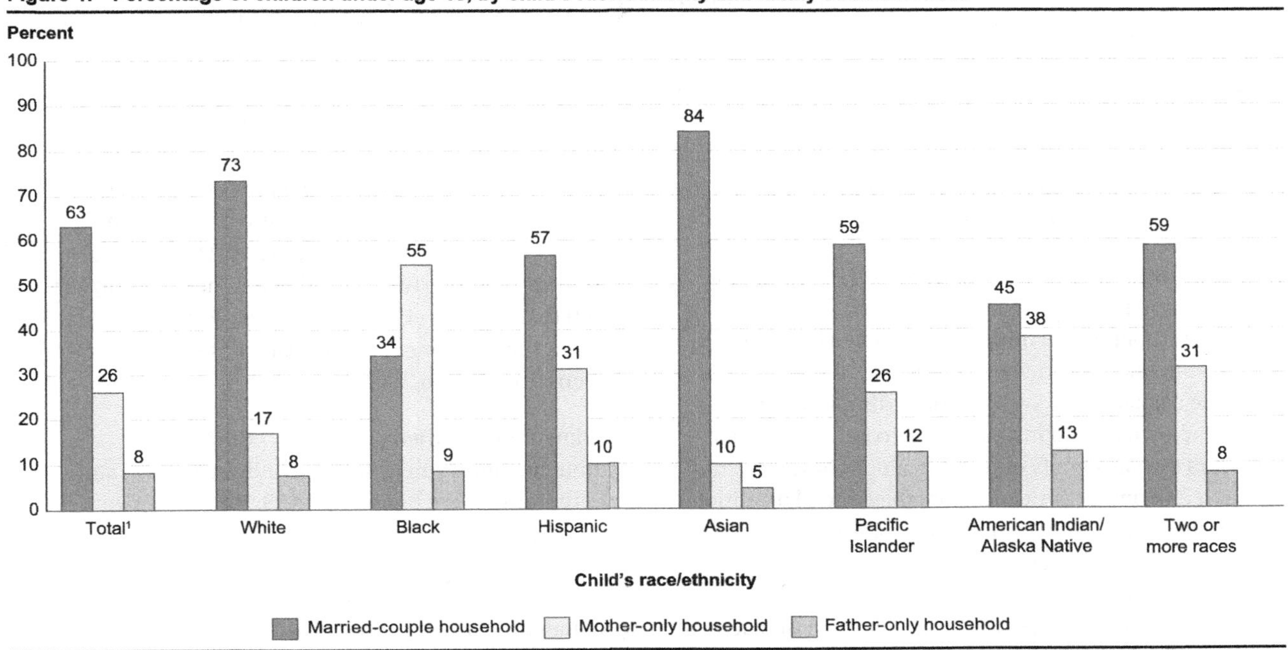

[1] Includes respondents who wrote in some other race that was not included as an option on the questionnaire.

NOTE: Data do not include foster children, children in unrelated subfamilies, children living in group quarters, and children who were reported as the householder or spouse of the householder. A "mother-only household" has a female householder, with no spouse present (i.e., the householder is unmarried or the spouse is not in the household), while a "father-only household" has a male householder, with no spouse present. Includes all children who live either with their parent(s) or with a householder to whom they are related by birth, marriage, or adoption (except a child who is the spouse of the householder). Children are classified by their parents' marital status or, if no parents are present in the household, by the marital status of the householder who is related to the children. The householder is the person (or one of the people) who owns or rents (maintains) the housing unit. Race categories exclude persons of Hispanic ethnicity. Although rounded numbers are displayed, the figures are based on unrounded data. Detail does not sum to 100 percent because the "All other children" category is not reported.

SOURCE: U.S. Department of Commerce, Census Bureau, American Community Survey (ACS), 2019. See *Digest of Education Statistics 2020*, table 102.20.

Preprimary, Elementary, and Secondary Education

Many factors contribute to the condition of an education system: who is served by the system, the contexts in which those students are served, what resources are available, and what outcomes are achieved. In large part, the first three of these factors are shaped by whether schooling is optional or mandatory. This section of the Condition of Education Indicator System focuses on compulsory schooling (and preparation for compulsory schooling): preprimary, elementary, and secondary education.

First, this section considers who is served by describing the school-age population, preprimary enrollment rates, and students' learning needs. Students come to school from different socioeconomic, racial/ethnic, and linguistic backgrounds and may have disabilities that require adjustments to instruction. Second, this section considers the variety of contexts in which these students are served—from the type of school they attend (traditional public, charter, private, or home school) to number and characteristics of the peers they share their classrooms with. Next, this section describes educational resources: namely, the training, experience, and number of teachers and the level and sources of education funding. Finally, this section considers key outcomes of compulsory schooling in the United States, including achievement and high school graduation.

Preprimary Education

Formal schooling, including preschool and kindergarten, are important components of early childhood services. In 2019, about 61 percent of 3- to 5-year-olds were enrolled in school (defined as having attended school—nursery or preschool, kindergarten, elementary school, or home school—in the 3 months preceding the survey). The enrollment rate was lower for 3- to 4-year-olds than for 5-year-olds (49 vs. 86 percent) (figure 2). The percentage of 3- to 4-year-olds who were enrolled in school was higher in 2019 than in 2010 (49 vs. 48 percent). For 5-year-olds, however, the enrollment rate in 2019 was not measurably different from that in 2010.

Enrollment rates varied by parents' educational attainment, employment status, family structure, and poverty status. For example, in 2019, the enrollment rates across age groups were generally higher for children whose parents had higher levels of educational attainment. Specifically, among 3- to 4-year-olds, the enrollment rate ranged from 35 percent for those with no parents who had completed high school to 60 percent for those with at least one parent who had attained a bachelor's or higher degree. A similar pattern can be observed for the enrollment rates of 5-year-olds, which

Figure 2. Percentage of 3- to 5-year-olds enrolled in school, by age group: 2010 through 2019

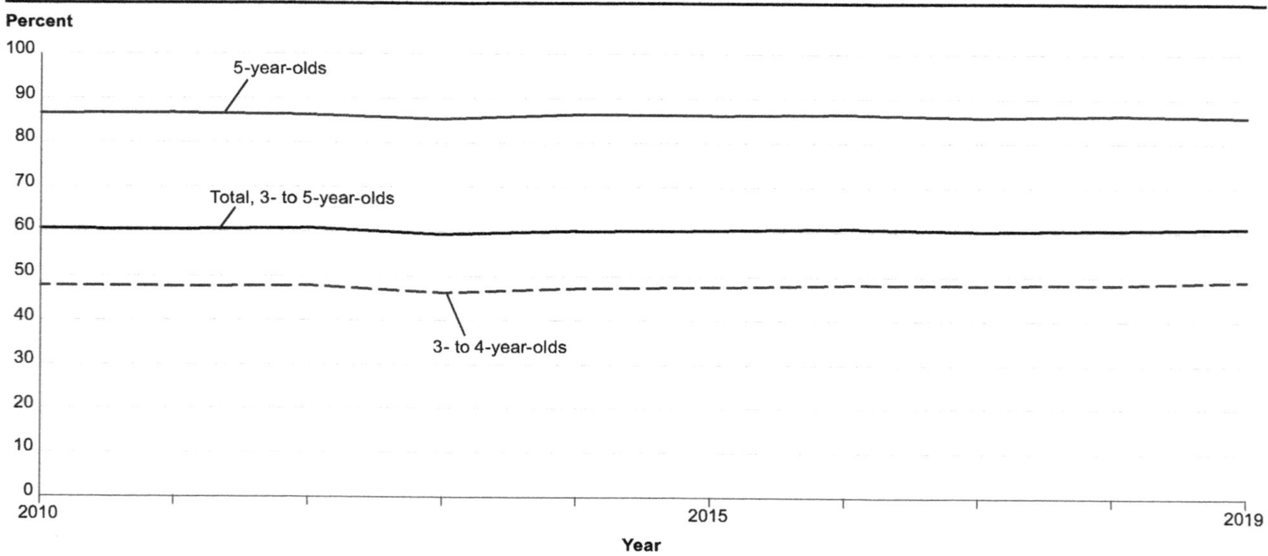

NOTE: Data are based on sample surveys of the entire population residing within the United States, including those living in group quarters (e.g., shelters, healthcare facilities, or correctional facilities).
SOURCE: U.S. Department of Commerce, Census Bureau, American Community Survey (ACS), 2010 through 2019. See *Digest of Education Statistics 2020*, table 202.20.

ranged from 78 percent for those with no parents who had completed high school to 90 percent for those whose parents had attained a bachelor's or higher degree (*Preschool and Kindergarten Enrollment*).

School Choice

Across the United States, an evolving school choice landscape reflects changes in the accessibility and desirability of an array of education options, including traditional and nontraditional public schools, private schools, and homeschooling. Over the past decade, traditional public schools and public charter schools have experienced different trends in enrollment (figure 3). Between fall 2009 and fall 2018, traditional public school enrollment decreased by 0.4 million; while public charter school enrollment increased steadily, more than doubling from 1.6 million students in fall 2009 to 3.3 million students in fall 2018. As a result of these concurrent trends, the percentage of all public school students who attended public charter schools increased from 3 to 7 percent over this period (*Public Charter School Enrollment*).

Private school enrollment in fall 2017 (5.7 million) was higher than in fall 2009 (5.5 million).[16] The percentage of total elementary and secondary students who were enrolled in private schools remained at 10 percent between fall 2009 and fall 2017 (*Private School Enrollment*).

Figure 3. School enrollment, by school type: Selected years, fall 2009 through fall 2018

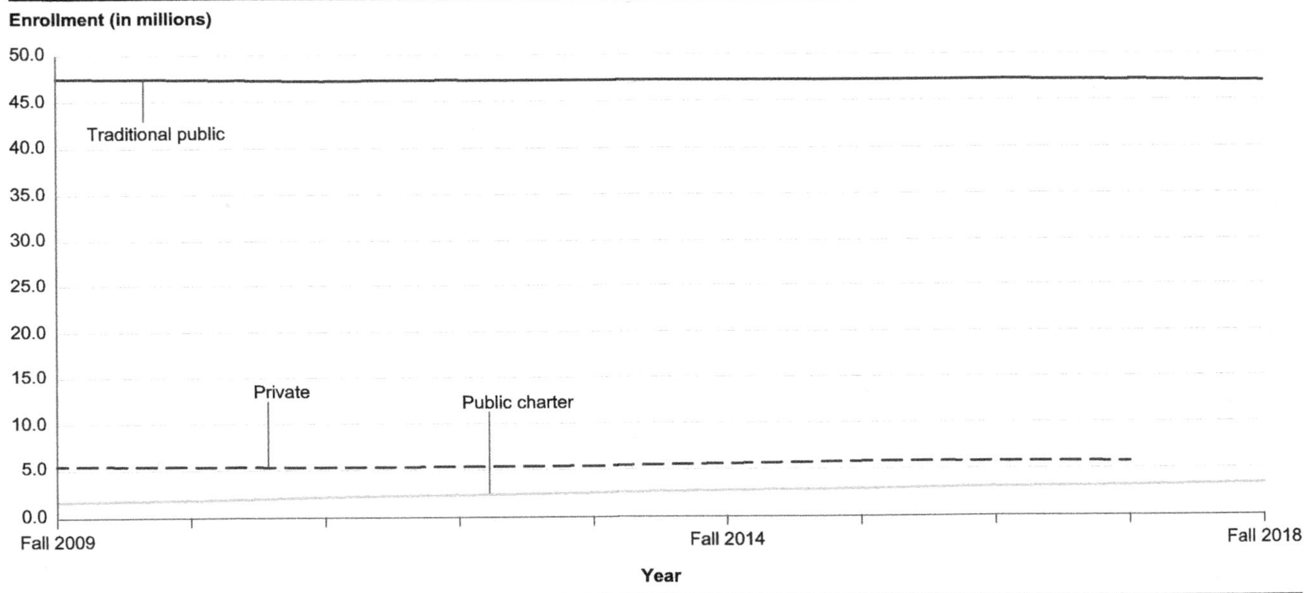

NOTE: Data in this figure represent the 50 states and the District of Columbia. Private school enrollment excludes prekindergarten students not enrolled in schools that offer kindergarten or higher grades.
SOURCE: U.S. Department of Education, National Center for Education Statistics, Common Core of Data (CCD), "Public Elementary/Secondary School Universe Survey," 2009–10 through 2018–19. Private School Universe Survey (PSS), 2009–10 through 2017–18. See *Digest of Education Statistics 2017*, *2018*, *2019*, and *2020*, table 216.20 and *Digest of Education Statistics 2020*, table 205.20

[16] Data on private schools are not available for fall 2018. Private school data are collected every 2 years, with the last data collection being 2017-18.

Racial/Ethnic Enrollment in Public Schools

In fall 2018, of the 50.7 million students enrolled in public elementary and secondary schools, 47 percent were White (a decrease from 54 percent in 2009), 15 percent were Black (a decrease from 17 percent), and 27 percent were Hispanic (an increase from 22 percent) (figure 4).[17] These compositional changes reflect divergent enrollment trends among these groups between fall 2009 and fall 2018. Between these years, public school enrollments among White students decreased from 26.7 million to 23.8 million, and the number of Black students decreased from 8.2 million to 7.7 million. In contrast, the number of Hispanic students increased from 11.0 million to 13.8 million.

In both fall 2009 and fall 2018, Asian students accounted for 5 percent of public elementary and secondary enrollment, and American Indian/Alaska Native students accounted for 1 percent. In fall 2018, Pacific Islander students accounted for less than one-half of 1 percent of public elementary and secondary enrollment, and students who were of Two or more races accounted for 4 percent (*Racial/Ethnic Enrollment in Public Schools*).[18]

Figure 4. Percentage distribution of students enrolled in public elementary and secondary schools, by race/ethnicity: Fall 2009 and fall 2018

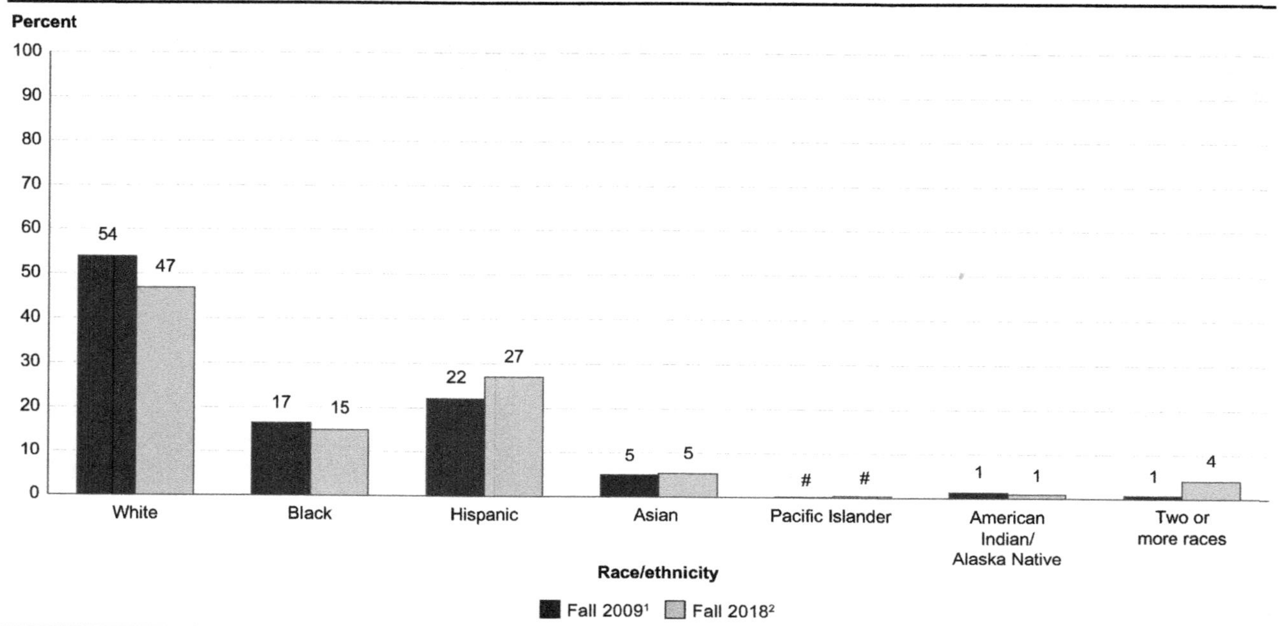

Rounds to zero.
[1] For fall 2009, data on students who were Pacific Islander and of Two or more races were reported by only a small number of states. Therefore, the data are not comparable to figures for 2018.
[2] Includes imputations for prekindergarten enrollment in California and Oregon.
NOTE: Data are for the 50 states and the District of Columbia. Race categories exclude persons of Hispanic ethnicity. Detail may not sum to totals because of rounding. Although rounded numbers are displayed, the figures are based on unrounded data.
SOURCE: U.S. Department of Education, National Center for Education Statistics, Common Core of Data (CCD), "State Nonfiscal Survey of Public Elementary and Secondary Education," 2009–10 and 2018–19. See *Digest of Education Statistics 2020*, table 203.50.

[17] Enrollments reflect aggregate totals reported by states, which differ from data reported by schools.

[18] In fall 2009, Pacific Islander students accounted for less than one-half of 1 percent of public elementary and secondary enrollment, and students who were of Two or more races accounted for 1 percent. However, for this year, data on these students were reported by only a small number of states; therefore, the data are not comparable with figures for fall 2018.

Students With Disabilities

From school year 2009-10 through 2019-20, the number of students served by the Individuals with Disabilities Education Act (IDEA)[19] increased from 6.5 million to 7.3 million and the percentage served increased from 13 percent of total public school enrollment to 14 percent of total public school enrollment.[20] In 2019-20, some 33 percent of all students who received special education services had specific learning disabilities,[21] 19 percent had speech or language impairments,[22] and 15 percent had other health impairments[23] (figure 5) (*Students With Disabilities*).

Figure 5. Percentage distribution of students ages 3–21 served under the Individuals with Disabilities Education Act (IDEA), by disability type: School year 2019–20

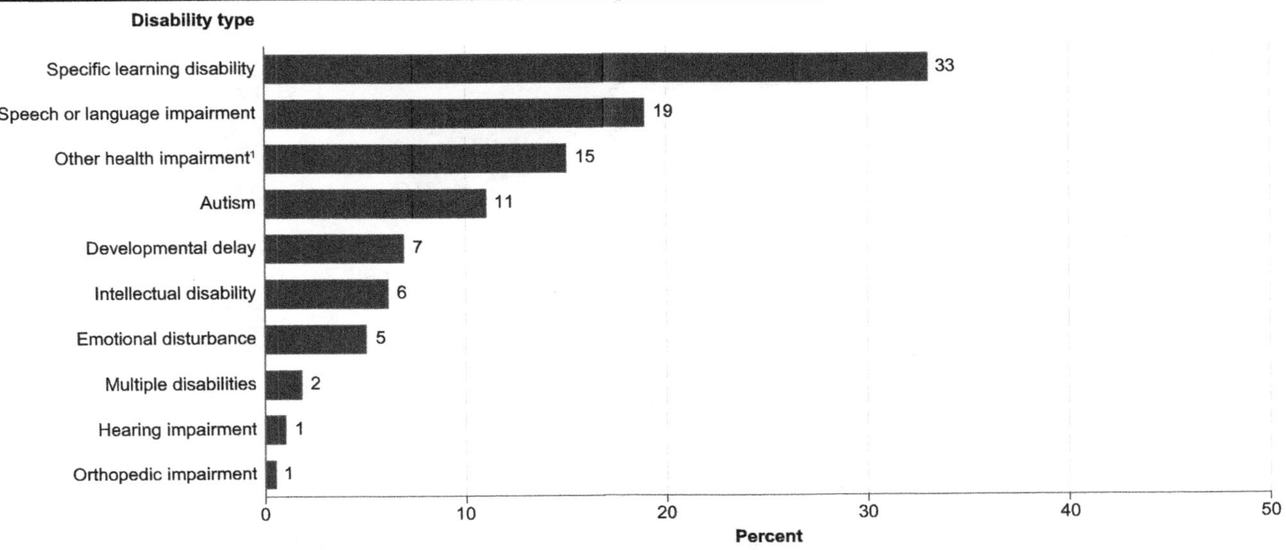

[1] Other health impairments include having limited strength, vitality, or alertness due to chronic or acute health problems such as a heart condition, tuberculosis, rheumatic fever, nephritis, asthma, sickle cell anemia, hemophilia, epilepsy, lead poisoning, leukemia, or diabetes.
NOTE: Data are for the 50 states and the District of Columbia only. Visual impairment, traumatic brain injury, and deaf-blindness are not shown because they each account for less than 0.5 percent of students served under IDEA. Due to categories not shown, detail does not sum to 100 percent. Although rounded numbers are displayed, the figures are based on unrounded data.
SOURCE: U.S. Department of Education, Office of Special Education Programs, Individuals with Disabilities Education Act (IDEA) database, retrieved February 2, 2021, from https://www2.ed.gov/programs/osepidea/618-data/state-level-data-files/index.html#bcc. See *Digest of Education Statistics 2020*, table 204.30.

[19] Enacted in 1975, the Individuals with Disabilities Education Act (IDEA), formerly known as the Education for All Handicapped Children Act, mandates the provision of a free and appropriate public school education for eligible students ages 3-21.

[20] Totals presented in this indicator include imputations for states for which data were unavailable. See reference tables in the *Digest of Education Statistics* for more information. Data for students ages 3-21 and 6-21 served under IDEA are for the 50 states and the District of Columbia only. Number of children served as a percent of total enrollment is based on total public school enrollment in prekindergarten through grade 12. Enrollment data for 2019-20 are projected.

[21] A specific learning disability is a disorder in one or more of the basic psychological processes involved in understanding or using language, spoken or written, that may manifest itself in an imperfect ability to listen, think, speak, read, write, spell, or do mathematical calculations.

[22] Speech or language impairments is defined as a communication disorder such as stuttering, impaired articulation, a language impairment, or a voice impairment that adversely affects a child's educational performance.

[23] Other health impairments include having limited strength, vitality, or alertness due to chronic or acute health problems such as a heart condition, tuberculosis, rheumatic fever, nephritis, asthma, sickle cell anemia, hemophilia, epilepsy, lead poisoning, leukemia, or diabetes.

English Language Learners

Students who are identified as English language learners (ELLs) can participate in language assistance programs to help ensure that they attain English proficiency and meet the academic content and achievement standards that all students are expected to meet. Participation in these types of programs can improve students' English language proficiency, which in turn has been associated with improved educational outcomes.[24] The percentage of public school students in the United States who were ELLs was higher in fall 2018 (10.2 percent, or 5.0 million students) than in fall 2010 (9.2 percent, or 4.5 million students).[25]

Figure 6. Percentage of public school students who were English language learners, by state: Fall 2018

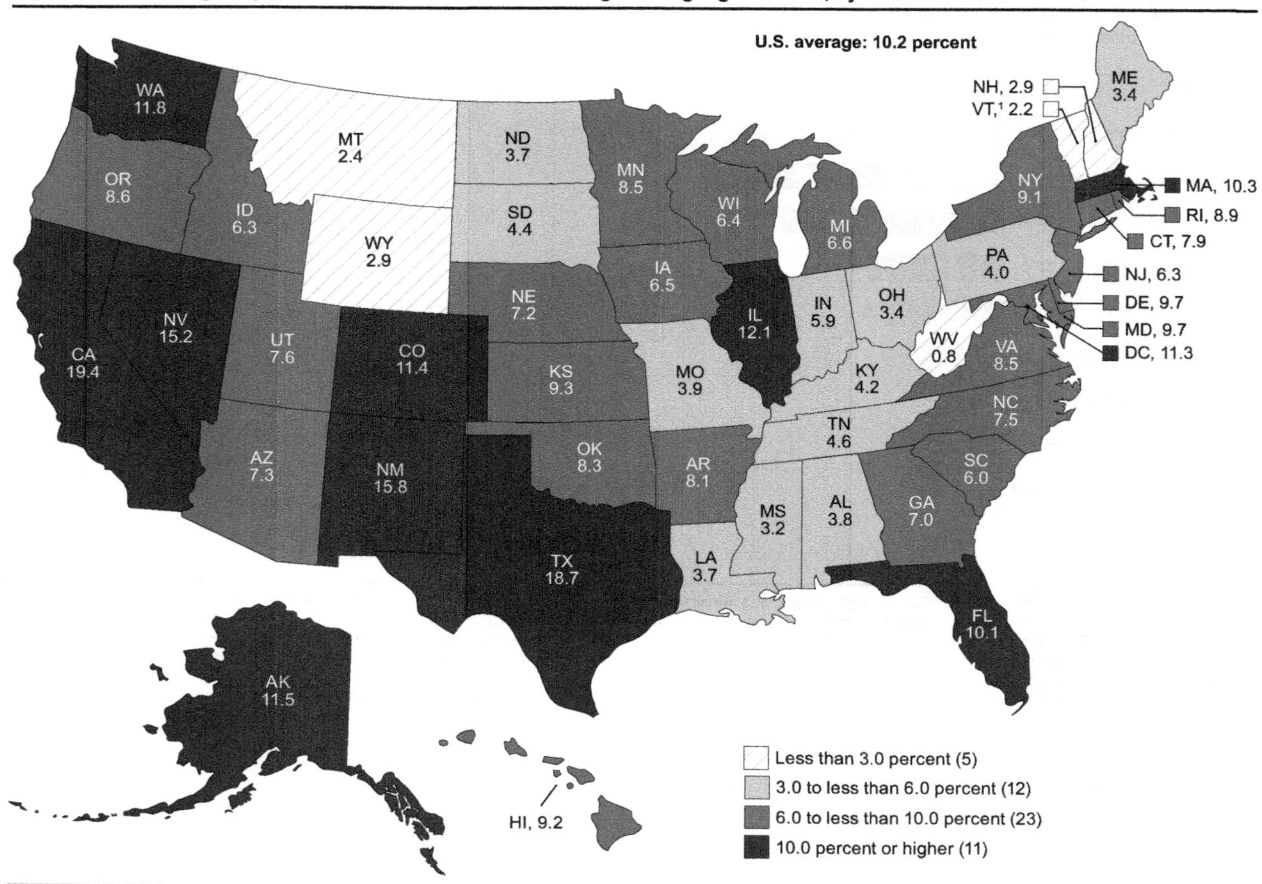

[1] Includes imputation for nonreported data from Vermont.
NOTE: U.S. average is for the 50 states and the District of Columbia. Categorizations are based on unrounded percentages.
SOURCE: U.S. Department of Education, National Center for Education Statistics, Common Core of Data (CCD), "Local Education Agency Universe Survey," 2018–19. See *Digest of Education Statistics 2020*, table 204.20.

[24] Genesee, F., Lindholm-Leary, K., Saunders, W., and Christian, D. (2005). English Language Learners in U.S. Schools: An Overview of Research Findings. *Journal of Education for Students Placed at Risk, 10*(4): 363-385. Retrieved December 8, 2020, from https://doi.org/10.1207/s15327671espr1004_2.

[25] For 2014 and earlier years, data on the total number of ELLs enrolled in public schools and on the percentage of public school students who were ELLs include only those ELL students who participated in ELL programs. Starting with 2015, data include all ELL students, regardless of program participation. Due to this change in definition, comparisons between 2018 and earlier years should be interpreted with caution. For all years, data do not include students who were formerly identified as ELLs but later obtained English language proficiency.

In fall 2018, the percentage of students who were identified as ELLs ranged from 1 percent in West Virginia to 19 percent in California. The percentage of public school students who were ELLs was 10.0 percent or more in 10 states, most of which were located in the West, and the District of Columbia.[26] The states were Alaska, California, Colorado, Florida, Illinois, Massachusetts, Nevada, New Mexico, Texas, and Washington. In contrast, the percentage of students who were ELLs was less than 3.0 percent in five states: Wyoming, New Hampshire, Montana, Vermont, and West Virginia (figure 6).

In fall 2018, there were about 3.8 million Hispanic ELL public school students, constituting over three-quarters (77.6 percent) of ELL student enrollment overall.[27] Asian students were the next largest racial/ethnic group among ELLs, with 528,700 students (10.7 percent of ELL students). In addition, there were 331,900 White ELL students (6.7 percent of ELL students) and 218,000 Black ELL students (4.4 percent of ELL students). In each of the other racial/ethnic groups for which data were collected (Pacific Islanders, American Indians/Alaska Natives, and individuals of Two or more races), fewer than 40,000 students were identified as ELLs. In addition, 766,600 ELL students were identified as students with disabilities in fall 2018, representing 15.3 percent of the total ELL student enrollment (English Language Learners in Public Schools).

Children's Internet Access at Home

In 2019, some 95 percent of 3- to 18-year-olds had home internet access: 88 percent had access through a computer, and 6 percent had access only through a smartphone.[28] The remaining 5 percent had no internet access at home. The percentage of 3- to 18-year-olds with home internet access were higher for those whose parents had attained higher levels of education and higher for those in higher income families (figure 7). For instance, in 2019, the percentage with home internet access was highest for those whose parents had attained a bachelor's or higher degree (99 percent) and lowest for those whose parents had less than a high school credential (83 percent).

The percentages of 3- to 18-year-olds with home internet access also varied across racial/ethnic groups. For instance, in 2019, the percentage with home internet access was highest for those who were Asian (99 percent) and lowest for those who were American Indian/Alaska Native (83 percent). In addition, the percentages with home internet access were higher for those who were of Two or more races (97 percent) and White (96 percent) than for those who were Hispanic (92 percent), Black (91 percent), and Pacific Islander (90 percent) (Children's Internet Access at Home).

Figure 7. Percentage of 3- to 18-year-olds who had home internet access, by parental education: 2018

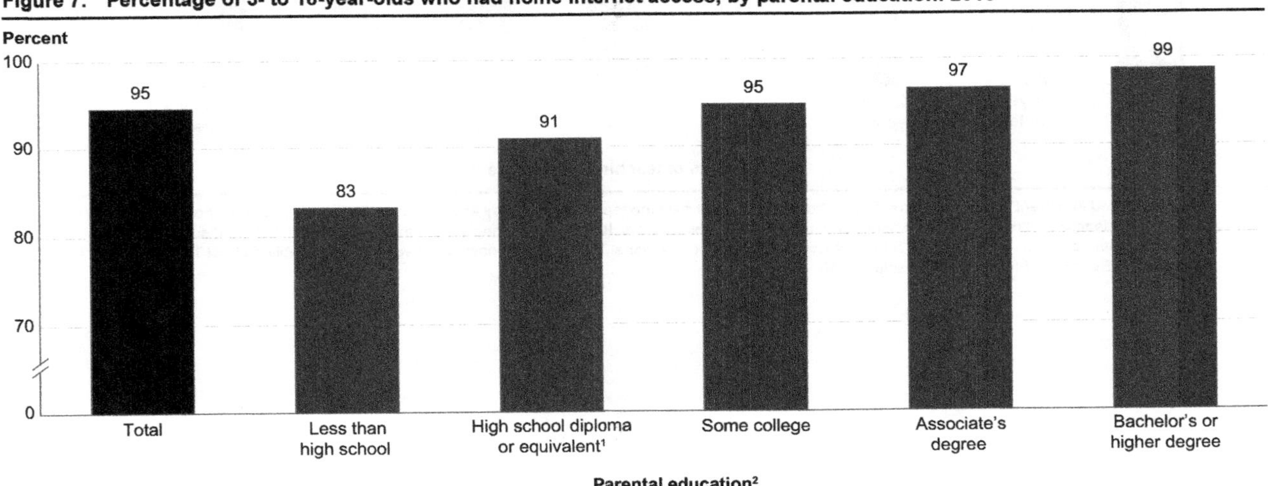

[1] Includes those who completed high school through equivalency credentials, such as the GED.
[2] Highest education level of any parent residing with the 3- to 18-year-olds (including an adoptive or stepparent). Includes only 3- to 18-year-olds who resided with at least one of their parents.
NOTE: Includes only 3- to 18-year-olds living in households (respondents living in group quarters such as shelters, healthcare facilities, or correctional facilities were not asked about internet access). Race categories exclude persons of Hispanic ethnicity. Although rounded numbers are displayed, the figures are based on unrounded data.
SOURCE: U.S. Department of Commerce, Census Bureau, American Community Survey (ACS), 2018. See *Digest of Education Statistics 2019*, table 702.12.

[26] Categorizations are based on unrounded percentages.
[27] The number of Hispanic ELL students is larger than the number of ELL students who speak Spanish. Home language data may be missing for some Hispanic ELL students. In addition, some Hispanic ELL students may report that they speak a language other than Spanish at home (such as a language that is indigenous to Latin America).

[28] Detail does not sum to totals because of rounding.

Public School Teachers

In the 2017-18 school year, there were 3.5 million full- and part-time public school teachers,[29] including 1.8 million elementary school teachers and 1.8 million secondary school teachers. In that year, some 90 percent of public school teachers held a regular or standard state teaching certificate or advanced professional certificate, 4 percent held a provisional or temporary certificate, 3 percent held a probationary certificate, 2 percent held no certification, and 1 percent held a waiver or emergency certificate. As for the racial/ethnic and sex distribution of public school teachers in 2018, a majority were White (79 percent) and a majority were female (76 percent).

In 2017-18, the average base salary (in current 2017-18 dollars) for full-time public school teachers was $57,900 (figure 8).[30] Average base salaries, in current 2017-18 dollars, ranged from $42,800 for teachers with 1 year or less of experience to $70,500 for teachers with 30 or more years of experience. Higher educational attainment was associated with higher average base salaries for full-time public school teachers who held at least a bachelor's degree (*Characteristics of Public School Teachers*).

Figure 8. Average base salary for full-time teachers in public elementary and secondary schools, by years of full- and part-time teaching experience: 2017–18

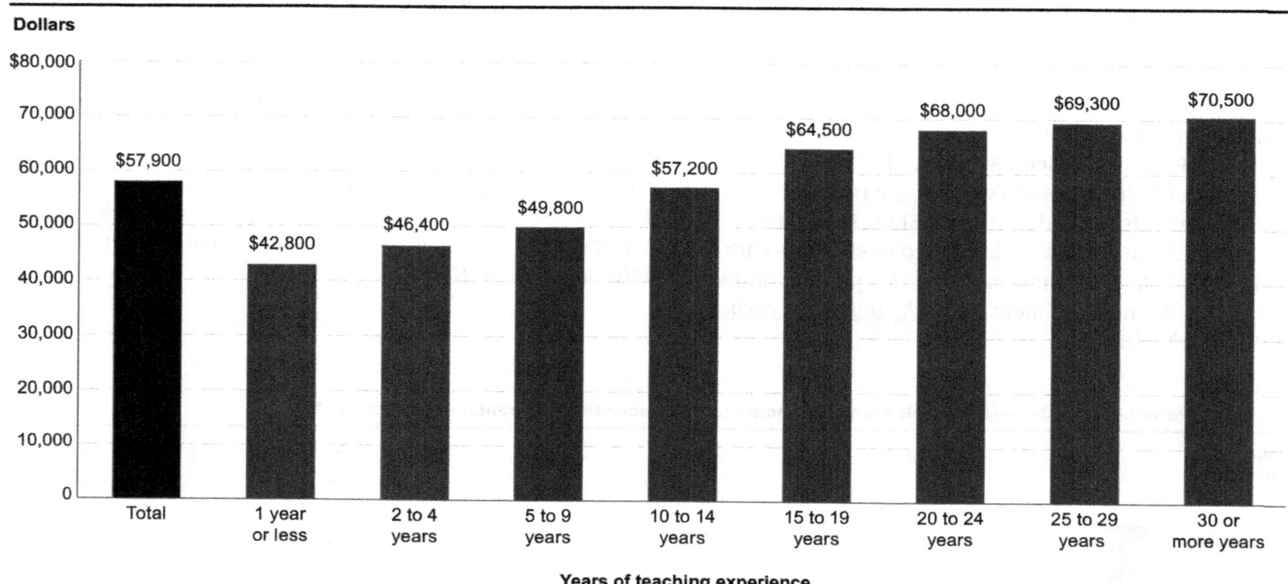

NOTE: Amounts presented in current 2017–18 dollars. Estimates are for regular full-time teachers only; they exclude other staff even when they have full-time teaching duties (regular part-time teachers, itinerant teachers, long-term substitutes, administrators, library media specialists, other professional staff, and support staff).
SOURCE: U.S. Department of Education, National Center for Education Statistics, National Teacher and Principal Survey (NTPS), "Public School Teacher Data File," 2017–18. See *Digest of Education Statistics 2020*, table 211.10.

[29] All data except those on school enrollment are based on a head count of full-time and part-time teachers rather than on the number of full-time equivalent teachers.

[30] Salary data are presented for regular, full-time public school teachers only; the data exclude other staff even when they have full-time teaching duties (regular part-time teachers, itinerant teachers, long-term substitutes, administrators, library media specialists, other professional staff, and support staff).

National Assessments

The National Assessment of Educational Progress (NAEP) assesses student performance in reading at grades 4, 8, and 12 in both public and private schools across the nation. In 2019, some 35 percent of 4th-grade students and 34 percent of 8th-grade students performed at or above *NAEP Proficient*. The average reading scores were 220 and 263 for 4th- and 8th-grade students, respectively.[31]

These scores can be disaggregated by the poverty level of the school students attended and by students' English language learner (ELL) status. In 2019, the average reading score for 4th-grade students in high-poverty schools (206) was lower than the scores for 4th-grade students in mid-high poverty schools (217), mid-low poverty schools (227), and low-poverty schools (240) (figure 9).[32] In the same year, the reading score for 4th-grade ELL students (191) was 33 points lower than the score for their non-ELL peers (224) (*Reading Performance*).

For mathematics, 41 percent of 4th-grade students and 34 percent of 8th-grade students performed at or above the *NAEP Proficient* level in 2019. The average mathematics score was 241 for 4th-grade students and 282 for 8th-grade students.[33]

Figure 9. Average National Assessment of Educational Progress (NAEP) reading scale scores of 4th-grade students, by selected characteristics: 2019

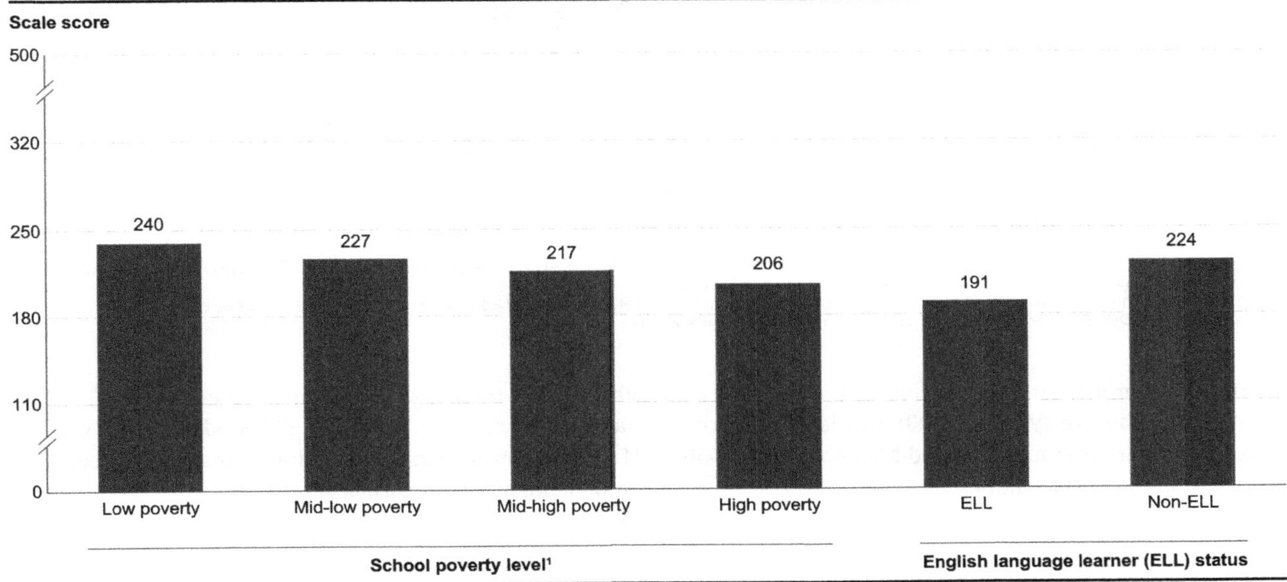

[1] High-poverty schools are defined as schools where 76 to 100 percent of the students are eligible for free or reduced-price lunch (FRPL); mid-high poverty schools are schools where 51 to 75 percent of the students are eligible for FRPL; mid-low poverty schools are schools where 26 to 50 percent of the students are eligible for FRPL; and low-poverty schools are schools where 25 percent or less of the students are eligible for FRPL. For more information on eligibility for FRPL and its relationship to poverty, see the NCES blog post "Free or reduced price lunch: A proxy for poverty?" The nonresponse rate for free or reduced-price lunch was greater than 15 percent but not greater than 50 percent.

NOTE: Includes public, private, Bureau of Indian Education, and Department of Defense Education Activity schools. The reading scale scores range from 0 to 500. Although rounded numbers are displayed, the figures are based on unrounded data.

SOURCE: U.S. Department of Education, National Center for Education Statistics, National Assessment of Educational Progress (NAEP), 2019 Reading Assessments, NAEP Data Explorer. See *Digest of Education Statistics 2019*, table 221.12.

[31] For 2019 Grade 12 NAEP results, see https://www.nationsreportcard.gov/reading/nation/scores/?grade=12.

[32] High-poverty schools are defined as schools where 76 to 100 percent of the students are eligible for free or reduced-price lunch (FRPL); mid-high poverty schools are schools where 51 to 75 percent of the students are eligible for FRPL; mid-low poverty schools are schools where 26 to 50 percent of the students are eligible for FRPL; and low-poverty schools are schools where 25 percent or less of the students are eligible for FRPL.

[33] For 2019 Grade 12 NAEP results, see https://www.nationsreportcard.gov/mathematics/nation/scores/?grade=12.

Figure 10. Average National Assessment of Educational Progress (NAEP) mathematics scale scores of 4th-grade students, by selected characteristics: 2019

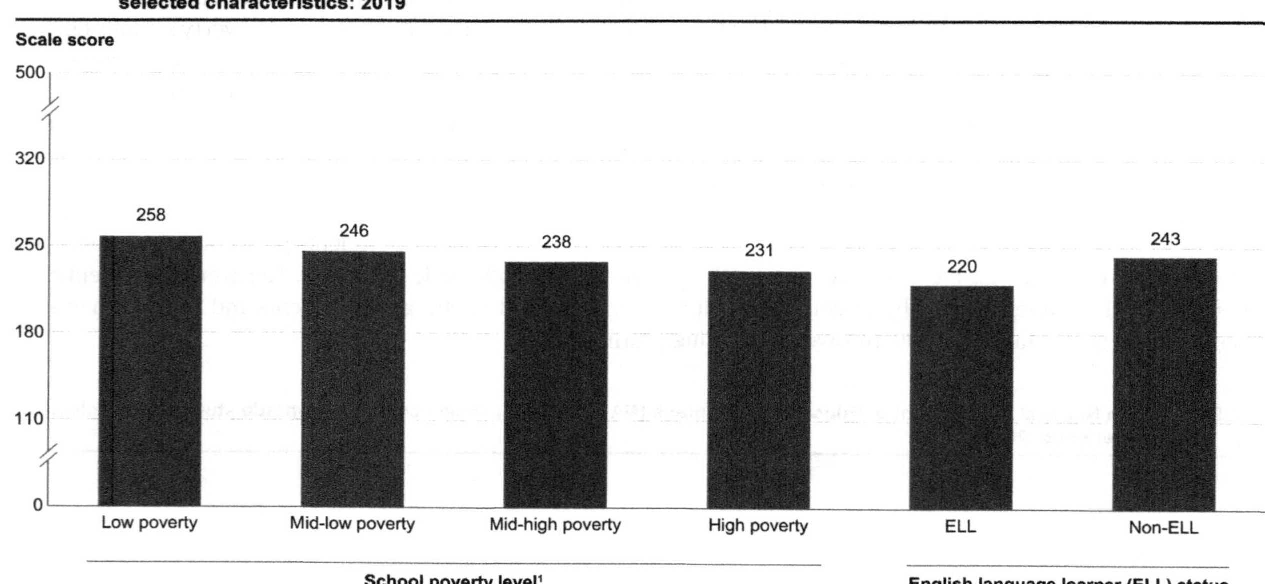

[1] High-poverty schools are defined as schools where 76 to 100 percent of the students are eligible for free or reduced-price lunch (FRPL); mid-high poverty schools are schools where 51 to 75 percent of the students are eligible for FRPL; mid-low poverty schools are schools where 26 to 50 percent of the students are eligible for FRPL; and low-poverty schools are schools where 25 percent or less of the students are eligible for FRPL. For more information on eligibility for FRPL and its relationship to poverty, see the NCES blog post "Free or reduced price lunch: A proxy for poverty?" The nonresponse rate for free or reduced-price lunch was greater than 15 percent but not greater than 50 percent.

NOTE: Includes public, private, Bureau of Indian Education, and Department of Defense Education Activity schools. The mathematics scale scores range from 0 to 500. Although rounded numbers are displayed, the figures are based on unrounded data.

SOURCE: U.S. Department of Education, National Center for Education Statistics, National Assessment of Educational Progress (NAEP), 2019 mathematics Assessments, NAEP Data Explorer. See *Digest of Education Statistics 2019*, table 222.12.

In 2019, the average mathematics score for 4th-grade students in high-poverty schools (231) was lower than the scores for 4th-grade students in mid-high poverty schools (238), mid-low poverty schools (246), and low-poverty schools (258) (figure 10). Additionally, the average mathematics score for 4th-grade ELL students (220) was 24 points[34] lower than the score for their non-ELL peers (243) (*Mathematics Performance*).

[34] Although rounded numbers are displayed, the underlying calculations are based on unrounded data.

High School Persistence and Completion

The adjusted cohort graduation rate (ACGR) is the percentage of students in a "cohort" of first-time 9th-graders who graduate with a regular high school diploma within 4 years.[35] The U.S. average ACGR for public high school students increased over the first 9 years it was collected, from 79 percent in 2010-11 to 86 percent in 2018-19. In 2018-19, the ACGRs for American Indian/Alaska Native (74 percent), Black (80 percent), and Hispanic (82 percent) public high school students were below the U.S. average of 86 percent (figure 11). The ACGRs for White (89 percent) and Asian/Pacific Islander (93 percent) students were above the U.S. average (*Public High School Graduation Rates*).

Figure 11. Adjusted cohort graduation rate (ACGR) for public high school students, by race/ethnicity: 2018–19

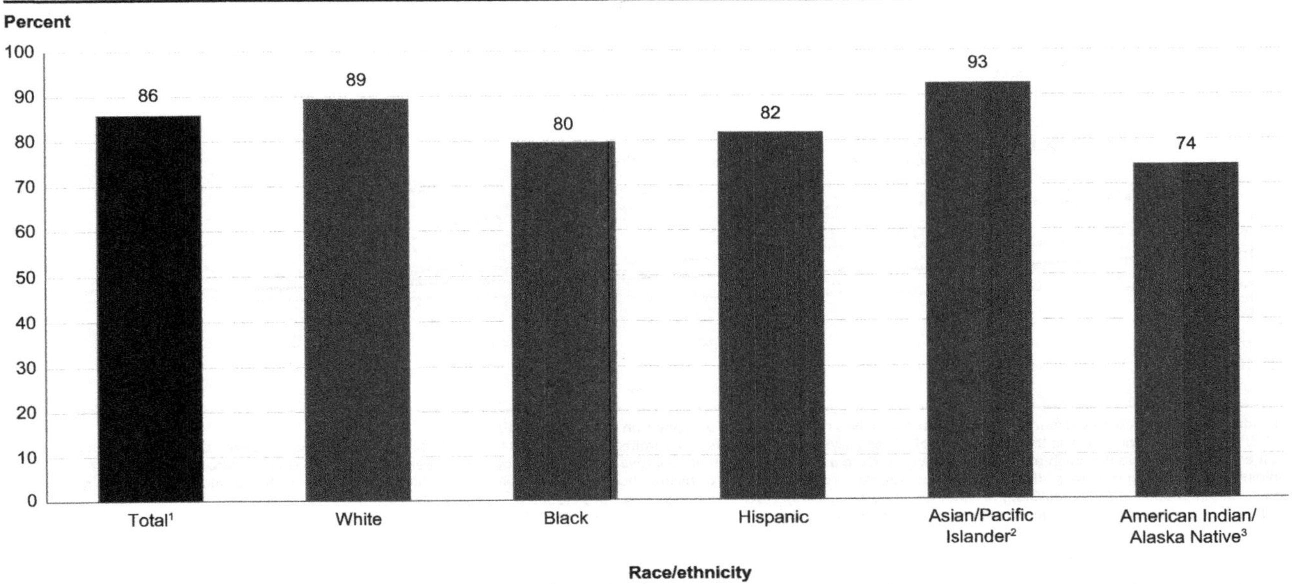

[1] Includes other race/ethnicity categories not separately shown.
[2] Reporting practices for data on Asian and Pacific Islander students vary by state. Asian/Pacific Islander data in this indicator represent either the value reported by the state for the "Asian/Pacific Islander" group or an aggregation of separate values reported by the state for "Asian" and "Pacific Islander." "Asian/Pacific Islander" includes the "Filipino" group, which only California and Hawaii report separately.
[3] Estimated assuming a count of zero American Indian/Alaska Native students for Hawaii.
NOTE: The ACGR is the percentage of public high school freshmen who graduate with a regular diploma within 4 years of starting ninth grade. The total ACGR is for the 50 states and the District of Columbia. Race categories exclude persons of Hispanic ethnicity.
SOURCE: U.S. Department of Education, Office of Elementary and Secondary Education, Consolidated State Performance Report, 2018–19; and National Center for Education Statistics, ED*Facts* file 150, Data Group 695, and ED*Facts* file 151, Data Group 696, 2018–19. See *Digest of Education Statistics 2020*, table 219.46.

[35] State education agencies calculate the ACGR by identifying the "cohort" of first-time 9th-graders in a particular school year. The cohort is then adjusted by adding any students who immigrate from another country or transfer into the cohort after 9th grade and subtracting any students who transfer out, emigrate to another country, or die.

Figure 12. Status dropout rates of 16- to 24-year-olds, by race/ethnicity: 2010 through 2019

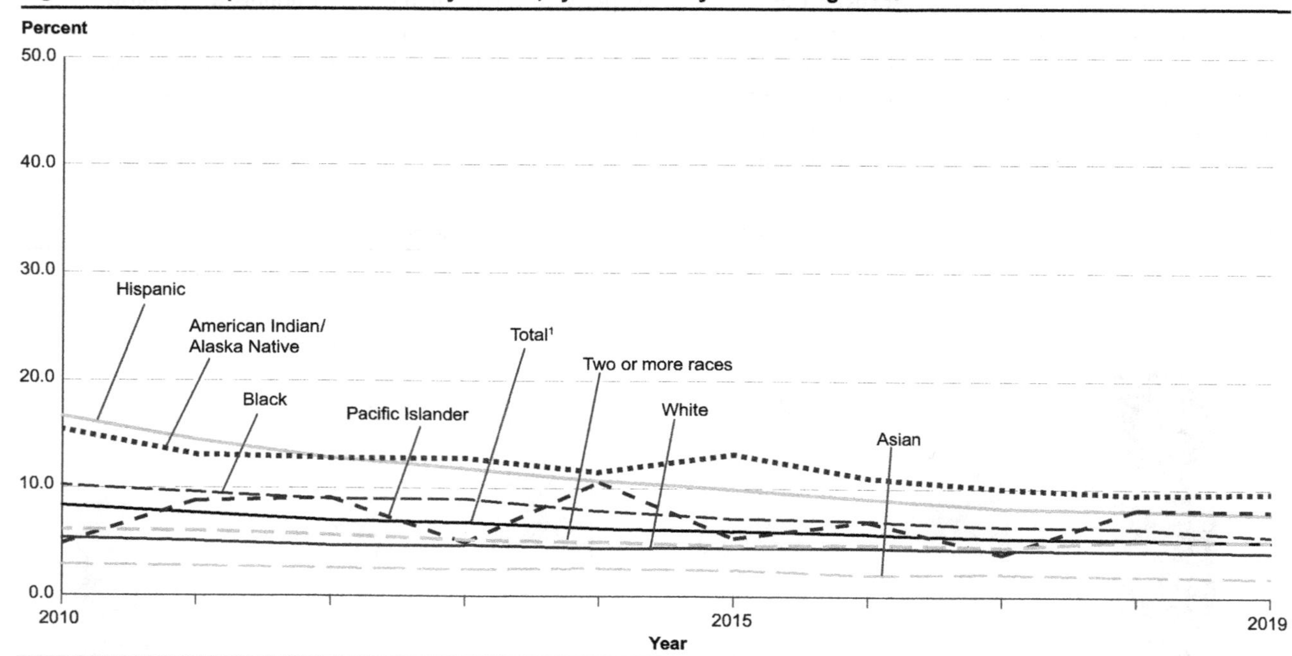

[1] Includes respondents who wrote in some other race that was not included as an option on the questionnaire.
NOTE: The status dropout rate is the percentage of 16- to 24-year-olds who are not enrolled in school and have not earned a high school credential (either a diploma or an equivalency credential such as a GED certificate). Data are based on sample surveys of the entire population residing within the United States, including both noninstitutionalized persons (e.g., those living in households, college housing, or military housing located within the United States) and institutionalized persons (e.g., those living in prisons, nursing facilities, or other healthcare facilities). Race categories exclude persons of Hispanic ethnicity.
SOURCE: U.S. Department of Commerce, Census Bureau, American Community Survey (ACS), 2010 through 2019. See *Digest of Education Statistics 2020*, table 219.80.

The *status dropout rate* represents the percentage of 16- to 24-year-olds who are not enrolled in school and have not earned a high school credential (either a diploma or an equivalency credential such as a GED certificate). In 2019, there were 2.0 million status dropouts between the ages of 16 and 24, and the overall status dropout rate was 5.1 percent. The overall status dropout rate decreased from 8.3 percent in 2010 to 5.1 percent in 2019 (figure 12). During this time, the status dropout rate declined for 16- to 24-year-olds who were Hispanic (from 16.7 to 7.7 percent), American Indian/Alaska Native (from 15.4 to 9.6 percent), Black (from 10.3 to 5.6 percent), White (from 5.3 to 4.1 percent), Asian (from 2.8 to 1.8 percent), and of Two or more races (from 6.1 to 5.1 percent). There was no measurable difference between the status dropout rates in 2010 and 2019 for those who were Pacific Islander (*Status Dropout Rates*).

School Finances

In school year 2017-18, elementary and secondary public school revenues totaled $761 billion in constant 2019-20 dollars. Of this total, 8 percent, or $59 billion, were from federal sources; 47 percent, or $357 billion, were from state sources; and 45 percent, or $345 billion, were from local sources.[36] Between 2009-10 and 2017-18, public school revenues increased by 8 percent in constant 2019-20 dollars, while public school enrollment increased by 3 percent (*Public School Revenue Sources*).

Total expenditures for public elementary and secondary schools in the United States in 2017-18 amounted to $762 billion,[37] or $14,891 per public school pupil enrolled in the fall (in constant 2019-20 dollars). Total expenditures included $13,118 per pupil on current expenditures, $1,376 per pupil on capital outlay, and $397 per pupil on interest on school debt. Current expenditures per pupil–which include salaries, employee benefits, purchased services, tuition, supplies, and other expenditures–were 4 percent higher in 2017-18 than in 2009-10 ($13,118 vs. $12,623), after adjusting for inflation (figure 13) (*Public School Expenditures*).

Figure 13. Current expenditures, capital outlay, and interest on school debt per pupil in fall enrollment in public elementary and secondary schools: 2009–10 through 2017–18

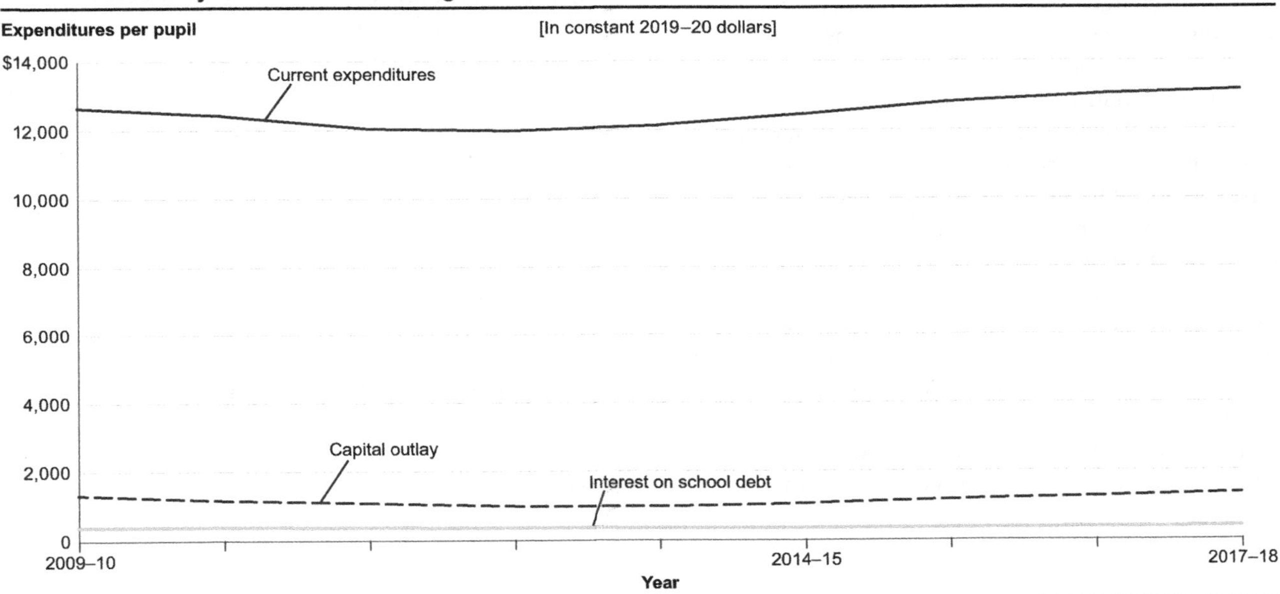

NOTE: Data in this figure represent the 50 states and the District of Columbia. "Current expenditures," "Capital outlay," and "Interest on school debt" are subcategories of total expenditures. Current expenditures includes salaries, employee benefits, purchased services, tuition, supplies, and other expenditures. Capital outlay includes expenditures for property and for buildings and alterations completed by school district staff or contractors. Expenditures are reported in constant 2019–20 dollars, based on the Consumer Price Index (CPI). Some data have been revised from previous figures. Excludes expenditures for state education agencies.
SOURCE: U.S. Department of Education, National Center for Education Statistics, Common Core of Data (CCD), "National Public Education Financial Survey," 2009–10 through 2017–18; CCD, "State Nonfiscal Survey of Public Elementary/Secondary Education," 2009–10 through 2017–18. See *Digest of Education Statistics 2019*, table 105.30, and *Digest of Education Statistics 2020*, tables 236.10, 236.55, and 236.60.

[36] Local revenues include revenues from such sources as local property and nonproperty taxes, investments, and student activities such as textbook sales, transportation and tuition fees, and food service revenues. Local revenues also include revenues from intermediate sources (education agencies with fundraising capabilities that operate between the state and local government levels).

[37] The $762 billion is the total expenditure, while $761 billion in the paragraph above is the total revenue.

Postsecondary Education

In the United States, many students continue their education after completing compulsory schooling by pursuing postsecondary credentials. Just like compulsory education, the condition of the postsecondary education system can be characterized by the students it serves, the contexts they learn in, the resources available to them, and the outcomes they achieve. However, because postsecondary education is not mandatory, the question of whom this system serves takes on a different nature. Accordingly, this section of the Condition of Education Indicator System begins by assessing postsecondary enrollments rates and attendance status, both overall and by student characteristics. Once enrolled, postsecondary students find themselves in a variety of institutional contexts–characterized by the types of degrees awarded, institutional control (public or private), and whether the private institutions are operated on a nonprofit or for-profit basis. Importantly, these different contexts offer students different resources, in terms of the programs available, the faculty and staff who teach them, and the quantity and quality of financial aid available. As additional background for understanding the provision of these resources, information is also provided on postsecondary expenditures and revenues, including tuition charged to students. Finally, the Condition of Education Indicator System considers several postsecondary outcomes, including persistence, degree completion, and degree fields, as well as differences in these outcomes by student and institutional characteristics.

In this *Report on the Condition of Education*, data on postsecondary enrollments, financial aid, degree fields and degree completion, changes in the institutional landscape, and faculty characteristics are highlighted.

Postsecondary Enrollment

Of the 3.2 million high school completers who graduated in the first 9 months of 2019, some 2.1 million, or 66 percent, were enrolled in college in October 2019. This annual percentage of high school completers who are enrolled in 2- or 4-year institutions within the specified time frame is known as the *immediate college enrollment rate*. These immediate college enrollment rates differ by student race/ethnicity. In 2019, the immediate college enrollment rate for Asian students (82 percent) was higher than the rates for White (69 percent), Hispanic (64 percent), and Black (57 percent) students, and the rate for White students was also higher than the rate for Black students.[38] For White, Asian, and Hispanic students, the immediate college enrollment rates were not measurably different between 2019 and 2010 (figure 14). However, for Black students, the immediate college enrollment rate was lower in 2019 (57 percent) than in 2010 (66 percent) (Immediate College Enrollment Rate).

[38] Due to some short-term data fluctuations associated with small sample sizes, estimates for the racial/ethnic groups shown were calculated based on 3-year moving averages, with the following exception: the percentages for 2019 were calculated based on a 2-year moving average (an average of 2018 and 2019). Other racial/ethnic groups are not discussed separately.

Figure 14. Immediate college enrollment rate of high school completers, by race/ethnicity: 2010 through 2019

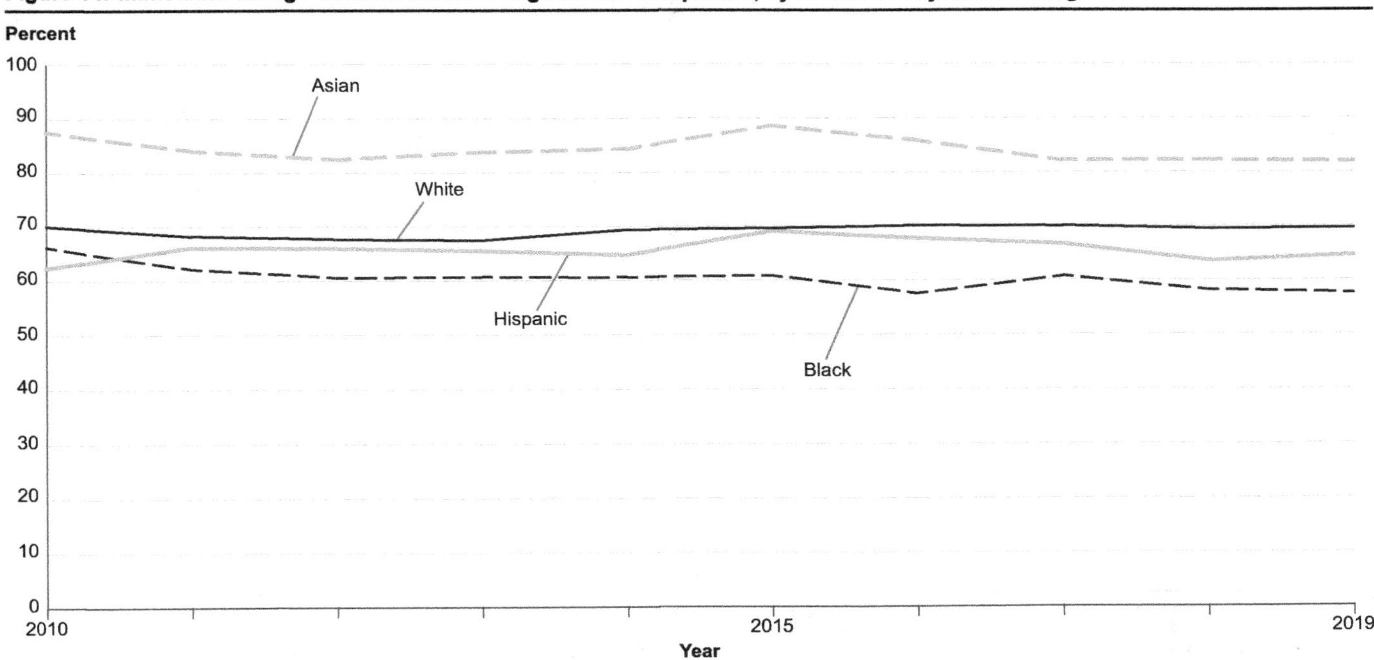

NOTE: *Immediate college enrollment rate* is defined as the annual percentage of high school completers who are enrolled in 2- or 4-year institutions in the October immediately following high school completion. High school completers include 16- to 24-year-olds who graduated with a high school diploma as well as those who completed a GED or other high school equivalency credential. Due to some short-term data fluctuations associated with small sample sizes, percentages for racial/ethnic groups shown were calculated based on 3-year moving averages, with the following exception: the percentages for 2019 were calculated based on a 2-year moving average (an average of 2018 and 2019). Other racial/ethnic groups are not shown separately. Race categories exclude persons of Hispanic ethnicity.
SOURCE: U.S. Department of Commerce, Census Bureau, Current Population Survey (CPS), October Supplement, 2010 through 2019. See *Digest of Education Statistics 2020*, table 302.20.

Figure 15. Undergraduate enrollment in degree-granting postsecondary institutions, by attendance status: Fall 2009 through fall 2019

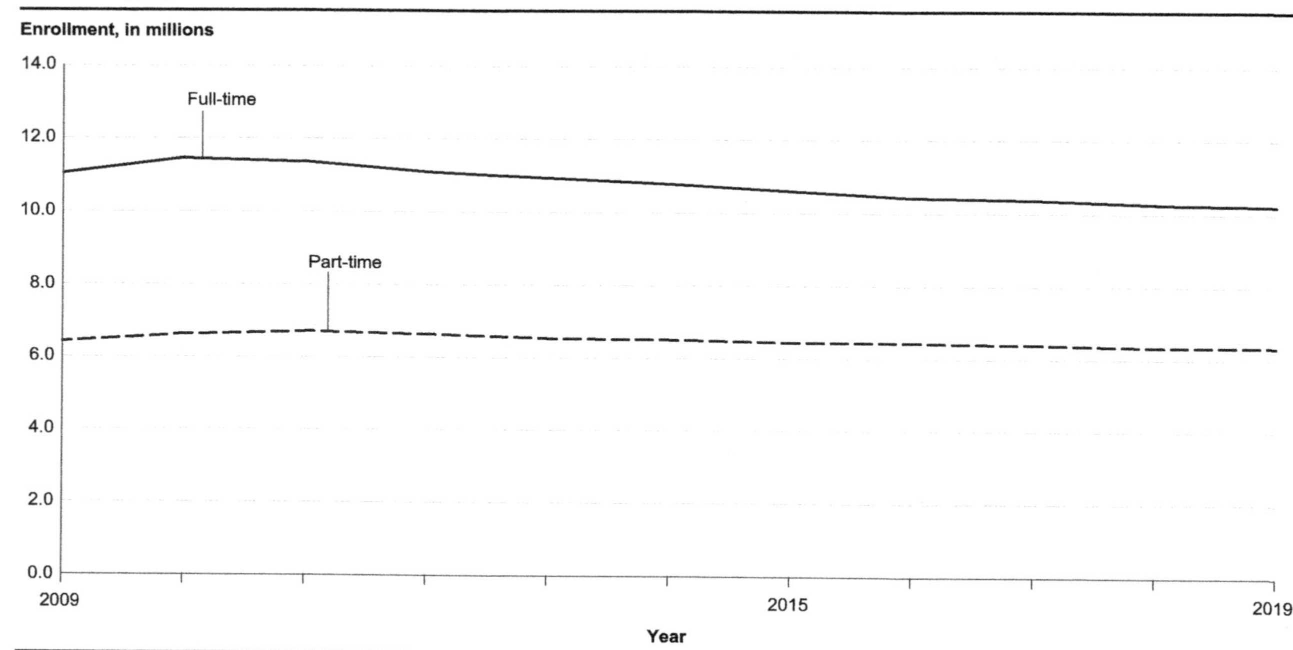

NOTE: Data are for the 50 states and the District of Columbia. Degree-granting institutions grant associate's or higher degrees and participate in Title IV federal financial aid programs. Some data have been revised from previously published figures.
SOURCE: U.S. Department of Education, National Center for Education Statistics, Integrated Postsecondary Education Data System (IPEDS), Spring 2010 through Spring 2020, Fall Enrollment component. See *Digest of Education Statistics 2020*, table 303.70.

Although the overall immediate college enrollment rate did not differ between 2010 and 2019, total undergraduate enrollment decreased by 5 percent between 2009 and 2019 (from 17.5 million to 16.6 million students): full-time enrollment decreased by 7 percent (from 11.0 million to 10.2 million students) and part-time enrollment decreased by 1 percent (from 6.4 million to 6.3 million students). (figure 15). On the other hand, total enrollment in postbaccalaureate programs (such as master's and doctoral programs[39]) increased by 8 percent (from 2.8 million to 3.1 million students) (Undergraduate Enrollment and Postbaccalaureate Enrollment).

In fall 2019, some 66 percent (11.0 million students) of the total undergraduate population were enrolled at 4-year institutions; the remaining 34 percent (5.6 million students) were enrolled in 2-year institutions. Between 2009 and 2019, enrollment increased by 10 percent at 4-year institutions (from 9.9 million to 11.0 million students) and decreased by 26 percent at 2-year institutions (from 7.5 million to 5.6 million students)[40] (Undergraduate Enrollment).

Postsecondary Institutions

In academic year 2018-19, there were approximately 3,700 degree-granting institutions in the United States with first-year undergraduates: 2,300 were 4-year institutions offering programs at the bachelor's or higher degree level and 1,300 were 2-year institutions offering associate's degrees and other certificates.

For all institutional controls,[41] the number of 4-year institutions was higher in 2018-19 than in 2000-01, while the number of 2-year institutions was lower (figure 16). For private for-profit institutions at both levels, these differences include fluctuations over the period. Between 2000-01 and 2012-13, the number of private for-profit 4-year institutions more than tripled, from 210 to 710.

[39] Doctoral programs include programs formerly referred to as "first professional" programs, such as law degrees (JD) and medical (MD) or dental (DDS) degrees.

[40] Some of the shift in enrollment patterns for 2-year and 4-year institutions during this period is likely explained by 2-year institutions' beginning to offer 4-year degree programs, which caused their classification to change. In 2019, some 893,300 undergraduate students were enrolled in 4-year institutions that were classified as 2-year institutions in 2009. These students could be enrolled in either 2- or 4-year programs.

[41] Institutional control refers to the classification of institutions of elementary/secondary or postsecondary education by whether the institution is operated by publicly elected or appointed officials and derives its primary support from public funds (public control) or is operated by privately elected or appointed officials and derives its major source of funds from private sources (private control).

Figure 16. Number of degree-granting institutions with first-year undergraduates, by level and control of institution: Academic years 2000–01, 2012–13, and 2018–19

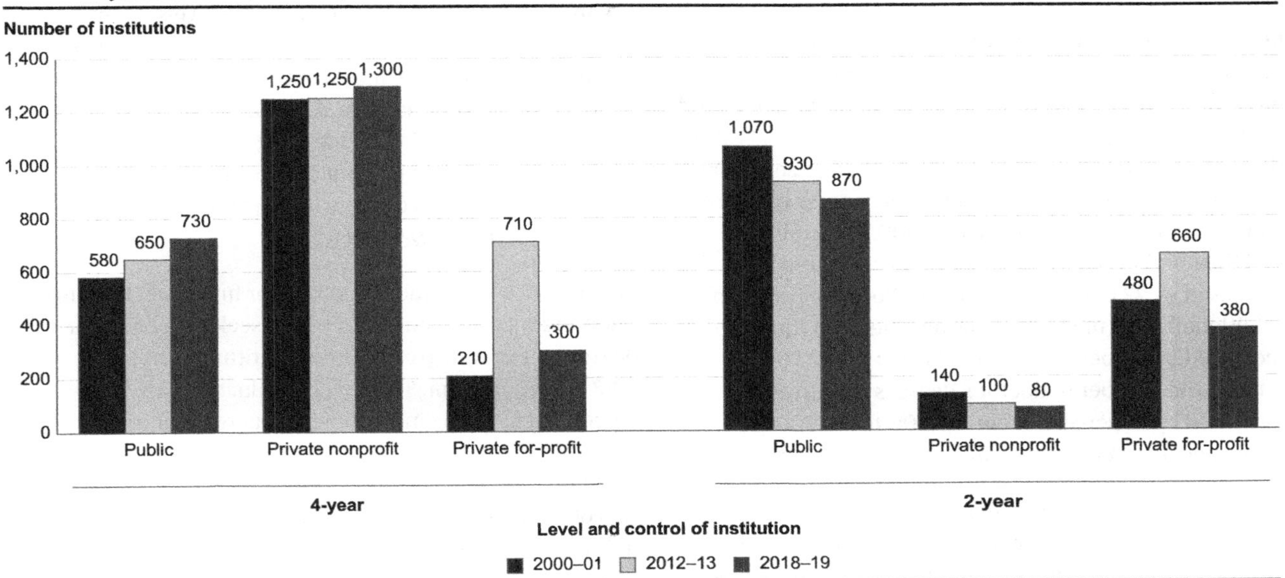

NOTE: Degree-granting institutions grant associate's or higher degrees and participate in Title IV federal financial aid programs. Excludes institutions not enrolling any first-time degree/certificate-seeking undergraduates. Although rounded numbers are displayed, the figures are based on unrounded data.
SOURCE: U.S. Department of Education, National Center for Education Statistics, Integrated Postsecondary Education Data System (IPEDS), Fall 2000 and Fall 2012, Institutional Characteristics component; and Winter 2018–19, Admissions component. See *Digest of Education Statistics 2013*, table 305.30; and *Digest of Education Statistics 2019*, table 305.30.

After peaking in 2012-13, the number of private for-profit 4-year institutions declined to 300 in 2018-19, which was 45 percent higher than the number of such institutions in 2000-01. Among 2-year institutions, the number of private for-profit institutions increased by 37 percent, from 480 to 660, and then declined by 42 percent to 380 in 2018-19. Overall, the number of private for-profit 2-year institutions was 21 percent lower in 2018-19 than in 2000-01 (*Characteristics of Degree-Granting Postsecondary Institutions*).

Faculty and Staff

In fall 2018, of the 1.5 million faculty[42] in degree-granting postsecondary institutions, 54 percent were full time and 46 percent were part time. The number of full-time faculty increased by 9 percent (from 762,100 to 832,100) from fall 2011 to fall 2018. In comparison, the number of part-time faculty decreased by 7 percent (from 762,400 to 710,500) between 2011 and 2018.

Of all full-time faculty in degree-granting postsecondary institutions in fall 2018, some 40 percent were White males; 35 percent were White females; 7 percent were Asian/Pacific Islander males; 5 percent were Asian/Pacific Islander females; and 3 percent each were Black males, Black females, Hispanic males, and Hispanic females.[43] Those who were American Indian/Alaska Native and those who were of Two or more races each made up 1 percent or less of full-time faculty. Compared to faculty overall, White males (53 percent) and Asian/Pacific Islander males (8 percent) made up a relatively larger percentage of full-time professors (*Characteristics of Postsecondary Faculty*).

[42] Faculty include professors, associate professors, assistant professors, instructors, lecturers, assisting professors, adjunct professors, and interim professors.

[43] Percentages are based on full-time faculty whose race/ethnicity was known. Race/ethnicity was not collected for nonresident aliens.

Completions and Graduation Rates

Between 2009-10 and 2018-19, the number of undergraduate and graduate awards conferred generally increased (figure 17). The number of certificates conferred below the associate's level was 7 percent higher in 2018-19 than in 2009-10 (1.0 million vs. 935,700). Between 2009-10 and 2018-19, the number of associate's degrees conferred increased by 22 percent (from 848,900 to 1.0 million), and the number of bachelor's degrees conferred also increased by 22 percent (from 1.6 million to 2.0 million). Additionally, the number of master's degrees conferred increased by 20 percent (from 693,300 to 833,700). Finally, the number of doctor's degrees conferred increased by 18 percent (from 158,600 to 187,600) (Postsecondary Certificates and Degrees Conferred).

In 2018-19, business[44] and health professions and related programs were among the most common fields for degrees awarded at the associate's (11 and 18 percent, respectively), bachelor's (19 and 12 percent, respectively), and master's (24 and 16 percent, respectively) degree levels. Health professions and related programs (44 percent of degrees conferred) was also the most common field at the doctoral degree level. Additionally, in 2018-19, STEM[45] fields made up 8 percent of associate's degrees, 21 percent of bachelor's degrees, 17 percent of master's degrees, and 16 percent of doctor's degrees (Undergraduate Degree Fields and Graduate Degree Fields).

The overall 6-year graduation rate for first-time, full-time undergraduate students who began seeking a bachelor's degree at 4-year degree-granting institutions in fall 2013 was 63 percent. The 6-year graduation rate was 62 percent at public institutions, 68 percent at private nonprofit institutions, and 26 percent at private for-profit institutions. The overall 6-year graduation rate was 66 percent for females and 60 percent for males (Undergraduate Retention and Graduation Rates).

Figure 17. Number of certificates and degrees conferred by postsecondary institutions, by award level: 2009–10 through 2018–19

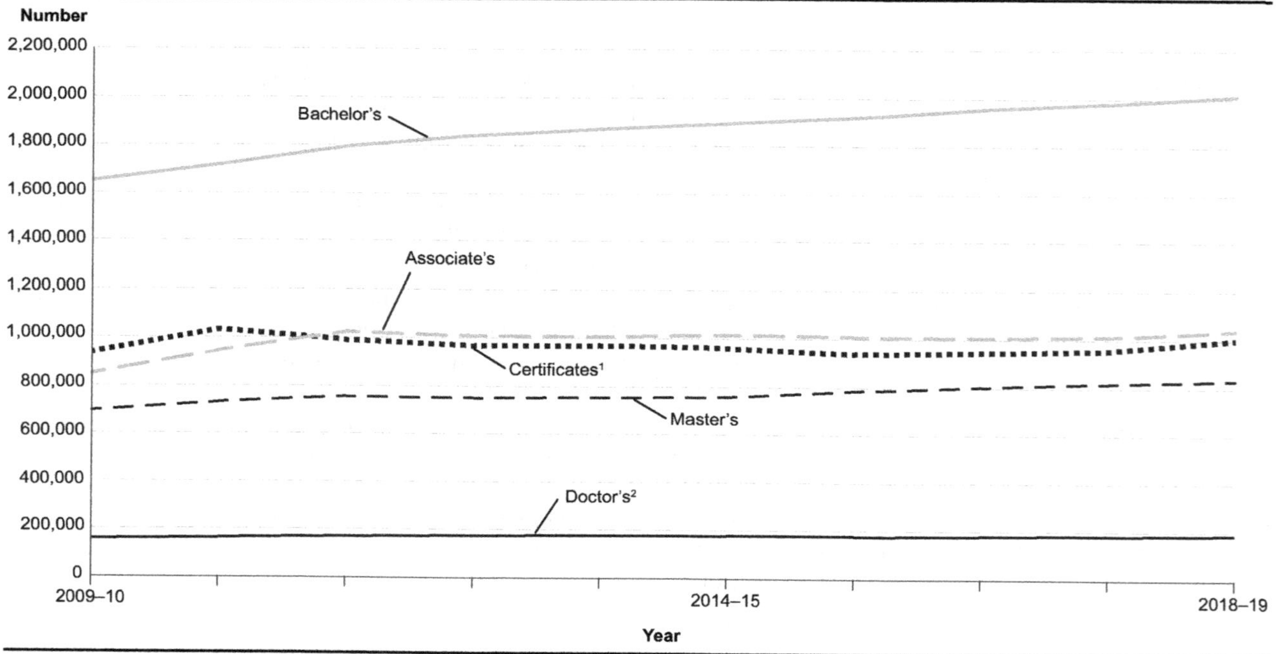

[1]Data are for certificates below the associate's degree level.
[2]Includes Ph.D., Ed.D., and comparable degrees at the doctoral level. Includes most degrees formerly classified as first-professional, such as M.D., D.D.S., and law degrees.
NOTE: Data in this figure represent the 50 states and the District of Columbia. Data are for postsecondary institutions participating in Title IV federal financial aid programs. Degree counts are limited to degree-granting institutions; certificate counts include both degree- and non-degree-granting institutions. Some data have been revised from previously published figures.
SOURCE: U.S. Department of Education, National Center for Education Statistics, Integrated Postsecondary Education Data System (IPEDS), Fall 2010 through Fall 2019, Completions component. See *Digest of Education Statistics 2020*, table 318.40.

---

[44] Personal and culinary services have been added to the definition of "business" for associate's degree data in order to be consistent with the definition of "business" for bachelor's degree data. "Business" is defined as business, management, marketing, and related support services, as well as personal and culinary services.

[45] Science, technology, engineering, and mathematics (STEM) fields include biological and biomedical sciences (excluding health professionals); computer and information sciences; engineering and engineering technologies; mathematics and statistics; and physical sciences and science technologies.

Finances and Resources

In academic year 2018-19, the average net price of attendance (total cost minus grant and scholarship aid) for first-time, full-time undergraduate students attending 4-year institutions was $13,900 at public institutions, compared with $27,200 at private nonprofit institutions and $23,800 at private for-profit institutions (in constant 2019-20 dollars) (figure 18) (Price of Attending an Undergraduate Institution).

Figure 18. Average total cost, grant and scholarship aid, and net price for first-time, full-time degree/certificate-seeking undergraduate students awarded Title IV aid, by level and control of institution: Academic year 2018–19

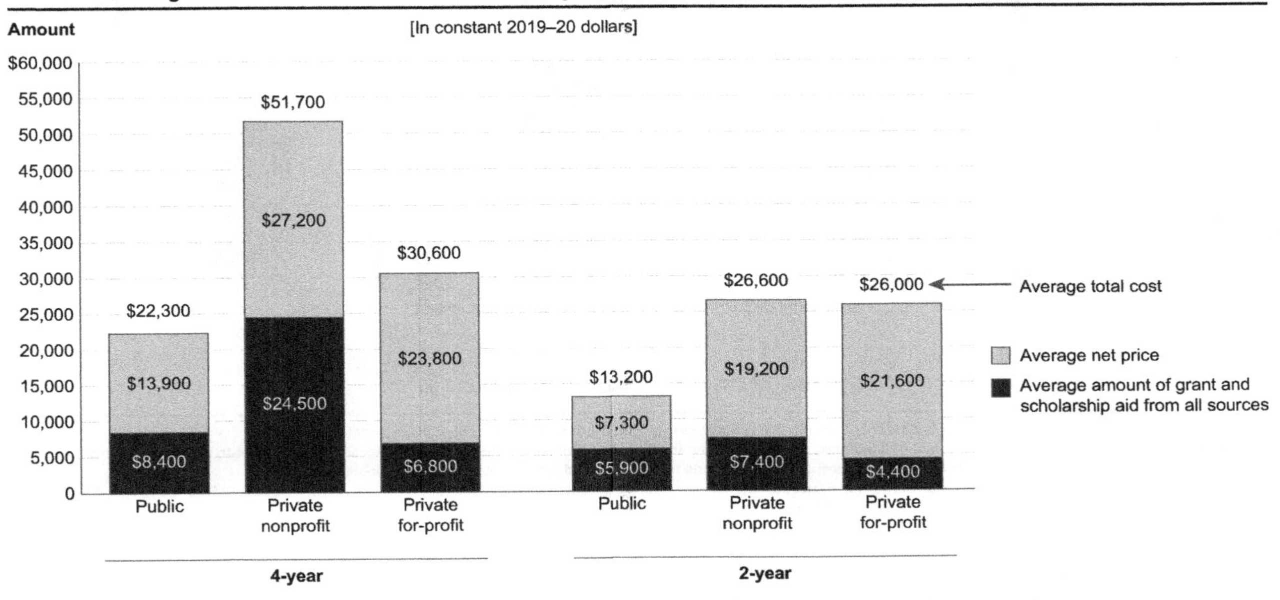

NOTE: Data are for the 50 states and the District of Columbia. Excludes students who previously attended another postsecondary institution or who began their studies on a part-time basis. Average net price is calculated here as the average total cost of attendance minus average grant and scholarship aid. Includes only first-time, full-time students who paid the in-district or in-state tuition rate and who were awarded Title IV aid. Excludes students who were not awarded any Title IV aid. Title IV aid includes grant aid, work-study aid, and loan aid. Grant and scholarship aid consists of federal Title IV grants, as well as other grant or scholarship aid from the federal government, state or local governments, or institutional sources. Data are weighted by the number of students at the institution who were awarded Title IV aid. Constant dollars are based on the Consumer Price Index, prepared by the Bureau of Labor Statistics, U.S. Department of Labor, adjusted to an academic-year basis. Although rounded numbers are displayed, the figures are based on unrounded data. Detail may not sum to totals because of rounding.
SOURCE: U.S. Department of Education, National Center for Education Statistics, Integrated Postsecondary Education Data System (IPEDS), Winter 2019–20, Student Financial Aid component. See *Digest of Education Statistics 2020*, table 331.30.

Grants and loans are the major forms of federal financial aid for first-time, full-time degree/certificate-seeking undergraduate students.[46] In academic year 2018-19, the percentage of first-time, full-time degree/certificate-seeking undergraduate students at 4-year institutions who were awarded specific types of financial aid varied according to institutional control. The percentages of students awarded aid in the form of federal grants and student loans were highest at private for-profit institutions (65 and 70 percent, respectively), the percentage of students awarded state or local aid was highest at public institutions (38 percent), and the percentage of students awarded institutional grants was highest at private nonprofit institutions (83 percent) (figure 19) (Sources of Financial Aid).

[46] Grants and loans are distinct forms of financial aid—loans typically have to be repaid whereas grants do not.

Figure 19. Percentage of first-time, full-time undergraduate students awarded financial aid at 4-year degree-granting postsecondary institutions, by type of financial aid and control of institution: Academic year 2018–19

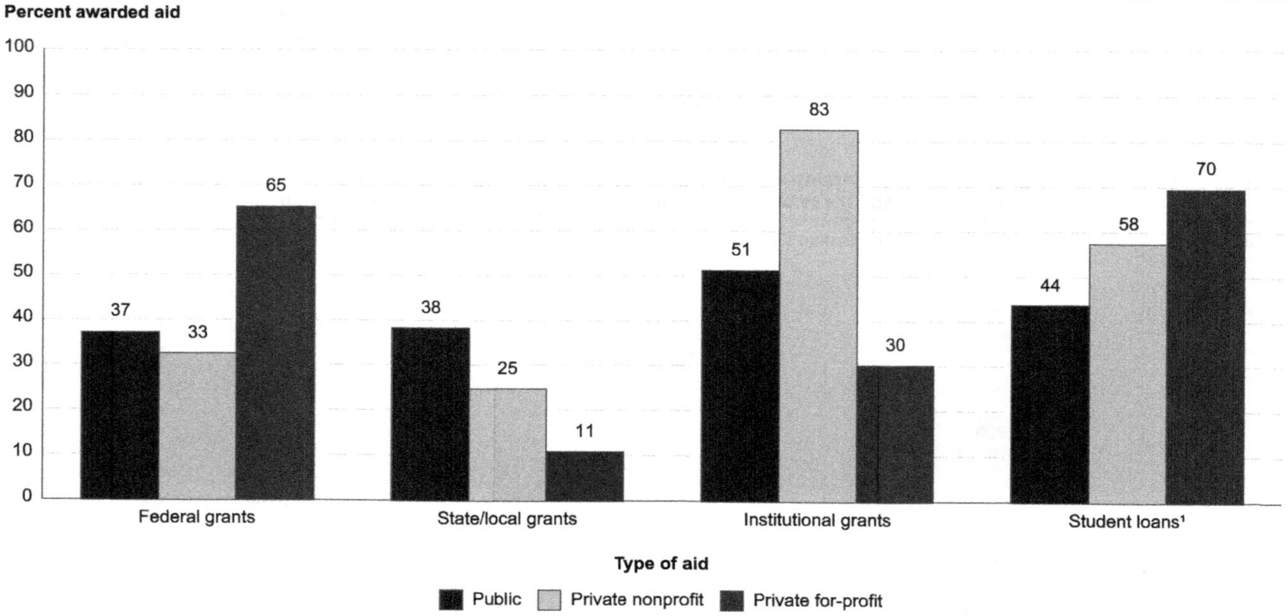

Type of aid	Public	Private nonprofit	Private for-profit
Federal grants	37	33	65
State/local grants	38	25	11
Institutional grants	51	83	30
Student loans[1]	44	58	70

Percent awarded aid; Type of aid

[1] Student loans include only loans made directly to students; they do not include Parent PLUS Loans or other loans made directly to parents.
NOTE: Data represent the 50 states and the District of Columbia. Degree-granting institutions grant associate's or higher degrees and participate in Title IV federal financial aid programs. Student financial aid includes any federal and private loans to students and federal, state/local, and institutional grants.
SOURCE: U.S. Department of Education, National Center for Education Statistics, Integrated Postsecondary Education Data System (IPEDS), Winter 2019–20, Student Financial Aid component. See *Digest of Education Statistics 2020*, table 331.20.

In 2018-19, total revenues at degree-granting postsecondary institutions in the United States were $672 billion (in current dollars). Total revenues were $416 billion at public institutions, $242 billion at private nonprofit institutions, and $14 billion at private for-profit institutions. The primary sources[47] of revenue for degree-granting postsecondary institutions in 2018-19 were tuition and fees; investments;[48] and government grants, contracts, and appropriations; and auxiliary enterprises.[49] Public institutions received the largest proportion of their revenues from government sources (including federal, state, and local government[50] grants, contracts, and appropriations), which constituted 41 percent of their overall revenues, while student tuition and fees constituted the largest primary source of revenue at private for-profit institutions (91 percent). At private nonprofit institutions, the category of all other revenue sources (including gifts, capital or private grants and contracts, hospital revenue, sales and services of educational activities, and other revenue) constituted 36 percent of overall revenues, and student tuition and fees constituted 32 percent of overall revenues (Postsecondary Institution Revenues).

In 2018-19, degree-granting postsecondary institutions in the United States[51] spent $632 billion (in current dollars). Total expenses were $401 billion at public institutions, $219 billion at private nonprofit institutions, and $12 billion at private for-profit institutions. In 2018-19, instruction expenses per full-time-equivalent (FTE) student (in constant 2019-20 dollars) was the largest expense category at public institutions ($11,010) and private nonprofit institutions ($19,150). At private for-profit institutions, the combined category of academic support, student services, and institutional support expenses was the largest category of expenses per FTE student ($10,930) (Postsecondary Institution Expenses).

[47] Revenues from all other sources are grouped into a broad "other" category. This category includes gifts, capital or private grants and contracts, hospital revenue, sales and services of educational activities, and other revenue.

[48] Investments/investment returns are aggregate amounts of dividends, interest, royalties, rent, and gains or losses from both fair-value adjustments and trades of institutions' investments and/or endowments.

[49] Auxiliary enterprises, such as residence halls and food services, are essentially self-supporting operations of institutions that furnish a service to students, faculty, or staff.

[50] Private grants and contracts are included in local government revenues at public institutions.

[51] Data represent the 50 states and the District of Columbia.

Population Characteristics and Economic Outcomes

Individuals' levels of educational attainment are related to economic outcomes. As such, this section of the Condition of Education Indicator System first reports educational attainment in the United States. The remainder of indicators in this section of the Condition of Education Indicator System examine further the relationship between educational attainment and labor force outcomes, such as median earnings and unemployment rates.

Rates of educational attainment have increased at all levels in the United States between 2010 and 2020. Generally, those with higher educational attainments had higher median earnings in 2019 and had higher rates of employment in March 2020.

Educational Attainment of Young Adults

Between 2010 and 2020, educational attainment rates among 25- to 29-year-olds increased at each attainment level.[52] During this period, the percentage who had completed at least high school increased from 89 to 95 percent, the percentage with an associate's or higher degree increased from 41 to 50 percent, the percentage with a bachelor's or higher degree increased from 32 to 39 percent, and the percentage with a master's or higher degree increased from 7 to 9 percent (figure 20).

In general, educational attainment rates during this time period increased for both male and female 25- to 29-year-olds as well as for those of various racial/ethnic groups. For example, the percentages who had completed at least high school increased for those who were Asian (from 94 to 97 percent), White (from 95 to 96 percent), Black (from 90 to 95 percent), and Hispanic (from 69 to 90 percent) during this period. Similarly, the percentages of individuals who had attained a bachelor's or higher degree increased between 2010 and 2020 for those who were Asian (from 56 to 72 percent), White (from 39 to 45 percent), Black (from 19 to 28 percent), and Hispanic (from 13 to 25 percent) (Educational Attainment of Young Adults).

Figure 20. Percentage of 25- to 29-year-olds, by educational attainment and sex: 2010 and 2020

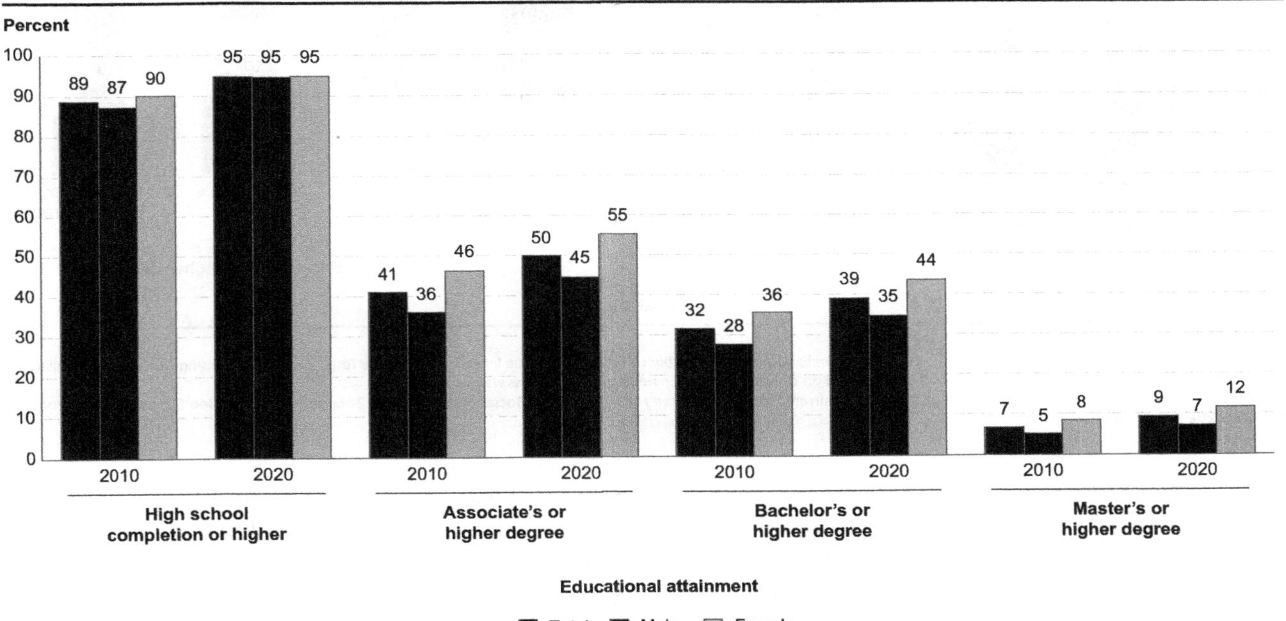

NOTE: Data were collected in March of each year and are based on sample surveys of the noninstitutionalized population, which excludes persons living in institutions (e.g., prisons or nursing facilities); data include military personnel who live in households with civilians, but exclude those who live in military barracks. High school completion includes those who graduated from high school with a diploma as well as those who completed high school through equivalency programs, such as a GED program. Caution should be used when comparing 2020 estimates to those of prior years due to the impact that the coronavirus pandemic had on interviewing and response rates in 2020. For additional information about the impact of the coronavirus pandemic on the Current Population Survey data collection, please see https://www2.census.gov/programs-surveys/cps/techdocs/cpsmar20.pdf. Although rounded numbers are displayed, the figures are based on unrounded data.
SOURCE: U.S. Department of Commerce, Census Bureau, Current Population Survey (CPS), Annual Social and Economic Supplement, 2010 and 2020. See *Digest of Education Statistics 2020*, table 104.20.

[52] *Educational attainment* refers to the highest level of education completed by the time of the survey (reported here as high school completion or higher, an associate's or higher degree, a bachelor's or higher degree, or a master's or higher degree).

Economic Outcomes

In March 2020, the employment rate was higher for those with higher levels of educational attainment. For example, the employment rate was highest for 25- to 34-year-olds with a bachelor's or higher degree (86 percent). The employment rate for those with some college (78 percent) was higher than the rate for those who had only completed high school (69 percent), which was higher than the employment rate for those who had not completed high school (57 percent). The same pattern was observed among both sexes. For example, the employment rate for females was highest for those with a bachelor's or higher degree (83 percent) and lowest for those who had not completed high school (41 percent). These data reference the period of early pandemic-related labor market impacts, just prior to the first major U.S. business and school closures (*Employment and Unemployment Rates by Educational Attainment*).

Figure 21. Median annual earnings of full-time, year-round workers ages 25–34, by educational attainment: 2019

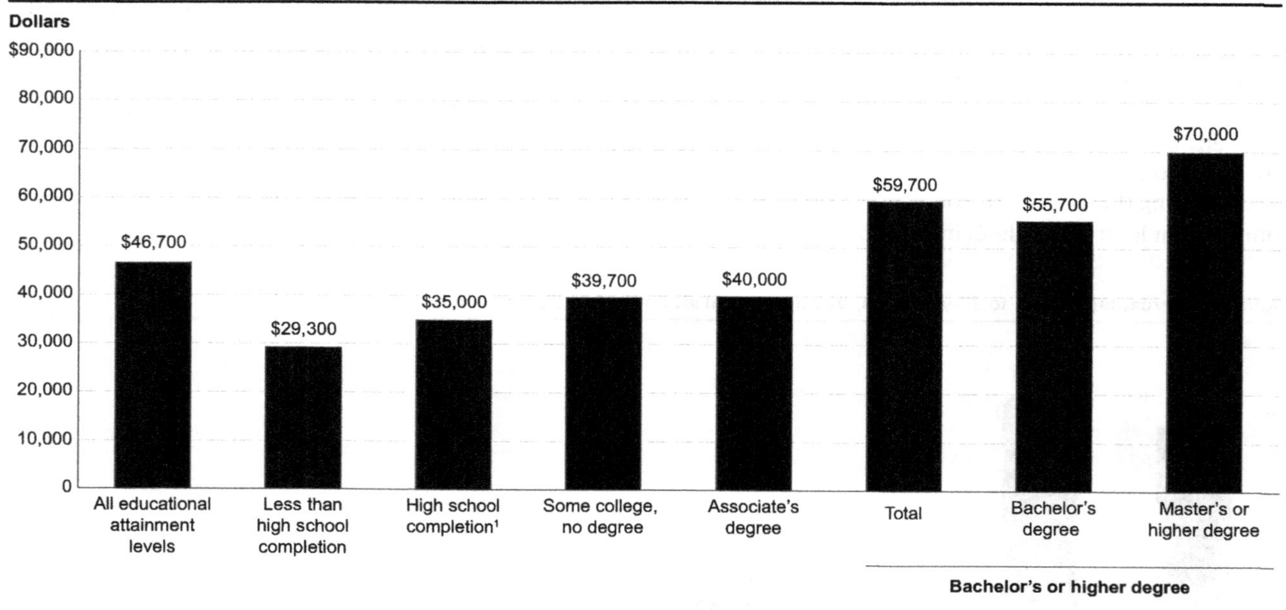

[1] Includes equivalency credentials, such as the GED.
NOTE: Data are based on sample surveys of the noninstitutionalized population, which excludes persons living in institutions (e.g., prisons or nursing facilities) and military barracks. *Full-time, year-round* workers are those who worked 35 or more hours per week for 50 or more weeks per year.
SOURCE: U.S. Department of Commerce, Census Bureau, Current Population Survey (CPS), Annual Social and Economic Supplement, 2020. See *Digest of Education Statistics 2020*, table 502.30.

For 25- to 34-year-olds who worked full time, year round, higher educational attainment was also associated with higher median earnings. This pattern was consistent from 2010 through 2019. For example, in 2019 the median earnings of those with a master's or higher degree ($70,000) were 26 percent higher than the earnings of those with a bachelor's degree ($55,700), and the median earnings of those with a bachelor's degree were 59 percent higher than the earnings of those who completed high school ($35,000) (figure 21) (*Annual Earnings by Educational Attainment*).

International Comparisons

Another way to assess the condition of education in the United States is to benchmark our performance on key indicators against peer countries. The indicators in this section of the Condition of Education Indicator System compare the U.S. education system to the education systems in other countries with respect to enrollment rates, student performance on international assessments, education expenditures, and educational attainment. This *Report on the Condition of Education* highlights key findings on international assessments and attainment.

The United States scored in the top 25 percent of participating education systems in both mathematics and science at both the 4th and 8th grade levels according to the 2019 Trends in International Mathematics and Science Study (TIMSS). Additionally, with more than 90 percent of 25- to 64-year-olds having completed a high school degree,[53] the United States was among the top 6 out of 35 countries in 2019 reporting data on educational attainment rates to the Organization for Economic Cooperation and Development.

Assessments

The Trends in International Mathematics and Science Study (TIMSS) is an international comparative study that has measured trends in mathematics and science achievement at 4th and 8th grade every 4 years since 1995. In 2019, TIMSS mathematics and science data were collected by 64 education systems at 4th grade and 46 education systems at 8th grade.

At grade 4, both the U.S. average mathematics score (535) and the U.S. average science score (539) in 2019 were higher than the TIMSS scale centerpoint (500 for both assessments).[54] In mathematics, 14 education systems had higher average mathematics scores than the United States, 7 had scores that were not measurably different, and 42 education systems had lower average scores. In science, 7 education systems had higher average science scores than the United States, 9 had scores that were not measurably different, and 47 education systems had lower average scores.

Similarly, at grade 8, both the U.S. average mathematics score (515) and the U.S. average science score (522) in 2019 were higher than the TIMSS scale centerpoint (500 for both assessments). In mathematics, 10 education systems had higher average mathematics scores than the United States, 7 had scores that were not measurably different, and 28 education systems had lower average scores (figure 22). In science, 10 education systems had higher average science scores than the United States, 9 had scores that were not measurably different, and 26 education systems had lower average scores (figure 23) (International Comparisons: Mathematics and Science Achievement at Grades 4 and 8).

[53] In this section, *high school degree* refers to degrees classified as ISCED 2011 level 3, which generally corresponds to high school completion in the United States, with some exceptions.

[54] TIMSS scores are reported on a scale from 0 to 1,000, with a scale centerpoint set at 500 and the standard deviation set at 100. The TIMSS scale centerpoint represents the mean of the overall achievement distribution in 1995. The TIMSS scale is the same in each administration; thus, a value of 500 in 2019 equals 500 in 1995 when that was the international average.

Figure 22. Average scores and 10th and 90th percentile scores of 8th-grade students on the TIMSS mathematics scale and percentile score gaps, by education system: 2019

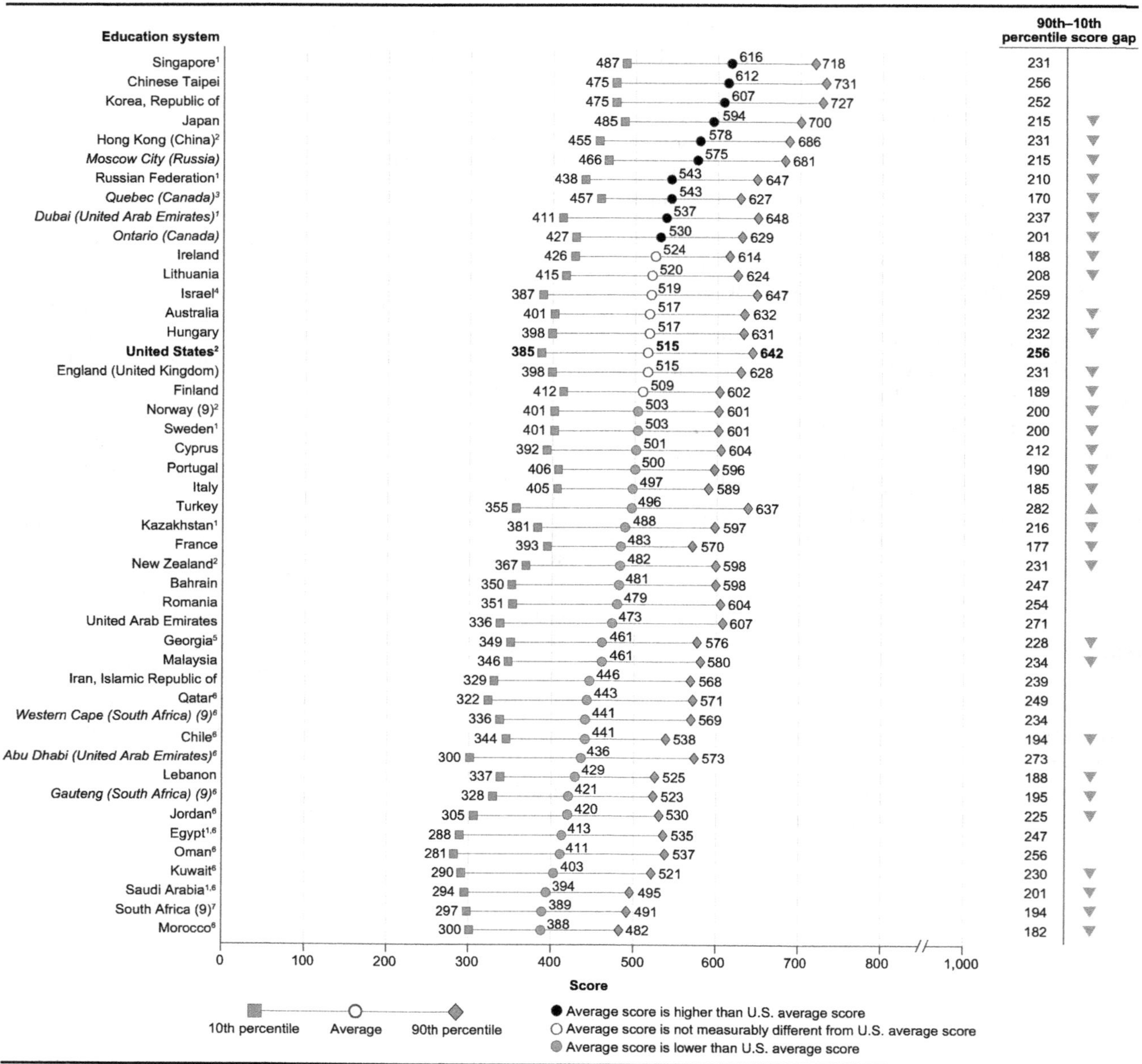

▲ 90th to 10th percentile score gap is higher than the U.S. score gap.
▼ 90th to 10th percentile score gap is lower than the U.S. score gap.

[1] National Defined Population covers 90 to 95 percent of the National Target Population, as defined by TIMSS.
[2] Met guidelines for sample participation rates only after replacement schools were included.
[3] Nearly satisfied guidelines for sample participation rates after replacement schools were included.
[4] National Defined Population covers less than 90 percent of the National Target Population (but at least 77 percent), as defined by TIMSS.
[5] National Target Population does not include all of the International Target Population, as defined by TIMSS.
[6] Reservations about reliability because the percentage of students with achievement too low for estimation exceeds 15 percent but does not exceed 25 percent.
[7] Reservations about reliability because the percentage of students with achievement too low for estimation exceeds 25 percent.

NOTE: In addition to average scores, this figure shows the scores for the (a) 10th percentile—the bottom 10 percent of students; and (b) 90th percentile—the top 10 percent of students. The percentile ranges are specific to each education system's distribution of scores, enabling users to compare scores across education systems. Education systems are ordered by average score. Education systems that are not countries are designated by their country in parentheses. Benchmarking participants are indicated with italics. For education systems with a "(9)" after their name, 9 indicates the years of formal schooling; these education systems chose to administer TIMSS at a different grade than other education systems (8 years of formal schooling). The TIMSS scale centerpoint is set at 500 and represents the mean of the overall achievement distribution in 1995. The standard deviation is set to 100. The TIMSS scale is the same in each administration (0 to 1,000 points); thus, a value of 500 in 2019 equals 500 in 1995. Although rounded numbers are displayed, data shown are based on unrounded estimates.

SOURCE: International Association for the Evaluation of Educational Achievement (IEA), Trends in International Mathematics and Science Study (TIMSS), 2019. See *TIMSS 2019 U.S. Highlights Web Report*, table M2b.

Figure 23. Average scores and 10th and 90th percentile scores of 8th-grade students on the TIMSS science scale and percentile score gaps, by education system: 2019

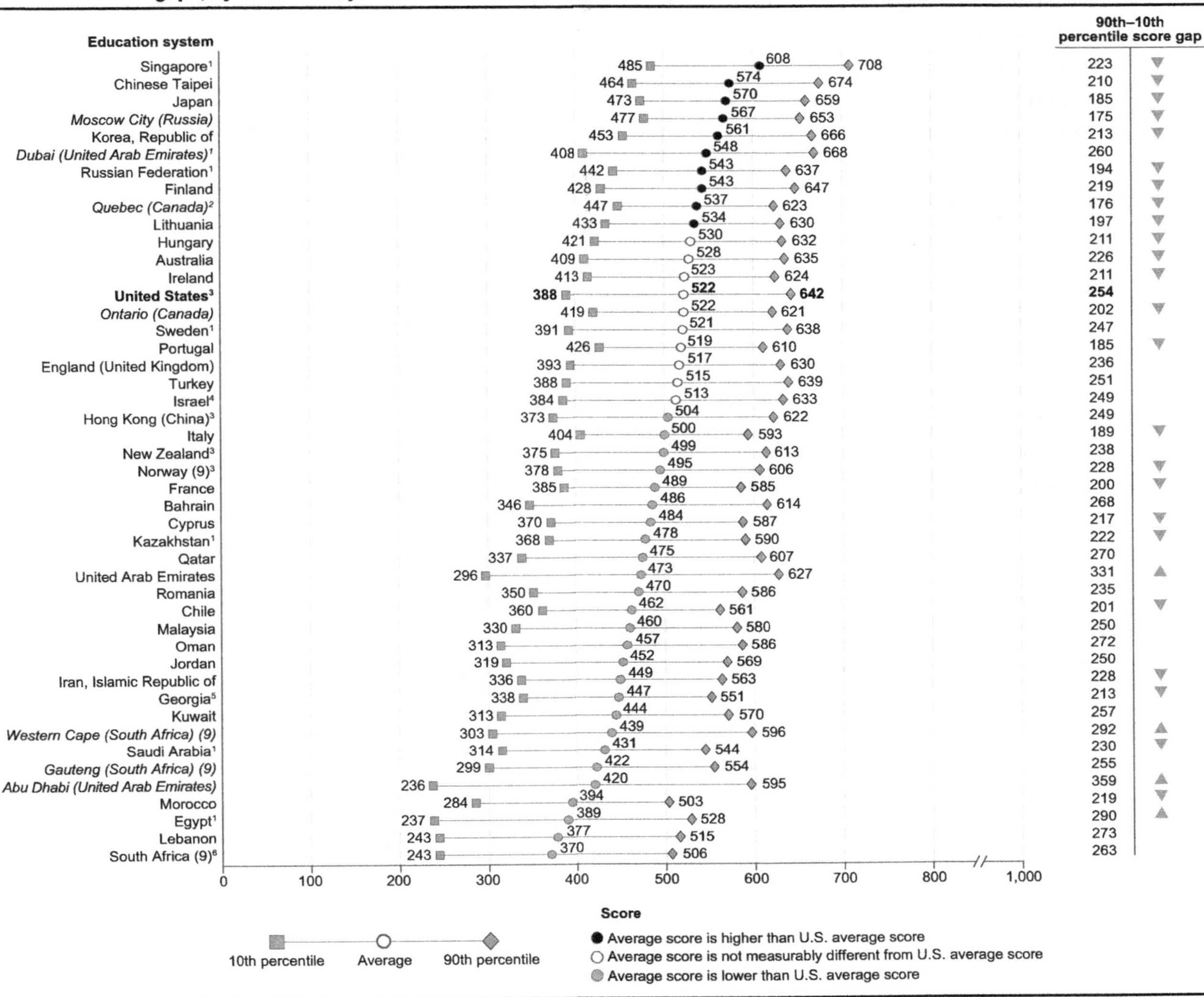

▲ 90th to 10th percentile score gap is higher than the U.S. score gap.
▼ 90th to 10th percentile score gap is lower than the U.S. score gap.
[1] National Defined Population covers 90 to 95 percent of the National Target Population, as defined by TIMSS.
[2] Nearly satisfied guidelines for sample participation rates after replacement schools were included.
[3] Met guidelines for sample participation rates only after replacement schools were included.
[4] National Defined Population covers less than 90 percent of the National Target Population (but at least 77 percent), as defined by TIMSS.
[5] National Target Population does not include all of the International Target Population, as defined by TIMSS.
[6] Reservations about reliability because the percentage of students with achievement too low for estimation exceeds 15 percent but does not exceed 25 percent.
NOTE: In addition to average scores, this figure shows the scores for the (a) 10th percentile—the bottom 10 percent of students; and (b) 90th percentile—the top 10 percent of students. The percentile ranges are specific to each education system's distribution of scores, enabling users to compare scores across education systems. Education systems are ordered by average score. Education systems that are not countries are designated by their country in parentheses. Benchmarking participants are indicated with italics. For education systems with a "(9)" after their name, 9 indicates the years of formal schooling; these education systems chose to administer TIMSS at a different grade than other education systems (8 years of formal schooling). The TIMSS scale centerpoint is set at 500 and represents the mean of the overall achievement distribution in 1995. The standard deviation is set to 100. The TIMSS scale is the same in each administration (0 to 1,000 points); thus, a value of 500 in 2019 equals 500 in 1995. Although rounded numbers are displayed, data shown are based on unrounded estimates.
SOURCE: International Association for the Evaluation of Educational Achievement (IEA), Trends in International Mathematics and Science Study (TIMSS), 2019. See *TIMSS 2019 U.S. Highlights Web Report*, table S2b.

Attainment

In 2019, some 91 percent of 25- to 64-year-olds in the United States had a high school diploma or its equivalent. In comparison, the average rate for the Organization for Economic Cooperation and Development (OECD) member countries was 80 percent. Among the 35 countries for which the OECD reported 2019 data on high school completion rates, the percentages of 25- to 64-year-olds who had completed high school ranged from 40 percent in Mexico to 90 percent or more in eight countries (Estonia, Finland, the United States, the Slovak Republic, Canada, Poland, Lithuania, and the Czech Republic).

Additionally, 48 percent of 25- to 64-year-olds in the United States had obtained a postsecondary degree, compared with the OECD average of 38 percent. Among the 36 countries for which the OECD reported 2019 data on postsecondary attainment rates, the percentages earning any postsecondary degree ranged from less than 20 percent in Mexico and Italy to 50 percent or more in five countries (Korea, Israel, Luxembourg, Japan and Canada). Nineteen countries, including the United States, reported that 40 percent or more in this age range had earned any postsecondary degree as of 2019.

For 25- to 34-year-olds–that is, the younger age group whose educational attainment is likely to reflect more recent shifts in educational and economic systems–the OECD average percentage who had completed high school rose from 82 to 85 percent between 2010 and 2019, while the corresponding percentage for the United States increased from 88 to 93 percent. In addition, the OECD average percentage with any postsecondary degree rose from 38 percent in 2010 to 45 percent in 2019, while the corresponding percentage in the United States rose from 42 to 50 percent (*International Educational Attainment*).

Irwin, V., J. Zhang, X. Wang, et al. "Report on the Condition of Education 2021." National Center for Education Statistics, May 25, 2021. https://nces.ed.gov/pubs2021/2021144.pdf. Accessed August 9, 2021.

Report on Indicators of School Crime and Safety: 2020

NCES 2021-092
U.S. DEPARTMENT OF EDUCATION

NCJ 300772
U.S. DEPARTMENT OF JUSTICE
OFFICE OF JUSTICE PROGRAMS

A Publication of the National Center for Education Statistics at IES

Violent Deaths and School Shootings

Violent deaths and shootings at schools are rare but tragic events with far-reaching effects on the school population and surrounding community. Based on the most recent data released by the School-Associated Violent Death Surveillance System (SAVD-SS), there were a total of 56 school-associated violent deaths[2] in the United States in the 2017-18 school year,[3] which included 46 homicides, 9 suicides, and 1 legal intervention death.[4] Of these 56 school-associated violent deaths, 35 were homicides and 8 were suicides of school-age youth (ages 5-18). (Violent Deaths at School and Away From School and School Shootings)

In the K-12 School Shooting Database (K-12 SSDB), school shootings are defined as incidents in which a gun is brandished or fired on school property or a bullet hits school property for any reason, regardless of the number of victims, time of day, day of the week, or reason. Between 2000-01 and 2019-20, the number of school shootings with casualties per year at public and private elementary and secondary schools ranged from 11 to 75 (figure 1).[5] In 2019-20, there were a total of 75 school shootings with casualties, including 27 school shootings with deaths and 48 school shootings with injuries only. In addition, there were 37 reported school shootings with no casualties in 2019-20. The majority of school shootings (including those with and without casualties) occurred at high schools.[6] (Violent Deaths at School and Away From School and School Shootings)

Figure 1. Number of school shootings with casualties at public and private elementary and secondary schools: 2000–01 through 2019–20

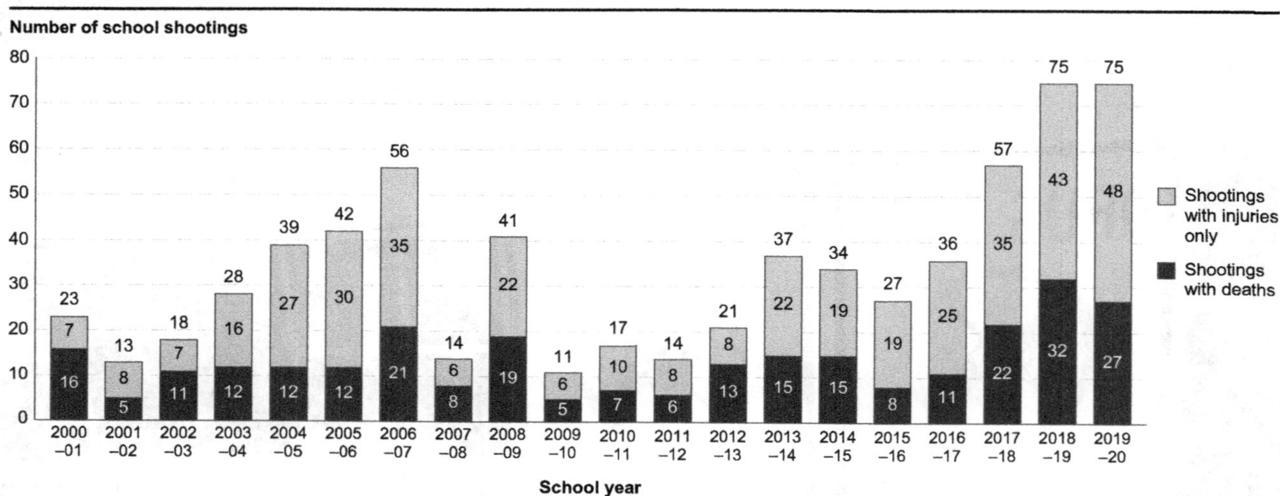

NOTE: "School shootings" include all incidents in which a gun is brandished or fired or a bullet hits school property for any reason, regardless of the number of victims (including zero), time, day of the week, or reason (e.g., planned attack, accidental, domestic violence, gang-related). Data in this figure were generated using a database that aims to compile information on school shootings from publicly available sources into a single comprehensive resource. For information on database methodology, see *K–12 School Shooting Database: Research Methodology* (https://www.chds.us/ssdb/resources/uploads/2020/09/CHDS-K12-SSDB-Research-Methods-Sept-2020.pdf). Due to school closures caused by the coronavirus pandemic, caution should be used when comparing 2019–20 data with data from earlier years. Some data have been revised from previously published figures.
SOURCE: U.S. Department of Defense, Naval Postgraduate School, Center for Homeland Defense and Security, K–12 School Shooting Database. Retrieved September 4, 2019, from https://www.chds.us/ssdb/. See *Digest of Education Statistics 2020*, table 228.12.

[2] The SAVD-SS defines a school-associated violent death as "a homicide, suicide, or legal intervention death (involving a law enforcement officer), in which the fatal injury occurred on the campus of a functioning elementary or secondary school in the United States." School-associated violent deaths also include those that occurred while the victim was on the way to or from regular sessions at school or while the victim was attending or traveling to or from an official school-sponsored event. Victims of school-associated violent deaths may include not only students and staff members but also others at school, such as students' parents and community members.

[3] Defined as the period from July 1, 2017, through June 30, 2018.

[4] Data are subject to change until law enforcement reports have been obtained and interviews with school and law enforcement officials have been completed. The details learned during the interviews can occasionally change the classification of a case.

[5] Due to school closures caused by the coronavirus pandemic, caution should be used when comparing 2019-20 data with data from earlier years.

[6] Includes other schools ending in grade 12.

Criminal Victimization Experienced by Students

Data from the National Crime Victimization Survey (NCVS) provide insights on nonfatal criminal victimization experienced by students ages 12-18, according to students' own reports. Nonfatal criminal victimization includes theft[7] and violent victimization, the latter of which includes rape, sexual assault, robbery, aggravated assault, and simple assault. In 2019, students ages 12-18 experienced 764,600 victimizations at school[8] and 509,300 victimizations away from school. This translates to a rate of 30 victimizations per 1,000 students at school, which was higher than the rate of 20 victimizations per 1,000 students away from school (figure 2). Both the at-school rate and the away-from-school rate represent a decrease of more than 80 percent from 1992. (*Incidence of Victimization at School and Away From School*)

According to data from the School Crime Supplement (SCS) to NCVS,[9] the total percentage of students ages 12-18 who reported being victimized at school during the previous 6 months decreased from 4 percent in 2009 to 2 percent in 2019. Specifically, SCS data indicate that, in 2019, about 2 percent of students reported theft[10] and 1 percent reported violent victimization. (*Prevalence of Criminal Victimization at School*)

In 2019, the percentage of students ages 12-18 who reported any victimization at school during the previous 6 months was higher for 6th-, 7th-, 9th-, and 10th-graders (3 percent each) than for 12th-graders (1 percent); the percentage was also higher for students of Two or more races (7 percent) than for Hispanic students (2 percent) and higher for students enrolled in schools in cities (3 percent) than for students enrolled in schools in suburban areas (2 percent; figure 3). A higher percentage of male students than of female students reported any victimization at school (3 vs. 2 percent), which was driven largely by a higher percentage of male students reporting violent victimization (2 percent vs. less than 1 percent). (*Prevalence of Criminal Victimization at School*)

[7] "Theft" includes attempted and completed purse-snatching, completed pickpocketing, and all attempted and completed thefts, with the exception of motor vehicle thefts. Theft does not include robbery, which involves the threat or use of force and is classified as a violent crime.

[8] "At school" is defined to include in the school building, on school property, on a school bus, and going to and from school.

[9] Respondent eligibility differs slightly in the NCVS and SCS. For example, students who are exclusively homeschooled are able to complete the NCVS but not the SCS. Thus, the calculation of estimates presented in this paragraph is based on a subset of the student sample used to calculate the estimates presented in the previous paragraph.

[10] Although the total percentage of students ages 12-18 who reported being victimized (which includes theft and violent victimization) and the percentage who reported theft both rounded to 2 percent in 2019, about 2.5 percent reported being victimized and 1.5 percent reported theft.

Figure 2. Rate of nonfatal victimization against students ages 12–18 per 1,000 students, by location: 1992 through 2019

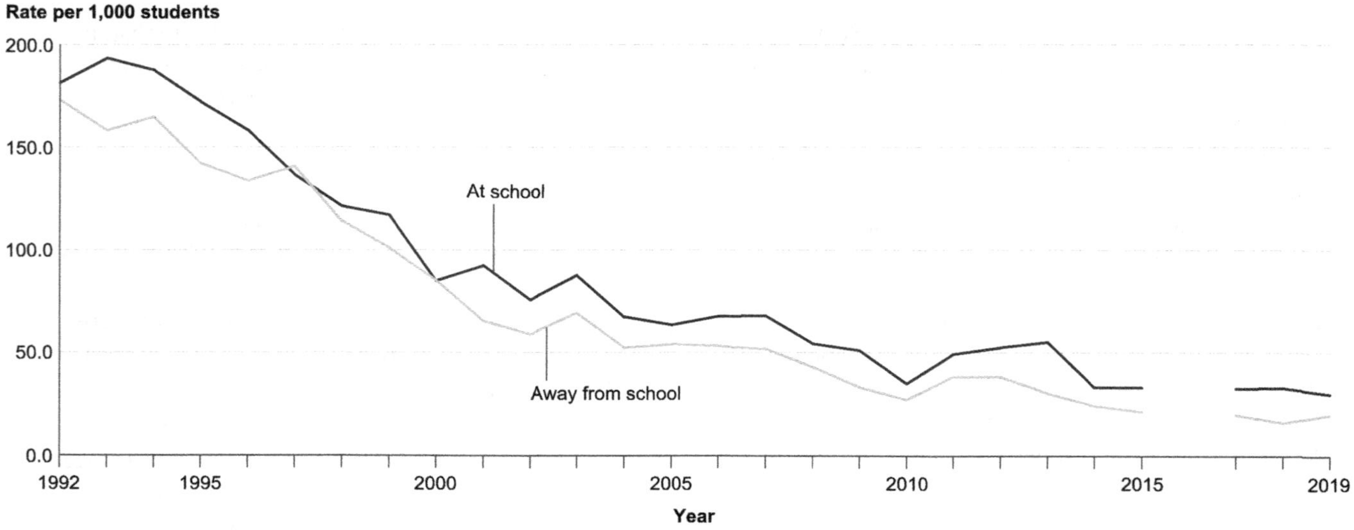

NOTE: Every 10 years, the National Crime Victimization Survey (NCVS) sample is redesigned to reflect changes in the population. Due to the sample redesign and other methodological changes implemented in 2006, use caution when comparing 2006 estimates with other years. Due to a sample increase and redesign in 2016, victimization estimates among youth in 2016 were not comparable to estimates for other years. Nonfatal victimization includes theft, rape, sexual assault, robbery, aggravated assault, and simple assault. "At school" includes in the school building, on school property, and on the way to or from school. The population size for students ages 12–18 was 25,528,100 in 2019. Estimates may vary from previously published reports.

SOURCE: U.S. Department of Justice, Bureau of Justice Statistics, National Crime Victimization Survey (NCVS), 1992 through 2019. See *Digest of Education Statistics 2020*, table 228.20.

Figure 3. Percentage of students ages 12–18 who reported criminal victimization at school during the previous 6 months, by selected student and school characteristics: 2019

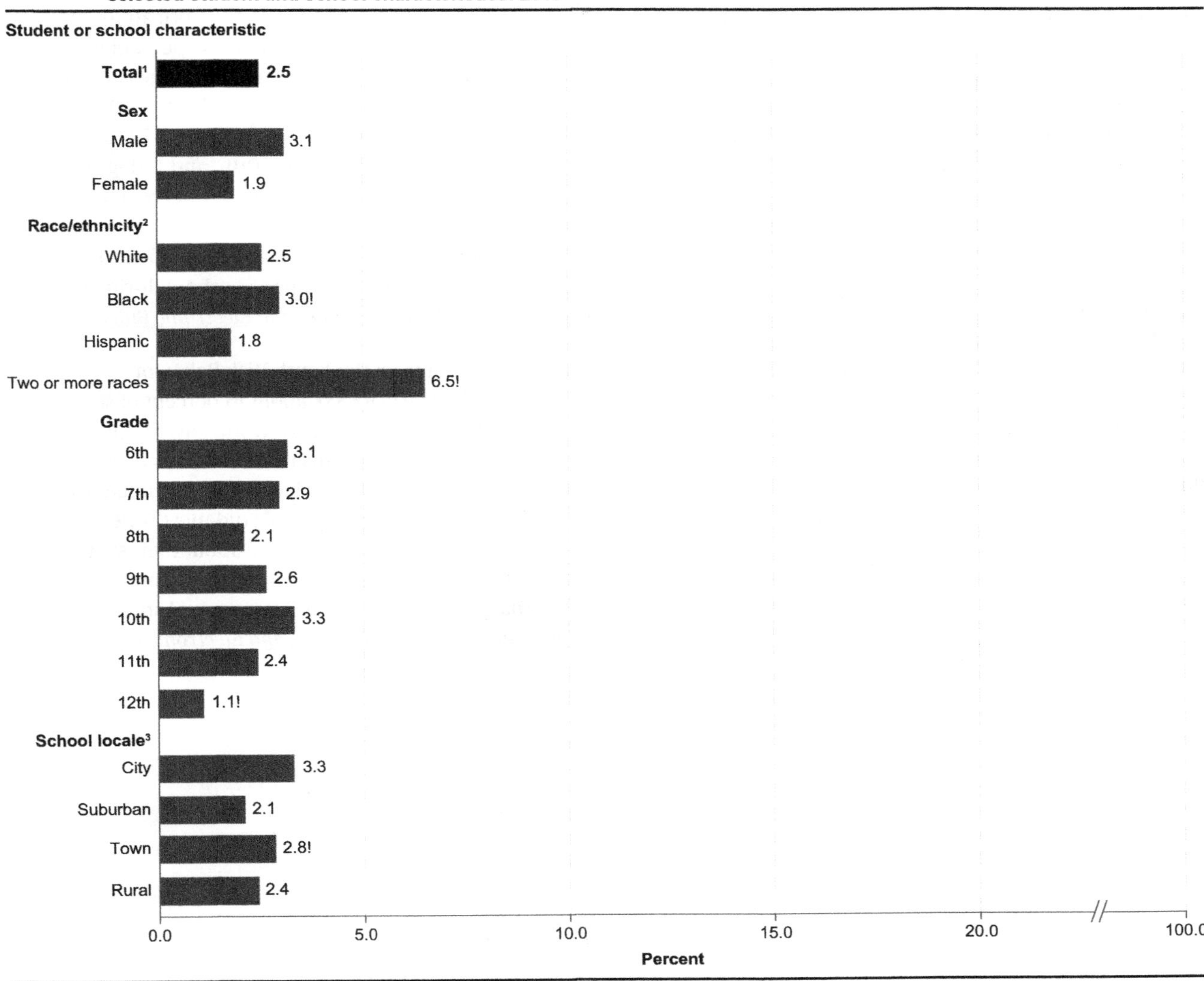

! Interpret data with caution. The coefficient of variation (CV) for this estimate is between 30 and 50 percent.
[1] Total includes race categories not separately shown.
[2] Race categories exclude persons of Hispanic ethnicity. Data for Asian, Pacific Islander, and American Indian/Alaska Native students did not meet reporting standards in 2019; therefore, data for these three groups are not shown.
[3] Excludes students with missing information about the school characteristic.
NOTE: Criminal victimization includes theft and violent victimization. "At school" includes in the school building, on school property, on a school bus, and going to and from school.
SOURCE: U.S. Department of Justice, Bureau of Justice Statistics, School Crime Supplement (SCS) to the National Crime Victimization Survey, 2019. See *Digest of Education Statistics 2020*, table 228.30.

Student Reports of Bullying Victimization

Another type of student victimization that is important to understand is bullying. Previous research has found that students who are bullied are more likely to experience depression and anxiety, have more health complaints, and skip or drop out of school (Swearer and Hymel 2015; Hornor 2018). The involvement of young bullying victims in recent suicides and school shootings has also heightened concerns regarding the public health implications of bullying (Hornor 2018).

According to data from the SCS, about 22 percent of students ages 12-18 reported being bullied[11] at school during the school year in 2019, which was lower than the percentage who reported being bullied in 2009 (28 percent). Students' reports of being bullied varied based on student and school characteristics in 2019 (figure 4). For instance, a higher percentage of female students than of male students reported being bullied at school during the school year (25 vs. 19 percent). The percentage of students who reported being bullied at school during the school year was higher for students of Two or more races (37 percent) than for White students (25 percent) and Black students (22 percent); all these percentages were in turn higher than the percentage of Asian students (13 percent). Higher percentages of 6th-, 7th-, and 8th-graders reported being bullied at school during the school year in 2019 (ranging from 27 to 28 percent), compared with 9th-, 10th-, and 12th-graders (ranging from 16 to 19 percent). A higher percentage of students enrolled in schools in rural areas (28 percent) than in schools in other locales (ranging from 21 to 22 percent) reported being bullied at school during the school year. (Bullying at School and Electronic Bullying)

According to data from the Youth Risk Behavior Surveillance System (YRBSS), about 16 percent of students in grades 9-12 reported being electronically[12] bullied during the previous 12 months in 2019. The percentage of students who reported being electronically bullied was higher for gay, lesbian, or bisexual students (27 percent) than for students who were not sure about their sexual identity (19 percent), and both percentages were higher than the percentage for heterosexual students (14 percent).[13] (Bullying at School and Electronic Bullying)

[11] "Bullying" includes students who reported that another student had made fun of them, called them names, or insulted them; spread rumors about them; threatened them with harm; tried to make them do something they did not want to do; excluded them from activities on purpose; destroyed their property on purpose; or pushed, shoved, tripped, or spit on them. In the total for students bullied at school, students who reported more than one type of bullying were counted only once.

[12] Being electronically bullied includes "being bullied through e-mail, chat rooms, instant messaging, websites, or texting" for 2011 through 2015, and "being bullied through texting, Instagram, Facebook, or other social media" for 2017 and 2019.

[13] Since 2015, the YRBSS has included a question on students' sexual identity by asking students in grades 9-12 which of the following best described them—"heterosexual (straight)," "gay or lesbian," "bisexual," or "not sure." In this report, students who identified as "gay or lesbian" or "bisexual" are discussed together as the "gay, lesbian, or bisexual" group. Students were not asked whether they identified as transgender on the YRBSS.

Figure 4. Percentage of students ages 12–18 who reported being bullied at school during the school year, by selected student and school characteristics: 2019

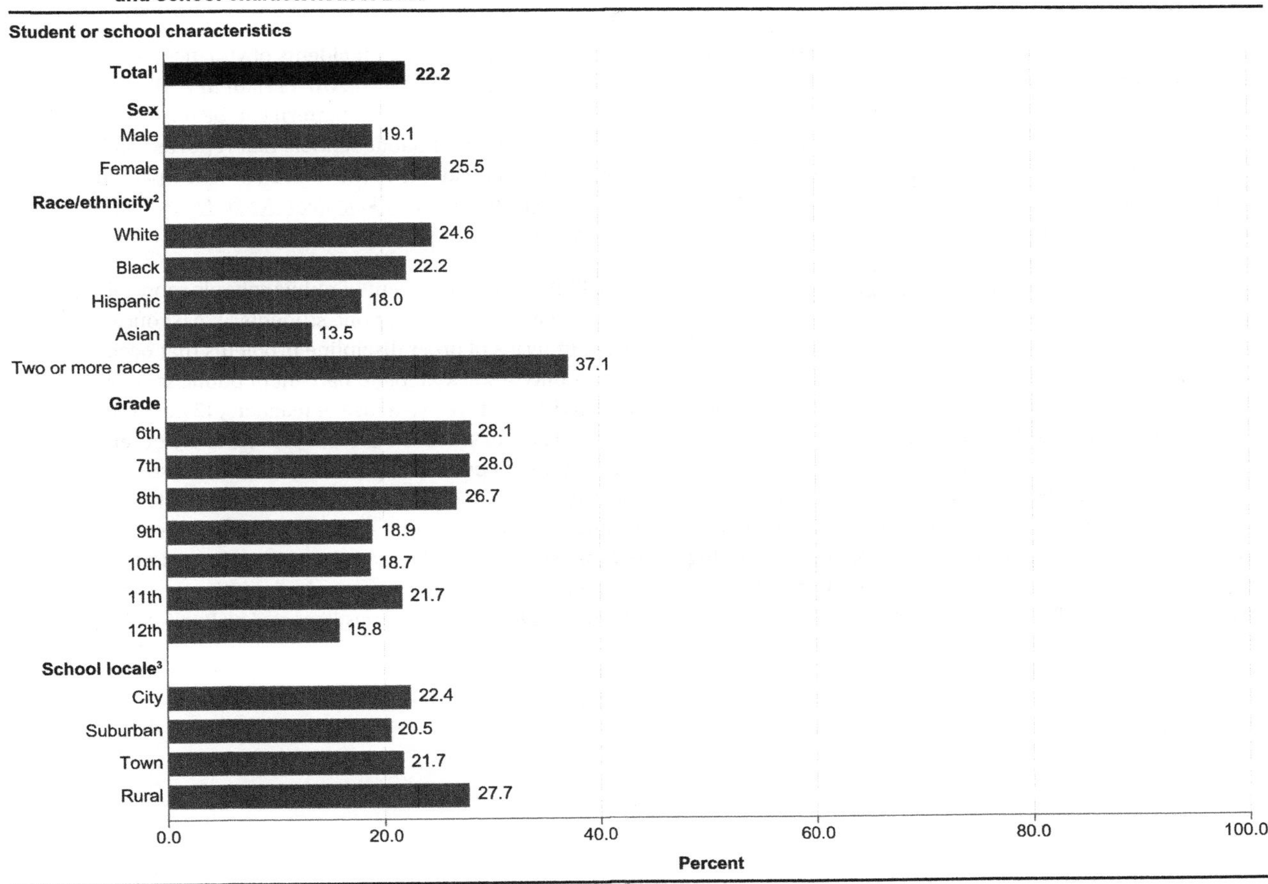

[1] Total includes race categories not separately shown.
[2] Race categories exclude persons of Hispanic ethnicity. Data for Pacific Islander and American Indian/Alaska Native students did not meet reporting standards in 2019; therefore, data for these two groups are not shown.
[3] Excludes students with missing information about the school characteristic.
NOTE: "At school" includes in the school building, on school property, on a school bus, and going to and from school. Although rounded numbers are displayed, the figures are based on unrounded data.
SOURCE: U.S. Department of Justice, Bureau of Justice Statistics, School Crime Supplement (SCS) to the National Crime Victimization Survey, 2019. See *Digest of Education Statistics 2020*, table 230.40.

Incidents and Discipline Problems Reported by Public Schools

Incidents and discipline problems recorded by schools are important measures of the school environment. The School Survey on Crime and Safety (SSOCS) asked public school principals to report the numbers of various types of criminal incidents that occurred at their school[14] and to indicate how often certain disciplinary problems happened in their school.[15] Such school-reported data can complement those data covering similar issues based on students' experience and observation, such as those collected through SCS and YRBSS.

During the 2017-18 school year, 80 percent of public schools recorded that one or more incidents of violence, theft, or other crimes[16] had taken place, amounting to 1.4 million incidents or a rate of 29 incidents per 1,000 students enrolled. During the same school year, 47 percent of schools reported one or more incidents of violence, theft, or other crimes to the police, amounting to 422,800 incidents, or a rate of 9 incidents per 1,000 students enrolled. The percentage of public schools that recorded one or more incidents of violence, theft, or other crimes was lower in 2017-18 than in 2009-10 (80 vs. 85 percent); the same pattern can be observed for the percentage of public schools that reported one or more criminal incidents to the police (47 vs. 60 percent). (Violent and Other Criminal Incidents Recorded by Public Schools and Those Reported to the Police)

In 2017-18, about 14 percent of public schools reported that bullying[17] occurred among students at least once a week. In terms of other discipline problems that occurred at least once a week, about 6 percent of public schools reported student verbal abuse of teachers; 12 percent reported acts of student disrespect for teachers other than verbal abuse; 3 percent reported widespread disorder in the classroom; 3 percent reported racial/ethnic tensions among students; 1 percent reported sexual harassment[18] of other students; and 1 percent reported harassment of other students based on sexual orientation or gender identity.[19] (Discipline Problems Reported by Public Schools)

[14] In SSOCS, "at school" was defined for respondents as including activities that happen in school buildings, on school grounds, on school buses, and at places that hold school-sponsored events or activities. In the survey questions about criminal incidents, respondents were instructed to include incidents that occurred before, during, or after normal school hours or when school activities or events were in session.

[15] Respondents were instructed to include discipline problems only for those times that were during normal school hours or when school activities or events were in session.

[16] "Violent incidents" include "serious violent incidents" as well as physical attacks or fights without a weapon and threat of physical attacks without a weapon. "Serious violent incidents" include rape, sexual assault other than rape, physical attacks or fights with a weapon, threat of physical attacks with a weapon, and robbery with or without a weapon. Theft or larceny refers to taking things worth over $10 without personal confrontation. "Other incidents" include possession of a firearm or explosive device; possession of a knife or sharp object; distribution, possession, or use of illegal drugs or alcohol; inappropriate distribution, possession, or use of prescription drugs; and vandalism.

[17] The SSOCS questionnaire defines bullying as "any unwanted aggressive behavior(s) by another youth or group of youths that involves an observed or perceived power imbalance and is repeated multiple times or is highly likely to be repeated. Bullying occurs among youth who are not siblings or current dating partners."

[18] Harassment is defined as "conduct that is unwelcome and denies or limits a student's ability to participate in or benefit from a school's education program. All students can be victims of harassment and the harasser can share the same characteristics of the victim. The conduct can be verbal, nonverbal, or physical and can take many forms, including verbal acts and name-calling, as well as nonverbal conduct, such as graphic and written statements, or conduct that is physically threatening, harmful, or humiliating."

[19] Sexual orientation means one's "emotional or physical attraction to the same and/or opposite sex." Gender identity means one's "inner sense of one's own gender, which may or may not match the sex assigned at birth."

Gangs and Hate-Related Speech

Another measure of the school environment is the extent of unfavorable conditions, such as the presence of gangs and hate-related[20] words and graffiti. These data are captured in the SCS based on student reports of conditions at school during the school year.

In 2019, of students ages 12–18, about 9 percent reported a gang presence at their school during the school year, 7 percent reported being called hate-related words, and 23 percent reported seeing hate-related graffiti (figure 5). These unfavorable conditions were less prevalent than they were a decade prior in 2009, when 20 percent of students reported a gang presence, 9 percent reported being called hate-related words, and 29 percent reported seeing hate-related graffiti. (*Students' Reports of Gangs at School*; *Students' Reports of Hate-Related Words and Hate-Related Graffiti*)

In 2019, there were differences in the reports of these unfavorable conditions by student and school characteristics. For instance, higher percentages of 9th- through 12th-graders (ranging from 10 to 12 percent) than of 6th- through 8th-graders (ranging from 5 to 6 percent) reported observing a gang presence at their school. In contrast, the percentages of students who reported being called a hate-related word at school were lower for 10th- and 12th-graders (5 and 4 percent, respectively) than for 7th- and 8th-graders (8 and 9 percent, respectively), and there were no measurable differences by students' grade level in the percentage of students who reported seeing hate-related graffiti at school. (*Students' Reports of Gangs at School*; *Students' Reports of Hate-Related Words and Hate-Related Graffiti*)

Students who reported being called hate-related words at school during the school year were asked to indicate whether the derogatory word they were called referred to their race, ethnicity, religion, disability, gender, or sexual orientation. In 2019, race was the most frequently reported characteristic referred to by hate-related words. A lower percentage of White students (2 percent) than of students of any other race/ethnicity for which data were available reported being called a hate-related word referring to their race (ranging from 4 percent of Hispanic students to 9 percent of students of Two or more races). (*Students' Reports of Hate-Related Words and Hate-Related Graffiti*)

Figure 5. Percentage of students ages 12–18 who reported a gang presence, being called hate-related words, and seeing hate-related graffiti at school during the school year: Selected years, 2009 through 2019

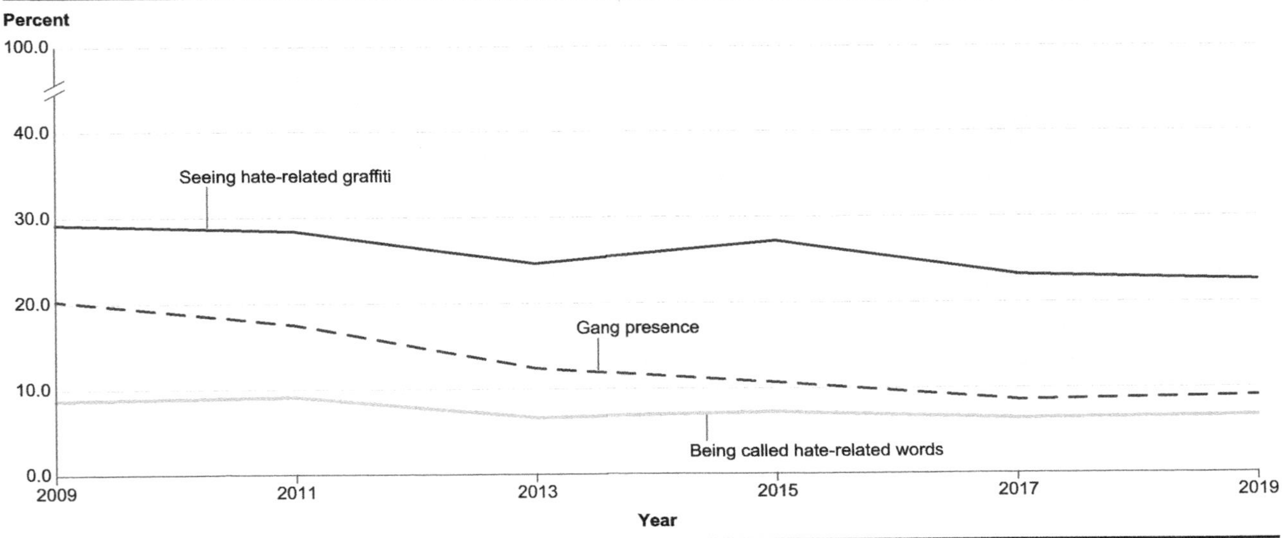

NOTE: "At school" includes in the school building, on school property, on a school bus, and going to and from school. "Hate-related" refers to derogatory terms used by others in reference to students' personal characteristics.
SOURCE: U.S. Department of Justice, Bureau of Justice Statistics, School Crime Supplement (SCS) to the National Crime Victimization Survey, 2009 through 2019. See *Digest of Education Statistics 2020*, tables 230.20 and 230.30.

Fights, Weapons, and Illegal Substances

Guns, fights, alcohol, and drugs are other indicators of disorder and incivility at school. Using data mostly from the YRBSS, these indicators examine how the prevalence of these issues has changed over the past decade and whether there are differences by student characteristics such as gender, race/ethnicity, sexual identity, and grade level.

The YRBSS asked students in grades 9-12 about their involvement in physical fights, both anywhere[21] and on school property, during the 12 months preceding the survey. Involvement in physical fights includes both aggressors and unwilling participants or victims. The percentage of students in grades 9-12 who reported having been in a physical fight anywhere during the previous 12 months was lower in 2019 than in 2009 (22 vs. 31 percent), and the percentage who reported having been in a physical fight on school property in the previous 12 months was also lower in 2019 than in 2009 (8 vs. 11 percent). The percentage of students who reported having been in a physical fight on school property during the previous 12 months in 2019 was higher for male students than for female students (11 vs. 4 percent); higher for students who were American Indian/Alaska Native (19 percent), Black (15 percent), and of Two or more races (11 percent) than for students who were White (6 percent) and Asian (5 percent; figure 6); higher for Black students than for students of Two or more races and Hispanic students (8 percent); and higher for 9th-graders (11 percent) and 10th-graders (8 percent) than for 11th-graders and 12th-graders (6 percent each). There were no measurable differences by sexual identity in the percentages of students who reported having been involved in a physical fight on school property in 2019. (*Physical Fights on School Property and Anywhere*)

Figure 6. Percentage of students in grades 9–12 who reported having been in a physical fight at least one time during the previous 12 months, by race/ethnicity and location: 2019

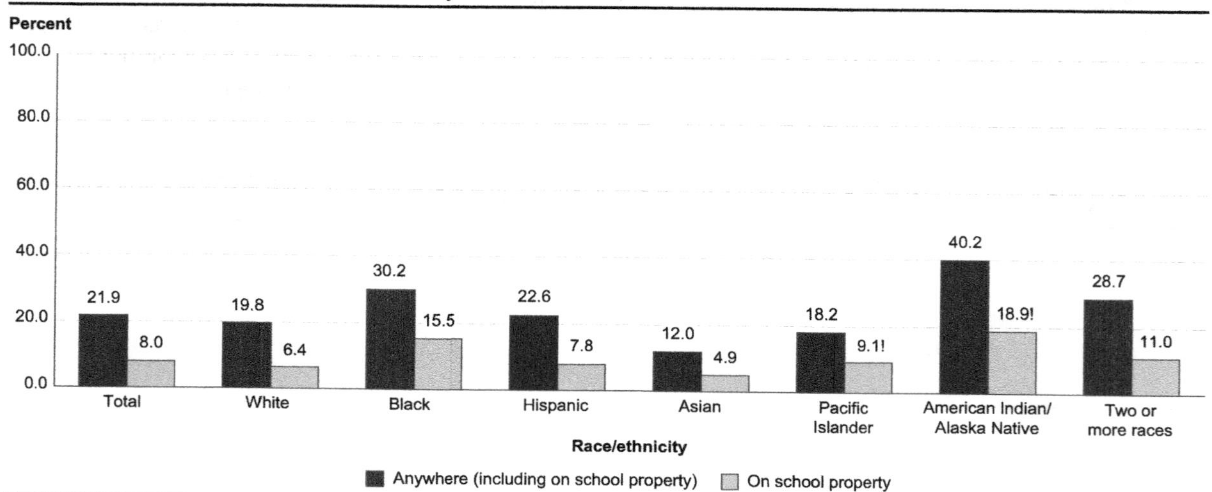

! Interpret data with caution. The coefficient of variation (CV) for this estimate is between 30 and 50 percent.
NOTE: The term "anywhere" is not used in the Youth Risk Behavior Surveillance System (YRBSS) questionnaire; students were simply asked how many times in the past 12 months they had been in a physical fight. In the question asking students about physical fights at school, "on school property" was not defined for respondents. Race categories exclude persons of Hispanic ethnicity.
SOURCE: Centers for Disease Control and Prevention, Division of Adolescent and School Health, Youth Risk Behavior Surveillance System (YRBSS), 2019. See *Digest of Education Statistics 2020*, table 231.10.

[21] "Anywhere" includes occurrences on school property. The term "anywhere" is not used in the YRBSS, and the survey did not define "on school property" for respondents.

On the topic of weapons, data are available for the percentages of students in grades 9–12 who reported carrying a weapon[22] anywhere and on school property during the previous 30 days and for the percentage of students who reported having been threatened or injured with a weapon on school property during the previous 12 months. An examination of these data over the past decade shows that, between 2009 and 2019, the percentage of students in grades 9–12 who reported carrying a weapon anywhere during the previous 30 days decreased (from 17 to 13 percent), as did the percentage of students who reported carrying a weapon on school property (decreased from 6 to 3 percent; figure 7). However, for threats and injuries with weapons on school property, there was not a consistent trend from 2009 to 2019. The percentage of students who reported being threatened or injured with a weapon on school property during the previous 12 months decreased from 8 percent in 2009 to 6 percent in 2017; in 2019 (7 percent), however, the percentage was higher than that in 2017 and not measurably different from the percentage in 2009. (Students Carrying Weapons on School Property and Anywhere and Students' Access to Firearms; Threats and Injuries With Weapons on School Property)

Figure 7. Percentage of students in grades 9–12 who reported carrying a weapon at least 1 day anywhere and on school property during the previous 30 days, and percentage who reported being threatened or injured with a weapon on school property at least one time during the previous 12 months: 2009, 2017, and 2019

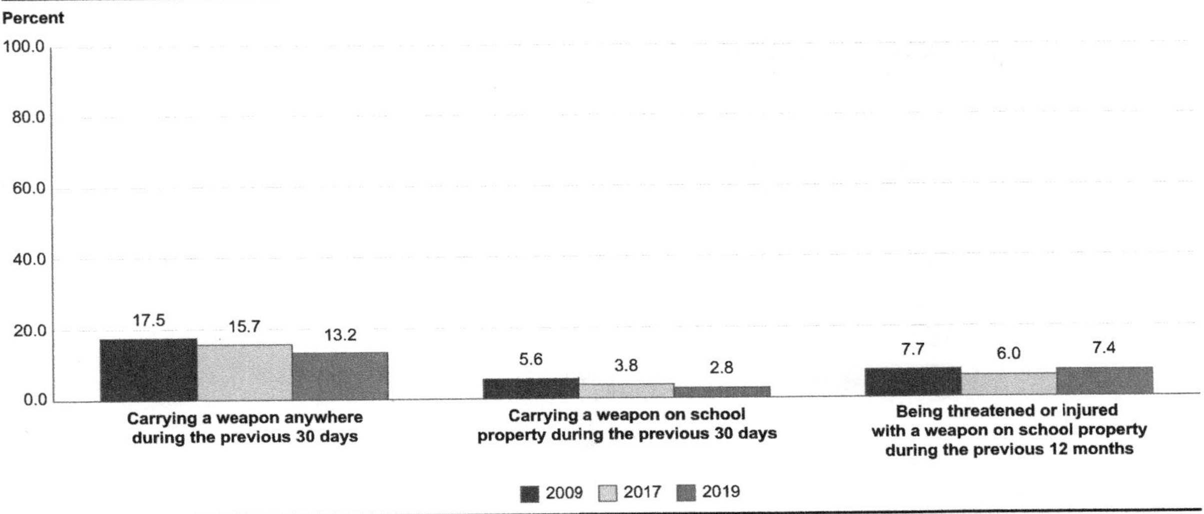

NOTE: Examples of weapons provided for respondents include guns, knives, or clubs. The term "anywhere" is not used in the Youth Risk Behavior Surveillance System (YRBSS) questionnaire; students were simply asked how many days they carried a weapon during the past 30 days. "On school property" was not defined for respondents.
SOURCE: Centers for Disease Control and Prevention, Division of Adolescent and School Health, Youth Risk Behavior Surveillance System (YRBSS), 2009, 2017, and 2019. See *Digest of Education Statistics 2020*, tables 228.40 and 231.40.

[22] Examples of weapons provided for respondents include guns, knives, or clubs.

In the United States, the purchase or public possession of alcohol anywhere is illegal until age 21, except in the company of a parent or legal-age spouse in certain states. Adolescent alcohol use is associated with various negative educational and health outcomes (French and Maclean 2006; Mason et al. 2010; Schilling et al. 2009). The percentage of students in grades 9-12 who reported using alcohol on at least 1 day during the previous 30 days decreased from 42 to 29 percent between 2009 and 2019. In 2019, the percentage of students in grades 9-12 reporting this behavior was lower for male students than for female students (26 vs. 32 percent; figure 8); lower for Asian students (14 percent) and Black students (17 percent) than for students of all other racial/ethnic groups; and lower for heterosexual students (29 percent) and students who were not sure about their sexual identity (25 percent) than for gay, lesbian, or bisexual students (34 percent). In 2019, the percentage of students in grades 9-12 who reported using alcohol on at least 1 day during the previous 30 days increased with grade level. (Students' Use of Alcohol)

Figure 8. Percentage of students in grades 9–12 who reported using alcohol at least 1 day during the previous 30 days, by selected student characteristics: 2019

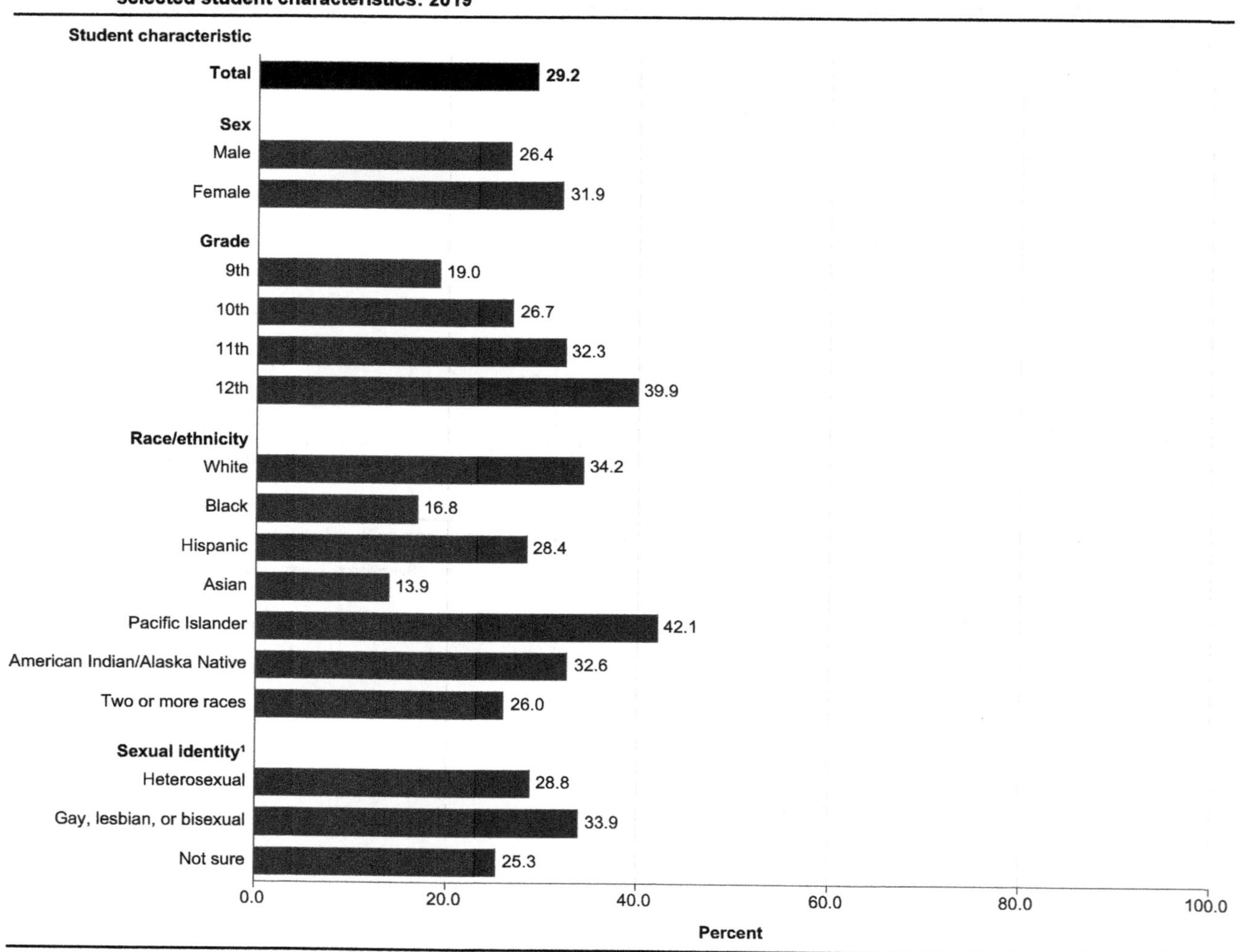

[1] Students were asked which of the following—"heterosexual (straight)," "gay or lesbian," "bisexual," or "not sure"—best described them.

NOTE: Race categories exclude persons of Hispanic ethnicity.

SOURCE: Centers for Disease Control and Prevention, Division of Adolescent and School Health, Youth Risk Behavior Surveillance System (YRBSS), 2019. See *Digest of Education Statistics 2020*, table 232.10.

The YRBSS asked students in grades 9-12 about their current use of marijuana anywhere as well as the availability of illegal drugs on school property. In 2019, about 22 percent of students in grades 9-12 reported using marijuana at least one time during the previous 30 days; the percentage of students who reported that someone had offered, sold, or given them an illegal drug on school property in the previous 12 months was also 22 percent in 2019. These percentages were not measurably different from their corresponding percentages in 2009.

In 2019, student reports of marijuana use and illegal drug availability varied by student characteristics. For instance, an examination of the data on the availability of illegal drugs on school property reveals differences by student race/ethnicity and sexual identity. Higher percentages of students of Two or more races (28 percent) and Hispanic students (27 percent) than of Black students (21 percent) and White students (20 percent) reported that illegal drugs were offered, sold, or given to them on school property (figure 9); all these percentages were higher than the corresponding percentage of Asian students (14 percent). Additionally, a higher percentage of gay, lesbian, or bisexual students (30 percent) than of students who were not sure about their sexual identity (24 percent) and students who were heterosexual (21 percent) reported that illegal drugs were offered, sold, or given to them on school property in 2019. (Marijuana Use and Illegal Drug Availability)

Figure 9. Percentage of students in grades 9–12 who reported that illegal drugs were made available to them on school property during the previous 12 months, by race/ethnicity and sexual identity: 2019

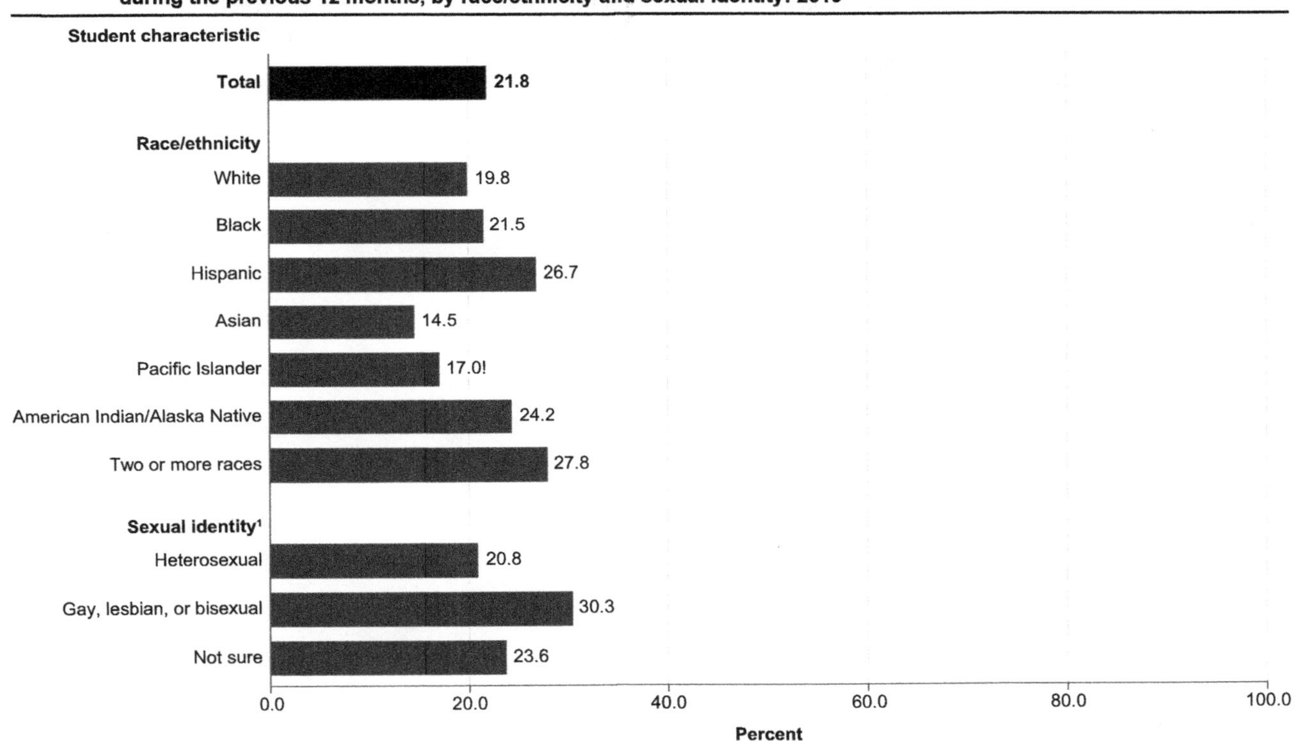

! Interpret data with caution. The coefficient of variation (CV) for this estimate is between 30 and 50 percent.
[1] Students were asked which of the following—"heterosexual (straight)," "gay or lesbian," "bisexual," or "not sure"—best described them.
NOTE: Students were asked if anyone offered, sold, or gave them an illegal drug on school property during the previous 12 months. "On school property" was not defined for respondents. Race categories exclude persons of Hispanic ethnicity.
SOURCE: Centers for Disease Control and Prevention, Division of Adolescent and School Health, Youth Risk Behavior Surveillance System (YRBSS), 2019. See *Digest of Education Statistics 2020*, table 232.70.

Student Perceptions of School Safety

The SCS collected data on student perceptions of school safety by asking students ages 12-18 about their fear of attack or harm at and away from school. In 2019, about 5 percent of students ages 12-18 reported that they had been afraid of attack or harm[23] at school during the school year, which was higher than the percentage of students who reported that they had been afraid of attack or harm away from school (3 percent; figure 10). The percentages of students who reported being afraid of attack or harm at school and away from school in 2019 were not measurably different from those in 2009. The SCS also asked students whether they avoided one or more places in school[24] because they were fearful that someone might attack or harm them. In 2019, the percentage of students who reported avoiding one or more places in school during the school year because they thought someone might attack or harm them was 5 percent, which was higher than the percentage who did so in 2009 (4 percent). (*Students' Perceptions of Personal Safety at School and Away From School*; *Students' Reports of Avoiding School Activities or Classes or Specific Places in School*)

In 2019, there were some measurable differences by student and school characteristics in the percentages of students ages 12-18 who reported fear and avoidance. For example, the percentage of students who reported avoiding one or more places in school because of fear of attack or harm was higher for students of Two or more races (11 percent) than for Hispanic (5 percent), Asian (4 percent), and White (4 percent) students; higher for Black students (7 percent) than for White students; and higher for 7th-, 8th-, and 9th-graders (5, 6, and 7 percent, respectively) than for 12th-graders (3 percent). The percentage of students who reported avoiding one or more places in school was higher for those enrolled in schools in cities than for those enrolled in schools in rural areas (6 vs. 4 percent). In addition, a higher percentage of public school students than of private school students reported avoiding one or more places in school (5 vs. 2 percent). (*Students' Reports of Avoiding School Activities or Classes or Specific Places in School*)

---

[23] Students were asked if they were "never," "almost never," "sometimes," or "most of the time" afraid that someone would attack or harm them at school or away from school. Students responding "sometimes" or "most of the time" were considered afraid.

[24] "Avoided one or more places in school" includes avoiding entrance to the school, hallways or stairs in school, parts of the school cafeteria, any school restrooms, and other places inside the school building. Students who reported avoiding multiple places in school were counted only once in the total for students avoiding one or more places.

Figure 10. Percentage of students ages 12–18 who reported being afraid of attack or harm during the school year, and percentage who reported avoiding one or more places in school because of fear of attack or harm during the school year: 2019

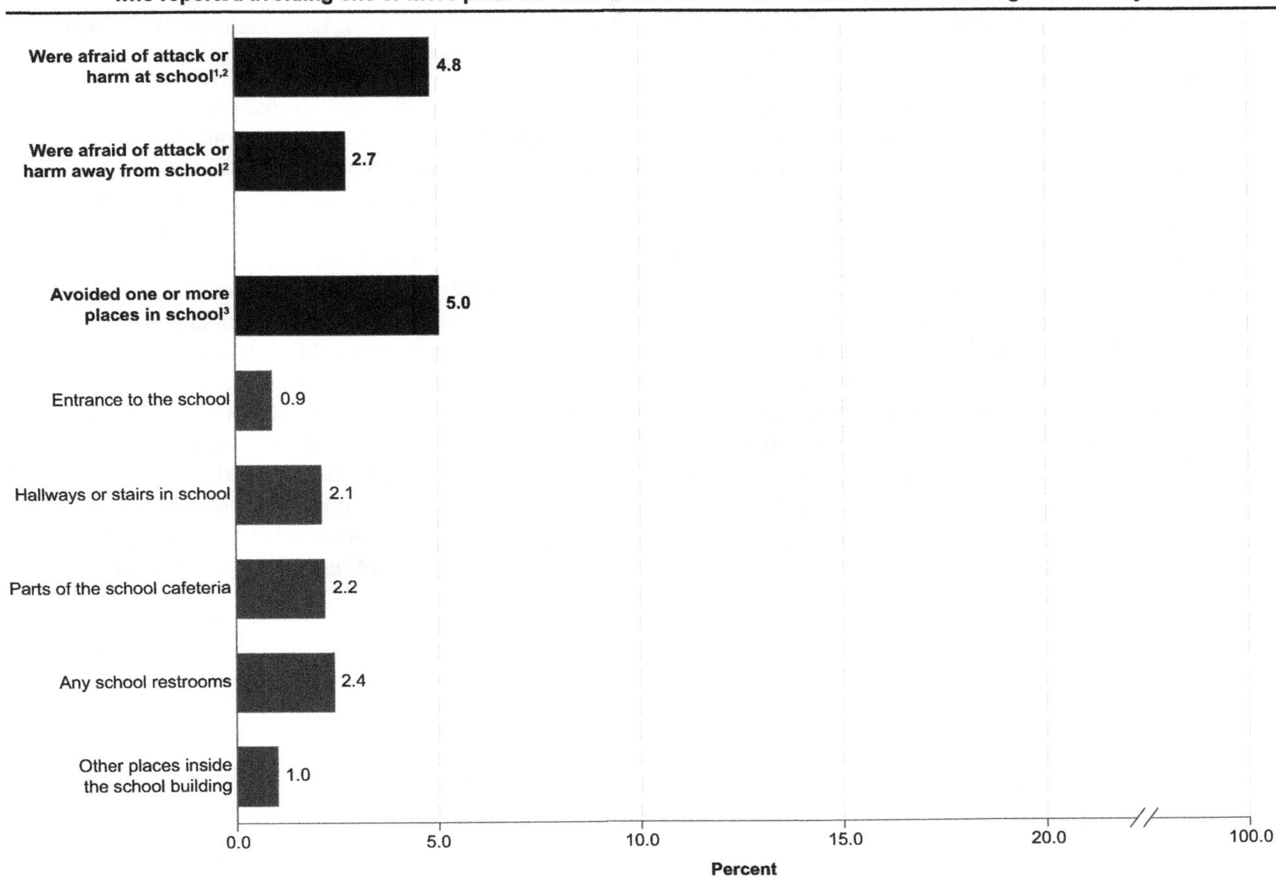

[1] "At school" includes in the school building, on school property, on a school bus, and going to and from school.

[2] Students were asked if they were "never," "almost never," "sometimes," or "most of the time" afraid that someone would attack or harm them at school or away from school. Students responding "sometimes" or "most of the time" were considered afraid.

[3] Students who reported avoiding multiple places in school were counted only once in the total for students avoiding one or more places.

SOURCE: U.S. Department of Justice, Bureau of Justice Statistics, School Crime Supplement (SCS) to the National Crime Victimization Survey, 2019. See *Digest of Education Statistics 2020*, tables 230.70 and 230.80.

Teacher Reports of Victimization and School Order

In addition to evaluating student reports of victimization and perceptions about personal safety at school, it is also important to understand issues of school order and safety from the perspective of teachers. According to data on public school teachers[25] from the 2015-16 National Teacher and Principal Survey (NTPS), threats of injury were more common than actual physical attacks. Additionally, both percentages were higher in 2015-16 than in 2007-08: the percentage of public school teachers who reported being threatened with injury by a student from their school was 10 percent in 2015-16, compared with 8 percent in 2007-08; the percentage who reported being physically attacked by a student from their school was 6 percent in 2015-16, compared with 4 percent in 2007-08.[26] During the 2015-16 school year, a higher percentage of elementary public school teachers than of secondary public school teachers reported being threatened with injury (11 vs. 9 percent) or being physically attacked (9 vs. 2 percent) by a student from their school (figure 11).[27] (*Teachers Threatened With Injury or Physically Attacked by Students*)

In the Teaching and Learning International Survey (TALIS) administered in 2018, lower secondary teachers (grades 7-9 in the United States) were asked to rate their ability to manage student classroom behaviors, including controlling disruptive behavior in the classroom, making expectations about student behavior clear, getting students to follow classroom rules, and calming a student who is disruptive or noisy. Eighty percent or more of lower secondary teachers in public schools in the United States reported that they were able to manage various aspects of student behavior quite a bit or a lot in 2018.[28] Lower percentages of teachers with less than 3 years of teaching experience than of teachers with more years of teaching experience, in general, reported being able to manage various aspects of student behavior quite a bit or a lot. (*Teachers' Reports on Managing Classroom Behaviors*)

[25] Public school teachers surveyed by NTPS include those that teach both in traditional public and public charter schools.

[26] The 2007-08 data were collected in the Schools and Staffing Survey (SASS). The NTPS was designed to allow comparisons with SASS data.

[27] Instructional level divides teachers into elementary or secondary based on a combination of grades taught, main teaching assignment, and structure of teachers' class(es), rather than the level of school in which teachers taught. Teachers with only ungraded classes were classified based on their main teaching assignment and the structure of their class(es). Among teachers with regularly graded classes, elementary teachers generally include those teaching prekindergarten through grade 6 and those teaching multiple grades, with a preponderance of grades taught being kindergarten through grade 6. In general, secondary teachers include those teaching any of grades 7 through 12 and those teaching multiple grades, with a preponderance of grades taught being grades 7 through 12 and usually with no grade taught being lower than grade 5.

[28] Teachers were asked "In your teaching, to what extent can you do the following?" For each item, teachers could select one option: "not at all," "to some extent," "quite a bit," or "a lot." This report combines the percentages for "quite a bit" and "a lot."

Figure 11. Percentage of public school teachers who reported that they were threatened with injury or that they were physically attacked by a student from their school during the previous 12 months, by instructional level: School year 2015–16

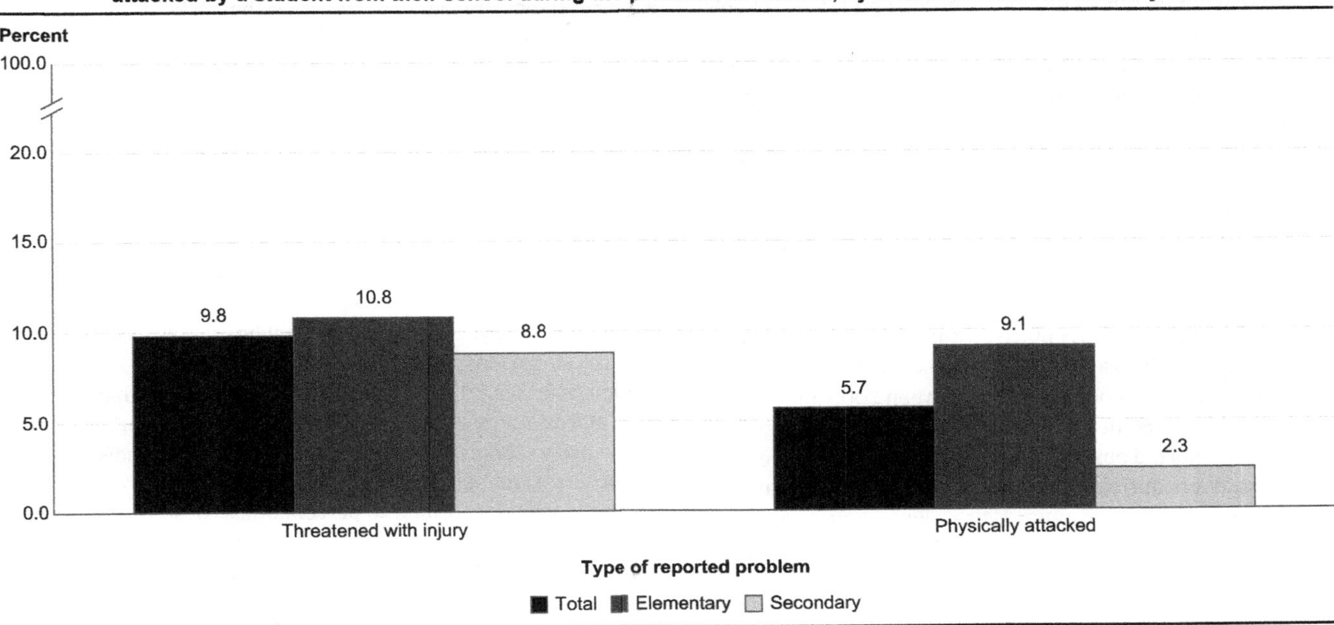

NOTE: Teachers who taught only prekindergarten students are excluded. Includes teachers in both traditional public schools and public charter schools. Instructional level divides teachers into elementary or secondary based on a combination of grades taught, main teaching assignment, and structure of teachers' class(es), rather than the level of school in which teachers taught. Teachers with only ungraded classes were classified based on their main teaching assignment and the structure of their class(es). Among teachers with regularly graded classes, elementary teachers generally include those teaching prekindergarten through grade 6 and those teaching multiple grades, with a preponderance of grades taught being kindergarten through grade 6. In general, secondary teachers include those teaching any of grades 7 through 12 and those teaching multiple grades, with a preponderance of grades taught being grades 7 through 12 and usually with no grade taught being lower than grade 5.
SOURCE: National Teacher and Principal Survey (NTPS), "Public School Teacher Data File," 2015–16. See *Digest of Education Statistics 2020*, table 228.70.

Discipline, Safety, and Security Practices

To maintain school discipline, order, and safety, schools across the United States have implemented preventive and responsive measures. In the SCS, students ages 12-18 were asked whether their schools used certain safety and security measures. In 2019, about 94 percent of students reported a written code of student conduct, and 89 percent reported the presence of school staff (other than security guards or assigned police officers) or other adults supervising the hallway. However, both measures were less prevalent compared with a decade prior in 2009 (96 and 91 percent, respectively; figure 12). In contrast, the percentage of students who reported observing the use of one or more security cameras to monitor the school increased between 2009 and 2019 (from 70 to 86 percent), as did the percentages of students who reported observing the use of locked entrance or exit doors during the day (from 64 to 85 percent) and the presence of security guards or assigned police officers (from 68 to 75 percent). (*Students' Reports of Safety and Security Measures Observed at School*)

In addition to student reports collected through SCS, data on school practices were collected through SSOCS by asking public school principals about their school's use of safety and security measures, whether their school had written procedures for responding to certain scenarios, and the number of disciplinary actions their school had taken against students for specific offenses. In 2017-18, about 94 percent of public schools reported they had a written plan for procedures to be performed in the event of a natural disaster, 92 percent reported plans for an active shooter, and 91 percent reported plans for bomb threats or incidents. About 46 percent of public schools reported that they had a written plan for procedures to be performed in the event of a pandemic disease.[29] In the same school year, 35 percent of public schools took at least one serious disciplinary action[30] for specific student offenses.[31] The percentage of public schools that took at least one serious disciplinary action was lower for primary schools (17 percent) than for middle schools (58 percent) and high schools (76 percent); it was also lower for schools in which 25 percent or less of students were eligible for free or reduced-price lunch (FRPL) (23 percent) than for schools in which higher percentages of students were eligible for FRPL (36 to 39 percent). (*Serious Disciplinary Actions Taken by Public Schools*; *Safety and Security Practices at Public Schools*)

---

[29]For more information, see the NCES blog post "The Prevalence of Written Plans for a Pandemic Disease Scenario in Public Schools."

[30]Serious disciplinary actions refer to those more exclusionary actions and are defined to include out-of-school suspensions lasting 5 or more days but less than the remainder of the school year; removals with no continuing services for at least the remainder of the school year; and transfers to specialized schools for disciplinary reasons.

[31]Offenses listed on the questionnaire included physical attacks or fights; distribution, possession, or use of alcohol; distribution, possession, or use of illegal drugs; use or possession of a firearm or explosive device; and use or possession of a weapon other than a firearm or explosive device.

Figure 12. Percentage of students ages 12–18 who reported various safety and security measures at school: 2009 and 2019

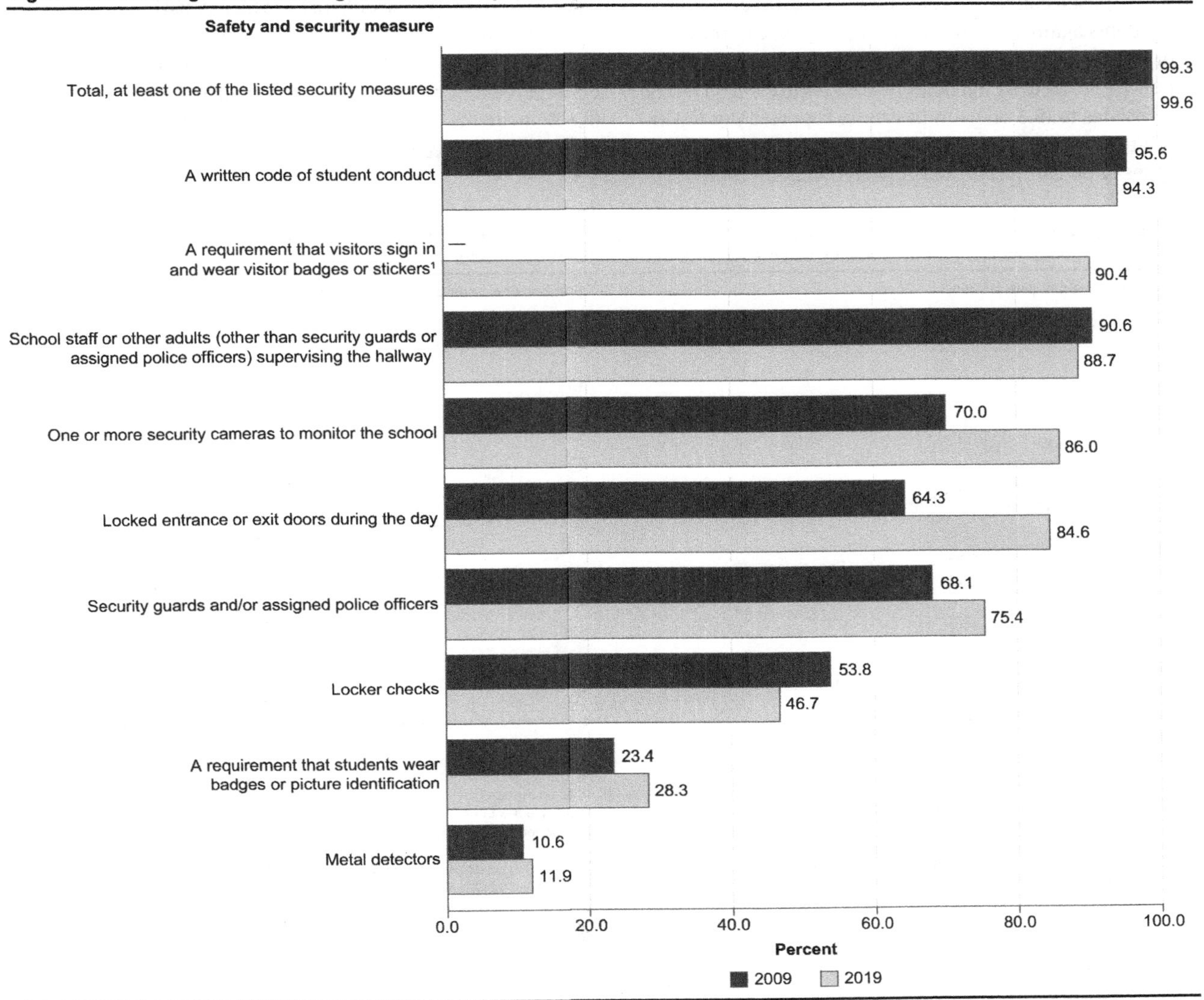

— Not available.

[1] Prior to 2015, the question asked simply whether the school had "a requirement that visitors sign in." As of 2015, the question has also included the requirement that visitors wear badges or stickers. Data for 2009 have been omitted because the change in questionnaire wording may affect comparability of the data over time.

NOTE: "At school" includes in the school building, on school property, on a school bus, and going to and from school.

SOURCE: U.S. Department of Justice, Bureau of Justice Statistics, School Crime Supplement (SCS) to the National Crime Victimization Survey, 2009 and 2019. See *Digest of Education Statistics 2020*, table 233.80.

Postsecondary Campus Safety and Security

At the postsecondary level, a total of 28,500 criminal incidents against persons and property on campuses of postsecondary institutions were reported to police and security agencies in 2018 (figure 13).[32] This translates to 19.5 on-campus crimes reported per 10,000 full-time-equivalent (FTE) students.[33] Among the various types of on-campus crimes reported in 2018, there were 12,300 forcible sex offenses, which constituted 43 percent of all criminal incidents. Other commonly reported crimes included burglaries[34] (9,600 incidents, or 34 percent of crimes) and motor vehicle thefts (3,100 incidents, or 11 percent of crimes). (Criminal Incidents at Postsecondary Institutions)

Figure 13. Number of on-campus crimes reported and number per 10,000 full-time-equivalent (FTE) students in degree-granting postsecondary institutions, by selected type of crime: 2009 through 2018

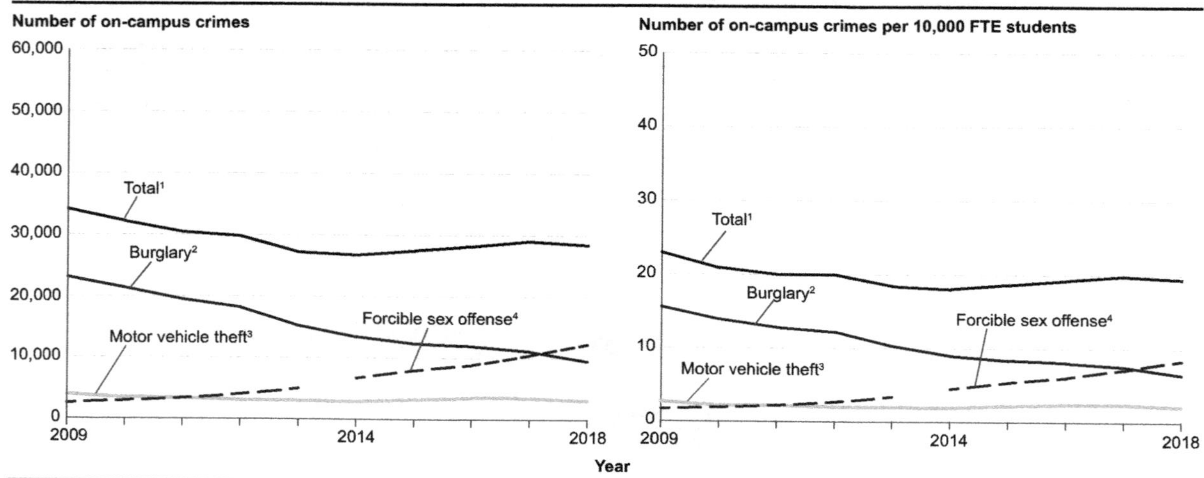

¹ Includes other reported crimes not separately shown.
² Unlawful entry of a structure to commit a felony or theft.
³ Theft or attempted theft of a motor vehicle.
⁴ Any sexual act directed against another person forcibly and/or against that person's will. Data on reported forcible sex offenses have been collected differently since 2014. Beginning in 2014, schools were asked to report the numbers of two different types of forcible sex offenses, rape and fondling, and these were added together to reach the total number of reported forcible sex offenses. In years prior to 2014, schools only reported a total number of reported forcible sex offenses, with no breakouts for specific types of offenses.

NOTE: Data are for degree-granting institutions, which are institutions that grant associate's or higher degrees and participate in Title IV federal financial aid programs. Some institutions that report *Jeanne Clery Disclosure of Campus Security Policy and Campus Crime Statistics Act* data—specifically, non-degree-granting institutions and institutions outside of the 50 states and the District of Columbia—are excluded from this figure. Crimes include incidents involving students, staff, and on-campus guests. Excludes off-campus crimes even if they involve college students or staff. Some data have been revised from previously published figures.

SOURCE: U.S. Department of Education, Office of Postsecondary Education, Campus Safety and Security Reporting System, 2009 through 2018; and National Center for Education Statistics, Integrated Postsecondary Education Data System (IPEDS), Spring 2010 through Spring 2019, Fall Enrollment component. See *Digest of Education Statistics 2020*, tables 329.10 and 329.20.

[32] The *Jeanne Clery Disclosure of Campus Security Policy and Campus Crime Statistics Act of 1990 (Clery Act)* specifies seven types of crimes that all Title IV institutions are required to report through the Campus Safety and Security Survey: murder, sex offenses (forcible and nonforcible), robbery, aggravated assault, burglary, motor vehicle theft, and arson.

[33] The base of 10,000 FTE students includes students who are enrolled exclusively in distance learning courses and who may not be physically present on campus.

[34] Refers to the unlawful entry of a structure to commit a felony or theft.

An examination of postsecondary crime data over the past decade reveals that the overall number of reported on-campus crimes was lower in 2018 than in 2009 (28,500 vs. 34,100 incidents; figure 13). In addition, the rate of crime, or the number of crimes per 10,000 FTE students, was also lower in 2018 than in 2009 (19.5 vs. 23.0 incidents per 10,000 FTE students). However, the number of reported forcible sex offenses on campus increased from 2,500 in 2009 to 12,300 in 2018 (a 383 percent increase).[35] Although changes in the reporting guidelines for forcible sex offenses in 2014[36] likely contributed to the largest single-year percentage increase in that year (36 percent, from 5,000 to 6,800), the number of reported forcible sex offenses on campus continued to increase steadily between 2014 and 2018, from 6,800 to 12,300 (an 82 percent increase, or an average increase of about 16 percent per year). (*Criminal Incidents at Postsecondary Institutions*)

A hate crime is a criminal offense that is motivated, in whole or in part, by the perpetrator's bias against the victim(s) based on race, ethnicity, religion, sexual orientation, gender, gender identity, or disability.[37]

In 2018, of the criminal incidents that occurred on the campuses of postsecondary institutions and were reported to police or security agencies, 814 incidents were classified as hate crimes. The three most common types of hate crimes reported by institutions were destruction, damage, and vandalism (345 incidents); intimidation (337 incidents); and simple assault (75 incidents; figure 14). (*Hate Crime Incidents at Postsecondary Institutions*)

Race, sexual orientation, and religion were the top three categories of motivating bias associated with hate crimes at postsecondary institutions in 2018. Eighty percent of the total reported on-campus hate crimes in 2018 were motivated by these three categories of bias. Race was the motivating bias in 43 percent of reported hate crimes (347 incidents), while an additional 11 percent (88 incidents) were motivated by ethnicity. Sexual orientation was the motivating bias in 22 percent of reported hate crimes (176 incidents), and religion was the motivating bias in 16 percent of reported hate crimes (128 incidents). (*Hate Crime Incidents at Postsecondary Institutions*)

---

[35] The rate for forcible sex offenses increased from 1.7 per 10,000 students in 2009 to 8.4 per 10,000 students in 2018.

[36] In years prior to 2014, schools only reported a total number of forcible sex offenses, with no breakouts for specific types of offenses. Beginning in 2014, schools were asked to report the numbers of two different types of forcible sex offenses–rape and fondling–and these were added together to reach the total number of reported forcible sex offenses. For instance, 6,700 rapes and 5,600 fondling incidents were reported in 2018.

[37] In addition to reporting data on hate-related incidents for the seven types of crimes already specified in the *Clery Act*, a 2008 amendment to the *Clery Act* requires campuses to report hate-related incidents for four additional types of crimes: simple assault; larceny; intimidation; and destruction, damage, and vandalism.

Figure 14. Number of on-campus hate crimes at degree-granting postsecondary institutions, by selected types of crime: 2018

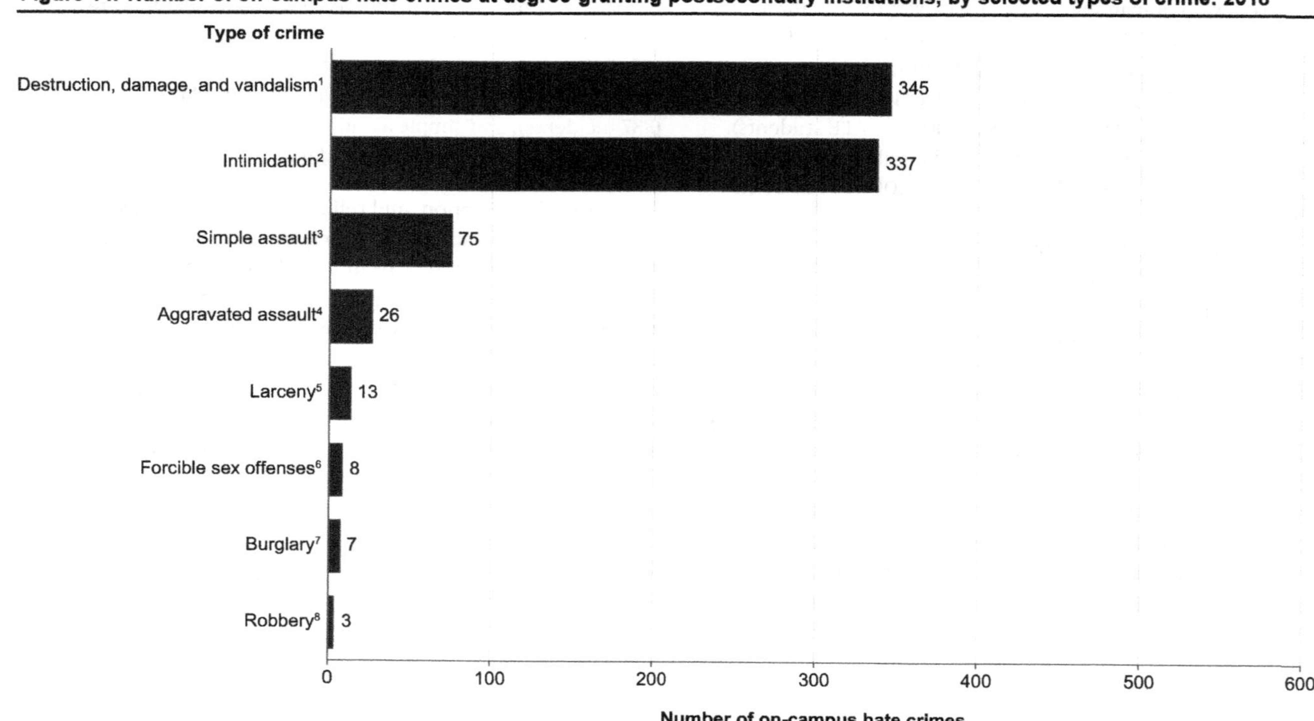

[1] Willfully or maliciously destroying, damaging, defacing, or otherwise injuring real or personal property without the consent of the owner or the person having custody or control of it.
[2] Placing another person in reasonable fear of bodily harm through the use of threatening words and/or other conduct, but without displaying a weapon or subjecting the victim to actual physical attack.
[3] Physical attack by one person upon another where neither the offender displays a weapon nor the victim suffers obvious severe or aggravated bodily injury involving apparent broken bones, loss of teeth, possible internal injury, severe laceration, or loss of consciousness.
[4] Attack upon a person for the purpose of inflicting severe or aggravated bodily injury.
[5] Unlawful taking, carrying, leading, or riding away of property from the possession of another.
[6] Any sexual act directed against another person forcibly and/or against that person's will.
[7] Unlawful entry of a structure to commit a felony or theft.
[8] Taking or attempting to take anything of value using actual or threatened force or violence.

NOTE: Data are for degree-granting institutions, which are institutions that grant associate's or higher degrees and participate in Title IV federal financial aid programs. Some institutions that report *Clery Act* data—specifically, non-degree-granting institutions and institutions outside of the 50 states and the District of Columbia—are excluded. A hate crime is a criminal offense that is motivated, in whole or in part, by the perpetrator's bias against a group of people based on their race, ethnicity, religion, sexual orientation, gender, gender identity, or disability. Includes on-campus incidents involving students, staff, and guests. Excludes off-campus crimes and arrests even if they involve students or staff. There was no arson, murder, or motor vehicle theft classified as hate crime in 2018.

SOURCE: U.S. Department of Education, Office of Postsecondary Education, Campus Safety and Security Reporting System, 2018. See *Digest of Education Statistics 2020*, table 329.30.

References

French, M.T., and Maclean, J.C. (2006). Underage Alcohol Use, Delinquency, and Criminal Activity. *Health Economics, 15*(12): 1261-1281. Retrieved November 30, 2020, from https://onlinelibrary.wiley.com/doi/abs/10.1002/hec.1126.

Hornor, G. (2018). Bullying: What the PNP Needs to Know. *Journal of Pediatric Health Care, 32*(4): 399-408.

Mason, W.A., Hitch, J.E., Kosterman, R., McCarty, C.A., Herrenkohl, T.I., and Hawkins, J.D. (2010). Growth in Adolescent Delinquency and Alcohol Use in Relation to Young Adult Crime, Alcohol Use Disorders, and Risky Sex: A Comparison of Youth From Low- Versus Middle-Income Backgrounds. *The Journal of Child Psychology and Psychiatry, 51*(12): 1377-1385. Retrieved November 10, 2020, from https://onlinelibrary.wiley.com/doi/full/10.1111/j.1469-7610.2010.02292.x.

Schilling, E.A., Aseltine, R.H., Jr., Glanovsky, J.L., James, A., and Jacobs, D. (2009). Adolescent Alcohol Use, Suicidal Ideation, and Suicide Attempts. *Journal of Adolescent Health, 44*(4): 335-341. Retrieved November 10, 2020, from https://www.sciencedirect.com/science/article/pii/S1054139X08003376.

Swearer, S.M., and Hymel, S. (2015). Understanding the Psychology of Bullying: Moving Toward a Social-Ecological Diathesis-Stress Model. *American Psychologist, 70*(4): 344-353.

Irwin, Veronique, Ke Wang, Jiashan Cui, Jizhi Zhang, and Alexandra Thompson. "Report on Indicators of School Crime and Safety: 2020." National Center for Education Statistics and Bureau of Justice Statistics, July 14, 2021. https://nces.ed.gov/pubs2021/2021092.pdf. Accessed August 9, 2021.

School Choice in the United States: 2019

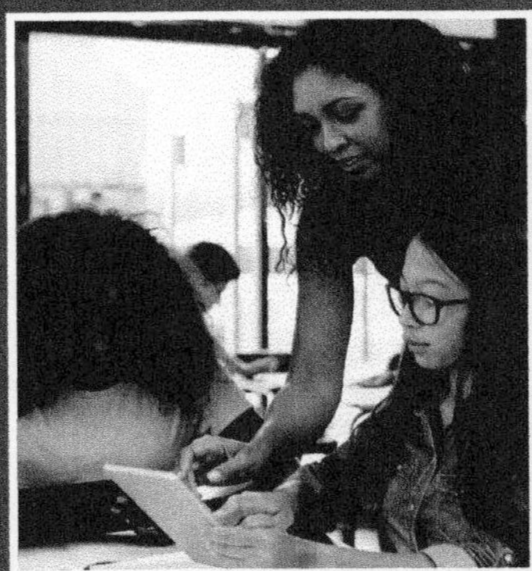

NCES 2019-106

U.S. DEPARTMENT OF EDUCATION

Indicator 1

School Enrollment Over Time

The percentage of students enrolled in assigned public schools in 2016 (69 percent) was lower than the percentage in 1999 (74 percent), while the percentage of students who were enrolled in chosen public schools (19 percent) and the percentage of homeschooled students (3 percent) were both higher in 2016 than the corresponding percentages in 1999 (14 and 2 percent, respectively). The percentage of students enrolled in private schools in 2016 (9 percent) was not measurably different from the percentage in 1999.

This indicator discusses enrollment changes among various types of elementary and secondary schools, as well as changes in the number of students who are homeschooled. Data for this indicator come from the Common Core of Data (CCD), the Private School Universe Survey (PSS), and the Parent and Family Involvement in Education (PFI) Survey of the National Household Education Surveys Program (NHES).

Enrollment Patterns in Various School Choice Options From 1999 to 2016

Figure 1.1. Percentage distribution of students ages 5 through 17 attending kindergarten through 12th grade, by school type or participation in homeschooling: Selected years, 1999 through 2016

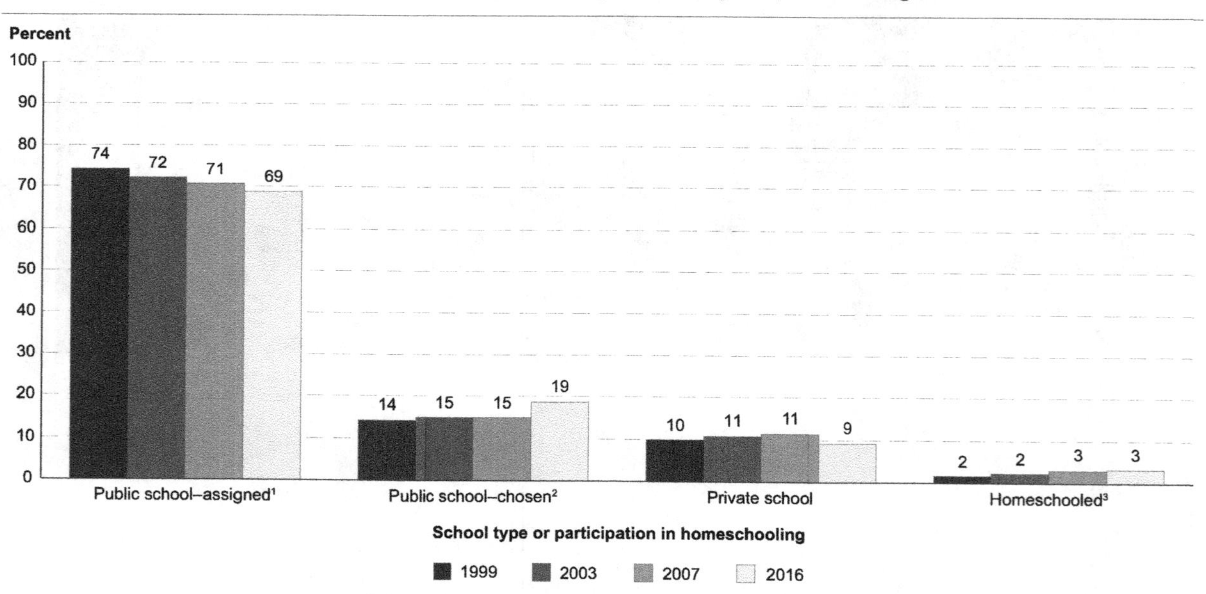

[1] A student is considered to be attending an assigned public school if the parent indicates that the school is the student's "regularly assigned" school.
[2] A student is considered to be attending a chosen public school if the parent indicates that the school is not the student's regularly assigned school (e.g., a traditional public school located outside the assignment boundary based on the student's residence) or if the student is attending a charter school or a magnet school.
[3] Students are considered to be homeschooled if their parents reported them being schooled at home instead of at a public or private school, if their enrollment in public or private schools did not exceed 25 hours a week, and if they were not being homeschooled only due to a temporary illness.
NOTE: While National Household Education Surveys Program (NHES) administrations in 1999, 2003, and 2007 were administered via telephone with an interviewer, NHES:2016 used self-administered paper-and-pencil questionnaires that were mailed to respondents. Measurable differences between estimates for 2016 and estimates for the earlier years in this figure could reflect actual changes in the population, or the changes could be due to the mode change from telephone to mail. Detail may not sum to totals because of rounding. Data are based on parent reports. Although rounded numbers are displayed, the figures are based on unrounded data.
SOURCE: U.S. Department of Education, National Center for Education Statistics, Parent Survey and Parent and Family Involvement in Education Survey of the National Household Education Surveys Program (Parent-NHES:1999 and PFI-NHES:2003, 2007, and 2016).

Data from the NHES PFI survey reveal patterns in student enrollment in assigned and chosen public schools, private schools, as well as in homeschooling. Based on parent reports, these enrollment data include students ages 5 through 17. A student is considered to be attending an assigned public school if the parent indicates that the school is the student's "regularly assigned" school. A student is considered to be attending a chosen public school if the parent indicates that the school is not the student's regularly assigned school (e.g., a traditional public school located outside the assignment boundary based on the student's residence, a charter school, or a magnet school). Private schools are controlled by an individual or organization other than a government agency and are usually not supported primarily by public funds. Students are considered to be homeschooled if their parents reported them being schooled at home instead of at a public or private school, if their enrollment in public or private schools did not exceed 25 hours a week, and if they were not being homeschooled only due to a temporary illness.

Based on 2016 data from the NHES, 69 percent of students ages 5 to 17 attending kindergarten through grade 12 were enrolled in assigned public schools, while 19 percent were enrolled in chosen public schools and 9 percent were enrolled in private schools. In addition, 3 percent of 5- to 17-year-olds were reported by their parents as being homeschooled. The percentage of students enrolled in assigned public schools in 2016 was lower than the percentage in 1999 (74 percent). In contrast, the percentage of students enrolled in chosen public schools and the percentage of homeschooled students were both higher in 2016 than the corresponding percentages were in 1999 (14 and 2 percent, respectively). The percentage of students enrolled in private schools in 2016 (9 percent) was not measurably different from the percentage in 1999.

Traditional Public and Public Charter School Enrollment Trends: 2000 to 2016

Table 1.1. Traditional public and public charter school enrollment, by school level: Fall 2000 and fall 2016

Public charter status and level	Enrollment, fall 2000	Enrollment, fall 2016	Percent change in enrollment, 2000 to 2016
Traditional public, total	46,612,000	47,264,000	1.4
Elementary	30,424,000	30,621,000	0.6
Secondary	14,959,000	15,294,000	2.2
Combined elementary/secondary	1,149,000	1,342,000	16.7
Public charter, total	448,000	3,010,000	571.4
Elementary	249,000	1,512,000	506.9
Secondary	80,000	504,000	533.6
Combined elementary/secondary	117,000	994,000	746.9

NOTE: Elementary schools include schools beginning with grade 6 or below and with no grade higher than 8. Secondary schools include schools with no grade lower than 7. Combined elementary/secondary schools include schools beginning with grade 6 or below and ending with grade 9 or above. Total includes enrollment in schools without grade spans that are not separately shown.
SOURCE: U.S. Department of Education, National Center for Education Statistics, Common Core of Data (CCD), "Public Elementary/Secondary School Universe Survey," 2000–01 and 2016–17.

The number of students enrolled in public elementary and secondary schools can be calculated using data from the CCD. Based on administrative universe data, the CCD categorizes public schools as either traditional or charter public schools. Public charter schools are publicly funded schools that are typically governed by a group or organization under a legislative contract (or charter) with the state, district, or other entity. Traditional public schools include all publicly funded schools other than public charter schools. Since data on parental choice of a program or school other than the assigned public school are not available in the school-based administrative data, the traditional public school category also includes chosen public schools that are not charter schools.

Figure 1.2. Traditional public school enrollment, by school level: Selected years, fall 2000 through fall 2016

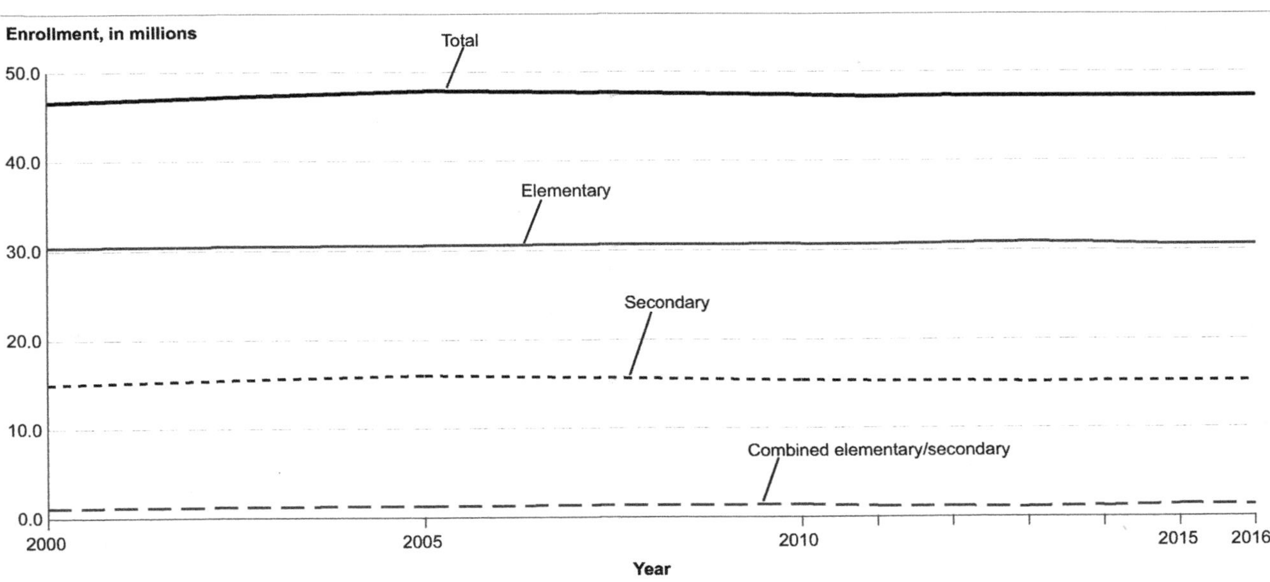

NOTE: Elementary schools include schools beginning with grade 6 or below and with no grade higher than 8. Secondary schools include schools with no grade lower than 7. Combined elementary/secondary schools include schools beginning with grade 6 or below and ending with grade 9 or above. Total includes enrollment in schools without grade spans that are not separately shown.
SOURCE: U.S. Department of Education, National Center for Education Statistics, Common Core of Data (CCD), "Public Elementary/Secondary School Universe Survey," selected years, 2000–01 through 2016–17.

Enrollment in traditional public elementary and secondary schools increased from 46.6 million students in 2000 to 47.9 million students in 2005, then decreased to 47.3 million students in 2016. Overall, total enrollment in traditional public schools was 1 percent higher in 2016 than in 2000. The numbers of students enrolled in traditional public schools were higher in 2016 than in 2000 for all school levels: enrollment in elementary schools was 1 percent higher (from 30.4 million to 30.6 million students); enrollment in secondary schools was 2 percent higher (from 15.0 million to 15.3 million students); and enrollment in combined elementary/secondary schools was 17 percent higher (from 1.1 million to 1.3 million students).[1] Of those 47.3 million students enrolled in traditional public schools in 2016, some 65 percent were enrolled in elementary schools, 32 percent were enrolled in secondary schools, and 3 percent were enrolled in combined elementary/secondary schools.

Figure 1.3. Public charter school enrollment, by school level: Selected years, fall 2000 through fall 2016

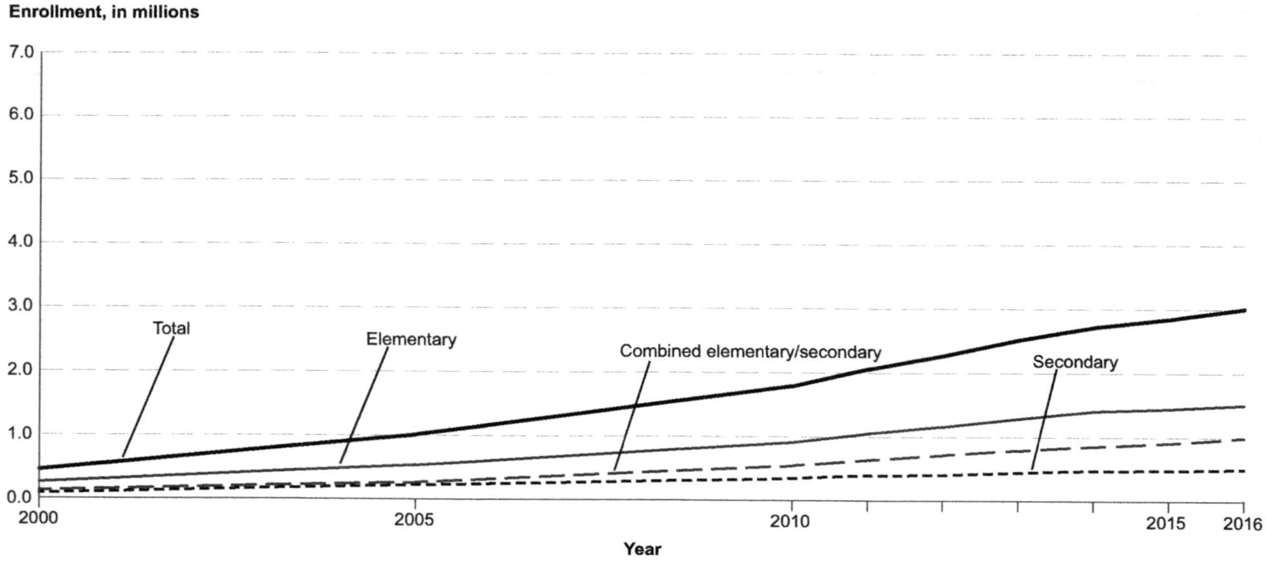

Enrollment, in millions

7.0
6.0
5.0
4.0
3.0
2.0
1.0
0.0

Total
Elementary
Combined elementary/secondary
Secondary

2000 2005 2010 2015 2016

Year

NOTE: Elementary schools include schools beginning with grade 6 or below and with no grade higher than 8. Secondary schools include schools with no grade lower than 7. Combined elementary/secondary schools include schools beginning with grade 6 or below and ending with grade 9 or above. Total includes enrollment in schools without grade spans that are not separately shown.
SOURCE: U.S. Department of Education, National Center for Education Statistics, Common Core of Data (CCD), "Public Elementary/Secondary School Universe Survey," selected years, 2000–01 through 2016–17.

Public charter school enrollment increased much more rapidly than enrollment in traditional public schools, growing from 0.4 million students in fall 2000 to 3.0 million students in fall 2016, an overall increase of 2.6 million students. During this period, public charter school enrollment increased across school levels. From fall 2000 to fall 2016, enrollment increased by more than 5 times in elementary schools (from 0.2 million to 1.5 million students) and secondary schools (from 0.1 million to 0.5 million students) and by more than 7 times in combined elementary/secondary schools (from 0.1 million to 1.0 million students). Of those 3.0 million students enrolled in public charter schools in 2016, some 50 percent were enrolled in elementary schools, 17 percent were enrolled in secondary schools, and 33 percent were enrolled in combined elementary/secondary schools.

Private School Enrollment Trends: 1999 to 2015

Figure 1.4. Private school enrollment, by grade level: Fall 1999 through fall 2015

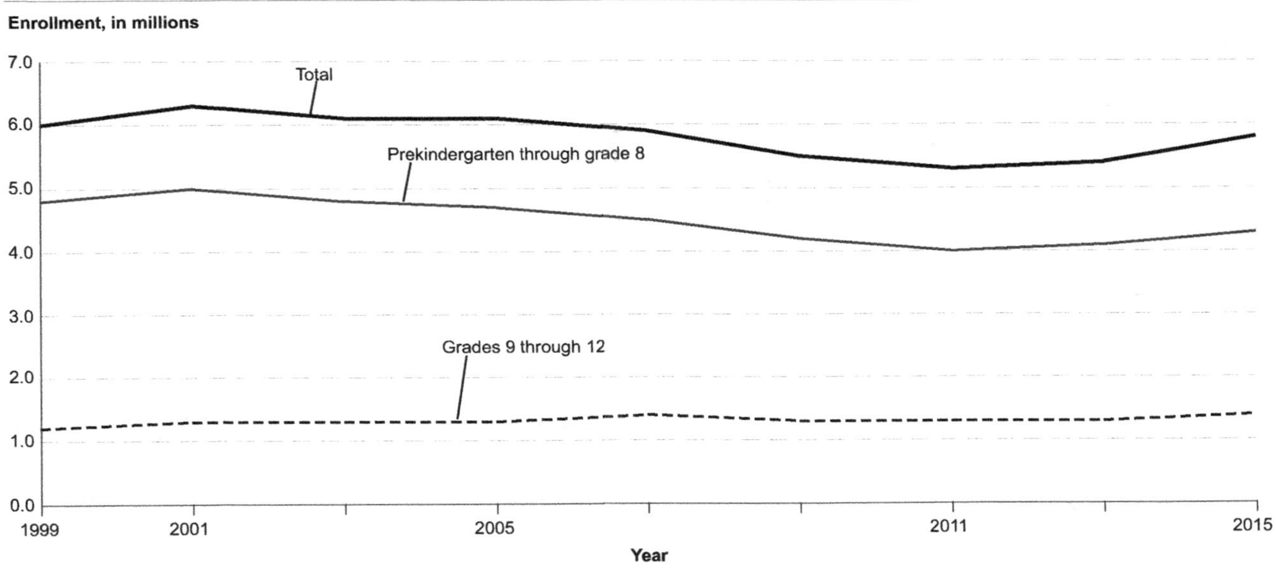

NOTE: Includes enrollment in prekindergarten through grade 12 in schools that offer kindergarten or higher grades. Total private school enrollment includes ungraded students. Ungraded students are prorated into prekindergarten through grade 8 and grades 9 through 12.
SOURCE: U.S. Department of Education, National Center for Education Statistics, Private School Universe Survey (PSS), 1999–2000 through 2015–16.

Private elementary and secondary school enrollment is calculated using data from the PSS. Private school enrollment in prekindergarten through grade 12 includes schools that offer kindergarten or higher grades. About 5.8 million students were enrolled in private elementary and secondary schools in fall 2015, an overall decrease of 0.3 million students (or 4 percent) from fall 1999 (6.0 million students). Enrollment in prekindergarten through grade 8 followed a similar pattern: it decreased by 10 percent, from 4.8 million students in fall 1999 to 4.3 million students in fall 2015. However, enrollment in grades 9 through 12 was 18 percent higher in fall 2015 (1.4 million students) than in fall 1999 (1.2 million students). Of those 5.8 million students enrolled in private elementary and secondary schools in 2015, some 75 percent were enrolled in prekindergarten through grade 8, and 25 percent were enrolled in grades 9 through 12.

Homeschool Enrollment Trends: 1999 to 2016

Figure 1.5. Number of homeschooled students ages 5 through 17 with a grade equivalent of kindergarten through 12th grade, by grade equivalent: Selected years, 1999 through 2016

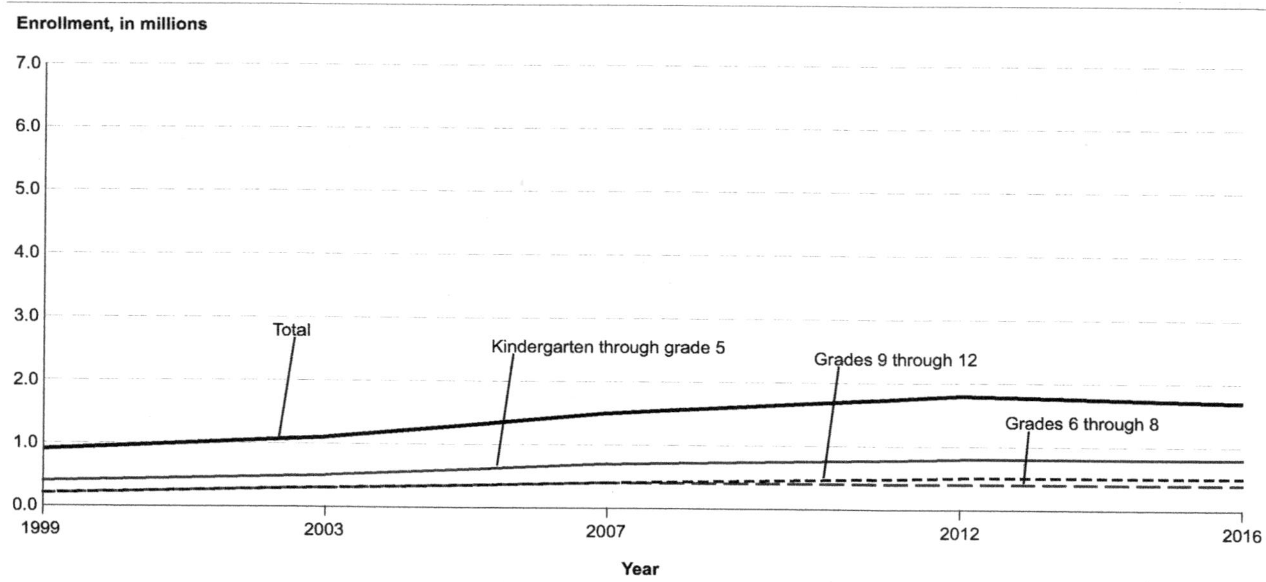

NOTE: Students are considered to be homeschooled if their parents reported them being schooled at home instead of at a public or private school, if their enrollment in public or private schools did not exceed 25 hours a week, and if they were not being homeschooled only due to a temporary illness. Homeschooled students include children ages 5 to 17 with a grade equivalent of kindergarten through grade 12. Students whose grade equivalent was "ungraded" were excluded from the grade analysis. While National Household Education Surveys Program (NHES) administrations prior to 2012 were administered via telephone with an interviewer, NHES:2012 and NHES:2016 used self-administered paper-and-pencil questionnaires that were mailed to respondents. Measurable differences between estimates for years prior to 2012 and estimates for later years could reflect actual changes in the population, or the changes could be due to the mode change from telephone to mail. The National Center for Education Statistics uses a statistical adjustment for estimates of homeschoolers in 2012. For more information about this adjustment, please see *Homeschooling in the United States: 2012* (NCES 2016-096REV).
SOURCE: U.S. Department of Education, National Center for Education Statistics, Parent Survey and Parent and Family Involvement in Education Survey of the National Household Education Surveys Program (Parent-NHES:1999 and PFI-NHES:2003, 2007, 2012, and 2016).

Data on homeschooled students come from the NHES PFI survey. Homeschooled students include children ages 5 to 17 with a grade equivalent of kindergarten through grade 12. The number of homeschooled students in 2016 (1.7 million) was almost double the number in 1999 (0.9 million). The numbers of homeschooled students have increased in all grade equivalent levels. From 1999 to 2016, the numbers of homeschooled students increased by 79 percent for students with a grade equivalent of kindergarten through grade 5 (from 0.4 million to 0.8 million), by 114 percent for students with a grade equivalent of grade 6 through grade 8 (from 0.2 million to 0.4 million), and by 124 percent for students with a grade equivalent of grade 9 through grade 12 (from 0.2 million to 0.5 million). Of the 1.7 million homeschooled students in 2016, some 45 percent had a grade equivalent of kindergarten through grade 5, some 24 percent had a grade equivalent of grades 6 through 8, and the remaining 31 percent had a grade equivalent of grades 9 through 12.

Endnotes:

[1] Elementary schools include schools beginning with grade 6 or below and with no grade higher than 8. Secondary schools include schools with no grade lower than 7. Combined elementary/secondary schools include schools beginning with grade 6 or below and ending with grade 9 or above.

Reference tables: Tables 1.1, 1.2, 1.3, and 1.4

Indicator 2

Public Schools and Enrollment

In fall 2016, a higher percentage of public charter school students than of traditional public school students were Black (26 vs. 15 percent) and Hispanic (33 vs. 26 percent), while a higher percentage of traditional public school students than of public charter school students were White (49 vs. 32 percent) and Asian/Pacific Islander (6 vs. 4 percent).

In fall 2016, about 47.3 million (94 percent) public school students attended traditional public schools and 3.0 million (6 percent) attended public charter schools.[1] Traditional public schools accounted for 93 percent (91,100) of all public schools, while public charter schools accounted for 7 percent (7,000). The pupil/teacher ratio was 16.1 at traditional public schools and 17.8 at public charter schools.[2] The number of public charter schools and their enrollments have increased substantially in recent years. The number of public charter schools increased by 252 percent (from 2,000 to 7,000) between fall 2001 and fall 2016, compared with a slight decrease of less than 1 percent for traditional public schools. The enrollment of public charter schools increased by 571 percent (from 0.4 million to 3.0 million) during the same period, compared with an increase of 1 percent for traditional public schools. This indicator uses the Common Core of Data to examine the characteristics of traditional and charter public schools and their students.

Figure 2.1. Percentage of all public school students enrolled in public charter schools, by state: Fall 2016

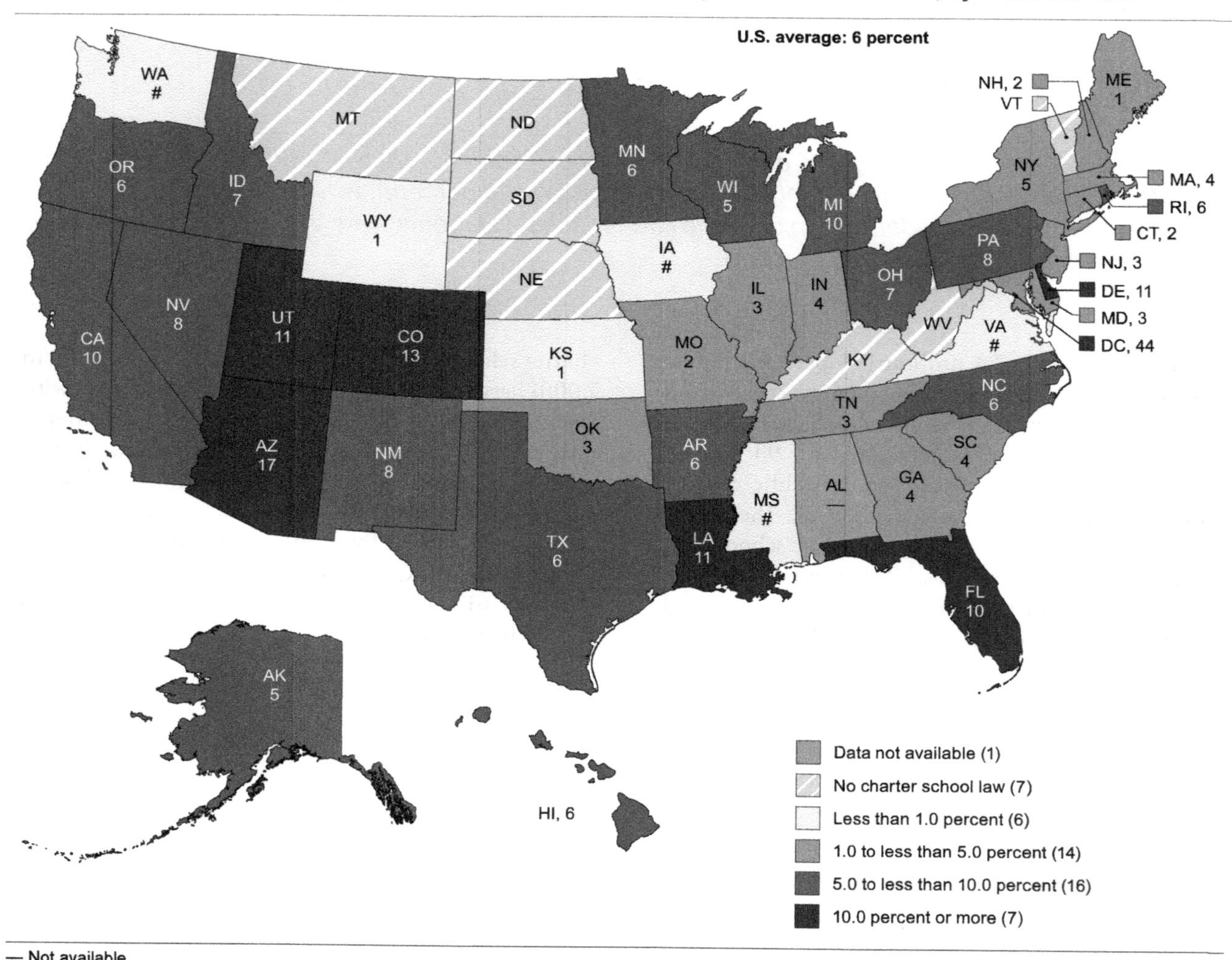

— Not available.
Rounds to zero.
NOTE: Categorizations are based on unrounded percentages.
SOURCE: U.S. Department of Education, National Center for Education Statistics, Common Core of Data (CCD), "Public Elementary/Secondary School Universe Survey," 2016–17.

As of fall 2016, charter school legislation had been passed in 43 states and the District of Columbia. Seven states (Kentucky, Montana, Nebraska, North Dakota, South Dakota, Vermont, and West Virginia) had not passed public charter school legislation by that time. Even among those states with charter school legislation, the laws varied from state to state with respect to issues such as the entities that could authorize charter schools and the required teacher qualifications.[3] Of the 44 jurisdictions with legislative approval for public charter schools as of fall 2016,[4] the District of Columbia had the highest percentage of public school students enrolled in charter schools (44 percent), followed by Arizona (17 percent) and Colorado (13 percent). In contrast, less than 1 percent of public school students were enrolled in charter schools in Iowa, Kansas, Mississippi, Virginia, Washington, and Wyoming.

Figure 2.2. Percentage distribution of students in traditional public schools and public charter schools, by race/ethnicity, and percentage of traditional public schools and public charter schools, by racial/ethnic concentration: 2016–17

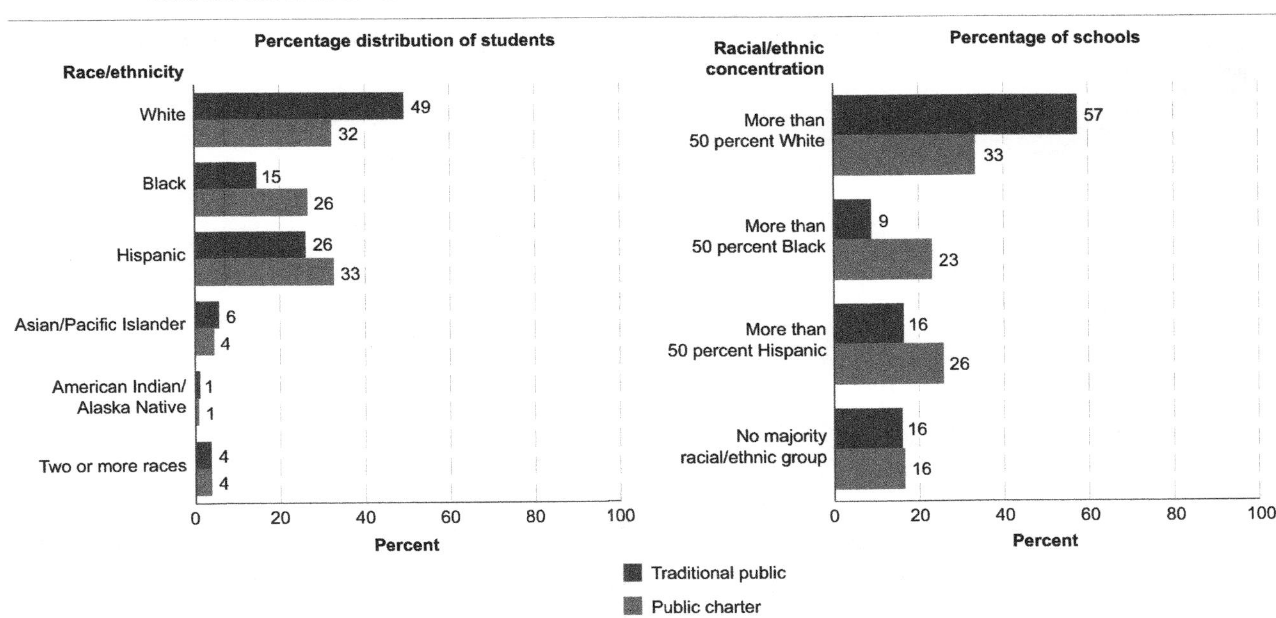

NOTE: Detail may not sum to totals because of rounding. Race categories exclude persons of Hispanic ethnicity. Schools with other racial/ethnic concentrations, such as those with enrollment that is more than 50 percent Asian, Pacific Islander, American Indian/Alaska Native, or Two or more races, are not shown. Although rounded numbers are displayed, the figures are based on unrounded data.
SOURCE: U.S. Department of Education, National Center for Education Statistics, Common Core of Data (CCD), "Public Elementary/Secondary School Universe Survey," 2016–17.

In fall 2016, a higher percentage of traditional public school students than of public charter school students were White (49 vs. 32 percent) or Asian/Pacific Islander (6 vs. 4 percent). In contrast, a higher percentage of public charter school students than of traditional public school students were Black (26 vs. 15 percent) or Hispanic (33 vs. 26 percent). For both traditional public schools and public charter schools, 4 percent of their enrolled students were of Two or more races and 1 percent were American Indian/Alaska Native.

Consistent with these patterns, a higher percentage of traditional public schools than of public charter schools had more than 50 percent White enrollment (57 vs. 33 percent) in fall 2016, while a higher percentage of public charter schools than of traditional public schools had more than 50 percent Black enrollment (23 vs. 9 percent) and more than 50 percent Hispanic enrollment (26 vs. 16 percent). The percentage of schools with no majority racial/ethnic group was 16 percent each for traditional public schools and public charter schools.

Figure 2.3. Percentage distribution of students in traditional public schools and public charter schools and percentage distribution of traditional public schools and public charter schools, by percentage of students in school eligible for free or reduced-price lunch: 2016–17

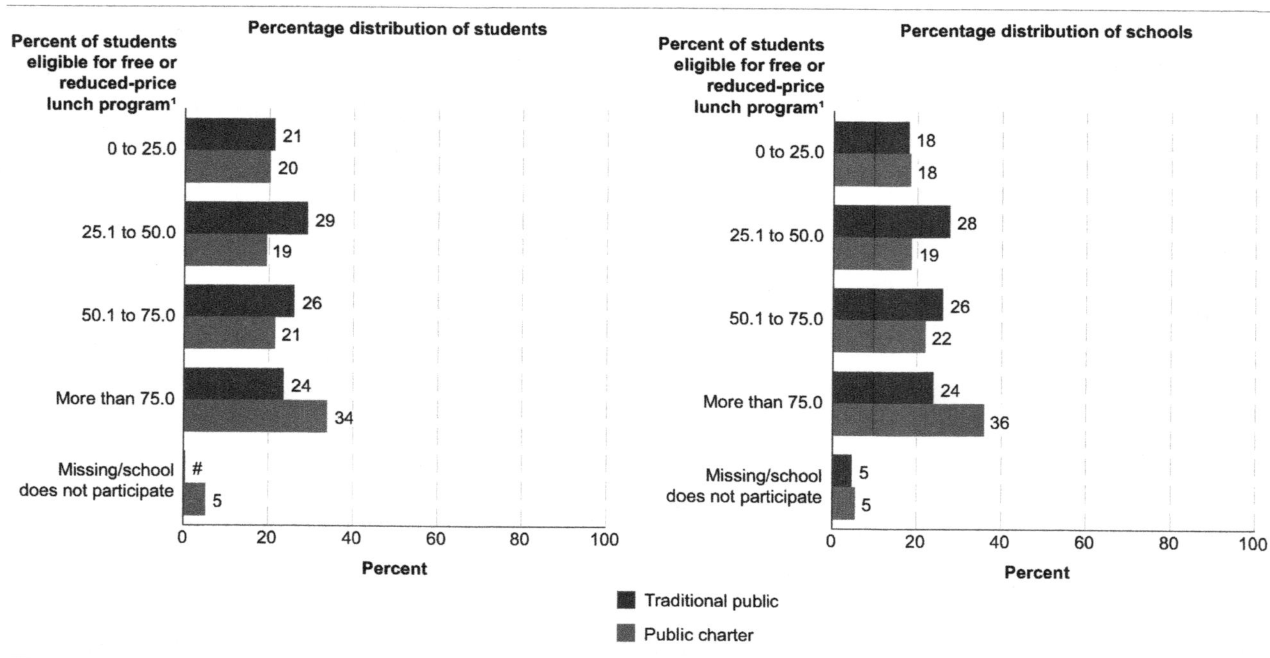

Rounds to zero.

[1] The National School Lunch Program is a federally assisted meal program. To be eligible for free lunch under the program, a student must be from a household with an income at or below 130 percent of the poverty threshold; to be eligible for reduced-price lunch, a student must be from a household with an income between 130 percent and 185 percent of the poverty threshold. In addition, children may qualify for free or reduced-price school lunches through participation in other federal programs or through the Community Eligibility provisions.

NOTE: Detail may not sum to totals because of rounding. Although rounded numbers are displayed, the figures are based on unrounded data.

SOURCE: U.S. Department of Education, National Center for Education Statistics, Common Core of Data (CCD), "Public Elementary/Secondary School Universe Survey," 2016–17.

Schools in which more than 75 percent of students qualify for free or reduced-price lunch (FRPL) under the National School Lunch Program are considered high-poverty schools. Those in which 25 percent or less of students qualify for FRPL are considered low-poverty schools. Compared with traditional public school students, a higher percentage of public charter school students in fall 2016 were enrolled in high-poverty schools (34 vs. 24 percent) and a lower percentage were enrolled in low-poverty schools (20 vs. 21 percent).[5]

Similar to the pattern observed for students, a higher percentage of public charter schools than of traditional public schools were considered high-poverty schools in fall 2016 (36 vs. 24 percent). However, the percentage of public charter schools considered low-poverty schools was 0.3 of a percentage point higher than the percentage of traditional public schools.[6]

Figure 2.4. Percentage distribution of traditional public schools and public charter schools, by school level and enrollment size: 2016–17

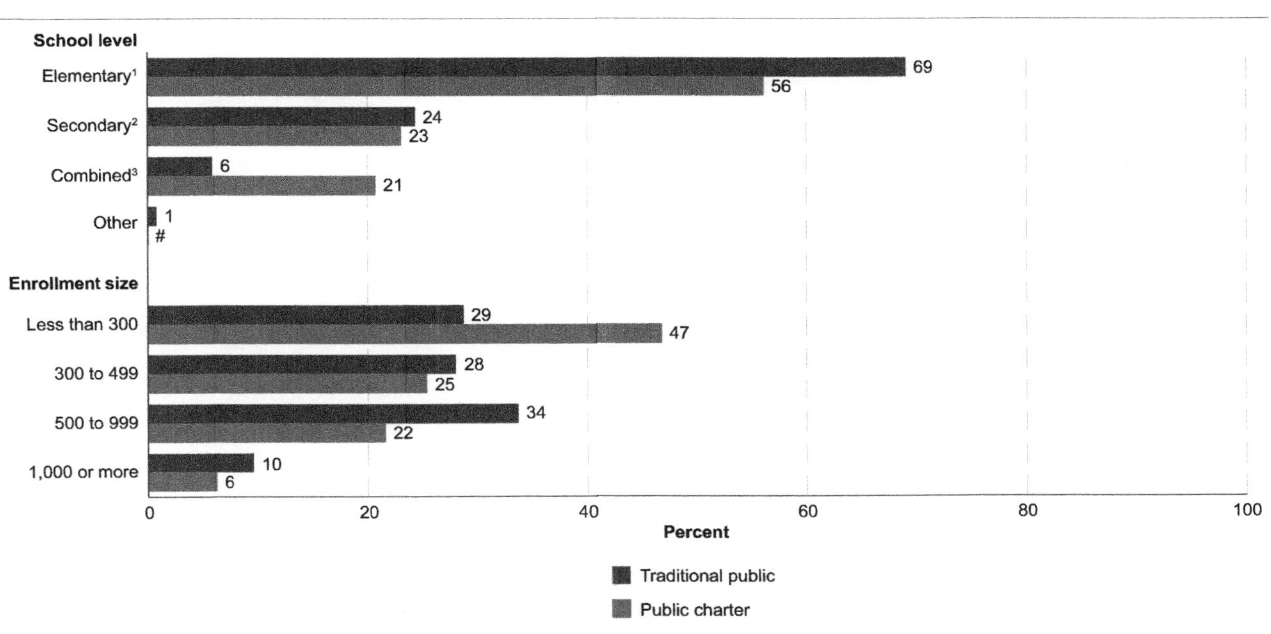

Rounds to zero.
[1] Includes schools beginning with grade 6 or below and with no grade higher than 8.
[2] Includes schools with no grade lower than 7.
[3] Includes schools beginning with grade 6 or below and ending with grade 9 or above.
NOTE: Detail may not sum to totals because of rounding. Although rounded numbers are displayed, the figures are based on unrounded data.
SOURCE: U.S. Department of Education, National Center for Education Statistics, Common Core of Data (CCD), "Public Elementary/Secondary School Universe Survey," 2016–17.

In fall 2016, a higher percentage of traditional public schools than of public charter schools were elementary schools (69 vs. 56 percent) and secondary schools (24 vs. 23 percent). In comparison, a higher percentage of public charter schools than of traditional public schools were combined elementary/secondary schools (21 vs. 6 percent).

Almost half (47 percent) of public charter schools in fall 2016 had an enrollment of less than 300, compared with 29 percent of traditional public schools. Schools of larger sizes (those with an enrollment of 300 to 499, 500 to 999, or 1,000 or more) were more prevalent among traditional public schools than among public charter schools. For instance, 34 percent of traditional public schools had an enrollment of 500 to 999, compared with 22 percent of public charter schools.

Figure 2.5. Percentage distribution of traditional public schools and public charter schools, by school locale and region: 2016–17

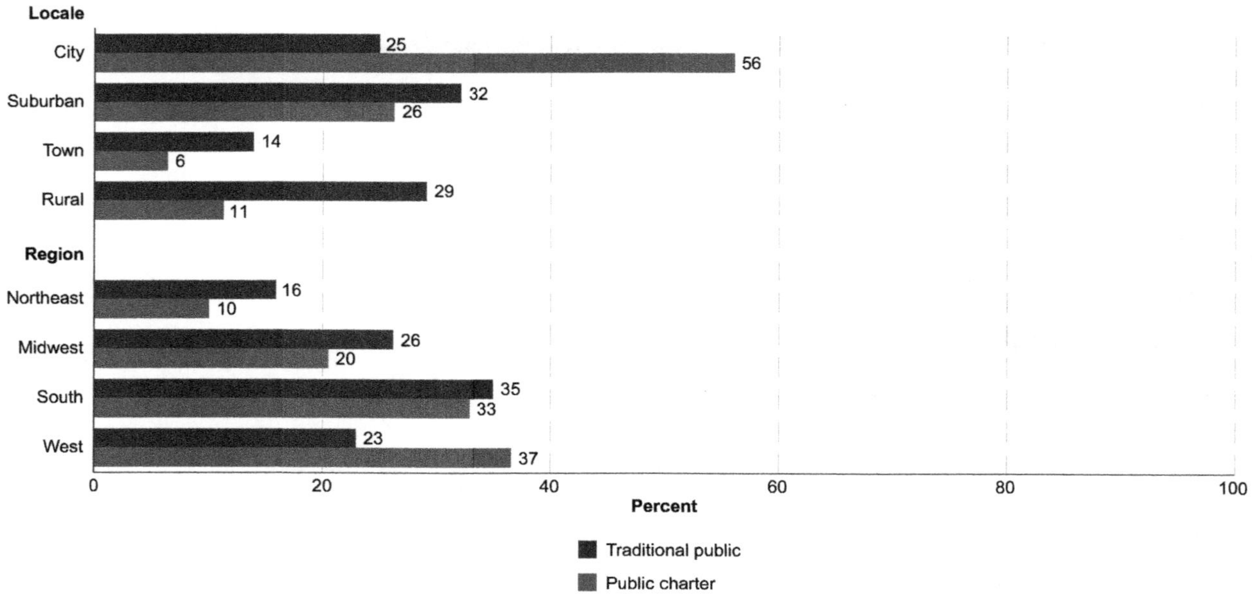

Locale
City 25 56
Suburban 32 26
Town 14 6
Rural 29 11
Region
Northeast 16 10
Midwest 26 20
South 35 33
West 23 37
0 20 40 60 80 100
Percent
Traditional public
Public charter

NOTE: Detail may not sum to totals because of rounding. Although rounded numbers are displayed, the figures are based on unrounded data.
SOURCE: U.S. Department of Education, National Center for Education Statistics, Common Core of Data (CCD), "Public Elementary/Secondary School Universe Survey," 2016–17.

In fall 2016, over half (56 percent) of public charter schools were located in cities, compared with 25 percent of traditional public schools. The percentages of traditional public schools in other locales (suburban areas, towns, and rural areas) were all higher than the percentages of public charter schools. For instance, 29 percent of traditional public schools were located in rural areas, compared with 11 percent of public charter schools.

With respect to region, a higher percentage of public charter schools than of traditional public schools in fall 2016 were located in the West (37 vs. 23 percent) while a higher percentage of traditional public schools than of public charter schools were located in the Northeast (16 vs. 10 percent), Midwest (26 vs. 20 percent), and South (35 vs. 33 percent).

Endnotes:

[1] For a definition of traditional public and public charter schools, see *Indicator 1*. For more information on the growth of traditional public school and public charter school enrollment over time, also see *Indicator 1*.

[2] Pupil/teacher ratio is based on schools that reported both enrollment and teacher data

[3] Wixom, M.A. (2018). *50-State Comparison: Charter School Policies*. Denver, CO: Education Commission of the States. Retrieved January 9, 2019, from https://www.ecs.org/charter-school-policies/.

[4] Data on fall enrollment in public charter schools were not available for Alabama in 2016.

[5] In fall 2016, some 5 percent of public charter school students and less than 1 percent of traditional public school students were enrolled in schools that did not participate in FRPL or had missing data.

[6] In fall 2016, some 5 percent each of public charter schools and traditional public schools did not participate in FRPL or had missing data.

Reference tables: Tables 2.1 and 2.2

Indicator 3

Private Schools and Enrollment

In fall 2015, some 5.8 million students (10.2 percent of all elementary and secondary students) were enrolled in private elementary and secondary schools. Thirty-six percent of private school students were enrolled in Catholic schools, 13 percent were enrolled in conservative Christian schools, 10 percent were enrolled in affiliated religious schools, 16 percent were enrolled in unaffiliated religious schools, and 24 percent were enrolled in nonsectarian schools.

Private elementary and secondary schools are educational institutions that are not primarily supported by public funds. In fall 2015, some 5.8 million students were enrolled in private elementary and secondary schools, accounting for 10.2 percent of all elementary and secondary school enrollment. The pupil/teacher ratio was 11.9 at private schools, which was lower than the ratio of 16.2 at public schools. This indicator describes the characteristics of students enrolled in private elementary and secondary schools, with a focus on how these characteristics vary by religious orientation of the schools. Data come from the Private School Universe Survey (PSS).

This indicator groups private schools into the following five categories based on the school's religious orientation: Catholic, conservative Christian, affiliated religious (schools that are affiliated with denominations other than Catholic or conservative Christian), unaffiliated religious (schools that have a religious orientation or purpose but are not affiliated with any specific denomination), and nonsectarian (schools that are not religiously affiliated). In fall 2015, of the 34,600 private elementary and secondary schools in the United States, 20 percent were Catholic schools, 12 percent were conservative Christian schools, 9 percent were affiliated religious schools, 26 percent were unaffiliated religious schools, and 33 percent were nonsectarian schools. Of the 5.8 million students enrolled in private elementary and secondary schools, 36 percent were enrolled in Catholic schools, 13 percent were enrolled in conservative Christian schools, 10 percent were enrolled in affiliated religious schools, 16 percent were enrolled in unaffiliated religious schools, and 24 percent were enrolled in nonsectarian schools.[1]

Figure 3.1. Percentage distribution of elementary and secondary enrollment, by private school religious orientation, public school type, and student race/ethnicity: Fall 2015

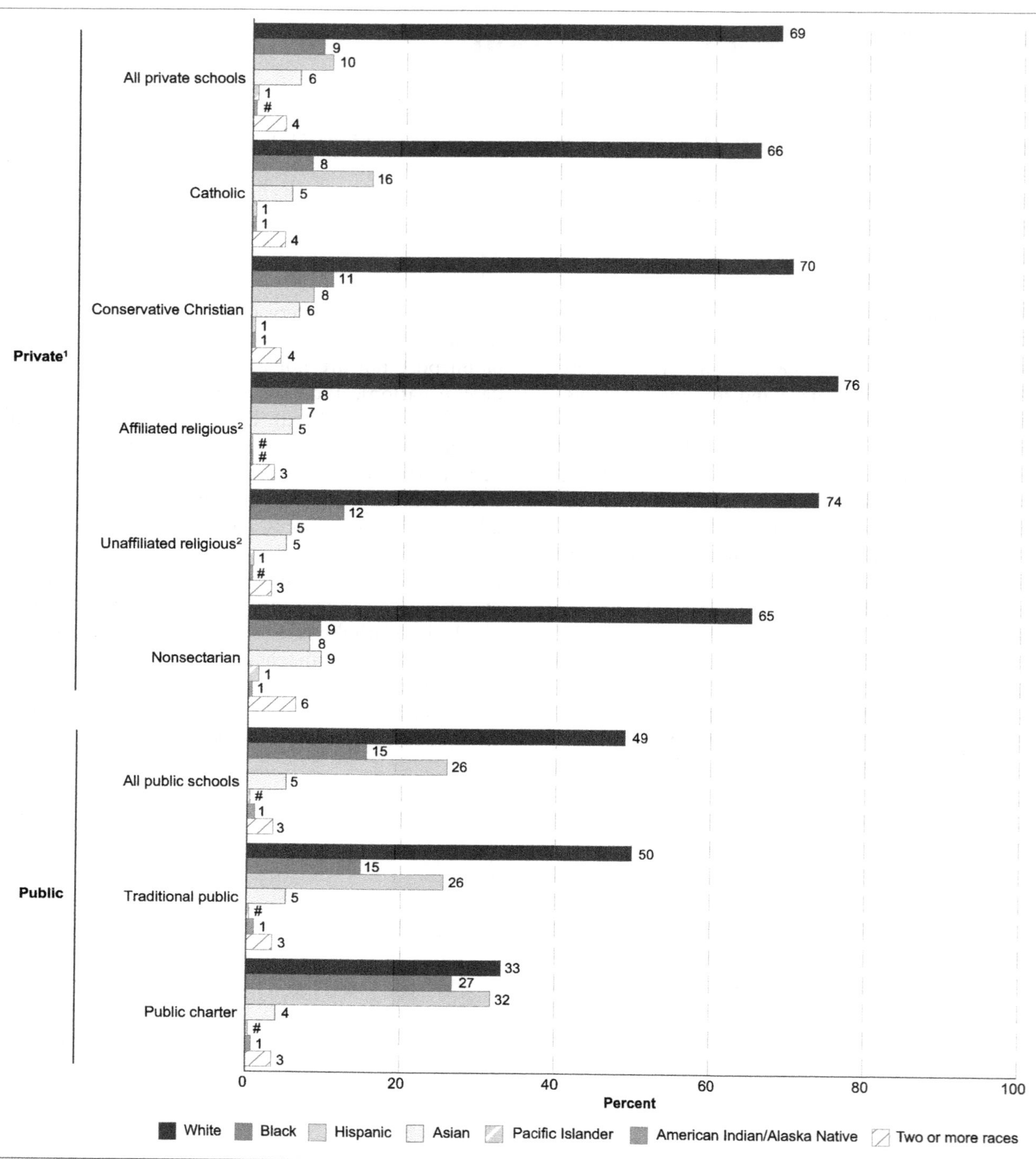

Rounds to zero.

[1] Race/ethnicity was not collected for prekindergarten students at private schools (846,900 out of 5,750,520 students in 2015), thus this figure only includes private enrollment in kindergarten through grade 12. Percentage distribution is based on the students for whom race/ethnicity was reported.

[2] Affiliated religious schools belong to associations of schools with a specific religious orientation other than Catholic or conservative Christian. Unaffiliated religious schools have a religious orientation or purpose but are not classified as Catholic, conservative Christian, or affiliated.

NOTE: Race categories exclude persons of Hispanic ethnicity. Detail may not sum to totals because of rounding. Although rounded numbers are displayed, the figures are based on unrounded data.

SOURCE: U.S. Department of Education, National Center for Education Statistics, Private School Universe Survey (PSS), 2015–16; and Common Core of Data (CCD), "Public Elementary/Secondary School Universe Survey," 2015–16.

In fall 2015, some 69 percent of all private elementary and secondary students were White, 9 percent were Black, 10 percent were Hispanic, 6 percent were Asian, 1 percent were Pacific Islander, one-half of 1 percent were American Indian/Alaska Native, and 4 percent were of Two or more races. In comparison, 50 percent of traditional public school students in fall 2015 were White, 15 percent were Black, 26 percent were Hispanic, 5 percent were Asian, less than one-half of 1 percent were Pacific Islander, 1 percent were American Indian/Alaska Native, and 3 percent were of Two or more races. For public charter school students, 33 percent were White, 27 percent were Black, 32 percent were Hispanic, 4 percent were Asian, less than one-half of 1 percent were Pacific Islander, 1 percent were American Indian/Alaska Native, and 3 percent were of Two or more races.[2] Similar to the overall pattern for all private elementary and secondary students, White students constituted the largest share of enrollment across all five categories of private schools: Catholic (66 percent), conservative Christian (70 percent), affiliated religious (76 percent), unaffiliated religious (74 percent), and nonsectarian (65 percent). Black students made up the second-largest share of enrollment at conservative Christian schools (11 percent), affiliated religious schools (8 percent), and unaffiliated religious schools (12 percent); Hispanic students made up the second-largest share of enrollment at Catholic schools (16 percent). The percentages of students who were Asian or of Two or more races were larger at nonsectarian schools (9 and 6 percent, respectively) than at schools with a religious orientation. Pacific Islander and American Indian/Alaska Native students each made up 1 percent or less of the enrollment across all five categories of private schools.

Figure 3.2. Percentage distribution of private school enrollment in prekindergarten through grade 12, for each school religious orientation, by school level: Fall 2015

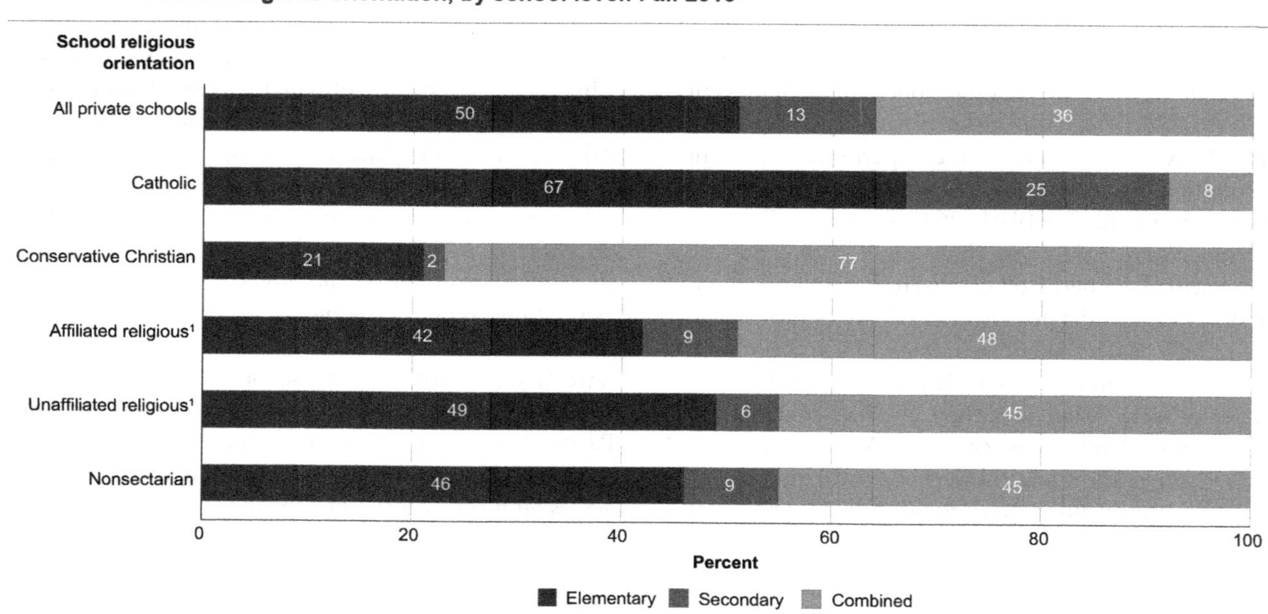

[1] Affiliated religious schools belong to associations of schools with a specific religious orientation other than Catholic or conservative Christian. Unaffiliated religious schools have a religious orientation or purpose but are not classified as Catholic, conservative Christian, or affiliated.
NOTE: Includes enrollment in prekindergarten through grade 12; excludes enrollment in schools that only offer prekindergarten. Elementary schools have grade 6 or lower and no grade higher than 8. Secondary schools have no grade lower than 7. Combined schools include those that have grades lower than 7 and higher than 8, as well as those that do not classify students by grade level. Detail may not sum to totals because of rounding. Although rounded numbers are displayed, the figures are based on unrounded data.
SOURCE: U.S. Department of Education, National Center for Education Statistics, Private School Universe Survey (PSS), 2015–16.

In fall 2015, half of all private elementary and secondary students (50 percent) were at elementary schools, 13 percent were at secondary schools, and 36 percent were at combined elementary and secondary schools. The share of students at elementary schools was highest at Catholic schools (67 percent) and lowest at conservative Christian schools (21 percent). A quarter of Catholic school students (25 percent) attended secondary schools, while 9 percent each of affiliated religious and nonsectarian school students, 6 percent of unaffiliated religious school students, and 2 percent of conservative Christian school students did so. In comparison, the share of students at combined schools was lowest at Catholic schools (8 percent) and highest at conservative Christian schools (77 percent).

Figure 3.3. Percentage distribution of private school enrollment in prekindergarten through grade 12, for each school religious orientation, by school enrollment: Fall 2015

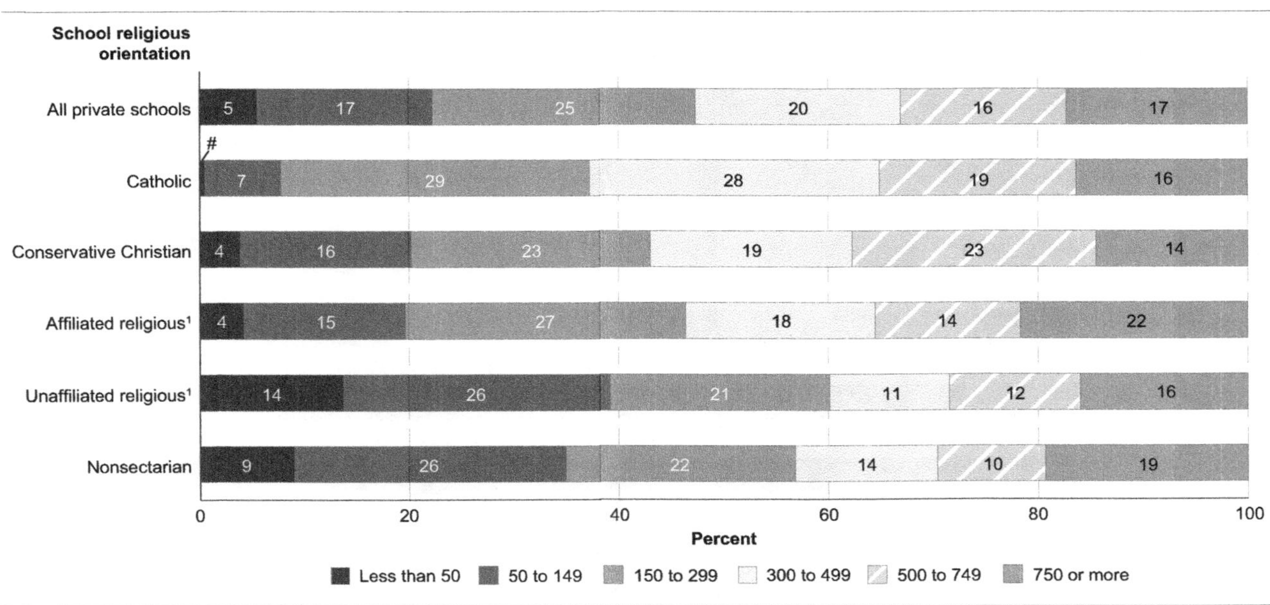

Rounds to zero.

[1] Affiliated religious schools belong to associations of schools with a specific religious orientation other than Catholic or conservative Christian. Unaffiliated religious schools have a religious orientation or purpose but are not classified as Catholic, conservative Christian, or affiliated.

NOTE: Includes enrollment in prekindergarten through grade 12; excludes enrollment in schools that only offer prekindergarten. Detail may not sum to totals because of rounding. Although rounded numbers are displayed, the figures are based on unrounded data.

SOURCE: U.S. Department of Education, National Center for Education Statistics, Private School Universe Survey (PSS), 2015–16.

On average, private schools were smaller than public schools. In fall 2015, the average private school had 166 students and the average public school had 526 students.[3] In fall 2015, some 5 percent of all private elementary and secondary students were enrolled in schools with less than 50 students, 17 percent were enrolled in schools with 50 to 149 students, 25 percent were enrolled in schools with 150 to 299 students, 20 percent were enrolled in schools with 300 to 499 students, 16 percent were enrolled in schools with 500 to 749 students, and 17 percent were enrolled in schools with 750 or more students. The share of students enrolled in schools with less than 50 students was lowest for Catholic school students (one-half of 1 percent) and highest for unaffiliated religious school students (14 percent). In contrast, the share of students enrolled in schools with 300 to 499 students was highest for Catholic school students (28 percent) and lowest for unaffiliated religious school students (11 percent). Twenty-two percent of affiliated religious school students and 19 percent of nonsectarian school students were enrolled in schools with 750 or more students, compared with 16 percent each of Catholic and unaffiliated religious school students and 14 percent of conservative Christian school students.

Figure 3.4. Percentage distribution of private school enrollment in prekindergarten through grade 12, for each school religious orientation, by school locale: Fall 2015

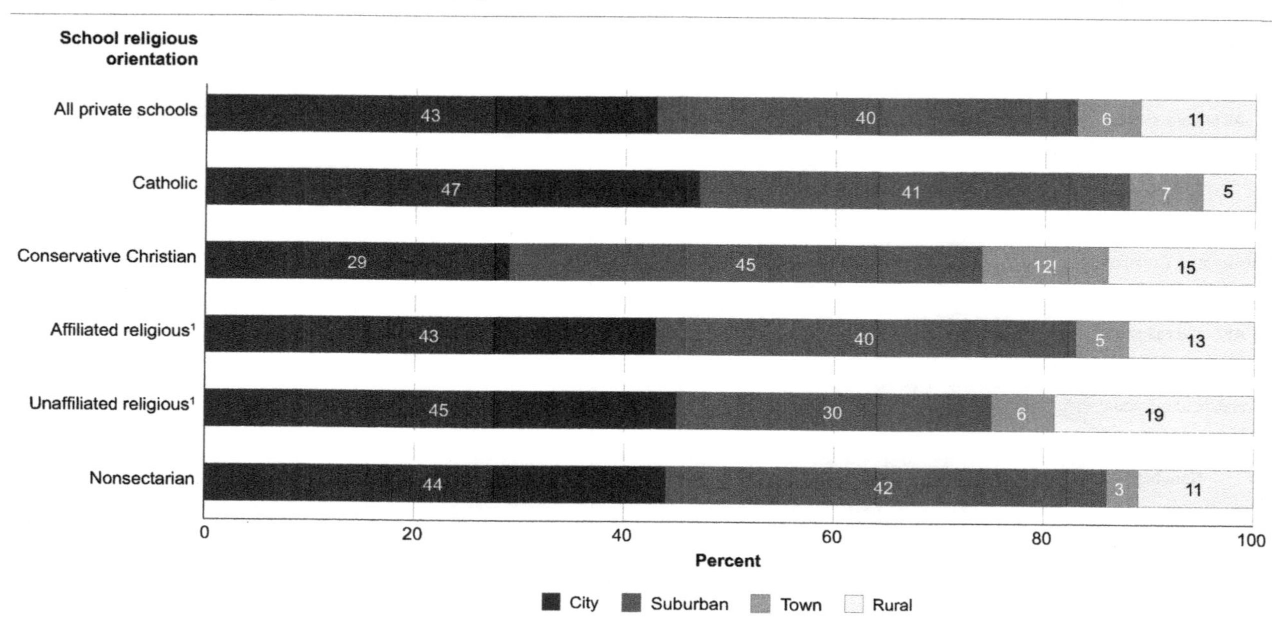

! Interpret data with caution. The coefficient of variation (CV) for this estimate is between 30 and 50 percent.
[1] Affiliated religious schools belong to associations of schools with a specific religious orientation other than Catholic or conservative Christian. Unaffiliated religious schools have a religious orientation or purpose but are not classified as Catholic, conservative Christian, or affiliated.
NOTE: Includes enrollment in prekindergarten through grade 12; excludes enrollment in schools that only offer prekindergarten. Detail may not sum to totals because of rounding. Although rounded numbers are displayed, the figures are based on unrounded data.
SOURCE: U.S. Department of Education, National Center for Education Statistics, Private School Universe Survey (PSS), 2015–16.

In fall 2015, some 43 percent of all private elementary and secondary students were enrolled in schools in cities, 40 percent were enrolled in schools in suburban areas, 6 percent were enrolled in schools in towns, and 11 percent were enrolled in schools in rural areas. The percentage of students enrolled in schools in cities was lower for public elementary and secondary students (30 percent) than for private elementary and secondary students, while the percentages of public elementary and secondary students enrolled in schools in towns (11 percent) and in rural areas (19 percent) were higher than the percentages for private elementary and secondary students.[4] In 2015, the distribution of private elementary and secondary students by school locale varied by school religious orientation. The share of students enrolled in schools in cities was lower at conservative Christian schools (29 percent) than at schools of any other religious orientation; this percentage was also lower at affiliated religious schools (43 percent) and nonsectarian schools (44 percent) than at Catholic schools (47 percent). The share of students enrolled in schools in suburban areas was lower at unaffiliated religious schools (30 percent) than at schools of any other religious orientation, and the share of students enrolled in schools in towns was lowest at nonsectarian schools (3 percent). The share of students enrolled in schools in rural areas was lowest at Catholic schools (5 percent); this percentage was also lower at nonsectarian schools (11 percent) than at conservative Christian schools (15 percent) and unaffiliated religious schools (19 percent).

Table 3.1. Number and percentage of private school students enrolled in prekindergarten through grade 12, for each affiliation of school enrolling 50,000 or more students: Fall 2015

Religious affiliation of school	Number of students	Percent of all private school students[1]
Roman Catholic	2,082,700	36
Christian (no specific denomination)	876,400	15
Jewish	334,400	6
Baptist	239,200	4
Lutheran Church—Missouri Synod	158,300	3
Episcopal	103,700	2
Amish	68,800 !	1 !
Presbyterian	56,100	1
Seventh-Day Adventist	53,300	1

! Interpret data with caution. The coefficient of variation (CV) for this estimate is between 30 and 50 percent.
[1] Detail does not sum to 100 percent because not all categories are reported.
NOTE: Includes enrollment in prekindergarten through grade 12; excludes enrollment in schools that only offer prekindergarten.
SOURCE: U.S. Department of Education, National Center for Education Statistics, Private School Universe Survey (PSS), 2015–16.

An analysis of schools with specific religious affiliations provides more detailed information about private school enrollment. In 2015, schools with nine religious affiliations accounted for 69 percent of the total private elementary and secondary school enrollment, and each of these types of schools enrolled 50,000 or more students: Roman Catholic (2,082,700 students), Christian, no specific denomination (876,400 students), Jewish (334,400 students), Baptist (239,200 students), Lutheran Church—Missouri Synod (158,300 students), Episcopal (103,700 students), Amish (68,800 students), Presbyterian (56,100 students), and Seventh-Day Adventist (53,300 students). Between 1999 and 2015, most affiliations experienced changes in student enrollment of more than 10 percent. For instance, enrollment in Roman Catholic schools was 22 percent lower in 2015 than in 1999 (2,660,400 students), while enrollment in Christian schools with no specific denomination was 44 percent higher in 2015 than in 1999 (609,200 students) and enrollment in Jewish schools was 68 percent higher in 2015 than in 1999 (198,600 students).[5]

Endnotes:

[1] Detail does not sum to 100 percent because of rounding.
[2] Data presented in this indicator on traditional public and public charter schools come from the fall 2015 data collection to provide a comparison with fall 2015 data on private schools. More recent data on traditional public and public charter schools are presented in *Indicator 2*.
[3] See tables 3.5 and 3.3, respectively, for the average enrollment sizes of private and public schools.
[4] See table 3.3 for the percentage distribution of public school enrollment by locale.
[5] See table 3.5 for the fall 1999 student enrollment for each religious affiliation.

Reference tables: Tables 3.1, 3.2, 3.3, 3.4, and 3.5

Indicator 4

Household Characteristics of Students in Public and Private Schools

In 2016, the percentage of students in grades 1 through 12 living in poor households was higher for chosen public school students (19 percent) and assigned public school students (18 percent) than for private school students (8 percent).

This indicator examines student enrollment in assigned public, chosen public, and private schools by selected household characteristics, including the number of parents in the household, the highest education level of parents, and the poverty status of the household.[1] Estimates are based on students enrolled in grades 1 through 12 in public and private schools, and they exclude homeschooled students. Data come from the Parent and Family Involvement in Education (PFI) questionnaire of the National Household Education Surveys Program (NHES). For information on the student and school characteristics for students enrolled in public and private schools, see *Indicators 2* and *3* of this report.

Figure 4.1. Percentage distribution of students enrolled in grades 1 through 12, by school type and number of parents in the household: 2016

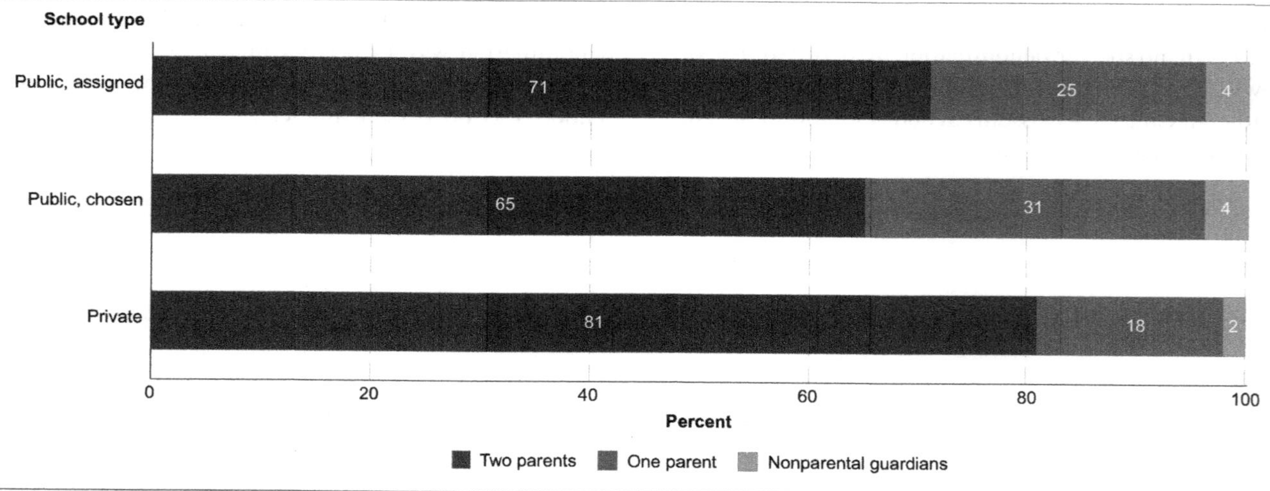

NOTE: Data exclude homeschooled children. Detail may not sum to totals because of rounding. Although rounded numbers are displayed, the figures are based on unrounded data.
SOURCE: U.S. Department of Education, National Center for Education Statistics, Parent and Family Involvement in Education Survey of the National Household Education Surveys Program (PFI-NHES:2016).

In 2016, the percentage of students in grades 1 through 12 who lived in two-parent households was lowest for chosen public school students (65 percent), followed by assigned public school students (71 percent), and was highest for private school students (81 percent). In contrast, the percentage of students who lived in one-parent households was highest for chosen public school students (31 percent), followed by assigned public school students (25 percent), and was lowest for private school students (18 percent). For students enrolled in each of the three types of schools, 4 percent or less lived in households with only nonparental guardians, and this percentage was higher for assigned and chosen public school students (4 percent each) than for private school students (2 percent).

Figure 4.2. Percentage distribution of students enrolled in grades 1 through 12, by school type and highest education level of parents: 2016

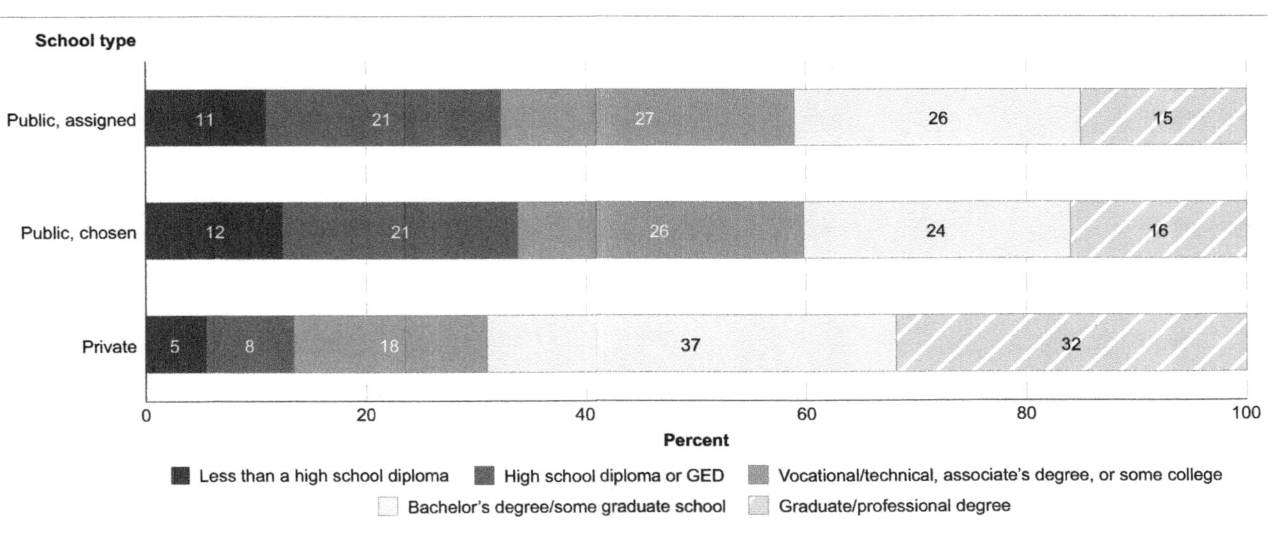

NOTE: Data exclude homeschooled children. Detail may not sum to totals because of rounding. Although rounded numbers are displayed, the figures are based on unrounded data.
SOURCE: U.S. Department of Education, National Center for Education Statistics, Parent and Family Involvement in Education Survey of the National Household Education Surveys Program (PFI-NHES:2016).

In 2016, higher percentages of assigned and chosen public school students than of private school students in grades 1 through 12 had parents whose highest education level was less than a high school diploma, a high school diploma or GED, or some college (some college also includes parents with a vocational/technical diploma or an associate's degree). For example, 12 percent of chosen public school students and 11 percent of assigned public school students had parents who did not complete high school, compared with 5 percent of private school students. In contrast, lower percentages of assigned and chosen public school students than of private school students had parents whose highest education level was a bachelor's degree[2] or a graduate/professional degree. For example, 15 percent of assigned public school students and 16 percent of chosen public school students had parents who had completed a graduate/professional degree, compared with 32 percent of private school students.

Figure 4.3. Percentage distribution of students enrolled in grades 1 through 12, by school type and poverty status of household: 2016

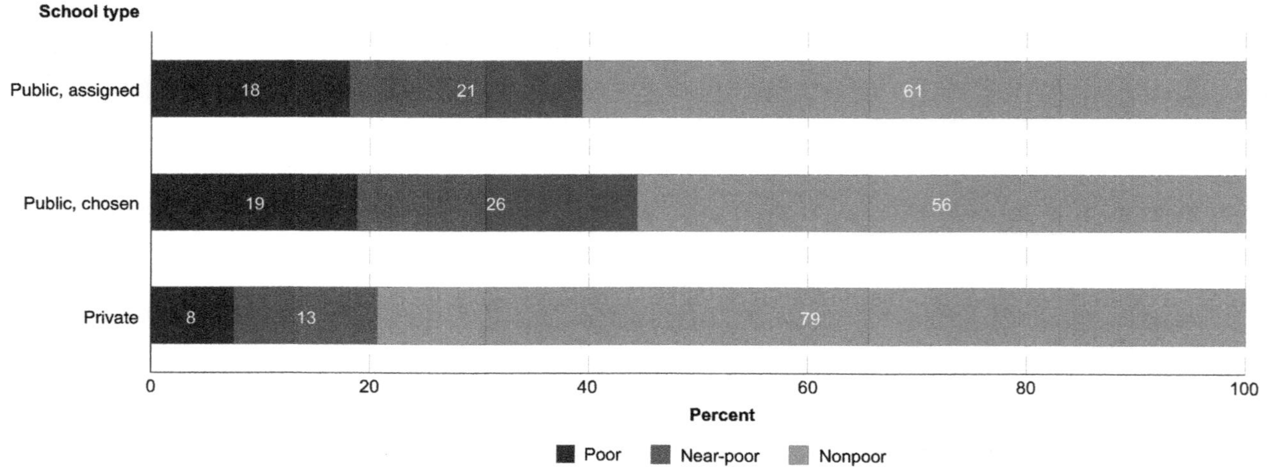

School type	Poor	Near-poor	Nonpoor
Public, assigned	18	21	61
Public, chosen	19	26	56
Private	8	13	79

Percent

NOTE: Data exclude homeschooled children. Poor children are those whose family incomes were below the U.S. Census Bureau's poverty threshold in the year prior to data collection; near-poor children are those whose family incomes ranged from the poverty threshold to 199 percent of the poverty threshold; and nonpoor children are those whose family incomes were at or above 200 percent of the poverty threshold. The poverty threshold is a dollar amount that varies depending on a family's size and composition and is updated annually to account for inflation. In 2015, for example, the poverty threshold for a family of four with two children was $24,036. Survey respondents are asked to select the range within which their income falls, rather than giving the exact amount of their income; therefore, the measure of poverty status is an approximation. Detail may not sum to totals because of rounding.
SOURCE: U.S. Department of Education, National Center for Education Statistics, Parent and Family Involvement in Education Survey of the National Household Education Surveys Program (PFI-NHES:2016).

In 2016, the percentage of students in grades 1 through 12 living in poor households[3] was higher for chosen public school students (19 percent) and assigned public school students (18 percent) than for private school students (8 percent). The percentage of students living in near-poor households was highest for chosen public school students (26 percent), followed by assigned public school students (21 percent), and was lowest for private school students (13 percent). In contrast, the percentage of students living in nonpoor households was lowest for chosen public school students (56 percent), followed by assigned public school students (61 percent), and was highest for private school students (79 percent).

Endnotes:

[1] A student is considered to be attending an assigned public school if the parent indicates that the school is the student's "regularly assigned" school. A student is considered to be attending a chosen public school if the parent indicates that the school is not the student's regularly assigned school (e.g., a traditional public school located outside the assignment boundary based on the student's residence, a charter school, or a magnet school).

[2] Includes parents with some graduate school education but no graduate/professional degree.

[3] Poor children are those whose family incomes were below the U.S. Census Bureau's poverty threshold in the year prior to data collection; near-poor children are those whose family incomes ranged from the poverty threshold to 199 percent of the poverty threshold; and nonpoor children are those whose family incomes were at or above 200 percent of the poverty threshold. The poverty threshold is a dollar amount that varies depending on a family's size and composition and is updated annually to account for inflation. In 2015, for example, the poverty threshold for a family of four with two children was $24,036. Survey respondents are asked to select the range within which their income falls, rather than giving the exact amount of their income; therefore, the measure of poverty status is an approximation.

Reference tables: Table 4.1

Indicator 5

Homeschooling

In 2016, the percentage of students who were homeschooled was higher for those living in households with three or more children (4.7 percent) than for those who were the only child in the household (2.7 percent) and for those living in households with two children (2.3 percent).

Students are considered to be homeschooled if their parents reported them being schooled at home instead of at a public or private school, if their enrollment in public or private schools did not exceed 25 hours a week, and if they were not being homeschooled only due to a temporary illness. Homeschooled students include children ages 5 to 17 with a grade equivalent of kindergarten through grade 12. The number of homeschooled students increased from 850,000 in 1999 to 1,690,000 in 2016, and the percentage of students who were homeschooled increased from 1.7 percent to 3.3 percent over the same time period (see *Indicator 1*). This indicator describes characteristics of students who were homeschooled in 2016 and the reasons parents chose to homeschool their children. Data come from the Parent and Family Involvement in Education (PFI) questionnaire of the National Household Education Survey (NHES).

Figure 5.1. Percentage of homeschooled students ages 5 through 17 with a grade equivalent of kindergarten through grade 12, by student's race/ethnicity and grade equivalent: 2016

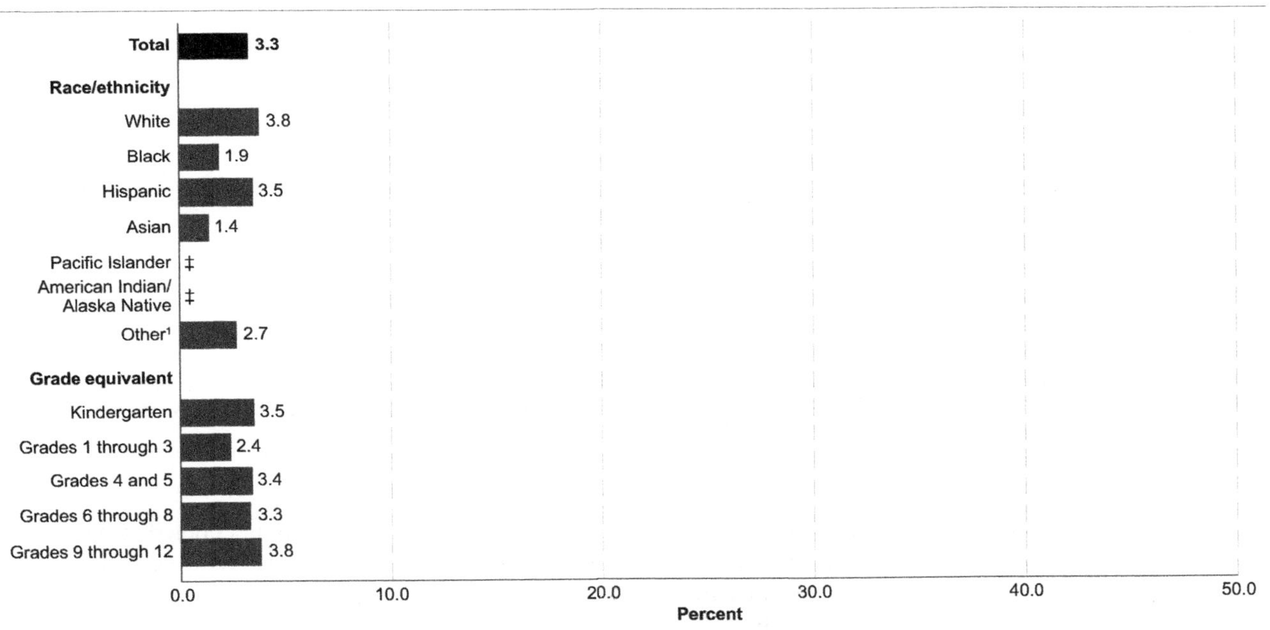

‡ Reporting standards not met (too few cases for a reliable estimate).

[1] Includes Two or more races and race/ethnicity not reported.

NOTE: Students are considered to be homeschooled if their parents reported them being schooled at home instead of at a public or private school, if their enrollment in public or private schools did not exceed 25 hours a week, and if they were not being homeschooled only due to a temporary illness. Although rounded numbers are displayed, the figures are based on unrounded data.

SOURCE: U.S. Department of Education, National Center for Education Statistics, Parent and Family Involvement in Education Survey of the National Household Education Surveys Program (PFI-NHES:2016).

In 2016, about 3.3 percent of children ages 5 to 17 with a grade equivalent of kindergarten through grade 12 were homeschooled, as reported by their parents. The percentage of students who were homeschooled was higher for White (3.8 percent) and Hispanic (3.5 percent) students than for Black (1.9 percent) and Asian (1.4 percent) students. A higher percentage of students whose grade equivalent was 9th through 12th grade were homeschooled (3.8 percent) compared with the percentage of students whose grade equivalent was 1st through 3rd grade (2.4 percent). No measurable differences in the percentages of students who were homeschooled were observed either by students' sex or by students' parent-reported disability status.

The percentage of students who were homeschooled was higher in 2016 than in 1999 for White and Hispanic students and for students whose grade equivalents were from 1st through 12th grade.[1] The percentage of students who were homeschooled was also higher in 2016 than in 1999 for both males and females and for both students who did and those who did not have a disability.

Figure 5.2. Percentage of homeschooled students ages 5 through 17 with a grade equivalent of kindergarten through grade 12, by locale and region: 2016

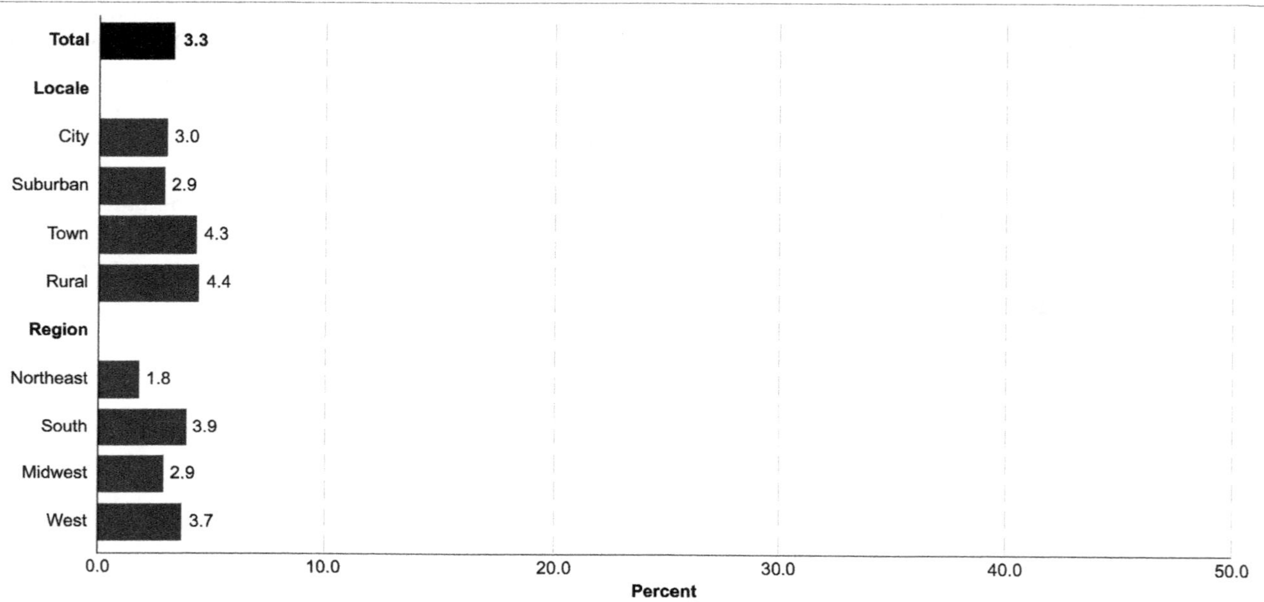

NOTE: Students are considered to be homeschooled if their parents reported them being schooled at home instead of at a public or private school, if their enrollment in public or private schools did not exceed 25 hours a week, and if they were not being homeschooled only due to a temporary illness. Although rounded numbers are displayed, the figures are based on unrounded data.
SOURCE: U.S. Department of Education, National Center for Education Statistics, Parent and Family Involvement in Education Survey of the National Household Education Surveys Program (PFI-NHES:2016).

The percentage of students who were homeschooled in 2016 varied by the locale in which they lived. A higher percentage of students who lived in rural areas (4.4 percent) than of those who lived in cities (3.0 percent) and suburban areas (2.9 percent) were homeschooled. The percentage of students living in towns who were homeschooled (4.3 percent) was not measurably different from the percentages of students living in other locales who were homeschooled. Higher percentages of students in the South and in the West than in the Northeast were homeschooled (3.9 percent in the South, 3.7 percent in the West vs. 1.8 percent in the Northeast). The percentage of students in the Midwest who were homeschooled (2.9 percent) was not measurably different from the percentages of students in other regions who were homeschooled.

The percentage of students who were homeschooled was higher in 2016 than in 1999 for students living in the South, Midwest, and West regions.

Figure 5.3. Percentage of homeschooled students ages 5 through 17 with a grade equivalent of kindergarten through grade 12, by selected family/household characteristics: 2016

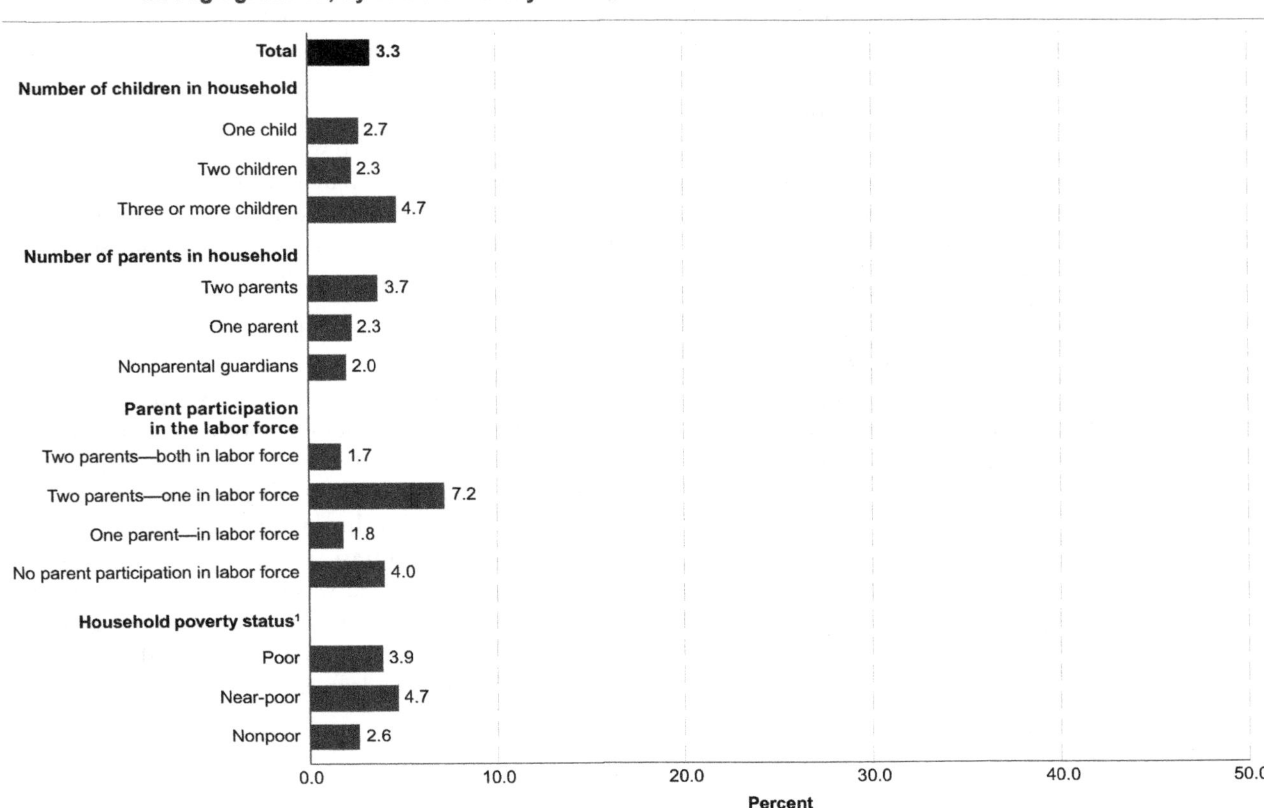

[1] Poor children are those whose family incomes were below the U.S. Census Bureau's poverty threshold in the year prior to data collection, near-poor children are those whose family incomes ranged from the poverty threshold to 199 percent of the poverty threshold, and nonpoor children are those whose family incomes were at or above 200 percent of the poverty threshold. The poverty threshold is a dollar amount that varies depending on a family's size and composition and is updated annually to account for inflation. In 2015, for example, the poverty threshold for a family of four with two children was $24,036. Survey respondents are asked to select the range within which their income falls, rather than giving the exact amount of their income; therefore, the measure of poverty status is an approximation.

NOTE: Students are considered to be homeschooled if their parents reported them being schooled at home instead of at a public or private school, if their enrollment in public or private schools did not exceed 25 hours a week, and if they were not being homeschooled only due to a temporary illness. Although rounded numbers are displayed, the figures are based on unrounded data.

SOURCE: U.S. Department of Education, National Center for Education Statistics, Parent and Family Involvement in Education Survey of the National Household Education Surveys Program (PFI-NHES:2016).

In 2016, the percentage of students who were homeschooled was higher for those living in households with three or more children (4.7 percent) than for those who were the only child in the household (2.7 percent) and for those living in households with two children (2.3 percent). Also, the percentage of students who were homeschooled was higher for those who had two parents living in the household (3.7 percent), compared with those who had one parent (2.3 percent) or who had only nonparental guardians (2.0 percent) in the household.

The percentage of students who were homeschooled was higher in 2016 than in 1999 for each of the number of children household groups. The percentage of students who were homeschooled was also higher in 2016 than in 1999 for students living in two-parent households and for those living in single-parent households.

The percentage of students who were homeschooled also varied by parent participation in the labor force and family income level. The percentage of students who were homeschooled in 2016 was highest for those who had two parents, one of whom was in the labor force (7.2 percent), and next highest for students who had no parent in the labor force (4.0 percent). Lower percentages of students who were homeschooled were from two-parent households with both parents in the labor force (1.7 percent) and from one-parent households with the parent in the labor force (1.8 percent). The percentages of students who were homeschooled were also higher for those who were poor[2] (3.9 percent) and near poor (4.7 percent) than for those who were nonpoor (2.6 percent). No measurable differences were observed for the percentage of students who were homeschooled in relation to their parents' educational attainment.

The percentage of students who were homeschooled was higher in 2016 than in 1999 for students in all labor force and family income level groups. The percentage of students who were homeschooled was also higher in 2016 than in 1999 for students whose parents' educational attainment was a high school diploma or GED or vocational/technical, an associate's degree, or some college. In contrast, the percentage of students who were homeschooled was not measurably different between 2016 and 1999 for students whose parents' educational attainment was a bachelor's degree[3] or a graduate/professional degree.[4]

Figure 5.4. Percentage of homeschooled students ages 5 through 17 with a grade equivalent of kindergarten through grade 12 whose parents identified each listed reason as their most important reason for homeschooling: 2016

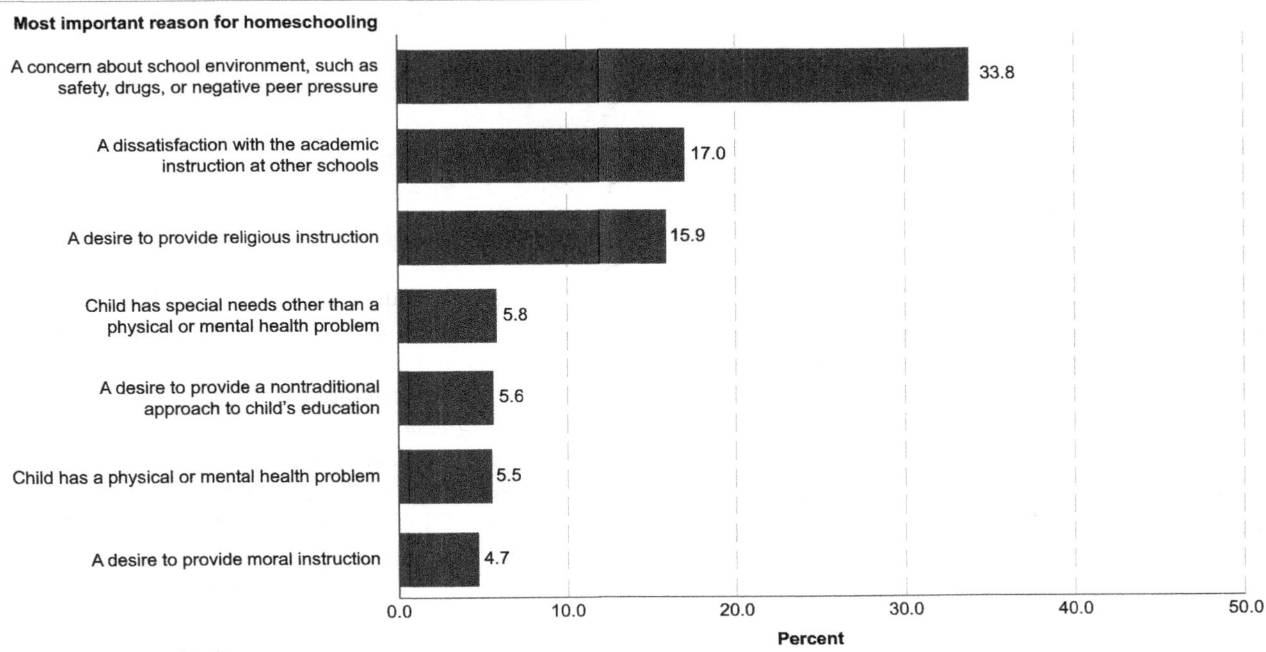

NOTE: Students are considered to be homeschooled if their parents reported them being schooled at home instead of at a public or private school, if their enrollment in public or private schools did not exceed 25 hours a week, and if they were not being homeschooled only due to a temporary illness. In addition to selecting listed reasons, parents could also write in "another reason." About 11 percent of parents wrote in another reason for homeschooling as the most important one; other reasons included family time, finances, travel, and a more flexible schedule.

SOURCE: U.S. Department of Education, National Center for Education Statistics, Parent and Family Involvement in Education Survey of the National Household Education Surveys Program (PFI-NHES:2016).

In 2016, parents of homeschooled students were asked to identify the most important reason for choosing to homeschool their child. The reason for choosing homeschooling that was reported as the most important by the highest percentage of homeschooled students' parents was a concern about school environment, such as safety, drugs, or negative peer pressure (34 percent). The two other reasons for homeschooling frequently cited as most important by students' parents were dissatisfaction with the academic instruction at their schools (17 percent) and a desire to provide religious instruction (16 percent).

Endnotes:

[1] See tables 5.1 and 5.3 for the 1999 data referenced in this indicator.

[2] Poor children are those whose family incomes were below the U.S. Census Bureau's poverty threshold in the year prior to data collection, near-poor children are those whose family incomes ranged from the poverty threshold to 199 percent of the poverty threshold, and nonpoor children are those whose family incomes were at or above 200 percent of the poverty threshold. The poverty threshold is a dollar amount that varies depending on a family's size and composition and is updated annually to account for inflation. In 2015, for example, the poverty threshold for a family of four with two children was $24,036. Survey respondents were asked to select the range within which their income fell, rather than to give the exact amount of their income; therefore, the measure of poverty status is an approximation.

[3] Includes parents with some graduate school education.

[4] A comparison was not conducted for students whose parents' educational attainment was less than a high school diploma/GED, because the 1999 data did not meet reporting standards.

Reference tables: Tables 5.1, 5.2, and 5.3

Indicator 6

Reading and Mathematics Performance

In 2017, no measurable differences in average 8th-grade reading and mathematics scores on the National Assessment of Educational Progress (NAEP) were observed between students in traditional public and public charter schools. This pattern persisted after taking into account how differences in parents' educational attainment were related to the assessment scores.

The National Assessment of Educational Progress (NAEP) assesses student academic performance at grades 4, 8, and 12 in both public and private schools across the nation. Using data collected in the NAEP 2017 reading and mathematics administrations, this indicator describes student assessment scores in 4th and 8th grade for students enrolled in traditional public schools and public charter schools.[1] The NAEP reading and mathematics scores range from 0 to 500 for both grade levels.[2]

Achievement score differences between students who were enrolled in traditional public and public charter schools could be influenced by factors other than school type, including socioeconomic background characteristics such as parents' educational attainment. In addition, enrollment in different types of schools varies by socioeconomic background.[3] Thus, it is important that explorations of how student achievement varies by school type account for these factors. This indicator reports findings from bivariate (*t* test) comparisons of 8th-grade reading and mathematics scores for students in traditional public and public charter schools, as well as multiple regression analyses that compare scores after controlling for parents' educational attainment. For each subject area, a regression analysis was conducted using the NAEP Data Explorer (NDE). For the analysis, which included all public school students, the dependent variable was the reading or mathematics score and the independent variables were public school type (traditional vs. charter) and parents' highest educational attainment. More complex relationships cannot be reported, and the available data do not allow controls for other student and school characteristics that research has shown are substantively correlated with student assessment scores and school type.[4] In addition, regression analyses were not possible for 4th-grade scores because students did not report on their parents' educational attainment.

Figure 6.1. Average National Assessment of Educational Progress (NAEP) reading scale score of 8th- and 4th-graders in traditional public and public charter schools: 2017

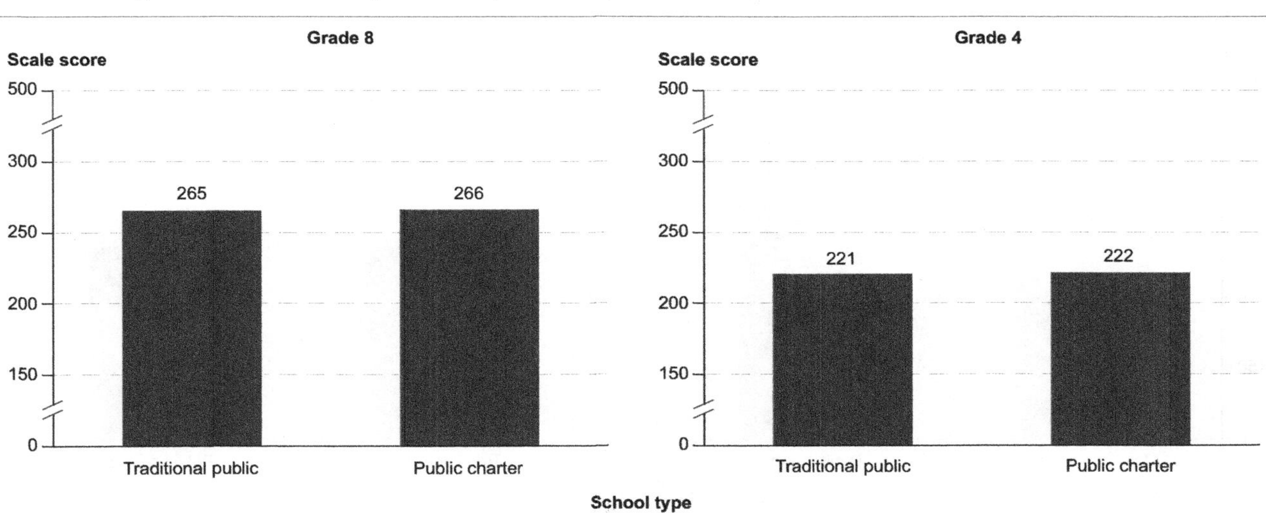

NOTE: While both the 8th- and 4th-grade scores are reported on a scale from 0 to 500, the scale scores are independent of each other—8th-grade results are not comparable to 4th-grade results. This is because the assessments increase in complexity and difficulty at each higher grade level, with the result that they measure different skills at the different grades, even though a progression is implied. Includes students tested with accommodations (11 percent of all 8th-graders and 12 percent of all 4th-graders); excludes only those students with disabilities and English language learners who were unable to be tested even with accommodations (2 percent of all students at both grades). Although rounded numbers are displayed, the figures are based on unrounded data.
SOURCE: U.S. Department of Education, National Center for Education Statistics, National Assessment of Educational Progress (NAEP), 2017 Reading Assessment, retrieved January 8, 2018, from the Main NAEP Data Explorer (https://nces.ed.gov/nationsreportcard/naepdata/).

In 2017, no measurable differences were observed between the average 8th-grade reading scores of students in traditional public (265) and public charter schools (266). This pattern was consistent with results from the regression analysis of 8th-grade scores, in which no measurable differences were observed between the scores of students in traditional public and public charter schools, after controlling for parents' educational attainment.

Bivariate comparisons of average reading scores in grade 4 by school type were consistent with the patterns observed in grade 8. In 2017, no measurable differences were observed between the 4th-grade reading scores of students in traditional public (221) and public charter schools (222).

Figure 6.2. Average National Assessment of Educational Progress (NAEP) mathematics scale score of 8th- and 4th-graders in traditional public and public charter schools: 2017

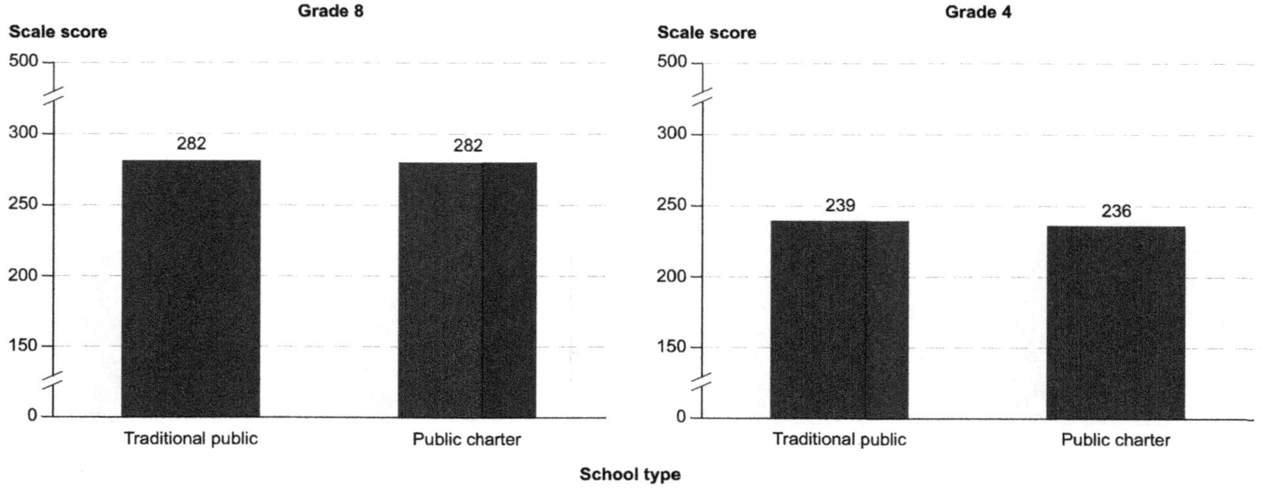

NOTE: While both the 8th- and 4th-grade scores are reported on a scale from 0 to 500, the scale scores are independent of each other—8th-grade results are not comparable to 4th-grade results. This is because the assessments increase in complexity and difficulty at each higher grade level, with the result that they measure different skills at the different grades, even though a progression is implied. Includes students tested with accommodations (12 percent of all 8th-graders and 12 percent of all 4th-graders); excludes only those students with disabilities and English language learners who were unable to be tested even with accommodations (2 percent of all students at both grades). Although rounded numbers are displayed, the figures are based on unrounded data.
SOURCE: U.S. Department of Education, National Center for Education Statistics, National Assessment of Educational Progress (NAEP), 2017 Mathematics Assessment, retrieved January 8, 2018, from the Main NAEP Data Explorer (https://nces.ed.gov/nationsreportcard/naepdata/).

In 2017, no measurable differences were observed between the average 8th-grade mathematics scores of students in traditional public and public charter schools (282 each). This pattern was consistent with results from the regression analysis of 8th-grade scores, in which no measurable differences were observed between the scores of students in traditional public and public charter schools, after controlling for parents' educational attainment.

Bivariate comparisons of average mathematics scores in grade 4 by school type were consistent with the patterns observed in grade 8. In 2017, no measurable differences were observed between the 4th-grade mathematics scores of students in traditional public (239) and public charter schools (236).

Endnotes:

[1] In the 2017 NAEP Nations Report Card, results for private schools overall and for non-Catholic private schools were suppressed because these schools did not meet NAEP statistical and reporting standards requiring a school response rate of at least 70 percent. Response rates for private schools overall were 61 percent at grade 4 and 60 percent at grade 8.

[2] While both the 4th- and 8th-grade scores are reported on a scale from 0 to 500, the scale scores are independent of each other—4th-grade results are not comparable to 8th-grade results. This is because the assessments increase in complexity and difficulty at each higher grade level, with the result that they measure different skills at the different grades, even though a progression is implied.

[3] For example, as noted in *Indicator 4*, the percentage of students whose family incomes were at or above 200 percent of the poverty threshold was lowest for students attending chosen public schools (56 percent), followed by students attending assigned public schools (61 percent), and was highest for students attending private schools (79 percent).

[4] See *The 2017 Mathematics & Reading Assessments Highlighted Results for the Nation, States, and Districts at Grades 4 and 8* (NCES 2018-037) (https://www.nationsreportcard.gov/reading_math_2017_highlights/) for more information on score differences associated with student and school characteristics.

Reference tables: Tables 6.1 and 6.2

Indicator 7

School Crime and Safety for Public and Private School Students

In 2017, a higher percentage of public school students ages 12–18 than of private school students in the same age group reported knowing of a gang presence at school (9 vs. 2 percent), seeing hate-related graffiti at school (25 vs. 6 percent), and being called hate-related words at school (7 vs. 4 percent) during the school year.

Measures of school crime and safety provide important insight into school climate. The School Crime Supplement (SCS) to the National Crime Victimization Survey collected data from students ages 12–18 who were enrolled in public and private schools on various aspects of school crime and safety, including: knowing of gang presence[1] at school,[2] seeing hate-related graffiti at school, being called hate-related words at school, and being bullied[3] at school. Although differences may exist among specific types of public and private schools, this indicator focuses on the overall differences between public and private school students' reports of these incidents as well as trends in the gaps between these groups over time.

Figure 7.1. Percentage of students ages 12–18 who reported that gangs were present at school during the school year, by school type: Selected years, 2001 through 2017

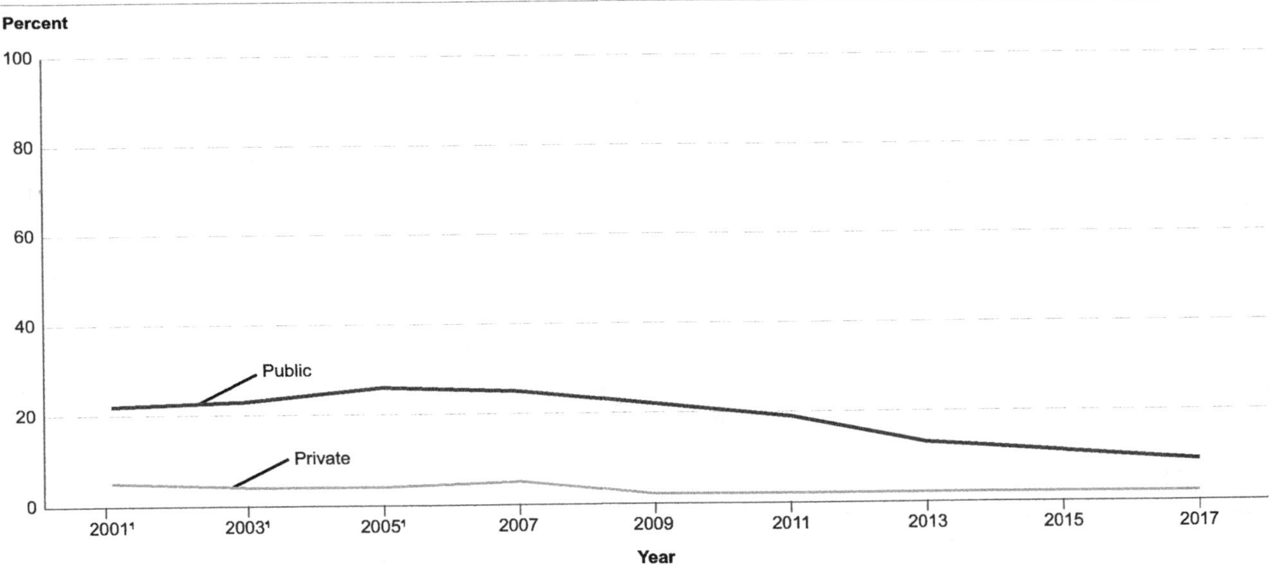

¹ In 2005 and prior years, the period covered by the survey question was "during the last 6 months," whereas the period was "during this school year" beginning in 2007. Cognitive testing showed that estimates for earlier years are comparable to those for 2007 and later years.
NOTE: All gangs, whether or not they are involved in violent or illegal activity, are included. "At school" includes in the school building, on school property, on a school bus, and going to and from school.
SOURCE: U.S. Department of Justice, Bureau of Justice Statistics, School Crime Supplement (SCS) to the National Crime Victimization Survey, 2001 through 2017.

In 2017, a higher percentage of public school students ages 12–18 than of private school students in the same age group reported that gangs were present at their school during the school year (9 vs. 2 percent). The same pattern was observed in every survey year since 2001. Between 2001 and 2017, the percentage of students who reported a gang presence at their school decreased for both public school students (from 22 to 9 percent) and private school students (from 5 to 2 percent). Since the decrease was larger for public school students (13 percentage points) than for private school students (3 percentage points), the gap between public and private school students was smaller in 2017 (8 percentage points) than in 2001 (17 percentage points).

Figure 7.2. Percentage of students ages 12–18 who reported seeing hate-related graffiti at school during the school year, by school type: Selected years, 2001 through 2017

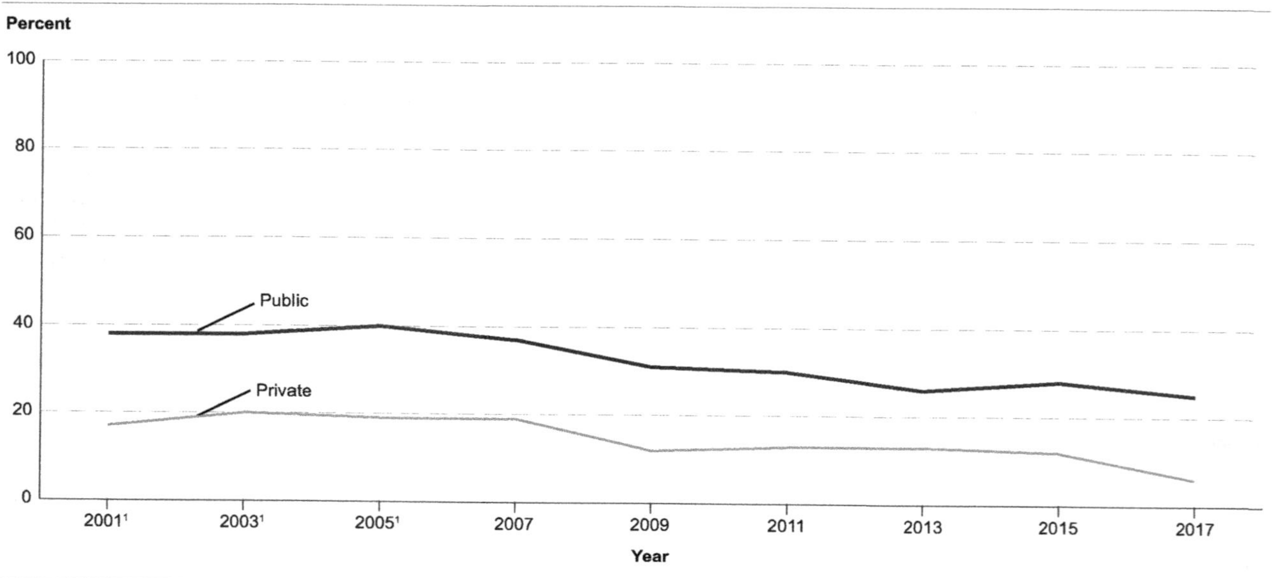

[1] In 2005 and prior years, the period covered by the survey question was "during the last 6 months," whereas the period was "during this school year" beginning in 2007. Cognitive testing showed that estimates for earlier years are comparable to those for 2007 and later years.

NOTE: "At school" includes in the school building, on school property, on a school bus, and going to and from school. "Hate-related" refers to derogatory terms used by others in reference to students' personal characteristics.

SOURCE: U.S. Department of Justice, Bureau of Justice Statistics, School Crime Supplement (SCS) to the National Crime Victimization Survey, 2001 through 2017.

Approximately 25 percent of public school students ages 12–18 reported seeing hate-related graffiti at school—that is, hate-related words or symbols written in classrooms, bathrooms, or hallways or on the outside of the school building—in 2017. In comparison, 6 percent of private school students ages 12–18 reported seeing hate-related graffiti at school. While the percentages of public and private school students who reported seeing hate-related graffiti at school both decreased between 2001 and 2017 (from 38 to 25 percent and from 17 to 6 percent, respectively), the percentage reported by public school students was higher than the percentage reported by private school students in every survey year during this period. Additionally, the gap between the percentages reported by public and private school students did not change measurably between 2001 and 2017.

Figure 7.3. Percentage of students ages 12–18 who reported being called hate-related words at school during the school year, by school type: Selected years, 2001 through 2017

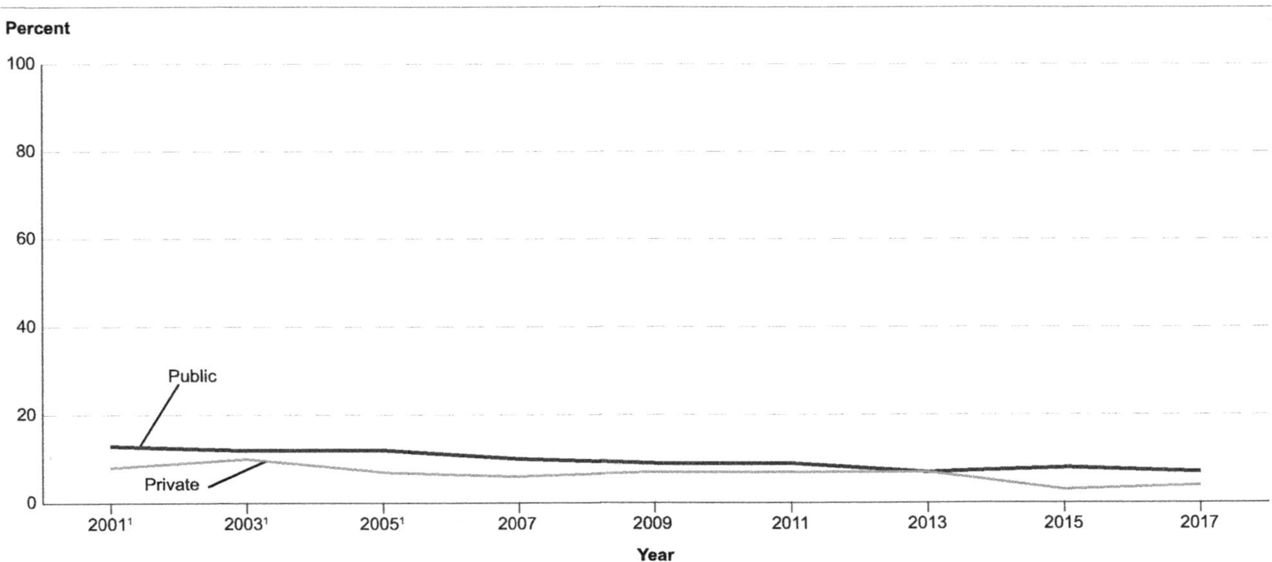

[1] In 2005 and prior years, the period covered by the survey question was "during the last 6 months," whereas the period was "during this school year" beginning in 2007. Cognitive testing showed that estimates for earlier years are comparable to those for 2007 and later years.
NOTE: "At school" includes in the school building, on school property, on a school bus, and going to and from school. "Hate-related" refers to derogatory terms used by others in reference to students' personal characteristics.
SOURCE: U.S. Department of Justice, Bureau of Justice Statistics, School Crime Supplement (SCS) to the National Crime Victimization Survey, 2001 through 2017.

The SCS also asked students ages 12–18 whether someone at school had called them an insulting or bad name having to do with their race, ethnicity, religion, disability, gender, or sexual orientation. In 2017, a higher percentage of public school students than of private school students reported being called hate-related words at school during the school year (7 vs. 4 percent); this pattern was also observed in 2001, 2005, 2007, and 2015. Between 2001 and 2017, the percentage of public school students who reported being called hate-related words at school decreased from 13 to 7 percent and the percentage for private school students decreased from 8 to 4 percent. The gap between the percentages reported by public and private school students in 2017 was not measurably different from the gap in 2001.

Figure 7.4. Percentage of students ages 12–18 who reported being bullied at school during the school year, by school type: Selected years, 2005 through 2017

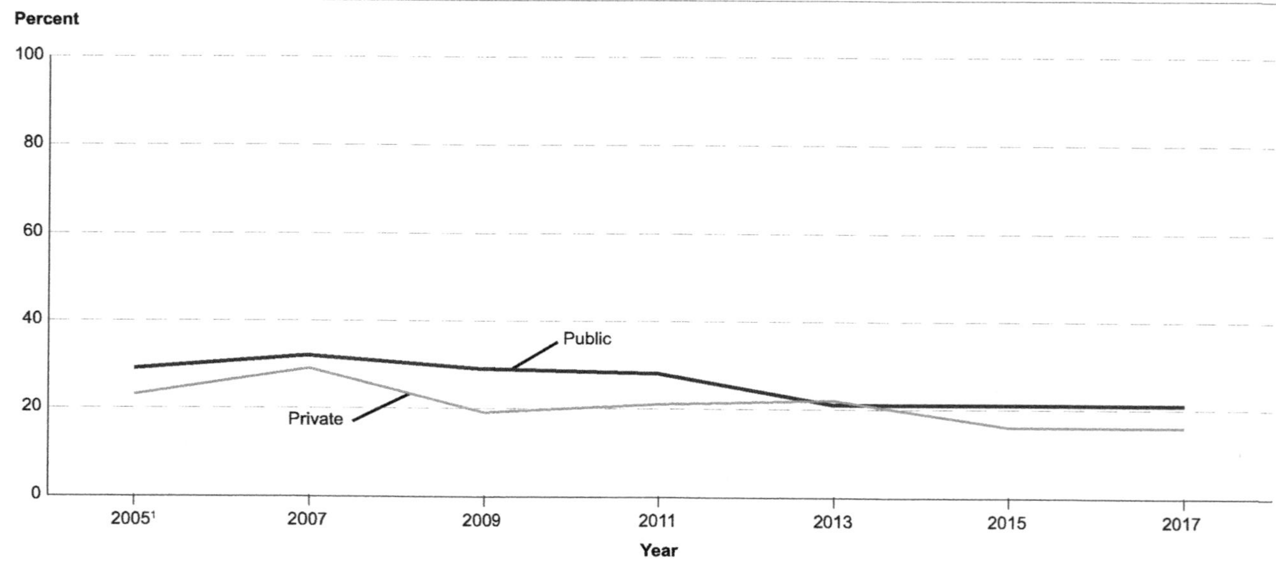

[1] In 2005, the period covered by the survey question was "during the last 6 months," whereas the period was "during this school year" beginning in 2007. Cognitive testing showed that estimates for earlier years are comparable to those for 2007 and later years.
NOTE: "At school" includes in the school building, on school property, on a school bus, and going to and from school.
SOURCE: U.S. Department of Justice, Bureau of Justice Statistics, School Crime Supplement (SCS) to the National Crime Victimization Survey, 2005 through 2017.

In 2017, about 21 percent of public school students ages 12–18 reported being bullied at school during the school year. This was not measurably different from the percentage of private school students who reported being bullied (16 percent).[4] Between 2005 and 2017, the percentage of public school students who reported being bullied at school decreased from 29 to 21 percent.[5] The percentage of private school students who reported being bullied at school was also lower in 2017 than in 2005 (16 vs. 23 percent); however, there was no clear pattern of consistent decrease during this period.

Endnotes:

[1] All gangs, regardless of whether or not they were involved in violent or illegal activity, were included.
[2] "At school" includes in the school building, on school property, on a school bus, and going to and from school.
[3] "Bullying" includes students who reported that another student had made fun of them, called them names, or insulted them; spread rumors about them; threatened them with harm; tried to make them do something they did not want to do; excluded them from activities on purpose; destroyed their property on purpose; or pushed, shoved, tripped, or spit on them. In the total for students bullied at school, students who reported more than one type of bullying were counted only once.
[4] The apparent difference between these estimates was not measurably different due to the confidence interval around the estimates.
[5] Data from prior to 2005 are excluded from this time series analysis due to a significant redesign of the bullying items in 2005.

Reference tables: Tables 7.1, 7.2, and 7.3

Indicator 8

Parental Choice and Satisfaction

In 2016, a higher percentage of students who lived in cities (53 percent) than of those who lived in suburbs (37 percent), towns (36 percent), and rural areas (32 percent) had parents who reported that public school choice was available.

Parental choices about the school their children will attend depend on the options that are available. This indicator examines differences in the choices parents make and their satisfaction with their children's school. Data come from the Parent and Family Involvement in Education questionnaire of the National Household Education Surveys Program (NHES). NHES asked parents about their perception of the availability of public school choice in their school district, whether they considered schools other than the one in which their children were currently enrolled, if the school in which their children were enrolled was their first choice, and if they had moved to a neighborhood so their children could attend a particular school. NHES also asked parents how satisfied they were with their children's school and teachers, the school's academic standards and order and discipline, and the school staff's interaction with parents.

Figure 8.1. Percentage of students enrolled in grades 1 through 12 whose parents reported having public school choice, by household locale and region: 2016

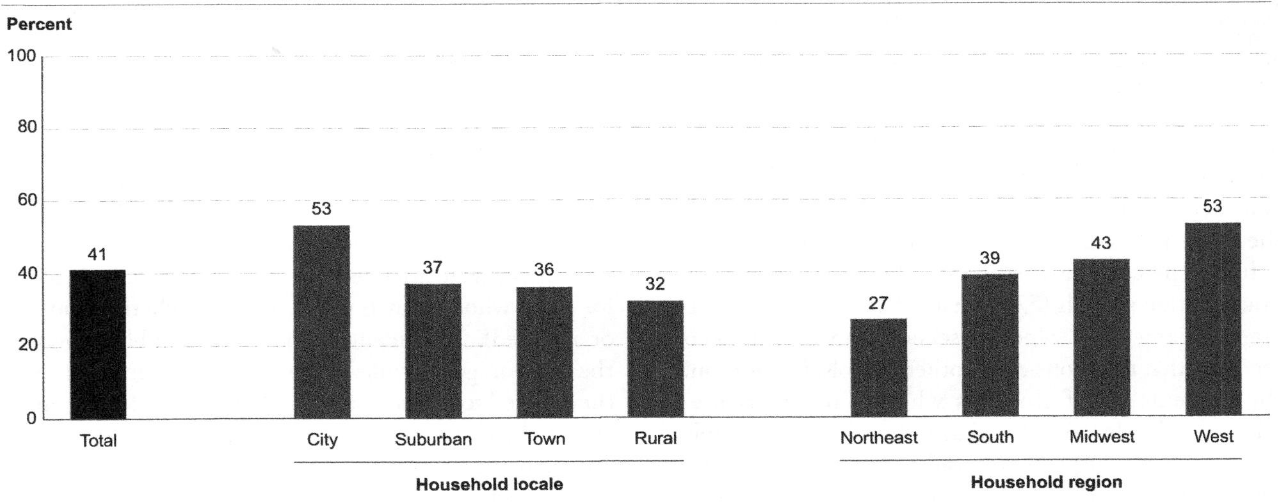

NOTE: Data exclude homeschooled children.
SOURCE: U.S. Department of Education, National Center for Education Statistics, Parent and Family Involvement in Education Survey of the National Household Education Surveys Program (PFI-NHES:2016).

In 2016, about 41 percent of students enrolled in grades 1 through 12 had parents who reported that public school choice was available to them. Public school choice was more common in some places than others. For example, a higher percentage of students who lived in cities (53 percent) than of students who lived in suburban areas (37 percent), towns (36 percent), and rural areas (32 percent) had parents who reported that public school choice was available. Additionally, the percentage of students whose parents reported that public school choice was available was highest for students in the West (53 percent), followed by students in the Midwest (43 percent), the South (39 percent), and the Northeast (27 percent).

Figure 8.2. Percentage of students enrolled in grades 1 through 12 whose parents considered other schools, reported current school was their first choice, or moved to their current neighborhood for the public school, by school type: 2016

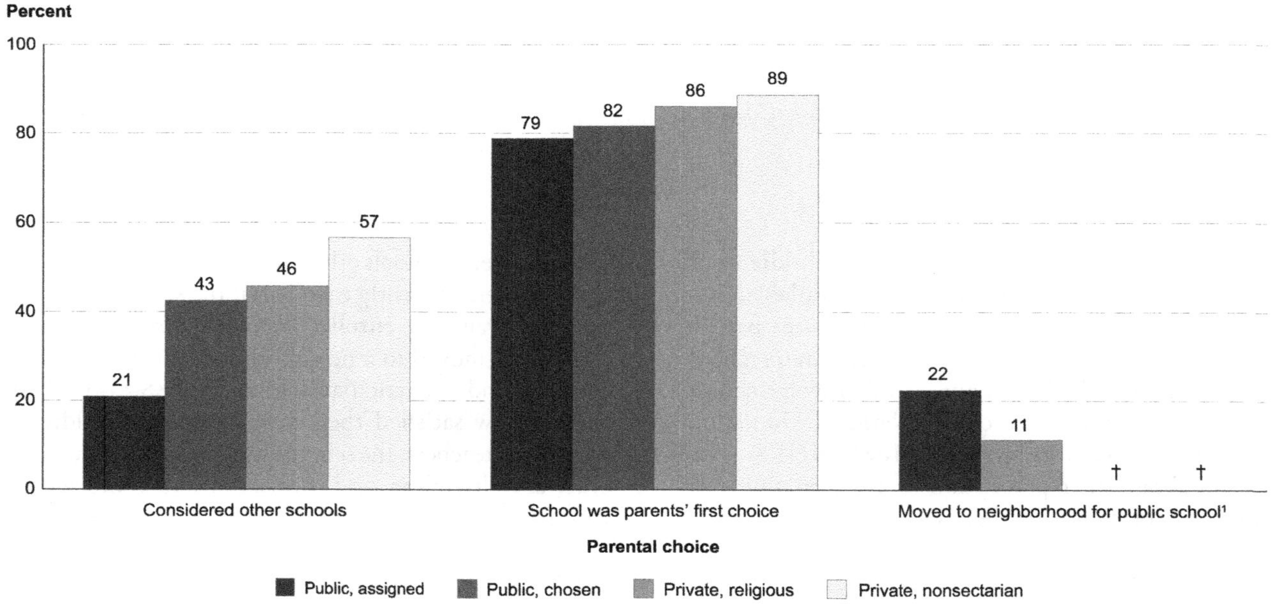

† Not applicable.
[1] Includes public school students only. Private school students are excluded.
NOTE: Data exclude homeschooled children.
SOURCE: U.S. Department of Education, National Center for Education Statistics, Parent and Family Involvement in Education Survey of the National Household Education Surveys Program (PFI-NHES:2016).

The percentage of students enrolled in grades 1 through 12 in 2016 whose parents reported that they considered other schools for their children differed by the type of school their children currently attended. A higher percentage of students who attended private, nonsectarian schools (57 percent) than of students who attended any other types of schools had parents who reported that they considered other schools. In addition, the percentages of students who attended private, religious schools (46 percent) and chosen public schools (43 percent) whose parents considered other schools were higher than the percentage of students who attended their assigned public school (21 percent).[1] The percentage of students whose parents reported that the school their children attended was their first choice was higher for students who attended private, nonsectarian schools and for students who attended private, religious schools than for those who attended public schools (whether chosen or assigned). Of students who attended public schools, the percentage of students whose parents reported that they moved to the neighborhood so their children could attend their current school was higher for students who attended their assigned schools (22 percent) than for students who attended chosen schools (11 percent).

Figure 8.3. Percentage of students enrolled in grades 1 through 12 whose parents considered other schools, reported current school was their first choice, or moved to their current neighborhood for the public school, by family poverty status: 2016

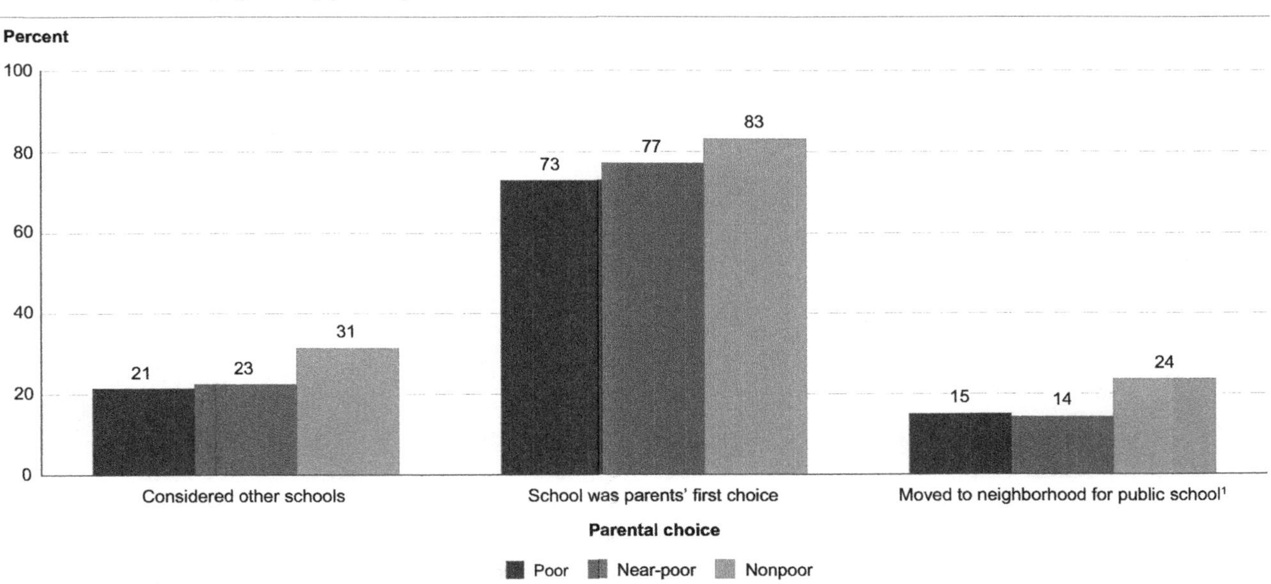

[1] Includes public school students only. Private school students are excluded.
NOTE: Data exclude homeschooled children.
SOURCE: U.S. Department of Education, National Center for Education Statistics, Parent and Family Involvement in Education Survey of the National Household Education Surveys Program (PFI-NHES:2016).

Parental decisions about schools also differed by family poverty status. In 2016, a higher percentage of students enrolled in grades 1 through 12 from nonpoor households (31 percent) than of students from near-poor households (23 percent) or poor households (21 percent) had parents who reported that they considered other schools. Similarly, higher percentages of students from nonpoor households than of students from near-poor or poor households had parents who reported that the school their children attended was their first choice and that they moved to the neighborhood so their children could attend their current public school.

Figure 8.4. Percentage of students enrolled in grades 1 through 12 whose parents considered other schools, reported current school was their first choice, or moved to their current neighborhood for the public school, by highest education level of parents: 2016

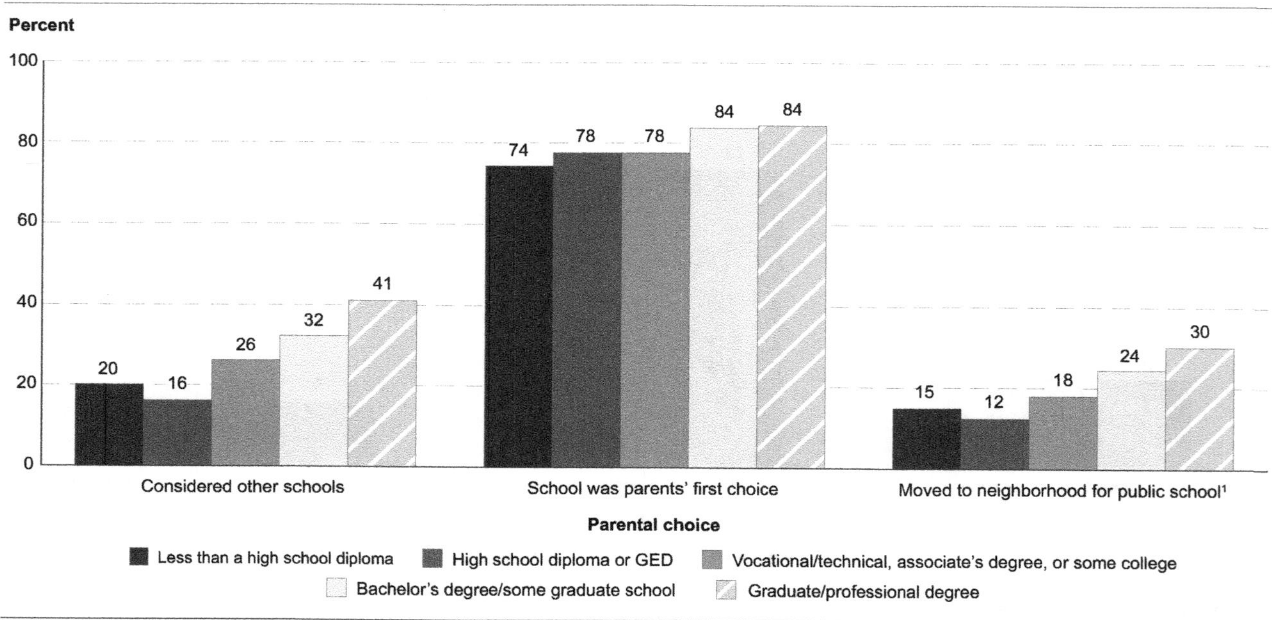

[1] Includes public school students only. Private school students are excluded.
NOTE: Data exclude homeschooled children. Although rounded numbers are displayed, the figures are based on unrounded data.
SOURCE: U.S. Department of Education, National Center for Education Statistics, Parent and Family Involvement in Education Survey of the National Household Education Surveys Program (PFI-NHES:2016).

In 2016, the percentages of students whose parents reported that they considered other schools, that the school their children attended was their first choice, and that they moved to the neighborhood so their children could attend their current public school were higher at each subsequent level of parental educational attainment, with some exceptions. For any of the three parental choices, there were no measurable differences between the percentages for students whose parents' highest level of educational attainment was less than a high school diploma and students whose parents' highest level of educational attainment was a high school diploma or GED.

In 2016, a higher percentage of Black students enrolled in grades 1 through 12 (31 percent) than of White students (26 percent) and Asian students (25 percent) had parents who reported that they considered other schools.[2] A higher percentage of White students (84 percent) than of Asian students (80 percent) and Hispanic students (78 percent) had parents who reported that the school their children attended was their first choice. Additionally, the percentage of Black students whose parents reported that the school their children attended was their first choice (70 percent) was lower than the percentages of White, Asian, and Hispanic students. Higher percentages of Asian students (27 percent) and White students (22 percent) than of Hispanic students (17 percent) and Black students (14 percent) had parents who reported that they moved to the neighborhood so their children could attend their current public school.

Figure 8.5. Percentage of students enrolled in grades 3 through 12 whose parents were very satisfied with various aspects of their children's schools, by school type: 2016

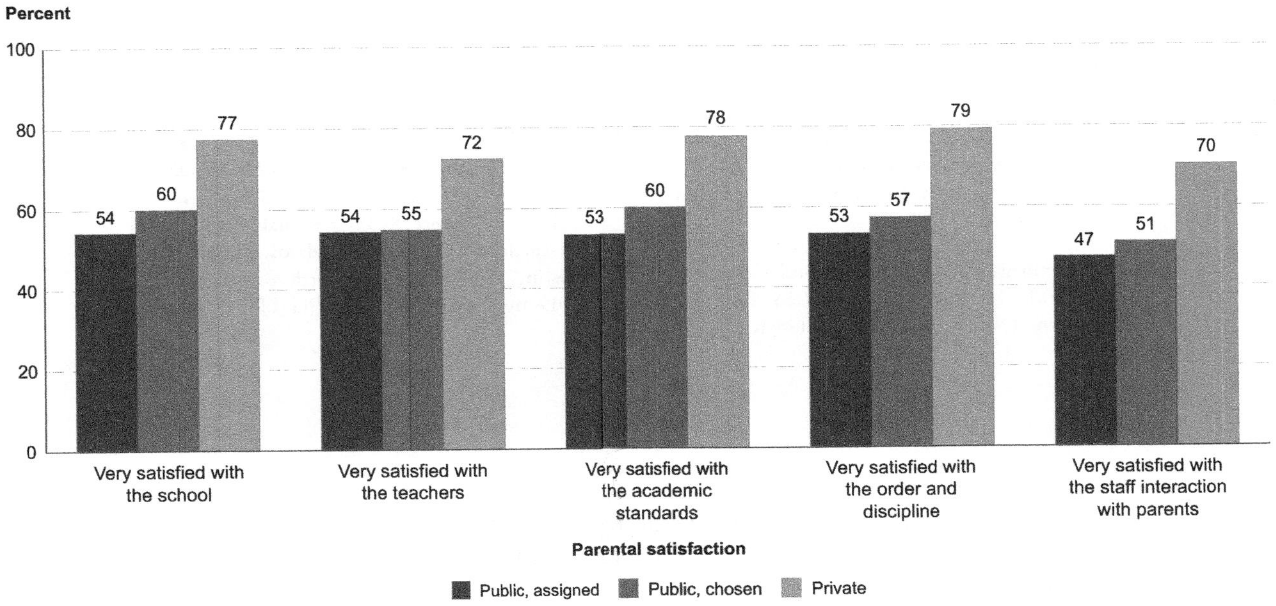

Parental satisfaction	Public, assigned	Public, chosen	Private
Very satisfied with the school	54	60	77
Very satisfied with the teachers	54	55	72
Very satisfied with the academic standards	53	60	78
Very satisfied with the order and discipline	53	57	79
Very satisfied with the staff interaction with parents	47	51	70

NOTE: Data exclude homeschooled children.
SOURCE: U.S. Department of Education, National Center for Education Statistics, Parent and Family Involvement in Education Survey of the National Household Education Surveys Program (PFI-NHES:2016).

Parents' satisfaction with different aspects of their children's school differed based on the type of school their children attended. Of students enrolled in grades 3 through 12 in 2016, a higher percentage of students who attended private schools (77 percent) than of students who attended chosen public schools (60 percent) or assigned public schools (54 percent) had parents who reported that they were very satisfied with the school. The percentage was also higher for those attending chosen public schools than assigned public schools. This same pattern was evident in parental satisfaction with academic standards, order and discipline, and staff interaction with parents. Additionally, a higher percentage of students who attended private schools (72 percent) than of students who attended chosen public schools (55 percent) and assigned public schools (54 percent) had parents who reported that they were very satisfied with the teachers at the school, but there was no measurable difference between the percentages for chosen and assigned public schools.

Endnotes:

[1] A student is considered to be attending an assigned public school if the parent indicates that the school is the student's "regularly assigned" school; a student is considered to be attending a chosen public school if the parent indicates that the school is not the student's regularly assigned school (e.g., a traditional public school located outside the assignment boundary based on the student's residence, a charter school, or a magnet school).

[2] See table 8.1 for school choice information by student race/ethnicity.

Reference tables: Tables 8.1 and 8.2

References

Schneider, M., Teske, P., and Marschall, M. (2000). *Choosing Schools: Consumer Choice and the Quality of American Schools*. Princeton, NJ: Princeton University Press.

U.S. Department of Education, National Center for Education Statistics. (2003). *NCES Statistical Standards* (NCES 2003-601). Washington, DC.

Wang, J., Schweig, J.D., and Herman, J.L. (2014). *Is There a Magnet School Effect? Using Meta-Analysis to Explore Variation in Magnet School Success* (CRESST Report 843). National Center for Research on Evaluation, Standards, and Student Testing. Los Angeles, CA. Retrieved February 7, 2019, from https://eric.ed.gov/?id=ED565781.

Wang, K., A. Rathbun, and L. Musu. "School Choice in the United States: 2019." National Center for Education Statistics, September 25, 2019. https://nces.ed.gov/pubs2019/2019106.pdf. Accessed August 10, 2021.

General

A Better Chance
253 W 35th Street
15th Floor
New York, NY 10001
646-346-1310
800-562-7865
Fax: 646-346-1311
admissions@abetterchance.org
www.abetterchance.org
A Better Chance is an organization whose mission is to increase the number of well-educated young people of color through the creation of educational opportunities for students in grades 6-12.

Founded: 1963

Francisco Tezen, President & CEO
Benjamin Bingman-Tennant, National Director, Programs

ASPIRA Association
1220 L Street NW
Suite 701
Washington, DC 20005
info@aspira.org
www.aspira.org
The ASPIRA Association promotes the empowerment of the Puerto Rican and Latino community by developing and nurturing the leadership, intellectual, and cultural potential of its youth so that they may contribute to their communities. Some of ASPIRA's services include career and college counseling, financial aid, educational advocacy, leadership training and more.

Founded: 1961

Ronald Blackburn, President & CEO
John Villamil-Casanova, EVP & CIO

Accelerated Christian Education Canada (ACE)
105 Anson Street
Southport, MB R0H-1N0
204-428-5332
800-976-7226
Fax: 204-428-5386
info@acecanada.net
www.acecanada.net
Offers individualized learning options for children, such as homeschooling, inspired by the basic values of Christianity.

Founded: 1974

Alfred MacLaren, Manager

Accessibility and Disability Resource Center
University Community Center
730 College Avenue
Norman, OK 73019
405-325-3852
Fax: 405-325-4491
adrc@ou.edu
www.ou.edu/adrc
The ADRC at The University of Oklahoma offers services and supports to students with disabilities. Services include accomodations, digital accessibility, campus accessibility maps and employee resources.

Chelle' Guttery, Ph.D, Director
Cathy Ellison, Administrative Coordinator

American Academy of Pediatrics (AAP)
345 Park Boulevard
Itasca, IL 60143
800-433-9016
Fax: 847-434-8000
mcc@aap.org
www.aap.org
Organization of pediatricians committed to serving children and adolescents to ensure their optimal physical, mental and social health. The organization offers its members professional resources, publications, conferences, advocacy and other resources to help them advance their practice.

Mark Del Monte, JD, CEO & Executive VP
Christine Bork, MBA, Chief Development Officer

6 American Academy of Special Education Professionals (AASEP)
3642 E Sunnydale Drive
Chandler Heights, AZ 85142
800-754-4421
Fax: 800-424-0371
membership@aasep.org
www.aasep.org
The Academy promotes collaboration among professionals in the field of special education, and encourages professional development among members through networking, research, publications, and membership benefits.

Roger Pierangelo, Ph.D, Executive Director
George Giuliani, Ph.D, Executive Director

7 American Council for Rural Special Education (ACRES)
West Virginia University
509 Allen Hall
PO Box 6122
Morgantown, WV 26506-6122
304-293-3450
acres-sped@mail.wvu.edu
www.acres-sped.org
The organization is comprised of special educators, general educators, related service providers, administrators, teacher trainers, researchers and parents committed to the enhancement of services for students and individuals living in rural communities in America.

Founded: 1981

Mark Butler, Chair
Anthony Menendez, Secretary

8 American Council of Trustees and Alumni (ACTA)
1730 M Street NW
Suite 600
Washington, DC 20036-4525
202-467-6787
888-258-6648
Fax: 202-467-6784
info@goacta.org
www.goacta.org
An independent, non-profit organization working with alumni, trustees, and education leaders to support liberal arts education, uphold high academic standards and safeguard the free exchange of ideas on campus.

Founded: 1995

Michael B. Poliakoff, Ph.D, President
Lauri Kempson, Senior Vice President

9 American Council on Education
1 Dupont Circle NW
Washington, DC 20036
202-939-9300
comments@ace.nche.edu
www.acenet.edu
Represents accredited degree-granting colleges and universities directly and through national and regional higher education associations. The council's mission is to advance education and serve as an advocate for adult education.

Ted Mitchell, President
Kara Freeman, Chief Operating Officer

10 American Driver and Traffic Safety Education Association (ADTSEA)
Highway Safety Services
1434 Trim Tree Road
Indiana, PA 15701
724-801-8246
Fax: 724-349-5042
office@adtsea.org
www.adtsea.org
The purpose of the American Driver and Traffic Safety Education Association is to promote quality traffic safety education by publishing policies and guidelines. The association also offers conferences, workshops, seminars, consulting services and educational materials.

Brett Robinson, Executive Director
Leslie Robinson, Office Manager

11 American Federation of Teachers (AFT)
555 New Jersey Avenue NW
Washington, DC 20001
202-879-4400
online@aft.org
www.aft.org
The American Federation of Teachers is a union of professionals devoted to ensuring access to economic opportunity and quality public education, healthcare and public services for the students and families within their communities. The federation offers resources on topics such as immigration, retirement, public services and more. AFT is an affiliated international union of the AFL-CIO.

Founded: 1916

Randi Weingarten, President
Evelyn DeJesus, Executive Vice President

12 American Montessori Society (AMS)
116 East 16th Street
New York, NY 10003-2163
212-358-1250
Fax: 212-358-1256
ams@amshq.org
www.amshq.org
The Society advocates for quality Montessori education by offering services such as an information center for its members, the media, and the public; teacher resources; research and professional development events.

Founded: 1960

Munir Shivji, Executive Director
Gina Taliaferro Lofquist, Senior Director, Education

13 American School Health Association
501 N Morton Street
Suite 110
Bloomington, IN 47404
202-854-1721
info@ashaweb.org
www.ashaweb.org
A non-profit organization founded to protect and improve the health and well-being of children and youth by supporting comprehensive school health programs.

Jeanie Alter, Executive Director
Kaitlyn Celis, Manager, Membership Services

14 American Society for Engineering Education (ASEE)
1818 N Street NW
Suite 600
Washington, DC 20036-2479
202-331-3500
Fax: 202-265-8504
board@asee.org
www.asee.org

A nonprofit organization of individuals and institutions committed to promoting the fields of engineering and engineering technology. The society develops policies and programs for engineering faculty members and offers publications, events, fellowships, job postings and more.

Founded: 1893

Norman Fortenberry, Executive Director
Patti Greenawalt, Managing Dir., Members

15 **Association Montessori International / USA (AMI USA)**
1421 Prince Street
Suite 350
Alexandria, VA 22314
703-746-9919
montessori@amiusa.org
www.amiusa.org
Applies the principles of Dr. Montessori to the education of children. The association oversees conferences and events, consultation programs, membership opportunities, training centers and other initiatives connected to the education field.

Founded: 1929

Ayize Sabater, Executive Director
Lynne Breitenstein-Aliberti, Director, Member Operations

16 **Association for Business Communication (ABC)**
PO Box 304
Natural Bridge Station, VA 24579-0304
540-231-8460
abcoffice@businesscommunication.org
www.businesscommunication.org
International, interdisciplinary organization engaged in fostering excellence in business communication scholarship, research, education and practice. The association offers resources, publications, conferences and membership benefits.

Founded: 1936

Jim Dubinsky, Ph.D, Executive Director
Marilyn Buerkens, Office Manager

17 **Association for Experiential Education**
2315 18th Street S
Saint Petersburg, FL 33712
303-440-8844
www.aee.org
Aims to advance experiential education by creating an accessible community for experiential education professionals.

Sherry Bagley, Executive Director
Steve Pace, Director, Accreditations

18 **Association for Interdisciplinary Studies (AIS)**
Oakland University
371 Wilson Boulevard
521 Wilson Hall
Rochester, MI 48309-4452
ais@interdisciplinarystudies.org
www.interdisciplinarystudies.org
The Association for Interdisciplinary Studies is an interdisciplinary professional organization dedicated to promoting the interchange of ideas among scholars and administrators in the arts and science fields on intellectual and organizational issues.

Founded: 1979

Jennifer J. Dellner, President
Khadijah O. Miller, Ph.D, Vice President, Relations

19 **Association for Play Therapy (APT)**
401 Clovis Avenue
Suite 107
Clovis, CA 93612
559-298-3400
Fax: 559-298-3410
info@a4pt.org
www.a4pt.org
The Association for Play Therapy promotes the value of play, play therapy and credentialed play therapists to advance the psychosocial development and mental health of all people. The association also sponsors and supports programs, services and related activities that promote public understanding of play therapy.

Founded: 1982

Kathryn Lebby, President & CEO
Diane Leon, Vice President & COO

20 **Association for Supervision & Curriculum Development (ASCD)**
1703 N Beauregard Street
Alexandria, VA 22311-1714
press@ascd.org
www.ascd.org
A membership organization that develops programs, products, and services essential to the way educators learn, teach, and lead.

Founded: 1943

Ranjit Sidhu, CEO & Executive Director
Dana Shanks-Williams, Chief Financial Officer

21 **Association of American Educators (AAE)**
25909 Pala Place
Suite 330
Mission Viejo, CA 92691
949-595-7979
800-704-7799
Fax: 949-595-7970
www.aaeteachers.org
Provides professional benefits and services to educators, including liability insurance, scholarships and grants, and professional resources.

Founded: 1994

Gary Beckner, Chair & President Emeritus
Colin Sharkey, Executive Director

22 **Association of State Supervisors of Mathematics (ASSM)**
517 Paint Brush Drive
Johnson City, TX 78636
www.assm.wildapricot.org
The Association of State Supervisors of Mathematics is an organization whose members provide supervising and consulting services in the area of mathematics. Its membership is made up of current or previous state or provincial supervisors of mathematics.

Founded: 1961

Joleigh Honey, President
Denise Schulz, Secretary

23 **Association of Teacher Educators (ATE)**
11350 Random Hills Road
Suite 800, PMB 6
Fairfax, VA 22030
703-659-1708
Fax: 703-595-4792
info@ate1.org
www.ate1.org
The mission of the Association of Teacher Educators is to improve the effectiveness of teacher education through leadership in the development of training programs. The association analyzes issues and practices relating to professional development and provides opportunities for the personal and professional growth of Association members.

Founded: 1920

Alisa Chapman, Executive Director
John McIntyre, Director, Meetings

24 **Attention Deficit Disorder Association (ADDA)**
PO Box 103
Denver, PA 17517
800-939-1019
Fax: 800-939-1019
info@add.org
www.add.org
The Attention Deficit Disorder Association (ADDA) is an adult ADHD organization providing information, resources and networking opportunities to help adults with Attention Deficit/Hyperactivity Disorder (AD/HD) lead better lives. The organization is entirely virtual, with no physical offices or staff.

Duane Gordon, President
Michael Phillips, Treasurer

25 **Awards and Personalization Association**
8735 W Higgins Road
Suite 300
Chicago, IL 60631
847-375-4800
Fax: 847-375-6480
info@awardspersonalization.org
www.awardspersonalization.org
The purpose of the Awards and Personalization Association is to advance the capabilities and growth of businesses whose primary focus is the manufacture, distribution or sales of awards and recognition goods and services.

Louise Ristau, CAE, Executive Director
Liz Giannini, Senior Operations Manager

26 **CHADD: Children & Adults with Attention Deficit/Hyperactivity Disorder**
4221 Forbes Boulevard
Suite 270
Lanham, MD 20706
301-306-7070
Fax: 301-306-7090
customer_service@chadd.org
www.chadd.org
National nonprofit organization offering advocacy, education and support for patients and parents of children with attention deficit disorders. The organization maintains support groups, provides a forum for continuing education about ADHD, and offers a national resource center.

Founded: 1987

Patricia M. Hudak, President
Bob O'Malley, Treasurer

27 **Canadian Association for Astrological Education**
226 Cromwell Avenue
Oshawa, ON L1J-4T8
905-725-9179
thecaae@gmail.com
www.thecaae.com
Offers a curriculum for the study of astrology and its applications covering the areas of relationships, vocation, horary astrology, consulting, mathematical techniques and chart rectification.

Founded: 1993

Joan Ann Evelyn, President
Nicole Kujtan, Treasurer

Canadian Association for Prior Learning Assessment (CAPLA)

PO Box 56001
RPO Minto Place
Ottawa, ON K1R-7Z1
613-860-1747
Fax: 705-878-5018
www.capla.ca
National advocate for recognizing prior learning in Canada. Members include adult learners, researchers, employers, academic and training institutions and more.

Founded: 1994

Andy Brown, Chair
Mary Harrison, Vice Chair

Canadian Association for Studies in Indigenous Education (CASIE)

www.casieaceea.org
Promotes the study of Indigenous education by offering platforms for dialogue, connecting professionals and students with a shared interest in the subject and encouraging scholary work. Constituent association of the Canadian Society for the Study of Education.

Aubrey Hanson, Ph.D, Co-President
Dustin Louie, Ph.D, Co-President

Canadian Association for Teacher Education

info@cate-acfe.ca
www.cate-acfe.ca
Promotes the study of teacher education through publications, scholarly research, conferences and dialogues.

Cathryn Smith, President
Leyton Schnellert, Vice President

Canadian Association for the Study of Adult Education (CASAE)

260 Dalhousie Street
Suite 204
Ottawa, ON K1N-7E4
613-241-0018
Fax: 613-241-0019
casae.aceea@csse.ca
www.casae-aceea.ca
Organization supporting adult education scholarship through publications on practice as well as through conferences and other resources.

Founded: 1981

Hongxia Shan, President
Tim Howard, Permanent Secretariat

2 Canadian Association of University Teachers (CAUT)

2705 Queensview Drive
Ottawa, ON K2B-8K2
613-276-9030
Fax: 613-614-5334
acppu@caut.ca
www.caut.ca
National advocate for academic professionals, providing lobbying services for its members as well as research and publications touching upon academic freedom and other relevant issues.

Founded: 1951

Brenda Austin-Smith, President
David Robinson, Executive Director

3 Center for Civic Education

5115 Douglas Fir Road
Suite J
Calabasas, CA 91302
818-591-9321
cce@civiced.org
www.civiced.org
Nonprofit, nonpartisan educational corporation dedicated to fostering the development of informed, responsible participation in civic life by citizens. The center aims to help students understand how constitutional democracy works, as well as democratic procedures for making decisions.

Christopher R. Riano, President
Mia Nagawiecki, Vice President

34 Center for Parent Information and Resources (CPIR)

c/o SPAN
35 Halsey Street
4th Floor
Newark, NJ 07102
973-642-8100
mrodriguez@spanadvocacy.org
www.parentcenterhub.org
The center provides information to Parent Centers serving children with disabilities and their families. Some of the services offered by the center include research material, workspaces for exchange of resources between centers and an e-newsletter.

Carolyn Hayer, Director
Myriam Alizo, Assistant Project Director

35 Center on Education Policy (CEP)

2100 Pennsylvania Avenue NW
Suite 310
Washington, DC 20052
202-994-9050
Fax: 202-994-8859
www.cep-dc.org
Provides research and information about public education so that Americans can see the role public education plays in a democracy, and understand the conflicting perceptions about the system. The long term goal of the center is to improve upon existing systems.

Founded: 1995

36 Childhood Education International

1100 15th Street NW
4th Floor
Washington, DC 20005
202-372-9986
800-423-3563
www.ceinternational1892.org
The association promotes and supports the education, development, and well-being of children, from birth through adolescence. It also seeks to influence the professional growth of educators and the efforts of others who are committed to the needs of children in a changing society.

Founded: 1892

Diane Whitehead, Chief Executive Officer
Michelle Allen, Director, Operations

37 Co-Operative Education and Work-Integrated Learning Canada (CEWIL)

150 Eglinton Avenue E
Suite 402
Toronto, ON M4P-1E8
416-483-3311
cewil@cewilcanada.ca
www.cewilcanada.ca
Voice for post-secondary Co-operative Education in Canada. The association promotes national standards, offers a forum for practitioners to network and provides informational resources and professional development opportunities for those working in the co-op education field.

Cara Krezek, President
Scott Daniels, Secretary

38 Constitutional Rights Foundation (CRF)

601 S Kingsley Drive
Los Angeles, CA 90005
213-487-5590
crf@crf-usa.org
www.crf-usa.org
The mission of the foundation is to help youth gain a deeper understanding of citizenship through values expressed in the Constitution and its Bill of Rights, and educate them to become active and responsible participants in society. The two main areas of focus are Law and Government and Civic Participation.

Amanda Susskind, President
Keri Doggett, Vice President, Programming

39 Cooperative Education and Internship Association (CEIA)

PO Box 42506
Cincinnati, OH 45242
513-793-2342
Fax: 513-793-0463
info@ceiainc.org
www.ceiainc.org
The association is nonprofit and member-driven, consisting of educators, employers, researchers, students, and partner agencies.

Founded: 1963

Peggy Harrier, Executive Director

40 Council for Advancement and Support of Education (CASE)

1201 Eye Street NW
Washington, DC 20005
202-328-2273
Fax: 202-387-4973
membersupportcenter@case.org
www.case.org
An international membership association that provides educational institutions with knowledge, standards, advocacy and training designed to strengthen alumni relations, communications, fundraising, marketing and allied professionals. CASE helps members raise funds for campus projects, produce recruitment materials, market their institutions to prospective students, diversify the profession and foster public support of education.

Founded: 1974

Sue Cunningham, President & CEO
Rob Moore, VP, Communications

41 Council for Christian Colleges and Universities (CCCU)

321 Eighth Street NE
Washington, DC 20002
202-546-8713
council@cccu.org
www.cccu.org
Association dedicated to advancing the cause of Christ-centered higher education by ensuring scholarships, programs and services embody the Christian values and spirit.

Founded: 1976

Shirley V. Hoogstra, JD, President
Mandi Bolton, Chief Financial Officer

42 Council for Exceptional Children (CEC)

3100 Clarendon Boulevard
Suite 600
Arlington, VA 22201-5332
888-232-7733
service@exceptionalchildren.org
www.exceptionalchildren.org
The Council for Exceptional Children works to improve the educational success of indi-

viduals with disabilities and/or unique gifts and talents.

Founded: 1922

Chad Rummel, Executive Director
Craig Evans, Chief Financial Officer

43 Council for the Accreditation of Educator Preparation (CAEP)

1140 19th Street NW
Suite 400
Washington, DC 20036
202-223-0077
caep@caepnet.org
www.caepnet.org
Professional accrediting organization for schools, colleges and departments of education as well as alternative educators. The focus is P-12 student education.

Founded: 1954

Christopher A. Koch, President
Malina Monaco, Vice President

44 Council of Graduate Schools (CGS)

1 Dupont Circle NW
Suite 230
Washington, DC 20036
202-223-3791
Fax: 202-331-7157
general_inquiries@cgs.nche.edu
www.cgsnet.org
The Council of Graduate Schools represents the graduate dean community. The council seeks to advance graduate education and research through advocacy in policy, innovative research and the development of best practices.

Suzanne T. Ortega, President
Keith Peregonov, Vice President, Operations

45 Council of Independent Colleges (CIC)

1 Dupont Circle NW
Suite 320
Washington, DC 20036-1142
202-466-7230
Fax: 202-466-7238
cic@cic.nche.edu
www.cic.edu
The Council of Independent Colleges is an association of nonprofit independent colleges and universities. The mission of the council is to advance excellence in schools, support leadership in school communities, and educate the public on the benefits of private higher education. The council also offers its members conferences, seminars, and other programs that help institutions to improve and to increase their visibility.

Founded: 1956

Marjorie Hass, President
Harold V. Hartley III, Senior Vice President

46 Council of Urban Boards of Education (CUBE)

National School Boards Association
1680 Duke Street
2nd Floor
Alexandria, VA 22314-3493
703-838-6722
Fax: 703-683-7590
info@nsba.org
www.nsba.org
Seeks to create opportunities for urban school board professionals, so that they may strive for equity in public education.

Viola M. Garcia, President
Chip Slaven, Interim Executive Director

47 EMPath: Economic Mobility Pathways

308 Congress Street
5th Floor
Boston, MA 02210
617-259-2900
info@empathways.org
www.empathways.org
EMPath supports governments and nonprofit organizations in serving low-income families by offering programs, research and advocacy. Their aim is to empower families so that people can increase their income, secure permanent housing, attain education, and break out of the cycle of poverty.

Elisabeth D. Babcock, MCRP, Ph.D, President & CEO
Mary D. Coleman, Senior Vice President & COO

48 Easterseals

141 W Jackson Boulevard
Suite 1400A
Chicago, IL 60604
312-726-6200
800-221-6827
Fax: 312-726-1494
info@easterseals.com
www.easterseals.com
Easter Seals provides services, education, outreach, and advocacy to people living with autism and other disabilities so they can learn and live as a part of their communities.

Founded: 1919

Angela F. Williams, President & CEO
Glenda Oakley, Chief Financial Officer

49 EdCan Network

60 St. Clair Avenue E
Suite 703
Toronto, ON M4T-1N5
416-591-6300
866-803-9549
Fax: 416-591-5345
info@edcan.ca
www.edcan.ca
The EdCan Network is the leading independent national bilingual voice in Canadian K-12 education. EdCan Network connects policy, research and practice through bilingual research, events and publications to offer a deeper perspective to help educators make sense of some of the most complex issues facing Canadian public education today.

Max Cooke, Chief Executive Officer
Mia San Jose, Operations Manager

50 Education Commission of the States

700 Broadway
Suite 810
Denver, CO 80203
303-299-3600
ecs@ecs.org
www.ecs.org
The Commision's mission is to help states develop effective policy and practice for public education by providing data, research, analysis and leadership; and by facilitating collaboration, the exchange of ideas among the states and long-range strategic thinking.

Jeremy Anderson, President

51 Education Development Center (EDC)

43 Foundry Avenue
Waltham, MA 02453-8313
617-969-7100
Fax: 617-969-5979
contact@edc.org
www.edc.org
The Education Development Center designs and evaluates programs addressing some of the world's challenges in education, health and economic opportunity. The center's mission is to improve education, health promotion and care, workforce preparation, communications technologies and civic engagement in communities.

Founded: 1958

David Offensend, President & CEO
Siobhan Murphy, Chief Operating Officer

52 Education Writers Association (EWA)

1825 K Street NW
Suite 200
Washington, DC 20006
202-452-9830
www.ewa.org
The Education Writers Association works to strengthen the community of education writers by offering programs, training, information, support, and recognition.

Caroline W. Hendrie, Executive Director
Kim Clark, Deputy Director

53 Education, Training and Research Associates (ETR)

5619 Scotts Valley Drive
Suite 140
Scotts Valley, CA 95066
800-620-8884
Fax: 831-438-4284
www.etr.org
Education, Training and Research Associates is a nonprofit dedicated to providing solutions in the areas of health and education. Their mission is to improve health and increase opportunities for youth and communities through research, publications, information resources and programs.

Vignetta Charles, Chief Executive Officer
Eric Blanke, Chief Operating Officer

54 Excelencia in Education

1156 15th Street NW
Suite 1001
Washington, DC 20005
202-785-7350
contact@edexcelencia.org
www.edexcelencia.org
Nonprofit organization working to support the acedemic success of Latino students in higher education. Goals are met through the promotion of education policies and provision of data on the educational status of Latinos.

Founded: 2004

Sarita E. Brown, President
Deborah A. Santiago, Chief Executive Officer

55 FHI 360

359 Blackwell Street
Suite 200
Durham, NC 27701
919-544-7040
Fax: 919-544-7261
eec@fhi360.org
www.fhi360.org
A nonprofit organization that develops programs and materials promoting bias-free learning in school and after school. Some services offered include quality assurance, research, data analysis, monitoring and evaluation, training and technical assistance, and more.

Patrick C. Fine, MEd, Chief Executive Officer
Deborah Kennedy-Iraheta, MA, Chief Operating Officer

56 Facing History and Ourselves

16 Hurd Road
Brookline, MA 02445

617-232-1595
800-856-9039
Fax: 617-232-0281
info@facinghistory.org
www.facinghistory.org
Facing History is an international nonprofit that helps teachers and students link the past to moral choices they face today. Some of the subjects examined include racism, prejudice and antisemitism.

Founded: 1976

Roger Brooks, President & CEO
Abby Weiss, Chief Program Officer

Foundation for Student Communication
Princeton University
48 University Place
Suite 305
Princeton, NJ 08544
info@businesstoday.org
www.businesstoday.org
The Foundation for Student Communication works to create a platform for business leaders both current and future to make connections. Interactions are encouraged through magazines, conferences, Seminar Series events, and Online Journal blog posts. Run by Princeton University students.

Founded: 1968

Sowon Lee, President
Richard Qiu, Director, Finance

Friends Council on Education
1507 Cherry Street
Philadelphia, PA 19102
215-241-7245
Fax: 267-519-5317
info@friendscouncil.org
www.friendscouncil.org
A national organization of Quaker schools which assists teachers, students and families by providing publications and programs supporting Quaker values in the classroom and in the life of the school community. Programs include peer networks, workshops, seminars, pilgrimages and more.

Founded: 1931

Drew Smith, Executive Director
Betsy Torg, Director, Development

Girls Inc.
120 Wall Street
18th Floor
New York, NY 10005
212-509-2000
Fax: 212-509-8708
communications@girlsinc.org
www.girlsinc.org
A national nonprofit youth organization dedicated to inspiring all girls to develop into healthy, educated, and independent adults. Programs offered touch upon the areas of media and economic literacy, leadership, relationships and more.

Founded: 1864

Stephanie J. Hull, President & CEO
Pat Driscoll, Chief Operating Officer

Global Council for Science and the Environment (GCSE)
1776 Eye Street NW
Suite 750
Washington, DC 20006
gcse@gcseglobal.org
www.gcseglobal.org
Nonprofit organization seeking to improve the scientific basis of environmental decision-making through fostering collaboration between leaders in the areas of interdisciplinary research, education, policy, and business.

Founded: 1990

Michelle Wyman, Executive Director
Erica Goldman, Ph.D, Deputy Director

61 **Global Exploration for Educators Organization (GEEO)**
700 East Main Street
Suite 100
Norristown, PA 19401
877-600-0105
travel@geeo.org
www.geeo.org
A nonprofit organization dedicated to encouraging and assisting teachers to travel abroad to broaden their knowledge and enrich the education of their own students upon returning to the classroom. The organization provides travel incentives, professional development credits, educational resources and more.

Founded: 2007

Jesse Weisz, Founder & Executive Director
Cindy Beecher, Program Manager

62 **Higher Learning Commission**
230 S LaSalle Street
Suite 7-500
Chicago, IL 60604-1411
312-621-7440
800-621-7440
Fax: 312-263-7462
info@hlcommission.org
www.hlcommission.org
Higher Learning Commission (HLC) is an independent corporation responsible for accrediting degree-granting post-secondary educational institutions in the United States.

Founded: 1895

Barbara Gellman-Danley, President
Eric Martin, Executive Vice President

63 **Independent Schools Association of the Southwest (ISAS)**
2626 Cole Avenue
Suite 300
Dallas, TX 75204
432-684-9550
Fax: 432-684-9401
webmaster@isasw.org
www.isasw.org
A voluntary membership association of private schools. The central purpose of the association is to encourage, support and develop the highest standard for independent schools of the region and to recognize by formal accreditation those schools in which these standards are maintained.

Founded: 1955

Scott Griggs, Executive Director
Heather Junker, Director, Programs

64 **Institute for Educational Leadership (IEL)**
4301 Connecticut Avenue NW
Suite 100
Washington, DC 20008
202-822-8405
Fax: 202-872-4050
iel@iel.org
www.iel.org
The vision of the Institute for Educational Leadership is to encourage leadership in all levels of society, inspiring those such as policymakers, administrators, and practitioners to develop youth for higher education, careers and citizenship.

Founded: 1964

Jose Munoz, Interim Director
Maame Appiah, Vice President, Finance

65 **Institute for Sport and Social Justice (ISSJ)**
PO Box 621419
Orlando, FL 32762-1419
407-823-4770
www.sportandsocialjustice.org
Formerly known as the National Consortium for Academics and Sports, the Institute seeks to use the power and appeal of sports as a tool with which to positively affect social change. Their services cover the areas of sports, diversity, education, social justice and ethical leadership.

Founded: 1985

Delise O'Meally, Chief Executive Officer
Jeffrey O'Brien, Vice President

66 **InterAction - American Council for Voluntary International Action**
1400 16th Street NW
Suite 210
Washington, DC 20036
202-667-8227
ia@interaction.org
www.interaction.org
InterAction is an alliance of U.S. based international nongovernmental organizations using its collective voice to shape important policy decisions on disaster relief and long term development issues including foreign assistance, the environment, women, health, education and agriculture.

Founded: 1984

Sam Worthington, Chief Executive Officer
Noam Unger, Vice President, Development

67 **Jewish Educators Assembly (JEA)**
Broadway & Locust Avenue
PO Box 413
Cedarhurst, NY 11516
516-569-2537
jewisheducators@aol.com
www.jewisheducators.org
Promotes excellence among educators committed to Conservative Jewish education by advancing professionalism, encouraging leadership, providing advocacy and certification, encouraging lifelong learning and building community.

Edward Edelstein, Executive Director

68 **John Dewey Society (JDS)**
PO Box 4056
Fresno, CA 93744
jdssecretary@gmail.com
www.johndeweysociety.org
The society fosters John Dewey's commitment to the use of critical and reflective intelligence to find solutions to problems in education and culture. The society also offers conferences, journals, books and resources.

Founded: 1935

Sarah Stitzlein, President
Becky L. Noel Smith, Secretary-Treasurer

69 **Learning Disabilities Association of America (LDA)**
4068 Mount Royal Boulevard
Suite 224B
Allison Park, PA 15101
412-341-1515
info@ldaamerica.org
www.ldaamerica.org
The Learning Disabilities Association of America is a national network of service providers supporting individuals with learning disabilities, their families and the professionals who work with them. The association of-

fers learning resources, advocacy services and conferences.

Founded: 1963

Cindy Cipoletti, Executive Director
Nina DelPrato, Administrative Manager

70 Lutheran Education Association (LEA)
7400 Augusta Street
River Forest, IL 60305
708-209-3343
Fax: 708-209-3458
lea@lea.org
www.lea.org
Seeks to spark ideas, thoughts and practices among Lutherans. The Lutheran Education Association links, equips and affirms educators and workers in ministry for the purpose of maintaining the Lutheran understanding of Scriptures and the Christian faith.

Jonathan Laabs, Ed.D, Executive Director
Edward C. Grube, LL.D, Director, Communications

71 MATRIX: Parent Network and Resource Center
2400 Las Gallinas Avenue
Suite 115
San Rafael, CA 94903-1454
415-884-3535
800-578-2592
Fax: 415-884-3555
info@matrixparents.org
www.matrixparents.org
Matrix provides training and information to parents of children with disabilities of all kinds (physical, cognitive, emotional or learning). The Matrix network consists of parent training and info centers, family empowerment centers and family resource centers.

Founded: 1983

Steve Diamond, Executive Director
Kimberly Grady, Development Director

72 McREL International
4601 DTC Boulevard
Suite 500
Denver, CO 80237-2596
303-337-0990
800-858-6830
info@mcrel.org
www.mcrel.org
Provides educators with research-based, practical guidance on the issues and challenges facing education today. Some services offered include customized consulting, professional learning and instructional coaching, leadership development, personnel evaluation, data analysis and program evaluation and more.

Founded: 1966

Bryan Goodwin, CEO & President
Kris Rouleau, Dir., Learning Services

73 Montana Empowerment Center
221 Parkway Drive
Kalispell, MT 59901
877-870-1190
www.mtempowermentcenter.org
Provides resources and assistance to Montana parents and educators of children with disabilities.

Founded: 2018

Rebecca Bogden-Richards, Executive Director

74 Music Teachers National Association (MTNA)
600 Vine Street
Suite 1710
Cincinnati, OH 45202
513-421-1420
888-512-5278
Fax: 513-421-2503
mtnanet@mtna.org
www.mtna.org
Advances the value of music study and music making to society while supporting the careers and professionalism of teachers of music. The association also provides networking opportunities, continuing education, conferences, certification, publications, grants and more.

Gary L. Ingle, Executive Director & CEO
Brian Shepard, Chief Operating Officer

75 National Academy of Education (NAEd)
500 5th Street NW
Washington, DC 20001
202-334-2341
info@naeducation.org
www.naeducation.org
Advances quality education research and its use in policy formation and practice. The academy also offers professional development fellowship programs.

Founded: 1965

Gregory White, Executive Director
Amy Berman, Deputy Director

76 National Alliance of Black School Educators (NABSE)
PO Box 176
Troy, NY 12181
833-762-2731
info@nabse.org
www.nabse.org
Nonprofit organization devoted to furthering the academic success of the nation's children, with an emphasis on children of African descent. NABSE is dedicated to improving both the educational experiences and accomplishments of African American youth through the development and use of instructional and motivational methods that lead to higher achievement.

Founded: 1970

Michael McFarland, President
Geneva A. Stark Pittman, Treasurer

77 National Association for Gifted Children (NAGC)
1300 I Street NW
Suite 400E
Washington, DC 20005
202-785-4268
nagc@nagc.org
www.nagc.org
Organization of parents, teachers, educators and other professionals committed to addressing the unique needs of children and youth with demonstrated gifts and talents. The organization's mission is to help children develop through education, advocacy, community building and research.

John Segota, Executive Director
Andrew Bassett, Director, Administration

78 National Association for Year-Round Education (NAYRE)
www.nayre.org
The National Association for Year-Round Education promotes year-round education by providing services on time and learning. The association provides publications, encourages research, and presents a clearing-house of information on the benefits of year-round education.

David Hornak, Executive Director

79 National Association for the Legal Support of Alternative Schools (NALSAS)
18520 NW 67th Avenue
Suite 188
Miami, FL 33015
800-456-7784
educate@nalsas.org
www.nalsas.org
The National Association for the Legal Support of Alternative Schools was originally designed to help interested persons/organizations locate, evaluate, and create viable alternatives to traditional schooling approaches, such as home study. The association now offers a Certificate of Accreditation for homeschooling programs and other members.

Founded: 1973

Ed Nagel, Chief Executive Officer

80 National Association of Career Colleges (NACC)
99 - 4338 Innes Road
Ottawa, ON K4A-3W3
613-800-0340
info@nacc.ca
www.nacc.ca
Organization bringing together professionals from career colleges to develop the programs that serve their students. Some services offered by the association include curriculums, professional development for instructors, conferences and resources for students and colleges.

Founded: 1896

Michael Sangster, Chief Executive Officer
Holly McKnight, Director, Education

81 National Association of Catholic School Teachers (NACST)
3070 Bristol Pike
Building 2, Suite 101
Bensalem, PA 19020
800-996-2278
nacst.nacst@verizon.net
www.nacst.com
The National Association of Catholic School Teachers unifies, advises and assists Catholic school teachers in matters of collective bargaining.

Founded: 1978

Rita C. Schwartz, President

82 National Association of Federally Impacted Schools (NAFIS)
Hall of the States
400 N Capitol Street NW
Suite 290
Washington, DC 20001
202-624-5455
info@nafisdc.org
www.nafisdc.org
Corporation of school districts throughout the country organized primarily to educate Congress on Impact Aid. The association works to ensure that the needs of federally connected children are met with adequate federal funds.

Hilary Goldmann, Executive Director
Leslie Finnan, Director, Policy & Advocacy

83 National Association of Parents with Children in Special Education (NAPCSE)
3642 E Sunnydale Drive
Chandler Heights, AZ 85142
800-754-4421
Fax: 800-424-0371

contact@napcse.org
www.napcse.org
National membership organization devoted to providing support to parents of children with special needs.

George Giuliani, President

National Association of Special Education Teachers (NASET)

1250 Connecticut Avenue NW
Suite 200
Washington, DC 20036
800-754-4421
Fax: 800-754-4421
contactus@naset.org
www.naset.org
TheÿNational Association of Special Education Teachersÿis the only national membership organization dedicated to meeting the needs of special education teachers and those preparing for the field of special education teaching. NASET offers publications, membership benefits and a career center.

Roger Pierangelo, Ph.D, Co-Executive Director
George Giuliani, Ph.D, Co-Executive Director

National Association of State Boards of Education (NASBE)

123 North Pitt Street
Suite 350
Alexandria, VA 22314
703-684-4000
boards@nasbe.org
www.nasbe.org
The National Association of State Boards of Education works to strengthen state leadership in educational policymaking, promote excellence in education, advocate for equal opportunity, and assure continued support for public education.

Founded: 1958

Robert Hull, President & CEO
Sharon Cannon, Director, Operations

86 National Association of State Student Council Executive Directors (NASSCED)

www.nassced.net
NASSCED members work with state student council associations to further develop student leaders.

Roberta Bittel, President
Ben Schanck, Vice President

87 National Board for Professional Teaching Standards

1525 Wilson Boulevard
Suite 700
Arlington, VA 22209
703-465-2700
www.nbpts.org
The mission of the National Board for Professional Teaching Standards is to improve the quality of teaching and learning by developing professional standards for accomplished teaching, certifying teachers who meet those standards and integrating certified teachers into educational reform efforts.

Founded: 1987

Peggy Brookins, NBCT, President & CEO
Joe Doctor, Chief Operating Officer

88 National Catholic Educational Association (NCEA)

407 Bicksler Square SE
Leesburg, VA 20175-3773
571-257-0010
info@ncea.org
www.ncea.org
Rooted in the Gospel of Jesus Christ, the National Catholic Educational Association is a professional membership organization that provides leadership, direction and service to fulfill the teaching mission of Catholic schools.

Lincoln Snyder, President & CEO
Margaret Kaplow, Director, Marketing

89 National Center for Learning Disabilities (NCLD)

1220 L Street NW
Suite 100
Washington, DC 20005
301-966-2234
info@ncld.org
www.ncld.org
The National Center for Learning Disabilities works to ensure that the nation's children, adolescents and adults with learning disabilities have every opportunity to succeed in school, work and life. NCLD provides advocacy services, programs and research to fulfill this purpose.

Founded: 1977

Lindsay E. Jones, Esq., President & CEO
Kena Mayberry, Chief Operating Officer

90 National Center for School Engagement (NCSE)

Pueblo, CO
719-248-8669
www.schoolengagement.org
Provides training and technical assistance, research and evaluation to school districts, law enforcement agencies, courts, as well as state and federal agencies to encourage students to succeed in school. Special attention is given to at-risk students and the prevention of truancy, the dropout rate, and bullying.

Terri Martinez-McGraw, Co-Director
Jodi Heilbrunn, Co-Director

91 National Coalition of Independent Scholars (NCIS)

125 Putney Road
Battleboro, VT 05301
info@ncis.org
www.ncis.org
Nonprofit corporation providing information for the creation of local organizations of independent scholars. The coalition seeks to improve access to research institutions and libraries, offer grants to members, provide information and advice about fellowships and publishing and more.

Founded: 1989

Amanda Haste, President
Kathleen Stein-Smith, Communications Officer

92 National Council for Black Studies (NCBS)

PO Box 14359
Cincinnati, OH 45250
513-769-2092
info@ncbsonline.org
www.ncbsonline.org
Promotes academic excellence and social responsibility in the discipline of Africana/Black Studies through the production and dissemination of knowledge, professional development and training, and advocacy for social change and social justice.

Founded: 1975

Amilcar Shabazz, Ph.D, President
Alphonso Simpson, Ph.D, Vice President

93 National Council for Higher Education (NCHE)

National Education Association
1201 16th Street NW
Washington, DC 20036-3290
202-833-4000
Fax: 202-822-7974
www.nea.org/home/32959.htm
Independent membership organization of the National Education Association, dedicated to higher education members of the parent association.

DeWayne Sheaffer, President
Alec Thomson, Vice President

94 National Council of Urban Education Associations (NCUEA)

National Education Association (NEA)
1201 16th Street NW
Washington, DC 20036-3290
202-833-4000
Fax: 202-822-7974
www.nea.org/home/66472.htm
NCUEA is a caucus of local affiliates of the National Education Association (NEA), dedicated to strengthening and making NEA more responsive to member needs. NCUEA works to develop public education in urban schools by supporting local associations, leaders and members on issues around advocacy, diversity, communication, human rights and more.

Brent McKim, President
Shannon Rasmussen, Vice President

95 National Council on Measurement in Education (NCME)

19 Mantua Road
Mount Royal, NJ 08061
856-284-3700
Fax: 856-423-3420
ncme@talley.com
www.ncme.org
The National Council on Measurement in Education is a professional organization for individuals involved in the work of educational measurement (such as assessment and testing). Council members include university faculty; test developers; state and federal testing and research directors, and testing specialists working in various fields. The council aims to develop educational measurement methods so that they can be more effective.

Derek Briggs, President
Deborah Harris, Vice President

96 National Council on Rehabilitation Education (NCRE)

1099 E Champlain Drive
Suite A, 137
Fresno, CA 93720
559-906-0787
info@ncre.org
www.ncre.org
A professional organization of educators dedicated to serving persons with disabilities through education and research. The council works to maintain excellence in the field of rehabilitation by addressing issues around training priorities, federal funding, and research activities.

Founded: 1955

Mona Robinson, Ph.D, CRC, President
Allison Fleming, Ph.D, CRC, First Vice President

97 National Council on Student Development (NCSD)

NCSD National Office
301 Largo Road
Largo, MD 20774

ncsd.aacc@gmail.com
www.ncsd-aacc.com
The council's mission is to promote knowledge, expertise and professional development opportunities for student development professionals through advocacy and education.

Scheherazade W. Forman, President
Keziah Owens-Colon, Secretary

98 National Education Association (NEA)
National Education Association
1201 16th Street NW
Washington, DC 20036-3290
202-833-4000
Fax: 202-822-7974
www.nea.org
An organization made up of professional employees with the mission of advocating for public education, from pre-school to university programs, to ensure success of students. Some areas covered within their services include debt, educational funding, legislative action, human and civil rights, teaching strategies, grants and events and more.

Founded: 1857

Becky Pringle, President
Kim A. Anderson, Executive Director

99 National Education Association-Retired
National Education Association
1201 16th Street NW
Washington, DC 20036-3290
202-833-4000
Fax: 202-822-7974
www.nea.org/retired
NEA-Retired serves the needs of retired education employees. Some services offered by the program include the improvement of retirement pensions, intergenerational programs and activities and political action.

Sarah Borgman, President
Jean Dobashi, Vice President

100 National Educational Association of Disabled Students (NEADS)
Carleton University
1125 Colonel by Drive
Room 514, Unicentre
Ottawa, ON K1S-5B6
613-380-8065
877-670-1256
Fax: 613-369-4391
info@neads.ca
www.neads.ca
Advocates for accessible education and employment for disabled graduates. The association provides support in the form of research, resources, projects, financial aid and more services offered to their members.

Founded: 1986

Frank Smith, National Coordinator
Daniel Patterson, Communications Officer

101 National Organization for Student Success (NOSS)
PO Box 963
Northport, AL 35476
205-331-5997
acook@thenoss.org
www.thenoss.org
Formerly known as the National Association for Developmental Education, the organization seeks to improve the theory and practice of developmental education and the professional skills of developmental educators as well as develop programs.

Annette Cook, Contact

102 National Organization on Disability (NOD)
77 Water Street
13th Floor
New York, NY 10005
646-505-1191
Fax: 646-505-1184
info@nod.org
www.nod.org
The National Organization on Disability is a nonprofit organization promoting the participation of people with disabilities in society. The organization works with employers and educational institutions to create strategies for disability inclusion.

Founded: 1982

Carol Glazer, President
Moeena Das, Chief of Staff

103 National Rural Education Association (NREA)
615 McCallie Avenue
Hunter Hall 212
Chattanooga, TN 37421
423-425-4539
allen-pratt@utc.edu
www.nrea.net
Organization made up of rural school administrators, teachers, board members, regional service agency personnel, researchers, business and industry representatives. The organization serves the educational needs of those living in rural communities.

Founded: 1907

Jon Habben, President
Allen Pratt, Ed.D, Executive Director

104 National School Boards Association (NSBA)
1680 Duke Street
2nd Floor
Alexandria, VA 22314-3493
703-838-6722
Fax: 703-683-7590
info@nsba.org
www.nsba.org
Nonprofit collective of state associations of school boards advocating for excellence in public education in the United States.

Viola M. Garcia, President
Chip Slaven, Interim Executive Director

105 National School Public Relations Association (NSPRA)
15948 Derwood Road
Rockville, MD 20855
301-519-0496
Fax: 301-519-0494
info@nspra.org
www.nspra.org
Provides communication training and services to school leaders with the aim of advancing education through responsible public relations. The association also offers resource and research files, contacts in the corporate communication industry, workshops and seminars.

Founded: 1935

Barbara Hunter, Executive Director
Mellissa Braham, Associate Director

106 National Society for Experiential Education (NSEE)
19 Mantua Road
Mount Royal, NJ 08061
856-423-3427
Fax: 856-423-3420
nsee@talley.com
www.nsee.org
The National Society for Experiential Education is a nonprofit membership association of educators, businesses and community leaders interested in the development and improvement of experiential education programs nationwide.

Founded: 1971

Haley Brust, Executive Director
Denise Smith, Membership Services Manager

107 National Student Council (NatStuCo)
1904 Association Drive
Reston, VA 20191-1537
703-860-0200
800-253-7746
Fax: 703-860-3422
natstuco@natstuco.org
www.natstuco.org
Promotes student participation within school communities, encourages development of new student councils, assists state associations of student councils, provides leadership training for council members and advisors and encourages healthy living for young people.

Founded: 1931

108 National Student Exchange (NSE)
2613 Northridge Parkway
Suite 106
Ames, IA 50010
515-450-5529
info@nse.org
www.nse.org
The National Student Exchange is a program offering undergraduate study opportunities across regional, provincial, and cultural borders. NSE students gain insight into the historical and cultural makeup of different regions, improve their communication skills with individuals from different backgrounds and prepare themselves to live and work in a culturally diverse society.

Founded: 1968

Debra Sanborn, President
Leah Holmberg, Program Coordinator

109 National Women's Studies Association (NWSA)
PO Box 221136
Chicago, IL 60622
773-524-1807
nwsaoffice@nwsa.org
www.nwsa.org
The National Women's Studies Association supports the production of educational materials on the subject of women and gender. Their mission is to demonstrate the value of women's studies and feminist scholarship in education.

Founded: 1977

Karsonya Wise Whitehead, President
Jennifer Ash, Interim Executive Director

110 Nechi Institute: Centre of Indigenous Learning
Nechi Institute
PO Box 2039, Station Main
St. Albert, AB T8N-2G3
800-459-1884
Fax: 780-458-1883
nechi@nechi.com
www.nechi.com
Offers accredited programs for Indigenous training, research and health. Nechi provides counselors, health care workers, social workers, educators, government agencies and other support agencies with knowledge and tools to help

them address the issues faced by Indigenous people.

Marilyn Buffalo, Chief Executive Officer
Barbara Paul, Registrar

New England School Development Council (NESDEC)

28 Lord Road
Marlborough, MA 01752
508-481-9444
Fax: 508-481-5655
nesdec@nesdec.org
www.nesdec.org
Nonprofit educational organization helping schools to achieve and maintain high performance standards by providing planning and management, professional development, legal assistance, research and publications services.

Founded: 1946

Arthur L. Bettencourt, Ed.D, Executive Director
Danielle Chin, Business Manager

2 New Meridian

9390 Research Boulevard
Kaleido II, Suite 310
Austin, TX 78759-0001
512-399-3440
info@newmeridiancorp.org
www.newmeridiancorp.org
Develops a set of tests and assessments for students across the country as well as provides resources to support educators.

Arthur VanderVeen, Chief Executive Officer
Gina Rivera, Chief Operating Officer

3 North American Association for Environmental Education (NAAEE)

1725 Desales Street NW
Suite 401
Washington, DC 20036
202-419-0412
info@naaee.org
www.naaee.org
Teaches children and adults how to learn about and investigate their environment and to make intelligent, informed decisions about how they can take care of it. Environmental literacy and social engagement is fostered through education. NAAEE also offers consultation services, research, an affiliate network, policy initiatives, certification and more.

Judy Braus, Executive Director
Sarah Bodor, Director, Policy

4 North American Association of Educational Negotiators (NAEN)

423 Allen Road
Porter Corners, NY 12859
518-369-5779
execdir@naen.org
www.naen.org
Improves the knowledge and performance of K-12 school district, community college, and university management negotiators by advancing their professional status, providing a forum for communication, and encouraging information exchanges with others in the same profession.

James B. Fernow, President
Rachel M. Rissetto, Executive Director

15 North American Students of Cooperation (NASCO)

2150 S Canalport Avenue
Suite 2A-11
Chicago, IL 60608
773-404-2667
info@nasco.coop
www.nasco.coop
Organizes and educates affordable group equity co-ops to promote a community oriented cooperative movement. The association provides education and technical assistance to its members, as well as public education about the co-op movement and spirit.

Founded: 1968

Elizabeth Anderson, Director, Education
Katherine Jennings, Director, Operations

116 Northwest Commission on Colleges and Universities (NWCCU)

8060 165th Avenue NE
Suite 200
Redmond, WA 98052
425-558-4224
Fax: 205-525-9848
info@nwccu.org
www.nwccu.org
The mission of the Northwest Commission on Colleges and Universities is to assure educational quality and enhance institutional effectiveness of higher education schools in the Northwest region through the application of accreditation criteria and evaluation procedures.

Sonny Ramaswamy, President
Pamela Goad, Executive Vice President

117 Oakland School

128 Oakland Farm Way
Troy, VA 22974
434-293-9059
information@oaklandschool.net
www.oaklandschool.net
Private boarding and day school specializing in helping students with learning difficulties. Oakland School provides an individualized academic program focused on reading, writing, math and study skills. It is a school for children ages 6 - 13 years old. A variety of recreational activities, including horseback riding, are also offered on a farm for Fall/Winter and Summer Programs.

Carol Williams, Head of School

118 Oklahoma State University - Education Outreach

Oklahoma State University
106 Nancy Randolph Davis
Stillwater, OK 74078
405-744-5053
contact.ehs@okstate.edu
www.education.okstate.edu/outreach
Education Outreach provides courses and academic programs as well as support and services to educators. It also encourages collaboration between the college and other communities. Some programs offered by Education Outreach include faculty-led study abroad trips, distance learning, non-credit courses and professional development opportunities.

119 PACER Center

8161 Normandale Boulevard
Bloomington, MN 55437
952-838-9000
800-537-2237
Fax: 952-838-0199
pacer@pacer.org
www.pacer.org
PACER Center serves children, youth, and young adults with disabilities, with the goal of improving their quality of life and creating opportunities. The center fosters a supportive environment where parents can help parents and receive the education and programs they need to continue supporting their children in every stage of their lives.

Founded: 1977

Paula F. Goldberg, Executive Director

120 Peace & Justice Studies Association (PJSA)

1421 37th Street NW
Suite 130
Washington, DC 20057
202-681-2057
info@peacejusticestudies.org
www.peacejusticestudies.org
Brings together academics, K-12 teachers and grassroots activists to explore alternatives to violence and share strategies for social justice and social change. PJSA also serves as a professional association for scholars in the field of peace and conflict resolution studies, and is a member of the International Peace Research Association.

Founded: 2001

Michael Loadenthal, Executive Director

121 Public Relations Student Society of America (PRSSA)

120 Wall Street
21st Floor
New York, NY 10005
212-460-1474
Fax: 212-995-0757
prssa@prsa.org
www.prssa.prsa.org
The Public Relations Student Society of America is an organization dedicated to serving students interested in public relations and communications. PRSSA advocates for high academic standards, ethical principles and diversity in the field, while offering professional development and networking opportunities to students.

Founded: 1967

Jeneen Garcia, Senior VP, Programming
Jessica Espinal, Manager, Student Programs

122 Religious Education Association (REA)

1 East Erie Street
Suite 525, PMB 4274
Chicago, IL 60611
804-905-8573
info@religiouseducation.net
www.religiouseducation.net
Creates opportunities for exploring and advancing the interconnected practices of scholarship, research, teaching, and leadership in faith communities, academic institutions, and the wider world community.

Founded: 1903

Lakisha Lockhart, Executive Secretary

123 STEM Education Coalition

777 6th Street NW
Suite 510
Washington, DC 20001
info@stemedcoalition.org
www.stemedcoalition.org
Works to raise awareness in congress, the Administration, and other organizations about the critical role that STEM education plays in ensuring the economic and technological expertise of the U.S. in the global marketplace.

James Brown, Executive Director
Austin Hall, Director, Policy

124 Sexuality Information & Education Council of the United States

1012 14th Street NW
Suite 305
Washington, DC 20005

202-265-2405
Fax: 202-462-2340
info@siecus.org
www.siecus.org
Promotes sexuality education for people of all ages, protects sexual rights, and expands access to sexual health services. The council trains educators, advocates for sound public policies related to sexuality, and provides information and resources on a host of sexuality topics.

Founded: 1964

Christine Soyong Harley, President & CEO
Gail Cowan, Development Director

125 **Smarter Balanced Assessment Consortium**
sb@smarterbalanced.org
www.smarterbalanced.org
Smarter Balancedÿis a public agency offering an online assessment system informed by thousands of educators and aligned to theÿCommon Core State Standards (CCSS). The agency also offers tools for educators to improve teaching and learning in the classroom.

Tony Alpert, Executive Director
Christyan Mitchell, Chief Operating Officer

126 **Society for Research in Child Development**
1825 K Street NW
Suite 325
Washington, DC 20006
202-800-0677
info@srcd.org
www.srcd.org
The Society for Research in Child Development is a membership association that advances developmental science and promotes its use to improve human lives.

Founded: 1933

Saima K. Hedrick, MPH, CAE, Executive Director
Kelly R. Fisher, Ph.d, Director, Policy

127 **Society for the Advancement of Excellence in Education (SAEE)**
www.saee.ca
Provides non-partisan education research and information to policy-makers, education partners and the public in order to encourage higher performance throughout Canada's public education system. Operations have wound down, but the group's online archive is still available.

Founded: 1996

128 **Solution Tree**
555 N Morton Street
Bloomington, IN 47404
812-336-7700
800-733-6786
Fax: 812-336-7790
info@solutiontree.com
www.solutiontree.com
Strives to be the premier provider of books, videos, multimedia resources, and professional development opportunities designed to help educators throughout the world realize continuous school improvement and connect with youth at risk.

Founded: 1998

Ed Ackerman, President & COO
Jeffrey C. Jones, Chief Executive Officer

129 **Summit Vision**
8111 Schott Road
Westerville, OH 43081
614-403-3891
www.summit-vision.com
Summit Vision believes that through the use of adventure and experiential learning tools, people can develop valuable skills and traits such as problem-solving, conflict resolution, decision-making, leadership, perseverance and empathy. Services offered include play days, camp and fitness programs.

Founded: 1997

Trey McBane, President
Karen Burke, Office Manager

130 **Teach Plus**
27-43 Wormwood Street
Suite 410
Boston, MA 02210
info@teachplus.org
www.teachplus.org
Offers programs to support teachers in making policy changes for the betterment of the education system for all.

Roberto J. Rodriguez, President & CEO
Michael Savoy, Ph.D, Vice President, Programs

131 **The Association of Boarding Schools (TABS)**
1 N Pack Square
Suite 301
Asheville, NC 28801
828-258-5354
Fax: 828-258-6428
questions@tabs.org
www.boardingschools.com
The association promotes awareness and understanding of boarding schools with the goal of expanding the pool of applicants for member institutions. The association also offers resources for educators seeking training, research, guidance and support on all issues pertaining to the residential school experience.

Founded: 1975

Pete Upham, Executive Director
Brett Fuhrman, VP, Finance & Operations

132 **The Gifted Child Society**
70 Hilltop Road
Suite 3015
Ramsey, NJ 07446-1155
201-444-6530
Fax: 201-444-9099
admin@gifted.org
www.gifted.org
Nonprofit organization providing educational enrichment and support services specifically designed for gifted children. Programs offered include workshops, day camps, IQ testing services, parent and guardian education and training for professionals and school educators.

Founded: 1957

D'Arcy Natale, Managing Director
Tom Nikolaidis, Curriculum Manager

133 **The Jewish Federations of North America (JFNA)**
25 Broadway
17th Floor
New York, NY 10004
212-284-6500
info@jewishfederations.org
www.jewishfederations.org
The Jewish Federations of North America is made up of Federations and communities dedicated to serving the Jewish communities of North America by offering education, funding for services, advocacy, crisis relief and more.

Mark Wilf, Chair
Eric D. Fingerhut, President & CEO

134 **US Israel Education Association**
www.usieducation.org
Provides resources to help build connections between the U.S. and Israeli leaders by offering educational tours and briefings about the systems of Israeli government.

Heather Johnston, Executive Director
Ari Sacher, Director, Education

135 **Wilderness Education Association (WEA)**
151 NC Highway 9
Suite B
Black Mountain, NC 28711
971-208-5751
nationaloffice@weainfo.org
www.weainfo.org
The Wilderness Education Association is a nonprofit organization whose purpose is to educate the general public and outdoor leaders in the appropriate use of wildlands and protected areas by developing and implementing educational programs and by forming strategic alliances with federal land management agencies, conservation groups and all organizations that are affected by wildlands.

Founded: 1977

Ryan B. Carlson, Executive Director
Kevin Earhart Sutton, Office Administrator

136 **World Association for Cooperative Education (WACE)**
University of Waterloo
200 University Avenue W
Waterloo, ON N2L-3G1
admin@waceinc.org
www.waceinc.org
Devoted to fostering Cooperative & Work-Integrated Education around the world.

Founded: 1983

Maurits van Rooijen, Co-Chair
Sampan Silapanad, Co-Chair

137 **World Council for Curriculum and Instruction (WCCI)**
WCCI Secretariat
Alliant International University
10455 Pomerado Road
San Diego, CA 92131
858-864-4057
wcci@alliant.edu
www.wcci-international.org
A transnational educational organization with the goal of creating a just and peaceful world community through support of education and community development programs. The organization also has a special status with Economic and Social Council (ECOSOC) of the UN and UNESCO.

Founded: 1970

Swee-Hin Toh, President
Estela Matriano, Executive Director

Administration

138 **American Association of Collegiate Registrars & Admissions Officers (AACRAO)**
1108 16th Street NW
Suite 400
Washington, DC 20036
202-293-9161
Fax: 202-872-8857

communications@aacrao.org
www.aacrao.org
Nonprofit professional organization bringing together those who work in higher education from around the world. The association provides professional development, guidelines, and professional standards to be used in the areas of records management, admissions, enrollment, information technology and student services.

Tiffany Robinson, President
Melanie Gottlieb, Interim Executive Director

9 American Association of School Administrators (AASA)

1615 Duke Street
Alexandria, VA 22314
703-528-0700
Fax: 703-841-1543
info@aasa.org
www.aasa.org
The mission of the American Association of School Administrators is to support and develop effective school system leaders who are dedicated to ensuring the quality of public education.

Daniel A. Domenech, Executive Director
Chuck Woodruff, Chief Operating Officer

0 American Association of University Administrators (AAUA)

10 Church Road
Wallingford, PA 19086
814-460-6498
Fax: 610-565-8089
dking@aaua.org
www.aaua.org
The mission of the American Association of University Administrators is to develop and advance superior standards for the profession of higher education administration.

Founded: 1970

Christine Cavanaugh, Chair
Dan L. King, President & CEO

1 American Finance Association (AFA)

University of Utah
1655 E Campus Center Drive
Salt Lake City, UT 84112
jim.schallheim@business.utah.edu
www.afajof.org
Association working to promote awareness about financial economics. It aims to improve public understanding of financial problems, distribute knowledge through written and other media and to enourage finance as an educational study.

John Graham, President
James Schallheim, Exec. Secretary & Treasurer

42 Association for Supervision & Curriculum Development (ASCD)

1703 N Beauregard Street
Alexandria, VA 22311-1714
press@ascd.org
www.ascd.org
A membership organization that develops programs, products, and services essential to the way educators learn, teach, and lead.

Founded: 1943

Ranjit Sidhu, CEO & Executive Director
Dana Shanks-Williams, Chief Financial Officer

43 Association of Arts Administration Educators (AAAE)

PO Box 25094
Providence, RI 02905
hello@artsadministration.org
www.artsadministration.org
The Association of Arts Administration Educators is an international organization representing college and university graduate and undergraduate programs in arts administration. Through their programs, the association offers students opportunities to develop knowledge and skills in arts leadership, management, entrepreneurship, cultural policy and more.

Founded: 1975

Haley Carlson, Programs/Operations Manager

144 Association of College Administration Professionals (ACAP)

PO Box 1389
Staunton, VA 24402
540-885-1873
Fax: 540-885-6133
www.acap.webstarts.com
The Association of College Administration Professionals provides career development services to college and university administrators. Among these services are monthly newsletters, articles and surveys, job postings and annual conferences.

Founded: 1995

145 Association of School Business Officials (ABSO) International

44790 Maynard Square
Suite 200
Ashburn, VA 20147
866-682-2729
Fax: 703-478-0205
asboreq@asbointl.org
www.asbointl.org
Provides programs and services that promote high standards for school business management procedures and which support professional development. Among the services offered are certification options, scholarships, legislative resources, a global network and advocacy.

Founded: 1910

David Lewis, Executive Director
Siobhan McMahon, CAE, Chief Operations Officer

146 Association of University Programs in Health Administration (AUPHA)

1730 M Street NW
Suite 407
Washington, DC 20036
202-763-7283
aupha@aupha.org
www.aupha.org
The Association of University Programs in Health Administration is a global network of colleges, universities, faculty, individuals and organizations united by the goal of improving healthcare delivery through development in healthcare management and policy education. Some programs offered by AUPHA include baccalaureate, master's and doctoral degree programs in health administration education, workshops and international programs.

Daniel Gentry, President & CEO
Jaime E. Stephens, Vice President & COO

147 Canadian Association of Principals (CAP)

300 Earl Grey Drive
Suite 220
Ottawa, ON K2T-1C1
613-839-0768
info@cdnprincipals.com
www.cdnprincipals.com
National organization advocating on behalf of school principals and vice principals with the goal of improving education for students. The association offers journals, reports and conferences for its members to get together and share ideas.

Founded: 1977

Terry MacIsaac, President

148 Council for the Accreditation of Educator Preparation (CAEP)

1140 19th Street NW
Suite 400
Washington, DC 20036
202-223-0077
caep@caepnet.org
www.caepnet.org
Formerly the National Council for Accreditation of Teacher Education (nCATE) and the Teacher Education Accreditation Council (TEAC), the Council seeks to support the development of educators through evidence-based accreditation with the aim of improving P-12 student learning.

Founded: 1954

Christopher A. Koch, President
Malina Monaco, Vice President

149 Council for the Advancement of Standards in Higher Education (CAS)

2598 East Sunrise Boulevard
Suite 2104
Fort Lauderdale, FL 33304
800-889-7270
executive_director@cas.edu
www.cas.edu
The Council for the Advancement of Standards in Higher Education (CAS) promotes collaboration within campus and creates standards for conduct in student affairs, student services, and student development programs.

Founded: 1979

Dan Bureau, President
Doreen Murner, Executive Director

150 Council of Chief State School Officers (CCSSO)

1 Massachusetts Avenue NW
Suite 700
Washington, DC 20001
202-336-7000
www.ccsso.org
Nonprofit organization of education leaders providing leadership, advocacy, and technical assistance to resolve issues related to education. The council envisions a system of schooling in each state that ensures high standards of performance and prepares students to succeed as productive members of society.

Carissa Moffat Miller, Ph.D, Chief Executive Officer
Scott Norton, Ph.D, Dep. Exec. Dir., Programs

151 Council of Higher Education Management Associations (CHEMA)

NACUBO
1110 Vermont Avenue NW
Suite 800
Washington, DC 20005-3593
202-861-2517
srodney@nacubo.org
www.chemanet.org
The Council of Higher Education Management Associations is an informal assembly of management-oriented higher education associations in the U.S. and Canada. CHEMA members share information and experiences, and collaborate on projects in order to better

serve the colleges and universities they represent.

Founded: 1971

Sterlicia Rodney, Contact

152 Independent Schools Association of the Central States (ISACS)
55 W Wacker Drive
Suite 701
Chicago, IL 60601
312-750-1190
Fax: 312-750-1193
info@isacs.org
www.isacs.org
The purpose of ISACS is to promote the development of strong learning communities characterized by high achievements, social responsibility, and independence of governance, programs and policies. ISACS provides professional development opportunities, consulting services, resources on the subject of independent school operations and networking events.

Mary Menacho, Executive Director
Karen Zeitlin, Director, Programs

153 NASPA - Student Affairs Administrators in Higher Education
111 K Street NE
10th Floor
Washington, DC 20002
202-265-7500
office@naspa.org
www.naspa.org
Association dedicated to supporting the student affairs administration profession. Services, programs and knowledge are provided by the association for the purpose of cultivating student success in colleges and universities.

Founded: 1919

Kevin Kruger, President
Stephanie Gordon, VP, Professional Development

154 National Association for Gifted Children (NAGC)
1300 I Street NW
Suite 400E
Washington, DC 20005
202-785-4268
nagc@nagc.org
www.nagc.org
Organization of parents, teachers, educators and other professionals committed to addressing the unique needs of children and youth with demonstrated gifts and talents. The organization's mission is to help children develop through education, advocacy, community building and research.

John Segota, Executive Director
Andrew Bassett, Director, Administration

155 National Association of College and University Business Officers (NACUBO)
1110 Vermont Avenue NW
Suite 800
Washington, DC 20005
202-861-2500
support@nacubo.org
www.nacubo.org
Membership organization representing 1,700+ colleges and universities across the U.S.

Susan Scroggins, Chair
Susan Whealler Johnston, President & CEO

156 National Association of Elementary School Principals (NAESP)
1615 Duke Street
Alexandria, VA 22314
703-684-3345
800-386-2377
Fax: 703-549-5568
naesp@naesp.org
www.naesp.org
Professional organization serving elementary and middle school principals and other education leaders. The association offers advocacy, conferences, a learning center and other services to prepare leaders for success in their work with children, families and communities.

Founded: 1921

L. Earl Franks, Ed.D, CAE, Executive Director
Nikki Sparks, Director, Operations

157 National Association of Private Special Education Centers (NAPSEC)
777 6th Street NW
11th Floor
Washington, DC 20001
202-434-8225
napsec@napsec.org
www.napsec.org
Provides support for private services offered to students with disabilities. Members include those who provide intervention services, schools, residential therapeutic centers, postsecondary and adult living programs and more.

Founded: 1971

Chris Tabakin, President
Danielle Johnson, Executive Director & CEO

158 National Association of Secondary School Principals (NASSP)
1904 Association Drive
Reston, VA 20191-1537
703-860-0200
800-253-7746
Fax: 703-860-3422
www.nassp.org
Promotes excellence in school leadership and provides members with a wide variety of programs and services to assist them in administration, supervision, curriculum planning, and effective staff development.

Founded: 1916

Ronn Nozoe, Chief Executive Officer

159 National Association of State Directors of Special Education (NASDSE)
1800 Diagonal Road
Suite 600
Alexandria, VA 22314
703-519-3800
www.nasdse.org
A nonprofit corporation that promotes and supports education programs for students with disabilities in the United States and outlying areas. The association does this by building connections with providers of policies, educational and other programs serving individuals with disabilities.

Founded: 1938

John Eisenberg, Executive Director
Valerie Williams, Dir., Government Relations

160 National Association of State Directors of Adult Education (NASDAE)
822 Guilford Avenue
Suite 170
Baltimore, MD 21202
202-499-4201
ptyler@nasdae.org
www.nasdae.org
The mission of the organization is to assist adult education staff in their professional development, attend to their public policy needs and establish and disseminate information on the field.

Founded: 1990

Sheryl Hart, Chair
Patricia Tyler, Executive Director

161 National Association of Student Financial Aid Administrators (NASFAA)
1801 Pennsylvania Avenue NW
Suite 850
Washington, DC 20006-3606
202-785-0453
Fax: 202-785-1487
info@nasfaa.org
www.nasfaa.org
Nonprofit corporation of postsecondary institutions, individuals, agencies and students interested in promoting the effective administration of student financial aid in the United States. The association provides advocacy, training, courses, technical supports, research, resources for councelors and more.

Brent Tener, National Chair
Justin Draeger, President & CEO

162 National Center for the Improvement of Educational Assessment
31 Mount Vernon Street
Dover, NH 03820
603-516-7900
Fax: 603-516-7910
www.nciea.org
The Center for Assessment strives to improve the assessment processes for education to enhance practices and ensure accountability in compliance with the Every Student Succeeds Act (ESSA). The center offers assessment systems, a library and conferences.

Scott Marion, Executive Director
Chris Domaleski, Associate Director

163 National Center on Educational Outcomes (NCEO)
University of Minnesota
150 Pillsbury Drive SE
207 Pattee Hall
Minneapolis, MN 55455
612-626-1530
Fax: 612-624-0879
nceo@umn.edu
www.nceo.info
The National Center on Educational Outcomes was established to provide national leadership in designing and building educational assessments and accountability systems that appropriately monitor educational results for all students, including students with disabilities and English Language Learners.

Founded: 1990

Sheryl Lazarus, Ph.D, Director
Kristin Liu, Ph.D, Assistant Director

164 National Orientation Directors Association (NODA)
1200 Washington Avenue S
Suite 215
Minneapolis, MN 55415
612-301-6632
866-521-6632
Fax: 612-624-2628
noda@umn.edu
www.nodaweb.org

The mission of the National Orientation Directors Association is to provide education, leadership and professional development in the fields of college student orientation, transition and retention.

Karnell McConnell-Black, President
Joyce Holl, Executive Director

5 National Policy Board for Educational Administration (NPBEA)

1904 Association Drive
Reston, VA 20191
wilsonj@npbea.org
www.npbea.org
The National Policy Board for Educational Administration is a national consortium of major stakeholders in educational leadership and policy. The purpose of the Board is to provide a forum for collaborative actions by organizations interested in the advancement of school and school-system leadership.

Jacquelyn Wilson, Executive Director

6 National School Safety Center (NSSC)

30200 Agoura Road
Suite 260
Agoura Hills, CA 91301
805-373-9977
info@schoolsafety.us
www.schoolsafety.us
Advocates for safe, secure and peaceful schools worldwide as well as the prevention of school crime and violence. The center provides schools with information, resources, consultation and training services neccessary to ensure safe environments.

Founded: 1984

Ronald D. Stephens, Executive Director

67 Pearson's Clinical Assessment Group

19500 Bulverde Road
Suite 201
San Antonio, TX 78259-3701
800-627-7271
Fax: 800-232-1223
clinicalcustomersupport@pearson.com
www.pearsonassessments.com
Offers tools to assist professionals in various fields, including schools, to promote effective education via assessments, research and innovative technologies.

Bob Whelan, President

68 The Heads Network

102 Wentworth Avenue
Nashville, TN 37215
615-533-6022
swade@headsnetwork.org
www.headsnetwork.org
Provides a forum for school leaders to learn from each other in the interest of the education and employment of girls and young women.

Founded: 1920

Margaret Wade, Executive Director

Early Childhood Education

69 Association for Early Learning Leaders

1250 S Capital of Texas Highway
Building 3, Suite 400
Austin, TX 78746
800-537-1118
info@earlylearningleaders.org
www.earlylearningleaders.org
The Association for Early Learning Leaders is a nonprofit organization serving administrators and directors of early education programs by offering accreditation information, conferences, online training and more.

Founded: 1984

Ronald McGuckin, President
Lori Buxton, Managing Director

170 Association to Benefit Children (ABC)

419 E 86th Street
New York, NY 10028
212-845-3821
Fax: 212-426-9488
abc@a-b-c.org
www.a-b-c.org
The Association to Benefit Childrenÿis dedicated to helping create quality of life for disadvantaged children and their families through compassionate programs designed to break the cycles of abuse, neglect, sickness and homelessness. Some of their services include supportive housing, family programs, mental health supports and early childhood education.

Founded: 1986

Gretchen Buchenholz, Executive Director
Eri Noguchi, Chief Operating Officer

171 Building Blocks for Literacy

Stern Center for Language and Learning
183 Talcott Road
Suite 101
Williston, VT 05495
802-878-2332
Fax: 802-878-0230
learning@sterncenter.org
www.buildingblocksforliteracy.org
Promotes early literacy skills for children in child care and preschool by providing certification, research, professional development and a video Family Forum online.

Founded: 1997

172 Child Care Aware of America

1515 N Courthouse Road
2nd Floor
Arlington, VA 22201
800-424-2246
info@childcareaware.org
www.childcareaware.org
Child Care Aware is a hub of information for parents and child care providers covering topics such as types of childcare, financial assistance, military assistance, programs, training for professionals, videos and newsletters.

Lynette M. Fraga, Ph.D, Chief Executive Officer
Michelle McCready, M.P.P., Dep. Executive Officer

173 Children's Place Association

700 N Sacramento Boulevard
Suite 300
Chicago, IL 60612
312-733-9954
Fax: 312-243-7653
www.childrens-place.org
The Children's Place Association provides assistance to primarily low income families and children in Chicago, Illinois. The Association is focused on education, health, family, and financial stability and facilitates early childhood education, offering home based, and center based education initiatives at their Arthur E. Jones Early Childhood Care and Learning Center.

Founded: 1991

Cathy Krieger, LCSW, MA, MBA, President & CEO
John Sweeney, MBA, Deputy Executive Director

174 Division for Early Childhood

PO Box 662089
Los Angeles, CA 90066
310-428-7209
Fax: 855-678-1989
dec@dec-sped.org
www.dec-sped.org
The Division for Early Childhood (DEC) works to promote policy and implement evidence-based practices that support the development of young children ages 0-8. The DEC is focused on helping children at risk for developmental delays and disabilities. It is a division of the Council for Exceptional Children.

Peggy Kemp, Executive Director
Diana Stanfill, Associate Director

175 Early Childhood Technical Assistance Center (ECTA)

ECTA Center
517 S Greensboro Street
Carrboro, NC 27510
919-962-2001
Fax: 919-966-7463
ectacenter@unc.edu
www.ectacenter.org
The Early Childhood Technical Assistance Center works to improve early childhood special education service systems by creating recommended practices and monitoring effectiveness of early intervention programs.

Christina Kasprzak, Co-Director
Megan Vinh, Co-Director

176 Exchange Press

7700 A Street
Lincoln, NE 68510
425-883-9394
800-221-2864
Fax: 402-467-6118
info@exchangepress.com
www.childcareexchange.com
Promotes the exchange of ideas among leaders in early childhood programs worldwide through magazine, books, training products, training seminars and international conferences. Some topics covered include administration, environments, family, social and emotional development, and teaching.

Kayley Cooper, Marketing Manager

177 HighScope Educational Research Foundation

600 N River Street
Ypsilanti, MI 48198
800-587-5639
info@highscope.org
www.highscope.org
HighScope Educational Research Foundation is an independent nonprofit research, development, and outreach organization. The foundation supports early childhood education including the professional development of individuals in the field.

Founded: 1970

Alejandra Barraza, Ph.D, President
Kimberly Diamond-Berry, Ph.D, Director, Research Policy

178 Military Child Education Coalition (MCEC)
909 Mountain Lion Circle
Harker Heights, TX 76548
254-953-1923
Fax: 254-953-1925
info@militarychild.org
www.militarychild.org
The Military Child Education Coalition is a nonprofit, international organization dedicated to equal and quality education for military children who are affected by mobility, family separation, and transition. The MCEC conducts research, develops resources, and maintains and fosters connections with school districts to facilitate communication.

Rebecca Porter, Ph.D, President & CEO
Tim Farrell, Senior Vice President & COO

179 National AfterSchool Association (NAA)
2961A Hunter Mill Road
Suite 626
Oakton, VA 22124
info@naaweb.org
www.naaweb.org
The National AfterSchool Association develops programs and provides after school education for children and youth in grades K-12. The NAA is a membership association comprised of individuals who work with children and provided extended learning opportunities.

Gina Warner, President & CEO
Heidi Ham, VP, Programs & Strategy

180 National Association for the Education of Homeless Children and Youth (NAEHCY)
4325 First Avenue
Suite 247
Tucker, GA 30085
404-530-9538
info@naehcy.org
www.naehcy.org
Professional organization dedicated to meeting the educational needs of children and youth experiencing homelessness. The association provides professional development, resources, advocacy and training for those interested in supporting the academic success of children and youth challenged by homelessness.

Jimiyu Evans, President
Tisha Tallman, Executive Director

181 National Association of Early Childhood Specialists in State Departments of Education
information@naecs-sde.org
www.naecs-sde.org
The National Association of Early Childhood Specialists in State Departments of Education (NAECS-SDE) promotes quality early childhood education through the improvement of instruction, curriculum, and administration of programs.

Founded: 1972

Noel Kelty, President
Robin Wilkins, Vice President

182 National Association of Family Child Care (NAFCC)
700 12th Street NW
Suite 700
Washington, DC 20005
202-796-5700
nafcc@nafcc.org
www.nafcc.org
The National Association for Family Child Care is a nonprofit membership association representing early childhood care providers throughout the United States. The association offers public policy advocacy, conferences and accreditation opportunities for professionals.

Lanette Dumas, Executive Director

183 National Child Care Association (NCCA)
PO Box 2948
Merrifield, VA 22116
877-537-6222
ncca@necpa.net
www.nationalchildcare.org
The National Child Care Association advocates for policies and regulations that positively impact children.

Cindy Lehnhoff, Director

184 National Head Start Association (NHSA)
1651 Prince Street
Alexandria, VA 22314
703-739-0875
866-677-8724
www.nhsa.org
The National Head Start Association is a nonprofit organization committed to supporting the needs of at risk children through policy change.

Founded: 1974

Yasmina Vinci, Executive Director
Thomas Sheridan, Deputy Director

185 National Institute for Early Education Research (NIEER)
Rutgers, The State University of New Jersey
73 Easton Avenue
New Brunswick, NJ 08901-1879
848-932-4350
Fax: 732-932-4360
info@nieer.org
www.nieer.org
The National Institute for Early Education Research (NIEER) provides independent research based information to support quality, effective early childhood education.

Founded: 2002

W. Steven Barnett, Sr. Co-Director & Founder
Ellen Frede, Sr. Co-Director

186 Southern Early Childhood Association (SECA)
PO Box 8109
Jacksonville, AR 72078
501-221-1648
www.seca.info
The Southern Early Childhood Association (SECA) provides a network for communication among childhood educators including preschool, kindergarten, primary teachers, administrators, and individuals interested in early childhood education.

Founded: 1948

Debbie Ferguson, President

Elementary Education

187 American Student Council Association (ASCA)
National Assoc. of Elementary School Principals
1615 Duke Street
Alexandria, VA 22314
703-684-3345
800-386-2377
Fax: 703-549-5568
naesp@naesp.org
www.naesp.org
A program of the Association of Elementary School Principals, the ASCA promotes and supports student councils across the U.S.

Founded: 1987

L. Earl Franks, Ed.D, CAE, Executive Director
Nikki Sparks, Director, Operations

188 Center for Play Therapy (CPT)
425 S Welch Street
Complex 2
Denton, TX 76203
940-565-3864
Fax: 940-565-4461
cpt@unt.edu
www.cpt.unt.edu
Encourages the development and emotional growth of children through play therapy and a positive interpersonal relationship with a therapist trained in play therapy. The center also provides training, research, publications, counseling services and literature on the field.

Founded: 1987

Dee Ray, Director
Gabby Mendez, Administrative Coordinator

189 National Association for the Education of Young Children (NAEYC)
1401 H Street NW
Suite 600
Washington, DC 20005
202-232-8777
800-424-2460
help@naeyc.org
www.naeyc.org
Supports those interested in serving and acting on behalf of the educational needs and rights of young children. The association engages in advancing practice, policy, and research in the field through accreditation programs and conferences.

Rhian Evans Allvin, Chief Executive Officer
Jill Stasz Harris, Chief Operating Officer

190 Voyager Sopris Learning
Cambium Learning Group
17855 Dallas Parkway
Suite 400
Dallas, TX 75287
800-547-6747
Fax: 888-819-7767
www.voyagersopris.com
Voyager Sopris Learning is a provider of solutions and professional development services to pre-K-12 students and educators.

Founded: 1994

Nick Gaehde, President

Employment

191 English Language Program
Center for Intercultural Education & Development
3300 Whitehaven Street NW
Suite 1000
Washington, DC 20007

800-308-7649
fellow@elprograms.org
www.elprograms.org
A program of the U.S Department of State, the English Language Programs sends United States English teachers abroad to US embassies to assist in delivering and maintaining quality English language programs.

Founded: 1969

Magda Potocka, Program Director
Toni Hull, Associate Director

2 Graphic Arts Education & Research Foundation
1899 Preston White Drive
Reston, VA 20191
703-264-7200
The Graphic Arts Education and Research Foundation (GAERF) is dedicated to advancing knowledge and education in graphic communications through programs that support workforce development.

Founded: 1983

3 Health Occupations Students of America
HOSA - Future Health Professionals
548 Silicon Drive
Suite 101
Southlake, TX 76092
800-321-4672
info@hosa.org
www.hosa.org
An international student organization, HOSA works to enhance the quality of healthcare through the promotion of career opportunities in the healthcare industry.

Founded: 1976

Jim Koeninger, Ph.D, Executive Director
Karen Koeninger, Deputy Executive Director

4 Mountain Pacific Association of Colleges & Employers (MPACE)
808 R Street
Suite 209
Sacramento, CA 95811
916-231-2140
Fax: 916-231-2141
staff@mpace.org
www.mpace.org
Comprised of career services professionals and employers, the Mountain Pacific Association of Colleges and Employers works with its members to help college students obtain jobs and internships.

Espie Santiago, President
Catherine Smith, CAE, Executive Director

95 National Association of Colleges and Employers (NACE)
62 Highland Avenue
Bethlehem, PA 18017
610-868-1421
customerservice@naceweb.org
www.naceweb.org
The National Association of Colleges and Employers connects college career services professionals with universities, colleges, and recruiting professionals. NACE provides information on employment, hiring trends, hiring practices, and student attitudes and outcomes.

Founded: 1956

David Ong, President
Shawn VanDerziel, Executive Director

96 National Association of Professional Employer Organizations (NAPEO)
707 N Saint Asaph Street
Alexandria, VA 22314
703-836-0466
Fax: 703-836-0976
info@napeo.org
www.napeo.org
The National Association of Professional Employer Organizations represents the PEO industry, advocating for the interests of PEOs at all levels of government.

Founded: 1984

Pat Cleary, President & CEO
Melissa Viscovich, CAE, Senior Vice President & COO

197 National Business Education Association (NBEA)
1914 Association Drive
Suite 203
Reston, VA 20191
703-860-8300
Fax: 703-860-4483
nbea@nbea.org
www.nbea.org
The National Business Education Association works to support individuals and groups who instruct, administer, research, and spread information regarding business. NBEA advances the professional interests of its members through programs that enhance professional growth and development.

Joe McClary, Executive Director
Jeri Werner, Operations Manager

198 National Student Employment Association (NSEA)
2 Great Falls Plaza
Unit 767
Auburn, ME 04212
512-423-1417
nsea@nsea.info
www.nsea.info
The National Student Employment Association is a student employment association providing professional development and employment opportunities for college students. Membership is open to any individual with an interest in hiring students.

Bridget Schwartz, President
Shirley Govindasamy, Board Relations Coordinator

199 Southern Business Education Association (SBEA)
National Business Education Association
1914 Association Drive
Suite 203
Reston, VA 20191-1596
www.sbeaonline.org
Professional organization of business educators from 12 southern states.

Marie Coleman, Ph.D, President
Jennifer Stubblefield, Director, Membership

Guidance & Counseling

200 American Association of Sex Educators, Counselors & Therapists
35 E Wacker Drive
Suite 850
Chicago, IL 60601
202-449-1099
Fax: 202-216-9646
info@aasect.org
www.aasect.org
The American Association of Sexuality Educators, Counselors and Therapists (AASECT) promotes sexual health through the development and advancement of the sexual therapy, counseling, and education fields.

Founded: 1967

Kellie Braband, Executive Director
Jessica Gonzalez, Certification & CE Manager

201 American College Counseling Association
1101 N Delaware Street
Indianapolis, IN 46202
855-220-8760
office@collegecounseling.org
www.collegecounseling.org
Primarily working in a higher education setting, the American College Counseling Association (ACCA) is comprised of mental health professionals and student members working to foster student development. The ACCA works to support and enhance college counselling, promote ethical practice, and facilitate communication among college counselors.

Founded: 1991

Andrew Lee, President

202 American College Personnel Association
One Dupont Circle NW
Suite 300
Washington, DC 20036
202-835-2272
Fax: 202-827-0601
info@acpa.nche.edu
www.myacpa.org
The American College Personnel Association (ACPA) works to advance student affairs and engage students in activities. The ACPA represents 1,200 private and public institutions with 7,500 members across the United States and the globe.

Founded: 1924

Chris Moody, Executive Director
Tricia Fechter Gates, Deputy Executive Director

203 American Counseling Association
6101 Stevenson Avenue
Suite 600
Alexandria, VA 22304
703-823-9800
800-347-6647
Fax: 800-473-2329
acamemberservices@counseling.org
www.counseling.org
A nonprofit professional and educational organization, the American Counseling Association (ACA) represents professional counselors working to grow and enhance the counseling profession.

Founded: 1952

Richard Yep, Chief Executive Officer
Brandi McIntyre, Governance Exec. Office Mgr.

204 American School Counselor Association
1101 King Street
Suite 310
Alexandria, VA 22314
703-683-2722
asca@schoolcounselor.org
www.schoolcounselor.org
The American School Counselor Association (ASCA) supports counselors at every level of education and works to promote professionalism and ethical practice. The ASCA offers its members professional development opportunities, provides current information re-

lated to professionalism, and supports research and evaluation in school counseling.

Jill Cook, Executive Director
Deirdra Williams Hawkes, Director, Programs

205 Association for Financial Counseling & Planning Education
79 S State Street
Suite D3
Westerville, OH 43081
614-368-1055
www.afcpe.org
A nonprofit organization, the Association for Financial Counseling & Planning Education (AFCPE) provides supports for professionals who offer counseling regarding financial planning to individuals and families. The AFCPE works with the government, military, and other organizations to establish policy that sets standards in the financial counseling, planning, and education fields.

Rebecca Wiggins, Executive Director
Rachael DeLeon, Senior Dir., Member Services

206 Association for University and College Counseling Center Directors
1101 N Delaware Street
Suite 200
Indianapolis, IN 46202
317-635-4755
Fax: 317-635-4757
office@aucccd.org
www.aucccd.org
The Association for University and College Counseling Center Directors (AUCCCD) is a professional organization working to encourage the development and success of directors. The AUCCCD supports higher education by advocating for collegiate mental health.

Founded: 1950

David Reetz, Ph.D, President
Steve Sprinkle, Ph.D, Treasurer

207 Association of Educational Therapists
7044 S 13th Street
Oak Creek, WI 53154
414-908-4949
customercare@aetonline.org
www.aetonline.org
The Association of Educational Therapists (AET) offers leadership, certification, and training for Educational Therapists. The AET promotes the ethical practice and sets standards in the Educational Therapy field.

Kaye Ragland, President

208 Canadian Education and Research Institute for Counselling
Foundation House
2 St Clair Avenue East
Suite 300
Toronto, ON M4T-2T5
416-929-2510
admin@ceric.ca
www.ceric.ca
A charitable organization dedicated to promoting the study of career counseling and career development. Some services offered by the organization include funds for projects, training programs for career professionals, publications and research.

Riz Ibrahim, Executive Director
Sharon Ferriss, Senior Director, Marketing

209 Council for Accreditation of Counseling & Related Educational Programs
500 Montgomery Street
Suite 350
Alexandria, VA 22314
703-535-5990
Fax: 703-739-6209
www.cacrep.org
An accrediting organization, the CACREP sets standards to promote excellence and enhance professional preparation among counseling and related educational programs. The CACREP works collaboratively with other organizations that are focused on accreditation.

Founded: 1981

Amy Milsom, Chair
Earl Grey-Brooks, Vice Chair

210 Higher Education Consultants Association
PO Box 9636
Spokane, WA 99209
800-662-6775
www.hecaonline.org
The Higher Education Consultants Association (HECA) is a professional organization focused on independent college admissions consulting.

Founded: 1997

Pauline Godfrey, President
Todd Weaver, Treasurer

211 International Accreditation of Counseling Services
101 S Whiting Street
Suite 211
Alexandria, VA 22304
703-823-9840
admin@iacsinc.org
www.iacsinc.org
Offering accreditation to university, four-year college, and two-year community college counseling services, the IACS encourages counseling programs to provide and meet excellent professional standards.

Cindy Cook, President
Nancy E. Roncketti, Executive Director

212 National Association of School Psychologists
4340 East West Highway
Suite 402
Bethesda, MD 20814
301-657-0270
866-331-6277
Fax: 301-657-0275
www.nasponline.org
The National Association of School Psychologists (NASP) represents over 25,000 school psychologists, psychology students, and related professionals. The NASP works to promote effective school psychology practices that fosters students' learning, behavior, and mental health.

Kathleen Minke, Executive Director
Laura Benson, Chief Operating Officer

International

213 Academic Travel Abroad
1155 Connecticut Avenue NW
Suite 300
Washington, DC 20036
800-556-7896
info@academic-travel.com
www.academic-travel.com
Academic Travel Abroad is an educational travel provider for organizations, and university undergraduate programs across the United States.

Founded: 1950

Kate Simpson, President
Mark Lenhart, Executive Director

214 Academy for International School Heads
14780 Highway 145
Dolores, CO 81323
720-890-6097
office@academyish.org
www.academyish.org
The Academy for International School Heads (AISH) is a nonprofit organization providing a forum of communication and support for the Head or Deputy Head of international schools.

Founded: 1999

Andy Page-Smith, Chief Executive Officer
Shere Holleman, Administrative Coordinator

215 Alberta Association of Recreation Facility Personnel (AARFP)
312 3rd Street W, Unit B
PO Box 100
Cochrane, AB T4C-1A4
403-851-7626
888-253-7544
office@aarfp.com
www.aarfp.com
The Alberta Association of Recreation Facility Personnel is a provincial nonprofit organization providing education, training, and consultation for people involved in recreation and recreation operations.

Founded: 1978

Laurie Darvill, Executive Director
Shawntel Dickinson, Administrative Coordinator

216 Alberta Council on Admissions and Transfer
Commercial Place
10155 - 102 Street
11th Floor
Edmonton, AB T5J-4L5
780-643-1890
Fax: 780-422-3688
acat@gov.ab.ca
www.acat.alberta.ca
The Alberta Council on Admissions and Transfer works cooperatively with postsecondary institutions, develops policies, guidelines, and procedures to ensure the effective transition of transfer agreements between institutions.

Founded: 1974

217 American Councils for International Education
1828 L Street NW
Suite 1200
Washington, DC 20036
202-833-7522
Fax: 202-833-7523
info@americancouncils.org
www.americancouncils.org
American Councils for International Education is dedicated to creating educational opportunities, such as international academic exchange, for individuals and institutions to facilitate a better understanding of culture and global political, economic, and social challenges.

Founded: 1974

David P. Patton, President & CEO
Lisa Choate, Executive Vice President

218 Association for Asian Studies
825 Victors Way
Suite 310
Ann Arbor, MI 48108

734-665-2490
Fax: 734-665-3801
info@asianstudies.org
www.asianstudies.org
A scholarly nonprofit professional organization, the Association for Asian Studies (AAS) is focused on the study of Asia, through the AAS' publications, resources, regional conferences, and annual conferences, the association provides members with professional development and networking opportunities. Membership is open to any individual interested in Asia.

Founded: 1941

Hilary Finchum-Sung, Executive Director
Michelle Hodges, Chief Financial Officer

9 Association for Canadian Education Resources

12 Helene Street N
Unit 1003
Mississauga, ON L5G-3B5
905-891-6004
office@acer-acre.ca
www.acer-acre.ca
The Association for Canadian Educational Resources (ACER) develops and offers programs and resources to educate individuals in environmental sciences. Programs are specifically focused on climate change.

Alice Casselman, President
Nimesha Basnayaka, Program Manager

20 Association for Canadian Studies in the United States (ACSUS)

Bridgewater State University
25 Park Terrace
Bridgewater, MA 02325
508-531-2688
www.acsus.org
The Association for Canadian Studies in the United States is a member based organization dedicated to fostering awareness and understanding of Canada and the relationship it has with the US.

Christopher Kirkey, President
Christina Keppie, Vice President

21 Association for Learning Environments

11445 E Via Linda
Suite 2-440
Scottsdale, AZ 85259
480-391-0840
www.a4le.org
Formerly the CEFPI, the Association for Learning Environments is focused on improving the environments in which children learn.

Philip J. Poinelli, Chair
William S. Bradley, Vice Chair

22 Association for the Advancement of International Education

15 Roszel Road
PO Box 3496
Princeton, NJ 08543-3496
609-716-7441
www.aaie.org
The Association for the Advancement of International Education (AAIE) is committed to developing and improving international education. Through the exchange of information and the establishment of professional networks, the AAIE works with educational institutions to promote the international exchange of ideas and research.

Founded: 1966

Mark E. Ulfers, Executive Director
Gerri-Ann Friedman, Manager, Marketing

223 Association of American Schools in South America

1911 NW 150 Avenue
Suite 101
Pembroke Pines, FL 33028
954-436-4034
Fax: 954-436-4092
www.aassa.com
A regional membership organization of American International schools in South America, the Association of American Schools in South America works to develop a better understanding of international education and to improve teaching techniques among Association schools.

Founded: 1977

Dereck Rhoads, Executive Director
Adam Slaton, Chief Learning Officer

224 Association of American Schools of Central America

www.aascaonline.net
The Association of American Schools of Central America advocates for United States style education in Central America. AASCA is for the betterment of social responsibility, learning, professional growth, and international mindedness for member schools.

Founded: 1990

Liliana Jenkins, President
Ron Vair, Vice President & Treasurer

225 Association of Christian Schools International

731 Chapel Hills Drive
Colorado Springs, CO 80920
719-367-5391
800-367-0798
communications@acsi.org
www.acsi.org
The Association of Christian Schools International promotes Christian education and provides training and resources to Christian schools and educators.

Larry Taylor, President
Kevin Buelke, Chief Finance Officer

226 Association of International Education Administrators

811 Ninth Street
Suite 215
Durham, NC 27705
919-893-4980
855-725-2432
info@aieaworld.org
www.aieaworld.org
The Association of International Education Administrators (AIEA) is a member based organization comprised of institutional leaders working to advance international components of higher education.

Founded: 1982

David Fleshler, President
Darla K. Deardorff, Executive Director

227 Atlantic Provinces Special Education Authority

5940 South Street
Halifax, NS B3H-1S6
902-424-8500
Fax: 902-423-8700
apsea@apsea.ca
www.apsea.ca
The Atlantic Provinces Special Education Authority (APSEA) is an interprovincial agency serving the educational needs of individuals with visual and hearing impairments in New Brunswick, Newfoundland and Labrador, Nova Scotia, and Prince Edward Island.

Founded: 1975

Lisa Doucet, Superintendent
Wade Tattrie, Director, Finance & Admin.

228 Canadian Accredited Independent Schools

PO Box 56
Jordan, ON L0R-1S0
905-684-5658
tnolan@cais.ca
www.cais.ca
A national network of member schools, the Canadian Accredited Independent Schools (CAIS) supports collaborative efforts in leadership, education, management, and governance.

Founded: 1981

Patti MacDonald, Executive Director
Tracey Nolan, Executive Assistant

229 Canadian Association of Communicators in Education

105-300 Greenbank Road
Ottawa, ON K2H-0B6
613-241-9333
members@cace-acace.org
www.cace-acace.org
The Canadian Association of Communications in Education (CACE) is committed to encouraging communication in education. CACE provides resources for educational marketing and communication professionals to ensure effective communication.

Founded: 1984

Dale Burgos, President
Candace Denison, Executive Director

230 Canadian Bureau for International Education

220 Laurier Avenue W
Suite 1550
Ottawa, ON K1P-5Z9
613-237-4820
Fax: 613-237-1073
communication@cbie.ca
www.cbie.ca
National nonprofit membership organization engaged in providing services for international learners. Services include forums for educational exchanges, scholarships, awards and internships, technical assistance and more.

Founded: 1966

Larissa Bezo, President & CEO
Karen Dalkie, Vice President, Development

231 Canadian Council for the Advancement of Education

The Woolen Mill
4 Cataraqui Street
Suite 310
Kingston, ON K7K-1Z7
613-531-9213
Fax: 613-531-0626
admin@ccaecanada.org
www.ccaecanada.org
The Canadian Council for the Advancement of Education (CCAE) is an organization working to promote excellence in education advancement through professional learning opportunities. The CCAE provides programs covering new trends and techniques designed to meet the needs of the 4,400 members.

Mark Hazlett, President & CEO
Tara Sandler, Dir., Strategic Education

232 **Canadian Society for the Study of Education**
260 Dalhousie Street
Suite 204
Ottawa, ON K1N-7E4
613-241-0018
Fax: 613-241-0019
csse-scee@csse.ca
www.csse-scee.ca
The Canadian Society for the Study of Education (CSSE) is an organization comprised of professors, students, researchers, and practitioners in education. The CSSE represents individuals who create educational knowledge, prepare teachers and leaders, and apply research in schools.
Founded: 1972
Jacqueline Ottmann, President
Ruth Kane, Secretary-Treasurer

233 **Commonwealth of Learning**
4710 Kingsway
Suite 2500
Burnaby, BC V5H-4M2
604-775-8200
Fax: 604-775-8210
info@col.org
www.col.org
The Commonwealth of Learning (COL) is an intergovernmental organization dedicated to the development and sharing of open learning and distance education knowledge, resources, and technologies. The COL was established by the Commonwealth Heads of Government.
Founded: 1987
Asha S. Kanwar, President & CEO
Venkataraman Balaji, Vice President

234 **Comparative and International Education Society**
University of Pittsburgh
230 S Bouquet Street
5100 Posvar Hall
Pittsburgh, PA 15260
oed@cies.us
www.cies.us
The Comparative and International Education Society (CIES) facilitates cross-cultural understanding, scholarship, academic achievement, and societal development through the study of the different facets of international education. The Society has over 2,500 members.
Founded: 1956
M. Najeeb Shafiq, Executive Director
Rose Wooten, Business Manager

235 **Consortium for Educational Resources on Islamic Studies**
University of Pittsburgh
4100 Posvar Hall
Pittsburgh, PA 15260
412-648-2113
Fax: 412-624-4672
cerisnet@gmail.com
www.cerisnet.pitt.edu
The Consortium for Educational Resources on Islamic Studies (CERIS) is a collaborative effort of academic, nonprofit, and religious organizations in Ohio, Pennsylvania, and West Virginia working to develop and disseminate information on Islamic Studies.
Rachel Sternfeld, President
Elaine Linn, Executive Director

236 **Cordell Hull Foundation for International Education**
45 Rockefeller Plaza
20th Floor
New York, NY 10111
dir@cordellhull.org
www.cordellhull.org
A nonprofit organization that works to improve foreign relations through teacher exchange.
Founded: 1951
Marianne Mason, Director

237 **Council of Ministers of Education, Canada**
95 St. Clair Avenue W
Suite 1106
Toronto, ON M4V-1N6
416-962-8100
Fax: 416-962-2800
information@cmec.ca
www.cmec.ca
The Council of Ministers of Education, Canada (CMEC) is an intergovernmental organization providing a forum of communication to discuss policy issues, consult with national and federal education organizations, and a tool to undertake activities and educational projects.
Founded: 1967
Chantal C. Beaulieu, Executive Director

238 **Council on International Educational Exchange**
300 Fore Street
Portland, ME 04101
207-553-4000
contact@ciee.org
www.ciee.org
The Council on International Educational Exchange (CIEE) offers study abroad, work exchange, and professional development programs to foster understanding, respect and the exchange of ideas and experiences between cultures.
Founded: 1947
James P. Pellow, Ed.D, President & CEO
Tim Propp, Chief Operating Officer

239 **Cultural Vistas**
1250 H Street NW
Suite 300
Washington, DC 20005
212-497-3500
info@culturalvistas.org
www.culturalvistas.org
Cultural Vistas promotes cultural understanding and collaboration through international exchange.
Founded: 1963
Jennifer Clinton, Ph.D, President & CEO
Megan Bah, Chief Financial Officer

240 **Graphic Communications Education Association**
PO Box 2544
Paso Robles, CA 93447
info@gceaonline.org
www.gceaonline.org
The Graphic Communications Education Association (GCEA) is a nonprofit organization focused on sharing theories, principles, techniques and processes with educators and industry professionals.
John Craft, President
Dina Vees, Treasurer

241 **IREX**
1275 K Street NW
Suite 600
Washington, DC 20005
202-628-8188
Fax: 202-628-8189
communications@irex.org
www.irex.org
IREX (International Research and Exchanges Board) is an independent, nonprofit organization committed to building a more inclusive world through equal access to quality education and information.
Founded: 1968
Kristin M. Lord, President & CEO
Mike Graham, Chief Financial Officer

242 **Institute of Cultural Affairs**
4750 N Sheridan Road
Chicago, IL 60640
773-769-6363
Fax: 773-944-1582
communications@ica-usa.org
www.ica-usa.org
The Institute of Cultural Affairs advocates for an equal and just society, working to strengthen communities and individuals through a variety of programs.
Founded: 1962
Phil Waitzman, Interim Executive Director

243 **Institute of International Education**
One World Trade Center
36th Floor
New York, NY 10007
212-883-8200
www.iie.org
The Institute of International Education (IIE) is committed to advancing international education and access to education across the globe. Through international exchange programs, the IIE promotes closer educational ties between the people of the United States and other countries.
Founded: 1919
Allan E. Goodman, President & CEO
Jason Czyz, Executive Vice President

244 **International Association Of Medical Science Educators**
IAMSE c/o JulNet Solutions LLC
1014 6th Avenue
Huntington, WV 25701
304-522-1270
Fax: 304-523-9700
support@iamse.org
www.iamse.org
A professional development society, the International Association of Medical Science Educators advances medical education through faculty development.
Founded: 1988
Julie K. Hewett, CMP, CAE, Association Manager
Danielle Inscoe, Managing Director

245 **International Association for Continuing Education & Training**
21670 Ridgetop Circle
Suite 170
Sterling, VA 20166
703-763-0705
Fax: 703-738-7194
info@iacet.org
www.iacet.org
The International Association for Continuing Education and Training (IACET) is a nonprofit organization working to advance the global workforce through accreditation.
Casandra Blassingame, Chief Executive Officer
Amy Starchville, Director, Operations

6 International Association for the Exchange of Students for Technical Experience
Cultural Vistas
1250 H Street NW
Suite 300
Washington, DC 20005
212-497-3500
iaeste@culturalvistas.org
www.culturalvistas.org
A program of Cultural Vistas, International Association for the Exchange of Students for Technical Experiences (IAESTE) supports international exchange of students gaining technical work experience.

7 International Baccalaureate
7501 Wisconsin Avenue West
Suite 200
Bethesda, MD 20814
301-202-3000
Fax: 301-202-3003
support@ibo.org
www.ibo.org
The International Baccalaureate (IB) is a nonprofit educational foundation working to develop the intellectual, personal, emotional, and social skills of youth ages 3-19 through education programs.

Founded: 1968

Sally Holloway, Deputy Director General
Anton Beguin, Chief Assessment Officer

8 International Education Council
777 6th Street NW
Suite 510
Washington, DC 20001
202-841-1873
contact@internationaleducationcouncil.org
www.internationaleducationcouncil.org
The International Education Council (IEC) is a nonprofit association focused on issues and policies affecting international education.

Cara Piperni, President
Harrison Wadsworth, Executive Director

9 International Education Exchange Council
San Francisco State University
1600 Holloway Avenue
Cesar Chavez Student Center Room T-125
San Francisco, CA 94132
415-405-0743
marketing@sfsuieec.com
www.sfsuieec.com
A program of San Francisco State University, the International Education Exchange Council, is a student run organization working to encourage international education through student exchange, study abroad programs, and the sharing of cultural experiences.

Noah Kuchins, Advisor

50 International Schools Services
15 Roszel Road
PO Box 5910
Princeton, NJ 08543
609-452-0990
www.iss.edu
International Schools Services is a nonprofit educational organization providing comprehensive and customized services to schools and educators. The organization recruits international teachers and helps to develop international schools.

Founded: 1955

Liz Duffy, President
Kristin Evins, Chief Administration Officer

251 International Society for Business Education
PO Box 84
Madison, WI 53954
www.siec-isbe.org
The International Society of Business Education is an international network of individuals, businesses, and organizations working to connect business and education.

Founded: 1901

Evelyn Meyer, International President
Lila Waldman, General Secretary

252 International Studies Association
362 Fairfield Way
Unit 4013
Storrs, CT 06269-4013
isa@isanet.org
www.isanet.org
The International Studies Association (ISA) is a global organization promoting the study, education, and exchange of information centered on international studies. The ISA has over 7,000 members.

Founded: 1959

Kristian Skrede Gleditsch, President
Mark A. Boyer, Executive Director

253 NAFSA: Association of International Educators
1425 K Street NW
Suite 1200
Washington, DC 20005
202-737-3699
inbox@nafsa.org
www.nafsa.org
NAFSA: Association of International Educators is an organization of individuals committed to facilitating international education, exchange, and global workforce development. NAFSA supports international educators, institutions, and organizations through training, professional development and networking opportunities, and advocating for international education.

Founded: 1948

Esther D. Brimmer, Executive Director & CEO
Dorothea Antonio, Deputy Executive Director

254 National Registration Center for Study Abroad
PO Box 1393
Milwaukee, WI 53201
414-278-0631
Fax: 414-271-8884
study@nrcsa.com
www.nrcsa.com
Working to foster international understanding, the National Registration Center for Study Abroad (NRCSA) supports international educational exchanges for individuals of all ages.

Founded: 1968

255 Odyssey of the Mind
Creative Competitions, Inc.
406 Ganttown Road
Sewell, NJ 08080
856-256-2797
Fax: 856-256-2798
info@odysseyofthemind.com
www.odysseyofthemind.com
An educational program that provides creative problem-solving activities for students from kindergarten through college. With creative and imaginative paths to problem solving, students learn skills that will provide them with the ability to solve problems for a lifetime.

Samuel Micklus, Founder

256 Ontario Cooperative Education Association
35 Reynar Drive
Quispamsis, NB E2G-1J9
ocea@rogers.com
www.ocea.on.ca
The Ontario Cooperative Education Association (OCEA) is a nonprofit working to provide leadership and professional development opportunities for its members.

Barbara Omland, Chair
Julia VanderWeerden, Treasurer

257 Opportunities Industrialization Centers International
1875 Connecticut Avenue NW
10th Floor
Washington, DC 20009
202-846-6798
info@oici.org
www.oici.org
OIC International is dedicated to alleviating poverty through workforce development and education.

Crispian Kirk, President & CEO

258 People to People International
2405 Grand Boulevard
Suite 500
Kansas City, MO 64108
816-531-4701
800-676-7874
Fax: 816-561-7502
ptpi@ptpi.org
www.ptpi.org
People to People International is committed to fostering cultural understanding and friendship through education, cultural, and humanitarian activities and the exchange of ideas and experiences.

Founded: 1956

Merrill Eisenhower Atwater, Chief Executive Officer
Nicole Randall, Senior Vice President

259 Phi Delta Kappa International
1820 N Fort Myer Drive
Suite 320
Arlington, VA 22209
800-766-1156
info@pdkintl.org
www.pdkintl.org
PDK International is a professional association comprised of educational associations working to facilitate connection between educators and leaders.

Joshua P. Starr, Ed.D, Chief Executive Officer
Albert Chen, M.E., Chief Operating Officer

260 TESOL International Association
1925 Ballenger Avenue
Suite 550
Alexandria, VA 22314-6820
703-518-2500
888-891-0041
Fax: 703-691-5327
members@tesol.org
www.tesol.org
An international association, TESOL advocates for quality English teaching through professional development, research, and standard setting.

Rosa Aronson, Interim Executive Director
Juliet Mason, Director, Membership

261 Tri-Association - The Association of American Schools
www.tri-association.org
The Tri-Association is a nonprofit organization dedicated to improving the quality of teaching and learning opportunities for schools in the region. The Association is supported by the United States State Department, Office of Overseas Schools, and covers schools located in Central America, Colombia-Caribbean, and Mexico.
Liliana Jenkins, President
Michael W. Adams, Executive Director

262 World Learning
1015 15th Street NW
7th Floor
Washington, DC 20005
202-408-5420
Fax: 202-408-5397
info@worldlearning.org
www.worldlearning.org
A nonprofit organization using education, development, and exchange programs, World Learning teaches educators ways in which to help students learn. With programs designed to improve education established in over 100 countries, World Learning helps to strengthen communities and institutions.
Carol Jenkins, President & CEO
Kote Lomidze, CPA, CFO & CAO

263 iEARN
475 Riverside Drive
Suite 450
New York, NY 10115
ec@iearn.org
www.iearn.org
iEARN is an international education and resource network using online and communication technology to foster safe communication between schools, youth organizations, and students.
Founded: 1988
Stefanie Ortiz-Cidlik, Executive Director
Ligaya Beebe, Program Manager

Language Arts

264 Academic Language Therapy Association (ALTA)
PO Box 152075
Austin, TX 78715-2075
512-488-9897
Fax: 512-851-1433
office@altaread.org
www.altaread.org
The Academic Language Therapy Association is a national nonprofit working to establish, maintain, and promote the standards of Certified Academic Language Therapists.
Founded: 1986
Lynne Fitzhugh, Ph.D, President
Paul Entzminger, Secretary

265 Accrediting Council on Education in Journalism and Mass Communications
University of Mississippi
201 Bishop Hall
PO Box 1848
University, MS 38677-1848
662-915-5550
www.acejmc.org
The Accrediting Council on Education in Journalism and Mass Communication promotes excellence in the professional education of journalism and mass communication, specifically education that is focused on incorporating technology into the professional field.
Patricia Thompson, Executive Director
Candace Oswalt, Project Coordinator

266 American Association of Teachers of French
302 N Granite Street
Marion, IL 62959-2346
815-310-0490
Fax: 815-310-5754
aatf@frenchteachers.org
www.frenchteachers.org
The American Association of Teachers of French (AATF) is a national association of French teachers with the goal of promoting the teaching and learning of the French language and French-speaking cultures and civilizations throughout North America. Currently, AATF has 70 active chapters across the United States.
Founded: 1927
Anne Jensen, President
Jayne Abrate, Executive Director

267 American Comparative Literature Association
323 E Wacker Drive
Suite 642
Chicago, IL 60601
312-600-8072
info@acla.org
www.acla.org
The American Comparative Literature Association (ACLA) is comprised of scholars whose work promotes cross-cultural literacy.
Founded: 1960
Shu-mei Shih, President
Dina Al-Kassim, Secretary-Treasurer

268 American Council on the Teaching of Foreign Languages
1001 N Fairfax Street
Suite 200
Alexandria, VA 22314
703-894-2900
headquarters@actfl.org
www.actfl.org
An individual membership organization of language educators and administrators, the American Council on the Teaching of Foreign Languages (ACTFL) works to improve and support the teaching and learning of all languages.
Founded: 1967
Howie Berman, Executive Director
MacKenzie Arbogust, Director, Finance

269 American Speech-Language-Hearing Association
2200 Research Boulevard
Rockville, MD 20850-3289
301-296-5700
800-498-2071
Fax: 301-296-8580
www.asha.org
The American Speech-Language-Hearing Association (ASHA) is a national association committed to supporting audiologists, speech-language pathologists, and speech, language, and hearing scientists by advancing science, setting standards, and advocating for those who work to make effective communication accessible for all.
Founded: 1925
A. Lynn Williams, President
Arlene A. Pietranton, Chief Executive Officer

270 Association for Education in Journalism and Mass Communication
234 Outlet Pointe Boulevard
Suite A
Columbia, SC 29210-5667
803-798-0271
Fax: 803-772-3509
aejmchq@aol.com
www.aejmc.org
The Association for Education in Journalism and Mass Communication is a nonprofit association working to foster, encourage, and facilitate excellence in journalism and mass communication education.
Founded: 1912
Tim P. Vos, President
Amanda Caldwell, Interim Executive Director

271 Center for Applied Linguistics
4646 40th Street NW
Washington, DC 20016-1859
202-362-0700
Fax: 202-362-3740
info@cal.org
www.cal.org
The Center for Applied Linguistics (CAL), is a nonprofit organization dedicated to promoting language and cultural understanding as it relates to access and equality in education.
Joel Gomez, Ed.D, President & CEO
Keira Ballantyne, Ph.D, Vice President, Programs

272 Children's Literature Assembly
info@childrensliteratureassembly.org
www.childrensliteratureassembly.org
Part of the National Council of Teachers of English, the Children's Literature Assembly (CLA) advocates for the presence of literature in the lives of youth. The CLA provides a forum for the exchange of information among teachers and works cooperatively with organizations to promote literature.
Ruth Lowery, President
Xenia Hadjioannou, Vice President

273 Children's Literature Association
3525 Piedmont Road
Building 5, Suite 300
Atlanta, GA 30305
630-571-4520
Fax: 708-876-5598
info@childlitassn.org
www.childlitassn.org
The Children's Literature Association (ChLA) is a nonprofit association dedicated to the academic study of children's literature. Members include scholars, critics, professors, students, teachers, and librarians.
Founded: 1973
Elisabeth Rose Gruner, President
Althea Tait, Vice President

274 International Dyslexia Association
40 York Road
4th Floor
Baltimore, MD 21204
410-296-0232
Fax: 410-321-5069
info@dyslexiaida.org
www.dyslexiaida.org
The International Dyslexia Association (IDA) is a nonprofit, educational organization dedicated to promoting literacy and education for individuals with dyslexia.
Sonja Banks, Chief Executive Officer
David Holste, Chief Financial Officer

5 **Journalism Education Association**
828 Mid-Campus Drive South
105 Kedzie Hall
Manhattan, KS 66506-1505
785-532-5532
Fax: 785-532-5563
staff@jea.org
www.jea.org
A nonprofit organization providing training and resources for educators teaching journalism. The Association offers national certification and publishes print and online resources for its members.

Founded: 1924

Sarah Nichols, MJE, President
Kelly Glasscock, CJE, Executive Director

6 **Modern Language Association**
85 Broad Street
Suite 500
New York, NY 10004-2434
646-576-5000
Fax: 646-576-5160
help@mla.org
www.mla.org
The Modern Language Association (MLA) provides a forum of communication for its members to discuss scholarly information and exchange teaching experiences in the field of humanities.

Founded: 1883

Paula M. Krebs, Executive Director
Dennis Looney, Director, Programs

7 **National Association for Bilingual Education**
1775 I Street NW
Suite 1150
Washington, DC 20006
240-450-3700
www.nabe.org
The National Association for Bilingual Education (NABE) is a nonprofit, membership organization dedicated to advocating for equal education for bilingual and multilingual students. NABE provides bilingual educators with resources, works to improve instruction, and helps to secure funding for programs serving children limited English proficiency.

Founded: 1975

Santiago V. Wood, Ed.D, National Executive Director
Nilda M. Aguirre, ED.S., Deputy Executive Director

78 **National Association for Poetry Therapy**
19001 S Richfield Avenue
Suite 20
Green Valley, AZ 85614
naptadmin@poetrytherapy.org
www.poetrytherapy.org
An international nonprofit organization, the National Association for Poetry Therapy (NAPT) promotes growth and healing through language, including the written word, symbols, and stories.

Marianela Medrano, President
Barbara Kreisberg, Vice President

79 **National Council of Teachers of English**
340 N Neil Street
Suite 104
Champaign, IL 61820
217-328-3870
877-369-6283
Fax: 217-328-9645
customerservice@ncte.org
www.ncte.org
The National Council of Teachers of English (NCTE) promotes literacy through the learning and teaching of English. The NCTE is a communication tool for English educators to connect with their peers and exchange information to improve literacy.

Founded: 1911

Alfredo Celedon Lujan, President
Emily Kirkpatrick, Executive Director

280 **National Federation of Modern Language Teachers Association**
1809 Saint Andrews Place
Lincoln, NE 68512
www.nfmlta.org
The National Federation of Modern Language Teachers Association (NFMLTA) is dedicated to the improvement of the teaching of languages, literature, and culture across the United States. The NFMLTA improves teaching primarily through the publishing of The Modern Language Journal.

Founded: 1916

Dr. Danko Sipka, President

281 **National Network for Early Language Learning**
info@nnell.org
www.nnell.org
Focused on K-8 education, the National Network for Early Language (NNELL) advocates for high quality education among elementary school students. The NNELL provides leadership and resources for educators, parents, and policymakers.

Founded: 1987

Michelle Olah, President
Jessica King, Treasurer

282 **ReadWriteThink**
c/o National Council of Teachers of English
340 N Neil Street
Suite 104
Champaign, IL 61820
www.readwritethink.org
ReadWriteThink provides free language and reading instructional material to educators, parents, and afterschool professionals.

283 **Sigma Tau Delta, International English Honor Society**
Northern Illinois University
Department of English
711 N First Street
DeKalb, IL 60115
815-981-9974
sigmatd@niu.edu
www.english.org
Main purpose is to confer distinction upon students of the English language and literature in undergraduate, graduate and professional studies. Sigma Tau Dalta also recognizes the accomplishments of professional writers who have contributed to the fields of language and literature.

Founded: 1924

William C. Johnson, Ph.D, Executive Director
Natasha McPartlin, Director, Operations

284 **Teachers & Writers Collaborative**
540 President Street
3rd Floor
New York, NY 11215
212-691-6590
Fax: 212-675-0171
info@twc.org
www.twc.org
The Teachers & Writers Collaborative (T&W) works to educate teachers and students through programs and publications focused on creative writing. Programs include writing workshops for students, professional development opportunities for educators, and poetry competitions.

Founded: 1967

Asari Beale, Executive Director
Nancy L. Weber, Education Director

Library Services

285 **American Association of Law Libraries**
105 West Adams Street
Suite 3300
Chicago, IL 60603
312-939-4764
Fax: 312-431-1097
www.aallnet.org
The American Association of Law Libraries (AALL) is dedicated to supporting the professional development and recognition of law librarianship.

Founded: 1906

Diane Rodriguez, President
Elizabeth Adelman, Vice President

286 **American Council on Education Library & Information Service**
1 Dupont Circle NW
Washington, DC 20036
202-939-9300
comments@ace.nche.edu
www.acenet.edu
The council seeks to provide leadership and a unifying voice on key higher education issues and to influence public policy through advocacy, research, and program initiatives.

Ted Mitchell, President
Kara Freeman, Chief Operating Officer

287 **American Indian Library Association**
PO Box 41296
San Jose, CA 95160
ailawebsite@gmail.com
www.ailanet.org
The American Indian Library Association (AILA) is dedicated to providing the library related needs of American Indians and Alaska Natives. The Association is membership based, comprised of individuals and institutions wishing to support the development and improvement of Indian library, cultural, and informational services in schools. The AILA is an affiliate of the American Library Association.

Founded: 1979

Cindy Hohl, President
Heather Devine-Hardy, Executive Director

288 **American Library Association (ALA)**
225 N Michigan Avenue
Suite 1300
Chicago, IL 60601
312-944-6780
800-545-2433
Fax: 312-440-9374
ala@ala.org
www.ala.org
The American Library Association promotes and develops the profession of librarianship and information services. The ALA is the oldest and largest library association in the world.

Founded: 1876

Tracie D. Hall, Executive Director
Cheryl Malden, Program Officer

289 American Theological Library Association
200 South Wacker Drive
Suite 3100
Chicago, IL 60606-5877
872-310-4200
888-665-2852
www.atla.com
The American Theological Library Association (ATLA) works to develop the study of theology and religion through fostering the improvement of theological and religious studies libraries and librarianship.

Founded: 1946

Brenda Bailey-Hainer, Executive Director
Gillian Harrison Cain, Director, Member Programs

290 Art Libraries Society of North America
4 Lan Drive
Suite 310
Westford, MA 01886
978-674-6211
customercare@arlisna.org
www.arlisna.org
The Art Libraries Society of North America (ARLIS/NA) provides a forum for communication between art professionals, organizations, and art libraries.

Founded: 1972

Mark Pompelia, President
Cambria Happ, Executive Director

291 Asian American Curriculum Project
529 East Third Avenue
San Mateo, CA 94401
650-375-8286
Fax: 650-375-8797
www.asianamericanbooks.wordpress.com
The Asian American Curriculum Project (AACP) is a nonprofit educational organization working to educate the public about the Asian American experience through books. The AACP provides a collection of Asian American books, with materials including literature, folk tales, posters, magazines, tapes, reference books, and dictionaries.

Founded: 1969

Florence M. Hongo, President & General Manager
Leonard D. Chan, Vice President

292 Asian Pacific American Librarians Association
PO Box 1598
San Pedro, CA 90733
www.apalaweb.org
A nonprofit organization, the Asian Pacific American Librarians Association (APALA) is a communication tool for Asian Pacific American librarians and libraries to discuss problems, exchange ideas, and recruit and mentor Asian Pacific American librarians.

Founded: 1980

Ray Pun, President
Lessa Pelayo-Lozada, Executive Director

293 Association for Library & Information Science Education
4 Lan Drive
Suite 310
Westford, MA 01886
978-674-6190
office@alise.org
www.alise.org
The Association for Library and Information Science Education (ALISE) promotes the advancement of research, teaching, and service for educators and scholars in the Library and Information Science field. ALISE is comprised of 500 individual members and 60 institutions.

Cambria Happ, Executive Director
Mega Subramaniam, Director, Programming

294 Association of Research Libraries
21 Dupont Circle NW
Suite 800
Washington, DC 20036
202-296-2296
Fax: 202-872-0884
webmgr@arl.org
www.arl.org
The Association of Research Libraries (ARL) is a nonprofit organization working to influence scholarly communication and public policies that affect research libraries. The ARL is comprised of 125 research libraries.

Founded: 1932

Mary Lee Kennedy, Executive Director
Jessica Aiwuyor, Senior Dir., Communications

295 Black Caucus of the American Library Association
PO Box 174
New York, NY 10159-0174
info@bcala.org
www.bcala.org
The Black Caucus of the American Library Association (BCALA) supports the development, promotion, and improvement of library resources for the African American community.

Founded: 1969

Shauntee Burns-Simpson, President
Nichelle M. Hayes, Vice President

296 Center for Research Libraries
6050 S Kenwood Avenue
Chicago, IL 60637-2804
773-955-4545
800-621-6044
Fax: 773-955-4339
www.crl.edu
An association of university, college, and independent research libraries, the Center for Research Libraries (CRL), provides primary resource material that supports research and quality teaching in all subjects.

Founded: 1949

Deborah Jakubs, Chair
Adriene Lim, Vice Chair

297 Institute of Museum and Library Services
955 L'Enfant Plaza North SW
Suite 4000
Washington, DC 20024-2135
202-653-4657
imlsinfo@imls.gov
www.imls.gov
The Institute of Museum and Library Services (IMLS) is committed to proving leadership through research, policy making, and the funding of libraries and museums.

Crosby Kemper, Director

298 International Association of School Librarianship
PO Box 684
Jefferson City, MO 65102
573-635-2173
Fax: 573-635-2858
iasl@c2cpro.solutions
www.iasl-online.org
The International Association of School Librarianship (IASL) provides a forum for individuals to promote effective school library programs as a tool in the educational process.

Katy Manck, President
Jill Hancock, Executive Director

299 Pro LiBRA Associates, Inc.
436 Springfield Avenue
Summit, NJ 07901-2618
908-918-0077
800-262-0070
Fax: 908-918-0977
staffing@prolibra.com
www.prolibra.com
Pro LiBRA is a library service company involved in staffing libraries and information centers.

300 Southeastern Library Association
SELA Administrative Services
PO Box 30703
Savannah, GA 31410
912-999-7979
selaadminservices@selaonline.org
www.selaonline.org
Provides a forum for discussing library education and leadership for the expansion of public library services. The association also offers information in the areas of reference and public services, resources and technical services, school and children's librarians and more.

Melissa Dennis, President
Vicki Gregory, Treasurer

301 Utah Library Association (ULA)
PO Box 708155
Sandy, UT 84070
801-494-3860
www.ula.org
The mission of the Utah Library Association is to serve the professional development and educational needs of its members and to provide leadership and direction in developing and improving library and information services in Utah.

Founded: 1912

Rita Christensen, President
Mindy Hale, Executive Director

Mathematics

302 American Institute of Mathematics
600 East Brokaw Road
San Jose, CA 95112-1006
408-350-2088
conrey@aimath.org
www.aimath.org
The American Institute of Mathematics (AIM) is dedicated to advancing mathematical knowledge and increased participation in the mathematical sciences at every level.

Founded: 1994

Brian Conrey, Executive Director
Estelle Basor, Deputy Director

303 American Mathematical Association of Two-Year Colleges
Southwest Tennessee Community College
5983 Macon Cove
Memphis, TN 38134
901-333-5643
Fax: 901-333-6251
amatyc@amatyc.org
www.amatyc.org
The American Mathematical Association of Two-Year College (AMATYC) provides a forum for the improvement of mathematical instruction in the first two years of college. The AMATYC offers professional development opportunities for

educators through conferences, workshops, and publications.

Founded: 1974

Kathryn Kozak, President
Barbra Steinhurst, Treasurer

4 Association for Symbolic Logic
University Of Connecticut
341 Mansfield Road
U-1009
Storrs, CT 06269-1009
860-486-3989
Fax: 860-486-4238
asl@uconn.edu
www.aslonline.org
An international organization, the Association for Symbolic Logic is dedicated to supporting research in logic. The Association provides a forum for the discussion of scholarly work.

Founded: 1936

Julia Knight, President
Phokion Kolaitis, Vice President

5 Association for Women in Mathematics
PO Box 40876
Providence, RI 02940
401-455-4042
awm@awm-math.org
www.awm-math.org
The Association for Women in Mathematics (AWM) is a nonprofit organization supporting women and girls to study and have careers in mathematical sciences.

Founded: 1971

Darla Kremer, Executive Director
Samantha Faria, Managing Director

6 Association of Mathematics Teacher Educators
c/o Michigan Technological University
1400 Townsend Drive
Houghton, MI 49931
906-487-1126
www.amte.net
The Association of Mathematics Teacher Educators is a professional organization devoted to the improvement of education for K-12 teachers of mathematics. The association offers professional learning opportunities, conferences, publications, job listings and more.

Founded: 1991

Megan Burton, President
Shari Stockero, Executive Director

07 Institute for Operations Research and the Management Sciences
5521 Research Park Drive
Suite 200
Catonsville, MD 21228
443-757-3500
800-446-3676
Fax: 443-757-3515
informs@informs.org
www.informs.org
The Institute for Operations Research and the Management Sciences (INFORMS) is an international association comprised of professionals in operations research and analytics. INFORMS works to advance the profession of operations research through conferences, competitions, networking opportunities, and development services.

Stephen Graves, President
Elena Gerstmann, Executive Director

308 Mathematical Association of America
1529 18th Street NW
Washington, DC 20036-1358
202-387-5200
800-741-9415
Fax: 202-265-2384
maahq@maa.org
www.maa.org
The Mathematical Association of America (MAA) is dedicated to advance mathematical sciences at the collegiate level.

Michael Pearson, Executive Director
Deirdre Longacher Smeltzer, Senior Director, Programs

309 National Academy of Sciences
500 Fifth Street NW
Washington, DC 20001
202-334-2000
www.nasonline.org
The National Academy of Sciences (NAS) is a private nonprofit society of scholars that offers independent objective advice related to science and technology. Members of NAS are active contributors in the international scientific community.

Founded: 1863

Marcia McNutt, President
Ken Fulton, Executive Director

310 National Council of Supervisors of Mathematics
PO Box 3406
Englewood, CO 80155
303-317-6595
Fax: 303-200-7099
office@mathedleadership.org
www.mathedleadership.org
The National Council of Supervisors of Mathematics (NCSM) is an organization providing professional development opportunities to education leaders, with the goal of preparing them to better support student academic success.

Mona Toncheff, President
Shawn Towle, First Vice President

311 National Council of Teachers of Mathematics
1906 Association Drive
Reston, VA 20191-1502
703-620-9840
800-235-7566
Fax: 703-476-2970
nctm@nctm.org
www.nctm.org
The National Council of Teachers of Mathematics (NCTM) supports and advocates for the increased quality in mathematic teaching. The NCTM has over 60,000 members and 230 affiliates across the United States and Canada.

Founded: 1920

Ken Krehbiel, Executive Director
David Barnes, Associate Executive Director

312 Society for Industrial and Applied Mathematics
3600 Market Street
6th Floor
Philadelphia, PA 19104-2688
215-382-9800
800-447-7426
Fax: 215-386-7999
membership@siam.org
www.siam.org
The Society for Industrials and Applied Mathematics (SIAM) facilitates connection and interaction between mathematics, scientific, and technological communities. SIAM provides members with activities, conferences, and publishes books and journals.

Founded: 1951

Suzanne L. Weekes, Executive Director

313 Society for Mathematical Biology
membership@smb.org
www.smb.org
An international organization, the Society for Mathematical Biology (SMB) promotes interaction between the mathematical and biological sciences. Through the development and dissemination of research, the SMB works to further science and math by hosting an annual meeting and the publication of research.

Founded: 1973

Heiko Enderling, President
Gibin Powathil, Secretary

314 Society of Actuaries
475 North Martingale Road
Suite 600
Schaumburg, IL 60173
847-706-3500
888-697-3900
Fax: 847-706-3599
customerservice@soa.org
www.soa.org
The Society of Actuaries (SOA) is an educational and research organization dedicated to advancing actuarial knowledge.

Founded: 1889

Roy Goldman, President
Gregory W. Heidrich, Chief Executive Officer

Music & Art

315 American Art Therapy Association
4875 Eisenhower Avenue
Suite 240
Alexandria, VA 22304
703-548-5860
888-290-0878
Fax: 703-783-8468
info@arttherapy.org
www.arttherapy.org
The American Art Therapy Association is a nonprofit organization is committed to the increased access and expansion of professional art therapists. The Association provides members with resources and networking opportunities to further the field of art therapy and encourages the highest quality of art therapy services.

Cynthia Woodruff, Executive Director
Barbara Florence, Director, Events & Education

316 American Dance Therapy Association
230 Washington Avenue Extension
Suite 101
Albany, NY 12203-3539
518-704-3636
Fax: 518-463-8656
info@adta.org
www.adta.org
The American Dance Therapy Association (ADTA) works to support the profession of dance and movement therapy. The ADTA provides communication among dance and movement therapists and related professions.

Founded: 1966

Michelle Lavoy, Operations Manager
Lauren Hoyt, Office Administrator

317 **American Guild of Music**
PO Box 599
Warren, MI 48090
248-686-1975
www.americanguild.org
An international organization, the American Guild of Music is dedicated to advancing the study of music and the promotion of artistic, educational, recreational, and commercial music. Membership to the Guild is open to music teachers, music store owners, teaching staff, music publishers, instrument manufacturers and music students.

Gina Selvaggi, President
Julie Kopasz, 1st Vice President

318 **American Musicological Society**
20 Cooper Square
Floor 2
New York, NY 10003
212-992-6340
877-679-7648
Fax: 877-679-7648
ams@amsmusicology.org
www.amsmusicology.org
The American Musicological Society's purpose is to advance scholarship in the various fields of music through research, learning, and teaching. To do this, it produces publications, holds an annual meeting, supports books in musicology, and offers a broad array of grants, fellowships, and awards throughout a year.

Founded: 1934

Siovahn Walker, Executive Director
Katie VanDerMeer, Office Manager

319 **Americana Music Association**
PO Box 128077
Nashville, TN 37212
615-386-6936
Fax: 615-386-6937
info@americanamusic.org
www.americanamusic.org
The Americana Music Association is a professional trade organization advocating for the authentic voice of American Roots Music around the world.

Founded: 1999

Jed Hilly, Executive Director
Danna Strong, Director, Education

320 **Arts Education Partnership**
700 Broadway Street
Suite 810
Denver, CO 80203
202-844-6281
www.aep-arts.org
Through research, policy and procedure, the Arts Education Partnership is a network of organizations dedicated to advancing and advocating for equal access to the arts in education.

Founded: 1995

Jamie Kasper, Director
Mary Dell'Erba, Senior Project Manager

321 **Association for Public Art**
1528 Walnut Street
Suite 1000
Philadelphia, PA 19102-3627
215-546-7550
Fax: 215-546-2363
apa@associationforpublicart.org
www.associationforpublicart.org
The Association for Public Art (APA) is a nonprofit civic organization dedicated to integrating public art and urban design in Philadelphia.

Founded: 1872

Penny Balkin Bach, Executive Director
Laura S. Griffith, Deputy Director

322 **Civic Music Association**
900 Keosauqua Way
Suite 113
Des Moines, IA 50309
515-280-4020
info@civicmusic.org
www.civicmusic.org
The Civic Music Association works to engage the central Iowa community with musical performances.

Founded: 1925

323 **College Art Association**
50 Broadway
21st Floor
New York, NY 10004
212-691-1051
Fax: 212-627-2381
nyoffice@collegeart.org
www.collegeart.org
The College Art Association (CAA) promotes the visual arts through practice and intellectual engagement.

Founded: 1911

Isimeme Omogbai, Executive Director & CEO
Denali Kemper, Development Officer

324 **Country Music Association**
35 Music Square E
Suite 201
Nashville, TN 37203
615-244-2840
info@cmaworld.com
www.cmaworld.com
The Country Music Association (CMA) is a trade association dedicated to promoting country music. The CMA has over 7,600 members of industry professionals, representative of the business.

Founded: 1958

Sarah Trahern, Chief Executive Officer
Amy Smartt, Senior VP, Administration

325 **Educational Theatre Association**
4805 Montgomery Road
Suite 400
Cincinnati, OH 45212
513-421-3900
Fax: 513-421-7077
info@schooltheatre.org
www.schooltheatre.org
The Education Theatre Association is a national nonprofit organization working to recognize, educate, influence the lives of individuals through theatre. The association offers Theatre Education Pro, a professional learning portal.

Founded: 1929

Julie Cohen Theobald, Executive Director
Allison Dolan, Chief Content Officer

326 **Future Music Oregon**
University of Oregon
School of Music & Dance
1225 University of Oregon
Eugene, OR 97403-1225
541-346-5652
www.music.uoregon.edu
Future Music Oregon is dedicated to the exploration of sound and its creation.

Jeffrey Stolet, Director

327 **International Technology and Engineering Educators Association**
1914 Association Drive
Suite 201
Reston, VA 20191-1539
703-860-2100
Fax: 703-860-0353
iteea@iteea.org
www.iteea.org
The International Technology and Engineering Educators Association (ITEEA) promotes technological literacy through leadership, professional development, and publications. ITEEA supports the teaching of, and those who teach, technology and engineering.

Steven A. Barbato, Executive Director
Kathleen de la Paz, Communications Director

328 **National Art Education Association**
901 Prince Street
Alexandria, VA 22314
703-860-8000
800-299-8321
Fax: 703-860-2960
info@arteducators.org
www.arteducators.org
The National Art Education Association is a membership organization open to visual arts educators. The Association advocates for balanced learning of the visual arts by qualified art educators.

Founded: 1947

Mario R. Rossero, Executive Director
A.J. Calbert, Chief Operations Officer

329 **National Association for Music Education**
1806 Robert Fulton Drive
Reston, VA 20191
703-860-4000
800-336-3768
Fax: 888-275-6362
memberservices@nafme.org
www.nafme.org
The National Association for Music Education (NAfME) advocates at the local, state, and national level for all aspects of music education. NAfMe provides resources for teachers, parents, and administrators, and hosts professional development events.

Founded: 1907

Christopher Woodside, Executive Director
Elizabeth Lasko, Director, Membership

330 **National Association of Schools of Music**
11250 Roger Bacon Drive
Suite 21
Reston, VA 20190-5248
703-437-0700
Fax: 703-437-6312
info@arts-accredit.org
www.nasm.arts-accredit.org
An organization of schools, conservatories, colleges, and universities, the National Association of Schools of Music (NASM) establishes national standards for undergraduate and graduate degrees.

Founded: 1924

Karen P. Moynahan, Executive Director

331 **National Dance Education Organization**
8609 Second Avenue
Suite 203-B
Silver Spring, MD 20910
301-585-2880
membership@ndeo.org
www.ndeo.org
The National Dance Education Organization (NDEO) is a nonprofit organization working to further dance education centered in the arts. The NDEO provides it members with a network of re-

sources, support, and professional development opportunities.

Founded: 1998

Susan McGreevy-Nichols, Executive Director
Melissa Greenblatt, Managing Director

2 National Guild for Community Arts Education

520 8th Avenue
Suite 302
New York, NY 10018
212-268-3337
guildinfo@nationalguild.org
www.nationalguild.org
The National Guild for Community Arts Education advocates for equal and accessible arts education for all. The Guild provides support for community art educators and members, including community schools, art and cultural centers, preparatory programs, performing art companies, museums, and parks and recreation departments.

Founded: 1937

Adam Johnston, Deputy Director, Operations
Heather Ikemire, Deputy Director, Learning

3 National Institute of Art and Disabilities

551 23rd Street
Richmond, CA 94804
510-620-0290
www.niadart.org
The National Institute of Art and Disabilities is an art studio dedicated to the promotion of independent living for individuals with disabilities.

Amanda Eicher, Executive Director
Arden Fredman, Dir., Community Programs

Physical Education

34 American Canoe Association

ACA Canoe-Kayak-SUP-Raft Rescue
PO Box 7996
Fredericksburg, VA 22404
540-907-4460
aca@americancanoe.org
www.americancanoe.org
The American Canoe Association (ACA) is a national nonprofit working to provide education and programs related to all aspects of paddling. The ACA promotes the stewardship and protection of paddling environments, and paddlesport competition.

Founded: 1880

Robin Pope, President
Beth Spilman, Interim Executive Director

35 International Council for Health, Physical Education, Recreation, Sport, and Dance

1900 Association Drive
Reston, VA 20191-1598
703-476-3462
Fax: 703-476-9527
ichper@aahperd.org
www.ichpersd.org
The International Council for Health, Physical Education, Recreation, Sport, and Dance (ICHPERD-SD), is a membership organization of professors, teachers, researchers, coaches, educators, and administrators in the fields of health and physical activity.

36 National Alliance for Youth Sports

2050 Vista Parkway
West Palm Beach, FL 33411
561-684-1141
800-688-5437
Fax: 561-684-2546
nays@nays.org
www.nays.org
The National Alliance for Youth Sports (NAYS) provides programs, services, and resources to support and advocate for safe and positive sports for children.

Founded: 1981

John Engh, Executive Director
Yolanda Williams, Senior Director

337 National Association for Kinesiology in Higher Education

PO Box 397117
Cambridge, MA 02139
info@nakhe.org
www.nakhe.org
The National Association for Kinesiology in Higher Education works to foster leadership in kinesiology administration and policy in relation to teaching and scholarship in higher education.

Tara Tietjen-Smith, President
Carrie Sampson Moore, Executive Director

338 National Association of Collegiate Directors of Athletics

24651 Detroit Road
Westlake, OH 44145
440-892-4000
Fax: 440-892-4007
membership@nacda.com
www.nacda.com
The National Association of Collegiate Directors of Athletics (NACDA) is a professional association of individuals in the field of athletics administration. The NACDA provides its members with professional educational and networking opportunities and is a forum for the exchange of information.

Founded: 1965

Bob Vecchione, Chief Executive Officer
Pat Manak, Senior Executive VP

339 National Athletic Trainers' Association

1620 Valwood Parkway
Suite 115
Carrollton, TX 75006
214-637-6282
800-879-6282
Fax: 214-637-2206
www.nata.org
The National Athletic Trainers' Association (NATA) is a membership association comprised of certified athletic trainers. NATA works to support and advocate for the recognition of athletic therapy as an essential practice that can advance healthcare.

Founded: 1950

Dave Saddler, Executive Director
Tamesha Logan, Associate Executive Director

340 National Collegiate Athletic Association

700 W Washington Street
PO Box 6222
Indianapolis, IN 46206-6222
317-917-6222
Fax: 317-917-6888
www.ncaa.org
The National Collegiate Athletic Association supports the long-term success of college athletes.

Mark Emmert, President

341 President's Council on Fitness, Sports & Nutrition

1101 Wootton Parkway
Suite 420
Rockville, MD 20852
fitness@hhs.gov
www.fitness.gov
The President's Council on Fitness, Sports & Nutrition (PCFSN) is dedicated to encouraging Americans in the adoption of a healthy lifestyle, including physical activity and good nutrition. The Council creates programs and campaigns focused on motivating people of all ages.

Founded: 1956

Kristina Harder, Executive Director

342 Shape America - Society of Health and Physical Educators

PO Box 225
Annapolis Junction, MD 20701
703-476-3400
800-213-7193
Fax: 703-476-9527
askmembership@shapeamerica.org
www.shapeamerica.org
A nonprofit, member organization of health and physical educators, Shape America works to advance and promote physical education and activity. The organization provides programs and resources to support health and physical educators at every level, advocating for school health and physical education throughout the United States. Shape America has helped to implement the Presidential Youth Fitness Program, Active Schools and the Jump Rope For Heart/Hoops for Heart programs.

Founded: 1885

Terri Drain, President
Stephanie A. Morris, Chief Executive Officer

343 Women's Sports Foundation

247 West 30th Street
5th Floor
New York, NY 10001
800-227-3988
info@womenssportsfoundation.org
www.womenssportsfoundation.org
An educational organization, the Women's Sports Foundation is dedicated to advancing the lives of women and girls of all ages through sport and physical activity.

Founded: 1974

Dr. Deborah Antoine, Chief Executive Officer
Aleia Taylor, Chief Marketing Officer

Reading

344 Center for Applied Linguistics

4646 40th Street NW
Washington, DC 20016-1859
202-362-0700
Fax: 202-362-3740
info@cal.org
www.cal.org
The Center for Applied Linguistics (CAL), is a nonprofit organization dedicated to promoting language and cultural understanding as it relates to access and equality in education.

Joel Gomez, Ed.D, President & CEO
Keira Ballantyne, Ph.D, Vice President, Programs

345 **College Reading & Learning Association**
7044 S 13th Street
Oak Creek, WI 53154
414-908-4961
customercare@crla.net
www.crla.net
The College Reading & Learning Association (CRLA) is dedicated to providing a forum for the exchange of ideas, methods, and information to improve student learning. The CRLA membership is comprised of, and open to professionals active in the fields of reading, learning assistance, developmental education, tutoring, and mentoring at the college/adult level.

Sonya Armstrong, President
Nicole Cheever, Certification Administrator

346 **International Literacy Association**
PO Box 8139
Newark, DE 19714-8139
302-731-1600
800-336-7323
Fax: 302-731-1057
customerservice@reading.org
www.literacyworldwide.org
An advocacy and membership organization, the International Literacy Association (ILA) fosters and encourages educators, students, and leaders to make literacy accessible for everyone. The ILA has a membership of more than 300,000 literacy educators in 128 countries.

Marcie Craig Post, Executive Director
Becky Fetterolf, Director, Program Content

347 **National Summer Learning Association**
1701 Pennsylvania Avenue NW
Suite 200
Washington, DC 20006
410-856-1370
Fax: 410-856-1383
www.summerlearning.org
The National Summer Learning Association (NSLA) is a national nonprofit organization focused on closing the education gap by providing summer learning opportunities for youth. The NSLA works with other national organizations to bring awareness and advocate for excellence in education for all.

Founded: 1992

Aaron Philip Dworkin, Chief Executive Officer
Brodrick Clarke, Vice President, Programs

348 **Organization of Teacher Educators in Literacy**
www.oter.coedu.usf.edu
A special interest group of the International Literacy Association, the Organization of Teacher Educators in Literacy (OTEL) provides a forum for members to communicate to debate and discuss issues and ways to improve reading instruction.

349 **ProLiteracy**
101 Wyoming Street
Syracuse, NY 13204
315-422-9121
888-528-2224
Fax: 315-422-6369
info@proliteracy.org
www.proliteracy.org
ProLiteracy is a membership organization advocating and providing literacy and basic education to adults across both nationally and internationally. ProLiteracy supports 1,000 programs providing adult literacy instruction, advocates for the awareness, funding, and support for literacy, provides professional development, and produces many instructional tools for students.

Kevin Morgan, President & CEO
Lara Pimentel, Senior Dir., Development

350 **Reach Out and Read**
89 South Street
Suite 201
Boston, MA 02111
617-455-0600
info@reachoutandread.org
www.reachoutandread.org
A nonprofit organization working to incorporate books into pediatric care. Reach Out and Read encourages families to read aloud together.

Founded: 1989

Brian Gallagher, M.P.A., Chief Executive Officer
Perri Klass, M.D., F.A.A.P., National Medical Director

351 **Reading Recovery Council of North America**
150 E Wilson Bridge Road
Suite 200
Worthington, OH 43085
614-310-7323
877-883-7323
info@readingrecovery.org
www.readingrecovery.org
The Reading Recovery Council of North America is a nonprofit organization of Reading Recovery, offering opportunities for leadership and professional development.

Billy Molasso, Executive Director
Sally Ann DeBolt, Dir., Educational Events

352 **Reading to Kids**
1600 Sawtelle Boulevard
Suite 210
Los Angeles, CA 90025
310-479-7455
Fax: 310-479-7435
info@readingtokids.org
www.readingtokids.org
Reading to Kids is dedicated to helping and inspiring underserved children through reading. The organization hosts monthly reading clubs, and offers parents training tools to encourage reading at home.

Founded: 1999

Charlie Orchard, Managing Director
Talethe Collins, Program Coordinator

353 **Women's National Book Association**
PO Box 237
FDR Station
New York, NY 10150
866-610-9622
info@wnba-books.org
www.wnba-books.org
The Women's National Book Association (WNBA) is an national organization dedicated to connecting, educating, and advocating for the literary community. The WNBA has 12 chapters across the United States, and is made up of women and men who work with and value books.

Founded: 1917

Natalie Obando-Desai, President
Linda Rosen, Secretary

Secondary Education

354 **American Association for Adult and Continuing Education**
2900 Delk Road
Suite 700, PMB 321
Marietta, GA 30067
678-271-4319
Fax: 404-393-9506
office@aaace.org
www.aaace.org
The American Association for Adult and Continuing Education (AAACE) is a nonprofit organization dedicated to providing leadership in the field of adult and continuing education. The AAACE works to expand opportunities for adult development through research, information, and practice.

Founded: 1982

Terry Dougherty, Managing Director
Ellen Shea, Conference Manager

355 **American Association of Colleges for Teacher Education**
1602 L Street NW
Suite 601
Washington, DC 20036
202-293-2450
Fax: 202-457-8095
aacte@aacte.org
www.aacte.org
The American Association of Colleges for Teacher Education (AACTE) advocates for high quality, evidence based educator preparation programs. AACTE represents over 800 postsecondary institutions, working to ensure that educators are prepared to teach at all levels.

Lynn M. Gangone, President & CEO
Jacqueline Rodriguez, Vice President, Research

356 **American Driver and Traffic Safety Education Association (ADTSEA)**
Highway Safety Services
1434 Trim Tree Road
Indiana, PA 15701
724-801-8246
Fax: 724-349-5042
office@adtsea.org
www.adtsea.org
The purpose of the American Driver and Traffic Safety Education Association is to promote quality traffic safety education by publishing policies and guidelines. The association also offers conferences, workshops, seminars, consulting services and educational materials.

Brett Robinson, Executive Director
Leslie Robinson, Office Manager

357 **Association for Institutional Research**
1435 Piedmont Drive E
Suite 211
Tallahassee, FL 32308
850-385-4155
Fax: 850-385-5180
air@airweb.org
www.airweb.org
The Association for Institutional Research (AIR) is an association of higher education professionals working in the institutional research, assessment, and planning education fields. AIR provides its members with professional development opportunities and educational resources, working to support the process of collecting, analyzing, and converting data to aid in higher education decision information.

Christine Keller, Executive Director & CEO
Jason Lewis, Deputy Director & CFO

358 **Association for Middle Level Education**
2550 Corporate Exchange Drive
Suite 324
Columbus, OH 43231

614-895-4730
800-528-6672
Fax: 614-895-4750
info@amle.org
www.amle.org
The Association for Middle Level Education is committed to meeting the educational and developmental needs of young adolescents by providing educators with the knowledge and resources to help them improve their services. The association offers workshops, publications and informational material.

Stephanie Simpson, Chief Executive Officer
Derek Neal, Chief Operating Officer

9 Association for Supervision & Curriculum Development (ASCD)
1703 N Beauregard Street
Alexandria, VA 22311-1714
press@ascd.org
www.ascd.org
A membership organization that develops programs, products, and services essential to the way educators learn, teach, and lead.

Founded: 1943

Ranjit Sidhu, CEO & Executive Director
Dana Shanks-Williams, Chief Financial Officer

0 Close Up Foundation
1330 Braddock Place
Suite 400
Alexandria, VA 22314
703-706-3300
info@closeup.org
www.closeup.org
Close Up works to inform all citizens of their democratic rights and responsibilities. Close Up partners with schools, educators, and organizations to implement programs and develop skills to engage citizens in democracy.

Founded: 1971

Timothy S. Davis, Chief Executive Officer
Eric Adydan, President & COO

1 College Board
250 Vesey Street
New York, NY 10281
212-713-8000
www.collegeboard.org
A nonprofit organization, the College Board is dedicated to expanding access to higher education by connecting students to college opportunities and programs, including an Advanced Placement Program, and SAT practice.

Founded: 1900

David Coleman, Chief Executive Officer
Jeremy Singer, President

62 National Alliance for Secondary Education and Transition
University of Minnesota
150 Pillsbury Drive SE
6 Pattee Hall
Minneapolis, MN 55455
ncset@umn.edu
www.nasetalliance.org
The National Alliance for Secondary Education and Transition (NASET) is a national coalition representing education and career organizations and advocacy groups focused on policy development and professional practice. NASET works in 5 areas, schooling, career preparatory experiences, youth development and leadership, family involvement and connecting activities.

Founded: 2003

363 National Business Education Association (NBEA)
1914 Association Drive
Suite 203
Reston, VA 20191
703-860-8300
Fax: 703-860-4483
nbea@nbea.org
www.nbea.org
The National Business Education Association works to support individuals and groups who instruct, administer, research, and spread information regarding business. NBEA advances the professional interests of its members through programs that enhance professional growth and development.

Joe McClary, Executive Director
Jeri Werner, Operations Manager

364 National Parent Teacher Association
1250 N Pitt Street
Alexandria, VA 22314
703-518-1200
800-307-4782
Fax: 703-836-0942
info@pta.org
www.pta.org
The National PTA is a nonprofit organization dedicated to the educational success of children, and parent involvement in schools.

Founded: 1897

Nathan R. Monell, Executive Director
Kristen Johnson, Director, Education

Science

365 Academy of Applied Science
University of New Hampshire
Leitzel Center
PO Box 705
Contoocook, NH 03229
603-862-3401
young.inventors@unh.edu
www.aas-world.org
The Academy of Applied Science offers science, technology, engineering, and math programs for students. The Young Inventors' Program, a program of the AAS, is a K-12 project-based learning curriculum that teaches students STEM principles and skill development through hands-on learning, research, and testing.

Sheldon Apsell, Chair
Christina White, Program Director

366 American Association for the Advancement of Science
1200 New York Avenue NW
Washington, DC 20005
202-326-6400
www.aaas.org
A nonprofit organization dedicated to the advancement of science. The American Association for the Advancement of Science (AAAS) is the largest multidisciplinary scientific society, with international membership.

Founded: 1848

Sudip Parikh, Chief Executive Officer
Tanisha Lewis, Chief Financial Officer

367 American Association of Physics Teachers
1 Physics Ellipse
College Park, MD 20740-3845
301-209-3311
Fax: 301-209-0845
eo@aapt.org
www.aapt.org
The American Association of Physics Teachers (AAPT) works to spread and improve physics knowledge and education through teaching.

Founded: 1930

Beth A. Cunningham, Executive Officer
Robert C. Hilborn, Associate Executive Officer

368 American Dairy Science Association
1800 S Oak Street
Suite 100
Champaign, IL 61820-6974
217-356-5146
Fax: 217-398-4119
adsa@assochq.org
www.adsa.org
The American Dairy Science Association (ADSA) works to advance the dairy industry. The ADSA is an international organization comprised of diary educators, scientists, and industry representatives.

Founded: 1906

Paul Kindstedt, President
Normand St-Pierre, Vice President

369 American Indian Science & Engineering Society (AISES)
6321 Riverside Plaza Lane NW
Unit A
Albuquerque, NM 87120
505-765-1052
Fax: 505-765-5608
info@aises.org
www.aises.org
The American Indian Science and Engineering Society is a national, nonprofit organization focused on substantially increasing the representation of American Indians, Alaska Natives, Native Hawaiians, Pacific Islanders, First Nations and other indigenous peoples of North America in science, technology, engineering and math (STEM) studies and careers.

Sarah EchoHawk, Chief Executive Officer
Kellie Jewett-Fernandez, Chief Development Officer

370 American Medical Student Association
25050 Riding Plaza
Suite 130, Box 632
Chantilly, VA 20152
703-620-6600
800-767-2266
Fax: 703-620-6445
members@amsa.org
www.amsa.org
A student run national organization, the American Medical Student Association (AMSA), works to advocate for, and represent the concerns of physicians in training.

Founded: 1950

Jamie Thayer Scates, Chief Executive Officer
Jennifer Salehi, Chief Administrative Officer

371 American Society for Clinical Laboratory Science
1861 International Drive
Suite 200
McLean, VA 22102
571-748-3770
ascls@ascls.org
www.ascls.org
The American Society for Clinical Laboratory Science (ASCLS) is dedicated to impacting healthcare through the assurance of

excellence in the practice of laboratory medicine.

Founded: 1936

Jim Flanigan, CAE, Executive Vice President
Andrea Hickey, MLS(ASCP), Director, Membership

372 American Society of Nephrology

1401 H Street NW
Suite 900
Washington, DC 20005
202-640-4660
Fax: 202-637-9793
email@asn-online.org
www.asn-online.org
The American Society of Nephrology (ASN) is dedicated to preventing, treating and curing kidney disease. With nearly 15,000 physicians and scientists making up its membership, the ASN advocates policy makers on the importance of kidney health.

Susan E. Quaggin, MD, FASN, President
Keisha L. Gibson, MD, MPH, FASN, Treasurer

373 Association for Information Science and Technology

8555 16th Street
Suite 850
Silver Spring, MD 20910
301-495-0900
asist@asist.org
www.asist.org
A professional organization, the Association for Information Science and Technology (ASIS&T) works to bring together the practice of science and scientific research. Through the professional exchange of information, career development, research dissemination, and education, ASIS&T is committed to advancing information sciences.

Founded: 1937

Lydia Middleton, MBA, CAE, Executive Director
Terrence Curtiss, Director, Membership

374 Association for Science Teacher Education (ASTE)

3451 S 5th Avenue
Whitehall, PA 18052
484-547-6046
executivedirector@theaste.org
www.theaste.org
The Association for Science Teacher Education works to promote leadership and support for those involved in the development of teachers of science. It offers an annual meeting, as well as three professional journals: Journal of Science Teacher Education (JSTE), Innovations in Science Teacher Education, and Contemporary Issues in Technology and Teacher Education (Science section).

Debi Hanuscin, President
Kate Popejoy, Executive Director

375 Association for the Advancement of Computing in Education

PO Box 719
Waynesville, NC 28786
828-246-9558
Fax: 828-246-9557
info@aace.org
www.aace.org
The Association for the Advancement of Computing in Education (AACE) is an international nonprofit association working to advance information technology and E-learning in education. The AACE offers conferences, publications, a digital library, and career center to provide professional growth opportunities for its members.

Founded: 1981

Gary H. Marks, Chief Executive Officer

376 Association of Science and Technology Centers

818 Connecticut Avenue NW
7th Floor
Washington, DC 20006-2734
202-783-7200
Fax: 202-783-7207
info@astc.org
www.astc.org
Represents, supports, and offers programming opportunities for science centers, museums, nature centers, aquariums, planetarium, zoos, and botanical gardens. The ASTC represents more than 500 members, sponsors an annual conference, and offers learning opportunities.

Founded: 1973

Christofer Nelson, President & CEO
Melissa Ballard, Director, Programs

377 California Biomedical Research Association

PO Box 19340
Sacramento, CA 95819-0340
916-558-1515
www.ca-biomed.org
The California Biomedical Research Association (CBRA) an organization promoting and supporting biomedical research, and conducting public outreach on the role of research and medical care. The CBRA is comprised of academic institutions, voluntary health agencies, hospitals, nonprofit medical research institutions, and pharmaceutical companies based in California, Nevada, and the greater western region.

Amanda Carson Banks, President

378 Canadian Association for Medical Education

2733 Lancaster Road
Suite 100
Ottawa, ON K1B-0A9
613-730-0687
Fax: 613-730-1196
came@afmc.ca
www.came-acem.ca
Organization of medical educators dedicated to promoting excellence in the field through advocacy, publications, professional development workshops and networking.

Dr. Shelley Ross, President
Dr. Marcus Law, Treasurer

379 Energy Education Group

The California Study, Inc.
664 Hilary Drive
Tiburon, CA 94920
415-435-4574
24hrcleanpower@gmail.com
www.energyforkeeps.org
A division of The California Study, Inc. the Energy Education Group is a nonprofit organization working to educate people on electricity and where it comes from.

Marilyn Nemzer, Executive Director

380 Entomological Society of America

3 Park Place
Suite 307
Annapolis, MD 21401-3722
301-731-4535
esa@entsoc.org
www.entsoc.org
The Entomological Society of America (ESA) is a nonprofit professional society working to advance the professional and scientific needs of entomologists.

Founded: 1889

Chris Stelzig, Executive Director
Rosina Romano, Director, Membership

381 Geothermal Education Office

664 Hilary Drive
Tiburon, CA 94920
Fax: 415-435-7737
24hrcleanpower@gmail.com
www.geothermaleducation.org
The Geothermal Education Office (GEO) is a nonprofit organization dedicated to promoting and producing information about geothermal resources and its uses as a clean sustainable energy.

Marliyn Nemzer, Executive Director

382 Green Communities Canada

1545 Monaghan Road
Peterborough, ON K9J-5N3
705-745-7479
Fax: 705-745-7294
info@greencommunitiescanada.org
www.greencommunitiescanada.org
National association of community organizations working to spread awareness about environmental health and reduce negative impacts on the environment through programs and initiatives.

Brianna Salmon, Executive Director
Se Keohane, Director, Finance

383 History of Science Society

University of Notre Dame
440 Geddes Hall
Notre Dame, IN 46556
574-631-1194
Fax: 574-631-1533
info@hssonline.org
www.hssonline.org
The History of Science Society is dedicated to understanding the relationship between history, science, technology, and medicine. The society has 3,000 members made up of individuals and institutions.

Founded: 1924

Jan Golinski, President
John Paul Gutierrez, Executive Director

384 Institute for Earth Education

PO Box 115
Greenville, WV 24945
304-832-6404
Fax: 304-832-6077
info@ieetree.org
www.ieetree.org
The Institute for Earth Education (IEE) is an international nonprofit organization dedicated to earth education. The IEE creates and implements programs to promote interpretation, education and contemplation of earth education.

Founded: 1974

385 National Association for Research in Science Teaching

11130 Sunrise Valley Drive
Suite 350
Reston, VA 20191
703-234-4082
Fax: 703-234-4147
info@narst.org
www.narst.org
The National Association for Research in Science Teaching (NARST) is an international organization working to improve the teaching and learning of science through research. NARST promotes science literacy by encouraging and supporting research into the teaching and learning of science, disseminating research findings, and working

with other educational and scientific societies to influence educational policies.

Founded: 1928

Renee Schwartz, President
Jerome Shaw, Secretary-Treasurer

6 National Association of Biology Teachers
PO Box 3363
Warrenton, VA 20188
703-264-9696
888-501-6228
Fax: 202-962-3939
office@nabt.org
www.nabt.org
The National Association of Biology Teachers (NABT) supports educators to ensure students receive the highest quality of biology and life science education. The NABT represents teachers, students, and science organizations and is committed to the professional development of educators, through pedagogy, relevant and scientifically sound instructional content, and advocating for biology teachers.

Founded: 1938

Julie Angle, President
Jaclyn Reeves-Pepin, Executive Director

7 National Association of Geoscience Teachers
c/o Science Education Resource Center
200 Division Street
Suite 210
Northfield, MN 55057
507-222-4368
Fax: 507-222-5175
nagtservice@nagt.org
www.nagt.org
The National Association of Geoscience Teachers (NAGT) is dedicated to improving geoscience education. NAGT membership is comprised of K-12 teachers, college and university faculty members, museums, and science centers.

Founded: 1938

Anne Egger, Executive Director
Amy Collette, Business Manager

38 National Center for Science Education
230 Grand Avenue
Suite 101
Oakland, CA 94610
510-601-7203
Fax: 510-788-7971
info@ncse.ngo
www.ncse.ngo
A nonprofit organization, the National Center for Science Education (NCSE) supports the accurate teaching of evolution and climate change. The NCSE works with teachers, scientists and communities to ensure scientific topics are taught without ideological interference.

Ann Reid, Executive Director
Glenn Branch, Deputy Director

89 National Earth Science Teachers Association
PO Box 271654
Fort Collins, CO 80527
nestaadmn@gmail.com
www.nestanet.org
The National Earth Science Teachers Association (NESTA) is a nonprofit, educational organization dedicated to advancing K-12, Earth and Space Science education in formal and informal settings.

Founded: 1983

Richard Jones, President
Missy Holzer, Secretary

390 National Science Teaching Association
1840 Wilson Boulevard
Arlington, VA 22201
703-243-7100
Fax: 703-243-7177
membership@nsta.org
www.nsta.org
The National Science Teaching Association (NSTA) is an international organization dedicated to improving and promoting excellence and innovation in science teaching.

Founded: 1944

Dr. Eric J. Pyle, President
Dr. Erika Shugart, Executive Director

391 School Science and Mathematics Association
Oklahoma State University
245 Willard Hall
Stillwater, OK 74078-1003
office@ssma.org
www.ssma.org
The School Science and Mathematics Association (SSMA) is a professional community of educators and researchers promoting scholarship, research, and practices that improve social science, mathematics, and STEM.

Founded: 1901

Stephanie Hathcock, Co-Executive Director
Toni Ivey, Co-Executive Director

392 Society for Science & the Public
1719 N Street NW
Washington, DC 20036
202-785-2255
society@societyforscience.org
www.societyforscience.org
A nonprofit membership organization, the Society for Science & the Public, is focused on, and dedicated to, expanding scientific literacy, effective STEM education, and research. The Society, formerly known as Science Service, advances science through information, education, and inspiration.

Founded: 1921

Maya Ajmera, President & CEO
Michele Glidden, Chief Program Officer

393 Soil Science Society of America
5585 Guilford Road
Madison, WI 53711-5801
608-273-8080
Fax: 608-273-2021
www.soils.org
The Soil Science Society of America (SSSA) is an international scientific society dedicated to fostering the dissemination and implementation of sustainable soil practices. The SSSA provides information about soil as it relates to crop production, environmental quality, ecosystems, waste management, recycling, and wise land use.

Founded: 1936

Luther Smith, Interim CEO
Sara Uttech, Director, Governance

Social Studies

394 American Association of Geographers
PO Box 73158
Washington, DC 20056
202-234-1450
Fax: 202-234-2744
membership@aag.org
www.aag.org
The American Association of Geographers (AAG) is a nonprofit, educational and scientific organization dedicated to the advancement of geography. The AAG provides a forum for its members and scholars to discuss theory, methods, and the practice of geography.

Founded: 1904

Gary Langham, Executive Director
Candida Mannozzi, Director, Operations

395 American Geographical Society
121 6th Avenue
Suite 6
New York, NY 10013
917-745-8354
ags@americangeo.org
www.americangeo.org
The American Geographical Society (AGS) advances and promotes geographic thinking in business, government, academic and social sectors. Their mission is to enhance the nation's geographic literacy and foster sound public policy, national security, and global wellbeing.ÿ

Founded: 1851

Marie Price, President
John Konarski, Chief Executive Officer

396 American Political Science Association
1527 New Hampshire Avenue NW
Washington, DC 20036-1203
202-483-2512
Fax: 202-483-2657
apsa@apsanet.org
www.apsanet.org
A professional organization, the American Political Science Association (APSA) promotes the study of political science. The APSA is comprised of 12,000 members from over 100 countries working to bring together political scientists from a wide range of fields for scholarly research, the increase of academic and non-academic opportunities, and strengthening the professional environment of political science.

Founded: 1903

Steven Rathgeb Smith, Executive Director
Betsy Super, Deputy Director

397 Canadian Association for Social Work Education
110 Didsbury Road
Suite M014
Kanata, ON K2T-0C2
services@caswe-acfts.ca
www.caswe-acfts.ca
A national nonprofit association comprised of faculties and school departments engaged in providing social work education. The association promotes excellence in the field by offering accreditation options, programs, research, a publication and an annual conference.

Billie Allan, President
Carole Carpot, Executive Director

398 **Canadian Association of Social Workers**
383 Parkdale Avenue
Suite 402
Ottawa, ON K2G-4W1
613-729-6668
casw@casw-acts.ca
www.casw-acts.ca
National organization engaged in overseeing general and financial policies that affect social work, as well as providing information and services for the development of social workers and their profession.

Founded: 1926

Fred Phelps, Executive Director
Sally Guy, Director, Policy & Strategy

399 **Council for Economic Education**
122 East 42nd Street
Suite 1012
New York, NY 10168
212-827-3600
Fax: 212-827-3610
info@councilforeconed.org
www.councilforeconed.org
The Council for Economic Education (CEE) is focused on the economic and financial education of students from K-12. The Council works to educate teachers by providing curriculum tools and pedagogical support in order to ensure youth are equipped to achieve financial and economic independence.

Nan J. Morrison, President & CEO
Sally Wood, COO & CFO

400 **Council of State Social Studies Specialists**
National Council for the Social Studies
8555 16th Street
Suite 500
Silver Spring, MD 20910
www.cs4.socialstudies.org/home
The Council of State Social Studies Specialists is a forum for the exchange of ideas between social studies specialists from different states and various state departments of education.

Founded: 1965

Scott Abbott, President
Linda Burrows, Treasurer

401 **Foundation for Teaching Economics**
260 Russell Boulevard
Suite B
Davis, CA 95616
530-757-4630
Fax: 530-757-4636
information@fte.org
www.fte.org
The Foundation for Teaching Economics is a nonprofit corporation working to introduce youth to economic, national, and international issues. The Foundation promotes the increased quality of economic education, provides workshops, and offers teachers tools to become more effective educators.

Founded: 1975

Roger Ream, President
Ted Tucker, Executive Director

402 **National Council for Geographic Education**
8555 16th Street
Suite 500
Silver Spring, MD 20910
833-465-6243
info@ncge.org
www.ncge.org
The National Council for Geographic Education (NCGE) is a nonprofit organization dedicated to promoting excellence among the geography teacher profession. The NCGE supports educators and students from kindergarten to university, with the council conducting and gathering research, producing journals, providing professional development opportunities, and organizing an annual conference.

Founded: 1915

Jeff Lash, President
Charles D. Regan, Executive Director

403 **National Council for the Social Studies**
8555 16th Street
Suite 500
Silver Spring, MD 20910
301-588-1800
800-296-7840
www.socialstudies.org
The National Council for the Social Studies (NCSS) advocates and supports social studies education. The Council is the largest professional association in the United States, and its membership is represented by K-12 teachers, college and university professors, and curriculum designers.

Founded: 1921

Lawrence M. Paska, Executive Director
Joy D. Lindsey, Director, Membership

404 **National Council on Public History**
425 University Boulevard
Cavanaugh Hall 127
Indianapolis, IN 46202-5140
317-274-2716
Fax: 317-278-5230
ncph@iupui.edu
www.ncph.org
A membership association, the National Council on Public History (NCPH) works to establish professional standards, ethics, and practices, to encourage collaboration between historians and the public. The NCPH provides professional development and networking opportunities, and supports history education.

Founded: 1980

Stephanie Rowe, Executive Director
Meghan Hillman, Program Manager

405 **New England History Teachers Association**
Dean College
99 Main Street
Franklin, MA 02038
info@nehta.org
www.nehta.org
The New England History Teachers Association (NEHTA) provides teachers and students with academic opportunities to engage in history and social studies discussions through conferences, publications, and awards.

Founded: 1897

Stephen Armstrong, President
Kristen Borges, Treasurer

406 **Oral History Association**
Middle Tennessee State University
Peck Hall 217
Box 193
Murfreesboro, TN 37132
615-898-2544
oha@oralhistory.org
www.oralhistory.org
The Oral History Association (OHA) is dedicated to promoting the value of oral history. OHA advocates policy makers, educators, and historians to foster the collections, preservation, and dissemination of oral history.

Founded: 1966

Kristine M. McCusker, Co-Executive Director
Louis Kyriakoudes, Co-Executive Director

407 **Society for History Education**
1250 N Bellflower Boulevard
Long Beach, CA 90840-1601
562-985-2573
info@thehistoryteacher.org
www.societyforhistoryeducation.org
The Society for History Education (SHE) is a nonprofit organization working to improve the learning experience in the classroom. SHE organizes and publishes the journal The History Teacher and is an affiliate of the American Historical Association.

Eileen Luhr, President
Elisa Herrera, Director

408 **Street Law**
Street Law, Inc.
1010 Wayne Avenue
Suite 870
Silver Spring, MD 20910
301-589-1130
Fax: 301-589-1131
learnmore@streetlaw.org
www.streetlaw.org
Street Law is a nonprofit organization that creates classroom and community programs focused on law, democracy, and human rights. Programs are created for teachers, lawyers, law students, non-governmental organizations, and law enforcement officers.

Founded: 1972

Ashok Regmi, Executive Director
Jos, Ar,valo, Chief Financial Officer

409 **The Africa-America Institute**
60 E 42nd Street
Suite 1700
New York, NY 10165-6222
212-949-5666
aainy@aaionline.org
www.aaionline.org
The Africa-America Institute (AAI) is an international education and policy organization working to foster engagement between Africa and America. The AAI seeks to advance higher education and the professional development of Africans, and raises funds to provide scholarships for under resourced students to attend African universities.

Founded: 1953

Kofi Appenteng, President & CEO
Steven B. Pfeiffer, Chair

410 **Western History Association**
University of Kansas, History Department
1445 Jayhawk Boulevard
3650 Wescoe Hall
Lawrence, KS 66045
785-864-0860
wha@westernhistory.org
www.westernhistory.org
The Western History Association (WHA) promotes the study of North American Western History. The WHA is comprised of historians, with 1,200 active members.

Founded: 1961

Elaine Nelson, Executive Director
Paige Mitchell, Office & Events Coordinator

World History Association (WHA)
Northeastern University
Department of History
360 Huntington Avenue
Boston, MA 02115
617-373-6818
Fax: 617-373-2661
info@thewha.org
www.thewha.org
The World History Association promotes the teaching, research, and publication of world history.

Laura J. Mitchell, President
Jonathan T. Reynolds, Vice President

Technology in Education

2 **American Technical Education Association**
ATEA
Dunwoody College of Technology
818 Dunwoody Boulevard
Minneapolis, MN 55403
612-381-3315
info@ateaonline.org
www.ateaonline.org
International organization dedicated to the professional growth and development of postsecondary educators and industrial trainers. The American Technical Education Association provides leadership and networking opportunities with others working in the field.

Sandra Krebsbach, Executive Director

3 **Association for Career & Technical Education (ACTE)**
1410 King Street
Alexandria, VA 22314
800-826-9972
Fax: 703-683-7424
acte@acteonline.org
www.acteonline.org
The Association for Career and Technical Education is the largest national education association working to prepare youth and adults for their careers through the advancement of education.

Founded: 1926

LeAnn Wilson, Executive Director
Steve DeWitt, Deputy Executive Director

14 **Association for Educational Communications & Technology**
320 W 8th Street
Suite 101
Bloomington, IN 47404-3745
812-335-7675
877-677-2328
aect@aect.org
www.aect.org
The Association for Educational Communications and Technology (AECT) is a professional organization of educators dedicated to improving instruction through technology. AECT provides a forum for the exchange and dispersal of information between its members; with its members instrumental in the study, planning, application, and production of communications media for instruction.

Xun Ge, President
Ellen Wagner, Interim Executive Director

15 **Association for the Advancement of Computing in Education**
PO Box 719
Waynesville, NC 28786
828-246-9558
Fax: 828-246-9557
info@aace.org
www.aace.org
The Association for the Advancement of Computing in Education (AACE) is an international nonprofit association working to advance information technology and E-learning in education. The AACE offers conferences, publications, a digital library, and career center to provide professional growth opportunities for its members.

Founded: 1981

Gary H. Marks, Chief Executive Officer

416 **CUE**
CUE, Inc.
877 Ygnacio Valley Road
Suite 200
Walnut Creek, CA 94596
925-478-3460
Fax: 925-934-6799
cueinc@cue.org
www.cue.org
CUE is a nonprofit membership and educational corporation working to inspire learners and educators through community, personalized learning, technology, leadership development, and the advocating of educational opportunities. CUE is open to all education disciplines from preschool to college.

Founded: 1978

Mike Vollmert, Interim Executive Director
Joe Marquez, Dir., Academic Innovation

417 **Canadian Network for Innovation in Education**
CNIE/RCIE
204, 260 Dalhousie
Ottawa, ON K1N-7E4
613-241-0018
Fax: 613-241-0019
hello@cnie-rcie.ca
www.cnie-rcie.ca
National organization dedicated to supporting innovation in Canadian education of all levels. Services offered to members include conferences, publications and platforms for conversations about the use of technology in education.

Cindy Ives, President
Saul Carliner, Vice President

418 **Center for Children & Technology**
96 Morton Street
7th Floor
New York, NY 10014
212-807-4200
Fax: 212-633-8804
www.cct.edc.org
The Center for Children & Technology (CCT) researches how technology influences and enhances teaching. CCT uses a range of research tools, including classroom based research studies and international evaluations to understand the role of technology in education.

Founded: 1980

Shelley Pasnik, Director & Senior VP
Bill Tally, Managing Project Director

419 **Center for Educational Leadership & Technology**
65 Boston Post Road W
Suite 200
Marlborough, MA 01752
508-624-4474
Fax: 508-624-6565
info@celtcorp.com
www.celtcorp.com
The Center for Educational Leadership and Technology (CELT) offers research, planning, and implementation services for educational institutions; including private and public schools, education agencies, education departments, universities and colleges, national education associations, and educational foundations. CELT is primarily focused on designing learner-centered data systems.

John Phillipo, Chief Executive Officer

420 **Center for Educational Technologies**
316 Washington Avenue
Wheeling, WV 26003-6243
304-243-2388
800-624-6992
Fax: 304-243-2497
www.cet.edu
The Center for Education Technologies creates curriculum supplements to improve the teaching and learning of science, technology, engineering, and math. The Center works with federal and state agencies, foundations, school districts, corporations, and educators by offering outreach, professional development, and onsite and distance learning opportunities.

421 **Consortium for School Networking**
1325 G Street NW
Suite 420
Washington, DC 20005
202-470-2784
membership@cosn.org
www.cosn.org
CoSN is a professional association working to advocate for the use of technology to improve teaching and learning in K-12 classrooms.

Keith R. Krueger, CAE, Chief Executive Officer
Robert Duke, CAE, Chief Operating Officer

422 **Consortium of College and University Media Centers**
201 E Main Street
Suite 1405
Lexington, KY 40507
859-514-9185
ccumc@ccumc.org
www.ccumc.org
The Consortium of College and University Media Centers (CCUMC) advocates for the accessibility of educational media, technology, and pedagogy. In addition, the CCUMC works to provide leadership and a forum for the exchange of information to the providers of media content, academic technology, and learning institutions.

Kristy Howard, Executive Director
Emily Glass, Manager, Education & Events

423 **DANEnet**
128 E Olin Avenue
Suite 66
Madison, WI 53713
608-274-3107
info@danenet.org
www.danenet.org
A nonprofit organization offering on-site technical support, training, planning and consulting services to community agencies and science education groups in Dane County.

Founded: 1994

Shawn Steen, Executive Director

424 **EDUCAUSE**
4845 Pearl E Circle
Suite 118, PMB 43761
Boulder, CO 80301-6112
303-449-4430
Fax: 303-440-0461

info@educause.edu
www.educause.edu
EDUCAUSE is a nonprofit association dedicated to improving and optimizing the impact of IT on higher education. EDUCAUSE is focused on building the IT profession, connecting and facilitating collaboration among IT professionals, research, and data analysis.

John O'Brien, President & CEO
Mairead Martin, Chief Information Officer

425 IMAGE Center
300 E Joppa Road
Suite 312
Towson, MD 21286
410-982-6311
Fax: 443-470-8593
info@imagemd.org
www.imagemd.org
IMAGE Center provides solutions and services to help individuals with disabilities lead productive and independent lives.

Mike Bullis, Executive Director

426 Innovations in Special Education Technology
The Council for Exceptional Children
3100 Clarendon Boulevard
Suite 600
Arlington, VA 22201-5332
www.isetcec.org
A division of the Council for Exceptional Children, Innovations in Special Education Technology (ISET) specializes in providing innovative technology-based solutions to educators, professionals, and members of families.

Tara Kaczorowski, President
Alexandra Hollingshead, Vice President

427 Instructional Technology Council
19 Mantua Road
Mount Royal, NJ 08061
856-423-0258
Fax: 856-423-3420
director@itcnetwork.org
www.itcnetwork.org
The Instructional Technology Council (ITC) is a nonprofit organization dedicated to advocating collaborating, researching, and the sharing of innovative educational technologies to its network of e-Learning providers with the purpose of advancing distance education.

Founded: *1977*

Andrea Taylor, Executive Director

428 International Society for Technology in Education
2111 Wilson Boulevard
Suite 300
Arlington, VA 22201
503-342-2848
800-336-5191
Fax: 541-302-3778
iste@iste.org
www.iste.org
Provides leadership and services to improve teaching and learning by advancing the effective use of technology in education.

Rand Hansen, President
Richard Culatta, Chief Executive Officer

429 International Technology and Engineering Educators Association
1914 Association Drive
Suite 201
Reston, VA 20191-1539
703-860-2100
Fax: 703-860-0353
iteea@iteea.org
www.iteea.org
The International Technology and Engineering Educators Association (ITEEA) promotes technological literacy through leadership, professional development, and publications. ITEEA supports the teaching of, and those who teach, technology and engineering.

Steven A. Barbato, Executive Director
Kathleen de la Paz, Communications Director

430 Learning Guild
120 Stony Point Road
Suite 210
Santa Rosa, CA 95401
707-566-8990
Fax: 707-566-8963
service@learningguild.com
www.learningguild.com
The Learning Guild is a member organization that produces conferences, online events, online training courses, eBooks, research reports, and a Learning Solutions Magazine. The Guild is source of information and a network for eLearning professionals.

David Holcombe, President & CEO
David Kelly, EVP & Executive Director

431 National Association of Media and Technology Centers
PO Box 378
West Milton, PA 17886
570-701-4202
Fax: 570-710-4202
www.namtc.org
The National Association of Media and Technology Centers (NAMTC) provides leadership opportunities, instructional technology, and professional development to foster the use of media and technology in education. Membership to NAMTC is open to regional, K-12, and higher education instructional technology media centers and commercial vendors.

Danielle O'Connor, President
Geoff Craven, Executive Director

432 National Center for Technology Innovation
American Institutes for Research
1400 Crystal Drive
10th Floor
Arlington, VA 22202
202-403-5000
Fax: 202-403-5000
nationaltechcenterorg@gmail.com
www.nationaltechcenter.org
A program of the American Institutes for Research, the National Center for Technology Innovation (NCTI) works to advance learning opportunities for individuals with disabilities by promoting technological innovation. NCTI supports researchers, product developers, manufacturers, and publishers to create and commercialize technology products for students.

433 National Center for Technology Planning
PO Box 2393
Tupelo, MS 38803
662-844-9630
Fax: 662-844-9630
www.nctp.com
The National Center for Technology Planning (NCTP) provides a forum for the collection and exchange of information related to technology planning.

Dr. Larry S. Anderson, Founder & Director

434 National Coalition for Technology in Education and Training
www.nctet.org
The National Coalition for Technology in Education and Training (NCTET) is a nonprofit organization promoting the use of technology to improve education and training.

Founded: *1993*

Jon Bernstein, Executive Director

435 Online Learning Consortium
6 Liberty Square
Suite 2309
Boston, MA 02109
617-716-1414
customerservice@onlinelearning-c.org
www.onlinelearningconsortium.org
Online Learning Consortium works to advance the quality of online learning through professional development, instruction, research, best-practice publications and connections to online learning organizations worldwide.

Founded: *1992*

Mary Niemiec, President
Elizabeth Ciabocchi, Vice President

436 State Educational Technology Directors Association
PO Box 10
Glen Burnie, MD 21060
202-715-6636
www.setda.org
The State Educational Technology Directors Association (SETDA) is a nonprofit association dedicated to representing and supporting the use of technology in teaching and learning.

Julia Fallon, Executive Director
Tera Daniels, Director, Operations

437 Technology Student Association
1904 Association Drive
Reston, VA 20191-1540
703-860-9000
888-860-9010
Fax: 703-738-7486
general@tsaweb.org
www.tsaweb.org
The Technology Student Association (TSA) works to promote personal development, leadership, and career opportunities in STEM. The TSA is open to students who are currently enrolled or were enrolled in technology education courses.

Rosanne T. White, Executive Director

438 United States Distance Learning Association
10 G Street NE
Suite 600
Washington, DC 20002
202-248-5023
info@usdla.org
www.usdla.org
The United States Distance Learning Association (USDLA) supports distance learning research and development across the United States.

Founded: *1987*

Dr. Reggie Smith III, Executive Director & CEO

439 WICHE Cooperative for Educational Technologies
3035 Center Green Drive
Suite 200
Boulder, CO 80301-2204

303-541-0231
wcetinfo@wiche.edu
www.wcet.wiche.edu
WICHE Cooperative for Educational Technologies (WCET) is a national nonprofit working to bring together higher education institutions, organizations, and companies to improve the quality and reach of e-Learning programs. In addition, WCET promotes the adoption of effective practices and policies that advance technology in education.

Founded: 1989

Russ Poulin, Executive Director
Van Davis, Chief Strategy Officer

Alabama

0 **Alabama Business Education Association (ABEA)**
National Business Education Association
1914 Association Drive
Reston, VA 20191-1596
703-860-8300
Fax: 703-620-4483
jonesmp@vestavia.k12.al.us
www.albusinessed.org
A professional association for business and marketing educators at the secondary and post-secondary levels. The association encourages professional growth among business teachers through events and networking.

Lanette Fargason, President
Morgan Jones, Membership Director

1 **Alabama Commission on Higher Education (ACHE)**
100 N Union Street
Suite 782
Montgomery, AL 36104-3758
334-242-1998
Fax: 334-242-2269
deborah.nettles@ache.alabama.gov
www.ache.alabama.gov
Coordinating board in the State of Alabama responsible for providing information on the state's education programs, colleges and universities, financial aid assistance programs, grants, scholarships, continuing education programs and career opportunities.

Jim Purcell, Ph.D, Executive Director
Robin McGill, Ph.D, Director, Instruction

42 **Alabama Education Association (AEA)**
422 Dexter Avenue
Montgomery, AL 36104
334-834-9790
800-392-5839
Fax: 334-262-8377
myaea@alaedu.org
www.myaea.org
Serves as an advocate for Alabama teachers and takes a lead role in the advancement of equitable and quality public education. The association provides legal assistance, member benefits and professional development resources.

Amy Marlowe, Interim Executive Director
Theron Stokes, Esq., Associate Executive Director

43 **Alabama Library Association (ALLA)**
6030 Monticello Drive
Montgomery, AL 36117
334-414-0113
allibraryassoc@gmail.com
www.allanet.org
Nonprofit corporation formed to encourage and promote the welfare of libraries and professional interests of librarians in Alabama. The association provides leadership for the development, advocacy and improvement of library services.

Founded: 1904

Daniel Tackett, President

444 **Alabama Public Library Service (APLS)**
6030 Monticello Drive
Montgomery, AL 36117
334-213-3900
800-723-8459
www.aplsws1.apls.state.al.us/aplsnew
The Alabama Public Library Service manages state funds provided by the State Legislature in making library services available to the citizens of Alabama, including those who are blind or disabled.

Ronald A Snider, District 1 Director
Angelia Stokes, District 2 Director

445 **Alabama State Council on the Arts**
201 Monroe Street
suite 110
Montgomery, AL 36130-1800
334-242-4076
Fax: 334-240-3269
staff@arts.alabama.gov
www.arts.state.al.us
Promotes high-quality education in the arts. Areas covered include literary arts, performing arts, visual arts, community arts and more.

Elliot A Knight, Ph.D, Executive Director
Andrew Henley, Deputy Director

446 **Alabama State Department of Education - Teaching and Learning Improvement Division**
50 N Ripley Street
PO Box 302101
Montgomery, AL 36104
334-694-4900
www.alsde.edu/div/dtl/Pages/home.aspx
The Teaching and Learning Improvement Division is responsible for implementing Alabama's strategic PLAN 2020, to ensure that graduating students receive the kind of education that would make them college or career ready.

Eric G Mackey, Ed.D, Superintendent, Education
Daniel Boyd, Ph.D, Deputy Superintendent

Alaska

447 **Alaska Association of School Librarians (AKASL)**
c/o Alaska Library Association
PO Box 81084
Fairbanks, AK 99708
akasl.president@gmail.com
www.akasl.org
Advances high standards for the school librarian profession and library information programs in the schools of Alaska. The association offers grants and awards, as well as development programs.

Janet Madsen, President
Jessica Tonnies, Secretary

448 **Alaska Commission on Postsecondary Education (ACPE)**
ACPE
PO Box 110505
Juneau, AK 99811
907-465-2962
800-441-2962
Fax: 907-465-5316
ACPE@alaska.gov
www.acpe.alaska.gov
Provides information on the state's education programs, colleges and universities, financial aid assistance programs, grants, scholarships, continuing education programs and career opportunities.

Stephanie Butler, Executive Director
Kerry Thomas, Director, Operations

449 **Alaska Education of Homeless Children and Youth Program**
Alaska Dept. of Education & Early Development
801 W 10th Street
Suite 200
Juneau, AK 99811-0500
907-465-8704
877-854-5437
Fax: 907-465-4156
eed.webmaster@alaska.gov
www.education.alaska.gov/esea/titlex-c
Ensures that all homeless children and youth have equal access to the same free, appropriate public education.

Sheila Box, Youth Program Manager

450 **Alaska Library Association (AkLA)**
PO Box 81084
Fairbanks, AK 99708
907-543-4571
pfadasiak@alaska.edu
www.akla.org
Provides leadership and advocacy for the educational and political concerns of the library community in Alaska. The association encourages cooperation among libraries and related groups, safeguards intellectual freedom, and promotes access to information for all Alaskans.

Deborah Rinio, President
Paul Adasiak, Secretary

451 **Alaska Native Knowledge Network (ANKN)**
University of Alaska Fairbanks
PO Box 756730
Fairbanks, AK 99775-6730
907-474-1902
Fax: 907-474-1957
www.ankn.uaf.edu
Assists Native people, government agencies, educators and the public by compiling and exchanging information related to Alaska Native knowledge systems and ways of knowing.

452 **Anchorage Education Association (AEA)**
4100 Spenard Road
Anchorage, AK 99517
president@anchorageea.net
www.anchorageea.org
Supports and represents teachers in Anchorage.

Tom Klaameyer, President
Marnie Hartill, Vice President, Programs

Arizona

453 **Arizona Commission for Postsecondary Education**
2020 N Central Avenue
Suite 650
Phoenix, AZ 85004
602-258-2435
Fax: 602-258-2483
acpe@azhighered.gov
www.highered.az.gov

Provides information on the state's education programs, colleges and universities, financial aid assistance programs, continuing education programs and career opportunities.

April L Osborn, Ph.D, Executive Director
Cathy Guthrie, Business Manager

454 Arizona Commission on the Arts
417 W Roosevelt Street
Phoenix, AZ 85003-1326
602-771-6501
Fax: 602-256-0282
info@azarts.gov
www.azarts.gov
Promotes high-quality education in the arts by offering grants and development programs as well as publications to cultivate arts communities and make arts activities accessible.

Jaime Dempsey, Executive Director
Kim McCreary, Fiscal Office Manager

455 Arizona Library Association (AzLA)
1645 W Valencia Road
Suite 109-432
Tuscon, AZ 85746
602-614-2841
admin@azla.org
www.azla.org
Promotes library service and librarianship in the state of Arizona. The accociation provides continuing education to school librarians, advocacy, job listings, awards and more.

Founded: 1926

Corey Christians, President
Amber Kent, Secretary

456 Arizona School Boards Association (ASBA)
2100 N Central Avenue
Suite 200
Phoenix, AZ 85004
602-254-1100
800-238-4701
asba-information@azsba.org
www.azsba.org
Nonprofit organization providing training, legislative advocacy, leadership and other services to public schools in Arizona.

Timothy L Ogle, Ph.D, Executive Director
Tracey Benson, Associate Executive Director

457 Arizona State Library, Archives and Public Records
State Librarian & Library Services Director
1700 W Washington Street
7th Floor
Phoenix, AZ 85007
602-542-6200
www.azlibrary.gov
Offers archives and records management, books in accessible formats for those with visual disabilities, research materials, publications and a digital library and museum containing public records.

Holly Henley, State Librarian
Ted Hale, Director, Archives & Records

458 Arizona State Office of Homeless Education
1535 W Jefferson Street
Bin 31
Phoenix, AZ 85007
602-542-4963
800-352-4558
Fax: 602-542-5175
homeless@azed.gov
Ensures that all homeless children and youth have equal access to the same free, appropriate public education. The office offers programs and training for those interested in the cause.

Alexis Clermont, State Homeless Coordinator

Arkansas

459 Arkansas Arts Council
1100 N Street
Little Rock, AR 72201
501-324-9150
Fax: 501-324-9207
info@arkansasarts.com
www.arkansasarts.org
Advances the arts in Arkansas by providing services and funding for arts programs (literary, performing or visual).

Founded: 1966

Patrick Ralston, Director
Jess Anthony, Grant Programs Manager

460 Arkansas Business Education Association (ABEA)
AR
ahutson2110@gmail.com
www.abea.us
A professional association comprised of secondary and post secondary business and marketing educators, with the mission of developing quality education in the business field.

Founded: 1954

Carole Anderson, President
Angie Hutson, Executive Director

461 Arkansas Department of Higher Education (ADHE)
423 Main Street
Suite 400
Little Rock, AR 72201
501-371-2000
communications@adhe.edu
www.adhe.edu
Provides information on the state's education programs, colleges and universities, financial aid and grants.

Maria Markham, Ph.D, Director
Nick Fuller, Deputy Director

462 Arkansas Education Association (AEA)
1500 W 4th Street
Little Rock, AR 72201
501-375-4611
800-632-0624
Fax: 501-375-4620
www.aeaonline.org
Advocates for education professionals and unites members and the state to ensure that public education prepares students to succeed in a diverse world.

Tracey-Ann Nelson, Executive Director
Charles Evans, Associate Executive Director

463 Arkansas Library Association (ArLA)
National Park College
101 College Drive
Hot Springs, AR 71913
501-313-1398
info@arlib.org
www.arlib.org
Furthers the professional development of library staff members, fosters communication and cooperation among librarians and trustees, increases library visibility and serves as an advocate for librarians and libraries.

Founded: 1911

Crystal Gates, President
Lynn Valetutti, Treasurer

464 Arkansas State Education for Homeless Children and Youth
4 Capitol Mall
Mail Slot 26
Little Rock, AR 72201
501-683-5428
Fax: 501-682-5136
www.dese.ade.arkansas.gov/divisions
Provides programs to ensure that all homeless children and youth have equal access to free public education.

Dana Davis, Program Advisor

California

465 Association for Environmental and Outdoor Education (AEOE)
2066 N Capitol Avenue
Suite 3028
San Jose, CA 95132
510-214-6406
info@aeoe.org
www.aeoe.org
The Association for Environmental and Outdoor Education is a nonprofit organization whose mission is to advance the impact of environmental and outdoor education in California. AEOE serves as the primary professional organization for environmental and outdoor education in California, providing programs and practitioners with tools, resources, and expertise through annual regional and statewide conferences, as well as an active online community.

Founded: 1954

Reed Schneider, President & Chair
Estrella Risinger, Executive Director

466 California Arts Council
1300 I Street
Suite 930
Sacramento, CA 95814
916-322-6555
800-201-6201
Fax: 916-322-6575
info@arts.ca.gov
www.cac.ca.gov
Promotes education in the arts through funding, programs, internships, research, policy development, workshops and more.

Anne Bown-Crawford, Executive Director
Ayanna L Kiburi, M.P.H., Deputy Director

467 California Association for Bilingual Education (CABE)
20888 Amar Road
Walnut, CA 91789-5054
626-814-4441
Fax: 626-814-4640
info@gocabe.org
www.gocabe.org
Nonprofit organization dedicated to supporting bilingual education for students in California by offering services to teachers, administrators, parents and others.

Founded: 1976

Jan Gustafson Corea, Chief Executive Officer
Cynthia Vasquez Petitt, Deputy Director

8 **California Business Education Association (CBEA)**
PO Box 588
Ridgecrest, CA 93556
760-608-3983
cbeaquestions@cbeaonline.org
www.cbeaonline.org
The mission of the California Business Education Association is to recognize and promote excellence in business disciplines.

Joseph Gaestel, President
Frank Timpone, Treasurer

9 **California Classical Association-Northern Section**
Convent and Stuart Hall
1715 Octavia Street
San Francisco, CA 94109
ccanorth@gmail.com
www.ccanorth.org
Funds support programs to enrich and promote Classical Studies.

Founded: 1969

Gillian McIntosh, President
David Jacobson, Treasurer

0 **California Foundation for Agriculture in the Classroom**
2300 River Plaza Drive
Suite 220
Sacramento, CA 95833-3293
916-561-5625
800-700-2482
Fax: 916-561-5697
info@learnaboutag.org
www.learnaboutag.org
The foundation's mission is to educate California's youth about the value of agriculture in their daily lives. The foundation offers programs, teaching resources, grants and professional training for educators.

Judy Culbertson, Executive Director
Liz Baskins, Outreach Program Coordinator

71 **California Kindergarten Association**
1014 Chippendale Way
Roseville, CA 95661
916-780-5331
Fax: 916-780-5330
cka@ckanet.org
www.ckanet.org
Promotes best practices and professionalism in teaching, in order to foster children's early learning and development.

Gennie Gorback, President
Cristiana Tibbats, Administrative Manager

72 **California Library Association (CLA)**
1055 E Colorado Boulevard
5th Floor
Pasadena, CA 91106
626-204-4071
info@cla-net.org
www.cla-net.org
Provides supports and development services for libraries, librarianship and the library community. The association also offers resources for learning about new ideas and technology.

Beth Wrenn-Estes, Business Manager
Lauren Takeda, Special Projects Coordinator

73 **California Reading Association**
638 Camino De Los Mares
Suite H130/476
San Clemente, CA 92673
949-547-6664
Fax: 949-481-8163
www.californiareading.org
An independent, self-governing organization dedicated to increasing literacy in California. Members include educators working in the fields of language arts education in all levels of the school system. The association offers advocacy, policy information, assessment standards and more.

Jody Anderson, President
Kathy Belanger, Administrative Director

474 **California School Library Association (CSLA)**
6444 E Spring Street
Suite 237
Long Beach, CA 90815-1553
888-655-8480
Fax: 888-655-8480
info@csla.net
www.csla.net
Organization made up of librarians, teachers, paraprofessionals, coordinators of curriculum and others involved in the education system. The organization offers advocacy, publications, events and resources to support the education of all California students.

Katie McNamara, President
Kathie Maier, Administrative Assistant

475 **California State Homeless Education**
1430 N Street
Sacramento, CA 95814-5901
916-319-0800
866-856-8214
homelessED@cde.ca.gov
www.cde.ca.gov/sp/hs
The program offers information and resources to ensure that all homeless children and youth have equal access to free, appropriate public education.

Leanne Wheeler, Consultant
Kathy Dobson, Executive Office

476 **California Student Aid Commission**
PO Box 419026
Rancho Cordova, CA 95741-9026
888-224-7268
Fax: 916-464-8002
studentsupport@csac.ca.gov
www.csac.ca.gov
Provides information on the state's education programs, colleges and universities, financial aid assistance programs, continuing education and career opportunities.

Marlene L Garcia, Executive Director
Virginia Jo Dunlap, Chief Deputy Director

477 **California Teachers Association (CTA)**
1705 Murchison Drive
Burlingame, CA 94010
650-697-1400
Fax: 650-552-5002
membership@cta.org
www.cta.org
Protects and promotes the well-being of California teachers by improving the conditions of teaching and learning and advancing the cause of universal education. The association offers professional development opportunities, resources for parents, publications, legal services and more.

E Toby Boyd, President
Gail Gregorio, Interim Executive Director

478 **Federal Reserve Bank of San Francisco Education Advisory Group**
101 Market Street
San Francisco, CA 94105
415-974-2000
800-227-4133
publicweb.sf@sf.frb.org
www.frbsf.org
The Education Advisory Group is made up of 20 high school and community college educators from around the 12th District. The group works with the SF Fed's Education & Outreach Department to review ideas, teaching activities, FRBSF education resources, the use of technology and the subject of Federal Reserve and the U.S. economy.

Mary C Daly, President & CEO
Deborah M Awai, SVP & Sr. Outreach Officer

479 **Northern California WestEd**
730 Harrison Street
San Francisco, CA 94107
415-565-3000
877-493-7833
Fax: 415-565-3012
www.wested.org
WestEd's Assessment and Standards Development Services program has helped shape effective assessment and accountability systems nationwide. WestEd is a nonprofit research, development, and service agency working with education and other communities to promote excellence and equity in education for all students - regardless of their circumstances.

Founded: 1995

Glen H Harvey, Chief Executive Officer
Matthew Nathan, Senior Director, Development

Colorado

480 **Colorado Association of Libraries (CAL)**
PO Box 740905
Arvada, CO 80006-0905
303-463-6400
cal@cal-webs.org
www.cal-webs.org
The Colorado Association of Libraries (CAL) advocates for quality library services, supports access to information and fosters the professional development of its members.

Ryan F Buller, President
Anne Holland, Secretary

481 **Colorado Business Educators (CBE)**
CO
dmsierra@dcsdk12.org
www.cbeducators.webs.com
Supports business educators in Colorado with curriculum material and career networking.

Bradley Hughes, President
Dennis Sierra, Program Coordinator

482 **Colorado Community College System (CCCS)**
9101 E Lowry Boulevard
Denver, CO 80230-6011
303-620-4000
sarah.kane@cccs.edu
www.cccs.edu
The Colorado Community College System (CCCS) comprises the state's largest system of higher education. CCCS provides accessible, responsive learning environments that facilitate the achievement of educational, professional and personal goals.

Bryon McClenney, Ph.D, President
Joe Garcia, Chancellor

483 **Colorado Creative Industries (CCI)**
1600 Broadway
Suite 2500
Denver, CO 80202
303-892-3840
Fax: 303-892-3848
oedit_creativeindustries@state.co.us
www.coloradocreativeindustries.org
Organization whose mission is to promote creative industries in Colorado to develop the economy, create jobs and enhance quality of life. Services offered by them include arts programs, arts spaces, education and grants.

Tim Schultz, Chair
Margaret Hunt, Executive Director

484 **Colorado Department of Higher Education (CCHE)**
1600 Broadway
Suite 2200
Denver, CO 80202
303-862-3001
Fax: 303-996-1329
departmentofhighereducation@dhe.state.co.us
www.highered.colorado.gov
Provides information on the state's education programs, colleges and universities, financial aid assistance programs, grants, continuing education programs and career opportunities.

Angie Paccione, Ph.D, Executive Director
Inta Morris, Chief Operating Officer

485 **Colorado Education Association (CEA)**
1500 Grant Street
Denver, CO 80203
303-837-1500
800-332-5939
www.coloradoea.org
The Colorado Education Association is a voluntary membership organization of K-12 teachers and education support professionals, retired educators and students interested in the field of teaching. The association provides advocacy, public education and networking.

Founded: 1875

Amie Baca-Ohlert, President
Kathy Rendon, Executive Director

486 **Colorado State Education for Homeless Children and Youth**
Colorado Department of Education
201 E Colfax Avenue
Denver, CO 80203
303-866-6600
Fax: 303-830-0793
wrenick_k@cde.state.co.us
www.cde.state.co.us/dropoutprevention/homeless_index
Ensures that all homeless children and youth have equal access to free, appropriate public education.

Kerry Wrenick, State Coordinator

Connecticut

487 **Connecticut Business & Industry Association (CBIA)**
350 Church Street
Hartford, CT 06103
860-244-1900
www.cbia.com
Serves as an advocate for the general business and industry community in Connecticut. The association promotes a business climate that is globally competitive and encourages communication and cooperation among businesses.

Chris DiPentima, Chair
Jennifer Morgan DelMonico, Vice Chair

488 **Connecticut Culture and Tourism Advisory Committee**
c/o Office of the Arts
450 Columbus Boulevard
Suite 5
Hartford, CT 06103
860-500-2360
Elizabeth.Shapiro@ct.gov
www.portal.ct.gov/DECD
Provides advice to the the Department of Economic and Community Development's offices of Arts, Tourism and Preservation on artistic and cultural matters.

W Michael P Price, Chair
Elizabeth Shapiro, Director, Arts

489 **Connecticut Education Association (CEA)**
Capitol Place
21 Oak Street
Hartford, CT 06106
860-525-5641
800-842-4316
Fax: 860-725-6323
info@cea.org
www.cea.org
The Connecticut Education Association advocates for teachers and public education by lobbying legislators for the resources public schools need and campaigning for high system standards.

Donald E Williams, Jr, Executive Director
Ray Rossomando, Director, Policy & Research

490 **Connecticut Office of Higher Education**
450 Columbus Boulevard
Suite 707
Hartford, CT 06103-1841
860-947-1800
Fax: 860-947-1310
HDao@ctohe.org
www.ctohe.org
Provides information on the state's education programs, colleges and universities, financial aid assistance programs, grants, continuing education programs and career opportunities. The office also offers advocacy for students, taxpayers and postsecondary schools.

Timothy D Larson, Executive Director
Mark French, Director, Financial Aid

491 **Connecticut State Education for Homeless Children and Youth**
450 Columbus Boulevard
Hartford, CT 06103-1841
860-807-2058
Fax: 860-807-2127
louis.tallarita@ct.gov
www.portal.ct.gov/SDE/Homeless/Homeless-Education
Ensures that all homeless children and youth have equal access to free, appropriate public education.

Louis Tallarita, Contact

Delaware

492 **Delaware Division of Libraries**
121 Martin Luther King Jr. Blvd N
Dover, DE 19901
302-739-4748
800-282-8696
Fax: 302-739-6787
mary.e.bradley@state.de.us
www.libraries.delaware.gov
Provides leadership and support for the development of Delaware's libraries by ensuring accessibility to library resources for all.

Annie Norman, Ph.D, Director
Beth-Ann Ryan, Deputy Director

493 **Delaware Division of the Arts**
820 N French Street
4th Floor
Wilmington, DE 19801
302-577-8278
Fax: 302-577-6561
delarts@state.de.us
www.arts.delaware.gov
Works to cultivate and support the arts in Delaware by offering grants, programs, education and access to arts for all citizens.

Paul Weagraff, Director

494 **Delaware Higher Education Office**
The Townsend Building
401 Federal Street
Suite 2
Dover, DE 19901
302-735-4120
800-292-7935
Fax: 302-739-5894
dheo@doe.k12.de.us
www.doe.k12.de.us/domain/226
Provides information and financial assistance to students and their families to make postsecondary education more accessible.

Adrian Peoples, Education Associate

495 **Delaware Library Association (DLA)**
121 Martin Luther King Jr. Blvd. N
Dover, DE 19901
302-257-3014
dla@lib.de.us
www.dla.lib.de.us
Promotes the profession of librarianship and provides library information and media services to the people of Delaware through a unified library community.

Alison Wessel, President
Marlowe Bogino, Secretary

496 **Delaware State Education Association (DSEA)**
DSEA
136 E Water Street
Dover, DE 19901
866-734-5834
Fax: 302-674-8499
execdirector@dsea.org
www.dsea.org
The Delaware State Education Association is a union of public school employees that advocates for the rights and interests of its members and outstanding public education for all students.

Founded: 1919

Jeff Taschner, Executive Director
Patricia McGonigle, Assistant Executive Director

7 **Delaware State Local Homeless Education for Children and Youth**
Collette Education Resource Center
35 Commerce Way
Suite 1
Dover, DE 19904
302-735-4000
Fax: 302-739-3092
dedoe@doe.k12.de.us
www.doe.k12.de.us/domain/362
Ensures that all homeless children and youth have equal access to public education by monitoring school enrollment, attendance and the identification of homeless youth.

John H Hulse, State Coordinator

District of Columbia

8 **Associates for Renewal in Education (ARE)**
Brenda Strong Nixon Community Complex
45 P Street NW
Washington, DC 20001
202-483-9424
Fax: 202-667-5299
info@areinc.org
www.areinc.org
A multi-project agency working to improve the quality of life and education of the young people of the District of Columbia, with an emphasis on at risk youth and under-served populations. The organization offers intervention, education and employment skills training towards this purpose.

Founded: 1971

Iris Bond-Gill, Chair
Dayna Nokes-Minor, President & CEO

9 **District of Columbia Commission on the Arts and Humanities (CAH)**
200 I Street SE
Washington, DC 20003
202-724-5613
Fax: 202-727-4135
cah@dc.gov
www.dcarts.dc.gov
Provides grants, professional opportunities, education and relevant programming to individuals involved in the arts so they may learn and contribute to the culture with their works.

Terrie Rouse-Rosario, Executive Director
Kennisha Rainge, Chief of Staff

0 **District of Columbia Library Association (DCLA)**
50 Massachusetts Avenue SE
PO Box 1653
Washington, DC 20002
202-872-1112
dclamembers@gmail.com
www.dcla.org
Provides library services to the residents of D.C. and represents the region at the Council of the American Library Association. The District of Columbia Library Association offers networking events, advocacy, job support and library resources.

Tracy Sumler, President
Lisa Massengale, Membership Director

01 **District of Columbia Office of the State Superintendent of Education (OSSE)**
1050 First Street NE
Washington, DC 20002
202-727-6436
osse@dc.gov
www.osse.dc.gov
The mission of the agency is to foster excellence in education for the residents of DC by offering programs and services to develop standards and increase accessibility.

Hanseul Kang, State Superintendent
Shana Young, Chief of Staff

Florida

502 **Florida Association for Media in Education (FAME)**
PO Box 941169
Maitland, FL 32794-1169
863-585-6802
FAME@floridamediaed.org
www.floridamediaed.org
Association advocating for student access to library media programs as well as offering services to school librarians. Services include professional development programs, resources and the promotion of technology-integration initiatives.

Lorraine Stinson, President
Amelia Zukoski, Treasurer

503 **Florida Business Technology Education Association**
561-310-0515
sslarsen@bellsouth.net
www.fbtea.org
Fosters business education in the state of Florida by offering professional development services, leadership and education.

MeMe Hall, President
Susan Larsen, Treasurer

504 **Florida Division of Cultural Affairs**
329 N Meridian Street
Tallahassee, FL 32301
850-245-6470
Fax: 850-245-6454
www.dos.myflorida.com/cultural
The state agency of Florida committed to promoting the arts by offering programming, exhibitions, jobs and resources.

Founded: 1977

Sandy Shaughnessy, Division Director
Gaylen Phillips, Arts Administrator

505 **Florida Education Association (FEA)**
213 S Adams Street
Tallahassee, FL 32301
888-807-8007
Fax: 850-201-2800
Tammy.Manning@floridaea.org
www.feaweb.org
Advocates for the right to a free, quality public education for all. The association advances the professional growth, development and status of all who serve the students in Florida's public schools, by offering them advocacy, legal services and training opportunities.

Fedrick Ingram, President
Andrew Spar, Vice President

506 **Florida Library Association (FLA)**
541 E Tennessee Street
Suite 103
Tallahassee, FL 32308
850-270-9205
admin@flalib.org
www.flalib.org
The Florida Library Association develops programs and undertakes activities to stregnthen libraries and the field of librarianship. FLA provides opportunities for librarians and support staff in Florida to advance their skills so that they can continue to be effective in the new information age.

Lisa O'Donnell, CAE, Executive Director
Karen Layton, Membership & Events Manager

507 **Florida State Office of Student Financial Assistance (OSFA)**
1940 N Monroe Street
Suite 70
Tallahassee, FL 32303-4759
850-410-5200
800-366-3475
OSFAStudentLoans@fldoe.org
www.floridastudentfinancialaid.org
Serves as a guarantor for the Federal Family Education Loan Program and the administrator of Florida's scholarship and grant programs. The office aims to make higher education more accessible and provides financial aid information to parents and students.

Levis Hughes, Bureau Chief
Brian Underhill, State Scholarships & Grants

Georgia

508 **Georgia Association of Educators (GAE)**
100 Crescent Center Parkway
Suite 500
Tucker, GA 30084
678-837-1100
chris.baumann@gae.org
www.pv.gae2.org
The Georgia Association of Educators is a professional organization serving public education professionals, through legal supports, programs and resources.

Tyra Ann Holt, Finance Director
Karen Henderson, Executive Assistant

509 **Georgia Business Education Association (GBEA)**
alex.collins@screven.k12.ga.us
www.gbea-online.org
Serves individuals and groups involved in instruction, administration, research and dissemination of information related to business. Teachers are given the opportunity to network with others working in the field and to develop their professional skills through conferences.

Vershondra Glover, President
Alex Collins, Vice President

510 **Georgia Council for the Arts (GCA)**
Techonology Square
75 Fifth Street NW
Suite 1200
Atlanta, GA 30308
404-962-4078
Fax: 404-685-2788
EMurray@georgia.org
www.gaarts.org
Supports the arts in Georgia by providing grants, programs and education services to artists.

Karen L Paty, Executive Director
Tina Lilly, Director, Grants Program

511 **Georgia Library Association (GLA)**
PO Box 30324
Savannah, GA 31410
912-376-9155
membership.gla@gmail.com
www.gla.georgialibraries.org

Provides support and encouragement for libraries to advance the educational, cultural and economic life of the state.

Laura Burtle, President
Ben Bryson, Treasurer

512 Georgia Parent Teacher Association
114 Baker Street NE
Atlanta, GA 30308-3366
404-659-0214
800-782-8632
gapta@bellsouth.net
www.georgiapta.org
An organization representing the needs of children, families and communities by advocating for the education, engagement and empowerment of every child in the state of Georgia.

Dawn Stastny, President
Diane Jacobi, Secretary

513 Georgia Public Library Service
2872 Woodcock Boulevard
Suite 250
Atlanta, GA 30341
404-235-7200
dhakes@georgialibraries.org
www.georgialibraries.org
Provides support services to develop the libraries of Georgia, which includes offering leadership support, resources, technology services, publications, advocacy and more.

Julie Walker, State Librarian
Wendy Cornelisen, Assistant State Librarian

514 Georgia State Education for Homeless Children and Youth
Georgia Department of Education
205 Jesse Hill Jr Drive SE
Atlanta, GA 30334
404-651-7555
Fax: 404-344-4526
emcghee@doe.k12.ga.us
www.gadoe.org
Ensures that all homeless children and youth have equal access to appropriate public education. This mission is promoted through the McKinney-Vento Education for Homeless Children and Youth program, which identifies the challenges unique to the experience of homeless youth and recommends solutions.

Eric McGhee, Grants Program Manager
Erica Glenn, Program Consultant

515 Georgia Student Finance Commission (GSFC)
2082 E Exchange Place
Tucker, GA 30084
770-724-9003
800-505-4732
Fax: 770-724-9089
www.gsfc.georgia.gov
Provides information on the state's student financial aid assistance programs, grants and scholarships to students and their families to help in the process of school enrollment.

Founded: 1965

Caylee Noggle, President

Hawaii

516 Hawaii Business Education Association (HBEA)
Leeward Community College
96-045 Ala Ike Street
Pearl City, HI 96782-3393
www.hbea.org
The Hawaii Business Education Association is devoted exclusively to serving individuals and groups teaching in the fields of business and information technology. The association provides conferences and other professional improvement opportunities to its members.

Evelyn Wong, Treasurer

517 Hawaii Education Association (HEA)
1953 S Beretania Street
Suite 5C
Honolulu, HI 96826
808-949-6657
866-653-9372
Fax: 808-944-2032
hea.office@hawaiieducationassociation.org
www.hawaiieducationassociation.org
Strengthens and supports quality education for all through the enrichment and development of future, current and retired educators. The association offers a variety of scholarships to educators and student teachers alongside other member benefits.

Founded: 1921

June Motokawa, President
Joan Husted, Vice President

518 Hawaii Library Association
PO Box 4441
Honolulu, HI 96812-4441
hawaii.library.association@gmail.com
www.hawaiilibraryassociation.weebly.com
Promotes library service and librarianship in Hawaii through programs, resources and education.

Michael Aldrich, President
Jessica Hogan, Secretary

519 Hawaii State Education for Homeless Children and Youth
Hawai'i State Department of Education
1390 Miller Street
Honolulu, HI 96813
808-305-9869
866-927-7095
doe_info@hawaiidoe.org
www.hawaiipublicschools.org
Ensures that children experiencing homelessness have access to public education.

Christina M Kishimoto, Superintendent
Heidi Armstrong, Asst. Supt., Student Support

520 Hawaii State Foundation on Culture and the Arts (SFCA)
250 S Hotel Street
2nd Floor
Honolulu, HI 96813
808-586-0300
hawaiisfca@hawaii.gov
www.sfca.hawaii.gov
Promotes the development of culture and the arts in Hawaii through grants, programs, education and more.

Jonathan Johnson, Executive Director
Margaret Lui, Secretary

521 Hawaii State Teachers Association (HSTA)
1200 Ala Kapuna Street
Honolulu, HI 96819
808-833-2711
Fax: 808-839-7106
kkerr@hsta.org
www.hsta.org
Supports the professional roles of teachers, advocates for teachers' interests, and assures quality education for Hawaii's youth.

Corey Rosenlee, President
Wilbert Holck, Executive Director

Idaho

522 Idaho Commission for Libraries (ICFL)
325 W State Street
Boise, ID 83702
208-334-2150
800-458-3271
Fax: 208-334-4016
jeannie.standal@libraries.idaho.gov
www.libraries.idaho.gov
The mission of the Idaho Commission for Libraries is to develop libraries in Idaho through funding, programs, policy guidance and events.

Ann Joslin, State Librarian
Stephanie Bailey-White, Deputy State Librarian

523 Idaho Commission on the Arts
2410 Old Penitentiary Road
Boise, ID 83712
208-334-2119
800-278-3863
info@arts.idaho.gov
www.arts.idaho.gov
Promotes the arts in Idaho by providing arts education, guidelines for teachers of art, programs and advocacy.

Michael Faison, Executive Director
Stuart Weiser, Deputy Director

524 Idaho Education Association (IEA)
620 N 6th Street
PO Box 2638
Boise, ID 83701
208-344-1341
800-727-9922
Fax: 208-336-6967
iea-mbc@idahoea.org
www.idahoea.org
Advocates for the professional and personal well-being of its members and the vision of excellence in public education. Members consist of education professionals and students.

Kari Overall, President
Paul Humbleton, Interim Executive Director

525 Idaho Library Association (ILA)
4911 N Shirley Avenue
Boise, ID 83703
208-334-2150
Fax: 208-334-4016
www.idaholibraries.org
Supports the library community in Idaho and encourages both students and professionals to engage with the services that libraries offer.

Founded: 1969

Katherine Lovan, Co-President
LeAnn Gelskey, Co-President

526 Idaho State Homeless Children and Youths Title IX-A
650 W State Street
Boise, ID 83702
208-332-6904
800-432-4601
Fax: 208-334-2228

speck@sde.idaho.gov
www.sde.idaho.gov/federal-programs/home less
Ensures that all homeless children and youth have access to public education, transportation and services.

Susan Peck, Coordinator
Karen Seay, Director, Federal Programs

Illinois

7 Association of Illinois School Library Educators (AISLE)
PO Box 1326
Galesburg, IL 61402-1326
309-341-1099
Fax: 309-341-2070
execsecretary@islma.org
www.aisled.org
Formerly the Illinois School Library Media Association, the organization promotes student interaction and continuing education of school library media specialists, as well as collaboration among parents, community members, teachers and administrators as they prepare students for life-long learning.

Founded: 1988

Becky Robinson, Executive Secretary
Caroline Campbell, Financial Secretary

8 Illinois Arts Council Agency
James R. Thompson Center
100 W Randolph Street
Suite 10-500
Chicago, IL 60601
312-814-6750
800-237-6994
iac.info@illinois.gov
www.arts.illinois.gov
Responsible for developing the state's public arts policy, creating culturally diverse programs and approving grants to support the arts sector and arts education.

Founded: 1965

Joshua Davis, Executive Director
Yazoo Hall, Chief of Operations

29 Illinois Association of Private Special Education Centers (IAPSEC)
IL
ssover@coveschool.org
www.iapsec.org
A nonprofit organization consisting of private schools serving Illinois children with exceptional needs and working to maintain the quality of special education through the setting of high standards of care.

Sally Sover, President
Karoline Dean, Secretary

30 Illinois Association of School Administrators (IASA)
2648 Beechler Court
Springfield, IL 62703-7305
217-753-2213
Fax: 217-753-2240
jgillespie@iasaedu.org
www.iasaedu.org
The state's advocacy organization for school administrators. The association supports excellence in education by offering its memembers professional development opportunities, leadership summits, member benefits, programs and more.

Founded: 1946

Brent Clark, Ph.D, Executive Director
Richard J Voltz, Ph.D, Assoc. Dir., Prof. Dev.

531 Illinois Association of School Business Officials (Illinois ASBO)
Northern Illinois University
108 Carroll Avenue
DeKalb, IL 60115
815-753-1276
Fax: 815-516-0184
jwarner@iasbo.org
www.iasbo.org
Provides its members a range of professional development activities and services in relation to the school business management profession.

Michael A Jacoby, Ed.D., SFO, CAE, Executive Director & CEO
Susan P Bertrand, MBA, CAE, Deputy Director & COO

532 Illinois Business Education Association (IBEA)
3610 Hennepin Drive
Joliet, IL 60431
815-483-4056
www.ibea.org
Association supporting the profession of business education by offering conferences, information, scholarships and reports.

Gary Hutchinson, Executive Director

533 Illinois Citizen Corps
2200 S Dirksen Parkway
Springfield, IL 62703
217-558-1334
Fax: 217-558-1335
www.illinois.gov
Works to strenthen citizens through education, training, and volunteer services with the aim of making communities safer and stronger. The Illinois Citizen Corps offers training for disaster relief response and other emergency situations that threaten the well-being of communities.

Michelle Hanneken, Program Manager

534 Illinois Education Association (IEA)
100 E Edwards Street
Springfield, IL 62704
217-544-0706
844-432-1800
ieaconnect@ieanea.org
www.ieanea.org
An association of teachers, higher education faculty and staff, educational support professionals, retired educators and students preparing to enter the teaching field. Services offered to members include professional development options, legal assistance, grants, advocacy and a host of member benefits.

Founded: 1853

Kathi Griffin, President
Al Llorens, Vice President

535 Illinois Homeless Education Program
100 N 1st Street
Springfield, IL 62777-0001
217-782-5270
www.isbe.net/Pages/Homeless.aspx
The purpose of the program is to ensures that all homeless children and youth have equal access to public education.

Vicki Hodges, Program Contact

536 Illinois Library Association (ILA)
33 W Grand Avenue
Suite 401
Chicago, IL 60654-6799
312-644-1896
Fax: 312-644-1899
ila@ila.org
www.ila.org
The association provides leadership for the development, promotion and improvement of library services in Illinois and for the library community in order to enhance learning and ensure access to information for all. Services offerred by the association include conferences, publications, legislative advocacy and a reading program.

Founded: 1896

Diane Foote, Executive Director
Cynthia M Robinson, Deputy Director

537 Illinois Student Assistance Commission (ISAC)
1755 Lake Cook Road
Deerfield, IL 60015-5209
800-899-4722
Fax: 847-831-8549
isac.studentservices@isac.illinois.gov
www.isac.org
Provides information on the state's education programs, with an emphasis on student financial aid assistance.

Founded: 1957

Eric Zarnikow, Executive Director
Carol Cook, Managing Dir., Programs

Indiana

538 Indiana Arts Commission (IAC)
100 N Senate Avenue
Room N505
Indianapolis, IN 46204
317-232-1268
800-743-3333
Fax: 317-232-5595
lricci@iac.in.gov
www.in.gov/arts
Provides leadership, advocacy, programs and public stewardship of artistic resources for citizens of Indiana. The commission's long term goal is to shape the cultural, economic and educational climate of Indiana for the better.

Lewis C Ricci, Executive Director
Miah Michaelsen, Deputy Director

539 Indiana Association of School Business Officials (IASBO)
1 N Capitol Avenue
Suite 1215
Indianapolis, IN 46204-2095
317-639-3586
dcosterison@indiana-asbo.org
www.indiana-asbo.org
The Indiana Association of School Business Officials is a professional organization which promotes the advancement of those involved in school business affairs such as finance, accounting, purchasing, maintenance and operations, human resources, facilities and grounds, food service, technology and transportation.

Dennis L Costerison, Executive Director
Ella Adamson, Member Services Admin

540 Indiana Business Education Association (IBEA)
PO Box 3361
Carmel, IN 46082
765-484-4511
Fax: 765-489-4333
khirschy@sacs.k12.in.us
www.sites.google.com/site/indianaibea/abo ut/home
Professional association of business educators, administrators and leaders with the mission of promoting business education. The

association offers professional development opportunities, news and courses.

Brian Wolfe, President
Julie Olschalager, Membership Director

541 Indiana Commission for Higher Education
101 W Ohio Street
Suite 300
Indianapolis, IN 46204-4206
317-464-4400
Fax: 317-464-4410
tlubbers@che.in.gov
www.in.gov/che/2376.htm
The commission's mission is to plan and coordinate Indiana's system of post-high school education, review budget appropriation requests, and handle other matters related to public institutions.

Founded: 1971

Teresa Lubbers, Commissioner
Dominick Chase, Associate Commissioner & CFO

542 Indiana Library Federation (ILF)
941 E 86th Street
Suite 260
Indianapolis, IN 46240
317-257-2040
askus@ilfonline.org
www.ilfonline.org
Works to advance library services of Indiana through member services such as technical assistance, mentoring programs, networking, advocacy and professional development opportunities for those working in the field.

Lucinda Nord, Executive Director
Tisa Davis, Mananger, Communications

543 Indiana State Teachers Association (ISTA)
150 W Market Street
Suite 900
Indianapolis, IN 46204
317-263-3400
844-275-4782
Fax: 317-655-3700
askista@ista-in.org
www.ista-in.org
Provides the resources necessary to enable people to effectively advocate for public schools and the education profession. Topics covered include compensation, working conditions, professional development and student well-being.

Daniel Holub, Executive Director
Jennifer Clutter, Director, Finance

Iowa

544 Iowa Arts Council
State Historical Building
600 E Locust Street
Des Moines, IA 50319
515-281-5111
www.iowaculture.gov/arts
Responsible for encouraging creativity by giving artists opportunities for growth and development, including public spaces to share their talents.

Founded: 1967

Lindsay Keast, Program Coordinator
Liesl Voges, Community Development

545 Iowa Business Education Association (IBEA)
IA
webmaster@ibeaonline.org
www.ibeaonline.org
Works to discover and serve the needs of business educators in Iowa. The association offers research, awards, workshops, conferences and professional development programs.

Dara Knudtson, President
Sandy Warning, Executive Secretary

546 Iowa College Student Aid Commission
475 SW 5th Street
Suite D
Des Moines, IA 50309
515-725-3400
877-272-4456
Provides information on the state's student financial aid assistance programs to increase the success of youth as they engage in higher education.

Founded: 1963

Kathleen Mulholland, Ph.D, Chair
Doug Shull, Vice Chair

547 Iowa Library Association (ILA)
6919 Vista Drive
West Des Moines, IA 50266
515-282-8192
800-452-5507
agalstad@coralville.org
www.iowalibraryassociation.org
The Iowa Library Association advocates for quality library services for all Iowans and provides leadership, education and support for members.

Founded: 1890

548 Iowa State Education Association (ISEA)
777 Third Street
Des Moines, IA 50309
800-445-9358
communications@isea.org
www.isea.org
Supports educators and other school staff by offering advocacy, professional development resources and member benefits. The association's mission is to improve public school education for all.

Mary Jane Cobb, Executive Director
Drew Gosselink, Assoc. Exec. Dir., Business

549 Iowa State Education for Homeless Children and Youth
400 E 14th Street
Des Moines, IA 50319-0146
515-402-2736
Fax: 515-242-5988
carolyn.cobb@iowa.gov
www.educateiowa.gov
Seeks to ensure that all homeless children and youth have access to public education regardless of their circumstances.

Carolyn Cobb, Consultant

Kansas

550 Kansas Association of School Librarians (KASL)
KS
kasltechcommittee@gmail.com
www.ksschoollibrarians.org
An organization of school librarians in the state of Kansas that provides advocacy, education, workshops and networking for the development of library services and library media specialists.

Martha House, President
Rachel Hodges, Secretary

551 Kansas Board of Regents
1000 SW Jackson Street
Suite 520
Topeka, KS 66612-1368
785-430-4240
Fax: 785-430-4233
scholars@ksbor.org
www.kansasregents.org
Functions as the govering board of the state's universities as well as coordinating board for public higher education institutions in Kansas. The board administers student financial aid, adult education and other education programs.

Founded: 1925

Blake Flanders, President & CEO
Daniel Archer, VP, Academic Affairs

552 Kansas Business Education Association (KBEA)
KS
michael.moseley@usd262.net
www.ksbea.org
Fosters business education in the state of Kansas by offering professional development programs and information to help business teachers increase their skills.

Barbara Railsback, President
Michael Moseley, Secretary

553 Kansas Creative Arts Industries Commission (CAIC)
Kansas Department of Commerce
1000 SW Jackson Street
Suite 100
Topeka, KS 66612-1354
785-296-2178
Fax: 785-296-4989
peter.jasso@ks.gov
www.kansascommerce.gov/about-us/commissions-partners
Supports the creative industries sector in Kansas by offering funding, grants, arts education and integration programs.

Peter Jasso, Director

554 Kansas Library Association (KLA)
Northwest Kansas Library System
2 Washington Sqare
Norton, KS 67654
785-877-5148
kansaslibraryassociation@yahoo.com
www.kslibassoc.org
Offers professional development opportunities for the library community of Kansas as well as information materials covering the issues that affect libraries, including policies and bylaws.

Laurel Little, President
Bethanie O'Dell, Secretary

555 Kansas National Education Association (KNEA)
715 SW 10th Avenue
Topeka, KS 66612-1686
785-232-8271
Fax: 785-232-6012
KNEAnews@knea.org
www.knea.org
Association of educators, school administrators and those studying to get into the teaching field. The association offers programs and services to promote public schools and the teaching profession, while developing its members professionally.

Founded: 1863

Mark Farr, President
Kevin Riemann, Executive Director

6 Kansas State Educating Homeless Children and Youth

Kansas State Department of Education
900 SW Jackson Street
Topeka, KS 66612
785-296-6714
mruhlman@ksde.org
www.ksde.org
Offers assistance to districts so they could better serve their homeless youth and children by ensuring equal access to public education without barriers. Areas covered include law, policy, dispute resolution and data on homelessness.

Maureen Ruhlman, Education Program Consultant

7 Mountain-Plains Business Education Association (M-PBEA)

lrhenneberg@gmail.com
www.mpbea.org
The Mountain-Plains Business Education Association is an affiliate of the National Business Education Association (NBEA), a professional organization serving individuals and groups engaged in instruction, administration, research, and dissemination of information related to business. Some services offered by them include professional publications, business conventions, networking opportunities and advocacy.

Matt Maw, President
Lori Henneberg, Executive Secretary

Kentucky

58 Kentucky Arts Council (KAC)

1025 Capital Center Drive
3rd Floor
Frankfort, KY 40601
502-564-3757
888-833-2787
Fax: 502-564-2839
Christopher.Cathers@ky.gov
www.artscouncil.ky.gov
The Kentucky Arts Council is the state government agency responsible for developing and promoting the arts in Kentucky. The agency creates opportunities for people to find value in the arts, participate in the arts and benefit from the arts through programs, grants and services.

Chris Cathers, Executive Director
Samuel Lockridge, Director, Arts Education

59 Kentucky Department for Libraries and Archives (KDLA)

300 Coffee Tree Road
Frankfort, KY 40601
502-564-8300
renita.van@ky.gov
www.kdla.ky.gov
A collection of library resources, including government records, research materials, historical records and more. The department also offers information for libraries (programs, policies, funding and development).

Stacey Whitehouse, Executive Secretary
Renita Van, Administrative Specialist

60 Kentucky Education for Homeless Children and Youth

Kentucky Department of Education
300 Sower Boulevard
5th Floor
Frankfort, KY 40601
502-564-3791
Fax: 502-564-8149
melissa.ferrell@education.ky.gov
www.education.ky.gov/federal/progs/txc
Initiative to ensure that all homeless youth and children of Kentucky have access to public education.

Melissa Farrell, Contact

561 Kentucky Higher Education Assistance Authority (KHEAA)

PO Box 798
Frankfort, KY 40602-0798
502-696-7200
800-928-8926
Fax: 502-696-7496
verification@kheaa.com
www.kheaa.com
Public corporation and government agency responsible for administering financial aid programs and offering information on higher education programs in Kentucky.

Founded: 1966

Carl Rollins, Ph.D, Executive Director
Erin Klarer, VP, Government Relations

562 Kentucky Library Association (KLA)

5932 Timber Ridge Drive
Suite 101
Prospect, KY 40059
502-223-5322
Fax: 502-223-4937
info@kylibasn.org
www.klaonline.org
Provides leadership, conferences and information to support libraries, information services and the profession of librarianship.

Kandace Rogers, President
John T Underwood, Executive Director

563 Kentucky School Media Association (KSMA)

G.C. Burkhead Elementa
521 Charlemagne Boulevard
Elizabethtown, KY 42701
270-769-5983
infosci@uky.edu
www.uky.edu/OtherOrgs/KSMA/ksma5.htm
Promotes the use of school library media by offering professional development activities to library media specialists.

Christine McIntosh, President
Becky Stephens, Treasurer

Louisiana

564 ADVANCE Program for Young Scholars

175 Sam Sibley Drive
Suite 5671
Natchitoches, LA 71457
318-357-4500
NSUAdvance@nsula.edu
www.advance.nsula.edu
ADVANCE is a residential program for talented youth in Louisiana, offering a specialized curriculum for students grades 8 through 12. The program also offers recreational and social activities.

Harriette Palmer, Associate Director

565 Louisiana Association of Business Educators (LABE)

Hebertd@Nsula.Edu
www.laabe.weebly.com
The mission of the association is to support business educators in the state of Louisiana by facilitating information sharing between professionals.

Dustin Hebert, Ph.D, President
Lauren Cart, Vice President

566 Louisiana Association of Educators (LAE)

8322 One Calais Avenue
Baton Rouge, LA 70809
225-343-9243
877-452-3477
advocacycenter@lae.org
www.lae.org
A membership organization dedicated to improving the education profession through advocacy, professional development opportunities and membership benefits.

Kenton Cooper, Executive Director
Craig Carter, Ph.D, Director, Membership

567 Louisiana Association of School Business Officials (LASBO)

620 Florida Street
Suite 210
Baton Rouge, LA 70801
225-343-2776
Fax: 225-344-1137
info@lasbo.org
www.lasbo.org
Nonprofit professional association made up of school administrators working in the areas of business and operations. The association offers a certification program, networking opportunities and scholarships to promote excellence in the practice of public school business administration.

Founded: 1965

Lesia Casanovas, President
Matt Dugas, CPA, Vice President

568 Louisiana Division of the Arts

1051 N 3rd Street
Room 405
Baton Rouge, LA 70802
225-342-8180
Fax: 225-342-8173
arts@crt.la.gov
www.crt.state.la.us/cultural-development/ar ts
Responsible for offering arts programs, education, grants, services and supports towards the purpose of developing arts and culture in Louisiana.

Founded: 1977

Cheryl Castille, Executive Director
Erica Anderson, Director, Grants & Programs

569 Louisiana Education for Homeless Children and Youth

Louisiana Department of Education
1201 N 3rd Street
Baton Rouge, LA 70802-5243
877-453-2721
ldoecommunciations@la.gov
www.louisianabelieves.com
The Louisiana Education for Homeless Children and Youths Program is a grant provided to fund services and supports for students experiencing homelessness.

John White, Superintendent of Education
Ken Bradford, Asst. Sup., Student Ops.

570 Louisiana Library Association (LLA)

1190 Meramec Station Road
Suite 207
Ballwin, MO 63021
972-851-8000
Fax: 972-991-6061

lla@amigos.org
www.llaonline.org
The mission of the Louisiana Library Association is to promote library interests of Louisiana by offering news about the profession, resources, advocacy, scholarships and networking events to interested professionals.

Founded: 1925

Donald Smith, President
Lauren Bordelon, Secretary

571 Louisiana Office of Student Financial Assistance (LOSFA)
602 N 5th Street
Baton Rouge, LA 70802
225-219-1012
800-259-5626
Fax: 225-208-1496
custserv@la.gov
www.osfa.la.gov
Offers information to students preparing to enroll in post-secondary education, with emphasis on matters of financial assistance.

Sujuan W Boutt,, Ed.D, Executive Director
Deborah Paul, Director, Scholarships

Maine

572 Maine Arts Commission
193 State Street
Augusta, ME 04333-0025
207-287-2724
Fax: 207-287-2725
mainearts.info@maine.gov
www.mainearts.maine.gov
The Commission seeks to engage all sectors both public and private to support the arts, while offering services to artists such as grants, conferences, funding, internships, education and more.

Julie A Richard, Executive Director
Argy Nestor, Director, Arts Education

573 Maine Association of School Libraries (MASL)
64 State House Station
Augusta, ME 04333-0064
maslibraries@gmail.com
www.maslibraries.org
The association works to advance the library profession by supporting library programs and personnel through scholarships, advocacy, continuing education for librarians and more.

Jennifer Stanbro, President
Megal Blakemore, Treasurer

574 Maine Education Association (MEA)
35 Community Drive
Augusta, ME 04330
207-622-5866
Fax: 207-623-2129
www.maineea.org
Represents education professionals in the state of Maine.

Founded: 1859

Paula Voelker, Executive Director
Krystyna Dzialo, Deputy Executive Director

575 Maine Education for Homeless Children and Youth
Maine Department of Education
23 State House Station
Augusta, ME 04333-0023
207-624-6637
Fax: 207-624-6700
gayle.erdheim@maine.gov
www.maine.gov/doe/homeless
An initiative to help homeless students succeed in school with minimal disruptions due to living circumstances.

Gayle Erdheim, Consultant & Team Leader

576 Maine Library Association (MLA)
MLA Business Office
93 Saco Avenue
Old Orchard Beach, ME 04064
207-730-3028
mainelibrary@gmail.com
www.mainelibraries.org
The purpose of the Maine Library Association is to promote and enhance the value of libraries and librarianship, to foster cooperation among library professionals, and to ensure that information is accessible to all citizens.

Founded: 1891

Jenna Blake Davis, Executive Director

Maryland

577 Maryland Commission on Public Art
c/o Maryland State Arts Council
175 W Ostend Street
Suite E
Baltimore, MD 21230
410-767-6555
800-735-2258
www.msac.org
The Commission ensures that public art is included in all state-funded consutrction projects.

Catherine Leggett, Chair

578 Maryland Higher Education Commission (MHEC)
6 N Liberty Street
Baltimore, MD 21201
410-767-3300
800-974-0203
Fax: 410-332-0270
mdhighered@mhec.state.md.us
www.mhec.state.md.us
Responsible for administering financial aid programs for students and establishing policies and regulations for universities, colleges and career schools within the state.

James D Fielder, Jr., Ph.D, Higher Education Secretary
Emily A A Dow, Ph.D, Asst. Sec., Academic Affairs

579 Maryland Homeless Education Assistance
Department of Education
200 West Baltimore Street
Baltimore, MD 21201-2595
410-767-0314
Valerie.Ashton-Thomas@maryland.gov
www.marylandpublicschools.org
Ensures that homeless children in Maryland have access to education resources.

Valerie Ashton-Thomas, Coordinator

580 Maryland Library Association (MLA)
1401 Hollins Street
Baltimore, MD 21223
410-947-5090
Fax: 410-947-5089
mla@mdlib.org
www.mdlib.org
Maryland Library Association provides leadership for those who are committed to libraries by offering them opportunities for professional development and communication and by advocating on behalf of the issues related to librarianship and library services.

Founded: 1923

Andrea Berstler, President
Margaret Carty, Executive Director

581 Maryland State Arts Council
175 W Ostend Street
Suite E
Baltimore, MD 21230
410-767-6555
800-735-2258
www.msac.org
Provides supports such as grants and programs to artists and organizations with the goal of developing the arts in Maryland.

Ken Skrzesz, Executive Director
Dana Parsons, Director, Grants

582 Maryland State Education Association (MSEA)
140 Main Street
Annapolis, MD 21401
443-433-3676
dhelfman@mseanea.org
www.marylandeducators.org
Consists of teachers, education administrators, specialists and students. The mission of the association is to improve public education in Maryland by offering career development opportunities, legal supports, testing and resources.

Cheryl Bost, President
David Helfman, Executive Director

583 Maryland State Library Agency
22 S Calhoun Street
Baltimore, MD 21223
667-219-4800
Fax: 667-219-4798
md.statelibrary@maryland.gov
www.marylandlibraries.org
Responsible for administering funds and creating programs that advance the libraries of Maryland. Formerly known as the Division of Library Development and Services.

Founded: 1968

Irene M Padilla, State Librarian

Massachusetts

584 Massachusetts Board of Library Commissioners
98 N Washington Street
Suite 401
Boston, MA 02114
617-725-1860
800-952-7403
Fax: 617-725-0140
answers@mblc.state.ma.us
www.mblc.state.ma.us
Government agency responsible for organizing, developing and coordinating library services throughout the Commonwealth. The agency administers programs and sets policies towards improving the overall function of Massachusetts libraries.

James Lonergan, Director
Celeste Bruno, Communications Director

585 Massachusetts Business Educators Association (MBEA)
MA

jbelisle@mbea-ma.org
www.mbea-ma.org
Supports business education professionals in the state of Massachusetts by offering conferences, programs and policy development.

Jacqueline Prester, President
Jennifer Belisle, Secretary

6 **Massachusetts Cultural Council**
10 St. James Avenue
3rd Floor
Boston, MA 02116-3803
617-858-2700
800-232-0960
Fax: 617-727-0044
mcc@art.state.ma.us
www.massculturalcouncil.org
State agency promoting the arts and sciences through grant programs, partnerships and services offered to cultural organizations, schools, communities and artists.

Anita Walker, Executive Director
Jen Lawless, Operations Director

7 **Massachusetts Department of Higher Education (DHE)**
1 Ashburton Place
Room 1401
Boston, MA 02108
617-994-6950
Fax: 617-727-0955
kabel@bhe.mass.edu
www.mass.edu
Provides information about student financial aid, colleges and universities to the citizens of Massachusetts. The Massachusetts Department of Higher Education is responsible for execution of policies set out by the Board of Higher Education for the purpose of coordinating the Commonwealth's higher education system.

Carlos Santiago, Commissioner
Clantha McCurcy, Ph.D, Sr. Dep. Comm., Access

8 **Massachusetts Library Association**
PO Box 404
Malden, MA 02148
781-698-7764
Fax: 781-998-0393
manager@masslib.org
www.masslib.org
Supports the Massachusetts library community by providing leadership, advocacy, professional development programs, conferences, networking opportunities and more.

Esme Green, President
Nora Blake, Vice President

89 **Massachusetts Office for the Education of Homeless Children and Youth**
75 Pleasant Street
Malden, MA 02148-4906
781-338-6330
Fax: 781-338-3090
sslautterback@doe.mass.edu
www.doe.mass.edu/mv
Responsible for ensuring that homeless children and youth have access to education and are given the neccessary services to help them overcome barriers.

Sarah Slautterback, State Coordinator

90 **Massachusetts Teachers Association (MTA)**
2 Heritage Drive
8th Floor
Quincy, MA 02171-2119
617-878-8000
800-392-6175
Fax: 617-742-7046
contactus@massteacher.org
www.massteacher.org
The Massachusetts Teachers Association is a union dedicated to improving the workplace for all education employees and protecting their rights. The association is governed by democratic principles.

Lisa Gallatin, Executive Director-Treasurer
Suzanne Wall, Director, Higher Education

591 **New England Library Association (NELA)**
55 N Main Street
Unit 49
Belchertown, MA 01007
413-813-5254
rscheier@nelib.org
www.nelib.org
Provides educational and leadership opportunities for library staff to support library services in New England.

Founded: 1963

Susan Edmonds, President
Robert Scheier, Administrator

Michigan

592 **Michigan Association for Media in Education (MAME)**
1407 Rensen Street
Lansing, MI 48910
517-394-2808
Fax: 517-492-3878
mame@mimame.org
www.mimame.org
The Michigan Association for Media in Education is an independent, professional association of library media specialists dedicated to developing educational, literary and technological excellence in the library/media services of Michigan's schools.

Cat Kerns, President
Teri Belcher, Executive Secretary

593 **Michigan Association of School Administrators (MASA)**
1001 Centennial Way
Suite 300
Lansing, MI 48917-9279
517-327-5910
Fax: 517-327-0779
www.gomasa.org
Professional organization serving school leaders of Michigan by offering legal services, publications, professional development opportunities and resources so they can better serve students.

Chris Wigent, Executive Director
Tina Kerr, Ph.D, Deputy Executive Director

594 **Michigan Council for Arts and Cultural Affairs (MCACA)**
Michigan Economic Development Corporation
300 N Washington Square
Lansing, MI 48913
888-522-0103
www.michiganbusiness.org/arts
Supports the arts in Michigan by providing opportunities for visibility, supporting arts education and providing grants.

Alison Watson, Director
Chad Swan-Badgero, Manager, Arts Education

595 **Michigan Education Association (MEA)**
1216 Kendale Boulevard
East Lansing, MI 48823
517-332-6551
800-292-1934
Fax: 517-337-4024
webmaster@mea.org
www.mea.org
A self-governing education association representing teachers, faculty and education support staff throughout Michigan. The association offers its members advocacy, professional development events, financial services and information so they can better serve their communities.

Paula Herbart, President
Michael Shoudy, Executive Director

596 **Michigan Education for Homeless Children and Youth**
608 W Allegan Street
PO Box 30008
Lansing, MI 48909
517-373-3324
www.michigan.gov/homeless
A branch in the Michigan Department of Education responsible for providing access to education for children and youth experiencing homelessness.

Michael Rice, State Superintendent

597 **Michigan Elementary & Middle School Principals Association (MEMSPA)**
1980 N College Road
Mason, MI 48854
517-694-8955
Fax: 517-694-8945
www.memspa.org
Professional organization serving elementary and middle level principals as they deliver quality educational experiences to the students of Michigan. The association provides leadership, legislative advocacy, professional development and guidance to its members.

Paul Liabenow, Executive Director
Syndee Malek, Associate Executive Director

598 **Michigan Library Association (MLA)**
3410 Belle Chase Way
Suite 100
Lansing, MI 48911
517-394-2774
mla@milibraries.org
www.milibraries.org
The Michigan Library Association is a professional organization dedicated to the support of its members through advocacy and professional development events, the advancement of librarianship and the promotion of quality library service for all Michigan citizens.

Deborah E Mikula, Executive Director
Romy Fitschen, Associate Executive Director

599 **Michigan Office of Postsecondary Financial Planning**
Michigan Department of Treasury
PO Box 30462
Lansing, MI 48909-7962
888-447-2687
mistudentaid@michigan.gov
www.michigan.gov/mistudentaid
MI Student Aid provides access to student financial resources and information available

for students in Michigan to encourage the pursuit of higher education.

Rachael Eubanks, State Treasurer
Anne Wohlfert, Bureau Administrator

Minnesota

600 Education Minnesota
41 Sherburne Avenue
St. Paul, MN 55103
651-227-9541
800-652-9073
Fax: 651-292-4802
webmaster@edmn.org
www.educationminnesota.org
Education Minnesota is an advocate for educators and public education in the state. Its main function is that of a union that helps teachers gain professional development, nagotiate job contracts and more.

Denise Specht, President
Sara Gjerdrum, Executive Director

601 Minnesota Library Association (MLA)
400 S 4th Street
Suite 754E
Minneapolis, MN 55415
612-294-6549
mla@management-hq.com
www.mnlibraryassociation.org
Facilitates educational opportunities, upholds ethical standards and forms connections between the library community and other groups.

Founded: 1891

Leslie Jones, Executive Director
Ashley Driste, Events Manager

602 Minnesota Marketing - Business - Information Technology Educators (MN MBITE)
MN
mbeionline@gmail.com
www.mbei-online.org
A professional organization for business educators working in the areas of marketing, accounting, information technology and graphic design. The organization provides advocacy, professional development and networking opportunities to its members.

Justin Wittrock, President
Dean Breuer, State Secretary

603 Minnesota PTA
7800 Metro Parkway
Suite 300
Bloomington, MN 55425
952-767-4909
mnpta@mnpta.org
www.mnpta.org
Minnesota PTA aims to support and advocate for children and youth in school, educate parents and teachers on issues affecting children and youth and encourage parent participation in the school system.

Founded: 1922

Heather Starks, President
JC St. Onge-Holm, Secretary

604 Minnesota School Boards Association (MSBA)
1900 W Jefferson Avenue
Saint Peter, MN 56082-3015
507-934-2450
800-324-4459
Fax: 507-931-1515
www.mnmsba.org
The purpose of the Association is to support, promote and enhance the work of public school boards.

Kirk Schneidawind, Executive Director
Gary Lee, Deputy Executive Director

605 Minnesota State Arts Board
Park Square Court
400 Sibley Street
Suite 200
Saint Paul, MN 55101-1928
651-539-2650
800-866-2787
Fax: 651-215-1602
msab@arts.state.mn.us
www.arts.state.mn.us
State agency supporting the arts in Minnesota by providing grants and encouraging creativity.

Sue Gens, Executive Director
David White, Director, Finance & Grants

606 Office of Higher Education
1450 Energy Park Drive
Suite 350
Saint Paul, MN 55108-5227
651-642-0567
800-657-3866
Fax: 651-642-0675
info.ohe@state.mn.us
www.ohe.state.mn.us
The Minnesota Office of Higher Education is a state agency responsible for providing financial aid programs to students as well as giving them the information they need when applying to higher education institutions.

Dennis Olson, Commissioner
Winnie Sullivan, Deputy Commissioner

Mississippi

607 Mississippi Arts Commission
Woolfolk Building
501 NW Street
Suite 1101A
Jackson, MS 39201
601-359-6030
Fax: 601-359-6008
www.arts.ms.gov
Supports the arts in Mississippi by offering grant programs to nonprofit organizations and artists.

Malcolm White, Executive Director
Larry Morrisey, Deputy Director

608 Mississippi Association of Educators (MAE)
775 N State Street
Jackson, MS 39202
601-354-4463
Fax: 601-352-7054
fholmes@nea.org
www.maetoday.org
The Mississippi Association of Educators supports teachers, higher education faculty and students by offering professional development programs, advocacy and membership benefits.

Tyrone C Hendrix, Executive Director
Hannah Orlansky, Director, Communications

609 Mississippi Business Education Association (MBEA)
Biloxi High School
1845 Tribe Drive
Biloxi, MS 39532
carole.deere@biloxischools.net
www.msmbea1950.wordpress.com
Professional organization for business educators of Mississippi. The association supports the development of business and technology education.

Founded: 1950

Debbie Wilson, President
Carole Deere, State Membership Director

610 Mississippi Education for Homeless Children and Youth
Mississippi Department of Education
PO Box 771
Jackson, MS 39205-0771
601-359-3499
Fax: 601-359-2587
qransburg@mdek12.org
www.mdek12.org/OFP/Title-IX-Part-A
Serves youth and children who are experiencing homelessness by helping them access education.

Quentin Ransburg, Executive Director
Arthur Goss, Assistant

611 Mississippi Institutions of Higher Learning
3825 Ridgewood Road
Jackson, MS 39211
601-432-6198
800-327-2980
questions@ihl.state.ms.us
www.mississippi.edu
Responsible for regulating student affairs among various other sectors.

Alfred Rankins, Jr., Ph.D., Commissioner
Marcus Thompson, Deputy Commissioner

612 Mississippi Library Association (MLA)
PO Box 13687
Jackson, MS 39236-3687
601-981-4586
Fax: 601-981-4501
info@misslib.org
www.misslib.org
Provides professional leadership for the development, promotion, and improvement of library and information services in Mississippi. The association also provides advocacy and conferences to stregnthen the profession of librarianship.

Founded: 1909

Sarah Crisler-Ruskey, President
Paula Bass, Administrator

613 Mississippi Library Commission (MLC)
3881 Eastwood Drive
Jackson, MS 39211
601-432-4111
800-647-7542
Fax: 601-432-4480
mslib@mlc.lib.ms.us
www.mlc.lib.ms.us
Provides information services for libraries on the subjects of technology and libary development so that all citizens of Mississippi would be able to access these resources.

Founded: 1926

Hulen Bivins, Executive Director
David Collins, Grant Program Director

Missouri

614 Missouri Arts Council
815 Olive Street
Suite 16
Saint Louis, MO 63101-1503
314-340-6845
866-407-4752
Fax: 314-340-7215
moarts@ded.mo.gov
www.missouriartscouncil.org
The Missouri Arts Council is the state agency dedicated to supporting the arts in the state through

programming, arts education, grants, events and advocacy.

Founded: 1965

Michael Donovan, Executive Director
Kathleen Morrissey, Assistant Director

5 Missouri Association of Elementary School Principals (MAESP)
3550 Amazonas Drive
Jefferson City, MO 65109
573-638-2460
Fax: 573-556-6270
maesp@maesp.com
www.maesp.com
A statewide professional association made up of elementary and middle school principals and educators that aspire to become principals. Services offered by the association to its members include legal advice and professional development opportunities.

Michael L Schooley, Ph.D, Executive Director
Scott Kimble, Director, Advocacy

6 Missouri Association of Secondary School Principals (MoASSP)
2409 W Ash Street
Columbia, MO 65203-0045
573-445-5071
Fax: 573-445-6416
gstevens@moassp.org
www.moassp.org
The mission of the Missouri Association of Secondary School Principals is to improve secondary education by offering professional development programs and workshops to the leaders of schools (principals and school administrator). The association provides information and leadership, promotes high educational standards and addresses state educational issues.

Ed Gettemeier, Co-President
Marc Spunaugle, Co-President

17 Missouri Business Education Association (MBEA)
MO
573-522-6540
andrew.reynolds@catnet.gen.mo.us
www.mbea.weebly.com
The mission of the association is to promote the professional growth of those working in the field of business education.

Michelle Yocom, President
Andrew Reynolds, Secretary

18 Missouri Department of Higher Education (MDHE)
205 Jefferson Street
PO Box 1469
Jefferson City, MO 65102-1469
573-751-2361
800-473-6757
Fax: 573-751-6635
www.dhe.mo.gov
The mission of the Missouri Department of Higher Education is to coordinate higher education policy and promote enrollment in Missouri 's public education institutions. The Department offers information to help students and families plan for college as well as development strategies for institutions.

Zora Mulligan, Commissioner

19 Missouri Education for Homeless Children and Youth
205 Jefferson Street
Jefferson City, MO 65101
573-522-8763
Fax: 573-526-6698
Donna.Cash@dese.mo.gov
www.dese.mo.gov
Responsible for ensuring homeless children and youth have access to education regardless of their circumstances.

Donna Cash, Homeless State Coordinator

620 Missouri Library Association (MLA)
1190 Meramec Station Road
Suite 207
Ballwin, MO 63021-6902
573-449-4627
Fax: 573-449-4655
mla@amigos.org
www.molib.org
A nonprofit educational organization dedicated to promoting library service and the profession of librarianship.

Founded: 1900

Erin Gray, President
Meredith McCarthy, Membership Chair

621 Missouri National Education Association (MNEA)
1810 E Elm Street
Jefferson City, MO 65101
573-634-3202
800-392-0236
Fax: 573-634-5646
deeann.aull@mnea.org
www.mnea.org
The Missouri National Education Association is an advocate for public schools and their students and employees. The association offers educational conferences and workshops for educators, legal services and advocacy.

DeeAnn Aull, Executive Director
Ann Jarrett, Dir., Teaching & Learning

622 Missouri PTA (MOPTA)
2101 Burlington Street
Columbia, MO 65202
573-445-4161
Fax: 573-445-4163
office@mopta.org
www.mopta.org
Provides programs, activities and advocacy for children and youth of Missouri. The PTA works to ensure the health, welfare, safety and education of all.

Carla White, President
Paula McKinney, Secretary

623 Missouri State Teachers Association (MSTA)
407 S 6th Street
Columbia, MO 65201
573-442-3127
800-392-0532
membercare@msta.org
www.msta.org
A grassroots organization of local community teachers associations. The mission of the association is to meet the needs of educators in Missouri by offering resources such as professional development, grants, learning standards and more.

Bruce Moe, Executive Director
Todd Fuller, Director, Marketing

Montana

624 Montana Arts Council
830 N Warren Street
PO Box 202201
Helena, MT 59620-2201
406-444-6430
800-282-3092
Fax: 406-444-6548
mac@mt.gov
www.art.mt.gov
State agency responsible for developing the arts in Montana. The agency offers funding, programs, advocacy and education towards realizing this mission.

Tatiana Gant, Executive Director
Monica Grable, Director, Arts Education

625 Montana Association for Career and Technical Education (Montana ACTE)
406-967-2540
mbranger@huntley.k12.mt.us
www.montanaacte.org
Supports members of the career and technical education community as the state affiliate of the national Association for Career and Technical Education (ACTE)

Carla Leligdowicz, President
Mark Branger, Executive Director

626 Montana Association of County School Superintendents (MACSS)
School Administrators of Montana
900 N Montana Avenue
Suite A-4
Helena, MT 59601
406-442-2510
Fax: 406-442-2518
cmaloney@bsb.mt.gov
www.sammt.org/macss
Organization of school superintendents offering services and educational leadership in Montana.

Cathy Maloney, President
Pam Birkeland, Secretary

627 Montana Association of Elementary and Middle School Principals (MAEMSP)
School Administrators of Montana
900 N Montana Avenue
Suite A-4
Helena, MT 59601
406-442-2510
Fax: 406-442-2518
www.sammt.org/maemsp
State affiliate for the national organization, the National Association of Elementary School Principals (NAESP).

Shelley Andres, President
Nicole Trahan, Vice President

628 Montana Association of School Superintendents (MASS)
School Administrators of Montana
900 N Montana Avenue
Suite A-4
Helena, MT 59601
406-442-2510
Fax: 406-442-2518
www.sammt.org/mass
Local affiliate for the national organization, the American Association of School Administrators (AASA).

Casey Klasna, President

629 Montana Association of Secondary School Principals (MASSP)
School Administrators of Montana
900 N Montana Avenue
Suite A-4
Helena, MT 59601
406-442-2510
Fax: 406-442-2518
www.sammt.org/massp

Represents the interests of middle and secondary school educators.

Justin Helvik, President
Shawn Hendrickson, Vice President

630 **Montana Business Education Association (MBEA)**
Dutton/Brady High School
101 2nd Street NE
Dutton, MT 59433
www.mbea.info
Serves business educators by offering them opportunities for growth in their profession.

Casey Donahue, President
Laurie Koepplin, Secretary

631 **Montana Council of Administrators of Special Education (MCASE)**
School Administrators of Montana
900 N Montana Avenue
Suite A-4
Helena, MT 59601
406-442-2510
Fax: 406-442-2518
www.sammt.org/mcase
Local affiliate of the national organization, the Council of Administrators for Special Education (CASE).

Sean Maharg, President
Jenny Malloy, Secretary

632 **Montana Education for Homeless Children and Youth**
Office of Public Instruction
PO Box 202501
Helena, MT 59620-2501
406-444-2036
888-231-9393
hdenny@mt.gov
www.opi.mt.gov
A program that seeks to make education accessible for children and youth experiencing homelessness.

Heather Denny, Education Coordinator
Sheri Harlow, Administrative Assistant

633 **Montana Educational Technologists Association (META)**
School Administrators of Montana
900 N Montana Avenue
Suite A-4
Helena, MT 59601
406-442-2510
Fax: 406-442-2518
www.sammt.org/meta
Supports and advocates for educational technologists in the state of Montana.

Everett Holm, President

634 **Montana Library Association (MLA)**
5176 N Valle Dorado
Kingman, AZ 86409
406-579-3121
debkmla@hotmail.com
www.mtlib.org
Works to develop and promote library services and librarianship in Montana through advocacy, conferences and grants.

Debbi Kramer, Executive Director
Matt Beckstrom, Postmaster

635 **School Administrators of Montana (SAM)**
900 N Montana Avenue
Suite A-4
Helena, MT 59601
406-442-2510
Fax: 406-442-2518
samkm@sammt.org
www.sammt.org
Represents and advocates for school administrators in Montana.

Founded: 1970

Kirk Miller, Executive Director
Gary Wagner, Director, Operations

Nebraska

636 **Nebraska Arts Council**
1004 Farnam Street
Omaha, NE 68102
402-595-2122
800-341-4067
Fax: 402-742-1110
nac.info@nebraska.gov
www.artscouncil.nebraska.gov
Dedicated to promoting and cultivating the arts in Nebraska through grants, leadership, advocacy, education and exhibitions.

Founded: 1974

Suzanne Wise, Executive Director
Mike Markey, Deputy Director

637 **Nebraska Education for Homeless Children and Youth**
301 Centennial Mall S
PO Box 94987
Lincoln, NE 68509-4987
402-471-2295
Fax: 402-471-0117
denise.fisher@nebraska.gov
www.education.ne.gov/federalprograms/title-vii-b
Reponsible for implementing the guidelines of the McKinney-Vento Homeless Assistance Act and creating services so that homeless children and youth may access public education.

Cathy Mohnike, Consultant

638 **Nebraska Library Association (NLA)**
c/o Executive Director
PO Box 21756
Lincoln, NE 68542-1756
402-826-2636
nlaexecutivedirector@nebraskalibraries.org
www.nebraskalibraries.org
The Nebraska Library Association supports and promotes all libraries and library services in the state through advocacy and professional development programs.

Michael Straatmann, President
Bailey Halbur, Secretary

639 **Nebraska Library Commission**
The Atrium
1200 N Street
Suite 120
Lincoln, NE 68508-2023
402-471-2045
800-307-2665
Fax: 402-471-2083
www.nlc.nebraska.gov
Part of the state's executive branch. The commission is responsible for the promotion and coordination of Nebraska libraries and library services through funding of programs, accreditation, training, accessible technology and more.

Founded: 1901

Rod Wagner, Library Commission Director
Tessa Terry, Communications Coordinator

640 **Nebraska State Business Education Association (NSBEA)**
Mid-Plains Community College South Campus
501 West State Farm Road
North Platte, NE 69101
308-535-3735
dwolken@lps.org
www.nsbea.org
Fosters education in business, marketing and information technology within the state of Nebraska by offering professional growth opportunities, networking and guidance.

Cathy Nutt, President
Deb Wolken, State Membership Director

641 **Nebraska State Education Association (NSEA)**
605 S 14th Street
Suite 200
Lincoln, NE 68508
402-475-7611
800-742-0047
Fax: 402-475-2630
maddie.fennell@nsea.org
www.nsea.org
A member-directed union of professional educators and education support professionals dedicated to advocating for all education professionals in Nebraska.

Maddie Fennell, Executive Director
Neal Clayburn, Associate Executive Director

Nevada

642 **Nevada Arts Council**
716 N Carson Street
Suite A
Carson City, NV 89701
775-687-6680
Fax: 775-687-6688
www.nvculture.org
State agency supporting the arts in Nevada through grants, programs, education, arts promotion, publications and various other resources.

Julia Arger, Chair
Tony Manfredi, Executive Director

643 **Nevada Education for Homeless Children and Youth**
700 E 5th Street
Suite 113
Carson City, NV 89701
775-687-9235
Fax: 775-687-9250
www.nde.doe.nv.gov
Offers assistance to homeless children and youth so that they may access public education.

Michael Walker, State Coordinator
Cyekeia Lee, Higher Education Specialist

644 **Nevada Library Association**
cornm@lvccld.org
www.nevadalibraries.org
The purpose of the association is to promote library services of Nevada through advocacy, events and membership resources.

Amy Dodson, President
Mayra Corn, Executive Secretary

645 **Nevada State Education Association**
3511 E Harmon Avenue
Las Vegas, NV 89121
702-733-7330
800-248-6732
Fax: 702-733-6004
contact.nsea@nsea-nv.org
www.nsea-nv.org
Advocates for the professional rights and economic security of its members, while also serving

as a voice for excellence in public education in Nevada.

Ruben Murillo, Jr., President
Brian Lee, Executive Director

New Hampshire

6 **New Hampshire Business Education Association**
200 Derry Road
Hudson, NH 03051
www.nhbea.com
Fosters business education in the state of New Hampshire by offering members opportunities to develop their skills and network with others working in the business education field.

Steve Foster, President
Michael Magoon, Vice President

7 **New Hampshire Education Association**
9 S Spring Street
Concord, NH 03301-2425
603-224-7751
866-556-3264
Fax: 603-224-2648
members@nhnea.org
www.neanh.org
The mission of the association is to strengthen and support public education by providing public school educators with the resources they need to develop their skills. The association also provides services for the children of New Hampshire so they can succeed in school.

Founded: 1857

Megan Tuttle, President
Rick Trombly, Executive Director

8 **New Hampshire Education for Homeless Children and Youth**
New Hampshire Department of Education
101 Pleasant Street
Concord, NH 03301-3494
603-271-6055
Fax: 603-271-2760
Kristine.Braman@doe.nh.gov
www.education.nh.gov
Provides resources and services to districts, schools and people in need of assistance so they can understand the regulations relating to the rights of homeless children and youth and thereby better serve these individuals.

Lynda Thistle-Elliott, Director
Kristine Braman, Program Assistant

49 **New Hampshire Higher Education Commission**
New Hampshire Department of Education
101 Pleasant Street
Concord, NH 03301-3494
603-271-0257
Patricia.Edes@doe.nh.gov
www.education.nh.gov/highered
The mission of the commission is to offer leadership and services in support of equal educational opportunities for the people of New Hampshire. Its divisions cover areas such as student assessment, educational technology, school health and safety, special education and more.

Todd J Leach, Ph.D, Chair
Patti Edes, Program Specialist IV

50 **New Hampshire Library Association**
c/o New Hampshire State Library
20 Park Street
Concord, NH 03301-6314
603-249-0645
kgabert@wadleighlibrary.org
www.nhlibrarians.org
The association is made up of library professionals working to advocate on behalf of the interests of its members, increase public awareness of library services, support the professional development of its members and encourage communication among professionals.

Marilyn Borgendale, President
Matthew Gunby, Secretary

651 **New Hampshire State Council on the Arts**
19 Pillsbury Street
1st Floor
Concord, NH 03301
603-271-2789
800-735-2964
Fax: 603-271-3584
julianne.gadoury@nh.gov
www.nh.gov/nharts
Supports the arts in New Hampshire through grants, arts education and other services.

Ginnie Lupi, Director
Julianne Gadoury, Grants Coordinator

New Jersey

652 **New Jersey Education Association (NJEA)**
180 W State Street
Trenton, NJ 08608
609-599-4561
Fax: 609-392-6321
www.njea.org
The mission of the New Jersey Education Association is to advance and protect the rights and interests of its members and promote excellence in public education. The association offers advocacy, training, grants and professional development in support of educators.

Edward J Richardson, Executive Director
Steve Swetsky, Assistant Executive Director

653 **New Jersey Education for Homeless Children and Youth**
New Jersey Department of Education
PO Box 500
Trenton, NJ 08625-0500
609-984-4974
Fax: 609-292-1211
McKinney.Vento@doe.nj.gov
www.nj.gov/education/homeless/index.html
Provides resources for parents, students and schools in order to make public education more accessible to young people experiencing homelessness.

Danielle Anderson Thomas, State Coordinator

654 **New Jersey Higher Education Student Assistance Authority (HESAA)**
PO Box 545
Trenton, NJ 08625-0545
609-584-4480
800-792-8670
Fax: 609-588-7389
Client_Services@hesaa.org
www.hesaa.org
State agency with the mission of providing information on higher education matters (such as financial aid) to students and families in order to assist them in planning academic futures.

David J Socolow, Executive Director
Hanifa L Barnes, Esq., Chief of Staff

655 **New Jersey Library Association (NJLA)**
PO Box 1534
Trenton, NJ 08607
609-394-8032
Fax: 609-394-8164
ptumulty@njla.org
www.njla.org
Advocates for the advancement of library services for the residents of New Jersey, provides continuing education and networking opportunities for librarians and promotes access to library services for all.

Founded: 1890

Tonya Garcia, President
Patricia Tumulty, Executive Director

656 **New Jersey School-Age Care Coalition (NJSACC)**
208 Lenox Avenue
Westfield, NJ 07090
908-789-0259
Fax: 908-789-4237
sac@njsacc.org
www.njsacc.org
Promotes out-of-school time programs and upholds the New Jersey Quality Afterschool Standards. The organization provides training, conferences and technical assistance for program development. It also works to improve State regulations and legislation to ensure that students have access to programs within their communities.

Diane Genco, Executive Director
Lee McDermott Schaefer, Policy Director

657 **New Jersey State Council on the Arts**
33 W State Street
4th Floor
Trenton, NJ 08608
609-292-6130
Feedback@sos.nj.gov
www.nj.gov/state/njsca/dos_njsca_about.html
Supports the arts in New Jersey by offering services, programs and grants to artists as well as by supporting arts education.

Founded: 1966

Allison Tratner, Executive Director
Danielle Bursk, Director, Artist Services

658 **New Jersey State Department of Education Learning Resource Centers**
NJ Department of Education
PO Box 500
Trenton, NJ 08625-0500
609-292-4469
877-900-6960
Fax: 609-777-2077
communications@doe.state.nj.us
www.nj.gov/education/lrc/services.htm
Provides in-service workshops, information, publications, training, conferences, consultations and technical assistance to educators and families of students with disabilities.

New Mexico

659 **National Education Association of New Mexico**
2007 Botulph
Santa Fe, NM 87505
505-982-1916
Fax: 505-982-6719
neanmsf@gmail.com
www.nea-nm.org
Engaged in ensuring excellence in public education by advocating for the rights of stu-

dents and education employees in New Mexico.

Betty Patterson, President
Charles Goodmacher, Director, Media Relations

660 New Mexico Arts
Bataan Memorial Building
407 Galisteo Street
Suite 270
Santa Fe, NM 87501
505-827-6490
800-879-4278
Fax: 505-827-6043
cynthiar.gonzales@state.nm.us
www.nmarts.org
A division of the Department of Cultural Affairs responsible for supporting the arts in New Mexico by funding arts services and programs.

Loie Fecteau, Executive Director
Phyllis Kennedy, Program Coordinator

661 New Mexico Higher Education Department
2044 Galisteo Street
Suite 4
Santa Fe, NM 87505-2100
505-476-8400
800-279-9777
Fax: 505-476-8453
Patrick.Lucero2@state.nm.us
www.hed.state.nm.us
Provides information on topics and issues related to higher education such as continuing education, grants, student financial aid options, credit transfers, information for school administrators and research data.

Barbara Damron, Cabinet Secretary
Robert McEntyre, Public Information Officer

662 New Mexico Library Association (NMLA)
PO Box 26074
Albuquerque, NM 87125
505-400-7309
Fax: 505-544-5740
contact@nmla.org
www.nmla.org
The New Mexico Library Association is a nonprofit organization dedicated to the support and promotion of libraries and library personnel through education, grants, conferences and legislative advocacy.

Lynette Schurdevin, President
Karla Hunt, Secretary

New York

663 Business Teachers Association of New York State (BTA)
NY
treasurer@btanys.org
www.btanys.org
The Business Teachers Association of New York State provides networking, support and professional growth opportunities for business educators so they may effectively educate their students.

Francine Martella, President
Melinda McCarthy, Treasurer

664 New York Education for Homeless Children and Youth (NY-TEACHES)
151 West 30th Street
5th Floor
New York, NY 10001
800-388-2014
Fax: 212-807-6872
info@nysteachs.org
www.nysteachs.org
The New York State Technical and Education Assistance Center for Homeless Students provides support for young people experiencing homelessness by educating schools, social service providers, parents and others about the rights of these youth to access education.

Jennifer Pringle, JD, Project Director
Michelle Frank, JD, Assistant Director

665 New York Library Association (NYLA)
6021 State Farm Road
Guilderland, NY 12084
518-432-6952
Fax: 518-427-1697
info@nyla.org
www.nyla.org
Provides support in the form of advocacy and professional development events to libraries and library staff in New York. The association also acts as a voice on library matters to media and policymakers.

Founded: 1890

Jeremy Johannesen, Executive Director
Lois Powell, Dir., Membership Services

666 New York State Council on the Arts (NYSCA)
300 Park Avenue S
10th Floor
New York, NY 10010
212-459-8800
info@arts.ny.gov
www.nysca.org
Dedicated to preserving and supporting the arts in New York through grants, advisory support and public education on the value the arts brings to communities.

Mara Manus, Executive Director
Ronni Reich, Director, Public Information

667 New York State Higher Education Services Corporation (HESC)
99 Washington Avenue
Albany, NY 12255
518-473-1574
888-697-4372
Fax: 518-474-2839
Teresa.Gehrer@hesc.ny.gov
www.hesc.ny.gov
The corporation is the agency of New York state responsible for administering and offering information on financial assistance available to students applying for higher education.

Guillermo Linares, Ph.D, President

668 New York State United Teachers (NYSUT)
800 Troy-Schenectady Road
Latham, NY 12110
518-213-6000
800-342-9810
mediarel@nysut.org
www.nysut.org
New York State United Teachers is a union of health care and education professionals dedicated to improving the professional and personal lives of its members and their families by advocating for excellence in education and healthcare for all New York citizens.

Andrew Pallotta, President
Jolene T. DiBrango, Executive Vice President

669 Tribeca Learning Center-PS 150
334 Greenwich Street
New York, NY 10013
212-732-4392
Fax: 212-766-5895
Info@ps150.net
www.ps150.net
Tribeca Learning Center, PS 150 nurtures the development of students in all aspects of their lives through a curriculum that integrates arts, sciences, math, language and physical education.

Jenny Bonnet, Principal
Christine Walford, School Secretary

North Carolina

670 North Carolina Arts Council
Department of Natural & Cultural Resources
4632 Mail Service Center
Raleigh, NC 27699-4600
919-807-6500
Fax: 919-807-6532
ncarts@ncdcr.gov
www.ncarts.org
Dedicated to developing the arts in North Carolina by providing education, grants, leadership and other resources useful for artists.

Stephen Hill, Chair
Wayne Martin, Executive Director

671 North Carolina Association for Career and Technical Education
NCACTE
7021 Goshen Road
Oxford, NC 27565
919-693-3962
Fax: 877-663-1146
tony.bello@gmail.com
www.ncacteonline.org
The association aims to act as a central agency, bringing together professionals working in various kinds of career and technical education in order to expand and promote the fields.

Carol Harper, President
Ruth Huff, Executive Director

672 North Carolina Association of Educators (NCAE)
700 S Salisbury Street
Raleigh, NC 27601
919-832-3000
800-662-7924
Fax: 919-829-1626
derevana.leach@ncae.org
www.ncae.org
The mission of the association is to advocate for members and students with the goal of enhancing public education and the education profession.

Mark Jewell, President
Rachelle Johnson, Executive Director

673 North Carolina Business Education Association (NCBEA)
jtucker@centurylink.net
www.ncbea.org
NCBEA works to promote and improve the quality of business education through membership meetings and strives to create programs useful for the development of business educators in North Carolina.

Madeline Tucker, President
Janis Tucker, Secretary

4 **North Carolina Department of Public Instruction (DPI)**
Education Building
301 N Wilmington Street
Raleigh, NC 27601-2825
919-807-3300
Fax: 919-807-3445
information@dpi.nc.gov
www.ncpublicschools.org
The North Carolina Department of Public Instruction (DPI) is the agency responsible for implementing the State's public school laws and the State Board of Education's policies and procedures relating to pre-kindergarten through 12th grade public education. The agency provides leadership and services to local public school districts to assist in developing the areas of curriculum, assessments and instruction.

Mark Johnson, State Superintendent
Adam Levinson, Chief Financial Officer

5 **North Carolina Homeless Education Program**
The SERVE Center at UNCG
PO Box 5367
Greensboro, NC 27435
336-315-7400
800-659-3204
Fax: 336-315-7457
lphillip@serve.org
www.serve.uncg.edu/hepnc/about.php
Ensures that young people experiencing homelessness in North Carolina have the resources they need to access education.

Lisa Phillips, State Coordinator
Patricia Lentz, Program Specialist

6 **North Carolina Library Association (NCLA)**
1841 Capital Boulevard
Raleigh, NC 27604
919-839-6252
Fax: 888-977-3143
nclaonline@gmail.com
www.nclaonline.org
Statewide organization intent on promoting libraries, intellectual freedom, library services and library professions in North Carolina.

Rodney Lippard, President
Julie Humphrey, Secretary

77 **North Carolina State Education Assistance Authority**
10 TW Alexander Drive
Research Triangle Park, NC 27709
919-549-8614
Fax: 919-549-8481
www.ncseaa.edu
Provides services such as student financial assistance programs and information on financial assistance options for citizens of North Carolina.

James O Roberts, Chair
Elizabeth V McDuffie, Executive Director

North Dakota

78 **North Dakota Council on the Arts**
1600 E Century Avenue
Suite 6
Bismarck, ND 58503-0649
701-328-7590
Fax: 701-328-7595
comserv@nd.gov
www.nd.gov/arts
State agency with the mission of developing and promoting the arts in North Dakota through programs, education, grants and opportunities for professional development of artists.

Founded: 1967

Beth G Klingenstein, Ph.D, Executive Director
Robin Bosch, Administrative Officer

679 **North Dakota Education for Homeless Children and Youth**
North Dakota Department of Public Instruction
600 E Boulevard Avenue
Dept. 201
Bismarck, ND 58505-0440
701-328-3544
esteckler@nd.gov
www.nd.gov
Aims to ensure that youth and children experiencing homelessness have access to public education.

Beth Larson-Steckler, State Homeless Coordinator
Heidi Merkel, Contact

680 **North Dakota Library Association**
PO Box 1595
Bismarck, ND 58502-1595
lwest@cityoffargo.com
www.ndla.info
The North Dakota Library Association is concerned with the right of all citizens of North Dakota to access library collections and services in their state.

Lesley Allan, President
Lori West, Professional Development

681 **North Dakota United (NDU)**
301 N 4th Street
Bismarck, ND 58501
701-223-0450
800-369-6332
Fax: 701-224-8535
comments@ndunited.org
www.ndunited.org
Works to provide public education and services to the citizens of North Dakota. Some services offered by the group include acting as a union to represent the rights of employees, support for improvement of institutions and professional development opportunities for members.

Nick Archuleta, President
Karen Christensen, Vice President of Education

Ohio

682 **Ohio Arts Council**
Rhodes State Office Tower
30 E Broad Street
33rd Floor
Columbus, OH 43215-3414
614-466-2613
Fax: 614-466-4494
communications@oac.ohio.gov
www.oac.ohio.gov
State agency supporting the arts in Ohio by offering grants, programs and other resources for artists and their supporters.

Geraldine Warner, Chair
Donna S Collins, Executive Director

683 **Ohio Association of School Business Officials**
8050 N High Street
Suite 170
Columbus, OH 43235
614-431-9116
844-838-5395
Fax: 614-431-9137
callie@oasbo-ohio.org
www.oasbo-ohio.org
The Ohio Association of School Business Officials is a nonprofit educational management organization dedicated to learning, utilizing and sharing the best methods and technology for school business administration.

Jim Rowan, Executive Director
Debbie Trzeciak, Chief Financial Officer

684 **Ohio Association of Secondary School Administrators**
8050 N High Street
Suite 180
Columbus, OH 43235-6484
614-430-8311
Fax: 614-430-8315
info@oassa.org
www.oassa.org
The Ohio Association of Secondary School Administrators is dedicated to advocating for the welfare of its members, while offering leadership, professional development and legislative influence.

Timothy Freeman, Executive Director
Heather Powell, Associate Executive Director

685 **Ohio Education for Homeless Children and Youth**
Ohio Department of Education
25 S Front Street
Mail Stop 404
Columbus, OH 43215
614-387-7725
Fax: 614-387-0963
Susannah.wayland@education.ohio.gov
www.education.ohio.gov
Represents initiatives and programs created to ensure that children and youth experiencing homelessness have access to education.

Susannah Wayland, Education Coordinator
Shannon D Teague, Assistant Director

686 **Ohio Library Council**
1105 Schrock Road
Suite 440
Columbus, OH 43229
614-410-8092
Fax: 614-410-8098
olc@olc.org
www.olc.org
The Ohio Library Council is the statewide professional association representing the interests of Ohio's public libraries and library staff. The council offers support for development of libraries through advocacy, education and collaboration.

Andrew Mangels, Chair
Douglas Evans, Executive Director

687 **Ohio Technology and Engineering Educators Association**
330-494-1100
tdouce@getsetsite.org
www.oteea.org
The mission of the Ohio Technology and Engineering Educators Association is to improve technological literacy for all Ohio students by providing professional development and networking opportunities to educators, as well as advocacy and public education on the value of technological literacy.

Richard F Miller, President
Victor Stefan, Executive Director

Oklahoma

688 Oklahoma Arts Council
Jim Thorpe Building
2101 N Lincoln Boulevard
Suite 640
Oklahoma City, OK 73105
405-521-2931
Fax: 405-521-6418
okarts@arts.ok.gov
www.arts.ok.gov
The Oklahoma Arts Council is responsible for helping to develop the arts in Oklahoma through grants, education, programs and initiatives.

Phyllis Stough, Chair
Amber Sharples, Executive Director

689 Oklahoma Department of Libraries
Allen Wright Memorial Library
200 NE 18th Street
Oklahoma City, OK 73105-3298
405-521-2502
Fax: 405-525-7804
info@libraries.ok.gov
www.libraries.ok.gov
Official state library of Oklahoma responsible for serving the state government's records management needs, assisting in developing libraries, coordinating projects and serving the public with programs and learning resources.

Melody Kellogg, Director
Vicki Sullivan, Deputy Director

690 Oklahoma Education Association (OEA)
323 E Madison Street
PO Box 18485
Oklahoma City, OK 73154
405-528-7785
800-522-8091
Fax: 405-524-0350
rkennedy@okea.org
www.okea.org
The Oklahoma Education Association (OEA) supports public education as the cornerstone of a democratic society. The association is comprised of public school teachers, counselors, administrators and others playing supporting roles in the education field. Some services offered by the association include legislative advocacy, professional development and other resources.

Alicia Priest, President
David DuVall, Executive Director

691 Oklahoma Education for Homeless Children and Youth
PO Box 36609
Oklahoma City, OK 73136
405-587-0106
Fax: 405-587-0642
webmaster@okcps.org
www.okcps.org
Initiative to offer supports for homeless children and youth, with the aim of making education more accessible to them.

Kathy Brown, Homeless Coordinator
Bryan Coleman, Assistant

692 Oklahoma Library Association (OLA)
PO Box 6550
Edmond, OK 73083
405-525-5100
Fax: 405-525-5103
exec_director@oklibs.org
www.oklibs.org
The Oklahoma Library Association supports libraries, library services and librarianship in Oklahoma. Members include library staff, library trustees, students, volunteers and others. The association offers advocacy, conferences and leadership resources.

Linda Pye, President
Natalie Currie, Secretary

Oregon

693 AFT-Oregon (American Federation of Teachers-Oregon)
10228 SW Capitol Hwy
Portland, OR 97219-6809
971-888-5665
aftoregon@aft-oregon.org
www.or.aft.org
Charted in 1952, AFT-Oregon, a state affiliate of the American Federation of Teachers, AFL-CIO, is a non-profit organization representing some 16,000 faculty and classified workers in K-12 and higher education, as well as child care workers. AFT-Oregon works with other unions and community groups to advocate for quality education and health care for all people in Oregon.

Jaime Rodriguez, President
Karen Bartholomew, Operations Specialist

694 Education of Homeless Children and Youth Program
255 Capitol St NE
Salem, OR 97310-0203
503-947-5781
Fax: 503-378-5156
dona.bolt@state.or.us
www.oregon.gov/ode
Ensures homless children and youth in Oregon have free access to education.

Dona Bolt, Education Specialist

695 Oregon Arts Commission
775 Summer St NE
Suite 200
Salem, OR 97301-1280
503-986-0082
Fax: 503-986-0082
www.oregonartscommission.org
Supports and funds creative initiatives in Oregon.

Brian Rogers, Executive Director
Kat Bell, Grants & Office Coordinator

696 Oregon Association of Student Councils (OASC)
707 13th Street SE
Suite 100
Salem, OR 97301-4035
503-480-7206
Fax: 503-581-9840
sara@oasc.org
www.oasc.org
The Oregon Association of Student Councils is a non-profit member association, serving middle and high schools throughout the state. It provides leadership development to both students and advisors and is sponsored by the Confederation of Oregon School Administrators.

Ben Bowman, Chair
Sara S Nilles, Executive Director

697 Oregon Education Association (OEA)
6900 SW Atlanta Street
Portland, OR 97223
503-684-3300
800-858-5505
Fax: 503-684-8063
www.oregoned.org
The mission of the Oregon Education Association (OEA) is to assure quality public education for every student in Oregon by providing a strong, positive voice for school employees. OEA's school funding priority, established in December 2002, seeks to restore stable and adequate funding for Oregon's schools and community colleges so that all Oregon students have access to a quality public education.

John Larson, President
Jim Fotter, Executive Director

698 Oregon Library Association (OLA)
PO Box 3067
La Grande, OR 97850-2042
541-962-5824
ola@olaweb.org
www.olaweb.org
The mission of the Oregon Library Association is to promote and advance library service through public and professional education and cooperation. Holds a conference in March and publishes two journals.

Elaine Hirsch, President
Kathy Street, Secretary

699 Oregon Student Assistance Commission (OSAC)
1500 Valley River Drive
Suite 100
Eugene, OR 97401
541-687-7400
800-452-8807
Fax: 541-687-7414
www.oregonstudentaid.gov

Juan Baez-Arevalo, Director
Susan Degen, Manager, State Grants

Pennsylvania

700 Office of Postsecondary Higher Education
333 Market St
Harrisburg, PA 17126-0333
717-787-5041
Fax: 717-772-3622

701 Pennsylvania Council on the Arts
215 Finance Building
Harrisburg, PA 17120
717-787-6883
Fax: 717-783-2538
www.pacouncilonthearts.org

702 Pennsylvania Library Association (PaLA)
220 Cumberland Parkway
Suite 10
Mechanicsburg, PA 17055
717-766-7663
800-622-3308
Fax: 717-766-5440
glenn@palibraries.org
www.palibraries.org
The Pennsylvania Library Association (PaLA) is a professional non-profit organization with strong volunteer leadership, dedicated to the support of its members, to the advancement of librarianship, and to the improvement and promotion of quality library service for citizens of the Commonwealth.

Glenn Miller, Executive Director
Mary O Garm, President

3 **Pennsylvania School Librarians Association**
9 Saint James Avenue
Somerville, MA 02144
617-628-4451
www.psla.org
Provides school librarians/media specialists with educational opportunities and current information through publications, workshops, seminars and conferences
Marg Foster, Secretary
Nancy S Latanision, President

4 **Pennsylvania State Education Association (PSEA)**
400 N 3rd Street
PO Box 1724
Harrisburg, PA 17105-1724
717-255-7000
800-944-7732
Fax: 717-255-7124
www.psea.org
PSEA's mission is to advocate for quality public education and our members through collective action. PSEA is a member-driven organization, headed by elected officers, an executive director and a board of directors.
James P Testerman, President
John F Springer, Executive Director

5 **Reading Education Association (REA)**
125 Morgantown Road
Suite 2
Reading, PA 19611
610-374-7101
www.readingea.com
The Reading Education Association (REA) represents the educators and students of Reading, Pennsylvania. REA advocates for the equal education and educational opportunities for the school district of Reading.
Priscilla Knight, Office Manager

Rhode Island

6 **Higher Education Assistance Authority**
560 Jefferson Blvd
Suite 100
Warwick, RI 02886-1304
401-736-1100
800-922-9855
Fax: 401-732-3541
www.riheaa.org

7 **National Education Association Rhode Island (NEARI)**
99 Bald Hill Road
Cranston, RI 02920
401-463-9630
Fax: 401-463-5337
RWalsh@nea.org
www.neari.org/matriarch/default.asp
The NEA Rhode Island is both a union and a professional organization.
Robert A Walsh Jr, Executive Director
Vincent P Santaniello, Deputy Executive Director

08 **Rhode Island Association of School Business Officials**
600 Mount Pleasant Avenue
Building #16, RIC
Providence, RI 02908
401-272-9811
Fax: 401-272-9834
www.riasp.org
Is an umbrella association serving elementary, middle level, and high school leaders from all across Rhode Island. Affiliated with both the National Association of Elementary School Principals (NAESP) and the National Association of Secondary School Principals (NASSP)
Norma Cole, President
Arlene Miguel, Secretary

709 **Rhode Island Educational Media Association**
6946 Camp Avenue
Suite 402
North Kingstown, RI 02852
401-398-7500
Fax: 401-886-0855
www@ride.ri.net
RINET provides complete Internet solutions for organizations that serve children, such as schools, libraries, municipalities, as well as high quality technology programs and services in support of K-12 teaching, learning and administration
Founded: 1999
Mike Mello, Membership Chairman
Sharon Hussey, Executive Director

710 **Rhode Island Library Association**
PO Box 6765
Providence, RI 02940
401-943-9080
Fax: 401-946-5079
book_n@yahoo.com
The Rhode Island Library Association is a profesional association of Librarians, Library Staff, Trustees, and library supporters whose purpose is to promote the profession of librarianship and to improve the visibility, accessibility, responsiveness and effectiveness of library and information services throughout Rhode Island.
Christopher Laroux, President
Laura Marlane, Vice President

711 **State Council on the Arts**
One Capitol Hill
Providence, RI 02908
401-222-3880
Fax: 401-222-3018
www.arts.ri.gov

South Carolina

712 **Education for Homeless Children and Youth**
1429 Senate St
Suite 1114-E
Columbia, SC 29201
803-734-3215
Fax: 803-734-3043
www.ed.sc.gov/

713 **South Carolina Arts Commission**
1800 Gervais St
Columbia, SC 29201
803-734-8696
Fax: 803-734-8526

714 **South Carolina Commission on Higher Education**
1333 Main St
Suite 200
Columbia, SC 29201
803-737-2260
877-349-7183
Fax: 803-737-2297
www.che.sc.gov

715 **South Carolina Education Association (SCEA)**
421 Zimalcrest Drive
Columbia, SC 29210
803-772-6553
800-422-7232
Fax: 803-772-0922
help@thescea.org
www.thescea.org/
Professional association for educators in South Carolina.
Aaron Wallace, Executive Director
Carolyn Randolph, Assistant Executive Director

716 **South Carolina Library Association**
PO Box 1763
Columbia, SC 29202
803-252-1087
scla@capconsc.com
www.scla.org
Informs members of issues and provides training and networking opportunities.
Megan Palmer, President
Danielle Robinson, Treasurer

South Dakota

717 **Education for Homeless Children and Youth**
700 Governors Dr
Pierre, SD 57501
605-773-6400
Fax: 605-773-3782

718 **Mountain Plains Library Association (MPLA)**
14293 West Center Drive
Lakewood, CO 80228
303-985-7795
mpla_execsecretary@operamail.com
www.mpla.us
The Mountain Plains Library Association (MPLA) is a twelve state association of librarians, library paraprofessionals and friends of libraries in Arizona, Colorado, Kansas, Montana, Nebraska, Nevada, New Mexico, North Dakota, Oklahoma, South Dakota, Utah and Wyoming. Its purpose is to promote the development of librarians and libraries by providing significant educational and networking opportunities. Holds conferences in September, October and November. Also publishes a newsletter.
Judy Zelenski, Interim Executive Secretary
Dan Chaney, MPLA Webmaster

719 **South Dakota Arts Council**
711 E Wells Ave
Pierre, SD 57501-3369
605-773-3301
800-952-3625
Fax: 605-773-5657
www.artscouncil.sd.gov

720 **South Dakota Education Association (SDEA)**
441 E Capitol Avenue
Pierre, SD 57501
605-224-9263
800-529-0090
Fax: 605-224-5810
Bryce.Healy@sdea.org
www.sdea.org/
The South Dakota Education Association/SDEA advocates new directions for public education, providing professional

services that benefit students, schools and the public.

Bryce Healy, Executive Director
Paul McCorkle, CFO/CIO

721 South Dakota Library Association
28363 472nd Ave
Worthing, SD 57707
605-343-3750
www.sdlibraryassociation.org
The SD Library Association strives to promote library service of the highest quality for present and potential SD library users; to provide opportunities for professional involvement of all persons engaged in any phase of librarianship within the state; and to further the professional development of SD librarians, trustees, and library employees.

Jan Brue Enright, President
Laura Olson, Secretary/Treasurer

Tennessee

722 Education for Homeless Children and Youth
710 James Robertson Parkway
Nashville, TN 37243-0379
615-532-6309
Fax: 615-253-5706

723 Tennessee Arts Commission
401 Charlotte Ave
Nasville, TN 37243-0780
615-532-5934
Fax: 615-741-8559
www.arts.state.tn.us

724 Tennessee Association of Secondary School Principals (TASSP)
2671 Bebe Branch Lane
Knoxville, TN 37928
423-309-6187
866-737-2777
Fax: 865-687-2341
www.tnassp.org/
The mission of the Tennessee Association of Secondary School Principals is: to promote professional standards of practice for secondary school administrators; provide high quality professional development experiences for rural, urban, and suburban administrators, statewide, based on their common and unique professional development needs; and advocate on behalf of secondary administrators in their efforts to provide high quality education for all students.

Dana Finch, President
Tommy Everette, Executive Director

725 Tennessee Higher Education Commission
404 James Robertson Parkway
Suite 1900
Nashville, TN 37243-0830
615-741-3605
Fax: 615-741-6230

726 Tennessee Library Association
PO Box 241074
Memphis, TN 38124-1074
901-485-6952
Fax: 615-269-1807
arhuggins1@comcast.net
www.tnla.org
Promote the establishment, maintenance, and support of adequate library services for all people of the state.

Annelle R Huggins, Executive Director
Dinah Harris, President

727 Tennessee School Boards Association
525 Brick Church Park Drive
Nashville, TN 37207
615-815-3900
www.tsba.net
The mission of the Tennessee School Boards Association is to assist school boards in effectively governing school districts.

Founded: 1953

Tammy Grissom, Executive Director
Ben Torres, Assistant Executive Director

Texas

728 Texas Association of Secondary School Principals (TASSP)
1833 S IH-35
Austin, TX 78741
512-443-2100
Fax: 512-442-3343
www.tassp.org/
TASSP provides proactive leadership to systemically change schools into learning communities in which all students and other participants achieve their full potential as life long learners in a diverse and changing society.

Bob Alvey, President
Tom Leyden, Associate Executive Director

729 Texas Commission on the Arts
PO Box 13406
Austin, TX 78711-3406
512-463-5535
800-252-9415
Fax: 512-475-2699
www.arts.state.tx.us

730 Texas Higher Education Coordinating Board
PO Box 12788
Austin, TX 78711-2788
512-427-6101
800-242-3062
Fax: 512-427-6127
www.thecb.state.tx.us

731 Texas Homeless Education Office
2901 N IH35
Austin, TX 78722
512-475-8765
800-446-3142
Fax: 512-471-6193

732 Texas Library Association (TLA)
3355 Bee Cave Road
Suite 401
Austin, TX 78746-6763
512-328-1518
800-580-2852
Fax: 512-328-8852
tla@txla.org
www.txla.org
The Texas Library Association is a professional organization that promotes librarianship and library service in Texas. Through legislative advocacy, continuing education events, and networking channels, TLA offers members opportunities for service to the profession as well as for personal growth.

Patricia H Smith, Executive Director
Gloria Meraz, Communications Director

Utah

733 Education for Homeless Children and Youth
250 East 500 S
PO Box 144200
Salt Lake City, UT 84114-4200
801-538-7975
Fax: 801-538-7991
www.schools.utah.gov

734 Utah Arts Council
617 East South Temple
Salt Lake City, UT 84102
801-320-9794
Fax: 801-533-3210
www.arts.utah.gov

735 Utah Education Association (UEA)
875 E 5180 S
Murray, UT 84107-5299
801-266-4461
800-594-8996
Fax: 801-265-2249
mark.mickelsen@utea.org
The mission of the Utah Education Association (UEA) is to advance the cause of public education in partnership with others: strengthen the teaching profession, promote quality schools for Utah's children, and advocate the well-being of members.

Kim Campbell, President
Mark Mickelsen, Executive Director

736 Utah State Library Division
250 North 1950 W
Suite A
Salt Lake City, UT 84116-7901
801-715-6777
800-433-1479
Fax: 801-715-6767

737 Utah System of Higher Education
60 South 400 W
Salt Lake City, UT 84101-1284
801-321-7103
Fax: 801-321-7156
www.utahsbr.edu

Vermont

738 Education for Homeless Children and Youth
120 State St
Montpelier, VT 05620-2501
802-828-5148
Fax: 802-828-0573
www.education.vermont.gov/new/html/pgm_homeless.html

739 Vermont Arts Council
136 State St
Montpelier, VT 05633-6001
802-828-3778
Fax: 802-828-3363
www.vermontartscouncil.org

740 Vermont Department of Libraries
109 State St
Montpelier, VT 05609-0601
802-828-3261
Fax: 802-828-2199
www.libraries.vermont.gov

1 Vermont Library Association
PO Box 803
Burlington, VT 05402
802-388-3845
Fax: 802-388-4367
www.vermontlibraries.org
The Vermont Library Association is an educational Organization working to develop, promote, and improve library and information services and librarianship in the state of Vermont.

Judah S Hamer, President
David Clark, Chapter Councilor

2 Vermont National Education Association (VTNEA)
10 Wheelock Street
Montpelier, VT 05602-3737
802-223-6375
800-649-6375
Fax: 802-223-1253
vtnea@together.net
www.vtnea.org/
The Vermont National Education Association is a voluntary organization of 11,000 Vermont teachers and education support professionals, their purpose being to make sure that members have a satisfying work environment where they are acknowledged for the work they perform and where the work they perform helps students do their best.

Joel D Cook, Executive Director
Darren M Allen, Communications Director

3 Vermont Student Assistance Corporation
10 East Allen St
PO Box 2000
Winooski, VT 05404-2601
www.vsac.org

4 Volunteers for Peace
131 Main Street
Suite 201
Burlington, VT 05401
802-598-0052
vfp@vfp.org
www.vfp.org
Volunteers for Peace promotes intercultural education and volunteer opportunities abroad so that people from diverse backgrounds can learn to work together to develop communities.

Tom Sherman, President
Matt Messier, Executive Director

Virginia

45 Child Development Resources (CDR)
150 Point O'Woods Road
Williamsburg, VA 23188
757-566-3300
Fax: 757-566-8977
info@cdr.org
www.cdr.org
A comprehensive resource for physicians, teachers, and parents covering questions about infants or toddlers. Areas served are Williamsburg, James City County, York County, and Poquoson, Virginia. Services include early intervention for children with disabilities and/or at-risk children.

Founded: 1965

Paul Scott, Executive Director
Carla Javier, Dir., Children's Services

46 Division of Student Leadership Services
701 East Franklin Streetÿ
Richmond, VA 23288-0001
804-285-2829
Fax: 804-285-1379
www.vaprincipals.org
Organization that sponsors the Virginia Student Councils Association; the Virginia Association of Honor Societies; and the Virginia Association of Student Activity Advisers.

Dr. Randy Barrack, President

747 Education for Homeless Children and Youth
PO Box 8795
Williamsburg, VA 23187-8795
757-221-4002
877-455-3412
Fax: 757-221-5300
www.wm.edu/hope

748 Organization of Virginia Homeschoolers
PO Box 5131
Charlottesville, VA 22905
866-513-6173
Fax: 804-946-2263
info@vahomeschoolers.org
www.vahomeschoolers.org
The Organization of Virginia Homeschoolers' most effective action is screening legislation for potential impact on homeschoolers. We pay attention to a large list of topics: home instruction statute, tutor provision, religious exemption provision, driver training, truancy, curfews, tax credits, and more.

Parrish Mort, President
Kenneth L Payne, Executive Director

749 Southern Association of Colleges & Schools
SACS Commission on Colleges
1866 Southern Lane
Decatur, GA 30033
404-679-4500
questions@sacscoc.org
www.sacscoc.org
Public and private school accreditation organization serving the southern states.

Belle S. Wheelan, Ph.D, President

750 State Council of Higher Education for Virginia
101 North 14th St
Richmond, VA 23219
804-225-2600
Fax: 804-225-2604
www.schev.edu

751 Virginia Alliance for Arts Education
PO Box 70232
Richmond, VA 23255-0232
804-740-7865
Fax: 804-828-2335
To promote aesthetic and creative art education for the development of the individual at all levels in the commonwealth of Virginia. To assist teachers in improving the quality of art education. To organize and conduct panels, forums, lectures, and tours for art educators and the general public on art and art instruction. To keep the public informed of the arts through whatever means are available.

Founded: 1974

Margaret Edwards, Division Director

752 Virginia Association for Health, Physical Education, Recreation & Dance
817 W Franklin Street
Box 842037
Richmond, VA 23284-2037
800-918-9899
Fax: 800-918-9899
www.vahperd.org
VAHPERD is a professional association of educators that advocate quality programs in health, physical education, recreation, dance and sport. The association seeks to facilitate the professional growth and educational practices and legislation that will impact the profession.

Judith Clark, President

753 Virginia Association for Supervision and Curriculum Development
33074 Clay Street
Hopewell, VA 23860
804-458-9554
vascd1@verizon.net
www.vaascd.org/
VASCD is an organization committed to excellence in education by providing programs and services that promote quality instruction for lifelong learning.

Linda Hyslop, Executive Director
Judy Lam, Administrative Coordinator

754 Virginia Association for the Education ofthe Gifted
PO Box 26212
Richmond, VA 23260-6212
804-355-5945
Fax: 804-355-5137
vagifted@comcast.net
www.vagifted.org
The Virginia Association for the Gifted supports research in gifted education and advocates specialized preparation for educators of the gifted. The association disseminates information, maintains a statewide network of communication, and cooperates with organizations and agencies to improve the quality of education in the Commonwealth of Virginia.

Liz Nelson, Executive Director

755 Virginia Association of Elementary School Principals
1805 Chantilly Street
Richmond, VA 23230
804-355-6791
www.vaesp.net
Nonprofit professional association advocating for public education and equal educational opportunities. Promotes leadership of school administrators and principals, and provides professional development opportunities.

Casey L. Conger, President
Jim Baldwin, Executive Director

756 Virginia Association of Independent Specialized Education Facilities
919 E Main Street
Suite 1150
Richmond, VA 23219
804-643-2776
Fax: 866-232-0034
www.vaisef.org
An association of private providers of specialized education and services for youth with special needs and their families.

William P. Elwood, Executive Director

757 Virginia Association of Independent Schools
9100 Arboretum Parkway
Suite 310
Richmond, VA 23236
804-282-3592
Fax: 804-282-3596
info@vais.org
www.vais.org

The Virginia Association of Independent Schools is a service organization that promotes educational, ethical and professional excellence. Through its school evaluation/accreditation program, attention to professional development and insistence on integrity, the Association safeguards the interests of its member schools.

Betsy Johnson Hunroe, Executive Director
Ellen Bostic, Director, Operations

758 Virginia Association of School Superintendents
1805 Chantilly Street
PO Box 400265
Richmond, VA ÿ2323-4265
Fax: 434-982-2942
www.vass.edschool.virginia.edu/
The Virginia Association of School Superintendents (VASS) is a professional organization dedicated to the mission of providing leadership and advocacy for public school education throughout the Commonwealth of Virginia.

J Andrew Stamp, Associate Executive Director
Alfred R Butler IV, Executive Director

759 Virginia Association of School Business Officials
Williamsburg-James City County Public Schools
PO Box 8783
Williamsburg, VA 23187-8783
757-253-6748
Fax: 757-253-0173
www.vasbo.org/
The mission of the Virginia Association of School Business Officials is to promote the highest standards of school business practices for its membership through professional development, continuing education, networking, and legislative impact.

David C Papenfuse, Division Director

760 Virginia Association of School Personnel Administrators
800 E City Hall Avenue
Norfolk, VA 23510-2723
757-340-1217
Fax: 757-340-1889
www.vaspa.org/
The Virginia Association of School Personnel Administrators helps personnel/human resources professionals improve their administrative skills and grow extensively in their profession.

Eddid P Antoine II, Division Director
Barbara Warren Jones, President

761 Virginia Commission for the Arts
223 Governor St
Richmond, VA 23219-2010
804-225-3132
Fax: 804-225-4327

762 Virginia Congress of Parents & Teachers
1027 Wilmer Avenue
Richmond, VA 23227-2419
804-264-1234
866-482-497
Fax: 804-264-4014
info@vapta.org
www.vapta.org
The Virginia Congress of Parents and Teachers, better known as the Virginia PTA is a volunteer child advocacy association working for ALL children and youth in the Commonwealth of Virginia.

Melissa S Nehrbass, President
Eugene A Goldberg, Executive Director

763 Virginia Consortium of Administrators for Education of the Gifted
RR 5 Box 680
Farmville, VA 23901-9011
804-225-2884
Fax: 814-692-3163
www.vagifted.org

Catherine Cottrell, Division Director

764 Virginia Council for Private Education
P.O. Box 29255
Richmond, VA 23242
804-423-6435
Fax: 804-423-6436
office@vcpe.org
www.vcpe.org
The Virginia Council for Private Education (VCPE) oversees accreditation of nonpublic preschool, elementary and secondary schools in the Commonwealth.

Grace T. Creasey, M.Ed., Executive Director
Dana Heller, Director of Operations

765 Virginia Council of Administrators of Special Education
Franklin County Public Schools
25 Bernard Road
Rocky Mount, VA 24151
703-493-0280
Fax: 540-483-5806
The Virginia Council of Administrators of Special Education is a professional organization that promotes professional leadership through the provision of collegial support and current information on recommended instructional practices as well as local, state and national trends in Special Education for professionals who serve students with disabilities in order to improve the quality and delivery of special education services in Virginia's public Schools

Dr. Sheila Bailey, President
Wyllys VanDerwerker, President-Elect

766 Virginia Council of Teachers of Mathematics
1033 Backwoods Road
Virginia Beach, VA 23455-6617
757-671-7316
www.vctm.org/
The purpose of the Virginia Council of Teachers of Mathematics is to stimulate an active interest in mathematics, to provide an interchange of ideas in the teaching of mathematics, to promote the improvement of mathematics education in Virginia, to provide leadership in the professional development of teachers, to provide resources for teachers and to facilitate cooperation among mathematics organizations at the local, state and national levels

Ellen Smith Hook, Division Director
Ian Shenk, President

767 Virginia Council on Economic Education
301 W Main Street
Box 844000
Richmond, VA 23284-4000
804-828-1627
Fax: 804-828-7215
shfinley@vcu.edu
www.vcee.org
Goal is for students to understand our economy and develop the life-long decision-making skills they need to be effective, informed citizens, consumers, savers, investors, producers and employees.

Yvonne Toms Allmond, Senior Vice President
Sallie Garrett, Contact

768 Virginia Education Association
116 S 3rd Street
Richmond, VA 23219
804-648-5801
800-552-9554
Fax: 804-775-8379
kboitnott@veanea.org
www.veanea.org/
VEA is a statewide community of more than 60,000 teachers and school support professionals working for the betterment of public education in the Commonwealth. First organized in 1863, VEA has consistently advocated for quality instruction and curriculum, adequate funding, and excellent working conditions for Virginia public employees.

Robert Whitehead, Executive Director
Kitty Boitnott, President

769 Virginia Educational Media Association
PO Box 2743
Fairfax, VA 22031-2743
703-764-0719
Fax: 703-272-3643
Aim is to promote literacy, information access and evaluation, love of literature, effective use of technology, collaboration in the teaching and learning process, intellectual freedom, professional growth, instructional leadership and lifelong learning.

Jean Remler, Executive Director
Terri Britt, President

770 Virginia Educational Research Association
3354 Taleen Court
Annandale, VA 22003-1161
703-698-1325
Fax: 703-698-0587
www.va-edresearch.org
The mission of the Educational Research Service is to improve the education of children and youth by providing educators and the public with timely and reliable research and information.

Dr. Edith Carter, Assistant Professor
Michaeline M Powell, President

771 Virginia High School League
1642 State Farm Boulevard
Charlottesville, VA 22911-8609
434-977-8475
Fax: 434-977-5943
ktillry@vhsl.org
www.vhsl.org
The Virginia High School League is an alliance of Virginia's public high schools that promotes education, leadership, sportsmanship, character and citizenship for students by establishing and maintaining high standards for school activities and competitions.

Craig Barbrow, President
Susan Bechtol, Chairman

772 Virginia Library Association
PO Box 56312
Virginia Beach, VA 23503-0277
757-583-0041
Fax: 757-583-5041
www.vla.org
The Virginia Library Association is a statewide organization whose purpose is to develop, promote, and improve library and information services and the profession of librarianship in order to advance literacy and learning and to ensure ac-

cess to information in the Commonwealth of Virginia.

Linda Hahne, Executive Director

3 **Virginia Middle School Association**
11138 Marsh Road
Bealeton, VA 22712-9360
703-439-3207
Fax: 540-439-2051
www.vmsa.org/

Lisa Norris, President
Virginia Jones, President Elect

4 **Virginia School Boards Association**
200 Hansen Road
Charlottesville, VA 22911
434-295-8722
Fax: 434-295-8785
www.vsba.org
The Virginia School Boards Association is a voluntary, nonpartisan association whose primary mission is the advancement of education through the unique American tradition of local citizen control of, and accountability for, the Commonwealth's public schools.

Gina Patterson, Executive Director
Jessica Blythe, Director, Communications

5 **Virginia Student Councils Association**
4909 Cutshaw Avenue
Richmond, VA 23230
804-355-2777
Fax: 804-285-1379
rbarrack@vassp.org
www.vassp.org/vsca.html
Assist school principals and assistant principals in providing leadership to their schools and communities for the purpose of improving the education of Virginia's youth.

Randy D Barrack, Executive Director
Lawrence W Lenz, President

6 **Virginia Vocational Association**
10259 Lakeridge Square Court
Suite G
Ashland, VA 23005-8159
804-365-4556

Jean Holbrook, President
Kathy Williams, Executive Director

77 **Voices for Virginia's Children**
701 E Franklin Street
Suite 807
Richmond, VA 23219
804-649-0184
Fax: 804-649-0161
info@vakids.org
www.vakids.org
Independent organization advocating for better lives and futures for the children and youth of Virginia. The organization makes recommendations for policy solutions, advises policymakers and develops leadership in support of policy initiatives.

Founded: 1994

Jamie Dyke Clancey, Board Chair
Margaret Nimmo Holland, Executive Director

Washington

78 **Jewish Federation of Greater Seattle**
6th Avenue & Lenora Street
Seattle, WA 98121
206-443-5400
Fax: 206-770-6363
info@jewishinseattle.org
www.jewishinseattle.org
Works to sustain a vibrant Jewish cimmunity that is connected locally, in Israel and worldwide. The federation also serves the needs of the Jewish comunity in Puget Sound region by offering human services, education, and cultural opportunities.

Founded: 1928

Nancy B Greer, President & CEO
Karen Parry, Director, Development

779 **Washington Education Association**
32032 Weyerhaeuser Way S
PO Box 9100
Federal Way, WA 98001-9687
253-941-6700
800-622-3393
www.washingtonea.org
The mission of the Washington Education Association is to advance the professional interests of its members in order to make public education the best it can be for students, staff and communities

John Donaghy, Executive Director
Rod Regan, Director

780 **Washington Library Association**
PO Box 33808
Seattle, WA 98133
206-823-1138
info@wla.org
www.wla.org
The Washington Library Association provides the leadership needed to develop, improve and promote library services so that all Washington residents can benefit from these services to further their education and enhance their skills.

Kate Laughlin, Executive Director

781 **Washington State Arts Commission**
PO Box 42675
Olympia, WA 98504-2675
360-753-3860
Fax: 360-586-5351
www.arts.wa.gov

782 **Washington State Higher Education Coordinating Board**
917 Lakeridge Way
PO Box 43430
Olympia, WA 98504-3430
360-753-7800
Fax: 360-753-7808

West Virginia

783 **Edvantia**
1031 Quarrier Street
PO Box 1348
Charleston, WV 25325-1348
304-347-0400
800-624-9120
Fax: 304-347-0487
info@edvantia.org
www.edvantia.org
Edvantia is a nonprofit corporation committed to helping client-partners improve education and meet federal and state mandates. Schools, districts, and state education agencies-as well as publishers and service providers-rely on Edvantia's core capabilities in research, evaluation, professional development, and technical assistance to help them succeed.

Nancy Balow, Author
Patricia Hammer, Director of Communications
Carolyn Luzader, Communications Specialist

784 **West Virginia Division of Culture and History**
The Culture Center Capitol Complex
199 Kanawha Boulevard E
Charleston, WV 25305-0300
604-558-0240
Fax: 304-558-3560
www.wvculture.org
The West Virginia Division of Culture and History works to identify, preserve, protect, and promote the art, culture, and artifacts of West Virginia.

Randall Reid-Smith, Commissioner
Caryn Gresham, Deputy Commissioner

785 **West Virginia Education Association**
1558 Quarrier Street
Charleston, WV 25311
304-346-5315
800-642-8261
Fax: 304-346-4325
mail@wvea.org
www.wvea.org
The West Virginia Education Association (WVEA) is a voluntary membership organization dedicated to advocating for education employees and the public education system. The WVEA has 15,000 members, 100 local affiliates, and is associated with the National Education Association.

David Haney, Executive Director
Ladonna Campbell, Secretary

786 **West Virginia Higher Education Policy Commission**
1018 Kanawha Boulevard E
Suite 700
Charleston, WV 25301
304-558-0699
Fax: 304-558-1011
molly.george@wvhepc.edu
www.hepc.wvnet.edu
The West Virginia Higher Education Commission develops policy for West Virginia's four-year colleges and universities.

Paul L. Hill, Chancellor

787 **West Virginia Library Association**
WV
www.wvla.org
The West Virginia Library Association (WVLA) promotes library services and librarianship in West Virginia.

Founded: 1914

Brenna Call, President
Kelly Funkhouser, Executive Director

788 **West Virginia Library Commission**
Culture Center, Building 9
1900 Kanawha Boulevard E
Charleston, WV 25305
304-558-2041
800-642-9021
www.librarycommission.lib.wv.us
The West Virginia Library Commission is focused on improving library and information services.

Karen Goff, Executive secretary
Jennifer Johnson, Admin Services Director

Wisconsin

789 **Division for Libraries and Technology**
Wisconsin Department of Public Instruction
125 S Webster St
Madison, WI 53707

608-266-3390
800-441-4563
www.dpi.wi.gov/dltcl
The Division for Libraries and Technology provides learning and information needs to Wisconsin citizens.

Tony Evers, State Superintendent

790 Wisconsin Arts Board
201 West Washington Avenue
PO Box 8690
Madison, WI 53708-8690
608-266-0190
Fax: 608-267-0380
www.artsboard.wisconsin.gov
A state agency, the Wisconsin Arts Board fosters arts, creativity, art education, community, and economic development and serves as a cultural resource for Wisconsin.

George Tzougros, Executive Director
Karen Goeschko, Assistant Director, Programs

791 Wisconsin Education Association Council
33 Nob Hill Drive
PO Box 8003
Madison, WI 53708-8003
608-276-7711
800-362-8034
Fax: 608-276-8203
www.weac.org
The Wisconsin Education Association Council (WEAC) is statewide educational organization representing public education employees including teachers, counselors, librarians, education support professionals, and university students studying to be teachers. WEAC supports a range of policies, reforms, and development opportunities designed to better public education.

Founded: 1853

Ron Martin, President
Peggy Wirtz-Olsen, Vice President

792 Wisconsin Higher Educational Aids Board
131 W Wilson Street, Suite 902
PO Box 7885
Madison, WI 53703-7885
608-267-2206
Fax: 607-267-2808
HEABmail@wi.gov
www.heab.state.wi.us
The Higher Educational Aids Board (HEAB) manages the states student financial aid system for residents in Wisconsin attending higher education institutions. HEAB provides financial aid programs, including grants, scholarships, and loan programs.

John Reinemann, Executive Secretary
Cassie Weisensel, Operations Program Associate

793 Wisconsin Library Association
4610 South Biltmore Lane
Suite 100
Madison, WI 53718-2153
608-245-3640
Fax: 608-245-3646
wla@wisconsinlibraries.org
www.wla.wisconsinlibraries.org
The Wisconsin Library Association advocates for and supports libraries, and library workers in the state of Wisconsin.

Plumer Lovelace, Executive Director
Vanessa Mauss, Membership Coordinator

Wyoming

794 Wyoming Arts Council (WAC)
Barrett Building
2301 Central Avenue
2nd Floor
Cheyenne, WY 82002
307-777-7742
michael.lange@wyo.gov
www.wyoarts.state.wy.us
The Wyoming Arts Council invests in resources that promote excellence in the arts; providing grants, and programs, and through partnerships the Council funds art projects across the state.

Michael Lange, Executive Director
Rachel Clifton, Assistant Director

795 Wyoming Education Association (WEA)
115 E 22nd Street
Suite 1
Cheyenne, WY 82001-3795
307-634-7991
Fax: 800-778-8161
rsniffin@wyoea.org
www.wyoea.org
The Wyoming Education Association is dedicated to improving public education in the state of Wyoming. The WEA works at all levels of education, in schools, colleges, and universities and facilitates the improvement in teaching and learning. The Association has more than 6,300 members.

Founded: 1892

Ron Sniffin, Executive Director
Kathy Vetter, President

796 Wyoming Library Association (WLA)
PO Box 1387
Cheyenne, WY 82003
307-632-7622
lauragrott@gmail.com
www.wyla.org
The Wyoming Library Association works to support, promote and educate the community on libraries, libraniship, and services provided by libraries in Wyoming.

Laura Grott, Executive Secrerary

797 Wyoming School Boards Association (WSBA)
2323 Pioneer Avenue
Cheyenne, WY 82001
307-634-1112
Fax: 307-634-1114
wsba@wsba-wy.org
www.wsba-wy.org
The Wyoming School Boards Association represents local school boards advocating for improved educational opportunities in Wyoming public schools. Through resource sharing members of the WSBA provides educational services to students that would be otherwise economically unfeasible.

Brian Farmer, Executive Director
Richard Strahorn, Director, Member Services

International

8 **AISA School Leaders' Retreat and Educators Conference**
Association of International Schools in Africa
Peponi Road
PO Box 14103, Nairobi
Kenya 00800
254-20-2697442
Fax: 254-20-4183272
info@aisa.or.ke
www.aisa.or.ke
Facilitates communications, cooperation, and professional growth among member schools. Promotes intercultural understanding and friendships as well as facilitating collaboration between its members, host country schools, and other regional and professional groups.
Annual/October
Peter Bateman, Executive Director

9 **Association for Experiential Education Annual Conference**
2315 18th Street S
Saint Petersburg, FL 33712
303-440-8844
www.aee.org
Annual international and regional conference dedicated to promoting, defining, developing, and applying the theories and practices of experiential education.
November
1,200 attendees
Sherry Bagley, Executive Director
Steve Pace, Director, Accreditations

0 **CIEE Annual Conference**
Council on International Educational Exchange
300 Fore Street
Portland, ME 04101
207-553-4000
conference@ciee.org
www.ciee.org
Open to study-abroad advisors, administrators, faculty and other international education professionals. The conference is an opportunity to share ideas, keep up with developments in the field, and meet with colleagues from around the world.
November
James P. Pellow, Ed.D, President & CEO
Tim Propp, Chief Operating Officer

1 **Center for Critical Thinking and Moral Critique International Conference**
Foundation for Critical Thinking
PO Box 196
Tomales, CA 94971
707-878-9100
800-833-3645
Fax: 707-878-9111
cct@criticalthinking.org
www.criticalthinking.org
Over 1,200 educators participate to discuss critical thinking and educational change.
Dr. Linda Elder, Senior Fellow
Dr. Gerald Nosich, Senior Fellow

02 **Council for Advancement and Support of Education (CASE)**
1201 Eye Street NW
Washington, DC 20005
202-328-2273
Fax: 202-387-4973
membersupportcenter@case.org
www.case.org
Offers numerous opportunities in the United States, Canada, Mexico, mainland Europe, and the United Kingdom to network with colleagues.
Fall/Winter
Sue Cunningham, President & CEO
Rob Moore, VP, Communications

803 **Council for Learning Disabilities International Conference**
11184 Antioch Road
PO Box 405
Overland Park, KS 66210
913-491-1011
Fax: 913-491-1011
www.council-for-learning-disabilities.org
Intensive interaction with and among professional educators and top LD researchers. Concise, informative and interesting forums on topics from effective instruction to self-reliance are presented by well-known professionals from across the country and around the world.
October
35 booths with 800 attendees
Joseph Morgan, President
Linda Nease, Executive Director

804 **Council of British Independent Schools in the European Communities Annual Conference**
St. Mary's University Palace
Strawberry Hill
Twickenham, UK TW1-4SX
44(0) 208 240 4142
Fax: 44(0) 208 240 4255
excecutive.director@cobis.org.uk
www.cobis.org.uk
Conference for members of senior management educational teams.
May
75 attendees and 20 exhibits
Colin Bell, Executive Director
Suzanne Howarth, Membership

805 **Early Education Leaders' Summit**
Association of Christian Schools International
731 Chapel Hills Drive
Colorado Springs, CO 80920
719-367-5391
800-367-0798
communications@acsi.org
www.acsi.org
Leadership training for early educators.
Larry Taylor, President
Kevin Buelke, Chief Finance Officer

806 **Early Educators' Conference**
Association of Christian Schools International
731 Chapel Hills Drive
Colorado Springs, CO 80920
719-367-5391
800-367-0798
communications@acsi.org
www.acsi.org
Professional development for early educators.
Larry Taylor, President
Kevin Buelke, Chief Finance Officer

807 **European Council of International Schools**
146 Buckingham Palace Road
Fourth Floor
London, UK SW1W-9TR
+44 0 20 7824 7040
Fax: +44 0 20 7824 7041
ecis@ecis.org
www.ecis.org
Support professional development, curriculum and instruction, leadership and good governance in international schools located in Europe and around the world.
April, November
Michelle Clue, Conference Coordinator
Jean Vahey, Executive Director

808 **Foundation for Student Communication International Conference**
Princeton University
48 University Place
Suite 305
Princeton, NJ 08544
info@businesstoday.org
www.businesstoday.org
The conference connects leading graduates from around the world with global business leaders.
Annual
Sowon Lee, President
Richard Qiu, Director, Finance

809 **Hort School: Conference of the Association of American Schools**
International School of Panama
P.O. Box 0819-02588
Panama City
507-293-3000
Fax: 507-266-7808
www.isp.edu.pa
Educates and inspires our students to reach their full potential and contribute to the world by providing an exemplary English language education enriched by our multicultural community.
October
600 attendees and 35 exhibits
Rajiv Bhat, Director
Terry McCoy, President

810 **International Association of Teachers of English as a Foreign Language**
Darwin College
University of Kent
Canterbury, Kent, UK CT2-7NY
44-1227-824430
Fax: 44-1227-824431
www.iatefl.org
Plenary sessions by eminent practitioners, a large number of workshops, talks and round tables given by other speakers, an ELT Resources Exhibition and Pre-Conference Events organized by Special Interest Groups.
April
80 booths with 1500 attendees
Alison Medland, Conference Organizer
Glenda Smart, Executive Director

811 **International Awards & Personalization Expo Trade Show**
8735 W Higgins Road
Suite 300
Chicago, IL 60631
847-375-4800
Fax: 847-375-6480
info@awardspersonalization.org
www.awardspersonalization.org
The International Awards & Personalization Expo offers opportunities for business leaders to learn about processes and products, experience hands-on training, and connect with industry colleagues on the subject of custom awards manufacturing.
February
Louise Ristau, CAE, Executive Director
Liz Giannini, Senior Operations Manager

812 International Awards Market
Awards and Recognition Association
4700 W Lake Avenue
Glenview, IL 60025
847-375-4800
800-344-2148
Fax: 888-374-7257
info@ara.org
www.ara.org
Providing outstanding business and educational opportunities for both retailers and suppliers. Retailers can view the latest industry products, take advantage of special show offers and benefit from a full educational program.
Feb, March, Nov
200 booths with 6,000 attendees
Lori Warren, President

813 International Conference
World Association for Symphonic Bands & Ensembles
1037 Mill Street
San Luis Obispo, CA 93401
805-541-8000
Fax: 805-543-9498
www.wasbe.org
WASBE is a nonprofit, international association open to individuals, institutions, and industries interested in symphonic bands and wind ensembles. Dedicated to enhancing the quality of the wind band throughout the world and exposing its members to new worlds of repertoire, musical culture, people and places.
Every 2 years
Bert Aalders, President

814 International Congress for School Effectiveness & Improvement
International Congress Secretariat
86 Ellison Road
Springwood
Australia NSW-2777
61 2 4751 7974
Fax: 61 2 4751 7974
admin@icsei.net
www.icsei.net
The purpose of building and using an expanded base for advancing research, practice and policy in the area of school effectiveness and improvement. The Congress offers the opportunity to exchange information and networking for the educational community.
January
500 attendees
Dr. Lorna Earl, President
Dr. Alma Harris, President Elect

815 International Dyslexia Association Annual Conference
40 York Road
4th Floor
Baltimore, MD 21204-2044
410-296-0232
800-ABC-D123
Fax: 410-321-5069
info@interdys.org
www.interdys.org
Provide the most comprehensive range of information and services that address the full scope of dyslexia and related difficulties in learning to read and write.
November
3000 attendees
Darnella Parks, Conference Manager
Kristen Penczek, Conference Director

816 International Exhibit
National Institute for Staff & Organizational Dev.
University of Texas
1912 Speedway, Stop D5600
Austin, TX 78712-1607
512-471-7545
Fax: 512-471-9426
www.nisod.org
The largest international conference to focus specifically on the celebration of teaching, learning, and leadership excellence.
May
1500 attendees
Sheryl Powell, Conference Director

817 International Listening Association Annual Convention
International Listening Association
Box 164
Belle Plaine, MN 56011
952-594-5697
Convention topics cover broad spectrum of listening practice and research. Papers, panels, courses, practice and workshops can be found at the convention in effort to network, spread research and new practices in effetcive listening training,
June
Dr. Nanette Johnson-Curiskis, Executive Director
Debra Worthington, Convention Planner

818 International Multicultural Institute (IMCI) Annual Conference
International Multicultural Institute
595 6th Street
Brooklyn, NY 11215
718-832-8625
www.imciglobal.org
Brings together practitioners from across the country and around the world to explore diversity and multiculturalism in both personal and professional contexts. Leaders from academia, business, and government present the latest thinking and action on diversity issues to conference participants.
June
Nancy J. Di Dia, Executive Director
Margaret Regan, President

819 International Reading Association Annual Convention
800 Barksdale Road
PO Box 8139
Newark, DE 19714-8139
302-731-1600
800-336-7323
Fax: 302-731-1057
customerservice@reading.org
www.reading.org
Contains exhibitors involved in various lectures and workshops dealing with illiteracy, literature and some library science courses.
May
800 booths with 13M attendees
Carrice C. Cummins, President
Marcie Craig Post, Executive Director

820 International Technology and Engineering Educators Association Conference
1914 Association Drive
Suite 201
Reston, VA 20191-1539
703-860-2100
Fax: 703-860-0353
iteea@iteea.org
www.iteea.org
Provides teachers with new and exciting ideas for educating students of all grade levels. The conference gives educators an opportunity for better understanding of the constant changes that take place in technology education.
150 booths with 2,200+ attendees
Steven A. Barbato, Executive Director
Kaitlin Blackborow, Meeting & Event Manager

821 International Trombone Festival
International Trombone Association
PO Box 441
Coppell, TX 75019
888-684-2361
Fax: 888-684-2362
www.trombone.net
Annual festival giving trombonists the opportunity to meet and share with other trombonists for performances, lectures, exhibits, competitions and more.
June
John Drew, President
Jon Bohls, Festivals Director

822 Learning Disabilities Association of America International Conference
4068 Mount Royal Boulevard
Suite 224B
Allison Park, PA 15101
412-341-1515
info@ldaamerica.org
www.ldaamerica.org
The conference connects adults with learning disabilities, educators, social workers, counselors, parents, researchers, attorneys, advocates and more.
Cindy Cipoletti, Executive Director
Nina DelPrato, Administrative Manager

National

823 AAUW National Convention
American Association of University Women
1111 16th Street NW
Washington, DC 20036
202-785-7700
800-326-2289
Fax: 202-872-1425
convention@aauw.org
www.aauw.org
The nation's leading voice promoting education and equity for women and girls. Speakers, panels and workshops allow for networking with other AAUW members and explore opportunities to further empower women.
Katie Broendel, Media/PR Manager
Christy Jones, Membership Director

824 ASCD Annual Conference
Association for Supervision & Curriculum Develop.
1703 N Beauregard Street
Alexandria, VA 22311-1714
press@ascd.org
www.ascd.org
Explores best practices, strategies, and skills for educators.
12000 attendees
Ranjit Sidhu, CEO & Executive Director
Dana Shanks-Williams, Chief Financial Officer

825 ASCD Leadership Summit
Association for Supervision & Curriculum Develop.
1703 N Beauregard Street
Alexandria, VA 22311-1714

press@ascd.org
www.ascd.org
The focus of the conference is on instructional leadership, leveraging resources, and leading and supporting students and adults.

Ranjit Sidhu, CEO & Executive Director
Dana Shanks-Williams, Chief Financial Officer

6 AZLA Conference
Arizona Library Association
1645 W Valencia Road
Suite 109-432
Tuscon, AZ 85746
602-614-2841
admin@azla.org
www.azla.org
Advance the education advantages of the state through libraries, and to promote general interest in library extension (traveling libraries). Sometimes conference is a joint venture between two libraries.

November
90+ booths with 2,000 attendees

Christine Dykgraaf, Conference Chair

7 AdvancED
National Study of School Evaluation
9115 Westside Parkway
Alpharetta, GA 30009-4958
678-392-2285
888-413-3669
Fax: 847-995-9088
contactus@advanc-ed.org
www.advanc-ed.org
Annual international summit held in Washington, DC. Share research on best educational practices, research based products. Research helps shape educational policy and strengthen learning practices worldwide.

November

Dr. Mark A Elgart, President/CEO

8 American Association for Employment in Education Annual Conference
American Association for Employment in Education
947 E. Johnstown Rd.
#170
Gahanna, OH 43230
614-485-1111
800-678-6010
Fax: 360-244-7802
aaee@osu.edu
www.aaee.org
Disseminate information on the educational marketplace, and job search process. Promote ethical standards and practices in the employment process. Promote dialogue and cooperation among institutions which prepare educators and institutions which provide employment opportunities.

November
20 booths with 150-200 attendees

Doug Peden, Executive Director
Diana Sanchez, Nat'l Conference Prog. Chair

29 American Association of Colleges for Teacher Education Annual Meeting
1602 L Street NW
Suite 601
Washington, DC 20036
202-293-2450
Fax: 202-457-8095
aacte@aacte.org
www.aacte.org
Learning event for educator preparation professionals. Oppportunities for networking, advancing understanding of new concepts and theories, hear new research and discover innovative practices and programs.

Lynn M. Gangone, President & CEO
Matthew Wales, Vice President, Events

830 American Association of Physics Teachers National Meeting
1 Physics Ellipse
College Park, MD 20740-3845
301-209-3311
Fax: 301-209-0845
eo@aapt.org
www.aapt.org
Gives members the opportunity to network, discuss innovations in teaching methods and share the results of research about teaching and learning.

Beth A. Cunningham, Executive Officer
Tiffany M. Hayes, Director, Conferences

831 American Association of School Librarians National Conference
American Library Association
225 N Michigan Avenue
Suite 1300
Chicago, IL 60601
312-280-4382
800-545-2433
Fax: 312-280-5276
aasl@ala.org
www.ala.org/aasl
An open conference holding seminars, workshops and tours of local libraries and facilities.

3,000 attendees

Sylvia Knight Norton, Executive Director
Allison Cline, Deputy Executive Director

832 American Association of Sexuality Educators, Counselors & Therapists Conference
35 E Wacker Drive
Suite 850
Chicago, IL 60601
202-499-1099
Fax: 202-216-9646
info@aasect.org
www.aasect.org
Facilitate productive discussions about identity and human sexuality; encourage interdisciplinary, intergenerational and cross-cultural collaboration and networking of current sexual health topics; provide opportunities for developing and refining skills in sexuality education, therapy, counseling and research.

50 booths with 400-500 attendees

Kellie Braband, Executive Director
Jessica Gonzalez, Certification & CE Manager

833 American Association of Teachers of French Convention
American Association of Teachers of French
302 N Granite Street
Marion, IL 62959-2346
815-310-0490
Fax: 815-310-5754
aatf@frenchteachers.org
www.frenchteachers.org
Conventions regularly occur in French-speaking areas. Representing the French language in North America and to encourage the dissemination, both in the schools and in the general public, of knowledge concerning all aspects of the culture and civilization of France and the French-speaking world.

July

Anne Jensen, President
Jayne Abrate, Executive Director

834 American Camp Association National Conference
American Camp Association
5000 State Road 67 N
Martinsville, IN 46151-7902
765-342-8456
800-428-2267
Fax: 765-342-2065
conference@ACAcamps.org
www.acacamps.org
Largest national camp conference hosted in the United States. Focuses on professional development, networking and commerce.

February
175 booths with 1500 attendees

Peg Smith, CEO
Kim Bruno, Marketing Manager

835 American Council on Education Annual Meeting
American Council on Education
1 Dupont Circle NW
Washington, DC 20036
202-939-9300
annualmeeting@ace.nche.edu
www.acenet.edu
Brings together higher education leaders from all sectors. The American Council on Education annual meeting is seen as the go-to event to network with colleagues, hear about emerging trends from national thought leaders and learn about new approaches to campus challenges.

March
74 booths

Ted Mitchell, President
Kara Freeman, Chief Operating Officer

836 American Council on the Teaching of Foreign Languages Annual Conference
1001 N Fairfax Street
Suite 200
Alexandria, VA 22314
703-894-2900
headquarters@actfl.org
www.actfl.org
Professional development opportunities, including pre and post convention workshops and sessions focused on all aspects of teaching and learning languages and cultures.

November
250 booths with 6,000+ attendees

Howie Berman, Executive Director
Julia Richardson, Director, Conventions

837 American Counseling Association Annual Conference
American Counseling Association
6101 Stevenson Avenue
Suite 600
Alexandria, VA 22304
703-823-9800
800-347-6647
Fax: 800-473-2329
acamemberservices@counseling.org
www.counseling.org
Education sessions, speakers, mental health training and time and space for networking

with other professionals in the mental health field.

4000 attendees

Richard Yep, Chief Executive Officer
Brandi McIntyre, Governance Exec. Office Mgr.

838 American Educational Research Association Annual Brown Lecture
American Educational Research Association
1430 K Street NW
Suite 1200
Washington, DC 20005
202-238-3200
Fax: 202-238-3250
communications@aera.net
www.aera.net
Features lectures on the vital role research plays in improving equality and equity in education.

October

Felice J. Levine, Executive Director
Lori Diane Hill, Assoc. Exec. Dir., Programs

839 American Indian Science & Engineering Society Annual Conference
6321 Riverside Plaza Lane NW
Unit A
Albuquerque, NM 87120
505-765-1052
Fax: 505-765-5608
info@aises.org
www.aises.org
The American Indian Science and Engineering Society is a national, nonprofit organization focused on substantially increasing the representation of American Indians, Alaska Natives, Native Hawaiians, Pacific Islanders, First Nations and other indigenous peoples of North America in science, technology, engineering and math (STEM) studies and careers. Provides an opportunity for networking, educational workshops, a career fair, showcasing academic research and study.

Sarah EchoHawk, Chief Executive Officer
Kellie Jewett-Fernandez, Chief Development Officer

840 American Library Association (ALA) Annual Conference & Exhibition
American Library Association
225 N Michigan Avenue
Suite 1300
Chicago, IL 60601
312-944-6780
800-545-2433
Fax: 312-440-9374
ala@ala.org
www.ala.org
Programs, updates, conversations about key issues like digital content, e-books, technology in libraries, books, leadership, literacy advocacy, community engagement and library marketing. Also provides networking opportunities.

20000+ attendees

Tracie D. Hall, Executive Director
Cheryl Malden, Program Officer

841 American Mathematical Society
American Mathematical Society
201 Charles Street
Providence, RI 02904-2294
401-455-4000
800-321-4267
Fax: 401-331-3842
meet@ams.org
www.ams.org
Advance mathematical achievement, encouraging research and provide communication necessary to progress in the field. Preserve, supplement and utilize the results of the research of mathematicians throughout the world.

January

Dr. Donald McClure, Executive Director
Penny Pina, Director Meetings/Conference

842 American Montessori Society Conference
116 East 16th Street
New York, NY 10003-2163
212-358-1250
Fax: 212-358-1256
ams@amshq.org
www.conference.amshq.org
Promotes quality Montessori education for all children from birth to 18 years of age. Conference participants share knowledge and research and strengthen bonds while creating new networks. Conference workshops address curriculum, socio-emotional development, leadership, public policy, research and more.

March

Munir Shivji, Executive Director
Gina Taliaferro Lofquist, Senior Director, Education

843 American Psychological Association Annual Conference
750 1st Street NE
Washington, DC 20002-4242
202-336-5500
800-374-2721
Fax: 202-336-6123
convention@apa.org
A national conference attended by psychologists from around the world. The conference has workshops, lectures, discussions, roundtables and symposiums.

August

13,000 attendees

Donald N Bersoff, Ph.D, JD, President

844 American Public Health Association Annual Meeting
American Public Health Association
800 I Street NW
Washington, DC 20001-3710
202-777-2742
Fax: 202-777-2534
anna.keller@apha.org
www.apha.org
The premier platform to share successes and failures, discover exceptional best practices and learn from expert colleagues and the latest research in the field.

November
650 booths with 13000 attendees

Georges C. Benjamin, Executive Director
James E. Dale, CoA Chair

845 American School Health Association School Health Conference
501 N Morton Street
Suite 110
Bloomington, IN 47404
202-854-1721
info@ashaweb.org
www.ashaweb.org
Attendees include school nurses, health educators, health counselors, physicians and students. During the conference, presentations are made by ASHA members, government officials and health education professionals covering a variety of issues centered around child and adolescent health.

October
40 booths with 500 attendees

Jeanie Alter, Executive Director
Kaitlyn Celis, Manager, Membership Services

846 American Speech-Language-Hearing Association Annual Convention
2200 Research Boulevard
Rockville, MD 20850-3289
301-296-5700
800-498-2071
Fax: 301-296-8580
www.asha.org
A scientific and professional conference of speech-language pathology, audiology and other professionals. Opportunity to learn about latest evidence based research, enhance clinical skills, improve technique and gain new tools and resources to advance career.

Annual
November
400 booths with 12,000 attendees

A. Lynn Williams, President
Arlene A. Pietranton, Chief Executive Officer

847 American Technical Education Association Annual Conference
ATEA
Dunwoody College of Technology
818 Dunwoody Boulevard
Minneapolis, MN 55403
612-381-3315
info@ateaonline.org
www.ateaonline.org
Administrators, directors and faculty of various technical institutes, junior colleges, universities and colleges. Topics cover all aspects of computer assisted instruction, distance education and technical education. Professional development opportunity for all involved in postsecondary technical education.

Sandra Krebsbach, Executive Director

848 Annual Effective Schools Conference
7227 North 16th Street
Suite 190
Phoenix, AZ 85020
866-626-7556
Fax: 888-756-7628
now@4aplus.com
Latest research and methods for creating successful educational environments where all students can reach their academic potential. Gain valuable hands-on experience, learn proven implementation strategies and hear from some of the greatest minds in the field.

March

Amber Countiss
Annie Hanks

849 Annual International Conference on ADHD
4221 Forbes Boulevard
Suite 270
Lanham, MD 20706
301-306-7070
Fax: 301-306-7090
customer_service@chadd.org
www.chadd.org/conference
The conference features research, practice, and public information on ADHD. It brings together children and adults with ADHD, clinicians, edu-

cators, researchers, coaches, organizers, advocates, and others.

November
60 booths

Patricia M. Hudak, President
Hermoine Wellman, Director, Meetings & Events

0 Annual NAEN Conference
North American Assoc. of Educational Negotiators
423 Allen Road
Porter Corners, NY 12859
518-369-5779
execdir@naen.org
www.naen.org
Conference on collective bargaining for educational professionals.

James B. Fernow, President
Rachel M. Rissetto, Executive Director

1 Association for Behavior Analysis International Annual Convention
Association for Behavior Analysis International
550 W Centre Avenue
Portage, MI 49024
269-492-9310
www.abainternational.org
Psychologists, psychology faculty and students, counselors and social workers are among the attendees of this conference offering over 25 exhibitors. The conference is research and education oriented.

43 booths

Maria E. Malott, Chief Executive Officer

2 Association for Behavioral and Cognitive Therapies Annual Convention
305 7th Avenue
16th Floor
New York, NY 10001-6008
212-647-1890
Fax: 212-647-1865
www.abct.org
Provide participants with clinical knowledge of specific issues or new research in the field, networking possibilities, clinical roundtable, panel discussions on training and symposia of the presentation of data or research.

November
2,000 attendees

Mary Ellen Brown, Education/Mtg Services Dir.
Mary Jane Eimer, Executive Director

53 Association for Education Finance and Policy
6703 Madison Creek
Columbia, MO 65203
573-814-9878
Fax: 314-256-2831
info@aefpweb.org
www.aefpweb.org
The conference theme changes yearly; this year the focus is education renewal and reform and the fact that domestic policy and global economic competition challenge our education system. The conference will present, discuss and evaluate the latest research on education topics and current reforms and policy directions.

March
3000 attendees

Deborah Cunningham, President
Angela M. Hull, Executive Director

854 Association for Education in Journalism and Mass Communication Conference
234 Outlet Pointe Boulevard
Suite A
Columbia, SC 29210-5667
803-798-0271
Fax: 803-772-3509
aejmchq@aol.com
www.aejmc.org
Featuring the latest in technology as well as special sessions on teaching, research and public service in the various components of journalism and mass communication.

August
1,500 attendees

Tim P. Vos, President
Amanda Caldwell, Interim Executive Director

855 Association for Interdisciplinary Studies Annual Conference
Oakland University
371 Wilson Boulevard
521 Wilson Hall
Rochester, MI 48309-4452
ais@interdisciplinarystudies.org
www.interdisciplinarystudies.org

October

Jennifer J. Dellner, President
Khadijah O. Miller, Ph.D, Vice President, Relations

856 Association for Persons with Severe Handicaps Annual Conference
1001 Connecticut Ave NW
Suite 235
Washington, DC 20036
202-540-9020
Fax: 202-540-9019
info@tash.org
www.tash.org
Provides a forum for individuals with disabilities, families, researchers, educators, scholars, and others to create dialogue around creating action for social and systems reform.

December
2,500 attendees

Barbara Trader, Executive Director

857 Association for Play Therapy Conference
Association for Play Therapy
401 Clovis Avenue
Suite 107
Clovis, CA 93612
559-298-3400
Fax: 559-298-3410
info@a4pt.org
www.a4pt.org
Major interdisciplinary event for Play Therapists wishing to earn continuing education credits, network with popular authors, speakers and vendors and enjoy extra curricular activities with peers.

October

Kathryn Lebby, President & CEO
Diane Leon, Vice President & COO

858 Association for Science Teacher Education International Conference
Association for Science Teacher Education
3451 S 5th Avenue
Whitehall, PA 18052
484-547-6046
executivedirector@theaste.org
www.theaste.org
Offers programs in science, mathematics and environmental education with a wide variety of teachers and professors attending.

Debi Hanuscin, President
Kate Popejoy, Executive Director

859 Association for the Education of Gifted Underachieving Students Conference
6 Wildwood Street
Burlington, MA 01803
651-962-5385
aegusquestions@gmail.com
www.aegus1.org
Attended by teachers, professors, administrators and social workers, this conference deals with cultural awareness and education of the disabled and gifted students.

April

Lois Baldwin, President
Terry Neu, Vice President

860 Association for the Study of Higher Education
University Of Nevada
4505 S. Maryland Parkway
453068
Las Vegas, NV 89154-3068
702-895-2737
Fax: 702-895-4269
ashe@unlv.edu
www.ashe.ws
The primary mission of the association for the Study of Higher Education (ASHE) is to foster scholarly inquiry of the highest standards of excellence for the purpose of increasing knowledge about and the understanding of higher education. This achieved through an annual scholarly conference, peer-reviewed publications, and various events and opportunities throughout the year.

November

Jason P. Guilbeau, Executive Director

861 Association of American Colleges & Universities Annual Meeting
Association of American Colleges & Universities
1818 R Street NW
Washington, DC 20009-1604
202-387-3760
Fax: 202-265-9532
www.aacu.org
Bringing together college educators from across institutional types, disciplines, and departments. Providing participants with innovative ideas and practices, and shaping the direction of their educational reform efforts.

January
1,200 attendees

Carol Geary, President

862 Association of Community College Trustees Conference
1233 20th Street NW
Suite 301
Washington, DC 20036-2907
202-775-4667
Fax: 202-223-1297
acctinfo@acct.org
www.acct.org
Exists to develop effective lay governing board leadership to strengthen the capacity of community colleges to achieve their missions on behalf of their communities.

1500+ attendees

J. Noah Brown, President/CEO
Lila Farmer, Conference Logistics Coord.

863 Association of Mathematics Teacher Educators Annual Conference
c/o Michigan Technological University
1400 Townsend Drive
Houghton, MI 49931
906-487-1126
www.amte.net
Annual conference for mathematics educators to come together and exchange the latest research and practice findings applicable to their fields of study.
February
Megan Burton, President
Shari Stockero, Executive Director

864 Association of Science and Technology Centers Annual Conference
Association of Science and Technology Centers
818 Connecticut Avenue NW
7th Floor
Washington, DC 20006-2734
202-783-7200
Fax: 202-783-7207
conference@astc.org
www.astc.org
Conference for professionals in science and technology centers across North America and the world.
October
2,600 attendees
Christofer Nelson, President & CEO
Melissa Ballard, Director, Programs

865 Association of Teacher Educators Annual Meeting
11350 Random Hills Road
Suite 800, PMB 6
Fairfax, VA 22030
703-659-1708
Fax: 703-595-4792
info@ate1.org
www.ate1.org
Alisa Chapman, Executive Director
John McIntyre, Director, Meetings

866 COSA School Law Seminar
National School Boards Association
1680 Duke Street
2nd Floor
Alexandria, VA 22314-3493
703-838-6722
Fax: 703-683-7590
info@nsba.org
www.nsba.org
Insights and advice are given to attorneys representing K-12 public school boards.
Viola M. Garcia, President
Chip Slaven, Interim Executive Director

867 CUBE Annual Conference
National School Boards Association
1680 Duke Street
2nd Floor
Alexandria, VA 22314-3493
703-838-6722
Fax: 703-683-7590
info@nsba.org
www.nsba.org
Annual conference of the Council of Urban Boards of Education, a council of the National School Boards Association.
September
Viola M. Garcia, President
Chip Slaven, Interim Executive Director

868 Center for Appalachian Studies Annual Conference
Appalachian Studies Center
One John Marshall Drive
Huntington, WV 25755-0918
304-696-2904
mthomas@marshall.edu
www.appalachianstudies.org
Central theme each year about some facet of Appalachia- communities, landscapes, evoulution of their work together-history, etc.
March
Katherine Ledford, Conference Chair
Mary Thomas, Executive Director

869 Center on Disabilities Conference
Students with Disabilities Resources
1811 Nordhoff
Bayramian Hall 110
Northridge, CA 91330-8264
818-677-1200
conference@csun.edu
www.csun.edu/cod
Provides a setting for researchers, practitioners, exhibitors, end users, speakers and participants to share knowledge and best practices in the field of assistive technology.
March
130 booths with 4800 attendees
Wayne Fernades, Mktg/Events Manager
Sandy Plotin, Managing Director

870 Choristers Guild's National Festival & Directors' Conference
Choristers Guild
12404 Park Central Drive
Suite 100
Dallas, TX 75251-1802
469-398-3606
800-246-7478
Fax: 469-398-3611
conferences@mailcg.org
www.choristersguild.org
Enables leaders to nurture the spiritual and musical growth of children and youth.
June
Jim Rindelaub, Director
Eve Hehn, Conferences

871 Closing the Gap
526 Main Street
PO Box 68
Henderson, MN 56044-0068
507-248-3294
Fax: 507-248-3810
info@closingthegap.com
www.closingthegap.com
Conference themes change yearly. Always focus on technology and howit changes—primarily with assistive technology.
October
150+ booths with 2400 attendees
Jan Latzke, Conference Registration
Connie Kneip, VP/General Manager

872 Conference for Advancement of Mathematics Teaching
Texas Education Agency
PO Box 200669
Austin, TX 78720-0669
512-335-2268
Fax: 512-335-8517
camt@camtonline.org
www.camtonline.org
Exhibits educational materials useful to mathematics teachers; education of the use of technology on the classroom and effective use of manipulative materials in the classroom.
July
175 booths with 7.5M-8M attendees
Joyce Polanco, Program Chair

873 Conference for Community Arts Education
520 8th Avenue
Suite 302
New York, NY 10018
212-268-3337
guildinfo@nationalguild.org
www.nationalguild.org
Brings together arts educators and leaders to share knowledge, network, and advance accessibility of arts education.
Adam Johnston, Deputy Director, Operations
Heather Ikemire, Deputy Director, Learning

874 Cooperative Education and Internship Association Conference
Cooperative Education and Internship Association
PO Box 42506
Cincinnati, OH 45242
513-793-2342
Fax: 513-793-0463
info@ceiainc.org
www.ceiainc.org
Conference aimed at practitioners and researchers from colleges, as well as employers.
Peggy Harrier, Executive Director

875 Council for Exceptional Children Annual Convention
The Council for Exceptional Children
2900 Crystal Drive
Suite 100
Arlington, VA 22202-3557
888-232-7733
service@cec.sped.org
www.cecconvention.org
The convention & expo is a special education professional development event. The event features educational sessions, opportunities to network with others working with children and learn about new and pending legislation, as well as a chance to explore cutting edge products and services.
February
Craig Evans, CMA, Executive Director
Carol Serrano, Dir., Conventions & Meetings

876 EDUCAUSE Annual Conference
4845 Pearl E Circle
Suite 118, PMB 43761
Boulder, CO 80301-6112
303-449-4430
Fax: 303-440-0461
info@educause.edu
www.educause.edu
Provides opportunity for educators to network with colleagues and learn form each other by sharing experience, ideas and information through presentations and sessions.
October
4,000+ attendees and 180 exhibits
John O'Brien, President & CEO
Mairead Martin, Chief Information Officer

877 Education Market Association
8380 Colesville Road
Silver Spring, MD 20910
301-495-0240
800-395-5550
Fax: 301-495-3330
www.edmarket.org

Lists 1,500 member dealers and manufacturers representatives for school supplies, equipment and instructional materials.

March
1200 booths with 5,000 attendees and 700 exhibits

Adrienne Dayton, VP of Marketing/Communicatio
Jim McGarry, President/ CEO

8 Educational Publishing Summit
Association of Educational Publishers
300 Martin Luther King Blvd.
Suite 200
Wilmington, DE 19801
302-295-8350
Fax: 302-656-2918
mail@aepweb.org
www.aepweb.org
Presents a range of informative and practical sessions that address all issues relating to the development and distribution of high-quality learning resources.

June

Charlene F Gaynor, CEO
JoAnn McDevitt, VP Sales/Mrktg/Business Dev.

9 Educational Theatre Association Conference
Educational Theatre Association
4805 Montgomery Road
Suite 400
Cincinnati, OH 45212
513-421-3900
Fax: 513-421-7077
info@schooltheatre.org
www.schooltheatre.org
Supports the association's mission by supporting educators through networking opportunities, educational workshops, speakers and resources that can enrich students' educational experience.

September
2,400 attendees

Julie Cohen Theobald, Executive Director
Allison Dolan, Chief Content Officer

0 GCSE Annual Conference
Global Council for Science and the Environment
1776 Eye Street NW
Suite 750
Washington, DC 20006
gcse@gcseglobal.org
www.gcseglobal.org
The Global Council for Science and the Environment is a nonprofit organization seeking to improve the scientific basis of environmental decision-making through fostering collaboration between leaders in the areas of interdisciplinary research, education, policy, and business.

Michelle Wyman, Executive Director
Erica Goldman, Ph.D, Deputy Director

81 INFOCOMM Tradeshow
InfoComm International
11242 Waples Mill Road
Suite 200
Fairfax, VA 22030
703-273-7200
800-659-7469
Fax: 703-273-5924
www.infocommshow.org
Designed for professionals in the audiovisual, information communications and system integration industries. Attendees can explore audiovisual products and services from the industry's leading manufacturers, and there are educational seminars, workshops and labs taught with a focus on technology, trends and the best practices in the country.

June

David Labuskes, Executive Director
Jason McGraw, Sr. VP Expositions

882 Independent Education Consultants Association Conference
3251 Old Lee Highway
Suite 510
Fairfax, VA 22030-1504
703-591-4850
800-888-4322
Fax: 703-591-4860
info@IECAonline.com
www.IECAonline.com
Attended by consultants, school, college and program admissions officers, administrators and staff and related service companies. Workshops and discussions led by leaders in their fields including specialists in educational trends, college admissions and boarding school issues, adolescent development, learning differences and emotional disorders and treatments.

Spring & Fall
400 booths with 800 attendees

Mark H Sklarow, Executive Director
Rachel King, Conference Manager

883 International Performance Improvement Conference
Int'l Society for Performance Improvement
1400 Spring Street
Suite 260
Silver Spring, MD 20910
301-587-8570
info@ispi.org
www.ispi.org
Provides educational opportunities with sessions in multiple formats across multiple tracks, keynote presentations, networking opportunities with other performance minded professionals across the spectrum of performance improvement disciplines.

April
60 booths with 1500 attendees

Nancy Crain Burns, President
Rose Baker, Treasurer

884 Iteachk
Staff Development for Educators
10 Sharon Road
PO Box 577
Peterborough, NH 03458
603-924-9621
800-462-1478
Fax: 800-337-9929
www.sde.com
Explore new technology engaging teachers and students, new games and tools for students, meet and learn from nation's top kindergarten experts, use strategies right away and network with others.

Jim Grant, Executive Director/Founder
Terra Tarango, President

885 Journalism Education Association National Convention
828 Mid-Campus Drive South
105 Kedzie Hall
Manhattan, KS 66506-1505
785-532-5532
Fax: 785-532-5563
staff@jea.org
www.jea.org
Semiannual gathering of high school journalists and advisers to discuss topics relevant to the profession of journalism, to network and to participate in professional learning workshops.

November

Sarah Nichols, MJE, President
Kelly Glasscock, CJE, Executive Director

886 Lutheran School Administrators Conference
Lutheran Education Association
7400 Augusta Street
River Forest, IL 60305
708-209-3343
Fax: 708-209-3458
lea@lea.org
www.lea.org
Conference features workshops, sectionals, plenary sessions, and a learning mall for administrators of schools.

Jonathan Laabs, Ed.D, Executive Director
Edward C. Grube, LL.D, Director, Communications

887 MEMSPA Annual State Conference
Michigan Elementary & Middle School Principals
Association
1980 N College Road
Mason, MI 48854
517-694-8955
Fax: 517-694-8945
www.memspa.org
Professional association for elementary & middle level principals.

Paul Liabenow, Executive Director
Syndee Malek, Associate Executive Director

888 MTNA National Conference
Music Teachers National Association
600 Vine Street
Suite 1710
Cincinnati, OH 45202
513-421-1420
888-512-5278
Fax: 513-421-2503
mtnanet@mtna.org
www.mtna.org/conference
Brings together representatives of the Music Teachers National Association. The conference features performances by students, classes, technology and informational sessions, pedagogy sessions, an exhibit hall and more.

March

Gary L. Ingle, Executive Director & CEO
Brian Shepard, Chief Operating Officer

889 Minnesota School Boards Association Leadership Conference
Minnesota School Boards Association
1900 W Jefferson Avenue
Saint Peter, MN 56082-3015
507-934-2450
800-324-4459
Fax: 507-931-1515
www.mnmsba.org
The purpose of the Association is to support, promote and enhance the work of public school boards.

January
200+ booths with 2,000+ attendees

Kirk Schneidawind, Executive Director
Gary Lee, Deputy Executive Director

890 Modern Language Association Convention
85 Broad Street
Suite 500
New York, NY 10004-2434
646-576-5000
Fax: 646-576-5160

convention@mla.org
www.mla.org
Opportunity for members to share scholarly findings and teaching experience and discuss trends in the field.

January
2000+ attendees

Paula M. Krebs, Executive Director
Dennis Looney, Director, Programs

891 NAAEE Annual Conference
North American Assoc. for Environmental Education
1725 Desales Street NW
Suite 401
Washington, DC 20036
202-419-0412
info@naaee.org
www.naaee.org
Promotes environmental education in the classroom and public, shares the latest research and information.

October

Judy Braus, Executive Director
Lori Mann, Director, Conferences

892 NABSE Annual Conference
National Alliance of Black School Educators
PO Box 176
Troy, NY 12181
833-762-2731
info@nabse.org
www.nabse.org
Offers educational workshops, plenary sessions, informative presentations, public forums, networking and fellowship.

November
300 booths with 6,000 attendees

Michael McFarland, President
Geneva A. Stark Pittman, Treasurer

893 NAESP Pre-K-8 Principals Conference
National Assoc. of Elementary School Principals
1615 Duke Street
Alexandria, VA 22314
703-684-3345
800-386-2377
Fax: 703-549-5568
naesp@naesp.org
www.naesp.org
Conference for Pre-K-8 principals to connect with peers, learn the best practices within their profession and prepare for the challenges ahead. Some topics that will be covered include Leading Learning Communities, Technology and Social Media, Arts Education and High Leverage Leadership.

July

L. Earl Franks, Ed.D, CAE, Executive Director
Nikki Sparks, Director, Operations

894 NAEYC Annual Conference
Nat'l Assoc. for the Education of Young Children
1401 H Street NW
Suite 600
Washington, DC 20005
202-232-8777
800-424-2460
help@naeyc.org
www.naeyc.org
Conference for teachers, program administrators, students, and researchers, featuring current trends and research in early education.

Rhian Evans Allvin, Chief Executive Officer
Jill Stasz Harris, Chief Operating Officer

895 NAFSA: Association of International Educators Annual Conference & Expo
1425 K Street NW
Suite 1200
Washington, DC 20005
202-737-3699
inbox@nafsa.org
www.nafsa.org
Annual meeting of professionals in the field of international education, for training workshops, educational sessions, networking opportunities and special events.

150 booths with 8,500 attendees

Esther D. Brimmer, Executive Director & CEO
Dorothea Antonio, Deputy Executive Director

896 NASPA Annual Conference
NASPA
111 K Street NE
10th Floor
Washington, DC 20002
202-265-7500
office@naspa.org
www.naspa.org
Exchange ideas with peers, earn continuing education credits, build new partnerships with vendors, gain tools and ideas and remain current on issues.

Annual
March
5000 attendees

Kevin Kruger, President
Stephanie Gordon, VP, Professional Development

897 NBEA Annual Convention
National Business Education Association
1914 Association Drive
Suite 203
Reston, VA 20191
703-860-8300
Fax: 703-860-4483
nbea@nbea.org
www.nbea.org
The National Business Education Association works to support individuals and groups who instruct, administer, research, and spread information regarding business. NBEA advances the professional interests of its members through programs that enhance professional growth and development.

March/April

Joe McClary, Executive Director
Jeri Werner, Operations Manager

898 NCEA Convention & Expo
National Catholic Educational Association
407 Bicksler Square SE
Leesburg, VA 20175-3773
571-257-0010
info@ncea.org
www.ncea.org
Attendees represent all aspects of Catholic and faith based education from pre-school to universities, to local parishes and more. Provides development sessions, departmental meetings, special events in order to gain knowledge and network with fellow colleagues.

Annually
April

Lincoln Snyder, President & CEO
Margaret Kaplow, Director, Marketing

899 NEA National Leadership Summit
National Education Association
1201 16th Street NW
Washington, DC 20036-3290
202-833-4000
Fax: 202-822-7974
www.nea.org/leadershipsummit
Meant to empower NEA members and leaders, encouraging them to develop their leadership knowledge and skills. There are interactive sessions and workshops exploring issues faced by the public education system.

March

Becky Pringle, President
Kim A. Anderson, Executive Director

900 NELA Annual Conference
New England Library Association
55 N Main Street
Unit 49
Belchertown, MA 01007
413-813-5254
rscheier@nelib.org
www.nelib.org
Bringing together librarians from New England in a forum to educate and network.

600 attendees

Robert Scheier, Administrator
Megan Bishop, Events Coordinator

901 NJLA Annual Conference
New Jersey Library Association
PO Box 1534
Trenton, NJ 08607
609-394-8032
Fax: 609-394-8164
ptumulty@njla.org
www.njlaconference.info

May
1139 attendees

Patricia A Tumulty, Executive Director

902 NOSS Conference
PO Box 963
Northport, AL 35476
205-331-5997
acook@thenoss.org
www.thenade.org
Conference for developmental education topics.

Annette Cook, Contact

903 NSBA Advocacy Institute
National School Boards Association
1680 Duke Street
2nd Floor
Alexandria, VA 22314-3493
703-838-6722
Fax: 703-683-7590
info@nsba.org
www.nsba.org
Meeting of school board members on Capitol Hill to shape legislative decisions around education.

February

Viola M. Garcia, President
Chip Slaven, Interim Executive Director

904 NSBA Annual Conference and Exposition
National School Boards Association
1680 Duke Street
2nd Floor
Alexandria, VA 22314-3493

703-838-6722
Fax: 703-683-7590
registration@nsba.org
www.nsba.org
The nation's largest policy and training conference for local education officials on national and federal issues affecting public schools in the U.S.

April
7,000 attendees and 300 exhibits

Viola M. Garcia, President
Chip Slaven, Interim Executive Director

5 NSEE Annual Conference
National Society for Experiential Education
19 Mantua Road
Mount Royal, NJ 08061
856-423-3427
Fax: 856-423-3420
nsee@talley.com
www.nsee.org
The purpose of the conference is to foster the effective use of experience as an integral part of education, in order to empower learners and promote the common good.

September

Haley Brust, Executive Director
Wendy Stevens, Meeting Manager

6 NSTA Annual Conference
National Science Teaching Association
1840 Wilson Boulevard
Arlington, VA 22201
703-243-7100
Fax: 703-243-7177
conferences@nsta.org
www.nsta.org
To promote excellence and innovation in science teaching and learning for all. Discover strategies for improving science teaching and learning, engage in professional discussions, receive the latest information of science education and network with colleagues from across the country and the globe.

Dr. Eric J. Pyle, President
Dr. Erika Shugart, Executive Director

7 National Academy Foundation NEXT
National Academy Foundation
218 West 40th Street
5th Floor
New York, NY 10018
212-635-2400
Fax: 212-635-2409
www.naf.org
Formerly the Institute for Staff Development, NEXT is a professional learning experience that will ignite innovation and spread effective practices across

July

JD Hoye, President
David Moore, Sr. VP Programs

08 National Art Education Association National Convention
National Art Education Association
901 Prince Street
Alexandria, VA 22314
703-860-8000
800-299-8321
Fax: 703-860-2960
info@arteducators.org
www.arteducators.org
Provides substantive professional development services that include the advancement of knowledge in all sessions, events and activities for the purpose of improving visual arts instruction in American schools.

March
171 booths with 5,000 attendees

Mario R. Rossero, Executive Director
A.J. Calbert, Chief Operations Officer

909 National Association Of State Directors Of Special Education Conference
NASDSE
1800 Diagonal Road
Suite 600
Alexandria, VA 22314
703-519-3800
www.nasdse.org
Multiple presentations, annual business meeting for state directors and networking opportunities.

October

John Eisenberg, Executive Director
Valerie Williams, Dir., Government Relations

910 National Association for Bilingual Education Conference
1775 I Street NW
Suite 1150
Washington, DC 20006
240-450-3700
www.nabe.org
Contains publishers and Fortune 500 companies displaying educational materials and multi-media products. Educational materials, products and services for use in linguistically and culturally diverse learning environments.

350 booths with 2,000+ attendees

Santiago V. Wood, Ed.D, National Executive Director
Nilda M. Aguirre, ED.S., Deputy Executive Director

911 National Association for College Admission Counseling Conference
Nat'l Association for College Admission Counseling
1050 N Highland Street
Suite 400
Arlington, VA 22201-2818
703-836-2222
800-822-6285
Fax: 703-243-9375
info@nacacnet.org
www.nacacnet.org
Membership association offering information to counselors and guidance professionals working in the college admissions office.

September
142 booths with 4,000 attendees

Joyce E. Smith, CEO
Bethany Blue Chirico, Director of Conference/Mtgs

912 National Association for Girls and Women in Sports Yearly Conference
1900 Association Drive
Reston, VA 20191-1598
703-476-3543
800-213-7193
Fax: 703-476-4566
nagws@aahperd.org
www.aahperd.org/nagws
An association providing information for girls and women in sports.

March/April
280 booths with 6,000 attendees

Lynda Ransdell, President
Sandra K. Sims, VP of Programs/Convention

913 National Association for Multicultural Education
NAME National Office
2100 M Street
Suite 170-245
Washington, DC 20037
202-628-6263
Fax: 202-628-6264
name@nameorg.org
www.nameorg.org
Opportunity to build networks, confront challenges and renews sense of possibility and hope in making schools and societies a better place through community advocacy and multicultural education.

Bette Tate Beaver, Executive Director

914 National Association for Music Education National Conference
National Association for Music Education (NAFME)
1806 Robert Fulton Drive
Reston, VA 20191
703-860-4000
800-336-3768
Fax: 888-275-6362
memberservices@nafme.org
www.nafme.org
Opportunities to network with peers from across the United States, professional development sessions giving tools and techniques for use in classrooms, receptions and keynote speakers.

Christopher Woodside, Executive Director
Elizabeth Lasko, Director, Membership

915 National Association of Biology Teachers Conference
PO Box 3363
Warrenton, VA 20188
703-264-9696
888-501-6228
Fax: 202-962-3939
office@nabt.org
www.nabt.org
Speakers, hands-on workshops, informative sessions on teaching biology.

November
140 booths with 1,700 attendees

Julie Angle, President
Jaclyn Reeves-Pepin, Executive Director

916 National Association of Independent Schools Conference
National Association of Independent Schools
1129 20th Street NW
Suite 800
Washington, DC 20036-3425
202-973-9700
Fax: 888-316-3862
annualconference@nais.org
www.nais.org
New ways to cultivate leadership in independent schools- for administrators, faculty and students- with workshops and speakers.

February/March
166 booths with 4000 attendees

Patrick Bassett, President
Amy Ahart, Director Annual Conference

917 National Association of Private Special Education Centers Conference
777 6th Street NW
11th Floor
Washington, DC 20001
202-434-8225
napsec@napsec.org
www.napsec.org

An annual conference for administrators of private programs serving people with disabilities.

Chris Tabakin, President
Danielle Johnson, Executive Director & CEO

918 National Association of School Psychologists Annual Convention
4340 East West Highway
Suite 402
Bethesda, MD 20814
301-657-0270
866-331-6277
Fax: 301-657-0275
www.nasponline.org
Gathering of school psychologists and related professionals, offering workshops, seminars, symposia, papers, presentations and exhibits on educational psychology topics.

100 booths with 4000 attendees

Kathleen Minke, Executive Director
Laura Benson, Chief Operating Officer

919 National Association of State Directors of Teacher Education and Certification Conference
1629 K Street NW
Suite 300
Washington, DC 20006
202-204-2208
Fax: 202-204-2210
NASDTEC is the National Association of State Directors of Teacher Education and Certification. It is the organization that represents professional standards boards and commissions and state departments of education in all 50 states.

June

Phillip S. Rogers, Executive Director

920 National Association of Student Financial Aid Administrators National Conference
1801 Pennsylvania Avenue NW
Suite 850
Washington, DC 20006-3606
202-785-0453
Fax: 202-785-1487
info@nasfaa.org
www.nasfaa.org/conference
Provides opportunities to learn and teach best practices in student financial aid, discover new products and services, network with others in the field and more.

June
2,300 attendees

Brent Tener, National Chair
Justin Draeger, President & CEO

921 National Black Child Development Institute Annual Conference
1313 L Street NW
Suite 110
Washington, DC 20005-4110
202-833-2220
800-556-2234
Fax: 202-833-8222
www.nbcdi.org
Educators and professionals in early care and education; elementary and secondary education and administration; child welfare and youth development; research; and local, state and federal policy convene to gain knowledge and acquire skills needed to ensure a quality future for all children and youth.

October

Felicia DeHaney, Pd.D, President/CEO
Keami Harris, Director of Programs

922 National Coalition for Aviation and Space Education
Omni Rosen Hotel
Orlando, FL
334-953-5095
mail@ncase.info
www.ncase.info
Provides educators with the tools that make classroom learning fun.

April

923 National Coalition of ESEA Title 1 Parents
310 Pennsylvania Ave. SE
3rd Floor
Washington, DC 20003
205-923-7955
Fax: 205-925-5403
Annual In-Service Professional Development conference on current education laws, legislation and educational issues with the assistance of the Department of Education.

October

Ernestine Thomas, President

924 National Conference on Student Services
Magna Publications
2718 Dryden Drive
Madison, WI 53704
608-246-3590
800-206-4805
Fax: 608-246-3597
www.magnapubs.com
Build strong foundation as a student leader, secure leadership skills and experience a possibly life-changing event.

April
35 booths with 500 attendees

Susan Liimata, Conference Manager
Catherine Stover, Managing Editor

925 National Council on Alcoholism & Drug Abuse
9355 Olive Boulevard
St. Louis, MO 63132
314-962-3456
Fax: 314-968-7394
info@ncada-stl.org
www.ncada-stl.org
A not-for-profit community health agency serving the metropolitan St. Louis area, provides educational materials on substance abuse and addiction, information and referral services, prevention and intervention.

Jim Murphy, President
Jenny Armbruster, Director, Community Services

926 National Dropout Prevention Network Conference
Clemson University
209 Martin Street
Clemson, SC 29631-1555
864-656-2599
864-656-2675
Fax: 864-656-0136
ndpc@clemson.edu
www.dropoutprevention.org
Networking opportunity for educators and counselors who work with at-risk students. Some subject areas that will be covered include absenteeism, workforce development, parent and family engagement, arts studies, alternative education and more.

October

Denise Gianforcaro, Registration
Debra Andrews, Coordination

927 National Education Association Annual Meeting
National Education Association
1201 16th Street NW
Washington, DC 20036-3290
202-833-4000
Fax: 202-822-7974
www.ra.nea.org
A general conference that addresses all facets and concerns of the educator.

June/July

Becky Pringle, President
Kim A. Anderson, Executive Director

928 National Forum to Advance Rural Education
National Rural Education Association
615 McCallie Avenue
Hunter Hall 212
Chattanooga, TN 37421
423-425-4539
allen-pratt@utc.edu
www.nrea.net
The National Forum to Advance Rural Education addresses issues that affect rural educators.

November
35 booths

Jon Habben, President
Allen Pratt, Ed.D, Executive Director

929 National Head Start Association Annual Conference
1651 Prince Street
Alexandria, VA 22314
703-739-0875
866-677-8724
www.nhsa.org
Seeks to advance program development and policy as well as promote training of the Head Start program professionals.

April

Yasmina Vinci, Executive Director
Kadejah Pearson, Manager, Conference & Events

930 National Parent Teacher Association Annual Convention & Expo
1250 N Pitt Street
Alexandria, VA 22314
703-518-1200
800-307-4782
Fax: 703-836-0942
info@pta.org
www.pta.org
Addresses parent-teacher involvement in education. Includes lectures, workshops and seminars for parents and professionals.

June

Nathan R. Monell, Executive Director
Kristen Johnson, Director, Education

931 National Reading Styles Institute Conference
PO Box 737
Syosset, NY 11791-3933
512-224-4555
800-331-3117
Fax: 516-921-5591
readingstyle@nrsi.com
www.nrsi.com
This conference addresses reading instruction and the problems of illiteracy.

July

Juliet Carbo, Conference Contact

2 **National Rehabilitation Education Conference**
National Council on Rehabilitation Education
1099 E Champlain Drive
Suite A, 137
Fresno, CA 93720
559-906-0787
info@ncre.org
www.ncre.org
A conference for professionals involved in training, recruiting, hiring and enhancing the development of rehabilitation counselors. Themes include evaluation processes, legislation and policy, employment, student development, inclusion and equity, career counseling and more.
Spring & Fall
Mona Robinson, Ph.D, CRC, President
Allison Fleming, Ph.D, CRC, First Vice President

3 **National Student Assistance Conference**
1270 Rakin Drive
Suite F
Troy, MI 48033-2843
800-453-7733
Fax: 800-499-5718
Learn to maintain and improve safe, drug free schools, student assistance programs. Develop skills to implement the Principles of Effectiveness. Choose from workshops and skill building sessions.

4 **National Women's History Project Annual Conference**
730 Second Street #469
PO Box 469
Santa Rosa, CA 95402
707-636-2888
Fax: 707-636-2909
nwhp1980@gmail.com
www.nwhp.org
Posters, reference books, curriculum materials and biographies of American women in all subjects for grades K-12.
July
72 attendees
Molly Murphy MacGregor, Executive Director/ Chair
Shona Rocco, Financial Manager

35 **Natural Learning Institute Seminar**
54385 Pine Crest Ave
Idyllwild, CA 92549
951-691-0139
Fax: 951-659-0242
www.naturallearninginstitute.org
Linda Hargan, President

36 **Neag Center for Gifted Education and Talent Development Conference**
University of Connecticut
2131 Hillside Road
Unit 3007
Storrs, CT 06269-3007
860-486-4826
Fax: 860-486-2900
www.gifted.uconn.edu
Provides educators with research based practical strategies for engagement and enrichment learning for all students, as well as meeting the needs of gifted and talented students.
Annual
JoAnn Easton, Confratute

937 **New Learning Technologies**
Society for Applied Learning Technology
50 Culpeper Street
Warrenton, VA 20186
540-347-0055
800-457-6812
Fax: 540-349-3169
info@lti.org
www.salt.org
To provide a comprehensive overview of the latest in research, design, and development in order to furnish attendees information on systems that are applicable to their organizations.

938 **New Learning Technologies Conference**
Society for Applied Learning Technology
50 Culpeper Street
Warrenton, VA 20186
540-347-0055
800-457-6812
Fax: 540-349-3169
info@lti.org
www.salt.org
For over 30 years the Society has sponsored conferences which are educational in nature and bring together senior professionals from government, industry, academia and the military to present the latest developments in the field of learning and training technologies.
August
20 booths with 400 attendees
Raymond G Fox, President

939 **North American Montessori Teachers' Association**
13693 Butternnut Road
Burton, OH 44021
440-834-4011
Fax: 440-834-4016
staff@montessori-namta.org
www.montessori-namta.org/
Professional organization for Montessori teachers and administrators. Services include The NAMTA Journal and other publications, videos and slide shows. Conferences in January and March.
David J Kahn, Executive Director

940 **Parents as Teachers National Center Conference**
2228 Ball Drive
Saint Louis, MO 63146
314-432-4330
Fax: 314-432-8963
patnc@patnc.org
www.patnc.org
An international early childhood parent education and family support program designed to enhance child development and school achievement through parent education accessible to all families. Serves families throughout pregnancy and until their child enters kindergarten, usually age 5.
April-May
40 booths with 1400+ attendees
Susan S Stepleton, President/CEO
Cheryl Dyle-Palmer, Director Operations

941 **ProLiteracy Conference on Adult Education**
ProLiteracy
101 Wyoming Street
Syracuse, NY 13204
315-422-9121
888-528-2224
Fax: 315-422-6369
info@proliteracy.org
www.proliteracy.org
Brings together adult literacy practitioners, educators and advocates to share new ideas in the field of adult literacy.
Kevin Morgan, President & CEO
Lara Pimentel, Senior Dir., Development

942 **Reidy Interactive Lecture Series**
Center for Assessment
31 Mount Vernon Street
Dover, NH 03820
603-516-7900
Fax: 603-516-7910
www.nciea.org
The goal is to discuss timely topics in educational assessment.
September
Scott Marion, Executive Director
Chris Domaleski, Associate Director

943 **Retention in Education Today for All Indigenous Nations**
ConferencePROS
University of Oklahoma
1639 Cross Center Drive, Suite 101
Norman, OK 73072
405-325-3760
800-203-5494
Fax: 405-325-7075
lasmith@ou.edu
www.conferencepros.com
National conference designed to discuss and share retention strategies for indigenous students.
Laurie Smith, Manager/ Projects Director
Richard Feinberg, Media Specialist Manager

944 **STEMtech Conference**
League for Innovation in the Community College
4505 East Chandler Boulevard
Suite 250
Phoenix, AZ 85048
480-705-8200
Fax: 480-705-8201
harris@league.org
www.league.org
Emphasizes student success in science, technology, engineering and mathematices (STEM) at all levels.
October
3,000 attendees
Robin Piccilliri, Meeting Planner

945 **School Equipment Show**
830 Colesville Road
Suite 250
Silver Spring, MD 20910-3297
301-495-0240
800-395-5550
Fax: 301-495-3330
www.nnsea.org
Annual show featuring exhibits from manufacturers of school equipment such as bleachers, classroom furniture, lockers, playground and athletic equipment, computer hardware, software, etc.
February
Elizabeth Bradley, Conference Contact

946 **Sexual Assault and Harassment on Campus Conference**
c/o Sexual Conference
PO Box 1338
Holmes Beach, FL 34218-1338
800-537-4903
www.ed.mtu.edu
Topics include gender based hate crime, sexual assault investigators, generational legacy of rape, innovations in the military, sexual harassment in K-12, updates on date-rape

drugs and many more. Hosted by the Hyatt Orlando Hotel in Kissimmee, Florida.

Karen McLaughlin, Conference Co-Chair
Alan McEvoy, Conference Co-Chair

947 Society for Research in Child Development Biennial Meeting
1825 K Street NW
Suite 325
Washington, DC 20006
202-800-0677
biennialmeeting@srcd.org
www.srcd.org
Provides a forum and networking opportunities for attendees, as well as furthers the Society's goal of promoting the understanding of child development through research.

March/April

Saima K. Hedrick, MPH, CAE, Executive Director
Anne Perdue, Director, Meetings & Events

948 TESOL International Convention & English Language Expo
TESOL International Association
1925 Ballenger Avenue
Suite 550
Alexandria, VA 22314-6820
703-518-2500
888-891-0041
Fax: 703-691-5327
members@tesol.org
www.tesol.org
Offers professional development opportunities to English language educators from across the globe.

4,000 attendees

Rosa Aronson, Interim Executive Director
Lisa Dyson, Director, Strategic Events

949 Teacher Link: An Interactive National Teleconference
Center for the Study of Small/Rural Schools
555 E Constitution Street
Room 138
Norman, OK 73072-7820
405-325-1450
Fax: 405-325-7075
jcsimmons@ou.edu
www.cssrs.ou.edu
Prevention Series

Spring
5 booths with 100 attendees

Jan C Simmons, Program Director

950 Teaching for Intelligence Conference
SkyLight
2626 S Clearbrook Drive
Arlington Heights, IL 60005
847-290-6600
800-348-4474
Fax: 877-260-2530
www.iriskylight.com
Focuses on student achievement, brain-based learning and multiple intelligences.

April

951 Technology & Learning Schooltech Exposition & Conference
212-615-6030
www.SchoolTechExpo.com
Over 150 targeted sessions specifically designed for all education professionals: technology directors, teachers, principals, superintendents and district administrators.

952 Technology Student Conference
Technology Student Association
1914 Association Drive
Reston, VA 20191-1538
703-860-9000
Fax: 703-758-4852
Devoted to the needs of technology education students and supported by educators, parents, and business leaders who believe in the need for a technologically literate society.

June
2,500 attendees

Rosanne White, Conference Manager

953 Technology, Reading & Learning Difficulties Conference
International Reading Association
19 Calvert Court
Piedmont, CA 94611
510-594-1249
888-594-1249
Fax: 510-594-1838
www.trld.com
Focuses on ways to use technology for reading, learning difficulties, staff development, adult literacy, and more.

January

954 The Heads Network Annual Conference
The Heads Network
102 Wentworth Avenue
Nashville, TN 37215
615-533-6022
swade@headsnetwork.org
www.headsnetwork.org
Discussions around innovation and trends relating to the education and employment of girls and young women.

Margaret Wade, Executive Director

955 Training of Trainers Seminar
Active Parenting Publishers
1220 Kennestone Circle
Suite 130
Marietta, GA 30066-6022
770-429-0565
800-825-0060
Fax: 770-429-0334
cservice@activeparenting.com
www.activeparenting.com
Delivers quality education programs for parents, children and teachers to schools, hospitals, social services organizations, churches and the corporate market.

Michael H. Popkin, Ph.D., Founder/ President
Micole Mason, Training Coordinator

956 USC Summer Superintendents' Conference
University of Southern California, School of Ed.
Waite Philips Hall, Room 901
Los Angeles, CA 90089-0031
213-740-2182
Fax: 213-749-2707
www.usc.edu
A select group of educational leaders nationwide engaged in reform practices offer discussions with nationally renowned speakers; tour innovative schools; and network with colleagues from the United States, Great Britain and Australia.

Lawrence O Picus, Conference Director
Carolyn Bryant, Conference Coordinator

Northeast

957 Clonlara School Annual Conference Home Educators
Clonlara Home Based Education Programs
1289 Jewett Street
Ann Arbor, MI 48104-6201
734-769-4511
Fax: 734-769-9629
info@clonlara.org
www.clonlara.org
Clonlara School is committed to illuminating educational rights and freedoms through our actions and deep dedication to human rights and dignity.

June
300 attendees

Terri Wheeler, Associate Director

958 Connecticut Library Association
234 Court St.
Middletown, CT 06457
860-346-2444
Fax: 860-344-9199
cla@ctlibrarians.org
www.ctlibraryassociation.org/index.php?bypass Cookie=1
Holds a conference in April and publishes a journal.

April
1000 attendees and 100 exhibits

Dawn La Valle, President
Beth A Crowley, VP/ President Elect

959 Hoosier Science Teachers Association Annual Meeting
5007 W 14th Street
Indianapolis, IN 46224-6503
317-244-7238
Fax: 317-486-4838
Papers, workshops, demonstrations and presentations in each area of science.

February
78 booths

Edward Frazer, Conference Contact

960 Illinois Library Association Annual Conference
Illinois Library Association
33 W Grand Avenue
Suite 401
Chicago, IL 60654-6799
312-644-1896
Fax: 312-644-1899
ila@ila.org
www.ila.org/events/annual-conference
A conference exploring the topic of library services, featuring authors and special speakers interested in discussing how people can better their communities.

October

Diane Foote, Executive Director
Cynthia M Robinson, Deputy Director

961 Illinois Vocational Association Conference
230 Broadway
Suite 150
Springfield, IL 62701-1138
217-585-9430
Fax: 217-544-0208
Equipment and supplies, publications, teaching aids, computers and food services.

February
75 booths with 600 attendees

Karen Riddle, Conference Contact

2 New Jersey School Boards Association Annual Meeting
413 W State Street
PO Box 909
Trenton, NJ 08605-0909
609-695-7600
888-886-5722
Fax: 609-695-0413
www.njsba.org
School/office supplies, furniture, equipment, counseling services and more.
October
630 booths with 9,000 attendees
Wendy L. Wilson, Conference Contact

3 New York State Council of Student Superintendents Forum
111 Washington Avenue
Suite 104
Albany, NY 12210-2210
518-449-1063
Fax: 518-426-2229
Offers educational products and related services.
February
12 booths
Dr. Claire Brown, Conference Contact

4 Ohio Library Council Convention and Expo
Ohio Library Council
1105 Schrock Road
Suite 440
Columbus, OH 43229
614-410-8092
Fax: 614-410-8098
olc@olc.org
www.olc.org
Explors strategies to maintain a balance between traditional practices and the use of innovations such as digital materials.
October
Andrew Mangels, Chair
Douglas Evans, Executive Director

5 Ohio School Boards Association Capital Conference & Trade Show
Greater Columbus Convention Center
400 N. High St.
Columbus, OH 43215
614-891-6466
www.conference.ohioschoolboards.org
Provides school officials from Ohio an opportunity to gain information about products, equipment, materials and services.
November
425 booths
Richard Lewis, Conference Contact

6 Satellites and Education Conference
189 Schmucker Science Center
W Chester University
West Chester, PA 19383
610-436-1000
Fax: 610-436-2790
www.sated.org
The Satellite Educators Association was established in 1988 as a professional society to promote the innovative use of satellite technology in education and disseminate information nationally to all members.
March
15 booths with 200 attendees
Nancy McIntyre, Director

67 UNI Overseas Recruiting Fair
University of Northern Iowa Career Services
102 Gilchrist Hall
Cedar Falls, IA 50614-0390
319-273-2083
Fax: 319-273-6998
overseas.placement@uni.edu
www.uni.edu/placement/overseas
About 160 recruiters from 120 schools in 80 countries recruit at this fair for certified K-12 educators.
February
Tracy Roling, Coordinator

968 Wisconsin Vocational Association Conference
44 E Mifflin Street
Suite 104
Madison, WI 53703-2800
608-283-2595
Fax: 608-283-2589
Trade and industry vendor equipment and book publishers.
April
50 booths
Linda Stemper, Conference Contact

Northwest

969 Montana High School Association Conference
1 S Dakota Street
Helena, MT 59601-5111
406-442-6010
School athletic merchandise.
January
15 booths
Dan Freund, Conference Contact

970 Nebraska School Boards Association Annual Conference
140 S 16th Street
Lincoln, NE 68508-1805
402-475-4951
Fax: 402-475-4961
60 booths exhibiting products and services directed at the public school market.
November
60 booths
Burma Kroger, Conference Contact

971 North Dakota Vocational Educational Planning Conference
State Capitol
600 East Boulevard Avenue, Dept. 270
Bismarck, ND 58505-610
701-328-3180
Fax: 701-328-1255
cte@nd.gov
www.nd.gov/cte/
August
30 booths
Ernest Breznay, Conference Contact

972 Pacific Northwest Library Association
Boise Public Library
715 Capitol Boulevard
Boise, ID 83702
208-384-4026
Fax: 208-384-4156
www.pnla.org
Oldest regional library association in the United States and the only binational association in North America.
Honore Bray, President
Gwendolyn Haley, First VP/President-Elect

973 WA-ACTE Career and Technical Exhibition for Career and Technical Education
Washington Association for Career & Tech Education
PO Box 315
Olympia, WA 98507-0315
360-786-9286
Fax: 360-357-1491
wa-acte@wa-acte.org
www.wa-acte.org
August
40 booths with 1,000 attendees
Tim Knue, Executive Director
Tess Alviso, Executive Assistant

Southeast

974 Association for Continuing Higher Education Conference
Trident Technical College
PO Box 118067
Charleston, SC 29423-8067
843-722-5546
Fax: 843-574-6470
15 tabletops.
October
Dr. Wayne Whelan, Executive VP

975 Center for Play Therapy Summer Institute
425 S Welch Street
Complex 2
Denton, TX 76203
940-565-3864
Fax: 940-565-4461
cpt@unt.edu
www.cpt.unt.edu/summer-institute
Conference for practitioners and educators to gain play therapy training experience through didactic and experiential learning components.
June
Dee Ray, Director
Gabby Mendez, Administrative Coordinator

976 Missouri Library Association Conference
Missouri Library Association
1190 Meramec Station Road
Suite 207
Ballwin, MO 63021-6902
573-449-4627
Fax: 573-449-4655
mla@amigos.org
www.molib.org/conference
The conference covers topics such as grant writing, graph making and development strategies. It features programming that supports libraries and the librarian profession.
October
Tiffany Mautino, Conference Coordinator
Katie McDonald, Conference Coordinator

977 National Youth-At-Risk Conference
Georgia Southern University
1332 Southern Drive
Statesboro, GA 30458
912-478-4636
Fax: 912-681-0306
www.academics.georgiasouthern.edu
Stresses education and development for professionals working with at-risk students.
February
Sybil Fickle, Conference Contact

Southwest

978 **CBEA Conference**
PO Box 588
Ridgecrest, CA 93556
760-608-3983
cbeaquestions@cbeaonline.org
www.cbeaonline.org
Conference features computer workshops, information sessions, speakers, exhibitions, tours and more.

Bi-Annual
November
200 attendees

Karen O'Connor, Conference Chair

979 **Children's Literature Festival**
Department of Library Science
Sam Houston State University
PO Box 2236
Huntsville, TX 77341-2236
936-294-1614
Fax: 936-294-3780
This annual event is sponsored by the Department of Library Science at Sam Houston State University.

980 **Colorado Library Association Conference (CALCON)**
PO Box 740905
Arvada, CO 80006-0905
303-463-6400
cal@cal-webs.org
www.cal-webs.org

September
60 booths with 450 attendees

Ryan F Buller, President
Anne Holland, Secretary

981 **Phoenix Learning Resources Conference**
12 W 31st Street
New York, NY 10001-4415
212-629-3887
800-221-1274
Fax: 212-629-5648
Supplemental and remedial reading and language arts programs for early childhood, K-12, and adult literacy programs.

Alexander Burke, President
John Rothermich, Executive VP

982 **Southwest Association College and University Housing Officers**
624 W. University Drive
Suite 418
Denton, TX 76204
936-294-1812
Fax: 936-294-1920
swacuho@gmail.com
www.swacuho.org
Products and services for college and university housing.

Febuary/March
45 booths

Diane Brittingham, President

983 **Texas Classroom Teachers Association Conference**
PO Box 1489
Austin, TX 78767-1489
512-477-9415
Fax: 512-469-9527
www.tcta.org
Educational materials, fundraising and jewelry.

February
150 booths

Jan Lanfear, Conference Contact

984 **Texas Library Association Conference**
3355 Bee Cave Road
Suite 401
Austin, TX 78746-6763
512-328-1518
800-580-2852
Fax: 512-328-8852
www.txla.org
Established in 1902 to promote and improve library services in Texas.

March
750 booths with 6,000 attendees

Sharon Amastae, President
Patricia H. Smith, Executive Director

985 **Texas Vocational Home Economics Teachers Association Conference**
3737 Executive Center Drive
Suite 210
Austin, TX 78731-1633
512-794-8370

July/August

Terry Green, Conference Contact

986 **Western History Association Annual Conference**
University of Kansas, History Department
1445 Jayhawk Boulevard
3650 Wescoe Hall
Lawrence, KS 66045
785-864-0860
wha@westernhistory.org
www.westernhistory.org
Features panels, workshops, sessions and discussions about the North American West.

October
45 booths

Elaine Nelson, Executive Director
Paige Mitchell, Office & Events Coordinator

General

7 **Accuracy Temporary Services Incorporated**
20674 Hall Road
Clinton Township, MI 48038
248-399-0220
800-297-2119
Fax: 586-465-9481
www.atsprojectsuccess.com
Educational consultant for public and private schools.

Howard Weaver, President

8 **Add Vantage Learning Incorporated**
6805 Route 202
New Hope, PA 18938
800-230-2213
Fax: 215-579-8391
www.vantagelearning.com/
Management and educational consultant for the general public.

Jim Pepitone, Chairman

9 **Advance Infant Development Program**
2232 D Street
Suite 203
LaVerne, CA 91750-5409
909-593-3935
Fax: 909-593-7969
Business and educational consultant for general trade.

Diane Hinds, President
Jeanine Coleman, Executive Director

0 **American International Schools**
2203 Franklin Road SW
Roanoak, VA 24014-1109
852-233-3812
Fax: 852-233-5276
American International School is pledged to preparing students to contribute to an increasingly international and interdependent world. AIS strives to provide an atmosphere conducive to building interpersonal relationships and global awareness. AIS is committed to working closely with students and families to attain academic excellence and to inspire the growth of well-rounded individuals.

Andrew Hurst, President
Lewis C Smith Jr, Executive VP

1 **Area Cooperative Educational Services**
350 State Street
North Haven, CT 06473
203-498-6800
Fax: 203-498-6817
acesinfo@aces.org
www.aces.org
ACES is the regional educational service center for twenty-five school districts in south central Connecticut.

Erika Forte, Assistant Executive Director
Thomas M. Danehy Ed.D., Executive Director

92 **Aspira of Penna**
2726 N 6th Street
Philadelphia, PA 19133-2714
215-229-1226
Educational consultant for educational institutions.

Oscar Cardona, President

993 **Association for Refining Cross-Cultured International**
Japanese American Cultural Center
244 S San Pedro Street
Suite 505
Los Angeles, CA 90012
213-620-0696
Fax: 213-620-0930
www.arcint.com
Educational consultants for international studies.

Chiey Nomura, Director

994 **Association of Christian Schools International**
731 Chapel Hills Drive
Colorado Springs, CO 80920
719-367-5391
800-367-0798
communications@acsi.org
www.acsi.org
Educational consultant for Christian Schools.

Larry Taylor, President
Kevin Buelke, Chief Finance Officer

995 **Basics Plus**
921 Aris Avenue
Suite C
Metairie, LA 70005-2200
504-832-5111
Fax: 504-832-5110
Educational consultants.

Scott Green, President

996 **Beacon Education Management**
112 Turnpike Road
Suite 107
Westborough, MA 01581
508-836-4461
800-789-1258
Fax: 508-836-2604
www.beaconedu.com
A K-12, education services company that offers contracted management services to public schools and charter school boards. Currently operating 27 charter schools in Massachusetts, Michigan, Missouri and North Carolina.

997 **Bluegrass Regional Recycling Corporation**
540 Recycle Drive
Richmond, KY 40475
859-626-9117
Fax: 859-233-7787
www.thebrrc.com
Consultants for educational, training, and services for governments and school systems.

Douglas Castle, Chairman

998 **CPM Educational Program**
1233 Noonan Drive
Sacramento, CA 95822-2569
916-446-9936
Fax: 916-444-5263
www.cpm.org
Educational and training consultants for school districts.

Karen Wootton, Executive Director
Paul Chmelik, Director

999 **Caldwell Flores Winters**
2187 Newcastle Avenue
Suite 201
Cardiff, CA 92007-1848
760-634-4239
800-273-4239
Fax: 760-436-7357
cfw@cfwinc.com
www.cfwinc.com/index.html
Offers educational counsel to school districts.

Ernesto Flores, President
Scott Gaudineer, AIA, Program Executive

1000 **Career Evaluation Systems**
1024 N Oakley Boulevard
Suite 4
Chicago, IL 60622-3586
773-772-9595
800-448-7552
Fax: 773-772-5010
Testing instruments for vocational evaluation.

1001 **Carnegie Foundation for the Advancement of Teaching**
51 Vista Lane
Stanford, CA 94305
650-566-5100
Fax: 650-326-0278
publications@carnegiefoundation.org
www.carnegiefoundation.org/
Educational consultant for the educational field.

Tom Payzant, Chair
Anthony S Bryk, President

1002 **Carney Sandoe & Associates**
44 Bromfield Street
Boston, MA 02108-4608
617-542-0260
800-225-7986
Fax: 617-542-9400
www.carneysandoe.com/
Educational consultant for private schools.

James H Carney, Chairman/President
Jonathan Ball, Managinf Associate

1003 **Carter/Tardola Associates**
419 Pleasant Street
Suite 307
Beloit, WI 53511
608-365-3163
Fax: 608-365-5961
www.carter-tardola.com/
Evaluates program, administration, staff, resource and time organization, and utilization of resources. Proposal development, language skills development, diversity training.

Betty Tardola, Educational Consultant

1004 **Center for Educational Innovation**
28 West 44th Street
Suite 300
New York, NY 10036-6600
212-302-8800
Fax: 212-302-0088
info@the-cei.org
www.the-cei.org
Educational consultant for private and commercial accounts.

Seymour Fliegel, President
John Falco, Vice President

1005 **Center for Resource Management**
1861 E. Beaumont Circle
Salt Lake City, UT 84121
801-509-5308
Fax: 603-427-6983
info@crm.org
www.crm.org
Employment, human resources, educational, development, training, computer software, organizational and management consultants for Human Service Agencies and Educational Institutions/ Schools.

Paul Parker, President
Colleen Parker, VP/ Office Manager

1006 **Child Like Consulting Limited**
700 E Rambling Drive
Wellington, FL 33414-5010
561-798-5847
800-487-6725
Fax: 866-468-4555
Training in literacy, music, classroom and learning center management.

1007 **Children's Educational Opportunity Foundation**
P.O Box 59
South Glastonbury, CT 06073
860-430-2756
855-326-4935
Fax: 479-273-9362
Educational consultant for institutions.
Mark R. Rousseau, President
Mary Jane Sullivan, Executive Director

1008 **Childs Consulting Associates**
514 Lakeside Drive
P O Box 550
Mackinaw City, MI 49701
231-436-4099
Fax: 231-436-4101
www.childs.com
Educational, schools and technology consultants for schools, banking and automotive industries.
John W Childs, President
Sheryl Childs, Executive Assistant

1009 **Classroom**
245 Fifth Avenue
Room 1901
New York, NY 10016-8728
212-545-8400
800-258-0640
Fax: 212-481-7178
www.classroominc.org
Technology based curriculum and teacher professional development for middle school and high school use.
Lewis W Bernard, Chairman
Lisa Holton, President

1010 **Coalition of Essential Schools**
482 Congress Street
Suite 500A
Portland, ME 04101
401-426-9638
Fax: 510-433-1455
info@essentialschools.org
www.essentialschools.org
The Coalition of Essential Schools (CES) is a leading comprehensive school reform organization, fundamentally changing the way people think about teaching and learning and transforming American education.
Hudi Podolsky, Executive Director

1011 **College Board**
250 Vesey Street
New York, NY 10281
212-713-8000
www.collegeboard.org
Educational, research, testing and financial consultant for learning institutions and students.
David Coleman, Chief Executive Officer
Jeremy Singer, President

1012 **College Bound**
17316 Edwards Road
Suite 180
Cerritos, CA 90703
562-860-2127
Fax: 562-407-2131
info@collegeboundca.org
Educational consultants.
Janice Criddle, Chair
Denise McLeod, Vice Chair

1013 **Community Connections**
1865 W Broad Street
Suite C
Athens, GA 30606
706-353-1313
800-924-5085
Fax: 706-353-1375
www.communityconnection211.org
Educational consultant for the general public.
Ashley Harp, President
Julia Weckbeck, Vice President

1014 **Community Foundation for Jewish Education**
30 S Wells-216
Chicago, IL 60606
312-673-3270
Fax: 312-913-1763
www.cfje.org
Educational consultant for the general public and schools.
Howard Swibel, President

1015 **Connecting Link**
387 Coopers Pond Drive
Suite 1
Lawrenceville, GA 30044-5231
770-979-5804
Fax: 770-931-6831
Business and educational consultants for teachers.
Dr. Bernard F Cleveland, President

1016 **Conover Company**
4 Brookwood Court
Appleton, WI 54914-8618
920-231-4667
800-933-1933
Fax: 800-933-1943
sales@conovercompany.com
www.conovercompany.com
Training and setting up workplace literacy programs; emotional intelligence assessment and skill enhancement; functional literacy software, career exploration and assessment software
Rebecca Schmitz, Member

1017 **Consortium on Reading Excellence**
1300 Clay Street
Suite 600
Oakland, CA 94612-1923
888-249-6165
Fax: 510-540-4242
orders@corelearn.com
www.corelearn.com
Educational consultant for public and private schools.
Bill Honig, President
Linda Diamond, CEO

1018 **Continuous Learning Group Limited Liability Company**
500 Cherrington Parkway
Suite 350
Pittsburgh, PA 15108
412-269-7240
Fax: 412-269-7247
info@clg.com
www.clg.com
Educational consultants.
Steve Jacobs, Non-Executive Chairman
Vikesh Mahendroo, President & CEO

1019 **Corporate Design Foundation**
20 Park Plaza
Suite 400
Boston, MA 02116-4303
617-566-7676
admin@cdf.org
www.cdf.org
Educational consultant for universities and colleges.
Peter G Lawrence, Chairman

1020 **Corporate University Enterprise**
909 North Washington Street
Suite 310
Alexandria, VA 22314
703-848-0070
866-848-1675
Fax: 703-848-0071
www.cuenterprise.com
Corporate University Enterprise, Inc. is and educational consulting firm designed to bring a strategic approach to workforce education in both private and public organizations. The company was incorporated in 1998 and has since served clients throughout the United States, Europe, and Asia.
Teresa Sayasithsena, Vice President
Karen Barley, President

1021 **Council for Aid to Education**
215 Lexington Avenue
Floor 16
New York, NY 10016-1599
212-661-5800
Fax: 212-661-9766
www.cae.org
Non-profit educational consultant for government and commercial concerns.
Roger W Benjamin, President
James Hundley, Executive Vice President

1022 **Council on Occupational Education**
7840 Roswell Road
Suite 325
Atlanta, GA 30350-1903
770-396-3898
800-917-2081
Fax: 770-396-3790
bowmanh@council.org
www.council.org
Managerial and educational consultant for post secondary technical education institutions.
Al Salazar, Chair
James Spruel, Vice Chair

1023 **Creative Learning Consultants**
1990 Market Road
Marion, IL 62959-1906
800-729-5137
Fax: 800-844-0455
info@piecesoflearning.com
www.piecesoflearning.com
Educational consulting for school districts, teachers, book stores and parents.
Stanley Balsamo, Secretary/Treasurer
Kathy Balsamo, President

1024 **Creative Learning Systems**
2065 S Escondido Blvd
Suite 108
Escondido, CA 92025
800-458-2880
Fax: 858-592-7055
info@creativelearningsystems.com
www.creativelearningsystems.com
Educational consulting firm.
Matt Dickstein, Chief Executive Officer

1025 **Dawson Education Cooperative**
711 Clinton Street
Suite 201
Arkadelphia, AR 71923-5921

870-246-3077
Fax: 870-246-5892
www.dawson.dsc.k12.ar.us
Educational consulting group.

Nathan Gills, President
Ron Wright, Director

26 Dawson Education Service Cooperative
711 Clinton Street
Suite 201
Arkadelphia, AR 71923-5921
870-246-3077
Fax: 870-246-5892
Educational and organizational consultants for school districts

Ron Wright, Director
Beth Neel, Assisstant Director

27 Designs for Learning
2233 University Ave W
Suite 450
St. Paul, MN 55114-1634
651-645-0200
Fax: 651-645-0240
dalley@designlearn.net
www.designlearn.net
Educational consultants for primary schools and the private sector.

David Alley, Chair
Pamela Meade, President

28 Direct Instructional Support Systems
535 Lakeview Plaza Blvd.
Suite B
Worthington, OH 43085-4146
614-846-8946
Fax: 614-846-1794
Educational consultant for public and private agencies.

Gary Moore, President

29 Dr. Anthony A Cacossa
4300 N Charles Street
Apartment 9B
Baltimore, MD 21218-1052
410-889-1806
Fax: 410-889-1806
Assists schools in marketing academic programs that offer internship opportunities.

30 E.P.P.A. Consulting
1116 Comanche Trail
Georgetown, KY 40324-1071
502-370-6341
eppa@juno.com
Provider of strategic and operational planning consulting services.

Theo R Leverenz, Ph.D, Contact, Owner

031 EPIE Institute: Educational Products Information Exchange Institute
103 West Montauk Highway
PO Box 590
Hampton Bays, NY 11946-4006
631-728-9100
www.epie.org
Curriculum development, training and evaluation of education products.

032 East Bay Educational Collaborative
317 Market Street
Warren, RI 02885
401-245-4998
Fax: 401-245-9332
Karen.corr@ebecri.org
www.ebecri.org
Business and educational consultant for member school districts.

Kathryn Crowley, Chair
Gerald Kowalczyk, Executive Director

1033 East Central Educational Service Center
1601 Indiana Avenue
Connersville, IN 47331
765-825-1247
Fax: 765-825-2532
www.ecesc.k12.in.us
Educational services for school districts in East Central Indiana.

William J Harrison, Executive Director

1034 Edge Learning Institute
4807 Rockside Rd.
Ste. 720
Z, OH 44131-3320
216-674-1085
888-892-0300
Fax: 216-674-8204
info@legacycultures.com
www.legacycultures.com
Educational consultants for the general public, commercial concerns, government agencies and school districts.

Paul Meshanko, President & CEO
Todd Costello, VP Business Operations

1035 Edison Schools
485 Lexington Avenue
2nd Floor
New York, NY 10017
212-419-1600
Fax: 212-419-1746
information@edisonlearning.com
The country's largest private manager of public schools. Implemented its design in 79 public schools, including 36 charter schools, which it operates under management contracts with local school districts and charter school boards.

Jeff Wahl, President, CEO

1036 Education Concepts
9861 Strausser Street
Canal Fulton, OH 44614
330-497-1055
Fax: 330-966-8000
Professional development programs for early childhood educators.

1037 Education Data
1305 E Waterman
Witchata, KS 67211
800-248-4135
Expertise in organizational needs assessments.

1038 Education Development Center (EDC)
43 Foundry Avenue
Waltham, MA 02453-8313
617-969-7100
Fax: 617-969-5979
contact@edc.org
www.edc.org
The Education Development Center designs and evaluates programs addressing some of the world's challenges in education, health and economic opportunity. The center's mission is to improve education, health promotion and care, workforce preparation, communications technologies and civic engagement in communities.

David Offensend, President & CEO
Siobhan Murphy, Chief Operating Officer

1039 Education Management Consulting LLC
49 Coryell Street
Lambertville, NJ 08530
609-397-8989
800-291-0199
Fax: 609-397-1999
Consultation for schools on special education and administration consultation for lawyers working on education and school related issues.

Dr. Edward F Dragan, President

1040 Educational Consultants of Oxford
10431 Highway 51 S
Courtland, MS 38620
601-563-8954
All areas of educational information services, tutoring, scholarship information, and non-traditional and overseas training.

1041 Educational Credential Evaluators
101 W. Pleasant St. Suite 200
PO Box 514070
Milwaukee, WI 53212-3963
414-289-3400
Fax: 414-289-3411
www.ece.org
Evaluates foreign educational credentials.

James Frey, President
Margit Schatzman, VP

1042 Educational Data Service
236 Midland Avenue
Saddle Brook, NJ 07663-4604
973-340-8800
Fax: 973-340-0078
www.ed-data.com
Educational and school consulting for Boards of Education.

Gil Wohl, President
Alan Wohl, Chairman

1043 Educational Information & Resource Center
900 Hollydell Drive
Sewell, NJ 08080
856-582-7000
Fax: 856-582-4206
www.eirc.org
Programs and consulting services for schools, on many topics from teaching techniques to technical assistance.

Rena Alpert, Board of Director
Jack Hill, Board of Director

1044 Educational Resources
6847 Corral Circle
Sarasota, FL 34243
651-592-3688
www.eduresources.org
Nonprofit educational organization seeking to promote understanding between different ethnic and religious groups through programs, lectures, curriculums and trips abroad.

Steven L Derfler, Founder

1045 Educational Services Company
3535 East 96th Street
Suite 126
Indianapolis, IN 46240-1754
317-818-3535
888-351-3535
Fax: 317-818-3533
Educational and management consulting for primary and secondary schools.

Douglas Cassman, President
William McMaster, Secretary

1046 Educational Specialties
9923 S Wood Street
Chicago, IL 60643-1809
773-445-1000
Fax: 773-445-5574

Educational consultant for schools.

Elois W Steward, President

1047 Educational Systems for the Future
11415 Georgetown Circle
Tampa, FL 33625-1560
813-814-1192
Fax: 813-814-1193
Development of teaching skills, training needs analysis, and training management.

Dr. Mary Sullivan Esseff, President & Director
Dr. Peter J Esseff, Vice President

1048 Educational Technology Design Consultants
100 Allentown Parkway
Suite 110
Allen, TX 75002
972-727-1234
Fax: 972-727-1491
www.etdc.com/html/about_us.html
Developing system design for virtual campus control and support.

1049 Educational Testing Service
1800 K Street, NW,
Suite 900
Washington, DC 20006-0001
202-659-0616
Fax: 202-659-8075
etsinfo@ets.org
www.ets.org
Educational and professional consulting for schools.

Kurt M. Landgraf, President
Sharon Robison, COO, Senior VP

1050 Edusystems Export
820 Wisconsin Street
Walworth, WI 53184-9765
262-275-5761
Fax: 262-275-2009
Expertise in educational systems.

1051 Effective Schools Products
PO Box 1337
Okemos, MI 48805-5983
517-349-8841
800-827-8041
Fax: 517-349-8852
Publishing consultants for schools, teachers, directors of planning and others in this field.

Ruth Lezotte, PhD, President
Dr. Carmen Granto, Superintendent

1052 Effective Training Solutions
93 Linden Street
Oakland, CA 94607-1447
510-834-1901
800-949-5035
Fax: 510-834-1905
www.trainingsuccess.com
Design and implementation of training strategies. Proficiency training-performance improvement training.

Ingrid Gudenas, CEO

1053 Efficacy Institute
182 Felton Street
Waltham, MA 02453-4134
781-547-6060
Fax: 781-547-6077
info@efficacy.org
www.efficacy.org
Non-profit, educational consultants for educational and community service institutions.

Dr Jeff Howard, Chair
Barbara M. Logan, Vice President

1054 Emerging Technology Consultants
216 Heritage Lane
New Brighton, MN 55112
651-639-3973
Fax: 651-639-3973
Serves as a connection between technology producers and the education and training industries.

Richard Pollak, Chief Executive Officer
Rubyanna Pollak, President

1055 Epistemological Engineering
5269 Miles Avenue
Oakland, CA 94618-1044
510-653-3377
866-341-3377
Fax: 866-879-7797
publications@eeps.com
www.eeps.com
Educational consultants.

Tim Erickson, President

1056 Examiner Corporation
600 Marshall Avenue
Suite 100
St. Paul, MN 55102-1723
651-451-7360
800-395-6840
Fax: 651-451-6563
examine@xmn.com
www.xmn.com
Educational and certification evaluation instruments.

Gary C Brown, President
Michelle Smith, Sales and Marketing

1057 Excell Education Centers
3807 Wilshire Boulevard
Los Angeles, CA 90010-3101
213-386-1953
Educational and planning consultants.

Raymond Hahl, Owner

1058 FPMI Communications
707 Fiber Street NW
Huntsville, AL 35801-5833
256-539-1850
Fax: 256-539-0911
Educational management consulting.

1059 First District Resa
201 West Lee Street
P.O. Box 780
Brooklet, GA 30415
912-842-5000
Fax: 912-842-5161
www.fdresa.org
Educational consultants for the general public and commercial concerns.

Dr. Whit Myers, Executive Director
Donna Mangrum, Chief Financial Officer

1060 Foundation for Educational Innovation
401 M Street SW
2nd Floor, Suite 1
Washington, DC 20024-2610
202-554-7400
Fax: 202-554-7401
Educational consultant for educational/school systems.

Archie Prioleau, President

1061 George Dehne & Associates
33 Main Street
Suite F
Old Saybrook, CT 06475
843-971-9088
860-388-3958
Fax: 843-971-7759
george@dehne.com
www.dehne.com
Educational and business consultants for commercial concerns and colleges.

George Dehne, President
Christopher Topher Small, Executive Vice President

1062 Health Outreach Project
825 Cascade Avenue
Atlanta, GA 30331-8362
404-755-6700
Educational consultants.

Sandra McDonald, President

1063 Higher Education Consortium
2233 University Avenue W
Suite 210
St. Paul, MN 55114
651-287-3300
Fax: 651-659-9421
hecua@hecua.org
www.hecua.org
Educational consultants.

Jenny Keyser, Executive Director
Patrick Mulvihill, Director of Operations

1064 Highlands Program
PO Box 76168
Atlanta, GA 30358-3915
404-497-0835
Educational consultants for educational institutions, corporations and consumers.

Don Hutcheson, President

1065 Howard Greene Associates
60 Post Road West
Westport, CT 06880-4208
203-226-4257
Fax: 203-226-5595
counseling@howardgreeneassociates.com
www.greenesguides.com
Educational consultants for school systems and individuals.

Howard R Greene, President & Founder
Ginger F.C. Miller, Director

1066 Huntley Pascoe
19125 N Creek Parkway
Bothel, WA 98011-8035
425-485-0900
Fax: 425-487-1825
Educational consultant for architects, utility companies, computer facilities, school districts and hospitals.

Roger Huntley, President

1067 Ingraham Dancu Associates
121 Bald Cypress Court
Pawleys Island, SC 29585
843-235-8709
Fax: 843-235-3422
dedancu@ingrahamdancu.com
www.ingrahamdancu.com
Development planning for educational and industrial clients.

Daniel E. Dancu, PhD, President

1068 Innovative Learning Group
514 East Fourth Street
Royal Oak, MI 48067
248-544-1568
Fax: 248-544-2159
www.innovativelg.com
Educational consultants for schools and the general public.

Lisa Toenniges, Owner/ CEO

69 Innovative Programming Systems
9001poplar Bridge Road
Bloomington, MN 55437
612-835-1290
Development of instructional and training programs.

70 Insight
12 S 6th Street
Suite 510
Minneapolis, MN 55402-1510
612-338-5777
Educational consultants for commercial concerns.
Mark Kovatch, President

71 Institute for Academic Excellence
901 Deming Way
Suite 301
Madison, WI 53717-1964
608-664-0965
Fax: 608-664-382
Educational consultants for K-12 schools.
John Hickey, Chairman

72 Institute for Development of Educational Activities
259 Regency Ridge
Dayton, OH 45459
937-434-6969
Fax: 937-434-5203
ideadayton@aol.com
www.idea.com
Assistance for administrators and teachers of elementary and secondary schools.

73 Institute for Global Ethics
6824 University Avenue
Middleton, WI 53562
608-204-5902
888-607-0883
ethics@globalethics.org
www.globalethics.org
Mission-driven organization aimed at providing the practical tools to build ethical environments and cultures at home, school, the workplace and in society. The organization offers consulting, seminars, research and grants towards realizing this mission.
Anthony J Gray, President & CEO
Iakovos Balassi, Project Manager

74 Interface Network
321 SW 4th Avenue
Suite 502
Portland, OR 97204-2323
503-222-2702
Fax: 503-222-7503
www.info@leaderEd.com
Educational consultant for the United States Department of Education, businesses, school districts and other governmental agencies.

075 International Center for Leadership in Education
1587 Route 146
Rexford, NY 12148
518-399-2776
Fax: 518-399-7607
info@leadered.com
www.leadered.com
Educational consultants for educational institutions, governments and commercial concerns.
Willard R Daggett, Chairman
Susan A. Gendron, President

076 International Schools Association
1033 Diego Drive South
BOCA RATON, FL 33428
561-883-3854
39-011-645-967
Fax: 561-483-2004
Fax: 39-011-643-298
info@isaschools.org
www.isaschools.org
Provides advisory and consultative services to its international and internationally minded member schools, as well as to other organizations in the field of education, such as UNESCO. The Association promotes innovations in international education, conducts conferences and workshops and publishes various educational materials.
Luis Martinez-Zorzo, Chairman
Freida Pilus, Vice Chairman

1077 J&Kalb Associates
300 Pelham Road
Suite 5K
New Rochelle, NY 10805
914-636-6154
Consulting experience to school districts.

1078 JBS International
5515 Security Lane
Suite 800
North Bethesda, MD 20852-5007
301-495-1080
Fax: 650-348-0260
info@jbsinternational.com
www.jbsinternational.com
Educational, data, market analysis, statistical and research consultants for US Government Agencies.
Jerri Shaw, Co-CEO/ President
Gail Bassin, Co-CEO/ CFO

1079 JCB/Early Childhood Education Consultant Service
813 Woodchuck Place
Bear, DE 19701
302-836-8505
Program design and cross-cultural staff development through seminars.

1080 JJ Jones Consultants
1206 Harrison Avenue
Oxford, MS 38655-3904
662-234-6755
Educational consultant for high school and college students.
JJ Jones, Owner

1081 JP Associates Incorporated
131 Foster Avenue
Valley Stream, NY 11580-4726
516-561-7803
Fax: 516-561-4066
Educational consultant for schools.
Jane Dinapoli, President

1082 Janet Hart Heinicke
1302 W Boston Avenue
Indianola, IA 50125
515-961-8933
Fax: 515-961-8903
Development of new programs and maintenance strategies.

1083 Jewish Learning Venture
7607 Old York Road
Melrose Park, PA 19027-3010
215-320-036
Fax: 215-635-8946
info@jewishlearningventure.org
www.jewishlearningventure.org
Educational consultants.
Rabbi Philip Warmflash, Executive Director
Elana Rivel, Associate Director

1084 Jobs for California Graduates
2525 O Street
Merced, CA 95340-3634
209-385-8466
Educational consultants for high school students.
Obie Obrien, Director

1085 John McLaughlin Company
1524 S Summit Avenue
Sioux Falls, SD 57105
605-332-4900
Fax: 605-339-1662
Advises companies regarding private-sector activities in K-12 and higher education.
John Laughlin, Owner

1086 Johnson & Johnson Associates
3970 Chain Bridge Road
Fairfax, VA 22030-3316
703-359-5969
800-899-6363
Fax: 703-359-5971
info@jjaconsultants.com
www.jjaconsultants.com
Educational consultants for governmental agencies and commercial concerns.
Dr. Johnson Edosomwan, President/CEO

1087 Joseph & Edna Josephson Institute
9841 Airport Blvd.
Suite 300
Los Angeles, CA 90045-6621
310-846-4800
800-711-2670
Fax: 310-846-4858
www.charactercounts.org
Educational consultant for organizations, government, businesses and the general public.
Scott Raecker, Chairman
Robert Holmes, Vice Chairman

1088 Kaludis Consulting Group
1050 Connecticut Avenue NW
10th Floor
Washington, DC 20036
202-772-3120
Fax: 202-331-1428
info@kaludisconsulting.com
www.kaludisconsulting.com
Educational consultants for colleges and universities.
George Kaludis, President/Chairman
Barry M Cohen, Senior Vice President

1089 Kentucky Association of School Administrators
87 C Michael Davenport Boulevard
Frankfort, KY 40601
800-928-5272
www.kasa.org
Professional association representing school administrators across the state of Kentucky.
Rhonda Caldwell, Executive Director
Wanda Darland, Associate Director

1090 Kleiner & Associates
8636 SE 75th Place
Mercer Island, WA 98040-5235
206-236-0608
Educational consultants for public and private institutions.
Charles Kleiner, Owner

1091 Lawrence A Heller Associates
324 Freeport Road
Pittsburgh, PA 15238-3422
412-820-0670
Fax: 412-820-0669
Development and implementation of educational programs.

1092 Leona Group
7878 N. 16th St
Suite 150
Phoenix, AZ 85020
602-953-2933
Fax: 602-953-0831
www.leonagroup.com
Currently manages more than 40 school sites in Michigan, Arizona, Ohio and Indiana

Wieland Wettstein, Chairman
Dr. Bill Coats, CEO

1093 Linkage
200 Wheeler Road
3rd Floor South Tower
Burlington, MA 01803-7305
781-402-5555
Fax: 781-402-5556
info@linkageinc.com
www.linkageinc.com
Linkage, Inc. is a global organizational development company that specializes in leadership development.

Phil Harkins, Executive Chairman
Harley Ostis, President & CEO

1094 Logical Systems
605 East 1st Street
Suite 101
Rome, GA 30161-3109
706-234-9896
Fax: 706-290-0998
www.logsysinc.com
Educational consultants for school districts.

Francis Ranwez, President

1095 Los Angeles Educational Alliance for Restructuring Now
445 S Figueroa Street
Los Angeles, CA 90071
323-255-3276
Fax: 213-626-5830
asant@ccf-la.org
Educational consulting for school systems.

Mary Chambers, Vice President
Michael Roos, President

1096 Louisiana Children's Research Center for Development & Learning
1 Galleria Blvd.
Suite 903
Metairie, LA 70001-3036
504-840-9786
Fax: 504-840-9968
learn@cdl.org
www.cdl.org
Educational consultants for the general public.

Frank Williams, Chairman
Gregory N. Rattler, Vice Chairman

1097 MK & Company
132 Bronte Street
San Francisco, CA 94110
415-826-5923
Program development and project management for educational products, services and organizations.

1098 MPR Associates
3040 East Cornwallis Road
Post Office Box 12194
Research Triangle Park, NC 27709-2194
510-849-4942
Fax: 510-849-0794
Educational consultants for governmental, educational and commercial concerns including law firms.

Gary Hoachlander, President

1099 Magi Educational Services Incorporated
7-11 Broadway
Suite 402
White Plains, NY 10601-3546
914-682-1861
Fax: 914-682-1760
Educational consultant for educational institutions.

Dr. Ronald Szczypkowski, President

1100 Management Concepts
8230 Leesburg Pike
Suite 800
Tysons Corner, VA 22182-2639
703-790-9595
888-545-8571
Fax: 703-790-1371
info@managementconcepts.com
www.managementconcepts.com
Educational consultants for commercial and governmental concerns.

Stephen L. Maier, President
Thomas F. Dungan lll, CEO

1101 Management Simulations
55 E Monroe
Chicago, IL 60093-1250
312-477-7200
877-477-8787
welcome@capsim.com
www.capsim.com
Educational consultants for commercial concerns and universities.

Daniel Smith, President
Shridhar Sampath, General Manager

1102 Marketing Education Resource Center
1375 King Avenue
PO Box 12279
Columbus, OH 43212-2220
614-486-6708
800-448-0398
Fax: 614-486-1819
www.mbaresearch.org
Educational, development and curriculum consulting for high schools and post secondary schools.

Trey Michael, Chair
James R Gleason Ph.D., President, CEO

1103 Maryland Educational Opportunity Center
2305 N. Charles St.
Suite 101
Baltimore, MD 21218
410-728-3400
888-245-2774
Fax: 410-523-6340
edhoward@meoconline.com
www.meoconline.com
Consultant services for educational institutions.

Ellen Howard, Executive Director
Lynn Drummond, Associate Director

1104 Maryland Elco Incorporated Educational Funding Company
4740 Chevy Chase Drive
Chevy Chase, MD 20815-6461
301-654-8677
Fax: 301-654-7750
info@efconline.com
www.efconline.com
Educational, accounting and billing consultants for service and vocational schools and businesses.

Nicholas Cokinos, Chairman
John Cokinos, President

1105 Mason Associates
142 N Mountain Avenue
Montclair, NJ 07042
201-744-9143
Educational services for independent secondary schools, colleges and universities.

1106 Matrix Media Distribution
28310 Roadside Drive
Suite 237
Agoura, CA 91301-4951
818-865-3470
Educational consultant for the educational market.

Paul Luttrell, President

1107 McKenzie Group
1100 17th Street NW
Suite 1100
Washington, DC 20036-4638
202-466-1111
Fax: 202-466-3363
Educational consultant for commercial concerns and government.

Floretta D McKenzie, President

1108 Measurement
423 Morris Street
Durham, NC 27701-2128
919-683-2413
Fax: 919-425-7726
www.measurementinc.com
Educational, research, testing and printing consultant for schools, state governments and private businesses.

Dr. Henry H Scherich, President
Dr. Michael B Bunch, Senior Vice President

1109 Measurement Learning Consultants
80920 Highway 10
Tolovana Park, OR 97145
503-436-1464
Business, educational, testing and development consultants for the general public and commercial concerns such as schools.

Albert G Bennyworth, Partner

1110 Merrimack Education Center
101 Mill Road
Chelmsford, MA 01824-4844
978-256-3985
Fax: 978-937-5585
www.mec.edu
Educational consultant for educational facilities.

John Barranco, Executive Director

1111 Michigan Education Council
40440 Palmer Road
Canton, MI 48188-2034
734-729-1000
Fax: 734-729-1004
Educational consultant for individuals.

Dawud Tauhidi, Director

1112 Midas Consulting Group
4600 S Syracuse Street
Suite 900
Denver, CO 80237
303-256-6500
Fax: 866-790-9500
info@midasconsultinggroup.com
Educational consultant for schools, universities, training centers and government agencies.

Michael Blimes, Executive Consultant

1113 Miller, Cook & Associates
1606 Bellview Avenue
Suite 1
Roanoke, VA 24014-4923
540-345-4393
800-591-1141

Fax: 239-394-2652
info@millercook.com
www.millercook.com
Educational consultants for colleges and universities.

William B Miller, President
Catherine R. Cook, Chief Executive Officer

14 Model Classroom
4095 173rd Place SW
Bellvue, WA 98008-5929
425-746-0331
Educational consultant for school districts, commercial concerns and the Department of Education.

Cheryl Avena, Owner

15 Modern Educational Systems
15 Limestone Terrace
Ridgefield, CT 06877-2621
203-431-4144
Educational consultant for schools.

Edward T McCormick, President

16 Modern Red Schoolhouse Institute
1901 21st Avenue
South Nashville, TN 37212-1502
615-320-8804
888-275-6774
Fax: 615-320-5366
Educational consultant for school districts.

Sally B Kilgore, President

17 Montana School Boards Association
863 Great Northern Blvd.
Suite 301
Helena, MT 59601-5156
406-442-2180
Fax: 406-442-2194
www.mtsba.org
Training, educational and school districts consultant for school boards.

Charles Wilson, President
Lance Melton, Executive Director

18 Montgomery Intermediate Unit 23
1605 West Main Street
Suite B
Norristown, PA 19403-3268
610-539-8550
Fax: 610-539-5073
webmaster@mciu.org
www.mciu.org
Educational consultants for professional associations, groups and student organizations.

Marc Lieberson, President

19 Moore Express
865 Pancheri Drive
Idaho Falls, ID 83402
208-523-6276
Educational consultant for public school districts, state and local governments and commercial concerns.

Lawry Wilde, President

20 Mosaica Education
45 Broadway
17th Floor
New York, NY 10006
212-232-0305
Fax: 212-232-0309
www.mosaicaeducation.com
Manages public schools either under contract with local school districts or funded directly by states under charter school laws that permit private management.

Gene Eidelman, President
Michael J Connelly, Chief Executive Officer

1121 Multicorp
1912 Avenue K
Suite 210
Plano, TX 75074-5960
972-551-8899
Computer and educational consultant.

Fred Sammet, Chairman

1122 National Center on Education & the Economy
2121 K Street NW
Suite 700
Washington, DC 20037-4507
202-379-1800
Fax: 202-293-1560
info@ncee.org
www.ncee.org
Educational consultant for schools.

Marc S Tucker, President
Betsy Brown Ruzzi, Vice President

1123 National Evaluation Systems
30 Gatehouse Road
PO Box 226
Amherst, MA 01004
Fax: 413-256-8221
Educational testing, test development, and assessment for education agencies.

1124 National Heritage Academies
3850 Broadmoor Avenue SE
Suite 201
Grand Rapids, MI 49512
877-223-6402
Fax: 616-575-6801
info@heritageacademies.com
www.nhaschools.com
Manages 22 charter academies (K-8) in Michigan and North Carolina.

2007, Author
Harry Hurlburt, President, CEO
Todd McKee, Chief Academic Officer

1125 National Reading Styles Institute
PO Box 737
Syosset, NY 11791
516-921-5500
800-331-3117
Fax: 516-921-5591
readingstyle@nrsi.com
www.nrsi.com
Educational consultants for schools and educators.

Marie Carbo, Executive Director

1126 National School Safety and Security Services
PO Box 110123
Cleveland, OH 44111
216-251-3067
ken@schoolsecurity.org
www.schoolsecurity.org
National consulting firm specializing in school security and crisis preparedness training, security assessments, and related safety consulting for K-12 schools, law enforcement, and other youth safety providers.

Kenneth S Trump, President/CEO
Dr. Asia Jones, Director

1127 Noel/Levitz Centers
2350 Oakdale Blvd.
Coralville, IA 52241-9581
319-626-8380
800-876-1117
Fax: 319-626-8388
ContactUs@noellevitz.com
Educational consultant for colleges and universities.

Tom Williams, President/CEO

1128 Ome Resa
2230 Sunset Boulevard
Steubenville, OH 43952-1349
740-283-2050
Fax: 740-283-1500
angie.underwood@omeresa.net
www.omeresa.net
Educational consultants for school districts.

Dave Hire, Chair
John Wilson, Vice Chair

1129 Oosting & Associates
200 Seaboard Lane
Franklin, TN 37067-8237
615-771-7706
Fax: 615-771-7810
Educational consultants for colleges and universities.

Dr. Kenneth Oosting, President

1130 Pamela Joy
1049 Whipple Avenue
Suite A
Redwood City, CA 94062-1414
650-368-9968
Fax: 650-368-2794
Educational consultants for schools.

Pamela Joy, Owner

1131 Parsifal Systems
155 N Craig Street
Pittsburgh, PA 15213
412-682-8080
Fax: 412-682-6291
Educational consultants for commercial concerns and schools.

Marcia Morton, President

1132 Paul H Rosendahl, PHD
240 Mohouli Street
Hilo, HI 96720-2445
808-935-5233
Fax: 808-961-6998
Science, archaeology, historical, resources and management consultant for developers, government agencies, educational institutions, groups and individuals.

Paul H Rosendahl, Owner

1133 Perfect PC Technologies
15012 Red Hill Avenue
Tustin, CA 92780-6524
714-258-0800
Computer consultants for commercial concerns, schools and institutions.

Neil Lin, President

1134 Performa
124 N Broadway
De Pere, WI 54115
920-336-9929
Fax: 920-336-2899
www.performainc.com
Planning and facility consultants for higher education, manufacturing and government agencies.

Doug Page, President
Jeff Kanzelberger, CEO

1135 Poetry Alive!
70 Woodfin Place
Suite WW4C
Asheville, NC 28801
828-255-7636
800-476-8172
Fax: 828-232-1045
poetry@poetryalive.com
www.poetryalive.com
Educational consultants for commercial concerns and school systems.

Bob Falls, President

1136 Post Secondary Educational Assistance
500 Century Park South
Suite 200
Birmingham, AL 35226-3920
205-930-4930
Fax: 205-930-4905
Educational consultant for commercial concerns.
Kenneth Horne, President

1137 Prevention Service
7614 Morningstar Avenue
Harrisburg, PA 17112-4226
717-651-9510
Educational consultant for corporations, private health clubs, school districts and other organizations.
Mark Everest, President

1138 Princeton Review
2315 Broadway
2nd Floor
New York, NY 10024-4332
212-874-8282
888-955-4600
Fax: 212-874-0775
www.princetonreview.com
Educational consultants for commercial concerns.
John Katzman, President

1139 Priority Computer Services
6561 Lonewolf Drive
Suite 110
South Bend, IN 46628
574-236-5979
866-661-9049
priority@pcserv-inc.com
www.prioritycomputer.biz
Computer consultant for commercial education.
Ben Hahaj, President

1140 Prism Computer Corporation
2 Park Plaza
Suite 1060
Irvine, CA 92614-8520
800-774-7622
Fax: 949-553-6559
Educational consultant for manufacturers, government agencies and colleges.
Micheal A Ellis, President

1141 Professional Computer Systems
849 SE Greenville Avenue
Winchester, IN 47394-8441
765-584-2288
Fax: 765-584-1283
www.pcswin.com
Computer consultants for businesses, schools and municipalities.
Steve Barnes, President

1142 Professional Development Institute
280 S County Road
Suite 427
Longwood, FL 32750-5468
407-834-5224
Educational consultants for US Department of Transportation and commercial concerns.
Elsom Eldridge, Jr, President

1143 Profiles
507 Highland Avenue
Iowa City, IA 52240-4516
319-354-7600
Fax: 319-354-6813
Educational consultants for school districts and commercial concerns.
Douglas Paul, President

1144 Pyramid Educational Consultants
13 Garfield Way
Newark, DE 19713
302-368-2515
888-732-7462
Fax: 302-368-2516
www.pecsusa.com
Educational consultant for general trade, historical commissions and other public bodies.
Andrew Bondy, President
Lori A Frost, Vice President

1145 Quality Education Development
41 Central Park West
New York, NY 10023
212-724-3335
800-724-2215
Fax: 212-724-4913
info@qedconsulting.com
Structures courses that promote knowledge and understanding through interactive learning, and communication programs.

1146 Quantum Performance Group
5050 Rushmore Road
Palmyra, NY 14522-9414
315-986-9200
Educational consultant for commercial concerns, including schools.
Dr. Mark Blazey, President

1147 Rebus
4111 Jackson Road
Ann Arbor, MI 48103-1827
734-668-4870
Fax: 734-913-4750
Educational consultant for schools and school districts.
Linda Borgsdorf, President

1148 Records Consultants
10826 Gulfdale Street
San Antonio, TX 78216-3607
210-366-4127
Fax: 210-366-0776
Educational consultant for school districts and municipalities.
Lang Glotfelty, President

1149 Regional Learning Service of Central New York
770 James Street Office
Syracuse, NY 13203-1644
315-446-0500
Fax: 315-446-5869
Educational consultants for commercial concerns.
Rebecca Livengood, Executive Director

1150 Reinventing Your School Board
Aspen Group International,Inc
PO Box 260301
Highlands Ranch, CO 80163-0301
303-478-0125
Fax: 208-248-6084
Linda Dawson, Contact
Dr. Randy Quinn, Contact

1151 Relearning by Design
447 Forcina Hall
PO Box 7718
Ewing, NJ 08628-0718
609-771-2921
Fax: 609-637-5130
info@relearning.org
www.relearning.org
Grant Wiggins, Author/Editor
Jacquelyn Nance, Chair

1152 Research Assessment Management
816 Camarillo Springs Road
Camarillo, CA 93012-9441
805-987-5538
Fax: 805-987-2868
Educational consultants for governmental agencies and commercial concerns.
Adrienne McCollum, PhD, President

1153 Robert E Nelson Associates
120 Oak Brook Center
Suite 208
Oak Brook, IL 60523
630-954-5585
Fax: 630-954-5606
Consulting for private colleges, universities and secondary schools.

1154 Rookey Associates
1740 Little York Xing
Little York, NY 13087
607-749-2325
Educational consultant for school districts, public utility companies and the government.
Ernest J Rookey, President

1155 Root Learning
810 W S Boundary Street
Perrysburg, OH 43551-5200
419-874-0077
Fax: 419-874-4801
Business, educational, employment consultant for commercial concerns.
Randall Root, Chairman/CEO

1156 School Management Study Group
1649 Lone Peoh Drive
Salt Lake City, UT 84117
801-277-3725
Fax: 801-277-4547
Organization seeking to promote improvement of schools and to involve educators in critical school problems.
Donald Thomas, President
Dale Holden, Associate

1157 SchoolMatch by Public Priority Systems
2200 Lane Woods Drive
Columbus, OH 43221
973-831-1757
www.schoolmatch.com
An educational consultant for private and public schools.
William L. Bainbridge, Ph.D., FACFE, President/ CEO

1158 Sensa of New Jersey
110 Mohawk Trail
Wayne, NJ 07470-5030
973-831-1757
An educational consultant for private and public schools.
John Pinto, President

1159 Shirley Handy
4151 Wild Lilac Drive
Turlock, CA 95382-8308
209-668-4142
Fax: 209-668-1855
www.n-e-n.com
Educational consultants for school districts and teachers.
Shirley Handy, Owner

60 Sidney Kreppel
704 E Benita Boulevard
Vestal, NY 13850-2629
607-754-6870
Educational consultants.
Sidney Kreppel, Owner

61 Solutions Skills
545 E Tennessee Street
Tallahassee, FL 32308-4981
850-681-6543
Fax: 850-681-6543
www.solutionskills.com
Business and educational consultants for state and governments, educational, medical and legal publishing companies.
Randall Vickers, President

62 Special Education Service Agency
3501 Denali Street
Suite 101
Anchorage, AK 99503-1068
907-563-8284
877-890-9269
Fax: 907-562-0545
sesa@sesa.org
www.sesa.org
Educational consultant for school districts.
Nancy Nagarkar, Executive Director
Laraine Adams, Secretary

63 Sports Management Group
918 Parker Street
Suite A-13
Berkeley, CA 94710
510-849-3090
Fax: 510-849-3094
Educational consulting for universities.
Lauren Livingston, President

64 Stewart Howe Alumni Service of New York
3109 N Triphammer Road
Lansing, NY 14882
607-533-9200
Fax: 607-533-9218
programs@stewarthowe.com
www.stewarthowe.com
Educational consultants for college organizations.
Peter McChesney, Director
Mike Duesing, Managing Partner

65 Strategies for Educational Change
11 Whitby Court
Mount Holly, NJ 08060
609-261-1702
Development of programs for youths at risk.

66 Success for All Foundation
300 E. Joppa Road
Suite 500
Baltimore, MD 21286
410-616-2300
800-548-4998
Fax: 410-324-4444
sfainfo@successforall.net
A not-for-profit organization dedicated to the development, evaluation and dissemination of proven reform models for preschool, elementary and middle schools.
Nancy Madden, Ph.D., CEO

167 Teachers Curriculum Institute
P.O. Box 1327
Rancho Cordova, CA 95741
916-366-3686
800-497-6138
Fax: 800-343-6828
www.teachtci.com
Educational consultant for schools and teachers.
Bert Bower, President/ CEO
Amy Larson, Chief Operating Officer

1168 Teachers Service Association
1107 E Lincoln Avenue
Orange, CA 92865-1939
714-282-6342
Educational consultants for schools and teachers.
Richard Ghysels, Secretary Treasurer

1169 Tech Ed Services
One World Trade Center
8th Floor
Long Beach, CA 90831
562-869-1913
800-832-4411
Fax: 562-869-5673
info@techedservices.com
www.techedservices.com
Computer, planning and training consultant for k-12 educators and adult educators.
Patricia K Sanford, President/ CEO
Brenna Terrones, TES Senior Specialist

1170 Technical Education Research Centers
2067 Massachusetts Avenue
Cambridge, MA 02140-1340
617-873-9600
Fax: 617-873-9601
contactus@terc.edu
www.terc.edu
Educational consultant for the National Science Foundation and the Department of Education.
Arthur Nelson, Founder
George E. Hein, Chairman

1171 Tesseract Group
18 W 27th Street
11th Floor
New York, NY 10001
212-481-8304
Fax: 212-481-8306
www.tesseractllc.com
An integrated education management company, serving private and public charter elementary, middle and high schools in six states.
Erica Payne, Founder

1172 Timothy Anderson Dovetail Consulting
936 Nantasket Avenue
Hull, MA 02045-1453
781-925-3078
Fax: 781-925-9830
Educational consultant for businesses.
Eric Anderson, Owner

1173 University Research
7200 Wisconsin Avenue
Suite 600
Bethesda, MD 20814-4811
301-654-8338
Fax: 301-941-8427
www.urc-chs.com
Educational consultants for the federal government along with other government and private sectors.
Barbara N. Turner, President

1174 University of Georgia-Instructional Technology
630 Aderhold Hall
Athens, GA 30602
706-542-4110
Fax: 706-542-4240
www.coe.uga.edu
Instructional design and development.
Aurthur M. Horne, Dean
Pedro R Portes, Professor

1175 Uplinc
48 Capital Drive
West Springfield, MA 01089
413-693-0700
www.uplinc.com
Computer consultants for commercial, general public and educational concerns.
Ron Marino, President

1176 William A Ewing & Company
505 S Main Street
Suite 700
Orange, CA 92868
714-245-1850
Fax: 714-456-1755
ewingo@aol.com
www.members.aol.com/ewingo
Expertise in compensation and classification.

1177 Wisconsin Technical College System Foundation
1 Foundation Circle
Waunakee, WI 53597-8914
608-849-2400
Fax: 608-849-2468
foundation@wtcsf.tec.wi.us
www.wtcsf.tec.wi.us
Educational consultant for educational institutions and businesses.
Loren Brumm, Executive Director

Africa

1178 Alexandra House School
King George V Avenue
Floreal
Mauritius
230-696-4108
Fax: 230-696-4108
admin@alexandrahouseschool.com
www.alexandrahouseschool.com
A private English Primary day school in Mauritius for boys and girls between 4 and 11 years of age. Cater for approximately 100 children and provide a British curriculum with a strong international flavour.
M Wrenn-Beejadhur, Principal

1179 American International School-Dhaka
United Nations Road Baridhara
Dhaka
Bangladesh
880-2-882-2414
Fax: 880-2-883-3175
www.ais-dhaka.net
Provides a program based on American educational principles to students from an international community, creates an academic and social environment that challenges students to achieve their potential, become life-long learners and contribute to changing global society.
Kyra Buchko, President
Diane Lindsey, Vice President

1180 American International School-Johannesburg
Private Bag X 4
Bryanston 2021
Republic of South Africa
011 464 1505
Fax: 27-11-464-1327
info@aisj-jhb.com
www.aisj-jhb.com
Serves a diverse community of students from around the world and provides a challenging education emphasizing academic excellence through a collaborative partnership with families and staff. Our program inspires and prepares the students to become responsible world citizens with a passion for life long learning.
Andy Page-Smith, Director
Ellinor Parkes, Admissions Coordinator

1181 American International School-Zambia
PO Box 31617
Lusaka
Zambia
260-211-260509 (10
Fax: 260-211-260-538
www.aislusaka.org
Committed to being a leading IB World School, offering a balanced, academically rigorous and internationally recognized college preparatory education and seeks to enable its students to become successful, lifelong learners, as well as humane, self-directed, confident and well-rounded individuals.
Chris Mulind, Director
Jim Anderson, Secondary Principal

1182 American School of Kinshasa
Unit 31550
APO AE
09828
243-884-6619
Fax: 243-884-1161
irene.epp@gmail.com
rawing on the strengths of a committed and culturally diverse community, The American School of Kinshasa aims to provide a high quality American primary and secondary education for English speaking students living in the Democratic Republic of Congo
Irene Epp, Superintendent
Fiona M Merali, Business Manager

1183 American School-Tangier
Rue Christophe Colomb
Tangier 9000
Morocco
212-39 93 98 27/28
Fax: 212-39 94 75 35
www.theamericanschooloftangier.com/
An independent, coeducational day and boarding school which offers an educational program from prekindergarten through grade 12 for students of all nationalities.
Brian Horvath, Head of School

1184 American School-Yaounde
BP 7475
Yaounde
Cameroon
237-2223-0421
Fax: 237-2223-6011
school@asoy.org
www.asoy.org
Ensures that all students achieve high academic success, demonstrate critical thinking skills, and become responsible and compassionate, global citizens prepared for their next stage in life; as gained through an enriched, American curriculum and offered in a challenging, secure, and diverse environment.
Paul Sheppard, School Director

1185 Arundel School
28 Arundel School Road
PO Box MP 91 Mount Pleasant
Harere, Zimbabwe
263-4-302121
head@arundel.ac.zw
www.arundel.ac.zw
School providing an active educational program, which encompasses excellence in culture, sports and personal development.
P. Makoni, Head
K Shawatu, Deputy Head

1186 Arusha International School
PO Box 733
Moshi, Kilimanjaro
Tanzania
255-27-275-5004
Fax: 255-27-275-2877
www.ismoshi.org
Offers a fully accredited, academically rigorous international education for students of ages three to nineteen years old.
Barry Sutherland, CEO
Bob Woods, Director

1187 Asmara International Community School
117-19 Street, #6
PO Box 4941, Asmara
Eritrea
291-1-161-705
Fax: 291-1-161-705
johnston@gmail.com
www.aicsasmara.com
Grade levels pre K-12.
Paul Johnston, Director

1188 Banda School
PO Box 24722
Nairobi
Kenya 00502
254-20-8891220/260
Fax: 254-20-8890004
www.bandaschool.com
Meet the educational needs of children living in and around Nairobi whose parents required a Preparatory School education for their children but who did not wish them to go to boarding school overseas.
Michael D Dickson, Headmaster
W Rutter, Deputy Head

1189 Bishop Mackenzie International Schools
PO Box 102
Lilongwe
Malawi
265-1-756-364
Fax: 265-1-751-374
The mission of the school is to prepare students to become responsible, self-reliant, contributing and productive citizens of our ever-changing world.
Peter Todd, Director
Janette Johnson, Primary Head Teacher

1190 Braeburn High School
Kisongo Campus
Gitanga Road
PO Box 45112 GPO Nairobi
Kenya 00100
254-20-5018000
Fax: 254-20-3872310
andy.hill@braeburn.ac.ke
www.braeburn.com
This is a co-educational international boarding school following the British National Curriculum (University of Cambridge International General Certificate of Secondary Education Examinations IGCSE), with boarding options.
R E Diaper, Principal
Mr. Terry L. K. Childs, CEO

1191 Braeburn School
Gitanga Road
PO Box 45112 GPO Nairobi
Kenya 00100
254-722 68557
Fax: 254-2-572310
www.braeburn.com
This school caters to close to 600 children from 61 different countries.
R E Diaper, Principal
Mr. Terry L. K. Childs, CEO

1192 British International School Cairo
km 38, Cairo-Alex Desert Road
Beverly Hills, 6th of October
Egypt, EG
202-3859-2000
Fax: 202-3859-1720
info@bisc.edu.eg
www.bisc.edu.eg
The School was established in 1976 to provide a balanced and challenging education based on British principles and curricula to meet the needs of the children of the expatriate British and Anglo-Egyptian communities; children from the Commonwealth and other countries with educational systems based upon British standards; children of the English-speaking Egyptian community and other nationalities tied to British-type schooling.
Simon O'Grady, Assistant
Ahmed Ezz, Principal

1193 British School-Lom
BP 20050
Lome
Togo

228-222-606
Fax: 228-222-498
admin@bsl.tg
www.bsl.tg
We value not only academic success but encourage talent of all kinds, whether in academic studies, art, drama, music or games; and that we take the position that the pupil who is kind and helpful, who has a positive attitude to school life and fellow pupils, is considered every bit as worthwhile as the brilliant scholar, artist or athlete.

94 British School-Lom,

228-226-46-06
Fax: 228-226-49-89
This school offers an English based curriculum for 120 day students and 95 boarding students (110 boys; 105 girls), ages 4-18. The school is an independent, co-educational day and boarding school. External exams from the University of London and Cambridge-UK plus International Baccalaureate (IB) is offered. Applications needed to teach include science, pre-school, French, math, social sciences, administration, Spanish, reading, German, English and physical education.

95 British Yeoward School

Parque Taoro
Tenerife
Spain, ES 38400
00-34-922-384685
Fax: 00-34-922-37-35-65
The International British Yeoward School provides a high quality British education for children of all ages in an open, multi-cultural environment; allowing each child to achieve their full potential in a positive learning community

Karen Hernandez, Head of Primary Grades
Alan Halstead, Head of School

96 Broadhurst Primary School

Private Bag BR 114 Broadhurst
Garborone
Botswana, BW
267-3971-221
Fax: 267-307987
broadhurst@info.bw
www.info.bw
To create, together with the family, a caring environment of learning and experience, in which children may develop their potential to the full, may acquire the knowledge and skills to equip them for living, may experience the best that the human spirit has achieved, may develop respect for themselves, for other people and the world around them and have the courage to make a difference to future

Rehana Khan, Head Teacher
Michael Eisen, Deputy Headteacher

97 Brookhouse Preparatory School

PO Box 24987- 00502
Nairobi
Kenya
254-20-2430260
Fax: 254-20-891641
info@brookhouse.ac.ke
www.brookhouse.ac.ke
Provides education in general computer literacy.

Eric Mulind, School Coordinator

198 Cairo American College

PO Box 39
Maadi 11431
Cairo, EG 11431
20-2-755-5505
Fax: 20-2-2519-6584
support@cacegypt.org
www.cacegypt.org
Cairo American College is a world class learning environment that affirms the voice, passions and talents of students and inspires them to use their hearts and minds as global citizens.

Nivine Captan-Amr, Board Chair
Elizabeth Bredin, Secretary

1199 Casablanca American School

Route de la Mecque,Lotissement Ougo
Casablanca, Morocco 20150
212-22-214-115
Fax: 212-22-212-488
cas@cas.ac.ma
www.cas.ac.ma
To offer the best possible U.S. and international university preparatory education program, curriculum and instruction for its students.

Simohamed Erroussafi, President
Karima Abisourour, Vice President

1200 Cavina School

PO Box 43090
Nairobi
Kenya
254-2-3866011
Fax: 254-2-3866676
cavina@iconnect.co.ke
www.cavina.ac.ke
Cavina aims to develop many qualities in the children who come through her gates - academic excellence, an inquiring mind, a sense of moral and social responsibility, and most of all a recognition of their relationship with their Creator who has revealed Himself through His son Jesus.

Massie Bloofield, Headmaster/Managing Director

1201 Dakar Academy

BP 3189 Route des Peres Maristes
Dakar, Senegal
West Africa
221-33-832-06-82
Fax: 221-33-832-17-21
office@dakar-academy.org
www.dakar-academy.org
Dakar Academy exists to partner in the advancement of the Kingdom of God through serving missionary families by providing education services for their children

Charlie Campbell, Chairman
Joseph Rosa, Director

1202 Greensteds School

Private Bag
Nakuru
Kenya
254 50 50770
Fax: 254 50 50775
office@greenstedsschool.com
www.greenstedsschool.com/
An international school for boys and girls.

MP Bentley, Headmaster

1203 Harare International School

66 Pendennis Road
Mount Pleasant
Harare, Zimbabwe
(263 4) 870514/5
Fax: 263-4-883-371
his@his.ac.zw
www.his-zim.com
Grade levels prekindergarten through twelfth, with enrollment of 376.

Marcel Gerrmann, Board Chair
Shannon Brauchli, Vice Chair

1204 Hillcrest Secondary School

PO Box 24819
Nairobi
Kenya 00502
254-20-882-222
Fax: 254-20-882-350
admin@hillcrest.ac.ke
www.hillcrest.ac.ke/secondary/
Mixed boarding school.

Christopher Drew, Head Teacher

1205 International Community School-Addis Ababa

PO Box 70282
Addis Adaba
Ethiopia
251-11-3-711-544
Fax: 251-11-371-0722
info@icsaddis.edu.et
www.icsaddis.edu.et/
An independent, coeducational day school which offers an educational program from prekindergarten through grade 12 for students of all nationalities.

Jim Laney, Director

1206 International School-Kenya

PO Box 14103
Nairobi
Kenya 00800
254-20-418-3622
Fax: 254-20-418-3272
info@isk.ac.ke
www.isk.ac.ke
Students from many backgrounds go to this school, which prepares them for successful transitions to other schools and universities around the world, offering both a North American Hogh School Diploma as well as the International Baccalaureate Diploma to its graduates.

John Roberts, Director
Jodi Lake, Curriculum Coordinator

1207 International School-Moshi

PO Box 733
Moshi, Kilimanjaro
Tanzania
255-27-275-5004
Fax: 255-27-275-2877
school@ismoshi.org
www.ismoshi.org
The school inspires individuals to be lifelong learners in a global community.

Bob Woods, Director of ISM
Keiron White, Head, Moshi Campus

1208 International School-Tanganyika

United Nations Road
PO Box 2651, Dar es Salaam
Tanzania
255-22-2151817/8
Fax: 255-22-2152077
ist@raha.com
www.istafrica.com
IST aspires to provide an outstanding international education. We value and respect cultural diversity and embrace the people and natural environment of Tanzania. Within this safe, secure and caring community students reach their full potential as citizens of the world.

David Shawver, Director
Nazir Thawer, General Manager

1209 John F Kennedy International School

CH-3792 Saanen
Switzerland
41-033-744-1372
Fax: 41- 033-744-8982

lovell@jfk.ch
www.jfk.ch
Boarding day school for boys and girls aged 5-14 years.

William Lovell, Co-Director
Sandra Lovell, Co-Director

1210 Kabira International School

PO Box 34249
Kampala
Uganda
256-0414-530-472
Fax: 256-0414-543-444
office@kisu.com
Grade levels Pre-K through 8, school year - September - July

Emma Whitney, Admissions
Elaine Whelen, Principal

1211 Kestrel Manor School

Ring Road Westlands
PO Box 14489, Nairobi
Kenya 00200
254-20-3740-311
Coeducational school for children Kindergarten through secondary schooling.

1212 Khartoum American School

PO Box 699
Khartoum
Sudan
249-15-577-0105
Fax: 249-183-512044
kas@krtams.org
www.krtams.org
An independent, coeducational day school which offers an educational program from prekindergarten through grade 12 for students of all nationalities.

Gregory Hughes, Superintendent
Brad Waugh, Principal

1213 Kigali International School

Caisse Sociale Estates, Gaculiro
BP 6558
Kigali, Rwanda
250-0783307282
Fax: 250-72128
office.kics@gmail.com
www.kicsrw.org
Non-profit, co-educational day school

Bryan Hixson, Chairman
Mark Thiessen, Vice Chairman

1214 Kingsgate English Medium Primary School

Box 169
Mafeteng, 900 Lesotho
Africa
Kingsgate is the only non-denominational primary school in the district. The curriculum is English-based offered to a total of 460 day students (240 boys; 220 girls), PreK-7. Overseas teachers are welcome with the length of stay being one year, with housing provided. Applications needed to teach include pre-school and reading.

M Makhothe, Principal

1215 Kisumu International School

PO Box 1276
Kisumu
Kenya
254-35-21678
www.kisumu.braeburn.com
This school is located on the shores of Lake Victoria and offers a unique education to students of all nationalities and cultural backgrounds. The total enrollment of the school is 35 day students, in grades K-7. The school does participate in the teacher exchange programs, with the length of stay being two years with housing provided by the school. Applications needed to teach include science, preschool, math, social sciences, English and physical education.

Neena Sharma, Principal

1216 Lincoln Community School

American Embassy Accra
N126/21 Dedeibaa Street
Abelemkpe, Accra
Ghana, West Africa
233 30 277 4018
Fax: 233 302 78 09 85
headofschool@lincoln.edu.gh
www.lincoln.edu.gh
is committed to inspiring students to achieve the highest standards of intellectual and personal development through a stimulating and comprehensive program.

Dennis Larkin, Head of School
Sanjay Rughani Tanzanian, President

1217 Lincoln International School of Uganda

PO Box 4200
Kampala
Uganda
256-41-4200374/8/9
Fax: 256-41-200303
dtodd@isumail.ac.ug
Grade levels Pre-K through 12, school year August - June

Daniel Todd, Dean of Studied/Admission
Jim Campbell, Chairman

1218 Maru A Pula School

Plot 4725
Maruapula Way
Botswana 00045
267-391-2953
Fax: 267-397-3338
principal.map@gmail.com
www.maruapula.org/
Maru-a-Pula is a dynamic, world-class school rooted in Botswana. We offer a rigorous curriculum that prepares students for entry to highly selective universities and to pursue challenging careers. Through programmes emphasizing self-discipline and community service, each student learns personal and social responsibility.

Andrew S Taylor, Principal

1219 Mombasa Academy

PO Box 86487
Mombasa
Kenya, KE
254-11-471629
Fax: 254-11-221484
www.msaacademy.com
Our aim is to help our pupils to reach their true potential. Within the academic and extra-curricular frameworks, staff offer pupils considerable personal support; warm and productive working relations are a distinguishing feature of our community and are instrumental in helping each girl and boy on the road towards maturity and self-fulfillment

Kishor Joshi, Headmaster
FJ Bentley, Founder

1220 Northside Primary School

PO Box 897
Gaborone
Botswana
267-395-2440
Fax: 267-395-3573
www.northsideschool.net
In Gaborone, Botswana, Northside Primary School provides education in English and serves the needs of primary school children of all nationalities.

Mandy Watson, Headteacher

1221 Nsansa School

PO Box 70322
Ndola
Zambia
26-2-611753
Fax: 26-2-618465
This school offers an English curriculum to 185 day students (96 boys; 124 girls), in grades K-7. Length of stay for overseas teachers is one year with housing provided. Student/teacher ratio is 20:1.

Nel Mather, Principal

1222 Peterhouse

Private Bag 3741
Marondera
Zimbabwe
263 (0)279 - 22200
Fax: 263 (0)279 - 24200
www.peterhouse.org
This Anglican school offers an English based curriculum for 19 day students and 790 boarding students (535 boys; 255 girls), in Form I-Form VI. The school is willing to participate in a teacher exchange program with the length of stay being one year, with housing provided. Applications needed to teach include science, math, and physical education.

JB Calderwood, Rector

1223 Rabat American School

1 Bis Rue Emir Ibn Abdelkade
Agdal, Rabat
Morocco 10000
212-537-671-476
Fax: 212-537-670
Fax: 212-537-670-963
info@ras.ma
www.ras.ma
We provide our students with a breadth of experiences which encourage them to realize their full potential and allow them to acquire the knowledge, skills, character, and confidence to contribute positively and responsibly to an ever-changing, interconnected world.

Paul W Johnson, Director

1224 Rift Valley Academy

PO Box 80
Kijabe, 00220
Kenya
254-20-3246-249
Fax: 254-20-3246-111
rva@rva.org
www.rva.org
RVA is a Christian boarding school located in central Kenya. The academy, a branch of Africa Inland Mission International, exists to provide a quality education in a nurturing environment for the children of missionaries serving in Africa.

Roy E Entwistle, Principal
Tim Cook, Superintendent

1225 Rosslyn Academy

PO Box 14146
Nairobi
Kenya 00800
254-20-263-5294
Fax: 254-20-263-5281
info@rosslynacademy.com
www.rosslynacademy.com
The purpose of Rosslyn Academy is to provide a K-12 North American and Christian-oriented educational program for children of missionaries. Rosslyn also welcomes children from privately

sponsored families who are in sympathy with the philosophy of the school.

Phil Dow, Superintendent
Don McGavran, Director of Operations

26 Sandford English Community School

PO Box 30056 MA
Addis Ababa
Ethiopia
251-11-123-38-92
Fax: 251-11-123-3728
admission@sandfordschool.org
www.sandfordschool.org
A co-educational, non-boarding, nursery to pre University institution. Its committed to providing a standard of education that is accepted within Ethiopia and by the international community.

Jon D P Lane, Head of Primary School
Tsegaye Kassa, Senior Manager

227 Schutz American School

51 Schutz Street
PO Box 1000
Alexandria, Egypt 21111
(20) (3) 576-2205
Fax: (20) (3) 576-0229
www.schutzschool.org.eg
A single campus houses PreK-3 through grade twelve in two main classroom buildings and an auditorium/ classroom complex, as well as the administrative center, dining room, resident staff housing, clinic, art room, computer labs, libraries and snack bar. Sports facilities on the campus include basketball, volleyball, tennis and football courts, a half-size grass soccer pitch, and a swimming pool and weight training room.

Dr Joyce Lujan, Head of School
Nathan Walker, Upper School Principal

228 Sifundzani School

PO Box A286, Swazi Plaza
Mbabane
Swaziland
268-404-2465
Fax: 268-404-0320
sifundzani@realnet.co.sz
A coeducational day school which offers an educational program from grades 1 through 10 for students of all nationalities.

Ella Magongo, Principal

229 Sir Harry Johnston Primary School

Kalimbuka Road
Zomba PO Box 52
Malawi
265-1525280
Fax: 265 888202374

Una Barras-Hargan, Headteacher

230 St. Barnabas College

34 Langeberg Avenue Bostmont Johann
PO Box 88188 Newclare
South Africa 02112
011-27-474-2055
Fax: 011-27-474-2249
theronn@stbarnabas.co.za
www.stbarnabas.co.za
St Barnabas College is a co-educational secondary school in Johannesburg. It is well known as a centre of excellence. The school's mission is to provide quality secondary education to young people, the main criterion for admission being intellectual potential and the motivation to succeed.

Glynn Blignaut, Headmaster
Faizel Panker, Deputy Headmaster

1231 St. Mary's School

Rhapta Road, PO Box 40580- 00100
Nairobi
Kenya
254-020-4444569
Fax: 254-020-4446191
info@stmarys.ac.ke
www.stmarys.ac.ke
We are a Catholic Private School committed to our international character in the provision of a spiritual, intellectual and physical education. We aim at developing the gifts of the young in an atmosphere which encourages the ethos of self-expression and mutual respect with a view to their facing the future responsibly, with confidence and courage.

John Awiti, Head of School
Rosemary Abuodha Omogo, Deputy Principal

1232 St. Paul's College

St. Paul's United Theological College
Po Private Bag
Limuru
Kenya 00217
254 - 20 - 2020505
Fax: 254-66-73033
www.stpaulslimuru.ac.ke/
The school prepares men and women for ministry in the Christian Church and present day society.

Samuel Kobia, Chancellor
Joseph Galgalo, Vice Chancellor

1233 Tigoni Girls Academy

Box 10
Limuru
Kenya
This Academy is a small, closely knit community of individuals from different cultures in which physical, emotional, creative and intellectual development is fortified in all aspects of daily life. Total enrollment is 40 boarding students, ages 11-16. Applications from overseas include science, math, social sciences, French, Spanish and English. Length of stay for overseas teachers is 2 years with housing provided. The Academy is affiliated with the Church of England.

Duncan Kelly, Principal

1234 Waterford-Kamhlaba United World College

PO Box 52
Mbabane
Swaziland
011-268-422-0866
Fax: 011-268-422-0088
admissions@waterford.sz
www.waterford.sz/index.php
This school offers a curriculum based in English for 181 day students and 295 boarding (251 boys; 226 girls), in grades 6-12. Overseas teachers length of stay is three years with housing provided. Applications needed to teach include math, English, and physical education.

Laurence Nodder, Principal
Bruce Wells, Deputy Principal

1235 Westwood International School

PO Box 2446
Gabarone
Botswana
011-267-390-6736
Fax: 011-267-390-6734
westwood-admissions@info.bw
www.westwoodis.com
Westwood International School shall provide students with a quality international education that shall effectively prepare them for access to tertiary study and the world of work, and enable them to confidently meet future challenges as life long learners

Phyllis Hildebrandt, Principal
Michael Francis, Director

1236 Windhoek International School

Private Bag
Windhoek
Namibia 16007
264-61-241-783
Fax: 264-61-243-127
www.wis.edu.na
The Windhoek International School prepares its students to be inquiring, knowledgeable and caring participants in the global arena through an international curriculum of the highest standard. WIS embraces the diversity of its students from the international community and Namibia, in an atmosphere of mutual respect, tolerance and educational enrichment for all

Catherine O'Connor-Smith, Secretary
Neville Field, Chairperson

Asia, Pacific Rim & Australia

1237 Aiyura International Primary School

PO Box 407
Ukarumpa Papua
New Guinea

Perry Bradford, Principal

1238 Ake Panya International School

158/1 Moo 3 Hangdong-Samoeng Road
Banpong, Hangdong, Chiang Mai 50230
Thailand
66-53-36-5303
Fax: 66-53-365-304
akepanya@cm.ksc.co.th
Grade levels 1-12, school year August - June

Barry Sutherland, Headmaster
Holly Shaw, Director of Studies

1239 Alotau International Primary School

PO Box 154
Alotau, Milne Bay Province
Papua New Guinea
675-641-1078
Fax: 675-641-1627
www.iea.ac.pg

Lucy Kula, Principal

1240 Amelia Earhart Intermediate School

Unit 5166
APO AP 96368
Okinawa
011-81-611-734-132
Fax: 011-81-611-734-720
Success in Education is a Partnership in Responsibility characterized by the opportunities and the guidance necessary to motivate learners, the desire and ability to be successful in human interactions, to access and process information, and to accept personal responsibility for all decisions made throughout one's lifetime.

Deborah Carlson, Principal

1241 American International School-Dhaka

P.O. Box: 6106
Gulshan, Dhaka 1212
Bangladesh
880-2-882-2452
Fax: 880-2-882-3175
www.ais-dhaka.net
Provides a program based on American educational principles to students from an inter-

national community, creates an academic and social environment that challenges students to achieve their potential, become life-long learners and contribute to changing global society.

Richard Boerner, Superintendent
Kyra Buchko, President

1242 American International School-Guangzhou

No 3 Yan Yu Street S
Ersha Island, Yuexiu District
Guangzhou PR China 51010
86-20-8735-3392
Fax: 86-20-8735-3339
admissions@aisgz.org
www.aisgz.org/
Prepares students for entrance into the very best universities in the world is enhanced by being in the cultural center of Guangzhou and Southern China.

Joseph Stucker, Director
Katherine Farrell, Chair

1243 American School-Bombay

SF 2 G Block
Bandra Kurla Complex
Mumbai 400 0
91 22 6772 7272ÿ
Fax: 91 22 6252 6666
admissions@asbindia.org
www.asbindia.org
ASB delivers a dynamic educational program that encourages each student to achieve her or his highest potential. While ASB is a U.S. style school, the Indian setting and multi-national community, representing over 51 countries, brings children who have varied experiences together to learn in a rich and unique environment

Paul M Fochtman, Superintendent

1244 American School-Guangzhou (China)

Number 3 Yan Yu Street S
Ersha Island, Yuexiu District
Guangzhou, China 51010
8620-8735-3393
Fax: 8620-8735-3339
admissions@aisgz.org
www.aisgz.org/
An independent, coeducational day school which offers an educational program from kindergarten through grade 12

Joseph Stucker, Director
Paul Wood, Principal

1245 American School-Japan

1-1 Nomizu 1
Chofu-shi, Tokyo
Japan 182-0
0422-34-5300
Fax: 0422-34-5303
www.asij.ac.jp
The American School in Japan is a private, coeducational day school which offers an educational program from nursery through grade 12 for students of all nationalities, but it primarily serves the American community living in the Tokyo area. The school was founded in 1902. The school year comprises 2 semesters extending from September to January and January to June.

Ed Ladd, Headmaster

1246 Aoba International School

2-10-34 Aobadai
Meguro-Ku, Tokyo
Japan 153-0-42
03-3461-1442
Fax: 81-3-3463-9873
meguro@aobajapan.jp
www.aobaonline.jp
A co-educational school located on campuses in Meguro and Suginami. Over 550 students are enrolled in classes from pre-kindergarten to grade nine.

Neal Dilk, Head of School
Chiharu Uemura, VP

1247 Ashgabat International School

Berzengi, Ata Turk Street
Ashgabat
Turkmenistan
386-12-007870
Fax: 386-12-007871
ashgabat@qsi.org
Offers high quality education in the English language for elementary students from three years through thirteen years of age.

Brad Goth, Director

1248 Bali International School

PO Box 3259
Denpasar
Bali, Indonesia
62-361-288-770
Fax: 62-361-285-103
admin@baliis.net
www.baliinternationalschool.com
Provides educational excellence in a supportive, secure environment, preparing students to thrive and succeed as responsible citizens in a changing world. Offers the three IB Programs (PYP, MYP and DP) and is accredited by WASC.

Chris Akin, Director
Russell McGrath, PS-12 Assistant Principal

1249 Bandung Alliance International School

Jalan Bujanggamanik Kav 2
Kota Baru Parahyangan
Bandung, Indonesia 40553
62-22-8681-3949
Fax: 62-22-8681-3953
info@baisedu.org
www.baisedu.org
BAIS operates as a private non-profit school to serve the international community. BAIS provides quality education in the traditions of classic, conservative ethics and values.

Pete Simano, Director
Charity Lamertha, Elementary Principal

1250 Bandung International School

Jl Suria Sumantri No 61
Bandung
West Java, Indonesia 40164
62-22-201-4995
Fax: 62-22-201-2688
At Bandung International Scholl, it is our vision to be a preeminent school providing world class secular education in the English language to the children of expatriates and others while maintaining strong links with the Indonesian community

Henri Behelmans, Head of School
Mark Holland, Chair

1251 Bangalore International School

Geddalahalli, Hennur Bagalur Road
Kothanur Post
Bangalore, India 560 0
91-802-846-5060
Fax: 91-802-846-5059
www.bangaloreinternationalschool.com
Provides internationally recognized standards of education with an India ethos and enable students to fulfill their potential in a culturally rich atmosphere.

Anuradha Monga, Principal

1252 Bangkok Patana School

643 Lasalle road Sukhumvit 105 Bang
Bangkok, Thailand 10260
6602-398-0200
Fax: 6602-399-3179
reception@patana.ac.th
www.patana.ac.th
We are an academically directed school, focussed on our commitment to offer all of our students the best intellectual and physical preparation for higher education.

Tej Bunnag, Chairman
Kulvadee Siribhadra, Director

1253 Beijing BISS International School

No 17, Area 4 An Zhen Xi Li
Chaoyang District, Beijing
China 10002
86-10-6443-3151
Fax: 86-10-6443-3156
Admissions@biss.com.cn
www.biss.com.cn
To educate and empower our students to attain personal excellence and positively impact the world.

Chan Ching Oi, CEO
Ettie Zilber, Head of School

1254 Bob Hope Primary School

Unit 5166
APO AP 96368-5166
Okinawa, Japan 96368-5166
11-81-611-734-0093
Fax: 11-81-98-934-6806
bhps.okinawa@pac.dodea.edu
The Bob Hope Primary School community is committed to teaching basic skills using developmentally appropriate strategies.

Jim Journey, Principal
Luldes Giraud, Vice Principal

1255 Bogor Expatriate School

PO Box 258
Jalan Papandayan 7, Bogor 16151
Indonesia
62-251-324360
Fax: 62-251-328512
Mission is to provide opportunities to foster positive attitudes towards learning.

Chris Rawlins, Head of School
Lance Kelly, Principal

1256 Bontang International School

15 Roszel Road
Po Box 5910
Princeton, NJ 08543
62-548551176
iss@iss.edu
An international school with an English/Japanese based curriculum for twenty day students (6 boys; 14 girls), grades PreK-8. Student/teacher ration 5:1.

Roger Hove, Executive Vice President

1257 Brent International School-Manila

Brentville Subdivision
Mamplasan, Bian, Laguna
Philippines 04024
63 (049) 511-4330
Fax: 632-633-8420
webmaster@brent.edu.ph
www.brent.edu.ph
Brent Schools, in a Christian ecumenical environment in the Philippines, are committed to develop individual students as responsible global citizens and leaders in their respective communities, with a multicultural and international perspective, and

equipped for entry to colleges and universities throughout the world.

Dick B Robbins, Headmaster
Jeffrey W Hammett, Deputy Headmaster

58 Brent School
Brent Road
PO Box 35, Baguio City
Philippines 02600
63 (074) 442-3628
Fax: 63 (074) 442-2260
webmaster@brent.edu.ph
www.brentschoolbaguio.com
Brent Schools, in a Christian ecumenical environment in the Philippines, are committed to develop individual students as responsible global citizens and leaders in their respective communities, with a multicultural and international perspective, and equipped for entry to colleges and universities throughout the world.

Dick B Robbins, Headmaster
Ursula Banga-an Daoey, Deputy Head

.59 British International School
Bintayo Jaya Sektor IX JI
Raya Jomabang Ciledug Pondok Aren
Jakarta, ID 15227
62-21-745-1670
Fax: 62-21-745-1671
enquiries@bis.or.id
www.bis.or.id
The new premises and facilities enable the school to excel further in the range of opportunities and experiences that can be offered to its students.

Christian Barkei, Principal
Brian Dallamore, Chairman

.60 British School Manila
36th Street University Park Forth B
Fort Bonifacio Global City
Taguig, PH
63 2 860 4800
Fax: 63 2 860 4900
admissions@britishschoolmanila.org
www.britishschoolmanila.org
The British School Manila will deliver the highest standard of education in the Philippines for British children and for English speaking children of other nationalities The British School Manila provides outstanding education for English speaking children of all nationalities aged 3-18, based on an adapted form of the National Curriculum of England, and the I.B. Diploma

Chris Mantz, Head of School
Glenn Hardy, Head of Primary School

261 British School-Muscat
PO Box 1907
Ruwi
Oman 00112
00968ÿ24600842ÿ
Fax: 00968 24601062
www.britishschoolmuscat.com
The Vision of the British School-Muscat is to offer the highest quality British education to children of wide ranging abilities and nationalities. It values cultural diversity and provides a caring, innovative and stimulating environment, realizing the full potential and celebrating the success of every student. The School's curriculum will also develop the child as a whole person, provide them with learning-to-learn skills and will prepare them to lead a successful life in an inter-cultural wor

Kai Vacher, Principal
Deirdre Selway, Registrar

1262 Calcutta International School Society
18 Lee Road
Calcutta 700 020
India
www.calcuttais.edu.in
This school offers an English-based curriculum to 480 day students (230 boys; 250 girls), grades Nursery-12. CIS follows GCE London Curriculum. The cultures represented by the student body include expatriates, NRIs, local children. The student body is mainly Indians. Highly qualified individuals offering excellent results. The school is willing to participate in a teacher exchange program with the length of stay being 1-2 years, with no housing provided.

N Chatterjee, Principal
L Chaturvedi, Faculty Head

1263 Caltex American School
CPI Rumbal
Pekanbaru, Sumatra Riau
Indonesia
62-765-995-501
Fax: 62-765-996-321
Grade level preK through 8.

Daniel Hovde, Superintendent

1264 Camberwell Grammar School
55 Mout Albert Road
Canterbury 3126, Victoria
Australia
61 3 9835 1777
Fax: 61 3 9836 0752
registrar@cgs.vic.edu.au
www.cgs.vic.edu.au
Independent boys school.

CF Black, Principal

1265 Canadian Academy
4-1 Koyo Cho Naka
Higashinada-Ku, Kobe
Japan 658-0-32
81-78-857-0100
Fax: 81-78-857-3250
www.canacad.ac.jp/canacad/welcome.html
Canadian Academy inspires students to inquire, reflect, and choose to compassionately impact the world throughout their lives.

Fred Wesson, Headmaster
Charles Kite, Assistant Headmaster

1266 Canadian School-India
14/1 Kodigehalli Main Road
Sahakar Nagar, Bangalore 560 092
India
91-80-343-8414
Fax: 91-80-343-6488
Grade levels K-13, school year August - June

T Alf Mallin, Principal

1267 Canberra Grammar School
40 Monaro Crescent
Red Hill
Australia ACT 2
02-6260-9700
Fax: 02-6260-9701
headmaster@cgs.act.edu.au
www.cgs.act.edu.au
To develop a cultured man, ready for today's world and the future, balanced in intellectual, spiritual, emotional and physical aspects, with a love of learning and a willingness to serve fellow students and the wider community

Justin Garrick, Headmaster
Alan Ball, Head of Senior School

1268 Carmel School-Hong Kong
10 Borrett Road
Mid-Levels
Hong Kong
852-2964-1600
Fax: 852-2813-4121
admin@carmel.edu.hk
www.carmel.edu.hk
Carmel School is committed to providing children living in Hong Kong with the highest international standard of secular and Jewish education. Through small classes and individual attention, the school offers a supportive environment that develops students' confidence, imagination and skills, in both academic and social spheres.

Edwin Epstein, Head of School
Kaisha Chow, Operations Director

1269 Casa Montessori Internationale
17 Palm Avenue Forbes Park Makati
Etro Manila D-3117
Philippines
Pre-nursery, nursery and kindergarten classes.

Carina Lebron, Principal

1270 Cebu International School
Banilad Road
PO Box 735, Cebu City 6000
Philippines
(63 32)ÿ401-1900
Fax: (63 32) 401-1904
www.cis.edu.ph/main.aspx
The primary aim of Cebu International School is to develop well-balanced global citizens who are intelligent, dynamic, respectful of universal moral values within a multicultural environment, and able to cope responsibly in an ever-changing interdependent world.

Deidre Fischer, Superintendent
Jenny Basa, Dean of Student Services

1271 Central Java Inter-Mission School
Jl Nakula Sadewa Raya Number 55
Salatiga, Jateng
Indonesia 50722
62-298-311673
Fax: 62-298-321609
office@mountainviewics.org
Primary intent of the school is that all students be thoroughly exposed to Scripture and that they find and sustain a vital relationship to Jesus Christ through Holy Spirit.

Willliam J Webb III, Superintendent
Kirk Thornton, Assistant Superintendent

1272 Central Primary School
Winston Churchill Avenue
Port Vila
Republic of Vanuatu
678-23122
Fax: 678-22526
central@vanuatu.com.vu
www.central.herts.sch.uk
Meet the needs of children from most countries and to provide an equivalent level of education for local children in an 'English as a First Language' context.

John Path, Chairman
John Lee Solomon, PEO

1273 Chiang Mai International School
PO Box 38
13 Chetupon Road
Thailand, TH 50000
665-324-2027
Fax: 665-324-2455
info@cmis.ac.th
www.cmis.ac.th

Encourage the development of students' abilities in critical, analytical, and independent thinking, demonstrated in fluent oral and written communication.

Lance Potter, Principal
Sinturong Pannavalee, Director

1274 Chinese International School
1 Hau Yuen Path
Braemar Hill, Hong Kong
China
852-2510-7288
Fax: 852-2510-7488
cis_info@cis.edu.hk
www.cis.edu.hk
Committed to the achievement of academic excellence and is characterized and enriched by its dual-language program in Chinese and English.

Theodore S Faunce, Headmaster
Li Bin, Deputy Head of School

1275 Chittagong Grammar School
Sarson Valley, 448/B Joynagar,
Chiottagong
Bangladesh
88-031-632900
cgslower@hotmail.com
Dedicated to the total growth and development of each student. Provides the students a broad, challenging and sound education to enable children to achieve the highest standards of which they are capable.

Afran Sanchita, Teacher
Akther Sharmin, Teacher

1276 Colombo International School
28, Gregory's Road
Colombo 7
Sri Lanka
94-11-269-7587
Fax: 94-11-269-9592
management@cis.lk
www.cis.lk
English medium co-educational day school with separate Infant, Junior and Secondary sections.

M.J. Chappell, Principal
Armyne Wirasinha, Chairman

1277 Concordia International School-Shanghai
999 Mingyue Road, Jinqiao,Pudong
Shanghai
201206, China
86-21-5899-0380
Fax: 86-21-5899-1685
Concordia's vision to offer academic excellence in a faith-based, caring community finds its roots in the 150-year educational tradition of the Lutheran Church-Missouri Synod.

James Koerschen, Head of School
Carol Ann Tonn-Bourg, Director of Admissions

1278 Cummings Elementary School
Unit 5039
APO AP
Japan 96319-5039
81-3117-66-2226
Fax: 81-3117-62-5110
pcumming@pac.dodea.edu
We, the community of Cummings Elementary School, are committed to guiding our students to become successful learners and responsible citizens in an ever-changing world

Scott Sterry, Principal

1279 Dalat School
11200 Penang
Tanjung Bunga
Malaysia
60-4-899-2105
Fax: 60-4-890-2141
info@dalat.org
www.dalat.org
The mission of Dalat International School is to prepare young people to live fully for God in a rapidly changing world by enabling them to understand, evaluate, and reconcile that world with the foundation of God's unchanging values.

Karl Steinkamp, Director
Fred Colburn, High School Principal

1280 Dover Court Prep School
Dover Road
Singapore, 139644
Singapore
65-67757664
Fax: 65-67774165
www.dovercourt.org
To teach goals of the learning process, which is facilitated through encouraging pupils to pose and solve problems, take risks, demonstrate responsible attitudes and behaviour, adopt a critical and self-evaluative approach to their work.

Maureen Roach, Director
Catherine Alliott, Chief Executive Officer

1281 Ela Beach International School
PO Box 1137
Boroko
Papua New Guinea
675-325-2183
Fax: 675-325-7925
This school consists of 262 boys and 222 girl day students in PreK-Grade 6. The length of stay for overseas teachers is three years with housing provided. School enrollment is made up of 260 PNG children, 224 non PNG children, overseas and PNG staff team teaching in mixed age group classrooms.

Bruce E Mackinlay, Principal

1282 Elsternwick Campus-Wesley College
577 Street Kilda Road
Melbourne
Australia 03004
61-3-8102-6100
Fax: 61 3 8102 6054
stkildaroad@wesleycollege.net
www.wesleycollege.net
Wesley College is a coeducational school of the Uniting Church which has enriched the lives of thousands of young people, since it opened on 18 January 1866 as a boy's boarding school. In its 140 year history, it has experienced the influence of 14 principals, each of whom has in turn, enriched the life of the College.

Jack Moshakis, Executive Director
Helen Drennen, Principal

1283 Faisalabad Grammar School
Kohinoor Nagar
Faisalabad 728593
Pakistan
www.fgschools.edu.pk
This Islamic school offers a curriculum taught in both English and Urdu to 2,000 day students (1,000 boys; 1,000 girls), in Junior Nursery up to eighteen years of age. The school runs 50% of classes in Matriculation Streams Local, and 50% in 'O' and 'A' level University of Cambridge UK examinations. Applications needed to teach include science, math, English and computers, with the length of stay for overseas teachers being one year.

RY Saigol Sarfraz, Principal
N Akhtar, VP

1284 Faith Academy
MCPO Box 2016
Makati City
Philippines 00706
11-632-248-5000
Fax: 63-2-658-0026
vanguard@faith.edu.ph
www.faith.edu.ph
Faith Academy envisions expanding children's educational delivery options to meet the needs of the missions enterprise throughout Asia.

Tom Hardeman, Superintendent
Mike Hause, Deputy Superindentent

1285 French International School
165 Blue Pool
Happy Valley, SAR, Hong Kong
China
852-257-76217
Fax: 852-257-79658
www.fis.edu.hk
To provide, together with families, a nurturing, culturally diverse community that inspires our young people to realize their true potential as confident, independent learners and responsible global citizens with moral values and integrity.

Francis Cauet, Headmaster
Samuel Hureau, Administrator

1286 Fukuoka International School
3-18-50 Momochi
Sawara-ku, Fukuoka
Japan 00814-6
81-92-841-7601
Fax: 81-92-841-7602
www.fis.ed.jp
To create a dynamic learning environment in which students can be educated in high international academic standards. We strive to be a model of unity in diversity in which the individual is respected in each student is challenged at his/her own level.

Linda Gush, Head of School
Daniel Habel, Dean of Students

1287 Garden International School
16 Jalan Kiara 3, Off Jalan Bukit K
Kuala Lumpur
Malaysia 50480
011-60-3-6209-6888
Fax: 011-60-3-6201-2468
admissions@gardenschool.edu.my
www.gardenschool.edu.my
Grade levels Pre-K through eleventh.

Simon Mann, Principal
Dato' Loy Teik Ngan, Chairman

1288 Geelong Grammar School-Glamorgan
14 Douglas Street
Toorak, Victoria
Australia 03142
011-61-3-9829-1444
Fax: 011-61-3-9826-2829
toorakcampus@ggs.vic.edu.au
www.ggs.vic.edu.au
Geelong Grammar School offers an exceptional Australian education. Our students are girls and boys who see the richness of the world through confident eyes.

Lisa Marchetti, Fundraising Coordinator
Stephen Meek, Principal

1289 German Swiss International School
11 Guildford Road, The Peak
Hong Kong
China

011-852-2849-6216
Fax: 011-852-2849-6347
gsis@gsis.edu.hk
www.gsis.edu.hk
Encourage and foster the talents of our students - as well-rounded individuals, responsible team members and open-minded citizens of the 21st century.

Hans PeterÿNaef, COO
Jens-Peter Green, Principal

90 Glenunga International High School

99 L'Estrange Street
Glenuga
South Australia 05064
011-61-8-8379-5629
Fax: 011-61-8-8338-2518
glenunga@gihs.sa.edu.au
www.gihs.sa.edu.au
Grade levels 8-12.

Wendy Johnson, Principal
Jeremy Cogan, Deputy Principal

91 Good Hope School-Kowloon

303 Clear Water Bay Road
Kowloon
Hong Kong
011-852- 2321-0250
Fax: 011-852- 2324-8242
goodhope@ghs.edu.hk
www.ghs.edu.hk
Provides equal opportunities to develop their moral, intellectual, physical, social, emotional and artistic aspects of life.

Pauline Yuen, Supervisor
Paul Chow, Principal

92 Goroka International School

PO Box 845
Goroka EHP
Papua New Guinea
011-675-732-1452
Fax: 011-675-732-2146
www.iea.ac.pg
Provide education of a high academic standard from early childhood to grade 12

James M Masa, Principal

93 Hebron School-Lushington Hall

Lushington Hall, Ootacamund
Tamil Nadu
India 64300
11-91-42-3244-2372
Fax: 11-91-42-3244-1295
admin@hebronooty.org
www.hebronooty.org
Independent, international Christian school.

Mark Noonan, Principal

294 Hillcrest International School

PO Box 249
Sentani 99352
Papua, Indonesia
011-62-967-591460
Fax: 011-62-967-592673
HIS is a Christian international school. Teachers must raise their own support, normally with a mission. Enrollment consists of 97 day students and 24 boarding (53 boys; 68 girls), in grades K-12.

Margaret Hartzler, Director
Ryan Kennedy, Director

295 Hiroshima International School

3-49-1 Kurakake
Asakita-Ku
Hiroshima, Japan 739-1
011-81-82-843-4111
Fax: 011-81-82-843-6399
info@hiroshima-is.ac.jp
www.hiroshima-is.ac.jp
The Hiroshima International School is an independent, coeducational day school which offers educational programs from preschool through grade 12. The school year comprises 2 semesters extending from early September to mid-June.

Peter MacKenzie, Principal

1296 Hokkaido International School

1-55, 5-Jo, 19-Chome
Hirahishi, Toyohira-Ku
Sapporo, Japan 062-0
011-81-11-816-5000
Fax: 011-81-11-816-2500
his@his.ac.jp
www.his.ac.jp
A private, coeducational day and boarding school which offers an America-style education from preschool through grade 12.

Michael Branson, Headmaster
Eri Kashiwabara, Business Manager

1297 Hong Kong International School

1 Red Hill Road
Tai Tam, Hong Kong
Republic of China
011-852-3149-7000
Fax: 011-852-2813-8740
Advancement@hkis.edu.hkÿ
www.hkis.edu.hk
The Hong Kong International School is a private, Christian, coeducational day school which offers an educational program from pre-primary through grade 12 for students of all nationalities and religious backgrounds. The school year comprises 2 semesters extending approximately from August 19 to January 16 and from January 19 to June 12.

Doug Werth, Chair
David Condon, Head of School

1298 Ikego Elementary School

PSC 474 Box 300
FPO, AP
Japan 96351-300
011-81-46-806-8320
Fax: 011-81-46-806-8324
principal_ikegoes@pac.dodea.edu
Provides developmentally-appropriate learning experiences that teaches, problem solving, critical thinking, make responsible choices.

Scott Finlay, Principal

1299 International Christian School

1 On Muk Lane
Shek Mun
N.T. Hong Kong
011-852-3920 0010
Fax: 011-852-2336-6114
ics@ics.edu.hk
www.ics.edu.hk
International Christian School is an exceptional school for a number of reasons. Every ICS graduate has enrolled in a college or university somewhere in the world.

Jack Young, Board Chair
Noel Chu, Executive Assistant

1300 International Community School

1225 The Parkland Road
Khwaeng Bangna, Khet Bangna Bangkok
Thailand 10260
011-66-2-338-0777
Fax: 011-66-2-338-0778
www.icsbangkok.com
Based on the Bible, in partnership with parents, we teach the whole student to know and apply wisdom for the good of our world and the glory of God.

Darren Gentry, Headmaster
Gary Opfer, High School Principal

1301 International School Manila

University Parkway
Fort Bonifacio Global City, Taguig
Philippines 01634
011-63-2-840-8400
Fax: 011-63-2-840-8405
International School Manila is an independent international school whose structure, traditions and style emanate from the United States and whose curriculum and methodology reflect the best in worldwide educational research and practice. Our school is diverse and dynamic, and our students have the highest aspirations for their education and future lives.

William Brown, High School Principal
David Toze, Superintendent

1302 International School of the Sacred Heart

4-3-1 Hiroo, Shibuya-ku
Tokyo
Japan 150-0
011-81-3-3400-3951
Fax: 011-81-3-3400-3496
info@issh.ac.jp
www.issh.ac.jp
ISSH is a multicultural Catholic school that warmly welcomes students and families from many faiths. The Pre-Kindergarten and Kindergarten classes for 3, 4 and 5 year olds are for boys and girls, while grades 1-12 are for girls only.

Yvonne Hayes, Headmistress
Charmaine Young, High School Principal

1303 International School-Bangkok

39/7 Soi Nichada Thani,Samakee Road
Nonthaburi
Thailand 11120
011-66-2-963-5800
Fax: 011-66-2-583-5432
www.isb.ac.th
Our Vision states that our students will make extraordinary academic progress. They become smart about their own learning processes, understanding what does and does not work for them as learners.

Dr Bill Gerritz, Head of School
Dr Ugo Costessi, Deputy Head of School/CFO

1304 International School-Beijing

10 An Hua Street
Shunyi District,,Beijing
China 10131
86-10-8046-2345
Fax: 86-10-8046-2001
isb-info@isb.bj.edu.cn
www.isb.bj.edu.cn
Educate and inspire students to reach their unique potential and contribute positively to society by providing a world class education enriched by diversity and the Chinese culture.

Thomas Hawkins, Head of School
Rodney Fagg, High School Principal

1305 International School-Eastern Seaboard

PO Box 6
Banglamung, Chonburi
Thailand 20150
(6638) 372 591
Fax: (6638) 372 950
ise@ise.ac.th
www.ise.ac.th
Prepare an international student population for higher education and lifelong learning by emphasizing higher level thinking skills, effective communication, global responsibilities, and personal wellness within a

cooperative and supportive school community.

Robert Brewitt, Superintendent
Heather Naro, Elementary Principal

1306 International School-Fiji
PO Box 10828
Laucala Beach Estate, Suva
Fiji Islands
11-679-3393-560
Fax: 11-679-3340-017
info@international.school.fj
www.international.school.fj
An independent co-educational day school offering pre-school, primary and secondary education and offers excellent education and a caring and nurturing environment for young people. The curriculum includes International Baccalaureate (Primary Years Programme, Middle Years Programme, Diploma Programme), University of Cambridge - International General Certificate of Secondary Education and the Australian Capital Territory Year 12 Certificate and University Admissions Index (UAI).

Dianne Korare, Principal
Sera Brown, Registrar

1307 International School-Ho Chi Minh City
16 Vo Truong Toan St
An Phu Ward, District 2, Ho Ci Minh City
Vietnam
84-8-898-9100
Fax: 84 (8) 3 519-4110
admissions@ishcmc.edu.vn
www.ishcmc.com
The school provides and teaches the students about intellectual, emotional, social, creative, linguistic, cultural, moral, aesthetic and physical needs of each students. The school seeks to involve parents in the education of their children through regular communication.

Sean O'Maonaigh, Headmaster
Chris Byrne, Admissions/Marketing

1308 International School-Kuala Lumpur
PO Box 12645
Kuala Lumpur
Malaysia 50784
603-4259-5600
Fax: 603-4257-9044
iskl@iskl.edu.my
www.iskl.edu.my
Offers its students a superior education to prepare them to be responsible world citizens who think creatively, reason critically, communicate effectively and learn enthusiastically throughout life.

Paul Chmelik, Headmaster
Amina O'Kane, Admissions Director

1309 International School-Lae
PO Box 2130
Lae, Morobe
Papua New Guinea 00411
011-675-479-1425
Fax: 011-675-472-3485
Offers high quality education, from ages 18 months to grade 8. The curriculum prepares students for national and international success.

Neal Mather, Principal

1310 International School-Manila
Univeristy Parkway
Fort Bonifacio, Taguig City
Philippines 01634
632-840-8488
Fax: 632-840-8489
www.ismanila.org
An independent international school whose structure, traditions and style emanate from the United States. It aims to build a community of reflective learners who are passionate, caring and responsible contributors to the world in which we live.

Ray Dempsey, President
David Toze, Superintendent

1311 International School-Penang-Uplands
Jalan Sungai Satu
Batu Feringgi, Penang
Malaysia 11100
011-604-8819-777
Fax: 011-604-8819-778
info@uplands.org
www.uplands.org
Uplands aims to provide excellent international education for students of all nationalities in a challenging multi-cultural environment. It favours methods of teaching which foster the joys of learning, discovery and enquiry, aiming to nurture students into thinking, learning, caring and striving to meet the needs of a better world.

John Horsfall, Acting Principal
M R Chandran, Chair

1312 International School-Phnom Penh, Cambodia
146 Norodom Boulevard
PO Box 138, Phnom Penh
Cambodia
855-23-213-103
Fax: 855-23-213-104
ispp@ispp.edu.kh
www.ispp.edu.kh
ISPP empowers students, in a caring international environment, to achieve their potential by pursuing personal and academic excellence, and to grow as responsible global citizens who celebrate diversity.

Barry Sutherland, Director
Laura Watson, Chairperson

1313 International School-Phnom Penh-Cambodia
146 Norodom Boulevard
PO Box 138, Phnom Penh
Cambodia
855-23-213-103
Fax: 855-23-361-002
ispp@ispp.edu.kh
www.ispp.edu.kh
ISPP empowers students, in a caring international environment, to achieve their potential by pursuing personal and academic excellence, and to grow as responsible global citizens who celebrate diversity.

Barry Sutherland, Director
Laura Watson, Chairperson

1314 International School-Pusan
798 Nae-ri, Gijang-eup
Gijang-gun, Busan 619-902
South Korea
82 51 742-3332
Fax: 82 51 742 3375
enquiries@bifskorea.org
www.isbusan.org
The school possess a caring, family-like ethos, giving the children a high level of self-confidence and esteem, and teaching them tolerance and respect for other cultures.

Stephen Palmer, Principal
Thomas Walker, Chairman

1315 International School-Ulaanbaatar
Four Seasons Garden, Khan-Uul Distr
1st Khoroo, PO Box 36/10
Ulaanbaatar, Mongolia 17032
976-70160010
Fax: 976-70160012
administration@isumongolia.edu.mn
www.isumongolia.edu.mn
The International School of Ulaanbaatar seeks to offer the best educational system possible, based on an international curriculum.

Gregory Rayl, Director
Tuul Arildii, Deputy Director

1316 Island School
20 Borrett Road
Mid Levels
Hong Kong
852-2524-7135
Fax: 852-2840-1673
www.island.edu.hk
An international, co-educational, comprehensive school, providing secondary education for children of all nations who can benefit from an education through the medium of English.

Pinder Wong, Council Chairman
Chris Binge, Principal

1317 Ivanhoe Grammar School
PO Box 91
The Ridgeway, Ivanhoe, Victoria
Australia 03079
61 3 9490 1877
Fax: 61 3 9497 4060
info@ivanhoe.com.au
www.igs.vic.edu.au
Our mission is to be a community of learning that develops in students the skills and values that will prepare them for the challenges and responsibilities of adult citizenship.

Roderick D Fraser, Principal
Andrew Sloane, Head of School

1318 JN Darby Elementary School
PSC 485 Box 99
FPO, AP
Japan 96321
011-81-956-50-8800
Fax: 011-81-956-50-8804
Darby_ES@pac.dodea.edu
www.darby-es.pac.dodea.edu/
The Darby Community promotes academic and social excellence so all students can become positive contributors to society.

Joy Jaramillo, Principal

1319 Jakarta International School
PO Box 1078/JKS
Jakarta 12010
Indonesia
(62-21) 750-3644
Fax: 62-21-765-7852
JIS is a place where people from almost 60 countries come together to share ideas, experiences and values.

Tim Carr, Head of School

1320 Japan International School
7-5-1 Hikarigaoka
Shibuya-Ku, Tokyo 168-0081
Japan
81-3-3335-6620
Fax: 81-3-3332-6930
hikarigaoka@aobajapan.jp
www.aobaonline.jp/
Student of all nationalities, and religions are welcome.

Charles S Barton, Headmaster

21 John McGlashan College
2 Pilkington Street
Maori Hill, Dunedin
New Zealand
03-467-6620
Fax: 03-467-6622
www.mcglashan.school.nz
ohn McGlashan College is an integrated, Year 7-13, secondary school for boys. The roll comprises approximately 380 dayboys from Dunedin city and its surrounds and 110 boarders, most of whom come from rural Otago and Southland. In addition, up to 20 international students are enrolled each year

K Michael Corkery, Principal
Neil Garry, Deputy Principal

22 Kansai Christian School
282-2 Oaza Misato, Heguri-cho, Ikom
Nara Ken 636-0904
Japan
0745-45-6422
Fax: 011-81-745-45-6422
office@kansaichristianschool.com
www.kansaichristianschool.com
Kansai Christian School was established in 1970 to provide a general education in a Christian environment for children of the evangelical missionary community

Albert Greeff, Principal

23 Kaohsiung American School
35 Sheng Li Road
Tzuo-Ying District (813)
Taiwan
886-7-583-0112
Fax: 886-7-582-4536
dchang@kas.kh.edu.tw
Kaohsiung American School (KAS) is a private, non-profit Pre-K - 12 institution with 330 students offering college preparatory programs leading to a U.S. high school diploma. It is located in Kaohsiung, a city of 1.5 million in southwestern Taiwan.

Tom Farrell, Superintendent
Deborah Taylor, Assistant Director

24 Kellett School
2 Wah Lok Path
Wah Fu, Pokfulam
Hong Kong
852-2551-8234
Fax: 852-2875-0262
admissions@kellettschool.com
www.kellettschool.com
Kellett School is an independent non-for-profit school catering to the English-speaking children living in Hong Kong. The school is operated by Kellett School Association Limited through a Board of Governors; seven of whom are parents, elected by the Association, and the remaining three are ex-officio members. All parents become members of the Association.

Ann McDonald, Principal

325 Kilmore International School
40 White Street
Kilmore, Victoria
Australia 03764
61-357-822-211
Fax: 61-357-822-525
info@kilmore.vic.edu.au
www.kilmore.vic.edu.au
The Kilmore International School is an independent, non-denominational, co-educational boarding and day school for academically motivated students undertaking their secondary education (Years 7-12 inclusive).

John Settle, Principal

1326 Kinabalu International School
PO Box 12080
88822 Kota Kinabalu, Sabah
Malaysia
608-822-4526
Fax: 608-824-4203
www.kis.edu.my
This school offers an English-based curriculum for 100 day students (50 boys; 50 girls), ages 3-13 years.

1973 pages

Stuart McLay, Principal
Elis Ho, Office Manager

1327 King George V School
2 Tin Kwong Road
Homantin, Kowloon
Hong Kong
852-2711-3029
Fax: 852-2760-7116
office@kgv.edu.hk
www.kgv.edu.hk
Non selective secondary school which provides a broad.

Ed Wickins, Principal
Richard Bradford, Vice Principal

1328 Kitakyushu International School
Yahata Higashi-ku, Takami 2,
Shinnittetsu, Shijo, Kitakyushu
Japan
81-93-652-0682
This school offers an English based curriculum for 8 day students (2 boys; 6 girls), in kindergarten through elementary. The school is always looking for dedicated and qualified teachers to teach children and adults in school and preschool (especially female teachers). Applications needed include preschool and English.

Ann Ratnayake, Principal

1329 Kodaikanal International School
Seven Roads Junction, PO Box 25
Kodaikanal, Tamil Nadu
India 624 1-0101
91-4542-247-500
Fax: 91-4542-241-109
contact@Kis.in
www.kis.in
Kodaikanal Internationa lSchool is an autonomous residential school with a broad college-oriented curriculum, serving young people from a wide diversity of cultures. The School's academic program is intentionally set within a community life based on the life and teaching of Jesus Christ and devoted to service in India and the whole human community.

Geoffrey Fisher, Principal
Gregg Faddegon, Vice Principal

1330 Kooralbyn International School
Shop 1, 29 Wellington Bundock Drive
Kooralbyn QLD 4285
Australia
61-7-5544-6111
Fax: 61-7-5544-6702
www.tkis.qld.edu.au
Aims to provide students with a broad liberal education.

Geoff Mills, Principal

1331 Kowloon Junior School
20 Perth Street
Ho Man Tin, Kowloon
Hong Kong
852-2714-5279
Fax: 852 2760 4438
office@kjs.edu.hk
www.kjs.edu.hk
Primary students learn English, math, science, technology, history, geography, art, music and physical education.

Mark Cripps, Principal
Deborah Graham, ESF Representative

1332 Kyoto International School
Kitatawara-cho,Nakadachiuri-sagaru
Yoshiyamachi-Dori, Kamigyo-ku, Kyoto
Japan 00602-8247
81-75-451-1022
Fax: 81-75-451-1023
kis@kyotointernationalschool.org
www.kyoto-is.org
Independent day school, offering education from Preschool level through to Middle School

Annette Levy, Head of School
Amanda Gillis-Furutaku, Board Chair

1333 Lahore American School
American Consulate General Lahore
15 Upper Mall, Canal Bank
Lahore
Pakistan 54000
92-42-576-2406
Fax: 92-42-571-1901
las@las.edu.pk
www.las.edu.pk
An independent, coeducational day school which offers an educational program from nursery through grade 12 for students of all nationalities.

Kathryn Cochran, Superintendent
Imran Aslam, Board Chair

1334 Lanna International School Thailand
300 Grandview Moo 10
Chiang-Mai to Hang Dong, T Mae-hea, A. M
Thailand 50100
66-53-806-231
Fax: 66-53-271-159
head@lannaist.ac.th
www.lannaist.ac.th
t is the goal of Lanna International School to prepare its students to be responsible world citizens who demonstrate a commitment to life-long learning and the application of that learning to the improvement of self, and local and global communities.

Roy Lewis, Head of School
Ajarn Kannika, School Director

1335 Lincoln School
PO Box 2673
Rabi Bhawan, Kathmandu
Nepal
977-1-4270482
Fax: 977-142-7268
Fax: 977-1-4272685
info@lsnepal.com.np
www.lsnepal.com
is an independent, international school in Kathmandu, Nepal with an American Curriculum

Allan Bredy, Director
Craig Baker, Principal

1336 Malacca Expatriate School
2443-C Jalan Batang Tiga
Tanjung Kling, Melaka
Malaysia 76400
011-60-6-315-4970
Fax: 011-60-6-315-4970
Mission is provide a high standard of learning. The students benefit from a high level of individual attention because of their low student to teacher ratio.

Susheila Samuel, Principal

1337 Marist Brothers International School
1-2-1 Chimori-cho
Suma-ku, Kobe
Japan 654-0
011-81-787-326266
Fax: 011-81-787-326268
www.marist.ac.jp
The philosophy of MBIS is designed to awaken students to the realities of life and to prepare them for the future. school aims to give to each student a well-rounded education incorporating the academic, moral, social and physical aspects of life.

Ed Fitzgerald, Principal
Geraldo de Couto, Vice Principal

1338 Matthew C Perry Elementary School
PSC 561 Box 1874
FPO Iwakuni 96310 0019
Japan
011-81-827-79-3447
Fax: 011-81-827-79-6490
principal.perryes@pac.dodea.edu
www.perry-es.pac.dodea.edu/
Committed to promoting student achievement in a positive safe environment. It provides a quality education for every student based on the needs of each child.

Shelia Cary, Principal
Christopher Racek, Asst. Principal

1339 Matthew C Perry Middle & High School
PSC 561 Box 1874
FPO Iwakuni 96310 1874
Japan
011-81-827-79-5449
Fax: 011-81-827-79-4600
principal.perryhs@pac.dodea.edu
www.perry-es.pac.dodea.edu/

Morgan Nugent, Principal
Robert Funk, Assistant Principal

1340 Mentone Boys Grammar School
63 Venice Street
Mentone, Victoria
Australia 03194
011-61-3-9584-4211
Fax: 011-61-3-9581-3290
enquiry@mentonegrammar.net
www.mentonegrammar.net
We are a school for boys and girls providing a flexible and sensitive approach which considers what boys and girls need at various stages of their development.

Mal Cater, Principal
Simon Appel, Chairman

1341 Mercedes College
540 Fullarton Road
Springfield 5062
South Australia
011-61-8-8372-3200
Fax: 011-61-8-8379-9540
Mercedes College, in Adelaide, South Australia, is a Reception to Year 12 Catholic co-educational school in the Mercy tradition.

Peter Daw, Principal
Steve Bowley, Business Manager

1342 Methodist Ladies College
207 Barkers Road Kew
Victoria 3101
Australia
011-61-3-9274-6333
Fax: 011-61-3-9819-2345
college@mlc.vic.edu.au
www.mlc.vic.edu.au
This college prepares its students for the world of tomorrow by liberating their talents through challenge, enrichment, and opportunity in a supportive Christian environment. Committed to technology and to student initiated learning so each girl from year five onward works with her personal computer to understand the present and shape the future. Total enrollment: 2,135 day students; 105 boarding. Grade range K-12. The school is willing to participate in a teacher exchange program.

Rosa Swtorelli, Principal
Louise Adler, Chairperson

1343 Minsk International School
DOS/Administrative Officer
7010 Minsk Place
Washington, DC 20521-7010
375-172-343-035
Fax: 375-172-343-035
An independent, coeducational day school which offers an educational program from kindergarten through grade 8 for students of all nationalities. Enrollment 11.

Stanley Harrison Orr, Director

1344 Moreguina International Primary School
PO Box 438
Konedobu Papua
New Guinea

Wayne Coleman, Principal

1345 Morrison Christian Academy
136-1 Shui Nan Road
Taichung 40679
Taiwan, TW 40679
11-886-4-2297-3927
Fax: 11-886-4-2292-1174
mcgillt@mca.org.tw
www.mca.org.tw
Morrison Academy exists to meet the educational needs of the children of missionaries throughout Taiwan, helping fulfill Christ's commission to go into all the world. Morrison seeks to provide a Christ-centered school culture where all students, from missionary and non-missionary families, experience a Biblically-integrated quality education. Therefore, Morrison structures learning so that students may develop the knowledge, discernment, and ability to dynamically impact their world as Christian

Tim McGill, Superintendent
Matt Strange, Director of Curriculum

1346 Mount Hagen International School
PO Box 945
Mount Hagen
Papua New Guinea
675-542-1964
Fax: 675-542-1840
www.iea.ac.pg
It is envisaged that students enrolled at the Mount Hagen International School will always remain encouraged by their schooling. They will earn an education of International standard, their learning will be contextualized within Papua New Guinea culture, and they will learn how to become productive members of their community

Bruce Imatana, Principal

1347 Mt Zaagham International School
PT Freeport
Tembagapura W Papua
Indonesia
62 901 407876
Fax: 62 901 403170
Grade levels Pre-K through 98, school year September - June. Two campuses Tembagapura and Kuala Kencana

Barney Latham, Superintendent
Richard Ledger, Principal

1348 Murray International School
PO Box 1137
Boroko
Papua New Guinea
675-325-2183
Fax: 675-325-7925
Non-profit, private, co-educational day school that provides quality international standard education for the expatriate and local community in Port Moresby.

Suzanne Savage, Principal
Marlene Filippi, Deputy Principal

1349 Murree Christian School
Jhika Gali, Murree Hills
Punjab
Pakistan 47180
0092-513-410321
Fax: 0092-513-411668
mcs@mcs.org.pk
www.mcs.org.pk
This school offers an English-based curriculum for 20 day students and 140 boarding students (75 boys; 85 girls), in grades K-12. Murree Christian School educates the children of missionaries from 14 different countries working in Pakistan and the region. Living allowances rather than salaries are awarded. Overseas teacher stay is two years with housing provided by the school.

Phil Billing, Director
Linda Fisher, HS Faculty Head

1350 Mussoorie International School
Srinagar Estate, Mussoorie 248179
Uttarakhand
India
91-135-2632007
Fax: 91-135-2631160
misadmission@gmail.com
www.misindia.net
One of the leading residential educational institutions for girls and is recognized for its progressive education with a definite account on India culture and traditions.

HK Rawal, Principal
A. Ghosh, Headmaster

1351 Nagoya International School
2686 Minamihara, Nakashidami
Moriyama-ku, Nagoya, 463-0002
Japan
81-52-736-2025
Fax: 81-52-736-3883
info@nis.ac.jp
Envisions a school community devoted to developing the skills, attitudes, and values that allow students to realize their full potential, lead lives of purpose, and become responsible, global citizens.

Rob Risch, Headmaster

1352 Narrabundah College
Jerrabomberra Avenue
Narrabundah, ACT 2604
Australia
61-2-6205-6999
Fax: 61-2-6205-6969
laura.beacroft@cbit.net.au
www.narrabundahc.act.edu.au
This college is a government college for years 11 and 12 students - the final two years of secondary education. It offers a challenging curriculum in a caring environment and meets the needs of an international community.

Steve Kyburz, Head of School
Laura Beacroft, Board Chair

53 New International School of Thailand
36 Sukhumvit Soi 15
Bangkok, TH 10110
66-2651-2065
Fax: 66-2253-3800
nist@nist.ac.th
www.nist.ac.th
Co-educational, day school, IBO World School

Simon Leslie, Headmaster
Adrian Watts, Deputy Head

54 Nile C Kinnick High School
PSC 473 Box 95
FPO, AP
96349-95
011-81-46816-7392
Fax: 011-81-46-816-7278
Kinnick_Principal@pac.dodea.edu
The mission of Nile C. Kinnick High School is to challenge students to maximize potential in order to prepare them to be responsible and productive citizens in an ever-changing world.

Lorenzo Brown, Principal

55 Nishimachi International School
2-14-7 Moto Azabu
Minato-ku Tokyo
Japan 106-0-46
81-3-3451-5520
Fax: 81-3-3456-0197
www.nishimachi.ac.jp
Offers a dual-language, multicultural program ro 430 student k-9.

Terence Christian, Headmaster

56 Okinawa Christian School International
1835 Zakimi, Yomitan-son
Okinawa 904-0301
Japan
81-098-958-3000
800-446-6423
Fax: 81-098-958-6279
info@ocsi.org
www.ocsi.org
Provides a major educational support base for the international community living on Okinawa.

Rich Barnett, Contact
Randel J Hadley, Superintendent

357 Osaka International School
4-4-16 Onohara Nishi
Mino-shi, Osaka, 562-0032
Japan
81-72-727-5050
Fax: 81-72-727-5055
addmissions@senri.ed.jp
www.senri.ed.jp
OIS is an English-language-based, preK-12 grade coeducational college-preparatory school.

John Searle, Head of School

358 Osaka YMCA International High School
6-7-34 Benten Minato-ku
Osaka 552-0007
Japan
06-4395-1002
Fax: 06-4395-1004
general-inquiry@oyis.org
www.oyis.org
OYIS strives to be a leading provider of international education for the citizens and residents of Osaka and its environs.

John Murphy, Principal

1359 Osan American High School
Unit 2037
APO AP 96278-0005
Korea
011-82-31-661-9076
Fax: 011-82-31-661-9121
PRINCIPAL.OSANHS@pac.dodea.edu
Provides student with successful, productive and rewarding educational experiences.

Timothy Erickson, Principal
Truly Schramm, Assistant Principal

1360 Osan Elementary School
Unit 2037
APO, AP 96278-2037
Korea
011-82-31-661-6912
Fax: 011-82-31-661-5733
Provides quality and challenging educational opportunities for all students to become critical thinkers, life-long learners, and productive citizens in a global society.

Mia Plourde, Secretary
David Petree, Principal

1361 Overseas Children's School
PO Box 9, Pelawatte
Battaramulla
Sri Lanka
94 11 2784920-2
Fax: 94-11-2784999
admin@osc.lk
www.osc.lk
OSC develops the whole person as a responsible learner striving for personal excellence within a culturally diverse school

Areta Williams, Head of School
Jerry Huxtable, Chair

1362 Overseas Family School
25 F Paterson Road
Singapore 23851
65-6738-0211
Fax: 65-6733-8825
executive_director@ofs.edu.sg
www.ofs.edu.sg
To focus on the individual needs of every student and to provide a supportive atmosphere designed to help students achieve personal academic goals.

David Perry, Chairman
Irene Wong, Executive Director

1363 Overseas School of Colombo
Pelawatte
PO Box 9, Battaranmulla
Sri Lanka
94 11 2784920-2
Fax: 94 11 2784999
admin@osc.lk
www.osc.lk
OSC develops the whole person as a responsible learner striving for personal excellence within a culturally diverse school.

Areta Williams, Head of School
Jerry Huxtable, Chair

1364 Pacific Harbour International School
PO Box 50
Pacific Harbour, Deuba
Fiji Islands
679-450-0005
Fax: 679-450-566
www.isbi.com

Janet Tuni, Principal

1365 Pasir Ridge International
Unocal-po Box 3-tampines S
Balikpapan 9152
Singapore
62-542-543-474
Fax: 62-542-767-126
Grade levels preK through 8.

Kathryn Carter-Golden PhD, Principal

1366 Peak School
20 Plunketts Road
The Peak
Hong Kong
852-2849 7211
Fax: 852-2849 7151
office@peakschool.net
www.ps.edu.hk
Helping promote a better understanding of Americans on the part of the peoples served

Annette Ainsworth, Principal/Secretary
Bill Garnett, Vice Principal

1367 Phuket International Preparatory School
115/15 Moo 7 Thepkasattri Road
Thepkasattri, Thalang, Phuket 83110
Thailand
66 (0)76 336 000
Fax: 66 (0)76 336 081
www.phuketinternationalacademy.com

Agnes Hebler, Principal

1368 Popondetta International School
PO Box 10
Popondetta, Papua
New Guinea

Michael Whitting, Principal

1369 Prahram Campus-Wesley College
577 St Kilda Road-Prahran
Melbourne
Australia
61 3 8102 6100
Fax: 61 3 8102 6054
stkildaroad@wesleycollege.net
www.wesleycollege.net

AB Conabere, Principal

1370 Pusan American School
Do DOS
Pusan 96259
South Korea
82-51-801-7528
Fax: 82-51-803-1729

Alexia Venglek, Principal

1371 Pusan Elementary & High School
Unit 15625
APO AP 96259-0005, Pusan
Korea
82-52-801-7528
Fax: 82-51-803-1729

1372 QSI International School-Phuket
Box 432 A Muang
Phuket 83000
Thailand
66-076-354-077
Fax: 66-76-354077
phuket@qsi.org
www.qsi.org
To keep this urge to learn alive in every child in QSI schools. Our schools are established to provide in the English language a quality education for students in the cities we serve.

Khun Janrita Hnobnorb, Administrative Coordinator
Alan Siporin, Director

1373 QSI International School-Zhuhai
No. 168 Anning Road
Xianzhou District
Zuhai, China 51900
86-756-815-6134
Fax: 86-756-8189021
zhuhai@qsi.org
www.qsi.org

To keep this urge to learn alive in every child in QSI schools. Our schools are established to provide in the English language a quality education for students in the cities we serve.

Matthew Farwell, Director

1374 Quarry Bay School
6 Hau Yuen Path Braemar Hill
North Point, Hong Kong
China
852 2566 4242ÿ
Fax: 852 2887 9849
debra.gardiner@qbs.edu.hk
www.qbs.edu.hk
Our aim is to encourage in our children the enjoyment of learning by providing activities both in and outside the classroom which help to develop confident, happy and successful individuals.

Mina Dunstan, Principal

1375 Rabaul International School
PO Box 855
Rabaul Enbp, Papua
New Guinea
675-982-8770
Fax: 675-982-8770

Ian Smith, Principal

1376 Richard E Byrd Elementary School
PSC 472 Box 12
FPO
Japan, AP 96348-12
011-81-45-281-4815
Fax: 011-81-45-281-4870
Richard E. . Byrd envisions a school unbound by traditional school concepts of time, location and age requirements. Byrd Elementary School will provide all students with vast opportunities for learning and civic involvement

Gwen Baxter-Oakley, Principal

1377 Robert D Edgren High School
Unit 5040
APO
Japan, AP 96319-5040
011-81-176-77-4377
Fax: 011-81-176-77-4959
Committed to helping students develop academically, socially, physically and emotionally in a global community.

Gerogia Watters, Principal

1378 Ruamrudee International School
6 Ramkamhaeng 184 Road
Minburi, Bangkok
Thailand 10510
66-2-518-0320
Fax: 66-2-518-0334
info@rism.ac.th
www.rism.ac.th/risweb
Grade levels K-12, school year August - June

Fr. Leo Travis, Director
Dave Parsons HS Principal

1379 Saigon South International School
Tan Phong Ward
Ho Chi Minh City
Vietnam
(84-8) 5413-0901
Fax: (84-8) 5413-0902
info@ssis.edu.vn
Saigon South International School is a college preparatory school committed to the intellectual and personal development of each student in preparation for a purposeful life as a global citizen.

Robert Crowther, Headmaster
Charles Barton, Head of School

1380 Saint Maur International School
83 Yamate-cho, Naka-ku
Yokohama
Japan, 231-8654
81-(0)45-641-5751
Fax: 81-(0)45-641-6688
office@stmaur.ac.jp
www.stmaur.ac.jp
International School in Japan providing Pre-school, Elementary and Secondary education for international students, bringing together people from different cultures and faiths.

Catherine Osias Endo, School Head
Richard Rucci, Director of Admissions

1381 Sancta Maria International School
41 Karasawa Minami-ku
Yokohama
Japan

Sr Mary Elizabeth Doll, Principal

1382 School at Tembagapura
PO Box 616 Cairns
Queensland 4870
Australia

Bruce Goforth, Principal

1383 Scots PGC College
60 Oxenham Street
Warwick, QLD
Australia 04370
61 7 4666 9811
Fax: 61 7 4666 9812
postbox@scotspgc.qld.edu.au
www.scotspgc.qld.edu.au
Our philosophy of schooling rests squarely on the belief that a true education encourages young people to question and explore, to develop a strong sense of personal identity, to strive to achieve one's best, and to value the act of serving without losing one's desire to lead.

Michael Harding, Principal
Nigel Grant, Director of Learning

1384 Seisen International School
12-15 Yoga 1-chome
Setagaya-Ku, Tokyo
Japan 158-0-97
03-3704-2661
Fax: 033701-1033
www.seisen.com
Seisen International School seeks to provide a happy, stable and secure environment in which students are prepared through teaching and example, to live in a world of tremendous challenge and rapid change.

Concesa Martin, Headmistress

1385 Semarang International School
Asad Ave-Mohammedpur
Semarang, Central Java
Indonesia 50254
62-24-8311-424
Fax: 62-24-8311-994
info@semarangis.or.id
www.semarangis.or.id
Offer Semarang 's international community high quality and affordable education based on the International Baccalaureate Organization's Primary Years Programme, (PYP) philosophy. Provide an educational and motivational base from which each pupil may take his or her place with confidence in any school in any country in the medium of English.

Barry Burns, Principal

1386 Seoul Academy
988-5, Daechi-dong
Kangamku Seoul
Korea 135-2
82-02-554-1690
Fax: 82-2-562-0451
sais5541690@hanmail.net
www.seoulacademy.net/
Grade levels pre-K through eighth.

Thomas O'Connor, Director

1387 Seoul British School
55 Yonhi Dong Sudaemun Ku
Seoul
Korea
822-330-3100
www.seoulforeign.org

Richard Schlueter, Principal

1388 Seoul Elementary School
Unit 15549
APO, AP
Korea 96205-5549
011-82-2-7916-4613
Fax: 011-82-2-793-6925
principal.seoules@pac.dodea.edu
Provides standards based instruction in a safe learning environment which fosters independent thinking and respects cultural diversity through collaboration among staff, students, parents and community

Catherine Yurica, Principal

1389 Seoul Foreign School
55 Yonhi-Dong Sodaemun-Gu
Seoul
Korea 120-8-113
82-2-330-3100
Fax: 82-2-335-1857
sfsoffice@seoulforeign.org
As has been true throughout our history, Seoul Foreign School is committed to academic excellence. Our rigorous college preparatory curriculum - which includes the International Baccalaureate diploma program - and our dynamic learning environment challenge students to achieve their full intellectual potential. Equally, we cherish Christian values which encourage our students to develop strong character, live and work with integrity, and accept responsibility for themselves and others.

John Engstrom, Head of School
Barry Benger, Director Human Resources

1390 Seoul High School
Unit 15549
APO, AP
South Korea 96205-5549
011+82-2-7918-5261
Fax: 011+82-2-7918-8822
Seoul American High School is located on Yongsan Army Base in the center of Seoul, Korea. The school complex is comprised of eight buildings containing over 60 classrooms and special purpose rooms.

Richard Schlueter, Principal

1391 Shanghai American School
258 Jin Feng Lu
Huacao Town, Minhang Dist. Shanghai
China 20110
86-21-6221-1445
Fax: 86-21-6221-1269
admission@saschina.org
www.saschina.org
Shanghai American School, in partnership with parents, fosters the development of each student's personal potential through a balance of the aca-

demic, physical, social, emotional and ethical aspects of life. SAS provides a challenging American core curriculum with an international perspective that inspires a passion for learning and intellectual vitality.

Kerry Jacobson, Superintendent
Andrew Torris, Deputy Superintendent

92 Shatin College
3 Lai Wo Lane
Sha Tin
Hong Kong
852 26991811
Fax: 852 26950592
info@shatincollege.edu.hk
www.shatincollege.edu.hk
Independent, coeducational, secondary school within the English Schools Foundation

David Cottam, Principal
Grahame Carder, Chairman

393 Shatin Junior College
3A Lai Wo Lane
Fo Tan, New Terretories
Hong Kong
852 2692 2721
Fax: 852 2602 5572
info@sjs.esf.edu.hk
www.sjs.edu.hk/
At Sha Tin Junior School we aim to provide a secure and happy environment in which a child can develop their academic, social and physical potential to the full.

Perry Tunesi, Principal

394 Shirley Lanham Elementary School
PSC 477 Box 38
FPO AP
Japan 96306-5
011-81-467-63-3664
Fax: 011-81-467-63-4476
Principal.lanhames@pac.dodea.edu
We are preparing all students to be responsible, positive contributors within a diverse, global community.

Dave Russell, Principal

395 Singapore American School
40 Woodlands Street 41
Singapore 73854
65-6363-3403
Fax: 65-6363-3408
communications@sas.edu.sg
www.sas.edu.sg
The Singapore American School is committed to providing each student an exemplary American educational experience with an international perspective.

Brent Mutsch, Superintendent

396 Sollars Elementary School
Unit 5041
APO, AP
Japan 96319-5041
011-81-176-77-3933
Fax: 011-81-176-77-3873
PRINCIPAL.SOLLARSES@pac.dodea.edu

Dana Chandler, Principal

397 South Island School
50 Nam Fung Road
Aberdeen
Hong Kong
852-255- 931
Fax: 852-255- 881
sis@mail.sis.edu.hk
www.sis.edu.hk
School Aims to develop students' confidence, self-esteem and a range of positive values and personal qualities and to produce enthusiastic, active, independent and lifelong learners.

Graham Silverthorne, Principal
Roberta Kam, Admission

1398 St. Andrews International School-Bangkok
Pridi Banomyong 20/1
Sukhumvit Soi 71, Prakanong, Bangkok
Thailand 10110
(+66) 23 81 23 87-
Fax: (+66) 23 91 52 27
www.standrews.ac.th/
Our mission is to provide an inclusive, international education in a happy, supportive and stimulating environment, where all the needs of the individual learner are met and students are inspired to achieve their full potential enabling them to become responsible global citizens

Paul Schofield, Head of School
Jamsai Anuvongchareon, Director

1399 St. Christopher's School
10 Nunn Road
Penang
Malaysia 10350
604-226-3589
Fax: 604-226-4340
principal@scips.org.my
www.scips.org.my
St. Christopher's International Primary School of Penang, caters for expatriates' and also Malaysian children. It is located in one of the most sought after residential areas on the island of Penang Malaysia.

John G Jones, Principal

1400 St. John's International School
Ladprao
Bangkok
Thailand 10900
662-513-8575
Fax: +66 2 513 5273
sjiadmin@stjohn.ac.th
www.international.stjohn.ac.th
A holistic British style school preparing students of all nationalities to become life long learners and effective communicators in the global community.

Chainarong Monthienvic, Principal

1401 St. Joseph International School
5-16-10 Shibamata, Katsushika-ku
Tokyo
Japan 125-0
035-694-4550
schray@stjoseph-k.org
www.stjoseph-k.org
Coeducational day/boarding school, preschool through grade 12.

James Mueller, Principal
Thomas Schray, Head Teacher

1402 St. Joseph's International Primary School
177 Currie Street
Nambour
New Guinea
54 -19 -22
www.stjosephsnambour.qld.edu.au

Barbara D'Arbon, Principal

1403 St. Mary's International School
1-6-19 Seta Setagaya-ku
Tokyo
Japan 158-8
813-370- 341
Fax: 813-370- 195
michelj@smis.ac.jp
www.smis.ac.jp
St. Mary's is committed to educating boys to be lifelong learners of good character who demonstrate academic, physical, artistic, and moral excellence, respect for religious and cultural beliefs, and responsibility as international citizens.

Michel Jutras, Headmaster
Br Lawrence G Lambert, Elementary School Principal

1404 St. Michael's International School
17-2 Nakayamate-dori 3-chome
Chuo-ku, Kobe-shi 650-0004
Japan
81-78-231-8885
Fax: 81-78-231-8899
head@smis.org
www.smis.org
Provides a distinctive Primary education within a positive culture of academic excellence and caring family community.

Aileen Pardon, Principal
Paul Grisewood, Head of School

1405 St. Stephen's International School
998 Viphavadi Rangsit Road
Lad Yao, Chatuchak, Bangkok
Thailand 10900
66-2-5130270
Fax: 66-2-9303307
info@sis.edu
www.sis.edu
To encourage all students in their studies, personal life and in all their interactions to strive for excellence on their journey to becoming effective and compassionate citizens and leaders. Our goal is to nurture a culture and a community of learners creating a unique East meets West environment .

Richard A Ralphs, School Director
Gary Rodbard, Principal

1406 St. Xavier's Greenherald School
Asad Ave-Mohammedpur
Dhaka 1207
Bangladesh

Mary Imelda, Principal

1407 Stearley Heights Elementary School
Unit 5166
APO Kadena 96368 5166
Okinawa 36368
001-81-611-694-452
Fax: 001-81- 98-934-681
Stearley-Heights.Principal@pac.dodea.edu
www.stearley-es.pac.dodea.edu

Thomas Godbold, Principal

1408 Sullivans Elementary School
PSC 473, Box 96
Yokosuka 96349 0096
Japan
011-81-468-16-7336
Fax: 011-81-468-16-7865
www.sullivans-es.pac.dodea.edu

Walter Wilhoit, Principal

1409 Surabaya International School
CitraRaya International Village
Citra Raya, Lakarsantri
Tromol Pos 2/SBDK, Surabaya
Indonesia 60225
62-31-741-4300
Fax: 62-31-741-4334
sisadmin@sisedu.net
www.sisedu.net
The Surabaya International School Community is committed to developing the social, emotional, physical, creative, and intellectual abilities necessary for its students to become reasoning, responsible, contributing,

successful members of our global community.

Larry Jones, Superintendent
Christopher Burke, Chairperson

1410 TEDA International School-Tianjin
Number 72 Third Avenue Teda
Tianjin, CN 30045
86 -2 6-2261
Fax: 86 -2 6-0018
www.tedainternationalschool.net
provide outstanding education to the students of all nationalities.

Nick Bowley, Director
Joseph Azmeh, Headmaster

1411 Tabubil International School
PO Box 408 Tabubil
Tabubil
Papua New Guinea
675-548-9233
Fax: 675-542-9641
To provides a high quality international school education catering to the varied needs of Tabubil's multicultural mining community. The school employs a well motivated and productive staff, with good working conditions and a high degree of community involvement

SE Walker, Principal

1412 Taegu Elementary & High School
Unit 15623
APO Taegu 96218 0005
Korea

Leon Rivers, Principal

1413 Taipei American School
800 Chung Shan N Road Section 6
Taipei
Taiwan 11152
886-2-287-39900
Fax: 886-2-287-31641
admissions@tas.edu.tw
www.tas.edu.tw
Our mission is to inspire each student to be a confident, creative, caring and moral individual prepared to adapt and succeed anywhere in a rapidly changing world. We provide an American-based education with a global perspective that results in a love of learning, academic excellence, a balanced life, and service to others.

Sharon D Hennessy, Superintendent
Ira B Weislow, Business Manager

1414 Tanglin Trust Schools
95 Portsdown Road
Singapore 13929
65-67780711
Fax: 65-67775862
admissions@tts.edu.sg
www.tts.edu.sg
Our vision is to be the premier school, providing the highest quality learning experiences for 3 to 18 year olds, and cultivating strong relationships in an environment where the individual is important. Our students enjoy a rich and stimulating all-round education which prepares them thoroughly for life in a rapidly-changing and competitive world.

Ronald Stones, Head of School
Peter Derby-Crook, CEO

1415 Thai-Chinese International School
101/177 Moo 7 Soi Mooban Bangpleeni
Prasertsin Road Bangplee Yai
Samutprakarn, TH 10540
66-2-260-8202
tcis@schoolmail.com
www.tcis.ac.th
provide an education which allows each student to develop his/her full being in all areas of human development, academic, physical, emotional, spiritual and social, to interact as critical and compassionate thinkers, and to become a responsible member of our global society.

1416 Timbertop Campus
Timbertop PB-Mansfield
Victoria 3722
Australia
61 3 5733 6777
Fax: 61 3 5777 5772
timbertop@ggs.vic.edu.au
www.ggs.vic.edu.au/Contact.aspx

Stephen Meek, Principal

1417 Traill Preparatory School
34-36 S01
18 Ramkhamheng Road, Huamark
Bangkok
Thailand
660-271- 877
Fax: 660-271- 854
www.traillschool.ac.th

AM Traill, Principal

1418 Ukarumpa High School
PO Box 406
Ukarumpa Via Lae, Papua
New Guinea
675-737-4498
Fax: 675-737-4618
www.ukarumpainternationalschool.org

Steve Walker, Principal

1419 United Nations International School-Hanoi
Phu Thuong Ward Lac Long Quan Road
Tay Ho District
Veitnam, VN
(84 4) 3758 1551
Fax: (84 4) 3758 1542
info@unishanoi.org
www.unishanoi.org
A private, nonprofit, English language, coeducational day school which offers an educational program from prekindergarten through grade 12 for the expatriate community of Hanoi.

Chip Barder, Head of School

1420 United World College-SE Asia
1207 Dover Road
PO Box 15, Singapore 9111
Singapore 13965
65 6775 5344
Fax: 65 6778 5846
info@uwcsea.edu.sg
www.uwcsea.edu.sg
The United World College Movement makes education a force to unite people, nations and cultures for peace and a sustainable future. We educate individuals to take responsibility for shaping a better world

Julian Whiteley, Head of College
Geraint Jones, Assistant Head of College

1421 University Vacancies in Australia
Australian Vice-Chancellors' Committee
GPO Box 1142
Canberra City
Australia
61-02-6285-8200
Fax: 60-02-6285-8211
contact@universitiesaustralia.edu.au
Universities Australia was established on 22 May 2007 as the industry peak body representing the university sector.

G Withers, Chief Executive Officer
P Rodely, Committee Executive Officer

1422 Vientiane International School
PO Box 3180
Phonesavanh Road, Saphanthong Tai Villag
Lao PDR
856 21 486001
Fax: 856 21 486009
contact@ourvis.com
www.vislao.com
Vientiane International School (VIS) is an independent, nonprofit day school offering an international-standard curriculum from Preschool through Grade 12. VIS is an IB World School.

Jane McGee, Director
Glenn Lawler, Primary Principal

1423 Wellesley College
PO Box 41037
Eastbourne, Lower Hutt 5047, Wellington
New Zealand
64 -56 -03
Fax: 64 -56 -28
office@wellesley.school.nz
www.wellesley.school.nz
Wellesley is a full independent primary day school for boys from Year 0 (aged five) to Year 8.

Warren Owen, Principal
Charlotte Gendall, Board member

1424 Wesley International School
Kotak Pos 275
Malang, East Java
Indonesia 65101
62-341-586410
Fax: 62-341-586413
wesley@wesleyinterschool.org
www.wesleyinterschool.org
Our mission at Wesley International School is to provide students with a Christ-centered education: one that inspires them to live a Godly life, that instills a biblical worldview, and produces academic excellence-an education that will prepare our students to impact and bless their world with knowledge, insight, action and love

Paul Richardson, HS Principal
Jonathan Heath, Director

1425 Western Academy of Beijing
PO Box 8547
10 Lai Guang Ying dong Lu, Beijing 10010
China
86-10-8456-4155
Fax: 86 10 6433-3974
wabinfo@wab.edu
www.wab.edu
The Western Academy of Beijing offers a challenging and caring, community based educational environment in which students are active participants in the learning process

Robert Landau, Director
Karen O'Connell, Deputy Chair

1426 Wewak International Primary School
PO Box 354
Wewak Esp, Papua
New Guinea

Darian Sullavan, Principal

1427 Woodstock School
Mussoorie
Uttarakhand
India 24817
91-135-632-610
Fax: 91-135-632-885
mail@woodstock.ac.in
www.woodstock.ac.in

Woodstock aims to develop responsible global citizens and leaders by providing a world-class international education, rooted in its Christian heritage and values, for a diverse group of students, especially from families in Christian or public service, in an Indian Himalayan environment

David Laurenson, Principal
Thomas Chandy, President

428 Xiamen International School
262 Xingbei San Lu, Xinglin
Jimei, Xiamen, Fujian
China
86-592-625-6581
Fax: 86-592-625-6584
askxis@xischina.com
www.xischina.com
Develops confident, knowledgeable students who enjoy life-long learning, demonstrate global awareness and contribute compassionately to the world around them.

Paul Raschke, Headmaster
Yuan Yuan Deng, Vice Chairman

429 Yew Chung Shanghai International School
18 W Rong Hua Road, Gubei New Area
Shanghai
China 20110
(8621) 6219 5910
Fax: (8621) 6219 0675
enquiry@ycef.com
www.ycis-sh.com
Provide an all-round education that nurtures the whole person - spiritual, academic, physical, social and emotional that includes relationships with others.

Andrew Mellor, Co-Principal
Julie Zheng, Co-Principal

430 Yogyakarta International School
P.O. Box 1175
Yogyakarta 55011, Jalan Cendrawasih No.1
Indonesia
62-274-625965
Fax: 62-274-625966
www.yis-edu.org/
Operates as a not for profit social foundation and is overseen by a School Board made up of both parents and non-parents.

Chris Scott, Principal

431 Yokohama International School
258 Yamate-cho Naka-ku
Yokohama
Japan 231-0
81-45-622-0084
Fax: 81-45-621-0379
yis@yis.ac.jp
www.yis.ac.jp
Provides the highest-quality, balanced education to internationally minded students in an inquiring and supportive environment.

Simon Taylor, Headmaster
John Inge, Chairman

432 Yokota High School
DoDDS P J YH Unit 5072
APO AP
Japan 96328-5072
011-81-3117-55-701
Fax: 011-81-3117-55-722
Yokota High School, working in partnership with the family and local community, provides a safe, academically-inspiring environment in which all students will develop to their maximum potential as life-long learners and responsible participants in an ever-changing global society.

Darrell Mood, Principal

1433 Yokota West Elementary School
DoDDS P J YW Unit 5072
APO AP
Japan 96328-5072
011-81-3117-55-761
Fax: 011-81-3117-55-573

Sharon Carter, Principal

1434 Yonggwang Foreign School
Ceii Site Office
PO Box 9, Yonggwang-Kun 513-880
Korea

Eleanor Jones, Principal

1435 Zama Junior High & High School
USA Garrison, Camp Zama
APO, Honshu 96343 0005
Japan

Samuel Menniti, Principal

1436 Zukeran Elementary School
Unit 35017
FPO AP
Japan 96379-5017
011-81-611-7452576
Fax: 011-81-098-892-795
Zukeran.Principal@pac.dodea.edu
Zukeran Elementary School shares the vision of creating a community of learners actively engaged in the pursuit of the knowledge, skills and experiences necessary to empower all children to meet the challenges of the 21st century.

Cindy Templeton, Principal
Roger Reade, Assistant Principal

Central & South America

1437 Academia Cotopaxi American International School
De las Higuerillas y Alondras
Quito
Ecuador
593-2-246-7411
Fax: 593-2-244-5195
info@cotopaxi.k12.ec
www.cotopaxi.k12.ec
Premier English-language school from early childhood through secondary school.

Kurt Kywi, President
Robert Moss, Vice President

1438 American Cooperative School
Lawton 20
Paramaribo
Suriname
597-49-9461
Fax: 597-498-853
www.acslp.org
A private, coeducational day school which offers an educational program from prekindergarten through grade 12 for students of all nationalities.

Frank Martens, Administrator

1439 American Elementary & High School
Caixa Postal 7432
01064-970, Sao Paulo
Brazil
55-11-3842-2499
Fax: 55-11-3842-9358
A private, coeducational day school which offers a full college-preparatory educational program from preschool through grade 12 for students of all nationalities.

Dr Gunther Brandt, Principal

1440 American International School-Bolivia
Casilla 5309
Cochabamba
Bolivia
591-4-428-8577
Fax: 591-4-428-8576
administracion@aisb.edu.bo
www.aisb.edu.bo
The American International School of Bolivia was founded in 1993 as an international, non-governmental, co-educational day school. The AIS/B educational system covers from Early Childhood education up to the IB program in grades 11 and 12 for students representing all nationalities and socio-economical levels.

Dr Silke Marina Scholer, Director General
Tatiana Jimenez BA, Chief Administrator

1441 American International School-Lincoln Buenos Aires
Andres Ferreyra 4073
B1637 AOS La Lucila, Buenos Aires
Argentina
(54)(11) 4851-1700
Fax: 54-11-479-02117
pacha_c@lincoln.edu.ar
www.lincoln.edu.ar
Provides education based on United States accredited curriculum in an environment of academic excellence that develops ethical, responsible and globally conscious world citizens.

Phil T Joslin, Superintendent

1442 American School
PO Box (01) 35
El Salvador
503-26-38-330
Fax: 503-26-38-385
recruiting@amschool.edu.sv
www.amschool.edu.sv
Founded in 1946 and is an independent, international, coeducational, college-preparatory institution

Yolanda de Lopez, Director of Admissions

1443 American School Foundation AC
Bondojito 215
Colonia Las Americas
Mexico City, Mexico 01120
52-55-5227-4900
Fax: 52-55-5273-4357
asf@asf.edu.mx
www.asf.edu.mx
is an academically rigorous, international, university preparatory school, which offers students from diverse backgrounds the best of American independent education

Julie Hellmund, Director

1444 American School Foundation-Guadalajara
Colomos 2100, Coronel Providencia
Guadalajara, Jalisco
Mexico 44640
52 (33) 3648-0299
Fax: 52-33-3817-3356
asfg@asfg.mx
www.asfg.mx
Educating students in a bilingual, bicultural and secular environment to be purposeful learners, critical and creative thinkers, effective communicators and community contributors, based on a foundation of honor, freedom and commitment

David McGrath, Principal
Jabet Heinze, Superintendent

1445 American School Foundation-Monterrey
Ave. Ignacio Morones Prieto No. 150
Col. San Isidro, Santa Catarina, N.L.
Nuevo Leon, Mexico 66190
(52)-81-5000-4400
Fax: (52)-81-5000-4428
www.asfm.edu.mx
A private, nonprofit, coeducational day school which offers an educational program from nursery through grade 12 for students of all nationalities.
Dr. Jeffrey Keller, Superintendent

1446 American School-Belo Horizonte
Avenida Deputado Cristovan Chiaradia 120
Caixa Postal 1701
Bairro Buritis, Belo Horizonte
30575-440
Brazil
55-31-378-6700
Fax: 55-31-378-6878
eabh@eabh.com.br
www.eabh.com.
A coeducational, private day school which offers an educational program from prekindergarten through grade 12 for students of all nationalities.
Sid Stewart, Principal

1447 American School-Brasilia
SGAS 605
Bloco E, Lotes 34/37
Brasilia,DF,Brazil 70200-650
55 (61) 3442-9700
Fax: 55 (61) 3442-9729
www.eabdf.br
A private, coeducational day school which offers an educational program from prekindergarten through grade 12 for students of all nationalities
Barry Dequanne, Headmaster
Beth Lopez, Lower School Principal

1448 American School-Campinas
Rua Cajamar, 35 - Jardim Alto da Ba
Campinas- SP
Brazil 13090
55 19 2102-1000
Fax: 55 19 2102-1016
www.escolaamericanadecampinas.com.br
Steve Herrara, Superintendent

1449 American School-Durango
Francisw Sarabia #416 Pte
Durango 34000
Mexico
(618) 813-36-36
Fax: (618) 811-28-39
www.cadurango.edu.mx
Dr Jorge O Nelson, Principal

1450 American School-Guatemala
11 Calle 1579 Zona 15 Vista Hermosa
Guatemala
Guatemala
502-690-
Fax: 502-698-
director@cag.edu.gt
www.cag.edu.gt
is to educate independent, critical-thinking, responsible, bilingual individuals prepared to meet the challenges of the future
Robert Gronniger, General Director
Edward Langlais, High School Principal

1451 American School-Guayaquil
PO Box 3304
Guayaquill
Ecuador
593-4-255-503
Fax: 593-4-250-453
www.americanschool.edu.ec
Grade levels K-12, school year April - January
Francisco Andrade, Interim General Director
Patricia Ayala de Coronel, HS Principal

1452 American School-Laguna Verde
Veracruz, Mexico
Maurice H Blum, Principal

1453 American School-Lima
Apartado 18-0977
Lima 18
Peru
51-14-35-0890
Fax: 51 1 619-9301
fdr@amersol.edu.pe
www.amersol.edu.pe
is to empower our students to pursue their passion for learning, lead lives of integrity and create socially responsible solutions.
Caron Kluznik, Superintendent

1454 American School-Pachuca
Valle de Anahuac S/N Valle de San J
ZC: 42083 Pachuca de Soto Hidalgo
Mexico
01-771 713 9608
Fax: 52-771-85077
admisiones@americana.edu.mx
www.americana.edu.mx/
Grade levels prekindergarten through ninth.
Nic,foro Ramirez, General Director

1455 American School-Puebla
Apartado 665
Puebla
Mexico
www.cap.edu.mx/english/
Dr Arthur W Chaffee, Principal

1456 American School-Puerto Vallarta
PO Box 2-280
Puerto Vallarta, Jalisco 48300
Mexico
52 322-221-1525
Fax: (52) 322-226-7677
Info@aspv.edu.mx
www.aspv.edu.mx
Gerald Selitzer, Director

1457 American School-Recife
408 Se Souza Street
Boa Viagem
Brazil 51030-60
55 81 3341.4716
Fax: 55-81-341-0142
info@ear.com.br
www.ear.com.br
A private, coeducational day school which offers an instructional program from prekindergarten through grade 12 for students of all nationalities.
George Takacks, Superintendent

1458 American School-Tampico
Hidalgo # 100
Tancol, Tampico
Mexico
52-12-272-081
Fax: 52-12-280-080
racevedo@ats.edu.mx
www.ats.edu.mx
Grade levels N through tenth.
Emma deSalazar, Headmaster

1459 American School-Torreon
Paseo del Algodn y Boulevard Carlo
Fracc Los Viedos Torren, Coahuila
Mexico 27019
871ÿ222 51 00 TO 0
Fax: 871 733 26 68
www.cat.mx
A prestigious center of academic excellence dedicated to creating life-long learners and ethical leaders in a global and changing world.
Makhlouf Ouyed, Director General
Martha Martinez, Business Manager

1460 Anglo American School
PO Box 3188-1000
San Jose
Costa Rica
506-279-2626
Fax: 506-279-7894
www.aas.ru
Grade levels Pre-K through 6, school year February - November
Virginia Hine Barrantes, Principal

1461 Anglo Colombian School
Apaptado Aereo 253393
Bogota
Colombia
www.anglocolombiano.edu.co
David Toze, Principal

1462 Anglo-American School
Calle 37
Avenida Central, 1000 San Jose
Costa Rica
495-231-447
www.aas.ru
Virginia Hine, Principal

1463 Antofagasta International School
Avda. Jaime Guzman Errazurz #04300
Antofagasta
Chile
56 - 55 - 694900
Fax: 56 - 55 - 694912
ais@ais.cl
www.ais.cl
A Pre-Kindergarten through 12th grade educational institution that is dedicated to offering a challenging, English-based curriculum to its students.
Carlos Ignacio Figueroa Ahumada, Principal
Carlos Arturo Calussen Calvo, Chairman

1464 Asociacion Colegio Granadino
AA 2138
Manizales, Caldas
Colombia
57-68-745-774
Fax: 57-68-746-066
www.granadino.edu.co
Grade levels Pre-K through 12, school year August - June
Gonzalo Arango, General Director

1465 Asociacion Escuelas Lincoln
Andres Ferreyra 4073
B1636 AOS La Lucila, Buenos Aires
Argentina
(54)(11) 4851-1700
Fax: 54-11-4790-2117
www.lincoln.edu.ar
Provide an education based on United States accredited curriculum
Phil Joslin, Superintendent
Claudia Pacha, Admissions

1466 Balboa Elementary School
Unit 9025
APO Balboa 34002
Panama

818-241-1801
www.gusd.net

Susan Beattie, Principal

67 Balboa High School
Unit 9025
APO Balboa 34002
Panama
818-241-1801
www.gusd.net

Ernest Holland, Principal

68 Barker College
91 Pacific Highway
Hornsby
NSW, Australia, 2077
61-2-9847-8399
Fax: 61-2-9847-8009
reception@barker.nsw.edu.au
www.barker.college
Barker College is an Anglican day and boarding school. In 2016, the School announced plans to become fully coeducational by 2022.

Phillip Heath, Head of Barker College
Peter Berkley, Chair

69 Belgrano Day School
Juramento 3035
Ciudad de Buenos Aires
Argentina c1428
54 -1 -81
Fax: 54 -1 -786
rrpp@bdsnet.com.ar
www.bds.edu.ar
We cooperate with the family to offer bilingual education quality for the training of future leaders and citizens of the world committed to the common good, free, responsible, creative and respectful of diversity and dissent.

Maria Matilde V Green, President
Carol Halle, Faculty Head

70 Bilingue School Isaac Newton
Chihuahua, Mexico

Lauya Gonzalez Valenzula, Principal

71 British American School
AA 4368
Barranquilla
Colombia 28277
704-341-3236
www.britishschoolofcharlotte.org

Rafael Ortegon Rocha, Principal

472 British School-Costa Rica
PO Box 8184-1000
San Jose
Costa Rica 02232-7833
50 - 2 -0 0
Fax: 50 - 2 -2 7
britsch@racsa.co.cr
www.thebritishschoolofcostarica.com/

David John Lloyd, Principal

473 British School-Venezuela
Sector 8 and Sector 12
Panchkula
India 13410
91-172-5028556
www.thebritishschool.org
aims to provide education with global standards. This will not only make students studying in the school eligible for higher education in the institutions across the world but also give NRI's settled abroad, an opportunity to send their children to such schools to have a better idea of the social system back home.

TBS Panchkula, Principal
U Sethi, Board Member

1474 Buenos Aires International Christian Academy
Red de Escuelas Mundiales Cristiana
Av Libertador General San Mart-n 2170
Buenos Aires, AR 01646
5411 4549 1300
Fax: 5411 4549 1300
info@baica.com
www.baica.com
Our school is unique in that we are home to both Argentineans and the expat community.

Andy Simon, Principal
Robert Newman, Director

1475 Caribbean International School
Box 1594
Cristobal Colon
Panama
507-445-0933
www.cis.edu.pa

Anderson, Principal

1476 Centro Cultural Brazil-Elementary School
Rua Jorge Tibirica 5
11100 Santos, Sao Paulo
Brazil

Newton Antionio Martin, Principal

1477 Cochabamba Cooperative School
Casilla 1395
Cochabamba
Bolivia 01395
591-42-987-61
Fax: 591-42-329-06
www.ccs.edu.bo
President

Provide attendees

Carl Wieburg, Director
Jos Leonis, Manager

1478 Colegio Abraham Lincoln
Calle 170, # 51A-81
SedePrimaria Avenue Calle 170 #65-31
Columbia
571-676-7360
www.abrahamlincoln.edu.co
Promoting human development within a humanistic philosophy and pruricultural.

Amparo Rueda, Director

1479 Colegio Americano De Guayaquil
Juan Tanca Marengo Avenue PO Box 33
Guayaquil
Ecuador
593-4-255-03
Fax: 593-4-250-453
info@colegioamericano.edu.ec
www.colegioamericano.edu.ec
Provide an education with the highest standards of quality, thus contributing to the improvement of our society.

Stanley Whitman, Principal
Francisco Andrade, Association President

1480 Colegio Anglo Colombiano
Avenida 19 # 152A-48
Bogota
, DC
571-259-5700
admissions@anglocolombiano.edu.co
www.anglocolombiano.edu.co
Our purpose is to educate human beings with open minds, real social awareness and the power of critical thinking.

David Toze, Principal
Catherine Cushnan, Admission

1481 Colegio Bilingue Juan Enrigue
Pestalozzi AC
Veracruz
Mexico

Michael S Garber, Principal

1482 Colegio Bolivar
Calle 5 Number 122-21 V-a Pance
Cali
Colombia
(57-2) 684 8600
Fax: 57-2-555-2041
cbinfo@colegiobolivar.edu.co
www.colegiobolivar.edu.co
Colegio Bolivar is an educational community whose mission is to educate its students in a bilingual, democratic environment to be autonomous, and to demonstrate a spirit of inquiry and collaboration, a commitment to excellence, and the highest aspirations for the welfare of both the individual and society.

Joseph Nagy, Director
Richard Martin, Dean of Students

1483 Colegio Columbo Britanico
Apartado Aereo 5774
Cali
Colombia
www.colombobritanico.edu.co

Ian Watson, Principal

1484 Colegio Gran Breta¤a
Cra 51 #215-20
Bogot
Colombia
57-1-676-0391
Fax: 57-1-676-0426
admissions@cgb.edu.co
www.cgb.edu.co
School teaching primary and secondary grade levels.

Robert Tomalin, Director
Fiorella Rocha, Director, Marketing

1485 Colegio Granadino
AA 2138 Manizales
Colombia
57-6-874-57-74
Fax: 57-6-874-60-66
www.granadino.edu.co
Early Childhood, Elementary, Middle School and High School

Gonzalo Arango, Principal
Robert Sims, Director

1486 Colegio Interamericano de la Montana
Boulevard La Montana
Finca El Socorro, Zona 16
Guatemala, GT 01016
502 2200.2990
Fax: 502-3-641-779
www.interamericano.edu.gt
The mission of Colegio Interamericano is to prepare its students for life and for studies anywhere in the world, by orienting them towards being responsible members of society.

Dr Michael Farr, General Director
Griselda de Amezquita, Head of Human Resources

1487 Colegio Jorge Washington
Zona Norte, Anillo Vial Km.12
Cartagena
Colombia, CO
57-5-673 5505
Fax: 57-5-665-6447
www.cojowa.edu.co
The mission of the George Washington School is to form bilingual and bicultural citizens who possess high ethical values and

commitment to the search for academic excellence and success in life.

Pete Nonnenkamp, Director
Maritza Garcia, Assistant Director

1488 Colegio Karl C Parrish
Kilometer 2 Antigua Via a Puerto Co
Barranquilla
Colombia, CO 52962
57-5-359-8929
Fax: 57-5-359-8828
mail@kcparrish.edu.co
www.kcparrish.edu.co
strives to provide an environment that results in students displaying personal integrity and character in their relationships both within and outside the school.

Laura Horbal Rebolledo, Director
Hectalina Donado, Elementary School Principal

1489 Colegio Montelibano
AA 6823 Cerromatoso
Montelibano, Bogota
Colombia

Francisco Cajiao, Principal

1490 Colegio Nueva Granada
Carrera 2 Este Number 70-20
Bogota
Colombia, CO
57-1-2123511
Fax: 57-1-211-3720
www.cng.edu
Prepare tomorrow's leaders by educating the mind, nurturing the spirit, and strengthening the body.

Barry McCombs PhD, Director
Michael Adams, Deputy Director

1491 Colegio Peterson SC
Apartado Postal 10-900
DF 11000
Mexico
52-5-81-30-11-4
Fax: 52-5-81-31-38-5

Marvin Peterson, Principal

1492 Colegio San Marcus
61 Ourense
Buenas Aires
Argentina 32004
988-247-4
Fax: 988- 39-5
csmarcos@csmarcos.com
www.csmarcos.com
Collegio San Marcos was established in 1988, when it began its first year of dentures, being recognized by the Galician regional government, as accredited Vocational Training Second Grade, under the Order of May 20, 1988 of the Department of Education and University (DOG num.110 June 1988).

Susana Raffo, Principal

1493 Colegio Ward
Hector Coucheiro 599
1706 DF Sarmiento, Ramos Mejia
Buenos Aires, Argentina
541- 46-8 03
info@ward.edu.ar
www.ward.edu.ar

Ruben Carlos Urcola, Principal
Daniel Campagna, Director

1494 Costa Rica Academy
Apartado Postal 4941
San Jose 1000
Costa Rica
506-239-03-76
Fax: 506-239-06-25
A private, coeducational school which offers an educational program from prekindergarten through grade 12 for students of all nationalities.

William D Rose, BS, Med, Principal

1495 Cotopaxi Academy
PO Box 17-11-6510
Quito
Ecuador
593-2-246-7411
Fax: 593-2-244-5195
info@cotopaxi.k12.ec
www.cotopaxi.k12.ec
Premier English-language early childhood through secondary school in Ecuador. The internationally recognized program is aggressively sought out by all National and International parents who truly want to join a partnership to provide the very best education possible for their children.

Eddie Wexler, Principal
Kurt Kywi, President

1496 Country Day School
Apartado 1139 - 1250
Escazu
Costa Rica
(506) 2289 - 0919
Fax: (506) 2228 - 2076
www.cds.ed.cr
CDS is an American School serving an international population. Accredited by the Middle States Association of Colleges and Schools in the United States, and by the Costa Rican Ministry of Education

Gloria Doll, Director
Maria Fernanda Cardona, Admissions Coordinator

1497 Crandon Institute
Casilla Correo 445
Montevideo
Uruguay
248- 33-5
www.crandon.edu.uy
This school offers a curriculum taught in Spanish for 2,000 day students (700 boys; 1,300 girls), in high school through junior college level (home economics, commercial). The school, affiliated with the Methodist church, employs 300 teachers.

Marcos Rocchietti, Principal

1498 Curundu Elementary School
Unit 0925
APO Curundu 34002 0005
Panama

Clifford Drexler, Principal

1499 Curundu Junior High School
Unit 0925
APO Curundu 34002 0005
Panama

Charles Renno, Principal

1500 Edron Academy-Calz Al Desierto
Desierto de los Leones 5578
Mexico City 01740
Mexico
5-585-30-49
Fax: 5-585-28-46

Richard Gilby Travers, Principal

1501 El Abra School
Phelps Dodge Corporation
Calama
Chile
56-55-313-600
Fax: 56-55-315-182
elabraschool@hotmail.com
Grade levels K-11, school year August - June

Margaret Maclean, Head of School

1502 English School
AA 51284
Bogota
Colombia

Leonard Mabe, Principal

1503 Escola Americana do Rio de Janeiro
Estrada Da Gavea 132
Rio de Janeiro
Brazil 22451-263
(916) 458-5932
Fax: 55-21-259-4722
www.earj.com.br
Escola Americana motivates engaged learners to become independent critical thinkers in a multicultural community.

Dr Dennis Klumpp, Principal
Caren Addis, Director of Admissions

1504 Escola Maria Imaculada
Rua Vig rio Joao de Pontes, 537, Ch
Sao Paulo
Brazil 04748
551- 2-01 7
Fax: 551- 55-1 77
www.chapelschool.com/

Gerald Gates, Principal

1505 Escuela Anaco
Avenue Jose Antonio Anzoategui, KM
Anaco
Venezuela
58 -82 -22 2
Offers a United States High School Diploma with a full schooling program from Day Care through Grade 12. Also have on-line courses to enhance our program. Uses the best of the educational standards of the states of California, New York, and Virginia.

Francene Conte, Principal
Bill Kralovec, Director

1506 Escuela Bilingue Santa Barbara
Apartado 342-El Marchito
San Pedro Sila
Honduras
504-659-3053
Fax: 504-659-3059
Grade levels preK through 8.

John P Leddy, Principal

1507 Escuela Bilingue Valle De Sula
Apartado 735
San Pedro Sula
Honduras

Carole A Black, Principal

1508 Escuela International Sampedrana
Col Gracias A Dios 500 mts W Hospit
San Pedro Sula
Honduras
504-566-2722
Fax: 504-566-1458
eperez@seishn.com
EIS seeks to be the premier school in the city of San Pedro Sula, the country of Honduras and region of Central America through the use of best teaching practices with the goal of reaching all of its students.

Gregorg E Werner, Principal
Ronald Vair, Superintendent

09 Escuela Las Palmas
Apartdo 6-2637
Panama
797-530-
www.cmpuentealto.cl
Aleida Molina, Principal

10 Foreign Students School
Avenue Station B
#6617-6615 Esquina 70
Miramar Havana City, Cuba
Gillian P Greenwood, Principal

11 Fort Clayton Elementary School
2000 Park Place Avenue
APO, Fort Clayton 34004 0005
Panama, TX
817-814-5400
www.lilybclayton.org
Barbara Seni, Principal

12 Fort Kobbe Elementary School
Unit 0714
APO, Fort Kobbe 34001 0005
Panama
Dr Vinita Swenty, Principal

13 Fundacion Colegio Americano de Quito
Manuel Benigno Cueva N80 - 190 Urba
PO Box 17-01-157, Carcel,n, Quito
Ecuador, DC
(593) 2 3976 300
Fax: 593-2-472-972
dirgeneral@fcaq.k12.ec
www.fcaq.k12.ec
Grade levels Pre-K through 12, school year September - June.
Susan Barbara, Director General

14 George Washington School
Apartado Aereo 2899
Cartagena
Colombia
57-5-665-3396
Fax: 57-5-665-6447
A private, coeducational day school which offers and educational program from prekindergarten through grade 12 for students of all nationalities.
Steven Fields, Principal

15 Grange School
Casilla 218
Correo 12, Santiago
Chile
56 2 25981500
admissions@grange.cl
www.grange.cl
Places great importance on the idea of 'fair play', a concept with connotations of sportsmanship, rule obedience, and honesty
Rachid Benammar, Headmaster

16 Greengates School
Avenue Circumbalacion Pte 102
Baliones De San Mateo, Naucalpah
Edo de Mexico, Mexico 53200
52-55-5373-0088
Fax: 52-55-5373-0765
www.greengates.edu.mx
Grade levels prekindergarten through twelfth.
Susan E Mayer, Principal

17 Howard Elementary School
805 Long Hollow Pike
Gallatin
Panama, TN 37066
615-452-3025
Jean Lamb, Principal

1518 Inst Tecnologico De Estudios
Apartado Postal 28B
Chihuahua
Mexico
528- 83-8 20
www.itesm.edu
Hector Chavrez Barron, Principal

1519 International Preparatory School
PO Box 20015-LC
Santiago
Chile
56-2-321-5800
Fax: 56-2-321-5821
www.internationalpreparatoryschool.com
Grade levels Pre-K through 12, school year March - December
Lesley Easton-Allen, Headmistress
Pamela Thomson, Curriculum Coordinator

1520 International School Nido de Aguilas
Avenida El Rodeo 14200
Santiago
Chile
56 2 2339 8100
mail@nido.cl
www.nido.cl
The International School Nido de Aguilas offers an English language-based, liberal arts education, influenced by U.S. and Chilean thought and tradition, that prepares students to be eloquent communicators and impactful stewards of a rapidly changing world.
David B. Perry, Headmaster

1521 International School-Curitiba
Av Dr Eug^nio Bertolli
3900 Santa Felicidade, Curitiba, Paran˜
Brazil 18241
413-525-7400
Fax: 413-525-7499
www.iscbrazil.com
It is a private, nonprofit, self-governed school that serves students and families from our local and international community; offers a U.S. based curriculum in English with American, Brazilian and International Baccalaureate diplomas; commits to academic and personal excellence and prepares students for universities around the world.
Elizabeth Mello, Principal 1-12
Bill Pearson, Superintendent

1522 International School-La Paz
CC1075870 Villa Dolores
La Paz, Cordoba
Argentina
LH Sullivan, Principal

1523 International School-Panama
PO Box 0819-02588
El Dorado
Panama
(507) 293-3000
Fax: 507-266-7808
www.isp.edu.pa
A private, coeducational day school which offers an educational program from prekindergarten through grade 12 for students of all nationalities.
Rajiv Bhatt, Director
Jania Jacob, Business Manager

1524 Karl C Parrish School
Km 2 Antigua via a Puerto
Barranquilla
Colombia
(57-5) 3598929
Fax: 57-5-3598828
mail@kcparrish.edu.co
www.kcparrish.edu.co
Karl C. Parrish is a private, non-sectarian, non-profit elementary and secondary school that is open to children of all nationalities.
Laura H Rebolledo, Director

1525 Liceo Pino Verde
Vereda Los Planes kilometro 5
V¡a Cerritos Entrada 16, El Tigre
Colombia
963-379368
info@liceopinoverde.edu.co
www.liceopinoverde.edu.co
This school teaches English as a second language; builds strong human values; develops logical thinking skills and prepares students for the world of technology and communication. Enrollment consists of 110 day students (57 boys; 53 girls, in grades PK-12. Overseas teachers are welcome to apply with the length of stay being two years, with housing provided. Applications needed to teach include science, math and English.
Luz Stella Rios Patino, Principal

1526 Limon School
P.O. Box 249
847 F Avenue
Limon, CO 80828
719-775-2350
Fax: 719-775-9052
www.limonbadgers.com
strive to provide a safe environment and develop responsible and productive citizens who have the knowledge and skills to seize their chosen opportunities
Chris Selle, Principal

1527 Lincoln International Academy
PO Box 52-7444
Miami, FL 33152
1 (305) 395-4825ÿ
lincoln@lincoln.edu.ni
www.lincoln.edu.ni
instilling in them solid Christian and human virtues as taught by the Catholic faith, challenging them to reach their full intellectual capacity and achieve a high integral academic excellence in order to face the challenges of today's world. providing them with English instruction while preserving our Hispanic-Nicaraguan culture.
Henningston Hammond, Operation Manager
Adolfo Gonzalez, General Director

1528 Mackay School
Vicuna Mackenna 700
Renaca
Chile
563-223- 660
Fax: 563-223- 667
www.mackay.cl
Nigel William Blackbur, Principal

1529 Marian Baker School
Apartado 4269
San Jose
Costa Rica 01000
560-273-3426
Fax: 506-273-4609
www.mbs.ed.cr/
Marian Baker School (MBS) is an International English speaking school educating preschool through high school students.
Linda Niehaus, Director
Bonnie Heigold, Business Manager

1530 Marymount School
1026 Fifth Avenue
Barranquilla
Colombia, NY 10028
212-744-4486
Fax: 212-744-0163
www.marymountnyc.org
Dr. Kathleen Cunniffe, Principal

1531 Metropolitan School
7281 Sarah Avenue
Maplewood, MO 63143
314-644-0850
The School is dedicated to providing a highly individualized educational experience for middle and senior high school students whose potential has not been recognized and/or meaningfully challenged in traditional school settings.
Judi Thomas, Head of School

1532 Modern American School
Cerro del Hombre 18
Col. Romero de Terreros
Mexico
565-476-
www.modernamerican.edu.mx
To provide our students with the educational elements which will promote the optimum development of the intellect, instill social awareness and emotional sensitivity, encourage artistic creativity, and emphasize physical well-being, aiming for excellence toward future success

1533 Northlands Day School
Roma 1210
1636 Olivos, Buenos Aires
Argentina
541-147-1 84
Fax: 541- 47-1 84
www.northlands.org.ar/
This bilingual day school for girls offers modern facilities, sports, etc. on a spacious campus. Languages spoken include English and Spanish and total enrollment is 1,100 students, ranging in grade from K1-12. Overseas teachers are accepted, with the length of stay being 2-6 years with housing provided.
Susan Brooke Jackson, MA, Principal

1534 Our Lady of Mercy School
Rua Visconde de Caravelas
48, Botafogo, Rio de Janeiro
Brazil
336-722-7204
www.ourladyofmercyschool.org
Our Lady of Mercy School is an American Catholic English speaking school whose main purpose is to educate the whole student towards global understanding.
Charles Lyndaker, Superintendent

1535 Pan American Christian Academy
1730 Link Road
04829-310 Sao Paulo
Brazil
480.471.5339
Fax: 55-11-59289591
info@paca.com.br
www.paca.com.br
American international school located in the city of Sao Paulo, working with 350 students from different parts of the world with an American-style pre-school through high school education. Since 1960, we've served the local and international community of Sao Paulo.
Micheal Epp, Superintendent

1536 Pan American School-Bahia
Caixa Postal 231
Salvador
Brazil, SA 40901-970
55-71-3368-8400
Fax: 55-71-3368-8441
info@escolapanamericana.com
www.escolapanamericana.com
A private, coeducational day school which offers a program from preschool through grade 12 for students of all nationalities.
Mary Jo Heatherington, PhD, Superintendent

1537 Pan American School-Costa Rica
Apartado 474
Monterrey
Costa Rica, NL 64000
(81) 83-42-07-78
Fax: (81) 83-40-27-49
www.pas.edu.mx
Offer excellent educational programs in English that foster the integral development of students.
Robert Arpee, Director

1538 Pan American School-Monterrey
Hidalgo 656 Pte
Apartado Postal 474, Monterrey 64000
Mexico
(81) 83-42-07-78
www.pas.edu.mx
This school offers an English curriculum for 1,393 day students and 100 boarding students (709 boys; 684 girls), grades preschool through nine. The school is willing to participate in a teacher exchange program with the length of stay being one year. Applications needed to teach include science, preschool, math, reading, English, and physical education.
Tobert L Arpee, Principal
Lenor Arpee, Faculty Head

1539 Pan American School-Porto Alegre
Rua Joao Paetzel 440
91 330 Porto Alegre
Brazil
555- 33-4 58
www.panamerican.com.br
Jennifer Sughrue, Principal

1540 Panama Canal College
Unit 0925
APO Balboa 34002 0005
Panama

1541 Prescott Anglo American School
PO Box 1036
Arequipa
Peru
www.prescott.edu.pe
This school offers a Spanish/English curriculum for 1,050 day students (450 boys; 600 girls) in grades K-12. Students are taught English three hours a day, so they can reach an intermediate level in grade 9, and high intermediate in grades 11-12.
Jorge Pachecot, Principal

1542 Redland School
272 Military Road
Cremorne
Chile, NS 02090
612-990- 313
Fax: 612-990- 322
www.redlands.nsw.edu.au
This school offers an English/Spanish curriculum to 820 day students (420 boys; 400 girls), in grades PreK-12. The student body is mostly Chilean and 90% of the teachers are Chilean. However, overseas teachers are welcome, with the applications being pre-school and English.
Richard Collingwood-Selby, Principal

1543 Reydon School for Girls
5178 Cruz Chica
Sierras de Cordoba, Cordoba
Argentina
NJ Milman, Principal

1544 Saint George's School
Carrera 92 No 156-88, Suba
Bogota
Colombia
057-168- 917
sanjorge@sgs.edu.co
www.sgs.edu.co
Mary De Acosta, Principal

1545 Santa Cruz Cooperative School
Barrio Las Palmas Calle Barcelona #
Casilla 753 Santa Cruz
Bolivia
(591) (3) 353-0808
Fax: (591) (3) 352-6993
william.j.mckelligott@gmail.com
www.sccs.edu.bo
College preparatory school equipping students with the necessary skills and values to be citizens and leaders for the 21st century. Preparing students to become productive citizens, leaders and life-long learners.
William J McKelligott, Director General
Hugo Paz, Board Director

1546 Santa Margarita School
22062 Antonio ParkwayÿÿRancho Santa
Surco, Lima
Peru, CA 92688
949-766-6000
www.smhs.org
Guillermo Descalzi, Principal

1547 St. Albans College
110 Clearwater Road
Lynnwood Glen Pretoria
South Africa
271-234- 122
Fax: 271-236- 191
www.stalbanscollege.com
St Alban's College is a learning community of boys, staff and parents. We are forward looking, committed to quality and service, and we pursue innovative strategies and encourage personal responsibility in the interest of all-round development of the boy as he journeys towards manhood.
Tom Hamilton, Headmaster
Carlos Palermo, Faculty Director

1548 St. Andrew's Scots School
Rosales 2809
Olivos
Argentina 01636
54-114-799-8318
Fax: 54-114-799-8318
admissions@sanandres.esc.edu.ar
www.sanandres.esc.edu.ar
St. Andrew's Scots School aims to graduate responsible citizens committed to serving Argentina and contributing to its equitable development through a well-balanced, bilingual education which meets high international standards and fosters a joy for learning.
Gabriel Rshaid, Headmaster
Ana Repila, Admissions Director

1549 St. Catherine's School
Carbajal 3250
1426 Capital Federal, Buenos Aires
Argentina

54-114-552-4353
Fax: 54-114-554-4113
www.redeseducacion.com.ar
Pre-K through 12, school year March-December
Mabel Manzitti, Principal

1550 St. George's College
Guido 800 CP
Quilmes, Buenos Aires
Argentina 01878
(5411) 4254-8237
Fax: 54-11-425-30030
info@stgeorge.com.ar
www.stgeorge.com.ar
Our mission is to provide students of varying abilities and backgrounds between the ages of 3 - 18 with a bilingual, fully integrated education of the highest calibre in order that they may develop their potential to the full in an appropriately resourced co-educational environment which nurtures individual development, independent thinking and the highest moral standards.
Derek Pringle, Headmaster
Peter Ashton, Deputy Headmaster

1551 St. Hilda's College
Cowley Place Oxford
OX4 1DY
England
44-1865-276884
Fax: 44-1865-276816
www.st-hildas.ox.ac.uk
To promote the education of women within Oxford University and the tradition of excellence in women's education which it pioneered.
Sheila Forbes, Principal
Lucia Nixon, Senior Tutor

1552 St. John School
Casilla 284
Concepcion
Chile
www.sjs.org
St. John School is a bilingual school that caters to children from PK through grade twelve. The student body includes 1,170 day students (580 boys and 590 girls). The school does participate in teacher exchange programs with the length of stay for teachers being two years. The languages spoken include Spanish and English and the student/teacher ratio is 10:1.
Chris Pugh, Principal

1553 St. Margaret's British School-Girls
Calle Saint Margaret
150 Lomas de Montemar
Chile
451-00 -
admissions@stmargarets.cl
www.stmargarets.cl
St. Margarets objective is to protect in its pupil its motto: Recte Fac Nec Time (Do Right , Fear not) This implies assigning value to great ideals, acting fairly and courteously, having sound judgement, enriched understanding, a discipline manner and making responsible use of their freedom.
Margery Byrne, Principal
Avril Cooper, Headmistress

1554 St. Paul's School
325 Pleasant Street
Concord, NH 03301-2591
603-229-4600
www.sps.edu
St. Paul's School is a fully residential academic community that pursues the highest ideals of scholarship. We strive to challenge our students intellectually and morally - to nurture a love for learning and a commitment to engage as servant leaders in a complex world.
Richardo Pons, Principal
William R Matthews, Jr, Rector

1555 St. Pauls School
1600 St Paul's Drive
Clearwater, FL 33764
727-536-2756
Fax: 727-531-2276
www.st.pauls.edu
To educate and inspire young minds in a challenging and nurturing community of learning.
AH Thurn, Principal
Angel W Kytle, Head of the School

1556 St. Peter's School
Pacheco 715
1640 Martinez, Buenos Aires
Argentina
www.st.peterspanchgani.org
Joy Headland, Principal

1557 Teaching Opportunities in Latin America for US Citizens
Organization of American States
17th & Constitution Avenue NW
Washington, DC 20036
202-458-3000
Fax: 202-458-3967
Supports teaching abroad opportunities.

1558 The American School Foundation of Monterrey
Ave. Ignacio Morones Prieto No. 150
Santa Catarina, N.L., C.P.
Mexico, MX 66190
(52)-81-5000-4400
Fax: (52)-81-5000-4428
www.asfm.edu.mx
providing the type of learning environment which will prepare its students to successfully assume their role in the international community during the current millennium.
Jeff Keller, Superintendent
Jeff Farrington, Principal

1559 The British School, Rio de Janeiro
R Real Grandeza 99
Botafogo, Rio de Janeiro
Brazil, BR 22281-30
55 21 2539-2717
Fax: 55 21 2244-5591
edu@britishschool.g12.br
www.britishschool.g12.br
The British School aims to develop responsible, well-informed, open-minded, confident and caring individuals by providing an educational community within which all pupils are motivated to realize their full potential through a challenging British-based education in a non-discriminatory and bi-cultural environment.
John Nixon, Director
Claudia Ribeiro, Finance & Admin Manager

1560 Uruguayan American School
Av Saldon de Rodriguez
Montevideo
Uruguay 11500-3360
598-2-600-7681
Fax: 598-2-606-1935
www.uas.edu.uy
Uruguayan American School is to provide, together with the family, a balanced college preparatory education. UAS integrates a US style curriculum with Uruguayan studies to equip our national and international students to be successful in a diverse, ever changing world
Mike Schramm, Director
Cecilia Burgueo, UP Coordinator

1561 William T Sampson
Elementary & High School
PSC 1005 Box 49
FPO, Guantanamo Bay 09593 0005
Cuba

Eastern Europe

1562 American Academy Larnaca
Gregory Afxentious Avenue
PO Box 40112, Larnaca
Cyprus 06301
357-248-5400
Fax: 357-246-1046
info@academy.ac.cy
www.academy.ac.cy
Non-profit making school that is supported by an active multi-functional operation to achieve its core purpose: pre-school to University entrance education of the highest standard. It is a private, selective, co-educational, independent school, registered under the Private Schools' Law, 1971, of the Republic of Cyprus and uniquely, is run by its own graduates.
Doros Neocleous, Principal
Tom Widdows, Director

1563 American College of Sofia
PO Box 873
Sofia
Bulgaria, 1000
(359-2) 434 10 10
Fax: (359-2) 434 10 09
acs@acsbg.org
www.acs.bg
The American College of Sofia integrates the values and best practices of American pedagogy with the rich educational traditions of Bulgaria and Europe. The college aims to develop critical thinking, leadership and collaboration among multi-talented students of various social, cultural, economic and geographic backgrounds.
Richard T Ewing, Jr, Ph.D, President
Maria Angelova, Deputy Director

1564 American International School-Bucharest
Sos Pipera-Tunari 196
Voluntari Jud Ilfov 077190
Romania
40-21-2044300
Fax: 40-21-2044306
office@aisb.ro
www.aisb.ro
The American International School of Bucharest is a multicultural and international learning community, located in Romania. English is the principal language of instruction.
David Ottaviano Ed D, Director
Tamara Shreve, Elementary Principal

1565 American International School-Budapest
PO Box 53
Budapest
Hungary 01525
36 26 556 000
Fax: 36 26 556 003
www.aisb.hu
The American International School of Budapest (AISB) is a private and independent co-educational day school governed by a

Board of Directors elected and appointed from the parent community. Established in 1973 by the United States Embassy to serve United States Government employees' dependents, AISB currently serves the needs of a rapidly expanding international population, including children of the local and expatriate business and diplomatic communities.

Ray Holliday Bersegeay, School Director
Larry Kinde, Chairman

1566 American International School-Cyprus
PO Box 23847, 11 Kassos Street
1086 Nisocia
Cyprus
357-22-316345
Fax: 357-22-316549
aisc@aisc.ac.cy
www.aisc.ac.cy
Founded in 1987, a private, coeducational, college preparatory day school providing a first class American and international university preparatory education within the Cyprus local community that incorporates a Greek as a First Language program for our Cypriot students.

Michelle Kleiss, Director
Terry Wolfson, Principal

1567 American International School-Krakow
Lusina ul. sw. Floriana 57
30-698 Krak¢w
Poland
48 12 270-1409
Fax: 48 12 270-1409
director@iskonline.org
Affiliated with the American School of Warsaw, AISK is an independent, coeducational day school which offers an educational program from preschool through grade 8 for students of all nationalities.

Ellen Deitsch Stern, Director

1568 American International School-Vienna
Salmannsdorfer Strasse 47
A-1190 Vienna
Austria
43-1-40-132-0
Fax: 43-1-40-132-5
info@ais.at
www.ais.at
Provide a culture of educational excellence, a nurturing environment, and an atmosphere of open communication and aims to prepare a diverse student body for higher education; to inspire the youth to realize their potential; to foster life-long learning, tolerance, personal integrity, and democratic values; and to prepare students to become responsible adults, with respect for different cultures and beliefs.

Carol Kluznik, Director
Gail McMillan, HS Principal

1569 American School of Bucharest
Sos Pipera-Tunari 196
Voluntari Jud Ilfov
Romania 07719
40-21-2044300
Fax: 40-21-2044306
office@aisb.ro
www.aisb.ro
An independent, international, coeducational day school which offers an educational program from prekindergarten through grade 12 for students of all nationalities.

David Ottaviano, Director
Jeri Guthrie Corn, Chair

1570 Asuncion Christian Academy
Avenida Santisimo Sacramento
1181 Casilla 1562
Asuncion, Paraguay-1209
011-595-21-607-378
Fax: 011-595-21-604-855
aca@aca.edu.py
www.acaknights.org/
Asuncion Christian Academy believes that the best education to prepare a student for adult life is an education based upon the truth of God's Word and having a growing and personal relationship with Jesus Christ.

Bethany Abreu, Director

1571 Falcon School
PO Box 23640
Nicosia
Cyprus 01685
357 22 424781
Fax: 357 22 313764
falconschool@cytanet.com.cy
www.falconschool.ac.cy/default.asp?id=261

Nikolas Michael Ieride, Principal

1572 Gimnazija Bezigrad
Periceva ulica 4
PO Box 2504
Ljubljana 01001-1001
Fax: 010-044-
info@gimb.org
www.gimb.org
Assistance to parents in raising gifted children to full and productive adulthood

Cyril Dominko, Principal
Janez Sustersic, Director

1573 International Elementary School-Estonia
Juhkentali 18
Tallinn
Estonia 10132
372-666-4380
Fax: 372-666-4383
office@ise.edu.ee
www.ise.edu.ee
Provide high-quality, international education; maximize personal potential; develop life-long learners who appreciate diversity; foster active, compassionate world citizens

Don Fitzmahan, Director
Terje Akke, PYP Coordinator

1574 International School-Belgrade
Temisvarska 19
Belgrade
Serbia 11040
381 11 206-9999
Fax: 381 11 206-9940
isb@isb.rs
www.isb.rs
An independent, coeducational day school which offers an educational program from kindergarten through grade 8 for students of all nationalities.

Dr. Eric Sands, Director
Sanja Ilic, Admissions Director

1575 International School-Budapest
P.O. Box 53
Budapest
Hungary 01525
36 26 556 000
Fax: 36 26 556 003
admissions@aisb.hu
www.aisb.hu
Grade levels N-8, school year August - June

Ray Holliday-Bersegeay, Director

1576 International School-Estonia
Juhkentali 18
Tallinn
Estonia 10132
372-666-4380
Fax: 372-666-4383
office@ise.edu.ee
www.ise.edu.ee
Provides high-quality, international education, maximize personal potential, develop life-long learners who appreciate diversity and foster active, compassionate world citizens.

Don Fitzmahan, Terje
Akke PYP Coordinator

1577 International School-Latvia
Viestura iela 6a
Jurmala
Latvia LV 20
(+371) 6775 5146
Fax: (+371) 6775 5009
merliha@isl.edu.lv
www.isl.edu.lv
Offers English-language, academically challenging programmes designed to develop life-long learners who are critical, creative and open-minded thinkers prepared and motivated to meet the diverse challenges of an ever-changing environment; act with integrity and responsibility locally and globally to transform their world in positive ways and appreciate and respect human diversity.

Larry Molacek, Director
Kevin Reimer, Deputy Director

1578 International School-Paphos
100 Aristotelous Savva Avenue
PO Box 62018, Paphos
Cyprus 08025
26 821700ÿ
Fax: 26 942541
info@isop-ed.org
www.isop-ed.org
The school caters for the needs of children from Kindergarten to Year 13. Its mission is to serve each and every one of the pupils as part of our school family and as an individual.

Litsa Olympiou, Headmistress

1579 International School-Prague
Nebusicka 700
164 00 Prague 6
Czech Republic
420 2 2038 4111
Fax: 420-2-2038-4555
ispmail@isp.cz
www.isp.cz
Educates students to be responsible, productive, ethical and healthy citizens with the ability to think creatively, reason critically, and communicate effectively through a variety of educational philosophies and methods, combining the best methodology and practices from a variety of national systems with an international perspective.

Rajiv Bhatt, Director
Barry Freckmann, Business Manager

1580 International Teachers Service
47 Papakyriazi Street
Larissa, Greece
41-253856
Fax: 41-251022
A recruitment service for teachers of English in Greece. Must have a BA/BS in education preferably English and/or EFL training or past experience in EFL and be a native speaker of English.

Fani Karatzou

81 Kiev International School
3A Svyatoshinsky Provuluk
Kyiv
Ukraine 03115
380-44-452-2792
Fax: 380-44-452-2998
kiev@qsi.org
www.qsi.org
Kyiv International School, a private non-profit institution

Scott D'Alterio, Director
David Pera, Director Instruction

82 Limassol Grammar-Junior School
10 Manoli Kalomiri & Theklas Lisiot
PO Box 51340
Limassol, Cyprus 03504
357-257-7933
Fax: 357-257-7818
junior@grammarschool.com.cy
The primary goal of the Grammar School is to provide its students with a solidly grounded liberal education. Thus, it seeks to encourage the intellectual, spiritual, and physical development of its students.

EWP Foley, Principal
Demetris Gregoriou, Director

583 Logos School of English Education
33-35 Yialousa Street
PO Box 51075 Limassol
Cyprus 03501
357-25336061
Fax: 357-25335578
Principal@Logos.ac.cy
www.logos.ac.cy

Gary Love, Principal

584 Magyar British International School
H-1519 Budapest
PO Box 219, Budapest
Hungary
361-466-9794
www.bisb.hu

Mary E Pazsit, Principal

585 Melkonian Educational Institute
PO Box 1907
Nicosia
Cyprus
www.englishschool.ac.cy/?link=contact.php

An Armenian boarding school with high academic standards.

S Bedikan, Principal

586 Private English Junior School
P.O Box 23575
Nicosia
Cyprus 01684
357-22 -9930
Fax: 357-22 -9930
info@englishschool.ac.cy
www.englishschool.ac.cy/?link=contact.ph

Vassos Hajierou, BA, Principal

587 QSI International School-Bratislava
Karloveska 64
Bratislava
Slovak Republic 842-2
421-2-6542-2844
Fax: 421-2-6541-1646
bratislava@qsi.org
www.qsi.org
To keep this urge to learn alive in every child in QSI schools. Our schools are established to provide in the English language a quality education for students in the cities we serve.

Britt Brantley, Director

1588 QSI International School-Ljubljana
Dolgi most 6A
1000 Ljubljana
Solvenia
386-1-2441750
Fax: 386-1-2441754
ljubljana@qsi.org
www.qsi.org
To keep this urge to learn alive in every child in QSI schools. Our schools are established to provide in the English language a quality education for students in the cities we serve.

Jay Loftin, Director

1589 QSI International School-Tbilisi
Village Zurgovani
Tbilisi
Republic of Georgia
995-32-53767
Fax: 995-32-322607
tbilisi@qsi.org
www.qsi.org
To keep this urge to learn alive in every child in QSI schools. Our schools are established to provide in the English language a quality education for students in the cities we serve.

James Rehberg, Director

1590 QSI International School-Yerevan
PO Box 82, Ashtarok Highway
Yerevan
Republic of Armenia 37501
374-10-349130
Fax: 374-10-397599
yerevan@qsi.org
www.qsi.org
To keep this urge to learn alive in every child in QSI schools. Our schools are established to provide in the English language a quality education for students in the cities we serve.

Douglas Shippert, Director

Middle East

1591 ACI & SEV Elementary School
Inonu Caddesi No 476
Goztepe, Izmir
Turkey 35290
90-232-285-3401
Fax: 90-232-246-1674
www.aci.k12.tr
Contribute to the growth of individuals who combine self-confidence with a firm sense of personal, social, and environmental responsibility. Enable students to be strong bilinguals in English and Turkish, well-educated adults, lifelong learners, and efficient communicators, who have developed skills, accountability, and attitudes for leading a fulfilling life and for serving their country and humanity.

Charles C Hanna, Director
Anet Gomel, Turkish First Vice Principal

1592 Abdul Hamid Sharaf School
PO Box 6008
Amman
Jordan 11118
962-615-2418
Fax: 962-651-2462
ahss@go.com.jo
www.ahss.edu.jo
A private, coeducational, K-12 day school serving the needs of a diverse group of students, international and local. Languages of instruction for the basic subjects are Arabic and English.

Sue Dahdah, Director

1593 Abquaiq Academy
PO Box 31677
Al-Khobar
Saudi Arabia 31952
966-3 5-6 04
Fax: 966-3 5-6 23
abqaiq@isgdh.org
The sole purpose of the school is for serving the educational needs of children from expatriate families.

Vineeta Dambal, Administrator/Principal

1594 Al Ain English Speaking School
PO Box 17939
Al Ain
United Arab Emirates
00971-3-7678636
Fax: 00971-3-767-1973
school@aaess.sch.ae
www.aaess.com
Al Ain English Speaking School is a member of the Association of British Schools in the Middle East and the Incorporated Association of Preparatory Schools (UK). The basic curriculum is that of the National Curriculum of England.

Peter Hodge, Principal

1595 Al Bayan Bilingual School
PO Box 24472
Safat 13105
Kuwait
965 2227 - 5000
Fax: 965 2227 - 5002
bbsjadm@bbs.edu.kw
www.bbs.edu.kw
A non-profit Arabic-English university preparatory educational institution, which fosters an environment for students to develop the intellectual qualities, ethical values, and positive attitudes required for effective participation and leadership in the overall development of Kuwait and the rapidly changing world.

Brian L McCauley, Director

1596 Al Khubairat Community School
PO Box 4001
Abu Dhabi
United Arab Emirates
971-244- 228
Fax: 971-244-6819
www.britishschool.sch.ae
British curriculum school for children aged 3 to 18.It is a non-profit school administered by a Board consisting of parent representatives and nominees of the British Ambassador.

Paul Coackley, Principal

1597 Al Rabeeh School
PO Box 41807
Abu Dhabi
United Arab Emirates
971 2 4482856
Fax: 971 2 4482854
www.alrabeeh.sch.ae/

HJ Kadri, Principal

1598 Al-Nouri English School
PO Box 46901
Fahaheel
Kuwait

PD Oldfield, Principal

1599 Al-Worood School
PO Box 46673
Abu Dhabi
United Arab Emirates
971-2-444-7655
Fax: 971-2-444-9732
www.alworood.sch.ae/alworood/StaticContentDetails.asp

Grade levels N-12, school year September - June

Ahmed Osman, Academic Principal
Abdulla Al Nuwais, President

1600 American Collegiate Institute
Inonu Caddesi #476 Goztepe
Izmir
Turkey 35290
90-232-285-3401
Fax: 90-232-246-4128
www.aci.k12.tr
Offers a 1 + 4 year academic program. Students enter the school based upon a competitive national high-school entrance exam needing to improve their English language skills go into the intensive English one-year preparatory program before entering the school's rigorous four-year educational program.

Charles C Hanna, Director
Anet Gomel, First Vice Principal

1601 American Community School
Rue de Paris, Jel El Bahr
PO Box 11-8129, Riad El Solh
Beirut, Lebanon 01107-2260
961-1-374-370
Fax: 961-1-366-050
www.acs.edu.lb
Founded in 1905, an independent, non-profit, non-sectarian, pre-K-12 coeducational day school.

George Damon, Headmaster
David Warren, Deputy Headmaster

1602 American Community School-Abu Dhabi
PO Box 42114
Abu Dhabi
United Arab Emirates
971-2-681-5115
Fax: 971-2-681-6006
acs@acs.sch.ae
www.acs.sch.ae
The mission is to empower and inspire all students to define and shape their futures, pursue their dreams and contribute to society.

Dr George Robinson, Superintendent
Waheeda Al Tamimi, Administrative Assistant

1603 American Community School-Beirut
Rue de Paris, Jel El Bahr
PO Box 11-8129, Riad El Solh
Beirut, Lebanon 01107-2260
961-1-374-370
Fax: 961-1-366-050
www.acs.edu.lb
Founded in 1905, an independent, non-profit, non-sectarian, pre-K-12 coeducational day school. It draws students from both the Lebanese and international communities in Lebanon and embraces diversity in race, gender, religion, national origin and economic background.

Dr George Robinson, Superintendent
David Warren, Deputy Headmaster

1604 American International School
PO Box 22090
Doha
Qatar
974-445-0150
Fax: 974-445-0157
info@asd.edu.qa
www.asd.edu.qa
The American School of Doha is an independent, U.S. accredited, college preparatory school, committed to provide the highest standard of educational excellence, through an enriched American curriculum.

Deborah Welch, Director
Michael Shahen, High School Principal

1605 American International School-Abu Dhabi
PO Box 5992
Abu Dhabi
United Arab Emirates
971-2-444-4333
Fax: 971-2-444-4005
admissions@aisa.sch.ae
www.aisa.sch.ae
Founded in 1995 to serve the needs of the local and expatriate residents of Abu Dhabi who want their children to pursue both American and International Baccalaureate curricula in an international setting.

Gareth Jones, Director
Abdulla Al-Hashly, Chairman

1606 American International School-Israel
PO Box 484, 65 Hashomron St
Even Yehuda
Israel 40500
972-9-890-1000
Fax: 972-9-890-1001
www.wbais.org/~joomla/index.php?option=com_frontpage&
An independent, coeducational day school which offers an educational program from kindergarten through grade 12 for students of all nationalities.

Richard Detwiler, Principal

1607 American International School-Kuwait
PO Box 3267
Salmiya
Kuwait 22033
(965) 22255155
Fax: (965) 22255156
www.aiskuwait.org
Grade levels kindergarten through twelfth.

Samera Al Rayes, Owner/Director
Noreen Hawley, Superintendent

1608 American International School-Muscat
PO Box 584
Azaiba Postal Code 130
Sultanate of Oman
968 24 595 180
Fax: 968 24 503 815
www.taism.com
Pursues academic excellence for students in the international community through an American-based education that develops ethical, responsible, and globally conscious life-long learners.

Kevin Schafer, Director
Keith Boniface, High School Principal

1609 American International School-Riyadh
PO Box 990
Riyadh
Saudi Arabia 11421
966-1-491-4270
Fax: 966-1-491-7101
registration@ais-r.edu.sa
www.aisr.org
As a school committed to excellence, we will educate and inspire our students to be responsible, productive and ethical world citizens with the skills and passion to think creatively, reason critically, communicate effectively and learn continuously. We will accomplish this in an American educational environment characterized by high measurable standards and a clearly defined, appropriately interrelated college preparatory curriculum, implemented by a superior staff in partnership with parents a

Dr. Dennis Larkin, Superintendent

1610 American School-Doha
PO Box 22090
Doha
Qatar
974-4459-1500
Fax: 974-4459-1570
www.asd.edu.qa
is an independent, U.S. accredited, college preparatory school, committed to provide the highest standard of educational excellence, through an enriched American curriculum

Deborah Welch, Director
Colin Boudreau, High School Principal

1611 American School-Kuwait
PO Box 6735
Hawalli
Kuwait 32040
965-266-4341
Fax: 965-265-0438
ask@ask.edu.kw
www.ask.edu.kw
It is a privately owned, independent coeducational day school which offers a general academic curriculum for students of all nationalities

Bernard Mitchell, Superintendent
Fawsi Hasan, Arabic Studies Principal

1612 American-British Academy
PO Box 372
Medinat Al Sultan Qaboos
Sultanate of Oman PC 11
968-24603646
Fax: 968-24603544
admin@abaoman.edu.om
www.abaoman.edu.om
Provides an international education of the highest quality to enable students to be confident, responsible, caring life-long learners.

Mona Nashman-Smith, Superintendent
Rod Harding, Director of Operations

1613 Amman Baccalaureate School
PO Box 441
Sweileh Amman
Jordan 11910
962-6-541-1191/7
Fax: 962-6-541-2603
info@abs.edu.jo
www.abs.edu.jo
A coeducational and non-profit school which caters to students aged 3-18 years that offers an academically rigorous programme, enriched by extensive co-curricular activities, that culminates in the International Baccalaureate Diploma or Certificates.

Stuart Bryan, Principal
Robert Jones, Vice-Principal

1614 Anglican International School-Jerusalem
82 Rechov Haneviim
PO Box 191 Jerusalem
Israel 91001
972-2-567-7200
Fax: 972-2-538-474
www.aisj.co.il
An internationally accredited, pre-Kindergarten to Grade 12 [ages 3-18] school. It creates student-focused academic and educational environment which aspires to achieve excellence.

Owen Hoskin, Director
Matthew Dufty, Deputy Principal

15 Ankara Elementary & High School
PSC 89 Unit 7010
APO, Ankara 09822 7010
Turkey
011-90-312-287-253
Fax: 011-90-312-285-179
AnkaraEHS.Principal@eu.dodea.edu
www.anka-ehs.eu.dodea.edu/

Kathleen Reiss, Principal
Rosie Uluer, Assistant Principal

16 Arab Unity School
PO Box 10563
Rashidiya, Dubai
United Arab Emirates
971-4-886-226
Fax: 971 4 2886321
www.arabunityschool.com
Provide an equal opportunity, to all students, to develop their intellectual faculties and to awaken their latent, creative talents, irrespective of their ethnic background.

Zainab A Taher, Founder Director

17 Baghdad International School
PO Box 571
Baghdad
Iraq

Amen A Rihani, Principal

18 Bahrain Bayan School
PO Box 32411
Isa Town
Bahrain
973-682-227
Fax: 973-780-019
bayanschool@bayan.edu.bh
www.bayanschool.edu.bh
A bilingual, coeducational, college preparatory school with an international curriculum and faculty. It aims to preserve the tenets of Arabic /Islamic values, to assist students to a depth of cross-cultural knowledge and to promote the global perspective necessary for future world citizens.

Dr Nakhle Wehbe, Director General
Gilbert Daoura, Operations Manager

619 Bahrain Elementary & High School
Psc 451 Box 690
FPO Bahrain
Bahrain 09834-5200
973 1772-7828
Fax: 973 1772-8583
www.bahr-ehs.eu.dodea.edu/
Grade levels K-12.

Gail Anderson, Principal

620 Bahrain School
PO Box 934
Juffair
Bahrain
973 1772-7828
Fax: 973 1772-8583
BahrainEHS.Principal@eu.dodea.edu
www.bahr-ehs.eu.dodea.edu/
To provide a safe environment in which our students are challenged to their maximum potential as responsible members of a multi-cultural society.

Gail Anderson, Principal
Laura Bleck, Assistant Principal

621 Bilkent University Preparatory School-Bilkent International School
East Campus
Bilkent Ankara
Turkey 06800
90 312 290 53 61
Fax: 90 312 266 49 63
BUPS serves the educational needs of selected Turkish students while BIS serves the needs of selected international students in the Ankara area.

James Swetz, Director
Dan Keller, Associate Director

1622 Bishop's School
PO Box 2001
Amman
Jordan
962-6-653668
This Episcopal boy's school, founded in 1936, teaches both the Jordanian Curricula and the London University General Certification of Education Curriculum. Total enrollment is 855 day students in grades 1-12. Length of stay for teachers is one year with no housing provided. Languages spoken are English and Arabic.

Najib F Elfarr, Principal
Jamil Ismair, Faculty Head

1623 British Aircraft Corp School
PO Box 3843
Riyadh
Saudi Arabia

MR Pound, Principal

1624 British Embassy Study Group
Sehit Ersan Caddesi 46A, 06680
Cankaya Ankara
Turkey 06680
90 (312) 468 6563
Fax: 90 (312) 468 6239
BESG is a co-educational primary school with 135 children aged between 3 and 11, representing nearly 26 countries. We are known as a friendly and caring British school, which values a holistic approach to education

Dawn Akyurek, Head Teacher
Katie Vincent, Deputy Head Teacher

1625 British International School-Istanbul
Dilhayat Sokak No:18 Etiler
Istanbul
Turkey, TR
90 (0) 212 257 51
Fax: 90-0-212-257 53 33
www.bis.k12.tr
The British International School Istanbul (BISI) provides a wide range of educational choices for international families. We are a private, coeducational school providing British-style international education for 520 students of 40 nationalities between the ages of 2r and 18.

Graham Pheby, Principal
Roger Short, Governor of the School

1626 Cairo American College
PO Box 39
Maadi 11431
Cairo, EG 11431
(20-2) 2755-5507
Fax: 20-2-519-6584
support@cacegypt.org
www.cacegypt.org
Cairo American College is a world class learning environment that affirms the voice, passions and talents of students and inspires them to use their hearts and minds as global citizens.

Nivine Captan-Amr, Board Chair
Elizabeth Bredin, Secretary

1627 Cambridge High School
PO Box 60835
Dubai
United Arab Emirates
971 - 4 282 4646
Fax: 971 - 4 282 4109

David Mcaughlin, Principal
Nigel Cropley, Vice Principal

1628 Continental School (Sais British)
PO Box 6453
Jeddah 21442
Saudi Arabia
966-269-9001
Fax: 966-269-9194
www.continentalschool.com
Inspire in students a love of learning using a child centered, British style of education. Strive for excellence, recognizing, celebrating and encouraging a spirit of internationalism.

Bruce Gamwell, Director
Marina Alibhai, Registrar

1629 Dhahran Academy International School Group
PO Box 31677
Al Khobar 31952
Saudi Arabia 31952
966-3-330-0555
Fax: 966-3-330-2450
info@isgdh.org
www.isgdh.org
Grades preSchool-11, enrollment 994.

Norma Hudson, Superintendent

1630 Dhahran Central School
PO Box 31677
Dhahran 31311
Saudi Arabia 31952
966-3-330-0555
Fax: 966-3-330-2450
info@isgdh.org
www.isgdh.org

Norma Hudson, Principal

1631 Dhahran Hills School
PO Box 31677
Dhahran 31311
Saudi Arabia 31952
966-3-330-0555
Fax: 966-3-330-2450
info@isgdh.org
www.isgdh.org

Norma Hudson, Principal

1632 Doha College-English Speaking
PO Box 7660
Doha Qatar
Arabian Gulf
974-806-770
Fax: 974-806-311
dess@dess.org
www.dess.org
An independent, coeducational day school which offers an educational program from children of all nationalities from kindergarten through grade12.

E Goodwin, Principal
Emad Turkman, Chairman

1633 Doha English Speaking School
PO Box 7660
Doha
Qatar
(974) 44592750
Fax: ÿ(974) 44592761
dess@dess.org
www.dess.org
Create a happy, secure, stimulating and supportive learning environment

Emad Turkman, Chairman
Eddie Liptrot, Head Teacher

1634 Doha Independent School
PO Box 5404
Doha Qatar
Arabian Gulf
SJ Williams, Principal

1635 Emirates International School
PO Box 6446
Dubai
United Arab Emirates
971-4-348-9804
Fax: 971-4-348-2813
mail@eischools.ae
www.eischools.ae
We offer a broad international education, in English, designed for local and expatriate students, that promotes excellence in all academic activities. It is our mission to enhance the educational, social and physical development of our students encouraging them to think analytically and creatively in preparation for the next stage of their education.
Daryle Russell, EdD, Headmaster
Jason Kirwin, HS Principal

1636 English School-Fahaheel
PO Box 7209
Fahaheel
Kuwait 64003
096-023-1010
Fax: 096-023-1054
esf@skee.com
www.skee.com
The English School Fahaheel recognizes the need for all students to be made aware of the demands placed upon them for Further Education and the world of work.
Ibrahim J Shuhaiber, Chairman
John J MacGregor, Principal

1637 English School-Kuwait
PO Box 379
Safat
Kuwait 13004
965-256-7205
Fax: 965-256-7147
www.tes.edu.kw
The English School was founded in 1953 under the auspices of the British Embassy and is the longest established school in Kuwait catering for the expatriate community. The School operates as a not-for-profit independent co-educational establishment providing the highest standards in education for children of Pre-Preparatory and Preparatory School age.
William James Strath, Principal
Richard Davis, Chair

1638 English Speaking School
PO Box 2002
Dubai
United Arab Emirates
974-445- 275
Fax: 974-445- 276
www.dessdxb.com
The school opened in 1963 in the upstairs room of a villa where expatriate workers were housed. There was one class which was taught by parents and a British Officer called Flight Lieutenant F. Loughman.
Bernadette McCarty, Principal
David Hammond, Headteacher

1639 Enka Okullari-Enka Schools
Sadi Gulcelik Spor Sitesi
Istinye, Istanbul
Turkey 34460
90-212-276-05-4547
Fax: 90-212-286-59-3035
Enka Schools provide an international education for our students. We have a well qualified and passionate group of teachers from Turkey and overseas. Most of our students are Turkish while some of them have international backgrounds.
Darlene Fisher, Director
Ayten Yilmaz, Preschool Principal

1640 Gulf English School
PO Box 2440
Doha
Qatar
974-445-8 77
Fax: 974-448-1 25
info@gulfenglishschool.com
www.gulfenglishschool.com
Provide a positive and stimulating environment which facilitates individual learning, encourages experimentation, and develops critical thinking and problem solving skills. We must enable each student to achieve his or her best in the pursuit of academic excellence, and give them the confidence to be independent thinkers, able to assume responsibility and leadership and to take their place in the wider world
Paul Andrews, Principal
Tim Brosnan, Faculty Head

1641 Habara School
PO Box 26510
Bahrain
973-172- 173
www.ameinfo.com
PM Wrench, Principal

1642 IBN Khuldoon National School
Po Box 20511
Manama
Bahrain
973-16-687-073
Fax: 973-17-689-028
info@ikns.edu.bh
www.ikns.edu.bh
This IBN school is a private, fee paying, non-profit, coeducational, accredited middle states school. The curriculum offered to the 1,210 day students (630 boys and 580 girls) in grades K-12, is English/Arabic. The school is willing to participate in a teacher exchange program with the applications needed being science, math, social sciences, pre-school and English.
Kamal Abdel-Nour, President
Ghada R Bou Zeineddine, Principal

1643 Incirlik Elementary School
Unit 7180 Box 270
APO AE 09824
Turkey
011-90-322-316-310
Fax: 011-90-322-332-757
IncirlikEHS.Principal@eu.dodea.edu
www.inci-ehs.eu.dodea.edu/
Mary Davis, Principal

1644 Incirlik High School
Unit 7180 Box 270
APO AE 09824
Turkey
011-90-322-316-310
Fax: 011-90-322-332-757
IncirlikEHS.Principal@eu.dodea.edu
www.inci-ehs.eu.dodea.edu/
Dr. Donald Torrey, Principal

1645 Infant School-House #45
Khalil Kando Gardens Road, 5651
Manama
Bahrain
Maria Stiles, Principal

1646 International Community School
PO Box 2002
Amman
Jordan 11181
962-6 5-2 10
Fax: 962-6 5-2 71
office@ics-amman.edu.jo
Ours is a school where people matter. ~We want good results for each student, according to his or her own abilities in the classroom, in sport , music, drama or art.
John Light, Principal
Sue Hill, Primary Head

1647 International School of Choueifat
PO Box 7212
Abu Dhabi
United Arab Emirates
971-2-446-1444
Fax: 971-2-446-1048
iscad@sabis.net
www.iscad-sabis.net
Over the last 27 years hundreds of students have graduated from The International Schools of Choueifat in the region and then graduated from top universities in the world. In the UK, these universities include Oxford, Cambridge, LSE, Bristol, Edinburgh, Bath, Birmingham, Liverpool, The Imperial College of Science and Technology and all other Colleges of London University.
Marilyn Abu-Esber, Director

1648 Istanbul International Community School
Karaagac Mahallesi, G 72 Sokak No:1
Buyukcekmece , Istanbul
Turkey 34866
90-212-857-8264
Fax: 90-212-857-8270
www.iics.k12.tr
Through its challenging curriculum and strong staff-student relationships, IICS provides a caring environment that inspires each student to excel and to be inquisitive, creative, compassionate, balanced and internationally-minded.
Peter Welch, Headmaster
Sean Murphy, Primary Principal

1649 Izmir Elementary & High School
PSC 88
APO, Izmir 09821 0005
Turkey
Terry Emerson, Principal

1650 Jeddah Preparatory School
British Consulate, Box 6316
Jeddah 21442 Saudi Arabia
265-235-
Fax: 065-183-
registrar@jpgs.org
www.jpgs.org/
John GF Parsons, Principal

1651 Jubail British Academy
PO Box 10059 Madinat Al Jubail
Jubail 31961
Saudi Arabia
966.3.341.7550
Fax: 966.3.341.6990
mmcdougall@isgdh.org
www.isg-jubail.org/
Norman Edwards, Principal

52 Jumeirah English Speaking School
PO Box 24942, Dubai
United Arab Emirates
971-4-394-5515
Fax: 971-4-394-3531
jess@jess.sch.ae
www.jess.sch.ae

CA Branson, Headmaster
RD Stokoe, Director

53 King Faisal School
PO Box 94558, Riyadh 11614
Saudia Arabia
966-1-482-0802
Fax: 966-1-482-1521
Grade levels preK-12, enrollment 600.

Mohammed Al-Humood, Director General

54 Koc School
PK 60-Tuzla
Istanbul
Turkey 34941
(90)216 585 6200
Fax: 90-216-304-1048
info@kocschool.k12.tr
www.kocschool.k12.tr
The goal of KoO School is to be respected nationally and internationally as a model K-12 school, offering an educational program of the highest academic and ethical standards.

Suna Kirac, Chairman

55 Kuwait English School
PO Box 8640
Salmiya 22057
Kuwait
256-552-
Fax: 256-293-
keschool@kes.edu.kw
www.kes.edu.kw/?page_id=69

Craig Halsall, Principal

656 Mohammed Ali Othman School
PO Box 5713
Taiz Yeman
Arab Republic
967-422-3671
Fax: 967-4 2-1495
www.maoschool.dx.am
Mohammed Ali Othman School is a well established school which has been running for over thirty years. At present it has around a thousand students from the Foundation Stage through to Year 12

Abdulla Ahmad, Principal
Fowzia Abdo Saeed, Deputy Head

657 Nadeen Nursery & Infant School
PO Box 26367
Adliya
Bahrain
973-177- 888
Fax: 973-177- 888
www.nadeenschool.info/
Nadeen School is dedicated to providing a caring, nurturing, and stimulating environment in which all children can learn and thrive. All of our students are treated with respect, care, and with the utmost sensitivity to their individual needs and requirements.

Pauline Puri, Principal

658 New English School
PO Box 6156
Hawalli
Kuwait, KW 32036
[00965] 25318060
Fax: [00965] 25319924
admin@neskt.com
www.neskt.com
Private, co-educational day-school to offer a British style curriculum from Kindergarten to 'A' level.

Tareq S Rajab, Founder

1659 Pakistan International School-Peshawar
23 Sahibzada Abdual Qayyum Road
University Town
Peshawar
92-441-4428
Fax: 92-441-7272
www.isbi.com
An independent, coeducaional day school which offers an educational program from prekindergarten through grade 8 and supervised correspondence study for the high school grades for all expatriate nationalities.

Angela Coleridge, Principal

1660 Rahmaniah-Taif-Acad International School
American Consulate General, Dhahran
District Saudi Arabia
03 -30 -555
Fax: 03 -30 -450
www.isgdh.org

Dean May, Principal

1661 Ras Al Khaimah English Speaking School
PO Box 975
Ras Al Khaimah
United Arab Emirates
971-7-362-441
Fax: 971-7-362-445
www.rakess.net

Roy Burrows, Principal

1662 Ras Tanura School
PO Box 6140
Ras Tanura
Saudi Arabia 31311
067-367-
david.weston@aramco.com
www.saudiaramco.com

David Weston, Principal

1663 Sanaa International School
PO Box 2002
Sanaa
Yemen
967-1-370192
Fax: 967-1-370-193
qsi-sanaa@qsi.org
www.qsi.org
Sanaa International School, a non-profit institution that opened in September 1971 offers a high quality education in the English language for pre-school, elementary, and secondary students. The Campus is located on 34 acres on the outskirts of Sanaa constructed and entered in September 1978.

Mr. Philip Weirich, Director

1664 Saudi Arabian International British School
PO Box 85769
Riyadh
Saudi Arabia 11612
966- 12-8 23
Fax: 966- 12-8 23
principal@britishschoolriyadh.com
www.britishschoolriyadh.com
Improve standards of teaching, learning and citizenship within a safe and secure environment. Our Mission Statement and School Improvement Plan provide the direction for the future development of our pupils and the continuous improvement of our school.

Peter Wiles, Acting Principal
Terry Sayce, Chairman

1665 Saudi Arabian International School-Dhahran
SAIS-DD, Box 677
Dhahran International Airport
Dhahran 31932, Saudi Arabia
996-3-330-0555
Fax: 966-3-330-0555
www.isgdh.org/

Dr. Leo Ruberto, Principal

1666 Saudi Arabian International School-Riyadh
PO Box 990
Riyadh
Kingdom of Saudi Arabia 11421
966-1-491-4270
Fax: 966-1-491-7101
registration@ais-r.edu.sa
www.aisr.org
Educate and inspire our students to be responsible, productive and ethical world citizens with the skills and passion to think creatively, reason critically, communicate effectively and learn continuously. We will accomplish this in an American educational environment characterized by high measurable standards and a clearly defined, appropriately interrelated college preparatory curriculum, implemented by a superior staff in partnership with parents and community.

Daryle Russell, EdD, Principal
Brian Matthews, Superintendent

1667 Saudia-Saudi Arabian International School
PO Box 167, CC 100
Jeddah 21231
Saudi Arabia

John Hazelton, Principal

1668 Sharjah English School
PO Box 1600
Sharjah
United Arab Emirates
971-655- 930
Fax: 971- 55- 930
www.seschool.ae
Not for profit school. It is self-supporting and financed by fees paid by parents for the education of their children.

David Throp, Principal
Jenefer Race, Primary Headteacher

1669 Sharjah Public School
PO Box 6125, Sharjah
United Arab Emirates
971-652- 124
www.sharjahpublicschool.ae

Nazim Khan, Principal

1670 St. Mary's Catholic High School
PO Box 52232
Dubai
United Arab Emirates
009-104-3370
Fax: 009-104-3368
maryscol@emirates.net.ae
www.stmarysdubai.com
St. Mary's Catholic High School is reputed for its high standards in academic work and also in the standards of discipline which we try to inspire in the children.

Sr Anne Marie Quigg, Principal
U D'Souza, Vice Principal

1671 Sultan's School
PO Box 665
Seeb
Sultanate of Oman 00121
968-24 -367
Fax: 968-24 -362
www.sultansschool.org
The Sultan's School is a co-educational school offering a bilingual Arabic-English education from early childhood to pre-university.
Anthony J Cashin, Principal

1672 Sunshine School
2 Dutcher Avenue
Pawling, NY 12564
845-855-9238
Fax: 845-855-0222
Our goal is to provide a quality pre-school education for young children. We do this by addressing both the social and the intellectual development of the child.
David Brinded, Principal

1673 Tarsus American College and SEV Primary
Cengiz Topel Cd Caminur Mah 201 Sk
Tarsus/Mersin
Turkey 33440
90-324-613-5402
Fax: 90-324-624-6347
info@tac.k12.tr
www.tac.k12.tr
The mission of Tarsus American Schools is to contribute to the growth of individuals who combine self-confidence with a firm sense of personal and social responsibility.
Bernard Mitchell, PhD, Superintendent
Jale Sever, Primary School Principal

1674 Universal American School
PO Box 17035
Khalidiya
Kuwait 72451
965-562-0297/561
Fax: 965-562-5343
uas@qualitynet.net
www.uas.edu.kw
The Universal American School is a private, college-preparatory, N-12 school serving a multinational student body from the diverse populations residing in Kuwait
Nora Al-Ghanim, Administrative Director
Mike Church, Assistant Principal

1675 Uskudar American Academy
Vakif Sokak Number 1
Baglarbasi Istanbul
Turkey, TR
90-216-310-6823
Fax: 90-216-333-1818
wshepard@uaa.k12.tr
www.uaa.k12.tr
The mission of SEV/ABH Schools is to contribute to the growth of individuals who combine self-confidence with a firm sense of personal, social, and environmental responsibility. We aim to enable our students to be strong bilinguals in English and Turkish, well-educated adults, lifelong learners, and efficient communicators, who have developed skills, accountability, and attitudes for leading a fulfilling life and for serving their country and humanity
Whitman Shepard, Director
Dilek Yakar, Primary Principal

1676 Walworth Barbour American International School in Israel
65 Hashomron Street
PO Box 484
Israel 40500
972-9-961-8100
Fax: 972-9-961-8111
Through a rigorous and dynamic American international curriculum, AIS, a private secular school in Israel, inspires each student to cultivate a respect for diversity, develop a passion for life-long learning, achieve academic potential, assume leadership, contribute actively to society, and resolve conflict through dialogue and understanding
Robert A Sills, Superintendent
John Chere, Chairman

Western Europe

1677 AC Montessori Kids
Route De Renipont 4
Lasne B-1380
Belgium
32-2-633-6652
Fax: 32-2-633-6652
A bilingual English/French Montessori School for children aged18 months - 12 years.
Laurence Randoux, Director
Mark Ciepers, Director

1678 AFCENT Elementary & High School
Unit 21606
APO AE 09703
Brunssum, Netherlands
www.afcent.org

1679 Abbotsholme School
Rocester (Uttoxeter, Staffordshire)
ST14 5BS
England
01889-590217
Fax: 01889-590001
admissions@abbotsholme.co.uk
www.abbotsholme.com
This interdenominational school offers an English-based curriculum for 78 day students and 166 boarding (152 boys; 92 girls), in grades 7-13.
Darrell J Farrant, MA, FRSA, Principal
Steve Fairclough, Head

1680 Academy-English Prep School
Apartado 1300 Palma D Mallorca
525 W 17th Street Bloomington
Spain, IN 47404
812-333-2882
Fax: 812-339-2253
www.theprepschool.info
CA Walker, Principal

1681 Ackworth School, Ackworth
Pontefract, West Yorkshire
England WF7 7
0977-611401
admissions@ackworthschool.com
www.ackworthschool.com
This school offers an English-based curriculum to 264 day students and 111 boarding students (180 boys; 195 girls), ages 11-18 years of age.
Peter J Simpson, Head
Jeffrey Swales, Deputy Head, Curriculum

1682 Alconbury Elementary School
Unit 5570 Box 60
APO AE 09470
Great Britain
011-44-1480-843620
Fax: 011-44-1480-843172
AlconburyES.Principal@eu.dodea.edu
To provide a safe and productive learning environment in which all students reach their fullest potential by developing knowledge and skills.
Teddy Emerson, Principal

1683 Alconbury High School
Unit 5570 Box 60
APO AE 09470
Great Britain
441- 80-4 36
Fax: 441- 80-4 31
To develop healthy, adaptable, independently thinking, and socially responsible members of the global community.
Teddy Emerson, Principal
Lance Posey, Assistant Principal

1684 Alexander M Patch Elementary School
Unit 30401
APO AE 09107
Germany
071- 68- 520
Fax: 071- 68- 713
www.patch-es.eu.dodea.edu
Provide a standards-based curriculum that develops lifelong learners and promotes highest student achievement in partnership with our community.
Robert Allen, Principal
Ronald Lathrop, Assistant. Principal

1685 Alexander M Patch High School
Unit 30401
APO AE 09107-0401
Germany
071- 68- 520
Fax: 071- 68- 713
Prepares all students to exceed challenging academic standards, know how to learn, communicate effectively, and make responsible decisions so that they can be continuous learners and productive citizens in a diverse society.
Robert Allen, Principal
Ronald Lathrop, Assistant. Principal

1686 Alfred T Mahan Elementary School
PSC 1003 Box 48
FPO Keflavik 09728
Iceland
Jan Long, Principal

1687 Alfred T Mahan High School
PSC 1003 Box 52
FPO Keflavik 09728 0352
Iceland
M Deatherage, Principal

1688 Amberg Elementary School
CMR 414
APO, Amberg 09173 0005
Germany
Letcher Connell, Principal

1689 Ambrit Rome International School
Via Filippo Tajani, 50
Rome, Italy 00149
39-06-559-5305
ambrit@ambrit-rome.com
www.ambrit-rome.com
Grade levels Pre-K through 8, school year September - June
Bernard C. Mullane, Director
Giovanni Piccolo, Vice Director

90 American College-Greece
6 Gravias Street
Aghia Paraskevi
Athens, Greece GR-15
30-1-600-9800
Fax: 30-1-600-9811
info@acg.edu
www.acg.edu
Founded in 1875, combining the best of American education with the intellectual and cultural heritage of Greece, provide a unique foundation for international educational excellence.

David G Horner, President
Nicholas Jiavaras, Executive Vice President

91 American Community School-Cobham
Heywood, Portsmouth Road
Cobham, Surrey
United Kingdom KT11
44-1932-869-744
Fax: 44-1932-869-789
hayoub@acs-england.co.uk
www.acs-england.co.uk
Promotes a high standard of scholarship, responsibility, and citizenship in a supportive, international community.

Tom Lehman, Head of School
Heidi Ayoub, Dean of Admissions

92 American Community School-Egham
Woodlee London Road (A30)
Egham, Surrey
United Kingdom TW20
44-1784-430-611
Fax: 44-1784-430-626
jlove@acs-england.co.uk
www.acs-england.co.uk
Promotes high standards of scholarship, responsibility and citizenship in a supportive, international community

Julia Love, Dean of Admissions
Moyra Hadley, Head of School

693 American Community School-Hillingdon
108 Vine Lane
Hillingdon, Middlesex
United Kingdom UB10
44-189-581-3734
Fax: 44-189-581-0634
HillingdonAdmissions@acs-england.co.uk
www.acs-england.co.uk
Foundes in 1978, has endeavoured to provide a quality education for a multi-national community in the London area.

Ginger Apple, Head of School
Rudianne Soltis, Dean of Admissions

694 American Community Schools
108 Vine Court
Hillingdon, Uxbridge, Middlesex
UB100BE
England
44-189-581-3734
Fax: 44-189-581-0634
hmulkey@acs-england.co.uk
This school serves the needs of the international business families in Greater London. Programs are nonsectarian, coeducational day schools with lower, middle and high school divisions offering coordinate college preparatory curricula from pre-kindergarten through grade twelve.

Paul Berg, Headmaster

1695 American Community Schools-Athens
129 Aghias Paraskevis Avenue and Ka
Halandri, Athens
Greece 15343
301-639-3200
Fax: 301-639-0051
gialamas@acs.gr
www.acs.gr
Provides a student-centered environment where individuals excel academically and develop intellectually, socially and ethically to thrive as healthy, responsible members of global society.

Stefanos Gialamas, President
Steve Kakaris, Business Manager

1696 American Embassy School-Reykjavik
Lngul nu 8
210 Gardab'r
Iceland
354-590-3106
Fax: 354-590-3110
isi@internationalschool.is
www.internationalschool.is
The International School of Iceland (ISI) is a private elementary school housed in an Icelandic public school, Sjÿlandssk›li. The school offers an international educational program to children in grades 1-7.

Berta Faber, Headmistress
Hanna Hilmarsdottir, Assistant Headmistress

1697 American International School-Carinthia
Friesacher Strasse 3 Audio ICC
A-9330 Althofen
Austria
www.cic-network.at

Ron Presswood, Principal

1698 American International School-Florence
Villa le Tavernule - via del Carota
Bagno a Ripoli, Florence
Italy, VA 50012
39-055-646-1007
Fax: 39-055-644-226
admin.tav@isfitaly.org
www.isfitaly.org
Business Manager

Provide attendees

Christopher Maggio, Head of School
Marie Jos , Manzini

1699 American International School-Genoa
Via Quarto 13-C
Genoa
Italy 16148
39-010-386-528
Fax: 39-010-398-700
www.aisge.it
Provides students of internationally- minded families with a high quality education in the English language, from Pre-School through to the 12th Grade.

Sheldon Friedman, Director
Raffaele Boccardo, President

1700 American International School-Lisbon
Rua Antonio Dos Reis, 95
Linho, 2710-301 Sintra
Portugal
351-21-923-98-00
Fax: 351-21-923-98-26
www.ecis.org
An independent, coeducational day school which offers an educational program from early childhood through grade 12 for student of all nationalities.

Blannie M Curtis, Director

1701 American International School-Rotterdam
Verhulstlaan 21
3055 WJ Rotterdam
Netherlands
31-10-422-5351
Fax: 31-10-422-4075
queries@aisr.nl
www.aisr.nl
Provides a comprehensive program of learning, with well-qualified and experienced faculty who prepare students Pre-School through Grade 12 for the ever-changing world in which we live.

Brian Atkins, Director
Anne-Marie Blitz, Elementary Principal

1702 American International School-Salzburg
Moosstrasse 106
Salzburg A-5020
Austria
43-662-824-617
Fax: 43-662-824-555
www.ais-salzburg.at
A boarding and day school committed to the college-preparatory education of conscientious young men and women. The academic and boarding programs nurture the students' intellectual growth and artistic potential, as well as their social, physical, and personal development.

Paul McLean, Headmaster
Felicia Gundringer, Admissions Coordinator

1703 American International School-Vienna
Salmannsdorfer Strasse 47
A-1190 Vienna
Austria
43-1-401-320
Fax: 43-1-401-325
info@ais.at
www.ais.at
Provide a culture of educational excellence, a nurturing environment, and an atmosphere of open communication and aims to prepare a diverse student body for higher education; to inspire the youth to realize their potential; to foster life-long learning, tolerance, personal integrity, and democratic values; and to prepare students to become responsible adults, with respect for different cultures and beliefs.

Ellen Stern, Director
Dr Greg Moncada, HS Principal

1704 American Overseas School-Rome
Via Cassia 811
Rome, IT 00189
39-06-3326-4841
Fax: 39-06-3326-2608
aosr@aosr.org
www.aosr.org
An independent, coeducational day school for students of all nationalities in prekindergarten through grade 13 and offers a boarding program for select students in grades 9-12.

Beth Kempler, Head of School

1705 American School of the Hague
Rijksstraatweg 200
2241 BX Wassenaar
The Netherlands

31-70-512-1060
Fax: 31-70-511-2400
info@ash.nl
www.ash.nl
educates students to excel in critical inquiry, creative thinking, clear communication, and commitment to others.

Paul De Minico, Superintendent
Douglas Buckley, Chair

1706 American School-Barcelona
Jaume Balmes 7
Esplugues de Llobregat
Spain 08950
34-93-371-4016
Fax: 34-93-473-4787
fully develop each student's unique potential by providing a high quality American/Spanish curriculum in an English-language based, respectful and diverse environment

Nancy Boyd, Elementary School Principal
Bill Volckok, Secondary School Principal

1707 American School-Bilbao
Soparda Bidea 10
Berang (Bizkaia)
Spain 48640
34-94-668-0860
Fax: 34-94-668-0452
asob@asob.es
www.asob.es/en
s a private, non-profit, International School, Offers students an American-style educational programme taught in English. The curriculum has an international focus and leads to the American High School Diploma

Roger West, Director

1708 American School-Las Palmas
Carretera de los Hoyos, Km 1.7
Las Palmas de Gran Canaria
Las Palmas, Spain 35017
34-928-430-023
Fax: 34-928-430-017
www.aslp.org
Supports students in becoming life long learners in the tradition of American education

Linnah Sanab, Director
Conchita Neyra, Assistant Director

1709 American School-London
One Waverly Place
London
United Kingdom NW8 0
44-207-449-1200
Fax: 44-207-449-1350
admissions@asl.org
www.asl.org
is to develop the intellect and character of each student by providing an outstanding American education with a global perspective.

Jodi Coats, Dean of Admissions

1710 American School-Madrid
Apartado 80
Madrid
Spain 28080
34-91-740-1900
Fax: 34-91-357-2678
info@asmadrid.org
Grade levels Pre-K through 12, school year September - June

Robert Thompson, Director
William O'Hale, Headmaster

1711 American School-Milan
Via K Marx 14
Noverasco di Opera, Milan
Italy 20090
39-02-530-001
Fax: 39-02-576-06274
director@asmilan.org
www.asmilan.org
s to provide a fulfilling educational environment where learners can discover and develop their capacities and achieve personal excellence.

Alen P Austen, Director
Samer Khoury, High School Principal

1712 American School-Paris
41, rue Pasteur
Saint Cloud
France 92210
33-1-411-28282
Fax: 33-1-460-22390
webteam@asparis.fr
www.asparis.org
We develop lifelong learners with an international focus who use their social, thinking and problem-solving skills to contribute constructively to a changing global society

Pilar Cabeza de Vaca, Headmistress
Jack Davis, Head of the School

1713 American School-Valencia
Avenida Sierra Calderona 29
Urb Los Monasterios, Puzol
Spain 46530
34-96-140-5412
Fax: 34-96-140-5039
asvalencia@asvalencia.org
www.asvalencia.org
An international, private, bilingual, university- preparatory school that provides a broad and balanced curriculum in a safe and positive learning environment that encourages students to seek challenges.

Saara Tatem, Director
Ildefonso Segura, Financial Director

1714 American School-the Hague
Rijkstraatweg 200
BX Wassenaar
Netherlands 02241
31-70-514-0113
Fax: 31-70-511-2400
info@ash.nl
www.ash.nl
Educates students to excel in critical inquiry, creative thinking, clear communication, and commitment to others.

Rick Spradling, Director

1715 Anatolia College
PO Box 21021
Pylea Thessaloniki
Greece 55510
30-31-398-201
Fax: 30-31-327-500
www.anatolia.edu.gr
Offers undergraduate and graduate programs of study characterized by reasoned and open inquiry, acquisition of the breadth and depth of knowledge associated with traditional university curricula, and achievement of the highest possible standards in student-centered teaching and faculty scholarship, with emphasis on individual growth.

Richard L Jackson, President
Panayiotis Kanellis, Executive Vice President

1716 Anglo-American School-Moscow
American Embassy
Itainen Puistotie 14
Finland 00140
7-095-231-4488
Fax: 7-095-231-4477
director@aas.ru
www.aas.ru
An international learning community where students, teachers and parents demand excellence and engagement from one another.

Drew Alexander, Director
Nicolette Kirk, Admissions Officer

1717 Anglo-American School-St. Petersburg
c/o American Embassy
Itainen Puistotie 14, Box L, Helsinki
Finland
7-812-320-8925
Fax: 7-812-320-8926
nastia.smirnova@aas.ru
An international learning community where students, teachers and parents demand excellence and engagement from one another.

Ronald Gleason, Principal
Ellen D Stren, Director

1718 Ansbach Elementary School
Unit 28614 APO AE 09177
Germany
011-49 -802
Fax: 011-46 -802
Provides many excellent opportunities to encouage and support all students intellectual, physical, social, emotional and creative developments and prepare them to meet the challengges of a dynamic and diverse world community.

Essie Grant, Principal

1719 Ansbach High School
Unit 28614
APO AE 09177
Germany
49-9802-223
Fax: 49-9802-1496
AnsbachHS.Principal@eu.dodea.edu
A public school serving the children of American Army units.

Jennifer Rowland, Principal

1720 Antwerp International School
Veltwijcklaan 180
2180 Ekeren-Antwerpen
Belgium
32-3-543-9300
Fax: 32-3-541-8201
ais@ais-antwerp.be
www.ais-antwerp.be
Educates young people to be responsible, caring, and productive members of a democratic society in a global community, and to prepare them for continued education. It promotes integrity, self-realization, mutual respect and understanding in a multi-cultural environment of students and teachers.

Alun Cooper, Headmaster

1721 Argonner Elementary School
Unit 20193 Box 0015
APO, Hanau 09165 0015
Germany

Christine Holsten, Principal

1722 Athens College
420 Madison Avenue
New York, NY 10017
212-697-7071
Fax: 212-697-7093
www.athenscollege.org
The mission of Athens College is to provide, by international standards, the highest quality education to the most deserving candidates and to culti-

vate in its students those habits of mind, body, and spirit necessary for responsible citizenship in GReece and the world; moral courage, intellectual discipline, compassion, and an unswerving devotion to justice and truth. Our goal is to instill in our students, by teaching and by example, a strong sense of measure.

Walter McCanny Eggleston, Principal
Dr Nicholas G Bacopoulos, President

23 Aviano Elementary School
Unit 6210 Box 180
APO, AE 09604-0180
Italy
011-39-0434-660921
avianoes.principal@eu.dodea.edu

Lillian Hiyama, Principal
Phyllis Fuglaar, Assistant Principal

24 Aviano High School
Unit 6210 Box 180
APO, AE 09604-0180
Italy
632-567-
Fax: 390- 34-6 09
avianohs.principal@eu.dodea.edu

Debra K Johnson, Principal

25 BEPS 2 Limal International School
23 Avenue Franklin Roosevelt
Brussels
Belgium 01050
32-10-417-227
Fax: 32-2-687-2968
info@beps.com
www.beps.com
The schools share a common philosophy and approach to education. An average class size of 16 allows for a high level of individual attention in a caring and supportive environment.

Charles A Gellar, Head
Henny de Waal, Headmistress

726 Babenhausen Elementary School
CMR 426 Unit 20219
APO, Babenhausen 09089 0005
Germany

Ida Rhodes, Principal

727 Bad Kissingen Elementary School
CMR 464
APO, Bad Kissingen 09226 0005
Germany

Beatrice McWaters, Principal

728 Bad Kreuznach Elementary School
CMR 441
APO, Bad Kreuznach 09525 0005
Germany

Peter Grenier, Principal

729 Bad Kreuznach High School
Unit 24324
APO, Bad Krueznach 09252 0005
Germany

Jennifer Beckwith, Principal

730 Bad Nauheim Elementary School
Unit 21103
APO, Bad Nauheim 09074 0005
Germany

Raymond Burkard, Principal

731 Badminton School
Westbury-on-Trym, Bristol
BS9 3BA
England
0272-623141
The school combines excellent facilities and teaching standards with a friendly atmosphere and a strong emphasis on pastoral care. Badminton is also focused on ensuring that girls realise their potential so that they can be capable of achieving whatever they want to be when they leave school.

Jan Scarrow, Headmistress

1732 Bamberg Elementary School
USAG Bamberg, Unit 27539
APO AE 09139
Germany
469-761-
Fax: 095- 31-15
BambergES.Principal@eu.dodea.edu

John G Rhyne, Principal

1733 Bamberg High School
Unit 27539
APO AE 09139
Germany
469-088-
BambergHS.Principal@eu.dodea.edu
www.bamb-hs.eu.dodea.edu/
Preparing all students to achieve success and personal fulfillment in a dynamic global environment.

Dominick Calabria, Principal
Richard Jimenez, Assistant Principal

1734 Barrow Hills School
Roke Lane
Witley, Godalming
Surrey, England GU8 5
01428-683639
Fax: 01428-683639
www.barrowhills.org.uk

Michael Connolly, Headmaster

1735 Baumholder High School
Unit 23816 Box 30
APO, AE 09034-0034
Germany
011-49 -783
Fax: 011-49 -783
BaumholderHS.Principal@eu.dodea.edu

Danny Robinson, Principal
Patrick McDonald, Assistant Principal

1736 Bavarian International School
Haputstrasse 1
Schloss Haimbausen
Haimhausen, Germany 85778
49-8133-9170
Fax: 49-8133-917-135
k.lippacher@bis-school.com
www.bis-school.com
Inspiring young minds and challenging young individuals to achieve their intellectual and personal potential within a caring international environment

Bryan Nixon, Director

1737 Bedales School
Church Road Steep
Petersfield Hampshire
England, UK GU32-2DG
01730-300100
Fax: 01730-300500
admin@bedales.org.uk
www.bedales.org.uk
Bedales School is a coeducational independent day and boarding school in Hampshire, comprising a Pre-prep, Dunannie (ages 3-8); Prep, Dunhurst (ages 8-13); and Bedales itself (ages 13-180).

Magnus Bashaarat, Head of Bedales
Louise Wilson, Sr. Deputy, Operations

1738 Bedford School
De Parys Avenue Bedford
England, UK MK40
44-0-1234-362200
Fax: 44-0-1234-362283
info@bedfordschool.org.uk
www.bedfordschool.org.uk
We pride ourselves on the pursuit of excellence, on encouraging boys to develop their talent, discover new interests and prepare for the world beyond school.

John Moule, Head Master

1739 Bedgebury School
Goudhurst
Cranbrook
Kent TN17
0580-211954
www.bedgeburyschool.co.uk
Our goal at Bell Bedgebury is a simple one - to offer all our students the best possible preparation for their future educational careers.

Eric Squires, Headmaster
David Morse, Principal

1740 Belgium Antwerp International School
Veltwijcklaan 180
Ekeren-Antwerp
Belgium 02180
32-3-543-9300
Fax: 32-3-541-8201
ais@ais-antwerp.be
www.ais-antwerp.be
The school is concerned with the student's social, physical, emotional and intellectual development. It is committed to excellence and to providing the best possible opportunities for growth for each student.

Alun Cooper, Headmaster
Matthew Cox, Elementary School Principal

1741 Benjamin Franklin International School
Martorell i Pena 9
Barcelona
Spain 08017
34-93-434-2380
Fax: 34-93-417-3633
www.bfis.org
We view education as an opportunity for children to live fully and become global citizens able to build a more humane world.

David Penberg, Director
James Duval, Elementary Principal

1742 Berlin International School
Lentzeallee 8/14
Berlin
Germany 14195
49-30-790-00370
Fax: 49-30-3790-00370
office@berlin-international-school.de
www.berlin-international-school.de
Berlin International School is a private, non-profit, non-denominational day school offering student-centered learning to international and local students from pre-school through university entrance preparation.

Hubert Keulers, Acting Director
Michael Cunningham, Principal

1743 Berlin Potsdam International School
Am Hochwald 30, Haus 2
14 532 Kleinmachnow
Germany
49-332-086-760
Fax: 49-332-086-7612
www.bpis.de
Grade levels N-12, school year August - June

Stephen Middlebrook, Director

1744 Bitburg Elementary School
52 MSG/CCSE-B Unit 3820 Box 45
APO, AE
Germany 09126-45
119-661-
Fax: 119- 61-
BitburgES.Principal@eu.dodea.edu
Joseph Lovett, Principal

1745 Bitburg High School
52 MSG/CCSH-B Unit 3820 Box 50
APO, AE
Germany 09126-50
065-692-
Fax: 065- 90-0
webmaster@eu.dodea.edu
David W Carlisle, Principal
Jennifer Remoy, Assistant Principal

1746 Bitburg Middle School
52 MSG/CCSM-B Unit 3820 Box 55
APO, AE
Germany 09126
561-946-3200
Fax: 065-611-2091
webmaster@eu.dodea.edu
Douglas Carlson, Principal

1747 Bjorn's International School
Gartnerivej 5
Copenhagen
Denmark 02100
453-929-2937
Fax: 453-929-1938
www.b-i-s.dk
Lea Kroghly, Principal

1748 Black Forest Academy
Postfach 1109
Kandern
Germany 79396
49-7626-91610
Fax: 49-7626-8821
www.bfacademy.com
Black Forest Academy's vision is globally-minded Christians changing their world for Christ.
George Durance, Principal
Tim Shuman, Director

1749 Bloxham School
Bloxham
Banbury
Oxfordshire, UK OX15
01295-720206
Fax: 01295-721897
registar@bloxhamschool.com
www.bloxhamschool.com
As the largest group of Church of England Schools in the UK, Woodard was established in 1847 and today is known for providing academic excellence and an unrivalled supportive environment where individuals can flourish.
Mark Allbrook, Headmaster
B Hurst, Chairman

1750 Blue Coat School
Birmingham Street
Walsall
West Midlands, UK WS1 2
0121-456-3966
Brian Bissell, Principal
Ken Yeates, Headteacher

1751 Boeblingen Elementary School
Unit 30401
APO
AE 09107
070-1 1-2715
Fax: 070-1 2-1368
To inspire curiosity and ambition for life-long learning in every student.
Dale Moore, Principal
Toufy Haddad, Assistant Principal

1752 Bonn International School
Martin-Luther-King Strasse 14
Bonn
Germany 53175
49-228-308-540
Fax: 49-228-308-5420
www.bis.bonn.org
The mission of Bonn International School is to inspire and empower students, aged 3-19, to become balanced, responsible global citizens who are successful, independent thinkers with a passion for learning.
Peter Murphy, Director
Diane Lewthwaite, Secondary School Principal

1753 Bordeaux International School
252 rue Jadaique
Bordeaux
France 33000
33-557-870-211
Fax: 33-556-790-047
bis@bordeaux-school.com
www.bordeaux-school.com
Conveniently located in the centre of historic Bordeaux, the school is purpose-built around a secure, enclosed and partially covered courtyard, which provides a space for pupils across the school to socialise with each other.
Christine Cussac, Head Teacher

1754 Brillantmont International School
16, avenue Charles-Secretan
Lausanne
Switzerland, CH 01005
41-21-310-0400
Fax: 41-21-320-8417
info@brillantmont.ch
www.brillantmont.ch
Brillantmont International School houses some 100 boarding boys and girls and about 50 day students.
Philippe Pasche, Director
Geraldine Boland, Deputy Director

1755 British Council School-Madrid
Prado de Somosaguas
Pozuelo de Alarc›n
Madrid, UK 28223
34-91-337-3500
Fax: 34-91-337-3573
general.enquiries@britishcouncil.org
www.britishcouncil.org
The British Council School is one of the leading bilingual, bi-cultural schools in the world, offering the very best of British and Spanish education. The school is divided into three departments (Early Years, Primary and Secondary) and offers education from children aged three to eighteen years old.
Jack Cushman, Principal
Norman Roddom, Head of School

1756 British Kindergarten
Ctra Del La Coruna Km 17
Las Rozas, 28230 Madrid
Spain
Mary Jane Maybury, Principal

1757 British Primary School
Stationsstraat 3 Vossem
Tervuren, BE 03080
32-2-767-3098
Fax: 32-2-767-0351
www.isftervuren.org
Our aim at St Paul's is to provide 'The Best Possible Start in Life '. We offer a secure, nurturing and truly caring environment for children, whether settling into a new country or going to school for the first time.
Katie Tyrie, Headteacher
Bruce Guy, Financial Manager

1758 British Primary School-Stockholm
Vossem
182 68 Djursholm
Sweden
468-755-2375
www.britishinternationalprimaryschool.se
Gaye Elliot, Principal

1759 British School-Amsterdam
Anthonie van Dijckstraat 1
Amsterdam, ME 01077
31-20-347-1111
Fax: 31-20-347-1222
Our school is commited to providing the best possible eduction for our students. This is achieved in a calm, friendly, purposeful learning environment. Our strong and experieced team of teaching professionals are supported with excellent resources and facilities.
John Light, Principal
K McCarthy, Chairman

1760 British School-Bern
Hintere Dorfgasse 20
Gumligen
Switzerland 03073
41-31-951-2358
Fax: 41-31-951-1710
britishschool@bluewin.ch
www.britishschool.ch
We aim to provide a high quality programme for children of all abilities that promotes the social, emotional, cognitive, moral, physical and aesthetic development of each child
Enid Potts, Head Teacher/Administrator
Joe Quinn, Support Staff

1761 British School-Brussels
Leuvensesteenweg 19
Tervuren
Belgium, BE 03080
322-767-4700
Fax: 322-767-8070
reception@britishschool.be
www.britishschool.be
The British School of Brussels, situated 30 minutes from the city centre on a beautiful campus, offers a British education to International families in the heart of Europe, with pupils from some 70 nationalities on roll.
Roland Chant, Principal
Brenda Despontin, Principal

1762 British School-Netherlands
Wheatfields
Tarwekamp 3
Netherlands 02592
071-616958
Fax: 071-617144
www.britishschool.nl
BSN provides the opportunity of becoming part of a student community defined by an ethos of mutual understanding and cultural harmony. We have high expectations of our students, so whilst appreciating the difference in the ability and achievement of individual children within the classroom, we expect the same high level of behaviour from all. Good behaviour, manners and a respect for

teachers and other adults are everyday expectations of our students.

Martin Coles, Principal
Nigel Collins, Assistant Principal

63 British School-Oslo
PO Box 7531, Skillebekk 0205
Oslo 2
Norway

Margaret Stark, Principal

64 British School-Paris
21B Lavant Street
Petersfield
Hampshire GU32-3EL
01-34-80-45-94
Fax: 01-39-76-12-69
ecis@ecis.org
www.ecis.org
The European Council of International Schools (ECIS) is a collaborative network promoting the ideals and best practice of international education.

Pilar Cabeza de Vaca, Executive Director
Mary Langford de Donoso, Deputy Executive Director

65 Bromsgrove School
Worcester Road
Bromsgrove
Worcestershire B61-7DU
44-0-1527-579679
Fax: 44-0-1527-576177
headmaster@bromsgrove-school.co.uk
www.bromsgrove-school.co.uk
This school offers an English curriculum to 840 day students and 350 boarding (700 boys; 490 girls), ages 3 to 18. The curriculum is English based but french, german and Spanish are also taught. Teachers from overseas are welcome with the length of stay being 1-2 years. Applications needed to teach include science, French, math, Spanish, reading, German, English and physical education.

Chris Edwards, Headmaster
John Rogers, Foundation Director

766 Brooke House College
Market Harborough Leicestershire
Leicestershire
England LE16-7AU
44-0-1852-462452
Fax: 44-0-1858-462487
enquiries@brookehouse.com
www.brookehouse.com
Brooke House College is a co-educational, international boarding college, specialising in preparing students from all over the globe, and from Britain, for entrance to the most prestigious universities to which they can aspire in both the U.K. and U.S.A

K Anderton, Academic Tutor
A Burditt, Diploma Personal Assistant

767 Brussels American School
Unit 8100 Box 13
APO AE 09714-9998
Belgium, BE
320-271-9552
Fax: 302-717-9577
BrusselsEHS.Principal@eu.dodea.edu
Brussels American School (BAS) serves students in Kindergarten through Grade 12. The elementary section of the school consists of Kindergarten through Grade 5. It is housed in one of the four major buildings and has a playground and special learning facilities. Grades 6-8 serve as transitional grades between the elementary and secondary programs; students attend classes in both the elementary and high school buildings

Walter G Seely, Principal
Cheryl A Aeillo, Assistant Principal

1768 Brussels English Primary School
23 Avenue Franklin Roosevelt
Brussels
Belgium 01050
62-010-41-72-27
Fax: 62-010-40-10-43
info@beps.com
www.beps.com
Offering the Primary Years Programme, a prestigious programme supported by many international schools around the world (ages 3 to 11).

Henny de Waal, Head of School
Dominique Floridor, Secretary

1769 Bryanston School
Blandford
Dorset
UK DT11-0PX
0258-452411
development@bryanston.co.uk
www.bryanston.co.uk
Bryanston they are those which encourage independence, individuality, and thinking, as well as being able to learn from living in a loving community which fast becomes, and remains, a family

Paul Speakman, Treasurer
Robert Ware, Chair

1770 Buckswood Grange International School
Broomham Hall Rye Road Guestling
Nr Hastings E Suxxex
England TN35-4LT
44-182-574-7000
Fax: 44-182-576-5010
achieve@buckswood.co.uk
www.buckswood.co.uk
A multinational boarding school for British and foreign students which combines the British curriculum with specialist EFL tution and close attention to social skills in an international environment.

Michael Reiser, Principal
David Walker, Marketing Manager

1771 Butzbach Elementary School
CMR 452 Box 5500
APO, Butzbach 09045 0005
Germany

Carl Ford, Principal

1772 Byron Elementary School
202 New Dunbar Road
Byron, GA 31008
478-956-5020
Fax: 478-956-5910
www.bes.peachschools.org
Our teachers are dedicated, hard working educators who are life learners themselves. An enriched, standards-based instruction is provided through collegial partnerships and staff development. Teachers continue to refine their instructional skills through book study discussions, grade level meetings, and attending various workshops.

Martin Dannelly, Principal
Dennis Teresia, Assistant Principal

1773 CIV International School-Sophia Antipolis
BP 97, 190 rue Frederic Mistral
Sophia Antipolis 06902
France
33-4-929-65224
Fax: 33-4-936-52215
www.civissa.org
Grade levels 1-12, school year September-June

Andrew Derry, Head of Section

1774 Calpe College International School
Cta de Cadiz Km 171
29670 Malaga
Spain
95-278-1479
Fax: 95-278-9416
www.calpeschool.com

Luis Proetta, Principal

1775 Campion School
PO Box 67484
Pallini GR-15302
Greece
301-813-5901
Fax: 301-813-6492
dbaker@hol.gr
www.campionschool.in

Dennis MacKinnon, Principal

1776 Canadian College Italy-The Renaissance School
59 Macamo Courte
Maple, Ontario
Canada L6A-1G1
905-508-7108
800-422-0548
Fax: 905-508-5480
cciren@rogers.com
A unique source of highest-quality English-language education, preparing students for university entrance in the U.S.A., U.K., Canada and Europe, become one of the pre-eminent high school boarding schools in Europe. Graduates from CCI's founding years earned acceptances, and a variety of scholarships

1777 Cascais International School
Rua Das Faias, Lt 7 Torre
2750 Cascais
Portugal
www.icsc.pt
An international nursery school, founded in 1996, that caters to children ages 1-6 years on a fulltime or part-time basis. The first language of the school is English and Portuguese is the second. Many other languages are spoken throughout the school. Offers an individual approach, flexible hours and transport. Total enrollment is 75 day students (45 boys; 30 girls).

Evan Lerven Sixma, Principal

1778 Castelli Elementary School
Via Dei Laghi, 8.60
Ligetta Di Marinus, Ag, 00047 Marina
Italy
39-06-9366-1311
Fax: 39-06-9366-1311
www.castelli-international.it

Diana Jaworska, Principal

1779 Castelli International School
Via Degli Scozzesi
13-Grottaferrata
Rome, Italy
39-06-943-15779
Fax: 39-06-943-15779
maryac@castelli-international.it
www.castelli-international.it/
To provide a stimulating educational environment for international families living south of Rome and in the Castelli Romani area. CIS believes that the children, being naturally curious, are eager to learn, and that

they learn best through inquiry, experience, and trial and error

Marianne Palladino, BA, MA, PhD, Director of Studies

1780 Casterton School
Kirkby Lonsdale, Via Carnforth
Lancashire, United Kingdom LA6-2SG
052-42-71202
admissions@castertonschool.co.uk
One of the most established academic girls boarding and day schools in the UK, with a national and international reputation.

P McLaughlin, Headmaster
G A Sykes, Deputy Head

1781 Caxton College
Ctra De Barcelona S/N 46530
Puzol Valencia
Spain
34-96-146-4500
Fax: 34-96142-0930
caxton@caxtoncollege.com
www.caxtoncollege.com
Aim to provide pupils with the skills necessary to form independent opinions enabling them to make personal decisions in response to situations which will arise in their lives.

Amparo Gil, Principal
Marta Gil, Vice Principal

1782 Center Academy
92 St John's Hill Battersea
London SW11 1SH
England
071-821-5760
www.centeracademy.com
To provide students with a learning environment that facilitates the development of self-confidence, motivation, and academic skills, and gives students the opportunity to achieve success in life.

Robert Detweiler, Principal
Mack R Hicks, Founder and Chairman

1783 Centre International De Valbonne
Civ-bp 097 06902 Sophia
Antipolis Cedex
France
33-4-929-652-24
Fax: 33-4-936-522-15
www.civfrance.com

Ian Hill, Principal

1784 Charters-Ancaster School
Penland Road, Bexhill on Sea
TN40 2JQ
England
0424-730499
Boarding girls ages eleven to eighteen; day school for boys three to eight and girls three-eighteen.

K Lewis, MA, Headmaster

1785 Children's House
Kornbergvegen 23-4050 Sola
Stavanger
Norway
www.hr.umich.edu

Christine Grov, Principal

1786 Cite Scolaire International De Lyon
2 Place De Montreal
69007 Lyon
France
33-04-78-69-60-06
Fax: 33-04-78-69-60-36
csi-lyon-gerland@ac-lyon.fr
www.csilyon.fr
Grade levels 1-12.

Donna Galiana, Director

1787 Cobham Hall
Cobham (Nr Gravesend, Kent)
DA12 3BL
England, UK
0474-82-3371
enquiries@cobhamhall.com
www.cobhamhall.com
Boarding and Day School for girls aged 11-18, ascribing to the Round Square philospophy of education and personal development.

Maggie Roberts, BA, M.Ed., PGCE, Headmistress
J Shelley, Registrar

1788 Colegio Ecole
Santa Rosa 12
Lugo Llanera
Asturias 33690
985- 77-8
ecole1@colegioecole.com
www.colegioecole.com

Patrick Wilson, Principal

1789 Colegio International-Meres
Apartado 107
33080 Oviedo, Asturias
Spain
985-792-427
Fax: 985-794-582
www.colegiomeres.com

Belen Orejas Fernandez, Principal

1790 Colegio International-Vilamoura
Apt 856, 8125 Vilamoura
Loule Algarve
Portugal
www.civ.com

Lawrence James, Principal

1791 College Du Leman International School
74 Route De Sauverny
CH-1290 Versoix, Geneva
Switzerland
41-22-775-5555
Fax: 41-22-775-5559
admissions@cdl.ch
www.cdl.ch
Grade levels include N-13 with an enrollment of 1700.

Francis Clivaz, General Director
Cedric Chaffois, Director of Admission

1792 College International-Fontainebleau
48 Rue Guerin 77300
Fontainebleau
France
01-64-22-11-77
Fax: 01-64-23-43-17
glenyskennedy@compuserve.com
www.fontainebleau.fr

Mrs. G Kennedy, Principal

1793 College Lycee Cevenol International
43400 Le Chambon sur Lignon
France
04-71-59-72-52
Fax: 04-71-65-87-38
www.lecevenol.org
he CollSge Lyc,e International C,venol (a private establishment under a contract of state sponsorship since 1971) today welcomes boarders and day students of local, regional, national and international origins.

Christiane Minssen, Principal
Robert Lassey, Headmaster

1794 Copenhagen International School
Hellerupvej 22-26
2900 Hellerup
Denmark
45-39-463-300
Fax: 45-39-612-230
www.cis-edu.dk
Develop the potential of each student in a stimulating environment of cultural diversity, academic excellence and mutual respect.

Peter Wellby, Director
Simon Watson, Senior School Principal

1795 Croughton High School
Unit 5485 Box 15
APO Croughton, 09494 0005
Great Britain

Dr. Charles Recesso, Principal

1796 Danube International School
Josef Gall-Gassee 2
1020 Vienna
Austria
00-43-1-720-3110
Fax: 43-1-720-3110-40
DIS started off life in 1992 in Schrutkagasse in the 13th District. The school had another name, then - 'Pawen International Community School' that now houses a Rudolf Steiner school

Peter Harding, Director
Sabine Biber-Brussmann, Registrar

1797 Darmstadt Elementary School
CMR 431
APO, Darmstadt 09175 0005
Germany

Sherry Templeton, Principal

1798 Darmstadt Junior High School
CMR 431
APO, Darmstadt 09175 0005
Germany

Daniel Basarich, Principal

1799 De Blijberg
Graaf Florisstraat 56
Rotterdam
Netherlands 3032C
010-448-2266
Fax: 010-448-2270
deblijberg_international@hotmail.com
www.international.blijberg.nl

Barbera Everaars, Director
Bart Loman, Director

1800 Dean Close School
Lansdown Road
Cheltenham
England GL51
0242-522640
squirrels@deanclose.org.uk
Aim to provide a rich variety of opportunities that will enable your son or daughter to develop in confidence and independance within our happy and caring community.

Sue Bennett, Headmistress
Anthony R Barchand, Faculty Head

1801 Dexheim Elementary School
Unit 24027
APO, Dexheim 09110 0005
Germany

Gary Waltner, Principal

02 Downside School
Stratton-on-the-Fosse, Bath (Avon)
Radstock Bath
England, UK BA3
0761-232-206
admin@downside.co.uk
www.downside.co.uk
Downside is an independent Catholic co-educational boarding school for pupils aged 9 to 18.

Dom Leo Maidlow Davis, Head Master
AR Hobbs, Deputy Head Master

03 Dresden International School
Annenstr 9
D-01067 Dresden
Germany
49-351-3400428
Fax: 49-351-3400430
www.dresden-is.de
Committed to the aim of continuous improvement, which has been such a feature of the school since it opened in 1996.

Chrissie Sorenson, Director
Steve Ellis, Secondary School Principal

04 ECC International School
Jacob Jordaensstraat 85-87
2018 Antwerp
Belgium

Dr. X Nieberding, Principal

05 Ecole Active Bilingue
70 rue du Theatre
Paris
France 75015
01-44-37-00-80
Fax: 01-45-79-06-66
info@eabjm.net
www.eabjm.org
An associated UNESCO school, EABJM is also contractually part of the French national education system. The high school prepares students for the French Baccalaureate, the French Baccalaureate with Option Internationale, or the International Baccalaureate. An official testing site for the SAT, EABJM is also accredited by the College Entrance Examination Board and the Cambridge University Local Examination Syndicate.

Danielle Monod, Principal

806 Ecole Active Bilingue Jeannine Manuel
70 rue du Theatre
75015 Paris
France 75015
45-44-37-00-80
Fax: 01-45-79-06-66
Grade levels k-12.

Elizabeth Zeboulon, Directrice

807 Ecole D'Humanite
CH-6085 Hasliberg-Goldern
Switzerland
41-33-972-9292
Fax: 41-33-972-9211
us.office@ecole.ch
www.ecole.ch
150 boys and girls, aged 6 to 20 and faculty live in small family-style groups. International, inter-racial student body. Main language is German, with special classes for beginners.

Kathleen Hennessy, Interim Director
Arsheles Curturils, Director

1808 Ecole Des Roches & Fleuris
3961 Bluche
Valais
Switzerland

Marcel Clivez, Principal

1809 Ecole Lemania
Chemin de Preville 3
CP500 1001 Lausanne
Switzerland
41-0-21-320-15-01
Fax: 41-0-21-312-67-00
info@lemania.com
www.lemania.com
This international college represents over 65 nationalities offering French and English intensive courses, summer programs, American academic studies at graduate and undergraduate levels, sports and cultural activities, and accommodation in boarding school. Total enrollment: 800 day students; 100 boarding (450 boys; 450 girls), in grades 1-10.

M JP du Pasquier, Principal

1810 Ecole Nouvelle Preparatoire
Route Du Lac 22, Ch-1094
Paudex
Switzerland

Marc Desmet, Principal

1811 Ecole Nouvelle de la Suisse Romande
Ch de Rovereaz 20, CP-161
CH-1000 Lausanne 12
Switzerland
41-21-654-65-00
Fax: 41-21-654-65-05
info@ensr.ch
www.ensr.ch
The mission of the school is to prepare its students

Isabel Matos, Director Administrative/Fina
Beth Krasna, President

1812 Edinburgh American School
29 Chester Street
Edinburgh EH37EN
Scotland
013-155- 460
Fax: 013-162- 499
www.edinburghacademy.org.uk

AW Morris, Principal

1813 Edradour School
Edradour House - Pitlochry
Perthshire PH165JW,
Scotland

JPA Romanes, Principal

1814 El Plantio International School Valencia
Urbanizacion El Plantio
Calle 233, N36, La Canada, Paterna
Spain
96-132-14-10
Fax: 96-132-18-41
www.plantiointernational.com
To educate young people who can adapt to their environment and therefore our objective is based on providing our students with the necessary skills to enable a better knowledge of the modem world and maximising the ability to communicate in an ever-changing and broadening society.

Anthony C Nelson, Principal

1815 Ellerslie School
Abbey Road, Malvern
WR14 3HF
England
0684-575701
www.ellerslie.school.nz

Elizabeth M Baker, BA, Headmaster

1816 English Junior School
Lilla Danska Vagen 1
412 74 Gothenburg
Sweden
31-401819

Patricia Gabrielsson, Principal

1817 English Kindergarten
Valenjanpolku 2
05880 Hyvinkaa
Finland

Riva Rentto, Principal

1818 English Montessori School
C/ de la Salle S/N
Aravaca, Madrid
Spain 28023
91-357-26-67
Fax: 91-307-15-43
t.e.m.s@teleline.es
www.englishmontessorischool.com
Each year of school up to and including Year 10 at The English Montessori School is validated with the Spanish Educational System. The importance of this is that a students entering or leaving the school can transfer to the equivalent level in any other school.

Elaine Fitzpatrick, Headmistress
Milagros Alonso, Director

1819 English School-Helsinki
Mantytie 14
Helinski
Finland 00270
358-9-477-1123
Fax: 358-9-477-1980
english.school@edu.hel.fi
www.eschool.edu.hel.fi
The English School is a private, national language school based on Christian values. The Ministry of Education has placed a special responsibility on the school to familiarize the students with Finnish and English languages as well as the culture of Finnish and Anglo-Saxon language areas.

Erkki Lehto, Principal
Riitta Volanen, Secretary

1820 English School-Los Olivos
Avda Pino Panera 25, 46110 Godella
Valencia
Spain 46110
96-363-99-38
Fax: 96-364-48-63

Jane Rodriguez, Principal

1821 European Business & Management School
Frederik de Merodestraat, 12-16
Antwerp
Belgium 02600
323-218-8182
Fax: 323-218-5868
Once a year, European Business and Management School organizes a cross-cultural business tour, providing our students with another opportunity to strengthen their competencies in global thinking in international business.

Luc Van Meli, Director

1822 European School-Brussels I
Avenue Du Vert Chasseur 46
Brussels
Belgium 01180
02-374-58-44

The European Schools fulfil a task that national schools are unable to fulfil: to teach pupils from different countries in their respective mother tongues and to instil in them the cultural values of their home country room a European perspective.

J Marshall, Principal
Kari Kivinen, Director

1823 European School-Italy
Via Montello 118
21100 Varese
Italy
32 -297-5990
www.ec.europa.eu
Jorg Hoffman, Principal

1824 Evangelical Christian Academy
Calle La Manda 47
Camarma de Esteruelas, Madrid
Spain 28816
34-91-741-2900
Fax: 34-91-320-8606
secretary@ecaspain.com
www.ecaspain.com
The vision drives every facet of ECA's existence. ECA offers a challenging, college preparatory curriculum in an American-based system. Students at ECA study Bible each year, and a Christian worldview is integrated into every aspect of the curriculum.
Beth Hornish, Principal
Scot Musser, Business Manager

1825 Feltwell Elementary School
CCSE/F Unit 5185 Box 315
APO AE
Great Britain 09461-5315
011-44 -842
Fax: 018-2 8-7931
feltwell.attendance@eu.dodea.edu
School where teachers, parents, and community share the responsibility for each child's learning.
Tom LaRue, Principal

1826 Frankfurt International School
An der Waldlust 15
Oberursel
Germany 61440
49-6171-2020
Fax: 49-6171-202384
admissions@fis.edu
www.fis.edu
To be the leading culturally diverse and family-oriented international school with English as the principal language of instruction. We inspire young individuals to develop their intellect, creativity and character to grow into adaptable, socially responsible global citizens by ensuring a dynamic, 21st-century, inquiry-driven education of the highest standard.
Jutta Kuehne, Director
Mark Ulfers, Head of School

1827 Frederiksborg Gymnasium
Carlsbergvej 15
3400 Hillerod
Denmark
800-055-7314
Fax: 482- 07-1
post@frborg-gymhf.dk
Peter Kuhlman, Principal

1828 Friends School
Saffron Walden, Essex
England CB11
0642-722141
Friends' School strives to be a unique community where the potential and talent of each individual is realised within a friendly and challenging environment based on Quaker principles.
Graham Wigley, Head

1829 Gaeta Elementary & Middle School
PSC Box 811
FPO Gaeta 09609 0005
Italy
Dr. Robert Kirkpatrick, Principal

1830 Garmisch Elementary School
Unit 24511
APO AE, Garmisch
Germany 09053
440-261-
Fax: 088-176-949
GarmischEMS.Webmaster@eu.dodea.edu
To provide a challenging curriculum in an atmosphere respectful of individual needs and cultural diversity. All students will learn the academic and social skills necessary for their future success.
Debbie Strong, Principal

1831 Geilenkirchen Elementary School
Unit 8045
APO AE, Geilenkirchen 09104 0005
Germany 09104
024-1 9- 308
Fax: 024-1 9- 308
GeilenkirchenES.Webmaster@eu.dodea.edu
www.geil-es.eu.dodea.edu/
Educating our students to be responsible, productive and ethical citizens with the skills to think creatively, reason critically, communicate effectively and learn continuously.
James V Dierendonck, Principal

1832 Gelnhausen Elementary School
CMR 465
APO, Gelnhausen 09076 0005
Germany
Jim Harrison, Principal

1833 Geneva English School
36 Route de Malagny
1294 Genthod
Switzerland
41-22-755-18-55
Fax: 41-22-779-14-29
admin@genevaenglishschool.ch
www.geneva-english-school.ch
A private, nonprofit primary school that is owned and managed by an association which is composed of parents whose children attend the school. The main objective of the school is to offer education on British lines for children of primary school age living in or near Geneva, and to prepare them for secondary education in any English-speaking school.
Denis Unsworth, Principal
Gareth Davies, Headmaster

1834 Giessen Elementary School
414th BSB GSN, Unit 20911
APO, Giessen 09169 0005
Germany
496-414-6265
496-414-8333
www.aoshs.org
Mary Ann Burkard, Principal

1835 Giessen High School
414th BSB GSB, Unit 20911
APO, Giessen 09169 0005
Germany
496-414-6266
www.aoshs.org
Gordon Gartner, Principal

1836 Grafenwoehr Elementary School
Unit 28127
APO AE
Germany 09114-8127
964-183-7133
Fax: 964- 32-4ÿ
GrafenwoehrES.Principal@eu.dodea.edu
To maintain a meaningful partnership with the community through which physical well being, cognitive growth, and emotional support are provided to all learners.
Crystal Bailey, Principal
David Eldredge, Assistant Principal

1837 Greenwood Garden School
Via Vito Sinisi 5
Rome
Italy
39-06-332-66703
Fax: 39-06-332-66703
greenwoodgarden@libero.it
www.greenwoodgardenschool.com
An international pre-school and kindergarten for children aging from 2-6 with teaching being done in English by mother-tongue educators experienced with young children
Donna Seibert, Directress

1838 Gstaad International School
Ahorn
Gstaad
Switzerland CH-37
41-33-744-2373
Fax: 41-33-744-3578
gis@gstaad.ch
www.gstaadschool.ch
The school's mission includes the building of endurance and stamina in both academics and sports, as well as stimulating personal achievement by teaching the values of respect, gratitude, humour and real caring for others. Students are continually presented with challenges and the opportunities to achieve where perhaps before they thought impossible.
Alain Souperbiet, Director

1839 Haagsche School Vereeniging
Nassaulaan 26
Den Haag-2514
003-170-363
info@hsvdenhaag.nl
www.hsvdenhaag.nl
HM Jongeling, Principal
Lorraine Dean, Director

1840 Hainerberg Elementary School
Unit 29647 Box 0086
APO AE, Wiesbaden
Germany 09096-86
337-516-
Fax: 011-49 -11 7
Wiesbadenes.principal@eu.dodea.edu
Provide exemplary educational programs that inspire and prepare all students for success in a global environment.
Maren James, Principal

1841 Halvorsen Tunner Elementary and Middle School
Unit 7565
APO, Rhein Main 09050 0005
Germany
Julie Gaski, Principal

1842 Hanau High School
Unit 20235
APO, Hanau 09165 0005
Germany
Allen Davenport, Principal

1843 Hanau Middle School
Unit 20193
APO, Hanau 09165 0016
Germany
Robert Sennett, Principal

1844 Harrow School
5 High Street
Harrow on the Hill
England HA1 3
01-423-2366
harrow@harrowschool.org.uk
www.harrowschool.org.uk
Barnaby Lenon, Headmaster

1845 Hatherop Castle School
Hatherop, Cirencester
England GL7 3
028-575-206
Paul Easterbrook, Headmaster

1846 Heidelberg High School
Unit 29237
APO AE
Germany 09102
370-800-
Fax: 062-213- 587
Kevin J Brewer, Principal

1847 Heidelberg Middle School
Unit 29237
APO AE
Germany 09102
221-338-9310
Donald Johnson, Principal

1848 Hellenic-American Education Foundation Athens College-Psychico College
15 Stefanou Delta
Psychico
Greece 154 5
30-1-671-2771
Fax: 30-1-674-8156
info@haef.gr
www.haef.gr
Grade levels 1-12, school year September - June
David William Rupp, President

1849 Helsingin Suomalainen
Isonnevantie 8
Helinski, Finland 00320
358- 47-1
www.syk.fi
Helsingin Suomalainen Yhteiskoulu (SYK) is an independent coeducational, which prepares its students either for the national matriculation exam or the International Baccalaureate, both of which give a student general university entry qualifications.
Anja-Liisa Alanko, Principal

1850 Het Nederlands Lyceum
Wijndaelerduin 1
Hague, Netherlands 02554
070-338-4567
Fax: 070-328-2049
primary@ishthehague.nl
www.ishthehague.nl
Offers young people of all nationalities between the ages of 4 and 18 top quality international education in a caring environment, which aim for academic success and encourage sporting and creative abilities in a community based on honesty, fairness, open-mindedness and tolerance.
Graeme Scott, Principal Primary School

1851 Het Rijnlands Lyceum
Appollolaan 1 2341 BA
Oegstgeest
Netherlands
31-3771-5155640
administratie@rijnlandslyceum-rlo.nl
www.rlo.nl
Lyceum is a state subsidized school with an international department offering IBMYP and IB. Offers an English/Dutch spoken curriculum to 1,190 day students and 60 boarding (650 boys; 600 girls), in grades 6 through 12. Student/teacher ratio is 15:1, and the school is willing to participate in a teacher exchange program, however, housing will not be provided by the school.
Drs LE Timmerman, Principal

1852 Hillhouse Montessori School
Avenida Alfonso Xiii 30 Y 34
Madrid 2
Spain
www.houseonthehill.com.sg
Judy Amick, Principal

1853 Hohenfels Elementary School
Unit 28214
APO AE
Germany 09173
466-400-ÿ
Fax: 094-2 8-32
Olaf Zwicker, Principal

1854 Hohenfels High School
CMR 414
APO, AE
Germany 09173
094-2 -9096
Fax: 094-2 8- 316
Daniel J Mendoza, Principal

1855 Holmwood House
Chitts Hill, Lexden
Colchester, Essex
England CO3 9
44-0-1904-626183
Fax: 44-0-1904-670899
hst@holmwood.essex.sch.uk
www.holmwood.essex.sch.uk
Holmwood House is an independent coeducational day and boarding preparatory school. The total enrollment of the school is 310 day students and 50 boarding students (240 boys and 120 girls), ages 4 1/2 to 13 1/2.
Alexander Mitchell, Headmaster

1856 Hvitfeldtska Gymnasiet
Rektorsgatan 2, SE-411 33
Goteborg
Sweden
46-31-367-0623
Fax: 46-31-367-0602
agneta.santesson@educ.goteborg.se
State school, founded 1647, offers the International Baccalaureate curriculum to a total enrollment of 90 girls and 90 boys, in grades 10-12.
Christen Holmstrom, Principal
Agneta Santesson, Deputy Headmaster

1857 Illesheim Elementary and Middle School
CMR 416 Box J
APO, Hohenfels 09140 0005
Germany
49-9841-8408
Fax: 49-9841-8987
Donald J Ness, Principal

1858 Independent Bonn International School
Tulpenbaumweg 42
Bonn 53177
Germany
49-228-32-31-66
Fax: 49-228-32-39-58
ibis@ibis-school.com
www.ibis-school.com
IBIS is an international primary school.
Irene Bolik, Headteacher

1859 Independent Schools Information Service
Grosveror Gardens House 35-37
Frosvernor Gardens, London SW1W 0BS
England
020-77981575
Fax: 020-77981561
national@isis.org.uk
www.isis.org.uk
Provides information on 1400 elementary and secondary schools in the United Kingdom and Ireland.
David J Woodhead

1860 Innsbruck International High School
Schonger, Austria A-6141
0-5225-4201
Fax: 0-5225-4202
An accredited coeducational boarding and day school. The school offers an American college preparatory high school curriculum for grades 9-12.
Gunther Wenko, Director
John E Wenrick, Headmaster

1861 Institut Alpin Le Vieux Chalet
1837 Chateau D'oex
Switzerland
212-338-9743
Fax: 212-949-7534
Jean Bach, Principal

1862 Institut Auf Dem Rosenberg
Hohenweg 60-9000 St Gallen
Switzerland
417- 27-0777
Fax: 417- 27- 982
info@instrosenberg.ch
www.instrosenberg.ch
Felicitas Scharli, Principal

1863 Institut Chateau Beau-Cedre
57 Av De Chillion
CH-1820 Territet Montreux
Switzerland
41-21-963-5341
Fax: 41-21-963-4783
This Institut is an exclusive boarding and finishing international school for girls. American high school with a general culture section for 30 boarding students in grades 9 through twelve. Languages spoken include French and English and the student/teacher ratio is 1:6.
Pierre Gay, Principal

1864 Institut Le Champ Des Pesses
1618 Chatel-st-denis
Montreux
Switzerland
PL Racloz, Principal

1865 Institut Le Rosey
Chateau du Rosey
1180 Rolle
Switzerland
41-21-822-5500
Fax: 41-21-822-5555
www.rosey.ch
Le Rosey's philosophy is inspired by what Harvard educationalist Howard Gardner has called multiple intelligences: its aim is to develop all Roseans' talents through academic, sporting and artistic programs.
Philippe Gudin, General Director
Michael Gray, Headmaster

1866 Institut Montana Bugerbug-American Schools
Zugerberg
CH 6300 Zug
Switzerland
41-41-711-1722
Fax: 41-41-711-5465
Grade levels include 7-13 with a total enrollment of 111.
Daniel Fredez, Director

1867 Institut Monte Rosa
57, Ave de Chillon,
CH-1820 Territet/Montreux
Switzerland
021-963-5341
Fax: 021-963-4783
info@monterosa.ch
www.monterosa.ch
Bernhard Gademann, BS, MS, Principal

1868 Inter-Community School
Strubenacher 3 Postfach
Zumikon
Switzerland 08126
41-1-919-8300
Fax: 41-1-919-8320
www.icsz.ch
The Inter-Community School is committed to providing a supportive and enabling learning environment in which all members of the community are challenged to achieve their individual potential, encouraged to pursue their passions, and expected to fulfil their responsibilities
Michael Matthews, Head of School
Martin Hall, Secondary Principal

1869 International Academy
Via di Grottarossa 295
00189 Rome
Italy
39-340-731-4195
info@internationalacademy.in
www.internationalacademy.in
Joan Bafaloukas Bulgarini, Principal

1870 International College Spain
C/Vereda Norte 3
La Moraleja, Madrid
Spain 28109
34-91-650-2398
Fax: 34-91-650-1035
admissions@icsmadrid.org
The philosophy of the school is to provide students with a high quality international education which places a strong emphasis on fostering respect for the world's nations and cultures.
Terry Hedger, Director
Hubert Keulers, Head of Primary School

1871 International Management Institute
Garden Square Building, Block-C Laa
Antwerp
Belgium 02610
32-3-21-85-431
Fax: 32-3-21-85-868
www.timi.edu
Our vision is to empower our students in terms of all the faculties required to pursue a career in the competitive globalized world. The focus of our curriculum is to enhance the learning perspective through customized modules and simulation exercises from globally renowned academicians and professionals.
Luc Van Mele, Director

1872 International Preparatory School
Rua Do Boror 12 Carcavelos
2775 Parede
Portugal
56-2-321-5800
Fax: 56-2-321-5821
www.tipschool.com

1873 International School Beverweerd
Beverweerdseweg 60, 3985 RE
Werkhoven
Netherlands
03437-1341
Fax: 03437-2079
Ray Kern, BA, MA, Principal

1874 International School-Algarve
Apartado 80 Porches 8400
Lagoa Algarve
Portugal
www.algarveschool.com
Peter Maddison, Principal

1875 International School-Amsterdam
PO Box 920
AX Amstelveen
The Netherlands 01180
31-20-347-1111
Fax: 31-20-347-1222
info@isa.nl
www.isa.nl
The International School of Amsterdam (ISA) was founded in 1964 to serve the educational needs of the children of the international community living in and around Amsterdam. ISA is a nonsectarian, non-profit coeducational day school, enrolling students in Pre-School through Grade 12 (from 3 to 18 years of age).
Dr Edward Greene, Director
Sarah Grace, Head of Lower School

1876 International School-Basel
Fleischbachstrasse 2
4153 Reinach BL
Switzerland
41-61-426-96-26
Fax: 41-61-426-96-25
www.isbasel.ch
mission of the International School Basel is to provide an international education to the highest recognized academic standards
Geoff Tomlinson, Principal

1877 International School-Bergen
Sandslihaugen 30
Sandsli, Bergen
Norway 5254
47 55306330
post@isob.no
www.isbergen.no
Provides an education for the children of expatriate oil company personnel in Bergen and attracts further corporate investment in the Bergen area.
Paul McKenzie, Director

1878 International School-Berne
170 Mattenstrasse
Gumligen
Switzerland 03073
41-31-951-2358
Fax: 41-31-951-1710
office@isberne.ch
www.isberne.ch
Creative learning community for students from all over the world, within the framework of the three International Baccalaureate Programmes, guided by ISBerne teachers and staff, students aged 3 - 18 have the opportunity to become open-minded, principled, knowledgeable, confident lifelong learners and multilingual citizens of the world, who respect themselves and others.
Kevin Page, Director
Cory Etchberger, Chair

1879 International School-Brussels
Kattenberg 19
Brussels 1170
Belguim
32-2-661-4211
Fax: 32-2-661-4200
admissions@isb.be
www.isb.be
Offers a challenging, inclusive international education designed to give every student opportunities for success within and beyond our school.
Kevin Bartlett, Director
Andrei Teixeira, Chairman

1880 International School-Cartagena
Manga Club Cp 30385 Cartagena
Los Belones Murcia
Spain
34-68-175000
www.cartagenainternationalschool.com
Robert Risch, Principal

1881 International School-Curacao
PO Box 3090
Koninginnelaan Emmastad, Curacao
Netherlands Antilles
599-9-737-3633
Fax: 599-90737-3142
www.isc.an
Offers a rigorous academic program in order to prepare students planning to pursue higher learning at colleges and universities around the world. The School's curriculum includes International Baccalaureate (IB) coursework that allows students the opportunity to receive the IB Diploma.
Margie Elhage, Director
Rene Romer, President

1882 International School-Dusseldorf
Niederrheinstrasse 336
Dusseldorf
Germany 40489
49-211-94066-799
Fax: 49-211-4080-744
www.isdedu.eu
Provide the students of the International School of D□sseldorf with the best possible program of academic and personal development in a challenging and supportive environment.
Neil A McWilliam, Director
Michael Coffey, Senior School Principal

1883 International School-Eerde
Kasteellaan 1
PJ Ommen
The Netherlands 07731
031-0529-451452
Fax: 031-0529-456377
www.eerde.nl

Offers numerous programmes tailored to the individual needs of each student, including children with learning difficulties and dyslexia, as well as highly gifted children. Eerde carefully monitors the personal, academic, athletic and creative development of each individual student ages 4 to 19.

Herman Voogd, Principal

884 International School-Friuli
Via Delle Grazie 1/A
Pordenone 33170
Italy
www.udineis.org

Susan Clarke, Principal

885 International School-Geneva
62 route de Chene
Geneva
Switzerland CH-12
41-22-787-2400
Fax: 41-22-787-2410
administration@ecolint.ch
www.ecolint.ch
Aims to provide a distinctive high quality international education that prepares pupils for membership of a world community based on mutual understanding, tolerance and shared humanitarian values.

Nicholas Tate, Director General
John Douglas, Director

886 International School-Hamburg
Hemmingstedter Weg 130
Hamburg
Germany 22609
040(0)8000 50 200
info@ishamburg.org
www.international-school-hamburg.de
A co-educational day school enrolling students from Primary 1 (age 3) to Grade 12. The school was founded in 1957 as the first international school in Germany.

Andrew Cross, Head of School
Jaki Graham, Junior School Principal

887 International School-Hannover Region
Bruchmeisterstrasse 6
Hannover
Germany D-301
49-511-27041650
Fax: 49-511-557934
adminoffice@is-hr.de
www.is-hr.de
Provides a high quality, balanced educational program in the English language for children of internationally-minded families.Offer a dynamic environment where each student is challenged and supported to become a dedicated learner for life and a contributing member of the local and global community.

Patricia Baier, Director
Steffen Stegeman, Business Manager

888 International School-Helsinki
Selkamerenkatu 11
Helsinki
Finland 00180
358-9-686-6160
Fax: 358-9-685-6699
mainoffice@ish.edu.hel.fi
www.ish.edu.hel.fi
Office Manager

Provide attendees

Bob Woods, Headmaster
Therese Thibault, Director

1889 International School-Iita
PMB 5320
Ibadan
Nigeria CR9 3
iita@cgiar.org
www.iita.org
Provide a comprehensive, international curriculum in an environment which promotes confidence, caring and understanding, and prepares our students for successful learning here and in schools around the world.

Neil Jackson, Principal

1890 International School-Lausanne
Chemin de la Grangette 2
Le Mont-sur-Lausanne
Switzerland CH -
41-21-728-1733
Fax: 41-21-728-7868
info@isl.ch
www.isl.ch
The school is committed to excellence in education, it strives to fulfill the unique potential of each student in a supportive and challenging holistic learning environment that prepares the student for continuing education and an active and responsible role in a multicultural world.

Lyn Cheetham, Director
John Ivett, Assistant Director

1891 International School-Le Chaperon Rouge
3963 Crans Sur Sierre
Crans/Montana
Switzerland
41-27-4812-500
Fax: 41-27-4812-502

Prosper Bagnoud, Principal

1892 International School-London
139 Gunnersbury Avenue
London
England W3 8L
44-20-8992-5823
Fax: 44-20-8993-7012
Aims to maximize the achievement of its students throughout the curriculum and in personal and social fields. Drawing on the rich variety of cultures represented at the school, ISL aims to develop in each student a global outlook which seeks to understand and appreciate the attitudes and values of others.

Amin Makarem, Director
Sergio Pawel, Deputy Head, Curriculum

1893 International School-Lyon
80 chemin du Grand Roule
Ste-Foy-LSs-Lyon
France F-691
47 -86 -190
Fax: 47 -86 -198
info@islyon.org
www.islyon.org
The school's curriculum is based on the programmes and pedagogy of the International Baccalaureate Organization which aims to develop in the students the skills, values and knowledge that will help them to become responsible citizens in an increasingly interconnected world.

Donna Philip, Director
Michael Ford, Curriculum Coordinator

1894 International School-Naples
Viale della Liberazione, 1
Bagnoli, Napoli 80125
Italy
39-081-721-2037
Fax: 39-081-570-0248
info@isnaples.it
www.isnaples.it
Provide a nurturing environment where students can grow intellectually, socially, psychologically and physically. Through a dedicated partnership of parents and educators, we strive to prepare our students to become productive, global citizens of the twenty-first century.

Josephine Sessa, Principal
Patricia Montesano, Vice Principal

1895 International School-Nice
15 Avenue Claude Debussy
Nice
France 06200
33-493-210-400
Fax: 33-493-216-911
www.isn-nice.org
The school offers Pre-Kindergarten through grade 12 instruction and college preparatory education and provides an intellectually challenging programme of studies which aims to promote analytic understanding with an integrated view of the various academic disciplines and to encourage creativity and self-expression. Serves both the international community and local families who wish to offer their children an education in English, which is both international and versatile.

Wylie Michael, Director

1896 International School-Paris
6 Rue Beethoven
Paris
France 75016
33-1-422-40954
Fax: 33-1-452-71593
www.isparis.edu
ISP create a challenging and motivating English-speaking environment where students and staff from around the world use the programs of the International Baccalaureate Organisation and work in harmony to develop every student's full intellectual and human potential.

Audrey Peverelli, Headmaster
Catherine Hard, Head of Admissions

1897 International School-Sotogrande
Apartado 15
Sotogrande San Roque Cadiz
Spain 11310
34-956-79-59-02
Fax: 34-956-79-48-16
www.sis.ac
Our school is a learning organisation with a passion for learning. Learning is a complex process and it is vitally important that our teachers know how pupils learn best and that they create exciting opportunities for learning to take place.

Geroge O'Brien, Headmaster
Christopher TJ Charleson, Head of School

1898 International School-Stavanger
Treskeveien 3
Hafrsfjord
Norway 04043
47-51-559-100
Fax: 47-51-552-962
www.isstavanger.no
The International School of Stavanger is dedicated to providing its students with an English language education in a supportive, academically stimulating, and multi-cultural environment.

Linda Duevel, PhD, Director
Gareth Jones, High School Principal

1899 International School-Stockholm
Johannesgatan 18
Stockholm SE-111 38
Sweden
46-8-412-4000
Fax: 46-8-412-4001
www.intsch.se
SIS vision is to enable students to learn, develop, grow, and fulfill their potential in an international environment, which is student-centered, safe, nurturing and rich with opportunities to learn.
Chris Mockrish, Principal
Richard Mast, Director

1900 International School-Stuttgart
Sigmaringer Street 257
Stuttgart
Germany 70597
49-7-11-76-9600-0
Fax: 49-7-11-76-9600-0
iss@issev.de
www.international-school-stuttgart.de
The International School of Stuttgart provides students of internationally-minded families with a high quality, English language education.
Timothy Kelley, Director
Sarah Kupke, Head of School

1901 International School-Trieste
Via Conconello 16 Opicina
Trieste Friuli - Venezia Giulia
Italy 34151
39-040-211-452
Fax: 39-040-213-122
istrieste@interbusiness.it
www.istrieste.org
It is our mission to provide students from the international and local community with a broad, balanced education using English both in curricular and extra-curricular life of the school.
Peter Metzger, Principal
Jim Pastore, Director

1902 International School-Turin
Vicolo Tiziano 10
Moncalieri
Italy 10024
391- 45-9
Fax: 39 -11 -43 2
www.acat-ist.it
The school's goal is to create self-motivated, independent learners who strive for excellence. The school community feels that this is best achieved in an environment which fosters trust and respect between the educational staff and the student body, demands accountability and team-work, while inspiring a general sense of well-being and self-confidence.
George Selby, BA, MA, Principal

1903 International School-Venice
Via Terraglio 30
Mestre, Venice
Italy 30174
04 -98 -711
Fax: 04 -98 -001
info@isvenice.com
www.isvenice.com
The fundamental aim of The International School of Venice is to give its pupils a bilingual education and an intellectual education based on tolerance, open-mindedness and an acceptance of diversity.
John Millerchip, Principal

1904 International School-Zug
Walterswil
Baar 6340
Switzerland
41-41-768-1188
Fax: 41-41-768-1189
www.iszl.ch
Grade levels include preK-8 with a total enrollment of 354.
Martin Latter, Head of School

1905 International Schule-Berlin, Potsdam
Seestrasse 45
14467 Potsdam
Germany
49-332-086-760
Fax: 49-332-086-7612
This school offers an English curriculum to 157 day students (87 boys and 64 girls) in grades PreK-12. Applications needed to teach include science, pre-school, math, social sciences, reading, English and physical education.
Matthias Truper, Principal

1906 International Secondary School-Eindhoven
Venetiestraat 43
RM Eindhoven
Netherlands 05632
040-413600
isse@issehv.nl
By striving for excellence in education and by engaging with the international community, the ISSE seeks to be an asset to Eindhoven and the Noord-Brabant region.
JM Westerhout, Principal
M Watts, Acting Head of School

1907 Internationale Schule Frankfurt-Rhein-Main
Strasse zur Internationalen Schule
Frankfurt
Germany 65931
49-69-954-3190
Fax: 49-69-954-31920
isf@sabis.net
www.isf-net.de
ISF Internationale Schule-Rhein-Main, as a member of the SABISr School Network, is academically oriented without being highly selective.
Angus Slesser, School Director
Carl Bistany, Managing Director

1908 Interskolen
Engtoften 22
8260 Viby J
Denmark
45-8611-4560
Fax: 45-8614-9670
adm@interskolen.dk
www.interskolen.dk
Coeducational day program for ages five to seventeen.
Tommy Schou Christesen, Principal

1909 John F Kennedy International School
CH-3792 Saanen
Switzerland 03792
41-33-744-1372
Fax: 41-33-744-8982
lovell@jfk.ch
www.jfk.ch
Boarding day school for boys and girls aged 5-14 years.
William Lovell, Co-Director
Sandra Lovell, Co-Director

1910 John F Kennedy School-Berlin
Teltower Damm 87-93
Berlin
Germany 14167
49-30-6321-5711
Fax: 49-30-6321-6377
jfks-el-adm@t-online.de
www.jfks.de
The John F. Kennedy School is a bilingual, bicultural German-American tuition-free public school.
Herr Ulrich Schurmann, Managing Principal
HR Roth, German Principal

1911 Joppenhof/Jeanne D'arc Clg
PO Box 4050, 6202 Rb Maastricht
Netherlands
47 -77 -000
www.paguro.net
L Spronck, Principal

1912 Kaiserslautern Elementary School
Unit 3240 Box 425
APO
Germany, AE 09021
080- -520
063- 99-46
Fax: 063- 58-06
Bariett Prince, Principal

1913 Kaiserslautern High School
Unit 3240 Box 425
APO
Germany, AE 09021
801- 1-20
063- 99-47
Fax: 063- 99-46
Bariett Prince, Principal
Richard Nicholson, Assistant Principal

1914 Kaiserslautern Middle School
Unit 3240 Box 425
APO
Germany, AE 09021
802- 1-20
063- 99-48
Fax: 063- 99-25
Bariett Prince, Principal
Marion Sutton, Assistant Principal

1915 Kendale Primary International School
Via Gradoli 86, Via Cassia Km 10300
00189 Rome
Italy
39-06-332-676-08
Fax: 39-06-332-676-08
kendale@diesis.com
www.diesis.com/kendale
Veronica Said Tani, Principal

1916 Kensington School
Carrer Dels Cavallers 31-33 Pedralb
Barcelona
Spain 08034
930-345-
Fax: 938-006-
info@kensingtonschoolbcn.com
www.kensingtonschoolbcn.com
EP Giles, Principal

1917 King Fahad Academy
Bromyard Avenue, Acton
London
United Kingdom W3-7HD9
020-7259-3350
academy@thekfa.org.uk
www.thekfa.org.uk
The idea for the establishment of an academy that caters for the educational needs of the Saudi Arabian, Arab and Muslim communities in the UK

took its genesis in the creation of the King Fahad Academy in London in 1985 AD/1405 H

Dr. Ibtissam Al-Bassam, Dean
Mohammed Bin Na Al Saud, Chairman

18 King's College
Paseo de los Andes, 35
Soto De Viuelas, Madrid
Spain
91-803-48-00
Fax: 91-803-65-57
info@kingscollege.es
www.kingscollege.es
to sustain and develop an educational environment in which all students are able to fulfil their maximum potential, both as individuals and as members of a community.

CA Clark, Principal
David Johnson, Headmaster

19 Kitzingen Elementary School
Unit 26124
APO, Kitzingen 09031 0005
Germany

Fred Paesel, Principal

20 Kleine Brogel Elementary School
701 MUNSS
Unit 8150, APO AE
Belgium 09719
001-179-2527
Fax: 001-179-0091
terry.emerson@eu.dodea.edu

Terry Emerson, Principal

21 La Chataigneraie International School
Geneva La Chataigneraie, 1297
1208 Geneva
Switzerland
122-787-2400
www.ecolint.ch

Michael Lee, Principal

922 La Maddalena Elementary School
PSC 816 Box 1755
FPO, La Maddalena, Sardinia 09612 0005
Italy
907-897- 820
www.aoshs.org

Janice Barber, Principal

923 Lajes Elementary School
Unit 7725
APO AE
Portugal 09720
351-295-5741
Fax: 011-351-295

Mary Waller, Principal

924 Lajes High School
Unit 7725
APO AE
Portugal 09720
351-295-5741
Fax: 351-295-5425

Virginia Briggs, Principal

925 Lakenheath Elementary School
Unit 5185 Box 40
APO AE
Great Britain 09464-8540
016-805-3072
Fax: 016-8 5-3943
Lakenheath Elementary School serves the US Military overseas as part of the Department of Defense Dependent Schools

Charles Yahres, Principal
Rhonda Bennett, Assistant Principal

1926 Lakenheath High School
Unit 5185 Box 45
APO AE
Great Britain 09461-8545
044- 01- 852
Fax: 044- 01- 853
lakenheathhs.attendance@eu.dodea.edu
Lakenheath High School (LHS) serves three U.S. Air Force bases located in the East Anglia region of England; about 1.5 hours drive northeast of London. LHS is coeducational.

Kent Worford, Principal
Barbara Lee, Assistant Principal

1927 Lakenheath Middle School
Unit 5185 Box 55
APO AE
Great Britain 09461-8555
011-44 -638
Fax: 226-737-
LakenheathMS.Principal@eu.dodea.edu

Mary Zimmerman-Bayer, Principal
D J LaFon, Assistant Principal

1928 Lancing College
Lancing, West Sussex
BN15 ORW
England
0273-452213
Fax: 01273-464720
admissions@lancing.org.uk
www.lancingcollege.co.uk
One of Britain's leading independent schools for boys and girls aged 13 to 18

Jonathan W J Gillespie, Headmaster
Harry Brunjes, Chairman

1929 Landstuhl Elementary and Middle School
CMR 402
APO AE
Germany 09180-402
637-192-6508
Fax: 637-192-6514
LandstuhlEMS.Principal@eu.dodea.edu

Susan Ransom, Principal
Stephen Austin, Assistant Principal

1930 Leighton Park School
Shinfield Road
Reading RG2 7DH
England
4-118-987-9600
Fax: 44-118-987-9625
info@leightonpark.com
www.leightonpark.com
Life at Leighton Park reflects the school's Quaker foundation and is influenced by Quaker thinking and practice. We seek to create a community of tolerance and understanding within which a balance between discipline, especially self-discipline, freedom and exploration is maintained.

John Dunston, Headmaster
Elizabeth Thomas, Deputy Head

1931 Leipzig International School
Konneritzstrasse 47
Leipzig
Germany 04229
49-341-421-0574
Fax: 49-341-421-2154
admin@intschool-leipzig.com
www.intschool-leipzig.com
The Leipzig International School provides a quality education conducted primarily in English for children of all nationalities and cultures living in the Leipzig region. We seek to give all students the opportunity to discover and develop their intellectual, creative, social and physical potential to the full.

Michael Webster, Headmaster
Clemens Gerteiser, Commercial Editor

1932 Lennen Bilingual School
65 Quai d'Orsay
Paris
France 75007
01-47-05-66-55
Fax: 01-47-05-17-18
www.lennenbilingual.com
This school teaches a curriculum in English and French to 120 day students. The school is willing to participate in a teacher exchange program with the length of stay being one year, with no housing provided by the school. Bilingual education is offered in the preschool and grade school (until Grade 3).

Michelle Lennen, Principal

1933 Leys School
The Leys School
Cambridge CB2 7AD
England
44-1223-508-900
Fax: 44-1223-505-333
office@theleys.net
The Leys is one of England's premier independent schools.

Mark Slater, Headmaster

1934 Leysin American School
1854 Leysin
Switzerland
41-24-493-3777
Fax: 41-24-493-3790
admissions@las.ch
www.las.ch
At the core of Leysin American School is a guiding set of principles and beliefs that set the highest standards for our efforts every day.

Steven Oh, Executive Director
Vladimir Kuskovski, Headmaster

1935 Livorno Elementary School
Unit 31301 Box 65
APO, Livorno 09613 0005
Italy
www.livo-ems.eu.dodea.edu

Dr. Robert Kethcart, Principal

1936 Livorno High School
Unit 31301 Box 65
APO, Livorno 09613 0005
Italy, AE 09613-5

Dr. Frank Calvano, Principal

1937 London Central High School
PSC 821 Box 119
APO, High Wycombe 09421 0005
Great Britain, AE 09421-5
www.londoncentral.org

Dr. Charles Recesso, Principal

1938 Lorentz International School
Groningensingel 1245, 6835HZ
Arnhem
Netherlands
31-26-320-0110
Fax: 31-26-320-0113

Jan M Meens, Principal

1939 Lusitania International College Foundation
Apartado 328
8600 Lagos
Portugal

Krisine Byrne, Principal

1940 Lyce International-American Section
BP 230, rue du Fer A Cheval
St Germain-En-Laye, 78104 Cedex
France
033-051-7485
Fax: 139-100-914
pursues this mission through a rigorous and rewarding American curriculum which culminates in the French Baccalaureate with International Option, as well as through a broad and enriching co-curricular program including such activities as drama, community service, sports and student publications.
Sean Lynch, Director
Beth Heudebourg, President

1941 Lycee Francais De Belgique
9 Avenue Du Lycee Francais
1180 Brussels
Belgium
02-374-58-78
www.lyceefrancais-jmonnet.be
Jean-Claude Giudicelli, Principal

1942 Lyc,e International-American Section
33-1-345-17485
Fax: 33-1-308-70049
Grade levels Pre-K through 12, school year September - June

1943 Malvern College
College Road, Malvern
Worcestershire WR14 3DF
England
01684-581-500
www.malverncollege.org.uk
Boarding school.
Antony Clark, Headmaster

1944 Mannheim Elementary School
Unit 29938
APO AE
09086
380-4705
Fax: 0621-723-905
esmannattend@eu.dodea.edu
Dr. Ardelle Hamilton PhD, Principal
Dr. Ellen Minette, Assistant Principal

1945 Mannheim High School
Unit 29939
APO AE
09267
380-409-
Fax: 062- 73-901
MannheimHS.Principal@eu.dodea.edu
is to equip all students to be conscientiously contributing citizens through a challenging curriculum and effective instruction
Sharon O'Donnell, Principal

1946 Margaret Danyers College
N Downs Road, Cheadle Hulme
Cheadle SK8 5HA
England
061-485-4372
Harry Tomlinson, BA, MA, MS, Headmaster

1947 Mark Twain Elementary School
Unit 29237
APO, Heidelberg 09102 0005
Germany 80909
www.mtwain.k12.ca.us
Joseph Newbury, Principal

1948 Marymount International School-Rome
Via di Villa Lauchli 180
00191 Rome
Italy
33-1-462-41051
Fax: 33-1-463-70750
marymount@marymountrome.org
www.marymountrome.org/
Marymount International School provides an education based on Christian values. Marymount is dedicated to fostering individual dignity in an atmosphere of love and respect in which students, faculty, staff and parents work and pray together.
Anne Marie Clancy, Headmistress

1949 Marymount International School-United Kingdom
George Road
Kingston upon Thames, Surrey, KT2 7PE
Surrey , United Kingdom KT2 7
44-20-8949-0571
Fax: 44-20-8336-2485
admissions@marymount.kingston.sch.uk
Marymount London is a vibrant and dynamic learning community where all are respected and encouraged to contribute,committed to developing individuals.
Cathleen Fagan, Headmistress

1950 Mattlidens Gymnasium
Mattliden 1
02230 Esbo
Finland
09 -16 -30 5
Fax: 09 -16 -30 5
www.mattliden.fi/gym/
Mattlidens Gymnasium is a coeducational Swedish-speaking upper secondary school
Tom Ginman, Headmaster

1951 Mayenne English School
Chateau les Courges 53420
Chailland
France
J Braillard, Principal

1952 Menwith Hill Estates & Middle School
PSC 45 Unit 8435
APO, High Wycombe 09468 0005
Great Britain
142-377-7778
Fax: 142-377-0236
Dr. Arnold Watland, Principal

1953 Millfield School
Butleigh Road Street
Somerset
England BA16-0YD
145-844-2291
office@millfieldschool.com
www.millfieldschool.com
With its outstanding facilities, a staff:pupil ratio of 1:7.5, an extraordinary range of academic courses and the unrivalled strength of its extra-curricular programme, Millfield strives to achieve all these aims. It also seeks to move with the times whilst maintaining the important traditions of good manners, discipline and respect for others
Craig Considine, Headmaster
Adrian E White, Chairman of the Governors

1954 Monkton Combe School
Church Lane
Monkton Combe, Bath
England BA2-7HG
01225-721102
Fax: 01225-721208
reception@monkton.org.uk
www.monktoncombeschool.com
Boarding and day school for girls and boys ages two to nineteen.
Chris Stafford, Headmaster
Richard Backhouse, Principal

1955 Monti Parioli English School
Via Monti Parioli 50
00197 Rome
Italy
Lynette Surtees, Principal

1956 Mougins School
615 Avenue Maurice Donat
CS 12180, 06252 Mougins Cedex
France
33-4-93-90-15-47
Fax: 33-4-93-75-31-40
information@mougins-school.com
www.mougins-school.com
The School has a capacity of 550 students, large enough to provide a stimulating environment and small enough to retain a caring family atmosphere. With over 40 nationalities, the School is culturally rich and aims to encourage pupils to develop morally, emotionally, culturally, intellectually and physically.
Brian G Hickmore, Headmaster
Johanna Povall, Deputy Head

1957 Mountainview School
Bosch 35-6331 Hunenberg
Switzerland
Brenda Moors, Principal

1958 Munich International School
Schloss Buchhof
Starnberg
Germany 82319
49-8151-366-100
Fax: 49-8151-366-109
admissions@mis-munich.de
www.mis-munich.de
MIS caters for the physical, social, emotional and educational development of its children by providing a student-centred, inquiry-based learning environment which fosters an appreciation in its students of their cultural heritage and the cultural richness of the global community.
Mary Sepalla, Head of School
Maha Kattoura, Chairman

1959 Naples Elementary School
PSC 808 Box 39
FPO, AE
Italy 09618
011-39 -8108
Fax: 011-39 -8108
NaplesES.Principal@eu.dodea.edu
Dr. Jacqueline Hulbert, Principal

1960 Naples High School
PSC 808 Box 15
FPO, AE
Italy 09618
011-39 -8108
Fax: 011-39 -8108
NaplesHS.Principal@eu.dodea.edu
Students will be prepared to be critical thinkers, effective communicators, and accountable members in a global society.
Carl Albrecht, Principal

1961 Neubruecke Elementary School
Unit 23825
APO, Neubruecke 09034 0005
Germany
Margaret Hoffman-Otto, Principal

1962 Neuchatel Junior College
44 Victoria Street
Suite 1310
Toronto, ON M5C-1Y2
038-25-27-00
800-263-2923
Fax: 038-24-42-59
info@neuchatel.org
www.njc.ch
To provide students a rigorous university preparatory programme in a culturally rich and multi-lingual European setting where learning through educational travel, engagement with world affairs and service to others fosters personal growth and leadership.
Norman Southward, Principal
Dayle Leishman, Director

1963 New School Rome
Via Della Camilluccia 669
Roma
Italy 00135
39-329-4269
info@newschoolrome.com
www.newschoolrome.com
The School is a non-profit making organisation run by the Academic Council (all staff and seven student representatives) which also elects the headteacher, and by the Executive Council (three elected teachers and four elected parents).
Josette Fusco, Head Teacher
Richard Lydiker, Executive Chairman

1964 Newton College
Av Ricardo El as Aparicio 240
La Molina
Lima-Peru, PE
511-479-0460
Fax: 511-479-0430
college@newton.edu.pe
www.newton.edu.pe
Newton College is an Anglo-Peruvian, co-educational, bilingual, day school for students aged 2 to 18.
David Few, Principal

1965 Norra Reals Gymnasium
Roslagsgatan 1
Stockholm
Sweden 113 5
087-420-
Fax: 087-328-
www.norrareal.stockholm.se
Offers two preparatory study programs: the science and social science.
Per Engback, Principal
Maria Sellberg, Assistant Principal

1966 Numont School
C/ Parma 16
Madrid
Spain 28043
349-130-0243
Fax: 349-759-
numont@telefonica.net
Provide a warm, happy and challenging atmosphere where children can derive pleasure from learning and achieving their personal goals. The emphasis is on the individual, so that all of the children, regardless of strengths and weaknesses, colour, creed or sex, feel valued and able to reach their full potential.
Margaret Ann Swanson, Principal

1967 Oak House School
Sant Pere Claver 12-18
Barcelona
Spain 08017
349-325- 402
Fax: 349-325- 402
sec@oakhouseschool.com
www.oakhouseschool.com
The training of students both personal and social is one of the main objectives of the educational work.
Teresa Armadans, Director of Finance
VicenØ Orobitg, Information Technology

1968 Oakham School
Chapel Close
Market Place
Oakham,Rutland, UK LE15
44-0-1572-758758
Fax: 44-0-1572-758595
www.oakham.rutland.sch.uk
A pioneer of full co-education, a boarding and day school for boys and girls aged 10 to 18 years that has become widely known for developing new ideas and making them work to the benefit of all Oakham's pupils.
Joseph AF Spence, Headmaster
Jon Wills, Registrar

1969 Oporto British School
Rua Da Cerca 326/338
PORTO
Portugal 4150-
226-666-
school@obs.edu.pt
www.obs.edu.pt
As the oldest British School in Continental Europe, the Oporto British School is committed to providing a high quality international education for its students.
Mark Rogers, Principal
David Butcher, Headmaster

1970 Oslo American School
Gml Ringeriksv 53, 1340 Bekkestua
Oslo
Norway 05507
www.oasalumni.org
James Mcneil, Principal

1971 Panterra American School
Via Ventre D'oca 41, Fontanella
Pescara 65131
Italy
Virginia Simpson, Principal

1972 Paris American Academy
277 Rue Street Jacques
Paris
France 75005
001-449-
Fax: 01 -4 4- 99
To create and maintain a system of higher education that contributes to the transformation of students into
Peter Carman, President/Executive Director
Jean-Michel Ageron-Blanc, General Director

1973 Patrick Henry Elementary School
Unit 29237
APO, Heidelberg
Germany, AE 09102
388-905-
Fax: 062-1 7-5 49
PatrickHenryES.Principal@eu.dodea.edu
To educate all children by providing a nurturing environment and standards-based curriculum dedicated to meeting he diverse needs of every child.
Russ Claus, Principal
Marie Granger, Assistant Principal

1974 Perse School
Hills Road
Cambridge CB2 8QF
England
0223-248127
office@perse.co.uk
www.perse.co.uk
Edward Elliott, Head of Politics
Dan Cross, Deputy Head

1975 Pinewood Schools of Thessaloniki
PO Box 21001
555 10 Pilea
Greece
30-31-301-221
Fax: 30-31-323-196
pinewood@spark.net.gr
www.pinepeaceschool.k12.vi
Independent, coeducational schools which offer an educational program from prekindergarten through grade 12 and boarding facilities from grade 7 though grade 12 for students of all nationalities. The school year comprises 2 semesters extending from September to January and from January to June.
Peter B Baiter, Director

1976 Pordenone Elementary School
PSC 1
Aviano
Italy
39-0434-28462
Fax: 39-0434-28761
D Jean Waddell, Principal

1977 Priory School
West Bank, Dorking
Surrey RH4 3DG
England
130-688-7337
Fax: 130-688-8715
enquiries@staff.priorycofe.surrey.sch.uk
www.priorycofe.surrey.sch.uk
To provide an educational environment which encourages pupils to become confident, competent, self-reliant and happy members of society, fully prepared for adult life and the world of work
A C Sohatski, Headteacher
M Pinchin, Senior Deputy Headteacher

1978 Queen Elizabeth School
Queen's Road, Barnet
Hertfordshire
England, UK EN5 4
020-844-0464
Fax: 020-844-0750
enquiries@qebarnet.co.uk
www.qebarnet.co.uk
To produce boys who are confident, able and responsible.
John Marincowitz, Headmaster

1979 Queens College the English School
Juan De Saridakis 64
Palma de Malorca
Spain
809-393-2153
www.qc.cuny.edu
This Methodist affiliated school offers an English-based curriculum to a total of 1,200 female students, grades K1-12. The school does recruit from overseas, offering three year contracts with housing provided for one week at the beginning of the contract, while they find accommodations. Applications

needed to teach include science, pre-school, French, math, Spanish, English and physical education.
Philip Cash, Principal

1980 Rainbow Elementary School
Unit 28614 Box 0040
APO, Ansbach 09177 0005
Germany
407-320-8450
www.rainbow.scps.k12.fl.us
Thomas Murdock, Principal

1981 Ramstein Elementary School
Unit 3240 Box 430
APO AE
Germany 09094
067-014-0 39
Fax: 067- 15- 835
To provide a quality education for eligible minor dipendents of DoD military and civilian personnel stationed overseas.
Kathy Downs, Principal

1982 Ramstein High School
Unit 3240 Box 445
APO AE
Germany 09094-445
067-1 4-6095
Fax: 067-1 4-9 86
To provide a varied and challenging curriculum that will allow students to be life-long learners and responsible participants in a global community.
Greg Hatch, Principal

1983 Ramstein Intermediate School
Unit 3240 Box 600
APO AE
Germany 09094-600
067-1 4-6023
Fax: 067-1 5-238
To provide an educational environment designed to maximize the potential of all Students.
Stanley B Caldwell, Principal

1984 Ramstein Junior High School
86 SPTG CCSI R, Unit 3240 Box 455
APO, Ramstein 09094 0005
Germany
Richard Snell, Principal

1985 Rathdown School
Upper Glenageary Road Glenageary
Co Dublin
Ireland
01-853133
admin@rathdownschool.ie
www.rathdownschool.ie/contact_us.php
Our aim is to offer a high-quality, modern, challenging and liberal education. In an inclusive and friendly environment, Rathdown School hopes to foster a love of learning which will enable each student to develop her own unique potential. Our purpose is to support and promote the student's academic, cultural, sporting, creative, musical and spiritual capabilities.
Barbara Ennis, Principal

1986 Rikkyo School in England
Guildford Road, Rudgwick, W Sussex
RH12 3BE
Great Britain
014-3 8-2107
Fax: 014-3 8-2535
eikoku@rikkyo.w-sussex.sch.uk
www.rikkyo.co.uk
M Usuki, Principal

1987 Riverside School
Walterswil
6340 Baar
Switzerland
41-41-724-5690
Fax: 41-41-724-5692
office.zug@iszl.ch
www.iszl.ch
The International School of Zug and Luzern (ISZL) provides a high quality Pre-School to Grade 12 international education to day students resident in the Cantons of central Switzerland.
Dominic Currer, Director
Elaine Tomlinson, Headmaster

1988 Robinson Barracks Elementary School
Unit 30401
APO
Germany, AE 09107
491-119-
Fax: 071- 85- 473
RobinsonBarracksES.Principal@eu.dodea.edu
The Robinson Barrack's school community provides a respectful environment where all members learn to recognize their strengths and gain confidence to become lifelong learners and leaders in an ever-changing world.
Shirley Sheck, Principal

1989 Rome International School
Via Panama 25
00198 Rome
Italy
039-06 -4482
Fax: 039-06 -4482
office@romeinternationalschool.it
www.romeinternationalschool.it
Provides a nurturing environment, in which children of all nationalities and faiths can explore and respect their own and each other's cultural and religious heritage.
Patricia Martin-Smith, Principal Primary School
Ivano Boragine, Managing Director

1990 Rosall School
Fleetwood
Lancashire
United Kingdom FY7 8
012- 37- 420
Fax: 012- 37- 205
Providing a unique educational experience we offer a wide ranging choice of curriculums underpinned by a commitment to academic excellence.
RDW Rhodes, Principal
GSH Penelley, Faculty Head

1991 Rosemead
East Street, Littlehampton
BN17 6AL
England
0903-716065
J Bevis, BA, Headmaster

1992 Rota Elementary School
PSC 819 Box 19
FPO AE 09645 0019
Spain
345-624-
Fax: 011-34 -56 8
rotaes.principal@eu.dodea.edu
Provides a standards-based educational program, which creates lifelong learners and responsible citizens.
Charles Callahan, Principal

1993 Rota High School
PSC 819 Box 63
FPO AE 09645 0005
Spain
345-624-
Fax: 011-34 -56 8
RotaHS.Principal@eu.dodea.edu
Lynne Michael, Principal

1994 Roudybush Foreign Service School
Place des Arcades, Sauveterre de Rouergue (Averyon)
France
This European school prepares men for the foreign service.
Franklin Roudybush, AB, MA, Headmaster

1995 Rugby School
Rugby, Warwickshire
United Kingdom CV22
44-178-854-3465
Fax: 44-178-856-9124
enquiries@rugbyschool.net
www.rugbyschool.net
Rugby School is an educational community whose philosophy embraces the challenges of academic excellence, spiritual awareness, responsibility and leadership, friendships and relationships and participation in a wide variety of activities
Patrick Derham, Headmaster
SK Fletcher, Deputy Head

1996 Runnymede College School
Calle Salvia 30
28109 La Moraleja, Madrid
Spain
34-91-650-8302
Fax: 34-91-650-8236
office@runnymede-college.com
www.runnymede-college.com
Provides an all-round, academic, liberal humanist education to all students regardless of their sex, race, religion or nationality. There is no religious instruction.
Frank M Powell, Headmaster
FJ Murphy, Deputy Head

1997 Rygaards International School
Bernstorffsvej 54, DK-2900
Hellerup
Denmark
45-39-62-10-53
Fax: 45-39-62-10-81
admin@rygaards.com
www.rygaards.com
Rygaards School is a private, Christian/Catholic, co-educational establishment. It is recognised by and subject to, Danish law and receives a subsidy from the Danish State.
Mathias Jepsen, Principal
Charles Dalton, Headmaster

1998 Salzburg International Preparatory School
Moosstrasse 106
A-5020 Salzburg
Austria
662-844485
Fax: 662-847711
A coeducational boarding school offering an American college preparatory high school curriculum for grades 7 to 12 as well as a post graduate course.

1999 Schiller Academy
51-55 Waterloo Road
London, SE1 8TX
United Kingdom
44-207-928-1372
Fax: 44-207-928-8089

Grade levels 9-12, school year August - June

George Selby, Headmaster
Renee Miller, Director Studies

2000 Schools of England, Wales, Scotland & Ireland
J. Burrow & Company
Imperial House, Lypiatt Road
Cheltenham 50201
England

2001 Schweinfurt American Elementary School
CMR 457
AP, AE
Germany 09033
09721-81893
Fax: 09721-803905
schweinfurtes.principal@eu.dodea.edu
The mission of Schweinfurt Elementary School is to help all students become respectful, responsible citizens and life-long learners.

Wilma Holt, Principal
Beverly Erdmann, Assistant Principal

2002 Schweinfurt Middle School
CMR 457
AP, AE
Germany 09033-5
354-681-1800
Fax: 097-1 8-363
Schweinfurt Middle School will engage all students in meaningful experiences that develop 21st Century Skills, preparing them to be successful and responsible citizens in a technological, global society.

Dr George P Carpenter, Principal

2003 Sembach Elementary School
Unit 4240 Box 325
APO, AE
Germany 09136
063- 67-0
Fax: 063-271-
SembachES.Principal@eu.dodea.edu

Monica Harvey, Principal

2004 Sembach Middle School
Unit 4240 Box 320
APO, AE
Germany 09136
063- 67-0
Fax: 063-271-
SembachMS.Principal@eu.dodea.edu

Bonnie B Hannan, Principal

2005 Sevenoaks School
Sevenoaks
Kent TN13 IHU
England
44 -017-245
Fax: 44 -017-245
enq@sevenoaksschool.org
www.sevenoaksschool.org
Sevenoaks School is an independent, co-educational boarding and day school, set in 100 acres in the heart of Southeast England. Half an hour from Central London, and half an hour from Gatwick International Airport, we are situated on the edge of Sevenoaks, overlooking the 15th century deer park of the Knole Estate.

Katy Ricks, Head of School
Tony Evans, Chairman

2006 Sevilla Elementary & Junior High School
496 ABS DODDS Unit 6585
APO Moron AB 09643 0005
Spain

Robert Ludwig, Principal

2007 Shape Elementary School
Unit 21420
APO, AE
Belgium 09705
011-32 -5044
Fax: 011-32 -31
ShapeES.Principal@eu.dodea.edu
It is the mission of SHAPE Elementary School to educate all students in an integrated, multi-cultural environment to become productive thinkers, to achieve their maximum physical and mental potential, and to be literate, responsible members of a global society through excellence in teaching and learning.

Charlene Leister, Principal
Miles Shea, Assistant Principal

2008 Shape High School
Unit 21420
APO, AE
Belgium 09705
011-32 -5044
Fax: 011-32 -31
david.tran@eu.dodea.edu

David Tran, Principal
Arlena Ray, Assistant Principal

2009 Shape International School
Avenue de Reijkjavik 717
SHAPE
Belgium 07010
65-44-52-83
Performs the operational duties previously undertaken by Allied Command Europe and Allied Command Atlantic

Jacques Laurent, Principal

2010 Sidcot School
Winscombe
N Somerset BS25 1PD
England
44-193-484-3102
Fax: 44-193-484-4181
addmissions@sidcot.org.uk
www.sidcot.org.uk
This friendly school with an international enrollment of 277 day students and 149 boarding students (255 boys; 171 girls), in grades K-12, is set in over one hundred acres of Somerset countryside. The school offers an English-based curriculum and the student/teacher ratio is 10:1.

John Walmsley, Headteacher
Ross Wallis, Head of Art

2011 Sierra Bernia School
La Caneta s/n
Alfaz del Pi Alicante
Spain 03580
96-687-51-49
Fax: 96-687-36-33
duncan@ctv.es
www.sierraberniaschool.com/news.php
Forefront of modern education. Combining both traditional and innovative methods of teaching made possible by the wealth and immense knowledge base of its fully qualified teaching body

Duncan Allan, Owner/Director
Iain Macinnes, Headteacher

2012 Sigonella Elementary & High School
PSC 824 Box 2630
FPO Signoella, Sicily 09627 2630
Italy
624-440-
www.sigo-es.eu.dodea.edu/

Dr. Peter Price, Principal

2013 Sigtunaskolan Humanistiska Laroverket
Manfred Bjorkquists Alle 6
Box 508, Sigtuna
Sweden 19328
46-8-592-57100
Fax: 46-8-592-57250
info@sshl.se
www.sshl.se
Grade levels include 7-12 with an enrollment of 543.

Kent Edberg, Principal
Rune Svaninger, Director

2014 Sir James Henderson School
Via Pisani Dossi 16
Milano
Italy 20134
39-02-264-13310
Fax: 39-02-264-13515
www.sjhschool.com
To ensure that its diverse student body grows to its full potential as independent learners in a caring British and international community, uniting the best of British educational tradition with the values, practices and beliefs of the International Baccalaureate

Stephen Anson, Principal
Jim Noble, Chairman

2015 Skagerak Gymnas
PO Box 1545-Veloy
3206 Sandefjord
Norway
473-345-6500
www.skagerak.org

Elisabeth Norr, Principal

2016 Smith Elementary School
Unit 23814 Box 30
APO, AE
Germany 09034-3814
067-783-5693
Fax: 067-783-8874
SmithES.Principal@eu.dodea.edu

Kent Bassett, Principal

2017 Southlands English School
Via Teleclide 40
Casalapalocco, Rome
Italy 00124
39 -605-5039
Fax: 06 -091-7192
www.southlands.it
Our aim is to give you a flavour of the quality educational experience available at Southlands and encourage you to visit the school so you can see for yourself the happy, successful community that Southlands nurtures.

Deryck M Wilson, Principal

2018 Spangdahlem Elementary School
52 MSG/CCSE S, Unit 3640 Box 50
APO, AE
Germany 09126-4050
065-056- 688
Fax: 065-056- 710
SpnagdahlemES.Principal@eu.dodea.edu

Richard R Alix, Principal

2019 Spangdahlem Middle School
52 CSG CCSM, Unit 3640 Box 45
APO, AE
Germany 09126-4045
065-506- 725
Fax: 065-506-0279
SpangdahlemMS.Principal@eu.dodea.ed
u
Spangdhalem Middle School promotes high achievement and lifelong learning for all students through positive interactions and standards-based educational program.
Joseph Malloy, Principal

2020 Sportfield Elementary School
Unit 20193 Box 0014
APO, Hanau
Germany, AE 09165-14
John O'Reilly, Jr, Principal

2021 St. Andrew's College
19 Carillon Avenue
Newtown NSW
Australia 02042
02-9626-1999
principalassist@standrewscollege.edu.au
www.standrewscollege.edu.au
St Andrew's is proud of its reputation as a leading academic institution, fostering leaders within the community and moulding the leaders of tomorrow. The College places emphasis on academic and intellectual development and excellence as core to the development of the individual.
Wayne Erickson, Principal
Donna Wiemann, Development Manager

2022 St. Anne's School
Jarama 9
Madrid 2
Spain
www.stannes.edu.in
Margaret Raines, Principal

2023 St. Anthony's International College
Camino de Coin km 53.5
Mijas-Costa, Malaga
Spain 29649
00 -09 -247
Fax: 00 -09 -046
info@stanthonyscollege.com
www.stanthonyscollege.com
The school with its friendly, family atmosphere provides opportunities for our students to achieve their best. Trying not to cater just for high achievers we endeavour, through a broad and balanced education, to find courses for all abilities.

2024 St. Catherine's British School
PO Box 51019
Kifissia 145 10 Athens
Greece
301- 8-97
Fax: 301- 8-64
www.stcatherines.gr
The school endeavors to foster a love of learning through a well taught, appropriately challenging, clearly defined and balanced curriculum. Our aim is to fully develop intellectual, social, physical and creative potential, giving students the foundatin to develop into sensitive, informed, and capable global citizens of the future.
Michael Toman, Principal
R Morton, Headmaster & CEO

2025 St. Christopher School
Barrington Road, Letchworth
Hertfordshire SG6 3JZ
England
0462-679301
Fax: 0462-481578
school.admin@stchris.co.uk
www.stchris.co.uk
St Christopher has a distinctive ethos, based on the development of each child's individuality whilst teaching a sense of responsibility towards others, towards the School and towards the local and global community.
Richard Palmer, Head of School
Emma-Kate Henry, Deputy Head of St Christophe

2026 St. Clare's Oxford
139 Banbury Road
Oxford OX2 7AL
England
44-186-555-2031
Fax: 44-186-551-3359
admissions@stclares.ac.uk
www.stclares.ac.uk
St. Clare's welcomes students and staff of all nationalities and cultures who will benefit from, and contribute to, our learning community. Living and studying together, we learn from one another. We are enriched and challenged by a diversity of views and ideas.
Paula Holloway, Principal
Tom Walsh, Vice Principal

2027 St. David's School
Justin Hall, Beckenham Road
West Wickham BR4 0QS
England
01784-252494
Fax: 01784-252494
office@stdavidsschool.com
www.sdsw.org
Boarding school for girls ages nine to eighteen; day school for girls ages four to eighteen.
Judith G Osborne, BA, Headmaster

2028 St. Dominic's International School
Outeiro de Polima-Arneiro
2785-816 Sao Domingos da Rana
Portugal
351-21-448-0550
351-214-5505
Fax: 351-21-444-3027
school@dominics-int.org
www.dominics-int.org
Our school mission is to offer an international education of the highest calibre enriched and enlivened by the Dominican tradition of study and education; promoting the development of each student's potential: physical, emotional, social, intellectual, moral and spiritual.
Maria do Rosÿri Empis, Principal
Manuel Lucas, President of Supervision

2029 St. Dominic's Sixth Form College
Mount Park Avenue Harrow on the Hil
Middlesex HA1 3HX
England
020-84228084
208-422-3759
Fax: 020-8422-3759
stdoms@stdoms.ac.uk
www.stdoms.ac.uk
St. Dominic's is a Roman Catholic Sixth Form College committed to the pesonal and spiritual growth of all its members based on Christian values, academic excellence and high quality pastoral care.
Patrick Harty, Principal

2030 St. Georges English School
Via Cassia Km 16
La Storta Rome
Italy 00123
06-3790141
Fax: 06-3792490
www.stgeorge.school.it
To develop the individual talents of young people and teach them to relate the experience of the classroom to the realities of the world outside.
Martyn Hales, Principal

2031 St. Georges School
Vila Goncalve, Quinta Loureiras
2750 Cascais
Portugal
112-602-4645
www.sgs.edu.in
MPB Hoare, Principal

2032 St. Georges School-Switzerland
Chemin de St Georges 19
Clarens Montreux
Switzerland 01815
21-964-34-11
Fax: 21-964-49-32
www.st-georges.ch
St. George's School encourages students to lift their eyes and recognise positive qualities within themselves and others and to nurture a caring and dynamic attitude in today's demanding world.
Dr Ilya V Eigenbrot, Principal
Francis Kahn, President of Directors

2033 St. Gerard's School
Thornhill Road, Bray Co Wicklow
Republic of Ireland
353-001-2821
Fax: 353-001-2821
www.stgerards.ie
To provide an opportunity for each student to realise his or her potential in all areas: academic, moral, personal, physical, social, spiritual and sporting.
Tom Geraghty, Headmaster
Victor Drummy, Deputy Principal

2034 St. Helen's School
Eastbury Road Northwood, Middlesex
England HA6-3AS
09274-28511
Fax: 0923-835824
enquiries@sthn.co.uk
www.sthn.co.uk
We aim to give every pupil an academic, innovative and stimulating education, developing her intellectual, creative and physical talents to the full. We provide a friendly, supportive and well-ordered environment in which every girl is treated as an individual and where integrity, personal responsibility and respect for others are highly valued.
YA Burne, Principal

2035 St. John's International School
Dreve Richelle 146
Waterloo
Belguim 01410
32-2-352-0610
Fax: 32-2-352-0630
www.stjohns.be
we exist to provide an English-speaking education that emphasizes Christian values, encourages academic excellence and stimulates social development within a culturally diverse environment. St. John's is also a caring environment where students are encouraged to reach their full potential, prepared to think globally, with a commitment to justice and challenged to act responsibly in a consistently changing society.
Joseph Doenges, Director
Judith Hoskins, Director Admissions

36 St. Mary's School
Rhapta Road, PO Box 40580- 00100
Nairobi
Kenya
0990-23721
info@stmarys.ac.ke
www.stmarys.ac.ke
We are a Catholic Private School committed to our international character in the provision of a spiritual, intellectual and physical education. We aim at developing the gifts of the young in an atmosphere which encourages the ethos of self-expression and mutual respect with a view to their facing the future responsibly, with confidence and courage.
M Mark Orchard, IBVM, BA, Principal

37 St. Michael's School
Otford Court
Otford TN14 5SA
England
095-92-2137
Keith Crombie, Headmaster

38 St. Stephen's School
Via Aventina 3
Rome
Italy 00153
39-06-575-0605
Fax: 39-06-574-1941
www.ststephens-rome.com
Philip Allen, Headmaster
Lesley Murphey, Head of the School

39 Stavenger British School
Gauselbakken 107
4032 Gausel
Norway
475-195-0250
www.biss.no
Zelma Roisli, Principal

40 Stover School
Newton Abbot
Devon
England TQ12
0626-54505
351-214-5505
mail@stover.co.uk
www.stover.co.uk
Susan Bradley, Principal

041 Stowe School
Stowe
Buckingham
England MK18
44-1280-818000
351-214-5505
Fax: 44-1280-818181
enquiries@stowe.co.uk
www.stowe.co.uk
Our vision for Stowe, a co-educational independent boarding and day school in the heart of the English countryside, is of a school that delivers the highest academic and cultural achievement; and a school that continues to foster the development of Stoics who are as original and individual as their school.
Anthony Wallersteiner, Headmaster
GM Hornby, Faculty Head

042 Summerfield School SRL
Via Tito Poggi 21 Divino Amore
00134 Rome
Italy
Vivien Franceschini, Principal

043 Summerhill School
Westward Ho
Leiston, Suffolk
England IP16
0728-830540
zoe@summerhillschool.co.uk
www.summerhillschool.co.uk
A S Neill's Summerhill School, a co-educational boarding school in Suffolk, England, is the original alternative 'free' school. Founded in 1921, it continues to be an influential model for progressive, democratic education around the world.
Zoe Readhead, Principal

2044 Sunny View School
C/ Teruel No 32, Cerro del Toril
Torremolinos Malaga
Spain 29620
345-283-
Fax: 345-272-
www.sunnyviewschool.com
Sunny View is a privately owned day school, which accepts students of all nationalities from the age of 3 years to 18 years. It is a long-established International School.
Jane Barbadillo, Principal
David McConnell, HS Principal

2045 Sutton Park School
St Fintan's Road
Sutton, Dublin 13
Ireland
353-1-832-2940
Fax: 353-1-832-5929
info@sps.ie
www.suttonparkschool.com
Sutton Park School aims to provide its pupils with an educational environment that is intellectually, physically and culturally challenging, so that they can grow into balanced, mature and confident adults.
Laurence J Finnegan, Chief Executive
Michael Moretta, Head of School

2046 Sutton Valence School
Maidstone
Kent
England ME17
0622-842281
enquiries@svs.org.uk
www.svs.org.uk
Our aim today is to give our girls and boys an excellent all round education in an atmosphere of togetherness and trust, where day and boarding pupils benefit from the same supportive ethos.
Joe Davies, Headmaster
Kathy Webster, Admissions Officer

2047 Swans School
Capricho s/n
Marbella, Malaga
Spain 29600
95 -77 -248
Fax: 95 -77 -431
info@swansschool.net
Swans' motto is Constancy and Truth.
TJ Swan, Principal
Nick Lee, Head Teacher

2048 TASIS Hellenic International School
PO Box 51051
Kifissia Gr-145 10
Greece
30-1-623-3888
Fax: 30-1-623-3160
info@tasis.edu.gr
www.tasis.com
Grade levels Pre-K through 12, school year September - June
Basile Daskalakis, President

2049 TASIS The American School in England
Coldharbour Lane
Thorpe, Surrey, TW20 8TE
England
44-1932-565-252
Fax: 44-1932-564-644
ukadmissions@tasis.com
www.tasis.com
Grade levels Pre-K through 12, school year August - June
Barry Breen, Headmaster

2050 Taunus International Montessori School
Altkonigstrasse 1 6370
Oberursel
Germany
496-171-9133
www.tims-frankfurt.com
Kathleen Hauer, Principal

2051 Teach in Great Britain
5 Netherhall Gardens
London, NW3, England
www.teachaway.com

2052 The International School-Aberdeen
Pitfodels House, North Deeside Road
Pitodels, Cults, Aberdeen
Scotland, UK AB15-9PN
44 1224 730300
admin@isa.aberdeen.sch.uk
www.isa.aberdeen.sch.uk
The International School of Aberdeen (ISA) is an independent, non-profit school (K-12) that delivers excellence in education. We do this through a safe and caring learning environment where students are challenged to reach their maximum potential through academic success and personal growth, becoming socially responsible and active global citizens.
Nicholas Little, Head of School
Don Newbury, Elementary Principal

2053 Thessaloniki International High School & Pinewood Elementary School
PO Box 21001
555 10 Pilea, Thessaloniki
Greece
30-31-301-221
Fax: 30-31-323-196
Grades preK-12, enrollment 256.
Peter B Baiter, Director

2054 Thomas Jefferson School
4100 South Lindbergh Boulevard
Saint Louis
Missouri, MO 63127
314-843-4151
www.tjs.org
The mission of Thomas Jefferson School is to give its students the strongest possible academic background, responsibility for their own learning, a concern for other people, and the resources to live happily as adults and become active contributors to society
William C Rowe, Head of School
Susan S Stepleton, Chair, Board of Trustees

2055 United Nations Nursery School
40 Rue Pierre Guerin
75016 Paris
France
33-1-452-72024
Fax: 33-1-428-87146
www.unns.net
Pre-K and kindergarten levels.
Brigitte Weill, Directrice

2056 United World College-Adriatic
Via Treste 29
Duino (TS)
Italy 34011
39 -40 -7391
Fax: 39 -40 -7392
www.uwcad.it
The United World Colleges offer students of all races and creeds the opportunity of developing international understanding through programmes which combine high quality academic study and activities which encourage
DB Sutcliffe, Principal
David Sutcliffe, Headmaster

2057 United World College-Atlantic
St Donats Castle Llantwit
Major S Glamorgan
United Kingdom
441- 46-9 90
www.atlanticcollege.org
a sense of adventure and social responsibility
Colin Jenkins, Principal

2058 Vajont Elementary School
PSC 1
Aviano
Italy
427-701553
Nick Suida, Principal

2059 Verdala International School
Fort Pembroke
Pembroke, STJ 14
Malta
356-332-361
Fax: 356-372-387
vis@maltanet.net
www.verdala.org
An independent, coeducational day and boarding school which offers an educational program from play school through grade 12 for students of all nationalities.
Adam Pleasance, Headmaster
Charles Zerafa, Business Manager

2060 Verona Elementary School
1011 Lee Highway
Verona, VA 24482
540-248-0141
Fax: 540-248-0562
www.augusta.k12.va.us
Marguerite McDonald, Principal

2061 Vicenza Elementary School
Unit 31401 Box 11
APO, Vicenza
Italy 09630-5
011-390-444
Fax: 011-39 -444
VicenzaES.Principal@eu.dodea.edu
Increase student achievement, we are committed to improving our children's ability to communicate in writing across all curricular areas, and to reason mathematically.
Martha Parsons, Principal

2062 Vicenza High School
Unit 31401 Box 11
APO, Vicenza
Italy 09630
011-390-444
Fax: 011-39 -444
VicenzaHS.Principal@eu.dodea.edu
www.vice-hs.eu.dodea.edu/
Lauri Kenney, Principal
Chris Beane, Assistant Principal

2063 Vicenza International School
Viale Trento 141
Vicenza 36100
Italy
39-0444-288-475
Fax: 39-0444-963-633
Grade levels 11-13, school year September - June
Dionigio Tanello, PhD, Director

2064 Vienna Christian School
Wagramerstrasse 175
Panthgasse 6A
Wien, Austria A-122
43-1-25122-501
351-214-5505
office@vcs-austria.org
www.viennachristianschool.org/
VCS is an international school with a United States-based curriculum.
Ken Norman, Director
Nancy L Deibert, Athletic Director/PE

2065 Vienna International School
Strasse der Menschenrechte 1
Vienna, Austria 01220
43-1-203-5595
Fax: 43-1-203-0366
www.vis.ac.at
To serve the children of the United Nations and diplomatic community in Vienna. It is also open to children of the international business community and of Austrian families.
James S Walbran, Director
Neil Tomalin, Head Primary School

2066 Vilseck Elementary School
Unit 28040
APO, Vilseck
Germany 09112-14
011-490-662
Fax: 011-490-662
VilseckES.Principal@eu.dodea.edu
www.vils-es.eu.dodea.edu/
Vilseck Elementary School prepares students for lifelong learning within a safe, nurturing environment. Honoring the uniqueness of our military community, we foster respect for all people and for cultural diversity
Hammack, Principal, Assistant Principal

2067 Vilseck High School
Unit 20841
APO, Vilseck
Germany 09112-5
011-490-662
Fax: 011-490-662
Duane.Werner@eu.dodea.edu
www.vils-hs.eu.dodea.edu/
VHS is home to approximately 520 students, grades 9-12, who have the opportunity to participate in Engaged Learning projects in academic areas. They have a wide range of choices in elective areas to include art, band, chorus, German, Spanish, home economics and technical education.
Duane Werner, Principal

2068 Violen School, International Department
Violenstraat 3, 1214
CJ Hilversum
Netherlands
035-621-6053
www.ipsviolen.nl
This school offers an enrollment of 240 day students (125 boys and 115 girls), in grades K through 6. The primary education is in the English language for international mobile families, set up and supported by the Dutch government.
Atse R Spoor, Principal

2069 Vogelweh Elementary School
Unit 3240 Box 435
APO
Germany, AE 09021
011-49 -3109
Fax: 011-49 -3105
Vogelweh Elementary School is committed to creating an environment that supports lifelong learning in order for students to be successful in a global society.
Donna E Donaldson, Principal
Janie Page, Assistant Principal

2070 Volkel Elementary School
752 MUNSS Unit 6790
APO, Volkel 09717 5018
Netherlands
www.aoshs.org
Claudia Holtzclaw, Principal

2071 Westwing School
Kyneton House
Thornbury BS122JZ
England
0454-412311
www.westwing.dvusd.org
Marjorie Crane, MA, Headmaster

2072 Wetzel Elementary School
Unit 23815
APO, Baumholder 09034 0005
Germany
Robert Richards, Principal

2073 Wiesbaden Middle School
Unit 29647
APO, AE
Germany 09096
011-049- 110
Fax: 011-049- 110
wiesbadenMS.Webmaster@eu.dodea.edu
The entire WMS community strives to provide a positive school climate through which all students can mature socially, academically and physically, while developing a lifelong love of learning.
Alexia Venglik, Principal

2074 Wolfert Van Borselen
Bredewater 24, Postbus 501
2700 AM Zoetermeer
Netherlands
www.wolfert.nl/
Gilles Schuilenburg, Principal

2075 Worksop College
Worksop, Nottinghamshire
S80 3AP
England
0909-472391
www.worksopcollege.notts.sch.uk/
Worksop College was founded as St Cuthbert's School in 1890 by Nathaniel Woodard. As a parish priest working in London in the 1840s Woodard was dismayed by the ignorance of the middle classes and believed that there was a need for something comparable to the National School's Christian schools for the poor in order to serve the needs of the trade classes.
Roy Collard, Headmaster

2076 Worms Elementary School
CMR 455
APO, Worms 09058 0005
Germany

011-490-662
www.wikimapia.org
Charles Raglan, Principal

77 Wuerzburg Elementary School
CMR 475 Box 6
APO, Wuerzburg 09244 6627
Germany
011-490-662
www.wikimapia.org
Dee Ann Edwards, Principal

78 Wuerzburg High School
CMR 475 Box 8
APO, Wuerzburg 09036 0005
Germany
011-490-662
www.wikimapia.org
Robert Kubarek, Principal

79 Wuerzburg Middle School
CMR 475 Box 7
APO, Wuerzburg 09036 0005
Germany
011-490-662
www.wikimapia.org
Karen Kroon, Principal

80 Zurich International School
Steinacherstrasse 140
8820 Wadenswill
Switzerland
41-43-833-2222
Fax: 41-43-833-2223
www.zis.ch
Zurich International School is a co-educational international day school in the Zurich area for students aged 3 to 18 and is fully accredited by both the Council of International Schools and the New England Association of Schools and Colleges and is an IB World School.
Peter C Mott, Director
Jennifer Saxe, Director Development

West Indies & Caribbean

081 American School-Santo Domingo
Apartado 20212
Santo Domingo
Dominican Republic
809-565-7946
809-549-5841
info@assd.edu.do
www.assd.edu.do
The American School of Santo Domingo provides all students with quality educational opportunities to make life long learners while fostering moral values and physical development.
Lourdes Tomas, School Director

082 Aquinas College
1607 Robinson Road SE
Grand Rapids, MI 49506-1799
616-632-8900
www.aquinas.edu
Emphasizes career preparation with a focus on leadership and service to others.
Vincent Ferguson, Principal

083 Belair School
43 Decarteret Road
Mandeville
Jamaica
1-876-962-2168
Fax: 1-876-962-3396
admissions@belairschool.com
www.belairschool.com
The Belair School seeks to promote the academic, social and emotional development of students and a value system of integrity through an integrated curriculum, so that students will become self-assured and responsible citizens.
Sylvan Shields, Director

2084 Bermuda High School
19 Richmond Road
Pembroke
Bermuda HM 08
1-441-295-6153
Fax: 1-441-295-2754
info@bhs.bm
www.bhs.bm
This girls school offers an English-based curriculum for 620 total day students in grades 1-12.
Tracy Renaud, Primary Head
Shanna-Lee Kerr, Primary Assistant

2085 Bermuda Institute-SDA
234 Middle Road
Southampton
Bermuda SN BX
441-238-1566
www.bermudainstitute.bm
The Bermuda Institute family exists to show children Jesus, nurture their love for Him and others, teach them to think, and empower them to serve.
Lois Tucker, Principal
Kathleen Allers, Elementary Vice Principal

2086 Bishop Anstey Junior School
Ariapita Road
Port of Spain
Trinidad and Tobago
868-624-1177
admin@bishopansteyjunior.edu.tt
www.bishopansteyjunior.edu.tt
To stimulate learning within the spiritual, academic, social , cultural and sporting disciplines aimed at developing rounded individuals, within an environment that allows the flexibility to cope with the challenges of the changing education landscape.
Grace Campbell, Principal

2087 Capitol Christian School
C-11 #3 Urb Real Santo Domingo
Dominican Republic
916-856-5630
Fax: 916-856-5609
www.ccscougars.org
Stacy Lee Blossom, Principal

2088 Ecole Flamboyant
PO Box 1744-A Schweitzer Hosp
Port-au-Prince
Haiti
509-381-141/2
Fax: 509-381-141
William Dunn, Principal

2089 International School-Aruba
Wayaca 238 A
Aruba
Dutch Caribbean
297-845-365
Fax: 297-847-341
info@isaruba.com
www.isaruba.com
A nonprofit, coeducational English-speaking day school serving students from prekindergarten to grade 12.
Paul D Sibley, Headmaster
Mary B Sibley, Academic Dean/Counselor

2090 International School-Curacao
PO Box 3090
Koninginnelaan Emmastad, Curacao
Netherlands Antilles
5-999-737-3633
Fax: 5-999-737-3142
Offers a rigorous academic program in order to prepare students planning to pursue higher learning at colleges and universities around the world. The School's curriculum includes International Baccalaureate (IB) coursework that allows students the opportunity to receive the IB Diploma.
Margie Elhage PhD, Director
Rene Romer, President

2091 International School-West Indies
PO Box 278 Leeward
Providenciales
British West Indies
Alison Hodges, Principal

2092 Kingsway Academy
PO Box N-4378
Nassau
Bahamas
242-324-6887
Fax: 242-393-6917
www.kingswayacademy.com
Kingsway Academy endeavours to provide children with a sound education that is thoroughly Christian in its outlook and practices - Training Children in the King's Way .
Carol Harrison, Principal

2093 Mount Saint Agnes Academy
PO Box HM 1004
Hamilton HMDX
Bermuda
441-292-4134
Fax: 441-295-7265
msaoffice@msa.bm
www.msa.bm
The Mission of Mount Saint Agnes Academy is to provide quality education in a caring, Christian environment. Belief in Christ and fidelity to the Roman Catholic Church form the foundation upon which all academic learning and social interaction take place. To this end we make a strong commitment to recognize each child as an individual and to help him/her to develop according to his/her own potential in order to become a responsible member of the community
Sue Moench, Principal
Margaret DiGiacomo, Assistant Principal

2094 Queens College
PO Box N7127
Nassau
Bahamas
242-393-1666
Fax: 242-393-3248
info@qchenceforth.com
www.qchenceforth.com
Our interests lie not only in academic excellence but also in raising well-rounded, courteous, spiritually grounded global citizens.
Andrea Gibson, Principal

2095 Saltus Cavendish School
PO Box DV 209
Devonshire DV BX
Bermuda
441-236-3215
Fax: 441-292-0438
www.saltus.bm
Saltus Grammar School is a co-educational, independent day school of excellent reputation. It is the premier independent school in

Bermuda and is well known in the international community.

Susan Furr, Headteacher
Stephanie Queary, Secretary

2096 St. Andrew's School
16 Valleton Avenue
Marraval Trinidad West Indies
Trinidad and Tobago
868-622-2630
Fax: 868-628-1857
principal@standrews.edu.tt
www.standrews.edu.tt
St. Andrew's is a progressive school that produces a caring, confident and responsible child. St. Andrew's also supports the development of social and moral values that allow the child to appreciate and respect diversity.

Sandra Farinha, Principal
Paula Moses, Vice Principal

2097 St. Anne's Parish School
PO Box SS6256
Nassau
Bahamas
868-622-2631
Fax: 868-628-1858
www.standrewsindia.com

Rev. Patrick Adderley, Principal

2098 St. John's College
PO Box N4858
Nassau
Bahamas
868-622-2632
Fax: 868-628-1859
www.standrewsindia.com

Arlene Ferguson, Principal

2099 St. Paul's Methodist College
PO Box F897
Freeport
Grand Bahamas
814-237-2163
www.stpaulsc.org

Annette Poitier, Principal

2100 Sunland Lutheran School
PO Box F2469
Freeport
Bahamas

J Pinder, Principal

2101 Tapion School
PO Box 511 La Toc
Castries, St Lucia
West Indies
758-452-2902
Fax: 758-453-0582
tapionsch@candw.lc
The Tapion School will endeavour to produce individuals who would be empowered to meet the demands of a changing society.

Laurena Primus, Principal
Margaret Francois, Administration Officer

U.S. Branches

2102 Aisha Mohammed International School
Washington, DC 20521-1
www.joh.cam.ac.uk

Daryl Barker, Principal

2103 Albania Tirana International School
DOS/Administrative Officer
9510 Tirana Place
Washington, DC 20521-9510
355-436-5239
qsialb@albaniaonline.net
www.www1.qsi.org/alb
Provides a quality education in the English language for expatriates living in Tirana and Albanian citizens who want their children to be educated in English.

Scott D'Alterio, Director
Sotiraq Trebicka, Administrative Coordinator

2104 Alexander Muss High School Israel
78 Randall Avenue
Rockville Centre, NY 11570
212-472-9300
800-327-5980
Fax: 212-472-9301
info@amiie.org
www.amiie.org
Provide a superior Israel education experience to learners of all ages in Israel and within communities throughout North America and abroad. The Institute promotes, builds and strengthens lifelong bonds between Jews and Israel through education, experiences and understanding.

Gideon Shavit, CEO
Chaim Fischgrund, Headmaster

2105 Almaty International School
DOS/Administrative Officer
7030 Almaty Place
Washington, DC 20521-7030
Grades preK-12, enrollment 169.

Robert B Draper, Director

2106 American School
Col Lomas del Guijarro Avenue Repœb
Tegucigalpa
Honduras 02134
504-239-3333
Fax: 504-239-6162
www.amschool.org
Provides a student-centered, enriching, college-preparatory education that emphasizes social responsibility in a safe, bicultural, and disciplined learning environment.

Liliana F Jenkins, Superintendent
David Mendoza, Business Administrator

2107 American Cooperative School
Calle 10 y Pasaje Kantutas, Calacot
c/o American Embassy, La Paz, Bolivia
La Paz, Bolivia
519-2-792-302
Fax: 591-2-797-218
acs@acslp.org
www.acslp.org
Offers college prepatory North American education that enables our graduates to enter the best universities in the United States, Canada, Europe and Latin America.

Matthew Kirby, Superintendent
Robert Boni, Chair

2108 American Cooperative School of Tunis
6360 Tunis Place
Washington, DC 20521-6360
216-71-760-905
Fax: 216-71-761-412
www.acst.net

Dennis Sheehan, Superintendent

2109 American Embassy School
Department of State/AES
9000 New Delhi Place
Washington, DC 20521-9000
91-11-611-7140
Fax: 91-11-687-3320
aesindia@aes.ac.in
www.serve.com/aesndi
Grade levels Pre-K through 12, school year August - May

Rob Mochrish, PhD, Director

2110 American Embassy School of New Delhi
Chandragupta Marg
Chanakyapuri, New Delhi
India 11002
91-11-611-7140
Fax: 91-11-687-3320
www.aes.ac.in
Serves students from the United States and other nations. It provides a quality American education that enables students to be inspired learners and responsible global citizens through the collaboration of a dedicated faculty and a supportive community.

Dr Robert Hetzel, Director
Linda McGinnis, Secretary, AES School Board

2111 American International School of Nouakchott
DOS/Administrative Officer
2430 Nouakchott Place
Washington, DC 20521-2430
222-2-52967
Fax: 222-2-52967
aisnsahara@yahoo.com
www.aisn.mr
At the American International School of Nouakchott, a partnership of educators and parents is committed to providing our culturally diverse students a safe, nurturing and respectful learning environment. We promote academic achievement through a curriculum founded on an American educational philosophy.

Sharon Orlins PhD, Director

2112 American International School-Abuja
DOS/Administrative Officer
8300 Abuja Place
Washington, DC 20521-8300
234-9-413-4464
Fax: 234-9-413-4464
www.aisabuja.com
Provide a quality education, utilizing an American curriculum for students of all nationalities from preschool through 12th grade.

Amy Uzoewulu, Director
Peter Williams, Primary Principal

2113 American International School-Bamako
DOS/Administrative Officer
2050 Bamako Place
Washington, DC 20189-2050
223-222-4738
Fax: 223-222-0853
aisb@aisbmali.org
www.aisbmali.org
An independent, coeducational day school which offers an educational program from prekindergarten through grade 10. Supervised study using the University of Nebraska High School correspondence courses for grades 12 may also be arranged.

David Henry, Director
Rob Van Doeselaar, Chairman

2114 American International School-Chennai
100 Feet Road
Taramani
Chennai 00600-113
91-44-499-0881
Fax: 91-44-466-0636

HeadofSchool@aisch.org
www.aisch.org
Embraces international diversity and strives to provide an academically challenging environment in order to foster intellectual curiosity and a sense of responsibility in our students. To fully educate the whole person, we are committed to cultivating lifelong learners and balanced, service-oriented citizens, who are thereby prepared to positively contribute in a globally competitive world.

Barry Clough, Head of School
Dr James R Fellabaum, High School Principal

15 American International School-Costa Rica
Interlink 249
PO Box 02-5635
Miami, FL 33102
506-229-3256
Fax: 506-223-9062
www.aiscr.com
A private, non-profit school that was founded in 1970 under the name of Costa Rica Academy. AIS serves approximately 200 students from pre-school through 12th grade.

Austin Briggs Jr, Headmaster
Neli Santiago, Principal

16 American International School-Freetown
Department of State/MGT
2160 Freetown Place
Washington, DC 20521-2160
232-22-232-480
Fax: 232-22-225-471
aisfinfo@yahoo.com
www.aisfreetown.websiteanimal.com
A private, non-profit, PreK-8th grade school providing an American curriculum to a multinational community in Freetown, Sierra Leone.

Ndye Njie, Director
Nielette Gordon, Administrative Assistant

17 American International School-Kingston
1a Olivier Road
Kingston 8
Jamaica
876-977-3625
Fax: 876-977-3625
aiskoff@cwjamaica.com
www.aisk.com
A non-profit, non-sectarian, private day school funded by tuition income receiving small annual grants from the U.S. Government through it Office of Overseas Schools.

Sean Goudie, Director
Anna Wallace, Lower School Coordinator

118 American International School-Lesotho
DOS/Administrative Officer
2340 Maseru Place
Washington, DC 20521-2340
266-322-987
Fax: 266-311-963
An independent, coeducational day school which offers an American education from preschool through grade 8. The school was founded in 1991 to serve the needs of the American community and other students seeking an English-language education.

Harvey Cohen, Principal

119 American International School-Libreville
2270 Libreville Place
Washington, DC 20521-2270
241-76-20-03
Fax: 241-74-55-07
aisl@internetgabon.com
www.aisa.or.ke

Paul Sicard, Director

2120 American International School-Lome
DOS/Administrative Officer
2300 Lome Place
Washington, DC 20521-2300
www.aisa.or.ke
Established in 1967 as a private, coeducational day school offering an educational program to students of all nationalities in pre-kindergarten through grade 8.

Clover Afokpa, Director
Warace Tchamsi, Administrative Assistant

2121 American International School-Lusaka
PO Box 31617
Lusaka
Zambia
260-1-260-509
Fax: 260-1-260-538
www.aislusaka.org
Committed to being a leading IB World School, offering a balanced, academically rigorous and internationally recognized college preparatory education.

Chris Muller, Director
Shirley Mee, Business Manager

2122 American International School-Mozambique
DOS/Administrative Officer
2330 Maputo Place
Washington, DC 20521-2330
258-1-49-1994
Fax: 258-1-49-0596
www.aisa.or.ke

Don Reeser, Director

2123 American International School-N'Djamena
DOS/Administrative Officer
2410 N'Djamena Place
Washington, DC 20521-2410
235-52-2103
Fax: 235-51-5654
www.aisa.or.ke

Gay Mickle, Director

2124 American International School-Nouakchott
2430 Nouakchott Place
Washington, DC 20521-2430
222-2-52967
Fax: 222-2-52967
aisnsahara@yahoo.com
Committed to provide culturally diverse students a safe, nurturing and respectful learning environment and promotes academic achievement through a curriculum founded on an American educational philosophy.

Sharon Orlins PhD, Director

2125 American Nicaraguan School
c/o American Embassy
Unit No 2710 Box 7, APO AA 34021
Washington, DC 20521-3240
505-278-0029
Fax: 505-267-3088
www.ans.edu.ni
A private, nonsectarian coeducaitonal day school which offers an educaional program from prekindergarten through grade 12 for students of all nationalities.

Fredy Ramirez, Elementary School Principal
Joseph Azmeh, Secondary Principal

2126 American Samoa Department of Education
Pago Pago
American Samoa 96799
011-684-633-5237
Fax: 011-684-633-5733
www.doe.as
Is to ensure student success by providing high quality teaching and learning opportunities to all our children

Sili K Sataua

2127 American School Honduras
American Embassy Tegucigalpa
Department of State
Washington, DC 20521-3480
504-239-333
Fax: 504-239-6162
admin_assistant@asamadagascar.org
www.amschool.org
A private, coeducational day school which offers an educational program from nursery through grade 12 for students of all nationalities.

James Szoka, Principal

2128 American School of Bombay
SF2, G Block
Bandra-Kurla Complex Road
Bandra (E), Mumbai, 400098

91-22-6772-7272
personnel@asbindia.org
www.asbindia.org
International school in Mumbai with the mission of empowering and developing its students so they can gain the skills and inspiration they need to succeed in their goals. The school is a coeducational independent day school teaching children from Pre-K through Grade 12.

Craig Johnson, Superintendent
Alok Parashar, Chief Operating Officer

2129 American School-Algiers
American Embassy Algiers
Washington, DC 20520-1
202-265-2800
Fax: 202-667-2174

Richard Gillogly, Principal

2130 American School-Antananarivo
2040 Antananarivo Place
Dulles, VA 20189-2040
261-20-22-420-39
Fax: 261-20-22-345-39
miasaadm@gmail.com
www.asamadagascar.org
As the only English language institution in Madagascar offering a K-12 diploma program, we challenge our students to actively engage with the exceptional educational opportunities that are available to them in our school.

Jay Long, Director

2131 American School-Asuncion
Avenida Esapaa 1175
PO Box 10093
Asuncion, Paraguay
595-21-600-476
Fax: 595-21-603-518
asagator@asa.edu.py
www.asa.edu.py
A bilingual learning community of International and Paraguayan families, is to prepare

responsible proactive world citizens in a student-centered, caring environment through a college preparatory program that adheres to the highest U.S. and Paraguayan standards of excellence

Dennis Klumpp, Director
David Warken, Elementary Principal

2132 American School-Dschang

Washington, DC 20521-1

Jane French, Principal

2133 American School-Guatemala

11 Calle 1579 Zona 1511 calle 15-79
Guatemala
Guatemala
502-236- 079
Fax: 502-236- 833
www.cag.edu.gt
The school's goal is to educate independent, critical-thinking, responsible, bilingual individuals prepared to meet the challenges of the future.

Tracy Berry-Lazo, General Director
Fabio Corvaglia, High School Principal

2134 American School-Niamey

DOS/Administrative Officer
2420 Niamey Place
Dulles, VA 20189-2420
227-723-942
Fax: 227-723-457
asniger@intnet.ne
A coeducational day school offering an educational program from prekindergarten through grade 9, and 10-12 correspondence.

Deborah M Robinson, Director

2135 American School-Port Gentil

1100 Louisiana Street
Suite 2500
Houston, TX 77002-5215

Keith Marriott, Principal

2136 American School-Tegucigalpa

Coronel Lomas del Guijarro
Avenue Repœblica Dominicana Calle Costa
Tegucigalpa, Honduras
504-239-3333
Fax: 504-239-6162
www.amschool.org
Provides a Student Centered, enriching, college-preparatory education that emphasizes social responsibility in a safe, bicultural, and disciplined learning enviroment

James Shepherd, Principal
Liliana Jerkins, Superintendent

2137 American School-Warsaw

Ul Warszawska 202
Konstancin-Jeziorna
Poland 05520
48-22-651-9611
Fax: 48-22-642-1506
admissions@asw.waw.pl
www.asw.waw.pl
Offers a rigorous, supportive and balanced PK-12 program in English for the international community of Warsaw that is driven by a strong commitment to prepare students for lives as responsible world citizens

Tony Gerlicz, Director
Rebecca Brown, Finance/Operations Director

2138 American School-Yaounde

BP 7475
Yaounde
Cameroon
234-223-0421
Fax: 237-223-6011
school@asoy.org
www.asoy.org
Ensures that all students achieve high academic success, demonstrate critical thinking skills, and become responsible and compassionate, global citizens prepared for their next stage in life; as gained through an enriched, American curriculum and offered in a challenging, secure, and diverse environment.

Nanci Shaw, School Director

2139 American-Nicaraguan School

Frente al Club Lomas de Monserrat
PO Box 2670, Managua
Nicaragua
505-2-782-565
Fax: 505-2-673-088
elementary@ans.edu.ni
www.ans.edu.ni
Provides its multicultural student community with a US-accredited college preparatory program, based on democratic and universal values, that develops critical thinkers and ethical individuals capable of realizing their leadership potential by making meaningful contributions to society.

Stan Key, Director General
Roberto Cardenal, Director of Finance

2140 Amoco Galeota School

PO Box 4381
Houston, TX 77210-4381

Barbara Punch, Principal

2141 Andersen Elementary & Middle School

Unit 14057
APO, Mariana Islands 96543 4057
Guam

2142 Anzoategui International School

PO Box 020010, M-42
Jet Cargo International
Miami, FL 33102-10
58-82-22683
Fax: 58-82-22683
aishead@telcel.net.ve
Grade levels Pre-K through 12, school year August - June

Jorge Nelson EdD, Superintendent

2143 Armenia QSI International School-Yerevan

DOS/Administrative Officer
7020 Yerevan Place
Washington, DC 20521-7020
374-1-391-030
Fax: 374-1-151-438
qsiy@arminco.com
www.qsi.org
An independent, coeducational day school which offers an educational program from preschool (3-4 years) through grade 12 for students of all nationalities. Enrollment 45.

Arthur W Hudson, Director

2144 Atlanta International School

2890 N Fulton Drive NE
Atlanta, GA 30305-3155
404-841-3840
Fax: 404-841-3873
www.aischool.org
Continuing to develop and deserve a worldwide reputation as an exemplary center of teaching and learning, a school that achieves and sets, within the framework of the International Baccalaureate.Maintaining an optimal size composition of faculty and students so that opportunities for individual learning, mutual understanding, and community feeling are maximized.

Robert Brindley, Headmaster
Charlotte Smith, Executive Assistant

2145 Awty International School

7455 Awty School Lane
Houston, TX 77055-7222
713-686-4850
Fax: 713-686-4956
admissions@awty.org
www.awty.org
Grade level prekindergarten through twelfth, with total enrollment of 900 students.

David Watson, Headmaster
John Ransom, Chairman

2146 Azerbaijan Baku International School

Darnagul Qasabasi Street Ajami Nakc
Block 3097
Baku, Azerbaijan 01108
994-12-90-63-52
Fax: 994-12-90-63-51
baku@qsi.org
www.qsi.org
the primary purpose of the school is to meet the needs of the children in Baku who require this type of education with a view to continuing their education in their home countries with a minimum of adjustment problems.

Scott Root, Director
Arthur W Hudson, Director

2147 Baku International School

Darnagul Qasabasi Street Ajami Nakc
Block 3097
Baku, Azerbaijan, AZ 01108
994-12-656352
Fax: 991-12-4105951
baku@qsi.org
www.qsi.org
the primary purpose of the school is to meet the needs of the children in Baku who require this type of education with a view to continuing their education in their home countries with a minimum of adjustment problems.

Scott Root, Director
Arthur W Hudson, Director

2148 Ball Brothers Foundation

222 S Mulberry Street
Muncie, IN 47305
765-741-5500
Fax: 765-741-5518
info@ballfdn.org
www.ballfdn.org
The Foundation's primary focus is Muncie and East Central Indiana.The Foundation has been a philanthropic leader, serving as initiator, convener, and catalyst among donors and nonprofit organizations. Within Muncie, the Foundation seeks to forge active partnerships with effective nonprofit agencies by providing consultation and financial support to promote their success.

Jud Fisher, Executive Director/ COO
John W Fisher, Chairman & President

2149 Banjul American Embassy School

2070 Banjul Place
Dulles, VA 20189-2070
220-495-920
Fax: 220-497-181
baes@qanet.gm
The school demonstrates U.S. education abroad to a multi-ethnic, multi-cultural, diverse student body and otherwise increases mutual understanding through its emphasis on an American-based curriculum, use of American textbooks and sup-

plemental materials, and its teaching staff, of whom four are American nationals trained in American universities.

Dianne Zemichael, Director
Leah Moore, Administrative Secretary

50 Bingham Academy Ethiopia

SIM International
PO Box 4937
Addis Ababa, Ethiopia
East Africa
251-11 -791
Fax: 251-11 -791
director@binghamacademy.net
www.binghamacademy.net
The purpose of Bingham Academy is to provide high quality, culturally sensitive education, within a Christian environment, which challenges each student to impact the world for God's glory.

Murray Overton, Director

51 Bishkek International School

14A Tynystanova Street
Bishkek
Kyrgyzstan 72005
996-312-66-35-03
Fax: 996-312-66-35-03
bishkek@qsi.org
www.qsi.org
The primary purpose of the school is to meet the needs of the children in Bishkek who require this type of education with a view to continuing their education in their home countries with a minimum of adjustment problems.

MaryKay Gudkova, Director

52 Bosnia-Herzegovina QSI International School Sarajevo

Omladinska #12
Vogosca-Saravejo
Bosnia & Herzegovina 71320
387-33-434-756
Fax: 387-33-434-756
saravejo@qsi.org
www.qsi.org
The primary purpose of the school is to meet the needs of the expatriate children living in Sarajevo who require this type of education.

Jay Hamric, Director
Arthur W Hudson, Director

153 Bratislava American International School

American Embassy Bratislava
Karloveska 64
Bratislava
Slovak Republic 842-2
421-7-722-844
Fax: 721-7-722-844
bratislava@qsi.org
www.qsi.sk
The primary purpose of the school is to meet the needs of the children in Bratislava who require this type of education with a view to continuing their education in their home countries with a minimum of adjustment problems.

Ronald Adams, Principal
Matthew Lake, Director

154 Bulgaria Anglo-American School-Sofia

DOS/Administrative Officer
5740 Sophia Place
Washington, DC 20521-5740
359-2-974-4575
Fax: 359-2-974-4483
aasregist@infotel.bg
An independent, coeducational day school which offers an educational program from prekindergarten through grade 8 for students of all nationalities. The school year comprises 2 semesters extending from August to December and from January to June. Enrollment 140.

Brian M Garton, Director
Arthur W Hudson, Director

2155 Burma International School Yangon

DOS/Administrative Officer
4250 Rangoon Place
Washington, DC 20521-4250
95-1-512-793/795
Fax: 95-1-525-020
www.internationalschoolyangon.org
Grades PK-12, enrollment 331.

Merry Wade, Director

2156 Burns Family Foundation

410 N Michigan Avenue
Room 1600
Chicago, IL 60611-4213
Offers support in secondary school education, higher education and youth services.

2157 Caribbean American School

5 Gates Court
Cranbury, NJ 08512-2926
509-257-7961
www.isbi.com

Ernestine Rochelle, Principal
Ernestine Roche Robinson, Director

2158 Caribbean-American School

PO Box 407139
Lynx Air
Ft Lauderdale, FL 33340-7139
509-257-7961
www.isbi.com
Grade levels Pre-K through 12, school year September - June

Ernestine Roche Robinson, Director
Ernestine Rochelle, Principal

2159 Chinese American International School

150 Oak Street
San Francisco, CA 94102
415-865-6000
Fax: 415-865-6089
caishead@aol.com
www.cais.org
Educates students for academic excellence, moral character and international perspective through immersion in American and Chinese culture and language.

Andrew W Corcoran, Executive Director

2160 Colegio Albania

PO Box 25573
Miami, FL 33102-5573

Eric Spindler, Principal

2161 Colegio Corazon de Maria

Ferrer y Ferrer-Santiago Igles
San Juan
Puerto Rico

M Cyril Stauss, Principal

2162 Colegio De Parvulos

263 Calle San Sebastian
San Juan 00901-1205
Puerto Rico

Maria Dolores Vice, Principal

2163 Colegio Del Buen Pastor

Camino Alejandrino Km 3.4
Rio Piedras 00927
Puerto Rico
www.colegiobuenpastor.com

Adria M Borges, Principal

2164 Colegio Del Sagrado Corazon

Obispado Final Urb La Alhambra
Ponce 00731
Puerto Rico
556- 14-2
www.sagradocorazon.edu.co

Joan G Dedapena, Principal

2165 Colegio Espiritu Santo

Box 191715 San Juan
Puerto Rico 00019-1715
787-754-0555
Fax: 754-715-

Carmen Jovet, Principal

2166 Colegio Inmaculada

Carr Militar 2 Km 49.6
Manati 00674
Puerto Rico
www.colegioinmaculada.es

Sor Nichlasa Maderea, Principal

2167 Colegio Inmaculada Concepcion

2 Calle Isabela
Guayanilla 00656-1703
Puerto Rico
www.colegioinmaculada.es

Sor Alejandrina Torres, Principal

2168 Colegio Internacional-Carabobo

VLN 1010
PO Box 025685
Miami, FL 33102-5685
58-41-421-807
Fax: 58-41-426-510
admin@cic-valencia.org.ve
www.cic-valencia.org.ve
To develop young men and women of character through an international college-preparatory program, in English, based on high intellectual and moral standards

Frank Anderson, Superintendent
Joe Walker, Director

2169 Colegio Internacional-Caracas

PAKMAIL 6030
PO Box 025323
Miami, FL 33102-5304
58-2-945-0444
Fax: 58-2-945-0533
cic@cic-caracas.org
www.cic-caracas.org
Colegio Internacional de Caracas is an English-medium, Pre-Nursery to Grade 12 school dedicated to the intellectual and personal development of each student in a caring and supportive environment. CIC offers a challenging program to prepare an international student body to excel in a variety of the world's finest schools and universities.

Alan Benson, Superintendent
Carmen Sweeting, Director of Academics

2170 Colegio Internacional-Puerto La Cruz

11010 NW 30th Street
Suite 104
Miami, FL 33172-5032
58-281-277-6051
Fax: 58-281-274-1134
ciplc@telcel.net.ve
Inspiring students to learn and serve by cultivating each student's full potential as an effective communicator, problem solver, and contributing global citizen.

Mike Martell, Superintendent
Frank Capuccio, Administrative Assistant

2171 **Colegio La Inmaculada**
1711 Ave Ponce De Leon
San Juan 00909-1905
Puerto Rico
787-754-0555
Fax: 754-715-
www.colegioinmaculada.es
Sor Teresa Del Rio, Principal

2172 **Colegio La Milagrosa**
107 Calle De Diego
San Juan 00925-3303
Puerto Rico
787-754-0555
Fax: 754-715-
www.colegioinmaculada.es
Maria Flores, Principal

2173 **Colegio Lourdes**
Box 190847
San Juan, PR 00919-847
787-767-6106
Fax: 787-767-5282
clourdes@coqui.net
www.colegiolourdes.net
Forming strong Christian faith and critical, able to make a commitment within the society and the church that is open to the realities and needs of his time, able to integrate into an attitude of service in a democratic society, as understand and explain the Preamble to the Constitution of Puerto Rico.
Paz Asiain, Director
Thalia Lopez, Principal

2174 **Colegio Madre Cabrini**
1564 Calle Encarnacion
San Juan 00920-4739
Puerto Rico
787-792-6180
Anne Marie Gavin, Principal

2175 **Colegio Maria Auxiliadora**
PO Box 797
Carolina 00986-0797
Puerto Rico
787-792-6181
Leles Rodriguez, Principal

2176 **Colegio Marista**
Final Santa Ana Alt Torrimar
Guaynabo 00969
Puerto Rico
www.marista.org.br
Hilario Martinez, Principal

2177 **Colegio Marista El Salvador**
PO Box 462
Manati 00674-0462
Puerto Rico
www.marista.org.br
Hnio Efrain Romo, Principal

2178 **Colegio Mater Salvatoris**
RR 3 Box 3080
San Juan 00926-9601
Puerto Rico
821- 99- 963
Fax: 821- 99- 973
www.matersalvatoris.org
Maria Luisa Benito, Principal

2179 **Colegio Notre Dame Nivel**
PO Box 967
Caguas 00726-0967
Puerto Rico
Francisca Suarez, Principal

2180 **Colegio Nuestra Senora de La Caridad**
PO Box 1164
Caparra Heigh 00920
Puerto Rico
www.colegiosdepr.com
Madre Esperanza Sanchez, Principal

2181 **Colegio Nuestra Senora de La Merced**
PO Box 4048
San Juan 00936-4048
Puerto Rico
Ivette Lopez, Principal

2182 **Colegio Nuestra Senora de Lourdes**
1050 Demetrio Odaly-Country Club
Rio Piedras 00924
Puerto Rico
Rita Manzano, Principal

2183 **Colegio Nuestra Senora de Valvanera**
53 Calle Jose I Quinton # 53
Coamo 00769-3108
Puerto Rico
Cruz Victor Colon, Principal

2184 **Colegio Nuestra Senora del Carmen**
RR 2, Box 9KK, Carr Trujillo Alt
Rio Piedras 00721
Puerto Rico
Candida Arrieta, Principal

2185 **Colegio Nuestra Senora del Pilar**
PO Box 387
Canovanas 00729-0387
Puerto Rico
Sor Leonilda Mallo, Principal

2186 **Colegio Nuestra Senora del Rosario**
Aa7 Calle 5
Bayamon 00959-3719
Puerto Rico
341-425-9781
www.maristasrosario.com
Theresita Miranda, Principal

2187 **Colegio Nuestra Sra del Rosario**
PO Box 1334
Ciales 00638-0414
Puerto Rico
787-871-1318
Fax: 787-871-5797
Parrochial School - Prekindergarten to 9th grade.
Angel Mendoza, Principal
Padre Gabriel M Jorres, Director

2188 **Colegio Padre Berrios**
PO Box 7717
San Juan 00916-7717
Puerto Rico
www.colegiopadreberrios.webs.com
Sor Enedina Santos, Principal

2189 **Colegio Parroquial San Jose**
PO Box 7718
San Juan 00916-7718
Puerto Rico 00644
www.colegiopadreberrios.webs.com
Sor Enedina Santos, Principal

2190 **Colegio Ponceno**
PO Box 7718
San Juan 00916-7718
Puerto Rico 00644
809-848-2525
www.colegiopadreberrios.webs.com
Sor Enedina Santos, Principal

2191 **Colegio Reina de Los Angeles**
M-19 Calle Frontera
San Juan, PR 00926
787-761-7455
Fax: 787-761-7440
Train Students education with a focus on physical, moral, intellectual, religious and social development within a framework of faith.
Victorina Ortega, Principal
Juana F Gomez, Director

2192 **Colegio Rosa Bell**
Calle Oviedo Number 42
Torrimar-Guaynabo, PR 00966
787-781-4240
Fax: 787-792-5415
www.rosabell.wordpress.com
The purpose of a good education is to maximize the capabilities of the individual: intellectually, socially, emotionally and physically.
Rose Rodriquez, Director
Miguel Arzola-Barris, Executive Director

2193 **Colegio Sacred Heart**
Palma Real Urb, Univ Gardens
San Juan 00927
Puerto Rico
Paul Marie, CSB, Principal

2194 **Colegio Sagrada Familia**
7 Hostos
Ponce
Puerto Rico 00731
www.safa.edu.uy
Sor Pilar Becerra, Principal

2195 **Colegio Sagrados Corazones**
A Esmeralda Urb, Ponce De Leon
Guaynabo 00969
Puerto Rico
Ana Arce de Marrer, Principal

2196 **Colegio San Agustin**
PO Box 4263
Bayamon 00958-1263
Puerto Rico
www.csa.edu.ph
Georgina Ortiz, Principal

2197 **Colegio San Antonio**
PO Box 21350
San Juan 00928-1350
Puerto Rico
809-764-0090
www.colegio-san-antonio.org
Rev. Paul S Brodie, Principal

2198 **Colegio San Antonio Abad**
PO Box 729
Humacao 00792-0729
Puerto Rico
809-764-0090
www.colegio-san-antonio.org
Padre Eduardo Torrella, Principal

2199 **Colegio San Benito**
PO Box 728
Humacao 00792-0728
Puerto Rico
Hermana Carmen Davila, Principal

00 Colegio San Conrado (K-12)
PO Box 7111
Ponce 00732-7111
Puerto Rico
Fax: 787-841-7303
Sister Nildred Rodriguez, Principal
Sister Wilma de Echevarria, Assistant Principal

01 Colegio San Felipe
566 Ave San Luis # 673
Arecibo 00612-3600
Puerto Rico
809-878-3532
www.colegiosanfelipe.edu.mx
Veronica Oravec, Principal

02 Colegio San Francisco De Asis
PO Box 789
Barranquitas
Puerto Rico 00794
787-857-2123
Fax: 787-857-2123
Founded in August 7, 1985
Hermana Maria Carbonell, Principal
Carlos Colon-Bernadi, Director

03 Colegio San Gabriel
Gpo Box 347
San Juan 00936
Puerto Rico
www.sangabriel.cl
Sor Antonia Garatachea, Principal

204 Colegio San Ignacio de Loyola
Urb Santa Mar a, 1940 Calle Saœco
San Juan
Puerto Rico 00927
787-765-3814
Fax: 787-758-4145
www.sanignacio.org
Dr Luis O Pino, Principal
Mario Alberto Torres, President

205 Colegio San Jose
PO Box 21300
San Juan
Puerto Rico 00928-1300
787-751-8177
Fax: 787-767-7146
sanjose@csj-rpi.org
www.csj-rpi.org
Bro Francisco T Gonzalez, Principal
Sra Elaine Torrens, Vice Principal

206 Colegio San Juan Bautista
PO Box E
Orocovis 00720
Puerto Rico
787-751-8177
Fax: 787-767-7146
www.colegiosanjuanbautista.com
Sor Maria Antonia Miya, Principal

207 Colegio San Juan Bosco
PO Box 14367
San Juan 00916-4367
Puerto Rico
www.sanjuanboscosalamanca.eu
Rev. P Jose Luis Gomez, Principal

208 Colegio San Luis Rey
43 Final SE, Urb Reparto Metro
San Juan 00921
Puerto Rico
Rosario Maria, Principal

2209 Colegio San Miguel
GPO Box 1714
San Juan 00936
Puerto Rico
www.sanluisrey.edu.co
Elvira Gonzalez, Principal

2210 Colegio San Rafael
PO Box 301
Quebradillas 00678-0301
Puerto Rico

2211 Colegio San Vicente Ferrer
PO Box 455
Catano 00963-0455
Puerto Rico
Maria Soledad Colon, Principal

2212 Colegio San Vicente de Paul
Calle Bolivar 709, Parada 24
San Juan
Puerto Rico 00909
787-727-4273
Fax: 787-728-2263
www.csvp-sj.org
Dra Isabel C Machado, Principal
P Evaristo Oliveras, Director

2213 Colegio Santa Clara
Via 14-2JL-456 Villa Fontana
Carolina 00983
Puerto Rico
www.colegiostaclara.com
Elsie Mujica, Principal

2214 Colegio Santa Cruz
PO Box 235
Trujillo Alto 00977-0235
Puerto Rico
113-024-5197
www.santacruz.g12.br
Maria Ramon Santiago, Principal

2215 Colegio Santa Gema
PO Box 1705
Carolina 00984-1705
Puerto Rico
491-711-5093
www.colegio-santagema.es
Lilia Luna De Anaya, Principal

2216 Colegio Santa Rita
Calle 9, Apartado 1557
Bayamon 00958
Puerto Rico
www.colegiosantarita.com.br
Elba N Villalba, Principal

2217 Colegio Santa Rosa
Calle Marti, 15 Esquina Maceo
Bayamon 00961
Puerto Rico
www.colegiosantarosa-pa.com.br
Ana Josefa Colon, Principal

2218 Colegio Santa Teresita
342 Victoria
Ponce 00731
Puerto Rico
015-278-1202
www.santateresita.edu.pe
Mary Terence, Principal

2219 Colegio Santiago Apostol
Calle 23 Bloque 23 #17, Urb Sierra Bayamon
Puerto Rico 00961
787-786- 917
Fax: 787-269-3965
Hilda Velazquez, Principal

2220 Colegio Santisimo Rosario
PO Box 26
Yauco 00698-0026
Puerto Rico
Judith Negron, Principal

2221 Colegio Santo Domingo
192 Calle Comerio
Bayamon 00959-5358
Puerto Rico
www.colegiosantodomingo.edu.do
Pura Huyke, Principal

2222 Colegio Santo Nino de Praga
PO Box 25
Penuelas 00624-0025
Puerto Rico
Aminta Santos, Principal

2223 Colegio Santos Angeles Custod
3 Sicilia Urb, San Jose
San Juan 00923
Puerto Rico
www.angelescustodios.com
Roberto Rivera, Principal

2224 Colegio de La Salle
PO Box 518
Bayamon 00960-0518
Puerto Rico
www.colsalle.edu.co
Wilfredo Perez De, Principal

2225 Commandant Gade Special Education School
St. Thomas, Virgin Islands 00801
Miss Jeanne Richards, Principal

2226 Community United Methodist School
PO Box 681
Frederiksted 00841-0681
Virgin Islands
Marva Oneal, Principal

2227 Country Day
RR 1 Box 6199
Kingshill, VI 00850
340-778-1974
Fax: 340-779-3331
www.stxcountryday.com
An independent, multicultural, college preparatory educational community set on a 34-acre tropical campus.
William Sinfield, Headmaster
Mariska Nurse, Dean of Guidance

2228 Croatia American International School-Zagreb
Vocarska 106
10 000 Zagreb
Croatia-5080
385-1-4680-133
Fax: 385-1-4680-171
asz@asz.hr
www.aisz.hr
Grades K-8, enrollment 112.
Robin Heslip, Director

2229 Dallas International School
6039 Churchill Way
Dallas, TX 75230
972-991-6379
Fax: 972-991-6608
www.dallasinternationalschool.org

DIS students will have the skills to continue their studies at universities in the United States or abroad and launch a professional career which will take advantage of all the opportunities created by globalization

Mea Ahlberg, Director of Admissions
MylSne Dumont, Middle School Coordinator

2230 Dominican Child Development Center
PO Box 5668
Agana
Guam 96910
617-477-7228
Fax: 671-472-4782
Kindergarten and nursery school.

Lednor Flores, Principal

2231 Dorado Academy
Urb Dorado del Mar Calle Madre Perl
Dorado
Puerto Rico 00646
787-796-2180
Fax: 787-796-7398
mescabi@doradoacademy.org
www.doradoacademy.org
Its objective is to provide to all students an education that reflects the school's philosophy. The teachers strive to implement by instruction the school's philosophy and meet instructional goals and objectives.

Liutma Caballero, Principal
Nancy Escabi, Headmaster

2232 Dwight School
291 Central Park W
New York, NY 10024
212-724-7524
Fax: 212-724-2539
admissions@dwight.edu
www.dwight.edu
Dwight's rigorous IB program and world-class faculty prepare a future generation of well-educated and ethical global leaders who will seek to create an environment of equality and respect for all human beings.

Marina Bernstein, Director Admissions
Alyson Waldman, Associate Director

2233 Educare
4235 Reserve Road
Unit 202
Lexington, KY 40514
859-396-7087
Fax: 859-201-1064
www.educare.org
To inspire children to achieve their very best; to educate children in character and leadership by drawing out their hidden character traits and leadership qualities.

Sara Connell, Principal

2234 Episcopal Cathedral School
PO Box 13305
Santurce
Puerto Rico 00908-3305
787-721-5478
Fax: 787-724-6668
www.gocougars.com
Founded in 1946.

Gary J DeHope, Director

2235 Escole Tout Petit
PO Box 1248
San Juan 00902
Puerto Rico

Vivian Aviles, Principal

2236 Escuela Beata Imelda
PO Box 804
Guanica 00653-0804
Puerto Rico

P Salvador Barber, Principal

2237 Escuela Bella Vista
Avenido Cecilio Acosta Calle 67 Ent
Maracaibo
Venezuela
58-61-966-696
Fax: 58-61-969-417
ebvnet@ebv.org.ve
www.ebv.org.ve
At EBV we offer an internationally enriched accredited U.S. program that prepares our students to participate actively, independently, cooperatively, and effectively in a multicultural, multilingual world. It is our commitment to educate each student to his/her maximum potential.

Steve Sibley, Superintendent
Todd Zukewich, High School Principal

2238 Escuela Campo Alegre
8424 NW 56th Street
Suite CCS 00007
Miami, FL 33166
58-2-993-3230
Fax: 58-2-993-0219
info@eca.com.ve
www.eca.com.ve
ECA seeks to inspire its students toward the highest standards and expectations through a stimulating and comprehensive program of intellectual and personal development.

Bambi Betts, Director
Phil Redwine, Principal

2239 Escuela Campo Alegre-Venezuela
8424 NW 56th Street
Suite CCS00007
Miami, FL 33166
58-2-993-7135
Fax: 58-2-993-0219
info@eca.com.ve
www.eca.com.ve
A private, coeducational day school offering a program for students from prekindergarten through grade 12.

Phil Redwine, Principal

2240 Escuela Caribe Vista School
8424 NW 56th Street
Suite CCS00007
Miami, FL 33166
765-668-4009
info@eca.com.ve
www.eca.com.ve

Phil Redwine, Principal

2241 Escuela Las Morochas
Apartado Postal # 235
Ciudad Ojeda, Estado Zulia
Venezuela
58-265-6315-539
Fax: 58-265-6315-539
Escuela Las Morochas is an English medium international school that offers a challenging U.S. education that encourages students to be life-long learners and responsible global citizens.

Jeff Trudeau, Director
Zulay Marcano, Assistant Secretary

2242 Escuela Nuestra Senora Del Carmen
PO Box 116, Playa De Ponce
Ponce 00731
Puerto Rico 00731
266-282-
Fax: 266-253-

Paquita Alvarado, Principal

2243 Escuela Superior Catolica
PO Box 4245
Bayamon 00958-1245
Puerto Rico

Eledis Diaz, Principal

2244 Fajardo Academy
55 Calle Federico Garcia
PO Box 1146, Fajardo 00648
Puerto Rico
809-863-1001
www.fajardoacademy.org

Miguel A Rivera, BA, MA, MEd, Principal

2245 Freewill Baptist School
PO Box 6265
Christiansted 00823-6265
Virgin Islands
www.freewillschool.com

Joe Postlewaite, Principal

2246 French-American International School
150 Oak Street
San Francisco, CA 94102
415-558-2000
Fax: 415-558-2024
fais@fais-ihs.org
Grade levels preK-12, with total student enrollment of 813.

Jane Camblin, Head of School

2247 George D Robinson School
5 Nairn Condado
Santurce 00907
Puerto Rico
845-344-2292

Daniel W Sheehan, Principal

2248 Georgetown American School
3170 Georgetown Place
Washington, DC 20521-3170
592-225-1595
Fax: 592-226-1459

Thurston Riehl, Director

2249 Georgia QSI International School-Tbilisi
Village Zurgovani
Tbilisi
Republic of Georgia
995-32-982909
Fax: 995-32-322-607
tbilisi@qsi.org
www.qsi.org
A private non-profit organization, organizes and operates schools of excellence, identifies quality educators for these schools, and provides educational consulting services

Scott D'Alterio, Director
David Pera, Director Instruction

2250 Glynn Christian School
Club 6, Christian Hill
St Croix, Kingshill 00851
Virgin Islands
340-778-1932
www.virginislandsdailynews.com

Muriel Francis, Principal

2251 Good Hope School-St. Croix
Estate Good Hope Frederiksted
St Croix 00840
Virgin Islands
340-778-1932
www.virginislandsdailynews.com

Tanya L Nichols, Principal

52 Good Shepherd School
PO Box 1069
St Croix, Kingshill 00851
Virgin Islands 00851
340-772-2280
Fax: 340-772-1021
www.virginislandsdailynews.com

Mary Ellen Mcencil, Director
Susan P Eversley, Assistant Director

53 Grace Baptist Academy
7815 Shallowford Road
Chattanooga, TN 37421
423-892-8223
Fax: 423-892-1194
www.gracechatt.org

Helen Yasper, Principal

54 Guam Adventist Academy
1200 Aguilar Road
Yoa
Guam 96915
617-789-1515
Fax: 617-789-3547
Office@GAAsda.org
www.gaasda.org
Learn about God and His character through Bible study, aided by the study of nature and E.G. White's writings. Develop a personal friendship with Jesus Christ

John N Youngberg, Principal
Dori Talon, Accountant

55 Guam Department of Education
PSC 455 Box 192
FPO, Mariana Islands 96540 1192
Guam 96915-1054
011-671-475-0457
Fax: 011-671-472-5003
www.gdoe.net
Develop a personal friendship with Jesus Christ

Rosie R Tainatongo, Director

56 Guam High School
PSC 455 Box 192
FPO, Mariana Islands 96540 1192
Guam 96915-1054
671-475-0462
Fax: 671-472-5003
www.gdoe.net

Rosie R Tainatongo, Director

257 Guam S Elementary & Middle School
PSC 455 Box 192
FPO, Mariana Islands 96540 1192
Guam 96915-1054
671-475-0462
Fax: 671-472-5003
www.gdoe.net

Rosie R Tainatongo, Director

258 Guamani School
PO Box 3000
Guayama
Puerto Rico 00785
787-864-6880
Fax: 787-866-4947
edelgado@guamani.com
www.guamani.com
A private non-profit, co-educational, non-sectarian school committed in offering an English-based academic college preparatory program geared in preparing students to become knowledgeable and responsible individuals for today's changing society.

Eduardo Delgado, Director
Pedro A Dominguez, Administrator

2259 Harvest Christian Academy
PO Box 23189
Barrigada
Guam 96921
671-477-6341
Fax: 671-477-7136
www.harvestministries.net
Harvest Christian Academy is a K-12th grade school. It is a ministry of Harvest Baptist Church.

John McGraw, Principal

2260 Hogar Colegio La Milagrosa
Ave Cotto 987 Barrio Cotto
Arecibo 00612
Puerto Rico 00612
787-878-0341
www.hogarcolegiolamilagrosa.com

Sor Trinidad Ibizarry, Principal

2261 India American Embassy School-New Delhi
Chandragupta Marg Chanakyapuri
New Delhi
India 11002
91-11-611-7140
Fax: 91-11-687-3320
aesindia@aes.ac.in
www.aes.ac.in
The American Embassy School serves students from the United States and other nations. It provides a quality American education that enables students to be inspired learners and responsible global citizens through the collaboration of a dedicated faculty and a supportive community.

Bob Hetzel, Director

2262 Inter-American Academy
Suite 8227
6964 NW 50th Street
Miami, FL 33166-5632
593-4-871-790
Fax: 593-4-873-358

Dr. Bruce Goforth, Executive Director

2263 International Community School-Abidjan
DOS/Administrative Officer
2010 Abidjan Place
Washington, DC 20521-2010
225-22-47-11-52
Fax: 225-22-47-19-96
American style curriculum from kindergarten through grade 12 for children of all nationalities.

Rob Mockrish, Director

2264 International High School-Yangon
4250 Rangoon Place
Department of State
Washington, DC 20521-4250
95-1-512-793
Fax: 95-1-525-020

Merry Wade, Director

2265 International School of Port-of-Spain
#POS 1369 1601 NW 97th Avenue
PO Box 025307
Miami, FL 33102-5307
868-632-4591
Fax: 868-632-4595
www.isps.edu.tt
ISPS will provide an outstanding educational programme for both international and resident families who want their children to pursue higher education.

Eric Larson, Director
John Horsfall, High School Principal

2266 International School-Conakry
2110 Conakry Place
Washington, DC 20521-2110
224-12-661-535
Fax: 224-41-15-22
isc@biasy.net
A private, coeducational school offering an educational program from pre-kindergarten through grade 12 for children from expatriate and host country families. Develop pupils' academic knowledge; learning, thinking, social, and communication skills; international attitudes; and appreciation for cultural diversity.

Greg Hughes, Director
Robert Merritt, Management Officer

2267 International School-Dakar
BP 5136
Dakar
Senegal
221-033- 250
Fax: 221-033- 250
admin_isd@orange.sn
An independent English-medium international school, which offers, in a nurturing environment, a rigorous, US-based, PK-12 curriculum enriched to reflect the needs and diversity of its international student body and faculty.

Wayne Rutherford, Director

2268 International School-Grenada
Washington, DC 20521-1
www.international-schoolfriends.com

Mary Delaney Dunn, Principal

2269 International School-Havana
Department of State
18 Street, 315 and 5th Avenue
Miramar, Havana City
Cuba 10600
053- 02- 281
Fax: 530-020-2740
office@ish.co.cu
The school offer high quality education to the children of the expatriate community in Cuba. Serves and can admit students who have a foreign (non-Cuban) citizenship, and are temporarily living in Cuba with their parent(s) or guardian(s), and as such form part of the diplomatic or expatriate non-diplomatic community in the country.

Ian Morris, Principal
Richard Fluit, Head, Secondary School

2270 International School-Islamabad
H-9/1, PO Box 1124
Islamabad
Pakistan 44000
92-51-434-950
Fax: 92-51-440-193
school@isoi.edu.pk
www.isoi.edu.pk
Offers an American- based curriculum to students of over 29 nationalities.

Rose C Puffer, Superintendent

2271 International School-Ouagadougou
s/c Ambassade des, Etats Unis
01 BP35, Ouagadougou
Burkina Faso
226-36-21-43
Fax: 226-36-22-28
iso@iso.bf
www.iso.bf
ISO strives to cultivate a student's intellect and character in an English-speaking environment, offering strong academic programs and promoting cultural understanding.

Larry Ethier, Director
Kim Overton, Curriculum Coordinator

2272 International School-Port of Spain
1601 NW 97th Avenue
PO Box 025307
Miami, FL 33102-5307
868-633-4777
Fax: 868-632-4595
www.isps.edu.tt
Provides a college preparatory, holistic education for children in grades pre-kindergarten through grade 12, providing them with the skills, knowledge, and values necessary to be productive individuals in an interdependent world.
Eric Larson, Director
Jackie Fung-Kee-Fung, Admission Director/PR

2273 International School-Sfax
Brit Gas 1100 Louisiana
Houston, TX 77002
Sidney Norris, Principal

2274 International School-Yangon
20 Shwe Taungyar
Bahan Township, Yangon
Myanmar-1
512-93 -
Fax: 95 - 52-020
We inspire students with a challenging, international education, based on an American curriculum, in a nurturing learning environment that promotes respondibility and respect. We aim to develop socially engaged, self-motivated, creative, compassionate individuals who will be a force for positive change in their communities and the world.
DJ Condon, Middle/High School Principal
Dennis MacKinnon, Director

2275 Izmir American Institute
Friends-850 Third Avenue
18th Floor
New York, NY 10022
232-355-0555
www.aci.k12.tr
Richard Curtis, Principal

2276 John F Kennedy School-Queretaro
Sabinos #272, Jurica
Queretaro
Mexico 76100
442-218-0075
Fax: 442-218-1784
admissions@jfk.edu.mx
www.jfk.edu.mx
The American School of Queretaro, is to provide the whole individual an opportunity for high quality U.S. type, bilingual education that recognizes individual talents and encourages lifelong learning
Dr. Francisco Galicia, Principal
Mirtha Stappung, General Director

2277 Jordan American Community School
PO Box 310, Dahiat Al-Amir Rashid
Amman 11831
Jordan
962-6-581-3944
Fax: 962-6-582-3357
school@acsamman.edu.jo
www.acsamman.edu.jo
ACS is fully accredited K-12 by the Middle States Association of Colleges and Schools and is a member in good standing of NESA, the Near East South Asia Association of Overseas Schools
Dr. Gray Duckett, Superintendent

2278 Karachi American Society School
American Consulate General Karachi
610 Karachi Place
Washington, DC 20521-6150
92-21-453-909619
Fax: 92-21-453-7305
www.kas.edu.pk
David Holmer, Principal

2279 Kongeus Grade School
44-46 Gade
St Thomas 00802
Virgin Islands 00802
Veronica Miller, Principal

2280 Lincoln International School-Kampala
Co of State
Washington, DC 20521-1
Margaret Bell, Principal

2281 Lincoln School
Lincoln School 565-20
PO Box 025331
Miami, FL 33102-5331
506-224- 660
Fax: 506-224- 670
www.lincoln.ed.cr
offer an integrated education, using English as the primary language of instruction, to motivate a continuing search for excellence and stimulate students to fully develop their potential to become responsible, enterprising, creative, open-minded citizens with solid ethical values, committed to democracy, and capable of being successful in a multicultural, global society.
Charles Prince, Principal

2282 Lincoln-Marti Schools
2700 SW 8 Street
Miami, FL 33135
305-643-4888
877-874-1999
Fax: 305-649-2767
info@lincoln-marti.com
www.lincolnmarti.com
Lincoln-Mart is an institution dedicated to educating the future of our community, both academically and socially.
Demitrio Perez, President

2283 Little People's Learning Center
9605 SE 7th Street
Vancouver, WA 98664
360-892-7570
info@lplc.net
www.lplc.net/home.html
Daphne Maynard, Principal
Becky Dolan, Director

2284 Little School House
47 Kongens Gade
St Thomas 00802
Virgin Islands
416-303-7282
Carol Struiell, Principal

2285 Luanda International School
Rua da Talatona Caixa 1566
Barrio da Talatona Luanda Sul Samba
Republica de Angola
244-2-44-3416
Fax: 244-2-44-3416
officesec@lisluanda.com
www.lisluanda.com
offers a balanced, academically challenging, English language education to the international community of Luanda, designed to develop individuals who are both independent learners and international citizens.
Anthony Baron, Director
Di Atkinson, Senior Administrator

2286 Lutheran Parish School
#1 Lille Taarne Gade
Charlotte Aml 00802
Puerto Rico 00802
Nancy Gotwalt, Principal

2287 Manor School
236 La Grande Princesse
Christiansted, VI 00820-4449
340-718-1448
Fax: 340-718-3651
is dedicated to personal and academic growth in an extended-family environment. We promote academic confidence, creativity, community involvement and citizenship, a sense of respon-sibility, and positive decision- making. We strive to ensure that our graduates are person-ally and academically prepared to succeed in their future endeavors.
Judith C Gadd, Headmistress
Hanley Hamed, Office Manager

2288 Maranatha Christian Academy
9201 75th Avenue N
Brooklyn Park, MN 55428
612- 58- 285
Fax: 763-315-7294
www.maranathachristianacademy.org
is to offer a pre-kindergarten through 12th grade traditional classroom education providing a quality educational experience, which encourages and enables students to mature spiritually, intellectually, physically, emotionally, and socially in accordanc
Rev. Gary Sprunger, Principal
Brian Sullivan, Chief Administrator

2289 Martin De Porress Academy
621 Elmont Road
Elmont, NY 11003
516-502-2840
Fax: 516-502-2841
sfagin@mdp.org
www.mdp.org/
The Martin De Porress Academy program provides academic instruction based upon the NY State Learning Standards as well as hands on experiences in business enterprises, performing arts, home improvement skills, life skills, culinary arts, maintenance services and community services.
Raymond R Blixt, Executive Director
Philip E Chance, Assistant Executive Director

2290 Montessori House of Children
572 Dunholme Way
Suite 103
Sunnyvale, CA 94086
408-749-1602
Our program is based on the premise that every child is an individual with his own needs and abilities. All children need affection and friendliness. They require affirmation, encouragement and understanding
William Myers, Principal
Priya Medelberg, Founder-Director

2291 Moravian School
4313 Green Pond Road
Bethlehem
Virgin Islands
610-868-4744
www.moravianacademy.org
This Moravian affiliated school offers a curriculum based in English for 200 day students (96 boys; 104 girls), in grades K-6. The school is willing to participate in a teacher exchange program,

with the length of stay being one year, with housing provided. Applications include science, Spanish and computer skills.

Condon L Joseph, Principal

92 Morrocoy International

MUN 4051
PO Box 025352
Miami, FL 33102-5352
58-286-9520016
Fax: 58-286-9521861
kempenich@telcel.net.ve
Grade levels Pre-K through 10, school year August - June

Michael Kempenich, Headmaster

93 Mount Carmel Elementary School

PO Box 7830
Agat 96928 0830
Guam-b830
256-852-7187
Fax: 256-852-0039
This Catholic school offers an English (primary) curriculum for 206 day students (100 boys; 106 girls), in Kinder 4 - 8th grade. Overseas teachers are accepted, with the length of stay being one year. Applications needed to teach include reading, English and counseling/counselor.

Bernadette Quintanilla, Sr, SSND, Principal
Augustin Gumataotao, Administrator

94 Nazarene Christian School

385 Hazel Mill Road
Asheville, NC 28806
828-252-9713
www.ashevillefirstnazarene.org
The Nazarene International Center provides support services to more than 1.2 million members worshiping in more than 11,800 churches in the United States, Canada, and 135 other world areas

Peggy Neighbors, Administrator

95 Nepal Lincoln School

Kathmandu (LS)
Department of State
Washington, DC 20521-6190
977-1-270-482
Fax: 977-1-272-685
info@lsnepal.com.np
Lincoln School is an independent, international school in Kathmandu, Nepal with an American Curriculum. We are committed to nurture of the individual student, excellence in all spheres of achievement, pursuit of personal responsibility, appreciation of diversity, and love of learning

Allan Bredy, Director
Craig Baker, Principal

296 Northern Mariana Islands Department of Education

PO Box 501370 CK
Siapan, MP 96950
011-670-664-3720
Fax: 011-670-664-3798

Rita Hocog Inos, Commissioner

297 Notre Dame High School

480 S San Miguel Street
Talofofo
Guam 96930-4699
671-789-1676
www.ndhs.org
Notre Dame is a co-educational, year-round high school run by the School Sisters of Notre Dame. This Roman Catholic affiliated school offers a curriculum in English for 191 day students and 9 boarding (32 boys; 168 girls), in grades 9-12. Student/teacher ratio is 10:1, and the applications needed to teach include science, math, social sciences, and English.

Regina Paulino, SSND, Principal

2298 Nuestra Senora de La Altagracia

672 Calle Felipe Gutierrez #672
San Juan 00924-2225
Puerto Rico

2299 Nuestra Senora de La Providencia

PO Box 11610
San Juan 00922-1610
Puerto Rico

2300 Okinawa Christian School

1835 Zakimi
Yomitan, Okinawa
Japan 904-0
098-958-3000
Fax: 098-958-6279
info@ocsi.org
www.ocsi.org
A non-denominational mission whose purpose is to partner with families of the international community of Okinawa by offering an excellent Christian education in the English language.

Paul Gieschen, Principal

2301 Open Classroom

PO Box 4046
St Thomas 00803
Virgin Islands 00803
805-904-5931
805-289-1817
Fax: 852- 54- 133

Janie Lang, Principal

2302 Osaka International School

4-16 Onohar Nishi 4-Chome
Mino, Osaki, 562-0032
Japan
072-727-5050
Fax: 072-727-5055
www.senri.ed.jp
OIS is an english-language-based, preK-12 grade coeducational college-preparatory school.

John Searle, Head of School

2303 Palache Bilingual School

PO Box 1832
Arecibo 00613-1832
Puerto Rico

Rev. David Valez, Principal

2304 Peace Corp

1111 20th Street NW
Washington, DC 20526
202-692-1470
800-424-8580
Fax: 202-692-1897
psa@peacecorps.gov
www.peacecorps.gov
Helping the people of interested countries in meeting their need for trained men and women. Helping promote a better understanding of Americans on the part of the peoples served

2305 Pine Peace School

PO Box 1657
St John, VI 00831
340-776-6595
An independent, non-profit, English language school that serves students without regard to sex, race, religion, or nationality.

Beth Knight, Headmistress

2306 Ponce Baptist Academy

72 Calle 1 Belgica
Ponce 00731
Puerto Rico

Vivian Medina, Principal

2307 Prophecy Elementary School

PO Box 10497
APO St Thomas 00801-3497
Virgin Islands 00801
340-775-7223
Fax: 340-714-5354
www.prophecyacademy.net
Church of God of Prophecy Academy, Inc. offers a Christian atmosphere which develops the physical, spiritual, intellectual and the social skills of every student. Our primary purpose is to help train students while teaching them the Christian way of life.

Anne E Bramble-Johnson, Principal
VeronaCeleste Hutchinson, Secretary/Office Manager

2308 Puerto Rico Department of Education

PO Box 190759
San Juan
Puerto Rico 00919-759
787-759-2000

Cesar A Rey-Hernandez, Secretary

2309 QSI International School-Chisinau

18 Anton Crihan Street
Chisinau
Moldova 20521-7080
373-24-2366
chisinau@qsi.org
www.qsi.org
To keep this urge to learn alive in every child in QSI schools. Our schools are established to provide in the English language a quality education for students in the cities we serve.

Sandra Smith, Director

2310 QSI International School-Skopje

Inlindenska BB, Reon 55
1000 Skopie
Macedonia 20521-7120
389-91-367-678
Fax: 389-91-362-250
skopje@qsi.org
www.qsi.org
To keep this urge to learn alive in every child in QSI schools. Our schools are established to provide in the English language a quality education for students in the cities we serve.

Robert Tower, Director
Aleksandar Kostadinovski, Finance Manager

2311 QSI International School-Vladivostok

DOS/Administrative Officer
5880 Vladivostok Place
Washington, DC 20521-5880
7-4232-321-292
Fax: 7-4232-313-684
www.qsi.org
Grades preK-9, enrollment 18.

Harold M Strom Jr, Director

2312 Rainbow Development Center

PO Box 7618
Christiansted 00823-7618
Virgin Islands
408-215-1386
www.rainbowccc.com

Gloria Henry, Principal

2313 Rainbow Learning Institute
PO Box 75
Christiansted 00821-0075
Virgin Islands
408-215-1386
www.rainbowccc.com
Alda Lockhart, Principal

2314 Rainbow School
PO Box 422
Charlotte Aml 00801
Virgin Islands
408-215-1386
www.rainbowccc.com
Louise Thomas, Principal

2315 Robinson School
5 Nairn Street Condado
San Juan 00907
Puerto Rico 00907
1-787-728-6767
Fax: 1-787-727-7736
robinson_school@hotmail.com
www.robinsonschool.org
The Heart of Educational Excellence. Robinson offers its students a solid foundation for their future academic and career pursuits.
Giberto Quintana, Executive Director
Hugh Andrews, President

2316 Roosevelt Roads Elementary School
PO Box 420132
Roosevelt Roads 00742-0132
Puerto Rico
787-865-3073
Fax: 787-865-4891
www.netdial.caribe.net

2317 Roosevelt Roads Middle & High School
PO Box 420131
Roosevelt Roads 00742-0131
Puerto Rico
787-865-4000
Fax: 787-865-4893
Waynna James, Principal

2318 Saint Anthony School
529 Chalan San Antonio
Tamuning
Guam 96913
671-647-1140
Fax: 471-649-7130
A Catholic co-educational elementary school in the Archdiocese of Agana, exists to educate the whole person by providing a rich integrated curriculum served by enabling adults.
Doris San Agustin, Principal
Elizabeth E San Nicolas, Vice-Principal

2319 Saint Eheresas Elementary School
2701 Indian Mound Trail
Coral Gables
American Samoa
305-446-1738
Fax: 305-446-2877
www.cotlf.org
Sister Katherine, Principal

2320 Saint Francis Elementary School
2701 Indian Mound Trail
Coral Gables
American Samoa, ÿF
305-446-1738
Fax: 305-446-2877
www.cotlf.org
Sister Gaynor Ana, Principal

2321 Saint John's School
911 N Marine Corps Drive
Tumon Bay 96913
Guam
671-646-8080
Fax: 617-649-6791
St. John's students on average score in the top 20% on national scholastic achievement tests in all academic subjects in all grades K-12, a tangible result of an integrated academic program supported by a dedicated faculty, many with advanced degrees in their respective areas of instruction
Glenn Chapin, Headmaster
Imelda D Santos, Dean of Students

2322 Saint John's School, Puerto Rico
1454-66 Ashford Avenue
San Juan 00907
Puerto Rico
787-728-5343
Fax: 787-268-1454
www.sjspr.org
Saint John's School is a college preparatory, nonsectarian, coeducational day school founded in 1915. The school, located in a residential area of the Condado, has an enrollment of approximately 750 students from preschool to grade twelve. 84% come from Hispanic backgrounds, 8% percent from diverse backgrounds and 8% from the continental United States. With the exception of Spanish and French classes, instruction is in English.
Louis R Christiansen, Principal
Barry Farnham, Headmaster

2323 Saints Peter & Paul High School
900 High Street
Easton, MD
410-822-2275
Fax: 410-822-1767
jnemeth@ssppeaston.org
www.ssppeaston.org
Saints Peter and Paul High School is a parochial, Catholic, college preparatory school.
James Nemeth, Principal
Carolyn Hayman, Administrative Assistant

2324 Samoa Baptist Academy
Tafuna
Pago Pago 96799
American Samoa
Janice Yerton, Principal

2325 San Carlos & Bishop McManus High School
PO Box Loo 9, Yumet
Aguadilla 00605
Puerto Rico
504-246-5121
questions@bishopmcmanus.ws
www.bishopmcmanus.ws
Nydia U Nieves, Principal

2326 San Vincente Elementary School
San Vincente School Drive
Soledad
Puerto Rico 96913
671-734-4242
This campus is on five acres of outside Barrigada Village. The average enrollment of 460 students consists of 234 boys and 226 girls in grades PreK-8. SVS holds a Certificate of Accreditation from the Western Association of Schools and Colleges until 1998. Length of stay for overseas teachers is two years, with housing provided. Applications needed to teach include English and physical education.
Adrian Cristobal, Principal
Tarcisia Sablan SSND, Faculty Head

2327 Santa Barbara School
274A W Santa Barbara Avenue
Dededo
Guam 96929
671-632-5578
Fax: 671-632-1414
To ensure that each student is given the opportunity to realize his or her full potential according to God's design by recognizing and affirming the gifts of each child.
Sr Jeanette Mar Pangelinan, Principal
Sr Maria Rosari Gaite, Vice Principal

2328 Santiago Christian School
PO Box 5600
Santiago
Dominican Republic, FL 33310-5600
809-570-6140
www.santiagochristianschool.org
Lloyd Haglund, Principal

2329 School and Chapel for the Deaf
HC-01 Buzon 7111
Luquillo
Puerto Rico 00773
787-889-3488
cscdluquillo@gmail.com
www.cscdluquillo.com
Teaches the Deaf for Christ, preschool-adult; provides unpaid internship opportunities for those interested in Deaf ministry
Lourdes Vargas, President
Elisabeth Hoke, Director, Education

2330 School of the Good Shepherd
1069 Kinghill
St Croix 00851
Virgin Islands 00851
www.goodshepherdtvm.org
Linda Navarro, Principal

2331 Seventh Day Adventist
PO Box 7909
St Thomas 00801-0909
Virgin Islands
Josiah Maynard, Principal

2332 Shekou International School
Jing Shan Villas, Nan Hai Road Shek
Guangdong Province
China 51806
86-755-2669-3669
Fax: 86-755-2667-4099
sis@sis.org.cn
www.sis.org.cn
Shekou International School follows a rigorous college preparatory US style curriculum and is dedicated to meeting the outcomes of the Expected Student Learning Results.
Robert Dunseth, Director
Jennifer Lees, Curriculum Coordinator

2333 Slovak Republic QSI International School of Bratislava
Karloveska 64
Bratislava
Slovak Republic 84220
421-2-6541-1636
Fax: 421-2-6541-1646
bratislava@qsi.org
www.qsi.sk
THE PRIMARY PURPOSE of the school is to meet the needs of the children in Bratislava who require this type of education with a view to con-

tinuing their education in their home countries with a minimum of adjustment problems.

Ronald Adams, Principal
Matthew Lake, Director

34 Slovenia QSI International School-Ljubljana
Dolgi Most 6A
Ljubljana
Slovenia 01000
386-1-439-6300
Fax: 386-1-439-6305
bratislava@qsi.org
www.qsi.org
THE PRIMARY PURPOSE of the school is to meet the needs of the children in Ljubljana who require this type of education with a view to continuing their education in their home countries with a minimum of adjustment problems.

Ronald Adams, Principal
Matthew Lake, Director

35 South Pacific Academy
PO Box 520
Pago Pago 96799 0520
American Samoa
644-237-4072

Tina Senrud, Principal

36 Southern Peru Staff Schools-Peru
180 Maiden Lane
New York, NY 10038-4925
www.isbi.com

John Dansdill, Principal

337 St. Croix Christian Academy
26-28 Golden Rock, Christiansted, S
PO Box 716
Virgin Islands, US 00821
340-718-4974
Fax: 340-718-6768
stccacademy@vipowernet.net
The mission of the school is to foster knowledge of God and to give the children a solid academic foundation, along with effective Christian training.

Linus Gittens, Principal

338 St. Croix Country Day School
Rt-01, Box 6199
Kingshill
Virgin Islands, US 00850
1-340-778-1974
Fax: 1-340-779-3331
It is dedicated to providing students with an enriched and challenging education, encouraging them to love learning, grow as individuals and be prepared for a productive and responsible future.

Bill Sinfield, Headmaster
Susan Gibbons, Business Manager

339 St. Croix Moravian School
PO Box 117
St Thomas 00801
Virgin Islands
www.aavirginislands.org

Condon L Joseph, Principal

340 St. Croix SDA School
PO Box 930
Kingshill 00851-0930
Virgin Islands

Peter Archer, Principal

2341 St. Joseph High School
PO Box 517
Frederiksted 00841-0517
Virgin Islands

Kevin Marin, Principal

2342 St. Patrick School
PO Box 988
Frderiksted 00841-0988
Virgin Islands
www.spsasansol.com

Juliette Clarke, Principal

2343 St. Peter & Paul Elementary School
PO Box 1706
St Thomas 00803
Virgin Islands
www.sppschool.org

Annamay Komment, Principal

2344 Sunbeam
36 Hospital Ground
St Thomas 00803
Virgin Islands
202-427-2383
Fax: 202-426-0308
www.sunbeaminfo.com

Ione Leonard, Principal

2345 Syria Damascus Community School
6110 Damascus Place
Dulles, VA 20189-6110
963-11-333-0331
Fax: 963-11-332-1457
dcs-dam@net.sy
An independent, coeducational day school which offers an American educational program from preschool through grade 12 for students of all nationalities.

John Gates, Director
Maura Connelly, Chairman

2346 Tashkent International School
7117 Tashkent Place
Dulles, VA 20189-7110
998-71-191-9671
Fax: 998-71-120-6621
office@tashschool.org
www.tashschool.org
To provide a high academic standard of education, educating students to become ethical, responsible, productive citizens of the world with the skills to think creatively, reason critically, and to communicate effectively

John Thomas, Director

2347 Teaching in Austria
Austrian Institute
11 E 52nd Street
New York, NY 10022-5301
212-579-5165

2348 Temple Christian School
PO Box 3009
Agana 96910
Guam 96910

Rev. Ray Fagan, Principal

2349 Tirana International School-Albania
Kutia Postare
Tirana
Albania, DC 01527-9510
355-4-365-239
Fax: 335-4-227-734
tirana@qsi.org
www.qsi.org
The school's educational philosophy, which includes a personalized approach to instruction, leads to teaching for mastery.

Ronald Adams, Principal
Matthew Lake, Director

2350 Trinity Christian School
1231 East Pleasant Run Road
Yiga 96929 0343
Cedar Hill, TX 75104
972-291-2505
Fax: 972-291-4739
www.trinitychristianschool.com
Being a Christian school means we assist parents in fulfilling their divine responsibility to thoroughly train each child to obey God in every area of life and make him or her a true disciple of Jesus Christ. Our program is designed to challenge and educate students of good moral character who are in the middle to upper range of academic ability

Kathleen L Watts, Superintendent
Rhonda Parker, Executive Assistant

2351 Turkmenistan Ashgabat International School
Box 2002
7070 Ashgabat Place
Washington, DC 20521-7070
967-1-234-437
Fax: 967-1-234-438
Grades K-11, enrollment 75.

Scott Root, Director

2352 Ukraine Kiev International School-An American Institution
EOS/Administrative Officer
5850 Kiev Place
Washington, DC 20521-5850
380-44-452-2792
Fax: 380-44-452-2998
www.kis.net.ua
An independent, coeducational day school which offers an educational program from prekindergarten through high school for students of all nationalities.

E Michael Tewalthomas, Director

2353 United Nations International School
24-50 FDR Drive
New York, NY 10010-4046
212-584-3071
admissions@unis.org
www.unis.org
The United Nations International School provides an international education that emphasizes academic excellence within a caring community for prekindergarten through twelfth grade students from the United Nations, as well as from other families seeking a similar education for their children.

Dan Brenner, Executive Director
Susan Enzer, Executive Assistant

2354 University del Sagrado Corazon
PO Box 12383
San Juan
Puerto Rico 00914-383
787-728-1515
www.sagrado.edu

2355 Uruguayan American School
Av Saldœn de Rodriguez
Montevideo
Uruguay, DC 11500-3360
598-2-600-7681
Fax: 598-2-600-1935
www.uas.edu.uy
Uruguayan American School is to provide, together with the family, a balanced college preparatory education. UAS integrates a US style curriculum with Uruguayan studies to equip our national and international students to be successful in a diverse, ever changing world

Thomas Oden, Director
Cecilia Burgueo, UP Coordinator

2356 Uruguayan American School-Montevideo
Av Saldœn de Rodriguez
Montevideo
Uruguay, DC 11500-3360
598-2-600-7681
Fax: 598-2-606-1935
www.uas.edu.uy
Uruguayan American School is to provide, together with the family, a balanced college preparatory education. UAS integrates a US style curriculum with Uruguayan studies to equip our national and international students to be successful in a diverse, ever changing world
Thomas Oden, Director
Cecilia Burgueo, UP Coordinator

2357 Uzbekistan Tashkent International School
38 Sarikul Street
Tashkent, Uzbekistan 10000
998-71-191-9671
Fax: 998-71-120-6621
office@tashschool.org
www.tashschool.org
Tashkent International School (TIS), an IB World School, is a private, not for profit, independent, co-educational day school governed by a Board of Directors elected and appointed from the parent community. TIS offers an American based international curriculum from Kindergarten - grade 12. TIS is an IB World School offering: the full International Baccalaureate Diploma in grades 11 - 12, the Primary Years Program for Kindergarten - grade 5, and is a candidate school for the Middle Years Program
Kevin Glass, Director
John Zohrab, Treasurer

2358 Venezuela Colegio Internacional-Carabobo
PO Box 025685
Miami, FL 33102-5685
58-41-426-551
Fax: 58-41-426-510
www.cic-valencia.org.ve
Colegio Internacional de Carabobo (CIC) is a school dedicated to the development of the whole child. Our teachers are innovative, skilled, and dedicated. Creativity and self-esteem are essential qualities for students to develop as they ascend the academic ladder.
Frank Anderson, Superintendent
Joe Walker, Director

2359 Venezuela Escuela Campo Alegre
8424 NW 56th Street
Suite CCS 00007
Miami, FL 33166
58-2-993-7135
Fax: 58-2-993-0219
www.eca.com.ve
Escuela Campo Alegre is a private non-profit English language school, designed primarily to serve the needs of the children from ages 3-18 of its shareholding members.
Jean K Vahey, Superintendent

2360 Venezuela International School-Caracas
Pakmail 6030
PO Box 025304
Miami, FL 33102-5304
58-2-945-0422
Fax: 58-2-945-0533
Colegio Internacional de Caracas is an English-medium, Pre-Nursery to Grade 12 school dedicated to the intellectual and personal development of each student in a caring and supportive environment.
Alan Benson, Superintendent

2361 Virgin Island Montessori School
6936 Vessup Lane
Saint Thomas, VI 00802
340-775-6360
Fax: 340-775-3080
www.vimontessori.com/
Virgin Islands Montessori School and International Academy offers a unique environment and learning experience to over 200 students from two years of age through High School
Shournagh Mcweeney, Administrator
Michael Bornn, President

2362 Virgin Islands Department of Education
44-46 Kongens Gade
Saint Thomas, Virgin Islands 00802
340-774-2810
Fax: 340-774-7153
www.doe.vi/
The mission of the Department of Education is to provide the Territory's students with an education that makes them competitive with their peers in the rest of the Caribbean,the United States, and the World; take advantage of our uniqueness of being geographically Caribbean and politically American; integrate all discipline; and educate the whole child.
LaVerne Terry, Commissioner
Donna Frett-Gregory, Assistant Commissioner

2363 Washington International School
3100 Macomb Street NW
Washington, DC 20008-3324
202-243-1800
Fax: 202-243-1802
admissions@wis.edu
www.wis.edu
Washington International School (WIS) is a coeducational day school offering 890 students a challenging curriculum and rich language program from Pre-Kindergarten through Grade 12
Clayton W. Lewis, Head of School
Sandra Bourne, Middle School Principal

2364 We Care Child Development Center
PO Box 818
Christiansted 00821-0818
Virgin Islands
www.utexas.edu
Pauline Canton, Principal

2365 Wesleyan Academy
PO Box 1489
Guaynabo
Puerto Rico 00970-1489
787-008-
Fax: 787-790-0730
www.wesleyanacademy.org
We are a nonprofit, private, coeducational, English Christian school providing a Pre-Pre Kinder through Twelfth grade college preparatory education.
Jack Mann, Principal

2366 Yakistan International School-Karachi
DOS/Administrative Officer
6150 Karachi Place
Washington, DC 20521-6150
92-21-453-9096
Fax: 92-21-454-7305
ameschl@cyber.net.pk
www.isk.edu.pk
Grades N-12, enrollment 338.
Glen Shapin, Superintendent

2367 Zion Academy
7629 199th Street SW
Lynnwood, WA 98036
425-640-3311
info@zionacademy.com
www.zionacademy.com
Zion Academy is a fully accredited private school. Consists of students that wish to work at home and desire complete oversight and administrative services.
Evelyn Williams, Principal
Marigene Lindsey, Founder and Headmaster

International

2368 Center for Strategic and International Studies
1616 Rhode Island Avenue NW
Washington, DC 20036
202-887-0200
Fax: 202-775-3199
books@csis.org
www.csis.org
Provides strategic insights and policy solutions to decisionmakers in government, international institutions, the private sector and civil society.
John J Hamre, President & CEO
Thomas J Pritzker, Chairman

2369 Council for International Exchange of Scholars
3007 Tilden Street NW
Suite 5-L
Washington, DC 20008-3009
202-686-4000
Fax: 202-362-3442
www.cies.org
Helped administer the Fulbright Scholar Program on behalf of the United States Department of State, Bureau of Educational and Cultural Affairs.
Michael A Brintnall, Executive Director
Judy Pehrson, Director External Relations

2370 Defense Language Institute-English Language Branch
US Civil Service Commission, San Antonio Area
2235 Andrews Avenue
Lackland, TX 78236-5514
210-671-3783
Fax: 210-671-5362
www.dlielc.org
The DLIELC is a Department of Defense (DOD) agency responsible for the management and operation of the Defense English Language Program (DELP) to train international military and civilian personnel to speak and teach English, manage the English as a second language program for the US military

2371 EF Educational Tours
2 Education Cir
Cambridge, MA 02141
800-637-8222
www.eftours.com
EF Educational Tours helps educators enrich classroom learing with international group travel. Students learn from experiencing the world's historic, cultural and natural sights.
Shane Steffens, President
Amar Dhotar, CPA, CA, Finance Manager

72 Education Information Services which Employ Americans
Education Information Services
PO Box 620662
Newton, MA 02462-662
781-433-0125
Fax: 781-237-2842
www.alis.alberta.ca
Devoted to helping Americans who wish to teach in American overseas schools and International Schools in which English is the primary teaching language. Supports those wishing to teach English as a second language. Publish papers covering every country in the world, list of recruiting fairs, internships, volunteers, jobs, summer overseas jobs.
Frederic B Viaux, President

73 Educational Information Services
PO Box 662
Newtown Lower Falls, MA 02162
617-964-4555
www.fulbright.jp
Offers information on employment opportunities including books, periodicals and more for the teaching professional who wishes to teach in American overseas schools, international schools, language (ESL) schools, and Department of Defense Dependencies Schools (DODDS).
Frederick B Viaux, President
Michelle V Curtin, Editor

74 Educational Placement Sources-US
Education Information Services/Instant Alert
PO Box 620662
Newton, MA 02462-662
617-433-0125
Lists 100 organizations in the United States that find positions for teachers, educational administrators, counselors and other professionals. Listings are classified by type, listed alphabetically and offer all contact information.
4 pages Annual
FB Viaux, President

375 Educational Staffing Program
International Schools Services
15 Roszel Road
PO Box 5910
Princeton, NJ 08543
609-452-0990
www.iss.edu
The Educational Staffing Program provides overseas school community services for the recruitment of educational staff.
Liz Duffy, President
Kristin Evins, Chief Administration Officer

376 European Council of International Schools
21B Lavant Street
Petersfield, Hampshire GU3 23EL
United Kingdom GU32
44-0-1730-268244
Fax: 44-0-1730-267914
ecis@ecis.org
www.ecis.org
The European Council of International Schools (ECIS) is a collaborative network promoting the ideals and best practice of international education.
T Michael Maybury, Executive Secretary
Pilar Cabeza de Vaca, CEO

377 FRS National Teacher Agency
PO Box 298
Seymour, TN 37865-298
865-577-8143
www.ffiec.gov
Offers employment options to educators in the United States and abroad.

2378 Foreign Faculty and Administrative Openings
Education Information Services
PO Box 620662
Newton, MA 02462-662
617-433-0125
150 specific openings in administration, counseling, library and other professional positions for American teachers in American schools overseas and in international schools in which teaching language is English.
15 pages Every 6 Weeks
FB Viaux, Coordinating Education

2379 Fulbright Teacher Exchange
600 Maryland Avenue SouthWest
Suite 320
Washington, DC 20024-2520
202-314-3520
800-726-0479
Fax: 202-479-6806
www.fulbrightexchanges.org
An organization that offers opportunities for two-year college faculty and secondary school teachers who would like to exchange with teachers in Eastern or Western Europe, Latin America, Australia, Africa, and Canada. To qualify, teachers must be US citizens, have three years full-time teaching experience and be employed in a full-time academic position.

2380 International Educators Cooperative
212 Alcott Road
East Falmouth, MA 02536-6803
508-540-8173
Fax: 508-540-8173
www.icemenlo.com
In addition to year round recruitment, International Educators Cooperative hosts Recruitment Centers in the United States each year.
Dr. Lou Fuccillo, Director

2381 National Association of Teachers' Agencies
National Association of Teachers' Agencies
799 Kings Highway
Fairfield, CT 06432
203-333-0611
Fax: 203-334-7224
fairfieldteachers@snet.net
www.jobsforteachers.com
Provides placement services for those seeking professional positions at all levels of teaching/administration/support services worldwide.
Mark King, Secretary/Treasurer

2382 National Council of Independent Schools' Associations
1129ÿ20th Street
PO Box 324
Australia
06-282-3488
Fax: 06-282-2926
www.nais.org
Services include career placement.
Fergus Thomson, President

2383 Overseas Employment Opportunities for Educators
Department of Defense, Office of Dependent Schools
2461 Eisenhower Avenue
Alexandria, VA 22331-3000
703-325-0867
This publication tells about teaching jobs in 250 schools operated for children of US military and civilian personnel stationed overseas. Applicants usually must qualify in two subject areas.

2384 Recruiting Fairs for Overseas Teaching
Education Information Services/Instant Alert
PO Box 620662
Newton, MA 02462-662
781-433-0125
Fax: 781-237-2842
Recruiting fairs and sponsors in the US and elsewhere for American educators who wish to teach outside of the United States.
FB Viaux, Coordinating Education

2385 UNI Overseas Recruiting Fair
University of Northern Iowa
102 Gilchrist Hall
Cedar Falls, IA 50614-390
319-273-2083
Fax: 319-273-6998
overseas.placement@uni.edu
www.uni.edu/placement/overseas
UNI is home to the oldest international recruitment event in the world. The event began in 1976 after the UNI Career Services staff and several school headmasters recognized the need for more efficient and cost-effective recruitment techniques. It became readily apparent that UNI was meeting a need for school recruiters and interested educators all over the globe. In addition to inventing the international recruitment fair, UNI developed fact sheets, credential files, vacancy listings, referral
February
Brian Atkins, Advisory Board
Susan Barba, Advisory Board

2386 WorldTeach
Center for International Development
79 John F Kennedy Street
Box 122
Cambridge, MA 02138
617-495-5527
800-483-2240
Fax: 617-495-1599
info@worldteach.org
www.worldteach.org
WorldTeach is a non-profit, non-governmental organization that provides opportunities for individuals to make a meaningful contribution to international education by living and working as volunteer teachers in developing countries
Laurie Roberts Belton, Executive Director
Eric Weiss, Program Manager

Alabama

2387 Auburn University at Montgomery Library
PO Box 244023
Montgomery, AL 36124-4023
334-244-3649
Fax: 334-244-3720
www.aumnicat.aum.edu
Member of The Foundation Center network, maintaining a collection of private foundation tax returns which provide information on the scope of grants dispensed by that particular foundation.
R Best, Dean Administration
T Bailey, ILL/ Reference

2388 Benjamin & Roberta Russell Educational and Charitable Foundation
PO Box 272
Alexander City, AL 35010-0272
256-329-4224
Offers giving in the areas of higher and public education, youth programs and a hospital.
James D Nabors, Executive Director

2389 Birmingham Public Library
Government Documents
2100 Park Place
Birmingham, AL 35203-2794
205-226-3600
Fax: 205-226-3729
www.bplonline.org
Member of The Foundation Center network, maintaining a collection of private foundation tax returns which provide information on the scope of grants dispensed by that particular foundation.

2390 Carolina Lawson Ivey Memorial Foundation
PO Box 340
Smiths, AL 36877-0340
334-826-5760
Scholarships are offered to college juniors and seniors who are pursuing careers of teaching social studies in middle or secondary grades. The grants are also offered to teachers in Alabama and west Georgia for curriculum planning and development, in-service training, the development of instructional materials for use in elementary and secondary schools, and other projects that focus on the cultural approach method of teaching.

2391 Huntsville Public Library
915 Monroe Street SW
Huntsville, AL 35801-5007
256-532-5940
www.hpl.lib.al.us/
Member of The Foundation Center network, maintaining a collection of private foundation tax returns which provide information on the scope of grants dispensed by that particular foundation.
Donna B Schremser, Library Director

2392 JL Bedsole Foundation
PO Box 1137
Mobile, AL 36633-1137
251-432-3369
Fax: 251-432-1134
www.jlbedsolefoundation.org
The foundation's primary interest is the support of educational institutions within the state of Alabama and civic and economic development which is limited to the geographical area of Southwest Alabama. The arts, social service and health programs receive limited grants. Organizations or projects outside of the State of Alabama are not considered for funding by the Foundation.
Mabel B Ward, Executive Director
Scott A Morton, Assistant Director

2393 Mildred Weedon Blount Educational and Charitable Foundation
PO Box 607
Tallassee, AL 36078-0007
334-283-4931
Support for Catholic schools, public schools and a scholarship fund for secondary school students.
Arnold B Dopson, Executive Director

2394 Mitchell Foundation
PO Box 1126
Mobile, AL 36633
251-432-1711
Fax: 334-432-1712
www.cgmf.org
Places an emphasis on secondary and higher education, social services programs, youth agencies, and aid for the handicapped.
Augustine Meaher, Executive Director
Marilu Hastings, Director

2395 University of South Alabama
307 University Boulevard
Mobile, AL 36688-0002
251-460-7025
Fax: 251-460-7636
www.library.southalabama.edu
Richard Wood, Dean of Libraries

Alaska

2396 University of Alaska-Anchorage Library
3211 Providence Drive
Anchorage, AK 99508-8000
907-786-1848
Fax: 907-786-6050
www.lib.uaa.alaska.edu
Member of The Foundation Center network, maintaining a collection of private foundation tax returns which provide information on the scope of grants dispensed by that particular foundation.
Stephen J Rollins, Dean of Library

Arizona

2397 Arizona Department of Education
1535 W Jefferson Street
Phoenix, AZ 85007
602-542-5393
800-352-4558
Fax: 602-542-5440
www.ade.state.az.us
Implements procedures that ensure the proper allocation, distribution, and expenditure of all federal and state funds administerd by the department. The following links to our web pages contain information pertaining to educational grants funded from the state or federal programs.
Tom Horne, Superintendent

2398 Arizona Governor's Committee on Employment of People with Disabilities
Samaritan Rehabilitation Institute
1012 E Willetta Street
Phoenix, AZ 85006-3047
602-239-4762
Fax: 602-239-5256
Jim Bruzewski, Executive Director

2399 Education Services
Arizona Department of Education
1535 W Jefferson Street
Phoenix, AZ 85007-3280
602-364-1961
Fax: 602-542-5440
Provides quality services and resources to schools, parent groups, government agencies, and community groups to enable them to achieve their goals.
Lillie Sly, Associate Superintendent

2400 Evo-Ora Foundation
2525 E Broadway Boulevard
Suite 111
Tucson, AZ 85716-5398
Giving is primarily aimed at education, especially Catholic high schools and universities.

2401 Flinn Foundation
1802 N Central Avenue
Suite 2300
Phoenix, AZ 85012-2513
602-744-6800
Fax: 602-744-6815
info@flinn.org
www.flinn.org
Supports nonprofit organizations in the state of Arizona for programs in health care, as well as an annual awards competition for Arizona's principal arts institutions and a college scholarship program for Arizona high school graduates. Scholarship provides expenses for four years, two summers of study-related travel abroad and other benefits.
John W Murphy, Executive Director

2402 Phoenix Public Library
Business & Sciences Department
12 E McDowell Road
Phoenix, AZ 85004-1627
602-262-4636
Fax: 602-261-8836
www.phxlib.org
Member of The Foundation Center network, maintaining a collection of private foundation tax returns which provide information on the scope of grants dispensed by that particular foundation.

2403 Special Programs
721 Broadway
12th Floor
New York, NY 10003
212-998-1800
tisch.special.info@nyu.edu
Tom Horne, Superintendent

2404 Support Services
Arizona Department of Education
1535 W Jefferson Street
Phoenix, AZ 85007-3280
602-542-5393
Fax: 602-542-5440
Rachel Arroyo, School Finance

2405 Vocational Technological Education
Arizona Department of Education
1535 W Jefferson Street
Phoenix, AZ 85007-3280
602-542-5393
Fax: 602-542-5440
Tom Horne, Superintendent

Arkansas

06 Charles A Frueauff Foundation
200 River Market Avenue
Suite 100
Little Rock, AR 72201-3848
501-324-2233
www.frueauff.org
Will review proposals from private four-year colleges and universities.

David Frueauff, President
Sue Frueauff, Chief Administrative Officer

07 Northwest Arkansas Community College
Borham Library
One College Drive
Bentonville, AR 72904-7397
479-636-9222
800-995-6922
www.nwacc.edu
Member of The Foundation Center network, maintaining a collection of private foundation tax returns which provide information on the scope of grants dispensed by that particular foundation.

Daniel Shewmaker, Secretary
Ric Clifford, Chairman

408 Roy and Christine Sturgis Charitable and Educational Trust
PO Box 92
Malvern, AR 72104-0092
501-337-5109
Giving is offered to Baptist and Methodist organizations, including schools, churches and higher and secondary education.

Katie Speer, Executive Director

409 The Jones Center For Families
922 East Emma Avenue
Springdale, AR 72765
479-756-8090
www.thejonescenter.net
Focuses funds on education, medical resources and religious organizations in Arkansas.

HG Frost Jr, Executive Director
Grace Donoho, Director Of Education

410 Walton Family Foundation
125 W Central Avenue
Room 217 Po Box 2030
Bentonville, AR 72712-5248
479-464-1570
Fax: 479-464-1580
www.wffhome.com
Offers giving for systemic reform of primary education (K-12) and early childhood development.

Stewart T Springfield, Executive Director

411 William C & Theodosia Murphy Nolan Foundation
200 N Jefferson Avenue
Suite 308
El Dorado, AR 71730-5853
870-863-7118
Fax: 870-863-6528
Supports education and the arts (historic preservation, arts centers) as well as religious welfare and youth organizations in Northern Louisiana and Southern Arkansas.

William C Nolan, Executive Director

412 Winthrop Rockefeller Foundation
225 East Markham Street
Suite 200
Little Rock, AR 72201-3999
501-376-6854
Fax: 501-374-4797
webfeedback@wrfoundation.org
www.wrfoundation.org
Dedicated to improving the quality of life and education in Arkansas. Grants go to schools that work to involve teachers and parents in making decisions; to universities and local schools to strengthen both levels of education; and for projects that promote stakeholder participation in the development of educational policy.

Sherece Y West, President
Jackie Cox-New, Sr Program Officer

California

2413 Ahmanson Foundation
9215 Wilshire Boulevard
Beverly Hills, CA 90210-5538
310-278-0770
info@theahmansonfoundation.org
Concentrates mainly on education, health and social services in Southern California.

Lee E Walcott, Executive Director
William H Ahmanson, President

2414 Alice Tweed Tuohy Foundation
205 E Carrillo Street
Suite 219
Santa Barbara, CA 93101-7186
805-962-6430
Priority consideration is given to applications from organizations serving: young people; education; selected areas of interest in health care and medicine; and community affairs.

Harris W Seed, President
Eleanor Van Cott, Executive VP

2415 Arrillaga Foundation
2560 Mission College Boulevard
Suite 101
Santa Clara, CA 95054-1217
408-980-0130
Fax: 408-988-4893
Giving is aimed at secondary schools and higher education in the state of California.

John Arrillaga, Executive Director

2416 Atkinson Foundation
1720 So.Amphlett Blvd
Suite 100
San Mateo, CA 94402-2710
650-357-1101
atkinfdn@aol.com
www.atkinsonfdn.org
Provides opportunities for people in San Mateo County, California to reach their highest potential and to improve the quality of their lives and to assist educational institutions and supporting organizations with the implementation of effective programs that reach and serve their target populations.

Elizabeth H Curtis, Administrator

2417 BankAmerica Foundation
Bank of America Center
PO Box 37000
San Francisco, CA 94137-0001
800-678-2632
Fax: 818-507-4023
www.bankamerica.com
Fields of interest include arts/cultural programs, higher education, community development and general federated giving programs.

Elizabeth Nachbaur, Program Director

2418 Bechtel Group Corporate Giving Program
Po Box 193965
San Francisco, CA 94119-3965
415-768-5974
Offers support for higher education and programs related to engineering and construction, math and science in grades K-12 and general charitable programs.

Kathryn M Bandarrae, Executive Director

2419 Bernard Osher Foundation
One Ferry Building
Suite 255
San Francisco, CA 94111
415-861-5587
Fax: 415-677-5868
nagle@osherfoundation.org
www.osherfoundation.org
Funds in the arts, post-secondary education and environmental education on San Francisco and Alameda Counties.

Patricia Nagle, Sr VP
Jeanie Hirokane, Corporate Secretary and Exec

2420 Boys-Viva Supermarkets Foundation
955 Carrillo Drive
Suite 103
Los Angeles, CA 90048-5400
Wide range of support for education of school-aged children, especially the at-risk population, tutoring, and social opportunities.

Fred Snowden, Executive Director

2421 California Community Foundation
221 S Figueroa Street
Suite 400
Los Angeles, CA 90012-1638
213-413-4130
Fax: 213-383-2046
www.calfund.org
Improving human condition through nonprofit agencies in Los Angeles County. Integral parts of eligible proposals are, hosting conferences, incurring debt, individuals, sectarian purposes or regranting.

Judy Spiegel, Sr VP of Programs
Antonia Hernandez, President/CEO

2422 Carrie Estelle Doheny Foundation
707 Wilshire Boulevard
Suite 4960
Los Angeles, CA 90017-2659
213-488-1122
Fax: 213-488-1544
www.dohenyfoundation.org
This foundation funds a myriad of organizations ranging from the education and medicine field to public health and science areas.

Robert A Smith III, Executive Director

2423 Dan Murphy Foundation
PO Box 711267
Los Angeles, CA 90071-9767
213-623-3120
Fax: 213-623-1421
Funds Roman Catholic institutions, with a primary interest in religious orders and schools.

Daniel J Donohue, Executive Director

2424 David & Lucile Packard Foundation
343 Second Street
Los Altos Hills, CA 94022-3643
650-948-7658
Fax: 650-941-3151
www.packard.org
Concentrates on four categories: education, the arts, conservation and child health. Also

allocates funds to companies interested in public improvement and public policy.

Colburn S Wilbur, Executive Director

2425 Evelyn & Walter Haas Jr Fund
114 Sansome Street
Suite 600
San Francisco, CA 94104
415-856-1400
Fax: 415-856-1500
www.haasjr.org
Interested in strengthening neighborhoods, communities, and human services. Funds mainly in San Francisco Bay Area.

Ira Hirschfield, President
Clayton Juan, Grants Administrator

2426 Foundation Center-San Francisco
312 Sutter Street
Suite 606
San Francisco, CA 94108-4314
415-397-0902
Fax: 415-397-7670
www.fdncenter.org
One of five Foundation Centers nationwide, the Foundation Center - San Francisco is a library which collects information on private foundations, corporate philanthropy, nonprofit management, fundraising and other topics of interest to nonprofit organization representatives.

Melissa A Berman, President & CEO
John Colborn, Vice President

2427 Foundations Focus
Marin Community Foundation
5 Hamilton Landing
Suite 200
Novato, CA 94949
415-464-2500
Fax: 415-464-2555
www.marincf.org
Grants support projects that benefit residents of Marin County, CA.

Don Jen, Program Officer/Education
Thomas Peters, President/CEO

2428 Francis H Clougherty Charitable Trust
500 Newport Center Drive
Suite 910
Newport Beach, CA 92660-7009
Offers grants in the areas of elementary, secondary school and higher education in Southern California.

2429 Freitas Foundation
C/O Fiduciary Resources
874 Fourth St
Suite D
San Rafael, CA 94901-3246
Offers giving in the areas of elementary and secondary education, as well as theological education.

Margaret Boyden, Executive Director

2430 Fritz B Burns Foundation
4001 W Alameda Avenue
Suite 201
Burbank, CA 91505-4338
818-840-8802
Fax: 818-840-0468
Grants are primarily focused on education, hospitals and medical research organizations.

Joseph E Rawlinson, Executive Director

2431 George Frederick Jewett Foundation
235 Montgomery Street
Suite 612
San Francisco, CA 94104-2915
415-421-1351
Fax: 415-421-1351
Concerns itself mainly with voluntary, nonprofit organizations that promote human welfare.

2432 Grant & Resource Center of Northern California
2280 Benton Drive, Building C
Suite A
Redding, CA 96003
530-244-1219
Fax: 530-244-0905
Member of The Foundation Center network, maintaining a collection of private foundation tax returns which provide information on the scope of grants dispensed by that particular foundation.

2433 Greenville Foundation
PO Box 4667
Scottsdale, AZ 85261-4667
707-938-9377
Fax: 707-939-9311
This foundation focuses its support on education, the environment and human rights. The main focus of the educational grants lie within the areas of elementary, secondary and higher education.

Virginia Hubbell, Executive Director
Virginia Hubbell, Administrator

2434 HN & Frances C Berger Foundation
PO Box 3064
Arcadia, CA 91006
626-447-3351
www.hnberger.org
Provides scholarships and endowments to colleges and universities.

Ronald M Auen, President/CEO
Christopher M McGuire, Vice President of Programs

2435 Henry J Kaiser Family Foundation
Quadrus
2400 Sand Hill Road
Menlo Park, CA 94025-6941
650-854-9400
Fax: 650-854-4800
www.kff.org
Concentrates on health care, minority groups and South Africa.

Drew Altman, President/CEO
Susan V Berresford, Former President

2436 Hon Foundation
25200 La Paz Road
Suite 210
Laguna Hills, CA 92653-5110
949-586-4400
Offers giving in the areas of elementary, secondary and higher education in the states of Hawaii and California.

2437 Hugh & Hazel Darling Foundation
520 S Grand Avenue
7th Floor
Los Angeles, CA 90071-2645
213-683-5200
Fax: 213-627-7795
Supports education in California with special emphasis on legal education; no grants to individuals; grants only to 501(c)(3) organizations.

Richard L Stack, Trustee

2438 Ingraham Memorial Fund
C/O Emrys J. Ross
301 E Colorado Boulevard
Suite 900
Pasadena, CA 91101-1916
626-796-9123
Offers giving in the areas of elementary, secondary and higher education, as well as theological education in Claremont and Pasadena, California.

2439 James G Boswell Foundation
101 W Walnut Street
Pasadena, CA 91103-3636
626-583-3000
Fax: 626-583-3090
Funds hospitals, pre-college private schools, public broadcasting and youth organizations.

James G Boswell II, Chairman
Sherman Railsback, EVP/COO

2440 James Irvine Foundation
575 Market Street
Suite 3400
San Francisco, CA 94105-1017
415-777-2244
Fax: 415-777-0869
www.irvine.org
Giving is primarily aimed at the areas of education, youth and health.

James E Canales, President/CEO
Kristin Nelson, Executive Assistant

2441 James S Copley Foundation
7776 Ivanhoe Avenue #1530
La Jolla, CA 92037-4520
858-454-0411
Fax: 858-729-7629
Support is offered for higher and secondary education, child development, cultural programs and community services.

Anita A Baumgardner, Executive Director

2442 John Jewett & H Chandler Garland Foundation
PO Box 550
Pasadena, CA 91102-0550
Support given primarily for secondary and higher education, social services and cultural and historical programs.

GE Morrow, Executive Director

2443 Joseph Drown Foundation
1999 Avenue of the Stars
Suite 2330
Los Angeles, CA 90067-4611
310-277-4488
Fax: 310-277-4573
www.jdrown.org
The Foundation's goal is to assist individuals in becoming successful, self-sustaining, contributing citizens. The foundation is interested in programs that break down any barrier that prevents a person from continuing to grow and learn.

Norman Obrow, Executive Director

2444 Jules & Doris Stein Foundation
PO Box 30
Beverly Hills, CA 90213-0030
213-276-2101
Supports charitable organizations.

2445 Julio R Gallo Foundation
PO Box 1130
Modesto, CA 95353-1130
209-579-3373
Offers grants and support to secondary schools and higher education universities.

Sam Gallo, Chairman

46 Kenneth T & Eileen L Norris Foundation

11 Golden Shore Street
Suite 450
Long Beach, CA 90802-4214
562-435-8444
Fax: 562-436-0584
grants@ktn.org
www.norrisfoundation.org
Funding categories include medical, education/science, youth, cultural and community.

Ronald Barnes, Executive Director

47 Koret Foundation

33 New Montgomery Street
Suite 1090
San Francisco, CA 94105-4526
415-882-7740
Fax: 415-882-7775
sandyedwards@koretfoundation.org
www.koretfoundation.org
Funding includes; public policy and selected programs in K-12 public education, higher education, youth programs, Jewish studies at colleges and universities, and Jewish education. The geographical area for grant-making is the San Francisco Bay area.

Tad Taube, President
Susan Koret, Board Chair

48 Lane Family Charitable Trust

500 Almer Road
Apartment 301
Burlingame, CA 94010-3966
Offers giving in the areas of secondary schools and higher education facilities in California.

Ralph Lane, Trustee
Joan Lane, Trustee

449 Levi Strauss Foundation

1155 Battery Street
Floor 7
San Francisco, CA 94111-1230
415-501-6000
Fax: 415-501-7112
www.levistrauss.com
Grants are made in four areas: AIDS prevention and care; economic empowerment; youth empowerment; and social justice. Grants are limited to communities where Levi Strauss and Company has plants or customer service centers.

Theresa Fay-Buslillos, Executive Director

450 Louise M Davies Foundation

180 Montgomery St
Suite 1616
San Francisco, CA 94104-4235
Offers giving in the areas of elementary, secondary and higher education, as well as scholarship funding for California students.

Donald Crawford Jr, Executive Director

451 Lowell Berry Foundation

3685 Mount Diablo Boulevard
Suite 269
Lafayette, CA 94549
925-284-4427
Fax: 925-284-4332
www.lowellberryfoundation.org
Assists Christian ministry at local church levels.

Debbie Coombe, Office Manager
Larry R Langdon, President

452 Luke B Hancock Foundation

360 Bryant Street
Palo Alto, CA 94301-1409
650-321-5536
Fax: 650-321-0697
Provides funding for programs which promote the well being of children and youth. Priority is given to programs which address the needs of youth who are at risk of school failure. Additional funding is provided for early childhood development, music education and homeless families.

Ruth M Ramel, Executive Director

2453 Margaret E Oser Foundation

1911 Lyon Court
Santa Rosa, CA 95403-0974
949-553-4202
Offers grants in the areas of elementary and secondary and higher education, which will benefit women.

Carl Mitchell, Executive Director

2454 Marin Community Foundation

5 Hamilton Landing
Suite 200
Novato, CA 94949-1736
415-461-3333
Fax: 415-464-2555
www.marincf.org
Established as a nonprofit public benefit corporation to engage in educational and philanthropic activities in Marin County, California.

Thomas Peterson, President&CEO
Julie Absey, Vice President

2455 Mary A Crocker Trust

233 Post Street
Floor 2
San Francisco, CA 94108-5003
415-982-0138
Fax: 415-982-0141
staff@mactrust.org
www.mactrust.org
Giving is aimed at precollegiate education, as well as conservation and environmental programs.

Barbaree Jernigan, Executive Director

2456 Maurice Amado Foundation

3940 Laurel Canyon Boulevard
Suite 809
Studio City, CA 91604
818-980-9190
Fax: 818-980-9190
Concentrates on the Jewish heritage.

Pam Kaizer, Executive Director

2457 McConnell Foundation

PO Box 492050
800 Shasta View Drive
Redding, CA 96003
530-226-6200
Fax: 530-226-6210
www.mcconnellfoundation.org
Interested in cultural, community and health care related projects.

Ana Diaz, Program Assistant

2458 McKesson Foundation

1 Post Street
San Francisco, CA 94104-5203
415-983-8300
www.mckesson.com/foundation.html
Giving is primarily to programs for junior high school students and for emergency services such as food and shelter.

Marcia M Argyris, Executive Director

2459 Milken Family Foundation

C/O Foundations of the Milken Families
1250 4th Street
Floor 6
Santa Monica, CA 90401-1353
310-570-4800
Fax: 310-570-4801
www.mff.org
Offers support to the educational community to reward educational innovators, stimulate creativity among students, involve parents and other citizens in the school system, and help disadvantaged youth.

Dr. Julius Lesner, Executive Director
Lowell Milken, Chairman & Co Founder

2460 Miranda Lux Foundation

57 Post Street
Suite 510
San Francisco, CA 94104-5020
415-981-2966
admin@mirandalux.org
www.mirandalux.org
Offers support to promising proposals for pre-school through junior college programs in the fields of pre-vocational and vocational education and training.

Kenneth Blum, Executive Director

2461 Northern California Grantmakers

625 Market Street
3rd Floor
San Francisco, CA 94105
415-777-4111
Fax: 415-777-1714
ncg@ncg.org
www.ncg.org
Northern California Grantmakers is an association of foundations, corporate contributions programs and other private grantmakers. Its mission is to jpromote the well being of people and their communities in balance with a healthy environment by the thoughtful and creative use of private wealth and resources for the public benefit. To this end, NCG works to enhance the effectiveness of philanthropy, including nonprofit organizations, government, business, media, academia and the public at large.

Colin Lacon, President

2462 Pacific Telesis Group Corporate Giving Program

130 Kearny Street
San Francisco, CA 94108-4818
415-394-3000
Primary areas of interest include K-12 education reform, education of minorities, women and disabled individuals in the math, science, engineering, education and MBA fields; and specific K-12 issues such as dropouts, information technology and parent involvement.

Jere A Jacobs, Executive Director

2463 Peninsula Community Foundation

11742 Jefferson Avenue
Suite 350
Newport News, VA 23606-3049
757-327-0862
Fax: 757-327-0865
www.pcfvirginia.org
Serving a population from Daly City to Mountain View, the foundations focus is on children and youth, adult services, programs serving homeless families and children, prevention of homelessness and civic and public benefit grants.

Sterling K Speirn, Executive Director
Gregory F Lawson, President

2464 Peter Norton Family Foundation

225 Arizona Avenue
Floor 2
Santa Monica, CA 90401-1243
310-576-7700
Fax: 310-576-7701

Offers giving in the areas of early childhood education, elementary school education, higher education, childrens services and AIDS research.

Anne Etheridge, ED, Executive Director

2465 RCM Capital Management Charitable Fund
4 Embarcadero Center
Suite 2900
San Francisco, CA 94111-4189
415-954-5474
Fax: 415-954-8200
www.rcm.com
Giving is offered in many areas including youth development, early childhood education and elementary education.

Jami Weinman, Executive Director

2466 Ralph M Parsons Foundation
888 West Sixth Street
Suite 700
Los Angeles, CA 90017-5600
213-362-7600
Fax: 213-482-8878
www.rmpf.org
Giving is focused on higher and pre-collegiate education, with an emphasis on engineering, technology, and science; social impact programs serving families, children and the elderly; health programs targeting underserved populations; civic and cultural programs.

Wendy G Hoppe, Executive Director
Walter B Rose, Vice Chairman

2467 Riordan Foundation
PO Box 491190
Los Angeles, CA 90049-3110
310-472-2020
Fax: 310-472-1414
www.riordanfoundation.org
Priorities of the foundation include early childhood literacy, youth programs, leadership programs, job training, direct medical services to young children, and cyclical, targeted mini-grants. When determining levels of support, priority is always given to programs which impact young children.

Jessica Flores, President
Jaime Kalenik, Program Coordinator

2468 Royal Barney Hogan Foundation
PMB 220,3000 S.Hulen
Ste 124
Forth Worth, TX
RoyalHoganFoundation@yahoo.com
Offers grants specifically for secondary education in the state of California.

Jacque Hogan, President/Treasurer
Robert L Towery, Secretary/Chief Executive Of

2469 SH Cowell Foundation
595 Market Street
Suite 950
San Francisco, CA 94105-4303
415-397-0285
Fax: 415-986-6786
www.shcowell.org
Offers support for educational programs, including pre-school and primary public educational programs.

JD Erickson, Executive Director
Anna Alpers, President

2470 Sacramento Regional Foundation
555 Capitol Mall
Suite 550
Sacramento, CA 95814-4502
916-492-6510
Fax: 916-492-6515
Primary interests of this foundation include the arts, humanities and education.

Stephen F Boutin, President
Janice Gow Pettey, CEO

2471 San Diego Foundation
2508 Historic Decatur Rd
Suite 200
San Diego, CA 92106-2434
619-235-2300
Fax: 619-239-1710
info@sdfoundation.org
www.sdfoundation.org
Offers grants in the areas of social services with emphasis on children and families, education and health for San Diego County.

Robert A Kelly, President/CEO
Rebecca Reichmann, VP Programs

2472 San Francisco Foundation
225 Bush Street
Suite 500
San Francisco, CA 94104-4224
415-733-8500
Fax: 415-477-2783
rec@sff.org
www.sff.org
Addresses community needs in the areas of community health, education, arts and culture, neighborhood revitalization, and environmental justice. Works to support families and communities to help children and youth succeed in school and provide opportunities for them to become confident, caring and contributing adults.

Sandra R Hernandez MD, CEO
Sara Ying Kelley, Director Public Affairs

2473 Santa Barbara Foundation
1111 Chapala Street
Suite 200
Santa Barbara, CA 93101-2780
805-963-1873
Fax: 805-966-2345
www.sbfoundation.org
Offers a student aid program with no interest-1/2 loan and 1/2 scholarship. Funding limited to long-term Santa Barbara County residents.

Claudia Armann, Program Officer
Peter MacDougall, Chairman

2474 Sega Youth Education & Health Foundation
255 Shoreline Drive
Suite 200
Redwood City, CA 94065-1428
Offers support only to organizations that address and promote youth education and health issues.

Trizia Carpenter, Executive Director

2475 Sidney Stern Memorial Trust
PO Box 893
Pacific Palisades, CA 90272-0893
310-459-2117
info@sidneysternmemorialtrust.org
www.sidneysternmemorialtrust.org
Funding offered includes education, community action groups, the arts and the disabled.

2476 Sol & Clara Kest Family Foundation
5150 Overland Avenue
Culver City, CA 90230-4914
213-204-2050
Offers support for Jewish organizations in the areas of education.

Sol Kest, Executive Director

2477 Szekely Family Foundation
3232 Dove Street
San Diego, CA 92103
619-295-2372
Offers giving in the areas of early childhood education, child development, elementary education, higher education, and adult and continuing education.

Deborah Szekely, Executive Director

2478 Thomas & Dorothy Leavey Foundation
10100 Santa Monica Boulevard
Suite 610
Los Angeles, CA 90067
310-551-9936
Focus is placed on college scholarships, medical research, youth groups and programs, and secondary and higher education purposes.

J Thomas McCarthy, Executive Director

2479 Times Mirror Foundation
202 West First Street
Los Angeles, CA 90012
213-237-3945
Fax: 213-237-2116
Giving is largely for higher education purposes including liberal arts and business education.

Cassandra Malry, Executive Director

2480 Timken-Sturgis Foundation
7421 Eads Avenue
La Jolla, CA 92037-5037
619-454-2252
Offers support for education in Southern California and Nevada.

Joannie Barrancotto, Executive Director

2481 Toyota USA Foundation
19001 S Western Avenue
Torrance, CA 90501-1106
310-715-7486
800-331-4331
Fax: 310-468-7814
www.toyota.com/foundation
Supports K-12 education programs, with strong emphasis on math and science.

William Pauli, National Manager

2482 Turst Funds Incorporated
100 Broadway Street
Floor 3
San Francisco, CA 94111-1404
415-434-3323
Offers grants for Catholic Schools, including elementary and secondary education, in the San Francisco Bay Area.

James T Healy, President

2483 Ventura County Community Foundation
Funding & Information Resource Center
4001 Mission Oaks Blvd
Suite 150
Camarillo, CA 93012-8504
805-988-0196
Fax: 805-484-2700
vccf@vccf.org
www.vccf.org
Member of The Foundation Center network, maintaining a collection of private foundation tax returns which provide information on the scope of grants dispensed by that particular foundation.

Gary E Erickson, President/CEO
Virginia Weber, Program Officer

2484 WM Keck Foundation
550 S Hope Street
Suite 2500
Los Angeles, CA 90071
213-680-3833
Fax: 213-614-0934

info@wmkeck.org
www.wmkeck.org
The Foundation also gives some consideration, limited to Southern California, for the support of arts and culture, civic and community services, health care and precollegiate education. The foundation's grant-making is focused primarily on pioneering research efforts in the areas of science, engineering and medical research, and on higher education, including liberal arts.

Dorothy Fleisher, Program Director
Allison Keller, Executive Director and Chief

85 Walter & Elise Haas Fund

1 Lombard Street
Suite 305
San Francisco, CA 94111-1130
415-398-4474
Fax: 415-986-4779
www.haassr.org
Supports education, arts, environment, human services, humanities and public affairs; is especially in projects which have a wide impact within their respective fields through enhancing public education and access to information, serving a central organizing role, addressing public policy, demonstrating creative approaches toward meeting human needs, or supporting the work of a major institution in the field.

Pamela H David, Executive Director
Peter E Hass Jr, President

486 Walter S Johnson Foundation

1660 Bush Street
Suite 300
San Francisco, CA 94025-3447
415-561-6540
Fax: 415-561-6477
www.wsjf.org
Giving is centered on education in public schools and social service agencies concerned with the quality of public education in Northern California and Washoe County, Nevada.

Pancho Chang, Executive Director

487 Wayne & Gladys Valley Foundation

1939 Harrison Street
Suite 510
Oakland, CA 94612-3535
510-466-6060
Fax: 510-466-6067
Supports four areas: education, medical research, community services and special projects.

Michael D Desler, Executive Director

488 Weingart Foundation

1055 W 7th Street
Suite 3200
Los Angeles, CA 90017-2509
213-688-7799
Fax: 213-688-1515
www.weingartfnd.org
Offers support for community services including a student loan program.

William C Allen, Chairman & CEO
Fred J Ali, President/Chief Adm. Officer

489 Wells Fargo Foundation

550 California Street
7th Floor MAC A0112-073
San Francisco, CA 94104
415-396-5830
Fax: 415-975-6260
www.wellsfargo.com
Offers support for elementary school education, secondary school education and community development.

Tim Hanlon, Executive Director

2490 Wilbur D May Foundation

C/O Brookhill Corporation
2716 Ocean Park Boulevard
Suite 2011
Santa Monica, CA 90405
Gives to youth organizations and hospitals.

2491 William & Flora Hewlett Foundation

2121 Sand Hill Road
Menlo Park, CA 94025-3448
650-234-4500
Fax: 650-234-4501
www.hewlett.org
The Hewlett Foundation concentrates its resources on the performing arts, education, population issues, environmental issues, conflict resolution and family and community development. Grants in the education program, specifically the elementary and secondary education part of it, are limited to K-12 areas in California programs, with primary emphasis on public schools in the San Francisco Bay area. The program favors schools, school districts and universities.

Larry Kramer, President
Walter B Hewlett, Chairman

2492 William C Bannerman Foundation

9255 Sunset Boulevard
Suite 400
West Hollywood, CA 90069
310-273-9933
Fax: 310-273-9931
Offers grants in the fields of elementary school, secondary schools, education, human services and youth programs K-12 in Los Angeles County, Adult Education and Vocational Training.

Elliot Ponchick, President

2493 Y&H Soda Foundation

1635 School Street
Moraga, CA 94556
925-631-1133
Fax: 925-631-0248
www.yhsodafoundation.org
Offers support in the areas of early childhood education, child development, elementary education and vocational and higher education.

Bob Uyeki, Executive Director

2494 Zellerbach Family Fund

575 Market Street
Suite 2950
San Francisco, CA 94105-4318
415-421-2629
Fax: 415-421-6713
www.zellerbachfamilyfoundation.org
Provides funds to nonprofit organizations in the San Francisco Bay Area.

Cindy Rambo, Executive Director
Linda Avidan, Program Director

Colorado

2495 Adolph Coors Foundation

4100 East Mississippi Avenue
Suite 1850
Denver, CO 80246
303-388-1636
Fax: 303-388-1684
www.adolphcoors.org
Giving is primarily offered for programs with an emphasis on education, human services, youth and health.

Sally W Rippey, Executive Director
Jeanne L Bistranin, Program Officers

2496 Boettcher Foundation

600 17th Street
Suite 2210
Denver, CO 80202-5422
303-534-1937
800-323-9640
www.boettcherfoundation.org
Offers grants to educational institutions, with an emphasis on scholarships and fellowships.

Timothy W Schultz, President/Executive Director

2497 Denver Foundation

55 Madison Street
8th Floor
Denver, CO 80206
303-300-1790
Fax: 303-300-6547
www.denverfoundation.org
The Foundation serves as the steward and the administrator of the endowment, charged with investing its earned income in programs that meet the community's growing and changing needs. The Foundation has a solid history of supporting a broad array of community efforts. Grants are awarded to nonprofit organizations that touch nearly every meaningful artistic, cultural, civic, educational, human service and health interest of metro Denver's citizens.

David Miller, President/CEO
Betsy Mangone, VP Philanthropic Services

2498 El Pomar Foundation

10 Lake Circle
Colorado Springs, CO 80906-4201
719-633-7733
800-554-7711
Fax: 719-577-5702
www.elpomar.org
Founded in 1937, the philosophy of this foundation is simply to help foster a climate for excellence in Colorado's third sector, the nonprofit community, as well as the foundation's own responsibility to improve the quality of life for all residents of Colorado. The foundation gives grants to the arts and humanities, civic and community, education, health, human services, and youth in community service.

William J Hybl, Executive Director

2499 Gates Foundation

500 Fifth Avenue North
Seattle, WA 98109
206-709-3100
info@gatesfoundation.org
www.gatesfoundation.org
The purpose of this foundation is to aid, assist, encourage, initiate, or carry on activities that will promote the health, well-being, security and broad education of all people. Because of a deep concern for and confidence in the future of Colorado, the foundation will invest primarily in institutions and programs that will enhance the quality of life for those who live and work in the state.

Thomas C Stokes, Executive Director

2500 Ruth & Vernon Taylor Foundation

518 17th Street
Suite 1670
Denver, CO 80202
303-893-5284
Fax: 303-893-8263

Offers support for education, the arts, human services and conservation.

Friday A Green, Executive Director

2501 US West Foundation
915 Memorial Drive
Manitowoc, WI 54220
920-684-6110
Fax: 920-684-7381
info@westfoundation.us
www.westfoundation.us
Grants are given in the areas of health and human services, including programs for youth, early childhood, elementary, secondary, higher and other.

Janet Rash, Executive Director
Thomas Bare, President

Connecticut

2502 Aetna Foundation
151 Farmington Avenue
Hartford, CT 06156-0001
860-273-0123
Fax: 860-273-4764
www.aetna.com/foundation/
Aetna gives grants in various areas that improve the community and its citizens. Certain areas include; children's health, education for at-risk students, and community initiatives. Geographic emphasis is placed on organizations and initiatives in Aetna's Greater Hartford headquarters communities; organizations in select communities across the country where Aetna has a significant local presence; and national organizations that can influence state, local or federal policies and programs.

Marilda L Gandara, President
Dave Wilmont, Executive Assistant

2503 Community Foundation of Greater New Haven
70 Audubon Street
New Haven, CT 06510-1248
203-777-2386
Fax: 203-787-6584
contactus@cfgnh.org
www.cfgnh.org
Offers a wide variety of giving with an emphasis on social services, youth services, AIDS research and education.

William W Ginsberg, President/CEO
Ronda Maddox, Administrative Assistant

2504 Connecticut Mutual Financial Services
140 Garden Street
Hartford, CT 06154-0200
860-987-6500
Giving is aimed at education, primarily higher education, equal opportunity programs and social services.

Astrida R Olds, Executive Director

2505 Emily Hall Tremaine Foundation
171 Orange Street
New Haven, CT 06510
203-639-5544
www.tremainefoundation.org
The Tremaine Foundation funds projects that seek to provide solutions for problems in the educational areas of art, environment and learning differences.

Michelle Knapik, President
Heather Pontonio, Senior Program Director

2506 Hartford Foundation for Public Giving
10 Columbus Boulevard
8th Floor
Hartford, CT 06106-2693
860-548-1888
Fax: 860-524-8346
www.hfpg.org
Offers grants for demonstration programs and capital purposes with emphasis on educational institutions, social services and cultural programs.

Michael R Bangser, Executive Director
Edward Forand Jr, Chairman

2507 Loctite Corporate Contributions Program
Hartford Square North
10 Columbus Boulevard
5th Floor
Hartford, CT 06106-1976
860-571-5100
Fax: 860-571-5430
Offers support in various fields of interest including funding for educational programs for inner city youths in grades K-12.

Kiren Cooley, Corporate Contributions

2508 Louis Calder Foundation
125 Elm Street
New Canaan, CT 06840
203-966-8925
Fax: 203-966-5785
www.louiscalderfdn.org
Offers support to organizations who promote education, health and welfare of children and youth in New York City.

Holly Nuechterlein, Program Manager

2509 Sherman Fairchild Foundation
71 Arch Street
Greenwich, CT 06830-6544
203-661-9360
Fax: 203-661-9360
Offers grants in higher education, fine arts and cultural institutions.

Patricia A Lydon, Executive Director

2510 Smart Family Foundation
74 Pin Oak Lane
Wilton, CT 06897-1329
203-834-0400
Fax: 203-834-0412
The foundation is interested in educational projects that focus on primary and secondary school children.

Raymond Smart, Executive Director

2511 Worthington Family Foundation
P.O Box 4311
Traverse City, MI 49685
203-255-9400
www.worthington-family-foundation.org
Offers grants in the areas of elementary school education and secondary school education in Connecticut.

Worthington Johnson, Executive Director
Ruth Worthington, President

Delaware

2512 Crystal Trust
Po Box 39
Montchanin, DE 19710-0039
302-651-0533
Grants are awarded for higher and secondary education and social and family services.

Stephen C Doberstein, Executive Director

2513 HW Buckner Charitable Residuary Trust
JP Morgan Services
PO Box 8714
Wilmington, DE 19899-8714
302-633-1900
Focuses giving on educational and cultural organizations in New York, Rhode Island and Massachusetts.

2514 Longwood Foundation
100 W 10th Street
Suite 1109
Wilmington, DE 19801-1694
302-654-2477
Fax: 302-654-2323
Limited grants are offered to educational institutions and cultural programs.

David D Wakefield, Executive Director

District of Columbia

2515 Abe Wouk Foundation
3255 N Street NW
Washington, DC 20007-2845
Offers grants in elementary, secondary education and federated giving programs.

Herman Wouk, Executive Director

2516 Eugene & Agnes E Meyer Foundation
1250 Connecticut Avenue
Suite 800
Washington, DC 20036-2215
202-483-8294
Fax: 202-328-6850
www.meyerfoundation.org
Offers grants in the areas of development and housing, education and community services, arts and humanities, law and justice, health and mental health.

Julie L Rogers, President
Barbara Krumsiek, Chairman

2517 Foundation Center-District of Columbia
1627 K Street NW
3rd Floor
Washington, DC 20006-1708
202-331-1400
Fax: 202-331-1739
Member of The Foundation Center network, maintaining a collection of private foundation tax returns which provide information on the scope of grants dispensed to nonprofit organizations by those particular foundations.

2518 Foundation for the National Capitol Region
1201 15th Street NW
Suite 420
Washington, DC 20005
202-955-5890
Fax: 202-955-8084
www.cfncr.org
Grants are focused on organization strengthening and regional collaboration. The Foundation wishes to foster collaborations that identify, address, and increase awareness of regional issues, as well as help strengthen the region's existing nonprofit organizations to improve their financial stability. The Foundation welcomes requests from organizations serving the Greater Washington area that are tax-exempt under Section 501(c)(3) of the Internal Revenue Code.

Terry Lee Freeman, President

19 Gilbert & Jaylee Mead Family Foundation
2700 Virginia Avenue NW #701
Washington, DC 20037-1908
202-338-0208
Offers support for education (K-12), the performing arts and community service programs for Washington, DC, Montgomery County, Maryland, and Geneva, Switzerland.
Linda Smith, Executive Director

20 Hitachi Foundation
1509 22nd Street NW
Washington, DC 20037-1073
202-457-0588
Fax: 202-296-1098
The majority of projects supported by the foundation: promote collaboration across sectors and among institutions, organizations and individuals; reflect multi-or-interdisciplinary perspectives; respect and value diversity of thought, action, and ethnicity. Grants are given in the areas of community development, education, global citizenship and program related investments.
Barbara Dyer, President/CEO

521 Morris & Gwendolyn Cafritz Foundation
1825 K Street NW
Suite 1400
Washington, DC 20006-1202
202-223-3100
Fax: 202-296-7567
www.cafritzfoundation.org
Gives grants to organizations in the metropolitan area, focusing on arts, humanities and scholarships.
Sara Cofrin, Program Assistant
Michael Bigley, Program Officer

522 Public Welfare Foundation
1200 U Street NW
Washington, DC 20009-4443
202-965-1800
Fax: 202-265-8851
info@publicwelfare.org
www.publicwelfare.org
Offers grants to grass roots organizations in the US and abroad with emphasis on the environment and education.
Larry Kressley, Executive Director
Teresa Langston, Director Of Programs

523 Washington Post Company Educational Foundation
1150 15th Street NW
Washington, DC 20071-0002
202-334-6000
Offers support for pre-college and higher education including student scholarships and awards for academic excellence.
Eric Grant, Director Contributions

Florida

524 Applebaum Foundation
1111 Biscaynees Boulevard
Tower 3, Room 853
North Miami, FL 33181
Offers an emphasis on higher education.

525 Benedict Foundation for Independent Schools
607 Lantana Lane
Vero Beach, FL 32963-2315
Support is offered primarily for independent secondary schools that have been members of the National Association of Independent Schools for ten consecutive years.
Nancy H Benedict, Executive Director
Davis M Benedict, Vice President & Director

2526 Chatlos Foundation
PO Box 915048
Longwood, FL 32791-5048
407-862-5077
Fax: 407-862-0708
www.chatlos.org
Bible colleges and seminaries, liberal arts colleges, vocation and domestic education, medical education; children, elderly, disabled and learning disabled. The Foundation is non-receptive to primary or secondary education, the arts, medical research, individual churches. No direct scholarship support to individuals.
William J Chatlos, Executive Director

2527 Citibank of Florida Corporate Giving Program
8750 Doral Boulevard
7th Floor
Miami, FL 33718
305-599-5775
Fax: 305-599-5520
Offers support for K-12 education for at-risk children. Funding is also available through the program for housing and community development in the state of Florida.
Susan Yarosz, Executive Director

2528 Dade Community Foundation
200 S Biscayne Boulevard
Suite 505
Miami, FL 33131-2343
305-371-2711
Fax: 305-371-5342
www.dadecommunityfoundation.org
Offers support for projects in the fields of education, arts and culture.
Ruth Shack, Executive Director

2529 Innovating Worthy Projects Foundation
Lakeview Corporate Center
4045 Sheridan Avenue
Miami, FL 33140-2904
305-861-5352
Fax: 305-868-4293
info@IWPF.org
www.iwpf.org
Offers grants and support for education in the areas of childhood education and elementary education.
Dr. Irving Packer, Executive Director

2530 Jacksonville Public Library
Business, Science & Documents
303 N Laura St
Jacksonville, FL 32202-3374
904-630-2665
Fax: 904-630-2431
www.jpl.coj.net
Member of The Foundation Center network, maintaining a collection of private foundation tax returns which provide information on the scope of grants dispensed by that particular foundation.
Gretchen Mitchell, Business/Science Department

2531 Jessie Ball duPont Fund
One Independent Drive
Suite 1400
Jacksonville, FL 32202-5011
904-353-0890
800-252-3452
Fax: 904-353-3870
smagill@dupontfund.org
www.dupontfund.org
Grants limited to those institutions to which the donor contributed personally during the five year period ending December 31, 1964. Among the 325 institutions eligible to recieve funds are higher and secondary education intitutions, cultural and historic preservation programs, social services organizations, hospitals, health agencies, churches and church-related organizations and youth agencies.
Dr. Sherry P Magill, President
JoAnn Bennett, Director Administration

2532 Joseph & Rae Gann Charitable Foundation
10185 Collins Avenue
Apartment 317
Bal Harbour, FL 33154-1606
Offers support in the areas of elementary, secondary and theological education.

2533 Orlando Public Library-Orange County Library System
Social Sciences Department
101 E Central Boulivard
Orlando, FL 32801-2471
407-835-7323
Fax: 407-835-7646
Member of The Foundation Center network, maintaining a collection on microfiche of Florida private foundation tax returns which provide information on the scope of grants dispensed by that particular foundation. Other available resources include directories of foundations, guide to funding, and materials on successful grant acquisition. FC Search Foundation Center CD Rom.
Angela C Jacobe, Head Social Science Dpt

2534 Peter D & Eleanore Kleist Foundation
12734 Kenwood Lane
Suite 89
Fort Myers, FL 33907-5638
Support is given to secondary school education and higher education.
Peter D Kleist, Executive Director

2535 Robert G Friedman Foundation
76 Isla Bahia Drive
Fort Lauderdale, FL 33316-2331
Giving is offered to elementary and high schools, with minor support to indigent individuals and charitable activities.
Robert G Friedman, Executive Director

2536 Southwest Florida Community Foundation
8771 College Parkway
Suite 201
Fort Myers, FL 33919
239-274-5900
Fax: 239-274-5930
swflcfo@earthlink.net
www.floridacommunity.com
Offers grants and support in the areas of education, higher education, children and youth services and general charitable giving to Lee, Charlotte, Hendry, Glades, and Collier Counties, Florida.
Paul B Flynn, Executive Director
Carol McLaughlin, Program Director

2537 Student Help and Assistance Program to Education
C/O Michael Bienes
141 Bay Colony Drive
Fort Lauderdale, FL 33308-2024

Offers grants and support in the areas of elementary and secondary education, music and dance.

2538 **Thomas & Irene Kirbo Charitable Trust**
550 Water St
Suite 1327
Jacksonville, FL 32202-5113
904-354-7212
Favors smaller colleges in Florida and Georgia.
Murray Jenks, Executive Director

2539 **Thompson Publishing Group**
PO Box 26185
Tampa, FL 33623
800-876-0226
www.grants.thompson.com
Assists education administrators and grant seekers in successful fundraising in the public and private sectors.
Joel M Drucker, Executive Director

Georgia

2540 **Atlanta-Fulton Public Library**
Foundation Collection/Ivan Allen Department
1 Margaret Mitchell Square NW
Atlanta, GA 30303-1089
404-730-1700
Fax: 404-730-1990
www.af.public.lib.ga.us.org
Member of The Foundation Center network, maintaining a collection of private foundation tax returns which provide information on the scope of grants dispensed by that particular foundation.

2541 **BellSouth Foundation**
C/O BellSouth Corporation
1155 Peachtree Street NE
Sutie 7H08
Atlanta, GA 30309-3600
404-249-2396
Fax: 404-249-5696
www.bellsouthfoundation.org
The foundation's purpose is to improve education in the South and to address the problem of the inadequate schooling in the region.
Mary D Boehm, President
Beverly Fleming, Administrative Assistant

2542 **Bradley Foundation**
1241 North Franklin Place
Milwaukee, WI 53202-2901
414-291-9915
Fax: 414-291-9991
www.bradleyfdn.org
Focuses on higher educational facilities, elementary and secondary education, human services and federated giving programs.
Terry Considine, Chairman

2543 **Callaway Foundation**
209 W Broome Street
#790
Lagrange, GA 30241-3101
706-884-7348
Fax: 706-884-0201
www.callawayfoundation.org
Offers giving in the areas of elementary, higher and secondary education, including libraries and community giving.
JT Gresham, Executive Director

2544 **Coca-Cola Foundation**
Po Box 1734
Atlanta, GA 30301
404-676-2568
Fax: 404-676-8804
Committed to serving communities through education. The foundation supports programs for early childhood education, elementary and secondary schools, public and private colleges and universities, teacher training, adult learning and global education programs, among others.
Donald R Greene, Executive Director

2545 **J Bulow Campbell Foundation**
3050 Peachtree Road
Suite 270
Atlanta, GA 30305
404-658-9066
Fax: 404-659-4802
www.jbcf.org
The purpose of this foundation is to offer grants and support to privately supported education, human welfare, youth services and the arts in the state of Georgia.
John W Stephenson, Executive Director

2546 **JK Gholston Trust**
C/O NationsBank of Georgia
PO Box 992
Athens, GA 30603-0992
706-357-6271
Support is offered to elementary school and higher education facilities in the Comer, Georgia area.
Janey M Cooley, Executive Director

2547 **John & Mary Franklin Foundation**
C/O Bank South N.A.
PO Box 4956
Atlanta, GA 30302
404-521-7397
Offers grants in secondary school/education, higher education and youth services.
Virlyn Moore Sr, Executive Director

2548 **John H & Wilhelmina D Harland Charitable Foundation**
2 Piedmont Center NE
Suite 710
Atlanta, GA 30305-1502
404-264-9912
Fax: 404-266-8834
info@harlandfoundation.org
www.harlandfoundation.org
Children and higher education.
Jane G Hardesty, Executive Director
Gail G Byers, Grants Manager

2549 **Joseph B Whitehead Foundation**
191 Peachtree Street NE
Suite 3540
Atlanta, GA 30303-2916
404-522-6755
Fax: 404-522-7026
fdns@woodruff.org
www.jbwhitehead.org
Offers grants in education, cultural programs, the arts and civic affairs.
Charles H McTier, Executive Director
James B William, Chairman

2550 **Lettie Pate Evans Foundation**
191 Peachtree Street NE
Suite 3540
Atlanta, GA 30303-2916
404-522-6755
Fax: 404-522-7026
fdns@woodruff.org
www.lpevans.org
Offers grants in the areas of higher education, and support for educational and cultural institutions.
Charles H McTier, Executive Director
James B William, Chairman

2551 **McCamish Foundation**
1 Buckhead Loop NE #3060
Atlanta, GA 30326-1528
Offers grants for conservation and educational institutions.

2552 **Metropolitan Atlanta Community Foundation**
50 Hurt Plaza
Suite 449
Atlanta, GA 30303
404-688-5525
Fax: 404-688-3060
www.atlcf.org
This foundation was organized for the administration of funds placed in trust for the purposes of improving education, community development and civic health of the 19-county metropolitan area of Atlanta.
Winsome Hawkins Sr, Executive Director
Alicia Phillip, President

2553 **Mill Creek Foundation**
4400 Braselton Hwy
Hoschton, GA 30548-0190
478-237-0101
Fax: 478-237-6187
www.mccef.org
The foundation's primary interests are educational programs in all levels of study in Emanuel County, Georgia.
James H Morgan, Executive Director

2554 **Mills Bee Lane Memorial Foundation**
Nations Bank of Georgia
PO Box 9626
Savannah, GA 31412-9626
Offers support in various areas of education, including higher, secondary, and elementary.

2555 **Peyton Anderson Foundation**
577 Mulberry Street
Suite 830
Macon, GA 31201
478-743-5359
Fax: 912-742-5201
grants@pafdn.org
www.peytonanderson.org
Supports organizations and programs that center on elementary education, higher education, adult education, literacy and basic skills and youth services, in Bibb County, Georgia only.
Juanita T Jordan, Executive Director
Karen Lambert, President

2556 **Rich Foundation**
11 Piedmont Avenue NE
Atlanta, GA 30303
404-262-2266
Funds are allocated to social services, health, the arts and education.
Anne Berg, Executive Director

2557 **Robert & Polly Dunn Foundation**
PO Box 723194
Atlanta, GA 31139-0194
404-816-2883
Fax: 404-237-2150
Offers support in the areas of child development, education, higher education, and children and youth services.
Karen C Wilbanks, Executive Director

2558 **Sapelo Foundation**
4503 New Jesup Highway
Brunswick, GA 31520

912-265-0520
Fax: 912-265-1888
info@sapelofoundation.org
www.sapelofoundation.org
Promotes social change affecting rural communities, the environment and vulnerable people in Georgia. The foundation offers a scholarship program as well as grants to students of McIntosh County, Georgia.

Christine Reeves Strigaro, Executive Director
Seandra Pope, Trustee

59 Tull Charitable Foundation
50 Hurt Plaza SE
Suite 1245
Atlanta, GA 30303-2916
404-659-7079
www.tullfoundation.org
Offers support to secondary schools, elementary schools and higher education facilities in the state of Georgia.

Barbara Cleveland, Executive Director

560 Warren P & Ava F Sewell Foundation
PO Box 645
Bremen, GA 30110-0645
Offers support in elementary school, secondary school education and religion.

Jack Worley, Executive Director

Hawaii

561 Barbara Cox Anthony Foundation
1132 Bishop Street #120
Honolulu, HI 96813-2807
Offers support to secondary schools, higher education, and human service organizations in Hawaii.

Barner Anthony, Executive Director

562 Cooke Foundation
827 Fort Street Mall
Honolulu, HI 96813
808-537-6333
888-731-3863
Fax: 808-521-6286
foundations@hcf-hawaii.org
www.hawaiicommunityfoundation.org
The environment, the arts, education and social services are the priority areas for this foundation.

Lisa Schiff, Private Foundation Service
Samuel Cooke, President & Trustee

563 Harold KL Castle Foundation
1197 Auloa Road
Kailua, HI 96734-2835
808-263-7073
Fax: 808-261-6918
www.castlefoundation.org
Grants are given in the area of education, community and cultural/community affairs.

Terrence R George, Executive Director
H Mitchell D'Olier, President

564 Hawaiian Electric Industries Charitable Foundation
PO Box 730
Honolulu, HI 96808-0730
808-532-5862
www.hei.com
Offers support for education, including higher education, business education, educational associations and secondary schools.

Scott Shirai, Executive Director
Robert F Clark, President

2565 James & Abigail Campbell Foundation
1001 Kamokila Boulevard
Kapolei, HI 96707-2014
808-674-3167
Fax: 808-674-3349
keolal@jamescampbell.com
www.campbellfamilyfoundation.org
Offers support in education for schools and educational programs related to literacy or job training in Hawaii.

Theresia McMurdo, Public Relations
D. Keola Lloyd, Grants Manager

2566 Oceanic Cablevision Foundation
200 Akamainui Street
Mililani, HI 96789-3999
808-625-8359
Offers support in a variety of areas with an emphasis on education, especially early childhood and cultural programs.

Kit Beuret, Executive Director

2567 Samuel N & Mary Castle Foundation
733 Bishop Street
Suite 1275
Honolulu, HI 96813-2912
808-522-1101
Fax: 808-522-1103
acastle@aloha.net
www.fdncenter.org
Funding is offered in the areas of education, human services and the arts for the state of Hawaii.

Annually

Al Castle, Executive Director

2568 University of Hawaii
Hamilton Library
2550 The Mall
Honolulu, HI 96822-2233
808-956-7214
Fax: 808-956-5968
Member of The Foundation Center network, maintaining a collection of private foundation tax returns which provide information on the scope of grants dispensed by that particular foundation.

Idaho

2569 Boise Public Library
715 S Capitol Boulevard
Boise, ID 83702-7115
208-384-4076
www.boisepubliclibrary.org
Member of The Foundation Center network, maintaining a collection of private foundation tax returns which provide information on the scope of grants dispensed by that particular foundation.

2570 The Whittenberger Foundation
PO Box 1073
Caldwell, ID 83606-1073
www.whittenberger.org
Provides funding for projects and initiatives that seek to improve quality of life for children and young people. Fields of interest to the foundation include education, arts and culture, health, social welfare, recreation and the environment.

Scott Gipson, Chair
Elaine Carpenter, Vice Chair

2571 Walter & Leona Dufresne Foundation
1150 W State Street
Boise, ID 83702-5327
Offers support in the areas of secondary school education and higher education.

Royce Chigbrow, Executive Director

Illinois

2572 Ameritech Foundation
30 S Wacker Drive
Floor 34
Chicago, IL 60606-7487
312-750-5223
Fax: 312-207-1098
A foundation that offers grants to elementary school/education, secondary school/education and higher education.

Michael E Kuhlin, Executive Director

2573 Awards and Recognition Industry Educational Foundation (ARIEF)
8735 W Higgins Road
Suite 300
Chicago, IL 60631
847-375-4800
Fax: 847-375-6480
info@awardspersonalization.org
www.awardspersonalization.org
Nonprofit organization supporting education and research in the awards and recognition industry, primarily through scholarships and an annual auction.

Louise Ristau, CAE, Executive Director
Liz Giannini, Senior Operations Manager

2574 Carus Corporate Contributions Program
315 5th Street
Peru, IL 61354-2859
815-223-1500
Offers support for higher, secondary, elementary and early childhood education.

Robert J Wilmot, Executive Director

2575 Chauncey & Marion Deering McCormick Foundation
410 N Michigan Avenue
Suite 590
Chicago, IL 60611-4220
312-644-6720
Preschool education, journalism and the improvement of socio-economic condition of Metropolitan Chicago are the main areas of giving for this foundation.

Charles E Schroeder, Executive Director

2576 Chicago Community Trust
225 North Michigan Avenue
Suite 2200
Chicago, IL 60601-1088
312-616-8000
Fax: 312-616-7955
www.cct.org
A community foundation that offers support for general operating projects and specific programs and projects in areas including child development, education and higher education.

Sandy Chears, Grants Manager
Terry Mazany, President

2577 Coleman Foundation
651 West Washington Boulevard
Suite 306
Chicago, IL 60661-2515
312-902-7120
Fax: 312-902-7124
info@colemanfoundation.org
www.colemanfoundation.org
A nonprofit, private foundation established in the state of Illinois in 1951. Major areas of

support include health, educational, cultural, scientific and social programs. Grants generally focus on organizations within the Midwest and particularly within the state of Illinois and the Chicago Metropolitan area. No grants are made for programs outside of the United States. Ongoing support is not available, continuing programs must indicate how they will be sustained in the future.

Rosa Janus, Program Manager
Michael W Hennessy, President/CEO

2578 Dellora A & Lester J Norris Foundation
PO Box 4325
Saint Charles, IL 60174-9075
630-377-4111
Education, health and social services are the main concerns of this foundation, with Illinois, Colorado and Florida being their priority.

Eugene W Butler, Executive Director

2579 Dillon Foundation
PO Box 454
Boulder, MT 59632-0537
406-980-1588
info@dillonfoundation.org
www.dillonfoundation.org
Offers support for educational purposes, including higher education and community services.

Peter W Dillon, Executive Director

2580 Dr. Scholl Foundation
1033 Skokie Boulevard
Suite 230
Northbrook, IL 60062
847-559-7430
www.drschollfoundation.com
Applications for grants are considered in the following areas: private education at all levels including elementary, secondary schools, colleges and universities and medical and nursing institutions; general charitable organizations and programs, including grants to hospitals and programs for children, developmentally disabled and senior citizens; civic, cultural, social services, health care, economic and religious activities.

Pamela Scholl, Executive Director

2581 Evanston Public Library
1703 Orrington Avenue
Evanston, IL 60201-3886
847-866-0300
Fax: 847-866-0313
Member of The Foundation Center network, maintaining a collection of private foundation tax returns which provide information on the scope of grants dispensed by that particular foundation.

Neal J Ney, Director

2582 Farny R Wurlitzer Foundation
PO Box 418
Sycamore, IL 60178-0418
Offers support in the areas of education, including programs for minorities, early childhood, elementary and secondary institutions, music education and organizations.

William A Rolfing, Executive Director

2583 Grover Hermann Foundation
1000 Hill Grove
Suite 200
Western Springs, IL 60558-6306
708-246-8331
Focus of giving is on higher education and private schooling activities.

Paul K Rhoads, Executive Director

2584 Joyce Foundation
70 W Madison Street
Suite 2750
Chicago, IL 60602
312-782-2464
Fax: 312-782-4160
info@joycefdn.org
www.joycefdn.org
Based in Chicago with assets of $1 billion, the Joyce foundation supports efforts to strengthen public policies in ways that improve the quality of life in the Great Lakes region. Last year the foundation made nearly $17 million in grants to groups working to inprove public education in Chicago, Cleveland, Detroit and Milwaukee.

Ellen Alberding, President

2585 Lloyd A Fry Foundation
120 S Lasalle Street
Suite 1950
Chicago, IL 60603-3419
312-580-0310
Fax: 312-580-0980
www.fryfoundation.org
The foundation primarily supports education, higher education, the performing arts, and social service organizations.

Unmi Song, Executive Director

2586 Northern Trust Company Charitable Trust
Community Affairs Division
50 S Lasalle Street
Chicago, IL 60603-1006
312-630-6000
www.ntrs.com
Offers grants in the areas of community development, education and early childhood education.

Marjorie W Lundy, Executive Director

2587 Palmer Foundation
734 15th Street NW
Suite 600
Washington, DC 20005
202-595-1020
Fax: 202-833-5540
admin@thepalmerfoundation.org
www.thepalmerfoundation.org
Offers grants in elementary and secondary education, as well as youth services and Protestant churches.

2588 Philip H Corboy Foundation
33 N Dearborn Street
Chicago, IL 60602-2502
312-346-3191
www.corboydemetrio.com
Offers grants in the areas of elementary, secondary, law school education and health care.

2589 Polk Brothers Foundation
20 W Kinzie Street
Suite 1100
Chicago, IL 60610-4600
312-527-4684
Fax: 312-527-4681
www.polkbrosfdn.org
Offers grants for new or ongoing programs to organizations whose work is based in the areas of education, social services and health care.

Nikki W Stein, Executive Director
Shiela A Robinson, Grants Administrator

2590 Prince Charitable Trust
303 West Madison Street
Suite 1900
Chicago, IL 60606-7407
312-419-8700
Fax: 312-419-8558
Offers support for cultural programs, public school programming and social service organizations.

Benna B Wilde, Managing Director
Sharon L Robison, Grants Manager

2591 Regenstein Foundation
8600 W Bryn Mawr Avenue
Suite 705N
Chicago, IL 60631-3579
773-693-6464
Fax: 773-693-2480
Offers grants for educational and general charitable institutions within the metropolitan Chicago area and the state of Illinois.

Joseph Regenstein Jr, Executive Director

2592 Richard H Driehaus Foundation
333 N Michigan Avenue
Suite 510
Chicago, IL 60601-1604
312-641-5772
Fax: 312-641-5736
www.driehausfoundation.org
Offers support in elementary, secondary and higher education in the state of Illinois.

Susan Fischer, Executive Director
Peter Handler, Program Director

2593 Robert R McCormick Tribune Foundation
435 N Michigan Avenue
Suite 770
Chicago, IL 60611-4066
312-222-3512
Fax: 312-222-3523
www.rrmtf.org
Offers contributions for private higher education and rehabilitation services.

Nicholas Goodban, Senior VP/Philanthropy
Richard A Behrenhausen, President/CEO

2594 Sears-Roebuck Foundation
Sears Tower
Department 903-BSC 51-02
Chicago, IL 60684
312-875-8337
The foundation focuses its giving primarily on projects that address education and volunteerism.

Paula A Banke, Executive Director

2595 Spencer Foundation
875 N Michigan Avenue
Suite 3930
Chicago, IL 60611-1803
312-337-7000
Fax: 312-337-0282
www.spencer.org
Supports research aimed at the practice of understanding and expanding knowledge in the area of education.

Michael McPherson, President

2596 Sulzer Family Foundation
1940 W Irving Park Road
Chicago, IL 60613-2437
312-321-4700
Offers giving for education, including higher, secondary, elementary and adult education in the areas of Chicago, Illinois.

John J Hoellen, Executive Director

97 United Airlines Foundation
1800 Massachusetts Avenue
Suite 400
Washington, DC 20036-0919
847-952-5714
www.unfoundation.org
Offers a wide variety of support programs with an emphasis on education and educational reform.
Eileen Younglove, Executive Director
Timothy E Wirth, President

98 Valenti Charitable Foundation
Valenti Builders
PO Box 2534
Rancho Santa Fe, CA 92067-3311
858-759-9239
Fax: 858-759-1319
Irene@valentifoundation.org
www.valentifoundation.org
Offers support in elementary education, secondary school education, higher education and children and youth services.
Valenti Sr Trustee, Executive Director

Indiana

99 Allen County Public Library
900 Library Plaza
Fort Wayne, IN 46802-3699
260-421-1200
Fax: 260-421-1386
www.acpl.lib.in.us
Member of The Foundation Center network, maintaining a collection of private foundation tax returns which provide information on the scope of grants dispensed by that particular foundation.

600 Arvin Foundation
1 Noblitt Plaza #3000
Columbus, IN 47201-6079
812-379-3207
Fax: 812-379-3688
Giving is offered primarily to primary, secondary and higher education and technical training.
E Fred Meyer, Executive Director

601 Clowes Fund
320 N Meridian Street Suite 316
The Chamber of Commerce Building
Indianapolis, IN 46204-1722
800-943-7209
Fax: 800-943-7286
www.clowesfund.org
Offers giving for higher and secondary education; the performing arts; marine biology and social service organizations.
Elizabeth Casselman, Executive Director
Alexander W Clowes, President

602 Dekko Foundation
PO Box 548
Kendallville, IN 46755-0548
260-347-1278
Fax: 260-347-7103
Offers support for all levels of education and human service organizations.
Linda Speakman, Executive Director

603 Eli Lilly & Company Corporate Contribution Program
Lilly Corporate Center D.C. 1627
Indianapolis, IN 46285
317-276-2000
Offers support in the areas of secondary school/education, higher education and health care programs.
Thomas King, President

2604 Foellinger Foundation
520 E Berry Street
Fort Wayne, IN 46802-2002
260-422-2900
Fax: 260-422-9436
info@foellinger.org
www.foellinger.org
Giving is aimed at higher education and other secondary and elementary projects, community programs and social service organizations.
Harry V Owen, Executive Director

2605 Indianapolis Foundation
615 N Alabama Street
Suite 119
Indianapolis, IN 46204-1498
317-634-2423
Fax: 317-684-0943
Offers support in the areas of education and neighborhood services.
Kenneth Gladish, Executive Director

2606 John W Anderson Foundation
402 Wall Street
Valparaiso, IN 46383-2562
219-462-4611
Fax: 219-531-8954
Offers grants in the areas of higher education, youth programs, human services, and arts and humanities. Grants are limited primarily to Northwest Indian organizations.
William Vinovich, Vice Chairman/Trustee

2607 Lilly Endowment
2801 N Meridian Street
Indianapolis, IN 46208-0068
317-924-5471
Fax: 317-926-4431
www.lillyendowment.org
Supports the causes of religion, education and community development. Although the Endowment supports efforts of national significance, especially in the field of religion, it is primarily committed to its hometown, Indianapolis, and home state, Indiana.
Sue Ellen Walker, Communications Associate

2608 Moore Foundation
1661 Page Mill Road
Palo Alto, CA 94304-2158
317-848-2013
Fax: 317-571-0744
info@moore.org
www.moore.org
Offers support in elementary school and secondary school education, higher education, business school education and youth services in Indiana.
Eileen C Ryan, Executive Director
Gordon Moore, Chairman

2609 W Brooks Fortune Foundation
7933 Beaumont Green W Drive
Indianapolis, IN 46250-1652
317-842-1303
Support is limited to education-related programs in Indiana.
William Brooks Fortune, Executive Director

Iowa

2610 Cedar Rapids Public Library
Funding Information Center
500 1st Street SE
Cedar Rapids, IA 52401-2095
319-398-5123
Fax: 319-398-0476
www.crlibrary.org
Member of The Foundation Center network, maintaining a collection of private foundation tax returns which provide information on the scope of grants dispensed by that particular foundation.
Tamara Glise, Public Services Manager
Eileen C Ryan, Executive Director

2611 RJ McElroy Trust
425 Cedar Street
Suite 312
Waterloo, IA 50701
312
www.mcelroytrust.org
The trust funds grants to educational youth programs in the northeast quarter of Iowa. The trust guidelines do not include grants to individuals.
Linda L Klinger, Executive Director

Kansas

2612 Mary Jo Williams Charitable Trust
PO Box 660075
Dallas, TX 75266-0075
866-866-7509
Offers support in the areas of early childhood education, higher education, and children and youth services.
Michael E Collins, Executive Director

2613 Sprint Foundation
2330 Shawnee Mission Parkway
Westwood, KS 66205-2090
913-624-3343
www.sprint.com
Offers grants in a variety of areas with an emphasis on education, including business education, secondary education and higher education.
Don G Forsythe, Executive Director

2614 Wichita Public Library
223 S Main Street
Wichita, KS 67202-3795
316-261-8500
Fax: 316-262-4540
Member of The Foundation Center network, maintaining a collection of private foundation tax returns which provide information on the scope of grants dispensed by that particular foundation.

Kentucky

2615 Ashland Incorporated Foundation
50 E River Center Boulevard
Covington, KY 41012
859-815-3630
Fax: 859-815-4496
www.ashland.com
Offers support to educational organizations, colleges and universities, as well as giving an employee matching gift program to higher education and community funding.
James O'Brien, CEO

2616 Gheens Foundation
401 W Main Street
Suite 705
Louisville, KY 40202
502-584-4650
Fax: 502-584-4652
www.gheensfoundation.org

The foundation's support is aimed at higher and secondary education, ongoing teacher education, and social service agencies.

James N Davis, Executive Director
William G Duncan, Secretary

2617 James Graham Brown Foundation
4350 Brownsboro Road
Suite 200
Louisville, KY 40207
502-896-2440
Fax: 502-896-1774
info@jgbf.org
www.jgbf.org
Offers grants in the areas of higher education and social services.

Mason Rummel, Executive Director
Dodie L McKenzie, Program Officer

2618 Louisville Free Public Library
301 York Street
Louisville, KY 40203-2257
502-574-1611
Fax: 502-574-1657
www.lfpl.org
Member of The Foundation Center network, maintaining a collection of private foundation tax returns which provide information on the scope of grants dispensed by that particular foundation.

2619 Margaret Hall Foundation
6685 Walnutwood Circle
Baltimore, MD 21212-1727
443-708-3548
Awards grants and scholarships to private, nonprofit secondary schools for innovative programming.

Helen R Burg, Executive Director

2620 VV Cooke Foundation Corporation
220 Mount Mercy Drive
Pewee Valley, KY 40056-9068
502-241-0303
Offers support in education and youth services with an emphasis on Baptist church and school support.

John B Gray, Executive Director

Louisiana

2621 Baton Rouge Area Foundation
402 N 4th Street
Baton Rouge, LA 70802
225-387-6126
877-387-6126
Fax: 225-387-6153
www.braf.org
Offers grants in the area of elementary and secondary education and health.

John G Davies, President

2622 Booth-Bricker Fund
826 Union Street
Suite 300
New Orleans, LA 70112-1421
504-581-2430
Fax: 504-566-4785
Does not have a formal grant procedure or grant application form; nor does it publish an annual report. The Booth-Bricker Fund makes contributions for the purposes of promoting, developing and fostering religious, charitable, scientific, literary or educational programs, primarily in the state of Louisiana. It does not make contributions to individuals.

Gray S Parker, Chairman

2623 East Baton Rouge Parish Library
Centroplex Branch Grants Collection
7711 Goodwood Boulevard
Baton Rouge, LA 70806
225-231-3750
www.ebrpl.com
Member of The Foundation Center network, maintaining a collection of private foundation tax returns which provide information on the scope of grants dispensed by that particular foundation.

2624 Fred B & Ruth B Zigler Foundation
Zigler Foundation
PO Box 986
Zigler Building
Jennings, LA 70546-0986
337-824-2413
Fax: 337-824-2414
Offers support to higher, secondary and primary education.

Julie G Berry, President
Marie Romero, Secretary

2625 New Orleans Public Library
Business & Science Division
219 Loyola Avenue
New Orleans, LA 70112-2044
504-529-7323
Fax: 504-596-2609
www.nutrias.org
Member of The Foundation Center network, maintaining a collection of private foundation tax returns which provide information on the scope of grants dispensed by that particular foundation.

2626 Shreve Memorial Library
424 Texas Street
Shreveport, LA 71101-5452
318-226-5897
Fax: 318-226-4780
webmaster@shreve-lib.org
www.shreve-lib.org
Member of The Foundation Center network, maintaining a collection of private Louisiana foundation tax returns which provide information on the scope of grants dispensed by that particular foundation.

Carlos Colon, Reference Supervisor

Maine

2627 Clarence E Mulford Trust
PO Box 290
Fryeburg, ME 04037-0290
207-935-2061
Fax: 207-935-3939
Offers grants to charitable, educational and scientific organizations for the purpose of improving education.

David R Hastings II, Executive Director

2628 Harold Alfond Trust
C/O Dexter Shoe Company
Two Monument Square
Portland, ME 04101-0353
207-828-7999
www.haroldalfondfoundation.org
Grants are offered to secondary and higher education in Maine and Maryland.

Keith Burden, Executive Director

Maryland

2629 Abell Foundation
111 S Calvert Street
Suite 2300
Baltimore, MD 21202-6182
410-547-1300
Fax: 410-539-6579
abell@abell.org
www.abell.org
The foundation supports education with an emphasis on public education, including early childhood and elementary, research, and minority education.

Robert C Embry Jr, Executive Director
Ellen Mullan, Controller

2630 Aegon USA
1111 N Charles Street
Baltimore, MD 21201-5505
410-576-4571
Fax: 410-347-8685
www.aegonins.com
Offers grants in elementary school, secondary school, higher education and medical school education.

Larry G Brown, Executive Director

2631 Clarence Manger & Audrey Cordero Plitt Trust
C/O First National Bank of Maryland
25 S Charles St
Baltimore, MD 21201-3330
410-566-0914
Offers grants to educational institutions for student loans and scholarships.

Mary M Kirgan, Executive Director

2632 Clark-Winchcole Foundation
Air Rights Building
3 Bethesda Metro Center
Suite 550
Bethesda, MD 20814
301-654-3607
Fax: 301-654-3140
Offers grants in the areas of higher education and social service agencies.

Laura E Philips, Executive Director

2633 Commonwealth Foundation
9737 Colesville Road
Suite 800
Silver Spring, MD 20910
301-495-4400
Offers grants in the areas of early childhood education, child development, elementary schools, secondary schools and youth services.

Barbara Bainum, Executive Director

2634 Dresher Foundation
4940 Campbell Boulevard
Suite 110
Baltimore, MD 21236
410-933-0384
www.jdgraphicdesign.com/dresher/dresherfoundation/
Offers giving in the areas of elementary school, early childhood education, meals on wheels, and food distribution.

2635 Edward E Ford Foundation
66 Pearl Street
Suite 322
Portland, ME 04101
207-774-2346
Fax: 207-774-2348
office@eeford.org
www.eeford.org

Offers giving to secondary schools and private education in the US and its protectorates.

Robert Hallett, Executive Director

36 Enoch Pratt Free Library
Social Science & History Department
400 Cathedral Street
Baltimore, MD 21201-4484
301-396-5430
www.pratt.lib.md.us
Member of The Foundation Center network, maintaining a collection of private foundation tax returns which provide information on the scope of grants dispensed by that particular foundation.

37 France-Merrick Foundation
The Exchange
2 Hamill Rd,Quadrangle East
Suite 302
Baltimore, MD 21210-2139
410-464-2004
Fax: 410-832-5704
Offers grants in the areas of public education, private and higher education, health, social services and cultural activities.

Frederick W Lafferty, Executive Director

38 Grayce B Kerr Fund
117 Bay Street
Easton, MD 21601-2769
410-822-6652
Fax: 410-822-4546
office@gbkf.org
www.gbkf.org
The major area of interest to the fund is education, including higher, elementary and early childhood education for the state of Maryland with focus on the Eastern Shore Counties.

Margaret van den Berg, Administrative Assistant
John R Valliant, President

639 Henry & Ruth Blaustein Rosenberg Foundation
Blaustein Building
10 East Baltimore Street
Suite 1111
Baltimore, MD 21202
410-347-7201
Fax: 410-347-7210
info@blaufund.org
www.blaufund.org
Offers grants in the areas of secondary and higher education.

Betsy F Ringel, Executive Director
Henry A Rosenberg Jr, President

640 James M Johnston Trust for Charitable and Educational Purposes
2 Wisconsin Circle
Suite 600
Chevy Chase, MD 20815-7003
301-907-0135
Grants are given to higher and secondary educational institutions located in Washington, DC and North Carolina.

Julie Sanders, Executive Director

641 John W Kluge Foundation
15004 Sunflower CT
Rockville, MD 20853-0174
301-929-9340
Offers grants in higher education and secondary education.

642 Marion I & Henry J Knott Foundation
3904 Hickory Avenue
Baltimore, MD 21211-1834
410-235-7068
Fax: 410-889-2577
info@knottfoundation.org
www.knottfoundation.org
Grantmaking limited to private nonsectarian schools and Catholic schools geographically located within the Archdiocese of Baltimore, Maryland.

Greg Cantori, Executive Director

2643 Robert G & Anne M Merrick Foundation
The Exchange
1122 Kenilworth Drive
Suite 118
Baltimore, MD 21204-2142
410-832-5700
Fax: 410-832-5704
Offers grants for public education, higher education and social services.

Frederick W Lafferty, Executive Director

Massachusetts

2644 Associated Grantmakers of Massachusetts
55 Court Street
Suite 520
Boston, MA 02108-4304
617-426-2606
Fax: 617-426-2849
www.agmconnect.org
Member of The Foundation Center network, maintaining a collection of private foundation tax returns which provide information on the scope of grants dispensed by that particular foundation.

Ron Ancrum, President
Martha Moore, Director Center Philanthropy

2645 Boston Foundation
75 Arlington Street
10th Floor
Boston, MA 02116-4407
617-338-1700
Fax: 617-338-1604
www.tbf.org
Supports local educational, social and housing programs and institutions.

Paul Grogan, President

2646 Boston Globe Foundation II
135 Morrissey Boulevard
Boston, MA 02107
617-929-2895
Fax: 617-929-7889
The foundation's highest priority is community based agencies which understand, represent and are part of the following populations; children and youth with disabilities, children and youth with AIDS, refugees, low-birth weight babies, pregnant and nursing mothers and incarcerated youth.

Suzanne W Maas, Executive Director
Leah P Bailey

2647 Boston Public Library
Social Sciences Reference
700 Boylston Street
Boston, MA 02116-2813
617-536-5400
www.bpl.org
Member of The Foundation Center network, maintaining a collection of private foundation tax returns which provide information on the scope of grants dispensed by that particular foundation.

Bernard Margolis, President

2648 Dean Foundation for Little Children
C/O Boston Safe Deposit & Trust Company
PO Box 185
Pittsburgh, PA 15230-0185
Giving is centered on little children age twelve and under for the care and relief of destitute children. Provides support for preschools, day care, summer camps and other programs.

Nancy Criscitiello, Executive Director

2649 Hyams Foundation
50 Federal Street
Floor 9
Boston, MA 02110-2210
617-426-5600
Fax: 617-426-5696
www.hyamsfoundation.org
The foundation seeks to promote understanding and appreciation of diversity, including race, ethnicity, gender, sexual orientation, age, physical ability, class and religion. The foundation's primary objective is to meet the needs of low-income and other underserved populations, striving to address the causes of those needs, whenever possible. Foundation supports low-income communities in their efforts to identify their own problems, solve these problems and improve people's lives.

Elizabeth B Smith, Executive Director
Angela Brown, Director of Programs

2650 Irene E & George A Davis Foundation
C/O Ann T Keiser
1 Monarch Place
Suite 1450
Springfield, MA 01144-1300
413-734-8336
Fax: 413-734-7845
info@davisfdn.org
www.davisfdn.org
Education and social service organizations and programs in Western Massachusetts are the primary concern of this foundation.

Mary E Walachy, Executive Director

2651 James G Martin Memorial Trust
122 Pond Street
Jamaica Plain, MA 02130-2714
Giving is centered on elementary education and higher education in Massachusetts.

Ms Martin, Executive Director

2652 Jessie B Cox Charitable Trust
Grants Management Association
60 State Street
Boston, MA 02109-1899
617-227-7940
Fax: 617-227-0781
This trust makes grants for projects which will address important social issues in the trust's fields of interest and for which adequate funding from other sources cannot be obtained. The trust funds projects in New England in the areas of health, education and the environment. The trustees look to support special projects which will assist the applicants to achieve their long-range organizational goals.

Michaelle Larkins, Executive Director
Susan M Fish, Grants Administrator

2653 LG Balfour Foundation
Fleet Bank of Massachusetts
75 State Street
Boston, MA 02109-1775
617-346-4000
Offers support for scholarships and innovative projects designed to eliminate barriers

and improve access to education for all potentially qualified students.

Kerry Herliney, Executive Director

2654 Little Family Foundation
33 Broad Street
Suite 10
Boston, MA 02109-4216
617-723-6771
Fax: 617-723-7107
Offers scholarships at various business schools and Junior Achievement programs in secondary schools.

Arthur D Little, Executive Director

2655 Rogers Family Foundation
10 Clay Street
Suite 200
Oakland, CA 94067-4501
510-899-7918
Fax: 978-685-1588
www.rogersfoundation.org
Offers support in the areas of secondary and higher education in the Lawrence, Massachusetts area.

Kathleen Rogers, President
Nicole Taylor, Secretary/Treasurer

2656 State Street Foundation
225 Franklin Street
12th Floor
Boston, MA 02110
617-664-1937
www.statestreet.com
Offers grants to organizations that help improve the quality of life in the greater Boston area. Interest includes human services, public and secondary education, vocational education, and arts and culture programs.

Madison Thompson, Executive Director

2657 Sudbury Foundation
326 Concord Road
Sudbury, MA 01776-1843
978-443-0849
Fax: 978-579-9536
www.sudburyfoundation.org
Offers college scholarships to local high school seniors who meet eligibility criteria.

Marilyn Martino, Executive Director
Tricia Brunner, Grants Administrator

2658 Trustees of the Ayer Home
PO Box 1865
Lowell, MA 01853-1865
978-452-5914
Fax: 978-452-5914
Funding (greater Lowell, MA only) educational programs (RLF, SMARTS). Primary interests are women and children.

D Donahue, Assistant Treasurer

2659 Weld Foundation
Peter Loring/Janice Palumbo
Loring, Wolcott & Coolidge
30 Congress Street
Boston, MA 02110-2409
617-523-6531
Fax: 617-523-6535
Grants are offered in the areas of elementary, secondary and higher education in Massachusetts.

2660 Western Massachusetts Funding Resource Center
65 Elliot Street
Springfield, MA 01105-1713
413-732-3175
Fax: 413-452-0618
www.diospringfield.org/wmfrc.html
Member of The Foundation Center network, maintaining a collection of private foundation tax returns which provide information on the scope of grants dispensed by that particular foundation.

Kathleen Dowd, Director
Jean Los, Administrative Assistant

2661 William E Schrafft & Bertha E Schrafft Charitable Trust
77 Summer Street
Boston, MA 02110
617-457-7327
www.schrafftcharitable.org
Giving is primarily allocated to educational programs in the Boston metropolitan area.

Arthur H Parker, Trustee
Lavinia B Chase, Trustee

2662 Woodstock Corporation
Woodstock Corporation
27 School Street
Suite 200
Boston, MA 02108-2301
617-227-0600
Fax: 617-523-0229
info@woodstockcorp.com
www.woodstockcorp.com
Offers support in the area of secondary school education in the state of Massachusetts.

2663 Worcester Public Library
Grants Resource Center
3 Salem Square
Worcester, MA 01608
508-799-1655
Fax: 508-799-1652
www.worcpublib.org
Member of The Foundation Center network, maintaining a collection of private foundation tax returns which provide information on the scope of grants dispensed by that particular foundation.

J Peck, Director Grants Resource

Michigan

2664 Alex & Marie Manoogian Foundation
21001 Van Born Road
Taylor, MI 48180-1340
313-274-7400
Fax: 313-792-6657
Supports higher and secondary education, cultural programs and human service organizations.

Alex Manoogian, Executive Director

2665 Charles Stewart Mott Foundation
Office of Proposal Entry
503 S Saginaw Street
Suite 1200
Flint, MI 48502-1851
810-238-5651
800-645-1766
Fax: 810-237-4857
www.mott.org
Grants are given to nonprofit organizations with an emphasis on programs of volunteerism, at-risk youth, environmental protection, economic development and education.

2666 Chrysler Corporate Giving Program
12000 Chrysler Drive
Detroit, MI 48288-0001
810-576-5741
Offers support for education, especially secondary education and leadership development.

Lynn A Feldhouse, Executive Director

2667 Community Foundation for Southeastern Michigan
333 W Fort Street
Suite 2010
Detroit, MI 48226-3134
313-961-6675
Fax: 313-961-2886
www.cfsem.org
Supports projects in the areas of education, culture and social services.

Mariam C Noland, President

2668 Community Foundation of Greater Flint
500 South Saginaw Street
Flint, MI 48502-2013
810-767-8270
Fax: 810-767-0496
cfgf@cfgf.org
www.cfgf.org
A community foundation that makes grants to benefit residents of Genessee County, Michigan. Areas of interest include: arts, education, environment, community services and health and social services.

Kathi Horton, President
Evan M Albert, VP Program

2669 Cronin Foundation
203 E Michigan Avenue
Marshall, MI 49068-1545
616-781-9851
Fax: 616-781-2070
Offers support to expand educational, social and cultural needs of the community within the Marshall, Michigan school district.

Joseph E Schroeder, Executive Director

2670 Detroit Edison Foundation
2000 2nd Avenue
Room 1046
Detroit, MI 48226-1279
313-235-9271
Fax: 313-237-9271
Offers support for all levels of education, and local community social services and cultural organizations in Southeast Michigan.

Katharine W Hunt, Executive Director

2671 Ford Motor Company Fund
One American Road
PO Box 1899
Dearborn, MI 48126-2798
888-313-0102
Fax: 313-337-6680
www.ford.com
Ford Motor Company Fund continues the legacy of Henry Ford's commitment to innovative education at all levels. We remain dedicated to creating and enriching educational opportunities, especially in the areas of science, engineering, math and business, while promoting diversity in education.

Sandra E Ulsh, President
Jim Graham, Manager Education Programs

2672 Frey Foundation
40 Pearl Street NW
Suite 1100
Grand Rapids, MI 49503-3023
616-451-0303
Fax: 616-451-8481
www.freyfdn.org
Awards grants and supports the needs of children in their early years, support for environmental ed-

ucation and protection of our natural resources.

Milton W Rohwer, President
Teresa J Crawford, Grants Manager

673 General Motors Foundation
PO Box 33170
Detroit, MI 48232-5170
313-556-4260
www.gm.com/company/gmability/philanthropy
Offers support for higher education, cultural programs and civic affairs.

Ronald L Theis, Executive Director

674 Grand Rapids Foundation
185 Oakes St SW
Grand Rapids, MI 49503
616-454-1751
Fax: 616-454-6455
grfound@grfoundation.org
www.grfoundation.org
A community foundation established in 1922. The foundation actively serves the people of Kent County by administering funds it receives and by making philanthropic grants to non-profit organizations in response to community needs. Various educational scholarships are offered on the basis of a competitive process which considers academic achievement, extracurricular activities, a statement of one's own personal aspirations and educational goals, and financial need. Kent County Residency required.

Ruth Bishop, Program Associate-Education
Diana Sieger, President

675 Harry A & Margaret D Towsley Foundation
3055 Plymouth Road
Suite 200
Ann Arbor, MI 48105-3208
312-662-6777
Areas of support include pre-school education, social services, and continuing education.

Margaret Ann Riecker, Executive Director

676 Henry Ford Centennial Library
Adult Services
16301 Michigan Avenue
Dearborn, MI 48126-2792
313-943-2330
Fax: 313-943-3063
Member of The Foundation Center network, maintaining a collection of private foundation tax returns which provide information on the scope of grants dispensed by that particular foundation.

677 Herbert H & Grace A Dow Foundation
1018 W Main Street
Midland, MI 48640-4292
989-631-3699
Fax: 989-631-0675
www.hhdowfdn.org
Limited to organizations within Michigan. Has charter goals to improve the educational, religious, economic and cultural lives of Michigan's people.

Margaret Ann Riescker, President
Elysa M Rogers, Assistant VP

678 Herrick Foundation
150 W Jefferson Avenue
Suite 2500
Detroit, MI 48226-4415
313-496-7585
Offers grants to colleges and universities, health agencies and social service organizations.

Dolores de Galleford, Executive Director

2679 Kresge Foundation
3215 W Big Beaver Road
Troy, MI 48084
248-643-9630
Fax: 313-643-0588
www.kresge.org
Giving is aimed at areas of interest including arts and humanities, social services and public policy.

John E Marshall III, Executive Director
Sandra McAlister Ambrozy, Senior Program Officer

2680 Malpass Foundation
PO Box 1206
East Jordan, MI 49727-1206
Offers giving in the areas of education and community development.

William J Lorne, Executive Director

2681 McGregor Fund
333 W Fort Street
Suite 2090
Detroit, MI 48226-3134
313-963-3495
Fax: 313-963-3512
info@mcgregorfund.org
www.mcgregorfund.org
Social services, health and education grants awarded to organizations located in Ohio, primarily the Detroit area.

C David Campbell, President
Kate Levin Markel, Program Officer

2682 Michigan State University Libraries
Social Sciences/Humanities
366 W Circle Drive
East Lansing, MI 48824
517-353-8700
Fax: 517-432-3532
www.lib.msu.edu
Member of The Foundation Center network, maintaining a collection of private foundation tax returns which provide information on the scope of grants dispensed by that particular foundation.

2683 Richard & Helen DeVos Foundation
190 Muncie NW
Suite 500
Grand Rapids, MI 49503
616-454-4114
Fax: 616-454-4654
Strong geographical preference to Western Michigan. Funding includes Christian education, cultural, community, education (not an individual basis) and government services. Donations are also made on a national level to organizations based in Washington, DC.

Stephanie Roy, Executive Director

2684 Rollin M Gerstacker Foundation
PO Box 1945
Midland, MI 48641-1945
989-631-6097
Fax: 517-832-8842
Primary purpose of this foundation is to carry on, indefinitely, financial aid to charities concentrated in the states of Michigan and Ohio. Grants are given in the areas of community support, schools, education, social services, music and the arts, youth activities, health care and research, churches and other areas.

Carl A Gerstacker, Executive Director

2685 Steelcase Foundation
PO Box 1967, CH-4E
Grand Rapids, MI 49501-1967
616-246-4695
Fax: 616-475-2200
www.steelcase.com
Offers support for human services and education, to improve the quality of life for children, the elderly and the disabled in the areas where there are manufacturing plants.

Susan Broman, Executive Director

2686 Wayne State University
Purdy-Kresge Library
5265 Cass Avenue
Detroit, MI 48202-3930
313-577-6424
www.lib.wayne.edu
Member of The Foundation Center network, maintaining a collection of private foundation tax returns which provide information on the scope of grants dispensed by that particular foundation.

2687 Whirlpool Foundation
2000 N M 63
MD 3106
Benton Harbor, MI 49022-2692
269-923-5584
Fax: 269-925-0154
www.whirlpoolcorp.com
Giving centers on learning, cultural diversity, adult education, and scholarships for children of corporation employees.

Ddaniel Hopp, President & Chairman
Pamela Silcox, Operations Manager

Minnesota

2688 Andersen Foundation
Andersen Corporation
100 4th Avenue N
Bayport, MN 55003-1058
651-264-5150
Fax: 651-264-5537
Grants are given in the areas of higher education, health, youth and the arts in Minnesota.

2689 Bush Foundation
E-900 First National Bank Building
332 Minnesota Street
Saint Paul, MN 55101-1314
651-227-0891
Fax: 651-297-6485
www.bushfoundation.org
The foundation is predominantly a regional grantmaking foundation, with broad interests in education, human services, health, arts and humanities and in the development of leadership.

Anita M Pampusch, President
John Archabal, Senior Program Officer

2690 Cargill Foundation
PO Box 9300
Minneapolis, MN 55440-9300
952-742-4311
Fax: 612-742-7224
www.cargill.com
Offers grants in the areas of education, health, human service organizations, arts and cultural programs and social service agencies.

Audrey Tulberg, Executive Director

2691 Charles & Ellora Alliss Educational Foundation
800 Nicollet Mall
Minneapolis, MN 55402-1314

612-303-4411
Fax: 651-244-0860
allissfoundation@usbank.com
www.allissfoundation.org
The foundation is organized exclusively for support of the education of young people, up to and including the period of post-graduate study. As a matter of policy, the foundation generally has limited its program to universities and colleges located in Minnesota. Grants are made to such institutions in support of undergraduate scholarship programs administered by their student aid offices. The foundation makes no direct grants to individuals.

John Bultena, Executive Director
Anita M Pampusch, Board of Trustee

2692 Duluth Public Library
520 W Superior Street
Duluth, MN 55802-1578
218-723-3802
Fax: 218-723-3815
www.duluth.lib.mn.us
Member of The Foundation Center network, maintaining a collection of private foundation tax returns which provide information on the scope of grants dispensed by that particular foundation.

Elizabeth Kelly, Library Director

2693 FR Bigelow Foundation
Center 55th Street East
Suite 600
St. Paul, MN 55101-1797
651-224-5463
800-875-6167
Fax: 651-224-8123
www.frbigelow.org
Offers support in early childhood education, elementary and secondary education, higher and adult education and human services.

Richard B Heydinger, Chair
Carleen K Rhodes, Secretary

2694 First Bank System Foundation
PO Box 522
Minneapolis, MN 55480-0522
612-973-2440
Offers support for public elementary and secondary education, arts and cultural programs.

Cheryl L Rantala, Executive Director

2695 Hiawatha Education Foundation
360 Vila Street
Winona, MN 55987-1500
507-453-5550
Giving is centered on Catholic high schools and colleges, as well as awarding scholarships to college-bound high school graduates.

Robert Kierlin, Executive Director

2696 IA O'Shaughnessy Foundation
2001 Killebrew Drive
Suite 120
Bloomington, MN 55425-0704
952-698-0959
Fax: 952-698-0959
Giving is centered on cultural programs, secondary and higher education, human services and medical programs.

John Bultena, Executive Director
John F O'Shaughnessy, President

2697 Marbrook Foundation
730 2nd Avenue
Suite 1300
Minneapolis, MN 55402
612-752-1783
Fax: 612-752-1780
www.marbrookfoundation.org
Offers grants in the areas of the environment, the arts, social empowerment, spiritual endeavors, basic human needs and health.

Annual Report

Julie S Hara, Executive Director

2698 Medtronic Foundation
7000 Central Avenue NE
Minneapolis, MN 55432-3576
763-514-4000
800-328-2518
Fax: 763-514-8410
www.medtronic.com
Offers grants in the areas of education (especially at the pre-college level), community funding and social services.

Penny Hunt, Executive Director

2699 Minneapolis Foundation
800 Ids Center 80 S 8th Street
Minneapolis, MN 55402
612-672-3878
Fax: 612-672-3846
www.minneapolisfoundation.org
The foundation strives to strengthen the community for the benefit of all citizens. Grants are awarded for the purposes of achieving this goal in the areas of early childhood education, child development, and education.

Karen Kelley-Ariwoola, VP Community Philanthropy

2700 Minneapolis Public Library
Music, Art, Sociology & Humanities
250 S Marquette
Minneapolis, MN 55401-2188
612-630-6000
Fax: 612-630-6220
www.mplib.org
Member of The Foundation Center network, maintaining a collection of private foundation tax returns which provide information on the scope of grants dispensed by that particular foundation.

Katherine G Hadle, Director

2701 Otto Bremer Foundation
445 Minnesota Street
Suite 2250
Saint Paul, MN 55101-2135
651-227-8036
888-291-1123
Fax: 651-312-3665
www.ottobremer.org
Offers support for post-secondary education, human services and community affairs.

John Kostishack, Executive Director
Karen Starr, Senior Program Officer

2702 Saint Paul Foundation
55 Fifth Street East
Suite 600
St. Paul, MN 55101-1797
651-224-5463
800-875-6167
Fax: 651-224-8123
info@saintpaulfoundation.org
www.saintpaulfoundation.org
Offers support for educational, charitable and cultural purposes of a public nature.

Carleen K Rhodes, President
Mindy K Molumby, Grants Administrator

2703 TCF Foundation
Code EXO-02-C
200 Lake Street
East Wayzata, MN 55391-1693
952-745-2757
Fax: 612-661-8554
www.tcfexpress.com
Giving is primarily for education through grants and employee matching gifts, including secondary schools, higher education and organizations that increase public knowledge.

Neil I Whitehouse, Executive Director

Mississippi

2704 Foundation for the Mid South
134 East Amite Street
Jackson, MS 39201
601-355-8167
Fax: 601-355-6499
www.fndmidsouth.org
Makes grants in the area of education, as well as economic development and families and children.

George Penick, Executive Director
Kay Kelly Arnold, Vice Chairman

2705 Jackson-Hinds Library System
300 N State Street
Jackson, MS 39201-1705
601-968-5811
www.jhlibrary.com
Member of The Foundation Center network, maintaining a collection of private foundation tax returns which provide information on the scope of grants dispensed by that particular foundation.

Carolyn McCallum, Executive Director

2706 Mississippi Power Foundation
PO Box 4079
Gulfport, MS 39502-4079
228-864-1211
www.mississippipower.com
The foundation is dedicated to the improvement and enhancement of education in Mississippi from kindergarten to twelfth grade.

Huntley Biggs, Executive Director

2707 Phil Hardin Foundation
2750 North Park Drive
Meridian, MS 39305-5800
601-483-4282
Fax: 601-483-5665
info@philhardin.org
www.philhardin.org
Offers giving in Mississippi for schools and educational institutions and programs.

C Thompson Wacaster, Executive Director

Missouri

2708 Ameren Corporation Charitable Trust
Ameren Corporation
PO Box 66149
MC 100
Saint Louis, MO 63166-6149
314-554-2789
877-426-3736
Fax: 314-554-2888
sbell@ameren.com
www.ameren.com
Offers giving in the areas of education, environment, youth and seniors; giving restricted to nonprofits located in Ameren service area in Missouri and Illinois.

Annually

Susan M Bell, Sr Community Relations
Otis Cowan, Community Relations Manger

'09 Clearinghouse for Midcontinent Foundations
University of Missouri
5110 Cherry Street
Suite 310
Kansas City, MO 64110-2426
816-253-1176
Fax: 816-235-5727
Member of The Foundation Center network, maintaining a collection of private foundation tax returns which provide information on the scope of grants dispensed by that particular foundation.

'10 Danforth Foundation
205 E Butterfield Road
Suite 410
Elmhurst, IL 60126-2733
630-501-1235
Fax: 314-588-0035
This foundation is aimed at enhancing human life through activities which emphasize the theme of improvement in teaching and learning. Serves the pre-collegiate education through grantmaking and program activities.
Dr. Bruce J Anderson, President

'11 Enid & Crosby Kemper Foundation
C/O UMB Bank, N.A.
PO Box 419692
Kansas City, MO 64141-6692
816-860-7711
Fax: 816-860-5690
Giving is primarily allocated to organizations and programs focusing on educational and cultural needs.
Stephen J Campbell, Executive Director

'12 Hall Family Foundation
Charitable & Crown Investment - 323
PO Box 419580
Kansas City, MO 64141-6580
816-274-8516
Fax: 816-274-8547
www.hallfamilyfoundation.org
Offers grants in the areas of all levels of education, performing and visual arts, community development, and children, youth and families.
William S Berkley, President & CEO
David A Warm, Executive Director

713 James S McDonnell Foundation
1034 S Brentwood Boulevard
Suite 1850
Saint Louis, MO 63117-1284
314-721-1532
Fax: 314-721-7421
www.jsmf.org
Foundation Program, Cognitive Studies for Educational Practice, funding available through competition in broadly announced requests for proposals. Program grant guidelines are announced in 3 year cycles.
John T Bruer, President
Cheryl A Washington, Grants Manager

714 Kansas City Public Library
14 West 10th Street
Kansas City, MO 64105
816-701-3400
Fax: 816-701-3401
www.kclibrary.org
Member of The Foundation Center network, maintaining a collection of private foundation tax returns which provide information on the scope of grants dispensed by that particular foundation.
Jonathan Kemper, President
David Mayta, Vice President

2715 Mary Ranken Jordan & Ettie A Jordan Charitable Foundation
Mercantile Bank
PO Box 387
Saint Louis, MO 63166-0387
314-231-7626
Giving is limited to charitable institutions with an emphasis on secondary education and cultural programs, as well as higher education and social services.
Fred Arnold, Executive Director

2716 McDonnell Douglas Foundation
PO Box 419692
M S 10203
Kansas City, MO 64141-6692
314-234-0360
Fax: 314-232-7654
Offers various grants with an emphasis on higher and other education and community funding.
AM Bailey, Executive Director

2717 Monsanto Fund
800 N Lindbergh Boulevard
Saint Louis, MO 63167-0001
314-694-1000
Fax: 314-694-7658
monsanto.fund@monsanto.com
www.monsanto.com
Giving is offered primarily in the area of education, specifically science and math.
Deborah J Patterson, President

Montana

2718 Eastern Montana College Library
Special Collections-Grants
1500 N 30th Street
Billings, MT 59101-0245
406-657-1662
800-565-6782
Fax: 406-657-2037
www.msubillings.edu/library
Member of The Foundation Center network, maintaining a collection of private foundation tax returns which provide information on the scope of grants dispensed by that particular foundation.
Joan Bares, Grants Manager

2719 Montana State Library
Library Services
1500 University Drive
Billings, MT 59101-4542
406-657-2011
800-565-6782
Fax: 406-444-5612
www.msl.state.mt.us/
Member of The Foundation Center network, maintaining a collection of private foundation tax returns which provide information on the scope of grants dispensed by that particular foundation.
Barbara Duke, Administrative Assistant

Nebraska

2720 Dr. CC & Mabel L Criss Memorial Foundation
US Bank
PO Box 64713
Saint Paul, MN 55614-0713
800-441-2117
Fax: 402-348-6666
Offers support for educational and scientific purposes, including higher education.

2721 Thomas D Buckley Trust
PO Box 647
Chappell, NE 69129-0647
308-874-2212
Fax: 308-874-3491
Offers giving in the areas of education, health care and youth and religion. Grants awarded in Chappell, NE, community and surrounding area.
Connie Loos, Secretary

2722 W Dale Clark Library
Social Sciences Department
215 S 15th Street
Omaha, NE 68102-1601
402-444-4826
Fax: 402-444-4504
www.omahapubliclibrary.org
Member of The Foundation Center network, maintaining a collection of private foundation tax returns which provide information on the scope of grants dispensed by that particular foundation.
Angela Green-Garland, President
Arun K Agarwal, Vice President

Nevada

2723 Conrad N Hilton Foundation
30440 Agoura Road
Agoura Hills, CA 91301-1988
818-851-3700
Fax: 775-323-4150
www.hiltonfoundation.org
Founded in 1944 as a Trust, this foundation is dedicated to fulfilling and expanding Conrad Hilton's philanthropic vision by carrying out grantmaking activities. The foundation's giving is focused primarily in two areas: the alleviation of human suffering, particularly among disadvantaged children; and the human services works of the Catholic Sisters through a separate entity as described under Major Projects (supportive housing, disabled, education and prevention of domestic violence).
Donald H Hubbs, Executive Director
Steven M Hilton, President

2724 Cord Foundation
E.L. Cord Foundation Center For Learning Literacy
1664 N Virginia Street
Reno, NV 89557-0208
775-784-4951
Fax: 775-784-4758
www.unr.edu/cll
Offers support for secondary and higher education, including youth organizations and cultural programs.
Donald Bear, Director/Professor

2725 Donald W Reynolds Foundation
1701 Village Center Circle
Las Vegas, NV 89134-6303
702-804-6000
Fax: 702-804-6099
Devotes funds to further the cause of free press and journalism education.
Fred Smith, Chairman
Wes Smith, Vice-Chairman

2726 EL Wiegand Foundation
Wiegand Center
165 W Liberty Street
Reno, NV 89501-1915
775-333-0310
Fax: 775-333-0314
Offers grants in of culture and the arts, organizations, health and medical institutions,

with an emphasis on Roman Catholic organizations.

Kristen A Avansino, Executive Director

2727 Las Vegas-Clark County
Library District
7060 W Windmill Lane
Las Vegas, NV 89113-2030
702-382-5280
Fax: 702-382-5491
www.lvccld.org
Member of The Foundation Center network, maintaining a collection of private foundation tax returns which provide information on the scope of grants dispensed by that particular foundation.

Daniel L Walters, Executive Director
Kelly Benavidez, Chairman

2728 Washoe County Library
301 S Center Street
Reno, NV 89501-2102
775-327-8300
Fax: 775-327-8341
www.washoe.lib.nv.us/
Member of The Foundation Center network, maintaining a collection of private foundation tax returns which provide information on the scope of grants dispensed by that particular foundation.

Fred Lokken, Chairman

New Hampshire

2729 Lincolnshire
Liberty Lane
Hampton, NH 03842
Giving is primarily for secondary school education, business school education and recreation.

William Coffey, Executive Director

2730 New Hampshire Charitable Foundation
37 Pleasant Street
Concord, NH 03301-4005
603-225-6641
Fax: 603-225-1700
info@nhcf.org
www.nhcf.org
Offers grants for charitable and educational purposes including college scholarships, existing charitable organizations, child welfare, community services, health and social services and new programs that emphasize programs rather than capital needs.

Racheal Stuart, VP Program

2731 Plymouth State College
Herbert H. Lamson Library
17 High Street
Plymouth, NH 03264-1595
603-535-2258
Fax: 603-535-2445
www.plymouth.edu/psc/library
Member of The Foundation Center network, maintaining a collection of private foundation tax returns which provide information on the scope of grants dispensed by that particular foundation.

New Jersey

2732 Community Foundation of New Jersey
Knox Hill Road
PO Box 338
Morristown, NJ 07963-0338
973-267-5533
Fax: 973-267-2903
cfnj@bellatlantic.net
www.cfnj.org
Offers support for programs that offer a path of solution of community problems in the areas of education, leadership development and human services.

Hans Dekker, President

2733 Fund for New Jersey
Kilmer Square
One Palmer Square East
Suite 303
Princeton, NJ 08542-1242
609-356-0241
Fax: 732-220-8654
www.fundfornj.org
Offers grants on projects which provide the basis of action in education, AIDS research, minorities/immigrants, public policy and community development.

Mark M Murphy, Executive Director
Kiki Jamieson, President

2734 Hoechst Celanese Foundation
Route 202-206 N
PO Box 2500
Somerville, NJ 08876
908-522-7500
Fax: 908-598-4424
Provides support for education, particularly in the sciences.

Lewis F Alpaugh, Executive Director

2735 Honeywell Foundation
101 Columbia Road
Morristown, NJ 07962-4658
973-455-2000
877-841-2840
Fax: 973-455-4807
Offers support for education, including fellowship and scholarship aid to colleges.

2736 Hyde & Watson Foundation
31-F Mountain Boulevard
Warren, NJ 07059-1454
908-753-3700
Fax: 908-753-0004
hydeandwatson@yahoo.com
Support of capital projects of lasting value which tend to increase quality, capacity, or efficiency of a grantee's programs or services, such as purchase or relocation of facilities, capital equipment, instructive materials development, and certain medical research areas. Broad fields include health, education, religion, social services, arts, and humanities. Geographic areas served include the New York City Metropolitan region and primarily Essex, Union, and Morris Counties in New Jersey.

Hunter W Corbin, President

2737 Mary Owen Borden Memorial Foundation
160 Hodge Road
Princeton, NJ 08540-3014
609-924-3637
Fax: 609-252-9472
Offers grants in the areas of childhood education, child development, education, conservation and health and human services.

Thomas Borden, Executive Director

2738 Merck Company Foundation
1 Merck Drive #100
Whitehouse Station, NJ 08889-0100
908-423-2042
www.merck.com
Offers support of education, primarily medical through community programs, grants and matching gift programs for colleges and secondary education.

John R Taylor, Executive Director
Kenneth C Fraizer, Chairman,President& CEO

2739 Prudential Foundation
Prudential Plaza
751 Broad Street
Floor 15
Newark, NJ 07102-3714
973-802-4791
www.prudential.com
Focus is on children and youth for services that can better their lives. Grants are made in the areas of education, health and human services, community and urban development, business and civic affairs, culture and the arts. Emphasis is placed on programs that serve the city of Newark and the surrounding New Jersey urban centers, programs in cities where The Prudential has a substantial presence and national programs that further the company's objectives.

Barbara L Halaburda, Executive Director

2740 Turrell Fund
21 Van Vleck Street
Montclair, NJ 07042-2358
973-783-9358
Fax: 973-783-9283
turrell@turrellfund.org
Offers grants to organizations and agencies that are dedicated to the care of children and youth under twelve years of age, with an emphasis on education, early childhood education, delinquency prevention and child and youth services.

E Belvin Williams, Executive Director

2741 Victoria Foundation
31 Mulberry Street
5th Floor
Newark, NJ 07102
973-792-9200
Fax: 793-792-1300
cmcfarvic@aol.com
www.victoriafoundation.org
Grants are limited to Newark, New Jersey in the following areas: elementary and secondary education, after school enrichment programs, teacher training and academic enrichment.

Catherine M McFarland, Executive Officer
Nancy K Zimmerman, Senior Program Officer

2742 Warner-Lambert Charitable Foundation
201 Tabor Road
Morris Plains, NJ 07950-2614
212-573-2323
Fax: 212-573-7851
Grants are given in the areas of education, health care, culture and the arts. Supports higher institutions of learning which concentrate on pharmacy, medicine, dentistry, the sciences and mathematics. Current support is aimed at the higher levels of education, but the foundation has begun to place more of its attention on the growing needs that impact elementary and secondary training.

Evelyn Self, Community Affairs
Richard Keelty, VP Investor Affair

2743 Wilf Family Foundation
820 Morris Tpke
Short Hills, NJ 07078-2619
973-467-5000

Awards grants in the areas of Jewish higher education and religion.

Joseph Wilf, Executive Director

New Mexico

44 Dale J Bellamah Foundation
PO Box 36600
Albuquerque, NM 87176-6600
858-756-1154
Fax: 858-756-3856
Offers grants for higher education including military academies, hospitals and social service organizations.

AF Potenziani, Executive Director

45 New Mexico State Library
Information Services
1209 Camino Carlos Rey
Santa Fe, NM 87507
505-476-9700
Fax: 505-476-9701
Member of The Foundation Center network, maintaining a collection of private foundation tax returns which provide information on the scope of grants dispensed by that particular foundation.

46 RD & Joan Dale Hubbard Foundation
PO Box 1679
Ruidoso Downs, NM 88346-1679
505-378-4142
Giving is offered in the areas of childhood education, elementary, secondary and higher education as well as other cultural programs.

Jim Stoddard, Executive Director

New York

747 Achelis Foundation
767 3rd Avenue
4th Floor
New York, NY 10017-2023
212-644-0322
Fax: 212-759-6510
main@achelis-bodman-fnds.org
Grants include biomedical research at Rockefeller University, rebuilding the Hayden Planetarium at the American Museum of Natural History, support for the arts and culture, the charter school movement, youth organizations, and special efforts to curb father absence and strengthen family life with awards.

Russell P Pennoyer, President
Joseph S Dolan, Executive Director

748 Adrian & Jessie Archbold Charitable Trust
401 East 60th Street
New York, NY 10022
212-371-1152
Eastern United States educational institutions and health care service organizations are the main recipients of the Trust.

Myra Mahon, Executive Director

749 Alfred P Sloan Foundation
630 5th Avenue
Suite 2550
New York, NY 10111-0100
212-649-1649
Fax: 212-757-5117
www.sloan.org
A nonprofit foundation offering Sloan Research Fellowships which are awarded in chemistry, computer science, economics, mathematics, neuroscience and physics. These are competitive grants given to young faculty members with high research potential on the recommendation of department heads and other senior scientists.

Ralph E Gomory, President

2750 Altman Foundation
521 5th Avenue
35th Floor
New York, NY 10175
212-682-0970
info@altman.org
www.altmanfoundation.org
In education, the Altman Foundation supports programs that identify, sponsor and tutor talented disadvantaged youngsters and help them to obtain educations in non-public and independent schools. The Foundation awards grants only in New York State with an almost-exclusive focus on the five boroughs of New York City. The Foundation does not award grants or scholarships to individuals.

Karen L Rosa, VP/Executive Director

2751 Ambrose Monell Foundation
C/O Fulton, Duncombe & Rowe
1 Rockefeller Plaza
Room 301
New York, NY 10020-2002
212-586-0700
Fax: 212-245-1863
www.monellvetlesen.org
Broad range of allocation including education, social service, cultural organizations and the environment.

Ambrose K Monell, Executive Director
George Rowe, President,Treasurer and Dire

2752 American Express Foundation
American Express Company
World Financial Center
New York, NY 10285
212-640-5661
The foundation's giving focuses on three areas including community service, education and employment.

Mary Beth Salerno, Executive Director
Angela Woods, Philanthropic Program

2753 Andrew W Mellon Foundation
140 E 62nd Street
New York, NY 10065-8187
212-838-8400
Fax: 212-888-4172
www.mellon.org
Offers grants in the areas of higher education, cultural affairs and public affairs.

W.Taylor Revely, President
Lewis W Bernard, Chairman

2754 Arnold Bernhard Foundation
220 E 42nd Street
Floor 6
New York, NY 10017-5806
212-907-1500
Offers funding in the areas of education with the emphasis placed on college and universities as well as college preparatory schools.

Jean B Buttner, Executive Director

2755 Atran Foundation
23-25 East 21st Street
3rd Floor
New York, NY 10010
212-505-9677
Offers grants and funding to nonprofit educational and religious organizations.

2756 Beatrice P Delany Charitable Trust
The Chase Manhattan Bank
1211 Avenue of the Americas
34th Floor
New York, NY 10036
212-935-9935
Giving is offered for education, especially higher education and religion.

John HF Enteman, Executive Director

2757 Bodman Foundation
767 3rd Avenue
4th Floor
New York, NY 10017-2023
212-644-0322
Fax: 212-759-6510
main@achelis-bodman-fnds.org
Grants include biomedical research at Rockefeller University, building the Congo Gorilla Forest Education Center at the Bronx Zoo through the Wildlife Conservation Society, rebuilding of the Hayden Planetarium for Science and Technology at the American Museum of Natural History, support for Symphony Space, the charter school movement, youth organizations, and the Rutgers University Foundation.

John N Irwin III, Chairman
John B Krieger, Executive Director

2758 Bristol-Myers Squibb Foundation
345 Park Avenue
Floor 43
New York, NY 10154-0004
212-546-4331
www.bms.com
Offers support for elementary and secondary school, math and science education reform, civic affairs and health care.

Cindy Johnson, Executive Director
Lamberto Andreotti, Chief Executive Officer

2759 Buffalo & Erie County Public Library
History Department
Lafayette Square
Buffalo, NY 14203
716-858-8900
Fax: 716-858-6211
www.buffalolib.org
Member of The Foundation Center network, maintaining a collection of private foundation tax returns which provide information on the scope of grants dispensed by that particular foundation.

Michael C Mahaney, Director

2760 Caleb C & Julia W Dula Educational & Charitable Foundation
C/O Chemical Bank
112 S Hanley RD
St Louis, MO 63105-3418
212-270-9066
Offers grants to charities with an emphasis on secondary and higher education.

G Price-Fitch, Executive Director

2761 Capital Cities-ABC Corporate Giving Program
77 W 66th St
New York, NY 10023-6201
212-456-7498
Fax: 212-456-7909
Offers support in adult education, literary and basic skills, reading, and AIDS research.

Bernadette Longford Williams, Executive Director

2762 Carl & Lily Pforzheimer Foundation
950 Third Ave
30th Floor
New York, NY 10022-2705
212-764-0655
Offers support primarily for higher and secondary education, cultural programs, public administration, and health care.
Carl H Pforzheimer III, Executive Director

2763 Carnegie Corporation of New York
437 Madison Avenue
New York, NY 10022-7001
212-374-3200
Fax: 212-754-4073
www.carnegie.org
The foundation has several program goals including education and healthy development of children and youth, including early childhood health and education, early adolescence educational achievement, science education and education reform.
Janet L Robinson, President
Kurt L Schmoke, Vice-Chairman

2764 Chase Manhattan Corporation Philanthropy Department
1 Chase Manhattan Plaza
Floor 9
New York, NY 10005-1401
212-552-7087
Offers support to various organizations to enhance the well-being of the communities Chase Manahattan serves. Grants are awarded in the areas of education, youth services, community and economic development, homeless, library science, health care and housing development.
Steven Gelston, Executive Director

2765 Christian A Johnson Endeavor Foundation
1060 Park Avenue
New York, NY 10128-1008
212-534-6620
Offers support to private institutions of higher education at the baccalaureate level and on educational outreach programs.
Wilmot H Kidd, Executive Director

2766 Cleveland H Dodge Foundation
420 Lexington Avenue
Suite 2331
New York, NY 10170-3292
212-972-2800
Fax: 212-972-1049
www.chdodgefoundation.org
Bestows funding for nonprofit organizations aimed at improving higher education and youth organizations.
William D Rueckert, President
Bayard Dodge, Vice-President

2767 Cowles Charitable Trust
P.O Box 219
Rumson, NJ 07760
732-936-9826
www.www1.mville.edu/Grants/GrantDescriptionPages/Cowles.htm
Funding for higher education and cultural organizations.
Gardner Cowles, President

2768 Daisy Marquis Jones Foundation
1600 S Avenue
Suite 250
Rochester, NY 14620-3921
585-461-4950
Fax: 585-461-9752
mail@dmjf.org
www.dmjf.org
Offers grants for nonprofit organizations focusing on improving the lives of children, youth and the elderly, in Monroe and Yates counties in New York State.
Donald W Whitney, President
Marless A Honan, Administrative Assistant

2769 DeWitt Wallace-Reader's Digest Fund
5 Penn Plaza
7th Floor
New York, NY 10001-9301
212-251-9700
Fax: 212-679-6990
The mission of this foundation is to invest in programs and projects that enhance the quality of educational and career development opportunities for all school-age youth.
M Christine De Vita, President

2770 Edna McConnell Clark Foundation
415 Madison Avenue
10th Floor
New York, NY 10017
212-551-9100
Fax: 212-421-9325
www.emcf.org
Supports select youth, serving organizations working with children 9-24 during the non-school hours.
Michael Bailin, President

2771 Edward John Noble Foundation
32 E 57th Street
Floor 19
New York, NY 10022-2513
212-759-4212
Fax: 212-888-4531
Offers grants to major cultural organizations in New York City, especially for arts educational programs and management training internships.
June Noble Larkin, Chairman

2772 Edward W Hazen Foundation
333 Seventh Avenue
14 th Floor
New York, NY 10001
212-889-3034
Fax: 212-889-3039
hazen@hazenfoundation.org
www.hazenfoundation.org
The foundation focuses giving on public education and youth development in the area of public education.
Lori Bezahler, President
Sonia Jarvis, Chairman

2773 Edwin Gould Foundation for Children
126 East 31st Street
New York, NY 10016
212-251-0907
Fax: 212-982-6886
Supports projects that promote the welfare and education of children. Interests lies in early childhood education, higher education, children and youth services and family services.
Michael W Osheowitz, Executive Director

2774 Elaine E & Frank T Powers Jr Foundation
81 Skunks Misery Road
Locust Valley, NY 11560-1306
Offers support in the areas of secondary and higher education as well as youth services.

2775 Elmer & Mamdouha Bobst Foundation
Elmer Holmes Bobst Library, NYU
70 Washington Square S
New York, NY 10012-1019
212-998-2440
Fax: 212-995-4070
Offers grants and funding in the areas of youth, community development and the arts.

2776 Equitable Foundation
3rd Floor Champaca II Building
162 L.P Leviste Street, Salcedo Village
Makati City 10019-6018
mail@equitablefoundation.com
www.equitablefoundation.com
Offers grants in the areas of secondary school education, arts, community services, art and cultural programs, and higher education.
Kathleen A Carlson, Executive Director
Darlene Ramos, Administrative Assistant

2777 Ford Foundation
320 E 43rd Street
New York, NY 10017-4890
212-573-5000
Fax: 212-351-3677
www.fordfound.org
Offers grants to advance public well-being and educational opportunities. Grants are given in the areas of education, secondary school/education, early childhood education, development services, human services, citizenship, academics and more.
Barron M Tenny, Secretary
Luis Ubinas, President

2778 Frances & Benjamin Benenson Foundation
C/O Door County Community Foundation
P.O. Box 802
Sturgeon Bay, WI 54235-1006
920-746-1786
Fax: 212-755-0021
www.benensoncapital.com
Offers grants in elementary/secondary education, higher education and human services.
Cynthia Green Colin, Executive Director

2779 George F Baker Trust
C/O JPMorgan Chase Bank
N.A Philanthropic Services
270 Park Avenue
New York, NY 10017
212-473-1587
Fax: 212-464-2305
jonathan.q.horowitz@jpmchase.com
Offers giving in the areas of higher and secondary education, social services, civic affairs and international affairs.
Monica J Neal, Vice President

2780 George Link Jr Foundation
10 Rockefeller Plaza
16th Floor
New York, NY 10020
212-713-7654
Fax: 212-645-4055
Giving is primarily centered on higher education, secondary school/education and medical research.
Eve Weiss, Executive Director

2781 Gladys & Roland Harriman Foundation
51 Madison Avenue
30 th Floor
New York, NY 10010-1202
212-489-7700
Fax: 212-581-9541
hlf1@hluce.org

Giving is centered on education and support for youth and social service agencies.

Michael Gilligan, President
Margaret B Fitzgerald, Chairman

82 Glady Brooks Foundation

1055 Franklin Avenue
Garden City, NY 11530
212-943-3217
www.gladysbrooksfoundation.org
The purpose of this foundation is to provide for the intellectual, moral and physical welfare of the people of this country by establishing and supporting nonprofit libraries, educational institutions, hospitals and clinics. In the area of education, grant applications will be considered generally for (a) educational endowments to fund scholarships based solely on leadership and academic ability of the student; (b) endowments to support salaries of educators.

Harman Hawkins, Chairman
Robert E Hill, Executive Director

'83 Green Fund

14 E 60th Street
Suite 702
New York, NY 10022-1006
212-755-2445
Fax: 212-755-0021
Offers grants in the area of higher and secondary education.

Cynthia Green Colin, Executive Director

'84 Hagedorn Fund

C/O JPMorgan Private Bank
Private Foundation Services
270 Park Avenue, 16th floor
New York, NY 10017
212-473-1587
Fax: 212-464-2304
g.horowitz@jpmorgan.com
www.fdnweb.org
Offers support for higher and secondary education, youth agencies and social service agencies.

Jonathan Horowitz, Program Officer

785 Hasbro Children's Foundation

10 Rockefeller Plaza
16th Floor
New York, NY 10020
212-713-7654
888-836-7025
Fax: 212-645-4055
www.hasbro.org
Offers support to improve the quality of life for children. Areas of interest include education, AIDS research, literacy, special education, and youth services.

Eve Weiss, Executive Director

786 Henry Luce Foundation

51 Madison Avenue, 30th Floor
New York, NY 10010
212-489-7700
Fax: 212-581-9541
hlf1@hluce.org
www.hluce.org
Offers grants for specific programs and projects in the areas of higher education and scholarship, social sciences at private colleges and universities, American arts and public affairs.

Michael Gilligan, President
Ellen Holtzman, Program Director

787 Herman Goldman Foundation

61 Broadway
Floor 18
New York, NY 10006-2701
212-797-9090
Fax: 212-797-9161
This foundation offers grants in the areas of social, legal and organizational approaches to aid for deprived or handicapped people; education for new or improved counseling for effective pre-school, vocational, and paraprofessional training; and the arts.

Richard K Baron, Executive Director

2788 Hess Foundation

1185 Avenue of the Americas
New York, NY 10036-2601
212-997-8500
Fax: 212-536-8390
webmaster@hess.com
www.hess.com
Offers grants that focus on higher education, performing arts, and welfare organizations.

Leon Hess, Executive Director

2789 Horace W Goldsmith Foundation

375 Park Avenue
Suite 1602
New York, NY 10152-1699
212-319-8700
800-319-2881
Fax: 212-319-2881
Offers giving and support for education, higher education, cultural programs and museums.

James C Slaughter, Executive Director

2790 IBM Corporate Support Program

Old Orchard Road
Armonk, NY 10504
914-765-1900
The mission of this fund is to improve the areas and the communities that IBM operates in. Grants are awarded in various areas including early childhood education, elementary education, secondary education, business school/education, and engineering school/education.

Stanley Litow, Executive Director

2791 JI Foundation

C/O Patterson, Belknap, Webb & Tyler
1133 Avenue of the Americas
New York, NY 10036
212-336-2000
Offers grants in the areas of elementary education, higher education, and general charitable giving.

2792 JP Morgan Charitable Trust

60 Wall Street
Floor 46
New York, NY 10005-2836
212-648-9673
Offers support in the area of education, housing, economic development, advocacy and international affairs.

Roberta Ruocco, Executive Director

2793 Joukowsky Family Foundation

410 Park Avenue
Suite 1610
New York, NY 10022-4407
212-355-3151
Fax: 212-355-3147
www.joukowsky.org
Giving is focused on higher and secondary education.

Nina J Koprulu, Director/President
Emily R Kessler, Executive Director

2794 Julia R & Estelle L Foundation

1 HSBC Center
Suite 3650
Buffalo, NY 14203-1217
716-856-9490
Fax: 716-856-9493
www.oisheifdt.org
This fund offers grants in the areas of higher and secondary education, medical research, social services and support agencies.

Thomas E Baker, President
James M Wadsworth, Chairman

2795 Leon Lowenstein Foundation

575 Madison Avenue
New York, NY 10022-3613
212-605-0444
Fax: 212-688-0134
Support is given for New York City public education and medical research.

John F Van Gorder, Executive Director

2796 Levittown Public Library

1 Bluegrass Lane
Levittown, NY 11756-1292
516-579-8585
Fax: 516-735-3168
www.nassaulibrary.org/levtown/
Member of The Foundation Center network, maintaining a collection of private foundation tax returns which provide information on the scope of grants dispensed by that particular foundation.

Margaret Santer, President

2797 Louis & Anne Abrons Foundation

C/O First Manhattan Company
437 Madison Avenue
New York, NY 10022-7001
212-756-3376
Fax: 212-832-6698
Offers support in the areas of education, improvement programs, environmental and cultural projects.

Richard Abrons, Executive Director

2798 Margaret L Wendt Foundation

40 Fountain Plaza
Suite 277
Buffalo, NY 14202-2200
716-855-2146
Fax: 716-855-2149
Offers various grants with an emphasis on education, the arts and social services in Buffalo and Western New York.

Robert J Kresse, Executive Director

2799 New York Foundation

10 East 34th Street
10 th Floor
New York, NY 10016-2996
212-594-8009
Fax: 212-594-5918
www.nyf.org
Provides support for the implementation of programs that offer support for the quality of life including educational services, health organizations, centers and services, civil rights, public policy, research and more.

Maria Mottola, Executive Director
Melissa Hall, Operations Manager

2800 Palisades Educational Foundation

C/O Gibney, Anthony & Flaherty
665 5th Avenue
Floor 2
New York, NY 10022-5305
Offers support for secondary and higher education in New York, New Jersey and Connecticut.

Ralph F Anthony, Executive Director

2801 Robert Sterling Clark Foundation

135 E 64th Street
New York, NY 10065-7307

212-288-8900
Fax: 212-288-1033
rscf@rsclark.org
www.rsclark.org
For more than 15 years, this foundation has provided support to New York City's cultural community. During this time, the Foundation has tried to structure a grants program so that it is flexible and meets the needs of the institutions and organizations. Grants are given in the areas of cultural institutions, arts advocacy, family planning services and supporting new initiatives in the area of arts and education.

Margaret C Ayers, President
James A Smith, Chairman

2802 Rochester Public Library
Business, Economics & Law
115 S Avenue
Rochester, NY 14604-1896
585-428-8045
Fax: 585-428-8353
Member of The Foundation Center network, maintaining a collection of private foundation tax returns which provide information on the scope of grants dispensed by that particular foundation.

Emeterio M Otero, President

2803 Ronald S Lauder Foundation
Rykestrasse 53
10405 Berlin
Berlin 10153-0023
212-572-6966
www.lauderfoundation.com
Offers giving in the areas of elementary/secondary education, human services and religion.

Marjorie S Federbush, Executive Director
Ronald S Lauder, Chairman & President

2804 SH & Helen R Scheuer Family Foundation
350 5th Avenue
Suite 3410
New York, NY 10118-0110
212-947-9009
Fax: 212-947-9770
Offers support in the areas of higher education, welfare funding and cultural programs.

2805 Samuel & May Rudin Foundation
345 Park Avenue
New York, NY 10154-0004
212-407-2544
Fax: 212-407-2540
Offers support for higher education, social services, religious welfare agencies, hospitals and cultural programs.

Susan H Rapaport, Executive Director

2806 Seth Sprague Educational and Charitable Foundation
C/O U.S. Trust Company of New York
114 W 47th Street
New York, NY 10036-1510
212-852-3683
Fax: 212-852-3377
Offers support in the areas of education, culture, the arts, human services, community development and government/public administration.

Maureen Augusciak, Executive Director

2807 Starr Foundation
399 Park Avenue
17th Floor
New York, NY 10022-0002
212-909-3600
Fax: 212-750-3536
Support is given for educational projects with an emphasis on higher education, including scholarships under specific programs.

Ta Chun Hsu, Executive Director
Florence A Davis, President

2808 Tiger Foundation
101 Park Avenue
47th Floor
New York, NY 10178-0002
212-984-2565
Fax: 212-949-9778
info@tigerfoundation.org
www.tigerfoundation.org
Support is given primarily for early childhood education, youth programs and job training.

Phoebe Boyer, Executive Director

2809 Tisch Foundation
667 Madison Avenue
New York, NY 10021-8029
212-545-2000
Support is given in the area of education, especially higher education, and includes institutions in Israel and research-related programs.

Laurence A Tisch, Executive Director

2810 Travelers Group
388 Greenwich Street
New York, NY 10013-2375
212-816-8000
Fax: 212-816-5944
The main purpose of this foundation is to support public education, offering grants in the communities that the company serves.

Dee Topol, Executive Director

2811 White Plains Public Library
100 Martine Avenue
White Plains, NY 10601-2599
914-422-1400
Fax: 914-422-1462
www.whiteplainslibrary.org
Member of The Foundation Center network, maintaining a collection of private foundation tax returns which provide information on the scope of grants dispensed by that particular foundation.

2812 William Randolph Hearst Foundation
300 West 57th Street
26th Floor
New York, NY 10019-3741
212-649-3750
Fax: 212-586-1917
heart.ny@hearstfdn.org
www.hearstfdn.org
Offers support to programs that aid priority-level and minority groups, educational programs especially private secondary and higher education, health systems and cultural programs.

Paul Dinovitz, Executive Director
Ligia Cravo, Senior Program Officer

2813 William T Grant Foundation
570 Lexington Avenue
Floor 18
New York, NY 10022-6837
212-752-0071
Fax: 212-752-1398
info@wtgrantfdn.org
www.wtgrantfoundation.org
The goal of the foundation is to help create a society that values people and helps them to reach their potenial. The Foundation is interested in environmentally friendly approaches

Edward Seidman, Senior VP Programs
Robert Granger, President

North Carolina

2814 AE Finley Foundation
P.O. Box 98266
Raleigh, NC 27624-8266
919-782-0565
Fax: 919-782-6978
Private foundation contributing and supporting to charitable, scientific, literary, religious and educational organizations. It endeavors to contribute to soundly managed and operated qualifying organizations which fundamentally give service with a broad scope and impact, aid all kinds of people and contribute materially to the general welfare.

Robert C Brown, Executive Director

2815 Cannon Foundation
PO Box 548
Concord, NC 28026-0548
704-786-8216
Fax: 704-785-2052
info@cannonfoundation.org
www.thecannonfoundationinc.org
Offers support for higher and secondary education, cultural programs, and grants to social service and youth agencies.

Frank Davis, Executive Director
William C Cannon Jr, President

2816 Dickson Foundation
301 S Tryon Street
Suite 1800
Charlotte, NC 28202
704-372-5404
Fax: 704-372-6409
Main focus is on areas of education & healthcare. Considers funding programs in the Southeast.

Susan Patterson, Secretary/Treasurer

2817 Duke Endowment
100 N Tryon Street
Suite 3500
Charlotte, NC 28202-4012
704-376-0291
Fax: 704-376-9336
www.dukeendowment.org
Support is given to higher education, children and youth services, churches and hospitals.

Eugene W Cochrane Jr, Executive Director
Minor M Shaw, Chairman

2818 First Union University
Two 1st Union Center
Charlotte, NC 28288
704-374-6868
Fax: 704-374-4147
Offers support for higher education and special programs for public elementary and secondary schools.

Ann D Thomas, Executive Director

2819 Foundation for the Carolinas
220 N Tryon Street
Charlotte, NC 28202
704-973-4500
800-973-7244
Fax: 704-376-1243
www.fftc.org
Offers support for education, the arts and health in North Carolina and South Carolina.

Ron Carter, President/CEO
Catherine P Bessant, Chairman

20 Kathleen Price and Joseph M Bryan Family Foundation
3101 N Elm Street
Greensboro, NC 27408-3184
336-288-5455
Grants are primarily offered in the fields of higher, secondary, and early childhood education.
William Massey, Executive Director

21 Mary Reynolds Babcock Foundation
2920 Reynolda Road
Winston Salem, NC 27106-4618
336-748-9222
Fax: 336-777-0095
www.mrbf.org
This foundation traditionally provides funds to programs in education, social services, the environment, the arts and citizen participation in the development of public policy. The foundation prefers to fund programs of two kinds: those particularly sensitive to the changing and emerging needs of society and those addressing society's oldest needs in new and imaginative ways.
Gayle W Dorman, Executive Director
Sandra H Mikush, Assitant Director

22 Non-Profit Resource Center/Pack Memorial Library
Learning Resources Center
67 Haywood Street
Asheville, NC 28801-4897
828-254-4960
Fax: 828-251-2258
Cooperating collection of the Foundation Center. Other resources for non-profit organizations are also available.
Ed Sheary, Library Director

23 State Library of North Carolina
Government & Business Services
109 E Jones Street
Raleigh, NC 27601-2806
919-807-7450
Fax: 919-733-5679
Member of The Foundation Center network, maintaining a collection of private foundation tax returns which provide information on the scope of grants dispensed by that particular foundation.

24 William R Kenan Jr Charitable Trust
Kenan Center
PO Box 3858
Chapel Hill, NC 27515-3858
919-962-0343
Fax: 919-962-3331
The focus of this foundation is on education, primarily at private institutions in the US. The emphasis now is on national literacy and the importance of early childhood education. Grants have just established an institute for the arts and an institute for engineering, technology and science. No grants are given to individuals for scholarships, for research or other special projects or for medical, public health or social welfare projects. This Trust does not accept unsolicited requests.
William C Friday, Executive Director

825 Winston-Salem Foundation
860 W 5th Street
Winston Salem, NC 27101-2506
336-725-2382
Fax: 336-727-0581
www.wsfoundation.org
Educational grants and loans to residents of Forsyth County, North Carolina in most areas.
Scott Wierman, President
Donna Rader, VP Grants & Programs

2826 Z Smith Reynolds Foundation
102 West Third Street
Suite 1110
Winston Salem, NC 27101-3940
336-725-7541
800-443-8319
Fax: 336-725-6069
www.zsr.org
Grants are limited to the state of North Carolina. General purpose foundation provides for their current priorities including community economic development, women's issues, minority issues, environment and pre-collegiate education. No grants are given to individuals.
Thomas W Ross, Executive Director

North Dakota

2827 Myra Foundation
PO Box 13536
Grand Forks, ND 58208-3536
701-775-9420
jbotsford@myrafoundation.org
www.myrafoundation.org
Offers grants in the areas of secondary school, and higher education to residents of Grand Forks County, North Dakota.
Edward C Gillig, Executive Director

2828 Tom & Frances Leach Foundation
1720 Burnt Boat Drive
PO Box 1136
Bismarck, ND 58502-1136
701-255-0479
www.leachfoundation.org
Offers grants in the areas of higher and other education in North Dakota.
Clement C Weber, Executive Director

Ohio

2829 Akron Community Foundation
345 W Cedar Street
Akron, OH 44307-2407
330-376-8522
Fax: 330-376-0202
acf_fund@ix.netcom.com
www.akroncommunityfdn.org
The foundation receives donations to permanent endowment and makes grants to qualified nonprofit organizations within Summit County, Ohio.
Jody Bacon, President

2830 American Foundation Corporation
720 National City Bank Building
Cleveland, OH 44114
216-241-6664
Fax: 216-241-6693
Offers support in the areas of higher and secondary education, the arts and community funds.
Maria G Muth, Executive Director

2831 Burton D Morgan Foundation
22 Aurora Street
Hudson, OH 44236-1500
330-655-1660
Fax: 330-655-1673
admin@bdmorganfdn.org
www.bdmorganfdn.org
The foundation's present areas of interest include economics, education, mental health and organizations principally located in Northeast Ohio. No grants are made to individuals and few grants are made to social service organizations.
Deborah D Hoover, President
Denise M Griggs, Chief Financial Officer

2832 Dayton Foundation
500 Kettering Tower
Dayton, OH 45423-1395
937-222-0410
Fax: 937-222-0636
info@daytonfoundation.org
www.daytonfoundation.org
Educational and community service grants.
Michael M Parks, President
Ellen S Ireland, Vice-Chairman

2833 Eva L & Joseph M Bruening Foundation
1422 Euclid Avenue
Suite 966
Cleveland, OH 44115-1952
216-621-2632
Fax: 216-621-8198
www.fmscleveland.com/bruening
Support is offered in the fields of education, early childhood education, education fund-raising, higher education, youth services and health agencies.
Janet E Narten, Executive Director
Karen Noster, Chairman

2834 GAR Foundation
Andrew Jackson House
277 East Mill Street
Akron, OH 44308-1828
330-576-2926
800-686-2825
Fax: 330-437-2843
info@garfdn.org
Established in 1967 as a charitable trust, the foundation offers grants to organizations located primarily in Akron, Ohio area or, secondarily, in Northeastern Ohio or elsewhere in the United States at the discretion of the Distribution Committee. Grants for research projects of educational or scientific institutions, capital improvement projects, or matching campaigns are the priorities of this foundation.
Richard A Chenoweth, Executive Director
Robert W Briggs, Co-Trustee

2835 George Gund Foundation
1845 Guildhall Building
45 Prospect Avenue
West Cleveland, OH 44115
216-241-3114
Fax: 216-241-6560
info@gundfdn.org
www.gundfdn.org
The primary interest of this foundation is in educational projects, with an emphasis on inventive movements in teaching and learning, and on increasing educational opportunities for the disadvantaged.
David Abbott, Executive Director
Marcia Egbert, Senior Program Officer

2836 Hoover Foundation
101 E Maple Street
North Canton, OH 44720-2517
330-499-9499
Fax: 330-497-5065

Offers grants for elementary education, secondary and higher education and youth agencies.

LR Hoover, Executive Director
Annette Bravard, Vice President of Marketing

2837 Kettering Fund
1480 Kettering Tower
Dayton, OH 45423-1001
937-228-1021
888-719-1185
www.cfketteringfamilies.com
Support is offered for social and educational studies and research as well as community development and cultural programs.

Judith M Thompson, Executive Director

2838 Kulas Foundation
Tower City Center
50 Public Square
Suite 600
Cleveland, OH 44113-2267
216-623-4770
Fax: 216-623-4773
www.fdncenter.org/grantmaker/kulas/
A major general interest foundation, but with an emphasis on music. Giving is limited to Cuyahoga County and its surrounding area. Provides support to musical educational programs at Baldwin Wallace College, Case Western Reserve University and Cleveland Institute of Music. Also provides tickets to cultural programs to students in 16 colleges and universities in the area. The Foundation does not provide grants or loans to individuals. Support is geared to local primary and secondary schools.

Nancy W McCann, President/Treasurer

2839 Louise H & David S Ingalls Foundation
20600 Chagrin Boulevard
Suite 301
Shaker Heights, OH 44122-5334
216-921-6000
Offers support to organizations whose primary interest in the improvement of the educational, physical and mental condition of humanity throughout the world. Grants are given in secondary, elementary, and educational research.

Jane W Watson, Executive Director

2840 Louise Taft Semple Foundation
425 Walnut Street
Suite 1800
Cincinnati, OH 45202-3948
513-381-2838
Fax: 513-381-0205
Support is offered in the areas of secondary school/education, higher education, human services and health care organizations.

Dudley S Taft, Executive Director

2841 Martha Holden Jennings Foundation
Advisory & Distribution Committee Office
1228 Euclid Avenue
Suite 710
Cleveland, OH 44115-1831
216-589-5700
Fax: 216-589-5730
www.mhjf.org
The purpose of this foundation is to foster the development of young people to the maximum possible extent through improving the quality of teaching in secular elementary and secondary schools.

William T Hiller, Executive Director
Kathy L Kooyman, Grants Manager

2842 Mead Corporation Foundation
Courthouse Plz NE
Dayton, OH 45463-0001
937-495-3883
Fax: 937-495-4103
Grants are given to elementary, secondary, higher and minority education.

Ronald F Budzik, Executive Director

2843 Nord Family Foundation
747 Milan Avenue
Amherst, OH 44001
440-984-3939
Fax: 440-984-3934
www.nordff.org
Offers support for a variety of programs, including giving for early childhood, secondary, and higher education, social services, cultural affairs and civic activities.

David R Ashenhurst, Executive Director

2844 Ohio Bell Telephone Contribution Program
45 Erieview Plaza
Room 870
Cleveland, OH 44114-1814
216-822-4445
800-257-0902
Offers support of elementary school/education, secondary school/education, higher education, literacy and basic skills.

William W Boag Jr, Executive Director

2845 Ohio State Library Foundation Center
Kent H. Smith Library
1480 West Lane Avenue
Columbus, OH 43221-2001
614-292-2141
Member of The Foundation Center network, maintaining a collection of private foundation tax returns which provide information on the scope of grants dispensed by that particular foundation.

John B Gerlach, Chairman & CEO
Martin Murrer, Vice-Chairman

2846 Owens-Corning Foundation
PO Box 1688
Toledo, OH 43603-1688
419-248-8000
Fax: 419-325-4273
Offers support for education, including religious schools and science and technology programs.

Emerson J Ross, Executive Director

2847 Procter & Gamble Fund
200 West Fourth Street
Cincinnati, OH 45202-2775
513-241-2880
Fax: 513-983-8250
info@gcfdn.org
www.gcfdn.org
Always considers the interests of the company's employees helping in the community, the arts, improving of schools and universities and to meet the needs of the less-fortunate neighbors. Some donations into the education program include grants to the United Negro College Fund, The National Hispanic Scholarship Fund, The Leadership Conference on Civil Rights Education Fund and more than 600 colleges and universities.

RL Wehling, President
G Talbot, VP

2848 Public Library of Cincinnati
Grants Resource Center
800 Vine Street #Library
Cincinnati, OH 45202-2009
513-369-6900
Fax: 513-665-3384
www.cincinnatilibrary.org
Member of The Foundation Center network, maintaining a collection of private foundation tax returns which provide information on the scope of grants dispensed by that particular foundation.

Kimber L Fender, Director

2849 Thomas J Emery Memorial
Frost & Jacobs
201 E 5th Street
Suite 2500
Cincinnati, OH 45202-4113
513-621-3124
Offers support in secondary school/education, higher education, health care, human services and arts/cultural programs.

Henry W Hobson Jr, Executive Director

2850 Timken Foundation of Canton
200 Market Avenue N
Suite 210
Canton, OH 44702-1622
330-452-1144
Fax: 330-455-1752
Offers support to promote the broad civic betterment including the areas of education, conservation and recreation. Grants restricted to caption projects only.

Don D Dickes, Secretary
Nancy Kuvdsen

2851 Wolfe Associates
34 S 3rd Street
Columbus, OH 43215-4201
614-461-5220
Fax: 614-469-6126
The foundation supports those organizations whose programs educate the individual and cultivate the individual's ability to participate in and contribute to the community or which enhance the quality of life which the community can offer to its citizens. The foundation has six general program areas in which it focuses its support: health and medicine, religion, education, culture, community service and environment.

AK Pierce Jr, Executive Director

Oklahoma

2852 Grace & Franklin Bernsen Foundation
15 W 6th Street
Suite 1308
Tulsa, OK 74119-5407
918-584-4711
Fax: 918-584-4713
gfbersen@aol.com
www.bernsen.org
The foundation is limited by its policies to support of nonprofit organizations within the metropolitan area of Tulsa. The foundation discourages applications for general support or reduction of debt or for continuing or additional support for the same programs, although a single grant may cover several years. No grant is made to individuals or for the benefit of specific individuals and the applications must be received before the twelfth of each month.

John Strong Jr, Trustee

53 Mervin Bovaird Foundation
100 W 5th Street
Suite 800
Tulsa, OK 74103-4291
918-583-1777
Fax: 918-592-5809
Awards scholarships to the University of Tulsa. Recipients are selected by Tulsa Area high schools and by Tulsa Junior College. No individual grants are made.

R Casey Cooper, President

54 Oklahoma City University
Dulaney Brown Library
2501 N Blackwelder Avenue
Oklahoma City, OK 73106-1493
405-521-5000
Fax: 405-521-5291
www.okcu.edu
Member of The Foundation Center network, maintaining a collection of private foundation tax returns which provide information on the scope of grants dispensed by that particular foundation.

Victoria Swinney, Director

55 Public Service Company of Oklahoma Corporate Giving Program
212 E 6th Street #201
Tulsa, OK 74119-1295
918-586-0420
Offers support in the areas of elementary, secondary and higher education.

Mary Polfer, Executive Director

56 Samuel Roberts Noble Foundation
2510 Sam Noble Parkway
Ardmore, OK 73401-2180
580-223-5810
Fax: 580-224-6380
www.noble.org
Offers support in the areas of higher education, agricultural research, human services and educational grants for health research pertaining to degenerative diseases, cancer and for health delivery systems.

Michael A Cawley, Executive Director
Emily Bynum, Administrative Assistant

Oregon

857 Collins Foundation
1618 SW 1st Avenue
Suite 305
Portland, OR 97201-5708
503-227-7171
Fax: 503-295-3794
www.collinsfoundation.org
Offers general support with an emphasis on higher education, hospices and health agencies, youth programs and arts and culture.

Cynthia G Adams, Executive Vice President
Cindy Knowles, Director Of Programs

858 Ford Family Foundation
1600 NW Stewart Parkway
Roseburg, OR 97471-1957
541-957-5574
Fax: 541-957-5720
info@tfff.org
www.tfff.org
Giving is centered on education, youth organizations and human service programs in Oregon and Siskiyou County in California.

Bart Howard, Director Scholarship Program
Sarah Reeve, Scholarship Program Officer

2859 Meyer Memorial Trust
425 NW 10th Avenue
Suite 400
Portland, OR 97209
503-228-5512
Fax: 503-228-5840
mmt@mmt.org
www.mmt.org
The Trust operates three different funding programs, all of which are restricted primarily to Oregon: 1) a broad-based General Purpose program that provides funds for education, arts, and humanities, health, social welfare, community development, and other activities; 2) a Small Grants program that provides up to $12,000 for small projects in the general purpose categories; and 3) the Support for Teacher Initiatives program, which provides grants of up to $7,000- to teachers.

Doug Stamm, Executive Director
Cathie Glennon, Executive Assistant

2860 Multnomah County Library
Government Documents
801 SW 10th Avenue
Portland, OR 97205-2597
503-988-5123
Fax: 503-988-8014
www.multcolib.org
Member of The Foundation Center network, maintaining a collection of private foundation tax returns which provide information on the scope of grants dispensed by that particular foundation.

2861 Oregon Community Foundation
1221 SW Yamhill
Suite 100
Portland, OR 97205
503-227-6846
Fax: 503-274-7771
www.ocfl.org
The purpose of this foundation is to improve the cultural, educational and social needs in all levels of society throughout the state of Oregon.

Gregory A Chaille, Executive Director

2862 Tektronix Foundation
PO Box 1000
Wilsonville, OR 97070-1000
503-627-7111
www.tek.com
Offers support for education, especially science, math and engineering, and some limited art grants.

Jill Kirk, Executive Director

Pennsylvania

2863 Alcoa Foundation
201 Isabella Street
Pittsburgh, PA 15212-5858
412-553-4545
Fax: 412-553-4498
www.alcoa.com
Grants are given for education, arts and cultural programs.

F Worth Hobbs, Executive Director

2864 Annenberg Foundation
St. David's Center
2000 Avenue of the Stars
Suite 1000 S
Los Angeles, CA 90067-5293
310-209-4560
Fax: 310-209-1631
info@annenbergfoundation.org
www.annenbergfoundation.org
Primary support is given to childhood and K-12 education.

Dr. Gail C Levin Sr, Executive Director
Wallis Annenberg, Chairman

2865 Arcadia Foundation
105 E Logan Street
Norristown, PA 19401-3058
215-275-8460
www.arcadiafoundation.org
Gives only in Eastern Pennsylvania, no personal scholarships, accepts proposals only between June 1-August 15. These will be considered for the following calendar year. Proposal has to be no more than 2 pages long and longer submissions will be discarded. Must have a copy of the IRS tax-identified letter with no other enclosures.

Marilyn Lee Steinbright, Executive Director

2866 Audrey Hillman Fisher Foundation
2000 Grant Building
Pittsburgh, PA 15219
412-338-3466
Fax: 412-338-3463
Offers support for secondary school/education, higher education, rehabilitation, science and engineering.

Ronald W Wertz, Executive Director

2867 Bayer Corporation
100 Bayer Court
Pittsburgh, PA 15205
412-777-2000
Fax: 412-777-3468
www.bayerus.com/about/community/
Support is given primarily in education, especially science programs, chemistry and the arts.

Rebecca Lucore, Executive Director

2868 Buhl Foundation
650 Smithfield Street
Pittsburgh, PA 15222-1207
412-566-2711
Fax: 412-566-2714
buhl@buhlfoundation.org
www.buhlfoundation.org
Grants are given to colleges and universities, secondary schools and educational associations, community educational and training programs, and other community programs offering health and education to the community. Grants are not made for building funds, overhead costs, accumulated deficits, ordinary operating budgets, general fund-raising campaigns, loans, scholarships and fellowships, other foundations, nationally funded organized groups or individuals.

Dr. Doreen Boyce, President

2869 Connelly Foundation
One Tower Bridge
Suite 1450
West Conshohocken, PA 19428-2873
610-834-3222
Fax: 610-834-0866
www.connellyfdn.org
Offers support for education, health, human service, culture and civic programs to non-profit organizations located in the city of Philadelphia and the greater Delaware Valley region.

Victoria K Flaville, VP Administration
Josephine C Mandeville, President/CEO

2870 Eden Hall Foundation
Pittsburgh Office And Research Park
600 Grant Street
Suite 3232
Pittsburgh, PA 15219

412-642-6697
Fax: 412-642-6698
www.edenhallfdn.org
This foundation offers support for higher education, social welfare and the improvement of conditions of the poor and needy.

Sylvia V Fields, Program Director
George C Greer, Chairman/President

2871 Erie County Library System
160 E Front Street
Erie, PA 16507-1554
814-451-6927
Fax: 814-451-6969
Member of The Foundation Center network, maintaining a collection of private foundation tax returns which provide information on the scope of grants dispensed by that particular foundation.

2872 Foundation Center-Carnegie Library of Pittsburgh
Foundation Collection
4400 Forbes Avenue
Pittsburgh, PA 15213-4080
412-622-6277
Fax: 412-454-7001
foundati@carnegielibrary.org
Member of the Foundation Center network, of cooperating collections; providing current, factual information about grants and grantmaking organizations, and other aspects of philanthropy to the local nonprofit community.

Jim Lutton, Manager
Herb Elish, Director

2873 HJ Heinz Company Foundation
PO Box 57
Pittsburgh, PA 15230-0057
412-456-5772
Fax: 412-456-7859
www.heinz.com/jsp/foundation.jsp
Offers support for higher education, employee matching gifts, social service agencies and cultural programs.

Loretta M Oken, Executive Director

2874 John McShain Charities
540 N 17th Street
Philadelphia, PA 19130-3988
215-564-2322
Offers support for higher and secondary education, Roman Catholic church support and social welfare.

Mary McShain, Executive Director

2875 Mary Hillman Jennings Foundation
625 Stanwix Street
Apt 2203
Pittsburgh, PA 15222-1408
412-434-5606
Fax: 412-434-5907
Offers grants to schools, youth agencies, and hospitals and health associations.

Paul Euwer Jr, Executive Director

2876 McCune Foundation
750 Six PPG Place
Pittsburgh, PA 15222
412-644-8779
Fax: 412-644-8059
The foundation provides support to independent higher education and human services.

Henry S Beukema, Executive Director

2877 Pew Charitable Trusts
One Commerce Square
2005 Market Street
Suite 1700
Philadelphia, PA 19103-7077
215-575-9050
Fax: 215-575-4939
info@pewtrusts.org
www.pewtrusts.com
Offers support for education (including theology), arts culture, as well as public policy and religion.

Rebecca W Rimel, Executive Director
Robert H Campbell, Board of Director

2878 Richard King Mellon Foundation
One Mellon Bank Center
500 Grant Street
Suite 4106
Pittsburgh, PA 15219-2502
412-392-2800
Fax: 412-392-2837
www.fdncenter.org/grantmaker/rkmellon/
Offers local grant programs with an emphasis on education, social services and the environment.

Seward Prosser Mellon, Trustee/President
Bruce King Mell Henderson, President

2879 Rockwell International Corporation Trust
625 Liberty Avenue
Pittsburgh, PA 15222-3110
414-212-5200
Fax: 414-212-5201
Offers support in the areas of K-12 math and science education, and higher education in the field of engineering and science.

William R Fitz, Executive Director

2880 Samuel S Fels Fund
1528 Walnut Street
Suite 1002
Philadelphia, PA 19102-5308
215-731-9455
Fax: 215-731-9457
www.samfels.org
Offers grants in continuing support that help prevent, lessen or resolve contemporary social problems including education, arts/cultural programs, and community development.

Helen Cunningham, Executive Director
Robin N Culmer, Office Administrator

2881 Sarah Scaife Foundation
Three Mellon Bank Center
301 Grant Street
Suite 3900
Pittsburgh, PA 15219-6401
412-392-2900
www.scaife.com
Offers grants in the areas of education and community development.

Joanne B Beyer, Executive Director
Michael W Gleba, Executive Vice President

2882 Shore Fund
C/O Melton Bank N.A.
PO Box 185
Pittsburgh, PA 15230-0185
412-234-4695
Fax: 412-234-3551
Although the foundation appreciates funding opportunities within the field of education, most grants given out have been to schools with which the foundation's trustees have been personally involved.

Helen M Collins, Executive Director

2883 Stackpole-Hall Foundation
44 S Saint Marys Street
Saint Marys, PA 15857-1667
814-834-1845
Fax: 814-834-1869
stackpolehall@windstream.net
www.stackpolehall.org
Offers support for higher education and secondary education, literacy and vocational projects, social services, arts and cultural programs, and community development.

William C Conrad, Executive Director

2884 United States Steel Foundation
600 Grant Street
Suite 639
Pittsburgh, PA 15219-2800
412-433-5237
Fax: 412-433-2792
Grants are awarded for capital development, special projects or operating needs. Support is limited to organizations within the United States, with preference to those in the US Steel Corporation's operating areas. US Steel does not award grants for religious purposes. Additionally, grants are not awarded for conferences, seminars or symposia, travel, publication of papers, books or magazines, or production of films, videotapes or other audiovisual materials.

Craig D Mallick, General Manager
Pamela E DiNardo, Program Administrator

2885 William Penn Foundation
2 Logan Square11th Floor
100 North 18th Street
Philadelphia, PA 19103-2757
215-988-1830
Fax: 215-988-1823
grants@williampennfoundation.org
www.williampennfoundation.org
The foundation supports culture, environment, human development, including programs for youth and elderly, education, including early childhood, secondary, elementary and higher.

Kathryn J Engebretson, President
Bergen Bruce, Director of Finance and Admi

Rhode Island

2886 Champlin Foundations
2000 Chapel View Boulevard
Suite 350
Cranston, RI 02920
401-944-9200
Fax: 401-944-9299
Offers giving in the areas of higher, secondary and other education. Exclusively in Rhode Island.

David A King, Executive Director
Jonathan K Farnum, Distribution Committee Membe

2887 Providence Public Library
Reference Department
150 Empire Street
Providence, RI 02903-3219
401-455-8000
www.provlib.org
Member of The Foundation Center network, maintaining a collection of private foundation tax returns which provide information on the scope of grants dispensed by that particular foundation.

Dale Thompson, Director
Robert K Taylor, Chairman

2888 Rhode Island Foundation
One Union Station
Providence, RI 02903-4630
401-274-4564
Fax: 401-331-8085
www.rifoundation.org

Promotes charitable activities which tend to improve the living conditions and well-being of the residents of Rhode Island.

Ned Handy, President
David M Hirsch, Chairman

South Carolina

2889 Charleston County Library
68 Calhoun Street
Charleston, SC 29401
843-805-6930
Fax: 843-727-3741
www.ccpl.org
Member of The Foundation Center network, maintaining a collection of private foundation tax returns which provide information on the scope of grants dispensed by that particular foundation.

Janet Segal, Chairperson
Harlan Greene, Chairperson

2890 South Carolina State Library
1500 Senate Street
Columbia, SC 29201-3815
803-734-8666
Fax: 803-734-8676
www.state.sc.us/scsl/
Member of The Foundation Center network, maintaining a collection of private foundation tax returns which provide information on the scope of grants dispensed by that particular foundation.

James B Johnson Jr, Director

South Dakota

2891 South Dakota Community Foundation
1714 North Lincoln Ave
Box 296
Pierre, SD 57501-3159
605-224-1025
800-888-1842
Fax: 605-224-5364
www.sdcommunityfoundation.org
The mission of the foundation is to promote philanthropy, receive and administer charitable gifts and invest in a wide range of programs promoting the social and economic well being of the people of the South Dakota. Grants given in South Dakota only.

Bob Sutton, President
Stephanie Judson, Administrative Vice Presiden

2892 South Dakota State Library
Reference Department
800 Governors Drive
Pierre, SD 57501-2294
605-773-5070
Fax: 605-773-4950
www.sdstatelibrary.com
Member of The Foundation Center network, maintaining a collection of private foundation tax returns which provide information on the scope of grants dispensed by that particular foundation.

Tennessee

2893 Benwood Foundation
736 Market Street
Suite 1600
Chattanooga, TN 37402-4803
423-267-4311
Fax: 423-267-9049
www.benwood.org
The general purpose of this foundation is to support such religious, charitable, scientific, literary and educational activities as will promote the advancement of mankind in any part of the United States of America. It should be recognized by all prospective grantees that while the foundation is not limited to the Chattanooga, Tennessee area, the bulk of the grants are made to organizations in the immediate area.

Jean R McDaniel, Executive Director
Sarah Morgan, President

2894 Christy-Houston Foundation
1296 Dow Street
Murfreesboro, TN 37130-2413
615-898-1140
Fax: 615-895-9524
Offers grants for education, arts, culture and health care to residents and organizations of Rutherford County, Tennessee.

James R Arnhart, Executive Director

2895 Frist Foundation
3100 West End Avenue
Suite 1200
Nashville, TN 37203
615-292-3868
Fax: 615-292-5843
www.fristfoundation.org
Broad general-purposed charitable foundation whose grants are restricted primarily to Nashville.

Peter F Bird Jr, President/CEO
Thomas F Frist Jr, Chairman

2896 JR Hyde Foundation
17 West Pontotoc Ave
Suite 200
Memphis, TN 38103-0084
901-685-3400
Fax: 901-683-7478
info@hydefoundation.org
www.hydefoundation.org
Offers grants for higher education, including scholarships for the children of Malone and Hyde employees, community funds, secondary education and youth services.

JR Hyde III, Executive Director

2897 Lyndhurst Foundation
517 E 5th Street
Chattanooga, TN 37403-1826
423-756-0767
Fax: 423-756-0770
www.lyndhurstfoundation.org
Support local arts and culture and downtown revitalzation efforts in Chattanooga. Support the protection and enhancement of the natural environment of the Southern Appalachian Region. Support the elementary and secondary public schools in Chattanooga.

Jack E Murrah, President

2898 Nashville Public Library
Business Information Division
615 Church Street
Nashville, TN 37219
615-862-5800
www.library.nashville.org
Member of The Foundation Center network, maintaining a collection of private foundation tax returns which provide information on the scope of grants dispensed by that particular foundation.

Keith B Simmons, Board Chair

2899 Plough Foundation
6410 Poplar Avenue
Suite 710
Memphis, TN 38119-5736
901-761-9180
Fax: 901-761-6186
Offers grants for community projects, including a community fund, early childhood and elementary education, social service agencies and the arts.

Noris R Haynes Jr, Executive Director

2900 RJ Maclellan Charitable Trust
Provident Building
Suite 501
Chattanooga, TN 37402
423-755-1366
Supports higher and theological education, social services and youth programs.

Hugh O Maclellan Jr, Executive Director

Texas

2901 Albert & Ethel Herzstein Charitable Foundation
6131 Westview Drive
Houston, TX 77055-5421
713-681-7868
Fax: 713-681-3652
www.herzsteinfoundation.org
Concentrates support on temples and medical research with grants offered to medical schools.

L Michael Hajtman, President
Nathan H Topek, Chairman

2902 Burlington Northern Foundation
3800 Continental Plaza
777 Main Street
Fort Worth, TX 76102
817-352-6425
Fax: 817-352-7924
The major channel of philanthropy for Burlington Northern and its subsidiaries. The foundation administers a consistent contribution program in recognition of the company's opportunity to support and improve the general welfare and quality of life in communities it serves.

Beverly Edwards, President
Becky Blankenship, Grant Administrator

2903 Burnett Foundation
801 Cherry Street
Suite 1400
Fort Worth, TX 76102-6814
817-877-3344
Fax: 817-338-0448
Focus is on Fort Worth and Santa Fe, NM, seeking to be a positive force in the community, supporting the energy and creativity that exist in the nonprofit sector, and building capacity in organizations and people in the fields of education, health, community affairs, human services and arts and humanities.

Thomas F Beech, Executive Director

2904 Cooper Industries Foundation
PO Box 4446
Houston, TX 77210-4446
713-209-8400
Fax: 713-209-8982
www.cooperindustries.com
The policy of this foundation is to carry out the responsibilities of corporate citizenship, by supporting nonprofit organizations in areas where employees are located, which best serve the educational, health, welfare, civic, cultural and social needs of the foundation's

communities. All gifts are consistent with the company's objectives to enhance the quality of life and to honor the principles and freedoms that have enabled the company to prosper and grow. Average Grant: $5,000.

Victoria Guennewig, President
Jennifer L Evans, Secretary

2905 Corpus Christi State University
Library-Reference Department
805 Comanche
Corpus Christi, TX 78401
361-880-7000
Fax: 361-880-7005
Member of The Foundation Center network, maintaining a collection of private foundation tax returns which provide information on the scope of grants dispensed by that particular foundation.

Denise Landry

2906 Cullen Foundation
601 Jefferson Street
Floor 40
Houston, TX 77002-7900
713-651-8837
Fax: 713-651-2374
www.cullenfdn.org
Supports educational, medical purposes, community funds and conservation.

Alan M Stewart, Executive Director
Sue A Alexander, Grants Administrator

2907 Dallas Public Library
Urban Information
1515 Young Street
Dallas, TX 75201-5499
214-670-1400
Fax: 214-670-1451
www.dallaslibrary.org
Member of The Foundation Center network, maintaining a collection of private foundation tax returns which provide information on the scope of grants dispensed by that particular foundation.

2908 El Paso Community Foundation
333 North Oregon St
2nd Floor
El Paso, TX 79901
915-533-4020
Fax: 915-532-0716
www.epcf.org
Grants to 501(c)(3) organizations in the El Paso geographic area. Fields of interest are arts and humanities, education, environment, health and disabilities, human services and civic benefits. No grants to individuals are offered.

Janice Windle, President
Virginia Martinez, Executive VP

2909 Ellwood Foundation
PO Box 52482
Houston, TX 77052-2482
713-739-0763
Scholarships for social services and education.

H Wayne Hightower, Executive Director

2910 Eugene McDermott Foundation
1155 Union Circle
Suite 311580
Denton, TX 76203-5017
940-369-5200
Fax: 940-369-5248
www.tshaonline.org
Offers support primarily for higher and secondary education, health, cultural programs, and general community interests.

Eugene McDermott, Executive Director
Laurie E Jasinski, Research Editor

2911 Ewing Halsell Foundation
711 Navarro Street
Suite 535
San Antonio, TX 78205-1786
210-223-2649
Fax: 210-271-9089
www.ewinghalsell.org
Offers grants in the areas of art and cultural programs, education, medical research, human services and youth services.

Jackie Moczygemba

2912 Exxon Education Foundation
5959 Las Colinas Boulevard
Irving, TX 75039-2298
972-444-1106
Fax: 972-444-1405
Grants are given in the areas of environment, education, public information and policy research, united appeals and federated drives, health, civic and community service organizations, minority and women-oriented service organizations, arts, museums and historical associations. In the education area grants are awarded to mathematics education programs, elementary and secondary school improvement programs, undergraduate general education programs, research, training and support programs.

EF Ahnert, Executive Director

2913 Fondren Foundation
7 TCT 37
PO Box 2558
Houston, TX 77252
713-236-4403
Provides support in various areas of interest with an emphasis on higher and secondary education, social services and cultural organizations.

Melanie Scioneaus, Executive Director

2914 George Foundation
310 Morton Street
PMB Suite C
Richmond, TX 77469-3135
281-342-6109
Fax: 281-341-7635
www.thegeorgefoundation.org
Offers giving for religious, educational, charitable or scientific purposes.

Roland Adamson, Executive Director
Sandra Thompson, Chief Financial Officer

2915 Gordon & Mary Cain Foundation
8 E Greenway Plaza
Suite 702
Houston, TX 77046-0892
713-960-9283
Fax: 713-877-1824
The foundation is not limited to education but does contribute a large amount to that area. For a company to apply for a grant they must offer a statement of purpose or a summary of the project needing funding; budget with balance sheet, fund balance, distribution of funds, audited statement and number of employees; latest copy of IRS tax-exempt status letter 501(c)(3); current projects needing funding with amounts needed for entire project and the amount of the grant being requested.

James D Weaver, Executive Director

2916 Haggar Foundation
6113 Lemmon Avenue
Dallas, TX 75209-5715
214-352-8481
Fax: 214-956-4446
Offers support in various areas with an emphasis on higher and secondary education, including a program for children of company employees.

Mary Vaughan Rumble, Executive Director

2917 Hobby Foundation
2131 San Felipe Street
Houston, TX 77019-5620
713-521-4694
Fax: 713-521-3950
Offers grants to educational facilities in the state of Texas.

Oveta Culp Hobby, Executive Director

2918 Houston Endowment
600 Travis Street
Suite 6400
Houston, TX 77002-3000
713-238-8100
Fax: 713-238-8101
www.houstonendowment.org
Offers support for charitable, religious or educational organizations.

H Joe Nelson III, Executive Director
Ann B Stern, President

2919 Houston Public Library
Bibliographic Information Center
500 McKinney Street
Houston, TX 77002-2534
832-238-9640
Fax: 832-393-1383
www.hpl.lib.tx.us/hpl/hplhome
Member of The Foundation Center network, maintaining a collection of private foundation tax returns which provide information on the scope of grants dispensed by that particular foundation.

2920 James R Dougherty Jr Foundation
PO Box 640
Beeville, TX 78104-0640
361-358-3560
Fax: 361-358-9693
Offers support for Roman Catholic church-related industries including education, higher, secondary and other education.

Hugh Grove Jr, Executive Director

2921 Leland Fikes Foundation
3050 Lincoln Plaza
500 N Akard
Dallas, TX 75201
214-754-0144
Fax: 214-855-1245
Giving is focused on education, youth services, family planning, public interest and cultural programs.

Nancy Solana, Executive Director

2922 MD Anderson Foundation
1515 Holcombe Blvd
Houston, TX 77030-2558
713-658-2316
www.mdanderson.org
The purpose of this foundation is to improve lives in the areas of health care, education, human service, youth and research.

John W Lowrie, Executive Director

2923 Meadows Foundation
3003 Swiss Avenue
Wilson Historic Block
Dallas, TX 75204-6049
214-826-9431
800-826-9431
Fax: 214-824-0642

besterline@mfi.org
www.mfi.org
Support is given in the area of arts and culture, civic and public affairs , education, health, including mental health, and human services.

Bruce Esterline, VP Grants
Carol Stabler, Director Communications

24 Moody Foundation
2302 Post Office Street
Suite 704
Galveston, TX 77550-1994
409-797-1500
Fax: 409-763-5564
info@moodyf.org
www.moodyf.org
Provides major support for two foundation-initiated projects: the Transitional Learning Center, a residential rehabilitation and research facility for the treatment of traumatic brain injury, and Moody Gardens, a world-class education and recreation complex that includes a 1-acre enclosed rainforest, the area's largest aquarium, a space museum, IMAX theater, and the Moody Hospitality Institute.

Peter M Moore, Grants Director
Robert L Moody, Sr.Chiarman

25 Paul & Mary Haas Foundation
PO Box 2928
Corpus Christi, TX 78403-2928
361-887-6955
Offers scholastic grants to graduating high school seniors from Corpus Christi, Texas. The student must have above average grades and ability to prove financial need. The Foundation asks that the senior contact them in the Fall of his/her senior year in order to begin the in-house application process. The grant is a maximum of $1,500 per semester and is renewable for a total of eight semesters if the student maintains a 3.0 GPA. The student may attend college or university of his choice.

Karen Wesson, Executive Director

926 Perot Foundation
12377 Merit Drive
Suite 1700
Dallas, TX 75251-2239
972-788-3000
Fax: 972-788-3091
Educational grants, medical research funding and grantmaking for the arts and cultural organizations.

Bette Perot, Executive Director

927 RW Fair Foundation
PO Box 689
Tyler, TX 75710-0689
903-592-3811
Grants are given for secondary and higher education, church-related programs and legal education.

Wilton H Fair, Executive Director

928 Sid W Richardson Foundation
309 Main Street
Fort Worth, TX 76102-4006
817-336-0494
Fax: 817-332-2176
www.sidrichardson.org
This foundation was established for the purpose of supporting organizations that serve the people of Texas. Grants are given in the areas of education, health, the arts and human services.

Valleau Wilkie Jr, Executive Director

2929 Strake Foundation
712 Main Street
Suite 3300
Houston, TX 77002-3210
713-546-2400
Fax: 713-216-2401
Foundation gives primarily in Texas in the areas of operating budgets, continuing support, annual campaigns, special projects, research, matching funds and general purposes.

George W Strake Jr, Executive Director

2930 Trull Foundation
404 4th Street
Palacios, TX 77465-4812
361-972-5241
Fax: 361-972-1109
www.trullfoundation.org
1. A concern for the needs of the Palacios, Matagorda county are, where the foundation has its roots. Local health care, the senior center, and other local projects were considered and supported. 2. A concern for children and families. Grants are given to direct and channel lives away from child abuse, neglect from hunger, and poverty. 3. A concern for those persons and families devastated by the effects of substance abuse.

Gail Purvis, Executive Director
Lucja White, Administrative Assistant

Utah

2931 Marriner S Eccles Foundation
79 S Main Street
Salt Lake City, UT 84111-1901
801-246-5155
General support for Utah's human services, education and the arts programs.

Erma E Hogan, Executive Director

2932 Ruth Eleanor Bamberger and John Ernest Bamberger Memorial Foundation
136 S Main Street
Salt Lake City, UT 84101-1690
801-364-2045
Fax: 801-322-5284
bambergermemfdn@qwestoffice.net
www.ruthandjohnbambergermemorialfdn.org
Offers support for secondary education, especially undergraduate scholarships for student nurses and for schools.

William H Olwell, Executive Director

2933 Salt Lake City Public Library
210 East 400 south
Salt Lake City, UT 84111-3280
801-524-8200
Fax: 801-524-8272
www.slcpl.lib.ut.us
Member of The Foundation Center network, maintaining a collection of private foundation tax returns which provide information on the scope of grants dispensed by that particular foundation.

Dana Tumtowsky, Comm Relations Coordinator
Nancy Tessman, Director

Vermont

2934 Vermont Community Foundation
PO Box 30
Three Court Street
Middlebury, VT 05753-0030
802-388-3355
Fax: 802-388-3398
www.vermontcf.org
Offers support for the arts and education, the environment, preservation of the community, public affairs and more for the betterment of Vermont.

David F Finney, President/CEO
John Killacky, Executive Director

2935 Vermont Department of Libraries
Reference Services
109 State Street
Montpelier, VT 05609-0001
802-828-3268
Fax: 802-828-2199
www.dol.state.vt.us
Member of The Foundation Center network, maintaining a collection of private foundation tax returns which provide information on the scope of grants dispensed by that particular foundation.

2936 William T & Marie J Henderson Foundation
PO Box 600
Stowe, VT 05672-0600
Offers grants in the areas of elementary and secondary education.

William T Henderson, Executive Director

Virginia

2937 Beazley Foundation
3720 Brighton Street
Portsmouth, VA 23707-3902
757-393-1605
Fax: 757-393-4708
info@beazleyfoundation.org
www.beazleyfoundation.org
The purpose of this foundation to further the causes of charity, education and religion. Offers support for higher, secondary and medical education, youth agencies, community agencies and development.

Judge Richard S Bray, President
Donna M Russell, Associate Director

2938 Flagler Foundation
PO Box 644
Richmond, VA 23205
804-648-5033
Offers support for secondary and higher education, cultural programs and restoration.

Lawrence Lewis Jr, Executive Director

2939 Hampton Public Library
22 Lincoln Street
Hampton, VA 23669-4200
757-727-6315
Fax: 757-728-3037
council@hampton.gov
www.hampton.va.us
Member of The Foundation Center network, maintaining a collection of private foundation tax returns which provide information on the scope of grants dispensed by that particular foundation.

Molly Joseph Ward, Mayor
George E Wallace, Vice Mayor

2940 Jeffress Memorial Trust
Bank Of America Private Bank
Po Box 8795
Williamsburg, VA 23187-8795
804-788-3698
Fax: 804-788-2700
Funds research in higher education.

Richard B Brandt, Advisor

2941 **Kentland Foundation**
267 Kentlands Boulevard
Gaithesrsburg, MD 20878-5442
301-926-6636
info@kentlands.org
www.kentlands.org
Focuses on civic affairs organizations and education.
Helene Walker, Executive Director

2942 **Longview Foundation for Education in World Affairs/International Understanding**
1069 West Broad Street
Suite 801
Falls Church, VA 22046
301-681-0899
Fax: 301-681-0925
globaled@longviewfdn.org
www.longviewfdn.org
Offers grants and scholarships with an emphasis on pre-collegiate education, primarily elementary education, and also supports teacher education.
Betsy Devlin-Foltz, Director
Stevenson McIlvaine, President

2943 **NAESP Foundation**
National Assoc. of Elementary School Principals
1615 Duke Street
Alexandria, VA 22314
703-684-3345
800-386-2377
Fax: 703-549-5568
naesp@naesp.org
www.naesp.org
The Foundation aims to advance excellence, innovation, and equity in schools through funding professional development for principals.
L. Earl Franks, Ed.D, CAE, Executive Director
Nikki Sparks, Director, Operations

2944 **Richmond Public Library**
Business, Science & Technology Department
3100 Ellwood Avenue
Richmond, VA 23221-2193
804-646-1139
Fax: 804-646-4757
www.richmondpubliclibrary.org
Member of The Foundation Center network, maintaining a collection of private foundation tax returns which provide information on the scope of grants dispensed by that particular foundation.
Peter Blake, Chairman
Brenda Drew, Vice-Chairman

2945 **Virginia Foundation for Educational Leadership**
2204 Recreation Drive
Virginia Beach, VA 23456-6178
757-430-2412
Fax: 757-430-3247
George E McGovern, Division Director

Washington

2946 **Comstock Foundation**
3010 Gull Road
Kalamazoo, MI 49048
269-250-8900
Fax: 269-250-8901
www.comstockps.org
The Foundation contributes only to 501(c)(3) organizations, limited to Spokane County and its environs. In the field of general education, Comstock Foundation favors grants only to private institutions of higher learning, and no grants are made to individuals.
Horton Herman, Trustee
Charles M Leslie, Trustee

2947 **Foster Foundation**
13 Central Way
Kirland, WA 98033
206-726-1815
info@thefosterfoundation.org
www.thefosterfoundation.org
Offers support in art, culture, higher education, adult education, literacy and basic reading, health care and children and youth services.
Jill Goodsell, Executive Director

2948 **MJ Murdock Charitable Trust**
703 Broadway Street
Suite 701
Vancouver, WA 98660-3308
360-694-8415
Fax: 360-694-1819
Offers support primarily for special projects of private organizations in the areas of education, higher education, human services and program development.
John Van Zytveld, Senior Program Director

2949 **Seattle Foundation**
1200 5th Avenue
Suite 1300
Seattle, WA 98101-3151
206-622-2294
Fax: 206-622-7673
www.seattlefoundation.org
A community foundation that facilitates charitable giving; administers charitable funds, trusts and bequests; and distributes grants to non-profit organizations that are making a positive difference in our community. Grants are awarded to organizations working in areas that include social service, children and youth, civic, culture, elderly, conservation, education and health/rehabilitation.
Phyllis J Campbell, President/CEO
Molly Stearns, Senior Vice President

2950 **Seattle Public Library**
Science, Social Science
1000 4th Avenue
Seattle, WA 98104-1109
206-386-4636
Fax: 206-386-4634
www.spl.org
Member of The Foundation Center network, maintaining a collection of private foundation tax returns which provide information on the scope of grants dispensed by that particular foundation.

2951 **Spokane Public Library**
Funding Information Center
906 West Main Street
Spokane, WA 99201-0903
509-444-5300
Fax: 509-444-5365
www.spokanelibrary.org
Member of The Foundation Center network, maintaining a collection of private foundation tax returns which provide information on the scope of grants dispensed by that particular foundation.
Pat Partovi, Director

West Virginia

2952 **Clay Foundation**
1426 Kanawha Boulevard E
Charleston, WV 25301-3084
304-344-8656
Fax: 304-344-3805
Private charitable foundation making grants for health, education and programs for the aging or disadvantaged children.
Charles M Avampao, Executive Director

2953 **Kanawha County Public Library**
123 Capitol Street
Charleston, WV 25301-2686
304-343-4646
Fax: 304-348-6530
www.kanawha.lib.wv.us
Member of The Foundation Center network, maintaining a collection of private foundation tax returns which provide information on the scope of grants dispensed by that particular foundation.
Michael Albert, President
Elizabeth O Lord, First Vice President

2954 **Phyllis A Beneke Scholarship Fund**
Security National Bank & Trust Company
PO Box 511
Wheeling, WV 26003-0064
Offers support and scholarships for secondary education.
GP Schramm Sr, Executive Director

Wisconsin

2955 **Faye McBeath Foundation**
101 W Pleasant Street
Suite 210
Milwaukee, WI 53212-3157
414-272-2626
Fax: 414-272-6235
The purpose of the foundation is to provide Wisconsin people the best in education, child welfare, homes and care for the elderly and research in civics and government.
Scott E Gelzer, Executive Director
Aileen Mayer, Executive Assistant

2956 **Lynde & Harry Bradley Foundation**
1241 N Franklin Place
Milwaukee, WI 53202-2901
414-291-9915
Fax: 414-291-9991
www.bradleyfdn.org
The Foundation encourages projects that focus on cultivating a renewed, healthier and more vigorous sense of citizenship among the American people, and among peoples of all nations, as well. Grants are awarded to organizations and institutions exempt from federal taxation under Section 501(c)(3) and publicly supported under section 509(a), favor projects which are not normally financed by public tax funds, consider requests from religious organizations and institutions as well.
Michael W Grebe, President/CEO
Terry Considine, Chairman

2957 **Marquette University Memorial Library**
1355 West Wisconsin Avenue
Milwaukee, WI 53233-2287
414-288-7556
Fax: 414-288-5324
www.marquette.edu/library/
Member of The Foundation Center network, maintaining a collection of private foundation tax returns which provide information on the scope of grants dispensed by that particular foundation.

58 Siebert Lutheran Foundation
300 N Corporate Dr
Suite 200
Brookfield, WI 53045-1392
262-754-9160
Fax: 262-754-9162
contactus@siebertfoundation.org
www.siebertfoundation.org
Offers support in elementary and secondary, higher education and early childhood education.

Ronald D Jones, President
Deborah Engel, Administrative Assistant

59 University of Wisconsin-Madison
Memorial Library
728 State Street
Madison, WI 53706-1418
608-262-3242
Fax: 608-262-8569
grantsinfo@library.wisc.edu
Member of The Foundation Center network, maintaining a collection of private foundation tax returns which provide information on the scope of grants dispensed by that particular foundation.

Wyoming

60 Natrona County Public Library
307 E 2nd Street
Casper, WY 82601-2598
307-237-4935
Fax: 307-266-3734
www.library.natrona.net
Member of The Foundation Center network, maintaining a collection of private foundation tax returns which provide information on the scope of grants dispensed by that particular foundation.

Grants, Federal & Private

61 American Honda Foundation
PO Box 2205
Torrance, CA 90509-2205
310-781-4090
Fax: 310-781-4270
www.hondacorporate.com/community
Offers support for national organizations whose areas of interest include youth and scientific education. Grants reach private elementary, secondary, higher, vocational and scientific education.

Kathryn A Carey, Manager

962 Awards for University Administrators and Librarians
Association of Commonwealth Universities
John Foster House
36 Gordon Square
London WC1H OPF, England
171 3878572
Fax: 171 3872655
pubinfo@acu.ac.uk
Lists approximately 40 sources of financial assistance for administrative and library staff for universities worldwide. Includes name, address, phone, fax, tenure place and length, amount of aid, requirements for eligibility and application procedure, and frequency and number of grants available.

40 pages Biennial
ISSN: 0964-2714

Moira Hunter, Editor

2963 Awards for University Teachers and Research Workers
Association of Commonwealth Universities
36 Gordon Square
London
WC1H OPF, England
44-20-7380-6700
Fax: 44-20-7387-2655
Lists approximately 740 awards open to university teachers and research workers in one country for research, study visits or teaching at a university in another country. Offers fellowships, visiting professorships and lectureships and travel grants.

364 pages Biennial
ISSN: 0964-2706

2964 Educational Foundation of America
55 Walls Drive
Fairfield, CT 06824-3515
203-226-6498
Fax: 203-227-0424
Funds projects in arts, education and programs benefiting Native Americans.

Diane M Allison, Executive Director
Lynn P Babicka, President

2965 Foundation Center
79 5th Avenue
Floor 8
New York, NY 10003-3076
212-620-4230
Fax: 212-807-3677
A national service organization which disseminates information on private giving through public service programs, publications, and through a national network of library reference collections for free public use. Over 100 network members have sets of private foundation information returns, and the New York, Washington, DC, Cleveland and San Francisco reference collections operated by the Foundation offer a wide variety of services and collections of information on foundations and grants.

Cheryl Loe, Director Of Communications
Laura Cascio, Fulfillment Management

2966 GTE Foundation
PO Box 152257
Irving, TX 75015-2257
972-507-5434
Fax: 972-615-4310
www.gte.com
The emphasis of giving for the foundation is on higher education in math, science and technology. It also sponsors scholarships and supports community funds and social service agencies that emphasize literacy training.

Maureen Gorman, VP

2967 George I Alden Trust
370 Main Street
Worcester, MA 01608-1714
508-459-8005
Fax: 508-459-8305
trustees@aldentrust.org
www.aldentrust.org
Gives to higher education organizations and facilities with an emphasis on scholarship endowments.

Francis H Dewey III, Executive Director
Warner S Fletcher, Chairman

2968 Gershowitz Grant and Evaluation Services
505 Merle Hay Tower
Des Moines, IA 50310
515-270-1718
Fax: 515-270-8325
gershowitz@netins.net
To give schools an edge in funding their technology programs

Michael V Gershowitz, PhD
Steve Panyan, PhD

2969 Grants and Contracts Service
Department of Education/Regional Office Building
7th & D Streets
Suite 3124
Washington, DC 20202-0001
202-401-2000
Fax: 202-260-7225
To support improvements in teaching and learning and to help meet special needs of schools and students in elementary and secondary education

Gary J Rasmussen, Director

2970 Grantsmanship Center
PO Box 17220
Los Angeles, CA 90017-0220
213-482-9860
Fax: 213-482-9863
norton@tgci.com
www.tgci.com
The world's oldest and largest training organization for the nonprofit sector. Since it was founded in 1972, the has trained trains more than 75,000 staff members of public and private agencies; training provided includes grantsmanship, program management and fundraising. Center also produces publications on grantsmanship, fundraising, planning, management and personnel issues for nonprofit agencies.

Norton Kiritz, President

2971 John S & James L Knight Foundation
Wachovia Financial Center
Suite 3300
200south Biscayne Boulevard
Miami, FL 33131-2349
305-908-2600
Fax: 305-908-2698
web@knightfoundation.org
www.knightfdn.org
The foundation makes national grants in journalism, education and the field of arts and culture. It also supports organizations in communities where the Knight brothers were involved in publishing newspapers but is wholly separate from and independent of those newspapers.

James D Spaniolo, Executive Director

2972 National Academy of Education - Spencer Postdoctoral Fellowship
500 5th Street NW
Washington, DC 20001
202-334-2341
info@naeducation.org
www.naeducation.org
The Spencer Postdoctoral Fellowship is designed to promote scholarship in the United States and abroad on matters relevant to the improvement of education in all its forms.

Gregory White, Executive Director
Amy Berman, Deputy Director

2973 National Academy of Education - Spencer Dissertation Fellowship
500 5th Street NW
Washington, DC 20001
202-334-2341
info@naeducation.org
www.naeducation.org
The Spencer Dissertation Fellowship aims to inspire scholars from across disciplines and

fields to research new ways of improving education.

Gregory White, Executive Director
Amy Berman, Deputy Director

2974 National Science Foundation
2415 Eisenhower Avenue
Alexandria, VA 22314
703-292-5111
info@nsf.gov
www.nsf.gov
Offers grants, workshops and curricula for all grade levels.

Sethuraman Panchanathan, Director

2975 Trust to Reach Education Excellence
1904 Association Drive
Reston, VA 20191-1537
703-860-0200
800-253-7746
Fax: 703-476-5432
tree@principals.org
Founded to make grants to educators and students who would ordinarily not have access to outstanding NASSP programs, such as camps, programs and workshops on leadership, technology and school reform.

Dr. Anne Miller, Executive Director

2976 Union Carbide Foundation
39 Old Ridgebury Road
Danbury, CT 06817-0001
203-794-6945
Fax: 203-794-7031
www.unioncarbide.com
Offers grants in the areas of elementary and secondary education, with an emphasis on systemic reform; higher education with a focus on science and engineering; and environmental protection awareness.

Nancy W Deibler, Executive Director

2977 United States Institute of Peace
2301 Constitution Avenue
Washington, DC 20037
202-457-1700
Fax: 202-429-6063
www.usip.org
Includes grants, fellowships, a National Peace Essay Contest for high school students and teacher training institutes.

Richard H Solomon, President
Judy Ansley, Board of Director

2978 United States-Japan Foundation
145 E 32nd Street
Floor 12
New York, NY 10016-6055
212-481-8753
Fax: 212-481-8762
info@us-jf.org
www.us-jf.org
A nonprofit, philanthropic organization with the principal mission of promoting a greater mutual knowledge between United States and Japan and to contribute to a strengthened understanding of important public policy issues of interest to both countries. Currently the focus is on precollegiate education, policy studies, and communications and public opinion.

2979 Westinghouse Foundation
Westinghouse Electric Corporation
Po Box 355
ECE 575C
Pittsburgh, PA 15230-0355
412-374-6824
Fax: 412-642-4874
www.westinghousenuclear.com
Makes charitable contributions to community priorities primarily where Westinghouse has a presence. Areas of emphasis include: education, health and welfare, culture and the arts and civic and social grants. Support for education is central to Westinghouse's contributions program, particularly higher education in the areas of engineering, applied science and business. Also encourages educational programs that strengthen public schools through enhanced student learning opportunities.

G Reynolds Clark, Executive Director

2980 Xerox Foundation
800 Long Ridge Road #1600
Stamford, CT 06902-1227
203-968-3445
www.xerox.com
Offers giving in the areas of higher education to prepare qualified men and women for careers in business, government and education.

Joseph M Cahalan, Executive Director

Fundraising

2981 A&L Fund Raising
29 Carriage Drive
South Windsor, CT 06074-1140
860-242-2476
800-286-7247
Offers many successful fundraising programs including Christmas gifts, designer gift wraps from Ashley Taylor and Geoffrey Boehm chocolates. A&L sells only the highest quality items at affordable prices with great service to schools and organizations.

Anita Brown

2982 A+ Enterprises
1426 Route 33
Hamilton Square, NJ 08690-1704
609-587-1765
800-321-1765
A promotional corporation offering a variety of fundraising programs for schools and educational institutions, ranging from Christmas campaigns to chocolates, as well as magnets and gift campaigns.

2983 Aid for Education
CD Publications
8204 Fenton Street
Sliver Spring, MD 20910
301-588-6380
800-666-6380
Fax: 301-588-0519
afe@cdpublications.com
www.cdpublications.com

18 pages Newsletter
ISSN: 1058-1324

Frank Kimko, Editor

2984 All Sports
21 Round Hill Road
Wethersfield, CT 06109
860-721-0273
800-829-0273
Fax: 860-257-9609
www.graduationshirts.com
Fundraising and school promotion company offering crew sweatshirts, hoods, tees, jackets, caps, gymwear and specialty signature shirts for graduating classes.

Wally Schultz, Owner

2985 Art to Remember
5535 Macy Drive
Indianapolis, IN 46235
317-826-0870
800-895-8777
Fax: 317-823-2822
www.arttoremember.com
Raises funds for art departments and special school programs.

2986 Childrens Youth Funding Report
CD Publications
8204 Fenton Street
Sliver Spring, MD 20910
301-588-6380
800-666-6380
Fax: 301-588-6385
cye@cdpublications.com
Detailed coverage of federal and private grant opportunities and legislative initiatives effecting childrens programs in such areas as child welfare, education healthcare.

18 pages Monthly

Steve Albright, Editor

2987 Disability Rights Education & Defense Fund
3075 Adeline Street
Suite 210
Berkeley, CA 94703
510-644-2555
Fax: 510-841-8645
info@dredf.org
www.dredf.org
The Disability Rights Education and Defense Fund works to advance the civil and human rights of people with disabilities through legal advocacy, training, education, public policy and legislative development.

Claudia Center, President & Chair
Susan Henderson, Executive Director

2988 Dutch Mill Bulbs
212 Piper Cir
Annville, PA 17003
800-533-8824
Fax: 800-556-0539
info@dutchmillbulbs.com
www.dutchmillbulbs.com
Raises funds for organizations, including high schools, by selling Spring and Fall flower bulbs.

Jeffrey E Ellenberger, President

2989 E-S Sports Screenprint Specialists
47 Jackson Street
Holyoke, MA 01040-5512
413-534-5634
800-833-3171
Fax: 413-538-8648
Scholastic Spirit Division offers screenprinted T-shirts, sweatshirts, shorts and apparel. This program offers schools and organizations an easy way to increase school spirit with no risk, no minimum orders and prompt delivery.

Aaron Porchelli, Division Director

2990 Fundraising USA
1395 State Route 23
Butler, NJ 07405-1736
973-283-1946
800-428-6178
Fundraiser offering a variety of programs for schools and organizations including Walk-A-Thons. This program is fast becoming the most popular way for schools to raise money. The walks are designed to take place at your own school, and children are not responsible for collecting any money. Fundraising USA collects all donations through the mail.

91 Gold Medal Products
10700 Medallion Drive
Cincinnati, OH 45241-4807
513-769-7676
800-543-0862
Fax: 513-769-8500
info@gmpopcorn.com
www.gmpopcorn.com
Offers a full line of fundraising products popcorn poppers and supplies and programs including candy, clothing and sports programs for schools and colleges.

Chris Petroff
Dan Kroeger, President

92 Human-i-Tees
400 Columbus Avenue
Valhalla, NY 10595-1335
800-275-2638
Fax: 914-745-1799
www.humanitees.com
Environmental T-shirt fundraisers that provide large profits while raising environmental awareness for thousands of school, youth and service organizations across the country.

93 Hummel Sweets
PO Box 232
Forestville, MD 20747
800-998-8115
Offer fundraising programs with 45% to 50% profit.

94 M&M Mars Fundraising
800 High Street
Hackettstown, NJ 07840-1552
908-852-1000
Fax: 908-850-2734
Offers America's favorite candies for fundraising programs throughout the year.

95 QSP
Subsidiary of the Reader's Digest Association
PO Box 2003
Ridgefield, CT 06877-0903
203-756-3022
800-667-2536
Fax: 800-844-3568
customerservice@qsp.ca
www.qsp.ca
For twenty-seven years, this fundraiser has helped students raise more than $900,000,000 for extracurricular programs and projects that are essential to a meaningful, well-rounded education. With QSP programs, students earn money to fund worthwhile projects and learn about the business world at the same time. QSP offers various fundraising programs including: Family Reading Programs; The Music Package; Delightful Edibles; and The Parade of Gifts.

Robert L Metivier, Sales Manager

996 Sally Foster Gift Wrap
PO Box 539
Duncan, SC 29334-0539
800-552-5875
Fax: 800-343-0809
Fundraiser offers gift wrap packages to schools. Offers high quality merchandise, including the heaviest papers and foils available. This proven two-week program is quick, easy and profitable offering your school or organization the opportunity to raise thousands of dollars to buy computers, books, athletic equipment and more. Organizations and schools keep 50% of all the profits, and there are no up-front costs or risks.

Mark Metcalfe, Sr VP

2997 School Identifications
Chas. E. Petrie Comapny
PO Box 527
Woodburn, OR 97071-0012
503-982-0757
800-772-0798
Fax: 503-981-3038
info@schoolidents.com
www.schoolidents.com
An easy fundraising project for schools, offering school identification cards and tags for students.

2998 School Memories Collection
Fundcraft Publishing
PO Box 340
Collierville, TN 38027
901-853-7070
800-853-1363
Fax: 901-853-6196
info@fundcraft.com
www.schoolmemories.com
Memory books with games and activities.

Chris Bradley, Marketing Director

2999 Sports Shoes & Apparel
3 Moulton Drive
Londonderry, NH 03053-4061
603-437-7844
800-537-7844
Fax: 603-437-2300
Offers customized sweatshirts, T-shirts and beach towels at group discount, with several complete fund raising programs being available as well. Beach towels for fundraising.

Bill McMahon, Regional Manager

3000 Steve Wronker's Funny Business
39 Boswell Road
W Hartford, CT 06107-3708
860-233-6716
800-929-swfb
Fax: 860-561-8910
Comedy and educational magic shows available for preschool and elementary school aged children. Award winning programs such as The Magic of Books and Magic from Around the World are available for any size audience. For middle schools and high schools, comedy hypnosis is a perfect venue for entertainment as a fundraising program, for high school after-prom parties, graduation parties, or just for an evening's entertainment.

Steve Wronker

3001 T-Shirt People/Wearhouse
10722 Hanna Street
Beltsville, MD 20705-2123
301-937-4843
800-638-7070
Fax: 301-937-2916
www.t-shirtpeople.com
Fundraiser offering customized T-shirts to boost school spirit, raise funds, instill school pride and save money.

3002 Troll Book Fairs
100 Corporate Drive
Mahwah, NJ 07430-2041
201-529-4000
Fax: 201-529-8282
A profit-making program designed to introduce children to the wonderful world of books.

3003 Union Pen Company
166 Wallins Corner Road
Amsterdam, NY 12010
800-203-9917
Fax: 800-688-4877
unionpen@aol.com
www.unionpen.com
This company offers advertising gifts including customized pens and key chains that will increase confidence, school spirit and community goodwill in education. Group discounts are available.

Matt Roberts, General Manager
Morton Tenny, President

3004 www.positivepins.com
802 E 6th Streetve
PO Box 52528
Tulsa, OK 74152
918-587-2405
800-282-0085
Fax: 918-382-0906
pinrus@aol.com
Fundraising organization used by educational organizations. Designer and manufacturer of lapel pins used for employee service, appreciation, volunteer recognition, donor incentives and recognition, public relations and spirit.

Bern L Gentry, President
Michelle Anderson, VP

Scholarships & Financial Aid

3005 AFL-CIO Guide to Union Sponsored Scholarships, Awards & Student Aid
AFL-CIO
1100 1st St NE
Suite 850
Washington, DC 20002-4104
202-637-5000
www.unionplus.org
Lists international and national unions, local unions, state federations and labor councils offering scholarships, awards or financial aid to students.

100 pages Annual

3006 American-Scandinavian Foundation
58 Park Avenue at 38th Street
New York, NY 10016
212-779-3587
info@amscan.org
www.amscan.org
The Foundation provides information, scholarships and grants on the study programs in Scandinavia.

Edward P. Gallagher, President
Steven B. Peri, Deputy Chairman

3007 Arts Scholarships
Jewish Foundation for Education of Women
430 Park Ave
Suite 3A
Highland Park, IL 60035-1827
212-288-3931
Fax: 212-288-5798
fdnscholar@aol.com
www.scholarships.com
These scholarships are being offered at the Julliard School, Tisch School, of the Arts at New York University, and the Manhattan School of Music to qualified students enrolled in their programs. Faculty members will select recipients.

Marge Goldwater, Executive Director

3008 CUNY Teacher Incentive Program
Jewish Foundation for Education of Women
135 E 64th Street
New York, NY 10019-1827
212-288-3931
Fax: 212-288-5798
fdnscholar@aol.com
www.jfew.org

Provide stipends to CUNY graduates who are studying for a master's degree in education and interested in a teaching career in the New York City public school system. Contact the office of the Vice Chancellor for Academic Affairs at CUNY for further information.

Marge Goldwater, Executive Director

3009 College Board

250 Vesey Street
New York, NY 10281
212-713-8000
www.collegeboard.org

The College Board is a national nonprofit membership association that supports educational transitions through programs and services in assessment, guidance, admission, placement, financial aid, and educational reform.

David Coleman, Chief Executive Officer
Jeremy Singer, President

3010 Dissertation Fellowships in the Humanities

Jewish Foundation for Education of Women
135 E 64th Street
New York, NY 10065-1827
212-288-3931
Fax: 212-288-5798
fdnscholar@aol.com
www.jfew.org

A small number of fellowships will be awarded through the CUNY Graduate Center to qualified applicants.

Marge Goldwater, Executive Director

3011 George & Mary Kremer Foundation

1100 5th Avenue S
Suite 411
Naples, FL 34102-7415
941-261-2367
Fax: 941-261-1494
www.kremerfoundation.com

Provides scholarship funding for needy children in elementary Catholic schools throughout the Continental United States.

Mary Anderson Goddard, Director
Sister MT Ballrach, Assistant Director

3012 Intel Science Talent Search Scolarship

1719 N Street NW
Washington, DC 20036-2888
202-785-2255
Fax: 202-785-1243
www.sciserv.org

Offers a variety of services to teachers and students, including Intel Science Talent Search Scholarship competition, science fairs and publications.

3013 Jewish Foundation for Education of Women

Jewish Foundation for Education of Women
135 E 64th Street
New York, NY 10019-1827
212-288-3931
Fax: 212-288-5798
fdnscholar@aol.com
www.jfew.org

The Jewish Foundation for Education of Women is a private, nonsectarian foundation providing scholarships to women for higher education in the New York City area. A variety of specific programs are available. Most programs are administered collaboratively with area schools and organizations; the Foundation's mission is to help women of all ages attain the education and training needed to make them productive, economically independent members of the community.

Marge Goldwater, Executive Director
Sharon L Weinberg, Chairman

3014 Octameron Associates

P.O Box 2748
Alexandria, VA 22301-0748
703-836-5480
Fax: 703-836-5650
info@octameron.com
www.octameron.com

Octameron is a publishing and consulting firm with over 25 years experience in financial aid and admissions.

Anna Leider, Publisher

3015 Scholarship America

One Scholarship Way
Saint Peter, MN 56082-1556
507-931-1682
800-537-4180
Fax: 507-931-9250
dsnatoff@aol.com
www.dollarsforscholars.org

Provides community volunteers with the tools and support to create, develop and sustain legally constituted community-based scholarship foundations. Over 15,000 volunteers are active on 760 Dollars for Scholars chapter boards and committees throughout the United States. In addition, 20,000 high school youth and community residents are active in fund-raising events and academic support programs. Since the late 1950's, over 155,000 students have received Dollars for Scholars scholarships.

David Bach, VP
Susan Ponwith, President&CEO

3016 Scholarships in the Health Professions

Jewish Foundation for Education of Women
135 E 64th Street
New York, NY 10021
212-288-3931
Fax: 212-288-5798
fdnscholar@aol.com
www.jfew.org

Provides scholarships to emigres from the former Soviet Union who are studying medicine, dentistry, nursing, pharmacy, OT, PT, dental hygiene, and physician assistanceship.

Marge Goldwater, Executive Director

Federal Listings

17 Accounting & Financial Management Services
U.S. Department of Education
400 Maryland Avenue, SW
Washington, DC 20202-0001
800-872-5327
Fax: 202-401-0207
www.www2.ed.gov

Arne Duncan, Secretary of Education
Emma Vadehra, Chief of Staff

18 Assistance to States Division
U.S. Department of Education
400 Maryland Avenue, SW
Washington, DC 20202
202-401-2000
800-872-5327
Fax: 202-260-7225
www.www2.ed.gov

Arne Duncan, Secretary of Education
Emma Vadehra, Chief of Staff

19 Brody Professional Development
Brody Communications Ltd.
115 West Avenue
Suite 114
Jenkintown, PA 19046
215-886-1688
Fax: 215-886-1699
info@brodypro.com
www.brodypro.com
Brody offers tailored training programs, executive coaching and presentations in the areas of communication skills and professional development.

Miryam Roddy, Manager of Maximum Exposure

20 Compensatory Education Program
US Department of Education
400 Maryland Avenue SW
Washington, DC 20202
202-401-2000
800-872-5327
Fax: 202-260-7764
www.ed.gov

Emma Vadehra, Chief of Staff
Richard Culatta, Director, Education Tech

021 Elementary Secondary Bilingual & Research Branch
U.S. Department of Education
400 Maryland Avenue, SW
Suite 3653
Washington, DC 20202
202-401-0113
800-872-5327
Fax: 202-260-7225
www.www2.ed.gov

Arne Duncan, Secretary of Education
Emma Vadehra, Chief of Staff

022 Elementary, Secondary & Vocational Analysis
U.S. Department of Education
400 Maryland Avenue SW
3043 Main Building
Washington, DC 20202-0001
202-401-0318
800-872-5327
Fax: 202-260-7225
www.www2.ed.gov

Arne Duncan, Secretary of Education
Emma Vadehra, Chief of Staff

3023 Management Services
U.S. Department of Education
400 Maryland Avenue SW
Washington, DC 20202-0001
202-401-0500
800-872-5327
Fax: 202-260-7225
www.www2.ed.gov

Arne Duncan, Secretary of Education
Emma Vadehra, Chief of Staff

3024 National Center for Education Statistics
1990 K Street NW
8th & 9th Floors
Washington, DC 20006
202-502-7300
Fax: 202-502-7466
www.nces.ed.gov

Sean P. Jack Buckley, Commissioner

3025 National Council on Disability
1331 F Street NW
Suite 850
Washington, DC 20004-1107
202-272-2004
Fax: 202-272-2022
ncd@ncd.gov
www.ncd.gov/
An independent federal agency comprised of 15 members appointed by the President and confirmed by the Senate.

Jonathan M. Young, Ph.D., Chairman
Aaron Bishop, Executive Director

3026 National Institute of Child Health and Human Development
Bldg.31, Room 2A32, MSC 2425
31 Center Drive
Bethesda, MD 20892-2425
800-370-2943
Fax: 866-760-5947
NICHDInformationResourceCenter@mail.nih.gov
www.nichd.nih.gov
Develops research to solve problems in the physical and mental evolution of development. Including some of the most emotionally draining disorders, learning disabilities, behavioral disabilities, birth defects and infant mortality. Acts as a clearinghouse of materials, information and referrals and more.

Ellie Brown Hochman, Administrative Officer
Brenda Hanning, Program Management Officer

3027 National Library of Education
U.S. Department of Education
400 Maryland Avenue, SW
Washington, DC 20202
202-401-2000
800-872-5327
Fax: 202-401-0547
library@ed.gov
www.ed.gov

Emma Vadehra, Chief of Staff
Richard Culatta, Director, Education Tech

3028 National Trust for Historic Preservation: Office of Education Initiatives
The Watergate Office Building
2600 Virginia Avenue, Suite 1000
Washington, DC 20037
202-588-6000
800-944-6847
Fax: 202-588-6038
info@savingplaces.org
Teaching with Historic Places, a program offered by the National Park Service's National Register of Historic Places, and the National Trust for Historic Preservation Press.

Stephanie Meeks, President & CEO
Tabitha Almquist, Chief of Staff

3030 Office for Civil Rights
U.S. Department of Education
400 Maryland Avenue SW
Lyndon Baines Johnson Dept of Ed Bldg.
Washington, DC 20202-1100
202-401-2000
800-872-5327
Fax: 202-453-6012
ocr@ed.gov
www.ed.gov

Emma Vadehra, Chief of Staff
Richard Culatta, Director, Education Tech

3031 Office of Bilingual Education and Minority Languages Affairs
U.S. Department of Education
400 Maryland Avenue SW
Washington, DC 20202-6510
202-401-2000
800-872-5327
Fax: 202-260-7225
www.ed.gov

Emma Vadehra, Chief of Staff
Richard Culatta, Director, Education Tech

3032 Office of Elementary & Secondary Education
U.S. Department of Education
400 Maryland Avenue SW
Washington, DC 20202
202-401-2000
800-872-5327
Fax: 202-205-0310
oese@ed.gov
www.ed.gov

Emma Vadehra, Chief of Staff
Richard Culatta, Director, Education Tech

3033 Office of Indian Education
U.S. Department of Education
400 Maryland Avenue SW
LBJ Building, 3E205
Washington, DC 20202-6335
202-401-2000
800-872-5327
Fax: 202-260-7779
indian.education@ed.gov
www.ed.gov

Emma Vadehra, Chief of Staff
Richard Culatta, Director, Education Tech

3034 Office of Legislation & Congressional Affairs
U.S. Department of Education
400 Maryland Avenue SW
Washington, DC 20202-3100
202-401-2000
800-872-5327
Fax: 202-401-1438
olca@ed.gov
www.ed.gov

Emma Vadehra, Chief of Staff
Richard Culatta, Director, Education Tech

olca@ed.gov
www.ed.gov

Emma Vadehra, Chief of Staff
Richard Culatta, Director, Education Tech

3035 Office of Migrant Education
U.S. Department of Education
400 Maryland Avenue SW
Room 3E317 FOB-6
Washington, DC 20202-6135
202-401-2000
800-872-5327
Fax: 202-205-0089
www.ed.gov

Emma Vadehra, Chief of Staff
Richard Culatta, Director, Education Tech

3036 Office of Overseas Schools
US Department of State
Room H328, SA-1
Washington, DC 20522-0132
202-261-8200
Fax: 202-261-8224
OverseasSchools@state.gov
www.state.gov
Maintains detailed information on 190 overseas elementary and secondary schools which receive some assistance from the US Department of State. These schools provide an American-type education which prepares students for schools, colleges and universities in the United States.

Dr. Keith D Miller, Director

3037 Office of Planning, Evaluation and Policy Development
U.S. Department of Education
400 Maryland Avenue SW
Suite 4022
Washington, DC 20201-0001
202-401-2000
800-872-5327
Fax: 202-260-7225
www.ed.gov

Emma Vadehra, Chief of Staff
Richard Culatta, Director, Education Tech

3038 Office of Special Education Programs
Department of Education/3086 Mary E. Switzer Bldg.
600 Independence Avenue SW
Washington, DC 20202-2570
202-205-5507
Fax: 202-260-7225
thomas_hehir@ed.gov
www.ed.gov

Thomas Hehir, Director

3039 Office of Student Financial Assistance Programs
U.S. Department of Education
400 Maryland Avenue SW
Washington, DC 20202-0001
202-401-2000
800-872-5327
www.ed.gov

Emma Vadehra, Chief of Staff
Richard Culatta, Director, Education Tech

3040 Planning & Evaluation Service
U.S. Department of Education
400 Maryland Avenue, SW
Washington, DC 20202
202-401-2000
800-872-5327
Fax: 202-260-7225
www.ed.gov

Emma Vadehra, Chief of Staff
Richard Culatta, Director, Education Tech

3041 Rehabilitation Services Administration
U.S. Department of Education
400 Maryland Avenue SW
Washington, DC 20202-2800
202-401-2000
800-872-5327
Fax: 202-260-7225
www.ed.gov

Emma Vadehra, Chief of Staff
Richard Culatta, Director, Education Tech

3042 Research to Practice Division
U.S. Department of Education
Ofc of Special Ed/Rehabilitative Sv
400 Maryland Avenue SW
Washington, DC 20202-7100
202-401-2000
800-872-5327
www.ed.gov

Emma Vadehra, Chief of Staff
Richard Culatta, Director, Education Tech

3043 School Assistance Division
U.S. Department of Education
400 Maryland Avenue, SW
Washington, DC 20202-2141
202-260-2270
800-872-5327
Fax: 202-260-7225
www.www2.ed.gov

Arne Duncan, Secretary of Education
Emma Vadehra, Chief of Staff

3044 School Improvement Grants
U.S. Department Of Education
400 Maryland Avenue SW
Washington, DC 20202
202-401-2000
800-872-5327
www.ed.gov

Emma Vadehra, Chief of Staff
Richard Culatta, Director, Education Tech

3045 School Improvement Programs-Equity and Educational Excellence Division
U.S. Department of Education
400 Maryland Avenue, SW
Washington, DC 20202-2141
202-260-3693
800-872-5327
Fax: 202-260-7225
www.www2.ed.gov

Arne Duncan, Secretary of Education
Emma Vadehra, Chief of Staff

3046 School Improvement Programs-Safe and Drug Free Schools
Office of Safe and Drug Free Schools
400 Maryland Avenue, SW
Washington, DC 20202
202-245-7896
800-872-5327
Fax: 202-485-0013
osdfs.safeschl@ed.gov
www.ed.gov
Works to promote safe schools that are free from drug abuse and violence.

Arne Duncan, Secretary of Education
Emma Vadehra, Chief of Staff

3047 US Department of Defense Dependents Schools
2461 Eisenhower Avenue
Alexandria, VA 22331-3000
571-325-0867

Marilyn Witcher

3048 US Department of Education
400 Maryland Avenue SW
Washington, DC 20202
800-872-5327
Fax: 202-401-0689
customerservice@inet.ed.gov
www.ed.gov
Ensures equal access to education and promotes educational excellence for all Americans.

Arne Duncan, Secretary of Education
Emma Vadehra, Chief of Staff

3049 Vocational & Adult Education
U.S. Department of Education
400 Maryland Avenue, SW
Washington, DC 20202
202-205-5451
800-872-5327
Fax: 202-260-7225
www.www2.ed.gov

Arne Duncan, Secretary of Education
Emma Vadehra, Chief of Staff

3050 Washington DC Department of Education
825 N Capitol Street NE
Suite 900
Washington, DC 20202-4210
202-442-5885
Fax: 202-442-5026

Paul L Varce, Superintendent

Alabama

3051 Alabama State Department of Education
50 N Ripley Street
PO Box 302101
Montgomery, AL 36104
334-242-9700
www.alsde.edu
Mission is to provide a state system of education which is committed to academic excellence and which provides education of the highest quality to all Alabama students, preparing them for the 21st century. For certification information contact the Alabama certification office at 334-242-9977.

Dr. Joseph B Morton, State Superintendent of Ed.
Dr. Craig Pouncey, Deputy State Superintendent

3052 General Counsel
Alabama Department of Education
50 N Ripley Street
PO Box 302101
Montgomery, AL 36130-0624
334-242-9700
www.alsde.edu
Provides legal counsel to the State Superintendent of Education, State Board of Education and State Department of Education.

Larry Craven, General Counsel
Juliana Teixeira Dean, Associate General Counsel

3053 Instructional Services
Alabama Department of Education
50 N Ripley Street
P.O. Box 302101?
Montgomery, AL 36104

334-242-9700
Fax: 334-242-9708
www.alsde.edu

Charlie G Williams, Assistant Superintendent

054 Professional Services
Alabama Department of Education
50 N Ripley Street
P.O. Box 302101?
Montgomery, AL 36104
334-242-9700
Fax: 334-242-9708
www.alsde.edu

Eddie R Johnson, Assistant Superintendent

055 Rehabilitation Services
Alabama Department of Rehabilitation Services
602 S. Lawrence St.
Montgomery, AL 36104
334-293-7500
800-441-7607
Fax: 334-293-7383
www.rehab.alabama.gov
State agency that provides and services and assistance to Alabama's children and adults with disabilities and their families.

Steve Shrivers, Commissioner

056 Special Education Services
Alabama Department of Education
50 N Ripley Street
P.O. Box 302101?
Montgomery, AL 36104
334-242-9700
Fax: 334-242-9192
www.alsde.edu

Bill East, Division Director

057 Student Instructional Services
Alabama Department of Education
50 N Ripley Street
P.O. Box 302101?
Montgomery, AL 36104
334-242-9700
Fax: 334-242-9708
www.alsde.edu

Martha V Beckett, Assistant Superintendent

058 Superintendent
Alabama Department of Education
50 N Ripley Street
P.O. Box 302101?
Montgomery, AL 36104
334-242-9700
Fax: 334-242-9708
www.alsde.edu

Ed Richardson, Superintendent

059 Vocational Education
Alabama Department of Education
50 N Ripley Street
P.O. Box 302101?
Montgomery, AL 36104
334-242-9700
Fax: 334-353-8861
www.alsde.edu

Stephen B Franks, Division Director

Alaska

060 Alaska Commission on Postsecondary Education (ACPE)
ACPE
PO Box 110505
Juneau, AK 99811
907-465-2962
800-441-2962
Fax: 907-465-5316
ACPE@alaska.gov
www.acpe.alaska.gov
Provides information on the state's education programs, colleges and universities, financial aid assistance programs, grants, scholarships, continuing education programs and career opportunities.

Stephanie Butler, Executive Director
Kerry Thomas, Director, Operations

3061 Alaska Department of Education Administrative Services
801 W 10th Street
Suite 200
Juneau, AK 99801-1894
907-465-2802
Fax: 907-465-4156
For certification information visit www.eed.state.ak.us/TeacherCertification/ or contact 907-465-2831.

Shirley J Halloway, Commissioner

3062 Alaska Department of Education & Early Development
801 W 10th Street, Suite 200
PO Box 110500
Juneau, AK 99811-500
907-465-2800
Fax: 907-465-4156
eed.webmaster@alaska.gov

Gerald Covey, Commissioner

3063 Libraries, Archives & Museums
PO Box 110571
333 Willoughby Avenue
Juneau, AK 99811-0571
907-465-2910
Fax: 907-465-2151
eed.webmaster@alaska.gov
Summer reading programs

Linda Thibodeau, Director
Bob Banghart, Chief Curator

3064 School Finance & Data Management
Alaska Department of Education & Early Development
801 W 10th Street, Suite 200
PO Box 110500
Juneau, AK 99811-0500
907-465-2800
Fax: 907-465-4156
eed.webmaster@alaska.gov
www.eed.state.ak.us
Public school funding programs

Cynthia Curran, Director
Paul Prussing, Deputy Director

3065 Teaching And Learning Support Program
Alaska Department of Education & Early Development
801 W 10th Street, Suite 200
PO Box 110500
Juneau, AK 99811-0500
907-465-2800
Fax: 907-465-4156
eed.webmaster@alaska.gov
www.eed.state.ak.us
To improve students performance as well as the administering of a variety of federal, state and private programs that provide support to school district staff across the state.

Cynthia Curran, Director
Paul Prussing, Deputy Director

3066 Vocational Rehabilitation
Alaska Department of Labor & Workforce Development
801 W 10th Street
Suite A
Juneau, AK 99801-1894
907-465-2814
800-478-2815
Fax: 907-465-2856
dawn.duval@alaska.gov
www.labor.state.ak.us
Helping individuals with disabilities to find employment

Cheryl Walsh, Director
John Cannon, Chairperson

Arkansas

3067 Arkansas Department of Education
4 Capitol Mall
Room 403-A
Little Rock, AR 72201-1071
501-682-4475
virginia.hill@arkansas.gov
www.arkansased.org
Mission is to provide the highest quality leadership, service, and support to school districts and schools in order that they may provide equitable, quality education for all to ensure that all public schools comply with the standards.

Samuel Ledbetter, Chair
Abby Cress, Administrative Analyst

3068 Arkansas Department of Education: Special Education
4 Capitol Mall
Room 403-A
Little Rock, AR 72201-1071
501-682-4475
www.arkansased.org

Samuel Ledbetter, Chair
Abby Cress, Administrative Analyst

3069 Federal Programs
Arkansas Department of Education
4 Capitol Mall
Room 403-A
Little Rock, AR 72201-1011
501-682-4475
www.arkansased.org

Samuel Ledbetter, Chair
Abby Cress, Administrative Analyst

California

3070 California Department of Education
1430 N Street
Sacramento, CA 95814-5901
916-319-0800
Fax: 916-657-4975
EHughes@cde.ca.gov.
www.cde.ca.gov
Works to encourage the highest achievement for students by defining the knowledge, concepts and skills that students should aquire in each grade level.

Tom Torlakson, St Superintendent Public Ins
Richard Zeiger, Chief Deputy Superintendent

3071 California Department of Education's Educational Resources Catalog
CDE Press Sales
1430 N Street
Suite 3207
Sacramento, CA 95814-5901
916-319-0800
800-995-4099
Fax: 916-323-0823
www.cde.ca.gov
Offers new techniques and fresh perspectives in handbooks, guides, videos and more.

Tom Torlakson, St Superintendent Public Ins

3072 California Department of Special Education
1430 N Street
Sacramento, CA 95814-5901
913-319-0800
Fax: 916-327-3516
EHughes@cde.ca.gov
www.cde.ca.gov
Resources and information that serve the unique needs of persons with disabilities by helping them to meet or exceed high standards of achievement in both academic and nonacademic skills.

Tom Torlakson, St Superintendent Public Ins

3073 Curriculum & Instructional Leadership Branch
California Department of Education
1430 N Street
Sacramento, CA 95814-5901
916-319-0800
www.cde.ca.gov
Works to improve students academic achievements

Tom Torlakson, St Superintendent Public Ins

3074 Region 9: Education Department
San Diego COE
6401 Linda Vista Road
Suite 321
North San Diego, CA 92111
858-569-5304
Part of a statewide system of school support established to meet state and federal requirements, the support system works within county offices offering intensive and sustained assistance to local schools and educational agencies receiving Title I funds, helping to increase the opportunity for all student's to meet the state academic content standards.

David Brashear, Director

3075 Specialized Programs Branch
California Department of Education
1430 N Street
Sacramento, CA 95814-5901
916-319-0800
EHughes@cde.ca.gov
www.cde.ca.gov
Works to ensure that all children have the opportunity to obtain high-quality education.

Tom Torlakson, St Superintendent Public Ins
Mary Payne, District/School Improvement

Colorado

3076 Colorado Department of Education
201 E Colfax Avenue
Denver, CO 80203-1799
303-866-6600
Fax: 303-866-6938
www.cde.state.co.us
For certification information visit www.cde.state.co.us/index_license.htm or contact 303-866-6628.

William T Moloney, Commissioner

3077 Educator Licensing Unit
Colorado Department of Education
201 E Colfax Avenue
Denver, CO 80203-1704
303-866-6628
Fax: 303-866-6866
Licensing applications for educators, career and technical education. Issues educators licenses, reviews content, induction/professional development and disciplinary actions

Ed Almon, Educator Licensing

3078 Office of Federal Program Administration
Colorado Department of Education
1560 Broadway
Suite 1450
Denver, CO 80202-5149
303-866-6600
Fax: 303-866-6637
Administers funds under the elementary and secondary education act as well as a variety of other state and federal competitive awards and grants with the main goal to help all students to reach proficiency in English language arts, mathematics and reading.

Patrick Chapman, Executive Director
Lynn Bamberry, Director

3079 State Library
Colorado Department of Education
201 E Colfax Avenue
Room 309
Denver, CO 80203-1704
303-866-6900
Fax: 303-866-6940
www.cde.state.co.us
Provides leadership and expertise in library related activities and policies and provides assistance to public and academic schools.

Eugene Hainer, Assistant Commissioner
Sharon Morris, Director

3080 Supplemental Educational Services
Colorado Department of Education
1560 Broadway
Suite 1450
Denver, CO 80202
303-866-6600
Fax: 303-866-6637
medler_l@cde.state.co.us
www.cde.state.co.us
SES offers tutoring outside the regular school day that is designed to increase the academic achievement in reading/mathematics and language arts to low-income students in low-income schools

Patrick Chapman, Executive Director
Lisa Medler, Title IIA Coordinator

Connecticut

3081 Connecticut Early Childhood Unit
Connecticut State Department of Education
165 Capital Avenue
Hartford, CT 06106
860-713-6740
Fax: 860-713-7018
Offers programs for children, infants and toddlers with disabilities.

Steven Adamowski, Superintendent

3082 Connecticut Governor's Committee on Employment of the Handicapped
Labor Department Building
200 Constitution Ave. NW
Washington, DC 20210
860-263-6774
866-4 U-A DO
Fax: 860-263-6039
www.dol.gov

3083 Connecticut State Department of Education
165 Capitol Avenue
Hartford, CT 06106
860-713-6543
Fax: 860-722-8502
www.sde.ct.gov

Steven Adamowski, Superintendent

3084 Education Programs & Services
Connecticut Department of Education
25 Industrial Park Road
Middletown, CT 06457-1520
860-807-2005
Fax: 860-635-7125

Theodore S Sergi, Division Director

3085 Finance & Grants Department
Connecticut State Department of Education
Grants Management
165 Capitol Avenue
Hartford, CT 06106
860-713-0466
Fax: 860-713-7046
www.sde.ct.gov

Eugene Croce, Manager
Candace Madison, Secretary

3086 Office of State Coordinator of Vocational Education for Disabled Students
Vocational Prgs. for the Disabled & Disadvantaged
PO Box 2219
Hartford, CT 06145
860-807-2001
Fax: 860-807-2196

3087 Teaching & Learning Division
Connecticut State Department of Education
165 Capital Avenue
Hartford, CT 06106-1659
860-713-6740
Fax: 860-713-7018
ciquest@ct.gov
www.sde.ct.gov

George Coleman, Acting Commissioner

3088 Vocational-Technical School Systems
Connecticut Technical High School System
25 Industrial Park Road
Middletown, CT 06457-1520
800-822-6832
Fax: 860-807-2196
cthsinternet@ct.gov
www.cttech.org

Patricia Ciccone, Superintendent
Robert Lombardi, Assistant

Delaware

89 Assessments & Accountability Branch Delaware Department of Education
The Townsend Building
401 Federal Street, Suite 2
Dover, DE 19901-3639
302-735-4000
Fax: 302-739-4654
www.doe.k12.de.us

Mark T. Murphy, Secretary of Education
Mary Kate McLaughlin, Chief of Staff

90 Delaware Department of Education
The Townsend Building
401 Federal Street, Suite 2
Dover, DE 19901-3639
302-735-4000
Fax: 302-739-4654
dedoe@doe.k12.de.us
www.doe.k12.de.us
Our mission is to promote the highest quality education for every Delaware student by providing visionary leadership and superior service.

Mark T. Murphy, Secretary of Education
Mary Kate McLaughlin, Chief of Staff

91 Delaware Department of Education: Administrative Services
The Townsend Building
401 Federal Street, Suite 2
Dover, DE 19901-3639
302-735-4000
Fax: 302-739-4654
dedoe@doe.k12.de.us
www.doe.k12.de.us

Mark T. Murphy, Secretary of Education
Mary Kate McLaughlin, Chief of Staff

92 Improvement & Assistance Branch Delaware Department of Education
The Townsend Building
401 Federal Street, Suite 2
Dover, DE 19901-3639
302-735-4000
Fax: 302-739-4654
dedoe@doe.k12.de.us
www.doe.k12.de.us

Mark T. Murphy, Secretary of Education
Mary Kate McLaughlin, Chief of Staff

District of Columbia

093 DC Office of Special Education
District of Columbia Public Schools
441 4th Street, NW, 700S
Washington, DC 20001
202-727-0252
Fax: 202-727-9385
ocp@dc.gov
www.ocp.dc.gov

Nancy Hapeman, Interim Director
Yinka Alao, Chief of Staff

094 District of Columbia Department of Education
441 4th Street, NW, 700S
Washington, DC 20001
202-727-0252
Fax: 202-727-9385
ocp@dc.gov
www.ocp.dc.gov

Nancy Hapeman, Interim Director
Yinka Alao, Chief of Staff

Florida

3095 Florida Department of Education
Turlington Building Suite 1514
325 West Gaines Street
Tallahassee, FL 32399
850-245-0505
Fax: 850-245-9667
commissioner@fldoe.org
www.fldoe.org
Offers information on community colleges, vocational education, public schools, human resources, financial assistance, adult education and more.

Pam Stewart, Commissioner/Fl. Dept of Ed
Kathy Hebda, Chief of Staff

Georgia

3096 Georgia Department of Education
2054 Twin Towers East
205 Jesse Hill Jr. Drive SE
Atlanta, GA 30334
404-656-2800
800-311-3627
Fax: 404-651-6867
askdoe@doe.k12.ga.us
www.gadoe.org
Among many other features, this organization offers agriculture education, federal programs, Leadership Development Academy, school and community nutrition progams, Spanish language and cultural program, technology/career (vocational) education and more.

Richard Woods, Superintendent
Sue Goodman, Manager

Hawaii

3097 Career & Technical Education Center
University of Hawaii
Lunalilo Portable 1
Lower Campus Road
Honolulu, HI 96822-2489
808-956-7461
Fax: 808-956-9096
hicte@hawaii.edu
www.hawaii.edu/cte

Angela Meixell, Interim Director
Sherilyn Lau, Education Specialist

3098 Hawaii Department of Education
1390 Miller Street
PO Box 2360
Honolulu, HI 96813
808-586-3230
Fax: 808-586-3234
doe_info@notes.k12.hi.us
www.hawaiipublicschools.org

Kathryn Matayoshi, Superintendent
Ronn Nozoe, Deputy Superitendent

3099 Information & Telecommunications Services Branch
Hawaii Department of Education
1390 Miller St., Room 417
PO Box 2360
Honolulu, HI 96813
808-586-3230
Fax: 808-586-3234
doe_info@notes.k12.hi.us
www.hawaiipublicschools.org

Kathryn Matayoshi, Superintendent
Ronn Nozoe, Deputy Superitendent

3100 Office of Curriculum, Instruction and Student Support
Hawaii Department of Education
Queen Liliuokalani Bldg, Rm 316
1390 Miller St,
Honolulu, HI 96813
808-586-3446
Fax: 808-586-3429
doe_info@notes.k12.hi.us

Kathryn Matayoshi, Superintendent
Leila Hayashida, Acting Assis Superintendent

3101 Special Education Department
Hawaii Department of Education
1390 Miller Street
Ofc Curriculum/Instruction/Student Supp.
Honolulu, HI 96813
808-586-3230
Fax: 808-586-3234
doe_info@notes.k12.hi.us
www.hawaiipublicschools.org

Kathryn Matayoshi, Superintendent
Ronn Nozoe, Deputy Superitendent

3102 State Public Library System
Hawaii State Public Library System
478 South King Street
Honolulu, HI 96813-2901
808-586-3617
Fax: 808-586-3314
www.hawaii.sdp.sirsi.net

Richard P. Burns, State Librarian

Idaho

3103 Idaho State Department of Education
650 West State Street
PO Box 83720
Boise, ID 83720-0027
208-332-6800
800-432-4601
Fax: 208-334-2228
infosuperintendent@sde.idaho.gov
www.sde.idaho.gov

Tom Luna, Superintendent
Sherri Ybarra, Superitendent

3104 Special Education Division
Idaho State Department of Education
650 W. State Street
PO Box 83720
Boise, ID 83720-0027
208-332-6806
Fax: 208-334-2228
infosuperintendent@sde.idaho.gov
www.sde.idaho.gov
Committed to empower people with disabilities with appropriate resources to make informed choices about their futures.

Sherri Ybarra, Superitendent
Casandra Myers, Administrative Assistant

Illinois

3105 Educator & School Development
Illinois Department of Education
100 N. 1st Street
Springfield, IL 62777
217-782-4321
866-262-6663
www.isbe.state.il.us

Dr. Christopher Koch, State Superintendent
Gery J. Chico, Board Chair

3106 Educator Certification
Illinois Department of Education
100 N. 1st Street
Springfield, IL 62777
217-782-4321
866-262-6663
www.isbe.state.il.us
Dr. Christopher Koch, State Superintendent
Gery J. Chico, Board Chair

3107 Finance & Support Services
Illinois Department of Education
100 N. 1st Street
Springfield, IL 62777
217-782-4321
866-262-6663
finance@isbe.net
www.isbe.state.il.us
Dr. Christopher Koch, State Superintendent
Gery J. Chico, Board Chair

3108 Illinois Department of Education
100 N 1st Street
Springfield, IL 62777
217-782-4321
866-262-6663
www.isbe.state.il.us
Dr. Christopher Koch, State Superintendent
Gery J. Chico, Board Chair

3109 School Finance
Illinois State Department of Education
100 N. 1st Street
Springfield, IL 62777
217-782-4321
866-262-6663
finance@isbe.net
www.isbe.state.il.us
Dr. Christopher Koch, State Superintendent
Gery J. Chico, Board Chair

3110 School Improvement & Assessment Services
Illinois State Board of Education
100 N 1st Street
Springfield, IL 62777
217-782-4321
866-262-6663
www.isbe.state.il.us
Chris Koch, Superintendent
Gery J. Chico, Board Chair

3111 Special Education
Illinois State Board of Education
100 N 1st Street
Springfield, IL 62777
217-782-4321
866-262-6663
Dr. Christopher Koch, State Superintendent
Gery J. Chico, Board Chair

Indiana

3112 Center for School Assessment & Research
Indiana Department of Education
South Tower, Suite 600
115 W. Washington Street
Indianapolis, IN 46204-2203
317-232-6610
Fax: 317-232-8004
webmaster@doe.in.gov
www.doe.in.gov
Glenda Ritz, Superitendent

3113 Community Relations & Special Populations
Indiana Department of Education
South Tower, Suite 600
115 W. Washington Street
Indianapolis, IN 46204-2203
317-232-6610
Fax: 317-232-8004
webmaster@doe.in.gov
www.doe.in.gov
Glenda Ritz, Superitendent

3114 External Affairs
Indiana Department of Education
South Tower, Suite 600
115 W. Washington Street
Indianapolis, IN 46204-2203
317-232-6610
Fax: 317-232-8004
webmaster@doe.in.gov
www.doe.in.gov
Glenda Ritz, Superitendent

3115 Indiana Department of Education
South Tower, Suite 600
115 W. Washington Street
Indianapolis, IN 46204-2798
317-232-6610
Fax: 317-232-8004
webmaster@doe.in.gov
www.doe.in.gov
For certification information visit www.in.gov/psb or contact 866-542-3672.
Glenda Ritz, Superitendent

3116 Office of Legal Affairs
Indiana Department of Education
South Tower, Suite 600
115 W. Washington Street
Indianapolis, IN 46204-2203
317-232-6610
Fax: 317-232-8004
webmaster@doe.in.gov
www.doe.in.gov
Glenda Ritz, Superitendent

3117 Office of School Financial Management
Indiana Department of Education
South Tower, Suite 600
115 W. Washington Street
Indianapolis, IN 46204-2203
317-232-6610
Fax: 317-232-8004
webmaster@doe.in.gov
www.doe.in.gov
Glenda Ritz, Superitendent

3118 Office of the Deputy Superintendent
Indiana Department of Education
South Tower, Suite 600
115 W. Washington Street
Indianapolis, IN 46204-2203
317-232-6610
Fax: 317-232-8004
webmaster@doe.in.gov
www.doe.in.gov
Glenda Ritz, Superitendent

3119 School Improvement & Performance Center
Indiana Department of Education
South Tower, Suite 600
115 W. Washington Street
Indianapolis, IN 46204-2203
317-232-6610
Fax: 317-232-8004
webmaster@doe.in.gov
www.doe.in.gov
Glenda Ritz, Superitendent

Iowa

3120 Community Colleges Division
Iowa Department of Education
400 E. 14th Street
Des Moines, IA 50319-0146
515-281-5294
Fax: 515-281-5988
www.educateiowa.gov
Brad Buck, Director
Jeremy Varner, Administrator

3121 Division of Library Services
Iowa Department of Education
400 E. 14th Street
Des Moines, IA 50319-0146
515-281-5294
Fax: 515-281-5988
www.educateiowa.gov
Brad Buck, Director
Jeremy Varner, Administrator

3122 Educational Services for Children & Families
Iowa Department of Education
400 E. 14th Street
Des Moines, IA 50319-0146
515-281-5294
Fax: 515-281-5988
www.educateiowa.gov
Brad Buck, Director
Jeremy Varner, Administrator

3123 Elementary & Secondary Education
Iowa Department of Education
400 E. 14th Street
Des Moines, IA 50319-0146
515-281-5294
Fax: 515-281-5988
www.educateiowa.gov
Strives for higher levels of learning and achievement for students in public elementary and secondary schools
Brad Buck, Director
Jeremy Varner, Administrator

3124 Financial & Information Services
Iowa Department of Education
400 E. 14th Street
Des Moines, IA 50319-0146
515-281-5294
Fax: 515-242-5988
www.educateiowa.gov
Brad Buck, Director
Jeremy Varner, Administrator

3125 Iowa Department of Education
Iowa Department of Education
400 E. 14th Street
Des Moines, IA 50319-0146
515-281-5294
Fax: 515-281-5988
www.educateiowa.gov
Serves the students of Iowa by providing leadership and resources for schools, area education agencies and community colleges. For certification information visit www.state.ia.us/boee or contact 515-281-3245.
Brad Buck, Director
Jeremy Varner, Administrator

3126 Iowa Public Television
Iowa Department of Education
400 E. 14th Street
Des Moines, IA 50319-0146

515-281-5294
Fax: 515-281-5988
www.educateiowa.gov

Brad Buck, Director
Jeremy Varner, Administrator

127 Vocational Rehabilitation Services
Iowa Department of Education
400 E. 14th Street
Des Moines, IA 50319-0146
515-281-5294
Fax: 515-281-5988
www.educateiowa.gov

Brad Buck, Director
Jeremy Varner, Administrator

Kansas

128 Kansas Department of Education
Kansas State Department of Education
900 SW Jackson Street
Topeka, KS 66612-1212
785-296-3201
Fax: 785-796-7933
contact@ksde.org
www.ksde.org

Dr. Diane DeBacker, Commissioner of Education
Brad Neuenswander, Interim Commissioner

129 Office of the Commissioner
Kansas State Department of Education
900 SW Jackson Street
Topeka, KS 66612-1212
785-296-3201
Fax: 785-296-7933
contact@ksde.org
www.ksde.org

Dr. Diane DeBacker, Commissioner of Education
Brad Neuenswander, Interim Commissioner

130 Special Education Services Department
Kansas State Department of Education
900 SW Jackson Street
Topeka, KS 66612-1212
785-296-3201
Fax: 785-296-7933
contact@ksde.org
www.ksde.org

Dr. Diane DeBacker, Commissioner of Education
Brad Neuenswander, Interim Commissioner

131 Teacher Education & Licensure
Kansas State Department of Education
900 SW Jackson Street
Topeka, KS 66612-1212
785-296-3201
Fax: 785-296-7933
contact@ksde.org
www.ksde.org

Dr. Diane DeBacher, Commissioner of Education
Brad Neuenswander, Interim Commissioner

Kentucky

132 Communications Services
Kentucky Department of Education
500 Mero Street
Frankfort, KY 40601-1957
502-564-4770
andrew.liaupsin@education.ky.gov
www.education.ky.gov

Terry Holliday, Ph.D, Commissioner of Education
Rebecca Blessing, General Counsel

3133 Curriculum, Assessment & Accountability Council
Kentucky Department of Education
??Capital Plaza Tower
500 Mero St.
Frankfort, KY 40601-1957
502-564-4770
Fax: 502-564-7749
rebecca.blessing@education.ky.gov
www.education.ky.gov/Pages/default.aspx

Terry Holliday, Ph.D, Commissioner of Education
Rebecca Blessing, General Counsel

3134 Education Technology Office
Kentucky Department of Education
500 Mero Street
16th Floor CPT
Frankfort, KY 40601-1957
502-564-4770
rebecca.blessing@education.ky.gov
www.education.ky.gov/Pages/default.aspx

Terry Holliday, Ph.D, Commissioner of Education
Rebecca Blessing, General Counsel

3135 Kentucky Department of Education
Kentucky Department of Education
500 Mero Street
Capital Plaza Tower
Frankfort, KY 40601-1957
502-564-4770
Fax: 502-564-5680
rebecca.blessing@education.ky.gov
www.education.ky.gov/Pages/default.aspx
For certification information visit www.kyepsb.net or contact 502-573-4606.

Terry Holliday PhD, Commissioner of Education
Rebecca Blessing, General Counsel

3136 Regional Services Centers
Kentucky Department of Education
500 Mero Street
18th Floor CPT
Frankfort, KY 40601-1957
502-564-4770
rebecca.blessing@education.ky.gov
www.education.ky.gov/Pages/default.aspx

Terry Holliday, Ph.D, Commissioner of Education
Rebecca Blessing, General Counsel

3137 Special Education Services
Kentucky Department of Education
500 Mero Street
8th Floor
Frankfort, KY 40601-1957
502-564-4770
Fax: 502-564-6721
rebecca.blessing@education.ky.gov
www.education.ky.gov/Pages/default.aspx

Terry Holliday, Ph.D, Commissioner of Education
Rebecca Blessing, General Counsel

3138 Teacher Education & Certification
Kentucky Department of Education
500 Mero Street
17th Floor
Frankfort, KY 40601-1957
502-564-4770
rebecca.blessing@education.ky.gov
www.education.ky.gov/Pages/default.aspx

Terry Holliday, Ph.D, Commissioner of Education
Rebecca Blessing, General Counsel

Louisiana

3139 Academic Programs Office
Louisiana Department of Education
1201 North Third Streetÿ
PO Box 94064
Baton Rouge, LA 70804-9064
877-453-2721
Fax: 225-342-0193
customerservice@la.gov
www.louisianabelieves.com

Paul Pastorek, State Superintendent of Educ
Rene Greer, Director, Public Affairs

3140 Louisiana Department of Education
1201 North Third Streetÿ
PO Box 94064
Baton Rouge, LA 70804-9064
504-342-3607
877-453-2721
Fax: 225-342-0193
www.louisianabelieves.com
Provides leadership and enacts policies that result in improved academic achievement and responsible citizenship for all students. For certification information visit www.louisianaschools.net or contact 225-342-3490.

Cecil J Picard, Superintendent

3141 Management & Finance Office
Louisana State Department of Education
1201 North Third Streetÿ
PO Box 94064
Baton Rouge, LA 70804-9064
225-342-3617
877-453-2721
Fax: 225-219-7538
www.louisianabelieves.com

Marlyn J Langley, Deputy Superintendent

3142 Office of Educator Support
Louisiana Department of Education
1201 North Third Streetÿ
PO Box 94064
Baton Rouge, LA 70804-9064
877-453-2721
Fax: 225-342-0193
customerservice@la.gov
www.louisianabelieves.com

Paul Pastorek, State Superintendent of Educ
Karen Burke, Acting Asst. Superintendent

3143 Special Education Services
Louisiana Department of Education
1201 North Third Streetÿ
PO Box 94064
Baton Rouge, LA 70804-9064
877-453-2721
Fax: 225-342-0193
customerservice@la.gov
www.louisianabelieves.com

Paul Pastorek, State Superintendent of Educ
Rene Greer, Director, Public Affairs

3144 **Standards, Assessments & Accountability**
Louisiana Department of Education
1201 North Third Streetÿ
PO Box 94064
Baton Rouge, LA 70804-9064
877-453-2721
Fax: 225-342-3600
customerservice@la.gov
www.louisianabelieves.com

Paul Pastorek, State Superintendent of Educ
Scott Norton, Assistant Superintendent

Maine

3145 **Administrator and Teacher Certification**
Maine Department of Education
Certification Office
23 State House Station
Augusta, ME 04333-0023
207-624-6600
Fax: 207-624-6700
commish.doe@maine.gov
www.maine.gov

Jim Rier, Commissioner
Charlene Tucker, Team Coordinator

3146 **Adult Education**
Maine Department of Education
23 State House Station
Augusta, ME 04333-0023
207-624-6600
Fax: 207-624-6700
commish.doe@maine.gov
www.maine.gov

Jim Rier, Commissioner
Charlene Tucker, Team Coordinator

3147 **Maine Department of Education**
23 State House Station
Augusta, ME 04333-0023
207-624-6600
Fax: 207-624-6700
commish.doe@maine.gov
www.maine.gov

Jim Rier, Commissioner
Charlene Tucker, Team Coordinator

Maryland

3148 **Career & Technology Education**
Maryland State Department of Education
200 W Baltimore Street
Baltimore, MD 21201-2595
410-767-0100
888-246-0016
Fax: 410-333-2099
pmikos@msde.state.md.us
www.marylandpublicschools.org

Pat Mikos, Program Manager
Kimberlee Schultz, Public Affair Officer

3149 **Certification & Accreditation**
Maryland State Department of Education
200 W. Baltimore Street
Baltimore, MD 21201-2595
410-767-0100
888-246-0016
www.marylandpublicschools.org

Nancy S. Grasmick, St Superintendent of Schools
Kimberlee Schultz, Public Affair Officer

3150 **Instruction Division**
Maryland State Department of Education
200 W Baltimore Street
Baltimore, MD 21201-2595
410-767-0100
888-246-0016
www.marylandpublicschools.org

Mary Cary, Assistant Superintendent
Kimberlee Schultz, Public Affair Officer

3151 **Library Development & Services**
Maryland State Department of Education
200 West Baltimore Street
Baltimore, MD 21201-2595
410-767-0100
888-246-0016
www.marylandpublicschools.org

Irene Padilla, Asst St Superintendent Lib.
Kimberlee Schultz, Public Affair Officer

3152 **Maryland Department of Education**
Maryland State Department of Education
200 W Baltimore Street
Baltimore, MD 21201-2595
410-767-0100
888-246-0016
Fax: 410-333-6033
www.marylandpublicschools.org
Mission of MSDE is to provide leadership, support, and accountability for effective systems of public education, library services and rehabilitation services. For certification information visit www.certification.msde.state.md.us or contact 410-767-0412.

Nancy S Grasmick, Superintendent
Kimberlee Schultz, Public Affair Officer

3153 **Office of Special Education and Rehabilitative Services**
U.S. Department of Education
400 Maryland Avenue SW
Washington, DC 20202-7100
202-245-7459
www.ed.gov

Melody Musgrove, Director
Bill Wolf, Acting Deputy Director

3154 **Special Education/Early Intervention Services Division**
Maryland State Department of Education
200 W Baltimore Street
9th Floor
Baltimore, MD 21201-2595
410-767-0100
888-246-0016
Fax: 410-333-8165
www.marylandpublicschools.org

Nancy S. Grasmick, St Superintendent of Schools
Kimberlee Schultz, Public Affair Officer

Massachusetts

3155 **Massachusetts Department of Education**
75 Pleasant Streetÿ
Malden, MA 02148-4906
781-338-3000
Fax: 781-338-3770
boe@doe.mass.edu
www.doe.mass.edu

David P Driscoll, Commissioner

3156 **Massachusetts Department of Educational Improvement**
75 Pleasant Streetÿ
Malden, MA 02148-4906
781-388-3300
Fax: 781-338-3770
boe@doe.mass.edu
www.doe.mass.edu

Andrea Perrault, Division Director

3157 **Region 1: Education Department**
J.W. McCormick Post Office & Courthouse
540 McCormick Courthouse
Boston, MA 02109-4557
617-223-9317
Fax: 617-223-9324

Michael Sentance

Michigan

3158 **Administrative Services Office**
Michigan Department of Education
608 W Allegan Street
Lansing, MI 48933-1524
517-373-3324
877-932-6424
Fax: 517-335-4565
www.michigan.gov

Rick Snyder, Governor

3159 **Adult Extended Learning Office**
Michigan Department of Education
608 W Allegan Street
Lansing, MI 48933-1524
517-373-3324
877-932-6424
Fax: 517-335-4565
www.michigan.gov

Rick Snyder, Governor

3160 **Career & Technical Education**
Michigan Department of Education
608 W Allegan Street
Lansing, MI 48933-1524
517-373-3324
877-932-6424
Fax: 517-373-8776
www.michigan.gov

Rick Snyder, Governor

3161 **Higher Education Management Office**
Michigan Department of Education
608 W Allegan Street
Lansing, MI 48933-1524
517-373-3324
877-932-6424
Fax: 517-373-2759
www.michigan.gov

Rick Snyder, Governor

3162 **Instructional Programs**
Michigan Department of Education
608 W Allegan Street
Lansing, MI 48933-1524
517-373-3324
877-932-6424
Fax: 517-335-4565
www.michigan.gov

Rick Snyder, Governor

3163 **Michigan Department of Education**
Michigan Department of Education
608 W Allegan Street
PO Box 30008
Lansing, MI 48909
517-373-3324
877-932-6424
Fax: 517-335-4565
MDEweb@michigan.gov
www.michigan.gov/mde

Rick Snyder, Governor

64 Office of School Management
Michigan Department of Education
608 W Allegan Street
Lansing, MI 48933-1524
517-373-3324
877-932-6424
Fax: 517-335-4565
www.michigan.gov
Rick Snyder, Governor

65 Office of the Superintendent
Michigan Department of Education
608 W Allegan Street
Lansing, MI 48933-1524
517-373-3324
877-932-6424
Fax: 517-335-4565
www.michigan.gov
Rick Snyder, Governor

66 Postsecondary Services
Michigan Department of Education
608 W Allegan Street
Lansing, MI 48909
517-373-3324
877-932-6424
Fax: 517-335-4565
www.michigan.gov
Rick Snyder, Governor

67 School Program Quality
Michigan Department of Education
608 W Allegan Street
Lansing, MI 48933-1524
517-373-3324
877-932-6424
Fax: 517-373-4565
www.michigan.gov
Rick Snyder, Governor

68 Special Education
Michigan Department of Education
608 W Allegan Street
Lansing, MI 48933-1524
517-373-3324
877-932-6424
Fax: 581-733-5456
www.michigan.gov
Rick Snyder, Governor

169 Student Financial Assistance
Michigan Department of Education
608 W Allegan Street
Lansing, MI 48933-1524
517-373-3324
877-932-6424
Fax: 517-335-4565
www.michigan.gov
Rick Snyder, Governor

170 Teacher & Administrative Preparation
Michigan Department of Education
608 W Allegan Street
Lansing, MI 48933-1524
514-373-3324
877-932-6424
Fax: 517-335-4565
www.michigan.gov
Rick Snyder, Governor

Minnesota

171 Data & Technology
Minnesota Department of Education
1500 Highway 36 West
Roseville, MN 55113-2233
651-582-8200
mde.commissioner@state.mn.us
www.education.state.mn.us/mde
Brenda Cassellius, Commissioner
Charlene Briner, Chief of Staff

3172 Data Management
Minnesota Department of Education
1500 Highway 36 West
Roseville, MN 55113
651-582-8200
Fax: 651-582-8873
mde.commissioner@state.mn.us
www.education.state.mn.us/mde
Brenda Cassellius, Commissioner
Charlene Briner, Chief of Staff

3173 Education Funding
Minnesota Department of Education
1500 Highway 36 West
Roseville, MN 55113-2233
651-582-8200
mde.commissioner@state.mn.us
www.education.state.mn.us/mde
Brenda Cassellius, Commissioner
Charlene Briner, Chief of Staff

3174 Financial Conditions & Aids Payment
Minnesota Department of Education
1500 Highway 36 West
Roseville, MN 55113-2233
651-582-8200
mde.commissioner@state.mn.us
www.education.state.mn.us/mde
Brenda Cassellius, Commissioner
Charlene Briner, Chief of Staff

3175 Government Relations
Minnesota Department of Education
1500 Highway 36 West
Roseville, MN 55113-2233
651-582-8200
mde.commissioner@state.mn.us
www.education.state.mn.us/mde
Brenda Cassellius, Commissioner
Charlene Briner, Chief of Staff

3176 Human Resources Office
Minnesota Department of Education
1500 Highway 36 West
Roseville, MN 55113-2233
651-582-8200
mde.commissioner@state.mn.us
www.education.state.mn.us/mde
Brenda Cassellius, Commissioner
Charlene Briner, Chief of Staff

3177 Minnesota Department of Children, Families & Learning
Minnesota Department of Education
1500 Highway 36 W
Roseville, MN 55113-4266
651-582-8200
Fax: 651-582-8724
mde.commissioner@state.mn.us
www.education.state.mn.us/mde
Works to help communities to measurably improve the well-being of children through programs that focus on education, community services, prevention, and the preparation of young people for the world of work. All department efforts emphasize the achievement of positive results for children and their families.
Brenda Cassellius, Commissioner
Charlene Briner, Chief of Staff

3178 Minnesota Department of Education
Minnesota Department of Education
1500 Highway 36 W
Roseville, MN 55113-4266
651-582-8200
Fax: 651-582-8724
mde.commissioner@state.mn.us
www.education.state.mn.us
Brenda Cassellius, Commissioner
Charlene Briner, Chief of Staff

3179 Residential Schools
Minnesota Department of Education
1500 Highway 36 West
Roseville, MN 55113-2233
651-582-8200
mde.commissioner@state.mn.us
www.education.state.mn.us/mde
Brenda Cassellius, Commissioner
Charlene Briner, Chief of Staff

Mississippi

3180 Community Outreach Services
Mississippi Department of Education
PO Box 771
Jackson, MS 39205-0771
601-359-3513
Fax: 601-359-3033
www.mde.k12.ms.us
Sarah Beard, Division Director

3181 Educational Innovations
Mississippi Department of Education
PO Box 771
Jackson, MS 39205-0771
601-359-3513
Fax: 601-359-2587
www.mde.k12.ms.us
David Robinson, Division Director

3182 External Relations
Mississippi Department of Education
PO Box 771
372 Central High Building
Jackson, MS 39205-0771
601-359-3513
Fax: 601-359-3033
www.mde.k12.ms.us
Andrew P Mullins, Division Director

3183 Management Information Systems
Mississippi Department of Education
PO Box 771
Jackson, MS 39205-0771
601-359-3513
Fax: 601-359-3033
www.mde.k12.ms.us
Rusty Purvis, Division Director

3184 Mississippi Department of Education
Mississippi Department of Education
359 NW Street
PO Box 771
Jackson, MS 39205-0771
601-359-3513
Fax: 601-359-3242
www.mde.k12.ms.us
Dr.Henry Johnson, Superintendent

3185 Mississippi Employment Security Commission
Mississippi Department of Education
PO Box 771
Jackson, MS 39205-0771
601-359-3513
Fax: 601-961-7405
www.mde.k12.ms.us

3186 Office of Accountability
Mississippi Department of Education
PO Box 771
Jackson, MS 39205-0771
601-359-3513
Fax: 601-359-1748
www.mde.k12.ms.us
Judy Rhodes, Division Director

3187 Vocational Technical Education
Mississippi Department of Education
359 NW Street
PO Box 771
Jackson, MS 39205-0771
601-359-3513
Fax: 601-359-3989
Samuel McGee, Division Director

Missouri

3188 Deputy Commissioner
Missouri Department of Education
205 Jefferson Street
PO Box 480 Floor 6
Jefferson City, MO 65101-0480
573-751-4212
Fax: 573-751-1179
www.dese.mo.gov
Margie Vandeven, Commissioner

3189 Division of Instruction
Missouri Department of Education
205 Jefferson Street
Floor 6
Jefferson City, MO 65101-0480
573-751-4212
Fax: 573-751-8613
www.dese.mo.gov
Margie Vandeven, Commissioner

3190 Missouri Department of Education
Missouri Department of Education
205 Jefferson Street, 6th Floor
PO Box 480
Jefferson City, MO 65101-0480
573-751-4212
Fax: 573-751-8613
www.dese.mo.gov
A team of dedicated individuals working for the continuous improvement of education and services for all citizens. We believe that we can make a positive difference in the quality of life for all Missourians by providing exceptional service to students, educators, schools and citizens.
Margie Vandeven, Commissioner

3191 Region 7: Education Department
Missouri Department of Education
10220 NW Executive Hills Boulevard
Kansas City, MO 64153-2312
816-891-7972
Fax: 816-891-7972
www.dese.mo.gov
Margie Vandeven, Commissioner

3192 Special Education Division
Missouri Department of Education
205 Jefferson Street
PO Box 480 Floor 6
Jefferson City, MO 65101-0480
573-751-4212
Fax: 573-751-8613
communications@dese.mo.gov
www.dese.mo.gov
Margie Vandeven, Commissioner

3193 Urban & Teacher Education
Missouri Department of Education
205 Jefferson Street
Floor 6
Jefferson City, MO 65101-0480
573-751-4212
Fax: 573-751-8613
communications@dese.mo.gov
www.dese.mo.gov
Margie Vandeven, Commissioner

3194 Vocational & Adult Education
Missouri Department of Education
205 Jefferson Street, 5th Floor
PO Box 480
Jefferson City, MO 65101-0480
573-751-4212
Fax: 573-751-8613
communications@dese.mo.gov
www.dese.mo.gov
Margie Vandeven, Commissioner

3195 Vocational Rehabilitation
Missouri Department of Education
205 Jefferson Street
PO Box 480
Jefferson City, MO 65101-0480
573-751-4212
Fax: 573-751-8613
communications@dese.mo.gov
www.dese.mo.gov
Margie Vandeven, Commissioner

Montana

3196 Accreditation & Curriculum Services Department
Montana Department of Education
106 State Capitol
PO Box 200113
Helena, MT 59620-113
406-444-2511
Fax: 406-444-2701
www.mt.gov/education
Steve Bullock, Governor

3197 Division of Information-Technology Support
Montana Department of Education
106 State Capitol
PO Box 200113
Helena, MT 59620-113
406-444-2511
Fax: 406-444-2701
www.mt.gov/education
Steve Bullock, Governor

3198 Montana Department of Education
Montana Department of Education
1227 11th Avenue
PO Box 200113
Helena, MT 59620-113
406-444-2511
Fax: 406-444-2701
www.mt.gov/education
For certification information visit www.opi.state.mt.us or contact 406-444-3150.
Steve Bullock, Governor

3199 Operations Department
Montana Department of Education
106 State Capitol
PO Box 200113
Helena, MT 59620-113
406-444-2511
Fax: 406-444-2701
www.mt.gov/education
Steve Bullock, Governor

Nebraska

3200 Administrative Services Office
Nebraska Department of Education
301 Centennial Mall S
Lincoln, NE 68508-2529
402-471-2295
Fax: 402-471-6351
www.education.ne.gov
To provide quality services and support in the areas of finance human resource management continuous quality improvement, office/building services,and technical assistant.
Mike Stefkovich, Division Director

3201 Division of Education Services
Nebraska Department of Education
301 Centennial Mall S
Lincoln, NE 68508-2529
402-471-2783
Fax: 402-471-0117
www.education.ne.gov
Marge Harouff, Division Director

3202 Nebraska Department of Education
Nebraska Department of Education
301 Centennial Mall S
PO Box 94987
Lincoln, NE 68509-4987
402-471-5020
Fax: 402-471-4433
www.education.ne.gov
Douglas D Christensen, Commissioner

3203 Rehabilitation Services Division
Nebraska Department of Education
301 Centennial Mall S 6th Floor
PO Box 94987
Lincoln, NE 68509-2529
402-471-3649
877-637-3422
Fax: 402-471-0788
www.education.ne.gov
Frank C Lloyd, Director

Nevada

3204 Administrative & Financial Services
Nevada Department of Education
700 E. Fifth Street
Carson City, NV 89701-4204
775-687-9200
888-590-6726
Fax: 775-687-9101
www.doe.nv.gov
Dale A.R. Erquiaga, Superintendent
Steve Canavero, Ph.D., Deputy Superintendent

3205 Instructional Services Division
Nevada Department of Education
700 E. Fifth Street
Carson City, NV 89701-4204
775-687-9200
Fax: 775-687-9101
www.doe.nv.gov
Dale A.R. Erquiaga, Superintendent
Steve Canavero, Ph.D., Deputy Superintendent

3206 Nevada Department of Education
700 E 5th Street
Carson City, NV 89701-5096
775-687-9200
Fax: 775-687-9101
www.doe.nv.gov

Mission is to lead Nevada's citizens in accomplishing lifelong learning and educational excellence.

Dale A.R. Erquiaga, Superintendent
Steve Canavero, Ph.D., Deputy Superintendent

New Hampshire

207 Information Services
New Hampshire Department of Education
101 Pleasent Street
Concord, NH 03301-3860
603-271-3494
Fax: 603-271-1953
www.education.nh.gov
New Hampshire schools enrollment, financial, assessment information.

Virginia M. Barry, Commissioner
Paul K. Leather, Deputy Commissioner

208 New Hampshire Department of Education
New Hampshire Department of Education
101 Pleasant Street
State Office Park S
Concord, NH 03301-3860
603-271-3494
800-339-9900
Fax: 603-271-1953
www.education.nh.gov
Mission is to provide educational leadership and services which promote equal educational opportunities and quality practices and programs than enable New Hampshire residents to become fully productive members of society.

Virginia M. Barry, Commissioner
Paul K. Leather, Deputy Commissioner

209 New Hampshire Division of Instructional Services
New Hampshire Department of Education
101 Pleasant Street
Concord, NH 03301-3860
603-271-3494
Fax: 603-271-1953
www.education.nh.gov

Virginia M. Barry, Commissioner
Paul K. Leather, Deputy Commissioner

210 Standards & Certification Division
New Hampshire Department of Education
101 Pleasant St
Concord, NH 03301-3860
603-271-3494
Fax: 603-271-1953
www.education.nh.gov

Virginia M. Barry, Commissioner
Paul K. Leather, Deputy Commissioner

New Jersey

211 New Jersey Department of Education
New Jersey Department of Education
100 Riverview Plaza
PO Box 500
Trenton, NJ 08625-0500
609-292-4450
877-900-6960
Fax: 609-777-4099
www.state.nj.us/education
Develops and implements policies that address the major education issues in New Jersey. The State Board will engage in an effort to ensure that all children receive a quality public education that prepares them to succeed as responsible, productive citizens in a global society.

David C. Hespe, Commissioner
Bari Anhalt Erlichson, Chief Performance Officer

3212 New Jersey Department of Education: Finance
New Jersey Department of Education
100 Riverview Plaza
PO Box 500
Trenton, NJ 08625-0500
609-292-4421
877-900-6960
Fax: 609-292-6794
www.state.nj.us/education

David C. Hespe, Commissioner
Bari Anhalt Erlichson, Chief Performance Officer

3213 New Jersey Division of Special Education
New Jersey Department of Education
100 Riverview Plaza
PO Box 500
Trenton, NJ 08625-0500
609-292-0147
877-900-6960
Fax: 609-984-8422
www.state.nj.us/education

David C. Hespe, Commissioner
Bari Anhalt Erlichson, Chief Performance Officer

3214 New Jersey State Library
New Jersey Department of Education
PO Box 520
Trenton, NJ 08625-0500
609-292-6200
877-900-6960
Fax: 609-292-2746
nblake@njstatelib.org
www.state.nj.us/education

David C. Hespe, Commissioner
Bari Anhalt Erlichson, Chief Performance Officer

3215 Professional Development & Licensing
New Jersey Department of Education
PO Box 500
Trenton, NJ 08625-0500
609-292-2070
877-900-6960
Fax: 609-292-3768
www.state.nj.us/education

David C. Hespe, Commissioner
Bari Anhalt Erlichson, Chief Performance Officer

3216 Urban & Field Services
New Jersey Department of Education
100 Riverview Plaza
PO Box 520
Trenton, NJ 08625-0500
609-292-4442
877-900-6960
Fax: 609-292-3830
www.state.nj.us/education

David C. Hespe, Commissioner
Bari Anhalt Erlichson, Chief Performance Officer

New Mexico

3217 Agency Support
New Mexico Department of Education
300 Don Gaspar
Education Building
Santa Fe, NM 87501-2786
505-827-5800
www.ped.state.nm.us/ped

Tres Giron, Division Director

3218 Learning Services
New Mexico Department of Education
300 Don Gaspar
Education Building
Santa Fe, NM 87501
505-827-5800
Fax: 505-827-6689
www.ped.state.nm.us/ped

Albert Zamora, Division Director

3219 New Mexico Department of Education
New Mexico Department of Education
300 Don Gaspar
Education Building
Santa Fe, NM 87501-2786
505-827-5800
Fax: 505-827-6520
www.ped.state.nm.us/ped

Michael J Davis, Superintendent

3220 New Mexico Department of School-Transportation & Support Services
New Mexico Department of Education
300 Don Gaspar
Education Building
Santa Fe, NM 87501
505-827-5800
www.ped.state.nm.us/ped

Susan Brown, Division Director

3221 School Management Accountability
New Mexico Department of Education
300 Don Gaspar
Education Building
Santa Fe, NM 87501
505-827-5800
Fax: 505-827-6689
www.ped.state.nm.us/ped

Michael J Davis, Division Director

3222 Vocational Education
New Mexico Department of Education
300 Don Gaspar
Education Building
Santa Fe, NM 87501
505-827-5800
www.ped.state.nm.us/ped

Tom Trujillo, Division Director

New York

3223 Cultural Education
New York Department of Education
89 Washington Avenue
Albany, NY 12234
518-474-3852
Fax: 518-474-2718
SiteSupport@mail.nysed.gov
www.nysed.gov

Carole F Huxley, Division Director

3224 **Elementary, Middle & Secondary Education**
New York Department of Education
89 Washington Avenue
Albany, NY 12234-0001
518-474-3852
Fax: 518-474-2718
SiteSupport@mail.nysed.gov
www.nysed.gov
James Kadamus, Deputy

3225 **Higher & Professional Education**
New York Department of Education
89 Washington Avenue
Albany, NY 12234-0001
518-474-3852
Fax: 518-474-2718
SiteSupport@mail.nysed.gov
www.nysed.gov
Johanna Duncan-Poitier, Deputy Commissioner

3226 **New York Department of Education**
New York Department of Education
89 Washington Avenue
Albany, NY 12234
518-474-3852
Fax: 518-473-4909
SiteSupport@mail.nysed.gov
www.nysed.gov
Richard P Mills, President

3227 **Professional Responsibility Office**
New York Department of Education
89 Washington Avenue
Albany, NY 12234-2643
518-474-3852
Fax: 518-485-9361
SiteSupport@mail.nysed.gov
www.nysed.gov

3228 **Region 2: Education Department**
New York Department of Education
89 Washington Avenue
Albany, NY 12234
518-474-3852
Fax: 212-264-4427
SiteSupport@mail.nysed.gov
www.nysed.gov

3229 **Vocational & Educational Services for Disabled**
New York Department of Education
89 Washington Avenue
Albany, NY 12234
518-474-3852
800-272-5448
Fax: 518-457-4562
SiteSupport@mail.nysed.gov
www.nysed.gov
David Segalla, Regional Coordinator

North Carolina

3230 **Auxiliary Services**
North Carolina Department of Education
301 N Wilmington Street
Raleigh, NC 27601-2825
919-807-3300
Fax: 919-733-5279
www.ncpublicschools.org
Charles Weaver, Division Director

3231 **Financial & Personnel Services**
North Carolina Department of Education
301 N Wilmington Street
Raleigh, NC 27601-2825
919-807-3300
www.ncpublicschools.org
James O Barber, Division Director

3232 **North Carolina Department of Education**
North Carolina Department of Education
301 N Wilmington Street
Raleigh, NC 27601-2825
919-807-3300
Fax: 919-807-3279
www.ncpublicschools.org
Bob R Etheridge, Division Director

3233 **North Carolina Department of Instructional Services**
North Carolina Department of Education
301 N Wilmington Street
Raleigh, NC 27601-2825
919-807-3300
Fax: 919-807-3279
www.ncpublicschools.org
Henry Johnson, Division Director

3234 **Staff Development & Technical Assistance**
North Carolina Department of Education
301 N Wilmington Street
Raleigh, NC 27601-2825
919-807-3300
www.ncpublicschools.org
Nancy Davis, Division Director

North Dakota

3235 **North Dakota Department of Education**
North Dakota Department of Education
600 E Boulevard Avenue
Dept. 201
Bismarck, ND 58505-0440
701-328-2260
Fax: 701-328-2461
dpi@nd.gov
www.dpi.state.nd.us
Wayne G Sanstead, Superintendent
Kirsten Baesler, State Superintendent

3236 **North Dakota Department of Public Instruction Division**
North Dakota Department of Education
600 E Boulevard Avenue
Dept. 201
Bismarck, ND 58505-0440
701-328-2260
Fax: 701-328-2461
dpi@nd.gov
www.dpi.state.nd.us
Kirsten Baesler, State Superintendent

3237 **North Dakota State Board for Vocational & Technical Education**
North Dakota Department of Education
600 E Boulevard Avenue
Dept. 201
Bismarck, ND 58505-0440
701-328-2260
Fax: 701-328-2461
dpi@nd.gov
www.dpi.state.nd.us
Kirsten Baesler, State Superintendent
Reuben Guenthner, Division Director

3238 **Study & State Film Library**
North Dakota Department of Education
600 E Boulevard Avenue
Dept. 201
Bismarck, ND 58505-0440
701-328-2260
dpi@nd.gov
www.dpi.state.nd.us
Kirsten Baesler, State Superintendent
Robert Stone, Division Director

Ohio

3239 **Blind School**
Ohio Department of Education
25 S Front Street
Columbus, OH 43215-4131
614-466-3641
877-644-6338
Fax: 614-752-1713
contact.center@education.ohio.gov
www.education.ohio.gov
Richard A. Ross, Superitendent
Tom Gunlock, President

3240 **Curriculum, Instruction & Professional Development**
Ohio Department of Education
25 S Front Street
Columbus, OH 43215-4131
614-466-2761
877-644-6338
Fax: 704-992-5168
contact.center@education.ohio.gov
www.education.ohio.gov
Richard A. Ross, Superitendent
Tom Gunlock, President

3241 **Early Childhood Education**
Ohio Department of Education
25 S Front Street
Columbus, OH 43215-4131
614-466-0224
877-644-6338
Fax: 614-728-2338
contact.center@education.ohio.gov
www.education.ohio.gov
Richard A. Ross, Superitendent
Tom Gunlock, President

3242 **Federal Assistance**
Ohio Department of Education
25 S Front Street
Columbus, OH 43215-4131
614-466-4161
877-644-6338
Fax: 704-992-5168
contact.center@education.ohio.gov
www.education.ohio.gov
Richard A. Ross, Superitendent
Tom Gunlock, President

3243 **Ohio Department of Education**
Ohio Department of Education
25 S Front Street
7th Floor
Columbus, OH 43215-4183
614-466-7578
877-644-6338
Fax: 614-728-4781
contact.center@education.ohio.gov
www.education.ohio.gov
Works in partnership with school districts to assure high achievements for all learners, promote a safe and orderly learning environment, provide leadership, support, and build capacity, and provide support to school districts particularly those who need it most.
Richard A. Ross, Superitendent
Tom Gunlock, President

44 Personnel Services
Ohio Department of Education
25 S Front Street
Columbus, OH 43215-4131
614-466-3763
877-644-6338
Fax: 704-992-5168
contact.center@education.ohio.gov
www.education.ohio.gov
Richard A. Ross, Superitendent
Tom Gunlock, President

45 School Finance
Ohio Department of Education
25 S Front Street
Columbus, OH 43215-4183
614-466-6266
877-644-6338
Fax: 704-992-5168
contact.center@education.ohio.gov
www.education.ohio.gov
Richard A. Ross, Superitendent
Tom Gunlock, President

246 School Food Service
Ohio Department of Education
25 S Front Street
Columbus, OH 43215-4131
614-466-2945
877-644-6338
Fax: 704-992-5168
contact.center@education.ohio.gov
www.education.ohio.gov
Richard A. Ross, Superitendent
Tom Gunlock, President

247 School for the Deaf
Ohio Department of Education
25 S Front Street
Columbus, OH 43215-4131
614-466-3641
877-644-6338
Fax: 704-992-5168
contact.center@education.ohio.gov
www.education.ohio.gov
Richard A. Ross, Superitendent
Tom Gunlock, President

248 Special Education
Ohio Department of Education
25 S Front Street
Worthington, OH 43085
614-466-2650
877-644-6338
Fax: 704-992-5168
contact.center@education.ohio.gov
www.education.ohio.gov
Richard A. Ross, Superitendent
Tom Gunlock, President

249 Student Development
Ohio Department of Education
25 S Front Street
Columbus, OH 43215-4131
614-466-3641
877-644-6338
Fax: 704-992-5168
contact.center@education.ohio.gov
www.education.ohio.gov
Richard A. Ross, Superitendent
Tom Gunlock, President

250 Teacher Education & Certification
Ohio Department of Education
25 S Front Street
Columbus, OH 43215-4131
614-466-3430
877-644-6338
Fax: 704-992-5168
contact.center@education.ohio.gov
www.education.ohio.gov
Richard A. Ross, Superitendent
Tom Gunlock, President

3251 Vocational & Career Education
Ohio Department of Education
25 S Front Street
Columbus, OH 43215-4131
614-466-3430
877-644-6338
Fax: 704-992-5168
contact.center@education.ohio.gov
www.education.ohio.gov
Richard A. Ross, Superitendent
Tom Gunlock, President

Oklahoma

3252 Accreditation & Standards Division
Oklahoma State Department of Education
2500 N Lincoln Boulevard
Oklahoma City, OK 73105-4599
405-521-3301
Fax: 405-521-6205
sdeservicedesk@sde.ok.gov
www.ok.gov/sde
Joy Hofmeister, Superitendent
Liz Young, Executive Assistant

3253 Federal/Special/Collaboration Services
Oklahoma State Department of Education
2500 N Lincoln Boulevard
Oklahoma City, OK 73105-4599
405-521-3301
Fax: 405-521-6205
sdeservicedesk@sde.ok.gov
www.ok.gov/sde
Joy Hofmeister, Superitendent
Liz Young, Executive Assistant

3254 Oklahoma Department of Career and Technology Education
Oklahoma Department of Career and Technology Educa
1500 W 7th Avenue
Stillwater, OK 74074-4398
405-377-2000
Fax: 405-743-5541
Paula.Bowles@careertech.ok.gov
www.okcareertech.org
Roy Peters Jr, Division Director
Paula Bowles, Chief Comm Officer/ CMO

3255 Oklahoma Department of Education
Oklahoma State Department of Education
2500 N Lincoln Boulevard
Hodge Education Building
Oklahoma City, OK 73105-4599
405-521-3301
Fax: 405-521-6205
sdeservicedesk@sde.ok.gov
www.ok.gov/sde
Joy Hofmeister, Superitendent
Liz Young, Executive Assistant

3256 Oklahoma Department of Education; Financial Services
Oklahoma State Department of Education
2500 N Lincoln Boulevard
Oklahoma City, OK 73105-4599
405-521-3301
Fax: 405-521-6205
sdeservicedesk@sde.ok.gov
www.ok.gov/sde
Joy Hofmeister, Superitendent
Liz Young, Executive Assistant

3257 Professional Services
Oklahoma State Department of Education
2500 N Lincoln Boulevard
Oklahoma City, OK 73105-4599
405-521-3301
Fax: 405-521-6205
sdeservicedesk@sde.ok.gov
www.ok.gov/sde
Joy Hofmeister, Superitendent
Liz Young, Executive Assistant

3258 School Improvement
Oklahoma State Department of Education
2500 N Lincoln Boulevard
Oklahoma City, OK 73105-4599
405-521-3301
Fax: 405-521-6205
sdeservicedesk@sde.ok.gov
www.ok.gov/sde
Joy Hofmeister, Superitendent
Liz Young, Executive Assistant

Oregon

3259 Assessment & Evaluation
Oregon Department of Education
255 Capitol Street NE
Salem, OR 97310-0203
503-378-3600
Fax: 503-378-5156
ode.frontdesk@ode.state.or.us
www.ode.state.or.us
Rob Saxton, Deputy Superintendent

3260 Community College Services
Oregon Department of Education
225 Capitol Street NE
Salem, OR 97310-1341
503-378-3600
Fax: 503-378-5156
ode.frontdesk@ode.state.or.us
www.ode.state.or.us
Rob Saxton, Deputy Superintendent

3261 Compensatory Education Office
Oregon Department of Education
225 Capitol Street NE
Salem, OR 97310-1341
503-378-3569
Fax: 503-378-5156
ode.frontdesk@ode.state.or.us
www.ode.state.or.us
Rob Saxton, Deputy Superintendent

3262 Deputy Superintendent Office
Oregon Department of Education
225 Capitol Street NE
Salem, OR 97310-1341
503-378-3573
Fax: 503-378-5156
ode.frontdesk@ode.state.or.us
www.ode.state.or.us
Rob Saxton, Deputy Superintendent

3263 Early Childhood Council
Oregon Department of Education
225 Capitol Street NE
Salem, OR 97310-1341
503-378-5585
Fax: 503-378-5156
ode.frontdesk@ode.state.or.us
www.ode.state.or.us
Rob Saxton, Deputy Superintendent

3264 Government Relations
Oregon Department of Education
225 Capitol Street NE
Salem, OR 97310-1341

503-378-8549
Fax: 503-378-5156
ode.frontdesk@ode.state.or.us
www.ode.state.or.us

Rob Saxton, Deputy Superitendent

3265 Management Services
Oregon Department of Education
225 Capitol Street NE
Salem, OR 97310-1341
503-378-8549
Fax: 503-378-5156
ode.frontdesk@ode.state.or.us
www.ode.state.or.us

Rob Saxton, Deputy Superitendent

3266 Office of Field, Curriculum & Instruction Services
Oregon Department of Education
225 Capitol Street NE
Salem, OR 97310-1341
503-378-8004
Fax: 503-378-5156
ode.frontdesk@ode.state.or.us
www.ode.state.or.us

Rob Saxton, Deputy Superitendent

3267 Oregon Department of Education
Oregon Department of Education
225 Capitol Street NE
Salem, OR 97310-0203
503-378-3569
Fax: 503-378-5156
ode.frontdesk@ode.state.or.us
www.ode.state.or.us

Rob Saxton, Deputy Superitendent

3268 Professional Technical Education
Oregon Department of Education
225 Capitol Street NE
Salem, OR 97310-1341
503-378-3584
Fax: 503-378-5156
ode.frontdesk@ode.state.or.us
www.ode.state.or.us

Rob Saxton, Deputy Superitendent

3269 Special Education
Oregon Department of Education
225 Capitol Street NE
Salem, OR 97310-1341
503-378-3600
Fax: 503-378-5156
ode.frontdesk@ode.state.or.us
www.ode.state.or.us

Rob Saxton, Deputy Superitendent

3270 Student Services Office
Oregon Department of Education
225 Capitol Street NE
Salem, OR 97310-1341
503-378-5585
Fax: 503-378-5156
ode.frontdesk@ode.state.or.us
www.ode.state.or.us

Rob Saxton, Deputy Superitendent

3271 Twenty First Century Schools Council
Oregon Department of Education
225 Capitol Street NE
Salem, OR 97310-1341
503-378-3600
Fax: 503-378-5156
ode.frontdesk@ode.state.or.us

Rob Saxton, Deputy Superitendent

Pennsylvania

3272 Chief Counsel
Pennsylvania Department of Education
333 Market Street
Harrisburg, PA 17126-2210
717-783-6788
Fax: 717-783-0347
www.education.state.pa.us

Carolyn Dumaresq, Acting Secretary

3273 Chief of Staff Office
Pennsylvania Department of Education
333 Market Street
Harrisburg, PA 17126-2210
717-783-6788
Fax: 717-787-7222
www.education.state.pa.us

Carolyn Dumaresq, Acting Secretary

3274 Higher Education/Postsecondary Office
Pennsylvania Department of Education
333 Market Street
Harrisburg, PA 17126-2210
717-783-6788
Fax: 717-783-0583
www.education.state.pa.us

Carolyn Dumaresq, Acting Secretary

3275 Office of Elementary and Secondary Education
Pennsylvania Department of Education
333 Market Street
5th Floor
Harrisburg, PA 17126
717-783-6788
Fax: 717-783-6802
dhaines@state.pa.us
www.education.state.pa.us

Carolyn Dumaresq, Acting Secretary

3276 Office of the Comptroller
Pennsylvania Department of Education
333 Market Street
Harrisburg, PA 17126-2210
717-783-6788
Fax: 717-787-3593
www.education.state.pa.us

Carolyn Dumaresq, Acting Secretary

3277 Pennsylvania Department of Education
Pennsylvania Department of Education
333 Market Street
Harrisburg, PA 17126
717-783-6788
Fax: 717-787-7222
www.education.state.pa.us

Carolyn Dumaresq, Acting Secretary

3278 Region 3: Education Department
Pennsylvania Department of Education
333 Market Street
Harrisburg, PA 17126-3309
717-783-6788
www.education.state.pa.us

Carolyn Dumaresq, Acting Secretary

Rhode Island

3279 Career & Technical Education
Rhode Island Department of Education
255 Westminster Street
Providence, RI 02903-3414
401-222-4600
Fax: 401-222-2537
www.ride.ri.gov

Deborah Gist, Commissioner
Andy Andrade, Commissioner Support

3280 Equity & Access Office
Rhode Island Department of Education
255 Westminster Street
Providence, RI 02903-3414
401-222-4600
Fax: 401-222-2537
www.ride.ri.gov

Deborah Gist, Commissioner
Andy Andrade, Commissioner Support

3281 Human Resource Development
Rhode Island Department of Education
255 Westminster Street
Providence, RI 02903-3414
401-222-4600
Fax: 401-222-2537
www.ride.ri.gov

Deborah Gist, Commissioner
Andy Andrade, Commissioner Support

3282 Instruction Office
Rhode Island Department of Education
255 Westminster Street
Providence, RI 02903-3414
401-222-4600
Fax: 401-222-2537
www.ride.ri.gov

Deborah Gist, Commissioner
Andy Andrade, Commissioner Support

3283 Office of Finance
Rhode Island Department of Education
255 Westminster Street
Providence, RI 02903-3414
401-222-4600
Fax: 401-222-2537
www.ride.ri.gov

Deborah Gist, Commissioner
Andy Andrade, Commissioner Support

3284 Outcomes & Assessment Office
Rhode Island Department of Education
255 Westminster Street
Providence, RI 02903-3414
401-222-4600
Fax: 401-222-2537
www.ride.ri.gov

Deborah Gist, Commissioner
Andy Andrade, Commissioner Support

3285 Resource Development
Rhode Island Department of Education
255 Westminster Street
Providence, RI 02903-3414
401-222-4600
Fax: 401-222-6033
www.ride.ri.gov

Deborah Gist, Commissioner
Andy Andrade, Commissioner Support

3286 Rhode Island Department of Education
Rhode Island Department of Education
255 Westminster Street
Providence, RI 02903
401-222-4600
Fax: 401-222-6178
ride0001@ride.ri.net
www.ride.ri.gov
Goal of all our work is to improve student performance and help all students meet or exceed a high level of performance. Standards, instruction, and assessment intertwine to provide a system that ensures a strong education for our students.

Deborah Gist, Commissioner
Andy Andrade, Commissioner Support

287 School Food Services Administration
Rhode Island Department of Education
255 Westminster Street
Providence, RI 02903-3414
401-222-4600
Fax: 401-222-3080
www.ride.ri.gov

Deborah Gist, Commissioner
Andy Andrade, Commissioner Support

288 Special Needs Office
Rhode Island Department of Education
255 Westminster Street
Providence, RI 02903-3414
401-456-9331
Fax: 401-456-8699
www.ride.ri.gov

Deborah Gist, Commissioner
Andy Andrade, Commissioner Support

289 Teacher Education & Certification Office
Rhode Island Department of Education
255 Westminster Street
Providence, RI 02903-3414
401-222-4600
Fax: 401-222-2048
www.ride.ri.gov

Deborah Gist, Commissioner
Andy Andrade, Commissioner Support

South Carolina

290 Budgets & Planning
South Carolina Department of Education
1429 Senate Street
Suite 950
Columbia, SC 29201-3730
803-734-8500
Fax: 803-734-0645
SCSuptED@ed.sc.gov
www.ed.sc.gov

Molly Spearman, Superitendent

291 Communications Services
South Carolina Department of Education
1429 Senate Street
Columbia, SC 29201-3730
803-734-8500
Fax: 803-734-3389
SCSuptED@ed.sc.gov
www.ed.sc.gov

Molly Spearman, Superitendent

292 General Counsel
South Carolina Department of Education
1429 Senate Street
Columbia, SC 29201-3730
803-734-8500
Fax: 803-734-4384
SCSuptED@ed.sc.gov
www.ed.sc.gov

Molly Spearman, Superitendent

293 Internal Administration
South Carolina Department of Education
1429 Senate Street
Columbia, SC 29201-3730
803-734-8500
Fax: 803-734-6225
SCSuptED@ed.sc.gov
www.ed.sc.gov

Molly Spearman, Superitendent

294 Policy & Planning
South Carolina Department of Education
1429 Senate Street
Columbia, SC 29201-3730
803-734-8500
Fax: 803-734-8624
SCSuptED@ed.sc.gov
www.ed.sc.gov

Molly Spearman, Superitendent

3295 South Carolina Department of Education
South Carolina Department of Education
1429 Senate Street
Columbia, SC 29201
803-734-8500
Fax: 803-734-3389
SCSuptED@ed.sc.gov
www.ed.sc.gov
Provides leadership and services to ensure a system of public education in which all students become educated, responsible, and contributing citizens. For certification information visit www.myscschools.com or contact 803-734-5280.

Molly Spearman, Superitendent

3296 Support Services
South Carolina Department of Education
1429 Senate Street
Columbia, SC 29201-3730
803-734-8500
Fax: 803-734-8254
SCSuptED@ed.sc.gov
www.ed.sc.gov

Molly Spearman, Superitendent

South Dakota

3297 Finance & Management
South Dakota Department of Education
800 Governors Drive
Pierre, SD 57501-2291
605-773-3248
Fax: 605-773-6139
www.doe.sd.gov

Stacy Krusemark, Division Director

3298 Services for Education
South Dakota Department of Education
800 Governors Drive
Pierre, SD 57501-2291
605-773-4699
Fax: 605-773-3782
www.doe.sd.gov

Donlynn Rice, Division Director

3299 South Dakota Department of Education & Cultural Affairs
South Dakota Department of Education
800 Governors Drive
Pierre, SD 57501-2291
605-773-2291
Fax: 605-773-6139
www.doe.sd.gov
Advocates for education, facilitate the delivery of statewide educational and cultural services, and promote efficient, appropriate, and quality educational opportunities for all persons residing in South Dakota.

Ray Christensen, Secretary
Patrick Keating, Division Director

3300 South Dakota State Historical Society
South Dakota Dept of Education & Cultural Affairs
800 Governors Drive
Pierre, SD 57501-2291
605-773-3458
Fax: 605-773-6041
www.doe.sd.gov
Program areas: Archaeology, archives, historic preservation, museum, research, and publishing

Jay D Vogt, History Manager

3301 Special Education Office
South Dakota Department of Education
800 Governors Drive
Pierre, SD 57501-2291
605-773-3678
Fax: 605-773-3782
www.doe.sd.gov

Michelle Powers, Division Director

Tennessee

3302 Special Education
Tennessee Department of Education
710 James Robertson Parkway
6th Floor
Nashville, TN 37243-5158
615-741-2851
Fax: 615-532-9412
www.tn.gov

Kevin S. Huffman, Commissioner
Kathleen Airhart, Deputy Commissioner

3303 Teaching and Learning
Tennessee Department of Education
710 James Robertson Parkway
5th Floor
Nashville, TN 37243-5158
615-532-6195
Fax: 615-741-1837
wprotoe@mail.state.tn.us
www.tn.gov

Kevin S. Huffman, Commissioner
Kathleen Airhart, Deputy Commissioner

3304 Tennessee Department of Education
Tennessee Department of Education
710 James Robertson Parkway
6th Floor
Nashville, TN 37243-5158
615-741-2731
Fax: 615-741-6236
jwalters@mail.state.tn.us
www.tn.gov

Kevin S. Huffman, Commissioner
Kathleen Airhart, Deputy Commissioner

3305 Vocational Education
Tennessee Department of Education
710 James Robertson Parkway
4th Floor
Nashville, TN 37243-5158
615-532-2800
Fax: 615-532-8226
www.tn.gov

Kevin S. Huffman, Commissioner
Kathleen Airhart, Deputy Commissioner

Texas

3306 Accountability Reporting and Research
Texas Education Agency
1701 N. Congress Avenue
WBT Building Room 3-111
Austin, TX 78701-1494
512-463-9734
Fax: 512-463-9838
www.tea.texas.gov

Rick Perry, Commissioner

3307 Chief Counsel
Texas Department of Education
1701 N. Congress Avenue
Austin, TX 78701-1402
512-463-9734
Fax: 512-463-9838
www.tea.texas.gov
Rick Perry, Commissioner

3308 Continuing Education
Texas Education Agency
1701 N. Congress Avenue
Austin, TX 78701-1402
512-463-9734
Fax: 512-463-9838
www.tea.texas.gov
Rick Perry, Commissioner

3309 Curriculum Development & Textbooks
Texas Department of Education
1701 N. Congress Avenue
Austin, TX 78701-1402
512-463-9734
Fax: 512-463-9838
www.tea.texas.gov
Rick Perry, Commissioner

3310 Curriculum, Assessment & Professional Development
Texas Department of Education
1701 N. Congress Avenue
Austin, TX 78701-1402
512-463-9734
Fax: 512-463-9838
www.tea.texas.gov
Rick Perry, Commissioner

3311 Curriculum, Assessment and Technology
Texas Department of Education
1701 N. Congress Avenue
Austin, TX 78701-1402
512-463-9734
Fax: 512-463-9838
www.tea.texas.gov
Rick Perry, Commissioner

3312 Education of Special Populations & Adults
Texas Department of Education
1701 N. Congress Avenue
Austin, TX 78701-1402
512-463-9734
Fax: 512-463-9838
www.tea.texas.gov
Rick Perry, Commissioner

3313 Field Services
Texas Department of Education
1701 N. Congress Avenue
Austin, TX 78701-1402
512-463-9734
Fax: 512-463-9838
www.tea.texas.gov
Rick Perry, Commissioner

3314 Internal Operations
Texas Department of Education
1701 N. Congress Avenue
Austin, TX 78701-1402
512-463-9734
Fax: 512-463-9838
www.tea.texas.gov
Rick Perry, Commissioner

3315 Operations & School Support
Texas Department of Education
1701 N. Congress Avenue
Austin, TX 78701-1494
512-463-9734
Fax: 512-463-9838
www.tea.texas.gov
Rick Perry, Commissioner

3316 Permanent School Fund
Texas Department of Education
1701 N. Congress Avenue
Room 5-120
Austin, TX 78701-1402
512-463-9734
Fax: 512-463-9838
www.tea.texas.gov
Rick Perry, Commissioner

3317 Region 6: Education Department
Texas Department of Education
1200 Main Tower
Dallas, TX 75202-4325
512-463-9734
Fax: 512-463-9838
www.tea.texas.gov
Rick Perry, Commissioner

3318 Texas Department of Education
Texas Department of Education
1701 N Congress Avenue
William B Travis Building
Austin, TX 78701-1494
512-463-9734
Fax: 512-463-9838
www.tea.texas.gov
Rick Perry, Commissioner

Utah

3319 Applied Technology Education Services
Utah Department of Education
250 E 500 S
PO Box 144200
Salt Lake City, UT 84111-3204
801-538-7840
Fax: 801-538-7868
www.schools.utah.gov
State agency for career and technical education.
Rod Brems, Associate Superintendent
Mark Peterson, Director

3320 Instructional Services Division
Utah Department of Education
250 E 500 S
PO Box 144200
Salt Lake City, UT 84111-3204
801-538-7515
Fax: 801-538-7768
www.schools.utah.gov
Jerry P Peterson, Division Director
Mark Peterson, Director

3321 Schools for the Deaf & Blind
Utah Department of Education
250 E 500 S
PO Box 144200
Salt Lake City, UT 84111-3204
801-629-4700
Fax: 801-629-4896
www.schools.utah.gov
Wayne Glaus, Division Director
Mark Peterson, Director

3322 Utah Office of Education
Utah Department of Education
250 E 500 South
PO Box 144200
Salt Lake City, UT 84111-3204
801-538-7510
Fax: 801-538-7768
www.schools.utah.gov
Steven O Laing, Superintendent
Mark Peterson, Director

3323 Utah Office of Education; Agency Services Division
Utah Department of Education
250 E 500 S
PO Box 144200
Salt Lake City, UT 84114-4200
801-538-7500
Fax: 801-538-7768
www.schools.utah.gov
Patrick Ogden, Associate Superintendent
Mark Peterson, Director

Vermont

3324 Career & Lifelong Learning
Vermont Department of Education
120 State Street
Montpelier, VT 05620-0001
802-479-1030
Fax: 802-828-3146
AOE.EdInfo@state.vt.us
www.education.vermont.gov
Rebecca Holcombe, Secretary
John Fischer, Deputy Secretary

3325 Core Services
Vermont Department of Education
120 State Street
Montpelier, VT 05620-0001
802-479-1030
Fax: 802-828-3140
AOE.EdInfo@state.vt.us
www.education.vermont.gov
Rebecca Holcombe, Secretary
John Fischer, Deputy Secretary

3326 Family & School Support
Vermont Department of Education
120 State Street
Montpelier, VT 05620-0001
802-479-1030
Fax: 802-828-3140
AOE.EdInfo@state.vt.us
www.education.vermont.gov
Rebecca Holcombe, Secretary
John Fischer, Deputy Secretary

3327 Financial Management Team
Vermont Department of Education
120 State Street
Montpelier, VT 05620-0001
802-479-1030
Fax: 802-828-3140
AOE.EdInfo@state.vt.us
www.education.vermont.gov
Rebecca Holcombe, Secretary
John Fischer, Deputy Secretary

3328 School Development & Information
Vermont Department of Education
120 State Street
Montpelier, VT 05620-0001
802-479-1030
Fax: 802-828-3140
AOE.EdInfo@state.vt.us
www.education.vermont.gov
Rebecca Holcombe, Secretary
John Fischer, Deputy Secretary

3329 Teaching & Learning
Vermont Department of Education
120 State Street
Montpelier, VT 05620-0001

802-479-1030
Fax: 802-828-3140
AOE.EdInfo@state.vt.us
www.education.vermont.gov

Rebecca Holcombe, Secretary
John Fischer, Deputy Secretary

330 Vermont Department of Education
Vermont Department of Education
120 State Street
Montpelier, VT 05620-0001
802-479-1030
Fax: 802-828-3140
AOE.EdInfo@state.vt.us
www.education.vermont.gov
For certification information visit www.pen.k12.va.us or contact 804-225-2022.

Rebecca Holcombe, Secretary
John Fischer, Deputy Secretary

331 Vermont Special Education
Vermont Department of Education
120 State Street
Montpelier, VT 05620-0001
802-479-1030
www.education.vermont.gov

Rebecca Holcombe, Secretary
John Fischer, Deputy Secretary

Virginia

332 Administrative Services
Virginia Department of Education
14th & Franklin Streets
PO Box 2120
Richmond, VA 23218
804-225-3252
Fax: 804-786-5828
www.doe.virginia.gov

Steven R. Staples, Superitendent

333 Policy, Assessment, Research & Information Systems
Virginia Department of Education
101 N 4th Street
PO Box 2120
Richmond, VA 23218-2120
804-225-2102
800-292-3820
Fax: 804-371-8978
www.doe.virginia.gov

Steven R. Staples, Superitendent

334 Student Services
Virginia Department of Education
14th & Franklin Streets
PO Box 2120
Richmond, VA 23218
804-225-2757
Fax: 804-786-5828
www.doe.virginia.gov

Steven R. Staples, Superitendent

335 Virginia Centers for Community Education
Virginia Department of Education
101 N 4th Street
PO Box 2120
Richmond, VA 23218-2120
804-225-2293
Fax: 804-786-5828
www.doe.virginia.gov

Steven R. Staples, Superitendent

3336 Virginia Department of Education
Virginia Department of Education
James Monroe Building
101 N 14th Street
Richmond, VA 23219
804-225-2023
800-292-3820
Fax: 804-371-2099
www.doe.virginia.gov

Steven R. Staples, Superitendent

Washington

3337 Region 10: Education Department
US Department of Education
915 2nd Avenue
Room 3362
Seattle, WA 98174-1001
206-220-7800
Fax: 202-220-7806
www.ed.gov

3338 Washington Department of Education
Washington State Board of Education
600 Washington Street SE
P.O. Box 47206
Olympia, WA 98504-7200
360-725-6025
Fax: 360-753-6712
sbe@k12.wa.us
www.sbe.wa.gov

Theresa Bergeson, Superintendent
Isabelÿ Munoz-Colon, Chair

3339 Washington Department of Education; Instruction Program
Washington State Board of Education
600 Washington Street SE
P.O. Box 47206
Olympia, WA 98504-7200
360-725-6025
Fax: 360-586-0247
sbe@k12.wa.us
www.sbe.wa.gov

John Pearson, Division Director
Isabelÿ Munoz-Colon, Chair

3340 Washington Department of Education; Commission on Student Learning Administration
Washington State Board of Education
600 Washington Street SE
P.O. Box 47206
Olympia, WA 98504-7200
360-725-6025
Fax: 360-664-3028
sbe@k12.wa.us
www.sbe.wa.gov

Terry Bergeson, Division Director
Isabelÿ Munoz-Colon, Chair

3341 Washington Department of Education; Executive Services
Washington State Board of Education
600 Washington Street SE
P.O. Box 47206
Olympia, WA 98504-7200
360-725-6025
Fax: 360-753-6754
sbe@k12.wa.us
www.sbe.wa.gov

Ken Kanikeberg, Division Director
Isabelÿ Munoz-Colon, Chair

3342 Washington Department of Education; School Business & Administrative Services
Washington State Board of Education
600 Washington Street SE
P.O. Box 47206
Olympia, WA 98504-7200
360-725-6025
sbe@k12.wa.us
www.sbe.wa.gov

David Moberly, Division Director
Isabelÿ Munoz-Colon, Chair

West Virginia

3343 Division of Administrative Services
West Virginia Department of Education
1900 Kanawha Boulevard E
Building 6
Charleston, WV 25305-0009
304-558-2441
Fax: 304-558-8867
www.wvde.state.wv.us

Carolyn Arrington, Division Director

3344 Research, Accountability & Professional
West Virginia Department of Education
1900 Kanawha Boulevard E
Building 6
Charleston, WV 25305-0009
304-558-3762
Fax: 304-558-8867
www.wvde.state.wv.us

William J Luff Jr, Division Director

3345 Student Services & Instructional Services
West Virginia Department of Education
1900 Kanawha Boulevard E
Building 6
Charleston, WV 25305-0009
304-558-2691
Fax: 304-558-8867
www.wvde.state.wv.us

Keith Smith, Division Director

3346 Technical & Adult Education Services
West Virginia Department of Education
1900 Kanawha Boulevard E
Building 6
Charleston, WV 25305-0009
304-558-2346
Fax: 304-558-8867
www.wvde.state.wv.us

Adam Sponaugle, Division Director

3347 West Virginia Department of Education
West Virginia Department of Education
1900 Kanawha Boulevard E
Building 6, Room B-358
Charleston, WV 25305-0330
304-558-2681
Fax: 304-558-0048
The constitutional mission is to provide supervision of the K-12 education system.

David Stewart, Superintendent
Audrey Horne, President

Wisconsin

3348 **Division for Learning Support: Equity & Advocacy**
Wisconsin Department of Education
125 S Webster Street
PO Box 7841
Madison, WI 53707-7841
608-266-3390
800-441-4563
Fax: 608-267-3746
www.dpi.wi.gov
Tony Evers, Superintendent
Carolyn Stanford-Taylor, Division Director

3349 **Instructional Services Division**
Wisconsin Department of Education
125 S Webster Street
PO Box 7841
Madison, WI 53707-7841
608-266-3390
800-441-4563
Fax: 608-267-3746
www.dpi.wi.gov
Tony Evers, Superintendent
Pauline Nikolay, Division Director

3350 **Library Services Division**
Wisconsin Department of Education
2109 S. Stoughton Road
PO Box 7841
Madison, WI 53707-7841
608-266-3390
800-441-4563
Fax: 608-267-3746
www.dpi.wi.gov
Tony Evers, Superintendent
William Wilson, Division Director

3351 **School Financial Resources & Management**
Wisconsin Department of Education
125 S Webster Street
PO Box 7841
Madison, WI 53707-7841
608-266-3390
800-441-4563
Fax: 608-267-3746
www.dpi.wi.gov
Tony Evers, Superintendent
Bambi Statz, Division Director

3352 **Wisconsin College System Technical**
Wisconsin Department of Education
125 S Webster Street
PO Box 7841
Madison, WI 53707-7841
608-266-3390
800-441-4563
Fax: 608-266-1285
www.dpi.wi.gov
Tony Evers, Superintendent
Richard Carpenter, President

3353 **Wisconsin Department of Public Instruction**
Wisconsin Department of Education
125 S Webster Street
PO Box 7841
Madison, WI 53707-7841
608-266-3390
800-441-4563
Fax: 608-266-5188
statesuperintendent@dpi.wi.gov
www.dpi.wi.gov
Tony Evers, Superintendent
Mike Thompson, Deputy State Superintendent

Wyoming

3354 **Accounting, Personnel & School Finance Unit**
Wyoming Department of Education
2300 Capitol Avenue
Hathaway Building, 2nd Floor
Cheyenne, WY 82002-2060
307-777-7675
Fax: 307-777-6234
www.edu.wyoming.gov
Ron Micheli, Chairman
Barry Nimmo, Division Director

3355 **Applied Data & Technology Unit**
Wyoming Department of Education
2300 Capitol Avenue
Hathaway Building, 2nd Floor
Cheyenne, WY 82002-2060
307-777-7675
Fax: 307-777-6234
www.edu.wyoming.gov
Ron Micheli, Chairman
Steven King, Division Director

3356 **Services for Individuals with Hearing Loss**
Wyoming Department of Education
2300 Capitol Avenue
Hathaway Building, 2nd Floor
Cheyenne, WY 82002-2060
307-777-7675
Fax: 307-777-6234
www.edu.wyoming.gov
Ron Micheli, Chairman
Tim Sanger, Division Director

3357 **Support Programs & Quality Results Division**
Wyoming Department of Education
2300 Capitol Avenue
Hathaway Building, 2nd Floor
Cheyenne, WY 82002-2060
307-777-7675
Fax: 307-777-6234
www.edu.wyoming.gov
Ron Micheli, Chairman
Dr. Alan Sheinker, Division Director

3358 **Wyoming Department of Education**
Wyoming Department of Education
2300 Capitol Avenue
Hathaway Building, 2nd Floor
Cheyenne, WY 82002-2060
307-777-7675
Fax: 307-777-6234
www.edu.wyoming.gov
Dr.Trent Blankenship, Superintendent
Ron Micheli, Chairman

Associations

3359 American Association of Colleges for Teacher Education
1602 L Street NW
Suite 601
Washington, DC 20036
202-293-2450
Fax: 202-457-8095
aacte@aacte.org
www.aacte.org
A national alliance of educator preparation programs dedicated to the highest quality professional development of teachers and school leaders in order to enhance PK-12 student learning.

Lynn M. Gangone, President & CEO
Jacqueline Rodriguez, Vice President, Research

3360 American Association of Higher Education
12110 Grandview Road
Grandview, MO 64030
816-765-5551
Fax: 855-252-7622
admin@aahea.org
www.aahea.org
The individual membership organization that promotes the changes higher education must make to ensure its effectiveness in a complex, interconnected world. The association equips individuals and institutions committed to such changes with the knowledge they need to bring those changes about.

Robert Kohley, Office Manager

3361 American Educational Research Association
1430 K Street NW
Suite 1200
Washington, DC 20005
202-238-3200
Fax: 202-238-3250
communications@aera.net
www.aera.net
Supports the improvement of the educational process through the encouragement of scholarly inquiry related to education, and the practical application of research results. The association also holds an annual conference and publishes books, videos and magazines.

Felice J. Levine, Executive Director
Lori Diane Hill, Assoc. Exec. Dir., Programs

3362 American Educational Studies Association
www.educationalstudies.org
An international learned society for students, teachers, research scholars, and administrators who are interested in the foundations of education. A society primarily comprised of college and university professors who teach and research in the field of education utilizing one or more of the liberal arts disciplines of philosophy, history, politics, sociology, anthropology, or economics as well as comparative/international and cultural studies.

Sandra Spickard Prettyman, Interim Executive Director
Jennifer Stoops, Director, Communications

3363 Association for Middle Level Education
2550 Corporate Exchange Drive
Suite 324
Columbus, OH 43231
614-895-4730
800-528-6672
Fax: 614-895-4750
info@amle.org
www.amle.org
Committed to the educational and developmental needs of young adolescents.

Stephanie Simpson, Chief Executive Officer
Derek Neal, Chief Operating Officer

3364 Association for Talent Development
1640 King Street
Box 1443
Alexandria, VA 22313-1443
703-683-8100
800-628-2783
Fax: 703-683-1523
customercare@td.org
www.td.org
Dedicated to workplace learning and supporting the knowledge and skill development of employees around the world.

Jim Caprara, Chair
Tony Bingham, President & CEO

3365 Association of Teacher Educators (ATE)
11350 Random Hills Road
Suite 800, PMB 6
Fairfax, VA 22030
703-659-1708
Fax: 703-595-4792
info@ate1.org
www.ate1.org
The mission of the Association of Teacher Educators is to improve the effectiveness of teacher education through leadership in the development of training programs. The association analyzes issues and practices relating to professional development and provides opportunities for the personal and professional growth of Association members.

Alisa Chapman, Executive Director
John McIntyre, Director, Meetings

3366 Canadian Association for University Continuing Education (CAUCE)
University of Saskatchewan
Williams Building
221 Cumberland Avenue N
Saskatoon, SK S7N-1M3
306-966-5604
Fax: 306-966-5590
cauce.secretariat@usask.ca
www.cauce-aepuc.ca
Association of professionals working in the field of university continuing education in Canada. The association offers services and resources for the development of its members and their careers.

Sheila LeBlanc, President
Coral Sawchyn, Manager

3367 Center for Rural Studies
University of Vermont
146 University Place
206 Morrill Hall
Burlington, VT 05405
crs@uvm.edu
www.uvm.edu/crs
A nonprofit, fee-for-service research and resource center that works with people and communities to address social, economic, and resource-based challenges. CRS supports the research and teaching missions of the university through its work in applied research, community outreach, program evaluation, and consulting services.

Jane Kolodinsky, Director
Elisa Ziglar, Business Manager

3368 Council for Learning Disabilities
11184 Antioch Road
PO Box 405
Overland Park, KS 66210
913-491-1011
Fax: 913-491-1011
www.council-for-learning-disabilities.org
An international organization that promotes evidence-based teaching, collaboration, research, leadership, and advocacy. Comprised of professionals who represent diverse disciplines and are committed to enhancing the education and quality of life for individuals with learning disabilities and others who experience challenges in learning.

Joseph Morgan, President
Linda Nease, Executive Director

3369 Council of Administrators of Special Education
1675 E Seminole Street
Suite L1
Springfield, MO 65804
417-427-7720
Fax: 417-427-6520
office@casecec.org
www.casecec.org
An international professional educational organization which is affiliated with the Council for Exceptional Children (CEC) whose members are dedicated to the enhancement of the worth, dignity, potential, and uniqueness of each individual in society.

Erin Maguire, President
Phyllis Wolfram, Executive Director

3370 Distance Education Accrediting Commission
1101 17th Street NW
Suite 808
Washington, DC 20036
202-234-5100
info@deac.org
www.deac.org
A voluntary, non-governmental, educational organization that was founded to promote sound educational standards and ethical business practices within the correspondence field.

Leah Matthews, Executive Director
Nan Ridgeway, Director, Accreditation

3371 Institute for Educational Leadership (IEL)
4301 Connecticut Avenue NW
Suite 100
Washington, DC 20008
202-822-8405
Fax: 202-872-4050
iel@iel.org
www.iel.org
The vision of the Institute for Educational Leadership is to encourage leadership in all levels of society, inspiring those such as policymakers, administrators, and practitioners to develop youth for higher education, careers and citizenship.

Jose Munoz, Interim Director
Maame Appiah, Vice President, Finance

3372 International Council on Education for Teaching
University Boulevard
Laredo, TX 78041
956-326-2420
Fax: 956-326-2419
contact@icet4u.org
www.icet4u.org
An international association of policy and decision-makers in education, government and business dedicated to global development through education. ICET provides programs

and services that give its members access to a worldwide resource base of organizations, programs, specialized consultative services and research and training opportunities at the university level.

Carol Hordatt Gentles, Chair
James O'Meara, President

3373 Learning Forward
504 S Locust Street
Oxford, OH 45056
513-523-6029
800-727-7288
Fax: 513-523-0638
office@learningforward.org
www.learningforward.org
The largest non-profit professional association committed to ensuring success for all students through staff development and school improvement. The purpose of the NSDC is that every educator engages in effective professional learning every day so every student achieves.

Denise Glyn Borders, President & CEO
Michael Lanham, COO & CFO

3374 Learning for Life
1325 W Walnut Hill Lane
Irving, TX 75038
972-580-2433
lfl@lflmail.org
www.learningforlife.org
A character education program designed to support schools and community-based organizations in their efforts toward preparing youth to successfully handle the complexities of today's society.

Tim Anderson, National Director
Anissa Hicks, Project Manager

3375 National Association for Professional Development Schools
1300 Pennsylvania Avenue NW
Suite 190-611
Washington, DC 20004
855-936-2737
info@napds.org
www.napds.org
To advance the education profession by supporting Professional Development Schools. The Professional Development School (PDS) movement aims to cultivate an environment that sees universities and PK-12 schools working together mutually.

Rebecca West Burns, President
Melissa A. Baker, Secretary

3376 National Association of State Directors of Teacher Education & Certification
1629 K Street NW
Suite 300
Washington, DC 20006
202-204-2208
support@nasdtec.org
www.nasdtec.org
The organization that represents professional standards boards and commissions and state departments of education in all 50 states, the District of Columbia, the Department of Defense Education Activity, Guam, and the Canadian province of Ontario.

Phillip S. Rogers, Executive Director
Mike Carr, Development Coordinator

3377 National Commission for Health Education Credentialing
1541 Alta Drive
Suite 303
Whitehall, PA 18052-5642
484-223-0770
888-624-3248
Fax: 800-813-0727
www.nchec.org
Aims to enhance the professional practice of health education by upholding standards in health education certifications.

Linda Lysoby, Executive Director
Melissa Opp, Deputy Executive Director

3378 National Women's Studies Association (NWSA)
PO Box 221136
Chicago, IL 60622
773-524-1807
nwsaoffice@nwsa.org
www.nwsa.org
The National Women's Studies Association supports the production of educational materials on the subject of women and gender. Their mission is to demonstrate the value of women's studies and feminist scholarship in education.

Karsonya Wise Whitehead, President
Jennifer Ash, Interim Executive Director

3379 Search Associates
admin@searchassociates.com
www.searchassociates.com
Search Associates helps place over 3,000 teachers, administrators and interns in international schools throughout the world each year.

Jessica D. Magagna, Chief Executive Officer
George Entwistle, Dir., Consulting Services

3380 The Center For The Future of Teaching and Learning
WestEd
730 Harrison Street
San Francisco, CA 94107
415-565-3000
877-493-7833
Fax: 415-565-3012
www.wested.org
A not-for-profit organization dedicated to strengthening teacher development policy and practice.

Tracy Huebner, Director

Awards & Honors

3381 Distinguished Teaching Awards
National Science Teaching Association
1840 Wilson Boulevard
Arlington, VA 22201
703-243-7100
Fax: 703-243-7177
awards@nsta.org
www.nsta.org
Awards NSTA members who have made extraordinary contributions to the science education field.

Dr. Eric J. Pyle, President
Dr. Erika Shugart, Executive Director

3382 Magna Awards
National School Boards Association
1680 Duke Street
Floor 2
Alexandria, VA 22314-3493
703-838-6722
Fax: 703-683-7590
info@nsba.org
www.nsba.org
Recognizes school district programs that help increase student achievement.

Chip Slaven, Interim CEO
Verjeana McCotter-Jacobs, Chief Transformation Officer

3383 NAPDS Awards
Nat'l Assn. for Professional Development Schools
1300 Pennsylvania Avenue NW
Suite 190-611
Washington, DC 20004
855-936-2737
info@napds.org
www.napds.org
The National Association for Professional Development Schools (NAPDS) offers four annual awards to members and their institutions: the Exemplary PDS Achievement Award; the Outstanding Doctoral Dissertation Award; the Emerging PDS Leader Award; and the Jason Kinsey Award.

Rebecca West Burns, President
Melissa A. Baker, Secretary

3384 NSTA Fellow Award
National Science Teaching Association
1840 Wilson Boulevard
Arlington, VA 22201
703-243-7100
Fax: 703-243-7177
awards@nsta.org
www.nsta.org
This award recognizes NSTA members who have made extraordinary contributions to science education through personal commitment to education, specifically science teaching or science; educational endeavors and original work that position recipients as exemplary leaders in their field; significant contributions to the profession that reflect dedication to NSTA as well the entire educational community.

Dr. Eric J. Pyle, President
Dr. Erika Shugart, Executive Director

3385 NSTA Legacy Award
National Science Teaching Association
1840 Wilson Boulevard
Arlington, VA 22201
703-243-7100
Fax: 703-243-7177
awards@nsta.org
www.nsta.org
This NSTA award posthumously recognizes long-standing members of NSTA for significant lifelong service to NSTA and contributions to science education.

Dr. Eric J. Pyle, President
Dr. Erika Shugart, Executive Director

3386 National Teachers Hall of Fame
Emporia State University
1 Kellogg Circle
Campus Box 4017
Emporia, KS 66801
620-341-5660
hallfame@emporia.edu
www.nthf.org
The mission of The National Teachers Hall of Fame is to recognize and honor exceptional career teachers, encourage excellence in teaching, and preserve the rich heritage of the teaching profession in the United States.

Jackie Vietti, Chair
Carol Strickland, Executive Director

3387 Presidential Awards for Excellence in Mathematics and Science Teaching
National Science Foundation
2415 Eisenhower Avenue
Alexandria, VA 22314
info@paemst.org
www.paemst.org

This award is the nation's highest commendation for K-12 math and science teachers. Up to 108 teachers are recognized annually with this prestigious award.

88 Sanford N. McDonnell Award for Lifetime Achievement in Character Education
Character Education Partnership
PO Box 650307
Sterling, VA 20165
202-296-7743
www.character.org
Honors any individual who has made a significant impact on the field of character education.

Arthur Schwartz, President
Dean D'Ambrosi, Executive Vice President

89 Senior Researcher Award
Society for Research in Music Education, NAfME
1806 Robert Fulton Drive
Reston, VA 20191
703-860-4000
800-336-3768
Fax: 888-275-6362
memberservices@nafme.org
www.nafme.org
For recognition of a significant scholarly achievement maintained over a period of years.

Carlos Abril, Chair

Conferences

90 AACRAO Annual Meeting
American Assoc of Collegiate Registrars/Admissions
1108 16th Street NW
Suite 400
Washington, DC 20036
202-293-9161
Fax: 202-872-8857
meetings@aacrao.org
www.aacrao.org
The meeting features workshops, sessions, roundtables and networking opportunities for those interested in learning more about education administration.

April
2,000 attendees

Tiffany Robinson, President
Melanie Gottlieb, Interim Executive Director

391 AASA National Conference on Education
American Association of School Administrators
1615 Duke Street
Alexandria, VA 22314
703-528-0700
Fax: 703-841-1543
info@aasa.org
www.aasa.org
Where America's school leaders go for a vision of the future in public education; to explore new thinking, new products, new services and new technologies.

February

Daniel A. Domenech, Executive Director
Chuck Woodruff, Chief Operating Officer

392 ACE Fellows Program
American Council on Education
1 Dupont Circle NW
Washington, DC 20036
202-939-9300
comments@ace.nche.edu
www.acenet.edu
The nation's premier higher education leadership development program in preparing senior leaders to serve American colleges and universities. Enables participants to immerse themselves in the culture, policies, and decision-making processes of another institution.

Ted Mitchell, President
Kara Freeman, Chief Operating Officer

3393 AFT Convention
American Federation of Teachers
555 New Jersey Avenue NW
Washington, DC 20001
202-879-4400
online@aft.org
www.aft.org/convention
The AFT represents 1.7 million teachers, school support staff, higher education faculty and staff, health care professionals, and state and municipal employees. AFT is an affiliated international union of the AFL-CIO.

Randi Weingarten, President
Evelyn DeJesus, Executive Vice President

3394 Association for Educational Communications & Technology Annual Convention
Assn. for Educational Communications & Technology
320 W 8th Street
Suite 101
Bloomington, IN 47404-3745
812-335-7675
877-677-2328
aect@aect.org
www.aect.org
Provide leadership in educational communications and technology by linking a wide range of professionals holding a common interest in the use of educational technology and its application learning process.

November

Xun Ge, President
Ellen Wagner, Interim Executive Director

3395 Association for Library & Information Science Education Annual Conference
Assn. for Library & Information Science Education
4 Lan Drive
Suite 310
Westford, MA 01886
978-674-6190
office@alise.org
www.alise.org
Promotes excellence in education for library and information sciences as a means of increasing library services.

Cambria Happ, Executive Director
Mega Subramaniam, Director, Programming

3396 Association for Middle Level Education Annual Conference
Association for Middle Level Education
2550 Corporate Exchange Drive
Suite 324
Columbus, OH 43231
614-895-4730
800-528-6672
Fax: 614-895-4750
info@amle.org
www.amle.org
Professional development opportunities for educators.

Stephanie Simpson, Chief Executive Officer
Derek Neal, Chief Operating Officer

3397 Association for Talent Development International Conference & Exposition
Association for Talent Development
1640 King Street
Box 1443
Alexandria, VA 22313-1443
703-683-8100
800-628-2783
Fax: 703-683-1523
customercare@td.org
www.td.org
This premier event for workplace learning and performance professionals welcomes attendees from more than 70 countries. The conference features 200+ educational sessions from industry leading experts, and a world-class EXPO filled with the latest products and services available from top suppliers.

Jim Caprara, Chair
Tony Bingham, President & CEO

3398 Association of Mathematics Teachers of New York State (AMTNYS) Annual Fall Conference
www.amtnys.org

October-November

Ellen Falk, President
Laurie Rosborough, Executive Secretary

3399 Association of Texas Professional Educators Summit
Association of Texas Professional Educators
305 E Huntland Drive
Suite 300
Austin, TX 78752
800-777-2873
Fax: 512-467-2203
info@atpe.org
www.atpe.org
Provides leadership training and networking opportunities.

Shannon J. Holmes, Ed.D, Executive Director
Amanda Bernstein, SHRM-CP, Director, Operations

3400 Association of Wisconsin School Administrators Conference
Association of Wisconsin School Administrators
4797 Hayes Road
Suite 103
Madison, WI 53704
608-241-0300
Fax: 608-249-4973
awsa@awsa.org
www.awsa.org
The Association of Wisconsin School Administrators exists to coordinate the collective interests and needs of school administrators and to enhance their professional growth and competency for the purpose of improving the quality of educational opportunities for the youth of Wisconsin.

October
60 booths

Jim Lynch, Executive Director
Joe Schroeder, Associate Executive Director

3401 CSBA Education Conference & Trade Show
California School Boards Association
3251 Beacon Boulevard
West Sacramento, CA 95691
800-266-3382
csba@csba.org
www.csba.org

Premier continuing education program - delivering practical solutions to help governance teams from districts and county offices of education improve student learning and achievement.

December
200 booths

Vernon M. Billy, Executive Director & CEO
Troy Flint, Chief Information Officer

3402 California Council for Adult Education Conference
California Council for Adult Education
PO Box 4646
Whittier, CA 90607
888-542-2231
membership@ccaestate.org
www.ccaestate.org

1,200 attendees

Adriana Sanchez-Aldana, Executive Director
James Hayes, Office Manager

3403 California Kindergarten Conference
California Kindergarten Association
1014 Chippendale Way
Roseville, CA 95661
916-780-5331
Fax: 916-780-5330
cka@ckanet.org
www.ckanet.org
Promotes best practices and professionalism in teaching, in order to foster children's early learning and development.

Gennie Gorback, President
Cristiana Tibbats, Administrative Manager

3404 Central States Conference on the Teaching of Foreign Languages Conference
PO Box 404
Ishpeming, MI 49849
csctfl.exec.director@gmail.com
www.csctfl.wildapricot.org
Foreign language organization serving a number of states through annual spring conferences featuring approximately 140 workshops and sessions on the subject of second-language learning and teaching.

March

Jason Jolley, Chair
Jill Woerner, Vice Chair

3405 Council for Advancement and Support of Education (CASE)
1201 Eye Street NW
Washington, DC 20005
202-328-2273
Fax: 202-387-4973
membersupportcenter@case.org
www.case.org
Offers numerous opportunities in the United States, Canada, Mexico, mainland Europe, and the United Kingdom to network with colleagues.

Fall/Winter

Sue Cunningham, President & CEO
Rob Moore, VP, Communications

3406 Florida Association for Career & Technical Education Conference & Trade Show
Florida Assn. for Career & Technical Education
1220 N Paul Russell Road
Tallahassee, FL 32301
850-878-6860
Fax: 850-878-5476
www.facte.org

July

Amy McAllister, President
Marsan Carr, Executive Director

3407 Florida Association of School Administrators Conference
206B S Monroe Street
Tallahassee, FL 32301
850-224-3626
Fax: 850-224-3892
www.fasa.net
Panels, keynote speakers, sessions and more.

Michele White, Executive Director
Armon'da Davis, Director, Communications

3408 Foundation for Critical Thinking Annual Conference
PO Box 196
Tomales, CA 94971
707-878-9100
800-833-3645
Fax: 707-878-9111
cct@criticalthinking.org
www.criticalthinking.org
Provides a unique opportunity to improve understanding of critical thinking, as well as one's ability to foster it in the classroom and other aspects in work/life.

Dr. Linda Elder, Senior Fellow
Dr. Gerald Nosich, Senior Fellow

3409 Higher Learning Commission Annual Conference
Higher Learning Commission
230 S LaSalle Street
Suite 7-500
Chicago, IL 60604-1411
312-621-7440
800-621-7440
Fax: 312-263-7462
info@hlcommission.org
www.hlcommission.org
Provides opportunities for administrators, faculty and staff of HLC member institutions to exchange information and ideas with fellow colleagues.

Barbara Gellman-Danley, President
Eric Martin, Executive Vice President

3410 ISBA/IAPSS Annual Conference
Indiana School Boards Association
1 N Capitol Avenue
Suite 1215
Indianapolis, IN 46204
317-639-0330
info@isba-ind.org
www.isba-ind.org
Jointy sponsored by the Indiana School Boards Association and Indiana Association of Public School Superintendents. A comprehensive program designed by the ISBA and IAPSS that brings the latest information and some of the most informed experts on current topics in education.

Terry Spradlin, Executive Director
Julie Slavens, Director, Policy Services

3411 ISTE Annual Conference & Exposition
International Society for Technology in Education
2111 Wilson Boulevard
Suite 300
Arlington, VA 22201
503-342-2848
800-336-5191
Fax: 541-302-3778
iste@iste.org
www.iste.org
A forum in which to learn, exchange, and survey the field of educational technology.

Rand Hansen, President
Richard Culatta, Chief Executive Officer

3412 Illinois Assistant Principal & Dean Summit
Illinois Principals Association
2940 Baker Drive
Springfield, IL 62703
217-525-1383
Fax: 217-525-7264
support@ilprincipals.org
www.ilprincipals.org
Where assistant principals and deans attend annually to hear outstanding educational leaders; participate in educational sessions and to network with colleagues across the state.

120 booths with 200 attendees

Jason Leahy, Executive Director
Brian D. Schwartz, Deputy Executive Director

3413 Illinois Association of School Boards Joint Annual Conference
Illinois Association of School Boards
2921 Baker Drive
Springfield, IL 62703-5929
217-528-9688
www.iasb.com
The event is open to local school board members, superintendents and secretaries, school administrators, state and regional educators and officials, school attorneys, university professors, exhibitors, and guests.

November
235 booths with 9500+ attendees

Thomas Bertrand, Executive Director
Jennifer Feld, Chief Financial Officer

3414 International Association for Social Science Information Service & Technology Conference
www.iassistdata.org
IASSIST is an international organization of professionals working with information technology and data services to support research and teaching in the social sciences. Its members work in a variety of settings, including data archives, statistical agencies, research centers, libraries, academic departments, government departments, and non-profit organizations.

May-June

San Cannon, President
Robin Rice, Vice President

3415 Iowa Association of School Boards Annual Convention
Iowa Association of School Boards
6000 Grand Avenue
Des Moines, IA 50312
515-288-1991
800-795-4272
Fax: 515-243-4992
www.ia-sb.org
IASB is an organization of elected school board members dedicated to assisting school boards in achieving their goal of excellence and equity in public education.

Lisa Bartusek, Executive Director

3416 Iowa Council of Teachers of Mathematics Conference
Iowa Council of Teachers of Mathematics
PO Box 445
Gowrie, IA 50543
www.iowamath.org

Math teachers conference.

Lori Mueller, President
Deb Tvrdik, Treasurer

417 Iowa Reading Association Conference

Iowa Reading Association
705 South Wilson
Jefferson, IA 50129
515-370-5857
iowareading@gmail.com
www.iowareading.org
Nationally prominent speakers, published authors, and experienced instructors will anchor the conference, sharing current research and creative reading strategies.

Lauriel Weekly, Co-President
Dani Woodman, Co-President

418 Kansas Association of School Boards Convention

1420 SW Arrowhead Road
Topeka, KS 66604
785-273-3600
www.kasb.org
An annual event connecting education leaders across the state of Kansas.

70 booths

John Heim, Executive Director
Brian Jordan, Deputy Executive Director

419 Kentucky Association of School Administrators Annual Leadership Institute

87 C Michael Davenport Boulevard
Frankfort, KY 40601
800-928-5272
www.kasa.org
Connects school leaders and industry partners from across the state to exchange ideas through networking, education sessions, and business solutions.

Rhonda Caldwell, Executive Director
Wanda Darland, Associate Director

420 Kentucky School Boards Association Annual Conference

Kentucky School Boards Association
260 Democrat Drive
Frankfort, KY 40601
800-372-2962
Fax: 502-695-5451
www.ksba.org
Information sessions, keynote speakers, and networking opportunities for board members, superintendents, and other education leaders.

1,000 attendees

Davonna Page, President
Kerri Schelling, Executive Director

421 Lilly Conferences on Evidence-Based Teaching and Learning

Int'l Teaching Learning Cooperative (ITLC)
5015 Southpark Drive
Suite 210
Durham, NC 27713
919-270-6306
registrar@lillyconferences.com
www.lillyconferences.com
A series of five annual conferences presenting the scholarship of teaching and learning. Teacher-scholars from across the U.S. and internationally gather to share innovative pedagogies and discuss questions, challenges, and insights about teaching and learning.

Todd Zakrajsek, President

3422 Louisiana School Boards Association Annual Convention

Louisiana School Boards Association
620 Florida Street
Suite 100
Baton Rouge, LA 70801
225-769-3191
Fax: 225-769-6108
www.lsba.com

Janet Pope, Executive Director
Stefanie Alsbury, Business Manager

3423 Maine Principals Association Conference

50 Industrial Drive
Augusta, ME 04330
207-622-0217
Fax: 207-622-1513
mpa@mpa.cc
www.mpa.cc
To assure a quality education for all students, promote the principalship.

Michael R. Burnham, Exec. Dir., Interscholastic
Holly D. Couturier, Exec. Dir., Professional

3424 Massachusetts Association of School Committees (MASC) Conference

One McKinley Square
Boston, MA 02109
617-523-8454
800-392-6023
www.masc.org

Glenn Koocher, Executive Director
Sam Cheesman, Director, Operations

3425 Michigan Association of School Boards Annual Leadership Conference

Michigan Association of School Boards
1001 Centennial Way
Suite 400
Lansing, MI 48917-8249
517-327-5900
Fax: 517-327-0775
info@masb.org
www.masb.org
The premier leadership event that features nationally acclaimed speakers addressing current education topics.

110 booths with 500 attendees and 110 exhibits

Don Wotruba, Executive Director
Kent Cartwright, Deputy Director

3426 Michigan Elementary & Middle School Principals Annual Conference

Michigan Elementary & Middle School Principals
Association
1980 N College Road
Mason, MI 48854
517-694-8955
Fax: 517-694-8945
www.memspa.org
Professional association for elementary & middle level principals.

Paul Liabenow, Executive Director
Syndee Malek, Associate Executive Director

3427 Michigan Science Teachers Association Annual Conference

Michigan Science Teachers Association
2501 Jolly Road
Suite 110
Okemos, MI 48864
734-973-0433
Fax: 734-677-3287
info@msta-mich.org
www.msta-mich.org
A conference that aims to supply science teachers with information and research.

Holly McGoran, President
Betty Crowder, Executive Director

3428 Mid-South Educational Research Association Annual Meeting

2100 Forest Hills Boulevard
Haughton, LA 71037
info@msera.org
www.msera.org
Focuses on assessment and involvement in education by releasing research and statistics.

Teresa Clark, President
Randy Parker, Executive Director

3429 Middle States Council for Social Studies Annual Conference

National Council for the Social Studies
8555 16th Street
Suite 500
Silver Spring, MD 20910
president.mscss@gmail.com
www.midstatescouncil.org
Seeks to develop and implement new curriculum into the social studies area.

Carolyn vanRoden, President
Scott Bacon, Treasurer

3430 Minnesota Association of School Administrators Conference

1884 Como Avenue
Saint Paul, MN 55108
651-645-6272
866-444-5251
Fax: 651-645-7518
members@mnasa.org
www.mnasa.org
Seeks to establish the statewide agenda for children, serve as the preeminent voice for public education and empower members through quality services and support.

Deb Henton, Executive Director
Mia Urick, Dir., Professional Learning

3431 Minnesota School Boards Association Leadership Conference

Minnesota School Boards Association
1900 W Jefferson Avenue
Saint Peter, MN 56082-3015
507-934-2450
800-324-4459
Fax: 507-931-1515
www.mnmsba.org
The purpose of the Association is to support, promote and enhance the work of public school boards.

January
200+ booths with 2,000+ attendees

Kirk Schneidawind, Executive Director
Gary Lee, Deputy Executive Director

3432 Missouri School Boards Association Annual Conference

Missouri School Boards Association
2100 I-70 Drive SW
Columbia, MO 65203
573-445-9920
800-221-6722
Fax: 573-445-9981
www.mosba.org

125 booths

Melissa Randol, Executive Director
Brent Ghan, Deputy Executive Director

3433 Missouri State Teachers Association Convention

407 S 6th Street
Columbia, MO 65201

573-442-3127
800-392-0532
membercare@msta.org
www.msta.org
The convention features an assembly of delegates, committee progress reports and an open discussion on issues facing the education profession.

November

Bruce Moe, Executive Director
Todd Fuller, Director, Marketing

3434 Montana Principals Conference
School Administrators of Montana
900 N Montana Avenue
Suite A-4
Helena, MT 59601
406-442-2510
Fax: 406-442-2518
www.sammt.org
Combined conference of the Montana Association of Elementary and Middle School Principals (MAEMSP) and the Montana Association of Secondary School Principals (MASSP).

January

3435 NAAEE Annual Conference
North American Assoc. for Environmental Education
1725 Desales Street NW
Suite 401
Washington, DC 20036
202-419-0412
info@naaee.org
www.naaee.org
Conference for environmental education professionals, offering networking, learning, and discussion of best practices, while fostering innovation.

October

Judy Braus, Executive Director
Lori Mann, Director, Conferences

3436 NCASA Conference on Educational Leadership
North Carolina Assn. of School Administrators
107 Glenwood Avenue
Raleigh, NC 27603
919-828-1426
Fax: 919-828-6099
info@ncasa.net
www.ncasa.net
Connects school administrators from across the state to receive timely information and updates. Information sessions, keynote presentations, panel discussions, networking opportunities, and more are available.

March-April
40 booths

Katherine Joyce, Executive Director
Karen Owens, Assistant Executive Director

3437 NCTM Annual Meeting & Exposition
National Council of Teachers of Mathematics
1906 Association Drive
Reston, VA 20191-1502
703-620-9840
800-235-7566
Fax: 703-476-2970
nctm@nctm.org
www.nctm.org
Covers topics like differentiated instruction, common core standards, intervention, technology and more.

Ken Krehbiel, Executive Director
David Barnes, Associate Executive Director

3438 NEA National Leadership Summit
National Education Association
1201 16th Street NW
Washington, DC 20036-3290
202-833-4000
Fax: 202-822-7974
www.nea.org/leadershipsummit
Meant to empower NEA members and leaders, encouraging them to develop their leadership knowledge and skills. There are interactive sessions and workshops exploring issues faced by the public education system.

March

Becky Pringle, President
Kim A. Anderson, Executive Director

3439 NSTA National Conference
National Science Teaching Association
1840 Wilson Boulevard
Arlington, VA 22201
703-243-7100
Fax: 703-243-7177
conferences@nsta.org
www.nsta.org

Dr. Eric J. Pyle, President
Dr. Erika Shugart, Executive Director

3440 National Association for Professional Development Schools Annual Conference
Nat'l Assn. for Professional Development Schools
1300 Pennsylvania Avenue NW
Suite 190-611
Washington, DC 20004
855-936-2737
info@napds.org
www.napds.org
Brings together school and university partnerships from across the country to discuss challenges, share tools and strategies, and connect with other PDS professionals.

Rebecca West Burns, President
Melissa A. Baker, Secretary

3441 National Association of State Boards of Education Annual Conference
123 North Pitt Street
Suite 350
Alexandria, VA 22314
703-684-4000
boards@nasbe.org
www.nasbe.org
Speakers cover topics such as ESSA implementation, education equity and excellence, leadership development, school funding, personalized learning and more.

October

Robert Hull, President & CEO
Sharon Cannon, Director, Operations

3442 National Association of State Boards of Education Legislative Conference
123 North Pitt Street
Suite 350
Alexandria, VA 22314
703-684-4000
boards@nasbe.org
www.nasbe.org
Provides a chance for members to engage with members of Congress, officials from the federal Department of Education, and others.

March

Robert Hull, President & CEO
Sharon Cannon, Director, Operations

3443 National Career Development Association Conference
National Career Development Association
305 N Beech Circle
Broken Arrow, OK 74012
918-663-7060
Fax: 918-663-7058
webeditor@ncda.org
www.ncda.org

Deneen Pennington, Executive Director
Natalie Scrimsher, Director, Membership

3444 National Council for Geographic Education Annual Conference
National Council for Geographic Education
8555 16th Street
Suite 500
Silver Spring, MD 20910
833-465-6243
info@ncge.org
www.ncge.org
Where geography educators from across the country and around the world meet to exchange ideas, research, resources, and best practices in geography education.

45 booths with 800 attendees

Jeff Lash, President
Charles D. Regan, Executive Director

3445 National Council for History Education Conference
National Council for History Education
13940 Cedar Road
Suite 393
University Heights, OH 44118
240-696-6600
nche@nche.net
www.nche.net
Brings together history professionals to tackle issues concerning history education.

March-April
750 attendees and 75 exhibits

Grace Leatherman, Executive Director
Sarah Drake Brown, Associate Director

3446 National Council for the Social Studies Annual Conference
National Council for the Social Studies
8555 16th Street
Suite 500
Silver Spring, MD 20910
301-588-1800
800-296-7840
www.socialstudies.org
Provides new ideas, resources, techniques, and skills focusing on social studies education. Features more than 400 sessions, workshops, presentations, speakers and panels, and social events.

Lawrence M. Paska, Executive Director
David Bailor, Director, Meetings

3447 National Council of Teachers of English Annual Convention
National Council of Teachers of English
340 N Neil Street
Suite 104
Champaign, IL 61820
217-328-3870
877-369-6283
Fax: 217-328-9645
customerservice@ncte.org
www.ncte.org

Brings together educators, experts, authors, administrators, publishers and others to discuss the profession of teaching.

Alfredo Celedon Lujan, President
Emily Kirkpatrick, Executive Director

3448 National Education Association Annual Meeting
National Education Association
1201 16th Street NW
Washington, DC 20036-3290
202-833-4000
Fax: 202-822-7974
www.ra.nea.org
A general conference that addresses all facets and concerns of the educator.

June/July

Becky Pringle, President
Kim A. Anderson, Executive Director

3449 National Principals Conference
National Assn. of Secondary School Principals
1904 Association Drive
Reston, VA 20191-1537
703-860-0200
800-253-7746
Fax: 703-860-3422
info@principalsconference.org
www.principalsconference.org
Offers programming addressing the needs and challenges of K-12 school leaders.

July
290 booths

Ronn Nozoe, Chief Executive Officer

3450 New England League of Middle Schools Annual Conference
New England League of Middle Schools
PO Box 887
Georgetown, MA 01833
877-402-7627
nelms@nelms.org
www.nelms.org

Jeff Rodman, Executive Director
Mary Jean Fawcett, Assistant Executive Director

3451 New Mexico School Boards Association Conference
New Mexico School Boards Association
300 Galisteo Street
Suite 204
Santa Fe, NM 87501
505-983-5041
Fax: 505-983-2450
nmsba@nmsba.org
www.nmsba.org
The New Mexico School Boards Association aspires to be recognized as the premier source of development and support for local boards of education in New Mexico.

20 booths

Joe Guillen, Executive Director
Lorraine Vigil, Program Director

3452 New York State Council of School Superintendents Leadership Summit
7 Elk Street
3rd Floor
Albany, NY 12207
518-449-1063
Fax: 518-426-2229
www.nyscoss.org
Provides members with opportunities to expand their expertise and knowledge in educational administration through keynote addresses, discussions, meetings, workshops, and networking.

Charles S. Dedrick, Executive Director
Vreneli G. Banks, Associate Director

3453 New York State School Boards Association Annual Convention & Expo
New York State School Boards Association
24 Century Hill Drive
Suite 200
Latham, NY 12110-2125
518-783-0200
Fax: 518-783-0211
info@nyssba.org
www.nyssba.org
Provides school board professionals with opportunities to learn, network with peers, and hear about the latest products and services impacting education.

October

Fred J. Langstaff, President
Robert Schneider, Executive Director

3454 New York State United Teachers Representative Assembly
800 Troy-Schenectady Road
Latham, NY 12110
518-213-6000
800-342-9810
mediarel@nysut.org
www.nysut.org

April-May

Andrew Pallotta, President
Jolene T. DiBrango, Executive Vice President

3455 North American Association of Summer Sessions Regional Conferences
North Carolina State University
2016 Harris Hall
Campus 7302
Raleigh, NC 27695-7302
919-515-2261
naass@naass.org
www.naass.org

Troy Hargrove, President

3456 Northeast Conference on the Teaching of Foreign Languages Conference
2400 Main Street
Buffalo, NY 14214
info@nectfl.org
www.nectfl.org
NECTFL aspires to serve the diverse community of language professionals through responsive leadership in its outreach activities and its annual conference.

April-May
160 booths with 2,500 attendees

Christopher Gwin, Chair
John D. Carlino, Executive Director

3457 Northwest Commission on Colleges and Universities Annual Conference
8060 165th Avenue NE
Suite 200
Redmond, WA 98052
425-558-4224
Fax: 205-525-9848
info@nwccu.org
www.nwccu.org

Sonny Ramaswamy, President
Pamela Goad, Executive Vice President

3458 Ohio Association of Secondary School Administrators Conference
Ohio Assn. of Secondary School Administrators
8050 N High Street
Suite 180
Columbus, OH 43235-6484
614-430-8311
Fax: 614-430-8315
info@oassa.org
www.oassa.org
Offers school administrators the opportunity to network with colleagues while gaining valuable information.

Timothy Freeman, Executive Director
Heather Powell, Associate Executive Director

3459 Ohio Business Teachers Association Conference
Columbus State Community College
550 E Spring Street
Columbus, OH 43215
www.obta-ohio.org
Promote among educators the desire to find better techniques and methods in an effort to improve instruction in the field of business so that students are well prepared to take their place in the business world.

October
40 booths

Jennifer Jorrey, President
Lisa Briggs, Treasurer

3460 Oklahoma State School Boards Association Education Leadership Conference
Oklahoma State School Boards Association
2801 N Lincoln Boulevard
Suite 125
Oklahoma City, OK 73105
405-528-3571
888-528-3571
Fax: 405-528-5695
www.ossba.org
Unites education leaders from across the state and offers information sessions, speaker presentations, and exhibits.

August

Shawn Hime, Executive Director
Joe Siano, Associate Executive Director

3461 Oregon School Boards Association Annual Convention
Oregon School Boards Association
1201 Court Street NE
Suite 400
Salem, OR 97301
503-588-2800
800-578-6722
Fax: 503-588-2813
info@osba.org
www.osba.org
To improve student achievement through advocacy, leadership and services to Oregon public school boards.

Jim Green, Executive Director
Mary Paulson, Deputy Executive Director

3462 PASA-PSBA School Leadership Conference
Pennsylvania School Boards Association
400 Bent Creek Boulevard
Mechanicsburg, PA 17050-1873
www.paschoolleaders.org
A multi-day conference for school leaders across the state. Co-hosted by the Pennsylvania Association of School Administrators (PASA) and the Pennsylvania School Boards Association (PSBA).

3463 PDK International Conference
Phi Delta Kappa International
1820 N Fort Myer Drive
Suite 320
Arlington, VA 22209
800-766-1156
info@pdkintl.org
www.pdkintl.org

Professional development opportunities for educators and administrators.

Joshua P. Starr, Ed.D, Chief Executive Officer
Albert Chen, M.E., Chief Operating Officer

3464 Pacific Northwest Council for Languages Annual Conference
1329 11th Ct SW
Olympia, WA 98502
www.pncfl.org
The Pacific Northwest Council for Languages unites, serves, and supports all world language educators in Alaska, Idaho, Montana, Oregon, Washington, and Wyoming.

Lynn Johnston, President
Lauren Kiolet, Executive Director

3465 Pennsylvania Council for the Social Studies Conference
Pennsylvania Bar Association
222 Paxson Avenue
Glenside, PA 19038
www.pcssonline.org
The PCSS promotes quality Social Studies education from kindergarten to higher learning by advocating the Social Studies at all levels of education in Pennsylvania.

October
50 booths with 500 attendees

Rachel Finley Bowman, President
David Keller Trevaskis, Executive Secretary

3466 Pennsylvania Science Teachers Association Conference
www.pascience.org
Work towards the advancement, improvement, and coordination of science education in all areas of science at all educational levels.

70 booths

Samantha Ramaswamy, President
Robert Cohen, Vice President

3467 School Administrators of Iowa Conference
School Administrators of Iowa
12199 Stratford Drive
Clive, IA 50325
515-267-1115
Fax: 515-267-1066
www.sai-iowa.org

August

Brad Buck, President
Jason Toenges, Vice President

3468 Science Teachers Association of New York State Annual Conference
PO Box 2121
Liverpool, NY 13089-2121
webmaster@stanys.org
www.stanys.org

Shelly Hinchliffe, President
Maureen Smith, Vice President

3469 South Carolina Library Association Conference
South Carolina Library Association
PO Box 1763
Columbia, SC 29202
803-252-1087
scla@capconsc.com
www.scla.org

October
125 booths with 350 attendees

Megan Palmer, President
Danielle Robinson, Treasurer

3470 Southern Association of Colleges & Schools Annual Meeting
SACS Commission on Colleges
1866 Southern Lane
Decatur, GA 30033
404-679-4500
questions@sacscoc.org
www.sacscoc.org

Belle S. Wheelan, Ph.D, President

3471 Southern Early Childhood Annual Conference
Southern Early Childhood Association
PO Box 8109
Jacksonville, AR 72078
501-221-1648
www.seca.info
Southern Early Childhood Association unites preschool, kindergarten, and primary educators and administrators, as well as other staff members working with and for families.

February

Debbie Ferguson, President

3472 TASA/TASB Convention
Texas Association of School Boards
PO Box 400
Austin, TX 78767-0400
512-467-0222
800-580-8272
tasb@tasb.org
www.tasb.org
Offers school board members and school administrators the opportunity to earn continuing education credit, hear keynote speakers, explore a tradeshow with hundreds of exhibitors, and network with more than 6,000 public school officials.

September-October

James B. Crow, Executive Director
Dan Troxell, Deputy Executive Director

3473 Tennessee School Boards Association Leadership Conference & Annual Convention
525 Brick Church Park Drive
Nashville, TN 37207
615-815-3900
www.tsba.net
Features speakers, clinics, and workshops.

November

Tammy Grissom, Executive Director
Ben Torres, Assistant Executive Director

3474 Texas State Teachers Association
8716 N Mopac Expressway
Austin, TX 78759
512-476-5355
www.tsta.org
The Texas State Teachers Association seeks to unite, organize and empower public education advocates to shape public education in Texas. Conferences include ESP Statewide Conference, Summer Academy, and Regional Leadership Academies.

Ovidia Molina, President
Richard Kouri, Executive Director

3475 The Center Annual Conference for Teachers of Linguistically & Culturally Diverse Students
The Center: Resources for Teaching & Learning
2626 S Clearbrook Drive
Arlington Heights, IL 60005-4626
224-366-8500
www.thecenterweb.org
A conference for administrators and teachers of English-language learners.

Ronald Perlman, President
Lisa Groff, Chief Financial Officer

3476 USA Kansas Annual Conference
United School Administrators of Kansas
1420 SW Arrowhead Road
Suite 100
Topeka, KS 66604
785-232-6566
Fax: 785-232-9776
usaoffice@usakansas.org
www.usakansas.org
Offers quality professional development opportunities for education administrators and leaders.

G.A. Buie, Executive Director
Jerry Henn, Assistant Executive Director

3477 University Professional & Continuing Education Association Annual Conference
Univ. Professional & Continuing Education Assn.
One Dupont Circle
Suite 330
Washington, DC 20036
202-659-3130
info@upcea.edu
www.upcea.edu
Gathering of higher education professionals who develop, implement, and promote professional and continuing education and online learning in North America.

April
70 booths with 1,000 attendees

Robert Hansen, Chief Executive Officer
Amy Heitzman, Chief Learning Officer

3478 VAIS Conference
Virginia Association of Independent Schools
9100 Arboretum Parkway
Suite 310
Richmond, VA 23236
804-282-3592
Fax: 804-282-3596
info@vais.org
www.vais.org
The Virginia Association of Independent Schools is a service organization that promotes educational, ethical and professional excellence. Through its school evaluation/accreditation program, attention to professional development and insistence on integrity, the Association safeguards the interests of its member schools.

November
1,500 attendees

Betsy Johnson Hunroe, Executive Director
Ellen Bostic, Director, Operations

3479 Virginia ASCD Conference
Virginia ASCD
2516 Old Lynchburg Road
North Garden, VA 22959
434-466-7466
www.vascd.org
Features keynote speakers, sessions, and networking opportunities for educators.

December
30 booths with 600 attendees

Laurie McCullough, Executive Director
Beverly Winter, Office Manager

3480 Virginia Association of Elementary School Principals Conference
Virginia Assn. of Elementary School Principals
1805 Chantilly Street
Richmond, VA 23230
804-355-6791
www.vaesp.net
Nonprofit professional association advocating for public education and equal educational opportunities. Promotes leadership of school administrators and principals, and provides professional development opportunities.
50 booths with 300 attendees
Casey L. Conger, President
Jim Baldwin, Executive Director

3481 Virginia School Boards Association Annual Convention
Virginia School Boards Association
200 Hansen Road
Charlottesville, VA 22911
434-295-8722
Fax: 434-295-8785
www.vsba.org
A convention for school board members, superintendents, and school division staff from across Virginia.
November
Gina Patterson, Executive Director
Jessica Blythe, Director, Communications

3482 Wisconsin Association of School Boards Annual Conference
Wisconsin Association of School Boards
122 W Washington Avenue
Suite 400
Madison, WI 53703
608-257-2622
877-705-4422
Fax: 608-257-8386
info@wasb.org
www.wasb.org
The WASB provides background and support for elected school leaders as they do the difficult work of democracy: weighing and balancing the unique values of their communities.
370 booths with 3,000 attendees
John Ashley, Executive Director

3483 Wisconsin Association of School District Administrators Conference
Wisconsin Assn. of School District Administrators
4797 Hayes Road
Suite 201
Madison, WI 53704
608-242-1090
Fax: 608-242-1290
www.wasda.org
The premiere collaborative leadership association, serves superintendents by providing professional support and expanding their capacity to be effective, innovative leaders.
70 booths
Jon Bales, Executive Director
Barb Sramek, Dir., Prof. Development

Directories & Handbooks

3484 A Competency Based Framework for Health Education Specialists
Nat'l Comm. for Health Education Credentialing
1541 Alta Drive
Suite 303
Whitehall, PA 18052-5642
484-223-0770
888-624-3248
Fax: 800-813-0727
www.nchec.org
Serves as a framework for professional preparation, credentialing, and professional development for health education professionals.
Linda Lysoby, Executive Director
Melissa Opp, Deputy Executive Director

3485 Appropriate Inclusion and Paraprofessionals
National Education Association
1201 16th Street NW
Washington, DC 20036-3290
202-833-4000
Fax: 202-822-7974
www.nea.org
A book offering information on mainstreaming disabled students and the work of paraprofessionals in the education process.
Becky Pringle, President
Kim A. Anderson, Executive Director

3486 Assessing Student Performance: Exploring the Purpose and Limits of Testing
Jossey-Bass
1 Montgomery Street
Suite 1200
San Francisco, CA 94104
415-433-1740
josseybasseducation@wiley.com
www.josseybass.com
Clarifies the limits of testing in an assessment system. Analyzes problematic practices in test design and formats that prevent students from explaining their answers by showing that assessment is more than testing and intellectual performance is more than right answers.
336 pages Softcover
ISBN: 0-7879-5047-5

3487 Assessment
Master Teacher
1 Leadership Lane
PO Box 1207
Manhattan, KS 66505-1207
800-669-9633
orders@masterteacher.com
www.masterteacher.com
Provides strategies for testing, grading, giving feedback, and conducting fair assessments.
Nikki Warnick, Chief Executive Officer

3488 Association for Continuing Higher Education Directory
2900 Delk Road
Suite 700, PMB 321
Marietta, GA 30067
423-251-5100
admin@acheinc.org
www.acheinc.org
Dedicated to promoting lifelong learning and excellence in continuing higher education. Encourage professional development, research and exchange of information for its members and continuing higher education as a means of enhancing and improving society.
Amy Johnson, President
Susan Elkins, Vice President

3489 Association for Talent Development Directory
Association for Talent Development
1640 King Street
Box 1443
Alexandria, VA 22313-1443
703-683-8100
800-628-2783
Fax: 703-683-1523
customercare@td.org
www.td.org
Offers an online directory of learning and development providers, as well as an online directory of academic degree programs.
Jim Caprara, Chair
Tony Bingham, President & CEO

3490 Before the School Bell Rings
Phi Delta Kappa International
1820 N Fort Myer Drive
Suite 320
Arlington, VA 22209
800-766-1156
info@pdkintl.org
www.pdkintl.org
Early childhood teachers and administrators, childcare providers and parents will enjoy and learn from this practical, insightful book.
84 pages Paperback
Carol B. Hillman, Author
Joshua P. Starr, Ed.D, Chief Executive Officer
Albert Chen, M.E., Chief Operating Officer

3491 Beyond Tracking: Finding Success in Inclusive Schools
Phi Delta Kappa International
1820 N Fort Myer Drive
Suite 320
Arlington, VA 22209
800-766-1156
info@pdkintl.org
www.pdkintl.org
Research data, practical ideas and reports from educators involved in untracking schools.
293 pages Hardcover
Harbison Pool and Jane A. Page, Author
Joshua P. Starr, Ed.D, Chief Executive Officer
Albert Chen, M.E., Chief Operating Officer

3492 Book of Metaphors, Volume II
Kendall Hunt Publishing Company
4050 Westmark Drive
PO Box 1840
Dubuque, IA 52004-1840
800-228-0810
corpinfo@kendallhunt.com
www.kendallhunt.com
A compilation of presentations designed to enhance learning for those participating in adventure-based programs. Practitioners share how they prepare experiences for presentations.
256 pages Paperback
ISBN: 0-7872-0306-8

3493 Brief Legal Guide for the Independent Music Teacher
Music Teachers National Association
600 Vine Street
Suite 1710
Cincinnati, OH 45202
513-421-1420
888-512-5278
Fax: 513-421-2503
mtnanet@mtna.org
www.mtna.org
Offering insights into the most common legal issues faced by independent music teachers.
Gary L. Ingle, Executive Director & CEO
Brian Shepard, Chief Operating Officer

3494 Contracting Out: Strategies for Fighting Back
National Education Association
1201 16th Street NW
Washington, DC 20036-3290
202-833-4000
Fax: 202-822-7974
www.nea.org

Becky Pringle, President
Kim A. Anderson, Executive Director

3495 Creating the Environment to Maximize Student Learning
Master Teacher
1 Leadership Lane
PO Box 1207
Manhattan, KS 66505-1207
800-669-9633
orders@masterteacher.com
www.masterteacher.com
Helps teachers create a classroom environment that advances student learning.

Nikki Warnick, Chief Executive Officer

3496 Directory of Curriculum Materials Centers and Collections
Assn. of College & Research Libraries, ALA
225 N Michigan Avenue
Suite 1300
Chicago, IL 60601-7616
312-280-2523
800-545-2433
Fax: 312-280-2520
acrl@ala.org
www.ala.org/acrl
Listing of centers that have collections of curriculum materials to aid in supporting teacher education programs.

Kara Malenfant, Interim Executive Director
Gena Parsons-Diamond, Program Officer

3497 Education Full Text
EBSCO
10 Estes Street
Ipswich, MA 01938
978-356-6500
Fax: 978-356-6565
information@ebsco.com
www.ebsco.com
A database consisting of education journals, including open access, non-open access, and peer reviewed journals.

Tim Collins, Chief Executive Officer

3498 Eleven Principles Framework for Schools: A Guide to Cultivating a Character-Inspired Culture
Character Education Partnership
PO Box 650307
Sterling, VA 20165
202-296-7743
www.character.org
A framework for building supportive school cultures that focus on character development.

Arthur Schwartz, President
Dean D'Ambrosi, Executive Vice President

3499 Ethical Issues in Experiential Education
Kendall Hunt Publishing Company
4050 Westmark Drive
PO Box 1840
Dubuque, IA 52004-1840
800-228-0810
corpinfo@kendallhunt.com
www.kendallhunt.com
An examination of ethical issues in the field of adventure programming and experiential education. Topics include ethical theory, informed consent, sexual issues, student rights, environmental concerns and programming practices.

144 pages

3500 Finishing Strong: The Last 60 Days of the School Year
Master Teacher
1 Leadership Lane
PO Box 1207
Manhattan, KS 66505-1207
800-669-9633
orders@masterteacher.com
www.masterteacher.com
Provides advice for finishing the school year strong.

Robert L. DeBruyn, Author
Nikki Warnick, Chief Executive Officer

3501 Great Classroom Management
Master Teacher
1 Leadership Lane
PO Box 1207
Manhattan, KS 66505-1207
800-669-9633
orders@masterteacher.com
www.masterteacher.com
Helps teachers develop structures, routines, and strategies for managing a classroom successfully.

Robert L. DeBruyn, Author
Nikki Warnick, Chief Executive Officer

3502 How to Raise Test Scores
Corwin Press
2455 Teller Road
Thousand Oaks, CA 91320
800-233-9936
Fax: 800-417-2466
order@corwin.com
www.corwin.com
Provides teachers with strategies designed to help students achieve success in the classroom.

30 pages Softcover

Robin Fogarty, Author

3503 Inclusion Facilitator Book
Master Teacher
1 Leadership Lane
PO Box 1207
Manhattan, KS 66505-1207
800-669-9633
orders@masterteacher.com
www.masterteacher.com
Offers practical help for regular classroom teachers and special education teachers in meeting the challenges of inclusion.

Wendy Dover, Author
Nikki Warnick, Chief Executive Officer

3504 Keeping the Momentum Strong in the Critical Middle of the School Year
Master Teacher
1 Leadership Lane
PO Box 1207
Manhattan, KS 66505-1207
800-669-9633
orders@masterteacher.com
www.masterteacher.com
Offers advice to help teachers keep the momentum strong in the middle of the school year.

Robert L. DeBruyn, Author
Nikki Warnick, Chief Executive Officer

3505 Law of Teacher Evaluation: A Self-Assessment Handbook
Phi Delta Kappa International
1820 N Fort Myer Drive
Suite 320
Arlington, VA 22209
800-766-1156
info@pdkintl.org
www.pdkintl.org
Provides a concise, authoritative overview of US state statutes, regulations and guidelines regarding the performance evaluation of educators.

51 pages Paperback

Perry A. Zirkel, Author
Joshua P. Starr, Ed.D, Chief Executive Officer
Albert Chen, M.E., Chief Operating Officer

3506 Libraries Unlimited
ABC-CLIO
147 Castilian Drive
Santa Barbara, CA 93117
805-968-1911
800-368-6868
Fax: 866-270-3856
customerservice@abc-clio.com
www.abc-clio.com
Produces publications for academic, public, school, and special libraries.

3507 Life Skills Training
National Health Promotion Associates
711 Westchester Avenue
White Plains, NY 10604
914-421-2525
800-293-4969
Fax: 914-421-2007
lstinfo@nhpamail.com
www.lifeskillstraining.com
Botvin LifeSkills Training (LST) is a research-validated substance abuse prevention program proven to reduce the risks of alcohol, tobacco, drug abuse, and violence by targeting the major social and psychological factors that promote the initiation of substance use and other risky behaviors.

Gilbert J. Botvin, President

3508 List of Regional, Professional & Specialized Accrediting Association
Educational Information Services
PO Box 662
Newton Lower Falls, MA 02162
617-964-4555
A list of those associations involved in accreditation for the education fields.

3509 MacMillan Guide to Correspondence Study
MacMillan Publishers
16365 James Madison Highway
Gordonsville, VA 22942
888-330-8477
Fax: 800-672-2054
press.inquiries@macmillan.com
www.us.macmillan.com
Contaings a list of accredited and non-accredited institutions offering independent study programs.

782 pages

3510 Making Every Lesson Highly Effective
Master Teacher
1 Leadership Lane
PO Box 1207
Manhattan, KS 66505-1207
800-669-9633
orders@masterteacher.com
www.masterteacher.com
Guidance and strategies for structuring lessons and ensuring student success in the classroom.

Nikki Warnick, Chief Executive Officer

511 Middle Grades Education in an Era of Reform
Academy for Educational Development
1255 23rd Street NW
Washington, DC 20037-1125
202-884-8800
Fax: 202-884-8400
Reviews middle-grades educational reform policies and practices.

512 NASDTEC Knowledge Base
Nat'l Assn. of State Dir. of Teacher Education
1629 K Street NW
Suite 300
Washington, DC 20006
202-204-2208
support@nasdtec.org
www.nasdtec.org
Provides state-specific information about the preparation and licensure of education professionals.

Phillip S. Rogers, Executive Director
Mike Carr, Development Coordinator

513 Orators & Philosophers: A History of the Idea of Liberal Education
College Board
250 Vesey Street
New York, NY 10281
212-713-8000
www.collegeboard.org
A cogent study of the historical evolution of the idea of liberal education. The book portrays this evolution as a struggle between two contending points of view, one oratorical and the other philosophical.

308 pages

Bruce A. Kimball, Author
David Coleman, Chief Executive Officer
Jeremy Singer, President

514 Paraeducator's Guide to Supporting Modifications
Master Teacher
1 Leadership Lane
PO Box 1207
Manhattan, KS 66505-1207
800-669-9633
orders@masterteacher.com
www.masterteacher.com
A guide for helping paraeducators provide appropriate modifications for students with all types of special needs.

Nikki Warnick, Chief Executive Officer

515 Personal Planner and Training Guide for the Paraeducator
Master Teacher
1 Leadership Lane
PO Box 1207
Manhattan, KS 66505-1207
800-669-9633
orders@masterteacher.com
www.masterteacher.com
Offers strategies designed to help paraeducators work effectively with students and teachers.

Wendy Dover, Author
Nikki Warnick, Chief Executive Officer

516 Professional Learning Communities at Work
Solution Tree
555 N Morton Street
Bloomington, IN 47404
812-336-7700
800-733-6786
Fax: 812-336-7790
info@solutiontree.com
www.solutiontree.com
This publication provides specific, practical, how-to information on the best practices in use in schools through the US and Canada for curriculum development, teacher preparation, school leadership, professional development programs, school-parent partnerships, assessment practices and much more.

Ed Ackerman, President & COO
Jeffrey C. Jones, Chief Executive Officer

3517 Programs for Preparing Individuals for Careers in Special Education
Council for Exceptional Children
3100 Clarendon Boulevard
Suite 600
Arlington, VA 22201-5332
888-232-7733
service@exceptionalchildren.org
www.exceptionalchildren.org
This directory offers over 600 colleges and universities with programs in special education. Information includes institution name, address, contact person, telephone, fax, Internet, accreditation status, size of faculty, level of program, and areas of specialty.

256 pages

Chad Rummel, Executive Director
Craig Evans, Chief Financial Officer

3518 Quality School Teacher
HarperCollins Publishers
195 Broadway
New York, NY 10007
212-207-7000
800-242-7737
hello@harpercollins.com
www.harpercollins.com
Provides the specifics that classroom teachers are asking for as they begin the move to quality schools. It is written for educators who are trying to give up the old system of boss-managing, and to create classrooms that produce quality work.

144 pages

William Glasser, Author

3519 Requirements for Certification of Teachers & Counselors
University of Chicago Press
5801 S Ellis Avenue
Floor 4
Chicago, IL 60637-5418
312-702-7700
800-621-2736
Fax: 800-621-8476
A list of state and local departments of education for requirements including teachers, counselors, librarians, and administrators for elementary and secondary schools.

256 pages Annual
ISBN: 0-226-42850-8

Elizabeth Kaye, Author
John Tryneski, Coordinating Education

3520 Research for Better Schools Publications
123 South Broad Street
Philadelphia, PA 19109-2471
215-568-6150
Fax: 215-568-7260
info@rbs.org
www.rbs.org
RBS is a private, nonprofit educational organization funded primarily through grants and contracts from the U.S. Department of Education, the National Science Foundation, Mid-Atlantic state departments of education, institutions of higher education, foundations, and school districts.

Dr. Keith M Kershner, Executive Director
Rev. John F Bloh, President

3521 Resources for Teaching Middle School Science
National Academy Press
901 D Street SW
Suite 704B
Washington, DC 20024-403
202-633-2966
Fax: 202-287-7309
shulers@si.edu
www.nsrconline.org
The NSRC is an intermediary organization that bridges research on how children learn with best practices for the classroom.

496 pages

National Science Resources Center, Author
Sally Goetz Shuler, Executive Director
Tanya Miller, Executive Assistant

3522 Restructuring in the Classroom: Teaching, Learning, and School Organization
Jossey-Bass
1 Montgomery Street
Suite 1200
San Francisco, CA 94104
415-433-1740
josseybasseducation@wiley.com
www.josseybass.com
Teaching, learning and school organization.

288 pages Hardcover
ISBN: 0-7879-0239-1

Richard Elmore, Penelope Peterson, Sarah McCarthey, Author

3523 Revolution Revisited: Effective Schools and Systemic Reform
Phi Delta Kappa International
1820 N Fort Myer Drive
Suite 320
Arlington, VA 22209
800-766-1156
info@pdkintl.org
www.pdkintl.org
The authors examine the Effective Schools movement of the past quarter century as a school reform philosophy and renewal process for today and for the coming years.

132 pages Paperback

B.O. Taylor and P. Bullard, Author
Joshua P. Starr, Ed.D, Chief Executive Officer
Albert Chen, M.E., Chief Operating Officer

3524 Seminar Information Service
250 El Camino Real
Suite 112
Tustin, CA 92780-4469
714-508-0340
877-736-4636
Fax: 714-734-8027
www.seminarinformation.com
In 1981, Catherine Bellizzi and Mona Piontkowski founded Seminar Information Service, Inc. (SIS). Their idea was to fill a void - thousands of seminars were taking place, but there wasn't any one central source to tell someone where and when they were being held.

1,000 pages Annual

Mona Pointkowski, Co-Founder
Catherine Bellizzi, Co-Founder

3525 Starting Strong in the First 60 Days of the School Year
Master Teacher
1 Leadership Lane
PO Box 1207
Manhattan, KS 66505-1207
800-669-9633
orders@masterteacher.com
www.masterteacher.com
A guide designed to help teachers and teacher mentors develop a strong learning environment for the beginning of the school year.
Robert L. DeBruyn, Author
Nikki Warnick, Chief Executive Officer

3526 Substitute Teacher Training Guide
Master Teacher
1 Leadership Lane
PO Box 1207
Manhattan, KS 66505-1207
800-669-9633
orders@masterteacher.com
www.masterteacher.com
Practical learning guide for substitute teachers.
John Eller, Author
Nikki Warnick, Chief Executive Officer

3527 Teacher Created Resources
Teacher Created Resources
6421 Industry Way
Westminster, CA 92683-3652
888-343-4335
800-662-4321
Fax: 800-525-1524
custserv@teachercreated.com
www.teachercreated.com
We publish quality resource books at the early childhood, elementary, and middle school levels. Our books cover all aspects of the curriculum—language arts, social studies, math, science, technology, and the arts.
Ina Levin, Managing Editor
Karen Goldfluss, Managing Editor

3528 Teacher Reference Centre
University of British Columbia
1961 E Mall
Vancouver, BC V6T-1Z1
604-822-6375
Fax: 604-822-3893
www.resources.library.ubc.ca
Provides indexing and abstracts for teacher and administrator journals and magazines.

3529 Teacher's Guide for Working with Paraeducators
Master Teacher
1 Leadership Lane
PO Box 1207
Manhattan, KS 66505-1207
800-669-9633
orders@masterteacher.com
www.masterteacher.com
Provides teachers with strategies for working with and supervising paraeducators.
Nikki Warnick, Chief Executive Officer

3530 Teachers as Leaders
Phi Delta Kappa International
1820 N Fort Myer Drive
Suite 320
Arlington, VA 22209
800-766-1156
info@pdkintl.org
www.pdkintl.org
Examines teacher recruitment, retention, professional development and leadership. The central theme of these twenty essays is excellence in education and how to achieve it.
320 pages Hardcover
Donovan R. Walling, Author
Joshua P. Starr, Ed.D, Chief Executive Officer
Albert Chen, M.E., Chief Operating Officer

3531 Teachers in Publishing
Pike Publishing Company
221 Town Center W
Suite 112
Santa Maria, CA 93458-5083
Editorial, research, sales, consulting, in office positions or travel to learn teachers' needs and instruct new texts.

3532 Teaching About Islam & Muslims in the Public School Classroom
9300 Gardenia Avenue
#B3
Fountain Valley, CA 92708-2253
714-839-2929
Fax: 714-839-2714
117 pages
ISBN: 1-930109-008
Susan Douglas, Author
Shabbir Mansuri, Founding Director

3533 Teaching as the Learning Profession: Handbookof Policy and Practice
Jossey-Bass/Pfeiffer
989 Market Street
San Francisco, CA 94103-1741
415-433-1740
Fax: 415-433-0499
Provides the best essays about the status of teaching, and the contributing writers are among the best thinkers in education today.
426 pages Hardcover
Linda Darling-Hammond, Editor
Gary Sykes, Editor

3534 The Health Education Specialist: A Companion Guide for Professional Excellence
Nat'l Comm. for Health Education Credentialing
1541 Alta Drive
Suite 303
Whitehall, PA 18052-5642
484-223-0770
888-624-3248
Fax: 800-813-0727
www.nchec.org
Linda Lysoby, Executive Director
Melissa Opp, Deputy Executive Director

3535 The Principal's Playbook to Making Every Day Count
Master Teacher
1 Leadership Lane
PO Box 1207
Manhattan, KS 66505-1207
800-669-9633
orders@masterteacher.com
www.masterteacher.com
Leadership strategies, communications tips, lessons, and techniques for school principals.
Nikki Warnick, Chief Executive Officer

3536 Theory of Experiential Education
Kendall Hunt Publishing Company
4050 Westmark Drive
PO Box 1840
Dubuque, IA 52004-1840
800-228-0810
corpinfo@kendallhunt.com
www.kendallhunt.com
This groundbreaking resource looks at the theoretical foundations of experiential education from philosophical, historical, psychological, social and ethical perspectives.
496 pages
ISBN: 0-7872-0262-2

3537 Time to Teach, Time to Learn: Changing the Pace of School
1615 Duke Street
Alexandria, VA 22314
703-528-0700
800-360-6332
Fax: 413-774-1129
info@aasa.org
Giving students the chance to learn and their teachers the chance to teach.
322 pages Softcover
Chip Wood, Author

3538 Top Quality School Process (TQSP)
National School Services
390 Holbrook Drive
Wheeling, IL 60090-5812
847-541-2768
800-262-4511
Fax: 847-541-2553
A customized School Improvement Program that incorporates input from all stakeholders in the educational process to establish baseline data, implement a continuous process of school improvement, and select quality programs for professional development.

3539 US Department of Education: Office of Educational Research & Improvement
National Library of Education
555 New Jersey Avenue NW
Washington, DC 20208-5573
202-219-2230
Fax: 202-219-2030
www.www2.ed.gov/pubs/TeachersGuide/oeri.html
Offers a variety of publications for professional development. The list of sources includes statistical reports, topical reports and effective programs, schools and practices.
John Blake, Reference/Information
Nancy Cavanaugh, Collection Development

3540 Welcome to Teaching and our Schools
Master Teacher
1 Leadership Lane
PO Box 1207
Manhattan, KS 66505-1207
800-669-9633
orders@masterteacher.com
www.masterteacher.com
Sets the stage for teachers so that they can have an enthusiastic and successful year in the classroom.
Robert L. DeBruyn, Author
Nikki Warnick, Chief Executive Officer

3541 Winning with Parents
Master Teacher
1 Leadership Lane
PO Box 1207
Manhattan, KS 66505-1207
800-669-9633
orders@masterteacher.com
www.masterteacher.com
A learning guide designed to help teachers build professional relationships with parents to maximize student learning.
Robert L. DeBruyn, Author
Nikki Warnick, Chief Executive Officer

542 World Exchange Program Directory
Center for U.N. Studies, GPO Box 2786
Ramna
Dacca 1000, Bangladesh
Offers listings, by geographical location, of exchange programs available to United States and abroad students. Listings include all contact information, schedules, fields and levels of study and bilingual information.
Biennial

543 You Can Handle Them All
Master Teacher
1 Leadership Lane
PO Box 1207
Manhattan, KS 66505-1207
800-669-9633
orders@masterteacher.com
www.masterteacher.com
Outlines 136 student behaviors and suggested techniques for managing each behavior.
Robert L. DeBruyn; Jack L. Larson, Author
Nikki Warnick, Chief Executive Officer

Periodicals

544 ATEA Journal
ATEA
Dunwoody College of Technology
818 Dunwoody Boulevard
Minneapolis, MN 55403
612-381-3315
www.ateaonline.org
Official journal of the American Technical Education Association, dedicated to topics related to postsecondary technical education.
Nasser Razek, Editor

545 Action in Teacher Education
Association of Teacher Educators
11350 Random Hills Road
Suite 800, PMB 6
Fairfax, VA 22030
703-659-1708
Fax: 703-595-4792
info@ate1.org
www.ate1.org
The official publication of the Association of Teacher Educators, serving as a forum for the exchange of information and ideas related to the improvement of teacher education at all levels.
Quarterly
ISSN: 0162-6620
Amanda Rudolph, Co-Editor
Heather Olson Beal, Co-Editor

546 American Educator
American Federation of Teachers
555 New Jersey Avenue NW
Washington, DC 20001
202-879-4420
ae@aft.org
www.aft.org/ae
The professional journal of the American Federation of Teachers is a quarterly magazine covering research and subjects related to K-12 education.
Quarterly
Lisa Hansel, Chief Publications Editor
Jennifer Dubin, Managing Editor

547 Education & Treatment of Children
Association for Behavior Analysis International
550 W Centre Avenue
Portage, MI 49024
269-492-9310
www.abainternational.org
A journal devoted to the dissemination of information concerning behavioral assessments or interventions for children and youth with emotional or behavioral problems.
Quarterly
Claire St. Peter, Editor-in-Chief

3548 Exceptional Children (EC)
Council for Exceptional Children
3100 Clarendon Boulevard
Suite 600
Arlington, VA 22201-5332
888-232-7733
service@exceptionalchildren.org
www.exceptionalchildren.org
Offers research and perspectives on topical issues in special education.
Quarterly
Chad Rummel, Executive Director
Craig Evans, Chief Financial Officer

3549 Extensions
HighScope Educational Research Foundation
600 N River Street
Ypsilanti, MI 48198
800-587-5639
info@highscope.org
www.highscope.org
Online archive of HighScope Educational Research Foundation's Extensions newsletter, which offered a teacher guide for users of the HighScope curriculum. Articles on classroom strategies, training techniques, problem-solving ideas, and news from the field, as well as training data.
Alejandra Barraza, Ph.D, President
Kimberly Diamond-Berry, Ph.D, Director, Research Policy

3550 GuildNotes Newsletter
National Guild of Community Arts Education
520 8th Avenue
Suite 302
New York, NY 10018
212-268-3337
guildinfo@nationalguild.org
www.nationalguild.org
Monthly
Adam Johnston, Deputy Director, Operations
Heather Ikemire, Deputy Director, Learning

3551 Ideas & Perspectives
ISM Independent School Management
2207 Concord Pike
Suite 417
Wilmington, DE 19803
302-656-4944
Fax: 302-656-0647
www.isminc.com
Outlines strategies and solutions for private school administrators and leaders.
Roxanne S. Higgins, President
Weldon Burge, Editor

3552 In Your Corner
Master Teacher
1 Leadership Lane
PO Box 1207
Manhattan, KS 66505-1207
800-669-9633
orders@masterteacher.com
www.masterteacher.com
A newsletter providing leadership solutions for K-12 educators.
Nikki Warnick, Chief Executive Officer

3553 Intervention in School and Clinic
Hammill Institute on Disabilities
1301 W 25th Street
Suite 300
Austin, TX 78705-4248
512-451-3521
Fax: 512-451-3728
www.hammill-institute.org
The hands-on how-to resource for teachers and clinicians working with individuals with learning disabilities or behavior disorders.
5x Year
ISSN: 1053-4512
Randall Boone, Editor
Kyle Higgins, Editor

3554 Journal of Classroom Interaction
University of Houston
College of Education
442 Farish Hall
Houston, TX 77204-5026
713-743-8677
jci@uh.edu
www.jciuh.org
The journal is a semi-annual publication devoted to empirical investigations and theoretical papers dealing with observation techniques, research on student and teacher behavior, and other issues relevant to the domain of classroom interaction.
H. Jerome Freiberg, Editor

3555 Journal of Economic Education
Taylor & Francis
530 Walnut Street
Suite 850
Philadelphia, PA 19106
215-625-8900
Fax: 215-207-0050
www.taylorandfrancis.com
The Journal of Economic Education offers original articles on innovations in and evaluations of teaching techniques, materials, and programs in economics.
Quarterly
ISSN: 0022-0485
Sam Allgood, Co-Editor
KimMarie McGoldrick, Co-Editor

3556 Journal of Experiential Education
Association for Experiental Education
2315 18th Street S
Saint Petersburg, FL 33712
303-440-8844
www.aee.org
Publishes refereed articles on experiential education.
Quarterly
ISSN: 1053-8259
Jayson Seaman, Editor

3557 Journal of Teacher Education
American Assn. of Colleges for Teacher Education
1602 L Street NW
Suite 601
Washington, DC 20036
202-293-2450
Fax: 202-457-8095
aacte@aacte.org
www.aacte.org
Articles, editorials, and commentaries focusing on policy, practice, and research pertaining to teacher preparation.
Cheryl Craig, Co-Editor
Valerie Hill Jackson, Co-Editor

3558 Journal of Technology Education
Int'l Technology & Engineering Educators Assn.
1914 Association Drive
Suite 201
Reston, VA 20191-1539
703-860-2100
Fax: 703-860-0353
iteea@iteea.org
www.iteea.org
Scholarly journal serving as a forum for discussion of technology education.

Steven A. Barbato, Executive Director
Kathleen de la Paz, Communications Director

3559 Journal on Excellence in College Teaching
Miami University
Oxford, OH 45056
513-529-9265
wentzegw@miamioh.edu
www.celt.miamioh.edu/ject
A peer-reviewed journal published by and for faculty at colleges and universities to increase student learning through effective teaching, interest in and enthusiasm for the profession of teaching, and communication among faculty about their classroom experiences.

Quarterly
ISSN: 1052-4800

Gregg Wentzell, Editor-in-Chief

3560 Journalism Education Today Magazine
Journalism Education Association
828 Mid-Campus Drive South
105 Kedzie Hall
Manhattan, KS 66506-1505
785-532-5532
Fax: 785-532-5563
staff@jea.org
www.jea.org
A publication providing educational perspectives on the subjects of teaching, scholastic media strategy, pedagogical updates, journalism research and more to the members of the Journalism Education Association.

Bradley Wilson, Ph.D, Editor

3561 Michigan Education
University of Michigan School of Education
610 E University Avenue
Ann Arbor, MI 48109-1259
734-764-9470
www.soe.umich.edu
Magazine of the University of Michigan School of Education.

3562 PDS Partners: Bringing Research to Practice
Nat'l Assn. for Professional Development Schools
1300 Pennsylvania Avenue NW
Suite 190-611
Washington, DC 20004
855-936-2737
info@napds.org
www.napds.org
Provides information about research and practice related to school-university partnerships and the Professional Development School model.

2x Year

Eva Garin, Co-Editor
Drew Polly, Co-Editor

3563 Performance Improvement Journal
Int'l Society for Performance Improvement
1400 Spring Street
Suite 260
Silver Spring, MD 20910
301-587-8570
info@ispi.org
www.ispi.org
Presents the latest ideas and approaches for performance improvement.

Monthly
ISSN: 1090-8811

Nancy Crain Burns, Editor

3564 Preventing School Failure
Taylor & Francis
530 Walnut Street
Suite 850
Philadelphia, PA 19106
215-625-8900
Fax: 215-207-0050
www.taylorandfrancis.com
A journal for educators and parents seeking strategies to promote the success of students who have learning and behavior problems. It includes practical examples of programs and practices that help children and youth in schools, clinics, correctional institutions, and other settings. Articles are written by educators and concern teaching children with various kinds of special needs.

Quarterly
ISSN: 1045-988X

William H. Evans, Executive Editor
Robert A. Gable, Executive Editor

3565 Rural Educator
National Rural Education Association
615 McCallie Avenue
Hunter Hall 212
Chattanooga, TN 37421
423-425-4539
www.nrea.net
Official journal of the NREA. A nationally recognized publication that features timely and informative articles written by leading rural educators from all levels of education.

3x Year
ISSN: 0273-446X

Devon Brenner, Co-Editor
Erin McHenry-Sorber, Co-Editor

3566 School-University Partnerships
Nat'l Assn. for Professional Development Schools
1300 Pennsylvania Avenue NW
Suite 190-611
Washington, DC 20004
855-936-2737
info@napds.org
www.napds.org
Publishes research on school-university partnerships and the Professional Development School philosophy.

2x Year

Seth Parsons, Co-Editor
Mandy Bean, Co-Editor

3567 TEACHING Exceptional Children (TEC)
Council for Exceptional Children
3100 Clarendon Boulevard
Suite 600
Arlington, VA 22201-5332
888-232-7733
service@exceptionalchildren.org
www.exceptionalchildren.org
Contains current information about special education teaching and learning, plus materials for classroom use.

6 Issues/Year

Chad Rummel, Executive Director
Craig Evans, Chief Financial Officer

3568 TEDLines Newsletter
The Council for Exceptional Children
3100 Clarendon Boulevard
Suite 600
Arlington, VA 22201-5332
888-232-7733
www.tedcec.org
Newsletter of the Teacher Education Division offering information about TED activities, upcoming events, current trends and practices, state and national legislation, recently published materials and practical information of interest to persons involved in the preparation and continuing professional development of effective professionals in special education and related service fields.

3x Year

Ruby Owiny, President
Karen Voytecki, Executive Director

3569 TESOL Journal: A Journal of Teaching and Classroom Research
TESOL International Association
1925 Ballenger Avenue
Suite 550
Alexandria, VA 22314-6820
703-518-2500
888-891-0041
Fax: 703-691-5327
tj@tesol.org
www.tesol.org
Publishes articles on current theory and research in the field of English education to speakers of other languages.

50 pages Quarterly

Youngjoo Yi, Editor
Peter Sayer, Editor

3570 Teacher Education and Special Education
The Council for Exceptional Children
3100 Clarendon Boulevard
Suite 600
Arlington, VA 22201-5332
888-232-7733
www.tedcec.org
Contains information on current research, exemplary practices, timely issues, legislation, book reviews, and new programs and materials relative to the preparation and continuing professional development of effective professionals in special education and related service fields. A publication of the Teacher Education Division of the Council for Exceptional Children.

Quarterly

Cynthia Griffin, Co-Editor
Melinda Leko, Co-Editor

3571 Teaching Education
Taylor & Francis
530 Walnut Street
Suite 850
Philadelphia, PA 19106
215-625-8900
Fax: 215-207-0050
www.taylorandfrancis.com
Publishes articles on issues related to the professional education of teachers.

Quarterly
ISSN: 1047-6210

Dennis Sumara, Co-Editor
Julianne Moss, Co-Editor

72 Techniques: Connecting Education and Careers
Association for Career and Technical Education
1410 King Street
Alexandria, VA 22314
800-826-9972
Fax: 703-683-7424
acte@acteonline.org
www.acteonline.org
To provide leadership in developing an educated, prepared, adaptable and competitive workforce.

LeAnn Wilson, Executive Director
Steve DeWitt, Deputy Executive Director

573 Technology and Engineering Teacher
Int'l Technology & Engineering Educators Assn.
1914 Association Drive
Suite 201
Reston, VA 20191-1539
703-860-2100
Fax: 703-860-0353
iteea@iteea.org
www.iteea.org
A peer-reviewed journal for elementary, junior high, middle, and high school teachers, as well as teacher educators. Publishes articles on trends, news, activities, and other information surrounding technology and engineering education.

8x Year

Steven A. Barbato, Executive Director
Kathleen de la Paz, Communications Director

574 The New Educator
Association of Teacher Educators
11350 Random Hills Road
Suite 800, PMB 6
Fairfax, VA 22030
703-659-1708
Fax: 703-595-4792
info@ate1.org
www.ate1.org
Focuses on the issues facing teacher educators, teacher education programs, and school systems.

Quarterly
ISSN: 1547-688X

Megan Blumenreich, Editor-in-Chief

575 The Source
ISM Independent School Management
2207 Concord Pike
Suite 417
Wilmington, DE 19803
302-656-4944
Fax: 302-656-0647
www.isminc.com
A weekly newsletter from ISM. Provides information about the latest news and trends impacting private-independent schools.

Roxanne S. Higgins, President

576 Today's Catholic Teacher
Bayard Inc.
1 Montauk Avenue
Suite 200
New London, CT 06320
800-321-0411
www.bayardfaithresources.com
Today's Catholic Teacher magazine is written for teachers in Catholic schools. Each issue is filled with information designed to help teachers succeed in the classroom.

3577 UPCEA Weekly Briefing
Univ. Professional & Continuing Education Assn.
One Dupont Circle
Suite 330
Washington, DC 20036
202-659-3130
info@upcea.edu
www.upcea.edu
Provides professional, continuing, and online education news, as well as information about events and association news.

Robert Hansen, Chief Executive Officer
Amy Heitzman, Chief Learning Officer

Software, Hardware & Internet Resources

3578 Ayotree
1515 E Colorado Boulevard
Pasadena, CA 91106
www.ayotree.com
School management software that utilizes a secure cloud-based system.

3579 Blackboard
11720 Plaza America Drive
11th Floor
Reston, VA 20190
www.blackboard.com
Offers teaching and learning solutions, including Blackboard Learn, a learning management system.

Bill Ballhaus, Chair, President & CEO
Tim Tomlinson, Chief Product Officer

3580 Common Curriculum
8 Market Place
Suite 300
Baltimore, MD 21202
833-394-7526
www.commoncurriculum.com
Digital lesson and unit planning platform.

Scott Messinger, Co-Founder
Robbie Earle, Co-Founder

3581 Dyknow
www.dyknow.com
Classroom management software for teachers.

3582 Education World
75 Mill Street
Colchester, CT 06415
www.educationworld.com
An online resource for teachers, administrators, and school staff.

3583 Gradekeeper
dethier@gradekeeper.com
www.gradekeeper.com
Computes grades and generates seating charts, progress reports, and more.

3584 Instructure
6330 S 3000 E
Suite 700
Salt Lake City, UT 84121
800-203-6755
info@instructure.com
www.instructure.com
Education technology company offering a variety of learning platforms, including Canvas Learning Management System.

Steve Daly, Chief Executive Officer
Mitch Benson, Chief Product Officer

3585 KQED Teach
KQED
50 Beale Street
5th Floor
San Francisco, CA 94105
415-864-2000
teach@kqed.org
www.teach.kqed.org
Online professional learning platform focused on teaching digital media literacy skills to educators.

3586 Learning for Justice
Southern Poverty Law Center
400 Washington Avenue
Montgomery, AL 36104
www.learningforjustice.org
Provides free resources to K-12 educators with the goal of creating and fostering inclusive school communities where all children and youth are respected and valued.

Jalaya Liles Dunn, Director
Hoyt J. Phillips III, Deputy Director

3587 National Professional Resources Inc.
6586 Hypoluxo Road
Suite 180
Lake Worth, FL 33467
239-631-2253
800-453-7461
Fax: 239-631-2259
orders@nprinc.com
www.nprinc.com
Produces videos/DVDs and publishes books on the most significant and current topical areas in the educational arena.

Robert M. Hanson, Chief Executive Officer
Helene Hanson, Vice President

3588 Original E-Z Grader Corp.
PO Box 23698
Chagrin Falls, OH 44023
800-732-4018
Fax: 800-689-2772
ezgrader@voyager.net
www.ezgrader.com
Products for grading papers, calculating weighted grades, and more.

3589 PBS LearningMedia
Public Broadcasting Service (PBS)
1225 S Clark Street
Arlington, VA 22202
www.pbslearningmedia.org
Free teaching resources including videos, lesson plans, interactive lessons, and more.

Paula Kerger, President & CEO
Jonathan Barzilay, Chief Operating Officer

3590 PowerSchool
150 Parkshore Drive
Folsom, CA 95630
877-873-1550
Fax: 916-596-0950
sales@powerschool.com
www.powerschool.com
Provider of cloud-based software for K-12 education, including Schoology Learning and PowerSchool SIS.

Hardeep Gulati, Chief Executive Officer
Marcy Daniel, Chief Product Officer

3591 Renaissance
2911 Peach Street
PO Box 8036
Wisconsin Rapids, WI 54495-8036
715-424-3636
800-338-4204
answers@renaissance.com
www.renaissance.com
Learning analytics solutions for educators.

Chris Bauleke, Chief Executive Officer
Todd Brekhus, Chief Product Officer

3592 **SimpleK12**
www.simplek12.com
Online training and professional development for teachers.

3593 **TeacherVision**
PO Box 51660
Boston, MA 02205
800-498-3264
www.teachervision.com
Resources for K-12 teachers.

3594 **Teachers Pay Teachers**
111 E 18th Street
11th Floor
New York, NY 10003
support@teacherspayteachers.com
www.teacherspayteachers.com
An online marketplace for teachers to buy and sell instructional materials and access digital tools.

3595 **Teaching Channel**
2805 Dodd Road
Suite 200
Eagan, MN 55121
www.teachingchannel.com
Offers a library of over 1,400 videos to help teachers learn new techniques and improve their teaching practices.

3596 **WeAreTeachers**
101 JFK Parkway
Short Hills, NJ 07078
973-921-5500
www.weareteachers.com
Articles, ideas, and resources for teachers.

3597 **k12jobs.com**
PO Box 210811
West Palm Beach, FL 33421
www.k12jobs.com
To provide schools with an efficient and cost-effective recruiting tool, providing service and opportunities to institutions and job seekers alike.

3598 **www.aasa.org**
American Association of School Administrators
1615 Duke Street
Alexandria, VA 22314
703-528-0700
Fax: 703-841-1543
info@aasa.org
www.aasa.org
Supports and develops effective school system leaders who are dedicated to the highest quality public education for all children.

Daniel A. Domenech, Executive Director
Chuck Woodruff, Chief Operating Officer

3599 **www.classbuilder.com**
www.classbuilder.com
An online tool for creating quizzes, tests, and assessments.

3600 **www.ed.gov/teaching/resources**
U.S. Department of Education
400 Maryland Avenue SW
Washington, DC 20202
800-872-5327
www.ed.gov/teaching/resources
Free educational resources.

3601 **www.gsn.org**
Global SchoolNet Foundation
270 N El Camino Real
Suite 395
Encinitas, CA 92024
760-635-0001
www.globalschoolnet.org
Collaborative projects, communication tools and professional development.

Yvonne Marie Andres, President
John St. Clair, Vice President

3602 **www.imagescape.com**
5121 N Ravenswood Avenue
Chicago, IL 60640
877-275-9144
www.imagescape.com

3603 **www.learninga-z.com**
1840 E River Road
Suite 320
Tucson, AZ 85718
520-232-5000
866-889-3729
Fax: 520-327-9934
www.learninga-z.com
LearningPage provides a collection of professionally produced instructional materials and resources.

3604 **www.makeworksheets.com**
www.makeworksheets.com
Enables teachers to create worksheets and lesson plans.

3605 **www.rhlschool.com**
RHL School
www.rhlschool.com
Free ready to use quality worksheets for teaching, reinforcement, and review.

3606 **www.teachingjobs.com**
510-508-7386
info@teachingjobs.com
www.teachingjobs.com
Connects education employers and job seekers.

Training Materials

3607 **At-Risk Students: Identification and Assistance Strategies**
Center for the Study of Small/Rural Schools
555 E Constitution Street
Room 138
Norman, OK 73072-7820
405-325-1450
Fax: 405-325-7075
jcsimmons@ou.edu
www.cssrs.ou.edu
The Center for the Study of Small/Rural Schools is a cooperative effort between the University of Oklahoma's Colleges of Education and Continuing Education. Endorsed by the National Rural Education Association as one of its five recognized rural education research

Video

Jan C Simmons, Program Director

3608 **Building Better Learners Online Course**
Master Teacher
1 Leadership Lane
PO Box 1207
Manhattan, KS 66505-1207
800-669-9633
orders@masterteacher.com
www.masterteacher.com
A 3-hour course designed to help teachers develop key learning skills in students.

Nikki Warnick, Chief Executive Officer

3609 **Building an Environment of Respect and High Expectations Online Course**
Master Teacher
1 Leadership Lane
PO Box 1207
Manhattan, KS 66505-1207
800-669-9633
orders@masterteacher.com
www.masterteacher.com
Offers strategies for creating a positive, respectful, student-centered learning environment.

Nikki Warnick, Chief Executive Officer

3610 **Character Education Online Training**
Master Teacher
1 Leadership Lane
PO Box 1207
Manhattan, KS 66505-1207
800-669-9633
orders@masterteacher.com
www.masterteacher.com
Provides 24 courses to help teachers incorporate character education into the classroom.

Nikki Warnick, Chief Executive Officer

3611 **Cisco Educational Archives**
University of North Carolina at Chapel Hill
170 W Tasman Drive
Po Box 1207
San Jose, CA 95134-3455
408-526-4000
800-553-6387
www.cisco.com
Focus on business operations, product innovation and design, and customer solutions. We develop products with minimal environmental impact and extend our technology to reduce environmental footprints globally.

John T Chambers, Chairman / CEO
Frank Calderoni, Executive VP/CFO

3612 **Clinical Play Therapy Videos: Child-Centered Developmental & Relationship Play Therapy**
425 S Welch Street
Complex 2
Denton, TX 76203
940-565-3864
Fax: 940-565-4461
cpt@unt.edu
www.cpt.unt.edu
Encourage the unique development and emotional growth of children through the process of play therapy, a dynamic interpersonal relationship between a child and a therapist trained in play therapy procedures.

Dee Ray, Director
Gabby Mendez, Administrative Coordinator

3613 **Conflict Resolution Strategies in Schools**
Center for the Study of Small/Rural Schools
555 E Constitution Street
Room 138
Norman, OK 73072-7820
405-325-1450
Fax: 405-325-7075
jcsimmons@ou.edu
www.cssrs.ou.edu
Series IV

Video

Jan C Simmons, Program Director

3614 **Conover Company**
4 Brookwood Court
Appleton, WI 54914-8618
800-933-1933
Fax: 800-933-1943
sales@conovercompany.com
www.conovercompany.com
Developing training programs for industry. Provide off-the-shelf as well as custom sales and marketing, training, presentation, and application

programs that connect learning to the workplace

Rebecca Schmitz, Member

3615 Cooperative Learning Strategies
Center for the Study of Small/Rural Schools
555 E Constitution Street
Room 138
Norman, OK 73072-7820
405-325-1450
Fax: 405-325-7075
jcsimmons@ou.edu
www.cssrs.ou.edu
Series I

Video

Jan C Simmons, Program Director

3616 Crisis Management in Schools
Center for the Study of Small/Rural Schools
555 E Constitution Street
Room 138
Norman, OK 73072-7820
405-325-1450
Fax: 405-325-7075
jcsimmons@ou.edu
www.cssrs.ou.edu
Series IV

Video

Jan C Simmons, Program Director

3617 Curriculum Alignment: Improving Student Learning
Center for the Study of Small/Rural Schools
555 E Constitution Street
Room 138
Norman, OK 73072-7820
405-325-1450
Fax: 405-325-7075
jcsimmons@ou.edu
www.cssrs.ou.edu
Series I

Video

Jan C Simmons, Program Director

3618 Datacad
20 Tower Lane
P.O. Box 815
Simsbury, CT 6070
860-217-0490
800-394-2231
Fax: 860-217-1866
info@datacad.com
www.datacad.com
DATACAD's product development, sales, and marketing activities are managed at the corporate headquarters in Avon, Connecticut

Mark F Madura, President/CEO
David A Giessleman, Senior Vice President and CT

3619 Educational Productions Inc
7101 Wisconsin Avenue
Suite 700
Bethesda, MD 20814
800-950-4949
800-637-3652
Fax: 301-634-0826
custserv@edpro.com
www.teachingstrategies.com
To increase the skills and understanding of the adults who work with, teach and care for young children.

Linda Freedman, President
Rae Latham, Vice-President

3620 Effectively Managing the Classroom Online Course
Master Teacher
1 Leadership Lane
PO Box 1207
Manhattan, KS 66505-1207
800-669-9633
orders@masterteacher.com
www.masterteacher.com
Strategies and techniques to help teachers limit disruptions and effectively manage the classroom.

Nikki Warnick, Chief Executive Officer

3621 Eleven Principles of Effective Character Education
Character Education Partnership
PO Box 650307
Sterling, VA 20165
202-296-7743
www.character.org
Leading the nation in helping schools develop people of good character for a just and compassionate society.

Arthur Schwartz, President
Dean D'Ambrosi, Executive Vice President

3622 English Language Learners Online Training
Master Teacher
1 Leadership Lane
PO Box 1207
Manhattan, KS 66505-1207
800-669-9633
orders@masterteacher.com
www.masterteacher.com
Offers 17 online courses that focus on teaching strategies for teachers helping English language learners succeed in the classroom.

Nikki Warnick, Chief Executive Officer

3623 Eye on Education
7625 Empire Drive
Florence, KY 41042-2919
888-299-5350
800-634-7064
Fax: 914-833-0761
orders@taylorandfrancis.com
www.routledge.com
Books on performance-based learning and assessment.

3624 Hearlihy & Company
Po Box 1708
Pittsburg, KS 66762-1747
866-622-1003
Fax: 800-443-2260
orders@hearlihy.com
www.hearlihy.com
Training and installation for schools purchasing modular labratories.

Kevin Bolte, Contact

3625 How to Teach Online Series
Master Teacher
1 Leadership Lane
PO Box 1207
Manhattan, KS 66505-1207
800-669-9633
orders@masterteacher.com
www.masterteacher.com
Courses to help teachers teach effectively in online and blended learning environments.

Nikki Warnick, Chief Executive Officer

3626 Improving Parent/Educator Relationships
Center for the Study of Small/Rural Schools
555 E Constitution Street
Room 138
Norman, OK 73072-7820
405-325-1450
Fax: 405-325-7075
jcsimmons@ou.edu
www.cssrs.ou.edu
Series I

Video

Jan C Simmons, Program Director

3627 Improving Student Thinking in the Content Area
Center for the Study of Small/Rural Schools
555 E Constitution Street
Room 138
Norman, OK 73072-7820
405-325-1450
Fax: 405-325-7075
jcsimmons@ou.edu
www.cssrs.ou.edu
Series II

Video

Jan C Simmons, Program Director

3628 Inclusion Online Training
Master Teacher
1 Leadership Lane
PO Box 1207
Manhattan, KS 66505-1207
800-669-9633
orders@masterteacher.com
www.masterteacher.com
Provides 40 courses and a resource library designed to help general education teachers work successfully with students with diverse learning needs.

Nikki Warnick, Chief Executive Officer

3629 International Clearinghouse for the Advancement of Science Teaching
University of Maryland
Benjamin Building
Room 226
College Park, MD 20742-1100
301-405-1000
Fax: 301-314-9055
www.umd.edu
Provides curriculum information about science and mathematics teaching.

Wallace D. Loh, President
Mary Ann Rankin, Vice President

3630 Managing Students Without Coercion
Center for the Study of Small/Rural Schools
555 E Constitution Street
Room 138
Norman, OK 73072-7820
405-325-1450
Fax: 405-325-7075
jcsimmons@ou.edu
www.cssrs.ou.edu
Series II

Video

Jan C Simmons, Program Director

3631 Meaningful and Effective Assessment Online Course
Master Teacher
1 Leadership Lane
PO Box 1207
Manhattan, KS 66505-1207
800-669-9633
orders@masterteacher.com
www.masterteacher.com
Helps teachers develop strategies for effective assessment.

Nikki Warnick, Chief Executive Officer

3632 Meeting the Needs of Diverse Learners Online Course
Master Teacher
1 Leadership Lane
PO Box 1207
Manhattan, KS 66505-1207
800-669-9633
orders@masterteacher.com
www.masterteacher.com
Helps teachers implement strategies to make lessons accessible to all students.
Nikki Warnick, Chief Executive Officer

3633 Multicultural Education: Teaching to Diversity
Center for the Study of Small/Rural Schools
555 E Constitution Street
Room 138
Norman, OK 73072-7820
405-325-1450
Fax: 405-325-7075
jcsimmons@ou.edu
www.cssrs.ou.edu
Series II
Video
Jan C Simmons, Program Director

3634 Outcome-Based Education: Making it Work
Center for the Study of Small/Rural Schools
555 E Constitution Street
Room 138
Norman, OK 73072-7820
405-325-1450
Fax: 405-325-7075
jcsimmons@ou.edu
www.cssrs.ou.edu
Series III
Video
Jan C Simmons, Program Director

3635 Overview of Prevention: A Social Change Model
Center for the Study of Small/Rural Schools
555 E Constitution Street
Room 138
Norman, OK 73072-7820
405-325-1450
Fax: 405-325-7075
jcsimmons@ou.edu
www.cssrs.ou.edu
Prevention Series
Video
Jan C Simmons, Program Director

3636 Paraeducator Online Training
Master Teacher
1 Leadership Lane
PO Box 1207
Manhattan, KS 66505-1207
800-669-9633
orders@masterteacher.com
www.masterteacher.com
Offers 140 training and assessment courses for paraeducators.
Nikki Warnick, Chief Executive Officer

3637 Positioning for High-Quality Student Engagement Online Course
Master Teacher
1 Leadership Lane
PO Box 1207
Manhattan, KS 66505-1207
800-669-9633
orders@masterteacher.com
www.masterteacher.com
Provides strategies to help teachers fully engage students in learning activities.
Nikki Warnick, Chief Executive Officer

3638 Powerful Instructional Strategies Online Course
Master Teacher
1 Leadership Lane
PO Box 1207
Manhattan, KS 66505-1207
800-669-9633
orders@masterteacher.com
www.masterteacher.com
A 3-hour course that helps teachers structure powerful and challenging lessons.
Nikki Warnick, Chief Executive Officer

3639 Quality School
Center for the Study of Small/Rural Schools
555 E Constitution Street
Room 138
Norman, OK 73072-7820
405-325-1450
Fax: 405-325-7075
jcsimmons@ou.edu
www.cssrs.ou.edu
Series II
Video
Jan C Simmons, Program Director

3640 SAP Today
Performance Resource Press
1270 Rankin Drive
Suite F
Troy, MI 48083-2843
800-453-7733
Fax: 800-499-5718
Overview offers the basics of student assistance.

3641 Site-Based Management
Center for the Study of Small/Rural Schools
555 E Constitution Street
Room 138
Norman, OK 73072-7820
405-325-1450
Fax: 405-325-7075
jcsimmons@ou.edu
www.cssrs.ou.edu
Series III
Video
Jan C Simmons, Program Director

3642 Social and Emotional Learning Series
Master Teacher
1 Leadership Lane
PO Box 1207
Manhattan, KS 66505-1207
800-669-9633
orders@masterteacher.com
www.masterteacher.com
Eighteen courses providing techniques to help teachers develop social and emotional skills in students.
Nikki Warnick, Chief Executive Officer

3643 Solutions to Bridge The Learning Loss Gap
Master Teacher
1 Leadership Lane
PO Box 1207
Manhattan, KS 66505-1207
800-669-9633
orders@masterteacher.com
www.masterteacher.com
Provides teacher strategies to help struggling students reengage their learning.
Nikki Warnick, Chief Executive Officer

3644 Strategic Planning for Outcome-Based Education
Center for the Study of Small/Rural Schools
555 E Constitution Street
Room 138
Norman, OK 73072-7820
405-325-1450
Fax: 405-325-7075
jcsimmons@ou.edu
www.cssrs.ou.edu
Series II
Video
Jan C Simmons, Program Director

3645 Strengthening the Family: An Overview of a Holistic Family Wellness Model
Center for the Study of Small/Rural Schools
555 E Constitution Street
Room 138
Norman, OK 73072-7820
405-325-1450
Fax: 405-325-7075
jcsimmons@ou.edu
www.cssrs.ou.edu
Prevention Series
Video
Jan C Simmons, Program Director

3646 Substitute Teacher Online Training
Master Teacher
1 Leadership Lane
PO Box 1207
Manhattan, KS 66505-1207
800-669-9633
orders@masterteacher.com
www.masterteacher.com
Offers 25 self-paced courses for substitute teachers.
Nikki Warnick, Chief Executive Officer

3647 Superintendent/School Board Relationships
Center for the Study of Small/Rural Schools
555 E Constitution Street
Room 138
Norman, OK 73072-7820
405-325-1450
Fax: 405-325-7075
jcsimmons@ou.edu
www.cssrs.ou.edu
Series I
Video
Jan C Simmons, Program Director

3648 Support Staff Online Training
Master Teacher
1 Leadership Lane
PO Box 1207
Manhattan, KS 66505-1207
800-669-9633
orders@masterteacher.com
www.masterteacher.com
Courses for school staff members.
Nikki Warnick, Chief Executive Officer

3649 TQM: Implementing Quality Management in Your School
Center for the Study of Small/Rural Schools
555 E Constitution Street
Room 138
Norman, OK 73072-7820
405-325-1450
Fax: 405-325-7075
jcsimmons@ou.edu
www.cssrs.ou.edu
Series III
Video
Jan C Simmons, Program Director

50 Teachers as Heros
Center for the Study of Small/Rural Schools
555 E Constitution Street
Room 138
Norman, OK 73072-7820
405-325-1450
Fax: 405-325-7075
jcsimmons@ou.edu
www.cssrs.ou.edu
Series IV
Video
Jan C Simmons, Program Director

51 Teaching for Intelligent Behavior
Center for the Study of Small/Rural Schools
555 E Constitution Street
Room 138
Norman, OK 73072-7820
405-325-1450
Fax: 405-325-7075
jcsimmons@ou.edu
www.cssrs.ou.edu
Series IV
Video
Jan C Simmons, Program Director

52 Understanding Behavior Online Courses
Master Teacher
1 Leadership Lane
PO Box 1207
Manhattan, KS 66505-1207
800-669-9633
orders@masterteacher.com
www.masterteacher.com
Four courses designed to hone the behavior management skills of teachers.
Nikki Warnick, Chief Executive Officer

653 Voices in the Hall: High School Principals at Work
Phi Delta Kappa International
1820 N Fort Myer Drive
Suite 320
Arlington, VA 22209
800-766-1156
info@pdkintl.org
www.pdkintl.org
William E. Webster, Author
Joshua P. Starr, Ed.D, Chief Executive Officer
Albert Chen, M.E., Chief Operating Officer

654 Wavelength
4753 N Broadway
Suite 818
Chicago, IL 60640
773-784-1012
877-528-47 2
Fax: 773-784-1079
info@wavelengthinc.com
www.wavelengthinc.com
Wavelength offers a fresh perspective on the key challenges in education today. Our programs are founded on the tenet that humor heals and enlightens. Of course, we also realized that by focusing our humor on education, we'd never run out of material

655 Winning Attitudes and Beliefs for Success Online Course
Master Teacher
1 Leadership Lane
PO Box 1207
Manhattan, KS 66505-1207
800-669-9633
orders@masterteacher.com
www.masterteacher.com
Focuses on the professional responsibilities of teachers, including classroom leadership, student and parent relationships, attitudes, and more.
Nikki Warnick, Chief Executive Officer

Workshops & Programs

3656 ACE Fellows Program
American Council on Education
1 Dupont Circle NW
Washington, DC 20036
202-939-9300
comments@ace.nche.edu
www.acenet.edu
Provides comprehensive leadership development for senior faculty and administrators of universities and colleges. Offers seminars, case studies, team-based projects, and networking opportunities.
Ted Mitchell, President
Kara Freeman, Chief Operating Officer

3657 ART New England Workshops
Massachusetts College of Art and Design
Office of Continuing Education
621 Huntington Avenue
Boston, MA 02115-5801
jknight@massart.edu
www.ane.massart.edu
Offers painting, drawing, photography, jewelry making, sculpting, computer imaging, and ceramics workshops.
Joe Doucette, Administrator
Jackie Knight, Program Manager

3658 Annual Conductor's Institute of South Carolina
PO Box 6891
Columbia, SC 29260
803-960-9237
conductorsinstituteofsc@gmail.com
www.theconductorsinstitute.com
The Conductor's Institute of South Carolina brings aspiring and experienced conductors to study with guest conductors and composers.
Donald Portnoy, Director

3659 Anti-Bullying & Cyber-Intimidation Program
Learning for Life
1325 W Walnut Hill Lane
Irving, TX 75038
972-580-2433
lfl@lflmail.org
www.learningforlife.org
Provides learning and professional development tools to help create safe learning environments for all students.
Tim Anderson, National Director
Anissa Hicks, Project Manager

3660 Ball State University
2000 W University Avenue
Muncie, IN 47306
765-289-1241
800-382-8540
askus@bsu.edu
www.bsu.edu
Ball State University's mission is to engage students in educational, research, and creative endeavors and empower them to have fulfilling careers. The university offers about 120 major programs and 100 graduate degrees.
Geoffrey S. Mearns, President

3661 BetterLesson
955 Massachusetts Avenue
Suite 300
Cambridge, MA 02139
617-329-9130
inquiries@betterlesson.com
www.betterlesson.com
Workshops and coaching services for teachers, instructors, and administrators.
Matthew Kennard, Chief Executive Officer
Ed Rayner, Chief Financial Officer

3662 Boxlight
1045 Progress Circle
Lawrenceville, GA 30043
866-972-1549
www.mimio.boxlight.com
Offers education training and professional development solutions, including certifications, online courses, workshops, and customized programs.
Michael Pope, Chair & CEO

3663 Bryant and Stratton College
1259 Central Avenue
Albany, NY 12205
518-437-1802
www.bryantstratton.edu
Bryant and Stratton College aims to help students develop meaningful career skills in a concise, contemporary and effective manner - providing graduates with the marketable job skills they need to succeed in an increasingly competitive marketplace.
Francis J. Felser, President & CEO

3664 Center for Educational Leadership - Trinity University
Trinity University
1 Trinity Place
San Antonio, TX 78212-7200
210-999-7501
800-874-6489
education@trinity.edu
www.trinity.edu
Offers three degree programs (Teacher, Principal, and School Psychology), as well as pre-college and network programs.
Angela Breidenstein, Interim Chair

3665 Center for Global Education and Experience - Augsburg University
Augsburg University
2211 Riverside Avenue
Campus Box 307
Minneapolis, MN 55454
612-330-1159
globaled@augsburg.edu
www.ww..augsburg.edu/global
To provide cross-cultural educational opportunities in order to foster critical analysis of local and global conditions so that personal and systemic change takes place, leading to a more just and sustainable world.
Leah Spinosa de Vega, Director, Global Initiatives

3666 Center for Image Processing in Education
1155 15TH STREET NW
SUITE 700
Washington, DC 20005-3750
202-721-9200
800-322-9884
Fax: 202-721-9250
CIPE promotes computer-aided visualization as a tool for inquiry-based learning. In support of that mission, it develops instructional materials and conducts workshops that use digital image analysis and geographic information systems technologies as platforms for

teaching about science, mathematics, and technology.

Greg Lebedev, Chair
Karen Karrigan, Vice Chair

3667 Center for Learning Connections
Edmonds College
20000 68th Avenue W
Lynnwood, WA 98036
425-640-1852
www.ce.edmonds.edu
The mission of the Center for Learning Connections is to prepare learners to manage change and create successful futures.

Cal Crow, Program Director

3668 Center for Occupational Research & Development
4901 Bosque Boulevard
Suite 200
Waco, TX 76710
254-772-8756
info@cord.org
www.cord.org
The Center for Occupational Research and Development (CORD) is a national non-profit organization dedicated to leading change in education.

Hope Cotner, President
Ron Schwartinsky, Vice President, Finance

3669 Center for Play Therapy Fall Conference
425 S Welch Street
Complex 2
Denton, TX 76203
940-565-3864
Fax: 940-565-4461
cpt@unt.edu
www.cpt.unt.edu
Features a one day workshop led by a recognized authority in the field of play therapy. This workshop enables professionals in the field of mental health to broaden their knowledge and clinical skills in play therapy.

September

Dee Ray, Director
Gabby Mendez, Administrative Coordinator

3670 Champions Daily Living Skills Program
Learning for Life
1325 W Walnut Hill Lane
Irving, TX 75038
972-580-2433
lfl@lflmail.org
www.learningforlife.org
Provides educators with lesson plans designed to teach social, personal, life, and self-concept skills to students with special needs.

Tim Anderson, National Director
Anissa Hicks, Project Manager

3671 Champions Transition Program
Learning for Life
1325 W Walnut Hill Lane
Irving, TX 75038
972-580-2433
lfl@lflmail.org
www.learningforlife.org
Helps school districts, teachers, and parents prepare students with special needs for independence.

Tim Anderson, National Director
Anissa Hicks, Project Manager

3672 College of the Ozarks
100 Opportunity Avenue
Point Lookout, MO 65726
800-222-0525
webmaster@cofo.edu
www.cofo.edu
A four-year liberal arts institution dedicated to providing Christian education for youth.

Jerry C. Davis, President

3673 Curriculum Center - Office of Educational Services
Southern Illinois University Carbondale
1263 Lincoln Drive
Suite 114
Carbondale, IL 62901-6899
618-453-2121
Fax: 217-786-3020
www.coas.siu.edu
Programs in vocational areas, career awareness, career development, integration, technology, tech preparation.

Mickey A.ÿ Latour, Dean

3674 Darryl L. Sink & Associates
1 Cielo Vista Place
Monterey, CA 93940
831-649-8384
Fax: 831-649-3914
jane@dsink.com
www.dsink.com
DSA designs and develops learning solutions for businesses, government agencies, and non-profit organizations. It offers training development services, workshops, and resources.

Darryl Sink, President
Jane Sink, Vice President, Marketing

3675 DeVry University
1200 E Diehl Road
Naperville, IL 60563
602-216-7700
877-496-9050
www.devry.edu
Subjects include communications, technology, graphic communications, healthcare, business, liberal arts, and training and development.

Tom Monahan, President & CEO

3676 Depco
689 S. Hwy. 69
PO Box 178
Pittsburg, KS 66762
620-231-0019
800-767-1062
Fax: 620-231-0024
www.depcollc.com
DEPCO (Dependable Education Products Company) was introduced as a manufacturers' representative organization, which represented manufacturers of vocational education products

3677 Eastern Illinois University School of Technology
1014 Klehm Hall
600 Lincoln Avenue
Charleston, IL 61920-3099
217-581-3226
Fax: 217-581-6607
www.eiu.edu/tech/
Subjects include manufacturing, construction, electronics, graphic communications, training and development.

Austin Cheney, Chair
Rendong Bai, Associate Professor

3678 Edison Welding Institute
EWI
1250 Arthur E Adams Drive
Columbus, OH 43221-3585
614-688-5000
Fax: 614-688-5001
info@ewi.org
www.ewi.org
The NJC's mission is to enhance the life-cycle affordability and mission capability of critical Navy weapon systems through the implementation of materials joining technology

Richard Rogovin, Chair
Henry Cialone, President/ CEO

3679 Education Northwest
1417 NW Everett Street
Suite 310
Portland, OR 97209
800-547-6339
www.educationnorthwest.org
The mission of Education Northwest is to solve educational challenges and improve learning. Services include webinars, consulting and professional development, research, and evaluation services.

Patty Wood, Chief Executive Officer
Jeff Strickler, Chief Operating Officer

3680 Educational Summit
The Principals' Center
20 Nassau Street
Suite 211
Princeton, NJ 8542-4509
609-497-1907
Fax: 609-497-1927
An educational summit held in August for school principals to explore, debate and design new models for schooling in America with implications for choice, charters and the community.

3681 Electronics Industries Alliance/CEA
2500 Wilson Boulevard
Arlington, VA 22201-3834
703-907-7670
Fax: 703-907-7968
www.CEMAweb.org
Electronics workshops.

3682 Elementary Education Professional Development School
Pennsylvania State University
228 Chambers Building
Pennsylvania State University
University Park, PA 16802
814-865-0488
n78@psu.edu
www.ed.psu.edu
The first goal is to enhance the educational experiences of all children. The second goal focuses on ensuring high quality field experiences for new teachers.

David H. Monk, Dean
Greg J. Kelly, Associate Dean

3683 Eleven Principles Workshop
Character Education Partnership
PO Box 650307
Sterling, VA 20165
202-296-7743
www.character.org
Coaches teachers, school leaders, and district coordinators on how to incorporate the 11 Principles Framework into their school environments.

Arthur Schwartz, President
Dean D'Ambrosi, Executive Vice President

3684 Emco Maier Corporation
46850 Magellan Drive
Unit 160
Novi, MI 48377-2448
248-313-2700
Fax: 248-313-2701

info@emcomaier-usa.com
www.emco-world.us
The EMCO success story began in 1947 with the production of conventional lathes. In the years to follow, EMCO repeatedly impressed the market with extraordinary, innovative solutions.

Josh Dack, Sales Manager
Karen Fahy, Sales/Marketing Coordinator

685 Energy Concepts
1001 Cottonwood Drive NEÿ
PO Box 628
Willmar, MN 56201
320-235-9079
800-621-1247
Fax: 847-837-8171
info@energyconceptsinc.com
www.energyconceptsinc.com
Subjects include material science technology, principles of technology year I&II.

686 Fastech
1750 Westfield Drive
Findlay, OH 45840
419-425-2233
Fax: 419-425-9431
info@fastechinc.net
www.fastechinc.net
Subjects include mastercam training, and FMMT CD's.

Roger J. Darr, President

687 Festo Corporation
395 Moreland Road
PO Box 18023
Hauppauge, NY 11788
631-435-0800
Fax: 631-435-8026
customer.service@us.festo.com
www.festo-usa.com
Subjects include fluid power, PLC, industrial automation.

Fred Zieram, Sales Manager
Petra Milks, Product Coordinator

688 Foundation for Critical Thinking
PO Box 196
Tomales, CA 94971
707-878-9100
800-833-3645
Fax: 707-878-9111
cct@criticalthinking.org
www.criticalthinking.org
The Foundation creates events and resources designed to help educators improve their instruction. Materials developed through the Foundation for Critical Thinking include books, thinker's guides, videos, and other teaching and learning resources.

Dr. Linda Elder, Senior Fellow
Dr. Gerald Nosich, Senior Fellow

689 Four State Regional Technology Conference
Pittsburg State University
College of Technology
1701 S Broadway
Pittsburg, KS 66762
620-235-7000
800-854-7488
Fax: 620-235-4343
tbaldwin@pittstate.edu
www.pittstate.edu
Subjects include educational technology and technology management.

November
30 booths with 250 attendees

Tom Baldwin, Dean, College of Technology
Steve Scott, President

3690 Graduate Programs for Professional Educators
North Central Association of Colleges & Schools
Walden University
155 5th Avenue S
Minneaoplis, MN 55401
800-444-6795
Fax: 941-498-4266
www.northcentralassociation.org
Both the MS and PhD in Education allow study from home or work. The Master of Science in Education serves classroom teachers and the PhD in education serves the advanced learning needs of educators from a wide range that serves practice fields and levels.

Benny Gooden, President
David Ho, Vice President

3691 Grand Canyon University College of Education
3300 W Camelback Road
Phoenix, AZ 85017-3030
602-639-7500
800-800-9776
Fax: 312-263-7462
cmosby@gcu.edu
www.gcu.edu
Prepares learners to become global citizens, critical thinkers, effective communicators, and responsible leaders by providing an academically challenging, values-based curriculum from the context of our Christian heritage.

Brain Mueler, President/ CEO
Stan Meyer, Chief Operating Officer

3692 Harvard Graduate School of Education
13 Appian Way
Longfellow Hall, 5th Floor
Cambridge, MA 02138
617-496-9139
800-545-1849
Fax: 617-496-8051
ppe@gse.harvard.edu
www.gse.harvard.edu/ppe
Offers degree programs and professional education programs, including early childhood, K-12, higher education, and online programs.

Bridget Long, Dean

3693 Harvard Institute for School Leadership
Harvard Graduate School of Education
Appian Way
Fifth Floor
Cambridge, MA 2138
617-495-3572
800-545-1849
Fax: 617-496-8051
webeditor@gse.harvard.edu
www.gse.harvard.edu/ppe
An intensive residential program for leadership teams from school districts. Participants will gain new perspectives on the processes and goals of school reform and practical skills for leading change in their districts.

July

3694 Hobart Institute of Welding Technology
400 Trade Square East
Troy, OH 45373
800-332-9448
Fax: 937-332-9550
info@welding.orgÿ
www.welding.org
Preparation course for CWI/CWE exams. Instructor course devoted to welding theory and hand-son practice.

Elmer Swank, Contact

3695 Indiana University-Purdue University of Indianapolis, IUPUI
Department of Construction Technology
420 University Blvd.
ET 209
Indianapolis, IN 46202-5160
317-274-5555
Fax: 317-274-4567
askiu@iu.edu
www.iupui.edu
Subjects include architectural technology, civil engineering technology, construction technology, interior design.

Charles R. Bantz, Chancellor
Nasser H. Paydar, Executive Vice Chancellor

3696 Industrial Training Institute
3385 Wheeling Road
Lancaster, OH 43130
740-687-5262
800-638-4180
Fax: 740-687-5262
drbillstevens1@msn.com
Subjects include basic electricity, motors, controls, PLC's, NEC and process control; custom designed training and consulting.

3697 Institute of Higher Education
General Board of Higher Education & Ministry/UMC
1001 19th Avenue S
P. O. ÿBox 340007
Nashville, TN 37203-7
615-340-7400
Fax: 615-340-7379
scu@gbhem.org
www.gbhem.org
An annual seminar for administrators and faculty of United Methodist-related educational institutions addressing current themes related to the college's mission.

June
125 attendees

James E. Dorff, President
Lanther Marie Mills, Vice President

3698 Interdisciplinary Academic & Character Development Program
Learning for Life
1325 W Walnut Hill Lane
Irving, TX 75038
972-580-2433
lfl@lflmail.org
www.learningforlife.org
Provides educators with lesson plans that integrate character development and life skills practice into the classroom.

Tim Anderson, National Director
Anissa Hicks, Project Manager

3699 International Curriculum Management Audit Center
Phi Delta Kappa International
1820 N Fort Myer Drive
Suite 320
Arlington, VA 22209
800-766-1156
info@pdkintl.org
www.pdkintl.org

Joshua P. Starr, Ed.D, Chief Executive Officer
Albert Chen, M.E., Chief Operating Officer

3700 International Graduate School
Berne University
35 Center Street
Suite 18
Wolfeboro Falls, NH 03896-1080
603-569-8648
866-755-5557
Fax: 603-569-4052

Doctoral Degrees in one to two years, Specialist Diplomas in six to twelve months in: business, education (all specialties), government, health services, international relations, psychology, religion, social work and human services.

3701 International Workshops

187 Aqua View Road
Cedarburg, WI 53012
262-377-7062
Fax: 262-377-7096
thintz@internationalworkshops.org
www.internationalworkshops.org
International Workshops creates an international community of artists and teachers in a site that combines touristic and cultural interest.

400 attendees

Tori Hintz, Manager
Gerald F Fischbach, Director

3702 Island Drafting & Technical Institute

128 Broadway
Amityville, NY 11701-2704
631-691-8733
Fax: 631-691-8738
info@idti.edu
www.idti.edu
Our aim is to graduate students well-trained and technically qualified so that they may enter their chosen field or continue their education at the baccalaureate or higher level.

John G Diliberto, VP

3703 Janice Borla Vocal Jazz Camp

N Central College, Music Department
30 N Brainard Street
Naperville, IL 60540
630-416-3911
Fax: 630-416-6249
jborla@aol.com
www.janiceborlavocaljazzcamp.org
The camp's mission is to enable jazz vocalists to develop and enhance their individual performing skills and musical creativity, regardless of prior experience level, by studying with and attending performances of professional artists actively engaged in the field of jazz performance.

Janice Borla, Director
Jay Clayton, Faculty

3704 Jefferson State Community College

2601 Carson Road
Birmingham, AL 35215
205-853-1200
800-239-5900
Fax: 205-856-8572
www.jeffstateonline.com
Certificate and degree programs in automated manufacturing, electromechanical systems, industrial maintenance, and CAD.

3705 July in Rensselaer

St Joseph's College, Graduate Dept
PO Box 984
Rensselaer, IN 47978
219-866-6352
Fax: 219-866-6102
Solo, ensemble, liturgy, accompanying, history, improvisation, private lessons, technique, repertoire, sight reading, workshops, theory and sacred choral music.

Rev. James Challancin, Director

3706 K'nex Education Division

2990 Bergey Road
PO Box 700
Hatfield, PA 19440
888-ABC-KNEX
Fax: 215-996-4222
abcknex@knex.com
www.knexeducation.com
Introductory, set specific, regional and design your own professional development programs offered for any/all K-12 technology, math and science sets.

3707 Kaleidoscope

Consulting Psychologists Press
3803 E Bayshore Road
Palo Alto, CA 94303-4300
800-624-1765
Fax: 650-969-8608
An institute for educators that develops insights into teaching styles and learning styles; administers and interprets the Myers-Briggs Type Indicator (personality inventory); learn new techniques to help children understand and value their unique qualities; create and deliver lessons that enlighten all students and more.

July

3708 Kent State University

375 Terrace Drive
Van Deusen Hall
Kent, OH 44242
330-672-2892
Fax: 330-672-2894
lepps@kent.edu
Subjects include aeronautics, electronics, manufacturing engineering, computer technology, and automotive engineering technology.

Verna Fitzsimmons, Interim Dean
Isaac Richmond Nettey, Associate Dean

3709 Kentucky State University

400 East Main Street
Frankfort, KY 40601
502-597-6000
Fax: 502-227-6236
webadmin@kysu.edu
www.kysu.edu
Associates in applied science in drafting and design technology and applied science in electronics technology.

Mary Evans Sias, President
Stephen Mason, Executive Assistant

3710 Kodaly Teaching Certification Program

DePaul University, School of Music
804 West Belden Avenue
Chicago, IL 60614
773-325-4355
Fax: 773-325-7263
Music education, pedagogy and workshops.

Robert Krueger, Director Operations

3711 Lab Volt Systems

1710 State Highway 34
Farmingdale, NJ 07727
732-938-2000
800-522-2658
Fax: 732-774-8573
us@labvolt.com
www.labvolt.com
Global leader in the design and manufacture of hands-on training laboratories for public education, industry, and the military.

Eric Maynard, Contact

3712 Learners Edge

2805 Dodd Road
Suite 200
Eagan, MN 55121
952-469-3454
866-665-3713
Fax: 952-658-1150
www.learnersedge.com
Online continuing education and professional development courses for teachers.

Jim Hall, Chief Executive Officer
Wendy Amato, Chief Academic Officer

3713 Learning & The Enneagram

National Enneagram Institute at Milton Academy
230 Atherton Street
Milton, MA 02186-2424
617-898-1798
Fax: 617-898-1712
An educational enterprise dedicated to guiding individuals and organizations in the most responsible and effective format for their needs. Programs include exploration of what every educator needs to know; why we learn in the way we do; and how we teach.

July

Regina Pyle, Coordinator

3714 Learning Materials Workshop

58 Henry Street
Burlington, VT 05401
800-693-7164
Fax: 802-862-8399
info@learningmaterialswork.com
www.learningmaterialswork.com
Learning Materials Workshop Blocks are learning tools in the hands of young children. They are open-ended, yet carefully designed in a variety of colors, sizes, shapes, and textures that stimulate and develop perpetual, motor, and language skills. Learning Materials Workships are designed for early childhood/primary grade teachers, paraprofessionals, curriculum coordinators, special education teachers, ESL teachers, and teachers of the gifted and talented to help develop the learning process.

Karen Hewitt, President

3715 Light Machines

444 E Industrial Park Avenue
Manchester, NH 03109-5317
800-221-2763
Fax: 603-625-2137
www.lightmachines.com
Subjects include demonstrations and comprehensive training on CNC routers, turning machines and milling machines, and CAD/CAM software.

3716 MPulse Maintenance Software

PO Box 22906
Eugene, OR 97402
541-302-6677
800-944-1796
Fax: 541-302-6680
info@mpulsesoftware.com
www.mpulsesoftware.com
Deliver simply better EAM / CMMS software that is easier to use and faster to implement. Keep it affordable by controlling the cost of sales and marketing. Design it to keep up with their needs today, their challenges of tomorrow, while maintaining the history of what they did yesterday. And do it better than anyone else

Steve Brous, President & CEO

3717 Marcraft International Corporation

1350 Spaulding Ave
Suite 302
Kennwick, WA 99352
509-374-1951
800-441-6006
Fax: 509-374-9250

sales@marcraft.com
www.marcraft.com
s to develop exceptional products for effectively teaching and training people the technical IT, computer, and electronics training skills in demand today and in the future.

Robert Krug, National Sales Manager

718 Maryland Center for Career and Technology Education
1415 Key Highway
Baltimore, MD 21230
410-685-1648
Fax: 410-685-0032
Subjects include technology education and occupational education certification.

719 Millersville University
PO Box 1002
1 South George Street
Millersvile, PA 17551
717-872-3011
800-426-4553
Fax: 877-327-8132
www.millersville.edu
With a student population of 7,259 undergraduate and 1,047 graduate students, Millersville University offers all the advantages you would expect from a university: competitive programs, great facilities, a diverse student community and a variety of campus programming all offered in an accessible, intimate and close-knit atmosphere more frequently found at a smaller college

Michael G Warfel, Chairman
Paul G Wedel, Vice Chairman

720 Missouri National Education Association Workshops & Conferences
Missouri National Education Association
1810 E Elm Street
Jefferson City, MO 65101
573-634-3202
800-392-0236
Fax: 573-634-5646
deeann.aull@mnea.org
www.mnea.org
Offers workshops, support programs, webinars, training sessions, conferences and more.

DeeAnn Aull, Executive Director
Ann Jarrett, Dir., Teaching & Learning

721 Morehead State University
150 University Boulevard
Morehead, KY 40351
606-783-2221
Fax: 606-783-5000
admissions@moreheadstate.edu
Morehead State University was founded upon and continues to embrace the ideal that all persons should have opportunity to participate in higher education. With immense pride in its past and great promise for its future, the University intends to emerge in the first decade of the 21st century as an even stronger institution recognized for superb teaching and learning with exemplary programs in teacher education, space-related science and technology, entrepreneurship, visual and performing arts, r

Beth Patrick, Vice President
Dayna Seelig, Special Assistant to the Pre

722 Musikgarten
507 Arlington Street
Greensboro, NC 27406
336-272-5303
800-216-6864
Fax: 336-272-0581
musgarten@aol.com
www.musikgarten.org
Early childhood music education workshops teaching music and understanding children.

Lorna Heyge, President

3723 NCSS Summer Workshops
National Council for the Social Studies
8555 16th Street
Suite 500
Silver Spring, MD 20910
301-588-1800
800-296-7840
www.socialstudies.org
Provides educational programs for social studies professionals.

Lawrence M. Paska, Executive Director
Joy D. Lindsey, Director, Membership

3724 NEA Aspiring Educators Program
National Education Association
1201 16th Street NW
Washington, DC 20036-3290
202-833-4000
Fax: 202-822-7974
www.nea.org/home/1600.htm
Strives to promote community partnerships; foster leadership through pre-professional opportunities and peer mentoring; promote membership among diverse populations; supplement teacher-education training; promote national accreditation of teacher-education training and more.

Becky Pringle, President
Kim A. Anderson, Executive Director

3725 National Center for Construction Education & Research
13614 Progress Boulevard
Alachua, FL 32615
386-518-6500
888-622-3720
Fax: 386-518-6303
info@nccer.org
www.nccer.org
Our mission is to build a safe, productive, and sustainable workforce of craft professionals.

Don Whyte, President
Cathy Tyler, Executive Assistant

3726 National Computer Systems
4401 L Street NW
Suite 550
Edina, MN 55435
612-995-8997
800-328-6172
Fax: 952-830-8564
www.ncsus.net
Programs offer skills to teach technology in the classroom.

3727 National Head Start Association (NHSA)
1651 Prince Street
Alexandria, VA 22314
703-739-0875
866-677-8724
www.nhsa.org
Nonprofit organization offering professional development training to those working with at risk children.

Yasmina Vinci, Executive Director
Thomas Sheridan, Deputy Director

3728 Northern Arizona University
South San Francisco Street
Flagstaff, AZ 86011
928-523-9011
Fax: 520-523-6395
www.nau.edu
Provide an outstanding undergraduate residential education strengthened by research, graduate and professional programs, and sophisticated methods of distance delivery.

John D Haeger, President
Tracy Cooper, Lab Assistant

3729 Ohio Public School Employees Association
6805 Oak Creek Drive
Columbus, OH 43229-1591
614-890-4770
800-786-2773
www.oapse.org
Provides leadership training sessions.

Lois Carson, President
Joseph R. Rugola, Executive Director

3730 Orff-Schulwerk Teacher Certification Program
DePaul University, School of Music
804 West Belden Avenue
Chicago, IL 60614
773-325-7260
Fax: 773-325-7264
Music education, pedagogy and workshops.

Judy Bundra, Associate Dean

3731 Owens Community College
PO Box 10000
Toledo, OH 43699-1947
567-661-7000
800-466-9367
Fax: 419-661-7664
www.owens.edu
We believe in serving our students and our communities. Your success is our misssion.

Diana H Talmage, Chairman
R J Molter, Vice Chair

3732 PBS Digital Innovators
Public Broadcasting Service (PBS)
1225 S Clark Street
Arlington, VA 22202
www.pbs.org/education/digitalinnovators
Professional development program for PreK-12 educators.

Paula Kerger, President & CEO
Jonathan Barzilay, Chief Operating Officer

3733 Paideia Group
608 Garden Leaf Court
St. Louis, MO 63011
636-220-9300
Fax: 919-932-3905
www.paideiagroup.com
To help people understand what it means to be customer-focused. Participants focus on the skills, attitudes, and automatic behaviors that must be developed to reach a common goal of becoming a customer-focused organization.

Beth Symes, Principal and Founder

3734 Pamela Sims & Associates
54 Mozart Crescent
Brampton, Ontario
Canada L6Y-2W7
905-455-7331
888-610-7467
Fax: 905-455-0207
loveofkids@aol.com
www.pamelasims.com
Seminars and workshops for educators and parents.

Pamela Sims, President
Kelly Smith, Marketing Director

3735 Pennsylvania State University-Workforce Education & Development Program
411D Keller Building
University Park, PA 16802

814-863-3858
Fax: 814-863-7532
eifl@psu.edu
www.ed.psu.edu
To promote excellence, opportunity, and leadership among professionals in the workforce education and development field including, but not limited to, those employed in secondary or postsecondary education institutions, social services industries, and employee groups and private businesses.

Edgar I Farmer, Department Head
Judith A Kolb, Professor-in-Charge

3736 Performance Learning Systems
72 Lone Oak Drive
Cadiz, KY 42211
270-522-2000
866-757-2527
Fax: 270-522-2010
info@plsweb.com
www.plsweb.com
The mission of Performance Learning Systems, Inc. is to enhance education through the development of educational services.

Jackie Futrell, Resource Manager
Stephen G Barkley, Master teacher-of-teachers

3737 Piano Workshop
Goshen College
1700 S Main Street
Goshen, IN 46526
574-535-7000
Fax: 574-535-7949
www.goshen.edu/music/Piano%20Workshop/Main
The Goshen College Piano Workshop and Academy comprises lectures, master classes and recital performances presented by distinguished clinicians, composers and performers. Teachers participating in the Workshop hear inspiring lectures relevant to piano pedagogy, performance and literature.

Beverly K Lapp, Associate Professor of Music

3738 Pittsburg State University
College of Technology
1701 S Broadway
Pittsburg, KS 66762
620-231-7000
800-854-7488
Fax: 620-235-4343
psuinfo@pittstate.edu
www.pittstate.edu
A comprehensive regional university, provides undergraduate and graduate programs and services to the people of southeast Kansas, but also to others who seek the benefits offered.

Bruce Dallman, Dean, College of Technology
Steve Scott, President

3739 Polaroid Education Program
565 Technology Square
#3B
Cambridge, MA 02139-3539
781-386-2000
Fax: 781-386-3925
This program offers workshops for professional educators, preK-12; the Visual Learning Workshop and an Instant Image Portfolio Workshop.

3740 Principals' Center
Harvard Graduate School of Education
13 Appian Way
5th Floor
Cambridge, MA 02138
617-384-7482
principals@gse.harvard.edu
www.gse.harvard.edu/principals
Professional development programs for educators.

3741 Professional Development Institutes
Center for Professional Development & Services
2730 University Boulevard
Suite 301
Kensington, MD 20895
301-949-1771
800-766-1156
Fax: 301-949-5441
www.pditraining.net
Offers a wide variety of courses for Real Estate professionals around the US to meet their pre-licensing, post-licensing, and continuing education needs. Also offers non-credit courses on Technology, Business, Accounting, and Project Management, among others to further any career.

3742 Professional Development Workshops
Rebus
4111 Jackson Road
Ann Arbor, MI 48103
734-668-4870
800-435-3085
Fax: 734-668-4728
Workshops that promote success by assessing children in the context of active learning.

June/July

Sam Meisels, CEO
Linda Borgsdorf, President

3743 Robert McNeel & Associates
3670 Woodland Park Avenue N
Seattle, WA 98103
206-545-7000
Fax: 206-545-7321
www.en.na.mcneel.com
3D modeling workshop for design, drafting, graphics, and technology educators.

3744 Rockford Systems
4620 Hydraulic Road
Rockford, IL 61109-2695
815-874-7891
800-922-7533
Fax: 815-874-6144
sales@rockfordsystems.com
www.rockfordsystems.com
Machine safegaurding seminar for technology educators.

3745 SUNY College at Oswego
7060 Route 104
Oswego, NY 13126-3599
315-312-2500
Fax: 315-312-2863
stanley@oswego.edu
www.oswego.edu
The chief goal of the Oswego College Foundation, Inc. is to raise and manage private support to advance SUNY Oswego's mission.

October
26 booths with 350-400 attendees

Deborah F Stanley, President
Howard Gordon, Executive Assistant to Presi

3746 School of Music
Georgia State University
PO Box 4097
Atlanta, GA 30302-4097
404-413-5900
Fax: 404-413-5910
music@gsu.edu
www.music.gsu.edu
The mission of the School of Music is to provide a comprehensive, rigorous, and innovative academic program that is consistent with the urban context and mission of Georgia State University, and that serves the pursuit of artistic, professional, and scholarly excellence through experiences of lasting value to all stakeholders.

W Dwight Coleman, Director
Robert J Ambrose, Associate Director

3747 Southern Polytechnic State University
1100 S Marietta Parkway
Marietta, GA 30060-2896
678-915-7778
800-635-3204
Fax: 678-915-7490
coned@spsu.edu
Specialize in the delivery of comprehensive real-world training on a grand scale. Whether it be High-Tech, Business Professional or Engineering

3748 Southwestern Oklahoma State University
Industrial and Engineering Technology Department
100 Campus Drive
Weatherford, OK 73096
580-774-3063
Fax: 580-774-3795
admissions@swosu.edu
www.swosu.edu
The mission of Southwestern Oklahoma State University is to provide educational opportunities in higher education that meet the needs of the state and region; contribute to the educational, economic, and cultural environment; and support scholarly activity.

Gary Bell, Chair
Jeff Short, Program Coordinator

3749 Specialized Solutions
24703 US Highway 19-N
Suite 200
Clearwater, FL 33763
240-252-5070
888-840-2378
Fax: 877-200-5959
Technology based training and certification self study programs.

Sheri Nash, Contact

3750 Staff Development Workshops & Training Sessions
National School Conference Institute
PO Box 37527
Phoenix, AZ 85069-7527
602-371-8655
Fax: 602-371-8790
Offers twenty relevant and leading edge programs including curriculum instruction assessment, restructuring your school, improving student performance and gifted at-risk students. Ten monthly sessions of each program are available, with monthly feedback to follow-up. Accelerates restructuring efforts and also offers graduate credit.

3751 Storytelling for Educational Enrichment The Magic of Storytelling
2709 Oak Haven Drive
San Marcos, TX 78666-5065
512-392-0669
800-322-3199
Fax: 512-392-9660
krieger@corridor.net
Teacher in-service and training in storytelling and puppetry for teachers of Pre-K through third grades. The Magic of Storytelling is for all ages and levels, specializing in original stories of enlightenment and environmental education. Over

ten years experiences with many national and regional conferences and training.

Cherie Krieger, President

752 Summer Institute in Siena

University of Siena-S/American Universities
595 Prospect Road
Waterbury, CT 06706
203-754-5741
Fax: 203-753-8105
www.sienamusic.org
Programs offered in cooperation with the University of Siena-S and American Universities and Colleges. The program in Siena Italy is open to qualified graduates, undergraduates, professionals, teachers, 19 years of age or above. Special diploma; credit or non-credit; in-service credit; auditions; trips to Rome, Florence, Assisi, Venice, Pisa, three days in Switzerland; a Puccini Opera.

Joseph Del Principe, Music Director

753 Supplemental Instruction, Supervisor Workshops

University of Missouri-Kansas City
5100 Rockhill Road
SASS 210
Kansas City, MO 64110-2499
816-235-1174
Fax: 816-235-5156
cad@umkc.edu
Supplemental Instruction (SI) is an academic assistance program that utilizes peer-assisted study sessions.

Kim Wilcox, Coordinator of Training
Glen Jacobs, Executive Director

754 Synergy Learning

Synergy Learning
PO Box 206
Putney, VT 05346
802-387-3065
www.synergylearning.org
Provides on-site workshops, courses, and other professional development experiences for K-8 educators.

Casey Murrow, Executive Director

755 Syracuse University Disability Studies

805 S Crouse Avenue
105 Hoople Building
Syracuse, NY 13244-2280
315-443-4486
Fax: 315-443-0193
sudcc@syr.edu
www.disabilitystudies.syr.edu
Promotes its mission of inclusion by developing and sponsoring academic programs and courses, conferences and publications, research and training programs, and public education and advocacy efforts on behalf of, and with, people with disabilities.

Diane R Wiener, Ph.D, LMSW, Director

756 THE Institute & Knowvation

1105 Media 9201 Oakdale Avenue
Suite 101
Chatsworth, CA 91311
818-734-1520
800-840-0003
Fax: 818-734-1522
kodell@1105media.com
www.thejournal.com/institute
T.H.E. Institute believes that in order for students to be successful in the 21st century, technology must be an integral part of every aspect of education.

Geoffrey H Fletcher, Executive Director

3757 TUV Product Service

Westendstra e 199
Munich, MA D-806
49 -9 5-91 0
800-TUV-0123
Fax: 978-762-7637
info@tuev-sued.de
www.tuvglobal.com
As process partners with comprehensive industry knowledge our teams of specialists provide early consultation and continuous guidance, thus achieving the optimisation of technology, systems and expertise

Axel Stepken, Chief Executive Officer
Manfred Bayerlein, Chief Operations Officer

3758 Teacher Education Institute

1079 W Morse Boulevard
Suite A
Winter Park, FL 32789-3751
800-331-2208
Fax: 800-370-2600
tei@teachereducation.com
www.teachereducation.com
TEI was founded in 1981 to meet the needs of classroom teachers for quality education and training in practical, proven skills and methods that make a tangible and positive difference in their relationships and interactions with students and colleagues.

Vince Welsh, President

3759 Teachers College: Columbia University

Center for Technology & School Change
525 W 120th Street
New York, NY 10027
212-678-3000
Fax: 212-678-4048
webcomments@tc.columbia.edu
www.tc.columbia.edu
bring educational opportunities to all members of society, and whose faculty and students, time and again during more than a century of leadership, have demonstrated the power of ideas to change the world.

Howard Budin, Director Center for Technolo
Susan H Fuhrman, President

3760 Technology Training for Educators

Astronauts Memorial Foundation
Kennedy Space Center
, FL 32899
321-452-2887
800-792-3494
Fax: 321-452-6244
www.amfcse.org
Microsoft NT Administration; Technology Specialist; Management of Technology; Advanced Technology Specialist.

3761 Thomson Delmar Learning

10650 Toebben Drive
Independence, KY 41051
518-464-3500
800-354-9706
Fax: 518-464-7000
www.solutions.cengage.com/brands/Delmar/
Subjects include welding, HVAC-R, electrical, electronics, automotive, CADD and drafting, construction, blueprint reading, and fire science.

Josef Blumenfeld, Senior Vice President
Lindsay Stanley, Senior Director

3762 Tooling University

3615 Superior Avenue
Building 44,6th Floor
Cleveland, OH 44114-3898
216-706-6600
866-706-8665
Fax: 216-706-6601
info@toolingu.com
www.toolingu.com
Toolingu.com is the leading online training provider focused on the unique needs of manufacturers. Our roots are in manufacturing, and our business started by recognizing the industry's specific needs

Gene Jones, Director Marketing

3763 Total Quality Schools Workshop

Pennsylvania State University
302F Rackley Building
University Park, PA 16802
814-843-3765
hli@psu.edu
www.ed.psu.edu
Designed for public school educators at the state, national, and international level, this training program provides information in the philosophy, tools, and techniques of total quality management in education. The three day-six week program focuses on leadership, reform models, and education decision making.

William Hartman, Director

3764 University of Arkansas at Little Rock

2801 S University Avenue
Little Rock, AR 72204-1099
501-683-7302
Fax: 501-683-7304
admissions@ualr.edu
www.ualr.edu
With more than 100 programs of study, UALR has an academic program to suit your interests. We offer everything from computer science to fine arts, and we're sure you will find your niche on our campus

Sandra Bates, President
Tammy Starks, Vice President

3765 University of Central Florida

3100 Technology Parkway
Suite 264
Orlando, FL 32826-3281
407-823-4910
Fax: 407-207-4911
distrib@ucf.edu
www.distrib.ucf.edu
The University of Central Florida is one of the most dynamic universities in the country. Offering 223 degree programs, it has become an academic and research leader in numerous fields, such as optics, modeling and simulation, engineering and computer science, business administration, education, science, hospitality management and digital media.

John C Hitt, President/Corporate Secretar
John Schell, Vice President

3766 University of Michigan-Dearborn Center for Corporate & Professional Development

4901 Evergreen Road
CCPD-2000
Dearborn, MI 48128-2406
313-593-5000
Fax: 313-593-5111
info@umich.edu
www.umd.umich.edu
We offer undergraduate, graduate, and professional education to a diverse, highly motivated, and talented student body. Our programs are responsive to the changing needs of society; relevant to the goals of our students and community partners; rich in opportunities for independent and collaborative study, research, and practical application; and reflective of the traditions of excellence,

innovation, and leadership that distinguish the University of Michigan

Daniel Little, Chancellor
Ray Metz, Chief of Staff

3767 **Wavelength**
4753 N Broadway
Suite 808
Chicago, IL 60640
773-784-1012
877-528-47 2
Fax: 773-784-1079
www.wavelengthinc.com
Wavelength offers a fresh perspective on the key challenges in education today. Our programs are founded on the tenet that humor heals and enlightens.

3768 **Wids Learning Design System**
1 Foundation Circle
Waunakee, WI 53597
800-677-9437
800-821-6313
Fax: 608-849-2468
info@wids.org
www.wids.org
WIDS strives to enhance the quality of learning through the development, implementation, support, and continuous improvement of the WIDS Learning Design System, a comprehensive methodology, supported by application and professional development tools, for designing and planning performance-based assessment learning and teaching.

Lisa Laabs, Office Manager
Judy Neill, Director

3769 **Workforce Education and Development**
Southern Illinois University Carbondale
475 Clocktower Drive
Mailcode 4605
Carbondale, IL 62901-4605
618-453-3321
Fax: 618-453-1909
wed@siu.edu
www.wed.siu.edu/Public/
The Department of Workforce Education and Development is one of the largest education, training, and development departments in the United States. A recent external evaluation team recognized the Department as among the top ten in the nation.

Keith Waugh, Associate Professor/Chairman

Directories & Handbooks / General

70 106 Ways Parents Can Help Students Achieve

American Association of School Administrators
1615 Duke Street
Alexandria, VA 22314
703-528-0700
Fax: 703-841-1543
info@aasa.org
www.aasa.org
Provides parents with useful information about the importance of parental involvement, concrete ways to work with children and schools to promote success, and a list of resources for further reading.

Set of 10
ISBN: 0-8108-4220-5

771 A Personal Planner & Training Guide for the Substitute Teacher

Master Teacher
One Leadership Lane
PO Box 1207
Manhattan, KS 66502-1207
800-669-9633
Fax: 800-669-1132
www.masterteacher.com
Helps substitute teachers set the tone for a positive experience.

90 pages
ISBN: 0-914607-89-8

John Eller, Author

772 Academic Year & Summer Programs Abroad

American Institute for Foreign Study
1 High Ridge Park
Stamford, CT 06905-5504
203-399-5000
866-906-2437
Fax: 203-399-5590
info@aifs.com
www.aifs.com
Offers school names, addresses, courses offered, tuition and fee information.

224 pages Annual

Cyril Taylor, Founder/ Chairman
William L. Gertz, President/ CEO

773 Accredited Institutions of Postsecondary Education

MacMillan Publishing Company
1633 Broadway
New York, NY 10019
212-654-8500
888-247-8269
Fax: 800-835-3202
www.ope.ed.gov/accreditation/
Lists over 5,000 accredited institutions and programs for postsecondary education in the United States.

600 pages Annual

774 Activities and Strategies for Connecting Kids with Kids: Elementary Edition

Master Teacher
One Leadership Lane
PO Box 1207
Manhattan, KS 66502-1207
800-669-9633
Fax: 800-669-1132
www.masterteacher.com
Activities, lesson plans, and strategies that celebrate each student's individual differences while developing cooperation, tolerance, understanding, sharing and caring.

159 pages
ISBN: 0-914607-74-X

3775 Activities and Strategies for Connecting Kids with Kids: Secondary Edition

Master Teacher
One Leadership Lane
PO Box 1207
Manhattan, KS 66502-1207
800-669-9633
Fax: 800-669-1132
www.masterteacher.com
Activities, lesson plans, and strategies that celebrate each student's individual differences while developing cooperation, tolerance, understanding, sharing and caring.

136 pages
ISBN: 0-914607-75-8

3776 American School Directory

PO Box 20002
Murfreesboro, TN 37129
866-273-2797
Fax: 800-929-3408
support@asddataservices.com
www.asd.com
More than 104,000 school sites are loaded with pictures, art, calendars, menus, local links and notes from students, parents and alumni. Choose the school by name, state list, or by ASD number.

3777 Amusing and Unorthodox Definitions

Careers/Consultants Consultants in Education
3050 Palm Aire Drive N
#310
Pompano Beach, FL 33069
954-974-5477
Fax: 954-974-5477
carconed@aol.com
Collection of amusing and unorthodox definitions. The meanings, purposes and implications assigned to the words appearing here will delight audiences, enliven conversations and keep you chuckling.

ISBN: 0-7392-0089-5
ISSN: 99-94623

Dr. Robert M Bookbinder, President/Author

3778 Associated Schools Project in Education for International Co-operation

UNESCO Associated Schools Project Network
7 Place de Fontenoy
75352 Paris 07 SP
France
33 -0 1-45 6
1-45681000
www.unesco.org
Lists 1,970 secondary and primary schools, teacher training institutions and nursery schools in 95 countries that participate in the UNESCO Associated School Project.

200 pages Annual

3779 Awakening Brilliance: How to Inspire Children to Become Successful Learners

Pamela Sims & Associates
54 Mozart Crescent
Canada L6Y 2W7
905-455-7331
888-610-7467
Fax: 905-455-0207
loveofkids@aol.com
Seminars and workshops for educators and parents. Upcoming workshops include themes of awakening students' potential and team leadership skills.

248 pages Paperback
ISBN: 0-9651126-0-8

Pamela Sims, Author/Editor
Kelly Smith, Marketing Director

3780 Beyond the Bake Sale

Master Teacher
One Leadership Lane
PO Box 1207
Manhattan, KS 66502-1207
800-669-9633
Fax: 800-669-1132
www.masterteacher.com
A notebook containing 101 detailed plans that not only provide you with fundraising ideas, but get you started, keep you on track, and lead your team through the finishing touches.

101 pages
ISBN: 1-58992-119-4

3781 Cabells Directory of Publishing Opportunities in Educational Curriculum & Methods

Cabell Publishing Company
Box 5428
Tobe Hahn Station
Beaumont, TX 77726
409-898-0575
Fax: 409-866-9554
info@cabells.com
www.cabells.com
Provides information on editor's contact information, manuscript guidelines, acceptance rate, review information and circulation data for over 350 academic journals.

799 pages Annual
ISBN: 0-911753-27-3

David WE Cabell, Editor
Deborah L English, Editor

3782 Cadet Gray: Your Guide to Military Schools-Military Colleges & Cadet Programs

Reference Desk Books
PO Box 22925
Santa Barbara, CA 93121
805-772-8806
This is a comprehensive reference book which describes 55 American military schools, grade schools, high schools, junior colleges, senior colleges, and the federal service academies. Descriptions include school histories, academic requirements, military environment, extracurricular activities and costs.

Publication Date: 1990 212 pages
ISBN: 0-962574-90-2

3783 Carnegie Communications, LLC

Porter Sargent Publishers
2 LAN Drive
Suite 100
Westford, MA 01886-3028
978-692-5092
800-342-7470
Fax: 978-692-4174
info@carnegiecomm.com
www.carnegiecomm.com
Lists and authoritatively describes 800 elementary and secondary schools in 130 countries. Written for the educator, personnel advisor, student and parent as well as diplomatic and corporate officials, this unique guide is an indispensable reference for Amer-

ican students seeking preparatory schooling overseas. Hardcover.

Publication Date: 1991 544 pages BiAnnual

Joe Moore, President/ CEO
Meghan Dalesandro, EVP, Operation

3784 Character Education Kit: 36 Weeks of Success: Elementary Edition

Master Teacher
One Leadership Lane
PO Box 1207
Manhattan, KS 66502-1207
800-669-9633
Fax: 800-669-1132
www.masterteacher.com
Takes the guesswork out of delivering your character education message by providing you with all the pieces of a well-rounded program including important components for 36 character traits.

428 pages
ISBN: 1-58992-096-1

3785 Choosing Your Independent School in the United Kingdom & Ireland

Independent Schools Information Service
56 Buckingham Gate
London SW1E 6AG
England
71-63087934
1,400 independent schools in the United Kingdom and Ireland with contact information, entry requirements, fees, scholarships available, subjects and exam boards.

293 pages Annual/September

3786 Classroom Teacher's Guide for Working with Paraeducators

Master Teacher
One Leadership Lane
PO Box 1207
Manhattan, KS 66502-1207
800-669-9633
Fax: 800-669-1132
www.masterteacher.com
This workbook includes numerous forms that allow teachers to communicate more effectively to paras the vital information they will need in working with special students.

60 pages
ISBN: 1-58992-127-5

Wendy Dover, Author

3787 Commonwealth Universities Yearbook

Association of Commonwealth Universities
20-24 Tavistock Square
London WC1H 0PF
England
207-380-6700
44-20-7380-6700
Fax: 207-387-2655
Fax: 44-20-738-2655
info@acu.ac.uk
www.acu.ac.uk
Offers information on over 700 university institutions of recognized academic standing in 36 Commonwealth countries or regions, including Africa, Asia, Australia, Britain, Canada and the Pacific.

2,600 pages Annual
ISBN: 0-85143-188-7
ISSN: 0069-7745

Olive Mugenda, Chairman
Jan Thomas, Vice Chairman

3788 Community Engagement: Guidelines for Excellence

North American Assoc. for Environmental Education
1725 Desales Street NW
Suite 401
Washington, DC 20036
202-419-0412
info@naaee.org
www.naaee.org
A set of guidelines designed to help environmental educators create inclusive environments for their communities.

3789 Complete Learning Disabilities Directory

Grey House Publishing
5979 North Elm Avenue
Suite 113
Millerton, NY 12546
518-789-8700
800-562-2139
Fax: 518-789-0556
books@greyhouse.com
www.greyhouse.com
A one-stop sourcebook for people of all ages with learning disabilities and those who work with them. This comprehensive database in print includes information about associations and organizations, schools, government agencies, testing materials, camps, books, newsletters and more.

800 pages Annual/Softcover
ISBN: 1-59237-049-7

Leslie Mackenzie, Publisher
Richard Gottlieb, Editor

3790 Computer and Web Resources for People with Disabilities

Alliance for Technology Access/Hunter House
1119 Old Humboldt Road
Suite 240
Jackson, TN 38305
731-554-5282
800-914-3017
Fax: 731-554-5283
www.ataccess.org
This directory shows how America's forty-five million people with disabilities can potentially benefit from using computer technology to achieve goals and change their lives. Written by experts in the field, this important work provides a comprehensive, step-by-step guide to approaching computer innovations. It explains how to identify the appropriate technology, how to seek funding, how to set it up and what to consider.

Publication Date: 1996 400 pages Paperback/CD ROM
ISBN: 0-89793-433-4

James Allison, President
Bob Van der Linde, Vice President

3791 Conservation Education and Outreach Techniques

North American Assoc. for Environmental Education
1725 Desales Street NW
Suite 401
Washington, DC 20036
202-419-0412
info@naaee.org
www.naaee.org
Presents the theory and practice for creating effective education and outreach programmes for conservation.

3792 Cornocopia of Concise Quotations

Careers/Consultants Consultants in Education
3050 Palm Aire Drive N
#310
Pompano Beach, FL 33069
954-974-5477
Fax: 954-974-5477
carconed@aol.com
Wealth of practical reminders of the enduring ideas. The book furthers humane understandings by gathering and preserving the wisdom of the wise and experienced.

ISBN: 0-7392-0275-8
ISSN: 99-95201

Dr. Robert M Bookbinder, President

3793 Digest of Supreme Court Decisions

Phi Delta Kappa International
1820 N Fort Myer Drive
Suite 320
Arlington, VA 22209
800-766-1156
info@pdkintl.org
www.pdkintl.org
Designed as a ready reference, this edition of a popular digest provides a concise set of individual summaries of cases decided by the Supreme Court. Fully indexed.

256 pages Paperback

Perry A. Zirkel, Author
Joshua P. Starr, Ed.D, Chief Executive Officer
Albert Chen, M.E., Chief Operating Officer

3794 Directory for Exceptional Children

Porter Sargent Publishers, Inc.
2 LAN Drive
Suite 100
Westford, MA 01886-3028
978-692-5092
800-342-7470
Fax: 617-523-1021
info@portersargent.com
www.portersargent.com
A comprehensive survey of 2,500 schools, facilities and organizations across the country serving children and young adults with developmental, physical and medical disabilities. With 15 distinct chapters covering a range of disabilities, this work is an invaluable aid to parents and professionals seeking the optimal environment for special-needs children. Hardcover.

Publication Date: 1994 1152 pages BiAnnual
ISSN: 0070-5012

Dan McKeever, Senior Editor

3795 Directory of Central Agencies for Jewish Education

Jewish Education Service of North America
247 West 37th Street
5th Floor
New York, NY 10018
212-284-6882
Fax: 212-284-6951
www.jesna.org
Offers educational resources for professionals in Jewish education, including general education information, materials and services.

Cass Gottlieb, Chair
Sandra Gold, Vice Chair

3796 Directory of College Cooperative Education Programs

World Association for Cooperative Education
University of Waterloo
200 University Avenue W
Waterloo, ON N2L-3G1
admin@waceinc.org
www.waceinc.org
A publication providing detailed information on cooperative education programs at 460 colleges throughout the United States, originally pub-

lished by the former National Commission for Cooperative Education, which merged with the World Association for Cooperative Education in 2010.

219 pages

Maurits van Rooijen, Co-Chair
Sampan Silapanad, Co-Chair

97 Directory of ERIC Information Service Providers

Educational Resources Information Ctr./Access ERIC
1600 Research Boulevard
Rockville, MD 20850-3172
301-656-9723
www.eric.ed.gov
Offers information on more than 1,000 government agencies, nonprofit and profit organizations, individuals and foreign organizations that provide access to ERIC microfiche collections, search services and abstract journal collections.

100 pages Biennial

798 Directory of Graduate Programs

Graduate Record Examinations Program/ETS
PO Box 6000
Princeton, NJ 08541-6000
609-771-7670
866-473-4373
Fax: 610-290-8975
www.ets.org/gre
Accredited institutions that offer graduate degrees.

1,400 pages 4 Volumes

799 Directory of International Internships: A World of Opportunities

International Studies & Programs
Michigan State University
427 N. Shaw Lane, Room 207
East Lansing, MI 48824-1035
517-353-2350
Fax: 517-353-7254
gliozzo@msu.edu
www.isp.msu.edu
A directory containing information about a wide range of overseas internship oppotunities. Over 500 entries of international internships sponsored by educational institutions, government agencies, and private organizations. There are indexes of topics in geographical areas listed by countries and geographical areas listed by topic.

Adedayo Adekson, Assistant Dean
Deandra Beck, Associate Dean

800 Directory of Overseas Educational Advising Centers

College Board
250 Vesey Street
New York, NY 10281
212-713-8000
www.collegeboard.org
This directory has been developed as a means through which institutions of higher education can communicate directly with overseas education advisers and through which advisers can communicate more directly with each other.

165 pages

David Coleman, Chief Executive Officer
Jeremy Singer, President

801 Directory of Postsecondary Institutions

National Center for Education Statistics
K Street NW
Washington, DC 20006
202-502-7300
877-4ED-PUBS
Fax: 301-470-1244
edpubs@inet.ed.gov
Postsecondary institutions in the US, Puerto Rico, Virgin Islands and territories in the Pacific United States. Two volumes: Volume I Degree-Granting Institutions, Volume II Non-Degree-Granting Institutions.

Publication Date: 1990 500 pages Biennial

3802 Directory of Youth Exchange Programs

UN Educational, Scientific & Cultural Association
Youth Division, 1 Rue Miollis
Paris F-75015
France
1-4563842
Offers about 370 nonprofit organizations and governmental agencies in 95 countries that organize youth and student exchanges, study tours and correspondence exchanges.

Publication Date: 1992 225 pages

3803 Diversity, Accessibility and Quality

College Board
250 Vesey Street
New York, NY 10281
212-713-8000
www.collegeboard.org
This overview is designed to examine aspects of US education that have particular importance in programs of student exchange.

Publication Date: 1995 47 pages
ISBN: 0-874474-24-8

David Coleman, Chief Executive Officer
Jeremy Singer, President

3804 ERIC - Education Resources Information Center

655 15th Street NW
Suite 500
Washington, DC 20005
800-538-3742
ericrequest@ed.gov
www.eric.ed.gov
The mission of the center is to provide a comprehensive, easy-to-use, searchable, Internet-based bibliographic and full-text database of education research and information that meets the requirements of the Education Sciences Reform Act of 2002.

Publication Date: 1965

3805 Education Sourcebook: Basic Information about National Education Expectations and Goals

Omnigraphics
155 West Congress
Suite 200
Detroit, MI 48226
313-961-1340
800-234-1340
Fax: 313-961-1383
contact@omnigraphics.com
www.omnigraphics.com
A collection of education-related documents and articles for parents and students.

1123 pages
ISBN: 0-7808-0179-2

Jeanne Gough, Author
Paul Rogers, Publicity Associate

3806 Educational Placement Sources-Abroad

Education Information Services/Instant Alert
PO Box 620662
Newton, MA 02462-0662
617-433-0125
Lists 150 organizations, arranged by type, in the United States and abroad that place English-speaking teachers and education administrators in positions abroad.

19 pages Annual

FB Viaux, President

3807 Educational Rankings Annual

Gale Group
27500 Drake Road
Farmington Hills, MI 48331-3535
248-699-GALE
800-877-4253
Fax: 877-363-4253
galeord@galegroup.com
www.cengage.com
Top 10 lists from popular and scholarly periodicals, government publications, and others. The lists cover all facets of education.

890 pages Annual Hardcover
ISBN: 0-7876-7419-2

Lynn C Hattendorf Westney, Author
Josef Blumenfeld, Senior Vice President
Lindsay Stanley, Senior Director

3808 Educational Resources Catalog

CDE Press
1430 N Street
PO Box 271
Sacramento, CA 95814-0271
916-445-1260
800-995-4099
Fax: 916-323-0823
www.cde.ca.gov
Resource catalog from the California Department of Education.

3809 Educator's Desk Reference: A Sourcebook of Educational Information & Research

MacMillan Publishing Company
1633 Broadway
New York, NY 10019
212-654-8500
Fax: 800-835-3202
Directory includes national and regional education organizations.

Publication Date: 1989

3810 Educator's Scrapbook

Careers/Consultants Consultants in Education
3050 Palm Aire Drive N
#310
Pompano Beach, FL 33069
954-974-5477
Fax: 954-974-5477
carconed@aol.com
Collection of education morsels offered to those who who would seek to redefine and clarify the aims and purposes of today's education. The book attepts to help its readers refocus upon the real purposes of education and their relationships to current education practices.

ISBN: 0-9703623-0-7
ISSN: 00-93185

Dr. Robert M Bookbinder, President

3811 Educators Guide to FREE Computer Materials and Internet Resources

Educators Progress Service
214 Center Street
Beaver Dam, WI 53956-1408
920-210-3684
888-951-4469
Fax: 920-326-3127
info@monumentalhosting.com
www.monumentalhosting.com

Lists and describes almost 2000 web sites of educational value. Available in two grade specific editions.

317 pages Annual
ISBN: 87708-362-2

Kathy Nehmer, President

3812 Educators Guide to FREE Films, Filmstrips and Slides
Educators Progress Service
214 Center Street
Beaver Dam, WI 53956-1408
920-210-3684
888-951-4469
Fax: 920-326-3127
info@monumentalhosting.com
www.monumentalhosting.com
Lists and describes free and free-loan films, filmstrips, slides, and audiotapes for all age levels.

135 pages Annual
ISBN: 87708-400-9

Kathy Nehmer, President

3813 Educators Guide to FREE Multicultural Material
Educators Progress Service
214 Center Street
Beaver Dam, WI 53956-1408
920-210-3684
888-951-4469
Fax: 920-326-3127
info@monumentalhosting.com
www.monumentalhosting.com
Lists and describes FREE films, videotapes, filmstrips, slides, web sites, and hundreds of free printed materials in the field of multicultural and diversity education for all age levels.

198 pages Annual
ISBN: 87708-412-2

Kathy Nehmer, President

3814 El-Hi Textbooks and Serials in Print
RR Bowker Reed Reference
2104 21st Avenue South
Birmingham, NJ 35223-1541
205-870-4693
Fax: 908-665-6688
www.frankflemingart.com
Listing of about 995 publishers of elementary and secondary level textbooks and related teaching materials.

Annual

3815 Environmental Education Materials: Guidelines for Excellence
North American Assoc. for Environmental Education
1725 Desales Street NW
Suite 401
Washington, DC 20036
202-419-0412
info@naaee.org
www.naaee.org
A set of recommendations for developing and selecting environmental education materials.

23 pages

3816 Evaluating Your Environmental Education Programs: A Workbook for Practitioners
North American Assoc. for Environmental Education
1725 Desales Street NW
Suite 401
Washington, DC 20036
202-419-0412
info@naaee.org
www.naaee.org
Walks readers through designing and conducting an evaluation.

ISBN: 1-884008-15-3

3817 Family Services Report
CD Publictions
8204 Fenton Street
Sliver Spring, MD 20910
301-588-6380
855-237-1396
Fax: 301-588-0519
info@cdpublications.com
Private grants for family service programs

18 pages
ISSN: 1524-9484

Ray Sweeney, Editor
Mary Crompton, Publisher

3818 Fifty State Educational Directories
Career Guidance Foundation
1327 E. Kemper Rd
Suite 3000
Cincinnati, OH 45246-1906
513-834-8780
Fax: 513-834-8779
www.collegesource.com
A collection on microfiche consisting of reproductions of the state educational directories published by each individual state department of education.

3819 Funny School Excuses
Careers/Consultants Consultants in Education
3050 Palm Aire Drive N
#310
Pompano Beach, FL 33069
954-974-5477
Fax: 954-974-5477
carconed@aol.com
Collection of illustrations, cartoons and excuses gathered from authentic notes written by parents and sometimes their children. The book is wonderfully entertaining and recommended for its unusual humor, variety, and revelations of human nature.

ISBN: 0-7392-0309-6
ISSN: 99-95349

Dr. Robert M Bookbinder, President

3820 Ganley's Catholic Schools in America
Fisher Publishing Company
PO Box 15070
Sun City West, AZ 85376-5070
623-328-8326
800-759-7615
Fax: 480-657-9422
publisher@ganleyscatholicschools.com
www.ganleyscatholicschool.com
Comprehensive listings on all Catholic Schools in America. Listings include phone numbers, addresses, names of administrators, number of students, complete diocesan, state, regional and national statistics. Includes an extensive analysis of demographic trends within Catholic elementary and secondary education, prepared by the National Catholic Education Association.

450+ pages Annual/June
ISBN: 1-558331-59-0

Millard T Fischer, Publisher

3821 Graduate & Undergraduate Programs & Courses in Middle East Studies in the US, Canada
Middle East Studies Association of North America
University of Arizona
633 Third Ave
New York, NY 10017-6795
520-697-1505
Fax: 520-626-9095
www.acls.org

Pauline Yu, President
Steven C. Wheatley, Vice President

3822 Guide to International Exchange, Community Service & Travel for Persons with Disabilities
Mobility International USA
132 E. Broadway
Suite 343
Eugene, OR 97401
541-343-1284
Fax: 541-343-6812
info@miusa.org
www.miusa.org
This directory lists an impressive array of information regarding international study, living, travel, funding and contact organizations for people with disabilities.

Publication Date: 1981
ISBN: 1-880034-24-7

Susan Sygall, Chief Executive Officer
Cerise Roth-Vinson, Chief Operating Officer

3823 Guide to Summer Camps & Schools
Porter Sargent Publishers
2 LAN Drive
Suite 100
Westford, MA 01886-3028
978-692-5092
800-342-7470
Fax: 617-523-1021
info@portersargent.com
www.portersargent.com
Covers the broad spectrum of recreational and educational summer opportunities. Current facts from 1,500 camps and schools, as well as programs for those with special needs or learning disabilities, makes the guide a comprehensive and convenient resource.

816 pages Biannual
ISBN: 0-875581-33-1

HJ Lane Coordinating Editor, Author
J Yonce, General Manager
Daniel McKeever, Sr Editor

3824 Guidelines for Effective Character Education Through Sports
Character Education Partnership
PO Box 650307
Sterling, VA 20165
202-296-7743
www.character.org
Guidelines for turning sports and physical education programs into the powerful, positive forces they should be.

Arthur Schwartz, President
Dean D'Ambrosi, Executive Vice President

3825 HEATH Resource Center at the National Youth Transitions Center
HEATH Resource Center
2134 G Street NW
Suite 308
Washington, DC 20052-0001
202-973-0904
800-544-3284
Fax: 202-973-0908
www.heath.gwu.edu
A national clearinghouse on postsecondary education for people with disabilities, managed by the George Washington University Graduate

School and the HSC Foundation. HEATH develops training modules and publishes resource papers, fact sheets, directories, and website information. The center also fosters a network of professionals in disability issues.

Publication Date: 2000

Joan Kester, Ph.D, Principal Investigator
Christopher Nace, Research Assistant

3826 Handbook of Private Schools

Porter Sargent Publishers
2 LAN Drive
Suite 100
Westford, MA 01886-3028
978-692-5092
800-342-7470
Fax: 617-523-1021
www.portersargent.com
Continuing a tradition that began in 1915, this handbook provides optimal guidance in the choice of educational environments and opportunities for students. Totally revised and updated, this 83rd edition presents current facts on 1,700 elementary and secondary boarding and day schools across the United States. Complete statistical data on enrollments, tuition, graduates, administrators and faculty have been compiled and objectively reported. Hardcover.

1472 pages Annual
ISBN: 0-875581-44-7

J Yonce, General Manager
Daniel McKeever, Sr Editor

3827 Handbook of United Methodist-Related Schools, Colleges, Universities & Theological Schools

General Board of Higher Education & Ministry/UMC
1001 19th Avenue
PO Box 340007
Nashville, TN 37203-0007
615-340-7400
Fax: 615-340-7379
scu@gbhem.org
www.gbhem.org
Includes two pages of information about each of United Methodist's 123 institutions, a chart indicating major areas of study, information about United Methodist loan and scholarship programs, as well as information about how to select a college. Published every four years.

344 pages Paperback

James E. Dorff, President
Lanther Marie Mills, Vice President

3828 Hidden America

Place in the Woods
3900 Glenwood Avenue
Golden Valley, MN 55422-5302
763-374-2120
Fax: 952-593-5593
placewoods@aol.com
Set of five reference-essay books on American minorities (African America; Hispanic America, the People (Native Americans); American women; My Own Book! classroom reference for elementary through secondary).

36+ pages Paperback Book

Roger Hammer, Publisher

3829 Higher Education Directory

Higher Education Publications
1801 Robert Fulton Drive
Suite 555
Reston, VA 20191-5499
571-313-0478
888-349-7715
Fax: 571-313-0526
info@hepinc.com
www.hepinc.com
Lists over 4,364 degree granting colleges and universities accredited by approved agencies, recognized by the US Secretary of Education successor to the Department of Education's: Education Directory, Colleges and Universities and Council for Higher Education Accreditation (CHEA).

Publication Date: 1994 1,040 pages Annual/Paperback
ISBN: 0-914927-44-2
ISSN: 0736-0197

Jeanne Burke, Editor
Fred Hafner JR, Vice President Operations

3830 Higher Education Opportunities for Women & Minorities: Annotated Selections

U.S. Office of Postsecondary Education
400 Maryland Avenue SW
Room 3915
Washington, DC 20202-0001
202-708-9180
Programs of public and private organizations and state and federal government agencies that offer loans, scholarships and fellowship opportunities for women and minorities.

143 pages Biennial

3831 Home from Home (Educational Exchange Programs)

Central Bureau for Educational Visits & Exchanges
10 Spring Gardens
London, SW1A 2BN, England
171-389-4004
Fax: 171-389-4426
150 organizations and agencies worldwide that arrange stays with families for paying guests or on an exchange basis. Organizations are geographically listed including a description of program, costs, insurance information, overseas representation and language instruction.

216 pages

3832 Homeschooler's Guide to FREE Teaching Aids

Educators Progress Service
214 Center Street
Beaver Dam, WI 53956-1408
920-210-3684
888-951-4469
Fax: 920-326-3127
info@monumentalhosting.com
www.monumentalhosting.com
Lists and describes free print materials specifically available to homeschoolers with students of all age levels.

277 pages
ISBN: 87708-375-4

Kathy Nehmer, President

3833 Homeschooler's Guide to FREE Videotapes

Educators Progress Service
214 Center Street
Beaver Dam, WI 53956-1408
920-210-3684
888-951-4469
Fax: 920-326-3127
info@monumentalhosting.com
www.monumentalhosting.com
Lists and describes free and free-loan videotapes specifically available to homeschoolers with students of all age levels.

248 pages Annual
ISBN: 87708-411-4

Kathy Nehmer, President

3834 ISS Directory of International Schools

International Schools Services
15 Roszel Road
PO Box 5910
Princeton, NJ 08543
609-452-0990
www.iss.edu
A comprehensive guide to American and international schools around the world. The Directory is carefully researched and compiled to include current and complete information on over 600 international schools.

Liz Duffy, President
Kristin Evins, Chief Administration Officer

3835 Inclusion Guide for Handling Chronically Disruptive Behavior

Master Teacher
One Leadership Lane
PO Box 1207
Manhattan, KS 66502-1207
800-669-9633
Fax: 800-669-1132
www.masterteacher.com
A comprehensive process for ensuring that no disruptive behavior is tolerated, no student is turned away, and all students are served.

150 pages
ISBN: 0-914607-40-5

Teresa VanDover, Author

3836 Incorporating Multiple Intelligences into the Curriculum and into the Classroom: Elementary

Master Teacher
One Leadership Lane
PO Box 1207
Manhattan, KS 66502-1207
800-669-9633
Fax: 800-669-1132
www.masterteacher.com
Contains lesson plans and teaching methods that address the needs of students and help them identify their strengths according to the domains of multiple intelligences.

181 pages
ISBN: 0-914607-63-4

3837 Incorporating Multiple Intelligences into the Curriculum and into the Classroom: Secondary

Master Teacher
One Leadership Lane
PO Box 1207
Manhattan, KS 66502-1207
800-669-9633
Fax: 800-669-1132
www.masterteacher.com
Contains lesson plans and teaching methods that address the needs of students and help them identify their strengths according to the domains of multiple intelligences.

147 pages
ISBN: 0-914607-64-2

3838 Independent Study Catalog

Peterson's Guides
PO Box 2123
Princeton, NJ 08543-2123
800-338-3282
Fax: 609-896-4531
A comprehensive listing of over 10,000 correspondence course offerings at 100 accredited colleges and universities nationwide, for those seeking the flexibility and convenience of at-home study.

293 pages
ISBN: 1-560794-60-7

3839 International Federation of Organizations for School Correspondence/Exchange
FIOCES
29, rue d'ulm, F-75230 Paris
F-75230 Paris
France
Governmental agencies and other organizations concerned with scholastic correspondence and student exchange programs.
Publication Date: 1991 3 pages

3840 International Schools Directory
European Council of International Schools
Fourth Floor, 146 Buckingham Palace
London, SW1W 9TR
United Kingdom
44 -0 2- 782
1730-268244
Fax: 1730-267914
ecis@ecis.org
www.ecis.org
Over 420 ECIS schools in more than 90 countries; 300 affiliated colleges and universities worldwide; educational publishers and equipment suppliers.
Publication Date: 1965 550 pages Annual
Kevin J. Ruth, Ph.D., Executive Director
Darlene Fisher, People & Programmes Lead

3841 International Study Telecom Directory
WorldWide Classroom
PO Box 1166
Milwaukee, WI 53201-1166
414-224-3476
Fax: 414-224-3466
info@worldwide.edu
www.worldwide.edu
Comprehensive directory for locating educational resources both internationally and throughout the US Provides contact information on educational institutions including address, phone, fax, e-mail and URL. New icon system offers additional information on the type of programs offered. Resource guide at beginning includes useful web sites, airline and car rental contact numbers, currency converters, international organizations and international publications.
Mike Witley, President
Stacy Hargarten, Classroom Publications

3842 International Voluntary Service Directory
Volunteers for Peace
1034 Tiffany Road
Belmont, VT 05730
802-259-2759
Fax: 802-259-2922
vfp@vfp.org
www.vfp.org
Comprehensive listing of over 3,400 workcamps in 100 countries around the world. Organized by country.
289 pages Annual
ISBN: 0-945617-20-B
Peter Coldwell, Director

3843 International Who's Who in Education
International Biographical Centre/Melrose Press
3 Regal Lane, Soham, Ely
Cambridgeshire CB7 5BA
United Kingdom
353-721091
Lists about 5,000 persons at all levels of teaching and educational administration.
1,000 pages

3844 International Yearbook of Education: Education in the World
UN Educational, Scientific & Cultural Assn.
7, place de Fontenoy
F-75700 Paris
France
1-45681000
Describes and offers information on educational systems worldwide.
Publication Date: 1989 200 pages

3845 Job Search Handbook for Educators
American Association for Employment in Education
P.O. Box 510
Sycamore, IL 60178
614-485-1111
Fax: 360-244-7802
info@aaee.org
www.aaee.org
100-page handbook including articles and information on applications, cover letters, resumes, references, networking, professional appearance, social media, portfolios, interviewing, employment options, skills, salary, and demand for K-12 educators.
Tim Neubert, Executive Director
Cindy Holland, Board President

3846 K-12 Environmental Education: Guidelines for Excellence
North American Assoc. for Environmental Education
1725 Desales Street NW
Suite 401
Washington, DC 20036
202-419-0412
info@naaee.org
www.naaee.org
Provides guidelines for effective environmental education programs and curricula.

3847 Legal Basics: A Handbook for Educators
Phi Delta Kappa International
1820 N Fort Myer Drive
Suite 320
Arlington, VA 22209
800-766-1156
info@pdkintl.org
www.pdkintl.org
Superintendents, principals, counselors, teachers, and paraprofessionals need to pay close attention to their actions in schools and classrooms because, from a legal standpoint, those settings may contain hazardous conditions. Legal Basics points out the pitfalls and how to avoid them.
120 pages Paperback
Evelyn B. Kelly, Author
Joshua P. Starr, Ed.D, Chief Executive Officer
Albert Chen, M.E., Chief Operating Officer

3848 Lesson Plans and Modifications for Inclusion and Collaborative Classrooms
Master Teacher
One Leadership Lane
PO Box 1207
Manhattan, KS 66502-1207
800-669-9633
Fax: 800-669-1132
www.masterteacher.com
Each modification is a complete lesson plan that gives the teacher a description of the activity and objetive the materials need and a step-by-step guide of how to carry out the learning process.
Publication Date: 1969 242 pages
ISBN: 0-914607-37-5

3849 Lesson Plans for Character Education: Elementary Edition
Master Teacher
One Leadership Lane
PO Box 1207
Manhattan, KS 66502-1207
800-669-9633
Fax: 800-669-1132
www.masterteacher.com
Gives you more than 140 practical lessons developed and tested by teachers across the curriculum and in all grade levels.
Publication Date: 1969 207 pages
ISBN: 0-914607-53-7

3850 List of Over 70 Higher Education Association
Educational Information Services
PO Box 662
Newton Lower Falls, MA 02162
617-964-4555
Provides descriptions and contact information on associations for individuals in higher education.

3851 List of State Boards of Higher Education
Educational Information Services
PO Box 662
Newton Lower Falls, MA 02162
617-964-4555
A compilation of the boards of education for all the states in the union.

3852 List of State Community & Junior College Board Offices
Educational Information Services
PO Box 662
Newton Lower Falls, MA 02162
617-964-4555
A list of the board officers and state officers within community, junior and university institutions.

3853 MDR School Directory
Market Data Retrieval
6 Armstrong Road
Suite 301
Shelton, CT 06484-6216
203-926-4800
800-333-8802
Fax: 203-929-5253
mdrinfo@dnb.com
www.mdreducation.com
MDR's school directories provide comprehensive data on every public school district and school throughout the United States and the District of Columbia. Each state directory contains current names and job titles of key decision makers, school and district addresses, phone numbers, current enrollments and much more. The content is also available on CD-ROM and diskette.
Publication Date: 1969 51 Volume Set
Aaron Stibel, GM, CEO MDR Education
Kristina James, Director of Marketing

3854 Minority Student Guide to American Colleges
Paoli Publishing
P.O. Box 190
Suite 287
Paoli, IN 47454-1553
812-723-2572
Fax: 812-723-2592
www.paolinewsrepublican.com

Covers colleges, military schools, and financial aid information for minority students.

89 pages

3855 Monograph 1: Using a Logic Model to Review and Analyze an Environmental Education Program
North American Assoc. for Environmental Education
1725 Desales Street NW
Suite 401
Washington, DC 20036
202-419-0412
info@naaee.org
www.naaee.org
Reviews and analyzes a long-standing and well-documented environmental education program.

72 pages
ISBN: 1-884008-86-0

3856 Monograph 2: Preparing Effective Environmental Educators
North American Assoc. for Environmental Education
1725 Desales Street NW
Suite 401
Washington, DC 20036
202-419-0412
info@naaee.org
www.naaee.org
Focuses on the methods used to prepare those who teach environmental education.

89 pages

3857 NAFSA's Guide to Education Abroad for Advisers & Administrators
NAFSA: Association of International Educators
1425 K Street NW
Suite 1200
Washington, DC 20005
202-737-3699
inbox@nafsa.org
www.nafsa.org

Esther D. Brimmer, Executive Director & CEO
Dorothea Antonio, Deputy Executive Director

3858 NEA Almanac of Higher Education
National Education Association
1201 16th Street NW
Washington, DC 20036-3290
202-833-4000
Fax: 202-822-7974
www.nea.org
Provides NEA members with broad information on higher education in the U.S., including salaries/benefits, economic conditions, workload, bargaining trends, and information on non-faculty professionals.

ISSN: 0743-670X

Becky Pringle, President
Kim A. Anderson, Executive Director

3859 NSEE Perspectives
National Society for Experiential Education
19 Mantua Road
Mount Royal, NJ 08061
856-423-3427
Fax: 856-423-3420
nsee@talley.com
www.nsee.org
Book exploring the theory and practice of experiential education and conflicting opinions on the meaning of the common good within service learning and civic engagement.

John S. Duley, Author

3860 National Directory of Children, Youth & Families Services
Contexo Media
9737 Washingtonian Blvd
Suite 200
Gaithersburg, MD 20878
800-334-5724
Fax: 301-287-2535
Organized by state and county, this directory lists over 30,000 organizations and 46,000 contacts that focus on helping anyone who is committed to providing the best possible service to our nation's at-risk children, youth and families.

Publication Date: 0 1456 pages Annually

Treavor Peterson, President
Kim Luna, Product Manager

3861 National Guide to Educational Credit for Training Programs
American Council on Education
1 Dupont Circle NW
Washington, DC 20036
202-939-9300
comments@ace.nche.edu
www.acenet.edu
More than 4,500 courses offered by over 280 government agencies, business firms and nonprofit groups.

Ted Mitchell, President
Kara Freeman, Chief Operating Officer

3862 New England Association of Schools and Colleges
New England Association of Schools and Colleges
3 Burlington Woods Drive
Suite 100
Burlington, MA 01803-1433
781-425-7700
855-886-3272
Fax: 781-425-1001
www.neasc.org
Listing of over 1,575 institutions of higher education, public and independent schools and vocational-technical schools in New England.

Publication Date: 1885 65 pages Annual

Mary Lyons, Chair
William L. Burke III, Secretary-Treasurerÿ

3863 Nonformal Environmental Education Programs: Guidelines for Excellence
North American Assoc. for Environmental Education
1725 Desales Street NW
Suite 401
Washington, DC 20036
202-419-0412
info@naaee.org
www.naaee.org
A set of recommendations for developing and administering high quality nonformal environmental education programs.

3864 Overseas American-Sponsored Elementary and Secondary Schools
US Department of State, Office Overseas Schools
2201 C Street NW
Washington, DC 20520
202-647-4000
Fax: 202-261-8224
www.state.gov/m/a/os
Lists nearly 180 independent schools overseas and 10 regional associations of schools.

30 pages Annual

Antony Blinken, Deputy Secretary

3865 Paradigm Lost: Leading America Beyond Its Fear of Educational Change
American Association of School Administrators
1615 Duke Street
Alexandria, VA 22314
703-528-0700
Fax: 703-841-1543
info@aasa.org
www.aasa.org
Explores the beliefs and assumptions upon which schools operate; provides powerful and practical insights and improvement strategies.

Publication Date: 1998 158 pages
ISBN: 0-87652-232-5

3866 Patterson's American Education
Educational Directories Inc
Po Box 68097
Schaumburg, IL 60168-97
847-891-1250
800-357-6183
Fax: 847-891-0945
www.ediusa.com
Lists more than 11,000 public school districts; 300 parochial superintendents; 400 territorial schools; 400 state department of education personnel; and 400 educational associations in one easy to use consistent format. Arranged alphabetically by state then by city. City listings include the city name, telephone area code, city population, county name, public school district name, enrollment, grade range, superintendent's name, address and phone number. Index of secondary schools included.

Publication Date: 1904 974 pages Annual
ISBN: 0-9771602-3-8
ISSN: 0079-0230

Linda Moody, Office Manager

3867 Patterson's Schools Classified
Educational Directories Inc.
1025 W Wise Road
PO Box 68097
Schaumburg, IL 60168-97
847-891-1250
800-357-6183
Fax: 847-891-0945
www.ediusa.org
Contains 7,000 accredited postsecondary schools, the broadest assortment available in a single directory. Universities, colleges, community colleges, junior colleges, career schools and teaching hospitals are co-mingled under 50 academic disciplines but retain their school type identification. School professional accreditation is shown in 32 classifications. The basic entry includes school name, mailing address and contact person, with additional descriptive material supplied by the school.

Publication Date: 1904 302 pages Annual
ISBN: 0-9771602-2-X

Wayne Moody, Coordinating Education

3868 Peterson's Competitive Colleges
Peterson's, A Nelnet Company
Princeton Pike Corporate Center
461 From Road
Paramus, NJ 07652
609-896-1800
800-338-3282
Fax: 402-458-3042

support@petersons.com
www.petersons.com
The most trusted source of advice for excellent students searching for high-quality schools. Provides objective criteria to compare more than 440 leading colleges and universities.

Publication Date: 1975 524 pages
ISBN: 1-560795-98-0

3869 Peterson's Guide to Four-Year Colleges
Peterson's, A Nelnet Company
Princeton Pike Corporate Center
461 From Road
Paramus, NJ 07652
609-896-1800
800-338-3282
Fax: 402-458-3042
support@petersons.com
www.petersons.com
Includes descriptions of over 2,000 colleges, providing guidance on selecting the right school, getting in and financial aid.

Publication Date: 1975 2,922 pages

3870 Peterson's Guide to Two-Year Colleges
Peterson's, A Nelnet Company
Princeton Pike Corporate Center
461 From Road
Paramus, NJ 07652
609-896-1800
800-338-3282
Fax: 402-458-3042
support@petersons.com
www.petersons.com
The only two-year college guide available, this new and expanded directory is the most complete source of information on institutions that grant an associate as their highest degree.

Publication Date: 1975 712 pages
ISBN: 1-560796-05-7

3871 Peterson's Regional College Guide Set
Peterson's, A Nelnet Company
Princeton Pike Corporate Center
461 From Road
Paramus, NJ 07652
609-896-1800
800-338-3282
Fax: 402-458-3042
support@petersons.com
www.petersons.com
Six individual regional guides that help students compare colleges in a specific geographic area.

Publication Date: 1975

3872 Power of Public Engagement Book Set
Master Teacher
One Leadership Lane
PO Box 1207
Manhattan, KS 66502-1207
800-669-9633
Fax: 800-669-1132
www.masterteacher.com
Learn how to engage your community to make the changes needed to ensure the best education for its children.

Publication Date: 1969
ISBN: 1-58992-128-3

William G O'Callaghan Jr, Author

3873 Private Independent Schools
Bunting & Lyon
238 N Main Street
Wallingford, CT 06492-3728
203-269-3333
Fax: 203-269-5697
BuntingandLyon@aol.com
www.macraesbluebook.com
Provides information on more than 1,100 elementary and secondary private schools and summer programs in the United States and abroad. This annual guide, now in its 56th edition, is the most concise, current resource available on private school programs.

Publication Date: 1996 644 pages Annual Hardcover
ISBN: 0-913094-56-0
ISSN: 0079-5399

Peter G Bunting, Publisher

3874 Private School Law in America
Progressive Business Publications
370 Technology Drive
Malvern, PA 19355
610-695-8600
800-220-5000
Fax: 610-647-8089
customer_service@pbp.com
www.pbp.com
An up-to-date compilation of summarized federal and state appellate court decisions which affect private education. The full legal citation is supplied for each case. A brief introductory note on the American judicial system is provided along with updated appendices of recent US Supreme Court cases and recently published law review articles. Also included are portions of the US Constitution which are most frequently cited in private education cases.

Publication Date: 1959 500 pages Annually
ISBN: 0-939675-80-3

Ed Satell, Founder

3875 Professional Development of Environmental Educators: Guidelines for Excellence
North American Assoc. for Environmental Education
1725 Desales Street NW
Suite 401
Washington, DC 20036
202-419-0412
info@naaee.org
www.naaee.org
Recommendations about the basic knowledge and abilities educators need to provide high quality environmental education.

3876 Public Schooling in America: A Reference Handbook
ABC-CLIO
147 Castilian Drive
Santa Barbara, CA 93117
805-968-1911
800-368-6868
Fax: 866-270-3856
customerservice@abc-clio.com
www.abc-clio.com
Discusses the history of public education in the U.S. and major issues facing the public school system.

Hardcover
ISBN: 0-87436-595-5

Richard D. Van Scotter, Author

3877 Public Schools USA: A Comparative Guide to School Districts
Peterson's, A Nelnet Company
Princeton Pike Corporate Center
461 From Road
Paramus, NJ 07652
609-896-1800
800-338-3282
Fax: 402-458-3042
support@petersons.com
www.petersons.com
Lists over 400 school districts in 52 metropolitan areas throughout the United States.

Publication Date: 1975 490 pages Annual

Charles Hampton Harrison, Author

3878 School Foodservice Who's Who
Information Central
PO Box 3900
Prescott, AZ 86302-3900
520-778-1513
Listing of over 2,500 food service programs in public and Catholic school systems.

110 pages Triennial

3879 School Guide
School Guide Publications
210 N Avenue
New Rochelle, NY 10801-6402
914-632-7771
800-433-7771
Fax: 914-632-3412
mridder@schoolguides.com
www.schoolguides.com
Listing of over 3,000 colleges, vocational schools and nursing schools in the US.

Publication Date: 1886 280 pages Annual/Paperback
ISBN: 1-893275-30-2

Janette Aiello, Editor

3880 Schools of Character
Character Education Partnership
PO Box 650307
Sterling, VA 20165
202-296-7743
www.character.org

Arthur Schwartz, President
Dean D'Ambrosi, Executive Vice President

3881 Schools-Business & Vocational Directory
American Business Directories
5711 S 86th Circle
Omaha, NE 68127-4146
402-593-4600
888-999-1307
Fax: 402-331-5481
www.americanbusinessandservicedirectory.com
A complete listing of business and vocational schools nationwide. Includes phone numbers, contact names, employee sizes and more.

Annual

Jerry Venner, Coordinating Education

3882 Theory & Practice of Experiential Education
Association for Experiential Education
2315 18th Street S
Saint Petersburg, FL 33712
303-440-8844
www.aee.org

Publication Date: 2008 578 pages Paperback
ISBN: 0-929361-17-8

Sherry Bagley, Executive Director
Steve Pace, Director, Accreditations

3883 Treasury of Noteworthy Proverbs
Morris Publishing
P.O. Box 2110
Kearney, NE 68848
954-974-5477
800-650-7888
Fax: 308-237-0263
carconed@aol.com
www.morrispublishing.com
Tapestry of maxims, aphorisims, and pithy sayings. A revealing picture of the wisdom, philosophy, and humor of the people of this and many other nations throughout the world.
Publication Date: 1933
ISBN: 0-7392-0208-1
ISSN: 99-943-75
Dr. Robert M Bookbinder, President

3884 US Supreme Court Education Cases
Progressive Business Publications
370 Technology Drive
Malvern, PA 19355
610-695-8600
800-220-5000
Fax: 610-647-8089
customer_service@pbp.com
www.pbp.com
A compilation of summarized US Supreme Court decisions since 1954 which affect education. The full legal citation is supplied for each case. Also included are portions of the US Constitution which are most frequently cited in education cases.
Publication Date: 1959 Annually
Liz Webb, Senior Corporate Recruiter
Ed Satell, Founder

3885 VincentCurtis Educational Register
VincentCurtis
PO Box 724
Falmouth, MA 02541-0724
508-457-6473
Fax: 508-457-6499
register@vincentcurtis.com
An online guide to a variety of private boarding and day schools as well as resident summer programs in the United States, Canada and Europe. The guide includes articles, information and advice on the subject of independent education.
Publication Date: 1941
Stan Vincent, Editor

3886 Western Association of Schools and Colleges
Western Association of Schools and Colleges
533 Airport Boulevard
Suite 200
Burlingame, CA 94010-2009
650-696-1060
Fax: 650-696-1867
mail@acswasc.org
www.acswasc.org
Listing of schools and colleges in California, Hawaii, Guam, American Samoa and East Asia.
130 pages Annual
Fred Van Leuven, Executive Director
Marilyn S. George, Associate Executive Director

3887 What's Fair Got to Do With It
WestEd
730 Harrison Street
San Francisco, CA 94107
415-565-3000
877-493-7833
Fax: 415-565-3012
www.wested.org
A tool for professional development. Each case is a candid, dramatic, and highly readable first-person account that makes concrete the challenges of fairness, expectations, respect, and communication when people who share goals, perhaps, but not cultures, interact.
122 pages
ISBN: 0-914409-20-5

3888 Whole Nonprofit Catalog
Grantmanship Center
PO Box 17720
Los Angeles, CA 90017
213-482-9860
800-421-9512
Fax: 213-482-9863
Info@tgci.com
www.tgci.com
Offers information on training programs offered by the Center, publications and other services available to the nonprofit sector.
Publication Date: 1972
Cathleen Kiritz, President
Barbara Floersch, Executive Director

3889 Working Together: A Guide to Community-Based Educational Resources
Research, Advocacy & Legislation/Council of LaRaza
1126 16th Street, NW
Suite 600
Washington, DC 20036-4845
202-289-1380
comments@nclr.org
www.nclr.org
Listing of about 30 community-based organizations nationwide providing educational services to Hispanic Americans.
35 pages
Jorge A. Plasencia, Chair
Renata Soto, Vice Chair

3890 World of Learning
Gale Group
27500 Drake Road
Farmington Hills, MI 48331
248-699-4253
800-877-4253
Fax: 877-363-4253
www.cengage.com
Contains information for over 26,000 universities, colleges, schools of art and music, libraries, archives, learned societies, research institutes, museums and art galleries in more than 180 countries.

ISBN: 0-7876-5004-8
Michael E. Hansen, CEO
Fernando Bleichmar, Chief Strategy Officer

Directories & Handbooks / Administration

3891 American School & University - Who's Who Directory & Buyer's Guide
Prism Business Media
9800 Metcalf Avenue
Overland Park, KS 66212-2286
913-967-1960
Fax: 913-967-1905
jagron@asumag.com
www.asumag.com
Comprehensive directory of suppliers and products for facility needs; listings of architects by region; listing of associations affiliated with the education industry; article index for quick and easy reference; in-depth calendar of events.
Publication Date: 1928 Annual
Joe Agron, Editor-In-Chief
Gregg Herring, VP, Market Leader

3892 Bricker's International Directory
Peterson's, A Nelnet Company
Princeton Pike Corporate Center
461 From Road
Paramus, NJ 07652
609-896-1800
800-338-3282
Fax: 402-458-3042
support@petersons.com
www.petersons.com
Offers over 400 residential management development programs at academic institutions in the United States and abroad.
Publication Date: 1975 Annual

3893 Cabells Directory of Publishing Opportunities in Educational Psychology and Administration
Cabell Publishing Company
Box 5428
Tobe Hahn Station
Beaumont, TX 77726
409-898-0575
Fax: 409-866-9554
info@cabells.com
www.cabells.com
Provides information on editor contact information, manuscript guidelines, acceptance rate, review information and circulation data for over 225 academic journals.
Publication Date: 1978 799 pages Annual
ISBN: 0-911753-28-1
David WE Cabell, Editor
Deborah L English, Associate Editor

3894 Continuing Education Guide
Int'l Assoc. for Continuing Education & Training
21670 Ridgetop Circle
Suite 170
Sterling, VA 20166
703-763-0705
Fax: 703-738-7194
info@iacet.org
www.iacet.org
Explores how to interpret and use the Continuing Education Unit or other criteria used for continuing education programs. This guide, written by continuing education and training consultant, Louis Phillips, is a reference source complete with sample forms, charts, checklists and everything needed to evaluate a school's continuing education program.
Casandra Blassingame, Chief Executive Officer
Amy Starchville, Director, Operations

3895 Creating Quality Reform: Programs, Communities and Governance
Pearson Education Communications
1 Lake Street
Upper Saddle River, NJ 07458
201-236-7000
Fax: 877-260-2530
communications@pearsoned.com
www.pearsoned.com
Publication Date: 2002
J Thomas Owens, Editor
Jan C Simmons, Editor

3896 Deskbook Encyclopedia of American School Law
Progressive Business Publications
370 Technology Drive
Malvern, PA 19355

610-695-8600
800-220-5000
Fax: 610-647-8089
customer_service@pbp.com
www.pbp.com
An up-to-date compilation of summarized federal and state appellate court decisions which affect education. The full legal citation is supplied for each case with a brief introductory note on the American judicial system is provided along with updated appendices of recent US Supreme Court cases and recently published law review articles.

Publication Date: 1959 Annually

Liz Webb, Senior Corporate Recruiter
Ed Satell, Founder

3897 Developing a Character Education Program
Association for Supervision & Curriculum Develop.
1703 N Beauregard Street
Alexandria, VA 22311-1714
press@ascd.org
www.ascd.org

Henry Huffman, Author

3898 Development Education: A Directory of Non-Governmental Practitioners
U.N. Non-Governmental Liaison Service
Palais des Nations, CH 1211
Geneva 10
Switzerland
ngls@unctad.org
www.un-ngls.org
Lists about 800 national non-governmental organizations in industrialized countries and international non-governmental networks concerned with developmental education.

Publication Date: 1975 400 pages

Beth Peoch, Officer in Charge
David Vergari, Administration

3899 Directory of Chief Executive Officers of United Methodist Schools, Colleges & Universities
General Board of Higher Education & Ministry/UMC
1001 19th Avenue South
PO Box 340007
Nashville, TN 37203-0007
615-340-7406
Fax: 615-340-7379
scu@gbhem.org
www.gbhem.org
123 United Methodist educational institutions including theology schools, professional schools, two year colleges and colleges and universities with all contact information arranged by institution type. Paperback.

32 pages Annual

James E. Dorff, Presiden
Ianther Marie Mills, Vice President

3900 Directory of Organizations in Educational Management
ERIC Clearinghouse on Educational Management
1501 Kincaid Street
Eugene, OR 97403-1299
541-346-3053
800-438-8841
Fax: 541-346-3485
www.scholarsbank.uoregon.edu
Offers listings of 163 organizations in the field of educational management at the elementary and secondary school levels.

Dr. Philip Piele, Director
Stuart C Smith, Associate Director

3901 Educating for Character
Master Teacher
One Leadership Lane
PO Box 1207
Manhattan, KS 66502-1207
800-669-9633
Fax: 800-669-1132
www.masterteacher.com
Dr. Licona has developed a 12 point program that offers practical strategies designed to create a working coalition of parents, teachers and communities.

428 pages
ISBN: 0-553-37052-9

Thomas Lickona PhD, Author

3902 Educating for Character: How Our Schools Can Teach Respect and Responsibility
Random House
1745 Broadway
New York, NY 10019
212-782-9000
www.randomhousebooks.com

Publication Date: 1992 496 pages

Thomas Lickona, Author

3903 Education Budget Alert
Committee for Education Funding
1640 Rhode Island Ave., NW
Suite 600
Washington, DC 20036-2109
202-383-0083
Fax: 202-463-4803
jchang@cef.org
www.cef.org
Federal programs currently help over 63 million Americans to engage in formal learning. This guidebook explains what these programs do, what types of activities are supported, the reasons the federal government initiated these programs, and their level at funding.

Publication Date: 2012 150 pages Annually

Noelle Ellerson, President
Makese Motley, Vice-President

3904 Educational Consultants Directory
American Business and Service Directory
5711 S 86th Circle
PO Box 27347
Omaha, NE 68127
402-593-4600
800-555-6124
Fax: 402-331-5481
www.americanbusinessandservicedirectory.com
A list of more than 5,000 entries, including name, address, phone, size of advertisement, name of owner or manager and number of employees.

3905 Educational Dealer-Buyers' Guide Issue
Fahy-Williams Publishing
171 Reed St.
PO Box 1080
Geneva, NY 14456-2137
315-789-0458
800-344-0559
Fax: 315-789-4263
www.fwpi.com
List of approximately 2,000 suppliers of educational materials and equipment.

Annual

J. Kevin Fahy, Publisher
Tina Manzer, Editorial Director

3906 Executive Summary Set
Master Teacher
One Leadership Lane
PO Box 1207
Manhattan, KS 66502
800-669-9633
Fax: 800-669-1132
www.masterteacher.com
An easy, effective and practical way to orient new board members before they attend their first meeting. Executive Summary Sets cover the vital information board members must have in eight areas: tenets of education; powers and responsibilities; decision making; communication for maximum results; resource management; assessment of programs; assessment of personnel and conflict resolution.

Robert DeBruyn, Editor

3907 Hispanic Yearbook-Anuario Hispano
TIYM Publishing
8370 Greensboro Dr.
#1009
McLean, VA 22102
703-734-1632
Fax: 703-356-0787
TIYM@aol.com
This guide lists Hispanic organizations, publications, radio and TV stations, through not specifically for grant-giving purposes.

Publication Date: 1985 Annually

John O Zavala, COO
Ramon Palencia, Director PR

3908 Leading to Change: The Challenge of the New Superintendency
Jossey-Bass
1 Montgomery Street
Suite 1200
San Francisco, CA 94104
415-433-1740
josseybasseducation@wiley.com
www.josseybass.com
The challenge of the new superintendency.

Publication Date: 1814 352 pages
ISBN: 0-7879-0214-4

Susan Moore Johnson, Author

3909 Legal Basics: A Handbook for Educators
Phi Delta Kappa International
1820 N Fort Myer Drive
Suite 320
Arlington, VA 22209
800-766-1156
info@pdkintl.org
www.pdkintl.org
Superintendents, principals, counselors, teachers, and paraprofessionals need to pay close attention to their actions in schools and classrooms because, from a legal standpoint, those settings may contain hazardous conditions. Legal Basics points out the pitfalls and how to avoid them.

120 pages Paperback

Evelyn B. Kelly, Author
Joshua P. Starr, Ed.D, Chief Executive Officer
Albert Chen, M.E., Chief Operating Officer

3910 Lifeworld of Leadership: Creating Culture, Community, and Personal Meaning in Our Schools
Jossey-Bass
1 Montgomery Street
Suite 1200
San Francisco, CA 94104

415-433-1740
josseybasseducation@wiley.com
www.josseybass.com
Explores the crucial link between school improvement and school character.

Publication Date: 1814 240 pages Paperback
ISBN: 0-7879-7277-6

911 Looking at Schools: Instruments & Processes for School Analysis

Research for Better Schools
123 South Broad Street
Suite 1860
Philadelphia, PA 19109
215-568-6150
Fax: 215-568-7260
www.rbs.org
Thirty-five institutions that offer instruments and processes to assess the performance of students, teachers and administrators, school climate effectiveness and school-community relations.

Publication Date: 1966 140 pages

Carol Crociante, Executive Assistant
Keith M Kershner, Executive Director

912 Market Data Retrieval-National School Market Index

Market Data Retrieval
6 Armstrong Road
Suite 301
Shelton, CT 06484-0947
203-926-4800
800-333-8802
Fax: 203-929-5253
msubrizi@dnb.com
www.schooldata.com
An annual report on school spending patterns for instructional materials in the United States. The Index now in its twenty-fifth year of publication, lists the expenditures for instructional materials for all 15,000 US senior districts.

Publication Date: 1996
ISBN: 0-897708-25-3

Mike Subrizi, Marketing Director

913 National School Supply & Equipment Association Membership/Buyers' Guide Directory

Education Market Association
8380 Colesville Rd
Suite 250
Silver Spring, MD 20910
301-495-0240
800-395-5550
Fax: 301-495-3330
www.edmarket.org
Lists 1,500 member dealers, manufacturers and manufacturers' representatives for school supplies, equipment and instructional materials.

200 pages Annual

Adrienne Watts, Author
Jim McGarry, President/ CEO
Adrienne Dayton, VP, Marketing & Comm.

914 Proactive Leadership in the 21st Century

Master Teacher
One Leadership Lane
PO Box 1207
Manhattan, KS 66502-1207
800-669-9633
Fax: 800-669-1132
www.masterteacher.com
Contain the laws and principals of leadership and people management as they had never been defined and described before giving school administrators a set of guidelines that if followed would guarantee success.

ISBN: 0-914607-44-8

Robert L DeBruyn, Author

3915 QED's State School Guides

Quality Education Data
601 E. Marshall St
Suite 250
Sweet Springs, MO 65351
303-860-1832
800-776-6373
Fax: 660-335-4157
info@qeddata.com
www.qeddata.com
Complete directories of every US school district and public, Catholic and private school. Directories are available for individual states, geographic regions and the entire United States. Each directory includes names of district administrators, school principals and school librarians, as well as addresses, phone numbers and enrollment information. QED's State school guide also includes key demographic and instructional technology data for each district and school.

Publication Date: 1993 Yearly
ISBN: 0-887476-49-0

John F. Hood, President
Peter Long, CEO

3916 School Promotion, Publicity & Public Relations: Nothing but Benefits

Master Teacher
One Leadership Lane
PO Box 1207
Manhattan, KS 66502-1207
785-539-0555
800-669-9633
Fax: 785-539-7739
www.masterteacher.com
Contains the vital foundations an administrator must have to understand and implement a program of publicity, promotion and public relations, in a school or school district.

327 pages
ISBN: 0-914607-25-1

Tracey H DeBruyn, Author

3917 Schoolwide Discipline Strategies that Make a Difference in Teaching & Learning

Master Teacher
One Leadership Lane
PO Box 1207
Manhattan, KS 66502-1207
800-669-9633
Fax: 800-669-1132
www.masterteacher.com
This approach to discipline will help your school or district eliminate the dependecy on one individual, provide guidance for present and new teachers, allow disipline to become a K-12 program, an bring about consistancy in the handling of all student misbehaviors.

150 pages
ISBN: 1-58992-000-7

Larry Dixon, Author

3918 The Teaching Professor

Magna Publications
2718 Dryden Drive
Madison, WI 53704
608-246-3590
Fax: 608-246-3597
support@magnapubs.com
www.magnapubs.com
This newsletter has been a leading source of information and inspiration for educators committed to creating a better learning environment.

Publication Date: 1972 530 pages Paperback November
1000 attendees and 10+ exhibits

William Haight, President
Jody Glynn Patrick, Vice President

Directories & Handbooks / Early Childhood Education

3919 Early Childhood Environmental Education Programs: Guidelines for Excellence

North American Assoc. for Environmental Education
1725 Desales Street NW
Suite 401
Washington, DC 20036
202-419-0412
info@naaee.org
www.naaee.org
A set of recommendations for developing and administering high-quality early childhood environmental education programs.

Directories & Handbooks / Elementary Education

3920 Educational Impressions

P.O. Box 377
Franklin, NJ 07414-0377
973-423-4666
800-451-7450
Fax: 201-644-0907
www.edimpressions.com
Educational workbooks, activity books, literature guides, and audiovisuals. Grades K-8, with emphasis on intermediate and middle grades.

Paperback/Video/Audi

Neil Peller, Marketing Director
Lori Brown, Sales/Marketing

3921 Educators Guide to FREE Videotapes-Elementary/ Middle School Edition

Educators Progress Service
214 Center Street
Randolph, WI 53956-1408
920-326-3126
888-951-4469
Fax: 920-326-3127
epsinc@centurytel.net
www.freeteachingaids.com
Lists and describes free and free-loan videotapes for the elementary and middle school level.

Annual
ISBN: 0-877082-67-7

Kathy Nehmer, President

3922 Educators Guide to FREE Videotapes-Secondary Edition

Educators Progress Service
214 Center Street
Randolph, WI 53956-1408
920-326-3126
888-951-4469
Fax: 920-326-3127
epsinc@centurytel.net
www.freeteachingaids.com

Lists and describes free and free-loan videotapes for the elementary and middle school level.

Annual
ISBN: 0-877082-67-7

Kathy Nehmer, President

3923 Elementary Teachers Guide to FREE Curriculum Materials
Educators Progress Service
214 Center Street
Randolph, WI 53956-1408
920-326-3126
888-951-4469
Fax: 920-326-3127
epsinc@centurytel.net
www.freeteachingaids.com
Lists and describes free supplementary teaching aids for the elementary level.

Annual
ISBN: 0-877082-64-2

Kathy Nehmer, President

3924 KIDSNET Media Guide and News
KIDSNET
6856 Eastern Avenue NW
Suite 208
Washington, DC 20012
202-291-1400
Fax: 202-882-7315
www.kidsnet.org
Contains children's television, radio and video listings. Also lists related teaching materials and copyright guidelines.

150 pages Monthly

3925 Lesson Plans, Integrating Technology into the Classroom: Elementary Edition
Master Teacher
One Leadership Lane
PO Box 1207
Manhattan, KS 66502-1207
800-669-9633
Fax: 800-669-1132
www.masterteacher.com
Gives teachers practical lessons developed and tested by teachers across the curriculum, with students of all levels of ability in using technology.

Publication Date: 1969 130 pages
ISBN: 0-914607-59-6

3926 Nursery Schools & Kindergartens Directory
American Business Directories
5711 S 86th Circle
Omaha, NE 68127-4146
402-593-4600
888-999-1307
Fax: 402-331-5481
www.americanbusinessandservicedirectory.com
A geographical listing of 34,900 nursery schools and kindergartens including all contact information, first year in Yellow Pages and descriptions. Also available are regional editions and electronic formats.

Annual

Jerry Venner, Coordinating Education

3927 Parent Involvement Facilitator: Elementary Edition
Master Teacher
One Leadership Lane
PO Box 1207
Manhattan, KS 66502-1207
800-669-9633
Fax: 800-669-1132
www.masterteacher.com
Packed with ideas for you and your teachers to implement along with the exact steps for you to follow.

169 pages
ISBN: 0-914607-45-6

3928 Patterson's Elementary Education
Educational Directories Inc.
1025 W Wise Road
PO Box 68097
Schaumberg, IL 60168-97
847-891-1250
800-357-6183
Fax: 847-891-0945
A directory to more than 13,000 public school districts; 71,000 public, private and Catholic elementary and middle schools; 1,600 territorial schools; and 400 state department of education personnel in one easy to use consistent format. Arranged alphabetically by state then city. City listings include city name, telephone area code, city population, county name, public school district name, enrollment, grade range, superintendent's name, address and phone number.

Publication Date: 1994 870 pages Annual
ISBN: 0-910536-59-7

Douglas Moody, Coordinating Education

3929 Teaching Our Youngest-A Guide for Preschool Teachers and Child Care and Family Providers
ED Pubs
P.O. Box 22207
Alexandria, VA 22304-1398
877-4ED-PUBS
Fax: 703-605-6794
edpubs@inet.ed.gov
www.edpubs.org
This booklet draws from scientifically based research about what can be done to help children develop their language abilities, increase their knowledge, become familiar with books and other printed materials,learn letters and sounds, recognize numbers and learn to count.

Directories & Handbooks / Employment

3930 Cabell's Directory of Publishing Opportunities in Education
Cabell Publishing
Box 5428
Tobe Hahn Station
Beaumont, TX 77726-5428
409-898-0575
Fax: 409-866-9554
info@cabells.com
www.cabells.com
Includes list of more than 430 education journals that consider manuscripts for publication. Includes contact names and addresses for submitting manuscripts, topics considered, publication guidelines, fees, and circulation information.

Publication Date: 1978 1,200 pages

David WE Cabell, Editor
Deborah L English, Associate Editor

3931 Cabell's Directory of Publishing Opportunities in Accounting
Cabell Publishing Company
Box 5428
Tobe Hahn Station
Beaumont, TX 77726
409-898-0575
Fax: 409-866-9554
info@cabells.com
www.cabells.com
Contains information on 130 journal. Entries include manuscript guidelines for authors: editor's address, phone, fax and e-mail. Review process and the time required, acceptance rates, readership circulation and subscription prices. The Index classifies journals by 15 topics areas and provides information on type of review, acceptance rate and review time.

Publication Date: 1978 425 pages Annual
ISBN: 0-911753-13-3

David WE Cabell, Editor
Deborah L English, Editor

3932 Cabell's Directory of Publishing Opportunities in Economics & Finance
Cabell Publishing Company
Box 5428
Tobe Hahn Station
Beaumont, TX 77726-5428
409-898-0575
Fax: 409-866-9554
info@cabells.com
www.cabells.com
Contains information on 350 journals. Each journal entry includes manuscript guidelines for authors: editor's address, phone, fax and e-mail, review process and time required, acceptance rates, readership, circulation and subscription prices. The Index classifies journals by 15 topic areas and provides information on type of review, acceptance rate and review time.

Publication Date: 1978 1100 pages Annual
ISBN: 0-911753-14-1

David WE Cabell, Editor
Deborah L English, Associate Editor

3933 Cabells Directory of Publishing Opportunities in Management
Cabell Publishing Company
Box 5428
Tobe Hahn Station
Beaumont, TX 77726
409-898-0575
Fax: 409-866-9554
info@cabells.com
www.cabells.com
Provides editor contact information, acceptance rates, review information, manuscript guidelines and circulation data for over 540 academic journals.

Publication Date: 1978 648 pages
ISBN: 0-911753-15-X

David WE Cabell, Editor
Deborah L English, Associate Editor

3934 Career Book
VGM Career Books
4255 W Touhy Avenue
Lincolnwood, IL 60712
732-329-6991
Fax: 732-329-6994
Offers information on educational employment opportunities in America and abroad.

BiAnnual Hard/Paper

Joyce Lain Kennedy & Darryl Laramore, Author

3935 Career Information Center
MacMillan Publishers
16365 James Madison Highway
Gordonsville, VA 22942
888-330-8477
Fax: 800-672-2054
press.inquiries@macmillan.com
www.us.macmillan.com
Information on salaries and occupational outlooks for nearly 3,000 careers.

)36 Careers Information Officers in Local Authorities
Careers Research & Advisory Centre/Hobsons Pub.
Sheraton House, Castle Park
Cambridge CB3 0AX
England
44 -0 1-23 4
223-354551
enquiries@crac.org.uk
www.crac.org.uk
1,100 United Kingdom institutions offering collections of career information and audio-visual materials covering career opportunities and current job markets. Arranged alphabetically listing address, phone, contact name and titles, type of materials held and a description of the facilities.

Publication Date: 1964 165 pages 12.95 pounds

Ellen Pearce, Chief Executive
Alison Mitchell, Director of Development

)37 Certification and Accreditation Programs Directory
Gale Research
27500 Drake Road
Farmington Hills, MI 48331-3535
248-699-4253
800-877-4253
Fax: 877-363-4253
galeord@gale.com
www.cengage.com
Directory of private organizations that offer more than 1,700 voluntary certification programs and approximately 300 accreditation programs. Also on CD-ROM.

Publication Date: 1995 620 pages
ISSN: 1084-2128

Michael E. Hansen, CEO
Fernando Bleichmar, Chief Strategy Officer

)38 Council of British Independent Schools in the European Communities-Members Directory
Council of British International Schools
St Mary's University, Strawberry Hi
Twickenham, TW1 4SX
United Kingdom
44-1303-260857
Fax: 44-1303-260857
ceo@cobis.org.uk
www.cobis.org.uk

Annual

Colin Bell, CEO
Sarah Wooldridge, Finance Officer

)39 Directory of English Language Schools in Japan Hiring English Teachers
Information Career Opportunities Research Center
Box 1100, Station F
Toronto M4Y 2T7
Canada
416-925-8878
English-language schools in Japan.

15 pages Annual

)40 Directory of International Internships Michigan State University
MSU: Dean's Office of Int'l Studies and Programs
427 N. Shaw Lane
Room 207
East Lansing, MI 48824-1035
517-355-2350
Fax: 517-353-7254
infonew@isp.msu.edu
www.isp.msu.edu
International internships sponsored by academic institutions, private corporations and the federal government.

Publication Date: 1994 168 pages Paperback

Rachel Warner, Director of Communications
Julie Norton, Secretary

3941 Directory of Schools, Colleges, and Universities Overseas
Overseas Employment Services
EBSCO Industries
PO Box 1943
Birmingham, AL 35201
205-991-1330
Fax: 205-995-1582
Directory of 300 educational institutions worldwide that hire teachers to teach different subjects in English.

21 pages Annual

Leonard Simcoe, Editor

3942 Directory of Work and Study in Developing Countries
Vacation-Work Publishers
9 Park End Street
Oxford OX1 1HJ
England
865-241978
Offers information on about 420 organizations worldwide offering employment and study opportunities in over 100 developing countries.

215 pages

3943 Earn & Learn: Cooperative Education Opportunities
Octameron Associates
1900 Mount Vernon Avenue
PO Box 2748
Alexandria, VA 22301-0748
703-836-5480
Fax: 703-836-5650
info@octameron.com
www.octameron.com
Explains how students may participate in cooperative work-study education programs with federal government agencies.

Publication Date: 1997 48 pages BiAnnual
ISBN: 1-57509-023-6

3944 English in Asia: Teaching Tactics for New English Teachers
Global Press
350 Rhode Island Street
Suite 240
San Francisco, CA 94103-1135
415-570-9114
info@globalpressinstitute.org
www.globalpressinstitute.org
Directory covering 1,000 private English-language schools in Asia, to which applications can be sent to teach.

Publication Date: 1992 180 pages

Danforth Austin, Chairman
Cristi Hegranes, Secretary

3945 European Council of International Schools Directory
European Council of International Schools
Fourth Floor, 146 Buckingham Palace
London, SW1W 9TR, London
United Kingdom
004- 0-20 7
44-1730-26-8244
Fax: 44-1730-267914
ecis@ecis.org
www.ecis.org
More than 420 member elementary and secondary international schools in Europe and worldwide.

Publication Date: 1965 480 pages Annual

Kevin J Ruth, PhD, President
Darlene Fisher, People & Programmes Lead

3946 Faculty Exchange Center Directory and House Exchange Supplement
Faculty Exchange Center
University of Dayton
300 College Park
Dayton, OH 45469-3116
937-229-1000
info@udayton.edu
www.https://www.udayton.edu
Offers information for college and faculty members wishing to exchange positions and/or homes temporarily with faculty members at other institutions.

35 pages Annual

Steven D. Cobb, Chair
Rev. Martin A. Solma, Vice Chair

3947 Foreign Faculty and Administrative Openings
Education Information Services
PO Box 620662
Newton, MA 02462-0662
617-433-0125
150 specific openings in administration, counseling, library and other professional positions for American teachers in American schools overseas and in international schools in which teaching language is English.

15 pages Every 6 Weeks

FB Viaux, Coordinating Education

3948 Guide to Educational Opportunities in Japan
Embassy of Japan
2520 Massachusetts Avenue NW
Washington, DC 20008
202-238-6700
Fax: 202-328-2187
www.embjapan.org
This guide describes opportunities for study in Japan and outlines different forms of financial assistance.

3949 How to Create a Picture of Your Ideal Job or Next Career
Ten Speed Press
6001 Shellmound Street
Emeryville, CA 94608-0123
510-285-3000
800-841-BOOK
Fax: 510-285-2979
www.randomhouse.com
Offers handy tips on how to choose the right career, and then go out and get it.

Publication Date: 1989

Richard Nelson Bolles, Author

3950 Jobs Clearinghouse
Association for Experiential Education
2315 18th Street S
Saint Petersburg, FL 33712
303-440-8844
www.aee.org
An online directory of full-time, part-time, and seasonal employment and internship opportunities in the experiential education field.

Sherry Bagley, Executive Director
Steve Pace, Director, Accreditations

3951 Leading Educational Placement Sources in the US
Educational Information Services
PO Box 662
Newton Lower Falls, MA 02162
617-964-4555
An index of the host placement agencies in America for education professionals.

3952 List of Over 200 Executive Search Consulting Firms in the US
Educational Information Services
PO Box 662
Newton Lower Falls, MA 02162
617-964-4555
www.nypl.org
Covers companies with active search committees in America.

3953 List of Over 600 Personnel & Employment Agencies
Educational Information Services
PO Box 662
Newton Lower Falls, MA 02162
617-964-4555
www.nypl.org
Contains information on personnel and employment agencies.

3954 Living in China: A Guide to Studying, Teaching & Working in the PRC & Taiwan
China Books & Periodicals
360 Swift Avenue
Suite 48
South San Francisco, CA 94080
650-872-7076
800-818-2017
Fax: 650-872-7808
info@chinabooks.com
www.chinabooks.com
America's #1 source of publications about China since 1960.

284 pages Paperback
ISBN: 0835125823
November

Chellis Ying, Marketing Director
Chris Robyn, Senior Managing Editor

3955 Opening List in US Colleges, Public & Private Schools
Education Information Services/Instant Alert
PO Box 620662
Newton, MA 02462-0662
617-433-0125
Offers about 150 current professional openings in US colleges and public and private schools.

10 pages Every 6 weeks

FB Viaux, Coordinating Education

3956 Opening List of Professional Openings in American Overseas Schools
Education Information Services/Instant Alert
PO Box 620662
Newton, MA 02462-0662
617-433-0125
About 150 current professional openings for teachers, administrators, counselors, librarians and educational specialists in American overseas schools and international schools at which the teaching language is primarily English.

FB Viaux, Coordinating Education

3957 Overseas Employment Opportunities for Educators
Department of Defense, Office of Dependent Schools
4800 Mark Center Drive
Alexandria, VA 22350-1400
571-372-0590
www.dodea.edu
This publication tells about teaching jobs in 250 schools operated for children of US military and civilian personnel stationed overseas. Applicants usually must qualify in two subject areas.

3958 Private School, Community & Junior College Four Year Colleges & Universities
Educational Information Services
PO Box 662
Newton Lower Falls, MA 02162
617-964-4555
Names, addresses and phones for any state or region in the United States offering employment opportunities.

3959 Research, Study, Travel, & Work Abroad
US Government Publishing Office
710 North Capitol Street N.W.
Washington, DC 20401-1
202-512-1800
866-512-1800
Fax: 202-512-2104
ContactCenter@gpo.gov
www.gpo.gov

Publication Date: 1861

Davita Vance-Cooks, Director
Jim Bradley, Deputy Director

3960 Teaching Overseas
KSJ Publishing Company
PO Box 2311
Sebastopol, CA 95473-2311
A directory of information on how to find jobs teaching overseas.

Publication Date: 1992 89 pages 2nd Edition
ISBN: 0-962044-55-5

3961 VGM's Careers Encyclopedia
VGM Career Books/National Textbook Company
4255 W Touhy Avenue
Lincolnwood, IL 60646-1933
708-679-5500
A list of over 200 professional associations that provide career guidance information.

3962 Work Abroad: The Complete Guide to Finding a Job Overseas
Transitions Abroad
P.O. Box 1369
Amherst, MA 01004
413-992-6486
Fax: 802-442-4827
editor@transitionsabroad.com
www.transitionsabroad.com
Resource for finding both short- and long-term jobs abroad. Organized by region and country, includes websites and phone numbers.

Publication Date: 1977

Dr. Joanna Hubbs, President
Gregory Hubbs, Editor-in-Chief

3963 Workforce Preparation: An International Perspective
The Johns Hopkins University Press
2715 North Charles Street
Baltimore, MD 21218-4319
410-516-6989
800-530-9673
Fax: 410-516-8805
muse@press.jhu.edu
www.muse.jhu.edu
Excellent collection of material by 20 prominent educators describes efforts in developed and developing countries worldwide to prepare youth and adults for work.

Dean Smith, Director
Wendy Queen, Deputy Director

3964 World of Learning
Europa Publications
18 Bedford Square
London WC1B 3JN
England
00 -00 - 7 8
171-580-8236
Fax: 171-636-1664
www.europa.eu
Details over 26,000 educational, cultural and scientific institutions throughout the world, together with an exhaustive directory of over 150,000 people active within them.

2,072 pages Annual
ISBN: 0-946653-92-5

Directories & Handbooks / Financial Aid

3965 Catalog of Federal Domestic Assistance
Office of Management & Budget
Washington, DC 20402
www.https://www.cfda.gov/
Offers information from all federal agencies that have assistance programs (loans, scholarships and technical assistance as well as grants) and compiles these into the CFDA. The individual entries are grouped by Department of Agency and includes an excellent set of instructions and several indices. Indices allow the user to search for grants by subject matter, agency, deadline date or eligibility criteria.

3966 Chronicle Financial Aid Guide
Chronicle Guidance Publications
66 Aurora Street
Moravia, NY 13118-3569
315-497-0330
800-622-7284
Fax: 315-497-3359
customerservice@chronicleguidance.com
www.chronicleguidance.com
Financial aid programs offered primarily by noncollegiate organizations, independent and AFL-CIO affiliated labor unions and federal and state governments for high school seniors and undergraduate and graduate students.

Publication Date: 1938 460 pages Annual
ISBN: 1-5563-310-1

Janet Seemann, Author
Cheryl Fickeisen, President and CEO
Gary Fickeisen, Vice President

3967 College Costs and Financial Aid Handbook
College Board
250 Vesey Street
New York, NY 10281
212-713-8000
www.collegeboard.org
A step-by-step guide providing facts on costs plus financial aid and scholarship availability at 3,200 two- and four-year institutions.

David Coleman, Chief Executive Officer
Jeremy Singer, President

3968 College Financial Aid Annual
Arco/Macmillan
1633 Broadway
Floor 7
New York, NY 10019-6708
212-654-8933
Lists of private businesses, academic institutions and other organizations that provide awards and scholarships for financial aid; guide to federal and state financial aid.

3969 Directory of Educational Contests for Students K-12
ABC-CLIO
147 Castilian Drive
Santa Barbara, CA 93117
805-968-1911
800-368-6868
Fax: 866-270-3856
customerservice@abc-clio.com
www.abc-clio.com

3970 Directory of Financial Aid for Women
Reference Service Press
2310 Homestead Rd
Suite C1 #219
Los Altos, CA 94024
650-861-3170
Fax: 650-861-3171
rspinfo@aol.com
www.rspfunding.com
Offers information on more than 1,500 scholarships, fellowships, loan sources, grants, awards and internships.
490 pages
Gail Schlachter, President
R. David Weber, Editor-in-Chief

3971 Directory of Institutional Projects Funded by Office of Educational Research
U.S. Office of Educational Research & Improvement
555 New Jersey Avenue NW
Washington, DC 20208-5573
202-219-2079
Fax: 202-219-2135
www.https://www2.ed.gov/pubs/TeachersGuide/oeri.html
Publication Date: 1990 60 pages

3972 Directory of International Grants & Fellowships in the Health Sciences
National Institutes of Health
9000 Rockville Pike
Building 31, Room B2C29
Bethesda, MD 20892-2220
301-496-4000
Fax: 301-594-1211
NIHinfo@od.nih.gov
www.nih.gov
Fellowships and grants listed separately in this guide. Each listing includes a complete program description with contact information.
Publication Date: 1887
Francis S. Collins, M.D., Ph.D., Director

3973 Don't Miss Out: The Ambitous Students Guide to Financial Aid
Octameron Associates
1900 Mt Vernon Avenue
P.O. Box 2748
Alexandria, VA 22301-0748
703-836-5480
Fax: 703-836-5650
www.octameron.com
Publication Date: 0 192 pages Anually

3974 Fellowships in International Affairs-A Guide to Opportunities in the US & Abroad
Lynne Rienner Publishing
1800 30th Street
Suite 314
Boulder, CO 80301
303-444-6684
Fax: 303-444-0824
www.rienner.com
This guide lists fellowships meant to encourage women to pursue careers in international security.
Publication Date: 1984

3975 Fellowships, Scholarships and Related Opportunities
Center for International Ed./University of TN
1620 Melrose Avenue
University of Tennessee
Knoxville, TN 37996-3531
865-974-3177
Fax: 865-974-2985
international@utk.edu
www.international.utk.edu
140 grants, scholarships and fellowships available to citizens of the United States for study or research abroad.
50 pages Biennial

3976 Financial Aid for Research & Creative Activities Abroad
Reference Service Press
2310 Homestead Rd
Suite C1 #219
Los Altos, CA 94024
650-861-3170
Fax: 650-861-3171
www.rspfunding.com
This book lists opportunities fir high school students and undergraduates, graduates, postdoctoral students, professionals and others.
432 pages
ISBN: 1588410625
Gail Schlachter, President
R.David Weber, Editor-in-Chief

3977 Financial Aid for Study Abroad: a Manual for Advisers & Administrators
NAFSA: Association of International Educators
1425 K Street NW
Suite 1200
Washington, DC 20005
202-737-3699
inbox@nafsa.org
www.nafsa.org
105 pages
Esther D. Brimmer, Executive Director & CEO
Dorothea Antonio, Deputy Executive Director

3978 Foundation Grants to Individuals
Foundation Center
79 Fifth Avenue/16th Street
New York, NY 10003-3076
212-260-4230
Fax: 212-807-3677
www.foundationcenter.org
Features current information for grant seekers.
Publication Date: 1956
Melissa Berman, President and CEO
Patrick Collins, CFO

3979 Free Money for College: Fifth Edition
Facts On File
132 West 31st Street
17th Floor
New York, NY 10001
800-322-8755
custserv@factsonfile.com
www.factsonfile.com
1,000 grants and scholarships.
Publication Date: 1999 240 pages Annual
Hardcover
ISBN: 081603947X
Laurie Blum, Author
Laurie Likoff, Editorial Director

3980 Free Money for Foreign Study: A Guide to 1,000 Grants for Study Abroad
Facts On File
132 West 31st Street
17th Floor
New York, NY 10001
800-322-8755
custserv@factsonfile.com
www.factsonfile.com
Lists organizations and institutions worldwide offering scholarships and grants for study outside the United States.
262 pages
Laurie Likoff, Editorial Director

3981 Fund Your Way Through College: Uncovering 1,100 Opportunities in Aid
Visible Ink Press/Gale Research
43311 Joy Road
#414
Canton, MI 48187-2075
734-667-3211
Fax: 734-667-4311
www.visibleinkpress.com
1,100 scholarships, grants, loans, awards and prizes for undergraduate students.
470 pages

3982 German-American Scholarship Guide-Exchange Opportunities for Historians and Social Scientist
German Historical Institute
1607 New Hampshire Avenue NW
Washington, DC 20009-2562
202-387-3355
Fax: 202-387-6437
www.ghi-dc.org
This guide is divided into two sections: scholarships for study and research in the US and scholarships for study and research in Germany.
Hartmut Berghoff, Director
Uwe Spiekmann, Deputy Director

3983 Getting Funded: The Complete Guide to Writing Grant Proposals
Continuing Education Press
400 W First St
Chico, CA 95929-0250
530-898-6105
866-647-7377
Fax: 530-898-6105
rce@csuchico.edu
www.rce.csuchico.edu
A step-by-step guide to writing successful grants and proposals. An indispensible reference for experienced and first-time grant writers alike.
180 pages Paperback
ISBN: 0-87678-071-0
Mary Hall, Author
Debra Barger, Administration
Joe Picard, Director

3984 Graduate Scholarship Book
Pearson Education
1 Lake Street
Upper Saddle River, NJ 07458
201-909-6200
Fax: 201-767-5029
www.pearsoned.com
A complete guide to scholarships, grants and loans for graduate and professional study.
441 pages Biennial

3985 Grant Writing Beyond The Basics: Proven Strategies Professionals Use To Make Proposals
Continuing Education Press
400 W First St
Chico, CA 95929-0250
530-898-6105
866-647-7377
Fax: 530-898-6105
rce@csuchico.edu
www.rce.csuchico.edu
Designed to inspire those with grant writing experience who want to take their development strategies to the next level.
128 pages Paperback
ISBN: 0-87678-117-2
Michael K Wells, Author
Debra Barger, Administration
Joe Picard, Director

3986 Grants & Awards Available to American Writers
PEN American Center
588 Broadway
Suite 303
New York, NY 10012
212-334-1660
Fax: 212-334-2181
www.pen.org
Includes a full program description and is then broken down by type of writing. Awards for work in a particular country are listed alphabetically by country.
340 pages Paperback
ISBN: 0-934638-20-9
Peter Godwinÿ, President
John Troubh, Executive Vice-President

3987 Grants Register
MacMillan Publishers
16365 James Madison Highway
Gordonsville, VA 22942
888-330-8477
Fax: 800-672-2054
press.inquiries@macmillan.com
www.us.macmillan.com
This directory offers a comprehensive list of programs organized alphabetically with special attention to eligibility requirements. Index by subject.

3988 Grants, Fellowships, & Prizes of Interest to Historians
American Historical Association
400 A Street SE
Washington, DC 20003-3889
202-544-2422
Fax: 202-544-8307
aha@theaha.org
www.historians.org
This guide offers information on awards for historians from undergraduate to postgraduate grants, fellowships, prizes, internships and awards.
Publication Date: 1884
Jim Grossman, Executive Director
Shatha Almutawa, Associate Editor

3989 Guide to Department of Education Programs
US Department of Education
400 Maryland Avenue SW
Washington, DC 20202-0001
202-401-2000
800-872-5327
www.ed.gov
Programs of financial aid offered by the Department of Education.
Publication Date: 1980 35 pages Annual
Emma Vadehra, Chief of Staff
James Cole, Jr., General Counsel

3990 Harvard College Guide to Grants
Office of Career Services
Harvard University
54 Dunster Street
Cambridge, MA 02138
617-495-2595
Fax: 617-495-3584
www.ocs.fas.harvard.edu
This guide describes national and regional grants and fellowships for study in the US, study abroad and work and practical experience.
234 pages Paperback

3991 How to Find Out About Financial Aid & Funding
Reference Service Press
2310 Homestead Rd.
Suite C1 #219
Los Altos, CA 94024
650-861-3170
Fax: 650-861-3171
rspinfo@aol.com
www.rspfunding.com
Over 700 financial aid directories and Internet sites described and evaluated.
432 pages Hardcover
ISBN: 1588410935
Gail A Schlachter, Author
Gail Schlachter, President
R. David Weber, Editor-in-Chief

3992 International Foundation Directory
Europa Publications
11 New Fetter Lane
London
England EC4P 4EE
00 -00 - 7 8
44-0-20-7842-2110
Fax: 44-0-20-7842-2249
www.europa.eu
A world directory of international foundations, trusts and similar non-profit institutions. Provides detailed information on over 1,200 institutions in some 70 countries throughout the world.
Publication Date: 1994 736 pages
ISBN: 1-857430-01-8
Paul Kelly, Editorial Director

3993 International Scholarship Book: The Complete Guide to Financial Aid
Pearson Education
1 Lake Street
Upper Saddle River, NJ 07458
201-909-6200
Fax: 201-767-5029
www.pearsoned.com
Offers information on private organizations providing financial aid for university students interested in studying in foreign countries.
335 pages Cloth

3994 Journal of Student Financial Aid
University of Notre Dame
Office of Financial Aid
Notre Dame, IN 46556
574-631-5000
www.nd.edu
Offers a listing of private and federal sources of financial aid for college bound students.
3x Year
Rev. John I. Jenkins, President
Thomas G. Burish, Provost

3995 Loans and Grants from Uncle Sam
Octameron Associates
1900 Mount Vernon Avenue
PO Box 2748
Alexandria, VA 22301-0748
703-836-5480
Fax: 703-836-5650
Offers information on federal student loan and grant programs and state loan guarantee agencies.
72 pages Annual
ISBN: 1-57509-097-X
Anna Leider, Author

3996 Money for Film & Video Artists
American for the Art
1000 Vermont Avenue NW
6th Floor
Washington, DC 20005
202-371-2830
Fax: 202-371-0424
www.artsusa.org
The listings are organized by sponsoring organization and entries include basic application and program information.
Abel Lopez, Chair
Ramona Baker, Vice Chair

3997 Money for International Exchange in the Arts
American for the Art
1000 Vermont Avenue NW
6th Floor
Washington, DC 20005
202-371-2830
Fax: 202-371-0424
www.artsusa.org
A guide to the various resources available to support artists and arts organizations in international work.
Abel Lopez, Chair
Ramona Baker, Vice Chair

3998 Money for Visual Artists
America for the Art
1000 Vermont Avenue NW
6th Floor
Washington, DC 20005
202-371-2830
Fax: 202-371-0424
www.artsusa.org
Programs are listed alphabetically by sponsor with detailed program description.
Abel Lopez, Chair
Ramona Baker, Vice Chair

3999 National Association of State Scholarship and Grant Program Survey Report
National Association of State Scholarship Programs
8 W. 38TH ST
Suite 503
New York, NY 10018-1324
917-551-6770
contact@nas.org
www.nas.org

Listing of over 50 member state agencies administering scholarship and grant programs for student financial aid.

Publication Date: 1987 150 pages

Peter Wyatt Wood, President
Ashley Thorne, ExecutiveÿDirector

4000 National Association of Student Financial Aid Administrators Directory
1801 Pennsylvania Avenue NW
Suite 850
Washington, DC 20006-3606
202-785-0453
Fax: 202-785-1487
info@nasfaa.org
www.nasfaa.org/Directory_of_Associations
Offers information on institutions of postsecondary education and their financial aid administrators.

Brent Tener, National Chairÿ
Justin Draeger, President & CEO

4001 Need A Lift?
The American Legion
700 N Pennsylvania Street
P.O. Box 36460
Indianapolis, IN 46236-1050
317-630-1200
888-453-4466
Fax: 317-630-1381
emblem@legion.org
www.EMBLEM.legion.org
Sources of career, scholarship and loan information or assistance.

144 pages Annual/Paperback

Robert Caudell, Author

4002 Peterson's Grants for Graduate and Postdoctoral Study
Peterson's, A Nelnet Company
Princeton Pike Corporate Center
461 From Road
Paramus, NJ 07652
609-698-1800
800-338-3282
Fax: 402-458-3042
support@petersons.com
www.petersons.com
Only comprehensive source of current information on grants and fellowships exclusively for graduate and postdoctoral students.

Publication Date: 1998 5th Edition
ISBN: 1-560794-01-1

4003 Peterson's Sports Scholarships and College Athletic Programs
Peterson's, A Nelnet Company
Princeton Pike Corporate Center
461 From Road
Paramus, NJ 08648
609-896-1800
800-338-3282
Fax: 402-458-3042
support@petersons.com
www.petersons.com
A college-by-college look at scholarships designated exclusively for student athletes in 32 men's and women's sports.

Publication Date: 2004 624 pages 5th Edition
ISBN: 0768915244

4004 Scholarship Handbook
College Board
250 Vesey Street
New York, NY 10281
212-713-8000
www.collegeboard.org
Useful text for college-bound students, their families and guidance counselors. Offers more than 2,000 descriptions of national and state level award programs, public and private education loan programs, internship opportunities and more.

David Coleman, Chief Executive Officer
Jeremy Singer, President

4005 Scholarships for Emigres Training for Careers in Jewish Education
Jewish Foundation for Education of Women
135 E 64th Street
New York, NY 10065
212-288-3931
Fax: 212-288-5798
fdnscholar@aol.com
www.jfew.org
Open to emigres from the former Soviet Union who are pursuing careers in Jewish education. Candidates in Jewish education, rabbinical and cantorial studies, and Jewish studies are invited to write the Foundation.

Elizabeth Leiman Kraiem, Executive Director
Jill Weber Smith, Chair

4006 Scholarships, Fellowships and Loans
Gale Research
27500 Drake Road
Farmington Hills, MI 48231-5477
800-877-4253
Fax: 877-363-4253
www.cengage.com
Written especially for professionals, students, counselors, parents and others interested in education. This resource provides more than 3,700 sources of education-related financial aid and awards at all levels of study.

Publication Date: 1995 1,290 pages Annual
ISBN: 0-810391-14-7

Michael E. Hansen, CEO
Fernando Bleichmar, Chief Strategy Officer

4007 Student Guide
Federal Student Aid Information Center
PO Box 84
Washington, DC 20044-0084
800-433-3243
800-433-3243
www.https://studentaid.ed.gov
Describes the federal student aid programs, and general information about the eligibility criteria, application procedures and award levels, and lists important deadlines and phone numbers.

54 pages

John J McCarthy, Director

4008 Study Abroad
U.N. Educational, Scientific & Cultural Assn.
7, place de Fontenoy
F-75700 Paris
France
1-45681123
Listing of over 200,000 scholarships, fellowships and educational exchange opportunities offered for study in 124 countries.

1,300 pages Biennial

4009 Write Now: A Complete Self-Teaching Programfor Better Handwriting
Continuing Education Press
400 W First St
Chico, CA 95929-0250
530-898-6105
866-647-7377
Fax: 530-898-4020
rce@csuchico.edu
www.rce.csuchico.edu
A step-by-step guide to improving one's handwriting. Develop clean and legible italic handwriting with regular practice.

128 pages Paperback
ISBN: 0-87678-089-3

Barbara Getty & Inga Dubay, Author
Debra Barger, Administration
Joe Picard, Director

Directories & Handbooks / Guidance & Counseling

4010 Accredited Institutions of Postsecondary Education
MacMillan Publishers
16365 James Madison Highway
Gordonsville, VA 22942
888-330-8477
Fax: 800-672-2054
press.inquiries@macmillan.com
www.us.macmillan.com
Lists over 5,000 accredited institutions and programs for postsecondary education in the United States.

4011 Adolescent Pregnancy Prevention Clearinghouse
Children's Defense Fund Education & Youth Develop.
25 E Street NW
#400
Washington, DC 20001-2109
202-628-8787
800-233-1200
Fax: 202-662-3560
cdfinfo@childrensdefense.org
www.childrensdefense.org
Provides information and clarification on the connection between pregnancy and broader life questions for youth.

Marian Wright Edelman, President
Richard Gollub, Chief Financial Officer

4012 COLLEGESOURCE
Career Guidance Foundation
8090 Engineer Road
San Diego, CA 92111-1906
858-560-8051
800-854-2670
Fax: 858-278-8960
www.collegesource.org
CD-ROM and Web College Catalog Collection. Contains colleges and universitie's catalogs from throughout the US, over 2,600. Also a college search program that can be searched by major, tuition costs, and more. Foreign catalogs available.

Annette Crone, Account Coordinator
David Hunt, Account Coordinator

4013 Cabells Directory of Publishing Opportunities in Educational Psychology and Administration
Cabell Publishing Company
Box 5428
Tobe Hahn Station
Beaumont, TX 77726
409-898-0575
Fax: 409-866-9554
info@cabells.com
www.cabells.com
Provides information on editor contact information, manuscript guidelines, acceptance rate, review information and circulation data for over 225 academic journals.

Publication Date: 1978 799 pages Annual
ISBN: 0-911753-19-2

David WE Cabell, Editor
Deborah L English, Associate Editor

4014 Career & Vocational Counseling Directory
American Business Directories
5711 S 86th Circle
Omaha, NE 68127-4146
402-593-4600
888-999-1307
Fax: 402-331-5481
www.americanbusinessandservicedirectory.com
Nationwide listing of 3,300 companies/consultants available in print, computer magnetic tape and diskette, mailing labels, and index cards listing the name, address, phone, size of advertisement, contact person and number of employees.
Annual
Jerry Venner, Coordinating Education

4015 College Handbook
College Board
250 Vesey Street
New York, NY 10281
212-713-8000
www.collegeboard.org
Descriptions of 3,200 colleges and universities.
David Coleman, Chief Executive Officer
Jeremy Singer, President

4016 College Handbook Foreign Student Supplement
College Board
250 Vesey Street
New York, NY 10281
212-713-8000
www.collegeboard.org
Lists about 2,800 colleges and universities that are open to foreign students.
David Coleman, Chief Executive Officer
Jeremy Singer, President

4017 College Transfer Guide
School Guide Publications
210 N Avenue
New Rochelle, NY 10801-6402
914-632-7771
800-433-7771
Fax: 914-632-3412
mridder@schoolguides.com
www.schoolguides.com
Five hundred four-year colleges in the Northeast and Midwest that accept transfer students listing transfer requirements, deadlines, fees, enrollment, costs and contact information. Circulation, 60,000.
125 pages Annual/January

4018 Community College Exemplary Instructional Programs
Massachusetts Bay Community College Press
50 Oakland Street
Wellsley Hills, MA 02181
781-239-3000
Fax: 781-237-1061
www.massbay.edu
Community college programs identified as outstanding by the National Council of Instructional Administrators.
Publication Date: 1961
John O'Donnell, President

4019 Comparative Guide to American Colleges for Students, Parents & Counselors
HarperCollins
195 Broadway
New York, NY 10007-5244
212-207-7000
Fax: 212-207-7145
www.harpercollins.com
Accredited four-year colleges in the United States.
800 pages Cloth

4020 Directory of Play Therapy Training
University of North Texas
PO Box 310829
425 S. Welch St., Complex 2
Denton, TX 76203
940-565-3864
Fax: 940-565-4461
cpt@unt.edu
www.centerforplaytherapy.com
Provides training, research publications and serves as a clearinghouse for literature in the field.
Paperback
Rinda Thomas, Office Manager
Sue C Bratton, Center Director

4021 Educators Guide to FREE Guidance Materials
Educators Progress Service
214 Center Street
Randolph, WI 53956-1408
920-326-3126
888-951-4469
Fax: 920-326-3127
epsinc@centurytel.net
www.freeteachingaids.com
Lists and describes free films, videotapes, filmstrips, slides, web sites, and hundreds of free printed materials in the field of career education and guidance for all age levels.
190 pages Annual
ISBN: 87708-406-8
Kathy Nehmer, President

4022 Index of Majors and Graduate Degrees
College Board
250 Vesey Street
New York, NY 10281
212-713-8000
www.collegeboard.org
Includes descriptions of over 600 majors and identifies the 3,200 colleges, universities, and graduate schools that offer them.
David Coleman, Chief Executive Officer
Jeremy Singer, President

4023 Tests: a Comprehensive Reference for Psychology, Education & Business
PRO-ED
8700 Shoal Creek Boulevard
Austin, TX 78757-6897
512-451-3246
800-897-3202
Fax: 800-397-7633
general@proedinc.com
www.proedinc.com
This fifth edition groups updated information on approximately 2,000 assessment instruments into three primary classifications-psychology, education, and business-and 89 subcategories, enabling users to readily identify the tests that meet their assessment needs. Each entry contains a statement of the instrument's purpose, a concise description of the instrument, scoring procedures, cost, and publisher information.
Publication Date: 1991 809 pages Paperback/Hardcover
ISBN: 0-89079-709-9
Taddy Maddox, General Editor

4024 Vocational Biographies
Vocational Biographies
PO Box 31
Sauk Centre, MN 56378-0031
320-352-6516
800-255-0752
Fax: 320-352-5546
careers@vocbio.com
www.vocbio.com
Real life career success stories of persons in every walk of life that allow students to see a career through the eyes of a real person. New for 2005: Internet Access to 1001 Career Success Stories.
Toby Behnen, President
Roxann Behnen, Customer Service/Sales

4025 What Works and Doesn't With at Risk Students
BKS Publishing
3109 150th Place SE
Mill Creek, WA 98012-4864
425-745-3029
Fax: 425-337-4837
DocBlokk@aol.com
www.literacyfirst.com
Publication Date: 1919 162 pages Paperback
ISBN: 0-9656713-0-5
Jan Glaes, Author
Bill Blokker, Owner

4026 World of Play Therapy Literature
Center for Play Therapy
PO Box 311337
5308 Valley Ridge Plaza
Middleton, WI 53562
608-203-8646
Fax: 608-203-5872
www.playtherapymadison.com
Author and topical listings of over 6,000 books, dissertations, documents, and journal articles on play therapy, updated every two years.
Publication Date: 1995 306 pages
Landreth, Homeyer, Bratton, Kale, Hipl, Schumann, Author

Directories & Handbooks / Language Arts

4027 Classroom Strategies for the English Language Learner
Master Teacher
One Leadership Lane
PO Box 1207
Manhattan, KS 66502-1207
800-669-9633
Fax: 800-669-1132
www.masterteacher.com
A practical model for accelerating both oral language and literacy development, based on the latest research for effective instruction of both Native English speakers and English language learners.
266 pages
ISBN: 1-58992-068-6
Socrro Herrera EdD, Author

4028 Italic Handwriting Series-Book A
Continuing Education Press
400 W First St
Chico, CA 95929-0250

530-898-6105
866-647-7377
Fax: 530-898-4020
rce@csuchico.edu
www.rce.csuchico.edu
Book A is the first workbook of a seven-part series. Designed for the beginning reader and writer, it introduces the alphabet one letter at a time. Illustrated.

64 pages Paperback
ISBN: 0-87678-092-3

Barbara Getty & Inga Dubay, Author
Debra Barger, Administration
Joe Picard, Director

4029 Italic Handwriting Series-Book B
Continuing Education Press
400 W First St
Chico, CA 95929-0250
530-898-6105
866-647-7377
Fax: 530-898-4020
rce@csuchico.edu
www.rce.csuchico.edu
Book B is the second workbook of a seven-part series. Designed for the beginning reader and writer. Introduces words and sentences, lowercase and capitol print script, one letter per page. Illustrated.

59 pages Paperback
ISBN: 0-87678-093-1

Barbara Getty & Inga Dubay, Author
Debra Barger, Administration
Joe Picard, Director

4030 Italic Handwriting Series-Book C
Continuing Education Press
400 W First St
Chico, CA 95929-0250
530-898-6105
866-647-7377
Fax: 530-898-4020
rce@csuchico.edu
www.rce.csuchico.edu
Book C is the third workbook of a seven-part series. Covers basic italic and introduces the cursive. Words and sentences include days of week, months of year, modes of transportation, and tongue twisters. Illustrated.

60 pages Paperback
ISBN: 0-87678-094-X

Barbara Getty & Inga Dubay, Author
Debra Barger, Administration
Joe Picard, Director

4031 Italic Handwriting Series-Book D
Continuing Education Press
400 W First St
Chico, CA 95929-0250
530-898-6105
866-647-7377
Fax: 530-898-4020
rce@csuchico.edu
www.rce.csuchico.edu
Book D is the fourth workbook of a seven-part series. Reviews basic italic and covers the total cursive program. Includes prefixes, suffixes, capitalization, and playful poems. Explores history of the alphabet. Illustrated.

80 pages Paperback
ISBN: 0-87678-095-8

Barbara Getty & Inga Dubay, Author
Debra Barger, Administration
Joe Picard, Director

4032 Italic Handwriting Series-Book E
Continuing Education Press
400 W First St
Chico, CA 95929-0250
530-898-6105
866-647-7377
Fax: 530-898-4020
rce@csuchico.edu
www.rce.csuchico.edu
Book E is the fifth workbook of a seven-part series. Reviews basic italic and covers the total cursive program. Writing practice covers natural history— plants, volcanoes, cities. Explores history of the alphabet. Illustrated.

56 pages Paperback
ISBN: 0-87678-096-6

Barbara Getty & Inga Dubay, Author
Debra Barger, Administration
Joe Picard, Director

4033 Italic Handwriting Series-Book F
Continuing Education Press
400 W First St
Chico, CA 95929-0250
530-898-6105
866-647-7377
Fax: 530-898-4020
rce@csuchico.edu
www.rce.csuchico.edu
Book F is the sixth workbook of a seven-part series. Reviews basic italic and covers the total cursive program. Writing practice emphasizes figures of speech (e.g. homophones, puns, metaphors, acronyms). Explores history of the alphabet. Illustrated.

56 pages Paperback
ISBN: 0-87678-097-4

Barbara Getty & Inga Dubay, Author
Debra Barger, Administration
Joe Picard, Director

4034 Italic Handwriting Series-Book G
Continuing Education Press
400 W First St
Chico, CA 95929-0250
530-898-6105
866-647-7377
Fax: 530-898-4020
rce@csuchico.edu
www.rce.csuchico.edu
Book G is the seventh workbook of a seven-part series. A comprehensive self-instruction program in basic and cursive italic. Writing content follows a central theme-the history of our alphabet. Suitable for older students. Illustrated.

56 pages Paperback
ISBN: 0-87678-098-2

Barbara Getty & Inga Dubay, Author
Debra Barger, Administration
Joe Picard, Director

4035 Language Schools Directory
American Business Directories
5711 S 86th Circle
Omaha, NE 68127-4146
402-593-4600
888-999-1307
Fax: 402-331-5481
www.americanbusinessandservicedirectory.com
A listing of language schools, arranged by geographic location, offering contact information which is updated on a continual basis, and printed on request. Directory is also available in electronic formats.

Jerry Venner, Coordinating Education

4036 Picture Book Learning Volume-1
Picture Book Learning Inc.
PO Box 270075
Louisville, CO 80027
303-548-2809
todd@picturebooklearning.com
www.picturebooklearning.com
Teachers can use this fun method of teaching elementary children basic language arts skills through the use of picture books.

60 pages
ISBN: 0-9760725-0-5

Todd Osborne, Co-President
Corinne Osborne, Editor

4037 Process of Elimination - a Method of Teaching Basic Grammar - Teacher Ed
Scott & McCleary Publishing Company
2482 11th Street SW
PO Box 3830
Akron, OH 44314-0830
702-566-8756
800-765-3564
Fax: 702-568-1378
jscott7576@aol.com
www.scottmccleary.com
Series of 7 steps designed to teach basic grammar skills to students in middle grades through college. Available in a teacher edition and a student workbook.

50 pages
ISBN: 0-9636225-2-8
ISSN: 0-9636225-

Milton Metheny, Author
Janet Scott, Publisher
Sheila McCleary, Publisher

4038 Process of Elimination: A Method of Teaching Basic Grammar - Student Ed
Scott & McCleary Publishing Company
2482 11th Street SW
PO Box 3830
Akron, OH 44314-0830
702-566-8756
800-765-3564
Fax: 702-568-1378
jscott7576@aol.com
www.scottmccleary.com
Series of 7 steps designed to teach basic grammar skills to students in middle grades through college. Available in a teacher edition and a student workbook.

Milton Metheny, Author
Janet Scott, Publisher
Sheila McCleary, Publisher

4039 Put Reading First: The Research Building Blocks For Teaching Children To Read
ED Pubs
P.O. Box 22207
Alexandria, VA 22304-1398
877-4ED-PUBS
Fax: 703-605-6794
edpubs@inet.ed.gov
www.edpubs.org
Provides analysis and discussion in five areas of reading instruction: phonemic awareness, phonics, fluency, vocabulary and text comprehension.

4040 Write Now: A Complete Self Teaching Program for Better Handwriting
Continuing Education Press
400 W First St
Chico, CA 95929-0250
530-898-6105
866-647-7377
Fax: 530-898-4020
rce@csuchico.edu
www.rce.csuchico.edu
Finally, a handwriting improvement book for adults. Teach yourself to write legibly and retain it over time using this step-by-step guide to modern italic handwriting with complete instructions as well as practice exercises and

tips. The secret to legible handwriting is the absence of loops in letterform, making it easier to write and easier to read.

96 pages Paperback
ISBN: 0-87678-089-3

Barbara Getty & Inga Dubay, Author
Debra Barger, Administration
Joe Picard, Director

Directories & Handbooks / Library Services

4041 Directory of Manufacturers & Suppliers
Special Libraries Association
331 S Patrick Street
Alexandria, VA 22314-3501
703-647-4900
Fax: 703-647-4901
sla@sla.org
www.sla.org
The SLA network consists of nearly 15,000 librarians and information professionals who specialize in the arts, communication, business, social science, biomedical sciences, geosciences and environmental studies, and industry, business, research, educational and technical institutions, government, special departments of public and university libraries, newspapers, museums, and public or private organizations that provide or require specialized information.

Doug Newcomb, Deputy CEO
Linda Broussard, Chief Financial Officer

4042 Directory of Members of the Association for Library and Information Science Education
Assn. for Library & Information Science Education
4 Lan Drive
Suite 310
Westford, MA 01886
978-674-6190
office@alise.org
www.alise.org
The Directory is designed to serve as a handbook for the association, including a list of officers, committees, and interest groups and strategic planning information for the association. Also listed are graduate schools of library and information science and their faculty.

Cambria Happ, Executive Director
Mega Subramaniam, Director, Programming

4043 Libraries Unlimited
ABC-CLIO
147 Castilian Drive
Santa Barbara, CA 93117
805-968-1911
800-368-6868
Fax: 866-270-3856
customerservice@abc-clio.com
www.abc-clio.com
Catalog includes reference, collection development, library management, cataloging, and technology.

4044 Managing Info Tech in School Library Media Centers
Libraries Unlimited, ABC-CLIO
147 Castilian Drive
Santa Barbara, CA 93117
805-968-1911
800-368-6868
Fax: 866-270-3856
customerservice@abc-clio.com
www.abc-clio.com

Publication Date: 2000 290 pages Hardcover
ISBN: 1-56308-724-3

4045 Managing Media Services Theory and Practice
Libraries Unlimited, ABC-CLIO
147 Castilian Drive
Santa Barbara, CA 93117
805-968-1911
800-368-6868
Fax: 866-270-3856
customerservice@abc-clio.com
www.abc-clio.com

Publication Date: 2002 418 pages
ISBN: 1-56308-530-5

Directories & Handbooks / Music & Art

4046 College Guide for Visual Arts Majors
Peterson's, A Nelnet Company
Princeton Pike Corporate Center
461 From Road
Paramus, NJ 07652
609-896-1800
800-338-3282
Fax: 402-458-3042
support@petersons.com
www.petersons.com
Offers descriptions of over 700 accredited US colleges and universities, music conservatories, and art/design schools that grant undergraduate degrees in the areas of studio art.

Publication Date: 2006 404 pages
ISBN: 1-560795-36-0

4047 Community Outreach and Education for the Arts Handbook
Music Teachers National Association
PO Box 261452
Littleton, CO 80163-1452
303-565-5351
888-512-5278
Fax: 555-555-1212
mtnanet@mtaa.org
www.mtaa.org
Resource booklet for independent music teachers.

Paperback
March
150 booths with 2500 attendees

Chad Schwatbach, Pr/Marketing Associate

4048 Italic Letters
Continuing Education Press
400 W First St
Chico, CA 95929-0250
530-898-6105
866-647-7377
Fax: 530-898-4020
rce@csuchico.edu
www.rce.csuchico.edu
Italic Letters is for professional and amateur calligraphers, art teachers, and enthusiasts of the book arts. Numerous tips on letter shapes, spacing, slant, pen edge angle, and other secrets to handsome writing.

128 pages Paperback
ISBN: 0-87678-091-5

Barbara Getty & Inga Dubay, Author
Debra Barger, Administration
Joe Picard, Director

4049 Money for Film & Video Artists
American for the Art
1000 Vermont Avenue NW
6th Floor
Washington, DC 20005
202-371-2830
Fax: 202-371-0424
www.artsusa.org
The listings are organized by sponsoring organization and entries include basic application and program information.

Abel Lopez, Chair
Ramona Baker, Vice Chair

4050 Money for Visual Artists
America for the Art
1000 Vermont Avenue NW
12th Floor
Washington, DC 20005
202-371-2830
Fax: 202-371-0424
www.artsusa.org
Programs are listed alphabetically by sponsor with detailed program description.

Abel Lopez, Chair
Ramona Baker, Vice Chair

4051 School Arts
Davis Publications, Inc.
50 Portland Street
Worcester, MA 01608
800-533-2847
Fax: 508-753-3834
www.schoolartsdigital.com
Companies offering products, materials, and art education resources or programs that focus on the history of art, multicultural resources such as Fine Art, reproductions, CD-Roms, museum education, programs, slides, books, videos, exhibits, architecture, timelines, and resource kits.

Directories & Handbooks / Physical Education

4052 Educators Guide to FREE HPER Materials
Educators Progress Service
214 Center Street
Randolph, WI 53956-1408
920-326-3126
888-951-4469
Fax: 920-326-3127
epsinc@centurytel.net
www.freeteachingaids.com
Lists and describes free films, videotapes, filmstrips, slides, web sites, and hundreds of free printed materials in the field of health, physical education, and recreation for all age levels.

184 pages Annual
ISBN: 87708-407-6

Kathy Nehmer, President

Directories & Handbooks / Professional Development

4053 International Handbook for Cooperative and Work-Integrated Education
World Association for Cooperative Education
University of Waterloo
200 University Avenue W
Waterloo, ON N2L-3G1
admin@waceinc.org
www.waceinc.org
Sub-titled International Perspectives of Theory, Research and Practice, this handbook provides wide coverage of the areas of cooperative educa-

tion and work-integrated learning, with an emphasis on research-informed practice.

Richard K. Coll, Editor
Karsten E. Zegwaard, Editor

Directories & Handbooks / Reading

)54 Diagnostic Reading Inventory for Bilingual Students in Grades 1-8
Scott & McCleary Publishing Company
2482 11th Street SW
PO Box 3830
Akron, OH 44314-0830
702-566-8756
800-765-3564
Fax: 702-568-1378
jscott7576@aol.com
www.scottmccleary.com
Series of 13 tests designed to access reading performance. IRI, spelling, phonics, visual and auditory discrimination and listening comprehension are just some of the tests included.

155 pages
ISBN: 0-9636225-1-X

Janet M Scott, Co-Author
Sheila C McCleary, Co-Author

)55 Diagnostic Reading Inventory for Primary and Intermediate Grades K-8
Scott & McCleary Publishing Company
2482 11th Street SW
PO Box 3830
Akron, OH 44314-0830
702-566-8756
800-765-3564
Fax: 702-568-1378
jscott7576@aol.com
www.scottmccleary.com
Designed to assess reading performance in grades K-8. Tests include: word recognition, oral reading inventory, comprehension, listening comprehension, auditory and visual discrimination, auditory and visual memory, learning modalities inventory, phonics mastery tests, structural analysis, word association and a diagnostic spelling test.

260 pages
ISBN: 0-9636225-4-4

Janet M Scott, Co-Author
Sheila C McCleary, Co-Author

)56 Laubach Literacy Action Directory
Laubach Literacy Action
222 Waverly Avenue
Syracuse, NY 13244-2010
315-422-9121
888-528-2224
Fax: 315-422-6369
info@laubach.org
www.library.syr.edu
Listing of over 1,100 local literacy councils and associates who teach the Laubach Method.

Publication Date: 1955 90 pages Annual

)57 Ready to Read, Ready to Learn
ED Pubs
P.O. Box 22207
Alexandria, VA 22304-1398
703-605-6794
Fax: 703-605-6794
edpubs@inet.ed.gov
www.edpubs.org

4058 Tips for Reading Tutors
ED Pubs
P.O. Box 22207
Alexandria, VA 22304-1398
877-4ED-PUBS
Fax: 703-605-6794
edpubs@inet.ed.gov
Basic tips for reading tutors

Directories & Handbooks / Secondary Education

4059 College Board Guide to High Schools
College Board
250 Vesey Street
New York, NY 10281
212-713-8000
www.collegeboard.org
Offers listings and information on over 25,000 public and private high schools nationwide.

David Coleman, Chief Executive Officer
Jeremy Singer, President

4060 Compendium of Tertiary & Sixth Forum Colleges
SCOTVIC: S McDonald, Principal
Ridge College
Manchester
England
61-4277733
Offers listings of over 200 Sixth Form and Tertiary Colleges in the United Kingdom offering courses preparing secondary students for university study.

Publication Date: 1990 200 pages Biennial

4061 Directory of Public Elementary and Secondary Education Agencies
US National Center for Education Statistics
1990 K Street, NW
8th & 9th Floors
Washington, DC 20006-5651
202-502-7300
800-424-1616
Fax: 202-502-7466
www.nces.ed.gov
Directory of approximately 17,000 local education agencies that operate their own schools or pay tuition to other local education agencies.

400 pages Annual

Peggy G. Carr, Acting Commissioner
Lena McDowell, Contact

4062 Educators Guide to FREE Family and Consumer Education Materials
Educators Progress Service
214 Center Street
Randolph, WI 53956-1408
920-326-3126
888-951-4469
Fax: 920-326-3127
epsinc@centurytel.net
www.freeteachingaids.com
Lists and describes free films, videotapes, filmstrips, slides, web sites, and hundreds of free printed materials in the field of home econominics and consumer education for all age levels.

161 pages Annual
ISBN: 87708-408-4

Kathy Nehmer, President

4063 Focus on School
ABC-CLIO
147 Castilian Drive
Santa Barbara, CA 93117
805-968-1911
800-368-6868
Fax: 866-270-3856
customerservice@abc-clio.com
www.abc-clio.com
Hotlines, print and nonprint resources on education for young adults.

Publication Date: 1990

4064 Great Source Catalog
Great Source Education Group
PO Box 7050
Wilmington, MA 01887
800-289-4490
Fax: 800-289-3994
www.hmhco.com
Alternative, affordable, student-friendly K-12 materials to make teaching and learning fun for educators and students.

4065 Helping Your Child Succeed In School: Elementary and Secondary Editions
Master Teacher
One Leadership Lane
Manhattan, KS 66502-1207
785-539-0555
800-669-9633
Fax: 800-669-1132
www.masterteacher.com
Provides a way for school administrators to help parents help their children succeed in school. Published in English and Spanish.

Erica Paronson, Executive Editor

4066 Lesson Plans for Integrating Technology into the Classroom: Secondary Edition
Master Teacher
One Leadership Lane
PO Box 1207
Manhattan, KS 66502-1207
800-669-9633
Fax: 800-669-1132
www.masterteacher.com
Gives teachers practical lessons developed and tested by teachers across the curriculum, with students of all levels of ability in using technology.

104 pages
ISBN: 1-58992-152-6

4067 Lesson Plans for Problem-Based Learning: Secondary Edition
Master Teacher
One Leadership Lane
PO Box 1207
Manhattan, KS 66502-1207
800-669-9633
Fax: 800-669-1132
www.masterteacher.com
An instructional technique which organizes the curriculum around a major problem that students work to solve over the weeks or months.

117 pages
ISBN: 0-914607-87-1

4068 Lesson Plans for the Substitute Teacher: Secondary Edition
Master Teacher
One Leadership Lane
PO Box 1207
Manhattan, KS 66502-1207
800-669-9633
Fax: 800-669-1132
www.masterteacher.com
Gives you more than 100 lessons developed and tested by teachers across the curriculum and at all grade levels.

177 pages
ISBN: 1-58992-108-9

4069 Peterson's Private Secondary Schools
Peterson's, A Nelnet Company
Princeton Pike Corporate Center
461 From Road
Paramus, NJ 07652-2123
609-896-1800
800-338-3282
Fax: 402-458-3042
support@petersons.com
www.petersons.com
Listing of over 1,400 accredited and state-approved private secondary schools in the US and abroad.
1,300 pages Annual

4070 Secondary Teachers Guide to FREE Curriculum Materials
Educators Progress Service
214 Center Street
Randolph, WI 53956-1408
920-326-3126
888-951-4469
Fax: 920-326-3127
epsinc@centurytel.net
www.freeteachingaids.com
Lists and describes free supplementary teaching aids for the high school and college level.
296 pages Annual
ISBN: 87708-399-1
Kathy Nehmer, President

Directories & Handbooks / Science

4071 Earth Education: A New Beginning
Institute for Earth Education
Cedar Cove
PO Box 115
Greenville, WV 24945
304-832-6404
Fax: 304-832-6077
info@ieetree.org
www.eartheducation.org
This book proposes another direction-an alternative that many environmental leaders and teachers around the world have already taken. It is called The Earth Education Path, and anyone can follow it in developing a genuine program made up of magical learning adventures.
334 pages Paperback
ISBN: 0917011023
Steve Van Matre, Chairman

4072 Earthkeepers
Institute for Earth Education
Cedar Cove
PO Box 115
Greenville, WV 24945
304-832-6404
Fax: 304-832-6077
ieel@aol.com
www.eartheducation.org
This book will give you the best picture of what a complete earth education program involves. Even if you can't set up the complete Earthkeepers program, there are many activities you can use to build an earth education program in your own settting and situation.
108 pages Paperback
ISBN: 0917011015
Bruce Johnson, Chairman

4073 Educators Guide to FREE Science Materials
Educators Progress Service
214 Center Street
Randolph, WI 53956-1408
920-326-3126
888-951-4469
Fax: 920-326-3127
www.freeteachingaids.com
Lists and describes free films, videotapes, filmstrips, slides, web sites, and hundreds of free printed materials in the field of science for all age levels.
Annual
Kathy Nehmer, President

4074 K-6 Science and Math Catalog
Carolina Biological Supply Co.
2700 York Road
PO Box 6010
Burlington, NC 27216-6010
336-584-0381
800-334-5551
Fax: 336-538-6330
quotations@carolina.com
www.carolina.com
Service teaching materials for grades Pre K through 8, including charts, computers, software, books, living animals and plants, microscopes, microscope slides, models, teaching kits and more.
Publication Date: 1927

4075 Science for All Children; A Guide to Improving Science Education
National Academy Press
Smithsonian Information
P.O. Box 23293
Washington, DC 20026-3293
202-633-1000
Fax: 202-287-2070
info@si.edu
Provides concise and practical guidelines for implementing science education reform at local level, including the elements of an effective, inquiry-based, hands-on science program. Produced by the National Science Resources Center. Published by National Academy Press.
240 pages
ISBN: 0-309-05297-1
National Science Resources Center, Author
John McCarter Jr., Chair
Shirley Ann Jackson, Vice Chair

4076 Sunship Earth
Institute for Earth Education
Cedar Cove
PO Box 115
Greenville, WV 24945
304-832-6404
Fax: 304-832-6077
ieel@aol.com
www.eartheducation.org
Contains clear descriptions of key ecological concepts and concise reviews of important learning principals, plus over 200 additional pages of ideas, activities and guidelines for setting up a complete Sunship Earth Study Station.
265 pages Paperback
ISBN: 0876030460
Bruce Johnson, Chairman

4077 Sunship III
Institute for Earth Education
Cedar Cove
PO Box 115
Greenville, WV 24945
304-832-6404
Fax: 304-832-6077
ieel@aol.com
www.eartheducation.org
Examines perception and choice in our daily habits and routines. It is about exploration and discovery in the larger context of where and how we live, and examining alteratives and making sacrifices on behalf of a healthier home planet.
133 pages Paperback
ISBN: 0917011031
Bruce Johnson, Chairman

4078 UNESCO Sourcebook for Out-of-School Science & Technology Education
U.N. Educational, Scientific & Cultural Assn.
7, place de Fontenoy
F-75700 Paris
France
Offers information on science clubs, societies and congresses, science fairs and museums.
145 pages

Directories & Handbooks / Social Studies

4079 Directory of Central America Classroom Resources
Central American Resource Center
2845 West 7th Street
Los Angeles, CA 90005-2012
213-385-7800
Fax: 213-385-1094
info@carecen-la.org
www.carecen-la.org
Offers information on suppliers of education resource materials about Central America, including curricula, materials, directories and organizations providing related services.
Publication Date: 1990 200 pages
Angela Sanbrano, President
Gloria Annicchiarico, Vice President

4080 Educators Guide to FREE Social Studies Materials
Educators Progress Service
214 Center Street
Randolph, WI 53956-1408
920-326-3126
888-951-4469
Fax: 920-326-3127
www.freeteachingaids.com
Lists and describes free films, videotapes, filmstrips, slides, web sites, and hundreds of free printed materials in the field of social studies for all age levels.
287 pages Annual
ISBN: 87708-405-X
Kathy Nehmer, President

4081 Geography: A Resource Book for Secondary Schools
ABC-CLIO
147 Castilian Drive
Santa Barbara, CA 93117
805-968-1911
800-368-6868
Fax: 866-270-3856
customerservice@abc-clio.com
www.abc-clio.com
List of organizations and associations to use as resources for secondary education geography studies.

Directories & Handbooks / Technology in Education

4082 American Trade Schools Directory
Croner Publications
10951 Sorrento Valley Road
Suite 1D
San Diego, CA 92121
858-546-1954
800-441-4033
Fax: 858-546-1955
paul@croner.com
www.ww.croner.com
Loose leaf binder directory listing trade and technical schools throughout the United States, in alphabetical order, by state, then city, then school name.

411 pages
ISBN: 0-875140-02-5

Rosa Padilla, Office Manager

4083 Association for Educational Communications & Technology: Membership Directory
Assn. for Educational Communications & Technology
320 W 8th Street
Suite 101
Bloomington, IN 47404-3745
812-335-7675
877-677-2328
aect@aect.org
www.aect.org
Five thousand audiovisual and instructional materials specialists and school media specialists, with audio-visual and TV production personnel. Also listed are committees, task force divisions, auxiliary affiliates, state organizations and directory of corporate members.

Xun Ge, President
Ellen Wagner, Interim Executive Director

4084 Chronicle Vocational School Manual
Chronicle Guidance Publications
66 Aurora Street
Moravia, NY 13118-3569
315-497-0339
800-899-0454
Fax: 315-497-3359
customerservice@chronicleguidance.com
www.chronicleguidance.com
A geographical index of more than 3,500 vocational schools including all contact information, programs, admissions requirements, costs, financial aid programs and student services.

Publication Date: 1938 300 pages Annual
ISBN: 1-556312-50-4

Cheryl Fickeisen, President/ CEO
Gary Fickeisen, Vice President

4085 Directory of Public Vocational-Technical Schools & Institutes in the US
Media Marketing Group
Voorhees Town Center
220 Laurel Road
Voorhees, NJ 08043-0611
856-782-6000
Fax: 856-385-7155
www.2mg.com
Offers information on over 1,400 post secondary vocational and technical education programs in public education; private trade and technical schools are not included.

Publication Date: 1994 400 pages Biennial
ISBN: 0-933474-51-2

Frank Palmieri, President

4086 Directory of Vocational-Technical Schools
Media Marketing Group
Voorhees Town Center
220 Laurel Road
Voorhees, NJ 08043-0611
856-782-6000
Fax: 856-385-7155
Offers information on public, postsecondary schools offering degree and non-degree occupational education.

Publication Date: 1996 450 pages Biennial
ISBN: 0-933474-52-0

Frank Palmieri, President

4087 Educational Film & Video Locator
RR Bowker Reed Reference
121 Chanlon Road
New Providence, NJ 07974-1541
908-665-2834
Fax: 908-464-3553
www.sabre.org
Producers and distributors of educational films.

Publication Date: 1990

4088 Guide to Vocational and Technical Schools East & West
Peterson's, A Nelnet Company
Princeton Pike Corporare Center
461 From Road
Paramus, NJ 07652
609-896-1800
800-338-3282
Fax: 402-458-3042
support@petersons.com
www.petersons.com
These two directories cover the full range of training programs in over 240 career fields divided into the categories of Business, Technology, Trade, Personal Services, and Health Care. East edition covers East of Mississippi; West edition covers West of the Mississippi.

Publication Date: 2006 579 pages Per Volume

4089 Industrial Teacher Education Directory
National Assn. of Industrial Teacher Educators
University of Northern Iowa
Cedar Falls, IA 50614-0178
319-273-2561
Fax: 319-273-5818
www.uni.edu/indtech
Listing of about 2,800 industrial education faculty members at 250 universities and four-year colleges in the United States, Canada, Australia, Japan and Taiwan.

108 pages Annual

M Fahmy, Professor/Head of Department
Charles Johnson, Coordinator of Tech Ed. Prog

4090 Information Literacy: Essential Skills for the Information Age
Syracuse University
900 South Crouse Ave
Syracuse, NY 13244-0001
315-443-1870
800-464-9107
Fax: 315-443-5448
www.syr.edu
Traces history, development, and economic necessity of information literacy. Reports on related subject matter standards. Includes reports on the National Educational Goals (1991), the Secretary's Commission on Achieving Necessary Skills Report (1991), and the latest updates from ALA's Information Power (1998).

377 pages
ISBN: 0-937597-44-9

Richard L. Thompson, Chairman
Kenneth E. Goodman, Vice Chair

4091 Internet Resource Directory for Classroom Teachers
Regulus Communications
140 N 8th Street
Suite 201
Lincoln, NE 68508-1358
402-432-2680
www.regulus.com/
Directory offering information on all resources available on-line for classroom teachers, including e-mail addresses, Home Page URL's, phone and fax numbers, surface-mail addresses, classroom contacts and teaching resources. Available in paper and electronic formats.

Publication Date: 1996 272 pages Paper Format

Jane A Austin, Coordinating Education

4092 K-12 District Technology Coordinators
Quality Education Data
601 E. Marshall St
Suite 250
Sweet Springs, MO 65351-4715
303-860-1832
800-776-6373
Fax: 660-335-4157
info@qeddata.com
www.qeddata.com
The first in QED's National Educator Directories, this comprehensive directory of technology coordinators combines QED's exclusive database of technology and demographic data with names of technology coordinators in the 7,000 largest US school districts. The directory includes district phone number, number of students in the district, number of computers, student/computer ratio and predominant computer brand.

Publication Date: 1994 400 pages

Peter Long, CEO
John F. Hood, President

4093 NetLingo.Com
805-794-8687
info@netlingo.com
www.netlingo.com
An easy-to-understand dictionary of 10,000+ internet terms, plus every online acronym any user will ever need to know, this modern reference book is written by a woman using layman's language and is for international students, educators, industry professionals and online businesses and organizations.

Publication Date: 0
ISBN: 0-9706396-7-8

Erin Jansen, Author
Erin Jansen, Founder

4094 Quick-Source
AM Educational Publishing
P.O. Box 247
Suite D
Harrisonburg, VA 22801-3048
866-293-5313
800-296-5750
Fax: 540-433-5640
info@quicksourcelearning.com
www.https://www.quicksourcelearning.com/
Educational technology directory with over 1,100 names, addresses, phones/faxes, and brief descriptions of the products/services of

companies/organizations; supports major works/word processors (MS-DOS/MAC); conferences and other educational technology listings.

Annual/September

4095 Schools Industrial, Technical & Trade Directory

American Business Directories
5711 S 86th Circle
Omaha, NE 68127-4146
402-593-4600
888-999-1307
Fax: 402-331-5481
A geographical listing of over 3,750 schools with all contact information, size of advertisement and first year in Yellow Pages. Also available in electronic formats.

Annual

Jerry Venner, Coordinating Education

4096 TESS: The Educational Software Selector

EPIE Institute
103 W Montauk Highway
PO Box 590
Hampton Bays, NY 11946-4003
631-728-9100
Fax: 631-728-9228
A list of over 1,200 suppliers of educational software and over 18,000 educational software products (on CD-ROM) for pre-school through college information. Includes description of program, grade level data, price, platform and review citations.

Publication Date: 1967

Nancy Boland, Coordinating Education

4097 Tech Directions-Directory of Federal & Federal and State Officials Issue

Prakken Publications
416 Longshore Drive
PO Box 8623
Ann Arbor, MI 48107-8623
734-975-2800
Fax: 313-577-1672
www.https://www.techdirections.com
Listing of federal and state officials concerned with vocational, technical, industrial trade and technology education in the United States and Canada.

Annual

Susanne Peckham, Managing Editor
Pam Moore, Assistant Editor

4098 Technology in Public Schools

Quality Education Data
601 E. Marshall St
Suite 250
Sweet Springs, MO 65351-4715
303-860-1832
800-776-6373
Fax: 660-335-4157
www.qeddata.com
Annual survey of instructional technology represents more than 67% of all US K-12 students. Includes computer brand and processor type market share, CD-ROM, networks, LAN, modem, cable and in-depth internet access installed base information.

Publication Date: 1994 160 pages Yearly
ISBN: 0-88947-925-1

Peter Long, CEO
John F. Hood, President

Periodicals / General

4099 AACS Newsletter

American Association of Christian Schools
602 Belvoir Avenue
East Ridge, TN 37412-2221
423-629-4280
Fax: 423-622-7461
www.aacs.org
Association news offering the most up-to-date information relating to Christian education.

Publication Date: 1972 4 pages Monthly

Dr. Carl Herbster, Contact

4100 AAHE Bulletin

American Association for Higher Education
4505 S. Maryland Parkway
Box 453068
Las Vegas, NV 89154-3068
702-895-2737
Fax: 702-895-4269
ASHE@unlv.edu
www.ashe.ws
Electronic newsletter

16 pages Monthly

Kim Nehls, Ph.D, Executive Director
Holly Schneider, Conference Coordinator

4101 ACJS Today

Academy of Criminal Justice Services
7339 Hanover Parkway
Suite A
Greenbelta, MD 20770
301-446-6300
800-757-2257
Fax: 301-446-2819
www.acjs.org
Provides upcoming events, news releases, ACJS activities, ads, book reviews and miscellaneous information.

24-32 pages Quarterly

Brian Payne, President
Brandon Applegate, 1st Vice President

4102 ASCD Education Update

Association for Supervision & Curriculum Develop.
1703 N Beauregard Street
Alexandria, VA 22311-1714
press@ascd.org
www.ascd.org
News on contemporary education issues and information on ASCD programs.

Publication Date: 1943

Ranjit Sidhu, CEO & Executive Director
Dana Shanks-Williams, Chief Financial Officer

4103 ASSC Newsletter

Arkansas School Study Council
500 Woodlane Street
Suite 256
Little Rock, AR 72201
501-682-1010
Fax: 479-442-2038
www.sos.arkansas.gov
Monthly up-date on education, finance, new legislation, mandates for Arkansas public schools.

3-10 pages

Judith Crouch, Human Resources
Laura Labay, Public Affairs

4104 AV Guide Newsletter

Educational Screen
380 E NW Highway
Des Plaines, IL 60016-2201
847-298-6622
Fax: 847-390-0408
Provides concise and practical information on audiovisually oriented products with an emphasis on new ideas and methods of using learning media, including educational computer software.

Monthly
ISSN: 0091-360X

HS Gillette, Publisher
Natalie Ferguson, Editor

4105 Academe

American Association of University Professors
1133 Nineteenth Street, NW
Suite 200
Washington, DC 20036-3406
202-737-5900
Fax: 202-737-5526
aaup@aaup.org
www.aaup.org
A thoughtful and provocative review of developments affecting higher education faculty. With timely features and informative departments, Academe delivers the latest on the state of the profession, legal and legislative trends, and issues in academia.

BiMonthly

Lawrence Hanley, Editor, Author
Julie Schmid, Executive Director
Elona M. Jouben, Executive Assistant

4106 Aero Gramme

Alternative Education Resource Organizations
417 Roslyn Road
Roslyn Heights, NY 11577-2620
516-621-2195
800-769-4171
Fax: 516-625-3257
info@educationrevolution.org
www.educationrevolution.org
Networks all forms of educational alternatives, from public and private alternative schools to homeschooling.

Quarterly

Jerry Mintz, Director
Chri Mercogliano, Course Instructor

4107 Agenda: Jewish Education

Jewish Education Service of North America
247 West 37th Street
5th Floor
New York, NY 10018
212-284-6950
Fax: 212-284-6951
Seeks to create a community of discourse on issues of Jewish public policy dealing with Jewish education and the indications of policy options for the practice of Jewish education.

Quarterly
ISSN: 1072-1150

Cass Gottlieb, Chair
Sandra Gold, Vice Chair

4108 American Educational Research Journal

American Educational Research Association
1430 K Street NW
Suite 1200
Washington, DC 20005
202-238-3200
Fax: 202-238-3250
publications@aera.net
www.aera.net
Publishes articles that advance understandings of education and learning across all subfields and disciplines.

Ellen Goldring, Editor-in-Chief

4109 American Journal of Education
University of Chicago
5801 South Ellis Avenue
Chicago, IL 60637
773-702-1234
Fax: 773-702-6207
aje@uchicago.edu
www.uchicago.edu

Quarterly

Robert Dreeben and Zalman Usiskin, Author
Robert J. Zimmer, President
Eric D. Isaacs, Provost

4110 American Music Teacher (AMT)
Music Teachers National Association
600 Vine Street
Suite 1710
Cincinnati, OH 45202
513-421-1420
888-512-5278
Fax: 513-421-2503
amt@mtna.org
www.mtna.org
Official publication of the Music Teachers National Association, with articles, reviews and columns helping music teachers excel in the classroom.

Publication Date: 1951

Gary L. Ingle, Executive Director & CEO
Marcie Gerrietts Lindsey, Director, Publishing

4111 American Scholar
1785 Massachusetts Avenue NW
4th Floor
Washington, DC 20036-2117
202-265-3808
A general interest magazine that includes articles on science, literature, and book reviews.

Quarterly

Anne Fadiman, Editor

4112 American Students & Teachers Abroad
US Government Printing Office
732 N Capitol Street NW
Washington, DC 20401
202-512-1800
Fax: 202-512-2104

4113 Annual Report
Jessie Ball duPont Fund
One Dependent Drive
Suite 1400
Jacksonville, FL 32202-5011
904-353-0890
800-252-3452
Fax: 904-353-3870
contactus@dupontfund.org
www.dupontfund.org
Focused on a variety of good work aimed at growing the capacity of the nonprofit sector.

Publication Date: 0 Annually

4114 Association of Orthodox Jewish Teachers of the New York Public Schools
Association of Orthodox Jewish Teachers of the NY
1577 Coney Island Avenue
Brooklyn, NY 11230-4715
718-258-3585
Fax: 718-258-3586
www.aojt.org
Newsletter representing observant Jewish teachers in the New York City Public Schools.

Publication Date: 1963 8-12 pages Quarterly Newsletter

Nechemia Aaron Oberstein, President
Rachel B. Lieff, Vice President

4115 Between Classes-Elderhostel Catalog
Road Scholar
11 Avenue de Lafayette
Boston, MA 02111-1913
617-426-7788
Fax: 617-426-8351
www.roadscholar.org
Seasonal listings of elderhostel educational programs offered by educational cultural institutions in the US and 60 countries overseas.

120 pages Quarterly

Heather Baynes, Contact

4116 Blumenfeld Education Newsletter
PO Box 45161
Boise, ID 83711-5161
Providing knowledge to parents and educators who want to save children of America from destructive forces that endanger them. Children in public schools are at grave risk in 4 ways: academically, spiritually, morally, physically, and only a well-informed public will be able to reduce these risks.

8 pages

Peter F Watt, Publisher
Samuel L Blumenfeld, Editor

4117 Brighton Times
Brighton Academy/Foundation of Human Understanding
1121 NE 7th Street
PO Box 1000
Grants Pass, OR 97528-1421
541-474-6865
800-877-3227
Fax: 541-956-6705
www.https://www.fhu.com/aboutroy.html
Home schooling information.

Monthly

Cynthia Coumoyer, Contact

4118 Brochure of American-Sponsored Overseas Schools
Office of Overseas Schools, Department of State
Room H328
SA-1
Washington, DC 20522-132
202-261-8200
Fax: 202-261-8224
OverseasSchools@state.gov
www.state.gov

Dr. Keith D. Miller, Director
Antony Blinken, Deputy Secretary

4119 Business Today
Princeton University
48 University Place
Suite 305
Princeton, NJ 08544
info@businesstoday.org
www.businesstoday.org
Oldest program of the Foundation for Student Communication at Princeton University, with a distribution base of over 200,000 students and executives.

Publication Date: 1968 Bi-annual

Sowon Lee, President
Richard Qiu, Director, Finance

4120 Business-Education Insider
Heritage Foundation
214 Massachusetts Avenue NE
Washington, DC 20002-4999
202-546-4400
Fax: 202-546-8328
www.heritage.org
Deals with issues relating to the corporate/business world, and the effects it has on education.

Monthly

George Adams, Senior Production Specialist
David S. Addington, Group VP, Research

4121 CBE Report
Association for Community Based Education
1806 Vernon Street NW
PO BOX 70587
Washington, DC 20024-0587
202-462-6333
www.faqs.org
Educational institutions covering news, workshops and resources.

Monthly

4122 CEDS Communique
Council for Exceptional Children
3100 Clarendon Boulevard
Suite 600
Arlington, VA 22201-5332
888-232-7733
service@exceptionalchildren.org
www.exceptionalchildren.org
Reports on the activities of the Council for Educational Diagnostic Services and information about special programs, upcoming events, current trends and practices, and other topical matters.

Bi-Annual

4123 Center Focus
Center of Concern
1225 Otis Street NE
Washington, DC 20017-2516
202-635-2757
Fax: 202-832-9494
coc@coc.org
www.coc.org
Newsletters addressing the everchanging needs and concerns in the education field.

6 pages BiMonthly

Raymond W. Baker, President
Claire M. Cifaloglio, M.D., Pediatrician

4124 Center for Continuing Education of Women Newsletter
University of Michigan
Ann Arbor, MI 48109
734-763-1400
Fax: 734-936-1641
Association news focusing on the concerns of women in education.

4 pages

4125 Center for Parent Education Newsletter
81 Wyman Street
Wapham, MA 02160
617-964-2442
Offers information and tips to address parent involvement in the education of their children.

BiMonthly

4126 Change
Taylor & Francis
325 Chestnut Street
Suite 800
Philadelphia, PA 19106-1802

215-625-8900
800-365-9753
Fax: 202-296-5149
customer.service@taylorandfrancis.com
www.heldref.org
Perspectives on the critical issues shaping the world of higher education. It is not only issue-oriented and reflective, but challenges the status quo in higher education.

BiMonthly

Margaret A Miller, President
Theodore J Marchese, VP/Editor

4127 Chronicles of Quaker Education
Friends Council on Education
1507 Cherry Street
Philadelphia, PA 19102
215-241-7245
Fax: 267-519-5317
info@friendscouncil.org
www.friendscouncil.org
Print newsletter of the Friends Council on Education.

Drew Smith, Executive Director
Betsy Torg, Director, Development

4128 Clearing House: A Journal of Educational Research
Taylor & Francis
325 Chestnut Street
Suite 800
Philadelphia, PA 19106-1826
215-625-8900
800-365-9753
Fax: 202-296-5149
customer.service@taylorandfrancis.com
www.heldref.org
Each issue offers a variety of articles for teachers and administrators of middle schools and junior and senior high schools. It includes experiments, trends and accomplishments in courses, teaching methods, administrative procedures and school programs.

4 pages BiMonthly
ISSN: 0009-8655

Deborah N Cohen, Promotions Manager
Judy Cusick, Managing Editor

4129 Commuter Perspectives
National Clearinghouse for Commuter Programs
Western Illinois University
3300 River Drive
Moline, IL 61265-9634
309-762-8843
Fax: 301-314-9874
www.wiu.edu
A quarterly newsletter published by the National Clearinghouse for Commuter Programs for professionals who work for, with, and on behalf of commuter students.

8 pages Quarterly

Dr. Kristi Mindrup, Co-Director
Dr. Melissa Mahan, Co-Director

4130 Congressional Digest
301-528-7777
Fax: 301-634-3189
support@congressionaldigest.com
www.congressionaldigest.com
An independent, scholarly publication featuring debates within the U.S. Supreme Court, presented in a neutral manner.

Publication Date: 1921

Sarah Orrick, Editor

4131 ConneXions
Association of International Schools in Africa
Peponi Road
PO Box 14103, Nairobi
Kenya 00800
254- 20- 269
254-20-2697442
Fax: 254- 20- 418
Fax: 254-20-4183272
info@aisa.or.ke
www.aisa.or.ke
Published twice per year, ConneXions is AISA's print and online newsletter

Peter Bateman, Executive Director
Thomas Shearer, Chairperson

4132 Contemporary Education
Indiana State University, School of Education
200 North Seventh Street
Terre Haute, IN 47809-9989
877-856-8005
Fax: 812-856-8088
www.coe.indstate.edu
A readable and currently informative journal of topics in the mainstream of educational thought.

Quarterly
ISSN: 0010-7476

Todd Whitaker, Editor
Beth Whitaker, Editor

4133 Contemporary Issues in Technology and Teacher Education (CITE)
AMTE, c/o Meredith College
3800 Hillsborough Street
Raleigh, NC 27607
919-760-8240
Fax: 919-760-8763
harpersr@miamioh.edu
www.citejournal.org
An online, peer-reviewed journal including articles on the cross-section of teacher education and technology integration.

Quarterly

Michael D. Steele, President
Tim Hendrix, Executive Director

4134 Creativity Research Journal
Lawrence Erlbaum Associates
10 Industrial Avenue
Mahwah, NJ 07430-2262
201-258-2200
800-926-6579
Fax: 201-236-0072
www.erlbaum.com
A peer-reviewed journal covering a full range of approaches including behavioral, cognitive, clinical developmental, educational, social and organizational. Online access is available by visiting LEAonline.com

Quarterly
ISSN: 1040-0419

Mark A Runco, PhD., Editor

4135 Currents Magazine
Council for Advancement & Support of Education
1201 Eye Street NW
Washington, DC 20005
202-328-2273
Fax: 202-387-4973
membersupportcenter@case.org
www.case.org
Published nine times a year and distributed to professional members, Currents delivers essential information, insight and ideas that empower those who support education to master challenges and act decisively to create a better future for their institutions and the world.

Sue Cunningham, President & CEO
Rob Moore, VP, Communications

4136 DCDT Network Newsletter
Council for Exceptional Children
3100 Clarendon Boulevard
Suite 600
Arlington, VA 22201-5332
888-232-7733
service@exceptionalchildren.org
www.exceptionalchildren.org
Newsletter of the Division on Career Development and Transition. Provides the latest information on legislation, projects, resource materials and implementration strategies in the field of career development and transition for persons with disabilities and/or who are gifted. Carries information about Division activities, upcoming events, announcements and reports of particular interest to DCDT members.

3 Issues/Year

4137 DECA Dimensions
1908 Association Drive
Reston, VA 20191-1503
703-860-5000
Fax: 703-860-4013
info@deca.org
www.deca.org
An educational nonprofit association news management for marketing education students across the country, Canada, Guam and Puerto Rico. Offers information on DECA activities, leadership, business and career skills, which help develop future leaders in business, marketing and management.

36 pages Quarterly
ISSN: 1060-6106

Carol Lund, Author
Chuck Beatty, Project Manager
Cindy Allen, Director

4138 DLD Newsletter
Council for Exceptional Children
3100 Clarendon Boulevard
Suite 600
Arlington, VA 22201-5332
888-232-7733
service@exceptionalchildren.org
www.exceptionalchildren.org
Information concerning education and welfare of children and youth with learning disabilities, published by the Division for Learning Disabilities.

4139 Decision Line
Decision Sciences Institute
334 Melcher Hal
Suite 325
Houston, TX 77204-6021
713-743-4815
Fax: 713-743-8984
info@decisionsciences.org
www.decisionsciences.org
Contains articles on education, business and decision sciences as well as available positions and textbook advertising.

32 pages 5x Year

E. Powell Robinson, Jr., Interim Executive Director
Dana L. Evans, Program Director

4140 Desktop Presentations & Publishing
Doron & Associates
291 Farmington Avenue
Farmington, CT 6032-5421
860-677-8666
866-764-5378
Fax: 860-677-5839
dental_associates@sbcglobal.net

Computer generated presentations and visual aids for education and business.

16 pages BiMonthly

Tom Doron, Contact

141 Development and Alumni Relations Report

LRP Publications
360 Hiatt Drive
Suite 700
Palm Beach Gardens, FL 33418
561-622-6520
800-341-7874
Fax: 561-622-1375
custserve@lrp.com
www.lrp.com

Provides colleges and universities with innovative ideas for improving: alumni relations; the involvement of alumni in clubs and chapters; annual giving; endowment and capital campaigns; and planned giving. Plus, you can recieve free e-mail updates on crucial news affecting your job with your paid subscription.

Monthly Newsletter

Kenneth F. Kahn, President

142 Different Books

Place in the Woods
111 Third Avenue South
Suite 290
Minneapolis, MN 55401-5302
612-627-1970
Fax: 612-627-1980
ump@umn.edu
www.upress.umn.edu

Special imprint of books by, for and about persons on a different path. Features main characters with disabilities as heroes and heroines in storyline. For hi-lo reading in early elementary grades (3-7).

Publication Date: 1925 Paperback

Roger Hammer, Publisher

143 Directions

AFS Intercultural Programs USA
71 West 23rd Street
6th Floor
New York, NY 10010-4102
212-807-8686
Fax: 212-807-1001
www.afs.org

News of AFS US volunteers.

6 pages Monthly

Dr. Vincenzo Morlini, President/ CEO
Dr. Urs-Rainer von Arx, VP, CFO & Operation Officer

144 Disability Compliance for Higher Education

LRP Publications
360 Hiatt Drive
Suite 700
Palm Beach Gardens, FL 33418
561-622-6520
800-341-7874
Fax: 561-622-1375
custserve@lrp.com
www.lrp.com

Newsletter helps colleges determine if they're complying with the Americans with Disabilities Act (ADA) and Section 504 of the Rehabilitation Act- so they can avoid costly litigation. Gives tips on how to provide reasonable accommodations in test-taking, grading, admissions, and accessibility to programs and facilities.

Monthly
ISSN: 1086-1335

Edward Filo, Author
Kenneth F. Kahn, President

4145 Diversity 2000

Holocaust Resource Center
Kean College
1000 Morris Avenue
Union, NJ 07083

Offers ideas and issues on multicultural school education programs.

BiMonthly

Janice Kroposky, Director
Helen Walzer, Assistant Director

4146 ERIC/CRESS Bulletin

AEL, Inc.
102 E. Keefe Ave
Milwaukee, WI 53212-1348
414-265-7630
866-656-1486
Fax: 414-265-7628
sales@aelseating.com
www.https://www.aelseating.com

Announces new developments in the ERIC system nationally, and publications and events relevant to American Indians, Alaska Natives, Mexican Americans, migrants, outdoor education and rural, small schools.

3x Year Newsletter

Patricia Hammer Cahape, Associate Director

4147 Eagle Forum

Eagle Education Fund
P.O. BOX 17113
Fountain Hills, AZ 85269-8110
www.fhgeef.org

News on the Eagle Education Fund.

Quarterly

Ralph Norman, President
Pam McNeil, 1st Vice President

4148 EdPress News

PreK-12 Learning Group
325 Chestnut St.
Ste. 1110
Philadelphia, PA 19106
267-351-4310
Fax: 267-351-4317
www.aepweb.org

The Association supports the growth of educational publishing and it's positive effects on learning and teaching. EdPress provides information and analysis of markets and trends, education and legislative policy, learning and teaching research, and intellectual property. The Association also provides training and staff development programs, promotes supplemental learning resources as essential curriculum materials, and advocates on issues relevant to its constituents.

Jay Diskey, Executive Director
Stacey Pusey, Editorial Director

4149 Education

Project Innovation
1362 Santa Cruz Court
Chula Vista, CA 91910-7114
760-630-9938
rcassel5@aol.com
www.rcassel.com

Original investigations and theoretical articles dealing with education. Preference given to innovations, real or magical, which promise to improve learning.

160 pages Quarterly
ISSN: 0013-1172

Dr. Russell Cassel, Editor
Lan Mieu Cassel, Managing Editor

4150 Education Digest

Prakken Publications
PO Box 8623
3970 Varsity Drive
Ann Arbor, MI 48107-8623
734-975-2800
800-530-9673
Fax: 734-975-2787
www.eddigest.com

Offers outstanding articles condensed for quick review from over 200 magazines, monthlies, books, newsletters and journals, timely and important for professional educators and others interested in the field.

80 pages Monthly
ISSN: 0013-127X

George F Kennedy, Publisher
Kenneth Schroeder, Managing Editor

4151 Education Hotline

Editorial Projects in Education
6935 Arlington Road
Suite 100
Bethesda, MD 20814
301-280-3100
800-445-8250
Fax: 301-280-3250
ads@epe.org
www.edweek.org

Education newsletter.

4152 Education Newsletter Library Counterpoint

LRP Publications
360 Hiatt Drive
Suite 700
Palm Beach Gardens, FL 33418
561-622-6520
800-341-7874
Fax: 561-622-1375
custserve@lrp.com
www.lrp.com

Offers its readers concise, informative and timely articles covering innovative practices in special education. Covers: special education news from the states; updates on curriculum; developments in special education technology; classified ads; descriptions of new products and publications; and more.

On-Line

Kenneth F. Kahn, President

4153 Education Newsline

National Association of Christian Educators
PO Box 3200
Costa Mesa, CA 92628-3200
949-251-9333
www.naceoffice.com

Articles pertinent to public education for teachers and parents, current trends and solutions and the work of Citizens for Excellence in Education.

Publication Date: 1972 8 pages BiMonthly

Robert Simonds, Publisher
Kathi Hudson, Editor

4154 Education Northwest Newsletter

Education Northwest
1417 NW Everett Street
Suite 310
Portland, OR 97209
800-547-6339
www.educationnorthwest.org

E-newsletter containing information about news, products, and workshops from Education Northwest.

Patty Wood, Chief Executive Officer
Jeff Strickler, Chief Operating Officer

4155 Education Quarterly
New Jersey State Department of Education
100 Riverview Plaza
PO Box 500
Trenton, NJ 08625-500
877-900-6960
www.state.nj.us/education
New Jersey education information and updates.
6 pages Quarterly
Richard Vespucci, Contact

4156 Education USA
LRP Publications
360 Hiatt Drive
Suite 1106
Palm Beach Gardens, FL 33418
561-622-6520
800-341-7874
Fax: 561-622-1375
custserve@lrp.com
www.lrp.com
Offers information on court decisions, federal funding, the national debate over standards, education research, school finance, and more. Subscribers receive biweekly reports on Education Department policies on Title I, special education, bilingual education, drug-free schools and other issues affecting schools nationwide.
8-10 pages BiWeekly
Kenneth F. Kahn, President

4157 Education Update
Heritage Foundation
214 Massachusetts Avenue NE
Washington, DC 20002-4999
202-546-4400
Fax: 202-544-7330
www.heritage.org
Contains analyses of policy issues and trends in US education.

4158 Education Week
Editorial Projects in Education, Inc.
6935 Arlington Road
Suite 100
Bethesda, MD 20814-5233
301-280-3100
800-346-1834
Fax: 301-280-3250
ads@epe.org
www.edweek.org
For principals, superintendents, director, managers and other administrators.

4159 Education in Focus
Books for All Times
PO Box 2
Alexandria, VA 22313-0002
703-548-0457
jdavid@bfat.com
Examines failures and successes of public and private education by looking beneath the surface for answers and explanations.
6 pages BiAnnually
ISSN: 1049-7250
Joe David, Editor

4160 Educational Forum
University of Colorado-Denver, School of Education
PO Box 173364
Campus Box 106
Denver, CO 80217-3364
303-556-3402
Fax: 303-556-4479
www.ucdenver.edu
The university is recognized as one of the leading public universities in the nation and offers a broad range of academic opportunities to students.
Quarterly
Hank Brown, President
Michel Dahlin, Interim Vice President

4161 Educational Freedom Spotlight On Homeschooling
Clonlara Home Based Education Programs
1289 Jewett Street
Ann Arbor, MI 48104-6201
734-769-4511
Fax: 734-769-9629
www.clonlara.org
Clonlara School is committed to illuminating educational rights and freedoms through our actions and deep dedication to human rights and dignity.
12 pages Monthly
Susan Andrews, Editor
Carmen Amabile, Coordinator

4162 Educational Horizons
P. Lambda Theta, Int'l Honor & Professional Assn.
P.O. Box 7888
Bloomington, IN 47407-7888
812-339-1156
Fax: 812-339-0018
www.pilambda.org
Founded in the spirit of academic excellence in order to provide leadership in addressing educational, social and cultural issues of national and international significance and to enhance the status of educators by providing a recognized forum for sharing new perspectives, research findings and scholarly essays.
48 pages Quarterly
ISSN: 0013-175X
Dan Brown, Executive Director
Bill Bushaw, Chief Executive Officer

4163 Educational Researcher
American Educational Research Association
1430 K Street NW
Suite 1200
Washington, DC 20005
202-238-3200
Fax: 202-238-3250
publications@aera.net
www.aera.net
Publishes research news and commentary on events in the field of educational research and articles of a wide interest to anyone involved in education.
June Ahn, Co-Editor
Dana Thompson Dorsey, Co-Editor

4164 Educational Theory
University of Illinois at Urbana
901 West Illinois Street
Urbana, IL 61801-6925
217-333-0302
Fax: 217-244-3711
edtheory@uiuc.edu
www.illinois.edu
The purpose of this journal is to foster the continuing development of educational theory and encourage wide and effective discussion of theoretical problems with the educational profession. Publishes articles and studies in the foundations of education and in related disciplines outside the field of education which contribute to the advancement of education theory.
570 pages Quarterly
ISSN: 0013-2004
Nicholas C Burbules, Editor
Diane E Beckett, Business Manager

4165 Focus on Autism
Pro-Ed., Inc.
8700 Shoal Creek Boulevard
Austin, TX 78757-6897
512-451-3246
800-897-3202
Fax: 512-451-8542
www.proedinc.com
Hands-on tips, techniques, methods and ideas from top authorities for improving the quality of assessment, instruction and management.
Brenda Smith Myles, PhD, Editor

4166 Focus on Research
The Council for Exceptional Children
2900 Crystal Drive
Suite 100
Arlington, VA 22202-3557
888-232-7733
www.cecdr.org
Newsletter of the CEC's Division for Research. Contains member opinion articles, debates on research issues, descriptions and dates of specific projects, notices of funded program priorities in special education, the availability of research dollars, and the discussion of emerging issues that may affect research in special education.
2x Year

4167 Foreign Student Service Council
2263 12th Place NW
Washington, DC 20009-4405
202-232-4979
Non-profit organization dedicated to promoting understanding between international students and Americans.
Quarterly

4168 Fortune Education Program
2890 Gateway Oaks Drive
Suite 100
Sacramento, CA 95833-1872
916-924-8633
800-448-3399
Fax: 916-924-8664
www.fortuneschool.us
Professional program that offers 75% off the cover price of Fortune magazine, a free educator's desk reference, a free 2-page teaching guide, fast delivery, choice of billing options. Plus quality customer service.
Paulette Brown Hinds, Managing Partner
Carolyn Lawson, Chief Information Officer

4169 Forum
Educators for Social Responsibility
23 Garden Street
Cambridge, MA 02138-3623
617-492-1764
Fax: 617-864-5164
educators@esrnational.org
www.esrnational.org
Edited for educators concerned with teaching in the nuclear age.
12 pages Quarterly
Barry Berman, Chief Financial Officer
Deborah Childs-Bowen, Executive Director

4170 Fulbright News
American Friends Service Committee
1501 Cherry St.
Room 450
Philadelphia, PA 19102-2269

215-241-7000
Fax: 212-941-6291
www.https://afsc.org
A four page newsletter distributed 5 times a year to visiting Fulbright scholars in the New York area. Contains a scholar profile, information about activities, tips for living in the United States, events in the New York area, and relevant announcements.

4 pages

Kristen Pendleton, Publisher

171 GED Items

Adult Learning Center
1340 Braddock Place
7th Floor
Alexandria, VA 22314-1110
703-619-8027
www.acps.k12.va.us/adulted
Newsletter of the GED Testing Service with articles focusing on adult education programs, teaching tips, GED graduate success stories and administration of GED testing.

12 pages BiMonthly

172 Harvard Education Letter

Harvard Education Publishing Group
8 Story Street
1st Floor
Cambridge, MA 02138
617-495-3432
800-513-0763
Fax: 617-496-3584
www.edletter.org
Published by the Harvard Graduate School of Education and reports on current research and innovative practice in PreK-12.

Publication Date: 1985 8 pages Bi-Monthly
ISSN: 8755-3716

Douglas Clayton, Publisher
Nancy Walser, Editor

173 Help! I'm in Middle School... How Will I Survive?

Northern Research Station
11 Campus Blvd.
Suite 200
Newtown Square, PA 19073
610-557-4017
www.nrs.fs.fed.us/pubs
The goal of NRS Publications is the success of every child. We provide a varity of books, educational games, posters, educational dice, overhead tiles, science kits, the SHAPES parts of speech learning system and creative play toys to help meet that goal.

Merry L Gumm, President
Tanya L Hein, Vice President

174 Heritage Newsletter

Phi Delta Kappa International
1820 N Fort Myer Drive
Suite 320
Arlington, VA 22209
800-766-1156
info@pdkintl.org
www.pdkintl.org
News and updates on the latest activities of PDK International and the PDK Educational Foundation.

2x Year

Joshua P. Starr, Ed.D, Chief Executive Officer
Albert Chen, M.E., Chief Operating Officer

175 Higher Education & National Affairs

American Council on Education
1 Dupont Circle NW
Washington, DC 20036
202-939-9300
comments@ace.nche.edu
www.acenet.edu
National newsletter with Capitol Hill and Administration updates on issues that affect colleges and universities. Includes stories on the federal budget, student financial aid, tax laws, Education Department regulations and research, legal issues and minorities in higher education.

Ted Mitchell, President
Kara Freeman, Chief Operating Officer

4176 History of Education Quarterly

Indian University
School of Education
107 S. Indiana Ave.
Bloomington, IN 47405-7000
812-855-4848
Fax: 812-855-3631
www.iu.edu
Discusses current and historical movements in education.

Quarterly

Charles R. Bantz, Executive VP
MaryFrances McCourt, Senior VP, CFO

4177 Homeschooling Marketplace Newsletter

13106 Patrici Circle
Omaha, NE 68164
Offers information, strategies and tips for homeschooling.

Clarice Routh, Contact

4178 IDRA Newsletter

Intercultural Development Research Association
5835 Callaghan Road
Suite 101
San Antonio, TX 78228-1125
210-444-1710
Fax: 210-444-1714
feedback@idra.org
www.idra.org
Mini-journal covering topics in the education of minority, poor and language-minority students in public institutions. It provides research-based solutions and editorial materials for education.

Monthly

Maria Robledo Montecel, President & CEO
Abelardo Villarreal, Chief of Operations

4179 IEA Reporter

Idaho Education Association
620 N 6th Street
PO Box 2638
Boise, ID 83701
208-344-1341
800-727-9922
Fax: 208-336-6967
www.idahoea.org

Quarterly

Kari Overall, President
Paul Humbleton, Interim Executive Director

4180 Inclusive Education Programs

LRP Publications
360 Hiatt Drive
Suite 700
Palm Beach Gardens, FL 33418
561-622-6520
800-341-7874
Fax: 561-622-1375
custserve@lrp.com
www.lrp.com
Newsletter covers the legal and practical issues of educating children with disabilities in regular education environments. It provides practical, how-to-advice, real life examples, and concise case summaries of the most recent judicial case laws.

Monthly
ISSN: 1076-8548

Kenneth F. Kahn, President

4181 Innovative Higher Education

Kluwer Academic/Human Sciences Press
233 Spring Street
New York, NY 10013
212-620-8000
800-221-9369
Fax: 212-463-0742
www.wkpa.nl
Provides educators and scholars with the latest creative strategies, programs and innovations designed to meet contemporary challenges in higher education. Professionals throughout the world contribute high-quality papers on the changing rules of vocational and liberal arts education, the needs of adults reentering the education process, and the reconciliation of faculty desires to economic realities, among other topics.

Quarterly
ISSN: 0742-5627

Carol Bischoff, Publisher
Ronald Simpson, Editor

4182 Insight

Independent Education Consultants Association
3251 Old Lee Highway
Suite 510
Fairfax, VA 22030-1504
703-591-4850
800-888-4322
Fax: 703-591-4860
www.IECAonline.com
Publication of national professional association of educational counselors working in private practice. Association provides counseling in college, secondary schools, learning disabilities and wilderness therapy programs.

Rebecca Peek, Author
Gail Meyer, President
Pamela Jobin, Vice President

4183 Insights Magazine

Awards and Personalization Association
8735 W Higgins Road
Suite 300
Chicago, IL 60631
847-375-4800
Fax: 847-375-6480
info@awardspersonalization.org
www.awardspersonalization.org
Formerly known as Recognition Review, Insights is the leading voice of the awards, engraving and recognition industry.

Monthly

Louise Ristau, CAE, Executive Director
Bryan O'Donnell, Managing Editor

4184 International Debates

Congressional Digest Corp.
4416 East West Highway
Suite 400
Bethesda, MD 20814-4568
301-634-3113
800-637-9915
Fax: 301-634-3189
www.pro-and-con.org
An independent publication featuring global controversies in the United Nations and other international forums, pro and cons.

ISSN: 1542-0345

Delores Baisden, Assistant

4185 International Education
University of Tennessee
College of Education
Health & Human Services
Knoxville, TN 37996-3400
865-974-1000
Fax: 865-974-8718
scarey@utk.edu
www.utk.edu
Publishes articles related to various international topics.
Publication Date: 1997 BiAnnual/Paperback
ISSN: 0160-5429
Sue Carey, Managing Editor

4186 International Journal of Qualitive Studies in Education
Taylor & Francis Group, LLC Books
6000 Broken Sound Parkway, NW
Suite 300
Boca Raton, FL 33487
561-994-0555
Fax: 561-241-7856
orders@taylorandfrancis.com
www.tandF.co.uk/journals
Aims to enhance the theory of qualitative research in education.
6 Issues Per Year
Jim Scheurich, Editor
Angela Valenzuela, Editor

4187 International Volunteer
Volunteers for Peace
7 Kilburn Street
Suite 316
Burlington, VT 05401-9988
802-540-3060
Fax: 802-259-2922
info@vfp.org
www.vfp.org
Newsletter of Volunteers for Peace, which provides intercultural education and community services.
8 pages Annual
Peter Coldwell, Author
Megan Brook, Executive Director
Maddie Craig, Coordinator

4188 Issues in Integrative Studies
Association for Integrative Studies
Miami University
Oxford, OH 45056
513-529-2659
Fax: 513-529-5849
aisorg@muohio.edu
www.units.muohio.edu/aisorg
An annual, refereed professional journal for members.
ISBN: 1081-4760
Rick Szostak, Editor

4189 Journal of Behavioral Education
Kluwer Academic/Human Sciences Press
233 Spring Street
New York, NY 10013
212-620-8000
800-221-9369
Fax: 212-463-0742
www.wkpa.nl
Provides the first single-source forum for the publication of research on the application of behavioral principles and technology to education. Publishes original empirical research and brief reports covering behavioral education in regular, special and adult education settings. Subject populations include handicapped, at-risk, and non-handicapped students of all ages.
Quarterly
ISSN: 1053-0819
Carol Bischoff, Publisher
Christopher Skinner, Co-Editor

4190 Journal of Character Education
Character Education Partnership
PO Box 650307
Sterling, VA 20165
202-296-7743
Fax: 704-752-9113
www.character.org
Offers information about character education research, theory, practice, and opinion.
2x Year
Jacques S. Benninga, Co-Editor
Marvin W. Berkowitz, Co-Editor

4191 Journal of College and Character (JCC)
NASPA
111 K Street NE
10th Floor
Washington, DC 20002
202-265-7500
office@naspa.org
www.naspa.org
Professional journal with articles and research on ethics, values and character development in higher education settings.
Publication Date: 2000 Quarterly
Jon C. Dalton, Co-Editor
Pamela C. Crosby, Co-Editor

4192 Journal of Creative Behavior
Creative Kids Education Foundation
11726 San Vicente Blvd.
Suite 370
Los Angeles, CA 90049
310-234-8604
800-447-2774
Fax: 413-559-6615
creativekidsfoundation@gmail.com
www.creativekidseducationfoundation.org
Devoted to the serious general reader with vocational/avocational interests in the fields of creativity and problem solving. Its articles are authored not only by established writers in the field, but by up-and coming contributors as well. The criteria for selecting articles include reference, clarity, interest and overall quality.
Quarterly
Jama Laurent, President
Byron Adams, Professor of Music

4193 Journal of Curriculum Theorizing
Colgate University
Department of Education
13 Oak Drive
Hamilton, NY 13346
315-228-7000
Fax: 315-228-7998
www.colgate.edu
Analyzes and provides insights to curriculum movements and evolution.
Quarterly
JoAnne Pagano, Editor

4194 Journal of Disability Policy Studies
Pro-Ed., Inc.
8700 Shoal Creek Boulevard
Austin, TX 78757-6897
512-451-3246
800-897-3202
Fax: 512-302-8542
proed1@aol.com
www.proedinc.com
Devoted exclusively to disability policy topics and issues.
Quarterly Magazine
ISSN: 1044-2073
Craig R Fiedler, JD, PhD, Editor
Billie Jo Rylance, PhD, Editor

4195 Journal of Educational Research
Taylor & Francis
325 Chestnut Street
Suite 800
Philadelphia, PA 19106-1826
215-625-8900
800-354-1420
Fax: 202-296-5149
customer.service@taylorandfrancis.com
www.heldref.org
Since 1920, this journal has contributed to the advancement of educational practice in elementary and secondary schools. Authors experiment with new procedures, evaluate traditional practices, replicate previous research for validation and perform other work central to understanding and improving the education of today's students and teachers. This Journal is a valuable resource for teachers, counselors, supervisors, administrators, planners and educational researchers.
64 pages BiMonthly
ISSN: 0022-0671
Deborah Cohen, Promotions Editor

4196 Journal of Experimental Education
Taylor & Francis
325 Chestnut Street
Suite 800
Philadelphia, PA 19106-1826
215-625-8900
800-354-1420
Fax: 202-296-5149
customer.service@taylorandfrancis.com
www.heldref.org
Aims to improve educational practice by publishing basic and applied research studies using the range of quantitative and qualitative methodologies found in the behavioral, cognitive and social sciences. Published studies address all levels of schooling, from preschool through graduate and professional education, and various educational context, including public and private education in the United States and abroad.
96 pages Quarterly
Paige Jackson, Managing Editor

4197 Journal of Finance
American Finance Association, University of Utah
1655 E Campus Center Drive
Salt Lake City, UT 84112
editor@jfinance.org
www.afajof.org
Publishes research covering all major areas of finance.
Wendy Washburn, Assistant Editor

4198 Journal of Law and Education
University of South Carolina Law School
701 Main Street
Columbia, SC 29208
803-777-4155
Fax: 803-777-9405
lawweb@law.sc.edu
www.law.sc.edu
A periodical offering information on the newest laws and legislation affecting education.
Quarterly
Ronbert M. Wilcox, Dean
Jaclyn A. Cherry, Associate Dean

199 Journal of Learning Disabilities
Pro-Ed., Inc.
8700 Shoal Creek Boulevard
Austin, TX 78757-6897
512-451-3246
800-897-3202
Fax: 512-451-8542
proed1@aol.com
www.proedinc.com
Special series, feature articles and research articles.

Bi-Monthly Magazine
ISSN: 0022-2194

Wayne P Hresko, PhD, Editor-in-Chief

200 Journal of Negro Education
Howard University
2400 Sixth Street, NW
Washington, DC 20059-0001
202-806-6100
Fax: 202-806-8434
jne@howard.edu
www.howard.edu
A Howard University quarterly review of issues incident to the education of Black people; tracing educational developments and presenting research on issues confronting Black students in the US and around the world.

120+ pages Quarterly
ISSN: 0022-2984

D. Kamili Anderson, Associate Editor
Dr. Sylvia T. Johnson, Editor-in-Chief

201 Journal of Positive Behavior Interventions
Pro-Ed., Inc.
8700 Shoal Creek Boulevard
Austin, TX 78757-6897
512-451-3246
800-897-3202
Fax: 512-302-9129
www.proedinc.com
Sound, research-based principles of positive behavior support for use in home, school and community settings for people with challenges in behavioral adaptation.

Glen Dunlap, PhD, Editor
Robert L Koegel, PhD, Editor

202 Journal of Research and Development in Education
University of Georgia, College of Education
G3 Aderhold Hall
110 Carlton Street,
Athens, GA 30602
404-542-1154
www.coe.uga.edu
A magazine offering insight and experimental and theoretical studies in education.

Quarterly

Craig H. Kennedy, Dean
Laura Lee Bierema, Associate Dean

203 Journal of Research in Rural Education
University of Maine, College of Education
5766 Shibles Hall
Orono, ME 04469-5766
207-581-2493
Fax: 207-581-2423
www.umaine.edu
Publishes the results of educational research relevant to rural settings.

3x Year Journal

Theodore Coladarci, Editor
Sara Sheppard, Managing Editor

4204 Journal of School Health
American School Health Association
501 N Morton Street
Suite 110
Bloomington, IN 47404
202-854-1721
info@ashaweb.org
www.ashaweb.org
Contains material related to health promotion in school settings.

40 pages Monthly
ISSN: 0022-4391

Robert J. McDermott, Editor-in-Chief

4205 Journal of Special Education
Pro-Ed., Inc.
8700 Shoal Creek Boulevard
Austin, TX 78757-6897
512-451-3246
800-897-3202
Fax: 512-302-9129
www.proedinc.com
Timely, sound special education research.

Lynn S Fuchs, PhD, Editor
Douglas Fuchs, PhD, Editor

4206 Journal of Student Affairs Research and Practice (JSARP)
NASPA
111 K Street NE
10th Floor
Washington, DC 20002
202-265-7500
office@naspa.org
www.naspa.org
Specializes in current research in student affairs practice, with an emphasis on unconventional manuscripts.

Publication Date: 1963 5x Year

Bridget Turner Kelly, Executive Editor

4207 Journal of Urban & Cultural Studies
University of Massachusetts at Boston
Department of English
100 Morrissey Blvd.
Boston, MA 02125-3393
617-287-5000
Fax: 617-287-4000
www.umb.edu/
Explores various issues in education that deal with urban and cultural affairs.

Donaldo Macedo, Editor

4208 Journal of Women and Gender in Higher Education
NASPA
111 K Street NE
10th Floor
Washington, DC 20002
202-265-7500
office@naspa.org
www.naspa.org
Scholarly journal focused on gender-based experiences of students, faculty and staff.

Publication Date: 2008 3x Year

Margaret Sallee, Editor-in-Chief
Jeni Hart, Editor-in-Chief

4209 Kaleidoscope
Evansville-Vanderburgh School Corporation
951 Walnut St
Evansville, IN 47713-1821
812-435-8599
www.district.evscschools.com
A staff publication for and about employees of the Evansville-Vanderburgh School Corporation.

8 pages Monthly

Patti S Coleman, Contact

4210 LD Forum
Council for Learning Disabilities
11184 Antioch Road
PO Box 405
Overland Park, KS 66210
913-491-1011
Fax: 913-491-1011
www.council-for-learning-disabilities.org
Provides updated information and research on the activities of the Council for Learning Disabilities.

Bimonthly

Apryl Poch, Editor

4211 Learning Disability Quarterly
Council for Learning Disabilities
11184 Antioch Road
PO Box 405
Overland Park, KS 66210
913-491-1011
Fax: 913-491-1011
www.council-for-learning-disabilities.org
Aimed at learning disabled students, their parents and educators.

Quarterly

Diane P. Bryant, Editor

4212 Learning Point Magazine Laboratory
North Central Regional Educational Laboratory
1000 Thomas Jefferson Street NW
Suite 300
Washington, DC 20007-1447
202-403-5000
Fax: 202-403-5001
info@ncrel.org
www.ncrel.org
Applies research and technology to learning.

16 pages Quarterly

Jeri Nowakowski, Director

4213 Learning Unlimited Network of Oregon
31960 SE Chin Street
Boring, OR 97009-9708
503-663-5153
Cuts through all barriers to communication and learning; institutional, personal, physical, psychological, spiritual. It focuses on basic communication/language skills but sets no limits on means or tools, subjects or participants in seeking maximum balance and productivity for all.

10 pages 9x Year

Gene Lehman, Contact

4214 Let It Grow. Let It Grow. Let It Grow. Hands-on Activities to Explore the Planet Kingdom
NSR Publications
1482 51st Road
Douglass, KS 67039
620-986-5472
The goal of NSR Publication is the success of every child. We provide a variety of books, educational games, posters, educational dice, overhead tiles, science kits, the SHAPES parts of speech learning system and creative play toys to help meet that goal.

58 pages

Merry L Gumm, President
Tanya L Hein, Vice President

4215 Liberal Education
Association of American Colleges & Universities
1818 R Street NW
Washington, DC 20009-1604

202-387-3760
Fax: 202-265-9532
www.aacu-edu.org
Concentrates on issues currently affecting American higher education. Promotes and strengthens undergraduate curriculum, classroom teaching and learning, collaborative leadership, faculty leadership, diversity. Other publications on higher education include books, monographs, peer review, and on campus with women.

64 pages Quarterly
ISSN: 0024-1822

Kenneth P. Ruscio, Chair
Edward J. Ray, Vice Chair

4216 Link
AEL, Inc.
102 E. Keefe Ave
Milwaukee, WI 53212-1348
414-265-7630
866-656-1486
Fax: 414-265-7628
sales@aelseating.com
www.aelseating.com
A newsletter for educators providing research summaries, education news, and news of AEL products, services and events.

12 pages Quarterly Newsletter

Patricia Hammer Cahape, Associate Director

4217 Lisle-Interaction
433 W Sterns Street
Temperance, MI 48182-9568
734-847-7126
800-477-1538
Fax: 512-259-0392
www.lisleinternational.org
Reports on domestic and international programs, annual meetings and board meetings of the Lisle Fellowship which seeks to broaden global awareness and appreciation of different cultures. Occasional special articles on topics such as racism, book reviews. News of members are also included.

16 pages Quarterly

Mark Kinney, Executive Director
Dianne Brause, VP

4218 MEA Today
Montana Education Association
1232 E 6th Avenue
Helena, MT 59601-3927
406-442-4250
800-398-0826
Fax: 406-443-5081
www.mea-mft.org
National and state association news, legislative policies, and classroom features.

8 pages Monthly

Eric Feaver, President
Melanie Charlsonÿ, VP

4219 MTNA E-Journal
Music Teachers National Association
600 Vine Street
Suite 1710
Cincinnati, OH 45202
513-421-1420
888-512-5278
Fax: 513-421-2503
ejournal@mtna.org
www.mtna.org
Peer-reviewed online journal of the Music Teachers National Association, presenting scholarly research-oriented articles on music and the music teaching profession.

Gary L. Ingle, Executive Director & CEO
Marcie Gerrietts Lindsey, Director, Publishing

4220 Massachusetts Home Learning Association Newsletter
23 Mountain Street
Sharon, MA 02067-2234
781-784-8006
www.mhla.org
A source for information gleaned from all the major national magazines and many state newsletters. Calendar of events for Massachusetts homeschooling and several feature articles on legal, educational or familial issues.

24 pages Quarterly

Sharon Terry, Editor
Patrick Terry, Editor

4221 Mel Gabler's Newsletter
Educational Research Analysts
PO Box 7518
Longview, TX 75607-7518
972-753-5993
www.textbookreviews.org/
Educational information pertaining to curricula used in schools.

8 pages SemiAnnually

Mel Gabler, Publisher
Chad Rosenberger, Editor

4222 Minnesota Education Update
Office of Library Development & Services
200 West Baltimore Street
550 Cedar Street
Baltimore, MD 21201-2595
410-767-0444
Fax: 410-333-2507
www.marylandpublicschools.org
Policies and activities in elementary and secondary education in the state of Minnesota.

8 pages Monthly

Amber Massaquoi, Executive Assistant
Dennis Nangle, Branch Chief

4223 Missouri Schools
Missouri Department of Education
PO Box 480
Jefferson City, MO 65102-0480
573-751-4212
Fax: 573-751-8613
www.dese.mo.gov
State education policy.

28 pages BiMonthly

Margie Vandeven, Commissioner
Jay Nixon, Governor

4224 Momentum
National Catholic Educational Association
1005 North Glebe Road
Suite 525
Arlington, VA 22201
571-257-0010
Fax: 703-243-0025
Magazine of the National Catholic Educational Association, with articles on faith, strategies, technology and leadership.

Publication Date: 1970 Quarterly

Thomas W Burnford, D.Min., Ph.D, President & CEO

4225 Montana Schools
Montana Office of Public Instruction
State Capitol
Helena, MT 59620
406-444-3095
Fax: 406-444-2893
www.opi.mt.gov
Information about people and programs in the Montana education system.

12 pages 5x Year

Ellen Meloy

4226 Montessori Observer
International Montessori Society
9525 Georgia Avenue
Suite 200
Silver Spring, MD 20910
301-589-1127
800-301-3131
Fax: 301-920-0764
havis@imsmontessori.org
www.imsmontessori.org
Provides news and information about Montessori education and the work of the International Montessori Society.

Publication Date: 1979
ISSN: 0889-5643

Lee Havis, Editor

4227 NAEIR Advantage
Nat'l Assn. for Exchange of Industrial Resources
560 McClure Street
Galesburg, IL 61401-4286
309-343-0704
800-562-0955
Fax: 309-343-3519
www.naeir.org
News of the National Association for the Exchange of Industrial Resources, which collects donations of new excess inventory from corporations and redistributes them to American schools and nonprofits.

Publication Date: 1977 8 pages BiMonthly

Gary C Smith, President/CEO
Robert B. Gilstrap, Vice President/CFO

4228 NAEN Bulletin
North American Assoc. of Educational Negotiators
423 Allen Road
Porter Corners, NY 12859
518-369-5779
execdir@naen.org
www.naen.org
Association news and notes.

Members Only

James B. Fernow, President
Rachel M. Rissetto, Executive Director

4229 NAFSA Newsletter
NAFSA: Association of International Educators
1425 K Street NW
Suite 1200
Washington, DC 20005
202-737-3699
inbox@nafsa.org
www.nafsa.org
Publishes news and information related to international education and exchange.

Esther D. Brimmer, Executive Director & CEO
Dorothea Antonio, Deputy Executive Director

4230 NEA Higher Education Advocate
National Education Association
1201 16th Street NW
Washington, DC 20036-3290
202-833-4000
Fax: 202-822-7974
www.nea.org
Reports on NEA and general higher education news.

5x Year

Becky Pringle, President
Kim A. Anderson, Executive Director

231 NEA Today
National Education Association
1201 16th Street NW
Washington, DC 20036-3290
202-833-4000
Fax: 202-822-7974
www.nea.org/publications
Flagship publication of the National Education Association. Contains news and features of interest to classroom teachers and other employees of schools. A mobile app is also available.
Quarterly
Becky Pringle, President
Kim A. Anderson, Executive Director

232 NEA Today for NEA-Retired Members
National Education Association
1201 16th Street NW
Washington, DC 20036-3290
202-833-4000
Fax: 202-822-7974
www.nea.org/publications
Formerly known as This Active Life, the publication blends content from NEA Today with unique content aimed at retired educators.
Quarterly
Becky Pringle, President
Kim A. Anderson, Executive Director

233 NEWSLINKS
International Schools Services
15 Roszel Road
P.O. Box 5910
Princeton, NJ 08543
609-452-0990
Fax: 609-452-2690
newslinks@iss.edu
Regularly published newspaper of International Schools Services that is distributed free of charge to overseas teachers, school administrators and libraries, US universities, educational organizations, multinational corporations, school supply companies and educational publishers.
Publication Date: 1955 32-40 pages Quarterly
Liz Duffy, President
Kristin Evins, CFO

234 NJEA Review
New Jersey Education Association
180 W State Street
Trenton, NJ 08607-1211
609-599-4561
Fax: 609-392-6321
webmaster@njea.org
www.njea.org/njea-review
Monthly educational journal of the New Jersey Education Association which focuses on educational news and issues related to New Jersey public schools. Its readers are active and retired teaching staff members and support staff, administrators, board members, teacher education students, and others in New Jersey public schools and colleges.
Publication Date: 1927 80 pages Monthly
ISSN: 0027-6758
Steven Baker, Editorial Director
Patrick Rumaker, Editor

235 NREA News
National Rural Education Association
Colorado State University
Fort Collins, CO 80523
Fax: 970-491-1317
jnewlin@lamar.colostate.edu
www.colostate.edu
Keeps all members up-to-date on Association activities, events, rural education conferences and meetings, and research projects in progress.
Publication Date: 1870 8 pages Quarterly Newsletter
ISSN: 0273-4460
Joseph T Newlin, Editor

4236 NYSUT United
New York State United Teachers
800 Troy-Schenectady Road
Latham, NY 12110
518-213-6000
800-342-9810
united@nysutmail.org
www.nysut.org/news/nysut-united
Andrew Pallotta, President
Jolene T. DiBrango, Executive Vice President

4237 National Accrediting Commission of Cosmetology, Arts and Sciences
National Accrediting Commission of Cosmetology
4401 Ford Avenue
Suite 1300
Arlington, VA 22302-1432
703-600-7600
Fax: 703-379-2200
www.naccas.org
Information on accreditation, cosmetology schools and any federal regulations affecting accreditation and postsecondary education.
Publication Date: 1969 20 pages 6x Year
Tony Mirando, MS, DC, Executive Director
Eddie Broomfield, Asst. to Executive Director

4238 National Homeschool Association Newsletter
National Homeschool Association
PO Box 290
Hartland, MI 48353-0290
425-432-1544
Information on what's happening in the homeschooling community.
28 pages Quarterly

4239 National Monitor of Education
CA Monitor of Education
1331 Fairmount Avenue
Suite 61
El Cerrito, CA 94530
510-527-4430
Fax: 510-528-9833
jsod@aol.com
www.e-files.org
Supports traditional moral and academic values in education. Reports on litigation and reviews various education publications. Issues reported on include parents' rights and movement to restore basic academics.
8 pages Bi-Monthly/Paperback
Susan O'Donnell, Publisher
Susan Sweet, Newsletter Design

4240 New Hampshire Educator
National Education Association, New Hampshire
103 N State Street
Concord, NH 03301-2425
603-224-7751
Fax: 603-224-2648
www.neanh.org
Reports on the advancements in education in the state and nation and promotes the welfare of educators.
Publication Date: 1854 10 pages Monthly
Scott McGilvray, President
Megan Tuttle, Vice President

4241 New Images
METCO
55 Dimock Street
Boston, MA 02119-1029
617-427-1545
Mailed to METCO parents and educational institutions local and national.
4 pages Quarterly
JM Mitchell

4242 News N' Notes
NTID at Rochester Institute of Technology
52 Lomb Memorial Drive
Rochester, NY 14623
585-475-6400
gbuckley@ntid.rit.edu
www.ntid.rit.edu
Convention news, membership information, education legislation advocacy and personal contributions to the scholarly society.
Publication Date: 1829 12 pages Quarterly
Dr. Gerard J. Buckley, President
Bernard Hurwitz, J.D., Executive Assistant

4243 Non-Credit Learning News
Learning for All Seasons
6 Saddle Club Road
#579X
Lexington, MA 02420-2115
781-861-0379
Marketing information for directors and marketers of non-credit programs.
8 pages 10x Year
Susan Capon

4244 Notes from the Field
Jessie Ball duPont Fund
One Dependent Drive
Suite 1400
Jacksonville, FL 32202-5011
904-353-0890
800-252-3452
Fax: 904-353-3870
contactus@dupontfund.org
www.dupontfund.org
Provides information on the various organizations and institutes the Jessie Ball duPont Fund reaches out to every year.
Publication Date: 1977 3x
Sherry P. Magill, President
Mark D. Constantine, Senior Vice President

4245 Occupational Programs in California Community Colleges
Leo A Myer Associates/LAMA Books
2381 Sleepy Hollow Avenue
Hayward, CA 94545-3429
510-785-1091
888-452-6244
Fax: 510-785-1099
www.lamabooks.com
Writers and publishers of HVAC books.
186 pages Bi-Annually
ISBN: 0-88069
Steve Meyer, President

4246 Our Children: The National PTA Magazine
1250 N Pitt Street
Alexandria, VA 22314
703-518-1200
800-307-4782
Fax: 703-836-0942
info@pta.org
www.pta.org
Written by, for and about the National PTA. A nonprofit organization of parents, educators,

students, and other citizens active in their schools and communities.

Nathan R. Monell, Executive Director
Kristen Johnson, Director, Education

4247 PTA National Bulletin
National Association of Hebrew Day School PTA'S
160 Broadway
New York, NY 10038-4201
212-227-1000
Fax: 212-406-6934
Educational events in day school relating to PTA movement. News of national and regional groups.

Quarterly

4248 PTA in Pennsylvania
Pennsylvania PTA
4804 Derry Street
Harrisburg, PA 17111-3440
717-564-8985
Fax: 717-564-9046
info@papta.org
www.papta.org
Topical articles about issues affecting education and children, such as safety and health, AIDS, parents involvement and guidance, environmental concerns and special education.

24 pages Quarterly
ISSN: 1072-3242
250 attendees and 40-50 exhibits

Deborah Dunstone, President
Christine Harty, Secretary

4249 Parents as Teachers National Center
2228 Ball Drive
Saint Louis, MO 63146
314-432-4330
Fax: 314-432-8963
patnc@patnc.org
www.parentsasteachers.org
Provides information, training and technical assistance for those interested in adopting the home-school-community partnership program. Offers parents the information and support needed to give their children the best possible start in life.

Quarterly

Julie Robbens, Editor, Author
Scott Hippert, President/CEO
Cheryl Dyle-Palmer, M.A., EVP/ COO

4250 Passing Marks
San Bernadino City Unified School District
777 N F Street
San Bernardino, CA 92410
909-381-1250
Fax: 909-388-1451
www.sbcusd.k12.ca.us
Educational resume of school activities, covering instruction, personnel, administration, board of education, etc.

12 pages Monthly

Michael J. Gallo, President
Bobbie Perong, Vice President

4251 Pennsylvania Home Schoolers Newsletter
RR 2 Box 117
Kittanning, PA 16201-9311
724-783-6512
Fax: 724-783-6512
A support newsletter directed to homeschooling families in Pennsylvania. Articles, reviews of curriculum, advice, calendar, support group listing, children's writing section.

32 pages Quarterly

Howard Richman, Publisher
Susan Richman, Editor

4252 Pennsylvania State Education Association
400 N 3rd Street
PO Box 1724
Harrisburg, PA 17105-1724
717-255-7000
800-944-7732
Fax: 717-255-7124
www.psea.org

Publication Date: 1852 16 pages 9x Year
ISSN: 0896-6605

Michael J. Crossey, President
W. Gerard Oleksiak, Vice President

4253 Phi Delta Kappan
Phi Delta Kappa International
1820 N Fort Myer Drive
Suite 320
Arlington, VA 22209
800-766-1156
info@pdkintl.org
www.pdkintl.org
Advocates research-based school reform and covers professinal development, research, federal policy, and standards.

ISSN: 0031-7217

Rafael Heller, Editor

4254 Planning for Higher Education
Society for College and University Planning (SCUP)
1330 Eisenhower Place
Ann Arbor, MI 48108
734-669-3270
Fax: 734-661-0157
info@scup.org
www.scup.org/phe
A quarterly, peer-reviewed journal devoted to the advancement and application of the best planning practices for colleges and universities.

70+ pages Quarterly Journal
ISSN: 0736-0983
July
150 booths with 1,200 attendees and 150 exhibits

Ellen Stanton Milstone, Chair
Philip G. Stack, Vice Chair

4255 Policy & Practice
American Public Human Services Association
1133 19th Street, NW
Suite 400
Washington, DC 20036
202-682-0100
Fax: 202-289-6555
www.aphsa.org
This quarterly magazine presents a comprehensive look at issues important to public human services administrators. It also features a wide spectrum of views by the best thinkers in social policy.

Publication Date: 1930 52 pages Quarterly
ISSN: 1520-801X

Reggie Bicha, President
Tracy Wareing, Executive Director

4256 Population Educator
Population Connection
1400 16th Street NW
Suite 320
Washington, DC 20036-2215
202-332-2200
800-767-1956
Fax: 202-332-2302
poped@populationconnection.org
www.populationeducation.org
Offers population education news, classroom activities and workshop schedules for grades K-12.

4 pages Quarterly

Pamela Wasseman

4257 Public Education Alert
Public Education Association
39 W 32nd Street
New York, NY 10001-3803
212-868-1640
Fax: 212-302-0088
Provides information and consumer-oriented analysis of law policy issues and current developments in New York City public education. PEA Alert back issues; e-guide to New York City's public high school offering comparative data.

Ray Domanico, Publisher
Jessica Wolfe, Editor

4258 QUIN: Quarterly University International News
University of Minnesota, Office in Education
231 Pillsbury Drive S.E
Minneapolis, MN 55455-213
612-625-1915
800-752-1000
Fax: 612-624-1693
www.admissions.tc.umn.edu
International campus update for students, faculty, staff and the community.

TriQuarterly

Rachelle Hernandez, Associate Vice Provost

4259 R&D Alert Online
730 Harrison Street
San Francisco, CA 94107
415-565-3000
877-493-7833
Fax: 415-565-3012
www.wested.org
Provides regular updates on research and insights from WestEd's ongoing work in education and healthy development.

Glen H Harvey, Chief Executive Officer
Matthew Nathan, Senior Director, Development

4260 Reclaiming Children and Youth
Pro-Ed., Inc.
8700 Shoal Creek Boulevard
Austin, TX 78757-6897
512-451-3246
800-897-3202
Fax: 512-451-8542
general@proedinc.com
www.proedinc.com
Provides positive, creative solutions to professionals serving youth in conflict.

Quarterly Magazine

Nicholas J Long, PhD, Editor
Larry K Brendtro, PhD, Editor

4261 Recognition Review
Awards and Recognition Association
8735 W. Higgins Road
Suite 300
Chicago, IL 60631
847-375-4800
800-344-2148
Fax: 847-375-6480
info@ara.org
www.ara.org
Published monthly by the Awards and Recognition Association. Recognition Review is the lead-

ing voice of the awards, engraving and recognition industry.

Publication Date: 1964 Monthly

Jeanette Brewer Richardson, CRS, President
Louise Ristau, CAE, Executive Director

262 Regional Spotlight

Southern Regional Education Board
592 10th Street NW
Atlanta, GA 30318-5776
404-875-9211
Fax: 404-872-1477
www.sreb.org
News of educational interest directed to 15 SREB-member states.

9 pages

Steve Beshear, Chair
Dave Spence, President

263 Rehabilitation Research, Policy, and Education

National Council on Rehabilitation Education
1099 E Champlain Drive
Suite A, 137
Fresno, CA 93720
559-906-0787
info@ncre.org
www.ncre.org
The journal explores the subject of rehabilitation education. Topics covered include issues related to licensing, certification, accreditation, innovative methodology, employment trends, educational media and more.

Quarterly

David R. Strauser, Ph.D, Editor

264 Remedial and Special Education

Pro-Ed., Inc.
8700 Shoal Creek Boulevard
Austin, TX 78757-6897
512-451-3246
800-897-3202
Fax: 512-451-8542
general@proedinc.com
www.proedinc.com
Highest-quality interdisciplinary scholarship that bridges the gap between theory and practice involving the education of individuals for whom typical instruction is not effective.

Bi-Monthly Magazine
ISSN: 0741-9325

Edward A Polloway, EdD, Editor-in-Chief

265 Renaissance Educator

Renaissance Educational Associates
4817 N County Road 29
Loveland, CO 80538-9515
970-679-4300
Quarterly publication highlighting educators around the world who are revealing the effectiveness of integrity in education.

8 pages Quarterly

Kristy Clark

266 Research in Higher Education

Kluwer Academic/Human Sciences Press
233 Spring Street
New York, NY 10013
212-620-8000
800-221-9369
Fax: 212-463-0742
www.wkpa.nl
Essential source of new information for all concerned with the functioning of postsecondary educational institutions. Publishes original, quantitative research articles which contribute to an increased understanding of an institution, aid faculty in making more informed decisions about current or future operations, and improve the efficiency of an institution.

Bimonthly
ISSN: 0361-0365

Carol Bischoff, Publisher
John C Smart, Editor

4267 Research in the Schools

Mid-South Educational Research Association
2100 Forest Hills Boulevard
Haughton, LA 71037
info@msera.org
www.msera.org
A nationally refereed journal sponsored by the Mid-South Educational Research Association and Sam Houston State University. RITS publishes original contributions in the following areas: 1) Research in practice; 2) Topical articles; 3) Methods and techniques; 4) Assessment; and 5) Educational, policy, reform, and accountability, as well as other topics of interest.

2x Year
ISSN: 1085-5300

Anthony J. Onwuegbuzie, Co-Editor

4268 Review of Educational Research

American Educational Research Association
1430 K Street NW
Suite 1200
Washington, DC 20005
202-238-3200
Fax: 202-238-3250
publications@aera.net
www.aera.net
Publishes critical reviews of research literature about education.

Bimonthly

P. Karen Murphy, Editor

4269 Roeper Review: A Journal on Gifted Education

Roeper Institute
PO Box 329
Bloomfield Hills, MI 48303-0329
248-203-7321
Fax: 248-203-7310
tcross@bsu.edu
www.roeperreview.org
A journal that focuses on gifted and talented education, the Roeper Review applies the highest standards of peer review journalism to cover a broad range of issues. For professionals who work with teachers and for professionals who work directly with gifted and talented children and their families, the journal provides readable coverage of policy issues. Each issue covers one or more subjects. Regular departments include research reports and book reviews.

60-80 pages Quarterly
ISSN: 0278-3193

Tracy L Cross PhD, Editor
Vicki Rossbach, Subsciption

4270 Rural Educator: Journal for Rural and Small Schools

National Rural Education Association
Colorado State University
Fort Collins, CO 80523
970-491-7022
Fax: 970-491-1317
www.colostate.edu
Official journal of the NREA. A nationally recognized publication that features timely and informative articles written by leading rural educators from all levels of education. All NREA members are encouraged to submit research articles and items of general information for publication.

Publication Date: 1870 40 pages TriAnnual

Joseph T Newlin, Editor

4271 SEDL Letter

Southwestern Educational Development Laboratory
4700 Mueller Boulevard
Austin, TX 78723
512-476-6861
800-476-6861
Fax: 512-476-2286
information@sedl.org
www.sedl.org
A biannual letter that complements and draws on work and performed by SEDL under a variety of funding sources, including the US Department of Education and the US government.

Publication Date: 1960
ISBN: 520-7315

Linda Villarreal, Chair
Gwenneth Price-Picard, Vice Chair

4272 SKOLE: A Journal of Alternative Education

Down-To-Earth Books
72 Philip Street
Albany, NY 12202-1729
518-432-1578
Publishes articles, poems, and research by people engaged in alternative education.

200 pages SemiAnnually

Mary Leue

4273 Safety Forum

Safety Society
1900 Association Drive
Reston, VA 20191-1502
703-476-3440
Offers articles and up-to-date information on school safety.

4 pages TriQuarterly

Linda Moore

4274 School Bus Fleet

Bobit Business Media
3520 Challenger Street
Torrance, CA 90503
310-533-2400
Fax: 310-533-2512
info@schoolbusfleet.com
www.schoolbusfleet.com
Provides coverage of federal vehicle and education regulations that affect pupil transportation, policy and management issues as well as how to improve the safety of children riding yellow buses. Special sections cover transportation for students with disabilities.

Publication Date: 1956

James Blue, General Manager
Nicole Schlosser, Executive Editor

4275 School Foodservice & Nutrition

School Nutrition Association
1600 Duke Street
Floor 7
Alexandria, VA 22314-3421
703-739-3900
800-877-8822
Fax: 703-739-3915
www.schoolnutrition.org
For foodservice professionals presenting current articles on industry issues, management events, legislative issues, public relations programs and professional development news.

11x Year

Adrienne Gall Tufts, Editor

4276 School Health Action
American School Health Association
501 N Morton Street
Suite 110
Bloomington, IN 47404
202-854-1721
info@ashaweb.org
www.ashaweb.org
Provides information on topics that affect school health professionals.

Biweekly

Jeanie Alter, Executive Director
Kaitlyn Celis, Manager, Membership Services

4277 School Law Bulletin
Quinlan Publishing
23 Drydock Avenue
Boston, MA 02210-2336
617-542-0048
Covers cases and laws pertaining to schools.

8 pages Monthly

4278 School Safety
National School Safety Center
30200 Agoura Road
Suite 260
Agoura Hills, CA 91301
805-373-9977
info@schoolsafety.us
www.schoolsafety.us
Online archive of two former publications, the School Safety Newsjournal and the School Safety Update. They were intended for educators, law enforcers, judges and legislators on the prevention of drugs, gangs, weapons, bullying, discipline problems and vandalism; also on-site security and character development as they relate to students and schools.

Ronald D. Stephens, Executive Director

4279 School Transportation News
STN Media Company Inc.
P.O. Box 789
Redondo Beach, CA 90277
310-792-2226
Fax: 310-792-2231
bpaul@stnonline.com
www.stnonline.com
Covers school district and contractor fleets, special needs and prekindergarten transportation, Head Start, and more on a monthly basis. Reports developments affecting public school transportation supervisors and directors, state directors of school transportation, school bus contractors, special needs transportation, Head Start transportation, private school transportation, school business officials responsible for transportation and industry suppliers.

Publication Date: 1991 Magazine/Monthly 100 booths

Bill Paul, Author
Ryan Gray, Editor-in-Chief
Tony Corpin, Publisher

4280 School Zone
West Aurora Public Schools, District 129
80 S River Street
#14
Aurora, IL 60506-5178
630-844-4400
www.sd129.org
Informs the community of what is happening in their schools, with their students, and with their tax dollars.

4 pages 5x Year

Laurel Chivari

4281 Shaping the Future
Lutheran Education Association
7400 Augusta Street
River Forest, IL 60305
708-209-3343
Fax: 708-209-3458
lea@lea.org
www.lea.org/resources
Newsletter for LEA members to focus on the unique spiritual and professional needs of church workers and to celebrate life in the ministry. Resource information for the organization, upcoming events, encouragement for pre-planning.

3x Year

Jonathan Laabs, Ed.D, Executive Director
Edward C. Grube, LL.D, Director, Communications

4282 Sharing Space
Creative Urethanes, Children's Creative Response
PO Box 271
Nyack, NY 10960-0271
845-358-4601
Trains all those working with children to communicate positivity and cooperation.

12 pages TriAnnually

4283 Special Education Leadership
LifeWay Church Resources
One LifeWay Plaza
Nashville, TN 37234
615-251-2000
800-588-7222
Fax: 615-251-5933
www.lifeway.com
Covers special education issues relating to religious education.

Publication Date: 1891 52 pages Quarterly

Thom S. Rainer, President/ CEO
Brad Waggoner, Executive Vice President

4284 Special Educator
LRP Publications
360 Hiatt Drive
Palm Beach Gardens, FL 33418
703-516-7002
800-341-7874
Fax: 561-622-2423
custserve@lrp.com
www.lrp.com
Covers important issues in the field of special education, including such topics as law and administrative policy.

Publication Date: 1977 22 pages 22 Issues Per Year
ISSN: 1047-1618

Kenneth F. Kahn, President

4285 Star News
Jefferson Center for Character Education
PO Box 1283
Monrovia, CA 91017-1283
949-770-7602
Fax: 949-450-1100
Mission is to produce and promote programs to teach children the concepts, skills and behavior of good character, common core values, personal and civic responsibility, workforce readiness and citizenship.

Quarterly

Robert Jamieson, CEO
Sharon McClenahan, Administrative Assistant

4286 Statewise: Statistical & Research Newsletter
State Board of Education, Planning & Research
PO Box 1402
Dover, DE 19903-1402
302-736-4601
Fax: 302-739-4654
Statistical data relating to Delaware public schools.

2 pages

4287 Street Scenes
(APO Street College of Education
610 W 112th Street
New York, NY 10025-1898
212-222-6700
Fax: 212-222-6700
New ideas in education.

8 pages SemiAnnually

Renee Creange

4288 TSBA Journal
Tennessee School Boards Association
525 Brick Church Park Drive
Nashville, TN 37207
615-815-3900
www.tsba.net
Publishes articles on issues relating to local, state, and national education.

2x Year

Tammy Grissom, Executive Director
Ben Torres, Assistant Executive Director

4289 Teacher$ Talk
Teachers Insurance and Annuity Association
730 3rd Avenue
New York, NY 10017-3206
212-490-9000
Fax: 800-914-8922
www.tiaa-cref.org
Offers timely information and helpful hints about savings, investments, finance and insurance for teachers and educators.

Publication Date: 1918 Quarterly

Roger Ferguson, President/ CEO
Ron Pressman, EVP/ COO

4290 Telluride Newsletter
217 West Ave.
Ithaca, NY 14850
607-273-5011
Fax: 607-272-2667
telluride@tellurideassociation.org
www.tellurideassociation.org
News of interest to alumni of Telluride Association sponsored programs.

Publication Date: 1891 8 pages TriQuarterly

Eric Lemer

4291 Tennessee Education
University of Tennessee
College of Education
Knoxville, TN 37996-0001
865-974-5252
Fax: 865-974-8718
admissions@utk.edu
www.utk.edu
Publishes articles on topics related to K through higher education.

BiAnnually
ISSN: 0739-0408

Mary Lucal, Assistant Vice Chancellor

4292 The Independent Scholar (TIS)
National Coalition of Independent Scholars
125 Putney Road
Battleboro, VT 05301
tis@ncis.org
www.ncis.org

A peer-reviewed open-access journal for independent scholars.

Amanda Haste, President
Kathleen Stein-Smith, Communications Officer

293 The Leaflet
Higher Learning Commission
230 S LaSalle Street
Suite 7-500
Chicago, IL 60604-1411
312-621-7440
800-621-7440
Fax: 312-263-7462
info@hlcommission.org
www.hlcommission.org
Provides updates, news and resources pertaining to the Higher Learning Commission, as well as accreditation and the field of higher education.

Barbara Gellman-Danley, President
Eric Martin, Executive Vice President

294 The Sounds and Spelling Patterns of English: P Honics for Teachers and Parents
Oxton House Publishers, LLC
Po Box 209
Farmington, ME 04938
207-779-1923
800-539-7323
Fax: 207-779-0623
info@oxtonhouse.com
www.oxtonhouse.com
A clear, concise, practical, jargon-free overview of the sounds that make up the English language and the symbols that we use to represent them in writing. It includes a broad range of strategies for helping beginning readers develop fluent decoding skills.

62 pages

Jill Fulkerson, Representative, Colorado
Phillip Neill, Representative, Texas

295 Theory Into Practice
Ohio State University, College of Education
122 Ramseyer Hall
29 W Woodruff Avenue
Columbus, OH 43210
614-292-3407
Fax: 614-292-7900
tip@osu.edu
Nationally recognized for excellence in educational journalism; thematic format, providing comprehensive discussion of single topic with many diverse points of view.

Quarterly
ISSN: 0040-5841

Anita Woolfolk Hey, Author
Anita Woolfolk Hey, Editor

296 Thought & Action
National Education Association
1201 16th Street NW
Washington, DC 20036-3290
202-833-4000
Fax: 202-822-7974
www.subscribenea.com
The journal was published by the National Education Association from 1985-2018, and was a peer-reviewed journal of higher education, offering both theoretical and practical information. Copies are still available online.

Lily Eskelsen Garcia, President
John C Stocks, Executive Director

297 Three R'S for Teachers: Research, Reports & Reviews
Master Teacher
Po Box 1207
Manhattan, KS 66502
785-539-0555
800-669-9633
Fax: 800-669-1132
www.masterteacher.com
The publication that synthesizes the most recent educational research, data and trends on specific topics for teachers.

Publication Date: 1969 Quarterly

Dr. Joanna Hubbs, President
Gregory Hubbs, Editor-in-Chief

4298 Tidbits
Assn. for Legal Support of Alternative Schools
PO Box 2823
Santa Fe, NM 87504-2823
505-471-6928
Information and legal advice to those involved in non-public educational facilities.

12 pages Quarterly

Ed Nagel

4299 Transitions Abroad: The Guide to Learning, Living, & Working Abroad
Transitions Abroad
P.O. Box 1369
Amherst, MA 1004
413-992-6486
Fax: 802-442-4827
webeditor@TransitionsAbroad.com
www.transitionsabroad.com
This magazine contains articles and bibliographies on travel, study, teaching, internships and work abroad.

Publication Date: 1977 Bi-Monthly

4300 Unschoolers Network
Unschoolers Network
2 Smith Street
Farmingdale, NJ 07727
732-938-2473
UnNet@unschooling.org
www.unschooling.org/UnNet
Information and support for families teaching their children at home.

Publication Date: 1977 14 pages Monthly

Nancy Plent

4301 VSBA Newsletter
Vermont School Boards Association
2 Prospect Street
Montpelier, VT 05602
802-223-3580
800-244-8722
www.vtvsba.org
General information.

Publication Date: 1936 16 pages Monthly

Stephen Dale, Executive Director
Kerri Lamb, Operations Manager

4302 WACE Newsletter
World Association for Cooperative Education
University of Waterloo
200 University Avenue W
Waterloo, ON N2L-3G1
admin@waceinc.org
www.waceinc.org
Provides information on co-operative and work-integrated education developments across the globe.

Maurits van Rooijen, Co-Chair
Sampan Silapanad, Co-Chair

4303 WCER Highlights
Wisconsin Center for Education Research
1025 W Johnson Street
Suite 785
Madison, WI 53706
608-263-4200
Fax: 608-263-6448
uw-wcer@education.wisc.edu
www.wcer.wisc.edu
News about research conducted at the Wisconsin Center for Education Research.

Publication Date: 1964 8 pages Quarterly
ISSN: 1073-1882

Robert Mathieu, Director
Paul Baker, Specialist

4304 Western Journal of Black Studies
Washington State University
Heritage House
Pullman, WA 99164-0001
509-335-3564
888-468-6978
Fax: 509-335-8338
admissions@wsu.edu
www.wsu.edu
A journal which canvasses topical issues affecting Black studies and education.

Publication Date: 1890 Quarterly

Elson S. Floyd, Ph.D., President
Daniel J. Bernardo, Provost & EVP

4305 World Council for Gifted and Talented Children
Western Kentucky University
1906 College Heights Boulevard
Suite 11030
Bowling Green, KY 42101
270-745-4123
headquarters@world-gifted.org
www.world-gifted.org
Offers information and articles on gifted education for the professional.

4306 Young Audiences Newsletter
Young Audiences New York
One East 53rd Street
New York, NY 10128-1688
212-319-9269
Fax: 212-319-9272
info@yany.org
www.yany.org
Organization news of performing arts education programs in schools and communities.

Publication Date: 1952 Annual

Kim Greenberg, Chair
Robert Riesenberg, President

Periodicals / Administration

4307 AASA Journal of Scholarship and Practice
American Association of School Administrators
1615 Duke Street
Alexandria, VA 22314
703-528-0700
Fax: 703-841-1543
info@aasa.org
www.aasa.org
Published by the Leadership Development Office of the American Association of School Administrators, this refereed journal focuses on research and evidence-based practice.

Quarterly

Ken Mitchell, Ed.D, Editor

4308 ACCT Advisor
Association of Community College Trustees
1101 17th Street NW
Suite 300
Washington, DC 20036
202-775-4667
Fax: 202-223-1297

acctinfo@acct.org
www.acct.org
Provides news of association events, federal regulations, activities, state activities, legal issues and other news of interest to community college governing board members.

Robin M. Smith, Chair
Bakari Lee, Vice Chair

4309 AVA Update
Association for Volunteer Administration
PO Box 4584
Boulder, CO 80306-4584
303-447-0558
Information of value to administrators of volunteer services.

4 pages BiMonthly

Martha Martin

4310 Accreditation Fact Sheet
NAPNSC Accrediting Commission for Higher Education
182 Thompson Road
Grand Junction, CO 81503-2246
970-243-5441
Fax: 970-242-4392
Newsletter reporting on the origin, history, developments, procedures and changes of educational institution accreditation.

Annually

H. Earl Heusser, Author
H Earl Heusser, Executive Director

4311 Administrative Information Report
Nat'l Association of Secondary School Principles
1904 Association Drive
Reston, VA 20191-1537
703-860-0200
800-253-7746
Fax: 703-620-6534
www.principals.org
Offers school statistics and administrative updates for secondary school principals and management officers.

Publication Date: 1916 4 pages Monthly

G.A. Buie, President
JoAnn D. Bartoletti, Executive Director

4312 American School & University Magazine
Intertec Publishing
PO Box 12960
Overland Park, KS 66282-2960
913-967-1960
Fax: 913-967-1905
Directed at business and facilities administrators in the nation's public and private schools.

Monthly

Joe Agron, Editor

4313 American School Board Journal (ASBJ)
National School Boards Association
1680 Duke Street
2nd Floor
Alexandria, VA 22314-3493
703-838-6722
Fax: 703-683-7590
info@nsba.org
www.nsba.org
Published primarily for school board members and school system superintendents serving public elementary and secondary schools in the United States and Canada.

Publication Date: 1891 Bimonthly

Viola M. Garcia, President
Chip Slaven, Interim Executive Director

4314 Board
Master Teacher
PO Box 1207
Manhattan, KS 66502
785-539-0555
800-669-9633
Fax: 800-669-1132
www.masterteacher.com
Designed to be a continuous form of communication to help board members know and understand the duties, responsibilities, and commitments of the office; view the superintendent of schools as the educational leader; improve administrator-board working relationships; better understand the purpose of education; and work at their responsibilities in a prudent, calm, and rational manner.

Publication Date: 1969 Monthly

Dr. Joanna Hubbs, President
Gregory Hubbs, Editor-in-Chief

4315 Building Leadership Bulletin
2990 Baker Drive
Springfield, IL 62703-2800
217-525-1383
Fax: 217-525-7264
www.ipa.vsta.net
Topical, timely issues.

8 pages 11x Year

Julie Weichert, Associate Director

4316 Business Education Forum
National Business Education Association
1914 Association Drive
Suite 203
Reston, VA 20191
703-860-8300
Fax: 703-860-4483
nbea@nbea.org
www.nbea.org
A journal of distinctive articles dealing with current issues and trends, future directions and exemplary programs in business education at all instructional levels. Articles focus on international business, life-long learning, cultural diversity, critical thinking, economics, state-of-the-art technology and the latest research in the field.

Publication Date: 1939 200 pages Quarterly

Joe McClary, Executive Director
Jeri Werner, Operations Manager

4317 California Schools Magazine
California School Boards Association
3251 Beacon Boulevard
West Sacramento, CA 95691
800-266-3382
csba@csba.org
www.csba.org
For school board members, superintendents and school business managers responsible for the operation of California's public schools. Articles of interest to parents, teachers, community members and anyone else concerned with public education.

Quarterly
ISSN: 1081-8936

Vernon M. Billy, Executive Director & CEO
Troy Flint, Chief Information Officer

4318 Clearing House: A Journal of Educational Research
Heldref Publications
325 Chestnut Street
Suite 800
Philadelphia, PA 19106
215-625-8900
800-365-9753
Fax: 202-296-5149
customer.service@taylorandfrancis.com
www.heldref.org
Each issue offers a variety of articles for teachers and administrators of middle schools and junior and senior high schools. It includes experiments, trends and accomplishments in courses, teaching methods, administrative procedures and school programs.

4 pages BiMonthly
ISSN: 0009-8655

Deborah N Cohen, Promotions Manager
Judy Cusick, Managing Editor

4319 College & University (C&U) Journal
American Assoc of Collegiate Registrars/Admissions
1108 16th Street NW
Suite 400
Washington, DC 20036
202-293-9161
Fax: 202-872-8857
communications@aacrao.org
www.aacrao.org
Current issues, new techniques and technology are examined in this policy and research journal on higher education.

Quarterly

Tiffany Robinson, President
Melanie Gottlieb, Interim Executive Director

4320 Currents Magazine
Council for Advancement & Support of Education
1201 Eye Street NW
Washington, DC 20005
202-328-2273
Fax: 202-387-4973
membersupportcenter@case.org
www.case.org
Published nine times a year and distributed to professional members, Currents delivers essential information, insight and ideas that empower those who support education to master challenges and act decisively to create a better future for their institutions and the world.

Sue Cunningham, President & CEO
Rob Moore, VP, Communications

4321 ERS Spectrum
Educational Research Service
1001 N. Fairfax Street
Suite 500
Arlington, VA 22314-1587
703-243-2100
800-791-9308
Fax: 703-243-1985
www.ers.org
A quarterly journal of school research and information. Publishes practical research and information for school decisions. Authors include practicing administrators and other educators in local school districts.

Publication Date: 1958 48 pages Quarterly
ISSN: 0740-7874

Lester Strong, Chair
Christopher Curran, Vice Chair

4322 Education Daily
LRP Publications
360 Hiatt Drive
Palm Beach Gardens, FL 33418
703-516-7002
800-341-7874

Fax: 561-622-2423
custserve@lrp.com
www.lrp.com
News on national education policy. Offers daily reports of Education Department policies, initiatives and priorities— how they are developed and how they affect school programs.

Publication Date: 1977 6-8 pages Daily

Kenneth F. Kahn, President

323 Educational Administration Quarterly

University of Wisconsin, Milwaukee
PO Box 413
Milwaukee, WI 53201-0413
414-229-1122
Fax: 414-229-5300
www.www4.uwm.edu
Deals with administrative issues and policy.

Quarterly

Mark Mone, Chancellor
Johannes Britz, Provost/ Vice Chancellor

324 Electronic Learning

Scholastic
555 Broadway
New York, NY 10012-3919
212-343-6100
800-724-6527
Fax: 212-343-4801
Published for the administrative level, education professionals who are directly responsible for the implementing of electronic technology at the district, state and university levels.

8x Year

Lynn Diamond, Advertising Director
Therese Mageau, Editor

325 Enrollment Management Report

LRP Publications
360 Hiatt Drive
Palm Beach Gardens, FL 33418
703-516-7002
800-341-7874
Fax: 561-622-2423
custserve@lrp.com
www.lrp.com
Provides colleges and universities with solutions and strategies for recruitment, admissions, retention and financial aid. Reviews the latest trends, research studies and their findings and gives a profile on how other institutions are handling their enrollment management issues.

Publication Date: 1977 Monthly
ISSN: 1094-3757

Kenneth F. Kahn, President

326 Galileo For Superintendents And District Level Administrators

Master Teacher
Po Box 1207
Manhattan, KS 66505
785-539-0555
800-669-9633
Fax: 800-669-1132
www.masterteacher.com
The monthly web and print service provides direction & strategies for superintendents and district level administrators.

Publication Date: 1969 Monthly Newsletter

Dr. Joanna Hubbs, President
Gregory Hubbs, Editor-in-Chief

327 HR on Campus

LRP Publications
360 Hiatt Drive
Palm Beach Gardens, FL 33418
703-516-7002
800-341-7874
Fax: 561-622-2423
custserve@lrp.com
www.lrp.com
This monthly newsletter provides coverage of the latest and most inovative programs higher education institutions use to handle their human resource challenges. Plus, you can recieve free e-mail updates on crucial news affecting your job with your paid subscription.

Publication Date: 1977 Monthly
ISSN: 1098-9293

Kenneth F. Kahn, President

4328 IPA Newsletter

2990 Baker Drive
Springfield, IL 62703-2800
217-525-1383
Fax: 217-525-7264
www.ipa.vsta.net
Provides current information on Illinois principals and the profession.

8 pages 11x Year

David Turner, Author
Julie Weichert, Associate Director

4329 Integrated Pathways

Association of Integrative Studies
Miami University
Oxford, OH 45056
513-529-2659
Fax: 513-529-5849
rszostak@ualberta.ca
www.units.muohio.edu/aisorg
AIS news, including updates on AIS conferences, decisions of the AIS Board of Directors, and membership announcements. Published quarterly.

Publication Date: 1979
ISSN: 1081-647X

Rick Szostak, President
James Welch, Vice President, Development

4330 Journal of Education for Business

Heldref Publications
325 Chestnut Street
Suite 800
Philadelphia, PA 19106
215-625-8900
800-365-9753
Fax: 202-296-5149
customer.service@taylorandfrancis.com
www.heldref.org
Offers information to instructors, supervisors, and administrators at the secondary, postsecondary and collegiate levels. The journal features basic and applied research-based articles in accounting, communications, economics, finance, information systems, management, marketing and other business disciplines.

BiMonthly

4331 Keystone Schoolmaster Newsletter

Pennsylvania Assn. of Secondary School Principals
PO Box 39
122 Valley Road
Summerdale, PA 17093
717-732-4999
Fax: 717-732-4890
Reports achievements, honors, problems and innovations by officers and established authorities.

Publication Date: 1960 4 pages Monthly

Jacqueline Clarke Havrilla, President
Paul M. Healey, PhD, Executive Director

4332 Leading Edge

National School Public Relations Association
15948 Derwood Road
Rockville, MD 20855
301-519-0496
Fax: 301-519-0494
info@nspra.org
www.nspra.org
Newsletter for National School Public Relations Association chapter leaders.

Barbara Hunter, Executive Director
Mellissa Braham, Associate Director

4333 Legal Notes for Education

Progressive Business Publications
370 Technology Drive
Malvern, PA 19355
610-695-8600
800-220-5000
Fax: 610-647-8089
customer_service@pbp.com
www.pbp.com
Reports the latest school law cases and late-breaking legislation along with the most recent law review articles affecting education. Federal and state appellate court decisions are summarized and the full legal citation is supplied for each case.

Publication Date: 1959 Monthly

Ed Satell, Founder
Liz Webb, Human Resources

4334 Maintaining Safe Schools

LRP Publications
360 Hiatt Drive
Palm Beach Gardens, FL 33418
703-516-7002
800-341-7874
Fax: 561-622-2423
custserve@lrp.com
www.lrp.com
Focuses on the legal and practical issues involved in preventing and responding to violent acts by students in schools, and highlights successful violence prevention programs in school districts across the country. Offers strategies for mediation, discipline and crisis managment.

Publication Date: 1977 Monthly
ISSN: 1082-4774

Kenneth F. Kahn, President

4335 Managing School Business

LRP Publications
360 Hiatt Drive
Palm Beach Gardens, FL 33418
703-516-7002
800-341-7874
Fax: 561-622-2423
custserve@lrp.com
www.lrp.com
Newsletter provides school business managers with tips on how to solve the problems they face in managing finance, operations, personnel, and their own career.

Publication Date: 1977 Biweekly
ISSN: 1092-2229

Angela Childers, Author
Kenneth F. Kahn, President

4336 Memo to the President

American Assn. of State Colleges & Universities
1307 New York Avenue NW
5th Floor
Washington, DC 20005
202-293-7070
Fax: 202-296-5819
www.aascu.org
Monitors public policies at national, state and campus level on higher education issues.

Reports on activities of the Association and member institutions.

20 pages Monthly
November

J. Keith Motley, Chair
Muriel A. Howard, President

4337 National Faculty Forum
National Faculty of Humanities, Arts & Sciences
1676 Clifton Road NE
Atlanta, GA 30329-4050
404-727-5788
Offers administrative news and updates for persons in higher education.

TriQuarterly

4338 News of the Nation
American Association of School Administrators
1615 Duke Street
Alexandria, VA 22314
703-528-0700
Fax: 703-841-1543
info@aasa.org
www.aasa.org
Provides members with education news from across the U.S.

Juli Valentine, Editor

4339 OASCD Journal
Oklahoma Curriculum Development
3705 S. 98th East Avenue
Tulsa, OK 74146
918-627-4403
Fax: 918-627-4433
A refereed journal which prints contributions on curriculum theory and practices, leadership in education, staff development and supervision. The Editorial Board welcomes photographs, letters to the editor, program descriptions, interviews, research reports, theoretical pieces, reviews of books and non-print media, poetry, humor, cartoons, satire and children's art and writing, as well as expository articles.

Annual

Blaine Smith, Executive Secretary

4340 On Board
New York State School Boards Association
24 Century Hill Drive
Suite 200
Latham, NY 12110-2125
518-783-0200
Fax: 518-783-0211
info@nyssba.org
www.nyssba.org
Contains general educational news, state and federal legislative activity, legal and employee relations issues, commentary, issues in education, and successful education programs around the state.

Fred J. Langstaff, President
Robert Schneider, Executive Director

4341 Perspectives for Policymakers
New Jersey School Boards Association
413 W State Street
#909
Trenton, NJ 08618-5617
609-695-7600
888-88N-SBA
info@njsba.org
www.njsba.org
Each issue focuses on a specific topic in education providing background, activities and resources.

8 pages SemiAnnually

Donald Webster, Jr., President
Daniel T. Sinclair, VP, County Activities

4342 Planning & Changing
Illinois State University
College of Education
Campus Box 5300
Normal, IL 61790-5300
309-438-2399
Fax: 309-438-8683
www.coe.ilstu.edu/eafdept/pandc.htm
An educational leadership and policy journal. This journal attempts to disseminate timely and useful reports of practice and theory with particular emphasis on change, and planning in K-12 educational settings and higher education settings. Paperback.

Publication Date: 1857 64 pages Quarterly
ISSN: 0032-0684

Perry Schoon, Chair, College Faculty
Alan Bates, College Faculty

4343 Principal
Nat'l Association of Elementary School Principals
1615 Duke Street
Alexandria, VA 22314-3406
703-684-3345
Fax: 800-396-2377
A professional magazine edited for elementary and middle school principals and others interested in education.

5x Year

Leon E Greene, Editor
Louanne M Wheeler, Production Manager

4344 Principal Communicator
National School Public Relations Association
15948 Derwood Road
Rockville, MD 20855
301-519-0496
Fax: 301-519-0494
nspra@nspra.org
www.napra.org
Tips for building public relations people.

6 pages Monthly

Andy Grunig, Manager of Communications

4345 Private Education Law Report
Progressive Business Publications
370 Technology Drive
Malvern, PA 19355
610-695-8600
800-220-5000
Fax: 610-647-8089
customer_service@pbp.com
www.pbp.com
Reports the latest school law cases and late-breaking legislation along with the most recent law review articles affecting private education. Federal and state appellate court decisions are summarized and the full legal citation is supplied for each case.

Publication Date: 1959 Monthly

Ed Satell, Founder
Liz Webb, Human Resources

4346 Public Personnel Management
International Personnel Management Association
1617 Duke Street
Alexandria, VA 22314-3406
703-549-7100
Fax: 703-684-0948
Caters to those professionals in human resource management.

Quarterly

Sarah AI Shiffert, Editor

4347 Rural Educator-Journal for Rural and Small Schools
National Rural Education Association
Colorado State University
Fort Collins, CO 80523
970-491-7022
Fax: 970-491-1317
www.colostate.edu
Official journal of the NREA. A nationally recognized publication that features timely and informative articles written by leading rural educators from all levels of education. All NREA members are encouraged to submit research articles and items of general information for publication.

Publication Date: 1870 40 pages Quarterly Magazine
ISSN: 0273-446X

Joseph T Newlin, Editor

4348 School Administrator
American Association of School Administrators
1615 Duke Street
Alexandria, VA 22314
703-528-0700
Fax: 703-841-1543
info@aasa.org
www.aasa.org
Ensures the highest quality education systems for all learners through the support and development of leadership on the building, district and state levels.

Monthly

Jay Goldman, Editor

4349 School Business Affairs (SBA)
Association of School Business Officials Int'l
44790 Maynard Square
Suite 200
Ashburn, VA 20147
866-682-2729
Fax: 703-478-0205
asboreq@asbointl.org
www.asbointl.org
For school business administrators responsible for the administration and purchase of products and services for the schools.

11x Year

David Lewis, Executive Director
Siobhan McMahon, CAE, Chief Operations Officer

4350 School Business Leader
Association of School Business Officials Int'l
44790 Maynard Square
Suite 200
Ashburn, VA 20147
866-682-2729
Fax: 703-478-0205
asboreq@asbointl.org
www.asbointl.org
Leadership-focused newsletter of the Association of School Business Officials International, and is member-exclusive.

David Lewis, Executive Director
Siobhan McMahon, CAE, Chief Operations Officer

4351 School Law Briefings
LRP Publications
360 Hiatt Drive
Palm Beach Gardens, FL 33418
703-516-7002
800-341-7874
Fax: 561-622-2423

custserve@lrp.com
www.lrp.com
Gives you summaries of general education, special education, and early childhood court cases, as well as administrative hearings.

Publication Date: 1977 Monthly
ISSN: 1094-3749

Kenneth F. Kahn, President

352 School Law News
LRP Publications
360 Hiatt Drive
Palm Beach Gardens, FL 33418
703-516-7002
800-341-7874
Fax: 561-622-2423
custserve@lrp.com
www.lrp.com
Advises administrators to avoid legal pitfalls by monitoring education-related court action across the nation. With School Law News, administrators receive the latest information on issues like sexual harassment liability, special education, religion in the schools, affirmative action, youth violence, student-faculty rights, school finance, desegregation and much more.

Publication Date: 1977 8-10 pages Monthly

Kenneth F. Kahn, President

353 School Planning & Management
Peter Li Education Group
2621 Dryden Road
Suite 300
Dayton, OH 45439
937-293-1415
800-523-4625
Fax: 800-370-4450
For the business needs of school administrators featuring issues, ideas and technology at work in public, private and independent schools.

Monthly
ISSN: 1086-4628

Peter J Li, Publisher
Deborah Moore, Editor

354 Section 504 Compliance Advisor
LRP Publications
360 Hiatt Drive
Palm Beach Gardens, FL 33418
703-516-7002
800-341-7874
Fax: 561-622-2423
custserve@lrp.com
www.lrp.com
Newsletter examines the requirements of Section 504 of the Rehabilitation Act and analyzes their impact on disciplining students. Provides educators and administrators with detailed tips and advice to help them solve the discipline problems they face everyday and keep their policies and programs in compliance.

Publication Date: 1977 Monthly
ISSN: 1094-3730

Kenneth F. Kahn, President

355 Special Education Law Monthly
LRP Publications
360 Hiatt Drive
Palm Beach Gardens, FL 33418
703-516-7002
800-341-7874
Fax: 561-622-2423
custserve@lrp.com
www.lrp.com
Covers court decisions and administrative rulings affecting the education of students with disabilities.

Publication Date: 1977 Monthly
ISSN: 1094-3773

Kenneth F. Kahn, President

4356 Special Education Law Report
Progressive Business Publications
370 Technology Drive
Malvern, PA 19355
610-695-8600
800-220-5000
Fax: 610-647-8089
www.pbp.com
Reports the latest school law cases and late-breaking legislation along with the most recent law review articles affecting special education. Federal and state appellate court decisions are summarized and the full legal citation is supplied for each case.

Publication Date: 1959 Monthly

Ed Satell, Founder
Liz Webb, Human Resources

4357 Special Education Report
LRP Publications
360 Hiatt Drive
Palm Beach Gardens, FL 33418
703-516-7002
800-341-7874
Fax: 561-622-2423
custserve@lrp.com
www.lrp.com
The special education administrator's direct pipeline to federal legislation, regulation and funding of programs for children and youths with disabilities.

Publication Date: 1977 6-8 pages Monthly

Kenneth F. Kahn, President

4358 Strategic Enrollment Management (SEM) Quarterly
American Assoc of Collegiate Registrars/Admissions
1108 16th Street NW
Suite 400
Washington, DC 20036
202-293-9161
Fax: 202-872-8857
communications@aacrao.org
www.aacrao.org
Promotes research in innovative enrollment methods.

Quarterly

Tiffany Robinson, President
Melanie Gottlieb, Interim Executive Director

4359 Student Affairs Today
LRP Publications
360 Hiatt Drive
Palm Beach Gardens, FL 33418
703-516-7002
800-341-7874
Fax: 561-622-2423
custserve@lrp.com
www.lrp.com
Newsletter provides strategies and tips for handling higher education institutions' student affairs challenges and problems involving: sexual harassment, binge drinking, fraternity and sorority activities, student housing and more. Gives profiles of other colleges programs.

Publication Date: 1977 Monthly
ISSN: 1098-5166

Kenneth F. Kahn, President

4360 Superintendents Only Notebook
Master Teacher
Leadership Lane
PO Box 1207
Manhattan, KS 66502
800-669-9633
Fax: 800-669-1132
www.masterteacher.com
Offers superintendents hundreds of solid ideas to help their jobs run more smoothly. Written by practicing superintendents and business executives, this publication saves hundreds of hours of anguish over the course of the year.

Publication Date: 1969 Monthly

Dr. Joanna Hubbs, President
Gregory Hubbs, Editor-in-Chief

4361 THE Journal Technology Horizons in Education
T.H.E Journal
1105 Media
9201 Oakdale Ave., Suite 101
Chatsworth, CA 91311
818-734-1520
Fax: 818-734-1522
editorial@thejournal.com
www.thejournal.com
A forum for administrators and managers in school districts to share their experiences in the use of technology-based educational aids.

Publication Date: 1972

Rajeev Kapur, Chief Executive Officer
Henry Allain, Chief Operating Officer

4362 The Learning Professional
Learning Forward
504 S Locust Street
Oxford, OH 45056
513-523-6029
800-727-7288
Fax: 513-523-0638
office@learningforward.org
www.learningforward.org
Devoted to strengthening the knowledge and skills of education personnel.

6x Year

Denise Glyn Borders, President & CEO
Michael Lanham, COO & CFO

4363 Thrust for Educational Leadership
Association of California School Administrators
1029 J Street
Suite 500
Sacramento, CA 95814
916-444-3216
800-608-2272
Fax: 916-444-3739
rdelling@lausd.net
www.acsa.org
Designed for school administrators who must stay abreast of educational developments, management and personnel practices, social attitudes and issues that impact schools.

Publication Date: 1971 7x Year

Randall V. Delling, President
Ralph Gomez Porras, Vice President

4364 Title I Handbook
Thompson Publishing Group, Inc.
P.O. Box 41868
Austin, TX 78704
800-677-3789
Fax: 800-999-5661
service@thompson.com
www.titleionline.com
Two-volume looseleaf provides complete, up-to-date coverage of Title I, the largest federal program of aid for elementary and secondary education. The book contains all the laws, regulations and guidance needed to

sucessfully operate the grant program, and insightful articles on key Title I topics, ongoing budget coverage, and special reports on issues like Title I testing, schoolwide programs, and audits. Also included is a compilation of official Title I policy letters, found nowhere else.

Publication Date: 1972 1,500 pages Quarterly

Cheryl L. Sattler, Author
Jeannette Burke, Director, Product Marketing
Mark Reishus, Energy Regulation

4365 **Title I Monitor**
Thompson Publishing Group, Inc.
P.O. Box 41868
Austin, TX 78704
202-872-4000
800-677-3789
Fax: 800-999-5661
service@thompson.com
www.titleionline.com
This newsletter provides continuing coverage of Title I, the largest federal program of aid for elementary and secondary education. Title I is at the heart of the debate over education reform, and the Monitor ensures that educators have the most up-to-date information about developments in this ever-changing program. Breaking news about the Title I budget, new legislation and regulations, court cases and other issues.

Publication Date: 1972 Monthly
ISSN: 1086-2455

Cheryl L Sattler, Author
Jeannette Burke, Director, Product Marketing
Mark Reishus, Energy Regulation

4366 **Training Magazine**
Lakewood Publications
P.O. Box 247
27020 Noble Road
Excelsior, MN 55331
847-559-7596
800-328-4329
Fax: 847-559-7596
ntrn@omeda.com
www.trainingmag.com
Focuses on corporate training and employee development, as well as management and human performance issues.

Monthly

Mike Murrell, President/ Publisher
Bryan Powell, VP - Finance/Operations

Periodicals / Early Childhood Education

4367 **Child Development**
Arizona State University
University Drive and Mill Avenue
Tempe, AZ 85287
480-965-9011
Fax: 480-965-8544
www.asu.edu
Offers professionals working with children news on childhood education, books, reviews, questions and answers and professional articles of interest.

BiMonthly

Michael M. Crow, President
Morgan R. Olsen, VP, Business & Finance

4368 **Child Study Journal**
Buffalo State College
1300 Elmwood Avenue
Buffalo, NY 14222
716-878-4000
www.suny.buffalostate.edu
Articles of interest related to childhood education.

Publication Date: 1871 Quarterly

Katherine S. Conway-Turner, President

4369 **Childhood Education Innovations**
Childhood Education International
1100 15th Street NW
4th Floor
Washington, DC 20005
202-372-9986
800-423-3563
www.ceinternational1892.org
Features innovations in childhood education from schools around the world, seeking to address challenges faced by educators.

Publication Date: 1892

Diane Whitehead, Chief Executive Officer
Anne Bauer, Director, Publications

4370 **Children Today**
ACF Office of Public Affairs
370 L'Enfant Promenade, S.W.
4th Floor
Washington, DC 20447
202-401-9215
888-747-1861
Fax: 202-205-9688
www.acf.hhs.gov/office-of-public-affairs
An interdisciplinary magazine published by the Administration for Children and Families (ACF). The content is a mix of theory and practice, research and features, news and opinions for its audience.

Quarterly

Jeff Hild, Chief of Staff
Mark Greenberg, Assistant Secretary

4371 **Communication Disorders Quarterly**
Council for Exceptional Children
3100 Clarendon Boulevard
Suite 600
Arlington, VA 22201-5332
888-232-7733
service@exceptionalchildren.org
www.exceptionalchildren.org
Information concerning education and welfare of children with communication disorders.

Quarterly

4372 **Early Childhood Education Journal**
Kluwer Academic/Human Sciences Press
233 Spring Street
New York, NY 10013
212-620-8000
Fax: 212-463-0742
www.wkpa.nl
Provides professional guidance on instructional methods and materials, child development trends, funding and administrative issues and the politics of day care.

Quarterly
ISSN: 1082-3301

Carol Bischoff, Publisher
Mary Renck Jalongo, Editor

4373 **Early Childhood Report**
LRP Publications
360 Hiatt Drive
Palm Beach Gardens, FL 33418
703-516-7002
800-341-7874
Fax: 561-622-2423
custserve@lrp.com
www.lrp.com
Educational newsletter for parents and professionals involved at the local state and federal levels responsible for the design and implementation of early childhood programs.

Publication Date: 1977 Monthly
ISSN: 1058-6482

Kenneth F. Kahn, President

4374 **Early Childhood Research Quarterly**
Department of Individuals & Family Syudies
111 Alison Annex
University of Delaware
Newark, DE 19716
302-831-6500
Fax: 302-831-8776
hdfs-dept@udel.edu
www.hdfs.udel.edu
Addresses various topics in the development and education of young children.

Quarterly

Dr. Marion Hyson, Editor

4375 **Early Childhood Today**
Scholastic
555 Broadway
New York, NY 10012
212-343-6100
800-724-6527
Fax: 212-343-4801
www.scholastic.com
The magazine for all early childhood professionals working with infants to six-year-olds. Each issue provides child development information resources, staff development information and parent communication information.

Publication Date: 1920 8x Year
ISSN: 1070-1214

Richard Robinson, Chair/ President/ CEO
Maureen O'Connell, EVP/ CFO/ CAO

4376 **Helping Children Learn: Early Childhood Edition**
The Parent Institute
PO Box 7474
Fairfax Station, VA 22039-7474
800-756-5525
Fax: 800-216-3667
customer@parent-institute.com
www.parent-institute.com
Newsletter providing parents with tips on helping their children succeed in school.

9x Year

4377 **Highlights for Children**
Highlights for Children
PO Box 269
1800 Watermark Drive
Columbus, OH 43216-0269
888-372-6433
www.highlights.com/working-for-highlights
Magazine featuring Fun with a Purpose, to all children preschool to preteen. Features stories, hidden pictures, reading and thinking exercises, crafts, puzzles, and more.

Publication Date: 1946

Kent S. Johnson, CEO
Christine French Cully, Editor in Chief

4378 **Journal of Early Intervention**
Council for Exceptional Children
3100 Clarendon Boulevard
Suite 600
Arlington, VA 22201-5332
888-232-7733
service@exceptionalchildren.org
www.exceptionalchildren.org

Official Journal of the Division for Early Childhood of the Council for Exceptional Children.

Quarterly
ISSN: 1053-8151

Brian Boyd, Editor
Brian Reichow, Editor

4379 Journal of Research in Childhood Education
Childhood Education International
1100 15th Street NW
4th Floor
Washington, DC 20005
202-372-9986
800-423-3563
www.ceinternational1892.org
Current research in education and related fields. It is intended to advance knowledge and theory of the education of children, from infancy through early adolescence. The journal seeks to stimulate the exchange of research ideas through publication of: reports of empirical research; theroretical articles; ethnographic and case studies; cross-cultural studies and studies addressing international concerns; and participant observation studies.

Publication Date: 1892 142 pages
ISSN: 0256-8543

Diane Whitehead, Chief Executive Officer
Anne Bauer, Director, Publications

4380 Pre-K Today
Scholastic
555 Broadway
New York, NY 10012
212-343-6100
800-724-6527
Fax: 212-343-4801
www.scholastic.com
Edited to serve the needs of early childhood professionals, owners, directors, teachers and administrators in preschools and kindergarten.

Publication Date: 1920 8x Year

Richard Robinson, Chair/ President/ CEO
Maureen O'Connell, EVP/ CFO/ CAO

4381 Report on Preschool Programs
Business Publishers
2222 Sedwick Drive
Durham, NC 27713
301-587-6300
800-223-8720
Fax: 800-508-2592
custserv@bpinews.com
www.bpinews.com
Reports on information about Head Start regulations, federal funding policies, state trends in Pre-K and research news. Also covers information on grant and contract opportunities.

Publication Date: 1963 8 pages BiWeekly

Eric Easton, Publisher
Chuck Devarics, Editor

4382 SERVE Center at UNC Greensboro
5900 Summit Avenue
Suite 201
Greensboro, NC 27412
336-315-7400
800-755-3277
Fax: 336-315-7457
info@serve.org
www.serve.org
Its mission is to support and promote teaching and learning excellence in the Pre-Kindergarten to Grade 12 education community.

George Hancock, Executive Director

4383 The Active Learner
HighScope Educational Research Foundation
600 N River Street
Ypsilanti, MI 48198
800-587-5639
info@highscope.org
www.highscope.org
Early education journal of HighScope Educational Research Foundation, with teaching tips, activities, research and policies.

Alejandra Barraza, Ph.D, President
Kimberly Diamond-Berry, Ph.D, Director, Research Policy

4384 Topics in Early Childhood Special Education
Pro-Ed
8700 Shoal Creek Boulevard
Austin, TX 78757-6897
512-451-3246
800-897-3202
Fax: 512-451-8542
general@proedinc.com
www.proedinc.com
Provides program developers, advocates, researchers, higher education faculty and other leaders with the most current, relevant research on all aspects of early childhood education for children with special needs.

Judith J Carta, PhD, Editor

4385 Totline Newsletter
Frank Schaffer Publications
23740 Hawthorne Boulevard
Torrance, CA 90505
310-378-1137
800-421-5533
Fax: 800-837-7260
fspcustsrv@aol.com
www.frankschaffer.com
Creative activities for working with toddlers and preschool children.

32 pages BiMonthly

Periodicals / Elementary Education

4386 Childhood Education Innovations
Childhood Education International
1100 15th Street NW
4th Floor
Washington, DC 20005
202-372-9986
800-423-3563
www.ceinternational1892.org
Features innovations in childhood education from schools around the world, seeking to address challenges faced by educators.

Publication Date: 1892

Diane Whitehead, Chief Executive Officer
Anne Bauer, Director, Publications

4387 Children's Literature in Education
Kluwer Academic/Human Sciences Press
233 Spring Street
New York, NY 10013
212-620-8000
Fax: 212-463-0742
www.wkpa.nl
Source for stimulating articles and interviews on noted children's authors, incisive critiques of classic and contemporary writing for young readers, and original articles describing successful classroom reading projects. Offers timely reviews on a variety of reading-related topics for teachers and teachers-in-training, librarians, writers and interested parents.

Quarterly
ISSN: 0045-6713

Margaret Mackey & Geoff Fox, Editors, Author
Carol Bischoff, Publisher

4388 Creative Classroom
Creative Classroom Publishing
149 5th Avenue
12th Floor
New York, NY 10010
212-353-3639
Fax: 212-353-8030
A magazine for teachers of K-8, containing innovative ideas, activities, classroom management tips and information on contemporary social problems facing teachers and students.

BiMonthly

Susan Eveno, Editorial Director
Laura Axler, Associate Editor

4389 Educate@Eight
US Department of Education, Region VIII
1244 Speer Boulevard
Suite 310
Denver, CO 80204-3582
303-844-3544
Fax: 303-844-2524
www.ed.gov

8 pages

Helen Littlejohn, Author

4390 Elementary School Journal
University of Missouri
1507 E Broadway
Hillcrest Hall
Columbia, MO 65211
573-882-2121
www.missouri.edu
Academic journal publishing primarily original studies but also reviews of research and conceptual analyses for researchers and practitioners interested in elementary schooling. Emphasizes papers dealing with educational theory and research and their implications.

Publication Date: 1839 5x Year

R. Bowen lLoftin, Chancellor
Kenneth D. Dean, Interim Provost

4391 Elementary Teacher's Ideas and Materials Workshop
Princeton Educational Publishers
117 Cuttermill Road
NY, NY 11021-3101
516-466-9300
Articles on teaching for elementary schools.

16 pages 10x Year

Barry Pavelec

4392 Gifted Child Quarterly (GCQ)
National Association for Gifted Children
1300 I Street NW
Suite 400E
Washington, DC 20005
202-785-4268
nagc@nagc.org
www.nagc.org
Scholarly journal of the National Association for Gifted Children.

Quarterly

John Segota, Executive Director
Carolyn Kaye, Senior Manager, Publishing

4393 Helping Children Learn: Elementary School Edition
The Parent Institute
PO Box 7474
Fairfax Station, VA 22039-7474
800-756-5525
Fax: 800-216-3667
customer@parent-institute.com
www.parent-institute.com
Newsletter providing parents with tips on helping their children succeed in school.

9x Year

4394 Helping Children Learn: Middle School Edition
The Parent Institute
PO Box 7474
Fairfax Station, VA 22039-7474
800-756-5525
Fax: 800-216-3667
customer@parent-institute.com
www.parent-institute.com
Newsletter providing parents with tips on helping their children succeed in school.

9x Year

4395 Helping Your Child Succeed in Elementary School
Rowman & Littlfield Education
4501 Forbes Boulevard
Suite 200
NY, MD 20706
301-459-3366
Fax: 301-429-5748
customercare@rowman.com
www.rowmaneducation.com
Provides parents with useful information about the importance of parental involvement, concrete ways to work with children and schools to promote success, and a list of resources for further reading.

Tom Koerner, PhD, VP & Publisher
Dean Roxanis, Sr. Marketing Manager

4396 Highlights for Children
Highlights for Children
PO Box 269
1800 Watermark Drive
Columbus, OH 43216-0269
888-372-6433
Fax: 614-876-8564
www.highlights.com/working-for-highlights
Magazine featuring Fun with a Purpose, to all children preschool to preteen. Features stories, hidden pictures, reading and thinking exercises, crafts, puzzles, and more.

Publication Date: 1946

Kent S. Johnson, CEO
Christine French Cully, Editor in Chief

4397 Independent School
National Association of Independent Schools
1129 20th Street, NW
Suite 800
Washington, DC 20036-3425
202-973-9700
Fax: 888-316-3862
www.nais.org
Contains information and opinion about secondary and elementary education in general and independent education in particular.

TriAnnually

Thomas W Leonhardt, Editor
Kurt R Murphy, Advertising/Editor

4398 Instructor
Scholastic
555 Broadway
New York, NY 10012
212-343-6100
800-724-6527
Fax: 212-343-4801
www.scholastic.com
Edited for teachers, curriculum coordinators, principals and supervisors of primary grades through junior high school.

Publication Date: 1920 Monthly

Richard Robinson, Chair/ President/ CEO
Maureen O'Connell, EVP/ CFO/ CAO

4399 Journal of Research in Childhood Education
Childhood Education International
1100 15th Street NW
4th Floor
Washington, DC 20005
202-372-9986
800-423-3563
www.ceinternational1892.org
Current research in education and related fields. It is intended to advance knowledge and theory of the education of children, from infancy through early adolescence. The journal seeks to stimulate the exchange of research ideas through publication of: reports of empirical research; theroretical articles; ethnographic and case studies; cross-cultural studies and studies addressing international concerns; and participant observation studies.

Publication Date: 1892 142 pages
ISSN: 0256-8543

Diane Whitehead, Chief Executive Officer
Anne Bauer, Director, Publications

4400 Montessori Life
American Montessori Society
116 East 16th Street
New York, NY 10003-2163
212-358-1250
Fax: 212-358-1256
ams@amshq.org
www.amshq.org
Magazine for parents and educators.

Publication Date: 1960 Quarterly
ISSN: 1054-0040

Carey Jones, Co-Editor

4401 Parenting for High Potential (PHP)
National Association for Gifted Children
1300 I Street NW
Suite 400E
Washington, DC 20005
202-785-4268
nagc@nagc.org
www.nagc.org
Magazine of the National Association for Gifted Children, for parents.

Quarterly

John Segota, Executive Director
Carolyn Kaye, Senior Manager, Publishing

4402 Parents Make the Difference!
The Parent Institute
PO Box 7474
Fairfax Station, VA 22039-7474
800-756-5525
Fax: 800-216-3667
customer@parent-institute.com
www.parent-institute.com
Newsletter focusing on parent involvement in children's education. Focuses on parents of preschool-aged children.

9x Year

4403 Teaching K-8 Magazine
Early Years
40 Richards Avenue
Norwalk, CT 06854-2319
203-855-2650
800-249-9363
Fax: 203-855-2656
www.teachingk-8.com
Written for teachers in the elementary grades, kindergarten through eighth, offering classroom tested ideas and methods.

Monthly Magazine
ISSN: 0891-4508
November-December

Allen A Raymond, Publisher
Patricia Broderick, Editorial Director

4404 Teaching for High Potential (THP)
National Association for Gifted Children
1300 I Street NW
Suite 400E
Washington, DC 20005
202-785-4268
nagc@nagc.org
www.nagc.org
Magazine of the National Association for Gifted Children, for teachers.

Quarterly

John Segota, Executive Director
Carolyn Kaye, Senior Manager, Publishing

Periodicals / Employment

4405 AACE Careers Update
American Association for Career Education
2900 Amby Place
Hermosa Beach, CA 90254
310-376-7378
Fax: 310-376-2926
Connects careers, education and work through career education for all ages. Career awareness, exploration, decision making, and preparation. Employability, transitions, continuing education, paid and nonpaid work, occupations, career tips, resources, partnerships, conferences and workshops. Awards and recognition, trends and futures. A newsletter is published.

8+ pages Quarterly/Newsletter
ISBN: 1074-9551

Dr.Pat Nellor Wickwire, Author
Dr. Pat Nellor Wickwire, Editor

4406 Career Development and Transition for Exceptional Individuals
Council for Exceptional Children
3100 Clarendon Boulevard
Suite 600
Arlington, VA 22201-5332
888-232-7733
service@exceptionalchildren.org
www.exceptionalchildren.org
Contains articles dealing with the latest research activities, model programs, and issues in career development and transition planning for individuals with disabilities and/or who are gifted. Published by the Hammill Institute on Disabilities and SAGE Publishing in association with the Division on Career Development and Transition of The Council for Exceptional Children.

3 Issues/Year
ISSN: 2165-1434

Erik W. Carter, Editor
Valerie L. Mazzotti, Editor

4407 Career Education News
Diversified Learning
72300 Vallat Road
Rancho Mirage, CA 92270-3906
619-346-3336

Reports on programs, materials and training for career educators.

4 pages BiWeekly

Webster Wilson Jr, Publisher
Webster Wilson, Editor

4408 Careers Bridge Newsletter
St. Louis Public Schools
801 N. 11th Street
Saint Louis, MO 63101
314-231-3720
www.slps.org
Available to educators and business/community persons on collaborative activities and promotion of career and self-awareness education in preschool to grade 12.

BiMonthly

Dr. Kelvin Adams, Superintendent
Roger CayCe, Interim Chief of Staff

4409 Chronicle of Higher Education
Subscription Department
163 E. Center Street
Marion, OH 43302
740-387-0400
800-347-6969
www.marionstar.com
Newspaper published weekly advertising many teaching opportunities overseas.

Weekly

Adam Trabitz, Sales Director
Kelly Gearhart, Sales Manager

4410 Current Openings in Education in the USA
Education Information Services
100 Walnut Street
Newton, MA 02460
617-559-6000
www.newton.k12.ma.us
This publication is a booklet listing about 140 institutions or school systems, each with one to a dozen or more openings for teachers, librarians, counselors and other personnel.

15 pages Every 6 Weeks

F Viaux, Coordinating Education

4411 Education Jobs
National Education Service Center
PO Box 1279
Riverton, WY 82501-1279
307-856-0170
Offers information on employment in the education field.

Weekly

Lucretia Ficht, Contact

4412 Faculty, Staff & Administrative Openings in US Schools & Colleges
Educational Information Services
PO Box 662
Newton Lower Falls, MA 02162
617-964-4555
A listing of available positions in the educational system in the United States.

Monthly

4413 International Educator
The International Educator
PO Box 513
Cummaquid, MA 02637
508-790-1990
877-375-6668
Fax: 508-790-1922
tie@tieonline.com
www.tieonline.com/contact_us.cfm
A newspaper listing over 100 teaching positions overseas.

Publication Date: 1986 Quarterly

Daniel Lincoln, Editor
Nikki Gundry, Ad Sales Rep.

4414 Journal of Cooperative Education
University of Waterloo
200 University Avenue West
Waterloo, ON N2L 3
519-888-4567
519-885-1211
www.uwaterloo.ca
Dedicated to the publication of thoughtful and timely articles concerning work-integrated education. It invites manuscripts which are essays that analyze issues, reports of research, descriptions of innovative practices.

Publication Date: 1957 3x Year

Feridun Hamdullahpur, President/ Vice-Chancellor
Ian Orchard, VP Academic & Provost

4415 Journal of Vocational Education Research
Colorado State University
202 Education
Fort Collins, CO 80523
970-491-6835
Fax: 970-491-1317
www.colostate.edu
Publishes refereed articles dealing with research and research-related topics in vocational education. Manuscripts based on original investigations, comprehensive reviews of literature, research methodology and theoretical constructs in vocational education are encouraged.

Quarterly

Brian Cobb, Editor

4416 New Jersey Education Law Report
Whitaker Newsletters
313 S Avenue
#340
Fanwood, NJ 07023-1364
908-889-6336
800-359-6049
Fax: 908-889-6339
Court decisions and rulings on employment in New Jersey schools.

8 pages
ISSN: 0279-8557

Joel Whitaker, Publisher
Fred Rossu, Editor

4417 SkillsUSA Champions
SkillsUSA Inc.
14001 SkillsUSA Way
Leesburg, VA 20176-5494
703-777-8810
Fax: 703-777-8999
anyinfo@skillsusa.org
www.skillsusa.org
To individuals interested in cultivating leaderships skills, SkillsUSA is a dynamic resource that inspires and connects all members creating a virtual community through its revalent and useful content.

28 pages Quarterly
ISSN: 1040-4538

Ahmad Shawwal, President
Dalton Lee Crump, Vice President

4418 VEWAA Newsletter
Vocational Evaluation & Work Adjustment Assn.
1234 Haley Circle
Auburn University
Auburn, AL 36849
334-844-3800
www.vewaa.com
News and information about the practice of vocational evaluation and work adjustment.

8 pages Quarterly

Ronald Fru, Publisher
Clarence D Brown, Editor

4419 Views & Visions
Wisconsin Vocational Association
44 E Mifflin Street
Suite 104
Madison, WI 53703-2800
608-283-2595
Fax: 608-283-2589
For teachers of vocational and adult education.

8 pages BiMonthly

Linda Stemper

4420 Vocational Training News
Aston Publications
701 King Street
Suite 444
Alexandria, VA 22314-2944
703-683-4100
800-453-9397
Fax: 703-739-6517
Contains timely, useful reports on the federal Job Training Partnership Act and the Carl D Perkins Vocational Education Act. Other areas include literacy, private industry councils and training initiatives.

10 pages Weekly

Cynthia Carter, Publisher
Matthew Dembicki, Editor

Periodicals / Financial Aid

4421 American-Scandinavian Foundation Magazine
American-Scandinavian Foundation
58 Park Avenue
New York, NY 10016-5025
212-779-3587
info@amscan.org
www.amscan.org
Covers politics, culture and lifestyles of Denmark, Finland, Iceland, Norway and Sweden.

100 pages Quarterly Magazine

Edward P Gallagher, President
Christian Sonne, Deputy Chairman

4422 Education Grants Alert
LPR Publications
360 Hiatt Drive
Palm Beach Gardens, FL 33418-2944
703-516-7002
800-341-7874
Fax: 561-622-2423
custserve@lrp.com
www.lrp.com
Dedicated to helping schools increase funding for K-12 programs. This newsletter will uncover new and recurring grant competitions from federal agencies that fund school projects, plus scores of corporate and foundation sources.

Publication Date: 1977 Weekly

Kenneth F. Kahn, President

4423 Federal Research Report
Business Publishers
2222 Sedwick Drive
Durham, NC 27713
301-587-6300
800-223-8720
Fax: 800-508-2592

custserv@bpinews.com
www.bpinews.com
Identifies critical funding sources supplying administrator's with contact names, addresses, telephone numbers, RFP numbers and other vital details.

Publication Date: 1963 8 pages Weekly

Eric Easton, Publisher
Leonard Eiserer, Editor

4424 Foundation & Corporate Grants Alert
LRP Publishing
360 Hiatt Drive
Palm Beach Gardens, FL 33418
703-516-7002
800-341-7874
Fax: 561-622-2423
custserve@lrp.com
www.lrp.com
Offers information on funding trends, new foundations and hard-to-find regional funders. You'll also get to foundation and corporate funders from the inside, with foundation profiles and interviews with program officers.

Publication Date: 1977 Monthly

Kenneth F. Kahn, President

4425 Grants for School Districts Monthly
Quinlan Publishing
23 Drydock Avenue
Boston, MA 02210-2336
617-542-0048
Listing of grants available for schools across the country.

Monthly

4426 Informativo
LASPAU (Latin America Scholarship Program)
25 Mount Auburn Street
Suite 300
Cambridge, MA 02138-6095
617-495-5255
angelica_natera@harvard.edu
www.laspau.harvard.edu
Administers scholarships for staff members nominated by Latin American and Caribbean education and development organizations and other public and private sector entities.

Publication Date: 1964 8 pages SemiAnnually

Jeff Coburn, Chair
Fernando Reimers, Vice Chair

4427 NASFAA Newsletter
National Assn. of Student Financial Aid Admin.
1801 Pennsylvania Avenue NW
Suite 850
Washington, DC 20006-3606
202-785-0453
Fax: 202-785-1487
info@nasfaa.org
www.nasfaa.org/newsletter
News covering student financial aid legislation and regulations.

Brent Tener, National Chair
Justin Draeger, President & CEO

4428 United Student Aid Funds Newsletter
PO Box 6180
Indianapolis, IN 46206-6180
317-578-6094
USA Funds Education Loan products and services information.

8 pages BiMonthly

Nelson Scharadin, Publisher
Dena Weisbard, Editor

Periodicals / Guidance & Counseling

4429 Adolescence
Libra Publishers
3089C Clairemont Drive
San Diego, CA 92117-6802
858-571-1414
Fax: 858-571-1414
librapublishers@juno.com
Articles contributed by professionals spanning issues relating to teenage education, counseling and guidance. Paperback.

256 pages Quarterly
ISSN: 0001-8449

Jon Kroll, Editor
William Kroll, Author

4430 Adultspan Journal
American Counseling Association
6101 Stevenson Avenue
Suite 600
Alexandria, VA 22304
703-823-9800
800-347-6647
Fax: 800-473-2329
acamemberservices@counseling.org
www.counseling.org
Journal concerned with publishing current information on adult development and aging.

2x Year

Suzanne Degges-White, Editor

4431 American Journal of Sexuality Education
AASECT
35 E Wacker Drive
Suite 850
Chicago, IL 60601
202-449-1099
Fax: 202-216-9646
info@aasect.org
www.aasect.org
Provides information about current research and developments in sexuality education.

Quarterly
ISSN: 1554-6128

William J. Taverner, Editor-in-Chief

4432 Attention
CHADD
4221 Forbes Boulevard
Suite 270
Lanham, MD 20706
301-306-7070
Fax: 301-306-7090
customer_service@chadd.org
www.chadd.org
Magazine for children and adults with Attention Deficit/Hyperactivity Disorder, and their families.

Publication Date: 1987 48 pages Bi-Monthly
ISSN: 1551-0980

Patricia M. Hudak, President
Susan Buningh, MRE, Director, Communications

4433 Before You Can Discipline
Master Teacher
Leadership Lane
PO Box 1207
Manhattan, KS 66505-1207
800-669-9633
Fax: 800-669-1132
www.masterteacher.com
Understand exactly how student's primary and secondary needs can and do influence acceptable and unacceptable behavior. Develop professional attitudes toward discipline problems and learn the laws and principals of managing people.

Publication Date: 1969 170 pages
ISBN: 0-914607-03-0

Robert L DeBruyn, Author
Dr. Joanna Hubbs, President
Gregory Hubbs, Editor-in-Chief

4434 Career Development Quarterly
American Counseling Association
6101 Stevenson Avenue
Suite 600
Alexandria, VA 22304
703-823-9800
800-347-6647
Fax: 800-473-2329
acamemberservices@counseling.org
www.counseling.org
Publishes articles on career counseling, development, education, coaching, management, and more.

Quarterly

Paul J. Hartung, Editor

4435 Child Psychiatry & Human Development
Kluwer Academic/Human Sciences Press
233 Spring Street
New York, NY 10013
212-620-8000
800-221-9369
Fax: 212-463-0742
www.wkpa.nl
Interdisciplinary international journal serving the groups represented by child psychiatry, clinical child/pediatric/family psychology, pediatrics, social science, and human development. Publishes research on diagnosis, assessment, treatment, epidemiology, development, advocacy, training, cultural factors, ethics, policy, and professional issues as related to clinical disorders in children, adolescents and families.

Quarterly
ISSN: 0009-398X

Carol Bischoff, Publisher
Kenneth J Tarnowski, Editor

4436 Child Welfare
Child Welfare League of America
440 1st Street NW
Suite 310
Washington, DC 20001-2085
202-688-4200
Fax: 202-833-1689
cwla@cwla.org
www.cwla.org

Publication Date: 1920 BiMonthly

Joesph M. Costa, Chair
Julie Sweeney-Springwater, Vice Chair

4437 Child and Adolescent Social Work Journal
Kluwer Academic/Human Sciences Press
233 Spring Street
New York, NY 10013
212-620-8000
800-221-9369
Fax: 212-463-0742
www.wkpa.nl

Features original articles that focus on clinical social work practice with children, adolescents and their families. The journal addresses current issues in the field of social work drawn from theory, direct practice, research, and social policy, as well as focuses on problems affecting specific populations in special settings.

Bimonthly
ISSN: 0738-0151

Carol Bischoff, Publisher
Thomas Kenemore, Editor

438 College Board News
College Board
250 Vesey Street
New York, NY 10281
212-713-8000
www.collegeboard.org
Reports on the activities of the College Board. Its articles inform readers about the Board's services in such areas as high school, guidance, college admission, curriculum and placement, testing, financial aid, adult education and research.

David Coleman, Chief Executive Officer
Jeremy Singer, President

439 Counseling & Values
American Counseling Association
6101 Stevenson Avenue
Suite 600
Alexandria, VA 22304
703-823-9800
800-347-6647
Fax: 800-473-2329
acamemberservices@counseling.org
www.counseling.org
Editorial content focuses on the roles of values and religion in counseling and psychology.

Abigail H. Conley, Editor

440 Counseling Insider
American Counseling Association
6101 Stevenson Avenue
Suite 600
Alexandria, VA 22304
703-823-9800
800-347-6647
Fax: 800-473-2329
acamemberservices@counseling.org
www.counseling.org
Publishes the latest news in the counseling industry.

Biweekly

Richard Yep, Chief Executive Officer
Brandi McIntyre, Governance Exec. Office Mgr.

441 Counseling Today
American Counseling Association
6101 Stevenson Avenue
Suite 600
Alexandria, VA 22304
703-823-9800
800-347-6647
Fax: 800-473-2329
acamemberservices@counseling.org
www.counseling.org
Covers national and international counseling issues and reports legislative and governmental activities affecting counselors.

Monthly

Richard Yep, Chief Executive Officer
Brandi McIntyre, Governance Exec. Office Mgr.

4442 Counselor Education & Supervision
American Counseling Association
6101 Stevenson Avenue
Suite 600
Alexandria, VA 22304
703-823-9800
800-347-6647
Fax: 800-473-2329
acamemberservices@counseling.org
www.counseling.org
Covers counseling theories, techniques and skills, teaching and training.

Quarterly

Spencer G. Niles, Editor

4443 ERIC Clearinghouse on Counseling & Student Services
ERIC Clearinghouse on Counseling and Student Servi
201 Ferguson Building UNCG
Greensboro, NC 27412
910-334-4114
800-414-9769
Fax: 910-334-4116
Covers news about ERIC and the counseling clearinghouse and developments in the fields of education and counseling.

4 pages Quarterly

David Osher, Director
Mary Quinn, Deputy Director

4444 Educational & Psychological Measurement
Sage Publications
2455 Teller Road
Thousand Oaks, CA 91320
805-499-9774
800-818-7243
Fax: 800-583-2665
journals@sagepub.com
www.sagepub.com

Quarterly

Sara Miller Mccune, Founder/ Chairman
Blaise R. Simqu, President & CEO

4445 Family Relations
Miami University
501 E. High St.
Oxford, OH 45056
513-529-4909
Fax: 513-529-7270
www.miamioh.edu

Publication Date: 1809 Quarterly

Dr. David C. Hodge, President
Robin Parker, General Counsel

4446 Family Therapy: The Journal of the California Graduate School of Family Psychology
Libra Publishers
3089C Clairemont Drive
San Diego, CA 92117-6802
858-571-1414
Fax: 858-571-1414
Articles contributed by professionals spanning issues relating to teenage education, counseling and guidance. Paperback.

96 pages Quarterly
ISSN: 0091-6544

William Kroll, Editor

4447 Health & Social Work
National Association of Social Workers
750 First Street NE
Suite 800
Washington, DC 20002
202-408-8600
800-638-8799
Fax: 202-336-8311
membership@naswdc.org
www.socialworkers.org
Covers practice, innovation, research, legislation, policy , planning, and all the professional issues relevant to social work services in all levels of education.

Publication Date: 1955

Darrell P. Wheeler, PhD, MPH, ACSW, President
Angelo McClain, PhD, LICSW, CEO

4448 ICA Quarterly
Western Illinois University
1 University Circle
Macomb, IL 61455
309-298-1414
Fax: 309-298-3253
info@wiu.edu
www.wiu.edu
Official publication of the Illinois Counseling Association. Focus is on material of interest and value to professional counselors.

Publication Date: 1899 Quarterly

Dr. Jack Thomas, President
Dr. Kenneth Hawkinson, Provost & Academic VP

4449 International Journal of Play Therapy
Association for Play Therapy
401 Clovis Avenue
Suite 107
Clovis, CA 93612
559-298-3400
Fax: 559-298-3410
info@a4pt.org
www.a4pt.org
Peer-reviewed journal presenting scholarly articles on the subject of play therapy and related research, case studies, theoretical applications and current practices.

Quarterly
ISSN: 1555-6824

Franc Hudspeth, Editor

4450 Journal of Addictions & Offender Counseling
American Counseling Association
6101 Stevenson Avenue
Suite 600
Alexandria, VA 22304
703-823-9800
800-347-6647
Fax: 800-473-2329
acamemberservices@counseling.org
www.counseling.org
Publishes articles for professionals in the field of addictions and offender counseling, with focus on theory, research and practice surrounding prevention and treatment programs.

2x Year

John M. Laux, Editor

4451 Journal of Child and Adolescent Group Therapy
Kluwer Academic/Human Sciences Press
233 Spring Street
New York, NY 10013
212-620-8000
800-221-9369
Fax: 212-463-0742
www.wkpa.nl
Addresses the whole spectrum of professional issues relating to juvenile and parent group treatment. Promotes the exchange of new ideas from a wide variety of disciplines concerned with enhancing treatments for this special population. The multidisciplinary contributions include clinical reports, illustrations of new technical methods, and stud-

ies that contribute to the advancement of therapeutic results, as well as articles on theoretical issues, applications, and the group process.

Quarterly
ISSN: 1053-0800

Carol Bischoff, Publisher
Edward S Soo, Editor

4452 Journal of College Admission
Nat'l Association for College Admission Counseling
1050 N Highland Street
Suite 400
Alexandria, VA 22201
703-836-2222
800-822-6285
Fax: 703-243-9375
info@nacacnet.org
www.nacac.com
Membership association offering information to counselors and guidance professionals working in the college admissions office.

Publication Date: 1937 32 pages Quarterly
ISSN: 0734-6670

Elaina Loveland, Author
Jeff Fuller, President
Joyce E. Smith, CEO

4453 Journal of College Counseling
American Counseling Association
6101 Stevenson Avenue
Suite 600
Alexandria, VA 22304
703-823-9800
800-347-6647
Fax: 800-473-2329
acamemberservices@counseling.org
www.counseling.org
Publishes articles for counselors working in higher education.

3x Year

Oren M. Shefet, Editor

4454 Journal of Counseling & Development
American Counseling Association
6101 Stevenson Avenue
Suite 600
Alexandria, VA 22304
703-823-9800
800-347-6647
Fax: 800-473-2329
acamemberservices@counseling.org
www.counseling.org
A quarterly journal that publishes articles on counseling practice, theory, and research.

ISSN: 0748-9633

Matthew Lemberger-Truelove, Editor

4455 Journal of Drug Education
California State University
18111 Nordhoff Street
Northridge, CA 91330
818-677-1200
Fax: 818-677-2045
www.csun.edu
Offers information to counselors and guidance professionals dealing with areas of drug and substance abuse education in the school system.

Publication Date: 1958 Quarterly

Dianne F. Harrison, President
Colin Doanhue, VP & CFO

4456 Journal of Emotional and Behavioral Disorders
Pro-Ed
8700 Shoal Creek Boulevard
Austin, TX 78757-6897
512-451-3246
800-897-3202
Fax: 512-451-8542
general@proedinc.com
www.proedinc.com
Presents high-quality interdisciplinary scholarship in the area of emotional and behavioral disabilities. Explores issues including youth violence, emotional problems among minority children, long-term foster care placement, mental health services, social development and educational strategies.

Michael H Epstein, EdD, Editor
Douglas Cullinan, EdD, Editor

4457 Journal of Employment Counseling
American Counseling Association
6101 Stevenson Avenue
Suite 600
Alexandria, VA 22304
703-823-9800
800-347-6647
Fax: 800-473-2329
acamemberservices@counseling.org
www.counseling.org
Focuses on the theory, research and practice of employment counseling, as well as explores current problems and concerns of counselors in the field.

Quarterly

Mark Rehfuss, Editor

4458 Journal of Humanistic Counseling
American Counseling Association
6101 Stevenson Avenue
Suite 600
Alexandria, VA 22304
703-823-9800
800-347-6647
Fax: 800-473-2329
acamemberservices@counseling.org
www.counseling.org
Publishes research on humanistic counseling.

3x Year

Linwood G. Vereen, Editor

4459 Journal of Humanistic Education and Development
Ohio University
1 Ohio University
345 Baker University Center
Athens, OH 45701
740-593-1000
Fax: 740-593-0569
deanofstudents@ohio.edu
www.ohio.edu
Focuses on the humanities and promotes their place in the educational system.

Publication Date: 1786 Quarterly

David Brightbill, Chair
David A. Wolfort, Vice Chair

4460 Journal of Multicultural Counseling & Development
American Counseling Association
6101 Stevenson Avenue
Suite 600
Alexandria, VA 22304
703-823-9800
800-347-6647
Fax: 800-473-2329
acamemberservices@counseling.org
www.counseling.org
Focuses on research, theory, and program applications relevant to multicultural and ethnic minority interests in theh counseling and human development field.

Quarterly

Cirecie A. West-Olatunji, Editor

4461 NACAC Bulletin
Nat'l Association for College Admission Counseling
1050 N Highland Street
Suite 400
Alexandria, VA 22201
703-836-2222
800-822-6285
Fax: 703-243-9375
info@nacacnet.org
www.nacac.com
Membership association offering information to counselors and guidance professionals working in the college admissions office.

Publication Date: 1937 Monthly

Jeff Fuller, President
Joyce E. Smith, CEO

4462 NASW News
National Association of Social Workers
750 First Street NE
Suite 800
Washington, DC 20002
202-408-8600
800-638-8799
Fax: 301-206-7989
membership@naswdc.org
www.naswdc.org
Features in-depth coverage of developments in social work practice, news of national social policy developments, political and legislative news in social services, noteworthy achievements of social workers and association news.

Publication Date: 1955 Monthly

Darrell P. Wheeler, PhD, MPH, ACSW, President
Angelo McClain, PhD, LICSW, CEO

4463 National Coalition for Sex Equity in Education
PO Box 534
Annandale, NJ 08801
908-735-5045
Fax: 908-735-9674
info@ncsee.org
www.ncsee.org
The only national organization for gender equity specialists and educators. Individuals and organizations committed to reducing sex role stereotyping for females and males. Services include an annual national training conference, a quarterly newsletter and a membership directory. Members may join task forces dealing with equity related topics such as computer/technology issues, early childhood, male issues, sexual harassment prevention, sexual orientation and vocational issues.

Quarterly Newsletter

Theodora Martin, Business Manager

4464 Rehabilitation Counseling Bulletin
Pro-Ed
8700 Shoal Creek Boulevard
Austin, TX 78757-6897
512-451-3246
800-897-3202
Fax: 512-451-8542
general@proedinc.com
www.proedinc.com
International journal providing original empirical research, essays of a theoretical nature, methodological treatises and comprehensive reviews of

the literature, intensive case studies and research critiques.

Quarterly Magazine
ISSN: 0034-3552

Douglas Strohmer, PhD, Editor

4465 School Psychology Review
National Association of School Psychologists
4340 East West Highway
Suite 402
Bethesda, MD 20814
301-657-0270
866-331-6277
Fax: 301-657-0275
www.nasponline.org
Established in 1972, the School Psychology Review is a peer-reviewed academic journal, which encompasses a variety of issues about educational psychology.

170 pages Quarterly
ISSN: 0279-6015

Shane R. Jimerson, Editor

4466 Social Work Research Journal
National Association of Social Workers
750 First Street NE
Suite 800
Washington, DC 20002
202-408-8600
800-638-8799
Fax: 202-336-8311
membership@naswdc.org
www.socialworkers.org
Contains orginal research papers that contribute to knowledge about social work issues and problems. Topics include new technology, strategies and methods, and research results.

Publication Date: 1955 Quarterly
ISSN: 1070-5309

Darrell P. Wheeler, PhD, MPH, ACSW, President
Angelo McClain, PhD, LICSW, CEO

4467 Social Work in Education
National Association of Social Workers
750 First Street NE
Suite 800
Washington, DC 20002
202-408-8600
Fax: 202-336-8310
membership@naswdc.org
www.socialworkers.org
Covers practice, innovation, research, legislation, policy, planning, and all the professional issues relevant to social work services in all levels of education.

Publication Date: 1955

Darrell P. Wheeler, PhD, MPH, ACSW, President
Angelo McClain, PhD, LICSW, CEO

4468 SocialWork
National Association of Social Workers
750 First Street NE
Suite 800
Washington, DC 20002
202-408-8600
800-638-8799
Fax: 202-336-8311
membership@naswdc.org
www.socialworkers.org
Covers important research findings, critical analyses, practice issues, and information on current social issues such as AIDS, homelessness, and federal regulation of social programs. Case management, third-party reimbursement, credentialing, and other professional issues are addressed.

Publication Date: 1955

Darrell P. Wheeler, PhD, MPH, ACSW, President
Angelo McClain, PhD, LICSW, CEO

4469 The Elective
College Board
250 Vesey Street
New York, NY 10281
212-713-8000
www.collegeboard.org
A digital magazine focusing on key issues in education and the pathways to higher education.

David Coleman, Chief Executive Officer
Jeremy Singer, President

4470 Today's School Psychologist
LRP Publications
360 Hiatt Drive
Palm Beach Gardens, FL 33418
703-516-7002
800-341-7874
Fax: 561-622-2423
custserve@lrp.com
www.lrp.com/ed
An in-depth guide to a school psychologist's job, offering practical strategies and tips for handling day-to-day responsibilites, encouraging change, and improving professional standing and performance.

Publication Date: 1977 Monthly
ISSN: 1098-9277

Kenneth F. Kahn, President

4471 Washington Counseletter
Chronicle Guidance Publications
66 Aurora Street
Moravia, NY 13118-3569
315-497-0330
800-622-7284
Fax: 315-497-3359
customerservice@chronicleguidance.com
www.chronicleguidance.com
Monthly report highlighting federal, state, and local developments affecting the counseling and education professions. Items list events, programs, activities and publications of interest to counselors and educators.

Publication Date: 1938 8 pages 8x Year

Cheryl Fickeisen, President/ CEO
Gary Fickeisen, Vice President

Periodicals / Language Arts

4472 AATF National Bulletin
American Association of Teachers of French
302 N Granite Street
Marion, IL 62959-2346
815-310-0490
Fax: 815-310-5754
aatf@frenchteachers.org
www.frenchteachers.org
Announcements and short articles relating to the association on French language and cultural activities.

Quarterly

Anne Jensen, President
Jayne Abrate, Executive Director

4473 ACTFL Connection
American Council on the Teaching of Foreign Lang.
1001 N Fairfax Street
Suite 200
Alexandria, VA 22314
703-894-2900
headquarters@actfl.org
www.actfl.org
An e-newsletter containing timely information on matters of interest to foreign language educators.

Howie Berman, Executive Director
MacKenzie Arbogust, Director, Finance

4474 ADE Bulletin
Association of Departments of English
26 Broadway
Third Floor
New York, NY 10004-1789
646-576-5133
Fax: 646-835-4056
dlaurence@mla.org
www.ade.org
This bulletin concentrates on developments in scholarship, curriculum and teachers in English.

64 pages
ISSN: 0001-0888

David Laurence, Director
Doug Steward, Associate Director

4475 Beyond Words
1534 Wells Drive NE
Albuquerque, NM 87112-6383
505-275-2558
Offers information on literature, language arts and English for the teaching professional.

10x Year

4476 Bilingual Research Journal
National Association for Bilingual Education
1775 I Street NW
Suite 1150
Washington, DC 20006
240-450-3700
www.nabe.org
Journal published by National Association for Bilingual Education.

Publication Date: 1972 Quarterly
ISSN: 1523-5882

Maria E. Franquiz, Editor
Alba Ortiz, Editor

4477 Bilingual Review Press
Arizona State University
PO Box 877705
Tempe, AZ 85287-7705
480-965-8972
Fax: 480-965-0865
www.asu.edu
Offers information and reviews on books, materials and the latest technology available to bilingual educators.

3x Year

Gary D Keller, President

4478 CEA Forum
jmcdaniel30@radford.edu
www.journals.tdl.org
Online peer-reviewed journal publishing articles on professional issues and pedagogy related to the teaching of college English.

Jamie McDaniel, Editor
Morgan Ebbs, Assistant Editor

4479 Classroom Notes Plus
National Council of Teachers of English
340 N Neil Street
Suite 104
Champaign, IL 61820
217-328-3870
877-369-6283
Fax: 217-328-9645

customerservice@ncte.org
www.ncte.org
Features usable teaching ideas for teachers by teachers.

Alfredo Celedon Lujan, President
Emily Kirkpatrick, Executive Director

4480 College English
National Council of Teachers of English
340 N Neil Street
Suite 104
Champaign, IL 61820
217-328-3870
877-369-6283
Fax: 217-328-9645
collegeenglishjournal@gmail.com
www.ncte.org
Professional journal for college teachers of English.

Melissa Ianetta, Editor

4481 Communication Disorders Quarterly
Pro-Ed., Inc.
8700 Shoal Creek Boulevard
Austin, TX 78757-6897
512-451-3246
800-897-3202
Fax: 512-451-8542
general@proedinc.com
www.proedinc.com
Research, intervention and practice in speech, language and hearing.

Quarterly Magazine
ISSN: 1525-7401

Alejandro Brice, Editor

4482 Communication: Journalism Education Today
Truman High School
3301 S Noland Road
Independence, MO 64055
816-521-2710
Fax: 816-521-2913
www.sites.isdschools.org/truman
Provides educational perspectives to JEA members— mostly high schools journalism editors— on a wide variety of topics such as teaching/advising issues, scholastic media strategy, pedagogical updates, current journalism research and other professional and technological concerns.

Publication Date: 1964 Quarterly
ISBN: 1536
ISSN: 9129

Pam Boatright, President
Bradley Wilson, Editor

4483 Composition Studies Freshman English News
De Paul University
1 E. Jackson Blvd.
Chicago, IL 60604
312-362-8000
800-4DE-PAUL
Fax: 773-325-7328
dpcl@depaul.edu
www.depaul.edu/
Theoretical and practical articles on rhetorical theory.

Publication Date: 1898 44 pages SemiAnnually

Rev. Dennis H. Holtschneider, CM, EdD, President
Robert L. Kozoman, EVP

4484 Council-Grams
National Council of Teachers of English
340 N Neil Street
Suite 104
Champaign, IL 61820
217-328-3870
877-369-6283
Fax: 217-328-9645
customerservice@ncte.org
www.ncte.org
Offers information and updates in the areas of English, language arts and reading.

Alfredo Celedon Lujan, President
Emily Kirkpatrick, Executive Director

4485 Counterforce
Society for the Advancement of Good English
4501 Riverside Avenue
#30
Anderson, CA 96007-2759
530-365-8026
Offers updates and information for English teachers and professors.

Quarterly

4486 English Education
NYU Steinhardt
239 Greene Street
6th Floor
New York, NY 10003
212-998-5460
Fax: 212-998-4049
ce33@nyu.edu
www.steinhardt.nyu.edu/teachlearn/english
Offers information about educational programs for English teachers and professors to develop their skills for the classroom.

Maryrose Cordero, Operations Administrator
Cherrelle Hall, Department Administrator

4487 English Journal
National Council of Teachers of English
340 N Neil Street
Suite 104
Champaign, IL 61820
217-328-3870
877-369-6283
Fax: 217-328-9645
englishjournal@ncte.org
www.ncte.org
A journal for middle school and junior and senior high school English teachers.

6x Year
ISSN: 0013-8274

Toby Emert, Co-Editor
R. Joseph Rodriguez, Co-Editor

4488 English Leadership Quarterly
National Council of Teachers of English
340 N Neil Street
Suite 104
Champaign, IL 61820
217-328-3870
877-369-6283
Fax: 217-328-9645
elq@ncte.org
www.ncte.org
Teaching of English for secondary school English Department chairpersons.

Quarterly

Elaine Simos, Editor

4489 English for Specific Purposes
University of Michigan
500 South State Street
Ann Arbor, MI 48109
734-764-1817
Fax: 619-594-6530
sgrafton@umich.edu
www.umich.edu
Concerned with English education and its importance to the developing student.

Publication Date: 1817 3x Year

Janey Lack, Chair
Steve Grafton, President/ CEO

4490 Foreign Language Annals
American Council on the Teaching of Foreign Lang.
1001 N Fairfax Street
Suite 200
Alexandria, VA 22314
703-894-2900
headquarters@actfl.org
www.actfl.org
Dedicated to advancing all areas of the profession of foreign language teaching. It seeks primarily to serve the interests of teachers, administrators and researchers, regardless of educational level of the language with which they are concerned.

Publication Date: 1967 Quarterly

Howie Berman, Executive Director
MacKenzie Arbogust, Director, Finance

4491 INBOX Newsletter
National Council of Teachers of English
340 N Neil Street
Suite 104
Champaign, IL 61820
217-328-3870
877-369-6283
Fax: 217-328-9645
customerservice@ncte.org
www.ncte.org
Stories in English language arts education, ideas for teachers, and NCTE news.

Alfredo Celedon Lujan, President
Emily Kirkpatrick, Executive Director

4492 Journal of Basic Writing
City University of NY, Instructional Resource Ctr.
535 E 80th Street
New York, NY 10021-0767
212-794-5445
Fax: 212-794-5706
Publishes articles of theory, research and teaching practices related to basic writing. Articles are refereed by members of the Editorial Board and the editors.

Spring & Fall

Karen Greenberg, Editor
Trudy Smoke, Editor

4493 Journal of Teaching Writing
Indiana Teachers of Writing
425 University Boulevard CA 345
Indianapolis, IN 46202
317-274-4777
Fax: 317-278-1287
jtw@iupui.edu
www.iupui.edu/~jtw
A refereed journal for classroom teachers and researchers at all academic levels whose interest or emphasis is the teaching of writing. Appearing semiannually, JTW publishes articles on the theory, practice, and teaching of writing throughout the curriculum. Each issue covers a range of topics, from composition theory and discourse analysis to curriculum development and innovative teaching techniques. Contributors are reminded to tailor their writing for a diverse readership.

12-20 pages Semiannually

Dr. Kim Brian Lovejoy, Editor
Kay Halasek, Reviews Editor

4494 Journalism Quarterly
George Washington University
2121 Eye Street, NW
Washington, DC 20052

202-994-1000
Fax: 202-994-5806
www.gwu.edu
Information on all facets of writing and journalism for the student and educator.

Publication Date: 1821 Quarterly

Nelson A. Carbonell, Jr., Chair
Steven Knapp, President

495 Language & Speech
Kingston Press Services, Ltd.
43 Derwent Road, Whitton
Twickenham, Middlesex TW2 7HQ
United Kingdom
0-20-8893-3015
Fax: 208-893-3015
www.kingstonepress.com
Includes psychological research articles, speech perception, speech production, psycholinguistics and reading.

Quarterly

496 Language Arts
National Council of Teachers of English
340 N Neil Street
Suite 104
Champaign, IL 61820
217-328-3870
877-369-6283
Fax: 217-328-9645
languagearts@ncte.org
www.ncte.org
Journal for instructors in language arts at the elementary level.

6x Year

Rick Coppola, Co-Editor
Sandra L. Osorio, Co-Editor

497 Language, Speech & Hearing Services in School
Ohio State University
281 W. Lane Ave.
Columbus, OH 43210
614-292-OHIO
Fax: 614-292-7504
www.osu.edu
Interested in innovative technology and growth in language development in schools.

Jeffery Wadsworth, Chair
Ronald A. Ratner, Vice Chair

498 Merlyn's Pen: Fiction, Essays and Poems by America's Teens
11 South Angell St.
Suite 301
Providence, RI 02906
401-751-3766
800-247-2027
Fax: 401-751-3766
merlyn@merlynspen.org
www.merlynspen.com
Merlyns' Pen magazine is a selective publisher of model writing by America's students in grades 6-12. Products include Merlyn's Pen magazine (a reproducible annual magazine) and the American Teen Writer Series, collections of anthologized short fiction and nonfiction by brilliant teen writers. Used for models, inspiration, and instruction in literature and writing.

Publication Date: 1985 100 pages Annually
ISSN: 0882-2050

R. James Stahl, Editor

499 Modern Language Journal
Case Western Reserve University
10900 Euclid Ave.
Cleveland, OH 44106
216-368-2000
Fax: 216-368-2216
www.case.edu

Publication Date: 1826 Quarterly

Barbara R. Snyder, President
William A. Baeslack III, Provost & EVP

4500 NASILP Journal
Temple University
1801 N. Broad Street
Philadelphia, PA 19122
215-204-7000
www.temple.edu
Articles, news and book reviews on language instructional methodology.

Publication Date: 1884 12 pages SemiAnnually

Neil D. Theobald, President

4501 National Clearinghouse for Bilingual Education Newsletter
George Washington University
2121 Eye Street, NW
Washington, DC 20052
202-994-1000
800-321-6223
www.gwu.edu
Provides information to practitioners on the education of language minority students.

Publication Date: 1821 Weekly

Nelson A. Carbonell, Jr., Chair
Steven Knapp, President

4502 PCTE Bulletin
Williamsport Area Community College
One College Avenue
Williamsport, PA 17701
570-326-3761
800-367-9222
www.pct.edu
Focuses on Pennsylvania literacy issues.

Publication Date: 1970 SemiAnnually

Sen. Gene Yaw, Chair
Dave Jane Gilmour, Ph.D., President

4503 Perspectives
National Association for Bilingual Education
1775 I Street NW
Suite 1150
Washington, DC 20006
240-450-3700
www.nabe.org
Provides information about bilingual education programs.

Quarterly

Santiago V. Wood, Ed.D, National Executive Director
Nilda M. Aguirre, ED.S., Deputy Executive Director

4504 Quarterly Journal of Speech
National Communication Association
1765 N Street NW
Washington, DC 20036
202-464-4622
Fax: 202-464-4600
inbox@natcom.org
www.natcom.org
Main academic journal in the speech/communication field of education.

Publication Date: 1914 Quarterly

Carole Blair, President
Christina S. Beck, 1st VP

4505 Quarterly of the NWP
National Writing Project
2105 Bancroft Way
Suite 1042
Berkeley, CA 94720-1042
510-642-0963
Fax: 510-642-4545
nwp@nwp.org
www.writingproject.org
Journal on the research in and practice of teaching writing at all grade levels.

40 pages Quarterly Magazine
ISSN: 0896-3592

Art Peterson, Amy Bauman; Editors, Author
Judith Warren Little, Chair
Elyse Eidman-Aadahl, Executive Director

4506 Quill and Scroll
University of Iowa School of Journalism
100 Adler Journalism Builing
Iowa City, IA 52242
319-335-3457
Fax: 319-335-3989
quill-scroll@uiowa.edu
www.uiowa.edu
Founded and distributed for the purpose of encouraging and rewarding individual achievements in journalism and allied fields. This magazine is published bimonthly during the school year and has a variety of pamphlets and lists of publications available as resources.

BiMonthly

Richard P Johns, Executive Director

4507 Research in the Teaching of English
Harvard Graduate School of Education
Larsen Hall
Appian Way
Cambridge, MA 02138
617-495-3521
Fax: 617-495-0540
www.gse.harvard.edu
A research journal devoted to original research on the relationships between teaching and learning for language development in reading, writing and speaking at all age levels.

Publication Date: 1920 Quarterly

Sandra Stotsky, Editor

4508 Rhetoric Review
University of Arizona
Department of English
Tucson, AZ 85721
520-621-2211
Fax: 520-621-7397
www.arizona.edu
A journal of rhetoric and composition publishing scholarly and historical studies, theoretical and practical articles, views of the profession, review essays of professional books, personal essays about writing and poems.

Publication Date: 1885 200+ pages Quarterly
ISSN: 0735-0198

Ann Weaver Hart, President
Andrew DuMont, Executive Communication Mngr

4509 Studies in Second Language Acquisition
Cambridge University Press
1105 Atwater
Bloomington, IN 47401-5020
812-855-6874
Fax: 812-855-2386
ssla@indiana.edu
www.indiana.edu/~ssla
Referred journal devoted to problems and issues in second and foreign language acquisition of any language.

140 pages Quarterly Paperback
ISSN: 0272-2631

Albert Valdman, Editor

4510 **TESOL Journal: A Journal of Teaching and Classroom Research**
TESOL International Association
1925 Ballenger Avenue
Suite 550
Alexandria, VA 22314-6820
703-518-2500
888-891-0041
Fax: 703-691-5327
tj@tesol.org
www.tesol.org
Publishes articles on current theory and research in the field of English education to speakers of other languages.
50 pages Quarterly
Youngjoo Yi, Editor
Peter Sayer, Editor

4511 **TESOL Quarterly**
TESOL International Association
1925 Ballenger Avenue
Suite 550
Alexandria, VA 22314-6820
703-518-2500
888-891-0041
Fax: 703-691-5327
tq@tesol.org
www.tesol.org
TESOL Quarterly is a scholarly journal containing articles on academic research, theory, reports, reviews. Articles about linguistics, ethnographies, and more describe the theoretic basis for ESL/EFL teaching practices.
Quarterly
Charlene Polio, Editor
Peter De Costa, Editor

4512 **Writing Lab Newsletter**
Purdue University, Department of English
500 Oval Drive
W. Lafayette, IN 47907
765-494-3740
Fax: 765-494-3780
www.cla.purdue.edu/english
Monthly newsletter for readers involved in writing centers and/or one-to-one instruction in writing skills.
Publication Date: 1955 16 pages Monthly/Newsletter
ISSN: 1040-3779
Nancy Peterson, Department Head
Ryan Schneider, Dir. Of Graduate Studies

Periodicals / Library Services

4513 **ALA Editions Catalog**
American Library Association
225 N Michigan Avenue
Suite 1300
Chicago, IL 60601
312-944-6780
800-545-2433
Fax: 312-440-9374
ala@ala.org
www.ala.org
Contains over 1,000 job listings, news and reports on the latest technologies in 11 issues annually. Also scholarships, grants and awards are possibilities.
Annually
Tracie D. Hall, Executive Director
Cheryl Malden, Program Officer

4514 **American Libraries**
American Library Association
225 N Michigan Avenue
Suite 1300
Chicago, IL 60601
312-944-6780
800-545-2433
Fax: 312-440-9374
ala@ala.org
www.ala.org
The magazine of the American Library Association that is published six times a year and distributed to more than 65,000 individuals.
ISSN: 0002-9769
Sanhita SinhaRoy, Editor
Terra Dankowski, Managing Editor

4515 **Booklist**
American Library Association
225 N Michigan Avenue
Suite 1300
Chicago, IL 60601
312-944-6780
800-545-2433
Fax: 312-440-9374
ala@ala.org
www.ala.org
A guide to current print and audiovisual materials worthy of consideration for purchase by small and medium-sized public libraries and school library media centers.
Tracie D. Hall, Executive Director
Cheryl Malden, Program Officer

4516 **Catholic Library World**
Catholic Library Association
8550 United Plaza Blvd.
Baton Rouge, LA 19041-1412
225-408-4417
www.cathla.org
A periodical geared toward the professional librarian in order to keep them abreast of new publications, library development, association news and technology.
Publication Date: 1921 Quarterly
Sara R. Baron, President
Mary Kelleher, VP/ Treasurer

4517 **Choice**
ALA, Assn. of College & Research Libraries
575 Main Street
Suite 300
Middletown, CT 06457
860-347-6933
Fax: 860-346-8586
www.ala.org/acrl/choice
A magazine distributed to librarians and other organizations that analyzes various materials, offers book reviews and information on the latest technology available for the library acquisitions departments.
11x Year
Mark Cummings, Editor & Publisher
Bill Mickey, Editorial Director

4518 **ILA Reporter**
Illinois Library Association
33 W Grand Avenue
Suite 401
Chicago, IL 60654-6799
312-644-1896
Fax: 312-644-1899
ila@ila.org
www.ila.org/publications/ila-reporter
30 pages
ISSN: 0018-9979
Diane Foote, Executive Director
Tamara Jenkins, Manager, Communication

4519 **Information Technology & Libraries**
University of the Pacific
3601 Pacific Avenue
Stockton, CA 95211
209-946-2285
Fax: 209-946-2805
President@Pacific.edu
www.pacific.edu
Offers information on the latest technology, systems and electronics offered to the library market.
Quarterly
Pamela Eibeck, President
Ken Mullen, VP, Business & Finance

4520 **Journal of Education for Library and Information Sciences**
Kent State University
800 E. Summit St.
Kent, OH 44240
330-672-3000
Fax: 330-672-7965
info@kent.edu
www.kent.edu
The latest information on books, publications, electronics and technology for the librarian.
Publication Date: 1910 Quarterly
Beverly Warren, President
Edward G. Mahon, Vice President

4521 **Libraries & Culture**
University of Texas at Austin/Univ. of Texas Press
PO Box 7819
Austin, TX 78713-7819
512-471-3434
Fax: 512-232-7178
www.utexas.edu
An interdisciplinary journal that explores the significance of collections of recorded knowledge. Scholarly articles and book reviews cover international topics dealing with libraries, books, reviews, archives, personnel, and their history; for scholars, librarians, historians, readers interested in the history of books and libraries.
Publication Date: 1883 100 pages Quarterly
ISSN: 0894-8631
William Powers, Jr., President
Gregory L. Fenves, EVP & Provost

4522 **Library Collections, Acquisitions & Technical Services**
Pergamon Press, Elsevier Science
The Boulevard, Lanngford Lane
Kidlington, Oxford
United Kingdom
614-292-4738
Fax: 614-292-7859
deidrichs.1@osu.edu
www.elsvier.com
Offers information on policy, practice, and research on the collection management and technical service areas of libraries.
500 pages Quarterly
ISSN: 1464-9055
Carol Pitts Diedrichs, Editor

4523 **Library Issues: Briefings for Faculty and Administrators**
Mountainside Publishing Company
PO Box 8330
Ann Arbor, MI 48107

734-662-3925
Fax: 734-662-4450
www.libraryissues.com
Offers overviews of the trends and problems affecting campus libraries. Explained in layman's terms as they relate to faculty, administrators and the parent institution.

Publication Date: 1980 4-6 pages Bi-Monthly
ISSN: 0734-3035

Richard M. Dougherty, Editor
Ann P. Dougherty, Managing Editor

524 Library Quarterly
Indiana University, School of Library Science
1320 E. 10th Street
LI 011
Bloomington, IN 47405-3907
812-855-2018
888-335-7547
Fax: 812-855-6166
ilsmain@indiana.edu
www.ils.indiana.edu
Updates, information, statistics, book reviews and publications for librarians.

Quarterly

David Cole, Manager, IT Hardware
Jane M. Lewis, ILS Business Dir.

525 Library Resources & Technical Services
Columbia University, School of Library Sciences
116th Street and Broadway
New York, NY 10027
212-854-1754
Fax: 212-854-8951
askcuit@columbia.edu
www.columbia.edu

Publication Date: 1754 Quarterly

Lee C. Bollinger, President
John H. Coatsworth, Provost

526 Library Trends
Grad. School Library & Info. Science
501 E Daniel Street
MC-493
Champaign, IL 61820-6211
217-333-3280
Fax: 217-244-3302
dstroud@illinois.edu
www.lis.illinois.edu
A scholarly quarterly devoted to invited papers in library and information science. Each issue is devoted to a single theme.

208 pages Quarterly

Allen Renear, Chair
Carol Tilley, Chair, Admissions

527 Media & Methods Magazine
American Society of Educators
1429 Walnut Street
Philadelphia, PA 19102-3218
215-563-6005
Fax: 215-587-9706
info@media-methods.com
www.media-methods.com
Leading pragmatic magazine for K-12 educators and administrators. The focus is on how to integrate today's technologies and presentation tools into the curriculum. Very up-to-date and well respected national source publication. Loyal readers are media specialists, school librarians, technology coordinators, administrators and classroom teachers.

5x Year

Michele Sokoloff, Publisher
Christine Weiser, Editor

4528 NEWSletter
New Jersey Library Association
PO Box 1534
Trenton, NJ 08607
609-394-8032
Fax: 609-394-8164
newsletter_editor@njlamembers.org
www.njla.org/newsletter
Distributed to more than 1,800 members, serves as a vehicle for communication of library issues and activities among members of NJLA.

Quarterly

Patricia Tumulty, Executive Director

4529 Read, America!
Place in the Woods
3900 Glenwood Avenue
Golden Valley, MN 55422-5302
763-374-2120
Fax: 952-593-5593
readamerica10732@aol.com
News, book reviews, ideas for librarians and reading program leaders; short stories and poetry pages for adults and children; and an annual Read America! collection with selections of new books solicited from 350 publishers.

12 pages Quarterly Newsletter
ISSN: 0891-4214

Roger Hammer, Editor/Publisher

4530 School Library Journal
School Library Journal
123 William St., Suite 802
New York, NY 10038
646-380-0700
Fax: 646-380-0756
slj@mediasourceinc.com
www.schoollibraryjournal.com
For children, young adults and school librarians.

Kathy Ishizuka, Executive Editor
Rebecca T. Miller, Editor-in-Chief

4531 School Library Media Activities Monthly
LMS Associates
2205 West Division
Suite A-9
Arlington, TX 76012
301-685-8621
800-725-7377
lms@lmsassociates.com
www.lmsassociates.com

Monthly

Steve Langston, President
Michael Fiedler, GM/ Sales Rep.

4532 School Library Research
American Library Association
225 N Michigan Avenue
Suite 1300
Chicago, IL 60601
312-944-6780
800-545-2433
Fax: 312-440-9374
ala@ala.org
www.ala.org
Publishes research on the management, implementation, and evaluation of school library programs.

Elizabeth A. Burns, Ph.D, Co-Editor
Audrey Church, Ph.D, Co-Editor

4533 Southeastern Librarian (SELn)
SELA Administrative Services
PO Box 30703
Savannah, GA 31410
912-999-7979
selaadminservices@selaonline.org
www.selaonline.org
Publishes articles, announcements and news of professional interest to the library community in the southeast. The publication also represents a significant means for addressing the Association's research objective.

Melissa Dennis, President
Vicki Gregory, Treasurer

4534 Special Libraries
Special Libraries Association
331 South Patrick Street
Alexandria, VA 22314-3501
703-647-4900
Fax: 703-647-4901
www.sla.org
Includes information and manuscripts on the administration, organization and operation of special libraries.

Publication Date: 1909 Quarterly

Jill Strand, President
Linda Broussard, CFO

4535 Specialist
Special Libraries Association
1700 18th Street NW
Washington, DC 20009-2514
703-647-4900
Fax: 703-647-4901
www.sla.org
Contains news and information about the special library/information field.

Publication Date: 1909 Monthly

Jill Strand, President
Linda Broussard, CFO

4536 TLACast
Texas Library Association
3355 Bee Cave Road
Suite 401
Austin, TX 78746-6763
512-328-1518
800-580-2852
Fax: 512-328-8852
tla@txla.org
www.txla.org
The association's online newsletter that is published several times a year to keep members informed on TLA issues and events.

Publication Date: 1902

Sharon Amastae, President
Patricia H. Smith, Executive Director

4537 Teacher Librarian
301-805-2191
dlevitov@teacherlibrarian.com
www.teacherlibrarian.com
Professional journal targeted to the specific needs and concerns of librarians and teachers working with K-12 students. The focus is on the role of the school librarian, as an educator.

Deborah D. Levitov, Ph.D, Editor
Edward Kurdyla, Publisher

4538 Texas Library Journal
Texas Library Association
3355 Bee Cave Road
Suite 401
Austin, TX 78746-6763
512-328-1518
800-580-2852
Fax: 512-328-8852
tla@txla.org
www.txla.org

Publication Date: 1902
ISBN: 0040-4446

Sharon Amastae, President
Patricia H. Smith, Executive Director

Periodicals / Mathematics

4539 Focus on Learning Problems in Math
Center for Teaching/Learning Math
754 Old Connecticut Path
Framingham, MA 01701-7747
508-877-7895
Fax: 508-788-3600
mahesh@mathematicsforall.org
www.mathematicsforall.org
An interdisciplinary journal. Edited jointly by the Research Council for Diagnostic and Prescription Mathematics and the Center for Teaching/Learning of Mathematics. The objective of focus is to make available the current research, methods of identification, diagnosis, and remediation of learning problems in mathematics. Contribution from the fields of education psychology and mathematics having the potential to import on classroom or clinical practice are valued.
64-96 pages Quarterly
Mahesh Sharma, Editor/ Founder

4540 Illuminations Bright Ideas
National Council of Teachers of Mathematics
1906 Association Drive
Reston, VA 20191-1502
703-620-9840
800-235-7566
Fax: 703-476-2970
nctm@nctm.org
www.nctm.org
E-newsletter providing news and success stories of math teachers who use Illuminations resources in their classrooms.
7x Year
Ken Krehbiel, Executive Director
David Barnes, Associate Executive Director

4541 Journal for Research in Mathematics Education
National Council of Teachers of Mathematics
1906 Association Drive
Reston, VA 20191-1502
703-620-9840
800-235-7566
Fax: 703-476-2970
nctm@nctm.org
www.nctm.org
A forum for disciplined inquiry into the teaching and learning of math at all levels, from preschool through adult. Available in print or online version.
5x Year
ISSN: 0021-8251
Patricio Herbst, Editor

4542 Journal of Computers in Math & Science
PO Box 2966
Charlottesville, VA 22902-2966
804-973-3087
Fax: 703-997-8760
Quarterly

4543 Journal of Recreational Mathematics
4761 Bigger Road
Kettering, OH 45440-1829
631-691-1470
Fax: 631-691-1770
Promotes the creative practice of mathematics for educational learning.
Quarterly
Joseph S Madachy, Editor

4544 Math Notebook
Center for Teacher/Learning Math
754 Old Connecticut Path
Framingham, MA 01701-7747
508-877-7895
Fax: 508-788-3600
mahesh@mathematicsforall.org
www.mathematicsforall.org
A publication for teachers and parents to improve mathematics instruction.
4x/5x Year
Mahesh Sharma, Editor/ Founder

4545 Mathematics & Computer Education
MAYTC Journal
PO Box 158
Old Bethpage, NY 11804-0158
516-822-5475
Contains a variety of articles pertaining to the field of mathematics.
TriAnnually
George Miller, Editor

4546 Mathematics Teacher Educator
National Council of Teachers of Mathematics
1906 Association Drive
Reston, VA 20191-1502
703-620-9840
800-235-7566
Fax: 703-476-2970
nctm@nctm.org
www.nctm.org
Journal working to develop and strengthen the knowledge of mathematics teacher educators.
3x Year
ISSN: 2167-9789
Karen Hollebrands, Editor

4547 Mathematics Teacher: Learning & Teaching PK-12
National Council of Teachers of Mathematics
1906 Association Drive
Reston, VA 20191-1502
703-620-9840
800-235-7566
Fax: 703-476-2970
nctm@nctm.org
www.nctm.org
Devoted to the improvement of mathematics instruction.
Monthly
ISSN: 0025-5769
Angela T. Barlow, Editor-in-Chief

4548 Notices of the American Mathematical Society
American Mathematical Society
201 Charles Street
Providence, RI 2904-2294
401-455-4000
800-321-4267
Fax: 401-331-3842
www.ams.org
Announces programs, meetings, conferences and symposia of the AMS and other mathematical groups.
Publication Date: 1888 10x Year
David A. Vogan, Jr., President
Dr. Donald McClure, Executive Director

4549 Summing Up
National Council of Teachers of Mathematics
1906 Association Drive
Reston, VA 20191-1502
703-620-9840
800-235-7566
Fax: 703-476-2970
nctm@nctm.org
www.nctm.org
E-newsletter providing updates, news, resources and information about math education.
Monthly
Ken Krehbiel, Executive Director
David Barnes, Associate Executive Director

4550 The Math-Science Connector
School Science & Mathematics Association
Oklahoma State University
245 Willard Hall
Stillwater, OK 74078-1003
office@ssma.org
www.ssma.org
Newsletter of the School Science and Mathematics Association.
Stephanie Hathcock, Co-Executive Director
Toni Ivey, Co-Executive Director

Periodicals / Music & Art

4551 American Academy of Arts & Sciences Bulletin
American Academy of Arts & Sciences
136 Irving Street
Cambridge, MA 02138
617-576-5000
Fax: 617-576-5050
www.amacad.org
Covers current news of the Academy as well as developments in the arts and sciences.
Publication Date: 1780
Don M. Randel, Chair
Jonathan F. Fanton, President

4552 Art Education
National Art Education Association
901 Prince Street
Alexandria, VA 22314
703-860-8000
800-299-8321
Fax: 703-860-2960
info@arteducators.org
www.arteducators.org
A professional journal in the field of art education devoted to articles on all education levels.
6x Year
Mario R. Rossero, Executive Director
A.J. Calbert, Chief Operations Officer

4553 Arts & Activities
Arts & Activities Magazine
12345 World Trade Drive
San Diego, CA 92128
858-605-0242
subs@artsandactivities.com
www.artsandactivities.com
For classroom teachers, art teachers and other school personnel teaching visual art from kindergarten through college levels.
Monthly
ISSN: 0004-3931

4554 Arts Education Policy Review
Heldref Publications
325 Chestnut Street
Suite 800
Philadelphia, PA 19106
215-625-8900
800-365-9753
Fax: 202-296-5149

customer.service@taylorandfrancis.com
www.heldref.org
Discusses major policy issues concerning K-12 education in the various arts. The journal presents a variety of views rather than taking sides and emphasizes analytical exploration. Its goal is to produce the most insightful, comprehensive and rigorous exchange of ideas ever available on arts education. The candid discussions are a valuable resource for all those involved in the arts and concerned about their role in education.

40 pages BiWeekly
ISSN: 1063-2913

Leila Saad, Managing Editor

555 CCAS Newsletter
Council of Colleges of Arts & Sciences
c/o The College of William & Mary
PO Box 8795
Williamsburg, VA 23187-8795
757-221-1784
Fax: 757-221-1776
ccas@wm.edu
www.ccas.net
Membership newsletter to inform deans about arts and sciences issues in education.

Publication Date: 1965 4-10 pages BiMonthly

Timothy D. Johnston, President
Kate Conley, Treasurer

556 Choral Journal
American Choral Directors Association
PO Box 6310
Lawton, OK 73506-0310
903-935-7963
Fax: 903-934-8114
jmoore@etbu.edu
www.acda.org/page.asp%3Fpage%3Dwomenschoirhistory
Publishes scholarly, practical articles and regular columns of importance to professionals in the fields of choral music and music education. Articles explore conducting teachnique, rehearsal strategies, historical performance practice, choral music history and teaching materials.

Publication Date: 1980 Monthly

Amy Blosser, Chair
Karen Fulmer, President

557 Dramatics
Educational Theatre Association
4805 Montgomery Road
Suite 400
Cincinnati, OH 45212
513-421-3900
Fax: 513-421-7077
info@schooltheatre.org
www.schooltheatre.org
Online resource for the International Thespian Society. Published by the Educational Theatre Association.

Julie Cohen Theobald, Executive Director
Allison Dolan, Chief Content Officer

558 Flute Talk
The Instrumentalist
200 Northfield Road
Northfield, IL 60093
847-446-5000
888-446-6888
Fax: 847-446-6263
advertising@theinstrumentalist.com
www.theinstrumentalist.com
Published 10 times each year for flute teachers and intermediate or advanced students, with issues every month except June and August.

Monthly

4559 General Music Today
National Association for Music Education
1806 Robert Fulton Drive
Reston, VA 20191
703-860-4000
800-336-3768
Fax: 888-275-6362
memberservices@nafme.org
www.nafme.org
Publishes articles about issues concerning general music education professionals.

3x Year

4560 GuildNotes Newsletter
National Guild of Community Arts Education
520 8th Avenue
Suite 302
New York, NY 10018
212-268-3337
guildinfo@nationalguild.org
www.nationalguild.org

Monthly

Adam Johnston, Deputy Director, Operations
Heather Ikemire, Deputy Director, Learning

4561 Instrumentalist
The Instrumentalist
200 Northfield Road
Northfield, IL 60093
847-446-5000
888-446-6888
Fax: 847-446-6263
advertising@theinstrumentalist.com
www.theinstrumentalist.com
Published 12 times each year for band and orchestra directors and teachers of instruments in these groups.

Monthly

4562 Journal of Experiential Education
Association for Experiential Education
2315 18th Street S
Saint Petersburg, FL 33712
303-440-8844
www.aee.org
A professional journal that publishes articles in outdoor adventure programming, service learning, environmental education, therapeutic applications, research and theory, the creative arts, and much more.

Quarterly
ISSN: 1053-8259

Jayson Seaman, Editor

4563 Journal of Music Teacher Education
National Association for Music Education
1806 Robert Fulton Drive
Reston, VA 20191
703-860-4000
800-336-3768
Fax: 888-275-6362
memberservices@nafme.org
www.nafme.org
General interest articles and research articles on music teacher education.

3x Year

James R. Austin, Editor

4564 Journal of Research in Music Education
National Association for Music Education
1806 Robert Fulton Drive
Reston, VA 20191
703-860-4000
800-336-3768
Fax: 888-275-6362
memberservices@nafme.org
www.nafme.org
Information about research related to music teaching and learning.

Quarterly

Peter Miksza, Chair, Editorial Committee

4565 Journal of the American Musicological Society
American Musicological Society
20 Cooper Square
Floor 2
New York, NY 10003
212-992-6340
877-679-7648
Fax: 877-679-7648
ams@amsmusicology.org
www.amsmusicology.org
One of the premier journals in musicology, Journal of the American Musicological Society publishes scholarship from a broad array of musical inquiry.

ISSN: 0003-0139

Kevin C. Karnes, Editor-in-Chief

4566 Music Educators Journal
National Association for Music Education
1806 Robert Fulton Drive
Reston, VA 20191
703-860-4000
800-336-3768
Fax: 888-275-6362
memberservices@nafme.org
www.nafme.org
Offers informative, timely and accurate articles, editorials, and features to a national audience of music educators.

Quarterly
ISSN: 0027-4321

Ella Wilcox, Editor

4567 NAEA News
National Art Education Association
1806 Robert Fulton Drive
Suite 300
Reston, VA 20191
703-860-8000
Fax: 703-860-2960
info@arteducators.org
www.naea-reston.org
National, state and local news affecting visual arts education.

24 pages BiMonthly

Dr. Thomas Hatfield, Executive Director

4568 Piano Magazine
editor@claviercompanion.com
www.claviercompanion.com
Provides information on piano teaching, learning, and performing. Formerly Clavier Companion Magazine.

Pamela Pike, Editor-in-Chief

4569 SchoolArts
Davis Publications
50 Portland Street
Worcester, MA 01608
508-754-7201
800-533-2847
Fax: 508-791-3834
VSullivan@DavisArt.com
www.davisart.com
Davis has promoted and advocated for art education at both the local and national levels, providing good ideas for teachers and celebrating cultural diversity and the contributions of world cultures through a wide range of art forms.

Publication Date: 1901

Wyatt Wade, President
Valerie Sullivan, Publications

4570 SchoolArts Magazine
Davis Publications
50 Portland Street
Worcester, MA 01608
508-754-7201
800-533-2847
Fax: 508-791-3834
VSullivan@DavisArt.com
www.davisart.com
Aimed at art educators in public and private schools, elementary through high school. Articles offer ideas and information involving art media for the teaching profession and for use in classroom activities.
Publication Date: 1901 Monthly
ISSN: 0036-3463
Wyatt Wade, President
Valerie Sullivan, Publications

4571 Studies in Art Education
Louisiana State University, Dept. of Curriculum
Baton Rouge, LA 70803-0001
225-578-3202
Fax: 225-578-9135
webmaster@lsu.edu
www.lsu.edu
Reports on developments in art education.
Quarterly
Karen A Hamblen, Editor

4572 Ultimate Early Childhood Music Resource
Miss Jackie Music Company
10001 El Monte Street
Shawnee Mission, KS 66207-3631
913-381-3672
jsilberg@interserv.com
www.jackiesilberg.com
Designed to assist parents and teachers engaged in early childhood.
16 pages Quarterly
Jackie Weissman, Publisher
Emily Smith, Editor

4573 Update: Applications of Research in Music Education
National Association for Music Education
1806 Robert Fulton Drive
Reston, VA 20191
703-860-4000
800-336-3768
Fax: 888-275-6362
memberservices@nafme.org
www.nafme.org
Publishes reviews and articles on the findings of research in music teaching.
3x Year
Brian Silvey, Editor

Periodicals / Physical Education

4574 American Journal of Health Education
Shape America
PO Box 225
Annapolis Junction, MD 20701
703-476-3400
800-213-7193
Fax: 703-476-9527
askmembership@shapeamerica.org
www.shapeamerica.org
Articles for professionals working in health education.
James M. Eddy, Editor-in-Chief
Thomas Lawson, Editor

4575 Athletic Management
College Athletic Administrator
2488 N Triphammer Road
Ithaca, NY 14850
607-274-3209
Fax: 607-273-0701
www.athletics.ithaca.edu/staff.aspx
Offers information on how athletic managers can improve their operations, focusing on high school and college athletic departments.
BiMonthly
Andrea McClatchie, Operations and Events
Kathy Farley, Administrative Assistant

4576 Athletics Administration
Nat'l Assn. of Collegiate Dir. of Athletics
24651 Detroit Road
Westlake, OH 44145
440-892-4000
Fax: 440-892-4007
www.nacda.com
The official publication of the National Association of Collegiate Directors of Athletics (NACDA), Athletics Administration focuses on athletics facilities, new ideas in marketing, promotions, development, legal ramifications and other current issues in collegiate athletics administrations.
Quarterly
Bob Vecchione, Chief Executive Officer
Pat Manak, Senior Executive VP

4577 Et Cetera Newsletter
Shape America
PO Box 225
Annapolis Junction, MD 20701
703-476-3400
800-213-7193
Fax: 703-476-9527
askmembership@shapeamerica.org
www.shapeamerica.org
Provides timely news and information about the health and physical education field.
Biweekly
Terri Drain, President
Stephanie A. Morris, Chief Executive Officer

4578 Journal of Athletic Training
National Athletic Trainers' Association
1620 Valwood Parkway
Suite 115
Carrollton, TX 75006
214-637-6282
800-879-6282
Fax: 214-637-2206
www.nata.org
Research pertaining to the athletic training profession.
Monthly
Dave Saddler, Executive Director
Tamesha Logan, Associate Executive Director

4579 Journal of Environmental Education
Heldref Publications
325 Chestnut Street
Suite 800
Philadelphia, PA 19106
215-625-8900
800-365-9753
Fax: 202-296-5149
customer.service@taylorandfrancis.com
www.heldref.org
An excellent resource for department chairpersons and directors of programs in environmental, resources, and outdoor education.
48 pages Quarterly
ISSN: 0095-8964
B Alison Panko, Managing Editor

4580 Journal of Experiential Education
Association for Experiential Education
2315 18th Street S
Saint Petersburg, FL 33712
303-440-8844
www.aee.org
A professional journal that publishes articles in outdoor adventure programming, service learning, environmental education, therapeutic applications, research and theory, the creative arts, and much more.
Quarterly
ISSN: 1053-8259
Jayson Seaman, Editor

4581 Journal of Physical Education, Recreation and Dance
Shape America
PO Box 225
Annapolis Junction, MD 20701
703-476-3400
800-213-7193
Fax: 703-476-9527
askmembership@shapeamerica.org
www.shapeamerica.org
Presents new books, teaching aids, facilities, equipment, supplies, news of the profession and related groups.
Publication Date: 1986
ISSN: 0730-3084
Thomas Lawson, Editor

4582 Journal of Teaching in Physical Education
Human Kinetics Incorporation
PO Box 5076
Champaign, IL 61825-5076
217-351-5076
800-747-4457
Fax: 217-351-1549
info@hkusa.com
www.humankinetics.com/jtpe
Journal for in-service and pre-service teachers, teacher educators, and administrators, that presents research articles based on classroom and laboratory studies, descriptive and survey studies, summary and review articles, as well as discussions of current topics.
132 pages Quarterly
ISSN: 0273-5024
Brian Moore, Managing Editor
Skip Maier, Journals Division Dir.

4583 Marketing Recreation Classes
Learning Resources Network
P.O. Box 9
River Falls, WI 54022
715-426-9777
800-678-5376
Fax: 888-234-8633
info@lern.org
www.lern.org
Successful new class ideas and promotion techniques for recreation instructors.
8 pages Monthly
William A. Draves, President
Greg Marsello, VP, Development

4584 Momentum Magazine
Shape America
PO Box 225
Annapolis Junction, MD 20701
703-476-3400
800-213-7193
Fax: 703-476-9527

askmembership@shapeamerica.org
www.shapeamerica.org
Provides information, resources, news, and updates for the health and physical education community.

Terri Drain, President
Stephanie A. Morris, Chief Executive Officer

585 Physical Education Digest

Physical Education Update
11 Cerilli Crescent
Sudbury
Ontario, Ca P3E5R
705-805-9245
800-455-8782
Fax: 705-805-9245
www.physicaleducationupdate.com
Edited for physical educators and scholastic coaches. Condenses practical ideas from periodicals and books.

36 pages Quarterly
ISSN: 0843-2635

Dick Moss, Editor/ Publisher

586 Physical Educator

Arizona State University
University Drive and Mill Avenue
Tempe, AZ 85287
480-965-9011
Fax: 480-965-2569
www.asu.edu
Offers articles for the physical educator.

Quarterly

Michael M. Crow, President
Morgan R. Olsen, VP, Business & Finance

587 Quest

Louisiana State University/Dept. of Kinesiology
Huey Room 112
Baton Rouge, LA 70803-0001
225-388-2036
Fax: 225-388-3680
www.southeastern.edu
Publishes articles concerning issues critical to physical education in higher education. Its purpose is to stimulate professional development within the field.

Publication Date: 1925 Quarterly

Dr. John Crain, President
Dr. Tammy Bourg, Provost/ VP

588 Research Quarterly for Exercise & Sport

Shape America
PO Box 225
Annapolis Junction, MD 20701
703-476-3400
800-213-7193
Fax: 703-476-9527
askmembership@shapeamerica.org
www.shapeamerica.org
Publishes research on exercise, sport and human movement.

Mark Williams, Editor-in-Chief
Thomas Lawson, Editor

589 Strategies: A Journal for Physical & Sport Educators

Shape America
PO Box 225
Annapolis Junction, MD 20701
703-476-3400
800-213-7193
Fax: 703-476-9527
askmembership@shapeamerica.org
www.shapeamerica.org
Information and tips for sport and physical educators.

6x Year

Thomas Lawson, Editor

4590 Teaching Elementary Physical Education

Human Kinetics Publishers
1607 N Market Street
P.O. Box 5076
Champaign, IL 61820
217-351-5076
800-747-4457
Fax: 217-351-1459
info@hkusa.com
www.humankinetics.com
A resource for elementary physical educators, by physical educators. Each 32-page issue includes informative articles on current trends, teaching hints, activity ideas, current resources and events, and more.

32 pages BiMonthly Magazine
ISSN: 1045-4853

Brian Holding, CEO
Margery Robinson, Managing Editor

Periodicals / Professional Development

4591 Educational Leadership

Association for Supervision & Curriculum Develop.
1703 N Beauregard Street
Alexandria, VA 22311-1714
press@ascd.org
www.ascd.org
For educators by educators. With a circulation of 140,000, Educational Leadership is acknowledged throughout the world as an authoritative source of information about teaching and learning, new ideas and practices relevant to practicing educators, and the latest trends and issues affecting prekindergarten through higher education.

Publication Date: 1943

Anthony Rebora, Editor-in-Chief
Naomi Thiers, Managing Editor

4592 Exceptional Children (EC)

Council for Exceptional Children
3100 Clarendon Boulevard
Suite 600
Arlington, VA 22201-5332
888-232-7733
service@exceptionalchildren.org
www.exceptionalchildren.org
Offers research and perspectives on topical issues in special education.

6 Issues/Year

Chad Rummel, Executive Director
Craig Evans, Chief Financial Officer

4593 Experience Magazine

Cooperative Education and Internship Association
PO Box 42506
Cincinnati, OH 45242
513-793-2342
Fax: 513-793-0463
info@ceiainc.org
www.ceiainc.org
Official magazine of the Cooperative Education and Internship Association.

Peggy Harrier, Executive Director
Michael Sharp, Editor

4594 Innovations in Science Teacher Education

Association for Science Teacher Education
3451 S 5th Avenue
Whitehall, PA 18052
484-547-6046
istejournal@theaste.org
www.innovations.theaste.org
Principal journal of the Association for Science Teacher Education, with research and position papers offering insight into classroom methods, professional development, and teacher recruitment and retention.

Sarah Boesdorfer, Co-Editor-in-Chief
Rebekka Darner, Co-Editor-in-Chief

4595 Journal of Montessori Research

American Montessori Society
116 East 16th Street
New York, NY 10003-2163
212-358-1250
Fax: 212-358-1256
ams@amshq.org
www.amshq.org
Official online journal of the American Montessori Society.

Biannual
ISSN: 2378-3923

Angela K. Murray, Ph.D, Editor

4596 Journal of Science Teacher Education (JTSE)

Association for Science Teacher Education
3451 S 5th Avenue
Whitehall, PA 18052
360-961-1792
jste@theaste.org
www.theaste.org/publications/jste
Principal journal of the Association for Science Teacher Education, with research and position papers offering insight into classroom methods, professional development, and teacher recruitment and retention.

Todd Campbell, Co-Editor-in-Chief
Geeta Verma, Co-Editor-in-Chief

4597 Journal of the American Academy of Special Education Professionals (JAASEP)

AASEP
3642 E Sunnydale Drive
Chandler Heights, AZ 85142
800-754-4421
Fax: 800-424-0371
editor@aasep.org
www.aasep.org
Peer-reviewed online journal devoted to professional development of special education professionals.

ISSN: 2325-7466

Roger Pierangelo, Ph.D, Executive Director
George Giuliani, Ph.D, Executive Director

4598 MBEA Journal

Holmes Community College
412 West Ridgeland Avenue
Ridgeland, MS 39157
kmyricks@holmescc.edu
www.msmbea1950.wordpress.com
Official journal of the Mississippi Business Education Association.

Katrina Myricks, Journal Contact

4599 TEACHING Exceptional Children (TEC)

Council for Exceptional Children
3100 Clarendon Boulevard
Suite 600
Arlington, VA 22201-5332

888-232-7733
service@exceptionalchildren.org
www.exceptionalchildren.org
Contains current information about special education teaching and learning, plus materials for classroom use.

6 Issues/Year

Chad Rummel, Executive Director
Craig Evans, Chief Financial Officer

4600 The State Education Standard
123 North Pitt Street
Suite 350
Alexandria, VA 22314
703-684-4000
boards@nasbe.org
www.nasbe.org
Journal of the National Association of State Boards of Education, focused on policy development and implementation with regards to education.

Robert Hull, President & CEO
Valerie Norville, Editorial Director

4601 WestEd E-Bulletin
730 Harrison Street
San Francisco, CA 94107
415-565-3000
877-493-7833
Fax: 415-565-3012
www.wested.org
Provides regular information on research, resources, solutions, and job postings.

Glen H Harvey, Chief Executive Officer
Matthew Nathan, Senior Director, Development

Periodicals / Reading

4602 Beyond Words
20827 NW Cornell Rd.
Suite 500
Hillsboro, OR 97124
503-531-8700
Fax: 503-531-8773
www.beyondword.com
Offers information on literature, language arts and English for the teaching professional.

Publication Date: 1983 10x Year

Richard Cohn, President/ Publisher
Tim Schroeder, Chief Operating Officer

4603 Building Readers
The Parent Institute
PO Box 7474
Fairfax Station, VA 22039-7474
800-756-5525
Fax: 800-216-3667
customer@parent-institute.com
www.parent-institute.com
Focuses on parent involvement in children's reading education.

9x Year

4604 Christian Literacy Outreach
Christian Literacy Association
541 Perry Highway
Pittsburgh, PA 15229
412-364-3777
www.pghpresbytery.org
Association news offering membership information, convention news, books and articles for the Christian education professional.

Publication Date: 1975 4 pages Quarterly

Joseph Mosca

4605 Exercise Exchange
Appalachian State University
222 Duncan Hall
Boone, NC 28608
828-262-2000
Fax: 828-262-2128
admissions@appstate.edu
www.appstate.edu
Bi-annual journal which features classroom-tested approaches to the teaching of English language arts from middle school through college; articles are written by classroom practitioners.

Publication Date: 1899 BiAnnual
ISSN: 0531-531X

Dr. Randy Edwards, Chief of Staff
Melody C. Miller, Executive Assistant

4606 Forum for Reading
Fitchburg State College, Education Department
160 Pearl Street
Fitchburg, MA 01420-2697
978-665-3000
800-705-9692
admissions@fitchburgstate.edu
Offers articles, reviews, question and answer columns and more for educators and students.

Publication Date: 1894 2x Year

Dr. Ronald P. Colbert, Chair
Beth Lawrence, Secretary

4607 Journal of Adolescent & Adult Literacy
International Reading Association
800 Barksdale Road
Newark, DE 19711-3204
302-731-1600
800-336-7323
Fax: 302-731-1057
customerservice@reading.org
www.reading.org
Carries articles and departments for those who teach reading in adolescent and adult programs. Applied research, instructional techniques, program descriptions, training of teachers and professional issues.

Publication Date: 1956 80-96 pages 8x Year
ISSN: 1081-3004

Jill Lewis-Spector, President
Diane Barone, Vice President

4608 Journal of Reading Recovery
Reading Recovery Council of North America
150 E Wilson Bridge Road
Suite 200
Worthington, OH 43085
614-310-7323
877-883-7323
info@readingrecovery.org
www.readingrecovery.org
The Journal of Reading Recovery offers current information on Reading Recovery teaching theory, implementation and research on early intervention for beginning readers.

Patricia Scharer, Editor-in-Chief

4609 Laubach LitScape
Laubach Literacy Action
1320 Jamesville Avenue
Syracuse, NY 13210
315-422-9121
888-528-2224
Fax: 315-422-6369
info@laubach.org
www.laubach.org
Includes articles about national literacy activities as well as support and information on tutoring, resources, training, new readers, program management, and recruitment and retention of students and volunteers.

12 pages Quarterly

Linda Church, Managing Editor

4610 Literacy Advocate
Laubach Literacy Action
1320 Jamesville Avenue
Syracuse, NY 13210
315-422-9121
888-528-2224
Fax: 315-422-6369
www.laubach.org
Covers United States and international programs and membership activities.

8 pages Quarterly

Beth Kogut, Editor

4611 News for You
Laubach Literacy Action
1320 Jamesville Avenue
Syracuse, NY 13210
315-422-9121
888-528-2224
Fax: 315-422-6369
www.laubach.org
A newspaper for older teens and adults with special reading needs. Includes US and world news written at a 4th to 6th grade reading level.

4 pages Weekly
ISSN: 0884-3910

Heidi Stephens, Editor

4612 Phonics Institute
The Phonics Instuite
PO Box 98682
Steilacoom, WA 98388
253-588-3436
www.readingstore.com
Restoration of intensive phonics to beginning reading instruction.

8 pages 5x Year

4613 RIF Newsletter
Smithsonian Institution
PO Box 37012
SI Building, Room 153, MRC 010
Washington, DC 20013-7012
202-357-2888
Fax: 202-786-2564
info@si.edu
www.si.edu
Describes RIF's nationwide reading motivation program.

Publication Date: 1846 TriQuarterly

John W. McCarter, Jr., Chair
Shirley Ann Jackson, Vice Chair

4614 Read, America!
Place in the Woods
3900 Glenwood Avenue
Golden Valley, MN 55422-5302
763-374-2120
Fax: 952-593-5593
readamerica10732@aol.com
News, book reviews, ideas for librarians and reading program leaders; short stories and poetry pages for adults and children; and an annual Read America! collection with selections of new books solicited from 350 publishers.

12 pages Quarterly Newsletter
ISSN: 0891-4214

Roger Hammer, Editor/Publisher

4615 Reading Improvement
Project Innovation of Mobile
PO Box 8508
Mobile, AL 36608

251-610-8333
philfeldman@projectinnovation.com
www.projectinnovation.com
A journal dedicated to improving reading and literacy in America.

Quarterly

Phil Feldman, Ph.D, Editor

616 Reading Psychology
Texas A&M University, College of Education
Department of Education
College Station, TX 77843-0001
979-845-7093
Fax: 979-845-9663
www.tamu.edu/about/departments.html

Publication Date: 1862 Quarterly

Dr. Mark A. Hussey, President
Dr. Karan L. Watson, Provost/ EVP

617 Reading Research Quarterly
Ohio State University
281 W. Lane Ave.
Columbus, OH 43210
614-292-OHIO
Fax: 614-292-1816
www.osu.edu
Delves into reading ratings and special concerns in the field of literacy.

Quarterly

Jeffery Wadsworth, Chair
Ronald A. Rtaner, Vice Chair

618 Reading Research and Instruction
Appalachian State University, College of Education
Dept. of Curriculum & Instruction
Boone, NC 28608
828-262-2000
admissions@appstate.edu
www.appstate.edu

Publication Date: 1899 Quarterly

John C. Fennebresque, Chair
W. Louis Bissette, Jr., Vice Chair

619 Reading Teacher
International Reading Association
800 Barksdale Road
Newark, DE 19711-3204
302-731-1600
800-336-7323
Fax: 301-731-1057
customerservice@reading.org
www.reading.org
Carries articles and departments for those who teach reading in preschool and elementary schools. Applied research, instructional techniques, program descriptions, the training of teachers, professional issues and special feature reviews of children's books and ideas for classroom practice.

Publication Date: 1956 8x Year

Jill Lewis-Spector, President
Marcie Craig Post, Executive Director

620 Reading Today
International Reading Association
800 Barksdale Road
Newark, DE 19711-3204
302-731-1600
800-336-7323
Fax: 302-731-1057
customerservice@reading.org
www.reading.org
Edited for IRA individual and institutional members offering information for teachers, news of the education profession and information for and relating to parents, councils and international issues.

Publication Date: 1956 36-44 pages BiMonthly

Jill Lewis-Spector, President
Marcie Craig Post, Executive Director

4621 Recording for the Blind & Dyslexic
Learning Ally
20 Roszel Road
Princeton, NJ 08540
609-750-1830
800-221-4792
Fax: 609-750-9653
bvidialogue@LearningAlly.org
www.learningally.org
Textbooks on tape for students who cannot read standard print.

Publication Date: 1948

Andrew Friedman, President/ CEO
Jim Halliday, Executive Vice President

4622 Report on Literacy Programs
Business Publishers
2222 Sedwick Drive
Durham, NC 27713
301-587-6300
800-223-8720
Fax: 800-508-2592
custserv@bpinews.com
www.bpinews.com
Reports on the efforts of business and government to provide literacy training to adults— focusing on the effects of literacy on the workforce.

8-10 pages BiWeekly

Eric Easton, Publisher
Dave Speights, Editor

4623 Visual Literacy Review & Newsletter
International Visual Literacy Association
Virginia Tech
Old Security Building
Blacksburg, VA 24061
540-231-8992
jhethorn@udel.edu
www.ivla.org
Forum for sharing research and practice within an educational context in the area of visual communication.

8 pages BiMonthly

Janet Hethorn, President
Cindy Kovalik, Vice President

Periodicals / Secondary Education

4624 ACTIVITY
American College Testing
2201 Dodge
Iowa City, IA 52243-0001
319-337-1410
Fax: 319-337-1014
Distributed free of charge to more than 100,000 persons concerned with secondary and postsecondary education. ACT, an independent nonprofit organization provides a broad range of educational programs and services throughout this country and abroad.

Quarterly

Dan Lechay, Editor

4625 Adolescence
Libra Publishers
3089C Clairemont Drive
PNB 383
San Diego, CA 92117-6802
858-571-1414
Fax: 858-571-1414
Articles contributed by professionals spanning issues relating to teenage education, counseling and guidance. Paperback.

256 pages Quarterly
ISSN: 0001-8449

William Kroll, Editor

4626 American Secondary Education
Bowling Green State University
Education Room 531
Bowling Green, OH 43403-0001
419-372-2531
Fax: 419-372-8265
joelo@bgsu.edu
www.bgsu.edu
Serves those involved in secondary education— administrators, teachers, university personnel and others. Examines and reports on current issues in secondary education and provides readers with information on a wide range of topics that impact secondary education professionals. Professionals are provided with the most up-to-date theories and practices in their field.

Quarterly

Joel O'Dorisio, Chair
Allen Rogel, Vice Chair

4627 Child and Youth Care Forum
Kluwer Academic/Human Sciences Press
233 Spring Street
New York, NY 10013
212-620-8000
800-221-9369
Fax: 212-463-0742
Independent, professional publication committed to the improvement of child and youth care practice in a variety of day and residential settings and to the advancement of this field. Designed to serve child and youth care practitioners, their supervisors, and other personnel in child and youth care settings, the journal provides a channel of communication and debate including material on practice, selection and training, theory and research, and professional issues.

Bimonthly
ISSN: 1053-1890

Carol Bischoff, Publisher
Doug Magnuson, Co-Editor

4628 Family Therapy: The Journal of the California Graduate School of Family Psychology
Libra Publishers
3089C Clairemont Drive
PNB 383
San Diego, CA 92117-6802
858-571-1414
Fax: 858-571-1414
Articles contributed by professionals spanning issues relating to teenage education, counseling and guidance. Paperback.

96 pages Quarterly
ISSN: 0091-6544

William Kroll, Editor

4629 Helping Children Learn: High School Edition
The Parent Institute
PO Box 7474
Fairfax Station, VA 22039-7474
800-756-5525
Fax: 800-216-3667
customer@parent-institute.com
www.parent-institute.com
Newsletter providing parents with tips on helping their children succeed in school.

9x Year

4630 **High School Journal**
University of North Carolina
CB 3500 Peabody Hall
Chapel Hill, NC 27599-3500
919-966-1346
Fax: 919-962-1533
www.soe.unc.edu/hsj
The Journal publishes articles dealing with adolescent growth, development, interests, beliefs, values, learning, etc., as they effect school practice. In addition, it reports on research dealing with teacher, administrator and student interaction within the school setting. The audience is primarily secondary school teachers and administrators, as well as college level educators.
Publication Date: 1918 60 pages Quarterly
ISSN: 0018-1498
Zan Crowder, Editor
Hillary Parkhouse, Associate Editor

4631 **Independent School**
National Association of Independent Schools
1129 20th Street, NW
Suite 800
Washington, DC 20036-3425
202-973-9700
Fax: 888-316-3862
www.nais.org
Contains information and opinion about secondary and elementary education in general and independent education in particular.
TriAnnually
John E. Chubb, President
Kurt R Murphy, Advertising/Editor

4632 **Journal of At-Risk Issues**
Clemson University
209 Martin Street
Clemson, SC 29631-1555
864-656-2599
Fax: 864-656-0136
ndpc@clemson.edu
www.dropoutprevention.org
A journal published by the National Dropout Prevention Center/Network presenting research articles on the subject of dropout prevention and at-risk youth.
Publication Date: 0
Greg Hickman, Ph.D, Editor
Gary J Burkholder, Ph.D, Assistant Editor

4633 **NASSP Bulletin**
National Assn. of Secondary School Principals
1904 Association Drive
P.O. Box 417939
Reston, VA 20191-1537
703-860-0200
800-253-7746
Fax: 703-620-6534
nassp@nassp.org
www.principals.org
For administrators at the secondary school level dealing with subjects that range from the philosophical to the practical.
TriAnnual
G.A. Buie, President
Michael Allison, President Elect

4634 **Parents Still Make the Difference!**
The Parent Institute
PO Box 7474
Fairfax Station, VA 22039-7474
800-756-5525
Fax: 800-216-3667
customer@parent-institute.com
www.parent-institute.com
Newsletter focusing on parent involvement in children's education. Focuses on parents of children in grades 7-12.
9x Year

Periodicals / Science

4635 **American Biology Teacher**
National Association of Biology Teachers
PO Box 3363
Warrenton, VA 20188
703-264-9696
888-501-6228
Fax: 202-962-3939
abteditor@nabt.org
www.nabt.org
Articles for teachers of biology and life science.
9x Year
ISSN: 0002-7685
William F. McComas, Editor

4636 **AnthroNotes**
Smithsonian Information
PO Box 37012
SI Building, Room 153, MRC 010
Washington, DC 20013-7012
202-633-1000
Fax: 202-357-2208
info@si.edu
www.mnh.si.edu
Offers archeological, anthropological research in an engaging style.
20 pages
Ann Krupp, Editor

4637 **Appraisal: Science Books for Young People**
Children's Science Book Review Committee
Boston University
School of Education
Boston, MA 02215
617-353-4150
This is a journal dedicated to the review of science books for children and young adults. Now in its 27th year of publication, Appraisal reviews nearly all of the science books published yearly for pre-school through high-school age young people. Each book is examined by a children's librarian and by a specialist in its particular discipline.
Quarterly
Diane Holzheimer, Editor

4638 **CCAS Newsletter**
Council of Colleges of Arts & Sciences
PO Box 8795
Williamsburg, VA 23187-8795
757-221-1784
Fax: 757-221-1776
www.ccas.net
Membership newsletter to inform deans about arts and sciences issues in education.
Publication Date: 1965 4-10 pages Bi-Monthly
Dr. Anne-Marieÿ McCartan, Executive Director
Nichelle Wright, Office Specialist

4639 **Connected Science Learning**
National Science Teaching Association
1840 Wilson Boulevard
Arlington, VA 22201
703-243-7100
Fax: 703-243-7177
connectedscience@nsta.org
www.nsta.org
Focuses on programs and research that connect STEM education both in school and out of school settings.
Beth Murphy, Editor

4640 **Cream of the Crop**
California Foundation for Agriculture
2300 River Plaza Drive
Suite 220
Sacramento, CA 95833-3293
916-561-5625
800-700-2482
Fax: 916-561-5697
info@learnaboutag.org
www.LearnAboutAg.org
E-newsletter released monthly with articles about agriculture related resources, ideas, information and CFAITC event overviews.
Judy Culbertson, Executive Director
Mindy DeRohan, Project Coordinator

4641 **Dimensions Magazine**
Association of Science and Technology Centers
818 Connecticut Avenue NW
7th Floor
Washington, DC 20006-2734
202-783-7200
Fax: 202-783-7207
pubs@astc.org
www.astc.org
A digital publication offering articles on issues of interest for the science and technology centers and museums field.
Christofer Nelson, President & CEO
Melissa Ballard, Director, Programs

4642 **Hands On Agriculture**
California Foundation for Agriculture
2300 River Plaza Drive
Suite 220
Sacramento, CA 95833
916-561-5625
800-722-2482
Fax: 916-561-5697
www.LearnAboutAg.org
E-newsletter aimed at financial supporters of the California Foundation for Agriculture in the Classroom.
Judy Culbertson, Executive Director
Mindy DeRohan, Project Coordinator

4643 **Journal of College Science Teaching**
National Science Teaching Association
1840 Wilson Boulevard
Arlington, VA 22201
703-243-7100
Fax: 703-243-7177
jcst@nsta.org
www.nsta.org
Professional journal for college and university teachers of introductory and advanced science with special emphasis on interdisciplinary teaching of nonscience majors. Contains feature articles and departments including a science column, editorials, lab demonstrations, problem solving techniques and book reviews.
6x Year
David Wojnowski, Editor
Janna Palliser, Managing Editor

4644 **Journal of Environmental Education**
Taylor & Francis
325 Chestnut Street
Suite 800
Philadelphia, PA 19106
215-625-8900
800-354-1420
Fax: 202-296-5149
customer.service@taylorandfrancis.com
www.heldref.org

A vital research journal for everyone teaching about the environment. Each issue features case studies of relevant projects, evaluation of new research, and discussion of public policy and philosophy in the area of environmental education. The Journal is an excellent resource for department chairpersons and directors of programs in outdoor education.

Quarterly

Kerri P Kilbane, Editor

645 Journal of Research in Science Teaching
Wiley InterScience
Wiley Corporate Headquarters
111 River Street
Hoboken, NJ 07030-5774
866-465-3817
Fax: 201-748-5715
onlinelibrarysales@wiley.com
www.interscience.wiley.com

10x Year

646 NSTA Reports
National Science Teaching Association
1840 Wilson Boulevard
Arlington, VA 22201
703-243-7100
Fax: 703-243-7177
nstareports@nsta.org
www.nsta.org
E-newsletter providing news and information about science teaching and learning.

Weekly

Dr. Eric J. Pyle, President
Dr. Erika Shugart, Executive Director

647 Odyssey
Cobblestone Publishing
30 Grove Street
Suite C
Peterborough, NH 03458-1453
603-924-7209
800-821-0115
Fax: 603-924-7380
www.odysseymagazine.com
Secrets of science are probed with each theme issues's articles, interviews, activities and math puzzles. Astronomical concepts are experienced with Jack Horkheimer's Star Gazer cartoon and Night-Sky Navigation.

48 pages Monthly
ISSN: 0163-0946

Elizabeth E Lindstrom, Editor

648 Reports of the National Center for Science Education
National Center for Science Education
420 40th Streetÿ
Suite 2
Oakland, CA 94609-2688
510-601-7203
800-290-6006
Fax: 510-601-7204
info@ncse.com
www.ncseweb.org
An examination of issues and current events in science education with a focus on evolutionary science, and the evolution/creation controversy.

36-44 pages BiMonthly Newsletter
ISSN: 1064-2358

Brian Altersÿ, President
Lorne Trottier, Vice President/ Treasurer

649 Science Activities
Heldref Publications
325 Chestnut Street
Suite 800
Philadelphia, PA 19106
215-625-8900
800-365-9753
Fax: 202-296-5149
customer.service@taylorandfrancis.com
www.heldref.org
A storehouse of up-to-date creative science projects and curriculum ideas for the K-12 classroom teacher. A one-step source of experiments, projects and curriculum innovations in the biological, physical and behavioral sciences, the journal's ideas have been teacher tested, providing the best of actual classroom experiences. Regular departments feature news notes, computer news, book reviews and new products and resources for the classroom.

48 pages Quarterly
ISSN: 0036-8121

Betty Bernard, Managing Editor

4650 Science News Magazine
Society for Science & The Public
1719 N Street NW
Washington, DC 20036
202-785-2255
subscriptions@sciencenews.org
www.societyforscience.org
Information and programs in all areas of science.

Maya Ajmera, President, CEO & Publisher
Nancy Shute, Editor-in-Chief

4651 Science Scope
National Science Teaching Association
1840 Wilson Boulevard
Arlington, VA 22201
703-243-7100
Fax: 703-243-7177
scope@nsta.org
www.nsta.org
Specifically for middle-school and junior-high science teachers. Science Scope addresses the needs of both new and veteran teachers. The publication includes classroom activities, posters and teaching tips, along with educational theory on the way adolescents learn.

6x Year

Patty McGinnis, Editor
Caroline Barnes, Managing Editor

4652 Science Teacher
National Science Teaching Association
1840 Wilson Boulevard
Arlington, VA 22201
703-243-7100
Fax: 703-243-7177
tst@nsta.org
www.nsta.org
Professional journal for high school science teachers. Offers articles on a wide range of scientific topics, innovative teaching ideas and experiments, and current research news. Also offers reviews, posters, information on free or inexpensive materials, and more.

6x Year

Ann Haley Mackenzie, Editor
Peter Lindeman, Managing Editor

4653 Science and Children
National Science Teaching Association
1840 Wilson Boulevard
Arlington, VA 22201
703-243-7100
Fax: 703-243-7177
www.nsta.org
Dedicated to elementary science teaching. Provides lively how-to articles, helpful hints, software and book reviews, colorful posters and inserts, think pieces and on-the-scene reports from classroom teachers.

6x Year

Elizabeth Barrett-Zahn, Editor

4654 Sea Frontiers
International Oceanographic Foundation
4600 Rickenbacker Causeway
Key Biscayne, FL 33149-1031
305-361-4888
A general interest magazine about science education including underwater studies.

BiMonthly

Bonnie Gordon, Editor

4655 The Physics Teacher
American Association of Physics Teachers
1 Physics Ellipse
College Park, MD 20740-3845
301-209-3311
Fax: 301-209-0845
pubs@aapt.org
www.aapt.org
Published by the American Association of Physics Teachers and dedicated to the improvement of the teaching of introductory physics at all levels.

Beth A. Cunningham, Executive Officer
David H. Wolfe, Director, Communications

4656 The STEM Classroom
National Science Teaching Association
1840 Wilson Boulevard
Arlington, VA 22201
703-243-7100
Fax: 703-243-7177
membership@nsta.org
www.nsta.org
E-newsletter highlighting important issues in science and STEM education. Every issue has three versions (Elementary, Middle, and High School).

Monthly

Dr. Eric J. Pyle, President
Dr. Erika Shugart, Executive Director

4657 Universe in the Classroom
Astronomical Society of the Pacific
390 Ashton Avenue
San Francisco, CA 94112-1722
415-337-1100
Fax: 415-337-5205
astroed@astrosociety.org
www.astrosociety.org/uitc
On teaching astronomy in grades 3-12, including astronomical news, plain-English explanations, teaching resources and classroom activities.

8 pages Quarterly

Gordon Myers, President
Connie Walker, Vice President

4658 What's Growin' On?
California Foundation for Agriculture
2300 River Plaza Drive
Suite 220
Sacramento, CA 95833
916-561-5625
800-722-2482
Fax: 916-561-5697
www.LearnAboutAg.org
Educational newspaper highlighting the agriculture industry in California.

16 pages Annual

Judy Culbertson, Executive Director
Mindy DeRohan, Project Coordinator

Periodicals / Social Studies

4659 **American Sociological Review**
Pennsylvania State University
211 Oswald Tower, Department of Soc
University Park, PA 16802
814-865-2527
Fax: 814-863-7216
sociology@la.psu.edu
www.psu.edu/
Addresses most aspects of sociology in a general range of categories for academic and professional sociologists.
Bimonthly
David Baker, Professor of Education
Duane Alwin, Director

4660 **AnthroNotes**
Smithsonian Information
PO Box 37012
SI Building, Room 153, MRC 010
Washington, DC 20013-7012
202-633-1000
Fax: 202-357-2208
info@si.edu
www.mnh.si.edu
Offers archeological, anthropological research in an engaging style.

4661 **AppleSeeds**
Cobblestone Publishing
30 Grove Street
Suite C
Peterborough, NH 03458-1453
603-924-7209
800-821-0115
Fax: 603-924-7380
custsvc@cobblestonepub.com
www.cobblestonepub.com
A delightful way to develop love of non-fiction reading in grades 2-4. Full color articles, photographs, maps, activities that grab student and teacher interest. Children's doings and thinking around the world in Mail Bag.
Publication Date: 1973 32 pages Monthly
ISSN: 1099-7725
Susan Buckey, Barb Burt, Editors, Author
Lou Waryncia, Managing Editor

4662 **Boletin**
Center for the Teaching of the Americas
Immaculata College
Immaculata, PA 19345
610-647-4400
School teaching of the Americas.
Quarterly
Sr. Mary Consuela

4663 **California Weekly Explorer**
California Weekly Reporter
285 E Main Street
Suite 3
Tustin, CA 92780-4429
714-730-5991
Fax: 714-730-3548
Resources, events, awards and reviews relating to California history.
16 pages Weekly
Don Oliver

4664 **Calliope**
Cobblestone Publishing
30 Grove Street
Suite C
Peterborough, NH 03458-1453
603-924-7209
800-821-0115
Fax: 603-924-7380
custsvc@cobblestonepub.com
www.cobblestonepub.com
Invests in world history with reality not only through articles, stories and maps but also current events and resource lists. Calliope's themes are geared to topics studied in world history classrooms.
48 pages Monthly
ISSN: 1058-7086
Lou Waryncia, Managing Editor
Charles F Baker, Editors

4665 **Capitalism for Kids**
National Schools Commitee for Economic Education
250 East 73rd Street
Suite 12G
New York, NY 10021-8641
212-535-9534
Fax: 212-535-4167
www.nscee.org
Teaches young people about capitalism and the free enterprise system in a clear and entertaining styl. Disscusses the practical aspects of starting a small business.
247 pages
Edward H. Crane, Jr., Chairman
John G. Murphy, Ph.D, President

4666 **Cobblestone**
Cobblestone Publishing
30 Grove Street
Suite C
Peterborough, NH 03458-1453
603-924-7209
800-821-0115
Fax: 603-924-7380
custsvc@cobblestonepub.com
www.cobblestonepub.com
Blends sound information with excellent writing, a combination that parents and teachers appreciate. Cobblestone offers imaginative approaches to introduce young readers to the world of American history.
48 pages Monthly
ISSN: 0199-5197
Lou Waryncia, Managing Editor
Meg Chorlian, Editor

4667 **Colloquoy on Teaching World Affairs**
World Affairs Council of North California
312 Sutter Street
Suite 200
San Francisco, CA 94108-4311
415-293-4600
Fax: 415-982-5028
www.worldaffairs.org
Offers information, articles and updates for the history teacher.
3x Year
Peter J. Robertson, Chairman
Jane M. Wales, President/ CEO

4668 **Faces**
Cobblestone Publishing
30 Grove Street
Suite C
Peterborough, NH 03458-1453
603-924-7209
800-821-0115
Fax: 603-924-7380
www.cobblestonepub.com
The world is brought to the classroom through the faces of its people. World culture encourages young readers' perspectives through history, folk tales, news and activities.
48 pages Monthly
ISSN: 0749-1387
Lou Waryncia, Managing Editor
Elizabeth Crooker Carpentiere, Editor

4669 **Focus**
Freedoms Foundation at Valley Forge
PO Box 706
Valley Forge, PA 19482-0706
215-933-8825
800-896-5488
Fax: 610-935-0522
tsueta@ffvf.org
www.ffvf.org
Strives to teach America and promote responsible citizenship through educational programs and awards designed to recognize outstanding Americans.
6 pages Quarterly
Thomas M Sueat, Editor

4670 **Footsteps**
Cobblestone Publishing
30 Grove Street
Suite C
Peterborough, NH 03458-1453
603-924-7209
800-821-0115
Fax: 603-924-7380
www.cobblestonepub.com
Celebrates heritage of African Americans and explores their contributions to culture from colonial times to present. Courage, perserverance mark struggle for freedom and equality in articles, maps, photos, etc.
48 pages 9x Year
ISSN: 1521-5865
Lou Waryncia, Managing Editor
Charles Baker, Editor

4671 **History Matters Newsletter**
National Council for History Education
13940 Cedar Road
Suite 393
University Heights, OH 44118
240-696-6600
nche@nche.net
www.nche.net
Serves as a resource to help members improve the quality and quantity of history learning.
Monthly
Grace Leatherman, Executive Director
Sarah Drake Brown, Associate Director

4672 **Inquiry in Social Studies: Curriculum, Research & Instruction**
University of North Carolina-Charlotte
Dept of Curriculum & Instruction
Charlotte, NC 28223
704-547-4500
Fax: 704-547-4705
An annual journal of North Carolina Council for the Social Studies with a readership of 1,400.
Annual
John A Gretes, Editor
Jeff Passe, Editor

4673 **Journal of American History**
Organization of American Historians
112 N. Bryan Avenue
Bloomington, IN 47408-4141
812-855-7311
800-446-8923
Fax: 812-855-0696

Contains articles and essays concerning the study and investigation of American history.

Quarterly

Patricia Limerick, President
Jon Butler, President-Elect

4674 Journal of Economic Education
Heldref Publications
325 Chestnut Street
Suite 800
Philadelphia, PA 19106
215-625-8900
800-365-9753
Fax: 202-296-5149
customer.service@taylorandfrancis.com
www.heldref.org
Offers original articles on innovations in and evaluations of teaching techniques, materials and programs in economics.

Quarterly
ISSN: 0022-4085

4675 Journal of Geography
National Council for Geographic Education
8555 16th Street
Suite 500
Silver Spring, MD 20910
833-465-6243
info@ncge.org
www.ncge.org
Stresses the essential value of geographic education and knowledge in schools.

ISSN: 0022-1341

Meredith Marsh, Editor

4676 Magazine of History
Organizations of American History
112 N. Bryan Avenue
Bloomington, IN 47408-4141
812-855-7311
800-446-8923
Fax: 812-855-0696
oah@oah.org
www.oah.org
Includes informative articles, lesson plans, current historiography and reproducible classroom materials on a particular theme. In addition to topical articles, such columns as Dialogue, Studentspeak and History Headlines allow for the exchange of ideas from all levels of the profession.

70-90 pages Quarterly Magazine
ISSN: 0882-228X

Patricia Limerick, President
Jon Butler, President-Elect

4677 New England Journal of History
Bentley College
Dept of History
175 Forest Street
Waltham, MA 02452
781-891-2000
Fax: 781-891-2896
www.bentley.edu
Covers all aspects of American history for the professional and student.

3x Year

Gloria Cordes Larson, Esq., President
Victor Schlitzer, Director, Marketing & Adv.

4678 News & Views
Pennsylvania Council for the Social Studies
11533 Clematis Boulevard
Pittsburgh, PA 15235-3105
717-238-8768
lguru1@aol.com
www.pcss.org
Offers news, notes, and reviews of interest to social studies educators.

20 pages 5x Year
ISSN: 0894-8712

Jack Suskind, Executive Secretary
Leo R West, Editor

4679 Perspective
Association of Teachers of Latin American Studies
PO Box 620754
Flushing, NY 11362-0754
718-428-1237
Fax: 718-428-1237
Promotes the teaching of Latin America in US schools and colleges.

10 pages BiMonthly

Daniel Mugan

4680 Social Education
National Council for the Social Studies
8555 16th Street
Suite 500
Silver Spring, MD 20910
301-588-1800
800-296-7840
www.socialstudies.org
Journal for the social studies profession serving middle and high school and college and university teachers. Social Education features research on significant topics relating to social studies, lesson plans that can be applied to various disciplines, techniques for using teaching materials in the classroom and information on the latest instructional technology.

6x Year

Michael J. Simpson, Editor

4681 Social Studies
Heldref Publications
325 Chestnut Street
Suite 800
Philadelphia, PA 19106
215-625-8900
800-365-9753
Fax: 202-296-5149
customer.service@taylorandfrancis.com
www.heldref.org
Offers K-12 classroom teachers, teacher educators and curriculum administrators an independent forum for publishing their ideas about the teaching of social studies at all levels. The journal presents teachers' methods and classroom-tested suggestions for teaching social studies, history, geography and the social sciences.

48 pages BiMonthly

Helen Kress, Managing Editor

4682 Social Studies Journal
Pennsylvania Council for the Social Studies
11533 Clematis Boulevard
Pittsburgh, PA 15235-3105
717-238-8768
lguru1@aol.com
www.pcss.org
Delves into matters of social studies, history, research and statistics for the education professional and science community.

80 pages Annual

Leo R West, Editor
Dr. Saundra McKee, Editor

4683 Social Studies Professional
National Council for the Social Studies
8555 16th Street
Suite 500
Silver Spring, MD 20910
301-588-1800
800-296-7840
www.socialstudies.org
Newsletter focusing on strategies, tips and techniques for the social studies educator. New product announcements, professional development opportunities, association news, state and regional meetings.

Lawrence M. Paska, Executive Director
Michael Simpson, Director, Publications

4684 Social Studies and the Young Learner
National Council for the Social Studies
8555 16th Street
Suite 500
Silver Spring, MD 20910
301-588-1800
800-296-7840
www.socialstudies.org
This publication furthers creative teaching in grades K-6, meeting teachers' needs for new information and effective teaching activities.

Quarterly

Scott M. Waring, Editor

4685 Society For History Education/History Teacher
California State University - Long Beach
CSULB, 1250 Bellflower Blvd.
Long Beach, CA 90840-1601
562-985-2573
Fax: 562-985-5431
historytacherjournal@gmail.com
www.thehistoryteacher.org
The most widely recognized journal in the United States suppoting all areas of history education, pre-collegiate through university level, with practical and insightful professional analyses of both traditional and innovative teaching techniques.

150 pages Quarterly
ISSN: 0018-2745

Jane Dabel, Editor
Elisa Herrera, Executive Director

4686 Teaching Georgia Government Newsletter
Carl Vinson Institute of Government
201 N Milledge Avenue
Athens, GA 30602-5482
706-542-2736
Fax: 706-542-9301
www.cviog.uga.edu
Substantive and supplementary material for social studies teachers in Georgia. Topics of government, history, archaeology, geography, citizenship, etc. are covered. Publications available and upcoming social studies meetings in the state are also announced.

8 pages TriAnnually

Stacy Jones, Associate Director
Laura Meadows, Director

4687 Theory and Research in Social Education
National Council for the Social Studies
8555 16th Street
Suite 500
Silver Spring, MD 20910
301-588-1800
800-296-7840
www.socialstudies.org
Features articles covering a variety of topics: teacher training, learning theory, and child development research; instructional strategies; the relationship of the social sciences, philosophy, history and the arts to social education; models and theories used in develop-

ing social studies curriculum; and schemes for student participation and social action.

Quarterly
ISSN: 0093-3104

Wayne Journell, Editor

4688 Wall Street Journal - Classroom Edition
PO Box 7019
Chicopee, MA 01021
800-544-0522
Fax: 413-598-2332
classroom.edition@wsj.com
www.wsjclassroom.com
Monthly student newspaper, with stories drawn from the daily journal that show international, business, economic, and social issues affect students' lives and futures. The newspaper is supported by posters, monthly teacher guides, and videos. Regular features on careers, enterprise, marketing, personal finance and technology. Helps teachers prepare students for the world of work by combining timely articles with colorful graphics, etc.

Monthly

Krishnan Anantharamanz, Editor

4689 Women's History Project News
National Women's History Project
730 Second Street #469ÿ
PO Box 469
Santa Rosa, CA 95402
707-636-2888
Fax: 707-636-2909
nwhp1980@gmail.com
www.nwhp.org
Monthly E-mail newsletter about US women's history, for educators, researchers, program planners, and general women's history enthusiasts.

Monthly

Molly Murphy MacGregor, Chair/ Co-Founder
Shona Rocco, Financial Manager

Periodicals / Technology in Education

4690 Connections/EdTech News
Commonwealth of Learning
4710 Kingsway
Suite 2500
Burnaby, BC V5Hÿ-4M2
604-775-8200
Fax: 604-775-8210
info@col.org
www.col.org
Published three times per year, these newsletters provide a continually updated mailing list of over 9,000 government officials, education leaders and international agencies with information on COL's work with its partners as well as other developments worldwide.

Asha S. Kanwar, President & CEO
Venkataraman Balaji, Vice President

4691 E-School News
7920 Norfolk Avenue
Suite 900
Bethesda, MD 20814
301-913-0115
800-394-0115
Fax: 301-913-0119
ndavid@eschoolnews.com
www.eschoolnews.com
Monthly newspaper dedicated to providing news and information to help educators use technology to improve education.

Monthly

Gregs Downey, Publisher
Nancy David, Customer Relations Director

4692 EDUCAUSE Review
EDUCAUSE
4845 Pearl E Circle
Suite 118, PMB 43761
Boulder, CO 80301-6112
303-449-4430
Fax: 303-440-0461
info@educause.edu
www.educause.edu
Strategic policy advocacy; teaching and learning initiatives applied research; special interest collaboration communities; awards for leadership and exemplary practices; and extensive online information services.

ISSN: 1945-709X

John O'Brien, President & CEO
Mairead Martin, Chief Information Officer

4693 Education Technology News
Business Publishers
2222 Sedwick Drive
Durham, NC 27713
301-587-6300
800-223-8720
Fax: 800-508-2592
www.bpinews.com
Offers information on computer hardware, multimedia products, software applications, public and private funding and integration of technology into K-12 classrooms.

8 pages BiWeekly

Eric Easton, Publisher
Brian Love, Editorial Coordinato

4694 Educational Technology
700 E Palisade Avenue
Englewood Cliffs, NJ 07632-3040
201-871-4007
800-952-BOOK
Fax: 201-871-4009
Published since 1961, periodical covering the entire field of educational technology. Issues feature essays by leading authorities plus a Research Section. With many special issues covering aspects of the field in depth. Readers are found in some 120 countries.

9x Year

Lawrence Lipsitz, Editor

4695 Electronic Learning
Scholastic
555 Broadway
New York, NY 10012-3919
212-343-6100
800-724-6527
Fax: 212-343-4801
Published for the administrative level, education professionals who are directly responsible for the implementing of electronic technology at the district, state and university levels.

8x Year

Lynn Diamond, Advertising Director
Therese Mageau, Editor

4696 Electronic School
1680 Duke Street
Alexandria, VA 22314
703-838-6722
Fax: 703-683-7590
www.electronic-school.com
The school technology authority.

Cheryl S Williams, Director
Ann Lee Flynn, Director Education

4697 Information Searcher
Datasearch Group
14 Hadden Road
Scarsdale, NY 10583-3328
914-723-1995
Fax: 914-723-1995
Quarterly newsletter for the Internet and curriculum-technology integration in school.

32 pages

Pam Berger, President
Bill Berger, Treasurer

4698 International Journal on E-Learning
Assn. for the Adv. of Computing in Education
PO Box 719
Waynesville, NC 28786
828-246-9558
Fax: 828-246-9557
info@aace.org
www.aace.org
Discusses advances in technology and e-learning.

Quarterly
ISSN: 1537-2456

Gary H. Marks, Editor

4699 Journal of Computers in Mathematics and Science Teaching
Assn. for the Adv. of Computing in Education
PO Box 719
Waynesville, NC 28786
828-246-9558
Fax: 828-246-9557
info@aace.org
www.aace.org
Dedicated to information about the use of information technology in the teaching of mathematics and science.

Quarterly
ISSN: 0731-9258

Gary H. Marks, Editor

4700 Journal of Educational Technology Systems
58 New Mill Road
Smithtown, NY 11787-3342
516-632-8767
A compendium of articles submitted by professionals regarding the newest technology in the educational field.

Quarterly

Dr. Thomas Liao, Editor

4701 Journal of Information Systems Education
Bryant University
1150 Douglas Pike
Smithfield, RI 02917-1284
401-232-6000
800-622-7001
Fax: 401-232-6319
admission@bryant.edu
www.bryant.edu
Publishes original articles on current topics of special interest to Information Systems Educators and Trainers. Focus is applications-oriented articles describing curriculum, professional development or facilities issues. Topics include course projects/cases, lecture materials, curriculum design and/or implementation, workshops, faculty/student intern/extern programs,

hardware/software selection and industry relations.

Quarterly

Richard Glass, Contact

702 Journal of Interactive Learning Research

Assn. for the Adv. of Computing in Education
PO Box 719
Waynesville, NC 28786
828-246-9558
Fax: 828-246-9557
info@aace.org
www.aace.org
Publishes articles on the theory, design, implementation, and impact on education and training of interactive learning environments, including computer-based systems, interactive simulations, intelligent tutoring systems and more.

Quarterly
ISSN: 1093-023X

Gary H. Marks, Editor

703 Journal of Research on Technology in Education

International Society for Technology in Education
2111 Wilson Boulevard
Suite 300
Arlington, VA 22201
503-342-2848
800-336-5191
Fax: 541-302-3778
iste@iste.org
www.iste.org
A quarterly journal of original research and detailed system and project evaluations. It also defines the state of the art and future horizons of educational computing.

Quarterly

Albert Ritzhaupt, Editor-in-Chief
Kara Dawson, Co-Editor-in-Chief

704 Journal of Special Education Technology

The Council for Exceptional Children
1920 Association Drive
Reston, VA 20191-1589
703-620-3660
888-232-7733
Fax: 703-264-9494
cec@cec.sped.org
www.cecp.air.org/teams/stratpart/cec.asp
Provides professionals in the field with information on new technologies, current research, exemplary practices, relevant issues, legislative events and more concerning the availability and effective use of technology and media for individuals with disabilities and/or who are gifted.

Quarterly

Herbert Rieth, Editor

705 Matrix Newsletter

Department of CCTE, Teachers College/Communication
PO Box 8
New York, NY 10027-0008
212-678-3344
Fax: 212-678-8227
Newsletter describing activities and interests of Department of Communication, Computing and Technology.

14 pages SemiAnnually

Marie Sayer

4706 MultiMedia Schools

Information Today
143 Old Marlton Pike
Medford, NJ 08055-8750
609-654-6266
800-300-9868
Fax: 609-654-4309
custserv@infotoday.com
www.infotoday.com
A practical journal of multimedia, CD-Rom, online and Internet in K-12.

Thomas H Hogan, Publisher
Ferdi Serim, Editor

4707 National Forum of Instructional Technology Journal

McNeese State University
4205 Ryan Stree
Lake Charles, LA 70601-5915
337-475-5000
800-622-3352
Fax: 318-475-5467
www.mcneese.edu

Publication Date: 1939

Dr. J Mark Hunter, Editor

4708 Society for Applied Learning Technology

50 Culpeper Street
Warrenton, VA 20186
540-347-0055
800-457-6812
Fax: 540-349-3169
info@lti.org
www.salt.org

Publication Date: 1972 Quarterly

4709 TAM Connector

The Council for Exceptional Children
1920 Association Drive
Reston, VA 20191-1589
703-620-3660
888-232-7733
Fax: 703-264-9494
cec@cec.sped.org
Contains information about upcoming events, current trends and practices, state and national legislation, recently published materials and practical information relative to the availability and effective use of technology and media for individuals who are gifted or are disabled.

Quarterly

Cynthia Warger, Editor

4710 Tech Directions

Prakken Publications
275 Meity Drive
P.O. Box 8623
Ann Arbor, MI 48107-8623
734-975-2800
Fax: 734-975-2787
www.eddigest.com
Issues programs, projects for educators in career-technical and technology education and monthly features on technology, computers, tech careers.

Monthly
ISSN: 1062-9351

Tom Bowden, Managing Editor

4711 Technology & Learning

NewBay Media
28 East 28th Street
12th Floor
New York, NY 10016
212-378-0400
800-607-4410
Fax: 212-378-0470
www.techlearning.com
Product reviews; hard-hitting, straightforward editorial features; ideas on challenging classroom activities; and more. Tailor made to the special needs of a professional and an educator.

Publication Date: 2006 60-80 pages Monthly Magazine
ISSN: 1053-6728
March & October

Susan McLester, Author
Judy Salpeter, Editor-in-Chief
Jo-Ann McDevitt, Publisher

4712 Technology Integration for Teachers

Master Teacher
One Leadership Lane
PO Box 1207
Manhattan, KS 66502-1207
800-669-9633
Fax: 800-669-1132
www.masterteacher.com

4 pages Monthly

4713 Technology Teacher

International Technology Education Association
1914 Association Drive
Suite 201
Reston, VA 20191-1538
703-860-2100
Fax: 703-860-0353
Seeks to advance technological literacy through professional development activities and publications.

40 pages 8x Year

Kendall Starkweather, Executive Director
Kathleen de la Paz, Editor

4714 Technology in Education Newsletter

111 E 14th Street
#140
New York, NY 10003-4103
800-443-7432
This newsletter for K-12 educators and administrators, covers national trends of technology in education.

4715 Web Feet Guides

Thomson Gale
Thomson Gale World Headquarters
27500 Drake Road
Farmington Hills, MI 48331-3535
248-699-4253
800-877-4253
Fax: 877-363-4253
www.webfeetguides.com
The premier subject guides to the Internet, rigorously reviewed by librarians and educators, fully annotated, expanded and updated monthly. Appropriate for middle school through adult. Available in print, online, or MARC records. For more information, free trials and free samples.

Monthly

General

4716 **ABC Feelings Adage Publications**
Po Box 7280
Ketchum, ID 83340
208-788-5399
Fax: 208-788-4195
info@abcfeelings.com
www.abcfeelings.com
Interactive line of children's products that relate feelings to each letter of the alphabet. Encourages dialogue, understanding, communication, enhances self-esteem. Books, audiotape, poster, placemats, charts, activity cards, t-shirts and multicultural activity guides, floor puzzles,feelings dictionary, carpets.
Ages 3-10
Dr. Alexandra Delis-Abrams, President

4717 **ABDO Publishing Company**
P.O Box 398166
Minneapolis, MN 55439-5300
452-831-2120
800-800-1312
Fax: 800-862-3480
info@abdopublishing.com
www.abdopub.com
K-8 nonfiction books, including Abdo and Daughters imprint, high/low books for reluctant readers and Checkerboard Library with K-3 science, geography, and biographics for beginning readers. Sand Castle for pre-K to second grade, graduated reading program.
Jill Abdo Hansen, President
James Abdo, Publisher

4718 **ADL-A World of Difference Institute**
212-885-7700
education@adl.org
www.adl.org
Provider of anti-bias education materials and training for schools, universities, law enforcement agencies and community organizations.
Marvin D Nathan, National Chair
Jonathan Greenblatt, CEO & National Director

4719 **AGS**
4201 Woodland Road
Circle Pines, MN 55014-1796
763-786-4343
800-328-2560
Fax: 800-471-8457
Major test publisher and distributor of tests for literature, reading, English, mathematics, sciences, aptitude, and various other areas of education. Includes information on timing, scoring, teacher's guides and student's worksheets.

4720 **AIMS Education Foundation**
1595 S Chestnut Avenue
Fresno, CA 93702-4706
559-255-4094
888-733-2467
Fax: 559-255-6396
aimsed@fresno.edu
www.aimsedu.org
A nonprofit educational foundation that focuses on preparing materials for science and mathematics areas of education.

4721 **Ablex Publishing Corporation**
PO Box 811
Stamford, CT 06904-0811
201-767-8450
Fax: 201-767-8450
Publishes academic books and journals dealing with many different subject areas. Some of these include: education, linguistics, psychology, library science, computer and cognitive science, writing research and sociology.
Kristin K Butter, President

4722 **Acorn Naturalists**
155 El Camino Real
Tustin, CA 92780
714-838-4888
800-422-8886
Fax: 714-838-5309
www.acornnaturalists.com
Publishes and distributes science and environmental education materials for teachers, naturalists and outdoor educators. A complete catalog is available.
World Wildlife Fund, Author
Jennifer Rigby, Director
Mika Stonehawk, Operations Manager

4723 **Active Child**
PO Box 2346
Salem, OR 97308-2346
503-371-0865
Publishes creative curriculum for young children.

4724 **Active Learning**
10744 Hole Avenue
Riverside, CA 92505-2867
909-689-7022
Fax: 909-689-7142
Interactive learning center publishing materials for childhood education.

4725 **Active Parenting Publishers**
1220 Kennestone Circle
Suite 130
Marietta, GA 30066-6022
770-429-0565
800-825-0060
Fax: 770-429-0334
cservice@activeparenting.com
www.activeparenting.com
Produces and sells books and innovative video-based programs for use in parent education, self-esteem education and loss education groups/classes.

4726 **Addison-Wesley Publishing Company**
2725 Sand Hill Road
Menlo Park, CA 94025-7019
650-854-0300
Publisher and distributor of a wide range of fiction, nonfiction and textbooks for grades K-12 in the areas of mathematics, reading, language arts, science, social studies and counseling.

4727 **Advance Family Support & Education Program**
301 S Frio Street
Suite 103
San Antonio, TX 78207-4422
210-270-4630
Fax: 210-270-4612
Offers books and publications on counseling and support for the family, student and educator.

4728 **Alarion Press**
PO Box 1882
Boulder, CO 80306-1882
303-443-9039
800-523-9177
Fax: 303-443-9098
www.alarion.com
Video programs, posters, activities, manuals and workbooks dealing with History Through Art and Architecture for grades K-12.

4729 **Albert Whitman & Company**
250 South Northwest Highway
Suite 320
Park Ridge, IL 60068-2723
847-232-2800
800-255-7675
Fax: 847-581-0039
mail@awhitmanco.com
www.albertwhitman.com
Children's books.

4730 **Allyn & Bacon**
160 Gould Street
Needham Heights, MA 02194
781-455-1250
Fax: 781-455-1220
Publisher of college textbooks and professional reference books.

4731 **Alpha Publishing Company**
1910 Hidden Point Road
Annapolis, MD 21401-6002
410-757-5404
Educational materials for K-12 curricula.

4732 **American Association for State & Local History**
1717 Church Street
Nashville, TN 37203-2921
615-320-3203
Fax: 615-327-9013
www.aaslh.org
How-to books for anyone teaching history or social studies.

4733 **American Association of School Administrators (AASA)**
1615 Duke Street
Alexandria, VA 22314
703-528-0700
Fax: 703-841-1543
info@aasa.org
www.aasa.org
Publishes a variety of educational materials and resources on education administration. Topics covered include scholarship and practice, children's program publications, policy, news and media, district-level change and more.
Daniel A. Domenech, Executive Director
Chuck Woodruff, Chief Operating Officer

4734 **American Guidance Service**
4201 Woodland Road
Circle Pines, MN 55014-1796
612-786-4343
800-328-2560
Fax: 763-783-4658
Largest distributor of educational materials focusing on guidance counselors and educators in the field of counseling. Materials include books, pamphlets, workshops and information on substance abuse, childhood education, alcoholism, inner-city subjects and more.
Matt Keller, Marketing Director

4735 **American Institute of Physics**
2 Huntington Quadrangle
Suite 1NO1
Melville, NY 11747
516-576-2200
Fax: 516-349-9704
www.aip.org
Physics books.
Marc Brodsky, Executive Director

4736 **American Nuclear Society**
Outreach Department
555 N Kensington Avenue
La Grange Park, IL 60526-5592
708-352-6611
800-323-3044

Fax: 708-352-0499
outreach@ans.org
Nuclear science and technology, supplemental educational materials for grades K-12. Re-Actions newsletters.

737 American Physiological Society
9650 Rockville Pike
Bethesda, MD 20814-3991
301-530-7132
Fax: 301-634-7098
www.the-aps.org
Videotapes, tracking materials and free teacher resource packets.

738 American Technical Publishers
10100 Orland Parkway
Suite 200
Orland Parkway, IL 60467-5756
708-957-1100
800-323-3471
Fax: 708-957-1101
service@americantech.net
www.go2atp.com
Offers instructional materials for a variety of vocational and technical training areas.

739 American Water Works Association
6666 W Quincy Avenue
Denver, CO 80235-3098
303-794-7711
800-926-7337
Fax: 303-347-0804
www.awwa.org
Activity books, teacher guides and more on science education.

Gary McCoy, Director-at-large

740 Ampersand Press
750 Lake Street
Port Townsend, WA 98368
360-379-5187
800-624-4263
Fax: 360-379-0324
info@ampersandpress.com
www.ampersandpress.com
Nature and science educational games.

Lou Haller, Owner

741 Amsco School Publications
315 Hudson Street
New York, NY 10013-1085
212-886-6500
800-969-8398
Fax: 212-675-7010
www.amscopub.com
Basal textbooks, workbooks and supplementary materials for grades 7-12.

742 Anderson's Bookshops
123 West Jefferson
Naperville, IL 60540-3832
630-355-2665
Fax: 630-355-3470
www.andersonsbookshop.com
The very latest and best trade books to use in the classroom.

743 Annenberg/CPB Project
1301 Pennsylvania Avenue NW
Suite 302
Washington, DC 20004-2037
202-783-0500
Fax: 202-783-0333
order@learner.org
www.learner.org
Offers teaching resources in chemistry, geology, physics and environmental science.

Pete Neal, General Manager
Larisa M Kirgan, Operations Officer

4744 Art Image Publications
PO Box 160
Derby Line, VT 05830-0568
800-361-2598
Fax: 800-559-2598
www.artimagepublications.com
Offers various products including art appreciation kits, art image mini-kits and visual arts programs for grades K-12.

Rachel Ross, President
Rachel Ross, Art Educational Consultant

4745 Art Visuals
PO Box 925
Orem, UT 84059-0925
801-226-6115
Fax: 801-226-6115
Social studies and art history products including an Art History Timeline, 20 feet long that represents over 50 different styles, ranging from prehistoric to contemporary art; Modern Art Styles, set of 30 posters depicting 20th century styles; Multicultural Posters, Africa, India, China, Japan and the World of Islam, with 18 posters in each culture. Sets on women artists and African American Artists. Each set is printed on hard cardstock, laminated and ultraviolet protected.

Diane Asay, Owner

4746 Asian American Curriculum Project
529 East Third Avenue
San Mateo, CA 94401
650-375-8286
Fax: 650-375-8797
www.asianamericanbooks.wordpress.com
Develops, promotes and disseminates Asian-American books to schools and libraries.

Florence M. Hongo, President & General Manager
Leonard D. Chan, Vice President

4747 Association for Science Teacher Education (ASTE)
3451 S 5th Avenue
Whitehall, PA 18052
484-547-6046
executivedirector@theaste.org
www.theaste.org
The Association for Science Teacher Education works to promote leadership and support for those involved in the development of teachers of science. It offers an annual meeting, as well as three professional journals: Journal of Science Teacher Education (JSTE), Innovations in Science Teacher Education, and Contemporary Issues in Technology and Teacher Education (Science section).

Debi Hanuscin, President
Kate Popejoy, Executive Director

4748 Association for Supervision & Curriculum Development (ASCD)
1703 N Beauregard Street
Alexandria, VA 22311-1714
press@ascd.org
www.ascd.org
Publishers of educational leadership books, audios and videos focusing on teaching and learning in all subjects and grade levels.

Ranjit Sidhu, CEO & Executive Director
Dana Shanks-Williams, Chief Financial Officer

4749 Association of American Publishers
71 5th Avenue
Floor 12
New York, NY 10003
212-255-0200
Fax: 212-255-7007
www.publishers.org
Association for the book publishing industry.

4750 Atheneum Books for Children
MacMillan Publishing Company
1633 Broadway
New York, NY 10019
212-512-2000
Fax: 800-835-3202
Hardcover trade books for children and young adults.

4751 Australian Press-Down Under Books
15235 Brand Boulevard
Suite A107
Mission Hills, CA 91345-1423
818-837-3755
Big Books, models for writing, small books and teacher's ideas books from Australia.

4752 Avon Books
1350 Avenue of the Americas
New York, NY 10019-4702
212-481-5600
Fax: 212-532-2172
Focuses on middle grade paperbacks for the classroom and features authors such as Cleary, Avi, Borks, Hous, Reeder, Hobbs, Hahn, Taylor and Prish.

4753 Ballantine/Del Rey/Fawcett/Ivy
201 E 50th Street
New York, NY 10022-7703
212-782-9000
800-638-6460
Fax: 212-782-8438
Offer paperback books for middle school and junior and senior high.

4754 Barron's Educational Series
250 Wireless Boulevard
Hauppauge, NY 11788-3924
631-434-3311
800-645-3476
Fax: 631-434-3217
barrons@barronseduc.com
www.barronseduc.com
Educational books, including a full line of juvenile fiction and non-fiction, and titles for test prep and guidance, ESL, foreign language, art history and techniques, business, and reference.

Frederick Glasser, Director School/Library Sale

4755 Baylor College of Medicine
One Baylor Plaza
Houston, TX 77030
713-798-4951
Fax: 713-798-6521
www.bcm.edu
Offers materials and programs in the scientific area from Texas Scope, Sequence and Coordination projects.

Peter G Traber, President
Robert H Allen, Chairman

4756 Beech Tree Books
1350 Avenue of the Americas
New York, NY 10019-4702
212-261-6500
Fax: 212-261-6518
Curriculum offering reading materials, fiction and nonfiction titles.

4757 Black Butterfly Children's Books
625 Broadway
Floor 10
New York, NY 10012-2611
212-982-3158
A wide variety of books focusing on children, hardcover and paperback.

4758 **Blake Books**
2222 Beebee Street
San Luis Obispo, CA 93401-5505
805-543-7314
800-727-8550
Fax: 805-543-1150
Photo books on nature, endangered species, habitats, etc. for ages 10 and up.
Paige Torres, President

4759 **Bluestocking Press Catalog**
Bluestocking Press
PO Box 1014
Placerville, CA 95997-1014
530-622-8586
800-959-8586
Fax: 530-642-9222
Jane@bluestockingpress.com
www.bluestockingpress.com
Approximately 800 items with a concentration in American History, economics and law. That includes fiction, nonfiction, primary source material, historical documents, facsimile newspapers, historical music, hands-on-kits, audio history, coloring books and more.
Jane A Williams, Coordinating Editor

4760 **Boyds Mill Press**
815 Church Street
Honesdale, PA 18431-1889
570-253-1164
Fax: 570-253-0179
Publishes books for children from preschool to young adult.

4761 **BridgeWater Books**
100 Corporate Drive
Mahwah, NJ 07430-2041
Distinctive children's hardcover books featuring award-winning authors and illustrators, including Laurence Yep, Babette Cole, Joseph Bruchac and others. An imprint of Troll Associates.

4762 **Bright Ideas Charter School**
2507 Central Freeway East
Wichita Falls, TX 76302-5802
940-767-1561
Fax: 940-767-1904
lydiaplmr@aol.com
K-12 curriculum framework for educators struggling to move toward a global tomorrow.
Lynda Plummer, President

4763 **Brown & Benchmark Publishers**
25 Kessel Court
Madison, WI 63711
608-273-0040
College textbooks in language arts and reading.

4764 **Bureau for At-Risk Youth Guidance Channel**
Guidance Channel
135 Dupont Street
PO Box 760
Plainview, NY 11803-0760
516-349-5520
800-999-6884
Fax: 800-262-1886
info@at-risk.com
www.at-risk.com
Publisher and distributor of educational curriculums, videos, publications and products for at-risk youth and the counselors and others who work with them. Bureau products focus on areas such as violence and drug prevention, character education, parenting skills and more.
Sally Germain, Editor-in-Chief

4765 **Business Publishers**
PO Box 17592
Baltimore, MD 21297
301-587-6300
800-274-6737
Fax: 301-585-9075
Publishes education related materials.

4766 **CLEARVUE/eav**
6465 N Avondale Avenue
Chicago, IL 60631
773-775-9433
800-253-2788
Fax: 773-775-9855
www.clearvue.com
CLEARVUE/eav offers educators the largest line of curriculum-oriented media in the industry. CLEARVUE/eav programs have, and will continue to enhance students' interest, learning, motivation and skills.
Sarah M Lucas, Communications Coordinator
Kelli Campbell, VP

4767 **Calculators**
7409 Fremont Avenue S
Minneapolis, MN 55423-3971
800-533-9921
Fax: 612-866-9030
Calculators and calculator books for K thru college level instruction. Calculator products by Texas Instruments, Casio, Sharp and Hewlett-Packard.
Richard Nelson, President

4768 **Cambridge University Press**
Edinburgh Building
Shaftesbury Road
Cambridge, England CB22RU
Curriculum materials and textbooks for science education for grades K-12.

4769 **Candlewick Press**
2067 Massachusetts Avenue
Cambridge, MA 02140-1340
617-661-3330
Fax: 617-661-0565
High quality trade hardcover and paperback books for children and young adults.

4770 **Capstone Press**
151 Good Counsel Drive
Mankato, MN 56001-3143
952-224-0529
888-262-6135
Fax: 888-262-0705
timadsen@capstone-press.com
www.capstonepress.com
PreK-12 Nonfiction publisher
Tim Mandsen, Director Marketing

4771 **Careers/Consultants in Education Press**
3050 Palm Aire Drive N
#310
Pompano Beach, FL 33069
954-974-3511
Fax: 954-974-5477
carconed@aol.com
Current education job lists for teacher and administrator positions in schools and colleges. Plus nine differently titled desk/reference paperback books.
Dr. Robert M Bookbinder, President

4772 **Carolrhoda Books**
A Division of Lerner Publishing Group
241 1st Avenue N
Minneapolis, MN 55401-1607
612-332-3344
800-328-4929
Fax: 612-332-7615
www.lernerbooks.com
Fiction and nonfiction for readers K through grade 6. List includes picture books, biographies, nature and science titles, multicultural and introductory geography books, and fiction for beginning readers.
Rebecca Poole, Submissions Editor

4773 **Carson-Dellosa Publishing Company**
PO Box 35665
Greensboro, NC 27425-5665
336-632-0084
800-321-0943
Fax: 336-632-087
Textbooks, manuals, workbooks and materials aimed at increasing students reading skills.

4774 **Center for Play Therapy (CPT)**
425 S Welch Street
Complex 2
Denton, TX 76203
940-565-3864
Fax: 940-565-4461
cpt@unt.edu
www.cpt.unt.edu
Offers literature covering topics in the field of play therapy.
Dee Ray, Director
Gabby Mendez, Administrative Coordinator

4775 **Central Regional Educational Laboratory**
2550 S Parker Road
Suite 500
Aurora, CO 80014
303-337-0990
Fax: 303-337-3005
The Regional Educational Laboratories are educational research and development organizations supported by contracts with the US Education Department, Office of Educational Research and Improvement. Specialty area: curriculum, learning and instruction.
Dr. J Timothy Waters, Executive Director

4776 **Charles Scribner & Sons**
MacMillan Publishing Company
1633 Broadway
New York, NY 10019
212-632-4944
Fax: 800-835-3202
Hardcover trade books for children and young adults.

4777 **Chicago Board of Trade**
141 W Jackson Boulevard
Chicago, IL 60604-2992
312-435-3500
Educational materials including a new economics program entitled Commodity Challenge.

4778 **Children's Book Council**
12 West 37th Street
2nd Floor
New York, NY 10018-7480
212-966-1990
800-999-2160
Fax: 212-966-2073
www.cbcbooks.org
The Children's Book Council, Inc is the nonprofit trade association of publishers and packagers of trade books and related materials for children and young adults.
JoAnn Sabatino-Falkenstein, VP Marketing

4779 **Children's Press**
Grolier Publishing
90 Sherman Turnpike
Danbury, CT 06816
800-621-1115
Fax: 800-374-4329
Leading supplier of reference and children's nonfiction and fiction books.

780 Children's Press/Franklin Watts
PO Box 1330
Danbury, CT 06813-1330
203-797-3500
Fax: 203-797-3197
K-12 curriculum materials.

781 Children's Television Workshop
1 Lincoln Plaza
New York, NY 10023-7129
212-875-6809
Fax: 212-875-7388
Hands-on books for elementary school use in the area of science education.

Brenda Pilson, Review Coordinator
Elaine Israel, Editor-in-Chief

782 Chime Time
2440-C Pleasantdale Road
Atlanta, GA 30340-1562
770-662-5664
Early childhood products and publications.

783 Choices Education Project
Watson Institute for International Studies
Brown University
PO Box 1948
Providence, RI 02912-1948
401-863-3155
Fax: 401-863-1247
choices@brown.edu
www.choices.edu
Develops interactive, supplementary curriculum resources on current and historical international issues. Makes complex current and historic international issues accessible for secondary school students. Materials are low-cost, reproducible, updated annually.

Annually

784 Close Up Publishing
44 Canal Center Plaza
Alexandria, VA 22314-1592
800-765-3131
Fax: 703-706-3564
Offers textbooks, workbooks and other publications focusing on self-esteem, learning and counseling.

785 Cognitive Concepts
PO Box 1363
Evanston, IL 60204-1363
888-328-8199
Fax: 847-328-5881
www.cogcon.com
Leading provider of language and literacy software, books, internet services and staff development. Specialize in integrating technology with scientific principles and proven instructional methods to offer effective and affordable learning solutions for educators, specialists and families.

786 College Board
250 Vesey Street
New York, NY 10281
212-713-8000
www.collegeboard.org
Publishers of books of interest to educational researchers, policymakers, students, counselors, teachers; products to prepare students for college and test prep materials.

David Coleman, Chief Executive Officer
Jeremy Singer, President

787 Coloring Concepts
1732 Jefferson Street
Suite 7
Napa, CA 94559-1737
707-257-1516
800-257-1516
Fax: 707-253-2019
chris@coloringconcepts.com
www.coloringconcepts.com
Colorable active learning books for middle school through college that combine scientifically correct text with colorable illustrations to provide an enjoyable and educational experience that helps the user retain more information than during normal reading. Subjects include Anatomy, Marine Biology, Zoology, Botany, Human Evolution, Human Brain, Microbiology and biology.

Christopher Elson, Operations

4788 Comprehensive Health Education Foundation
22419 Pacific Hwy S
Seattle, WA 98198-5106
206-824-2907
800-833-6388
info@chef.org
www.chef.org
Primarily Health gives K-3 kids a dynamic, hands-on health program while teaching academic skills.

Larry Clark, President
Marvin Hamanishi, Vice President

4789 Computer Learning Foundation
PO Box 60007
Palo Alto, CA 94306-0007
408-720-8898
Fax: 408-730-1191
clf@computerlearning.org
Publishes books and videos on using technology.

4790 Computer Literacy Press
Computer Literacy Press
PO Box 562
Earlysville, VA 22936
513-600-3455
513-530-0110
Fax: 800-833-5413
Instructional materials using hands-on, step-by-step format, appropriate for courses in adult and continuing education, business education, computer literacy and applications, curriculum integration, Internet instruction, and training and staff development. Products are available for ranging from middle school through high school as well as post secondary, teacher training and adult/senior courses.

Robert First, President

4791 Concepts to Go
PO Box 10043
Berkeley, CA 94709-5043
510-848-3233
Fax: 510-486-1248
Develops and distributes manipulative activities for language arts and visual communications for ages 3-8.

4792 Congressional Quarterly
1414 22nd Street NW
Washington, DC 20037-1003
202-887-8500
Fax: 202-293-1487
Comprehensive publications and reference and paperback books pertaining to Congress, US Government and politics, the presidency, the Supreme Court, national affairs and current issues.

4793 Continental Press
520 E Bainbridge Street
Elizabethtown, PA 17022-2299
717-367-1836
800-233-0759
Fax: 717-367-5660
www.continentalpress.com
Publisher of print for PreK-12 (plus adult education). Programs relate to skill areas in reading, math, comprehension, phonics, etc. Producers of Testlynx Software.

4794 Cottonwood Press
107 Cameron Drive
Suite 398
Fort Collins, CO 80525
970-204-0715
800-864-4297
Fax: 970-204-0761
Publishes books focusing on teaching language arts and writing, grades 5-12.

Cheryl Thurston

4795 Council for Exceptional Children (CEC)
3100 Clarendon Boulevard
Suite 600
Arlington, VA 22201-5332
888-232-7733
service@exceptionalchildren.org
www.exceptionalchildren.org
The Council for Exceptional Children is a major publisher of special education literature and features an online catalogue of all publications.

Chad Rummel, Executive Director
Craig Evans, Chief Financial Officer

4796 Creative Teaching Press
Po Box 2723
Huntington Beach, CA 92647-0723
800-287-8879
Fax: 800-229-9929
customerservice@creativeteaching.com
www.creativeteaching.com
Offers language and literature-based books including Teaching Basic Skills through Literature, Literature-Based Homework Activities, I Can Read! I Can Write!, Multicultural Art Activities, Responding to Literature, and Linking Math and Literature.

Jim Connelly, President
Luella Connelly, Co-Founder

4797 Cricket Magazine Group
315 5th Street
Peru, IL 61354-2859
815-223-1500
Magazines of high quality children's literature.

4798 Curriculum Associates
PO Box 2001
North Billerica, MA 01862-0901
978-667-8000
800-225-0248
Fax: 800-366-1158
cainfo@curriculumassociates.com
www.curriculumassociates.com
Supplementary educational materials; cross-curriculum, language arts, reading, study skills, test preparation, diagnostic assessments, emergent readers, videos, and software.

4799 DC Heath & Company
125 Spring Street
Lexington, MA 02421-7801
781-862-6650
Publishes resources for all academic levels ranging from textbooks, fiction and nonfiction titles to business and college guides.

4800 DLM Teaching Resources
PO Box 4000
Allen, TX 75013-1302
972-248-6300
800-527-4747
Offers a variety of teacher's resources and guides for testing in all areas of education.

4801 **Dawn Publications**
14618 Tyler Foote Road
Nevada City, CA 95959-9316
530-478-7540
800-545-7475
Fax: 530-478-0112
Specializes in nature, children and health and healing books, tapes and videos and dedicated to helping people experience unity and harmony.
Bob Rinzler, Publisher
Glenn Hoveman, Editor

4802 **Delta Education**
80 Northwest Blvd.
Nashua, NH 03061-3000
800-258-1302
Fax: 800-282-9560
Science programs, materials and curriculum kits.

4803 **Dial Books for Young Readers**
345 Hudson Street
New York, NY 10014-3658
212-366-2800
Fax: 212-366-2938
www.penguinputnam.com
General hardcover, children's books, from toddler through young adult, fiction and nonfiction.

4804 **Didax Educational Resources**
PO Box 507
Rowley, MA 01969-0907
978-948-2340
800-458-0024
Fax: 978-948-2813
www.didaxinc.com
High quality educational materials featuring Unifix and hundreds of math and reading supplements.
Brian Scarlett, President
Martin Kennedy, VP

4805 **Dinah-Might Activities**
PO Box 39657
San Antonio, TX 78218-6657
210-698-0123
Fax: 210-698-0095
Learn how to integrate language arts, math, map and globe skills and more into a science curriculum. Books include The Big Book of Books and Activities, Organizing the Integrated Classroom, Write Your Own Thematic Units and Reading and Writing All Day Long.

4806 **Dinocardz Company**
146 5th Avenue
San Francisco, CA 94118-1310
415-751-5809
Dinosaur curriculums for grades 1-3 and 4-6.

4807 **Disney Press**
Disney Juvenile Publishing
114 5th Avenue
New York, NY 10011-5604
212-633-4400
Fax: 212-633-5929
Hardcover trade and library editions and paperback books for children, grades K-12.
Liisa-Ann Fink, President

4808 **Dominic Press**
1949 Kellogg Avenue
Carlsbad, CA 92008-6582
619-481-3838
Offers a range of materials for the Reading Recovery Program and Chapter 1 programs.

4809 **Dorling Kindorley Company**
95 Madison Avenue
New York, NY 10016
212-213-4800
Fax: 212-689-5254
Science books for all grade levels.

4810 **Dover Publications**
31 E 2nd Street
Mineola, NY 11501
516-294-7000
Fax: 516-742-6953
Fun and educational storybooks, coloring, activity, cut-and-assemble toy books, science for children.
Clarence Strowbridge, President

4811 **Dutton Children's Books**
375 Hudson Street
New York, NY 10014-3658
212-366-2000
Fax: 212-366-2948
General hardcover children's books from toddler through young adult, fiction and nonfiction.

4812 **DynEd International**
1350 Bayshore Highway
Suite 850
Burlingame, CA 94010
800-765-4375
Fax: 650-375-7017
www.dyned.com
Pre-K-adult listening and speaking skill development English language acquisition software.
Steven Kearney, Sales
Sue Young, Operations

4813 **EBSCO Publishing**
EBSCO Publishing
10 Estes Street
Ipswich, MA 01938
800-653-2726
Fax: 978-356-6565
information@ebscohost.com
www.ebscohost.com
Database and eBook provider for libraries and other institutions — more than 375 full-text and secondary research databases and more than 300,000 eBooks available via the EBSCOhost platform. EBSCO's content services K-12 students to public library patrons, from academic, corporate and medical researchers to clinicians and governments around the world.
Tim Collins, President
Sam Brooks, EVP Sales/Marketing

4814 **ERICAE Clearinghouse on Assessment & Evaluation**
University of Maryland
1129 Shriver Laboratory
Building 075
College Park, MD 20742-5701
301-405-7449
800-464-3742
Fax: 301-405-8134
feedback3@ericae.net
www.ericae.net
Provides information on topics pertaining to tests and other measurement devices, research design and methodology.

4815 **ETA - Math Catalog**
620 Lakeview Parkway
Vernon Hills, IL 60061-1828
847-816-5050
800-445-5985
Fax: 847-816-5066
www.etauniverse.com
Offers a full line of mathematics products, materials, books, textbooks and workbooks for grades K-12.
Mary Cooney, Product Development Manager
Monica Butler, Director Marketing

4816 **EVAN-Motor Corporation**
18 Lower Ragsdale Drive
Monterey, CA 93940-5728
831-649-5901
Fax: 800-777-4332
Resource materials for K-6 science educational programs.

4817 **Early Start-Fun Learning**
PO Box 350187
Jacksonville, FL 32235-0187
904-641-6138
Preschool materials for the educator.

4818 **Earth Foundation**
5151 Mitchelldale
B11
Houston, TX 77092-7200
713-686-9453
Fax: 713-686-6561
Join the largest active network of educators working to save endangered ecosystems and their species! Multi-disciplinary, hands-on curriculum and videos for the classroom.
Cynthia Everage, President

4819 **Editorial Projects in Education**
6935 Arlington Road
Suite 100
Bethesda, MD 20814-5233
301-280-3100
800-346-1834
Fax: 301-280-3250
customercare@epe.org
www.www2.edweek.org
Publishes various newsletters and publications in the fields of history and education.
Christopher B Swanson, Director
Carole Vinograd Bausell, Assistant Director

4820 **Edmark**
Riverdeep Inc.
100 Pine Street
Suite 1900
San Francisco, CA 94111
415-659-2000
888-242-6747
Fax: 415-659-2020
info@riverdeep.net
www.edmark.com
Develops innovative and effective educational materials for children.
Barry O'Callaghan, Chairman
Tony Mulderry, Executive Vice President

4821 **Education Center**
3515 W Market Street
Greensboro, NC 27403-1309
336-273-9409
Publishers of the Mailbox, teacher's helper magazines, learning centers clubs, classroom beautiful bulletin board clubs, the storybook club and more.

4822 **Education, Training and Research Associates (ETR)**
5619 Scotts Valley Drive
Suite 140
Scotts Valley, CA 95066
800-620-8884
Fax: 831-438-4284
www.etr.org
Education, Training and Research Associates is a nonprofit dedicated to providing solutions in the areas of health and education. Their mission is to improve health and increase opportunities for

youth and communities through research, publications, information resources and programs.

Vignetta Charles, Chief Executive Officer
Eric Blanke, Chief Operating Officer

323 Educational Marketer
SIMBA Information
11 Riverbend Drive
PO Box 4234
Stamford, CT 06907-0234
800-307-2529
Fax: 203-358-5824
Contains a range of print and electronic tools, including software and multimedia materials for educational institutions.

824 Educational Press Association of America
Glassboro State College
Glassboro, NJ 08028
609-445-7349
Offers various publications and bibliographic data focusing on all aspects of education.

825 Educational Productions
9000 SW Gemini Drive
Beaverton, OR 97008
503-644-7000
800-950-4949
Fax: 503-350-7000
custserv@edpro.com
www.edpro.com
Video training programs that help increase parenting skills and help every teacher meet performance standards. Offers training on preventing discipline problems, increasing parenting skills, supporting literacy efforts and more.

826 Educational Teaching Aids
620 Lakeview Pkwy
Vernon Hills, IL 60061-1838
847-816-5050
800-445-5985
Fax: 847-816-5066
Manipulatives to enhance understanding of basic concepts and to help bridge the gap between the concrete and the abstract.

827 Educators Progress Service
214 Center Street
Randolph, WI 53956
920-326-3127
888-951-4469
Fax: 920-326-3126
www.freeteachingaids.com
A complete spectrum of curriculum and mixed media resources for allgrade levels.

828 Educators Publishing Service
31 Smith Place
Cambridge, MA 02138-1089
617-547-6706
800-225-5750
Fax: 617-547-0412
www.epsbooks.com
Supplementary workbooks and teaching materials in reading, spelling, vocabulary, comprehension, and elementary math, as well as materials for assessment and learning differences.

829 Edumate-Educational Materials
2231 Morena Boulevard
San Diego, CA 92110-4134
619-275-7117
Multicultural and multilingual materials in the form of toys, puzzles, books, videos, music, visuals, games, dolls and teacher resources. Special emphasis on Spanish and other languages. Literature offered from North and South America.

Gustavo Blankenburg, President

4830 Ellis
406 W 10600 S
Suite 610
Salt Lake City, UT 84003
801-374-3424
888-756-1570
Fax: 801-374-3495
www.ellis.com
Publish software that teaches English.

4831 Encyclopaedia Britannica
333 N La Salle Street
Chicago, IL 60610
312-347-7159
800-323-1229
Fax: 312-294-2104
www.britannica.com
Books and related educational materials.

4832 Energy Learning Center
USCEA
1776 I Street NW
Suite 400
Washington, DC 20006-3700
703-741-5000
Fax: 703-741-6000
Energy learning materials.

4833 Essential Learning Products
PO Box 2590
Columbus, OH 43216-2590
800-357-3570
Fax: 614-487-2272
Publishers of phonics workbooks.

4834 Ethnic Arts & Facts
PO Box 20550
Oakland, CA 94620-0550
510-465-0451
888-278-5652
Fax: 510-465-7488
Kit titles include: Traditional Africa, Urban Africa, China, Guatemala, Peru, Huichol Indians of Mexico, Chinese Shadow Puppet Kit. African-American Music History Mini-Kit. Artifact kits/resource booklets designed to enhance appreciation of cultural diversity, improve geographic literacy and sharpen critical thinking and writing skills.

Susan Drexler, Curriculum Specialist

4835 Evan-Moor Corporation
18 Lower Ragsdale Drive
Monterey, CA 93940-5728
How to Make Books with Children and other fine teacher resources and reproducible materials for all curriculum areas grades PreK-6.

4836 Everyday Learning Corporation
PO Box 812960
Chicago, IL 60681-2960
800-382-7670
Fax: 312-233-7860
University of Chicago school mathematics project. Everyday Mathematics enriched curriculum for grades K-6.

4837 Exploratorium
3601 Lyon Street
San Francisco, CA 94123-1099
415-563-7337
Fax: 415-561-0307
www.exploratorium.edu
Exploratorium is dedicated to the formal and informal teaching of science using innovative interactive methods of inquiry. It publishes materials for educators and provides professional development opportunities both in print and online.

Quarterly/Monthly

4838 Extra Editions K-6 Math Supplements
PO Box 38
Urbana, IL 61803-0038
Fax: 614-794-0107
Special needs math supplements offering 70 single-topic units from K-6 that reach students your basic math program misses. Extra Editions newspaper-like format uses animation with a hands-on approach to show real life necessity for computational skills, time, money, problem solving, critical thinking, etc. Ideal for Chapter One, Peer-Tutoring, Parental Involvement, Home Use, and more.

Craig Rucker, General Manager
Earl Ockenga, Author/Owner

4839 F(G) Scholar
Future Graph
538 Street Road
Suite 200
Southhampton, PA 18966-3780
215-396-0721
Fax: 215-396-0724
A revolutionary program for teaching, learning and using math. This single program allows students and teachers easy answers to Algebra, Trigonometry, Pre-Calculus, Calculus, Statistics, Probability and more. It combines all of the power of a graphing calculator, spreadsheet, drawing tools, mathematics and programming/scripting language and much more, and makes it simple and fun to use.

4840 Facts on File
11 Penn Plaza
New York, NY 10001
212-967-8800
800-322-8755
Fax: 212-967-9196
llikoff@factsonfile.com
www.factsonfile.com
Reference books for teacher education, software, hardware and educational computer systems.

9 Hardcover Books

Laurie Likoff, Editorial Director

4841 Farrar, Straus & Giroux
19 Union Square W
New York, NY 10003-3304
212-741-6900
Fax: 212-633-9385
Children's, young adult and adult trade books in hardcover and paperback, including Sunburst Books, Aerial Miraso/libros juveniles and Hill and Wang.

4842 First Years
1 Kiddie Drive
Avon, MA 02322-1171
508-588-1220
Early childhood books, hardcover and paperback.

4843 Forbes Custom Publishing
60 5th Avenue
New York, NY 10011-8802
513-229-1000
800-355-9983
Fax: 800-451-3661
fcpinfo@forbes.com
Offers educators and teachers the opportunity to select unique teaching material to create a book designed specifically for their courses.

4844 Formac Distributing
5502 Atlantic Street
Halifax, NS E3HIG-4

902-421-7022
800-565-1905
Fax: 902-425-0166
Contemporary and historical fiction for ages 6-15. Multicultural themes featuring Degrassi Y/A series; first novel chapter books.

4845 Frank Schaffer Publications
3195 Wilson Drive NW
Grand Rapids, MI 49534
800-417-3261
Fax: 888-203-9361
www.frankschaffer.com
Best-selling supplemental materials including charts, literature notes, resource materials and more.

4846 Franklin Watts
Grolier Publishing
Sherman Turnpike
Danbury, CT 06816
800-621-1115
800-843-3749
Fax: 800-374-4329
Publisher of library bound books, paperback and Big Books for literature based, multicultural classrooms and school libraries.

4847 Free Spirit Publishing
217 Fifth Avenue North
Suite 200
Minneapolis, MN 55401-1299
612-338-2068
800-736-7323
Fax: 612-337-5050
Free Spirit is the leading publisher of learning tools that support young people's social and emotional health.

4848 Frog Publications
PO Box 280996
Tampa, FL 33682
813-935-5845
Fax: 813-935-3764
www.frog.com
An organized system of cooperative games for K-5 reading, language arts, thinking skills, math, social studies, Spanish and multicultural studies. Parental Involvement Program, Learning Centers, Test Preperation, Afterschool Program Materials. Drops in the Bucket daily practice books.

4849 Gareth Stevens
330 W Olive Street
Suite 100
Milwaukee, WI 53212
414-332-3520
800-542-2595
Fax: 414-336-0156
info@gsinc.com
www.garethstevens.com
Complete display of supplemental children's reading material for grades K-6, including our New World Almanac Library imprint grades 6-12.

Bi-Annually
ISSN: 0-8368

Mark Sachner, Author
Juanita Jones, Marketing Manager
Jonathan Strickland, National Sales Manager

4850 Goethe House New York
1014 5th Avenue
New York, NY 10028-0104
Teaching materials on Germany for the social studies classroom in elementary, middle and high schools.

4851 Goodheart-Willcox Publisher
18604 W Creek Drive
Tinley Park, IL 60477-6243
800-323-0440
Fax: 888-409-3900
custerv@goodheartwillcox.com
Comprehensive text designed to help young students learn about themselves, others, and the environment. Readers will develop skills in clothing, food, decision making, and life management. Case studies throughout allow students to apply learning to real-life situations.

4852 Greenhaven Press
PO Box 9187
Farmington Hills, MI 48333-9187
800-231-5163
800-231-5163
Fax: 248-699-8035
Publishers of the Opposing Viewpoints Series, presenting viewpoints in an objective, pro/con format on some of today's controversial subjects.

4853 Greenwillow Books
1350 Avenue of the Americas
New York, NY 10019-4702
212-261-6500
Fax: 212-261-6518
Offers publications for all reading levels.

4854 Grey House Publishing
4419 Route 22
PO Box 56
Amenia, NY 12501
518-789-8700
800-562-2139
Fax: 518-789-0556
books@greyhouse.com
www.greyhouse.com
Publisher of educational reference directories, and encyclopedias.

Richard Gottlieb, President
Leslie Mackenzie, Publisher

4855 Grolier Publishing
90 Sherman Turnpike
Danbury, CT 06816
203-797-3500
800-621-1115
Fax: 203-797-3197
Publisher of library bound and paperback books in the areas of social studies, science, reference, history, and biographies for schools and libraries for grades K-12.

4856 Gryphon House
Gryphon House
PO Box 275
Mount Rainier, MD 20712-0275
301-779-6200
Fax: 301-595-0051
info@ghbooks.com
Resource and activity books for early childhood teachers and directors.

Cathy Callootte, Marketing Director

4857 H. W. Wilson
Grey House Publishing
2 University Plaza
Suite 310
Hackensack, NJ 07601
844-630-6369
Fax: 201-968-0511
info@hwwilsoninprint.com
www.hwwilsoninprint.com
H. W. Wislon publishes database and reference resources to serve libraries, schools and corporations.

4858 Hands-On Prints
PO Box 5899-268
Berkeley, CA 94705
510-601-6279
Fax: 510-601-6278
Specializes in cultural and language materials for children with an emphasis on internationalism and multiculturalism.

Christina Cheung, President

4859 Hardcourt Religion Publishers
6277 Sea Harbor Drive
Orlando, FL 32887
563-557-3700
800-922-7696
Fax: 563-557-3719
Publishers of religion education materials for schools and parishes.

4860 Hazelden Educational Materials
PO Box 176
Center City, MN 55012-0176
651-257-4010
Fax: 651-213-4590
Educational publisher of materials supporting both students and faculty in areas of substance abuse and related topics.

4861 Heinemann
361 Hanover Street
Portsmouth, NH 03801-3959
603-431-7894
Fax: 203-750-9790
Holistic/student-centered publications, videotapes and workshops for parents, teachers and administrators.

4862 Henry Holt & Company
175 Fifth Avenue
New York, NY 10010
646-307-5095
800-628-9658
Fax: 212-633-0748
Books and materials for classroom teachers, grades 6-adult, including programs on science literacy.

4863 Henry Holt Books for Young Readers
115 W 18th Street
New York, NY 10011-4113
800-628-9658
Fax: 212-647-0490
Hardcover and paperback trade books for preschool through young adult, fiction and nonfiction. Also, big books and promotional materials are available.

4864 High Touch Learning
PO Box 754
Houston, MN 55943-0754
507-896-3500
800-255-0645
Fax: 507-896-3243
Classroom interactive learning maps promoting the hands-on approach to the teaching of social studies.

4865 HighScope Educational Research Foundation
600 N River Street
Ypsilanti, MI 48198
800-587-5639
info@highscope.org
www.highscope.org
Provides early childhood educational materials, with over 300 titles of books, videos, cassettes and CDs to choose from. Research and training materials as well as curriculum and development materials are based on the HighScope active learning approach.

Alejandra Barraza, Ph.D, President
Kimberly Diamond-Berry, Ph.D, Director, Research Policy

4866 Holiday House
425 Madison Avenue
New York, NY 10017-1110

212-688-0085
Fax: 212-688-0395
Hardcover and paperback children's books. General fiction and nonfiction, preschool through high school.

867 Hoover's
5800 Airport
Dallas, TX 78752-3812
512-374-4500
Fax: 512-374-4501
Everything educational, for the early childhood and K-12 market. As a partner for over 100 years, the company is eager to extend their commitment to produce quality, timely shipping and customer service to the public. Offer over 10,000 products for infants, toddlers, pre-school and school age educational needs.

868 Horn Book Guide
Horn Book
56 Roland Street
Suite 200
Boston, MA 02129
617-628-0225
800-325-1170
Fax: 617-628-0882
info@hbook.com
www.hbook.com
The most comprehensive review source of children's and young adult books available. Published each spring and fall, the Guide contains concise, critical reviews of almost every hardcover trade children's and young adult book published in the United States - nearly 2,000 books each issue.

BiAnnually
ISSN: 1044-405X

Anne Quirk, Marketing Manager
Roger Sutton, Editor

869 Houghton Mifflin Books for Children
222 Berkeley Street
Boston, MA 02116-3748
617-351-5000
800-225-3362
Fax: 617-351-1111
www.hmco.com
Wide variety of children's and young adult books, fiction and nonfiction.

870 Houghton Mifflin Company: School Division
222 Berkeley Street
Boston, MA 02116-3748
617-351-5000
Fax: 617-651-1106
Children's literature; K-12 reading and language arts print and software programs; and testing and evaluation for K-12.

871 Hyperion Books for Children
114 5th Avenue
New York, NY 10011-5604
212-633-4400
Fax: 212-633-5929
Children's books in paperback and hardcover editions.

872 ITP South-Western Publishing Company
5101 Madison Road
Cincinnati, OH 45227-1427
800-824-5179
Fax: 800-487-8488
Innovative instructional materials for teaching integrated science.

873 Idea Factory
10710 Dixon Drive
Riverview, FL 33569-7406
813-677-6727
Teacher resource books, science project ideas, materials and more for elementary and middle school teachers.

4874 Illinois Early Intervention Clearinghouse
University of Illinois at Urbana-Champaign
51 Gerty Drive
Champaign, IL 61820-7469
217-333-1386
877-275-3227
ecap@illinois.edu
www.eiclearinghouse.org
The Illinois Early Intervention Clearinghouse provides publications and information to the early childhood and parenting communities on topics relating to the development of children with special needs and their families.

Meghan Burke, Co-Principal Investigator
Amy Santos, Ph.D, Co-Principal Investigator

4875 Institute for Chemical Education
University of Wisconsin
1101 University Avenue
Madison, WI 53706-1322
608-262-3033
800-991-5534
Fax: 608-265-8094
ice@chem.wisc.edu
www.ice.chem.wisc.edu
Hands-on activities, publications, kits and videos.

4876 Institute for Educational Leadership - Resources
4301 Connecticut Avenue NW
Suite 100
Washington, DC 20008
202-822-8405
Fax: 202-872-4050
iel@iel.org
www.iel.org/resources
The Institute's list of resources on educational trends and policies is available to the public.

Jose Munoz, Interim Director
Maame Appiah, Vice President, Finance

4877 IntelliTools
1720 Corporate Circle
Petaluma, CA 94954
707-773-2000
800-899-6687
Fax: 707-773-2001
Provider of hardware and software giving students with special needs comprehensive access to learning.

4878 Intellimation
130 Cremona Drive
Santa Barbara, CA 93117-5599
805-968-2291
800-346-8355
Fax: 805-968-8899
Educational materials in all areas of curriculum for early learning through college level. Over 400 titles are available in video, and software and multimedia exclusively for the Macintosh. Free catalogs avaiable.

Karin Fisher, Marketing Associate
Marlene Carlyle, Marketing Supervisor

4879 Intercultural Press
100 City Hall Plaza
Suite 501
Boston, MA 02108
617-523-3801
888-273-2539
Fax: 617-523-3708
www.interculturalpress.com
Publishes over 100 titles.

Judy Carl-Hendrick, Managing Editor

4880 J Weston Walch, Publisher
PO Box 658
Portland, ME 04104-0658
207-772-2846
800-558-2846
Fax: 207-772-3105
www.walch.com
Walch Publishing is an independent, family-owned publisher of educational supplemental materials for grades 3 through 12 and adult makets.

4881 Jacaranda Designs
3000 Jefferson Street
Boulder, CO 80304-2638
707-374-2543
Fax: 707-374-2543
Authentic African children's books from Kenya, including modern concept stories for K-3 in bilingual editions, folktales, and traditional cultural stories for older readers. All books are written and illustrated by African Kenyans.

Carrie Jenkins Williams, President

4882 Jarrett Publishing Company
PO Box 1460
Ronkonkoma, NY 11779
631-981-4248
Fax: 631-588-4722
Offers a wide range of books for today's educational needs.

4883 JayJo Books
Guidance Channel
135 Dupont Street
PO Box 760
Plainview, NY 11803
516-349-5520
800-999-6884
Fax: 516-349-5521
jayjobooks@guidancechannel.com
www.jayjo.com
Publisher of books to help teachers, parents and children cope with chronic illnesses, special needs and health education in classroom, family and social settings.

Sally Germain, Editor-in-Chief

4884 John Wiley & Sons
111 River Street
Hoboken, NJ 07030-5774
201-748-6000
Fax: 201-748-6088
Publish science and nature books for children and adults.

4885 Jossey-Bass: An Imprint of Wiley
Jossey-Bass
1 Montgomery Street
Suite 1200
San Francisco, CA 94104
415-433-1740
josseybasseducation@wiley.com
www.josseybass.com
Creating educational incentives that work.

4886 Junior Achievement
1 Education Way
Colorado Springs, CO 80906-4477
719-540-8000
Fax: 719-540-6127
Provides business and economics-related materials and programs to students in grades K-12. All programs feature volunteers from the local business community. Materials are free, but available only from local Junior Achievement offices.

4887 Kaeden Corporation
PO Box 16190
19915 Lake Road
Rocky River, OH 44116
440-356-0030
800-890-7323
Fax: 440-356-5081
www.kaeden.com
Books for emergent readers at the K, 1 and 2 levels, ideal for Title 1 and Reading Recovery and other at-risk reading programs.
Laura Cowan, Sales Manager
Joan Hoyer, Office Manager

4888 Kane/Miller Book Publishers
PO Box 8515
La Jolla, CA 92038-0529
858-456-0540
Fax: 858-456-9641
info@kanemiller.com
www.kanemiller.com
English translation of foreign children's picture books. Distributors of Spanish language children's books.
Byron Parnell, Sales Manager
Kira Lynn, President

4889 Keep America Beautiful
1010 Washington Boulevard
Stamford, CT 06901
203-323-8987
Fax: 203-325-9199
info@kab.org
www.kab.org
K-12 curriculum specializing in litter prevention and environmental education. Education posters with lesson plans printed right on the back of each poster and school recycling guides.

4890 Kendall-Hunt Publishing Company
4050 Westmark Drive
PO Box 1840
Dubuque, IA 52004-1840
800-228-0810
www.kendallhunt.com
A leading custom publisher in the United States with over 6,000 titles in print. Kendall-Hunt publishes educational materials for kindergarten through college to continuing education creditation and distance learning courses.

4891 Knowledge Adventure
2377 Crenshaw Blvd
Suite 302
Torrance, CA 90501
310-533-3400
Fax: 310-533-3700
editorial@education.com
www.knowledgeadventure.com
Develops, publishes, and distributes best-selling multimedia educational software for use in both homes and schools.

4892 Knowledge Unlimited
PO Box 52
Madison, WI 53701-0052
800-356-2303
Fax: 608-831-1570
www.newscurrents.com
NewsCurrents, the most effective current events programs for grades 3-12. Now available on DVD or Online.

4893 Kraus International Publications
358 Saw Mill River Road
Millwood, NY 10546-1035
914-762-2200
800-223-8323
Fax: 914-762-1195
Offers teacher resource notebooks with complete resource information for teachers and administrators at all levels. Great for program planning, quick reference, inservice training. Also offers books on early childhood education, English/language arts, mathematics, science, health education and visual arts.
Barry Katzen, President

4894 Lake Education
AGS/Lake Publishing Company
500 Harbor Boulevard
Belmont, CA 94002-4075
650-592-1606
800-328-2560
Fax: 800-471-8457
Alternative learning materials for underachieving students grades 6-12, RSL and adult basic education. High interest, low readability fiction, adapted classic literature, lifeskills and curriculum materials to supplement and support many basal programs.
Phil Schlenter
Carol Hegarty, VP Editorial

4895 Langenseheidt Publishing
515 Valley Street
Maplewood, NJ 07040-1337
800-526-4953
Fax: 908-206-1104
www.hammondmap.com
World maps, atlases, general reference guides and CD-Roms.

4896 Lawrence Hall of Science
University of California
Berkeley, CA 94720
510-642-5132
Fax: 510-642-1055
www.lawrencehallofscience.org
Offers programs and materials in the field of science and math education for teachers, families and interested citizens. Exhibits include Equals, Family Math, CePUP and FOSS.
Linda Schneider, Marketing Manager
Mike Salter, Marketing/PR Associate

4897 Leap Frog Learning Materials
6401
Suite 100
Emeryville, CA 94608-1071
510-596-3333
800-701-5327
Learning materials, books, posters, games and toys for children.

4898 Learning Connection
19 Devane Street
Frostproof, FL 33843-2017
863-635-5610
800-338-2282
Fax: 863-635-4676
Thematic, literature-based units with award-winning books, media and hands-on for PK-12 including parent involvement, early childhood, bilingual, literacy, math, writing, science and multicultural.

4899 Learning Disabilities Association of America (LDA)
4068 Mount Royal Boulevard
Suite 224B
Allison Park, PA 15101
412-341-1515
info@ldaamerica.org
www.ldaamerica.org
The Learning Disabilities Association of America is a national network of service providers supporting individuals with learning disabilities, their families and the professionals who work with them. The association offers learning resources, advocacy services and conferences. The national office has a resource center with over 500 publications for sale. Publications explore the subject of disability, with emphasis on learning disabilities.
Cindy Cipoletti, Executive Director
Nina DelPrato, Administrative Manager

4900 Learning Links
2300 Marcus Avenue
New Hyde Park, NY 11042-1083
516-437-9075
800-724-2616
Fax: 516-437-5392
learningLx@aol.com
All you need for literature based instruction; Noveltie, study guides, thematic units books and more.

4901 Lee & Low Books
95 Madison Avenue
Suite 606
New York, NY 10016-3303
212-779-4400
Fax: 212-683-1894
www.leeandlow.com
A multicultural children's book publisher. Our primary focus is on picture books, especially stories set in contemporary America. Spanish language titles are available.
Craig Low, VP Publisher
Louise May, Executive Editor

4902 Leo A Myer Associates/LAMA Books
20956 Corsair Boulevard
Hayward, CA 94545-1002
510-785-1091
Fax: 510-785-1099
Writers and publishers of HVAC books.
Barbara Ragura, Marketing Assistant

4903 Lerner Publishing Group
A Division Lerner Publications Group
241 1st Avenue N
Minneapolis, MN 55401-1607
612-332-3344
800-328-4929
Fax: 612-332-7615
www.lernerbooks.com
Primarily nonfiction for readers of all grade levels. List includes titles encompassing nature, geography, natural and physical science, current events, ancient and modern history, world art, special interests, sports, world cultures, and numerous biography series. Some young adult and middle grade fiction.
Jennifer Martin, Submissions Editor

4904 Linden Tree Children's Records & Books
170 State Street
Los Altos Hills, CA 94022-2863
650-949-3390
Fax: 650-949-0346
Offers a wide variety of books, audio cassettes and records for children.

4905 Listening Library
One Park Avenue
Old Greenwich, CT 06870-1727
203-637-3616
800-243-4504
Fax: 800-454-0606
A producer of quality unabridged audiobooks for listeners of all ages. Specializing in children's literature and adult classics.
BiAnnually
Annette Imperati, Director Sales/Marketing

4906 Little, Brown & Company
3 Center Plaza
Boston, MA 02108-2084

617-227-0730
Fax: 617-263-2854
Trade books for children and young adults, hardcover and paper, including Sierra Club Books for Children.

907 Lodestar Books
375 Hudson Street
New York, NY 10014-3658
212-366-2000
General hardcover children's books from toddler through young adult, fiction and nonfiction.

908 Lothrop, Lee & Shepard Books
1350 Avenue of the Americas
New York, NY 10019-4702
212-261-6500
Fax: 212-261-6518
Children's books.

909 Lynne Rienner Publishing
1800 30th Street
Suite 314
Boulder, CO 80301
303-333-3003
800-803-8488
Fax: 303-333-4037
karen-hemmes@mindspring.com
www.fireflybooks.com
Publishes academic-level books with a focus on international and domestic social sciences.

Karen Hemmes, Publicist
Mary Kay Opicka, Publicist

910 MHS
PO Box 950
North Tonawanda, NY 14120-0950
416-492-2627
800-456-3003
Fax: 416-492-3343
www.mhs.com
Publishers and distributors of professional assessment materials.

Steven J Stein, PhD, President

911 MacMillan Learning
16365 James Madison Highway
Gordonsville, VA 22942
888-330-8477
Fax: 800-672-2054
orders@mpsvirginia.com
www.macmillanlearning.com
Offers educational content incorporating interactive teaching tools. A wide variety of subjects are covered such as Astronomy, Biochemistry, Communication, Economics, Nutrition and Health, English, Political Science, Psychology and more.

912 Macmillan Education
Springer Nature Group
1 New York Plaza
Suite 4600
New York, NY 10004-1562
800-777-4643
www.macmillaneducation.com
Publishes educational materials, such as English language teaching content and higher education content covering various subjects. They also offer a Spanish curriculum.

913 Macro Press
18242 Peters Court
Fountain Valley, CA 92708-5873
310-823-9556
Fax: 310-306-2296
Includes resources to conduct thematic hands-on science lessons and integrated curriculum; and, student materials offering a Scientist's Notebook and reading materials to integrate hands-on (grade specific) scientific thinking, problem solving and documenting skills to benefit all students. Nine award-winning K-6 teachers (200+ years combined experience) joined together to address the real needs of today's high student load.

Leigh Hoven Swenson, President

4914 Magna Publications
2718 Dryden Drive
Madison, WI 53704
608-227-8109
800-206-4805
Fax: 608-246-3597
www.magnapubs.com
Produces eight subscriptions newsletters in the field of higher education.

Carrie Jenson, Conference Manager
David Burns, Associate Publisher

4915 Major Educational Resources Corporation
10153 York Road
Suite 107
Hunt Valley, MD 21030-3340
800-989-5353
Multimedia curriculum tools for educators.

4916 Margaret K McElderry Books
1633 Broadway
New York, NY 10019
212-512-2000
Fax: 800-835-3202
Hardcover trade books for children and young adults.

4917 Mari
3215 Pico Boulevard
Santa Monica, CA 90405-4603
310-829-2212
800-955-9494
Fax: 310-829-2317
www.mariinc.com
The best literature learning materials for K-12. Offers Mini-Units for writing and critical thinking skills, Literature Extenders that extend literature across the curriculum and Basic Skills Through Literature that combine literature and skill work.

4918 MasterTeacher
Leadership Lane
PO Box 1207
Manhattan, KS 66505-1207
800-669-9633
Fax: 800-669-1132
www.masterteacher.com
A publisher of videotapes for the professional. Offers programs on inclusion, tests and testing, student motivation, discipline and more.

4919 MathSoft
101 Main Street
Cambridge, MA 02142
617-577-1017
800-628-4223
Fax: 617-577-8829
www.mathsoft.com
Provider of math, science and engineering software for business, academia, research and government.

4920 McCracken Educational Services
PO Box 3588
Blaine, WA 98231
360-332-1881
800-447-1462
Fax: 360-332-7332
www.mccrackened.com
Materials for beginning reading, writing and spelling. Big Books, manipulative materials, teacher resource books, spelling through phonics, posters and both audio and video tapes.

Robert & Marlene McCracken, Author

4921 McGraw Hill Children's Publishing
PO Box 1650
Grand Rapids, MI 49501-1650
616-363-1290
Fax: 800-543-2690
New self-esteem literature based reading and multicultural literature based reading.

4922 Mel Bay Publications
1734 Gilsinn Lane
Fenton, MO 63026
637-257-3970
800-863-5229
Fax: 636-257-5062
email@melbay.com
www.melbay.com
Music supply distributors.

William Bay, President
Joanne Wiggins, General Manager

4923 Merriam-Webster
47 Federal Street
#281
Springfield, MA 01105-3805
413-734-3134
Fax: 413-734-0257
A wide variety of titles for students and teachers of all grade levels.

4924 Millbrook Press
1251 Washington Avenue N
Minneapolis, MN 55401
203-740-2220
800-328-4929
Fax: 800-332-1132
www.millbrookpress.com
Exceptional nonfiction juvenile and young adult books for schools and public libraries.

4925 Milton Roy Company
820 Linden Avenue
Rochester, NY 14625-2710
716-248-4000
Teacher support materials, scientific kits and manuals.

4926 Mimosa Publications
90 New Montgomery Street
San Francisco, CA 94105-4501
415-982-5350
A language based K-3 math program featuring big books, language and activity based math topics and multicultural math activities.

4927 Model Technologies
2420 Van Layden Way
Modesto, CA 95356-2454
209-575-3445
Curriculum guides and scientific instruction kits.

4928 Mondo Publishing
980 Avenue Of The Americas
New York, NY 10018
Fax: 888-532-4492
mondopub@aol.com
www.mondopub.com
Offers multicultural big books and music cassettes: Folk Tales from Around the World series; Exploring Habitats series; and, Let's Write and Sing a Song, whole language activities through music.

4929 Morning Glory Press
6595 San Haroldo Way
Buena Park, CA 90620-3748
714-828-1998
888-612-8254

Fax: 714-828-2049
www.morninggloryPress.com
Publishes books and materials for teenage parents.

Quarterly

Jeanne Lindsay, President
Carole Blum, Promotion Director

4930 Music for Little People
PO Box 1460
Redway, CA 95560-1460
707-923-3991
Fax: 707-923-3241
Science and environmental education materials set to music for younger students.

4931 N&N Publishing Company
18 Montgomery Street
Middletown, NY 10940-5116
Low-cost texts and workbooks.

4932 NASP Publications
National Association of School Psychologists
4340 EW Highway
Suite 402
Bethesda, MD 20814
301-657-0270
Fax: 301-657-0275
center@naspweb.org
Over 100 hard-to-find books and videos centering on counseling, psychology and guidance for students.

Betty Somerville, President

4933 NCTM Educational Materials
National Council of Teachers of Mathematics
1906 Association Drive
Reston, VA 20191-1502
703-620-9840
800-235-7566
Fax: 703-476-2970
nctm@nctm.org
www.nctm.org
Publications, software, and information to improve the teaching and learning of mathematics.

Ken Krehbiel, Executive Director
David Barnes, Associate Executive Director

4934 NYSTROM
3333 N Elston Avenue
Chicago, IL 60618-5898
773-463-1144
800-621-8086
Fax: 773-463-0515
Maps, globes, hands-on geography and history materials.

4935 National Aeronautics & Space Administration
NASA Headquarters
300 E Street SW
Washington, DC 20546
202-358-0000
Fax: 202-358-3251
Over 10 different divisions offering a wide variety of classroom and educational materials in the areas of science, physics, aeronautics and more.

4936 National Center for Science Teaching & Learning/Eisenhower Clearinghouse
1929 Kenny Road
Columbus, OH 43210-1015
Collects and creates the most up-to-date listing of science and mathematics curriculum materials in the nation.

4937 National Council for the Social Studies
8555 Sixteenth Street
Suite 500
Silver Spring, MD 20910
301-588-1800
800-683-0812
Fax: 301-588-2049
sgriffin@ncss.org
www.ncss.org
Publishes books, videotapes and journals in the area of social education and social studies.

4938 National Council on Economic Education
1140 Avenue of the Americas
New York, NY 10036-5803
212-730-7007
Offers various programs including their latest, US History: Eyes on the Economy, a council program for secondary education teachers.

4939 National Geographic School Publishing
1145 17th Street NW
Washington, DC 20036
800-368-2728
Fax: 515-362-3366
Books, magazines, videos, and software in the areas of science, geography and social studies.

4940 National Geographic Society
PO Box 10041
Des Moines, IA 50340-0597
800-548-9797
Fax: 301-921-1575
www.nationalgeographic.com
Science materials, videos, CD-ROM's and telecommunications program.

4941 National Head Start Association (NHSA)
1651 Prince Street
Alexandria, VA 22314
703-739-0875
866-677-8724
www.nhsa.org
Nonprofit organization serving America's low-income children and families. The association publishes books, periodicals and resource guides on aspects of early education and practice.

Yasmina Vinci, Executive Director
Thomas Sheridan, Deputy Director

4942 National Textbook Company
4255 W Touhy Avenue
Lincolnwood, IL 60646-1975
847-679-5500
800-323-4900
Fax: 847-679-2494
Offers various textbooks for students grades K-college level.

4943 National Women's History Project
3343 Industrial Drive
Suite #4
Santa Rosa, CA 95403
707-636-2888
Fax: 707-636-2909
nwhp@aol.com
www.nwhp.org
Non-profit organization, the clearinghouse for information about multicultural US women's history. Initiated March as National Women's History Month; issues a catalog of women's history materials. Provides teacher-training nationwide; coordinates the Women's History Network; produces videos, posters, curriculum units and other curriculum materials.

Molly Murphy MacGregor, Exec. Dir./Co-Founder

4944 National Writing Project
University of California, Berkeley
2105 Bancroft Way
#1042
Berkeley, CA 94720-1042
510-642-6096
Fax: 510-642-4545
Technical reports and occasional paper series: a series of research reports and essays on the research in and practice of teaching writing at all grade levels.

4945 New Canaan Publishing Company
PO Box 752
New Canaan, CT 06840
203-966-3408
800-705-5698
Fax: 203-966-3408
www.newcanaanpublishing.com
Children's publications.

4946 New Press
38 Greene Street
4th Floor
New York, NY 10013
212-629-8802
Fax: 212-629-8617
Multicultural teaching materials, focusing on the social studies.

4947 NewsBank
5020 Tamiami Trail N
Suite 110
Naples, FL 34103-2837
941-263-6004
Electronic information services that support the science curriculum.

4948 North South Books
11 E 26th Street
17 Floor
New York, NY 10010-2007
212-706-4545
Fax: 212-706-4544
Publisher of quality children's books by authors and illustrators from around the world.

4949 Nystrom, Herff Jones
3333 N Elston Avenue
Chicago, IL 60618-5811
913-432-8100
Fax: 913-432-3958
Charts for earth, life and physical science for upper elementary and high school grades.

4950 Options Publishing
PO Box 1749
Merrimack, NH 03054
603-429-2698
800-782-7300
Fax: 603-424-4056
www.optionspublishing.com
Publishers of supplemental materials in reading, math and language arts.

Marty Furlong, VP

4951 Organization of American Historians
112 N Bryan Avenue
Bloomington, IN 47408-4136
812-855-7311
800-446-8923
Fax: 812-855-0696
oah@oah.org
www.oah.org
Offers various products and literature dealing with American history, as well as job registries,

Magazine of History, Journal of American History, OAH Newsletter, and more.

Damon Freeman, Marketing Manager
Michael Regoli, Publications Director

952 Oxton House Publishers, LLC
Po Box 209
Farmington, ME 04938
207-779-1923
800-539-7323
Fax: 207-779-0623
info@oxtonhouse.com
www.oxtonhouse.com
Publishes high quality, innovative, affordable materials for teaching, reading and mathematics and for dealing with learning disabilities.

William Berlinghoff, Managing Editor
Bobby Brown, Marketing Director

953 PF Collier
1315 W 22nd Street
Suite 250
Oak Brook, IL 60523-2061
A leading educational publisher for more than 110 years, creating the home learning center. Products include: Collier's Encyclopedia, Quickstart and Early Learning Fun.

954 PRO-ED
8700 Shoal Creek Boulevard
Austin, TX 78757-6897
512-451-3246
800-897-3202
Fax: 800-397-7633
info@proedinc.com
www.proedinc.com
A leading publisher of assessments, therapy materials and resource/reference books in the areas of speech, language, and hearing; psychology; special education; and occupational therapy.

955 Parenting Press
PO Box 75267
11065 5th Avenue NE
Seattle, WA 98125-0267
206-364-2900
800-992-6657
Fax: 206-364-0702
www.ParentingPress.com
Publishes books for parents, children, and professionals who work with them. Nonfiction books include topics on parenting, problem solving, dealing with feelings, safety, and special issues.

Carolyn J Threadgill, Publisher

956 Penguin USA
375 Hudson Street
New York, NY 10014-3658
212-366-2000
Fax: 212-366-2934
www.penguinputnam.com
Children's and adult hardcover and paperback general trade books, including classics and multiethnic literature.

957 Perfection Learning Corporation
Perfection Learning
10520 New York Avenue
Des Moines, IA 50322
303-333-3003
800-803-8488
Fax: 303-333-4037
karen-hemmes@mindspring.com
www.fireflybooks.com
Perfection Learning publishes high interest-low reading level fiction and non-fiction books for young adults.

Karen Hemmes, Publicist
Mary Kay Opicka, Publicist

4958 Perma Bound Books
E Vandalia Road
Jacksonville, IL 62650
217-243-5451
800-637-6581
Fax: 800-551-1169
Thematically arranged for K-12 classroom use with 480,000 titles available in durable Perma-Bound bindings; related library services also available.

Ben Mangum, President

4959 Personalizing the Past
1534 Addison Street
Berkeley, CA 94703-1454
415-388-9351
Museum quality artifact history kits complete with integrated lesson plan teachers guide. Copy-ready student worksheets, literature section, videos and audio tapes. United States and ancient world history.

4960 Perspectives on History Series
Discovery Enterprises, Ltd.
31 Laurelwood Drive
Carlisle, MA 01741
978-287-5401
800-729-1720
Fax: 978-287-5402
ushistorydocs@aol.com
Primary and secondary source materials for middle school to college levels; bibliographies; plays for grades 5-9 on American history topics. Educators curriculum guides for using primary source documents. 75-volumes of primary source documents on American history may be purchased individually or in sets. New Researching American History Series presents documents with summaries and vocabulary on each page (20 volumes) sold individually or in sets.

JoAnne Deitch, President

4961 Peytral Publications Inc
PO Box 1162
Minnetonka, MN 55345
952-949-8707
877-739-8725
Fax: 952-906-9777
www.peytral.com
Books and videos for educators.

Peggy Hammeken, Owner

4962 Phelps Publishing
PO Box 22401
Cleveland, OH 44122
216-752-4938
Fax: 216-752-4941
earl@phelpspublishing.com
www.phelpspublishing.com
Publisher of art instruction books for ages 8 to 108.

Earl Phelps, President

4963 Phoenix Learning Resources
12 W 31st Street
New York, NY 10001-4415
212-629-3887
800-221-1274
Fax: 212-629-5648
Phoenix Learning Resources provides all students with the skills to be successful, lifelong learners.

Alexander Burke, President
John Rothermich, Executive VP

4964 Pleasant Company Publications
8400 Fairway Pl
Middleton Branch, WI 53562-2554
608-836-4848
800-233-0264
Fax: 800-257-3865
The American Girls Collection historical fiction series.

4965 Pocket Books/Paramount Publishing
1230 Avenue of the Americas
New York, NY 10020-1513
212-698-7000
Books for children and young adults in hardcover and paperback originals and reprints of bestselling titles.

4966 Population Connection
1400 16th Street NW
Suite 320
Washington, DC 20036-2290
800-767-1956
Fax: 202-332-2302
poped@populationconnection.org
www.populationconnection.org
Curriculum materials for grades K-12 to teach students about population dynamics and their social, political and environmental effects in the United States and the world.

Pamela Wasserman, Director Education

4967 Prentice Hall School Division
340 Rancheros Drive
Suite 160
San Marcos, CA 92069
760-510-0222
Fax: 760-510-0230
Superb language arts textbooks and ancillaries for students grades 6-12.

4968 Prentice Hall School Division - Science
1 Lake Street
Upper Saddle River, NJ 07458
201-236-7000
Fax: 201-236-3381
Science textbooks and ancillaries for grades 6-12 and advanced placement students.

4969 Prentice Hall/Center for Applied Researchin Education
1 Lake Street
Upper Saddle River, NJ 07458
201-236-7000
Fax: 201-236-3381
Publisher of practical, time and work saving teaching/learning resources for PreK-12 teachers and specialists in all content areas.

4970 Project Learning Tree
American Forest Foundation
1111 19th Street NW
Suite 780
Washington, DC 20036-3603
202-463-2462
Fax: 202-463-2461
Pre-K through grade 12 curriculum materials containing hundreds of hands-on science activities. PLT uses the forest as a window into the natural world to increase students' understanding of our complex environment. Stimulates critical and creative thinking; develops the ability to make informed decisions on environmental issues; and instills the confidence and commitment to take action on them.

Kathy McGlauflin, President

4971 Prufrock Press
PO Box 8813
Waco, TX 76714
800-998-2208
Fax: 800-240-0333
www.prufrock.com
Exciting classroom products for gifted and talented education.

4972 Puffin Books
375 Hudson Street
New York, NY 10014-3658

212-366-2819
Fax: 212-366-2040
Offers the Puffin Teacher Club set.
Lisa Crosby, President

4973 RR Bowker
ProQuest Affiliate
121 Chanlon Road
New Providence, NJ 07974-1541
908-464-6800
Fax: 908-665-6688
A leading information provider to schools and libraries for over one hundred years, RR Bowker provides quality resources to help teachers and librarians make informed reading selections for children and young adults.

4974 Raintree/Steck-Vaughn
Harcourt Achieve
6277 Sea Harbor Drive
Orlando, FL 32887
800-531-5015
Fax: 800-699-9459
www.steck-vaughn.com
Reference materials for K-8 students and texts for underachieving students K-12.
Tim McEwen, President
Martijn Tel, Chief Financial Officer

4975 Rand McNally
8255 Central Park Avenue
Skokie, IL 60076-2970
847-674-2151
Cross-curricular products featuring reading/language arts in the social studies.

4976 Random House
201 E 50th Street
New York, NY 10022-7703
212-751-2600
Fax: 212-572-8700
Offers a line of science trade books for grades K-8.

4977 Random House/Bullseye/Alfred A Knopf/Crown Books for Young Readers
201 E 50th Street
New York, NY 10022-7703
212-751-2600
Fax: 212-572-8700
Publisher of hardcover books, paperbacks, books and cassettes and videos for children.

4978 Recorded Books
270 Skipjack Road
Prince Frederick, MD 20678-3410
800-638-1304
Professionally narrated, unabridged books on standard-play audio cassettes, classroom ideas and combinations of print book, cassettes and teacher's guides.
Linda Hirshman, President

4979 Redleaf Press
10 Yorkton Court
Saint Paul, MN 55117-1065
800-428-8309
Fax: 800-641-0115
jward@redleafpress.org
www.redleafpress.org
Publisher of curriculum, activity, and childrens books for early childhood professionals.
Sid Farrer, Editor In Chief
JoAnne Voltz, Marketing Manager

4980 Reference Desk Books
430 Quintana Road
Suite 146
Morro Bay, CA 93442-1948
805-772-8806
Offers a variety of books for the education professional.

4981 Rhythms Productions
PO Box 34485
Los Angeles, CA 90034-0485
310-836-4678
800-544-7244
Fax: 310-837-1534
Producer and publisher of songs and games for learning through music. Cassettes, CDs, books for birth through elementary featuring rhythms, puppet play, art activities, and more. Titles include Lullabies, Singing Games, Watch Me Grow series, Mr. Windbag concept stories, phonics, First Reader's Kit, Hear-See-Say-Do Musical Math series, Themes, and more. Also publishes a line of folk dances from elementary through adult.
Audio
Ruth White, President

4982 Richard C Owen Publishers
PO Box 585
Katonah, NY 10536
914-232-3903
800-336-5588
Fax: 914-232-3977
www.rcowen.com
Focus child-centered learning, Books for Young Learners, professional books, the Learning Network and Meet the Author series.
Mary Frundt, Marketing

4983 Riverside Publishing Company
425 Spring Lake Drive
Ithaca, IL 60143
630-467-7000
800-323-9540
Fax: 630-467-7192
www.riverpub.com
Offers a full line of reading materials, including fiction and nonfiction titles for all grade levels.

4984 Roots & Wings Educational Catalog-Australiafor Kids
PO Box 19678
Boulder, CO 80308-2678
303-776-4796
800-833-1787
Fax: 303-776-6090
www.rootsandwingscatalog.com/
www.australiaforkids.com
Catalog company providing materials for the education of the young child, specializing in the following topics: Australia, multiculturalism, parenting and families, teaching, special needs, environment and peace.
Susan Ely, President/Sales
Anne Wilson, VP/Marketing

4985 Rosen Publishing Group
29 E 21st Street
New York, NY 10010-6209
212-777-3017
800-237-9932
Fax: 888-436-4643
Nonfiction books on self-help and guidance for young adults. Books also available for reluctant readers on self-esteem, values and drug abuse prevention.

4986 Routledge/Europa Library Reference
Taylor & Francis Books
29 W 35 Street
New York, NY 10001-2299
212-216-7800
800-634-7064
Fax: 212-564-7854
reference@routledge-ny.com
Publisher of a wide range of print and online library reference titles, including the renowned Europa World Yearbook and the award-winning Routledge Encyclopedia of Philosophy (both available in online and print formats), Garland Encyclopedia of World Music, Routledge Religion and Society Encyclopedias, Chronological History of US Foreign Relations, and many other acclaimed resources.
Koren Thomas, Sr Marketing/Library Ref
Elizabeth Sheehan, Marketing/Library Reference

4987 Runestone Press
A Divisions of Lerner Publishing Group
241 1st Avenue N
Minneapolis, MN 55401-1607
612-332-3344
800-328-4929
Fax: 612-332-7615
www.lernerbooks.com
Nonfiction for readers in Grades 5 and up. Newly revised editions of previously out-of-print books. List includes Buried Worlds archaeology series and titles of Jewish and Native American interest. Complete catalog is available.
Harry J Lerner, President
Mary M Rodgers, Editorial Director

4988 Saddleback Educational
Three Watson
Irvine, CA 92618-2767
949-860-2500
800-637-8715
Fax: 888-734-4010
Supplementary curriculum materials for K-12 and adult students.

4989 SafeSpace Concepts
1424 N Post Oak Road
Houston, TX 77055-5401
713-956-0820
800-622-4289
Fax: 713-956-6416
safespacec@aol.com
www.safespaceconcepts.com
Manufactures young children's play equipment and furnishings.
Barbara Carlson, PhD, President
Jerry Johnson, Marketing Director

4990 Sage Publications
Sage Publications
2455 Teller Road
Thousand Oaks, CA 91320
303-333-3003
800-803-8488
Fax: 303-333-4037
karen-hemmes@mindspring.com
www.fireflybooks.com
Sage Publications publishes handbooks and guides with a focus on research and science.
Karen Hemmes, Publicist
Mary Kay Opicka, Publicist

4991 Salem Press
Grey House Publishing
2 University Plaza
Suite 310
Hackensack, NJ 07601
201-968-0500
800-221-1592
Fax: 201-968-0511
sales@salempress.com
www.salempress.com
Salem Press delivers award-winning literary, historical, medical and science reference content to

the public library, academic and high school markets.

Richard Gottlieb, President
Laura Mars, Editorial Director

4992 Santillana Publishing
901 W Walnut Street
Compton, CA 90220-5109
310-763-0455
800-245-8584
Fax: 305-591-9145
Publishers of K-12 and adult titles in Spanish.Imprints include: Altea, Alfagunea, Taurus and Aguilar.

Marla Norman, Publisher/Trade Book
Antonio de Marco, President

4993 Scholastic
555 Broadway
New York, NY 10012
212-343-6100
800-724-6527
Fax: 212-343-4801
www.scholastic.com
Publisher and distributor of children's books. Provides professional and classroom resources for K-12.

4994 School Book Fairs
PO Box 835105
Richardson, TX 75083
972-231-9838
A children's book publisher that provides distribution of leisure reading materials to elementary and middle schools through book fair fund-raising events via a North American network with 97 locations.

4995 Science Inquiry Enterprises
14358 Village View Lane
Chino Hills, CA 91709-1706
530-295-3338
Fax: 530-295-3334
Selected science teaching materials.

4996 Scott & McCleary Publishing Company
2482 11th Street SW
Akron, OH 44314-1712
702-566-8756
800-765-3564
Fax: 702-568-1378
jscott7576@aol.com
www.scottmccleary.com
Diagnostic reading and testing material.

Janet M Scott, Publisher
Sheila C McCleary, Publisher

4997 Scott Foresman Company
1900 E Lake Avenue
Glenview, IL 60025-2086
800-554-4411
Fax: 800-841-8939
Science tests and reading/language arts materials for teachers and students. Celebrate Reading! is the K-8 literature-based reading/integrated language arts program designed to meet the needs of all children. Book Festival is a literature learning center that offers teachers a collection of trade books for independent reading.

Bert Crossland, Reading Product Manager
Jim Fitzmaurice, VP Editor Group

4998 Sharpe Reference
M.E. Sharpe, Inc.
80 Business Park Drive
Armonk, NY 10504
914-273-1800
800-541-6563
Fax: 914-273-2106
custserv@mesharpe.com
www.mesharpe.com
Historical, political, geographical and art reference books.

Diana McDermott, Director Marketing

4999 Signet Classics
375 Hudson Street
New York, NY 10014-3658
212-366-2000
Fax: 212-366-2888
Publishes books on literature, poetry and reading.

5000 Silver Moon Press
160 5th Avenue
Suite 622
New York, NY 10010-7003
212-242-6499
800-874-3320
Fax: 212-242-6799
Informational and entertaining books for young readers. Subjects include history, multiculturalism and science.

5001 Simon & Schuster Children's Publishing
1230 Avenue of the Americas
New York, NY 10020
212-698-7000
Fax: 212-698-7007
Fiction and nonfiction, in hardcover and paperback editions, for preschool through young adult.

5002 Social Issues Resources Series
1100 Holland Drive
Boca Raton, FL 33487-2701
561-994-0079
Fax: 561-994-2014
Provides information systems in print format and CD-ROM format.

5003 Social Science Education Consortium
Box 21270
Boulder, CO 80308-4270
303-492-8154
Fax: 303-449-3925
www.ssecinc.org
Produces curriculum guides, instructional units and collections of lesson plans on US history, law-related education, global studies, public issues and geography. Develops projects for social studies teachers and evaluates social studies programs.

James Cooks, Executive Director
Laurel Singleton, Associate Director

5004 Social Studies School Service
10200 Jefferson Boulevard
Culver City, CA 90232-3598
310-839-2436
800-421-4246
Fax: 310-839-2249
access@socialstudies.com
www.socialstudies.com
Supplemental materials in all areas of social studies, language arts.

5005 Special Education & Rehabilitation Services
330 C Street
Washington, DC 20202
202-205-5465
Fax: 202-260-7225

Judith E Heuman, Assistant Secretary

5006 Speech Bin
1965 25th Avenue
Vero Beach, FL 32960-3000
561-770-0007
800-477-3324
Fax: 561-770-0006
Publisher and distributor of books and materials for professionals in rehabilitation, speech-language pathology, occupational and physical therapy, special education, and related fields. Major product lines include professional and children's books, computer software, diagnostic tests.

Jan J Binney, VP

5007 Stack the Deck Writing Program
PO Box 5352
Chicago, IL 60680-0429
312-675-1000
Fax: 312-765-0453
Composition textbooks, grades 1-12, plus computer software.

5008 Stenhouse Publishers
477 Congress Street
Suite 4B
Portland, ME 04101-3417
888-363-0566
Fax: 800-833-9164
www.stenhouse.com
Professional materials for teachers by teachers.

5009 Story Teller
PO Box 921
Salem, UT 84653-0921
801-423-2560
Fax: 801-423-2568
www.thestoryteller.com
Felt board stories books and educational sets.

Patti Gardner, VP Sales

5010 Summit Learning
7755 Rockwell Avenue
PO Box 755
Fort Atkinson, WI 53538-0755
800-777-8817
800-777-8817
Fax: 800-317-2194
www.summitlearning.com
Summit learning is a distributor of manipulative-based math and science materials, provides you with a carefully selected group of the most popular high-quality products at low prices.

Gary Otto, Marketing Manager

5011 Sunburst Technology
1550 Executive Drive
Elgin, IL 60123
914-747-3310
800-338-3457
Fax: 914-747-4109
www.sunburst.com
K-12 educational software, guidance and health materials, and online teacher resources.

5012 Sundance Publishing
234 Taylor Street
PO Box 1326
Littleton, MA 01460
978-486-9201
800-343-8204
Fax: 978-486-8759
A supplementary educational publisher of instructional materials for shared, guided, and independent reading, phonics, and comprehension skills for grades K-9. Some of its programs include AlphKids, SunLit Fluency, Popcorns and Little Readers. Its Second Chance Reading Program for below-level readers features high-interest titles, written for upper elementary/middle school students. It also distributes paperback editions of some of the most widely taught literature titles for grades K-1

Katherine Jasmine, VP Marketing

5013 **Synergistic Systems**
2297 Hunters Run Drive
Reston, VA 20191-2834
703-758-9213
Science education curriculum materials.

5014 **TASA**
PO Box 382
Brewster, NY 10509-0382
845-277-8100
800-800-2598
Fax: 845-277-3548
Degrees of Literacy Power Program; English Language Profiles, primary, standard and advanced DRP tests, Degrees of World Meaning Tests.

5015 **TL Clark Incorporated**
5111 SW Avenue
St. Louis, MO 63110
314-865-2525
800-859-3815
Fax: 314-865-2240
www.tlclarkinc.com
Educational products for grades Pre-K-3. Rest time products including cots and mats, sand and water play tubs, active play items including tunnels, tricycles and foam play items.

Jim Fleminla, President

5016 **TMC/Soundprints**
353 Main Avenue
Norwalk, CT 06851-1508
203-846-2274
800-228-7839
Fax: 203-846-1776
Children's story books for children ages 4 through 8 under the license of the Smithsonian Institute and the National Wildlife Federation. Each 32 page four color book highlights a unique aspect of the animal featured in the book so as to provide education while still being entertaining. Each book can be bought with an audiocassette read-a-long and plush toy. Over 80 books in print.

Ashley Anderson, Associate Publisher
Chelsea Shriver

5017 **Tambourine Books**
1350 Avenue of the Americas
New York, NY 10019-4702
212-261-6500
Fax: 212-261-6518
A wide variety of books to increase creativity and reading skills in students.

5018 **Taylor & Francis Publishers**
7625 Empire Drive
Florence, KY 41042
800-624-7064
Fax: 800-248-4724
Publisher of professional texts and references in several fields including the behavioral sciences; arts, humanities, social sciences, science technology and medicine.

Chris Smith, Customer Service Manager

5019 **Teacher's Friend Publications**
3240 Trade Center Drive
Riverside, CA 92507
909-682-4748
800-343-9680
Fax: 909-682-4680
Complete line of the original monthly and seasonal Creative Idea Books. Plus, two new cooperative-learning language series and much more.

Karen Sevaly, Author
Richard Sevaly, President/CEO
Kim Marsh, National Sales Manager

5020 **Teaching Comprehension: Strategies for Stories**
Oxton House Publishers, LLC
Po Box 209
Farmington, ME 04938
207-779-1923
800-539-7323
Fax: 207-779-0623
info@oxtonhouse.com
www.oxtonhouse.com
A detailed roadmap for providing students with effective strategies for comprehending and remembering stories. It includes story-line masters for helping students to organize their thinking and to accurately depict character and sequence events.

62 pages

William Berlinghoff, Managing Editor
Bobby Brown, Marketing Director

5021 **The Narrative Press**
4392 US Highway 26/85
Torrington, WY 82240
307-532-3495
Fax: 307-532-3495
mike.bond@narrativepress.com
www.narrativepress.com
Publisher of first person narratives of adventure and exploration, useful for teaching about the U.S. Western history covering mountain men and trappers, Asian history and African History. Also published by The Narrative Press are books on sea travel, autobiographies and California history.

Vickie Zimmer, Editor

5022 **Theme Connections**
Perfection Learning
PO Box 500
Logan, IA 51546-0500
800-831-4190
Fax: 712-644-2392
Features 135 best-selling literature titles and related theme libraries for students to develop lifelong learning strategies.

5023 **Ther-A-Play Products**
PO Box 2030
Lodi, CA 95241-2030
209-368-6787
800-308-6749
Fax: 209-365-2157
Children's books, play therapy books, sandplay and sandtray manipulatives, puppets, games, doll houses and furniture. Playmobile and educational toys, specializing in counselors' tools. Books on abuses, illness, death, behavior and parenting.

Madge Geiszler, Owner

5024 **Thomson Learning**
115 5th Avenue
New York, NY 10003-1004
212-979-2210
800-880-4253
Fax: 248-699-8061
Book publisher of library and classroom-oriented educational resources for children and young adults. Over 200 books are available in 30 different subjects.

5025 **Time-Life Books**
2000 Duke Street
Alexandria, VA 22314-3414
703-838-7000
Fax: 703-838-7166
A wide-ranging selection of quality reference and supplemental books for students from elementary to high school.

5026 **Tiny Thought Press**
1427 S Jackson Street
Louisville, KY 40208-2720
502-637-6916
Fax: 502-634-1693
Children's books that build character and self-esteem.

5027 **Tom Snyder Productions**
80 Coolidge Hill Road
Watertown, MA 02472
800-342-0236
Fax: 800-304-1254
Developer and publisher of educational software.

John McAndrews, Contact

5028 **Tor Books/Forge/SMP**
175 5th Avenue
New York, NY 10010-7703
212-388-0100
Fax: 212-388-0191
Science-fiction and fantasy children's books, mysteries, Westerns, general fiction and classics publications.

5029 **Tricycle Press**
PO Box 7123
Berkeley, CA 94707-0123
510-559-1600
800-841-2665
Fax: 510-559-1637
Publisher of books and posters for children ages 2-12 and their grown-ups. Catalog available.

Christine Longmuir, Publicity/Marketing

5030 **Troll Associates**
100 Corporate Drive
Mahwah, NJ 07430-2322
201-529-4000
Fax: 201-529-8282
Publisher of children's books and products, including paperbacks and hardcovers, special theme units, read-alongs, videos, software and big books.

5031 **Trumpet Club**
1540 Broadway
New York, NY 10036-4039
212-492-9595
School book club featuring hardcover and paperback books, in class text sets and author video visits.

5032 **Turn-the-Page Press**
203 Baldwin Avenue
Roseville, CA 95678-5104
916-786-8756
800-959-5549
Fax: 916-786-9261
Books, cassettes and videos focusing on early childhood education.

Michael Leeman, President

5033 **USA Today**
1000 Wilson Boulevard
Arlington, VA 22209-3901
703-276-3400
Fax: 703-854-2103
Educational programs focusing on social studies.

5034 **Upstart Books**
PO Box 800
Fort Atkinson, WI 53538-0800
920-563-9571
800-558-2110
Fax: 920-563-7395
Publishes teacher activity resources, reading activities, library and information seeking skills, Internet.

Matt Mulder, Director
Virginia Harrison, Editor

5035 Useful Learning
711 Meadow Lane Court
Apartment 12
Mount Vernon, IA 52314-1549
319-895-6155
800-962-3855
The Useful Spelling Textbook series for Grades 2-8, represents a curriculum based upon the scientific knowledge of research studies conducted during the past 80 years at The University of Iowa, Iowa City, IA. Incorporates the New Iowa Spelling Scale and is composed of qualitative curriculum, qualitative learning practices and qualitative instructional procedures.
Larry D. Zenor, PhD, President
Bradley M Loomer, PhD, Board Chairman

5036 VIDYA Books
PO Box 7788
Berkeley, CA 94707-0788
510-527-9932
Fax: 510-527-2936
Supplemental materials about India and the surrounding region for K-12 lesson plans.

5037 Viking Children's Books
375 Hudson Street
New York, NY 10014-3658
212-941-8780
General hardcover children's books, from toddler through young adult, fiction and nonfiction.

5038 Vision 23
Twenty-Third Publications
185 Willow Street
Mystic, CT 06355-2636
860-536-2611
Fax: 800-572-0788
A wide variety of children's products including books, games, clothing and toys.

5039 WH Freeman & Company
41 Madison Avenue
New York, NY 10010-2202
212-576-9400
Fax: 212-481-1891
Books relating to the world of mathematics.

5040 Wadsworth Publishing School Group
10 Davis Drive
Belmont, CA 94002-3002
650-595-2350
Fax: 800-522-4923
College and advanced placement/honors high school materials in biology, chemistry and environmental science.

5041 Walker & Company
104 Fifth Avenue
New York, NY 10011
212-727-8300
800-289-2553
Fax: 212-727-0984
www.walkerbooks.com
Hardcover and paperback trade titles for Pre-K-12th grade, including picture books, photo essays, fiction and nonfiction titles appropriate for every curriculum need.

5042 Warren Publishing House
11625-G Airport Road
Everett, WA 98204-3790
425-353-3100
New Totline Teaching Tales with related activities plus quality whole language teacher activity books including Alphabet Theme-A-Saurus and Piggyback Songs.

5043 Waterfront Books
85 Crescent Road
Burlington, VT 05401-4126
802-658-7477
800-639-6063
Fax: 802-860-1368
www.waterfrontbooks.com
Publishes and distributes books on special issues for children: barriers to learning, coping skills, mental health, prevention strategies, family/parenting, etc. for grades K-12. Titles include: The Divorce Workbook; Josh, a Boy with Dyslexia; What's a Virus, Anyway? The Kids' Book About AIDS and more.
Sherrill N Musty, Publisher
Michelle Russell, Order Fulfillment

5044 Web Feet Guides
Rock Hill Communications
14 Rock Hill Road
Bala Cynwyd, PA 19004
610-667-2040
888-762-5445
Fax: 610-667-2291
The premier subject guides to the Internet, rigorously reviewed by librarians and educators, fully annotated, expanded and updated monthly. Appropriate for middle school through adult. Available in print, online, or marc records. For more information, free trials and Web casts, and free interactive Web Quests for your K-8 students, visit our Web site.
Linda Smith, Marketing Coordinator

5045 West Educational Publishing
620 Opperman Drive
#645779
Saint Paul, MN 55123-1340
A leader in quality social studies textbooks and ancillaries for grades K-12.

5046 Western Psychological Services
12031 Wilshire Boulevard
Los Angeles, CA 90025-1251
310-478-2061
800-648-8857
Fax: 310-478-7838
www.wpspublish.com
Assessment tools for professionals in education, psychology and allied fields. Offer a variety of tests, books, software and therapeutic games.

5047 Wildlife Conservation Society
Bronx Zoo
Education Department
2300 Southern Boulevard
Bronx, NY 10460
718-220-5131
800-937-5131
Fax: 718-733-4460
sscheio@wes.org
www.wcs.com
Environmental science and conservation biology curriculum materials and information regarding teacher training programming for Grades K-12, on site or off site, nationally and locally. Science programming for grades pre-K-12 available on site.
Sydell Schein, Manager/Program Services
Ann Robinson, Director National Programs

5048 William Morrow & Company
1350 Avenue of the Americas
New York, NY 10019-4702
212-261-6500
Fax: 212-261-6518
High quality hardcover and paperback books for children.

5049 Winston Derek Publishers
101 French Landing Drive
Nashville, TN 37228-1511
615-321-0535
A cross section of African American books and educational materials, including preschool and primary grade books.

5050 Wisconsin State Reading Association
WSRA
909 Rock Ridge Road
Burlington, WI 53105
262-514-1450
Fax: 262-514-1450
wsra@wsra.org
www.wsra.org
The Wisconsin State Reading Association is a professional organization providing leadership, advocacy and expertise for those working in the field of literacy education.
La Tasha Fields, President
Colleen Pennell, First Vice President

5051 Wolfram Research, Inc.
100 Trade Center Drive
Champaign, IL 61820-7237
217-398-0700
800-965-3726
Fax: 217-398-0747
info@wolfram.com
www.wolfram.com
Offers mathematics publications, statistics and information to educators of grades K-12.
Stephen Wolfram, Founder/CEO
Jean Buck, Dir., Corp Communications

5052 Workman Publishing
708 Broadway
New York, NY 10003-9508
212-254-5900
Fax: 212-254-8098
Children's curriculum, books, textbooks, workbooks, fiction and nonfiction titles.

5053 World & I
News World Communications
2800 New York Avenue NE
Washington, DC 20002-1945
202-636-3365
800-822-2822
Fax: 202-832-5780
With over 40 articles each month, The World & I presents an enlightening look at our changing world through the eyes of noted scholars and experts covering current issues, the arts, science, book reviews, lifestyles, cultural perspectives, philosophical trends, and the millennium. For educators, students and libraries. Free teacher's guides year round. Also, online archives available at www.worldandi.com.
Charles Kim, Business Director

5054 World Association of Publishers, Manufacturers& Distributors
Worlddidac
Bollwerk 21, PO Box 8866 CH-3001
Berne
Switzerland
41-31-3121744
Fax: 41-31-3121744
info@worlddidac.org
A worldwide listing of over 330 publishers, manufacturers and distributors of educational materials. Listings include all contact information, products and school levels/grades.
160 pages Annual
Beat Jost, Coordinating Education

5055 World Bank
1818 H Street NW
Room T-8061
Washington, DC 20433-0002
202-477-1234
Fax: 202-477-6391
Maps, poster kits, case studies and videocassettes that teach about life in developing countries.

5056 World Book Educational Products
525 W Monroe Street
20th Floor
Chicago, IL 60661
312-729-5800
Fax: 312-729-5600
Reference books and the World Book Encyclopedia on CD-Rom.

5057 World Eagle
111 King Street
Littleton, MA 01460-1527
978-486-9180
800-854-8273
Fax: 978-486-9652
www.worldeagle.com
Publishes an online, social studies educational resource magazine: comparative data, graphs, maps and charts on world issues. Publishes world regional atlases, and supplies maps and curriculum materials.
Valentina Bardawil Powers, Author
Martine Crandall-Hollick, President

5058 World Resources Institute
10 G Street, NE
Suite 800
Washington, DC 20002
202-729-7600
Fax: 202-729-7610
The world Resources Institute is an envoronmental think tank that goes beyond research to create practical ways to protect the Earth and improve people's lives. our mission is to move human society to live in ways that protect Earth's environment for surrent and future generations.
Jonathan Lash, President

5059 World Scientific Publishing Company
27 Warren Street
Suite 401-402
Hackensack, NJ 07601
201-487-9655
Fax: 201-487-9695
wspc@wspc.com
www.wspc.com
This is one of the world's leading academic publishers. It now publishes more than 400 books and 100 journals a year in diverse fields of science technology, medicine, business and management.
Ruth Zhou, Marketing Executive

5060 Worth Publishers
33 Irving Plaza
New York, NY 10003-2332
212-475-6000
Fax: 212-689-2383
A balanced and comprehensive account of the U.S. past is accompanied by an extensive set of supplements.

5061 Wright Group
19201 120th Avenue NE
Bothell, WA 98011-9507
800-523-2371
Fax: 425-486-7704
www.wrightgroup.com
Supplementary program materials for reading education.

5062 Write Source Educational Publishing House
PO Box 460
Burlington, WI 53105-0460
262-763-8258
Fax: 262-763-2651
Publishes Writers Express, a writing, thinking and learning handbook series for grades 4 and 5. Also offer the latest editions of Write Source 2000 and Writers INC for grades 6-8 and 9-12.

5063 You Call This Living?
William Kingsley Publishing
3036 Big Oaks Drive
Garland, TX 75044
972-220-9959
seabed999@yahoo.com
www.billkingsley.com
The book explored the human condition and the need for a drastic overhaul of the educational system.
274 pages
ISBN: 978-578-12522
Bill Kingsley, Author
Bill Kingsley

5064 Zaner-Bloser K-8 Catalog
2200 W 5th Avenue
Columbus, OH 43215
614-486-0221
800-421-3018
Fax: 614-487-2699
www.zaner-bloser.com
Publisher of handwriting materials and reading, writing, spelling and study skills programs.
Robert Page, President

5065 Zephyr Press
814 North Franklin Street
Chicago, IL 60610-3109
312-337-5985
800-232-2187
Fax: 312-337-5985
www.zephyrpress.com
Zephyr Press publishes effective, state-of-the-art-teaching materials for classroom use.
Joey Tanner MEd, President

5066 ZooBooks
ZooBooks/Wildlife Education. Ltd.
12233 Thatcher Court
Poway, CA 92064-6880
619-513-7600
800-477-5034
Fax: 858-513-7660
www.zoobooks.com
Reference books offering fascinating insights into the world of wildlife. Created in collaboration with leading scientists and educators, these multi-volume Zoobooks make important facts and concepts about nature, habitat and wildlife understandable to children. From alligators to zebras, aquatic to exotic, each Zoobook is colorful, scientifically accurate and easy to read.

General

067 AVKO Educational Research Foundation
3084 Willard Road
Birch Run, MI 48415-9404
810-686-9283
Fax: 810-686-1101
avkoemail@aol.com
www.avko.org
Comprised of teachers and individuals interested in helping others learn to read and spell, while researching the causes of learning disabilities. The foundation develops reading training materials for individuals with dyslexia or other learning disabilities using a method involving audio, visual, kinesthetic and oral diagnosis and remediation.
Don McCabe, President/Research Director
Linda Heck, Vice President

068 Assistive Technology Clinics
Children's Hospital
1056 E 19th Avenue
#030
Denver, CO 80218-1007
303-861-6250
Fax: 303-764-8214
A diagnostic clinic providing evaluation, information and support to families with children with disabilities in the areas of seating and mobility. Offers augmentative communication and assistive technology access.
Tracey Kovach, Coordinator

069 Center for Equity and Excellence in Education
George Washington University
1555 Wilson Boulevard
Suite 515
Arlington, VA 22209-2004
703-528-3588
800-925-3223
Fax: 703-528-5973
Mission is to advance education reform so that all students achieve high standards. Operates under the umbrella of the Institute for Education Policy Studies within the Graduate School of Education and Human Development. Designs and conducts program evaluation for states, districts and schools and conducts program evalutaion, policy and applied research effecting equitable educational opportunities for all students.
Charlene Rivera, Executive Director
Kristina Anstrom, Assistant Director

070 Center for Learning
The Center for Learning
PO Box 910
2105 Evergreen Road
Villa Maria, PA 16155
724-964-8083
800-767-9090
Fax: 724-964-8992
customerservice@centerforlearning.org
www.centerforlearning.org
To improve education by writing and publishing values-based curriculum materials that enable teachers to foster student responsibility for learning

071 Center for Organization of Schools
Johns Hopkins University
2701 N Charles Street
Suite 300
Baltimore, MD 21218-2404
410-516-8800
Fax: 410-516-8890
mmaushard@csos.jhu.edu
www.csos.jhu.edu
Conduct research, development, evaluation, and dissemination of replicable strategies designed to transform low-performing schools so that al lstudents graduate ready for college, career and life. Products include curricula that help all students achieve at a high level. Programs in early learning; school, family and community partnerships; a financial literacy program called Stocks ain the Future, and the Baltimore Education Research Consotrium, plus Talent development Secondary reform
James McPartland, Co-Director
Mary Maushard, Communication Director

5072 Center for Public Education (CPE)
National School Boards Association
1680 Duke Street
2nd Floor
Alexandria, VA 22314-3493
703-838-6722
Fax: 703-683-7590
info@nsba.org
www.nsba.org
Provides research, data and analysis about public education, and seeks to improve student achievement.
Viola M. Garcia, President
Chip Slaven, Interim Executive Director

5073 Center for Research on the Context of Teaching
Stanford University
CERAS Building
4th Floor 520 Galvez Mall
Stanford, CA 94305-3084
650-725-1845
Fax: 650-736-2296
www.stanford.edu/group/CRC/
Conducts research on ways in which secondary school teaching and learning are affected by their contexts.
Milbrey W McLaughlin, Co-Director
Joan E Talbert, Co-Director

5074 Center for Safe Schools
National School Boards Association
1680 Duke Street
2nd Floor
Alexandria, VA 22314-3493
703-838-6722
Fax: 703-683-7590
info@nsba.org
www.nsba4safeschools.org
Seeks to ensure a safe and secure environment for all members of the public school community. Key areas are infrastructure, crisis and emergency management, whole child health, and cyber security.
Charlie Wilson, President
Thomas Gentzel, Executive Director & CEO

5075 Center for Social Organization of Schools
Johns Hopkins University
3003 N Charles Street
Suite 200
Baltimore, MD 21218-3888
410-516-8800
Fax: 410-516-8890
jmcpartland@csos.jhu.edu
Conduct programmatic research to improve the education system, as well as full-time support staff engaged in developing curricula and providing technical assistance to help schools use the Center's research.
Jim McPartland, Director
Mary Maushard, Communication Director

5076 Center for Technology in Education
Bank Street College of Education
6740 Alexander Bell Drive
Suite 302
Columbia, MD 21046-1898
410-516-9800
Fax: 410-516-9818
cte@jhu.edu
www.cte.jhu.edu
Improve the quality of life of children and youth, particularly those with special needs, through teaching, research, and leadership in the use of technology.
Jacqueline A Nunn, Director
K Lynne Harper Mainzer, Deputy Director

5077 Center for the Study of Reading
University of Illinois
158 Children's Research Center
51 Gerty Drive
Champaign, IL 61820
217-333-2552
Fax: 217-244-4501
csrrca@uiuc.edu
Conduct reading research and development must be to discover and put into practice the means for reaching children who are failing to read.
Richard C Anderson, Director
Kim Nguyen-Jahiel, Associate Director

5078 Center for the Study of Small/Rural Schools
University of Oklahoma
555 E Constitution Street
Suite 138
Norman, OK 73072-7820
405-325-1450
Fax: 405-325-7075
jcsimmons@ou.edu
www.cssrs.ou.edu
Assists small and rural schools in building and maintaining necessary knowledge bases, founded on state-of-the-art research in the areas of school improvement and reform, restructuring, staff development, administration, and teaching.
Jan C Simmons, Director

5079 Center on Families, Schools, Communities & Children's Learning
Northeastern University
50 Nightingale Hall
Boston, MA 02215
617-373-2595
Fax: 617-373-8924
Examines how families, communities and schools can work in partnership to promote children's motivation, learning and development, including disseminating information.
Nancy Ames, Vice President

5080 Center on Organization & Restructuring of Schools
1025 W Johnson Street
Madison, WI 53706-1706
608-263-7575
Fax: 608-263-6448
Focuses on restructuring K-12 schools in various areas of student development and progress.
Fred M Newman, Director

5081 Curriculum Research and Development Group
University of Hawaii
1776 University Avenue
Honolulu, HI 96822-2463
808-956-4969
800-799-8111
Fax: 808-956-6730

crdg@hawaii.edu
www.hawaii.edu/crdg
Conducts research and creates, evaluates, disseminates, and supports educational programs that serve students, teachers, parents, and other educators in grades preK-12.

Helen Au, Assistant Director
Dr. Kathleen F. Berg, Director

5082 Division for Research
The Council for Exceptional Children
2000 Broadway
Oakland, CA 94612
510-891-3400
www.dor.kaiser.org
The Division of Research aims to conduct, publish, and disseminate high-quality epidemiologic and health services research to improve the health and medical care of Kaiser Permanente members and the society at large.

Joe Selby, Director
Morris Collen, Founder

5083 Early Childhood Technical Assistance Center Resources
ECTA Center
517 S Greensboro Street
Carrboro, NC 27510
919-962-2001
Fax: 919-966-7463
ectacenter@unc.edu
www.ectacenter.org
Provides access to primary sources, research and reference materials for the benefit of those working in the special education system: administrators, researchers, policy makers, practitioners, families and advocates.

Christina Kasprzak, Co-Director
Megan Vinh, Co-Director

5084 Educational Information & Resource Center
Research Department
606 Delsea Drive
Sewell, NJ 08080-9399
856-582-7000
Fax: 856-582-4206
EIRC is committed to continuously improving the education, safety, physical and emotional health of children. EIRC meets this commitment by developing and delivering a comprehensive array of support services to those who teach, raise, care for and mentor children.

Charles Ivory, Executive Director
John Henry, Program Director

5085 Educational Research Service
1001 N Fairfax Street
Suite 500
Alexandria, VA 22314-1587
703-243-2100
800-791-9308
Fax: 703-243-1985
www.ers.org
For over 30 years Educational Research Service has been the nonprofit organization serving the research and information needs of the nation's K-12 education leaders and the public.

John C Draper EdD, CEO
Katherine A Behrens, Chief Operating Officer

5086 Educational Testing Service
Rosedale Road
Princeton, NJ 08541
609-921-9000
Fax: 609-734-5410
www.ets.org
To advance quality and equity in education by providing fair and valid assessments, research and related services. Our products and services measure knowledge and skills, promote learning and educational performance, and support education and professional development for all people worldwide.

Susan Keipper, Program Director
Kurt Landgraf, President and CEO

5087 Florida Atlantic University-Multifunctional Resource Center
1515 W Commercial Boulevard
Suite 303
Boco Raton, FL 33309-3095
561-297-3000
800-328-6721
Fax: 561-297-2141
Provides training and technical assistance to Title VII-funded classroom instructional projects and other programs serving limited-English proficient students.

Dr Ann C Willig, Director
Elaine Sherr, Research Assistant

5088 Information Center on Education
Eba Room 385
Albany, NY 12234-1
518-474-8716
Fax: 518-473-7737
Coordinates data collection procedures within the New York State Education Department.

Leonard Powell, Director

5089 Information Exchange
Maine State Library
64 State House Station
Augusta, ME 04333-64
207-287-5620
800-322-8899
Fax: 207-287-5624
Provides access to the latest education research and information for teachers.

Edna M Comstock, Director

5090 Institute for Research in Learning Disabilities
The University of Kansas
3060 Robert
Lawrence, KS 66045-1
785-864-4780
Fax: 785-864-5728
Although the focus of the Institute's research is children, they have a sizeable publication list with some of their research having relevance for adults.

5091 Instructional Materials Laboratory
University of Missouri-Columbia
8 London Hall
Columbia, MO 65211-2230
800-669-2465
800-669-2465
Fax: 573-882-1992
www.iml.missouri.edu/
Prepares and disseminates instructional materials for the vocational education community.

Dana Tannehill, Director
Richard Branton, Assistant Director

5092 Learning Research and Development Center
University of Pittsburgh
3939 O'Hara Street
Pittsburgh, PA 15260
412-624-7487
Fax: 412-624-3051
lrangel@pitt.edu
www.lrdc.pitt.edu
LRDC fosters an environment in which research initiatives relating to the science, practice, organization and technology of learning, teaching and training are born and thrive.

Charles Perfetti, Director
Alan Lesgold, Senior Scientist/Research Sc

5093 Life Lab Science Program
1156 High Street
Santa Cruz, CA 95064
831-459-2001
Fax: 831-459-3483
lifelab@lifelab.org
www.lifelab.org
Life Lab Science Program is nationally acknowledged as an expert leader in the development and dissemination of garden-centered educational programs.

Gail Harlamoff, Executive Director
Whitney Cohen, Education Director

5094 Merrimack Education Center
101 Mill Road
Chelmsford, MA 01824-4899
978-256-3985
Fax: 978-256-6890
www.mec.edu/
Merrimack Education Center (MEC) is a diversified educational and technological resource for schools, cities and towns and other non-profit organizations. MEC offers a broad range of special education, professional development, facilities management and technology programs and solutions.

John Barranco, Director

5095 Mid-Atlantic Regional Educational Laboratory
1301 Cecil B Moore Avenue
Philadelphia, PA 19122-6091
215-204-3000
Fax: 215-204-5130
robert.sullivan@temple.edu
www.temple.edu
The Regional Educational Laboratories are educational research and development organizations supported by contracts with the US Education Department. Specialty area: Education Leadership.

William Evans, Director

5096 Mid-Continent Regional Educational Laboratory
2550 S Parker Road
Suite 500
Aurora, CO 80014-1678
303-337-0990
Fax: 303-337-3005
Focuses on improvement of education practices in Colorado, Kansas, Missouri, Nebraska, Wyoming, North Dakota and South Dakota.

C. Lawrence Hutchins, Director

5097 Midwestern Regional Educational Laboratory
1900 Spring Road
Suite 300
Oak Brook, IL 60521
630-649-6500
Fax: 630-649-6700
nowakows@ncrel.org
The Regional Educational Laboratories are educational research and development organizations supported by contracts with the US Education Department, Office of Educational Research and Improvement. Specialty area: Technology.

Dr. Jeri Nowakowski, Executive Director

098 Missouri LINC
401 E Stewart Road
Columbia, MO 65211
573-882-2733
800-392-0533
Fax: 573-882-5071
Serves students with special needs through a resource and technical assistance center.
Linda Bradley, Director

099 NCDPI Homeless Education Program
Dixon Building
5900 Summit Avenue
Browns Summit, NC 27214
336-315-7491
Fax: 336-315-7457
lphillip@serve.org
www.hepnc.uncg.edu
The NCHEP ensures that children and youth experiencing homelessness in North Carolina have access and resources needed to enroll in and to be successful in school.
Lisa Phillips, State Coordinator

100 NEA Foundatrion for the Improvement of Education
1201 16th Street NW
Washington, DC 20036
202-822-7840
Fax: 202-822-7779
www.neafoundation.org
The NEA Foundation, through the unique strength of its partnership with educators, advances student achievement by investing in public education that will prepare each of America's children to learn and thrive in a rapidly changing world.
Aaron J Pope, Communications Associate
John I Wilson, Executive Director

101 National Black Child Development Institute
1313 L Street, NW
Suite 110
Washington, DC 20005-4110
202-833-2220
800-556-2234
Fax: 202-833-8222
moreinfo@nbcdi.org
www.nbcdi.org
NBCDI's mission is to improve and protect the quality of life of Black children and families.
Carol Brunson Day, President
Gillian Shurland, Contact

102 National Center for Improving Science Education
2000 L Street NW
Suite 616
Washington, DC 20036-4917
202-467-0652
Fax: 202-467-0659
Promotes change in state and local policies and practices in science curricula, teaching, and assessment.
Senta A Raizen, Director

103 National Center for Research in Mathematical Sciences Education
University of Wisconsin-Madison
1025 W Johnson Street
#557
Madison, WI 53706-1706
608-263-4285
Fax: 608-263-3406
Provides a research base for the reform of school mathematics.
Thomas A Romberg, Director

5104 National Center for Research in Vocational Education
University of California, Berkeley
2030 Addison Street
Suite 500
Berkeley, CA 94720-1674
510-642-4004
800-762-4093
Fax: 510-642-2124
The mission of the National Center for Research in Vocational Education (NCRVE) is to strengthen education to prepare all individuals for lasting and rewarding employment and lifelong learning.
David Stern, Director
Phyllis Hudecki, Associate Director

5105 National Center for Research on Teacher Learning
Michigan State University, College of Education
116 Erickson Hall
East Lansing, MI 48824-1034
517-355-9302
Fax: 517-432-2795
The NCRTL extended its findings about learning from students-as-learners to teachers-as-learners in order to understand how teachers learn to teach.
Robert E Floden, Director
G Williamson McDiarmid, Director

5106 National Center for Science Teaching & Learning
Ohio State University
1314 Kinnear Road
Columbus, OH 43212-1156
614-292-3339
Fax: 614-292-0263
Seeks to understand how non-curricular factors affect how science is taught in grades K-12.
Arthur L White, Director

5107 National Center for the Study of Privatizationin Education
525 W 120th Street
Box 181, 230 Thompson Hall
New York, NY 10027-6696
212-678-3259
Fax: 212-678-3474
ncspe@columbia.edu
www.ncspe.org
The goal of the National Center for the Study of Privatization in Education is to provide an independent, non-partisan source of analysis and information on privatization in education.
Henry M Levin, Director
Clive Belfield, Associate Director

5108 National Center on Education & the Economy
555 13th Street, NW
Suite 500 W
Washington, DC 20004
202-783-3668
888-361-6233
Fax: 202-783-3672
info@ncee.org
www.ncee.org
NCEE is committed not just to research, analysis and advocacy, but also to following through on its recommendations by creating the training, professional development, technical assistance and materials that professionals in the system need to implement the proposals we make.
Marc Tucker, President/Founder
Rich Moglia Cannon, Chief Financial Officer

5109 National Center on Education in the Inner Cities
Temple University
13th Street & Cecil B Moore Avenue
Philadelphia, PA 19122
215-893-8400
Fax: 215-735-9718
Conducts systematic studies of innovative initiatives for improving the quality and outcomes of schooling and broad-based efforts to strengthen and improve education.
Margaret C Wang, Director

5110 National Child Labor Committee
1501 Broadway
Suite 1908
New York, NY 10036-5592
212-840-1801
Fax: 212-768-0963
The National Child Labor Committee (NCLC) is a private, non-profit organization founded in 1904 and incorporated by an Act of Congress in 1907 with the mission of promoting the rights, awareness, dignity, well-being and education of children and youth as they relate to work and working.
Jeffrey F Newman, President/Executive Director
Erik Butler, President

5111 National Clearinghouse for Alcohol & Drug Information
PO Box 2345
Rockville, MD 20847-2345
240-221-4019
800-729-6686
Fax: 240-221-4292
SAMHSA's National Clearinghouse for Alcohol and Drug Information (NCADI) is the Nation's one-stop resource for information about substance abuse prevention and addiction treatment.
John Noble, Director

5112 National Clearinghouse for Bilingual Education
George Washington University
2011 Eye Street NW
Suite 300
Washington, DC 20006
202-467-0867
800-321-6223
Fax: 202-467-4283
askncela@ncela.gwu.edu
www.ncela.gwu.edu
OELA's National Clearinghouse collects, coordinates and conveys a broad range of research and resources in support of an inclusive approach to high quality education for ELLs.
Nancy Zelasko, Director
Minerva Gorena, Director

5113 National Clearinghouse for Information on Business Involvement in Education
National Association for Industry-Education Co-op
235 Hendricks Boulevard
Buffalo, NY 14226-3304
716-834-7047
Fax: 718-834-7047
Seeks to foster industry-education cooperation in the US and Canada in the areas of school improvement, career education and human resource/economic development.
Dr. Donald Clark, Director

5114 National Dropout Prevention Center
Clemson University
209 Martin Street
Clemson, SC 29631-1555

864-656-2599
Fax: 864-656-0136
ndpc@clemson.edu
www.dropoutprevention.org
Provides knowledge and promotes networking for researchers, practitioners, policymakers and families to increase opportunities for at-risk youth to help them succeed in high school.

Sandy Addis, Ph.D, Director
Jennie Cole, Research Associate

5115 National Information Center for Educational Media
PO Box 8640
Albuquerque, NM 87198-8640
505-998-0800
800-926-8328
Fax: 505-256-1080
mhlava@accessinn.com
www.nicem.com
The world's most comprehensive audiovisual database for over 35 years and a crucial reference tool for librarians, media specialists, training directors, faculty, teachers and researchers.

Marjorie Hlava, President
Jay Van Eman, Chief Executive Officer

5116 National Research Center on the Gifted & Talented
University of Connecticut
2131 Hillside Road
Unit 3007
Storrs, CT 06269-3007
860-486-4826
Fax: 860-486-2900
www.gifted.uconn.edu
Studies focusing on meeting the needs of gifted and talented youth have received national and international attention for over 40 years.

Joseph S Renzulli, Director
Phillip E Austin, President

5117 National Resource Center on Self-Care & School-Age Child Care
American Home Economics Association
1555 King Street
Alexandria, VA 22314-2738
703-706-4620
800-252-SAFE
Fax: 703-706-4663
Provides materials to parents, educators, child care professionals and others concerned about the number of latchkey children and about quality school-age child care.

Dr. Margaret Plantz, Director

5118 National School Boards Association Library
1680 Duke Street
2nd Floor
Alexandria, VA 22314-3493
703-838-6722
Fax: 703-683-7590
info@nsba.org
www.nsba.org
Maintains an up-to-date collection of resources concerning education issues, with an emphasis on school board policy issues. Publications include amicus briefs, reports, school law resources, conference presentations, surveys and newsletters.

Viola M. Garcia, President
Chip Slaven, Interim Executive Director

5119 National School Safety Center (NSSC)
30200 Agoura Road
Suite 260
Agoura Hills, CA 91301
805-373-9977
info@schoolsafety.us
www.schoolsafety.us
Serves as an advocate for safe schools and the prevention of school crime and violence. The center also offers research materials, statistics and books on the subject.

Ronald D. Stephens, Executive Director

5120 National Science Resources Center
901 D Street SW
Suite 704B
Washington, DC 20024
202-633-2966
Fax: 202-287-2070
nsrcinfo@si.edu
Intermediary organization that bridges research on how children learn with best practices for the classroom.

Sally Shuler, Executive Director
Jennifer Childress, Director

5121 North Central Regional Educational Laboratory
1120 East Diehl Road
Suite 200
Naperville, IL 60563-1486
630-649-6500
Fax: 630-649-6700
info@ncrel.org
www.ncrel.org
Being an educator is a great responsibility. At Learning Point Associates, we accept responsibility in order to deserve the trust that has been placed in us and our work

Gina Burkhard, Chief Executive Officer
Robert Davis, Chief Financial Officer

5122 Northeast Regional Center for Drug-Free Schools & Communities
12 Overton Avenue
Sayville, NY 11782-2437
718-340-7000
Fax: 516-589-7894
Works to support the prevention of alcohol and other drug use in the northeast region of the United States.

Dr. Gerald Edwards, Director

5123 Northeast and Islands Regional Educational Laboratory
222 Richmond Street
Suite 300
Providence, RI 02903
401-274-9548
800-521-9550
Fax: 401-421-7650
Promotes educational change to provide all students equitable opportunities to succeed. We advocate for populations whose access to excellent education has been limited or denied.

Oaxaca Schroder, Administrative Assistant
Sunitha Appikatla, Senior Programmer/Analyst

5124 Pacific Regional Educational Laboratory
1099 Alakea Street
Suite 2500
Honolulu, HI 96813
808-969-3482
Fax: 808-969-3483
The Regional Educational Laboratories are educational research and development organizations supported by contracts with the U.S. Education Department, Office of Educational Research and Improvement. Specialty area: Language and Cultural Diversity.

Dr. John Kofel, Executive Director

5125 Parent Educational Advocacy Training Center
100 N Washington Street
Suite 234
Falls Church, VA 22046-4523
703-923-0010
800-869-6782
Fax: 800-693-3514
partners@peatc.org
www.peatc.org
Mission is to build positive futures for children in Virginia by working collaboratively with families, schools and communities in order to improve opportunities for excellence in education and success in school and community life.

Michael Jefferson, President
Betsy McGuire, Vice President

5126 Parents as Teachers National Center
2228 Ball Drive
Saint Louis, MO 63146
314-432-4330
866-728-4968
Fax: 314-432-8963
info@parentsasteachers.org
To provide the information, support and encouragement parents need to help their children develop optimally during the crucial early years of life.

Sue Stepleton, President/CEO
Cheryl Dyle-Palmer, COO

5127 Public Education Fund Network
601 13th Street NW
Suite 710 S
Washington, DC 20005-3808
202-628-7460
Fax: 202-628-1893
To build public demand and mobilize resources for quality public education for all children through a national constituency of local education funds and individuals.

Wendy D Puriefoy, Director
Richard J. Vierk, Chairman

5128 Quality Education Data
1050 Seventeenth Street
Suite 1100
Denver, CO 80265
303-209-9400
800-525-5811
Fax: 303-209-9444
www.qeddata.com
Gathers information about K-12 schools, colleges and other educational institutions, offers an on-line database on education, directories of public and nonpublic schools and research reports.

Jeanne Hayes, President
Katie Bukovsky, Sales Executive

5129 Regional Educational Laboratory Northwest
Education Northwest
1417 NW Everett Street
Suite 310
Portland, OR 97209
800-547-6339
www.educationnorthwest.org
One of ten regional educational laboratories across the U.S., REL Northwest aims to improve the use of data and research in education practice through research, data analysis, and technical assistance. REL Northwest serves the states of Alaska, Idaho, Montana, Oregon, and Washing-

ton. It is funded by the U.S. Department of Education's Institute of Education Sciences.

Patty Wood, Chief Executive Officer
Jeff Strickler, Chief Operating Officer

130 Regional Laboratory for Educational Improvement of the Northeast
555 New Jersey Ave NW
Washington, DC 20208
800-347-4200
Fax: 781-481-1120
Seeks to improve education in Connecticut, Maine, Massachusetts, New Hampshire, New York, Rhode Island, Vermont, Puerto Rico and the Virgin Islands.

David P Crandall, Director

131 Research for Better Schools
112 N Broad Street
Philadelphia, PA 19102-2471
215-568-6150
Fax: 215-568-7260
info@rbs.org
www.rbs.org
RBS is a private, nonprofit educational organization funded primarily through grants and contracts from the U.S. Department of Education, the National Science Foundation, Mid-Atlantic state departments of education, institutions of higher education, foundations, and school districts.

Dr. Keith M Kershner, Executive Director
Rev. John F Bloh, President

132 SERVE Center
5900 Summit Avenue
Suite 201
Browns Summit, NC 27214
336-315-7400
800-755-3277
Fax: 336-315-7457
info@serve.org
www.serve.uncg.edu
Its mission is to support and promote teaching and learning excellence in the Pre-kindergarten to Grade 12 education community.

George Hancock, Executive Director
Carol Sanders, Director, Operations

133 SIGI PLUS
Educational Testing Service
105 Terry Drive
Suite 120
Newtown, PA 18940-1872
800-257-7444
Fax: 215-579-8589
A computerized career guidance program developed by Educational Testing Service. Covers all the major aspects of career decision making and planning through a carefully constructed system of nine separate but interrelated sections, including a Tech Prep module and Internet Hydrolink Connectivity.

Annie Schofer, Sales Manager

134 Satellite Educational Resources Consortium
939 S Stadium Road
Columbia, SC 29201-4724
803-252-2782
Fax: 803-252-5320
Seeks to expand educational opportunities by employing the latest telecommunication technologies to make quality education in math, science, and foreign languages available equally and cost-effectively to students regardless of their geographic location.

Wilbur H Hinton, Executive Director

5135 Scientific Learning
300 Frank H Ogawa Plaza
Suite 600
Oakland, CA 94612-2040
888-665-9707
Fax: 510-444-3580
customerservice@scilearn.com
www.scientificlearning.com
Scientific Learning bases their products and services on neuroscience research and scientifically validated efficacy and deliver them using the most efficient technologies. We also provide beneficial products and services to our customers that are easy to use and access.

Robert C Bowen, Chairman/CEO
Andy Myers, President/COO

5136 Smithsonian Institution/Office of Elementary& Secondary Education
PO Box 37012
SI Building, Room 153, MRC 010
Washington, DC 20013-7012
202-633- 100
Fax: 202-357-2116
info@si.edu
www.si.edu
Helps K-12 teachers incorporate museums and other community resources into their curricula.

Ann Bay, Director
G Wayne Clough, Secretary

5137 Society for Research in Child Development
1825 K Street NW
Suite 325
Washington, DC 20006
202-800-0677
info@srcd.org
www.srcd.org
The Society for Research in Child Development is a membership association that advances developmental science and promotes its use to improve human lives.

Saima K. Hedrick, MPH, CAE, Executive Director
Kelly R. Fisher, Ph.D, Director, Policy

5138 Southeast Regional Center for Drug-Free Schools & Communities
Spencerian Office Plaza
Louisville, KY 40292-1
502-588-0052
800-621-7372
Fax: 502-588-1782
Works to support the prevention of alcohol and drug use among youth in the Southeast region.

Nancy J Cunningham, Director

5139 Southern Regional Education Board
592 10th Street NW
Atlanta, GA 30318-5776
404-875-9211
Fax: 404-872-1477
evalutech@sreb.org
www.sreb.org
Nonprofit, nonpartisan organization that helps government and education leaders in its 16 member states work together to advance education and improve the social and economic life of the region.

Mark D Musick, Director
David S Spence, President

5140 Southwest Comprehensive Regional Assistance Center-Region IX
New Mexico Highlands University
121 Tijeras Avenue NE
Suite 2100
Albuquerque, NM 87102-3461
800-247-4269
Fax: 505-243-4456
National network of 15 technical assistance centers, funded through the US Department of Education, designed to support federally funded educational programs. Specifically, these centers will provide comprehensive training and technical assistance under the Improving America's Schools Act (IASA) to States, Tribes, community based organizations, local education agencies, schools and other recipients of funds under the Act.

Paul E Martinez EdD, Director

5141 Southwestern Educational Development Laboratory
4700 Mueller Boulevard
Austin, TX 78723
512-476-6861
800-476-6861
Fax: 512-476-2286
www.sedl.org
SEDL is a private, nonprofit corporation dedicated to fulfilling its mission with clients and other education stakeholders on a national, regional, state, and local basis through diverse and interrelated funding, partnerships, and projects.

Dr. Wesley A Hoover, President/ CEO
Vicki Dimock, Chief Program Officer

5142 Special Interest Group for Computer Science Education
Computer Science Department
University of Texas at Austin
Austin, TX 78712
512-471-9539
Fax: 512-471-8885
www.sigcse.org
Provides a forum for solving problems common in developing, implementing and evaluating computer science education programs and courses.

Nell B Dale, Director

5143 Stern Center for Language and Learning
183 Talcott Road
Suite 101
Williston, VT 05495
802-878-2332
Fax: 802-878-0230
www.sterncenter.org
Nonprofit research and education center devoted to helping learners of all abilities achieve their goals.

Laurie Quinn, President

5144 TACS/WRRC
1268 University of Oregon
Eugene, OR 97403
541-346-5641
Fax: 541-346-0322
www.wrrc.uoregon.edu/tacs
Supports state education agencies in their task of ensuring quality programs and services for children with disabilities and their families.

Richard Zeller, Co-Director
Caroline Moore, Project Director

5145 TERC
2067 Massachusetts Avenue
Cambridge, MA 2140-1340
617-873-9600
Fax: 617-873-9601
contactus@terc.edu
www.terc.edu
We imagine a future in which learners from diverse communities engage in creative, rig-

orous, and reflective inquiry as an integral part of their lives.

24 pages
ISSN: 0743-0221

Laurie Brennan, President
Nira Voss, Chief Financial Officer

5146 **UCLA Statistical Consulting**
University of California, Los Angeles
8130 MSB, UCLA
PO Box 951554
Los Angeles, CA 90095-1554
310-825-8299
Fax: 310-206-5658
www.ats.ucla.edu
Provides statistical consulting services to UCLA and off-campus students. The staff is faculty members, graduate students and the Department of Statistics. Specializes in the quantitative analysis of research problems in a wide variety of fields.

Debbie Barrera, Administrator
Richard Berk, Director

5147 **Wisconsin Center for Education Research**
Univ. of Wisconsin-Madison, School of Education
1025 W Johnson Street
Suite 785
Madison, WI 53706
webmaster@wcer.wisc.edu
www.wcer.wisc.edu
An education research center seeking to make advances in education policy and practice.

Audio Visual Materials

148 AGC/United Learning
Discovery Education
1560 Sherman Avenue
Suite 100
Evanston, IL 60201
847-328-6700
800-323-9084
Fax: 847-328-6706
www.discoveryed.com
A publisher/producer of educational videos and digital content K-College curriculum based.

Coni Rechner, Director Marketing
Ronald Reed, Sr. Vice President

149 Active Parenting Publishing
1220 Kennestone Circle
Suite 130
Marietta, GA 30066-6022
770-429-0565
800-825-0060
Fax: 770-429-0334
cservice@activeparenting.com
www.activeparenting.com
Videos and books on parenting, character education, substance abuse prevention, divorce and step-parenting, ADHD and more.

Dr. Michael H. Popkin, Founder

150 Allied Video Corporation
PO Box 702618
Tulsa, OK 74170-2618
918-587-6477
800-926-5892
Fax: 918-587-1550
Produces the educational video series, The Assistant Professor. Animations and three-dimensional graphics clearly illustrate concepts in mathematics, science and music. Companion supplementary materials are also available.

Video

Charles Brown, President

151 Altschul Group Corporation
1560 Sherman Avenue
Suite 100
Evanston, IL 60201-4817
800-323-9084
Video and film educational programs.

152 Ambrose Video Publishing Inc
145 West 45th Street
New York, NY 10036
212-768-7373
800-526-4663
Fax: 212-768-9282
customerservice@ambrosevideo.com
www.ambrosevideo.com
A leading distributor of broadcast quality documentation/educational videos to individuals (in the home) and schools, libraries and other institutions. The company also sells through catalog, sales staff and television advertising.

153 Anchor Audio
5931 Darwin Court
Carlsbad, CA 92008
310-784-2300
800-262-4671
Fax: 760-827-7105
sales@anchoraudio.com
www.anchoraudio.com
Various audio visual products for the school and library.

Alex Jacobs, VP, Sales
Nick Craig, Sales

5154 Association for Educational Communications & Technology
1025 Vermont Avenue NW
Suite 820
Washington, DC 20005-3516
202-347-7834
Offers a full line of videotapes and films for the various educational fields including language arts, science and social studies.

5155 BUILD Sucess Through the Values of Excellence
Center for the Study of Small/Rural Schools
555 E Constitution Street
Room 138
Norman, OK 73072-7820
405-325-1450
Fax: 405-325-7075
jcsimmons@ou.edu
www.cssrs.ou.edu
Series IV

Video

Jan C Simmons, Ph.D., Program Director

5156 Bergwall Productions
540 Baltimore Pike
Chadds Ford, PA 19317-9304
800-645-3565
Educational videotapes and films.

5157 Cedrus
1420 Buena Vista Avenue
McLean, VA 22101-3510
703-883-0986
Videodiscs, videocassettes and filmstrips for educational purposes.

5158 Cengage Learning
2493 Du Bridge Avenue
Irvine, CA 92606-5022
949-660-0727
800-233-7078
Fax: 949-660-0206
www.cengage.co.in/
Videos for students and professionals focused on child development, early childhood education, and the challenges facing many young children. Effective educational media for development specialists, regular and special education staff in elementary school, preschool teachers, childcare providers, health care workers and parents.

Dennis Timmerman, Sr Account Executive

5159 Character Education
Center for the Study of Small/Rural Schools
555 E Constitution Street
Room 138
Norman, OK 73072-7820
405-325-1450
Fax: 405-325-7075
jcsimmons@ou.edu
www.cssrs.ou.edu
Series IV

Video

Jan C Simmons, Ph.D., Program Director

5160 Chip Taylor Communications
2 East View Drive
Derry, NH 03038-5728
603-434-9262
800-876-2447
Fax: 603-432-2723
chip@chiptaylor.com
www.chiptaylor.com
Offers worldwide Digital and DVD program distribution for Broadcast, Digital, Theatrical, Education, Library, Museum, Institution, Organization, In-flight, At Sea, Medical, Business, Home and Retail markets.

Video

Chip Taylor, President

5161 Churchill Media
6677 N NW Highway
Chicago, IL 60631-1304
310-207-6600
800-334-7830
Fax: 800-624-1678
Videos, videodiscs and curriculum packages for schools and libraries.

5162 College Board
250 Vesey Street
New York, NY 10281
212-713-8000
www.collegeboard.org
Offers a variety of educational materials and publications focusing on college issues.

David Coleman, Chief Executive Officer
Jeremy Singer, President

5163 Computer Prompting & Captioning Company
1010 Rockville Pike
Suite 306
Rockville, MD 20852-3035
301-738-8487
800-977-6678
Fax: 301-738-8488
info@cpcweb.com
www.cpcweb.com
Closed captioning systems and service.

Sid Hoffman, Project Manager

5164 Crystal Productions
5320 Carpinteria Ave
Suite K
Carpinteria, CA 93013-2107
847-657-8144
800-255-8629
Fax: 800-657-8149
www.crystalproductions.com
Producer and distributor of educational resource material in art and sciences. Resources include videotapes, posters, books, videodiscs, CD-Rom, reproductions, games.

132 pages

Amy Woodworth, President

5165 Dukane Corporation
Audio Visual Products Division
2900 Dukane Drive
St Charles, IL 60174-3395
630-584-2300
Fax: 630-584-5156
www.dukane.com
Full line of audio visual products, LCD display panels, computer data projectors, overhead projectors, microfilm readers and silent and sound filmstrip projectors.

Michael W. Ritschdorff, President/ CEO
Terry Goldman, VP, Administration

5166 Early Advantage
270 Monroe Turnpike
P.O. Box 743
Fairfield, CT 6824-9853
888-248-0480
Fax: 800-409-9928
customerservice@early-advantage.com
Features the Muzzy video collection for teaching children beginning second language skills.

5167 Educational Video Group
291 S Wind Way
Greenwood, IN 46142-9190
317-888-6581
Fax: 317-888-5857
www.evgonline.com
Award-winning video programs and textbooks in education, presenting new offerings

in speech, government and historic documentaries.

Roger Cook, President

5168 English as a Second Language Video Series
Master Teacher
One Leadership Lane
PO Box 1207
Manhattan, KS 66502-1207
800-669-9633
Fax: 800-669-1132
www.masterteacher.com
Assessing the needs of culturally diverse learners, you will learn what must be done to evaluate the learning needs and progress of ESL students.

ISBN: 1-58992-045-7

5169 Fase Productions
4801 Wilshire Boulevard
Suite 215
Los Angeles, CA 90010-3813
213-965-8794
Educational videotapes and films.

5170 Films for Humanities & Sciences
PO Box 2053
Princeton, NJ 08543-2053
609-419-8000
800-257-5126
Fax: 609-419-8071
www.wiley.com
A leading publisher/distributor of over four thousand educational programs, including NOVA and TV Ontario, for school and college markets. Also a leader in the production and distribution of videotapes and videodiscs to the educational, institutional and government markets.

5171 First Steps/Concepts in Motivation
18105 Town Center Drive
Olney, MD 20832-1479
301-774-9429
800-947-8377
Educational videotapes and accessories promoting physical fitness for preschoolers and young children. Using choreographed dance movement, familiar and fun children's music, colorful mats, bean bags and rhythm sticks, First Steps teaches balance, gross and fine motor skills, rhythm, coordination, and primary learning skills.

Dale Rimmey, Marketing Director
Larry Rose, President/Owner

5172 Future of Rural Education
Center for the Study of Small/Rural Schools
555 E Constitution Street
Room 138
Norman, OK 73072-7820
405-325-1450
Fax: 405-325-7075
jcsimmons@ou.edu
www.cssrs.ou.edu
Series I

Video

Jan C Simmons, Ph.D., Program Director

5173 Gangs in Our Schools: Identification, Response, and Prevention Strategies
Center for the Study of Small/Rural Schools
555 E Constitution Street
Room 138
Norman, OK 73072-7820
405-325-1450
Fax: 405-325-7075
jcsimmons@ou.edu
www.cssrs.ou.edu
Series III

Video

Jan C Simmons, Ph.D., Program Director

5174 Guidance Associates
31 Pine View Road
PO Box 1000
Mount Kisco, NY 10549-7000
800-431-1242
Fax: 914-666-5319
willg1961@gmail.com
www.guidanceassociates.com
Curriculum based videos in health/guidance, social studies, math, science, English, the humanities and career education.

Will Goodman, President

5175 Health Connection
55 West Oak Ridge Drive
Hagerstown, MD 21740
800-548-8700
Fax: 888-294-8405
www.healthconnection.org
Tools for freedom from tobacco and other drugs.

5176 Human Relations Media
175 Tompkins Avenue
Pleasantville, NY 10570-3144
800-431-2050
Fax: 914-244-0485
Offers a wide variety of videotapes and videodiscs in the areas of guidance, social services, human relations, self-esteem and student services.

5177 INSIGHTS Visual Productions
374-A N Highway 101
Encinitas, CA 92024-2527
760-942-0528
Fax: 760-944-7793
Science video for K-12 and teacher training.

5178 INTELECOM Intelligent Telecommunications
150 E Colorado Boulevard
Suite 300
Pasadena, CA 91105-1937
626-796-7300
800-576-2988
Fax: 626-577-4282
www.intelecomonline.net
Videos and educational films.

Bob Miller, VP Marketing/Sale

5179 In Search of Character
Performance Resource Press
1270 Rankin Drive
Suite F
Troy, MI 48083-2843
800-453-7733
Fax: 800-499-5718
www.pronline.net
Character education videos.

5180 Instructional Resources Corporation
1819 Bay Ridge Avenue
Annapolis, MD 21403-2835
800-922-1711
Fax: 410-268-8320
American History Videodisc.

5181 Intermedia
5600 Rainier Ave S
Suite 203
Seattle, WA 98118
206-284-2995
800-553-8336
Fax: 206-283-0778
www.intermedia-inc.com
Distributes a wide range of high-quality, social interest videos on topics such as teen pregnancy prevention, substance abuse prevention, domestic violence, sexual harassment, dating violence, date rape, gang education, cultural diversity, AIDS prevention and teen patenting. Offer free 30 day previews of the programs which are developed to address the needs of educators who must deal with the pressing social problems of today.

Paperback/Video

Susan Hoffman, President
Ted Fitch, General Manager

5182 International Historic Films
3533 S Archer Avenue
Chicago, IL 60609-1135
773-927-2900
Fax: 773-927-9211
intrvdeo@ix.netcom.com
www.ihffilm.com
Military, political and social history of the 20th century.

Video/Audio

5183 January Productions
PO Box 66
Hawthorne, NJ 07507-0066
973-423-4666
800-451-7450
Fax: 973-423-5569
Educational videotapes, read-a-long books, and CD-Rom.

Paperback/Video/Audi

Lori Brown, Sales/Marketing

5184 Karol Media
375 Stewart Road
Hanover, PA 18706
570-822-8899
Fax: 570-822-8226
www.karolmedia.com
Science videos.

Carol Kincheloe, Founder
Mick Kincheloe, Founder

5185 Kimbo Educational
PO Box 477
Long Branch, NJ 07740-0477
732-229-4949
800-631-2187
service@kimboed.com
www.kimboeddownloads.com
Manufacturer of children's audio-musical learning fun. Also offers videos and music by other famous children's artists such as Raffi, Sharon, Lois and Bram.

Jim Kimble, President

5186 Leadership: Rethinking the Future
Center for the Study of Small/Rural Schools
555 E Constitution Street
Room 138
Norman, OK 73072-7820
405-325-1450
Fax: 405-325-7075
jcsimmons@ou.edu
www.cssrs.ou.edu
Series IV

Video

Jan C Simmons, Ph.D., Program Director

5187 MPC Multimedia Products Corp
1010 Sherman Avenue
Hamden, CT 06514
203-407-4623
800-243-2108
Fax: 203-407-4636
Over 5,000 most frequently requested high quality audio, visual and video products and materials

offered at deep discount prices. Manufacturer of high quality tape records,CD's record players, PA systems, headphones

148 pages BiAnnual

T. Guercia, Author
T Guercia, VP
A Melillo, Sales Manager

188 Main Street Foundations: Building Community Teams
Center for the Study of Small/Rural Schools
555 E Constitution Street
Room 138
Norman, OK 73072-7820
405-325-1450
Fax: 405-325-7075
jcsimmons@ou.edu
www.cssrs.ou.edu
Prevention Series

Video

Jan C Simmons, Ph.D., Program Director

189 Marshmedia
Marsh Media
P.O. Box 8082
Shawnee Mission, KS 66208-82
816-523-1059
800-821-3303
Fax: 816-333-7421
info@marshmedia.com
www.marshmedia.com
Children's educational videotapes, books and teaching guides.

32 pages Bi-Annual
ISBN: 1-55942-xxx

Joan K Marsh, President

190 Media Projects
5215 Homer Street
Dallas, TX 75206-6623
214-826-3863
Fax: 214-826-3919
mail@mediaprojects.org
www.mediaprojects.org
Educational videotapes in all areas of interest, including drug education, violence prevention, women's studies, history, youth issues and special education.

Allen Mondell, Director, Writer, Producer

191 Middle School: Why and How
Center for the Study of Small/Rural Schools
555 E Constitution Street
Room 138
Norman, OK 73072-7820
405-325-1450
Fax: 405-325-7075
jcsimmons@ou.edu
www.cssrs.ou.edu
Series III

Video

Jan C Simmons, Ph.D., Program Director

192 Multicultural Educations: Valuing Diversity
Center for the Study of Small/Rural Schools
555 E Constitution Street
Room 138
Norman, OK 73072-7820
405-325-1450
Fax: 405-325-7075
jcsimmons@ou.edu
www.cssrs.ou.edu
Series I

Video

Jan C Simmons, Ph.D., Program Director

193 NUVO, Ltd.
PO Box 1729
Chula Vista, CA 91912
619-426-8440
Fax: 619-691-1525
nuvoltd@aol.com
Produces and distributes how-to videotapes for teens and adults on beginning reading and decorative napkin folding useful in classroom instruction and individual practice. Also distributes two bilingual (Spanish/English) books by psychologist Dr. Jorge Espinoza.

5194 National Film Board
1251 Avenue of the Americas
New York, NY 10020-1104
800-542-2164
Fax: 845-774-2945
Educational films and videos ranging from documentaries on nature and science to social issues such as teen pregnancy.

5195 National Geographic School Publishing
PO Box 10579
Washington, DC 20090-8019
800-368-2728
Fax: 515-362-3366
Offers a wide variety of videodiscs, videotapes and educational materials in the area of social studies, geography, science and social sciences.

5196 PBS Video
1320 Braddock Pl
Alexandria, VA 22314-1649
703-739-5380
800-424-7963
Fax: 703-739-5269
Award-winning programs from PBS, public television's largest video distributors. Video and multimedia programming including interactive videodiscs for schools, colleges and libraries. The PBS Video Resource Catalog is organized into detailed subject categories.

5197 PICS Authentic Foreign Video
University of Iowa
270 International Center
Iowa City, IA 52242-1802
319-335-3500
800-373-PICS
Fax: 319-335-0280
webmaster@uiowa.edu
www.housing.uiowa.edu
Provides educators with authentic foreign language videos in French, German and Spanish on videotapes and videodisc. Also offers software to accompany the videodiscs as well as written materials in the form of transcripts and videoguides with pedagogical hints and tips.

Sally Mason, President
Anny Ewing, French Coll Editor

5198 Penton Overseas
2470 Impala Drive
Carlsbad, CA 92008-7226
800-748-5804
Fax: 760-431-8110
Educational videotapes and videodiscs in a wide variety of interests for classroom use.

5199 Phoenix Films/BFA Educ Media/Coronet/MII
Phoenix Learning Group
141 Millwell Dr.
Suite A
St. Louis, MO 63043
314-569-0211
800-221-1274
Fax: 314-569-2834
phoenixdealer@aol.com
www.phoenixlearninggroup.com
Educational multi-media - VHS, CD-Rom, DVD, streaming & broadcast.

Video

Kathy Longsworth, Vice President, Market Dev

5200 Presidential Classroom
2201 Old Ivy Road
P.O. Box 400406
Charlottesville, VA 22904
434-924-7236
800-441-6533
Fax: 434-982-2739
eriedel@presidentialclassroom.org
www.presidentialclassroom.org
Video of civic education programs in Washington, DC for high school juniors and seniors. Each one week program provides students with an inside view of the federal government in action and their role as responsible citizens and future leaders.

Annual
400 attendees

Jack Buechner, President/CEO
William Antholis, Director and CEOÿ

5201 Rainbow Educational Media Charles Clark Company
4540 Preslyn Drive
Raleigh, NC 27616
919-954-7550
800-331-4047
Fax: 919-954-7554
www.rainbowedumedia.com
Educational videocassettes and CD-Roms.

Karen C Francis, Business Analyst

5202 Rainbow Educational Video
170 Keyland Court
Bohemia, NY 11716-2638
800-331-4047
Producer and distributor of educational videos.

Wesley Clark, Marketing Director

5203 Reading & O'Reilly: The Wilton Programs
PO Box 302
Wilton, CT 06897-0302
800-458-4274
Producers and distributors of award-winning audiovisual educational programs in art appreciation, history, multicultural education, social studies and music. Titles include: African-American Art and the Take-a-Bow, musical production series. Free catalog is available of full product line.

Lee Reading, President
Gretchen O'Reilly, VP

5204 SAP Today
Performance Resource Press
1270 Rankin Drive
Suite F
Troy, MI 48083-2843
800-453-7733
Fax: 800-499-5718
www.store.amplifiedlifenetwork.com
Overview offers the basics of student assistance.

5205 SVE: Society for Visual Education
55 E Monroe Street
Suite 3400
Chicago, IL 60603-5710
312-849-9100
800-829-1900
Fax: 800-624-1678
Producer and distributor of curriculum based instructional materials including videodisc,

microcomputer software, video cassettes and filmstrips for grade levels PreK-12.

5206 Slow Learning Child Video Series
Master Teacher
One Leadership Lane
PO Box 1207
Manhattan, KS 66502-1207
800-669-9633
Fax: 800-669-1132
www.masterteacher.com
Provides a full understandging of the slow learning child and allows all educators to share in the excitment of teaching this invidual in ways that develop his or her emerging potenial to the fullest.

ISBN: 1-58992-157-0

Mildred Odom Bradley, Author

5207 Spoken Arts
PO Box 100
New Rochelle, NY 10802-0100
727-578-7600
Literature-based audio and visual products for library and K-12 classrooms.

5208 Teacher's Video Company
8150 S Krene Road
Tempe, AZ 85284
800-262-8837
Fax: 800-434-5638
Video for teachers.

5209 Teen Court: An Alternative Approach to Juvenile Justice
Center for the Study of Small/Rural Schools
555 E Constitution Street
Room 138
Norman, OK 73072-7820
405-325-1450
Fax: 405-325-7075
jcsimmons@ou.edu
www.cssrs.ou.edu
Prevention Series

Video

Jan C Simmons, Ph.D., Program Director

5210 Tools to Help Youth
529 S 7 Street
Suite 570
Minneapolis, MN 55415
800-328-0417
Fax: 612-342-2388
www.communityintervention.com
Books and videos on counseling, character education, anger management, life skills, and achohol, tobacco and other drug uses.

5211 Training Video Series for the Professional School Bus Driver
Master Teacher
One Leadership Lane
PO Box 1207
Manhattan, KS 66502-1207
800-669-9633
Fax: 800-669-1132
www.masterteacher.com
Will help you provide bus drivers with consistent direction and training for the many situations thay will encounter beyond driving safety.

ISBN: 1-58992-082-1

5212 True Colors
Center for the Study of Small/Rural Schools
555 E Constitution Street
Room 138
Norman, OK 73072-7820
405-325-1450
Fax: 405-325-7075
jcsimmons@ou.edu
www.cssrs.ou.edu
Series III

Video

Jan C Simmons, Ph.D., Program Director

5213 United Transparencies
435 Main Street
#104
Johnson City, NY 13790-1935
607-729-6512
800-477-6512
Fax: 607-729-4820
A full line of overhead transparencies for Junior-Senior high school and colleges and technical programs.

D Hetherington

5214 Video Project
145 9th Street
Suite 230
San Francisco, CA 94103
800-475-2638
Fax: 415-692-6223
support@videoproject.com
www.videoproject.org
Provides documentaries on critical social and global issues to classrooms and communities, in order to advance awareness and encourage action on important concerns.

Arlin Golden, Co-Director
Michael Kuehnert, Co-Director

5215 Weston Woods Studios
265 Post Road West
Westport, CT 06880
203-845-0197
800-243-5020
Fax: 203-845-0498
wstnwoods@aol.com
Audiovisual adaptations of classic children's literature.

Video

Cindy Cardozo, Marketing Coordinator

Classroom Materials

5216 ABC School Supply
3312 N Berkeley Lake Road NW
Duluth, GA 30096-3024
Instructional materials and supplies.

5217 ADP Lemco
5970 W Dannon Way
West Jordan, UT 84081
801-280-4000
800-575-3626
Fax: 801-280-4040
customerservice@adplemco.com
www.adplemco.com
Announcement boards, schedule boards, chalkboards, tackboard, marker boards, trophy cases, athletic equipment, gym divider curtains and basketball backstops.

David L Hall, Sr VP

5218 APCO
388 Grant Street SE
Atlanta, GA 30312-2227
404-688-9000
877-988-APCO
Fax: 404-577-3847
www.apcosigns.com
Classroom supplies including announcement and chalkboards.

Anne M Gallup

5219 AbleNet
2625 Patton Road
Roseville, MN 55113-1308
651-294-2200
800-322-0956
Fax: 651-294-2259
customerservice@ablenetinc.com
www.ablenetinc.com
Adaptive devices for students with disabilities from Pre-K through adult, as well as activities and games for students of all abilities.

Bill Sproull, Board Chairman
Jennifer Thalhuber, President/CEO

5220 Accounter Systems USA
1107 S Mannheim Road
Suite 305
Westchester, IL 60154-2560
800-229-8765
Sports timers and clocks and classroom supplies.

5221 Accu-Cut Systems
1035 E Dodge Street
Fremont, NE 68025
402-721-4134
800-288-1670
Fax: 402-721-5778
info@accucut.com
www.accucut.com
Manufacturer of die cutting machines dies.

5222 Airomat Corporation
2916 Engle Road
Fort Wayne, IN 46809-1198
260-747-7408
800-348-4905
Fax: 260-747-7409
airomat@airomat.com
www.airomat.com
Mats and matting.

Jody Feasel, VP
Janie Feasel, President/CEO

5223 Airspace USA
89 Patton Avenue
Asheville, NC 28801
828-258-1319
800-872-1319
Fax: 828-258-1390
www.airspacesolutions.com
Airspace Soft Center Play and Learn Systems provide a comprehensive range of play, learning and physical development opportunities using commercial grade and foam filled play equipment. Play manual provided.

Daniel Brenman, VP Sales/Marketing
Tracy Syxes, Administrator

5224 All Art Supplies
Art Supplies Wholesale
4 Enon Street
North Beverly, MA 01915
800-462-2420
Fax: 978-922-1495
info@allartsupplies.com
www.allartsupplies.com
Art supplies at wholesale prices.

5225 American Foam
HC 37 Box 317 H
Lewisburg, WV 24901
304-497-3000
800-344-8997
Fax: 304-497-3001
Carving blocks of foam.

5226 American Plastics Council
700 Second St., NE
Washington, DC 20002
202-249-7000
800-243-5790
Fax: 202-249-6100
www.plastics.org

Offers classroom materials on recycling and environmental education.

227 Anatomical Chart Company
8221 Kimball Avenue
Skokie, IL 60076-2956
847-679-4700
www.anatomical.com
Maps and charts for educational purposes.

228 Angels School Supply
600 E Colorado Boulevard
Pasadena, CA 91101-2006
626-584-0855
Fax: 626-584-0888
www.angelschoolsupply.com
School and classroom supplies.

Jennifer , Sales Representitive

229 Aol@School
22070 Broderick Drive
Dulles, VA 20166
888-468-3768
www.school.aol.com
Age-appropriate, high-quality educational content tailored for K-12 students and educators. Aol@School focuses and filters the Web for us, providing appropriate, developmental access to the vast educational resources on the internet.

230 Armada Art Materials
Armada Art Inc.
142 Berkeley Street
Boston, MA 02116
617-859-3800
800-435-0601
Fax: 617-859-3808
info@armadaart.com
www.armadaart.com

231 Art Materials Catalog
United Art and Education
PO Box 9219
Fort Wayne, IN 46899-9219
260-478-1121
800-322-3247
Fax: 800-858-3247
www.unitednow.com
Art materials.

232 Art Supplies Wholesale
4 Enon Street
North Beverly, MA 01915
800-462-2420
Fax: 978-922-1495
info@allartsupplies.com
www.allartsupplies.com
Wholesale art supplies.

233 Art to Remember
5535 Macy Drive
Indianapolis, IN 46235
317-826-0870
800-895-8777
Fax: 317-823-2822
info@arttoremember.com
www.arttoremember.com
A unique program that encourages your students' artisic creativity while providing an opportunity to raise funds for schools.

Patty Arbuckle, Program Coordinator
Kathy Robinson, Program Coordinator

234 Artix
PO Box 25008
Kelowna, BC V1W3Y
250-861-5345
800-665-5345
Papermaking kits.

235 Assessories by Velma
PO Box 2580
Shasta, CA 96087-2580
Multicultural education-related products.

5236 At-Risk Resources
135 Dupont Street
PO Box 760
Plainview, NY 11803-0706
800-999-6884
Fax: 800-262-1886
Dealing with drug violence prevention, character education, self-esteem, teen sexuality, dropout prevention, safe schoolks, career development, parenting crisis and trauma, and professional development.

5237 Atlas Track & Tennis
19495 SW Teton Avenue
Tualatin, OR 97062-8846
800-423-5875
Fax: 503-692-0491
Specialty sport surfaces; synthetic running tracks, tennis courts, and athletic flooring for schools.

5238 Audio Forum
69 Broad Street
Guildford, CT 06437
203-453-9794
Fax: 203-453-9774
info@audioforum.com
Cassettes, CD's and books for language study.

5239 Badge-A-Minit
345 N. Lewis Ave.
Oglesby, IL 61348
815-883-8822
800-223-4103
Fax: 815-883-9696
questions@badgeaminit.com
www.badgeaminit.com
Awards, trophies, emblems and badges for educational purposes.

5240 Bag Lady School Supplies
9212 Marina Pacifica Drive N
Long Beach, CA 90803-3886
Classroom supplies.

5241 Bale Company
PO Box 6400
Providence, RI 02940-6400
800-822-5350
Fax: 401-831-5500
www.bale.com
Awards, medals, pins, plaques and trophies.

5242 Bangor Cork Company
William & D Streets
Pen Argyl, PA 18072
610-863-9041
Fax: 610-863-6275
www.bangorcork.com
Announcement boards.

Janice Cory, Customer Services Rep

5243 Baumgarten's
144 Ottley Drive NE
Atlanta, GA 30324-4016
404-874-7675
800-247-5547
Fax: 800-255-5547
www.baumgartens.com
Products available include pencil sharpeners, pencil grips, pocket binders, disposable aprons, American flags, practical colorful clips, fastening devices in a variety of shapes and sizes, identification security items, lamination, magnifiers and key chains.

David Baumgarten, Vice President
Michael Lynch, National Sales Manager

5244 Best Manufacturing Sign Systems
1202 N. Park Avenue
PO Box 577
Montrose, CO 81401-3171
970-249-2378
800-235-2378
Fax: 970-249-0223
sales@bestsigns.com
www.bestsigns.com
Architectural and ADA signs, announcement boards.

Mary Phillips, Sales Manager

5245 Binney & Smith
1100 Church Lane
Easton, PA 18044-431
610-253-6271
800-CRA-YOLA
Fax: 610-250-5768
www.crayola.com
Crayons.

Mike Perry, President, CEO
Smith Holland, CFO, EVP

5246 Black History Month
Guidance Channel
135 Dupont Street
PO Box 760
Plainview, NY 44803-0706
800-999-6884
Fax: 800-262-1886
Products to celebrate Black history, multicultutral resources.

5247 Blackboard Resurfacing Company
50 N 7th Street
Bangor, PA 18013-1731
610-588-0965
Fax: 610-863-1997
Chalk and announcement boards.

Karin Karpinski, Administrative Assistant

5248 Bob's Big Pencils
1848 E 27th Street
Hays, KS 67601-2108
Large novelty pencils, plaques, bookends and many pencil related items.

5249 Book It!/Pizza Hut
9111 E Douglas Avenue
Wichita, KS 67207-1205
316-687-8401
National reading incentive program with materials, books and incentive display items to get students interested in reading.

5250 Borden
Home & Professional Products Group
180 E Broad Street
Columbus, OH 43215-3799
614-225-7479
Fax: 614-225-7167
Arts and crafts supplies, maintenance and repair supplies.

5251 Bulman Products
1650 Mc Reynolds Ave NW
Grand Rapids, MI 49504
616-363-4416
Fax: 616-363-0380
bulman@macatawa.com
www.bulmanproducts.com
Art craft paper.

5252 Bydee Art
8603 Yellow Oak Street
Austin, TX 78729-3739
512-474-4343
Fax: 512-474-5749
Prints, books, T-shirts with the Bydee People focusing on education.

5253 **C-Thru Ruler Company**
6 Britton Drive
Bloomfield, CT 06002-3632
860-243-0303
Fax: 860-243-1856
www.CThruRuler.com
Arts, crafts and classroom supplies.
Ross Zachs, Manager

5254 **CHEM/Lawrence Hall of Science**
University of California
1 Centennial Drive #5200
Berkeley, CA 94720-5200
510-642-6000
Fax: 510-642-1055
www.lawrencehallofscience.org
Activities for grades 5-6 and helps students understand the use of chemicals in our daily lives.
Elizabeth K. Stage, Director
Rena Dorph, Research

5255 **CORD Communications**
324 Kelly Street
Waco, TX 76710-5709
254-776-1822
Fax: 254-776-3906
Instructional materials for secondary and postsecondary applications in science education.

5256 **Califone International**
1145 Arroyo Avenue, # A
San Fernando, CA 91340
818-407-2400
800-722-0500
Fax: 877-402-2248
www.califone.com
Multisensory, supplemental curricula on magnetic cards for use with all Card Reader/Language master equipment.
Nelly Spievak, Sales Coordinator

5257 **Cardinal Industries**
PO Box 1430
Grundy, VA 24614-1430
276-935-4545
800-336-0551
Fax: 276-935-4970
Awards, emblems, trophies and badges.

5258 **Carousel Productions**
1100 Wilcrest Drive
Suite 100
Houston, TX 77042-1642
281-568-9300
Fax: 281-568-9498
Moments in History T-shirts, as well as other various educational gifts and products.

5259 **Cascade School Supplies**
1 Brown Street
PO Box 780
North Adams, MA 01247
800-628-5078
Fax: 866-298-6578
president@cascadeschoolsupplies.com
www.cascadeschoolsupplies.com
Offers a variety of school supplies and more.
Peter L. Cote, President

5260 **Celebrate Diversity**
Guidance Channel
135 Dupont Street
PO Box 760
Plainview, NY 44803-0706
800-999-6884
Fax: 800-262-1886
Educational resources that celebrate diversity.

5261 **Celebrate Earth Day**
Guidance Channel
135 Dupont Street
PO Box 760
Plainview, NY 44803-0706
800-999-6884
Fax: 800-262-1886
Educational resources for celebrating earth day.

5262 **Center Enterprises**
PO Box 33161
West Hartford, CT 06110
860-953-4423
Fax: 800-373-2923
Clifford individual curriculum and storybook stamp sets, individual, grading, curriculum based and Sweet Arts rubber stamp line, stamp pads, embossing inks and powders.

5263 **Center for Learning**
10200 Jefferson Blvd.
Box 802
Culver City, CA 90232
440-331-1404
800-421-4246
Fax: 800-944-5432
customerservice@centerforlearning.org
www.centerforlearning.org
Supplementary curriculum units for all grade levels in biography, language arts, novel/drama and social studies.

5264 **Center for Teaching International Relations**
University of Denver
2199 S. University Blvd.
Denver, CO 80208
303-871-3106
www.du.edu
Reproducible teaching activities and software promoting multicultural understanding and international relations in the classroom for grades K-adult.
Rebecca Chopp, Chancellor
Gregg Kvistad, Executive Vice Chancellor

5265 **Childcraft Education Corporation**
20 Kilmer Avenue
Edison, NJ 08817
732-572-6100
Distributes children's toys, products, materials and publications to schools.

5266 **Childswork/Childsplay**
The Guidence Channel
135 Dupont Street
PO Box 760
Plainview, NY 11803-0760
800-962-1141
Fax: 800-262-1886
www.childswork.com
Contains over 450 resources to address the social and emotional needs of children and adolescents.
Lawrence C Shapiro, PhD, President
Constance H Logan, Development Coordinator

5267 **Chroma**
205 Bucky Drive
Lititz, PA 17543
717-626-8866
800-257-8278
Fax: 717-626-9292
infousa@chromaonline.com
www.chromaonline.com
Tempera and acrylic paints.

5268 **Chroma-Vision Sign & Art System**
PO Box 434
Greensboro, NC 27402-0434
336-275-0602
Refillable and renewable felt tip markers used with non-toxic, water soluable, fast drying colors for making signs, posters, and general art work with no messy cleanup.
S Gray, President

5269 **Citizenship Through Sports and Fine Arts Curriculum**
National Federation of State High School Assoc.
PO Box 690
Indianapolis, IN 46206
317-972-6900
800-776-3462
Fax: 317-822-5700
www.nfhs.org
High school activities curriculum package that includes an introductory video, Rekindling the Spirit, along with the Overview booklet, plus two insightful books covering eight targets of the curriculum.
Tom Mezzanotte, President
Tom Welter, Presideny- Elect

5270 **Claridge Products & Equipment**
Claridge Products & Equipment
601 Highway 62-65 S
PO Box 910
Harrison, AR 72602-0910
870-743-2200
Fax: 870-743-1908
claridge@claridgeproducts.com
www.claridgeproducts.com
Claridge manufactures chalkboards, markerboards, bulletin boards, display and trophy cases, bulletin and directory board cabinets, easels, lecterns, speakers' stands, wood lecture units with matching credenzas and much more.
Terry McCutchen, Sales Manager

5271 **Collins & Aikman Floorcoverings**
311 Smith Industrial Boulevard
Dalton, GA 30722
800-248-2878
Fax: 706-259-2666
www.powerbond.com
An alternative to conventional carpet to improve indoor air quality and reduce maintenance cost. Powerboard floor covering.
T Ellis, General Manager/Edu Markets

5272 **Columbia Cascade Company**
1300 S.W. Sixth Avenue
Suite 310
Portland, OR 97201-3464
503-223-1157
800-547-1940
Fax: 503-223-4530
hq@timberform.com
www.timberform.com
Playground equipment and site furniture.
Dale Gordon, Sales Manager

5273 **Creative Artworks Factory**
19031 McGuire Road
Perris, CA 92570-8305
909-780-5950
Screenprinted T-shirts, posters and gifts for educational purposes.

5274 **Creative Educational Surplus**
9801 James Avenue S
#C
Bloomington, MN 55431-2919
Art and classroom materials.

5275 **Creative Shapes Etc.**
30 Bermar Park
Suite 1
Rochester, NY 14624
585-335-6619
Fax: 585-335-6070

info@creativeshapesetc.com
www.creativeshapesetc.com
Provides products for DIY craft, classroom decoration and bulletin boards, made entirely in the U.S.

276 Crown Mats & Matting
2100 Commerce Drive
Fremont, OH 43420-1048
419-332-5531
800-628-5463
Fax: 800-544-2806
sales@crown-mats.com
www.crown-mats.com
Mats, matting and flooring for schools.

Vincent J. DePhillipsy̌, President

277 Dahle USA
49 Vose Farm Road
Peterborough, NH 03458
603-924-0003
800-995-1379
Fax: 603-924-1616
Arts and crafts supplies, school and office products, office shreddars and more.

278 Designer Artwear I
8475 C-1 Highway 6 N
Houston, TX 77095
281-446-6641
Specialty clothing, accessories, etc. all educationally designed.

279 Dexter Educational Toys
Dexter Educational Toys, Inc.
PO Box 630861
Aventura, FL 33163-0861
305-931-7425
800-291-4515
Fax: 305-931-0552
dexterplay@bellsouth.net
www.dexterplay.com
Manufacturer and distributor of education material. Dress-ups for children 2-7 years. Multicultural hand puppets, finger puppets, head masks puppet theaters, rag dolls, dress-ups for teddy bears and dolls, cloth books, export manufacturing under special designs and orders.

Genny Silverstein, VP Secretary

280 Dick Blick Art Materials
PO Box 1267
Galesburg, IL 61402-1267
309-343-6181
800-723-2787
Fax: 800-621-8293
info@dickblick.com
www.dickblick.com
Classroom art supplies.

281 Dinorock Productions
407 Granville Drive
Silver Spring, MD 20901-3238
301-588-9300
Musical, Broadway puppet shows for early childhood fun and education.

282 Discovery Toys
12443 Pine Creek Road
Cerritos, CA 90703-2044
562-809-0331
800-341-8697
Fax: 562-809-0331
contact@discoverytoys.net
www.discoverytoyslink.com/elizabeth
Emphasizes child physical, social and educational development through creative play. Educational toys, games and books are available for all ages. Services include home demonstrations, fund raisers, phone and catalog orders. New Book of Knowledge Encyclopedia and patenting video tapes are also available.

Jerry Salerno, CEO
Jim Myers, COO

5283 Disney Educational Productions
500 S Buena Vista Street
Burbank, CA 91521-0001
800-777-8100
Creates and manufactures classroom aids for the educational field.

5284 Dixie Art Supplies
5440 Mounes St.
Suite 108
New Orleans, LA 70123-3290
504-733-6509
800-783-2612
Fax: 504-733-0668
artdixie@aol.com
www.dixieart.com
Fine art supplier.

5285 Dr. Playwell's Game Catalog
Guidance Channel
135 Dupont Street
PO Box 760
Plainview, NY 44803-0706
800-999-6884
Fax: 800-262-1886
Games that develop character and life skills.

5286 Draper
411 South Pearl Street
Spiceland, IN 47385
765-987-7999
800-238-7999
Fax: 765-987-7142
draper@draper.com
www.draperinc.com
Projection screens, video projector mounts and lifts, plasma display mounts, presentation easels, window shades and gymnasium equipment.

Chris Broome, Contract Market Manager
Bob Mathes, AV/Video Market Manager

5287 Draw Books
Peel Productions
PO Box 546
Columbus, NC 28722-0546
828-859-3879
800-345-6665
Fax: 801-365-9898
www.drawbooks.com
How-to-draw books for elementary and middle school.

Paperback
ISBN: 0-939217

5288 Dupont Company
Corlan Products
CRP-702
Wilmington, DE 19880
302-774-1000
800-436-7426
Fax: 800-417-1266
www.dupont.com/
Arts and crafts supplies.

5289 Durable Corporation
75 N Pleasant Street
Norwalk, OH 44857-1218
419-668-8138
800-419-8622
Fax: 800-537-6287
www.durablecorp.com
Furniture, classroom supplies, arts and crafts and educational products.

5290 Early Ed
3110 Sunrise Drive
Crown Point, IN 46307-8905
Teacher sweatshirts, cardigans, T-shirts, tote bags and jewelry.

5291 Education Department
Wildlife Conservation Society
2300 Southern Boulevard
Bronx, NY 10460
718-220-5100
800-937-5131
Fax: 718-733-4460
membership@wcs.org
www.wcs.org
Year round programs for school and general audience. Teacher training, grades K-12.

Sydell Schein, Manager/Program Services
Ann Robinson, Director/National Programs

5292 Educational Equipment Corporation of Ohio
845 Overholt Road
Kent, OH 44240-7529
330-673-4881
Fax: 330-673-4915
mkaufman@mkco.com
Chalkboards, tackboards, trophy cases, announcement boards.

Michael Kaufman, General Manager
Eric Baughman, Sales Manager

5293 Electronic Book Catalog
Franklin Learning Resources
1 Franklin Plaza
Burlington, NJ 08016-4908
800-BOO-MAN
Fax: 609-387-1787
Electronic translation machines, calculators and supplies.

5294 Ellison Educational Equipment
25862 Commercentre Drive
Lake Forest, CA 92630-8804
800-253-2238
Fax: 800-253-2240
europecustomerservices@ellison.com
www.ellison.com
Serves the educational and craft community with time-saving equipment, supplies and ideas.

5295 Endura Rubber Flooring
2 University Office Park
Waltham, MA 02453-3421
781-647-5375
Fax: 781-647-4543
Floorcoverings, mats and matting for schools.

5296 Fairgate Rule Company
3718 New York 9G
Sawkill Industrial Park
Rhinebeck, NY 12572
845-876-3063
Fax: 845-265-4128
sales@fairgate.com
www.fairgate.com
Arts and crafts supplies.

5297 Family Reading Night Kit
Renaissance Learning
2911 Peach Street
PO Box 8036
Wisconsin Rapids, WI 54495-8036
715-424-3636
800-338-4204
Fax: 715-424-4242
answers@renaissance.com
www.renlearn.com
Kit to start a family reading night where parents and children spent quality time together sharing enthusiasm over books.

Mary T. Minch, EVP, Finance, CFO
Samir Joglekar, EVP, Sales

5298 **Fascinating Folds**
PO Box 10070
Glendale, AZ 85318
602-375-9979
Fax: 602-375-9978
World's large supplier of origami and paper arts products.

5299 **Fiskars Corporation**
2537 Daniels St.
Madison, WI 53718
608-233-1649
866-348-5661
Fax: 608-294-4790
www.fiskars.com
School scissors.

5300 **Flipside Products**
7624 Reinhold Driveÿ
Cincinnati, OH 45237
513-527-4521
800-926-0704
Fax: 513-527-4526
info@flipsideproducts.com
www.flipsideproducts.com
Suppliers of certificates, awards, graduation supplies, dry erase boards, chalk boards, project sheets and more school-related and office products.
Bryan Sharpe, VP, Operations
Meghan O'Brien, Sales Coordinator

5301 **Fox Laminating Company**
84 Custer Street
W Hartford, CT 06110-1955
860-953-4884
800-433-2468
Fax: 860-953-1277
sales@foxlaminating.com
www.foxlam.com
Easy, simple, and inexpensive do-it-yourself laminators. A piece of paper can be laminated for just pennies. Badges, ID's and luggage tags can also be made. Also laminated plaques for awards, diplomas, and mission statements.
Joe Fox, President
John Mills, Marketing Manager

5302 **George F Cram Company**
PO Box 426
Indianapolis, IN 46206-0426
317-635-5564
Fax: 317-687-2845
Classroom geography maps, state maps, social studies skills and globes.

5303 **Gift-in-Kind Clearinghouse**
PO Box 850
Davidson, NC 28036-0850
704-892-7228
Fax: 704-892-3825
Educational and classroom supplies, computers and gifts for teachers.

5304 **Gold's Artworks**
2100 N Pine St.
Lumberton, NC 28358
910-739-9605
800-356-2306
Fax: 910-739-9605
www.goldsartworks.20m.com
Papermaking supplies.

5305 **Golden Artist Colors**
188 Bell Road
New Berlin, NY 13411-9527
607-847-6154
800-959-6543
Fax: 607-847-6767
goldenart@goldenpaints.com
www.goldenpaints.com
Acrylic paints.
Barbara Schindler, President/ COO
Mark Golden, CEO

5306 **Graphix**
5800 Pennsylvania Ave.
Maple Heights, OH 44137
216-581-9050
800-447-2349
Fax: 216-581-9041
info@grafixarts.com
www.grafixarts.com
Art and crafts supplies and a source for creative plastic films.
Tanya Lutz, National Sales Manager

5307 **Grolier Multimedial Encyclopedia**
Grolier Publishing
PO Box 1716
Danbury, CT 06816
203-797-3703
800-371-3908
Fax: 203-797-3899
Encyclopedia software.

5308 **Hands-On Equations**
Borenson & Associates
PO Box 3328
Allentown, PA 18106
610-398-6908
800-993-6284
Fax: 610-398-7863
info@borenson.com
www.borenson.com
System to teach algebraic concepts to elementary and middle school students.

5309 **Harrisville Designs**
Center Village
PO Box 806
Harrisville, NH 03450
603-827-3333
800-338-9415
Fax: 603-827-3335
www.harrisville.com
Award-winning weaving products for children.

5310 **Henry S Wolkins Company**
605 Myles Standish Boulevard
Taunton, MA 02780
800-233-1844
Fax: 877-965-5467
www.wolkins.com
Art and craft materials, teaching aids, early learning products, furniture, general school equipment.

5311 **Hooked on Phonics Classroom Edition**
665 3rd Street
Suite 225
San Francisco, CA 94107
714-437-3450
800-222-3334
www.hop.com
Program that teaches students to learn letters and sounds to decoding words, and then reading books.

5312 **Hydrus Galleries**
PO Box 4944
San Diego, CA 92164-4944
800-493-7299
Fax: 619-283-7466
www.hydra9.com
Curriculum-based classroom activities including papyrus outlines for students to paint.

5313 **Insect Lore**
PO Box 1535
Shafter, CA 93263
800-548-3284
Fax: 661-746-0334
livebug@insectlore.com
www.insectlore.com
Science materials for elementary and preschoolstudents.

5314 **J&A Handy-Crafts**
165 S Pennsylvania Avenue
Lindenhurst, NY 11757-5058
631-226-2400
888-252-1130
Fax: 631-226-2564
www.jacrafts.com
Arts, crafts and educational supplies.
Paul Siegelman, Marketing

5315 **Jiffy Printers Products**
35070 Maria Road
Cathedral City, CA 92234
760-321-7335
Fax: 760-770-1955
jiffyprod@aol.com
Adhesive wax sticks.
Ivan Zwelling, Owner

5316 **Key-Bak**
Division of West Coast Chain Manufacturing Co.
4245 Pacific Privado
Ontario, CA 91761
909-923-7800
800-685-2403
Fax: 909-923-0024
sales@keybak.com
www.keybak.com
Badges, awards and emblems for educational purposes.

5317 **Keyboard Instructor**
Advanced Keyboard Technology, Inc.
PO Box 2418
Paso Robles, CA 93447-2418
805-237-2055
Fax: 805-239-8973
Mobile keyboarding lab with individualized instruction.

5318 **Kids Percussion Buyer's Guide**
Percussion Marketing Council
PO Box 33252
Cleveland, OH 44133
440-582-7006
Fax: 440-230-1346
DLevine360@aol.com
www.playdrums.com
This guide is divided into two sections- recreational instruments and those for beginning traditional drummers.

5319 **Kids at Heart & School Art Materials**
PO Box 94082
Seattle, WA 98124-9482
Classroom and art materials.

5320 **Kidstamps**
PO Box 18699
Cleveland Heights, OH 44118-0699
216-291-6884
Fax: 216-291-6887
kidstamps@apk.net
www.kidstamps.com
Rubber stamps, T-shirts, bookplates and mugs designed by leading children's illustrators.

5321 **Knex Education Catalog**
Knex Education
2990 Bergey Road
PO Box 700
Hatfield, PA 19440-0700
800-KID-KNEX
email@knex.com
www.knexeducation.com

Hands-on, award-winning curriculum supported K-12 math, science and technology sets.

Joel Glickman, Chairman
Bob Glickman, Vice Chairman

5322 Lauri
PO Box 0263
Smethport, PA 16749
800-451-0520
Fax: 207-639-3555
Lacing puppets craft kits, crepe rubber picture puzzles, phonics kits and math manipulatives for pre- K and up. Catalog offers 200 manipulatives for early childhood.

5323 Learning Materials Workshop
58 Henry Streety
Burlington, VT 05401-3621
802-802-8399
800-693-7164
Fax: 802-862-0794
info@learningmaterialswork.com
www.learningmaterialswork.com
Designs and produces open-ended blocks and construction sets for early childhood classrooms. An education guide and video, as well as training workshops are offered.

Karen Hewitt, President/ Founder

5324 Learning Needs Catalog
Riverdeep Interactive Learning
PO Box 97021
Redmond, WA 98073-9721
800-362-2890
Hardware, software and print products designed for specialized student needs for Pre-K to grade 12.

5325 Learning Power and the Learning Power Workbook
Great Source Education Group
181 Ballardvale
Willmington, MA 01887
800-289-4490
Student materials for 8th and 9th grade critical thinking, study skills, life management, and other student success course.

218 pages
ISBN: 0-963813-33-1

5326 Learning Well
111 Kane Street
Baltimore, MD 21224-1728
800-645-6564
Fax: 800-413-7442
Drawing compass/ruler.

5327 Linray Enterprises
167 Corporation Road
Hyannis, MA 02601-2204
800-537-9752
Mats and matting for gym classes.

5328 Loew-Coenell
300 Gap Way
Erlanger, KY 41018-3160
866-227-9206
Fax: 201-836-7070
sales@loew-cornell.com
www.loew-cornell.com
Leader in art and craft brushes, painting accessories and artists'tools.

5329 Longstreth
28 Wells Road
Spring City, PA 19475-0475
610-495-7022
800-545-1329
Fax: 610-495-7023
www.longstreth.com
Awards, emblems, badges and trophies, sports timers and clocks.

5330 Love to Teach
693 Glacier Pass
Westerville, OH 43081-1295
614-899-2115
800-326-8361
Fax: 614-899-2070
www.lovetoteach.com
Gifts for teachers.

Linda Vollmer, Contact

5331 Lyra
78 Browne Street
Suite 3
Brookline, MA 02146
888-PEN-LYRA
mshoham@aol.com
Drawing supplies.

5332 MPI School & Instructional Supplies
PO Box 24155
Lansing, MI 48909-4155
517-393-0440
Fax: 517-393-8884
School and classroom supplies, arts and crafts.

5333 Magnetic Aids
201 Ann Street
P.O. Box 2502
Newburgh, NY 12550
845-863-1400
800-426-9624
Fax: 845-863-1490
info@magneticaids.com
www.magneticaids.com
Announcement and chalkboards, office supplies and equipment. Magnetic book supports.

Paul Pecka, VP Sales

5334 Mailer's Software
970 Calle Negocio
San Clemente, CA 92673-6201
949-492-7000
Fax: 949-589-5211
Charts, maps, globes and software for the classroom.

5335 Marsh Industries
Div. of Marsh Lumber Company
2301 E. High Avenue
PO Box 1000
New Philadelphia, OH 44663-5100
330-308-8667
800-426-4244
Fax: 330-308-5325
vpsales@marsh-ind.com
www.marsh-ind.com
Marker boards chalkboards, and tacknoards for new rennovative construction projects. Glass enclosed bulletin and directory boards. Map rail and accessories.

William Singhaus, Sales Manager

5336 Master Woodcraft
1312 College Street
Oxford, NC 27565
919-693-8811
800-333-2675
Fax: 919-693-1707
Announcement and classroom chalkboards, arts and craft supplies. Cork bulletin boards, dry erase melamine boards, easels, floor and table top.

J Moss, VP

5337 Material Science Technology
Energy Concepts
595 Bond Street
Lincolnshire, IL 60069
800-621-1247
Provides practical knowledge of the use and development of materials in todays world. Each unit combines theory with hands-on experience.

5338 Math Through the Ages: A Gentle History for Teachers and Others
Oxton Publishers, LLC
124 Main St., Suite 203
PO Box 209
Farmington, ME 04938
207-779-1923
800-539-7323
Fax: 207-779-0623
info@oxtonhouse.com
www.oxtonhouse.com
An easy-to-use tool for teachers who want some history for their math classes, this book contains 25 independent 4-to-6 page historical summaries of particular topics from elementary and secondary math, a 56-page overview and an extensive bibliography.

224 pages

William Berlinghoff, Managing Editor
Bobby Brown, Marketing Director

5339 Midwest Publishers Supply
4640 N Olcott Avenue
Harwood Heights, IL 60706
800-621-1507
Fax: 800-832-3189
info@mps-co.com
www.mps-co.com
Arts and crafts supplies.

Bonnie Cready, Sales Manager

5340 Miller Multiplex
1555 Larkin Williams Road
Fenton, MO 63026-3008
636-343-5700
800-325-3350
Fax: 636-326-1716
Announcement boards, classroom displays, charts and photography, books towers, posters, frames, kiosk displays, presentation displays.

12 pages Annually

Kathy Webster, Director Marketing

5341 Monsanto Company
800 N Lindbergh Boulevard
Saint Louis, MO 63167-0001
314-694-1000
Fax: 314-694-7625
www.monsanto.com
Arts and crafts supplies.

Hugh Grant, Chairman/ CEO
Brett D. Begemann, President/ COO

5342 MooreCo
2885 Lorraine Avenue
Temple, TX 76501-7402
254-778-4727
800-749-2258
Fax: 254-773-0500
support@moorecoinc.com
www.moorecoinc.com
Producer of visual display products including a complete line of chalk, marker, tack, bulletin, fabric and projection boards. Also offered in their catalogue are display and trophy cases, beginner boards, reversible boards, mobile easels, desk-top and floor carrels and early childhood products.

Greg Moore, President & CEO
Jonathan Vogelsang, Director, Educational Sales

5343 Morrison School Supplies
400 Industrial Road
San Carlos, CA 94070-6285
650-592-3000
800-950-4567

Fax: 650-592-1679
www.morrisonschoolsupplies.com
School supplies, classroom equipment, furniture and toys.

5344 Names Unlimited
2300 Spikes Lane
Lansing, MI 48906-3996
Chalkboard and markerboard slates and tablets.

5345 Nasco Education
901 Janesville Avenue
PO Box 901
Fort Atkinson, WI 53538-0901
920-563-2446
800-558-9595
Fax: 800-372-1236
custserv@enasco.com
www.Nascoeducation.com
Serving k-12 educators for over 78 years. Nasco's family of 14 catalogs of educational materials includes over 80,000 products in many areas: life skills, health, family and consumer science, physical activities and cooperative games, early childhood, arts & crafts, special education, math science STEAM, career and technical education and more.

Nedra Sadorf, CEO
Sarah Long, Category Manager Art

5346 National Educational Systems (NES)
National Educational Systems, Inc.
6333 De Zavala
Suite 106
San Antonio, TX 78249
800-231-4380
Fax: 210-699-4674
info@shopnes.com
www.shopnes.com
The National Educational Systems offers quality instructional materials and support services to its clients. NES works to provides clients with the latest in instructional material, bilingual materials, dual language, special needs, and teacher resources.

5347 National Teaching Aids
401 Hickory Street
PO Box 2121
Fort Collins, CO 80522
970-484-7445
800-289-9299
Fax: 970-484-1198
custserv@amep.com
www.hubbardscientific.com
Learning math, alphabet, and geography skills is easy with our Clever Catch Balls. These colorful 24-inch inflatable vinyl balls provide an excellent way for children to practice math, alphabet and geography skills. Excellent learning tool in organized classroom activities, on the playground, or at home.

Michael Warring, President
Candace Coffman, National Sales Manger

5348 New Hermes
2200 Northmont Parkway
Duluth, GA 30096
770-623-0331
800-843-7637
Fax: 770-814-7203
www.newhermes.com
Announcement boards, trophies, badges, emblems.

Gerard Guyard, Chairman

5349 Newbridge Discovery Station
33 Boston Post Road Westÿ
Suite 440
Marlborough, MA 1752
800-867-0307
Fax: 800-456-2419
www.newbridgeonline.com
Monthly quick tips and activities for teachers.

5350 Newbridge Jumbo Seasonal Patterns
PO Box 5267
Clifton, NJ 07015
Art projects, games, bulletin boards, flannel boards, story starters, learning center displays, costumes, masks and more for grades Pre K-3.

5351 NewsCurrents
Knowledge Unlimited
2320 Pleasant View Roadÿ
PO Box 52
Madison, WI 53701
608-836-6660
800-356-2303
Fax: 800-618-1570
csis@newscurrents.com
www.newscurrents.com
Current issues discussion programs for grades 3 and up.

5352 Original E-Z Grader
PO Box 23698
Chagrin Falls, OH 44023
800-732-4018
Fax: 800-689-2772
ezgrader@voyager.net
www.ezgrader.com
Electronic gradebook that computes percentage scores quickly and accurately.

5353 Partners in Learning Programs
1065 Bay Boulevard
Suite H
Chula Vista, CA 91911-1626
619-407-4744
Fax: 619-407-4755
Manufacturers and produces books, manuals, materials, supplies and gifts, such as banners for classroom purposes.

5354 Pearson Education Technologies
827 W Grove Avenue
Mesa, AZ 85210
520-615-7600
800-222-4543
Fax: 520-615-7601
SuccessMaker is a multimedia K-Adult learning system which includes math, reading, language arts and science courseware.

5355 Pentel of America
2715 Columbia Street
Torrance, CA 90503
310-320-3831
800-421-1419
Fax: 310-533-0697
www.pentel.com
Office supplies and equipment.

5356 Pin Man
Together Inc.
802 E 6th Street
PO Box 52528
Tulsa, OK 74105-3264
918-587-2405
800-282-0085
Fax: 918-382-0906
Manufacturer of custom designed lapel pins, totes for Chapter 1, reading, scholastic achievement, honor roll, parent involvement, staff awards and incentives with over 25,000 items available for imprint.

Bern Gentry, CEO

5357 PlayConcepts
2275 Huntington Drive
#305
San Marino, CA 91108-2640
800-261-2584
Fax: 626-795-1177
Creative, 3-D scenery that stimulates dramatic play. The scenes complement integrated curriculum. They are age and developmentally appropriate, non-biased, and effective for groups or individuals.

5358 Polyform Products Company
1901 Estes Avenue
Elk Grove Village, IL 60007
847-427-0020
Fax: 847-427-0020
polyform@sculpey.com
www.sculpey.com
Manufacturer of sculpey modeling clay.

5359 Presidential Classroom
2201 Old Ivy Road
P.O. Box 400406
Charlottesville, VA 22904
434-924-7236
800-441-6533
Fax: 434-982-2739
www.presidentialclassroom.org
Civic education programs in Washington, DC for high school juniors and seniors. Each one week program provides students with an inside view of the federal government in action and their role as responsible citizens and future leaders.

Jan-March, June+July
400 attendees

Jack Buechner, President/CEO
William Antholis, Director/ CEOÿ

5360 Professor Weissman's Software
Professor Weissman's Software
246 Crafton Avenue
Staten Island, NY 10314-4227
347-528-7837
Fax: 718-698-5219
mathprof@math911.com
www.math911.com
Algebra comic books, learn by example algebra flash cards, step-by-step software tutorials for algebra, trigonometry, precalculus, statistics, network versions for all software.

Martin Weissman, Owner
Keith Morse, VP

5361 Pumpkin Masters
PO Box 61456
Denver, CO 80206-8456
303-860-8006
Fax: 303-860-9826
Classroom pumpkin carving kits featuring whole language curriculum with safer and easier carving tools and patterns.

5362 Puppets on the Pier
Pier 39
Box H4
San Francisco, CA 94133
415-379-9544
800-443-4463
Fax: 415-379-9544
puppetshop@gmail.com
www.puppetdream.com
Puppets, arts, crafts and other creative educational products for children.

Arthur Partner

5363 Qwik-File Storage Systems
1000 Allview Drive
Crozet, VA 22932-3144
804-823-4351

Schedule boards and classroom supplies.

364 RC Musson Rubber Company
1320 East Archwood Avenue
P.O. Box 7038ÿ
Akron, OH 44306-2825
330-773-7651
800-321-3281
Fax: 330-773-3254
info@mussonrubber.com
www.mussonrubber.com
Rubber floorcoverings, mats and athletic matting.
Mark Reese, Customer Service Manager
Robert Segers, VP

365 RCA Rubber Company
1833 East Market St.ÿ
P.O. Box 9240
Akron, OH 44305-0240
330-784-1291
800-321-2340
Fax: 330-794-6446
www.rcarubber.com
Floorcoverings, athletic mats and more for the physical education class.

366 Reading is Fundamental
600 Maryland Avenue SW
Suite 600
Washington, DC 20024-2520
202-673-1641
Fax: 202-673-1633
Distributor of posters, bookmarks, and parent guide brochures.

367 Reconnecting Youth
National Educational Service
304 W Kirkwood Avenue
Suite 2
Bloomington, IN 47404-5132
812-336-7700
800-733-6786
Fax: 812-336-7790
Curriculum to help discouraged learners achieve in school, manage their anger, and decrease drug use, depression, and suicide risk. The program was piloted for five years with over 600 urban Northwestern public high school students with funding from the National Institute on Drug Abuse and the National Institute of Mental Health, and has since been successful in many educational settings.
3 Ring Binder Circul
ISBN: 1-879639-42-4
Jane St. John, Sales Marketing Director

368 Red Ribbon Resources
135 Dupont Street
PO Box 760
Plainview, NY 11803
800-646-7999
Fax: 800-262-1886
www.redribbonresources.com
Over 250 low cost giveaways to promote your safe and drug-free school and community.

369 Renaissance Graphic Arts
69 Steamwhistle Drive
Ivyland, PA 18974
215-357-5705
888-833-3398
Fax: 215-357-5258
pat@printmaking-materials.com
www.printmaking-materials.com
Tools, papers, plates, inks and assorted products necessary for printmaking.

370 Rock Paint Distributing Corporation
365 Sunnyside Drive
PO Box 482
Milton, WI 53563
608-868-6873
800-236-6873
Fax: 800-715-7625
handyart@handyart.com
www.handyart.com
Tempera paint, India ink, acrylic paint, block inc, washable paint, fabric paint.
Chuck Jackson, President

5371 S&S Worldwide
S&S Arts & Crafts
75 Mill Street
PO Box 513ÿ
Colchester, CT 06415-1263
860-537-3451
800-243-9232
Fax: 800-566-6678
cservice@ssww.com
www.ssww.com
Arts and crafts, classroom games and group paks.

5372 Safe & Drug Free Catalog
Performance Resource Press
1270 Rankin Drive
Suite F
Troy, MI 48083-2843
800-453-7733
Fax: 800-499-5718
www.pronline.net
Books, videos, CD-Roms, phamlets and posters toassist students with social skills, counseling, drug and violence prevention.

5373 Sakura of America
30780 San Clemente Street
Hayward, CA 94544-7131
510-475-8880
800-776-6257
Fax: 510-475-0973
express@sakuraofamerica.com
www.gellyroll.com
Producer of writing and drawing materials such as Gelly Roll Pens, Cray pas Oil pastels, Fantasia Watercolors, Pigma Micron Pens, Pentouch, Koi Watercolors, Pigma Pro Brush, Zentangle, Identipen, Microperm, Pigma Calligrapher and Mechanical Pencils.
Robert Kahre, National Accounts Manager
Julia Reed, Marketing Manager

5374 Sanford Corporation
A Lifetime of Color
2711 Washington Boulevard
Bellwood, IL 60104-1970
708-547-6650
800-323-0749
Fax: 708-547-6719
consumer.service@sanfordcorp.com
www.sanfordcorp.com
Writing instruments, art supplies.
Angela Nigl, Author
Sharon Meyers, PR Manager

5375 Sax Visual Art Resources
Sax Arts and Crafts
2725 S Moorland Road
bept. SA
New Berlin, WI 53151
800-558-6696
Fax: 800-328-4729
www.saxfcs.com
Variety of resources for slides, books, videos, fine art posters and CD-Roms.

5376 School Mate
PO Box 2225
Jackson, TN 38302
731-935-2000
Fax: 800-668-7610
Pre-school and elementary art products.

5377 SchoolMatters
Current
The Current Building
Colorado Springs, CO 80941-0001
800-525-7170
Fax: 800-993-3232
Offers a variety of creative classroom ideas including stickers, mugs, posters, signs and more for everyday and holidays and everyday of the year.

5378 Scott Sign Systems
7525 Pennsylvania Avenue
Suite 101
Sarasota, FL 34243
941-355-5171
800-237-9447
Fax: 941-351-1787
info@scottsigns.com
www.scottsigns.com
Educational supplies including announcement, letters, signs, graphics and chalkboards.
Kathy Hannon, Regional Sales Manager
Lisa Pyrcz, Account Mgr, Southeast/West

5379 Scratch-Art Company
PO Box 303
Avon, MA 02322
508-583-8085
800-377-9003
Fax: 508-583-8091
www.scratchart.com
Offers materials for drawing, sketching and rubbings.

5380 Sea Bay Game Company
77 Cliffwood Avenue, Suite 1-D
Cliffwood, NJ 07721
732-583-7902
800-568-0188
Fax: 732-583-7284
www.seabaygame.com
Manufacturer and distributor of products, games and creative play to nursery schools and preschools.

5381 Seton Identification Products
20 Thompson Road
PO Box 819
Branford, CT 06405-819
855-544-7992
800-243-6624
Fax: 800-345-7819
help@seton.com
www.seton.com
Manufacturer of all types of identification products including signs, tags, labels, traffic control, OSHA, ADA and much more.

5382 Sign Product Catalog
Scott Sign Systems, Inc.
7525 Pennsylvania Avenue
Suite 101
Sarasota, FL 34243
941-355-5171
800-237-9447
Fax: 941-351-1787
info@scottsigns.com
www.scottsigns.com
Educational supplies including announcement, letters, signs, graphics and chalkboards.
Kathy Hannon, Regional Sales Manager
Lisa Pyrcz, Account Mgr, Southeast/West

5383 Small Fry Originals
2700 S Westmoreland Road
Dallas, TX 75233-1312
214-330-8671
800-248-9443
Children's original artwork preserved in plastic plates and mugs.

5384 **Southwest Plastic Binding Corporation**
109 Millwell Court
Maryland Heights, MO 63043-2509
314-739-4400
800-325-3628
Fax: 800-942-2010
www.swbindinglaminating.com
Overhead transparencies, maps, charts and classroom supplies.

5385 **Spectrum Corporation**
10048 Easthaven Boulevard
Houston, TX 77075-3298
713-944-6200
800-392-5050
Fax: 713-944-1290
sherrig@specorp.com
www.spectrumstuff.com
Announcement boards, scoreboards and sports equipment, sports timers and clocks.

5386 **Speedball Art Products Company**
2301 Speedball Road
PO Box 5157
Statesville, NC 28677
704-838-1475
800-898-7224
Fax: 704-838-1472
www.speedballart.com
Art products for stamping, calligraphy, printmaking, drawing and painting.

Walt Glazer, CEO
Tonya Hill, Director of Sales

5387 **Sponge Stamp Magic**
525 S Anaheim Hills Road
Apartment C314
Anaheim, CA 92807-4726
Rubber stamps and games for classroom use.

5388 **Staedtler**
5725 McLaughlin Road
Mississauga, On L5R 3
905-501-9008
800-776-5544
Fax: 905-501-9117
info@staedtler.ca
www.staedtler-usa.com
Arts and crafts supplies, office supplies and equipment.

Dick Hoye, National Sales Manager

5389 **Sylvan Learning Systems**
1000 Lancaster Street
Baltimore, MD 21202
410-843-6828
888-779-5826
Fax: 410-783-3832
www.sylvanlearning.com
Provides public school academic programs that are traditional sylvan programs modified to fit the needs of individual school districts and performance guarantees.

Jody Madron, Contact

5390 **Tandy Leather Company**
PO Box 791
Fort Worth, TX 76101-0791
817-451-1480
Fax: 817-451-5254
Arts and crafts supplies, computer peripherals and systems.

5391 **Teacher Appreciation**
Guidance Channel
135 Dupont Street
PO Box 760
Plainview, NY 44803-0706
800-999-6884
Fax: 800-262-1886
Products for celebrating teacher appreciation week.

5392 **Teachers Store**
PO Box 24155
Lansing, MI 48909-4155
517-393-0440
Fax: 517-393-8884
School and classroom supplies, arts and crafts.

5393 **Texas Instruments**
12500 TI Boulevard
P.O. Box 660199
Dallas, TX 75243-4136
972-995-2011
800-336-5236
Fax: 972-995-4360
www.ti.com
Manufacturer of calculators.

Rich Templeton, Chairman/ President
Brian Crutcher, EVP, Business Operations

5394 **Triarco Arts & Crafts**
9900 13th Ave. N.
Suite 1015
Plymouth, MN 55441-5035
763-559-5590
800-328-3360
Fax: 736-559-2215
info@triarcoarts.com
www.etriarco.com
Art supplies.

5395 **Vanguard Crafts**
1081 E 48th Street
Brooklyn, NY 11234
718-377-5188
800-662-7238
Fax: 888-692-0056
Arts and crafts supplier.

5396 **Wagner Zip-Change**
3100 W Hirsch Avenue
Melrose Park, IL 60160-1741
708-681-4100
800-323-0744
Fax: 800-243-4924
sales@wagnerzip.com
www.wagnerzip.com
Non-lighted changeable letter message activity signs, changeable letters in all sizes and colors.

CJ Krasula, Marketing VP
Jim Leone, Sales Manager

5397 **Walker Display**
6520 Grand Avenue
P.O. Box 16955
Duluth, MN 55807-2242
218-624-8990
800-234-7614
Fax: 888-695-4647
www.walkerdisplay.com
Arts, crafts, classroom supplies and displays.

5398 **Wellness Reproductions**
Guidance Channel
135 Dupont Street
PO Box 760
Plainview, NY 44803-0706
800-999-6884
Fax: 800-262-1886
Mental and life skills educational materials.

5399 **What So Proudly We Hail**
1730 M Street NW
Suite 905
Washington, DC 20036
202-499-5267
cheryl@whatsoproudlywehail.org
www.whatsoproudlywehail.org
What So Proudly We Hail is an e-curriculum of literary resources to aid in the classroom education of American History, civics, social studies, and language arts. Resources are American based, with speeches, stories, songs, and anthology.

5400 **Wikki Stix One-of-a-Kind Creatables**
Omnicor
11034 N. 23rd Drive
#103
Phoenix, AZ 85029-4735
602-870-9937
800-869-4554
Fax: 602-870-9877
info@wikkistix.com
www.wikkistix.com
Unique, one-of-a-kind twistable, stickable, creatable, hands-on teaching tools. Ideal for Pre-K through 8 for science, language arts, math, arts and crafts, positive behavior rewards, rainy day recess, classroom display, diagrams and 3-D work. Self-stick; no glue needed.

Kem Clark, President
Gloria Porter, General Manager

5401 **Wilson Language Training**
47 Old Webster Road
Oxford, MA 1540
508-368-2399
800-899-8454
Fax: 508-368-2300
www.wilsonlanguage.com
Multisensory language program.

5402 **Wilton Art Appreciation Programs**
Reading & O'Reilley
PO Box 646
Botsford, CT 06404
203-270-6336
800-458-4274
Fax: 203-270-5569
www.wiltonart.com
Materials for art appreciation including CD-ROMS, videos, fine art prints, slides, workbooks, teacher' guides, lessons, puzzles and games.

Diana O'Neill, President

5403 **Young Explorers**
P.O. Box 3338
Chelmsford, MO 1824-938
800-239-7577
Fax: 888-876-8847
www.youngexplorers.com
Educational material for children.

Electronic Equipment

5404 **AIMS Multimedia**
9710 De Soto Avenue
Chatsworth, CA 91311-4409
818-773-4300
800-367-2467
Fax: 818-341-6700
info@aimsmultimedia.com
Film, video, laserdisc producer and distributor, offering a free catalog available materials. Also provides internet video streaming.

David Sherman, President
Biff Sherman, President

5405 **Advance Products Company**
1101 E Central Avenue
Wichita, KS 67214-3922
316-263-4231
Fax: 316-263-4245
Manufacturer of steel mobile projection and television tables, video cabinets, easels, computer

furniture, wall and ceiling TV mounts, and study tables and carrels.

Paul Keck

406 All American Scoreboards
Everbrite
401 South Main Street
Pardeeville, WI 53954
608-429-2121
800-356-8146
Fax: 877-505-9405
scoreboardsales@everbrite.com
www.allamericanscoreboards.com
Scoreboards.

Doug Winkelmann, Product Manager

407 American Time & Signal Company
140 3rd Avenue S
Dassel, MN 55325
800-328-8996
Fax: 800-789-1882
theclockexperts@atsclock.com
www.atsclock.com
Sports timers and clocks.

Jeff Baumgartner, CEO/ Owner

408 Arts & Entertainment Network
235 E 45th Street
Floor 9
New York, NY 10017-3354
212-210-1400
Fax: 212-210-9755
www.aenetworks.com
Cable network offering free educational programming to schools.

409 Barr Media/Films
12801 Schabarum Avenue
Irwindale, CA 91706-6808
626-338-7878
K-12 film, video and interactive Level I and III laserdisc programs.

410 C-SPAN Classroom
4000 N Capitol Street NW
Washington, DC 20001
202-737-3220
800-523-7586
Fax: 202-737-6226
www.c-span.org
C-SPAN School Bus travels through more than 80 communities during each school year. This bus is a mobile television production studio and learning center designed to give hands-on experience with C-SPAN's programming.

John Evans, CEO/ Chairman
Thomas O. Might, President/ CEO

411 CASIO
570 Mount Pleasant Avenue
Dover, NJ 07801-1631
973-361-5400
Fax: 570-868-6898
www.casio.com
Cameras, overhead projectors and electronics.

412 CASPR
100 Park Center Plaza
Suite 550
San Jose, CA 95113-2204
800-852-2777
www.caspr.com
Leader in the field of library automation for schools. Integrated library automation-cross platforms: Macintosh, Windows, Apple IIe/IIGS. Multimedia source.

Norman Kline, President

5413 Canon USA
1 Canon Plaza
Melville, NY 11747
631-330-5000
Fax: 516-328-5069
pr@cusa.canon.com
www.usa.canon.com/cusa/home
School equipment and supplies including a full line of electronics, cameras, calculators and other technology.

5414 Caulastics
5955 Mission Street
Daly City, CA 94014-1397
415-585-9600
Overhead projectors, transparencies and electronics.

5415 Cheshire Corporation
Cheshire Corporation
PO Box 61109
Denver, CO 80206-8109
303-333-3003
Fax: 303-333-4037
karen-hemmes@mindspring.com
Cheshire corporation is a publicist for book, video, CD-ROM and internet publishers in the school and library market.

Karen Hemmes, Publicist
Mary Kay Opicka, Publicist

5416 Chief Manufacturing
6436 City West Parkway
Eden Prairie, MN 55344
952-894-6280
800-582-6480
Fax: 877-894-6918
orders@chiefmfg.com
www.chiefmfg.com
Manufacturer of Communications Support Systems for audio visual and video equipment. Chief's product includes a full-line of mounts, electric lifts, carts, and accessories for LCD/DLP projectors, plasma displays and TV/monitors.

Liz Sorensen, Marketing Assistant
Sharon McCubbin, Marketing Manager

5417 Chisholm
7019 Realm Drive
San Jose, CA 95119-1321
408-329-4305
800-888-4210
info@chisholm.com
www.chisholm.com
Computer peripherals, overhead projectors and overhead transparencies.

5418 Daktronics
201 Daktronics Dr.ÿ
Brookings, SD 57006-5128
605-697-4300
800-325-8766
Fax: 605-697-4300
sales@daktronics.com
www.daktronics.com
Scoreboards, electronic message displays statistics software.

Gary Gramm, HSPR Market Manager

5419 Depco- Millennium 3000
3305 Airport Drive
PO Box 178
Pittsburg, KS 66762
316-231-0019
800-767-1062
Fax: 316-231-0024
www.depcoinc.com
Program tracks and schedules for you, the test taker delivers tests electronically, as well as, automatic final exams. There are workstation security features to help keep students focused on their activities.

5420 Discovery Networks
7700 Wisconsin Avenue
Bethesda, MD 20814-3578
301-986-0444
www.discovery.com
Manages and operates The Discovery Channel, offering the finest in nonfiction documentary programming, as well as The Learning Channel, representing a world of ideas to learners of all ages.

5421 Echolab
175 Bedford Street
Burlington, MA 01803-2794
781-273-1512
Fax: 978-250-3335
Cameras, equipment, projectors and electronics.

5422 Eiki International
Audio Visual/Video Products
26794 Vista Terrace Drive
Lake Forest, CA 92630
949-457-0200
Fax: 949-457-7878
Video projectors, overhead projectors and transparencies.

5423 Elmo Manufacturing Corporation
1478 Old Country Road
Plainview, NY 11803-5034
516-501-1400
800-947-3566
Fax: 516-501-0429
www.elmousa.com
Overhead projectors and transparencies.

5424 Fair-Play Scoreboards
1700 Delaware Avenue
Des Moines, IA 50317-2999
800-247-0265
Fax: 515-265-3364
sales@fair-play.com
www.fair-play.com
Scoreboards and sports equipment.

5425 Festo Corporation
395 Moreland Road
PO Box 18023
Hauppauge, NY 11788
631-435-0800
800-993-3786
Fax: 631-435-3847
product.support@us.festo.com
www.festo-usa.com

5426 General Audio-Visual
333 West Merrick Road
Valley Stream, NY 11580-5219
516-825-8500
Fax: 516-568-2057
www.gavi.com
Offers a full line of audio-visual equipment and supplies, cameras, projectors and various other electronics for the classroom.

5427 Hamilton Electronics
2003 W Fulton Street
Chicago, IL 60612-2365
312-421-5442
Fax: 312-421-0818
www.hamiltonbuhl.com
Electronics, equipment and supplies.

5428 JR Holcomb Company
3205 Harvard Avenue
Cleveland, OH 44101
216-341-3000
800-362-9907
Fax: 216-341-5151
A full line of electronics including calculators, overhead projectors and overhead transparencies.

5429 JVC Professional Products Company
41 Slater Drive
Elmwood Park, NJ 07407-1311
201-794-3900
Electronics line including cameras, projectors, transparencies and other technology for the classroom.

5430 Labelon Corporation
10 Chapin Street
Canandaigua, NY 14424-1589
585-394-6220
800-428-5566
Fax: 585-394-3154
www.labelon.com
Electronics, supplies and equipment for schools.

5431 Learning Channel
7700 Wisconsin Avenue
Bethesda, MD 20814
800-346-0032
Offers educational programming for schools.

5432 Learning Station/Hug-a-Chug Records
3950 Bristol Court
Melbourne, FL 32904-8712
321-728-8773
800-789-9990
Fax: 321-722-9121
thelearningstation@cfl.rr.com
www.learningstationmusic.com
Early childhood products including OMH, cassettes, CD's and videos. Also, the Learning Station performs children and family concerts and are internationally acclaimed for their concert/keynote presentations for early childhood conferences and other educational organizations.
Don Monopoli, President
Laurie Monopoli, VP

5433 Learning Well
2200 Marcus Avenue
#3759
New Hyde Park, NY 11042-1042
800-645-6564
Fax: 800-638-6499
Instructional material including computer and board games, videos, cassettes, audio tapes, theme units, manipulatives for grades PreK-8.
Mona Russo, President

5434 Leightronix
1125 N Cedar Rd
Mason, MI 48854
517-694-5589
800-243-5589
Fax: 517-694-1600
sales@leightronix.com
www.leightronix.com
Educational cable programming for schools and institutions.

5435 MCM Electronics
650 Congress Park Drive
Centerville, OH 45459
888-235-4692
800-543-4330
Fax: 800-765-6960
www.mcmelectronics.com
Offers a full line of electronics products and components for use in the classroom or at home. Over 40,000 parts.

5436 Magna Plan Corporation
71 Meadowbank Drive
Ottawa, On K2G0P
613-563-8727
800-361-1192
Fax: 518-298-2368
info@visualplanning.com
www.visualplanning.com
Overhead projectors.
Joseph P Josephson, Managing Director
Joel Boloten, Manager Consultation Service

5437 Mitsubishi Professional Electronics
200 Cottontail Lane
Somerset, NJ 08873-1231
732-560-4500
Fax: 732-560-4535
www.mitsubishielectric.com
Video projectors and electronics.

5438 Multi-Video
PO Box 35444
Charlotte, NC 28235-5444
704-563-4279
800-289-0111
Fax: 704-568-0219
Cameras, projectors and equipment.

5439 Naden Scoreboards
505 Fair Avenue
PO Box 636
Webster City, IA 50595-0636
515-832-4290
800-467-4290
Fax: 515-832-4293
www.naden.com
Electronic scoreboards for sports.
Russ Naden, President

5440 Navitar
200 Commerce Drive
Rochester, NY 14623
585-359-4000
800-828-6778
Fax: 585-359-4999
info@navitar.com
www.navitar.com
Overhead projectors and transparencies.
Julian Goldstein, Co-President
Jeremy Goldstein, Co-President

5441 Neumade Products Corporation
30 Pecks Lane
Newtown, CT 06470-2361
203-270-1100
Fax: 203-270-7778
neumadeGJ@aol.com
www.neumade.com
Overhead projectors, overhead transparencies, video projectors and electronics.
Gregory Jones, VP Sales

5442 Nevco Scoreboard Company
301 East Harris Avenue
Greenville, IL 62246-2151
618-664-0360
800-851-4040
Fax: 618-664-0398
sales@nevco.com
www.nevco.com
Nevco is a premier manufacturer and distributor of scoreboards, message centers and video displays.
G.D. Moore, President
Phil Robertson, Sales Manager

5443 Panasonic Communications & System Company
1 Panasonic Way
Secaucus, NJ 07094-2917
201-392-4818
800-524-1064
Fax: 201-392-4044
Cameras, projectors, equipment, players, CD-ROM equipment and school supplies.

5444 Quickset International
3650 Woodhead Drive
Northbrook, IL 60062-1895
800-247-6563
Fax: 847-498-1258
www.moogs3.com
Telecommunication equipment, cameras, projectors and electronics.

5445 RMF Products
1275 Paramount Pkwy.
PO Box 520
Batavia, IL 60510-0520
630-879-0020
Fax: 630-879-6749
info@rmfproducts.com
www.rmfproducts.com
Complete line of slide-related products including two and three-projector dissolve controls, programmers, multi-track tape recorders, audio-visual cables, remote controls and slide mounts.
Richard Frieders, President

5446 RTI-Research Technology International
4700 Chase
Lincolnwood, IL 60712-1689
847-677-3000
800-323-7520
Fax: 800-784-6733
sales@rtico.com
TapeChek Videotape Cleaner/Inspector/Rewinders make videotapes last longer and perform better. Find damage before tape is circulated. Also available is videotape/laser disc storage, shipping and care products.
Ray Short, President/ CEO
Tom Boyle, Senior VP, RTI Sales

5447 Recreation Equipment Unlimited
PO Box 4700
Pittsburgh, PA 15206-0700
412-731-3000
Fax: 412-731-3052
Scoreboards and sports/recreation equipment.

5448 Reliance Plastics & Packaging
25 Prospect Street
Newark, NJ 07105-3300
973-473-7200
Fax: 973-589-6440
Vinyl albums for audio or video cassettes, video discs, slides, floppy disks, CDs Protect, store and circulate valuable media properly.

5449 Resolution Technology
26000 Avenida Aeropuerto Spc 22
San Juan Capistrano, CA 92675-4736
949-661-6162
Fax: 949-661-0114
Video systems and videomicroscopy equipment.

5450 RobotiKits Direct
17141 Kingsview Avenue
Suite B
Carson, CA 90746-1207
310-515-6800
877-515-6652
Fax: 310-515-0927
info@owirobot.com
www.owirobot.com
New science and robotic kits for the millenium.
Craig Morioka, President
Armer Amante, General Manger

5451 S'Portable Scoreboards
3058 Alta Vista Drive
Fallbrook, CA 92028-8738
800-323-7745
Fax: 270-759-0066
Portable scoreboards, manual and electronic, sports timers and clocks.

452 SONY Broadcast Systems Product Division
1 Sony Drive
Park Ridge, NJ 07656
800-472-SONY
Interactive videodisc players for multimedia applications, VTRs, monitors, projection systems, video cameras, editing systems, printers and scanners, video presentation stands, audio cassette duplicators and video library systems.

453 Scott Resources/ Hubbard Scientific
National Training Aids
401 Hickory Street
PO Box 2121
Fort Collins, CO 80522-2121
970-484-7445
800-289-9299
Fax: 970-484-1198
custserv@amep.com
Microsilide system is a comprehensive, classroom-ready to help students learn. The microslide system combines superb photo-materials with detaled curriculum material and reproducible student activity sheets at an affrdable price.
Michael Warring, President
Candace Coffman, National Sales Manager

454 Shure Brothers
222 Hartrey Avenue
Evanston, IL 60202-3696
847-866-2200
Fax: 847-866-2551
Electronics, hardware and classroom supplies.

455 Swift Instruments
1190 N 4th Street
San Jose, CA 95112
408-293-2380
800-523-4544
Fax: 408-292-7967
Capture live or still microscopic images through your compound or stereo microscope and background sound images through your VCR or computer.

456 Tech World
Lab-Volt
PO Box 686
Farmingdale, NJ 07727
732-938-2000
800-522-8658
Fax: 732-774-8573
us@labvolt.com
www.labvolt.com
Tech World provides superior hands-on instruction using state-of-the-art technology and equipment. Lab-Volt also offers a full line of attractive, durable, and flexible modular classroom furniture.

457 Technical Education Systems
56 East End Drive
Gilberts, IL 60136
847-428-3085
800-451-2169
Fax: 847-428-3286
www.tii-tech.com
Hands-on application-oriented training systems integrating today's real world technologies in a flexible and easy-to-understand curriculum format.

458 Telex Communications
12000 Portland Avenue S
Burnsville, MN 55337
952-884-4051
800-828-6107
Fax: 952-884-0043
www.telex.com
Telex manufactures a variety of products for the educational market, including multimedia headphones, headsets and microphones; LCD computer and multimedia projection panels, group listening centers, video projectors, slide projectors, portable sound systems, wired and wireless intercoms, and wired and wireless microphones.
Dawn Wiome, Marketing Coordinator

5459 The Transcription Studio
The Transcription Studio, LLC
2267 Honolulu Ave
Suite 2
Montrose, CA 91020
818-248-3400
Fax: 818-846-8933
Operations@TranscriptionStudio.com
www.transcriptionstudio.com
We transcribe and provide closed-captioning services to the education and academic fields.
Jeff Zedlar, CEO
Deborah Hargreaves, Director of Operations

5460 Three M Visual Systems
3M Austin Center
6801 River Place Boulevard
Austin, TX 78726-4530
512-984-1800
800-328-1371
Fax: 512-984-6529
Overhead projectors, audiovisual carts and tables, and overhead transparencies.

5461 Tom Snyder Productions
100 Talcott Avenue
Watertown, MA 02472-5703
617-926-6000
800-342-0236
Fax: 800-304-1254
www.tomsnyder.com
Educational videotapes, videodiscs and computer programs.
Bridget Dalton, Ed.D., Author
Peggy Healy Stearns, Ph.D., Author

5462 Varitronics Systems
PO Box 234
Minneapolis, MN 55440
800-637-5461
Fax: 800-543-8966
Computer electronics, hardware, software and systems.

5463 Wholesale Educational Supplies
PO Box 120123
East Haven, CT 06512-0123
800-243-2518
Fax: 800-452-5956
Over 5,000 audio visual and video equipment and supplies offered at deep discount prices. Free 148 page catalog.
J Fields, President

Furniture & Equipment

5464 ASRS of America
304 Park Avenue South
11th Floor
New York, NY 10010
212-760-1607
Fax: 212-760-1614
info@elecompack.com
www.elecompack.com
Offers Elecompack, high density compact shelving which offers double storage capacity, automatic passive safety systems and custom front panels.
Walter M Kaufman

5465 Adden Furniture
710 Chelmsford Street
Lowell, MA 01851
978-454-7848
800-625-3876
Fax: 978-453-1449
Manufacturer of dormitory furniture, bookcases and shelving products.
Linda Kane, President
Patrick Furnari, CEO

5466 Air Technologies Corporation
25641 White Sands Street
Dana Point, CA 92629
949-661-5060
800-759-5060
Fax: 949-661-2454
ken@airtech.net
www.airtech.net
Develop and manufacture professional ergonomic computer products.

5467 Alma Industries
1300 Prospect Street
High Point, NC 27260-8329
336-578-5700
Fax: 336-578-0105
Bookcases and shelving for educational purposes.

5468 Angeles Group
9 Capper Drive
Dailey Industrial Park
Pacific, MO 63069
636-257-0533
800-346-6313
Fax: 636-257-5473
www.angeles-group.com
Housekeeping furniture and children play kitchen's made of durable and sturdy molded polyethylene. Baseline Furniture: tables, chairs, lockers, cubbies, bookcases, bookracks, silver rider trikes, spaceline cots, basic trikes, and bye bye buggies.
Tim Lynch, Director of Sales
David Curry, General Manager

5469 Anthro Corporation Technology Furniture
10450 SW Manhasset Dr.
Tualatin, OR 97062
503-691-2556
800-325-3841
Fax: 800-325-0045
www.anthro.com
Durable computer workstations and accessories; educational discounts; and dozens of shapes and sizes.
Shoaib Tureen, Co-Founder, President
Cathy Filgas, Co-Founder, VP-Sales

5470 Architectural Precast
10210 Winstead Lane
Cincinnati, OH 45246
513-772-4670
800-542-1738
Fax: 513-772-4672
est@archprecast.com
www.archprecast.com
Furniture, tables, playground equipment, desks.

5471 Blanton & Moore Company
PO Box 70
Barium Springs, NC 28010-0070
704-528-4506
Fax: 704-528-6519
www.blantonandmoore.com
Standard and custom library furniture crafted from fine hardwoods.
Billy Galliher, Manager Sales Administration

5472 Borroughs Corporation
3002 N Burdick Street
Kalamazoo, MI 49004-3483
616-342-0161
800-748-0227
Fax: 269-342-4161
www.borroughs.com
Bookcases and shelving products for educational purposes.

Zac Sweetland, VP, Sales
Tom Gambon, VP Finance & Administration

5473 Brady Office Machine Security
11056 S Bell Avenue
Chicago, IL 60643-3935
773-779-8349
800-326-8349
Fax: 773-779-9712
b.brady1060@aol.com
The Brady Office Machine Security physically protects all office machines, computer components, faxes, printers, VCRs, have wall and ceiling mounts for TVs.

Bernadette Brady, President
Don Brady, VP

5474 Bretford Manufacturing
9715 Soreng Avenue
Schiller Park, IL 60176-2186
540-678-2545
www.bretford.com
Manufacturer of a full line of AV and computer projection screens, television mounts, wood office furniture and a full line of combination wood shelving and steel library shelving.

5475 Brixey
13030 Inglewood Avenue
Suite 200
Hawthorne, CA 90250
310-263-7025
877-694-0752
Fax: 310-263-7250
brixey@brixey.com
www.brixey.com
Furniture for the classroom.

5476 Brodart Company, Automation Division
500 Arch Street
Williamsport, PA 17701
570-326-2461
800-233-8467
Fax: 570-326-1479
support@brodart.com
www.brodart.com
Brodart's Automation Division has been providing library systems, software, and services for over 25 years. Products include: library management systems, media management systems, Internet solutions, cataloged web sites, cataloging resource tools, union catalog solutions, public access catalogs, and bibliographic services.

Kasey Dibble, Marketing Coordinator
Sally Wilmoth, Director Marketing/Sales

5477 Buckstaff Company
Buckstaff Company
PO Box 2851
Oshkosh, WI 54903
920-235-5890
800-755-5890
Fax: 920-235-2018
sales@buckstaff.com
www.buckstaff.com
The premier manufacturer of library furniture in the United States. Quality and durability has been the Buckstaff trademark for 150 years.

Tom Mugerauer, Sales Manager, National

5478 Carpets for Kids Etc...
115 SE 9th Avenue
Portland, OR 97214-1301
503-232-1203
Fax: 503-232-1394
customerservice@carpetsforkids.com
www.carpetsforkids.com
Carpets, flooring and floorcoverings for educational purposes.

5479 Children's Factory
505 N Kirkwood Road
Saint Louis, MO 63122-3913
314-821-1441
Fax: 877-726-1714
Manufactures children's indoor play furniture.

5480 Children's Furniture Company
Gressco Ltd.
328 Moravian Valley Road
Waunakee, WI 53597-339
608-849-6300
800-345-3480
Fax: 608-849-6304
info@gresscoltd.com
www.gressco.com
Commercial quality furniture for children of all ages.

Robert Childers, President
Caroline Ashmore, Marketing/Sales

5481 Community Playthings
PO Box 901
Rifton, NY 12471-0901
800-777-4244
Fax: 800-336-5948
Unstructured maple toys and furniture including innovative products, especially for infants and toddlers.

5482 Continental Film
1466 Riverside Drive, Suite E
PO Box 5126
Chattanooga, TN 37406
423-622-1193
888-909-3456
Fax: 423-629-0853
www.continentalfilm.com
LCD projectors, distance learning systems, interactive white boards, document cameras.

Jim Webster, President
Courtney Sisk, VP

5483 Counterpoint
17237 Van Wagoner Road
Spring Lake, MI 49456-9702
800-628-1945
Fax: 616-847-3109
Audiovisual carts and tables.

5484 CyberStretch By Jazzercise
2460 Impala Drive
Carlsbad, CA 92010
760-476-1750
Fax: 760-602-7180
customercare@jazzercise.com
www.jazzercise.com
To foster and promote wellness through the production of free interactive software programs for business, government, educational and personal use.

Kathy Missett, Contact

5485 Da-Lite Screen Company
3100 North Detroit Street
Warsaw, IN 46582
574-267-8101
800-622-3737
Fax: 877-325-4832
info@da-lite.com
www.da-lite.com
Projection screens, monitor mounts, audiovisual carts and tables, overhead projectors and transparencies.

5486 DeFoe Furniture 4 Kids
910 S Grove Avenue
Ontario, CA 91761-8011
909-947-4459
Fax: 909-947-3377
Furniture, floorcoverings, toys, constructive playthings and more for children grades PreK-5.

5487 Decar Corporation
7615 University Avenue
Middleton Branch, WI 53562-3142
606-836-1911
Library shelving, storage facilities and furniture.

5488 DecoGard Products
Construction Specialties
Route 405
PO Box 400
Muncy, PA 17756
570-546-5941
Fax: 570-546-5169
Physical fitness and athletic floor coverings and mats.

5489 Engineering Steel Equipment Company
560 Central Drive
Suite 104
Virginia Beach, VA 23454
757-627-0762
Fax: 757-625-5754
Audiovisual carts and tables, bookcases and library shelving.

5490 Environments
PO Box 1348
Beaufort, SC 29901-1348
843-846-8155
800-348-4453
Fax: 843-846-2999
Publishes a catalog featuring equipment and materials for child care and early education. Offers durable and easy-to-maintain products with values that promote successful preschool, kindergarden, special needs and multi-age programs.

5491 Flagship Carpets
PO Box 1189
Chatsworth, GA 30705-1189
www.flagshipcarpets.com
Carpets, flooring and floorcoverings.

5492 Fleetwood Group
PO Box 1259
Holland, MI 49422-1259
616-396-1142
800-257-6390
Fax: 616-820-8300
Offers library and school furniture including shelving, check out desks and multimedia units.

5493 Fordham Equipment Company
3308 Edson Avenue
New York, NY 10469
718-379-7300
800-249-5922
Fax: 718-379-7312
Distributor and manufacturer of complete line of library supplies. Specialize in professional library shelving and furniture (wood and metal), mobile shelving and displayers. Catalog on request.

Al Robbins, President

5494 Good Sports
6031 Broad Street Mall
Pittsburgh, PA 15206-3009
412-661-9500
Mats, matting, floorcoverings and athletic training mats.

5495 Grafco
ERD
PO Box 71
Catasauqua, PA 18032-0071
800-367-6169
Fax: 610-782-0813
www.grafco.com
GRAFCO manufactures sturdy and durable computer furniture and tables designed for the educational environment.

Art Grafenberg, President

5496 Grammer
6989 N 55th Street
Suite A
Oakdale, MN 55128
651-770-6515
800-367-7328
Leading manufacturer and designer of ergonomically sound seating. Offers a chair designed especially for children.

5497 Greeting Tree
2709 Oak Haven Drive
San Marcos, TX 78666
512-392-0669
800-322-3199
Fax: 512-392-9660
Solid wood furniture for Reading Recovery, Reading Library, Primary and Early Childhood. Specializes in quality and customized furniture for today's classroom. Kitchen learning centers, storage units of all sizes and sorts, easels with over fourteen different display front possibilities.

BiAnnually

Cherie Krieger, Owner

5498 Gressco Ltd.
Gressco
328 Moravian Valley Road
PO Box 339
Waunakee, WI 53597-339
608-849-6300
800-345-3480
Fax: 608-849-6304
info@gresscoltd.com
www.gressco.com
Gressco is a supplier of a complete line of commercial children's HABA furniture and library displays for all types of medias. Kwik-case for the security protection of CDs, videos, and audiocassettes. Catalog available.

Caroline Ashmore, Marketing/Sales

5499 H Wilson Company
2245 Delany Road
Waukegan, IL 60087
708-339-5111
800-245-7224
Fax: 800-245-8224
info@hwilson.com
www.hwilson.com
Manufacturer of furniture for audio, video, and computers. Complete line of TV wall and ceiling mounts. Makers of the famous Tuffy color carts.

Matthew Glowiak, Director Sales/Marketing

5500 HON Company
200 Oak Street
Muscatine, IA 52761-4341
563-272-7100
800-466-8694
Fax: 563-264-7505
HONGSATeam@honcompany.com
www.hon.com
Bookcases and shelving units.

5501 Haworth
One Haworth Center
Holland, MI 49423-9576
616-393-3000
800-344-2600
Fax: 616-393-1570
www.haworth.com
Steel and wood desks, systems furniture, seating, files, bookcases, shelving units, and tables.

5502 Joy Carpets
104 West Forrest Road
Fort Oglethorpe, GA 30742-3675
706-866-3335
800-645-2787
Fax: 706-866-7928
joycarpets@joycarpets.com
www.joycarpets.com
Manufacturer of recreational and educational carpet for the classroom, home, or business. With a 10 year wear warranty, Class #1 Flammability rating, anti-stain and anti-bacterial treatment.

Joy Dobosh, Director Marketing

5503 KI
PO Box 8100
Green Bay, WI 54308-8100
920-468-8100
Fax: 920-468-2232
Library shelving, furniture, bookcases and more.

5504 Kensington Technology Group
2855 Campus Drive
San Mateo, CA 94403
650-572-2700
Fax: 650-572-9675
www.kensington.com
Offers several ergonomic mice.

5505 Kimball Office Furniture Company
1600 Royal Street
Jasper, IN 47549-1001
800-482-1818
800-482-1616
Fax: 812-482-8300
www.kimball.com
Bookcases, office equipment and shelving units for educational institutions.

5506 Lee Metal Products
PO Box 6
Littlestown, PA 17340-0006
717-359-4111
Fax: 717-359-4414
www.leemetal.com
Carts, tables, bookcases and storage cabinets.

Richard Kemper, President

5507 Library Bureau
172 Industrial Road
Fitchburg, MA 01420
978-345-7942
800-221-6638
Fax: 978-345-0188
melvil@librarybureau.com
www.librarybureau.com
Library shelving, bookcases, cabinets, circulation desks, carrels, computer workstations, upholstered seating.

Dennis Ruddy, Sr Project Manager

5508 Library Store
Library Store
112 E S Street
PO Box 0964
Tremont, IL 61568-964
309-925-5571
800-548-7204
Fax: 800-320-7706
customerservice@thelibrarystore.com
www.thelibrarystore.com
The Library Store offers through its full-line catalog, supplies and furniture items for librarians, schools, and churches. Free catalog available containing special product discounts.

Janice Smith, Marketing Director

5509 Little Tikes Company
2180 Barlow Road
Hudson, OH 44236-4199
330-656-3906
800-321-0183
Fax: 330-650-3221
www.littletikes.com
Offers a wide variety of furniture, educational games and toys and safety products for young children.

5510 Lucasey Manufacturing Company
2744 E 11th Street
Oakland, CA 94601-1429
510-534-1435
800-582-2739
Fax: 510-534-6828
www.lucasey.com
Audiovisual carts , tables, and TV mounts

Jan RenceTurnbull, National Accountant

5511 Lundia
600 Capitol Way
Jacksonville, IL 62650-1096
800-726-9663
Fax: 800-869-9663
www.lundiausa.com
Bookcases and shelving products, as well as furniture for educational institutions.

5512 Lyon Metal Products
PO Box 671
Aurora, IL 60507-0671
630-892-8941
800-433-8488
Fax: 630-892-8966
lyon@lyonworkspace.com
www.lyonworkspace.com
Bookcases and library shelving.

5513 Mateflex-Mele Corporation
2007 Beechgrove Place
Utica, NY 13501
315-733-1412
844-244-8464
Fax: 315-735-4372
www.mateflex.com
Manufacturers of Mateflex gymnasium flooring for basketball/gym courts. Mateflex II tennis court surfaces and Mateflex/Versaflex gridded safety floor tiles.

Gabe Martini, Sales Manager

5514 Microsoft Corporation
One Microsoft Way
Redmond, WA 98502-6399
425-882-8080
Fax: 206-703-2641
www.microsoft.com
Strives to produce innovative products and services that meet our costomers' evolving needs.

5515 Miller Multiplex
1610 Design Way
Dupo, IL 62239-1820
636-343-5700
800-325-3350
Fax: 618-286-6202
info@Miller-Group.com
www.multiplexdisplays.com
Announcement boards, classroom displays, charts and pghtography, books towers, post-

ers, frames, kiosk displays, presentation displays.

12 pages

Kathy Webster, Director Marketing

5516 ModuForm
ModuForm, Inc.
172 Industry Road
Fitchburg,, MA 01420
978-345-7942
800-221-6638
Fax: 978-345-0188
guestlog@moduform.com
www.moduform.com
Residence hall furniture, loung seating, tables, stacking chairs, fully upholstered seating.

Robert Kushnir, Nationals Sales Manager
Darlene Bailey, VP Sales/Marketing

5517 Morgan Buildings, Pools, Spas, RV's
12700 Hillcrest Rd Suite 278
PO Box 660280
Dallas, TX 75230
972-864-7300
800-935-0321
Fax: 972-864-7382
rmoran@morganusa.com
www.morganusa.com
Classrooms, campus and other buildings custom designed to meet your projects needs. Permanent and relocatable modular classrooms or complete custom facilities. Rent, lease or purchase options available.

5518 Norco Products
Division of USA McDonald Corporation
4985 Blue Mountain Road
PO Box 4227
Missoula, MT 59806
406-251-3800
800-662-2300
Fax: 406-251-3824
jim@norcoproducts.com
www.norcoproducts.com
Mobile cabinets, YRE funiture, tables, science labs, home economics displays, bookcases and shelving units, laboratory equipment, casework, cabinets, computer labs, podiums, award display cabinets, flags and flag poles.

Jim McDonald, President
Patti McDonald, Vice President

5519 Nova
421 W Industrial Avenue
PO Box 725
Effingham, IL 62401
800-730-6682
Fax: 800-940-6682
www.novadesk.com
Patented furniture solution for computer mounting incorporates the downward gaze, our visual system's natural way of viewing close objects. Scientific evidence indicates that viewing a computer monitor at a downward gaze angle is a better solution than with traditional monitor placement.

5520 Oscoda Plastics
5585 North Huron Avenue
PO Box 189
Oscoda, MI 48750
989-739-6900
800-544-9538
Fax: 800-548-7678
sales@oscodaplastics.com
www.protect-allflooring.com
Oscoda Plastics manufactures Protect-All Specialty Flooring from 100% recycled post-industrial vinyls. Protect-All is perfect for use in locker rooms, kitchen/walk-in cooler floors, fitness areas, weight rooms, gym floors, or as a temporary gym floor cover.

Joe Brinn, National Sales Manager
Rick Maybury, Sales Coordinator

5521 Palmer Snyder
201 High Street
Conneautville, PA 16406
814-587-6313
800-762-0415
Fax: 814-587-2375
Tables are built with the highest quality materials for long life and low maintenance. A complete range of rugged options.

5522 Paragon Furniture
2224 East Randol Mill Road
Arlington, TX 76011
817-633-3242
800-451-8546
Fax: 817-633-2733
customerservice@paragoninc.com
www.paragoninc.com
Offers a line of furniture for classroom, labs, science, and libraries.

Carl Brockway, VP Sales
Mark Hubbard, President

5523 Pawling Corporation
Borden Lane
Wassaic, NY 12592
845-373-9300
800-431-3456
Fax: 800-451-2200
sales@pawling.com
Pawling is an approved manufacturer by E&I cooperative buying for athletic flooring, traffic safety products, wall and corner protection and entrance mat systems.

Richard Meyer, Sales Manager

5524 Peerless Sales Company
1980 N Hawthorne Avenue
Melrose Park, IL 60160-1167
708-865-8870
Fax: 708-865-2941
Auidovisual carts and tables.

5525 RISO
300 Rosewood Drive
Suite 210
Danvers, MA 01923-4527
978-777-7377
800-876-7476
Fax: 978-777-2517
The Risograph digital printer offers high speed copy/duplicating at up to 130 pages per minute. A 50-sheet document feeder lets people print multi-page documents quickly and inexpensively. Specifically designed to handle medium run length jobs that are too strenuous for copiers. Offers various other products and office equipment available to the education community.

5526 Research Technology International
4700 Chase Avenue
Lincolnwood, IL 60646-1689
847-677-3000
800-323-7520
Fax: 847-677-1311
sales@rtico.com
www.ritco.com
Tape check, Video tape cleaner, disk chack optical, disc rejestor.

5527 Russ Bassett Company
8189 Byron Road
Whittier, CA 90606-2615
562-945-2445
800-350-2445
Fax: 562-698-8972
info@russbassett.com
www.russbassett.com
Shelving units, furniture and bookcases for educational institutions.

5528 SNAP-DRAPE
2045 Westgate Drive
Suite 100
Carrollton, TX 75006-5116
972-466-1030
800-527-5147
Fax: 800-230-1330
info@snapdrape.com
www.snapdrape.com
Table and stage skirting

Melissa Acton, Marketing/Sales Assistant

5529 Screen Works
2201 W Fulton Street
Chicago, IL 60612
312-243-8265
800-294-8111
Fax: 312-243-8290
screens@thescreenworks.com
www.thescreenworks.com
Manufacturers the E-Z Fold brand of portable projection screens and offers a full line of portable presentation accessories and services, including: an extensive screen rental inventory; audio-visula roll carts; lecterns and PaperStand flip charts. Custom screen sizes, screen surface cleaning and frame repair service also available.

David Hull, National Sales Manager

5530 Spacemaster Systems
155 W Central Avenue
Zeeland, MI 49464-1601
616-772-2406
Fax: 616-772-2100
Standard and Custom Shelving Systems and USEFUL AISLE Storage Systems.

5531 Spacesaver Corporation
1450 Janesville Avenue
Fort Atkinson, WI 53538-2798
920-563-6362
800-255-8170
Fax: 920-563-2702
info@spacesaver.com
www.spacesaver.com
Flexible Spacesaver custom designs high-density mobile storage systems. Will double your storage and filing capacity while increasing usable floor space. Store files, supplies, manuals, books, drawings, multi-media, etc.

5532 Synsor Corporation
1920 Merrill Creek Pkwy
Everett, WA 98203-5859
425-551-1300
800-426-0193
Fax: 425-551-1313
www.synsor.com
Offers a full line of educational furniture.

5533 Tab Products Company
1400 Page Mill Road
Palo Alto, CA 94304-1124
800-672-3109
Fax: 920-387-1802
Bookcases and shelving products for library/media centers.

5534 Tepromark International
206 Mosher Avenue
Woodmere, NY 11598-1662
516-569-4533
800-645-2622
Fax: 516-295-5991
Trolley Rail wall guards, corner guards, wall guards with hand rails, door plates, chair rolls,

kick plates, vinyl floor mats and carpet mats. All mats promote safety from slipping in wet areas.

Robert Rymers

5535 Tesco Industries
1038 E Hacienda Street
Bellville, TX 77418-2828
979-865-3176
800-699-5824
Fax: 979-865-9026
tesco@tesco-ind.com
www.tesco-ind.com
Bookcases and shelving units.

5536 Texwood Furniture
1353 N 2nd Street
Taylor, TX 76574
512-352-3000
888-878-0000
Fax: 512-352-3084
ajohnson@texwood.com
www.texwood.com
Wood library furniture, shelving, computer tables and circulation desks and early childhood furniture.

Andrea Johnson, Director Marketing
Dave Gaskers, VP Sales/Marketing

5537 Tot-Mate by Stevens Industries
704 West Main Street
Teutopolis, IL 62467-1212
217-857-7100
800-397-8687
Fax: 217-857-7101
timw@stevens.com
www.stevensind.com
Early learning furniture manufactured by Stevens Industries. Features include 16 color choices, plastic laminate surfacing, rounded corners, beveled edges, safe and strong designs. Items offered include change tables, storage shelving, book displays, teacher cabinets, housekeeping sets and locker cubbies.

Randy Ruholl, Sales Representative
Paul Jones, Customer Service

5538 University Products
University Products
517 Main Street
PO Box 101
Holyoke, MA 1040
413-532-3372
800-628-1912
Fax: 413-532-9281
info@universityproducts.com
www.universityproducts.com
University Products specializes in top-quality archival materials for conservation and preservation as well as library and media centers supplies, equipment, and furnishings.

Scott E. Magoon, President/ COO

5539 W. C. Heller & Company
Heller
201 W Wabash Avenue
Montpelier, OH 43543
419-485-3176
Fax: 419-485-8694
wcheller@hotmail.com
Complete line of wood library furniture in oak and birch, custom cabinetry and special modifications. Over 110 years in business.

Robert L Heller II, VP Sales

5540 Wheelit
PO Box 352800
Toledo, OH 43635-2800
419-531-4900
800-523-7508
Fax: 419-531-6415
Carts and storage containers.

5541 White Office Systems
50 Boright Avenue
Kenilworth, NJ 07033
908-272-6700
800-275-1442
Fax: 908-931-0840
www.whitesystems.com
Shelving, bookcases, furniture and products for libraries, media centers, schools and offices.

5542 Whitney Brothers Company
PO Box 644
Keene, NH 03431-0644
603-352-2610
Fax: 603-357-1559
www.whitneybros.com
Manufactures children's furniture products for preschools and day care centers.

5543 Winsted Corporation
10901 Hampshire Avenue S
Minneapolis, MN 55438
952-944-9050
800-447-2257
Fax: 800-421-3839
info@winsted.com
www.winsted.com
Video furniture, accessories, tape storage systems and lan rack systems.

Rich McPherson, Western Regional Manager
Kim Richter, Western Regional Manager

5544 Wood Designs
PO Box 1308
Monroe, NC 28111-1308
704-283-7508
800-247-8465
Fax: 704-289-1899
www.wooddesigns.org
Manufactures wooden educational equipment and teaching toys for early learning environments. Sold through school supply dealers and stores.

Dennis Gosney, President
Paul Schneider, VP Sales/Marketing

5545 Worden Company
199 E 17th Street
Holland, MI 49423
800-748-0561
Fax: 616-392-2542
info@wordencompany.com
www.wordencompany.com
Furniture for office, business, school or library.

Maintenance

5546 American Locker Security Systems
2701 Regent Blvd
Suite 200
DFW Airport, TX 75261
817-329-1600
800-828-9118
Fax: 817-421-8618
info@americanlocker.com
www.americanlocker.com
Lockers featuring coin operated lockers.

David L Henderson, VP/General Manager

5547 Atlantic Fitness Products
PO Box 300
Linthicum Hts, MD 21090-0300
410-859-3907
800-445-1855
www.atlanticfitnessproducts.com
School lockers and fitness/physical education products and equipment.

5548 Barco Products
24 N. Washington Ave.
Batavia, IL 60510
800-338-2697
sales@barcoproducts.com
www.barcoproducts.com
Maintenance and safety products made from recycled materials.

Cyril Matter, CEO
Judy Leonard, Marketing Manager

5549 Blaine Window Hardware
17319 Blaine Drive
Hagerstown, MD 21740
800-678-1919
Fax: 888-250-3960
parts@Blainewindow.com
www.blainewindow.com
Producers of window and door parts including window repair hardware, custom screens locker hardware, chair glides, panic exit hardware, balance systems, door closers and motorized operators.

David Crouse, President
Robert Slick, Purchasing Agent

5550 Bleacherman, M.A.R.S.
105 Mill Street
Corinth, NY 12822
518-654-9084
800-628-1332
Fax: 518-654-2232
School lockers.

5551 Burkel Equipment Company
14670 Hanks Drive
Red Bluff, CA 96080-9475
800-332-3993
School lockers, hardware and security equipment, maintenance and repair supplies.

5552 Chemtrol
Santa Barbara Control Systems
5375 Overpass Road
Santa Barbara, CA 93111-5879
800-621-2279
Fax: 805-683-1893
www.ccdc.ucsb.edu
Maintenance supplies for educational institutions.

Karl Johan Astrom, Mechanical Engineering
Bassam Bamieh, Mechanical Engineering

5553 Contact East
Stanley Supply & Services, Inc.
335 Willow Street
North Andover, MA 01845-5995
978-682-9844
800-225-5370
Fax: 800-743-8141
sales@contacteast.com
www.contacteast.com
Maintenance supplies and equipment.

5554 DeBourgh Manufacturing Company
27505 Otero Avenue
PO Box 981
La Junta, CO 81050
719-384-8161
800-328-8829
Fax: 719-384-7713
sales@debourgh.com
www.debourgh.com
Security equipment, hardware, storage and school lockers.

Ralph Malers, Employee

5555 Dow Corning Corporation
2200 W. Salzburg Rd.
PO Box 0994
Midland, MI 48686-0994

989-496-4000
Fax: 989-496-4572
www.dowcorning.com/content/publishedlit/Global_Fast_Facts.pd
Maintenance supplies and equipment.
Robert D. Hansen, President/ CEO
Cathy Yang, Global Media Relations,China

5556 Dri-Dek Corporation
Kendall Products
P.O. Box 8656
Naples, FL 34101
239-643-0448
800-348-2398
Fax: 800-828-4248
info@dri-dek.com
www.dri-dek.com
Oxy-BI vinyl compound in the Dri-Dek flooring systems helps halt the spread of infectious fungus and bacteria in areas with barefooted traffic. This compound makes Dri-Dek's anti-skid, self-draining surface ideal for use in the wettest conditions.

5557 Esmet
1406 5th Street SW
Canton, OH 44702
330-452-9132
800-321-0870
Fax: 330-452-2557
info@esmet.com
www.esmet.com
Lockers for the educational institution.

5558 Ex-Cell Metal Products
11240 Melrose Avenue
Franklin, IL 60131
847-451-0451
Fax: 847-451-0458
Maintenance supplies and repair equipment.

5559 Facilities Network
PO Box 868
Mahopac, NY 10541-0868
845-621-1664
School lockers and security system units.

5560 Fibersin Industries
37031 E Wisconsin Avenue
PO Box 88
Oconomowoc, WI 53066-88
262-567-4427
Fax: 262-567-4814
info@fiberesin.com
www.fiberesin.com
School lockers and maintenance supplies. Desks, cradenzas, bookcases for school adm. Tables for cafeteria and adm.

5561 Flagpole Components
4150A Kellway Circle
Addison, TX 75001
972-250-0893
800-634-4926
Fax: 972-380-5143
Maintenance and repair supplies and equipment.

5562 Flexi-Wall Systems
PO Box 89
208 Carolina Dr.
Liberty, SC 29657-0089
864-843-3104
800-843-5394
Fax: 864-843-9318
flexiwall@bellsouth.net
www.flexiwall.com/pages/home_page.htm
Maintenance and repair supplies for educational institutions.

5563 Flo-Pac Corporation
700 Washington Avenue N
Suite 400
Minneapolis, MN 55401-1130
612-332-6240
Fax: 612-344-1663
Maintenance and repair supplies.

5564 Four Rivers Software Systems
400 Penn Center Blvd
Suite 450
Pittsburgh, PA 15235
412-256-9020
Fax: 412-273-6420
www.frsoft.com
Maintenance and repair supplies, business and administrative software and supplies.
Pierre Harrison, Regional VP,Healthcare
M. Lynn O'Donnell, Dir. Of Marketing

5565 Friendly Systems
3878 Oak Lawn Avenue
#1008-300
Dallas, TX 75219-4460
972-857-0399
Maintenance and repair supplies.

5566 GE Capitol Modular Space
40 Liberty Boulevard
Malvern, PA 19355
610-225-2836
800-523-7918
Fax: 610-225-2762
www.modspace.com
School lockers, shelving and storage facilities.

5567 Glen Products
13765 Alton Parkway
Suite A
Irvine, CA 92618-1627
800-486-4455
Storage facilities, lockers and security systems.

5568 Global Occupational Safety
22 Harbor Park Drive
Port Washington, NY 11050-4650
516-625-4466
Safety storage facilities, shelving, lockers and hardware.

5569 Graffiti Gobbler Products
6428 Blarney Stone Court
Springfield, VA 22152-2106
800-486-2512
Educational maintenance and repair supplies and equipment.

5570 H&H Enterprises
PO Box 585
Grand Haven, MI 49417-9430
616-846-8972
800-878-7777
Fax: 616-846-1004
www.handhent.com
Maintenance and repair supplies.

5571 HAZ-STOR
75 Camrose Cres.
Underwood., Ql 4119
073-341-6200
800-727-2067
Fax: 073-341-6211
Manufacturer of pre-fabricated steel structures including hazardous material storage buildings and outdoor flammables lockers as well as waste compactors and drum crushers, secondary containment products and process shelters.
Roger Quinlan, National Sales Manager
Antoinette Balthazor, Marketing Coordinator

5572 HOST/Racine Industries
1405 16th Street
Racine, WI 53403-2249
800-558-9439
Fax: 262-637-1624
Maintenance and repair supplies.

5573 Hako Minuteman
14N845 U.S. Route 20
Pingree Grove, IL 60140
847-264-5400
Fax: 847-683-5207
www.minutemanintl.com
Maintenance and repair supplies for educational institutions.

5574 Haws Corporation
1455 Kleppe Ln
Sparks, NV 89431
775-359-4712
888-640-4297
Fax: 775-359-7424
haws@hawsco.com
www.hawsco.com
Manufacturer of drinking fountains, electric water coolers, emergency drench showers and eyewashes.
Tom White, President
Aaron Cross, Jr., VP of Operations

5575 Honeywell
Home & Building Control
PO Box 524
Minneapolis, MN 55440-0524
973-455-2001
Fax: 973-455-4807
Maintenance and cleaning products for educational purposes.

5576 Insta-Foam Products
2050 N Broadway Street
Joliet, IL 60435-2571
800-800-FOAM
Fax: 800-326-1054
Maintenance supplies, cleaning products and repair hardware.

5577 Interstate Coatings
1005 Highway 301 S
Wilson, NC 27895
800-533-7663
Hardware, repair, maintenance and cleaning supplies.

5578 J.A. Sexauer
PO Box 1000
White Plains, NY 10602
800-431-1872
Fax: 888-499-0441
www.casinovendors.com/vendor/j-a-sexauer
Cleaning and maintenance supplies for educational institutions.

5579 Karnak Corporation
330 Central Avenue
Clark, NJ 07066
732-388-0300
800-526-4236
Fax: 732-388-9422
www.karnakcorp.com/Contact.aspx
Maintenance and cleaning supplies.
Sarah J. Jelin, Chairwoman, President
John McDermott, Vice-Chairman

5580 Kool Seal
Unifex Professional Maintenance Products
1499 Enterprise Pkwy
Twinsburg, OH 44087-2241
800-321-0572
Fax: 330-425-9778
Maintenance, repair and cleaning supplies.

5581 LDSystems
407 Garden Oaks
Houston, TX 77018
713-695-9400
Fax: 713-695-8015
info@ldsystems.com
www.ldsystems.com
Environmentally-safe bottom pump air powered spray containers to dispense cleaning supplies such as window sprays, for cooling during workouts and general storage containers.

Dick Stark

5582 List Industries
401 Jim Moran Blvd.
PO Box 9601
Deerfield Beach, FL 33442
954-429-9155
800-776-1342
Fax: 954-428-3843
www.listindustries.com
School lockers and storage facilities.

JR List, President
Max H. List, Founder

5583 Maintenance
1051 W Liberty Street
Wooster, OH 44691-3307
330-264-6262
800-892-6701
Fax: 800-264-2578
Provides pavement maintenance products for parking lots, driveways, tennis courts, etc.

Robert E Huebner

5584 Master Bond
154 Hobart Street
Hackensack, NJ 07601
201-343-8983
Fax: 201-343-2132
main@masterbond.com
www.masterbond.com
Repair hardware, maintenance and cleaning products for schools.

Dr. Walter Brenne, Technical Director

5585 Master Builders
Admixture Division
23700 Chagrin Boulevard
Cleveland, OH 44122-5554
216-831-5500
Fax: 216-839-8815
School hardware, maintenance and repair supplies and equipment.

5586 Medart
Division of Carriage Industries
PO Box 435
Garrettsville, OH 44231-0435
662-453-2506
School lockers.

5587 Modular Hardware
8190 N Brookshire Court
Tucson, AZ 85741-4037
520-744-4424
800-533-0042
Fax: 800-533-7942
School hardware, for repair and maintenance purposes.

5588 Penco Products
1820 Stonehenge Drive
Greenville, NC 27858
610-666-0500
800-562-1000
Fax: 610-666-7561
general@pencoproducts.com
www.pencoproducts.com
School lockers.

L. Lewis Sagendorph, Founder
Sarah Crandell, Accounts Payable

5589 Permagile Industries
910 Manor Lane
Bay Shore, NY 11706-7512
516-349-1100
Maintenance and cleaning products and supplies.

5590 Powr-Flite Commercial Floor Care Equipment
3301 Wichita Court
Fort Worth, TX 76140
817-551-0700
800-880-2913
Fax: 817-551-0719
info@powr-flite.com
www.powrflite.com
School maintenance supplies focusing on floor care equipment products, accessories and parts.

Curtis Walton, Contact

5591 ProCoat Products
260 Centre Street
Suite D
Holbrook, MA 02343
781-767-2270
Fax: 781-767-2271
info@procoat.com
www.procoat.com
Designed to restore aged and discolored acoustical ceiling tiles. Acoustical and fire retarding qualities are maintained. Ceiling restoration is cost effective, time efficient and avoids solid waste disposal. Products available also for preventative maintenance programs.

Kenneth Woolf, Borad Chairman, Founder
Lisa Ploss, President

5592 Rack III High Security Bicycle Rack Company
675 Hartz Avenue
Suite 306
Danville, CA 94526-3859
800-733-1971
Lockers, bicycle racks, storage facilities and hardware.

5593 Republic Storage Systems Company
1038 Belden Avenue NE
Canton, OH 44705-1454
330-438-5800
800-477-1255
Fax: 330-454-7772
Storage facilities, containers, maintenance products, shelving and lockers.

John Berger, Co-Founder
Wilson Berger, Co-Founder

5594 Safety Storage
855 N. 5th Street
Charleston, IL 61920
800-344-6539
Fax: 831-637-7405
www.safetystorage.com
Equipment, supplies and storage containers for maintenance and educational purposes.

Lynn Dufek, CEO

5595 Salsbury Industries
1010 E 62nd Street
Los Angeles, CA 90001-1598
323-846-6700
800-624-5269
Fax: 323-846-6800
salsbury@mailboxes.com
www.mailboxes.com
School lockers, maintenance products and storage facilities.

5596 Servicemaster
Education Management Services
860 Ridge Lake Boulevard
Downers Grove, IL 60515
800-926-9700
A provider of facility management support services to education.

Mark A. Smith, Ed.D, President
Joshua T. Fischer, PhD, VP of Operations

5597 Sheffield Plastics
Bayer MaterialScience LLC
119 Salisbury Road
Sheffield, MA 01257
413-229-8711
800-628-5084
Fax: 413-229-8717
www.sheffieldplastics.com
Maintenance and cleaning products for schools.

5598 Southern Sport Surfaces
PO Box 1817
Cumming, GA 30028-1817
770-887-3508
800-346-1632
Maintenance and cleaning products for schools.

5599 System Works
3301 Windy Ridge Parkway
Marietta, GA 30067
770-952-8444
800-868-0497
Fax: 770-955-2977
Addresses the capacity, quality and safety requirements of maintenance operations. Comprehensive and interactive it maximizes maintenance resources, people, tools and replacement parts, for increased productivity and equipment reliability, reduced inventories and accurate cost accounting.

Karen Kharlead

5600 TENTEL Corporation
330 Industrial Drive # 4
Placerville, CA 95667
530-344-0183
800-538-6894
Fax: 530-344-0186
www.tentel.com
Cleaning, repair and maintenance products for educational institutions.

5601 Tiffin Systems
450 Wall Street
Tiffin, OH 44883-1366
419-447-8414
800-537-0983
Fax: 419-447-8512
mdysard@tiffinmetal.com
www.tiffinmetal.com
Lockers, storage containers and shelving.

Matt Dysard, President/ COO
Will Heddles, CEO

5602 Topog-E Gasket Company
1224 N Utica
Tulsa, OK 74110
918-587-6649
Fax: 918-587-6961
info@topog-e.com
www.topog-e.com
Maintenance supplies and products.

5603 Tru-Flex Recreational Coatings
Touraine Paints
1760 Revere Beach Pkwy
Everett, MA 02149-5906
800-325-0017
Maintenance, floor care, coatings and repair supplies for upkeep of schools and institutions.

5604 **Wagner Spray Tech Corporation**
1770 Fernbrook Lane N
Minneapolis, MN 55447
763-553-0759
Fax: 763-553-7288
www.wagnerspraytech.com
Maintenance supplies, floor care, cleaning and repair products and equipment.

5605 **Wilmar**
303 Harper Drive
Moorestown, NJ 08057
800-345-3335
800-345-3000
Fax: 800-220-3291
customercare@wilmar.com
www.wilmar.com
Maintenance and repair products, hardware and supplies.

5606 **Witt Company**
4454 Steel Place
Cincinnati, OH 45209-1184
513-979-3127
800-543-7417
Fax: 513-979-3134
Lockers, maintenance supplies and storage containers for educational purposes.

5607 **Zep Manufacturing**
1310 Seaboard Industrial Dr.
Atlanta, GA 30318
404-352-1680
877-428-9937
www.zep.com
Maintenance and cleaning supplies.

Scientific Equipment

5608 **Adventures Company**
435 Main Street
Johnson City, NY 13790-1935
607-729-6512
800-477-6512
Fax: 607-729-4820
A full line of supplies and equipment for science and technology education.

D Hetherington

5609 **Alfa Aesar**
26 Parkridge Rd
Ward Hill, MA 01835
978-521-6300
800-343-0660
Fax: 978-521-6350
www.alfa.com
Laboratory equipment and supplies.

5610 **American Chemical Society**
1155 16th Street NW
Washington, DC 20036
202-872-4600
800-333-9511
Fax: 202-833-7732
service@acs.org
www.@acs.org
Exhibits hands-on activities and programs for K-12 and college science curriculum.

Pat N. Confalone, Chair
Diane Grob Schmidt, President

5611 **Arbor Scientific**
PO Box 2750
Ann Arbor, MI 48106-2750
734-477-9370
800-367-6695
Fax: 734-477-9373
www.arborsci.com
Innovative products for Science Education.

56 pages Bi-Annual Catalog

Dave Barnes, Marketing Director

5612 **Astronomy to Go**
1115 Melrose Avenue
Melrose Park, PA 19027-3017
215-831-0485
Fax: 215-831-0486
astro2go@aol.com
Programs include Starlab Planetarium presentations, hands-on demonstrations, slides and lecture shows and energy observing sessions with our many telescopes. We are funded through our traveling museum shop which carries a large assortment of t-shirts, jewelry, gifts, books, and teaching supplies as well as an extensive selection of meterorites.

Bob Summerfield, Director/ Founder

5613 **CEM Corporation**
3100 Smith Farm Road
Matthews, NC 28104
704-821-7015
Fax: 704-821-7894
www.cem.com
Laboratory and scientific supplies, furniture, casework and equipment.

5614 **Carolina Biological Supply Company**
2700 York Road
Burlington, NC 27215-3398
336-584-0381
800-334-5551
Fax: 800-222-7112
carolina@carolina.com
www.carolina.com
Educational products for teachers and students of biology, molecular biology, biotechnology, chemistry, earth science, space science, physics, and mathematics. Carolina serves elementary schools through universities with living and preserved animals and plants, prepared microscope slides, microscopes, audiovisuals, books, charts, models, computer software, games, apparatus, and much more.

5615 **Challenger Center for Space Science Education**
422 1st St. SE
3rd Floor
Washington, DC 20003
202-827-1580
800-969-5747
Fax: 703-683-7546
www.challenger.org
Is a global not-for-profit education organization created in 1986 by familes of the astronauts tragically lost during the last flight of the Challenger Space Shuttle. Dedicated to the educaltional spirit of that mission, Challenger center develops Learning Centers and othe educational programs worldwide to continue the mission to engage students in science and math education

Dr. Lance Bush, President/ CEO
Steven Goldberg, CFO

5616 **ChronTrol Corporation**
7525-D Mission Gorge Rd.
San Diego, CA 92120
619-282-8686
800-854-1999
Fax: 619-563-6563
info@chrontrol.com
www.chrontrol.com
Scientific equipment, laboratory supplies and furniture.

5617 **Classic Modular Systems**
1911 Columbus Street
Two Rivers, WI 54241
414-793-2269
800-558-7625
Fax: 414-793-2896
info@classicmodular.com
www.classicmodular.com
Laboratory equipment, shelving, cabinets and markerboards.

Cathy Albers, Advertising Manager

5618 **Columbia University's Biosphere 2 Center**
Highway 77 & Biosphere Road
Oracle, AZ 85623
520-838-6155
Fax: 520-838-6136
www.b2science.org
Educational programs and products.

Pierre Meystre, Director
Joaquin Ruiz, Director

5619 **Connecticut Valley Biological Supply Company**
82 Valley Road
PO Box 326
Southampton, MA 01073
413-527-4030
800-628-7748
Fax: 800-355-6813
connval@ctvalleybio.com
www.connecticutvalleybiological.com
Cultures and specimens, instruments, equipment, hands-on kits, books, software, audiovisuals, models and charts for teaching botany, zoology, life science, anatomy, physiology, genetics, astronomy, entomology, microscopy, AP Biology, microbiology, horticulture, biotechnology, earth science, natural history and environmental science.

Marschall P. Lohr, Founder

5620 **Crow Canyon Archaeological Center**
23390 Road K
Cortez, CO 81321
970-565-8975
800-422-8975
Fax: 970-565-4859
webmanager@crowcanyon.org
www.crowcanyon.org
Experiential education programs in archaeology and Native American history. Programs offered for school groups, teachers and other adults.

ISBN: 0-7872-6748-1

M Elaine Davis and Marjorie R Connelly, Author
W. Bruce Milne, Chair
Barbara L. Schwietert, Vice-Chairman

5621 **Cuisenaire Company of America**
10 Bank Street
#5026
White Plains, NY 10606-1933
914-997-2600
Fax: 914-684-6137
Science materials and equipment.

5622 **DISCOVER Science Program**
105 Terry Drive
Suite 120
Newtown, PA 18940-1872
800-448-3399
Fax: 215-579-8589
Features the newest developments in a wide range of science topics and provides an easy way for teachers to stay current and up-to-date in the world of science. The DISCOVER Program offers the DISCOVER magazine at the lowest possible price.

623 Delta Biologicals
PO Box 26666
Tucson, AZ 85726-6666
520-790-7737
800-821-2502
Fax: 520-745-7888
customerservice@deltabio.com
www.deltabio.com
Products and supplies for science and biology educators for over 30 years. Preserves specimens, laboratory furniture, microscopes, anatomy models, balances and scales, dissection supplies, lab safety supplies, multimedia, plant presses.

Lynn Hugins, Marketing
Darlene Harris, Customer Service Manager

624 Delta Biologicals Catalog
PO Box 26666
Tucson, AZ 85726-6666
520-790-7737
800-821-2502
Fax: 520-745-7888
customerservice@deltabio.com
www.deltabio.com

96 pages

Lynn Hugins, Marketing
Darlene Harris, Customer Service Manager

625 Detecto Scale Corporation
203 E Daugherty Street
Webb City, MO 64870
417-673-4631
800-641-2008
Fax: 417-673-5001
detecto@cardet.com
www.detectoscale.com
Scientific equipment and supplies for educational laboratories.

Johnathan Sabo, VP Marketing

626 Dickson Company
930 S Westwood Avenue
Addison, IL 60101-4997
630-543-3747
800-757-3747
Fax: 800-676-0498
dicksoncsr@dicksondata.com
www.dicksondata.com
Laboratory instruments, electronics, furniture and equipment.

Mike Unger, President
Mark Kohlmeier, CFO

627 Donald K. Olson & Associates
PO Box 858
Bonsall, CA 92003-0858
Fax: 19-4 -
Mineral and fossil samples for educational purposes.

628 Dranetz Technologies
1000 New Durham Road
Edison, NJ 08818-4019
732-287-3680
800-372-6832
Fax: 732-287-9014
www.dranetz.com
Laboratory instruments, equipment and supplies.

629 Edmund Scientific - Scientifics Catalog
E726 Edscorp Building
Department 16A1
Barrington, NJ 08007
856-547-3488
Fax: 856-573-6295
Over 5,000 products including a wide selection of microscopes, telescopes, astronomy aids, fiber optic kits, demonstration optics, magnets and science discover products used in science fair projects.

Nancy McGonigle, President

5630 Educational Products
1342 N I35 E
Carrollton, TX 75006
972-245-9512
Fax: 972-245-5468
Science display boards, workshop materials and science fair accessories.

5631 Edwin H. Benz Company
73 Maplehurst Avenue
Providence, RI 02908
401-331-5650
Fax: 401-331-5685
engineering@benztesters.com
www.benztesters.com
Laboratory equipment.

Ted Benz, President

5632 Electro-Steam Generator Corporation
50 Indel Ave.
PO Box 438
Rancocas, NJ 08073-0438
609-288-9071
866-617-0764
Fax: 609-288-9078
www.electrosteam.com
Laboratory equipment and supplies. Manufacture steam generators for sterilizers, autoclaves, clean rooms, pure steam humidification, laboratories, steam rooms, and cleaning of all kinds.

Jack Harlin, Sales/Marketing Associate

5633 Estes-Cox Corporation
PO Box 227
Penrose, CO 81240-0227
719-372-6565
800-820-0202
Fax: 719-372-3217
webcs@centurims.com
www.esteseducator.com
Supplier of model rockets, engines and supporting videos, curriculums and educational publications for K-12.

Ann Grimm, Director Education

5634 FOTODYNE
950 Walnut Ridge Drive
Hartland, WI 53029
262-369-7000
800-362-3642
Fax: 262-369-7017
Biotechnology curriculum equipment.

Brian Walsh, President & Owner
Dennis Devitt, Board Member

5635 First Step Systems
PO Box 2304
Jackson, TN 38302-2304
800-831-0877
Fax: 216-361-0829
Developed an effective, safe and less expensive approach to blood exposure safety for schools and classrooms that both help comply with OSHA requirements and is easy to purchase and resupply.

Susan Staples, Account Manager
Renee Carr, Bid Support

5636 Fisher Scientific Company
1410 Wayne Avenue
Indiana, PA 15701-3940
724-357-1000
Fax: 724-357-1019
A full line of laboratory and scientific supplies and equipment for educational institutions.

5637 Fisher Scientific/EMD
3970 John Creek Court
Suite 500
Suwanee, GA 30024
770-871-4500
800-766-7000
Fax: 800-926-1166
Supplier of chemistry, biology and physics laboratory supplies and equipment.

5638 Fisons Instruments
8 Forge Parkway
Franklin, MA 02038-3157
978-524-1000
Laboratory equipment and instruments for the scientific classroom.

5639 Flinn Scientific
PO Box 219
Batavia, IL 60510
630-879-6900
800-452-1261
Fax: 866-452-1436
flinn@flinnsci.com
www.flinnsci.com
Laboratory safety supplies.

5640 Forestry Supplies
PO Box 8397
205 West Rankin St.
Jackson, MS 39284-8397
601-354-3565
800-647-5368
Fax: 800-543-4203
fsi@forestry-suppliers.com
www.forestry-suppliers.com
Field and lab equipment for earth, life and environmental sciences.

Ken Peacock, VP Marketing
Debbie Raddin, Education Specialist

5641 Frank Schaffer Publications
23740 Hawthorne Boulevard
Torrance, CA 90505-5927
310-378-1133
800-421-5565
Fax: 800-837-7260
Charts, animal posters, floor puzzles, resource books and more.

5642 Frey Scientific
PO Box 300
Nashua, NH 03061-3000
800-225-3739
Fax: 800-226-3739
www.freyscientific.com
Name brand scientific products including Energy Physics, Earth Science, Chemistry and Applied Science. Over 12,000 products and kits for grades 5-14 are available.

5643 Great Adventure Tours
1717 Old Topanga Canyon Road
Topanga, CA 90290-3934
800-642-3933
Educational science field trips and adventures.

5644 Guided Discoveries
PO Box 1360
Claremont, CA 91711
800-45 -423
Fax: 909-625-7305
www.guideddiscoveries.org
Outdoor educational science programs.

Ross Turner, President/ CEO/ Co-Founder
Kristi Turner, CFO/ Co-Founder

5645 HACH Company
PO Box 389
Loveland, CO 80539
970-669-3050
800-227-4224
Fax: 970-669-2932
www.hach.com
Water and soil test kits for field and laboratory work.

5646 Heathkit Educational Systems
455 Riverview Drive
Benton Harbor, MI 49022-5015
616-925-6000
800-253-0570
Fax: 616-925-3895
Electronics educational products from basic electricity to high-tech lasers and microscopes and beyond. Comprehensive line of different media to fit varied applications. Including Computer-Aided Instruction and Computer-Aided Troubleshooting services and Heathkit's PC Servicing, Troubleshooting and Networking courses.
Carolyn Feltner, Sales Coordinator
Patrick Beckett, Marketing Manager

5647 Holometrix
25 Wiggins Avenue
Bedford, MA 01730-2314
781-275-3300
Fax: 781-275-3705
Laboratory instruments.

5648 Howell Playground Equipment
3728 Salem Rd.
Enterprise, AL 36330
217-442-0482
800-239-1370
Fax: 334-347-9563
howellequipment@aol.com
www.primestripe.com
Playground equipment and bicycle racks.
Nina Payne, President

5649 Hubbard Scientific
PO Box 2121
401 Hickory St.
Fort Collins, CO 80522
970-484-7445
800-289-9299
Fax: 970-484-1198
custserv@amep.com
www.amep.com
Earth science and life science models, kits, globes and curriculum materials.

5650 Innova Corporation
115 George Lamb Road
Bernardston, MA 01337-9742
Science kits and globes.

5651 Insect Lore
PO Box 1535
Shafter, CA 93263
661-746-6047
800-548-3284
Fax: 661-746-0334
www.insectlore.com
Science and nature materials for preschool through grade 6. Raises butterflies, frogs, ladybugs and more. Features books, curriculum units, videos, puppet, posters, and other nature oriented products.

5652 Insights Visual Productions
PO Box 230644
Encinitas, CA 92023-0644
800-942-0528
Laboratory instruments, manuals, and supplies.

5653 Instron Corporation
100 Royall Street
Canton, MA 02021-1089
781-828-2500
Fax: 781-575-5776
www.instron.com
Laboratory and scientific equipment, supplies and furniture.

5654 Johnsonite
16910 Munn Road
Chagrin Falls, OH 44023
440-543-8916
800-899-8916
Fax: 440-543-8920
info@johnsonite.com
www.johnsonite.com/ContactUs.aspx
Physical education mats, matting and floors.

5655 Justrite Manufacturing Company
2454 E Dempster Street
Suite 300
Des Plaines, IL 60016
847-298-9250
800-798-9250
Fax: 847-298-9261
justrite@justritemfg.com
www.justritemfg.com
Supplies and equipment aimed at the scientific classroom or laboratory.

5656 KLM Bioscientific
8888 Clairemont Mesa Boulevard
Suite D
San Diego, CA 92123-1137
858-571-5562
Fax: 858-571-5587
www.labsuppliesUSA.com
A mail order company that provides high quality, reasonably priced, on time living and preserved biological specimens. The Biology Store also carries a wide range of instructional materials including books, charts, models and videos. Also available is a wide range of general labware.
Loli Victorio, President

5657 Ken-a-Vision Manufacturing Company
5615 Raytown Road
Kansas City, MO 64133-3388
816-353-4787
Fax: 816-358-5072
info@ken-a-vision.com
www.ken-a-vision.com
Video Flex, Vison Viewer, Pupil CAM, Microscopes and Microrojectors
Steve Dunn, Domestic/International Op.
Ben Hoke, Sales Manger

5658 Kepro Circuit Systems
3640 Scarlet Oak Boulevard
Kirkwood, MO 63122-6606
800-325-3878
Fax: 636-861-9109
Laboratory equipment.

5659 Kewaunee Scientific Corporation
2700 W Front Street
Statesville, NC 28677
704-873-7202
800-824-6626
Fax: 704-873-5160
humanresources@kewaunee.com
www.kewaunee.com
Developer of science and laboratory supplies such as casework, fume hoods, adaptable modular systems, moveable workstations and various other technical furniture.
David M Rausch, President & CEO
Thomas D Hull III, Vice President & CFO

5660 Knex Education Catalog
Knex Education
2990 Bergey Road
PO Box 700
Hatfield, PA 19440-0700
888-KID-KNEX
email@knex.com
www.knexeducation.com
Hands-on, award-winning curriculum supported K-12 math, science and technology sets.
Michael Araten, President

5661 Koffler Sales Company
785 Oakwood Road
Suite C-100
Lake Zurich, IL 60047-1524
847-438-1152
800-355-MATS
Fax: 847-438-1514
info@kofflersales.com
www.kofflersales.com
Floor mats, Matting and stair treads.
Ron Starr, President
Pat Starr, CEO

5662 Komodo Dragon
PO Box 822
The Dalles, OR 97058-0822
541-773-5808
Museum-quality fossils and minerals.

5663 Kreonite
715 E 10th Street N
Wichita, KS 67214-2918
316-263-1111
Fax: 316-263-6829
Laboratory equipment, furniture and hardware.

5664 Kruger & Eckels
1406 E Wilshire Avenue
Santa Ana, CA 92705
714-547-5165
Fax: 714-547-2009
www.krugerandeckels.com
Laboratory and scientific instruments for institutional or educational use.

5665 LEGO Data
PO Box 1600
Enfield, CT 06083-1600
860-749-2291
Fax: 860-763-7477
Curriculum programs and materials for science education.

5666 LINX System
Science Source
PO Box 727
Waldoboro, ME 04572-0727
207-832-6344
800-299-5469
Fax: 207-832-7281
www.thesciencesource.com
A building system that integrates science, mathematics and technology at the K-9 level.

5667 Lab Safety Supply
PO Box 1368
401 S Wright Rd.
Janesville, WI 53547-1368
608-754-2345
800-356-0783
Fax: 608-754-1806
custserv@labsafety.com
www.labsafety.com
Extensive variety of school products, including lab and safety apparel and floorcoverings.

5668 Lab Volt Systems
PO Box 686
Farmingdale, NJ 07727-0686
Educational materials and equipment for the science educator.

669 Lab-Aids
17 Colt Court
Ronkonkoma, NY 11779
631-737-1133
800-381-8003
Fax: 631-737-1286
mkt@lab-aids.com
www.lab-aids.com
Science kits, published curriculum materials.

John Weatherby, Sales/Marketing Director
David M Frank, President

670 Labconco Corporation
8811 Prospect Avenue
Kansas City, MO 64132-2696
816-333-8811
800-821-5525
Fax: 816-363-0130
labconco@labconco.com
www.labconco.com
Laboratory equipment and supplies.

Mark Schmitz, VP, Research & Engineering

671 Lakeside Manufacturing
1977 S Allis Street
Milwaukee, WI 53207-1295
414-481-3900
Fax: 414-481-9313
Laboratory and scientific instruments, equipment, furniture and supplies.

672 Lane Science Equipment Company
225 W 34th Street
Suite 1412
New York, NY 10122-1496
212-563-0663
Fax: 212-465-9440
Scientific equipment, technology and supplies.

673 Lasy USA
1309 Webster Avenue
Fort Collins, CO 80524-2756
800-444-2126
Fax: 970-221-4352
Building sets that encourage children to encounter technology through problem solving activities, planning, co-operation and perseverance. Allows students to build and learn programming skills in areas of communication, construction, manufacturing and transportation.

Dave Nayak

674 Learning Technologies
40 Cameron Avenue
Somerville, MA 02144-2404
617-628-1459
800-537-8703
Fax: 617-628-8606
starlab@starlab.com
www.starlab.com
STARLAB portable planetarium systems and the Project STAR hands-on science materials.

Jane Sadler, President

675 Leica Microsystems EAD
PO Box 123
Buffalo, NY 14240-0123
716-686-3000
Fax: 716-686-3085
Educational microscopes for elementary through university applications.

676 Life Technologies
7335 Executive Way
Frederick, MD 21704
240-379-4328
800-952-9166
Fax: 716-774-6727
Supplier of biology and cell culture products.

5677 Lyon Electric Company
1690 Brandywine Avenue
Chula Vista, CA 91911
619-216-3400
Fax: 619-216-3434
Electrical tabletop incubators for science classrooms and tabletop animal intensive care units, hatchers and brooders.

Caroline Vazquez, Sales Manager
Jose Madrigal, Marketing Manager

5678 Magnet Source
747 S Gilbert Street
Castle Rock, CO 80104
303-688-3966
888-525-3536
Fax: 303-688-5303
magnet@magnetsource.com
www.magnetsource.com
Educational magnetic products and magnetic toys designed to stimulate creativity and encourage exploration of science with fun magnets. Kits include experiments, fun games, activities and powerful magnets. Moo Magnets, rare earth magnets, horseshoes, and bulk magnets.

Jim Madsen, Sales Manager

5679 Meiji Techno America
Meiji Techno America
5895 Rue Ferrari
San Jose, CA 95138
408-226-3454
800-832-0060
Fax: 408-226-0900
info@meijitechno.com
www.meijitechno.com
A full line of elementary, secondary, grade school and college-level microscopes and accessories.

James J Dutkiewicz, General Manager

5680 Metrologic Instruments
Coles Road at Route 42
Blackwood, NJ 08012
800-436-3876
Fax: 856-228-0653
Manufactures low-power lasers and laser accessories for the classroom, a range of helium-neon lasers, a modulated VLD laser, optics lab, sandbox holography kit, speed of light lab, optics bench system and digital laser power meter, as well as a selection of pin carriers, mounting pins, lenses and mirrors. Sponsors the Physics Bowl, a yearly national physics competition for high school students by the American Association of Physics Teachers.

Betty Williams

5681 Modern School Supplies
PO Box 958
Hartford, CT 06143
860-243-2329
Fax: 800-934-7206
www.modernss.com
Products for hands-on science education.

5682 Mohon International
1600 Porter Court
Paris, TN 38242
731-642-4251
Fax: 731-642-4262
Classroom equipment and supplies, directed at the scientific classroom and laboratory.

5683 Museum Products Company
84 Route 27
Mystic, CT 06355-1226
860-536-6433
800-395-5400
Fax: 860-572-9589
museumprod@aol.com
Field guides, rock collections, environmental puzzles, posters, charts, books, magnets, magnifiers, microscopes and other lab equipment. Also weather simulators, physics demonstration, games, toys in space, animal track replicas and fossils. Free catalog.

John Bannister, President

5684 Nalge Company
PO Box 20365
Rochester, NY 14602-0365
585-586-8800
800-625-4327
Fax: 585-586-8987
Plastic labware and safety products for the scientific classroom.

5685 National Instruments
6504 Bridge Point Parkway
Austin, TX 78730-5039
512-794-0100
Fax: 512-683-5794
Laboratory/scientific instruments.

5686 National Optical & Scientific Instruments
6508 Tri-County Pkwy.
Schertz, TX 78154
210-590-7010
800-275-3716
Fax: 210-590-1104
natlopt@sbcglobal.net
www.nationaloptical.com
Wholesale distributor of national comppound, stero and digital miocroscopes for K-12 and college.

Michael Hart, Sales Manager
Cynthia Syverson-Mercer, Director

5687 Ohaus Corporation
19-A Chapin Road
Pine Brook, NJ 07058
973-377-9000
800-672-7722
Fax: 973-593-0359
www.distribuidoramuller.com.ar/equipos/ohaus/traveler.pdf
Scientific supplies and equipment for the classroom or laboratory.

5688 PASCO Scientific
10101 Foothills Boulevard
Roseville, CA 95747-7100
916-786-3800
800-772-8700
Fax: 916-786-7565
jbrown@pasco.com
US manufacturers of physics apparatus and probe warer that enable teachers to improve science literacy and meet the standards

Justine Brown, Copy Writer

5689 Quest Aerospace Education
350 E 18th Street
Yuma, AZ 85364
602-595-9506
Fax: 520-783-9534
A complete line of model rockets and related teaching materials.

5690 Resources for Teaching Elementary School Science
National Academy Press
Arts & Industries Bldg Room 1201
900 Jefferson Drive SW
Washington, DC 20560-0403
202-287-2063
Fax: 202-287-2070
outreach@nas.edu
www.si.edu
Resource guides for elementary, middle school, and high school science teachers. Annotated guides to hands-on, inquiry-centered

curriculum materials and sources of help in teaching science from kindergarten through sixth grades. Produced by the National Science Resources Center.

National Science Resources Center, Author
Douglas Lapp, Executive Director

5691 Rheometrics
1 Possumtown Road
Piscataway, NJ 08854-2100
732-560-8550
Laboratory/science supplies and equipment.

5692 SARUT
107 Horatio Street
New York, NY 10014-1569
212-691-9453
Science and nature-related educational tools.

5693 Safe-T-Rack Systems
4325 Dominguez Road
Suite A
Rocklin, CA 95677
916-632-1121
Fax: 916-632-1173
www.safe-t-racksystems.com
Laboratory furniture, safety storage containers and equipment.

5694 Sargent-Welch Scientific Company
PO Box 92912
Rochester, NY 14692-9012
847-459-6625
800-727-4368
Fax: 800-676-2540
www.sargentwelch.com
Models, books and instruments for the scientific classroom.

5695 Science Instruments Company
6122 Reisterstown Road
Baltimore, MD 21215-3423
410-358-7810
Develops, manufactures and markets unique hands-on programs in biotechnology, biomedical instrumentation, telecommunications, electronics and industrial controls.

5696 Science Source
86475 Gene Lasserre Blvd.
Yulee, FL 32097
904-225-5558
800-875-3214
Fax: 904-225-2228
info@sciencefirst.com
www.thesciencesource.com
Design technology books, teacher resource and student books on design and technology, design technology materials, equipment and supplies used in the construction of design challenges.

Michelle Winter, Sales/Marketing Support
Rudolf Graf, President

5697 Science for Today & Tomorrow
1840 E 12th Street
Mishawaka, IN 46544
574-258-5397
Fax: 574-258-5594
Hands-on science activities packaged for K-3 students.

5698 Scientific Laser Connection, Incorporated
5021 N 55th Avenue
Suite 10
Glendale, AZ 85301-7535
623-939-6711
877-668-7844
Fax: 623-939-3369
Laser education modules.

Don Morris, President
Travis Gatrin, Service

5699 Shain/Shop-Bilt
509 Hemlock Street
Philipsburg, PA 16866-2937
814-342-2820
Fax: 814-342-6180
Laboratory casework and cabinets.

5700 Sheldon Lab Systems
PO Box 836
Crystal Springs, MS 39059-0836
601-892-2731
Fax: 601-892-4364
Laboratory casework and technical equipment for K-12, college and university level.

5701 Skilcraft
CRAFT House Corporation
328 N Westwood Avenue
Toledo, OH 43607-3317
419-537-9090
Fax: 419-537-9160
Microchemistry sets.

5702 Skullduggery Kits
624 S B Street
Tustin, CA 92780-4318
800-336-7745
Fax: 714-832-1215
Social studies kits offers hands-on learning, art projects, complete lesson plans, authentic replicas, and challenging products designed for small groups of students with increasing levels of difficulty.

5703 Skulls Unlimited International
10313 S Sunnylane
Oklahoma City, OK 73160
405-794-9300
800-659-SKUL
Fax: 405-794-6985
sales@skullsunlimited.com
www.skullsunlimited.com
Leading supplier of specimen supplies to the educational community.

Jay Villemarette, President

5704 Society of Automotive Engineers
400 Commonwealth Drive
Warrendale, PA 15086-7511
724-776-4841
877-606-7323
Fax: 724-776-5760
www.sae.org
Award-winning science unit for grades 4-6.

Jamie Ferguson, Development Officer
Lori Gatmaitan, Director

5705 Southern Precision Instruments Company
3419 E Commerce Street
San Antonio, TX 78220-1322
210-212-5055
800-417-5055
Fax: 210-212-5062
Microscopes and microprojectors for grades K-1-K-12 and college levels. Stereo and compound microscopes, along with CCTV color systems.

Victor Spiroff, VP/General Manager

5706 Southland Instruments
17741 Metzler Lane
Unit A
Huntington Beach, CA 92647-6246
714-847-5007
Fax: 714-893-3613
Microscopes.

5707 Spectronics Corporation
956 Brush Hollow Road
Westbury, NY 11590
516-333-4840
800-274-8888
Fax: 800-491-6868
info@spectroline.com
www.spectroline.com
Laboratory and scientific classroom equipment, hardware and shelving.

Gloria Blusk, Manager Customer Service
Vincent McKenna, Publicist

5708 Spitz
700 Brandywine Drive
Chadds Ford, PA 19317
610-459-5200
Fax: 610-459-3830
spitz@spitzinc.com
www.spitzinc.com
Offers scientific and laboratory instruments and accessories.

Jon Shaw, President/ CEO
Paul Dailey, CFO

5709 Swift Instruments
1190 N 4th Street
San Jose, CA 95112-4946
408-293-2380
Educational microscopes and other laboratory instruments.

5710 TEDCO
498 S Washington Street
Hagerstown, IN 47346-1596
765-489-4527
800-654-6357
Fax: 765-489-5752
sales@tedcotoys.com
www.tedcotoys.com
Bill Nye Extreme Gyro, Prisms, Educational Toys Solar Science Kit.

Raplh Teetor, Founder
Marjorie Teetor, Owner

5711 Telaire Systems
6489 Calle Real
Goleta, CA 93117-1538
805-964-1699
Fax: 805-964-2129
Laboratory instruments and hardware.

5712 Tooltron Industries
103 Parkway
Boerne, TX 78006
830-249-8277
800-293-8134
Fax: 830-755-8134
easykut@gvtc.com
www.tooltron.com
Scientific hardware and laboratory equipment, including instruments and accessories. School scissors and craft supplies.

Thomas Love, Owner/VP Marketing

5713 Triops
PO Box 11369
Pensacola, FL 32524
850-479-4415
800-200-3466
Fax: 850-479-3315
triopsinc@aol.com
www.triops.com
Classroom activities and kits in environmental, ecological and biological sciences.

Dr. Eugene Hull, President
Peter Bender, Office Manager

714 Trippense Planetarium Company
Science First
86475 Gene Lasserre Blvd.
Yulee, FL 32097
904-225-5558
800-875-3214
Fax: 904-225-2228
info@sciencefirst.com
www.sciencefirst.com
Astronomy and earth science models and materials, including the Trippense planetarium, Elementary planetarium, Copernican and Ptolemic solar systems, Milky Way model, Explore Celestial Globes and the patented top quality educational astronomy models since 1905.

Kris Spors, Customer Service Manager
Nancy Bell, President

715 Unilab
967 Mabury Road
San Jose, CA 95133
800-288-9850
Fax: 408-975-1035
unilab@richnet.net
www.unilabinc.com
Designs and manufactures products for teaching science and technology.

Gerald A Beer, VP

716 Vibrac Corporation
16 Columbia Drive
PO Box 840
Amherst, NH 03031
603-882-6777
Fax: 603-886-3857
www.vibrac.com
Scientific instruments and hardware.

717 Wild Goose Company
5181 S 300 W
Murray, UT 84107-4709
801-466-1172
Hands-on science kits for elementary-aged students 3 and up and resource books for all levels of general science.

718 Wildlife Supply Company
86475 Gene Lasserre Blvd.
Yulee, FL 32097
904-225-9889
800-799-8115
Fax: 904-225-2228
goto@wildco.com
www.wildco.com
Aquatic sampling equipment including Fieldmaster Field Kits, Water Bottle Kits, Secchi Disks, line and messengers and a NEW Mini Ponar bottom grab. Also, a variety of professional Wildco bottom grabs, water bottles, plankton nets, hand corers and other materials.

Aaron Bell, Product Manager
Bruce Izard, Customer Service Manager

719 WoodKrafter Kits
PO Box 808
Yarmouth, ME 04096-0808
207-846-3722
Fax: 207-846-1019
Science kits, hands-on curriculum-based science kits for ages 4 and up, classroom packs, supplies and science materials also available.

Sports & Playground Equipment

720 American Playground Corporation
6406 Production Drive
Anderson, IN 46013-9408
765-642-0288
800-541-1602
Fax: 765-649-7162
www.american-playground.com
Playground equipment and supplies.

Julie Morson, Inside Sales Manager
Marty Bloyd, General Manager

5721 American Swing Products
9120 Double Diamond Parkway
Suite 1062
Reno, NV 89521
800-433-2573
800-433-2573
Fax: 775-883-2384
play@americanswing.com
www.americanswing.com
Producer of playground equipment and products such as swing seats, swing hangers, tire swivels, slides and more. Materials used include stainless steel and carbon steel.

Susan Simon, President
Karen Gonzalez, Office Manager

5722 BCI Burke Company
660 Van Dyne Road
PO Box 549
Fond Du Lac, WI 54936-0549
920-921-9220
800-266-1250
Fax: 920-921-9566
pr@bciburke.com
www.bciburke.com
Playground equipment.

5723 Backyard Dreams
Backyard Dreams Denver
5370 N Broadway
Denver, CO 80216
303-868-9916
info@backyard-dreams.com
www.backyard-dreams.com
Produces playground equipment such as AlleyOop Trampolines and Redwood Playsets.

Joey Delmore, Owner

5724 Belson Manufacturing
111 N River Road
North Aurora, IL 60542-1396
800-323-5664
Playground equipment.

5725 Colorado Time Systems
1551 E 11th Street
Loveland, CO 80537
970-667-1000
800-279-0111
Fax: 970-667-5876
www.coloradotime.com
Been the system of choice for sports timing and scoring. Has a timing system for almost every sport including swimming, basketball, football, baseball, track, soccer and most others. Has a wide variety of displays ranging from fixed digit scoreboards to animation LED boards to fullcolor video displays and ribbon boards.

Randy Flint, Sr Sales Representative
Rick Connell, CDS Sales Manager

5726 Constructive Playthings
Action For Children
1227 E 119th Street
Grandview, MO 64030-1178
312-823-1100
www.actforchildren.org/
Playground, recreational and indoor fun equipment for children grades PreK-3.

5727 Creative Outdoor Designs
142 Pond Drive
Lexington, SC 29073-8009
803-957-9259
Fax: 803-957-7152
Playground equipment.

5728 Curtis Marketing Corporation
2550 Rigel Road
Venice, FL 34293-3200
941-493-8085
Playground equipment.

5729 GameTime
150 PlayCore Dr. SE
Fort Payne, AL 35967
256-845-5610
800-235-2440
Fax: 256-845-9361
info@gametime.com
www.gametime.com
Playground equipment.

Doris Dellinger, Marketing Service Manager

5730 Gared Sports
9200 E 146th Street
Building A
Noblesville, IN 46060
317-774-9840
800-325-2682
Fax: 314-421-6014
koughton@garedholdings.com
www.garedsports.com
Gared offers a full line of basketball, volleyball, soccer and lacrosse equipment, as well as bleachers and seating for various types of indoor and outdoor facilities.

Laura St. George, VP, Sales & Marketing
Mark Cicotte, Team Dealer Sales Manager

5731 Gerstung/Gym-Thing
6308 Blair Hill Lane
Baltimore, MD 21209-2102
800-922-3575
Physical education mats, matting and floorcoverings.

5732 Grounds for Play
1050 Columbia Dr.
Carrollton, GA 30117
817-477-5482
800-552-7529
Fax: 817-477-1140
www.groundsforplay.com
Playground equipment, flooring, floorcoverings, play eviroment design, lanscape architecure, insatllation, and safety insepection.

Jim Dempsey, Senior VP
Emily Smith, Office Manager

5733 Iron Mountain Forge
One Iron Mountain Drive
Farmington, MO 63640
800-325-8828
Fax: 573-760-7441
Playground equipment.

5734 JCH International
978 E Hermitage Road NE
Rome, GA 30161-9641
800-328-9203
Coverings, mats and physical education matting.

5735 Jaypro
Jaypro Sports
976 Hartford Tpke
Waterford, CT 06385
860-447-3001
800-243-0533
Fax: 860-444-1779
info@jaypro.com
www.jaypro.com

Sports equipment.

Linda Andels, Marketing Manager
Bill Wild, VP Sales/Marketing

5736 **Kidstuff Playsystems**
5400 Miller Avenue
Gary, IN 46403-2844
800-255-0153
Fax: 219-938-3340
rhagelberg@kidstuffplaysystems.com
Preschool and grade school playground equipment, Health Trek Fitness Course, park site furnishings.

Dick Hagelberg, CEO

5737 **Kompan**
7717 New Market Street
Olympia, WA 98501
360-943-6374
800-426-9788
Fax: 360-943-5575
www.kompan.com
Unique playgrond equipment.

Tom Grover, Marketing Director

5738 **LA Steelcraft Products**
1975 Lincoln Avenue
Pasadena, CA 91103
626-798-7401
800-371-2438
Fax: 626-798-1482
info@lasteelcraft.com
www.lasteelcraft.com
Manufacturer of quality athletic, park and playground equipment for schools, parks and industry. Features indoor/outdoor fiberglass furniture, court and field equipment, site furnishings, bike racks, flagpoles, baseball and basketball backstops.

James D Holt, President
John C Gaudesi, COO

5739 **Landscape Structures**
PO Box 198
601 7th St.
Delano, MN 55328-0198
763-972-3391
888-4FU-LSI
Fax: 763-972-3185
www.playlsi.com
Playground equipment.

Bill Jannott, Board Member
Rick Jannott, Board Member

5740 **MMI-Federal Marketing Service**
PO Box 241367
Montgomery, AL 36124-1367
334-286-0700
Fax: 334-286-0711
Playground equipment, sports timers, clocks and school supplies.

5741 **Matworks**
Division of Janitex Rug Service Corporation
11900 Old Baltimore Pike
Beltsville, MD 20705-1265
800-523-5179
Fax: 301-595-0740
info@thematworks.com
www.thematworks.com
Mats, matting and floorcoverings for entrances, gymnasiums, and all other facilities where the potential for slip and fall exists.

Robert Burman, Chairman
Robert B. Collins, CEO and President

5742 **Miracle Recreation Equipment Company**
878 E Highway 60
PO Box 420
Monett, MO 65708-0420
417-235-6917
888-458-2752
Fax: 417-235-6816
www.miracle-recreation.com
Playground and recreation equipment.

5743 **National Teaching Aids**
401 Hickory Street
PO Box 2121
Fort Collins, CO 80522
970-484-7445
800-289-9299
Fax: 970-484-1198
bevans@amep.com
www.amep.com
Learning math, alphabet, and geography skills is easy with our Clever Catch Balls. These colorful 24-inch inflatable vinyl balls provide an excellent way for children to practice math, alphabet and geography skills. Excellent learning tool in organized classroom activities, on the playground, or at home.

Michael Warring, President
Candace Coffman, National Sales Manger

5744 **New Braunfels General Store International**
3150 Interstate H 35 S
New Braunfels, TX 78130-7927
830-620-4000
Fax: 830-620-0598
Playground equipment, supplies and classroom supplies.

5745 **Outback Play Centers**
1280 W Main Street
Sun Prairie, WI 53590-0010
608-825-2140
800-338-0522
Fax: 608-825-2114
Playground equipment.

Jack Garczynskl, President

5746 **Playground Environments**
22 Old Country Road
PO Box 578
Quogue, NY 11959
516-653-5465
800-662-0922
Fax: 516-653-2933
peplay@mindspring.com
www.ncsu.edu
Designs and manufactures integrated play and recreational areas for children, providing them with new experiences in a safe, accessible, educationally supportive and fun environment.

Suzanne Crocitto, Contact
Claire Dudley, Ass. Landscape Architect

5747 **Playworld Systems**
1000 Buffalo Road
Lewisburg, PA 17837-9795
570-522-9800
800-233-8404
Fax: 570-522-3030
info@PlayworldSystems.com
www.playworldsystems.com
Playground and recreational equipment.

Mathew M. Miller, Chief Executive Officer

5748 **Porter Athletic Equipment Company**
Porter Athletic Equipment Company
601 Mercury Drive
Champaign, IL 61822-9648
217-367-8438
800-637-3090
Fax: 217-367-8440
www.porterathletic.com
Athletic equipment, floorcoverings, mats and supplies.

Dan Morgan, VP Sales/Marketing

5749 **Quality Industries**
130 Jones Boulevardÿ
PO Box 765
La Vergne, TN 37086-0765
800-745-8613
Fax: 615-793-2347
Recycled plastic park and playground equipment.

5750 **Real ACT Prep Guide**
Peterson's, A Nelnet Company
Princeton Pike Corporate Center
2000 Lenox Drive PO Box 67005
Lawrenceville, NJ 08648
609-896-1800
800-338-3282
Fax: 609-896-4531
Familiarizes students with the test's format, reviews skills, and provides the all-important practice that helps build confidence.

621 pages
ISBN: 0-768919-75-4

Elaine Bender, Mark Weinfeld, et al., Author

5751 **Recreation Creations**
PO Box 955
Hillsdale, MI 49242-0955
517-439-0300
800-888-0977
Fax: 517-439-0303
www.rec-creations.com
Heavy duty park and playground equipment for school and public use. Equipment is both colorful and safe.

DC Shaneour

5752 **Roppe Corporation**
1602 N Union Street
Fostoria, OH 44830-1158
419-435-8546
800-537-9527
Fax: 419-435-1056
sales@roppe.com
www.roppe.com
Floorcoverings, mats and matting.

5753 **Safety Play**
10460 Roosevelt Boulevard
#295
St Petersburgh, FL 33716-3818
727-522-0061
888-878-0244
Fax: 727-522-0061
safetyplay@mindspring.com
www.safetyplay.net
Playground and recreational accident consultants. Experienced in insepctions, design, expert witness. Creators of Playground Safety Signs as required to be on the playground.

Scott Burmon, Contact

5754 **Sport Court**
5445 W Harold Gatty Dr.
Salt Lake City, UT 84116-1504
801-972-0260
800-421-8112
Fax: 801-401-3504
www.sportcourt.com

Sport flooring, portable flooring, outdoor-indoor educational institutions.

Finnika Lundmark, Director Marketing

755 Sport Floors
6651 Reese Road
PO Box 1478
Memphis, TN 38133-1478
901-452-9492
800-881-6440
Fax: 901-452-9250
www.sportsfloorsinc.com
Sport floors, flooring, floorcoverings, mats and matting.

756 Sportmaster
6031 Broad Street Mall
Pittsburgh, PA 15206-3009
412-243-5100
Fax: 412-731-3052
Playground equipment, sports timers and clocks.

757 Stackhouse Athletic Equipment Company
1450 McDonald St NE
Salem, OR 97301-6949
503-363-1840
800-285-3640
Fax: 503-363-0511
www.stackhouseathletic.com
Volleyball, soccer, football and baseball hardgoods.

Greg Henshaw, VP Marketing

758 Swedes Systems - HAGS Play USA
2180 Stratingham Drive
Dublin, OH 43016-8907
Fax: 614-889-9026
Playground safety consultants.

759 Ultra Play Systems
Parek Stuff
1675 Locust Streetÿ
Red Bud, IL 62278-1000
800-458-5872
www.ultraplay.com
Playground and recreational equipment.

760 Wausau Tile
PO Box 1520
Wausau, WI 54402-1520
715-359-3121
800-388-8728
Fax: 715-355-4627
wtile@wausautile.com
www.wausautile.com
Playground and recreation equipment.

Rob Geurink, Furnishings Division Manager

761 Wear Proof Mat Company
2156 W Fulton Street
Chicago, IL 60612-2392
312-733-4570
Fax: 800-322-7105
Mats, matting and floorcoverings for the physical education class.

762 Wolverine Sports
745 State Circle
Ann Arbor, MI 48108-1647
734-761-5690
800-521-2832
Fax: 800-654-4321
www.wolverinesports.com
Playground, sports and physical fitness furniture and equipment.

General

5763 A-V Online
National Information Center for Educational Media
4725 Indian School Road NE
Suite 100
Albuquerque, NM 87198-8640
505-265-3591
800-926-8328
Fax: 505-256-1080
info-request@nicem.com
www.nicem.com
A CD-ROM that contains over 400,000 citations with abstracts, to non-print educational materials for all educational levels. It is available on an annual subscription basis and comes with semiannual updates.
Lisa Savard, Marketing and Sales

5764 ACT
2201 N Dodge Street
PO Box 168
Iowa City, IA 52243-0168
319-337-1000
Fax: 319-339-3021
www.act.org
Help individuals and organizations make informed decisions about education and work.
Jon L. Erickson, President
Jon Whitmore, Chief Executive Officer

5765 AMX Corporation
3000 Research Drive
Richardson, TX 75243-5481
469-624-7400
800-222-0193
Fax: 972-624-7153
www.amx.com
Multiple products, equipment and supplies.
Rashid Skaf, President

5766 ASC Electronics
2 Kees Pl
Merrick, NY 11566-3625
516-623-3206
Fax: 516-378-2672
High tech multimedia system. Completely software driven, featuring interactive video, audio and data student drills. Novell network. System includes CD-ROM, laserdisc and digital voice card technology.

5767 Accelerated Math
Renaissance
2911 Peach Street
PO Box 8036
Wisconsin Rapids, WI 54495-8036
715-424-3636
800-338-4204
answers@renaissance.com
www.renaissance.com
Math management software that helps teachers increase student math achievement.
Chris Bauleke, Chief Executive Officer
Todd Brekhus, Chief Product Officer

5768 Accelerated Reader
Renaissance
2911 Peach Street
PO Box 8036
Wisconsin Rapids, WI 54495-8036
715-424-3636
800-338-4204
answers@renaissance.com
www.renaissance.com
Software program that helps teachers manage students' independent reading practice.
Chris Bauleke, Chief Executive Officer
Todd Brekhus, Chief Product Officer

5769 Actrix Systems
6315 San Ignacio Avenue
San Jose, CA 95119-1202
800-422-8749
Fax: 509-744-2851
Computer networks.

5770 Allen Communications
5 Triac Center
5th Floor
Salt Lake Cty, UT 84180
801-537-7800
Fax: 801-537-7805
Software.

5771 Alltech Electronics Company
602 Garrison Street
Oceanside, CA 92054-4865
760-721-0093
Fax: 760-732-1460
Computer hardware.

5772 Anchor Pad Products
Anchor Pad Products
11105 Dana Circle
Cypress, CA 90630-5133
714-799-4071
800-626-2467
Fax: 714-799-4094
www.anchorpad.com
Cost effective physical security systems for computers, computer peripherals and office equipment.
Kris Jones, Marketing Associate
Melanie Rustle, Marketing Associate

5773 Apple Computer
1 Infinite Loop
Cupertino, CA 95014-2084
408-996-1010
800-692-7753
Fax: 408-974-2786
www.apple.com
Offers a wide selection of software systems and programs for the student, educator, professional and classroom use. Program areas include reading, science, social studies, history, language arts, mathematics and more.
Tim Cook, CEO
Angela Ahrendts, Senior Vice Presidentÿ

5774 Ascom Timeplex
400 Chestnut Ridge Road
Woodcliff Lake, NJ 07675-7604
201-646-1571
Fax: 201-646-0485
Computer networks.

5775 BGS Systems
128 Technology Drive
Waltham, MA 02453-8909
617-891-0000
Facility planning and evaluation software.

5776 BLS Tutorsystems
5153 W Woodmill Drive
Wilmington, DE 19808-4067
800-545-7766
Computer software.

5777 Boxlight
1045 Progress Circle
Lawrenceville, GA 30043
866-972-1549
www.mimio.boxlight.com
Develops educational technology products to improve learning and engagement in the classroom.
Michael Pope, Chair & CEO

5778 Broderbund Software
500 Redwood Boulevard
Novato, CA 94947-6921
319-395-9626
800-223-8941
Fax: 319-395-7449
Educational software.

5779 Bulletin Boards for Busy Teachers
www.geocities.com/VisionTeacherwv/
Bulletin board tips and education links.

5780 CASL Software
6818 86th Street E
Puyallup, WA 98371-6450
206-845-7738
Educational software for schools and institutions in all areas of interest.

5781 CCU Software
PO Box 6724
Charleston, WV 25362-0724
800-843-5576
Fax: 800-321-4297
Educational software.

5782 CCV Software
5602 36th Street S
Fargo, ND 58104-6768
800-541-6078
Fax: 800-457-6953
All varieties of software and hardware for the educational fields of interest including language arts, math, social studies, science, history and more.

5783 Cambridge Development Laboratory
86 West Street
Waltham, MA 02451-1110
781-890-4640
800-637-0047
Fax: 781-890-2894
Meets all educational software needs in language arts, mathematics, science, social studies early learning and special education.

5784 Chariot Software Group
2645 Financial Court
Suite 1
San Diego, CA 92117-3002
858-270-0202
800-242-7468
Fax: 858-270-2027
info@chariot.com
www.chariot.com
Academic software.

5785 Child's Play Software
5785 Emporium Square
Columbus, OH 43231-2802
614-833-1836
Fax: 614-833-1837
Markets learning games and creative software to schools.

5786 Claris Corporation
5201 Patrick Henry Drive
Santa Clara, CA 95054-1171
800-747-7483
Educational software.

5787 Classroom Direct
20200 E 9 Mile Road
Saint Clair Shores, MI 48080-1791
800-777-3642
Fax: 800-628-6250
Full line of hardware and software for Mac, IBM and Apple II at discount prices.

5788 College Board/SAT
250 Vesey Street
New York, NY 10281

212-713-8000
www.collegeboard.org
David Coleman, Chief Executive Officer
Jeremy Singer, President

789 Computer City Direct
2000 Two Tandy Center
Fort Worth, TX 76102
800-538-0586
Hardware.

790 Computer Friends
10200 SW Eastridge Street
Portland, OR 97225
800-547-3303
Fax: 503-643-5379
www.cfriends.com
Computer hardware, software and networks, printer support products.
Jimmy Moglia, Marketing Director

791 Data Command
PO Box 548
Kankakee, IL 60901-0548
800-528-7390
Educational software.

792 Davidson & Associates
19840 Pioneer Avenue
Torrance, CA 90503-1690
800-545-7677
Educational software and systems.

793 Dell Computer Corporation
9595 Arboretum Boulevard
Austin, TX 78759-6337
512-338-4400
800-388-1450
Hardware.

794 Digital Divide Network
19 Duncan Street
Suite 505
Toronto, ON
416-977-9363
Fax: 416-352-1898
www.digitaldivide.net
Knowledge to help everyone succeed in the digital age.
Adam Clare, Lead Editor
Kristen Jordan, Project Coordinator

795 Digital Equipment Corporation
Educational Computer Systems Group
2 Iron Way
Marlboro, MA 01752
Computer hardware and networks.

796 Don Johnston Developmental Equipment
26799 West Commerce Drive
Suite 115
Volo, IL 60073-1190
847-740-0749
800-999-4660
Fax: 847-740-7326
info@donjohnston.com
www.donjohnston.com
Develops educational software for special needs. Products include the Ukandu Series for emergent literacy, LD, ESL, students Co-Writer and Write: OutLoud.

797 Edmark Corporation
6727 185th Avenue NE
PO Box 97021
Redmond, WA 98052-5037
425-556-8400
800-691-2986
Fax: 425-556-8430
Markets educational software.

5798 EduQuest, An IBM Company
PO Box 2150
Atlanta, GA 30301-2150
Offers exciting educational software in various fields of interest including history, social studies, reading, math and language arts, as well as computers.

5799 Educational Activities
1937 Grand Avenue
P.O. Box 87
Baldwin, NY 11510-2889
516-223-4666
800-797-3223
Fax: 516-623-9282
www.edact.com
Supplemental materials.
Carol Stern, VP
Roni Hofbauer, Office Manager

5800 Educational Resources
1550 Executive Drive
Elgin, IL 60123-9330
630-213-8681
Fax: 630-213-8681
The largest distributor of educational software and technology in the education market. Features Mac, APL, ligs and IBM school versions, lab packs, site licenses, networking and academic versions. Hardware, accessories and multimedia is also available.

5801 Electronic Specialists Inc.
75 Middlesex Ave
PO Box 389
Natick, MA 01760-0004
508-655-1532
810-225-4876
Fax: 508-653-0268
clipprx@ix.netcom.com
Computer and electronics, including networks and computer systems plus transformers and power converters.
Frank Stifter, President

5802 Environmental Systems Research Institute
380 New York Street
Redlands, CA 92373-8100
909-793-2853
888-377-4575
www.esri.com
Demonstrates a full range of geographic information system software products.
Jack Dangermond, Founder

5803 Eversan Inc.
34 Main Street
Whitesboro, NY 13492
315-736-3967
800-383-6060
Fax: 315-736-4058
www.eversan.com
Announcement boards, scoreboards and classroom supplies, sports timers and clocks.
Michelle Moran, Sales Representative
Elsa Kucherna, Sales Representative

5804 GAMCO Educational Materials
PO Box 1911
Big Spring, TX 79721-1911
800-351-1404
Publishes software in math, language arts, reading, social studies, early childhood education and teacher tools for Macintosh, Apple, IBM and MS-DOS compatible.

5805 Games2Learn
1936 East Deere Avenue
Suite 120
Santa Ana, CA 92705
714-751-4263
888-713-4263
Fax: 714-442-0869
www.games2learn.com
Develops, markets and provides children and adults with quality, fun, interactive educational products designed to increase their skills in language, math and general knowledge. Creator of The Phonics Game.

5806 Gateway Learning Corporation
665 3rd Street
Suite 225
San Francisco, CA 94107
800-544-7323
www.hop.com
Develop and sell innovative educational products for home learning.
Lionel Guerin, Chairman
Frederic Gagey, Chief Financial Officer

5807 Greene & Associates
1100 NW Loop 410
Suite 700
San Antonio, TX 78213-5857
210-366-8768
Fax: 210-366-0198
www.greeneandassociates.com
Educational software.
Barbara A. F. Greene, Chief Executive Officer

5808 Grolier
PO Box 1716
Danbury, CT 06816
800-371-3908
Fax: 800-456-4402
Multimedia software for education.

5809 Hubbell
Kellems Division
40 Waterview Drive
Shelton, CT 06378-2604
475-882-4800
800-288-6000
Fax: 203-882-4852
www.hubbell-wiring.com
Computer hardware, software, systems, and networks.

5810 Indiana Cash Drawer
1315 S Miller Street
Shelbyville, IN 46176-2424
317-398-6643
Fax: 317-392-0958
Computer peripherals.

5811 Ingenuity Works
325 Howe St
Suite 407
Vancouver, BC 98230-9702
604-484-8053
800-665-0667
Fax: 604-431-7996
information@ingenuityworks.com
www.ingenuityworks.com
Publishes K-12 educational software for classroom use. Key curriculum areas include geography, keyboarding, and math (K-9). Network and district licenses are available.
Brigetta , Director Marketing

5812 Instructional Design
WIDS-Worldwide Instructional Design System
1 Foundation Circle
Waunakee, WI 53597-8914
608-849-2411
800-677-9437
Fax: 608-849-2468
info@wids.org
www.wids.org
Performance-based curriculum design software and professional devlopment tools. Use software to write curriculum, implement

standards, create assessments, and build in learning styles. Excellent upfront online design tool.

Leah Osborn, Director
Terri Johnson, Associate Director

5813 Instructor
Scholastic
555 Broadway
New York, NY 10012-3919
212-343-6100
800-724-6527
Fax: 212-343-4801
www.scholastic.com/instructor
Edited for teachers, curriculum coordinators, principals and supervisors of primary grades through junior high school.

Monthly

Dick Robinson, President and CEO
Lynn Diamond, Advertising Director

5814 Jostens Learning Corporation
4920 Pacific Heights Boulevard
Suite 500
San Diego, CA 92121
858-587-0087
800-521-8538
Fax: 858-587-1629
Educational software and CD-ROM's.

5815 Journey Education
5212 Tennyson Pkwy.
Suite 130
Plano, TX 75024
800-876-3507
Fax: 972-245-3585
sales@journeyed.com
www.journeyed.com
Software for students.

5816 Ken Cook Education Systems
9929 W Silver Spring Drive
PO Box 25267
Milwaukee, WI 53225-1024
414-466-6060
800-362-2665
Fax: 414-466-0840
BoatingManuals@kencook.com
www.boatpubs.com
Classroom curricular software.

5817 Kensington Microwave
2855 Campus Drive
San Mateo, CA 94403-2510
650-572-2700
800-535-4242
Fax: 650-572-9675
www.kensington.com
Computer systems and peripherals.

5818 Lapis Technologies
1100 Marina Village Parkway
Alameda, CA 94501-1043
510-748-1600
Computer peripherals.

5819 Laser Learning Technologies
120 Lakeside Avenue
#3240
Seattle, WA 98122-6533
800-722-3505
Educational CD-ROM's and interactive videos.

5820 Lawrence Productions
6146 West Main St
Suite A
Kalamazoo, MI 49009-9687
269-903-2395
800-421-4157
Fax: 616-665-7060
www.lpi.com
More than 60 proven software titles for PreK to adult, covering problem solving, early learning and leadership skills.

5821 Learning Company
500 Redwood Boulevard
Novato, CA 94947
415-881-8000
800-825-4420
Fax: 877-864-2275
www.sphinxaur.com/learning-company/novato-ca/
School educational software.

5822 Library Corporation, Sales & Marketing
1501 Regency Way
Woodstock, GA 30189-5487
770-591-0089
Computer networks.

Gary Kirk, Branch Manager

5823 LinkNet
Introlink
1400 E Touhy Avenue
Suite 260
Des Plaines, IL 60018-3339
847-390-8700
Fax: 847-390-9435
Computer networks.

5824 MECC
6160 Summit Drive N
Minneapolis, MN 55430-2100
800-685-MECC
www.mecc.co
Educational software, hardware and overhead projectors.

5825 Mamopalire of Vermont
PO Box 24
Warren, VT 05674
802-496-4095
888-496-4094
Fax: 802-496-4096
bethumpd@wcvt.com
www.bethumpd.com
Provides quality educational books and board games for the whole family.

Rebecca Cahilly, President
Glenn Cahilly, CEO

5826 McGraw-Hill Education
PO Box 182605
Columbus, OH 43218
800-338-3987
Fax: 800-953-8691
hep_customer-service@mheducation.com
www.mheducation.com
Provides educational software for PreK-12 and higher education teaching as well as reference and trade publications for the medical, business and engineering professions.

David Levin, President & CEO
Angelo T DeGenaro, Chief Information Officer

5827 Microsoft Corporation
1 Microsoft Way
Redmond, WA 98052-8300
425-882-8080
Fax: 425-936-7329
www.microsoft.com
One of the largest publishers and distributors of educational software, hardware, equipment and supplies.

Bill Gates, Founder
Paul Allen, Founder

5828 Misty City Software
11866 Slater Avenue NE
Kirkland, WA 98034-4103
206-820-2219
800-795-0049
Fax: 425-820-4298
Publisher of Grade Machine, gradebook software for Macintosh, MS-DOS, and Apple II. Grade Machine used by thousands of teachers in hundreds of schools worldwide. Grade Machine has full-screen editing, flexible reports, large class capacity, excellent documentation and reasonable cost.

Roberta Spiro, Business Manager
Russell Cruickshanks, Sales Manager

5829 NCR Corporation
1700 S Patterson Boulevard
Dayton, OH 45479-0002
937-445-5000
Computer networks, systems (large, mini, micro, medium and personal).

5830 NetZero
2555 Townsgate Road
Westlake Village, CA 91361-2650
805-418-2020
Fax: 805-418-2075
www.netzero.com
Free Internet access.

5831 New Century Education Corporation
220 Old New Brunswick Road
P.O. Box 43052
Upper Montclair, NJ 07043
732-981-0820
800-833-6232
Fax: 732-981-0552
www.newcenturyeducation.org
ILS systems.

Janice Harrison, Marketing Representative

5832 OnLine Educator
A comprehensive archive of educational sites with useful search capabilities and descriptions of the sites.

5833 Online Computer Systems
1 Progress Drive
Horsham, PA 19044-3502
CD-ROM networking, CD-ROM titles and CD-ROM tower units.

5834 PBS LearningMedia
Public Broadcasting Service (PBS)
1225 S Clark Street
Arlington, VA 22202
www.pbslearningmedia.org
Free teaching resources including videos, lesson plans, interactive lessons, and more.

Paula Kerger, President & CEO
Jonathan Barzilay, Chief Operating Officer

5835 Parent Link
Parlant Technology
290 N University Avenue
PO Box 50240
Provo, UT 84605
801-373-9669
800-735-2930
Fax: 801-373-9697
info@parlant.com
www.parlant.com
School to home communication systems allow scholls to create messages — emails, telephone calls, web content, printed letters, about student information, grades, attendance, homework, and activities. Also provides inbound access via internet and telephone.

George Joeckel, Marketing

5836 Peopleware
1621 114th Avenue SE
Suite 120
Bellevue, WA 98004-6905

425-454-6444
Fax: 425-454-7634
Classroom curricular software.

837 Phillips Broadband Networks
100 Fairgrounds Drive
Manlius, NY 13104-2437
315-682-9105
Fax: 315-682-1022
Computer networks.

838 Pioneer New Media Technologies
2265 E 220th Street
Long Beach, CA 90810-1639
800-LAS-R ON
www.pioneerelectronics.com
DRM-604X CD-ROM mini-changer, world's fastest CD-ROM drive for multimedia. Also offers special packages including The Mystery Reading Bundle, CLD-V2400RB which includes the CLD-V2400 LaserDisc player, educator's remote control, UC-V109BC barcode reader and membership in the Pioneers in Learning Club and The Case of the Missing Mystery Writer videodisc from Houghton Mifflin.

839 Polaroid Corporation
575 Tech Square
Cambridge, MA 02139
781-386-2000
Fax: 781-386-3925
Computer repair, hardware and peripherals, equipment and various size systems.

840 Power Industries
37 Walnut Street
Wellsley Hills, MA 02181
800-395-5009
Educational software.

841 Quetzal Computers
1708 E 4th Street
Brooklyn, NY 11223-1925
718-375-1186
Computer systems and networks, peripherals and hardware.

842 RLS Groupware
Realtime Learning Systems
2700 Connecticut Avenue NW
Washington, DC 20008-5330
202-483-1510
Classroom curricular software.

843 Radio Shack
100 Throckmorton Street
Suite 1800
Ft. Worth, TX 76102
817-415-3700
Fax: 817-415-2335
Computer networks and peripherals.

Laura Moore, Sr VP Public Relations

844 Rose Electronics
10850 Wilcrest Drive
Suite 900
Houston, TX 77099-3599
281-933-7673
Fax: 281-933-0044
Computer peripherals and hardware.

845 SVE & Churchill Media
6677 N NW Highway
Chicago, IL 60631
773-775-9550
800-829-1900
Fax: 773-775-5091
Has brought innovative media technology into america's pre-K through high school classrooms. By producing programs to satisfy state curriculum standards, SVE consistantly provides educators with high-quality and award-winning videos, CD-ROMs, eLMods, and DVDs in science, social studies, English and health/guidance.

Sarah M Lucas, Communications Coordinator
Kelli Campbell, VP Marketing/Development

5846 School Cruiser
Time Cruiser Computing Corporation
9 Law Drive
3rd Floor, Ottawa, Ontario
Canada K1N 7G1
613-562-9847
877-450-9482
Fax: 613-562-4768
www.epals.com
School Cruiser provides online tools and resources to promote academic and community interaction. It lets you access and share school calenders, lesson plans, homework assignments, announcements and other school related information.

5847 School Specialty
PO Box 1579
Appleton, WI 54912-1579
1-419-589-1600
888-388-3224
Fax: 888-388-6344
orders@schoolspecialty.com
www.schoolspecialty.com
A classroom superstore that features the leading suppliers of educational products and services such as Crayola, 3M, Elmer's and more. The company also provides their own brands among educational resources such as instructional materials, playground equipment, art supplies, office supplies, furniture and more.

Joseph Yorio, President & CEO
Laura Vartanian, SVP, Human Resources

5848 SchoolHouse
The Encarta Lesson Collection and other educational resources.

5849 Seaman Nuclear Corporation
7315 S 1st Street
Oak Creek, WI 53154-2095
414-762-5100
Fax: 414-762-5106
Facility planning and evaluation software.

Scott C. Seamen, President
Todd Seaman, Vice President

5850 Skills Bank Corporation
7104 Ambassador Road
Suite 1
Baltimore, MD 21244-2732
800-451-5726
Educational manufacturing company offering computer and electronic resources, software, programs and systems focusing on home education and tutoring.

5851 Sleek Software Corporation
2404 Rutland Drive,Suite 600
P.O. Box 170100
Austin, TX 78717
512-833-0352
800-337-5335
Fax: 512-833-9718
info@sleek.com
www.sleek.com
Specializes in Algorithm-Based tutorial and test-generating software.

5852 Smartstuff Software
PO Box 82284
Portland, OR 97282-0284
415-763-4799
800-671-3999
Fax: 877-278-7456
Foolproof Security is a dual platform desktop security product that prevents unwanted changes to the desktop and a product line for the internet that protects browser settings, filters content, and allows guided activities.

5853 Society for Visual Education
1345 W Diversey Parkway
Chicago, IL 60614-1249
773-775-9550
Fax: 800-624-1678
Educational software dealing specifically with special education.

5854 SofterWare
132 Welsh Road
Suite 140
Horsham, PA 19044-2217
215-628-0400
800-220-4111
Fax: 215-628-0585
info@softerware.com
www.softerware.com
Offers software, support and administrative solutions to four markets: childcare centers, public and private schools, nonprofit organizations and institutions, and camps.

Nathan Relles, President and Co-Founder
Douglas Schoenberg, CEO/ Co-Founder

5855 SpecialNet
GTE Educational Network Services
5525 N Macarthur Boulevard
Suite 320
Irving, TX 75038-2600
214-518-8500
800-927-3000
Fax: 757-852-8277
Contains news and information on trends and developments in educational services and programs. Databases, bulletin boards, school packages, student/teacher packages, online magazines, distance learning, vocational education, school health, educational laws, and more.

5856 Student Software Guide
800-874-9001
Discounts on a variety of software materials.

5857 Sun Microsystems
2550 Garcia Avenue
#6-13
Mountain View, CA 94043-1100
714-643-2688
800-555-9786
Fax: 650-934-9776
Computer networks and peripherals.

5858 Sunburst/Wings for Learning
101 Castleton Street
Pleasantville, NY 10570-3405
914-747-3310
800-338-3457
Fax: 914-747-4109
Educational materials, including software, print materials, videotapes, videodisc and interdisciplinary packages.

5859 Support Systems International Corporation
136 S 2nd Street
Richmond, CA 94804-2110
510-234-9090
800-777-6269
Fax: 510-233-8888
Sales@FiberMailbox.com
www.fiberopticcableshop.com
Fiber optic patch cables, converters, and switches.

Ben Parsons, General Manager

5860 Surfside Software
PO Box 1112
East Orleans, MA 02643-1112
800-942-9008
Educational software.

5861 Target Vision
1160 Pittsford Victor Road
Suite K
Pittsford, NY 14534-3825
800-724-4044
Fax: 585-248-2354
TVI DeskTop expands your show directly to desktop PC utilizing existing LANS. View information by topics or as a screen saver. Features: graphic importing, VCR interface, advanced scheduling and more.

5862 Teacher Universe
5900 Hollis Street
Suite A
Emeryville, CA 94608
877-248-3224
Fax: 415-763-4917
info@teacheruniverse.com
www.teacheruniverse.com
Creates technology-rich solutions for improving the quality of life and work for teachers worldwide.

5863 Technolink Corporation
2609 Reach Rdÿ
Williamsport, PA 17701-4004
570-323-9057
Fax: 814-693-5901
sales@technolinkcorp.com
www.technolinkcorp.com
Computer systems and electronics.

5864 Tom Snyder Productions
100 Talcott Avenue
Watertown, MA 02472-5703
800-342-0236
Fax: 800-304-1254
www.tomsnyder.com
Educational CD-ROM products and Internet services for schools.

Tom Synder, Founder

5865 Tripp Lite
1111 West 35th Street
Chicago, IL 60610-4117
773-869-1111
international@tripplite.com
www.tripplite.com
Peripherals, hardware and computer systems.

Moti Shulak, Sales Representative

5866 True Basic
12 Commerce Avenue
West Lebanon, NH 03784-1669
800-436-2111
Fax: 603-298-7015
john@truebasic.com
www.truebasic.com
Educational software.

5867 U.S. Public School Universe Database
U.S. National Center for Education Statistics
555 New Jersey Avenue NW
Washington, DC 20001-2029
202-219-1335
85,000 public schools of elementary and secondary levels, public special education, vocational/technical education and alternative education schools.

5868 USA CityLink Project
USA CityLink Project
Floppies for Kiddies
4060 Highway 59
Mandevelle, LA 70471
985-898-2158
Fax: 985-892-8535
Collects used and promotional disketts from the masses for redistribution to school groups and nonprofits throughout the county.

Carol Blake, Contact

5869 Unisys
PO Box 500
Blue Bell, PA 19424-0001
215-986-3501
Fax: 215-986-3279
www.unisys.com
A full line of computers (sizes ranging from mini/micro to medium/large and personal).

Peter Altabef, President and CEO
Quincy Allen, Chief Marketing Officer

5870 Ventura Educational Systems
910 Ramona Avenue
P.O. Box 1622ÿ
Arroyo Grande, CA 93421-1622
805-473-7383
800-336-1022
Fax: 805-556-4469
sales@venturaes.com
www.venturaes.com
Publishers of curriculum based educational software for all grade levels, specializing in interactive math and science software. Programs include teacher's guide with student worksheets.

Fred Ventura, Software Developer
Marne Ventura, Teacher

5871 Viziflex Seels
406 N Midland Aveÿ
Saddle Brook, NJ 07663-6895
201-487-8080
800-627-7752
Fax: 201-487-3266
info@viziflex.com
www.viziflex.com
Peripherals, hardware and electronics, floorcoverings, mats and matting.

5872 Waterford Institute
1590 E 9400 S
Sandy, UT 84093-3009
801-349-2200
800-767-9976
Fax: 801-572-1667
www.waterford.org
Produces children's educational software for math and reading.

Dustin Heuston, Chairman
Benjamin Heuston, President and COO

5873 Web Connection
Education Week
6935 Arlington Road
Bethesda, MD 20814
301-280-3100
800-346-1834
ads@epe.org
www.edweek.org
Information about education suppliers.

Larry Berger, Chairman
Gina Burkhardt, Secretary

5874 Wiremold Company
60 Woodlawn Street
W Hartford, CT 06110-2383
800-243-8421
Computer networks and peripherals.

5875 Wisconsin Technical College System Foundation
4622 University Avenue
PO Box 7874
Madison, WI 53707-7874
608-266-1207
800-821-6313
Fax: 608-266-1690
foundation@wtcsf.tec.wi.us
www.wtcsystem.edu
Interactive videodiscs, self-paced instruction or with barcodes. Students learn faster, become more motivated and retain more information. Math, algebra and electronics courseware are also available.

Drew Petersen, President
John Schwantes, Vice President

5876 Word Associates
3226 Robincrest Drive
Northbrook, IL 60062-5125
847-291-1101
Fax: 847-291-0931
microlrn@aol.com
www.wordassociates.com
Software tutorials featuring lessons in question format, with tutorial and test mode. 15 titles include Math SAT, 2 English SAT; US Constitution Tutor; Phraze Maze; Geometry: Planely Simple, Concepts and Proofs, Right Triangles; Life Skills Math; Algebra; Reading: Myths and More Myths, Magic and Monsters; Economics; American History. Windows, Macintosh, CD's or disks.

Software

Myrna Helfand, President
Sherry Azaria, Marketing

5877 Ztek Company
PO Box 967
Lexington, KY 40588-1768
859-281-1611
800-247-1603
Fax: 859-281-1521
cs@ztek.com
www.ztek.com
Offers physics multimedia lessons on CD-ROM, DVD, videodisc and videotape. Also, carries Pioneer New Media DVD and videodisc players as well as Bretford Manufacturing's line of audio-visual furniture.

5878 ePALS.com
Classroom Exchange
World's largest online classroom community, connecting over 3 million students and teachers through 41,044 profiles.

5879 www.ericir.syr.edu
AskERIC
Ask a question about education and receive a personalized e-mail response in two business days.

5880 www.gsn.bilkent.edu.tr
Ballad of an EMail Terrorist
Global SchoolNet Foundation

One pitfall of the internet is danger of vulgarity and/or obscenity to a child via e-mail.

5881 www.suzyred.home.texas.net
The Little Red School House
Offers sections on music, writing, quotes, web quests, jokes, poetry, games, activities and more.

5882 www.FundRaising.Com
FundRaising.Com
800-443-5353
Internet fundraising company.

5883 www.abcteach.com
P.O. Box 1217
Union Lake, MI 48387-1217
Fax: 248-493-6565
support@abcteach.com

Offers ideas and activities for kids, parents, students and teachers. Features section on many topics in education, including writing, poetry, word searches, crosswords, games, maps, mazes and more.

5884 www.abctooncenter.com
ABC Toon Center
This family orientated site offers games, cartoons, storybook, theater, information stations and more. This site is open to children of differnt languages. Can be translated into Italian, French, Spanish, German and Russian.

5885 www.americatakingaction.com
America Taking Action
Provides every school with a free, 20 page website with resources for teachers, parents, students and the community. Created entirely by involved parents, teachers and community leaders as a public service.

5886 www.awesomelibrary.org
Awesome Library
Organizes the Web with 15,000 carefully reviewed resources, including the top 5 percent in education. Offers sections of mathematics, science, social studies, english, health, physical education, technology, languages, special education, the arts and more. Features a section involved with today's current issues facing our world, like pollution, gun control, tobacco, and other changing 'hot' topics. Site can be browsed in English, German, Spanish, French or Portuguese.

5887 www.bigchalk.com
Big Chalk-The Education Network
800-521-0600
Fax: 734-997-4268
Educational web site tailored to fit teachers' and students' needs.

5888 www.brunchbunch.org
Brunch Bunch
The foundation names all of the grants it makes after teachers who have demonstrated excellence. The foundation regularly makes significant grants to aid teachers' efforts.

5889 www.busycooks.com
BusyCooks.com
A hit with home economics teachers, enjoying free recipes and online cooking shows. Tapping into the experience of thousands to nuture your culinary creativity.

5890 www.chandra.harvard.edu
Chandra X-ray Observatory Center
60 Garden Street
Cambridge, MA 2138
617-496-7941
Fax: 617-495-7356
cxcpub@cfa.harvard.edu
Find teacher-developed, classroom-ready materials based on results from the Chandra mission. Classroom-ready activities, interactive games, activities, quizzes, and printable activities which will keep students absorbed with interest.

5891 www.cherrydale.com
Cherrydale Farms
707 N. Valley Forge Rd.
Lansdale, PA 19446
800-333-4525
Website offers company information, fund raising products and information, online mega mall, card shop, career opportunities and much more. Produces fine chocolates and confections. Many opportunities for schools to raise funds with various Cherrydale programs.

5892 www.cleverapple.com
Education Station
info@cleverapple.com
Offers links to many sites involved with education.

5893 www.edhelper.com
edhelper.com
Keeps you up to date with the latest educational news.

5894 www.education-world.com
Education World
75 Mill St.
Colchester, CT 6415
800-227-0831
webmaster@educationworld.com
Features and education-specific search engine with links to over 115,000 sites. Offers monthly reviews of other educational web sites, and other original content on a weekly basis.

5895 www.eduverse.com
Software developer building core technologies for powering international distance education. Features an online distance education engine, product information, news releases and more.

5896 www.efundraising.com
efundraising.com
C/O FedEx Trade Networks
156 Lawrence Paquette Ind'l Drive, PMW#
Champlain, NY 12919
866-825-2921
Fax: 877-275-8664
online@fundraising.com
Provides non-profit groups with quality products, low prices and superior service. Helping thousands of schools, youth sports teams and community groups reach their fundraising goals each year.

5897 www.embracingthechild.com
Embracing the Child
pk@embracingthechild.org
Educational resource for teachers and parents that provides a structural resource for home and classroom use, lesson planning, as well as a child-safe site, for children's research, classroom use and homework fulfillment.

5898 www.enc.org
ENC Learning Inc.
1585 Central Ave.
Ste C-5 #293
Summerville, SC 29483
614-378-4567
Fax: 843-832-2063
For math and science teachers-anywhere in the K-12 spectrum. This organization contains a wealth of information, activities, resources, and demonstrations for the sciences and math.

5899 www.englishhlp.com
English Help
englishhlpr@hotmail.com
This page is a walk through of Microsoft Power Point. The goal is to show in a few simple steps how to make your own website. Created by Rebecca Holland.

5900 www.expage.com/Just4teachers
Just 4 Teachers
The ultimate website for educators! Teaching tips, resources, themeunits, search engines, classroom management and sites for kids.

5901 www.fraboom.com
Fraboom
FR Productions, LLC
1427 NW Raleigh St
Portland, OR 97209
503-208-2315
support@fraboom.com
This site's tools let you specify areas within your state's standards and search for a list of 'Flying Rhinoceros' lessons that meet your criteria. Offers other information sources for teachers and students.

5902 www.globalschoolnet.org
Global SchoolNet Foundation
270 N. El Camino Real
Ste. 395
Encinitas, CA 92024
760-635-0001
Connects teachers, administrators, and parents with options and possibilities the Internet has to offer the schools of the world.

Dr. Yvonne Marie Andres, President
John St. Clair, Vice President

5903 www.gradebook.org/
The Classroom
Dedicated to the students and teachers of the world.

5904 www.homeworkspot.com
HomeworkSpot
A free online homework resource center developed by educators, students, parents and journalists for K-12 students. It simplifies the search for homework help, features a top-notch reference cetner, current events, virtual field trips and expeditions, extracurricular activities and study breaks, parent and teacher resources and much more.

5905 www.iearn.org
iEARN USA
Utilizes projects for students ages 6 through 19. Projects are concerned with the environment as well as arts, politics, and the health and welfare of all the Earth's citizens.

5906 www.jasonproject.org
Jason Project
Founded in 1989 as a tool for live, interactive programs for students in the fourth through eighth grades. Annual projects are funded through a variety of public corporations and governmental organizations.

Dr. Eleanor Smalley, EVP/ COO
Sean Smith, SVP/ CTO

5907 www.k12planet.com
Chancery Software
Chancery Software is announcing a new school to home extension that will provide student information systems to give parents, students, and educators access to accurate information about students in one, easy-to-use website.

5908 www.kiddsmart.com
Institute for Child Development
The ICD develops educational materials and resources designed to facilitate children's social and emotional development. Offers the previous materials as well as research summaries, lesson plans, training, workshops, games, multi-cultural materials and other resources to teachers, educational centers, parents, counselors, corporations, non-profits and others involved in the child-care professions.

5909 www.lessonplansearch.com
Lesson Plan Search
220 lesson plans from cooking to writing.

5910 www.lessonplanspage.com
HotChalk
1999 S. Bascom Avenue
Suite 1020
Campbell, CA 95008

888-468-2336
Fax: 408-608-1679
support@hotchalk.com
A collection of over 1,000 free lesson plans for teachers to use in their classrooms. Lesson plans are organized by subject and grade level.

5911 www.library.thinkquest.org
Think Quest Library of Entries
The Arti FAQS 2100 Project is designed to predict how art will influence our lives in the next hundred years. Students can use available data to make reasonable predictions for the future.

5912 www.ncspearson.com
NCS Pearson
NCS Pearson is at the forefront of the education space with curriculum, contant, tools, assessment, and interface to enterprise systems

5913 www.negaresa.org
Northeast Georgia RESA
keith.everson@negaresa.org
For teachers, electronic web-based grade book aplication eGRader 2000. Many educational resource links as well has discussion groups, a news and events section, and even links to online shopping.

Dr. Keith Everson, Executive Director
Debra Wallace, Business/ Finance Director

5914 www.netrover.com/~kingskid/108.html
Room 108
An educational activity center for kids. Offers lots of fun for children with educational focus; like songs, art, math, kids games, children's stories and much more. Sections with pen pal information, puzzles, crosswords, teachers store, spelling, kids sites, email, music, games and more.

5915 www.pcg.cyberbee.com
IwayNet Communications
614-294-9292
support@iwaynet.net
Offered to classes all over the world via the internet. Your class commits to exchanging picture postcards with all other participants. Appropriate for all ages, for public and private schools, for youth groups and for home- schools.

5916 www.pitt.edu
EdIndex
724-244-4939
poole@pitt.edu
A web resource for teachers and students, offers course information, MS Office tutorials, personal and professional pages, and more.

5917 www.riverdeep.net
Riverdeep Interactive Learning
617-351-5316
800-426-657
Sales_Support@hmhco.com
Riverdeep's interactive science, language and math arts programs deliver high quality educational experiences.

5918 www.safedayeducation.com
Safe Day Education
The leader in bully prevention and street proofing education for kids; safe dating preparation programs for teens; and re-empowerment and assault prevention training for women.

5919 www.safekids.com/child_safety.htm
SafeKids.Com
larry@safekids.com
Cyberspace is a fabulous tool for learning, but some of it can be exploitative and even criminal.

Larry Magid, Founder/ Editor

5920 www.sdcoe.k12.ca.us
Researches a coral reef and creates a diorama for The Cay by Theodore Taylor.

5921 www.shop2gether.com
Collective Publishing Service
We are committed to helping all schools buy better by shopping together. Building upon a scalable, dynamic procurement platform and group buying technology, we also provide a unique ecommerce system, delivering next generation procurement services over the Internet.

5922 www.spaceday.com
Space Day
Program engineered to build problem-solving and teamwork skills.

5923 www.specialednews.com
Special Education News
info@specialednews.com
Consists of breaking news stories from Washington and around the country. These stories are compliled together in the Special Education News letter is sent via e-mail once a week.

5924 www.straightscoop.org
Straight Scoop News Bureau
SSNB increases the frequency of anti-drug themes and messages in junior high and high school student media.

5925 www.tcta.org
Texas Classroom Teachers Association
PO Box 1489
Austin, TX 78767-1489
512-477-9415
888-879-8282
Fax: 512-469-9527
Compromised of Texas educators, provides interest for teachers everywhere. Education laws and codes are presented here.

Terrill Q. Littlejohn, President
Teresa Koehler, President-Elect

5926 www.teacherszone.com
TeachersZone.Com
Lesson plans, free stuff for teachers, contests, sites for kids, conferences and workshops, schools and organizations, job listings, products for school.

5927 www.teacherweb.com
TeacherWeb
PO BOX 06290
Chicago, IL 60606
TeacherWeb, your free personal website that's as easy to use as the bulletin board in your classroom. This site offers a secure, password-protected service.

5928 www.teachingheart.com
Teaching is A Work of Heart
Chock-full of ideas, projects, motivational thoughts, behavior ideas.

5929 www.thelearningworkshop.com
Learning Workshop.com
Services for teachers, students, and parents. For teachers online gradebooks and grade tracking, students can check their grades online, parents enjoy articles written expressly for them and a tutor search by zip code.

5930 www.tutorlist.com
TutorList.com
Offers information on tips on how to find and choose a tutor, what a tutor does, educational news and more.

5931 www.worksafeusa.org
WorkSafeUSA
Addresses the alarming injury and death rates experienced by America's adolescent workers. This non-profit site publishes and distributes A Teen Guide to Workplace Safety, available in English and Spanish.

5932 www1.hp.com
Hewlett-Packard Development Company
3000 Hanover Street
Palo Alto, CA 94304-1185
650-857-1501
Compaq is one of the leading corporations in educational technology, working on developing solutions that will connect students, teachers and the community.

Administration

5933 ASQC
611 E Wisconsin Avenue
Milwaukee, WI 53202-4695
800-248-1946
Fax: 414-272-1734
Business and administrative software.

5934 Anchor Pad
Anchor Pad Products
11105 Dana Cir
Cypress, CA 90630-5133
714-799-4071
800-626-2467
Fax: 714-799-4094
Computer and office security

Caroline Jones, COO
Melanie Ruste, Sales/Marketing Associate

5935 Applied Business Technologies
55 S.E. 2nd Avenue
Delray Beach, FL 33444
561-272-1232
800-683-6590
Fax: 610-359-9420
info@appliedcorp.com
Computer networks and administrative software.

5936 AskSam Systems
PO Box 1831
Perry, FL 32348
850-584-6590
800-800-1997
Fax: 850-584-7481
info@asksam.com
Business and administrative free form database software.

Dottie Sheffield, Sales Manager

5937 Autodesk Retail Products
1725 220th Street
Suite C101
Bothell, WA 98021-8809
425-487-2233
Fax: 425-486-1636
Administrative and business software.

5938 Avcom Systems
250 Cox Lane
PO Box 977
Cutchogue, NY 11935-1303
631-734-5080
800-645-1134
Fax: 631-734-7204

Supplies for making and mounting transparencies. Products includes economy and self-adhesive mounts; transparent rolls and sheets; markers, pens and cleaners; thermo, computer graphics and plain-paper copier transparency films and laminating supplies.

Joseph K Lukas

939 Bobbing Software
67 Country Oaks Drive
Buda, TX 78610-9338
800-688-6812
Administrative software and systems.

940 Bull HN Information Systems
285 Billerica Road
Chelmsford, MA 01824
978-294-6000
Fax: 978-244-0085
Computer networks, computers (large, medium, micro and mini), and supplies.

941 Bureau of Electronic Publishing
745 Alexander Road
#728
Princeton, NJ 08540-6343
973-808-2700
Administrative software, hardware and systems.

942 CRS
17440 Dallas Parkway
Suite 120
Dallas, TX 75287-7307
800-433-9239
Administrative software and systems.

943 Campus America
900 E Hill Avenue
Suite 205
Knoxville, TN 37915-2580
865-523-4477
877-536-0222
Fax: 617-492-9081
Computer supplies, equipment, systems and networks.

944 Century Consultants
150 Airport Road
Suite 1500
Lakewood, NJ 08701-3309
732-363-9300
Fax: 732-363-9374
Develops, markets, and services Oracle based web-enabled Management software, STAR_BASE, for school districts K-12.

945 Computer Resources
1037 Calef Highway
Barrington, NH 03825-0060
603-664-5811
888-641-9922
Fax: 603-664-5864
The Modular Management System for Schools is a school administrative software system designed to handle all student record keeping and course scheduling needs. A totally integrated modular system built around a central Student Master File. Additional modules handle student scheduling, grades, attendance and discipline reporting.

Raymond J Perreault, VP Marketing
Robert W Cook, National Sales Manager

946 Computer Supply People, The
N93 W14636 Whittaker Way
Menomonee Falls, WI 53051-1629
262-251-5511
800-242-2090
Fax: 262-251-4737
medmgt@computersupplypeople.com
www.computersupplypeople.com
Computer supplies, equipment and systems, Koss headphones.

John Schimberg, Education Sales

5947 Cyborg Systems
2 N Riverside Plaza
Chicago, IL 60606-2600
312-454-1865
Administrative and business software programs.

5948 Diskovery Educational Systems
1860 Old Okeechobee Road
Suite 105
West Palm Beach, FL 33409-5281
561-683-8410
800-331-5489
Fax: 561-683-8416
info@diskovery.com
www.diskovery.com
Computer supplies, equipment, and various size systems.

5949 Doron Precision Systems
Doron Precision Systems
150 Corporate Drive
PO Box 400
Binghamton, NY 13902-0400
607-772-1610
Fax: 607-772-6760
sales@doronprecision.com
www.doronprecision.com
Business and classroom curriculum software. Driving Simulation Systems and Entertainment Simulation Systems.

5950 Educational Data Center
180 De La Salle Drive
Romeoville, IL 60446-1895
800-451-7673
Fax: 815-838-9412
Administration software.

5951 EnrollForecast: K-12 Enrollment Forecasting Program
Association of School Business Officials Int'l
11401 N Shore Drive
Reston, VA 20190-4232
703-478-0405
Fax: 703-478-0205
A powerful planning tool that helps project student enrollment.

Peg D Kirkpatrick, Editor/Publisher
Robert Gluck, Managing Editor

5952 Epson America
3840 Kilroy Airport Way
Long Beach, CA 90806
800-289-7766
Webmaster@ea.epson.com
www.epson.com
Computer repair and peripherals.

John Lang, President/ CEO
Keith Kratzberg, SVP, Sales & Marketing

5953 FMJ/PAD.LOCK Computer Security Systems
520 W. Central Ave.
Brea, CA 92821
714-990-3218
800-872-9562
Fax: 714-990-5409
dealerinquiry@fmjpadlock.com
www.fmjpadlock.com
Computer peripherals, supplies and equipment.

Tom Separa

5954 Geist
Geist Manufacturing
1821 Yolande Avenue
Lincoln, NE 68521-1835
402-474-3400
800-432-3219
Fax: 402-474-4369
products@geistmfg.com
Power distribution for racks, cabinets and data centers.

Terri Rockeman, Customer Service Supervisor

5955 Global Computer Supplies
11 Harbor Park Drive
Port Washington, NY 11050-4622
516-625-6200
800-446-9662
Fax: 516-484-8533
www.globalcomputer.com
Computer supplies, equipment, hardware, software and systems.

5956 Harrington Software
658 Ridgewood Road
Maplewood, NJ 07040-2536
201-761-5914
Administrative and business software.

5957 Information Design
7009 S Potomac Street
Suite 110
Englewood, CO 80112
303-792-2990
800-776-2469
Fax: 303-792-2378
Administrative and business software including systems focusing on payroll, personnel, financial accounting, purchasing, budgeting, fixed asset accounting and salary administration.

5958 International Rotex
7171 Telegraph Road
Los Angeles, CA 90040-3227
800-648-1871
Computer supplies.

5959 Jay Klein Productions Grade Busters
118 N. Tejon St.
Suite 304
Colorado Springs, CO 80903
719-599-8786
Fax: 719-380-9997
A line of teacher productivity tools, the most highly recognized integrated gradebooks, attendance records, seating charts and scantron packages in K-12 education today (Mac, DOS, Windows, Apple II).

Jay A Klein, President
Angela C Wormley, Office Manager

5960 Jostens Learning Corporation
5521 Norman Center Drive
Minneapolis, MN 55437-1040
800-635-1429
The leading provider of comprehensive multimedia instruction, including hardware, software and service.

5961 MISCO Computer Supplies
1 Misco Plaza
Holmdel, NJ 07733-1033
800-876-4726
Computer supplies, networks, equipment and accessories.

5962 Mathematica
Wolfram Research, Inc.
100 Trade Centre Drive
Champaign, IL 61820-7237
217-398-0700
800-965-3726
Fax: 217-398-0747
info@wolfram.com
www.wolfram.com

Classroom curricular software and business/administrative software.

Stephen Wolfram, Founder/CEO
Jean Buck, Dir., Corp Communications

5963 MicroAnalytics
Student Transportation Systems
2300 Clarendon Boulevard
Suite 404
Arlington, VA 22201-3331
703-841-0414
Fax: 703-527-1693
Automates bus routing and scheduling for school districts with fleets of 5 to 500 buses. BUSTOPS is flexible, affordable and easy to use. Offers color maps and graphics, efficient routing, report writing, planning and more to improve your pupil transportation system.

Mary Buchanan, Sales Manager

5964 MicroLearn Tutorial Series
Word Associates
3226 Robincrest Drive
Northbrook, IL 60062-5125
847-291-1101
Fax: 847-291-0931
microlrn@aol.com
Software tutorials featuring lessons in question format, with tutorial and test mode. 15 titles include Math SAT, 2 English SAT; US Constitution Tutor; Phraze Maze; Geometry: Planely Simple, Concepts and Proofs, Right Triangles; Life Skills Math; Algebra; Reading: Myths and More Myths, Magic and Monsters; Economics; American History. Windows, Macintosh, CD's or disks.

Software

Myrna Helfand, President

5965 NCS Marketing
11000 Prairie Lakes Drive
Eden Prairie, MN 55344-3885
800-447-3269
Fax: 612-830-7788
www.ncspearson.com
OpScan optical mark reading scanners from NCS process data at speeds of up to 10,000 sheets per hour for improved accuracy and faster turnaround. Also provides software and scanning applications and services that manage student, financial, human resources, instructional and assessment information.

Sheryl Kyweriga

5966 National Computer Systems
11000 Prairie Lakes Drive
Minneapolis, MN 55440
800-447-3269
Fax: 952-830-8564
Administrative software and systems.

5967 Parlant Technologies
PO Box 50240
Provo, UT 84605
801-373-9669
800-735-2930
Fax: 801-373-9697
info@parlant.com
Administrative software and systems.

5968 Quill Corporation
P.O. Box 37600
Philadelphia, PA 19101-0600
847-634-4800
800-982-3400
Fax: 800-789-8955
www.quill.com
Computer and office supplies and equipment.

5969 Rauland Borg
1802 West Central Road
Mount Prospect, IL 60056
847-679-0900
Fax: 800-217-0977
www.rauland.com
Administrative software and systems.

Kidder's Rauland-Borg, President/ CEO
Peipert , SVP, Finance

5970 Rediker Administration Software
2 Wileraham Road
Hampden, MA 01036-9685
413-566-3463
800-213-9860
Fax: 413-566-2274
APSupport@rediker.com
www.rediker.com
School administrative software for the teaching professional.

Rich Rediker, CEO
Andrew Anderlonis, President

5971 Scantron Corporation
1313 Lone Oak Road
Eagan, MN 55121
949-639-7500
800-722-687
www.scantron.com
Computer peripherals, administrative software and services.

5972 SourceView Software International
PO Box 578
Concord, CA 94522-0578
925-825-1248
Classroom curricular, business and administrative software.

5973 Systems & Computer Technology Services
4 Country View Road
Malvern, PA 19355-1408
610-647-5930
Fax: 610-578-7778
Administrative and business software programs and services.

5974 Trapeze Software
8360 East Via de Ventura
Suite L-200
Scottsdale, AZ 85258
480-627-8400
Fax: 480-627-8411
info@trapezegroup.com
www.trapezegroup.com
Computerized bus routing, boundary planning and redistricting software and services, and AVL (automatic vehicle locator software).

Clint Rooley, Director of Sales

5975 University Research Company
7200 Wisconsin Avenue
Suite 600
Bethesda, MD 20814
301-654-8338
800-526-4972
Fax: 301-941-8427
www.urc-chs.com
Supplies Quiz-A-Matic electronics for quiz competitions.

Barbara N. Turner, President

5976 Velan
4153 24th Street
Suite 1
San Francisco, CA 94114-3667
415-949-9150
Administrative software and systems.

5977 WESTLAW
West Group
610 Opperman Drive
Eagan, MN 55123-1340
612-687-7000
800-937-8529
Fax: 651-687-5827
www.westlaw.com
Online service concerning the complete text of U.S. federal court decisions, state court decisions from all 50 states, regulations, specialized files, and texts dealing with education.

5978 www.teacherfiles.homestead.com/index~ns4
Homestead
800-986-0958
www.homestead.com
Offers sections on clip art, quotes, slogans, lesson plans, organizations, web quests, political involvement, grants, publications, special education, professional development, humor and more.

5979 www.abcteach.com
Abcteach
P.O. Box 1217
Union Lake, MI 48387-1217
Fax: 248-493-6565
support@abcteach.com
www.abcteach.com
Free printable materials for kids, parents, student teachers and teachers. Theme units, spelling word searches, research help, writing skills and much more.

5980 www.apple.com
PowerSchool
PowerSchool's web-based architecture makes it easy to learn and easy to use.

5981 www.atozteacherstuff.com
A to Z Teacher Stuff
webmaster@atozteacherstuff.com
www.atozteacherstuff.com
Features quick indexes to online lesson plans and teacher resources, educational sites for teachers, articles, teacher store and more.

5982 www.awesomelibrary.org
Awesome Library
www.awesomelibrary.org
Organizes the Web with 15,000 carefully reviewed resources, including the top 5 percent in education. Offers sections of mathematics, science, social studies, english, health, physical education, technology, languages, special education, the arts and more. Features a section involved with today's current issues facing our world, like pollution, gun control, tobacco, and other changing 'hot' topics. Site can be browsed in English, German, Spanish, French or Portuguese.

5983 www.easylobby.com
HID Global
611 Center Ridge Drive
Austin, TX 78753
www.hidglobal.com
The complete electronic visitor management system.

Denis H,bert, President/ CEO
Michele DeWitt, SVP, Human Resources

5984 www.fraboom.com
FR Productions, LLC
1427 NW Raleigh St
Portland, OR 97209
503-208-2315
support@fraboom.com
This site's tools let's you specify areas within your state's standards and search for a list of 'Flying Rhinoceros' lessons that meet your criteria. Offers other information sources for teachers and students.

985 www.fundraising.com
PO BOX 305142
Nashville, TN 37230-5142
800-443-5353
www.fundraising.com
Internet fundraising company.

986 www.hoagiesgifted.org
Hoagies Gifted Education Page
256 Eagleview Boulevard PMB 123
Exton, PA 19341
webmaster@hoagiesgifted.org
www.hoagiesgifted.org
Features the latest research on parenting and educating gifted children. Offers ideas, solutions and other things to try for parents of gifted children. Sections with world issues facing children and other important social topics.

Carolyn K. Founder/ Director

987 www.kiddsmart.com
Institute for Child Development
The ICD develops educational materials and resources designed to facilitate children's social and emotional development. Offers the previous materials as well as research summaries, lesson plans, training, workshops, games, multi-cultural materials and other resources to teachers, educational centers, parents, counselors, corporations, non-profits and others involved in the child-care professions.

988 www.nycteachers.com
NYCTeachers.com
www.nycteachers.com
Designed for NYC teachers that work within public school systems. Speaks out on controversial issues facing the broadening, funding, development, staffing and other concerns about public schools. Welcomes your suggestions and comments about the site and the issues involved.

989 www.songs4teachers.com
O'Flynn Consulting
c/o Mary Flynn
494 St. Vincent Street
Barrie, ON L4M 7
705-728-6528
Fax: 705-728-6528
mary@songs4teachers.com
www.songs4teachers.com
Offers many resources for teachers including songs made especially for your classroom. Sections with songs and activities for holidays, seasons and more. Features books and audios with 101 theme songs for use in the classroom or anywhere children gather to sing.

990 www.thecanadianteacher.com
The Canadian Teacher Marketplace
www.thecanadianteacher.com
Site where educators can find the latest links to free resources, materials, lesson plans, software, samples and computers. Some links are for Canadians only.

991 www.welligent.Com
Welligent
5205 Colley Avenue
Norfolk, VA 23508
888-317-5960
info@welligent.com
www.welligent.com
A web-based software program that improves student health management and your school's finances at the same time.

Early Childhood Education

5992 Jump Start Math for Kindergartners
Knowledge Adventure
Torrance, CA
800-545-7677
www.knowledgeadventure.com
The program covers important and essential kindergarten math skills such as, writing numbers, sorting, and problem solving/following directions.

David Lord, President/ CEO
Jim Czulewicz, Chief Revenue Officer

5993 Mindplay
4400 E. Broadway Blvd.
Suite 400
Tucson, AZ 85711
520-888-1800
800-221-7911
Fax: 520-888-7904
mail@mindplay.com
www.mindplay.com
Educational software focusing on early childhood education and adult literacy.

Stacie Johnson, Communication Coordinator
Judith Bliss, Founder/ Chairwoman

5994 Nordic Software
PO Box 5403
Lincoln, NE 68505
402-489-1557
800-306-6502
Fax: 402-489-1560
Specializes in developing and publishing educational software titles. Well-known for its software titles that make it easy for children to learn while playing on the computer. Develops and publishes elementary software products for the Macintosh and Windows platforms. Products include Turbo Math Facts, Clock Shop, Coin Critters, Language Explorer and Preschool Parade, and more.

Tammy Hurlbut, Finance/Operations

5995 Personalized Software
PO Box 359
Phoenix, OR 97535
541-535-8085
800-553-2312
Fax: 541-535-8889
info@childcaremanager.com
www.childcaremanager.com
Offers a full line of childcare management and development software programs.

5996 Science for Kids
9950 Concord Church Road
Lewisville, NC 27023-9720
336-945-9000
800-572-4362
Fax: 336-945-2500
sci4kids@aol.com
www.scienceforkids.com
Developers and publishers of CD-ROM science and early learning programs for children ages 5-14; for Macintosh and Windows computers; school and home programs available.

Charles Moyer, Executive VP

Elementary Education

5997 Educational Institutions Partnership Program
Defense Information Systems Agency
Automation Resources Information
701 S Courthouse Road
Arlington, VA 22204-2199
703-607-6900
Fax: 703-607-4371
Makes available used computer equipment for donation of transfer to eligible schools, including K-12 schools recognized by the US Department of Education, Universities, colleges, Minority Institutions and nonporfit groups.

5998 Houghton Mifflin Company
222 Berkeley Street
Boston, MA 02116-3748
617-351-5000
Fax: 617-351-1106
www.hmhco.com
Offers literature-based technology products for grades K-8 including CD's Story Time, a Macintosh based CD-ROM programs for grades 1 and 2 and Channel R.E.A.D., a videodisc series for grades 3-8.

Linda K. Zecher, President/ CEO/ Director
Eric Shuman, Chief Financial Officer

5999 Kid Keys 2.0
Knowledge Adventure
800-545-7677
schoolsales@jumpstart.com
www.knowledgeadventure.com
Keyboarding for grades K-2.

6000 Kinder Magic
1680 Meadowglen Lane
Encinitas, CA 92024-5652
760-632-6693
Fax: 760-632-9995
www.kindermagic.com
Educational software for ages 4-11.

Dr. Ilse Ortabasi, President

6001 Micrograms Publishing
9934 N Alpine Road
Suite 108
Machesney Park, IL 61115-8240
800-338-4726
Fax: 815-877-1482
www.micrograms.com
Micrograms develops educational software for schools and homes.

6002 Tudor Publishing Company
17218 Preston Road
Suite 400
Dallas, TX 75252-4018
Grade level evaluation (GLE) is a computer-adaptive assessment program for elementary and secondary students.

6003 Wordware Publishing
2320 Los Rios Boulevard
#200
Plano, TX 75074-8157
214-423-0090
Fax: 972-881-9147
Publisher of computer reference tutorials, regional Texas and Christian books. Educational division produces a diagnostic and remediation software for grade levels 3-8. Content covers over 3,000 objectives in reading, writing and math. Contact publisher for dealer information.

Eileen Schnett, Product Manager

6004 World Classroom
Global Learning Corporation
PO Box 201361
Arlington, TX 76006-1361
214-641-3356
800-866-4452
An educational telecommunications network that prepares students, K-12 to use real-life data to make real-life decisions about themselves and their environment. Participating countries have included Argentina, Austra-

lia, Belgium, Canada, Denmark, France, Germany, Hungary, Iceland, Indonesia, Kenya, Russia, Lithuania, Mexico, Singapore, Taiwan, the Netherlands, the United States and Zimbabwe.

6005 www.k-6educators....education/k-6 educators
About Education Elementary Educators

6006 www.etacuisenaire.com/index.htm
ETA hand2mind
500 Greenview Court
Vernon Hills, IL 60061
847-816-5050
800-288-9920
Fax: 800-875-9643
www.hand2mind.com
Over 5,000 manipulative-based education and supplemental materials for grades K-12.
Bill Chiasson, President
Dr. Barbara diSioudi, VP, Product Development

6007 www.wnet.org/wnetschool
wNet School
212-560-2713
www.wnet.org/education
Helps K-12 teachers by providing free standards based lesson plans, classroom activities, multimedia primers, online mentors, links to model technology schools, and more. Online workshops are also included in the WNET TV site.
Carole Wacey, Vice President
Christopher Brande, National Segment Producer

6008 www.cherrydale.com/
Cherrydale Farms
707 N. Valley Forge Rd.
Lansdale, PA 19446
800-333-4525
www.cherrydale.com
Website offers company information, fund raising products and information, online mega mall, card shop, career opportunities and much more. Produces fine chocolates and confections. Many opportunities for schools to raise funds with various Cherrydale programs.

6009 www.efundraising.com
Fundraising
C/O FedEx Trade Networks
156 Lawrence Paquette Ind'l Drive, PMW#
Champlain, NY 12919
866-825-2921
Fax: 877-275-8664
www.efundraising.com
Provides non-profit groups with quality products, low prices and superior service. Helping thousands of schools, youth sports teams and community groups reach their fundraising goals each year.

6010 www.hoagiesgifted.org
Hoagies' Gifted Education Page
256 Eagleview Boulevard PMB 123
Exton, PA 19341
webmaster@hoagiesgifted.org
www.hoagiesgifted.org
Features the latest research on parenting and educating gifted children. Offers ideas, solutions and other things to try for parents of gifted children. Sections with world issues facing children and other important social topics.
Carolyn K. Founder/ Director

6011 www.netrover.com/~kingskid/108.html
Room 108
www.netrover.com
An educational activity center for kids. Offers lots of fun for children with educational focus; like songs, art, math, kids games, children's stories and much more. Sections with pen pal information, puzzles, crosswords, teachers store, spelling, kids sites, email, music, games and more.

6012 www.netrox.net
Dr. Labush's Links to Learning
General links for teachers with internet help, coloring pages, and enrichment programs.

6013 www.primarygames.com
PrimaryGames.com
webmaster@primarygames.com
www.primarygames.com
Contains educational games for elementary students.

6014 www.usajobs.opm.gov/b1c.htm
Overseas Employment Info-Teachers

Employment

6015 AASA Job Bulletin
American Association of School Administrators
1615 Duke Street
Alexandria, VA 22314
860-437-5700
888-575-9675
clientserv@yourmembership.com
www.aasa.org
The Job Bulletin was made to help employers and job candidates save time finding one another.

6016 Educational Placement Service
90 S Cascade
Suite 1110
Colorado Springs, CO 80903
www.teacherjobs.com
Largest teacher placement service in the U.S.

6017 Teachers@Work
PO Box 430
Vail, CO 81658
970-476-5008
Fax: 970-476-1496
Electronic employment service designed to match the professional staffing needs of schools with teacher applicants.

6018 www.SchoolJobs.com
SchoolJobs.com
Provides principals, superintendents and other administrators the ability to market their job openings to a national pool of candidates, also gives educational professionals the chance to search for opportunities matching their skills.

6019 www.aasa.org
American Association of School Administrators
1615 Duke Street
Alexandria, VA 22314
703-528-0700
Fax: 703-841-1543
info@aasa.org
www.aasa.org
Leadership news online.

Guidance & Counseling

6020 Alcohol & Drug Prevention for Teachers, Law Enforcement & Parent Groups
PO Box 4656
Reading, PA 19606
610-582-2090
Fax: 610-404-0406
nodrugs@earthlink.net
www.nodrugs.com
Local organizations and international groups against drugs.

6021 Live Wire Media
P.O. Box 848
Mill Valley, CA 94942
415-564-9500
800-359-5437
Fax: 415-552-4087
sales@livewiremedia.com
www.livewiremedia.com/
Videos for youth guidance and character development, and teacher training.
Christine Hollander, Director Marketing

6022 Phillip Roy Multimedia Materials
PO Box 130
Indian Rocks Beach, FL 34635
727-593-2700
800-255-9085
Fax: 727-595-2685
ruth@philliproy.com
www.philliproy.com
Multimedia materials for use with alternative education, Chapter 1, dropout prevention, Even Start, Head Start, JTPA/PIC, special education students, at-risk students, transition to work programs. Focuses on basic skills, conflict resolution, remediation, vocational education, critical thinking skills, communication skills, reasoning and decision making skills. Materials can be duplicated networked at no cost.
Phil Padol, Consultant
Regina Jacques, Customer Support

6023 www.goodcharacter.com
2355 Westwood Boulevard
Suite 312
Los Angeles, CA 90084
800-359-5437
Fax: 415-552-4087
info@goodcharacter.com
www.goodcharacter.com
Teaching guides for K-12 character education, packed with discussion questions, assignments, and activities that can be used as lesson plans.

International

6024 FHI 360
359 Blackwell Street
Suite 200
Durham, NC 27701
919-544-7040
Fax: 919-544-7261
eec@fhi360.org
www.fhi360.org
Provides information on international exchange, fellowship and training.
Patrick C. Fine, MEd, Chief Executive Officer
Deborah Kennedy-Iraheta, MA, Chief Operating Officer

6025 www.asce.org
American Society of Civil Engineers
1801 Alexander Bell Drive
Reston, VA 20191
703-295-6300
800-548-2723
www.asce.org

This site lists scholarships and fellowships available only to ASCE members.

Robert D. Stevens, President
Dennis D. Truax, Treasurer

026 www.cie.uci.edu
International Opportunities Program
1100 Student Services II
Irvine, CA 92697-2475
949-824-6343
Fax: 949-824-9133
studyabroad@uci.edu
www.cie.uci.edu
Valuable links for exploring opportunities for study and research abroad.

Marcella Khelif, Associate Director
Sharon Parks, Assistant Director

027 www.ciee.org
Council on International Educational Exchange
300 Fore Street
Portland, ME 04101
207-553-4000
contact@ciee.org
www.ciee.org
Study abroad programs by region, work abroad opportunities, international volunteer projects and Council-administered financial aid and grant information.

James P. Pellow, Ed.D, President & CEO
Tim Propp, Chief Operating Officer

28 www.cies.org
Council for International Exchange of Scholars
1400 K Street, NW
Suite 700
Washington, DC 20005
202-686-4000
Fax: 202-686-4029
Scholars@iie.org
www.cies.org
Information on the Fulbright Senior Scholar Program which is made available to Fulbright alumni,grantees, prospective applicants and public at large.

Jeff Hopper, Director
Peter VanDerwater, Director of Outreach

29 www.daad.org
German Academic Exchange Service (DADD)
871 United Nations Plaza
New York, NY 10017
212-758-3223
Fax: 212-755-5780
daadny@daad.org
www.daad.org
Promotes international academic relations and contains links to research grants, summer language grants,annual grants, grants in German studies andspecial programs.

Dr. Nina Lemmens, Director
Peter Kerrigan, Deputy & Marketing Director

030 www.ed.gov
US Department of Education
400 Maryland Avenue, SW
Washington, DC 20202
800-872-5327
www.www2.ed.gov
This site describes programs and fellowships offered by the International Education and Graduate Programs office of the US Department of Education.

Arne Duncan, Secretary of Education
Emma Vadehra, Chief of Staff

6031 www.finaid.org
FinAid
A free, comprehensive, independent and ojective guide to student financial aid.

Mark Kantrowitz, Founder

6032 www.iie.org
Institute of International Education
One World Trade Center
36th Floor
New York, NY 10007
212-883-8200
www.iie.org
This site provides information regarding IIE's programs, services and resources, including the Fulbright Student Program.

Allan E. Goodman, President & CEO
Jason Czyz, Executive Vice President

6033 www.iiepassppport.org
Institute of International Education
One World Trade Center
36th Floor
New York, NY 10007
212-883-8200
www.iie.org
A student guide on the web to 5,000 learning opportunities worldwide.

Allan E. Goodman, President & CEO
Jason Czyz, Executive Vice President

6034 www.irex.org
International Research and Exchange Board
questions@finaid.org
www.finaid.org
Academic exchanges between the United States and Russia. Lists a variety of programs as well as grant and fellowship oppurtunities.

6035 www.isp.msu.edu/ncsa
Michigan State University
National Consortium for Study in Af in Africa

ncsa@msu.edu
Provides a comprehensive lists of sponsors for African exchange.

6036 www.istc.umn.edu/
University of Minnesota
International Study and Travel Center

Comprehensive and searchable links to study, work and travel abroad opportunities.

6037 www.languagetravel.com
Language Travel Magazine
Resource for finding study abroad language immersion courses.

6038 www.nsf.gov
National Science Foundation
2415 Eisenhower Avenue
Alexandria, VA 22314
703-292-5111
info@nsf.gov
www.nsf.gov
Encourages exchange in science and engineering. The site has international component, providing links with valuable information on fellowships, grants and awards, summer institutes, workshops, research and education projects, and international programs.

Sethuraman Panchanathan, Director

6039 www.si.edu/
Smithsonian Institution
600 Maryland Ave.
Suite 1005
Washington, DC 20024
202-633-5330
Fax: 202-633-5489
learning@si.edu
www.smithsonianeducation.org
Fellowships link to Smithsonian Oppurtunities for research and study.

Patricia Bartlett, Chief of Staff
Claudine Brown, Assistant Secretary

6040 www.studiesinaustralia.com/study
Studies in Australia
enquiries@studiesinaustralia.com
www.studiesinaustralia.com
Listing of study abroad oppurtunities in Australia, providing details of academic and training institutions and the programs they offer to prospective international students and education professionals.

Denis Whelan, Vice President of Sales
Elysia Singam, Advertising Copy Controller

6041 www.studyabroad.com/
StudyAbroad.com
3803 West Chester Pk.
Suite 125
Newtown Sq, PA 19073
484-766-2920
Fax: 610-499-9205
webmaster@studyabroad.com
www.studyabroad.com
Study abroad information resource listing study abroad programs worldwide.

6042 www.studyabroad.com/.
StudyAbroad.com
3803 West Chester Pk.
Suite 125
Newtown Sq, PA 19073
484-766-2920
Fax: 610-499-9205
webmaster@studyabroad.com
www.studyabroad.com
A commercial site with thousands of study abroad programs in over 100 countries with links to study abroad program home pages.

6043 www.ucis.pitt.edu/crees
University of Pittsburgh
Center for Russian/European Studies
4400 Wesley W. Posvar Hall, 230 South Bo
Pittsburgh, PA 15260
412-648-7407
Fax: 412-648-7002
crees@pitt.edu
www.ucis.pitt.edu/crees
Index of electronic resources for the student interested in Russian and European language and culture study.

Andrew Konitzer, Acting Director
Dawn Seckler, Acting Associate Director

6044 www.upenn.edu/oip/scholarships.html
University of Pennsylvania
Scholarships/Graduate Study Abroad

Provides links for graduate study abroad and scholarship opportunities.

6045 www.usc.edu
University of Southern California
Resources for Colleges and Universities in International Exchange

Links for browsing all aspects of international exchange, including study, research, work and teaching abroad, financial aid, grants and scholarships.

6046 www.usinfo.state/gov
US Department of State International Information Programs

Comprehensive desriptions of all IIP programs, sections on policy issues, global and regional issues and IIP publications.

6047 www.wes.org
World Education Services
Bowling Green Station
P.O. Box 5087
New York, NY 10274-5087
212-966-6311
Fax: 212-739-6100
www.wes.org
Features information on WES' foreign credentials evaluation services, world education workshops, and the journals World Education and News Reviews.

6048 www.world-arts-resources.com/
World Wide Arts Resources
P.O. Box 150
Granville, OH 43023
646-455-1425
www.wwar.com
Focuses solely on the arts, this site provides links for funding sources, university programs and arts organizations all over the world.

6049 www.yfu.org/
Youth for Understanding (YFU)
641 S Street, NW.
Suite 200
Washington, DC 20001
202-774-5200
www.yfuusa.org
Oppurtunities for young people around the world to spend a summer, semester or year with a host family in another country.

6050 wwww.sas.upenn.edu
African Studies Center, University of Pennsylvania
647 Williams Hall
255 S 36th Street
Philadelphia, PA 19104-6305
215-898-6971
Fax: 215-573-7379
www.africa.upenn.edu
Links to Africa-related internet sources, African Studies Association and UPenn African Studies Center.

Carol Muller, Ph.D, Director
Ali B. Ali-Dinar, Ph.D, Associate Director

Language Arts

6051 Advantage Learning Systems
Renaissance Learning
2911 Peach Street
Wisconsin Rapids, WI 54494
715-424-3636
800-338-4204
Fax: 715-424-4242
answers@renlearn.com
www.renlearn.com
Accelerated Reader software and manuals that motivate K-12 students to read more and better books. The program boosts reading scores and library circulation. Lets educators quickly and accurately assess student reading while motivating students to read more and better books.

John J. Lynch Jr., Chief Executive Officer
Mary T. Minch, EVP, Finance & CFO

6052 Bytes of Learning Incorporated
266 Elmwood Avenue #256
Buffalo, NY 14222
905-947-4646
800-465-6428
Fax: 905-475-8650
www.bytesoflearning.com
Single and site licensed software for Macintosh, Apple II, DOS and Windows-network compatible too. Keyboarding, language arts, career exploration and more on diskette and CD-ROM.

6053 Humanities Software
408 Columbia Street
#950
Hood River, OR 97031-2044
503-386-6737
800-245-6737
Fax: 541-386-1410
Over 150 whole language, literature-based language arts software titles for grades K-12.

Karen Withrow, Marketing Assistant
Charlotte Arnold, Marketing Director

6054 Teacher Support Software
3542 NW 97th Boulevard
Gainesville, FL 32606-7322
352-332-6404
800-228-2871
Fax: 352-332-6779
www.tssoftware.com
Language arts, Title 1, special ed, at-risk and ESL, curriculum-based networkable software for grades K-12. Vocabulary software that develops sight word recognition, provides basal correlated databases, tests reading comprehension, tracks student's progress and provides powerful teacher tools.

6055 Weaver Instructional Systems
6161 28th Street SE
Grand Rapids, MI 49546-6931
616-942-2891
800-634-8916
Fax: 616-942-1796
wisesoft@aol.com
www.wisesoft.com
Reading and language arts computer software programs for K-college.

6056 www.caslt.org
Canadian Association of Second Language Teachers
2490 Don Reid Drive
Ottawa, ON K1H 1
613-727-0994
877-727-0994
www.caslt.org
Promotes the advancement of second language education throughout Canada.

Guy Leclair, Executive Director
Diane Paquette, Finance Manager

6057 www.riverdeep.net
Riverdeep Interactive Learning
617-351-5316
800-426-6577
Sales_Support@hmhco.com
www.forms.hmhco.com
Riverdeep's interactive science, language and math arts programs deliver high quality educational experiences.

6058 www.signit2.com
Aylmer Press
Box 2302
Madison, WI 53701
608-441-5277
steve@signit2.com
www.signit2.com
Website hosted by Aylmer Press which produces video's to teach kids sign language as well as music.

6059 www.usajobs.opm.gov/b1c.html
Overseas Employment Info- Teachers
US Office of Personnel Management

Library Services

6060 American Econo-Clad Services
2101 N Topeka
Topeka, KS 66601
800-255-3502
Fax: 785-233-3129
A full service supplier of educational materials for the library, curriculum and software resource needs including MatchMaker, CD-ROM and ABLE (Analytically Budgeted Library Expenditures) computer systems.

6061 Anchor Audio Portable Sound Systems
5931 Darwin Court
Carlsbad, CA 92008
310-784-2300
800-262-4671
Fax: 760-827-7105
sales@anchoraudio.com
www.anchoraudio.com
Various audio visual products for the school and library.

Alex Jacobs, VP, Sales

6062 Baker & Taylor
2550 West Tyvola Road
Suite 300
Charlotte, NC 28217
704-998-3100
800-775-1800
www.baker-taylor.com
Nation's leading wholesale supplier of audio, computer software, books, videocassettes and other accessories to schools and libraries.

George F. Coe, President/ CEO
Jeff Leonard, Chief Financial Officer

6063 Brodart Company, Automation Division
500 Arch Street
Williamsport, PA 17701
570-326-2461
800-233-8467
Fax: 570-326-1479
support@brodart.com
www.brodart.com
Brodart's Automation Division has been providing library systems, software, and services for over 25 years. Products include: library management systems, media management systems, Internet solutions, cataloged web sites, catalog-ing resource tools, union catalog solutions, public access catalogs, and bibliographic services.

Kasey Dibble, Marketing Coordinator
Sally Wilmoth, Director Marketing/Sales

6064 Catalog Card Company
12219 Nicollet Avenue
Burnsville, MN 55337-1650
612-882-8558
800-442-7332
Fax: 785-290-1223
MARC records compatible with all software for retrospective conversions and new book orders. Catalog Card's conversion services include barcode labels to complement circulation software. MARC records generated from Dewey/Sears and Library of Congress databases are in standard USMARC or MicroLIF format.

065 Data Trek
5838 Edison Place
Carlsbad, CA 92008-6519
800-876-5484
Turn-key library automation systems and computer networks.

066 Demco
PO Box 7488
Madison, WI 53707-7488
800-356-1200
Fax: 800-245-1329
custserv@demco.com
www.demco.com
A leader in educational and library supplies for more than 80 years, Demco offers library audio and visual supplies and equipment plus display furniture.

067 Dewey Decimal Classification
OCLC Forest Press
6565 Frantz Road
Dublin, OH 43017-3395
614-764-6000
800-848-5878
Fax: 614-764-6096
oclc@oclc.org
www.oclc.org
OCLC Forest Press publishes the Dewey Decimal Classification (DDC) system and many related print and CD-ROM products that teach librarians and library users about the DDC.

Skip Prichard, Chief Executive Officer
Rick Schwieterman, Chief Financial Officer

068 Ebsco Subscription Services
International Headquarters
10 Estes Street
Ipswich, MA 01938
205-991-1480
800-653-2726
Fax: 978-356-6565
information@ebsco.com
www.ebsco.com
Periodical subscription and ordering and customer service equipment, computer and CD-ROM supplies, products and hardware for libraries.

Tim Collins, President
Sam Brooks, EVP

69 Electronic Bookshelf
5276 S Country Road, 700 W
Frankfort, IN 46041
765-324-2182
Fax: 765-324-2183
Reading motivation, testing management system and various computer systems and networks for educational purposes.

Rosalie Carter

70 Filette Keez Corporation/Colorworks Diskette Organizing System
3204 Channing Lane
Bedford, TX 76021-6506
817-283-5428
Produces ten filing inventions for classroom library, lab and district technology resources management. SelecTsideS folders store multimedia in Press-an-Inch Technology Slings and keep instruction, printouts, pamphlets and blackliners altogether. The diskette/CD portfolio color coordinates with the student/magazine Spbinder, plastic LaceLox fastener and all systems paper supplies: CD envelopes, storage box dividers, sheeted cards, perforated tractor labels and keys, available in 7 tech colors.

Roxanne Kay Harbert, Founder/President
Ray L Harbert, VP

6071 Follett School Solutions
1391 Corporate Drive
McHenry, IL 60050-7041
815-344-8700
800-323-3397
Fax: 800-807-3623
www.follettsoftware.com
Comprehensive, user-friendly circulation and catalog software for Windows, Mac OS, and MS-DOS systems-plus Internet technology, online periodical databases, outstanding customer support, and retrospective conversion services-all developed within the quality guidelines of Winnebago's ISO 9001 certification with TickIT accreditation.

6072 Follett Software Company
1391 Corporate Drive
McHenry, IL 60050-7041
815-344-8700
800-323-3397
Fax: 815-344-8774
marketing@fsc.follett.com
www.fsc.follett.com
Helping K-12 schools and districts create a vital library-to-classroom link to improve student achievement. FSC combines award-winning library automation with practical applications of the Internet. From OPAC data enhancement and easy-to-implement Internet technology to innovative information literacy solutions, FSC helps simplify resource management, increase access to resources inside and outside your collection and provide tools to integrate technology into the curriculum.

Patricia Yonushonis, Marketing Manager
Ann Reist, Conference Manager

6073 Foundation for Library Research
1200 Bigley Avenue
Charleston, WV 25302-3752
304-343-6480
Fax: 304-343-6489
The Automated Library Systems integrated library automation software.

Robert Evans

6074 Gaylord Brothers
PO Box 4901
Syracuse, NY 13221-4901
800-448-6160
Fax: 800-272-3412
www.gaylord.com
Library, AV supplies and equipment; security systems; and library furniture.

Tim Krein

6075 Highsmith Company
W5527 Highway 106
Fort Atkinson, WI 53538
414-563-9571
Catalog of microcomputer and multimedia curriculum products and software.

Barbara R Endl

6076 Information Access Company
362 Lakeside Drive
Foster City, CA 94404-1171
800-227-8431
Offers automation products and electronics for library/media centers.

6077 LePAC NET
Brodart Automation
500 Arch Street
Williamsport, PA 17701
570-326-2461
800-233-8467
Fax: 570-326-1479
support@brodart.com
www.brodart.com
Software for searching thousands of library databases with a single search. Schools can use to take multiple individual library databases and consolidate them, while deleting duplicate listings, into a union database.

Shawn Knight, Assistant Marketing Manager
Denise Macafee, Marketing Manager

6078 Library Corporation
Library Corporation
Research Park
Inwood, WV 25428-9733
304-229-0100
800-325-7759
Fax: 304-229-0295
info@TLCdelivers.com
www.tlcdelivers.com
Web-based library management systems allows patrons to have easy and immediate access to books and other library resources.

Annette Harwood Murphy, President/CEO/Chair
Calvin Whittington, Director, Finance & Admin

6079 Lingo Fun
International Software
PO Box 486
Westerville, OH 43086-0486
800-745-8258
Providers of microcomputer software including CD-ROM's for Macintosh and MPC, on-line dictionaries, translation assistants; teaching programs for elementary presentation, review and reinforcement, test preparation, and literary exploration.

6080 MARCIVE
PO Box 47508
San Antonio, TX 78265-7508
210-646-6161
800-531-7678
Fax: 210-646-0167
info@marcive.com
www.marcive.com
Economical, fast 100% conversion. Full MARC records with SEARS or LC headings. Free authorities processing smart barcode labels, reclassification, MARC Record enrichment

Robert Fleming, President
Scott Fleming, Chief Operating Officer

6081 Medianet/Dymaxion Research Limited
5515 Cogswell Street
Halifax, No B3J 1
902-422-1973
Fax: 902-421-1267
info@medianet.ns.ca
www.medianet.ns.ca
Medianet is the scheduling system for equipment and media that has consistently been rated as best in its class. Features include book library system integration, time-of-day booking, catalog production, WWW and touch tone phone booking by patrons.

Peter Mason, President

6082 Mitinet/Marc Software
PO Box 505
Bethany, MO 64424-0505
608-845-2300
800-824-6272
Fax: 660-425-3998
www.mitinet.com
Import/export USMARC, MICROLIF to USMARC conversions.

Bart Fitzgerald, Owner/ President
Cindy Beerkircher, Office Manager

6083 Orange Cherry Software
69 Westchester Avenue
PO Box 390
Pound Ridge, NY 10576-1702
914-764-4104
800-672-6002
Fax: 914-764-0104
Educational software products for libraries and media centers.
Biannual
Nicholas Vazzana, President

6084 Pearson Education
3001 Wayburne Drive
Burnbay
Canada V5G 4W3
604-294-1233
877-873-1550
Fax: 604-294-2225
proded@pearson.com
www.pearsonschoolsystems.com
Online catalog searches and checking materials in and out.

6085 Right on Programs
27 Bowdon Road
Suite B
Greenlawn, NY 11740
631-424-7777
Fax: 631-424-7207
riteonsoft@aol.com
Computer software for Windows and networks for library management including circulation, cataloging, periodicals, catalog cardmaking, inventory and thirty more. Used in more than 24,000 schools and libraries of all sizes.
D Farren, VP

6086 SOLINET, Southeastern Library Network
1438 W Peachtree Street NW
Suite 200
Atlanta, GA 30309-2955
404-892-0943
800-999-8558
Fax: 404-892-7879
information@solinet.net
www.solinet.net
SOLINET provides access, training and support for OCLC products and services; offers discounted library products and services, including licensed databases; provides electronic information solutions; workflow consulting, training and customized workshops; and supports a regional preservation of materials program.
Cathie Gharing, Marketing Coordinator
Liz Hornsby, Editor

6087 SirsiDynix
3300 North Ashton Blvd
Suite 500
Lehi, UT 84043
801-223-5200
800-288-8020
Fax: 801-331-7770
marketing@sirsidynix.com
www.sirsi.com
Unicorn Collection Management Systems are fully integrated UNIX-based library systems, automating all of a library's operation. Modules include: cataloging, authority control, public access, materials booking, circulation, academic reserves, acquisitions, serials control, reference database manager and electronic mail. Modules can be configured for all types and sizes of libraries.
Bill Davison, Chief Executive Officer
Scott Wheelhouse, SVP, Operations

6088 Social Issues Resources Series
PO Box 2348
Boca Raton, FL 33427
561-994-0079
800-521-0600
Fax: 561-994-4704
www.ars.sirs.com
Publisher of CD-ROM reference systems for PC and Macintosh computers. Databases of full-text articles carefully selected from 1,000 domestic and international sources. Also provides PC-compatible and stand-alone and network packages.
Paula Jackson, Marketing Director
Suzanne Panek, Customer Service

6089 TekData Systems Company
1111 W Park Avenue
Libertyville, IL 60048-2952
847-367-8800
Fax: 847-367-0235
tekdata@tekdata.com
www.tekdata.com
Scheduling and booking systems for intranets and internets.
Randy Kick, Sales Manager

6090 Three M Library Systems
Three M Center
Building 225-4N-14
St. Paul, MN 55144
800-328-0067
Fax: 800-223-5563
Materials Flow Management system is the first comprehensive system for optimizing the handling, processing and security of your library materials - from processing to checkout to check-in. The SelfCheck System and Staff Workstation automate the processing of virtually all of your library materials, while the Tattle-Tape Security Strips and Detection Systems help ensure the security of those materials.

6091 UMI
300 N Zeeb Road
Ann Arbor, MI 48103-1553
800-521-0600
Fax: 800-864-0019
Information products in microform, CD-ROM, online and magnetic tape.

6092 University Products
517 Main Street
#101
Holyoke, MA 01040-5514
413-532-3372
800-628-1912
Fax: 413-452-0618
info@universityproducts.com
www.universityproducts.com
Complete selection of library and media center supplies and equipment.
Juhn Dunpay

6093 WLN
PO Box 3888
Lacey, WA 98509-3888
360-923-4000
800-342-5956
Fax: 360-923-4009
School and media librarians experience 95% hit rates with WLN's LaserCat, CD-ROM database, a cataloging product and MARC record service.

6094 www.awesomelibrary.org
Awesome Library
www.awesomelibrary.org
Organizes the Web with 15,000 carefully reviewed resources, including the top 5 percent in education. Offers sections of mathematics, science, social studies, english, health, physical education, technology, languages, special education, the arts and more. Features a section involved with today's current issues facing our world, like pollution, gun control, tobacco, and other changing 'hot' topics. Site can be browsed in English, German, Spanish, French or Portuguese.

6095 www.techlearning.com
Technology & Learning
28 East 28th Street
12th floor
New York, NY 10016
212-378-0400
Fax: 212-378-0470
www.techlearning.com
Open 24 hours, every day of the week, with an extensive and up-to-date catalog of over 53,000 software and hardware products. Powerful search engine will help you find the right education-specific products.

Mathematics

6096 Accelerated Math
Renaissance Learning
2911 Peach Street
Wisconsin Rapids, WI 54494
715-424-3636
800-338-4204
Fax: 715-424-4242
answers@renlearn.com
www.renlearn.com
Accelerated Math provides 17 different reports, providing individualized, constructive feedback to students, parents, and teachers.
John J. Lynch Jr., Chief Executive Officer
Mary T. Minch, EVP, Finance & CFO

6097 Applied Mathematics Program
Prime Technology Corporation
PO Box 2407
Minneola, FL 34755-2407
352-394-7558
Fax: 352-394-3778
www.primetechnology.net
Provides students with comprehensive instruction in 11 math areas. In working with this program, students develop employment and life skills. The program will also lead the student to greater success on the mathematics sections of any standardized test.
Paul Scime, President

6098 CAE Software
3608 Shepherd Street
Chevy Chase, MD 20815-4132
301-907-9845
800-354-3462
Provides educational software for mathematics, grades 3-12. Simulations, tutorials, games, and problem solving. Titles include Mathematics Life Skills Services, Reading and Making Graphs Series, MathLab Series, Meaning of Fractions, Using Fractions and Using Decimals, ALG Football, GEO Pool and GEO Billiards, Paper Route, Mathematics Achievement Project, and others.
Alan R Chap, President

6099 EME Corporation
PO Box 1949
Stuart, FL 34995-1949
772-285-2131
800-848-2050
Fax: 561-219-2209
emecorp@aol.com
www.emescience.com
Publishers of award-winning science and math software, elementary through high school levels.

100 Logal Software
125 Cambridgepark Drive
Cambridge, MA 02140-2329
617-491-4440
Fax: 617-491-5855
Math and science products for high school through college.

Martha Cheng, President

101 MathType
Design Science
140 Pine Avenue
4th Floor
Long Beach, CA 90803-1502
562-432-2920
800-827-0685
Fax: 562-432-2857
info@dessci.com
www.dessci.com
Designed to make the creation of complex equations on a computer simple and fast. It works in conjunction with the software applications you already own, such as word processing programs, graphics programs, presentation programs, and web-authoring applications. Create research papers, tests, slides, books or web pages quickly and easily. MathType is the powerful, professional version of the Equation Editor in Microsoft Word, and Wordperfect.

Bruce Virga, EVP Sales/BD, COO
Paul R. Topping, President/ CEO

102 Mathematica
Wolfram Research, Inc.
100 Trade Center Drive
Champaign, IL 61820-7237
217-398-0700
800-965-3726
Fax: 217-398-0747
info@wolfram.com
www.wolfram.com
Mathematica is an indispensable tool for finding and communicating solutions quickly and easily.

Stephen Wolfram, Founder/CEO
Jean Buck, Dir., Corp Communications

103 MindTwister Math
Edmark Corporation
PO Box 97021
Redmond, WA 98073-9721
425-556-8400
800-691-2986
Fax: 425-556-8430
Software to help students in grade 3 and 4 build math fact fluency, practice mental math and improve estimating skills as they compete in a series of math challenges.

104 Multimedia - The Human Body
Sunburst Digital, Inc.
3150 W Higgins Rd
Ste 140
Hoffman Estates, IL 60169
914-747-3310
800-321-7511
Fax: 914-747-4109
service@sunburst.com
www.sunburst.com
Multimedia production of the intricate workings of the human body.

105 Texas Instruments
Consumer Relations
12500 TI Boulevard
Dallas, TX 75243
972-995-2011
800-842-2737
Fax: 972-917-0874
www.ti.com
Instructional calculators offer features matched to math concepts taught at each of conceptional development. Classroom accessories and teacher support programs that support the Texas Instruments products enhance instruction and learning. TI also offers a complete range of powerful notebook computers and laser printers for every need.

Rich Templeton, Chairman/ President/ CEO
Steve Anderson Analog, SVP

6106 William K. Bradford Publishing Company
35 Forest Ridge Road
Concord, MA 01742-5414
800-421-2009
Fax: 978-318-9500
www.wkbradford.com
Educational software for grades K-12. Especially math and grade book.

Hal Wexler, VP

6107 www.mathgoodies.com
Mrs. Glosser's Math Goodies
75 Mill Street
Colchester, CT 6415
914-736-0286
Fax: 866-776-9170
www.mathgoodies.com
Free educational site featuring interactive math lessons. Use a problem-solving approach and actively engage students in the learning process.

6108 www.mathstories.com
MathStories.com
1426 Pine Grove Way
San Jose, CA 95129
Customerservice@Mathstories.com
www.mathstories.com
The goal of this site is to help grade school children improve their math problem-solving and critical thinking skills. Offers over 4000 math word problems for children.

6109 www.riverdeep.net
Riverdeep Interactive Learning
617-351-5316
800-426-6577
Sales_Support@hmhco.com
Riverdeep's interactive science, language and math arts programs deliver high quality educational experiences.

6110 www.themathemagician.8m.com
The Mathemagician
310-452-0655
themathemagician_us@yahoo.com
www.themathemagician.8m.com
Offers the help of a real live person to help students correct and understand math and other home work problems.

Music & Art

6111 Harmonic Vision
1433 Rapids Trl
Nekoosa, WI 54457
715-325-3252
800-474-0903
Fax: 866-422-6686
www.harmonicvision.com
Leading musical education software to teach effectiveness of music in the home, school and studio.

6112 Midnight Play
Simon & Schuster Interactive
1230 Avenue of the Americas
New York, NY 10020
212-698-7000
800-793-9972
www.simonandschuster.com
Electronic picture book with an unusual look at creativity.

Carolyn Reidy, President/ CEO
Jon Anderson, EVP & Publisher

6113 Music Teacher Find
33 W 17th Street
10th Floor
New York, NY 10011
212-242-2464
www.MusicTeacherFind.com
Comprehensive Music Teacher Database designed to help music students find quality teachers in their neighborhood.

6114 Music and Guitar
www.nl-guitar.com
Original music programs for schools, courses and encounterswith music.

6115 Pure Gold Teaching Tools
PO Box 16622
Tuscon, AZ 85732
520-747-5600
866-692-6500
Fax: 520-571-9077
Exciting teaching methods and fabulous gifts for teachers, parents, students, pre-schoolers, homeschoolers and music therapists.

Heidi Goldman, President

6116 www.library.thinkquest.org
Think Quest
The Arti FAQS 2100 Project is designed to predict how art will influence our lives in the next hundred years. Students can use available data to make reasonable predictions for the future.

6117 www.members.truepath.com/headoftheclass
Head of The Class
Offers three galleries with clip art for teachers and children, several lesson plans, teaching tips, songs for teachers, lounge laughs, teacher tales and more.

6118 www.billharley.com
Round River Productions
301 Jacob Street
Seekonk, MA 2771
508-336-9703
800-682-9522
Fax: 508-336-2254
debbie@billharley.com
www.billharley.com
Humerous, yet meaningful songs which chronicle the lives of children at school and at home. His recordings of songs and stories can be used most effectively in the classroom as inspirational tools for the motivation of learning.

6119 www.sanford-artedventures.com
Sanford- A Lifetime of Color
800-323-0749
Teaches students about art and color theory while they play a game. Lessons plans, newsletter and product information.

6120 www.songs4teachers.com
O'Flynn Consulting
oflynn4@home.com
Offers many resources for teachers including songs made especially for your classroom. Sections with songs and activities for holidays, seasons and more. Features books and audios with 101 theme songs for use in the classroom or anywhere children gather to sing.

6121 www.ushistory.com
History Happens
www.songsabouthistory.com
Teaches integrating art, music, literature, science, math, library skills, and American history. The Primary source is stories from American history presented in musci video style.

Physical Education

6122 InfoUse
2560 9th Street
Suite 216
Berkeley, CA 94710-2557
510-549-6520
Fax: 510-549-6512
An award-winning, multimedia development and products firm, features CD-ROM, websites on health, education and disability. For training, education or presentations, our services include: research, instructional design, interface design, graphics, animation, content acquisition, videoing, analog and digital editing and evaluation. Products include SafeNet, (HIV prevention for fifth and sixth grade children), Place Math and Math Pad (math tools and lessons for students with disabilities).
Lewis E Kraus, VP
Susan Stoddard, President

6123 www.sports-media.org
Sports Media
www.sports-media.org
A tool for p.e. teachers, coaches, students and everyone who is interested in p.e./fitness and sports. Interactive p.e. lesson plans, sports pen-apls for the kids, European p.e. mailing list, and developing teaching skills in physical education.
Dr. Zan Gao, Editor-in-Chief
Guy Van Damme, Co-Chief editor

Reading

6124 Accelerated Reader
Renaissance Learning
2911 Peach Street
Wisconsin Rapids, WI 54494
715-424-3636
800-338-4204
Fax: 715-424-4242
answers@renlearn.com
www.renlearn.com
Helps teachers increase literature-based reading practice for all k-12 students
John J. Lynch Jr., Chief Executive Officer
Mary T. Minch, EVP, Finance & CFO

Secondary Education

6125 New York Times
New York, NY
646-698-8000
Fax: 646-698-8344
www.nytimes.com/learning
A resource for educators, parents and students in grades six through 12. Provides a daily lesson plan and comprehensive interactive resources based on newspaper content.
Katherine Schulte, Editor
Michael Gonchar, Deputy Editor

6126 Wm. C. Brown Communications
2460 Kerper Boulevard
Dubuque, IA 52001-2224
College textbooks, software, CD-ROM and more for grades 10-12.

6127 www.adulted.about.com/education/adulted
Adult/Continuing Education

6128 www.englishhlp.www5.50megs.com
English Help
englishhlpr@hotmail.com
This page is a walk through of Microsoft Power Point. The goal is to show in a few simple steps how to make your own website. Created by Rebecca Holland.

6129 www.number2.com
Number2.com
Currently offer SAT and GRE prep along with a vocabulary builder. Practice questions and word drill are adapted to the ability level of the user.

Science

6130 Academic Software Development Group
University of Maryland
University of Maryland
Computer Science Center
College Park, MD 20742-0001
301-405-5100
Fax: 301-405-0726
Offers BioQuest Library which is a set of peer-reviewed resources for science education.

6131 Accu-Weather
385 Science Park Road
State College, PA 16803-2215
814-237-0309
Fax: 814-238-1339
www.accuweather.com
Offers a telecommunications weather and oceanography database.
Dr. Joel N. Myers, Founder/ Chairman/ President
Barry Lee Myers, CEO

6132 AccuLab Products Group
614 Senic Drive
Suite 104
Modesto, CA 95350
209-522-8874
Fax: 209-522-8875
Science laboratory software.

6133 Learning Team
10 Long Pond Road
Armonk, NY 10504-2625
914-273-2226
800-793-TEAM
Fax: 914-273-2227
Offers CD-ROM, including MathFinder, Science Helper and Small Blue Planet and Redshift, the Learning Team edition.
Thomas Laster

6134 Problem Solving Concepts
611 N Capitol Avenue
Indianapolis, IN 46204-1205
317-267-9827
800-755-2150
Fax: 317-262-5044
Pro Solv provides students with a new approach to learning introductory physics problem solving techniques. Multi-experiential exercises with supporting text introduce students to relevant variables and their interrelations, principles, graphing and the development of problem solving skills through the quiz/tutorial mode.
Thomas D Feigenbaum, President
Gean R Shelor, Administrative Assistant

6135 Quantum Technology
PO Box 8252
Searcy, AR 72145-8252
A microcomputer database collection system that allows users to perform experiments in chemistry, biology and applied physics.

6136 SCI Technologies
SCI Technologies
2002 W. Huron St.
Chicago, IL 60612
312-243-1977
800-421-9881
Fax: 312-243-1972
create@scitechnologies.com
www.scitechnologies.com
A computer-based interface with an integrated hardware and software package that allows the focus of a science lab to shift from data collection to data analysis and experiment design.
Colleen Greenblatt, Sales Manager
Michelle Trexler, Event Coordinator

6137 Videodiscovery
1700 Westlake Avenue N
Suite 600
Seattle, WA 98109-3040
206-285-5400
800-548-3472
Fax: 206-285-9245
Publishers of award winning science videodiscs and multimedia software for kindergarten through post-secondary classes.

6138 www.kidsastronomy.com
KidsAstronomy.com
www.kidsastronomy.com
Offers information on astronomy, deep space, the solar system, space exploration, a teachers corner and more.

6139 www.riverdeep.net
Riverdeep Interactive Learning
617-351-5316
800-426-6577
Sales_Support@hmhco.com
Riverdeep's interactive science, language and math arts programs deliver high quality educational experiences.

Social Studies

6140 AccuNet/AP Multimedia Archive
AccuWeather, Inc.
385 Science Park Road
State College, PA 16803
814-235-8600
800-249-5389
Fax: 814-235-8669
apsupport@accuweather.com
www.ap.accuweather.com
The Photo Archive is an on-line database containing almost a half-million of Associated Press's current and historic images for the last 150 years.
Michael Warfield, Southeastern Sales Manager
Richard Towne, Northeastern Sales Manager

6141 Cengage Learning
10650 Toebben Drive
Independence, KY 41051
800-354-9706
Fax: 800-487-8488
order.samples@cengage.com
www.cengage.com

Offers CD-Rom information that offer students contextual understanding of the most commonly-studies persons, events and social movements in U.S. history; concepts, theories, discoveries and people involved in the study of science; current geopolitical data with cultural information on 200 nations of the world as well as all U.S. states and dependencies; poetry and literary information; and more in various databases for education.

Michael E. Hansen, Chief Executive Officer
Sandi Kirshner, Chief Marketing Officer

142 WorldView Software
11 Barby Lane
Plainview, NY 11803
516-681-1773
history@worldviewsoftware.com
www.worldviewsoftware.com
WorldView Software's interactive social studies programs for middle school and high school are comprehensive, curriculum-based tools that may be used along with or in place of textbooks. Each program contains Socratic learning sessions, writing activities, thousands of test or study questions (with explanations), and a plethora of resource material: biographies, chronologies, glossaries, original source documents and more.

Jerrold Kleinstein, President

143 www.faculty.acu.edu
M.I. Smart Program
Abilene Christian University
Abilene, TX 79699
325-674-2000
800-460-6228
www.acu.edu
Site designed for teacher and students. Offers electronic resources for historical and cultural geography. Features games, quizzes, trivia and virtual tours for students and thier teachers.

Dr. Phil Schubert, President
Steven Holley, Chief Financial Officer

Technology in Education

144 BLINKS.Net
PO Box 79321
Atlanta, GA 30357
404-243-5202
Fax: 404-241-4992
Fastest growing free Internet service provider and community portal for information and resources for the African American, Caribbean, Latino, and African markets.

145 Boyce Enterprises
360 Sharry Lane
Santa Maria, CA 93455
805-937-4353
Fax: 805-934-1765
Development of computer-based vocational curriculums.

146 Center for Educational Outreach and Innovation
Teachers College-Columbia University
525 W 120th Street
Box 132
New York, NY 10027
212-678-3000
800-209-1245
Fax: 212-678-8417
ceoi-mail@tc.columbia.edu
www.tc.columbia.edu
Lifelong learning programs, including distance learning courses, certificates and workshoops in education related topics.

Dr. Susan H. Fuhrman, President
Dr. Thomas James, Provost/ Dean

6147 Depco
3305 Airport Drive
PO Box 178
Pittsburg, KS 66762
316-231-0019
800-767-1062
Fax: 316-231-0024
www.depcoinc.com
Program tracks and schedules for you, the test taker delivers tests electronically, as well as, automatic final exams. There are workstation security features to help keep students focused on their activities.

6148 Dialog Information Services
Worldwide Headquaters
3460 Hillview Avenue
#10010
Palo Alto, CA 94304-1338
415-858-3785
800-334-2564
Fax: 650-858-7069
The world's most comprehensive online information source offering over 450 databases containing over 330 million articles, abstracts and citations - covering an unequaled variety of topics, with particular emphasis on news, business, science and technology. Dialog has offices throughout the United States and around the world.

6149 Distance Education Database
International Centre for Distance Learning
Open University, Walton Hall
Milton Keynes
England
441-085-3537
Fax: 441-086-4173
Contains information on distance education, including more than 22,000 distance-taught programs and courses in the Commonwealth of Learning, an organization created by the Commonwealth Heads of Government. On-line and CD-Rom versions of the database contain detailed information on over 30,000 distance-taught courses, 900 distance teaching instructions, and nearly 9,000 books, journals, reports and papers.

Keith Harry, Director

6150 EDUCAUSE
4845 Pearl E Circle
Suite 118, PMB 43761
Boulder, CO 80301-6112
303-449-4430
Fax: 303-440-0461
info@educause.edu
www.educause.edu
Aims to link practitioners in primary and secondary education through computer-mediated communications networks.

John O'Brien, President & CEO
Mairead Martin, Chief Information Officer

6151 Educational Structures
NCS Pearson
827 W Grove Avenue
Mesa, AZ 85210
800-736-4357
www.ncspearson.com
Features complete lesson plans and resources in social studies, mathematics, science, and language arts.

6152 Gibson Tech Ed
31500 Grape St. Bldg 3-364
Lake Elsinore, CA 92532
800-422-1100
Fax: 951-471-4981
www.gibsonteched.com
Educational materials to teach electronics, from middle, junior, high school and college.

Gary Gibson, Founder
Tim Gibson, President

6153 Grolier Interactive
Grolier Publishing
90 Sherman Turnpike
Danbury, CT 06816
800-371-3908
Fax: 800-456-4402
www.publishing.grolier.com
Instructional software including reference, science, mathematics, music, social studies, early learning, art and art history, language arts/literature.

6154 Heifner Communications
4451 Interstate 70 Drive NW
Columbia, MO 65202-3271
573-445-6163
800-445-6164
Fax: 512-527-2395
Offers educational-merit, cable-programming available via satellite. HCI Distance Learning systems are designed for dependable services and ease of operation and competitive prices.

Vicky Roberts

6155 In Focus
27700 B SW Parkway Avenue
Wilsonville, OR 97070-9215
503-685-8887
800-294-6400
Fax: 503-685-8887
LCD panels, video projectors and systems.

6156 JonesKnowledge.com
Jones Knowledge Group
9697 E Mineral Avenue
Centennial, CO 80112
800-350-6914
For administrators, that means and integrated solution-with no minimum commitment, or upfront investment. For instructors, it means getting your course online your way, without being a web expert, and for students it means, an accessible and convenient online experience.

6157 Mastercam
CNC Software
5717 Wollochet Drive NW
Suite 2A
Gig Harbor, WA 98335
800-275-6226
Fax: 253-858-6737
mcinfo@mastercam.com
www.mastercamedu.com

6158 Merit Audio Visual
Merit Software
121 West 27th Street
Suite 1200
New York, NY 10001
212-675-8567
800-753-6488
Fax: 646-351-0423
sales@meritsoftware.com
www.meritsoftware.com
Easy to use, interactive basic skills software for Windows 9x/ME/NT/2000/XP computers. Lessons for reading, writing, grammar and math with appropriate graphics for teens and adults.

Ben Weintraub, Marketing Manager

6159 National Information Center for Educational Media
4725 Indian School Road NE
Suite 100
Albuquerque, NM 87198-8640
505-265-3591
800-926-8328
Fax: 505-256-1080
NICEM maintains a comprehensive database describing educational media materials for all ages and subjects. It is available on CD-ROM and online.

Lisa Savard, Sales/Marketing Director

6160 NoRad Corporation
4455 Torrance Boulevard
#2806513
Torrance, CA 90503-4398
310-605-0808
Fax: 323-934-2101
Mini, personal, medium and large computer systems for educational institutions.

6161 Proxima Corporation
9440 Carroll Park Drive
San Diego, CA 92121
858-457-5500
800-294-6400
Fax: 503-685-7239
www.proxima.com
Proxima Corporation is a global leader in the multimedia projection market, providing world class presentation solutions to corporate enterprises, workgroups, mobile professionals, trainers, and professional public speakers.

Kim Gallagher, Public Relations Manager
Kathy Bankerd, Director Marketing Programs

6162 RB5X: Education's Personal Computer Robot
General Robotics Corporation
760 S Youngfield Court
Suite 8
Lakewood, CO 80228-2813
303-988-5636
800-422-4265
Fax: 303-988-5303
www.edurobot.com
RB5X: Education's Personal Computer Robot. All grade levels. Self learn, self teach, hands on modular system. Problem solving, basic learning skills, increases self-esteem. Expanable open-ended, motivation at its best.

Constant Brown, President

6163 SEAL
550 Spring Street
Naugatuck, CT 06770-1906
203-729-5201
Complete line of systems and electronics for schools.

6164 Sharp Electronics Corporation
LCD Products Group
Sharp Plaza
Mall Stop One
Mahwah, NJ 07430
201-529-8200
800-237-4277
Fax: 201-529-9636
aquosadvantage@sharpusa.com
www.sharpusa.com
Offers a full line of LCD-based video and computer multimedia projectors and projection panels for use in a wide range of educational applications. Sharp's product line also includes industrial VHS format VCRs, color TV monitors.

J Ganguzza, Director/Marketing

6165 The NCTA Foundation
25 Massachusetts Avenue NW
Suite 100
Washington, DC 20001
202-222-2300
webmaster@ncta.com
www.ncta.com
The foundation assists its member organizations by helping them develop programs to promote responsible and effective use of cable's broadband technology, services and content in learning and teaching. Some topics covered by them include the future of Wi-Fi, open Internet, protecting consumer privacy, preventing robocalls and more.

Michael Powell, President & CEO
Dave Pierce, Executive Director

6166 Valiant
80 Little Falls Road
Fairfield, NJ 07004
800-825-4268
Fax: 800-453-6338
sales@valiantnational.com
www.valiantnational.com
Distributors of LCD projection panels, P/A systems, overhead/slide and filmstrip projectors, cassette recorders, classroom record players, laser pointers, laminating equipment, lecturns, listening centers and headphones.

Sheldon Goldstein

6167 Vernier Software
13979 SW Millikan Way
Beaverton, OR 97005
503-277-2299
888-VER-ER
Fax: 503-277-2440
info@vernier.com
www.vernier.com
Laboratory interacting software for the Macintosh, IBM and Apple II.

6168 Websense
10240 Sorrento Valley Road
San Diego, CA 92121
858-320-8000
800-723-1166
Fax: 858-458-2950
www.websense.com
Internet filtering.

John R. McCormack, Chief Executive Officer
John Borgerding, President/ COO

6169 www.di...elearn/cs/eductechnology/index.htm
About Education Distance Learning

6170 www.futurekids.com
FUTUREKIDS School Technology Solutions
330 East 85th Street
New York, NY 10028
212-717-0110
Fax: 212-717-0259
info1@futurekidsnyc.com
www.futurekidsnyc.com
Helping schools use technology to transform education.

6171 www.online.uophx.edu
University of Phoenix Online
Offers you the convenience and flexibility of attending classes from your personal computer. Students are discussing issues, sharing ideas, testing theories, essentially enjoying all of the advantages of an on-campus degree programs. Interaction is included like e-mail, so you practice at your convenience.

6172 www.crossteccorp.com
NetOp
500 NE Spanish River Blvd.
Suite 201
Boca Raton, FL 33431
561-391-6560
800-675-0729
Fax: 561-391-5820
sales@crosstecsoftware.com
www.crossteccorp.com
A powerful combination of seven essential tools for networked classrooms. Based on the award winning technology of NetOp Remote Control and is easy-to-use software only solution.

6173 www.growsmartbrains.com
GrowSmartBrains.com
Website for parents and educators who want research based information and practical stradegies for raising children in a media age.

6174 www.zdnet.com
ZDNet
www.zdnet.com
Full-service destination for people looking to buy, use and learn more about technology.

Larry Dignan, Editor-in-Chief
David Grober, Senior Editor

6175 www.21ct.org
Twenty First Century Teachers Network
A nationwide, non-profit initiative of the McGuffey Project, dedicated to assisting k-12 teachers learn, use and effectively integrate technology in the curriculum for improved student learning.

6176 www.aboutonehandtyping.com/
One Hand Typing and Keyboarding Resources
740 Purdue Dr.
Claremont, CA 91711
909-398-1228
Fax: 408-228-8752
www.aboutonehandtyping.com
This site dishes up a blend of messages and stories, resources for one-hand typists, links to alternative keyboards, teaching links, and more.

6177 www.digitaldividenetwork.org
Digital Divide Network
c/o TakingITGlobal
19 Duncan Street, Suite 505
Toronto, ON M5H 3
416-977-9363
Fax: 416-352-1898
ddn@takingitglobal.org
The goal of bridging the divide is to use communications technology to help improve the quality of life of all communities and their citizens; provide them with the tools, skills and information they need to help them realize their socioeconomic, educational and cultural potential.

Adam Clare, Volunteer Lead Editor
Kirsten Jordan, DDN Project Coordinator

6178 www.getquizzed.com
GetQuizzed
Designed as a free service that provides a database that allows users to create, store and edit Multiple Choice or Question and Answer quizzes, under password protected conditions.

6179 www.guidetogeekdom.com
Guide to Geekdom
info@guidetogeekdom.com
www.guidetogeekdom.com
Designed especially for Homeschoolers, step-by-step lessons teach students how to use the computer and troubleshoot computer problems. Offers workbooks, sample lesson and more.

180 www.happyteachers.com
HappyTeachers.com
Information about technical and vocational education programs, products and curriculum.

181 www.integratingit.com
Integrating Information Technology for the Classroom, School, & District

Dedicated to providing the education community a place to find real world strategies, solutions, and resources for integrating technology. Organized by the perspective of the classroom teacher, the school administrator, and the district.

182 www.livetext.com
LiveText Curriculum Manager
1 W. Harris Avenue
2nd Floor
La Grange, IL 60525
866-548-3839
Fax: 708-588-1793
edu-solutions@livetext.com
www.livetext.com
Provides tools for engaged learning classroom projects and provides online professional development for teachers.

183 www.ncrel.org
North Central Regional Educational Laboratory
1120 East Diehl Road
Suite 200
Naperville, IL 60563-1486
Fax: 630-649-6730
info@ncrel.org
www.ncrel.org
Offers research results regarding the effective use of technology.
Gina Burkhardt, CEO
Sabrina Laine, Chief Officer, R&D

184 www.ncrtec.org
N Central Regional Technology in Education Consortiums

www.ncrtec.org
Provides a variety of tools and information to improve technology-related professional development programs.

Elementary Education

6185 Curriculum Associates
153 Rangeway Road
No. Billerica, MA 01862
978-667-8000
800-225-0248
Fax: 800-366-1158
www.curriculumassociates.com
Test preparation material with a guarantee of success; skill instruction and assessment.

Frank E. Ferguson, Chairman
Robert Waldron, Chief Executive Officer

6186 Diagnostic Reading Inventory for Primaryand Intermediate Grades K-8
Scott and McCleary Publishing Co.
PO Box 3830
Akron, OH 44314-0830
702-566-8756
800-765-3564
Fax: 702-568-1378
jscott7576@aol.com
A series of 13 tests at each grade level, 10 can be given in a group setting. 3 Forms of the IRI teacher friendly. Easy to administer.

Spiral Paperback
ISBN: 0-9636225-4-4

Janet M. Scott and Sheila C. McCeary, Author
Janet Scott, Co-Author
Sheila McCleary, Co-Author

6187 Lexia Learning Systems
200 Baker Ave Ext.
Concord, MA 01742
978-405-6200
800-435-3942
Fax: 978-287-0062
info@lexialearning.com
www.lexialearning.com
Reading software and assessment programs for children and adults, professional development programs for teachers, principals and administrators.

Elizabeth C. Crawford Brooke, VP, Education & Research
Collin Earnst, VP, Marketing

6188 National Study of School Evaluation
1699 E Woodfield Road
Suite 406
Schaumburg, IL 60173-4958
847-995-9080
800-843-6773
Fax: 847-995-9088
schoolimprovement@nsse.org
www.nsse.org
Provides educational leaders with state-of-the-art assessment and evaluation materials to enhance and promote student growth and school improvement.

Dr. Kathleen A. Fitzpatrick, Executive Director

6189 Pro-Ed, Inc.
8700 Shoal Creek Blvd
Austin, TX 78757-6897
800-897-3202
Fax: 800-397-7633
info@proedinc.com
www.linguisystems.com
Offers tests and print materials for speech language pathologists, teachers of the learning disabled, middle school language arts and reading teachers.

6190 STAR Early Literacy
Renaissance
2911 Peach Street
PO Box 8036
Wisconsin Rapids, WI 54495-8036
715-424-3636
800-338-4204
answers@renaissance.com
www.renaissance.com
Literacy and numeracy assessments for K-3 students.

Chris Bauleke, Chief Executive Officer
Todd Brekhus, Chief Product Officer

6191 Testing Miss Malarky
Bloomsbury Publishing Inc.
1385 Broadway
5th Floor
New York, NY 10018
212-419-5300
888-330-8477
Fax: 212-727-0984
ebookhelp@bloomsbury.com
www.bloomsbury.com
Author and artist exploit the mania that accompanies the classes first standardized test.

32 pages
ISBN: 0-8027-8737-1

Judy Finchler, Contact

Language Arts

6192 DRC/CTB
20 Ryan Ranch Road
Monterey, CA 93940
800-538-9547
Fax: 763-268-3000
A division of the Data Recognition Corporation and publisher of educational assessments such as K-12 achievement tests, early literacy assessment, language proficiency evaluation, adult basic skills tests and test management/instructional planning software.

Laurie Bauer, Test Development Specialist
Rob Mann, Director, DRC Info Systems

6193 SLEP Program Office
PO Box 6155
Princeton, NJ 08541-6155
Offers information on the Secondary Level English Proficiency Test.

Mathematics

6194 Psychological Assessment Resources
16204 North Florida Avenue
Lutz, FL 33549
813-961-2196
800-331-TEST
Fax: 800-727-9329
www.parinc.com
Catalog of professional testing resources.

6195 STAR Math
Renaissance
2911 Peach Street
PO Box 8036
Wisconsin Rapids, WI 54495-8036
715-424-3636
800-338-4204
answers@renaissance.com
www.renaissance.com
Computer-adaptive tests provide instructional levels, grade equivalents and percentile ranks.

Chris Bauleke, Chief Executive Officer
Todd Brekhus, Chief Product Officer

Music & Art

6196 A&F Video's Art Catalog
PO Box 264
Geneseo, NY 14454
New listing of titles for Art Teachers and Art Lovers.

6197 All Art Supplies
Art Supplies Wholesale
4 Enon Street
North Beverly, MA 01915
800-462-2420
Fax: 978-922-1495
info@allartsupplies.com
www.allartsupplies.com
Art supplies at wholesale prices.

6198 American Art Clay Company
6060 Guion Road
Indianapolis, IN 46254
317-244-6871
800-374-1600
Fax: 317-248-9300
salessupport@amaco.com
www.amaco.com
Provides ceramic materials and equipment.

6199 Arnold Grummer
PO Box 13245
Milwaukee, WI 53213
800-453-1485
Fax: 414-453-1495
www.arnoldgrummer.com
Products and information to meet most any papermaking need.

6200 Arrowmont School of Arts & Crafts
556 Parkway
Gainsburg, TN 37738
865-438-5860
Fax: 865-438-4101
www.arrowmont.org
The art school of tomorrow.

Marty Begalla, President
Susie Glenn, Vice President

6201 Art & Creative Materials Institute
99 Derby St.
Suite 200
Hingham, MA 02043
781-556-1044
Fax: 781-207-5550
www.acminet.org
A non-profit trade association whose memebers are manufacturers of art and creative materials. Sponsors a certification program to ensure that art materials are non-toxic or affixed with health warning labels where appropriate. Publishes a booklet on the safe use of art materials and a listing of products that are approved under its certification program. Both of these publications are free of charge.

Debbie Gustafson, Deputy Director
David H Baker, Executive Director

6202 Art Instruction Schools
3309 Broadway Street NW
Minneapolis, MN 55413
www.artists-ais.com

6203 Art to Remember
5535 Macy Drive
Indianapolis, IN 46235
317-826-0870
800-895-8777

Fax: 317-823-2822
info@arttoremember.com
www.arttoremember.com
A unique program that encourages your students' artistic creativity while providing an oppurtunity to raise funds for schools.

204 ArtSketchbook.com
487 Hulsetown Road
Campbell Hall, NY 10916
845-496-4709
www.artsketchbook.com
Provides instructions and work examples by an elementary student, secondary student and a professional artist.

205 Arts Institutes International
Education Management Corporation
210 Sixth Avenue
33rd Floor
Pittsburgh, PA 15222
888-624-0300
csprogramadmin@edmc.edu
www.artinstitutes.edu
Post-secondary career education. Offers associate's, bachelor's and non-degree programs in design, media arts, technology, culinary arts and fashion.

206 Museum Stamps
PO Box 356
New Canaan, CT 06840
800-659-2787
Fax: 203-966-2729
www.museumstamps.com
Rubber stamps of famous works of art, stamp accessories, classroom projects.

207 Music Ace 2
Harmonic Vision
1433 Rapids Trl
Nekoosa, WI 54457
715-325-3252
800-474-0903
Fax: 866-422-6686
www.harmonicvision.com
Introduces concepts such as standard notation, rhythm, melody, time signatures, harmony, intervals and more.

208 www.ilford.com
Ilford
www.ilford.com
Partners in imaging.

209 www.speedballart.com
2301 Speedball Road
Statesville, NC 28677
800-898-7224
www.speedballart.com
Speedball lesson plans and teaching aids for calligraphy, stamping, printmaking, drawing, painting and more.

Walt Glazer, Chief Executive

Reading

210 Advantage Learning Systems
2911 Peach Street
PO Box 8036
Wisconsin Rapids, WI 54495-8036
800-338-4204
Fax: 715-424-4242
www.advlearn.com
New computer-adaptive tests that assess student reading and math levels in just 15 minutes or less.

211 Educational Testing Service/Library
Test Collection
Rosedale Road
Princeton, NJ 08541
609-734-5686
Fax: 609-734-5410
Provides information on tests and related materials to those in research and advisory services and educational activities.

Janet Williams, President

6212 National Foundation for Dyslexia
4801 Hermitage Road
Richmond, VA 23227-3332
804-262-0586
800-SOS-READ
Provides screenings for schools or individuals and assists individuals with IEP's. Provides information about support groups and organizations and teacher training workshops.

Jo Powell, Executive Director

6213 Psychological Assessment Resources
16204 North Florida Avenue
Lutz, FL 33549
813-961-2196
800-331-TEST
Fax: 800-727-9329
www.parinc.com
Catalog of professional testing resources.

6214 STAR Reading
Renaissance
2911 Peach Street
PO Box 8036
Wisconsin Rapids, WI 54495-8036
715-424-3636
800-338-4204
answers@renaissance.com
www.renaissance.com
Computer-adaptive tests provide instructional levels, grade equivalents and percentile ranks.

Chris Bauleke, Chief Executive Officer
Todd Brekhus, Chief Product Officer

6215 www.voyagersopris.com
Cambium Learning Group
17855 Dallas Parkway
Suite 400
Dallas, TX 75287
www.voyagersopris.com
Improves performance in reading for those at different grade levels.

Secondary Education

6216 ACT
PO Box 4060
Iowa City, IA 52243-0001
319-337-1000
800-498-6065
Offers a full-service catalog of tests for intermediate and secondary schools organized by assessment, career and educational planning, study skills, surveys and research services.

Catalog

6217 American College Testing
ACT
2201 Dodge
#168
Iowa City, IA 52243-0001
319-337-1028
Fax: 319-337-1014
www.act.org
Provides educational assessment services to students and their parents, high schools, colleges and professional associations. Also workforce development services, including a network of ACT Centers and the Workkeys program.

Jon Whitmore, Chief Executive Officer
Janet E. Godwin, Chief Operating Officer

6218 American Council on Education: GED Testing Service
1919 M Street NW
Suite 600
Washington, DC 20036
877-392-6433
communications@gedtestingservice.com
www.gedtestingservice.com
A test delivered via computer to adult learners, to help them gain the skills and knowledge they need to be employable.

Randy Trask, President & CEO
Vicki Greene, VP, Operations

6219 CLEP Official Study Guide
College Board
250 Vesey Street
New York, NY 10281
212-713-8000
www.collegeboard.org
Includes practice questions, preparation suggestions and guides.

David Coleman, Chief Executive Officer
Jeremy Singer, President

6220 College-Bound Seniors
College Board
250 Vesey Street
New York, NY 10281
212-713-8000
www.collegeboard.org
Profile of SAT and achievement test takers, national report.

David Coleman, Chief Executive Officer
Jeremy Singer, President

6221 Educational Testing Service
660 Rosedale Road
Princeton, NJ 08541
609-921-9000
Fax: 609-734-5410
www.ets.org
Private educational measurement institution and a leader in educational research.

Susan Keipper, Program Director

6222 GED Testing Service
American Council on Education
1 Dupont Cir NW
Washington, DC 20036-1110
202-939-9490
877-392-6433
Fax: 202-775-8578
help@GEDtestingservice.com
www.gedtestingservice.com
The largest testing service in the United States. Maintains a full line of tests and testing resources for all areas of education and all grade levels K-college level testing.

Randy Trask, President/ CEO

6223 Master The GMAT
Peterson's, A Nelnet Company
461 From Road
Paramus, NJ 07652
609-896-1800
800-338-3282
Fax: 402-458-3042
custsvc@petersons.com
www.petersons.com
Helps test takers get ready, develop test-preparation strategies and manage test anxiety

constructively, whether they have seven weeks to prepare or just one day.

672 pages Book & Disk

Martinson, Author

6224 Master The SAT
Peterson's, A Nelnet Company
461 From Road
Paramus, NJ 07652
609-896-1800
800-338-3282
Fax: 402-458-3042
custsvc@petersons.com
www.petersons.com
Features easily accessible Red Alert sections offering essential tips for test-taking success. Provides students with the critical skills they need to tackle the SAT.

821 pages Book & Disk
ISBN: 1-560796-06-5

John Davenport Carris with Michael R. Crystal, Author

6225 National Center for Fair & Open Testing
P.O. Box 300204
Jamaica Plain, MA 02130
617-477-9792
Fax: 617-497-2224
www.fairtest.org
Dedicated to ensuring that America's students and workers are assessed using fair, accurate, relevant and open tests.

Cinthia Schuman, President

6226 National Study of School Evaluation
1699 E Woodfield Road
Suite 406
Schaumburg, IL 60173-4958
847-995-9080
800-843-6773
Fax: 847-995-9088
www.nsse.org
Provides educational leaders with state-of-the-art assessment and evaluation materials to enhance and promote student growth and school improvement.

Dr. Kathleen A. Fitzpatrick, Executive Director

6227 Official SAT Study Guide
College Board
250 Vesey Street
New York, NY 10281
212-713-8000
www.collegeboard.org
The authoritative preparation guide for students taking the SAT.

David Coleman, Chief Executive Officer
Jeremy Singer, President

6228 Official Study Guide for All SAT Subject Tests
College Board
250 Vesey Street
New York, NY 10281
212-713-8000
www.collegeboard.org
This preparation guide contains actual, previously administered tests across all SAT subject tests.

David Coleman, Chief Executive Officer
Jeremy Singer, President

6229 Official Study Guide for the New SAT
College Board
250 Vesey Street
New York, NY 10281
212-713-8000
www.collegeboard.org
Includes detailed descriptions of the SAT sections, targeted practice questions, practice essay questions, practice tests, reviews, test-taking tips and resources.

David Coleman, Chief Executive Officer
Jeremy Singer, President

6230 Panic Plan for the SAT
Peterson's, A Nelnet Company
461 From Road
Paramus, NJ 07652
609-896-1800
800-338-3282
Fax: 402-458-3042
custsvc@petersons.com
www.petersons.com
An excellent, two-week review, featuring actual questions from the SAT. Helps students make the most out of the limited time they have left to study.

368 pages
ISBN: 1-560794-32-1

Michael R Crystal, Author

6231 Pearson's Clinical Assessment Group
19500 Bulverde Road
Suite 201
San Antonio, TX 78259-3701
800-627-7271
Fax: 800-232-1223
clinicalcustomersupport@pearson.com
www.pearsonassessments.com
Provides assessment materials for teachers in all areas of curricula.

Bob Whelan, President

6232 Preventing School Failure
Taylor & Francis
325 Chestnut Street
Suite 800
Philadelphia, PA 19106
215-625-8900
800-354-1420
Fax: 202-296-5149
customer.service@taylorandfrancis.com
www.heldref.org
The articles cover a broad array of specific topics, from important technical aspects and adaptions of functional behavioral assessment to descriptions of projects in which functional behavioral assessment is being used to provide technical assistance to preschools, schools, and families who must deal eith children and adolescents who present serious challenging behaviors.

Quarterly
ISSN: 1045-988X

Sheldon Braaten, Executive Editor

6233 Psychometric Affiliates
PO Box 807
Murfreeboro, TN 37133
615-890-6296
Testing instruments for use by educational institutions.

Jeannette Heritage

6234 Registration Bulletin
College Board
250 Vesey Street
New York, NY 10281
212-713-8000
www.collegeboard.org
Available in five regional and a New York State edition, the Bulletin provides information on how to register for the SAT I and SAT II, and on how to use the related services.

David Coleman, Chief Executive Officer
Jeremy Singer, President

6235 Scholastic Testing Service
480 Meyer Road
Bensenville, IL 60106-1617
630-766-7150
800-642-6787
Fax: 630-766-8054
sts@ststesting.com
www.ststesting.com
Publisher of assessment materials from birth into adulthood, ability and achievement tests for kindergarten through grade twelve. Tests are also constructed on contract for educational agencies and school districts. Publish the Torrance Tests of Creative Thinking, Thinking Creatively in Action and Movement, the STS High School Placement Test and Educational Development Series.

OF Anderhalter, President
John D Kauffman, VP Marketing

6236 Taking the SAT I: Reasoning Test
College Board
250 Vesey Street
New York, NY 10281
212-713-8000
www.collegeboard.org
A complete guide for students who plan to take the SAT I: Reasoning Test.

David Coleman, Chief Executive Officer
Jeremy Singer, President

6237 TestSkills
College Board
250 Vesey Street
New York, NY 10281
212-713-8000
www.collegeboard.org
A preparation program for the PSAT/NMSQT that helps students sharpen skills and increase confidence needed to succeed on the tests.

David Coleman, Chief Executive Officer
Jeremy Singer, President

6238 The SAT Subject Tests Student Guide
College Board
250 Vesey Street
New York, NY 10281
212-713-8000
www.collegeboard.org
Provides information about the content and format of each of the SAT II: Subject Tests, as well as test-taking advice and sample questions.

David Coleman, Chief Executive Officer
Jeremy Singer, President

National, State, and Canadian Education Statistics

List of Reference Tables

All Levels of Education

Elementary and Secondary Education

Postsecondary Education

Outcomes of Education

Canadian Education Statistics

Table 104.10. Rates of high school completion and bachelor's degree attainment among persons age 25 and over, by race/ethnicity and sex: Selected years, 1910 through 2019

[Standard errors appear in parentheses]

Sex, high school or bachelor's degree attainment, and year	Total, percent of all persons age 25 and over	White[1]	Black[1]	Hispanic	Asian/Pacific Islander			American Indian/ Alaska Native	Two or more races
					Total	Asian	Pacific Islander		
1	2	3	4	5	6	7	8	9	10
Total									
High school completion or higher[2]									
1910[3]	13.5 (—)	— (†)	— (†)	— (†)	— (†)	— (†)	— (†)	— (†)	— (†)
1920[3]	16.4 (—)	— (†)	— (†)	— (†)	— (†)	— (†)	— (†)	— (†)	— (†)
1930[3]	19.1 (—)	— (†)	— (†)	— (†)	— (†)	— (†)	— (†)	— (†)	— (†)
1940	24.5 (—)	26.1 (—)	7.7 (—)	— (†)	— (†)	— (†)	— (†)	— (†)	— (†)
1950	34.3 (—)	36.4 (—)	13.7 (—)	— (†)	— (†)	— (†)	— (†)	— (†)	— (†)
1960	41.1 (—)	43.2 (—)	21.7 (—)	— (†)	— (†)	— (†)	— (†)	— (†)	— (†)
1970	55.2 (—)	57.4 (—)	36.1 (—)	— (†)	— (†)	— (†)	— (†)	— (†)	— (†)
1975	62.5 (—)	65.8 (—)	42.6 (—)	38.5 (—)	— (†)	— (†)	— (†)	— (†)	— (†)
1980	68.6 (0.20)	71.9 (0.21)	51.4 (0.81)	44.5 (1.18)	— (†)	— (†)	— (†)	— (†)	— (†)
1985	73.9 (0.18)	77.5 (0.19)	59.9 (0.74)	47.9 (0.99)	— (†)	— (†)	— (†)	— (†)	— (†)
1986	74.7 (0.18)	78.2 (0.19)	62.5 (0.72)	48.5 (0.96)	— (†)	— (†)	— (†)	— (†)	— (†)
1987	75.6 (0.17)	79.0 (0.18)	63.6 (0.71)	50.9 (0.94)	— (†)	— (†)	— (†)	— (†)	— (†)
1988	76.2 (0.17)	79.8 (0.18)	63.5 (0.70)	51.0 (0.92)	— (†)	— (†)	— (†)	— (†)	— (†)
1989	76.9 (0.17)	80.7 (0.18)	64.7 (0.69)	50.9 (0.89)	82.3 (1.17)	— (†)	— (†)	— (†)	— (†)
1990	77.6 (0.17)	81.4 (0.17)	66.2 (0.67)	50.8 (0.88)	84.2 (1.09)	— (†)	— (†)	— (†)	— (†)
1991	78.4 (0.16)	82.4 (0.17)	66.8 (0.66)	51.3 (0.86)	84.2 (1.05)	— (†)	— (†)	— (†)	— (†)
1992	79.4 (0.16)	83.4 (0.16)	67.7 (0.65)	52.6 (0.85)	83.7 (1.02)	— (†)	— (†)	— (†)	— (†)
1993	80.2 (0.16)	84.1 (0.16)	70.5 (0.63)	53.1 (0.83)	84.2 (1.00)	— (†)	— (†)	— (†)	— (†)
1994	80.9 (0.15)	84.9 (0.16)	73.0 (0.61)	53.3 (0.78)	84.8 (0.98)	— (†)	— (†)	— (†)	— (†)
1995	81.7 (0.15)	85.9 (0.16)	73.8 (0.61)	53.4 (0.78)	83.8 (1.06)	— (†)	— (†)	— (†)	— (†)
1996	81.7 (0.16)	86.0 (0.16)	74.6 (0.53)	53.1 (0.68)	83.5 (0.82)	— (†)	— (†)	— (†)	— (†)
1997	82.1 (0.14)	86.3 (0.15)	75.3 (0.52)	54.7 (0.54)	85.2 (0.75)	— (†)	— (†)	— (†)	— (†)
1998	82.8 (0.14)	87.1 (0.14)	76.4 (0.50)	55.5 (0.53)	84.9 (0.74)	— (†)	— (†)	— (†)	— (†)
1999	83.4 (0.14)	87.7 (0.14)	77.4 (0.49)	56.1 (0.52)	84.7 (0.73)	— (†)	— (†)	— (†)	— (†)
2000	84.1 (0.13)	88.4 (0.14)	78.9 (0.48)	57.0 (0.51)	85.7 (0.71)	— (†)	— (†)	— (†)	— (†)
2001	84.3 (0.13)	88.7 (0.13)	79.5 (0.47)	56.5 (0.50)	87.8 (0.60)	— (†)	— (†)	— (†)	— (†)
2002	84.1 (0.09)	88.7 (0.10)	79.2 (0.34)	57.0 (0.34)	87.7 (0.44)	— (†)	— (†)	— (†)	— (†)
2003	84.6 (0.09)	89.4 (0.09)	80.3 (0.33)	57.0 (0.33)	87.8 (0.43)	87.8 (0.44)	88.2 (1.87)	77.2 (1.64)	86.1 (0.97)
2004	85.2 (0.09)	90.0 (0.09)	81.1 (0.32)	58.4 (0.32)	86.9 (0.43)	86.9 (0.44)	88.5 (1.91)	77.8 (1.61)	87.2 (0.91)
2005	85.2 (0.14)	90.1 (0.16)	81.4 (0.44)	58.5 (0.53)	87.8 (0.62)	87.7 (0.62)	90.1 (2.69)	75.6 (2.02)	88.6 (0.83)
2006	85.5 (0.15)	90.5 (0.15)	81.2 (0.43)	59.3 (0.58)	87.5 (0.71)	87.5 (0.71)	85.7 (2.51)	78.5 (2.11)	88.1 (0.90)
2007	85.7 (0.15)	90.6 (0.15)	82.8 (0.39)	60.3 (0.56)	88.0 (0.79)	87.9 (0.81)	88.6 (2.30)	80.3 (2.27)	89.3 (0.87)
2008	86.6 (0.15)	91.5 (0.15)	83.3 (0.40)	62.3 (0.58)	89.0 (0.62)	88.8 (0.64)	94.4 (1.00)	78.4 (2.74)	89.5 (1.12)
2009	86.7 (0.15)	91.6 (0.15)	84.2 (0.44)	61.9 (0.56)	88.4 (0.61)	88.3 (0.63)	90.8 (1.76)	81.5 (1.83)	87.4 (0.96)
2010	87.1 (0.13)	92.1 (0.14)	84.6 (0.41)	62.9 (0.53)	89.1 (0.67)	89.1 (0.68)	90.2 (1.95)	80.8 (1.76)	88.9 (0.90)
2011	87.6 (0.13)	92.4 (0.14)	84.8 (0.41)	64.3 (0.54)	88.8 (0.55)	88.7 (0.57)	90.4 (1.61)	82.3 (1.77)	89.4 (1.00)
2012	87.6 (0.15)	92.5 (0.14)	85.7 (0.40)	65.0 (0.59)	89.1 (0.59)	89.0 (0.61)	91.6 (1.33)	81.8 (1.69)	91.0 (0.89)
2013	88.2 (0.14)	92.9 (0.13)	85.9 (0.42)	66.2 (0.52)	90.2 (0.51)	90.2 (0.53)	89.5 (1.72)	82.2 (1.68)	92.6 (0.75)
2014	88.3 (0.15)	93.1 (0.17)	86.7 (0.45)	66.5 (0.57)	89.5 (0.62)	89.5 (0.64)	88.8 (2.15)	81.0 (2.01)	93.3 (0.88)
2015	88.4 (0.12)	93.3 (0.13)	87.7 (0.37)	66.7 (0.48)	88.9 (0.49)	89.1 (0.51)	85.1 (2.04)	83.8 (1.64)	91.6 (0.87)
2016	89.1 (0.13)	93.8 (0.13)	87.7 (0.34)	68.5 (0.48)	90.7 (0.49)	90.6 (0.51)	93.3 (1.38)	84.7 (1.35)	92.8 (0.83)
2017	89.6 (0.12)	94.1 (0.13)	88.1 (0.37)	70.5 (0.47)	90.9 (0.47)	90.9 (0.49)	89.3 (2.03)	85.3 (1.36)	93.4 (0.71)
2018	89.8 (0.12)	94.3 (0.13)	88.6 (0.33)	71.6 (0.40)	90.6 (0.40)	90.6 (0.41)	90.6 (1.77)	83.6 (1.32)	93.2 (0.61)
2019	90.1 (0.12)	94.6 (0.11)	88.8 (0.38)	71.8 (0.48)	91.3 (0.45)	91.2 (0.46)	93.8 (1.32)	87.9 (1.31)	92.6 (0.84)
Bachelor's or higher degree[4]									
1910[3]	2.7 (—)	— (†)	— (†)	— (†)	— (†)	— (†)	— (†)	— (†)	— (†)
1920[3]	3.3 (—)	— (†)	— (†)	— (†)	— (†)	— (†)	— (†)	— (†)	— (†)
1930[3]	3.9 (—)	— (†)	— (†)	— (†)	— (†)	— (†)	— (†)	— (†)	— (†)
1940	4.6 (—)	4.9 (—)	1.3 (—)	— (†)	— (†)	— (†)	— (†)	— (†)	— (†)
1950	6.2 (—)	6.6 (—)	2.2 (—)	— (†)	— (†)	— (†)	— (†)	— (†)	— (†)
1960	7.7 (—)	8.1 (—)	3.5 (—)	— (†)	— (†)	— (†)	— (†)	— (†)	— (†)
1970	11.0 (—)	11.6 (—)	6.1 (—)	— (†)	— (†)	— (†)	— (†)	— (†)	— (†)
1975	13.9 (—)	14.9 (—)	6.4 (—)	6.6 (—)	— (†)	— (†)	— (†)	— (†)	— (†)
1980	17.0 (0.16)	18.4 (0.18)	7.9 (0.44)	7.6 (0.63)	— (†)	— (†)	— (†)	— (†)	— (†)
1985	19.4 (0.16)	20.8 (0.19)	11.1 (0.47)	8.5 (0.55)	— (†)	— (†)	— (†)	— (†)	— (†)
1986	19.4 (0.16)	20.9 (0.19)	10.9 (0.47)	8.4 (0.53)	— (†)	— (†)	— (†)	— (†)	— (†)
1987	19.9 (0.16)	21.4 (0.19)	10.8 (0.46)	8.6 (0.53)	— (†)	— (†)	— (†)	— (†)	— (†)
1988	20.3 (0.16)	21.8 (0.19)	11.2 (0.46)	10.0 (0.55)	— (†)	— (†)	— (†)	— (†)	— (†)
1989	21.1 (0.16)	22.8 (0.19)	11.7 (0.46)	9.9 (0.53)	41.5 (1.51)	— (†)	— (†)	— (†)	— (†)
1990	21.3 (0.16)	23.1 (0.19)	11.3 (0.45)	9.2 (0.51)	41.7 (1.47)	— (†)	— (†)	— (†)	— (†)
1991	21.4 (0.16)	23.3 (0.19)	11.5 (0.45)	9.7 (0.51)	40.3 (1.42)	— (†)	— (†)	— (†)	— (†)
1992	21.4 (0.16)	23.2 (0.19)	11.9 (0.45)	9.3 (0.49)	39.3 (1.35)	— (†)	— (†)	— (†)	— (†)
1993	21.9 (0.16)	23.8 (0.19)	12.2 (0.45)	9.0 (0.48)	42.1 (1.35)	— (†)	— (†)	— (†)	— (†)
1994	22.2 (0.16)	24.3 (0.19)	12.9 (0.46)	9.1 (0.45)	41.3 (1.34)	— (†)	— (†)	— (†)	— (†)
1995	23.0 (0.16)	25.4 (0.19)	13.3 (0.47)	9.3 (0.45)	38.5 (1.40)	— (†)	— (†)	— (†)	— (†)
1996	23.6 (0.17)	25.9 (0.20)	13.8 (0.42)	9.3 (0.40)	42.3 (1.09)	— (†)	— (†)	— (†)	— (†)
1997	23.9 (0.16)	26.2 (0.19)	13.3 (0.41)	10.3 (0.33)	42.6 (1.04)	— (†)	— (†)	— (†)	— (†)
1998	24.4 (0.16)	26.6 (0.19)	14.8 (0.42)	11.0 (0.33)	42.3 (1.02)	— (†)	— (†)	— (†)	— (†)
1999	25.2 (0.16)	27.7 (0.19)	15.5 (0.43)	10.9 (0.33)	42.4 (1.01)	— (†)	— (†)	— (†)	— (†)
2000	25.6 (0.16)	28.1 (0.19)	16.6 (0.44)	10.6 (0.32)	44.4 (1.00)	— (†)	— (†)	— (†)	— (†)
2001	26.1 (0.16)	28.6 (0.19)	16.1 (0.43)	11.2 (0.32)	48.0 (0.92)	— (†)	— (†)	— (†)	— (†)
2002	26.7 (0.11)	29.4 (0.14)	17.2 (0.31)	11.1 (0.21)	47.7 (0.66)	— (†)	— (†)	— (†)	— (†)
2003	27.2 (0.11)	30.0 (0.14)	17.4 (0.31)	11.4 (0.21)	48.8 (0.65)	50.0 (0.67)	27.0 (2.56)	12.6 (1.30)	22.0 (1.17)
2004	27.7 (0.11)	30.6 (0.14)	17.7 (0.31)	12.1 (0.21)	48.9 (0.64)	49.7 (0.66)	32.4 (2.81)	14.3 (1.36)	21.8 (1.13)
2005	27.7 (0.23)	30.6 (0.29)	17.6 (0.45)	12.0 (0.31)	49.3 (0.91)	50.4 (0.93)	24.6 (3.67)	14.5 (1.51)	23.2 (1.19)

See notes at end of table.

Table 104.10. Rates of high school completion and bachelor's degree attainment among persons age 25 and over, by race/ethnicity and sex: Selected years, 1910 through 2019—Continued

[Standard errors appear in parentheses]

Sex, high school or bachelor's degree attainment, and year	Total, percent of all persons age 25 and over	White[1]	Black[1]	Hispanic	Asian/Pacific Islander: Total	Asian/Pacific Islander: Asian	Asian/Pacific Islander: Pacific Islander	American Indian/ Alaska Native	Two or more races
1	2	3	4	5	6	7	8	9	10
2006	28.0 (0.20)	31.0 (0.25)	18.6 (0.47)	12.4 (0.32)	49.1 (1.04)	50.0 (1.06)	26.9 (3.42)	12.9 (1.60)	23.1 (1.28)
2007	28.7 (0.21)	31.8 (0.27)	18.7 (0.51)	12.7 (0.31)	51.2 (1.02)	52.5 (1.03)	23.8 (3.30)	13.1 (1.24)	23.7 (1.30)
2008	29.4 (0.21)	32.6 (0.26)	19.7 (0.51)	13.3 (0.29)	51.9 (0.95)	52.9 (0.97)	28.4 (2.86)	14.9 (1.52)	24.4 (1.36)
2009	29.5 (0.21)	32.9 (0.26)	19.4 (0.45)	13.2 (0.34)	51.6 (0.91)	52.8 (0.95)	28.3 (2.68)	17.5 (2.08)	25.5 (1.34)
2010	29.9 (0.19)	33.2 (0.24)	20.0 (0.51)	13.9 (0.31)	51.6 (1.04)	52.8 (1.09)	25.6 (2.89)	16.0 (1.77)	25.3 (1.30)
2011	30.4 (0.19)	34.0 (0.24)	20.2 (0.50)	14.1 (0.34)	49.5 (0.92)	50.8 (0.96)	22.1 (2.73)	16.1 (1.73)	27.4 (1.27)
2012	30.9 (0.21)	34.5 (0.27)	21.4 (0.53)	14.5 (0.35)	50.7 (0.92)	51.9 (0.94)	24.5 (2.75)	16.7 (1.82)	27.1 (1.34)
2013	31.7 (0.21)	35.2 (0.26)	22.0 (0.49)	15.1 (0.34)	52.5 (0.92)	53.9 (0.93)	25.6 (2.66)	15.4 (1.72)	30.6 (1.35)
2014	32.0 (0.27)	35.6 (0.35)	22.8 (0.66)	15.2 (0.39)	51.3 (1.00)	52.7 (1.02)	22.3 (3.27)	13.8 (1.43)	31.2 (1.81)
2015	32.5 (0.22)	36.2 (0.28)	22.9 (0.52)	15.5 (0.31)	52.9 (0.84)	54.4 (0.87)	22.8 (2.39)	19.8 (1.32)	30.6 (1.52)
2016	33.4 (0.24)	37.3 (0.31)	23.5 (0.46)	16.4 (0.40)	55.1 (0.87)	56.4 (0.89)	27.5 (2.92)	16.8 (1.39)	30.6 (1.52)
2017	34.2 (0.24)	38.1 (0.31)	24.3 (0.49)	17.2 (0.35)	53.9 (0.84)	55.4 (0.88)	25.1 (2.81)	20.5 (1.92)	32.6 (1.39)
2018	35.0 (0.26)	38.8 (0.34)	25.6 (0.53)	18.3 (0.37)	55.6 (0.81)	57.1 (0.80)	24.1 (2.34)	18.8 (1.72)	32.4 (1.40)
2019	36.0 (0.23)	40.1 (0.33)	26.3 (0.51)	18.8 (0.35)	57.3 (0.78)	58.6 (0.79)	28.1 (2.78)	16.8 (1.40)	34.1 (1.38)
Males									
High school completion or higher[2]									
1940	22.7 (—)	24.2 (—)	6.9 (—)	— (†)	— (†)	— (†)	— (†)	— (†)	— (†)
1950	32.6 (—)	34.6 (—)	12.6 (—)	— (†)	— (†)	— (†)	— (†)	— (†)	— (†)
1960	39.5 (—)	41.6 (—)	20.0 (—)	— (†)	— (†)	— (†)	— (†)	— (†)	— (†)
1970	55.0 (—)	57.2 (—)	35.4 (—)	— (†)	— (†)	— (†)	— (†)	— (†)	— (†)
1980	69.2 (0.29)	72.4 (0.31)	51.2 (1.21)	44.9 (1.71)	— (†)	— (†)	— (†)	— (†)	— (†)
1990	77.7 (0.24)	81.6 (0.25)	65.8 (1.01)	50.3 (1.25)	86.0 (1.49)	— (†)	— (†)	— (†)	— (†)
1995	81.7 (0.22)	86.0 (0.22)	73.5 (0.91)	52.9 (1.11)	85.8 (1.46)	— (†)	— (†)	— (†)	— (†)
1996	81.9 (0.23)	86.1 (0.23)	74.6 (0.80)	53.0 (0.97)	86.2 (1.10)	— (†)	— (†)	— (†)	— (†)
1997	82.0 (0.21)	86.3 (0.21)	73.8 (0.79)	54.9 (0.76)	87.5 (1.00)	— (†)	— (†)	— (†)	— (†)
1998	82.8 (0.20)	87.1 (0.21)	75.4 (0.77)	55.7 (0.74)	87.9 (0.98)	— (†)	— (†)	— (†)	— (†)
1999	83.4 (0.20)	87.7 (0.20)	77.2 (0.74)	56.0 (0.75)	86.9 (1.00)	— (†)	— (†)	— (†)	— (†)
2000	84.2 (0.19)	88.5 (0.20)	79.1 (0.72)	56.6 (0.73)	88.4 (0.94)	— (†)	— (†)	— (†)	— (†)
2001	84.4 (0.19)	88.6 (0.19)	80.6 (0.69)	55.6 (0.72)	90.6 (0.78)	— (†)	— (†)	— (†)	— (†)
2002	83.8 (0.14)	88.5 (0.14)	79.0 (0.51)	56.1 (0.48)	89.8 (0.58)	— (†)	— (†)	— (†)	— (†)
2003	84.1 (0.13)	89.0 (0.14)	79.9 (0.50)	56.3 (0.46)	89.8 (0.58)	89.8 (0.59)	89.8 (2.61)	76.5 (2.33)	87.2 (1.36)
2004	84.8 (0.13)	89.9 (0.13)	80.8 (0.49)	57.3 (0.45)	88.8 (0.59)	88.8 (0.60)	88.9 (2.65)	77.1 (2.31)	87.8 (1.29)
2005	84.9 (0.19)	89.9 (0.20)	81.4 (0.60)	57.9 (0.69)	90.4 (0.65)	90.5 (0.66)	88.5 (3.62)	75.6 (2.57)	89.0 (1.19)
2006	85.0 (0.20)	90.2 (0.21)	80.7 (0.63)	58.5 (0.77)	89.5 (0.84)	89.7 (0.86)	85.8 (3.10)	78.1 (2.77)	88.0 (1.36)
2007	85.0 (0.21)	90.2 (0.22)	82.5 (0.55)	58.2 (0.80)	90.0 (0.81)	90.1 (0.82)	88.1 (2.75)	78.3 (3.58)	89.4 (1.28)
2008	85.9 (0.19)	91.1 (0.20)	82.1 (0.61)	60.9 (0.72)	91.0 (0.66)	90.8 (0.69)	95.8 (1.40)	77.3 (3.37)	89.6 (1.21)
2009	86.2 (0.19)	91.4 (0.20)	84.2 (0.60)	60.6 (0.72)	90.8 (0.66)	90.7 (0.68)	92.1 (2.18)	80.0 (2.33)	87.3 (1.26)
2010	86.6 (0.17)	91.8 (0.19)	84.2 (0.57)	61.4 (0.68)	91.4 (0.78)	91.5 (0.79)	89.3 (2.84)	78.9 (2.46)	88.1 (1.36)
2011	87.1 (0.18)	92.0 (0.17)	84.2 (0.55)	63.6 (0.71)	90.6 (0.68)	90.6 (0.69)	91.5 (2.22)	80.6 (2.35)	88.1 (1.40)
2012	87.3 (0.19)	92.2 (0.18)	85.1 (0.56)	64.0 (0.73)	90.6 (0.68)	90.5 (0.70)	93.3 (1.84)	81.8 (2.39)	90.2 (1.45)
2013	87.6 (0.17)	92.7 (0.17)	84.9 (0.62)	64.6 (0.66)	91.6 (0.57)	91.7 (0.57)	89.3 (2.48)	81.0 (2.11)	93.3 (1.03)
2014	87.7 (0.19)	92.5 (0.22)	86.3 (0.58)	65.1 (0.74)	91.8 (0.70)	91.9 (0.72)	90.0 (2.68)	80.2 (2.30)	93.8 (1.08)
2015	88.0 (0.16)	93.0 (0.16)	87.2 (0.48)	65.5 (0.63)	90.9 (0.56)	91.3 (0.58)	84.9 (2.83)	81.9 (2.12)	92.5 (1.23)
2016	88.5 (0.17)	93.4 (0.19)	87.0 (0.51)	67.2 (0.63)	92.3 (0.58)	92.2 (0.60)	94.9 (1.58)	84.1 (2.07)	92.8 (1.15)
2017	89.1 (0.16)	93.7 (0.18)	87.4 (0.53)	69.5 (0.59)	92.5 (0.55)	92.7 (0.55)	89.1 (2.77)	83.0 (1.96)	93.2 (1.15)
2018	89.4 (0.16)	93.9 (0.18)	88.3 (0.48)	70.7 (0.53)	92.8 (0.48)	92.9 (0.49)	92.2 (2.31)	79.3 (1.93)	92.5 (1.02)
2019	89.6 (0.16)	94.2 (0.15)	88.1 (0.54)	70.8 (0.59)	92.8 (0.52)	92.8 (0.54)	93.3 (2.11)	84.1 (1.96)	91.0 (1.17)
Bachelor's or higher degree[4]									
1940	5.5 (—)	5.9 (—)	1.4 (—)	— (†)	— (†)	— (†)	— (†)	— (†)	— (†)
1950	7.3 (—)	7.9 (—)	2.1 (—)	— (†)	— (†)	— (†)	— (†)	— (†)	— (†)
1960	9.7 (—)	10.3 (—)	3.5 (—)	— (†)	— (†)	— (†)	— (†)	— (†)	— (†)
1970	14.1 (—)	15.0 (—)	6.8 (—)	— (†)	— (†)	— (†)	— (†)	— (†)	— (†)
1980	20.9 (0.26)	22.7 (0.29)	7.7 (0.65)	9.2 (0.99)	— (†)	— (†)	— (†)	— (†)	— (†)
1990	24.4 (0.25)	26.7 (0.28)	11.9 (0.69)	9.8 (0.74)	45.9 (2.14)	— (†)	— (†)	— (†)	— (†)
1995	26.0 (0.25)	28.9 (0.29)	13.7 (0.71)	10.1 (0.67)	42.3 (2.06)	— (†)	— (†)	— (†)	— (†)
1996	26.0 (0.26)	28.8 (0.30)	12.5 (0.61)	10.3 (0.59)	46.9 (1.59)	— (†)	— (†)	— (†)	— (†)
1997	26.2 (0.24)	29.0 (0.28)	12.5 (0.60)	10.6 (0.47)	48.0 (1.51)	— (†)	— (†)	— (†)	— (†)
1998	26.5 (0.24)	29.3 (0.28)	14.0 (0.62)	11.1 (0.47)	46.0 (1.50)	— (†)	— (†)	— (†)	— (†)
1999	27.5 (0.24)	30.6 (0.28)	14.3 (0.62)	10.7 (0.46)	46.3 (1.48)	— (†)	— (†)	— (†)	— (†)
2000	27.8 (0.24)	30.8 (0.28)	16.4 (0.65)	10.7 (0.45)	48.1 (1.47)	— (†)	— (†)	— (†)	— (†)
2001	28.0 (0.24)	30.9 (0.28)	15.9 (0.64)	11.1 (0.45)	52.9 (1.33)	— (†)	— (†)	— (†)	— (†)
2002	28.5 (0.17)	31.7 (0.20)	16.5 (0.47)	11.0 (0.30)	51.5 (0.96)	— (†)	— (†)	— (†)	— (†)
2003	28.9 (0.17)	32.3 (0.20)	16.8 (0.47)	11.2 (0.29)	52.8 (0.96)	54.2 (0.98)	25.7 (3.76)	13.1 (1.85)	21.9 (1.69)
2004	29.4 (0.17)	32.9 (0.20)	16.6 (0.46)	11.8 (0.30)	52.9 (0.93)	54.0 (0.95)	31.9 (3.94)	15.6 (1.99)	20.7 (1.60)
2005	28.9 (0.29)	32.4 (0.37)	16.0 (0.64)	11.8 (0.43)	53.0 (1.10)	54.3 (1.13)	25.1 (4.70)	17.0 (2.30)	23.1 (1.67)
2006	29.2 (0.24)	32.8 (0.31)	17.5 (0.63)	11.9 (0.40)	51.9 (1.33)	53.1 (1.35)	26.6 (4.67)	13.7 (2.07)	22.6 (1.75)
2007	29.5 (0.25)	33.2 (0.33)	18.1 (0.62)	11.8 (0.37)	54.2 (1.31)	55.8 (1.32)	19.2 (4.14)	12.7 (1.89)	21.5 (1.81)
2008	30.1 (0.25)	33.8 (0.33)	18.7 (0.67)	12.6 (0.39)	54.9 (1.24)	56.1 (1.24)	27.5 (3.64)	14.6 (2.15)	22.7 (1.62)
2009	30.1 (0.28)	33.9 (0.36)	17.9 (0.57)	12.5 (0.41)	54.8 (1.14)	56.5 (1.17)	23.0 (3.35)	16.1 (2.96)	24.4 (1.92)
2010	30.3 (0.23)	34.2 (0.30)	17.9 (0.59)	12.9 (0.37)	54.6 (1.26)	56.2 (1.30)	18.0 (3.74)	13.5 (2.61)	24.8 (1.86)
2011	30.8 (0.23)	35.0 (0.29)	18.4 (0.64)	13.1 (0.44)	52.4 (1.15)	54.0 (1.21)	19.1 (3.55)	14.1 (1.98)	25.7 (1.91)
2012	31.4 (0.27)	35.5 (0.33)	19.5 (0.62)	13.3 (0.45)	53.0 (1.26)	54.4 (1.29)	24.1 (3.34)	16.1 (2.27)	25.2 (1.85)
2013	32.0 (0.25)	36.0 (0.31)	20.2 (0.64)	13.9 (0.43)	55.1 (1.17)	56.9 (1.20)	23.1 (3.32)	14.0 (2.13)	29.0 (1.78)
2014	31.9 (0.32)	35.9 (0.41)	21.0 (0.88)	14.2 (0.51)	53.7 (1.33)	55.5 (1.34)	16.7 (3.42)	14.8 (2.46)	29.2 (2.56)
2015	32.3 (0.27)	36.3 (0.35)	21.1 (0.63)	14.3 (0.38)	55.6 (1.11)	57.3 (1.16)	24.4 (2.87)	18.1 (2.14)	27.2 (2.14)

See notes at end of table.

Table 104.10. Rates of high school completion and bachelor's degree attainment among persons age 25 and over, by race/ethnicity and sex: Selected years, 1910 through 2019—Continued

[Standard errors appear in parentheses]

Sex, high school or bachelor's degree attainment, and year	Total, percent of all persons age 25 and over	White[1]	Black[1]	Hispanic	Asian/Pacific Islander: Total	Asian/Pacific Islander: Asian	Asian/Pacific Islander: Pacific Islander	American Indian/ Alaska Native	Two or more races
1	2	3	4	5	6	7	8	9	10
2016	33.2 (0.29)	37.2 (0.37)	21.8 (0.62)	15.4 (0.48)	57.7 (1.05)	59.4 (1.10)	22.2 (3.65)	16.5 (1.87)	25.6 (2.06)
2017	33.7 (0.28)	37.8 (0.37)	22.6 (0.61)	15.8 (0.41)	55.7 (1.10)	57.2 (1.14)	26.2 (3.61)	17.7 (1.93)	30.3 (1.87)
2018	34.6 (0.30)	38.9 (0.40)	23.7 (0.73)	16.6 (0.45)	58.5 (1.01)	60.1 (1.02)	23.6 (3.59)	15.4 (1.78)	30.0 (2.05)
2019	35.4 (0.30)	39.9 (0.43)	24.4 (0.72)	16.9 (0.43)	59.4 (1.00)	60.9 (1.01)	24.8 (4.02)	12.9 (1.59)	31.1 (2.11)
Females									
High school completion or higher[2]									
1940	26.3 (—)	28.1 (—)	8.4 (—)	— (†)	— (†)	— (†)	— (†)	— (†)	— (†)
1950	36.0 (—)	38.2 (—)	14.7 (—)	— (†)	— (†)	— (†)	— (†)	— (†)	— (†)
1960	42.5 (—)	44.7 (—)	23.1 (—)	— (†)	— (†)	— (†)	— (†)	— (†)	— (†)
1970	55.4 (—)	57.7 (—)	36.6 (—)	— (†)	— (†)	— (†)	— (†)	— (†)	— (†)
1980	68.1 (0.28)	71.5 (0.30)	51.5 (1.08)	44.2 (1.63)	— (†)	— (†)	— (†)	— (†)	— (†)
1990	77.5 (0.23)	81.3 (0.24)	66.5 (0.90)	51.3 (1.23)	82.5 (1.57)	— (†)	— (†)	— (†)	— (†)
1995	81.6 (0.21)	85.8 (0.22)	74.1 (0.81)	53.8 (1.09)	81.9 (1.54)	— (†)	— (†)	— (†)	— (†)
1996	81.6 (0.22)	85.9 (0.22)	74.6 (0.71)	53.3 (0.97)	81.0 (1.21)	— (†)	— (†)	— (†)	— (†)
1997	82.2 (0.20)	86.3 (0.20)	76.5 (0.68)	54.6 (0.76)	82.9 (1.11)	— (†)	— (†)	— (†)	— (†)
1998	82.9 (0.19)	87.1 (0.20)	77.1 (0.67)	55.3 (0.75)	82.3 (1.09)	— (†)	— (†)	— (†)	— (†)
1999	83.3 (0.19)	87.6 (0.19)	77.5 (0.66)	56.3 (0.73)	82.8 (1.06)	— (†)	— (†)	— (†)	— (†)
2000	84.0 (0.19)	88.4 (0.19)	78.7 (0.64)	57.5 (0.71)	83.4 (1.03)	— (†)	— (†)	— (†)	— (†)
2001	84.2 (0.18)	88.8 (0.19)	78.6 (0.64)	57.4 (0.70)	85.2 (0.91)	— (†)	— (†)	— (†)	— (†)
2002	84.4 (0.13)	88.9 (0.13)	79.4 (0.45)	57.9 (0.48)	85.7 (0.64)	— (†)	— (†)	— (†)	— (†)
2003	85.0 (0.13)	89.7 (0.13)	80.7 (0.44)	57.8 (0.46)	86.1 (0.62)	86.1 (0.64)	86.9 (2.63)	77.9 (2.30)	85.1 (1.38)
2004	85.4 (0.12)	90.1 (0.12)	81.2 (0.43)	59.5 (0.46)	85.3 (0.63)	85.1 (0.64)	88.1 (2.76)	78.6 (2.24)	86.5 (1.29)
2005	85.5 (0.15)	90.3 (0.18)	81.5 (0.53)	59.1 (0.63)	85.4 (0.76)	85.2 (0.78)	91.7 (2.46)	75.6 (2.29)	88.1 (1.12)
2006	85.9 (0.16)	90.8 (0.17)	81.5 (0.51)	60.1 (0.59)	85.6 (0.82)	85.6 (0.81)	85.7 (3.08)	78.9 (2.18)	88.2 (1.11)
2007	86.4 (0.15)	91.0 (0.16)	83.0 (0.49)	62.5 (0.56)	86.1 (0.93)	86.0 (0.97)	89.1 (2.40)	81.9 (1.91)	89.2 (1.22)
2008	87.2 (0.17)	91.8 (0.18)	84.2 (0.49)	63.7 (0.61)	87.2 (0.75)	87.0 (0.78)	93.0 (1.57)	79.2 (2.95)	89.5 (1.53)
2009	87.1 (0.16)	91.9 (0.17)	84.2 (0.48)	63.3 (0.59)	86.4 (0.73)	86.3 (0.75)	89.7 (2.33)	82.7 (1.96)	87.6 (1.16)
2010	87.6 (0.15)	92.3 (0.17)	85.0 (0.46)	64.4 (0.59)	87.2 (0.72)	87.1 (0.75)	90.9 (2.41)	82.5 (1.95)	89.7 (1.13)
2011	88.0 (0.15)	92.8 (0.16)	85.3 (0.50)	65.1 (0.57)	87.1 (0.64)	87.0 (0.66)	89.5 (2.25)	83.8 (2.00)	90.7 (1.22)
2012	88.0 (0.17)	92.7 (0.18)	86.1 (0.46)	66.0 (0.65)	87.9 (0.64)	87.8 (0.66)	90.1 (2.11)	81.8 (1.84)	91.6 (1.13)
2013	88.6 (0.16)	93.2 (0.16)	86.6 (0.46)	67.9 (0.55)	89.0 (0.61)	88.9 (0.63)	89.6 (2.01)	83.1 (2.16)	92.0 (0.95)
2014	88.9 (0.17)	93.7 (0.20)	87.0 (0.55)	67.9 (0.61)	87.4 (0.76)	87.4 (0.77)	87.8 (2.98)	81.6 (2.78)	92.8 (1.28)
2015	88.8 (0.14)	93.5 (0.15)	88.2 (0.43)	67.8 (0.53)	87.1 (0.60)	87.2 (0.62)	85.3 (2.46)	85.6 (2.10)	90.9 (1.14)
2016	89.6 (0.14)	94.3 (0.15)	88.3 (0.39)	69.7 (0.53)	89.3 (0.55)	89.2 (0.56)	91.8 (2.26)	85.2 (1.69)	92.8 (1.07)
2017	90.0 (0.14)	94.5 (0.14)	88.6 (0.43)	71.6 (0.52)	89.4 (0.54)	89.4 (0.56)	89.5 (2.20)	87.2 (1.52)	93.6 (0.92)
2018	90.2 (0.13)	94.7 (0.15)	88.7 (0.41)	72.5 (0.48)	88.6 (0.51)	88.6 (0.52)	89.1 (2.77)	87.4 (1.51)	93.7 (0.86)
2019	90.5 (0.13)	95.0 (0.14)	89.3 (0.43)	72.8 (0.49)	90.0 (0.52)	89.8 (0.54)	94.2 (1.63)	91.3 (1.30)	93.9 (1.02)
Bachelor's or higher degree[4]									
1940	3.8 (—)	4.0 (—)	1.2 (—)	— (†)	— (†)	— (†)	— (†)	— (†)	— (†)
1950	5.2 (—)	5.4 (—)	2.4 (—)	— (†)	— (†)	— (†)	— (†)	— (†)	— (†)
1960	5.8 (—)	6.0 (—)	3.6 (—)	— (†)	— (†)	— (†)	— (†)	— (†)	— (†)
1970	8.2 (—)	8.6 (—)	5.6 (—)	— (†)	— (†)	— (†)	— (†)	— (†)	— (†)
1980	13.6 (0.20)	14.4 (0.23)	8.1 (0.59)	6.2 (0.79)	— (†)	— (†)	— (†)	— (†)	— (†)
1990	18.4 (0.21)	19.8 (0.25)	10.8 (0.59)	8.7 (0.69)	37.8 (2.01)	— (†)	— (†)	— (†)	— (†)
1995	20.2 (0.22)	22.1 (0.26)	13.0 (0.62)	8.4 (0.61)	35.0 (1.90)	— (†)	— (†)	— (†)	— (†)
1996	21.4 (0.23)	23.2 (0.27)	14.8 (0.58)	8.3 (0.53)	38.0 (1.50)	— (†)	— (†)	— (†)	— (†)
1997	21.7 (0.21)	23.7 (0.25)	14.0 (0.56)	10.1 (0.46)	37.4 (1.43)	— (†)	— (†)	— (†)	— (†)
1998	22.4 (0.21)	24.1 (0.25)	15.4 (0.58)	10.9 (0.47)	38.9 (1.39)	— (†)	— (†)	— (†)	— (†)
1999	23.1 (0.22)	25.0 (0.26)	16.5 (0.59)	11.0 (0.46)	39.0 (1.37)	— (†)	— (†)	— (†)	— (†)
2000	23.6 (0.22)	25.5 (0.26)	16.8 (0.59)	10.6 (0.44)	41.0 (1.37)	— (†)	— (†)	— (†)	— (†)
2001	24.3 (0.22)	26.5 (0.26)	16.3 (0.58)	11.3 (0.45)	43.4 (1.26)	— (†)	— (†)	— (†)	— (†)
2002	25.1 (0.15)	27.3 (0.19)	17.7 (0.42)	11.2 (0.31)	44.2 (0.91)	— (†)	— (†)	— (†)	— (†)
2003	25.7 (0.15)	27.9 (0.19)	18.0 (0.43)	11.6 (0.30)	45.3 (0.89)	46.3 (0.92)	28.0 (3.50)	12.2 (1.81)	22.2 (1.61)
2004	26.1 (0.15)	28.4 (0.19)	18.5 (0.43)	12.3 (0.31)	45.2 (0.88)	45.7 (0.90)	32.9 (4.01)	13.1 (1.84)	22.7 (1.59)
2005	26.5 (0.23)	28.9 (0.30)	18.9 (0.51)	12.1 (0.42)	46.0 (1.08)	46.8 (1.10)	24.1 (4.08)	12.2 (2.00)	23.3 (1.43)
2006	26.9 (0.22)	29.3 (0.28)	19.5 (0.55)	12.9 (0.39)	46.6 (1.11)	47.3 (1.15)	27.2 (4.03)	12.3 (1.81)	23.6 (1.70)
2007	28.0 (0.23)	30.6 (0.29)	19.2 (0.59)	13.7 (0.44)	48.6 (1.07)	49.5 (1.10)	27.9 (4.16)	13.4 (1.53)	25.8 (1.58)
2008	28.8 (0.24)	31.5 (0.29)	20.5 (0.58)	14.1 (0.37)	49.3 (0.99)	50.1 (1.02)	29.3 (3.82)	15.1 (1.75)	26.1 (1.92)
2009	29.1 (0.21)	31.9 (0.26)	20.6 (0.56)	14.0 (0.41)	48.8 (0.98)	49.7 (1.02)	32.9 (3.74)	18.8 (1.91)	26.6 (1.67)
2010	29.6 (0.21)	32.4 (0.26)	21.6 (0.63)	14.9 (0.42)	49.1 (1.12)	49.9 (1.19)	32.2 (4.11)	18.2 (1.83)	25.7 (1.59)
2011	30.1 (0.22)	33.1 (0.28)	21.7 (0.60)	15.2 (0.43)	47.0 (1.04)	48.0 (1.07)	24.7 (3.52)	17.9 (2.17)	28.9 (1.70)
2012	30.6 (0.23)	33.5 (0.30)	22.9 (0.61)	15.8 (0.45)	48.6 (0.93)	49.7 (0.94)	24.9 (3.70)	17.2 (2.13)	28.8 (1.88)
2013	31.4 (0.24)	34.4 (0.31)	23.4 (0.61)	16.2 (0.42)	50.2 (0.94)	51.3 (0.96)	28.0 (3.44)	16.6 (2.05)	32.0 (1.89)
2014	32.0 (0.32)	35.3 (0.42)	24.2 (0.75)	16.1 (0.50)	49.3 (1.12)	50.4 (1.15)	27.1 (4.38)	13.1 (1.92)	33.1 (2.08)
2015	32.7 (0.25)	36.1 (0.32)	24.3 (0.60)	16.6 (0.42)	50.4 (0.82)	51.8 (0.85)	21.3 (3.13)	21.3 (1.71)	33.4 (1.96)
2016	33.7 (0.27)	37.3 (0.32)	24.8 (0.54)	17.4 (0.47)	52.9 (0.96)	53.8 (0.97)	32.4 (3.94)	17.0 (1.78)	35.0 (2.17)
2017	34.6 (0.28)	38.3 (0.36)	25.7 (0.59)	18.6 (0.48)	52.3 (0.94)	53.8 (0.97)	24.2 (3.54)	22.9 (2.73)	34.6 (1.87)
2018	35.3 (0.30)	38.8 (0.37)	27.1 (0.63)	20.1 (0.47)	53.1 (0.90)	54.4 (0.88)	24.6 (3.34)	21.7 (2.26)	34.4 (1.84)
2019	36.6 (0.25)	40.3 (0.34)	27.9 (0.61)	20.8 (0.46)	55.4 (0.83)	56.6 (0.82)	30.8 (3.50)	20.2 (1.95)	36.8 (1.98)

—Not available.
†Not applicable.
[1]Includes persons of Hispanic ethnicity for years prior to 1980.
[2]Data for years prior to 1993 are for persons with 4 or more years of high school. Data for later years are for high school completers—i.e., those persons who graduated from high school with a diploma as well as those who completed high school through equivalency programs, such as a GED program.
[3]Estimates based on Census Bureau reverse projection of 1940 census data on education by age.
[4]Data for years prior to 1993 are for persons with 4 or more years of college.

NOTE: Prior to 2005, standard errors were computed using generalized variance function methodology rather than the more precise replicate weight methodology used in later years. For 1960 and prior years, data were collected in April. For later years, data were collected in March. Race categories exclude persons of Hispanic ethnicity except where otherwise noted.
SOURCE: U.S. Department of Commerce, Census Bureau, *U.S. Census of Population: 1960*, Vol. I, Part 1; J.K. Folger and C.B. Nam, *Education of the American Population* (1960 Census Monograph); Current Population Reports, Series P-20, various years; and Current Population Survey (CPS), Annual Social and Economic Supplement, 1970 through 2019. (This table was prepared October 2019.)

Table 104.20. Percentage of persons 25 to 29 years old with selected levels of educational attainment, by race/ethnicity and sex: Selected years, 1920 through 2019

[Standard errors appear in parentheses]

Sex, selected level of educational attainment, and year	Total	White[1]	Black[1]	Hispanic	Asian/Pacific Islander: Total	Asian/Pacific Islander: Asian	Asian/Pacific Islander: Pacific Islander	American Indian/ Alaska Native	Two or more races
1	2	3	4	5	6	7	8	9	10
Total									
High school completion or higher[2]									
1920[3]	— (†)	22.0 (—)	6.3 (—)	— (†)	— (†)	— (†)	— (†)	— (†)	— (†)
1940	38.1 (—)	41.2 (—)	12.3 (—)	— (†)	— (†)	— (†)	— (†)	— (†)	— (†)
1950	52.8 (—)	56.3 (—)	23.6 (—)	— (†)	— (†)	— (†)	— (†)	— (†)	— (†)
1960	60.7 (—)	63.7 (—)	38.6 (—)	— (†)	— (†)	— (†)	— (†)	— (†)	— (†)
1970	75.4 (—)	77.8 (—)	58.4 (—)	— (†)	— (†)	— (†)	— (†)	— (†)	— (†)
1980	85.4 (0.40)	89.2 (0.40)	76.7 (1.64)	58.0 (2.59)	— (†)	— (†)	— (†)	— (†)	— (†)
1990	85.7 (0.38)	90.1 (0.37)	81.7 (1.37)	58.2 (1.94)	91.5 (2.09)	— (†)	— (†)	— (†)	— (†)
1995	86.8 (0.39)	92.5 (0.36)	86.7 (1.23)	57.1 (1.80)	90.8 (2.26)	— (†)	— (†)	81.5 (6.97)	— (†)
2000	88.1 (0.37)	94.0 (0.33)	86.8 (1.13)	62.8 (1.22)	93.7 (1.27)	— (†)	— (†)	79.2 (5.19)	— (†)
2005	86.2 (0.42)	92.8 (0.39)	87.0 (1.03)	63.3 (1.32)	95.6 (0.88)	95.5 (0.92)	99.5 (0.54)	80.2 (4.77)	91.4 (1.93)
2006	86.4 (0.36)	93.4 (0.35)	86.3 (1.09)	63.2 (1.17)	96.4 (0.88)	96.6 (0.86)	93.4 (3.70)	79.8 (5.19)	89.3 (2.70)
2007	87.0 (0.36)	93.5 (0.33)	87.7 (1.16)	65.0 (1.06)	96.8 (0.91)	97.5 (0.73)	86.2 (7.36)	84.5 (4.41)	90.5 (2.19)
2008	87.8 (0.36)	93.7 (0.38)	87.5 (1.29)	68.3 (1.16)	95.9 (0.86)	95.8 (0.91)	97.5 (2.09)	86.7 (3.36)	94.2 (1.72)
2009	88.6 (0.36)	94.6 (0.33)	88.9 (0.98)	68.9 (1.16)	95.4 (0.91)	95.8 (0.95)	91.6 (3.46)	81.1 (4.26)	88.5 (2.40)
2010	88.8 (0.32)	94.5 (0.31)	89.6 (0.93)	69.4 (1.22)	93.7 (1.18)	94.0 (1.24)	89.7 (5.05)	89.9 (2.98)	88.5 (2.76)
2011	89.0 (0.34)	94.4 (0.34)	88.1 (0.98)	71.5 (1.12)	95.4 (0.87)	95.3 (0.91)	98.3 (1.23)	84.9 (3.95)	90.7 (2.15)
2012	89.7 (0.38)	94.6 (0.37)	88.5 (0.96)	75.0 (1.16)	96.2 (0.73)	96.1 (0.77)	98.6 (0.83)	84.5 (3.94)	92.8 (2.22)
2013	89.9 (0.35)	94.1 (0.35)	90.3 (0.92)	75.8 (1.10)	95.4 (0.77)	95.4 (0.81)	95.5 (2.71)	84.7 (3.47)	97.4 (1.11)
2014	90.8 (0.39)	95.6 (0.41)	91.9 (0.93)	74.7 (1.31)	96.6 (0.76)	96.6 (0.79)	96.0 (2.19)	83.9 (4.67)	96.0 (2.01)
2015	91.2 (0.31)	95.4 (0.32)	92.5 (0.78)	77.1 (1.02)	95.3 (0.92)	95.8 (0.87)	87.2 (6.60)	86.7 (2.65)	94.9 (1.54)
2016	91.7 (0.34)	95.2 (0.33)	91.1 (0.92)	80.6 (1.01)	96.7 (0.68)	96.8 (0.68)	94.0 (3.90)	84.5 (4.13)	94.8 (1.49)
2017	92.5 (0.32)	95.6 (0.30)	92.3 (0.89)	82.7 (0.92)	96.4 (0.76)	96.8 (0.76)	90.1 (4.96)	84.6 (4.34)	94.8 (2.01)
2018	92.9 (0.32)	95.6 (0.37)	92.0 (0.86)	85.2 (0.89)	97.0 (0.70)	97.5 (0.71)	90.7 (3.86)	89.1 (3.06)	93.3 (1.68)
2019	93.5 (0.29)	96.3 (0.32)	91.5 (0.91)	86.4 (0.80)	96.9 (0.71)	96.9 (0.76)	97.3 (2.00)	94.8 (2.27)	95.5 (1.76)
Associate's or higher degree									
1995	33.0 (0.54)	38.3 (0.67)	22.5 (1.52)	13.0 (1.23)	51.1 (3.91)	— (†)	— (†)	11.6! (5.75)	— (†)
2000	37.7 (0.55)	43.7 (0.70)	26.0 (1.47)	15.4 (0.91)	60.8 (2.55)	— (†)	— (†)	29.7 (5.84)	— (†)
2005	37.3 (0.56)	43.9 (0.77)	26.5 (1.43)	17.3 (0.91)	66.4 (2.14)	68.7 (2.17)	17.8! (6.08)	24.4 (4.13)	36.8 (3.99)
2006	37.6 (0.51)	45.1 (0.75)	25.3 (1.48)	16.1 (0.77)	66.7 (2.27)	68.6 (2.33)	33.5 (8.26)	18.2 (5.17)	31.6 (3.67)
2007	38.6 (0.55)	45.8 (0.77)	27.3 (1.36)	18.1 (0.77)	66.2 (2.08)	68.0 (2.11)	37.1 (8.93)	14.6 (4.27)	35.3 (3.80)
2008	39.7 (0.55)	47.6 (0.72)	27.6 (1.39)	18.7 (0.90)	65.1 (2.21)	66.9 (2.19)	35.3 (7.53)	20.9 (3.60)	33.5 (3.84)
2009	39.3 (0.58)	47.1 (0.83)	27.8 (1.43)	18.4 (0.89)	63.0 (2.21)	66.7 (2.23)	20.9 (5.84)	20.8 (4.05)	35.6 (3.76)
2010	41.1 (0.51)	48.9 (0.69)	29.4 (1.41)	20.5 (0.99)	60.5 (2.33)	63.4 (2.45)	22.0! (7.92)	28.9 (6.19)	36.9 (3.57)
2011	42.1 (0.65)	50.1 (0.85)	29.8 (1.50)	20.6 (0.87)	63.6 (2.36)	64.6 (2.35)	39.7 (9.75)	25.0 (4.52)	42.0 (4.33)
2012	42.8 (0.58)	49.9 (0.80)	31.6 (1.40)	22.7 (1.01)	66.3 (1.96)	68.3 (2.01)	32.4 (6.33)	23.6 (4.32)	47.6 (3.76)
2013	43.2 (0.57)	51.0 (0.79)	29.5 (1.42)	23.1 (0.87)	65.5 (1.93)	67.2 (1.96)	37.3 (7.84)	26.3 (5.70)	44.2 (3.81)
2014	44.1 (0.75)	51.9 (1.01)	32.0 (1.98)	23.4 (1.18)	67.8 (2.35)	70.3 (2.40)	‡ (†)	18.2 (4.23)	40.8 (4.46)
2015	45.7 (0.53)	54.0 (0.78)	31.1 (1.41)	25.7 (1.01)	68.9 (2.09)	71.7 (2.13)	24.9 (6.58)	22.3 (3.65)	38.4 (3.56)
2016	46.1 (0.62)	54.3 (0.82)	31.7 (1.46)	27.0 (1.19)	69.5 (2.07)	71.5 (2.15)	28.6 (8.03)	16.5 (3.47)	41.3 (4.10)
2017	46.1 (0.61)	53.5 (0.83)	32.7 (1.35)	27.7 (1.00)	68.0 (2.11)	69.9 (2.10)	35.8 (8.65)	27.1 (5.97)	45.6 (3.86)
2018	46.7 (0.65)	53.6 (0.89)	32.6 (1.54)	30.5 (1.17)	72.2 (1.90)	75.5 (1.83)	22.6 (5.98)	24.4 (4.14)	41.5 (3.50)
2019	49.1 (0.65)	55.7 (0.87)	39.6 (1.90)	31.3 (1.04)	75.0 (1.67)	77.5 (1.71)	36.5 (7.07)	22.7 (4.34)	44.7 (3.81)
Bachelor's or higher degree[4]									
1920[3]	— (†)	4.5 (—)	1.2 (—)	— (†)	— (†)	— (†)	— (†)	— (†)	— (†)
1940	5.9 (—)	6.4 (—)	1.6 (—)	— (†)	— (†)	— (†)	— (†)	— (†)	— (†)
1950	7.7 (—)	8.2 (—)	2.8 (—)	— (†)	— (†)	— (†)	— (†)	— (†)	— (†)
1960	11.0 (—)	11.8 (—)	5.4 (—)	— (†)	— (†)	— (†)	— (†)	— (†)	— (†)
1970	16.4 (—)	17.3 (—)	10.0 (—)	— (†)	— (†)	— (†)	— (†)	— (†)	— (†)
1980	22.5 (0.47)	25.0 (0.55)	11.6 (1.24)	7.7 (1.39)	— (†)	— (†)	— (†)	— (†)	— (†)
1990	23.2 (0.46)	26.4 (0.55)	13.4 (1.20)	8.1 (1.07)	43.0 (3.71)	— (†)	— (†)	— (†)	— (†)
1995	24.7 (0.49)	28.8 (0.62)	15.4 (1.31)	8.9 (1.04)	43.1 (3.87)	— (†)	— (†)	‡ (†)	— (†)
2000	29.1 (0.52)	34.0 (0.67)	17.8 (1.28)	9.7 (0.75)	54.3 (2.60)	— (†)	— (†)	15.9 (4.68)	— (†)
2005	28.8 (0.55)	34.5 (0.78)	17.6 (1.21)	11.2 (0.81)	60.0 (2.20)	62.1 (2.25)	17.0! (6.01)	16.4 (3.56)	28.0 (3.79)
2006	28.4 (0.52)	34.3 (0.78)	18.7 (1.33)	9.5 (0.66)	59.6 (2.39)	61.9 (2.44)	20.7! (6.70)	9.5! (4.26)	23.3 (3.14)
2007	29.6 (0.54)	35.5 (0.75)	19.5 (1.21)	11.6 (0.61)	59.4 (2.24)	61.5 (2.26)	26.5! (8.25)	6.4! (2.99)	26.3 (3.44)
2008	30.8 (0.51)	37.1 (0.70)	20.4 (1.35)	12.4 (0.69)	57.9 (2.26)	60.2 (2.32)	20.2! (6.75)	14.3 (3.17)	26.6 (3.75)
2009	30.6 (0.57)	37.2 (0.85)	18.9 (1.36)	12.2 (0.80)	56.4 (2.25)	60.3 (2.28)	12.5! (4.44)	15.9 (3.73)	29.7 (3.84)
2010	31.7 (0.51)	38.6 (0.72)	19.4 (1.20)	13.5 (0.80)	52.5 (2.32)	55.8 (2.47)	10.0! (4.40)	18.6 (4.80)	29.8 (3.22)
2011	32.2 (0.62)	39.2 (0.88)	20.1 (1.25)	12.8 (0.73)	56.0 (2.50)	57.2 (2.52)	28.8! (9.04)	17.3 (4.45)	32.4 (3.85)
2012	33.5 (0.58)	39.8 (0.78)	23.2 (1.38)	14.8 (0.90)	59.6 (2.17)	61.7 (2.24)	25.5 (6.12)	10.4 (2.87)	32.9 (3.72)
2013	33.6 (0.55)	40.4 (0.77)	20.5 (1.38)	15.7 (0.82)	58.0 (2.16)	60.1 (2.18)	24.7! (7.54)	16.6 (4.89)	29.6 (3.45)
2014	34.0 (0.75)	40.8 (1.05)	22.4 (1.82)	15.1 (0.97)	60.8 (2.44)	63.2 (2.50)	‡ (†)	5.6! (2.24)	32.4 (4.12)
2015	35.6 (0.55)	43.0 (0.83)	21.3 (1.33)	16.4 (0.78)	62.8 (2.25)	66.0 (2.27)	11.4! (4.64)	15.3 (3.21)	29.6 (3.62)
2016	36.1 (0.61)	42.9 (0.87)	22.7 (1.26)	18.7 (1.06)	63.5 (2.11)	65.6 (2.20)	20.4! (6.62)	10.2 (2.57)	28.3 (3.76)
2017	35.7 (0.63)	42.1 (0.88)	22.8 (1.37)	18.5 (0.82)	60.6 (2.22)	62.7 (2.28)	25.3 (7.04)	16.3! (5.22)	32.8 (3.84)
2018	37.0 (0.66)	43.5 (0.96)	22.6 (1.39)	20.7 (1.03)	67.1 (2.10)	70.5 (2.08)	15.1 (4.53)	15.5 (3.30)	26.9 (3.01)
2019	38.7 (0.62)	44.9 (0.88)	29.1 (1.64)	20.6 (0.86)	68.3 (1.94)	71.4 (1.96)	21.6 (6.22)	13.6 (3.59)	34.3 (3.68)

See notes at end of table.

Table 104.20. Percentage of persons 25 to 29 years old with selected levels of educational attainment, by race/ethnicity and sex: Selected years, 1920 through 2019—Continued

[Standard errors appear in parentheses]

Sex, selected level of educational attainment, and year	Total	White[1]	Black[1]	Hispanic	Asian/Pacific Islander: Total	Asian/Pacific Islander: Asian	Asian/Pacific Islander: Pacific Islander	American Indian/ Alaska Native	Two or more races
1	2	3	4	5	6	7	8	9	10
Master's or higher degree									
1995	4.5 (0.24)	5.3 (0.31)	1.8 (0.48)	1.6 (0.46)	10.9 (2.43)	— (†)	— (†)	‡ (†)	— (†)
2000	5.4 (0.26)	5.8 (0.33)	3.7 (0.63)	2.1 (0.36)	15.5 (1.89)	— (†)	— (†)	‡ (†)	— (†)
2005	6.3 (0.31)	7.5 (0.45)	2.6 (0.44)	2.1 (0.38)	16.9 (1.93)	17.5 (2.01)	‡ (†)	‡ (†)	7.0! (2.49)
2006	6.4 (0.29)	7.5 (0.42)	3.2 (0.58)	1.5 (0.25)	20.1 (2.00)	21.1 (2.10)	‡ (†)	‡ (†)	7.1 (1.83)
2007	6.3 (0.30)	7.6 (0.42)	3.5 (0.59)	1.5 (0.25)	17.5 (1.84)	18.5 (1.93)	‡ (†)	‡ (†)	6.2! (2.38)
2008	7.0 (0.28)	8.2 (0.40)	4.4 (0.64)	2.0 (0.28)	19.9 (1.84)	21.0 (1.96)	‡ (†)	‡ (†)	6.9! (2.57)
2009	7.4 (0.30)	8.9 (0.45)	4.2 (0.54)	1.9 (0.26)	21.1 (1.98)	22.9 (2.16)	‡ (†)	‡ (†)	6.5! (2.02)
2010	6.8 (0.26)	7.7 (0.38)	4.7 (0.60)	2.5 (0.37)	17.9 (1.87)	19.2 (1.99)	‡ (†)	‡ (†)	5.3! (1.63)
2011	6.9 (0.32)	8.1 (0.45)	4.0 (0.52)	2.7 (0.37)	16.7 (1.78)	17.5 (1.85)	‡ (†)	‡ (†)	6.1 (1.59)
2012	7.2 (0.35)	8.2 (0.51)	5.1 (0.66)	2.7 (0.36)	17.8 (1.85)	18.9 (1.92)	‡ (†)	2.6! (1.28)	4.1! (1.49)
2013	7.4 (0.31)	8.6 (0.50)	3.3 (0.50)	3.0 (0.37)	20.6 (1.73)	21.8 (1.79)	‡ (†)	‡ (†)	4.8! (1.54)
2014	7.6 (0.41)	9.0 (0.58)	3.9 (0.77)	2.9 (0.43)	17.9 (1.84)	18.8 (1.92)	‡ (†)	‡ (†)	7.1! (2.32)
2015	8.7 (0.33)	10.1 (0.51)	5.0 (0.60)	3.2 (0.41)	21.6 (1.85)	22.8 (1.97)	‡ (†)	‡ (†)	7.8 (1.79)
2016	9.2 (0.33)	10.5 (0.52)	5.2 (0.69)	4.1 (0.49)	23.8 (1.95)	24.9 (2.01)	‡ (†)	2.1! (0.85)	5.3! (1.74)
2017	9.2 (0.34)	10.1 (0.55)	5.5 (0.71)	3.9 (0.40)	24.5 (1.76)	25.6 (1.89)	‡ (†)	‡ (†)	5.0! (1.72)
2018	9.0 (0.36)	10.1 (0.62)	4.5 (0.65)	3.4 (0.43)	27.5 (1.87)	29.2 (1.98)	‡ (†)	‡ (†)	2.9! (1.44)
2019	9.4 (0.36)	10.3 (0.52)	6.2 (0.80)	3.4 (0.40)	27.1 (1.79)	28.9 (1.90)	‡ (†)	‡ (†)	10.4 (2.52)
Males									
High school completion or higher[2]									
1980	85.4 (0.49)	89.1 (0.48)	74.7 (1.97)	57.0 (3.45)	— (†)	— (†)	— (†)	— (†)	— (†)
1990	84.4 (0.56)	88.6 (0.57)	81.4 (2.03)	56.6 (2.69)	95.3 (1.78)	— (†)	— (†)	— (†)	— (†)
1995	86.3 (0.56)	92.0 (0.53)	88.4 (1.72)	55.7 (2.51)	90.5 (3.11)	— (†)	— (†)	83.6 (9.73)	— (†)
2000	86.7 (0.55)	92.9 (0.51)	87.6 (1.67)	59.2 (1.76)	92.1 (2.03)	— (†)	— (†)	68.5 (9.40)	— (†)
2005	85.0 (0.58)	91.8 (0.53)	86.6 (1.76)	63.2 (1.72)	96.8 (1.09)	96.7 (1.15)	99.1 (0.94)	73.0 (8.43)	89.1 (3.07)
2006	84.4 (0.54)	92.3 (0.52)	84.2 (2.02)	60.5 (1.64)	97.2 (1.01)	97.2 (1.06)	97.8 (1.60)	75.0 (6.34)	89.2 (3.81)
2007	84.9 (0.50)	92.7 (0.48)	87.4 (1.65)	60.5 (1.59)	95.9 (1.13)	96.3 (1.10)	‡ (†)	76.6 (8.90)	92.9 (2.64)
2008	85.8 (0.54)	92.6 (0.58)	85.7 (1.99)	65.6 (1.55)	95.6 (1.23)	95.4 (1.31)	100.0 (0.00)	90.5 (4.04)	92.7 (2.68)
2009	87.5 (0.51)	94.4 (0.46)	88.8 (1.56)	66.2 (1.54)	96.4 (1.17)	96.2 (1.25)	98.2 (1.81)	77.5 (8.59)	92.0 (3.01)
2010	87.4 (0.44)	94.6 (0.42)	87.9 (1.52)	65.7 (1.52)	93.8 (1.83)	93.5 (1.95)	98.2 (1.35)	93.2 (3.47)	87.9 (4.32)
2011	87.5 (0.49)	93.4 (0.48)	88.0 (1.43)	69.2 (1.62)	94.2 (1.30)	93.9 (1.36)	98.5 (1.46)	84.5 (5.28)	86.2 (4.41)
2012	88.4 (0.51)	93.8 (0.50)	86.2 (1.58)	73.3 (1.57)	96.1 (1.04)	96.0 (1.09)	97.3 (1.74)	82.8 (8.27)	91.0 (3.58)
2013	88.3 (0.52)	93.3 (0.53)	87.8 (1.60)	73.1 (1.64)	94.4 (1.12)	94.3 (1.21)	96.3 (3.04)	89.0 (3.25)	96.8 (1.77)
2014	90.1 (0.53)	95.4 (0.60)	93.5 (1.18)	72.4 (1.76)	96.1 (1.10)	96.1 (1.14)	‡ (†)	83.5 (7.17)	96.9 (2.02)
2015	90.5 (0.45)	95.1 (0.45)	91.8 (1.22)	75.7 (1.41)	95.9 (1.23)	97.1 (0.96)	75.8 (12.49)	83.2 (4.73)	98.0 (1.27)
2016	90.9 (0.46)	94.8 (0.44)	91.7 (1.19)	78.3 (1.34)	96.0 (1.06)	96.2 (1.05)	‡ (†)	84.4 (5.70)	98.1 (1.22)
2017	91.5 (0.48)	94.8 (0.46)	92.0 (1.19)	80.7 (1.31)	97.3 (0.77)	97.7 (0.75)	89.3 (6.87)	76.5 (8.11)	95.9 (2.38)
2018	91.9 (0.44)	95.0 (0.53)	90.7 (1.37)	83.4 (1.22)	97.1 (0.92)	97.6 (0.96)	89.3 (6.35)	82.9 (5.67)	92.8 (2.42)
2019	92.7 (0.39)	96.2 (0.42)	89.8 (1.41)	84.6 (1.11)	96.8 (0.98)	96.9 (1.00)	‡ (†)	92.1 (4.18)	93.8 (3.00)
Associate's or higher degree									
1995	32.1 (0.76)	37.1 (0.94)	23.5 (2.28)	11.6 (1.62)	49.8 (5.30)	— (†)	— (†)	‡ (†)	— (†)
2000	35.3 (0.78)	40.7 (0.98)	24.1 (2.16)	13.0 (1.20)	60.7 (3.68)	— (†)	— (†)	17.6! (7.71)	— (†)
2005	33.4 (0.74)	39.6 (1.05)	22.7 (1.77)	16.1 (1.12)	64.0 (3.16)	66.7 (3.19)	18.5! (7.78)	19.9! (7.06)	31.0 (5.10)
2006	33.8 (0.67)	41.5 (0.97)	21.3 (2.02)	12.8 (1.02)	65.4 (3.32)	67.9 (3.37)	25.6! (9.90)	18.9! (6.54)	28.4 (5.26)
2007	34.1 (0.76)	40.8 (1.01)	26.4 (2.06)	13.8 (0.96)	64.5 (3.04)	66.3 (3.12)	‡ (†)	14.9! (6.39)	30.8 (5.22)
2008	34.7 (0.72)	42.2 (0.98)	24.2 (2.16)	15.2 (1.05)	61.5 (3.23)	62.8 (3.21)	41.3 (11.71)	22.0! (6.95)	29.9 (4.62)
2009	34.5 (0.66)	41.8 (1.04)	21.9 (1.97)	15.9 (1.16)	63.0 (2.86)	66.6 (2.99)	17.4! (8.42)	17.1! (7.26)	31.7 (5.35)
2010	36.1 (0.68)	44.5 (0.98)	22.9 (2.16)	16.0 (1.20)	57.4 (3.12)	61.1 (3.27)	‡ (†)	30.1 (8.14)	31.5 (5.23)
2011	37.0 (0.88)	45.2 (1.17)	25.9 (2.24)	16.1 (1.18)	57.9 (3.40)	58.8 (3.48)	42.9 (12.13)	22.0 (5.29)	38.4 (7.04)
2012	38.2 (0.81)	44.8 (1.11)	25.3 (1.92)	20.6 (1.45)	63.4 (3.00)	65.5 (2.94)	28.8! (10.22)	15.7! (5.97)	46.3 (5.90)
2013	38.5 (0.69)	46.0 (1.03)	24.8 (1.76)	20.0 (1.20)	61.2 (2.74)	62.6 (2.80)	39.3 (11.03)	27.5 (7.59)	42.8 (5.00)
2014	39.4 (0.95)	47.4 (1.35)	28.9 (2.66)	18.2 (1.40)	63.5 (3.37)	66.0 (3.41)	‡ (†)	23.7! (8.06)	33.5 (6.67)
2015	41.3 (0.73)	49.3 (1.15)	24.6 (2.00)	22.7 (1.32)	67.1 (3.01)	69.5 (2.93)	26.0! (9.45)	17.7! (5.36)	37.7 (5.16)
2016	41.8 (0.87)	49.9 (1.19)	28.3 (2.21)	23.4 (1.56)	66.1 (2.83)	68.2 (2.90)	‡ (†)	13.7! (4.53)	27.7 (5.03)
2017	41.3 (0.86)	48.3 (1.22)	29.5 (2.22)	22.0 (1.33)	64.8 (2.85)	66.0 (2.88)	38.6! (11.88)	19.4! (7.61)	41.0 (5.82)
2018	42.0 (0.85)	47.8 (1.22)	29.1 (2.36)	27.3 (1.49)	71.2 (2.69)	74.1 (2.67)	21.2! (8.56)	15.6! (4.70)	34.9 (5.45)
2019	44.9 (0.86)	50.6 (1.15)	37.6 (2.75)	26.8 (1.41)	73.8 (2.46)	75.6 (2.55)	‡ (†)	16.1! (5.28)	45.2 (5.46)
Bachelor's or higher degree[4]									
1980	24.0 (0.59)	26.8 (0.69)	10.5 (1.39)	8.4 (1.94)	— (†)	— (†)	— (†)	— (†)	— (†)
1990	23.7 (0.65)	26.6 (0.79)	15.1 (1.87)	7.3 (1.41)	47.6 (4.19)	— (†)	— (†)	— (†)	— (†)
1995	24.5 (0.70)	28.4 (0.88)	17.4 (2.04)	7.8 (1.35)	42.0 (5.23)	— (†)	— (†)	‡ (†)	— (†)
2000	27.9 (0.73)	32.3 (0.93)	18.4 (1.96)	8.3 (0.98)	55.5 (3.74)	— (†)	— (†)	‡ (†)	— (†)
2005	25.5 (0.68)	30.7 (0.98)	14.2 (1.57)	10.2 (0.99)	58.5 (3.11)	61.0 (3.17)	17.2! (7.62)	14.5! (6.14)	24.5 (4.93)
2006	25.3 (0.67)	31.4 (0.98)	15.2 (1.66)	6.9 (0.70)	58.7 (3.46)	60.9 (3.52)	23.3! (9.77)	‡ (†)	20.8 (4.65)
2007	26.3 (0.72)	31.9 (0.98)	18.9 (1.86)	8.6 (0.71)	58.5 (3.45)	60.4 (3.54)	‡ (†)	‡ (†)	23.3 (4.88)
2008	26.8 (0.64)	32.6 (0.89)	19.0 (1.94)	10.0 (0.86)	54.1 (3.41)	55.8 (3.53)	26.1! (9.86)	17.7! (6.67)	25.7 (4.45)
2009	26.6 (0.66)	32.6 (1.04)	14.8 (1.82)	11.0 (1.04)	55.2 (3.07)	59.2 (3.24)	‡ (†)	15.2! (7.21)	24.6 (5.77)
2010	27.8 (0.68)	34.8 (0.96)	15.0 (1.72)	10.8 (1.06)	49.0 (3.12)	52.3 (3.31)	‡ (†)	18.9! (7.12)	24.9 (4.91)
2011	28.4 (0.82)	35.5 (1.16)	17.0 (1.83)	9.6 (0.90)	50.8 (3.42)	52.1 (3.55)	28.1! (11.40)	15.4! (4.80)	34.1 (6.62)
2012	29.8 (0.82)	36.0 (1.06)	19.1 (1.74)	12.5 (1.20)	55.0 (3.15)	56.9 (3.16)	24.3! (9.06)	‡ (†)	30.4 (5.43)
2013	30.2 (0.68)	37.1 (1.00)	17.4 (1.63)	13.1 (1.06)	53.0 (3.03)	55.1 (3.13)	19.0! (9.38)	16.8! (6.40)	29.3 (4.61)
2014	30.9 (0.93)	37.7 (1.36)	20.8 (2.40)	12.4 (1.22)	56.9 (3.55)	59.0 (3.59)	‡ (†)	‡ (†)	26.4 (6.13)
2015	32.4 (0.74)	39.5 (1.12)	17.6 (1.83)	14.5 (1.04)	60.9 (3.13)	63.8 (3.12)	‡ (†)	‡ (†)	26.7 (5.07)

See notes at end of table.

Table 104.20. Percentage of persons 25 to 29 years old with selected levels of educational attainment, by race/ethnicity and sex: Selected years, 1920 through 2019—Continued

[Standard errors appear in parentheses]

Sex, selected level of educational attainment, and year	Total	White[1]	Black[1]	Hispanic	Asian/Pacific Islander: Total	Asian/Pacific Islander: Asian	Asian/Pacific Islander: Pacific Islander	American Indian/ Alaska Native	Two or more races
1	2	3	4	5	6	7	8	9	10
2016	32.7 (0.80)	39.5 (1.20)	20.4 (1.87)	16.2 (1.31)	59.0 (2.86)	61.4 (2.98)	‡ (†)	7.8! (3.17)	19.7 (4.52)
2017	32.0 (0.81)	37.7 (1.19)	21.7 (1.79)	15.0 (1.13)	57.7 (2.92)	59.2 (3.00)	26.4! (10.58)	‡ (†)	26.1 (5.48)
2018	33.2 (0.85)	38.8 (1.32)	18.7 (1.95)	18.4 (1.34)	66.7 (2.97)	69.6 (2.97)	17.3! (8.00)	8.4! (3.50)	25.1 (4.93)
2019	35.7 (0.83)	40.8 (1.17)	28.3 (2.30)	18.2 (1.23)	67.6 (2.73)	70.1 (2.79)	‡ (†)	6.4! (3.12)	36.7 (5.14)
Master's or higher degree									
1995	4.9 (0.35)	5.6 (0.45)	2.2! (0.80)	2.0! (0.70)	12.6 (3.52)	— (†)	— (†)	‡ (†)	— (†)
2000	4.7 (0.34)	4.9 (0.43)	2.1! (0.72)	1.5 (0.43)	17.2 (2.85)	— (†)	— (†)	‡ (†)	— (†)
2005	5.2 (0.38)	6.2 (0.55)	1.1! (0.43)	1.7 (0.46)	19.7 (3.13)	20.5 (3.30)	‡ (†)	‡ (†)	‡ (†)
2006	5.1 (0.37)	5.8 (0.51)	1.7! (0.52)	1.1 (0.32)	20.5 (2.68)	21.8 (2.83)	‡ (†)	‡ (†)	5.9! (2.66)
2007	5.0 (0.39)	5.7 (0.50)	3.3 (0.99)	0.6! (0.19)	18.4 (2.89)	19.3 (3.00)	‡ (†)	‡ (†)	9.8! (4.28)
2008	5.3 (0.34)	5.9 (0.49)	3.4 (0.90)	1.2 (0.32)	20.9 (2.94)	22.1 (3.07)	‡ (†)	‡ (†)	7.8! (2.85)
2009	6.1 (0.37)	7.4 (0.60)	3.2 (0.73)	1.2 (0.28)	20.4 (2.48)	22.0 (2.69)	‡ (†)	‡ (†)	5.0! (2.38)
2010	5.2 (0.32)	6.3 (0.50)	2.9 (0.69)	1.5 (0.39)	15.0 (2.19)	16.2 (2.36)	‡ (†)	‡ (†)	‡ (†)
2011	5.1 (0.38)	5.9 (0.49)	1.9 (0.54)	1.8 (0.41)	18.0 (2.58)	19.1 (2.71)	‡ (†)	‡ (†)	‡ (†)
2012	5.6 (0.42)	6.3 (0.59)	2.7 (0.72)	2.4 (0.50)	16.2 (2.46)	17.2 (2.60)	‡ (†)	‡ (†)	‡ (†)
2013	5.7 (0.38)	6.3 (0.53)	1.5! (0.56)	2.1 (0.43)	20.8 (2.49)	22.1 (2.60)	‡ (†)	‡ (†)	5.9! (2.47)
2014	5.9 (0.51)	7.0 (0.72)	2.6! (0.82)	2.2 (0.52)	15.9 (2.56)	16.6 (2.65)	‡ (†)	‡ (†)	‡ (†)
2015	7.0 (0.40)	8.2 (0.62)	2.5 (0.75)	2.3 (0.56)	21.1 (2.65)	22.4 (2.78)	‡ (†)	‡ (†)	5.6! (2.37)
2016	7.2 (0.43)	8.7 (0.68)	3.9 (0.87)	2.1 (0.43)	19.7 (2.73)	20.6 (2.85)	‡ (†)	‡ (†)	‡ (†)
2017	7.8 (0.42)	8.5 (0.64)	3.9 (0.89)	2.8 (0.52)	24.3 (2.52)	25.4 (2.63)	‡ (†)	‡ (†)	‡ (†)
2018	7.3 (0.44)	7.7 (0.70)	2.8 (0.74)	3.1 (0.56)	27.0 (2.81)	28.6 (2.95)	‡ (†)	‡ (†)	‡ (†)
2019	7.7 (0.43)	8.0 (0.61)	3.8 (0.90)	2.2 (0.45)	29.1 (2.86)	30.3 (2.96)	‡ (†)	‡ (†)	11.7! (3.59)
Females									
High school completion or higher[2]									
1980	85.5 (0.48)	89.2 (0.48)	78.3 (1.71)	58.9 (3.38)	— (†)	— (†)	— (†)	— (†)	— (†)
1990	87.0 (0.51)	91.7 (0.49)	82.0 (1.85)	59.9 (2.79)	85.1 (2.82)	— (†)	— (†)	— (†)	— (†)
1995	87.4 (0.54)	93.0 (0.50)	85.3 (1.75)	58.7 (2.60)	91.2 (3.28)	— (†)	— (†)	79.6 (9.88)	— (†)
2000	89.4 (0.49)	95.2 (0.43)	86.2 (1.53)	66.4 (1.69)	95.2 (1.55)	— (†)	— (†)	86.3 (5.68)	— (†)
2005	87.4 (0.44)	93.8 (0.47)	87.3 (1.22)	63.4 (1.54)	94.6 (1.36)	94.4 (1.41)	‡ (†)	87.1 (5.12)	94.2 (2.26)
2006	88.5 (0.44)	94.6 (0.41)	88.0 (1.14)	66.6 (1.41)	95.6 (1.44)	96.0 (1.31)	‡ (†)	83.3 (6.55)	89.4 (3.81)
2007	89.1 (0.45)	94.2 (0.44)	87.9 (1.46)	70.7 (1.30)	97.7 (1.05)	98.5 (0.68)	86.0 (8.19)	90.2 (4.49)	87.9 (3.82)
2008	89.9 (0.39)	94.7 (0.44)	89.2 (1.43)	71.9 (1.34)	96.1 (1.12)	96.2 (1.18)	95.2 (4.01)	84.2 (4.68)	95.9 (2.44)
2009	89.8 (0.41)	94.8 (0.44)	89.0 (1.12)	72.5 (1.34)	94.5 (1.20)	95.3 (1.18)	86.2 (5.92)	83.4 (4.81)	84.8 (3.57)
2010	90.2 (0.39)	94.4 (0.42)	91.1 (0.96)	74.1 (1.53)	93.6 (1.25)	94.5 (1.27)	81.2 (9.50)	86.8 (4.80)	89.1 (3.55)
2011	90.7 (0.36)	95.5 (0.42)	88.2 (1.24)	74.3 (1.26)	96.6 (0.89)	96.6 (0.92)	‡ (†)	85.3 (6.02)	94.0 (2.52)
2012	91.1 (0.44)	95.3 (0.46)	90.6 (1.11)	76.9 (1.39)	96.3 (0.98)	96.1 (1.04)	100.0 (0.00)	85.8 (4.53)	94.7 (2.35)
2013	91.5 (0.38)	94.9 (0.43)	92.5 (0.95)	78.8 (1.17)	96.2 (0.96)	96.3 (1.01)	94.8 (2.88)	82.0 (5.40)	98.2 (1.15)
2014	91.5 (0.50)	95.9 (0.54)	90.5 (1.62)	77.4 (1.56)	97.1 (0.96)	97.1 (0.99)	‡ (†)	84.1 (6.05)	95.2 (3.44)
2015	91.8 (0.39)	95.8 (0.41)	93.2 (0.90)	78.6 (1.34)	94.8 (1.18)	94.6 (1.25)	96.7 (1.86)	89.3 (3.52)	91.5 (2.99)
2016	92.5 (0.40)	95.7 (0.41)	90.7 (1.33)	83.2 (1.22)	97.4 (0.76)	97.4 (0.79)	‡ (†)	84.6 (5.34)	91.5 (2.76)
2017	93.4 (0.34)	96.4 (0.39)	92.6 (1.22)	84.8 (1.04)	95.5 (1.10)	95.8 (1.16)	90.7 (4.70)	90.9 (3.70)	94.0 (3.24)
2018	94.0 (0.39)	96.3 (0.44)	93.2 (0.95)	87.2 (1.13)	97.0 (0.91)	97.4 (0.85)	91.8 (6.23)	95.1 (2.18)	93.8 (2.49)
2019	94.3 (0.36)	96.4 (0.41)	93.1 (1.06)	88.4 (0.98)	97.1 (0.95)	96.9 (1.02)	98.9 (1.09)	97.5 (1.87)	97.0 (1.69)
Associate's or higher degree									
1995	34.0 (0.77)	39.5 (0.95)	21.6 (2.03)	14.6 (1.86)	52.6 (5.77)	— (†)	— (†)	‡ (†)	— (†)
2000	40.1 (0.78)	46.6 (1.00)	27.5 (1.99)	17.7 (1.37)	60.8 (3.54)	— (†)	— (†)	37.7 (8.00)	— (†)
2005	41.3 (0.72)	48.2 (0.99)	29.8 (1.81)	18.8 (1.23)	68.5 (2.86)	70.4 (2.90)	‡ (†)	28.7 (6.96)	43.7 (6.04)
2006	41.5 (0.72)	48.8 (1.00)	28.8 (1.91)	20.3 (1.17)	68.0 (2.60)	69.4 (2.65)	‡ (†)	17.6! (6.91)	34.7 (5.09)
2007	43.2 (0.72)	50.8 (1.02)	28.0 (1.61)	23.5 (1.25)	67.7 (2.73)	69.6 (2.88)	42.5 (11.79)	14.5! (5.53)	40.2 (5.87)
2008	44.9 (0.77)	53.0 (1.00)	30.7 (1.79)	23.2 (1.43)	68.5 (2.80)	70.8 (2.82)	29.5! (9.83)	20.2 (4.14)	37.6 (5.73)
2009	44.4 (0.75)	52.5 (1.02)	33.0 (1.79)	21.7 (1.22)	63.0 (3.19)	66.8 (3.13)	23.6! (8.47)	23.3 (5.09)	39.8 (5.19)
2010	46.3 (0.71)	53.5 (0.92)	35.2 (1.77)	26.2 (1.48)	63.3 (2.68)	65.6 (2.80)	31.4! (13.43)	27.7 (8.27)	41.8 (5.08)
2011	47.4 (0.74)	55.2 (1.00)	33.3 (1.92)	26.2 (1.29)	69.1 (2.50)	70.2 (2.48)	‡ (†)	28.7 (7.46)	44.5 (5.08)
2012	47.4 (0.68)	55.0 (0.94)	37.0 (1.80)	25.1 (1.23)	69.1 (2.22)	71.0 (2.29)	36.1 (9.80)	29.2 (6.04)	49.0 (5.15)
2013	47.9 (0.77)	56.1 (0.99)	33.6 (1.99)	26.8 (1.30)	69.2 (2.29)	71.2 (2.33)	35.5 (10.28)	25.6 (7.48)	46.0 (6.22)
2014	48.9 (0.99)	56.5 (1.28)	34.8 (2.77)	29.4 (1.67)	71.5 (3.14)	74.1 (3.18)	‡ (†)	15.7! (5.27)	48.2 (6.06)
2015	50.1 (0.72)	58.7 (0.98)	36.9 (1.78)	29.0 (1.47)	70.7 (2.55)	73.8 (2.61)	24.0! (9.77)	25.8 (4.73)	39.2 (5.20)
2016	50.5 (0.71)	58.7 (0.95)	34.8 (1.73)	31.0 (1.51)	72.6 (2.49)	74.5 (2.56)	‡ (†)	18.9 (4.75)	54.5 (5.59)
2017	51.0 (0.73)	58.8 (1.04)	35.5 (1.69)	33.9 (1.34)	71.2 (2.77)	73.9 (2.71)	34.0! (10.51)	33.1 (7.83)	49.6 (5.82)
2018	51.5 (0.82)	59.6 (1.17)	35.8 (1.86)	34.2 (1.56)	73.1 (2.31)	76.9 (2.21)	23.6! (8.51)	32.8 (6.29)	48.2 (5.45)
2019	53.5 (0.77)	60.9 (1.12)	41.4 (2.20)	36.2 (1.44)	76.1 (2.03)	79.5 (2.12)	38.1 (8.05)	29.2 (6.55)	44.2 (5.30)
Bachelor's or higher degree[4]									
1980	21.0 (0.56)	23.2 (0.65)	12.4 (1.36)	6.9 (1.74)	— (†)	— (†)	— (†)	— (†)	— (†)
1990	22.8 (0.64)	26.2 (0.78)	11.9 (1.56)	9.1 (1.64)	37.4 (3.83)	— (†)	— (†)	— (†)	— (†)
1995	24.9 (0.70)	29.2 (0.89)	13.7 (1.70)	10.1 (1.59)	44.5 (5.74)	— (†)	— (†)	‡ (†)	— (†)
2000	30.1 (0.73)	35.8 (0.96)	17.4 (1.69)	11.0 (1.12)	53.1 (3.62)	— (†)	— (†)	19.1! (6.48)	— (†)
2005	32.2 (0.75)	38.2 (1.00)	20.5 (1.68)	12.4 (1.07)	61.4 (3.06)	63.1 (3.11)	‡ (†)	18.2! (6.43)	32.1 (5.70)
2006	31.6 (0.70)	37.2 (0.99)	21.7 (1.77)	12.8 (1.05)	60.4 (2.76)	62.8 (2.82)	‡ (†)	‡ (†)	25.7 (4.72)
2007	33.0 (0.72)	39.2 (1.03)	20.0 (1.38)	15.4 (1.10)	60.3 (2.83)	62.5 (2.88)	32.1! (11.09)	‡ (†)	29.6 (5.17)
2008	34.9 (0.71)	41.7 (0.98)	21.6 (1.57)	15.5 (1.11)	61.6 (2.67)	64.4 (2.71)	‡ (†)	12.2! (3.69)	27.7 (5.57)
2009	34.8 (0.78)	42.0 (1.12)	22.6 (1.75)	13.8 (1.09)	57.6 (3.00)	61.3 (3.03)	18.2! (6.42)	16.3 (4.42)	35.0 (5.07)
2010	35.7 (0.68)	42.4 (0.96)	23.3 (1.72)	16.8 (1.20)	55.8 (2.93)	58.9 (3.00)	‡ (†)	18.4! (6.68)	34.0 (4.96)

See notes at end of table.

Table 104.20. Percentage of persons 25 to 29 years old with selected levels of educational attainment, by race/ethnicity and sex: Selected years, 1920 through 2019—Continued

[Standard errors appear in parentheses]

Sex, selected level of educational attainment, and year	Total		White[1]		Black[1]		Hispanic		Asian/Pacific Islander						American Indian/Alaska Native		Two or more races	
									Total		Asian		Pacific Islander					
1	2		3		4		5		6		7		8		9		10	
2011	36.1	(0.71)	43.0	(1.03)	22.9	(1.62)	16.8	(1.10)	61.0	(2.74)	62.0	(2.75)	‡	(†)	19.7!	(6.64)	31.2	(4.36)
2012	37.2	(0.69)	43.6	(0.97)	26.7	(1.78)	17.4	(1.10)	64.0	(2.38)	66.2	(2.45)	26.8!	(9.73)	14.0!	(4.55)	35.5	(5.50)
2013	37.0	(0.71)	43.8	(0.95)	23.2	(2.03)	18.6	(1.10)	62.4	(2.51)	64.3	(2.54)	29.7!	(10.58)	16.4!	(6.57)	30.0	(5.26)
2014	37.2	(1.00)	43.9	(1.36)	23.8	(2.61)	18.3	(1.40)	64.3	(3.23)	66.9	(3.29)	‡	(†)	‡	(†)	38.4	(5.96)
2015	38.9	(0.74)	46.6	(1.06)	24.6	(1.72)	18.5	(1.21)	64.5	(2.74)	68.1	(2.73)	‡	(†)	21.8	(4.51)	32.9	(5.20)
2016	39.5	(0.75)	46.3	(1.03)	24.9	(1.55)	21.5	(1.44)	67.7	(2.66)	69.6	(2.72)	‡	(†)	12.2!	(4.00)	36.8	(5.55)
2017	39.3	(0.78)	46.5	(1.11)	23.8	(1.79)	22.4	(1.16)	63.5	(2.88)	66.3	(2.85)	24.6!	(9.17)	18.7!	(6.83)	38.5	(5.84)
2018	40.8	(0.84)	48.4	(1.24)	26.2	(1.81)	23.2	(1.43)	67.4	(2.60)	71.5	(2.55)	13.5!	(6.42)	22.5	(5.87)	28.7	(4.34)
2019	41.8	(0.76)	49.2	(1.14)	29.8	(1.97)	23.1	(1.26)	69.0	(2.38)	72.7	(2.38)	27.0!	(8.25)	20.6!	(6.21)	32.1	(4.87)
Master's or higher degree																		
1995	4.1	(0.32)	5.0	(0.42)	1.4!	(0.59)	1.2!	(0.58)	8.9!	(3.29)	—	(†)	—	(†)	‡	(†)	—	(†)
2000	6.2	(0.38)	6.7	(0.50)	4.9	(0.96)	2.7	(0.58)	13.9	(2.51)	—	(†)	—	(†)	‡	(†)	—	(†)
2005	7.3	(0.44)	8.8	(0.64)	4.0	(0.70)	2.6	(0.51)	14.4	(2.08)	15.0	(2.15)	‡	(†)	‡	(†)	10.0!	(4.26)
2006	7.8	(0.42)	9.2	(0.63)	4.5	(0.93)	2.0	(0.41)	19.7	(2.33)	20.4	(2.44)	‡	(†)	‡	(†)	8.3!	(2.89)
2007	7.6	(0.43)	9.4	(0.63)	3.7	(0.66)	2.6	(0.53)	16.5	(2.39)	17.7	(2.54)	‡	(†)	‡	(†)	‡	(†)
2008	8.7	(0.44)	10.4	(0.64)	5.2	(0.87)	2.9	(0.46)	18.9	(2.30)	19.9	(2.44)	‡	(†)	‡	(†)	‡	(†)
2009	8.8	(0.45)	10.4	(0.66)	5.1	(0.80)	2.7	(0.43)	21.7	(2.45)	23.7	(2.70)	‡	(†)	‡	(†)	7.9!	(2.84)
2010	8.5	(0.39)	9.2	(0.56)	6.2	(0.94)	3.8	(0.56)	20.6	(2.60)	21.8	(2.75)	‡	(†)	‡	(†)	10.0!	(3.06)
2011	8.8	(0.48)	10.4	(0.72)	5.8	(0.85)	3.8	(0.63)	15.4	(1.98)	15.9	(2.03)	‡	(†)	‡	(†)	9.9	(2.61)
2012	8.8	(0.45)	10.0	(0.67)	7.1	(1.00)	3.0	(0.45)	19.3	(2.23)	20.4	(2.31)	‡	(†)	‡	(†)	6.3!	(2.49)
2013	9.2	(0.44)	10.8	(0.71)	4.8	(0.74)	4.0	(0.59)	20.4	(1.91)	21.6	(2.00)	‡	(†)	‡	(†)	3.3!	(1.56)
2014	9.3	(0.56)	11.1	(0.84)	5.0	(1.17)	3.6	(0.63)	19.7	(2.33)	20.8	(2.47)	‡	(†)	‡	(†)	7.5!	(3.00)
2015	10.4	(0.51)	12.0	(0.73)	7.2	(0.98)	4.1	(0.60)	22.0	(2.51)	23.2	(2.67)	‡	(†)	‡	(†)	10.2!	(3.20)
2016	11.2	(0.51)	12.3	(0.74)	6.3	(1.02)	6.3	(0.89)	27.5	(2.51)	28.8	(2.58)	‡	(†)	‡	(†)	8.2!	(3.17)
2017	10.5	(0.49)	11.8	(0.75)	6.8	(1.06)	5.0	(0.67)	24.8	(2.38)	25.8	(2.54)	‡	(†)	‡	(†)	5.4!	(2.45)
2018	10.7	(0.50)	12.6	(0.83)	6.2	(1.02)	3.8	(0.54)	27.9	(2.40)	29.9	(2.56)	‡	(†)	‡	(†)	‡	(†)
2019	11.2	(0.55)	12.6	(0.81)	8.5	(1.23)	4.6	(0.62)	25.2	(2.27)	27.5	(2.47)	‡	(†)	‡	(†)	9.1!	(3.32)

—Not available.
†Not applicable.
!Interpret data with caution. The coefficient of variation (CV) for this estimate is between 30 and 50 percent.
‡Reporting standards not met. Either there are too few cases for a reliable estimate or the coefficient of variation (CV) is 50 percent or greater.
[1]Includes persons of Hispanic ethnicity for years prior to 1980.
[2]Data for years prior to 1993 are for persons with 4 or more years of high school. Data for later years are for high school completers—i.e., those persons who graduated from high school with a diploma as well as those who completed high school through equivalency programs, such as a GED program.
[3]Estimates based on Census Bureau reverse projection of 1940 census data on education by age.
[4]Data for years prior to 1993 are for persons with 4 or more years of college.

NOTE: Prior to 2005, standard errors were computed using generalized variance function methodology rather than the more precise replicate weight methodology used in later years. For 1960 and prior years, data were collected in April. For later years, data were collected in March. Data are based on sample surveys of the noninstitutionalized population, which excludes persons living in institutions (e.g., prisons or nursing facilities); data include military personnel who live in households with civilians, but exclude those who live in military barracks. Race categories exclude persons of Hispanic ethnicity except where otherwise noted.
SOURCE: U.S. Department of Commerce, Census Bureau, *U.S. Census of Population: 1960*, Vol. I, Part 1; J.K. Folger and C.B. Nam, *Education of the American Population* (1960 Census Monograph); Current Population Reports, Series P-20, various years; and Current Population Survey (CPS), Annual Social and Economic Supplement, 1970 through 2019. (This table was prepared October 2019.)

Table 104.30. Number of persons age 18 and over, by highest level of educational attainment, sex, race/ethnicity, and age: 2019

[Numbers in thousands. Standard errors appear in parentheses]

Sex, race/ethnicity, and age	Total	Elementary school (kindergarten–8th grade)	High school: 1 to 3 years	High school: 4 years, no completion	High school: Completion[1]	Postsecondary education: Some college, no degree	Postsecondary education: Associate's degree	Postsecondary education: Bachelor's degree	Postsecondary education: Master's degree	Postsecondary education: First-professional or doctor's degree
1	2	3	4	5	6	7	8	9	10	11
Total, 18 and over	**250,563 (112.1)**	**8,879 (181.5)**	**13,976 (200.9)**	**3,705 (110.2)**	**70,947 (532.4)**	**45,028 (382.6)**	**24,550 (281.7)**	**53,312 (433.1)**	**22,459 (248.4)**	**7,707 (163.9)**
18 and 19 years old	7,831 (86.2)	104 (16.5)	2,429 (65.7)	650 (36.7)	2,271 (66.4)	2,235 (70.3)	101 (16.0)	‡ (†)	‡ (†)	‡ (†)
20 to 24 years old	21,254 (30.8)	172 (23.8)	845 (47.6)	385 (34.2)	6,417 (151.0)	8,103 (151.1)	1,711 (71.8)	3,344 (112.1)	234 (27.9)	‡ (†)
25 years old and over	221,478 (50.3)	8,603 (173.6)	10,701 (176.5)	2,671 (91.0)	62,259 (463.1)	34,690 (330.2)	22,738 (265.5)	49,937 (397.8)	22,214 (246.3)	7,665 (160.5)
25 to 29 years old	23,277 (42.7)	357 (34.3)	857 (49.9)	297 (33.7)	6,089 (128.6)	4,243 (111.2)	2,416 (87.3)	6,823 (117.4)	1,803 (75.3)	392 (37.9)
30 to 34 years old	21,932 (39.0)	554 (36.8)	930 (48.1)	269 (26.0)	5,549 (107.6)	3,287 (82.9)	2,323 (76.4)	5,904 (107.1)	2,294 (69.5)	821 (51.2)
35 to 39 years old	21,443 (39.7)	684 (39.6)	1,085 (49.4)	245 (22.7)	5,184 (102.8)	2,984 (64.6)	2,274 (70.0)	5,515 (97.0)	2,643 (73.7)	829 (44.7)
40 to 49 years old	39,929 (54.4)	1,605 (65.0)	1,908 (69.3)	449 (36.8)	10,289 (173.2)	5,737 (110.1)	4,311 (97.5)	9,457 (152.8)	4,590 (108.8)	1,582 (66.3)
50 to 59 years old	41,518 (161.7)	1,571 (66.3)	2,040 (70.4)	607 (42.4)	12,205 (173.1)	6,429 (123.7)	4,521 (120.4)	8,839 (154.9)	3,983 (107.2)	1,323 (64.1)
60 to 64 years old	20,592 (147.3)	812 (44.5)	991 (52.1)	241 (23.4)	6,423 (148.9)	3,223 (92.1)	2,280 (78.2)	4,051 (102.1)	1,867 (71.0)	705 (46.5)
65 years old and over	52,788 (159.2)	3,019 (97.6)	2,890 (81.1)	563 (43.9)	16,519 (207.5)	8,787 (163.3)	4,613 (111.2)	9,348 (175.4)	5,034 (128.7)	2,013 (86.2)
Males, 18 and over	**121,301 (98.0)**	**4,458 (104.8)**	**7,156 (137.6)**	**2,003 (80.6)**	**36,076 (347.6)**	**21,500 (260.7)**	**10,758 (163.9)**	**25,206 (269.8)**	**9,721 (167.1)**	**4,423 (111.4)**
18 and 19 years old	3,890 (68.2)	50 (10.1)	1,274 (46.0)	367 (26.0)	1,167 (48.6)	976 (48.5)	‡ (†)	‡ (†)	‡ (†)	‡ (†)
20 to 24 years old	10,716 (30.5)	96 (15.9)	502 (33.6)	225 (25.3)	3,651 (101.0)	3,933 (94.5)	783 (44.5)	1,411 (72.2)	93 (17.3)	‡ (†)
25 years old and over	106,695 (50.8)	4,313 (102.3)	5,380 (120.1)	1,412 (65.3)	31,257 (307.9)	16,591 (222.8)	9,936 (159.5)	23,785 (253.9)	9,621 (166.0)	4,400 (110.6)
25 to 29 years old	11,792 (44.0)	210 (24.5)	466 (33.3)	182 (24.7)	3,416 (99.1)	2,227 (83.1)	1,079 (59.7)	3,302 (90.7)	734 (46.6)	176 (25.4)
30 to 34 years old	10,935 (38.9)	316 (26.8)	492 (30.7)	163 (20.4)	3,178 (81.0)	1,632 (61.4)	1,000 (51.1)	2,841 (78.3)	858 (41.3)	454 (39.4)
35 to 39 years old	10,629 (39.5)	373 (29.5)	611 (38.2)	134 (18.3)	2,951 (81.9)	1,512 (56.5)	1,018 (46.6)	2,566 (71.6)	1,068 (50.8)	396 (30.1)
40 to 49 years old	19,621 (54.5)	840 (44.1)	1,042 (53.6)	231 (23.8)	5,680 (117.2)	2,822 (75.6)	2,053 (62.0)	4,206 (93.3)	1,952 (62.6)	796 (42.4)
50 to 59 years old	19,976 (156.9)	838 (45.4)	1,093 (48.8)	329 (29.5)	6,173 (122.9)	2,957 (88.7)	1,935 (75.1)	4,137 (98.0)	1,755 (63.9)	760 (44.1)
60 to 64 years old	9,819 (140.9)	395 (29.6)	464 (36.6)	122 (18.6)	3,171 (100.5)	1,487 (62.9)	972 (48.3)	1,949 (75.2)	817 (49.6)	443 (32.7)
65 years old and over	23,923 (159.2)	1,341 (56.5)	1,213 (51.6)	252 (28.4)	6,689 (124.1)	3,953 (104.3)	1,879 (70.0)	4,783 (116.2)	2,437 (88.4)	1,376 (62.6)
Females, 18 and over	**129,262 (62.6)**	**4,421 (104.7)**	**6,820 (127.7)**	**1,702 (61.8)**	**34,872 (267.4)**	**23,528 (219.0)**	**13,792 (195.0)**	**28,106 (264.8)**	**12,738 (162.6)**	**3,284 (95.6)**
18 and 19 years old	3,941 (62.5)	‡ (†)	1,155 (46.5)	283 (22.8)	1,104 (43.8)	1,258 (52.3)	61 (12.7)	‡ (†)	‡ (†)	‡ (†)
20 to 24 years old	10,538 (3.5)	76 (16.2)	344 (32.2)	160 (22.5)	2,766 (88.3)	4,171 (96.2)	928 (51.9)	1,934 (73.8)	141 (20.9)	‡ (†)
25 years old and over	114,783 (11.5)	4,290 (98.4)	5,321 (105.7)	1,259 (51.7)	31,002 (246.9)	18,099 (206.8)	12,802 (183.5)	26,151 (245.3)	12,593 (160.2)	3,265 (93.5)
25 to 29 years old	11,485 (7.4)	147 (20.4)	391 (32.4)	116 (18.7)	2,674 (76.6)	2,015 (67.6)	1,337 (59.5)	3,521 (85.4)	1,069 (58.2)	216 (23.9)
30 to 34 years old	10,997 (3.9)	237 (23.5)	439 (32.5)	106 (16.2)	2,372 (62.6)	1,655 (53.0)	1,323 (51.1)	3,063 (69.6)	1,436 (54.0)	367 (28.1)
35 to 39 years old	10,814 (6.1)	312 (23.7)	475 (30.1)	111 (14.6)	2,232 (58.5)	1,472 (41.0)	1,256 (47.3)	2,949 (62.6)	1,574 (51.3)	433 (29.7)
40 to 49 years old	20,307 (4.0)	766 (37.0)	866 (38.2)	217 (24.0)	4,609 (90.6)	2,915 (71.6)	2,258 (73.0)	5,251 (105.8)	2,639 (80.7)	786 (41.6)
50 to 59 years old	21,542 (44.9)	734 (36.9)	947 (43.6)	278 (25.7)	6,032 (104.9)	3,472 (84.3)	2,586 (87.3)	4,702 (102.5)	2,228 (71.1)	563 (35.1)
60 to 64 years old	10,773 (44.9)	417 (26.4)	527 (37.7)	119 (17.7)	3,252 (85.6)	1,736 (60.0)	1,308 (54.5)	2,102 (62.4)	1,050 (53.2)	262 (27.9)
65 years old and over	28,865 (0.8)	1,678 (63.5)	1,678 (58.9)	311 (27.8)	9,830 (138.5)	4,834 (106.2)	2,735 (81.7)	4,565 (106.9)	2,597 (84.5)	637 (48.5)
White, 18 and over	**158,197 (130.4)**	**1,951 (92.5)**	**6,398 (139.4)**	**1,528 (73.3)**	**43,449 (423.1)**	**28,674 (293.6)**	**16,743 (244.1)**	**37,806 (356.7)**	**16,000 (223.0)**	**5,647 (152.3)**
18 and 19 years old	4,215 (65.2)	58 (13.7)	1,382 (49.7)	289 (25.3)	1,192 (52.9)	1,223 (54.3)	57 (12.3)	‡ (†)	‡ (†)	‡ (†)
20 to 24 years old	11,425 (42.3)	‡ (†)	317 (29.8)	109 (19.4)	3,163 (101.2)	4,533 (106.2)	980 (58.3)	2,150 (81.7)	104 (19.3)	‡ (†)
25 years old and over	142,557 (111.7)	1,856 (87.2)	4,699 (120.5)	1,131 (63.5)	39,094 (386.6)	22,918 (259.9)	15,707 (229.9)	35,642 (337.8)	15,897 (222.8)	5,614 (148.6)
25 to 29 years old	12,558 (40.6)	70 (16.9)	312 (31.3)	84 (16.7)	2,999 (93.0)	2,099 (81.6)	1,350 (66.7)	4,353 (95.2)	1,056 (60.2)	234 (31.1)
30 to 34 years old	12,333 (47.7)	105 (16.6)	311 (32.2)	91 (15.5)	2,688 (79.7)	1,795 (68.2)	1,400 (56.7)	3,902 (90.0)	1,470 (59.5)	572 (43.3)
35 to 39 years old	12,190 (45.1)	99 (16.4)	323 (28.5)	72 (14.4)	2,611 (71.5)	1,662 (52.6)	1,382 (57.3)	3,758 (82.5)	1,740 (64.2)	543 (36.4)
40 to 49 years old	23,196 (55.1)	178 (25.1)	620 (36.0)	144 (21.3)	5,539 (123.0)	3,499 (87.5)	2,884 (78.2)	6,301 (119.0)	2,990 (92.3)	1,040 (55.9)
50 to 59 years old	27,443 (143.3)	252 (28.0)	928 (49.8)	267 (30.0)	7,930 (159.1)	4,396 (101.3)	3,202 (106.3)	6,601 (135.5)	2,909 (88.0)	958 (55.0)
60 to 64 years old	14,620 (131.8)	159 (21.0)	499 (40.5)	151 (21.8)	4,584 (121.5)	2,313 (76.7)	1,788 (76.1)	3,091 (91.0)	1,447 (66.6)	588 (44.8)
65 years old and over	40,218 (152.0)	993 (61.7)	1,706 (66.3)	323 (35.8)	12,743 (183.0)	7,153 (147.4)	3,701 (100.4)	7,636 (165.1)	4,284 (118.0)	1,679 (80.2)
Black, 18 and over	**29,618 (83.0)**	**666 (46.6)**	**2,180 (76.8)**	**681 (51.6)**	**9,912 (163.2)**	**6,148 (125.3)**	**2,919 (87.5)**	**4,610 (112.4)**	**2,036 (73.5)**	**467 (37.8)**
18 and 19 years old	1,015 (31.7)	‡ (†)	306 (27.1)	98 (13.2)	340 (26.8)	244 (22.9)	‡ (†)	‡ (†)	‡ (†)	‡ (†)
20 to 24 years old	2,875 (28.6)	‡ (†)	130 (18.5)	‡ (†)	1,151 (55.1)	1,010 (52.5)	154 (23.0)	321 (32.7)	‡ (†)	‡ (†)
25 years old and over	25,728 (70.5)	633 (45.0)	1,744 (67.8)	516 (41.7)	8,422 (141.1)	4,894 (108.7)	2,754 (83.7)	4,285 (106.8)	2,015 (72.4)	466 (37.7)
25 to 29 years old	3,322 (27.7)	‡ (†)	185 (24.9)	‡ (†)	964 (54.8)	759 (46.9)	349 (35.0)	758 (45.6)	186 (25.7)	‡ (†)
30 to 34 years old	2,870 (24.4)	‡ (†)	108 (17.5)	‡ (†)	962 (45.5)	640 (36.8)	298 (27.4)	531 (36.7)	215 (21.9)	‡ (†)
35 to 39 years old	2,624 (23.4)	‡ (†)	144 (17.8)	58 (11.8)	778 (42.1)	501 (30.8)	343 (28.7)	472 (33.1)	250 (22.7)	63 (12.4)
40 to 49 years old	4,864 (29.6)	‡ (†)	225 (25.9)	81 (16.1)	1,538 (57.5)	881 (40.7)	519 (35.7)	918 (45.3)	518 (34.9)	134 (18.6)
50 to 59 years old	4,999 (56.7)	95 (17.9)	357 (31.8)	110 (17.5)	1,685 (56.3)	895 (41.8)	598 (38.2)	761 (43.4)	394 (33.3)	105 (19.9)
60 to 64 years old	2,247 (63.7)	52 (14.0)	206 (22.5)	‡ (†)	833 (46.9)	416 (26.9)	232 (21.7)	285 (24.2)	160 (20.3)	‡ (†)
65 years old and over	4,803 (39.2)	343 (28.9)	519 (31.9)	128 (16.3)	1,661 (51.4)	802 (41.7)	415 (27.3)	560 (35.3)	292 (24.8)	84 (14.5)

See notes at end of table.

Table 104.30. Number of persons age 18 and over, by highest level of educational attainment, sex, race/ethnicity, and age: 2019—Continued

[Numbers in thousands. Standard errors appear in parentheses]

Sex, race/ethnicity, and age	Total	Elementary school (kindergarten–8th grade)	High school: 1 to 3 years	High school: 4 years, no completion	High school: Completion[1]	Postsecondary education: Some college, no degree	Postsecondary education: Associate's degree	Postsecondary education: Bachelor's degree	Postsecondary education: Master's degree	Postsecondary education: First-professional or doctor's degree
1	2	3	4	5	6	7	8	9	10	11
Hispanic, 18 and over	**41,217 (49.2)**	**5,482 (129.1)**	**4,461 (114.8)**	**1,188 (58.7)**	**13,029 (159.4)**	**6,915 (111.2)**	**3,236 (85.6)**	**4,900 (110.6)**	**1,555 (57.9)**	**452 (30.9)**
18 and 19 years old	1,862 (44.1)	‡ (†)	549 (30.3)	196 (22.0)	544 (30.8)	518 (29.4)	‡ (†)	‡ (†)	‡ (†)	‡ (†)
20 to 24 years old	4,780 (8.8)	91 (13.9)	340 (28.9)	169 (20.8)	1,636 (55.0)	1,717 (54.1)	434 (28.8)	371 (31.5)	‡ (†)	‡ (†)
25 years old and over	34,575 (15.1)	5,367 (125.6)	3,572 (101.2)	823 (47.8)	10,848 (137.6)	4,680 (84.5)	2,775 (82.3)	4,527 (107.2)	1,532 (57.6)	452 (30.9)
25 to 29 years old	4,963 (31.3)	223 (25.6)	308 (25.9)	144 (19.8)	1,693 (54.5)	1,042 (46.5)	532 (35.5)	853 (42.5)	131 (17.3)	‡ (†)
30 to 34 years old	4,421 (30.1)	404 (30.3)	453 (31.2)	112 (16.5)	1,535 (50.1)	602 (32.4)	444 (33.2)	613 (39.2)	205 (23.1)	53 (10.3)
35 to 39 years old	4,480 (36.9)	530 (32.8)	564 (37.2)	91 (15.3)	1,434 (44.1)	585 (34.4)	383 (25.3)	596 (37.4)	244 (22.0)	54 (11.2)
40 to 49 years old	7,931 (51.8)	1,283 (55.5)	952 (50.6)	186 (18.4)	2,491 (70.1)	929 (43.6)	591 (34.1)	1,004 (47.1)	379 (32.6)	117 (16.3)
50 to 59 years old	5,992 (62.2)	1,095 (50.5)	607 (38.1)	185 (22.1)	1,806 (59.7)	757 (35.7)	424 (32.0)	747 (38.7)	301 (22.5)	70 (11.1)
60 to 64 years old	2,244 (50.7)	517 (34.4)	218 (21.7)	‡ (†)	630 (34.5)	305 (22.0)	145 (16.0)	264 (22.7)	95 (12.2)	‡ (†)
65 years old and over	4,544 (6.2)	1,314 (51.5)	470 (26.8)	72 (13.1)	1,258 (44.1)	460 (27.9)	255 (23.3)	452 (29.6)	178 (17.9)	85 (11.6)
Asian, 18 and over	**15,400 (105.1)**	**679 (44.8)**	**517 (40.7)**	**186 (21.8)**	**2,657 (85.2)**	**1,839 (62.2)**	**995 (51.3)**	**4,994 (106.6)**	**2,512 (88.7)**	**1,021 (51.3)**
18 and 19 years old	390 (23.0)	‡ (†)	92 (13.5)	‡ (†)	93 (14.6)	142 (15.4)	‡ (†)	‡ (†)	‡ (†)	‡ (†)
20 to 24 years old	1,327 (32.4)	‡ (†)	‡ (†)	‡ (†)	178 (21.5)	519 (33.5)	90 (16.3)	397 (35.3)	85 (17.4)	‡ (†)
25 years old and over	13,683 (99.1)	659 (42.6)	410 (38.4)	132 (17.9)	2,386 (80.2)	1,178 (50.9)	899 (47.4)	4,589 (101.6)	2,416 (82.8)	1,014 (51.3)
25 to 29 years old	1,646 (37.8)	‡ (†)	‡ (†)	‡ (†)	162 (20.7)	157 (19.2)	101 (18.3)	699 (37.3)	391 (30.9)	85 (15.4)
30 to 34 years old	1,659 (37.8)	‡ (†)	‡ (†)	‡ (†)	200 (22.1)	120 (17.0)	106 (15.4)	695 (39.5)	365 (29.6)	139 (18.6)
35 to 39 years old	1,596 (35.7)	‡ (†)	‡ (†)	‡ (†)	208 (22.1)	125 (17.5)	98 (14.3)	577 (31.7)	363 (26.7)	150 (18.8)
40 to 49 years old	2,970 (56.5)	87 (14.2)	69 (14.6)	‡ (†)	457 (31.2)	232 (24.1)	197 (22.3)	1,031 (49.3)	598 (36.2)	271 (23.6)
50 to 59 years old	2,255 (50.0)	118 (16.4)	97 (16.5)	‡ (†)	516 (35.3)	210 (21.3)	183 (19.6)	622 (33.1)	313 (27.6)	166 (18.8)
60 to 64 years old	1,115 (42.6)	80 (13.7)	‡ (†)	‡ (†)	242 (23.1)	106 (15.1)	55 (10.8)	373 (30.4)	150 (20.9)	55 (10.1)
65 years old and over	2,443 (37.9)	313 (26.7)	131 (18.1)	‡ (†)	601 (39.0)	229 (23.8)	158 (20.4)	592 (37.3)	235 (24.9)	149 (20.0)

†Not applicable.

‡Reporting standards not met. Either there are too few cases for a reliable estimate or the coefficient of variation (CV) is 50 percent or greater.

[1]Includes completion of high school through equivalency programs, such as a GED program.

NOTE: Total includes other racial/ethnic groups not shown separately. Race categories exclude persons of Hispanic ethnicity. Detail may not sum to totals because of rounding.

SOURCE: U.S. Department of Commerce, Census Bureau, Current Population Survey (CPS), Annual Social and Economic Supplement, 2019. (This table was prepared January 2020.)

Table 104.40. Percentage of persons 18 to 24 years old and age 25 and over, by educational attainment, race/ethnicity, and selected racial/ethnic subgroups: 2010 and 2018

[Standard errors appear in parentheses]

Year and race/ethnicity	18 to 24 years old							Age 25 and over					
		High school completion[1] or higher							High school completion[1] or higher				
				At least some college									
	Less than high school completion	Total, high school or higher	High school only	Total, at least some college	Some college, no degree	Associate's degree	Bachelor's or higher degree	Less than high school completion	Total, high school or higher	High school only	Some college, no degree	Associate's degree	Bachelor's or higher degree
1	2	3	4	5	6	7	8	9	10	11	12	13	14
2010													
Total[2]	**16.7 (0.10)**	**83.3 (0.10)**	**29.4 (0.10)**	**53.8 (0.11)**	**40.2 (0.13)**	**4.5 (0.05)**	**9.1 (0.08)**	**14.4 (0.04)**	**85.6 (0.04)**	**28.5 (0.04)**	**21.3 (0.03)**	**7.6 (0.02)**	**28.2 (0.06)**
White	11.8 (0.09)	88.2 (0.09)	28.5 (0.14)	59.7 (0.15)	43.0 (0.19)	5.2 (0.07)	11.5 (0.11)	9.3 (0.03)	90.7 (0.03)	29.3 (0.05)	21.9 (0.04)	8.1 (0.03)	31.4 (0.06)
Black	22.1 (0.25)	77.9 (0.25)	31.7 (0.35)	46.2 (0.35)	38.6 (0.34)	3.1 (0.12)	4.5 (0.14)	17.8 (0.10)	82.2 (0.10)	31.8 (0.12)	24.9 (0.13)	7.5 (0.07)	17.9 (0.10)
Hispanic	28.5 (0.33)	71.5 (0.33)	32.1 (0.25)	39.4 (0.29)	32.0 (0.26)	3.5 (0.10)	3.8 (0.11)	37.7 (0.17)	62.3 (0.17)	26.4 (0.10)	17.3 (0.10)	5.5 (0.06)	13.1 (0.11)
Cuban	17.7 (1.24)	82.3 (1.24)	30.8 (1.48)	51.5 (1.62)	35.7 (1.48)	7.7 (0.76)	8.1 (0.75)	23.6 (0.50)	76.4 (0.50)	28.7 (0.56)	16.3 (0.44)	7.7 (0.31)	23.6 (0.49)
Dominican	20.6 (1.21)	79.4 (1.21)	27.6 (1.38)	51.9 (1.58)	41.1 (1.68)	4.1 (0.56)	6.7 (0.78)	34.5 (0.76)	65.5 (0.76)	26.4 (0.76)	17.6 (0.54)	6.5 (0.35)	15.0 (0.57)
Mexican	30.5 (0.38)	69.5 (0.38)	33.3 (0.31)	36.2 (0.35)	30.3 (0.33)	3.0 (0.12)	2.8 (0.11)	43.4 (0.19)	56.6 (0.19)	26.2 (0.15)	16.4 (0.13)	4.6 (0.07)	9.4 (0.11)
Puerto Rican	23.8 (0.80)	76.2 (0.80)	32.9 (0.94)	43.3 (0.93)	34.2 (0.86)	3.9 (0.33)	5.1 (0.39)	25.5 (0.40)	74.5 (0.40)	29.8 (0.36)	20.7 (0.31)	7.7 (0.20)	16.3 (0.27)
Spaniard	13.5 (1.61)	86.5 (1.61)	26.4 (2.16)	60.1 (2.30)	45.9 (2.21)	4.4 (0.78)	9.8 (1.18)	11.7 (0.60)	88.3 (0.60)	21.7 (0.80)	27.4 (0.87)	8.6 (0.51)	30.7 (0.85)
Central American[3]	37.3 (1.03)	62.7 (1.03)	28.6 (0.86)	34.0 (0.92)	26.7 (0.79)	3.4 (0.33)	3.9 (0.35)	46.9 (0.49)	53.1 (0.49)	24.1 (0.40)	14.1 (0.30)	4.3 (0.17)	10.6 (0.28)
Costa Rican	13.4 (3.01)	86.6 (3.01)	24.3 (4.14)	62.3 (4.20)	43.5 (5.17)	12.8 (3.44)	5.9 ! (2.40)	17.8 (1.75)	82.2 (1.75)	22.4 (2.23)	23.5 (2.10)	8.4 (1.31)	27.9 (2.17)
Guatemalan	49.7 (1.85)	50.3 (1.85)	26.6 (1.79)	23.7 (1.46)	18.5 (1.12)	2.7 (0.59)	2.5 (0.42)	54.5 (0.94)	45.5 (0.94)	22.1 (0.75)	12.0 (0.56)	3.1 (0.30)	8.4 (0.51)
Honduran	43.8 (2.41)	56.2 (2.41)	25.7 (1.99)	30.5 (2.18)	24.2 (1.90)	1.9 (0.57)	4.3 (1.03)	47.5 (1.35)	52.5 (1.35)	25.7 (1.16)	12.6 (0.73)	4.4 (0.38)	9.8 (0.64)
Nicaraguan	19.5 (3.30)	80.5 (3.30)	32.2 (3.11)	48.4 (3.56)	32.3 (2.92)	10.6 (2.00)	5.5 (1.28)	27.5 (1.52)	72.5 (1.52)	27.0 (1.36)	20.5 (1.03)	7.6 (0.81)	17.3 (0.91)
Panamanian	12.8 (2.71)	87.2 (2.71)	29.7 (4.23)	57.5 (3.96)	47.5 (4.23)	4.0 ! (1.87)	5.9 ! (1.95)	7.9 (0.96)	92.1 (0.96)	23.7 (1.76)	28.4 (1.66)	9.1 (0.75)	30.9 (1.45)
Salvadoran	33.9 (1.48)	66.1 (1.48)	30.6 (1.23)	35.5 (1.42)	28.9 (1.41)	2.5 (0.43)	4.1 (0.56)	53.1 (0.68)	46.9 (0.68)	24.1 (0.66)	12.1 (0.48)	3.3 (0.26)	7.3 (0.30)
South American	15.1 (0.92)	84.9 (0.92)	26.8 (1.25)	58.1 (1.30)	44.6 (1.12)	5.1 (0.49)	8.4 (0.66)	16.6 (0.41)	83.4 (0.41)	25.4 (0.40)	20.0 (0.38)	7.8 (0.24)	30.2 (0.46)
Chilean	10.7 ! (3.37)	89.3 (3.37)	18.5 (4.92)	70.8 (5.44)	56.2 (5.73)	‡ (†)	11.8 ! (3.58)	9.8 (1.29)	90.2 (1.29)	25.7 (1.75)	19.1 (1.58)	10.6 (1.36)	34.7 (1.93)
Colombian	13.0 (1.45)	87.0 (1.45)	27.2 (2.07)	59.8 (2.39)	45.6 (2.28)	5.9 (1.04)	8.2 (1.12)	14.8 (0.61)	85.2 (0.61)	27.3 (0.74)	18.2 (0.65)	8.1 (0.44)	31.6 (0.82)
Ecuadorian	24.8 (3.00)	75.2 (3.00)	25.4 (2.25)	49.8 (2.88)	38.2 (2.75)	4.1 (1.02)	7.5 (1.48)	30.3 (1.07)	69.7 (1.07)	26.3 (0.84)	19.3 (0.80)	5.8 (0.43)	18.4 (0.88)
Peruvian	14.1 (1.81)	85.9 (1.81)	23.6 (2.01)	62.3 (2.47)	49.5 (2.35)	5.5 (1.01)	7.4 (1.09)	11.1 (0.74)	88.9 (0.74)	27.1 (1.05)	23.9 (0.77)	8.2 (0.63)	29.6 (1.26)
Venezuelan	9.1 (2.13)	90.9 (2.13)	27.8 (3.95)	63.1 (3.90)	44.0 (4.13)	5.8 (1.43)	13.4 (2.82)	6.8 (0.87)	93.2 (0.87)	14.1 (1.17)	18.0 (1.19)	11.5 (0.94)	49.6 (1.60)
Other South American	11.6 (1.79)	88.4 (1.79)	35.1 (3.44)	53.3 (3.35)	41.1 (3.19)	4.4 (1.26)	7.8 (1.82)	15.2 (0.95)	84.8 (0.95)	23.6 (1.07)	20.7 (0.98)	6.8 (0.52)	33.7 (1.30)
Other Hispanic	21.8 (1.16)	78.2 (1.16)	32.2 (1.61)	46.0 (1.43)	36.7 (1.29)	4.4 (0.62)	4.9 (0.66)	22.9 (0.69)	77.1 (0.69)	29.2 (0.66)	23.5 (0.66)	7.4 (0.30)	17.1 (0.54)
Asian	8.7 (0.29)	91.3 (0.29)	20.3 (0.40)	71.0 (0.43)	47.2 (0.55)	4.8 (0.23)	19.0 (0.37)	14.3 (0.15)	85.7 (0.15)	16.1 (0.16)	13.0 (0.14)	6.5 (0.10)	50.2 (0.23)
Chinese[4]	6.5 (0.58)	93.5 (0.58)	17.7 (0.88)	75.7 (1.04)	46.7 (1.14)	3.6 (0.35)	25.4 (0.93)	18.4 (0.33)	81.6 (0.33)	15.5 (0.29)	8.7 (0.25)	5.4 (0.17)	52.0 (0.38)
Filipino	7.1 (0.64)	92.9 (0.64)	22.6 (0.94)	70.4 (1.00)	49.5 (1.40)	7.0 (0.68)	13.9 (1.00)	7.7 (0.25)	92.3 (0.25)	14.7 (0.32)	19.7 (0.36)	9.0 (0.27)	48.9 (0.51)
Japanese	4.8 (1.19)	95.2 (1.19)	19.3 (2.27)	75.9 (2.70)	55.9 (3.25)	7.7 (1.41)	12.3 (1.97)	5.3 (0.38)	94.7 (0.38)	19.8 (0.61)	17.5 (0.60)	10.6 (0.43)	46.8 (0.76)
Korean	6.4 (0.80)	93.6 (0.80)	18.8 (1.30)	74.8 (1.31)	55.7 (1.63)	2.8 (0.46)	16.3 (1.11)	7.8 (0.32)	92.2 (0.32)	18.5 (0.56)	14.3 (0.43)	6.1 (0.29)	53.2 (0.73)
South Asian[5]	10.5 (0.72)	89.5 (0.72)	21.7 (0.95)	67.8 (1.08)	39.6 (1.33)	4.9 (0.48)	23.4 (1.07)	12.0 (0.28)	88.0 (0.28)	11.8 (0.32)	8.4 (0.24)	4.6 (0.17)	63.2 (0.44)
Asian Indian	7.6 (0.71)	92.4 (0.71)	16.0 (0.95)	76.4 (1.17)	39.3 (1.66)	5.0 (0.55)	32.1 (1.53)	8.8 (0.28)	91.2 (0.28)	9.1 (0.31)	6.8 (0.24)	4.1 (0.17)	71.2 (0.48)
Bangladeshi	12.9 ! (3.88)	87.1 (3.88)	14.3 (2.95)	72.7 (4.72)	48.0 (5.86)	9.3 ! (3.86)	15.4 (3.91)	17.3 (2.01)	82.7 (2.01)	17.3 (1.75)	8.1 (0.97)	8.2 (1.28)	49.1 (2.49)
Bhutanese	--- (†)	--- (†)	--- (†)	--- (†)	--- (†)	--- (†)	--- (†)	--- (†)	--- (†)	--- (†)	--- (†)	--- (†)	--- (†)
Nepalese	--- (†)	--- (†)	--- (†)	--- (†)	--- (†)	--- (†)	--- (†)	--- (†)	--- (†)	--- (†)	--- (†)	--- (†)	--- (†)
Pakistani	11.1 (1.64)	88.9 (1.64)	22.6 (2.44)	66.3 (3.07)	44.9 (3.17)	6.0 (1.28)	15.3 (2.26)	13.3 (0.97)	86.7 (0.97)	16.3 (1.16)	10.4 (0.92)	5.0 (0.58)	55.0 (1.64)
Southeast Asian	12.3 (0.77)	87.7 (0.77)	21.0 (0.87)	66.7 (0.98)	49.8 (1.13)	5.2 (0.57)	11.6 (0.69)	25.8 (0.48)	74.2 (0.48)	21.4 (0.42)	15.8 (0.38)	6.8 (0.20)	30.2 (0.55)
Burmese	--- (†)	--- (†)	--- (†)	--- (†)	--- (†)	--- (†)	--- (†)	--- (†)	--- (†)	--- (†)	--- (†)	--- (†)	--- (†)
Cambodian	19.0 (3.04)	81.0 (3.04)	35.7 (3.08)	45.4 (3.95)	35.8 (3.68)	3.2 ! (1.15)	6.4 ! (2.10)	33.4 (1.90)	66.6 (1.90)	27.9 (1.60)	16.4 (1.37)	6.2 (0.79)	16.1 (1.09)
Hmong	16.2 (2.92)	83.8 (2.92)	40.5 (3.71)	43.3 (3.72)	36.4 (3.33)	3.9 (1.16)	3.0 ! (0.93)	33.4 (2.10)	66.6 (2.10)	23.9 (2.10)	20.7 (1.87)	7.5 (1.16)	14.5 (1.42)
Laotian	14.6 (3.34)	85.4 (3.34)	28.6 (3.94)	56.8 (5.02)	46.4 (5.00)	5.7 ! (1.88)	4.7 ! (1.90)	30.9 (1.72)	69.1 (1.72)	29.0 (1.83)	20.2 (1.72)	6.3 (0.87)	13.5 (1.32)
Thai	14.1 ! (4.51)	85.9 (4.51)	17.3 (3.95)	68.7 (5.18)	44.4 (5.88)	5.3 ! (2.16)	19.0 (4.34)	15.8 (1.42)	84.2 (1.42)	19.1 (1.45)	12.7 (1.24)	8.3 (1.01)	44.1 (1.86)
Vietnamese	9.1 (0.88)	90.9 (0.88)	20.6 (1.18)	70.4 (1.38)	53.4 (1.54)	5.1 (0.78)	11.9 (0.89)	29.7 (0.62)	70.3 (0.62)	22.1 (0.57)	15.9 (0.43)	6.8 (0.27)	25.6 (0.65)
Other Southeast Asian[6]	9.1 ! (4.18)	90.9 (4.18)	24.1 (6.18)	66.8 (7.00)	49.1 (7.15)	‡ (†)	17.0 (4.64)	7.9 (1.63)	92.1 (1.63)	17.5 (2.24)	15.3 (2.02)	8.0 (1.32)	51.3 (2.82)
Other Asian	18.4 (1.77)	81.6 (1.77)	20.3 (1.54)	61.4 (2.05)	44.5 (2.19)	5.9 (1.10)	11.0 (1.33)	18.9 (0.83)	81.1 (0.83)	17.8 (0.95)	15.0 (0.82)	6.3 (0.49)	42.0 (1.27)
Pacific Islander	11.0 (1.49)	89.0 (1.49)	40.1 (2.39)	48.9 (2.63)	39.4 (2.91)	4.1 (1.01)	5.5 (1.22)	12.0 (0.78)	88.0 (0.78)	36.4 (1.48)	28.1 (1.38)	8.5 (0.73)	15.0 (0.88)
American Indian/Alaska Native	25.8 (0.99)	74.2 (0.99)	35.9 (1.04)	38.4 (1.14)	33.1 (1.15)	2.6 (0.43)	2.7 (0.41)	19.5 (0.41)	80.5 (0.41)	31.5 (0.52)	26.6 (0.48)	8.2 (0.29)	14.2 (0.37)
Some other race	18.6 (1.90)	81.4 (1.90)	28.3 (2.23)	53.1 (3.03)	32.7 (2.80)	4.9 (1.09)	15.5 (2.54)	16.9 (1.16)	83.1 (1.16)	22.7 (0.97)	18.7 (0.94)	6.8 (0.48)	34.9 (1.27)
Two or more races	15.5 (0.50)	84.5 (0.50)	30.8 (0.78)	53.7 (0.84)	41.8 (0.76)	4.2 (0.32)	7.7 (0.39)	11.8 (0.23)	88.2 (0.23)	24.0 (0.35)	26.3 (0.32)	8.8 (0.18)	29.1 (0.34)
White and Black	19.0 (1.17)	81.0 (1.17)	34.0 (1.35)	47.0 (1.54)	37.4 (1.53)	3.8 (0.58)	5.7 (0.84)	9.1 (0.68)	90.9 (0.68)	23.6 (0.89)	30.3 (1.19)	9.1 (0.68)	27.9 (1.03)
White and Asian	10.3 (0.84)	89.7 (0.84)	23.1 (1.39)	66.6 (1.53)	47.5 (1.66)	5.2 (0.62)	13.9 (0.94)	7.6 (0.46)	92.4 (0.46)	16.9 (0.67)	21.9 (0.68)	8.7 (0.46)	44.9 (0.83)
White and American Indian/ Alaska Native	19.2 (1.31)	80.8 (1.31)	33.5 (1.51)	47.3 (1.49)	38.8 (1.62)	3.7 (0.65)	4.9 (0.67)	14.9 (0.44)	85.1 (0.44)	28.7 (0.60)	27.5 (0.50)	9.0 (0.29)	19.9 (0.43)
Other Two or more races	13.9 (1.10)	86.1 (1.10)	32.9 (1.44)	53.2 (1.64)	43.1 (1.64)	3.9 (0.55)	6.2 (0.68)	12.3 (0.43)	87.7 (0.43)	23.8 (0.61)	26.2 (0.51)	8.6 (0.38)	29.2 (0.64)
2018													
Total[2]	**12.4 (0.08)**	**87.6 (0.08)**	**32.1 (0.13)**	**55.5 (0.13)**	**38.4 (0.16)**	**5.4 (0.06)**	**11.7 (0.10)**	**11.7 (0.04)**	**88.3 (0.04)**	**26.9 (0.05)**	**20.2 (0.03)**	**8.6 (0.02)**	**32.6 (0.07)**
White	10.3 (0.09)	89.7 (0.09)	30.9 (0.16)	58.8 (0.17)	38.6 (0.19)	6.0 (0.08)	14.2 (0.13)	6.9 (0.04)	93.1 (0.04)	26.9 (0.06)	20.7 (0.04)	9.2 (0.03)	36.3 (0.08)
Black	15.2 (0.27)	84.8 (0.27)	34.9 (0.37)	50.0 (0.39)	38.8 (0.41)	4.4 (0.15)	6.8 (0.20)	13.4 (0.09)	86.6 (0.09)	31.8 (0.14)	24.0 (0.12)	8.7 (0.08)	22.1 (0.14)
Hispanic	16.6 (0.20)	83.4 (0.20)	35.5 (0.25)	47.9 (0.27)	36.6 (0.26)	5.1 (0.14)	6.2 (0.14)	30.3 (0.15)	69.7 (0.15)	28.2 (0.11)	17.8 (0.10)	6.7 (0.06)	17.0 (0.12)
Cuban	12.0 (0.93)	88.0 (0.93)	30.7 (1.32)	57.3 (1.46)	34.9 (1.68)	10.3 (0.99)	12.0 (0.92)	18.0 (0.42)	82.0 (0.42)	28.8 (0.54)	15.6 (0.30)	8.9 (0.36)	28.7 (0.46)
Dominican	16.3 (1.15)	83.7 (1.15)	32.7 (1.28)	50.9 (1.49)	38.9 (1.33)	5.0 (0.63)	7.1 (0.73)	28.0 (0.63)	72.0 (0.63)	27.0 (0.58)	18.8 (0.54)	6.8 (0.30)	19.3 (0.56)
Mexican	16.1 (0.23)	83.9 (0.23)	37.0 (0.32)	46.9 (0.34)	37.0 (0.35)	4.7 (0.15)	5.1 (0.13)	34.9 (0.17)	65.1 (0.17)	29.1 (0.15)	17.5 (0.12)	5.9 (0.07)	12.6 (0.11)
Puerto Rican	16.3 (0.74)	83.7 (0.74)	36.6 (0.96)	47.2 (1.04)	34.4 (0.94)	5.0 (0.37)	7.8 (0.52)	19.3 (0.30)	80.7 (0.30)	29.9 (0.38)	21.0 (0.29)	9.1 (0.22)	20.7 (0.34)
Spaniard	10.7 (1.27)	89.3 (1.27)	27.0 (1.81)	62.3 (2.06)	40.5 (2.19)	6.1 (1.00)	15.7 (1.59)	8.5 (0.54)	91.5 (0.54)	20.8 (0.67)	23.1 (0.64)	9.3 (0.55)	38.2 (0.83)
Central American[3]	25.9 (0.89)	74.1 (0.89)	32.3 (0.81)	41.8 (0.82)	31.4 (0.76)	5.2 (0.34)	5.2 (0.37)	41.5 (0.44)	58.5 (0.44)	25.2 (0.35)	14.4 (0.30)	5.3 (0.17)	13.6 (0.29)
Costa Rican	6.9 ! (2.37)	93.1 (2.37)	38.2 (5.55)	54.9 (5.07)	37.3 (5.35)	7.0 ! (2.68)	10.6 ! (3.20)	16.0 (1.68)	84.0 (1.68)	25.2 (1.98)	22.0 (1.85)	7.8 (1.01)	29.0 (1.97)
Guatemalan	33.1 (1.69)	66.9 (1.69)	27.8 (1.53)	39.1 (1.46)	29.7 (1.34)	4.0 (0.63)	5.3 (0.67)	49.7 (0.92)	50.3 (0.92)	22.2 (0.70)	13.1 (0.58)	4.3 (0.33)	10.8 (0.53)
Honduran	30.1 (1.96)	69.9 (1.96)	33.1 (2.23)	36.8 (2.58)	27.8 (2.37)	4.7 (1.06)	4.3 (0.89)	44.0 (1.19)	56.0 (1.19)	26.1 (0.90)	12.6 (0.63)	4.2 (0.37)	13.1 (0.76)
Nicaraguan	9.9 (2.02)	90.1 (2.02)	33.4 (3.67)	56.8 (3.96)	37.5 (3.71)	10.5 (2.17)	8.8 (1.63)	21.9 (1.27)	78.1 (1.27)	27.1 (1.27)	17.9 (1.01)	9.5 (0.80)	23.6 (1.18)
Panamanian	10.7 (2.60)	89.3 (2.60)	30.3 (3.79)	59.1 (3.69)	43.6 (3.90)	6.5 ! (2.22)	8.9 (2.16)	6.8 (0.95)	93.2 (0.95)	22.6 (1.53)	23.2 (1.63)	12.3 (1.06)	35.0 (1.68)
Salvadoran	24.5 (1.20)	75.5 (1.20)	34.8 (1.19)	40.6 (1.23)	31.3 (1.08)	5.1 (0.47)	4.2 (0.49)	45.2 (0.66)	54.8 (0.66)	26.5 (0.54)	13.8 (0.43)	4.5 (0.24)	10.0 (0.36)
South American	10.1 (0.61)	89.9 (0.61)	27.6 (0.92)	62.3 (1.03)	42.2 (1.02)	6.8 (0.50)	13.3 (0.67)	12.4 (0.36)	87.6 (0.36)	23.6 (0.42)	18.6 (0.36)	8.8 (0.27)	36.6 (0.38)
Chilean	8.6 ! (3.49)	91.4 (3.49)	11.9 (3.31)	79.5 (4.25)	60.7 (4.72)	4.6 ! (2.14)	14.2 (3.90)	6.7 (1.13)	93.3 (1.13)	21.5 (2.12)	21.3 (1.42)	7.4 (0.87)	43.1 (1.95)
Colombian	10.3 (1.15)	89.7 (1.15)	27.4 (1.71)	62.3 (1.86)	38.6 (1.84)	7.7 (0.95)	15.9 (1.38)	11.8 (0.51)	88.2 (0.51)	25.5 (0.76)	18.0 (0.67)	9.4 (0.43)	35.3 (0.88)

[Standard errors appear in parentheses]

Year and race/ethnicity	18 to 24 years old: Less than high school completion	18 to 24 years old: High school completion[1] or higher: Total, high school or higher	18 to 24 years old: High school completion[1] or higher: High school only	18 to 24 years old: At least some college: Total, at least some college	18 to 24 years old: At least some college: Some college, no degree	18 to 24 years old: At least some college: Associate's degree	18 to 24 years old: At least some college: Bachelor's or higher degree	Age 25 and over: Less than high school completion	Age 25 and over: High school completion[1] or higher: Total, high school or higher	Age 25 and over: High school completion[1] or higher: High school only	Age 25 and over: High school completion[1] or higher: Some college, no degree	Age 25 and over: High school completion[1] or higher: Associate's degree	Age 25 and over: High school completion[1] or higher: Bachelor's or higher degree
1	2	3	4	5	6	7	8	9	10	11	12	13	14
Ecuadorian	11.5 (1.64)	88.5 (1.64)	30.0 (2.42)	58.5 (2.56)	42.9 (2.32)	6.1 (1.00)	9.6 (1.18)	24.2 (1.06)	75.8 (1.06)	25.7 (1.08)	18.9 (0.93)	7.7 (0.52)	23.5 (0.89)
Peruvian	10.5 (1.59)	89.5 (1.59)	28.3 (2.22)	61.2 (2.40)	43.1 (2.75)	5.7 (1.01)	12.4 (1.26)	8.9 (0.60)	91.1 (0.60)	26.5 (0.96)	22.7 (0.86)	9.2 (0.63)	32.7 (0.94)
Venezuelan	9.0 (1.94)	91.0 (1.94)	29.3 (3.40)	61.8 (3.45)	39.5 (3.31)	8.0 (2.33)	14.4 (2.09)	5.0 (0.70)	95.0 (0.70)	12.4 (0.84)	13.6 (0.77)	9.9 (0.85)	59.2 (1.39)
Other South American	8.4 (1.71)	91.6 (1.71)	27.3 (3.25)	64.4 (3.26)	46.6 (3.26)	6.1 (1.41)	11.6 (2.23)	11.3 (0.87)	88.7 (0.87)	23.7 (1.02)	17.4 (0.76)	8.0 (0.49)	39.6 (1.09)
Other Hispanic	17.1 (1.00)	82.9 (1.00)	34.9 (1.36)	47.9 (1.43)	38.2 (1.24)	4.6 (0.49)	5.1 (0.80)	21.4 (0.53)	78.6 (0.53)	31.0 (0.61)	21.6 (0.55)	7.2 (0.29)	18.8 (0.57)
Asian	7.0 (0.28)	93.0 (0.28)	21.8 (0.45)	71.2 (0.48)	42.4 (0.50)	4.8 (0.22)	24.0 (0.41)	12.3 (0.12)	87.7 (0.12)	14.3 (0.15)	11.3 (0.11)	6.7 (0.09)	55.3 (0.21)
Chinese[4]	5.0 (0.39)	95.0 (0.39)	20.0 (0.73)	74.9 (0.77)	42.2 (0.98)	2.7 (0.34)	30.0 (0.95)	15.2 (0.29)	84.8 (0.29)	13.9 (0.29)	7.8 (0.17)	5.5 (0.16)	57.6 (0.43)
Filipino	7.6 (0.63)	92.4 (0.63)	24.6 (1.26)	67.8 (1.45)	43.6 (1.43)	8.0 (0.77)	16.2 (1.02)	5.9 (0.22)	94.1 (0.22)	15.1 (0.34)	19.3 (0.31)	10.1 (0.28)	49.5 (0.50)
Japanese	5.4 (1.45)	94.6 (1.45)	22.8 (3.04)	71.8 (3.22)	47.7 (3.80)	5.1 (1.44)	19.1 (2.54)	4.6 (0.31)	95.4 (0.31)	17.3 (0.56)	14.5 (0.53)	10.8 (0.44)	52.8 (0.70)
Korean	6.7 (0.92)	93.3 (0.92)	19.4 (1.36)	73.9 (1.64)	46.4 (1.71)	3.4 (0.62)	24.0 (1.52)	7.4 (0.34)	92.6 (0.34)	15.5 (0.42)	12.3 (0.35)	5.7 (0.25)	59.1 (0.66)
South Asian[5]	6.7 (0.42)	93.3 (0.42)	19.0 (0.85)	74.3 (0.84)	40.1 (1.05)	4.6 (0.42)	29.5 (1.11)	9.0 (0.22)	91.0 (0.22)	8.8 (0.21)	6.4 (0.20)	4.2 (0.14)	71.7 (0.37)
Asian Indian	5.4 (0.47)	94.6 (0.47)	18.1 (0.90)	76.4 (0.87)	39.5 (1.25)	3.9 (0.42)	33.0 (1.26)	7.2 (0.21)	92.8 (0.21)	7.4 (0.21)	5.7 (0.20)	3.6 (0.14)	76.2 (0.42)
Bangladeshi	16.2 (3.82)	83.8 (3.82)	22.9 (3.70)	60.9 (4.42)	38.2 (4.34)	5.7 ! (2.12)	17.1 (3.33)	15.5 (1.49)	84.5 (1.49)	18.5 (1.76)	8.4 (1.05)	7.7 (1.16)	50.0 (2.18)
Bhutanese	‡ (†)	‡ (†)	‡ (†)	‡ (†)	‡ (†)	‡ (†)	‡ (†)	57.5 (6.79)	42.5 (6.79)	16.1 (4.31)	8.1 ! (2.68)	‡ (†)	17.2 (4.84)
Nepalese	13.9 ! (4.28)	86.1 (4.28)	23.6 (3.61)	62.6 (5.31)	43.5 (4.52)	7.5 ! (2.48)	11.5 (3.19)	29.6 (2.45)	70.4 (2.45)	16.9 (1.80)	7.2 (1.38)	6.6 (1.24)	39.7 (2.36)
Pakistani	6.7 (1.11)	93.3 (1.11)	20.2 (2.76)	73.1 (2.91)	43.4 (2.57)	7.4 (1.47)	22.2 (2.37)	13.5 (0.92)	86.5 (0.92)	14.8 (0.88)	10.6 (0.77)	6.8 (0.65)	54.2 (1.43)
Southeast Asian	10.4 (0.77)	89.6 (0.77)	26.3 (1.03)	63.2 (1.11)	42.8 (1.04)	5.9 (0.57)	14.5 (0.85)	25.3 (0.40)	74.7 (0.40)	21.8 (0.39)	14.7 (0.35)	8.0 (0.25)	30.2 (0.44)
Burmese	29.4 (4.53)	70.6 (4.53)	34.8 (4.61)	35.7 (5.16)	29.6 (5.29)	‡ (†)	4.3 ! (1.82)	49.6 (2.68)	50.4 (2.68)	19.5 (1.97)	9.3 (1.42)	3.6 (0.72)	18.0 (1.86)
Cambodian	15.3 (2.44)	84.7 (2.44)	35.1 (4.15)	49.6 (4.15)	32.4 (3.72)	4.9 (1.47)	12.3 (2.92)	28.2 (1.57)	71.8 (1.57)	29.3 (1.44)	15.7 (1.17)	7.4 (0.75)	19.5 (1.05)
Hmong	5.8 (1.42)	94.2 (1.42)	32.6 (3.87)	61.6 (4.06)	43.9 (3.68)	5.1 ! (1.70)	12.6 (2.28)	22.7 (1.43)	77.3 (1.43)	27.1 (1.89)	18.0 (1.42)	10.7 (1.07)	21.5 (1.70)
Laotian	10.3 ! (4.11)	89.7 (4.11)	36.2 (5.41)	53.5 (5.24)	37.9 (5.37)	‡ (†)	13.1 ! (4.83)	26.9 (1.44)	73.1 (1.44)	30.2 (1.75)	16.6 (1.30)	7.0 (0.82)	19.3 (1.41)
Thai	7.3 ! (2.50)	92.7 (2.50)	27.1 (4.77)	65.6 (5.11)	42.9 (4.84)	3.1 ! (1.45)	19.5 (3.22)	16.7 (1.32)	83.3 (1.32)	15.1 (1.23)	13.3 (1.13)	7.4 (0.73)	47.5 (1.98)
Vietnamese	9.4 (0.86)	90.6 (0.86)	22.4 (1.30)	68.2 (1.37)	45.7 (1.47)	6.8 (0.87)	15.7 (1.17)	25.1 (0.48)	74.9 (0.48)	20.5 (0.45)	14.7 (0.46)	8.1 (0.31)	31.6 (0.59)
Other Southeast Asian[6]	3.6 ! (1.68)	96.4 (1.68)	20.8 (4.13)	75.6 (4.73)	45.1 (5.41)	11.7 ! (4.12)	18.8 (3.66)	7.3 (1.38)	92.7 (1.38)	16.6 (2.05)	11.2 (1.60)	10.0 (1.78)	54.9 (2.60)
Other Asian	4.9 (0.87)	95.1 (0.87)	24.7 (2.13)	70.4 (2.04)	40.3 (2.50)	6.7 (1.31)	23.4 (2.07)	12.4 (0.86)	87.6 (0.86)	13.5 (0.82)	14.3 (0.79)	8.2 (0.55)	51.6 (1.21)
Pacific Islander	17.4 (2.17)	82.6 (2.17)	39.5 (2.91)	43.1 (3.33)	34.3 (2.98)	4.7 (1.33)	4.1 (1.15)	12.2 (0.85)	87.8 (0.85)	35.0 (1.11)	25.1 (0.94)	9.2 (0.65)	18.5 (0.91)
American Indian/Alaska Native	18.9 (1.07)	81.1 (1.07)	39.2 (1.13)	41.8 (1.45)	34.7 (1.30)	3.1 (0.38)	4.0 (0.47)	16.8 (0.37)	83.2 (0.37)	31.8 (0.44)	26.6 (0.43)	9.3 (0.27)	15.5 (0.34)
Some other race	13.0 (1.55)	87.0 (1.55)	30.7 (2.14)	56.4 (2.62)	38.7 (2.42)	6.5 (1.47)	11.2 (1.38)	13.9 (0.79)	86.1 (0.79)	23.2 (0.95)	19.2 (0.85)	7.9 (0.50)	35.7 (1.14)
Two or more races	13.5 (0.41)	86.5 (0.41)	32.3 (0.63)	54.1 (0.71)	39.0 (0.61)	4.6 (0.22)	10.6 (0.42)	8.0 (0.22)	92.0 (0.22)	21.5 (0.31)	25.0 (0.34)	9.6 (0.22)	35.9 (0.39)
White and Black	15.9 (0.74)	84.1 (0.74)	34.8 (1.15)	49.4 (1.30)	38.2 (1.20)	3.8 (0.39)	7.3 (0.64)	7.4 (0.36)	92.6 (0.36)	22.4 (0.71)	26.8 (0.75)	11.0 (0.57)	32.5 (0.74)
White and Asian	8.9 (0.81)	91.1 (0.81)	25.7 (1.06)	65.4 (1.18)	44.0 (1.27)	4.7 (0.51)	16.7 (0.89)	5.7 (0.35)	94.3 (0.35)	15.0 (0.56)	19.8 (0.55)	8.4 (0.42)	51.1 (0.75)
White and American Indian/ Alaska Native	18.1 (1.26)	81.9 (1.26)	36.0 (1.52)	45.9 (1.65)	34.4 (1.63)	4.8 (0.59)	6.7 (1.04)	10.1 (0.40)	89.9 (0.40)	27.0 (0.65)	28.0 (0.67)	9.8 (0.38)	25.1 (0.60)
Other Two or more races	11.4 (0.93)	88.6 (0.93)	33.2 (1.35)	55.4 (1.41)	37.7 (1.32)	5.7 (0.68)	12.0 (1.03)	8.5 (0.39)	91.5 (0.39)	21.6 (0.48)	25.7 (0.60)	9.5 (0.37)	34.7 (0.68)

—Not available.

†Not applicable.

!Interpret data with caution. The coefficient of variation (CV) for this estimate is between 30 and 50 percent.

‡Reporting standards not met. Either there were too few cases for a reliable estimate or the coefficient of variation (CV) is 50 percent or greater.

[1] High school completers include diploma recipients and those completing high school through alternative credentials, such as a GED.

[2] Total includes other racial/ethnic groups not shown separately.

[3] Includes other Central American subgroups not shown separately.

[4] Includes Taiwanese.

[5] In addition to the subgroups shown, also includes Sri Lankan.

[6] Consists of Indonesian and Malaysian.

NOTE: Data are based on sample surveys of the entire population in the given age range residing within the United States, including both noninstitutionalized persons (e.g., those living in households, college housing, or military housing located within the United States) and institutionalized persons (e.g., those living in prisons, nursing facilities, or other healthcare facilities). Race categories exclude persons of Hispanic ethnicity. Detail may not sum to totals because of rounding.

SOURCE: U.S. Department of Commerce, Census Bureau, American Community Survey (ACS), 2010 and 2018. (This table was prepared April 2020.)

Table 104.50. Persons age 25 and over who hold a bachelor's or higher degree, by sex, race/ethnicity, age group, and field of bachelor's degree: 2017

[Standard errors appear in parentheses]

Field of bachelor's degree	Total		Sex: Male		Sex: Female		Race/ethnicity: White		Black		Hispanic		Asian/ Pacific Islander		American Indian/ Alaska Native		Age: 25 to 29 years old		30 to 49 years old		50 years old and over	
1	2		3		4		5		6		7		8		9		10		11		12	
Total population, 25 and over (in thousands)	**221,310**	**(21.0)**	**106,905**	**(24.7)**	**114,406**	**(21.0)**	**143,646**	**(27.3)**	**25,835**	**(9.8)**	**33,490**	**(8.9)**	**13,124**	**(9.2)**	**1,342**	**(1.3)**	**23,029**	**(10.1)**	**84,099**	**(23.7)**	**114,182**	**(19.8)**
Percent of population with bachelor's degree	**32.0**	**(0.07)**	**31.4**	**(0.08)**	**32.6**	**(0.07)**	**35.8**	**(0.08)**	**21.6**	**(0.12)**	**16.0**	**(0.11)**	**53.2**	**(0.20)**	**15.0**	**(0.36)**	**34.3**	**(0.18)**	**35.9**	**(0.10)**	**28.7**	**(0.06)**
Bachelor's degree holders	Number (in thousands)																					
Total	**70,854**	**(164.9)**	**33,521**	**(87.4)**	**37,334**	**(87.7)**	**51,378**	**(110.8)**	**5,572**	**(31.1)**	**5,370**	**(39.3)**	**6,984**	**(27.5)**	**201**	**(5.5)**	**7,890**	**(42.2)**	**30,169**	**(84.5)**	**32,795**	**(76.3)**
Agriculture	715	(9.7)	468	(7.5)	247	(5.1)	598	(8.7)	24	(2.0)	35	(2.5)	47	(2.8)	‡	(†)	75	(3.5)	274	(6.3)	366	(6.0)
Architecture	507	(8.7)	340	(6.7)	167	(4.7)	339	(6.3)	26	(2.4)	63	(3.2)	68	(2.7)	‡	(†)	54	(3.6)	218	(6.1)	235	(5.8)
Business/management	14,355	(50.2)	7,912	(39.1)	6,443	(30.9)	10,231	(38.5)	1,300	(16.1)	1,225	(16.6)	1,313	(13.3)	41	(3.0)	1,381	(17.4)	6,378	(35.8)	6,596	(26.8)
Communications and communications technologies	2,737	(19.5)	1,129	(12.9)	1,608	(15.2)	2,087	(16.8)	244	(6.6)	213	(6.8)	133	(4.1)	6	(0.9)	427	(7.8)	1,424	(15.6)	886	(9.6)
Computer and information sciences	2,276	(20.1)	1,626	(16.4)	650	(9.4)	1,238	(12.3)	224	(7.0)	165	(5.6)	584	(9.8)	3	(0.6)	318	(8.6)	1,302	(15.0)	656	(9.8)
Criminal justice and fire protection	1,262	(15.1)	745	(10.1)	517	(10.5)	843	(11.6)	203	(6.4)	144	(5.3)	38	(2.5)	6	(0.9)	209	(6.4)	693	(10.9)	361	(6.4)
Education	8,973	(39.1)	2,129	(17.6)	6,844	(30.2)	7,255	(31.7)	677	(11.2)	577	(9.8)	325	(7.1)	35	(2.2)	559	(10.0)	2,775	(22.8)	5,639	(27.1)
Engineering and engineering technologies	6,357	(35.0)	5,359	(30.3)	998	(12.0)	4,076	(26.2)	310	(7.4)	548	(10.7)	1,294	(13.5)	11	(1.2)	705	(10.1)	2,657	(23.7)	2,995	(19.8)
English language and literature	2,254	(17.9)	762	(11.2)	1,492	(12.6)	1,807	(15.1)	124	(4.5)	110	(5.1)	162	(4.5)	4	(0.6)	217	(6.2)	920	(11.3)	1,117	(12.6)
Foreign languages, literatures, and linguistics	736	(10.7)	200	(5.2)	536	(9.9)	535	(9.6)	31	(2.8)	77	(3.5)	75	(2.9)	‡	(†)	75	(2.8)	291	(5.9)	369	(7.5)
Health sciences	5,365	(24.0)	954	(9.8)	4,411	(21.3)	3,792	(18.1)	482	(10.9)	356	(7.3)	622	(9.8)	18	(1.3)	618	(8.2)	2,252	(17.1)	2,496	(16.4)
Liberal arts and humanities	982	(12.7)	388	(7.9)	594	(9.3)	710	(10.1)	71	(3.4)	89	(3.6)	85	(3.7)	4	(0.9)	85	(3.6)	432	(7.8)	465	(7.1)
Mathematics/statistics	1,071	(12.2)	614	(8.3)	456	(8.1)	782	(10.0)	64	(3.1)	51	(3.1)	152	(4.6)	‡	(†)	107	(3.9)	375	(7.5)	589	(9.3)
Natural sciences (biological, environmental, and physical)	5,974	(40.0)	3,339	(25.7)	2,635	(23.0)	4,258	(28.0)	361	(9.3)	369	(7.4)	843	(10.2)	16	(1.5)	791	(13.3)	2,552	(25.9)	2,632	(18.0)
Philosophy/religion/theology	941	(13.5)	646	(10.1)	295	(6.8)	721	(10.4)	80	(3.8)	59	(3.1)	60	(3.2)	3	(0.6)	82	(3.7)	353	(7.6)	506	(7.7)
Psychology	3,403	(22.5)	1,024	(12.3)	2,380	(17.9)	2,462	(17.8)	333	(7.0)	312	(7.5)	201	(5.0)	10	(1.3)	482	(8.9)	1,607	(14.6)	1,314	(13.2)
Social sciences and history	6,638	(35.1)	3,701	(24.7)	2,937	(21.0)	4,990	(27.3)	485	(9.8)	471	(8.9)	528	(9.2)	16	(1.3)	743	(11.6)	2,767	(22.9)	3,129	(20.5)
Social work and public administration	1,005	(11.8)	220	(5.7)	785	(10.1)	652	(8.9)	182	(6.4)	97	(4.0)	48	(2.7)	6	(0.9)	115	(4.3)	437	(8.6)	453	(7.4)
Visual and performing arts	2,914	(21.0)	1,104	(13.8)	1,810	(16.7)	2,239	(18.1)	154	(6.0)	204	(5.9)	243	(6.5)	7	(1.0)	444	(9.7)	1,324	(16.8)	1,146	(11.6)
Other fields[1]	2,389	(18.6)	861	(11.3)	1,528	(13.0)	1,761	(15.2)	196	(6.5)	205	(5.1)	165	(4.9)	9	(1.1)	404	(9.1)	1,139	(14.6)	846	(11.5)
	Percentage distribution, by field																					
Total	**100.0**	**(†)**	**100.0**	**(†)**	**100.0**	**(†)**	**100.0**	**(†)**	**100.0**	**(†)**	**100.0**	**(†)**	**100.0**	**(†)**	**100.0**	**(†)**	**100.0**	**(†)**	**100.0**	**(†)**	**100.0**	**(†)**
Agriculture	1.0	(0.01)	1.4	(0.02)	0.7	(0.01)	1.2	(0.02)	0.4	(0.04)	0.7	(0.05)	0.7	(0.04)	1.0	(0.25)	0.9	(0.04)	0.9	(0.02)	1.1	(0.02)
Architecture	0.7	(0.01)	1.0	(0.02)	0.4	(0.01)	0.7	(0.01)	0.5	(0.04)	1.2	(0.06)	1.0	(0.04)	0.4!	(0.14)	0.7	(0.05)	0.7	(0.02)	0.7	(0.02)
Business/management	20.3	(0.06)	23.6	(0.10)	17.3	(0.08)	19.9	(0.06)	23.3	(0.26)	22.8	(0.28)	18.8	(0.17)	20.5	(1.30)	17.5	(0.19)	21.1	(0.12)	20.1	(0.07)
Communications and communications technologies	3.9	(0.03)	3.4	(0.04)	4.3	(0.04)	4.1	(0.03)	4.4	(0.12)	4.0	(0.12)	1.9	(0.06)	2.8	(0.45)	5.4	(0.10)	4.7	(0.05)	2.7	(0.03)
Computer and information sciences	3.2	(0.03)	4.9	(0.05)	1.7	(0.03)	2.4	(0.02)	4.0	(0.12)	3.1	(0.11)	8.4	(0.14)	1.7	(0.30)	4.0	(0.11)	4.3	(0.05)	2.0	(0.03)
Criminal justice and fire protection	1.8	(0.02)	2.2	(0.03)	1.4	(0.03)	1.6	(0.02)	3.7	(0.11)	2.7	(0.10)	0.5	(0.04)	3.2	(0.42)	2.6	(0.08)	2.3	(0.04)	1.1	(0.02)
Education	12.7	(0.04)	6.4	(0.05)	18.3	(0.06)	14.1	(0.05)	12.1	(0.20)	10.7	(0.17)	4.6	(0.10)	17.4	(0.97)	7.1	(0.12)	9.2	(0.07)	17.2	(0.06)
Engineering and engineering technologies	9.0	(0.04)	16.0	(0.08)	2.7	(0.03)	7.9	(0.05)	5.6	(0.13)	10.2	(0.18)	18.5	(0.18)	5.4	(0.60)	8.9	(0.12)	8.8	(0.07)	9.1	(0.05)
English language and literature	3.2	(0.02)	2.3	(0.03)	4.0	(0.03)	3.5	(0.03)	2.2	(0.08)	2.0	(0.09)	2.3	(0.06)	1.8	(0.28)	2.8	(0.08)	3.0	(0.04)	3.4	(0.04)
Foreign languages, literatures, and linguistics	1.0	(0.01)	0.6	(0.02)	1.4	(0.03)	1.0	(0.02)	0.6	(0.05)	1.4	(0.06)	1.1	(0.04)	0.7!	(0.22)	1.0	(0.04)	1.0	(0.02)	1.1	(0.02)
Health sciences	7.6	(0.03)	2.8	(0.03)	11.8	(0.06)	7.4	(0.03)	8.7	(0.19)	6.6	(0.13)	8.9	(0.13)	9.2	(0.64)	7.8	(0.10)	7.5	(0.06)	7.6	(0.05)
Liberal arts and humanities	1.4	(0.02)	1.2	(0.02)	1.6	(0.02)	1.4	(0.02)	1.3	(0.06)	1.7	(0.07)	1.2	(0.05)	2.1	(0.46)	1.1	(0.05)	1.4	(0.03)	1.4	(0.02)
Mathematics/statistics	1.5	(0.02)	1.8	(0.02)	1.2	(0.02)	1.5	(0.02)	1.1	(0.05)	0.9	(0.06)	2.2	(0.07)	0.9!	(0.27)	1.4	(0.05)	1.2	(0.02)	1.8	(0.03)
Natural sciences (biological, environmental, and physical)	8.4	(0.05)	10.0	(0.07)	7.1	(0.06)	8.3	(0.05)	6.5	(0.16)	6.9	(0.13)	12.1	(0.14)	8.0	(0.71)	10.0	(0.15)	8.5	(0.08)	8.0	(0.05)
Philosophy/religion/theology	1.3	(0.02)	1.9	(0.03)	0.8	(0.02)	1.4	(0.02)	1.4	(0.07)	1.1	(0.06)	0.9	(0.05)	1.4	(0.29)	1.0	(0.05)	1.2	(0.03)	1.5	(0.02)
Psychology	4.8	(0.03)	3.1	(0.04)	6.4	(0.04)	4.8	(0.03)	6.0	(0.12)	5.8	(0.13)	2.9	(0.07)	4.9	(0.63)	6.1	(0.11)	5.3	(0.05)	4.0	(0.04)
Social sciences and history	9.4	(0.04)	11.0	(0.07)	7.9	(0.05)	9.7	(0.05)	8.7	(0.17)	8.8	(0.15)	7.6	(0.13)	8.1	(0.64)	9.4	(0.13)	9.2	(0.07)	9.5	(0.06)
Social work and public administration	1.4	(0.02)	0.7	(0.02)	2.1	(0.03)	1.3	(0.02)	3.3	(0.11)	1.8	(0.07)	0.7	(0.04)	2.9	(0.43)	1.5	(0.06)	1.4	(0.03)	1.4	(0.02)
Visual and performing arts	4.1	(0.03)	3.3	(0.04)	4.8	(0.04)	4.4	(0.04)	2.8	(0.11)	3.8	(0.10)	3.5	(0.09)	3.4	(0.51)	5.6	(0.12)	4.4	(0.05)	3.5	(0.03)
Other fields[1]	3.4	(0.02)	2.6	(0.03)	4.1	(0.03)	3.4	(0.03)	3.5	(0.11)	3.8	(0.09)	2.4	(0.07)	4.3	(0.53)	5.1	(0.11)	3.8	(0.05)	2.6	(0.03)

†Not applicable.
!Interpret data with caution. The coefficient of variation (CV) for this estimate is between 30 and 50 percent.
‡Reporting standards not met (too few cases for a reliable estimate).
[1]Includes area, ethnic, and civilization studies; family and consumer sciences; library sciences; military sciences; multi/interdisciplinary studies; physical fitness, parks, recreation and leisure; precision production; transportation technologies; and other fields, not separately classified.
NOTE: Data are based on sample surveys of the entire population age 25 and over residing within the United States, including both noninstitutionalized persons (e.g., those living in households, college housing, or military housing located within the United States) and institutionalized persons (e.g., those living in prisons, nursing facilities, or other healthcare facilities). The first bachelor's degree major reported by respondents was used to classify their field of study, even though they were able to report a second bachelor's degree major and may possess advanced degrees in other fields. Totals include other racial/ethnic groups not separately shown. Race categories exclude persons of Hispanic ethnicity. Detail may not sum to totals because of rounding.
SOURCE: U.S. Department of Commerce, Census Bureau, American Community Survey (ACS), 2017. (This table was prepared May 2019.)

Table 104.70. Number and percentage distribution of children under age 18, by parents' highest level of educational attainment, child's age group and race/ethnicity, and household type: 2010 and 2019

[Standard errors appear in parentheses]

Year, age group, race/ethnicity, and household type	Total, all children under age 18 who resided with at least one parent[1]: Number (in thousands)		Total, all children under age 18 who resided with at least one parent[1]: Percentage distribution		Highest level of education attained by any parent residing with child[1]: Total, all levels		Less than high school completion		High school completion[2]		Some college, no degree		Associate's degree		Bachelor's or higher degree: Total		Bachelor's degree		Master's degree		Doctor's degree[3]	
1	2		3		4		5		6		7		8		9		10		11		12	
2010																						
Total	**70,581**	**(40.7)**	**100.0**	**(†)**	**100.0**	**(†)**	**11.6**	**(0.09)**	**20.4**	**(0.10)**	**22.9**	**(0.10)**	**9.7**	**(0.06)**	**35.3**	**(0.13)**	**20.4**	**(0.08)**	**10.2**	**(0.07)**	**4.8**	**(0.04)**
Age group																						
4 years old and under	19,360	(19.8)	27.4	(0.02)	100.0	(†)	12.8	(0.12)	20.6	(0.14)	22.8	(0.14)	8.5	(0.09)	35.3	(0.19)	19.9	(0.13)	10.5	(0.11)	4.9	(0.07)
5 to 17 years old	51,221	(32.7)	72.6	(0.02)	100.0	(†)	11.2	(0.10)	20.3	(0.12)	23.0	(0.12)	10.2	(0.07)	35.3	(0.13)	20.6	(0.09)	10.1	(0.07)	4.7	(0.05)
Race/ethnicity																						
White	38,158	(19.3)	54.1	(0.04)	100.0	(†)	4.2	(0.07)	17.1	(0.13)	22.1	(0.13)	11.1	(0.08)	45.5	(0.17)	26.0	(0.11)	13.3	(0.10)	6.1	(0.07)
Black	9,540	(28.6)	13.5	(0.04)	100.0	(†)	12.4	(0.23)	27.0	(0.33)	31.2	(0.31)	9.6	(0.17)	19.8	(0.25)	12.4	(0.20)	5.7	(0.14)	1.7	(0.07)
Hispanic	16,302	(21.2)	23.1	(0.02)	100.0	(†)	30.0	(0.28)	26.1	(0.24)	21.4	(0.20)	6.9	(0.12)	15.6	(0.19)	10.2	(0.14)	3.7	(0.08)	1.7	(0.05)
Asian	3,078	(13.5)	4.4	(0.02)	100.0	(†)	8.4	(0.27)	11.9	(0.36)	11.0	(0.27)	6.6	(0.24)	62.2	(0.51)	29.9	(0.48)	19.8	(0.31)	12.6	(0.28)
Pacific Islander	118	(3.5)	0.2	(0.00)	100.0	(†)	5.9	(1.25)	31.9	(2.68)	33.8	(2.95)	12.0	(1.71)	16.4	(1.73)	12.7	(1.63)	2.1	(0.53)	1.6 !	(0.50)
American Indian/Alaska Native	519	(7.9)	0.7	(0.01)	100.0	(†)	13.3	(0.95)	27.2	(0.96)	32.3	(1.14)	9.8	(0.72)	17.4	(0.76)	11.9	(0.67)	4.1	(0.39)	1.4	(0.23)
Some other race[4]	173	(7.0)	0.2	(0.01)	100.0	(†)	12.1	(1.70)	20.8	(1.69)	20.2	(1.24)	7.9	(0.97)	39.1	(2.20)	18.3	(1.72)	12.9	(1.45)	7.9	(0.89)
Two or more races	2,693	(25.5)	3.8	(0.04)	100.0	(†)	6.1	(0.23)	17.4	(0.33)	26.6	(0.44)	11.2	(0.31)	38.7	(0.42)	21.7	(0.45)	10.9	(0.31)	6.1	(0.24)
Household type, by race/ethnicity																						
Two-parent household	46,327	(79.6)	100.0	(†)	100.0	(†)	7.1	(0.08)	15.5	(0.11)	20.3	(0.11)	10.5	(0.07)	46.6	(0.16)	26.0	(0.11)	13.9	(0.09)	6.7	(0.06)
White	28,826	(58.4)	62.2	(0.09)	100.0	(†)	1.9	(0.06)	12.9	(0.12)	19.8	(0.14)	11.5	(0.10)	53.9	(0.18)	30.1	(0.13)	16.2	(0.11)	7.6	(0.09)
Black	3,197	(24.6)	6.9	(0.05)	100.0	(†)	2.8	(0.20)	17.5	(0.44)	28.5	(0.52)	12.4	(0.32)	38.8	(0.50)	22.4	(0.42)	12.2	(0.35)	4.2	(0.18)
Hispanic	9,680	(47.9)	20.9	(0.09)	100.0	(†)	25.0	(0.28)	24.6	(0.29)	21.4	(0.27)	7.9	(0.16)	21.1	(0.26)	13.4	(0.18)	5.2	(0.12)	2.5	(0.07)
Asian	2,617	(16.4)	5.7	(0.04)	100.0	(†)	6.7	(0.28)	10.2	(0.39)	9.7	(0.27)	6.3	(0.26)	67.1	(0.54)	31.2	(0.54)	21.9	(0.36)	14.0	(0.31)
Pacific Islander	79	(3.8)	0.2	(0.01)	100.0	(†)	2.9 !	(1.20)	30.6	(3.39)	31.7	(3.34)	13.5	(2.25)	21.3	(2.56)	16.7	(2.44)	2.6	(0.72)	2.0 !	(0.65)
American Indian/Alaska Native	244	(7.3)	0.5	(0.02)	100.0	(†)	3.9	(0.61)	20.4	(1.24)	35.3	(1.55)	13.8	(1.14)	26.6	(1.42)	17.3	(1.25)	7.0	(0.82)	2.3	(0.40)
Some other race[4]	112	(5.5)	0.2	(0.01)	100.0	(†)	6.2	(1.46)	16.8	(2.01)	16.5	(1.55)	7.4	(1.19)	53.1	(2.62)	23.4	(2.25)	18.4	(2.15)	11.3	(1.31)
Two or more races	1,571	(18.8)	3.4	(0.04)	100.0	(†)	1.6	(0.18)	10.6	(0.37)	21.3	(0.49)	11.8	(0.44)	54.7	(0.69)	29.1	(0.65)	16.1	(0.46)	9.5	(0.38)
Single-parent household	24,254	(90.2)	100.0	(†)	100.0	(†)	20.3	(0.18)	29.8	(0.19)	27.9	(0.19)	8.2	(0.10)	13.7	(0.13)	9.6	(0.12)	3.1	(0.06)	1.1	(0.03)
White	9,332	(56.0)	38.5	(0.15)	100.0	(†)	11.3	(0.19)	30.1	(0.26)	29.2	(0.27)	10.0	(0.18)	19.4	(0.22)	13.2	(0.19)	4.5	(0.12)	1.6	(0.06)
Black	6,343	(34.8)	26.2	(0.14)	100.0	(†)	17.2	(0.31)	31.8	(0.39)	32.6	(0.36)	8.2	(0.20)	10.2	(0.23)	7.4	(0.20)	2.4	(0.11)	0.5	(0.05)
Hispanic	6,622	(46.0)	27.3	(0.16)	100.0	(†)	37.4	(0.43)	28.2	(0.34)	21.3	(0.26)	5.5	(0.15)	7.6	(0.19)	5.5	(0.18)	1.4	(0.08)	0.6	(0.05)
Asian	460	(10.6)	1.9	(0.04)	100.0	(†)	18.5	(1.01)	21.5	(0.86)	18.0	(0.94)	8.0	(0.64)	33.9	(1.07)	22.2	(0.94)	7.5	(0.58)	4.3	(0.37)
Pacific Islander	39	(3.0)	0.2	(0.01)	100.0	(†)	12.0	(2.67)	34.6	(4.54)	37.9	(5.03)	9.1	(2.47)	6.4	(1.59)	4.6 !	(1.43)	‡	(†)	‡	(†)
American Indian/Alaska Native	275	(7.5)	1.1	(0.03)	100.0	(†)	21.8	(1.64)	33.1	(1.50)	29.6	(1.47)	6.3	(0.79)	9.2	(0.81)	7.1	(0.77)	1.5	(0.33)	0.6 !	(0.18)
Some other race[4]	61	(4.4)	0.3	(0.02)	100.0	(†)	22.9	(2.99)	28.1	(2.91)	27.0	(2.50)	8.7	(1.69)	13.3	(1.97)	8.9	(1.60)	2.8	(0.70)	‡	(†)
Two or more races	1,122	(19.8)	4.6	(0.08)	100.0	(†)	12.5	(0.50)	27.0	(0.69)	34.0	(0.72)	10.3	(0.43)	16.3	(0.57)	11.4	(0.48)	3.7	(0.28)	1.2	(0.18)
2019																						
Total	**68,940**	**(47.6)**	**100.0**	**(†)**	**100.0**	**(†)**	**9.0**	**(0.09)**	**18.7**	**(0.11)**	**19.6**	**(0.11)**	**10.1**	**(0.07)**	**42.6**	**(0.17)**	**22.7**	**(0.10)**	**13.9**	**(0.08)**	**6.0**	**(0.06)**
Age group																						
4 years old and under	18,454	(23.2)	26.8	(0.03)	100.0	(†)	8.2	(0.12)	19.3	(0.16)	20.1	(0.14)	9.2	(0.10)	43.2	(0.22)	23.1	(0.17)	13.9	(0.12)	6.3	(0.09)
5 to 17 years old	50,486	(42.0)	73.2	(0.03)	100.0	(†)	9.3	(0.10)	18.5	(0.12)	19.4	(0.13)	10.4	(0.07)	42.3	(0.17)	22.5	(0.11)	13.9	(0.09)	5.9	(0.06)
Race/ethnicity																						
White	34,755	(20.8)	50.4	(0.03)	100.0	(†)	3.3	(0.06)	14.1	(0.11)	17.7	(0.13)	11.0	(0.10)	53.9	(0.19)	28.3	(0.15)	17.8	(0.12)	7.8	(0.09)
Black	8,859	(37.2)	12.9	(0.05)	100.0	(†)	8.2	(0.19)	26.0	(0.36)	27.5	(0.37)	11.1	(0.23)	27.3	(0.32)	15.3	(0.25)	9.3	(0.20)	2.7	(0.13)
Hispanic	17,675	(21.2)	25.6	(0.02)	100.0	(†)	22.0	(0.25)	26.5	(0.22)	20.8	(0.21)	8.5	(0.13)	22.2	(0.25)	13.8	(0.18)	6.1	(0.12)	2.2	(0.07)
Asian	3,340	(17.5)	4.8	(0.02)	100.0	(†)	6.3	(0.25)	9.0	(0.26)	8.7	(0.26)	5.7	(0.19)	70.4	(0.49)	29.5	(0.41)	26.4	(0.37)	14.5	(0.25)
Pacific Islander	116	(5.6)	0.2	(0.01)	100.0	(†)	7.1	(1.62)	27.9	(2.51)	28.0	(2.58)	12.1	(1.72)	24.9	(2.66)	16.7	(2.32)	7.3	(1.42)	1.0 !	(0.39)
American Indian/Alaska Native	491	(8.0)	0.7	(0.01)	100.0	(†)	10.9	(0.86)	25.7	(1.27)	28.4	(1.04)	10.6	(0.65)	24.4	(0.93)	14.3	(0.77)	8.5	(0.62)	1.6	(0.27)
Some other race[4]	260	(9.3)	0.4	(0.01)	100.0	(†)	13.9	(1.56)	15.9	(1.46)	18.6	(1.48)	8.7	(1.03)	42.9	(1.54)	19.6	(1.47)	14.7	(1.14)	8.6	(0.78)
Two or more races	3,443	(29.9)	5.0	(0.04)	100.0	(†)	4.1	(0.20)	15.2	(0.36)	21.8	(0.38)	10.7	(0.30)	48.2	(0.45)	24.8	(0.38)	15.2	(0.36)	8.2	(0.23)
Household type, by race/ethnicity																						
Two-parent household	45,154	(77.3)	100.0	(†)	100.0	(†)	5.5	(0.09)	12.9	(0.11)	16.2	(0.11)	10.3	(0.08)	55.1	(0.19)	28.0	(0.13)	18.7	(0.11)	8.4	(0.08)
White	26,263	(59.1)	58.2	(0.10)	100.0	(†)	1.7	(0.05)	9.3	(0.11)	15.1	(0.13)	10.9	(0.11)	62.9	(0.19)	32.0	(0.18)	21.4	(0.14)	9.6	(0.11)
Black	3,166	(32.6)	7.0	(0.07)	100.0	(†)	2.5	(0.23)	15.0	(0.52)	21.1	(0.52)	12.6	(0.38)	48.8	(0.61)	24.8	(0.40)	18.1	(0.47)	5.9	(0.31)
Hispanic	10,311	(41.4)	22.8	(0.08)	100.0	(†)	17.0	(0.32)	23.6	(0.29)	20.0	(0.28)	9.4	(0.19)	30.0	(0.37)	17.8	(0.26)	8.8	(0.18)	3.3	(0.11)
Asian	2,867	(19.3)	6.4	(0.04)	100.0	(†)	5.1	(0.26)	7.5	(0.26)	6.9	(0.25)	5.0	(0.18)	75.6	(0.51)	30.3	(0.45)	29.1	(0.40)	16.1	(0.29)
Pacific Islander	72	(5.4)	0.2	(0.01)	100.0	(†)	‡	(†)	24.5	(3.44)	28.4	(3.41)	13.7	(2.81)	30.6	(3.70)	21.1	(3.28)	8.0	(1.74)	1.4 !	(0.59)
American Indian/Alaska Native	231	(6.9)	0.5	(0.02)	100.0	(†)	2.4	(0.48)	17.8	(1.46)	27.9	(1.65)	11.8	(1.00)	40.1	(1.72)	22.2	(1.34)	14.8	(1.16)	3.1	(0.54)
Some other race[4]	163	(7.6)	0.4	(0.02)	100.0	(†)	9.7	(1.69)	12.4	(1.64)	13.8	(1.85)	8.4	(1.43)	55.7	(2.13)	23.1	(1.96)	19.9	(1.68)	12.7	(1.18)
Two or more races	2,080	(24.0)	4.6	(0.05)	100.0	(†)	0.9	(0.12)	7.6	(0.35)	15.6	(0.43)	10.5	(0.38)	65.3	(0.48)	31.5	(0.52)	21.5	(0.45)	12.3	(0.38)
Single-parent household	23,786	(94.4)	100.0	(†)	100.0	(†)	15.8	(0.17)	29.8	(0.21)	26.0	(0.21)	9.7	(0.09)	18.7	(0.18)	12.5	(0.14)	4.8	(0.09)	1.4	(0.04)
White	8,492	(57.0)	35.7	(0.16)	100.0	(†)	8.2	(0.17)	28.7	(0.31)	25.7	(0.27)	11.3	(0.16)	26.1	(0.27)	17.2	(0.24)	6.8	(0.16)	2.2	(0.08)

[Standard errors appear in parentheses]

Year, age group, race/ethnicity, and household type	Total, all children under age 18 who resided with at least one parent[1]: Number (in thousands)	Total, all children under age 18 who resided with at least one parent[1]: Percentage distribution	Highest level of education attained by any parent residing with child[1]: Total, all levels	Less than high school completion	High school completion[2]	Some college, no degree	Associate's degree	Bachelor's or higher degree: Total	Bachelor's or higher degree: Bachelor's degree	Bachelor's or higher degree: Master's degree	Bachelor's or higher degree: Doctor's degree[3]
1	2	3	4	5	6	7	8	9	10	11	12
Black	5,693 (41.6)	23.9 (0.14)	100.0 (†)	11.4 (0.28)	32.1 (0.47)	31.0 (0.44)	10.2 (0.28)	15.3 (0.38)	10.0 (0.29)	4.4 (0.20)	0.9 (0.10)
Hispanic	7,364 (44.3)	31.0 (0.16)	100.0 (†)	29.1 (0.37)	30.6 (0.34)	21.9 (0.34)	7.3 (0.19)	11.2 (0.21)	8.2 (0.18)	2.3 (0.11)	0.6 (0.05)
Asian	473 (11.2)	2.0 (0.05)	100.0 (†)	13.4 (0.90)	18.0 (0.91)	19.6 (1.06)	10.0 (0.75)	38.9 (1.15)	24.3 (1.03)	9.8 (0.60)	4.8 (0.41)
Pacific Islander	44 (2.8)	0.2 (0.01)	100.0 (†)	14.0 (3.32)	33.4 (4.50)	27.4 (4.01)	9.5 ! (2.99)	15.8 (2.99)	9.5 (2.37)	6.0 ! (2.21)	‡ (†)
American Indian/Alaska Native	260 (6.5)	1.1 (0.03)	100.0 (†)	18.4 (1.50)	32.7 (1.90)	28.9 (1.48)	9.6 (0.92)	10.5 (0.94)	7.3 (0.79)	2.9 (0.47)	0.3 ! (0.14)
Some other race[4]	97 (5.4)	0.4 (0.02)	100.0 (†)	20.9 (3.07)	21.9 (2.57)	26.7 (2.39)	9.2 (1.56)	21.3 (2.25)	13.7 (2.11)	5.8 (1.29)	1.8 ! (0.60)
Two or more races	1,362 (21.9)	5.7 (0.10)	100.0 (†)	9.0 (0.49)	26.7 (0.67)	31.3 (0.74)	10.9 (0.46)	22.0 (0.62)	14.6 (0.52)	5.5 (0.34)	1.9 (0.17)

†Not applicable.

!Interpret data with caution. The coefficient of variation (CV) for this estimate is between 30 and 50 percent.

‡Reporting standards not met. Either there are too few cases for a reliable estimate or the coefficient of variation (CV) is 50 percent or greater.

[1] Parents include adoptive and stepparents, but exclude parents not residing in the same household as their children.

[2] Includes parents who completed high school through equivalency programs, such as a GED program.

[3] Includes parents with professional degrees.

[4] Respondents who wrote in some other race that was not included as an option on the questionnaire.

NOTE: Data are based on sample surveys of the entire population residing within the United States, but this table includes only children under age 18 who resided with at least one of their parents (including an adoptive or stepparent). Children in single-parent households resided with only one parent, while those in two-parent households resided with two parents. Race categories exclude persons of Hispanic ethnicity. Detail may not sum to totals because of rounding.

SOURCE: U.S. Department of Commerce, Census Bureau, American Community Survey (ACS), 2010 and 2019. (This table was prepared November 2020.)

Table 104.80. Percentage of persons 18 to 24 years old and age 25 and over, by educational attainment and state: 2000 and 2018

[Standard errors appear in parentheses]

State	Percent of 18- to 24-year-olds who were high school completers[1]		Percent of population 25 years old and over, by educational attainment											
			2000					2018						
			Less than high school completion	High school completion[1] or higher	Bachelor's or higher degree			Less than high school completion	High school completion[1] or higher		Bachelor's or higher degree			
	2000	2018			Total	Bachelor's degree	Graduate degree		Total	High school only	Total	Bachelor's degree	Graduate degree	
1	2	3	4	5	6	7	8	9	10	11	12	13	14	
United States	**74.7 (0.02)**	**87.6 (0.08)**	**19.6 (0.01)**	**80.4 (0.01)**	**24.4 (0.01)**	**15.5 (0.01)**	**8.9 (#)**	**11.7 (0.04)**	**88.3 (0.04)**	**26.9 (0.05)**	**32.6 (0.07)**	**20.0 (0.04)**	**12.7 (0.04)**	
Alabama	72.2 (0.15)	87.2 (0.70)	24.7 (0.06)	75.3 (0.06)	19.0 (0.05)	12.1 (0.04)	6.9 (0.03)	13.5 (0.28)	86.5 (0.28)	30.8 (0.31)	25.3 (0.34)	15.8 (0.28)	9.5 (0.23)	
Alaska	76.9 (0.40)	87.6 (1.67)	11.7 (0.12)	88.3 (0.12)	24.7 (0.16)	16.1 (0.13)	8.6 (0.10)	6.0 (0.52)	94.0 (0.52)	27.9 (0.95)	30.1 (1.13)	18.6 (0.88)	11.4 (0.79)	
Arizona	69.2 (0.19)	84.9 (0.71)	19.0 (0.06)	81.0 (0.06)	23.5 (0.07)	15.1 (0.06)	8.4 (0.04)	12.4 (0.17)	87.6 (0.17)	24.1 (0.24)	29.6 (0.26)	18.5 (0.21)	11.1 (0.17)	
Arkansas	75.4 (0.19)	88.5 (0.82)	24.7 (0.07)	75.3 (0.07)	16.7 (0.06)	11.0 (0.05)	5.7 (0.04)	12.7 (0.30)	87.3 (0.30)	34.3 (0.47)	23.3 (0.40)	14.8 (0.28)	8.5 (0.26)	
California	70.7 (0.07)	89.9 (0.17)	23.2 (0.03)	76.8 (0.03)	26.6 (0.03)	17.1 (0.02)	9.5 (0.02)	16.1 (0.09)	83.9 (0.09)	20.7 (0.09)	34.4 (0.11)	21.4 (0.10)	13.0 (0.09)	
Colorado	75.1 (0.15)	87.2 (0.63)	13.1 (0.05)	86.9 (0.05)	32.7 (0.06)	21.6 (0.06)	11.1 (0.04)	7.8 (0.19)	92.2 (0.19)	21.0 (0.34)	42.0 (0.29)	26.1 (0.27)	15.9 (0.22)	
Connecticut	78.2 (0.21)	90.3 (0.74)	16.0 (0.06)	84.0 (0.06)	31.4 (0.08)	18.1 (0.07)	13.3 (0.06)	9.2 (0.24)	90.8 (0.24)	27.0 (0.37)	39.7 (0.35)	21.8 (0.27)	17.9 (0.27)	
Delaware	77.6 (0.41)	86.2 (1.77)	17.4 (0.14)	82.6 (0.14)	25.0 (0.16)	15.6 (0.14)	9.4 (0.11)	10.4 (0.57)	89.6 (0.57)	32.9 (0.83)	31.2 (0.77)	18.2 (0.64)	13.0 (0.51)	
District of Columbia	79.4 (0.40)	90.4 (1.42)	22.2 (0.18)	77.8 (0.18)	39.1 (0.21)	18.1 (0.17)	21.0 (0.18)	8.2 (0.57)	91.8 (0.57)	16.9 (0.67)	60.2 (0.61)	25.4 (0.62)	34.8 (0.62)	
Florida	71.7 (0.11)	84.9 (0.37)	20.1 (0.04)	79.9 (0.04)	22.3 (0.04)	14.2 (0.03)	8.1 (0.02)	11.5 (0.09)	88.5 (0.09)	28.5 (0.16)	30.5 (0.15)	19.2 (0.14)	11.3 (0.09)	
Georgia	70.0 (0.15)	84.9 (0.42)	21.4 (0.05)	78.6 (0.05)	24.3 (0.05)	16.0 (0.05)	8.3 (0.04)	12.5 (0.18)	87.5 (0.18)	27.7 (0.21)	32.0 (0.21)	19.5 (0.19)	12.5 (0.16)	
Hawaii	85.8 (0.25)	90.0 (0.99)	15.4 (0.10)	84.6 (0.10)	26.2 (0.12)	17.8 (0.10)	8.4 (0.08)	8.3 (0.42)	91.7 (0.42)	26.9 (0.63)	33.2 (0.65)	21.7 (0.49)	11.5 (0.40)	
Idaho	77.3 (0.25)	84.6 (1.48)	15.3 (0.09)	84.7 (0.09)	21.7 (0.10)	14.9 (0.09)	6.8 (0.06)	9.3 (0.39)	90.7 (0.39)	28.2 (0.63)	27.4 (0.52)	18.4 (0.49)	9.0 (0.41)	
Illinois	76.0 (0.09)	88.4 (0.39)	18.6 (0.03)	81.4 (0.03)	26.1 (0.03)	16.6 (0.03)	9.5 (0.02)	10.6 (0.14)	89.4 (0.14)	26.2 (0.21)	35.2 (0.21)	21.1 (0.17)	14.0 (0.15)	
Indiana	76.5 (0.15)	84.1 (0.66)	17.9 (0.05)	82.1 (0.05)	19.4 (0.05)	12.2 (0.04)	7.2 (0.04)	11.2 (0.22)	88.8 (0.22)	33.2 (0.28)	26.9 (0.29)	17.2 (0.21)	9.7 (0.19)	
Iowa	81.4 (0.16)	88.6 (0.82)	13.9 (0.06)	86.1 (0.06)	21.2 (0.07)	14.7 (0.06)	6.5 (0.04)	7.8 (0.27)	92.2 (0.27)	31.0 (0.42)	28.6 (0.49)	19.4 (0.38)	9.2 (0.35)	
Kansas	78.3 (0.18)	88.6 (0.85)	14.0 (0.06)	86.0 (0.06)	25.8 (0.08)	17.1 (0.06)	8.7 (0.05)	9.1 (0.27)	90.9 (0.27)	25.6 (0.38)	33.4 (0.38)	20.9 (0.34)	12.5 (0.30)	
Kentucky	74.9 (0.15)	88.5 (0.75)	25.9 (0.06)	74.1 (0.06)	17.1 (0.05)	10.2 (0.04)	6.9 (0.03)	12.9 (0.28)	87.1 (0.28)	32.3 (0.31)	25.2 (0.30)	14.8 (0.23)	10.4 (0.22)	
Louisiana	72.3 (0.15)	83.5 (0.81)	25.2 (0.06)	74.8 (0.06)	18.7 (0.05)	12.2 (0.04)	6.5 (0.03)	14.0 (0.33)	86.0 (0.33)	34.6 (0.41)	24.3 (0.31)	15.9 (0.28)	8.4 (0.19)	
Maine	78.9 (0.28)	90.1 (1.23)	14.6 (0.08)	85.4 (0.08)	22.9 (0.10)	15.0 (0.09)	7.9 (0.06)	7.2 (0.43)	92.8 (0.43)	31.0 (0.67)	30.6 (0.62)	19.1 (0.48)	11.5 (0.44)	
Maryland	79.6 (0.16)	89.7 (0.58)	16.2 (0.05)	83.8 (0.05)	31.4 (0.07)	18.0 (0.06)	13.4 (0.05)	9.5 (0.21)	90.5 (0.21)	24.4 (0.31)	40.7 (0.33)	21.7 (0.26)	19.0 (0.28)	
Massachusetts	82.2 (0.13)	89.7 (0.47)	15.2 (0.05)	84.8 (0.05)	33.2 (0.06)	19.5 (0.05)	13.7 (0.04)	9.2 (0.18)	90.8 (0.18)	23.5 (0.28)	44.4 (0.28)	24.4 (0.23)	20.1 (0.22)	
Michigan	76.5 (0.10)	87.8 (0.48)	16.6 (0.03)	83.4 (0.03)	21.8 (0.04)	13.7 (0.03)	8.1 (0.02)	9.0 (0.16)	91.0 (0.16)	28.6 (0.22)	29.6 (0.27)	18.1 (0.20)	11.5 (0.16)	
Minnesota	79.3 (0.13)	88.5 (0.66)	12.1 (0.04)	87.9 (0.04)	27.4 (0.06)	19.1 (0.05)	8.3 (0.03)	6.6 (0.20)	93.4 (0.20)	24.0 (0.34)	37.2 (0.40)	24.2 (0.36)	13.0 (0.26)	
Mississippi	71.3 (0.18)	86.0 (0.94)	27.1 (0.08)	72.9 (0.08)	16.9 (0.06)	11.1 (0.05)	5.8 (0.04)	14.6 (0.34)	85.4 (0.34)	29.6 (0.45)	23.4 (0.43)	14.5 (0.34)	8.9 (0.26)	
Missouri	76.5 (0.13)	88.1 (0.60)	18.7 (0.05)	81.3 (0.05)	21.6 (0.05)	14.0 (0.04)	7.6 (0.03)	9.7 (0.22)	90.3 (0.22)	30.0 (0.26)	29.6 (0.26)	17.8 (0.27)	11.7 (0.19)	
Montana	78.6 (0.31)	87.5 (1.60)	12.8 (0.10)	87.2 (0.10)	24.4 (0.13)	17.2 (0.11)	7.2 (0.08)	6.6 (0.39)	93.4 (0.39)	28.3 (0.70)	30.4 (0.80)	20.0 (0.72)	10.4 (0.43)	
Nebraska	80.0 (0.21)	89.1 (1.04)	13.4 (0.07)	86.6 (0.07)	23.7 (0.09)	16.4 (0.08)	7.3 (0.06)	8.2 (0.24)	91.8 (0.24)	25.4 (0.55)	32.9 (0.53)	21.8 (0.43)	11.1 (0.36)	
Nevada	66.7 (0.32)	85.5 (0.97)	19.3 (0.10)	80.7 (0.10)	18.2 (0.10)	12.1 (0.08)	6.1 (0.06)	13.2 (0.29)	86.8 (0.29)	27.7 (0.46)	24.9 (0.41)	16.1 (0.33)	8.8 (0.25)	
New Hampshire	77.8 (0.29)	90.5 (1.17)	12.6 (0.08)	87.4 (0.08)	28.7 (0.11)	18.7 (0.10)	10.0 (0.07)	7.1 (0.31)	92.9 (0.31)	27.4 (0.54)	37.2 (0.59)	22.5 (0.52)	14.7 (0.42)	
New Jersey	76.3 (0.14)	89.5 (0.45)	17.9 (0.04)	82.1 (0.04)	29.8 (0.05)	18.8 (0.04)	11.0 (0.04)	9.9 (0.17)	90.1 (0.17)	26.3 (0.21)	40.6 (0.24)	24.5 (0.22)	16.1 (0.18)	
New Mexico	70.5 (0.24)	82.3 (1.57)	21.1 (0.09)	78.9 (0.09)	23.5 (0.09)	13.7 (0.07)	9.8 (0.06)	14.7 (0.43)	85.3 (0.43)	26.6 (0.52)	27.5 (0.50)	15.8 (0.39)	11.7 (0.34)	
New York	76.1 (0.09)	88.9 (0.31)	20.9 (0.03)	79.1 (0.03)	27.4 (0.04)	15.6 (0.03)	11.8 (0.03)	12.8 (0.12)	87.2 (0.12)	25.8 (0.16)	37.3 (0.18)	20.8 (0.15)	16.5 (0.14)	
North Carolina	74.2 (0.11)	87.1 (0.52)	21.9 (0.04)	78.1 (0.04)	22.5 (0.04)	15.3 (0.04)	7.2 (0.03)	11.7 (0.17)	88.3 (0.17)	25.4 (0.20)	31.9 (0.23)	20.5 (0.17)	11.4 (0.15)	
North Dakota	84.4 (0.24)	93.1 (1.03)	16.1 (0.10)	83.9 (0.10)	22.0 (0.12)	16.5 (0.10)	5.5 (0.06)	7.4 (0.51)	92.6 (0.51)	26.3 (0.80)	28.8 (1.00)	21.2 (0.87)	7.6 (0.40)	
Ohio	76.8 (0.09)	87.7 (0.38)	17.0 (0.03)	83.0 (0.03)	21.1 (0.03)	13.7 (0.03)	7.4 (0.02)	9.5 (0.13)	90.5 (0.13)	32.8 (0.21)	28.8 (0.21)	17.6 (0.15)	11.2 (0.16)	
Oklahoma	74.8 (0.16)	83.9 (0.91)	19.4 (0.06)	80.6 (0.06)	20.3 (0.06)	13.5 (0.05)	6.8 (0.04)	11.5 (0.28)	88.5 (0.28)	31.5 (0.41)	25.8 (0.38)	16.7 (0.33)	9.2 (0.28)	
Oregon	74.2 (0.17)	86.8 (0.76)	14.9 (0.05)	85.1 (0.05)	25.1 (0.06)	16.4 (0.06)	8.7 (0.04)	9.8 (0.26)	90.2 (0.26)	21.9 (0.35)	34.2 (0.38)	21.1 (0.32)	13.1 (0.26)	
Pennsylvania	79.8 (0.09)	88.2 (0.44)	18.1 (0.03)	81.9 (0.03)	22.4 (0.03)	14.0 (0.03)	8.4 (0.02)	8.9 (0.15)	91.1 (0.15)	34.9 (0.20)	31.8 (0.22)	19.0 (0.19)	12.9 (0.15)	
Rhode Island	81.3 (0.32)	91.3 (1.32)	22.0 (0.13)	78.0 (0.13)	25.6 (0.14)	15.9 (0.12)	9.7 (0.10)	11.2 (0.45)	88.8 (0.45)	28.4 (0.68)	34.5 (0.71)	20.0 (0.50)	14.5 (0.53)	
South Carolina	74.3 (0.18)	86.5 (0.70)	23.7 (0.07)	76.3 (0.07)	20.4 (0.07)	13.5 (0.06)	6.9 (0.04)	11.9 (0.25)	88.1 (0.25)	29.9 (0.36)	28.2 (0.31)	17.8 (0.27)	10.5 (0.19)	
South Dakota	78.2 (0.33)	83.7 (1.65)	15.4 (0.12)	84.6 (0.12)	21.5 (0.13)	15.5 (0.12)	6.0 (0.08)	7.8 (0.46)	92.2 (0.46)	30.5 (0.97)	28.9 (0.92)	20.1 (0.71)	8.7 (0.60)	
Tennessee	75.1 (0.16)	87.5 (0.58)	24.1 (0.06)	75.9 (0.06)	19.6 (0.06)	12.8 (0.05)	6.8 (0.03)	12.2 (0.20)	87.8 (0.20)	32.0 (0.28)	27.4 (0.29)	17.4 (0.20)	10.0 (0.21)	
Texas	68.6 (0.08)	85.6 (0.28)	24.3 (0.03)	75.7 (0.03)	23.2 (0.03)	15.6 (0.03)	7.6 (0.02)	16.1 (0.13)	83.9 (0.13)	25.0 (0.14)	30.3 (0.14)	19.6 (0.11)	10.7 (0.10)	
Utah	80.3 (0.16)	89.6 (0.70)	12.3 (0.07)	87.7 (0.07)	26.1 (0.09)	17.8 (0.08)	8.3 (0.06)	7.3 (0.33)	92.7 (0.33)	22.8 (0.44)	35.0 (0.51)	22.9 (0.38)	12.2 (0.33)	
Vermont	83.0 (0.28)	91.3 (1.85)	13.6 (0.10)	86.4 (0.10)	29.4 (0.13)	18.3 (0.11)	11.1 (0.09)	6.6 (0.61)	93.4 (0.61)	29.0 (0.81)	39.1 (1.00)	23.4 (0.83)	15.7 (0.58)	
Virginia	79.4 (0.13)	89.7 (0.46)	18.5 (0.05)	81.5 (0.05)	29.5 (0.06)	17.9 (0.05)	11.6 (0.04)	10.0 (0.17)	90.0 (0.17)	24.0 (0.24)	39.5 (0.29)	22.3 (0.26)	17.2 (0.22)	
Washington	75.3 (0.16)	87.2 (0.57)	12.9 (0.05)	87.1 (0.05)	27.7 (0.06)	18.4 (0.05)	9.3 (0.04)	8.4 (0.15)	91.6 (0.15)	21.8 (0.23)	36.7 (0.31)	22.7 (0.24)	13.9 (0.19)	
West Virginia	78.2 (0.22)	87.3 (1.26)	24.8 (0.09)	75.2 (0.09)	14.8 (0.07)	8.9 (0.06)	5.9 (0.05)	11.9 (0.39)	88.1 (0.39)	40.1 (0.59)	21.4 (0.56)	12.7 (0.38)	8.6 (0.32)	
Wisconsin	78.9 (0.13)	89.2 (0.52)	14.9 (0.04)	85.1 (0.04)	22.4 (0.05)	15.2 (0.04)	7.2 (0.03)	7.7 (0.19)	92.3 (0.19)	30.9 (0.32)	30.2 (0.37)	19.8 (0.28)	10.4 (0.21)	
Wyoming	79.0 (0.41)	88.2 (2.02)	12.1 (0.13)	87.9 (0.13)	21.9 (0.16)	14.9 (0.14)	7.0 (0.10)	7.3 (0.60)	92.7 (0.60)	28.9 (1.03)	27.0 (0.83)	17.3 (0.81)	9.7 (0.73)	

#Rounds to zero.

[1]High school completers include those graduating from high school with a diploma as well as those completing high school through equivalency programs, such as a GED program.

NOTE: Data for 2018 are based on sample surveys of the entire population in the given age range residing within the United States, including both noninstitutionalized persons (e.g., those living in households, college housing, or military housing located within the United States) and institutionalized persons (e.g., those living in prisons, nursing facilities, or other healthcare facilities), while data for 2000 are based on sample surveys of the population residing in individual housing units only. Caution should be used when comparing data between these two years. Detail may not sum to totals because of rounding.

SOURCE: U.S. Department of Commerce, Census Bureau, Census 2000 Summary File 3, retrieved October 11, 2006, from https://factfinder2.census.gov/faces/tableservices/jsf/pages/productview.xhtml?pid=DEC_00_SF3_QTP20&prodType=table; Census Briefs, *Educational Attainment: 2000*; and American Community Survey (ACS), 2018. (This table was prepared February 2020.)

Table 104.85. Rates of high school completion and bachelor's degree attainment among persons age 25 and over, by race/ethnicity and state: 2018

[Standard errors appear in parentheses]

State	Percent with high school completion[1] or higher						Percent with bachelor's or higher degree					
	Total[2]	White	Black	Hispanic	Asian	Two or more races	Total[2]	White	Black	Hispanic	Asian	Two or more races
1	2	3	4	5	6	7	8	9	10	11	12	13
United States	**88.3 (0.04)**	**93.1 (0.04)**	**86.6 (0.09)**	**69.7 (0.15)**	**87.7 (0.12)**	**92.0 (0.22)**	**32.6 (0.07)**	**36.3 (0.08)**	**22.1 (0.14)**	**17.0 (0.12)**	**55.3 (0.21)**	**35.9 (0.39)**
Alabama	86.5 (0.28)	88.6 (0.31)	83.4 (0.56)	65.9 (2.38)	84.3 (2.45)	88.2 (2.32)	25.3 (0.34)	28.0 (0.41)	17.2 (0.58)	18.3 (2.13)	52.9 (3.14)	25.6 (2.89)
Alaska	94.0 (0.52)	96.5 (0.48)	98.2 (1.53)	88.5 (4.23)	91.6 (3.68)	95.7 (1.78)	30.1 (1.13)	36.5 (1.39)	23.5 (6.04)	23.1 (4.42)	24.6 (4.05)	24.6 (3.95)
Arizona	87.6 (0.17)	94.6 (0.18)	89.8 (1.02)	71.3 (0.51)	89.3 (1.05)	93.7 (1.04)	29.6 (0.26)	36.0 (0.31)	25.0 (1.33)	13.7 (0.40)	57.7 (1.84)	37.7 (2.76)
Arkansas	87.3 (0.30)	89.5 (0.33)	86.2 (0.79)	59.7 (2.38)	88.7 (3.40)	85.3 (2.59)	23.3 (0.40)	25.0 (0.46)	16.8 (1.02)	11.5 (1.40)	44.3 (3.84)	20.4 (2.72)
California	83.9 (0.09)	95.1 (0.08)	91.0 (0.30)	66.1 (0.23)	88.4 (0.19)	93.4 (0.37)	34.4 (0.11)	44.6 (0.17)	27.0 (0.54)	13.6 (0.19)	53.8 (0.33)	41.9 (0.84)
Colorado	92.2 (0.19)	96.8 (0.14)	90.4 (1.14)	73.7 (0.79)	90.4 (0.98)	95.4 (0.84)	42.0 (0.29)	48.3 (0.32)	28.6 (1.94)	17.0 (0.64)	56.6 (1.54)	44.2 (2.24)
Connecticut	90.8 (0.24)	94.6 (0.23)	88.0 (0.83)	73.9 (1.10)	89.4 (1.04)	89.6 (2.38)	39.7 (0.35)	44.6 (0.43)	22.9 (1.19)	16.9 (0.82)	65.3 (1.70)	45.4 (4.54)
Delaware	89.6 (0.57)	93.2 (0.52)	88.7 (1.15)	61.9 (3.18)	85.3 (4.30)	89.2 (4.91)	31.2 (0.77)	34.2 (0.93)	22.1 (1.65)	17.2 (2.24)	55.2 (4.92)	23.4 (5.21)
District of Columbia	91.8 (0.57)	99.3 (0.23)	87.6 (1.05)	76.0 (3.32)	96.8 (1.72)	96.2 (1.82)	60.2 (0.61)	92.9 (0.62)	27.8 (1.29)	53.9 (3.67)	88.9 (2.61)	70.4 (5.35)
Florida	88.5 (0.09)	93.1 (0.12)	83.7 (0.41)	80.0 (0.28)	87.9 (0.63)	92.2 (0.88)	30.5 (0.15)	34.0 (0.17)	20.0 (0.48)	25.5 (0.29)	50.0 (1.16)	35.0 (1.57)
Georgia	87.5 (0.18)	90.8 (0.20)	87.6 (0.27)	61.8 (1.05)	87.1 (0.88)	92.6 (1.31)	32.0 (0.21)	35.9 (0.26)	24.6 (0.47)	18.1 (0.75)	56.4 (1.17)	39.5 (2.41)
Hawaii	91.7 (0.42)	97.1 (0.42)	95.8 (2.16)	89.1 (1.37)	88.9 (0.78)	95.3 (0.64)	33.2 (0.65)	44.1 (1.56)	30.8 (4.63)	27.2 (2.02)	35.0 (1.01)	26.3 (1.39)
Idaho	90.7 (0.39)	93.8 (0.34)	92.4 (5.30)	64.3 (2.56)	90.2 (3.78)	96.8 (1.73)	27.4 (0.52)	29.3 (0.56)	24.5 (7.26)	11.0 (1.42)	41.5 (5.73)	22.8 (4.37)
Illinois	89.4 (0.14)	94.2 (0.11)	86.7 (0.46)	69.2 (0.70)	90.9 (0.62)	91.5 (1.47)	35.2 (0.21)	39.5 (0.24)	22.1 (0.57)	14.4 (0.43)	66.4 (0.97)	41.0 (2.25)
Indiana	88.8 (0.22)	90.5 (0.21)	86.0 (0.74)	68.6 (1.81)	83.5 (1.94)	88.2 (2.08)	26.9 (0.29)	27.7 (0.33)	18.6 (0.90)	14.0 (1.07)	58.8 (2.45)	31.2 (2.68)
Iowa	92.2 (0.27)	94.3 (0.24)	81.5 (3.21)	62.1 (2.73)	82.3 (2.95)	93.1 (2.23)	28.6 (0.49)	29.4 (0.47)	12.0 (2.22)	14.3 (1.79)	48.0 (3.98)	26.6 (5.26)
Kansas	90.9 (0.27)	94.4 (0.26)	86.5 (1.83)	63.8 (1.68)	87.7 (2.08)	94.2 (1.57)	33.4 (0.38)	35.9 (0.45)	20.3 (2.07)	13.8 (1.29)	58.1 (2.42)	25.4 (3.29)
Kentucky	87.1 (0.28)	87.7 (0.27)	87.0 (0.98)	70.6 (2.65)	82.1 (2.61)	86.4 (2.35)	25.2 (0.30)	25.6 (0.33)	17.0 (1.25)	21.1 (2.30)	50.6 (3.39)	28.5 (3.78)
Louisiana	86.0 (0.33)	89.3 (0.32)	81.5 (0.57)	73.2 (1.90)	83.4 (2.09)	91.1 (2.15)	24.3 (0.31)	28.4 (0.43)	15.3 (0.48)	19.1 (1.61)	44.7 (2.86)	29.8 (2.86)
Maine	92.8 (0.43)	93.0 (0.44)	74.0 (11.31)	92.1 (2.27)	87.0 (4.35)	98.1 (1.24)	30.6 (0.62)	30.7 (0.61)	20.2! (7.30)	41.3 (6.33)	34.8 (6.26)	24.1 (5.34)
Maryland	90.5 (0.21)	94.2 (0.21)	90.0 (0.34)	68.5 (1.15)	89.9 (1.06)	92.4 (1.11)	40.7 (0.33)	46.3 (0.40)	30.0 (0.53)	23.3 (0.99)	64.4 (1.34)	43.2 (2.14)
Massachusetts	90.8 (0.18)	94.3 (0.18)	86.6 (0.83)	70.5 (0.85)	86.6 (0.80)	92.6 (1.57)	44.4 (0.28)	47.3 (0.31)	30.2 (1.07)	21.5 (0.86)	62.7 (1.24)	47.8 (2.63)
Michigan	91.0 (0.16)	92.8 (0.16)	86.2 (0.49)	75.1 (1.28)	89.8 (0.99)	88.2 (1.50)	29.6 (0.27)	30.7 (0.27)	17.8 (0.73)	19.7 (1.15)	65.5 (1.54)	26.8 (1.94)
Minnesota	93.4 (0.20)	96.0 (0.14)	81.7 (1.65)	70.6 (2.42)	84.0 (1.30)	91.7 (2.05)	37.2 (0.40)	38.5 (0.45)	23.0 (1.98)	21.9 (1.61)	48.1 (2.19)	35.3 (3.68)
Mississippi	85.4 (0.34)	88.4 (0.39)	81.4 (0.60)	68.0 (3.11)	88.8 (2.33)	88.1 (3.25)	23.4 (0.43)	27.2 (0.53)	16.7 (0.54)	17.8 (2.69)	47.4 (4.15)	33.5 (5.85)
Missouri	90.3 (0.22)	91.4 (0.21)	86.6 (0.78)	75.6 (1.93)	91.8 (1.32)	89.1 (2.10)	29.6 (0.26)	30.4 (0.33)	19.2 (0.93)	23.1 (1.42)	63.0 (2.72)	26.5 (2.12)
Montana	93.4 (0.39)	94.2 (0.40)	‡ (†)	90.3 (3.20)	80.9 (7.21)	88.8 (4.05)	30.4 (0.80)	31.4 (0.78)	‡ (†)	31.2 (7.44)	40.5 (11.17)	13.8 (3.51)
Nebraska	91.8 (0.24)	95.0 (0.22)	88.6 (2.13)	66.0 (2.15)	80.3 (3.10)	84.3 (4.77)	32.9 (0.53)	35.2 (0.55)	22.6 (3.13)	13.8 (1.65)	44.7 (4.58)	25.4 (4.45)
Nevada	86.8 (0.29)	93.9 (0.27)	89.5 (1.09)	67.3 (0.89)	90.3 (0.88)	91.9 (1.67)	24.9 (0.41)	29.6 (0.59)	17.3 (1.29)	11.6 (0.64)	38.3 (1.54)	28.4 (2.87)
New Hampshire	92.9 (0.31)	94.0 (0.30)	72.8 (5.01)	74.6 (3.34)	89.4 (2.42)	90.2 (4.02)	37.2 (0.59)	37.3 (0.61)	13.8! (4.81)	20.4 (3.30)	62.7 (3.85)	35.0 (5.51)
New Jersey	90.1 (0.17)	94.7 (0.14)	88.0 (0.55)	75.2 (0.63)	92.4 (0.39)	94.1 (0.95)	40.6 (0.24)	44.8 (0.29)	25.4 (0.71)	20.6 (0.52)	70.9 (0.74)	48.9 (2.15)
New Mexico	85.3 (0.43)	95.5 (0.28)	89.1 (3.37)	76.5 (0.84)	87.1 (3.02)	95.3 (1.68)	27.5 (0.50)	42.2 (0.78)	22.6 (3.61)	15.3 (0.64)	56.2 (4.40)	33.7 (4.10)
New York	87.2 (0.12)	93.5 (0.12)	84.7 (0.42)	71.7 (0.44)	80.0 (0.47)	89.9 (0.95)	37.3 (0.18)	43.5 (0.21)	25.0 (0.46)	20.1 (0.42)	48.5 (0.66)	44.8 (1.52)
North Carolina	88.3 (0.17)	91.7 (0.17)	86.6 (0.35)	62.7 (1.16)	86.5 (1.31)	90.2 (1.47)	31.9 (0.23)	35.8 (0.25)	21.4 (0.54)	16.2 (0.88)	58.6 (1.68)	34.2 (2.07)
North Dakota	92.6 (0.51)	94.1 (0.41)	80.4 (7.18)	86.6 (4.34)	67.6 (8.97)	91.0 (5.22)	28.8 (1.00)	29.8 (1.11)	23.3! (8.35)	19.4 (4.75)	38.2 (8.59)	23.2! (7.29)
Ohio	90.5 (0.13)	91.9 (0.13)	85.4 (0.57)	77.4 (1.26)	86.8 (1.18)	89.1 (1.50)	28.8 (0.21)	29.9 (0.21)	17.6 (0.57)	20.3 (1.28)	59.6 (1.67)	27.7 (1.75)
Oklahoma	88.5 (0.28)	91.3 (0.25)	90.6 (0.89)	61.7 (1.67)	86.0 (2.16)	89.3 (1.01)	25.8 (0.38)	28.3 (0.44)	19.4 (1.39)	9.9 (0.98)	53.5 (3.84)	25.2 (1.82)
Oregon	90.2 (0.26)	94.0 (0.22)	88.6 (2.22)	62.5 (1.58)	86.9 (1.29)	90.5 (1.43)	34.2 (0.38)	36.1 (0.42)	27.6 (2.61)	15.9 (0.96)	51.0 (1.88)	30.6 (1.95)
Pennsylvania	91.1 (0.15)	93.2 (0.10)	87.6 (0.59)	71.4 (1.03)	85.7 (1.03)	92.1 (1.25)	31.8 (0.22)	33.3 (0.24)	19.8 (0.79)	16.8 (0.79)	59.2 (1.36)	28.7 (2.17)
Rhode Island	88.8 (0.45)	91.7 (0.40)	87.7 (1.94)	73.6 (2.30)	86.5 (2.81)	88.8 (4.31)	34.5 (0.71)	37.9 (0.81)	23.6 (2.99)	16.1 (1.75)	45.7 (4.23)	35.3 (5.65)
South Carolina	88.1 (0.25)	91.0 (0.28)	83.5 (0.66)	69.2 (1.73)	91.7 (1.83)	90.2 (1.78)	28.2 (0.31)	33.0 (0.40)	15.6 (0.65)	18.3 (1.35)	52.4 (3.04)	31.5 (3.14)
South Dakota	92.2 (0.46)	94.7 (0.39)	76.1 (7.61)	68.5 (6.39)	68.3 (9.62)	83.8 (7.59)	28.9 (0.92)	31.1 (0.99)	12.1! (5.65)	15.0 (4.32)	44.5 (8.72)	25.8! (7.75)
Tennessee	87.8 (0.20)	89.4 (0.20)	85.9 (0.54)	65.0 (1.66)	83.4 (1.83)	90.6 (1.52)	27.4 (0.29)	28.7 (0.31)	20.0 (0.72)	17.4 (1.25)	51.4 (2.45)	35.7 (2.39)
Texas	83.9 (0.13)	94.4 (0.10)	90.0 (0.27)	66.7 (0.28)	87.7 (0.47)	93.7 (0.72)	30.3 (0.14)	39.3 (0.20)	25.1 (0.44)	15.1 (0.21)	59.8 (0.71)	39.6 (1.21)
Utah	92.7 (0.33)	95.7 (0.24)	88.5 (4.08)	73.7 (1.79)	91.4 (1.79)	96.2 (1.74)	35.0 (0.51)	37.8 (0.54)	22.5 (5.57)	16.6 (1.23)	51.1 (3.62)	35.5 (3.63)
Vermont	93.4 (0.61)	93.6 (0.61)	‡ (†)	89.0 (4.72)	90.1 (7.83)	85.6 (6.87)	39.1 (1.00)	38.2 (0.97)	‡ (†)	35.9 (8.92)	80.9 (6.90)	51.8 (10.40)
Virginia	90.0 (0.17)	93.1 (0.15)	86.1 (0.47)	72.0 (1.13)	90.7 (0.52)	92.2 (1.10)	39.5 (0.29)	43.0 (0.32)	24.5 (0.65)	24.9 (0.92)	63.5 (1.01)	39.6 (2.03)
Washington	91.6 (0.15)	95.2 (0.14)	90.0 (1.02)	66.8 (0.93)	89.6 (0.48)	94.0 (0.69)	36.7 (0.31)	37.9 (0.32)	27.3 (1.55)	16.2 (0.63)	55.0 (1.03)	36.7 (1.58)
West Virginia	88.1 (0.39)	88.0 (0.40)	91.4 (1.78)	76.2 (5.27)	98.7 (1.06)	82.0 (4.38)	21.4 (0.56)	21.4 (0.58)	13.4 (1.77)	24.4 (4.66)	61.6 (7.39)	18.3 (4.52)
Wisconsin	92.3 (0.19)	94.3 (0.16)	85.2 (1.10)	71.6 (1.77)	83.0 (2.13)	95.3 (1.65)	30.2 (0.37)	31.6 (0.37)	15.8 (1.45)	16.5 (1.34)	45.8 (2.92)	36.8 (3.72)
Wyoming	92.7 (0.60)	93.8 (0.53)	‡ (†)	81.0 (3.83)	‡ (†)	95.1 (3.64)	27.0 (0.83)	28.5 (0.94)	‡ (†)	10.1 (2.12)	‡ (†)	‡ (†)

†Not applicable.
!Interpret data with caution. The coefficient of variation (CV) for this estimate is between 30 and 50 percent.
‡Reporting standards not met. Either there are too few cases for a reliable estimate or the coefficient of variation (CV) is 50 percent or greater.
[1]Includes completion of high school through equivalency programs, such as a GED program.
[2]Total includes racial/ethnic groups not shown separately.

NOTE: Data are based on sample surveys of the entire population in the given age range residing within the United States, including both noninstitutionalized persons (e.g., those living in households, college housing, or military housing located within the United States) and institutionalized persons (e.g., those living in prisons, nursing facilities, or other healthcare facilities). Race categories exclude persons of Hispanic ethnicity.
SOURCE: U.S. Department of Commerce, Census Bureau, American Community Survey (ACS), 2018 (This table was prepared February 2020.)

Table 104.88. Number of persons age 25 and over and rates of high school completion and bachelor's degree attainment among persons in this age group, by sex and state: 2018

[Standard errors appear in parentheses]

State	Number of persons age 25 and over (in thousands)						Percent with high school completion[1] or higher						Percent with bachelor's or higher degree					
	Total		Male		Female		Total		Male		Female		Total		Male		Female	
1	2		3		4		5		6		7		8		9		10	
United States	**223,246**	**(53.4)**	**107,863**	**(31.2)**	**115,383**	**(32.6)**	**88.3**	**(0.04)**	**87.7**	**(0.05)**	**88.9**	**(0.05)**	**32.6**	**(0.07)**	**31.9**	**(0.07)**	**33.3**	**(0.08)**
Alabama	3,340	(3.9)	1,574	(3.4)	1,766	(3.3)	86.5	(0.28)	84.7	(0.40)	88.1	(0.31)	25.3	(0.34)	24.4	(0.39)	26.1	(0.44)
Alaska	484	(2.1)	253	(2.2)	231	(1.9)	94.0	(0.52)	94.0	(0.58)	93.9	(0.73)	30.1	(1.13)	26.7	(1.49)	33.8	(1.39)
Arizona	4,841	(3.5)	2,369	(2.7)	2,471	(2.7)	87.6	(0.17)	87.6	(0.28)	87.7	(0.23)	29.6	(0.26)	29.8	(0.35)	29.4	(0.33)
Arkansas	2,019	(3.6)	969	(3.3)	1,050	(2.3)	87.3	(0.30)	86.4	(0.44)	88.2	(0.36)	23.3	(0.40)	22.3	(0.49)	24.2	(0.53)
California	26,828	(8.4)	13,142	(6.2)	13,686	(6.3)	83.9	(0.09)	83.7	(0.11)	84.1	(0.12)	34.4	(0.11)	34.1	(0.13)	34.7	(0.16)
Colorado	3,898	(4.1)	1,938	(3.5)	1,961	(2.9)	92.2	(0.19)	91.9	(0.28)	92.4	(0.24)	42.0	(0.29)	41.0	(0.41)	43.0	(0.36)
Connecticut	2,493	(2.3)	1,188	(2.3)	1,305	(1.8)	90.8	(0.24)	90.1	(0.36)	91.5	(0.28)	39.7	(0.35)	38.8	(0.51)	40.5	(0.39)
Delaware	680	(1.5)	322	(1.2)	358	(1.2)	89.6	(0.57)	88.2	(0.72)	91.0	(0.69)	31.2	(0.77)	29.2	(0.98)	33.0	(1.02)
District of Columbia	501	(0.9)	235	(0.7)	266	(0.8)	91.8	(0.57)	91.9	(0.75)	91.6	(0.75)	60.2	(0.61)	61.4	(0.91)	59.3	(0.86)
Florida	15,301	(7.2)	7,330	(5.6)	7,971	(4.8)	88.5	(0.09)	87.8	(0.14)	89.1	(0.12)	30.5	(0.15)	30.3	(0.19)	30.6	(0.21)
Georgia	6,982	(6.2)	3,311	(4.5)	3,671	(4.1)	87.5	(0.18)	86.3	(0.26)	88.6	(0.21)	32.0	(0.21)	30.9	(0.23)	33.0	(0.30)
Hawaii	999	(2.0)	492	(1.6)	507	(1.4)	91.7	(0.42)	92.0	(0.52)	91.4	(0.50)	33.2	(0.65)	31.6	(0.84)	34.7	(0.77)
Idaho	1,144	(2.6)	565	(2.0)	579	(2.3)	90.7	(0.39)	89.8	(0.55)	91.6	(0.49)	27.4	(0.52)	27.5	(0.66)	27.3	(0.74)
Illinois	8,704	(6.0)	4,197	(4.9)	4,507	(4.3)	89.4	(0.14)	88.7	(0.20)	90.1	(0.18)	35.2	(0.21)	34.3	(0.27)	36.0	(0.26)
Indiana	4,470	(4.2)	2,157	(3.6)	2,313	(3.4)	88.8	(0.22)	88.2	(0.28)	89.3	(0.27)	26.9	(0.29)	26.3	(0.35)	27.5	(0.38)
Iowa	2,109	(3.4)	1,030	(2.8)	1,079	(3.1)	92.2	(0.27)	91.5	(0.40)	92.9	(0.29)	28.6	(0.49)	27.6	(0.64)	29.6	(0.54)
Kansas	1,910	(3.7)	936	(3.0)	975	(2.5)	90.9	(0.27)	90.0	(0.40)	91.8	(0.31)	33.4	(0.38)	32.0	(0.52)	34.7	(0.49)
Kentucky	3,041	(4.0)	1,464	(3.1)	1,578	(2.7)	87.1	(0.28)	85.9	(0.38)	88.1	(0.34)	25.2	(0.30)	24.0	(0.39)	26.2	(0.36)
Louisiana	3,123	(4.5)	1,488	(3.8)	1,635	(3.1)	86.0	(0.33)	84.4	(0.44)	87.5	(0.36)	24.3	(0.31)	22.2	(0.41)	26.2	(0.44)
Maine	985	(1.8)	472	(1.7)	513	(1.6)	92.8	(0.43)	92.1	(0.53)	93.5	(0.52)	30.6	(0.62)	28.1	(0.88)	33.0	(0.77)
Maryland	4,168	(3.9)	1,975	(2.5)	2,194	(3.1)	90.5	(0.21)	89.6	(0.30)	91.4	(0.26)	40.7	(0.33)	39.9	(0.44)	41.5	(0.37)
Massachusetts	4,839	(3.5)	2,309	(2.9)	2,530	(2.6)	90.8	(0.18)	90.4	(0.24)	91.1	(0.22)	44.4	(0.28)	44.1	(0.37)	44.8	(0.37)
Michigan	6,877	(4.9)	3,329	(4.5)	3,549	(4.6)	91.0	(0.16)	90.4	(0.21)	91.7	(0.19)	29.6	(0.27)	29.3	(0.34)	29.8	(0.32)
Minnesota	3,816	(5.7)	1,880	(5.2)	1,936	(4.4)	93.4	(0.20)	92.8	(0.30)	94.1	(0.27)	37.2	(0.40)	35.7	(0.44)	38.6	(0.53)
Mississippi	1,978	(4.1)	929	(2.9)	1,049	(2.7)	85.4	(0.34)	83.3	(0.43)	87.3	(0.42)	23.4	(0.43)	21.0	(0.50)	25.6	(0.51)
Missouri	4,183	(4.3)	2,007	(3.4)	2,177	(3.5)	90.3	(0.22)	89.8	(0.29)	90.9	(0.30)	29.6	(0.26)	28.7	(0.35)	30.4	(0.32)
Montana	739	(2.1)	367	(2.0)	372	(2.1)	93.4	(0.39)	92.9	(0.57)	93.9	(0.56)	30.4	(0.80)	28.7	(0.96)	32.0	(1.07)
Nebraska	1,270	(2.5)	623	(2.3)	646	(2.2)	91.8	(0.24)	90.9	(0.36)	92.7	(0.34)	32.9	(0.53)	31.8	(0.68)	33.9	(0.73)
Nevada	2,098	(2.2)	1,042	(1.6)	1,056	(1.5)	86.8	(0.29)	86.6	(0.35)	86.9	(0.38)	24.9	(0.41)	24.7	(0.52)	25.1	(0.50)
New Hampshire	971	(1.7)	476	(1.4)	495	(1.5)	92.9	(0.31)	92.0	(0.52)	93.8	(0.37)	37.2	(0.59)	36.1	(0.74)	38.1	(0.81)
New Jersey	6,185	(3.7)	2,959	(3.4)	3,226	(2.8)	90.1	(0.17)	89.7	(0.23)	90.4	(0.19)	40.6	(0.24)	40.1	(0.31)	40.9	(0.28)
New Mexico	1,412	(3.2)	689	(2.8)	723	(2.1)	85.3	(0.43)	83.8	(0.65)	86.7	(0.51)	27.5	(0.50)	26.8	(0.71)	28.1	(0.62)
New York	13,679	(5.3)	6,497	(4.7)	7,182	(4.3)	87.2	(0.12)	87.1	(0.16)	87.4	(0.16)	37.3	(0.18)	36.0	(0.26)	38.4	(0.22)
North Carolina	7,105	(5.9)	3,370	(5.2)	3,736	(4.5)	88.3	(0.17)	86.6	(0.27)	89.8	(0.18)	31.9	(0.23)	30.4	(0.30)	33.2	(0.30)
North Dakota	501	(2.5)	256	(2.2)	245	(1.9)	92.6	(0.51)	92.7	(0.69)	92.4	(0.66)	28.8	(1.00)	26.1	(1.20)	31.6	(1.34)
Ohio	8,032	(5.7)	3,861	(4.5)	4,171	(3.9)	90.5	(0.13)	90.0	(0.17)	91.0	(0.16)	28.8	(0.21)	28.3	(0.27)	29.4	(0.24)
Oklahoma	2,613	(4.4)	1,266	(3.7)	1,347	(3.5)	88.5	(0.28)	87.4	(0.34)	89.5	(0.38)	25.8	(0.38)	25.1	(0.49)	26.6	(0.46)
Oregon	2,958	(3.3)	1,447	(2.5)	1,511	(2.5)	90.2	(0.26)	89.1	(0.36)	91.3	(0.28)	34.2	(0.38)	33.5	(0.49)	34.9	(0.46)
Pennsylvania	8,996	(5.8)	4,320	(5.5)	4,676	(4.3)	91.1	(0.15)	90.8	(0.18)	91.5	(0.20)	31.8	(0.22)	31.4	(0.27)	32.2	(0.28)
Rhode Island	741	(1.4)	356	(1.5)	385	(1.0)	88.8	(0.45)	88.1	(0.61)	89.5	(0.58)	34.5	(0.71)	34.3	(0.83)	34.7	(0.97)
South Carolina	3,490	(3.9)	1,642	(3.3)	1,848	(3.0)	88.1	(0.25)	86.7	(0.36)	89.3	(0.30)	28.2	(0.31)	27.7	(0.44)	28.7	(0.40)
South Dakota	580	(2.3)	290	(2.0)	290	(2.1)	92.2	(0.46)	91.5	(0.64)	92.9	(0.61)	28.9	(0.92)	28.0	(1.11)	29.8	(1.24)
Tennessee	4,641	(4.7)	2,215	(3.7)	2,426	(3.2)	87.8	(0.20)	87.2	(0.25)	88.3	(0.25)	27.4	(0.29)	26.8	(0.33)	27.9	(0.37)
Texas	18,483	(8.8)	9,011	(6.6)	9,472	(5.7)	83.9	(0.13)	83.3	(0.18)	84.4	(0.14)	30.3	(0.14)	29.8	(0.17)	30.7	(0.19)
Utah	1,874	(2.6)	931	(2.2)	943	(2.6)	92.7	(0.33)	92.5	(0.42)	92.9	(0.38)	35.0	(0.51)	36.7	(0.66)	33.4	(0.64)
Vermont	448	(1.5)	217	(1.4)	231	(1.3)	93.4	(0.61)	92.1	(0.88)	94.6	(0.60)	39.1	(1.00)	35.8	(1.24)	42.2	(1.41)
Virginia	5,820	(5.7)	2,804	(5.0)	3,017	(3.7)	90.0	(0.17)	89.0	(0.24)	91.0	(0.20)	39.5	(0.29)	39.1	(0.33)	39.8	(0.39)
Washington	5,222	(4.2)	2,580	(3.9)	2,642	(3.1)	91.6	(0.15)	91.2	(0.22)	92.0	(0.20)	36.7	(0.31)	36.4	(0.37)	36.9	(0.35)
West Virginia	1,281	(2.3)	623	(1.6)	658	(1.7)	88.1	(0.39)	86.7	(0.54)	89.3	(0.51)	21.4	(0.56)	20.8	(0.67)	21.9	(0.71)
Wisconsin	3,999	(4.0)	1,962	(3.8)	2,037	(3.9)	92.3	(0.19)	91.5	(0.26)	93.1	(0.24)	30.2	(0.37)	28.6	(0.43)	31.7	(0.47)
Wyoming	394	(1.8)	200	(1.7)	194	(1.3)	92.7	(0.60)	92.5	(0.80)	93.0	(0.76)	27.0	(0.83)	25.6	(1.10)	28.4	(1.23)

[1] Includes completion of high school through equivalency programs, such as a GED program.

NOTE: Data are based on sample surveys of the entire population in the given age range residing within the United States, including both noninstitutionalized persons (e.g., those living in households, college housing, or military housing located within the United States) and institutionalized persons (e.g., those living in prisons, nursing facilities, or other healthcare facilities). Detail may not sum to totals because of rounding.

SOURCE: U.S. Department of Commerce, Census Bureau, American Community Survey (ACS), 2018. (This table was prepared February 2020.)

Table 203.10. Enrollment in public elementary and secondary schools, by level and grade: Selected years, fall 1980 through fall 2029

[In thousands]

		Elementary												Secondary					
Year	All grades	Total	Pre-kinder-garten	Kinder-garten	1st grade	2nd grade	3rd grade	4th grade	5th grade	6th grade	7th grade	8th grade	Un-graded	Total	9th grade	10th grade	11th grade	12th grade	Un-graded[1]
1	2	3	4	5	6	7	8	9	10	11	12	13	14	15	16	17	18	19	20
1980	40,877	27,647	96	2,593	2,894	2,800	2,893	3,107	3,130	3,038	3,085	3,086	924	13,231	3,377	3,368	3,195	2,925	366
1985	39,422	27,034	151	3,041	3,239	2,941	2,895	2,771	2,776	2,789	2,938	2,982	511	12,388	3,439	3,230	2,866	2,550	303
1990	41,217	29,876	303	3,306	3,499	3,327	3,297	3,248	3,197	3,110	3,067	2,979	541	11,341	3,169	2,896	2,612	2,381	284
1991	42,047	30,503	375	3,311	3,556	3,360	3,334	3,315	3,268	3,239	3,181	3,020	542	11,544	3,313	2,915	2,645	2,392	278
1992	42,823	31,086	505	3,313	3,542	3,431	3,361	3,342	3,325	3,303	3,299	3,129	536	11,737	3,352	3,027	2,656	2,431	272
1993	43,465	31,502	545	3,377	3,529	3,429	3,437	3,361	3,350	3,356	3,355	3,249	513	11,963	3,487	3,050	2,751	2,424	250
1994	44,111	31,896	603	3,444	3,593	3,440	3,439	3,426	3,372	3,381	3,404	3,302	492	12,215	3,604	3,131	2,748	2,488	244
1995	44,840	32,338	637	3,536	3,671	3,507	3,445	3,431	3,438	3,395	3,422	3,356	500	12,502	3,704	3,237	2,826	2,487	247
1996	45,611	32,762	670	3,532	3,770	3,600	3,524	3,454	3,453	3,494	3,464	3,403	399	12,849	3,801	3,323	2,930	2,586	208
1997	46,127	33,071	695	3,503	3,755	3,689	3,597	3,507	3,458	3,492	3,520	3,415	440	13,056	3,819	3,376	2,972	2,673	216
1998	46,539	33,344	729	3,443	3,727	3,681	3,696	3,592	3,520	3,497	3,530	3,480	449	13,195	3,856	3,382	3,021	2,722	214
1999	46,857	33,486	751	3,397	3,684	3,656	3,691	3,686	3,604	3,564	3,541	3,497	415	13,371	3,935	3,415	3,034	2,782	205
2000	47,204	33,686	776	3,382	3,636	3,634	3,676	3,711	3,707	3,663	3,629	3,538	334	13,517	3,963	3,491	3,083	2,803	177
2001	47,672	33,936	865	3,379	3,614	3,593	3,653	3,695	3,727	3,769	3,720	3,616	304	13,736	4,012	3,528	3,174	2,863	159
2002	48,183	34,114	915	3,434	3,594	3,565	3,623	3,669	3,711	3,788	3,821	3,709	285	14,069	4,105	3,584	3,229	2,990	161
2003	48,540	34,201	950	3,503	3,613	3,544	3,611	3,619	3,685	3,772	3,841	3,809	255	14,339	4,190	3,675	3,277	3,046	150
2004	48,795	34,178	990	3,544	3,663	3,560	3,580	3,612	3,635	3,735	3,818	3,825	215	14,618	4,281	3,750	3,369	3,094	122
2005	49,113	34,204	1,036	3,619	3,691	3,606	3,586	3,578	3,633	3,670	3,777	3,802	205	14,909	4,287	3,866	3,454	3,180	121
2006	49,316	34,235	1,084	3,631	3,751	3,641	3,627	3,586	3,602	3,660	3,716	3,766	170	15,081	4,260	3,882	3,551	3,277	110
2007	49,291	34,204	1,081	3,609	3,750	3,704	3,659	3,624	3,600	3,628	3,700	3,709	139	15,086	4,200	3,863	3,557	3,375	92
2008	49,266	34,286	1,180	3,640	3,708	3,699	3,708	3,647	3,629	3,614	3,653	3,692	117	14,980	4,123	3,822	3,548	3,400	87
2009	49,361	34,409	1,223	3,678	3,729	3,665	3,707	3,701	3,652	3,644	3,641	3,651	119	14,952	4,080	3,809	3,541	3,432	90
2010	49,484	34,625	1,279	3,682	3,754	3,701	3,686	3,711	3,718	3,682	3,676	3,659	77	14,860	4,008	3,800	3,538	3,472	42
2011	49,522	34,773	1,291	3,746	3,773	3,713	3,703	3,672	3,699	3,724	3,696	3,679	77	14,749	3,957	3,751	3,546	3,452	43
2012	49,771	35,018	1,307	3,831	3,824	3,729	3,719	3,690	3,673	3,723	3,746	3,699	76	14,753	3,975	3,730	3,528	3,477	43
2013	50,045	35,251	1,328	3,834	3,885	3,791	3,738	3,708	3,697	3,684	3,748	3,753	85	14,794	3,980	3,761	3,526	3,476	52
2014	50,313	35,370	1,369	3,772	3,863	3,857	3,806	3,719	3,719	3,710	3,710	3,757	87	14,943	4,033	3,794	3,568	3,496	52
2015[2]	50,438	35,388	1,402	3,713	3,768	3,842	3,869	3,793	3,733	3,731	3,732	3,719	87	15,050	4,019	3,846	3,598	3,537	49
2016[3]	50,615	35,477	1,426	3,699	3,694	3,761	3,874	3,858	3,814	3,754	3,761	3,749	88	15,138	3,986	3,860	3,669	3,571	52
2017[2]	50,686	35,496	1,471	3,684	3,667	3,684	3,788	3,859	3,877	3,827	3,777	3,772	89	15,190	3,996	3,834	3,677	3,631	52
	Projected																		
2018	50,650	35,443	1,474	3,691	3,639	3,658	3,709	3,777	3,872	3,893	3,852	3,789	89	15,206	4,021	3,843	3,652	3,639	52
2019	50,634	35,402	1,483	3,714	3,645	3,629	3,683	3,699	3,790	3,888	3,919	3,864	89	15,232	4,038	3,867	3,661	3,615	52
2020	50,654	35,293	1,489	3,728	3,665	3,636	3,654	3,672	3,711	3,805	3,914	3,931	88	15,361	4,119	3,884	3,683	3,623	52
2021	50,643	35,094	1,484	3,716	3,679	3,655	3,661	3,644	3,684	3,726	3,830	3,926	88	15,549	4,190	3,961	3,700	3,646	52
2022	50,721	35,019	1,517	3,798	3,667	3,669	3,680	3,650	3,656	3,700	3,750	3,842	88	15,703	4,185	4,030	3,773	3,662	53
2023	50,768	35,022	1,525	3,819	3,749	3,658	3,695	3,670	3,662	3,671	3,724	3,763	89	15,746	4,095	4,025	3,839	3,735	52
2024	50,758	35,123	1,532	3,838	3,769	3,739	3,683	3,684	3,682	3,677	3,695	3,736	89	15,635	4,010	3,939	3,834	3,799	52
2025	50,704	35,267	1,539	3,854	3,787	3,759	3,764	3,672	3,696	3,697	3,701	3,707	89	15,438	3,982	3,857	3,752	3,795	52
2026	50,672	35,452	1,545	3,868	3,804	3,777	3,785	3,753	3,685	3,711	3,721	3,713	90	15,220	3,951	3,829	3,674	3,714	52
2027	50,734	35,641	1,549	3,879	3,817	3,794	3,803	3,774	3,766	3,700	3,735	3,733	90	15,093	3,958	3,800	3,648	3,637	52
2028	50,885	35,818	1,552	3,888	3,828	3,807	3,820	3,792	3,786	3,782	3,724	3,748	91	15,067	3,979	3,806	3,620	3,610	52
2029	51,068	35,987	1,555	3,894	3,837	3,818	3,834	3,809	3,805	3,802	3,806	3,736	91	15,081	3,994	3,827	3,626	3,582	52

[1]Includes students reported as being enrolled in grade 13.

[2]The prekindergarten, elementary total, and "all grades" counts include imputations for prekindergarten enrollment in California and Oregon.

[3]The prekindergarten, elementary total, and "all grades" counts include imputations for prekindergarten enrollment in California.

NOTE: Due to changes in reporting and imputation practices, prekindergarten enrollment for years prior to 1992 represent an undercount compared to later years. The total ungraded counts of students were prorated to the elementary and secondary levels based on prior reports. Detail may not sum to totals because of rounding. Some data have been revised from previously published figures.

SOURCE: U.S. Department of Education, National Center for Education Statistics, *Statistics of Public Elementary and Secondary School Systems, 1980–81;* Common Core of Data (CCD), "State Nonfiscal Survey of Public Elementary/Secondary Education," 1985–86 through 2017–18; and National Elementary and Secondary Enrollment Projection Model, 1972 through 2029. (This table was prepared December 2019.)

Table 203.20. Enrollment in public elementary and secondary schools, by region, state, and jurisdiction: Selected years, fall 1990 through fall 2029

Region, state, and jurisdiction	Actual total enrollment													Percent change in total enrollment, 2012 to 2017	Projected enrollment						Percent change in total enrollment, 2017 to 2029
	Fall 1990	Fall 2000	Fall 2007	Fall 2008	Fall 2009	Fall 2010	Fall 2011	Fall 2012	Fall 2013	Fall 2014	Fall 2015[1]	Fall 2016[2]	Fall 2017[1]		Fall 2018	Fall 2019	Fall 2020	Fall 2021	Fall 2022	Fall 2029	
1	2	3	4	5	6	7	8	9	10	11	12	13	14	15	16	17	18	19	20	21	22
United States	**41,216,683**	**47,203,539**	**49,290,559**	**49,265,572**	**49,360,982**	**49,484,181**	**49,521,669**	**49,771,118**	**50,044,522**	**50,312,581**	**50,438,043**	**50,615,189**	**50,685,567**	**1.8**	**50,649,800**	**50,634,000**	**50,654,200**	**50,643,100**	**50,721,200**	**51,068,100**	**0.8**
Region																					
Northeast	7,281,763	8,222,127	8,122,022	8,052,985	8,092,029	8,071,335	7,953,981	7,959,128	7,961,243	7,979,856	7,933,762	7,959,304	7,946,536	-0.2	7,915,600	7,889,500	7,866,800	7,838,300	7,824,100	7,705,000	-3.0
Midwest	9,943,761	10,729,987	10,770,210	10,742,973	10,672,171	10,609,604	10,573,792	10,559,230	10,572,920	10,560,539	10,555,579	10,538,947	10,523,753	-0.3	10,488,200	10,455,400	10,437,400	10,413,800	10,400,300	10,300,900	-2.1
South	14,807,016	17,007,261	18,422,773	18,490,770	18,651,889	18,805,000	18,955,932	19,128,376	19,298,714	19,506,193	19,641,472	19,749,816	19,824,469	3.6	19,849,000	19,878,600	19,926,300	19,975,000	20,065,800	20,519,200	3.5
West	9,184,143	11,244,164	11,975,554	11,978,844	11,944,893	11,998,242	12,037,964	12,124,384	12,211,645	12,265,993	12,307,230	12,367,122	12,390,809	2.2	12,397,100	12,410,500	12,423,700	12,416,000	12,431,000	12,543,100	1.2
State																					
Alabama	721,806	739,992	742,919	745,668	748,889	755,552	744,621	744,637	746,204	744,164	743,789	744,930	742,444	-0.3	737,200	733,500	732,900	733,500	735,200	743,900	0.2
Alaska	113,903	133,356	131,029	130,662	131,661	132,104	131,167	131,489	130,944	131,176	132,477	132,737	132,872	1.1	133,200	133,500	134,100	134,600	135,500	138,100	4.0
Arizona	639,853	877,696	1,087,447	1,087,817	1,077,831	1,071,751	1,080,319	1,089,384	1,102,445	1,111,695	1,109,040	1,123,137	1,110,851	2.0	1,111,000	1,112,600	1,113,200	1,113,400	1,115,400	1,139,300	2.6
Arkansas	436,286	449,959	479,016	478,965	480,559	482,114	483,114	486,157	489,979	490,917	492,132	493,447	496,085	2.0	496,100	496,300	496,600	497,400	499,400	510,900	3.0
California	4,950,474	6,140,814	6,343,471	6,322,528	6,263,438	6,289,578	6,287,834	6,299,451	6,312,623	6,312,161	6,305,347	6,309,138	6,304,266	0.1	6,285,300	6,269,700	6,251,900	6,220,500	6,200,300	6,112,700	-3.0
Colorado	574,213	724,508	801,867	818,443	832,368	843,316	854,265	863,561	876,999	889,006	899,112	905,019	910,280	5.4	912,600	915,000	917,600	918,300	921,800	951,100	4.5
Connecticut	469,123	562,179	570,626	567,198	563,968	560,546	554,437	550,954	546,200	542,678	537,933	535,118	531,288	-3.6	524,300	517,900	511,900	505,600	501,100	478,000	-10.0
Delaware	99,658	114,676	122,574	125,430	126,801	129,403	128,946	129,026	131,687	134,042	134,847	136,264	136,293	5.6	136,900	137,500	138,000	138,200	138,800	138,800	1.8
District of Columbia	80,694	68,925	78,422	68,681	69,433	71,284	73,911	76,140	78,153	80,958	84,024	85,850	87,315	14.7	87,200	89,700	91,800	94,000	96,100	99,800	14.3
Florida	1,861,592	2,434,821	2,666,811	2,631,020	2,634,522	2,643,347	2,668,156	2,692,162	2,720,744	2,756,944	2,792,234	2,816,791	2,832,424	5.2	2,849,400	2,865,200	2,887,200	2,908,600	2,935,700	3,109,900	9.8
Georgia	1,151,687	1,444,937	1,649,589	1,655,792	1,667,685	1,677,067	1,685,016	1,703,332	1,723,909	1,744,437	1,757,237	1,764,346	1,768,642	3.8	1,767,200	1,765,600	1,765,900	1,767,200	1,770,700	1,785,300	0.9
Hawaii	171,708	184,360	179,897	179,478	180,196	179,601	182,706	184,760	186,825	182,384	181,995	181,550	180,837	-2.1	180,600	180,300	179,500	178,500	177,400	168,600	-6.8
Idaho	220,840	245,117	272,119	275,051	276,299	275,859	279,873	284,834	296,476	290,885	292,277	297,200	301,186	5.7	303,500	305,900	308,100	310,300	312,600	326,200	8.3
Illinois	1,821,407	2,048,792	2,112,805	2,119,707	2,104,175	2,091,654	2,083,097	2,072,880	2,066,990	2,050,239	2,041,779	2,026,718	2,005,153	-3.3	2,000,200	1,991,600	1,984,800	1,976,800	1,966,000	1,872,000	-6.6
Indiana	954,525	989,267	1,046,764	1,046,147	1,046,661	1,047,232	1,040,765	1,041,369	1,047,385	1,046,269	1,046,757	1,049,547	1,054,187	1.2	1,053,400	1,050,400	1,050,200	1,051,100	1,052,500	1,065,700	1.1
Iowa	483,652	495,080	485,115	487,559	491,842	495,775	495,870	499,825	502,964	505,311	508,014	509,831	511,850	2.4	511,700	512,600	513,800	514,100	516,400	521,800	1.9
Kansas	437,034	470,610	468,295	471,060	474,489	483,701	486,108	489,043	496,440	497,275	495,884	494,347	497,088	1.6	495,100	493,700	492,400	490,300	489,200	478,900	-3.7
Kentucky	636,401	665,850	666,225	670,030	680,089	673,128	681,987	685,167	677,389	688,640	686,598	684,017	680,978	-0.6	678,900	677,000	676,000	674,800	675,300	683,100	0.3
Louisiana	784,757	743,089	681,038	684,873	690,915	696,558	703,390	710,903	711,491	716,800	718,711	716,293	715,135	0.6	710,600	706,800	703,900	702,800	702,700	700,900	-2.0
Maine	215,149	207,037	196,245	192,935	189,225	189,077	188,969	185,739	183,995	182,470	181,613	180,512	180,473	-2.8	179,200	178,100	177,300	176,700	176,100	174,500	-3.3
Maryland	715,176	852,920	845,700	843,861	848,412	852,211	854,086	859,638	866,169	874,514	879,601	886,221	893,684	4.0	898,800	904,800	908,300	911,000	914,600	910,500	1.9
Massachusetts	834,314	975,150	962,958	958,910	957,053	955,563	953,369	954,773	955,739	955,844	964,026	964,514	964,791	1.0	963,100	960,800	958,400	955,100	953,600	945,400	-2.0
Michigan	1,584,431	1,720,626	1,692,739	1,659,921	1,649,082	1,587,067	1,573,537	1,555,370	1,548,841	1,537,922	1,536,231	1,528,666	1,516,398	-2.5	1,499,800	1,484,200	1,473,200	1,461,600	1,452,300	1,421,500	-6.3
Minnesota	756,374	854,340	837,578	836,048	837,053	838,037	839,738	845,404	850,973	857,235	864,384	875,021	884,944	4.7	892,200	897,200	903,300	907,800	912,200	929,300	5.0
Mississippi	502,417	497,871	494,122	491,962	492,481	490,526	490,619	493,650	492,586	490,917	487,200	483,150	478,321	-3.1	471,400	465,500	460,600	456,400	452,500	427,100	-10.7
Missouri	816,558	912,744	917,188	917,871	917,982	918,710	916,584	917,900	918,288	917,785	919,234	915,040	915,472	-0.3	913,100	911,800	911,700	911,100	912,600	918,100	0.3
Montana	152,974	154,875	142,823	141,899	141,807	141,693	142,349	142,908	144,129	144,532	145,319	146,375	149,474	4.6	150,400	151,500	152,400	153,100	154,100	159,500	6.7
Nebraska	274,081	286,199	291,244	292,590	295,368	298,500	301,296	303,505	307,677	312,635	316,014	319,194	323,766	6.7	325,900	328,300	330,400	331,900	333,800	345,700	6.8
Nevada	201,316	340,706	429,362	433,371	428,947	437,149	439,634	445,707	451,831	459,189	467,527	473,744	485,785	9.0	492,200	499,300	506,200	512,600	519,700	554,000	14.0
New Hampshire	172,785	208,461	200,772	197,934	197,140	194,711	191,900	188,974	186,310	184,670	182,425	180,888	179,433	-5.0	177,900	176,400	174,600	173,000	171,600	166,100	-7.4
New Jersey	1,089,646	1,313,405	1,382,348	1,381,420	1,396,029	1,402,548	1,356,431	1,372,203	1,370,295	1,400,579	1,408,845	1,410,421	1,408,102	2.6	1,402,200	1,396,800	1,392,000	1,385,600	1,381,300	1,353,100	-3.9
New Mexico	301,881	320,306	329,040	330,245	334,419	338,122	337,225	338,220	339,244	340,365	335,694	336,263	334,345	-1.1	330,600	327,200	323,700	320,100	317,000	294,200	-12.0
New York	2,598,337	2,882,188	2,765,435	2,740,592	2,766,052	2,734,955	2,704,718	2,710,703	2,732,770	2,741,185	2,711,626	2,729,776	2,724,663	0.5	2,718,900	2,715,500	2,710,800	2,704,500	2,704,400	2,661,500	-2.3
North Carolina	1,086,871	1,293,638	1,489,492	1,488,645	1,483,397	1,490,605	1,507,864	1,518,465	1,530,857	1,548,895	1,544,934	1,550,062	1,553,513	2.3	1,550,400	1,548,600	1,550,200	1,551,800	1,563,200	1,598,400	2.9
North Dakota	117,825	109,201	95,059	94,728	95,073	96,323	97,646	101,111	103,947	106,586	108,644	109,706	111,920	10.7	111,100	113,000	115,100	117,000	119,000	130,300	16.5
Ohio	1,771,089	1,835,049	1,827,184	1,817,163	1,764,297	1,754,191	1,740,030	1,729,916	1,724,111	1,724,810	1,716,585	1,710,143	1,704,399	-1.5	1,690,900	1,679,900	1,671,100	1,662,400	1,657,200	1,631,400	-4.3
Oklahoma	579,087	623,110	642,065	645,108	654,802	659,911	666,120	673,483	681,848	688,511	692,878	693,903	695,092	3.2	697,400	698,500	699,900	700,100	702,500	709,900	2.1
Oregon	472,394	546,231	565,586	575,393	582,839	570,720	568,208	587,564	593,000	601,318	608,825	606,277	608,014	3.5	610,200	612,600	616,200	619,000	623,000	637,100	4.8
Pennsylvania	1,667,834	1,814,311	1,801,971	1,775,029	1,785,993	1,793,284	1,771,395	1,763,677	1,755,236	1,743,160	1,717,414	1,727,497	1,726,809	-2.1	1,719,900	1,714,700	1,713,800	1,711,000	1,709,800	1,704,500	-1.3
Rhode Island	138,813	157,347	147,629	145,342	145,118	143,793	142,854	142,481	142,008	141,959	142,014	142,150	142,949	0.3	143,200	142,800	142,100	141,600	141,200	139,900	-2.1

See notes at end of table.

Table 203.20. Enrollment in public elementary and secondary schools, by region, state, and jurisdiction: Selected years, fall 1990 through fall 2029—Continued

Region, state, and jurisdiction	Actual total enrollment													Percent change in total enroll-ment, 2012 to 2017	Projected enrollment						Percent change in total enroll-ment, 2017 to 2029
	Fall 1990	Fall 2000	Fall 2007	Fall 2008	Fall 2009	Fall 2010	Fall 2011	Fall 2012	Fall 2013	Fall 2014	Fall 2015[1]	Fall 2016[2]	Fall 2017[1]		Fall 2018	Fall 2019	Fall 2020	Fall 2021	Fall 2022	Fall 2029	
1	2	3	4	5	6	7	8	9	10	11	12	13	14	15	16	17	18	19	20	21	22
South Carolina	622,112	677,411	712,317	718,113	723,143	725,838	727,186	735,998	745,657	756,523	763,533	771,250	777,507	5.6	780,200	783,800	787,900	792,500	797,700	812,500	4.5
South Dakota	129,164	128,603	121,606	126,429	123,713	126,128	128,016	130,471	130,890	133,040	134,253	136,302	137,823	5.6	139,000	140,500	142,000	143,200	144,500	149,800	8.7
Tennessee	824,595	909,161	964,259	971,950	972,549	987,422	999,693	993,496	993,556	995,475	1,001,235	1,001,562	1,001,967	0.9	1,000,200	999,000	1,000,200	1,002,300	1,006,800	1,043,600	4.2
Texas	3,382,887	4,059,619	4,674,832	4,752,148	4,850,210	4,935,715	5,000,470	5,077,659	5,153,702	5,233,765	5,301,477	5,360,849	5,401,341	6.4	5,425,200	5,447,000	5,468,800	5,488,000	5,517,300	5,674,500	5.1
Utah	446,652	481,485	576,244	559,778	571,586	585,552	598,832	613,279	625,461	635,577	647,870	659,801	668,274	9.0	675,400	681,700	687,800	692,300	697,700	736,700	10.2
Vermont	95,762	102,049	94,038	93,625	91,451	96,858	89,908	89,624	88,690	87,311	87,866	88,428	88,028	-1.8	87,000	86,500	85,900	85,300	85,000	82,000	-6.9
Virginia	998,601	1,144,915	1,230,857	1,235,795	1,245,340	1,251,440	1,257,883	1,265,419	1,273,825	1,280,381	1,283,590	1,287,026	1,291,462	2.1	1,292,600	1,293,900	1,295,600	1,297,000	1,299,900	1,323,800	2.5
Washington	839,709	1,004,770	1,030,247	1,037,018	1,035,347	1,043,788	1,045,453	1,051,694	1,058,936	1,073,638	1,087,030	1,101,711	1,110,367	5.6	1,118,400	1,127,800	1,139,700	1,150,600	1,163,700	1,234,000	11.1
West Virginia	322,389	286,367	282,535	282,729	282,662	282,879	282,870	283,044	280,958	280,310	277,452	273,855	272,266	-3.8	269,200	265,900	262,500	259,600	257,400	246,200	-9.6
Wisconsin	797,621	879,476	874,633	873,750	872,436	872,286	871,105	872,436	874,414	871,432	867,800	864,432	860,753	-1.3	855,700	852,100	849,500	846,300	844,700	836,200	-2.8
Wyoming	98,226	89,940	86,422	87,161	88,155	89,009	90,099	91,533	92,732	94,067	94,717	94,170	94,258	3.0	93,700	93,400	93,200	92,800	92,700	91,500	-3.0
Jurisdiction																					
Bureau of Indian Education	—	46,938	—	40,927	41,351	41,962	—	—	—	—	—	45,399	46,330	—	—	—	—	—	—	—	—
DoDEA[3]	—	107,755	84,795	84,781	—	—	—	—	—	—	74,970	—	—	—	—	—	—	—	—	—	—
Other jurisdictions																					
American Samoa	12,463	15,702	—	—	—	—	—	—	—	—	—	—	12,620	—	—	—	—	—	—	—	—
Guam	26,391	32,473	—	—	—	31,618	31,243	31,186	33,414	31,144	30,821	30,758	30,112	-3.4	—	—	—	—	—	—	—
Northern Marianas	6,449	10,004	11,299	10,913	10,961	11,105	11,011	10,646	10,638	—	—	—	—	—	—	—	—	—	—	—	—
Puerto Rico	644,734	612,725	526,565	503,635	493,393	473,735	452,740	434,609	423,934	410,950	379,818	365,181	346,096	-20.4	—	—	—	—	—	—	—
U.S. Virgin Islands	21,750	19,459	15,903	15,768	15,493	15,495	15,711	15,192	14,953	14,241	13,805	13,194	10,868	-28.5	—	—	—	—	—	—	—

—Not available.
[1]Includes imputations for prekindergarten enrollment in California and Oregon.
[2]Includes imputations for prekindergarten enrollment in California.
[3]DoDEA = Department of Defense Education Activity. Includes both domestic and overseas schools.

NOTE: Detail may not sum to totals because of rounding. Some data have been revised from previously published figures.
SOURCE: U.S. Department of Education, National Center for Education Statistics, Common Core of Data (CCD), "State Nonfiscal Survey of Public Elementary/Secondary Education," 1990–91 through 2017–18; and State Public Elementary and Secondary Enrollment Projection Model, 1980 through 2029. (This table was prepared December 2019.)

Table 203.25. Public school enrollment in prekindergarten through grade 8, by region, state, and jurisdiction: Selected years, fall 1990 through fall 2029

Region, state, and jurisdiction	Actual enrollment													Percent change in enroll-ment, 2013 to 2018	
	Fall 1990	Fall 2000	Fall 2008	Fall 2009	Fall 2010	Fall 2011	Fall 2012	Fall 2013	Fall 2014	Fall 2015	Fall 2016	Fall 2017	Fall 2018		Fa
1	2	3	4	5	6	7	8	9	10	11	12	13	14	15	
United States	**29,875,914**	**33,686,421**	**34,285,564**	**34,409,260**	**34,624,530**	**34,772,751**	**35,017,893**	**35,250,792**	**35,369,694**	**35,387,986**	**35,477,332**	**35,496,055**	**35,497,748**	**0.7**	**35,4**
Region															
Northeast	5,188,795	5,839,970	5,476,224	5,494,080	5,540,276	5,479,174	5,493,308	5,502,015	5,519,184	5,486,906	5,509,561	5,494,484	5,475,308	**-0.5**	5,4
Midwest	7,129,501	7,523,246	7,373,391	7,361,959	7,349,334	7,358,792	7,368,484	7,394,141	7,374,598	7,361,263	7,346,552	7,331,579	7,306,433	**-1.2**	7,2
South	10,858,800	12,314,176	13,166,980	13,300,643	13,434,553	13,578,211	13,711,284	13,830,129	13,917,451	13,951,194	13,995,096	14,033,899	14,069,319	**1.7**	14,0
West	6,698,818	8,009,029	8,268,969	8,252,578	8,300,367	8,356,574	8,444,817	8,524,507	8,558,461	8,588,623	8,626,123	8,636,093	8,646,688	**1.4**	8,6
State															
Alabama	527,097	538,634	528,078	529,394	533,612	527,006	527,434	527,499	523,096	521,607	522,292	523,057	523,523	**-0.8**	5
Alaska	85,297	94,442	89,263	90,824	91,990	92,057	93,069	92,714	92,745	93,789	94,164	94,618	93,642	**1.0**	
Arizona	479,046	640,564	771,749	760,420	751,992	759,494	767,734	775,280	780,123	775,446	783,905	777,744	793,964	**2.4**	7
Arkansas	313,505	318,023	341,603	344,209	345,808	346,022	347,631	349,709	349,174	349,817	350,297	352,513	351,719	**0.6**	3
California	3,613,734	4,407,035	4,306,258	4,264,022	4,293,968	4,308,447	4,331,807	4,357,989	4,360,241	4,361,930	4,367,509	4,357,267	4,321,648	**-0.8**	4,3
Colorado	419,910	516,566	580,304	591,378	601,077	610,854	617,510	627,619	634,363	638,203	639,519	639,875	637,758	**1.6**	6
Connecticut	347,396	406,445	392,218	389,964	387,475	383,377	380,709	377,162	374,888	370,877	368,843	365,546	362,125	**-4.0**	3
Delaware	72,606	80,801	86,811	87,710	90,279	90,624	91,004	93,204	94,696	95,002	95,760	95,390	96,753	**3.8**	
District of Columbia	61,282	53,692	50,779	51,656	53,548	56,195	58,273	60,379	62,997	64,955	66,798	68,142	69,581	**15.2**	
Florida	1,369,934	1,759,902	1,849,295	1,850,901	1,858,498	1,876,102	1,892,560	1,913,710	1,933,695	1,952,461	1,969,010	1,980,941	1,994,347	**4.2**	2,0
Georgia	849,082	1,059,983	1,185,684	1,194,751	1,202,479	1,211,250	1,222,289	1,233,877	1,242,832	1,243,372	1,245,574	1,246,608	1,245,461	**0.9**	1,2
Hawaii	122,840	132,293	125,910	127,477	127,525	131,005	133,590	135,925	131,307	131,593	131,141	130,255	130,402	**-4.1**	1
Idaho	160,091	170,421	193,554	194,728	194,144	198,064	202,203	209,333	205,460	205,857	208,561	210,927	216,919	**3.6**	2
Illinois	1,309,516	1,473,933	1,479,195	1,463,713	1,454,793	1,453,156	1,448,201	1,445,459	1,428,964	1,422,487	1,408,702	1,388,977	1,370,182	**-5.2**	1,3
Indiana	675,804	703,261	730,021	730,599	729,414	724,605	725,040	731,035	729,804	725,444	725,811	728,666	726,878	**-0.6**	7
Iowa	344,804	333,750	335,566	341,333	348,112	350,152	355,041	357,953	359,449	361,206	362,666	363,718	365,737	**2.2**	3
Kansas	319,648	323,157	331,079	332,997	342,927	347,129	349,695	355,929	355,305	352,910	351,447	353,430	353,649	**-0.6**	3
Kentucky	459,200	471,429	472,204	484,466	480,334	488,456	491,065	485,001	491,766	487,634	485,275	481,962	479,561	**-1.1**	4
Louisiana	586,202	546,579	504,213	509,883	512,266	518,802	524,792	523,310	522,009	520,134	516,206	514,159	511,587	**-2.2**	5
Maine	155,203	145,701	129,324	128,646	128,929	130,046	127,924	127,071	126,109	125,340	124,938	124,937	124,850	**-1.7**	1
Maryland	526,744	609,043	576,473	581,785	588,156	594,216	602,802	612,580	620,442	626,505	630,440	633,791	635,285	**3.7**	6
Massachusetts	604,234	702,575	666,538	666,551	666,402	666,314	667,267	668,261	666,910	669,129	669,178	668,415	665,324	**-0.4**	6
Michigan	1,144,878	1,222,482	1,118,569	1,114,611	1,075,584	1,070,873	1,061,930	1,060,065	1,051,722	1,052,418	1,047,414	1,037,784	1,031,332	**-2.7**	1,0
Minnesota	545,556	577,766	560,184	564,661	569,963	575,544	583,363	589,564	594,161	598,675	607,084	614,476	615,709	**4.4**	6
Mississippi	371,641	363,873	351,807	351,652	350,885	352,999	356,364	356,432	352,884	348,569	345,125	341,927	338,465	**-5.0**	3
Missouri	588,070	644,766	635,411	638,082	642,991	645,376	647,530	649,061	648,864	649,885	647,307	648,697	647,461	**-0.2**	6
Montana	111,169	105,226	96,869	97,868	98,491	99,725	100,819	101,991	102,716	103,497	104,337	106,075	106,357	**4.3**	1
Nebraska	198,080	195,486	202,912	206,860	210,292	213,504	215,432	219,122	222,671	224,364	226,051	228,831	230,122	**5.0**	2
Nevada	149,881	250,720	308,328	305,512	307,297	309,360	313,730	319,240	324,518	330,593	333,991	343,807	349,619	**9.5**	3
New Hampshire	126,301	147,121	132,995	132,768	131,576	129,632	128,169	126,933	125,845	124,305	123,602	122,657	121,965	**-3.9**	1
New Jersey	783,422	967,533	956,765	968,332	981,255	947,576	956,070	956,379	982,202	989,332	990,740	987,988	979,147	**2.4**	9
New Mexico	208,087	224,879	231,415	235,343	239,345	239,481	240,978	241,528	241,105	238,896	236,407	235,839	234,323	**-3.0**	2
New York	1,827,418	2,028,906	1,843,080	1,847,003	1,869,150	1,857,574	1,868,561	1,884,845	1,889,428	1,870,048	1,886,863	1,880,208	1,874,568	**-0.5**	1,8
North Carolina	783,132	945,470	1,058,926	1,053,801	1,058,409	1,074,063	1,080,090	1,089,594	1,092,368	1,080,536	1,080,196	1,080,861	1,087,608	**-0.2**	1,0
North Dakota	84,943	72,421	63,955	64,576	66,035	67,888	70,995	73,527	76,165	77,969	79,249	81,031	82,288	**11.9**	
Ohio	1,257,580	1,293,646	1,239,494	1,225,346	1,222,808	1,217,226	1,211,299	1,208,500	1,204,872	1,194,990	1,190,358	1,187,254	1,184,755	**-2.0**	1,1
Oklahoma	424,899	445,402	467,960	476,962	483,464	490,196	496,144	501,504	503,846	505,311	504,388	503,796	505,349	**0.8**	5
Oregon	340,243	379,264	395,421	404,451	392,601	391,310	409,325	414,405	421,561	427,227	425,768	427,690	428,997	**3.5**	4
Pennsylvania	1,172,164	1,257,824	1,194,327	1,200,446	1,209,766	1,204,850	1,204,732	1,201,169	1,193,762	1,176,868	1,183,671	1,182,944	1,186,383	**-1.2**	1,1
Rhode Island	101,797	113,545	97,983	98,184	97,734	97,659	97,809	98,738	99,067	99,143	98,871	98,737	98,461	**-0.3**	
South Carolina	452,033	493,226	507,602	512,124	515,581	519,389	527,350	533,822	539,800	542,753	547,928	553,414	556,875	**4.3**	5
South Dakota	95,165	87,838	87,477	85,745	87,936	90,529	93,204	94,251	95,739	97,011	98,712	99,878	100,700	**6.8**	1
Tennessee	598,111	668,123	684,549	686,668	701,707	712,749	711,525	709,668	707,067	709,394	708,027	710,398	716,021	**0.9**	7
Texas	2,510,955	2,943,047	3,446,511	3,520,348	3,586,609	3,636,852	3,690,146	3,742,266	3,783,324	3,809,025	3,835,671	3,852,952	3,868,443	**3.4**	3,8
Utah	324,982	333,104	404,469	413,343	424,979	434,536	444,202	451,332	456,667	463,567	471,213	475,107	479,370	**6.2**	4
Vermont	70,860	70,320	62,994	62,186	67,989	62,146	62,067	61,457	60,973	61,864	62,855	63,052	62,486	**1.7**	
Virginia	728,280	815,748	855,008	864,020	871,446	881,225	889,444	896,573	897,688	896,809	897,696	900,027	898,317	**0.2**	8
Washington	612,597	694,367	704,794	705,387	714,172	718,184	724,560	730,868	740,320	750,222	762,362	769,992	786,827	**7.7**	7
West Virginia	224,097	201,201	199,477	200,313	201,472	202,065	202,371	201,001	199,767	197,310	194,413	193,961	190,424	**-5.3**	1
Wisconsin	565,457	594,740	589,528	593,436	598,479	602,810	606,754	609,675	606,882	603,904	601,751	598,837	597,619	**-2.0**	5
Wyoming	70,941	60,148	60,635	61,825	62,786	64,057	65,290	66,283	67,335	67,803	67,246	66,897	66,862	**0.9**	
Bureau of Indian Education	---	35,746	30,612	31,381	31,985	---	---	---	---	---	34,132	35,064	32,632	---	
DoDEA[1]	---	89,996	69,186	---	---	---	---	---	---	61,355	58,942	57,975	58,483	---	
Other jurisdictions															
American Samoa	9,390	11,895	---	---	---	---	---	---	---	---	---	8,877	8,352	---	
Guam	19,276	23,698	---	---	21,561	21,223	21,166	23,301	21,112	20,765	20,621	20,227	20,183	**-13.4**	
Northern Marianas	4,918	7,809	7,816	7,743	7,688	7,703	7,396	7,340	---	---	---	---	---	---	
Puerto Rico	480,356	445,524	355,115	347,638	334,613	318,924	305,048	294,976	284,246	261,667	251,197	238,807	210,452	**-28.7**	
U.S. Virgin Islands	16,249	13,910	10,567	10,409	10,518	10,576	10,302	10,283	9,724	9,503	9,037	12,698	7,309	**-28.9**	

—Not available.

[1] DoDEA = Department of Defense Education Activity. Includes both domestic and overseas schools.

NOTE: The total ungraded counts of students were prorated to the elementary level (prekindergarten through grade 8) and the secondary level (grades 9 through 12) based on the distribution of elementary and secondary enrollment in the prior year. Projections in this table were calculated prior to the coronavirus pandemic and therefore do not take into account the actual or potential impacts of the pandemic. Detail may not sum to totals because of rounding. Some data have been revised from previously published figures.

SOURCE: U.S. Department of Education, National Center for Education Statistics, Common Core of Data (CCD), "State Nonfiscal Survey of Public Elementary/Secondary Education," 1990-91 through 2018-19; Department of Defense Education Activity (DoDEA) Data Center, Enrollment Data, 2016, 2017, and 2018, retrieved August 11, 2020,

Table 203.30. Public school enrollment in grades 9 through 12, by region, state, and jurisdiction: Selected years, fall 1990 through fall 2029

Region, state, and jurisdiction	Actual enrollment													Percent change in enroll-ment, 2013 to 2018	
	Fall 1990	Fall 2000	Fall 2008	Fall 2009	Fall 2010	Fall 2011	Fall 2012	Fall 2013	Fall 2014	Fall 2015	Fall 2016	Fall 2017	Fall 2018		Fa
1	2	3	4	5	6	7	8	9	10	11	12	13	14	15	
United States	11,340,769	13,517,118	14,980,008	14,951,722	14,859,651	14,748,918	14,753,225	14,793,730	14,942,887	15,050,057	15,137,857	15,189,512	15,196,313	2.7	15,2
Region															
Northeast	2,092,968	2,382,157	2,576,761	2,597,949	2,531,059	2,474,807	2,465,820	2,459,228	2,460,672	2,446,856	2,449,743	2,452,052	2,434,768	-1.0	2,4
Midwest	2,814,260	3,206,741	3,369,582	3,310,212	3,260,270	3,215,000	3,190,746	3,178,779	3,185,941	3,194,316	3,192,395	3,192,174	3,185,412	0.2	3,1
South	3,948,216	4,693,085	5,323,790	5,351,246	5,370,447	5,377,721	5,417,092	5,468,585	5,588,742	5,690,278	5,754,720	5,790,570	5,794,669	6.0	5,8
West	2,485,325	3,235,135	3,709,875	3,692,315	3,697,875	3,681,390	3,679,567	3,687,138	3,707,532	3,718,607	3,740,999	3,754,716	3,781,464	2.6	3,7
State															
Alabama	194,709	201,358	217,590	219,495	221,940	217,615	217,203	218,705	221,068	222,182	222,638	219,387	216,193	-1.1	2
Alaska	28,606	38,914	41,399	40,837	40,114	39,110	38,420	38,230	38,431	38,688	38,573	38,254	37,321	-2.4	
Arizona	160,807	237,132	316,068	317,411	319,759	320,825	321,650	327,165	331,572	333,594	339,232	333,107	347,547	6.2	3
Arkansas	122,781	131,936	137,362	136,350	136,306	137,092	138,526	140,270	141,743	142,315	143,150	143,572	143,572	2.4	1
California	1,336,740	1,733,779	2,016,270	1,999,416	1,995,610	1,979,387	1,967,644	1,954,634	1,951,920	1,943,417	1,941,629	1,946,999	1,951,086	-0.2	1,9
Colorado	154,303	207,942	238,139	240,990	242,239	243,411	246,051	249,380	254,643	260,909	265,500	270,405	273,778	9.8	2
Connecticut	121,727	155,734	174,980	174,004	173,071	171,060	170,245	169,038	167,790	167,056	166,275	165,742	164,509	-2.7	1
Delaware	27,052	33,875	38,619	39,091	39,124	38,322	38,022	38,483	39,346	39,845	40,504	40,903	41,652	8.2	
District of Columbia	19,412	15,233	17,902	17,777	17,736	17,716	17,867	17,774	17,961	19,069	19,052	19,173	18,912	6.4	
Florida	491,658	674,919	781,725	783,621	784,849	792,054	799,602	807,034	823,249	839,773	847,781	851,483	852,097	5.6	8
Georgia	302,605	384,954	470,108	472,934	474,588	473,766	481,043	490,032	501,605	513,865	518,772	522,034	521,741	6.5	5
Hawaii	48,868	52,067	53,568	52,719	52,076	51,701	51,170	50,900	51,077	50,402	50,409	50,582	50,876	0.0	
Idaho	60,749	74,696	81,497	81,571	81,715	81,809	82,631	87,143	85,425	86,420	88,639	90,259	93,603	7.4	
Illinois	511,891	574,859	640,512	640,462	636,861	629,941	624,679	621,531	621,275	619,292	618,016	616,176	612,145	-1.5	6
Indiana	278,721	286,006	316,126	316,062	317,818	316,160	316,329	316,350	316,465	321,313	323,736	325,521	328,828	3.9	3
Iowa	138,848	161,330	151,993	150,509	147,663	145,718	144,784	145,011	145,862	146,808	147,165	148,132	149,096	2.8	1
Kansas	117,386	147,453	139,981	141,492	140,774	138,979	139,348	140,511	141,970	142,974	142,900	143,658	144,084	2.5	1
Kentucky	177,201	194,421	197,826	195,623	192,794	193,531	194,102	192,388	196,874	198,964	198,742	199,016	198,260	3.1	1
Louisiana	198,555	196,510	180,660	181,032	184,292	184,588	186,111	188,181	194,791	198,577	200,087	200,976	200,196	6.4	1
Maine	59,946	61,336	63,611	60,579	60,148	58,923	57,815	56,924	56,361	56,273	55,574	55,536	55,611	-2.3	
Maryland	188,432	243,877	267,388	266,627	264,055	259,870	256,836	253,589	254,072	253,096	255,781	259,893	261,542	3.1	2
Massachusetts	230,080	272,575	292,372	290,502	289,161	287,055	287,506	287,478	288,934	294,897	295,336	296,376	296,973	3.3	2
Michigan	439,553	498,144	541,352	534,471	511,483	502,664	493,440	488,776	486,200	483,813	481,252	478,614	472,862	-3.3	4
Minnesota	210,818	276,574	275,864	272,392	268,074	264,194	262,041	261,409	263,074	265,709	267,937	270,468	273,595	4.7	2
Mississippi	130,776	133,998	140,155	140,829	139,641	137,620	137,286	136,154	138,033	138,631	138,025	136,394	132,833	-2.4	1
Missouri	228,488	267,978	282,460	279,900	275,719	271,208	270,370	269,227	268,921	269,349	267,733	266,775	265,980	-1.2	2
Montana	41,805	49,649	45,030	43,939	43,202	42,624	42,089	42,138	41,816	41,822	42,038	43,399	42,487	0.8	
Nebraska	76,001	90,713	89,678	88,508	88,208	87,792	88,073	88,555	89,964	91,650	93,143	94,935	96,270	8.7	
Nevada	51,435	89,986	125,043	123,435	129,852	130,274	131,977	132,591	134,671	136,934	139,753	141,978	143,021	7.9	1
New Hampshire	46,484	61,340	64,939	64,372	63,135	62,268	60,805	59,377	58,825	58,120	57,286	56,776	56,550	-4.8	
New Jersey	306,224	345,872	424,655	427,697	421,293	408,855	416,133	413,916	418,377	419,513	419,681	420,114	420,922	1.7	4
New Mexico	93,794	95,427	98,830	99,076	98,777	97,744	97,242	97,716	99,260	96,798	99,856	98,506	99,214	1.5	
New York	770,919	853,282	897,512	919,049	865,805	847,144	842,142	847,925	851,757	841,578	842,913	844,455	826,265	-2.6	8
North Carolina	303,739	348,168	429,719	429,596	432,196	433,801	438,375	441,263	456,527	464,398	469,866	472,652	464,889	5.4	4
North Dakota	32,882	36,780	30,773	30,497	30,288	29,758	30,116	30,420	30,421	30,675	30,457	30,889	31,557	3.7	
Ohio	513,509	541,403	577,669	538,951	531,383	522,804	518,617	515,611	519,938	521,595	519,785	517,145	511,007	-0.9	5
Oklahoma	154,188	177,708	177,148	177,840	176,447	175,924	177,339	180,344	184,665	187,567	189,515	191,296	193,542	7.3	1
Oregon	132,151	166,967	179,972	178,388	178,119	176,898	178,239	178,595	179,757	181,598	180,509	180,324	180,510	1.1	1
Pennsylvania	495,670	556,487	580,702	585,547	583,518	566,545	558,945	554,067	549,398	540,546	543,826	543,865	544,374	-1.7	5
Rhode Island	37,016	43,802	47,359	46,934	46,059	45,195	44,672	43,270	42,892	42,871	43,279	44,212	44,975	3.9	
South Carolina	170,079	184,185	210,511	211,019	210,257	207,797	208,648	211,835	216,723	220,780	223,322	224,093	224,007	5.7	2
South Dakota	33,999	40,765	38,952	37,968	38,192	37,487	37,267	36,639	37,301	37,242	37,590	37,945	38,275	4.5	
Tennessee	226,484	241,038	287,401	285,881	285,715	286,944	281,971	283,888	288,408	291,841	293,535	291,569	291,603	2.7	2
Texas	871,932	1,116,572	1,305,637	1,329,862	1,349,106	1,363,618	1,387,513	1,411,436	1,450,441	1,492,452	1,525,178	1,548,389	1,565,028	10.9	1,5
Utah	121,670	148,381	155,309	158,243	160,573	164,296	169,077	174,129	178,910	184,303	188,588	193,167	197,661	13.5	2
Vermont	24,902	31,729	30,631	29,265	28,869	27,762	27,557	27,233	26,338	26,002	25,573	24,976	24,588	-9.7	
Virginia	270,321	329,167	380,787	381,320	379,994	376,658	375,975	377,252	382,693	386,781	389,330	391,435	391,050	3.7	3
Washington	227,112	310,403	332,224	329,960	329,616	327,269	327,134	328,068	333,318	336,808	339,349	340,375	336,909	2.7	3
West Virginia	98,292	85,166	83,252	82,349	81,407	80,805	80,673	79,957	80,543	80,142	79,442	78,305	77,552	-3.0	
Wisconsin	232,164	284,736	284,222	279,000	273,807	268,295	265,682	264,739	264,550	263,896	262,681	261,916	261,714	-1.1	2
Wyoming	27,285	29,792	26,526	26,330	26,223	26,042	26,243	26,449	26,732	26,914	26,924	27,361	27,451	3.8	
Bureau of Indian Education	---	11,192	10,315	9,970	9,977	---	---	---	---	---	11,267	11,266	11,074	---	
DoDEA[1]	---	17,759	15,595	---	---	---	---	---	---	13,615	13,284	13,159	12,923	---	
Other jurisdictions															
American Samoa	3,073	3,807	---	---	---	---	---	---	---	---	---	3,743	3,754	---	
Guam	7,115	8,775	---	---	10,057	10,020	10,020	10,113	10,032	10,056	10,137	9,885	9,536	-5.7	
Northern Marianas	1,531	2,195	3,097	3,218	3,417	3,308	3,250	3,298	---	---	---	---	---	---	
Puerto Rico	164,378	167,201	148,520	145,755	139,122	133,816	129,561	128,958	126,704	118,151	113,984	107,289	96,830	-24.9	
U.S. Virgin Islands	5,501	5,549	5,201	5,084	4,977	5,135	4,890	4,670	4,517	4,302	4,157	3,441	3,409	-27.0	

—Not available.

[1] DoDEA = Department of Defense Education Activity. Includes both domestic and overseas schools.

NOTE: The total ungraded counts of students were prorated to the elementary level (prekindergarten through grade 8) and the secondary level (grades 9 through 12) based on the distribution of elementary and secondary enrollment in the prior year. In addition to students in grades 9 through 12 and ungraded secondary students, this table includes a small number of students reported as being enrolled in grade 13. Projections in this table were calculated prior to the coronavirus pandemic and therefore do not take into account the actual or potential impacts of the pandemic. Detail may not sum to totals because of rounding. Some data have been revised from previously published figures.

SOURCE: U.S. Department of Education, National Center for Education Statistics, Common Core of Data (CCD), "State Nonfiscal Survey of Public Elementary/Secondary Education," 1990-91 through 2018-19; Department of Defense Education Activity (DoDEA) Data Center, Enrollment Data, 2016, 2017, and 2018, retrieved August 11, 2020,

Table 203.40. Enrollment in public elementary and secondary schools, by level, grade, and state or jurisdiction: Fall 2017

State or jurisdiction	Total, all grades	Elementary												Secondary					
		Total	Prekindergarten	Kindergarten	Grade 1	Grade 2	Grade 3	Grade 4	Grade 5	Grade 6	Grade 7	Grade 8	Elementary ungraded	Total	Grade 9	Grade 10	Grade 11	Grade 12	Secondary ungraded[1]
1	2	3	4	5	6	7	8	9	10	11	12	13	14	15	16	17	18	19	20
United States	**50,685,567**	**35,496,055**	**1,471,216**	**3,684,238**	**3,667,166**	**3,684,091**	**3,787,970**	**3,859,475**	**3,877,267**	**3,827,023**	**3,776,565**	**3,772,276**	**88,768**	**15,189,512**	**3,995,574**	**3,833,718**	**3,676,753**	**3,631,450**	**52,017**
Alabama	742,444	523,057	15,520	54,985	56,414	55,606	57,526	58,541	57,928	55,711	55,600	55,226	0	219,387	57,301	55,318	53,920	52,848	0
Alaska	132,872	94,618	3,586	10,196	10,243	10,331	10,409	10,398	10,229	10,007	9,741	9,478	0	38,254	9,584	9,285	9,503	9,882	0
Arizona	1,110,851	777,744	14,124	79,520	80,377	81,200	84,933	88,092	88,849	87,512	86,544	86,287	306	333,107	86,236	83,999	78,514	84,330	28
Arkansas	496,085	352,513	16,827	36,942	36,820	36,915	37,797	38,800	38,844	36,305	36,431	36,631	201	143,572	37,758	37,245	35,387	33,097	85
California	6,304,266	4,357,267	83,853[2]	531,725	456,175	455,523	447,253	466,660	472,202	486,261	477,308	474,828	5,479	1,946,999	495,277	483,745	475,696	489,221	3,060
Colorado	910,280	639,875	33,048	63,574	64,967	65,616	67,991	69,784	69,821	69,321	67,899	67,854	0	270,405	70,017	67,140	65,136	68,112	0
Connecticut	531,288	365,546	18,579	36,225	36,783	36,848	38,020	38,873	40,145	39,621	40,142	40,310	0	165,742	43,232	41,092	40,616	40,802	0
Delaware	136,293	95,390	1,802	9,943	10,048	10,327	10,602	10,838	10,754	10,498	10,362	10,216	0	40,903	11,806	10,476	9,521	9,100	0
District of Columbia	87,315	68,142	12,727	7,465	7,222	6,820	6,602	6,339	6,159	5,270	4,971	4,567	0	19,173	6,085	4,725	4,259	4,104	0
Florida	2,832,424	1,980,941	61,241	200,185	207,590	207,609	226,346	220,504	215,793	219,942	210,658	211,073	0	851,483	219,313	216,578	212,640	202,952	0
Georgia	1,768,642	1,246,608	47,726	126,400	128,192	130,015	135,911	138,249	139,160	135,448	132,993	132,514	0	522,034	147,677	135,406	123,273	115,678	0
Hawaii	180,837	130,255	1,582	14,316	14,755	14,981	11,986	15,443	15,308	14,425	13,996	13,226	237	50,582	14,408	13,143	11,766	11,068	197
Idaho	301,186	210,927	2,845	21,111	22,148	22,376	23,146	24,003	24,147	23,732	24,005	23,414	0	90,259	23,599	22,935	22,210	21,512	3
Illinois	2,005,153	1,388,977	83,664	132,075	137,580	139,991	145,553	148,792	151,331	149,568	149,227	151,180	16	616,176	159,550	155,612	150,969	150,045	0
Indiana	1,054,187	728,666	19,198	77,944	76,301	76,468	78,722	80,111	80,201	79,338	78,616	80,163	1,604	325,521	80,535	80,799	83,712	80,475	0
Iowa	511,850	363,718	30,454	38,293	34,934	36,056	36,683	37,980	38,071	37,618	37,138	36,491	0	148,132	37,728	37,111	36,238	37,055	0
Kansas	497,088	353,430	21,281	35,661	35,554	36,462	36,888	37,687	37,715	36,808	36,210	36,269	2,895	143,658	37,510	35,904	34,718	34,437	1,089
Kentucky	680,978	481,962	29,493	44,058	50,518	49,479	51,350	52,328	52,669	51,102	50,249	50,293	423	199,016	53,687	50,822	48,739	45,593	175
Louisiana	715,135	514,159	27,491	53,070	54,585	53,478	55,396	55,835	55,456	53,698	52,928	52,222	0	200,976	56,596	51,715	47,551	45,114	0
Maine	180,473	124,937	5,617	12,586	12,569	12,688	13,246	13,343	13,727	13,513	13,852	13,796	0	55,536	13,814	13,846	13,946	13,930	0
Maryland	893,684	633,791	30,422	64,045	66,082	66,879	68,516	70,330	69,515	67,059	65,571	65,372	0	259,893	71,633	67,738	60,336	60,186	0
Massachusetts	964,791	668,415	30,684	66,122	68,195	68,491	70,416	72,620	73,012	71,892	71,705	72,860	2,418	296,376	77,572	74,170	72,950	71,684	0
Michigan	1,516,398	1,037,784	44,258	116,636	105,819	103,930	105,399	107,959	112,263	112,397	111,842	114,521	2,760	478,614	123,324	121,134	115,646	117,197	1,313
Minnesota	884,944	614,476	22,692	64,111	63,518	64,385	65,710	67,226	67,694	66,560	66,152	66,428	0	270,468	67,007	65,975	66,653	70,833	0
Mississippi	478,321	341,927	5,732	35,988	36,391	36,409	37,952	38,880	38,842	35,783	35,864	35,613	4,473	136,394	35,716	34,365	32,230	30,933	3,150
Missouri	915,472	648,697	33,054	66,010	66,399	67,231	69,041	70,749	71,042	69,214	68,224	67,733	0	266,775	69,398	67,397	65,697	64,283	0
Montana	149,474	106,075	2,321	11,702	11,407	11,144	11,559	11,971	11,721	11,804	11,239	11,207	0	43,399	11,556	11,245	10,667	9,931	0
Nebraska	323,766	228,831	17,513	23,232	22,892	23,559	24,173	24,169	22,553	23,661	23,357	23,722	0	94,935	23,832	23,747	23,007	24,349	0
Nevada	485,785	343,807	8,908	35,083	36,354	36,375	36,959	38,624	39,062	38,004	37,216	36,389	833	141,978	36,452	36,510	35,532	33,456	28
New Hampshire	179,433	122,657	3,907	11,419	12,745	12,514	13,003	13,456	13,694	13,801	13,895	14,223	0	56,776	14,992	14,567	13,779	13,435	3
New Jersey	1,408,102	987,988	64,351	91,077	94,920	95,253	98,425	99,443	100,606	99,986	99,191	100,919	43,817	420,114	103,655	100,781	99,613	98,845	17,220
New Mexico	334,345	235,839	9,689	23,709	24,166	24,309	25,880	26,363	26,248	25,343	25,304	24,828	0	98,506	28,522	25,597	22,814	21,573	0
New York	2,724,663	1,880,208	65,558	193,045	197,155	198,490	200,783	202,149	203,385	199,743	197,715	198,879	23,306	844,455	218,826	212,490	195,169	194,079	23,891
North Carolina	1,553,513	1,080,861	18,734	115,064	115,584	117,037	121,228	122,866	122,997	119,927	117,127	110,297	0	472,652	129,965	120,884	114,820	105,208	1,775
North Dakota	111,920	81,031	2,778	9,273	8,739	8,713	8,876	8,781	8,746	8,575	8,307	8,243	0	30,889	8,199	7,760	7,561	7,369	0
Ohio	1,704,399	1,187,254	38,310	123,036	123,188	123,921	131,207	128,118	130,839	129,831	128,323	130,481	0	517,145	141,280	133,705	120,359	121,801	0
Oklahoma	695,092	503,796	41,727	51,920	52,328	51,834	53,565	52,385	52,257	50,368	47,950	49,462	0	191,296	52,268	49,055	46,439	43,534	0
Oregon	608,014	427,690	27,330[2]	41,884	43,156	43,504	44,827	46,543	46,542	45,378	44,151	44,375	0	180,324	44,819	44,257	44,003	47,245	0
Pennsylvania	1,726,809	1,182,944	8,498	121,043	126,361	126,616	129,812	134,060	134,805	133,628	133,276	134,845	0	543,865	141,407	136,286	133,081	133,091	0
Rhode Island	142,949	98,737	2,477	10,006	10,297	10,434	10,583	11,003	11,119	10,913	10,853	11,052	0	44,212	11,580	11,470	10,867	10,295	0
South Carolina	777,507	553,414	27,006	55,598	57,183	57,012	60,334	60,890	61,389	59,112	57,857	57,033	0	224,093	63,516	57,755	52,722	50,100	0
South Dakota	137,823	99,878	3,393	11,720	10,432	10,494	10,655	10,966	10,921	10,677	10,516	10,104	0	37,945	10,600	9,649	8,913	8,783	0
Tennessee	1,001,967	710,398	28,379	75,482	74,633	74,145	74,844	78,085	78,681	76,941	75,058	74,150	0	291,569	75,784	74,234	72,053	69,498	0
Texas	5,401,341	3,852,952	256,222	371,638	388,650	394,381	409,998	413,843	414,412	402,634	402,512	398,662	0	1,548,389	433,521	397,573	372,052	345,243	0
Utah	668,274	475,107	15,904	47,591	49,791	50,429	51,635	52,970	53,368	51,951	50,841	50,627	0	193,167	50,184	48,968	47,499	46,516	0
Vermont	88,028	63,052	8,818	5,789	5,814	5,871	5,848	6,236	6,265	6,040	6,240	6,131	0	24,976	6,447	6,430	6,192	5,907	0
Virginia	1,291,462	900,027	33,617	91,002	94,312	94,166	96,946	99,305	99,548	97,617	96,633	96,881	0	391,435	103,925	99,531	94,858	93,121	0
Washington	1,110,367	769,992	15,754	80,917	82,843	83,077	85,583	87,366	86,667	83,947	82,040	81,798	0	340,375	83,131	82,138	83,214	91,892	0
West Virginia	272,266	193,961	16,665	19,521	19,402	19,150	19,659	20,069	20,218	19,539	19,780	19,958	0	78,305	21,317	20,164	18,547	18,277	0
Wisconsin	860,753	598,837	55,186	56,832	57,517	58,370	60,783	61,913	62,743	61,551	61,583	62,359	0	261,916	65,980	64,354	64,556	67,026	0
Wyoming	94,258	66,897	671	7,469	7,118	7,179	7,411	7,537	7,604	7,449	7,373	7,086	0	27,361	7,453	6,893	6,610	6,405	0

See notes at end of table.

Table 203.40. Enrollment in public elementary and secondary schools, by level, grade, and state or jurisdiction: Fall 2017—Continued

State or jurisdiction	Total, all grades	Elementary												Secondary						
		Total	Prekindergarten	Kindergarten	Grade 1	Grade 2	Grade 3	Grade 4	Grade 5	Grade 6	Grade 7	Grade 8	Elementary ungraded	Total	Grade 9	Grade 10	Grade 11	Grade 12	Secondary ungraded[1]
1	2	3	4	5	6	7	8	9	10	11	12	13	14	15	16	17	18	19	20
Bureau of Indian Education	46,330	35,064	—	4,601	4,064	3,899	3,931	3,962	3,774	3,756	3,614	3,463	0	11,266	3,315	2,990	2,470	2,491	0
DoDEA[3]	—	—	—	—	—	—	—	—	—	—	—	—	—	—	—	—	—	—	—
Other jurisdictions																			
American Samoa	12,620	8,877	1,128	729	800	817	850	845	855	873	1,010	970	0	3,743	1,007	946	982	808	0
Guam	30,112	20,227	602	1,953	2,153	2,164	2,181	2,327	2,315	2,139	2,159	2,234	0	9,885	2,888	2,834	2,350	1,813	0
Northern Marianas	—	—	—	—	—	—	—	—	—	—	—	—	—	—	—	—	—	—	—
Puerto Rico	346,096	238,807	2,536	22,189	25,701	24,247	25,082	25,360	25,827	25,754	27,494	26,186	8,431	107,289	25,865	26,222	25,627	25,064	4,511
U.S. Virgin Islands	10,868	7,427	—	732	745	780	898	865	833	848	955	771	0	3,441	1,196	875	676	694	0

—Not available.
[1]Includes students reported as being enrolled in grade 13.
[2]Inputed by the National Center for Education Statistics.
[3]DoDEA = Department of Defense Education Activity. Includes both domestic and overseas schools.

NOTE: The total ungraded counts of students were prorated to the elementary and secondary levels based on prior state reports of the percentage of elementary and of secondary ungraded students.
SOURCE: U.S. Department of Education, National Center for Education Statistics, Common Core of Data (CCD), "State Nonfiscal Survey of Public Elementary/Secondary Education," 2017–18. (This table was prepared August 2019.)

Table 203.50. Enrollment and percentage distribution of enrollment in public elementary and secondary schools, by race/ethnicity and region: Selected years, fall 1995 through fall 2029

Region and year	Enrollment (in thousands)								Percentage distribution							
	Total	White	Black	Hispanic	Asian	Pacific Islander	American Indian/ Alaska Native	Two or more races	Total	White	Black	Hispanic	Asian	Pacific Islander	American Indian/ Alaska Native	Two or more races
1	2	3	4	5	6	7	8	9	10	11	12	13	14	15	16	17
United States																
1995	44,840	29,044	7,551	6,072	1,668[1]	—	505	—	100.0	64.8	16.8	13.5	3.7[1]	—	1.1	—
2000	47,204	28,878	8,100	7,726	1,950[1]	—	550	—	100.0	61.2	17.2	16.4	4.1[1]	—	1.2	—
2001	47,672	28,735	8,177	8,169	2,028[1]	—	564	—	100.0	60.3	17.2	17.1	4.3[1]	—	1.2	—
2002	48,183	28,618	8,299	8,594	2,088[1]	—	583	—	100.0	59.4	17.2	17.8	4.3[1]	—	1.2	—
2003	48,540	28,442	8,349	9,011	2,145[1]	—	593	—	100.0	58.6	17.2	18.6	4.4[1]	—	1.2	—
2004	48,795	28,318	8,386	9,317	2,183[1]	—	591	—	100.0	58.0	17.2	19.1	4.5[1]	—	1.2	—
2005	49,113	28,005	8,445	9,787	2,279[1]	—	598	—	100.0	57.0	17.2	19.9	4.6[1]	—	1.2	—
2006	49,316	27,801	8,422	10,166	2,332[1]	—	595	—	100.0	56.4	17.1	20.6	4.7[1]	—	1.2	—
2007	49,291	27,454	8,392	10,454	2,396[1]	—	594	—	100.0	55.7	17.0	21.2	4.9[1]	—	1.2	—
2008	49,266	27,057	8,358	10,563	2,405	46	589	247[2]	100.0	54.9	17.0	21.4	4.9	0.1	1.2	0.5[2]
2009	49,361	26,702	8,245	10,991	2,435	49	601	338[2]	100.0	54.1	16.7	22.3	4.9	0.1	1.2	0.7[2]
2010	49,484	25,933	7,917	11,439	2,296	171	566	1,164	100.0	52.4	16.0	23.1	4.6	0.3	1.1	2.4
2011	49,522	25,602	7,827	11,759	2,334	179	547	1,272	100.0	51.7	15.8	23.7	4.7	0.4	1.1	2.6
2012	49,771	25,386	7,803	12,104	2,372	180	534	1,393	100.0	51.0	15.7	24.3	4.8	0.4	1.1	2.8
2013	50,045	25,160	7,805	12,452	2,417	176	523	1,511	100.0	50.3	15.6	24.9	4.8	0.4	1.0	3.0
2014	50,313	24,923	7,807	12,805	2,470	176	519	1,612	100.0	49.5	15.5	25.4	4.9	0.3	1.0	3.2
2015[3]	50,438	24,644	7,784	13,080	2,521	177	510	1,723	100.0	48.9	15.4	25.9	5.0	0.4	1.0	3.4
2016[4]	50,615	24,413	7,765	13,329	2,571	184	511	1,842	100.0	48.2	15.3	26.3	5.1	0.4	1.0	3.6
2017[3]	50,686	24,124	7,709	13,571	2,640	185	498	1,959	100.0	47.6	15.2	26.8	5.2	0.4	1.0	3.9
2018[5]	50,650	23,846	7,671	13,704	2,691	187	491	2,060	100.0	47.1	15.1	27.1	5.3	0.4	1.0	4.1
2019[5]	50,634	23,597	7,639	13,831	2,737	188	484	2,160	100.0	46.6	15.1	27.3	5.4	0.4	1.0	4.3
2020[5]	50,654	23,376	7,616	13,952	2,787	189	477	2,257	100.0	46.1	15.0	27.5	5.5	0.4	0.9	4.5
2021[5]	50,643	23,170	7,598	14,044	2,823	190	471	2,347	100.0	45.8	15.0	27.7	5.6	0.4	0.9	4.6
2022[5]	50,721	23,041	7,636	14,070	2,882	189	464	2,439	100.0	45.4	15.1	27.7	5.7	0.4	0.9	4.8
2023[5]	50,768	22,910	7,657	14,082	2,939	187	458	2,535	100.0	45.1	15.1	27.7	5.8	0.4	0.9	5.0
2024[5]	50,758	22,779	7,665	14,057	2,999	186	452	2,619	100.0	44.9	15.1	27.7	5.9	0.4	0.9	5.2
2025[5]	50,704	22,639	7,664	14,016	3,060	186	446	2,694	100.0	44.6	15.1	27.6	6.0	0.4	0.9	5.3
2026[5]	50,672	22,522	7,664	13,975	3,122	185	441	2,762	100.0	44.4	15.1	27.6	6.2	0.4	0.9	5.5
2027[5]	50,734	22,446	7,675	13,967	3,192	186	437	2,832	100.0	44.2	15.1	27.5	6.3	0.4	0.9	5.6
2028[5]	50,885	22,401	7,707	13,995	3,260	186	434	2,901	100.0	44.0	15.1	27.5	6.4	0.4	0.9	5.7
2029[5]	51,068	22,359	7,746	14,049	3,327	186	433	2,967	100.0	43.8	15.2	27.5	6.5	0.4	0.8	5.8
Northeast																
1995	7,894	5,497	1,202	878	295[1]	—	21	—	100.0	69.6	15.2	11.1	3.7[1]	—	0.3	—
2000	8,222	5,545	1,270	1,023	361[1]	—	24	—	100.0	67.4	15.4	12.4	4.4[1]	—	0.3	—
2005	8,240	5,317	1,282	1,189	425[1]	—	27	—	100.0	64.5	15.6	14.4	5.2[1]	—	0.3	—
2010	8,071	4,876	1,208	1,364	494	6	27	96	100.0	60.4	15.0	16.9	6.1	0.1	0.3	1.2
2014	7,980	4,507	1,155	1,566	538	7	28	179	100.0	56.5	14.5	19.6	6.7	0.1	0.4	2.2
2015	7,934	4,409	1,136	1,610	547	7	29	197	100.0	55.6	14.3	20.3	6.9	0.1	0.4	2.5
2016	7,959	4,345	1,132	1,668	558	13	30	214	100.0	54.6	14.2	21.0	7.0	0.2	0.4	2.7
2017	7,947	4,269	1,117	1,714	570	13	30	232	100.0	53.7	14.1	21.6	7.2	0.2	0.4	2.9
Midwest																
1995	10,512	8,335	1,450	438	197[1]	—	92	—	100.0	79.3	13.8	4.2	1.9[1]	—	0.9	—
2000	10,730	8,208	1,581	610	239[1]	—	92	—	100.0	76.5	14.7	5.7	2.2[1]	—	0.9	—
2005	10,819	7,950	1,654	836	283[1]	—	96	—	100.0	73.5	15.3	7.7	2.6[1]	—	0.9	—
2010	10,610	7,327	1,505	1,077	303	9	94	294	100.0	69.1	14.2	10.2	2.9	0.1	0.9	2.8
2014	10,561	7,037	1,459	1,249	338	11	86	380	100.0	66.6	13.8	11.8	3.2	0.1	0.8	3.6
2015	10,556	6,968	1,458	1,284	348	12	84	400	100.0	66.0	13.8	12.2	3.3	0.1	0.8	3.8
2016	10,539	6,893	1,449	1,312	360	12	86	426	100.0	65.4	13.8	12.4	3.4	0.1	0.8	4.0
2017	10,524	6,825	1,446	1,340	372	13	82	447	100.0	64.9	13.7	12.7	3.5	0.1	0.8	4.2
South																
1995	16,118	9,565	4,236	1,890	280[1]	—	148	—	100.0	59.3	26.3	11.7	1.7[1]	—	0.9	—
2000	17,007	9,501	4,516	2,468	352[1]	—	170	—	100.0	55.9	26.6	14.5	2.1[1]	—	1.0	—
2005	18,103	9,381	4,738	3,334	456[1]	—	194	—	100.0	51.8	26.2	18.4	2.5[1]	—	1.1	—
2010	18,805	8,869	4,545	4,206	533	22	207	424	100.0	47.2	24.2	22.4	2.8	0.1	1.1	2.3
2014	19,506	8,681	4,577	4,846	613	28	184	579	100.0	44.5	23.5	24.8	3.1	0.1	0.9	3.0
2015	19,641	8,601	4,583	4,994	637	29	181	615	100.0	43.8	23.3	25.4	3.2	0.1	0.9	3.1
2016	19,750	8,513	4,571	5,142	665	30	177	652	100.0	43.1	23.1	26.0	3.4	0.2	0.9	3.3
2017	19,824	8,439	4,555	5,249	689	32	174	688	100.0	42.6	23.0	26.5	3.5	0.2	0.9	3.5
West																
1995	10,316	5,648	662	2,866	896[1]	—	244	—	100.0	54.7	6.4	27.8	8.7[1]	—	2.4	—
2000	11,244	5,624	733	3,625	998[1]	—	264	—	100.0	50.0	6.5	32.2	8.9[1]	—	2.4	—
2005	11,951	5,356	771	4,428	1,115[1]	—	281	—	100.0	44.8	6.5	37.1	9.3[1]	—	2.4	—
2010	11,998	4,861	659	4,792	966	133	237	349	100.0	40.5	5.5	39.9	8.1	1.1	2.0	2.9
2014	12,266	4,698	616	5,144	982	130	221	475	100.0	38.3	5.0	41.9	8.0	1.1	1.8	3.9
2015[3]	12,307	4,665	606	5,192	988	129	216	511	100.0	37.9	4.9	42.2	8.0	1.1	1.8	4.2
2016[4]	12,367	4,662	612	5,208	989	128	217	550	100.0	37.7	5.0	42.1	8.0	1.0	1.8	4.4
2017[3]	12,391	4,592	592	5,268	1,009	127	211	592	100.0	37.1	4.8	42.5	8.1	1.0	1.7	4.8

—Not available.
[1]Includes Pacific Islanders.
[2]For this year, data on Pacific Islanders and students of Two or more races were reported by only a small number of states. Therefore, the data are not comparable to figures for 2010 and later years.
[3]Includes imputations for prekindergarten enrollment in California and Oregon.
[4]Includes imputations for prekindergarten enrollment in California.
[5]Projected.

NOTE: Race categories exclude persons of Hispanic ethnicity. Enrollment data for students not reported by race/ethnicity were prorated by state and grade to match state totals. Prior to 2008, data on students of Two or more races were not collected. Some data have been revised from previously published figures. Detail may not sum to totals because of rounding.
SOURCE: U.S. Department of Education, National Center for Education Statistics, Common Core of Data (CCD), "State Nonfiscal Survey of Public Elementary and Secondary Education," 1995–96 through 2017–18; and National Elementary and Secondary Enrollment by Race/Ethnicity Projection Model, 1972 through 2029. (This table was prepared December 2019.)

Table 203.60. Enrollment and percentage distribution of enrollment in public elementary and secondary schools, by race/ethnicity and level of education: Fall 1999 through fall 2029

Level of education and year	Enrollment (in thousands)									Percentage distribution								
	Total	White	Black	Hispanic	Asian/Pacific Islander: Total	Asian/Pacific Islander: Asian	Asian/Pacific Islander: Pacific Islander	American Indian/ Alaska Native	Two or more races	Total	White	Black	Hispanic	Asian/Pacific Islander: Total	Asian/Pacific Islander: Asian	Asian/Pacific Islander: Pacific Islander	American Indian/ Alaska Native	Two or more races
1	2	3	4	5	6	7	8	9	10	11	12	13	14	15	16	17	18	19
Total																		
1999	46,857	29,035	8,066	7,327	1,887	—	—	542	—	100.0	62.0	17.2	15.6	4.0	†	†	1.2	†
2000	47,204	28,878	8,100	7,726	1,950	—	—	550	—	100.0	61.2	17.2	16.4	4.1	†	†	1.2	†
2001	47,672	28,735	8,177	8,169	2,028	—	—	564	—	100.0	60.3	17.2	17.1	4.3	†	†	1.2	†
2002	48,183	28,618	8,299	8,594	2,088	—	—	583	—	100.0	59.4	17.2	17.8	4.3	†	†	1.2	†
2003	48,540	28,442	8,349	9,011	2,145	—	—	593	—	100.0	58.6	17.2	18.6	4.4	†	†	1.2	†
2004	48,795	28,318	8,386	9,317	2,183	—	—	591	—	100.0	58.0	17.2	19.1	4.5	†	†	1.2	†
2005	49,113	28,005	8,445	9,787	2,279	—	—	598	—	100.0	57.0	17.2	19.9	4.6	†	†	1.2	†
2006	49,316	27,801	8,422	10,166	2,332	—	—	595	—	100.0	56.4	17.1	20.6	4.7	†	†	1.2	†
2007	49,291	27,454	8,392	10,454	2,396	—	—	594	—	100.0	55.7	17.0	21.2	4.9	†	†	1.2	†
2008	49,266	27,057	8,358	10,563	2,451	2,405	46	589	247[1]	100.0	54.9	17.0	21.4	5.0	4.9	0.1	1.2	0.5[1]
2009	49,361	26,702	8,245	10,991	2,484	2,435	49	601	338[1]	100.0	54.1	16.7	22.3	5.0	4.9	0.1	1.2	0.7[1]
2010	49,484	25,933	7,917	11,439	2,466	2,296	171	566	1,164	100.0	52.4	16.0	23.1	5.0	4.6	0.3	1.1	2.4
2011	49,522	25,602	7,827	11,759	2,513	2,334	179	547	1,272	100.0	51.7	15.8	23.7	5.1	4.7	0.4	1.1	2.6
2012	49,771	25,386	7,803	12,104	2,552	2,372	180	534	1,393	100.0	51.0	15.7	24.3	5.1	4.8	0.4	1.1	2.8
2013	50,045	25,160	7,805	12,452	2,593	2,417	176	523	1,511	100.0	50.3	15.6	24.9	5.2	4.8	0.4	1.0	3.0
2014	50,313	24,923	7,807	12,805	2,646	2,470	176	519	1,612	100.0	49.5	15.5	25.4	5.3	4.9	0.3	1.0	3.2
2015[2]	50,438	24,644	7,784	13,080	2,697	2,521	177	510	1,723	100.0	48.9	15.4	25.9	5.3	5.0	0.4	1.0	3.4
2016[3]	50,615	24,413	7,765	13,329	2,756	2,571	184	511	1,842	100.0	48.2	15.3	26.3	5.4	5.1	0.4	1.0	3.6
2017[2]	50,686	24,124	7,709	13,571	2,825	2,640	185	498	1,959	100.0	47.6	15.2	26.8	5.6	5.2	0.4	1.0	3.9
2018[4]	50,650	23,846	7,671	13,704	2,878	2,691	187	491	2,060	100.0	47.1	15.1	27.1	5.7	5.3	0.4	1.0	4.1
2019[4]	50,634	23,597	7,639	13,831	2,925	2,737	188	484	2,160	100.0	46.6	15.1	27.3	5.8	5.4	0.4	1.0	4.3
2020[4]	50,654	23,376	7,616	13,952	2,976	2,787	189	477	2,257	100.0	46.1	15.0	27.5	5.9	5.5	0.4	0.9	4.5
2021[4]	50,643	23,170	7,598	14,044	3,013	2,823	190	471	2,347	100.0	45.8	15.0	27.7	5.9	5.6	0.4	0.9	4.6
2022[4]	50,721	23,041	7,636	14,070	3,071	2,882	189	464	2,439	100.0	45.4	15.1	27.7	6.1	5.7	0.4	0.9	4.8
2023[4]	50,768	22,910	7,657	14,082	3,126	2,939	187	458	2,535	100.0	45.1	15.1	27.7	6.2	5.8	0.4	0.9	5.0
2024[4]	50,758	22,779	7,665	14,057	3,185	2,999	186	452	2,619	100.0	44.9	15.1	27.7	6.3	5.9	0.4	0.9	5.2
2025[4]	50,704	22,639	7,664	14,016	3,246	3,060	186	446	2,694	100.0	44.6	15.1	27.6	6.4	6.0	0.4	0.9	5.3
2026[4]	50,672	22,522	7,664	13,975	3,307	3,122	185	441	2,762	100.0	44.4	15.1	27.6	6.5	6.2	0.4	0.9	5.5
2027[4]	50,734	22,446	7,675	13,967	3,378	3,192	186	437	2,832	100.0	44.2	15.1	27.5	6.7	6.3	0.4	0.9	5.6
2028[4]	50,885	22,401	7,707	13,995	3,446	3,260	186	434	2,901	100.0	44.0	15.1	27.5	6.8	6.4	0.4	0.9	5.7
2029[4]	51,068	22,359	7,746	14,049	3,514	3,327	186	433	2,967	100.0	43.8	15.2	27.5	6.9	6.5	0.4	0.8	5.8
Prekindergarten through grade 8																		
1999	33,486	20,327	5,952	5,512	1,303	—	—	391	—	100.0	60.7	17.8	16.5	3.9	†	†	1.2	†
2000	33,686	20,130	5,981	5,830	1,349	—	—	397	—	100.0	59.8	17.8	17.3	4.0	†	†	1.2	†
2001	33,936	19,960	6,004	6,159	1,409	—	—	405	—	100.0	58.8	17.7	18.1	4.2	†	†	1.2	†
2002	34,114	19,764	6,042	6,446	1,447	—	—	415	—	100.0	57.9	17.7	18.9	4.2	†	†	1.2	†
2003	34,201	19,558	6,015	6,729	1,483	—	—	415	—	100.0	57.2	17.6	19.7	4.3	†	†	1.2	†
2004	34,178	19,368	5,983	6,909	1,504	—	—	413	—	100.0	56.7	17.5	20.2	4.4	†	†	1.2	†
2005	34,204	19,051	5,954	7,216	1,569	—	—	412	—	100.0	55.7	17.4	21.1	4.6	†	†	1.2	†
2006	34,235	18,863	5,882	7,465	1,611	—	—	414	—	100.0	55.1	17.2	21.8	4.7	†	†	1.2	†
2007	34,204	18,679	5,821	7,632	1,660	—	—	412	—	100.0	54.6	17.0	22.3	4.9	†	†	1.2	†
2008	34,286	18,501	5,793	7,689	1,705	1,674	31	410	187[1]	100.0	54.0	16.9	22.4	5.0	4.9	0.1	1.2	0.5[1]
2009	34,409	18,316	5,713	7,977	1,730	1,697	33	419	254[1]	100.0	53.2	16.6	23.2	5.0	4.9	0.1	1.2	0.7[1]
2010	34,625	17,823	5,495	8,314	1,711	1,589	122	394	887	100.0	51.5	15.9	24.0	4.9	4.6	0.4	1.1	2.6
2011	34,773	17,654	5,470	8,558	1,744	1,616	128	384	963	100.0	50.8	15.7	24.6	5.0	4.6	0.4	1.1	2.8
2012	35,018	17,535	5,473	8,804	1,773	1,644	129	375	1,057	100.0	50.1	15.6	25.1	5.1	4.7	0.4	1.1	3.0
2013	35,251	17,390	5,483	9,054	1,809	1,683	126	367	1,148	100.0	49.3	15.6	25.7	5.1	4.8	0.4	1.0	3.3
2014	35,370	17,193	5,471	9,273	1,842	1,718	124	363	1,227	100.0	48.6	15.5	26.2	5.2	4.9	0.4	1.0	3.5
2015[2]	35,388	16,972	5,448	9,424	1,878	1,754	124	356	1,311	100.0	48.0	15.4	26.6	5.3	5.0	0.4	1.0	3.7
2016[3]	35,477	16,823	5,440	9,544	1,914	1,784	129	358	1,399	100.0	47.4	15.3	26.9	5.4	5.0	0.4	1.0	3.9
2017[2]	35,496	16,623	5,409	9,678	1,956	1,827	129	347	1,482	100.0	46.8	15.2	27.3	5.5	5.1	0.4	1.0	4.2
2018[4]	35,443	16,442	5,401	9,718	1,992	1,862	130	342	1,549	100.0	46.4	15.2	27.4	5.6	5.3	0.4	1.0	4.4
2019[4]	35,402	16,291	5,393	9,748	2,023	1,894	129	336	1,610	100.0	46.0	15.2	27.5	5.7	5.3	0.4	0.9	4.5
2020[4]	35,293	16,130	5,371	9,745	2,060	1,930	130	330	1,658	100.0	45.7	15.2	27.6	5.8	5.5	0.4	0.9	4.7
2021[4]	35,094	15,968	5,324	9,700	2,086	1,956	130	323	1,693	100.0	45.5	15.2	27.6	5.9	5.6	0.4	0.9	4.8
2022[4]	35,019	15,900	5,332	9,603	2,135	2,007	129	318	1,730	100.0	45.4	15.2	27.4	6.1	5.7	0.4	0.9	4.9
2023[4]	35,022	15,856	5,336	9,549	2,187	2,058	129	313	1,780	100.0	45.3	15.2	27.3	6.2	5.9	0.4	0.9	5.1
2024[4]	35,123	15,852	5,365	9,529	2,238	2,109	129	310	1,828	100.0	45.1	15.3	27.1	6.4	6.0	0.4	0.9	5.2
2025[4]	35,267	15,858	5,406	9,531	2,290	2,161	129	309	1,872	100.0	45.0	15.3	27.0	6.5	6.1	0.4	0.9	5.3
2026[4]	35,452	15,868	5,449	9,567	2,338	2,209	129	309	1,922	100.0	44.8	15.4	27.0	6.6	6.2	0.4	0.9	5.4
2027[4]	35,641	15,872	5,493	9,617	2,376	2,248	128	308	1,975	100.0	44.5	15.4	27.0	6.7	6.3	0.4	0.9	5.5
2028[4]	35,818	15,855	5,533	9,672	2,421	2,293	128	308	2,030	100.0	44.3	15.4	27.0	6.8	6.4	0.4	0.9	5.7
2029[4]	35,987	15,832	5,572	9,726	2,462	2,335	127	308	2,087	100.0	44.0	15.5	27.0	6.8	6.5	0.4	0.9	5.8

See notes at end of table.

Table 203.60. Enrollment and percentage distribution of enrollment in public elementary and secondary schools, by race/ethnicity and level of education: Fall 1999 through fall 2029—Continued

Level of education and year	Enrollment (in thousands)									Percentage distribution								
					Asian/Pacific Islander									Asian/Pacific Islander				
	Total	White	Black	Hispanic	Total	Asian	Pacific Islander	American Indian/ Alaska Native	Two or more races	Total	White	Black	Hispanic	Total	Asian	Pacific Islander	American Indian/ Alaska Native	Two or more races
1	2	3	4	5	6	7	8	9	10	11	12	13	14	15	16	17	18	19
Grades 9 through 12																		
1999	13,371	8,708	2,114	1,815	584	—	—	151	—	100.0	65.1	15.8	13.6	4.4	†	†	1.1	†
2000	13,517	8,747	2,119	1,896	601	—	—	153	—	100.0	64.7	15.7	14.0	4.4	†	†	1.1	†
2001	13,736	8,774	2,173	2,011	619	—	—	159	—	100.0	63.9	15.8	14.6	4.5	†	†	1.2	†
2002	14,069	8,854	2,257	2,148	642	—	—	168	—	100.0	62.9	16.0	15.3	4.6	†	†	1.2	†
2003	14,339	8,884	2,334	2,282	663	—	—	177	—	100.0	62.0	16.3	15.9	4.6	†	†	1.2	†
2004	14,618	8,950	2,403	2,408	679	—	—	178	—	100.0	61.2	16.4	16.5	4.6	†	†	1.2	†
2005	14,909	8,954	2,490	2,570	709	—	—	186	—	100.0	60.1	16.7	17.2	4.8	†	†	1.2	†
2006	15,081	8,938	2,540	2,701	720	—	—	181	—	100.0	59.3	16.8	17.9	4.8	†	†	1.2	†
2007	15,086	8,775	2,571	2,821	736	—	—	183	—	100.0	58.2	17.0	18.7	4.9	†	†	1.2	†
2008	14,980	8,556	2,565	2,874	746	731	15	179	59[1]	100.0	57.1	17.1	19.2	5.0	4.9	0.1	1.2	0.4[1]
2009	14,952	8,385	2,532	3,014	754	738	16	182	84[1]	100.0	56.1	16.9	20.2	5.0	4.9	0.1	1.2	0.6[1]
2010	14,860	8,109	2,422	3,125	755	707	49	171	277	100.0	54.6	16.3	21.0	5.1	4.8	0.3	1.2	1.9
2011	14,749	7,948	2,357	3,202	769	719	50	163	309	100.0	53.9	16.0	21.7	5.2	4.9	0.3	1.1	2.1
2012	14,753	7,851	2,330	3,300	779	727	51	158	335	100.0	53.2	15.8	22.4	5.3	4.9	0.3	1.1	2.3
2013	14,794	7,770	2,322	3,398	784	733	51	156	363	100.0	52.5	15.7	23.0	5.3	5.0	0.3	1.1	2.5
2014	14,943	7,730	2,336	3,532	804	753	52	156	385	100.0	51.7	15.6	23.6	5.4	5.0	0.3	1.0	2.6
2015[2]	15,050	7,672	2,336	3,656	819	767	52	154	412	100.0	51.0	15.5	24.3	5.4	5.1	0.3	1.0	2.7
2016[3]	15,138	7,590	2,324	3,786	842	787	55	153	443	100.0	50.1	15.4	25.0	5.6	5.2	0.4	1.0	2.9
2017[2]	15,190	7,501	2,300	3,892	869	813	56	150	477	100.0	49.4	15.1	25.6	5.7	5.4	0.4	1.0	3.1
2018[4]	15,206	7,405	2,270	3,986	885	829	57	149	511	100.0	48.7	14.9	26.2	5.8	5.4	0.4	1.0	3.4
2019[4]	15,232	7,305	2,245	4,083	902	843	58	147	550	100.0	48.0	14.7	26.8	5.9	5.5	0.4	1.0	3.6
2020[4]	15,361	7,245	2,245	4,208	916	857	59	147	600	100.0	47.2	14.6	27.4	6.0	5.6	0.4	1.0	3.9
2021[4]	15,549	7,202	2,274	4,345	927	867	60	148	654	100.0	46.3	14.6	27.9	6.0	5.6	0.4	0.9	4.2
2022[4]	15,703	7,142	2,304	4,467	935	875	60	146	709	100.0	45.5	14.7	28.5	6.0	5.6	0.4	0.9	4.5
2023[4]	15,746	7,054	2,321	4,533	939	881	58	145	755	100.0	44.8	14.7	28.8	6.0	5.6	0.4	0.9	4.8
2024[4]	15,635	6,927	2,300	4,528	947	889	58	141	791	100.0	44.3	14.7	29.0	6.1	5.7	0.4	0.9	5.1
2025[4]	15,438	6,781	2,259	4,485	956	899	57	136	821	100.0	43.9	14.6	29.0	6.2	5.8	0.4	0.9	5.3
2026[4]	15,220	6,655	2,214	4,408	970	913	56	132	841	100.0	43.7	14.5	29.0	6.4	6.0	0.4	0.9	5.5
2027[4]	15,093	6,574	2,182	4,349	1,001	944	58	129	858	100.0	43.6	14.5	28.8	6.6	6.3	0.4	0.9	5.7
2028[4]	15,067	6,546	2,173	4,323	1,026	967	58	126	872	100.0	43.4	14.4	28.7	6.8	6.4	0.4	0.8	5.8
2029[4]	15,081	6,527	2,174	4,323	1,052	993	59	125	880	100.0	43.3	14.4	28.7	7.0	6.6	0.4	0.8	5.8

—Not available.
†Not applicable.
[1]For this year, data on students of Two or more races were reported by only a small number of states. Therefore, the data are not comparable to figures for 2010 and later years.
[2]Includes imputations for prekindergarten enrollment in California and Oregon.
[3]Includes imputations for prekindergarten enrollment in California.
[4]Projected.
NOTE: Race categories exclude persons of Hispanic ethnicity. Enrollment data for students not reported by race/ethnicity were prorated by state and grade to match state totals. Prior to 2008, data on students of Two or more races were not collected. Total counts of ungraded students were prorated to prekindergarten through grade 8 and grades 9 through 12 based on prior reports. Some data have been revised from previously published figures. Detail may not sum to totals because of rounding.
SOURCE: U.S. Department of Education, National Center for Education Statistics, Common Core of Data (CCD), "State Nonfiscal Survey of Public Elementary and Secondary Education," 1998–99 through 2017–18; and National Elementary and Secondary Enrollment by Race/Ethnicity Projection Model, 1972 through 2029. (This table was prepared December 2019.)

Table 203.70. Percentage distribution of enrollment in public elementary and secondary schools, by race/ethnicity and state or jurisdiction: Fall 2000 and fall 2017

State or jurisdiction	Percentage distribution, fall 2000						Percentage distribution, fall 2017							
	Total	White	Black	Hispanic	Asian/ Pacific Islander	American Indian/ Alaska Native	Total	White	Black	Hispanic	Asian	Pacific Islander	American Indian/ Alaska Native	Two or more races
1	2	3	4	5	6	7	8	9	10	11	12	13	14	15
United States	**100.0**	**61.2**	**17.2**	**16.3**	**4.1**	**1.2**	**100.0**	**47.6**	**15.2**	**26.7**	**5.2**	**0.4**	**1.0**	**3.9**
Alabama	100.0	60.8	36.5	1.3	0.7	0.7	100.0	54.5	32.8	7.9	1.5	0.1	0.9	2.2
Alaska	100.0	61.5	4.6	3.4	5.5	25.0	100.0	47.6	2.9	6.7	5.9	2.9	22.9	11.1
Arizona	100.0	52.8	4.6	33.9	2.1	6.6	100.0	38.2	5.4	45.5	2.9	0.4	4.5	3.1
Arkansas	100.0	71.7	23.3	3.6	0.9	0.5	100.0	60.8	20.4	13.1	1.6	0.8	0.6	2.6
California	100.0	36.1	8.5	43.4	11.1	0.9	100.0	23.2	5.5	54.3	11.6	0.5	0.5	4.5
Colorado	100.0	68.2	5.7	22.0	2.9	1.2	100.0	53.4	4.6	33.7	3.2	0.3	0.7	4.2
Connecticut	100.0	70.1	13.7	13.1	2.8	0.3	100.0	53.6	12.8	24.8	5.1	0.1	0.3	3.3
Delaware	100.0	60.7	30.8	6.0	2.3	0.3	100.0	44.2	30.3	17.4	3.9	0.1	0.4	3.7
District of Columbia	100.0	4.5	84.6	9.2	1.6	0.1	100.0	11.1	68.5	16.3	1.6	0.1	0.2	2.2
Florida	100.0	53.3	25.2	19.4	1.9	0.3	100.0	38.0	22.1	33.1	2.7	0.2	0.3	3.5
Georgia	100.0	54.7	38.2	4.8	2.2	0.2	100.0	39.7	36.7	15.6	4.1	0.1	0.2	3.7
Hawaii	100.0	20.4	2.3	4.5	72.3	0.4	100.0	12.2	1.7	14.2	28.6	28.6	0.2	14.4
Idaho	100.0	86.0	0.7	10.7	1.2	1.4	100.0	75.4	1.1	18.1	1.2	0.3	1.1	2.7
Illinois	100.0	59.8	21.3	15.4	3.4	0.2	100.0	48.0	16.8	26.2	5.1	0.1	0.3	3.5
Indiana	100.0	83.6	11.7	3.5	1.0	0.2	100.0	67.9	12.6	11.9	2.4	0.1	0.2	4.9
Iowa	100.0	90.2	4.0	3.6	1.7	0.5	100.0	75.9	6.1	10.8	2.5	0.3	0.4	4.0
Kansas	100.0	78.7	8.9	8.9	2.2	1.3	100.0	64.2	6.9	19.8	2.8	0.2	1.0	5.2
Kentucky	100.0	87.5	10.7	1.0	0.6	0.2	100.0	76.8	10.5	6.7	1.8	0.1	0.1	3.9
Louisiana	100.0	48.9	47.8	1.4	1.3	0.6	100.0	44.7	43.6	6.9	1.6	0.1	0.7	2.5
Maine	100.0	96.5	1.2	0.6	1.0	0.7	100.0	89.3	3.6	2.2	1.5	0.1	0.8	2.5
Maryland	100.0	53.4	37.1	4.8	4.4	0.4	100.0	37.3	33.7	17.4	6.6	0.1	0.3	4.6
Massachusetts	100.0	76.1	8.5	10.7	4.4	0.3	100.0	60.2	9.0	20.0	6.8	0.1	0.2	3.6
Michigan	100.0	73.8	19.8	3.5	1.8	1.0	100.0	66.2	18.0	7.9	3.4	0.1	0.6	3.9
Minnesota	100.0	82.9	6.6	3.4	5.1	2.0	100.0	66.5	11.0	9.3	6.8	0.1	1.6	4.7
Mississippi	100.0	47.3	51.1	0.8	0.7	0.1	100.0	44.2	48.5	3.7	1.1	0.1	0.2	2.1
Missouri	100.0	79.3	17.4	1.8	1.2	0.3	100.0	71.1	15.9	6.4	2.0	0.3	0.4	3.9
Montana	100.0	86.2	0.6	1.7	1.0	10.5	100.0	78.3	0.9	4.6	0.8	0.2	11.6	3.6
Nebraska	100.0	83.0	6.7	7.3	1.5	1.5	100.0	66.5	6.7	18.8	2.8	0.1	1.4	3.8
Nevada	100.0	56.7	10.2	25.7	5.7	1.7	100.0	32.5	11.1	42.4	5.5	1.4	0.9	6.2
New Hampshire	100.0	95.5	1.1	1.8	1.3	0.2	100.0	85.5	2.0	5.6	3.3	0.1	0.3	3.3
New Jersey	100.0	60.3	17.9	15.3	6.3	0.2	100.0	43.6	15.3	28.7	10.0	0.2	0.1	2.0
New Mexico	100.0	35.3	2.4	50.2	1.1	11.1	100.0	23.2	1.9	61.7	1.1	0.1	10.0	1.9
New York	100.0	54.9	20.2	18.5	6.0	0.4	100.0	43.2	17.2	27.0	9.3	0.3	0.7	2.4
North Carolina	100.0	61.0	31.3	4.4	1.9	1.5	100.0	48.2	25.3	17.5	3.3	0.1	1.2	4.3
North Dakota	100.0	89.4	1.0	1.2	0.8	7.6	100.0	77.4	4.9	4.9	1.6	0.3	8.5	2.4
Ohio	100.0	80.7	16.3	1.7	1.1	0.1	100.0	69.9	16.6	5.7	2.4	0.1	0.1	5.2
Oklahoma	100.0	64.9	10.8	6.0	1.4	16.9	100.0	48.9	8.6	17.2	2.0	0.4	13.6	9.3
Oregon	100.0	80.4	2.9	10.5	4.0	2.1	100.0	62.4	2.3	23.0	4.0	0.7	1.3	6.1
Pennsylvania	100.0	78.2	15.1	4.5	2.0	0.1	100.0	65.8	14.7	11.4	3.9	0.1	0.2	3.9
Rhode Island	100.0	74.3	7.9	14.0	3.3	0.5	100.0	57.7	8.6	25.3	3.3	0.2	0.7	4.2
South Carolina	100.0	54.9	42.1	1.9	1.0	0.2	100.0	50.8	33.6	9.5	1.6	0.1	0.3	4.1
South Dakota	100.0	86.5	1.2	1.2	0.9	10.1	100.0	73.9	3.2	6.0	1.8	0.1	11.1	4.0
Tennessee	100.0	72.4	24.5	1.8	1.1	0.2	100.0	62.8	21.9	10.3	2.0	0.1	0.2	2.7
Texas	100.0	42.0	14.4	40.6	2.7	0.3	100.0	27.9	12.6	52.4	4.4	0.1	0.4	2.3
Utah	100.0	85.8	1.0	8.9	2.8	1.6	100.0	74.4	1.4	17.1	1.7	1.6	1.1	2.7
Vermont	100.0	96.3	1.1	0.6	1.4	0.6	100.0	90.2	2.1	2.0	2.0	0.1	0.2	3.5
Virginia	100.0	63.6	27.1	4.9	4.1	0.3	100.0	48.9	22.4	15.7	7.0	0.2	0.3	5.5
Washington	100.0	74.4	5.3	10.2	7.3	2.7	100.0	54.4	4.4	23.2	7.7	1.1	1.2	8.0
West Virginia	100.0	94.7	4.3	0.4	0.5	0.1	100.0	90.1	4.3	1.8	0.7	#	0.1	3.1
Wisconsin	100.0	80.7	10.0	4.5	3.3	1.4	100.0	69.9	9.2	12.0	4.0	0.1	1.1	3.8
Wyoming	100.0	87.9	1.2	6.9	0.9	3.1	100.0	77.9	1.1	13.7	0.8	0.1	3.7	2.6
Bureau of Indian Education	100.0	0.0	0.0	0.0	0.0	100.0	100.0	0.0	0.0	0.0	0.0	0.0	100.0	0.0
DoDEA[1]	100.0	56.9	23.1	11.4	7.9	0.8	—	—	—	—	—	—	—	—
Other jurisdictions														
American Samoa	100.0	0.0	0.0	0.0	100.0	0.0	100.0	0.1	#	#	0.4	99.4	#	0.0
Guam	100.0	1.7	0.3	0.2	97.7	0.1	100.0	0.6	0.1	0.1	22.3	74.3	0.1	2.5
Northern Marianas	100.0	0.3	#	0.0	99.7	0.0	—	—	—	—	—	—	—	—
Puerto Rico	100.0	0.0	0.0	100.0	0.0	0.0	100.0	0.1	#	99.8	#	#	0.1	0.0
U.S. Virgin Islands	100.0	0.8	85.8	13.1	0.2	0.1	100.0	1.7	77.0	20.2	0.6	0.1	0.1	0.3

—Not available.
#Rounds to zero.
[1]DoDEA = Department of Defense Education Activity. Includes both domestic and overseas schools.
NOTE: Percentage distribution based on students for whom race/ethnicity was reported, which may be less than the total number of students in the state. Race categories exclude persons of Hispanic ethnicity. Detail may not sum to totals because of rounding.

SOURCE: U.S. Department of Education, National Center for Education Statistics, Common Core of Data (CCD), "State Nonfiscal Survey of Public Elementary/Secondary Education," 2000–01 and 2017–18. (This table was prepared January 2020.)

Table 203.75. Enrollment and percentage distribution of enrollment in public schools, by family poverty rate of 5- to 17-year-olds living in the school district, student race/ethnicity, region, and school locale: 2017-18

Student race/ethnicity, region, and school locale	Enrollment					Percentage distribution of enrollment				
		Family poverty rate[1] of 5- to 17-year-olds[2] living in the school district					Family poverty rate[1] of 5- to 17-year-olds[2] living in the school district			
	Total	0 to 9.455 percent	9.456 to 15.905 percent	15.906 to 22.407 percent	22.408 percent or more	Total	0 to 9.455 percent	9.456 to 15.905 percent	15.906 to 22.407 percent	22.408 percent or more
1	2	3	4	5	6	7	8	9	10	11
Total	**50,250,033**	**12,541,168**	**12,495,250**	**12,261,881**	**12,951,734**	**100.0**	**25.0**	**24.9**	**24.4**	**25.8**
White	23,842,957	8,308,497	6,769,184	5,274,884	3,490,392	100.0	34.8	28.4	22.1	14.6
Black	7,696,585	743,434	1,426,103	1,961,593	3,565,455	100.0	9.7	18.5	25.5	46.3
Hispanic	13,433,268	1,777,796	2,892,572	3,929,772	4,833,128	100.0	13.2	21.5	29.3	36.0
Asian	2,618,712	1,076,623	657,219	417,166	467,704	100.0	41.1	25.1	15.9	17.9
Pacific Islander	183,283	27,241	95,423	37,317	23,302	100.0	14.9	52.1	20.4	12.7
American Indian/Alaska Native	491,330	55,052	107,326	121,080	207,872	100.0	11.2	21.8	24.6	42.3
Two or more races	1,937,255	552,450	546,693	474,335	363,777	100.0	28.5	28.2	24.5	18.8
Race unknown	46,643	75	730	45,734	104	100.0	0.2	1.6	98.1	0.2
Region										
Northeast	**7,934,060**	**3,071,124**	**1,633,086**	**991,919**	**2,237,931**	**100.0**	**38.7**	**20.6**	**12.5**	**28.2**
White	4,261,036	2,277,224	1,059,895	491,391	432,526	100.0	53.4	24.9	11.5	10.2
Black	1,115,187	146,220	182,918	153,321	632,728	100.0	13.1	16.4	13.7	56.7
Hispanic	1,712,472	287,551	269,439	281,191	874,291	100.0	16.8	15.7	16.4	51.1
Asian	569,733	261,113	59,489	31,755	217,376	100.0	45.8	10.4	5.6	38.2
Pacific Islander	13,475	3,666	2,216	987	6,606	100.0	27.2	16.4	7.3	49.0
American Indian/Alaska Native	30,207	5,190	5,104	3,209	16,704	100.0	17.2	16.9	10.6	55.3
Two or more races	231,841	90,087	54,000	30,060	57,694	100.0	38.9	23.3	13.0	24.9
Race unknown	109	73	25	5	6	100.0	67.0	22.9	4.6	5.5
Midwest	**8,516,808**	**3,040,910**	**2,400,703**	**1,695,761**	**1,379,434**	**100.0**	**35.7**	**28.2**	**19.9**	**16.2**
White	5,861,251	2,424,897	1,815,107	1,076,618	544,629	100.0	41.4	31.0	18.4	9.3
Black	1,107,651	156,816	167,456	246,011	537,368	100.0	14.2	15.1	22.2	48.5
Hispanic	814,280	190,689	229,981	228,998	164,612	100.0	23.4	28.2	28.1	20.2
Asian	269,988	133,106	61,126	36,289	39,467	100.0	49.3	22.6	13.4	14.6
Pacific Islander	10,579	2,882	3,262	2,755	1,680	100.0	27.2	30.8	26.0	15.9
American Indian/Alaska Native	76,084	12,821	20,907	19,539	22,817	100.0	16.9	27.5	25.7	30.0
Two or more races	375,867	119,699	102,329	84,978	68,861	100.0	31.8	27.2	22.6	18.3
Race unknown	1,108	0	535	573	0	100.0	0.0	48.3	51.7	0.0
South	**19,823,783**	**2,586,724**	**4,700,640**	**6,159,458**	**6,376,961**	**100.0**	**13.0**	**23.7**	**31.1**	**32.2**
White	8,438,073	1,390,201	2,333,488	2,690,149	2,024,235	100.0	16.5	27.7	31.9	24.0
Black	4,554,700	324,350	889,059	1,311,550	2,029,741	100.0	7.1	19.5	28.8	44.6
Hispanic	5,248,709	495,355	1,028,863	1,732,465	1,992,026	100.0	9.4	19.6	33.0	38.0
Asian	688,762	235,906	212,844	147,468	92,544	100.0	34.3	30.9	21.4	13.4
Pacific Islander	31,673	3,907	7,625	13,218	6,923	100.0	12.3	24.1	41.7	21.9
American Indian/Alaska Native	173,754	13,793	36,344	49,625	73,992	100.0	7.9	20.9	28.6	42.6
Two or more races	688,001	123,212	192,416	214,971	157,402	100.0	17.9	28.0	31.2	22.9
Race unknown	111	0	1	12	98	100.0	0.0	0.9	10.8	88.3
West	**13,975,382**	**3,842,410**	**3,760,821**	**3,414,743**	**2,957,408**	**100.0**	**27.5**	**26.9**	**24.4**	**21.2**
White	5,282,597	2,216,175	1,560,694	1,016,726	489,002	100.0	42.0	29.5	19.2	9.3
Black	919,047	116,048	186,670	250,711	365,618	100.0	12.6	20.3	27.3	39.8
Hispanic	5,657,807	804,201	1,364,289	1,687,118	1,802,199	100.0	14.2	24.1	29.8	31.9
Asian	1,090,229	446,498	323,760	201,654	118,317	100.0	41.0	29.7	18.5	10.9
Pacific Islander	127,556	16,786	82,320	20,357	8,093	100.0	13.2	64.5	16.0	6.3
American Indian/Alaska Native	211,285	23,248	44,971	48,707	94,359	100.0	11.0	21.3	23.1	44.7
Two or more races	641,546	219,452	197,948	144,326	79,820	100.0	34.2	30.9	22.5	12.4
Race unknown	45,315	2	169	45,144	0	100.0	#	0.4	99.6	0.0
School locale										
City	**15,925,912**	**1,777,744**	**2,589,539**	**4,375,049**	**7,183,580**	**100.0**	**11.2**	**16.3**	**27.5**	**45.1**
White	4,637,207	901,110	1,144,964	1,425,591	1,165,542	100.0	19.4	24.7	30.7	25.1
Black	3,540,268	124,678	261,029	894,276	2,260,285	100.0	3.5	7.4	25.3	63.8
Hispanic	5,858,525	355,300	809,826	1,569,627	3,123,772	100.0	6.1	13.8	26.8	53.3
Asian	1,053,594	274,788	194,354	196,255	388,197	100.0	26.1	18.4	18.6	36.8
Pacific Islander	61,152	5,490	18,595	21,074	15,993	100.0	9.0	30.4	34.5	26.2
American Indian/Alaska Native	112,360	11,335	24,035	36,903	40,087	100.0	10.1	21.4	32.8	35.7
Two or more races	631,959	105,034	136,734	200,584	189,607	100.0	16.6	21.6	31.7	30.0
Race unknown	30,847	9	2	30,739	97	100.0	#	#	99.6	0.3
Suburban	**21,483,887**	**8,623,754**	**6,338,434**	**4,443,742**	**2,077,957**	**100.0**	**40.1**	**29.5**	**20.7**	**9.7**
White	10,418,436	5,642,790	2,890,889	1,414,566	470,191	100.0	54.2	27.7	13.6	4.5
Black	2,995,727	562,433	999,255	854,898	579,141	100.0	18.8	33.4	28.5	19.3
Hispanic	5,553,818	1,230,642	1,634,579	1,784,515	904,082	100.0	22.2	29.4	32.1	16.3
Asian	1,420,673	758,511	423,856	187,632	50,674	100.0	53.4	29.8	13.2	3.6
Pacific Islander	104,967	19,152	71,963	10,741	3,111	100.0	18.2	68.6	10.2	3.0
American Indian/Alaska Native	92,057	29,076	31,583	23,337	8,061	100.0	31.6	34.3	25.4	8.8
Two or more races	883,704	381,089	286,284	153,635	62,696	100.0	43.1	32.4	17.4	7.1
Race unknown	14,505	61	25	14,418	1	100.0	0.4	0.2	99.4	#
Town	**5,487,936**	**702,496**	**1,540,260**	**1,552,055**	**1,693,125**	**100.0**	**12.8**	**28.1**	**28.3**	**30.9**
White	3,494,835	574,280	1,156,507	1,044,263	719,785	100.0	16.4	33.1	29.9	20.6
Black	484,328	15,320	41,543	83,354	344,111	100.0	3.2	8.6	17.2	71.0
Hispanic	1,120,420	69,888	240,571	317,850	492,111	100.0	6.2	21.5	28.4	43.9
Asian	64,490	12,537	19,202	16,783	15,968	100.0	19.4	29.8	26.0	24.8
Pacific Islander	9,838	1,177	2,657	3,758	2,246	100.0	12.0	27.0	38.2	22.8
American Indian/Alaska Native	122,496	6,651	24,146	28,135	63,564	100.0	5.4	19.7	23.0	51.9
Two or more races	191,525	22,642	55,634	57,909	55,340	100.0	11.8	29.0	30.2	28.9
Race unknown	4	1	0	3	0	100.0	25.0	0.0	75.0	0.0

Student race/ethnicity, region, and school locale	Enrollment: Total	Enrollment: Family poverty rate[1] of 5- to 17-year-olds[2] living in the school district: 0 to 9.455 percent	9.456 to 15.905 percent	15.906 to 22.407 percent	22.408 percent or more	Percentage distribution of enrollment: Total	Percentage distribution: Family poverty rate[1] of 5- to 17-year-olds[2] living in the school district: 0 to 9.455 percent	9.456 to 15.905 percent	15.906 to 22.407 percent	22.408 percent or more
1	2	3	4	5	6	7	8	9	10	11
Rural	**7,653,484**	**1,508,564**	**2,193,245**	**1,952,066**	**1,999,609**	**100.0**	**19.7**	**28.7**	**25.5**	**26.1**
White	5,519,664	1,248,320	1,703,272	1,431,351	1,136,721	100.0	22.6	30.9	25.9	20.6
Black	679,507	41,859	126,095	129,623	381,930	100.0	6.2	18.6	19.1	56.2
Hispanic	955,051	130,200	237,195	274,205	313,451	100.0	13.6	24.8	28.7	32.8
Asian	83,675	32,009	21,730	17,061	12,875	100.0	38.3	26.0	20.4	15.4
Pacific Islander	8,288	1,666	2,723	1,942	1,957	100.0	20.1	32.9	23.4	23.6
American Indian/Alaska Native	167,862	8,401	29,051	33,989	96,421	100.0	5.0	17.3	20.2	57.4
Two or more races	238,150	46,105	72,476	63,321	56,248	100.0	19.4	30.4	26.6	23.6
Race unknown	1,287	4	703	574	6	100.0	0.3	54.6	44.6	0.5

#Rounds to zero.

[1] A family is in poverty if its income falls below the Census Bureau's poverty threshold, which is a dollar amount that varies depending on a family's size and composition and is updated annually to account for inflation. In 2018, for example, the poverty threshold for a family of four with two children was $25,465. The family poverty rate of 5- to 17-year-olds is the percentage of children in this age group whose families are in poverty. Includes only children classified as "related" and "relevant" (see footnote 2). For additional information about poverty status, see https://www.census.gov/topics/income-poverty/poverty/guidance/poverty-measures.html.

[2] Includes only those children who live in households and meet both of the following conditions: (1) The children are related to the householder by birth, marriage, or adoption (except a child who is the spouse of the householder). The householder is the person (or one of the people) who owns or rents (maintains) the housing unit. (2) The children are relevant to the school district. Children are relevant if they reside within the geographical boundaries of the district and are at a grade level served by the district, even if they do not attend a school in the district.

NOTE: School enrollment data were obtained from the Common Core of Data and poverty rate data were obtained from the Census Bureau. To create the school district categories, public school districts were ranked and divided into quarters based on the family poverty rate of their 5- to 17-year-old population; the cut points between the four quarters were chosen so that, at the national level, each quarter contains approximately the same number of students. For the approximately 3 percent of public school students who attended charter or other special districts, no data were available on their school district's family poverty rate. The rate for their district was imputed to be the same as the rate for the county containing the zip code listed for their superintendent's location. This table excludes 7,494 enrolled children whose poverty status could not be determined. Race categories exclude persons of Hispanic ethnicity.

SOURCE: U.S. Department of Education, National Center for Education Statistics, Common Core of Data (CCD), "Local Education Agency Universe Survey," 2017–18; and Education Demographic and Geographic Estimates (EDGE), "Public School File," 2017-18. U.S. Department of Commerce, Census Bureau, Small Area Income and Poverty Estimates (SAIPE) Program, 2018 Poverty Estimates for School Districts. (This table was prepared December 2019.)

Table 203.80. Average daily attendance (ADA) in public elementary and secondary schools, by state or jurisdiction: Selected years, 1969-70 through 2017-18

State or jurisdiction	1969-70	1979-80	1989-90	1999-2000	2007-08	2008-09	2009-10	2010-11	2011-12	2012-13	2013-14	2014-15	2015-16	
1	2	3	4	5	6	7	8	9	10	11	12	13	14	
United States	**41,934,376**	**38,288,911**	**37,799,296**	**43,806,726**	**46,155,880**	**46,173,477**	**45,919,206**	**46,118,737**	**46,400,465**	**46,553,754**	**46,829,716**	**47,064,337**	**47,248,060**	**47,2**
Alabama	777,123	711,432	683,833	725,212	731,161	712,179	698,208	709,225	715,402	688,614	706,566	702,430	697,618	(
Alaska	72,489	79,945	98,213	122,412	119,882	119,330	120,118	119,949	119,799	119,873	119,381	119,515	120,554	:
Arizona	391,526	481,905	557,252	782,851	973,689	999,386	968,764	964,683	969,825	973,369	989,026	993,460	997,670	1,(
Arkansas	414,158	423,610	403,025	422,958	439,347	439,432	435,676	443,118	443,125	470,644	449,815	447,483	449,578	‹
California[1]	4,418,423	4,044,736	4,893,341	5,957,216	6,365,266	6,365,278	6,017,381[2]	6,029,786[2]	6,034,192[2]	6,021,550[2]	6,048,363[2]	6,037,651[2]	6,031,796[2]	6,(
Colorado	500,388	513,475	519,419	656,700	735,549	747,845	762,190	763,147	779,747	784,242	798,520	798,176	814,441	{
Connecticut	618,881	507,362	439,524	533,779	553,445	549,776	548,787	537,104	534,846	534,350	528,163	523,101	517,742	!
Delaware	120,819	94,058	89,838	106,444	116,472	119,092	119,879	121,959	122,864	124,676	127,887	127,834	128,145	:
District of Columbia	138,600	91,576	71,468	65,371	61,636	68,447	68,217	69,575	71,910	76,579	74,208	78,109	79,590	
Florida	1,312,693	1,464,461	1,646,583	2,175,453	2,494,397	2,468,060	2,493,694	2,541,022	2,575,910	2,600,989	2,651,391	2,702,807	2,743,908	2,:
Georgia	1,019,427	989,433	1,054,097	1,326,713	1,561,935	1,569,767	1,596,180	1,621,397	1,646,051	1,646,352	1,670,887	1,685,269	1,696,996	1,(
Hawaii	168,140	151,563	157,360	171,180	166,179	166,118	165,766	169,926	171,763	173,092	175,246	169,296	169,894	:
Idaho	170,920	189,199	203,987	230,828	255,523	258,712	262,238	263,001	263,377	264,786	270,279	272,069	275,800	:
Illinois	2,084,844	1,770,435	1,587,733	1,789,089	1,881,810	1,881,276	1,887,561	1,863,017	1,858,409	1,867,289	1,858,766	1,844,870	1,838,813	1,{
Indiana	1,111,043	983,444	884,568	929,281	969,976	973,342	976,503	976,225	976,337	977,509	976,479	977,322	978,065	ç
Iowa	624,403	510,081	450,224	471,384	492,922	451,403	455,579	459,613	462,585	471,263	471,430	472,459	478,081	‹
Kansas	470,296	382,019	388,986	426,853	418,751	418,495	435,745	443,131	454,740	453,778	454,681	462,512	468,413	‹
Kentucky	647,970	619,868	569,795	565,693	585,775	585,556	587,102	593,323	594,440	618,774	622,088	617,642	618,606	(
Louisiana	776,555	727,601	727,125	701,957	631,163	637,764	643,374	654,093	664,640	673,911	676,421	680,540	681,707	(
Maine	225,146	211,400	195,089	194,554	175,161	173,357	168,213	165,067	166,483	164,339	163,539	160,260	160,600	:
Maryland	785,989	686,336	620,617	791,133	793,881	793,333	795,577	798,953	803,656	806,686	815,029	819,316	825,311	{
Massachusetts	1,056,207	935,960	763,231	913,502	917,181	913,976	912,792	910,568	906,736	907,954	912,102	908,322	908,385	ç
Michigan	1,991,235	1,758,427	1,446,996	1,574,894	1,528,815	1,498,107	1,477,312	1,452,125	1,438,279	1,422,806	1,412,373	1,398,468	1,386,658	1,:
Minnesota	864,595	748,606	699,001	818,819	790,206	791,427	785,455	786,838	792,437	795,827	800,941	804,465	811,549	{
Mississippi	524,623	454,401	476,048	468,746	461,459	460,797	460,327	460,894	460,703	461,356	456,100	454,100	451,492	‹
Missouri	906,132	777,269	729,693	836,105	852,106	853,580	852,460	839,997	840,917	843,762	847,838	847,524	849,768	{
Montana	162,664	144,608	135,406	142,313	132,104	131,982	130,704	130,949	133,266	132,579	133,187	133,438	133,521	:
Nebraska	314,516	270,524	254,754	261,767	264,810	266,536	269,590	271,468	285,837	288,023	292,297	296,753	285,527	:
Nevada	113,421	134,995	173,149	305,067	395,355	406,792	405,097	406,965	411,919	419,638	428,067	434,102	443,236	‹
New Hampshire	140,203	154,187	154,915	200,283	195,383	192,890	191,969	188,913	185,947	183,571	181,193	179,730	177,850	:
New Jersey	1,322,124	1,140,111	997,561	1,222,438	1,340,220	1,342,419	1,343,405	1,339,012	1,340,367	1,336,336	1,334,583	1,347,085	1,337,581	1,:
New Mexico	259,997	253,453	290,245	323,963	326,034	327,562	331,152	334,272	335,165	335,773	334,150	334,609	335,855	:
New York	3,099,192	2,530,289	2,244,110	2,595,070	2,520,932	2,510,519	2,516,922	2,513,770	2,512,327	2,500,382	2,498,180	2,497,078	2,498,603	2,‹
North Carolina	1,104,295	1,072,150	1,012,274	1,185,737	1,364,608	1,374,267	1,366,164	1,377,899	1,393,621	1,400,981	1,417,740	1,428,903	1,440,703	1,‹
North Dakota	141,961	118,986	109,659	105,123	91,972	91,816	91,114	92,440	94,310	97,135	99,380	101,334	103,652	:
Ohio	2,246,282	1,849,283	1,584,735	1,659,903	1,660,981	1,628,515	1,609,008	1,601,188	1,605,571	1,587,878	1,583,866	1,646,831	1,640,370	1,(
Oklahoma	560,993	548,065	543,170	586,266	596,450	603,375	610,019	616,775	624,410	630,766	639,376	644,034	650,035	(
Oregon	436,736	418,593	419,771	479,321	515,834	518,119	515,644	517,373	518,896	520,326	525,879	525,668	526,205	!
Pennsylvania	2,169,225	1,808,630	1,524,839	1,684,913	1,693,569	1,680,772	1,661,990	1,668,916	1,659,616	1,649,205	1,640,755	1,630,013	1,628,088	1,(
Rhode Island	163,205	139,195	125,934	144,422	134,737	131,963	131,538	131,494	131,379	131,056	130,705	130,747	131,778	:
South Carolina	600,292	569,612	569,029	624,456	656,996	662,231	664,136	664,133	673,850	681,402	688,327	697,021	708,282	:
South Dakota	158,543	124,934	119,823	122,252	114,723	114,209	115,242	119,449	120,950	123,220	123,988	125,671	126,634	:
Tennessee	836,010	806,696	761,766	844,878	891,430	895,335	896,130	899,382	903,695	910,540	912,575	914,854	914,418	ç
Texas	2,432,420	2,608,817	3,075,333	3,706,550	4,322,975	4,393,893	4,473,236	4,551,084	4,634,133	4,699,372	4,780,788	4,855,323	4,924,806	4,ç
Utah	287,405	312,813	408,917	448,096	503,562	513,884	528,608	540,683	556,885	561,680	572,091	581,819	592,659	(
Vermont	97,772	95,045	87,832	98,894	89,880	87,931	86,378	85,501	85,184	84,326	84,187	82,792	82,759	
Virginia	995,580	955,105	989,197	1,195,123	1,150,316	1,154,689	1,159,105	1,165,907	1,177,274	1,180,497	1,191,090	1,217,977	1,220,932	1,:
Washington	764,735	710,929	755,141	925,696	947,791	953,719	960,084	965,191	964,255	968,149	974,361	984,754	996,086	1,(
West Virginia	372,278	353,264	301,947	273,277	267,989	269,623	268,872	270,961	273,355	273,305	270,744	259,951	257,716	:
Wisconsin	880,609	770,554	711,466	825,699	823,754	823,595	817,284	825,622	825,949	829,261	829,249	822,319	822,133	{
Wyoming	81,293	89,471	91,277	86,092	79,788	81,006	80,717	81,654	83,131	83,983	85,439	86,531	87,451	
Other jurisdictions														
American Samoa	---	---	11,448	15,102	14,646	14,646	14,403	15,451	15,541	13,355	13,028	12,439	11,208	
Guam	20,315	---	23,883	---	28,358	28,521	28,075	28,765	28,735	29,591	28,932	29,022	29,922	
Northern Marianas	---	---	6,809	8,712	9,927	9,815	9,900	9,965	9,731	9,564	9,545	9,436	9,298	
Puerto Rico	---	656,709	597,436	540,676	494,880	477,918	466,483	411,164	429,799	422,560	397,960	404,611	365,632	:
U.S. Virgin Islands	---	---	18,924	18,676	15,903	15,768	15,493	15,747	15,711	15,192	12,178	10,684	10,159	

—Not available.

[1] Data for California for 1989-90 and earlier years are not strictly comparable with those for other states because California's attendance figures included excused absences.

[2] Excludes average daily attendance for regional occupational programs and summer school programs that were reported in prior years.

NOTE: Some data have been revised from previously published figures.

SOURCE: U.S. Department of Education, National Center for Education Statistics, Statistics of State School Systems, 1969-70; Revenues and Expenditures for Public Elementary and Secondary Education, 1979-80; and Common Core of Data (CCD), "National Public Education Financial Survey," 1989-90 through 2017-18. (This table was prepared January 2021.)

Table 203.90. Average daily attendance (ADA) as a percentage of total enrollment, school day length, and school year length in public schools, by school level and state: 2007-08 and 2011-12

[Standard errors appear in parentheses]

State	2007-08		2011-12							
			Total elementary, secondary, and combined elementary/secondary schools				Elementary schools		Secondary schools	
	ADA as percent of enrollment	Average hours in school day	ADA as percent of enrollment	Average hours in school day	Average days in school year	Average hours in school year	ADA as percent of enrollment	Average hours in school day	ADA as percent of enrollment	Average hours in school day
1	2	3	4	5	6	7	8	9	10	11
United States	**93.1 (0.22)**	**6.6 (0.02)**	**93.9 (0.12)**	**6.7 (0.01)**	**179 (0.1)**	**1,203 (2.0)**	**94.9 (0.12)**	**6.7 (0.01)**	**91.7 (0.34)**	**6.7 (0.02)**
Alabama	93.8 (1.24)	7.0 (0.07)	94.4 (0.94)	7.0 (0.04)	181 (0.8)	1,271 (8.5)	95.3 (0.92)	7.1 (0.04)	94.6 (0.65)	6.9 (0.13)
Alaska	89.9 (1.22)	6.5 (0.05)	91.4 (1.19)	6.7 (0.17)	177 (1.3)	1,183 (37.3)	‡ (†)	‡ (†)	‡ (†)	‡ (†)
Arizona	89.0 (2.95)	6.4 (0.09)	91.7 (0.99)	6.7 (0.08)	179 (1.3)	1,201 (12.5)	93.5 (0.53)	6.9 (0.06)	87.9 (2.40)	6.5 (0.26)
Arkansas	91.8 (1.35)	6.9 (0.06)	94.2 (0.58)	7.0 (0.07)	180 (0.5)	1,261 (14.1)	94.7 (0.36)	7.0 (0.08)	92.9 (1.93)	6.9 (0.14)
California	93.2 (0.71)	6.2 (0.07)	93.1 (0.46)	6.2 (0.05)	180 (0.3)	1,121 (9.0)	94.7 (0.51)	6.3 (0.06)	89.7 (1.08)	6.3 (0.08)
Colorado	93.9 (0.44)	7.0 (0.05)	93.1 (0.71)	7.1 (0.06)	172 (1.4)	1,215 (7.7)	94.6 (0.59)	7.0 (0.07)	88.0 (2.57)	7.1 (0.10)
Connecticut	87.9 (2.98)	6.5 (0.09)	94.9 (0.47)	6.6 (0.04)	181 (0.1)	1,201 (7.5)	95.4 (0.61)	6.6 (0.05)	94.3 (0.33)	6.7 (0.09)
Delaware	89.8 (1.75)	6.7 (0.09)	93.5 (0.50)	7.0 (0.10)	182 (1.2)	1,269 (23.7)	94.1 (0.50)	7.0 (0.12)	93.8 (0.71)	7.0 (0.09)
District of Columbia	91.2 (1.27)	6.9 (0.21)	‡ (†)	‡ (†)	‡ (†)	‡ (†)	‡ (†)	‡ (†)	‡ (†)	‡ (†)
Florida	92.7 (0.74)	6.4 (0.08)	93.2 (0.52)	6.6 (0.06)	181 (1.2)	1,193 (14.2)	94.3 (0.49)	6.6 (0.08)	90.7 (0.84)	6.7 (0.09)
Georgia	93.3 (1.28)	6.8 (0.06)	94.3 (0.53)	7.0 (0.04)	178 (0.4)	1,242 (8.5)	95.0 (0.59)	6.9 (0.05)	‡ (†)	‡ (†)
Hawaii	90.7 (4.58)	6.3 (0.10)	‡ (†)	‡ (†)	‡ (†)	‡ (†)	‡ (†)	‡ (†)	‡ (†)	‡ (†)
Idaho	92.4 (2.27)	6.6 (0.09)	94.1 (1.01)	6.7 (0.13)	166 (5.1)	1,110 (21.7)	94.4 (0.75)	6.7 (0.08)	93.1 (0.83)	6.7 (0.20)
Illinois	94.0 (0.71)	6.5 (0.05)	94.1 (0.40)	6.5 (0.04)	176 (0.4)	1,151 (7.7)	95.1 (0.29)	6.5 (0.05)	92.4 (1.29)	6.8 (0.08)
Indiana	95.7 (0.51)	6.8 (0.06)	95.9 (0.20)	6.8 (0.05)	180 (0.1)	1,226 (9.1)	96.1 (0.25)	6.7 (0.05)	95.5 (0.31)	7.0 (0.07)
Iowa	94.8 (0.65)	6.9 (0.09)	95.7 (0.36)	6.7 (0.12)	180 (0.2)	1,213 (21.8)	96.4 (0.21)	6.9 (0.05)	93.6 (1.39)	6.3 (0.47)
Kansas	95.4 (0.52)	7.0 (0.07)	94.9 (0.42)	7.0 (0.03)	177 (2.6)	1,245 (17.9)	95.5 (0.53)	7.0 (0.04)	94.0 (0.42)	7.1 (0.04)
Kentucky	93.1 (1.89)	6.7 (0.06)	93.2 (1.33)	6.8 (0.06)	179 (1.0)	1,211 (11.6)	95.9 (0.22)	6.8 (0.07)	87.0 (4.87)	6.8 (0.14)
Louisiana	90.3 (2.31)	7.1 (0.08)	92.8 (0.70)	7.2 (0.07)	178 (1.1)	1,283 (10.7)	93.0 (0.88)	7.3 (0.07)	93.5 (0.42)	7.1 (0.14)
Maine	90.3 (2.41)	6.5 (0.06)	94.2 (0.73)	6.6 (0.06)	176 (0.2)	1,156 (10.7)	94.4 (1.00)	6.6 (0.07)	93.8 (0.45)	6.3 (0.08)
Maryland	94.1 (0.44)	6.6 (0.07)	‡ (†)	‡ (†)	‡ (†)	‡ (†)	‡ (†)	‡ (†)	‡ (†)	‡ (†)
Massachusetts	94.6 (0.58)	6.5 (0.05)	93.5 (0.62)	6.4 (0.07)	180 (0.2)	1,157 (13.3)	94.4 (0.63)	6.4 (0.07)	90.3 (2.55)	6.6 (0.05)
Michigan	93.0 (1.01)	6.6 (0.08)	91.6 (0.71)	6.8 (0.03)	177 (0.5)	1,196 (5.9)	92.3 (0.99)	6.8 (0.03)	89.4 (1.28)	6.7 (0.07)
Minnesota	93.1 (0.91)	6.3 (0.12)	93.1 (0.49)	6.4 (0.08)	173 (1.3)	1,111 (14.0)	96.1 (0.19)	6.6 (0.07)	89.5 (1.21)	6.0 (0.20)
Mississippi	92.1 (2.00)	7.0 (0.12)	94.4 (0.47)	7.2 (0.09)	181 (0.4)	1,312 (16.4)	94.9 (0.57)	7.3 (0.06)	93.7 (0.86)	7.2 (0.24)
Missouri	94.8 (0.26)	6.7 (0.05)	95.1 (0.20)	6.9 (0.03)	175 (0.3)	1,197 (5.3)	95.6 (0.24)	6.9 (0.04)	94.3 (0.24)	6.8 (0.11)
Montana	91.3 (1.39)	6.8 (0.05)	93.9 (0.81)	6.6 (0.06)	179 (0.4)	1,189 (11.2)	94.3 (0.79)	6.6 (0.09)	93.0 (0.48)	6.7 (0.08)
Nebraska	94.9 (1.21)	6.9 (0.08)	94.8 (0.60)	7.1 (0.05)	177 (1.0)	1,257 (9.6)	96.0 (0.53)	7.1 (0.04)	94.5 (0.66)	6.8 (0.19)
Nevada	93.5 (1.27)	6.3 (0.06)	93.9 (0.39)	6.5 (0.07)	180 (1.1)	1,164 (10.9)	94.5 (0.30)	6.4 (0.10)	93.9 (0.70)	6.5 (0.07)
New Hampshire	92.2 (1.75)	6.5 (0.06)	91.1 (2.86)	6.6 (0.05)	180 (0.3)	1,181 (10.3)	95.9 (0.45)	6.5 (0.07)	75.1 (12.63)	6.7 (0.05)
New Jersey	94.6 (0.59)	6.4 (0.05)	93.5 (1.13)	6.6 (0.06)	181 (0.2)	1,201 (11.8)	93.7 (1.40)	6.6 (0.07)	92.6 (1.29)	6.7 (0.07)
New Mexico	91.9 (1.76)	6.8 (0.08)	92.8 (0.80)	6.9 (0.09)	177 (0.6)	1,216 (15.7)	93.8 (0.80)	6.7 (0.08)	88.5 (2.41)	7.1 (0.14)
New York	92.7 (1.30)	6.6 (0.09)	92.7 (0.94)	6.6 (0.06)	182 (0.2)	1,206 (10.6)	93.6 (1.28)	6.6 (0.07)	90.0 (1.32)	6.8 (0.07)
North Carolina	92.6 (1.73)	6.7 (0.06)	94.7 (0.37)	6.9 (0.04)	181 (0.2)	1,240 (7.4)	95.2 (0.23)	6.8 (0.04)	‡ (†)	‡ (†)
North Dakota	95.9 (0.59)	6.6 (0.04)	95.2 (0.46)	6.5 (0.06)	177 (0.3)	1,159 (10.0)	96.4 (0.35)	6.4 (0.08)	95.5 (0.45)	6.6 (0.14)
Ohio	91.8 (2.01)	6.6 (0.10)	93.8 (0.48)	6.6 (0.03)	180 (0.5)	1,191 (6.2)	95.0 (0.30)	6.6 (0.04)	91.0 (1.45)	6.7 (0.07)
Oklahoma	92.1 (2.24)	6.6 (0.06)	94.4 (0.32)	6.7 (0.04)	174 (0.7)	1,176 (8.6)	94.9 (0.38)	6.7 (0.04)	93.3 (0.74)	6.8 (0.10)
Oregon	94.4 (0.59)	6.6 (0.06)	94.2 (0.40)	6.6 (0.05)	170 (0.9)	1,118 (7.9)	95.1 (0.29)	6.5 (0.06)	91.1 (1.41)	6.7 (0.06)
Pennsylvania	94.9 (0.39)	6.4 (0.12)	94.4 (0.29)	6.7 (0.05)	181 (0.3)	1,212 (9.5)	94.9 (0.38)	6.7 (0.06)	92.9 (0.56)	6.9 (0.14)
Rhode Island	93.7 (1.27)	6.3 (0.03)	94.6 (0.36)	6.4 (0.05)	180 (0.1)	1,150 (8.2)	95.1 (0.38)	6.3 (0.05)	‡ (†)	‡ (†)
South Carolina	94.9 (0.71)	6.9 (0.07)	95.6 (0.26)	7.0 (0.04)	181 (0.4)	1,263 (7.3)	96.2 (0.27)	6.9 (0.05)	93.9 (0.84)	7.1 (0.05)
South Dakota	93.6 (2.53)	6.8 (0.08)	96.1 (0.24)	7.0 (0.07)	170 (1.1)	1,180 (6.7)	96.7 (0.30)	6.9 (0.08)	93.6 (0.53)	6.9 (0.17)
Tennessee	94.9 (0.23)	7.0 (0.05)	94.6 (0.30)	7.1 (0.03)	179 (0.4)	1,272 (7.8)	95.0 (0.28)	7.1 (0.04)	94.2 (0.45)	7.0 (0.02)
Texas	94.1 (1.34)	7.2 (0.11)	95.2 (0.43)	7.3 (0.04)	179 (0.7)	1,297 (8.8)	95.9 (0.41)	7.3 (0.03)	94.8 (0.29)	7.3 (0.06)
Utah	91.4 (1.56)	6.3 (0.29)	93.3 (0.80)	6.5 (0.08)	179 (0.3)	1,165 (13.5)	94.4 (0.80)	6.5 (0.08)	93.6 (0.74)	6.6 (0.09)
Vermont	92.7 (3.39)	6.7 (0.07)	94.0 (0.95)	6.7 (0.04)	178 (0.3)	1,183 (7.2)	93.7 (1.30)	6.8 (0.04)	94.7 (0.35)	6.2 (0.12)
Virginia	94.7 (0.46)	6.6 (0.05)	95.0 (0.32)	6.6 (0.03)	185 (3.4)	1,222 (18.8)	95.8 (0.32)	6.7 (0.03)	93.3 (0.65)	6.6 (0.10)
Washington	82.9 (3.06)	6.2 (0.08)	92.2 (0.67)	6.3 (0.06)	179 (0.3)	1,129 (11.3)	94.3 (0.55)	6.4 (0.04)	88.0 (2.00)	6.1 (0.19)
West Virginia	94.0 (0.99)	6.9 (0.07)	94.9 (0.46)	7.0 (0.05)	181 (0.4)	1,272 (9.8)	96.2 (0.27)	7.0 (0.07)	89.8 (1.98)	7.3 (0.09)
Wisconsin	95.0 (0.57)	6.9 (0.04)	94.9 (0.31)	6.9 (0.11)	179 (0.2)	1,234 (19.2)	95.7 (0.21)	7.0 (0.03)	91.9 (1.08)	7.0 (0.12)
Wyoming	92.4 (1.15)	6.9 (0.05)	93.6 (0.81)	7.0 (0.04)	174 (0.5)	1,209 (6.5)	94.8 (0.78)	6.9 (0.05)	89.9 (2.19)	7.0 (0.08)

†Not applicable.

‡Reporting standards not met. Either the response rate is under 50 percent or there are too few cases for a reliable estimate.

NOTE: Averages reflect data reported by schools rather than state requirements. School-reported length of day may exceed state requirements, and there is a range of statistical error in reported estimates.

SOURCE: U.S. Department of Education, National Center for Education Statistics, Schools and Staffing Survey (SASS), "Public School Data File," 2007-08 and 2011-12. (This table was prepared May 2013.)

Table 205.10. Private elementary and secondary school enrollment and private enrollment as a percentage of total enrollment in public and private schools, by region and grade level: Selected years, fall 1995 through fall 2017

[Standard errors appear in parentheses]

Grade level and year	Total private enrollment		Private enrollment, by region							
			Northeast		Midwest		South		West	
	In thousands	Percent of total enrollment	In thousands	Percent of total enrollment in Northeast	In thousands	Percent of total enrollment in Midwest	In thousands	Percent of total enrollment in South	In thousands	Percent of total enrollment in West
1	2	3	4	5	6	7	8	9	10	11
Total, all grades										
1995	5,918 (31.8)	11.7 (0.06)	1,509 (18.8)	16.1 (0.17)	1,525 (14.2)	12.7 (0.10)	1,744 (12.8)	9.8 (0.07)	1,141 (11.5)	10.0 (0.09)
1997	5,944 (18.5)	11.4 (0.03)	1,496 (8.3)	15.6 (0.07)	1,528 (11.6)	12.5 (0.08)	1,804 (11.3)	9.8 (0.06)	1,116 (5.2)	9.4 (0.04)
1999	6,018 (30.2)	11.4 (0.05)	1,507 (7.9)	15.5 (0.07)	1,520 (10.3)	12.4 (0.07)	1,863 (26.7)	10.0 (0.13)	1,127 (5.4)	9.3 (0.04)
2001	6,320 (40.3)	11.7 (0.07)	1,581 (9.5)	16.1 (0.08)	1,556 (22.9)	12.6 (0.16)	1,975 (21.4)	10.3 (0.10)	1,208 (23.4)	9.6 (0.17)
2003	6,099 (41.2)	11.2 (0.07)	1,513 (25.8)	15.4 (0.22)	1,460 (15.1)	11.9 (0.11)	1,944 (21.0)	9.9 (0.10)	1,182 (19.1)	9.2 (0.14)
2005	6,073 (42.4)	11.0 (0.07)	1,430 (7.7)	14.8 (0.07)	1,434 (21.0)	11.7 (0.15)	1,976 (24.7)	9.9 (0.11)	1,234 (26.3)	9.5 (0.18)
2007	5,910 (28.4)	10.8 (0.05)	1,426 (11.0)	15.0 (0.10)	1,352 (8.3)	11.2 (0.06)	1,965 (21.5)	9.7 (0.10)	1,167 (12.3)	9.1 (0.09)
2009	5,488 (35.9)	10.1 (0.06)	1,310 (15.7)	14.1 (0.14)	1,296 (25.9)	10.9 (0.19)	1,842 (17.6)	9.0 (0.08)	1,041 (8.0)	8.1 (0.06)
2011	5,268 (24.9)	9.7 (0.04)	1,252 (18.0)	13.7 (0.17)	1,263 (17.1)	10.7 (0.13)	1,747 (2.6)	8.5 (0.01)	1,006 (0.4)	7.8 (#)
2013	5,396 (50.3)	9.8 (0.08)	1,201 (9.5)	13.2 (0.09)	1,326 (45.2)	11.2 (0.34)	1,840 (8.3)	8.7 (0.04)	1,028 (18.3)	7.8 (0.13)
2015	5,751 (85.7)	10.3 (0.14)	1,314 (37.3)	14.3 (0.35)	1,408 (54.5)	11.9 (0.40)	1,965 (53.2)	9.1 (0.22)	1,062 (12.5)	8.0 (0.09)
2017	5,720 (74.1)	10.2 (0.12)	1,229 (18.4)	13.6 (0.18)	1,378 (45.5)	11.7 (0.34)	2,030 (45.4)	9.3 (0.19)	1,082 (32.0)	8.1 (0.22)
Prekindergarten through grade 8										
1995	4,756 (28.4)	12.8 (0.07)	1,174 (16.8)	17.0 (0.20)	1,238 (13.5)	14.2 (0.13)	1,413 (11.9)	10.8 (0.08)	931 (9.2)	11.2 (0.10)
1997	4,759 (17.3)	12.6 (0.04)	1,165 (8.3)	16.7 (0.10)	1,235 (11.0)	14.1 (0.11)	1,449 (10.0)	10.8 (0.07)	909 (4.4)	10.6 (0.05)
1999	4,789 (23.1)	12.6 (0.05)	1,168 (7.5)	16.5 (0.09)	1,222 (8.4)	14.0 (0.08)	1,487 (19.6)	10.9 (0.13)	913 (4.4)	10.5 (0.04)
2001	5,023 (36.1)	12.9 (0.08)	1,216 (9.4)	17.2 (0.11)	1,253 (21.2)	14.3 (0.21)	1,584 (17.8)	11.3 (0.11)	969 (21.2)	10.8 (0.21)
2003	4,788 (30.3)	12.3 (0.07)	1,131 (7.8)	16.3 (0.09)	1,167 (13.6)	13.5 (0.14)	1,547 (18.6)	10.9 (0.12)	944 (18.1)	10.4 (0.18)
2005	4,724 (33.0)	12.2 (0.07)	1,063 (6.6)	15.8 (0.08)	1,142 (19.3)	13.4 (0.20)	1,551 (21.2)	10.8 (0.13)	969 (15.0)	10.6 (0.15)
2007	4,546 (21.9)	11.8 (0.05)	1,047 (6.3)	15.9 (0.08)	1,065 (7.7)	12.7 (0.08)	1,525 (17.7)	10.5 (0.11)	909 (8.1)	10.2 (0.08)
2009	4,179 (33.2)	10.9 (0.08)	938 (12.6)	14.6 (0.17)	1,016 (25.1)	12.2 (0.26)	1,424 (16.2)	9.7 (0.10)	802 (7.2)	9.0 (0.07)
2011	3,977 (18.2)	10.3 (0.04)	898 (12.8)	14.1 (0.17)	967 (12.8)	11.7 (0.14)	1,337 (1.8)	9.0 (0.01)	774 (0.3)	8.6 (#)
2013	4,084 (42.4)	10.4 (0.10)	859 (8.8)	13.5 (0.12)	1,036 (37.9)	12.4 (0.40)	1,403 (7.9)	9.2 (0.05)	786 (15.0)	8.6 (0.15)
2015	4,304 (69.2)	10.9 (0.16)	932 (27.8)	14.6 (0.37)	1,099 (48.9)	13.1 (0.51)	1,471 (38.4)	9.5 (0.23)	802 (12.2)	8.7 (0.12)
2017	4,252 (69.0)	10.8 (0.16)	860 (18.3)	13.7 (0.25)	1,062 (41.8)	12.8 (0.44)	1,525 (42.4)	9.8 (0.25)	805 (29.9)	8.6 (0.29)
Grades 9 through 12										
1995	1,163 (4.6)	8.6 (0.03)	335 (2.9)	13.4 (0.10)	287 (0.9)	8.6 (0.03)	331 (2.1)	7.1 (0.04)	209 (2.3)	6.9 (0.07)
1997	1,185 (2.4)	8.3 (0.02)	331 (0.5)	12.8 (0.02)	293 (0.7)	8.4 (0.02)	354 (1.7)	7.2 (0.03)	207 (1.2)	6.4 (0.04)
1999	1,229 (8.3)	8.4 (0.05)	340 (1.1)	12.9 (0.04)	299 (2.5)	8.5 (0.07)	376 (7.6)	7.5 (0.14)	215 (1.8)	6.3 (0.05)
2001	1,296 (6.7)	8.6 (0.04)	365 (0.8)	13.3 (0.03)	302 (2.0)	8.5 (0.05)	390 (4.4)	7.6 (0.08)	239 (4.5)	6.8 (0.12)
2003	1,311 (24.7)	8.4 (0.15)	382 (24.0)	13.3 (0.72)	294 (4.1)	8.2 (0.11)	397 (3.0)	7.4 (0.05)	238 (3.5)	6.4 (0.09)
2005	1,349 (18.1)	8.3 (0.10)	367 (1.7)	12.4 (0.05)	292 (5.0)	8.0 (0.13)	425 (7.2)	7.5 (0.12)	265 (15.7)	6.7 (0.37)
2007	1,364 (12.0)	8.3 (0.07)	379 (8.8)	12.8 (0.26)	287 (1.3)	7.8 (0.03)	440 (5.5)	7.6 (0.09)	257 (5.7)	6.6 (0.14)
2009	1,309 (6.5)	8.1 (0.04)	372 (5.7)	13.0 (0.17)	280 (2.2)	7.8 (0.06)	418 (1.7)	7.2 (0.03)	239 (1.1)	6.1 (0.03)
2011	1,291 (15.4)	8.1 (0.09)	353 (5.2)	12.6 (0.16)	295 (14.4)	8.4 (0.38)	411 (1.8)	7.1 (0.03)	232 (0.1)	5.9 (#)
2013	1,312 (14.9)	8.2 (0.09)	342 (0.8)	12.4 (0.03)	291 (13.1)	8.4 (0.35)	437 (1.3)	7.4 (0.02)	242 (7.0)	6.2 (0.17)
2015	1,446 (23.8)	8.8 (0.13)	382 (10.5)	13.7 (0.32)	309 (10.9)	8.8 (0.28)	494 (18.2)	8.0 (0.27)	261 (1.9)	6.6 (0.04)
2017	1,468 (17.4)	8.8 (0.10)	369 (1.3)	13.3 (0.04)	316 (7.5)	9.0 (0.20)	505 (15.2)	8.0 (0.22)	278 (3.4)	6.9 (0.08)

#Rounds to zero.
NOTE: Includes enrollment in prekindergarten through grade 12 in schools that offer kindergarten or higher grade. Ungraded students are prorated into prekindergarten through grade 8 and grades 9 through 12. Detail may not sum to totals because of rounding.

SOURCE: U.S. Department of Education, National Center for Education Statistics, Private School Universe Survey (PSS), 1995–96 through 2017–18; and Common Core of Data (CCD), "Public Elementary/Secondary School Universe Survey," 1995–96 through 2017–18. (This table was prepared August 2019.)

Table 205.15. Private elementary and secondary school enrollment, percentage distribution of private school enrollment, and private school enrollment as a percentage of total enrollment in public and private schools, by school orientation and grade: Selected years, fall 1999 through fall 2017

[Standard errors appear in parentheses]

Grade	1999		2005		2011		2013		2015		2017									
											Total		Catholic		Other religious		Nonsectarian			
1	2		3		4		5		6		7		8		9		10			
	Enrollment																			
Total, all grades	**6,018,280**	**(30,179)**	**6,073,240**	**(42,446)**	**5,268,090**	**(24,908)**	**5,395,740**	**(50,342)**	**5,750,520**	**(85,729)**	**5,719,990**	**(74,133)**	**2,137,330**	**(40,520)**	**2,188,240**	**(40,106)**	**1,394,420**	**(26,889)**		
Prekindergarten through grade 8	**4,788,990**	**(23,055)**	**4,724,310**	**(33,034)**	**3,976,960**	**(18,241)**	**4,083,860**	**(42,441)**	**4,304,470**	**(69,171)**	**4,251,960**	**(69,049)**	**1,478,040**	**(37,641)**	**1,727,280**	**(36,077)**	**1,046,640**	**(24,548)**		
Prekindergarten	763,790	(6,261)	926,430	(15,701)	773,240	(2,420)	819,320	(10,185)	846,920	(17,898)	821,830	(17,849)	175,660	(4,995)	330,470	(12,883)	315,710	(8,956)		
Kindergarten	593,690	(4,053)	547,590	(4,887)	449,820	(2,989)	461,730	(5,429)	466,470	(8,411)	456,880	(7,890)	144,990	(3,694)	186,250	(4,149)	125,630	(3,870)		
1st grade	472,110	(2,080)	421,120	(2,826)	348,730	(2,191)	357,860	(4,963)	373,850	(6,901)	361,030	(6,042)	137,970	(3,863)	156,640	(3,450)	66,410	(1,772)		
2nd grade	449,090	(2,248)	405,470	(2,659)	340,230	(2,008)	344,520	(4,887)	368,450	(6,625)	352,130	(5,906)	138,210	(3,904)	151,220	(3,214)	62,700	(1,563)		
3rd grade	436,730	(1,962)	398,120	(2,462)	336,150	(1,850)	338,840	(4,193)	364,290	(6,479)	354,400	(6,167)	141,640	(4,058)	149,980	(3,217)	62,780	(1,287)		
4th grade	425,140	(1,956)	391,530	(2,297)	328,950	(1,921)	337,440	(4,508)	357,820	(6,202)	355,650	(5,831)	142,810	(4,008)	149,900	(3,174)	62,950	(1,294)		
5th grade	407,590	(2,019)	389,720	(2,379)	330,390	(1,832)	337,950	(4,192)	354,710	(5,903)	358,720	(5,811)	145,550	(4,032)	146,790	(2,955)	66,380	(1,669)		
6th grade	403,110	(2,094)	393,220	(2,280)	341,690	(1,766)	344,960	(4,820)	372,750	(7,276)	374,200	(6,861)	148,490	(4,091)	151,830	(3,558)	73,870	(2,066)		
7th grade	384,140	(2,140)	390,550	(4,093)	336,770	(1,684)	343,370	(4,317)	367,920	(6,574)	370,920	(6,791)	147,790	(4,249)	146,020	(3,417)	77,100	(2,028)		
8th grade	369,580	(2,285)	387,720	(4,024)	336,670	(1,951)	343,500	(3,717)	363,840	(7,047)	374,210	(6,444)	148,740	(3,812)	145,060	(3,494)	80,410	(2,007)		
Elementary ungraded	84,000	(1,267)	72,830	(1,916)	54,300	(672)	54,380	(1,061)	67,440	(11,164)	72,000	(12,109)	6,190	(†)	13,130!	(4,668)	52,680	(11,179)		
Grades 9 through 12	**1,229,290**	**(8,260)**	**1,348,930**	**(18,073)**	**1,291,130**	**(15,396)**	**1,311,880**	**(14,936)**	**1,446,060**	**(23,777)**	**1,468,020**	**(17,378)**	**659,290**	**(15,189)**	**460,960**	**(6,962)**	**347,780**	**(4,172)**		
9th grade	336,220	(2,131)	356,130	(4,333)	329,600	(3,875)	333,610	(3,612)	367,810	(6,279)	373,950	(4,554)	168,010	(3,729)	120,140	(2,073)	85,800	(1,322)		
10th grade	313,310	(1,919)	348,190	(5,949)	324,540	(4,161)	330,710	(3,780)	367,250	(6,041)	365,940	(4,257)	165,130	(3,681)	116,280	(1,662)	84,530	(1,060)		
11th grade	294,650	(2,193)	326,260	(4,456)	318,310	(3,647)	324,680	(3,850)	356,150	(5,906)	364,600	(4,572)	163,880	(4,110)	113,570	(1,639)	87,150	(1,169)		
12th grade	280,380	(1,958)	315,290	(4,850)	314,500	(3,769)	319,720	(3,787)	348,600	(5,652)	359,030	(4,200)	162,050	(3,683)	109,540	(1,778)	87,440	(1,011)		
Secondary ungraded	4,720	(1,404)	3,070	(†)	4,180	(92)	3,160	(14)	6,240	(†)	4,500	(†)	210	(†)	1,430	(†)	2,860	(†)		
	Percentage distribution																			
Total, all grades	**100.0**	**(†)**	**100.0**	**(†)**	**100.0**	**(†)**	**100.0**	**(†)**	**100.0**	**(†)**	**100.0**	**(†)**	**100.0**	**(†)**	**100.0**	**(†)**	**100.0**	**(†)**		
Prekindergarten through grade 8	**79.6**	**(0.06)**	**77.8**	**(0.22)**	**75.5**	**(0.23)**	**75.7**	**(0.22)**	**74.9**	**(0.27)**	**74.3**	**(0.35)**	**69.2**	**(0.73)**	**78.9**	**(0.31)**	**75.1**	**(0.38)**		
Prekindergarten	12.7	(0.08)	15.3	(0.21)	14.7	(0.08)	15.2	(0.15)	14.7	(0.22)	14.4	(0.22)	8.2	(0.17)	15.1	(0.45)	22.6	(0.49)		
Kindergarten	9.9	(0.04)	9.0	(0.06)	8.5	(0.04)	8.6	(0.08)	8.1	(0.08)	8.0	(0.06)	6.8	(0.08)	8.5	(0.08)	9.0	(0.16)		
1st grade	7.8	(0.02)	6.9	(0.03)	6.6	(0.02)	6.6	(0.05)	6.5	(0.07)	6.3	(0.06)	6.5	(0.09)	7.2	(0.09)	4.8	(0.08)		
2nd grade	7.5	(0.01)	6.7	(0.03)	6.5	(0.02)	6.4	(0.05)	6.4	(0.06)	6.2	(0.05)	6.5	(0.09)	6.9	(0.07)	4.5	(0.08)		
3rd grade	7.3	(0.02)	6.6	(0.03)	6.4	(0.02)	6.3	(0.04)	6.3	(0.05)	6.2	(0.06)	6.6	(0.10)	6.9	(0.07)	4.5	(0.07)		
4th grade	7.1	(0.01)	6.4	(0.03)	6.2	(0.02)	6.3	(0.04)	6.2	(0.05)	6.2	(0.05)	6.7	(0.08)	6.9	(0.07)	4.5	(0.08)		
5th grade	6.8	(0.01)	6.4	(0.04)	6.3	(0.02)	6.3	(0.04)	6.2	(0.05)	6.3	(0.05)	6.8	(0.09)	6.7	(0.08)	4.8	(0.09)		
6th grade	6.7	(0.02)	6.5	(0.03)	6.5	(0.02)	6.4	(0.05)	6.5	(0.07)	6.5	(0.06)	6.9	(0.09)	6.9	(0.10)	5.3	(0.12)		
7th grade	6.4	(0.02)	6.4	(0.04)	6.4	(0.02)	6.4	(0.05)	6.4	(0.06)	6.5	(0.07)	6.9	(0.12)	6.7	(0.11)	5.5	(0.11)		
8th grade	6.1	(0.02)	6.4	(0.04)	6.4	(0.02)	6.4	(0.04)	6.3	(0.06)	6.5	(0.07)	7.0	(0.11)	6.6	(0.11)	5.8	(0.10)		
Elementary ungraded	1.4	(0.02)	1.2	(0.03)	1.0	(0.01)	1.0	(0.02)	1.2	(0.19)	1.3	(0.21)	0.3	(0.01)	0.6!	(0.21)	3.8	(0.77)		
Grades 9 through 12	**20.4**	**(0.06)**	**22.2**	**(0.22)**	**24.5**	**(0.23)**	**24.3**	**(0.22)**	**25.1**	**(0.27)**	**25.7**	**(0.35)**	**30.8**	**(0.73)**	**21.1**	**(0.31)**	**24.9**	**(0.38)**		
9th grade	5.6	(0.02)	5.9	(0.05)	6.3	(0.06)	6.2	(0.05)	6.4	(0.07)	6.5	(0.09)	7.9	(0.18)	5.5	(0.08)	6.2	(0.11)		
10th grade	5.2	(0.01)	5.7	(0.08)	6.2	(0.06)	6.1	(0.06)	6.4	(0.07)	6.4	(0.09)	7.7	(0.18)	5.3	(0.08)	6.1	(0.09)		
11th grade	4.9	(0.02)	5.4	(0.06)	6.0	(0.05)	6.0	(0.06)	6.2	(0.07)	6.4	(0.09)	7.7	(0.19)	5.2	(0.08)	6.3	(0.10)		
12th grade	4.7	(0.02)	5.2	(0.07)	6.0	(0.06)	5.9	(0.06)	6.1	(0.07)	6.3	(0.09)	7.6	(0.18)	5.0	(0.08)	6.3	(0.10)		
Secondary ungraded	0.1	(0.02)	0.1	(#)	0.1	(#)	0.1	(#)	0.1	(#)	0.1	(#)	#	(†)	0.1	(#)	0.2	(#)		

See notes at end of table.

Table 205.15. Private elementary and secondary school enrollment, percentage distribution of private school enrollment, and private enrollment as a percentage of total enrollment in public and private schools, by school orientation and grade: Selected years, fall 1999 through fall 2017—Continued

[Standard errors appear in parentheses]

Grade	1999	2005	2011	2013	2015	2017 Total	2017 Catholic	2017 Other religious	2017 Nonsectarian
1	2	3	4	5	6	7	8	9	10
	Private enrollment as a percent of total enrollment								
Total, all grades	**11.4 (0.05)**	**11.0 (0.07)**	**9.7 (0.04)**	**9.8 (0.08)**	**10.3 (0.14)**	**10.2 (0.12)**	**3.8 (0.07)**	**3.9 (0.07)**	**2.5 (0.05)**
Prekindergarten through grade 8	**12.6 (0.05)**	**12.2 (0.07)**	**10.3 (0.04)**	**10.4 (0.10)**	**10.9 (0.16)**	**10.8 (0.16)**	**3.7 (0.09)**	**4.4 (0.09)**	**2.7 (0.06)**
Prekindergarten	55.4 (0.20)	52.3 (0.42)	40.4 (0.08)	41.5 (0.30)	41.6 (0.51)	39.6 (0.52)	8.5 (0.23)	15.9 (0.51)	15.2 (0.37)
Kindergarten	14.9 (0.09)	13.2 (0.10)	10.7 (0.06)	10.8 (0.11)	11.2 (0.18)	11.0 (0.17)	3.5 (0.09)	4.5 (0.09)	3.0 (0.09)
1st grade	11.4 (0.04)	10.2 (0.06)	8.5 (0.08)	8.4 (0.11)	9.0 (0.15)	9.0 (0.14)	3.4 (0.09)	3.9 (0.08)	1.7 (0.04)
2nd grade	10.9 (0.05)	10.1 (0.06)	8.4 (0.05)	8.3 (0.11)	8.8 (0.14)	8.7 (0.13)	3.4 (0.09)	3.8 (0.08)	1.6 (0.04)
3rd grade	10.6 (0.04)	10.0 (0.06)	8.3 (0.05)	8.3 (0.09)	8.6 (0.14)	8.6 (0.14)	3.4 (0.09)	3.6 (0.07)	1.5 (0.03)
4th grade	10.3 (0.04)	9.9 (0.05)	8.2 (0.04)	8.4 (0.10)	8.6 (0.14)	8.4 (0.13)	3.4 (0.09)	3.6 (0.07)	1.5 (0.03)
5th grade	10.2 (0.05)	9.7 (0.05)	8.2 (0.04)	8.4 (0.10)	8.7 (0.13)	8.5 (0.13)	3.4 (0.09)	3.5 (0.07)	1.6 (0.04)
6th grade	10.2 (0.05)	9.7 (0.05)	8.4 (0.04)	8.6 (0.11)	9.1 (0.16)	8.9 (0.15)	3.5 (0.09)	3.6 (0.08)	1.8 (0.05)
7th grade	9.8 (0.05)	9.4 (0.09)	8.4 (0.04)	8.4 (0.10)	9.0 (0.15)	9.0 (0.15)	3.6 (0.10)	3.5 (0.08)	1.9 (0.05)
8th grade	9.5 (0.05)	9.3 (0.09)	8.4 (0.04)	8.4 (0.08)	8.9 (0.16)	9.0 (0.14)	3.6 (0.09)	3.5 (0.08)	1.9 (0.05)
Elementary ungraded	16.8 (0.21)	22.8 (0.46)	40.3 (0.30)	38.6 (0.46)	46.6 (4.19)	48.5 (4.26)	4.2 (†)	8.8! (2.98)	35.5 (5.03)
Grades 9 through 12	**8.4 (0.05)**	**8.3 (0.10)**	**8.1 (0.09)**	**8.2 (0.09)**	**8.8 (0.13)**	**8.8 (0.10)**	**4.0 (0.09)**	**2.8 (0.04)**	**2.1 (0.02)**
9th grade	7.9 (0.05)	7.7 (0.09)	7.7 (0.08)	7.8 (0.08)	8.4 (0.13)	8.6 (0.10)	3.9 (0.08)	2.8 (0.05)	2.0 (0.03)
10th grade	8.4 (0.05)	8.3 (0.13)	8.0 (0.09)	8.1 (0.09)	8.7 (0.13)	8.7 (0.09)	3.9 (0.08)	2.8 (0.04)	2.0 (0.02)
11th grade	8.8 (0.06)	8.6 (0.11)	8.3 (0.09)	8.5 (0.09)	9.0 (0.14)	9.1 (0.10)	4.1 (0.10)	2.8 (0.04)	2.2 (0.03)
12th grade	9.1 (0.06)	9.0 (0.13)	8.4 (0.09)	8.5 (0.09)	9.0 (0.13)	9.0 (0.10)	4.1 (0.09)	2.8 (0.04)	2.2 (0.02)
Secondary ungraded	3.6 (1.03)	3.2 (†)	9.5 (0.19)	6.8 (0.03)	11.7 (†)	8.7 (†)	0.4 (†)	2.8 (†)	5.5 (†)

†Not applicable.
#Rounds to zero.
NOTE: Includes enrollment in prekindergarten through grade 12 in schools that offer kindergarten or higher grade. Ungraded students are prorated into prekindergarten through grade 8 and grades 9 through 12. Detail may not sum to totals because of rounding.

SOURCE: U.S. Department of Education, National Center for Education Statistics, Private School Universe Survey (PSS), 1999–2000 through 2017–18; and Common Core of Data (CCD), "Public Elementary/Secondary School Universe Survey," 1999–2000 through 2017–18. (This table was prepared August 2019.)

Table 205.20. Enrollment and percentage distribution of students enrolled in private elementary and secondary schools, by school orientation and grade level: Selected years, fall 1995 through fall 2017

[Standard errors appear in parentheses]

Grade level and year	Total private enrollment	Catholic				Other religious				Nonsectarian
		Total	Parochial	Diocesan	Private	Total	Conservative Christian	Affiliated[1]	Unaffiliated[1]	
1	2	3	4	5	6	7	8	9	10	11
	Enrollment									
Total, all grades										
1995	5,918,040 (31,815)	2,660,450 (6,878)	1,458,990 (2,079)	850,560 (5,674)	350,900 (1,176)	2,094,690 (16,956)	786,660 (8,815)	697,280 (4,886)	610,750 (11,831)	1,162,900 (18,443)
1997	5,944,320 (18,543)	2,665,630 (5,472)	1,438,860 (5,331)	873,780 (761)	352,990 (1,405)	2,097,190 (13,733)	823,610 (7,342)	646,500 (3,104)	627,080 (11,133)	1,181,510 (12,013)
1999	6,018,280 (30,179)	2,660,420 (4,831)	1,397,570 (4,421)	880,650 (†)	382,190 (1,945)	2,193,370 (27,176)	871,060 (4,827)	646,280 (4,894)	676,030 (24,593)	1,164,500 (8,156)
2001	6,319,650 (40,272)	2,672,650 (12,460)	1,309,890 (5,626)	979,050 (6,976)	383,710 (3,152)	2,328,160 (17,281)	937,420 (6,070)	663,190 (8,636)	727,550 (13,303)	1,318,840 (27,300)
2003	6,099,220 (41,219)	2,520,120 (10,580)	1,183,250 (9,937)	963,140 (4,754)	373,740 (3,996)	2,228,230 (19,674)	889,710 (8,852)	650,530 (5,860)	688,000 (14,805)	1,350,870 (29,197)
2005	6,073,240 (42,446)	2,402,800 (9,293)	1,062,950 (6,355)	956,610 (6,325)	383,230 (3,996)	2,303,330 (22,368)	957,360 (9,561)	696,910 (6,677)	649,050 (14,200)	1,367,120 (27,558)
2007	5,910,210 (28,363)	2,308,150 (6,083)	945,860 (5,361)	969,940 (1,788)	392,340 (3,432)	2,283,210 (20,628)	883,180 (6,616)	527,040 (3,512)	872,990 (18,217)	1,318,850 (18,235)
2009	5,488,490 (35,857)	2,160,220 (3,494)	856,440 (3,088)	909,010 (4,393)	394,770 (1,087)	2,076,220 (32,751)	737,020 (1,891)	516,310 (4,366)	822,890 (31,180)	1,252,050 (8,849)
2011	5,268,090 (24,908)	2,087,870 (14,426)	804,410 (3,686)	899,810 (14,320)	383,650 (459)	1,991,950 (21,814)	730,570 (4,721)	565,340 (2,990)	696,040 (20,419)	1,188,270 (5,376)
2013	5,395,740 (50,342)	2,055,140 (37,142)	739,850 (18,829)	936,320 (32,000)	378,970 (980)	2,030,930 (30,090)	707,100 (7,544)	565,490 (5,884)	758,350 (28,152)	1,309,670 (14,800)
2015	5,750,520 (85,729)	2,082,660 (42,791)	716,120 (24,336)	960,590 (22,533)	405,950 (14,453)	2,268,820 (68,162)	760,790 (53,772)	587,490 (23,414)	920,550 (45,692)	1,399,030 (29,132)
2017	5,719,990 (74,133)	2,137,330 (40,520)	648,580 (26,112)	1,052,150 (32,312)	436,590 (7,204)	2,188,240 (40,106)	685,070 (13,085)	633,310 (24,576)	869,850 (30,669)	1,394,420 (26,889)
Prekindergarten through grade 8										
1995	4,755,540 (28,435)	2,041,990 (5,249)	1,368,340 (2,079)	575,190 (3,528)	98,460 (1,176)	1,752,510 (14,834)	651,050 (7,219)	574,820 (4,581)	526,630 (11,121)	961,040 (17,471)
1997	4,759,060 (17,323)	2,046,620 (5,469)	1,352,620 (5,331)	598,380 (761)	95,620 (1,393)	1,744,500 (12,194)	678,660 (5,957)	529,050 (2,504)	536,790 (10,120)	967,940 (11,050)
1999	4,788,990 (23,055)	2,033,900 (4,830)	1,317,300 (4,421)	607,860 (†)	108,740 (1,943)	1,818,260 (19,897)	713,020 (3,748)	529,280 (3,866)	575,970 (17,632)	936,820 (7,302)
2001	5,023,160 (36,096)	2,032,080 (10,751)	1,226,960 (4,494)	687,540 (6,976)	117,580 (2,978)	1,926,870 (15,459)	765,080 (5,110)	535,850 (7,370)	625,940 (12,240)	1,064,210 (24,703)
2003	4,788,070 (30,338)	1,886,530 (11,055)	1,108,320 (9,937)	670,910 (4,754)	107,300 (337)	1,835,930 (16,931)	722,460 (6,517)	519,310 (4,134)	594,160 (13,504)	1,065,620 (15,379)
2005	4,724,310 (33,034)	1,779,830 (9,318)	993,390 (6,355)	673,110 (6,286)	113,330 (2,896)	1,865,430 (19,380)	764,920 (8,028)	561,320 (5,730)	539,190 (12,633)	1,079,050 (15,497)
2007	4,545,910 (21,853)	1,685,220 (5,288)	878,830 (4,562)	688,260 (1,640)	118,130 (3,104)	1,833,540 (18,364)	698,930 (5,885)	417,610 (3,218)	717,000 (16,573)	1,027,150 (11,379)
2009	4,179,060 (33,168)	1,541,830 (3,250)	782,050 (3,085)	642,720 (846)	117,050 (578)	1,665,680 (30,216)	579,190 (1,685)	401,430 (3,952)	685,050 (28,928)	971,550 (8,113)
2011	3,976,960 (18,241)	1,481,620 (3,867)	737,090 (3,675)	630,970 (321)	113,560 (459)	1,583,610 (16,558)	568,150 (3,607)	443,780 (2,604)	571,690 (15,197)	911,730 (3,469)
2013	4,083,860 (42,441)	1,466,550 (27,646)	680,370 (18,826)	666,260 (20,228)	119,930 (843)	1,615,120 (29,311)	544,610 (5,638)	446,050 (5,316)	624,470 (27,948)	1,002,180 (11,849)
2015	4,304,470 (69,171)	1,487,620 (42,646)	662,670 (24,233)	677,540 (22,542)	147,410 (14,387)	1,771,440 (47,422)	576,570 (38,496)	445,620 (15,105)	749,250 (33,313)	1,045,410 (27,611)
2017	4,251,960 (69,049)	1,478,040 (37,641)	593,910 (24,950)	738,980 (27,007)	145,150 (7,204)	1,727,280 (36,077)	518,200 (10,946)	486,720 (19,828)	722,360 (29,984)	1,046,640 (24,548)
Grades 9 through 12										
1995	1,162,500 (4,625)	618,460 (2,786)	90,650 (†)	275,370 (2,786)	252,440 (†)	342,180 (3,174)	135,610 (2,338)	122,460 (645)	84,120 (1,720)	201,860 (1,495)
1997	1,185,260 (2,374)	619,010 (96)	86,240 (†)	275,400 (†)	257,370 (96)	352,690 (2,261)	144,950 (1,660)	117,450 (848)	90,290 (1,221)	213,560 (1,860)
1999	1,229,290 (8,260)	626,520 (70)	80,270 (†)	272,790 (†)	273,460 (70)	375,100 (7,920)	158,040 (1,640)	117,000 (1,237)	100,060 (7,461)	227,670 (2,208)
2001	1,296,480 (6,669)	640,570 (2,317)	82,930 (2,293)	291,520 (†)	266,130 (338)	401,290 (3,527)	172,340 (2,633)	127,340 (1,625)	101,600 (1,852)	254,620 (4,465)
2003	1,311,150 (24,733)	633,590 (3,888)	74,930 (†)	292,230 (†)	266,430 (3,888)	392,310 (4,195)	167,250 (3,144)	131,220 (1,924)	93,840 (2,031)	285,250 (23,952)
2005	1,348,930 (18,073)	622,970 (1,538)	69,560 (†)	283,510 (700)	269,900 (1,341)	437,900 (6,541)	192,440 (3,404)	135,590 (1,493)	109,860 (5,190)	288,070 (16,551)
2007	1,364,300 (11,958)	622,930 (1,377)	67,030 (1,201)	281,680 (566)	274,210 (364)	449,680 (3,796)	184,260 (1,768)	109,430 (374)	156,000 (3,052)	291,700 (11,156)
2009	1,309,430 (6,480)	618,390 (4,409)	74,380 (42)	266,290 (4,311)	277,720 (920)	410,540 (4,285)	157,830 (362)	114,880 (1,074)	137,840 (4,111)	280,500 (1,880)
2011	1,291,130 (15,396)	606,250 (14,313)	67,320 (10)	268,840 (14,313)	270,090 (†)	408,330 (5,747)	162,420 (1,349)	121,560 (513)	124,350 (5,792)	276,550 (3,485)
2013	1,311,880 (14,936)	588,580 (13,452)	59,480 (358)	270,060 (13,416)	259,040 (905)	415,810 (2,774)	162,490 (1,942)	119,440 (1,862)	133,880 (1,762)	307,490 (6,938)
2015	1,446,060 (23,777)	595,050 (2,166)	53,450 (1,662)	283,050 (38)	258,550 (1,388)	497,390 (23,622)	184,220 (15,411)	141,870 (9,045)	171,300 (16,438)	353,620 (5,530)
2017	1,468,020 (17,378)	659,290 (15,189)	54,670 (3,818)	313,180 (14,701)	291,440 (†)	460,960 (6,962)	166,870 (2,664)	146,600 (5,627)	147,490 (2,665)	347,780 (4,172)

See notes at end of table.

Table 205.20. Enrollment and percentage distribution of students enrolled in private elementary and secondary schools, by school orientation and grade level: Selected years, fall 1995 through fall 2017—Continued

[Standard errors appear in parentheses]

Grade level and year	Total private enrollment	Catholic				Other religious				Nonsectarian
		Total	Parochial	Diocesan	Private	Total	Conservative Christian	Affiliated[1]	Unaffiliated[1]	
1	2	3	4	5	6	7	8	9	10	11
	Percentage distribution									
Total, all grades										
1995	100.0 (†)	45.0 (0.19)	24.7 (0.13)	14.4 (0.08)	5.9 (0.03)	35.4 (0.19)	13.3 (0.12)	11.8 (0.08)	10.3 (0.18)	19.7 (0.23)
1997	100.0 (†)	44.8 (0.13)	24.2 (0.09)	14.7 (0.05)	5.9 (0.03)	35.3 (0.18)	13.9 (0.12)	10.9 (0.06)	10.5 (0.17)	19.9 (0.17)
1999	100.0 (†)	44.2 (0.24)	23.2 (0.14)	14.6 (0.07)	6.4 (0.04)	36.4 (0.28)	14.5 (0.09)	10.7 (0.08)	11.2 (0.36)	19.3 (0.11)
2001	100.0 (†)	42.3 (0.25)	20.7 (0.14)	15.5 (0.12)	6.1 (0.04)	36.8 (0.22)	14.8 (0.13)	10.5 (0.13)	11.5 (0.18)	20.9 (0.33)
2003	100.0 (†)	41.3 (0.27)	19.4 (0.17)	15.8 (0.14)	6.1 (0.07)	36.5 (0.25)	14.6 (0.13)	10.7 (0.10)	11.3 (0.22)	22.1 (0.36)
2005	100.0 (†)	39.6 (0.26)	17.5 (0.13)	15.8 (0.14)	6.3 (0.07)	37.9 (0.25)	15.8 (0.14)	11.5 (0.09)	10.7 (0.20)	22.5 (0.34)
2007	100.0 (†)	39.1 (0.20)	16.0 (0.11)	16.4 (0.09)	6.6 (0.06)	38.6 (0.25)	14.9 (0.12)	8.9 (0.06)	14.8 (0.26)	22.3 (0.25)
2009	100.0 (†)	39.4 (0.25)	15.6 (0.11)	16.6 (0.13)	7.2 (0.05)	37.8 (0.37)	13.4 (0.09)	9.4 (0.07)	15.0 (0.48)	22.8 (0.16)
2011	100.0 (†)	39.6 (0.25)	15.3 (0.09)	17.1 (0.25)	7.3 (0.04)	37.8 (0.28)	13.9 (0.09)	10.7 (0.08)	13.2 (0.34)	22.6 (0.15)
2013	100.0 (†)	38.1 (0.50)	13.7 (0.33)	17.4 (0.51)	7.0 (0.07)	37.6 (0.44)	13.1 (0.16)	10.5 (0.13)	14.1 (0.47)	24.3 (0.28)
2015	100.0 (†)	36.2 (0.66)	12.5 (0.38)	16.7 (0.40)	7.1 (0.24)	39.5 (0.80)	13.2 (0.85)	10.2 (0.39)	16.0 (0.73)	24.3 (0.51)
2017	100.0 (†)	37.4 (0.53)	11.3 (0.40)	18.4 (0.51)	7.6 (0.16)	38.3 (0.42)	12.0 (0.24)	11.1 (0.40)	15.2 (0.43)	24.4 (0.40)
Prekindergarten through grade 8										
1995	100.0 (†)	42.9 (0.20)	28.8 (0.17)	12.1 (0.06)	2.1 (0.02)	36.9 (0.22)	13.7 (0.13)	12.1 (0.09)	11.1 (0.21)	20.2 (0.28)
1997	100.0 (†)	43.0 (0.15)	28.4 (0.12)	12.6 (0.05)	2.0 (0.03)	36.7 (0.20)	14.3 (0.13)	11.1 (0.06)	11.3 (0.19)	20.3 (0.19)
1999	100.0 (†)	42.5 (0.23)	27.5 (0.16)	12.7 (0.06)	2.3 (0.04)	38.0 (0.26)	14.9 (0.09)	11.1 (0.07)	12.0 (0.32)	19.6 (0.12)
2001	100.0 (†)	40.5 (0.27)	24.4 (0.17)	13.7 (0.14)	2.3 (0.05)	38.4 (0.25)	15.2 (0.15)	10.7 (0.14)	12.5 (0.20)	21.2 (0.37)
2003	100.0 (†)	39.4 (0.25)	23.1 (0.18)	14.0 (0.13)	2.2 (0.01)	38.3 (0.23)	15.1 (0.12)	10.8 (0.09)	12.4 (0.24)	22.3 (0.22)
2005	100.0 (†)	37.7 (0.25)	21.0 (0.14)	14.2 (0.15)	2.4 (0.06)	39.5 (0.21)	16.2 (0.16)	11.9 (0.09)	11.4 (0.22)	22.8 (0.23)
2007	100.0 (†)	37.1 (0.20)	19.3 (0.13)	15.1 (0.09)	2.6 (0.07)	40.3 (0.27)	15.4 (0.14)	9.2 (0.07)	15.8 (0.30)	22.6 (0.21)
2009	100.0 (†)	36.9 (0.29)	18.7 (0.15)	15.4 (0.12)	2.8 (0.03)	39.9 (0.43)	13.9 (0.11)	9.6 (0.10)	16.4 (0.57)	23.2 (0.20)
2011	100.0 (†)	37.3 (0.18)	18.5 (0.11)	15.9 (0.08)	2.9 (0.02)	39.8 (0.24)	14.3 (0.08)	11.2 (0.08)	14.4 (0.32)	22.9 (0.11)
2013	100.0 (†)	35.9 (0.53)	16.7 (0.42)	16.3 (0.44)	2.9 (0.04)	39.5 (0.52)	13.3 (0.17)	10.9 (0.15)	15.3 (0.59)	24.5 (0.31)
2015	100.0 (†)	34.6 (0.78)	15.4 (0.48)	15.7 (0.50)	3.4 (0.31)	41.2 (0.81)	13.4 (0.82)	10.4 (0.35)	17.4 (0.73)	24.3 (0.61)
2017	100.0 (†)	34.8 (0.64)	14.0 (0.52)	17.4 (0.56)	3.4 (0.17)	40.6 (0.52)	12.2 (0.28)	11.4 (0.45)	17.0 (0.56)	24.6 (0.48)
Grades 9 through 12										
1995	100.0 (†)	53.2 (0.20)	7.8 (0.03)	23.7 (0.20)	21.7 (0.09)	29.4 (0.20)	11.7 (0.18)	10.5 (0.06)	7.2 (0.14)	17.4 (0.12)
1997	100.0 (†)	52.2 (0.10)	7.3 (0.01)	23.2 (0.05)	21.7 (0.04)	29.8 (0.16)	12.2 (0.13)	9.9 (0.08)	7.6 (0.10)	18.0 (0.14)
1999	100.0 (†)	51.0 (0.34)	6.5 (0.04)	22.2 (0.15)	22.2 (0.15)	30.5 (0.45)	12.9 (0.14)	9.5 (0.11)	8.1 (0.56)	18.5 (0.19)
2001	100.0 (†)	49.4 (0.26)	6.4 (0.17)	22.5 (0.12)	20.5 (0.10)	31.0 (0.19)	13.3 (0.17)	9.8 (0.12)	7.8 (0.13)	19.6 (0.28)
2003	100.0 (†)	48.3 (0.91)	5.7 (0.11)	22.3 (0.42)	20.3 (0.44)	29.9 (0.59)	12.8 (0.32)	10.0 (0.23)	7.2 (0.20)	21.8 (1.43)
2005	100.0 (†)	46.2 (0.60)	5.2 (0.07)	21.0 (0.28)	20.0 (0.27)	32.5 (0.52)	14.3 (0.28)	10.1 (0.16)	8.1 (0.37)	21.4 (0.97)
2007	100.0 (†)	45.7 (0.40)	4.9 (0.09)	20.6 (0.18)	20.1 (0.17)	33.0 (0.33)	13.5 (0.16)	8.0 (0.07)	11.4 (0.22)	21.4 (0.65)
2009	100.0 (†)	47.2 (0.25)	5.7 (0.03)	20.3 (0.27)	21.2 (0.12)	31.4 (0.25)	12.1 (0.06)	8.8 (0.08)	10.5 (0.28)	21.4 (0.15)
2011	100.0 (†)	47.0 (0.63)	5.2 (0.06)	20.8 (0.88)	20.9 (0.25)	31.6 (0.49)	12.6 (0.18)	9.4 (0.13)	9.6 (0.43)	21.4 (0.35)
2013	100.0 (†)	44.9 (0.64)	4.5 (0.06)	20.6 (0.83)	19.7 (0.24)	31.7 (0.42)	12.4 (0.19)	9.1 (0.17)	10.2 (0.19)	23.4 (0.47)
2015	100.0 (†)	41.1 (0.67)	3.7 (0.13)	19.6 (0.32)	17.9 (0.30)	34.4 (1.11)	12.7 (0.96)	9.8 (0.59)	11.8 (1.02)	24.5 (0.51)
2017	100.0 (†)	44.9 (0.63)	3.7 (0.25)	21.3 (0.80)	19.9 (0.24)	31.4 (0.46)	11.4 (0.21)	10.0 (0.36)	10.0 (0.19)	23.7 (0.34)

†Not applicable.
[1]Affiliated schools belong to associations of schools with a specific religious orientation other than Catholic or conservative Christian. Unaffiliated schools have a religious orientation or purpose but are not classified as Catholic, conservative Christian, or affiliated.

NOTE: Includes enrollment in prekindergarten through grade 12 in schools that offer kindergarten or higher grade. Ungraded students are prorated into prekindergarten through grade 8 and grades 9 through 12. Detail may not sum to totals because of rounding.
SOURCE: U.S. Department of Education, National Center for Education Statistics, Private School Universe Survey (PSS), 1995–96 through 2017–18. (This table was prepared August 2019.)

Table 205.30. Percentage distribution of students enrolled in private elementary and secondary schools, by school orientation and selected characteristics: Selected years, fall 2005 through fall 2017

[Standard errors appear in parentheses]

Selected characteristic	2005	2007	2009	2011	2013	2015	2017										
								Catholic				Other religious					
							Total	Total	Parochial	Diocesan	Private	Total	Conservative Christian	Affiliated[1]	Unaffiliated[1]	Nonsectarian
1	2	3	4	5	6	7	8	9	10	11	12	13	14	15	16	17
Total	**100.0 (†)**	**100.0 (†)**	**100.0 (†)**	**100.0 (†)**	**100.0 (†)**	**100.0 (†)**	**100.0 (†)**	**100.0 (†)**	**100.0 (†)**	**100.0 (†)**	**100.0 (†)**	**100.0 (†)**	**100.0 (†)**	**100.0 (†)**	**100.0 (†)**	**100.0 (†)**
School level[2]																
Elementary	56.8 (0.34)	54.6 (0.24)	53.5 (0.24)	52.7 (0.23)	52.8 (0.47)	50.3 (0.80)	49.8 (0.55)	63.0 (0.83)	86.0 (1.39)	66.3 (1.27)	21.0 (1.30)	39.7 (0.95)	21.9 (0.81)	41.0 (1.71)	52.7 (1.59)	45.3 (0.62)
Secondary	14.2 (0.34)	14.0 (0.17)	14.3 (0.11)	14.4 (0.25)	13.7 (0.19)	13.5 (0.20)	14.1 (0.32)	27.1 (0.77)	6.0 (0.25)	29.0 (1.24)	53.7 (0.89)	5.5 (0.13)	2.4 (0.05)	8.4 (0.34)	5.8 (0.29)	7.9 (0.18)
Combined	29.1 (0.29)	31.4 (0.25)	32.2 (0.21)	32.9 (0.21)	33.5 (0.48)	36.2 (0.88)	36.1 (0.46)	9.9 (0.42)	8.0 (1.41)	4.7 (0.21)	25.3 (0.42)	54.9 (0.92)	75.7 (0.82)	50.6 (1.93)	41.5 (1.41)	46.8 (0.62)
Student race/ethnicity[3]																
White	75.3 (0.10)	74.5 (0.17)	72.6 (0.20)	71.4 (0.14)	69.6 (0.31)	68.6 (0.34)	66.7 (0.40)	65.6 (0.48)	66.6 (0.96)	66.6 (0.78)	61.7 (0.12)	70.7 (0.50)	67.3 (0.39)	74.2 (1.24)	70.8 (0.96)	62.0 (0.62)
Black	9.6 (0.08)	9.8 (0.08)	9.2 (0.07)	8.9 (0.06)	9.3 (0.27)	9.3 (0.31)	9.3 (0.23)	7.6 (0.15)	6.3 (0.29)	7.5 (0.21)	9.8 (0.11)	10.4 (0.37)	11.6 (0.28)	8.7 (1.22)	10.8 (0.37)	10.2 (0.45)
Hispanic	9.2 (0.05)	9.6 (0.14)	9.4 (0.09)	9.8 (0.05)	10.2 (0.11)	10.4 (0.15)	11.3 (0.22)	15.7 (0.29)	16.1 (0.58)	15.4 (0.57)	15.6 (0.24)	8.0 (0.33)	9.2 (0.15)	6.6 (0.20)	8.0 (0.84)	9.0 (0.33)
Asian[4]	4.1 (0.05)	5.4 (0.07)	5.1 (0.05)	5.5 (0.03)	5.9 (0.05)	6.2 (0.06)	6.5 (0.15)	5.3 (0.07)	4.9 (0.18)	5.1 (0.12)	6.3 (0.09)	5.3 (0.16)	6.3 (0.22)	5.8 (0.20)	4.0 (0.35)	10.5 (0.45)
Pacific Islander[4]	— (†)	— (†)	0.6 (0.02)	0.6 (#)	0.7 (0.01)	0.7 (0.02)	0.8 (0.03)	0.7 (0.07)	0.8 (0.21)	0.6 (0.02)	0.8 (0.08)	0.9 (0.02)	0.7 (0.01)	0.3 (0.01)	1.6 (0.05)	0.9 (0.02)
American Indian/Alaska Native	1.8 (0.01)	0.6 (0.02)	0.4 (#)	0.5 (#)	0.5 (0.01)	0.5 (0.01)	0.5 (0.03)	0.5 (0.01)	0.5 (0.02)	0.4 (0.01)	0.9 (0.01)	0.5 (0.09)	0.6 (0.04)	0.3 (0.03)	0.6! (0.23)	0.6 (0.01)
Two or more races[4]	— (†)	— (†)	2.7 (0.02)	3.3 (0.01)	3.9 (0.03)	4.3 (0.08)	4.9 (0.06)	4.6 (0.08)	4.7 (0.18)	4.5 (0.09)	4.9 (0.08)	4.1 (0.13)	4.2 (0.25)	4.1 (0.26)	4.1 (0.18)	6.8 (0.09)
School enrollment																
Less than 50	4.5 (0.10)	4.4 (0.12)	5.4 (0.39)	4.6 (0.14)	5.4 (0.47)	5.5 (0.39)	4.9 (0.15)	0.4 (0.01)	0.3 (0.01)	0.2 (0.01)	0.7 (0.01)	7.1 (0.30)	4.5 (0.51)	3.2 (0.39)	12.0 (0.54)	8.2 (0.42)
50 to 149	16.7 (0.17)	16.6 (0.20)	17.3 (0.18)	16.8 (0.15)	17.1 (0.23)	16.8 (0.40)	16.2 (0.37)	7.4 (0.44)	7.3 (0.49)	8.3 (0.83)	5.3 (0.17)	18.3 (0.65)	16.0 (0.34)	13.5 (0.59)	23.6 (1.52)	26.3 (0.90)
150 to 299	26.6 (0.18)	26.0 (0.19)	25.9 (0.17)	26.2 (0.15)	25.5 (0.29)	25.1 (0.49)	25.2 (0.54)	28.9 (0.96)	40.2 (2.10)	28.8 (1.35)	12.5 (0.21)	24.2 (0.80)	24.5 (0.61)	23.6 (1.88)	24.3 (1.45)	21.1 (0.85)
300 to 499	21.1 (0.20)	21.2 (0.11)	21.0 (0.19)	21.0 (0.11)	20.4 (0.21)	19.5 (0.49)	20.3 (0.52)	25.8 (0.74)	28.2 (1.45)	26.5 (1.05)	20.4 (1.31)	18.6 (0.94)	21.6 (1.24)	20.1 (2.04)	15.3 (1.76)	14.3 (0.65)
500 to 749	15.0 (0.31)	14.6 (0.09)	14.0 (0.09)	15.0 (0.25)	14.5 (0.24)	15.8 (0.97)	14.8 (0.49)	19.4 (0.99)	17.6 (2.03)	19.0 (1.55)	23.1 (0.38)	12.8 (0.39)	15.7 (0.89)	14.7 (0.65)	9.1 (0.33)	10.9 (0.59)
750 or more	16.1 (0.24)	17.2 (0.24)	16.3 (0.12)	16.4 (0.29)	17.0 (0.54)	17.3 (0.29)	18.7 (0.34)	18.1 (0.44)	6.4 (0.26)	17.1 (0.76)	38.0 (0.63)	19.0 (0.54)	17.6 (0.34)	24.8 (1.68)	15.8 (0.56)	19.1 (0.37)
Region																
Northeast	23.5 (0.19)	24.1 (0.18)	23.9 (0.26)	23.8 (0.27)	22.3 (0.25)	22.9 (0.59)	21.5 (0.37)	22.5 (0.76)	19.4 (1.28)	21.4 (1.34)	29.7 (0.49)	18.2 (0.38)	7.1 (0.14)	24.3 (0.99)	22.5 (0.89)	25.1 (0.50)
Midwest	23.6 (0.30)	22.9 (0.15)	23.6 (0.38)	24.0 (0.26)	24.6 (0.64)	24.5 (0.77)	24.1 (0.65)	35.2 (1.01)	41.9 (2.12)	35.4 (1.47)	24.7 (0.41)	20.7 (0.94)	16.5 (0.76)	21.4 (2.04)	23.4 (1.99)	12.5 (0.56)
South	32.5 (0.33)	33.3 (0.26)	33.6 (0.29)	33.2 (0.16)	34.1 (0.33)	34.2 (0.73)	35.5 (0.63)	26.0 (0.84)	24.4 (1.76)	27.2 (1.56)	25.6 (1.22)	43.5 (0.93)	49.6 (0.96)	39.4 (2.05)	41.8 (1.69)	37.4 (0.89)
West	20.3 (0.36)	19.7 (0.19)	19.0 (0.17)	19.1 (0.09)	19.1 (0.32)	18.5 (0.33)	18.9 (0.51)	16.3 (0.31)	14.2 (0.61)	16.0 (0.50)	19.9 (0.35)	17.6 (0.55)	26.7 (0.81)	14.9 (0.67)	12.4 (1.21)	25.0 (1.17)
School locale																
City	41.3 (0.26)	41.1 (0.22)	41.0 (0.31)	41.5 (0.27)	42.5 (0.50)	43.0 (0.77)	43.1 (0.63)	46.1 (1.02)	44.2 (2.00)	44.8 (1.38)	52.1 (0.79)	40.0 (0.97)	33.0 (0.74)	45.4 (2.01)	41.5 (1.63)	43.3 (0.92)
Sburban	40.0 (0.35)	40.3 (0.22)	39.0 (0.34)	38.3 (0.20)	41.0 (0.44)	40.2 (0.82)	39.9 (0.58)	40.8 (1.01)	39.3 (1.82)	42.7 (1.55)	38.7 (0.64)	37.7 (0.79)	43.7 (0.96)	39.2 (1.55)	31.9 (1.22)	42.0 (0.79)
Town	7.2 (0.13)	7.0 (0.09)	7.1 (0.17)	6.8 (0.05)	6.3 (0.33)	6.2 (0.56)	6.5 (0.42)	8.7 (1.02)	12.5 (2.13)	9.3 (1.56)	1.8 (0.03)	5.8 (0.12)	6.9 (0.17)	5.0 (0.20)	5.4 (0.19)	4.2 (0.69)
Rural	11.5 (0.37)	11.6 (0.32)	12.9 (0.42)	13.4 (0.33)	10.1 (0.47)	10.7 (0.57)	10.5 (0.41)	4.3 (0.15)	4.0 (0.44)	3.2 (0.10)	7.4 (0.12)	16.5 (0.96)	16.3 (0.50)	10.3 (2.09)	21.3 (1.79)	10.5 (0.46)

—Not available.
†Not applicable.
#Rounds to zero.
!Interpret data with caution. The coefficient of variation (CV) for this estimate is between 30 and 50 percent.
[1]Affiliated schools belong to associations of schools with a specific religious orientation other than Catholic or conservative Christian. Unaffiliated schools have a religious orientation or purpose but are not classified as Catholic, conservative Christian, or affiliated.
[2]Elementary schools have grade 6 or lower and no grade higher than 8. Secondary schools have no grade lower than 7. Combined schools include those that have grades lower than 7 and higher than 8, as well as those that do not classify students by grade level.
[3]Race categories exclude persons of Hispanic ethnicity. Race/ethnicity was not collected for prekindergarten students (821,800 out of 5,719,990 students in 2017). Percentage distribution is based on the students for whom race/ethnicity was reported.
[4]Prior to 2009, Pacific Islander data are included with Asian data. Separate data on Pacific Islander students and data on students of Two or more races were not collected prior to 2009.
NOTE: Includes enrollment in prekindergarten through grade 12 in schools that offer kindergarten or higher grade. Detail may not sum to totals because of rounding.
SOURCE: U.S. Department of Education, National Center for Education Statistics, Private School Universe Survey (PSS), 2005–06 through 2017–18. (This table was prepared August 2019.)

Table 205.40. Number and percentage distribution of private elementary and secondary students, teachers, and schools, by orientation of school and selected characteristics: Fall 1999, fall 2009, and fall 2017

[Standard errors appear in parentheses]

Selected characteristic	Fall 1999 Total Number	Fall 1999 Total Percent	Fall 2009 Total Number	Fall 2009 Total Percent	Fall 2017 Total Number	Fall 2017 Total Percent	Fall 2017 Catholic Number	Fall 2017 Catholic Percent	Fall 2017 Other religious Number	Fall 2017 Other religious Percent	Fall 2017 Nonsectarian Number	Fall 2017 Nonsectarian Percent
1	2	3	4	5	6	7	8	9	10	11	12	13
Students[1]												
Total	**6,018,280 (30,179)**	**100.0 (†)**	**5,488,490 (35,857)**	**100.0 (†)**	**5,719,990 (74,133)**	**100.0 (†)**	**2,137,330 (40,520)**	**100.0 (†)**	**2,188,240 (40,106)**	**100.0 (†)**	**1,394,420 (26,889)**	**100.0 (†)**
School level[2]												
Elementary	3,595,020 (11,516)	59.7 (0.22)	2,937,090 (26,807)	53.5 (0.24)	2,846,020 (56,267)	49.8 (0.55)	1,346,850 (36,078)	63.0 (0.83)	867,760 (29,313)	39.7 (0.95)	631,410 (15,274)	45.3 (0.62)
Secondary	806,640 (2,395)	13.4 (0.08)	785,810 (4,810)	14.3 (0.11)	808,630 (16,013)	14.1 (0.32)	578,300 (15,841)	27.1 (0.77)	119,880 (1,910)	5.5 (0.13)	110,450 (1,338)	7.9 (0.18)
Combined	1,616,620 (23,949)	26.9 (0.28)	1,765,590 (15,909)	32.2 (0.21)	2,065,340 (35,992)	36.1 (0.46)	212,190 (9,771)	9.9 (0.42)	1,200,600 (27,105)	54.9 (0.92)	652,550 (16,618)	46.8 (0.62)
School enrollment												
Less than 50	238,980 (5,691)	4.0 (0.09)	296,000 (22,889)	5.4 (0.39)	277,530 (9,120)	4.9 (0.15)	7,490 (0)	0.4 (0.01)	155,760 (6,968)	7.1 (0.30)	114,280 (6,141)	8.2 (0.42)
50 to 149	939,110 (10,717)	15.6 (0.14)	950,050 (12,053)	17.3 (0.18)	924,490 (25,783)	16.2 (0.37)	157,680 (9,882)	7.4 (0.44)	399,970 (16,510)	18.3 (0.65)	366,830 (14,385)	26.3 (0.90)
150 to 299	1,615,970 (7,315)	26.9 (0.16)	1,423,220 (9,951)	25.9 (0.17)	1,441,670 (38,720)	25.2 (0.54)	618,050 (25,586)	28.9 (0.96)	529,270 (20,288)	24.2 (0.80)	294,350 (13,550)	21.1 (0.85)
300 to 499	1,419,360 (13,203)	23.6 (0.18)	1,154,950 (10,730)	21.0 (0.19)	1,158,950 (31,868)	20.3 (0.52)	551,610 (15,687)	25.8 (0.74)	407,920 (23,904)	18.6 (0.94)	199,410 (8,974)	14.3 (0.65)
500 to 749	917,670 (2,330)	15.2 (0.08)	768,540 (†)	14.0 (0.09)	848,140 (30,584)	14.8 (0.49)	415,130 (24,969)	19.4 (0.99)	280,450 (7,412)	12.8 (0.39)	152,570 (9,627)	10.9 (0.59)
750 or more	887,190 (18,232)	14.7 (0.26)	895,720 (6,538)	16.3 (0.12)	1,069,210 (19,363)	18.7 (0.34)	387,370 (†)	18.1 (0.44)	414,870 (12,135)	19.0 (0.54)	266,970 (6,355)	19.1 (0.37)
Student race/ethnicity[3]												
White	4,061,870 (24,242)	77.3 (0.12)	3,410,360 (31,067)	72.6 (0.20)	3,267,740 (46,018)	66.7 (0.40)	1,285,900 (30,147)	65.6 (0.48)	1,312,690 (26,032)	70.7 (0.50)	669,160 (10,377)	62.0 (0.62)
Black	494,530 (5,079)	9.4 (0.09)	430,970 (2,579)	9.2 (0.07)	453,670 (11,354)	9.3 (0.23)	149,800 (2,761)	7.6 (0.15)	193,510 (7,194)	10.4 (0.37)	110,360 (5,814)	10.2 (0.45)
Hispanic	435,890 (1,592)	8.3 (0.04)	443,290 (4,113)	9.4 (0.09)	552,000 (13,863)	11.3 (0.22)	307,230 (7,087)	15.7 (0.29)	148,190 (6,890)	8.0 (0.33)	96,580 (4,916)	9.0 (0.33)
Asian	239,510 (877)	4.6 (0.02)	239,320 (1,894)	5.1 (0.05)	315,970 (8,834)	6.5 (0.15)	104,030 (1,531)	5.3 (0.07)	98,660 (3,190)	5.3 (0.16)	113,270 (6,348)	10.5 (0.45)
Pacific Islander	[4] (†)	[4] (†)	28,020 (884)	0.6 (0.02)	40,960 (1,418)	0.8 (0.03)	13,510 (1,387)	0.7 (0.07)	17,590 (188)	0.9 (0.02)	9,860 (94)	0.9 (0.02)
American Indian/ Alaska Native	22,690 (164)	0.4 (#)	21,080 (162)	0.4 (#)	26,840 (1,659)	0.5 (0.03)	10,340 (126)	0.5 (0.01)	10,060 (1,650)	0.5 (0.09)	6,440 (117)	0.6 (0.01)
Two or more races	— (†)	— —	127,090 (781)	2.7 (0.02)	240,970 (3,881)	4.9 (0.06)	90,870 (1,792)	4.6 (0.08)	77,070 (2,904)	4.1 (0.13)	73,020 (1,049)	6.8 (0.09)
School locale												
City	— (†)	— (†)	2,252,780 (12,708)	41.0 (0.31)	2,463,590 (50,197)	43.1 (0.63)	985,600 (23,753)	46.1 (1.02)	874,720 (26,907)	40.0 (0.97)	603,270 (20,872)	43.3 (0.92)
Suburban	— (†)	— (†)	2,137,800 (20,891)	39.0 (0.34)	2,284,510 (35,510)	39.9 (0.58)	873,070 (26,231)	40.8 (1.01)	825,600 (16,957)	37.7 (0.79)	585,830 (11,623)	42.0 (0.79)
Town	— (†)	— (†)	387,920 (9,565)	7.1 (0.17)	371,150 (25,577)	6.5 (0.42)	186,510 (23,522)	8.7 (1.02)	125,930 (730)	5.8 (0.12)	58,710 (10,017)	4.2 (0.69)
Rural	— (†)	— (†)	709,990 (26,462)	12.9 (0.42)	600,740 (25,531)	10.5 (0.41)	92,150 (2,740)	4.3 (0.15)	361,990 (24,792)	16.5 (0.96)	146,590 (5,414)	10.5 (0.46)
Teachers[5]												
Total	**408,400 (2,977)**	**100.0 (†)**	**437,410 (3,222)**	**100.0 (†)**	**482,320 (5,669)**	**100.0 (†)**	**152,900 (2,961)**	**100.0 (†)**	**182,860 (3,057)**	**100.0 (†)**	**146,560 (2,539)**	**100.0 (†)**
School level[2]												
Elementary	200,910 (735)	49.2 (0.31)	194,480 (1,878)	44.5 (0.25)	200,120 (3,691)	41.5 (0.56)	88,590 (2,249)	57.9 (1.17)	60,840 (1,641)	33.3 (0.79)	50,700 (1,339)	34.6 (0.63)
Secondary	62,740 (229)	15.4 (0.12)	67,530 (553)	15.4 (0.14)	73,690 (2,330)	15.3 (0.48)	45,780 (2,271)	29.9 (1.23)	12,920 (443)	7.1 (0.26)	14,990 (276)	10.2 (0.24)
Combined	144,750 (2,682)	35.4 (0.41)	175,410 (1,853)	40.1 (0.26)	208,520 (3,496)	43.2 (0.47)	18,530 (653)	12.1 (0.41)	109,110 (2,639)	59.7 (0.82)	80,870 (1,787)	55.2 (0.64)
School enrollment												
Less than 50	25,970 (488)	6.4 (0.11)	34,120 (1,642)	7.8 (0.34)	35,760 (1,330)	7.4 (0.25)	1,100 (0)	0.7 (0.01)	19,020 (1,077)	10.4 (0.53)	15,640 (782)	10.7 (0.50)
50 to 149	70,800 (983)	17.3 (0.21)	82,460 (1,102)	18.9 (0.23)	85,130 (2,523)	17.6 (0.42)	15,010 (1,508)	9.8 (0.89)	34,680 (1,158)	19.0 (0.56)	35,440 (1,440)	24.2 (0.81)
150 to 299	102,240 (486)	25.0 (0.20)	107,490 (1,873)	24.6 (0.33)	114,100 (2,944)	23.7 (0.53)	43,360 (1,706)	28.4 (0.93)	41,420 (1,498)	22.6 (0.74)	29,330 (1,504)	20.0 (0.94)
300 to 499	90,010 (1,316)	22.0 (0.28)	86,850 (751)	19.9 (0.19)	91,470 (2,245)	19.0 (0.46)	37,920 (1,185)	24.8 (0.91)	31,580 (1,443)	17.3 (0.70)	21,970 (680)	15.0 (0.47)
500 to 749	57,930 (79)	14.2 (0.10)	56,920 (†)	13.0 (0.10)	68,790 (2,335)	14.3 (0.46)	28,290 (2,018)	18.5 (1.17)	23,260 (610)	12.7 (0.36)	17,240 (506)	11.8 (0.27)
750 or more	61,440 (2,143)	15.0 (0.45)	69,570 (566)	15.9 (0.13)	87,090 (1,768)	18.1 (0.34)	27,230 (†)	17.8 (0.43)	32,910 (1,244)	18.0 (0.61)	26,950 (553)	18.4 (0.31)
School locale												
City	— (†)	— (†)	176,740 (799)	40.4 (0.33)	206,880 (3,770)	42.9 (0.58)	69,920 (1,760)	45.7 (1.23)	73,510 (2,032)	40.2 (0.87)	63,450 (1,782)	43.3 (0.76)
Suburban	— (†)	— (†)	166,170 (2,463)	38.0 (0.41)	185,400 (2,704)	38.4 (0.53)	60,840 (2,145)	39.8 (1.23)	65,780 (1,336)	36.0 (0.74)	58,770 (1,342)	40.1 (0.64)
Town	— (†)	— (†)	30,390 (663)	6.9 (0.15)	31,410 (2,294)	6.5 (0.45)	14,830 (2,040)	9.7 (1.21)	10,910 (125)	6.0 (0.13)	5,660 (1,041)	3.9 (0.70)
Rural	— (†)	— (†)	64,120 (1,960)	14.7 (0.39)	58,640 (2,235)	12.2 (0.43)	7,310 (173)	4.8 (0.14)	32,660 (1,970)	17.9 (0.92)	18,670 (1,036)	12.7 (0.74)

See notes at end of table.

Table 205.40. Number and percentage distribution of private elementary and secondary students, teachers, and schools, by orientation of school and selected characteristics: Fall 1999, fall 2009, and fall 2017—Continued

[Standard errors appear in parentheses]

Selected characteristic	Fall 1999		Fall 2009		Fall 2017							
	Total		Total		Total		Catholic		Other religious		Nonsectarian	
	Number	Percent	Number	Percent	Number	Percent	Number	Percent	Number	Percent	Number	Percent
1	2	3	4	5	6	7	8	9	10	11	12	13
Schools												
Total	**33,000 (301)**	**100.0 (†)**	**33,370 (834)**	**100.0 (†)**	**32,460 (559)**	**100.0 (†)**	**7,050 (147)**	**100.0 (†)**	**14,500 (319)**	**100.0 (†)**	**10,910 (342)**	**100.0 (†)**
School level[2]												
Elementary	22,300 (242)	67.6 (0.43)	21,420 (745)	64.2 (0.70)	20,090 (460)	61.9 (0.82)	5,410 (134)	76.7 (0.78)	8,010 (329)	55.2 (1.53)	6,670 (241)	61.1 (1.18)
Secondary	2,540 (62)	7.7 (0.19)	2,780 (39)	8.3 (0.23)	2,840 (92)	8.8 (0.30)	1,130 (57)	16.1 (0.74)	810 (63)	5.6 (0.45)	900 (28)	8.2 (0.30)
Combined	8,150 (160)	24.7 (0.40)	9,160 (153)	27.5 (0.54)	9,530 (300)	29.3 (0.76)	510 (16)	7.2 (0.26)	5,680 (206)	39.1 (1.42)	3,340 (176)	30.6 (1.13)
School enrollment												
Less than 50	9,160 (210)	27.8 (0.44)	11,070 (801)	33.2 (1.61)	10,300 (323)	31.7 (0.67)	240 (0)	3.4 (0.07)	5,780 (207)	39.9 (0.93)	4,280 (259)	39.2 (1.46)
50 to 149	10,260 (134)	31.1 (0.29)	10,470 (154)	31.4 (0.81)	9,970 (261)	30.7 (0.57)	1,480 (76)	21.0 (0.92)	4,310 (165)	29.7 (0.78)	4,180 (162)	38.3 (1.28)
150 to 299	7,440 (34)	22.5 (0.21)	6,690 (46)	20.1 (0.49)	6,790 (196)	20.9 (0.54)	2,840 (113)	40.3 (1.11)	2,510 (97)	17.3 (0.70)	1,450 (79)	13.3 (0.68)
300 to 499	3,730 (41)	11.3 (0.13)	3,010 (30)	9.0 (0.24)	3,030 (89)	9.3 (0.27)	1,420 (37)	20.2 (0.62)	1,090 (73)	7.5 (0.50)	520 (22)	4.8 (0.25)
500 to 749	1,530 (3)	4.6 (0.04)	1,280 (†)	3.8 (0.10)	1,410 (51)	4.4 (0.17)	690 (42)	9.8 (0.56)	470 (12)	3.2 (0.11)	250 (16)	2.3 (0.17)
750 or more	870 (20)	2.6 (0.06)	850 (7)	2.5 (0.06)	950 (21)	2.9 (0.08)	370 (†)	5.2 (0.16)	350 (12)	2.4 (0.10)	230 (8)	2.1 (0.10)
Racial/ethnic enrollment concentration												
More than 50 percent White	26,490 (290)	80.3 (0.21)	25,110 (818)	75.2 (0.74)	23,250 (434)	71.6 (0.60)	5,180 (†)	73.6 (0.58)	10,940 (303)	75.4 (0.77)	7,120 (259)	65.3 (1.14)
More than 50 percent Black	2,660 (34)	8.0 (0.11)	2,640 (70)	7.9 (0.28)	2,220 (79)	6.8 (0.26)	290 (†)	4.1 (0.13)	1,240 (55)	8.5 (0.40)	690 (49)	6.3 (0.47)
More than 50 percent Hispanic	1,220 (20)	3.7 (0.07)	1,550 (72)	4.6 (0.23)	1,990 (153)	6.1 (0.42)	680 (†)	9.7 (0.32)	620 (100)	4.3 (0.68)	680 (90)	6.2 (0.74)
No racial/ethnic group more than 50 percent	2,150 (36)	6.5 (0.11)	3,300 (103)	9.9 (0.36)	4,080 (121)	12.6 (0.32)	790 (†)	11.2 (0.30)	1,350 (45)	9.3 (0.34)	1,940 (113)	17.8 (0.87)
School locale												
City	— (†)	— (†)	10,810 (171)	32.4 (0.88)	10,530 (221)	32.4 (0.61)	2,830 (69)	40.2 (0.99)	3,910 (117)	26.9 (0.93)	3,790 (128)	34.8 (0.98)
Suburban	— (†)	— (†)	11,610 (176)	34.8 (0.94)	12,150 (300)	37.4 (0.76)	2,660 (69)	37.7 (0.97)	4,420 (144)	30.5 (1.00)	5,070 (180)	46.5 (1.11)
Town	— (†)	— (†)	3,340 (154)	10.0 (0.50)	2,750 (150)	8.5 (0.43)	1,020 (110)	14.5 (1.35)	1,180 (43)	8.1 (0.36)	550 (92)	5.0 (0.77)
Rural	— (†)	— (†)	7,610 (799)	22.8 (1.86)	7,020 (336)	21.6 (0.86)	530 (35)	7.5 (0.48)	4,990 (301)	34.4 (1.47)	1,500 (148)	13.8 (1.19)

—Not available.
†Not applicable.
#Rounds to zero.
[1]Includes students in prekindergarten through grade 12 in schools that offer kindergarten or higher grade.
[2]Elementary schools have grade 6 or lower and no grade higher than 8. Secondary schools have no grade lower than 7. Combined schools include those that have grades lower than 7 and higher than 8, as well as those that do not classify students by grade level.
[3]Race/ethnicity was not collected for prekindergarten students (821,800 in fall 2017). Percentage distribution is based on the students for whom race/ethnicity was reported.
[4]For 1999, Pacific Islander students are included under Asian. Prior to 2009, data were not collected on Pacific Islander students as a separate category.
[5]Reported in full-time equivalents (FTE). Excludes teachers who teach only prekindergarten students.
NOTE: Tabulation includes schools that offer kindergarten or higher grade. Detail may not sum to totals because of rounding.
SOURCE: U.S. Department of Education, National Center for Education Statistics, Private School Universe Survey (PSS), 1999–2000, 2009–10, and 2017–18. (This table was prepared August 2019.)

Table 205.80. Private elementary and secondary schools, enrollment, teachers, and high school graduates, by state: Selected years, 2007 through 2017

[Standard errors appear in parentheses]

State	Schools, fall 2017	Enrollment in prekindergarten through grade 12: Fall 2007	Fall 2009	Fall 2011	Fall 2013	Fall 2015	Fall 2017	Teachers,[1] fall 2017	High school graduates, 2016–17
1	2	3	4	5	6	7	8	9	10
United States	32,460 (559)	5,910,210 (28,363)	5,488,490 (35,857)	5,268,090 (24,908)	5,395,740 (50,342)	5,750,520 (85,729)	5,719,990 (74,133)	482,320 (5,669)	348,230 (3,751)
Alabama	370 (35)	83,840 (103)	95,570 (11,745)	81,070 (49)	76,400 (295)	75,070 (†)	70,840 (2,360)	5,890 (212)	4,580 (35)
Alaska	50 (†)	4,990 (†)	7,510! (2,740)	5,170 (†)	5,080 (†)	5,540 (†)	4,470 (†)	410 (†)	‡ (†)
Arizona	330 (32)	64,910 (†)	55,390 (†)	53,120 (229)	55,070 (†)	56,610 (†)	56,800 (1,153)	4,300 (128)	3,570 (†)
Arkansas	230! (85)	40,120 (11,961)	28,900 (1,371)	29,930 (1,245)	30,340 (1,496)	37,930 (6,108)	30,530 (1,872)	2,460 (85)	1,680 (†)
California	3,340 (47)	703,810 (6,129)	623,150 (4,185)	608,070 (69)	596,160 (3,500)	627,170 (10,231)	643,010 (22,494)	51,490 (2,007)	41,310 (398)
Colorado	410 (62)	64,740 (†)	63,720 (3,486)	61,140 (148)	60,690 (4,498)	68,140 (9,589)	56,420 (2,338)	5,070 (529)	2,960 (62)
Connecticut	370 (38)	85,150 (9,241)	72,540 (464)	66,320 (142)	72,770 (8,293)	66,710 (2,671)	62,680 (4,763)	7,840 (1,070)	5,950 (†)
Delaware	160! (59)	32,520 (2,701)	26,640 (†)	25,090 (†)	23,640 (†)	19,660 (†)	28,130! (9,939)	2,530! (832)	1,390 (147)
District of Columbia	60 (†)	19,640 (†)	17,810 (†)	16,950 (†)	19,790 (277)	17,110 (1,939)	14,280 (†)	1,700 (†)	1,060 (†)
Florida	2,870 (271)	391,660 (6,123)	343,990 (1,023)	340,960 (230)	372,790 (2,812)	389,310 (207)	471,580 (26,070)	37,960 (2,449)	26,900 (215)
Georgia	840 (111)	157,430 (9,185)	150,300 (6,251)	138,080 (†)	150,360 (2,250)	189,630 (27,662)	166,310 (16,140)	14,990 (209)	10,100 (†)
Hawaii	130 (†)	37,300 (290)	37,130 (†)	37,530 (†)	33,820 (32)	45,600 (7,730)	40,840 (†)	3,570 (†)	3,510 (†)
Idaho	280 (81)	24,700! (11,608)	18,680 (4,814)	13,670 (193)	18,580 (3,090)	20,230 (3,947)	26,040 (5,656)	1,820 (441)	890 (129)
Illinois	1,350 (70)	312,270 (6,638)	289,720 (9,237)	271,030 (1,289)	281,360 (6,026)	280,440 (19,662)	258,280 (16,148)	19,200 (973)	14,450 (192)
Indiana	910 (118)	119,910 (2,284)	120,770 (5,919)	129,120 (12,177)	121,230 (3,928)	171,570 (4,510)	144,780 (16,314)	10,370 (1,117)	6,610 (291)
Iowa	320 (80)	47,820 (†)	45,160 (†)	63,840 (14,665)	56,150 (9,338)	70,870 (16,178)	51,040 (1,661)	4,030 (289)	2,810 (†)
Kansas	200 (†)	47,780 (2,414)	44,680 (1,668)	43,100 (1,640)	41,520 (3,286)	42,270 (†)	43,660 (†)	3,350 (†)	2,870 (†)
Kentucky	420 (79)	76,140 (2,074)	70,590 (2,132)	69,410 (12)	74,750 (4,226)	70,090 (†)	86,880 (19,678)	7,300 (1,962)	7,260! (2,868)
Louisiana	530 (71)	137,460 (†)	147,040 (9,890)	125,720 (108)	129,720 (2,606)	166,560 (33,949)	146,100 (16,303)	10,940 (1,060)	8,700 (164)
Maine	140 (†)	21,260 (143)	18,310 (†)	18,350 (†)	18,380 (272)	18,600 (†)	18,340 (†)	1,990 (†)	2,530 (†)
Maryland	750 (53)	165,760 (1,160)	145,690 (160)	137,450 (564)	143,530 (2,030)	142,630 (3,549)	157,180 (14,193)	14,050 (673)	9,830 (†)
Massachusetts	660 (22)	151,640 (2,516)	137,110 (1,169)	130,940 (1,596)	134,560 (943)	123,230 (865)	121,040 (658)	14,540 (61)	10,700 (†)
Michigan	840 (94)	159,100 (2,047)	153,230 (5,828)	135,580 (544)	141,590 (6,240)	172,130 (34,196)	147,650 (10,736)	10,940 (983)	7,930 (124)
Minnesota	810 (220)	101,740 (3,903)	89,530 (†)	87,620 (†)	85,260 (†)	75,630 (†)	128,690 (30,057)	9,640 (2,104)	6,260 (922)
Mississippi	200 (†)	55,270 (†)	54,650 (2,458)	52,060 (†)	50,330 (3,333)	43,580 (†)	47,450 (†)	3,800 (†)	3,030 (†)
Missouri	780 (182)	125,610 (3,685)	117,970 (2,065)	130,130 (8,715)	139,570 (25,980)	125,290 (8,723)	132,030 (16,277)	10,100 (1,442)	8,250 (401)
Montana	120 (†)	15,030! (5,465)	10,390 (1,221)	10,550 (†)	10,560 (521)	11,690 (†)	10,390 (†)	1,040 (†)	530 (†)
Nebraska	270 (53)	40,320 (†)	39,040 (†)	40,750 (†)	42,300 (†)	48,960 (5,442)	50,940 (7,667)	4,420! (1,451)	3,900! (1,348)
Nevada	140 (†)	29,820 (2,009)	25,060 (†)	26,130 (†)	21,980 (†)	23,910 (†)	26,330 (†)	1,830 (†)	1,330 (†)
New Hampshire	350 (97)	30,920 (†)	26,470 (†)	27,350 (†)	26,700 (†)	25,330 (†)	32,490 (7,282)	3,460 (983)	2,840 (343)
New Jersey	1,100 (83)	253,250 (5,016)	232,020 (16,536)	210,220 (1,211)	211,150 (4,607)	213,170 (13,684)	214,840 (12,022)	18,990 (564)	15,070 (†)
New Mexico	‡ (†)	27,290 (1,388)	23,730 (507)	22,680 (10)	21,750 (†)	22,230 (†)	‡ (†)	‡ (†)	1,080 (†)
New York	1,690 (4)	518,850 (7,196)	486,310 (5,211)	487,810 (19,574)	452,380 (901)	520,660 (16,620)	469,720 (2,192)	43,290 (118)	31,020 (†)
North Carolina	640 (9)	121,660 (2,226)	110,740 (1,851)	119,070 (†)	118,090 (492)	124,030 (†)	122,060 (3,653)	11,730 (254)	6,820 (28)
North Dakota	50 (†)	7,430 (†)	7,750 (†)	7,770 (†)	8,290 (†)	7,830 (†)	9,260 (†)	790 (†)	‡ (†)
Ohio	1,430 (186)	239,520 (2,741)	246,250 (24,214)	213,990 (3,419)	238,620 (19,487)	255,690 (40,837)	247,790 (24,684)	18,190 (1,508)	14,640 (730)
Oklahoma	150 (†)	40,320 (5,032)	34,000 (716)	35,750 (847)	32,740 (†)	32,160 (1,061)	31,550 (†)	2,790 (†)	1,770 (†)
Oregon	400 (49)	66,260 (5,188)	56,820 (3,502)	53,200 (†)	58,830 (3,109)	57,310 (†)	52,960 (787)	4,410 (394)	3,260 (197)
Pennsylvania	2,500 (126)	324,020 (6,253)	301,640 (5,036)	276,300 (3,668)	253,800 (756)	315,830 (38,974)	282,330 (13,928)	23,630 (793)	18,060 (244)
Rhode Island	110 (†)	28,260 (1,096)	24,940 (†)	25,420 (†)	22,180 (†)	20,620 (2,711)	18,770 (†)	1,750 (†)	1,780 (†)
South Carolina	390 (33)	71,430 (1,043)	62,320 (311)	60,890 (†)	65,350 (4,447)	62,830 (†)	65,200 (2,438)	5,620 (367)	3,260 (33)
South Dakota	80 (†)	12,280 (†)	11,470 (†)	12,490 (†)	9,950 (†)	10,740 (†)	12,170 (†)	1,000 (†)	690 (†)
Tennessee	490 (9)	117,540 (12,851)	98,310 (4,176)	92,430 (34)	93,990 (3,210)	91,950 (†)	99,110 (7,467)	9,200 (674)	7,790 (583)
Texas	2,090 (180)	296,540 (4,132)	313,360 (11,968)	285,320 (2,046)	312,640 (5,896)	351,270 (26,334)	347,430 (28,896)	31,300 (2,472)	17,390 (1,399)
Utah	150 (†)	20,860 (†)	21,990 (1,558)	18,660 (55)	23,310 (†)	21,140 (†)	22,650 (†)	1,820 (†)	1,690 (†)
Vermont	100 (†)	12,600 (232)	10,350 (†)	9,030 (†)	8,890 (†)	10,040 (†)	9,090 (†)	1,120 (†)	870 (†)
Virginia	820 (40)	143,140 (7,988)	128,140 (2,581)	123,780 (82)	131,330 (1,828)	140,350 (12,832)	131,290 (281)	11,710 (80)	7,440 (160)
Washington	620 (20)	104,070 (3,054)	94,340 (625)	93,630 (234)	119,730 (17,349)	100,140 (479)	99,620 (762)	7,870 (78)	4,330 (†)
West Virginia	120 (†)	14,980 (†)	13,860 (†)	13,430 (1)	14,350 (†)	14,780 (†)	14,310 (†)	1,280 (†)	860 (†)
Wisconsin	910 (67)	138,290 (1,597)	130,510 (†)	127,250 (†)	160,650 (32,980)	144,020 (11,405)	151,990 (15,852)	11,280 (896)	6,160 (†)
Wyoming	40 (†)	2,930 (†)	2,910 (†)	2,740 (†)	2,780 (†)	2,240 (†)	2,320 (†)	220 (†)	‡ (†)

†Not applicable.
!Interpret data with caution. The coefficient of variation (CV) for this estimate is between 30 and 50 percent.
‡Reporting standards not met. Either there are too few cases for a reliable estimate or the coefficient of variation (CV) is 50 percent or greater.
[1]Reported in full-time equivalents (FTE). Excludes teachers who teach only prekindergarten students.
NOTE: Includes special education, vocational/technical education, and alternative schools. Tabulation includes schools that offer kindergarten or higher grade. Includes enrollment of students in prekindergarten through grade 12 in schools that offer kindergarten or higher grade. Some state counts are based on a census of schools in that state rather than a sample; for these counts, standard errors are not applicable. Detail may not sum to totals because of rounding.
SOURCE: U.S. Department of Education, National Center for Education Statistics, Private School Universe Survey (PSS), 2007–08 through 2017–18. (This table was prepared August 2019.)

Table 206.10. Number and percentage of homeschooled students ages 5 through 17 with a grade equivalent of kindergarten through 12th grade, by selected child, parent, and household characteristics: Selected years, 1999 through 2016

[Standard errors appear in parentheses]

Selected child, parent, or household characteristic	1999				2003				2007				2012				2016			
	Number homeschooled[1] (in thousands)		Percent homeschooled[1]		Number homeschooled[1] (in thousands)		Percent homeschooled[1]		Number homeschooled[1] (in thousands)		Percent homeschooled[1]		Number homeschooled[1,2] (in thousands)		Percent homeschooled[1,2]		Number homeschooled[1] (in thousands)		Percent homeschooled[1]	
1	2		3		4		5		6		7		8		9		10		11	
Total	**850**	**(71.1)**	**1.7**	**(0.14)**	**1,096**	**(92.3)**	**2.2**	**(0.18)**	**1,520**	**(118.0)**	**3.0**	**(0.23)**	**1,773**	**(115.7)**	**3.4**	**(0.23)**	**1,690**	**(118.4)**	**3.3**	**(0.23)**
Sex of child																				
Male	417	(43.9)	1.6	(0.17)	569	(61.9)	2.2	(0.24)	639	(75.1)	2.4	(0.28)	875	(73.7)	3.3	(0.28)	807	(79.2)	3.0	(0.30)
Female	434	(46.1)	1.8	(0.19)	527	(58.2)	2.1	(0.23)	881	(97.4)	3.5	(0.39)	898	(80.3)	3.6	(0.32)	882	(74.8)	3.5	(0.29)
Race/ethnicity of child																				
White	640	(62.3)	2.0	(0.19)	843	(77.5)	2.7	(0.25)	1,171	(102.2)	3.9	(0.34)	1,205	(95.7)	4.5	(0.35)	998	(92.6)	3.8	(0.35)
Black	84	(24.8)	1.0	(0.31)	103!	(33.9)	1.3!	(0.42)	61!	(21.2)	0.8!	(0.28)	140	(37.1)	2.0	(0.52)	132	(27.6)	1.9	(0.39)
Hispanic	77	(17.7)	1.1	(0.25)	59!	(21.1)	0.7	(0.26)	147	(27.5)	1.5	(0.29)	265	(41.1)	2.3	(0.35)	444	(62.2)	3.5	(0.50)
Asian/Pacific Islander	‡	(†)	‡	(†)	‡	(†)	‡	(†)	‡	(†)	‡	(†)	73!	(21.9)	2.8!	(0.90)	44	(12.6)	1.4	(0.40)
Asian	—	(†)	—	(†)	—	(†)	—	(†)	‡	(†)	‡	(†)	‡	(†)	‡	(†)	42	(12.0)	1.4	(0.40)
Pacific Islander	—	(†)	—	(†)	—	(†)	—	(†)	‡	(†)	‡	(†)	‡	(†)	‡	(†)	‡	(†)	‡	(†)
American Indian/Alaska Native	‡	(†)	‡	(†)	‡	(†)	‡	(†)	‡	(†)	‡	(†)	‡	(†)	‡	(†)	‡	(†)	‡	(†)
Other[3]	16!	(6.4)	1.6!	(0.62)	59!	(26.9)	4.9!	(2.13)	111	(29.5)	4.8	(1.30)	82	(16.3)	3.2	(0.61)	69	(15.2)	2.7	(0.62)
Grade equivalent[4]																				
Kindergarten through grade 5	428	(48.1)	1.8	(0.20)	472	(55.3)	1.9	(0.23)	717	(83.8)	3.0	(0.36)	833	(84.8)	3.2	(0.33)	767	(74.4)	3.0	(0.29)
Kindergarten	92	(19.7)	2.4	(0.52)	‡	(†)	‡	(†)	‡	(†)	‡	(†)	212	(47.3)	4.0	(0.90)	181	(40.7)	3.5	(0.80)
Grades 1 through 3	199	(36.7)	1.6	(0.29)	214	(33.3)	1.8	(0.28)	406	(64.5)	3.4	(0.54)	353	(50.9)	2.9	(0.42)	300	(34.1)	2.4	(0.28)
Grades 4 and 5	136	(22.5)	1.7	(0.28)	160	(30.1)	1.9	(0.35)	197	(41.4)	2.5	(0.52)	268	(44.2)	3.2	(0.52)	287	(51.8)	3.4	(0.62)
Grades 6 through 8	186	(28.0)	1.6	(0.24)	302	(44.9)	2.4	(0.36)	371	(65.3)	3.0	(0.53)	424	(49.0)	3.5	(0.41)	398	(49.1)	3.3	(0.41)
Grades 9 through 12	235	(33.3)	1.7	(0.24)	315	(47.0)	2.3	(0.33)	422	(58.2)	2.8	(0.38)	516	(53.6)	3.8	(0.39)	525	(55.9)	3.8	(0.40)
Number of children in the household																				
One child	132	(18.0)	1.3	(0.17)	110	(22.3)	1.4	(0.27)	197	(32.5)	2.3	(0.38)	418	(29.6)	3.4	(0.23)	338	(35.5)	2.7	(0.27)
Two children	248	(28.4)	1.3	(0.15)	306	(45.1)	1.5	(0.22)	414	(67.2)	2.0	(0.32)	493	(51.5)	2.5	(0.26)	475	(55.3)	2.3	(0.27)
Three or more children	470	(63.9)	2.3	(0.31)	679	(80.2)	3.1	(0.36)	909	(102.4)	4.1	(0.46)	862	(88.4)	4.5	(0.47)	877	(84.8)	4.7	(0.45)
Number of parents in the household																				
Two parents	683	(68.3)	2.1	(0.21)	886	(82.7)	2.5	(0.23)	1,357	(111.5)	3.6	(0.30)	1,354	(104.2)	3.8	(0.29)	1,358	(103.7)	3.7	(0.28)
One parent	142	(25.0)	0.9	(0.16)	196	(42.6)	1.5	(0.32)	118	(28.4)	1.0	(0.24)	342	(51.6)	2.5	(0.37)	293	(38.4)	2.3	(0.30)
Nonparental guardians	25!	(14.4)	‡	(†)	‡	(†)	‡	(†)	‡	(†)	‡	(†)	77!	(31.9)	4.0!	(1.60)	38	(9.9)	2.0	(0.54)
Parent participation in the labor force																				
Two parents—both in labor force	237	(39.8)	1.0	(0.17)	274	(44.1)	1.1	(0.18)	518	(76.2)	2.0	(0.29)	588	(63.5)	2.5	(0.27)	427	(56.5)	1.7	(0.23)
Two parents—one in labor force	444	(53.9)	4.6	(0.55)	594	(73.7)	5.6	(0.67)	808	(94.3)	7.5	(0.82)	719	(76.3)	6.2	(0.65)	935	(87.8)	7.2	(0.68)
One parent in labor force	98	(21.8)	0.7	(0.16)	174	(39.8)	1.4	(0.33)	127	(29.5)	1.3	(0.30)	247	(40.9)	2.2	(0.36)	189	(29.6)	1.8	(0.29)
No parent participation in labor force	71	(18.8)	1.9	(0.48)	‡	(†)	‡	(†)	‡	(†)	‡	(†)	130	(31.9)	4.8	(1.15)	139	(23.9)	4.0	(0.72)
Highest education level of parents																				
High school diploma or less	160	(26.5)	0.9	(0.15)	269	(51.6)	1.7	(0.32)	208	(35.5)	1.5	(0.24)	560	(81.7)	3.4	(0.50)	510	(66.1)	3.3	(0.43)
Vocational/technical, associate's degree, or some college	287	(37.3)	1.9	(0.24)	338	(57.7)	2.1	(0.36)	559	(77.5)	3.8	(0.52)	525	(45.6)	3.4	(0.29)	418	(49.2)	3.1	(0.36)
Bachelor's degree/some graduate school	213	(36.2)	2.6	(0.42)	309	(48.5)	2.8	(0.45)	444	(64.7)	3.9	(0.57)	434	(51.4)	3.7	(0.43)	501	(64.0)	3.6	(0.45)
Graduate/professional degree	190	(39.8)	2.3	(0.46)	180	(41.6)	2.3	(0.55)	309	(50.0)	2.9	(0.46)	255	(27.3)	3.3	(0.36)	260	(30.7)	3.0	(0.35)
Household income[5]																				
$20,000 or less	184	(35.2)	1.5	(0.28)	164	(38.9)	1.8	(0.43)	186	(42.1)	2.2	(0.50)	219	(41.8)	2.9	(0.56)	184	(29.0)	2.9	(0.46)
$20,001 to $50,000	356	(42.9)	1.8	(0.22)	430	(60.3)	2.6	(0.36)	420	(59.8)	3.1	(0.42)	528	(65.5)	3.8	(0.47)	483	(59.4)	3.7	(0.46)
$50,001 to $75,000	162	(25.5)	1.9	(0.30)	264	(51.1)	2.4	(0.46)	414	(58.8)	4.0	(0.57)	370	(48.9)	3.9	(0.53)	435	(58.6)	4.8	(0.65)
$75,001 to $100,000	148	(26.5)	1.5	(0.28)	169	(42.9)	2.6	(0.66)	264	(57.2)	3.8	(0.83)	288	(47.3)	4.2	(0.69)	268	(38.4)	3.8	(0.55)
Over $100,000	—	(†)	—	(†)	‡	(†)	‡	(†)	236	(57.5)	2.0	(0.49)	367	(42.8)	2.7	(0.31)	319	(39.0)	1.9	(0.24)
Locale																				
City	—	(†)	—	(†)	—	(†)	—	(†)	327	(40.4)	2.0	(0.26)	493	(59.5)	3.3	(0.40)	493	(56.0)	3.0	(0.33)
Suburban	—	(†)	—	(†)	—	(†)	—	(†)	503	(78.8)	2.6	(0.41)	601	(66.8)	3.1	(0.34)	651	(76.2)	2.9	(0.33)
Town	—	(†)	—	(†)	—	(†)	—	(†)	168	(37.1)	3.0	(0.65)	127	(30.8)	2.6	(0.63)	177	(30.0)	4.3	(0.70)
Rural	—	(†)	—	(†)	—	(†)	—	(†)	523	(75.9)	4.9	(0.71)	552	(68.2)	4.5	(0.55)	368	(45.1)	4.4	(0.54)

—Not available.
†Not applicable.
!Interpret data with caution. The coefficient of variation (CV) for this estimate is between 30 and 50 percent.
‡Reporting standards not met (too few cases for a reliable estimate).
[1]Excludes students who were enrolled in school for more than 25 hours a week. Also excludes students who were homeschooled only due to a temporary illness.
[2]The National Center for Education Statistics uses a statistical adjustment for estimates of homeschoolers in 2012. For more information about this adjustment, please see *Homeschooling in the United States: 2012* (NCES 2016-096REV).
[3]Includes Two or more races and race/ethnicity not reported.
[4]Students whose grade equivalent was "ungraded" were excluded from the grade analysis. The percentage of students with an "ungraded" grade equivalent was 0.02 percent in 2003 and 2007. There were no students with an "ungraded" grade equivalent in 2012.
[5]For 1999, estimates combine the "$75,001 to $100,000" and "Over $100,000" categories.
NOTE: While National Household Education Surveys Program (NHES) administrations prior to 2012 were administered via telephone with an interviewer, NHES:2012 and NHES:2016 used self-administered paper-and-pencil questionnaires that were mailed to respondents. Measurable differences between estimates for years prior to 2012 and estimates for later years could reflect actual changes in the population, or the changes could be due to the mode change from telephone to mail. Race categories exclude persons of Hispanic ethnicity. Detail may not sum to totals because of rounding. Some data have been revised from previously published figures.
SOURCE: U.S. Department of Education, National Center for Education Statistics, Parent Survey and Parent and Family Involvement in Education Survey of the National Household Education Surveys Program (Parent-NHES:1999 and PFI-NHES:2003, 2007, 2012, and 2016). (This table was prepared February 2018.)

Table 206.20. Percentage distribution of students ages 5 through 17 attending kindergarten through 12th grade, by school type or participation in homeschooling and selected child, parent, and household characteristics: Selected years, 1999 through 2016

[Standard errors appear in parentheses]

Selected child, parent, or household characteristic	1999				2003				2007				
	Public school		Private school	Home-schooled[1]	Public school		Private school	Home-schooled[1]	Public school		Private school	Home-schooled[1]	Pu
	Assigned	Chosen			Assigned	Chosen			Assigned	Chosen			Assi
1	2	3	4	5	6	7	8	9	10	11	12	13	
Total	**74.1 (0.45)**	**14.3 (0.33)**	**10.0 (0.28)**	**1.7 (0.14)**	**72.1 (0.57)**	**15.0 (0.41)**	**10.8 (0.39)**	**2.2 (0.18)**	**70.6 (0.70)**	**15.0 (0.55)**	**11.4 (0.45)**	**3.0 (0.23)**	**68.8 (0**
Sex of child													
Male	74.8 (0.60)	13.9 (0.44)	9.7 (0.34)	1.6 (0.17)	72.1 (0.70)	15.0 (0.56)	10.7 (0.48)	2.2 (0.24)	70.7 (1.05)	15.3 (0.79)	11.5 (0.73)	2.4 (0.28)	69.6 (C
Female	73.4 (0.61)	14.6 (0.45)	10.3 (0.41)	1.8 (0.19)	72.1 (0.78)	14.9 (0.54)	10.8 (0.51)	2.1 (0.23)	70.5 (0.88)	14.7 (0.64)	11.2 (0.54)	3.5 (0.39)	68.0 (C
Race/ethnicity of child													
White	75.0 (0.54)	11.2 (0.35)	11.8 (0.39)	2.0 (0.19)	72.7 (0.67)	12.4 (0.47)	12.2 (0.48)	2.7 (0.25)	69.9 (0.80)	12.0 (0.46)	14.2 (0.61)	3.9 (0.34)	71.8 (C
Black	70.2 (1.24)	22.6 (1.22)	6.2 (0.47)	1.0 (0.31)	66.6 (1.49)	23.4 (1.45)	8.6 (0.85)	1.3! (0.42)	68.4 (2.30)	23.0 (2.20)	7.8 (1.33)	0.8! (0.28)	60.3 (2
Hispanic	76.0 (1.02)	17.6 (0.91)	5.2 (0.40)	1.1 (0.25)	77.2 (1.17)	15.0 (0.99)	7.1 (0.66)	0.7! (0.26)	74.6 (1.41)	17.5 (1.25)	6.3 (0.57)	1.5 (0.29)	66.8 (1
Asian/Pacific Islander	68.8 (3.13)	18.1 (2.74)	11.3 (1.68)	‡ (†)	65.8 (3.52)	19.1 (3.23)	14.0 (2.21)	‡ (†)	72.1 (3.22)	13.6 (2.10)	12.1 (2.08)	‡ (†)	69.2 (2
Asian	— (†)	— (†)	— (†)	— (†)	— (†)	— (†)	— (†)	— (†)	71.4 (3.15)	12.8 (2.11)	13.4 (2.25)	‡ (†)	69.4 (2
Pacific Islander	— (†)	— (†)	— (†)	— (†)	— (†)	— (†)	— (†)	— (†)	77.9 (11.74)	‡ (†)	‡ (†)	‡ (†)	63.2 (12
Other[3]	70.2 (2.90)	17.2 (2.50)	10.7 (1.96)	1.9 (0.56)	68.2 (3.75)	18.3 (2.87)	8.8 (2.14)	4.6! (1.76)	69.4 (2.83)	18.6 (2.41)	7.8 (1.22)	4.2 (1.13)	69.9 (1
Disability status of child as reported by parent													
Has a disability	74.8 (0.93)	15.3 (0.78)	8.0 (0.49)	1.8 (0.27)	72.4 (1.12)	16.2 (0.75)	9.2 (0.70)	2.2 (0.35)	72.7 (1.35)	14.0 (0.91)	10.5 (0.96)	2.7 (0.49)	69.0 (1
Does not have a disability	73.9 (0.51)	14.0 (0.36)	10.5 (0.34)	1.7 (0.16)	72.0 (0.67)	14.5 (0.51)	11.3 (0.44)	2.1 (0.21)	69.9 (0.76)	15.3 (0.63)	11.7 (0.48)	3.1 (0.28)	68.7 (C
Grade equivalent[4]													
Kindergarten through grade 5	71.5 (0.61)	15.1 (0.43)	11.6 (0.41)	1.8 (0.20)	70.1 (0.70)	16.2 (0.56)	11.8 (0.53)	1.9 (0.23)	68.5 (1.16)	16.2 (1.04)	12.2 (0.69)	3.0 (0.36)	70.0 (C
Kindergarten	66.2 (1.67)	15.4 (1.13)	15.9 (1.29)	2.4 (0.52)	69.0 (1.50)	15.5 (1.18)	12.8 (1.21)	2.7 (0.64)	66.4 (2.20)	14.7 (1.60)	15.8 (1.61)	‡ (†)	70.3 (2
Grades 1 through 3	72.2 (0.87)	15.3 (0.67)	10.9 (0.53)	1.6 (0.29)	70.0 (1.18)	16.2 (0.96)	12.1 (0.73)	1.8 (0.28)	68.4 (1.68)	15.9 (1.63)	12.3 (0.93)	3.4 (0.54)	69.5 (1
Grades 4 and 5	72.9 (1.17)	14.6 (0.79)	10.7 (0.77)	1.7 (0.28)	70.7 (1.12)	16.5 (0.96)	10.9 (0.76)	1.9 (0.35)	69.7 (1.62)	17.5 (1.34)	10.3 (1.08)	2.5 (0.52)	70.7 (1
Grades 6 through 8	77.4 (0.79)	11.5 (0.65)	9.5 (0.47)	1.6 (0.24)	73.3 (1.03)	14.1 (0.81)	10.2 (0.59)	2.4 (0.36)	74.4 (1.44)	11.6 (0.81)	11.0 (1.14)	3.0 (0.53)	68.9 (1
Grades 9 through 12	75.7 (0.75)	15.1 (0.60)	7.5 (0.44)	1.7 (0.24)	74.6 (0.97)	13.6 (0.76)	9.5 (0.63)	2.3 (0.33)	70.8 (1.07)	15.9 (0.84)	10.5 (0.75)	2.8 (0.38)	66.4 (C
Number of parents in the household													
Two parents	74.5 (0.54)	12.0 (0.35)	11.5 (0.37)	2.1 (0.21)	71.8 (0.67)	13.6 (0.51)	12.1 (0.47)	2.5 (0.23)	69.5 (0.73)	13.8 (0.49)	12.9 (0.52)	3.6 (0.30)	68.5 (C
One parent	73.5 (0.78)	18.2 (0.55)	7.3 (0.47)	0.9 (0.16)	72.9 (1.09)	18.0 (0.98)	7.6 (0.67)	1.5 (0.32)	73.6 (1.39)	17.2 (1.14)	8.1 (1.18)	1.0 (0.24)	68.9 (1
Nonparental guardians	71.6 (2.70)	21.9 (2.72)	5.1 (0.84)	‡ (†)	73.2 (3.05)	20.1 (2.59)	5.8 (1.36)	‡ (†)	72.2 (5.91)	23.0 (6.19)	2.6 (0.74)	‡ (†)	74.2 (2
Highest education level of parents													
Less than a high school diploma	79.1 (1.38)	18.0 (1.46)	2.7 (0.51)	‡ (†)	76.9 (2.06)	18.9 (1.76)	2.9! (1.18)	‡ (†)	83.5 (2.77)	11.9 (1.93)	‡ (†)	‡ (†)	71.7 (2
High school diploma or GED	79.0 (0.84)	14.3 (0.72)	5.6 (0.44)	1.1 (0.19)	77.8 (1.01)	15.5 (0.89)	4.9 (0.45)	1.8 (0.34)	79.3 (1.74)	15.1 (1.66)	3.8 (0.56)	1.8 (0.32)	73.9 (1
Vocational/technical, associate's degree, or some college	75.8 (0.72)	14.7 (0.63)	7.7 (0.40)	1.9 (0.24)	74.0 (0.97)	15.5 (0.74)	8.3 (0.58)	2.1 (0.36)	72.0 (1.03)	15.3 (0.99)	8.8 (0.70)	3.8 (0.52)	71.7 (C
Bachelor's degree/some graduate school	68.6 (1.06)	13.2 (0.75)	15.8 (0.75)	2.4 (0.37)	67.1 (1.00)	13.2 (0.84)	16.8 (0.90)	2.8 (0.45)	67.3 (1.28)	14.6 (1.11)	14.2 (0.85)	3.9 (0.57)	65.8 (1
Graduate/professional degree	65.0 (1.14)	12.4 (0.77)	20.2 (0.91)	2.4 (0.54)	63.6 (1.50)	13.5 (1.14)	20.5 (1.28)	2.3 (0.55)	59.3 (1.35)	16.0 (0.95)	21.8 (1.13)	2.9 (0.46)	61.5 (1
Poverty status of household[5]													
Poor	74.8 (1.16)	19.2 (1.06)	4.3 (0.50)	1.7 (0.34)	76.3 (1.28)	17.7 (1.10)	3.7 (0.67)	2.3 (0.58)	76.6 (2.48)	17.8 (2.35)	3.7 (1.04)	1.8 (0.40)	72.9 (1
Near-poor	76.8 (0.79)	15.3 (0.70)	5.9 (0.48)	2.0 (0.31)	75.1 (1.17)	16.0 (0.87)	5.9 (0.69)	3.1 (0.50)	73.8 (1.51)	16.8 (1.19)	5.3 (0.73)	4.1 (0.66)	68.6 (1
Nonpoor	72.5 (0.57)	11.8 (0.34)	14.0 (0.47)	1.6 (0.18)	69.8 (0.70)	13.8 (0.54)	14.6 (0.54)	1.8 (0.21)	67.9 (0.74)	13.6 (0.48)	15.5 (0.54)	3.0 (0.30)	67.7 (C
Locale													
City	— (†)	— (†)	— (†)	— (†)	— (†)	— (†)	— (†)	— (†)	61.7 (1.46)	22.1 (1.38)	14.2 (0.97)	2.0 (0.26)	57.7 (1
Suburban	— (†)	— (†)	— (†)	— (†)	— (†)	— (†)	— (†)	— (†)	72.7 (0.95)	11.8 (0.67)	12.8 (0.68)	2.6 (0.41)	71.2 (C
Town	— (†)	— (†)	— (†)	— (†)	— (†)	— (†)	— (†)	— (†)	77.3 (1.77)	12.4 (1.43)	7.1 (0.75)	3.0 (0.65)	78.6 (1
Rural	— (†)	— (†)	— (†)	— (†)	— (†)	— (†)	— (†)	— (†)	76.7 (1.36)	11.5 (1.03)	6.8 (1.09)	4.9 (0.71)	79.0 (1
Region													
Northeast	72.8 (1.06)	13.4 (0.78)	12.6 (0.63)	1.1 (0.30)	71.6 (1.42)	11.9 (1.02)	14.6 (1.03)	1.8! (0.58)	72.5 (1.42)	11.8 (1.11)	13.6 (0.98)	2.2 (0.47)	73.4 (1
South	75.4 (0.65)	13.2 (0.52)	9.3 (0.43)	2.0 (0.28)	74.2 (0.88)	14.9 (0.72)	8.3 (0.58)	2.6 (0.39)	71.9 (1.15)	13.6 (0.96)	10.8 (0.58)	3.8 (0.46)	67.5 (1
Midwest	74.3 (0.80)	13.4 (0.72)	10.9 (0.61)	1.4 (0.24)	69.9 (1.27)	14.4 (0.92)	13.8 (1.04)	2.0 (0.37)	70.8 (1.54)	14.2 (1.06)	12.8 (1.14)	2.2 (0.53)	71.0 (1
West	72.7 (0.95)	17.7 (0.73)	7.5 (0.49)	2.0 (0.34)	71.9 (1.07)	17.9 (0.97)	8.3 (0.59)	2.0 (0.34)	67.0 (1.40)	20.3 (1.17)	9.4 (0.75)	3.1 (0.42)	65.5 (1

—Not available.

†Not applicable.

!Interpret data with caution. The coefficient of variation (CV) for this estimate is between 30 and 50 percent.

‡Reporting standards not met. The coefficient of variation (CV) for this estimate is 50 percent or greater.

[1] Excludes students who were enrolled in school for more than 25 hours a week. Also excludes students who were homeschooled only due to a temporary illness.

[2] In 63 cases in 2016, questions about whether a student's school was assigned were not asked because parents reported the school as a private school, and it was only later identified as a public school based on administrative data. Due to the missing data on whether the school was assigned or chosen, these cases were excluded from the analysis of public chosen and assigned schools.

[3] Includes American Indian/Alaska Native, Two or more races, and race/ethnicity not reported.

[4] Students whose grade equivalent was "ungraded" were excluded from the grade analysis. The percentage of students with an "ungraded" grade equivalent was 0.03 percent in 1999 and 0.02 percent in 2003 and 2007.

[5] Poor children are those whose family incomes were below the Census Bureau's poverty threshold in the year prior to data collection; near-poor children are those whose family incomes ranged from the poverty threshold to 199 percent of the poverty threshold; and nonpoor children are those whose family incomes were at or above 200 percent of the poverty threshold. The poverty threshold is a dollar amount that varies depending on a family's size and composition and is updated annually to account for inflation. In 2015, for example, the poverty threshold for a family of four with two children was $24,036. Survey respondents are asked to select the range within which their income falls, rather than giving the exact amount of their income; therefore, the measure of poverty status is an approximation.

NOTE: Data are based on parent reports. While National Household Education Surveys Program (NHES) administrations in 1999, 2003, and 2007 were administered via telephone with an interviewer, NHES:2016 used self-administered paper-and-pencil questionnaires that were mailed to respondents. Measurable differences between estimates for 2016 and estimates for the earlier years in this table could reflect actual changes in the population, or the changes could be due to the mode change from telephone to mail. Race categories exclude persons of Hispanic ethnicity. Detail may not sum to totals because of rounding. Some data have been revised from previously published figures.

SOURCE: U.S. Department of Education, National Center for Education Statistics, Parent Survey and Parent and Family Involvement in Education Survey of the National Household Education Surveys Program (Parent-NHES:1999 and PFI-NHES:2003, 2007, and 2016). (This table was prepared February 2018.)

Table 206.30. Percentage distribution of students enrolled in grades 1 through 12, by public school type and charter status, private school orientation, and selected child and household characteristics: 2016

[Standard errors appear in parentheses]

Selected child or household characteristic and public school type	Total, all schools	Public school, total	Public school type[1]		Public school charter status		Private school, total	Private school orientation	
			Assigned	Chosen	Traditional[2]	Charter		Religious	Nonsectarian
1	2	3	4	5	6	7	8	9	10
Percentage distribution of all enrolled students, by school type and charter status	**100.0 (†)**	**90.5 (0.32)**	**70.6 (0.61)**	**19.8 (0.52)**	**85.9 (0.44)**	**4.6 (0.31)**	**9.5 (0.32)**	**7.6 (0.32)**	**1.9 (0.18)**
Percentage distribution of students in schools of each type or status, by characteristic									
Total, all students	**100.0 (†)**	**100.0 (†)**	**100.0 (†)**	**100.0 (†)**	**100.0 (†)**	**100.0 (†)**	**100.0 (†)**	**100.0 (†)**	**100.0 (†)**
Sex of child									
Male	51.8 (0.67)	52.0 (0.72)	52.2 (0.87)	51.2 (1.69)	52.0 (0.78)	51.4 (3.38)	50.3 (1.92)	50.2 (2.18)	50.9 (5.01)
Female	48.2 (0.67)	48.0 (0.72)	47.8 (0.87)	48.8 (1.69)	48.0 (0.78)	48.6 (3.38)	49.7 (1.92)	49.8 (2.18)	49.1 (5.01)
Race/ethnicity of child									
White	51.8 (0.41)	50.7 (0.44)	54.6 (0.57)	36.9 (1.19)	51.8 (0.47)	30.4 (2.85)	62.1 (1.85)	64.0 (2.15)	54.6 (5.02)
Black	14.3 (0.19)	14.5 (0.26)	12.1 (0.41)	23.2 (1.27)	13.9 (0.31)	26.2 (3.63)	12.2 (1.34)	12.3 (1.57)	11.6 (2.75)
Hispanic	23.8 (0.28)	24.7 (0.35)	23.3 (0.52)	29.9 (1.43)	24.1 (0.37)	36.0 (3.09)	15.0 (1.38)	15.4 (1.51)	13.5 (3.25)
Asian/Pacific Islander	5.7 (0.26)	5.6 (0.29)	5.6 (0.30)	5.7 (0.63)	5.6 (0.30)	4.7 (1.37)	6.3 (1.05)	4.4 (0.90)	13.7 (3.54)
Asian	5.4 (0.25)	5.3 (0.28)	5.3 (0.29)	5.3 (0.60)	5.4 (0.28)	4.0 (1.15)	6.0 (1.02)	4.1 (0.85)	13.7 (3.54)
Pacific Islander	0.3 (0.05)	0.3 (0.06)	0.2 (0.06)	0.4! (0.19)	0.2 (0.05)	‡ (†)	‡ (†)	‡ (†)	‡ (†)
Other[3]	4.5 (0.26)	4.5 (0.29)	4.5 (0.33)	4.3 (0.49)	4.6 (0.30)	2.7 (0.71)	4.4 (0.63)	3.9 (0.64)	6.7 (1.85)
Disability status of child as reported by parent									
Has a disability	16.9 (0.57)	17.3 (0.61)	17.4 (0.68)	17.0 (1.04)	17.3 (0.61)	15.9 (2.00)	13.3 (1.20)	12.7 (1.40)	15.8 (2.86)
Does not have a disability	83.1 (0.57)	82.7 (0.61)	82.6 (0.68)	83.0 (1.04)	82.7 (0.61)	84.1 (2.00)	86.7 (1.20)	87.3 (1.40)	84.2 (2.86)
Grade level									
Grades 1 through 5	43.5 (0.33)	43.6 (0.35)	44.2 (0.51)	41.3 (1.15)	43.2 (0.40)	51.6 (3.23)	42.7 (1.89)	43.2 (2.14)	40.9 (4.79)
Grades 6 through 8	25.2 (0.33)	24.9 (0.34)	25.3 (0.52)	23.8 (1.11)	24.8 (0.37)	27.9 (2.89)	27.4 (1.55)	27.8 (1.74)	25.8 (3.80)
Grades 9 through 12	31.3 (0.27)	31.5 (0.32)	30.5 (0.44)	34.8 (1.09)	32.0 (0.35)	20.5 (2.13)	29.9 (1.60)	29.0 (1.84)	33.4 (3.54)
Number of parents in the household									
Two parents	70.3 (0.51)	69.3 (0.57)	70.5 (0.72)	64.9 (1.34)	69.3 (0.57)	68.2 (3.61)	80.6 (1.52)	80.0 (1.71)	82.7 (2.59)
One parent	25.7 (0.55)	26.6 (0.62)	25.4 (0.73)	30.7 (1.29)	26.4 (0.62)	28.7 (3.43)	17.7 (1.46)	18.2 (1.67)	15.4 (2.46)
Nonparental guardians	3.9 (0.26)	4.2 (0.28)	4.1 (0.37)	4.5 (0.62)	4.2 (0.30)	3.0 (0.59)	1.8 (0.37)	1.8 (0.36)	‡ (†)
Highest education level of parents									
Less than a high school diploma	10.7 (0.30)	11.3 (0.34)	10.9 (0.44)	12.4 (1.13)	11.0 (0.35)	17.1 (3.53)	5.5 (1.27)	5.8 (1.37)	‡ (†)
High school diploma or GED	20.0 (0.27)	21.3 (0.30)	21.3 (0.48)	21.4 (1.28)	21.5 (0.36)	17.7 (3.26)	8.0 (1.43)	8.9 (1.62)	‡ (†)
Vocational/technical, associate's degree, or some college	25.7 (0.44)	26.6 (0.45)	26.7 (0.58)	26.0 (1.07)	26.7 (0.47)	25.0 (2.57)	17.5 (1.57)	19.5 (1.76)	9.7 (2.46)
Bachelor's degree/some graduate school	26.7 (0.46)	25.6 (0.47)	26.0 (0.60)	24.2 (0.99)	25.8 (0.50)	22.8 (1.96)	37.2 (1.60)	38.2 (1.89)	33.1 (3.76)
Graduate/professional degree	16.8 (0.18)	15.2 (0.19)	15.0 (0.27)	16.0 (0.78)	15.1 (0.19)	17.4 (1.87)	31.8 (1.68)	27.5 (1.75)	49.0 (5.11)
Poverty status of household[4]									
Poor	17.3 (0.42)	18.3 (0.47)	18.1 (0.50)	18.8 (1.26)	18.2 (0.46)	19.9 (2.80)	7.6 (1.36)	7.0 (1.38)	9.9! (4.05)
Near-poor	21.4 (0.45)	22.2 (0.51)	21.3 (0.59)	25.6 (1.50)	21.9 (0.52)	28.2 (4.09)	13.1 (1.59)	14.9 (1.90)	6.0 (1.70)
Nonpoor	61.4 (0.46)	59.5 (0.49)	60.6 (0.66)	55.6 (1.33)	59.9 (0.51)	51.8 (3.60)	79.3 (1.79)	78.1 (2.07)	84.1 (3.83)
Locale									
City	31.2 (0.74)	30.5 (0.79)	25.6 (0.80)	48.1 (1.58)	29.1 (0.74)	57.8 (3.20)	37.2 (1.76)	36.8 (2.02)	38.6 (3.24)
Suburban	44.5 (0.73)	44.1 (0.77)	46.0 (0.82)	37.7 (1.47)	44.6 (0.76)	34.8 (2.90)	48.1 (1.90)	47.9 (2.19)	48.6 (3.38)
Town	7.9 (0.37)	8.5 (0.40)	9.3 (0.47)	5.4 (0.56)	8.7 (0.42)	3.4 (0.95)	3.0 (0.42)	3.0 (0.49)	2.6! (0.89)
Rural	16.4 (0.42)	16.9 (0.45)	19.1 (0.51)	8.7 (0.66)	17.5 (0.46)	4.0 (1.14)	11.8 (1.19)	12.2 (1.33)	10.2 (2.42)
Region									
Northeast	19.9 (0.50)	19.3 (0.57)	20.8 (0.65)	13.8 (1.23)	19.4 (0.57)	16.8 (2.93)	26.1 (1.81)	25.0 (2.02)	30.4 (4.34)
South	23.9 (0.53)	24.0 (0.56)	23.2 (0.65)	26.8 (1.57)	24.4 (0.56)	16.7 (2.15)	23.3 (1.51)	21.8 (1.73)	29.2 (3.50)
Midwest	21.9 (0.55)	21.5 (0.60)	22.3 (0.66)	18.2 (1.42)	21.5 (0.58)	20.6 (3.61)	26.5 (1.65)	31.0 (1.83)	8.4 (1.65)
West	34.2 (0.63)	35.3 (0.68)	33.7 (0.79)	41.2 (1.73)	34.7 (0.71)	45.9 (3.25)	24.1 (1.59)	22.2 (1.82)	32.1 (3.71)
Public school type[1]									
Assigned	70.6 (0.61)	78.0 (0.57)	100.0 (†)	† (†)	82.1 (0.53)	100.0 (†)	† (†)	† (†)	† (†)
Chosen	19.8 (0.52)	21.8 (0.58)	† (†)	100.0 (†)	17.6 (0.54)	† (†)	† (†)	† (†)	† (†)

†Not applicable.
!Interpret data with caution. The coefficient of variation (CV) for this estimate is between 30 and 50 percent.
‡Reporting standards not met. The coefficient of variation (CV) for this estimate is 50 percent or greater.
[1]In 31 cases, questions about whether a student's school was assigned were not asked because parents reported the school as a private school, and it was only later identified as a public school based on administrative data. Due to the missing data on whether the school was assigned or chosen, these cases were included neither with assigned public schools nor with chosen public schools. These cases were included in the public school totals, however, and they could still be accurately classified as either traditional or charter schools based on administrative data.
[2]Includes all types of public noncharter schools.
[3]Includes American Indian/Alaska Native, Two or more races, and race/ethnicity not reported.
[4]Poor children are those whose family incomes were below the Census Bureau's poverty threshold in the year prior to data collection; near-poor children are those whose family incomes ranged from the poverty threshold to 199 percent of the poverty threshold; and nonpoor children are those whose family incomes were at or above 200 percent of the poverty threshold. The poverty threshold is a dollar amount that varies depending on a family's size and composition and is updated annually to account for inflation. In 2015, for example, the poverty threshold for a family of four with two children was $24,257. Survey respondents are asked to select the range within which their income falls, rather than giving the exact amount of their income; therefore, the measure of poverty status is an approximation.
NOTE: Data exclude homeschooled children. Race categories exclude persons of Hispanic ethnicity. Detail may not sum to totals because of rounding.
SOURCE: U.S. Department of Education, National Center for Education Statistics, Parent and Family Involvement in Education Survey of the National Household Education Surveys Program (PFI-NHES:2016). (This table was prepared February 2018.)

Table 206.40. Percentage of students enrolled in grades 1 through 12 whose parents reported having public school choice, considered other schools, reported current school was their first choice, or moved to their current neighborhood for the public school, by school type and selected child and household characteristics: 2016

[Standard errors appear in parentheses]

School type and selected child or household characteristic	Public choice available		Considered other schools		School was parent's first choice		Moved to neighborhood for public school[1]	
1	2		3		4		5	
Total	**41.2**	**(0.69)**	**27.7**	**(0.58)**	**80.1**	**(0.56)**	**20.0**	**(0.62)**
School type[2]								
Public, assigned	27.5	(0.82)	21.0	(0.66)	78.9	(0.64)	22.4	(0.70)
Public, chosen[3]	100.0	(0.00)	42.6	(1.50)	81.6	(1.29)	11.2	(1.07)
Private, religious	20.8	(1.65)	45.7	(2.20)	86.1	(1.78)	†	(†)
Private, nonsectarian	20.2	(3.18)	56.6	(3.64)	88.6	(2.90)	†	(†)
Sex of child								
Male	41.5	(0.98)	28.5	(0.86)	79.3	(0.83)	18.6	(0.85)
Female	40.8	(1.00)	26.9	(0.77)	81.0	(0.81)	21.5	(0.82)
Race/ethnicity of child								
White	35.7	(0.81)	26.0	(0.65)	84.1	(0.69)	22.3	(0.80)
Black	51.6	(2.20)	31.1	(1.91)	69.6	(2.41)	13.8	(1.47)
Hispanic	46.9	(1.62)	28.7	(1.34)	78.2	(1.35)	17.1	(1.31)
Asian/Pacific Islander	40.3	(2.24)	25.7	(1.96)	80.0	(1.85)	27.4	(2.28)
Asian	40.0	(2.33)	24.7	(1.91)	79.9	(1.91)	27.2	(2.37)
Pacific Islander	44.8	(11.83)	45.8	(12.32)	80.3	(10.12)	31.4 !	(13.93)
Other[4]	41.0	(2.91)	32.8	(2.47)	79.1	(2.00)	20.4	(2.21)
Disability status of child as reported by parent								
Has a disability	41.5	(1.51)	30.2	(1.43)	76.1	(1.64)	18.5	(1.35)
Does not have a disability	41.1	(0.75)	27.2	(0.58)	81.0	(0.64)	20.3	(0.64)
Grade level								
Grades 1 through 5	39.0	(1.19)	27.9	(0.97)	79.8	(0.93)	20.6	(1.00)
Grades 6 through 8	40.8	(1.29)	27.3	(1.20)	78.8	(1.29)	19.0	(1.06)
Grades 9 through 12	44.5	(0.88)	28.0	(0.90)	81.8	(0.78)	19.9	(0.83)
Number of parents in the household								
Two parents	40.6	(0.79)	28.6	(0.72)	82.1	(0.65)	20.4	(0.72)
One parent	42.3	(1.39)	26.8	(1.12)	76.3	(1.25)	19.9	(0.98)
Nonparental guardians	43.6	(3.88)	18.3	(2.64)	70.8	(4.07)	13.2	(2.76)
Highest education level of parents								
Less than a high school diploma	44.5	(2.54)	20.2	(2.54)	74.4	(2.98)	15.0	(2.14)
High school diploma or GED	42.0	(1.77)	16.2	(1.31)	77.6	(1.55)	12.4	(1.28)
Vocational/technical, associate's degree, or some college	41.6	(1.30)	26.3	(0.94)	77.7	(0.98)	18.0	(0.98)
Bachelor's degree/some graduate school	39.9	(1.20)	32.4	(0.99)	83.9	(1.02)	24.5	(1.10)
Graduate/professional degree	39.6	(1.10)	41.1	(1.13)	84.5	(0.90)	30.2	(1.30)
Poverty status of household[5]								
Poor	42.2	(1.92)	21.5	(1.61)	73.1	(2.00)	15.1	(1.37)
Near-poor	46.4	(1.79)	22.5	(1.29)	77.3	(1.47)	14.3	(1.42)
Nonpoor	39.1	(0.82)	31.3	(0.63)	83.1	(0.58)	23.6	(0.72)
Locale								
City	53.1	(1.21)	34.1	(1.28)	77.6	(1.11)	17.8	(1.03)
Suburban	37.1	(0.92)	28.5	(0.81)	80.3	(0.90)	24.4	(0.89)
Town	36.0	(2.34)	18.3	(2.11)	82.0	(2.07)	12.3	(1.50)
Rural	32.1	(1.50)	18.1	(1.13)	83.8	(1.34)	16.3	(1.31)
Region								
Northeast	27.0	(1.78)	26.0	(1.55)	80.2	(1.33)	20.4	(1.28)
South	38.9	(1.14)	28.0	(0.95)	77.1	(1.14)	21.0	(0.98)
Midwest	42.7	(1.53)	24.4	(1.21)	83.2	(1.08)	19.8	(1.25)
West	52.9	(1.49)	31.5	(1.27)	81.8	(1.06)	18.5	(1.27)

† Not applicable.

! Interpret data with caution. The coefficient of variation (CV) for this estimate is between 30 and 50 percent.

[1] This column shows percentages of public school students only. Private school students are excluded from the analysis.

[2] In 31 cases, questions about whether a student's public school was assigned were not asked because parents reported the school as a private school, and it was only later identified as a public school based on administrative data. Due to the missing data, these cases were excluded from the analysis of public chosen and assigned schools.

[3] Students who attended chosen public schools were automatically coded as "yes" for whether or not their district allowed public school choice.

[4] Includes American Indian/Alaska Native, Two or more races, and race/ethnicity not reported.

[5] Poor children are those whose family incomes were below the Census Bureau's poverty threshold in the year prior to data collection; near-poor children are those whose family incomes ranged from the poverty threshold to 199 percent of the poverty threshold; and nonpoor children are those whose family incomes were at or above 200 percent of the poverty threshold. The poverty threshold is a dollar amount that varies depending on a family's size and composition and is updated annually to account for inflation. In 2015, for example, the poverty threshold for a family of four with two children was $24,036. Survey respondents are asked to select the range within which their income falls, rather than giving the exact amount of their income; therefore, the measure of poverty status is an approximation.

NOTE: Data exclude homeschooled children. Race categories exclude persons of Hispanic ethnicity.

SOURCE: U.S. Department of Education, National Center for Education Statistics, Parent and Family Involvement in Education Survey of the National Household Education Surveys Program (PFI-NHES:2016). (This table was prepared January 2018.)

Table 206.50. Percentage of students enrolled in grades 3 through 12 whose parents were satisfied or dissatisfied with various aspects of their children's schools, by school type: Selected years, 2003 through 2016

[Standard errors appear in parentheses]

Parent satisfaction	2003				2007				2016			
	Public school			Private school	Public school			Private school	Public school			Private school
	Total	Assigned	Chosen		Total[1]	Assigned[1]	Chosen[1]		Total[1]	Assigned[1]	Chosen[1]	
1	2	3	4	5	6	7	8	9	10	11	12	13
Very satisfied												
School	55.4 (0.75)	53.7 (0.79)	64.2 (1.72)	75.7 (1.73)	54.0 (0.93)	52.1 (0.96)	62.1 (2.34)	78.6 (1.76)	55.4 (0.76)	54.2 (0.84)	59.9 (1.66)	77.2 (1.77)
Teachers	57.8 (0.73)	56.4 (0.74)	64.5 (1.62)	71.8 (1.55)	57.9 (0.80)	56.6 (0.88)	63.5 (2.32)	75.8 (1.69)	54.3 (0.70)	54.2 (0.86)	54.7 (1.63)	72.3 (1.52)
Academic standards	56.1 (0.73)	54.5 (0.78)	63.8 (1.75)	78.9 (1.62)	58.2 (0.80)	56.3 (0.84)	65.9 (2.09)	81.3 (1.59)	54.6 (0.80)	53.2 (0.86)	59.9 (1.85)	77.5 (1.71)
Order and discipline	57.4 (0.73)	55.9 (0.78)	64.8 (1.81)	80.9 (1.47)	56.2 (0.89)	55.0 (0.97)	60.9 (2.21)	82.2 (1.55)	54.1 (0.66)	53.3 (0.77)	57.2 (1.59)	79.1 (1.70)
Staff interaction with parents	— (†)	— (†)	— (†)	— (†)	49.5 (0.93)	47.7 (1.00)	56.7 (2.24)	74.9 (1.77)	48.0 (0.67)	47.2 (0.79)	51.0 (1.74)	70.2 (1.77)
Somewhat satisfied												
School	34.0 (0.66)	35.3 (0.74)	27.6 (1.40)	19.7 (1.66)	34.0 (0.75)	34.9 (0.82)	30.5 (2.01)	18.3 (1.62)	35.3 (0.73)	36.0 (0.77)	32.6 (1.71)	19.5 (1.70)
Teachers	34.4 (0.71)	35.4 (0.71)	29.3 (1.57)	23.6 (1.35)	33.3 (0.74)	34.1 (0.84)	29.8 (1.87)	21.6 (1.67)	37.3 (0.70)	37.1 (0.78)	38.3 (1.71)	23.7 (1.51)
Academic standards	34.3 (0.71)	35.4 (0.79)	29.1 (1.59)	16.8 (1.42)	31.8 (0.75)	32.7 (0.84)	28.2 (1.99)	16.4 (1.40)	36.6 (0.73)	37.5 (0.76)	33.5 (1.82)	19.5 (1.59)
Order and discipline	29.7 (0.65)	30.5 (0.72)	26.0 (1.67)	15.0 (1.42)	29.6 (0.81)	30.1 (0.85)	27.6 (2.57)	15.1 (1.45)	33.9 (0.61)	34.9 (0.71)	30.7 (1.44)	17.2 (1.62)
Staff interaction with parents	— (†)	— (†)	— (†)	— (†)	35.7 (0.82)	36.4 (0.92)	33.5 (2.03)	21.5 (1.71)	38.5 (0.73)	39.0 (0.83)	37.1 (1.67)	24.4 (1.63)
Somewhat dissatisfied												
School	7.1 (0.34)	7.4 (0.37)	5.6 (0.75)	3.5 (0.69)	7.9 (0.42)	8.4 (0.45)	5.5 (0.98)	2.7 (0.53)	6.9 (0.43)	7.3 (0.50)	5.4 (0.71)	2.6 (0.55)
Teachers	5.8 (0.34)	6.2 (0.38)	4.1 (0.52)	3.5 (0.69)	6.4 (0.45)	6.6 (0.48)	5.6 (1.11)	2.0 (0.54)	6.7 (0.37)	7.1 (0.43)	5.4 (0.77)	3.1 (0.56)
Academic standards	6.3 (0.32)	6.6 (0.37)	4.3 (0.56)	3.6 (0.71)	6.4 (0.41)	6.8 (0.47)	4.9 (0.83)	2.1 ! (0.63)	6.5 (0.33)	7.0 (0.39)	4.8 (0.61)	2.4 (0.52)
Order and discipline	7.4 (0.39)	7.8 (0.42)	5.0 (0.69)	2.5 (0.53)	8.3 (0.45)	8.6 (0.50)	7.0 (1.00)	2.2 (0.49)	7.9 (0.39)	7.6 (0.51)	8.9 (0.91)	3.1 (0.56)
Staff interaction with parents	— (†)	— (†)	— (†)	— (†)	9.9 (0.46)	10.7 (0.59)	6.7 (0.93)	2.4 (0.53)	9.8 (0.40)	10.1 (0.50)	9.0 (0.86)	4.5 (0.71)
Very dissatisfied												
School	3.4 (0.23)	3.6 (0.26)	2.6 (0.54)	1.1 ! (0.43)	4.1 (0.37)	4.6 (0.44)	1.8 (0.51)	0.4 ! (0.17)	2.5 (0.22)	2.5 (0.21)	2.1 (0.44)	0.7 ! (0.25)
Teachers	2.0 (0.15)	2.0 (0.16)	2.1 (0.45)	1.0 ! (0.48)	2.4 (0.31)	2.7 (0.39)	1.1 ! (0.34)	0.7 ! (0.25)	1.7 (0.21)	1.6 (0.21)	1.6 (0.38)	0.9 ! (0.29)
Academic standards	3.3 (0.23)	3.4 (0.28)	2.7 (0.59)	0.7 ! (0.32)	3.7 (0.35)	4.3 (0.43)	1.0 ! (0.30)	0.3 ! (0.13)	2.3 (0.20)	2.4 (0.22)	1.8 (0.36)	0.6 ! (0.23)
Order and discipline	5.5 (0.35)	5.8 (0.38)	4.2 (0.72)	1.6 ! (0.62)	5.9 (0.41)	8.6 (0.50)	4.5 (0.82)	‡ (†)	4.0 (0.37)	4.2 (0.43)	3.2 (0.49)	0.7 ! (0.23)
Staff interaction with parents	— (†)	— (†)	— (†)	— (†)	4.9 (0.42)	5.3 (0.48)	3.2 (0.62)	1.3 (0.38)	3.7 (0.30)	3.8 (0.34)	2.9 (0.69)	0.9 ! (0.29)

—Not available.

† Not applicable.

! Interpret data with caution. The coefficient of variation (CV) for this estimate is between 30 and 50 percent.

‡ Reporting standards not met. The coefficient of variation (CV) for this estimate is 50 percent or greater.

[1] In 68 cases in 2007 and 31 cases in 2016, questions about whether a student's school was assigned were not asked because parents reported the school as a private school, and it was only later identified as a public school based on administrative data. Due to the missing data on whether the school was assigned or chosen, these cases were included neither with assigned public schools nor with chosen public schools; however, they were included in the public school totals.

NOTE: Data exclude homeschooled children. While National Household Education Surveys Program (NHES) administrations in 2003 and 2007 were administered via telephone with an interviewer, NHES:2016 used self-administered paper-and-pencil questionnaires that were mailed to respondents. Measurable differences between estimates for 2016 and estimates for the earlier years in this table could reflect actual changes in the population, or the changes could be due to the mode change from telephone to mail. Detail may not sum to totals because of rounding.

SOURCE: U.S. Department of Education, National Center for Education Statistics, Parent and Family Involvement in Education Survey of the National Household Education Surveys Program (PFI-NHES:2003, 2007, and 2016). (This table was prepared February 2018.)

Table 208.10. Public elementary and secondary pupil/teacher ratios, by selected school characteristics: Selected years, fall 1990 through fall 2017

Selected school characteristic	1990	1995	1999	2000	2001	2002	2003	2004	2005	2006	2007	2008	2009	2010[1]	2011	2012	2013	2014	2015	2016	2017
1	2	3	4	5	6	7	8	9	10	11	12	13	14	15	16	17	18	19	20	21	22
All schools	**17.4**	**17.8**	**16.6**	**16.4**	**16.3**	**16.2**	**16.4**	**16.2**	**16.0**	**15.8**	**15.7**	**15.7**	**16.0**	**16.4**	**16.3**	**16.4**	**16.3**	**16.2**	**16.2**	**16.2**	**16.1**
Enrollment size of school																					
Under 300	14.0	14.1	13.3	13.1	12.9	12.8	13.0	12.8	12.7	12.7	12.7	12.5	12.6	12.9	12.8	12.8	12.7	12.7	12.8	12.8	12.7
300 to 499	17.0	17.1	15.8	15.5	15.4	15.3	15.5	15.2	15.0	14.9	15.0	14.8	15.2	15.4	15.4	15.5	15.4	15.3	15.3	15.2	15.2
500 to 999	18.0	18.2	16.8	16.7	16.5	16.5	16.6	16.4	16.2	15.9	15.9	15.9	16.3	16.7	16.7	16.7	16.7	16.5	16.5	16.5	16.4
1,000 to 1,499	17.9	18.7	17.6	17.4	17.4	17.4	17.6	17.3	16.9	16.7	16.5	16.5	16.8	17.3	17.1	17.1	17.1	16.9	16.9	17.0	16.8
1,500 or more	19.2	20.0	19.3	19.1	19.0	18.9	19.2	19.1	18.8	18.6	18.1	18.3	18.7	19.5	19.0	19.0	19.1	19.0	19.0	18.9	18.8
Type																					
Regular schools	17.6	17.9	16.7	16.5	16.4	16.3	16.5	16.3	16.1	15.9	15.8	15.8	16.1	16.5	16.4	16.5	16.5	16.3	16.3	16.3	16.2
Alternative	14.2	16.6	15.8	15.2	14.9	14.9	15.0	14.4	14.0	14.7	13.5	14.2	14.3	14.8	14.7	14.8	14.3	14.5	14.4	14.4	13.9
Special education	6.5	7.2	7.2	7.0	6.4	7.0	7.3	7.4	6.2	6.6	7.1	6.8	7.1	6.9	7.1	7.2	6.6	7.0	7.4	7.2	7.3
Vocational	13.0	12.7	13.0	12.7	12.7	9.9	10.3	11.5	12.0	13.3	11.3	10.7	10.2	11.7	11.8	11.6	11.8	11.8	11.9	11.8	11.7
Percent of students eligible for free or reduced-price lunch																					
25 percent or less	—	—	16.9	16.7	16.7	16.6	16.8	16.8	16.5	16.4	16.3	16.1	16.5	16.8	16.9	16.5	16.5	16.4	16.5	16.5	16.2
26 percent to 50 percent	—	—	16.4	16.2	16.1	16.2	16.4	16.2	16.1	15.8	15.7	15.7	16.1	16.5	16.2	16.4	16.3	16.2	16.2	16.1	16.0
51 percent to 75 percent	—	—	16.2	16.1	16.0	16.0	16.0	15.9	15.6	15.3	15.2	15.4	15.8	16.2	15.8	16.2	16.1	16.0	16.0	15.9	15.9
More than 75 percent	—	—	16.3	16.1	16.0	16.0	16.1	15.9	15.5	15.4	15.0	15.1	15.6	16.0	15.5	16.3	16.5	16.4	16.4	16.4	16.2
Level and size																					
Elementary schools	18.1	18.1	16.7	16.5	16.3	16.2	16.3	16.0	15.8	15.6	15.6	15.5	15.9	16.3	16.3	16.4	16.3	16.1	16.1	16.1	16.0
Regular	18.2	18.1	16.7	16.5	16.3	16.2	16.3	16.0	15.8	15.6	15.6	15.5	15.9	16.3	16.3	16.4	16.4	16.2	16.1	16.1	16.0
Under 300	16.0	15.7	14.6	14.4	14.1	13.9	14.0	13.7	13.6	13.5	13.7	13.5	13.7	14.0	14.0	14.0	14.0	13.8	13.8	13.7	13.8
300 to 499	17.6	17.5	16.1	15.8	15.6	15.5	15.6	15.3	15.2	15.1	15.2	15.0	15.4	15.6	15.7	15.7	15.6	15.5	15.4	15.4	15.3
500 to 999	18.8	18.6	17.1	16.9	16.8	16.7	16.8	16.5	16.3	16.0	16.0	16.0	16.5	16.9	16.9	17.0	17.0	16.7	16.7	16.7	16.5
1,000 to 1,499	19.5	19.7	18.3	18.1	18.0	18.0	18.1	17.7	17.2	17.0	16.7	16.8	17.2	17.8	17.7	17.8	17.7	17.5	17.4	17.4	17.3
1,500 or more	19.9	20.9	20.0	20.5	20.2	20.3	20.8	20.5	19.6	19.4	18.0	18.1	18.5	19.3	19.0	18.9	19.1	19.0	18.8	18.6	18.0
Secondary schools	16.6	17.6	16.8	16.6	16.6	16.7	16.9	16.8	16.6	16.4	16.3	16.2	16.4	16.8	16.5	16.6	16.6	16.6	16.6	16.6	16.5
Regular	16.7	17.7	16.9	16.7	16.7	16.8	17.0	16.9	16.8	16.6	16.4	16.3	16.6	16.9	16.7	16.7	16.7	16.7	16.7	16.7	16.6
Under 300	12.3	12.8	12.0	12.0	11.9	12.0	12.3	12.0	12.2	12.0	12.1	11.9	11.9	12.2	12.0	12.1	12.1	11.9	12.1	12.2	12.1
300 to 499	14.9	15.7	14.6	14.5	14.4	14.4	14.7	14.7	14.6	14.4	14.4	14.3	14.3	14.6	14.6	14.5	14.4	14.6	14.6	14.5	14.5
500 to 999	16.1	16.9	16.0	15.8	15.7	15.8	16.0	15.9	15.8	15.6	15.4	15.4	15.6	15.8	15.7	15.7	15.7	15.7	15.7	15.8	15.7
1,000 to 1,499	17.2	18.0	17.1	16.8	16.8	16.9	17.2	17.0	16.8	16.5	16.5	16.3	16.6	16.9	16.6	16.6	16.6	16.5	16.5	16.6	16.5
1,500 or more	19.3	20.0	19.2	18.9	18.8	18.8	19.0	19.0	18.8	18.5	18.2	18.2	18.6	19.3	18.8	18.9	18.9	18.9	18.7	18.7	18.6
Combined schools	14.5	15.0	13.4	13.7	13.4	13.5	13.8	13.9	14.1	14.7	13.4	13.9	14.0	15.4	14.4	14.4	14.7	14.2	15.2	15.0	14.8
Under 300	8.9	9.0	9.1	9.2	9.1	9.1	9.5	9.2	9.5	10.1	9.2	8.9	9.1	9.2	9.4	9.3	9.1	9.2	9.6	9.7	9.4
300 to 499	14.2	14.7	13.8	13.5	13.1	13.1	14.4	13.4	13.9	14.3	13.7	13.9	13.8	13.6	13.3	13.3	13.5	13.6	14.3	14.0	13.6
500 to 999	16.3	16.6	14.9	15.8	15.6	16.0	15.4	15.8	15.9	16.0	15.2	15.6	15.8	16.9	15.6	15.5	15.5	15.1	16.3	15.9	15.7
1,000 to 1,499	17.8	18.2	16.9	17.5	18.1	17.7	17.5	17.4	16.4	17.3	15.9	16.7	17.9	19.2	18.1	17.8	17.9	17.3	17.5	17.3	16.9
1,500 or more	17.7	19.6	19.2	18.6	18.9	19.1	19.2	18.7	20.0	20.3	18.0	21.7	21.7	25.7	23.4	23.3	24.7	20.9	23.6	22.9	22.9
Ungraded	6.4	6.9	5.3	7.0	6.3	6.8	9.6	8.0	7.7	7.2	7.3	5.5	8.5	5.3	6.0	5.9	3.0	8.1	9.0	5.1	5.7
Level, type, and percent of students eligible for free or reduced-price lunch																					
Elementary, regular																					
25 percent or less	—	—	17.1	16.9	16.7	16.5	16.7	16.6	16.4	16.2	16.2	16.0	16.4	16.8	16.6	16.5	16.5	16.3	16.4	16.3	16.1
26 to 50 percent	—	—	16.5	16.3	16.2	16.1	16.2	16.0	15.8	15.5	15.6	15.6	16.0	16.4	16.3	16.4	16.3	16.1	16.1	16.0	15.9
51 to 75 percent	—	—	16.3	16.2	16.1	16.0	16.0	15.7	15.5	15.1	15.2	15.2	15.7	16.0	15.9	16.2	16.1	15.8	15.8	15.8	15.7
More than 75 percent	—	—	16.6	16.4	16.2	16.1	16.3	16.0	15.6	15.4	15.1	15.2	15.8	16.1	15.7	16.5	16.6	16.5	16.4	16.4	16.3
Secondary, regular																					
25 percent or less	—	—	17.0	16.9	16.9	16.9	17.2	17.5	17.0	16.9	16.8	16.6	16.8	17.1	17.4	16.7	16.8	16.7	16.9	16.8	16.4
26 to 50 percent	—	—	16.6	16.4	16.3	16.5	16.9	16.9	16.8	16.4	16.4	16.2	16.5	16.8	16.4	16.6	16.5	16.5	16.6	16.6	16.5
51 to 75 percent	—	—	16.8	16.6	16.6	16.6	17.0	16.9	16.7	16.3	16.1	16.4	16.5	17.1	16.1	16.7	16.8	16.9	16.9	16.8	16.8
More than 75 percent	—	—	16.8	16.5	16.5	16.3	16.6	16.2	16.7	16.2	15.7	15.9	16.0	16.5	15.5	16.6	17.0	17.0	17.1	17.1	17.0

—Not available.
[1]Includes imputations for California and Wyoming.
NOTE: Includes only schools that reported both enrollment and teacher data. Ratios are based on data reported by schools and may differ from data reported in other tables that reflect aggregate totals reported by states.

SOURCE: U.S. Department of Education, National Center for Education Statistics, Common Core of Data (CCD), "Public Elementary/Secondary School Universe Survey," 1990–91 through 2017–18. (This table was prepared February 2020.)

Table 208.20. Public and private elementary and secondary teachers, enrollment, pupil/teacher ratios, and new teacher hires: Selected years, fall 1955 through fall 2029

Year	Teachers (in thousands)			Enrollment (in thousands)			Pupil/teacher ratio			Number of new teacher hires (in thousands)[1]		
	Total	Public	Private	Total	Public	Private	Total	Public	Private	Total	Public	Private
1	2	3	4	5	6	7	8	9	10	11	12	13
1955	1,286	1,141	145[2]	35,280	30,680	4,600[2]	27.4	26.9	31.7[2]	—	—	—
1960	1,600	1,408	192[2]	42,181	36,281	5,900[2]	26.4	25.8	30.7[2]	—	—	—
1965	1,933	1,710	223	48,473	42,173	6,300	25.1	24.7	28.3	—	—	—
1970	2,292	2,059	233	51,257	45,894	5,363	22.4	22.3	23.0	—	—	—
1975	2,453	2,198	255[2]	49,819	44,819	5,000[2]	20.3	20.4	19.6[2]	—	—	—
1976	2,457	2,189	268	49,478	44,311	5,167	20.1	20.2	19.3	—	—	—
1977	2,488	2,209	279	48,717	43,577	5,140	19.6	19.7	18.4	—	—	—
1978	2,479	2,207	272	47,637	42,551	5,086	19.2	19.3	18.7	—	—	—
1979	2,461	2,185	276[2]	46,651	41,651	5,000[2]	19.0	19.1	18.1[2]	—	—	—
1980	2,485	2,184	301	46,208	40,877	5,331	18.6	18.7	17.7	—	—	—
1981	2,440	2,127	313[2]	45,544	40,044	5,500[2]	18.7	18.8	17.6[2]	—	—	—
1982	2,458	2,133	325[2]	45,166	39,566	5,600[2]	18.4	18.6	17.2[2]	—	—	—
1983	2,476	2,139	337	44,967	39,252	5,715	18.2	18.4	17.0	—	—	—
1984	2,508	2,168	340[2]	44,908	39,208	5,700[2]	17.9	18.1	16.8[2]	—	—	—
1985	2,549	2,206	343	44,979	39,422	5,557	17.6	17.9	16.2	—	—	—
1986	2,592	2,244	348[2]	45,205	39,753	5,452[2]	17.4	17.7	15.7[2]	—	—	—
1987	2,631	2,279	352	45,488	40,008	5,479	17.3	17.6	15.6	—	—	—
1988	2,668	2,323	345[2]	45,430	40,189	5,242[2]	17.0	17.3	15.2[2]	—	—	—
1989	2,713	2,357	356	46,141	40,543	5,599	17.0	17.2	15.7	—	—	—
1990	2,759	2,398	361[2]	46,864	41,217	5,648[2]	17.0	17.2	15.6[2]	—	—	—
1991	2,797	2,432	365	47,728	42,047	5,681	17.1	17.3	15.6	—	—	—
1992	2,823	2,459	364[2]	48,694	42,823	5,870[2]	17.2	17.4	16.1[2]	—	—	—
1993	2,868	2,504	364	49,532	43,465	6,067	17.3	17.4	16.7	—	—	—
1994	2,922	2,552	370[2]	50,106	44,111	5,994[2]	17.1	17.3	16.2[2]	—	—	—
1995	2,974	2,598	376	50,759	44,840	5,918	17.1	17.3	15.7	—	—	—
1996	3,051	2,667	384[2]	51,544	45,611	5,933[2]	16.9	17.1	15.5[2]	—	—	—
1997	3,138	2,746	391	52,071	46,127	5,944	16.6	16.8	15.2	—	—	—
1998	3,230	2,830	400[2]	52,526	46,539	5,988[2]	16.3	16.4	15.0[2]	—	—	—
1999	3,319	2,911	408	52,875	46,857	6,018	15.9	16.1	14.7	305	222	83
2000	3,366	2,941	424[2]	53,373	47,204	6,169[2]	15.9	16.0	14.5[2]	—	—	—
2001	3,440	3,000	441	53,992	47,672	6,320	15.7	15.9	14.3	—	—	—
2002	3,476	3,034	442[2]	54,403	48,183	6,220[2]	15.7	15.9	14.1[2]	—	—	—
2003	3,490	3,049	441	54,639	48,540	6,099	15.7	15.9	13.8	311	236	74
2004	3,536	3,091	445[2]	54,882	48,795	6,087[2]	15.5	15.8	13.7[2]	—	—	—
2005	3,593	3,143	450	55,187	49,113	6,073	15.4	15.6	13.5	—	—	—
2006	3,622	3,166	456[2]	55,307	49,316	5,991[2]	15.3	15.6	13.2[2]	—	—	—
2007	3,656	3,200	456	55,201	49,291	5,910	15.1	15.4	13.0	327	246	80
2008	3,670	3,222	448[2]	54,973	49,266	5,707[2]	15.0	15.3	12.8[2]	—	—	—
2009	3,647	3,210	437	54,849	49,361	5,488	15.0	15.4	12.5	—	—	—
2010	3,512	3,099	413[2]	54,867	49,484	5,382[2]	15.6	16.0	13.0[2]	—	—	—
2011	3,508	3,103	405	54,790	49,522	5,268	15.6	16.0	13.0	241	173	68
2012	3,517	3,109	408[2]	55,104	49,771	5,333[2]	15.7	16.0	13.1[2]	—	—	—
2013	3,555	3,114	441	55,440	50,045	5,396	15.6	16.1	12.2	—	—	—
2014	3,594	3,132	461[2]	55,888	50,313	5,575[2]	15.6	16.1	12.1[2]	—	—	—
2015	3,633	3,151	482	56,189	50,438	5,751	15.5	16.0	11.9	325	218	107
2016	3,653	3,169	483[2]	56,369	50,615	5,754[2]	15.4	16.0	11.9[2]	351	257	94
2017	3,652	3,170	482	56,406	50,686	5,720	15.4	16.0	11.9	329	241	89
2018[3]	3,639	3,157	482	56,367	50,650	5,717	15.5	16.0	11.9	317	226	91
2019[3]	3,661	3,176	485	56,350	50,634	5,716	15.4	15.9	11.8	351	258	93
2020[3]	3,670	3,184	486	56,368	50,654	5,714	15.4	15.9	11.8	340	248	92
2021[3]	3,684	3,197	488	56,343	50,643	5,700	15.3	15.8	11.7	346	253	92
2022[3]	3,708	3,217	491	56,434	50,721	5,713	15.2	15.8	11.6	357	263	94
2023[3]	3,731	3,237	494	56,480	50,768	5,712	15.1	15.7	11.6	357	262	95
2024[3]	3,758	3,260	498	56,460	50,758	5,702	15.0	15.6	11.5	363	267	96
2025[3]	3,786	3,284	502	56,404	50,704	5,700	14.9	15.4	11.4	367	269	97
2026[3]	3,813	3,307	506	56,370	50,672	5,699	14.8	15.3	11.3	368	270	98
2027[3]	3,842	3,332	510	56,439	50,734	5,704	14.7	15.2	11.2	373	274	99
2028[3]	3,880	3,364	516	56,605	50,885	5,720	14.6	15.1	11.1	384	283	101
2029[3]	3,909	3,390	520	56,806	51,068	5,738	14.5	15.1	11.0	377	280	97

—Not available.

[1]A teacher is considered to be a new hire for a public or private school if the teacher had not taught in that control of school in the previous year. A teacher who moves from a public to private or a private to public school is considered a new teacher hire, but a teacher who moves from one public school to another public school or one private school to another private school is not considered a new teacher hire.

[2]Estimated.

[3]Projected.

NOTE: Data for teachers are expressed in full-time equivalents (FTE). Counts of private school teachers and enrollment include prekindergarten through grade 12 in schools offering kindergarten or higher grades. Counts of public school teachers and enrollment include prekindergarten through grade 12. The pupil/teacher ratio includes teachers for students with disabilities and other special teachers, while these teachers are generally excluded from class size calculations. Ratios for public schools reflect totals reported by states and differ from totals reported for schools or school districts. Some data have been revised from previously published figures. Detail may not sum to totals because of rounding.

SOURCE: U.S. Department of Education, National Center for Education Statistics, *Statistics of Public Elementary and Secondary Day Schools*, 1955–56 through 1980–81; *Statistics of Nonpublic Elementary and Secondary Schools*, 1955 through 1980; 1983–84, 1985–86, and 1987–88 Private School Survey; Common Core of Data (CCD), "State Nonfiscal Survey of Public Elementary/Secondary Education," 1981–82 through 2017–18; Private School Universe Survey (PSS), 1989–90 through 2017–18; Schools and Staffing Survey (SASS), "Public School Teacher Data File" and "Private School Teacher Data File," 1999–2000 through 2011–12; National Teacher and Principal Survey (NTPS), 2015–16; Elementary and Secondary Teacher Projection Model, 1973 through 2029; and New Teacher Hires Projection Model, 1988 through 2029. (This table was prepared December 2019.)

Table 208.30. Public elementary and secondary teachers, by level and state or jurisdiction: Selected years, fall 2000 through fall 2017

[In full-time equivalents]

State or jurisdiction	Fall 2000	Fall 2005	Fall 2010	Fall 2014	Fall 2015	Fall 2016				Fall 2017			
						Total	Elementary	Secondary	Ungraded	Total	Elementary	Secondary	Ungraded
1	2	3	4	5	6	7	8	9	10	11	12	13	14
United States	2,941,461[1]	3,143,003[1]	3,099,095[1]	3,132,351[1]	3,151,497[1]	3,169,499[1]	1,759,610[1]	1,232,805[1]	177,083[1]	3,169,750[1]	1,746,538[1]	1,233,360[1]	189,851[1]
Alabama	48,194[2]	57,757	49,363	42,737	40,766	42,533	22,476	20,057	0	41,802	22,301	19,501	0
Alaska	7,880	7,912	8,171	7,759	7,832	7,825	4,070	3,754	0	7,743	4,070	3,673	0
Arizona	44,438	51,376	50,031	48,124	47,944	48,220	33,135	15,085	0	47,868	33,299	14,569	0
Arkansas	31,947	32,997	34,273	35,430	35,804	35,730	18,317	14,768	2,645	35,800	18,177	14,862	2,760
California	298,021[2]	309,222[2]	260,806[2]	267,685[2]	263,475	271,287[2]	182,600[2]	86,140	2,547	271,523[2]	181,402[2]	85,849	4,272
Colorado	41,983	45,841	48,543	51,388	51,798	52,014	29,401	22,613	0	52,373	29,341	23,033	0
Connecticut	41,044	39,687	42,951	42,062	43,772	42,343	26,744	15,373	226	45,081	29,414	15,428	239
Delaware	7,469	7,998	8,933	9,649	8,962	9,208	4,678	4,530	0	9,399	4,788	4,611	0
District of Columbia	4,949	5,481[3]	5,925	6,565	6,789	6,727	3,990	2,713	24	6,659	4,078	2,581	0
Florida	132,030	158,962	175,609	180,442	182,586	186,339	76,301	67,849	42,190	186,128	75,746	67,474	42,908
Georgia	91,043	108,535	112,460	111,470	113,031	114,763	52,918	44,721	17,124	116,022	53,116	45,502	17,403
Hawaii	10,927	11,226	11,396	11,663	11,747	11,782	6,397	5,315	70	12,033	6,518	5,450	66
Idaho	13,714	14,521	15,673	15,609	15,656	16,204	7,648	8,556	0	16,592	7,764	8,828	0
Illinois	127,620	133,857	132,983	132,456[4]	129,948	128,893	90,125	38,506	263	128,204	89,854	38,018	332
Indiana	59,226	60,592	58,121[2]	56,547	57,675	60,162	31,163	28,999	0	61,018	31,621	29,398	0
Iowa	34,636	35,181	34,642	35,684	35,687	35,808	25,205	10,603	0	35,553	25,007	10,546	0
Kansas	32,742	33,608	34,644	37,659	40,035	36,193	18,496	17,697	0	36,387	18,729	17,658	0
Kentucky	39,589	42,413	42,042	41,586	41,902	42,029	24,772	10,058	7,199	42,064	24,701	10,092	7,270
Louisiana	49,915	44,660	48,655	46,340	58,469	48,408	32,806	15,602	0	40,281	27,409	12,872	0
Maine	16,559	16,684	15,384	14,937	14,857	14,750	10,284	4,467	0	14,760	10,329	4,431	0
Maryland	52,433	56,685	58,428	59,194	59,414	59,703	36,442	23,261	0	60,175	36,657	23,518	0
Massachusetts	67,432	73,596	68,754	71,859	71,969	72,413	47,382	25,031	0	73,381	47,733	25,648	0
Michigan	97,031	98,069	88,615	85,038	84,181	83,597	34,756	32,785	16,057	84,473	35,276	32,978	16,219
Minnesota	53,457	51,107	52,672	55,690	55,985	56,715	30,555	24,270	1,889	57,260	30,816	24,497	1,947
Mississippi	31,006	31,433	32,255	32,311	32,175	31,924	14,907	13,196	3,822	31,625	14,795	13,117	3,713
Missouri	64,735	67,076	66,735	67,356	67,635	67,926	35,235	32,691	0	68,496	35,725	32,771	0
Montana	10,411	10,369	10,361	10,234	10,412	10,555	7,391	3,127	36	10,515	7,383	3,097	35
Nebraska	20,983	21,359	22,345	22,988	23,308	23,611	15,221	8,390	0	23,771	15,321	8,450	0
Nevada	18,293	21,744	21,839	21,656	22,702	23,705	11,422	8,486	3,797	23,709	11,348	8,453	3,908
New Hampshire	14,341	15,536	15,365	14,773	14,770	14,760	9,761	4,999	0	14,589	9,859	4,730	0
New Jersey	99,061	112,673	110,202	115,067	114,968	115,729	61,286	37,911	16,532	115,496	61,197	37,635	16,664
New Mexico	21,042	22,021	22,437	22,411	21,722	21,331	9,454	8,123	3,754	21,092	9,387	7,960	3,745
New York	206,961	218,989	211,606	203,781	206,086	209,151	105,341	93,792	10,018	213,159	108,893	95,744	8,522
North Carolina	83,680	95,664	98,357	99,320	99,355	100,220	69,663	29,741	816	100,401	70,004	29,641	756
North Dakota	8,141	8,003	8,417	9,049	9,195	9,265	6,122	3,143	0	9,284	6,163	3,121	0
Ohio	118,361	117,982	109,282	106,526[3]	101,742	102,600	57,122	41,128	4,350	98,912	43,987	41,543	13,382
Oklahoma	41,318	41,833	41,278	42,073	42,452	41,090	23,119	17,970	0	41,597	23,643	17,954	0
Oregon	28,094	28,346	28,109	27,850	29,086	29,756	21,089	8,667	0	29,909	21,158	8,752	0
Pennsylvania	116,963	122,397	129,911	122,030	120,893	122,552	58,732	52,965	10,855	121,918	58,334	52,638	10,946
Rhode Island	10,645	14,180[2]	11,212	9,471	10,631	10,689	5,965	4,724	0	10,687	5,939	4,748	0
South Carolina	45,380	48,212	45,210	49,475	50,237	50,789	35,712	15,078	0	52,467	36,969	15,498	0
South Dakota	9,397	9,129	9,512	9,618	9,638	9,777	6,364	2,499	914	9,833	6,250	2,495	1,087
Tennessee	57,164	59,596	66,558	65,341	66,488	64,270	45,296	18,975	0	64,019	45,462	18,558	0
Texas	274,826	302,425	334,997	342,257	347,329	352,809	175,290	153,142	24,377	356,877	176,132	155,342	25,403
Utah	22,008	22,993	25,677	27,374[3]	28,348[3]	28,841[3]	14,050[3]	11,882[3]	2,909[3]	29,212[3]	14,230[3]	12,035[3]	2,946[3]
Vermont	8,414	8,851	8,382	8,276	8,338	8,187	3,326	2,736	2,124	8,313	3,176	2,745	2,392
Virginia	86,977[2]	103,944	70,947	89,968	90,255	91,628	42,155	49,473	0	85,936	37,097	48,840	0
Washington	51,098	53,508	53,934	59,555	57,942	58,815	32,242	24,507	2,067	60,183	33,057	24,810	2,316
West Virginia	20,930	19,940	20,338	20,029	19,664	19,356	9,168	10,167	21	19,239	9,951	9,083	205
Wisconsin	60,165	60,127	57,625	58,376[3]	58,185	59,011	29,429	29,125	457	58,598	28,986	29,198	414
Wyoming	6,783	6,706	7,127	7,615	7,653	7,506	4,089	3,417	0	7,335	3,948	3,387	0
Jurisdiction													
Bureau of Indian Education	—	—	—	—	—	—	—	—	—	—	—	—	—
DoDEA[5]	7,504	7,759	—	—	—	—	—	—	—	—	—	—	—
Other jurisdictions													
American Samoa	820	989	—	—	—	—	—	—	—	—	—	—	—
Guam	1,975	1,804	1,843	2,286	2,336	2,289	1,154	1,135	0	2,202	1,068	1,134	0
Northern Marianas	526	614	607	—	—	—	—	—	—	—	—	—	—
Puerto Rico	37,620	42,036	36,506	31,186	30,438	28,899	13,097	10,140	5,661	28,039	16,617	6,275	5,147
U.S. Virgin Islands	1,511	1,434	1,457	1,131	1,106	1,154	546	593	15	1,066	500	553	13

—Not available.
[1]Includes imputed values for states.
[2]Includes imputations to correct for underreporting of prekindergarten teachers.
[3]Imputed.
[4]Includes imputations to correct for underreporting of prekindergarten, kindergarten, and ungraded teachers.
[5]DoDEA = Department of Defense Education Activity. Includes both domestic and overseas schools.

NOTE: Distribution of elementary and secondary teachers determined by reporting units.

SOURCE: U.S. Department of Education, National Center for Education Statistics, Common Core of Data (CCD), "State Nonfiscal Survey of Public Elementary/Secondary Education," 2000–01 through 2017–18. (This table was prepared August 2019.)

Table 208.40. Public elementary and secondary teachers, enrollment, and pupil/teacher ratios, by state or jurisdiction: Selected years, fall 2000 through fall 2017

State or jurisdiction	Pupil/teacher ratio				Fall 2015			Fall 2016			Fall 2017		
	Fall 2000	Fall 2005	Fall 2010	Fall 2014	Teachers	Enrollment	Pupil/ teacher ratio	Teachers	Enrollment	Pupil/ teacher ratio	Teachers	Enrollment	Pupil/ teacher ratio
1	2	3	4	5	6	7	8	9	10	11	12	13	14
United States	**16.0**[1]	**15.6**[1]	**16.0**[1]	**16.1**[1]	**3,151,497**[1]	**50,438,043**[1]	**16.0**[1]	**3,169,499**[1]	**50,615,189**[1]	**16.0**[1]	**3,169,750**[1]	**50,685,567**[1]	**16.0**[1]
Alabama	15.4[2]	12.8	15.3	17.4	40,766	743,789	18.2	42,533	744,930	17.5	41,802	742,444	17.8
Alaska	16.9	16.8	16.2	16.9	7,832	132,477	16.9	7,825	132,737	17.0	7,743	132,872	17.2
Arizona	19.8	21.3	21.4	23.1	47,944	1,109,040	23.1	48,220	1,123,137	23.3	47,868	1,110,851	23.2
Arkansas	14.1	14.4	14.1	13.9	35,804	492,132	13.7	35,730	493,447	13.8	35,800	496,085	13.9
California	20.6[2]	20.8[2]	24.1[2]	23.6[2]	263,475	6,305,347[2]	23.9[2]	271,287[2]	6,309,138[2]	23.3[2]	271,523[2]	6,304,266[2]	23.2[2]
Colorado	17.3	17.0	17.4	17.3	51,798	899,112	17.4	52,014	905,019	17.4	52,373	910,280	17.4
Connecticut	13.7	14.5	13.1	12.9	43,772	537,933	12.3	42,343	535,118	12.6	45,081	531,288	11.8
Delaware	15.4	15.1	14.5	13.9	8,962	134,847	15.0	9,208	136,264	14.8	9,399	136,293	14.5
District of Columbia	13.9	14.0[3]	12.0	12.3	6,789	84,024	12.4	6,727	85,850	12.8	6,659	87,315	13.1
Florida	18.4	16.8	15.1	15.3	182,586	2,792,234	15.3	186,339	2,816,791	15.1	186,128	2,832,424	15.2
Georgia	15.9	14.7	14.9	15.6	113,031	1,757,237	15.5	114,763	1,764,346	15.4	116,022	1,768,642	15.2
Hawaii	16.9	16.3	15.8	15.6	11,747	181,995	15.5	11,782	181,550	15.4	12,033	180,837	15.0
Idaho	17.9	18.0	17.6	18.6	15,656	292,277	18.7	16,204	297,200	18.3	16,592	301,186	18.2
Illinois	16.1	15.8	15.7	15.5[4]	129,948	2,041,779	15.7	128,893	2,026,718	15.7	128,204	2,005,153	15.6
Indiana	16.7	17.1	18.0[2]	18.5	57,675	1,046,757	18.1	60,162	1,049,547	17.4	61,018	1,054,187	17.3
Iowa	14.3	13.7	14.3	14.2	35,687	508,014	14.2	35,808	509,831	14.2	35,553	511,850	14.4
Kansas	14.4	13.9	14.0	13.2	40,035	495,884	12.4	36,193	494,347	13.7	36,387	497,088	13.7
Kentucky	16.8	16.0	16.0	16.6	41,902	686,598	16.4	42,029	684,017	16.3	42,064	680,978	16.2
Louisiana	14.9	14.7	14.3	15.5	58,469	718,711	12.3	48,408	716,293	14.8	40,281	715,135	17.8
Maine	12.5	11.7	12.3	12.2	14,857	181,613	12.2	14,750	180,512	12.2	14,760	180,473	12.2
Maryland	16.3	15.2	14.6	14.8	59,414	879,601	14.8	59,703	886,221	14.8	60,175	893,684	14.9
Massachusetts	14.5	13.2	13.9	13.3	71,969	964,026	13.4	72,413	964,514	13.3	73,381	964,791	13.1
Michigan	17.7[2]	17.8	17.9	18.1	84,181	1,536,231	18.2	83,597	1,528,666	18.3	84,473	1,516,398	18.0
Minnesota	16.0	16.4	15.9	15.4	55,985	864,384	15.4	56,715	875,021	15.4	57,260	884,944	15.5
Mississippi	16.1	15.7	15.2	15.2	32,175	487,200	15.1	31,924	483,150	15.1	31,625	478,321	15.1
Missouri	14.1	13.7	13.8	13.6	67,635	919,234	13.6	67,926	915,040	13.5	68,496	915,472	13.4
Montana	14.9	14.0	13.7	14.1	10,412	145,319	14.0	10,555	146,375	13.9	10,515	149,474	14.2
Nebraska	13.6	13.4	13.4	13.6	23,308	316,014	13.6	23,611	319,194	13.5	23,771	323,766	13.6
Nevada	18.6	19.0	20.0	21.2	22,702	467,527	20.6	23,705	473,744	20.0	23,709	485,785	20.5
New Hampshire	14.5	13.2	12.7	12.5	14,770	182,425	12.4	14,760	180,888	12.3	14,589	179,433	12.3
New Jersey	13.3	12.4	12.7	12.2	114,968	1,408,845	12.3	115,729	1,410,421	12.2	115,496	1,408,102	12.2
New Mexico	15.2	14.8	15.1	15.2	21,722	335,694	15.5	21,331	336,263	15.8	21,092	334,345	15.9
New York	13.9	12.9	12.9	13.5	206,086	2,711,626	13.2	209,151	2,729,776	13.1	213,159	2,724,663	12.8
North Carolina	15.5	14.8	15.2	15.6	99,355	1,544,934	15.5	100,220	1,550,062	15.5	100,401	1,553,513	15.5
North Dakota	13.4	12.3	11.4	11.8	9,195	108,644	11.8	9,265	109,706	11.8	9,284	111,920	12.1
Ohio	15.5	15.6	16.1	16.2[3]	101,742	1,716,585	16.9	102,600	1,710,143	16.7	98,912	1,704,399	17.2
Oklahoma	15.1	15.2	16.0	16.4	42,452	692,878	16.3	41,090	693,903	16.9	41,597	695,092	16.7
Oregon	19.4	19.5	20.3	21.6	29,086	608,825[2]	20.9[2]	29,756	606,277[2]	20.4[2]	29,909	608,014[2]	20.3[2]
Pennsylvania	15.5	15.0	13.8	14.3	120,893	1,717,414	14.2	122,552	1,727,497	14.1	121,918	1,726,809	14.2
Rhode Island	14.8	10.8	12.8	15.0	10,631	142,014	13.4	10,689	142,150	13.3	10,687	142,949	13.4
South Carolina	14.9	14.6	16.1	15.3	50,237	763,533	15.2	50,789	771,250	15.2	52,467	777,507	14.8
South Dakota	13.7	13.4	13.3	13.8	9,638	134,253	13.9	9,777	136,302	13.9	9,833	137,823	14.0
Tennessee	15.9[2]	16.0	14.8	15.2	66,488	1,001,235	15.1	64,270	1,001,562	15.6	64,019	1,001,967	15.7
Texas	14.8	15.0	14.7	15.3	347,329	5,301,477	15.3	352,809	5,360,849	15.2	356,877	5,401,341	15.1
Utah	21.9	22.1	22.8	23.2[3]	28,348[3]	647,870	22.9[3]	28,841[3]	659,801	22.9	29,212[3]	668,274	22.9
Vermont	12.1	10.9	11.6	10.6	8,338	87,866	10.5	8,187	88,428	10.8	8,313	88,028	10.6
Virginia	13.2[2]	11.7	17.6	14.2	90,255	1,283,590	14.2	91,628	1,287,026	14.0	85,936	1,291,462	15.0
Washington	19.7	19.3	19.4	18.0	57,942	1,087,030	18.8	58,815	1,101,711	18.7	60,183	1,110,367	18.4
West Virginia	13.7	14.1	13.9	14.0	19,664	277,452	14.1	19,356	273,855	14.1	19,239	272,266	14.2
Wisconsin	14.6	14.6	15.1	14.9[3]	58,185	867,800	14.9	59,011	864,432	14.6	58,598	860,753	14.7
Wyoming	13.3	12.6	12.5	12.4	7,653	94,717	12.4	7,506	94,170	12.5	7,335	94,258	12.9
Jurisdiction													
Bureau of Indian Education	—	—	—	—	—	—	—	—	45,399	—	—	46,330	—
DoDEA[5]	14.4	11.7	—	—	—	74,970	—	—	—	—	—	71,134	—
Other jurisdictions													
American Samoa	19.1	16.6	—	—	—	—	—	—	—	—	—	12,620	—
Guam	16.4	—	17.2	13.6	2,336	30,821	13.2	2,289	30,758	13.4	2,202	30,112	13.7
Northern Marianas	19.0	19.1	18.3	—	—	—	—	—	—	—	—	—	—
Puerto Rico	16.3	13.4	13.0	13.2	30,438	379,818	12.5	28,899	365,181	12.6	28,039	346,096	12.3
U.S. Virgin Islands	12.9	11.7	10.6	12.6	1,106	13,805	12.5	1,154	13,194	11.4	1,066	16,139	15.1

—Not available.
[1]Includes imputed values for states.
[2]Includes imputations to correct for underreporting of prekindergarten teachers/enrollment.
[3]Imputed.
[4]Includes imputations to correct for underreporting of prekindergarten, kindergarten, and ungraded teachers.
[5]DoDEA = Department of Defense Education Activity. Includes both domestic and overseas schools.

NOTE: Teachers reported in full-time equivalents (FTE). Ratios reflect totals reported by states and differ from totals reported for schools or school districts.
SOURCE: U.S. Department of Education, National Center for Education Statistics, Common Core of Data (CCD), "State Nonfiscal Survey of Public Elementary/Secondary Education," 2000–01 through 2017–18. (This table was prepared February 2020.)

Table 209.10. Number and percentage distribution of teachers in public and private elementary and secondary schools, by selected teacher characteristics: Selected years, 1987–88 through 2017–18

[Standard errors appear in parentheses]

Selected teacher characteristic	Number of teachers (in thousands)							Percentage distribution of teachers						
	1987–88	1990–91	1999–2000	2003–04	2007–08	2011–12	2017–18	1987–88	1990–91	1999–2000	2003–04	2007–08	2011–12	2017–18
1	2	3	4	5	6	7	8	9	10	11	12	13	14	15
Public schools														
Total	**2,323 (13.2)**	**2,559 (20.7)**	**3,002 (19.4)**	**3,251 (29.2)**	**3,405 (44.0)**	**3,385 (41.4)**	**3,545 (23.5)**	**100.0 (†)**	**100.0 (†)**	**100.0 (†)**	**100.0 (†)**	**100.0 (†)**	**100.0 (†)**	**100.0 (†)**
Sex														
Male	685 (6.8)	719 (11.2)	754 (10.7)	813 (13.3)	821 (20.4)	802 (22.2)	834 (11.6)	29.5 (0.22)	28.1 (0.31)	25.1 (0.30)	25.0 (0.32)	24.1 (0.47)	23.7 (0.49)	23.5 (0.28)
Female	1,638 (10.1)	1,840 (14.7)	2,248 (16.0)	2,438 (23.5)	2,584 (34.6)	2,584 (30.5)	2,712 (20.2)	70.5 (0.22)	71.9 (0.31)	74.9 (0.30)	75.0 (0.32)	75.9 (0.47)	76.3 (0.49)	76.5 (0.28)
Race/ethnicity														
White[1]	2,018 (12.6)	2,214 (20.0)	2,532 (17.2)	2,702 (30.1)	2,829 (38.7)	2,773 (30.5)	2,811 (22.7)	86.9 (0.24)	86.5 (0.29)	84.3 (0.30)	83.1 (0.53)	83.1 (0.53)	81.9 (0.53)	79.3 (0.35)
Black[1]	191 (4.6)	212 (6.4)	228 (6.0)	257 (11.0)	239 (15.8)	231 (12.1)	239 (7.4)	8.2 (0.19)	8.3 (0.25)	7.6 (0.19)	7.9 (0.34)	7.0 (0.45)	6.8 (0.31)	6.7 (0.20)
Hispanic[1]	69 (2.6)	87 (4.5)	169 (6.4)	202 (11.3)	240 (16.6)	264 (13.4)	331 (9.2)	3.0 (0.11)	3.4 (0.17)	5.6 (0.20)	6.2 (0.34)	7.1 (0.46)	7.8 (0.37)	9.3 (0.26)
Asian[1,2]	21 (1.1)	27 (1.7)	48 (2.7)	42 (2.5)	42 (7.2)	61 (7.3)	75 (3.5)	0.9 (0.05)	1.0 (0.06)	1.6 (0.09)	1.3 (0.08)	1.2 (0.21)	1.8 (0.21)	2.1 (0.10)
Pacific Islander	— (†)	— (†)	— (†)	6 (0.8)	6 (1.3)	5 (1.4)	8 (1.0)	— (†)	— (†)	— (†)	0.2 (0.03)	0.2 (0.04)	0.1 (0.04)	0.2 (0.03)
American Indian/ Alaska Native[1]	24 (1.3)	20 (1.4)	26 (1.9)	17 (1.2)	17 (1.9)	17 (2.9)	18 (1.7)	1.0 (0.06)	0.8 (0.05)	0.9 (0.06)	0.5 (0.04)	0.5 (0.06)	0.5 (0.08)	0.5 (0.05)
Two or more races	— (†)	— (†)	— (†)	24 (2.2)	31 (2.9)	35 (3.7)	63 (3.1)	— (†)	— (†)	— (†)	0.7 (0.07)	0.9 (0.09)	1.0 (0.11)	1.8 (0.09)
Age														
Under 30	313 (5.0)	257 (5.7)	509 (9.2)	540 (27.4)	612 (22.4)	518 (15.9)	531 (9.4)	13.5 (0.19)	10.0 (0.23)	17.0 (0.28)	16.6 (0.84)	18.0 (0.61)	15.3 (0.44)	15.0 (0.24)
30 to 39	823 (7.7)	684 (10.8)	661 (9.8)	798 (14.5)	898 (16.8)	979 (19.3)	991 (12.9)	35.4 (0.30)	26.7 (0.35)	22.0 (0.29)	24.5 (0.38)	26.4 (0.39)	28.9 (0.53)	27.9 (0.29)
40 to 49	762 (7.4)	1,034 (13.3)	953 (10.3)	840 (14.3)	808 (19.2)	849 (19.2)	1,028 (12.3)	32.8 (0.25)	40.4 (0.37)	31.8 (0.32)	25.9 (0.38)	23.7 (0.47)	25.1 (0.51)	29.0 (0.32)
50 to 59	357 (5.7)	477 (8.6)	786 (12.6)	942 (26.0)	879 (21.1)	783 (20.5)	732 (11.6)	15.4 (0.23)	18.7 (0.29)	26.2 (0.35)	29.0 (0.74)	25.8 (0.51)	23.1 (0.49)	20.7 (0.29)
60 and over	68 (2.5)	107 (4.1)	93 (4.0)	131 (4.8)	207 (10.3)	256 (13.2)	263 (6.1)	2.9 (0.11)	4.2 (0.16)	3.1 (0.13)	4.0 (0.14)	6.1 (0.29)	7.6 (0.34)	7.4 (0.17)
Highest degree earned														
Less than bachelor's	15 (1.0)	17 (1.2)	20 (1.3)	35 (2.5)	27 (2.1)	128 (8.6)	97 (3.6)	0.7 (0.04)	0.7 (0.05)	0.7 (0.04)	1.1 (0.08)	0.8 (0.06)	3.8 (0.24)	2.7 (0.10)
Bachelor's	1,214 (9.8)	1,327 (11.7)	1,560 (15.8)	1,651 (22.8)	1,612 (28.8)	1,350 (21.1)	1,393 (15.8)	52.3 (0.28)	51.9 (0.31)	52.0 (0.40)	50.8 (0.56)	47.4 (0.59)	39.9 (0.52)	39.3 (0.36)
Master's	932 (8.5)	1,077 (13.5)	1,257 (13.9)	1,331 (21.7)	1,517 (27.8)	1,614 (29.1)	1,744 (17.5)	40.1 (0.30)	42.1 (0.34)	41.9 (0.38)	40.9 (0.56)	44.5 (0.55)	47.7 (0.57)	49.2 (0.36)
Education specialist[3]	146 (3.4)	118 (5.3)	143 (5.2)	195 (6.8)	218 (8.6)	257 (9.7)	271 (6.8)	6.3 (0.14)	4.6 (0.20)	4.7 (0.17)	6.0 (0.19)	6.4 (0.25)	7.6 (0.27)	7.6 (0.18)
Doctor's	16 (1.2)	20 (1.7)	22 (1.8)	38 (3.5)	30 (2.7)	37 (4.0)	41 (2.5)	0.7 (0.05)	0.8 (0.07)	0.7 (0.06)	1.2 (0.11)	0.9 (0.08)	1.1 (0.11)	1.2 (0.07)
Years of teaching experience														
Less than 3	145 (3.2)	185 (4.8)	325 (7.7)	339 (36.6)	392 (18.1)	244 (8.5)	318 (7.2)	6.2 (0.14)	7.2 (0.19)	10.8 (0.24)	10.4 (1.13)	11.5 (0.48)	7.2 (0.24)	9.0 (0.19)
3 to 9	568 (6.3)	596 (9.4)	854 (12.3)	1,043 (14.1)	1,125 (19.6)	1,104 (20.6)	1,003 (14.1)	24.4 (0.22)	23.3 (0.30)	28.5 (0.37)	32.1 (0.33)	33.0 (0.52)	32.6 (0.52)	28.3 (0.34)
10 to 20	1,072 (8.7)	1,056 (11.8)	865 (10.1)	946 (21.5)	1,017 (24.3)	1,265 (21.0)	1,416 (14.4)	46.1 (0.27)	41.3 (0.35)	28.8 (0.33)	29.1 (0.58)	29.9 (0.57)	37.4 (0.53)	39.9 (0.35)
Over 20	539 (6.1)	721 (10.6)	958 (13.5)	922 (27.9)	871 (23.9)	772 (23.8)	808 (11.8)	23.2 (0.23)	28.2 (0.30)	31.9 (0.36)	28.4 (0.81)	25.6 (0.62)	22.8 (0.54)	22.8 (0.29)
Level of instruction[4]														
Elementary	1,292 (9.5)	1,442 (11.8)	1,602 (13.5)	1,716 (25.8)	1,725 (37.1)	1,726 (20.2)	1,779 (24.5)	55.6 (0.33)	56.3 (0.40)	53.3 (0.42)	52.8 (0.66)	50.7 (0.91)	51.0 (0.65)	50.2 (0.62)
General	788 (7.4)	887 (10.6)	1,042 (12.5)	1,130 (29.8)	1,100 (26.5)	1,078 (22.1)	1,097 (17.3)	33.9 (0.29)	34.6 (0.39)	34.7 (0.41)	34.8 (0.86)	32.3 (0.70)	31.8 (0.71)	30.9 (0.45)
Arts/music	116 (3.0)	110 (4.3)	99 (3.7)	101 (5.3)	103 (6.6)	82 (5.4)	99 (4.2)	5.0 (0.13)	4.3 (0.17)	3.3 (0.12)	3.1 (0.17)	3.0 (0.19)	2.4 (0.16)	2.8 (0.11)
English	60 (2.3)	72 (3.8)	66 (3.8)	70 (5.1)	104 (9.9)	92 (6.9)	117 (4.6)	2.6 (0.10)	2.8 (0.14)	2.2 (0.13)	2.2 (0.16)	3.0 (0.29)	2.7 (0.21)	3.3 (0.13)
ESL/bilingual	18 (1.1)	20 (1.3)	28 (1.8)	25 (3.6)	24 (3.3)	51 (6.8)	48 (3.4)	0.8 (0.05)	0.8 (0.05)	0.9 (0.06)	0.8 (0.11)	0.7 (0.10)	1.5 (0.20)	1.4 (0.10)
Health/physical ed	56 (2.0)	66 (3.2)	57 (3.5)	73 (5.0)	63 (6.0)	79 (8.1)	65 (3.5)	2.4 (0.09)	2.6 (0.12)	1.9 (0.12)	2.2 (0.15)	1.8 (0.18)	2.3 (0.23)	1.8 (0.10)
Mathematics	31 (2.0)	30 (1.9)	23 (2.4)	19 (2.3)	28 (3.8)	32 (6.5)	36 (2.3)	1.3 (0.09)	1.2 (0.08)	0.8 (0.08)	0.6 (0.07)	0.8 (0.11)	0.9 (0.19)	1.0 (0.07)
Science	18 (1.5)	21 (1.9)	11 (1.3)	19 (3.0)	15 (3.4)	18 (3.3)	23 (1.8)	0.8 (0.06)	0.8 (0.07)	0.4 (0.04)	0.6 (0.09)	0.4 (0.10)	0.5 (0.10)	0.6 (0.05)
Special education	168 (3.9)	176 (5.9)	227 (5.6)	240 (20.6)	230 (13.0)	239 (10.3)	235 (6.3)	7.2 (0.16)	6.9 (0.23)	7.6 (0.18)	7.4 (0.63)	6.7 (0.37)	7.1 (0.31)	6.6 (0.17)
Other elementary	37 (2.4)	60 (3.2)	49 (3.5)	40 (3.5)	58 (4.2)	55 (5.2)	60 (3.0)	1.6 (0.10)	2.4 (0.12)	1.6 (0.12)	1.2 (0.11)	1.7 (0.12)	1.6 (0.15)	1.7 (0.08)
Secondary	1,031 (10.5)	1,118 (16.5)	1,401 (17.7)	1,534 (26.0)	1,680 (39.0)	1,659 (37.8)	1,766 (25.2)	44.4 (0.33)	43.7 (0.40)	46.7 (0.42)	47.2 (0.66)	49.3 (0.91)	49.0 (0.65)	49.8 (0.62)
Arts/music	73 (2.0)	74 (2.3)	110 (3.4)	112 (4.1)	121 (6.2)	121 (5.6)	130 (4.5)	3.1 (0.09)	2.9 (0.08)	3.7 (0.11)	3.4 (0.12)	3.6 (0.18)	3.6 (0.14)	3.7 (0.13)
English	171 (3.2)	195 (5.1)	245 (5.1)	269 (9.0)	306 (10.0)	289 (9.9)	294 (6.6)	7.4 (0.12)	7.6 (0.18)	8.2 (0.15)	8.3 (0.27)	9.0 (0.27)	8.5 (0.25)	8.3 (0.18)
ESL/bilingual	6 (0.5)	10 (0.7)	16 (1.2)	18 (2.5)	21 (2.5)	20 (2.4)	24 (1.9)	0.3 (0.02)	0.4 (0.03)	0.5 (0.04)	0.6 (0.08)	0.6 (0.07)	0.6 (0.07)	0.7 (0.05)
Foreign language	43 (1.2)	52 (2.4)	71 (2.4)	73 (3.3)	78 (5.0)	88 (4.5)	85 (3.5)	1.9 (0.05)	2.0 (0.09)	2.4 (0.08)	2.3 (0.10)	2.3 (0.14)	2.6 (0.12)	2.4 (0.10)
Health/physical ed	76 (2.4)	76 (2.2)	99 (3.1)	102 (4.3)	119 (5.7)	101 (3.9)	97 (3.2)	3.3 (0.10)	3.0 (0.08)	3.3 (0.10)	3.1 (0.12)	3.5 (0.16)	3.0 (0.11)	2.7 (0.09)
Mathematics	139 (2.5)	155 (4.3)	207 (4.5)	213 (5.5)	252 (9.1)	250 (7.5)	265 (6.6)	6.0 (0.10)	6.0 (0.15)	6.9 (0.14)	6.5 (0.17)	7.4 (0.25)	7.4 (0.19)	7.5 (0.18)
Science	115 (2.9)	128 (4.0)	169 (4.0)	189 (6.8)	195 (8.3)	209 (6.1)	220 (5.6)	4.9 (0.11)	5.0 (0.15)	5.6 (0.12)	5.8 (0.20)	5.7 (0.24)	6.2 (0.16)	6.2 (0.15)
Social studies	118 (2.4)	124 (3.3)	163 (4.4)	178 (5.7)	209 (9.9)	197 (6.3)	214 (5.2)	5.1 (0.10)	4.8 (0.12)	5.4 (0.14)	5.5 (0.16)	6.1 (0.27)	5.8 (0.16)	6.0 (0.14)
Special education	100 (2.2)	113 (3.5)	113 (2.8)	174 (7.5)	165 (9.7)	191 (12.2)	199 (5.5)	4.3 (0.09)	4.4 (0.13)	3.8 (0.09)	5.4 (0.23)	4.9 (0.28)	5.7 (0.32)	5.6 (0.15)
Vocational/technical	166 (3.0)	160 (3.7)	161 (3.5)	169 (5.7)	164 (6.3)	147 (5.7)	139 (4.4)	7.1 (0.12)	6.3 (0.12)	5.4 (0.10)	5.2 (0.17)	4.8 (0.17)	4.3 (0.16)	3.9 (0.12)
Other secondary	25 (1.3)	30 (1.5)	47 (2.0)	36 (2.1)	47 (3.4)	46 (4.0)	98 (3.9)	1.1 (0.06)	1.2 (0.06)	1.6 (0.07)	1.1 (0.06)	1.4 (0.10)	1.4 (0.12)	2.8 (0.11)

See notes at end of table.

Table 209.10. Number and percentage distribution of teachers in public and private elementary and secondary schools, by selected teacher characteristics: Selected years, 1987–88 through 2017–18—Continued

[Standard errors appear in parentheses]

Selected teacher characteristic	Number of teachers (in thousands)							Percentage distribution of teachers						
	1987–88	1990–91	1999–2000	2003–04	2007–08	2011–12	2017–18	1987–88	1990–91	1999–2000	2003–04	2007–08	2011–12	2017–18
1	2	3	4	5	6	7	8	9	10	11	12	13	14	15
Private schools														
Total	**307 (8.5)**	**356 (7.2)**	**449 (10.6)**	**467 (10.3)**	**490 (9.2)**	**465 (11.1)**	**509 (9.1)**	**100.0 (†)**	**100.0 (†)**	**100.0 (†)**	**100.0 (†)**	**100.0 (†)**	**100.0 (†)**	**100.0 (†)**
Sex														
Male	67 (3.3)	82 (3.3)	107 (3.8)	110 (8.4)	127 (4.6)	117 (6.9)	133 (4.1)	21.8 (0.86)	22.9 (0.74)	23.9 (0.48)	23.6 (1.93)	26.0 (0.78)	25.2 (1.33)	26.0 (0.63)
Female	240 (7.2)	275 (5.8)	342 (7.7)	357 (14.3)	362 (7.7)	348 (10.1)	377 (7.3)	78.2 (0.86)	77.1 (0.74)	76.1 (0.48)	76.4 (1.93)	74.0 (0.78)	74.8 (1.33)	74.0 (0.63)
Race/ethnicity														
White[1]	285 (8.3)	329 (7.0)	402 (9.6)	411 (12.0)	423 (8.8)	411 (11.1)	433 (8.3)	92.8 (0.50)	92.2 (0.46)	89.5 (0.42)	88.0 (0.99)	86.4 (0.80)	88.3 (0.69)	85.1 (0.61)
Black[1]	7 (0.8)	9 (1.0)	17 (1.4)	19 (2.9)	20 (2.2)	17 (2.4)	16 (1.5)	2.3 (0.27)	2.7 (0.28)	3.7 (0.29)	4.0 (0.65)	4.0 (0.44)	3.6 (0.54)	3.2 (0.29)
Hispanic[1]	9 (1.1)	12 (1.0)	21 (1.5)	23 (3.1)	29 (2.1)	24 (2.4)	37 (2.2)	2.8 (0.36)	3.3 (0.26)	4.7 (0.30)	4.8 (0.71)	5.9 (0.38)	5.2 (0.51)	7.2 (0.43)
Asian[1,2]	4 (0.8)	5 (0.6)	7 (0.6)	9 (1.0)	11 (1.5)	9 (1.4)	14 (1.4)	1.2 (0.26)	1.5 (0.18)	1.6 (0.14)	1.8 (0.20)	2.2 (0.29)	1.8 (0.31)	2.7 (0.27)
Pacific Islander	— (†)	— (†)	— (†)	‡ (†)	‡ (†)	‡ (†)	‡ (†)	— (†)	— (†)	— (†)	0.2! (0.07)	0.3! (0.14)	‡ (†)	0.1! (0.04)
American Indian/Alaska Native[1]	3 (0.4)	1 (0.3)	2 (0.4)	‡ (†)	‡ (†)	‡ (†)	‡ (†)	0.9 (0.12)	0.4 (0.09)	0.6 (0.08)	‡ (†)	‡ (†)	‡ (†)	0.3! (0.10)
Two or more races	— (†)	— (†)	— (†)	3! (1.4)	4 (0.6)	4 (0.9)	7 (0.9)	— (†)	— (†)	— (†)	0.6! (0.28)	0.7 (0.12)	0.8 (0.19)	1.3 (0.17)
Age														
Under 30	67 (2.6)	60 (2.2)	87 (3.1)	88 (3.7)	80 (3.9)	78 (6.8)	83 (3.5)	21.8 (0.77)	16.7 (0.61)	19.3 (0.43)	18.9 (0.78)	16.3 (0.67)	16.7 (1.48)	16.2 (0.65)
30 to 39	106 (3.6)	100 (4.0)	101 (3.2)	103 (5.8)	109 (5.2)	112 (6.2)	124 (4.1)	34.5 (0.81)	28.1 (0.78)	22.4 (0.50)	22.0 (1.36)	22.3 (0.91)	24.0 (1.07)	24.4 (0.66)
40 to 49	84 (3.4)	121 (3.1)	131 (4.2)	119 (7.1)	116 (3.6)	110 (6.3)	115 (4.0)	27.4 (0.78)	33.9 (0.74)	29.2 (0.62)	25.4 (1.41)	23.8 (0.65)	23.8 (1.06)	22.7 (0.68)
50 to 59	34 (2.2)	53 (2.3)	106 (3.2)	121 (11.1)	128 (4.5)	99 (5.0)	108 (3.8)	11.1 (0.57)	14.8 (0.55)	23.5 (0.46)	25.8 (2.07)	26.2 (0.87)	21.3 (1.06)	21.2 (0.64)
60 and over	16 (1.7)	23 (1.6)	25 (1.2)	37 (4.7)	56 (3.1)	66 (5.0)	79 (3.4)	5.3 (0.49)	6.4 (0.41)	5.7 (0.24)	8.0 (0.99)	11.5 (0.62)	14.2 (1.05)	15.5 (0.58)
Highest degree earned														
Less than bachelor's	13 (1.4)	23 (1.6)	33 (2.3)	43! (21.5)	40 (2.9)	39 (5.2)	51 (2.8)	4.4 (0.42)	6.4 (0.45)	7.3 (0.46)	9.2! (4.41)	8.1 (0.58)	8.4 (1.07)	10.0 (0.53)
Bachelor's	189 (5.1)	221 (5.7)	258 (5.8)	259 (11.2)	264 (6.8)	225 (6.7)	216 (5.3)	61.4 (0.75)	61.9 (0.90)	57.5 (0.64)	55.5 (2.90)	53.9 (0.95)	48.5 (1.37)	42.4 (0.83)
Master's	92 (3.8)	96 (3.1)	136 (4.5)	138 (6.1)	161 (5.3)	166 (7.5)	204 (5.9)	29.8 (0.73)	27.0 (0.71)	30.3 (0.58)	29.5 (1.35)	32.8 (0.84)	35.8 (1.16)	40.0 (0.80)
Education specialist[3]	9 (0.9)	11 (0.9)	14 (1.0)	17 (2.4)	14 (1.3)	23 (2.3)	25 (1.8)	3.0 (0.30)	2.9 (0.24)	3.1 (0.19)	3.6 (0.54)	2.8 (0.25)	5.0 (0.48)	4.8 (0.33)
Doctor's	4 (0.7)	6 (0.8)	8 (0.8)	10 (1.2)	12 (1.9)	11 (2.0)	14 (1.2)	1.5 (0.23)	1.8 (0.22)	1.8 (0.16)	2.2 (0.26)	2.4 (0.38)	2.3 (0.41)	2.8 (0.23)
Years of teaching experience														
Less than 3	38 (1.4)	47 (1.8)	73 (3.0)	71 (17.5)	72 (4.8)	52 (7.1)	62 (2.4)	12.4 (0.44)	13.2 (0.47)	16.3 (0.44)	15.2 (3.50)	14.7 (0.92)	11.2 (1.54)	12.1 (0.45)
3 to 9	111 (3.4)	123 (3.6)	144 (4.1)	162 (7.1)	163 (5.9)	150 (6.3)	152 (4.8)	36.1 (0.85)	34.6 (0.67)	32.0 (0.56)	34.6 (1.65)	33.2 (1.05)	32.3 (1.07)	29.8 (0.74)
10 to 20	109 (4.3)	122 (3.9)	137 (4.1)	130 (7.3)	133 (4.8)	147 (7.6)	167 (4.7)	35.6 (0.78)	34.4 (0.77)	30.6 (0.54)	27.9 (1.63)	27.1 (0.83)	31.6 (1.38)	32.9 (0.71)
Over 20	49 (2.8)	63 (2.8)	95 (2.8)	105 (7.0)	122 (4.7)	116 (7.2)	128 (4.2)	15.8 (0.65)	17.8 (0.73)	21.2 (0.47)	22.4 (1.62)	24.9 (0.88)	24.9 (1.44)	25.2 (0.67)
Level of instruction[4]														
Elementary	179 (5.6)	225 (4.7)	261 (5.8)	263 (17.5)	258 (6.5)	245 (9.3)	262 (6.1)	58.3 (0.92)	63.2 (0.72)	58.1 (0.66)	56.4 (3.06)	52.8 (1.03)	52.8 (1.67)	51.4 (0.85)
Secondary	128 (4.7)	131 (4.0)	188 (6.2)	204 (13.4)	231 (7.1)	219 (9.9)	247 (6.5)	41.7 (0.92)	36.8 (0.72)	41.9 (0.66)	43.6 (3.06)	47.2 (1.03)	47.2 (1.67)	48.6 (0.78)

—Not available.
†Not applicable.
!Interpret data with caution. The coefficient of variation (CV) for this estimate is between 30 and 50 percent.
‡Reporting standards not met. Either there are too few cases for a reliable estimate or the coefficient of variation (CV) is 50 percent or greater.
[1]Data for 1987–88 through 1999–2000 are only roughly comparable to data for later years, because the new category of Two or more races was introduced in 2003–04.
[2]Includes Pacific Islander for 1987–88 through 1999–2000.
[3]Education specialist degrees or certificates are generally awarded for 1 year's work beyond the master's level. Includes certificate of advanced graduate studies.
[4]Teachers were classified as elementary or secondary on the basis of the grades they taught, rather than on the level of the school in which they taught. In general, elementary teachers include those teaching prekindergarten through grade 6 and those teaching multiple grades, with a preponderance of grades taught being kindergarten through grade 6. In general, secondary teachers include those teaching any of grades 7 through 12 and those teaching multiple grades, with a preponderance of grades taught being grades 7 through 12 and usually with no grade taught being lower than grade 5.
NOTE: Excludes teachers who teach only prekindergarten. Data are based on a head count of full-time and part-time teachers rather than on the number of full-time-equivalent teachers reported in other tables. Detail may not sum to totals because of rounding and cell suppression. Race categories exclude persons of Hispanic ethnicity.
SOURCE: U.S. Department of Education, National Center for Education Statistics, Schools and Staffing Survey (SASS), "Public School Teacher Data File" and "Private School Teacher Data File," 1987–88 through 2011–12; SASS, "Charter School Teacher Data File," 1999–2000; and National Teacher and Principal Survey (NTPS), "Public School Teacher Data File" and "Private School Teacher Data File," 2017–18. (This table was prepared November 2019.)

Table 209.20. Number, highest degree, and years of teaching experience of teachers in public and private elementary and secondary schools, by selected teacher characteristics: Selected years, 1999–2000 through 2017–18

[Standard errors appear in parentheses]

Selected teacher characteristic	Number of teachers (in thousands)				Percent of teachers, by highest degree earned, 2017–18					Percent of teachers, by years of full-time and part-time teaching experience, 2017–18			
	1999–2000	2007–08	2011–12	2017–18	Less than bachelor's	Bachelor's	Master's	Education specialist[1]	Doctor's	Less than 3	3 to 9	10 to 20	Over 20
1	2	3	4	5	6	7	8	9	10	11	12	13	14
Public schools													
Total	**3,002 (19.4)**	**3,405 (44.0)**	**3,385 (41.4)**	**3,545 (23.5)**	**2.7 (0.10)**	**39.3 (0.36)**	**49.2 (0.36)**	**7.6 (0.18)**	**1.2 (0.07)**	**9.0 (0.19)**	**28.3 (0.34)**	**39.9 (0.35)**	**22.8 (0.29)**
Sex													
Male	754 (10.7)	821 (20.4)	802 (22.2)	834 (11.6)	4.0 (0.24)	39.0 (0.64)	49.6 (0.65)	5.7 (0.26)	1.7 (0.18)	8.9 (0.38)	27.4 (0.60)	40.6 (0.68)	23.2 (0.52)
Female	2,248 (16.0)	2,584 (34.6)	2,584 (30.5)	2,712 (20.2)	2.3 (0.11)	39.4 (0.39)	49.1 (0.40)	8.2 (0.22)	1.0 (0.07)	9.0 (0.21)	28.6 (0.39)	39.7 (0.40)	22.7 (0.38)
Race/ethnicity													
White[2]	2,532 (17.2)	2,829 (38.7)	2,773 (30.5)	2,811 (22.7)	2.6 (0.12)	38.6 (0.39)	50.4 (0.39)	7.4 (0.19)	1.0 (0.07)	8.3 (0.21)	27.3 (0.37)	40.1 (0.39)	24.3 (0.34)
Black[2]	228 (6.0)	239 (15.8)	231 (12.1)	239 (7.4)	3.0 (0.42)	32.9 (1.23)	50.7 (1.40)	11.3 (0.85)	2.1 (0.37)	10.8 (0.75)	30.3 (1.27)	38.7 (1.25)	20.2 (1.03)
Hispanic[2]	169 (6.4)	240 (16.6)	263 (13.4)	331 (9.2)	3.6 (0.41)	51.1 (1.20)	37.9 (1.06)	6.1 (0.49)	1.3 (0.20)	11.8 (0.71)	34.0 (0.99)	39.6 (1.03)	14.6 (0.75)
Asian[2,3]	48 (2.7)	42 (7.2)	61 (7.3)	75 (3.5)	1.7 (0.45)	29.0 (1.85)	55.1 (2.00)	11.3 (1.24)	2.8 (0.77)	12.0 (1.33)	31.1 (2.01)	42.1 (2.06)	14.8 (1.44)
Pacific Islander	— (†)	6 (1.3)	5 (1.4)	8 (1.0)	‡ (†)	44.2 (6.46)	38.6 (6.15)	8.7! (2.64)	‡ (†)	6.7! (2.41)	24.0 (5.02)	44.2 (6.58)	25.1 (5.45)
American Indian/Alaska Native[2]	26 (1.9)	17 (1.9)	17 (2.9)	18 (1.7)	5.3! (2.63)	51.6 (3.93)	36.2 (4.05)	6.2 (1.63)	‡ (†)	9.0 (2.03)	20.9 (2.68)	42.5 (4.31)	27.6 (3.92)
Two or more races	— (†)	31 (2.9)	35 (3.8)	63 (3.1)	3.2 (0.92)	40.8 (2.33)	47.0 (2.50)	7.8 (1.35)	1.2! (0.41)	12.5 (1.40)	35.5 (2.41)	34.6 (2.13)	17.4 (1.86)
Age													
Under 30	509 (9.2)	612 (22.4)	518 (15.9)	531 (9.4)	2.7 (0.29)	64.8 (0.88)	30.3 (0.85)	2.1 (0.24)	‡ (†)	37.1 (0.80)	62.8 (0.79)	‡ (†)	‡ (†)
30 to 39	661 (9.8)	898 (16.8)	979 (19.3)	991 (12.9)	2.2 (0.18)	37.9 (0.62)	52.9 (0.65)	6.5 (0.34)	0.6 (0.08)	6.7 (0.29)	42.9 (0.65)	50.3 (0.65)	‡ (†)
40 to 49	953 (10.3)	808 (19.2)	849 (19.2)	1,028 (12.3)	2.9 (0.19)	33.5 (0.60)	53.3 (0.67)	9.2 (0.34)	1.1 (0.12)	3.4 (0.23)	15.5 (0.45)	58.1 (0.57)	23.0 (0.49)
50 to 59	786 (12.6)	879 (21.1)	783 (20.5)	732 (11.6)	2.9 (0.25)	33.4 (0.69)	52.1 (0.75)	9.5 (0.40)	2.1 (0.22)	2.0 (0.19)	9.2 (0.39)	33.5 (0.68)	55.2 (0.72)
60 and over	93 (4.0)	207 (10.3)	256 (13.2)	263 (6.1)	3.6 (0.38)	32.1 (1.05)	49.2 (1.08)	12.0 (0.75)	3.1 (0.39)	1.7 (0.30)	6.5 (0.54)	28.2 (1.07)	63.6 (1.05)
Level of instruction[4]													
Elementary	1,602 (13.5)	1,725 (37.1)	1,726 (20.2)	1,779 (24.5)	2.1 (0.15)	42.6 (0.53)	47.1 (0.53)	7.6 (0.27)	0.7 (0.08)	9.4 (0.30)	29.2 (0.50)	39.0 (0.51)	22.4 (0.42)
General	1,019 (13.6)	1,100 (26.5)	1,078 (22.1)	1,097 (17.3)	2.1 (0.21)	45.0 (0.68)	45.5 (0.67)	6.9 (0.33)	0.5 (0.10)	9.4 (0.40)	28.8 (0.58)	39.9 (0.66)	21.9 (0.55)
Arts/music	[5] (†)	103 (6.6)	82 (5.4)	99 (4.2)	1.4 (0.34)	49.1 (2.12)	42.9 (2.10)	5.5 (0.90)	1.1! (0.53)	9.1 (1.12)	29.7 (1.94)	37.0 (2.15)	24.2 (1.77)
English	33 (2.8)	104 (9.9)	92 (6.9)	117 (4.6)	1.9 (0.50)	35.4 (1.78)	51.3 (1.84)	10.4 (1.01)	1.0! (0.39)	7.7 (1.02)	25.5 (1.64)	39.0 (1.77)	27.8 (1.54)
ESL/bilingual	[5] (†)	24 (3.3)	51 (6.8)	48 (3.4)	1.8! (0.81)	32.9 (3.15)	51.2 (3.15)	13.3 (2.03)	0.9! (0.35)	8.8 (1.52)	29.8 (3.27)	39.3 (3.26)	22.1 (2.76)
Health/physical ed	[5] (†)	63 (6.0)	79 (8.1)	65 (3.5)	5.1 (1.27)	50.2 (2.32)	41.5 (2.40)	3.0 (0.76)	‡ (†)	7.6 (1.25)	24.1 (2.07)	38.9 (2.59)	29.4 (2.24)
Mathematics	26 (2.5)	28 (3.8)	32 (6.5)	36 (2.3)	2.7! (0.88)	43.1 (3.17)	48.0 (3.31)	6.2 (1.60)	‡ (†)	7.5 (1.44)	31.2 (3.18)	41.4 (3.31)	19.8 (2.40)
Science	[5] (†)	15 (3.4)	18 (3.3)	23 (1.8)	4.3! (1.48)	45.8 (3.88)	44.9 (3.98)	3.8! (1.23)	‡ (†)	8.6! (2.62)	29.3 (3.61)	42.9 (3.52)	19.2 (3.37)
Special education	210 (5.8)	230 (13.0)	239 (10.3)	235 (6.3)	1.2 (0.23)	33.9 (1.34)	53.2 (1.40)	10.3 (0.82)	1.3 (0.35)	11.8 (0.82)	33.6 (1.29)	34.8 (1.31)	19.8 (1.05)
Other elementary	314 (8.4)	58 (4.2)	55 (5.2)	60 (3.0)	2.3 (0.49)	32.4 (2.47)	54.2 (2.66)	9.5 (1.38)	1.4! (0.65)	6.8 (1.23)	29.9 (2.31)	38.9 (2.46)	24.4 (2.08)
Secondary	1,401 (17.7)	1,680 (39.0)	1,659 (37.8)	1,766 (25.2)	3.4 (0.16)	36.0 (0.49)	51.3 (0.49)	7.7 (0.26)	1.6 (0.11)	8.6 (0.23)	27.4 (0.41)	40.9 (0.45)	23.2 (0.43)
Arts/music	[6] (†)	121 (6.2)	121 (5.6)	130 (4.5)	3.3 (0.69)	44.8 (1.58)	44.6 (1.59)	5.8 (0.72)	1.4 (0.28)	9.7 (1.03)	28.6 (1.39)	35.9 (1.31)	25.9 (1.38)
English	235 (5.0)	306 (10.0)	289 (9.9)	294 (6.6)	1.5 (0.28)	34.1 (0.98)	54.2 (0.95)	8.4 (0.64)	1.8 (0.27)	8.4 (0.55)	27.6 (0.98)	41.2 (1.06)	22.7 (0.87)
ESL/bilingual	[6] (†)	21 (2.5)	20 (2.4)	24 (1.9)	‡ (†)	24.0 (3.58)	58.1 (3.98)	14.7 (2.79)	1.7! (0.85)	6.8 (1.33)	25.8 (3.30)	43.7 (3.66)	23.6 (3.35)
Foreign language	[6] (†)	78 (5.0)	88 (4.5)	85 (3.5)	0.8 (0.22)	31.3 (1.89)	57.5 (1.90)	7.5 (0.99)	2.9 (0.65)	8.7 (1.47)	26.0 (1.62)	43.8 (1.93)	21.5 (1.55)
Health/physical ed	[6] (†)	119 (5.7)	101 (3.9)	97 (3.2)	2.8 (0.57)	45.0 (1.73)	47.7 (1.66)	4.0 (0.85)	0.4! (0.17)	5.6 (0.69)	22.3 (1.19)	41.7 (1.59)	30.4 (1.46)
Mathematics	191 (4.3)	252 (9.1)	250 (7.5)	265 (6.6)	2.5 (0.35)	37.5 (1.10)	53.1 (1.12)	5.8 (0.48)	1.1 (0.21)	8.9 (0.62)	28.3 (0.93)	40.9 (1.09)	21.8 (0.94)
Science	159 (3.7)	195 (8.3)	209 (6.1)	220 (5.6)	2.9 (0.41)	33.7 (1.27)	54.5 (1.32)	6.4 (0.64)	2.5 (0.32)	9.1 (0.67)	27.1 (1.12)	42.5 (1.20)	21.3 (1.05)
Social studies	147 (4.3)	209 (9.9)	197 (6.3)	214 (5.2)	2.2 (0.29)	35.9 (1.28)	53.3 (1.31)	6.8 (0.59)	1.8 (0.34)	8.0 (0.60)	27.3 (1.13)	42.8 (1.19)	21.9 (0.97)
Special education	99 (2.3)	165 (9.7)	191 (12.2)	199 (5.5)	2.6 (0.43)	30.7 (1.13)	50.9 (1.32)	14.6 (0.97)	1.2 (0.30)	9.3 (0.73)	30.6 (1.14)	37.3 (1.36)	22.8 (1.31)
Vocational/technical	125 (3.2)	164 (6.3)	147 (5.7)	139 (4.4)	14.4 (1.14)	37.8 (1.59)	40.1 (1.40)	6.0 (0.68)	1.7 (0.32)	9.3 (0.76)	27.6 (1.34)	40.9 (1.39)	22.2 (1.19)
Other secondary	443 (8.5)	47 (3.4)	46 (4.0)	98 (3.9)	4.3 (0.71)	37.6 (1.66)	49.0 (1.72)	8.4 (1.01)	0.7! (0.23)	7.6 (0.89)	23.5 (1.42)	41.4 (1.82)	27.6 (1.60)

See notes at end of table.

Table 209.20. Number, highest degree, and years of teaching experience of teachers in public and private elementary and secondary schools, by selected teacher characteristics: Selected years, 1999–2000 through 2017–18—Continued

[Standard errors appear in parentheses]

Selected teacher characteristic	Number of teachers (in thousands)				Percent of teachers, by highest degree earned, 2017–18					Percent of teachers, by years of full-time and part-time teaching experience, 2017–18			
	1999–2000	2007–08	2011–12	2017–18	Less than bachelor's	Bachelor's	Master's	Education specialist[1]	Doctor's	Less than 3	3 to 9	10 to 20	Over 20
1	2	3	4	5	6	7	8	9	10	11	12	13	14
Private schools													
Total	**449 (10.6)**	**490 (9.2)**	**465 (11.1)**	**509 (9.1)**	**10.0 (0.53)**	**42.4 (0.83)**	**40.0 (0.80)**	**4.8 (0.33)**	**2.8 (0.23)**	**12.1 (0.45)**	**29.8 (0.74)**	**32.9 (0.71)**	**25.2 (0.67)**
Sex													
Male	107 (3.8)	127 (4.6)	117 (6.9)	133 (4.1)	8.7 (0.87)	37.6 (1.39)	44.0 (1.42)	3.8 (0.53)	5.9 (0.65)	12.0 (0.90)	30.1 (1.32)	31.6 (1.21)	26.3 (1.25)
Female	342 (7.7)	362 (7.7)	348 (10.1)	377 (7.3)	10.4 (0.60)	44.1 (0.97)	38.5 (0.90)	5.2 (0.41)	1.7 (0.19)	12.2 (0.54)	29.7 (0.86)	33.3 (0.86)	24.8 (0.77)
Race/ethnicity													
White[2]	402 (9.6)	423 (8.8)	411 (11.1)	433 (8.3)	9.3 (0.57)	42.2 (0.89)	40.7 (0.86)	4.8 (0.36)	2.9 (0.25)	11.3 (0.49)	28.8 (0.81)	33.4 (0.78)	26.6 (0.73)
Black[2]	17 (1.4)	20 (2.2)	17 (2.4)	16 (1.5)	10.1 (2.26)	48.1 (4.12)	34.4 (3.77)	5.4! (1.71)	‡ (†)	16.2 (3.56)	35.6 (4.14)	30.9 (3.99)	17.3 (2.94)
Hispanic[2]	21 (1.5)	29 (2.1)	24 (2.4)	37 (2.2)	15.1 (2.07)	45.2 (2.70)	33.0 (2.78)	5.1 (1.37)	1.7! (0.53)	17.7 (2.31)	34.3 (2.78)	30.2 (2.64)	17.8 (2.44)
Asian	‡ (†)	11 (1.5)	9 (1.4)	14 (1.4)	10.0 (2.25)	37.2 (4.40)	44.1 (4.38)	‡ (†)	3.3! (1.41)	15.3 (2.69)	37.9 (4.12)	32.2 (4.21)	14.5 (3.49)
Pacific Islander	— (†)	‡ (†)	‡ (†)	‡ (†)	‡ (†)	‡ (†)	‡ (†)	‡ (†)	‡ (†)	‡ (†)	‡ (†)	‡ (†)	‡ (†)
American Indian/Alaska Native	‡ (†)	‡ (†)	‡ (†)	‡ (†)	‡ (†)	‡ (†)	‡ (†)	‡ (†)	‡ (†)	‡ (†)	‡ (†)	‡ (†)	‡ (†)
Two or more races	— (†)	4 (0.6)	4 (0.9)	7 (0.9)	12.5! (5.41)	43.4 (6.37)	37.9 (6.04)	‡ (†)	3.9! (1.75)	15.5! (5.38)	41.1 (6.64)	24.3 (5.49)	19.2 (4.34)
Age													
Under 30	87 (3.1)	80 (3.9)	78 (6.8)	83 (3.5)	26.5 (1.64)	46.7 (1.80)	25.3 (1.42)	1.4! (0.41)	‡ (†)	42.2 (1.87)	57.6 (1.87)	‡ (†)	‡ (†)
30 to 39	101 (3.2)	109 (5.2)	112 (6.2)	124 (4.1)	7.3 (0.88)	40.9 (1.44)	44.3 (1.52)	4.2 (0.56)	3.3 (0.49)	11.7 (0.98)	46.9 (1.53)	41.3 (1.60)	‡ (†)
40 to 49	131 (4.2)	116 (3.6)	110 (6.3)	115 (4.0)	5.0 (0.67)	43.1 (1.56)	43.9 (1.56)	5.4 (0.65)	2.6 (0.39)	5.9 (0.60)	23.8 (1.39)	53.8 (1.64)	16.5 (1.19)
50 to 59	106 (3.2)	128 (4.5)	99 (5.0)	108 (3.8)	7.9 (0.85)	42.8 (1.69)	39.6 (1.72)	6.4 (0.82)	3.3 (0.52)	3.6 (0.49)	12.3 (0.99)	36.6 (1.51)	47.5 (1.51)
60 and over	25 (1.2)	56 (3.1)	66 (5.0)	79 (3.4)	6.8 (1.14)	38.7 (1.92)	43.4 (1.95)	6.4 (0.88)	4.6 (0.80)	2.0 (0.53)	6.6 (1.05)	18.3 (1.43)	73.1 (1.75)
Level of instruction[4]													
Elementary	261 (5.8)	258 (6.5)	245 (9.3)	262 (6.1)	11.7 (0.76)	48.3 (1.20)	34.2 (1.12)	5.1 (0.51)	0.8 (0.18)	12.6 (0.69)	29.5 (1.07)	33.3 (1.07)	24.6 (0.96)
General	168 (4.0)	163 (3.9)	151 (7.0)	154 (4.7)	11.5 (0.91)	51.1 (1.51)	32.8 (1.36)	4.1 (0.60)	0.6! (0.20)	12.3 (0.97)	30.4 (1.35)	33.1 (1.39)	24.2 (1.21)
Arts/music	(5) (†)	20 (1.6)	20 (1.8)	23 (1.8)	8.0 (1.97)	47.5 (3.81)	41.9 (3.87)	1.9! (0.85)	‡ (†)	10.0 (2.05)	22.5 (3.03)	37.2 (3.65)	30.4 (3.60)
English	(5) (†)	13 (1.2)	16 (2.8)	12 (1.3)	13.1 (3.61)	38.1 (5.07)	33.3 (5.01)	14.5 (3.29)	‡ (†)	13.1 (3.25)	26.0 (4.37)	27.9 (3.98)	33.1 (4.74)
ESL/bilingual	(5) (†)	(5) (†)	(5) (†)	‡ (†)	‡ (†)	‡ (†)	‡ (†)	‡ (†)	‡ (†)	‡ (†)	‡ (†)	‡ (†)	‡ (†)
Health/physical ed	(5) (†)	14 (1.7)	11 (1.2)	13 (1.1)	10.3! (3.11)	57.9 (4.39)	27.0 (3.86)	4.4! (2.02)	‡ (†)	8.9 (2.26)	33.1 (4.34)	31.7 (4.33)	26.3 (3.96)
Mathematics	(5) (†)	7 (1.0)	6 (1.1)	8 (1.2)	15.0 (4.04)	56.2 (6.27)	24.0 (4.92)	4.0! (1.85)	‡ (†)	18.3 (4.59)	26.2 (5.11)	35.9 (7.62)	19.6 (4.94)
Science	(5) (†)	6 (0.8)	5 (1.0)	8 (1.0)	‡ (†)	55.1 (6.75)	38.3 (6.64)	‡ (†)	‡ (†)	‡ (†)	28.7 (6.12)	42.2 (7.22)	20.6 (4.46)
Special education	16 (1.6)	9 (1.0)	10 (1.9)	16 (1.7)	10.0 (2.84)	33.2 (3.66)	44.5 (3.75)	11.8 (2.52)	‡ (†)	16.1 (2.84)	42.0 (3.73)	19.8 (3.31)	22.1 (3.44)
Other elementary	77 (2.2)	27 (2.3)	25 (2.8)	26 (2.0)	18.8 (3.29)	37.7 (3.74)	34.9 (4.09)	6.3 (1.88)	2.2! (1.00)	15.1 (3.23)	24.2 (2.96)	39.0 (3.83)	21.8 (3.16)
Secondary	188 (6.2)	231 (7.1)	219 (9.9)	247 (6.5)	8.1 (0.55)	36.2 (0.98)	46.1 (1.07)	4.5 (0.40)	5.0 (0.40)	11.7 (0.64)	30.1 (0.99)	32.4 (0.93)	25.8 (0.90)
Arts/music	(6) (†)	19 (1.8)	21 (2.2)	24 (1.7)	10.3 (1.85)	41.7 (3.04)	39.4 (3.07)	4.7 (1.28)	3.8 (1.10)	10.4 (1.65)	31.3 (3.00)	35.4 (3.14)	22.9 (2.90)
English	33 (1.7)	39 (2.8)	39 (4.1)	43 (2.1)	6.1 (1.27)	32.3 (2.19)	52.6 (2.45)	4.7 (0.82)	4.2 (0.89)	10.3 (1.44)	31.8 (2.44)	33.0 (2.16)	24.9 (2.22)
ESL/bilingual	(6) (†)	(6) (†)	(6) (†)	‡ (†)	‡ (†)	‡ (†)	‡ (†)	‡ (†)	‡ (†)	‡ (†)	‡ (†)	‡ (†)	‡ (†)
Foreign language	(6) (†)	22 (2.6)	22 (3.5)	24 (1.7)	6.9 (1.45)	35.9 (3.15)	47.8 (3.30)	4.7 (1.37)	4.6 (0.89)	11.5 (2.17)	26.1 (3.07)	34.0 (3.04)	28.3 (2.96)
Health/physical ed	(6) (†)	12 (1.8)	10 (1.8)	10 (0.9)	13.3! (4.32)	47.2 (4.92)	36.2 (4.49)	‡ (†)	‡ (†)	‡ (†)	24.9 (3.94)	33.5 (4.56)	21.6 (3.99)
Mathematics	33 (1.6)	36 (2.6)	38 (5.1)	41 (2.0)	6.4 (1.17)	39.5 (2.44)	45.5 (2.65)	3.3! (1.13)	5.3 (1.13)	9.4 (1.48)	30.5 (2.35)	31.8 (2.26)	28.4 (2.36)
Science	23 (1.3)	31 (1.9)	28 (2.7)	31 (1.7)	7.2 (1.23)	37.9 (2.90)	43.3 (2.98)	2.8 (0.82)	8.8 (1.31)	11.4 (1.52)	32.2 (2.85)	29.3 (2.53)	27.1 (2.63)
Social studies	19 (1.1)	31 (2.6)	28 (2.9)	29 (1.6)	5.3 (1.23)	31.4 (2.73)	51.7 (2.99)	3.7 (0.99)	7.9 (1.59)	10.9 (1.60)	29.0 (2.61)	33.2 (2.84)	27.0 (2.42)
Special education	7 (1.0)	6 (1.0)	9 (1.5)	10 (1.4)	9.5 (2.15)	31.1 (4.01)	50.7 (4.01)	7.8 (2.05)	‡ (†)	12.4 (2.76)	37.8 (5.21)	32.7 (4.38)	17.1 (3.47)
Vocational/technical	4 (0.6)	5 (0.8)	5 (1.2)	5 (0.7)	13.8! (4.54)	44.4 (7.28)	30.9 (7.02)	7.7! (3.27)	‡ (†)	19.9 (5.06)	17.0! (5.80)	36.3 (5.93)	26.7 (5.30)
Other secondary	69 (2.6)	29 (2.3)	20 (2.2)	30 (1.7)	12.5 (2.03)	33.6 (2.69)	43.3 (2.61)	6.9 (1.45)	3.6 (0.86)	14.1 (1.86)	30.7 (2.47)	29.4 (2.17)	25.8 (2.43)

—Not available.
†Not applicable.
!Interpret data with caution. The coefficient of variation (CV) for this estimate is between 30 and 50 percent.
‡Reporting standards not met. Either there are too few cases for a reliable estimate or the coefficient of variation (CV) is 50 percent or greater.
[1]Education specialist degrees or certificates are generally awarded for 1 year's work beyond the master's level. Includes certificate of advanced graduate studies.
[2]Data for 1999–2000 are only roughly comparable to data for later years, because the new category of Two or more races was introduced in 2003–04.
[3]Includes Pacific Islander for 1999–2000.
[4]Teachers were classified as elementary or secondary on the basis of the grades they taught, rather than on the level of the school in which they taught. In general, elementary teachers include those teaching prekindergarten through grade 6 and those teaching multiple grades, with a preponderance of grades taught being kindergarten through grade 6. In general, secondary teachers include those teaching any of grades 7 through 12 and those teaching multiple grades, with a preponderance of grades taught being grades 7 through 12 and usually with no grade taught being lower than grade 5.
[5]Included under Other elementary.
[6]Included under Other secondary.
NOTE: Excludes teachers who teach only prekindergarten. Data are based on a head count of full-time and part-time teachers rather than on the number of full-time-equivalent teachers reported in other tables. Detail may not sum to totals because of rounding and cell suppression. Race categories exclude persons of Hispanic ethnicity.
SOURCE: U.S. Department of Education, National Center for Education Statistics, Schools and Staffing Survey (SASS), "Public School Teacher Data File" and "Private School Teacher Data File," 1999–2000, 2003–04, 2007–08, and 2011–12; SASS, "Charter School Teacher Data File," 1999–2000; and National Teacher and Principal Survey (NTPS), "Public School Teacher Data File" and "Private School Teacher File," 2017–18. (This table was prepared November 2019.)

Table 209.21. Number and percentage distribution of teachers in traditional public and public charter elementary and secondary schools, by instructional level and selected teacher and school characteristics: 2017-18

[Standard errors appear in parentheses]

Selected teacher or school characteristic	Number of teachers (in thousands)							Percentage distribution of teachers				
	Total			Elementary		Secondary		Total			Elementary	
	Total	Traditional public	Public charter	Traditional public	Public charter	Traditional public	Public charter	Total	Traditional public	Public charter	Traditional public	Public charter
1	2	3	4	5	6	7	8	9	10	11	12	13
Total	**3,545 (23.5)**	**3,340 (23.8)**	**206 (7.7)**	**1,678 (24.0)**	**101 (5.0)**	**1,662 (25.6)**	**104 (5.0)**	**100.0 (†)**	**100.0 (†)**	**100.0 (†)**	**100.0 (†)**	**100.0 (†)**
Sex												
Male	834 (11.6)	785 (11.5)	48 (2.4)	190 (6.1)	11 (0.8)	595 (11.8)	38 (2.1)	23.5 (0.28)	23.5 (0.29)	23.5 (0.82)	11.3 (0.32)	10.6 (0.73)
Female	2,712 (20.2)	2,555 (20.4)	157 (6.2)	1,487 (21.9)	91 (4.7)	1,067 (18.0)	66 (3.4)	76.5 (0.28)	76.5 (0.29)	76.5 (0.82)	88.7 (0.32)	89.4 (0.73)
Race/ethnicity												
White	2,811 (22.7)	2,671 (22.8)	140 (5.5)	1,332 (21.9)	70 (3.8)	1,339 (22.8)	70 (3.6)	79.3 (0.35)	80.0 (0.37)	68.0 (1.20)	79.4 (0.60)	69.1 (1.56)
Black	239 (7.4)	217 (7.4)	21 (1.9)	107 (5.7)	11 (1.3)	110 (5.1)	11 (1.2)	6.7 (0.20)	6.5 (0.21)	10.4 (0.79)	6.4 (0.33)	10.6 (1.13)
Hispanic	331 (9.2)	299 (9.0)	32 (2.2)	166 (7.4)	16 (1.5)	133 (5.4)	16 (1.5)	9.3 (0.26)	9.0 (0.26)	15.6 (0.90)	9.9 (0.41)	15.5 (1.26)
Asian	75 (3.5)	69 (3.5)	6 (0.7)	34 (2.8)	2 (0.4)	35 (2.3)	4 (0.5)	2.1 (0.10)	2.1 (0.10)	3.0 (0.31)	2.1 (0.16)	2.4 (0.40)
Pacific Islander	8 (1.0)	8 (1.0)	‡ (†)	4 (0.8)	‡ (†)	4 (0.6)	‡ (†)	0.2 (0.03)	0.2 (0.03)	0.4 (0.12)	0.2 (0.05)	‡ (†)
American Indian/Alaska Native	18 (1.7)	18 (1.7)	‡ (†)	10 (1.5)	‡ (†)	8 (0.9)	‡ (†)	0.5 (0.05)	0.5 (0.05)	0.4 ! (0.13)	0.6 (0.09)	‡ (†)
Two or more races	63 (3.1)	58 (3.1)	5 (0.4)	25 (2.1)	2 (0.3)	33 (2.2)	3 (0.4)	1.8 (0.09)	1.7 (0.09)	2.3 (0.21)	1.5 (0.13)	1.8 (0.28)
Age												
Under 30	531 (9.4)	482 (9.5)	49 (2.6)	254 (8.1)	26 (1.9)	228 (6.5)	23 (1.4)	15.0 (0.24)	14.4 (0.25)	23.9 (0.87)	15.1 (0.42)	25.8 (1.27)
30 to 39	991 (12.9)	926 (12.4)	65 (3.0)	471 (11.0)	31 (2.0)	455 (9.0)	34 (2.0)	27.9 (0.29)	27.7 (0.30)	31.4 (0.83)	28.1 (0.48)	30.1 (1.27)
40 to 49	1,028 (12.3)	979 (12.5)	49 (2.4)	499 (10.3)	25 (1.7)	480 (10.2)	24 (1.6)	29.0 (0.32)	29.3 (0.33)	23.9 (0.82)	29.7 (0.49)	25.1 (1.16)
50 to 59	732 (11.6)	702 (11.4)	31 (1.9)	341 (9.0)	15 (1.2)	360 (8.9)	16 (1.3)	20.7 (0.29)	21.0 (0.30)	14.9 (0.69)	20.3 (0.44)	14.3 (0.95)
60 and over	263 (6.1)	251 (6.0)	12 (1.0)	113 (4.0)	5 (0.6)	139 (4.7)	7 (0.8)	7.4 (0.17)	7.5 (0.18)	5.9 (0.42)	6.7 (0.24)	4.7 (0.53)
Highest degree earned												
Less than bachelor's	97 (3.6)	90 (3.5)	7 (0.9)	33 (2.5)	3 (0.7)	57 (2.9)	3 (0.5)	2.7 (0.10)	2.7 (0.10)	3.2 (0.40)	2.0 (0.15)	3.4 (0.64)
Bachelor's	1,393 (15.8)	1,290 (15.5)	103 (4.6)	702 (13.8)	55 (3.0)	587 (11.5)	49 (2.9)	39.3 (0.36)	38.6 (0.38)	50.3 (1.10)	41.9 (0.55)	54.0 (1.64)
Postbaccalaureate	2,056 (19.4)	1,960 (19.4)	95 (4.2)	942 (16.2)	43 (2.9)	1,018 (19.3)	52 (2.8)	58.0 (0.38)	58.7 (0.39)	46.4 (1.12)	56.2 (0.56)	42.7 (1.66)
Master's	1,744 (17.5)	1,665 (17.6)	79 (3.5)	801 (14.6)	36 (2.4)	863 (17.1)	43 (2.4)	49.2 (0.36)	49.8 (0.38)	38.6 (0.97)	47.8 (0.56)	35.6 (1.44)
Education specialist[1]	271 (6.8)	258 (6.7)	13 (1.2)	129 (5.0)	6 (0.9)	129 (4.8)	6 (0.7)	7.6 (0.18)	7.7 (0.19)	6.3 (0.53)	7.7 (0.28)	6.3 (0.84)
Doctor's	41 (2.5)	38 (2.5)	3 (0.4)	12 (1.5)	‡ (†)	26 (2.0)	2 (0.4)	1.2 (0.07)	1.1 (0.07)	1.6 (0.21)	0.7 (0.09)	0.8 (0.22)
Years of full-time and part-time teaching experience												
Less than 3	318 (7.2)	285 (6.9)	34 (2.0)	150 (5.8)	17 (1.4)	135 (4.7)	17 (1.2)	9.0 (0.19)	8.5 (0.19)	16.3 (0.76)	8.9 (0.31)	16.4 (1.13)
3 to 9	1,003 (14.1)	917 (14.0)	87 (3.9)	474 (11.4)	45 (2.5)	442 (9.4)	41 (2.3)	28.3 (0.34)	27.4 (0.36)	42.1 (0.94)	28.3 (0.51)	44.5 (1.35)
10 to 20	1,416 (14.4)	1,353 (14.1)	63 (2.8)	665 (12.6)	29 (2.0)	688 (13.2)	34 (2.1)	39.9 (0.35)	40.5 (0.36)	30.5 (0.90)	39.6 (0.52)	28.7 (1.25)
Over 20	808 (11.8)	785 (11.7)	23 (1.6)	389 (8.8)	11 (1.1)	397 (9.8)	12 (1.1)	22.8 (0.29)	23.5 (0.30)	11.1 (0.63)	23.2 (0.43)	10.4 (0.90)
Certification type[2]												
Regular	3,205 (22.0)	3,048 (21.9)	157 (6.1)	1,545 (22.6)	80 (4.3)	1,503 (23.4)	78 (4.0)	90.4 (0.19)	91.3 (0.19)	76.5 (0.90)	92.1 (0.26)	78.4 (1.21)
Probationary	108 (4.0)	98 (3.9)	9 (0.8)	46 (2.8)	5 (0.5)	52 (2.5)	5 (0.5)	3.0 (0.11)	2.9 (0.11)	4.5 (0.33)	2.8 (0.17)	4.6 (0.49)
Provisional or temporary	137 (4.7)	121 (4.4)	16 (1.4)	54 (3.1)	8 (0.8)	67 (3.1)	9 (1.0)	3.9 (0.13)	3.6 (0.13)	7.9 (0.58)	3.2 (0.18)	7.5 (0.74)
Waiver or emergency	35 (2.0)	31 (2.0)	4 (0.4)	11 (1.2)	2 (0.3)	20 (1.5)	2 (0.3)	1.0 (0.06)	0.9 (0.06)	1.8 (0.19)	0.6 (0.07)	1.8 (0.27)
No certification	61 (2.8)	41 (2.5)	19 (1.4)	22 (1.8)	8 (0.8)	19 (1.6)	11 (1.0)	1.7 (0.08)	1.2 (0.07)	9.4 (0.59)	1.3 (0.11)	7.7 (0.74)
School locale												
City	1,032 (19.6)	932 (18.6)	100 (5.4)	496 (16.0)	49 (3.3)	436 (14.2)	52 (3.3)	29.1 (0.50)	27.9 (0.51)	48.7 (2.04)	29.6 (0.84)	47.9 (2.61)
Suburban	1,374 (23.6)	1,305 (23.9)	69 (5.1)	636 (17.9)	33 (3.1)	669 (21.4)	36 (3.5)	38.7 (0.63)	39.1 (0.64)	33.3 (2.03)	37.9 (0.89)	32.3 (2.38)
Town	413 (12.1)	398 (11.8)	15 (2.2)	199 (8.9)	7 (1.6)	199 (9.0)	8 (1.5)	11.6 (0.33)	11.9 (0.35)	7.1 (1.05)	11.9 (0.51)	6.6 (1.50)
Rural	727 (18.6)	705 (18.0)	22 (3.0)	347 (12.6)	13 (2.1)	358 (12.7)	9 (1.4)	20.5 (0.51)	21.1 (0.53)	10.8 (1.43)	20.7 (0.72)	13.2 (1.97)
Percent of students eligible for free or reduced-price lunch												
0 to 25	665 (19.1)	642 (19.1)	24 (2.9)	300 (12.6)	12 (1.8)	342 (14.9)	12 (2.1)	18.8 (0.52)	19.2 (0.55)	11.4 (1.33)	17.9 (0.73)	11.4 (1.67)
26 to 50	947 (21.5)	907 (21.3)	40 (3.4)	384 (13.7)	17 (2.0)	523 (15.8)	22 (2.5)	26.7 (0.60)	27.2 (0.62)	19.3 (1.56)	22.9 (0.73)	17.1 (1.83)
51 to 75	817 (18.2)	779 (17.6)	38 (3.5)	390 (13.4)	21 (2.6)	389 (13.6)	17 (1.9)	23.0 (0.50)	23.3 (0.52)	18.5 (1.53)	23.3 (0.74)	20.9 (2.21)
76 to 100	1,029 (23.0)	952 (22.1)	77 (5.0)	583 (16.9)	39 (3.3)	370 (13.2)	38 (3.2)	29.0 (0.59)	28.5 (0.60)	37.4 (1.86)	34.7 (0.85)	38.0 (2.53)
School does not participate	87 (6.5)	60 (5.9)	27 (2.9)	21 (3.6)	13 (2.0)	39 (4.6)	15 (1.6)	2.5 (0.18)	1.8 (0.18)	13.3 (1.35)	1.3 (0.21)	12.7 (1.91)

†Not applicable.

!Interpret data with caution. The coefficient of variation (CV) for this estimate is between 30 and 50 percent

‡Reporting standards not met. Either there are too few cases for a reliable estimate or the coefficient of variation (CV) is 50 percent or greater.

[1] Education specialist degrees or certificates are generally awarded for 1 year's work beyond the master's level. Includes certificate of advanced graduate studies.

[2] Refers to certification of teachers to teach in the state where they are currently teaching. A teaching certificate is probationary if all requirements have been satisfied except completion of a probationary period. It is provisional or temporary if additional coursework, student teaching, or passage of a test is required to obtain regular certification. It is a waiver or emergency certificate if a certification program must be completed to continue teaching.

NOTE: Excludes teachers who teach only prekindergarten. Data are based on a head count of full-time and part-time teachers rather than on the number of full-time-equivalent teachers reported in other tables. Teachers were classified as elementary or secondary on the basis of the grades they taught, rather than on the level of the school in which they taught. In general, elementary teachers include those teaching prekindergarten through grade 6 and those teaching multiple grades, with a preponderance of grades taught being kindergarten through grade 6. In general, secondary teachers include those teaching any of grades 7 through 12 and those teaching multiple grades, with a preponderance of grades taught being grades 7 through 12 and usually with no grade taught being lower than grade 5. Detail may not sum to totals because of rounding and cell suppression. Race categories exclude persons of Hispanic ethnicity.

SOURCE: U.S. Department of Education, National Center for Education Statistics, National Teacher and Principal Survey (NTPS), "Public School Teacher Data File," 2017–18. (This table was prepared November 2019.)

Table 209.22. Number and percentage distribution of teachers in public elementary and secondary schools, by instructional level and selected teacher and school characteristics: 1999-2000 and 2017-18

[Standard errors appear in parentheses]

Selected teacher or school characteristic	Number of teachers (in thousands)												Percentage distribution of teachers											
	Total				Elementary				Secondary				Total				Elementary				Secondary			
	1999-2000		2017-18		1999-2000		2017-18		1999-2000		2017-18		1999-2000		2017-18		1999-2000		2017-18		1999-2000		
1	2		3		4		5		6		7		8		9		10		11		12		
Total	**3,002**	**(19.4)**	**3,545**	**(23.5)**	**1,602**	**(13.5)**	**1,779**	**(24.5)**	**1,401**	**(17.7)**	**1,766**	**(25.2)**	**100.0**	**(†)**	**100.0**	**(†)**	**100.0**	**(†)**	**100.0**	**(†)**	**100.0**	**(†)**	**100.0**	
Sex																								
Male	754	(10.7)	834	(11.6)	185	(5.4)	201	(6.2)	569	(9.3)	633	(11.9)	25.1	(0.30)	23.5	(0.28)	11.5	(0.32)	11.3	(0.31)	40.6	(0.44)	35.8	
Female	2,248	(16.0)	2,712	(20.2)	1,417	(12.7)	1,578	(22.4)	832	(12.5)	1,134	(17.6)	74.9	(0.30)	76.5	(0.28)	88.5	(0.32)	88.7	(0.31)	59.4	(0.44)	64.2	
Race/ethnicity																								
White[1]	2,532	(17.2)	2,811	(22.7)	1,342	(13.8)	1,402	(22.3)	1,190	(15.8)	1,409	(22.6)	84.3	(0.30)	79.3	(0.35)	83.8	(0.50)	78.8	(0.56)	85.0	(0.34)	79.8	
Black[1]	228	(6.0)	239	(7.4)	122	(5.2)	118	(5.7)	106	(3.5)	121	(5.1)	7.6	(0.19)	6.7	(0.20)	7.6	(0.32)	6.6	(0.31)	7.5	(0.24)	6.8	
Hispanic[1]	169	(6.4)	331	(9.2)	95	(5.2)	182	(7.4)	74	(4.1)	149	(5.4)	5.6	(0.20)	9.3	(0.26)	5.9	(0.32)	10.2	(0.39)	5.3	(0.27)	8.5	
Asian[1,2]	48	(2.7)	75	(3.5)	30	(2.3)	37	(2.8)	18	(1.2)	38	(2.3)	1.6	(0.09)	2.1	(0.10)	1.9	(0.15)	2.1	(0.15)	1.3	(0.08)	2.2	
Pacific Islander	---	(†)	8	(1.0)	---	(†)	4	(0.8)	---	(†)	4	(0.7)	---	(†)	0.2	(0.03)	---	(†)	0.2	(0.04)	---	(†)	0.2	
American Indian/ Alaska Native[1]	26	(1.9)	18	(1.7)	13	(1.5)	10	(1.5)	13	(0.8)	8	(0.9)	0.9	(0.06)	0.5	(0.05)	0.8	(0.09)	0.6	(0.08)	0.9	(0.06)	0.5	
Two or more races	---	(†)	63	(3.1)	---	(†)	26	(2.1)	---	(†)	36	(2.2)	---	(†)	1.8	(0.09)	---	(†)	1.5	(0.12)	---	(†)	2.0	
Age																								
Under 30	509	(9.2)	531	(9.4)	270	(7.7)	280	(8.3)	239	(5.4)	251	(6.5)	17.0	(0.28)	15.0	(0.24)	16.9	(0.46)	15.7	(0.40)	17.1	(0.30)	14.2	
30 to 39	661	(9.8)	991	(12.9)	362	(7.1)	502	(11.4)	298	(5.9)	489	(9.1)	22.0	(0.29)	27.9	(0.29)	22.6	(0.42)	28.2	(0.45)	21.3	(0.33)	27.7	
40 to 49	953	(10.3)	1,028	(12.3)	521	(8.8)	524	(10.2)	432	(7.3)	504	(10.2)	31.8	(0.32)	29.0	(0.32)	32.5	(0.52)	29.5	(0.46)	30.9	(0.35)	28.5	
50 to 59	786	(12.6)	732	(11.6)	396	(9.5)	356	(9.1)	390	(8.1)	376	(9.0)	26.2	(0.35)	20.7	(0.29)	24.7	(0.52)	20.0	(0.42)	27.8	(0.47)	21.3	
60 and over	93	(4.0)	263	(6.1)	52	(3.6)	118	(4.0)	41	(1.7)	146	(4.7)	3.1	(0.13)	7.4	(0.17)	3.2	(0.21)	6.6	(0.23)	2.9	(0.12)	8.3	
Highest degree earned																								
Less than bachelor's	20	(1.3)	97	(3.6)	4	(0.8)	37	(2.7)	16	(0.9)	60	(2.9)	0.7	(0.04)	2.7	(0.10)	0.2	(0.05)	2.1	(0.15)	1.2	(0.07)	3.4	
Bachelor's	1,560	(15.8)	1,393	(15.8)	872	(13.3)	757	(14.2)	688	(10.1)	636	(11.6)	52.0	(0.40)	39.3	(0.36)	54.4	(0.65)	42.6	(0.53)	49.2	(0.47)	36.0	
Postbaccalaureate	1,422	(15.2)	2,056	(19.4)	726	(11.6)	985	(16.5)	696	(12.0)	1,070	(19.1)	47.4	(0.41)	58.0	(0.38)	45.3	(0.65)	55.4	(0.53)	49.7	(0.48)	60.6	
Master's	1,257	(13.9)	1,744	(17.5)	645	(10.9)	838	(14.7)	613	(10.7)	907	(17.0)	41.9	(0.38)	49.2	(0.36)	40.3	(0.61)	47.1	(0.53)	43.7	(0.44)	51.3	
Education specialist[3]	143	(5.2)	271	(6.8)	74	(4.2)	135	(5.2)	68	(2.9)	136	(4.8)	4.7	(0.17)	7.6	(0.18)	4.6	(0.26)	7.6	(0.27)	4.9	(0.19)	7.7	
Doctor's	22	(1.8)	41	(2.5)	7	(1.3)	13	(1.5)	15	(1.1)	28	(2.0)	0.7	(0.06)	1.2	(0.07)	0.4	(0.08)	0.7	(0.08)	1.1	(0.08)	1.6	
Years of full-time and part-time teaching experience																								
Less than 3	325	(7.7)	318	(7.2)	171	(6.3)	167	(6.0)	154	(4.5)	152	(4.9)	10.8	(0.24)	9.0	(0.19)	10.7	(0.38)	9.4	(0.30)	11.0	(0.27)	8.6	
3 to 9	854	(12.3)	1,003	(14.1)	458	(9.2)	519	(11.9)	396	(8.0)	484	(9.1)	28.5	(0.37)	28.3	(0.34)	28.6	(0.51)	29.2	(0.50)	28.3	(0.50)	27.4	
10 to 20	865	(10.1)	1,416	(14.4)	484	(8.5)	694	(12.7)	381	(7.1)	722	(13.3)	28.8	(0.33)	39.9	(0.35)	30.2	(0.51)	39.0	(0.51)	27.2	(0.39)	40.9	
Over 20	958	(13.5)	808	(11.8)	489	(9.6)	399	(8.9)	469	(9.0)	409	(9.7)	31.9	(0.36)	22.8	(0.29)	30.5	(0.52)	22.4	(0.42)	33.5	(0.43)	23.2	
Certification type[4]																								
Regular	2,599	(18.6)	3,205	(22.0)	1,407	(13.3)	1,624	(23.1)	1,192	(16.1)	1,581	(23.2)	86.6	(0.22)	90.4	(0.19)	87.8	(0.38)	91.3	(0.27)	85.1	(0.33)	89.5	
Probationary	83	(3.0)	108	(4.0)	41	(2.8)	51	(2.9)	42	(2.0)	57	(2.6)	2.8	(0.10)	3.0	(0.11)	2.6	(0.17)	2.9	(0.16)	3.0	(0.14)	3.2	
Provisional or temporary	97	(4.2)	137	(4.7)	54	(3.7)	61	(3.2)	43	(2.1)	76	(3.3)	3.2	(0.14)	3.9	(0.13)	3.3	(0.23)	3.4	(0.18)	3.1	(0.14)	4.3	
Waiver or emergency	51	(2.7)	35	(2.0)	27	(2.2)	13	(1.2)	25	(1.5)	22	(1.5)	1.7	(0.09)	1.0	(0.06)	1.7	(0.14)	0.7	(0.07)	1.8	(0.10)	1.3	
No certification	173	(5.4)	61	(2.8)	74	(3.7)	30	(2.1)	99	(4.1)	31	(1.8)	5.8	(0.18)	1.7	(0.08)	4.6	(0.22)	1.7	(0.11)	7.1	(0.28)	1.7	
School classification																								
Traditional public	2,985	(19.5)	3,340	(23.8)	1,591	(13.5)	1,678	(24.0)	1,393	(17.7)	1,662	(25.6)	99.4	(0.01)	94.2	(0.22)	99.4	(0.01)	94.3	(0.28)	99.5	(0.02)	94.1	
Charter school	17	(0.3)	206	(7.7)	10	(0.2)	101	(5.0)	7	(0.2)	104	(5.0)	0.6	(0.01)	5.8	(0.22)	0.6	(0.01)	5.7	(0.28)	0.5	(0.02)	5.9	
School locale																								
City	---	(†)	1,032	(19.6)	---	(†)	545	(16.4)	---	(†)	487	(14.7)	---	(†)	29.1	(0.50)	---	(†)	30.6	(0.81)	---	(†)	27.6	
Suburban	---	(†)	1,374	(23.6)	---	(†)	668	(18.2)	---	(†)	705	(21.2)	---	(†)	38.7	(0.63)	---	(†)	37.6	(0.85)	---	(†)	39.9	
Town	---	(†)	413	(12.1)	---	(†)	206	(9.0)	---	(†)	207	(9.1)	---	(†)	11.6	(0.33)	---	(†)	11.6	(0.49)	---	(†)	11.7	
Rural	---	(†)	727	(18.6)	---	(†)	360	(13.0)	---	(†)	367	(12.9)	---	(†)	20.5	(0.51)	---	(†)	20.2	(0.70)	---	(†)	20.8	
Percent of students eligible for free or reduced-price lunch																								
0 to 25	1,117	(20.4)	665	(19.1)	463	(13.0)	312	(12.6)	653	(14.9)	354	(15.1)	37.2	(0.59)	18.8	(0.52)	28.9	(0.81)	17.5	(0.68)	46.6	(0.83)	20.0	
26 to 50	719	(18.4)	947	(21.5)	399	(13.2)	401	(13.8)	320	(10.4)	546	(15.8)	24.0	(0.60)	26.7	(0.60)	24.9	(0.79)	22.5	(0.69)	22.9	(0.73)	30.9	
51 to 75	463	(15.8)	817	(18.2)	294	(12.7)	411	(13.4)	169	(8.8)	405	(13.9)	15.4	(0.52)	23.0	(0.50)	18.4	(0.76)	23.1	(0.70)	12.1	(0.59)	23.0	
76 to 100	390	(13.2)	1,029	(23.0)	275	(12.0)	621	(17.2)	114	(6.7)	408	(13.9)	13.0	(0.42)	29.0	(0.59)	17.2	(0.72)	34.9	(0.82)	8.2	(0.47)	23.1	
School does not participate	314	(11.4)	87	(6.5)	170	(10.8)	34	(4.0)	144	(5.7)	53	(4.8)	10.5	(0.39)	2.5	(0.18)	10.6	(0.69)	1.9	(0.22)	10.3	(0.38)	3.0	

---Not available.

†Not applicable.

[1] Data for 1999-2000 are only roughly comparable to data for 2017-18, because the new category of Two or more races was introduced in 2003-04.

[2] Includes Pacific Islander for 1999-2000.

[3] Education specialist degrees or certificates are generally awarded for 1 year's work beyond the master's level. Includes certificate of advanced graduate studies.

[4] Refers to certification of teachers to teach in the state where they are currently teaching. A teaching certificate is probationary if all requirements have been satisfied except completion of a probationary period. It is provisional or temporary if additional coursework, student teaching, or passage of a test is required to obtain regular certification. It is a waiver or emergency certificate if a certification program must be completed to continue teaching.

NOTE: Excludes teachers who teach only prekindergarten. Data are based on a head count of full-time and part-time teachers rather than on the number of full-time-equivalent teachers reported in other tables. Teachers were classified as elementary or secondary on the basis of the grades they taught, rather than on the level of the school in which they taught. In general, elementary teachers include those teaching prekindergarten through grade 6 and those teaching multiple grades, with a preponderance of grades taught being kindergarten through grade 6. In general, secondary teachers include those teaching any of grades 7 through 12 and those teaching multiple grades, with a preponderance of grades taught being grades 7 through 12 and usually with no grade taught being lower than grade 5. Detail may not sum to totals because of rounding. Race categories exclude persons of Hispanic ethnicity.

SOURCE: U.S. Department of Education, National Center for Education Statistics, Schools and Staffing Survey (SASS), "Public School Teacher Data File," "Charter School Teacher Data File," "Public School Data File," and "Charter School Data File," 1999-2000; and National Teacher and Principal Survey (NTPS), "Public School Teacher Data File," 2017–18. (This table was prepared November 2019.)

Table 209.24. Number and percentage distribution of teachers in public elementary and secondary schools, by whether they entered teaching through an alternative route to certification program and selected teacher and school characteristics: 2017-18

[Standard errors appear in parentheses]

Selected teacher or school characteristic	Number of teachers (in thousands)						Percentage distribution of teachers, by teacher or school characteristic						Percentage distribution of teachers, by alternative route status					
	Total		Entered through alternative route program? Yes		No		Total		Entered through alternative route program? Yes		No		Total		Entered through alternative route program? Yes		No	
1	2		3		4		5		6		7		8		9		10	
Total	**3,545**	**(23.5)**	**659**	**(10.3)**	**2,886**	**(22.3)**	**100.0**	**(†)**	**100.0**	**(†)**	**100.0**	**(†)**	**100.0**	**(†)**	**18.6**	**(0.28)**	**81.4**	**(0.28)**
Sex																		
Male	834	(11.6)	215	(5.6)	618	(9.9)	23.5	(0.28)	32.6	(0.71)	21.4	(0.29)	100.0	(†)	25.8	(0.57)	74.2	(0.57)
Female	2,712	(20.2)	444	(8.6)	2,268	(19.2)	76.5	(0.28)	67.4	(0.71)	78.6	(0.29)	100.0	(†)	16.4	(0.30)	83.6	(0.30)
Race/ethnicity																		
White	2,811	(22.7)	438	(7.9)	2,373	(20.9)	79.3	(0.35)	66.5	(0.79)	82.2	(0.34)	100.0	(†)	15.6	(0.26)	84.4	(0.26)
Black	239	(7.4)	85	(4.1)	153	(5.8)	6.7	(0.20)	12.9	(0.56)	5.3	(0.19)	100.0	(†)	35.8	(1.32)	64.2	(1.32)
Hispanic	331	(9.2)	102	(4.6)	229	(7.2)	9.3	(0.26)	15.5	(0.62)	7.9	(0.25)	100.0	(†)	30.8	(1.06)	69.2	(1.06)
Asian	75	(3.5)	14	(1.2)	61	(3.3)	2.1	(0.10)	2.2	(0.18)	2.1	(0.11)	100.0	(†)	19.2	(1.52)	80.8	(1.52)
Pacific Islander	8	(1.0)	2	(0.5)	6	(0.9)	0.2	(0.03)	0.3	(0.08)	0.2	(0.03)	100.0	(†)	26.7	(5.70)	73.3	(5.70)
American Indian/Alaska Native	18	(1.7)	3	(0.8)	15	(1.5)	0.5	(0.05)	0.5	(0.12)	0.5	(0.05)	100.0	(†)	19.0	(3.72)	81.0	(3.72)
Two or more races	63	(3.1)	14	(1.2)	49	(2.7)	1.8	(0.09)	2.1	(0.19)	1.7	(0.09)	100.0	(†)	21.7	(1.72)	78.3	(1.72)
Main teaching assignment																		
Elementary education	1,153	(17.3)	139	(5.5)	1,014	(15.6)	32.5	(0.45)	21.2	(0.73)	35.1	(0.47)	100.0	(†)	12.1	(0.42)	87.9	(0.42)
Special education	433	(7.7)	80	(3.4)	353	(7.2)	12.2	(0.19)	12.2	(0.49)	12.2	(0.23)	100.0	(†)	18.5	(0.74)	81.5	(0.74)
Arts and music	229	(5.9)	35	(2.1)	195	(5.4)	6.5	(0.16)	5.2	(0.31)	6.7	(0.18)	100.0	(†)	15.1	(0.85)	84.9	(0.85)
English and language arts	412	(7.8)	76	(3.2)	336	(7.0)	11.6	(0.21)	11.5	(0.46)	11.6	(0.22)	100.0	(†)	18.5	(0.70)	81.5	(0.70)
English as a second language	72	(3.9)	17	(2.0)	55	(3.2)	2.0	(0.11)	2.6	(0.30)	1.9	(0.11)	100.0	(†)	23.7	(2.33)	76.3	(2.33)
Foreign languages	95	(3.6)	27	(1.9)	69	(3.1)	2.7	(0.10)	4.1	(0.28)	2.4	(0.10)	100.0	(†)	28.1	(1.65)	71.9	(1.65)
Health education	162	(4.4)	21	(1.8)	141	(4.2)	4.6	(0.12)	3.2	(0.27)	4.9	(0.14)	100.0	(†)	12.9	(1.06)	87.1	(1.06)
Mathematics and computer science	301	(6.6)	74	(3.3)	227	(5.5)	8.5	(0.18)	11.2	(0.47)	7.9	(0.19)	100.0	(†)	24.5	(0.91)	75.5	(0.91)
Natural sciences	242	(5.8)	71	(2.7)	171	(5.0)	6.8	(0.16)	10.8	(0.40)	5.9	(0.16)	100.0	(†)	29.3	(0.97)	70.7	(0.97)
Social sciences	224	(5.3)	42	(2.3)	182	(4.9)	6.3	(0.14)	6.4	(0.32)	6.3	(0.16)	100.0	(†)	18.8	(0.95)	81.2	(0.95)
Career or technical education	145	(4.5)	59	(2.9)	86	(3.3)	4.1	(0.13)	8.9	(0.40)	3.0	(0.11)	100.0	(†)	40.6	(1.47)	59.4	(1.47)
All others	76	(3.2)	18	(1.6)	58	(2.9)	2.2	(0.09)	2.8	(0.25)	2.0	(0.10)	100.0	(†)	24.2	(1.93)	75.8	(1.93)
School classification																		
Traditional public	3,340	(23.8)	607	(10.0)	2,733	(22.4)	94.2	(0.22)	92.0	(0.43)	94.7	(0.20)	100.0	(†)	18.2	(0.28)	81.8	(0.28)
Charter school	206	(7.7)	53	(2.9)	153	(5.8)	5.8	(0.22)	8.0	(0.43)	5.3	(0.20)	100.0	(†)	25.6	(0.96)	74.4	(0.96)
School level																		
Elementary	1,689	(25.8)	229	(7.2)	1,460	(23.2)	47.6	(0.66)	34.8	(0.90)	50.6	(0.69)	100.0	(†)	13.6	(0.37)	86.4	(0.37)
Middle	629	(18.9)	133	(6.2)	496	(15.3)	17.7	(0.52)	20.1	(0.90)	17.2	(0.52)	100.0	(†)	21.1	(0.73)	78.9	(0.73)
High	982	(24.8)	246	(8.2)	736	(20.1)	27.7	(0.66)	37.3	(1.11)	25.5	(0.66)	100.0	(†)	25.0	(0.61)	75.0	(0.61)
Combined	246	(9.2)	51	(2.7)	194	(7.5)	6.9	(0.26)	7.8	(0.40)	6.7	(0.26)	100.0	(†)	20.9	(0.78)	79.1	(0.78)
Percent of minority students in school[1]																		
Less than 10 percent	396	(11.8)	40	(2.7)	356	(10.8)	11.4	(0.34)	6.3	(0.42)	12.5	(0.38)	100.0	(†)	10.1	(0.60)	89.9	(0.60)
10 to 24 percent	625	(16.2)	80	(3.5)	545	(14.8)	18.0	(0.46)	12.5	(0.52)	19.2	(0.51)	100.0	(†)	12.8	(0.49)	87.2	(0.49)
25 to 49 percent	828	(19.0)	138	(5.2)	691	(16.6)	23.8	(0.56)	21.6	(0.79)	24.3	(0.59)	100.0	(†)	16.6	(0.52)	83.4	(0.52)
50 to 74 percent	683	(19.6)	128	(5.8)	555	(16.8)	19.6	(0.52)	20.1	(0.82)	19.5	(0.53)	100.0	(†)	18.7	(0.68)	81.3	(0.68)
75 to 89 percent	362	(14.0)	86	(5.0)	275	(11.2)	10.4	(0.39)	13.6	(0.73)	9.7	(0.38)	100.0	(†)	23.9	(1.01)	76.1	(1.01)
90 percent or more	587	(17.3)	166	(6.3)	421	(13.4)	16.9	(0.48)	26.0	(0.85)	14.8	(0.46)	100.0	(†)	28.3	(0.74)	71.7	(0.74)
School locale																		
City	1,032	(19.6)	231	(6.7)	801	(16.6)	29.1	(0.50)	35.0	(0.86)	27.8	(0.53)	100.0	(†)	22.4	(0.52)	77.6	(0.52)
Suburban	1,374	(23.6)	239	(7.6)	1,135	(21.4)	38.7	(0.63)	36.2	(0.97)	39.3	(0.67)	100.0	(†)	17.4	(0.50)	82.6	(0.50)
Town	413	(12.1)	62	(3.3)	351	(10.7)	11.6	(0.33)	9.4	(0.49)	12.1	(0.36)	100.0	(†)	15.0	(0.68)	85.0	(0.68)
Rural	727	(18.6)	127	(5.2)	600	(16.1)	20.5	(0.51)	19.3	(0.73)	20.8	(0.54)	100.0	(†)	17.5	(0.58)	82.5	(0.58)
Percent of students eligible for free or reduced-price lunch																		
0 to 25	665	(19.1)	93	(4.8)	572	(17.2)	18.8	(0.52)	14.1	(0.71)	19.8	(0.57)	100.0	(†)	14.0	(0.62)	86.0	(0.62)
26 to 50	947	(21.5)	152	(5.6)	794	(18.6)	26.7	(0.60)	23.1	(0.81)	27.5	(0.62)	100.0	(†)	16.1	(0.47)	83.9	(0.47)
51 to 75	817	(18.2)	157	(6.3)	660	(15.7)	23.0	(0.50)	23.8	(0.88)	22.9	(0.52)	100.0	(†)	19.2	(0.64)	80.8	(0.64)
76 to 100	1,029	(23.0)	237	(7.8)	792	(19.2)	29.0	(0.59)	36.0	(0.96)	27.4	(0.61)	100.0	(†)	23.1	(0.60)	76.9	(0.60)
School does not participate	87	(6.5)	20	(2.0)	68	(5.4)	2.5	(0.18)	3.0	(0.29)	2.3	(0.19)	100.0	(†)	22.5	(1.75)	77.5	(1.75)

†Not applicable.

[1] Excludes the 2 percent of teachers for whom the percentage of minority enrollment in the school was not available. Minority enrollment is the combined enrollment of students who are Black, Hispanic, Asian, Pacific Islander, American Indian/Alaska Native, and of Two or more races.

NOTE: Teachers were asked whether they entered teaching through an alternative route to certification program, which is a program that was designed to expedite the transition of nonteachers to a teaching career (for example, a state, district, or university alternative route to certification program). Data are based on a head count of full-time and part-time teachers rather than on the number of full-time-equivalent teachers reported in other tables. Detail may not sum to totals because of rounding. Race categories exclude persons of Hispanic ethnicity.

SOURCE: U.S. Department of Education, National Center for Education, National Teacher and Principal Survey (NTPS), "Public School Teacher Data File," 2017-18. (This table was prepared May 2020.)

Table 209.30. Highest degree earned, years of full-time teaching experience, and average class size for teachers in public elementary and secondary schools, by state: 2011–12

[Standard errors appear in parentheses]

State	Total number of teachers (in thousands)	Percent of teachers, by highest degree earned: Less than bachelor's	Bachelor's	Master's	Education specialist[2] or doctor's	Percent of teachers, by years of full-time teaching experience: Less than 3	3 to 9	10 to 20	Over 20	Average class size, by level of instruction[1]: Elementary	Secondary
1	2	3	4	5	6	7	8	9	10	11	12
United States	**3,385.2 (41.42)**	**3.8 (0.24)**	**39.9 (0.52)**	**47.7 (0.57)**	**8.7 (0.28)**	**9.0 (0.29)**	**33.3 (0.52)**	**36.4 (0.51)**	**21.3 (0.54)**	**21.2 (0.18)**	**26.8 (0.22)**
Alabama	45.0 (2.61)	3.8! (1.51)	34.5 (2.69)	52.8 (2.81)	8.9 (1.64)	8.0 (1.28)	30.9 (2.75)	39.2 (2.85)	21.9 (2.34)	19.2 (0.42)	27.4 (0.94)
Alaska	7.5 (0.70)	4.4! (1.78)	45.6 (4.44)	41.9 (4.01)	8.2 (2.37)	12.9 (3.30)	30.8 (4.15)	39.6 (4.16)	16.7 (3.76)	18.3 (1.35)	18.7 (1.22)
Arizona	61.7 (2.61)	4.6 (1.16)	44.4 (3.67)	44.1 (3.49)	6.9 (1.71)	16.4 (2.29)	38.0 (2.75)	28.5 (2.60)	17.2 (2.02)	24.1 (0.67)	27.7 (0.96)
Arkansas	37.7 (2.01)	3.7! (1.45)	54.7 (3.36)	35.0 (3.13)	6.6 (1.72)	11.5 (2.03)	28.9 (3.38)	32.3 (3.93)	27.3 (3.37)	20.4 (0.73)	25.4 (1.69)
California	285.5 (7.27)	4.8 (0.91)	43.4 (2.33)	39.2 (2.18)	12.7 (1.56)	9.4 (1.29)	29.1 (2.13)	42.3 (2.25)	19.1 (1.89)	25.0 (0.52)	32.0 (0.53)
Colorado	55.9 (3.14)	2.8! (1.00)	36.1 (3.51)	49.9 (4.26)	11.2 (2.79)	10.8 (2.25)	33.4 (3.50)	42.9 (3.96)	12.9 (2.51)	22.8 (1.29)	29.1 (1.25)
Connecticut	44.9 (2.51)	‡ (†)	15.3 (1.86)	64.4 (3.01)	17.7 (2.37)	10.0 (1.43)	29.1 (2.66)	37.1 (2.43)	23.8 (3.34)	19.6 (0.68)	22.0 (0.71)
Delaware	9.3 (0.70)	4.0! (1.50)	34.5 (4.36)	49.7 (4.55)	11.8 (2.85)	12.6 (3.31)	35.0 (3.59)	33.8 (4.04)	18.6 (2.75)	20.3 (0.82)	25.8 (2.09)
District of Columbia	‡ (†)	‡ (†)	‡ (†)	‡ (†)	‡ (†)	‡ (†)	‡ (†)	‡ (†)	‡ (†)	‡ (†)	‡ (†)
Florida	‡ (†)	‡ (†)	‡ (†)	‡ (†)	‡ (†)	‡ (†)	‡ (†)	‡ (†)	‡ (†)	‡ (†)	‡ (†)
Georgia	123.3 (3.97)	3.4! (1.15)	29.5 (3.48)	43.5 (3.79)	23.6 (3.00)	6.3 (1.70)	34.2 (3.42)	39.8 (3.34)	19.7 (2.58)	21.0 (0.91)	27.5 (1.42)
Hawaii	‡ (†)	‡ (†)	‡ (†)	‡ (†)	‡ (†)	‡ (†)	‡ (†)	‡ (†)	‡ (†)	‡ (†)	‡ (†)
Idaho	16.3 (1.83)	4.6 (1.37)	55.6 (3.30)	35.3 (3.18)	4.4 (1.20)	10.4 (1.93)	30.4 (3.18)	35.2 (3.02)	24.0 (2.89)	24.5 (0.63)	25.4 (2.13)
Illinois	140.9 (9.09)	2.7! (0.81)	32.6 (2.53)	57.8 (2.44)	7.0 (1.34)	9.3 (1.56)	36.4 (2.59)	34.4 (2.85)	20.0 (2.51)	22.9 (1.26)	27.7 (1.00)
Indiana	64.0 (2.98)	2.2 (0.52)	43.6 (3.04)	47.4 (3.29)	6.9 (1.45)	10.0 (1.92)	26.1 (2.42)	35.6 (3.01)	28.3 (3.02)	21.4 (0.45)	27.3 (1.07)
Iowa	36.1 (2.28)	3.5! (1.22)	52.8 (3.89)	39.7 (3.60)	4.1! (1.26)	8.8 (1.85)	29.0 (2.98)	33.0 (2.77)	29.2 (2.55)	20.3 (0.93)	27.4 (1.35)
Kansas	36.5 (2.27)	3.8 (0.83)	43.8 (3.52)	47.0 (3.66)	5.4 (1.38)	12.5 (2.98)	27.4 (3.00)	32.7 (3.15)	27.4 (2.83)	20.4 (0.86)	24.6 (1.21)
Kentucky	46.8 (2.51)	5.1 (1.22)	17.5 (2.24)	57.5 (2.58)	20.0 (2.11)	10.1 (1.83)	32.2 (2.82)	38.5 (2.81)	19.2 (2.02)	23.3 (1.92)	26.6 (1.09)
Louisiana	44.5 (2.39)	3.5! (1.72)	61.9 (3.12)	27.0 (2.68)	7.6 (1.55)	8.6 (1.51)	31.2 (3.13)	33.4 (3.31)	26.8 (3.10)	19.0 (0.80)	23.4 (0.78)
Maine	18.4 (0.90)	4.9! (1.60)	46.3 (3.41)	42.8 (3.30)	6.0 (1.36)	5.8 (1.47)	24.1 (2.57)	39.4 (3.32)	30.6 (2.81)	17.6 (0.64)	19.9 (1.76)
Maryland	‡ (†)	‡ (†)	‡ (†)	‡ (†)	‡ (†)	‡ (†)	‡ (†)	‡ (†)	‡ (†)	‡ (†)	‡ (†)
Massachusetts	79.2 (4.42)	3.9 (1.08)	21.8 (2.33)	67.5 (2.54)	6.8 (1.48)	12.4 (1.96)	33.4 (3.04)	36.8 (3.02)	17.4 (3.09)	19.9 (1.72)	24.5 (1.18)
Michigan	96.7 (3.73)	2.3 (0.55)	29.8 (2.50)	62.9 (2.52)	5.0 (1.40)	7.3 (1.00)	31.4 (2.68)	42.7 (2.44)	18.7 (2.12)	23.8 (0.93)	28.9 (0.81)
Minnesota	62.3 (2.99)	4.4 (0.77)	35.3 (2.06)	50.1 (1.87)	10.2 (1.40)	9.5 (1.20)	27.4 (2.05)	40.3 (2.14)	22.9 (2.00)	22.8 (0.70)	29.9 (0.86)
Mississippi	37.6 (2.11)	5.3 (1.45)	54.4 (3.87)	35.2 (3.57)	5.1 (1.51)	10.3 (1.97)	41.0 (3.45)	30.5 (3.35)	18.2 (3.18)	21.6 (1.01)	22.8 (1.15)
Missouri	68.7 (2.34)	4.4 (0.91)	33.3 (2.90)	57.5 (2.96)	4.8 (0.94)	10.4 (1.90)	35.3 (2.21)	35.2 (2.31)	19.2 (2.31)	20.2 (0.83)	26.8 (1.18)
Montana	12.4 (0.90)	6.4 (1.52)	55.2 (3.34)	34.6 (3.39)	3.8! (1.66)	9.6 (2.33)	31.3 (3.17)	30.5 (3.04)	28.6 (3.65)	18.9 (0.80)	21.7 (1.81)
Nebraska	23.9 (1.73)	5.5 (1.31)	44.9 (3.29)	45.9 (3.15)	3.7 (0.98)	10.6 (1.74)	27.2 (2.52)	34.6 (2.63)	27.6 (2.54)	17.9 (0.72)	23.5 (0.99)
Nevada	25.2 (2.63)	4.5! (1.85)	25.1 (3.92)	49.8 (4.26)	20.6 (3.23)	6.5! (2.17)	39.0 (4.02)	36.2 (4.29)	18.2 (3.55)	25.3 (1.41)	34.5 (1.54)
New Hampshire	15.7 (1.05)	3.0! (1.12)	40.2 (3.49)	48.7 (3.55)	8.1 (1.82)	8.1 (1.54)	32.8 (3.41)	31.5 (3.57)	27.5 (3.54)	20.4 (3.09)	21.7 (1.16)
New Jersey	125.2 (4.16)	3.0 (0.74)	48.5 (2.47)	40.8 (2.30)	7.6 (1.60)	7.3 (1.24)	35.4 (2.45)	37.4 (2.66)	20.0 (2.03)	18.5 (0.81)	23.9 (0.68)
New Mexico	21.7 (2.83)	4.3! (2.01)	43.3 (3.80)	42.1 (3.72)	10.3 (2.82)	8.0! (2.46)	30.9 (3.73)	40.3 (5.11)	20.8 (5.19)	19.8 (0.76)	23.7 (1.58)
New York	241.4 (14.58)	2.8! (1.00)	4.4 (1.09)	84.2 (1.56)	8.6 (1.32)	5.3 (1.38)	30.0 (2.81)	45.5 (2.35)	19.1 (2.41)	20.7 (1.36)	25.1 (0.96)
North Carolina	104.3 (5.71)	4.1! (1.57)	54.2 (3.16)	33.8 (2.80)	7.8 (1.84)	8.4 (1.52)	35.8 (3.13)	34.8 (3.05)	21.1 (2.74)	18.8 (0.65)	25.8 (1.25)
North Dakota	10.3 (0.74)	6.9 (1.63)	59.2 (3.08)	30.1 (2.60)	3.9 (1.13)	12.2 (2.09)	24.6 (3.06)	30.6 (3.28)	32.6 (3.45)	17.8 (0.60)	19.2 (1.41)
Ohio	122.1 (4.29)	5.3 (1.17)	24.0 (1.79)	64.5 (2.16)	6.2 (1.28)	7.1 (1.11)	28.8 (2.48)	40.8 (2.67)	23.3 (2.00)	21.3 (0.99)	26.7 (0.85)
Oklahoma	46.2 (2.49)	4.3 (1.04)	65.6 (2.66)	26.9 (2.56)	3.2! (1.12)	9.8 (1.84)	30.1 (2.58)	36.9 (2.93)	23.3 (2.27)	20.7 (0.56)	23.7 (0.88)
Oregon	31.8 (1.28)	4.2! (1.53)	26.3 (3.18)	59.8 (3.62)	9.7 (1.94)	7.2 (1.54)	37.0 (3.58)	35.6 (3.58)	20.2 (2.45)	26.4 (0.96)	30.0 (1.05)
Pennsylvania	148.8 (7.48)	4.5! (1.94)	32.9 (2.52)	53.9 (3.34)	8.7 (1.77)	6.2 (1.78)	37.0 (2.55)	35.8 (2.17)	21.0 (2.30)	22.4 (0.99)	25.2 (0.96)
Rhode Island	‡ (†)	‡ (†)	‡ (†)	‡ (†)	‡ (†)	‡ (†)	‡ (†)	‡ (†)	‡ (†)	‡ (†)	‡ (†)
South Carolina	51.8 (1.76)	3.0! (1.34)	28.8 (3.14)	57.9 (3.95)	10.3 (2.15)	8.4 (1.58)	30.5 (3.22)	32.3 (3.54)	28.9 (3.38)	19.1 (0.75)	26.0 (1.98)
South Dakota	10.8 (0.92)	2.3! (0.73)	68.8 (3.52)	26.6 (3.13)	2.3! (1.14)	8.8 (1.65)	24.6 (2.76)	32.9 (3.63)	33.7 (3.38)	20.4 (0.66)	22.3 (1.31)
Tennessee	76.5 (2.91)	4.4! (1.52)	35.1 (3.54)	46.3 (3.44)	14.2 (2.83)	10.6 (1.80)	34.0 (3.66)	34.1 (3.48)	21.3 (3.28)	17.7 (0.52)	26.9 (1.60)
Texas	350.8 (22.99)	3.3 (0.65)	66.4 (2.09)	25.8 (2.12)	4.6 (0.77)	8.9 (0.95)	40.4 (2.05)	31.1 (1.88)	19.7 (1.74)	18.2 (0.82)	26.9 (1.07)
Utah	27.9 (1.67)	4.2 (1.10)	56.8 (3.96)	27.3 (3.88)	11.7! (3.94)	15.0 (2.43)	39.9 (4.49)	25.6 (4.52)	19.5 (3.12)	27.4 (2.09)	31.5 (1.29)
Vermont	9.4 (0.34)	6.6 (1.46)	35.4 (2.78)	52.0 (2.87)	6.0 (1.59)	12.9 (1.60)	22.1 (2.38)	37.0 (2.56)	28.0 (2.73)	16.6 (0.40)	19.8 (1.25)
Virginia	88.5 (3.35)	3.3! (1.07)	47.5 (3.08)	41.6 (3.17)	7.6 (1.26)	9.1 (1.68)	31.5 (3.20)	34.2 (2.73)	25.2 (2.43)	20.4 (1.27)	23.8 (0.90)
Washington	55.5 (3.15)	2.9 (0.59)	23.1 (2.61)	62.9 (2.92)	11.1 (1.96)	6.2 (1.45)	32.2 (3.00)	34.8 (2.82)	26.8 (3.03)	23.7 (0.60)	29.7 (0.99)
West Virginia	24.2 (0.79)	3.1 (0.90)	46.6 (4.82)	43.2 (4.71)	7.1 (1.73)	12.0 (2.26)	31.2 (4.12)	30.5 (3.82)	26.3 (3.24)	18.7 (1.00)	24.0 (1.65)
Wisconsin	66.8 (3.42)	2.7 (0.79)	36.7 (2.96)	55.1 (2.98)	5.5 (1.41)	10.5 (1.67)	26.2 (3.12)	42.1 (3.24)	21.3 (2.73)	20.8 (0.55)	27.9 (0.95)
Wyoming	8.5 (0.57)	7.0! (3.08)	44.3 (4.47)	41.2 (4.18)	7.5! (2.74)	7.6! (2.62)	25.2 (4.09)	35.1 (3.73)	32.1 (4.30)	17.0 (1.05)	19.6 (1.22)

†Not applicable.

!Interpret data with caution. The coefficient of variation (CV) for this estimate is between 30 and 50 percent.

‡Reporting standards not met. Data may be suppressed because the response rate is under 50 percent, there are too few cases for a reliable estimate, or the coefficient of variation (CV) is 50 percent or greater.

[1]Elementary teachers are those who taught self-contained classes at the elementary level, and secondary teachers are those who taught departmentalized classes (e.g., science, art, social science, or other course subjects) at the secondary level. Teachers were classified as elementary or secondary on the basis of the grades they taught, rather than on the level of the school in which they taught. In general, elementary teachers include those teaching prekindergarten through grade 5 and those teaching multiple grades, with a preponderance of grades taught being kindergarten through grade 6. In general, secondary teachers include those teaching any of grades 7 through 12 and those teaching multiple grades, with a preponderance of grades taught being grades 7 through 12 and usually with no grade taught being lower than grade 5.

[2]Education specialist degrees or certificates are generally awarded for 1 year's work beyond the master's level. Includes certificate of advanced graduate studies.

NOTE: Data are based on a head count of all teachers rather than on the number of full-time-equivalent teachers appearing in other tables. Excludes prekindergarten teachers. Detail may not sum to totals because of rounding and cell suppression.

SOURCE: U.S. Department of Education, National Center for Education Statistics, Schools and Staffing Survey (SASS), "Public School Teacher Data File," 2011–12. (This table was prepared May 2013.)

Table 209.50. Percentage of public school teachers of grades 9 through 12, by field of main teaching assignment and selected demographic and educational characteristics: 2017-18

[Standard errors appear in parentheses]

Selected demographic or educational characteristic	Total	Field of main teaching assignment: Arts and music	English or language arts	Foreign languages	Health and physical education	Mathematics and computer science	Natural sciences	Social sciences	Special education	Vocational/ technical	All other
1	2	3	4	5	6	7	8	9	10	11	12
Number of teachers (in thousands)	1,167.3 (23.81)	95.7 (3.67)	169.0 (5.29)	70.1 (3.27)	65.8 (2.74)	167.9 (5.51)	141.5 (4.78)	140.0 (4.52)	134.7 (4.50)	122.4 (4.13)	60.2 (2.71)
Total	**100.0** (†)	**100.0** (†)	**100.0** (†)	**100.0** (†)	**100.0** (†)	**100.0** (†)	**100.0** (†)	**100.0** (†)	**100.0** (†)	**100.0** (†)	**100.0** (†)
Sex											
Male	40.0 (0.53)	41.8 (1.88)	23.2 (1.18)	21.8 (1.68)	66.3 (1.94)	40.1 (1.24)	43.6 (1.58)	61.3 (1.54)	25.0 (1.40)	45.1 (1.42)	40.9 (2.44)
Female	60.0 (0.53)	58.2 (1.88)	76.8 (1.18)	78.2 (1.68)	33.7 (1.94)	59.9 (1.24)	56.4 (1.58)	38.7 (1.54)	75.0 (1.40)	54.9 (1.42)	59.1 (2.44)
Race/ethnicity											
White	80.5 (0.59)	85.6 (1.23)	81.6 (1.04)	60.0 (2.10)	82.8 (1.54)	80.8 (1.20)	80.9 (1.30)	84.0 (1.09)	83.5 (1.10)	81.6 (1.32)	72.7 (2.00)
Black	6.2 (0.30)	4.4 (0.76)	6.9 (0.67)	2.5 (0.64)	7.6 (1.07)	6.2 (0.68)	5.5 (0.64)	4.7 (0.58)	6.6 (0.65)	9.0 (0.96)	8.5 (1.24)
Hispanic	8.1 (0.39)	5.0 (0.64)	7.1 (0.65)	29.7 (2.10)	6.5 (0.93)	7.2 (0.74)	6.9 (0.83)	6.9 (0.78)	5.6 (0.67)	5.9 (0.79)	11.6 (1.42)
Asian	2.3 (0.16)	1.9 (0.57)	1.7 (0.28)	5.8 (1.08)	0.9 (0.27)	3.3 (0.44)	3.3 (0.52)	1.2 (0.32)	1.4 (0.30)	1.1 (0.33)	2.5 ! (0.76)
Pacific Islander	0.3 (0.05)	‡ (†)	0.1 ! (0.04)	‡ (†)	‡ (†)	0.2 ! (0.09)	‡ (†)	0.3 ! (0.12)	0.4 ! (0.17)	‡ (†)	‡ (†)
American Indian/Alaska Native	0.5 (0.06)	0.4 ! (0.14)	0.2 ! (0.08)	‡ (†)	‡ (†)	0.4 ! (0.16)	0.5 ! (0.20)	0.9 ! (0.32)	0.6 (0.16)	0.4 ! (0.14)	0.7 (0.21)
Two or more races	2.1 (0.16)	2.5 (0.56)	2.4 (0.47)	1.4 ! (0.48)	1.6 ! (0.49)	1.9 (0.40)	2.5 (0.39)	2.0 (0.37)	1.9 (0.36)	1.7 (0.39)	3.2 (0.85)
Age											
Under 30	13.4 (0.35)	15.8 (1.25)	15.1 (0.94)	13.4 (2.14)	11.8 (1.20)	16.8 (1.02)	13.5 (1.03)	14.2 (1.01)	11.7 (1.12)	9.6 (0.89)	7.0 (1.05)
30 to 39	28.0 (0.42)	27.0 (1.66)	28.6 (1.13)	28.7 (1.95)	30.9 (1.69)	29.2 (1.35)	28.7 (1.38)	30.9 (1.39)	26.7 (1.36)	22.7 (1.21)	25.0 (2.28)
40 to 49	28.0 (0.48)	26.4 (1.74)	28.0 (1.16)	28.9 (1.99)	29.6 (1.79)	26.1 (1.20)	28.6 (1.40)	30.0 (1.28)	29.0 (1.41)	25.5 (1.31)	29.9 (2.22)
50 to 59	21.7 (0.46)	22.1 (1.56)	19.2 (1.08)	22.2 (1.81)	21.2 (1.57)	20.8 (1.17)	20.9 (1.18)	17.1 (1.14)	23.1 (1.29)	29.0 (1.44)	25.0 (1.94)
60 and over	8.9 (0.32)	8.7 (0.98)	9.1 (0.75)	6.9 (0.96)	6.6 (1.12)	7.0 (0.70)	8.3 (0.82)	7.8 (0.69)	9.6 (0.90)	13.2 (1.00)	13.0 (1.56)
Age at which first began to teach full time or part time											
25 or under	49.5 (0.63)	57.2 (1.81)	52.6 (1.40)	52.4 (2.22)	54.4 (2.10)	59.6 (1.39)	45.9 (1.61)	49.8 (1.39)	44.6 (1.39)	35.1 (1.49)	39.9 (2.16)
26 to 35	33.4 (0.52)	30.5 (1.65)	32.7 (1.32)	31.6 (1.98)	38.3 (2.04)	26.8 (1.22)	35.6 (1.41)	38.0 (1.39)	36.1 (1.32)	32.3 (1.36)	34.7 (2.09)
36 to 45	12.0 (0.33)	8.6 (0.94)	10.7 (0.78)	11.7 (1.60)	6.0 (0.81)	10.4 (0.76)	12.7 (1.04)	9.3 (0.80)	12.6 (0.94)	21.1 (1.33)	16.4 (1.61)
46 to 55	4.5 (0.22)	3.3 (0.66)	3.6 (0.51)	4.1 (0.71)	1.3 (0.34)	2.7 (0.38)	5.3 (0.61)	2.6 (0.49)	6.0 (0.76)	9.2 (0.87)	7.7 (1.15)
56 or over	0.6 (0.07)	0.3 ! (0.13)	0.4 ! (0.12)	‡ (†)	‡ (†)	0.5 ! (0.16)	0.5 ! (0.20)	0.3 ! (0.12)	0.6 ! (0.20)	2.4 (0.43)	1.3 ! (0.40)
Years of full-time and part-time teaching experience											
Less than 3	8.4 (0.27)	8.6 (0.96)	7.9 (0.68)	9.3 (1.70)	6.6 (0.94)	8.4 (0.74)	9.3 (0.86)	7.4 (0.71)	8.1 (0.85)	10.1 (0.82)	7.8 (0.99)
3 to 9	27.4 (0.49)	27.4 (1.54)	27.4 (1.24)	26.5 (1.85)	22.0 (1.39)	27.8 (1.17)	28.5 (1.38)	26.5 (1.32)	29.6 (1.35)	27.8 (1.45)	26.2 (2.01)
10 to 20	40.6 (0.50)	37.0 (1.69)	41.4 (1.35)	42.5 (2.18)	41.6 (1.98)	39.7 (1.30)	42.1 (1.49)	42.9 (1.49)	38.3 (1.58)	40.6 (1.49)	40.4 (2.39)
Over 20	23.6 (0.51)	27.0 (1.67)	23.4 (1.10)	21.8 (1.71)	29.8 (1.63)	24.1 (1.22)	20.2 (1.14)	23.1 (1.27)	23.9 (1.70)	21.5 (1.28)	25.6 (1.97)
Highest degree earned											
Less than bachelor's degree	4.0 (0.22)	2.9 (0.63)	1.7 (0.37)	0.9 (0.28)	2.9 (0.60)	2.6 (0.44)	3.2 (0.55)	2.3 (0.37)	3.1 (0.59)	16.0 (1.25)	4.4 (0.82)
Bachelor's degree	34.8 (0.65)	44.5 (1.84)	32.4 (1.35)	32.4 (2.02)	44.0 (2.06)	35.4 (1.39)	30.0 (1.53)	34.8 (1.59)	29.4 (1.36)	37.9 (1.69)	34.2 (2.28)
Master's degree	52.0 (0.62)	45.0 (1.87)	56.0 (1.37)	56.1 (2.11)	49.2 (2.09)	55.6 (1.44)	57.8 (1.62)	53.4 (1.65)	50.8 (1.55)	39.1 (1.45)	51.2 (2.31)
Education specialist[1]	7.6 (0.29)	6.2 (0.84)	8.3 (0.88)	7.3 (1.09)	3.4 (0.56)	5.3 (0.56)	6.2 (0.75)	7.5 (0.83)	15.7 (1.27)	5.3 (0.69)	9.2 (1.45)
Doctor's degree	1.7 (0.13)	1.3 (0.33)	1.6 (0.33)	3.3 (0.77)	0.6 ! (0.23)	1.2 (0.24)	2.8 (0.38)	2.0 (0.47)	0.9 (0.26)	1.6 (0.35)	1.1 ! (0.44)
Major field of study in bachelor's or higher degree[2]											
Arts and music	9.0 (0.29)	87.9 (1.20)	3.1 (0.45)	3.7 (0.74)	1.5 ! (0.47)	1.1 (0.21)	1.4 (0.38)	1.0 (0.27)	2.4 (0.47)	2.3 (0.50)	2.2 (0.49)
Education, elementary instruction	6.2 (0.24)	3.2 (0.64)	4.9 (0.54)	3.5 (0.62)	2.8 (0.79)	4.8 (0.54)	1.7 (0.30)	1.7 (0.32)	23.0 (1.43)	3.4 (0.48)	15.3 (1.27)
Education, secondary instruction	24.4 (0.52)	11.8 (1.31)	33.7 (1.66)	24.2 (1.89)	10.1 (1.22)	32.4 (1.25)	37.3 (1.42)	36.1 (1.42)	7.7 (0.77)	12.1 (0.98)	17.5 (1.67)
Education, special education	11.7 (0.33)	2.3 (0.59)	5.9 (0.56)	2.9 (0.66)	2.6 (0.49)	4.6 (0.65)	2.8 (0.52)	4.1 (0.68)	71.3 (1.31)	2.4 (0.43)	7.2 (1.13)
Education, other	17.3 (0.46)	11.3 (1.03)	18.8 (1.17)	19.6 (1.65)	18.1 (1.50)	18.1 (1.10)	14.8 (1.13)	20.7 (1.21)	17.9 (1.64)	15.5 (1.05)	17.6 (1.60)
English and language arts	16.4 (0.40)	5.2 (1.02)	75.9 (1.19)	14.4 (1.48)	3.4 (0.96)	2.4 (0.40)	1.2 (0.32)	4.6 (0.59)	12.1 (1.12)	3.9 (0.56)	21.7 (2.04)
Foreign languages	5.7 (0.26)	0.5 ! (0.19)	1.7 (0.31)	71.5 (1.89)	0.6 ! (0.23)	1.0 (0.26)	0.5 ! (0.15)	2.2 ! (0.80)	0.6 (0.18)	0.4 ! (0.16)	9.4 (1.59)
Health and physical education	7.9 (0.26)	1.4 ! (0.45)	1.3 (0.27)	2.1 (0.57)	80.0 (1.53)	2.0 (0.29)	3.8 (0.53)	4.3 (0.60)	7.1 (0.95)	4.1 (0.57)	8.9 (1.13)
Mathematics and computer science	10.4 (0.31)	‡ (†)	‡ (†)	2.1 ! (0.78)	0.8 ! (0.26)	62.0 (1.30)	3.1 (0.62)	0.6 ! (0.23)	2.1 (0.51)	3.2 (0.47)	4.6 (0.99)
Natural sciences	12.5 (0.33)	0.5 ! (0.19)	0.2 ! (0.08)	2.6 (0.60)	3.6 (0.92)	8.7 (0.74)	79.4 (1.20)	0.8 (0.24)	1.7 (0.36)	5.4 (0.70)	5.6 (0.99)
Social sciences	19.1 (0.43)	2.2 (0.46)	13.0 (1.02)	16.4 (1.56)	8.1 (1.23)	9.9 (0.83)	6.4 (0.67)	80.1 (1.19)	19.1 (1.27)	6.9 (0.82)	16.2 (1.60)
Vocational/technical education	12.0 (0.33)	4.0 (0.88)	3.9 (0.48)	6.3 (0.99)	4.2 (0.67)	10.4 (0.80)	6.6 (0.69)	4.6 (0.70)	7.1 (0.73)	59.2 (1.50)	12.7 (1.67)
Other field	13.6 (0.35)	7.6 (0.91)	14.2 (1.09)	17.6 (1.61)	13.7 (1.49)	12.4 (0.98)	9.4 (0.87)	10.8 (0.98)	15.3 (1.09)	12.3 (0.88)	34.3 (2.19)
No degree	4.0 (0.22)	2.9 (0.63)	1.7 (0.37)	0.9 (0.28)	2.9 (0.60)	2.6 (0.44)	3.2 (0.55)	2.3 (0.37)	3.1 (0.59)	16.0 (1.25)	4.4 (0.82)

†Not applicable.

!Interpret data with caution. The coefficient of variation (CV) for this estimate is between 30 and 50 percent.

‡Reporting standards not met. Either there are too few cases for a reliable estimate or the coefficient of variation (CV) is 50 percent or greater.

[1] Education specialist degrees or certificates are generally awarded for 1 year's work beyond the master's level. Includes certificates of advanced graduate studies.

[2] Data may sum to more than 100 percent because (1) a teacher who reported more than one major is represented in more than one field of study and (2) a teacher with multiple degrees in different fields of study is represented in more than one field of study.

NOTE: Race categories exclude persons of Hispanic ethnicity. Detail may not sum to totals because of rounding.

SOURCE: U.S. Department of Education, National Center for Education Statistics, National Teacher and Principal Survey (NTPS), "Public School Teacher Data File," 2017-18. (This table was prepared February 2020.)

Table 214.10. Number of public school districts and public and private elementary and secondary schools: Selected years, 1869–70 through 2017–18

School year	Regular public school districts[1]	Total, all public and private schools	Public schools[2]					Private schools[2,3]		
			Total, all public schools[4]	Total, schools with reported grade spans[5]	Schools with elementary grades		Schools with secondary grades	Total, all private schools[4]	Schools with elementary grades	Schools with secondary grades
					Total	One-teacher[6]				
1	2	3	4	5	6	7	8	9	10	11
1869–70	—	—	116,312	—	—	—	—	—	—	—
1879–80	—	—	178,122	—	—	—	—	—	—	—
1889–90	—	—	224,526	—	—	—	—	—	—	—
1899–1900	—	—	248,279	—	—	—	—	—	—	—
1909–10	—	—	265,474	—	—	212,448	—	—	—	—
1919–20	—	—	271,319	—	—	187,948	—	—	—	—
1929–30	—	—	248,117	—	238,306	148,712	23,930	—	9,275[7]	3,258[7]
1939–40	117,108[8]	—	226,762	—	—	113,600	—	—	11,306[7]	3,568[7]
1949–50	83,718[8]	—	—	—	128,225	59,652	24,542	—	10,375[7]	3,331[7]
1959–60	40,520[8]	—	—	—	91,853	20,213	25,784	—	13,574[7]	4,061[7]
1961–62	35,676[8]	125,634	107,260	—	81,910	13,333	25,350	18,374	14,762[7]	4,129[7]
1963–64	31,705[8]	—	104,015	—	77,584	9,895	26,431	—	—	4,451[7]
1965–66	26,983[8]	117,662	99,813	—	73,216	6,491	26,597	17,849[7]	15,340[7]	4,606[7]
1967–68	22,010[8]	—	—	94,197	70,879	4,146	27,011	—	—	—
1970–71	17,995[8]	—	—	89,372	65,800	1,815	25,352	—	14,372[7]	3,770[7]
1973–74	16,730[8]	—	—	88,655	65,070	1,365	25,906	—	—	—
1975–76	16,376[8]	—	88,597	87,034	63,242	1,166	25,330	—	—	—
1976–77	16,271[8]	—	—	86,501	62,644	1,111	25,378	19,910[7]	16,385[7]	5,904[7]
1978–79	16,014[8]	—	—	84,816	61,982	1,056	24,504	19,489[7]	16,097[7]	5,766[7]
1979–80	15,944[8]	—	87,004	—	—	—	—	—	—	—
1980–81	15,912[8]	106,746	85,982	83,688	61,069	921	24,362	20,764[7]	16,792[7]	5,678[7]
1982–83	15,824[8]	—	84,740	82,039	59,656	798	23,988	—	—	—
1983–84	15,747[8]	111,872	84,178	81,418	59,082	838	23,947	27,694	20,872	7,862
1984–85	—	—	84,007	81,147	58,827	825	23,916	—	—	—
1985–86	—	—	—	—	—	—	—	25,616	20,252	7,387
1986–87	15,713	—	83,421	82,316	60,811	763	23,481	—	—	—
1987–88	15,577	110,055	83,248	81,416	59,754	729	23,841	26,807	22,959	8,418
1988–89	15,376	—	83,165	81,579	60,176	583	23,638	—	—	—
1989–90	15,367	110,137	83,425	81,880	60,699	630	23,461	26,712	24,221	10,197
1990–91	15,358	109,228	84,538	82,475	61,340	617	23,460	24,690	22,223	8,989
1991–92	15,173	110,576	84,578	82,506	61,739	569	23,248	25,998	23,523	9,282
1992–93	15,025	—	84,497	82,896	62,225	430	23,220	—	—	—
1993–94	14,881	111,486	85,393	83,431	62,726	442	23,379	26,093	23,543	10,555
1994–95	14,772	—	86,221	84,476	63,572	458	23,668	—	—	—
1995–96	14,766	121,519	87,125	84,958	63,961	474	23,793	34,394	32,401	10,942
1996–97	14,841	—	88,223	86,092	64,785	487	24,287	—	—	—
1997–98	14,805	123,403	89,508	87,541	65,859	476	24,802	33,895	31,408	10,779
1998–99	14,891	—	90,874	89,259	67,183	463	25,797	—	—	—
1999–2000	14,928	125,007	92,012	90,538	68,173	423	26,407	32,995	30,457	10,693
2000–01	14,859	—	93,273	91,691	69,697	411	27,090	—	—	—
2001–02	14,559	130,007	94,112	92,696	70,516	408	27,468	35,895	33,191	11,846
2002–03	14,465	—	95,615	93,869	71,270	366	28,151	—	—	—
2003–04	14,383	130,407	95,726	93,977	71,195	376	28,219	34,681	31,988	11,188
2004–05	14,205	—	96,513	95,001	71,556	338	29,017	—	—	—
2005–06	14,166	132,436	97,382	95,731	71,733	326	29,705	35,054	32,127	12,184
2006–07	13,856	—	98,793	96,362	72,442	313	29,904	—	—	—
2007–08	13,838	132,656	98,916	97,654	73,011	288	30,542	33,740	30,808	11,870
2008–09	13,809	—	98,706	97,119	72,771	237	29,971	—	—	—
2009–10	13,625	132,183	98,817	97,521	72,870	217	30,381	33,366	30,590	11,941
2010–11	13,588	—	98,817	97,767	73,223	224	30,681	—	—	—
2011–12	13,567	129,189	98,328	97,357	73,000	205	30,668	30,861	28,184	11,165
2012–13	13,515	—	98,454	97,331	73,037	196	30,623	—	—	—
2013–14	13,491	131,890	98,271	97,290	73,223	193	30,256	33,619	30,919	11,110
2014–15	13,601	—	98,176	97,601	73,420	165	30,528	—	—	—
2015–16	13,584	132,853	98,277	97,586	73,546	197	30,828	34,576	31,630	12,669
2016–17	13,598	—	98,158	97,434	73,620	203	30,597	—	—	—
2017–18	13,551	130,930	98,469	97,568	73,686	188	30,160	32,461	29,616	12,371

—Not available.

[1]Regular districts exclude regional education service agencies and supervisory union administrative centers, state-operated agencies, federally operated agencies, and other types of local education agencies, such as independent charter schools.

[2]Schools with both elementary and secondary grades are included under elementary schools and also under secondary schools.

[3]Data for most years prior to 1976–77 are partly estimated. Prior to 1995–96, excludes schools with highest grade of kindergarten.

[4]Includes schools not classified by grade span, which are not shown separately.

[5]Includes elementary, secondary, and combined elementary/secondary schools.

[6]Excludes alternative schools, academies, hospitals, virtual schools, prisons, and juvenile detention facilities.

[7]These data cannot be compared directly with the data for years after 1980–81.

[8]Because of expanded survey coverage, data are not directly comparable with data for years after 1983–84.

SOURCE: U.S. Department of Education, National Center for Education Statistics, *Annual Report of the Commissioner of Education*, 1870 through 1910; *Biennial Survey of Education in the United States*, 1919–20 through 1949–50; *Statistics of State School Systems*, 1951–52 through 1967–68; *Statistics of Public Elementary and Secondary School Systems*, 1970–71 through 1980–81; *Statistics of Public and Nonpublic Elementary and Secondary Day Schools, 1968–69*; *Statistics of Nonpublic Elementary and Secondary Schools*, 1970–71; *Private Schools in American Education*; Schools and Staffing Survey (SASS), "Private School Questionnaire," 1987–88 and 1990–91; Private School Universe Survey (PSS), 1989–90 through 2017–18; and Common Core of Data (CCD), "Local Education Agency Universe Survey" and "Public Elementary/Secondary School Universe Survey," 1982–83 through 2017–18. (This table was prepared February 2020.)

Table 214.20. Number and percentage distribution of regular public school districts and students, by enrollment size of district: Selected years, 1979–80 through 2017–18

Year	Enrollment size of district									
	Total	25,000 or more	10,000 to 24,999	5,000 to 9,999	2,500 to 4,999	1,000 to 2,499	600 to 999	300 to 599	1 to 299	Size not reported
1	2	3	4	5	6	7	8	9	10	11
	Number of districts									
1979–80[1]	15,944	181	478	1,106	2,039	3,475	1,841	2,298	4,223	303
1989–90	15,367	179	479	913	1,937	3,547	1,801	2,283	3,910	318
1999–2000	14,928	238	579	1,036	2,068	3,457	1,814	2,081	3,298	357
2005–06	14,166	269	594	1,066	2,015	3,335	1,768	1,895	2,857	367
2006–07	13,856	275	598	1,066	2,006	3,334	1,730	1,898	2,685	264
2007–08	13,838	281	589	1,062	2,006	3,292	1,753	1,890	2,692	273
2008–09	13,809	280	594	1,049	1,995	3,272	1,766	1,886	2,721	246
2009–10	13,625	284	598	1,044	1,985	3,242	1,750	1,891	2,707	124
2010–11	13,588	282	600	1,052	1,975	3,224	1,738	1,887	2,687	143
2011–12	13,567	286	592	1,044	1,952	3,222	1,755	1,911	2,676	129
2012–13	13,515	290	588	1,048	1,924	3,227	1,751	1,908	2,678	101
2013–14	13,491	286	596	1,046	1,920	3,186	1,791	1,894	2,668	104
2014–15	13,601	288	609	1,046	1,898	3,221	1,766	1,880	2,687	206
2015–16	13,584	287	613	1,040	1,888	3,214	1,782	1,909	2,643	208
2016–17	13,598	287	613	1,044	1,908	3,236	1,776	1,926	2,647	161
2017–18	13,551	288	618	1,034	1,918	3,218	1,773	1,936	2,561	205
	Percentage distribution of districts									
1979–80[1]	100.0	1.1	3.0	6.9	12.8	21.8	11.5	14.4	26.5	1.9
1989–90	100.0	1.2	3.1	5.9	12.6	23.1	11.7	14.9	25.4	2.1
1999–2000	100.0	1.6	3.9	6.9	13.9	23.2	12.2	13.9	22.1	2.4
2005–06	100.0	1.9	4.2	7.5	14.2	23.5	12.5	13.4	20.2	2.6
2006–07	100.0	2.0	4.3	7.7	14.5	24.1	12.5	13.7	19.4	1.9
2007–08	100.0	2.0	4.3	7.7	14.5	23.8	12.7	13.7	19.5	2.0
2008–09	100.0	2.0	4.3	7.6	14.4	23.7	12.8	13.7	19.7	1.8
2009–10	100.0	2.1	4.4	7.7	14.6	23.8	12.8	13.9	19.9	0.9
2010–11	100.0	2.1	4.4	7.7	14.5	23.7	12.8	13.9	19.8	1.1
2011–12	100.0	2.1	4.4	7.7	14.4	23.7	12.9	14.1	19.7	1.0
2012–13	100.0	2.1	4.4	7.8	14.2	23.9	13.0	14.1	19.8	0.7
2013–14	100.0	2.1	4.4	7.8	14.2	23.6	13.3	14.0	19.8	0.8
2014–15	100.0	2.1	4.5	7.7	14.0	23.7	13.0	13.8	19.8	1.5
2015–16	100.0	2.1	4.5	7.7	13.9	23.7	13.1	14.1	19.5	1.5
2016–17	100.0	2.1	4.5	7.7	14.0	23.8	13.1	14.2	19.5	1.2
2017–18	100.0	2.1	4.6	7.6	14.2	23.7	13.1	14.3	18.9	1.5
	Number of students									
1979–80[1]	41,882,000	11,415,000	7,004,000	7,713,000	7,076,000	5,698,000	1,450,000	1,005,000	521,000	†
1989–90	40,069,756	11,209,889	7,107,362	6,347,103	6,731,334	5,763,282	1,402,623	997,434	510,729	†
1999–2000	46,318,635	14,886,636	8,656,672	7,120,704	7,244,407	5,620,962	1,426,280	911,127	451,847	†
2005–06	48,013,931	16,376,213	9,055,547	7,394,010	7,114,942	5,442,588	1,391,314	835,430	403,887	†
2006–07	48,105,666	16,496,573	9,083,944	7,395,889	7,092,532	5,433,770	1,363,287	840,032	399,639	†
2007–08	48,096,140	16,669,611	8,946,432	7,408,553	7,103,274	5,358,492	1,381,342	834,295	394,141	†
2008–09	48,033,126	16,634,807	9,043,665	7,324,565	7,079,061	5,329,406	1,392,110	832,262	397,250	†
2009–10	48,021,335	16,788,789	9,053,144	7,265,111	7,034,640	5,266,945	1,381,415	835,035	396,256	†
2010–11	48,059,830	16,803,247	9,150,912	7,318,413	6,973,720	5,215,389	1,372,759	833,764	391,626	†
2011–12	47,973,834	16,934,369	9,031,528	7,266,770	6,907,658	5,218,533	1,381,289	842,134	391,553	†
2012–13	48,033,002	17,101,040	8,967,874	7,300,285	6,817,724	5,232,487	1,377,490	841,150	394,952	†
2013–14	48,124,386	17,125,416	9,128,194	7,270,070	6,792,172	5,169,748	1,412,987	832,091	393,708	†
2014–15	48,390,432	17,267,232	9,275,438	7,270,961	6,740,298	5,214,007	1,393,249	831,703	397,544	†
2015–16	48,413,211	17,301,641	9,347,240	7,223,779	6,693,454	5,202,470	1,405,851	844,470	394,306	†
2016–17	48,599,865	17,353,942	9,363,219	7,274,211	6,748,580	5,214,673	1,397,636	851,548	396,056	†
2017–18	48,560,014	17,366,407	9,397,505	7,196,218	6,780,881	5,187,521	1,396,908	852,353	382,221	†
	Percentage distribution of students									
1979–80[1]	100.0	27.3	16.7	18.4	16.9	13.6	3.5	2.4	1.2	†
1989–90	100.0	28.0	17.7	15.8	16.8	14.4	3.5	2.5	1.3	†
1999–2000	100.0	32.1	18.7	15.4	15.6	12.1	3.1	2.0	1.0	†
2005–06	100.0	34.1	18.9	15.4	14.8	11.3	2.9	1.7	0.8	†
2006–07	100.0	34.3	18.9	15.4	14.7	11.3	2.8	1.7	0.8	†
2007–08	100.0	34.7	18.6	15.4	14.8	11.1	2.9	1.7	0.8	†
2008–09	100.0	34.6	18.8	15.2	14.7	11.1	2.9	1.7	0.8	†
2009–10	100.0	35.0	18.9	15.1	14.6	11.0	2.9	1.7	0.8	†
2010–11	100.0	35.0	19.0	15.2	14.5	10.9	2.9	1.7	0.8	†
2011–12	100.0	35.3	18.8	15.1	14.4	10.9	2.9	1.8	0.8	†
2012–13	100.0	35.6	18.7	15.2	14.2	10.9	2.9	1.8	0.8	†
2013–14	100.0	35.6	19.0	15.1	14.1	10.7	2.9	1.7	0.8	†
2014–15	100.0	35.7	19.2	15.0	13.9	10.8	2.9	1.7	0.8	†
2015–16	100.0	35.7	19.3	14.9	13.8	10.7	2.9	1.7	0.8	†
2016–17	100.0	35.7	19.3	15.0	13.9	10.7	2.9	1.8	0.8	†
2017–18	100.0	35.8	19.4	14.8	14.0	10.7	2.9	1.8	0.8	†

†Not applicable.
[1]Because of expanded survey coverage, data for 1979-89 are not directly comparable with figures for later years.
NOTE: Size not reported (column 11) includes school districts reporting enrollment of zero and school districts whose enrollment counts were suppressed because they failed data quality edits. Regular districts exclude regional education service agencies and supervisory union administrative centers, state-operated agencies, federally operated agencies, and other types of local education agencies, such as independent charter schools. Enrollment totals differ from other tables because this table represents data reported by regular school districts rather than states or schools. Detail may not sum to totals because of rounding.
SOURCE: U.S. Department of Education, National Center for Education Statistics, Common Core of Data (CCD), "Local Education Agency Universe Survey," 1979–80 through 2017–18. (This table was prepared March 2020.)

Table 214.30. Number of public elementary and secondary education agencies, by type of agency and state or jurisdiction: 2016–17 and 2017–18

State or jurisdiction	Total agencies		Type of agency: Regular school districts[1]		Regional education service agencies and supervisory union administrative centers		State-operated agencies		Federally operated agencies		Independent charter schools		Other agencies[2]	
	2016–17	2017–18	2016–17	2017–18	2016–17	2017–18	2016–17	2017–18	2016–17	2017–18	2016–17	2017–18	2016–17	2017–18
1	2	3	4	5	6	7	8	9	10	11	12	13	14	15
United States	**18,343**	**18,297**	**13,598**	**13,551**	**1,350**	**1,338**	**254**	**244**	**4**	**4**	**2,998**	**3,021**	**139**	**139**
Alabama	178	176	134	137	0	2	43	34	0	0	1	1	0	2
Alaska	54	54	53	53	0	0	1	1	0	0	0	0	0	0
Arizona	699	700	226	225	16	19	9	9	0	0	434	433	14	14
Arkansas	292	293	234	234	15	15	5	5	0	0	25	26	13	13
California	1,159	1,156	1,057	1,051	73	71	4	4	0	0	25	30	0	0
Colorado	267	270	178	178	83	86	4	4	0	0	2	2	0	0
Connecticut	205	205	169	169	6	6	6	6	0	0	24	24	0	0
Delaware	49	46	19	19	1	1	2	2	0	0	27	24	0	0
District of Columbia	61	63	1	1	0	0	1	1	0	0	59	61	0	0
Florida	76	77	67	67	0	0	2	2	0	0	2	3	5	5
Georgia	226	232	180	180	16	16	7	7	0	0	23	29	0	0
Hawaii	1	1	1	1	0	0	0	0	0	0	0	0	0	0
Idaho	160	162	115	115	2	2	3	3	0	0	40	42	0	0
Illinois	1,057	1,056	854	854	187	186	6	6	0	0	8	8	2	2
Indiana	423	427	294	294	30	29	4	3	0	0	93	99	2	2
Iowa	342	342	333	333	9	9	0	0	0	0	0	0	0	0
Kansas	317	317	307	307	0	0	10	10	0	0	0	0	0	0
Kentucky	186	186	173	173	9	9	3	3	0	0	0	0	1	1
Louisiana	185	201	69	69	0	0	6	7	0	0	105	121	5	4
Maine	268	271	249	252	8	8	2	2	0	0	9	9	0	0
Maryland	25	25	24	24	0	0	1	1	0	0	0	0	0	0
Massachusetts	431	432	326	326	26	25	1	1	0	0	78	80	0	0
Michigan	901	892	540	537	56	56	4	4	0	0	301	295	0	0
Minnesota	567	564	332	331	65	66	4	3	0	0	166	164	0	0
Mississippi	158	157	144	144	0	0	11	10	0	0	3	3	0	0
Missouri	566	566	518	518	0	0	6	6	0	0	38	38	4	4
Montana	487	485	401	399	77	77	4	4	0	0	0	0	5	5
Nebraska	284	279	245	244	34	30	5	5	0	0	0	0	0	0
Nevada	19	21	18	19	0	0	0	0	0	0	1	1	0	1
New Hampshire	301	305	180	180	97	101	0	0	0	0	24	24	0	0
New Jersey	678	681	565	567	20	21	4	4	0	0	88	89	1	0
New Mexico	157	151	89	89	0	0	6	6	0	0	62	56	0	0
New York[3]	999	1,011	689	689	37	37	6	6	0	0	267	279	0	0
North Carolina	306	314	115	117	1	1	4	4	3	3	167	173	16	16
North Dakota	226	225	178	178	45	44	3	3	0	0	0	0	0	0
Ohio	1,088	1,064	620	619	102	101	4	4	0	0	362	340	0	0
Oklahoma	600	595	513	512	0	0	3	3	0	0	31	28	53	52
Oregon	221	222	179	178	19	19	5	6	0	0	18	19	0	0
Pennsylvania	789	788	500	500	102	102	7	6	0	0	179	179	1	1
Rhode Island	63	63	32	32	4	4	8	8	0	0	19	19	0	0
South Carolina	101	101	84	84	11	11	3	3	0	0	1	1	2	2
South Dakota	167	166	150	149	14	14	3	3	0	0	0	0	0	0
Tennessee	146	147	146	147	0	0	0	0	0	0	0	0	0	0
Texas	1,228	1,225	1,025	1,025	20	20	3	3	0	0	180	177	0	0
Utah	156	160	41	41	4	4	3	2	0	0	108	113	0	0
Vermont	342	298	278	235	63	62	1	1	0	0	0	0	0	0
Virginia	222	210	130	132	71	57	20	20	1	1	0	0	0	0
Washington	332	334	299	299	10	10	0	0	0	0	8	10	15	15
West Virginia	57	57	55	55	0	0	2	2	0	0	0	0	0	0
Wisconsin	461	462	421	421	17	17	3	3	0	0	20	21	0	0
Wyoming	60	62	48	48	0	0	12	14	0	0	0	0	0	0
Jurisdiction														
Bureau of Indian Education	174	174	0	0	174	174	0	0	0	0	0	0	0	0
DoDEA[4]	8	—	0	0	0	0	0	0	8	—	0	0	0	0
Other jurisdictions														
American Samoa	1	1	1	1	0	0	0	0	0	0	0	0	0	0
Guam	1	1	1	1	0	0	0	0	0	0	0	0	0	0
Northern Marianas	—	—	—	—	—	—	—	—	—	—	—	—	—	—
Puerto Rico	1	1	1	1	0	0	0	0	0	0	0	0	0	0
U.S. Virgin Islands	2	2	2	2	0	0	0	0	0	0	0	0	0	0

—Not available.

[1]Includes both independent districts and those that are a dependent segment of a local government. Also includes components of supervisory unions that operate schools but share superintendent services with other districts.

[2]Includes public agencies that provide education but are not school districts, such as juvenile correctional institutions, sheriff's offices, hospitals, residential treatment centers, and university lab schools.

[3]New York City is counted as one school district.

[4]DoDEA = Department of Defense Education Activity. Includes both domestic and overseas schools.

SOURCE: U.S. Department of Education, National Center for Education Statistics, Common Core of Data (CCD), "Local Education Agency Universe Survey," 2016–17 and 2017–18. (This table was prepared February 2020.)

Table 214.40. Public elementary and secondary school enrollment, number of schools, and other selected characteristics, by locale: Fall 2014 through fall 2017

Enrollment, number of schools, and other characteristics	Total	City				Suburban				Town				Rural				Locale unknown
		Total	Large[1]	Mid-size[2]	Small[3]	Total	Large[4]	Mid-size[5]	Small[6]	Total	Fringe[7]	Distant[8]	Remote[9]	Total	Fringe[10]	Distant[11]	Remote[12]	
1	2	3	4	5	6	7	8	9	10	11	12	13	14	15	16	17	18	19
Fall 2014																		
Enrollment (in thousands)	50,010	15,235	8,042	3,319	3,874	19,882	17,072	1,821	989	5,680	1,436	2,694	1,549	9,213	5,310	2,881	1,022	†
Percentage distribution of enrollment, by race/ethnicity	100.0	100.0	100.0	100.0	100.0	100.0	100.0	100.0	100.0	100.0	100.0	100.0	100.0	100.0	100.0	100.0	100.0	†
White	49.6	29.5	20.4	32.5	45.8	50.6	48.7	60.7	64.4	64.2	67.8	65.4	58.9	71.6	66.9	79.6	73.3	†
Black	15.5	23.7	26.1	25.0	17.5	13.7	14.4	10.1	8.4	10.0	7.0	11.6	10.1	9.4	10.9	7.5	6.8	†
Hispanic	25.4	35.6	42.0	32.1	25.4	25.4	26.2	21.0	19.8	18.9	19.0	17.3	21.6	12.7	15.9	8.1	9.5	†
Asian	4.9	6.8	7.6	5.5	6.2	6.1	6.6	3.0	3.2	1.3	1.5	1.0	1.6	1.4	2.1	0.5	0.5	†
Pacific Islander	0.3	0.4	0.4	0.4	0.4	0.4	0.4	0.5	0.2	0.4	0.4	0.1	0.9	0.2	0.2	0.1	0.3	†
American Indian/Alaska Native	1.0	0.7	0.7	0.6	0.8	0.5	0.4	0.7	0.7	2.2	1.2	1.6	4.1	2.1	1.1	2.0	7.5	†
Two or more races	3.2	3.4	2.9	3.9	4.0	3.4	3.3	4.1	3.4	3.0	3.1	3.0	2.8	2.6	2.9	2.2	2.1	†
Students participating in English language learner (ELL) programs (in thousands)[13]	4,670	2,186	1,358	441	387	1,879	1,696	116	67	352	79	160	113	255	159	61	35	†
ELL program participants as a percent of enrollment[13]	9.3	13.8	16.2	12.2	10.2	8.8	9.1	6.2	6.7	6.2	5.9	5.9	6.8	3.5	4.5	2.2	3.6	†
Schools	98,176	26,560	13,870	5,745	6,945	31,099	25,966	3,217	1,916	13,391	2,949	6,299	4,143	27,126	10,422	10,315	6,389	†
Average school size[14]	525	591	593	599	579	655	673	579	537	445	500	448	398	350	528	286	165	†
Pupil/teacher ratio[15]	16.2	16.9	17.1	17.0	16.3	16.5	16.5	16.2	16.9	15.8	16.4	15.6	15.5	14.9	15.9	14.2	12.5	†
Enrollment (percentage distribution)	100.0	30.5	16.1	6.6	7.7	39.8	34.1	3.6	2.0	11.4	2.9	5.4	3.1	18.4	10.6	5.8	2.0	†
Schools (percentage distribution)	100.0	27.1	14.1	5.9	7.1	31.7	26.4	3.3	2.0	13.6	3.0	6.4	4.2	27.6	10.6	10.5	6.5	†
Fall 2015																		
Enrollment (in thousands)	50,112	15,276	8,276	3,368	3,632	19,903	17,095	1,819	989	5,630	1,422	2,670	1,538	9,303	5,434	2,855	1,014	3
Percentage distribution of enrollment, by race/ethnicity	100.0	100.0	100.0	100.0	100.0	100.0	100.0	100.0	100.0	100.0	100.0	100.0	100.0	100.0	100.0	100.0	100.0	100.0
White	48.9	29.1	20.2	32.6	46.0	49.7	47.8	59.9	63.6	63.6	67.1	64.8	58.3	70.8	65.9	79.3	73.1	48.7
Black	15.4	23.4	25.7	24.2	17.4	13.7	14.4	10.2	8.4	10.0	7.0	11.5	10.1	9.4	11.0	7.3	6.6	11.5
Hispanic	25.9	36.0	42.4	32.4	24.8	25.9	26.7	21.5	20.3	19.4	19.5	17.8	22.1	13.2	16.4	8.4	9.7	30.1
Asian	5.0	6.8	7.6	5.6	6.4	6.3	6.8	3.0	3.2	1.3	1.5	1.0	1.6	1.5	2.3	0.5	0.5	5.5
Pacific Islander	0.4	0.4	0.4	0.4	0.4	0.4	0.4	0.5	0.2	0.4	0.4	0.1	0.9	0.2	0.2	0.1	0.3	0.2
American Indian/Alaska Native	1.0	0.7	0.7	0.6	0.8	0.4	0.4	0.6	0.7	2.1	1.1	1.5	4.0	2.1	1.1	2.0	7.5	0.3
Two or more races	3.4	3.6	3.0	4.2	4.3	3.6	3.5	4.4	3.6	3.2	3.3	3.2	3.0	2.8	3.1	2.4	2.3	3.6
Number of English language learner (ELL) students (in thousands)[13]	4,795	2,217	1,402	452	363	1,941	1,754	119	68	365	81	164	120	272	173	64	36	#
ELL students as a percent of enrollment[13]	9.5	14.0	16.3	12.4	10.0	9.1	9.5	6.5	6.7	6.5	6.2	6.1	7.4	3.6	4.5	2.4	3.7	0.9
Schools	98,277	26,636	14,214	5,828	6,594	31,081	25,963	3,209	1,909	13,307	2,922	6,279	4,106	27,146	10,546	10,262	6,338	107
Average school size[14]	526	591	595	598	575	657	675	582	538	445	500	447	401	354	535	285	165	26
Pupil/teacher ratio[15]	16.2	16.8	17.1	16.8	16.3	16.5	16.5	16.4	16.8	15.8	16.3	15.7	15.4	14.9	15.9	14.3	12.5	11.8
Enrollment (percentage distribution)	100.0	30.5	16.5	6.7	7.2	39.7	34.1	3.6	2.0	11.2	2.8	5.3	3.1	18.6	10.8	5.7	2.0	#
Schools (percentage distribution)	100.0	27.1	14.5	5.9	6.7	31.6	26.4	3.3	1.9	13.5	3.0	6.4	4.2	27.6	10.7	10.4	6.4	0.1
Fall 2016																		
Enrollment (in thousands)	50,283	15,316	8,356	3,386	3,573	19,918	17,107	1,822	989	5,560	1,415	2,631	1,513	9,489	5,635	2,845	1,010	†
Percentage distribution of enrollment, by race/ethnicity	100.0	100.0	100.0	100.0	100.0	100.0	100.0	100.0	100.0	100.0	100.0	100.0	100.0	100.0	100.0	100.0	100.0	†
White	48.2	28.7	20.1	32.2	45.3	48.7	46.9	58.9	62.8	63.1	66.4	64.2	58.0	69.9	64.9	78.9	72.8	†
Black	15.3	23.2	25.3	23.9	17.4	13.6	14.3	10.3	8.3	9.9	7.0	11.3	10.0	9.4	11.0	7.2	6.4	†
Hispanic	26.4	36.4	42.5	33.3	25.0	26.5	27.3	22.1	20.8	19.8	19.9	18.3	22.2	13.8	17.2	8.7	9.8	†
Asian	5.1	6.9	7.8	5.2	6.4	6.4	7.0	3.1	3.3	1.3	1.5	1.0	1.6	1.6	2.4	0.5	0.5	†
Pacific Islander	0.4	0.4	0.4	0.4	0.4	0.4	0.4	0.4	0.2	0.4	0.4	0.1	0.9	0.2	0.3	0.1	0.3	†
American Indian/Alaska Native	1.0	0.7	0.7	0.6	0.8	0.4	0.4	0.6	0.6	2.1	1.1	1.6	4.1	2.0	1.0	2.0	7.7	†
Two or more races	3.6	3.8	3.2	4.4	4.6	3.9	3.8	4.7	3.9	3.4	3.6	3.4	3.2	3.0	3.3	2.6	2.5	†
Number of English language learner (ELL) students (in thousands)[13]	4,857	2,238	1,420	459	360	1,974	1,795	111	68	358	80	160	118	286	187	64	35	†
ELL students as a percent of enrollment[13]	9.6	14.0	16.2	12.4	10.1	9.3	9.7	6.3	6.9	6.5	6.4	6.0	7.4	3.8	4.7	2.4	3.6	†
Number of students with disabilities (in thousands)[13]	6,756	2,127	1,183	465	479	2,793	2,417	242	135	773	171	380	222	1,063	549	374	141	†
Students with disabilities as a percent of enrollment[13]	13.4	13.3	13.5	12.6	13.4	13.1	13.0	13.6	13.6	14.0	13.6	14.3	13.9	13.9	13.8	13.9	14.6	†

See notes at end of table.

Table 214.40. Public elementary and secondary school enrollment, number of schools, and other selected characteristics, by locale: Fall 2014 through fall 2017—Continued

Enrollment, number of schools, and other characteristics	Total	City				Suburban				Town				Rural				Locale unknown
		Total	Large[1]	Mid-size[2]	Small[3]	Total	Large[4]	Mid-size[5]	Small[6]	Total	Fringe[7]	Distant[8]	Remote[9]	Total	Fringe[10]	Distant[11]	Remote[12]	
1	2	3	4	5	6	7	8	9	10	11	12	13	14	15	16	17	18	19
Schools	98,169	26,658	14,315	5,865	6,478	31,068	25,950	3,218	1,900	13,148	2,912	6,205	4,031	27,295	10,791	10,193	6,311	†
Average school size[14]	528	591	596	597	574	656	674	580	538	444	500	446	399	358	541	285	165	†
Pupil/teacher ratio[15]	16.2	16.8	16.9	16.8	16.3	16.5	16.5	16.3	17.0	15.8	16.3	15.7	15.5	15.0	15.9	14.3	12.6	†
Enrollment (percentage distribution)	100.0	30.5	16.6	6.7	7.1	39.6	34.0	3.6	2.0	11.1	2.8	5.2	3.0	18.9	11.2	5.7	2.0	†
Schools (percentage distribution)	100.0	27.2	14.6	6.0	6.6	31.6	26.4	3.3	1.9	13.4	3.0	6.3	4.1	27.8	11.0	10.4	6.4	†
Fall 2017																		
Enrollment (in thousands)	50,345	15,283	8,386	3,313	3,584	19,939	17,123	1,826	990	5,522	1,409	2,614	1,500	9,601	5,755	2,841	1,005	†
Percentage distribution of enrollment, by race/ethnicity	100.0	100.0	100.0	100.0	100.0	100.0	100.0	100.0	100.0	100.0	100.0	100.0	100.0	100.0	100.0	100.0	100.0	†
White	47.6	28.4	20.1	31.7	44.6	47.9	46.0	58.0	62.0	62.6	65.8	63.7	57.6	69.2	64.0	78.5	72.6	†
Black	15.2	22.9	24.9	24.0	17.3	13.7	14.3	10.4	8.4	9.7	6.9	11.2	9.9	9.3	11.0	7.1	6.3	†
Hispanic	26.7	36.6	42.6	33.4	25.4	27.0	27.8	22.5	21.2	20.2	20.4	18.8	22.6	14.3	17.7	9.0	10.0	†
Asian	5.2	7.0	7.8	5.3	6.5	6.6	7.2	3.1	3.4	1.3	1.5	1.0	1.5	1.7	2.5	0.5	0.5	†
Pacific Islander	0.4	0.4	0.4	0.5	0.4	0.4	0.4	0.4	0.2	0.4	0.4	0.2	0.9	0.2	0.3	0.1	0.3	†
American Indian/Alaska Native	1.0	0.7	0.7	0.6	0.8	0.4	0.4	0.6	0.6	2.1	1.0	1.5	4.0	2.0	1.0	2.0	7.7	†
Two or more races	3.9	4.0	3.4	4.6	4.9	4.1	4.0	4.9	4.1	3.6	3.8	3.6	3.5	3.2	3.6	2.8	2.6	†
Number of English language learner (ELL) students (in thousands)[13]	4,953	2,275	1,451	456	367	2,015	1,831	116	68	360	80	163	117	303	196	68	39	†
ELL students as a percent of enrollment[13]	10.1	14.7	17.1	13.1	10.5	9.6	10.0	6.6	7.1	6.8	6.6	6.4	7.6	4.1	5.1	2.6	4.2	†
Number of students with disabilities (in thousands)[13]	6,953	2,195	1,227	468	499	2,870	2,481	252	137	789	173	390	226	1,100	564	389	147	†
Students with disabilities as a percent of enrollment[13]	13.8	13.8	14.0	13.1	13.9	13.4	13.3	13.9	14.0	14.4	13.9	14.7	14.2	14.4	14.2	14.4	15.0	†
Schools	98,480	26,781	14,564	5,731	6,486	31,217	26,112	3,208	1,897	13,098	2,890	6,198	4,010	27,384	10,943	10,175	6,266	†
Average school size[14]	528	589	588	599	580	657	674	586	543	445	502	445	400	362	546	286	165	†
Pupil/teacher ratio[15]	16.1	16.7	16.8	16.9	16.2	16.3	16.3	16.3	16.9	15.7	16.2	15.7	15.4	15.0	15.9	14.3	12.7	†
Enrollment (percentage distribution)	100.0	30.4	16.7	6.6	7.1	39.6	34.0	3.6	2.0	11.0	2.8	5.2	3.0	19.1	11.4	5.6	2.0	†
Schools (percentage distribution)	100.0	27.2	14.8	5.8	6.6	31.7	26.5	3.3	1.9	13.3	2.9	6.3	4.1	27.8	11.1	10.3	6.4	†

†Not applicable.
#Rounds to zero.
[1]Located inside an urbanized area and inside a principal city with a population of 250,000 or more.
[2]Located inside an urbanized area and inside a principal city with a population of at least 100,000, but less than 250,000.
[3]Located inside an urbanized area and inside a principal city with a population less than 100,000.
[4]Located inside an urbanized area and outside a principal city with a population of 250,000 or more.
[5]Located inside an urbanized area and outside a principal city with a population of at least 100,000, but less than 250,000.
[6]Located inside an urbanized area and outside a principal city with a population less than 100,000.
[7]Located inside an urban cluster that is 10 miles or less from an urbanized area.
[8]Located inside an urban cluster that is more than 10 but less than or equal to 35 miles from an urbanized area.
[9]Located inside an urban cluster that is more than 35 miles from an urbanized area.
[10]Located outside any urbanized area or urban cluster, but 5 miles or less from an urbanized area or 2.5 miles or less from an urban cluster.
[11]Located outside any urbanized area or urban cluster and more than 5 miles but less than or equal to 25 miles from an urbanized area, or more than 2.5 miles but less than or equal to 10 miles from an urban cluster.
[12]Located outside any urbanized area or urban cluster, more than 25 miles from an urbanized area, and more than 10 miles from an urban cluster.
[13]Data are based on locales of school districts rather than locales of schools as in the rest of the table. Data for 2014 and earlier years include only those ELL students who participated in ELL programs. Starting with 2015, data include all ELL students, regardless of program participation. Data exclude ELL students who are enrolled in prekindergarten.
[14]Average for schools reporting enrollment. Enrollment data were available for 95,230 out of 98,176 schools in 2014–15, 95,240 out of 98,277 schools in 2015–16, 95,306 out of 98,169 schools in 2016–17, and 95,265 out of 98,480 schools in 2017–18.
[15]Ratio for schools reporting both full-time-equivalent teachers and fall enrollment data.

NOTE: Detail may not sum to totals because of rounding. Race categories exclude persons of Hispanic ethnicity. Enrollment and ratios are based on data reported by schools and may differ from data reported in other tables that reflect aggregate totals reported by states.

SOURCE: U.S. Department of Education, National Center for Education Statistics, Common Core of Data (CCD), "Public Elementary/Secondary School Universe Survey," 2014–15, 2015–16, 2016–17, and 2017–18; CCD, "Local Education Agency Universe Survey," 2014–15, 2015–16, 2016–17, and 2017–18; and Education Demographic and Geographic Estimates (EDGE), "Public School File," 2015–16, 2016–17, and 2017–18. (This table was prepared November 2019.)

Table 215.30. Enrollment, poverty, and federal funds for the 120 largest school districts, by enrollment size in 2016: 2015-16 and fiscal year 2018

							Revenues by source of funds, 2015-16				Revenue from selected federal programs (in thousands), 2015-16						Federal Title I allocations (in federal fiscal year 2(			
Name of district	State	Rank order	Enrollment, fall 2016	5- to 17-year-old population, 2016	5- to 17-year-olds in poverty, 2016[1]	Poverty rate of 5- to 17-year-olds, 2016[1]	Total (in thousands)	Federal (in thousands)	Federal as a percent of total	Federal revenue per student[3]	Title I	School lunch	Individuals with Disabilities Education Act (IDEA)	Eisenhower math and science	Vocational education	Drug-free schools	Total	Basic Grants	Concentration Grants	Ta
1	2	3	4	5	6	7	8	9	10	11	12	13	14	15	16	17	18	19	20	
New York City	NY	1	984,462	1,245,611	328,553	26.4	$27,448,356	$1,739,101	6.3	$1,772	$656,226	$442,300	$291,052	$0	$13,209	$0	$786,291	$263,726	$63,591	$2
Los Angeles Unified	CA	2	633,621	715,436	194,823	27.2	10,329,380	1,091,400	10.6	1,707	356,168	368,564	125,629	38,351	7,877	0	426,351	128,870	31,074	
City of Chicago (SD 299)	IL	3	378,199	408,677	108,558	26.6	5,272,668	792,420	15.0	2,046	307,138	204,737	93,483	34,208	6,117	0	283,988	86,598	20,881	
Dade	FL	4	357,249	394,651	93,050	23.6	3,590,773	431,519	12.0	1,207	129,923	139,474	72,402	11,474	5,233	0	147,913	49,168	11,856	
Clark County	NV	5	326,953	367,926	69,496	18.9	3,220,684	277,628	8.6	852	93,953	105,672	43,115	5,706	4,008	0	106,449	36,988	8,919	
Broward	FL	6	271,852	295,468	48,843	16.5	2,607,068	278,292	10.7	1,034	63,140	83,798	57,031	9,849	2,872	0	74,139	25,870	6,238	
Houston ISD	TX	7	216,106	248,155	76,878	31.0	2,480,131	293,958	11.9	1,363	82,708	109,055	38,873	12,489	2,917	0	125,571	40,694	9,812	
Hillsborough	FL	8	214,386	228,744	43,271	18.9	2,098,358	308,427	14.7	1,455	70,281	84,928	45,151	8,465	2,883	0	65,509	23,144	5,581	
Orange	FL	9	200,674	213,379	44,506	20.9	2,253,016	219,981	9.8	1,117	62,310	80,993	39,806	7,004	2,499	0	66,586	23,484	5,663	
Palm Beach	FL	10	192,721	205,311	35,926	17.5	2,038,576	187,376	9.2	990	50,544	64,971	39,110	0	1,875	0	52,555	19,053	4,594	
Fairfax County	VA	11	187,467	197,292	13,070	6.6	2,733,933	126,061	4.6	678	18,754	34,053	33,107	2,445	1,710	0	23,210	8,290	1,999	
Hawaii Department of Education	HI	12	181,550	216,481	21,877	10.1	3,030,519	261,131	8.6	1,435	51,530	59,215	42,338	466	2,538	280	49,811	18,618	4,325	
Gwinnett County	GA	13	178,214	185,631	28,329	15.3	1,893,150	142,728	7.5	811	37,832	65,091	27,303	2,613	1,134	0	42,282	14,995	3,616	
Wake County	NC	14	160,467	190,315	19,440	10.2	1,380,356	109,144	7.9	691	26,914	30,191	31,734	2,757	0	0	28,950	10,336	2,491	
Montgomery County	MD	15	159,010	177,421	14,769	8.3	2,898,647	112,717	3.9	721	21,826	36,008	32,390	3,759	1,138	0	31,766	11,782	2,841	
Dallas ISD	TX	16	157,886	195,691	59,579	30.4	1,896,322	287,161	15.1	1,811	78,862	100,100	23,695	8,585	2,215	0	95,531	31,561	7,610	
Charlotte-Mecklenburg	NC	17	147,428	183,372	31,461	17.2	1,389,280	146,058	10.5	999	45,987	51,195	29,782	1,163	0	0	47,686	16,590	4,000	
Philadelphia City	PA	18	133,929	238,855	86,599	36.3	3,030,964	271,369	9.0	2,024	112,879	79,478	0	6,723	4,257	0	231,909	70,377	16,970	
Prince George's County	MD	19	130,814	144,242	17,574	12.2	2,206,548	145,009	6.6	1,125	36,153	56,104	28,191	4,257	39	0	38,354	14,023	3,381	
Duval	FL	20	129,479	147,336	28,913	19.6	1,211,671	150,524	12.4	1,165	39,064	47,889	36,787	5,070	1,294	0	42,289	15,701	3,750	
San Diego Unified	CA	21	128,040	138,882	25,011	18.0	1,790,524	151,427	8.5	1,170	35,955	49,465	24,725	8,279	1,103	0	44,091	15,904	3,835	
Cypress-Fairbanks ISD	TX	22	114,868	118,190	16,982	14.4	1,175,118	83,219	7.1	730	16,187	33,897	16,667	1,081	932	0	24,569	8,989	2,168	
Cobb County	GA	23	113,151	124,723	15,084	12.1	1,239,449	87,739	7.1	778	23,154	30,628	20,596	1,965	730	0	21,883	8,077	1,948	
Baltimore County	MD	24	112,139	130,717	13,929	10.7	1,782,381	102,256	5.7	920	26,382	31,245	25,992	3,425	941	0	30,632	11,397	2,748	
Shelby County	TN	25	111,403	132,312	44,897	33.9	1,218,671	212,572	17.4	1,857	64,329	79,600	26,140	0	2,068	1,155	70,761	23,816	5,743	
Northside ISD	TX	26	106,145	107,911	16,239	15.0	1,118,501	103,429	9.2	984	18,084	31,320	18,178	1,853	877	0	23,773	8,719	2,102	
Pinellas	FL	27	102,905	116,901	19,940	17.1	1,036,722	115,587	11.1	1,117	26,409	39,243	29,343	4,110	1,408	0	28,617	10,694	2,579	
Polk	FL	28	102,295	110,382	26,477	24.0	962,439	123,726	12.9	1,217	30,574	45,015	18,896	5,450	1,340	0	38,121	14,034	3,384	
DeKalb County	GA	29	101,284	115,181	28,144	24.4	1,194,250	121,738	10.2	1,201	40,696	43,005	28,170	3,544	1,093	0	42,484	15,064	3,632	
Jefferson County	KY	30	99,813	122,586	23,365	19.1	1,323,404	155,985	11.8	1,548	41,698	53,236	24,511	4,786	1,171	0	40,995	13,652	3,292	
Fulton County	GA	31	96,122	113,312	18,050	15.9	1,196,919	76,288	6.4	798	24,177	26,120	18,206	1,886	628	0	26,268	9,564	2,306	
Lee	FL	32	92,686	96,845	19,529	20.2	929,289	111,503	12.0	1,221	27,563	37,927	16,881	2,332	1,176	0	27,676	10,363	2,499	
Denver	CO	33	91,138	96,455	19,503	20.2	1,271,873	128,902	10.1	1,429	33,242	36,083	17,173	4,525	1,676	0	32,442	10,873	2,622	
Albuquerque	NM	34	90,651	112,667	23,996	21.3	1,021,201	102,693	10.1	1,134	29,733	22	17,787	0	1,535	0	38,271	13,083	3,155	
Prince William County	VA	35	89,345	90,603	7,770	8.6	1,110,691	60,078	5.4	684	10,645	27,010	13,587	733	728	0	12,391	4,917	1,186	
Fort Worth ISD	TX	36	87,428	94,508	28,946	30.6	963,004	136,873	14.2	1,572	39,262	41,590	14,267	5,880	1,047	0	43,144	15,291	3,687	
Jefferson County, No. R1	CO	37	86,371	86,109	6,117	7.1	929,179	50,952	5.5	587	11,256	13,650	15,592	2,058	405	0	9,015	3,577	862	
Davidson County	TN	38	85,163	98,704	22,632	22.9	1,004,078	114,198	11.4	1,334	31,282	47,021	21,049	0	1,296	1,136	33,968	12,068	2,910	
Austin ISD	TX	39	83,067	102,363	17,478	17.1	1,238,622	107,568	8.7	1,286	27,145	27,731	15,124	1,973	880	0	25,984	9,691	2,308	
Baltimore City	MD	40	82,354	89,009	27,470	30.9	1,420,023	160,881	11.3	1,923	52,749	49,872	22,568	5,999	1,487	0	62,633	22,279	5,372	
Anne Arundel County	MD	41	81,379	92,347	7,809	8.5	1,206,658	55,404	4.6	689	10,300	16,659	17,759	1,943	599	0	15,320	6,190	1,493	
Alpine	UT	42	78,957	87,585	6,253	7.1	603,204	32,485	5.4	422	5,589	9,595	11,011	957	633	0	8,565	3,367	804	
Loudoun County	VA	43	78,348	82,840	2,610	3.2	1,089,781	21,500	2.0	282	1,674	7,562	9,077	559	437	0	1,703	1,703	0	
Greenville, 01	SC	44	76,918	86,981	12,159	14.0	855,902	72,818	8.5	954	25,419	23,153	15,853	1,796	1,100	0	19,288	6,910	1,666	
Long Beach Unified	CA	45	76,428	84,056	19,563	23.3	1,075,291	110,337	10.3	1,418	29,141	30,867	14,964	5,325	728	0	34,261	12,576	3,032	
Milwaukee	WI	46	76,206	110,915	37,495	33.8	1,186,209	178,749	15.1	2,360	70,414	46,720	17,438	0	1,883	0	75,912	24,378	5,878	
Katy ISD	TX	47	75,428	67,757	6,399	9.4	835,819	45,898	5.5	629	5,952	11,582	11,340	529	404	0	7,879	3,396	374	
Fort Bend ISD	TX	48	74,146	90,019	9,879	11.0	758,885	45,181	6.0	618	9,526	11,481	11,907	1,367	548	0	13,753	5,320	1,283	
Brevard	FL	49	73,444	79,542	14,998	18.9	724,781	75,416	10.4	1,037	18,228	20,825	17,175	2,267	691	0	20,885	7,977	1,923	
Fresno Unified	CA	50	73,356	80,662	34,739	43.1	998,861	120,771	12.1	1,644	42,155	47,235	15,069	5,671	1,315	0	62,692	22,201	5,353	
Guilford County	NC	51	73,059	86,576	20,490	23.7	692,064	88,862	12.8	1,215	24,519	33,352	14,679	1,698	0	0	30,451	10,833	2,612	
Davis	UT	52	72,987	81,884	4,983	6.1	565,357	44,924	7.9	626	4,678	11,810	10,508	1,203	566	0	6,515	2,644	539	
Pasco	FL	53	72,493	77,344	12,760	16.5	698,805	72,438	10.4	1,027	14,751	24,279	16,635	1,836	607	0	17,529	6,798	1,639	
Aldine ISD	TX	54	69,768	66,271	22,388	33.8	758,420	101,027	13.3	1,435	26,952	40,183	12,975	2,260	770	0	33,002	11,851	2,857	
Granite	UT	55	69,580	83,404	10,403	12.5	557,620	62,079	11.1	886	14,342	23,182	11,924	2,087	1,026	0	15,286	5,505	1,327	
Virginia Beach City	VA	56	69,085	72,563	7,721	10.6	792,261	58,564	7.4	839	10,445	16,100	15,403	2,254	741	0	12,431	4,933	1,189	
Seminole	FL	57	67,808	72,393	8,965	12.4	636,054	54,132	8.5	808	11,828	19,604	12,698	1,841	556	0	11,756	4,769	1,150	
North East ISD	TX	58	67,531	79,190	11,312	14.3	733,799	55,786	7.6	823	12,479	18,888	11,459	1,254	642	0	15,974	6,074	1,465	
Douglas County, No. RE1	CO	59	67,470	70,114	1,750	2.5	682,388	18,449	2.7	276	1,657	3,796	8,616	529	147	0	984	984	0	
Washoe County	NV	60	66,671	72,321	10,876	15.0	661,369	71,496	10.8	1,075	16,928	16,893	10,280	1,946	699	12	14,085	5,885	1,419	
Mesa Unified	AZ	61	63,444	83,390	18,730	22.5	542,277	64,742	11.9	1,021	20,039	23,835	8,155	2,083	855	190	28,945	10,289	2,481	
Elk Grove Unified	CA	62	63,061	69,369	12,093	17.4	736,543	58,357	7.9	930	16,027	20,710	10,684	1,601	527	0	19,966	7,736	1,865	
Osceola	FL	63	63,031	61,371	13,740	22.4	602,465	72,832	12.1	1,177	18,837	28,752	11,568	2,027	812	0	18,771	7,234	1,744	
Volusia	FL	64	63,028	68,964	12,608	18.3	624,595	66,211	10.6	1,052	22,403	20,722	13,802	2,428	713	0	18,179	7,105	1,697	
Arlington ISD	TX	65	62,181	70,756	15,923	22.5	666,458	75,712	11.4	1,198	20,870	24,499	9,707	1,387	685	0	22,844	8,404	2,027	
Knox County	TN	66	60,372	70,385	11,257	16.0	538,759	54,877	10.2	910	16,672	20,849	13,830	0	837	0	16,158	6,086	1,468	
San Francisco Unified	CA	67	60,133	78,037	9,639	12.4	1,019,158	53,514	5.3	909	12,391	17,704	0	2,756	14	26	15,200	6,123	1,476	
Chesterfield County	VA	68	60,060	61,383	5,299	8.6	718,087	33,520	4.7	562	5,608	9,875	10,986	952	651	0	7,438	3,367	0	
Conroe ISD	TX	69	59,764	62,420	6,769	10.8	591,849	35,023	5.9	601	6,756	10,415	10,658	1,055	354	0	8,920	3,625	874	
El Paso ISD	TX	70	59,424	61,880	18,527	29.9	643,516	111,553	17.3	1,858	26,988	27,403	11,730	4,661	918	0	26,847	9,762	2,354	
Garland ISD	TX	71	57,133	62,916	11,977	19.0	597,799	54,476	9.1	947	12,978	21,297	9,602	1,107	620	0	16,749	6,337	1,528	
Mobile County	AL	72	56,628	66,870	19,514	29.2	564,939	78,217	13.8	1,358	24,171	31,594	15,858	3,753	960	443	29,181	10,344	2,494	
Pasadena ISD	TX	73	56,282	58,306	14,385	24.7	607,584	71,419	11.8	1,275	16,072	26,155	8,728	1,616	754	0	20,516	7,615	1,836	

Name of district	State	Rank order	Enroll-ment, fall 2016	5- to 17-year-old popu-lation, 2016	5- to 17-year-olds in poverty, 2016[1]	Poverty rate of 5- to 17-year-olds, 2016[1]	Revenues by source of funds, 2015-16: Total (in thousands)	Federal (in thousands)	Federal as a percent of total	Federal revenue per stu-dent[3]	Revenue from selected federal programs (in thousands), 2015-16: Title I	School lunch	Individuals with Disabilities Education Act (IDEA)	Eisen-hower math and science	Voca-tional educa-tion	Drug-free schools	Federal Title I allocations (in federal fiscal year 2(: Total	Basic Grants	Concen-tration Grants	Ta
1	2	3	4	5	6	7	8	9	10	11	12	13	14	15	16	17	18	19	20	
Frisco ISD	TX	74	55,923	43,248	1,579	3.7	574,629	12,497	2.2	234	1,099	4,146	4,122	121	222	0	842	842	0	
Howard County	MD	75	55,626	58,873	3,342	5.7	949,631	27,394	2.9	499	4,741	6,766	9,530	1,058	322	0	5,462	2,649	0	
Winston-Salem/Forsyth County	NC	76	55,228	64,492	14,495	22.5	503,819	62,956	12.5	1,145	18,949	18,960	14,749	1,388	0	0	21,021	7,741	1,849	
Cherry Creek, No. 5	CO	77	54,852	57,432	4,192	7.3	623,750	27,612	4.4	505	5,732	7,789	9,005	756	244	0	5,100	2,337	0	
Santa Ana Unified	CA	78	54,505	53,184	12,085	22.7	784,643	83,062	10.6	1,486	21,717	32,398	11,733	3,206	543	0	19,855	7,699	1,856	
Clayton County	GA	79	54,345	57,722	16,816	29.1	542,286	71,543	13.2	1,322	22,083	34,087	9,990	1,963	530	0	24,350	8,914	2,149	
Seattle	WA	80	54,215	66,075	6,627	10.0	881,789	52,833	6.0	991	14,410	9,378	13,585	486	360	0	11,812	4,455	1,074	
Plano ISD	TX	81	54,173	69,733	4,898	7.0	707,660	31,851	4.5	584	5,018	8,870	8,404	786	408	0	5,698	2,632	0	
Boston	MA	82	53,640	75,249	21,309	28.3	1,481,699	77,195	5.2	1,433	26,828	18,497	16,457	0	1,273	0	52,759	17,169	4,140	
Capistrano Unified	CA	83	53,613	61,792	4,019	6.5	556,213	23,256	4.2	432	4,739	4,943	9,604	912	287	0	5,138	2,561	0	
Jordan	UT	84	53,416	61,711	3,495	5.7	411,232	25,095	6.1	474	2,912	8,488	9,226	819	420	0	4,047	1,875	0	
Lewisville ISD	TX	85	53,257	64,833	5,137	7.9	615,597	32,773	5.3	613	4,076	11,054	8,383	591	376	0	5,928	2,729	0	
Corona-Norco Unified	CA	86	53,157	55,845	6,664	11.9	647,344	36,976	5.7	693	8,246	12,794	9,398	1,142	314	0	10,101	4,300	1,037	
San Bernardino City Unified	CA	87	53,152	55,421	20,868	37.7	716,242	72,318	10.1	1,357	28,113	26,990	8,698	2,787	647	0	37,081	13,530	3,263	
San Antonio ISD	TX	88	52,514	61,265	20,582	33.6	650,765	136,019	20.9	2,563	31,579	43,297	10,585	4,393	836	0	30,764	11,091	2,674	
Omaha	NE	89	52,344	65,240	11,932	18.3	687,093	96,897	14.1	1,865	34,778	24,842	14,695	4,336	1,047	0	27,444	9,529	2,276	
Atlanta	GA	90	51,927	58,615	19,520	33.3	903,489	82,444	9.1	1,601	38,069	24,030	9,512	6,372	597	0	28,811	10,484	2,557	
Klein ISD	TX	91	51,810	51,259	7,382	14.4	535,140	35,016	6.5	692	6,938	11,428	6,983	627	372	0	9,658	3,908	942	
Henrico County	VA	92	51,425	55,420	6,171	11.1	533,398	29,242	5.5	567	5,580	12,425	7,636	729	1,064	0	9,638	3,929	836	
Cumberland County	NC	93	51,194	54,197	14,042	25.9	436,794	65,548	15.0	1,281	14,115	21,149	9,872	2,481	0	0	20,743	7,591	1,830	
Wichita	KS	94	50,600	57,497	12,758	22.2	666,255	73,972	11.1	1,452	24,904	21,355	0	0	0	0	22,266	7,636	1,832	
Columbus City	OH	95	50,331	72,743	25,484	35.0	840,528	94,651	11.3	1,892	36,397	28,886	13,602	0	2,270	0	51,861	16,984	4,095	
Oakland Unified	CA	96	49,760	58,151	12,817	22.0	688,124	65,125	9.5	1,326	18,473	16,544	9,277	4,386	500	0	21,151	8,137	1,962	
San Juan Unified	CA	97	49,255	50,227	9,810	19.5	610,436	47,157	7.7	951	11,709	10,688	10,828	2,053	397	0	15,652	6,276	1,513	
Manatee	FL	98	48,884	52,635	9,982	19.0	491,872	55,102	11.2	1,140	14,734	19,598	10,650	23	803	0	13,236	5,289	1,275	
Jefferson Parish	LA	99	48,668	67,943	16,141	23.8	611,400	72,132	11.8	1,491	21,535	20,304	14,540	2,914	704	895	27,519	9,923	2,393	
Charleston, 01	SC	100	48,551	55,211	11,106	20.1	763,748	71,926	9.4	1,496	18,158	18,457	10,812	2,380	591	0	17,246	6,278	1,514	
District of Columbia	DC	101	48,462	77,386	21,997	28.4	1,329,719	154,922	11.7	3,205	29,450	25,496	9,053	6,185	2,358	321	50,946	18,434	4,445	
Round Rock ISD	TX	102	48,321	54,846	3,278	6.0	519,574	31,087	6.0	650	3,400	8,089	7,941	435	319	0	3,689	1,783	0	
Anchorage	AK	103	48,238	52,309	4,634	8.9	758,779	78,331	10.3	1,621	14,868	18,567	12,311	3,181	1,167	0	14,157	5,104	984	
Portland, SD1J	OR	104	48,173	56,467	7,235	12.8	697,501	54,051	7.7	1,118	12,975	11,191	14,185	2,743	470	0	12,164	4,560	1,100	
Tucson Unified	AZ	105	47,366	72,242	20,437	28.3	449,642	67,416	15.0	1,424	30,025	17,423	7,795	1,091	1,003	2,936	31,940	11,266	2,717	
Brownsville ISD	TX	106	46,880	46,381	18,449	39.8	555,104	102,330	18.4	2,143	26,320	38,949	8,357	2,629	787	0	28,135	10,275	2,454	
Sacramento City Unified	CA	107	46,815	52,925	13,719	25.9	645,019	76,733	11.9	1,638	18,414	21,969	9,811	3,458	1,222	0	23,040	8,777	2,116	
Collier	FL	108	46,416	47,497	8,103	17.1	571,140	53,751	9.4	1,169	17,122	17,171	9,553	1,429	575	0	10,460	4,311	1,036	
Alief ISD	TX	109	46,376	54,698	17,289	31.6	514,485	69,453	13.5	1,469	21,037	22,624	7,455	851	758	0	25,047	9,152	2,207	
Forsyth County	GA	110	46,238	48,680	2,654	5.5	471,715	16,236	3.4	367	2,675	4,912	6,180	427	206	0	2,850	1,428	0	
Socorro ISD	TX	111	45,927	42,950	10,640	24.8	439,467	46,901	10.7	1,036	10,623	20,712	6,156	1,147	521	0	14,541	5,588	1,347	
Detroit Public Schools	MI	112	45,455	124,278	57,539	46.3	838,553	193,905	23.1	4,160	98,109	42,071	9,804	0	1,269	0	127,607	39,342	10,027	
Hamilton County	TN	113	44,446	54,365	9,860	18.1	428,237	49,774	11.6	1,121	16,511	18,971	9,568	0	709	566	13,823	5,302	1,278	
Chandler Unified	AZ	114	44,352	46,562	4,932	10.6	350,971	20,423	5.8	480	5,173	6,564	5,070	609	419	0	5,687	2,684	0	
Garden Grove Unified	CA	115	44,223	49,336	9,904	20.1	647,198	51,880	8.0	1,146	12,985	18,669	8,870	2,137	510	230	15,752	6,309	1,521	
Rutherford County	TN	116	44,149	44,849	4,910	10.9	378,876	25,534	6.7	593	4,778	10,427	7,945	0	650	0	5,737	2,626	0	
Horry, 01	SC	117	43,991	44,231	11,581	26.2	543,802	42,444	7.8	983	14,500	15,036	9,301	1,290	633	0	17,971	6,502	1,568	
Killeen ISD	TX	118	43,782	42,827	7,806	18.2	439,981	102,083	23.2	2,360	8,054	14,527	6,063	1,054	446	0	10,655	4,270	1,020	
United ISD	TX	119	43,660	42,326	14,052	33.2	461,411	56,597	12.3	1,295	14,542	23,506	7,305	1,050	603	0	19,870	7,395	1,783	
Marion	FL	120	43,032	47,672	12,175	25.5	418,762	59,188	14.1	1,383	16,300	22,792	11,194	1,980	646	0	16,605	6,473	1,561	

[1] Poverty is defined based on the number of persons and related children in the family and their income. For information on poverty thresholds, see https://www.census.gov/data/tables/time-series/demo/income-poverty/historical-poverty-thresh

[2] Fiscal year 2018 Department of Education funds available for spending by school districts in the 2018-19 school year.

[3] Federal revenue per student is based on fall enrollment collected through the "Local Education Agency (School District) Finance Survey (F33)."

NOTE: Detail may not sum to totals because of rounding. ISD = independent school district.

SOURCE: U.S. Department of Education, National Center for Education Statistics, Common Core of Data (CCD), "Local Education Agency Universe Survey," 2016-17; "Local Education Agency (School District) Finance Survey (F33)," 2015-16; unpublished Department of Education budget data. U.S. Department of Commerce, Census Bureau, Small Area Income and Poverty Estimates (SAIPE) Program, 2016 Poverty Estimates for School Districts. (This table was prepared May 2019

Table 216.10. Public elementary and secondary schools, by level of school: Selected years, 1967–68 through 2017–18

Year	Total, all public schools	Schools with reported grade spans											Other schools[1]
			Elementary schools				Secondary schools						
		Total	Total[3]	Middle schools[4]	One-teacher schools	Other elementary schools	Total[5]	Junior high[6]	3-year or 4-year high schools	5-year or 6-year high schools	Other secondary schools	Combined elementary/ secondary schools[2]	
1	2	3	4	5	6	7	8	9	10	11	12	13	14
1967–68	—	94,197	67,186	—	4,146	63,040	23,318	7,437	10,751	4,650	480	3,693	—
1970–71	—	89,372	64,020	2,080	1,815	60,125	23,572	7,750	11,265	3,887	670	1,780	—
1972–73	—	88,864	62,942	2,308	1,475	59,159	23,919	7,878	11,550	3,962	529	2,003	—
1974–75	—	87,456	61,759	3,224	1,247	57,288	23,837	7,690	11,480	4,122	545	1,860	—
1975–76	88,597	87,034	61,704	3,916	1,166	56,622	23,792	7,521	11,572	4,113	586	1,538	1,563
1976–77	—	86,501	61,123	4,180	1,111	55,832	23,857	7,434	11,658	4,130	635	1,521	—
1978–79	—	84,816	60,312	5,879	1,056	53,377	22,834	6,282	11,410	4,429	713	1,670	—
1980–81	85,982	83,688	59,326	6,003	921	52,402	22,619	5,890	10,758	4,193	1,778	1,743	2,294
1982–83	84,740	82,039	58,051	6,875	798	50,378	22,383	5,948	11,678	4,067	690	1,605	2,701
1983–84	84,178	81,418	57,471	6,885	838	49,748	22,336	5,936	11,670	4,046	684	1,611	2,760
1984–85	84,007	81,147	57,231	6,893	825	49,513	22,320	5,916	11,671	4,021	712	1,596	2,860
1986–87	83,421	82,316	58,835	7,483	763	50,589	21,505	5,109	11,430	4,196	770	1,976	1,105[7]
1987–88	83,248	81,416	57,575	7,641	729	49,205	21,662	4,900	11,279	4,048	1,435	2,179	1,832[7]
1988–89	83,165	81,579	57,941	7,957	583	49,401	21,403	4,687	11,350	3,994	1,372	2,235	1,586[7]
1989–90	83,425	81,880	58,419	8,272	630	49,517	21,181	4,512	11,492	3,812	1,365	2,280	1,545[7]
1990–91	84,538	82,475	59,015	8,545	617	49,853	21,135	4,561	11,537	3,723	1,314	2,325	2,063
1991–92	84,578	82,506	59,258	8,829	569	49,860	20,767	4,298	11,528	3,699	1,242	2,481	2,072
1992–93	84,497	82,896	59,676	9,152	430	50,094	20,671	4,115	11,651	3,613	1,292	2,549	1,601
1993–94	85,393	83,431	60,052	9,573	442	50,037	20,705	3,970	11,858	3,595	1,282	2,674	1,962
1994–95	86,221	84,476	60,808	9,954	458	50,396	20,904	3,859	12,058	3,628	1,359	2,764	1,745
1995–96	87,125	84,958	61,165	10,205	474	50,486	20,997	3,743	12,168	3,621	1,465	2,796	2,167
1996–97	88,223	86,092	61,805	10,499	487	50,819	21,307	3,707	12,424	3,614	1,562	2,980	2,131
1997–98	89,508	87,541	62,739	10,944	476	51,319	21,682	3,599	12,734	3,611	1,738	3,120	1,967
1998–99	90,874	89,259	63,462	11,202	463	51,797	22,076	3,607	13,457	3,707	1,305	3,721	1,615
1999–2000	92,012	90,538	64,131	11,521	423	52,187	22,365	3,566	13,914	3,686	1,199	4,042	1,474
2000–01	93,273	91,691	64,601	11,696	411	52,494	21,994	3,318	13,793	3,974	909	5,096	1,582
2001–02	94,112	92,696	65,228	11,983	408	52,837	22,180	3,285	14,070	3,917	908	5,288	1,416
2002–03	95,615	93,869	65,718	12,174	366	53,178	22,599	3,263	14,330	4,017	989	5,552	1,746
2003–04	95,726	93,977	65,758	12,341	376	53,041	22,782	3,251	14,595	3,840	1,096	5,437	1,749
2004–05	96,513	95,001	65,984	12,530	338	53,116	23,445	3,250	14,854	3,945	1,396	5,572	1,512
2005–06	97,382	95,731	66,026	12,545	326	53,155	23,998	3,249	15,103	3,910	1,736	5,707	1,651
2006–07	98,793	96,362	66,458	12,773	313	53,372	23,920	3,112	15,043	4,048	1,717	5,984	2,431
2007–08	98,916	97,654	67,112	13,014	288	53,810	24,643	3,117	16,146	3,981	1,399	5,899	1,262
2008–09	98,706	97,119	67,148	13,060	237	53,851	24,348	3,037	16,246	3,761	1,304	5,623	1,587
2009–10	98,817	97,521	67,140	13,163	217	53,760	24,651	2,953	16,706	3,778	1,214	5,730	1,296
2010–11	98,817	97,767	67,086	13,045	224	53,817	24,544	2,855	16,321	4,047	1,321	6,137	1,050
2011–12	98,328	97,357	66,689	12,963	205	53,521	24,357	2,865	16,586	3,899	1,007	6,311	971
2012–13	98,454	97,331	66,708	13,064	196	53,448	24,294	2,816	16,393	3,875	1,210	6,329	1,123
2013–14	98,271	97,290	67,034	13,324	193	53,517	24,067	2,721	16,704	3,467	1,175	6,189	981
2014–15	98,176	97,601	67,073	13,250	165	53,658	24,181	2,706	16,603	3,585	1,287	6,347	575
2015–16	98,277	97,586	66,758	13,022	197	53,539	24,040	2,594	16,243	3,995	1,208	6,788	691
2016–17	98,158	97,434	66,837	13,253	203	53,381	23,814	2,527	16,514	3,523	1,250	6,783	724
2017–18	98,469	97,568	67,408	13,437	188	53,783	23,882	2,479	16,677	3,390	1,336	6,278	901

—Not available.
[1]Includes special education, alternative, and other schools not reported by grade span.
[2]Includes schools beginning with grade 6 or below and ending with grade 9 or above.
[3]Includes schools beginning with grade 6 or below and with no grade higher than 8.
[4]Includes schools with grade spans beginning with 4, 5, or 6 and ending with 6, 7, or 8.
[5]Includes schools with no grade lower than 7.
[6]Includes schools with grades 7 and 8 or grades 7 through 9.
[7]Because of revision in data collection procedures, figures not comparable to data for other years.
SOURCE: U.S. Department of Education, National Center for Education Statistics, *Statistics of State School Systems*, 1967–68 and 1975–76; *Statistics of Public Elementary and Secondary Day Schools*, 1970–71, 1972–73, 1974–75, and 1976–77 through 1980–81; and Common Core of Data (CCD), "Public Elementary/Secondary School Universe Survey," 1982–83 through 2017–18. (This table was prepared December 2019.)

Table 216.20. Number and enrollment of public elementary and secondary schools, by school level, type, and charter, magnet, and virtual status: Selected years, 1990–91 through 2017–18

School level, type, and charter, magnet, or virtual status	Number of schools										Fall enrollment									
	1990–91	2000–01	2005–06	2010–11	2012–13	2013–14	2014–15	2015–16	2016–17	2017–18	1990–91	2000–01	2005–06	2010–11	2012–13	2013–14	2014–15	2015–16	2016–17	2017–18
1	2	3	4	5	6	7	8	9	10	11	12	13	14	15	16	17	18	19	20	21
Total, all schools	**84,538**	**93,273**	**97,382**	**98,817**	**98,454**	**98,271**	**98,176**	**98,277**	**98,158**	**98,469**	**41,141,366**	**47,060,714**	**48,912,085**	**49,177,617**	**49,519,559**	**49,777,410**	**50,009,771**	**50,115,178**	**50,274,747**	**50,330,241**
School type																				
Regular	80,395	85,422	87,585	88,929	89,031	89,183	89,386	89,501	89,527	89,914	40,599,943	46,194,730	47,957,375	48,259,245	48,583,049	48,863,752	49,178,890	49,313,134	49,468,870	49,531,526
Special education	1,932	2,008	2,128	2,206	2,034	2,010	1,954	2,005	1,991	1,903	209,145	174,577	222,497	190,910	198,626	214,611	186,269	180,155	184,261	185,073
Vocational	1,060	1,025	1,221	1,485	1,403	1,380	1,387	1,396	1,391	1,467	198,117	199,669	217,621	164,013	160,207	148,447	147,550	146,321	146,601	147,516
Alternative[1]	1,151	4,818	6,448	6,197	5,986	5,698	5,449	5,375	5,249	5,185	134,161	491,738	514,592	563,449	577,677	550,600	497,062	475,568	475,015	466,126
School level and type																				
Elementary[2]	59,015	64,601	66,026	67,086	66,708	67,034	67,073	66,758	66,837	67,408	26,503,677	30,673,453	31,104,018	31,581,751	31,918,613	32,226,881	32,225,908	32,035,708	32,132,682	32,346,383
Regular	58,440	63,674	64,996	65,874	65,572	65,948	66,036	65,734	65,853	66,436	26,400,740	30,582,610	31,003,942	31,441,027	31,772,432	32,083,759	32,116,995	31,930,363	32,034,365	32,241,347
Special education	419	496	508	587	541	543	578	568	551	555	58,204	42,127	49,652	58,987	59,826	62,596	54,161	50,508	43,555	52,522
Vocational	31	8	8	16	15	7	6	5	5	4	17,686	2,409	1,713	3,495	3,734	1,791	1,749	1,729	1,960	1,831
Alternative[1]	125	423	514	609	580	536	453	451	428	413	27,047	46,307	48,711	78,242	82,621	78,735	53,003	53,108	52,802	50,683
Secondary[3]	21,135	21,994	23,998	24,544	24,294	24,067	24,181	24,040	23,814	23,816	13,569,787	15,038,171	16,219,309	15,692,610	15,670,275	15,640,128	15,731,561	15,748,184	15,798,446	15,759,707
Regular	19,459	18,456	19,252	19,449	19,479	19,411	19,441	19,325	19,264	19,171	13,313,097	14,567,969	15,685,032	15,197,786	15,161,226	15,167,671	15,270,834	15,296,173	15,355,391	15,324,419
Special education	165	219	368	359	333	331	339	313	316	296	11,913	12,607	42,696	27,990	28,235	28,312	24,729	21,929	21,700	21,710
Vocational	1,010	997	1,185	1,387	1,324	1,311	1,318	1,329	1,332	1,427	174,105	193,981	209,762	154,088	154,610	144,066	144,042	142,611	142,332	142,915
Alternative[1]	501	2,322	3,193	3,349	3,158	3,014	3,083	3,073	2,902	2,922	70,672	263,614	281,819	312,746	326,204	300,079	291,956	287,471	279,023	270,663
Combined elementary/ secondary[4]	2,325	5,096	5,707	6,137	6,329	6,189	6,347	6,788	6,783	6,344	925,887	1,266,778	1,526,186	1,897,712	1,926,786	1,898,252	2,049,039	2,329,346	2,335,618	2,216,403
Regular	1,784	2,780	3,121	3,363	3,558	3,446	3,713	4,236	4,236	3,936	855,814	1,007,368	1,263,952	1,620,031	1,649,010	1,611,918	1,790,208	2,085,918	2,078,659	1,965,052
Special education	376	715	735	964	935	940	935	923	907	877	43,992	86,253	91,966	99,120	107,295	111,958	106,500	107,658	112,826	105,334
Vocational	19	20	28	82	64	62	63	62	54	36	6,326	3,279	6,146	6,430	1,863	2,590	1,759	1,981	2,309	2,770
Alternative[1]	146	1,581	1,823	1,728	1,772	1,741	1,636	1,567	1,586	1,495	19,755	169,878	164,122	172,131	168,618	171,786	150,572	133,789	141,824	143,247
Other (not classified by grade span)	2,063	1,582	1,651	1,050	1,123	981	575	691	724	901	142,015	82,312	62,572	5,544	3,885	12,149	3,263	1,940	8,001	7,748
Regular	712	512	216	243	422	378	196	206	174	371	30,292	36,783	4,449	401	381	404	853	680	455	708
Special education	972	578	517	296	225	196	102	201	217	175	95,036	33,590	38,183	4,813	3,270	11,745	879	60	6,180	5,507
Vocational	0	0	0	0	0	0	0	0	0	0	0	0	0	0	0	0	0	0	0	0
Alternative[1]	379	492	918	511	476	407	277	284	333	355	16,687	11,939	19,940	330	234	0	1,531	1,200	1,366	1,533
Charter status and level																				
All charter schools[5]	—	1,993	3,780	5,274	6,079	6,465	6,747	6,855	7,011	7,193	—	448,343	1,012,906	1,787,091	2,269,435	2,522,022	2,721,786	2,845,322	3,010,287	3,143,269
Elementary[2]	—	1,011	1,969	2,866	3,388	3,634	3,851	3,854	3,934	4,064	—	249,101	532,217	905,575	1,156,075	1,288,568	1,405,015	1,448,523	1,511,812	1,601,350
Secondary[3]	—	467	1,057	1,368	1,465	1,522	1,563	1,576	1,618	1,667	—	79,588	219,627	341,534	399,921	443,423	467,231	482,296	504,301	539,890
Combined elementary/ secondary[4]	—	448	704	1,027	1,204	1,268	1,330	1,406	1,454	1,458	—	117,377	259,837	539,653	713,073	789,883	848,875	914,110	994,021	1,001,788
Other (not classified by grade span)	—	67	50	13	22	41	3	19	5	4	—	2,277	1,225	329	366	148	665	393	153	241
Magnet status and level																				
All magnet schools[5]	—	1,469	2,736	2,722	3,151	3,254	3,285	3,237	3,164	3,421	—	1,213,976	2,103,013	2,055,133	2,478,531	2,556,644	2,609,104	2,604,145	2,537,011	2,665,820
Elementary[2]	—	1,111	1,994	1,849	2,150	2,164	2,216	2,135	2,087	2,307	—	704,763	1,186,160	1,035,288	1,287,771	1,300,317	1,312,571	1,281,873	1,266,076	1,370,347
Secondary[3]	—	328	643	746	862	939	911	884	853	931	—	484,684	869,010	944,434	1,118,574	1,178,272	1,207,248	1,188,316	1,141,181	1,184,412
Combined elementary/ secondary[4]	—	29	80	103	121	133	142	203	205	165	—	24,529	47,509	75,411	72,148	78,055	89,277	133,956	129,752	111,056
Other (not classified by grade span)	—	1	19	24	18	18	16	15	19	18	—	0	334	0	38	0	8	0	2	5
Virtual status and level																				
All virtual schools[5,6]	—	—	—	—	—	477	576	592	562	656	—	—	—	—	—	200,343	229,608	234,148	212,311	278,783
Elementary[2]	—	—	—	—	—	65	77	74	68	77	—	—	—	—	—	14,277	19,341	19,064	14,669	20,941
Secondary[3]	—	—	—	—	—	100	132	144	132	159	—	—	—	—	—	18,625	29,303	32,535	23,355	36,505
Combined elementary/ secondary[4]	—	—	—	—	—	310	366	373	361	415	—	—	—	—	—	167,441	180,964	182,549	174,287	221,337
Other (not classified by grade span)	—	—	—	—	—	2	1	1	1	5	—	—	—	—	—	0	0	0	0	0

—Not available.

[1]Includes schools that provide nontraditional education, address needs of students that typically cannot be met in regular schools, serve as adjuncts to regular schools, or fall outside the categories of regular, special education, or vocational education.

[2]Includes schools beginning with grade 6 or below and with no grade higher than 8.

[3]Includes schools with no grade lower than 7.

[4]Includes schools beginning with grade 6 or below and ending with grade 9 or above.

[5]Magnet, charter, and virtual schools are also included under regular, special education, vocational, or alternative schools as appropriate.

[6]Virtual schools are defined as having instruction during which students and teachers are separated by time and/or location *and interact via internet-connected computers or other electronic devices.*

SOURCE: U.S. Department of Education, National Center for Education Statistics, Common Core of Data (CCD), "Public Elementary/Secondary School Universe Survey," 1990–91 through 2017–18. (This table was prepared November 2019.)

Table 216.30. Number and percentage distribution of public elementary and secondary students and schools, by traditional or charter school status and selected characteristics: Selected years, 1999–2000 through 2017–18

Selected characteristic	1999–2000			2000–01			2010–11			2017–18		
	Total, all public schools	Traditional (non-charter) schools	Charter schools	Total, all public schools	Traditional (non-charter) schools	Charter schools	Total, all public schools	Traditional (non-charter) schools	Charter schools	Total, all public schools	Traditional (non-charter) schools	Charter schools
1	2	3	4	5	6	7	8	9	10	11	12	13
Fall enrollment (in thousands)	46,689	46,350	340	47,061	46,612	448	49,178	47,391	1,787	50,330	47,187	3,143
Percentage distribution of students												
Sex	100.0	100.0	100.0	100.0	100.0	100.0	100.0	100.0	100.0	100.0	100.0	100.0
Male	51.4	51.4	51.1	51.4	51.4	51.2	51.4	51.4	49.5	51.4	51.5	49.6
Female	48.6	48.6	48.9	48.6	48.6	48.8	48.6	48.6	50.5	48.6	48.5	50.4
Race/ethnicity	100.0	100.0	100.0	100.0	100.0	100.0	100.0	100.0	100.0	100.0	100.0	100.0
White	61.8	61.9	42.5	61.0	61.2	42.7	52.5	53.1	36.2	47.6	48.7	32.1
Black	17.1	16.9	33.5	17.0	16.9	33.2	16.0	15.5	28.9	15.2	14.5	25.8
Hispanic	15.9	15.9	19.6	16.6	16.6	19.4	23.1	22.9	27.3	26.7	26.3	33.1
Asian/Pacific Islander	4.1	4.1	2.8	4.2	4.2	2.9	5.0	5.0	3.7	5.6	5.6	4.4
Asian	—	—	—	—	—	—	4.6	4.7	3.3	5.2	5.3	4.0
Pacific Islander	—	—	—	—	—	—	0.3	0.3	0.5	0.4	0.4	0.4
American Indian/Alaska Native	1.2	1.2	1.5	1.2	1.2	1.8	1.1	1.1	0.9	1.0	1.0	0.7
Two or more races	—	—	—	—	—	—	2.4	2.3	2.9	3.9	3.9	3.9
Percent of students eligible for free or reduced-price lunch program[1]	100.0	100.0	100.0	100.0	100.0	100.0	100.0	100.0	100.0	100.0	100.0	100.0
0 to 25.0	44.9	45.0	36.9	34.3	34.3	39.3	23.9	23.8	26.7	21.0	21.2	18.2
25.1 to 50.0	25.4	25.5	12.7	24.7	24.8	12.7	28.9	29.2	18.9	28.3	28.9	19.5
50.1 to 75.0	16.0	16.1	13.0	16.0	16.1	14.9	26.6	26.8	20.4	25.3	25.6	21.6
More than 75.0	12.2	12.2	14.3	12.4	12.4	14.7	20.1	19.7	30.7	24.8	24.2	34.5
Missing/school does not participate	1.4	1.2	23.2	12.5	12.4	18.4	0.5	0.4	3.2	0.6	0.2	6.2
Number of teachers	2,636,277	2,622,678	13,599	2,747,649	2,729,033	18,616	3,001,994	2,910,869	91,126	3,079,590	2,922,634	156,956
Pupil/teacher ratio[2]	16.6	16.6	18.8	16.4	16.4	18.2	16.4	16.4	18.0	16.1	16.0	17.7
Total number of schools	92,012	90,488	1,524	93,273	91,280	1,993	98,817	93,543	5,274	98,469	91,276	7,193
Percentage distribution of schools												
School level	100.0	100.0	100.0	100.0	100.0	100.0	100.0	100.0	100.0	100.0	100.0	100.0
Elementary[3]	69.7	70.0	54.6	69.3	69.7	50.7	67.9	68.7	54.3	68.5	69.4	56.5
Secondary[4]	24.3	24.3	25.9	23.6	23.6	23.4	24.8	24.8	25.9	24.3	24.3	23.2
Combined[5]	4.4	4.2	18.6	5.5	5.1	22.5	6.2	5.5	19.5	6.4	5.3	20.3
Ungraded	1.6	1.6	0.9	1.7	1.7	3.4	1.1	1.1	0.2	0.9	1.0	0.1
Size of enrollment	100.0	100.0	100.0	100.0	100.0	100.0	100.0	100.0	100.0	100.0	100.0	100.0
Less than 300	31.3	30.5	77.0	31.9	31.0	75.2	30.9	29.3	59.0	29.8	28.6	44.8
300 to 499	26.5	26.7	12.0	26.5	26.8	12.7	27.8	28.1	22.3	28.1	28.3	25.5
500 to 999	32.8	33.2	8.7	32.0	32.5	9.7	32.3	33.4	14.8	32.7	33.5	23.3
1,000 or more	9.5	9.7	2.4	9.6	9.8	2.4	9.0	9.3	3.9	9.4	9.6	6.3
Racial/ethnic concentration												
More than 50 percent White	70.9	71.2	51.1	70.2	70.6	51.6	60.4	61.7	38.4	54.8	56.6	32.3
More than 50 percent Black	11.1	10.8	26.5	11.1	10.8	25.1	10.7	9.8	25.4	9.8	8.7	22.8
More than 50 percent Hispanic	8.8	8.7	11.4	9.2	9.1	11.5	14.5	14.1	20.8	17.3	16.6	26.6
No majority racial/ethnic group	7.8	7.8	9.1	8.0	8.0	9.7	13.1	13.0	14.1	16.5	16.4	16.8
Percent of students eligible for free or reduced-price lunch program[1]	100.0	100.0	100.0	100.0	100.0	100.0	100.0	100.0	100.0	100.0	100.0	100.0
0 to 25.0	42.3	42.3	44.5	29.9	29.8	33.1	23.2	22.9	27.7	17.9	18.0	16.6
25.1 to 50.0	25.6	25.9	11.1	25.0	25.3	11.5	26.9	27.4	17.4	26.6	27.3	18.2
50.1 to 75.0	16.8	16.9	10.2	16.8	16.9	11.1	26.4	26.8	20.1	25.1	25.4	21.5
More than 75.0	11.9	11.9	12.4	12.2	12.2	13.1	21.3	20.7	33.1	25.8	24.9	37.0
Missing/school does not participate	3.3	3.0	21.9	16.2	15.8	31.1	2.2	2.3	1.7	4.6	4.4	6.6
Locale	—	—	—	—	—	—	100.0	100.0	100.0	100.0	100.0	100.0
City	—	—	—	—	—	—	26.2	24.5	55.5	27.2	24.9	56.1
Suburban	—	—	—	—	—	—	27.4	27.8	21.3	31.7	32.1	26.3
Town	—	—	—	—	—	—	14.0	14.4	7.6	13.3	13.9	6.1
Rural	—	—	—	—	—	—	32.3	33.3	15.6	27.8	29.1	11.5
Region	100.0	100.0	100.0	100.0	100.0	100.0	100.0	100.0	100.0	100.0	100.0	100.0
Northeast	16.1	16.3	7.2	16.2	16.3	10.9	15.5	15.9	9.5	15.2	15.6	10.1
Midwest	28.9	29.0	24.9	28.7	28.8	23.3	26.4	26.6	23.1	26.0	26.5	20.6
South	33.1	33.2	28.9	33.1	33.2	27.5	34.7	35.0	29.5	34.8	35.0	32.6
West	21.8	21.6	38.9	22.0	21.6	38.3	23.4	22.5	37.9	23.9	22.9	36.7

—Not available.
[1]The National School Lunch Program (NSLP) is a federally assisted meal program. To be eligible for free lunch under the program, a student must be from a household with an income at or below 130 percent of the poverty threshold; to be eligible for reduced-price lunch, a student must be from a household with an income between 130 percent and 185 percent of the poverty threshold. Data for 2017–18 include students whose NSLP eligibility has been determined through direct certification.
[2]Pupil/teacher ratio based on schools that reported both enrollment and teacher data.
[3]Includes schools beginning with grade 6 or below and with no grade higher than 8.
[4]Includes schools with no grade lower than 7.
[5]Includes schools beginning with grade 6 or below and ending with grade 9 or above.
NOTE: Detail may not sum to totals because of rounding. Race categories exclude persons of Hispanic ethnicity.
SOURCE: U.S. Department of Education, National Center for Education Statistics, Common Core of Data (CCD), "Public Elementary/Secondary School Universe Survey," 1999–2000 through 2017–18; and Education Demographic and Geographic Estimates (EDGE), "Public School File," 2017–18. (This table was prepared January 2020.)

Table 216.40. Number and percentage distribution of public elementary and secondary schools and enrollment, by level, type, and enrollment size of school: 2015–16, 2016–17, and 2017–18

	Number and percentage distribution of schools, by level and type						Enrollment totals and percentage distribution, by level and type of school[1]					
			Secondary[4]						Secondary[4]			
Enrollment size of school	Total[2]	Elementary[3]	All schools	Regular schools[7]	Combined elementary/secondary[5]	Other[6]	Total[2]	Elementary[3]	All schools	Regular schools[7]	Combined elementary/secondary[5]	Other[6]
1	2	3	4	5	6	7	8	9	10	11	12	13
2015–16												
Total	98,277	66,758	24,040	19,325	6,788	691	50,115,178	32,035,708	15,748,184	15,296,173	2,329,346	1,940
Percent[8]	**100.00**	**100.00**	**100.00**	**100.00**	**100.00**	**100.00**	**100.00**	**100.00**	**100.00**	**100.00**	**100.00**	**100.00**
Under 100	10.14	5.32	17.94	9.39	33.11	88.89	0.86	0.55	1.07	0.64	3.57	18.87
100 to 199	8.91	7.62	11.04	10.15	15.03	0.00	2.53	2.40	2.32	1.88	5.76	0.00
200 to 299	10.94	11.59	9.28	9.75	10.06	0.00	5.25	6.10	3.31	3.05	6.64	0.00
300 to 399	13.48	15.88	7.84	8.61	8.24	5.56	8.97	11.56	3.92	3.77	7.64	20.26
400 to 499	14.11	17.13	7.15	8.13	7.03	0.00	12.02	15.95	4.58	4.56	8.40	0.00
500 to 599	11.63	14.21	5.71	6.46	5.65	0.00	12.10	16.12	4.48	4.44	8.23	0.00
600 to 699	8.67	10.32	4.85	5.51	4.98	0.00	10.66	13.84	4.51	4.48	8.62	0.00
700 to 799	6.10	7.02	3.96	4.56	4.02	0.00	8.65	10.87	4.24	4.28	7.99	0.00
800 to 999	6.73	6.91	6.69	7.75	4.97	0.00	11.31	12.63	8.55	8.68	11.77	0.00
1,000 to 1,499	5.53	3.67	11.28	13.03	4.53	5.56	12.54	8.79	19.86	20.09	14.44	60.88
1,500 to 1,999	2.05	0.28	7.46	8.71	1.34	0.00	6.72	0.95	18.52	18.93	6.17	0.00
2,000 to 2,999	1.42	0.04	5.72	6.70	0.58	0.00	6.36	0.19	19.30	19.79	3.62	0.00
3,000 or more	0.29	#	1.07	1.25	0.45	0.00	2.03	0.04	5.34	5.41	7.16	0.00
Average enrollment[8]	526	482	698	797	376	108	526	482	698	797	376	108
2016–17												
Total	98,158	66,837	23,814	19,264	6,783	724	50,274,747	32,132,682	15,798,446	15,355,391	2,335,618	8,001
Percent[8]	**100.00**	**100.00**	**100.00**	**100.00**	**100.00**	**100.00**	**100.00**	**100.00**	**100.00**	**100.00**	**100.00**	**100.00**
Under 100	10.02	5.25	17.22	9.38	33.67	81.74	0.85	0.54	1.05	0.64	3.61	48.09
100 to 199	8.93	7.60	11.11	10.06	15.24	14.78	2.54	2.40	2.32	1.87	5.92	28.52
200 to 299	10.95	11.59	9.23	9.60	10.42	1.74	5.24	6.10	3.25	2.98	7.03	5.36
300 to 399	13.68	16.05	8.04	8.80	8.79	0.87	9.09	11.66	3.97	3.84	8.27	3.97
400 to 499	14.12	17.10	7.14	8.02	7.55	0.00	12.00	15.89	4.51	4.47	9.08	0.00
500 to 599	11.57	14.08	5.94	6.70	5.32	0.00	12.01	15.96	4.60	4.58	7.88	0.00
600 to 699	8.62	10.36	4.71	5.32	4.24	0.00	10.58	13.88	4.32	4.31	7.44	0.00
700 to 799	6.03	6.99	3.95	4.50	3.38	0.00	8.54	10.81	4.18	4.20	6.85	0.00
800 to 999	6.72	6.96	6.82	7.86	4.04	0.00	11.28	12.71	8.61	8.76	9.70	0.00
1,000 to 1,499	5.54	3.69	11.33	12.97	4.67	0.87	12.54	8.85	19.69	19.89	15.02	14.05
1,500 to 1,999	2.02	0.28	7.38	8.54	1.40	0.00	6.59	0.98	18.04	18.42	6.40	0.00
2,000 to 2,999	1.49	0.04	6.04	7.01	0.78	0.00	6.66	0.18	20.11	20.62	4.87	0.00
3,000 or more	0.29	0.01	1.08	1.24	0.51	0.00	2.08	0.04	5.35	5.42	7.93	0.00
Average enrollment[8]	528	483	708	802	371	70	528	483	708	802	371	70
2017–18												
Total	98,469	67,408	23,882	19,231	6,278	901	50,330,241	32,346,383	15,811,242	15,374,566	2,164,868	7,748
Percent[8]	**100.00**	**100.00**	**100.00**	**100.00**	**100.00**	**100.00**	**100.00**	**100.00**	**100.00**	**100.00**	**100.00**	**100.00**
Under 100	9.86	5.04	17.40	9.46	34.98	85.25	0.85	0.53	1.07	0.65	3.84	53.41
100 to 199	8.82	7.53	10.96	9.88	15.44	10.66	2.50	2.37	2.28	1.83	6.01	22.73
200 to 299	11.01	11.71	9.17	9.68	10.15	3.28	5.26	6.16	3.21	3.00	6.70	10.74
300 to 399	13.86	16.31	8.13	8.94	7.77	0.00	9.19	11.85	4.01	3.89	7.25	0.00
400 to 499	14.26	17.28	7.29	8.10	6.41	0.00	12.10	16.07	4.60	4.50	7.76	0.00
500 to 599	11.53	14.04	5.66	6.40	5.37	0.00	11.95	15.92	4.37	4.36	7.86	0.00
600 to 699	8.56	10.20	4.73	5.35	4.45	0.00	10.48	13.67	4.32	4.31	7.76	0.00
700 to 799	6.10	7.02	4.13	4.68	3.18	0.00	8.62	10.86	4.36	4.36	6.39	0.00
800 to 999	6.64	6.89	6.53	7.53	4.40	0.00	11.14	12.62	8.22	8.38	10.54	0.00
1,000 to 1,499	5.49	3.61	11.42	13.10	4.59	0.82	12.41	8.67	19.75	19.99	14.79	13.13
1,500 to 1,999	2.07	0.32	7.42	8.57	1.82	0.00	6.76	1.10	18.13	18.48	8.28	0.00
2,000 to 2,999	1.50	0.04	6.04	7.02	0.93	0.00	6.66	0.16	20.10	20.62	5.66	0.00
3,000 or more	0.30	#	1.13	1.30	0.50	0.00	2.08	0.02	5.58	5.63	7.16	0.00
Average enrollment[8]	528	483	709	804	372	64	528	483	709	804	372	64

#Rounds to zero.
[1]Because the data reflect reports by schools, totals differ from those in tables based on reports by states or school districts. Percentage distribution and average enrollment calculations exclude data for schools not reporting enrollment.
[2]Includes elementary, secondary, combined elementary/secondary, and other schools.
[3]Includes schools beginning with grade 6 or below and with no grade higher than 8.
[4]Includes schools with no grade lower than 7.
[5]Includes schools beginning with grade 6 or below and ending with grade 9 or above.
[6]Includes special education, alternative, and other schools not reported by grade span.
[7]Excludes special education schools, vocational schools, and alternative schools.
[8]Data are for schools reporting enrollments greater than zero. Enrollments greater than zero were reported for 95,240 out of 98,277 schools in 2015–16, 95,283 out of 98,158 in 2016–17, and 95,240 out of 98,469 in 2017–18.
NOTE: Detail may not sum to totals because of rounding.
SOURCE: U.S. Department of Education, National Center for Education Statistics, Common Core of Data (CCD), "Public Elementary/Secondary School Universe Survey," 2015–16, 2016–17, and 2017–18. (This table was prepared December 2019.)

Table 216.45. Average enrollment and percentage distribution of public elementary and secondary schools, by level, type, and enrollment size: Selected years, 1982–83 through 2017–18

Year	Average enrollment in schools, by level and type						Percentage distribution of schools, by enrollment size							
	Total[1]	Elementary[2]	Secondary[3]		Combined elementary/secondary[4]	Other[5]	Under 200	200 to 299	300 to 399	400 to 499	500 to 599	600 to 699	700 to 999	1,000 or more
			All schools	Regular schools[6]										
1	2	3	4	5	6	7	8	9	10	11	12	13	14	15
1982–83	478	399	719	—	478	142	21.9	13.8	15.5	13.1	10.2	7.1	10.2	8.3
1983–84	480	401	720	—	475	145	21.7	13.7	15.5	13.2	10.2	7.1	10.3	8.3
1984–85	482	403	721	—	476	146	21.5	13.6	15.5	13.2	10.3	7.1	10.4	8.4
1986–87	489	416	707	714	426	118	21.1	13.1	15.0	13.5	10.8	7.5	10.7	8.1
1987–88	490	424	695	711	420	122	20.3	12.9	14.9	13.8	11.1	7.8	11.2	8.0
1988–89	494	433	689	697	412	142	20.0	12.5	14.7	13.8	11.4	8.0	11.6	8.0
1989–90	493	441	669	689	402	142	19.8	12.2	14.5	13.7	11.5	8.3	12.0	7.9
1990–91	497	449	663	684	398	150	19.7	11.9	14.2	13.6	11.7	8.5	12.3	8.1
1991–92	507	458	677	717	407	152	19.1	11.7	14.1	13.5	11.8	8.6	12.8	8.5
1992–93	513	464	688	733	423	135	18.6	11.6	13.9	13.5	11.9	8.7	13.1	8.7
1993–94	518	468	693	748	418	136	18.6	11.5	13.6	13.5	11.7	8.8	13.3	9.0
1994–95	520	471	696	759	412	131	18.6	11.4	13.6	13.4	11.8	8.7	13.3	9.2
1995–96	525	476	703	771	401	136	18.5	11.2	13.5	13.4	11.8	8.8	13.4	9.4
1996–97	527	478	703	777	387	135	18.7	11.3	13.2	13.2	11.8	8.8	13.6	9.5
1997–98	525	478	699	779	374	121	19.3	11.2	13.1	13.3	11.6	8.6	13.4	9.6
1998–99	524	478	707	786	290	135	19.6	11.2	13.1	13.2	11.5	8.5	13.3	9.6
1999–2000	521	477	706	785	282	123	20.0	11.3	13.3	13.2	11.2	8.4	13.1	9.5
2000–01	519	477	714	795	274	136	20.4	11.4	13.2	13.3	11.0	8.2	12.9	9.6
2001–02	520	477	718	807	270	138	20.5	11.5	13.3	13.1	10.9	8.1	12.7	9.7
2002–03	519	476	720	813	265	136	20.7	11.6	13.4	13.0	10.9	8.1	12.4	9.8
2003–04	521	476	722	816	269	142	20.7	11.6	13.5	13.2	10.8	8.0	12.3	9.9
2004–05	521	474	713	815	298	143	20.7	11.6	13.5	13.2	10.8	8.1	12.2	9.9
2005–06	521	473	709	819	318	128	20.7	11.5	13.6	13.2	11.0	8.1	12.2	9.8
2006–07	521	473	711	818	325	138	20.3	11.5	13.8	13.4	11.0	8.2	12.2	9.6
2007–08	516	469	704	816	292	136	20.4	11.5	13.9	13.6	11.1	8.1	12.0	9.3
2008–09	517	470	704	807	308	177	20.0	11.4	13.8	13.9	11.3	8.3	12.2	9.1
2009–10	516	473	692	796	300	191	20.0	11.3	13.7	13.9	11.4	8.5	12.3	9.0
2010–11	517	475	684	790	343	57	19.8	11.0	13.9	13.9	11.5	8.5	12.5	9.0
2011–12	520	479	690	788	322	84	19.4	11.0	13.8	13.9	11.7	8.6	12.7	9.0
2012–13	522	481	689	785	337	84	19.3	10.9	13.6	13.9	11.7	8.6	12.8	9.1
2013–14	525	483	693	788	340	238	19.2	10.9	13.4	13.9	11.8	8.7	13.0	9.1
2014–15	525	483	694	791	354	131	19.2	10.9	13.4	13.9	11.8	8.6	12.9	9.2
2015–16	526	482	698	797	376	108	19.0	10.9	13.5	14.1	11.6	8.7	12.8	9.3
2016–17	528	483	708	802	371	70	19.0	11.0	13.7	14.1	11.6	8.6	12.8	9.3
2017–18	528	483	709	804	372	64	18.7	11.0	13.9	14.3	11.5	8.6	12.7	9.4

—Not available.
[1]Includes elementary, secondary, combined elementary/secondary, and other schools.
[2]Includes schools beginning with grade 6 or below and with no grade higher than 8.
[3]Includes schools with no grade lower than 7.
[4]Includes schools beginning with grade 6 or below and ending with grade 9 or above.
[5]Includes special education, alternative, and other schools not reported by grade span.
[6]Excludes special education schools, vocational schools, and alternative schools.

NOTE: Data reflect reports by schools rather than by states or school districts. Percentage distribution and average enrollment calculations include data only for schools reporting enrollments greater than zero. Enrollments greater than zero were reported for 95,240 out of 98,469 schools in 2017–18. Detail may not sum to totals because of rounding.
SOURCE: U.S. Department of Education, National Center for Education Statistics, Common Core of Data (CCD), "Public Elementary/Secondary School Universe Survey," 1982–83 through 2017–18. (This table was prepared December 2019.)

Table 216.50. Number and percentage distribution of public elementary and secondary school students, by percentage of minority enrollment in the school and student's racial/ethnic group: Selected years, fall 1995 through fall 2017

Year and racial/ ethnic group	Number of students in racial/ethnic group, by percent minority enrollment in the school							Percentage distribution of students in racial/ethnic group, by percent minority enrollment in the school						
	Total	Less than 10 percent	10 to 24 percent	25 to 49 percent	50 to 74 percent	75 to 89 percent	90 percent or more	Total	Less than 10 percent	10 to 24 percent	25 to 49 percent	50 to 74 percent	75 to 89 percent	90 percent or more
1	2	3	4	5	6	7	8	9	10	11	12	13	14	15
Total, 1995	**44,424,467**	**14,508,573**	**8,182,484**	**8,261,110**	**5,467,784**	**2,876,302**	**5,128,214**	**100.0**	**32.7**	**18.4**	**18.6**	**12.3**	**6.5**	**11.5**
White	28,736,961	13,939,633	6,812,196	5,246,785	2,094,440	499,884	144,023	100.0	48.5	23.7	18.3	7.3	1.7	0.5
Minority	15,687,506	568,940	1,370,288	3,014,325	3,373,344	2,376,418	4,984,191	100.0	3.6	8.7	19.2	21.5	15.1	31.8
Black	7,510,678	198,386	598,716	1,588,850	1,622,448	941,335	2,560,943	100.0	2.6	8.0	21.2	21.6	12.5	34.1
Hispanic	6,016,293	174,140	415,761	932,949	1,289,184	1,099,109	2,105,150	100.0	2.9	6.9	15.5	21.4	18.3	35.0
Asian/Pacific Islander	1,656,787	142,886	259,335	367,888	379,110	297,680	209,888	100.0	8.6	15.7	22.2	22.9	18.0	12.7
American Indian/ Alaska Native	503,748	53,528	96,476	124,638	82,602	38,294	108,210	100.0	10.6	19.2	24.7	16.4	7.6	21.5
Total, 2000	**46,120,425**	**12,761,478**	**8,736,252**	**8,760,300**	**6,013,131**	**3,472,083**	**6,377,181**	**100.0**	**27.7**	**18.9**	**19.0**	**13.0**	**7.5**	**13.8**
White	28,146,613	12,218,862	7,271,285	5,566,681	2,303,106	596,478	190,201	100.0	43.4	25.8	19.8	8.2	2.1	0.7
Minority	17,973,812	542,616	1,464,967	3,193,619	3,710,025	2,875,605	6,186,980	100.0	3.0	8.2	17.8	20.6	16.0	34.4
Black	7,854,032	178,185	561,488	1,485,130	1,652,393	1,043,907	2,932,929	100.0	2.3	7.1	18.9	21.0	13.3	37.3
Hispanic	7,649,728	181,685	505,612	1,121,809	1,542,982	1,432,639	2,865,001	100.0	2.4	6.6	14.7	20.2	18.7	37.5
Asian/Pacific Islander	1,924,875	132,813	295,437	441,769	423,175	353,395	278,286	100.0	6.9	15.3	23.0	22.0	18.4	14.5
American Indian/ Alaska Native	545,177	49,933	102,430	144,911	91,475	45,664	110,764	100.0	9.2	18.8	26.6	16.8	8.4	20.3
Total, 2005	**48,584,980**	**10,711,307**	**9,283,783**	**9,865,121**	**6,839,850**	**4,149,802**	**7,735,117**	**100.0**	**22.0**	**19.1**	**20.3**	**14.1**	**8.5**	**15.9**
White	27,742,612	10,208,608	7,720,632	6,259,485	2,604,846	707,603	241,438	100.0	36.8	27.8	22.6	9.4	2.6	0.9
Minority	20,842,368	502,699	1,563,151	3,605,636	4,235,004	3,442,199	7,493,679	100.0	2.4	7.5	17.3	20.3	16.5	36.0
Black	8,366,722	162,455	560,928	1,513,020	1,752,207	1,176,649	3,201,463	100.0	1.9	6.7	18.1	20.9	14.1	38.3
Hispanic	9,638,712	182,039	581,533	1,388,496	1,873,877	1,803,567	3,809,200	100.0	1.9	6.0	14.4	19.4	18.7	39.5
Asian/Pacific Islander	2,242,628	115,084	319,524	543,952	496,515	406,788	360,765	100.0	5.1	14.2	24.3	22.1	18.1	16.1
American Indian/ Alaska Native	594,306	43,121	101,166	160,168	112,405	55,195	122,251	100.0	7.3	17.0	27.0	18.9	9.3	20.6
Total, 2010	**49,212,031**	**7,395,549**	**9,177,649**	**11,236,328**	**7,904,340**	**4,718,126**	**8,780,039**	**100.0**	**15.0**	**18.6**	**22.8**	**16.1**	**9.6**	**17.8**
White	25,801,021	6,987,898	7,614,557	7,097,284	3,003,599	808,637	289,046	100.0	27.1	29.5	27.5	11.6	3.1	1.1
Minority	23,411,010	407,651	1,563,092	4,139,044	4,900,741	3,909,489	8,490,993	100.0	1.7	6.7	17.7	20.9	16.7	36.3
Black	7,873,809	95,108	415,807	1,335,674	1,697,727	1,236,333	3,093,160	100.0	1.2	5.3	17.0	21.6	15.7	39.3
Hispanic	11,367,157	142,927	583,019	1,654,084	2,238,071	2,063,492	4,685,564	100.0	1.3	5.1	14.6	19.7	18.2	41.2
Asian	2,281,908	63,974	259,910	585,447	552,633	390,731	429,213	100.0	2.8	11.4	25.7	24.2	17.1	18.8
Pacific Islander	169,678	4,958	13,772	27,478	32,241	41,652	49,577	100.0	2.9	8.1	16.2	19.0	24.5	29.2
American Indian/ Alaska Native	561,126	26,066	77,990	157,300	116,787	58,476	124,507	100.0	4.6	13.9	28.0	20.8	10.4	22.2
Two or more races	1,157,332	74,618	212,594	379,061	263,282	118,805	108,972	100.0	6.4	18.4	32.8	22.7	10.3	9.4
Total, 2015	**50,115,178**	**5,396,946**	**8,879,198**	**11,705,331**	**9,039,153**	**5,397,826**	**9,696,724**	**100.0**	**10.8**	**17.7**	**23.4**	**18.0**	**10.8**	**19.3**
White	24,505,632	5,072,523	7,350,271	7,372,017	3,444,117	927,072	339,632	100.0	20.7	30.0	30.1	14.1	3.8	1.4
Minority	25,609,546	324,423	1,528,927	4,333,314	5,595,036	4,470,754	9,357,092	100.0	1.3	6.0	16.9	21.8	17.5	36.5
Black	7,731,426	57,618	326,861	1,195,388	1,705,877	1,334,427	3,111,255	100.0	0.7	4.2	15.5	22.1	17.3	40.2
Hispanic	12,982,345	121,565	612,478	1,800,949	2,628,585	2,392,367	5,426,401	100.0	0.9	4.7	13.9	20.2	18.4	41.8
Asian	2,504,848	38,098	222,680	606,969	685,774	458,658	492,669	100.0	1.5	8.9	24.2	27.4	18.3	19.7
Pacific Islander	175,646	3,654	13,358	28,769	37,209	36,554	56,102	100.0	2.1	7.6	16.4	21.2	20.8	31.9
American Indian/ Alaska Native	504,365	15,229	54,626	136,002	109,499	58,998	130,011	100.0	3.0	10.8	27.0	21.7	11.7	25.8
Two or more races	1,710,916	88,259	298,924	565,237	428,092	189,750	140,654	100.0	5.2	17.5	33.0	25.0	11.1	8.2
Total, 2016	**50,274,747**	**5,022,678**	**8,774,358**	**11,786,119**	**9,298,054**	**5,573,066**	**9,820,472**	**100.0**	**10.0**	**17.5**	**23.4**	**18.5**	**11.1**	**19.5**
White	24,237,835	4,718,110	7,259,945	7,417,761	3,541,807	953,713	346,499	100.0	19.5	30.0	30.6	14.6	3.9	1.4
Minority	26,036,912	304,568	1,514,413	4,368,358	5,756,247	4,619,353	9,473,973	100.0	1.2	5.8	16.8	22.1	17.7	36.4
Black	7,698,283	51,649	309,819	1,168,994	1,714,844	1,360,977	3,092,000	100.0	0.7	4.0	15.2	22.3	17.7	40.2
Hispanic	13,262,558	114,844	615,713	1,823,154	2,708,043	2,475,126	5,525,678	100.0	0.9	4.6	13.7	20.4	18.7	41.7
Asian	2,560,906	32,890	213,564	612,963	720,640	472,524	508,325	100.0	1.3	8.3	23.9	28.1	18.5	19.8
Pacific Islander	183,415	3,708	13,567	29,378	38,580	38,780	59,402	100.0	2.0	7.4	16.0	21.0	21.1	32.4
American Indian/ Alaska Native	502,152	13,441	51,288	133,381	108,048	62,795	133,199	100.0	2.7	10.2	26.6	21.5	12.5	26.5
Two or more races	1,829,598	88,036	310,462	600,488	466,092	209,151	155,369	100.0	4.8	17.0	32.8	25.5	11.4	8.5
Total, 2017	**50,330,241**	**4,721,887**	**8,591,274**	**11,880,887**	**9,541,134**	**5,696,069**	**9,898,990**	**100.0**	**9.4**	**17.1**	**23.6**	**19.0**	**11.3**	**19.7**
White	23,976,394	4,432,804	7,106,209	7,478,286	3,630,789	975,815	352,491	100.0	18.5	29.6	31.2	15.1	4.1	1.5
Minority	26,353,847	289,083	1,485,065	4,402,601	5,910,345	4,720,254	9,546,499	100.0	1.1	5.6	16.7	22.4	17.9	36.2
Black	7,657,704	46,803	293,409	1,147,199	1,724,050	1,371,883	3,074,360	100.0	0.6	3.8	15.0	22.5	17.9	40.1
Hispanic	13,461,088	110,151	609,252	1,850,857	2,772,521	2,519,689	5,598,618	100.0	0.8	4.5	13.7	20.6	18.7	41.6
Asian	2,619,963	29,465	200,698	615,105	756,748	499,451	518,496	100.0	1.1	7.7	23.5	28.9	19.1	19.8
Pacific Islander	183,919	3,479	13,333	29,568	39,929	39,258	58,352	100.0	1.9	7.2	16.1	21.7	21.3	31.7
American Indian/ Alaska Native	490,714	11,993	47,979	129,037	108,045	63,294	130,366	100.0	2.4	9.8	26.3	22.0	12.9	26.6
Two or more races	1,940,459	87,192	320,394	630,835	509,052	226,679	166,307	100.0	4.5	16.5	32.5	26.2	11.7	8.6

NOTE: Data reflect racial/ethnic data reported by schools. Because some schools do not report complete racial/ethnic data, totals may differ from figures in other tables. Excludes 1995 data for Idaho and 2000 data for Tennessee because racial/ethnic data were not reported. Race categories exclude persons of Hispanic ethnicity. Detail may not sum to totals because of rounding.

SOURCE: U.S. Department of Education, National Center for Education Statistics, Common Core of Data (CCD), "Public Elementary/Secondary School Universe Survey," 1995–96 through 2017–18. (This table was prepared December 2019.)

Table 216.55. Number and percentage distribution of public elementary and secondary school students, by percentage of student's racial/ethnic group enrolled in the school and student's racial/ethnic group: Selected years, fall 1995 through fall 2017

Year and racial/ethnic group	Number of students in each racial/ethnic group, by percent of that racial/ethnic group in the school							Percentage distribution of students in each racial/ethnic group, by percent of that racial/ethnic group in the school						
	Total	Less than 10 percent	10 to 24 percent	25 to 49 percent	50 to 74 percent	75 to 89 percent	90 percent or more	Total	Less than 10 percent	10 to 24 percent	25 to 49 percent	50 to 74 percent	75 to 89 percent	90 percent or more
1	2	3	4	5	6	7	8	9	10	11	12	13	14	15
1995														
White	28,736,961	143,787	498,649	2,084,689	5,244,015	6,813,804	13,952,017	100.0	0.5	1.7	7.3	18.2	23.7	48.6
Black	7,510,678	657,403	1,119,556	1,873,303	1,386,802	811,898	1,661,716	100.0	8.8	14.9	24.9	18.5	10.8	22.1
Hispanic	6,016,293	646,364	847,792	1,359,649	1,360,020	874,878	927,590	100.0	10.7	14.1	22.6	22.6	14.5	15.4
Asian/Pacific Islander	1,656,787	703,101	435,495	301,984	135,001	67,558	13,648	100.0	42.4	26.3	18.2	8.1	4.1	0.8
American Indian/Alaska Native	503,748	223,244	75,019	63,070	39,200	15,084	88,131	100.0	44.3	14.9	12.5	7.8	3.0	17.5
2000														
White	28,146,613	189,779	595,137	2,294,232	5,556,108	7,279,301	12,232,056	100.0	0.7	2.1	8.2	19.7	25.9	43.5
Black	7,854,032	735,459	1,199,865	1,899,982	1,366,363	871,399	1,780,964	100.0	9.4	15.3	24.2	17.4	11.1	22.7
Hispanic	7,649,728	738,509	1,054,396	1,696,944	1,739,038	1,134,466	1,286,375	100.0	9.7	13.8	22.2	22.7	14.8	16.8
Asian/Pacific Islander	1,924,875	799,220	524,279	331,576	171,739	81,461	16,600	100.0	41.5	27.2	17.2	8.9	4.2	0.9
American Indian/Alaska Native	545,177	251,983	81,119	75,831	39,944	15,363	80,937	100.0	46.2	14.9	13.9	7.3	2.8	14.8
2005														
White	27,742,612	240,614	705,300	2,596,310	6,256,109	7,718,175	10,226,104	100.0	0.9	2.5	9.4	22.6	27.8	36.9
Black	8,366,722	849,399	1,396,670	2,004,856	1,453,759	884,663	1,777,375	100.0	10.2	16.7	24.0	17.4	10.6	21.2
Hispanic	9,638,712	848,160	1,316,558	2,071,303	2,218,616	1,545,322	1,638,753	100.0	8.8	13.7	21.5	23.0	16.0	17.0
Asian/Pacific Islander	2,242,628	925,411	616,762	363,562	214,304	100,845	21,744	100.0	41.3	27.5	16.2	9.6	4.5	1.0
American Indian/Alaska Native	594,306	276,846	86,978	84,665	43,272	21,275	81,270	100.0	46.6	14.6	14.2	7.3	3.6	13.7
2010														
White	25,801,021	288,136	807,107	2,991,928	7,090,581	7,620,071	7,003,198	100.0	1.1	3.1	11.6	27.5	29.5	27.1
Black	7,873,809	904,777	1,453,068	1,907,158	1,328,164	859,843	1,420,799	100.0	11.5	18.5	24.2	16.9	10.9	18.0
Hispanic	11,367,157	896,796	1,603,546	2,473,080	2,657,108	1,791,161	1,945,466	100.0	7.9	14.1	21.8	23.4	15.8	17.1
Asian	2,281,908	944,657	633,149	431,446	219,381	43,509	9,766	100.0	41.4	27.7	18.9	9.6	1.9	0.4
Pacific Islander	169,678	104,646	15,170	27,558	14,860	5,146	2,298	100.0	61.7	8.9	16.2	8.8	3.0	1.4
American Indian/Alaska Native	561,126	276,859	76,874	78,978	38,349	21,156	68,910	100.0	49.3	13.7	14.1	6.8	3.8	12.3
Two or more races	1,157,332	996,181	128,813	15,347	6,709	3,286	6,996	100.0	86.1	11.1	1.3	0.6	0.3	0.6
2015														
White	24,505,632	338,854	925,174	3,433,953	7,370,748	7,349,746	5,087,157	100.0	1.4	3.8	14.0	30.1	30.0	20.8
Black	7,731,426	926,749	1,501,089	1,921,738	1,359,513	867,967	1,154,370	100.0	12.0	19.4	24.9	17.6	11.2	14.9
Hispanic	12,982,345	917,357	1,853,764	2,853,336	3,113,283	2,063,469	2,181,136	100.0	7.1	14.3	22.0	24.0	15.9	16.8
Asian	2,504,848	958,423	688,104	525,789	264,939	51,494	16,099	100.0	38.3	27.5	21.0	10.6	2.1	0.6
Pacific Islander	175,646	115,753	16,543	26,626	12,225	4,398	101	100.0	65.9	9.4	15.2	7.0	2.5	0.1
American Indian/Alaska Native	504,365	244,771	70,672	70,002	31,830	20,554	66,536	100.0	48.5	14.0	13.9	6.3	4.1	13.2
Two or more races	1,710,916	1,441,131	257,234	9,985	1,644	915	7	100.0	84.2	15.0	0.6	0.1	0.1	#
2016														
White	24,237,835	345,391	951,004	3,526,424	7,414,830	7,269,692	4,730,494	100.0	1.4	3.9	14.5	30.6	30.0	19.5
Black	7,698,283	934,011	1,525,821	1,918,536	1,370,443	847,520	1,101,952	100.0	12.1	19.8	24.9	17.8	11.0	14.3
Hispanic	13,262,558	915,163	1,908,509	2,959,009	3,184,219	2,112,281	2,183,377	100.0	6.9	14.4	22.3	24.0	15.9	16.5
Asian	2,560,906	957,860	699,521	554,255	277,419	56,823	15,028	100.0	37.4	27.3	21.6	10.8	2.2	0.6
Pacific Islander	183,415	124,482	18,105	25,524	12,050	3,142	112	100.0	67.9	9.9	13.9	6.6	1.7	0.1
American Indian/Alaska Native	502,152	243,356	69,973	70,719	32,069	21,969	64,066	100.0	48.5	13.9	14.1	6.4	4.4	12.8
Two or more races	1,829,598	1,510,009	301,306	15,955	808	1,074	446	100.0	82.5	16.5	0.9	0.0	0.1	#
2017														
White	23,976,394	351,591	972,907	3,617,008	7,478,175	7,104,442	4,452,271	100.0	1.5	4.1	15.1	31.2	29.6	18.6
Black	7,657,704	937,456	1,540,064	1,930,181	1,347,953	841,625	1,060,425	100.0	12.2	20.1	25.2	17.6	11.0	13.8
Hispanic	13,461,088	909,319	1,958,390	3,020,258	3,251,806	2,108,336	2,212,979	100.0	6.8	14.5	22.4	24.2	15.7	16.4
Asian	2,619,963	960,701	714,338	574,139	292,198	64,730	13,857	100.0	36.7	27.3	21.9	11.2	2.5	0.5
Pacific Islander	183,919	127,122	18,381	23,397	11,678	3,237	104	100.0	69.1	10.0	12.7	6.3	1.8	0.1
American Indian/Alaska Native	490,714	239,389	68,775	65,205	32,948	20,172	64,225	100.0	48.8	14.0	13.3	6.7	4.1	13.1
Two or more races	1,940,459	1,573,163	343,041	21,498	2,752	0	5	100.0	81.1	17.7	1.1	0.1	0.0	#

#Rounds to zero.
NOTE: Data reflect racial/ethnic data reported by schools. Because some schools do not report complete racial/ethnic data, totals may differ from figures in other tables. Excludes 1995 data for Idaho and 2000 data for Tennessee because racial/ethnic data were not reported. Race categories exclude persons of Hispanic ethnicity. Detail may not sum to totals because of rounding.

SOURCE: U.S. Department of Education, National Center for Education Statistics, Common Core of Data (CCD), "Public Elementary/Secondary School Universe Survey," 1995–96 through 2017–18. (This table was prepared December 2019.)

Table 216.60. Number and percentage distribution of public school students, by percentage of students in school who are eligible for free or reduced-price lunch, school level, locale, and student race/ethnicity: Fall 2017

School level, locale, and student race/ethnicity	Number of students, by percent of students in school eligible for free or reduced-price lunch						Percentage distribution of students, by percent of students in school eligible for free or reduced-price lunch					
	Total	0 to 25.0 percent	25.1 to 50.0 percent	50.1 to 75.0 percent	More than 75.0 percent	Missing/ school does not participate	Total	0 to 25.0 percent	25.1 to 50.0 percent	50.1 to 75.0 percent	More than 75.0 percent	Missing/ school does not participate
1	2	3	4	5	6	7	8	9	10	11	12	13
Total	**50,330,241**	**10,575,788**	**14,236,362**	**12,740,656**	**12,491,910**	**285,525**	**100.0**	**21.0**	**28.3**	**25.3**	**24.8**	**0.6**
White	23,976,394	7,378,741	8,876,623	5,520,817	2,033,096	167,117	100.0	30.8	37.0	23.0	8.5	0.7
Black	7,657,704	567,654	1,438,606	2,159,919	3,457,276	34,249	100.0	7.4	18.8	28.2	45.1	0.4
Hispanic	13,461,088	1,097,002	2,476,376	3,839,382	5,996,254	52,074	100.0	8.1	18.4	28.5	44.5	0.4
Asian	2,619,963	1,013,918	673,157	513,707	403,943	15,238	100.0	38.7	25.7	19.6	15.4	0.6
Pacific Islander	183,919	22,183	51,720	64,784	44,348	884	100.0	12.1	28.1	35.2	24.1	0.5
American Indian/Alaska Native	490,714	40,556	109,998	133,764	202,716	3,680	100.0	8.3	22.4	27.3	41.3	0.7
Two or more races	1,940,459	455,734	609,882	508,283	354,277	12,283	100.0	23.5	31.4	26.2	18.3	0.6
School level[1]												
Elementary[2]	32,346,383	6,398,292	8,262,515	8,264,994	9,310,792	109,790	100.0	19.8	25.5	25.6	28.8	0.3
White	15,070,919	4,407,423	5,213,146	3,813,266	1,577,427	59,657	100.0	29.2	34.6	25.3	10.5	0.4
Black	4,976,996	310,931	786,604	1,308,539	2,554,563	16,359	100.0	6.2	15.8	26.3	51.3	0.3
Hispanic	8,847,659	663,432	1,401,848	2,335,243	4,426,259	20,877	100.0	7.5	15.8	26.4	50.0	0.2
Asian	1,672,851	674,378	384,908	315,435	291,864	6,266	100.0	40.3	23.0	18.9	17.4	0.4
Pacific Islander	113,715	12,792	26,892	40,366	33,319	346	100.0	11.2	23.6	35.5	29.3	0.3
American Indian/Alaska Native	304,152	21,452	56,800	84,578	140,243	1,079	100.0	7.1	18.7	27.8	46.1	0.4
Two or more races	1,360,091	307,884	392,317	367,567	287,117	5,206	100.0	22.6	28.8	27.0	21.1	0.4
Secondary[3]	15,811,242	3,802,293	5,429,067	3,891,915	2,618,320	69,647	100.0	24.0	34.3	24.6	16.6	0.4
White	7,867,081	2,715,719	3,325,684	1,418,598	363,107	43,973	100.0	34.5	42.3	18.0	4.6	0.6
Black	2,290,686	224,518	596,962	746,768	716,801	5,637	100.0	9.8	26.1	32.6	31.3	0.2
Hispanic	4,066,826	389,982	972,105	1,357,831	1,333,044	13,864	100.0	9.6	23.9	33.4	32.8	0.3
Asian	872,396	318,616	268,325	184,948	97,431	3,076	100.0	36.5	30.8	21.2	11.2	0.4
Pacific Islander	61,639	8,218	23,022	21,584	8,667	148	100.0	13.3	37.3	35.0	14.1	0.2
American Indian/Alaska Native	152,289	15,752	49,246	40,909	45,267	1,115	100.0	10.3	32.3	26.9	29.7	0.7
Two or more races	500,325	129,488	193,723	121,277	54,003	1,834	100.0	25.9	38.7	24.2	10.8	0.4
School locale												
City	15,282,104	1,877,136	3,169,673	3,735,112	6,408,206	91,977	100.0	12.3	20.7	24.4	41.9	0.6
White	4,335,254	1,081,252	1,492,990	1,049,836	671,185	39,991	100.0	24.9	34.4	24.2	15.5	0.9
Black	3,504,501	143,097	479,468	861,979	2,003,035	16,922	100.0	4.1	13.7	24.6	57.2	0.5
Hispanic	5,591,844	250,427	748,011	1,362,064	3,206,857	24,485	100.0	4.5	13.4	24.4	57.3	0.4
Asian	1,066,561	278,047	248,414	252,068	283,292	4,740	100.0	26.1	23.3	23.6	26.6	0.4
Pacific Islander	66,516	5,666	15,017	21,965	23,587	281	100.0	8.5	22.6	33.0	35.5	0.4
American Indian/Alaska Native	104,866	8,458	23,341	27,386	44,305	1,376	100.0	8.1	22.3	26.1	42.2	1.3
Two or more races	612,562	110,189	162,432	159,814	175,945	4,182	100.0	18.0	26.5	26.1	28.7	0.7
Suburban	19,928,348	6,364,619	5,651,985	4,301,976	3,491,758	118,010	100.0	31.9	28.4	21.6	17.5	0.6
White	9,541,064	4,421,808	3,174,211	1,411,315	460,394	73,336	100.0	46.3	33.3	14.8	4.8	0.8
Black	2,721,131	330,255	655,582	860,948	860,778	13,568	100.0	12.1	24.1	31.6	31.6	0.5
Hispanic	5,376,104	662,692	1,152,655	1,593,642	1,950,577	16,538	100.0	12.3	21.4	29.6	36.3	0.3
Asian	1,316,933	648,967	350,005	211,562	97,703	8,696	100.0	49.3	26.6	16.1	7.4	0.7
Pacific Islander	73,645	13,177	23,422	23,780	12,898	368	100.0	17.9	31.8	32.3	17.5	0.5
American Indian/Alaska Native	83,531	17,259	28,067	22,436	15,059	710	100.0	20.7	33.6	26.9	18.0	0.8
Two or more races	815,940	270,461	268,043	178,293	94,349	4,794	100.0	33.1	32.9	21.9	11.6	0.6
Town	5,522,279	509,799	1,903,810	1,941,965	1,135,097	31,608	100.0	9.2	34.5	35.2	20.6	0.6
White	3,456,185	422,645	1,473,381	1,189,836	347,423	22,900	100.0	12.2	42.6	34.4	10.1	0.7
Black	536,796	15,348	87,609	171,478	260,459	1,902	100.0	2.9	16.3	31.9	48.5	0.4
Hispanic	1,117,990	40,363	216,053	434,378	423,008	4,188	100.0	3.6	19.3	38.9	37.8	0.4
Asian	71,937	9,416	26,307	23,453	12,359	402	100.0	13.1	36.6	32.6	17.2	0.6
Pacific Islander	23,123	834	7,401	10,652	4,163	73	100.0	3.6	32.0	46.1	18.0	0.3
American Indian/Alaska Native	114,712	5,004	26,386	34,621	48,021	680	100.0	4.4	23.0	30.2	41.9	0.6
Two or more races	201,536	16,189	66,673	77,547	39,664	1,463	100.0	8.0	33.1	38.5	19.7	0.7
Rural	9,597,510	1,824,234	3,510,894	2,761,603	1,456,849	43,930	100.0	19.0	36.6	28.8	15.2	0.5
White	6,643,891	1,453,036	2,736,041	1,869,830	554,094	30,890	100.0	21.9	41.2	28.1	8.3	0.5
Black	895,276	78,954	215,947	265,514	333,004	1,857	100.0	8.8	24.1	29.7	37.2	0.2
Hispanic	1,375,150	143,520	359,657	449,298	415,812	6,863	100.0	10.4	26.2	32.7	30.2	0.5
Asian	164,532	77,488	48,431	26,624	10,589	1,400	100.0	47.1	29.4	16.2	6.4	0.9
Pacific Islander	20,635	2,506	5,880	8,387	3,700	162	100.0	12.1	28.5	40.6	17.9	0.8
American Indian/Alaska Native	187,605	9,835	32,204	49,321	95,331	914	100.0	5.2	17.2	26.3	50.8	0.5
Two or more races	310,421	58,895	112,734	92,629	44,319	1,844	100.0	19.0	36.3	29.8	14.3	0.6

[1]Combined elementary/secondary schools and schools not reported by grade span are not shown separately.
[2]Includes schools beginning with grade 6 or below and with no grade higher than 8.
[3]Includes schools with no grade lower than 7.
NOTE: Students with household incomes under 185 percent of the poverty threshold are eligible for free or reduced-price lunch under the National School Lunch Program (NSLP). In addition, some groups of children—such as foster children, children participating in the Head Start and Migrant Education programs, and children receiving services under the Runaway and Homeless Youth Act—are assumed to be categorically eligible to participate in the NSLP. Data include students whose NSLP eligibility has been determined through direct certification. Also, under the Community Eligibility option, some nonpoor children who attend school in a low-income area may participate if the district decides that it would be more efficient to provide free lunch to all children in the school. For more information, see https://www.fns.usda.gov/nslp. Race categories exclude persons of Hispanic ethnicity. Detail may not sum to totals because of rounding.
SOURCE: U.S. Department of Education, National Center for Education Statistics, Common Core of Data (CCD), "Public Elementary/Secondary School Universe Survey," 2017–18; and Education Demographic and Geographic Estimates (EDGE), "Public School File," 2017–18. (This table was prepared November 2019.)

Table 216.70. Public elementary and secondary schools, by level, type, and state or jurisdiction: 1990–91, 2000–01, 2010–11, and 2017–18

State or jurisdiction	Total, all schools, 1990–91	Total, all schools, 2000–01	Total, all schools, 2010–11	Schools by level, 2017–18: Total, all schools	Elementary[1]	Secondary[2]	Combined elementary/secondary[3]: Total	Prekindergarten, kindergarten, or grade 1 to grade 12	Other schools ending with grade 12	Other combined schools	Other[4]	Selected types of schools, 2017–18: Alternative[5]	Special education[5]	One-teacher schools[5]
1	2	3	4	5	6	7	8	9	10	11	12	13	14	15
United States	**84,538**	**93,273**	**98,817**	**98,469**	**67,408**	**23,882**	**6,278**	**3,267**	**2,509**	**502**	**901**	**5,185**	**1,903**	**188**
Alabama	1,297	1,517	1,600	1,474	922	399	149	96	49	4	4	63	23	0
Alaska	498	515	509	509	198	79	232	216	15	1	0	22	3	4
Arizona	1,049	1,724	2,265	2,330	1,391	762	162	89	58	15	15	59	20	4
Arkansas	1,098	1,138	1,110	1,086	689	373	23	8	10	5	1	5	4	0
California	7,913	8,773	10,124	10,319	7,028	2,488	651	503	139	9	152	1,075	155	34
Colorado	1,344	1,632	1,796	1,900	1,337	396	167	78	82	7	0	97	6	0
Connecticut	985	1,248	1,157	1,031	784	222	23	10	12	1	2	5	6	0
Delaware	173	191	214	227	165	38	19	11	5	3	5	6	19	0
District of Columbia	181	198	228	224	177	37	10	1	7	2	0	4	2	0
Florida	2,516	3,316	4,131	4,322	2,843	679	662	288	356	18	138	388	163	0
Georgia	1,734	1,946	2,449	2,307	1,775	457	68	17	38	13	7	39	19	0
Hawaii	235	261	289	292	212	53	27	22	3	2	0	1	1	0
Idaho	582	673	748	741	466	189	86	44	41	1	0	72	11	11
Illinois	4,239	4,342	4,361	4,241	3,086	989	73	19	49	5	93	144	113	1
Indiana	1,915	1,976	1,936	1,920	1,370	458	92	49	37	6	0	8	22	0
Iowa	1,588	1,534	1,436	1,322	935	348	39	4	35	0	0	17	3	1
Kansas	1,477	1,430	1,378	1,319	917	342	57	21	36	0	3	1	4	0
Kentucky	1,400	1,526	1,554	1,533	966	423	142	44	93	5	2	184	8	0
Louisiana	1,533	1,530	1,471	1,390	959	281	150	99	44	7	0	5	30	0
Maine	747	714	631	599	439	145	15	9	6	0	0	0	1	2
Maryland	1,220	1,383	1,449	1,420	1,120	240	48	19	23	6	12	44	37	0
Massachusetts	1,842	1,905	1,829	1,854	1,413	372	61	20	34	7	8	22	11	0
Michigan	3,313	3,998	3,877	3,730	2,272	959	453	257	188	8	46	378	269	5
Minnesota	1,590	2,362	2,392	2,525	1,379	851	292	140	140	12	3	493	314	0
Mississippi	972	1,030	1,083	1,060	614	329	44	36	7	1	73	67	0	0
Missouri	2,199	2,368	2,410	2,414	1,611	628	155	74	81	0	20	59	52	0
Montana	900	879	827	820	496	324	0	0	0	0	0	4	2	60
Nebraska	1,506	1,326	1,096	1,095	731	305	12	11	0	1	47	47	27	4
Nevada	354	511	645	691	513	127	50	17	28	5	1	32	14	14
New Hampshire	439	526	480	490	382	108	0	0	0	0	0	0	0	0
New Jersey	2,272	2,410	2,607	2,594	1,952	539	82	45	26	11	21	89	65	0
New Mexico	681	765	862	881	600	229	33	13	17	3	19	41	5	0
New York	4,010	4,336	4,757	4,795	3,286	1,121	385	175	154	56	3	53	133	0
North Carolina	1,955	2,207	2,567	2,647	1,939	553	155	73	63	19	0	73	25	0
North Dakota	663	579	516	516	305	178	0	0	0	0	33	0	32	7
Ohio	3,731	3,916	3,758	3,604	2,430	989	148	42	69	37	37	0	47	0
Oklahoma	1,880	1,821	1,785	1,800	1,234	564	2	1	1	0	0	5	4	0
Oregon	1,199	1,273	1,296	1,249	890	274	85	57	24	4	0	35	1	13
Pennsylvania	3,260	3,252	3,233	2,982	2,102	783	97	47	40	10	0	6	4	0
Rhode Island	309	328	317	317	241	70	6	5	1	0	0	2	1	0
South Carolina	1,097	1,127	1,214	1,255	933	282	40	13	22	5	0	12	7	0
South Dakota	802	769	710	697	442	240	15	8	7	0	0	30	12	12
Tennessee	1,543	1,624	1,784	1,782	1,351	351	80	30	40	10	0	19	16	0
Texas	5,991	7,519	8,732	8,905	6,156	2,076	673	274	242	157	0	874	12	0
Utah	714	793	1,016	1,051	688	282	81	42	10	29	0	29	59	0
Vermont	397	393	320	311	228	65	18	11	7	0	0	1	0	1
Virginia	1,811	1,969	2,175	2,113	1,490	436	35	25	10	0	152	125	33	0
Washington	1,936	2,305	2,338	2,425	1,583	625	217	135	71	11	0	312	89	3
West Virginia	1,015	840	757	730	544	155	31	11	19	1	0	33	3	0
Wisconsin	2,018	2,182	2,238	2,261	1,577	568	112	45	64	3	4	95	13	2
Wyoming	415	393	360	369	247	101	21	13	6	2	0	10	3	10
Jurisdiction														
Bureau of Indian Education	—	189	173	174	111	19	44	37	5	2	0	0	0	0
DoDEA[6]	—	227	191	—	—	—	—	—	—	—	—	—	—	—
Other jurisdictions														
American Samoa	30	31	28	28	22	6	0	0	0	0	0	0	0	0
Guam	35	38	40	—	—	—	—	—	—	—	—	—	—	—
Northern Marianas	26	29	30	41	34	7	0	0	0	0	0	1	0	—
Puerto Rico	1,619	1,543	1,473	1,121	855	182	60	7	26	27	24	0	17	0
U.S. Virgin Islands	33	36	32	28	19	9	0	0	0	0	0	0	0	0

—Not available.
[1]Includes schools beginning with grade 6 or below and with no grade higher than 8.
[2]Includes schools with no grade lower than 7.
[3]Includes schools beginning with grade 6 or below and ending with grade 9 or above.
[4]Includes schools not reported by grade span.
[5]Schools are also included under elementary, secondary, combined, or other as appropriate.
[6]DoDEA = Department of Defense Education Activity. Includes both domestic and overseas schools.
SOURCE: U.S. Department of Education, National Center for Education Statistics, Common Core of Data (CCD), "Public Elementary/Secondary School Universe Survey," 1990–91, 2000–01, 2010–11, and 2017–18. (This table was prepared December 2019.)

Table 216.75. Public elementary schools, by grade span, average school enrollment, and state or jurisdiction: 2017–18

State or jurisdiction	Total, all elementary schools	Total, all regular elementary schools[1]	Schools, by grade span: Prekindergarten, kindergarten, or grade 1 to grade 3 or 4	Prekindergarten, kindergarten, or grade 1 to grade 5	Prekindergarten, kindergarten, or grade 1 to grade 6	Prekindergarten, kindergarten, or grade 1 to grade 8	Grade 4, 5, or 6 to grade 6, 7, or 8	Other grade spans	Average school enrollment[2]: All elementary schools	Regular elementary schools[1]
1	2	3	4	5	6	7	8	9	10	11
United States	**67,408**	**66,436**	**4,985**	**25,906**	**9,470**	**6,826**	**13,437**	**6,784**	**483**	**487**
Alabama	922	913	95	288	140	62	215	122	498	500
Alaska	198	198	0	42	96	22	25	13	335	335
Arizona	1,391	1,374	48	236	376	484	174	73	505	507
Arkansas	689	687	129	142	154	7	153	104	450	452
California	7,028	6,882	118	2,569	2,043	1,068	1,057	173	545	553
Colorado	1,337	1,332	26	641	188	137	246	99	434	435
Connecticut	784	779	87	270	67	104	155	101	425	427
Delaware	165	156	14	83	4	7	38	19	538	553
District of Columbia	177	177	21	73	1	33	33	16	369	369
Florida	2,843	2,786	31	1,656	123	338	568	127	670	682
Georgia	1,775	1,774	36	1,060	22	42	464	151	684	684
Hawaii	212	212	0	87	85	10	28	2	534	534
Idaho	466	454	34	163	126	33	86	24	393	402
Illinois	3,086	3,058	283	774	285	660	580	504	426	429
Indiana	1,370	1,367	167	469	294	44	267	129	476	477
Iowa	935	934	112	322	137	10	226	128	355	355
Kansas	917	915	67	371	180	51	190	58	350	350
Kentucky	966	954	31	466	104	76	194	95	476	481
Louisiana	959	958	79	307	108	133	201	131	474	474
Maine	439	439	46	96	55	90	77	75	269	269
Maryland	1,120	1,107	11	685	51	102	222	49	558	563
Massachusetts	1,413	1,408	178	486	115	103	285	246	435	435
Michigan	2,272	2,175	218	760	185	246	453	410	421	424
Minnesota	1,379	1,201	115	433	238	80	274	239	427	468
Mississippi	614	614	69	140	87	40	153	125	495	495
Missouri	1,611	1,603	143	517	294	115	322	220	372	373
Montana	496	493	17	76	185	110	74	34	193	194
Nebraska	731	727	46	198	239	19	110	119	298	298
Nevada	513	504	11	283	72	32	98	17	633	643
New Hampshire	382	382	51	113	37	54	83	44	313	313
New Jersey	1,952	1,932	263	555	133	287	369	345	456	460
New Mexico	600	596	20	250	109	33	130	58	361	363
New York	3,286	3,262	287	1,293	343	292	716	355	514	516
North Carolina	1,939	1,927	77	1,100	53	141	468	100	527	530
North Dakota	305	305	13	88	95	67	33	9	247	247
Ohio	2,430	2,408	351	608	328	229	529	385	437	440
Oklahoma	1,234	1,230	82	308	157	275	257	155	387	387
Oregon	890	887	27	411	113	127	178	34	416	416
Pennsylvania	2,102	2,102	298	671	312	191	424	206	494	494
Rhode Island	241	240	35	103	17	3	50	33	391	392
South Carolina	933	931	45	479	33	49	230	97	567	568
South Dakota	442	432	29	128	57	95	107	26	218	220
Tennessee	1,351	1,342	179	528	48	180	327	89	504	506
Texas	6,156	6,047	607	2,933	430	149	1,381	656	570	577
Utah	688	651	5	124	433	33	45	48	541	562
Vermont	228	228	15	24	97	63	17	12	243	243
Virginia	1,490	1,490	40	845	148	11	311	135	578	578
Washington	1,583	1,504	62	736	248	84	315	138	457	473
West Virginia	544	543	70	251	28	39	113	43	349	350
Wisconsin	1,577	1,570	171	601	125	148	340	192	359	360
Wyoming	247	246	26	64	72	18	46	21	242	242
Jurisdiction										
Bureau of Indian Education	111	111	7	6	28	62	4	4	212	212
DoDEA[3]	—	—	—	—	—	—	—	—	—	—
Other jurisdictions										
American Samoa	22	22	0	0	0	22	0	0	349	349
Guam	34	34	0	24	0	0	8	2	595	595
Northern Marianas	—	—	—	—	—	—	—	—	—	—
Puerto Rico	855	854	10	449	79	183	125	9	263	263
U.S. Virgin Islands	19	19	1	1	14	1	2	0	326	326

—Not available.
[1]Excludes special education and alternative schools.
[2]Average for schools reporting enrollment data. Enrollment data were available for 67,010 out of 67,408 public elementary schools in 2017–18.
[3]DoDEA = Department of Defense Education Activity. Includes both domestic and overseas schools.

NOTE: Includes schools beginning with grade 6 or below and with no grade higher than 8. Excludes schools not reported by grade level, such as some special education schools for students with disabilities.
SOURCE: U.S. Department of Education, National Center for Education Statistics, Common Core of Data (CCD), "Public Elementary/Secondary School Universe Survey," 2017–18. (This table was prepared December 2019.)

Table 216.80. Public secondary schools, by grade span, average school enrollment, and state or jurisdiction: 2017–18

State or jurisdiction	Total, all secondary schools	Total, all regular secondary schools[1]	Schools, by grade span: Grades 7 and 8 or grades 7 to 9	Grades 7 to 12	Grades 8 to 12	Grades 9 to 12	Grades 10 to 12	Other spans ending with grade 12	Other grade spans	Vocational schools[2]	Average school enrollment[3]: All secondary schools	Regular secondary schools[1]
1	2	3	4	5	6	7	8	9	10	11	12	13
United States	**23,882**	**19,231**	**2,479**	**2,864**	**526**	**16,119**	**558**	**401**	**935**	**1,467**	**709**	**804**
Alabama	399	317	40	68	10	245	28	1	7	65	702	712
Alaska	79	62	12	19	2	41	2	2	1	3	448	525
Arizona	762	473	54	78	25	575	12	3	15	260	654	732
Arkansas	373	344	50	117	10	136	36	1	23	24	514	520
California	2,488	1,657	354	269	13	1,752	67	23	10	66	878	1,215
Colorado	396	336	35	42	2	299	4	2	12	7	669	748
Connecticut	222	201	29	4	3	182	2	2	0	17	772	798
Delaware	38	32	1	1	9	25	0	0	2	6	996	961
District of Columbia	37	33	0	0	2	33	0	0	2	0	429	462
Florida	679	508	18	32	28	558	6	20	17	50	1,293	1,585
Georgia	457	427	15	7	11	388	5	0	31	0	1,131	1,206
Hawaii	53	52	12	7	0	33	0	0	1	0	1,105	1,125
Idaho	189	142	26	33	1	124	5	0	0	6	526	653
Illinois	989	855	125	55	8	647	34	70	50	0	671	767
Indiana	458	436	72	74	8	275	11	8	10	28	818	827
Iowa	348	332	33	68	1	229	10	0	7	0	466	484
Kansas	342	339	34	96	3	207	1	1	0	0	456	459
Kentucky	423	236	26	35	6	227	5	5	119	122	684	858
Louisiana	281	260	28	39	54	141	12	0	7	11	730	759
Maine	145	117	8	17	1	92	0	0	27	27	459	463
Maryland	240	184	4	5	3	201	2	7	18	25	1,120	1,309
Massachusetts	372	318	28	36	13	283	5	6	1	37	810	830
Michigan	959	629	54	99	44	702	24	31	5	57	540	696
Minnesota	851	435	28	274	34	432	32	48	3	8	394	622
Mississippi	329	236	31	43	1	149	4	2	99	93	630	630
Missouri	628	551	57	174	2	367	13	8	7	63	542	544
Montana	324	321	153	0	0	171	0	0	0	0	158	159
Nebraska	305	294	25	157	1	115	1	6	0	0	380	380
Nevada	127	112	12	7	6	95	1	6	0	0	1,107	1,221
New Hampshire	108	108	13	0	0	93	1	0	1	0	549	549
New Jersey	539	406	54	38	12	409	6	6	14	69	832	1,027
New Mexico	229	207	32	26	2	149	8	0	12	0	465	498
New York	1,121	1,030	57	146	29	840	23	5	21	20	716	745
North Carolina	553	522	19	9	4	488	1	10	22	9	839	874
North Dakota	178	166	4	85	0	75	0	1	13	12	208	208
Ohio	989	915	128	142	41	624	16	20	18	73	597	606
Oklahoma	564	559	88	2	3	439	24	0	8	0	387	390
Oregon	274	250	25	40	4	203	1	1	0	0	645	695
Pennsylvania	783	694	96	153	11	502	13	2	6	84	807	815
Rhode Island	70	59	5	2	0	54	0	0	9	10	714	722
South Carolina	282	229	19	2	1	235	7	4	14	42	927	969
South Dakota	240	220	59	0	1	176	1	3	0	2	174	184
Tennessee	351	337	11	21	8	271	11	12	17	4	810	842
Texas	2,076	1,526	248	130	47	1,376	37	45	193	0	813	1,067
Utah	282	252	90	48	7	74	51	1	11	6	945	1,008
Vermont	65	49	7	17	0	41	0	0	0	15	469	479
Virginia	436	344	34	6	24	282	1	0	89	89	1,202	1,212
Washington	625	417	54	48	25	446	22	20	10	18	628	860
West Virginia	155	106	1	21	3	129	0	1	0	33	690	716
Wisconsin	568	498	54	57	3	420	13	18	3	6	487	536
Wyoming	101	98	17	15	0	69	0	0	0	0	325	334
Jurisdiction												
Bureau of Indian Education	19	19	1	4	2	12	0	0	0	0	337	337
DoDEA[4]	—	—	—	—	0	—	—	—	—	—	—	—
Other jurisdictions												
American Samoa	6	5	0	0	0	6	0	0	0	1	623	679
Guam	7	6	0	0	0	7	0	0	0	0	1,412	1,619
Northern Marianas	—	—	—	—	0	—	—	—	—	—	—	—
Puerto Rico	182	151	7	5	0	159	6	0	5	31	545	517
U.S. Virgin Islands	9	8	4	0	0	5	0	0	0	1	585	585

—Not available.
[1]Excludes vocational, special education, and alternative schools.
[2]Vocational schools are also included under appropriate grade span.
[3]Average for schools reporting enrollment data. Enrollment data were available for 22,293 out of 23,882 public secondary schools in 2017–18.
[4]DoDEA = Department of Defense Education Activity. Includes both domestic and overseas schools.

NOTE: Includes schools with no grade lower than 7. Excludes schools not reported by grade level, such as some special education schools for students with disabilities.
SOURCE: U.S. Department of Education, National Center for Education Statistics, Common Core of Data (CCD), "Public Elementary/Secondary School Universe Survey," 2017–18. (This table was prepared December 2019.)

Table 216.90. Public elementary and secondary charter schools and enrollment, and charter schools and enrollment as a percentage of total public schools and total enrollment in public schools, by state: Selected years, 2000–01 through 2017–18

State	Number of charter schools					Fall enrollment in charter schools					Charter schools as a percent of total public schools				Charter school enrollment as a percent of total fall enrollment in public schools			
	2000–01	2010–11	2015–16	2016–17	2017–18	2000–01	2010–11	2015–16	2016–17	2017–18	2000–01	2010–11	2016–17	2017–18	2000–01	2010–11	2016–17	2017–18
1	2	3	4	5	6	7	8	9	10	11	12	13	14	15	16	17	18	19
United States	**1,993**	**5,274**	**6,855**	**7,011**	**7,193**	**448,343**	**1,787,091**	**2,845,322**	**3,010,287**	**3,143,269**	**2.1**	**5.3**	**7.1**	**7.3**	**1.0**	**3.6**	**6.0**	**6.2**
Alabama	0	0	0	1	1	0	0	0	—	245	0.0	0.0	0.1	0.1	0.0	0.0	—	#
Alaska	19	27	28	28	29	2,594	5,751	6,343	6,677	7,007	3.7	5.3	5.5	5.7	1.9	4.4	5.0	5.3
Arizona	313	519	552	550	557	45,596	124,467	176,894	185,588	189,686	18.2	22.9	23.8	23.9	5.4	11.6	16.6	17.2
Arkansas	3	40	65	75	82	708	10,209	24,182	27,896	31,545	0.3	3.6	6.9	7.6	0.2	2.1	5.7	6.4
California	302	908	1,224	1,248	1,268	115,582	363,916	568,774	602,837	626,982	3.4	9.0	12.1	12.3	1.9	5.9	9.7	10.1
Colorado	77	168	226	238	250	20,155	74,685	108,793	114,694	120,739	4.7	9.4	12.6	13.2	2.8	8.9	12.7	13.3
Connecticut	16	18	24	24	24	2,429	5,139	9,132	9,573	10,187	1.3	1.6	1.9	2.3	0.4	0.9	1.8	2.0
Delaware	7	19	28	27	24	2,716	9,525	13,622	14,722	15,337	3.7	8.9	11.8	10.6	2.4	7.4	10.8	11.3
District of Columbia	33	97	109	110	111	—	26,910	35,798	37,151	38,696	16.7	42.5	49.3	49.6	—	37.8	43.7	44.8
Florida	148	458	653	655	654	26,893	154,703	270,953	283,560	295,814	4.5	11.1	15.7	15.1	1.1	5.9	10.1	10.4
Georgia	30	67	82	84	93	20,066	41,981	72,170	66,905	72,716	1.5	2.7	3.7	4.0	1.4	2.5	3.8	4.1
Hawaii	6	31	34	34	36	1,343	8,289	10,444	10,669	11,168	2.3	10.7	11.7	12.3	0.7	4.6	5.9	6.2
Idaho	9	40	54	57	59	1,083	15,330	19,381	20,579	21,070	1.3	5.3	7.7	8.0	0.4	5.6	6.9	7.0
Illinois	20	50	64	63	142	7,552	43,049	64,108	65,169	64,925	0.5	1.1	1.5	3.3	0.4	2.1	3.2	3.3
Indiana	0	60	88	93	99	0	22,472	39,671	43,079	47,089	0.0	3.1	4.8	5.2	0.0	2.2	4.1	4.5
Iowa	0	7	3	3	3	0	298	430	398	428	0.0	0.5	0.2	0.2	0.0	0.1	0.1	0.1
Kansas	1	25	10	10	10	67	4,618	3,186	3,159	3,191	0.1	1.8	0.8	0.8	#	1.0	0.6	0.7
Kentucky	0	0	0	0	0	0	0	0	0	0	0.0	0.0	0.0	0.0	0.0	0.0	0.0	0.0
Louisiana	19	78	138	151	150	3,212	29,199	74,030	79,022	80,726	1.2	5.3	10.8	10.8	0.4	4.2	11.0	11.3
Maine	1	0	7	9	11	154	0	1,518	1,955	2,240	0.1	0.0	1.5	1.8	0.1	0.0	1.1	1.3
Maryland	0	44	50	49	50	0	14,492	20,988	22,366	23,819	0.0	3.0	3.4	3.5	0.0	1.7	2.5	2.7
Massachusetts	41	63	81	78	80	13,712	28,422	40,199	42,596	45,238	2.2	3.4	4.2	4.3	1.4	3.0	4.5	4.7
Michigan	205	300	370	376	366	54,751	111,344	145,483	147,061	145,948	5.1	7.7	10.9	9.8	3.3	7.2	10.0	9.9
Minnesota	73	176	216	220	221	9,395	37,253	50,812	54,211	56,769	3.1	7.4	8.8	8.8	1.1	4.4	6.2	6.4
Mississippi	1	0	2	3	3	367	0	226	523	944	0.1	0.0	0.3	0.3	0.1	0.0	0.1	0.2
Missouri	21	53	70	72	68	7,061	20,076	21,619	22,803	23,624	0.9	2.2	3.0	2.8	0.8	2.2	2.5	2.6
Montana	0	0	0	0	0	0	0	0	0	0	0.0	0.0	0.0	0.0	0.0	0.0	0.0	0.0
Nebraska	0	0	0	0	0	0	0	0	0	0	0.0	0.0	0.0	0.0	0.0	0.0	0.0	0.0
Nevada	8	34	47	49	72	1,255	14,127	35,130	40,074	45,270	1.6	5.3	7.5	10.4	0.4	3.2	8.5	9.3
New Hampshire	0	14	31	31	31	0	983	3,011	3,422	3,543	0.0	2.9	6.3	6.3	0.0	0.5	1.9	2.0
New Jersey	53	76	89	88	89	10,179	24,591	41,026	46,274	49,447	2.2	2.9	3.4	3.4	0.8	1.8	3.4	3.6
New Mexico	10	81	99	99	97	1,335	15,290	22,079	25,139	26,116	1.3	9.4	11.4	11.0	0.4	4.6	7.6	7.8
New York	38	170	256	267	279	0	54,443	117,710	128,784	139,385	0.9	3.6	5.6	5.8	0.0	2.0	4.8	5.2
North Carolina	90	99	158	167	173	15,523	42,141	82,521	92,281	100,986	4.1	3.9	6.4	6.5	1.2	2.8	6.0	6.5
North Dakota	0	0	0	0	0	0	0	0	0	0	0.0	0.0	0.0	0.0	0.0	0.0	0.0	0.0
Ohio	66	339	373	362	340	14,745	96,669	118,603	116,279	113,162	1.7	9.0	10.1	9.4	0.8	5.5	6.8	6.6
Oklahoma	6	18	45	48	58	1,208	6,585	19,893	24,248	29,033	0.3	1.0	2.7	3.2	0.2	1.0	3.5	4.2
Oregon	12	108	126	124	127	559	20,372	30,728	32,323	33,677	0.9	8.3	10.0	10.2	0.1	3.7	5.7	5.9
Pennsylvania	65	145	175	179	179	18,981	90,613	130,940	132,979	137,712	2.0	4.5	6.0	6.0	1.0	5.1	7.8	8.1
Rhode Island	3	16	29	30	31	557	3,971	7,310	8,137	8,859	0.9	5.0	9.5	9.8	0.4	2.8	5.8	6.3
South Carolina	8	44	68	70	70	484	16,390	29,470	32,343	34,857	0.7	3.6	5.6	5.6	0.1	2.3	4.2	4.5
South Dakota	0	0	0	0	0	0	0	0	0	0	0.0	0.0	0.0	0.0	0.0	0.0	0.0	0.0
Tennessee	0	29	100	104	110	0	6,517	29,274	34,984	37,713	0.0	1.6	5.9	6.2	0.0	0.7	3.5	3.8
Texas	201	561	702	753	759	37,978	164,940	284,617	310,846	325,165	2.7	6.4	8.5	8.5	1.0	3.3	5.8	6.0
Utah	8	78	117	124	131	537	39,862	67,398	71,417	75,467	1.0	7.7	12.0	12.5	0.1	6.8	10.8	11.3
Vermont	0	0	0	0	0	0	0	0	0	0	0.0	0.0	0.0	0.0	0.0	0.0	0.0	0.0
Virginia	2	4	7	8	8	55	348	1,001	1,176	1,178	0.1	0.2	0.4	0.4	#	#	0.1	0.1
Washington	0	0	9	8	10	0	0	1,225	1,676	2,498	0.0	0.0	0.3	0.4	0.0	0.0	0.2	0.2
West Virginia	0	0	0	0	0	0	0	0	0	0	0.0	0.0	0.0	0.0	0.0	0.0	0.0	0.0
Wisconsin	78	207	242	237	233	9,511	36,863	44,162	44,209	42,499	3.6	9.2	10.5	10.3	1.1	4.2	5.1	4.9
Wyoming	0	3	4	5	5	0	258	468	503	569	0.0	0.8	1.3	1.4	0.0	0.3	0.5	0.6

—Not available.
#Rounds to zero.

SOURCE: U.S. Department of Education, National Center for Education Statistics, Common Core of Data (CCD), "Public Elementary/Secondary School Universe Survey," 2000–01 through 2017–18. (This table was prepared November 2019.)

Table 219.10. High school graduates, by sex and control of school; public high school averaged freshman graduation rate (AFGR); and total graduates as a ratio of 17-year-old population: Selected years, 1869–70 through 2029–30

School year	High school graduates							Public school AFGR[3]	Population 17 years old[4]	Graduates as a ratio of 17-year-old population[5]
		Sex		Control						
				Public[2]						
	Total[1]	Males	Females	Total	Males	Females	Private, total			
1	2	3	4	5	6	7	8	9	10	11
1869–70	16,000	7,064	8,936	—	—	—	—	—	815,000	2.0
1879–80	23,634	10,605	13,029	—	—	—	—	—	946,026	2.5
1889–90	43,731	18,549	25,182	21,882	—	—	21,849[6]	—	1,259,177	3.5
1899–1900	94,883	38,075	56,808	61,737	—	—	33,146[6]	—	1,489,146	6.4
1909–10	156,429	63,676	92,753	111,363	—	—	45,066[6]	—	1,786,240	8.8
1919–20	311,266	123,684	187,582	230,902	—	—	80,364[6]	—	1,855,173	16.8
1929–30	666,904	300,376	366,528	591,719	—	—	75,185[6]	—	2,295,822	29.0
1939–40	1,221,475	578,718	642,757	1,143,246	538,273	604,973	78,229[6]	—	2,403,074	50.8
1949–50	1,199,700	570,700	629,000	1,063,444	505,394	558,050	136,256[6]	—	2,034,450	59.0
1959–60	1,858,023	895,000	963,000	1,627,050	791,426	835,624	230,973	—	2,672,000	69.5
1969–70	2,888,639	1,430,000	1,459,000	2,588,639	1,285,895	1,302,744	300,000[6]	78.7	3,757,000	76.9
1975–76	3,142,120	1,552,000	1,590,000	2,837,129	1,401,064	1,436,065	304,991	74.9	4,272,000	73.6
1979–80	3,042,214	1,503,000	1,539,000	2,747,678	—	—	294,536	71.5	4,262,000	71.4
1985–86	2,642,616	—	—	2,382,616	—	—	260,000[6]	74.3	3,670,000	72.0
1986–87	2,693,803	—	—	2,428,803	—	—	265,000[6]	74.3	3,754,000	71.8
1987–88	2,773,020	—	—	2,500,020	—	—	273,000[6]	74.2	3,849,000	72.0
1988–89	2,743,743	—	—	2,458,800	—	—	284,943	73.4	3,842,000	71.4
1989–90[7]	2,574,162	—	—	2,320,337	—	—	253,825[8]	73.6	3,505,000	73.4
1990–91	2,492,988	—	—	2,234,893	—	—	258,095	73.7	3,417,913	72.9
1991–92	2,480,399	—	—	2,226,016	—	—	254,383[8]	74.2	3,398,884	73.0
1992–93	2,480,519	—	—	2,233,241	—	—	247,278	73.8	3,449,143	71.9
1993–94	2,463,849	—	—	2,220,849	—	—	243,000[6]	73.1	3,442,521	71.6
1994–95	2,519,084	—	—	2,273,541	—	—	245,543	71.8	3,635,803	69.3
1995–96	2,518,109	—	—	2,273,109	—	—	245,000[6]	71.0	3,640,132	69.2
1996–97	2,611,988	—	—	2,358,403	—	—	253,585	71.3	3,792,207	68.9
1997–98	2,704,050	—	—	2,439,050	1,187,647	1,251,403	265,000[6]	71.3	4,008,416	67.5
1998–99	2,758,655	—	—	2,485,630	1,212,924	1,272,706	273,025	71.1	3,917,885	70.4
1999–2000	2,832,844	—	—	2,553,844	1,241,631	1,312,213	279,000[6]	71.7	4,056,639	69.8
2000–01	2,847,973	—	—	2,569,200	1,251,931	1,317,269	278,773	71.7	4,023,686	70.8
2001–02	2,906,534	—	—	2,621,534	1,275,813	1,345,721	285,000[6]	72.6	4,023,968	72.2
2002–03	3,015,735	—	—	2,719,947	1,330,973	1,388,974	295,788	73.9	4,125,087	73.1
2003–04[7,9]	3,054,438	—	—	2,753,438	1,347,800	1,405,638	301,000[6]	74.3	4,113,074	74.3
2004–05	3,106,499	—	—	2,799,250	1,369,749	1,429,501	307,249	74.7	4,120,073	75.4
2005–06[7]	3,122,544	—	—	2,815,544	1,376,458	1,439,086	307,000[6]	73.4	4,200,554	74.3
2006–07	3,199,650	—	—	2,893,045	1,414,069	1,478,976	306,605	73.9	4,297,239	74.5
2007–08	3,312,337	—	—	3,001,337	1,467,180	1,534,157	311,000[6]	74.7	4,436,955	74.7
2008–09[7]	3,347,828	—	—	3,039,015	1,490,317	1,548,698	308,813	75.5	4,336,950	77.2
2009–10	3,435,022	—	—	3,128,022	1,542,684[10]	1,585,338[10]	307,000[6]	78.2	4,311,831	79.7
2010–11	3,449,940	—	—	3,144,100	1,552,981	1,591,113	305,840	79.6	4,367,816	79.0
2011–12	3,454,095	—	—	3,149,185	1,558,489	1,590,694	304,910[6]	80.8	4,294,110	80.4
2012–13	3,478,027	—	—	3,169,257	1,569,675	1,599,579	308,770	81.9	4,255,798	81.7
2013–14[11]	3,488,310	—	—	3,168,450	—	—	319,860	83.1	4,184,556	83.4
2014–15[12]	3,530,250	—	—	3,187,000	—	—	343,250	—	4,170,348	84.7
2015–16[11]	3,574,730	—	—	3,224,140	—	—	350,590	—	4,203,329	85.0
2016–17[12]	3,603,550	—	—	3,255,320	—	—	348,230	—	4,217,905	85.4
2017–18[11]	3,663,530	—	—	3,310,020	—	—	353,510	—	4,291,210	85.4
2018–19[11]	3,674,130	—	—	3,316,970	—	—	357,160	—	4,223,346	87.0
2019–20[11]	3,652,130	—	—	3,294,660	—	—	357,460	—	4,179,612	87.4
2020–21[11]	3,662,860	—	—	3,302,430	—	—	360,430	—	—	—
2021–22[11]	3,688,550	—	—	3,323,040	—	—	365,510	—	—	—
2022–23[11]	3,703,000	—	—	3,337,740	—	—	365,260	—	—	—
2023–24[11]	3,779,770	—	—	3,404,190	—	—	375,580	—	—	—
2024–25[11]	3,831,290	—	—	3,463,190	—	—	368,100	—	—	—
2025–26[11]	3,827,340	—	—	3,458,860	—	—	368,480	—	—	—
2026–27[11]	3,746,800	—	—	3,384,860	—	—	361,940	—	—	—
2027–28[11]	3,667,760	—	—	3,314,690	—	—	353,070	—	—	—
2028–29[11]	3,640,620	—	—	3,290,850	—	—	349,770	—	—	—
2029–30[11]	3,612,400	—	—	3,265,340	—	—	347,060	—	—	—

—Not available.
[1]Includes graduates of public and private schools.
[2]Includes estimates for states not reporting counts of graduates by sex. Data for 1929–30 and preceding years are from *Statistics of Public High Schools* and exclude graduates from high schools that failed to report to the Office of Education.
[3]The averaged freshman graduation rate provides an estimate of the percentage of students who receive a regular diploma within 4 years of entering ninth grade. The rate uses aggregate student enrollment data to estimate the size of an incoming freshman class and aggregate counts of the number of diplomas awarded 4 years later. Averaged freshman graduation rates in this table are based on reported totals of enrollment by grade and high school graduates, rather than on details reported by race/ethnicity.
[4]Derived from Current Population Reports, Series P-25. For years 1869–70 through 1989–90, 17-year-old population is an estimate of the October 17-year-old population based on July data. Data for 1990–91 and later years are October resident population estimates prepared by the Census Bureau.
[5]Based on persons of all ages graduating from high school in a given year divided by the 17-year-old population in the same year. This ratio allows for comparisons over time but does not provide a measure of graduation rates for incoming freshmen who form a cohort (or class) that is scheduled to graduate 4 years later. The ratio of high school graduates to the 17-year-old population differs from measures such as the AFGR (shown in column 9), which are designed to estimate high school cohort graduation rates.
[6]Estimated.
[7]Includes imputations for nonreporting states.
[8]Projected by private schools responding to the Private School Universe Survey.
[9]Includes estimates for public schools in New York and Wisconsin. Without estimates for these two states, the averaged freshman graduation rate for the remaining 48 states and the District of Columbia is 75.0 percent.
[10]Includes estimate for Connecticut, which did not report graduates by sex.
[11]Projected by the National Center for Education Statistics (NCES).
[12]Public school data are projected by NCES; private school data are actual.
NOTE: Includes graduates of regular day school programs. Excludes graduates of other programs, when separately reported, and recipients of high school equivalency certificates. Some data have been revised from previously published figures. Detail may not sum to totals because of rounding and adjustments to protect student privacy.
SOURCE: U.S. Department of Education, National Center for Education Statistics, *Annual Report of the Commissioner of Education*, 1870 through 1910; *Biennial Survey of Education in the United States*, 1919–20 through 1949–50; *Statistics of Public Elementary and Secondary School Systems*, 1958–59 through 1979–80; *Statistics of Nonpublic Elementary and Secondary Schools*, 1959 through 1980; Common Core of Data (CCD), "State Nonfiscal Survey of Public Elementary/Secondary Education," 1985–86 through 2009–10; "State Dropout and Completion Data File," 2005–06 through 2012–13; *Public School Graduates and Dropouts from the Common Core of Data*, 2007–08 and 2008–09; Private School Universe Survey (PSS), 1989 through 2017; and National High School Graduates Projection Model, 1972–73 through 2029–30. U.S. Department of Commerce, Census Bureau, Current Population Reports, Series P-25, Nos. 1000, 1022, 1045, 1057, 1059, 1092, and 1095; 2000 through 2009 Population Estimates, retrieved August 14, 2012, from https://www.census.gov/popest/data/national/asrh/2011/index.html; and 2010 through 2019 Population Estimates, retrieved November 29, 2019, from https://www.census.gov/data/datasets/time-series/demo/popest/2010s-national-detail.html#par_textimage_57373479. (This table was prepared December 2019.)

Table 219.20. Public high school graduates, by region, state, and jurisdiction: Selected years, 1980–81 through 2029–30

Region, state, and jurisdiction	Actual data						Projected data					
	1980–81	1989–90	1999–2000	2009–10	2011–12	2012–13	2013–14	2014–15	2015–16	2016–17	2017–18	2018–19
1	2	3	4	5	6	7	8	9	10	11	12	13
United States	**2,725,285**	**2,320,337**[1]	**2,553,844**	**3,128,022**	**3,149,185**	**3,169,257**	**3,168,450**	**3,187,000**	**3,224,140**	**3,255,320**	**3,310,020**	**3,316,970**
Region												
Northeast	593,727	446,045	453,814	556,400	554,705	555,202	546,910	543,080	545,820	551,480	553,700	550,610
Midwest	784,071	616,700	648,020	726,844	716,072	713,662	705,550	708,240	714,040	719,240	728,420	728,250
South	868,068	796,385	861,498	1,104,770	1,121,400	1,138,965	1,145,570	1,162,950	1,189,220	1,211,650	1,247,860	1,260,960
West	479,419	461,207	590,512	740,008	757,008	761,428	770,420	772,720	775,060	772,950	780,030	777,150
State												
Alabama	44,894	40,485	37,819	43,166	45,394	44,233	44,540	45,420	46,070	47,560	48,030	47,610
Alaska	5,343	5,386	6,615	8,245	7,989	7,860	7,720	7,860	7,840	7,910	8,030	7,910
Arizona	28,416	32,103	38,304	61,145	63,208	62,208	66,700	67,200	67,120	68,770	66,670	66,370
Arkansas	29,577	26,475	27,335	28,276	28,419	28,928	29,610	30,350	30,290	30,750	30,940	31,260
California	242,172	236,291	309,866	404,987	418,664	422,125	424,080	422,830	419,190	411,710	415,890	411,260
Colorado	35,897	32,967	38,924	49,321	50,087	50,968	51,310	51,450	53,310	54,060	55,560	56,330
Connecticut	38,369	27,878	31,562	34,495	38,681	38,722	37,860	37,160	37,420	37,890	37,850	37,310
Delaware	7,349	5,550	6,108	8,133	8,247	8,070	8,240	8,390	8,480	8,690	8,780	8,940
District of Columbia[2]	4,848	3,626	2,695	3,602	3,860	3,961	3,880	3,990	4,510	4,430	4,780	4,660
Florida	88,755	88,934	106,708	156,130	151,964	158,029	158,440	163,740	166,540	170,820	175,140	177,240
Georgia	62,963	56,605	62,563	91,561	90,582	92,416	94,380	97,420	100,070	102,050	105,810	107,740
Hawaii	11,472	10,325	10,437	10,998	11,360	10,790	11,050	10,760	10,860	10,690	11,180	10,550
Idaho	12,679	11,971	16,170	17,793	17,568	17,198	19,120	18,050	18,230	19,130	19,510	19,780
Illinois	136,795	108,119	111,835	139,035	139,575	139,228	137,640	140,520	140,850	141,250	142,720	142,810
Indiana	73,381	60,012	57,012	64,551	65,667	66,595	67,560	66,750	66,720	68,970	71,590	74,270
Iowa	42,635	31,796	33,926	34,462	33,230	32,548	32,590	32,450	32,700	32,850	33,280	33,050
Kansas	29,397	25,367	29,102	31,642	31,898	31,922	32,150	31,900	32,790	32,900	33,530	33,270
Kentucky	41,714	38,005	36,830	42,664	42,642	42,888	42,400	42,530	43,280	43,280	44,160	44,240
Louisiana	46,199	36,053	38,430	36,573	36,675	37,508	38,180	37,720	38,790	39,380	41,860	41,730
Maine	15,554	13,839	12,211	14,069	13,473	13,170	12,730	12,560	12,790	12,640	12,690	12,600
Maryland	54,050	41,566	47,849	59,078	58,811	58,896	58,120	57,650	57,490	57,290	59,120	58,430
Massachusetts	74,831	55,941[3]	52,950	64,462	65,157	66,360	65,200	65,790	68,630	68,610	69,250	69,610
Michigan	124,372	93,807	97,679	110,682	105,446	104,210	102,520	102,020	100,800	101,570	102,940	101,830
Minnesota	64,166	49,087	57,372	59,667	57,501	58,255	56,370	56,800	56,640	57,250	57,740	58,850
Mississippi	28,083	25,182	24,232	25,478	26,158	26,502	26,650	26,260	26,770	26,900	28,000	27,360
Missouri	60,359	48,957	52,848	63,994	61,313	61,407	60,900	60,590	61,600	60,890	61,380	60,990
Montana	11,634	9,370	10,903	10,075	9,750	9,369	9,470	9,390	9,320	9,380	9,480	9,850
Nebraska	21,411	17,664	20,149	19,370	20,464	20,442	20,580	20,650	21,090	21,130	21,800	21,900
Nevada	9,069	9,477	14,551	20,956	21,891	23,038	22,720	23,040	23,190	23,780	24,140	24,610
New Hampshire	11,552	10,766	11,829	15,034	14,426	14,262	13,790	13,520	13,600	13,160	13,100	12,910
New Jersey	93,168	69,824	74,420	96,225	93,819	96,490	95,220	95,250	97,130	97,990	98,320	97,940
New Mexico	17,915	14,884	18,031	18,595	20,315	19,232	18,590	19,530	19,480	19,770	19,900	19,730
New York	198,465	143,318	141,731	183,826	180,806	180,351	178,810	179,110	178,260	181,790	182,400	181,210
North Carolina	69,395	64,782	62,140	88,704	93,977	94,339	96,210	97,020	98,970	101,710	104,850	106,870
North Dakota	9,924	7,690	8,606	7,155	6,942	6,900	6,960	7,040	7,020	6,940	6,940	7,120
Ohio	143,503	114,513	111,668	123,437	123,135	122,491	119,520	120,940	125,050	126,590	126,900	125,270
Oklahoma	38,875	35,606	37,646	38,503	37,305	37,033	37,260	38,420	39,690	40,230	41,030	41,350
Oregon	28,729	25,473	30,151	34,671	34,261	33,899	34,440	34,800	35,650	34,700	34,540	34,920
Pennsylvania	144,645	110,527	113,959	131,182	131,733	129,777	127,200	123,560	121,840	123,990	124,750	123,070
Rhode Island	10,719	7,825	8,477	9,908	9,751	9,579	9,730	9,900	10,050	9,390	9,620	10,250
South Carolina	38,347	32,483	31,617	40,438	41,442	42,246	41,720	42,650	43,840	45,090	46,790	47,060
South Dakota	10,385	7,650	9,278	8,162	8,196	8,239	7,960	8,140	8,080	8,160	8,230	8,200
Tennessee	50,648	46,094	41,568	62,408	62,454	61,323	60,970	62,010	63,480	63,710	64,290	65,110
Texas	171,665	172,480	212,925	280,894	292,531	301,390	304,360	309,280	318,660	327,690	339,670	346,980
Utah	19,886	21,196	32,501	31,481	31,157	33,186	33,400	34,070	35,400	36,560	37,550	38,160
Vermont	6,424	6,127	6,675	7,199	6,859	6,491	6,360	6,240	6,090	6,010	5,740	5,700
Virginia	67,126	60,605	65,596	81,511	83,336	83,279	83,100	82,680	84,640	84,720	87,150	87,260
Washington	50,046	45,941	57,597	66,046	65,205	66,066	66,240	68,200	69,770	70,840	71,790	71,850
West Virginia	23,580	21,854	19,437	17,651	17,603	17,924	17,510	17,460	17,640	17,370	17,480	17,140
Wisconsin	67,743	52,038	58,545	64,687	62,705	61,425	60,810	60,460	60,710	60,740	61,380	60,700
Wyoming	6,161	5,823	6,462	5,695	5,553	5,489	5,590	5,550	5,700	5,660	5,790	5,840
Jurisdiction												
Bureau of Indian Education	—	—	—	—	—	—	—	—	—	—	—	—
DoDEA[4]	—	—	3,202	—	—	—	—	—	—	—	—	—
Other jurisdictions												
American Samoa	—	703	698	—	—	—	—	—	—	—	—	—
Guam	—	1,033	1,406	—	—	—	—	—	—	—	—	—
Northern Marianas	—	227	360	—	—	—	—	—	—	—	—	—
Puerto Rico	—	29,049	30,856	25,514	25,720	—	—	—	—	—	—	—
U.S. Virgin Islands	—	1,260	1,060	958	1,046	897	—	—	—	—	—	—

See notes at end of table.

Table 219.20. Public high school graduates, by region, state, and jurisdiction: Selected years, 1980–81 through 2029–30—Continued

Region, state, and jurisdiction	Projected data											
	2019–20	2020–21	2021–22	2022–23	2023–24	2024–25	2025–26	2026–27	2027–28	2028–29	2029–30	Percent change, 2012–13 to 2029–30
1	14	15	16	17	18	19	20	21	22	23	24	25
United States	**3,294,660**	**3,302,430**	**3,323,040**	**3,337,740**	**3,404,190**	**3,463,190**	**3,458,860**	**3,384,860**	**3,314,690**	**3,290,850**	**3,265,340**	**3.0**
Region												
Northeast	545,780	546,720	547,000	543,310	549,940	559,110	554,400	544,550	532,560	530,600	525,610	-5.3
Midwest	715,220	715,460	727,280	721,220	731,350	746,070	741,560	726,570	709,840	698,670	694,010	-2.8
South	1,255,600	1,250,440	1,255,270	1,272,010	1,302,070	1,339,300	1,346,460	1,323,500	1,280,680	1,270,240	1,262,520	10.8
West	778,050	789,810	793,490	801,200	820,840	818,720	816,440	790,240	791,620	791,350	783,210	2.9
State												
Alabama	45,440	44,150	44,470	44,640	44,970	46,610	46,950	46,080	44,370	44,160	43,750	-1.1
Alaska	7,710	7,700	7,740	7,860	8,060	8,230	8,450	8,460	8,400	8,270	8,210	4.4
Arizona	67,510	67,700	67,890	67,580	69,090	71,250	71,800	70,290	68,130	67,090	66,470	6.9
Arkansas	31,640	31,140	31,290	31,160	31,380	33,640	33,580	32,800	31,940	31,580	31,160	7.7
California	410,090	416,980	418,020	421,720	431,060	417,610	412,760	396,860	405,510	406,210	400,550	-5.1
Colorado	57,010	58,350	58,360	58,680	60,270	61,040	61,290	60,170	58,470	58,190	57,450	12.7
Connecticut	36,670	36,510	35,750	35,710	35,400	35,790	34,580	33,770	32,820	32,760	32,100	-17.1
Delaware	8,930	9,130	9,050	9,130	9,260	9,690	9,910	9,770	9,530	9,380	9,320	15.4
District of Columbia[2]	4,750	4,390	4,590	4,890	5,140	5,760	5,830	5,840	5,830	5,970	6,220	57.0
Florida	174,180	174,830	176,640	179,000	188,030	186,200	192,520	187,610	182,600	184,380	184,370	16.7
Georgia	107,290	105,750	106,870	107,910	110,690	113,680	113,570	111,590	107,580	106,390	104,890	13.5
Hawaii	10,820	10,840	10,930	11,070	11,150	11,410	11,400	8,750	10,850	10,600	10,580	-2.0
Idaho	19,960	19,940	20,410	21,160	21,290	22,100	22,250	21,790	21,410	21,440	21,390	24.3
Illinois	140,130	139,520	145,620	144,750	144,650	150,190	149,490	144,900	141,730	136,270	135,930	-2.4
Indiana	72,010	70,760	72,520	71,730	73,170	74,570	76,020	72,880	71,890	71,250	70,600	6.0
Iowa	33,300	33,780	33,660	34,460	35,300	35,980	36,020	34,960	34,490	33,520	33,090	1.7
Kansas	33,250	33,560	33,760	33,740	34,380	35,030	34,930	34,220	33,810	32,790	32,270	1.1
Kentucky	43,510	43,670	43,730	43,700	44,490	45,800	45,400	44,570	42,730	42,320	42,020	-2.0
Louisiana	41,500	39,860	40,290	40,330	40,760	42,750	42,100	41,430	39,400	39,020	38,690	3.2
Maine	12,310	12,190	12,420	12,490	12,350	12,590	12,340	12,280	11,830	11,760	11,590	-12.0
Maryland	60,940	61,140	61,920	62,350	64,270	66,460	67,230	65,980	64,730	64,490	63,770	8.3
Massachusetts	69,390	69,720	69,840	69,170	69,930	71,090	70,870	69,120	67,430	67,330	67,270	1.4
Michigan	97,340	97,200	97,780	94,520	95,430	96,050	92,160	89,790	88,410	89,440	88,440	-15.1
Minnesota	58,170	59,290	61,150	61,270	62,660	64,450	64,510	63,740	63,050	62,390	62,410	7.1
Mississippi	26,620	25,880	26,230	25,950	25,830	27,810	27,500	26,080	24,590	23,900	23,470	-11.4
Missouri	60,180	60,340	60,580	60,920	61,860	63,380	63,220	61,880	60,610	59,880	59,120	-3.7
Montana	10,110	10,310	10,420	10,460	11,030	10,980	11,240	10,860	10,480	10,740	10,630	13.5
Nebraska	22,390	22,880	23,350	23,120	23,640	22,600	24,330	24,460	23,980	23,490	23,690	15.9
Nevada	25,080	25,340	25,590	26,510	27,540	29,000	29,020	28,190	28,200	28,630	28,620	24.2
New Hampshire	13,010	12,740	12,780	12,490	12,520	12,450	12,260	11,930	11,490	11,770	11,650	-18.3
New Jersey	96,730	97,140	98,150	96,730	98,320	99,260	98,050	96,830	94,110	93,630	92,680	-3.9
New Mexico	19,540	19,430	19,380	19,710	19,730	20,150	20,240	19,840	18,430	18,050	17,630	-8.3
New York	182,650	182,770	181,350	181,310	183,920	187,960	186,630	184,630	181,070	178,810	177,180	-1.8
North Carolina	104,980	104,950	97,800	104,330	107,290	110,360	110,710	109,090	105,350	103,470	102,970	9.2
North Dakota	7,070	7,260	7,540	7,640	8,090	8,380	8,450	8,560	8,400	8,390	8,570	24.2
Ohio	123,090	122,280	121,570	119,450	122,070	123,670	121,360	121,300	115,910	114,420	113,900	-7.0
Oklahoma	41,390	42,270	42,160	40,930	43,180	44,880	44,840	44,530	43,390	42,170	42,060	13.6
Oregon	34,500	35,000	35,340	35,370	36,760	37,880	38,160	37,020	36,230	36,320	35,980	6.1
Pennsylvania	118,860	119,840	120,690	119,480	121,600	123,690	123,520	120,490	118,390	119,080	117,900	-9.2
Rhode Island	10,500	10,280	10,490	10,300	10,410	10,580	10,490	10,170	10,040	10,110	9,940	3.7
South Carolina	47,100	46,220	46,980	47,850	49,410	52,020	51,900	51,650	49,050	49,110	48,770	15.4
South Dakota	8,230	8,520	8,800	9,140	9,310	9,610	9,650	9,440	9,300	9,240	9,250	12.3
Tennessee	63,860	62,930	63,270	63,910	65,630	66,960	66,380	63,660	63,020	63,090	62,560	2.0
Texas	349,340	350,570	355,170	361,120	365,740	378,180	379,960	377,200	363,850	357,810	356,220	18.2
Utah	39,000	40,170	40,920	41,400	42,780	44,110	43,880	43,050	42,330	42,080	42,190	27.1
Vermont	5,670	5,530	5,540	5,640	5,490	5,700	5,670	5,330	5,380	5,360	5,290	-18.5
Virginia	87,080	87,070	88,330	88,640	90,150	92,180	91,980	89,990	87,630	88,000	87,480	5.0
Washington	70,920	72,030	72,530	73,490	75,810	78,550	79,670	78,850	77,280	77,980	77,960	18.0
West Virginia	17,070	16,500	16,500	16,180	15,860	16,320	16,070	15,660	15,090	14,980	14,820	-17.3
Wisconsin	60,060	60,090	60,970	60,490	60,800	62,160	61,430	60,440	58,260	57,590	56,710	-7.7
Wyoming	5,810	6,020	5,960	6,210	6,280	6,400	6,290	6,110	5,900	5,740	5,560	1.4
Jurisdiction												
Bureau of Indian Education	—	—	—	—	—	—	—	—	—	—	—	—
DoDEA[4]	—	—	—	—	—	—	—	—	—	—	—	—
Other jurisdictions												
American Samoa	—	—	—	—	—	—	—	—	—	—	—	—
Guam	—	—	—	—	—	—	—	—	—	—	—	—
Northern Marianas	—	—	—	—	—	—	—	—	—	—	—	—
Puerto Rico	—	—	—	—	—	—	—	—	—	—	—	—
U.S. Virgin Islands	—	—	—	—	—	—	—	—	—	—	—	—

—Not available.
[1]U.S. total includes estimates for nonreporting states.
[2]Beginning in 1989–90, graduates from adult programs are excluded.
[3]Projected data from NCES 91-490, *Projections of Education Statistics to 2002*.
[4]DoDEA = Department of Defense Education Activity. Includes both domestic and overseas schools.
NOTE: Data include regular diploma recipients, but exclude students receiving a certificate of attendance and persons receiving high school equivalency certificates. Some data have been revised from previously published figures. Detail may not sum to totals because of rounding.
SOURCE: U.S. Department of Education, National Center for Education Statistics, Common Core of Data (CCD), "State Nonfiscal Survey of Public Elementary/Secondary Education," 1981–82 through 2005–06; "State Dropout and Completion Data File," 2005–06 through 2012–13; and State High School Graduates Projection Model, 1980–81 through 2029–30. (This table was prepared December 2019.)

Table 219.30. Public high school graduates, by race/ethnicity: 1998–99 through 2029–30

Year	Number of high school graduates							Percentage distribution of graduates						
	Total	White	Black	Hispanic	Asian/ Pacific Islander	American Indian/ Alaska Native	Two or more races	Total	White	Black	Hispanic	Asian/ Pacific Islander	American Indian/ Alaska Native	Two or more races
1	2	3	4	5	6	7	8	9	10	11	12	13	14	15
1998–99	2,485,630	1,749,561	325,708	270,836	115,216	24,309	—	100.0	70.4	13.1	10.9	4.6	1.0	†
1999–2000	2,553,844	1,778,370	338,116	289,139	122,344	25,875	—	100.0	69.6	13.2	11.3	4.8	1.0	†
2000–01	2,569,200	1,775,036	339,578	301,740	126,465	26,381	—	100.0	69.1	13.2	11.7	4.9	1.0	†
2001–02	2,621,534	1,796,110	348,969	317,197	132,182	27,076	—	100.0	68.5	13.3	12.1	5.0	1.0	†
2002–03	2,719,947	1,856,454	359,920	340,182	135,588	27,803	—	100.0	68.3	13.2	12.5	5.0	1.0	†
2003–04	2,753,438	1,829,177	383,443	374,492	137,496	28,830	—	100.0	66.4	13.9	13.6	5.0	1.0	†
2004–05	2,799,250	1,855,198	385,987	383,714	143,729	30,622	—	100.0	66.3	13.8	13.7	5.1	1.1	†
2005–06	2,815,544	1,838,765	399,406	396,820	150,925	29,628	—	100.0	65.3	14.2	14.1	5.4	1.1	†
2006–07	2,893,045	1,868,056	418,113	421,036	154,837	31,003	—	100.0	64.6	14.5	14.6	5.4	1.1	†
2007–08	3,001,337	1,898,367	429,840	448,887	159,410	32,036	32,797[1]	100.0	63.3	14.3	15.0	5.3	1.1	1.1[1]
2008–09	3,039,015	1,883,382	451,384	481,698	163,575	32,213	26,763[1]	100.0	62.0	14.9	15.9	5.4	1.1	0.9[1]
2009–10	3,128,022	1,871,980	472,261	545,518	167,840	34,131	36,292[1]	100.0	59.8	15.1	17.4	5.4	1.1	1.2[1]
2010–11	3,144,100	1,835,332	471,461	583,907	168,875	32,768	51,748	100.0	58.4	15.0	18.6	5.4	1.0	1.6
2011–12	3,149,185	1,807,528	467,932	608,726	173,835	32,450	58,703	100.0	57.4	14.9	19.3	5.5	1.0	1.9
2012–13	3,169,257	1,791,147	461,919	640,413	179,101	31,100	65,569	100.0	56.5	14.6	20.2	5.7	1.0	2.1
2013–14[2]	3,168,450	1,765,670	441,190	678,020	181,550	30,120	71,890	100.0	55.7	13.9	21.4	5.7	1.0	2.3
2014–15[2]	3,187,000	1,746,730	446,000	703,430	184,780	29,990	76,060	100.0	54.8	14.0	22.1	5.8	0.9	2.4
2015–16[2]	3,224,140	1,742,530	451,780	731,860	184,660	30,160	83,160	100.0	54.0	14.0	22.7	5.7	0.9	2.6
2016–17[2]	3,255,320	1,737,890	455,260	755,350	186,390	30,120	90,310	100.0	53.4	14.0	23.2	5.7	0.9	2.8
2017–18[2]	3,310,020	1,733,070	461,460	787,440	200,160	29,920	97,970	100.0	52.4	13.9	23.8	6.0	0.9	3.0
2018–19[2]	3,316,970	1,708,880	457,520	816,590	201,210	29,420	103,350	100.0	51.5	13.8	24.6	6.1	0.9	3.1
2019–20[2]	3,294,660	1,669,470	450,140	833,680	203,790	28,640	108,950	100.0	50.7	13.7	25.3	6.2	0.9	3.3
2020–21[2]	3,302,430	1,659,350	438,840	847,220	210,500	28,010	118,520	100.0	50.2	13.3	25.7	6.4	0.8	3.6
2021–22[2]	3,323,040	1,644,960	437,670	867,260	215,970	28,630	128,550	100.0	49.5	13.2	26.1	6.5	0.9	3.9
2022–23[2]	3,337,740	1,619,670	437,020	897,540	216,500	28,350	138,660	100.0	48.5	13.1	26.9	6.5	0.8	4.2
2023–24[2]	3,404,190	1,617,130	448,210	938,810	217,600	28,450	154,000	100.0	47.5	13.2	27.6	6.4	0.8	4.5
2024–25[2]	3,463,190	1,621,480	460,190	964,330	220,810	28,420	167,960	100.0	46.8	13.3	27.8	6.4	0.8	4.8
2025–26[2]	3,458,860	1,593,110	461,810	974,170	224,280	27,780	177,720	100.0	46.1	13.4	28.2	6.5	0.8	5.1
2026–27[2]	3,384,860	1,545,340	453,610	957,640	220,380	27,160	180,730	100.0	45.7	13.4	28.3	6.5	0.8	5.3
2027–28[2]	3,314,690	1,503,860	435,320	937,280	225,420	25,930	186,900	100.0	45.4	13.1	28.3	6.8	0.8	5.6
2028–29[2]	3,290,850	1,486,770	428,000	927,090	229,260	24,670	195,070	100.0	45.2	13.0	28.2	7.0	0.7	5.9
2029–30[2]	3,265,340	1,475,140	425,170	908,160	237,300	24,420	195,160	100.0	45.2	13.0	27.8	7.3	0.7	6.0

—Not available.

†Not applicable.

[1]Data on students of Two or more races were not reported by all states; therefore, the data are not comparable to figures for 2010–11 and later years.

[2]Projected.

NOTE: Race categories exclude persons of Hispanic ethnicity. Prior to 2007–08, data on students of Two or more races were not collected separately. Some data have been revised from previously published figures. Detail may not sum to totals because of rounding and statistical methods used to prevent the identification of individual students.

SOURCE: U.S. Department of Education, National Center for Education Statistics, Common Core of Data (CCD), "State Nonfiscal Survey of Public Elementary/Secondary Education," 1981–82 through 2005–06; "State Dropout and Completion Data File," 2005–06 through 2012–13; and National Public High School Graduates by Race/Ethnicity Projections Model, 1995–96 through 2029–30. (This table was prepared December 2019.)

Table 219.32. Public high school graduates, by sex, race/ethnicity, and state or jurisdiction: 2012-13

State or jurisdiction	Total, male and female: Total	White	Black	Hispanic	Asian/Pacific Islander: Total	Asian	Pacific Islander	American Indian/ Alaska Native	Two or more races	Male: Total	White	Black	Hispanic	Asian/ Pacific Islander	American Indian/ Alaska Native	Two or more races	F: Total	White	Black
1	2	3	4	5	6	7	8	9	10	11	12	13	14	15	16	17	18	19	20
United States	**3,169,257**	**1,791,147**	**461,919**	**640,413**	**179,101**	**168,782**	**10,319**	**31,100**	**65,569**	**1,569,675**	**899,883**	**219,989**	**312,878**	**90,150**	**15,407**	**31,370**	**1,599,579**	**891,264**	**241,930**
Alabama	44,233	26,963	14,709	1,338	595	574	21	486	142	21,701	13,618	6,815	675	284	246	63	22,532	13,345	7,894
Alaska	7,860	4,428	271	482	725	567	158	1,495	459	3,945	2,224	133	238	379	738	233	3,915	2,204	138
Arizona	62,208	29,357	3,332	23,542	2,313	2,166	147	2,837	827	30,337	14,505	1,635	11,281	1,185	1,348	383	31,871	14,852	1,697
Arkansas	28,928	19,426	6,007	2,413	513	428	85	180	389	14,369	9,787	2,815	1,235	262	90	180	14,559	9,639	3,192
California	422,125	125,492	27,069	198,993	57,667	55,083	2,584	2,998	9,906	208,126	62,954	13,102	96,324	29,437	1,441	4,868	213,999	62,538	13,967
Colorado	50,968	31,552	2,441	13,219	1,916	1,797	119	432	1,408	25,170	15,703	1,234	6,434	911	213	675	25,798	15,849	1,207
Connecticut	38,722	25,828	4,758	5,838	1,707	1,642	65	142	449	19,435	13,084	2,368	2,859	831	75	218	19,287	12,744	2,390
Delaware	8,070	4,334	2,561	805	295	292	≤3	26	46	3,948	2,144	1,229	381	159	13	22	4,122	2,190	1,332
District of Columbia	3,961	142	3,028	422	59	54	5	7	303	1,732	64	1,285	192	26	≤3	164	2,228	78	1,743
Florida	158,029	73,953	32,454	42,010	4,804	4,652	152	629	4,179	77,301	36,500	15,484	20,638	2,372	326	1,981	80,728	37,453	16,970
Georgia	92,416	44,875	32,811	8,275	3,776	3,699	77	207	2,472	44,872	22,315	15,271	4,062	1,954	101	1,169	47,544	22,560	17,540
Hawaii	10,790	1,379	224	504	8,017	4,753	3,264	42	624	5,350	659	103	240	3,997	21	330	5,440	720	121
Idaho	17,198	13,883	199	2,375	329	258	71	198	214	8,524	6,914	102	1,137	168	99	104	8,674	6,969	97
Illinois	139,228	80,496	22,016	26,687	6,390	6,278	112	363	3,276	68,855	40,673	10,235	12,992	3,199	201	1,555	70,373	39,823	11,781
Indiana	66,595	51,519	6,877	4,643	1,209	1,176	33	223	2,124	32,674	25,530	3,150	2,263	593	106	1,032	33,921	25,989	3,727
Iowa	32,548	27,495	1,314	2,228	724	687	37	154	633	16,388	13,871	674	1,095	358	76	314	16,160	13,624	640
Kansas	31,922	22,933	2,235	4,352	801	756	45	369	1,232	16,057	11,654	1,125	2,131	396	196	555	15,865	11,279	1,110
Kentucky	42,888	35,865	4,581	1,236	577	550	27	119	510	21,653	18,215	2,237	609	297	56	239	21,235	17,650	2,344
Louisiana	37,508	19,635	15,307	1,259	747	722	25	272	288	17,728	9,529	6,974	600	379	130	116	19,780	10,106	8,333
Maine	13,170	12,175	319	191	294	284	10	92	99	6,660	6,162	157	104	145	47	45	6,510	6,013	162
Maryland	58,896	27,409	20,361	5,463	3,752	3,700	52	246	1,665	29,049	13,791	9,715	2,756	1,863	133	791	29,847	13,618	10,646
Massachusetts	66,360	47,254	5,870	7,941	3,874	3,800	74	153	1,268	33,048	23,642	2,859	3,937	1,934	82	594	33,312	23,612	3,011
Michigan	104,210	77,503	16,949	3,324	3,087	2,973	114	833	2,514	51,453	38,637	7,974	1,658	1,582	418	1,184	52,757	38,866	8,975
Minnesota	58,255	46,012	4,231	2,827	3,670	3,644	26	664	851	29,164	23,177	2,113	1,398	1,773	322	381	29,091	22,835	2,118
Mississippi	26,502	12,883	12,740	448	304	297	7	44	83	12,382	6,256	5,687	230	154	21	34	14,120	6,627	7,053
Missouri	61,407	47,112	9,671	2,317	1,273	1,202	71	283	751	31,258	24,158	4,764	1,172	666	142	356	30,149	22,954	4,907
Montana	9,369	8,041	65	281	128	109	19	738	116	4,794	4,122	34	154	60	366	58	4,575	3,919	31
Nebraska	20,442	15,329	1,264	2,666	413	393	20	230	540	10,340	7,815	615	1,318	207	124	261	10,102	7,514	649
Nevada	23,038	10,028	1,873	7,548	2,064	1,735	329	230	1,295	10,953	4,820	904	3,480	1,030	111	608	12,085	5,208	969
New Hampshire	14,262	13,022	261	457	353	344	9	37	132	7,176	6,569	143	214	175	15	60	7,086	6,453	118
New Jersey	96,490	54,591	14,930	17,711	8,788	8,555	233	111	359	48,698	27,864	7,409	8,736	4,453	48	188	47,792	26,727	7,521
New Mexico	19,232	5,509	426	10,628	303	288	15	2,146	220	9,390	2,745	218	5,114	155	1,054	104	9,842	2,764	208
New York[1]	180,351	98,641	30,059	33,532	16,496	16,295	201	785	838	88,740	49,507	14,149	16,174	8,169	376	365	91,611	49,134	15,910
North Carolina	94,339	52,914	25,497	9,078	2,568	2,482	86	1,301	2,981	46,526	26,687	12,125	4,412	1,239	660	1,403	47,813	26,227	13,372
North Dakota	6,900	6,051	164	134	103	92	11	417	31	3,486	3,073	81	70	56	194	12	3,414	2,978	83
Ohio	122,491	96,889	16,229	3,286	2,100	2,054	46	154	3,833	61,315	48,901	7,768	1,659	1,030	86	1,871	61,176	47,988	8,461
Oklahoma	37,033	21,386	3,434	3,601	928	857	71	6,441	1,243	18,444	10,761	1,670	1,756	450	3,205	602	18,589	10,625	1,764
Oregon	33,899	23,534	848	5,807	1,723	1,535	188	514	1,473	16,610	11,688	379	2,737	846	232	728	17,289	11,846	469
Pennsylvania	129,777	97,199	17,765	8,706	4,429	4,344	85	163	1,515	65,092	49,267	8,544	4,285	2,207	78	711	64,685	47,932	9,221
Rhode Island	9,579	6,582	770	1,740	298	282	16	36	153	4,749	3,305	371	842	141	19	71	4,830	3,277	399
South Carolina	42,246	23,802	14,769	2,070	707	647	60	123	775	20,566	11,845	6,945	1,022	351	65	338	21,680	11,957	7,824
South Dakota	8,239	7,025	209	229	149	144	5	543	83	4,147	3,553	104	101	75	274	40	4,092	3,472	105
Tennessee	61,323	42,682	14,509	2,800	1,185	1,113	72	147	—	30,378	21,452	6,836	1,408	601	82	—	30,943	21,230	7,673
Texas	301,390	104,466	38,772	139,783	12,044	11,650	394	1,311	5,014	151,002	53,036	19,177	69,495	6,174	701	2,419	150,388	51,430	19,595
Utah	33,186	26,757	402	4,100	1,135	669	466	373	419	16,436	13,259	212	1,994	613	165	193	16,750	13,498	190
Vermont	6,491	5,949	135	83	152	143	9	12	160	3,317	3,051	57	43	71	4	91	3,174	2,898	78
Virginia	83,279	47,825	18,565	8,055	5,293	5,183	110	265	3,276	41,383	24,168	8,820	4,000	2,710	130	1,555	41,896	23,657	9,745
Washington	66,066	43,132	2,905	10,092	5,826	5,380	446	740	3,371	32,368	21,235	1,416	4,860	2,865	381	1,611	33,698	21,897	1,489
West Virginia	17,924	16,572	917	174	134	131	≤3	19	105	9,033	8,344	475	84	69	13	48	8,891	8,228	442
Wisconsin	61,425	48,675	4,754	4,155	2,297	2,268	29	682	862	30,832	24,717	2,263	2,024	1,070	341	417	30,593	23,958	2,491
Wyoming	5,489	4,643	62	565	67	55	12	88	64	2,721	2,333	34	255	29	40	30	2,768	2,310	28
Bureau of Indian Education	—	—	—	—	—	—	—	—	—	—	—	—	—	—	—	—	—	—	—
DoD, overseas	—	—	—	—	—	—	—	—	—	—	—	—	—	—	—	—	—	—	—
DoD, domestic	—	—	—	—	—	—	—	—	—	—	—	—	—	—	—	—	—	—	—
Other jurisdictions																			
American Samoa	—	—	—	—	—	—	—	—	—	—	—	—	—	—	—	—	—	—	—
Guam	—	—	—	—	—	—	—	—	—	—	—	—	—	—	—	—	—	—	—
Northern Marianas	—	—	—	—	—	—	—	—	—	—	—	—	—	—	—	—	—	—	—
Puerto Rico	—	—	—	—	—	—	—	—	—	—	—	—	—	—	—	—	—	—	—
U.S. Virgin Islands	897	7	727	139	≤3	≤3	≤3	≤3	20	383	≤3	321	55	≤3	≤3	≤3	514	4	406

—Not available.

[1] Distribution of Asian and Pacific Islander students is estimated by the National Center for Education Statistics.

NOTE: Race categories exclude persons of Hispanic ethnicity. DoD = Department of Defense. To protect the confidentiality of individual students, small cell sizes have been bottom coded to less than or equal to three. Detail may not sum to totals because of statistical methods used to prevent the identification of individual students.

SOURCE: U.S. Department of Education, National Center for Education Statistics, Common Core of Data (CCD), "State Dropout and Completion Data File," 2012–13. (This table was prepared January 2016.)

Table 219.35. Public high school averaged freshman graduation rate (AFGR), by state or jurisdiction: Selected years, 1990-91 through 2012-13

State or jurisdiction	1990-91	1995-96	1999-2000	2000-01	2002-03	2003-04	2004-05	2005-06	2006-07	2007-08	2008-09	2009-10	2010-11	2011-12	2012-13
1	2	3	4	5	6	7	8	9	10	11	12	13	14	15	16
United States	**73.7**	**71.0**	**71.7**	**71.7**	**73.9**	**74.3** [1]	**74.7**	**73.4** [2]	**73.9**	**74.7**	**75.5** [2]	**78.2**	**79.6**	**80.8**	**81.9**
Alabama	69.8	62.7	64.1	63.7	64.7	65.0	65.9	66.2	67.1	69.0	69.9	71.8	76.1	75.1	74.2
Alaska	74.6	68.3	66.7	68.0	68.0	67.2	64.1	66.5	69.0	69.1	72.6	75.5	77.9	78.6	79.9
Arizona	76.7	60.8	63.6	74.2	75.9	66.8	84.7	70.5	69.6	70.7	72.5	74.7	78.9	77.3	76.5
Arkansas	76.6	74.2	74.6	73.9	76.6	76.8	75.7	80.4	74.4	76.4	74.0	75.0	77.0	78.1	80.1
California	69.6	67.6	71.7	71.6	74.1	73.9	74.6	69.2	70.7	71.2	71.0 [3]	78.2	79.7	81.7	83.6
Colorado	76.3	74.8	74.1	73.2	76.4	78.7	76.7	75.5	76.6	75.4	77.6	79.8	82.0	82.3	83.3
Connecticut	80.2	76.1	81.9	77.5	80.9	80.7	80.9	80.9	81.8	82.2	75.4	75.1	84.7	86.1	87.4
Delaware	72.5	70.4	66.8	71.0	73.0	72.9	73.0	76.3	71.9	72.1	73.7	75.5	76.1	77.1	77.0
District of Columbia	54.5	49.7	54.5	60.2	59.6	68.2	66.3	65.4 [4]	54.8	56.0	62.4	59.9	64.9	70.8	77.7
Florida	65.6	62.3	61.0	61.2	66.7	66.4	64.6	63.6	65.0	66.9	68.9	70.8	72.0	74.7	75.8
Georgia	70.3	61.9	59.7	58.7	60.8	61.2	61.7	62.4	64.1	65.4	67.8	69.9	69.6	69.6	70.5
Hawaii	75.9	74.5	70.9	68.3	71.3	72.6	75.1	75.5	75.4	76.0	75.3	75.4	73.7	77.9	78.0
Idaho	79.6	80.5	79.4	79.6	81.4	81.5	81.0	80.5	80.4	80.1	80.6	84.0	83.2	83.9	82.1
Illinois	76.6	75.2	76.3	75.6	75.9	80.3	79.4	79.7	79.5	80.4	77.7	81.9	80.0	82.1	82.7
Indiana	76.9	73.6	71.8	72.1	75.5	73.5	73.2	73.3	73.9	74.1	75.2	77.2	79.9	80.0	81.0
Iowa	84.4	84.3	83.1	82.8	85.3	85.8	86.6	86.9	86.5	86.4	85.7	87.9	89.0	89.3	89.4
Kansas	80.8	77.1	77.1	76.5	76.9	77.9	79.2	77.5	78.8	79.0	80.2	84.5	86.5	88.3	88.4
Kentucky	72.9	71.3	69.7	69.8	71.7	73.0	75.9	77.2	76.4	74.4	77.6	79.9	80.9	81.9	83.1
Louisiana	57.5	61.7	62.2	63.7	64.1	69.4	63.9	59.5	61.3	63.5	67.3	68.8	71.2	71.9	72.7
Maine	80.7	73.7	75.9	76.4	76.3	77.6	78.6	76.3	78.5	79.1 [5]	79.9 [5]	82.8 [6]	85.7	86.7	87.5
Maryland	77.5	78.3	77.6	78.7	79.2	79.5	79.3	79.9	80.0	80.4	80.1	82.2	83.8	84.5	85.6
Massachusetts	79.1	78.0	78.0	78.9	75.7	79.3	78.7	79.5	80.8	81.5	83.3	82.6	85.4	86.5	88.4
Michigan	72.1	71.4	75.3	75.4	74.0	72.5	73.0	72.2	77.0	76.3	75.3	75.9	74.7	77.5	78.3
Minnesota	90.8	86.1	84.9	83.6	84.8	84.7	85.9	86.2	86.5	86.4	87.4	88.2	89.2	88.4	91.0
Mississippi	63.3	59.7	59.4	59.7	62.7	62.7	63.3	63.5	63.5	63.9	62.0	63.8	68.5	67.3	68.4
Missouri	76.0	75.0	76.3	75.5	78.3	80.4	80.6	81.0	81.9	82.4	83.1	83.7	84.7	85.9	86.6
Montana	84.4	83.9	80.8	80.0	81.0	80.4	81.5	81.9	81.5	82.0	82.0	81.9	83.7	85.7	84.7
Nebraska	86.7	85.6	85.7	83.8	85.2	87.6	87.8	87.0	86.3	83.8	82.9	83.8	89.8	92.7	93.3
Nevada	77.0	65.8	69.7	70.0	72.3	57.4	55.8	55.8	54.2	56.3	56.3 [3]	57.8	58.7	59.5	67.5
New Hampshire	78.6	77.5	76.1	77.8	78.2	78.7	80.1	81.1	81.7	83.3	84.3	86.3	86.6	87.0	87.3
New Jersey	81.4	82.8	83.6	85.4	87.0	86.3	85.1	84.8	84.4	84.6	85.3	87.2	86.6	86.4	89.1
New Mexico	70.1	63.7	64.7	65.9	63.1	67.0	65.4	67.3	59.1	66.8	64.8	67.3	70.7	74.3	71.6
New York	66.1	63.6	61.8	61.5	60.9	60.9 [7]	65.3	67.4	68.9	70.9	73.5	76.0	77.6	77.1	78.5
North Carolina	71.3	66.5	65.8	66.5	70.1	71.4	72.6	71.8	68.6	72.8	75.1	76.9	76.8	78.7	80.5
North Dakota	87.6	89.5	86.0	85.4	86.4	86.1	86.3	82.2	83.1	83.8	87.4	88.4	90.2	91.1	91.4
Ohio	77.5	74.5	75.2	76.5	79.0	81.3	80.2	79.2	78.7	79.0	79.6	81.4	82.3	83.9	84.9
Oklahoma	76.5	75.6	75.8	75.8	76.0	77.0	76.9	77.8	77.8	78.0	77.3	78.5	79.9	79.3	79.4
Oregon	72.7	68.3	69.6	68.3	73.7	74.2	74.2	73.0	73.8	76.7	76.5	76.3	78.1	78.0	76.8
Pennsylvania	79.7	80.0	78.7	79.0	81.7	82.2	82.5	83.5 [4]	83.0	82.7	80.5	84.1	85.8	88.3	88.4
Rhode Island	75.0	72.7	72.8	73.5	77.7	75.9	78.4	77.8	78.4	76.4	75.3	76.4	76.6	77.1	79.0
South Carolina	66.6	60.9	58.6	56.5	59.7	60.6	60.1	61.0 [4]	58.9	62.2	66.0	68.2	69.0	71.6	74.2
South Dakota	83.8	84.5	77.6	77.4	83.0	83.7	82.3	84.5	82.5	84.4	81.7	81.8	81.6	83.1	83.8
Tennessee	69.8	66.6	59.5	59.0	63.4	66.1	68.5	70.7	72.6	74.9	77.4	80.4	81.1	83.6	82.4
Texas	72.2	66.1	71.0	70.8	75.5	76.7	74.0	72.5	71.9	73.1	75.4	78.9	81.4	83.0	83.6
Utah	77.5	76.9	82.5	81.6	80.2	83.0	84.4	78.6	76.6	74.3	79.4	78.6	78.5	77.6	81.6
Vermont	79.5	85.3	81.0	80.2	83.6	85.4	86.5	82.3	88.5	89.3	89.6	91.4	92.7	91.9	89.3
Virginia	76.2	76.2	76.9	77.5	80.6	79.3	79.6	74.5	75.5	77.0	78.4	81.2	82.7	83.9	84.8
Washington	75.7	75.5	73.7	69.2	74.2	74.6	75.0	72.9	74.8	71.9	73.7	77.2	79.0	79.2	80.4
West Virginia	76.6	77.0	76.7	75.9	75.7	76.9	77.3	76.9	78.2	77.3	77.0	78.3	78.1	80.3	81.5
Wisconsin	85.2	83.6	82.7	83.3	85.8	85.8 [7]	86.7	87.5	88.5	89.6	90.7	91.1	92.2	92.2	93.0
Wyoming	81.1	77.7	76.3	73.4	73.9	76.0	76.7	76.1	75.8	76.0	75.2	80.3	80.4	80.2	82.5
Other jurisdictions															
American Samoa	85.3	79.7	71.9	77.0	81.0	80.2	81.1	81.0	84.6	—	—	—	—	—	—
Guam	48.2	44.6	52.9	51.7	56.3	48.4	—	—	—	—	—	—	—	—	—
Northern Marianas	—	63.3	61.1	62.7	65.2	75.3	75.4	80.3	73.6	—	—	—	—	—	—
Puerto Rico	60.9	60.8	64.7	65.7	67.8	64.8	61.7	68.6	66.7	64.5	67.2	60.2	61.6	61.7	—
U.S. Virgin Islands	53.2	54.2	53.8	57.3	53.5	—	—	—	57.8	58.3	63.1	65.5	96.8	72.5	67.8

—Not available.

[1] Includes estimates for New York and Wisconsin. Without estimates for these two states, the averaged freshman graduation rate for the remaining 48 states and the District of Columbia is 75.0 percent.

[2] U.S. total includes estimates for nonreporting states.

[3] Estimated high school graduates from NCES 2011-312, *Public School Graduates and Dropouts from the Common Core of Data: School Year 2008-09.*

[4] Projected high school graduates from NCES 2009-062, *Projections of Education Statistics to 2018.*

[5] Includes 1,161 graduates in 2007-08 and 1,169 graduates in 2008-09 from private high schools that received a majority of their funding from public sources.

[6] Includes 1,419 fall 2006 9th-graders who attended publicly funded private schools that were not reported in the 2006-07 Common Core of Data, but were reported in data for later years.

[7] Estimated high school graduates from NCES 2006-606rev, *The Averaged Freshman Graduation Rate for Public High Schools From the Common Core of Data: School Years 2002-03 and 2003-04.*

NOTE: The averaged freshman graduation rate provides an estimate of the percentage of students who receive a regular diploma within 4 years of entering ninth grade. The rate uses aggregate student enrollment data to estimate the size of an incoming freshman class and aggregate counts of the number of diplomas awarded 4 years later. Averaged freshman graduation rates in this table are based on reported totals of enrollment by grade and high school graduates, rather than on details reported by race/ethnicity.

SOURCE: U.S. Department of Education, National Center for Education Statistics, Common Core of Data (CCD), "State Nonfiscal Survey of Public Elementary/Secondary Education," 1986-87 through 2010-11; "State Dropout and Completion Data File," 2005-06 through 2012-13; *The Averaged Freshman Graduation Rate for Public High Schools From the Common Core of Data: School Years 2002-03 and 2003-04*; *Public School Graduates and Dropouts from the Common Core of Data*, 2007-08 and 2008-09; and *Projections of Education Statistics to 2018*. (This table was prepared January 2016.)

Table 219.40. Public high school averaged freshman graduation rate (AFGR), by sex, race/ethnicity, and state or jurisdiction: 2012-13

State or jurisdiction	Total, male and female						Male						Female					
	Total[1]	White	Black	Hispanic	Asian/Pacific Islander	American Indian/Alaska Native	Total[1]	White	Black	Hispanic	Asian/Pacific Islander	American Indian/Alaska Native	Total[1]	White	Black	Hispanic	Asian/Pacific Islander	American Indian/Alaska Native
1	2	3	4	5	6	7	8	9	10	11	12	13	14	15	16	17	18	19
United States	**81.9**	**85.6**	**69.4**	**78.2**	**94.6**	**67.7**	**78.8**	**83.5**	**64.3**	**74.1**	**92.6**	**65.3**	**85.2**	**87.8**	**74.8**	**82.6**	**96.7**	**70.2**
Alabama	74.2	78.1	67.6	67.5	87.2	84.7	70.5	75.8	61.3	64.9	86.7	83.4	78.2	80.6	74.3	70.5	87.8	86.0
Alaska	79.9	82.3	74.7	87.6	94.1	68.6	77.7	80.7	67.3	87.7	92.1	64.7	82.2	83.9	83.6	87.6	96.5	72.8
Arizona	76.5	80.1	70.0	72.1	90.1	64.2	72.7	77.1	67.3	66.9	89.0	61.3	80.6	83.1	72.8	77.6	91.4	67.0
Arkansas	80.1	81.0	74.5	81.1	87.8	67.0	77.1	78.8	69.0	78.5	86.7	65.5	83.3	83.5	80.2	83.9	89.0	68.5
California	83.6	88.7	72.7	79.7	97.3	73.5	80.1	86.3	68.9	75.2	95.5	68.9	87.3	91.3	76.8	84.4	99.2	78.4
Colorado	83.3	84.5	68.7	77.7	90.4	62.7	79.8	81.7	66.5	73.0	87.2	60.3	87.0	87.6	71.1	82.7	93.5	65.2
Connecticut	87.4	90.4	76.6	77.7	100.0	79.5	84.9	89.1	72.0	73.0	99.6	80.1[2]	90.0	91.7	81.8	82.8	100.0	78.8[2]
Delaware	77.0	79.8	70.6	75.8	94.2	83.0[2]	72.7	76.1	65.2	71.8	92.8	‡	81.6	83.8	76.5	79.7	98.1	‡
District of Columbia	77.7	94.8	69.8	80.7	87.1[2]	‡	68.9	84.6[2]	59.8	76.8	82.9[2]	‡	86.2	100.0[2]	79.7	84.3	93.5[2]	‡
Florida	75.8	77.8	67.2	79.1	93.3	85.2	72.1	74.4	62.3	75.7	91.7	82.3	79.7	81.4	72.5	82.6	95.0	88.7
Georgia	70.5	76.5	63.7	64.4	90.8	66.9	66.5	73.3	58.0	60.9	89.3	63.3	74.9	79.8	69.6	68.1	92.5	70.8
Hawaii	78.0	57.5	70.6	84.8	79.8	57.0[2]	74.8	53.9	60.2	76.2	77.0	49.1[2]	81.4	61.3	82.8	94.4	82.9	67.7[2]
Idaho	82.1	82.4	77.3	78.7	88.8	55.2	79.8	80.0	84.5	75.1	87.8	55.1	84.5	84.8	71.0	82.2	89.8	55.2
Illinois	82.7	90.6	63.6	78.3	97.8	78.5	80.7	90.5	58.1	75.1	96.7	81.8	84.7	90.7	69.4	81.6	98.9	74.7
Indiana	81.0	83.1	66.4	85.7	99.2	92.7	77.0	79.8	59.3	80.2	96.8	89.6	85.2	86.6	73.9	91.6	100.0	95.6
Iowa	89.4	90.2	69.0	85.5	98.0	67.2	87.3	88.3	65.9	82.1	96.1	69.1	91.6	92.2	72.6	89.0	100.0	65.5
Kansas	88.4	89.6	75.5	85.9	95.9	68.8	86.3	88.6	73.6	79.8	94.2	68.1	90.6	90.6	77.5	92.7	97.5	69.6
Kentucky	83.1	83.4	79.5	86.8	99.7	100.0[2]	81.7	81.6	75.0	79.8	100.0	100.0[2]	86.6	85.4	84.4	94.9	99.0	100.0[2]
Louisiana	72.7	78.0	64.3	94.4	97.1	69.5	67.3	73.7	57.7	87.4	94.5	64.6	78.4	82.6	71.1	100.0	99.9	74.7
Maine	87.5	86.5	92.7	92.9	100.0	76.9	86.0	85.0	95.7	87.6	100.0	79.2[2]	89.1	88.2	90.0	100.0[2]	100.0	74.6[2]
Maryland	85.6	88.6	76.2	84.5	99.3	85.0	81.8	86.5	70.7	79.8	97.8	83.6	89.7	90.9	82.1	89.9	100.0	86.7
Massachusetts	88.4	90.9	87.0	72.7	100.0	67.6	86.1	89.3	81.2	69.6	100.0	71.5	90.8	92.6	93.4	76.0	100.0	63.6
Michigan	78.3	83.4	60.6	52.6	95.3	68.2	74.5	80.3	54.8	49.8	93.3	66.6	82.3	86.7	67.0	55.7	97.5	69.8
Minnesota	91.0	93.2	74.2	77.1	97.8	50.7	88.5	91.3	70.4	73.1	94.3	48.5	93.6	95.3	78.4	81.6	100.0	53.0
Mississippi	68.4	74.2	63.1	64.7	88.7	60.8[2]	63.1	70.5	56.4	62.5	85.1	52.6[2]	73.7	78.1	69.8	67.1	92.7	71.1[2]
Missouri	86.6	88.2	73.6	91.2	95.7	86.8	84.8	87.0	69.9	89.9	96.6	84.2	88.4	89.6	77.6	92.6	94.7	89.6
Montana	84.7	86.9	66.6[2]	94.6	92.3	60.1	83.7	85.8	66.7[2]	94.1	90.9[2]	59.1	85.8	88.0	66.4[2]	95.3	93.6[2]	61.2
Nebraska	93.3	94.6	71.3	90.7	93.4	65.5	91.3	93.4	67.4	85.7	90.5	66.0	95.5	95.9	75.5	96.1	96.6	64.9
Nevada	67.5	69.5	48.6	62.0	73.4	45.1	63.2	65.6	45.6	56.9	70.9	42.0	71.9	73.7	51.7	67.2	76.1	48.5
New Hampshire	87.3	86.7	85.9	87.0	97.3	68.5[2]	84.9	84.5	85.3	77.6	99.6	‡	89.8	89.1	86.8	97.3	95.2	71.0[2]
New Jersey	89.1	92.7	79.4	83.3	98.6	70.3	86.9	91.3	75.7	79.9	98.5	60.5[2]	91.4	94.3	83.4	86.8	98.8	80.2[2]
New Mexico	71.6	76.9	64.9	68.3	94.8	71.8	67.6	73.7	58.4	63.9	92.6	67.8	76.0	80.2	73.6	73.0	97.2	76.2
New York	78.5	87.1	65.2	66.4	90.9	71.9	76.1	87.1	60.5	62.1	86.1	65.2	81.0	87.1	70.1	70.9	96.1	79.4
North Carolina	80.5	83.4	69.7	79.9	91.9	76.3	76.6	80.8	64.3	74.7	89.5	72.5	84.7	86.2	75.4	85.7	94.3	80.6
North Dakota	91.4	93.8	100.0	85.4	100.0[2]	59.1	89.1	91.8	100.0[2]	89.7[2]	100.0[2]	54.5	93.8	95.8	100.0[2]	81.0[2]	100.0[2]	63.7
Ohio	84.9	89.4	65.2	85.7	98.8	73.9	82.7	87.7	60.5	84.0	96.5	81.6	87.3	91.1	70.3	87.6	100.0	66.0
Oklahoma	79.4	81.0	66.2	76.6	92.8	71.5	76.9	78.7	63.1	73.0	92.4	70.0	82.0	83.5	69.5	80.3	93.2	73.1
Oregon	76.8	76.7	66.4	76.0	87.3	56.5	73.2	73.7	59.9	70.3	86.2	49.2	80.6	80.0	72.7	82.0	88.4	64.3
Pennsylvania	88.4	90.8	76.4	77.4	100.0	68.4	86.0	89.2	71.7	73.2	100.0	63.0	91.0	92.6	81.2	81.9	100.0	74.3
Rhode Island	79.0	80.5	69.7	74.6	81.1	46.2[2]	75.3	77.2	64.0	70.4	77.8	53.3[2]	83.0	84.1	76.0	79.1	84.3	40.2[2]
South Carolina	74.2	78.2	66.3	74.7	86.3	57.4	69.4	74.4	60.0	70.7	85.6	56.2	79.5	82.3	73.1	79.0	87.0	58.8[2]
South Dakota	83.8	87.9	76.7	80.5	100.0	47.7	81.3	85.3	72.6	71.0	100.0[2]	47.9	86.3	90.7	81.4	90.1	100.0[2]	47.6
Tennessee	82.4	83.8	77.6	82.7	100.0	96.1	79.2	81.6	71.6	78.4	100.0	100.0[2]	85.8	86.2	83.8	87.5	100.0	85.2[2]
Texas	83.6	85.8	77.0	82.1	97.4	71.5	80.9	84.3	73.1	78.6	96.9	71.5	86.6	87.4	81.2	85.7	98.0	71.4
Utah	81.6	83.2	67.4	71.4	82.5	62.5	78.9	80.9	66.3	67.2	85.2	55.3	84.4	85.7	68.7	75.9	79.6	69.6
Vermont	89.3	89.2	88.0	97.3[2]	100.0	‡	88.9	88.9	79.2[2]	100.0[2]	100.0[2]	‡	89.7	89.6	95.9[2]	83.9[2]	100.0[2]	‡
Virginia	84.8	86.4	72.7	89.7	98.5	76.2	81.5	84.2	67.2	84.5	97.1	74.4	88.4	88.7	78.6	95.5	100.0	78.0
Washington	80.4	80.1	62.7	80.7	84.5	40.3	76.8	76.8	58.5	74.8	82.1	40.5	84.6	83.7	67.2	86.9	87.0	40.1
West Virginia	81.5	81.5	73.5	83.4	93.7	‡	79.7	79.7	73.5	80.0	92.8[2]	‡	83.3	83.5	73.5	86.8	99.0[2]	‡
Wisconsin	93.0	96.3	68.1	83.7	97.7	72.9	90.7	95.1	61.5	78.5	93.5	68.6	95.5	97.5	75.5	89.3	100.0	77.9
Wyoming	82.5	84.0	75.3[2]	77.9	100.0[2]	42.6	80.0	82.1	73.9[2]	69.4	‡	41.0[2]	85.0	85.9	77.1[2]	86.8	100.0[2]	44.2
Bureau of Indian Education	—	—	—	—	—	—	—	—	—	—	—	—	—	—	—	—	—	—
DoDEA, overseas	—	—	—	—	—	—	—	—	—	—	—	—	—	—	—	—	—	—
DoDEA, domestic	—	—	—	—	—	—	—	—	—	—	—	—	—	—	—	—	—	—
Other jurisdictions																		
American Samoa	—	—	—	—	—	—	—	—	—	—	—	—	—	—	—	—	—	—
Guam	—	—	—	—	—	—	—	—	—	—	—	—	—	—	—	—	—	—
Northern Marianas	—	—	—	—	—	—	—	—	—	—	—	—	—	—	—	—	—	—
Puerto Rico	—	—	—	—	—	—	—	—	—	—	—	—	—	—	—	—	—	—
U.S. Virgin Islands	67.8	‡	67.2	63.8	‡	‡	59.1	‡	59.6	54.5	‡	‡	76.1	‡	74.7	71.8	‡	‡

—Not available.

‡Reporting standards not met (too few cases).

[1] Total averaged freshman graduation rate (AFGR) is based on reported totals of enrollment by grade and high school graduates, rather than on details reported by race/ethnicity.

[2] AFGR is based on an estimate of 30 to 99 students entering ninth grade and may show large variation from year to year.

NOTE: The AFGR provides an estimate of the percentage of students who receive a regular diploma within 4 years of entering ninth grade. The rate uses aggregate student enrollment data to estimate the size of an incoming freshman class and aggregate counts of the number of diplomas awarded 4 years later. The enrollment data used in computing the AFGR for race/ethnicity categories include only students for whom race/ethnicity was reported. Race categories exclude persons of Hispanic ethnicity. DoDEA = Department of Defense Education Activity.

SOURCE: U.S. Department of Education, National Center for Education Statistics, Common Core of Data (CCD), "State Dropout and Completion Data File," 2012-13. (This table was prepared January 2016.)

Table 219.46. Public high school 4-year adjusted cohort graduation rate (ACGR), by selected student characteristics and state: 2010–11 through 2017–18

State	Total, ACGR for all students								ACGR for students with selected characteristics,[1] 2017–18													
									Race/ethnicity												
												Asian/Pacific Islander[5]									
	2010–11	2011–12	2012–13	2013–14	2014–15	2015–16	2016–17	2017–18	White	Black	Hispanic	Total	Asian	Pacific Islander	American Indian/ Alaska Native	Two or more races	Students with disabilities[2]	Limited English proficient[3]	Economically disadvantaged[4]	Homeless enrolled	Foster care
1	2	3	4	5	6	7	8	9	10	11	12	13	14	15	16	17	18	19	20	21	22
United States	**79**[6]	**80**[6]	**81**[7]	**82**	**83**	**84**	**85**	**85**	**89**	**79**	**81**	**92**	—	—	**74**[8]	—	**67**	**68**	**80**	—	—
Alabama[9]	72	75	80	86	89	87	89	90	92	88	88	94	94	85	90	91	68	64	84	78	77
Alaska	68	70	72	71	76	76	78	79	84	73	76	84	88	74	69	74	57	61	72	57	55
Arizona	78	76	75	76	77	80	78	79	83	74	76	89	90	76	68	75	68	47	73	52	45
Arkansas	81	84	85	87	85	87	88	89	91	86	86	88	95	73	84	90	85	83	87	81	74
California	76	79	80	81	82	83	83	83	87	73	81	93	94	81	71	73	66	68	80	69	53
Colorado	74	75	77	77	77	79	79	81	85	74	73	89	90	74	68	83	59	67	71	55	25
Connecticut	83	85	86	87	87	87	88	88	93	81	79	96	‡	>=90	85	88	65	67	80	70	48
Delaware	78	80	80	87	86	86	87	87	90	83	82	95	‡	>=50	76	91	69	69	78	83	62
District of Columbia	59	59	62	61	69	69	73	69	89	67	65	88	‡	‡	‡	>=90	47	56	59	44	46
Florida	71	75	76	76	78	81	82	86	89	81	85	96	96	89	80	87	77	75	82	74	50
Georgia	67	70	72	73	79	79	81	82	85	79	75	90	—	—	77	82	61	58	77	61	37
Hawaii	80	81	82	82	82	83	83	85	86	82	80	85	92	77	—	—	64	68	80	66	57
Idaho	—	—	—	77	79	80	80	81	82	71	76	83	86	72	61	74	59	76	72	58	47
Illinois	84	82	83	86	86	86	87	87	91	78	82	94	94	84	80	86	72	72	79	68	56
Indiana	86	86	87	88	87	87	84	88	90	79	84	95	96	83	84	85	73	69	85	82	68
Iowa	88	89	90	91	91	91	91	91	93	81	84	91	93	75	76	88	77	79	84	73	76
Kansas	83	85	86	86	86	86	87	87	90	79	81	93	93	81	79	86	80	81	80	68	61
Kentucky	—	—	86	88	88	89	90	90	92	82	83	95	95	85	89	88	75	70	88	84	—
Louisiana	71	72	74	75	78	79	78	81	86	78	68	92	92	76	89	81	59	36	76	60	35
Maine	84	85	86	87	88	87	87	87	87	78	83	92	‡	>=80	71	79	74	76	78	57	56
Maryland	83	84	85	86	87	88	88	87	93	85	72	96	97	84	90	90	67	51	79	67	59
Massachusetts	83	85	85	86	87	88	88	88	92	80	74	94	94	90	83	87	72	64	77	71	61
Michigan	74	76	77	79	80	80	80	81	84	70	74	91	91	87	70	75	58	71	70	57	40
Minnesota	77	78	80	81	82	82	83	83	88	67	67	87	87	76	51	72	62	66	70	47	—
Mississippi	75	75	76	78	81	82	83	84	88	81	79	93	‡	>=80	86	82	38	55	81	71	80
Missouri	81	84	86	87	88	89	88	89	92	80	85	92	—	—	87	88	76	71	82	76	69
Montana	82	84	84	85	86	86	86	86	89	80	79	90	93	76	68	82	77	63	78	66	75
Nebraska	86	88	89	90	89	89	89	89	93	78	81	82	‡	>=80	71	85	69	49	81	59	—
Nevada	62	63	71	70	71	74	81	83	86	72	82	92	94	84	80	83	66	76	81	76	46
New Hampshire	86	86	87	88	88	88	89	89	90	81	76	93	94	75	85	92	74	70	78	65	44
New Jersey	83	86	88	89	90	90	91	91	95	84	85	97	97	93	87	92	80	76	85	73	63
New Mexico	63	70	70	69	69	71	71	74	79	69	73	86	86	—	66	—	66	71	69	53	46
New York	77	77	77	78	79	80	82	82	90	73	72	89	89	77	69	84	57	31	76	56	61
North Carolina	78	80	83	84	86	86	87	86	90	83	80	93	—	—	84	84	69	68	80	67	73
North Dakota	86	87	88	87	87	88	87	88	91	76	75	89	—	—	72	—	69	68	75	52	71
Ohio	80	81	82	82	81	84	84	82	86	69	73	90	—	—	70	77	51	65	71	51	52
Oklahoma	—	—	85	83	83	82	83	82	83	77	79	86	87	74	81	84	58	61	75	67	61
Oregon	68	68	69	72	74	75	77	79	80	68	75	88	91	75	65	78	61	56	72	54	—
Pennsylvania	83	84	86	85	85	86	87	86	91	72	74	92	93	90	79	79	70	66	78	70	—
Rhode Island	77	77	80	81	83	83	84	84	87	83	77	91	‡	>=50	69	78	62	72	77	57	>=50
South Carolina	74	75	78	80	80	83	84	81	84	77	81	93	—	—	73	—	52	80	83	64	48
South Dakota	83	83	83	83	84	84	84	84	90	75	71	87	‡	>=80	50	80	63	77	69	60	—
Tennessee	86	87	86	87	88	89	90	90	93	84	83	95	95	91	90	—	73	71	84	75	67
Texas	86	88	88	88	89	89	90	90	94	87	88	96	96	86	85	91	78	77	87	80	63
Utah	76	80	83	84	85	85	86	87	89	76	78	89	92	85	77	87	70	70	77	—	—
Vermont	87	88	87	88	88	88	89	85	86	70	79	72	‡	‡	‡	80	68	58	76	60	—
Virginia	82	83	85	85	86	87	87	88	92	84	74	95	95	93	84	91	61	57	80	60	63
Washington	76	77	76	78	78	80	79	87	88	80	83	92	93	81	71	87	70	76	80	65	70
West Virginia	78	79	81	85	87	90	89	90	90	86	92	>=95	>=95	>=50	87	86	77	93	88	87	72
Wisconsin	87	88	88	89	88	88	89	90	94	70	82	91	‡	>=90	78	85	69	70	80	70	51
Wyoming	80	79	77	79	79	80	86	82	84	77	75	86	‡	>=50	59	78	63	61	70	62	—

See notes at end of table.

Table 219.46. Public high school 4-year adjusted cohort graduation rate (ACGR), by selected student characteristics and state: 2010–11 through 2017–18—Continued

—Not available.
‡Reporting standards not met (too few cases).
[1]The time when students are identified as having certain characteristics varies by state. Depending on the state, a student may be included in a category if the relevant characteristic is reported in 9th-grade data, if the characteristic is reported in 12th-grade data, or if it is reported at any point during the student's high school years.
[2]Students identified as children with disabilities under the Individuals with Disabilities Education Act (IDEA).
[3]Students who met the definition of limited English proficient students as outlined in the ED*Facts* workbook. For more information, see https://www2.ed.gov/about/inits/ed/edfacts/eden-workbook.html.
[4]Students who met the state criteria for classification as economically disadvantaged.
[5]States either report data for a combined "Asian/Pacific Islander" group or report the "Asian" and "Pacific Islander" groups separately. Total represents either a single value reported by the state for "Asian/Pacific Islander" or an aggregation of separate values reported for "Asian" and "Pacific Islander." "Asian/Pacific Islander" includes the "Filipino" group, which only California and Hawaii report separately.
[6]Includes imputed data for Idaho, Kentucky, and Oklahoma. Data were not available for these states because they had not yet started reporting ACGR data in 2010–11 and 2011–12.
[7]Includes imputed data for Idaho. Data were not available for Idaho because this state had not yet started reporting ACGR data in 2012–13.
[8]Estimated assuming a count of zero American Indian/Alaska Native students for Hawaii.
[9]Use data with caution. The Alabama State Department of Education has indicated that their ACGR data for some years was misstated. For more information, please see the following press release issued by the state: https://www.alsde.edu/sec/comm/News%20Releases/12-08-2016%20Graduation%20Rate%20Review.pdf.
NOTE: The adjusted cohort graduation rate (ACGR) is the percentage of public high school freshmen who graduate with a regular diploma within 4 years of starting 9th grade. Students who are entering 9th grade for the first time form a cohort for the graduating class. This cohort is "adjusted" by adding any students who subsequently transfer into the cohort and subtracting any students who subsequently transfer out, emigrate to another country, or die. Values preceded by the ">=" symbol have been "blurred" (rounded) to protect student privacy. Race categories exclude persons of Hispanic ethnicity.
SOURCE: U.S. Department of Education, Office of Elementary and Secondary Education, Consolidated State Performance Report, 2010–11 through 2017–18. (This table was prepared February 2020.)

Table 219.50. Number and percentage of 9th- to 12th-graders who dropped out of public schools (event dropout rate), by race/ethnicity, grade, and state or jurisdiction: 2009-10

State or jurisdiction	Percent of 9th- to 12th-graders who dropped out (event dropout rate), by race/ethnicity							Number and percent of 9th- to 12th-graders who dropped out (event dropout rate), by grade							
								Grade 9		Grade 10		Grade 11		Grade 12	
	Total	White	Black	Hispanic	Asian/Pacific Islander	American Indian/Alaska Native	Two or more races	Number of dropouts	Event dropout rate	Number of dropouts	Event dropout rate	Number of dropouts	Event dropout rate	Number of dropouts	Event dropout rate
1	2	3	4	5	6	7	8	9	10	11	12	13	14	15	16
United States	**3.4**	**2.3**	**5.5**	**5.0**	**1.9**	**6.7**	**‡**	**104,756**	**2.6**	**113,370**	**3.0**	**117,536**	**3.3**	**175,806**	**5.1**
Alabama	1.8	1.6	2.0	0.9	1.4	1.3	—	864	1.4	1,128	2.0	1,048	2.1	862	1.8
Alaska	6.9	5.1	6.4	6.1	4.8	11.6	9.6	404	4.0	551	5.5	1,014	9.3	851	8.7
Arizona	7.8	6.8	8.8	8.1	4.9	14.6	—	4,207	5.1	4,594	5.7	5,269	7.0	10,795	13.6
Arkansas	3.6	3.1	5.0	4.1	2.0	4.9	3.1	720	1.9	1,130	3.2	1,427	4.4	1,613	5.3
California	4.6	2.8	8.4	5.8	2.0	6.5	5.0	13,849	2.6	15,518	3.1	20,625	4.2	42,587	8.9
Colorado	5.3	3.2	8.6	9.9	2.4	10.1	—	1,957	3.1	2,216	3.7	3,045	5.3	5,673	9.7
Connecticut	3.0	1.4	6.8	6.9	1.1	3.0	—	1,316	2.8	1,127	2.6	1,452	3.4	1,299	3.2
Delaware	3.9	3.1	4.9	4.7	3.2	10.3	—	546	4.7	386	3.7	299	3.4	288	3.5
District of Columbia[1]	7.0	4.9	6.9	8.3	5.4	#	—	501	8.1	262	5.9	153	4.2	133	4.0
Florida	2.3	1.6	3.5	2.8	0.8	2.7	—	4,189	1.9	4,348	2.2	4,678	2.4	4,816	2.8
Georgia	3.8	3.1	4.6	4.3	1.5	4.2	3.4	5,800	4.0	5,095	4.2	4,074	3.8	2,800	2.9
Hawaii	5.2	6.4	7.9	5.9	4.7	9.0	—	562	3.7	816	5.7	726	5.8	632	6.0
Idaho	1.4	1.2	1.9	2.2	1.2	2.5	—	211	1.0	235	1.1	301	1.5	386	2.0
Illinois	2.9	1.8	5.7	3.8	0.9	3.0	—	3,482	2.0	5,287	3.1	3,970	2.7	5,801	4.0
Indiana	1.6	1.3	3.1	2.4	1.1	2.2	—	373	0.4	945	1.2	1,349	1.7	2,346	3.2
Iowa	3.4	2.8	9.1	6.9	2.1	8.9	4.9	363	1.0	713	1.9	1,276	3.5	2,747	7.1
Kansas	2.1	1.8	3.7	2.9	0.7	4.1	2.0	442	1.2	661	1.9	765	2.3	1,105	3.3
Kentucky	3.2	2.9	5.5	5.6	2.0	1.9	—	1,076	2.0	1,769	3.5	1,762	3.8	1,615	3.7
Louisiana	4.8	3.2	6.8	3.9	2.0	4.8	—	3,229	5.7	1,920	4.2	1,663	4.1	1,892	4.9
Maine	4.2	4.2	4.9	5.0	3.8	8.6	—	252	1.7	349	2.3	703	4.8	1,260	8.3
Maryland	2.7	2.0	3.4	4.2	0.9	3.2	—	1,998	2.7	2,029	3.0	1,686	2.7	1,369	2.2
Massachusetts	2.8	1.7	5.0	7.3	1.7	3.3	3.1	2,356	3.0	2,045	2.8	1,837	2.6	1,847	2.7
Michigan	4.3	2.7	9.2	6.2	3.1	5.4	—	4,305	3.1	6,661	4.9	5,318	4.2	6,699	5.3
Minnesota	1.6	1.0	3.9	4.2	1.6	5.7	—	337	0.5	453	0.7	796	1.2	2,752	3.7
Mississippi	7.4	5.6	9.3	5.9	2.8	4.6	#	2,399	6.0	2,651	7.3	2,339	7.3	2,023	7.0
Missouri	3.5	2.4	8.4	4.1	1.5	3.0	—	2,139	2.9	2,009	2.9	2,449	3.6	3,245	4.8
Montana	4.3	3.5	7.0	6.2	2.0	10.3	—	340	2.9	435	3.9	527	4.9	599	5.7
Nebraska	2.2	1.6	4.1	4.0	1.8	7.0	—	186	0.8	372	1.7	538	2.5	825	3.7
Nevada	4.5	3.4	6.5	5.4	3.1	4.7	—	790	2.3	1,389	4.0	1,294	4.4	2,071	8.0
New Hampshire	1.2	1.1	1.6	2.9	1.1	1.5	1.0	3	#	6	#	90	0.6	667	4.3
New Jersey	1.6	0.9	3.5	2.8	0.4	1.5	3.4	1,696	1.6	1,667	1.6	1,522	1.5	1,594	1.6
New Mexico	6.9	5.3	9.0	7.2	4.6	8.8	4.7	2,229	7.5	2,075	7.8	1,484	6.6	1,021	5.1
New York	3.6	1.7	6.5	5.9	2.4	5.6	—	7,354	3.1	8,222	3.5	6,674	3.4	8,931	4.7
North Carolina	4.7	4.0	5.4	6.1	2.0	6.1	—	6,553	5.1	5,535	4.9	4,769	4.8	3,338	3.8
North Dakota	2.2	1.7	2.6	3.5	0.9	7.5	—	40	0.5	174	2.3	207	2.7	259	3.4
Ohio	4.2	2.8	9.4	7.4	1.4	7.8	—	6,968	4.4	3,853	2.8	4,574	3.7	7,011	5.9
Oklahoma	2.4	2.1	3.3	3.5	1.1	2.5	—	949	1.9	1,062	2.3	1,188	2.8	1,086	2.7
Oregon	3.4	2.9	6.2	4.7	1.4	6.7	—	465	1.0	771	1.7	1,451	3.3	3,299	7.2
Pennsylvania	2.1	1.5	3.7	5.1	1.3	2.2	—	1,643	1.1	3,029	2.0	3,268	2.3	4,302	3.1
Rhode Island	4.6	3.8	6.6	6.8	4.5	8.5	—	573	4.4	613	5.0	509	4.7	471	4.4
South Carolina	3.0	2.7	3.3	3.6	1.3	5.6	—	1,691	2.7	1,811	3.3	1,547	3.2	1,220	2.7
South Dakota	2.6	1.6	3.4	5.2	2.7	10.5	—	184	1.8	267	2.7	258	2.8	291	3.3
Tennessee	2.7	1.8	4.9	3.3	1.2	2.7	—	1,370	1.8	1,579	2.1	1,790	2.6	2,843	4.3
Texas	2.7	1.2	4.2	3.6	0.5	3.6	—	6,945	1.8	8,253	2.5	6,824	2.2	14,048	4.8
Utah	2.6	2.1	3.8	5.5	2.8	5.7	—	207	0.5	555	1.4	927	2.3	2,444	6.1
Vermont	2.4	2.4	1.5	2.6	2.0	#	4.1	76	1.0	180	2.4	215	3.0	250	3.4
Virginia	2.1	1.4	3.0	4.6	1.2	1.6	—	1,741	1.7	1,857	1.9	1,934	2.1	2,467	2.8
Washington	4.2	3.6	6.1	5.8	3.0	8.2	—	2,881	3.4	2,792	3.4	3,472	4.4	4,815	5.8
West Virginia	4.0	4.0	4.6	4.6	0.5	3.6	1.9	809	3.4	848	4.1	839	4.4	798	4.3
Wisconsin	2.2	1.2	7.5	4.7	1.6	5.2	—	971	1.4	611	0.9	1,222	1.7	3,260	4.6
Wyoming	6.0	5.0	13.1	#	1.7	20.8	94.9	215	3.2	516	7.3	389	6.1	460	7.5
Bureau of Indian Education	—	—	—	—	—	—	—	—	—	—	—	—	—	—	—
DoD, overseas	—	—	—	—	—	—	—	—	—	—	—	—	—	—	—
DoD, domestic	—	—	—	—	—	—	—	—	—	—	—	—	—	—	—
Other jurisdictions															
American Samoa	—	—	—	—	—	—	—	—	—	—	—	—	—	—	—
Guam	—	—	—	—	—	—	—	—	—	—	—	—	—	—	—
Northern Marianas	—	—	—	—	—	—	—	—	—	—	—	—	—	—	—
Puerto Rico	—	—	—	—	—	—	—	—	—	—	—	—	—	—	—
U.S. Virgin Islands	5.5	#	5.3	7.4	#	#	—	122	7.2	68	5.5	53	4.7	38	3.7

—Not available.

#Rounds to zero.

‡Reporting standards not met (too few cases for a reliable estimate).

[1] Data were imputed based on prior year rates.

NOTE: Race categories exclude persons of Hispanic ethnicity. Event dropout rates measure the percentage of public school students in grades 9 through 12 who dropped out of school between one October and the next. Enrollment and dropout data for ungraded students were prorated into grades 9 through 12 based on the counts for graded students. DoD stands for Department of Defense.

SOURCE: U.S. Department of Education, National Center for Education Statistics, Common Core of Data (CCD), "State Dropout and Completion Data File," 2009-10. (This table was prepared November 2012.)

Table 219.55. Among 15- to 24-year-olds enrolled in grades 10 through 12, percentage who dropped out (event dropout rate), by sex and race/ethnicity: 1972 through 2018

[Standard errors appear in parentheses]

Year	Event dropout rate[1]											
			Sex				Race/ethnicity					
	Total[2]		Male		Female		White		Black		Hispanic	
1	2		3		4		5		6		7	
1972	6.1	(0.34)	5.9	(0.47)	6.3	(0.49)	5.3	(0.35)	9.6	(1.36)	11.2!	(3.70)
1973	6.3	(0.34)	6.8	(0.50)	5.7	(0.46)	5.5	(0.35)	10.0	(1.39)	10.0!	(3.50)
1974	6.7	(0.35)	7.4	(0.52)	6.0	(0.47)	5.8	(0.36)	11.6	(1.44)	9.9!	(3.34)
1975	5.8	(0.32)	5.4	(0.45)	6.1	(0.47)	5.1	(0.34)	8.7	(1.28)	10.9!	(3.30)
1976	5.9	(0.33)	6.6	(0.49)	5.2	(0.44)	5.6	(0.36)	7.4	(1.18)	7.3!	(2.71)
1977	6.5	(0.34)	6.9	(0.49)	6.1	(0.47)	6.1	(0.37)	8.6	(1.21)	7.8!	(2.79)
1978	6.7	(0.35)	7.5	(0.52)	5.9	(0.46)	5.8	(0.36)	10.2	(1.32)	12.3	(3.60)
1979	6.7	(0.35)	6.8	(0.50)	6.7	(0.49)	6.1	(0.37)	10.0	(1.34)	9.8!	(3.20)
1980	6.1	(0.33)	6.7	(0.49)	5.5	(0.45)	5.3	(0.35)	8.3	(1.22)	11.7	(3.36)
1981	5.9	(0.33)	6.0	(0.47)	5.8	(0.46)	4.9	(0.34)	9.7	(1.30)	10.7	(3.00)
1982	5.5	(0.34)	5.8	(0.50)	5.2	(0.47)	4.8	(0.37)	7.8	(1.23)	9.2!	(3.04)
1983	5.2	(0.34)	5.8	(0.50)	4.7	(0.46)	4.4	(0.36)	7.0	(1.20)	10.1!	(3.18)
1984	5.1	(0.34)	5.5	(0.50)	4.8	(0.47)	4.5	(0.37)	5.8	(1.08)	11.1	(3.28)
1985	5.3	(0.35)	5.4	(0.51)	5.1	(0.49)	4.4	(0.37)	7.8	(1.29)	9.8	(2.58)
1986	4.7	(0.33)	4.7	(0.46)	4.7	(0.46)	3.8	(0.34)	5.5	(1.08)	11.9	(2.70)
1987	4.1	(0.31)	4.4	(0.45)	3.8	(0.42)	3.6	(0.33)	6.4	(1.16)	5.6!	(1.94)
1988	4.8	(0.37)	5.4	(0.55)	4.6	(0.53)	4.4	(0.42)	6.3	(1.28)	11.0	(3.08)
1989	4.5	(0.35)	4.6	(0.50)	4.6	(0.50)	3.6	(0.37)	8.2	(1.40)	8.1	(2.43)
1990	4.0	(0.33)	4.2	(0.49)	4.1	(0.49)	3.5	(0.37)	5.2	(1.17)	8.4	(2.41)
1991	4.0	(0.33)	3.9	(0.47)	4.4	(0.51)	3.3	(0.37)	6.4	(1.27)	7.8	(2.33)
1992	4.4	(0.35)	3.9	(0.46)	4.9	(0.53)	3.7	(0.38)	5.0	(1.09)	8.2	(2.23)
1993	4.5	(0.36)	4.6	(0.51)	4.3	(0.50)	3.9	(0.40)	5.8	(1.20)	6.7!	(2.02)
1994	5.3	(0.37)	5.2	(0.51)	5.4	(0.53)	4.2	(0.40)	6.6	(1.21)	10.0	(2.18)
1995	5.7	(0.35)	6.2	(0.51)	5.3	(0.48)	4.5	(0.38)	6.4	(1.01)	12.4	(1.62)
1996	5.0	(0.34)	5.0	(0.48)	5.1	(0.49)	4.1	(0.38)	6.7	(1.05)	9.0	(1.49)
1997	4.6	(0.32)	5.0	(0.47)	4.1	(0.43)	3.6	(0.35)	5.0	(0.91)	9.5	(1.45)
1998	4.8	(0.33)	4.6	(0.45)	4.9	(0.47)	3.9	(0.36)	5.2	(0.91)	9.4	(1.46)
1999	5.0	(0.33)	4.6	(0.44)	5.4	(0.49)	4.0	(0.36)	6.5	(0.99)	7.8	(1.27)
2000	4.8	(0.33)	5.5	(0.49)	4.1	(0.43)	4.1	(0.37)	6.1	(1.00)	7.4	(1.24)
2001	5.0	(0.32)	5.6	(0.46)	4.3	(0.42)	4.1	(0.35)	6.3	(0.96)	8.8	(1.31)
2002	3.5	(0.27)	3.7	(0.39)	3.4	(0.37)	2.6	(0.28)	4.9	(0.87)	5.8	(1.01)
2003	4.0	(0.28)	4.2	(0.40)	3.8	(0.38)	3.2	(0.31)	4.8	(0.85)	7.1	(1.06)
2004	4.7	(0.30)	5.1	(0.44)	4.3	(0.41)	3.7	(0.34)	5.7	(0.94)	8.9	(1.20)
2005	3.8	(0.27)	4.2	(0.40)	3.4	(0.36)	2.8	(0.29)	7.3	(1.03)	5.0	(0.87)
2006	3.8	(0.27)	4.1	(0.39)	3.4	(0.36)	2.9	(0.30)	3.8	(0.77)	7.0	(1.01)
2007	3.5	(0.26)	3.7	(0.37)	3.3	(0.35)	2.2	(0.26)	4.5	(0.80)	6.0	(0.98)
2008	3.5	(0.26)	3.1	(0.34)	4.0	(0.39)	2.3	(0.27)	6.4	(0.94)	5.3	(0.85)
2009	3.4	(0.25)	3.5	(0.36)	3.4	(0.35)	2.4	(0.28)	4.8	(0.83)	5.8	(0.87)
2010	3.0	(0.26)	3.0	(0.36)	2.9	(0.35)	2.3	(0.29)	3.6	(0.88)	4.1	(0.73)
2011	3.4	(0.30)	3.6	(0.43)	3.1	(0.37)	2.7	(0.38)	4.4	(0.87)	4.6	(0.81)
2012	3.4	(0.32)	3.6	(0.48)	3.3	(0.49)	1.6	(0.24)	6.8	(1.35)	5.4	(0.93)
2013	4.7	(0.40)	4.8	(0.53)	4.5	(0.55)	4.3	(0.51)	5.8	(1.17)	5.7	(0.95)
2014	5.2	(0.38)	5.4	(0.58)	5.0	(0.53)	4.7	(0.43)	5.7	(1.21)	7.9	(1.05)
2015	4.9	(0.43)	5.1	(0.60)	4.6	(0.57)	3.8	(0.47)	6.8	(1.37)	6.2	(1.12)
2016	4.8	(0.36)	5.4	(0.57)	4.1	(0.52)	4.5	(0.45)	5.9	(1.19)	4.7	(0.76)
2017	4.7	(0.37)	5.4	(0.52)	3.9	(0.49)	3.9	(0.43)	5.5	(1.16)	6.5	(0.98)
2018	4.7	(0.43)	4.2	(0.48)	5.2	(0.66)	3.6	(0.50)	6.8	(1.35)	6.1	(1.03)

!Interpret data with caution. The coefficient of variation (CV) for this estimate is between 30 and 50 percent.

[1]The event dropout rate is the percentage of 15- to 24-year-olds in grades 10 through 12 who dropped out between one October and the next (e.g., the 2018 data refer to 10th- through 12th-graders who were enrolled in October 2017 but had dropped out by October 2018). Dropping out is defined as leaving school without a high school diploma or alternative credential such as a GED certificate.

[2]Includes other racial/ethnic groups not separately shown.

NOTE: Data are based on sample surveys of the civilian noninstitutionalized population, which excludes persons in the military and persons living in institutions (e.g., prisons or nursing facilities). Because of changes in data collection procedures, data for 1992 and later years may not be comparable with figures for prior years. Prior to 2010, standard errors were computed using generalized variance function methodology rather than the more precise replicate weight methodology used in later years. Race categories exclude persons of Hispanic ethnicity. Detail may not sum to totals because of rounding.

SOURCE: U.S. Department of Commerce, Census Bureau, Current Population Survey (CPS), October, 1972 through 2018. (This table was prepared October 2019.)

Table 219.57. Among 15- to 24-year-olds enrolled in grades 10 through 12, percentage who dropped out (event dropout rate), and number and percentage distribution of 15- to 24-year-olds in grades 10 through 12, by selected characteristics: Selected years, 2008 through 2018

[Standard errors appear in parentheses]

Selected characteristic	Event dropout rate[1]								2018							
									Number of 15- to 24-year-olds enrolled in grades 10 through 12 (in thousands)				Percentage distribution of 15- to 24-year-olds enrolled in grades 10 through 12			
	2008		2013		2017		2018		Total population[2]		Event dropouts only[3]		Total population[2]		Event dropouts only[3]	
1	2		3		4		5		6		7		8		9	
Total	**3.5**	**(0.26)**	**4.7**	**(0.40)**	**4.7**	**(0.37)**	**4.7**	**(0.43)**	**11,033**	**(155.2)**	**518**	**(46.0)**	**100.0**	**(†)**	**100.0**	**(†)**
Sex																
Male	3.1	(0.34)	4.8	(0.53)	5.4	(0.52)	4.2	(0.48)	5,646	(92.2)	236	(27.1)	51.2	(0.54)	45.6	(4.09)
Female	4.0	(0.39)	4.5	(0.55)	3.9	(0.49)	5.2	(0.66)	5,387	(103.5)	282	(34.9)	48.8	(0.54)	54.4	(4.09)
Race/ethnicity																
White	2.3	(0.27)	4.3	(0.51)	3.9	(0.43)	3.6	(0.50)	5,878	(110.2)	213	(29.4)	53.3	(0.61)	41.1	(4.52)
Black	6.4	(0.94)	5.8	(1.17)	5.5	(1.16)	6.8	(1.35)	1,508	(58.8)	‡	(†)	13.7	(0.51)	19.9	(3.73)
Hispanic	5.3	(0.85)	5.7	(0.95)	6.5	(0.98)	6.1	(1.03)	2,513	(65.3)	153	(26.4)	22.8	(0.64)	29.5	(4.32)
Asian	4.2!	(1.57)	1.8!	(0.78)	4.7!	(1.53)	4.7!	(1.79)	588	(47.8)	‡	(†)	5.3	(0.40)	5.4!	(2.03)
Pacific Islander	‡	(†)	‡	(†)	‡	(†)	‡	(†)	‡	(†)	‡	(†)	0.4	(0.10)	‡	(†)
American Indian/Alaska Native	‡	(†)	‡	(†)	4.4!	(1.86)	‡	(†)	100	(18.8)	‡	(†)	0.9	(0.17)	‡	(†)
Two or more races	‡	(†)	5.0!	(2.34)	‡	(†)	‡	(†)	399	(39.9)	‡	(†)	3.6	(0.34)	‡	(†)
Age[4]																
15 and 16	2.4	(0.40)	5.2	(0.73)	4.5	(0.64)	5.6	(0.94)	3,047	(96.6)	169	(27.2)	27.6	(0.69)	32.7	(4.11)
17	3.1	(0.41)	4.0	(0.62)	4.1	(0.55)	4.2	(0.59)	3,657	(70.3)	153	(21.9)	33.1	(0.55)	29.6	(3.53)
18	3.6	(0.50)	2.9	(0.58)	5.2	(0.79)	3.5	(0.64)	3,046	(72.6)	108	(19.4)	27.6	(0.54)	20.8	(3.22)
19	4.9	(1.11)	7.2	(1.61)	6.1!	(1.89)	6.5	(1.62)	877	(55.9)	‡	(†)	8.0	(0.49)	11.1	(2.87)
20 to 24	14.9	(2.79)	14.4	(3.41)	5.8!	(2.31)	7.5!	(2.71)	406	(47.3)	‡	(†)	3.7	(0.43)	5.9!	(2.04)
Recency of immigration[5]																
Born outside the United States	6.3	(1.49)	4.8	(1.24)	8.0	(1.72)	10.4	(2.48)	721	(50.1)	‡	(†)	6.5	(0.44)	14.5	(3.32)
Hispanic	7.2!	(2.18)	5.5!	(2.19)	5.9!	(2.27)	15.6	(4.53)	345	(35.7)	‡	(†)	3.1	(0.33)	10.4	(3.09)
Non-Hispanic	5.3!	(1.98)	4.1!	(1.52)	9.6	(2.53)	5.7!	(2.30)	376	(35.2)	‡	(†)	3.4	(0.31)	4.1!	(1.68)
First generation	2.5	(0.58)	4.4	(0.86)	4.2	(0.85)	6.4	(1.30)	2,208	(86.0)	142	(29.0)	20.0	(0.75)	27.4	(4.74)
Hispanic	3.6!	(1.11)	6.5	(1.48)	4.7	(1.17)	5.2	(1.21)	1,239	(62.4)	‡	(†)	11.2	(0.59)	12.5	(2.69)
Non-Hispanic	1.4!	(0.60)	1.9!	(0.74)	3.5	(1.04)	8.0	(2.20)	969	(62.5)	‡	(†)	8.8	(0.53)	14.9	(3.90)
Second or later generation	3.5	(0.29)	4.8	(0.46)	4.5	(0.45)	3.7	(0.40)	8,103	(150.5)	301	(32.0)	73.4	(0.78)	58.1	(4.98)
Hispanic	6.1	(1.47)	5.0	(1.16)	8.8	(1.93)	3.7!	(1.29)	929	(57.1)	‡	(†)	8.4	(0.51)	6.7!	(2.37)
Non-Hispanic	3.2	(0.29)	4.7	(0.47)	4.0	(0.40)	3.7	(0.43)	7,175	(144.9)	266	(30.4)	65.0	(0.80)	51.4	(4.81)
Disability status[6]																
With a disability	—	(†)	7.8!	(2.84)	6.2!	(2.10)	7.3	(1.83)	426	(39.8)	‡	(†)	3.9	(0.36)	6.0	(1.67)
Without a disability	—	(†)	4.6	(0.39)	4.6	(0.39)	4.6	(0.44)	10,607	(154.3)	487	(45.2)	96.1	(0.36)	94.0	(1.67)
Region																
Northeast	2.3	(0.50)	2.2	(0.57)	4.9	(1.01)	3.8	(0.99)	1,878	(86.6)	‡	(†)	17.0	(0.71)	13.7	(3.44)
Midwest	2.7	(0.47)	4.5	(0.85)	3.2	(0.63)	2.7	(0.57)	2,512	(85.0)	‡	(†)	22.8	(0.69)	13.2	(2.69)
South	4.3	(0.50)	5.8	(0.79)	5.2	(0.62)	5.6	(0.76)	4,016	(105.7)	225	(31.5)	36.4	(0.88)	43.4	(4.61)
West	4.1	(0.58)	4.9	(0.68)	5.1	(0.73)	5.8	(0.93)	2,627	(84.3)	154	(24.5)	23.8	(0.70)	29.6	(4.06)

—Not available.
†Not applicable.
!Interpret data with caution. The coefficient of variation (CV) for this estimate is between 30 and 50 percent.
‡Reporting standards not met. Either there are too few cases for a reliable estimate or the coefficient of variation (CV) is 50 percent or greater.
[1]The event dropout rate is the percentage of 15- to 24-year-olds in grades 10 through 12 who dropped out between one October and the next (e.g., the 2018 data refer to 10th- through 12th-graders who were enrolled in October 2017 but had dropped out by October 2018). Dropping out is defined as leaving school without a high school diploma or alternative credential such as a GED certificate.
[2]Includes all 15- to 24-year-olds who were enrolled in grades 10 through 12 in October 2017.
[3]Includes only those 15- to 24-year-olds who dropped out of grades 10 through 12 between October 2017 and October 2018. Dropping out is defined as leaving school without a high school diploma or alternative credential such as a GED certificate.
[4]Age at the time of data collection. A person's age at the time of dropping out may be 1 year younger, because the dropout event could occur at any time over the previous 12-month period.
[5]United States refers to the 50 states, the District of Columbia, Puerto Rico, American Samoa, Guam, the U.S. Virgin Islands, and the Northern Marianas. Children born abroad to U.S.-citizen parents are counted as born in the United States. Individuals defined as "first generation" were born in the United States, but one or both of their parents were born outside the United States. Individuals defined as "second generation or higher" were born in the United States, as were both of their parents.
[6]Individuals identified as having a disability reported difficulty with at least one of the following: hearing, seeing even when wearing glasses, walking or climbing stairs, dressing or bathing, doing errands alone, concentrating, remembering, or making decisions.
NOTE: Data are based on sample surveys of the civilian noninstitutionalized population, which excludes persons in the military and persons living in institutions (e.g., prisons or nursing facilities). Race categories exclude persons of Hispanic ethnicity. Detail may not sum to totals because of rounding. Prior to 2010, standard errors were computed using generalized variance function methodology rather than the more precise replicate weight methodology used in later years.
SOURCE: U.S. Department of Commerce, Census Bureau, Current Population Survey (CPS), October, 2008 through 2018. (This table was prepared October 2019.)

Table 219.60. Number and percentage of people taking, completing, and passing high school equivalency tests, by test taken and state or jurisdiction: 2013 and 2015

State or jurisdiction	General Educational Development (GED) test, 2013					High School Equivalency Test (HiSET), 2015					Test Assessing Secondary Completion (TASC), 2015				
	Total number of test takers[1]	Completers[2]		Passers[3]		Total number of test takers[1]	Completers[2]		Passers[3]		Total number of test takers[1]	Completers[2,4]		Passers[3,4]	
		Number completing test	Completion rate	Number passing test	Pass rate		Number completing test	Completion rate	Number passing test	Pass rate		Number completing test	Completion rate	Number passing test	Pass rate
1	2	3	4	5	6	7	8	9	10	11	12	13	14	15	16
United States	**816,213**	**713,960**	**87.5**	**540,535**	**75.7**	**61,600**	**47,329**	**77.4**	**27,318**	**57.7**	**49,618**	**43,547**	**87.8**	**26,060**	**59.8**
Alabama	17,189	16,621	96.7	10,560	63.5	—	—	—	—	—	—	—	—	—	—
Alaska	3,468	2,812	81.1	2,444	86.9	—	—	—	—	—	—	—	—	—	—
Arizona	23,808	20,664	86.8	16,313	78.9	—	—	—	—	—	—	—	—	—	—
Arkansas	8,245	8,063	97.8	6,923	85.9	—	—	—	—	—	—	—	—	—	—
California	64,983	57,422	88.4	44,864	78.1	12,007	8,815	73.4	4,459	50.0	—	—	—	—	—
Colorado	18,714	14,345	76.7	12,292	85.7	—	—	—	—	—	—	—	—	—	—
Connecticut	6,779	5,795	85.5	3,592	62.0	—	—	—	—	—	—	—	—	—	—
Delaware	1,281	1,272	99.3	1,160	91.2	—	—	—	—	—	—	—	—	—	—
District of Columbia	2,306	1,716	74.4	1,099	64.0	—	—	—	—	—	—	—	—	—	—
Florida	64,011	49,672	77.6	36,683	73.9	—	—	—	—	—	—	—	—	—	—
Georgia	32,705	28,732	87.9	22,178	77.2	—	—	—	—	—	—	—	—	—	—
Hawaii	1,402	1,339	95.5	1,137	84.9	179	162	90.5	83	51.2		—	—	—	—
Idaho	6,384	5,394	84.5	4,829	89.5	—	—	—	—	—	—	—	—	—	—
Illinois	35,998	32,590	90.5	22,675	69.6	—	—	—	—	—	—	—	—	—	—
Indiana	19,868	18,794	94.6	15,184	80.8	—	—	—	—	—	9,083	8,817	97.1	6,617	75.1
Iowa	5,485	4,330	78.9	4,260	98.4	3,084	1,890	61.3	1,537	81.3	—	—	—	—	—
Kansas	4,034	3,843	95.3	3,586	93.3	—	—	—	—	—	—	—	—	—	—
Kentucky	13,916	13,460	96.7	11,490	85.4	—	—	—	—	—	—	—	—	—	—
Louisiana	11,769	11,405	96.9	8,766	76.9	8,411	6,603	78.5	3,621	54.8	—	—	—	—	—
Maine	3,336	2,446	73.3	2,116	86.5	1,903	1,119	58.8	770	68.8	—	—	—	—	—
Maryland	11,034	9,403	85.2	6,388	67.9	—	—	—	—	—	—	—	—	—	—
Massachusetts	14,717	13,201	89.7	9,269	70.2	7,101	5,058	71.2	2,719	53.8	—	—	—	—	—
Michigan	22,233	18,029	81.1	13,641	75.7	—	—	—	—	—	—	—	—	—	—
Minnesota	12,094	10,143	83.9	8,753	86.3	—	—	—	—	—	—	—	—	—	—
Mississippi	14,087	12,982	92.2	8,479	65.3	—	—	—	—	—	—	—	—	—	—
Missouri	16,567	15,178	91.6	12,120	79.9	10,443	9,095	87.1	5,779	63.5	—	—	—	—	—
Montana	3,250	2,827	87.0	2,279	80.6	2,080	1,580	76.0	1,068	67.6	—	—	—	—	—
Nebraska	3,885	3,012	77.5	2,432	80.7	—	—	—	—	—	—	—	—	—	—
Nevada	6,946	6,677	96.1	4,979	74.6	3,003	2,594	86.4	1,420	54.7	215	191	88.8	105	55.0
New Hampshire	2,471	2,251	91.1	1,999	88.8	1,136	971	85.5	737	75.9	—	—	—	—	—
New Jersey	16,877	15,876	94.1	10,811	68.1	1,458	1,088	74.6	475	43.7	5,803	5,428	93.5	3,431	63.2
New Mexico	10,293	8,900	86.5	6,625	74.4	1,115	874	78.4	398	45.5	—	—	—	—	—
New York	56,635	52,934	93.5	31,282	59.1	—	—	—	—	—	29,822	25,901	86.9	13,437	51.9
North Carolina	30,957	25,163	81.3	20,780	82.6	744	403	54.2	206	51.1	—	—	—	—	—
North Dakota	2,009	1,512	75.3	1,322	87.4	—	—	—	—	—	—	—	—	—	—
Ohio	22,677	20,712	91.3	15,021	72.5	—	—	—	—	—	—	—	—	—	—
Oklahoma	10,349	9,448	91.3	7,368	78.0	252	174	69.0	83	47.7	—	—	—	—	—
Oregon	15,104	13,007	86.1	11,542	88.7	—	—	—	—	—	—	—	—	—	—
Pennsylvania	24,937	22,686	91.0	17,654	77.8	—	—	—	—	—	—	—	—	—	—
Rhode Island	3,147	2,799	88.9	2,363	84.4	—	—	—	—	—	—	—	—	—	—
South Carolina	13,135	11,761	89.5	8,713	74.1	—	—	—	—	—	—	—	—	—	—
South Dakota	2,027	1,215	59.9	1,100	90.5	—	—	—	—	—	—	—	—	—	—
Tennessee	16,184	15,322	94.7	11,334	74.0	7,086	6,001	84.7	3,165	52.7	—	—	—	—	—
Texas	58,235	50,826	87.3	37,338	73.5	—	—	—	—	—	—	—	—	—	—
Utah	6,253	5,821	93.1	5,212	89.5	—	—	—	—	—	—	—	—	—	—
Vermont	980	771	78.7	685	88.8	—	—	—	—	—	—	—	—	—	—
Virginia	23,904	21,264	89.0	15,773	74.2	—	—	—	—	—	—	—	—	—	—
Washington	22,734	18,474	81.3	15,865	85.9	—	—	—	—	—	—	—	—	—	—
West Virginia	6,611	5,649	85.4	4,638	82.1	—	—	—	—	—	4,695	3,210	68.4	2,470	77.0
Wisconsin	18,248	13,811	75.7	11,137	80.6	—	—	—	—	—	—	—	—	—	—
Wyoming	1,952	1,591	81.5	1,482	93.1	1,135	1,187	79.5	808	68.1	—	—	—	—	—
American Samoa	32	29	90.6	7	24.1	9	9	100.0	5	55.6	—	—	—	—	—
Guam	169	159	94.1	49	30.8	13	11	84.6	5	45.5	—	—	—	—	—
Northern Marianas	37	24	64.9	11	45.8	63	26	41.3	16	61.5	—	—	—	—	—
Puerto Rico	—	—	—	—	—	—	—	—	—	—	—	—	—	—	—
U.S. Virgin Islands	443	319	72.0	57	17.9	—	—	—	—	—	—	—	—	—	—

—Not available.

[1] Test takers are people who took any portion of the specified equivalency test (i.e., one or more content-area subtests) in the given year.

[2] Test completers are those test takers who had tested in all five content areas of the specified equivalency test by the end of the given year and who took their final content-area subtest in the given year. People completing their final subtest in the given year may have begun testing in an earlier year.

[3] Test passers are those test completers who met the minimum passing standard for the specified equivalency test. In order to receive a high school equivalency credential in some jurisdictions, test takers must meet additional requirements beyond passing an equivalency test.

[4] In New Jersey, New York, and West Virginia, TASC test takers who had already taken a GED subtest in a given content area were not required to take the same content area of the TASC test. In New Jersey, TASC test takers who had taken a HiSET subtest also were not required to take the same content area of the TASC test. TASC completers and passers in this table include only people who took TASC subtests for all content areas; those who took a combination of subtests from TASC and GED (or HiSET in New Jersey) are not included in the calculation of TASC completion and passing rates.

NOTE: The states and other jurisdictions decide which equivalency test(s) to offer. Detail may not sum to totals because of rounding.

SOURCE: American Council on Education, General Educational Development Testing Service, the GED Annual Statistical Report, 2013, retrieved June 28, 2017, from http://www.gedtestingservice.com/educators/historical-testing-data; Educational Testing Service, 2015 Annual Statistical Report on the HiSET Exam, retrieved June 28, 2017, from https://hiset.ets.org/s/pdf/2015_annual_statistical_report.pdf; Data Recognition Corporation, TASC Test 2015 Annual Statistical Report, retrieved June 28, 2017, from http://tasctest.com/pdfs/TASC_Test_2015_Annual_Statistical_Report.pdf. (This table was prepared June 2017.)

Table 219.65. High school completion rate of 18- to 24-year-olds not enrolled in high school (status completion rate), by sex and race/ethnicity: 1972 through 2018

[Standard errors appear in parentheses]

Year	Status completion rate[1]													
			Sex				Race/ethnicity							
	Total		Male		Female		White		Black		Hispanic		Asian[2]	
1	2		3		4		5		6		7		8	
1972	82.8	(0.36)	83.0	(0.52)	82.7	(0.49)	86.0	(0.36)	72.1	(1.45)	56.2	(3.67)	—	(†)
1973	83.7	(0.34)	84.0	(0.50)	83.4	(0.48)	87.0	(0.35)	71.6	(1.42)	58.7	(3.68)	—	(†)
1974	83.6	(0.34)	83.4	(0.50)	83.8	(0.47)	86.7	(0.35)	72.9	(1.41)	60.1	(3.40)	—	(†)
1975	83.8	(0.34)	84.1	(0.48)	83.6	(0.47)	87.2	(0.34)	70.2	(1.43)	62.2	(3.45)	—	(†)
1976	83.5	(0.33)	83.0	(0.49)	84.0	(0.46)	86.4	(0.34)	73.5	(1.36)	60.3	(3.36)	—	(†)
1977	83.6	(0.33)	82.8	(0.49)	84.4	(0.45)	86.7	(0.34)	73.9	(1.34)	58.6	(3.50)	—	(†)
1978	83.6	(0.33)	82.8	(0.48)	84.2	(0.45)	86.9	(0.34)	73.4	(1.33)	58.8	(3.21)	—	(†)
1979	83.1	(0.33)	82.1	(0.49)	84.0	(0.45)	86.5	(0.34)	72.6	(1.33)	58.5	(3.15)	—	(†)
1980	83.9	(0.32)	82.3	(0.48)	85.3	(0.43)	87.5	(0.33)	75.2	(1.28)	57.1	(2.99)	—	(†)
1981	83.8	(0.32)	82.0	(0.48)	85.4	(0.43)	87.1	(0.33)	76.7	(1.22)	59.1	(2.90)	—	(†)
1982	83.8	(0.34)	82.7	(0.50)	84.9	(0.46)	87.0	(0.35)	76.4	(1.28)	60.9	(2.61)	—	(†)
1983	83.9	(0.34)	82.1	(0.51)	85.6	(0.45)	87.4	(0.35)	76.8	(1.27)	59.4	(3.13)	—	(†)
1984	84.7	(0.34)	83.3	(0.50)	85.9	(0.45)	87.5	(0.35)	80.3	(1.19)	63.7	(3.03)	—	(†)
1985	85.4	(0.34)	84.0	(0.50)	86.7	(0.45)	88.2	(0.35)	81.0	(1.20)	66.6	(2.40)	—	(†)
1986	85.5	(0.34)	84.2	(0.51)	86.7	(0.45)	88.8	(0.35)	81.8	(1.19)	63.5	(2.30)	—	(†)
1987	84.7	(0.35)	83.6	(0.52)	85.8	(0.47)	87.7	(0.37)	81.9	(1.20)	65.1	(2.24)	—	(†)
1988	84.5	(0.39)	83.2	(0.58)	85.8	(0.52)	88.6	(0.40)	80.9	(1.35)	58.2	(2.56)	—	(†)
1989	84.7	(0.37)	83.2	(0.55)	86.2	(0.49)	89.0	(0.38)	81.9	(1.25)	59.4	(2.29)	89.3	(2.46)
1990	85.6	(0.36)	85.1	(0.53)	86.0	(0.50)	89.6	(0.37)	83.2	(1.22)	59.1	(2.35)	94.2	(1.72)
1991	84.9	(0.37)	83.8	(0.55)	85.9	(0.51)	89.4	(0.38)	82.5	(1.26)	56.5	(2.32)	95.2	(1.42)
1992	86.4	(0.36)	85.3	(0.53)	87.4	(0.49)	90.7	(0.36)	82.0	(1.26)	62.1	(2.32)	93.1	(1.73)
1993	86.2	(0.36)	85.4	(0.53)	86.9	(0.50)	90.1	(0.37)	81.9	(1.27)	64.4	(2.26)	93.9	(1.66)
1994	85.8	(0.36)	84.5	(0.53)	87.0	(0.49)	90.7	(0.36)	83.3	(1.19)	61.8	(2.06)	92.4	(1.83)
1995	85.0	(0.34)	84.3	(0.50)	85.7	(0.47)	89.5	(0.36)	84.1	(1.01)	62.6	(1.40)	94.8	(1.43)
1996	86.2	(0.35)	85.7	(0.50)	86.8	(0.48)	91.5	(0.34)	83.0	(1.08)	61.9	(1.49)	93.5	(1.24)
1997	85.9	(0.35)	84.6	(0.51)	87.2	(0.47)	90.5	(0.36)	82.0	(1.10)	66.7	(1.42)	90.6	(1.58)
1998	84.8	(0.36)	82.6	(0.53)	87.0	(0.47)	90.2	(0.36)	81.4	(1.11)	62.8	(1.37)	94.2	(1.22)
1999	85.9	(0.34)	84.8	(0.50)	87.0	(0.46)	91.2	(0.34)	83.5	(1.04)	63.4	(1.39)	94.0	(1.19)
2000	86.5	(0.33)	84.9	(0.49)	88.1	(0.44)	91.8	(0.33)	83.7	(1.01)	64.1	(1.36)	94.6	(1.13)
2001	86.5	(0.31)	84.6	(0.47)	88.3	(0.41)	91.1	(0.32)	85.7	(0.92)	65.7	(1.24)	96.1	(0.91)
2002	86.6	(0.31)	84.8	(0.46)	88.4	(0.41)	91.8	(0.31)	84.7	(0.95)	67.3	(1.15)	95.7	(0.89)
2003	87.1	(0.30)	85.1	(0.46)	89.2	(0.40)	91.9	(0.31)	85.0	(0.96)	69.2	(1.15)	94.8	(1.06)
2004	86.9	(0.30)	84.9	(0.46)	88.8	(0.40)	91.7	(0.31)	83.5	(0.98)	69.9	(1.12)	95.2	(1.00)
2005	87.6	(0.30)	85.4	(0.45)	89.8	(0.38)	92.3	(0.30)	86.0	(0.91)	70.3	(1.12)	96.0	(0.93)
2006	87.8	(0.29)	86.5	(0.43)	89.2	(0.39)	92.6	(0.30)	84.9	(0.93)	70.9	(1.11)	95.8	(0.95)
2007	89.0	(0.28)	87.4	(0.42)	90.6	(0.37)	93.5	(0.28)	88.8	(0.80)	72.7	(1.07)	92.8	(1.23)
2008	89.9	(0.27)	89.3	(0.39)	90.5	(0.37)	94.2	(0.26)	86.9	(0.86)	75.5	(1.03)	95.5	(1.01)
2009	89.8	(0.27)	88.3	(0.40)	91.2	(0.35)	93.8	(0.27)	87.1	(0.84)	76.8	(1.00)	97.6	(0.72)
2010	90.4	(0.35)	89.2	(0.53)	91.6	(0.38)	93.7	(0.38)	89.2	(1.08)	79.4	(1.21)	95.3	(1.26)
2011	90.8	(0.35)	89.9	(0.50)	91.8	(0.46)	93.8	(0.39)	90.1	(0.98)	82.2	(1.04)	94.1	(1.48)
2012	91.3	(0.33)	90.3	(0.47)	92.3	(0.45)	94.6	(0.38)	90.0	(1.01)	82.8	(1.02)	95.3	(1.24)
2013	92.0	(0.35)	91.4	(0.47)	92.6	(0.45)	94.3	(0.38)	91.5	(1.13)	85.0	(0.98)	96.3	(1.27)
2014	92.4	(0.32)	91.8	(0.46)	93.1	(0.38)	94.2	(0.40)	91.7	(0.91)	87.1	(0.88)	98.8	(0.47)
2015	93.0	(0.33)	92.5	(0.44)	93.4	(0.45)	94.7	(0.36)	91.9	(0.91)	88.4	(0.93)	97.3	(0.75)
2016	92.9	(0.32)	91.6	(0.46)	94.3	(0.37)	94.5	(0.36)	92.2	(1.02)	89.1	(0.81)	96.8	(0.75)
2017	93.3	(0.33)	92.3	(0.44)	94.3	(0.41)	94.8	(0.38)	93.8	(0.84)	88.3	(0.90)	98.6	(0.51)
2018	93.6	(0.32)	92.3	(0.46)	94.9	(0.39)	94.9	(0.37)	94.4	(0.85)	89.2	(0.85)	96.9	(0.92)

—Not available.
†Not applicable.
[1]The status completion rate is the number of 18- to 24-year-olds who are high school completers as a percentage of the total number of 18- to 24-year-olds who are not enrolled in high school or a lower level of education. High school completers include those with a high school diploma, as well as those with an alternative credential, such as a GED.
[2]Prior to 2003, Asian data include Pacific Islanders.
NOTE: Data are based on sample surveys of the civilian noninstitutionalized population, which excludes persons in the military and persons living in institutions (e.g., prisons or nursing facilities). Because of changes in data collection procedures, data for 1992 and later years may not be comparable with figures for prior years. Prior to 2010, standard errors were computed using generalized variance function methodology rather than the more precise replicate weight methodology used in later years. Race categories exclude persons of Hispanic ethnicity. Totals include other racial/ethnic groups not separately shown.
SOURCE: U.S. Department of Commerce, Census Bureau, Current Population Survey (CPS), October, 1972 through 2018. (This table was prepared November 2019.)

Table 219.67. High school completion rate of 18- to 24-year-olds not enrolled in high school (status completion rate), number of 18- to 24-year-olds not in high school, and number who are high school completers (status completers), by selected characteristics: Selected years, 2008 through 2018

[Standard errors appear in parentheses]

Selected characteristic	Status completion rate[1]								2018: Number of 18- to 24-year-olds not enrolled in high school (in thousands)				2018: Percentage distribution of 18- to 24-year-olds not enrolled in high school			
	2008		2013		2017		2018		Total population[2]		Status completers only[3]		Total population[2]		Status completers only[3]	
1	2		3		4		5		6		7		8		9	
Total	**89.9**	**(0.27)**	**92.0**	**(0.35)**	**93.3**	**(0.33)**	**93.6**	**(0.32)**	**27,713**	**(198.9)**	**25,950**	**(209.8)**	**100.0**	**(†)**	**100.0**	**(†)**
Sex																
Male	89.3	(0.39)	91.4	(0.47)	92.3	(0.44)	92.3	(0.46)	13,811	(111.7)	12,754	(125.5)	49.8	(0.16)	49.1	(0.23)
Female	90.5	(0.37)	92.6	(0.45)	94.3	(0.41)	94.9	(0.39)	13,902	(106.5)	13,196	(115.4)	50.2	(0.16)	50.9	(0.23)
Race/ethnicity																
White	94.2	(0.26)	94.3	(0.38)	94.8	(0.38)	94.9	(0.37)	14,887	(96.7)	14,134	(107.8)	53.7	(0.39)	54.5	(0.40)
Black	86.9	(0.86)	91.5	(1.13)	93.8	(0.84)	94.4	(0.85)	3,801	(89.9)	3,588	(91.5)	13.7	(0.26)	13.8	(0.29)
Hispanic	75.5	(1.03)	85.0	(0.98)	88.3	(0.90)	89.2	(0.85)	6,316	(80.9)	5,636	(87.8)	22.8	(0.22)	21.7	(0.27)
Asian	95.5	(1.01)	96.3	(1.27)	98.6	(0.51)	96.9	(0.92)	1,694	(55.5)	1,642	(55.7)	6.1	(0.18)	6.3	(0.19)
Pacific Islander	95.9	(3.99)	99.3	(0.79)	89.2	(7.65)	93.1	(4.39)	99	(18.3)	92	(17.3)	0.4	(0.07)	0.4	(0.07)
American Indian/Alaska Native	82.5	(4.03)	91.7	(2.97)	86.3	(3.21)	91.1	(2.21)	233	(31.7)	212	(30.4)	0.8	(0.11)	0.8	(0.12)
Two or more races	94.2	(1.72)	93.6	(1.83)	96.4	(1.28)	94.5	(1.85)	683	(40.3)	646	(41.3)	2.5	(0.15)	2.5	(0.16)
Race/ethnicity by sex																
Male																
White	93.6	(0.39)	93.8	(0.48)	94.3	(0.51)	93.9	(0.57)	7,461	(88.3)	7,008	(95.9)	54.0	(0.47)	54.9	(0.53)
Black	89.1	(1.15)	90.3	(1.41)	92.1	(1.48)	93.0	(1.19)	1,814	(48.7)	1,688	(51.6)	13.1	(0.31)	13.2	(0.36)
Hispanic	73.2	(1.48)	83.8	(1.35)	85.9	(1.22)	86.9	(1.19)	3,192	(48.7)	2,774	(56.1)	23.1	(0.33)	21.8	(0.40)
Asian	95.3	(1.49)	97.6	(1.17)	99.3	(0.41)	97.0	(1.17)	876	(34.8)	849	(37.2)	6.3	(0.24)	6.7	(0.27)
Pacific Islander	‡	(†)	‡	(†)	‡	(†)	‡	(†)	‡	(†)	‡	(†)	0.3!	(0.09)	0.3!	(0.09)
American Indian/Alaska Native	74.7	(7.04)	90.5	(6.44)	85.8	(5.00)	91.9	(3.13)	108	(20.3)	99	(19.5)	0.8	(0.15)	0.8	(0.15)
Two or more races	95.2	(2.18)	94.7	(2.65)	95.1	(2.14)	94.1	(2.99)	319	(37.0)	300	(37.3)	2.3	(0.27)	2.4	(0.30)
Female																
White	94.9	(0.35)	94.7	(0.45)	95.2	(0.49)	96.0	(0.46)	7,426	(67.6)	7,126	(71.5)	53.4	(0.69)	54.0	(0.70)
Black	85.0	(1.25)	92.6	(1.39)	95.3	(0.96)	95.7	(1.06)	1,987	(57.6)	1,901	(57.6)	14.3	(0.34)	14.4	(0.37)
Hispanic	77.9	(1.42)	86.2	(1.30)	90.7	(1.16)	91.6	(1.03)	3,124	(60.7)	2,862	(63.8)	22.5	(0.34)	21.7	(0.38)
Asian	95.6	(1.36)	94.9	(1.94)	97.9	(0.90)	96.8	(1.45)	818	(37.6)	793	(37.3)	5.9	(0.26)	6.0	(0.27)
Pacific Islander	‡	(†)	‡	(†)	‡	(†)	‡	(†)	‡	(†)	‡	(†)	0.4	(0.11)	0.4	(0.11)
American Indian/Alaska Native	88.2	(4.51)	92.5	(4.02)	87.0	(5.29)	90.4	(3.31)	125	(19.7)	113	(18.5)	0.9	(0.14)	0.9	(0.14)
Two or more races	93.1	(2.69)	92.5	(2.88)	97.4	(1.41)	94.9	(1.70)	364	(28.1)	346	(28.2)	2.6	(0.20)	2.6	(0.21)
Age																
18 and 19	89.0	(0.55)	91.4	(0.69)	90.6	(0.70)	91.4	(0.62)	6,802	(86.5)	6,218	(92.8)	24.5	(0.37)	24.0	(0.41)
20 and 21	91.0	(0.47)	92.4	(0.63)	94.2	(0.54)	94.3	(0.51)	8,185	(194.5)	7,720	(189.3)	29.5	(0.59)	29.8	(0.61)
22 to 24	89.7	(0.40)	92.1	(0.51)	94.2	(0.41)	94.4	(0.44)	12,725	(163.6)	12,011	(167.5)	45.9	(0.51)	46.3	(0.54)
Recency of immigration[4]																
Born outside the United States	73.9	(1.33)	82.2	(1.52)	86.6	(1.34)	87.2	(1.43)	2,780	(110.5)	2,425	(105.4)	10.0	(0.38)	9.3	(0.39)
Hispanic	59.0	(1.97)	71.8	(2.53)	78.1	(2.25)	79.1	(2.46)	1,296	(75.0)	1,025	(64.4)	4.7	(0.27)	3.9	(0.25)
Non-Hispanic	93.4	(1.15)	92.7	(1.50)	94.7	(1.23)	94.3	(1.39)	1,485	(82.0)	1,401	(83.3)	5.4	(0.29)	5.4	(0.31)
First generation	91.3	(0.73)	92.3	(0.86)	94.3	(0.75)	94.1	(0.79)	5,073	(135.8)	4,771	(134.2)	18.3	(0.47)	18.4	(0.49)
Hispanic	85.4	(1.51)	89.9	(1.29)	91.7	(1.18)	91.4	(1.22)	2,801	(94.5)	2,561	(91.4)	10.1	(0.33)	9.9	(0.34)
Non-Hispanic	96.4	(0.66)	95.5	(1.15)	97.9	(0.64)	97.3	(0.73)	2,272	(90.3)	2,210	(91.1)	8.2	(0.32)	8.5	(0.34)
Second generation or higher	92.0	(0.27)	93.3	(0.38)	94.1	(0.37)	94.4	(0.34)	19,860	(196.8)	18,754	(200.7)	71.7	(0.57)	72.3	(0.60)
Hispanic	84.0	(1.53)	88.7	(1.47)	90.8	(1.37)	92.4	(1.25)	2,219	(108.4)	2,051	(104.5)	8.0	(0.39)	7.9	(0.40)
Non-Hispanic	92.6	(0.27)	93.8	(0.38)	94.5	(0.37)	94.7	(0.36)	17,640	(163.2)	16,703	(171.6)	63.7	(0.47)	64.4	(0.52)
Disability[5]																
With a disability	—	(†)	81.3	(2.27)	84.8	(2.28)	84.7	(2.00)	1,104	(71.7)	935	(62.3)	4.0	(0.26)	3.6	(0.24)
Without a disability	—	(†)	92.4	(0.33)	93.6	(0.34)	94.0	(0.32)	26,609	(207.0)	25,014	(215.0)	96.0	(0.26)	96.4	(0.24)
Region																
Northeast	92.7	(0.56)	93.4	(0.79)	94.9	(0.64)	94.7	(0.82)	4,753	(149.8)	4,500	(150.4)	17.1	(0.52)	17.3	(0.56)
Midwest	90.3	(0.58)	93.2	(0.71)	93.3	(0.73)	93.0	(0.75)	5,649	(126.0)	5,256	(120.7)	20.4	(0.46)	20.3	(0.46)
South	89.1	(0.47)	91.2	(0.60)	92.8	(0.56)	93.5	(0.55)	10,770	(190.9)	10,071	(189.5)	38.9	(0.61)	38.8	(0.65)
West	88.7	(0.57)	91.2	(0.70)	93.1	(0.71)	93.6	(0.52)	6,542	(155.3)	6,123	(149.4)	23.6	(0.53)	23.6	(0.53)

—Not available.
†Not applicable.
‡Reporting standards not met (too few cases for a reliable estimate).
[1]The status completion rate is the number of 18- to 24-year-olds who are high school completers as a percentage of the total number of 18- to 24-year-olds who are not enrolled in high school or a lower level of education. High school completers include those with a high school diploma, as well as those with an alternative credential, such as a GED.
[2]Includes all 18- to 24-year-olds who are not enrolled in high school or a lower level of education.
[3]Status completers are 18- to 24-year-olds who are not enrolled in high school or a lower level of education and who also are high school completers—that is, have either a high school diploma or an alternative credential, such as a GED.
[4]United States refers to the 50 states, the District of Columbia, Puerto Rico, American Samoa, Guam, the U.S. Virgin Islands, and the Northern Marianas. Children born abroad to U.S.-citizen parents are counted as born in the United States. Individuals defined as "first generation" were born in the United States, but one or both of their parents were born outside the United States. Individuals defined as "second generation or higher" were born in the United States, as were both of their parents.
[5]Individuals identified as having a disability reported difficulty in at least one of the following: hearing, seeing even when wearing glasses, walking or climbing stairs, dressing or bathing, doing errands alone, concentrating, remembering, or making decisions.
NOTE: Data are based on sample surveys of the civilian noninstitutionalized population, which excludes persons in the military and persons living in institutions (e.g., prisons or nursing facilities). Race categories exclude persons of Hispanic ethnicity. Detail may not sum to totals because of rounding and the suppression of cells that do not meet National Center for Education Statistics reporting standards.
SOURCE: U.S. Department of Commerce, Census Bureau, Current Population Survey (CPS), October, 2008 through 2018. (This table was prepared October 2019.)

Table 219.70. Percentage of high school dropouts among persons 16 to 24 years old (status dropout rate), by sex and race/ethnicity: Selected years, 1960 through 2018

[Standard errors appear in parentheses]

Year	Total				Male				Female			
	All races/ ethnicities[1]	White	Black	Hispanic	All races/ ethnicities[1]	White	Black	Hispanic	All races/ ethnicities[1]	White	Black	Hispanic
1	2	3	4	5	6	7	8	9	10	11	12	13
1960[2]	27.2 (—)	— (†)	— (†)	— (†)	27.8 (—)	— (†)	— (†)	— (†)	26.7 (—)	— (†)	— (†)	— (†)
1967[3]	17.0 (—)	15.4 (—)	28.6 (—)	— (†)	16.5 (—)	14.7 (—)	30.6 (—)	— (†)	17.3 (—)	16.1 (—)	26.9 (—)	— (†)
1968[3]	16.2 (—)	14.7 (—)	27.4 (—)	— (†)	15.8 (—)	14.4 (—)	27.1 (—)	— (†)	16.5 (—)	15.0 (—)	27.6 (—)	— (†)
1969[3]	15.2 (—)	13.6 (—)	26.7 (—)	— (†)	14.3 (—)	12.6 (—)	26.9 (—)	— (†)	16.0 (—)	14.6 (—)	26.7 (—)	— (†)
1970[3]	15.0 (0.30)	13.2 (0.30)	27.9 (1.25)	— (†)	14.2 (0.42)	12.2 (0.43)	29.4 (1.87)	— (†)	15.7 (0.42)	14.1 (0.43)	26.6 (1.69)	— (†)
1971[3]	14.7 (0.29)	13.4 (0.30)	24.0 (1.17)	— (†)	14.2 (0.41)	12.6 (0.42)	25.5 (1.74)	— (†)	15.2 (0.41)	14.2 (0.42)	22.6 (1.58)	— (†)
1972	14.6 (0.28)	12.3 (0.29)	21.3 (1.09)	34.3 (2.93)	14.1 (0.40)	11.6 (0.41)	22.3 (1.63)	33.7 (4.26)	15.1 (0.40)	12.8 (0.42)	20.5 (1.48)	34.8 (4.03)
1973	14.1 (0.28)	11.6 (0.28)	22.2 (1.09)	33.5 (2.96)	13.7 (0.39)	11.5 (0.40)	21.5 (1.57)	30.4 (4.17)	14.5 (0.39)	11.8 (0.40)	22.8 (1.51)	36.4 (4.18)
1974	14.3 (0.28)	11.9 (0.28)	21.2 (1.07)	33.0 (2.74)	14.2 (0.39)	12.0 (0.41)	20.1 (1.55)	33.8 (3.94)	14.3 (0.39)	11.8 (0.40)	22.1 (1.49)	32.2 (3.82)
1975	13.9 (0.27)	11.4 (0.28)	22.9 (1.08)	29.2 (2.67)	13.3 (0.38)	11.0 (0.39)	23.0 (1.60)	26.7 (3.75)	14.5 (0.38)	11.8 (0.39)	22.9 (1.48)	31.6 (3.78)
1976	14.1 (0.27)	12.0 (0.28)	20.5 (1.03)	31.4 (2.66)	14.1 (0.39)	12.1 (0.40)	21.2 (1.53)	30.3 (3.88)	14.2 (0.38)	11.8 (0.39)	19.9 (1.39)	32.3 (3.64)
1977	14.1 (0.27)	11.9 (0.28)	19.8 (1.00)	33.0 (2.65)	14.5 (0.39)	12.6 (0.41)	19.5 (1.47)	31.6 (3.79)	13.8 (0.37)	11.2 (0.38)	20.0 (1.38)	34.3 (3.71)
1978	14.2 (0.27)	11.9 (0.28)	20.2 (1.01)	33.3 (2.62)	14.6 (0.39)	12.2 (0.40)	22.5 (1.54)	33.6 (3.77)	13.9 (0.37)	11.6 (0.39)	18.3 (1.32)	33.1 (3.65)
1979	14.6 (0.27)	12.0 (0.28)	21.1 (1.02)	33.8 (2.60)	15.0 (0.39)	12.6 (0.40)	22.4 (1.53)	33.0 (3.71)	14.2 (0.37)	11.5 (0.39)	20.0 (1.36)	34.5 (3.63)
1980	14.1 (0.27)	11.4 (0.27)	19.1 (0.98)	35.2 (2.47)	15.1 (0.39)	12.3 (0.40)	20.8 (1.48)	37.2 (3.57)	13.1 (0.36)	10.5 (0.37)	17.7 (1.29)	33.2 (3.42)
1981	13.9 (0.26)	11.3 (0.27)	18.4 (0.94)	33.2 (2.36)	15.1 (0.39)	12.5 (0.40)	19.9 (1.41)	36.0 (3.42)	12.8 (0.35)	10.2 (0.37)	17.1 (1.25)	30.4 (3.25)
1982	13.9 (0.28)	11.4 (0.29)	18.4 (0.99)	31.7 (2.51)	14.5 (0.40)	12.0 (0.43)	21.2 (1.52)	30.5 (3.57)	13.3 (0.38)	10.8 (0.40)	15.9 (1.28)	32.8 (3.53)
1983	13.7 (0.28)	11.1 (0.29)	18.0 (0.98)	31.6 (2.51)	14.9 (0.41)	12.2 (0.43)	19.9 (1.48)	34.3 (3.71)	12.5 (0.38)	10.1 (0.40)	16.2 (1.30)	29.1 (3.41)
1984	13.1 (0.28)	11.0 (0.29)	15.5 (0.93)	29.8 (2.49)	14.0 (0.41)	11.9 (0.43)	16.8 (1.39)	30.6 (3.62)	12.3 (0.38)	10.1 (0.40)	14.3 (1.24)	29.0 (3.42)
1985	12.6 (0.28)	10.4 (0.29)	15.2 (0.93)	27.6 (1.93)	13.4 (0.40)	11.1 (0.43)	16.1 (1.39)	29.9 (2.77)	11.8 (0.37)	9.8 (0.40)	14.3 (1.25)	25.2 (2.68)
1986	12.2 (0.27)	9.7 (0.29)	14.2 (0.91)	30.1 (1.88)	13.1 (0.40)	10.3 (0.42)	15.0 (1.36)	32.8 (2.67)	11.4 (0.37)	9.1 (0.39)	13.5 (1.23)	27.2 (2.64)
1987	12.6 (0.28)	10.4 (0.30)	14.1 (0.92)	28.6 (1.85)	13.2 (0.41)	10.8 (0.43)	15.0 (1.37)	29.1 (2.58)	12.1 (0.39)	10.0 (0.41)	13.3 (1.23)	28.1 (2.65)
1988	12.9 (0.31)	9.6 (0.32)	14.5 (1.01)	35.8 (2.17)	13.5 (0.45)	10.3 (0.47)	15.0 (1.50)	36.0 (3.02)	12.2 (0.42)	8.9 (0.43)	14.0 (1.38)	35.4 (3.13)
1989	12.6 (0.30)	9.4 (0.31)	13.9 (0.94)	33.0 (1.92)	13.6 (0.43)	10.3 (0.45)	14.9 (1.41)	34.4 (2.70)	11.7 (0.40)	8.5 (0.41)	13.0 (1.27)	31.6 (2.73)
1990	12.1 (0.29)	9.0 (0.30)	13.2 (0.94)	32.4 (1.91)	12.3 (0.42)	9.3 (0.44)	11.9 (1.30)	34.3 (2.71)	11.8 (0.41)	8.7 (0.42)	14.4 (1.34)	30.3 (2.70)
1991	12.5 (0.30)	8.9 (0.31)	13.6 (0.95)	35.3 (1.93)	13.0 (0.43)	8.9 (0.44)	13.5 (1.37)	39.2 (2.74)	11.9 (0.41)	8.9 (0.43)	13.7 (1.31)	31.1 (2.70)
1992[4]	11.0 (0.28)	7.7 (0.29)	13.7 (0.95)	29.4 (1.86)	11.3 (0.41)	8.0 (0.42)	12.5 (1.31)	32.1 (2.67)	10.7 (0.39)	7.4 (0.40)	14.8 (1.35)	26.6 (2.56)
1993[4]	11.0 (0.28)	7.9 (0.29)	13.6 (0.94)	27.5 (1.79)	11.2 (0.40)	8.2 (0.42)	12.6 (1.32)	28.1 (2.54)	10.9 (0.40)	7.6 (0.41)	14.4 (1.34)	26.9 (2.51)
1994[4]	11.4 (0.28)	7.7 (0.29)	12.6 (0.89)	30.0 (1.66)	12.3 (0.41)	8.0 (0.41)	14.1 (1.34)	31.6 (2.30)	10.6 (0.38)	7.5 (0.40)	11.3 (1.17)	28.1 (2.38)
1995[4]	12.0 (0.27)	8.6 (0.28)	12.1 (0.75)	30.0 (1.15)	12.2 (0.38)	9.0 (0.40)	11.1 (1.05)	30.0 (1.59)	11.7 (0.37)	8.2 (0.39)	12.9 (1.06)	30.0 (1.66)
1996[4]	11.1 (0.27)	7.3 (0.27)	13.0 (0.80)	29.4 (1.19)	11.4 (0.38)	7.3 (0.38)	13.5 (1.18)	30.3 (1.67)	10.9 (0.38)	7.3 (0.39)	12.5 (1.08)	28.3 (1.69)
1997[4]	11.0 (0.27)	7.6 (0.28)	13.4 (0.80)	25.3 (1.11)	11.9 (0.39)	8.5 (0.41)	13.3 (1.16)	27.0 (1.55)	10.1 (0.36)	6.7 (0.37)	13.5 (1.11)	23.4 (1.59)
1998[4]	11.8 (0.27)	7.7 (0.28)	13.8 (0.81)	29.5 (1.12)	13.3 (0.40)	8.6 (0.41)	15.5 (1.23)	33.5 (1.59)	10.3 (0.36)	6.9 (0.37)	12.2 (1.05)	25.0 (1.56)
1999[4]	11.2 (0.26)	7.3 (0.27)	12.6 (0.77)	28.6 (1.11)	11.9 (0.38)	7.7 (0.39)	12.1 (1.10)	31.0 (1.58)	10.5 (0.36)	6.9 (0.37)	13.0 (1.08)	26.0 (1.54)
2000[4]	10.9 (0.26)	6.9 (0.26)	13.1 (0.78)	27.8 (1.08)	12.0 (0.38)	7.0 (0.37)	15.3 (1.20)	31.8 (1.56)	9.9 (0.35)	6.9 (0.37)	11.1 (1.00)	23.5 (1.48)
2001[4]	10.7 (0.24)	7.3 (0.25)	10.9 (0.68)	27.0 (1.01)	12.2 (0.36)	7.9 (0.37)	13.0 (1.06)	31.6 (1.47)	9.3 (0.32)	6.7 (0.34)	9.0 (0.86)	22.1 (1.35)
2002[4]	10.5 (0.24)	6.5 (0.24)	11.3 (0.70)	25.7 (0.93)	11.8 (0.35)	6.7 (0.35)	12.8 (1.07)	29.6 (1.32)	9.2 (0.32)	6.3 (0.34)	9.9 (0.91)	21.2 (1.27)
2003[4,5]	9.9 (0.23)	6.3 (0.24)	10.9 (0.69)	23.5 (0.90)	11.3 (0.34)	7.1 (0.35)	12.5 (1.05)	26.7 (1.29)	8.4 (0.30)	5.6 (0.32)	9.5 (0.89)	20.1 (1.23)
2004[4,5]	10.3 (0.23)	6.8 (0.24)	11.8 (0.70)	23.8 (0.89)	11.6 (0.34)	7.1 (0.35)	13.5 (1.08)	28.5 (1.30)	9.0 (0.31)	6.4 (0.34)	10.2 (0.92)	18.5 (1.18)
2005[4,5]	9.4 (0.22)	6.0 (0.23)	10.4 (0.66)	22.4 (0.87)	10.8 (0.33)	6.6 (0.34)	12.0 (1.02)	26.4 (1.26)	8.0 (0.29)	5.3 (0.31)	9.0 (0.86)	18.1 (1.16)
2006[4,5]	9.3 (0.22)	5.8 (0.23)	10.7 (0.66)	22.1 (0.86)	10.3 (0.33)	6.4 (0.33)	9.7 (0.91)	25.7 (1.25)	8.3 (0.30)	5.3 (0.31)	11.7 (0.96)	18.1 (1.15)
2007[4,5]	8.7 (0.21)	5.3 (0.22)	8.4 (0.59)	21.4 (0.83)	9.8 (0.32)	6.0 (0.32)	8.0 (0.82)	24.7 (1.22)	7.7 (0.29)	4.5 (0.28)	8.8 (0.84)	18.0 (1.13)
2008[4,5]	8.0 (0.20)	4.8 (0.21)	9.9 (0.63)	18.3 (0.78)	8.5 (0.30)	5.4 (0.30)	8.7 (0.85)	19.9 (1.12)	7.5 (0.28)	4.2 (0.28)	11.1 (0.93)	16.7 (1.08)
2009[4,5]	8.1 (0.20)	5.2 (0.21)	9.3 (0.61)	17.6 (0.76)	9.1 (0.31)	6.3 (0.33)	10.6 (0.93)	19.0 (1.10)	7.0 (0.27)	4.1 (0.27)	8.1 (0.80)	16.1 (1.06)
2010[4,5]	7.4 (0.27)	5.1 (0.30)	8.0 (0.76)	15.1 (0.87)	8.5 (0.40)	5.9 (0.42)	9.5 (1.11)	17.3 (1.24)	6.3 (0.28)	4.2 (0.35)	6.7 (0.85)	12.8 (0.97)
2011[4,5]	7.1 (0.26)	5.0 (0.31)	7.3 (0.67)	13.6 (0.78)	7.7 (0.36)	5.4 (0.41)	8.3 (0.98)	14.6 (1.09)	6.5 (0.34)	4.6 (0.38)	6.4 (0.94)	12.4 (0.97)
2012[4,5]	6.6 (0.25)	4.3 (0.31)	7.5 (0.76)	12.7 (0.72)	7.3 (0.36)	4.8 (0.40)	8.1 (1.15)	13.9 (1.04)	5.9 (0.33)	3.8 (0.37)	7.0 (1.01)	11.3 (1.00)
2013[4,5]	6.8 (0.28)	5.1 (0.31)	7.3 (0.87)	11.7 (0.74)	7.2 (0.37)	5.5 (0.39)	8.2 (1.11)	12.6 (1.01)	6.3 (0.34)	4.7 (0.36)	6.6 (1.07)	10.8 (0.98)
2014[4,5]	6.5 (0.25)	5.2 (0.32)	7.4 (0.74)	10.6 (0.68)	7.1 (0.37)	5.7 (0.42)	7.1 (1.02)	11.8 (1.04)	5.9 (0.29)	4.8 (0.41)	7.7 (1.02)	9.3 (0.84)
2015[4,5]	5.9 (0.26)	4.6 (0.29)	6.5 (0.70)	9.2 (0.71)	6.3 (0.37)	5.0 (0.40)	6.4 (1.04)	9.9 (0.93)	5.4 (0.33)	4.1 (0.37)	6.5 (0.98)	8.4 (0.97)
2016[4,5]	6.1 (0.27)	5.2 (0.31)	6.2 (0.80)	8.6 (0.64)	7.1 (0.38)	5.8 (0.42)	8.2 (1.22)	10.1 (1.06)	5.1 (0.31)	4.6 (0.39)	4.3 (0.84)	7.0 (0.76)
2017[4,5]	5.8 (0.26)	4.6 (0.30)	5.7 (0.66)	9.5 (0.67)	6.6 (0.36)	5.0 (0.43)	7.0 (1.08)	11.5 (0.95)	5.0 (0.31)	4.3 (0.36)	4.4 (0.78)	7.4 (0.83)
2018[4,5]	5.7 (0.27)	4.5 (0.29)	5.8 (0.74)	9.0 (0.69)	6.3 (0.35)	5.1 (0.42)	6.0 (0.92)	10.4 (0.93)	5.1 (0.34)	3.8 (0.38)	5.6 (1.04)	7.5 (0.83)

—Not available.
†Not applicable.
[1]Includes other racial/ethnic groups not separately shown.
[2]Based on the April 1960 decennial census.
[3]For 1967 through 1971, White and Black include persons of Hispanic ethnicity.
[4]Because of changes in data collection procedures, data may not be comparable with figures for years prior to 1992.
[5]After 2002, White and Black exclude persons of Two or more races.

NOTE: Status dropouts are 16- to 24-year-olds who are not enrolled in school and who have not completed a high school program, regardless of when they left school. People who have received equivalency credentials, such as the GED, are counted as high school completers. All data except for 1960 are based on October counts. Data are based on sample surveys of the civilian noninstitutionalized population, which excludes persons in the military and persons living in institutions (e.g., prisons or nursing facilities). Prior to 2010, standard errors were computed using generalized variance function methodology rather than the more precise replicate weight methodology used in later years. Race categories exclude persons of Hispanic ethnicity except where otherwise noted.

SOURCE: U.S. Department of Commerce, Census Bureau, Current Population Survey (CPS), October, 1967 through 2018. (This table was prepared November 2019.)

Table 219.71. Population 16 to 24 years old and number of 16- to 24-year-old high school dropouts (status dropouts), by sex and race/ethnicity: Selected years, 1970 through 2019

[Standard errors appear in parentheses]

Year	Total				Male				Female			
	All races/ ethnicities[1]	White	Black	Hispanic	All races/ ethnicities[1]	White	Black	Hispanic	All races/ ethnicities[1]	White	Black	Hispanic
1	2	3	4	5	6	7	8	9	10	11	12	13
	Population 16 to 24 years old (in thousands)											
1970[2]	30,251 (260.7)	26,241 (245.8)	3,669 (93.6)	--- (†)	14,260 (175.6)	12,403 (165.7)	1,703 (62.5)	--- (†)	15,991 (177.3)	13,838 (167.3)	1,966 (63.7)	--- (†)
1975	34,700 (275.4)	27,867 (252.0)	4,310 (99.3)	1,962 (85.3)	16,925 (188.0)	13,711 (172.8)	1,992 (66.2)	940 (58.3)	17,775 (184.7)	14,157 (168.9)	2,319 (67.4)	1,022 (57.3)
1976	35,222 (277.0)	28,146 (253.1)	4,429 (100.2)	2,060 (87.1)	17,210 (189.3)	13,925 (173.9)	2,054 (66.9)	944 (58.4)	18,012 (185.6)	14,221 (169.2)	2,375 (67.9)	1,115 (59.4)
1977	35,658 (278.3)	28,393 (254.0)	4,516 (100.9)	2,123 (88.3)	17,431 (190.2)	14,027 (174.4)	2,086 (67.2)	1,018 (60.4)	18,227 (186.4)	14,366 (169.9)	2,430 (68.4)	1,106 (59.2)
1978	35,931 (279.1)	28,490 (254.3)	4,584 (101.4)	2,183 (89.3)	17,582 (190.8)	14,084 (174.7)	2,113 (67.5)	1,059 (61.5)	18,349 (186.9)	14,406 (170.1)	2,471 (68.8)	1,123 (59.6)
1979	36,131 (279.7)	28,602 (254.8)	4,618 (101.7)	2,242 (90.4)	17,708 (191.4)	14,172 (175.2)	2,128 (67.7)	1,085 (62.1)	18,423 (187.2)	14,430 (170.2)	2,490 (69.0)	1,157 (60.3)
1980	36,143 (279.7)	28,253 (253.5)	4,651 (101.9)	2,518 (95.0)	17,715 (191.4)	13,979 (174.2)	2,148 (67.9)	1,240 (65.8)	18,428 (187.2)	14,274 (169.5)	2,503 (69.1)	1,277 (62.8)
1981	36,945 (282.1)	28,483 (254.3)	4,895 (103.7)	2,684 (97.5)	18,167 (193.2)	14,111 (174.9)	2,286 (69.2)	1,333 (67.8)	18,778 (188.5)	14,372 (169.9)	2,608 (69.9)	1,352 (64.3)
1982	36,452 (296.5)	27,979 (266.7)	4,912 (109.6)	2,598 (102.1)	17,938 (203.2)	13,841 (183.3)	2,303 (73.3)	1,263 (70.3)	18,514 (198.1)	14,139 (178.4)	2,609 (73.9)	1,335 (67.9)
1983	35,884 (294.7)	27,385 (264.3)	4,907 (109.6)	2,587 (101.9)	17,712 (202.2)	13,616 (182.0)	2,329 (73.6)	1,242 (69.8)	18,172 (196.7)	13,769 (176.4)	2,578 (73.6)	1,345 (68.1)
1984	35,204 (292.6)	26,758 (261.8)	4,890 (109.5)	2,558 (101.4)	17,387 (200.8)	13,325 (180.4)	2,329 (73.6)	1,226 (69.4)	17,817 (195.3)	13,433 (174.7)	2,561 (73.5)	1,332 (67.8)
1985	34,382 (289.9)	25,772 (257.7)	4,749 (108.4)	2,887 (89.9)	16,892 (198.5)	12,715 (176.9)	2,239 (72.7)	1,472 (63.1)	17,490 (193.9)	13,057 (172.6)	2,510 (73.0)	1,415 (58.6)
1986	33,945 (288.4)	24,959 (254.2)	4,698 (108.0)	3,206 (93.7)	16,709 (197.7)	12,276 (174.3)	2,222 (72.5)	1,667 (66.4)	17,236 (192.9)	12,684 (170.5)	2,476 (72.7)	1,538 (60.5)
1987	33,452 (286.8)	24,479 (252.1)	4,631 (107.5)	3,234 (94.1)	16,458 (196.5)	12,058 (173.0)	2,176 (72.0)	1,680 (66.6)	16,994 (191.8)	12,420 (169.1)	2,455 (72.5)	1,554 (60.7)
1988	32,893 (310.4)	23,908 (272.0)	4,584 (116.7)	3,267 (105.6)	16,134 (212.5)	11,725 (186.3)	2,156 (78.2)	1,696 (74.7)	16,759 (207.9)	12,184 (182.7)	2,429 (78.7)	1,571 (68.2)
1989	32,007 (291.9)	22,947 (254.0)	4,593 (111.1)	3,459 (100.0)	15,783 (200.2)	11,314 (174.4)	2,193 (74.8)	1,783 (70.5)	16,224 (195.2)	11,634 (170.3)	2,399 (74.6)	1,676 (64.7)
1990	31,443 (289.8)	22,360 (251.1)	4,487 (110.2)	3,443 (99.8)	15,502 (198.8)	11,059 (172.7)	2,117 (73.9)	1,773 (70.4)	15,941 (193.8)	11,302 (168.2)	2,370 (74.3)	1,669 (64.6)
1991	31,171 (288.8)	21,883 (248.8)	4,475 (110.1)	3,519 (100.7)	15,408 (198.3)	10,819 (171.0)	2,126 (74.0)	1,829 (71.2)	15,763 (193.0)	11,064 (166.7)	2,350 (74.1)	1,690 (64.9)
1992[3]	30,944 (287.9)	21,697 (247.9)	4,527 (110.6)	3,476 (100.2)	15,375 (198.1)	10,826 (171.1)	2,169 (74.5)	1,760 (70.2)	15,569 (192.0)	10,871 (165.5)	2,358 (74.2)	1,716 (65.3)
1993[3]	30,845 (287.5)	21,499 (246.9)	4,536 (110.7)	3,595 (101.5)	15,355 (198.0)	10,742 (170.5)	2,179 (74.6)	1,802 (70.8)	15,490 (191.6)	10,757 (164.7)	2,357 (74.2)	1,793 (66.3)
1994[3]	32,560 (293.9)	22,080 (249.8)	4,805 (112.8)	4,411 (109.3)	16,304 (202.8)	11,016 (172.4)	2,298 (75.9)	2,355 (77.9)	16,257 (195.3)	11,064 (166.7)	2,507 (75.7)	2,056 (69.5)
1995[3]	32,379 (293.2)	21,991 (249.3)	4,732 (112.2)	4,485 (109.9)	16,208 (202.3)	11,062 (172.7)	2,236 (75.3)	2,338 (77.7)	16,170 (194.9)	10,929 (165.8)	2,496 (75.6)	2,147 (70.5)
1996[3]	32,452 (304.7)	21,527 (256.4)	4,745 (116.6)	4,481 (114.1)	16,296 (210.5)	10,836 (177.7)	2,251 (78.2)	2,313 (80.4)	16,156 (202.3)	10,690 (170.5)	2,494 (78.4)	2,168 (73.4)
1997[3]	32,960 (306.6)	21,800 (257.8)	4,847 (117.4)	4,660 (115.6)	16,619 (212.1)	11,001 (178.8)	2,308 (78.9)	2,487 (82.3)	16,341 (203.2)	10,799 (171.3)	2,540 (78.8)	2,173 (73.4)
1998[3]	33,445 (308.3)	21,920 (258.4)	4,893 (117.7)	5,034 (118.5)	16,854 (213.3)	11,067 (179.3)	2,305 (78.8)	2,683 (84.2)	16,592 (204.4)	10,854 (171.6)	2,588 (79.3)	2,351 (75.2)
1999[3]	34,169 (310.9)	22,408 (260.9)	4,939 (118.1)	5,060 (118.7)	17,106 (214.5)	11,325 (181.1)	2,336 (79.2)	2,603 (83.5)	17,063 (206.6)	11,084 (173.2)	2,603 (79.4)	2,457 (76.2)
2000[3]	34,568 (312.4)	22,574 (261.8)	5,058 (119.0)	5,237 (120.0)	17,402 (215.9)	11,390 (181.5)	2,417 (80.0)	2,725 (84.6)	17,166 (207.0)	11,184 (173.9)	2,641 (79.7)	2,513 (76.7)
2001[3]	35,167 (298.5)	22,874 (249.9)	5,119 (113.3)	5,344 (114.6)	17,663 (206.1)	11,598 (173.6)	2,418 (75.9)	2,744 (80.5)	17,504 (198.0)	11,276 (165.6)	2,701 (76.2)	2,601 (73.4)
2002[3]	35,495 (299.6)	22,358 (247.4)	4,991 (112.4)	6,120 (118.9)	17,893 (207.2)	11,183 (170.9)	2,375 (75.5)	3,281 (84.3)	17,602 (198.4)	11,175 (165.0)	2,617 (75.5)	2,838 (75.0)
2003[3,4]	36,017 (301.3)	22,565 (248.4)	4,973 (115.6)	6,103 (118.8)	18,099 (208.1)	11,329 (171.9)	2,385 (78.1)	3,214 (83.9)	17,918 (199.7)	11,236 (165.4)	2,588 (77.7)	2,888 (75.3)
2004[3,4]	36,504 (302.8)	22,654 (248.8)	5,048 (116.3)	6,301 (119.8)	18,406 (209.4)	11,395 (172.3)	2,425 (78.5)	3,326 (84.6)	18,097 (200.5)	11,259 (165.5)	2,623 (78.0)	2,975 (75.8)
2005[3,4]	36,761 (303.6)	22,806 (249.6)	5,111 (116.8)	6,364 (120.1)	18,547 (210.0)	11,492 (173.0)	2,457 (78.9)	3,341 (84.6)	18,214 (201.0)	11,314 (165.9)	2,654 (78.4)	3,023 (76.0)
2006[3,4]	37,047 (304.5)	22,863 (249.8)	5,260 (118.0)	6,439 (120.4)	18,707 (210.7)	11,537 (173.3)	2,573 (80.1)	3,357 (84.7)	18,340 (201.5)	11,327 (165.9)	2,688 (78.7)	3,083 (76.3)
2007[3,4]	37,480 (305.9)	22,962 (250.3)	5,363 (118.7)	6,632 (121.2)	18,940 (211.6)	11,641 (173.9)	2,639 (80.7)	3,447 (85.2)	18,541 (202.3)	11,320 (165.9)	2,724 (79.1)	3,186 (76.8)
2008[3,4]	37,569 (306.2)	22,956 (250.3)	5,387 (118.9)	6,721 (121.5)	18,948 (211.7)	11,628 (173.8)	2,616 (80.5)	3,472 (85.3)	18,621 (202.6)	11,328 (165.9)	2,771 (79.5)	3,249 (77.1)
2009[3,4]	37,616 (306.3)	22,809 (249.6)	5,445 (119.4)	6,809 (121.9)	18,949 (211.7)	11,542 (173.3)	2,633 (80.7)	3,497 (85.4)	18,667 (202.8)	11,267 (165.6)	2,812 (79.9)	3,313 (77.3)
2010[3,4]	37,949 (#)	22,607 (38.0)	5,450 (33.5)	7,193 (10.0)	19,126 (#)	11,437 (27.6)	2,609 (24.1)	3,714 (5.8)	18,823 (#)	11,170 (24.6)	2,841 (20.2)	3,479 (8.6)
2011[3,4]	38,205 (133.8)	22,359 (138.0)	5,444 (86.7)	7,656 (59.0)	19,430 (40.3)	11,290 (36.9)	2,627 (58.2)	4,123 (41.9)	18,775 (135.4)	11,068 (133.6)	2,817 (36.2)	3,533 (23.1)
2012[3,4]	38,800 (306.3)	21,708 (137.5)	5,540 (64.1)	8,201 (73.5)	19,557 (266.3)	10,963 (120.5)	2,699 (47.9)	4,241 (85.8)	19,243 (54.1)	10,745 (44.8)	2,841 (35.0)	3,959 (22.9)
2013[3,4]	38,804 (210.7)	21,542 (196.8)	5,570 (48.4)	8,263 (43.2)	19,561 (150.8)	10,911 (119.0)	2,708 (40.5)	4,248 (30.3)	19,243 (71.7)	10,631 (89.5)	2,863 (33.1)	4,015 (22.0)
2014[3,4]	38,650 (67.1)	21,290 (111.6)	5,590 (99.2)	8,345 (61.6)	19,484 (46.7)	10,775 (67.6)	2,739 (31.6)	4,278 (41.7)	19,166 (57.8)	10,515 (57.9)	2,851 (81.4)	4,066 (26.8)
2015[3,4]	38,491 (66.4)	21,161 (80.4)	5,502 (54.0)	8,412 (32.5)	19,392 (58.4)	10,715 (58.5)	2,703 (49.2)	4,280 (29.2)	19,099 (51.5)	10,446 (46.8)	2,799 (57.2)	4,132 (27.0)
2016[3,4]	38,367 (57.6)	20,887 (55.8)	5,378 (51.9)	8,512 (34.5)	19,338 (75.5)	10,582 (65.8)	2,639 (38.4)	4,321 (24.1)	19,030 (105.1)	10,305 (59.4)	2,740 (31.3)	4,191 (23.1)
2017[3,4]	38,079 (96.2)	20,501 (62.9)	5,311 (57.4)	8,568 (56.7)	19,177 (39.4)	10,429 (43.7)	2,572 (56.3)	4,338 (39.2)	18,902 (74.1)	10,073 (50.8)	2,738 (31.8)	4,230 (25.5)
2018[3,4]	37,962 (138.6)	20,234 (74.6)	5,263 (85.7)	8,724 (112.4)	19,107 (86.8)	10,251 (55.6)	2,577 (45.3)	4,423 (59.8)	18,856 (62.6)	9,983 (63.5)	2,686 (53.2)	4,301 (57.0)
2019[3,4]	37,734 (85.6)	19,996 (101.9)	5,080 (82.4)	8,798 (116.2)	18,963 (92.8)	10,148 (134.0)	2,466 (60.9)	4,444 (23.9)	18,770 (137.7)	9,848 (64.7)	2,613 (35.9)	4,354 (101.7)
	Number of 16- to 24-year-old (status) dropouts (in thousands)											
1970[2]	4,525 (90.1)	3,459 (79.6)	1,022 (46.0)	--- (†)	2,022 (60.5)	1,508 (52.9)	500 (31.8)	--- (†)	2,503 (66.7)	1,951 (59.5)	522 (33.2)	--- (†)
1975	4,824 (93.6)	3,185 (77.1)	987 (46.7)	573 (52.3)	2,248 (64.1)	1,509 (53.2)	457 (31.8)	251 (35.2)	2,577 (68.2)	1,676 (55.8)	530 (34.2)	323 (38.6)
1976	4,981 (95.0)	3,366 (79.1)	908 (45.5)	646 (54.7)	2,432 (66.4)	1,688 (55.9)	435 (31.4)	286 (36.7)	2,549 (67.9)	1,678 (55.9)	473 (33.0)	360 (40.6)
1977	5,031 (95.5)	3,374 (79.2)	893 (45.3)	701 (56.3)	2,519 (67.4)	1,767 (57.1)	407 (30.6)	322 (38.5)	2,512 (67.6)	1,607 (54.9)	487 (33.4)	379 (41.0)
1978	5,114 (96.2)	3,384 (79.3)	928 (46.1)	728 (57.2)	2,572 (68.1)	1,715 (56.4)	475 (32.5)	356 (39.9)	2,541 (68.0)	1,670 (55.8)	453 (32.6)	371 (41.0)
1979	5,265 (97.4)	3,433 (79.8)	975 (47.0)	758 (58.2)	2,650 (69.0)	1,779 (57.3)	477 (32.6)	358 (40.2)	2,614 (68.8)	1,653 (55.6)	499 (33.8)	400 (42.0)
1980	5,085 (96.0)	3,211 (77.5)	889 (45.4)	885 (62.2)	2,672 (69.2)	1,715 (56.3)	446 (31.8)	462 (44.2)	2,413 (66.5)	1,496 (53.2)	444 (32.4)	424 (43.7)
1981	5,143 (96.6)	3,232 (77.7)	901 (45.9)	891 (63.4)	2,746 (70.1)	1,762 (57.0)	454 (32.3)	480 (45.5)	2,397 (66.4)	1,470 (52.8)	447 (32.6)	411 (43.9)
1982	5,055 (101.5)	3,202 (81.9)	902 (48.6)	823 (65.3)	2,601 (72.5)	1,668 (58.9)	488 (35.1)	386 (45.0)	2,454 (71.0)	1,534 (56.9)	414 (33.4)	437 (47.2)
1983	4,905 (100.1)	3,053 (80.1)	882 (48.1)	816 (65.1)	2,631 (72.8)	1,661 (58.7)	463 (34.5)	426 (46.0)	2,274 (68.6)	1,392 (54.4)	418 (33.5)	391 (45.8)
1984	4,626 (97.5)	2,952 (78.8)	758 (45.3)	762 (63.6)	2,438 (70.4)	1,592 (57.6)	391 (32.3)	375 (44.4)	2,188 (67.4)	1,360 (53.8)	367 (31.8)	387 (45.6)
1985	4,324 (94.6)	2,688 (75.5)	719 (44.2)	797 (55.8)	2,264 (68.1)	1,406 (54.4)	360 (31.1)	440 (40.8)	2,060 (65.6)	1,282 (52.3)	360 (31.4)	357 (38.0)
1986	4,142 (92.8)	2,418 (71.9)	667 (42.8)	966 (60.4)	2,183 (67.0)	1,260 (51.7)	333 (30.1)	547 (44.6)	1,959 (64.1)	1,158 (49.9)	334 (30.4)	419 (40.6)
1987	4,230 (93.5)	2,538 (73.4)	653 (42.4)	926 (59.8)	2,169 (66.7)	1,299 (52.4)	326 (29.8)	490 (43.3)	2,061 (65.5)	1,239 (51.4)	327 (30.1)	437 (41.2)
1988	4,232 (101.8)	2,301 (76.5)	664 (46.5)	1,168 (71.0)	2,184 (72.9)	1,214 (55.3)	323 (32.3)	611 (51.3)	2,049 (71.1)	1,087 (52.8)	341 (33.4)	557 (49.2)
1989	4,038 (94.6)	2,152 (70.3)	639 (43.4)	1,142 (66.4)	2,145 (68.6)	1,160 (51.4)	327 (30.8)	613 (48.1)	1,893 (65.1)	991 (48.0)	312 (30.5)	529 (45.7)
1990	3,797 (92.0)	2,007 (68.1)	594 (42.0)	1,114 (65.9)	1,909 (65.2)	1,027 (48.6)	252 (27.6)	608 (48.0)	1,887 (65.0)	980 (47.6)	342 (31.7)	506 (45.1)
1991	3,881 (92.8)	1,953 (67.2)	609 (42.4)	1,241 (68.0)	2,001 (66.4)	967 (47.3)	288 (29.2)	717 (50.1)	1,880 (64.8)	985 (47.7)	321 (30.8)	525 (45.7)

[Standard errors appear in parentheses]

Year	Total				Male				Female			
	All races/ ethnicities[1]	White	Black	Hispanic	All races/ ethnicities[1]	White	Black	Hispanic	All races/ ethnicities[1]	White	Black	Hispanic
1	2	3	4	5	6	7	8	9	10	11	12	13
1992[3]	3,410 (87.7)	1,676 (62.6)	621 (42.8)	1,022 (64.5)	1,742 (62.6)	866 (45.0)	271 (28.5)	565 (47.0)	1,668 (61.5)	810 (43.6)	350 (31.9)	457 (43.9)
1993[3]	3,396 (87.5)	1,707 (63.1)	615 (42.7)	989 (64.3)	1,715 (62.2)	884 (45.4)	275 (28.7)	507 (45.8)	1,681 (61.6)	823 (43.9)	340 (31.5)	483 (45.1)
1994[3]	3,727 (91.5)	1,709 (63.2)	607 (42.6)	1,322 (73.0)	2,000 (66.7)	880 (45.3)	324 (30.8)	744 (54.2)	1,727 (62.6)	829 (44.1)	284 (29.3)	578 (48.9)
1995[3]	3,876 (86.5)	1,887 (61.5)	571 (35.3)	1,345 (51.6)	1,978 (61.7)	996 (44.6)	249 (23.4)	701 (37.2)	1,898 (60.6)	891 (42.4)	322 (26.4)	644 (35.7)
1996[3]	3,611 (87.1)	1,569 (58.7)	615 (37.9)	1,315 (53.2)	1,854 (62.3)	792 (41.7)	304 (26.5)	701 (38.6)	1,757 (60.9)	777 (41.3)	312 (27.0)	614 (36.6)
1997[3]	3,624 (87.4)	1,656 (60.2)	649 (38.8)	1,180 (51.8)	1,970 (64.1)	934 (45.0)	306 (26.7)	671 (38.6)	1,654 (59.3)	722 (39.9)	343 (28.2)	509 (34.5)
1998[3]	3,942 (90.7)	1,697 (60.9)	675 (39.5)	1,487 (56.5)	2,241 (67.8)	950 (45.3)	358 (28.5)	899 (42.7)	1,701 (60.1)	747 (40.6)	317 (27.3)	587 (36.6)
1999[3]	3,829 (89.7)	1,636 (59.9)	621 (38.1)	1,445 (56.1)	2,032 (65.1)	873 (43.7)	282 (25.8)	807 (41.2)	1,797 (61.7)	763 (41.0)	338 (28.1)	638 (37.9)
2000[3]	3,776 (89.2)	1,564 (58.7)	663 (39.3)	1,456 (56.6)	2,082 (65.8)	795 (41.8)	369 (28.9)	866 (42.4)	1,694 (60.1)	769 (41.2)	294 (26.4)	590 (37.1)
2001[3]	3,766 (84.6)	1,668 (57.4)	557 (34.6)	1,442 (53.8)	2,151 (63.4)	916 (42.4)	314 (25.7)	865 (40.3)	1,615 (55.9)	752 (38.7)	243 (23.1)	577 (35.1)
2002[3]	3,721 (84.2)	1,457 (53.9)	564 (34.7)	1,572 (56.6)	2,108 (63.0)	752 (38.7)	305 (25.3)	971 (43.3)	1,612 (55.9)	705 (37.5)	259 (23.7)	601 (36.1)
2003[3,4]	3,552 (82.6)	1,431 (53.4)	544 (34.2)	1,437 (54.9)	2,045 (62.2)	802 (39.8)	298 (25.1)	858 (41.5)	1,506 (54.2)	630 (35.6)	246 (23.2)	579 (35.6)
2004[3,4]	3,766 (84.8)	1,530 (55.1)	594 (35.5)	1,499 (56.0)	2,140 (63.5)	808 (40.0)	326 (26.1)	949 (43.1)	1,626 (56.2)	722 (37.9)	268 (24.1)	549 (35.1)
2005[3,4]	3,458 (81.7)	1,358 (52.2)	534 (33.9)	1,429 (55.1)	2,009 (61.8)	760 (38.9)	295 (25.0)	883 (42.2)	1,449 (53.3)	599 (34.8)	239 (22.9)	546 (35.0)
2006[3,4]	3,462 (81.8)	1,337 (51.8)	565 (34.9)	1,421 (55.1)	1,935 (60.8)	739 (38.4)	250 (23.3)	864 (42.0)	1,527 (54.6)	598 (34.7)	315 (25.9)	557 (35.4)
2007[3,4]	3,278 (79.8)	1,210 (49.4)	451 (31.6)	1,422 (55.4)	1,859 (59.8)	704 (37.5)	212 (21.7)	850 (41.9)	1,419 (52.8)	507 (32.1)	239 (22.9)	572 (35.9)
2008[3,4]	3,010 (76.8)	1,103 (47.3)	535 (34.1)	1,232 (52.5)	1,606 (56.0)	623 (35.4)	227 (22.3)	690 (39.0)	1,403 (52.6)	480 (31.3)	308 (25.7)	541 (35.2)
2009[3,4]	3,030 (77.0)	1,188 (49.0)	508 (33.3)	1,199 (52.1)	1,731 (57.9)	725 (38.0)	280 (24.5)	665 (38.4)	1,299 (50.7)	464 (30.8)	228 (22.5)	534 (35.1)
2010[3,4]	2,816 (100.8)	1,147 (67.9)	437 (41.5)	1,090 (62.3)	1,625 (77.3)	675 (48.4)	247 (29.2)	644 (46.2)	1,192 (53.0)	472 (38.7)	190 (24.1)	446 (33.9)
2011[3,4]	2,714 (99.1)	1,118 (68.1)	400 (37.5)	1,040 (60.1)	1,501 (69.9)	614 (46.0)	218 (26.4)	602 (44.9)	1,213 (64.6)	505 (42.9)	182 (27.2)	439 (34.0)
2012[3,4]	2,562 (101.1)	930 (67.7)	418 (42.3)	1,040 (59.0)	1,427 (74.2)	526 (43.8)	219 (31.2)	591 (46.1)	1,135 (63.8)	404 (39.4)	199 (28.9)	449 (39.6)
2013[3,4]	2,622 (109.3)	1,100 (66.7)	409 (48.4)	969 (61.2)	1,406 (73.6)	596 (42.8)	221 (29.9)	536 (43.1)	1,216 (66.0)	504 (38.5)	188 (31.1)	432 (39.5)
2014[3,4]	2,527 (94.9)	1,114 (68.1)	415 (42.8)	882 (57.4)	1,389 (71.1)	612 (44.6)	195 (27.9)	506 (45.4)	1,138 (55.7)	502 (43.2)	219 (30.5)	377 (33.9)
2015[3,4]	2,254 (99.1)	965 (61.5)	356 (38.2)	771 (59.8)	1,220 (70.8)	534 (43.4)	174 (28.2)	424 (40.2)	1,034 (63.3)	432 (38.7)	182 (28.1)	347 (40.2)
2016[3,4]	2,334 (102.8)	1,084 (64.8)	333 (43.4)	731 (54.3)	1,371 (74.2)	612 (43.6)	216 (32.5)	436 (45.5)	964 (58.3)	472 (40.2)	117 (23.3)	295 (32.3)
2017[3,4]	2,198 (101.5)	952 (62.0)	301 (35.4)	810 (57.4)	1,262 (69.0)	522 (45.8)	181 (27.9)	498 (41.3)	936 (59.0)	430 (36.4)	121 (21.6)	312 (35.1)
2018[3,4]	2,164 (102.0)	903 (59.6)	306 (39.0)	782 (61.1)	1,212 (67.1)	526 (42.9)	155 (23.6)	458 (41.9)	953 (63.7)	378 (37.6)	151 (28.2)	324 (36.1)
2019[3,4]	1,970 (87.3)	906 (66.9)	285 (34.7)	657 (54.4)	1,116 (64.9)	536 (47.2)	164 (26.6)	347 (35.7)	855 (58.4)	370 (38.2)	121 (21.8)	310 (36.3)

—Not available.

†Not applicable.

#Rounds to zero.

[1] Includes other racial/ethnic groups not separately shown.

[2] For 1970, White and Black include persons of Hispanic ethnicity.

[3] Because of changes in data collection procedures, data may not be comparable with figures for years prior to 1992.

[4] After 2002, White and Black exclude persons of Two or more races.

NOTE: Status dropouts are 16- to 24-year-olds who are not enrolled in school and who have not completed a high school program, regardless of when they left school. People who have received equivalency credentials, such as the GED, are counted as high school completers. All data are based on October counts. Data are based on sample surveys of the civilian noninstitutionalized population, which excludes persons in the military and persons living in institutions (e.g., prisons or nursing facilities). Prior to 2010, standard errors were computed using generalized variance function methodology rather than the more precise replicate weight methodology used in later years. Race categories exclude persons of Hispanic ethnicity except where otherwise noted. Detail may not sum to totals because of rounding.

SOURCE: U.S. Department of Commerce, Census Bureau, Current Population Survey (CPS), October, 1970 through 2019. (This table was prepared Januuary 2021.)

Table 219.73. Percentage of high school dropouts among persons 16 to 24 years old (status dropout rate) and number and percentage distribution of 16- to 24-year-olds, by selected characteristics: Selected years, 2009 through 2019

[Standard errors appear in parentheses]

Selected characteristic	Status dropout rate[1]								2019							
									Number of 16- to 24-year-olds (in thousands)				Percentage distribution of 16- to 24-year-olds			
	2009		2014		2018		2019		Total population[2]		Status dropouts only[3]		Total population[2]		Status dropouts only[3]	
1	2		3		4		5		6		7		8		9	
Total	**8.1**	**(0.20)**	**6.5**	**(0.25)**	**5.7**	**(0.27)**	**5.2**	**(0.23)**	**37,734**	**(85.6)**	**1,970**	**(87.3)**	**100.0**	**(†)**	**100.0**	**(†)**
Sex																
Male	9.1	(0.31)	7.1	(0.37)	6.3	(0.35)	5.9	(0.34)	18,963	(92.8)	1,116	(64.9)	50.3	(0.29)	56.6	(2.21)
Female	7.0	(0.27)	5.9	(0.29)	5.1	(0.34)	4.6	(0.31)	18,770	(137.7)	855	(58.4)	49.7	(0.29)	43.4	(2.21)
Race/ethnicity																
White	5.2	(0.21)	5.2	(0.32)	4.5	(0.29)	4.5	(0.33)	19,996	(101.9)	906	(66.9)	53.0	(0.32)	46.0	(2.59)
Black	9.3	(0.61)	7.4	(0.74)	5.8	(0.74)	5.6	(0.67)	5,080	(82.4)	285	(34.7)	13.5	(0.20)	14.5	(1.65)
Hispanic	17.6	(0.76)	10.6	(0.68)	9.0	(0.69)	7.5	(0.61)	8,798	(116.2)	657	(54.4)	23.3	(0.27)	33.3	(2.39)
Asian	2.1	(0.58)	1.0 !	(0.35)	4.1	(1.01)	2.6 !	(0.83)	2,208	(63.1)	‡	(†)	5.9	(0.17)	2.9 !	(0.94)
Pacific Islander	18.4	(5.42)	12.1 !	(6.05)	8.4 !	(3.97)	‡	(†)	110	(19.1)	‡	(†)	0.3	(0.05)	‡	(†)
American Indian/Alaska Native	13.2	(3.28)	15.7	(3.02)	5.9	(1.41)	5.6	(1.54)	367	(39.1)	‡	(†)	1.0	(0.10)	1.0	(0.30)
Two or more races	6.5	(1.41)	2.7	(0.80)	4.9 !	(1.49)	3.3 !	(1.06)	1,175	(47.4)	‡	(†)	3.1	(0.13)	1.9 !	(0.63)
Race/ethnicity by sex																
Male																
White	6.3	(0.33)	5.7	(0.42)	5.1	(0.42)	5.3	(0.45)	10,148	(134.0)	536	(47.2)	53.5	(0.49)	48.0	(2.93)
Black	10.6	(0.93)	7.1	(1.02)	6.0	(0.92)	6.6	(1.07)	2,466	(60.9)	164	(26.6)	13.0	(0.37)	14.7	(2.26)
Hispanic	19.0	(1.10)	11.8	(1.04)	10.4	(0.93)	7.8	(0.80)	4,444	(23.9)	347	(35.7)	23.4	(0.19)	31.1	(2.73)
Asian	‡	(†)	1.9 !	(0.66)	3.3 !	(1.04)	1.7 !	(0.77)	1,085	(29.0)	‡	(†)	5.7	(0.14)	1.6 !	(0.76)
Pacific Islander	26.9 !	(8.45)	‡	(†)	‡	(†)	‡	(†)	‡	(†)	‡	(†)	0.4	(0.08)	‡	(†)
American Indian/Alaska Native	12.3 !	(4.59)	13.7	(3.48)	4.8 !	(1.78)	7.5 !	(2.44)	191	(27.0)	‡	(†)	1.0	(0.14)	1.3 !	(0.43)
Two or more races	5.5 !	(1.86)	4.1 !	(1.45)	4.0 !	(1.89)	5.5 !	(1.94)	558	(32.5)	‡	(†)	2.9	(0.17)	2.8 !	(0.96)
Female																
White	4.1	(0.27)	4.8	(0.41)	3.8	(0.38)	3.8	(0.39)	9,848	(64.7)	370	(38.2)	52.5	(0.25)	43.3	(3.53)
Black	8.1	(0.80)	7.7	(1.02)	5.6	(1.04)	4.6	(0.83)	2,613	(35.9)	121	(21.8)	13.9	(0.17)	14.2	(2.24)
Hispanic	16.1	(1.06)	9.3	(0.84)	7.5	(0.83)	7.1	(0.83)	4,354	(101.7)	310	(36.3)	23.2	(0.38)	36.2	(3.55)
Asian	3.0 !	(0.99)	‡	(†)	4.8 !	(1.54)	3.5 !	(1.29)	1,123	(46.5)	‡	(†)	6.0	(0.28)	4.7 !	(1.71)
Pacific Islander	‡	(†)	‡	(†)	‡	(†)	‡	(†)	‡	(†)	‡	(†)	0.2	(0.06)	‡	(†)
American Indian/Alaska Native	14.1 !	(4.69)	18.1	(4.01)	7.1 !	(2.41)	‡	(†)	176	(24.7)	‡	(†)	0.9	(0.13)	‡	(†)
Two or more races	7.5	(2.10)	1.5 !	(0.72)	5.8 !	(2.03)	‡	(†)	617	(32.4)	‡	(†)	3.3	(0.17)	‡	(†)
Age																
16	2.7	(0.37)	5.2	(0.62)	5.0	(0.65)	5.7	(0.62)	4,154	(54.0)	236	(25.8)	11.0	(0.14)	12.0	(1.28)
17	4.4	(0.46)	5.2	(0.67)	6.7	(0.79)	5.2	(0.59)	4,237	(53.6)	220	(25.3)	11.2	(0.15)	11.2	(1.22)
18	7.8	(0.59)	7.0	(0.72)	6.1	(0.72)	6.1	(0.81)	4,055	(58.2)	249	(33.2)	10.7	(0.16)	12.6	(1.49)
19	9.3	(0.65)	7.2	(0.76)	6.5	(0.70)	5.5	(0.68)	4,251	(55.4)	233	(29.2)	11.3	(0.15)	11.8	(1.44)
20 to 24	9.7	(0.30)	6.8	(0.33)	5.4	(0.33)	4.9	(0.31)	21,037	(98.2)	1,033	(66.1)	55.8	(0.15)	52.4	(2.26)
Recency of immigration[4]																
Born outside the United States	20.7	(1.11)	12.4	(1.17)	11.4	(1.21)	8.6	(0.95)	3,264	(132.5)	281	(33.5)	8.7	(0.35)	14.3	(1.51)
Hispanic	32.0	(1.71)	22.0	(2.04)	19.0	(2.18)	14.2	(1.79)	1,510	(92.9)	214	(28.9)	4.0	(0.25)	10.9	(1.36)
Non-Hispanic	6.4	(1.01)	3.6	(0.93)	4.8	(1.08)	3.8	(1.10)	1,754	(96.4)	‡	(†)	4.6	(0.26)	3.4	(1.01)
First generation	7.5	(0.54)	4.9	(0.55)	5.6	(0.66)	5.1	(0.55)	7,181	(171.2)	363	(39.9)	19.0	(0.45)	18.4	(1.89)
Hispanic	11.1	(1.03)	6.8	(0.86)	7.1	(0.94)	6.4	(0.80)	3,958	(138.9)	254	(32.4)	10.5	(0.36)	12.9	(1.60)
Non-Hispanic	3.9	(0.56)	2.6	(0.60)	3.8	(0.83)	3.4	(0.73)	3,223	(136.1)	109	(24.3)	8.5	(0.36)	5.5	(1.20)
Second generation or higher	6.5	(0.21)	6.2	(0.28)	5.0	(0.28)	4.9	(0.26)	27,288	(171.5)	1,326	(70.4)	72.3	(0.45)	67.3	(2.13)
Hispanic	11.8	(1.13)	8.6	(1.18)	6.2	(1.01)	5.7	(0.84)	3,330	(126.9)	188	(28.3)	8.8	(0.33)	9.6	(1.39)
Non-Hispanic	6.1	(0.21)	5.9	(0.29)	4.8	(0.29)	4.7	(0.29)	23,958	(154.4)	1,138	(70.0)	63.5	(0.42)	57.7	(2.52)
Disability[5]																
With a disability	15.5	(1.44)	13.9	(1.59)	13.2	(1.52)	10.4	(1.45)	1,501	(74.0)	156	(23.2)	4.0	(0.20)	7.9	(1.19)
Without a disability	7.8	(0.21)	6.2	(0.24)	5.4	(0.27)	5.0	(0.24)	36,232	(113.3)	1,814	(87.8)	96.0	(0.20)	92.1	(1.19)
Region																
Northeast	7.1	(0.47)	5.3	(0.54)	5.1	(0.73)	4.9	(0.65)	6,412	(139.1)	311	(42.0)	17.0	(0.37)	15.8	(1.97)
Midwest	7.6	(0.44)	5.4	(0.52)	5.7	(0.56)	5.0	(0.58)	7,986	(161.8)	396	(46.6)	21.2	(0.43)	20.1	(2.13)
South	8.4	(0.36)	7.6	(0.49)	5.9	(0.44)	5.4	(0.39)	14,195	(210.5)	770	(56.0)	37.6	(0.53)	39.1	(2.29)
West	8.6	(0.44)	6.8	(0.55)	5.8	(0.48)	5.4	(0.49)	9,140	(151.2)	493	(45.6)	24.2	(0.40)	25.0	(2.17)

†Not applicable.

!Interpret data with caution. The coefficient of variation (CV) for this estimate is 30 percent or greater.

‡Reporting standards not met. Either there are too few cases for a reliable estimate or the coefficient of variation (CV) is 50 percent or greater.

[1] The status dropout rate is the percentage of 16- to 24-year-olds who are not enrolled in high school and who lack a high school credential. High school credentials include high school diplomas and alternative credentials, such as a GED certificate.

[2] Includes all 16- to 24-year-olds.

[3] Status dropouts are 16- to 24-year-olds who are not enrolled in high school and who lack a high school credential. High school credentials include high school diplomas and alternative credentials, such as a GED certificate.

[4] United States refers to the 50 states, the District of Columbia, Puerto Rico, American Samoa, Guam, the U.S. Virgin Islands, and the Northern Marianas. Children born abroad to U.S.-citizen parents are counted as born in the United States. Individuals defined as "first generation" were born in the United States, but one or both of their parents were born outside the United States. Individuals defined as "second generation or higher" were born in the United States, as were both of their parents.

[5] Individuals identified as having a disability reported difficulty in at least one of the following: hearing, seeing even when wearing glasses, walking or climbing stairs, dressing or bathing, doing errands alone, concentrating, remembering, or making decisions.

NOTE: Data are based on sample surveys of the civilian noninstitutionalized population, which excludes persons in the military and persons living in institutions (e.g., prisons or nursing facilities). Prior to 2010, standard errors were computed using generalized variance function methodology rather than the more precise replicate weight methodology used in later years. Race categories exclude persons of Hispanic ethnicity. Detail may not sum to totals because of rounding and the suppression of cells that do not meet National Center for Education Statistics reporting standards.

SOURCE: U.S. Department of Commerce, Census Bureau, Current Population Survey (CPS), October, 2009 through 2019. (This table was prepared January 2021.)

Table 219.75. Percentage of high school dropouts among persons 16 to 24 years old (status dropout rate) and percentage distribution of status dropouts, by labor force status and years of school completed: Selected years, 1970 through 2018

[Standard errors appear in parentheses]

Year	Status dropout rate	Percentage distribution of status dropouts, by labor force status[1]				Percentage distribution of status dropouts, by years of school completed				
		Total	In labor force		Not in labor force	Total	Less than 9 years	9 years	10 years	11 or 12 years
			Employed[2]	Unemployed						
1	2	3	4	5	6	7	8	9	10	11
1970	15.0 (0.30)	100.0 (†)	49.8 (1.08)	10.3 (0.66)	39.9 (1.06)	100.0 (†)	28.5 (0.98)	20.6 (0.87)	26.8 (0.96)	24.0 (0.92)
1975	13.9 (0.27)	100.0 (†)	46.0 (1.04)	15.6 (0.76)	38.4 (1.02)	100.0 (†)	23.5 (0.89)	21.1 (0.85)	27.5 (0.93)	27.9 (0.94)
1976	14.1 (0.27)	100.0 (†)	48.8 (1.03)	16.0 (0.75)	35.2 (0.98)	100.0 (†)	24.3 (0.88)	20.1 (0.82)	27.8 (0.92)	27.8 (0.92)
1977	14.1 (0.27)	100.0 (†)	52.9 (1.02)	13.6 (0.70)	33.6 (0.97)	100.0 (†)	24.3 (0.88)	21.7 (0.84)	27.3 (0.91)	26.6 (0.91)
1978	14.2 (0.27)	100.0 (†)	54.3 (1.01)	12.4 (0.67)	33.3 (0.96)	100.0 (†)	22.9 (0.85)	20.2 (0.81)	28.2 (0.91)	28.8 (0.92)
1979	14.6 (0.27)	100.0 (†)	54.0 (1.00)	12.7 (0.67)	33.3 (0.94)	100.0 (†)	22.6 (0.84)	21.0 (0.82)	28.6 (0.90)	27.8 (0.90)
1980	14.1 (0.27)	100.0 (†)	50.4 (1.02)	17.0 (0.77)	32.6 (0.95)	100.0 (†)	23.6 (0.86)	19.7 (0.81)	29.8 (0.93)	27.0 (0.90)
1981	13.9 (0.26)	100.0 (†)	49.8 (1.01)	18.3 (0.78)	31.9 (0.94)	100.0 (†)	24.3 (0.87)	18.6 (0.79)	30.2 (0.93)	26.9 (0.90)
1982	13.9 (0.28)	100.0 (†)	45.2 (1.08)	21.1 (0.88)	33.7 (1.02)	100.0 (†)	22.9 (0.91)	20.8 (0.88)	28.8 (0.98)	27.6 (0.97)
1983	13.7 (0.28)	100.0 (†)	48.4 (1.10)	18.2 (0.85)	33.4 (1.04)	100.0 (†)	23.0 (0.92)	19.3 (0.87)	28.8 (0.99)	28.8 (0.99)
1984	13.1 (0.28)	100.0 (†)	49.7 (1.13)	17.3 (0.86)	32.9 (1.06)	100.0 (†)	23.6 (0.96)	21.4 (0.93)	27.5 (1.01)	27.5 (1.01)
1985	12.6 (0.28)	100.0 (†)	50.1 (1.17)	17.5 (0.89)	32.4 (1.09)	100.0 (†)	23.9 (1.00)	21.0 (0.95)	27.9 (1.05)	27.2 (1.04)
1986	12.2 (0.27)	100.0 (†)	51.1 (1.19)	16.4 (0.88)	32.5 (1.12)	100.0 (†)	25.4 (1.04)	21.5 (0.98)	25.7 (1.04)	27.4 (1.07)
1987	12.6 (0.28)	100.0 (†)	52.4 (1.18)	13.6 (0.81)	34.0 (1.12)	100.0 (†)	25.9 (1.04)	20.7 (0.96)	26.0 (1.04)	27.5 (1.06)
1988	12.9 (0.31)	100.0 (†)	52.9 (1.29)	— (†)	— (†)	100.0 (†)	28.9 (1.17)	19.3 (1.02)	25.1 (1.12)	26.8 (1.14)
1989	12.6 (0.30)	100.0 (†)	53.2 (1.25)	13.8 (0.86)	33.0 (1.18)	100.0 (†)	29.4 (1.14)	20.8 (1.02)	24.9 (1.08)	25.0 (1.09)
1990	12.1 (0.29)	100.0 (†)	52.5 (1.29)	13.3 (0.88)	34.2 (1.23)	100.0 (†)	28.6 (1.17)	20.9 (1.05)	24.4 (1.11)	26.1 (1.14)
1991	12.5 (0.30)	100.0 (†)	47.5 (1.28)	15.8 (0.93)	36.7 (1.23)	100.0 (†)	28.6 (1.15)	20.5 (1.03)	26.1 (1.12)	24.9 (1.10)
1992[3]	11.0 (0.28)	100.0 (†)	47.6 (1.36)	15.0 (0.97)	37.4 (1.32)	100.0 (†)	21.6 (1.12)	17.5 (1.04)	24.4 (1.17)	36.5 (1.31)
1993[3]	11.0 (0.28)	100.0 (†)	48.7 (1.37)	12.8 (0.91)	38.5 (1.33)	100.0 (†)	20.5 (1.10)	16.6 (1.02)	24.1 (1.17)	38.8 (1.33)
1994[3]	11.4 (0.28)	100.0 (†)	49.5 (1.30)	13.0 (0.88)	37.5 (1.26)	100.0 (†)	23.9 (1.11)	16.2 (0.96)	20.3 (1.05)	39.6 (1.28)
1995[3]	12.0 (0.27)	100.0 (†)	48.9 (1.19)	14.2 (0.83)	37.0 (1.15)	100.0 (†)	22.2 (0.99)	17.0 (0.89)	22.5 (0.99)	38.3 (1.16)
1996[3]	11.1 (0.27)	100.0 (†)	47.3 (1.28)	15.0 (0.91)	37.7 (1.24)	100.0 (†)	20.3 (1.03)	17.7 (0.98)	22.6 (1.07)	39.4 (1.25)
1997[3]	11.0 (0.27)	100.0 (†)	53.3 (1.27)	13.2 (0.86)	33.5 (1.21)	100.0 (†)	19.9 (1.02)	15.7 (0.93)	22.3 (1.06)	42.1 (1.26)
1998[3]	11.8 (0.27)	100.0 (†)	55.1 (1.22)	10.3 (0.74)	34.6 (1.17)	100.0 (†)	21.0 (1.00)	14.9 (0.87)	21.4 (1.00)	42.6 (1.21)
1999[3]	11.2 (0.26)	100.0 (†)	55.6 (1.23)	10.0 (0.74)	34.4 (1.18)	100.0 (†)	22.2 (1.03)	16.3 (0.92)	22.5 (1.04)	39.0 (1.21)
2000[3]	10.9 (0.26)	100.0 (†)	56.9 (1.24)	12.3 (0.82)	30.8 (1.16)	100.0 (†)	21.5 (1.03)	15.3 (0.90)	23.1 (1.06)	40.0 (1.23)
2001[3]	10.7 (0.24)	100.0 (†)	58.3 (1.17)	14.8 (0.85)	26.9 (1.05)	100.0 (†)	18.4 (0.92)	16.8 (0.89)	23.8 (1.01)	40.9 (1.17)
2002[3]	10.5 (0.24)	100.0 (†)	57.4 (1.18)	13.3 (0.81)	29.2 (1.09)	100.0 (†)	22.8 (1.00)	17.1 (0.90)	21.3 (0.98)	38.9 (1.17)
2003[3]	9.9 (0.23)	100.0 (†)	53.5 (1.22)	13.7 (0.84)	32.9 (1.15)	100.0 (†)	21.2 (1.00)	18.2 (0.94)	20.7 (0.99)	40.0 (1.20)
2004[3]	10.3 (0.23)	100.0 (†)	53.0 (1.19)	14.3 (0.83)	32.7 (1.12)	100.0 (†)	21.4 (0.97)	15.9 (0.87)	22.5 (0.99)	40.3 (1.17)
2005[3]	9.4 (0.22)	100.0 (†)	56.9 (1.23)	11.9 (0.80)	31.2 (1.15)	100.0 (†)	18.9 (0.97)	16.8 (0.93)	21.4 (1.02)	42.9 (1.23)
2006[3]	9.3 (0.22)	100.0 (†)	56.4 (1.23)	11.7 (0.80)	32.0 (1.16)	100.0 (†)	22.1 (1.03)	13.4 (0.85)	20.7 (1.01)	43.9 (1.23)
2007[3]	8.7 (0.21)	100.0 (†)	55.5 (1.27)	11.2 (0.80)	33.3 (1.20)	100.0 (†)	21.2 (1.04)	16.9 (0.96)	22.9 (1.07)	39.0 (1.24)
2008[3]	8.0 (0.20)	100.0 (†)	46.8 (1.33)	16.3 (0.98)	36.9 (1.28)	100.0 (†)	18.4 (1.03)	15.2 (0.96)	23.8 (1.13)	42.6 (1.32)
2009[3]	8.1 (0.20)	100.0 (†)	43.2 (1.31)	19.9 (1.06)	36.9 (1.28)	100.0 (†)	17.7 (1.01)	13.6 (0.91)	24.4 (1.14)	44.3 (1.32)
2010[3]	7.4 (0.27)	100.0 (†)	45.8 (1.64)	18.7 (1.38)	35.5 (1.70)	100.0 (†)	19.2 (1.48)	13.1 (1.07)	22.5 (1.59)	45.2 (1.89)
2011[3]	7.1 (0.26)	100.0 (†)	49.8 (1.77)	16.0 (1.33)	34.2 (1.69)	100.0 (†)	18.1 (1.72)	12.9 (1.15)	21.2 (1.39)	47.7 (1.87)
2012[3]	6.6 (0.25)	100.0 (†)	44.8 (2.07)	18.1 (1.49)	37.1 (1.83)	100.0 (†)	18.3 (1.76)	10.2 (1.21)	21.9 (1.57)	49.6 (2.20)
2013[3]	6.8 (0.28)	100.0 (†)	41.1 (2.01)	16.8 (1.58)	42.1 (1.84)	100.0 (†)	18.3 (1.70)	13.3 (1.34)	21.1 (1.63)	47.4 (2.31)
2014[3]	6.5 (0.25)	100.0 (†)	44.7 (1.84)	17.0 (1.41)	38.3 (1.61)	100.0 (†)	15.0 (1.58)	13.7 (1.28)	21.3 (1.56)	50.0 (1.94)
2015[3]	5.9 (0.26)	100.0 (†)	41.7 (2.10)	14.2 (1.48)	44.1 (2.10)	100.0 (†)	14.5 (1.67)	13.9 (1.40)	21.3 (1.65)	50.2 (2.00)
2016[3]	6.1 (0.27)	100.0 (†)	46.6 (1.99)	13.9 (1.31)	39.6 (1.90)	100.0 (†)	17.6 (1.91)	10.8 (1.14)	21.9 (1.64)	49.7 (2.22)
2017[3]	5.8 (0.26)	100.0 (†)	46.7 (1.91)	8.3 (1.09)	44.9 (1.98)	100.0 (†)	21.0 (2.14)	9.8 (1.22)	20.3 (1.76)	49.0 (2.41)
2018[3]	5.7 (0.27)	100.0 (†)	50.7 (2.02)	8.5 (1.24)	40.8 (2.10)	100.0 (†)	17.0 (2.03)	10.3 (1.26)	20.6 (1.74)	52.0 (2.29)

—Not available.
†Not applicable.
[1]Data are not comparable to employment and unemployment rate data produced by the Bureau of Labor Statistics because the percentage distributions presented here include persons who are not in the labor force. The labor force consists of those who are employed and those who are unemployed (i.e., seeking employment); persons who are neither employed nor seeking employment are not in the labor force.
[2]Includes persons who were employed but not at work during the survey week.
[3]Because of changes in data collection procedures, data may not be comparable with figures for years prior to 1992.

NOTE: Status dropouts are 16- to 24-year-olds who are not enrolled in school and who have not completed a high school program, regardless of when they left school. People who have received equivalency credentials, such as the GED, are counted as high school completers. Data are based on sample surveys of the civilian noninstitutionalized population, which excludes persons in the military and persons living in institutions (e.g., prisons or nursing facilities). Prior to 2010, standard errors were computed using generalized variance function methodology rather than the more precise replicate weight methodology used in later years. Detail may not sum to totals because of rounding.
SOURCE: U.S. Department of Commerce, Census Bureau, Current Population Survey (CPS), October, 1970 through 2018. (This table was prepared November 2019.)

Table 219.80. Total number 16- to 24-year-old high school dropouts (status dropouts) and percentage of dropouts among persons 16 to 24 years old (status dropout rate), by selected characteristics: 2007 through 2019

[Standard errors appear in parentheses]

Selected characteristic	2007		2008		2009		2010		2011		2012		2013		2014		2015		2016		2017	
1		3		4		5		6		7		8		9		10		11		12		13
Total number of status dropouts (in thousands)	3,583	(25.9)	3,497	(31.2)	3,372	(30.4)	3,294	(31.5)	3,044	(26.2)	2,784	(26.9)	2,716	(24.7)	2,497	(21.5)	2,397	(21.1)	2,279	(23.1)	2,125	(19.5)
Status dropout rate																						
Total	**9.3**	**(0.06)**	**9.0**	**(0.08)**	**8.6**	**(0.08)**	**8.3**	**(0.08)**	**7.7**	**(0.06)**	**7.0**	**(0.07)**	**6.8**	**(0.06)**	**6.3**	**(0.05)**	**6.0**	**(0.05)**	**5.8**	**(0.06)**	**5.4**	**(0.05)**
Age																						
16	3.2	(0.11)	2.8	(0.10)	2.8	(0.10)	2.5	(0.09)	2.2	(0.09)	2.1	(0.08)	2.2	(0.08)	2.2	(0.10)	2.3	(0.09)	2.4	(0.10)	2.1	(0.08)
17	5.3	(0.15)	4.8	(0.12)	4.4	(0.12)	4.0	(0.12)	3.8	(0.11)	3.3	(0.12)	3.1	(0.09)	3.0	(0.12)	3.2	(0.10)	3.1	(0.11)	3.3	(0.11)
18	8.4	(0.18)	8.0	(0.17)	7.5	(0.17)	6.7	(0.14)	6.2	(0.15)	5.4	(0.14)	5.0	(0.17)	4.8	(0.15)	4.6	(0.13)	4.8	(0.13)	4.6	(0.13)
19	9.9	(0.19)	9.6	(0.20)	9.1	(0.20)	8.9	(0.19)	7.7	(0.15)	6.8	(0.13)	6.4	(0.16)	6.0	(0.18)	5.9	(0.15)	5.8	(0.15)	5.5	(0.14)
20–24	11.5	(0.09)	11.3	(0.11)	10.8	(0.11)	10.6	(0.10)	9.8	(0.10)	9.0	(0.09)	8.7	(0.09)	7.9	(0.07)	7.6	(0.08)	7.1	(0.09)	6.6	(0.07)
Race/ethnicity																						
White	6.1	(0.06)	5.9	(0.07)	5.6	(0.07)	5.3	(0.06)	5.1	(0.07)	4.7	(0.06)	4.7	(0.06)	4.4	(0.06)	4.5	(0.07)	4.5	(0.06)	4.3	(0.06)
Black	11.5	(0.18)	11.2	(0.17)	10.7	(0.18)	10.3	(0.17)	9.6	(0.18)	9.0	(0.18)	9.0	(0.19)	7.9	(0.17)	7.2	(0.15)	7.0	(0.17)	6.5	(0.16)
Hispanic	19.9	(0.21)	19.0	(0.23)	17.9	(0.22)	16.7	(0.26)	14.5	(0.19)	12.8	(0.18)	11.8	(0.20)	10.7	(0.15)	9.9	(0.16)	9.1	(0.17)	8.2	(0.15)
Asian	3.0	(0.19)	3.0	(0.18)	3.3	(0.17)	2.8	(0.16)	2.7	(0.14)	2.6	(0.14)	2.5	(0.16)	2.5	(0.14)	2.4	(0.15)	2.0	(0.14)	2.1	(0.15)
Pacific Islander	7.6	(1.23)	9.2	(1.54)	9.5	(1.45)	4.8	(0.95)	8.8	(1.62)	9.1	(1.45)	5.0	(1.03)	10.6	(1.66)	5.4	(1.58)	6.9	(1.01)	3.9	(1.03)
American Indian/Alaska Native	15.3	(0.94)	16.2	(0.80)	15.9	(0.83)	15.4	(0.80)	13.1	(0.75)	12.8	(0.71)	12.8	(0.76)	11.5	(0.77)	13.2	(0.78)	11.0	(0.68)	10.1	(0.62)
Some other race[1]	12.1	(1.37)	10.6	(1.30)	9.1	(1.48)	9.2	(1.42)	7.9	(1.52)	5.9	(0.89)	5.1	(1.13)	5.6	(1.03)	7.5	(1.15)	5.1	(1.09)	5.2	(1.08)
Two or more races	7.6	(0.41)	7.2	(0.39)	6.5	(0.36)	6.1	(0.30)	6.0	(0.33)	5.6	(0.25)	5.2	(0.28)	5.0	(0.26)	4.7	(0.22)	4.8	(0.26)	4.5	(0.25)
Sex and race/ethnicity																						
Male	10.9	(0.09)	10.5	(0.11)	10.1	(0.10)	10.0	(0.10)	9.0	(0.09)	8.2	(0.08)	8.0	(0.08)	7.2	(0.09)	7.0	(0.08)	6.8	(0.09)	6.4	(0.08)
White	6.8	(0.09)	6.6	(0.10)	6.3	(0.10)	6.1	(0.09)	5.8	(0.10)	5.4	(0.09)	5.4	(0.08)	5.0	(0.08)	5.1	(0.10)	5.2	(0.10)	4.9	(0.09)
Black	13.9	(0.29)	13.7	(0.23)	13.1	(0.27)	12.7	(0.26)	11.8	(0.25)	10.9	(0.26)	10.9	(0.27)	9.5	(0.22)	8.7	(0.22)	8.7	(0.22)	8.0	(0.24)
Hispanic	23.7	(0.30)	22.2	(0.33)	21.2	(0.31)	20.2	(0.34)	17.0	(0.27)	15.0	(0.23)	13.9	(0.26)	12.7	(0.23)	11.8	(0.21)	10.7	(0.25)	10.0	(0.21)
Asian	3.0	(0.26)	3.3	(0.26)	3.7	(0.26)	3.4	(0.25)	3.1	(0.19)	2.8	(0.24)	2.8	(0.19)	2.5	(0.19)	2.9	(0.22)	2.2	(0.19)	2.3	(0.22)
Pacific Islander	9.5	(2.13)	7.9	(1.76)	9.4	(2.06)	4.9	(1.05)	9.2	(2.10)	10.0	(1.74)	4.2	(1.00)	12.6	(2.45)	4.0 !	(1.27)	6.6	(1.54)	5.7 !	(1.91)
American Indian/Alaska Native	16.2	(1.18)	17.2	(1.11)	17.6	(1.20)	17.6	(1.34)	14.8	(1.12)	14.8	(1.06)	14.3	(1.11)	13.1	(1.14)	14.4	(1.03)	13.3	(1.10)	11.6	(0.97)
Some other race[1]	15.1	(2.17)	13.4	(1.84)	12.0	(2.43)	11.3	(2.16)	8.7	(2.04)	8.3	(1.49)	6.2	(1.75)	5.5	(1.36)	8.6	(1.73)	5.4	(1.57)	7.0	(1.83)
Two or more races	8.4	(0.63)	8.2	(0.52)	7.4	(0.56)	7.3	(0.49)	7.4	(0.57)	6.7	(0.43)	5.5	(0.43)	5.0	(0.34)	5.4	(0.36)	5.6	(0.37)	5.2	(0.41)
Female	7.6	(0.07)	7.5	(0.09)	7.1	(0.09)	6.6	(0.08)	6.2	(0.07)	5.7	(0.08)	5.6	(0.08)	5.2	(0.07)	5.0	(0.06)	4.7	(0.07)	4.4	(0.06)
White	5.3	(0.09)	5.2	(0.09)	4.9	(0.08)	4.5	(0.09)	4.3	(0.08)	4.0	(0.08)	4.0	(0.08)	3.9	(0.09)	3.9	(0.08)	3.7	(0.07)	3.6	(0.07)
Black	8.9	(0.25)	8.6	(0.24)	8.2	(0.21)	7.8	(0.23)	7.3	(0.22)	7.0	(0.21)	7.1	(0.23)	6.3	(0.21)	5.7	(0.20)	5.2	(0.23)	4.9	(0.18)
Hispanic	15.7	(0.25)	15.5	(0.26)	14.3	(0.26)	12.8	(0.27)	11.7	(0.23)	10.4	(0.23)	9.6	(0.23)	8.5	(0.20)	8.0	(0.20)	7.3	(0.20)	6.4	(0.19)
Asian	2.9	(0.22)	2.6	(0.21)	2.9	(0.28)	2.3	(0.20)	2.4	(0.18)	2.4	(0.20)	2.1	(0.22)	2.6	(0.21)	1.9	(0.19)	1.7	(0.18)	1.8	(0.19)
Pacific Islander	5.6	(1.42)	10.6	(2.17)	9.7	(2.00)	4.8 !	(1.60)	8.4	(2.11)	8.0 !	(2.41)	5.8 !	(1.76)	8.3	(1.64)	6.6 !	(2.46)	7.2	(1.50)	1.8 !	(0.70)
American Indian/Alaska Native	14.3	(1.27)	15.2	(1.08)	14.2	(1.17)	13.2	(1.14)	11.4	(0.86)	10.8	(0.95)	11.3	(0.96)	9.9	(0.93)	11.9	(1.15)	8.7	(0.85)	8.5	(0.90)
Some other race[1]	9.2	(1.69)	7.8	(1.68)	6.4	(1.60)	7.1	(1.69)	7.1	(2.08)	3.2	(0.79)	3.9	(1.16)	5.6	(1.48)	6.2	(1.73)	4.7	(1.29)	3.5	(0.92)
Two or more races	6.7	(0.66)	6.3	(0.48)	5.6	(0.43)	4.9	(0.41)	4.6	(0.41)	4.7	(0.34)	4.8	(0.36)	5.0	(0.39)	3.9	(0.31)	4.0	(0.34)	3.9	(0.31)
Institutionalized or noninstitutionalized status and race/ethnicity																						
Noninstitutionalized[2]	8.8	(0.06)	8.6	(0.07)	8.2	(0.08)	7.9	(0.08)	7.3	(0.06)	6.6	(0.07)	6.4	(0.06)	6.0	(0.05)	5.7	(0.05)	5.5	(0.06)	5.1	(0.05)
White	5.8	(0.06)	5.8	(0.07)	5.5	(0.07)	5.1	(0.06)	4.9	(0.07)	4.5	(0.06)	4.6	(0.06)	4.3	(0.06)	4.4	(0.07)	4.3	(0.06)	4.2	(0.06)
Black	10.0	(0.18)	10.0	(0.18)	9.4	(0.18)	9.1	(0.17)	8.5	(0.17)	7.9	(0.18)	7.9	(0.19)	6.8	(0.17)	6.2	(0.15)	6.1	(0.17)	5.5	(0.16)
Hispanic	19.4	(0.21)	18.6	(0.22)	17.5	(0.22)	16.3	(0.26)	14.1	(0.19)	12.4	(0.19)	11.5	(0.19)	10.4	(0.15)	9.5	(0.15)	8.7	(0.17)	8.0	(0.15)
Asian	2.8	(0.19)	2.9	(0.18)	3.2	(0.18)	2.8	(0.16)	2.7	(0.14)	2.6	(0.14)	2.4	(0.16)	2.5	(0.14)	2.4	(0.14)	2.0	(0.14)	2.1	(0.15)
Pacific Islander	7.5	(1.25)	9.1	(1.55)	8.7	(1.42)	4.5	(0.95)	8.8	(1.64)	8.8	(1.45)	5.0	(1.05)	10.2	(1.67)	5.3	(1.59)	6.9	(1.03)	3.3 !	(0.98)
American Indian/Alaska Native	14.8	(0.92)	15.7	(0.79)	15.3	(0.82)	14.9	(0.79)	12.6	(0.69)	12.4	(0.72)	12.0	(0.73)	11.3	(0.77)	12.6	(0.79)	10.4	(0.67)	9.7	(0.64)
Some other race[1]	12.0	(1.36)	10.5	(1.30)	9.1	(1.49)	9.0	(1.41)	7.9	(1.53)	5.8	(0.89)	4.7	(1.12)	5.4	(1.03)	7.3	(1.15)	5.0	(1.11)	5.0	(1.10)
Two or more races	7.2	(0.41)	6.8	(0.38)	6.1	(0.34)	5.8	(0.30)	5.7	(0.33)	5.5	(0.25)	5.0	(0.28)	4.8	(0.26)	4.4	(0.21)	4.5	(0.25)	4.3	(0.25)
Institutionalized[3]	45.9	(0.65)	40.6	(0.98)	40.1	(0.87)	37.4	(0.74)	35.4	(0.56)	35.4	(0.73)	36.0	(0.69)	33.1	(0.64)	34.6	(0.71)	33.7	(0.71)	32.4	(0.68)
White	39.8	(1.36)	30.6	(1.49)	31.2	(1.28)	28.8	(1.24)	26.9	(0.83)	25.9	(0.97)	26.6	(1.20)	23.9	(1.18)	24.6	(1.22)	26.0	(1.30)	25.1	(1.39)
Black	49.6	(1.11)	45.2	(1.27)	44.3	(1.28)	42.0	(1.05)	40.1	(1.04)	41.1	(1.17)	40.8	(1.12)	39.2	(1.12)	39.0	(1.06)	38.0	(1.45)	38.3	(1.14)
Hispanic	52.5	(1.60)	48.3	(1.79)	46.7	(1.56)	44.1	(1.51)	40.6	(1.22)	40.9	(1.55)	41.3	(1.61)	37.2	(1.30)	41.0	(1.63)	37.5	(1.50)	33.0	(1.44)
Asian	38.1	(6.16)	39.2	(5.76)	45.2	(9.23)	28.1	(6.20)	23.2	(6.25)	17.5 !	(7.42)	26.0 !	(8.09)	21.5 !	(10.04)	26.1 !	(7.98)	‡	(†)	‡	(†)
Pacific Islander	‡	(†)	‡	(†)	‡	(†)	‡	(†)	‡	(†)	‡	(†)	‡	(†)	‡	(†)	‡	(†)	‡	(†)	32.1 !	(12.36)
American Indian/Alaska Native	37.9	(6.15)	42.5	(6.91)	40.5	(5.54)	38.9	(6.46)	33.3	(6.83)	31.4	(5.39)	53.1	(7.63)	22.2	(5.70)	37.9	(6.08)	44.5	(6.02)	28.0	(5.96)
Some other race[1]	‡	(†)	‡	(†)	‡	(†)	‡	(†)	‡	(†)	‡	(†)	‡	(†)	‡	(†)	‡	(†)	‡	(†)	‡	(†)
Two or more races	29.6	(5.16)	38.0	(4.49)	30.2	(5.15)	23.3	(3.68)	30.5	(5.11)	19.0	(3.16)	22.9	(3.71)	20.8	(2.67)	24.5	(3.76)	28.4	(3.91)	26.4	(4.66)
Nativity and race/ethnicity																						
Native-born[4]	7.7	(0.05)	7.6	(0.07)	7.2	(0.06)	7.0	(0.06)	6.6	(0.06)	6.2	(0.06)	6.1	(0.06)	5.6	(0.05)	5.5	(0.06)	5.3	(0.05)	5.0	(0.05)
White	6.1	(0.07)	6.0	(0.07)	5.6	(0.07)	5.3	(0.06)	5.1	(0.07)	4.7	(0.06)	4.7	(0.06)	4.4	(0.06)	4.5	(0.07)	4.5	(0.06)	4.3	(0.06)
Black	11.7	(0.17)	11.4	(0.18)	10.9	(0.18)	10.5	(0.18)	9.9	(0.19)	9.2	(0.18)	9.1	(0.19)	8.0	(0.17)	7.3	(0.16)	7.1	(0.17)	6.6	(0.16)
Hispanic	11.8	(0.20)	11.4	(0.22)	10.9	(0.16)	10.4	(0.21)	9.5	(0.17)	9.0	(0.18)	8.5	(0.17)	7.9	(0.15)	7.6	(0.15)	7.0	(0.16)	6.4	(0.14)
Asian	2.3	(0.21)	2.5	(0.25)	2.5	(0.21)	2.0	(0.19)	1.7	(0.17)	1.9	(0.16)	1.7	(0.14)	1.8	(0.14)	1.5	(0.14)	1.0	(0.12)	1.5	(0.16)
Pacific Islander	6.6	(1.38)	8.1	(1.72)	8.6	(1.60)	4.6	(1.06)	6.0	(1.27)	6.9	(1.33)	3.6	(1.03)	7.5	(1.39)	5.1 !	(1.71)	4.8	(0.98)	3.1 !	(1.02)
American Indian/Alaska Native	15.4	(0.95)	16.3	(0.80)	15.9	(0.85)	15.5	(0.81)	13.2	(0.75)	12.9	(0.72)	12.9	(0.77)	11.4	(0.78)	13.1	(0.79)	10.9	(0.69)	10.1	(0.62)
Some other race[1]	11.8	(1.71)	9.9	(1.64)	8.6	(1.69)	6.1	(1.14)	6.3	(1.29)	4.4	(0.79)	5.9	(1.50)	4.0	(1.06)	6.4	(1.23)	4.9	(1.28)	3.6	(0.83)
Two or more races	7.6	(0.42)	7.3	(0.39)	6.5	(0.38)	6.1	(0.29)	5.8	(0.36)	5.6	(0.28)	5.2	(0.29)	5.0	(0.27)	4.6	(0.23)	4.8	(0.27)	4.5	(0.26)
Foreign-born	22.6	(0.27)	22.2	(0.29)	21.8	(0.31)	20.3	(0.32)	17.7	(0.29)	15.1	(0.26)	14.1	(0.29)	12.6	(0.26)	11.3	(0.25)	10.5	(0.24)	9.4	(0.28)
White	5.4	(0.40)	5.0	(0.44)	5.8	(0.52)	3.9	(0.36)	5.2	(0.42)	3.8	(0.36)	4.1	(0.41)	4.0	(0.36)	3.9	(0.39)	4.5	(0.49)	3.5	(0.35)
Black	8.0	(0.72)	8.1	(0.74)	7.6	(0.70)	6.7	(0.62)	5.6	(0.62)	6.1	(0.69)	7.4	(0.77)	5.9	(0.59)	6.4	(0.61)	5.9	(0.56)	5.4	(0.62)
Hispanic	35.5	(0.42)	36.1	(0.46)	34.5	(0.49)	32.7	(0.50)	29.1	(0.48)	25.4	(0.48)	23.6	(0.51)	21.1	(0.47)	19.1	(0.46)	17.5	(0.47)	16.1	(0.46)
Asian	3.7	(0.30)	3.5	(0.29)	4.3	(0.35)	3.9	(0.26)	3.8	(0.26)	3.4	(0.26)	3.3	(0.29)	3.5	(0.28)	3.5	(0.25)	3.1	(0.25)	2.8	(0.23)
Pacific Islander	11.9	(3.49)	12.8	(3.80)	14.8	(4.15)	6.1 !	(2.70)	22.6	(5.92)	21.6	(5.83)	13.5	(3.32)	23.8	(5.58)	7.7 !	(2.92)	19.4	(4.57)	9.6 !	(3.56)
American Indian/Alaska Native	‡	(†)	‡	(†)	‡	(†)	‡	(†)	‡	(†)	‡	(†)	‡	(†)	21.8 !	(7.44)	‡	(†)	‡	(†)	‡	(†)
Some other race[1]	12.6	(2.31)	12.0	(2.69)	10.8	(3.00)	15.5	(3.28)	11.6	(3.38)	9.1	(2.49)	2.7 !	(1.00)	10.9	(2.94)	10.5	(2.88)	6.0 !	(2.28)	11.5 !	(3.95)
Two or more races	5.7 !	(1.98)	6.1	(1.78)	6.9	(2.01)	7.2	(1.90)	9.3	(2.14)	6.5	(1.07)	4.8	(0.98)	5.4	(1.04)	5.0	(1.09)	4.9	(1.20)	5.3	(1.19)
English speaking ability																						

[Standard errors appear in parentheses]

Selected characteristic	2007		2008		2009		2010		2011		2012		2013		2014		2015		2016		2017	
1	3		4		5		6		7		8		9		10		11		12		13	
Spoke English at home or spoke English very well	7.6	(0.05)	7.5	(0.07)	7.2	(0.07)	6.9	(0.06)	6.5	(0.06)	6.1	(0.06)	6.0	(0.06)	5.5	(0.05)	5.3	(0.05)	5.2	(0.05)	4.9	(0.05)
Spoke a language other than English at home and spoke English less than very well	33.7	(0.40)	33.1	(0.48)	32.8	(0.41)	31.0	(0.43)	27.8	(0.45)	24.9	(0.43)	23.5	(0.53)	21.8	(0.47)	20.5	(0.41)	18.5	(0.42)	17.3	(0.48)
Disabilitiy status[5]																						
With a disability	18.4	(0.30)	18.9	(0.37)	18.1	(0.29)	17.4	(0.30)	15.8	(0.34)	15.4	(0.29)	15.2	(0.35)	13.9	(0.29)	12.6	(0.27)	12.4	(0.24)	12.1	(0.26)
Without a disability	8.6	(0.06)	8.4	(0.07)	8.1	(0.08)	7.8	(0.08)	7.2	(0.06)	6.5	(0.06)	6.3	(0.06)	5.8	(0.05)	5.6	(0.05)	5.3	(0.06)	5.0	(0.05)
Region																						
Northeast	7.1	(0.15)	6.6	(0.14)	6.8	(0.12)	6.3	(0.13)	6.1	(0.13)	5.6	(0.11)	5.4	(0.12)	5.2	(0.11)	4.8	(0.13)	4.7	(0.11)	4.5	(0.10)
Midwest	7.6	(0.15)	7.4	(0.14)	7.4	(0.13)	7.2	(0.12)	6.8	(0.12)	6.0	(0.12)	5.9	(0.12)	5.7	(0.10)	5.6	(0.11)	5.5	(0.14)	5.1	(0.11)
South	11.0	(0.11)	10.3	(0.11)	9.7	(0.13)	9.6	(0.13)	8.7	(0.11)	7.8	(0.10)	7.8	(0.11)	6.9	(0.10)	6.6	(0.10)	6.3	(0.10)	6.0	(0.09)
West	10.1	(0.14)	10.3	(0.15)	9.5	(0.14)	8.9	(0.14)	8.0	(0.12)	7.6	(0.10)	7.1	(0.10)	6.6	(0.10)	6.4	(0.10)	5.9	(0.10)	5.3	(0.10)

†Not applicable.

!Interpret data with caution. The coefficient of variation (CV) for this estimate is between 30 and 50 percent.

‡Reporting standards not met. Either there are too few cases for a reliable estimate or the coefficient of variation (CV) is 50 percent or greater.

[1] Respondents who wrote in some other race that was not included as an option on the questionnaire.

[2] Persons living in households as well as persons living in noninstitutionalized group quarters. Noninstitutionalized group quarters include college and university housing, military quarters, facilities for workers and religious groups, and temporary shelters for the homeless.

[3] Persons living in institutionalized group quarters, including adult and juvenile correctional facilities, nursing facilities, and other health care facilities.

[4] Includes those born in the 50 states, the District of Columbia, Puerto Rico, American Samoa, Guam, the U.S. Virgin Islands, and the Northern Marianas, as well as those born abroad to U.S.-citizen parents.

[5] A disability is a long-lasting physical, mental, or emotional condition that can make it difficult for a person to do activities such as walking, climbing stairs, dressing, bathing, learning, or remembering. The condition can also impede a person from being able to go outside the home alone or to work at a job or business. For more details, see https://www.census.gov/topics/health/disability/about/glossary.html.

NOTE: Status dropouts are 16- to 24-year-olds who are not enrolled in school and who have not completed a high school program, regardless of when they left school and whether they ever attended school in the United States. People who have received equivalency credentials, such as the GED, are counted as high school completers. Data are based on sample surveys of the entire population residing within the United States, including both noninstitutionalized persons (e.g., those living in households, college housing, or military housing located within the United States) and institutionalized persons (e.g., those living in prisons, nursing facilities, or other healthcare facilities). Estimates may differ from those in tables based on the Current Population Survey (CPS) because of differences in survey design and target populations. Some data have been revised from previously published figures. Race categories exclude persons of Hispanic ethnicity.

SOURCE: U.S. Department of Commerce, Census Bureau, American Community Survey (ACS), 2007 through 2019. (This table was prepared November 2020.)

Table 219.90. Number and percentage distribution of 14- through 21-year-old students served under Individuals with Disabilities Education Act (IDEA), Part B, who exited school, by exit reason, sex, race/ethnicity, age, and type of disability: 2016–17 and 2017–18

Year, sex, race/ethnicity, age, and type of disability	Exited school						Transferred to regular education[4]	Moved, known to be continuing[5]
	Total	Graduated with regular diploma	Received alternative certificate[1]	Reached maximum age[2]	Dropped out[3]	Died		
1	2	3	4	5	6	7	8	9
2016–17								
Total number	**413,353**	**293,096**	**42,857**	**5,219**	**70,636**	**1,545**	**64,962**	**157,645**
Percentage distribution of total	100.0	70.9	10.4	1.3	17.1	0.4	†	†
Number by sex								
Male	268,210	187,865	27,314	3,433	48,518	1,080	42,570	103,784
Female	145,140	105,229	15,543	1,786	22,117	465	22,392	53,860
Number by race/ethnicity								
White	203,362	151,159	19,663	2,357	29,433	750	36,414	72,481
Black	86,180	54,857	11,714	984	18,258	367	9,584	40,169
Hispanic	96,796	68,017	9,114	1,448	17,907	310	12,932	34,662
Asian	7,365	5,634	885	252	559	35	1,629	1,724
Pacific Islander	1,736	1,205	110	37	372	12	353	513
American Indian/Alaska Native	6,511	4,449	271	35	1,726	30	1,817	2,381
Two or more races	11,403	7,775	1,100	106	2,381	41	2,233	5,715
Number by age[6]								
14	3,468	18	2	†	3,236	211	16,805	36,133
15	5,989	64	40	†	5,647	238	15,302	36,814
16	18,179	4,876	455	†	12,536	312	15,179	36,156
17	172,682	141,114	11,815	1	19,428	324	11,406	27,703
18	149,070	115,314	15,630	1	17,919	206	4,601	14,061
19	34,341	20,738	5,735	10	7,730	128	1,006	4,414
20	16,986	7,563	5,037	1,242	3,062	82	457	1,686
21	12,638	3,409	4,143	3,964	1,078	44	206	678
Number by type of disability								
Autism	29,295	20,568	5,596	1,083	1,985	63	2,966	7,972
Deaf-blindness	77	42	19	9	4	3	3	34
Emotional disturbance	37,891	22,017	2,355	250	13,128	141	5,844	23,402
Hearing impairment	4,667	3,734	468	52	404	9	733	1,293
Intellectual disability	35,338	15,180	12,446	2,069	5,407	236	1,773	12,313
Multiple disabilities	8,506	3,878	2,684	649	969	326	404	2,671
Orthopedic impairment	2,697	1,730	562	149	198	58	246	528
Other health impairment[7]	71,481	53,396	4,940	279	12,558	308	11,463	30,029
Specific learning disability	207,649	159,563	12,910	540	34,282	354	31,558	73,438
Speech or language impairment	11,314	9,600	388	30	1,283	13	9,473	4,898
Traumatic brain injury	2,641	1,933	317	74	295	22	282	645
Visual impairment	1,797	1,455	172	35	123	12	217	422
2017–18								
Total number	**414,051**	**301,035**	**40,313**	**4,948**	**66,301**	**1,454**	**60,474**	**159,665**
Percentage distribution of total	100.0	72.7	9.7	1.2	16.0	0.4	†	†
Number by sex								
Male	268,660	192,705	26,156	3,251	45,541	1,007	39,673	104,974
Female	145,385	108,329	14,157	1,697	20,755	447	20,801	54,690
Number by race/ethnicity								
White	199,998	153,184	17,265	2,265	26,612	672	34,598	71,788
Black	86,203	56,745	10,651	832	17,602	373	8,209	39,870
Hispanic	99,834	70,593	10,245	1,399	17,311	286	12,445	36,992
Asian	7,623	6,017	816	248	508	34	1,565	1,859
Pacific Islander	1,779	1,209	102	43	415	10	432	512
American Indian/Alaska Native	6,229	4,429	225	48	1,493	34	1,088	2,508
Two or more races	12,385	8,858	1,009	113	2,360	45	2,137	6,136
Number by age[6]								
14	3,675	3	1	0	3,464	207	15,650	38,731
15	5,749	60	13	0	5,429	247	13,237	36,702
16	16,954	4,862	400	0	11,415	277	13,300	35,511
17	172,234	142,437	11,067	1	18,451	279	11,001	27,120
18	146,347	115,063	14,680	11	16,373	220	5,152	14,039
19	38,517	25,938	5,208	29	7,227	115	1,203	4,895
20	17,980	8,657	5,050	1,301	2,900	72	634	1,909
21	12,595	4,016	3,894	3,606	1,042	37	297	758

See notes at end of table.

Table 219.90. Number and percentage distribution of 14- through 21-year-old students served under Individuals with Disabilities Education Act (IDEA), Part B, who exited school, by exit reason, sex, race/ethnicity, age, and type of disability: 2016–17 and 2017–18—Continued

Year, sex, race/ethnicity, age, and type of disability	Exited school						Transferred to regular education[4]	Moved, known to be continuing[5]
	Total	Graduated with regular diploma	Received alternative certificate[1]	Reached maximum age[2]	Dropped out[3]	Died		
1	2	3	4	5	6	7	8	9
Number by type of disability								
Autism	32,617	23,494	5,837	1,113	2,090	83	3,196	9,385
Deaf-blindness	82	56	14	6	4	2	5	31
Emotional disturbance	36,754	22,204	2,238	246	11,934	132	5,159	22,299
Hearing impairment	4,502	3,753	353	45	340	11	691	1,230
Intellectual disability	35,194	16,760	11,136	1,967	5,141	190	1,600	12,583
Multiple disabilities	8,672	4,041	2,734	562	1,042	293	397	2,816
Orthopedic impairment	2,444	1,637	484	114	159	50	221	528
Other health impairment[7]	74,103	56,183	4,832	289	12,496	303	11,161	31,832
Specific learning disability	203,805	159,620	11,918	483	31,440	345	28,942	72,981
Speech or language impairment	11,429	9,820	303	30	1,256	20	8,647	4,897
Traumatic brain injury	2,667	1,990	321	66	274	16	256	663
Visual impairment	1,782	1,478	143	27	125	9	199	420

†Not applicable.

[1]Received a certificate of completion, modified diploma, or some similar document, but did not meet the same standards for graduation as those for students without disabilities.

[2]Each state determines its maximum age to receive special education services. At the time these data were collected, the maximum age across states generally ranged from 20 to 22 years old.

[3]"Dropped out" is defined as the total who were enrolled at some point in the reporting year, were not enrolled at the end of the reporting year, and did not exit for any of the other reasons described. Includes students previously categorized as "moved, not known to continue."

[4]"Transferred to regular education" was previously labeled "no longer receives special education."

[5]"Moved, known to be continuing" is the total number of students who moved out of the administrative area or transferred to another district and are known to be continuing in an educational program.

[6]Age data are as of fall of the school year, so some students may have been 1 year older at the time they exited school.

[7]Other health impairments include having limited strength, vitality, or alertness due to chronic or acute health problems such as a heart condition, tuberculosis, rheumatic fever, nephritis, asthma, sickle cell anemia, hemophilia, epilepsy, lead poisoning, leukemia, or diabetes.

NOTE: Data are for the 50 states, the District of Columbia, the Bureau of Indian Education, American Samoa, the Federated States of Micronesia, Guam, the Northern Marianas, Puerto Rico, the Republic of Palau, the Republic of the Marshall Islands, and the U.S. Virgin Islands. Includes imputations for missing or unavailable data from Illinois in 2016–17 and Vermont in 2017–18. Race categories exclude persons of Hispanic ethnicity. Detail may not sum to totals because of reporting anomalies and rounding.

SOURCE: U.S. Department of Education, Office of Special Education Programs, Individuals with Disabilities Education Act (IDEA) Section 618 Data Products: State Level Data Files. Retrieved February 20, 2020, from https://www2.ed.gov/programs/osepidea/618-data/state-level-data-files/index.html. (This table was prepared February 2020.)

Table 221.10. Average National Assessment of Educational Progress (NAEP) reading scale score, by sex, race/ethnicity, and grade: Selected years, 1992 through 2019

[Standard errors appear in parentheses]

Grade and year	All students	Sex: Average reading scale score: Male	Sex: Average reading scale score: Female	Sex: Gap between female and male score	Race/ethnicity: Average reading scale score: White	Black	Hispanic	Asian/Pacific Islander: Total	Asian[1]	Pacific Islander[1]	American Indian/ Alaska Native	Two or more races[1]	Gap between White and Black score	Gap between White and Hispanic score
1	2	3	4	5	6	7	8	9	10	11	12	13	14	15
Grade 4														
1992[2]	217 (0.9)	213 (1.2)	221 (1.0)	8 (1.6)	224 (1.2)	192 (1.7)	197 (2.6)	216 (2.9)	— (†)	— (†)	‡ (†)	— (†)	32 (2.1)	27 (2.9)
1994[2]	214 (1.0)	209 (1.3)	220 (1.1)	10 (1.7)	224 (1.3)	185 (1.8)	188 (3.4)	220 (3.8)	— (†)	— (†)	211 (6.6)	— (†)	38 (2.2)	35 (3.6)
1998	215 (1.1)	212 (1.3)	217 (1.3)	5 (1.8)	225 (1.0)	193 (1.9)	193 (3.2)	215 (5.6)	— (†)	— (†)	‡ (†)	— (†)	32 (2.2)	32 (3.3)
2000	213 (1.3)	208 (1.3)	219 (1.4)	11 (1.9)	224 (1.1)	190 (1.8)	190 (2.9)	225 (5.2)	— (†)	— (†)	214 (6.0)	— (†)	34 (2.1)	35 (3.1)
2002	219 (0.4)	215 (0.4)	222 (0.5)	6 (0.7)	229 (0.3)	199 (0.5)	201 (1.3)	224 (1.6)	— (†)	— (†)	207 (2.0)	— (†)	30 (0.6)	28 (1.4)
2003	218 (0.3)	215 (0.3)	222 (0.3)	7 (0.5)	229 (0.2)	198 (0.4)	200 (0.6)	226 (1.2)	— (†)	— (†)	202 (1.4)	— (†)	31 (0.5)	28 (0.6)
2005	219 (0.2)	216 (0.2)	222 (0.3)	6 (0.4)	229 (0.2)	200 (0.3)	203 (0.5)	229 (0.7)	— (†)	— (†)	204 (1.3)	— (†)	29 (0.4)	26 (0.5)
2007	221 (0.3)	218 (0.3)	224 (0.3)	7 (0.4)	231 (0.2)	203 (0.4)	205 (0.5)	232 (1.0)	— (†)	— (†)	203 (1.2)	— (†)	27 (0.5)	26 (0.6)
2009	221 (0.3)	218 (0.3)	224 (0.3)	7 (0.4)	230 (0.3)	205 (0.5)	205 (0.5)	235 (1.0)	— (†)	— (†)	204 (1.3)	— (†)	26 (0.6)	25 (0.6)
2011	221 (0.3)	218 (0.3)	225 (0.3)	7 (0.5)	231 (0.2)	205 (0.5)	206 (0.5)	235 (1.2)	236 (1.3)	216 (1.9)	202 (1.3)	227 (1.2)	25 (0.5)	24 (0.6)
2013	222 (0.3)	219 (0.3)	225 (0.3)	7 (0.5)	232 (0.3)	206 (0.5)	207 (0.5)	235 (1.1)	237 (1.1)	212 (2.5)	205 (1.3)	227 (1.0)	26 (0.6)	25 (0.6)
2015	223 (0.4)	219 (0.4)	226 (0.4)	7 (0.6)	232 (0.3)	206 (0.5)	208 (0.8)	239 (1.4)	241 (1.6)	215 (2.9)	205 (1.5)	227 (1.2)	26 (0.6)	24 (0.9)
2017	222 (0.3)	219 (0.3)	225 (0.3)	6 (0.4)	232 (0.3)	206 (0.5)	209 (0.5)	239 (0.9)	241 (1.0)	212 (2.7)	202 (1.8)	227 (0.9)	26 (0.6)	23 (0.5)
2019	220 (0.2)	217 (0.3)	224 (0.2)	7 (0.4)	230 (0.2)	204 (0.5)	209 (0.5)	237 (0.9)	239 (1.0)	212 (2.0)	204 (1.7)	226 (0.8)	27 (0.6)	21 (0.5)
Grade 8														
1992[2]	260 (0.9)	254 (1.1)	267 (1.0)	13 (1.5)	267 (1.1)	237 (1.7)	241 (1.6)	268 (3.9)	— (†)	— (†)	‡ (†)	— (†)	30 (2.0)	26 (2.0)
1994[2]	260 (0.8)	252 (1.0)	267 (1.0)	15 (1.4)	267 (1.0)	236 (1.8)	243 (1.2)	265 (3.0)	— (†)	— (†)	248 (4.7)	— (†)	30 (2.1)	24 (1.5)
1998	263 (0.8)	256 (1.0)	270 (0.8)	14 (1.3)	270 (0.9)	244 (1.2)	243 (1.7)	264 (7.1)	— (†)	— (†)	‡ (†)	— (†)	26 (1.5)	27 (1.9)
2000	— (†)	— (†)	— (†)	— (†)	— (†)	— (†)	— (†)	— (†)	— (†)	— (†)	— (†)	— (†)	— (†)	— (†)
2002	264 (0.4)	260 (0.5)	269 (0.5)	9 (0.7)	272 (0.4)	245 (0.7)	247 (0.8)	267 (1.7)	— (†)	— (†)	250 (3.5)	— (†)	27 (0.9)	26 (0.9)
2003	263 (0.3)	258 (0.3)	269 (0.3)	11 (0.4)	272 (0.2)	244 (0.5)	245 (0.7)	270 (1.1)	— (†)	— (†)	246 (3.0)	— (†)	28 (0.5)	27 (0.7)
2005	262 (0.2)	257 (0.2)	267 (0.2)	10 (0.3)	271 (0.2)	243 (0.4)	246 (0.4)	271 (0.8)	— (†)	— (†)	249 (1.4)	— (†)	28 (0.5)	25 (0.5)
2007	263 (0.2)	258 (0.3)	268 (0.3)	10 (0.4)	272 (0.2)	245 (0.4)	247 (0.4)	271 (1.1)	— (†)	— (†)	247 (1.2)	— (†)	27 (0.4)	25 (0.5)
2009	264 (0.3)	259 (0.3)	269 (0.3)	9 (0.5)	273 (0.2)	246 (0.4)	249 (0.6)	274 (1.1)	— (†)	— (†)	251 (1.2)	— (†)	26 (0.5)	24 (0.7)
2011	265 (0.2)	261 (0.3)	270 (0.2)	9 (0.4)	274 (0.2)	249 (0.5)	252 (0.5)	275 (1.0)	277 (1.0)	254 (2.2)	252 (1.2)	269 (1.2)	25 (0.5)	22 (0.5)
2013	268 (0.3)	263 (0.3)	273 (0.3)	10 (0.4)	276 (0.3)	250 (0.4)	256 (0.5)	280 (0.9)	282 (0.9)	259 (2.6)	251 (1.0)	271 (0.9)	26 (0.5)	21 (0.5)
2015	265 (0.2)	261 (0.2)	270 (0.3)	10 (0.4)	274 (0.2)	248 (0.5)	253 (0.4)	280 (1.3)	281 (1.3)	255 (2.4)	252 (1.7)	269 (1.1)	26 (0.5)	21 (0.5)
2017	267 (0.3)	262 (0.3)	272 (0.4)	10 (0.5)	275 (0.3)	249 (0.5)	255 (0.5)	282 (1.0)	284 (1.0)	255 (2.5)	253 (1.3)	272 (1.1)	25 (0.6)	19 (0.6)
2019	263 (0.3)	258 (0.3)	269 (0.3)	11 (0.5)	272 (0.3)	244 (0.5)	252 (0.6)	281 (0.9)	284 (0.9)	252 (2.3)	248 (1.6)	267 (0.9)	28 (0.5)	20 (0.6)
Grade 12														
1992[2]	292 (0.6)	287 (0.7)	297 (0.7)	10 (1.0)	297 (0.6)	273 (1.4)	279 (2.7)	290 (3.2)	— (†)	— (†)	‡ (†)	— (†)	24 (1.5)	19 (2.7)
1994[2]	287 (0.7)	280 (0.8)	294 (0.8)	14 (1.2)	293 (0.7)	265 (1.6)	270 (1.7)	278 (2.4)	— (†)	— (†)	274 (5.8)	— (†)	29 (1.8)	23 (1.9)
1998	290 (0.6)	282 (0.8)	298 (0.8)	16 (1.1)	297 (0.7)	269 (1.4)	275 (1.5)	287 (2.7)	— (†)	— (†)	‡ (†)	— (†)	27 (1.6)	22 (1.6)
2000	— (†)	— (†)	— (†)	— (†)	— (†)	— (†)	— (†)	— (†)	— (†)	— (†)	— (†)	— (†)	— (†)	— (†)
2002	287 (0.7)	279 (0.9)	295 (0.7)	16 (1.1)	292 (0.7)	267 (1.3)	273 (1.5)	286 (2.0)	— (†)	— (†)	‡ (†)	— (†)	25 (1.5)	20 (1.6)
2003	— (†)	— (†)	— (†)	— (†)	— (†)	— (†)	— (†)	— (†)	— (†)	— (†)	— (†)	— (†)	— (†)	— (†)
2005	286 (0.6)	279 (0.8)	292 (0.7)	13 (1.1)	293 (0.7)	267 (1.2)	272 (1.2)	287 (1.9)	— (†)	— (†)	279 (6.3)	— (†)	26 (1.4)	21 (1.4)
2007	— (†)	— (†)	— (†)	— (†)	— (†)	— (†)	— (†)	— (†)	— (†)	— (†)	— (†)	— (†)	— (†)	— (†)
2009	288 (0.7)	282 (0.7)	294 (0.8)	12 (1.1)	296 (0.6)	269 (1.1)	274 (1.0)	298 (2.4)	— (†)	— (†)	283 (3.7)	— (†)	27 (1.3)	22 (1.2)
2011	— (†)	— (†)	— (†)	— (†)	— (†)	— (†)	— (†)	— (†)	— (†)	— (†)	— (†)	— (†)	— (†)	— (†)
2013	288 (0.6)	284 (0.6)	293 (0.7)	10 (0.9)	297 (0.6)	268 (0.9)	276 (0.9)	296 (1.9)	296 (2.0)	289 (6.0)	277 (3.5)	291 (2.5)	30 (1.0)	22 (1.0)
2015	287 (0.5)	282 (0.6)	292 (0.7)	10 (1.0)	295 (0.7)	266 (1.1)	276 (0.9)	297 (2.1)	297 (2.1)	‡ (†)	279 (6.2)	295 (2.9)	30 (1.3)	20 (1.1)
2017	— (†)	— (†)	— (†)	— (†)	— (†)	— (†)	— (†)	— (†)	— (†)	— (†)	— (†)	— (†)	— (†)	— (†)
2019	— (†)	— (†)	— (†)	— (†)	— (†)	— (†)	— (†)	— (†)	— (†)	— (†)	— (†)	— (†)	— (†)	— (†)

—Not available.
†Not applicable.
‡Reporting standards not met. Either there are too few cases for a reliable estimate or the coefficient of variation (CV) is 50 percent or greater.
[1]Prior to 2011, separate data for Asian students, Pacific Islander students, and students of Two or more races were not collected.
[2]Accommodations were not permitted for this assessment.
NOTE: Scale ranges from 0 to 500. Includes public, private, Bureau of Indian Education, and Department of Defense Education Activity schools. For 1998 and later years, includes students tested with accommodations (2 to 14 percent of all students, depending on grade level and year); excludes only those students with disabilities and English language learners who were unable to be tested even with accommodations (2 to 6 percent of all students). Data on race/ethnicity are based on school reports. Race categories exclude persons of Hispanic ethnicity.
SOURCE: U.S. Department of Education, National Center for Education Statistics, National Assessment of Educational Progress (NAEP), 1992, 1994, 1998, 2000, 2002, 2003, 2005, 2007, 2009, 2011, 2013, 2015, 2017, and 2019 Reading Assessments, retrieved October 30, 2019, from the Main NAEP Data Explorer (https://nces.ed.gov/nationsreportcard/naepdata/). (This table was prepared October 2019.)

Table 221.12. Average National Assessment of Educational Progress (NAEP) reading scale score and percentage of students attaining NAEP reading achievement levels, by selected school and student characteristics and grade: Selected years, 1992 through 2019

[Standard errors appear in parentheses]

Grade and year	Percent of students in school eligible for free or reduced-price lunch: Average reading scale score[2]: 0 to 25 percent eligible (low poverty)	26 to 50 percent eligible	51 to 75 percent eligible	76 to 100 percent eligible (high poverty)	Gap between low-poverty and high-poverty score	English language learner (ELL) status: Average reading scale score[2]: ELL	Non-ELL	Gap between non-ELL and ELL score	Disability status[1]: Average reading scale score[2]: Identified as student with disability (SD)	Not identified as SD	Gap between non-SD and SD score	Percent of all students attaining NAEP reading achievement levels: Below *NAEP Basic*[3]	At or above *NAEP Basic*[3]: Total at or above *NAEP Basic*[3]	At *NAEP Basic*[3]	At or above *NAEP Proficient*[4]: Total at or above *NAEP Proficient*[4]	At *NAEP Proficient*[4]	At *NAEP Advanced*[5]
1	2	3	4	5	6	7	8	9	10	11	12	13	14	15	16	17	18
Grade 4																	
1992[6]	--- (†)	--- (†)	--- (†)	--- (†)	--- (†)	‡ (†)	‡ (†)	‡ (†)	‡ (†)	‡ (†)	‡ (†)	38 (1.1)	62 (1.1)	34 (0.9)	29 (1.2)	22 (0.9)	6 (0.6)
1994[6]	--- (†)	--- (†)	--- (†)	--- (†)	--- (†)	‡ (†)	‡ (†)	‡ (†)	‡ (†)	‡ (†)	‡ (†)	40 (1.0)	60 (1.0)	31 (0.7)	30 (1.1)	22 (0.8)	7 (0.7)
1998	231 (1.4)	218 (1.6)	205 (1.8)	187 (3.1)	44 (3.4)	174 (5.2)	217 (1.0)	43 (5.3)	176 (4.6)	217 (1.1)	41 (4.7)	40 (1.2)	60 (1.2)	30 (0.8)	29 (0.9)	22 (0.8)	7 (0.5)
2000	231 (1.5)	218 (1.3)	205 (2.1)	184 (2.8)	48 (3.2)	167 (5.2)	216 (1.1)	49 (5.3)	167 (4.8)	217 (1.2)	50 (4.9)	41 (1.4)	59 (1.4)	30 (1.1)	29 (1.1)	23 (1.0)	7 (0.6)
2002	233 (0.4)	221 (0.5)	210 (0.7)	196 (0.7)	37 (0.9)	183 (2.1)	221 (0.3)	38 (2.1)	187 (0.8)	221 (0.5)	34 (0.9)	36 (0.5)	64 (0.5)	32 (0.3)	31 (0.4)	24 (0.3)	7 (0.2)
2003	233 (0.4)	221 (0.5)	211 (0.5)	194 (0.5)	39 (0.7)	186 (0.8)	221 (0.3)	35 (0.8)	185 (0.6)	221 (0.3)	36 (0.6)	37 (0.3)	63 (0.3)	32 (0.2)	31 (0.3)	24 (0.3)	8 (0.1)
2005	234 (0.3)	221 (0.3)	211 (0.4)	197 (0.4)	37 (0.5)	187 (0.5)	222 (0.2)	35 (0.6)	190 (0.5)	222 (0.2)	32 (0.6)	36 (0.3)	64 (0.3)	33 (0.2)	31 (0.2)	24 (0.2)	8 (0.1)
2007	235 (0.4)	223 (0.4)	212 (0.4)	200 (0.5)	35 (0.7)	188 (0.6)	224 (0.3)	36 (0.6)	191 (0.6)	224 (0.3)	33 (0.7)	33 (0.3)	67 (0.3)	34 (0.2)	33 (0.3)	25 (0.2)	8 (0.2)
2009	237 (0.4)	223 (0.5)	215 (0.5)	202 (0.5)	35 (0.6)	188 (0.8)	224 (0.3)	36 (0.8)	190 (0.7)	224 (0.3)	35 (0.7)	33 (0.3)	67 (0.3)	34 (0.3)	33 (0.4)	25 (0.3)	8 (0.2)
2011	238 (0.5)	226 (0.5)	217 (0.4)	203 (0.5)	35 (0.7)	188 (0.8)	225 (0.3)	36 (0.9)	186 (0.5)	225 (0.3)	39 (0.6)	33 (0.3)	67 (0.3)	34 (0.2)	34 (0.4)	26 (0.3)	8 (0.2)
2013	240 (0.4)	227 (0.5)	218 (0.6)	203 (0.4)	37 (0.6)	187 (0.7)	226 (0.3)	38 (0.7)	184 (0.6)	227 (0.3)	42 (0.7)	32 (0.3)	68 (0.3)	33 (0.2)	35 (0.3)	27 (0.3)	8 (0.2)
2015	241 (0.5)	228 (0.5)	219 (0.6)	205 (0.6)	36 (0.8)	189 (1.1)	226 (0.3)	37 (1.1)	187 (0.7)	228 (0.3)	41 (0.8)	31 (0.4)	69 (0.4)	33 (0.3)	36 (0.4)	27 (0.3)	9 (0.2)
2017[7]	240 (0.6)	228 (0.6)	218 (0.6)	205 (0.5)	35 (0.8)	189 (0.8)	226 (0.3)	37 (0.9)	187 (0.5)	227 (0.3)	40 (0.6)	32 (0.3)	68 (0.3)	31 (0.3)	37 (0.3)	27 (0.3)	9 (0.2)
2019[7]	240 (0.5)	227 (0.4)	217 (0.4)	206 (1.0)	34 (1.1)	191 (0.7)	224 (0.2)	33 (0.7)	184 (0.6)	226 (0.2)	42 (0.7)	34 (0.3)	66 (0.3)	31 (0.3)	35 (0.3)	26 (0.2)	9 (0.1)
Grade 8																	
1992[6]	--- (†)	--- (†)	--- (†)	--- (†)	--- (†)	‡ (†)	‡ (†)	‡ (†)	‡ (†)	‡ (†)	‡ (†)	31 (1.0)	69 (1.0)	40 (0.7)	29 (1.1)	26 (1.0)	3 (0.3)
1994[6]	--- (†)	--- (†)	--- (†)	--- (†)	--- (†)	‡ (†)	‡ (†)	‡ (†)	‡ (†)	‡ (†)	‡ (†)	30 (0.9)	70 (0.9)	40 (0.7)	30 (0.9)	27 (0.8)	3 (0.3)
1998	273 (1.1)	262 (1.3)	252 (2.1)	240 (1.8)	33 (2.1)	218 (2.5)	264 (0.7)	46 (2.6)	224 (3.7)	266 (0.7)	42 (3.7)	27 (0.8)	73 (0.8)	41 (0.9)	32 (1.1)	30 (0.9)	3 (0.3)
2000	--- (†)	--- (†)	--- (†)	--- (†)	--- (†)	--- (†)	--- (†)	--- (†)	--- (†)	--- (†)	--- (†)	--- (†)	--- (†)	--- (†)	--- (†)	--- (†)	--- (†)
2002	276 (0.6)	264 (0.6)	254 (0.8)	240 (1.1)	36 (1.3)	224 (1.4)	266 (0.4)	42 (1.4)	228 (1.0)	268 (0.4)	39 (1.0)	25 (0.5)	75 (0.5)	43 (0.4)	33 (0.5)	30 (0.5)	3 (0.2)
2003	275 (0.4)	263 (0.4)	253 (0.6)	239 (1.0)	36 (1.1)	222 (1.5)	265 (0.3)	43 (1.5)	225 (0.6)	267 (0.3)	42 (0.6)	26 (0.3)	74 (0.3)	42 (0.2)	32 (0.3)	29 (0.2)	3 (0.1)
2005	274 (0.3)	262 (0.3)	252 (0.4)	240 (0.6)	34 (0.7)	224 (0.9)	264 (0.2)	40 (0.9)	227 (0.5)	266 (0.2)	39 (0.5)	27 (0.2)	73 (0.2)	42 (0.2)	31 (0.2)	28 (0.2)	3 (0.1)
2007	275 (0.4)	263 (0.4)	253 (0.5)	241 (0.7)	34 (0.8)	223 (1.1)	265 (0.2)	42 (1.1)	227 (0.6)	266 (0.2)	39 (0.6)	26 (0.2)	74 (0.2)	43 (0.2)	31 (0.2)	28 (0.2)	3 (0.1)
2009	277 (0.5)	265 (0.4)	256 (0.6)	243 (0.7)	34 (0.8)	219 (1.0)	266 (0.2)	47 (1.0)	230 (0.6)	267 (0.3)	37 (0.7)	25 (0.3)	75 (0.3)	43 (0.4)	32 (0.4)	30 (0.4)	3 (0.1)
2011	279 (0.4)	268 (0.4)	258 (0.5)	247 (0.5)	32 (0.7)	224 (1.0)	267 (0.2)	44 (1.0)	231 (0.5)	269 (0.2)	38 (0.6)	24 (0.3)	76 (0.3)	42 (0.3)	34 (0.3)	30 (0.2)	3 (0.1)
2013	282 (0.5)	270 (0.5)	261 (0.4)	249 (0.5)	33 (0.7)	225 (0.9)	270 (0.2)	45 (1.0)	232 (0.6)	272 (0.2)	39 (0.7)	22 (0.3)	78 (0.3)	42 (0.3)	36 (0.3)	32 (0.3)	4 (0.1)
2015	281 (0.5)	269 (0.5)	261 (0.6)	248 (0.6)	33 (0.8)	223 (0.9)	268 (0.2)	45 (0.9)	230 (0.6)	270 (0.2)	40 (0.6)	24 (0.3)	76 (0.3)	42 (0.3)	34 (0.3)	31 (0.3)	4 (0.1)
2017[7]	281 (0.5)	270 (0.4)	261 (0.5)	250 (0.5)	31 (0.7)	226 (0.8)	269 (0.3)	43 (0.8)	232 (0.6)	271 (0.3)	39 (0.6)	24 (0.3)	76 (0.3)	40 (0.3)	36 (0.3)	32 (0.3)	4 (0.1)
2019[7]	279 (0.5)	268 (0.6)	259 (0.6)	249 (0.9)	30 (1.0)	221 (0.9)	266 (0.3)	45 (0.9)	229 (0.6)	268 (0.3)	39 (0.6)	27 (0.3)	73 (0.3)	39 (0.3)	34 (0.3)	29 (0.3)	4 (0.1)
Grade 12																	
1992[6]	--- (†)	--- (†)	--- (†)	--- (†)	--- (†)	‡ (†)	‡ (†)	‡ (†)	‡ (†)	‡ (†)	‡ (†)	20 (0.6)	80 (0.6)	39 (0.7)	40 (0.8)	36 (0.8)	4 (0.3)
1994[6]	--- (†)	--- (†)	--- (†)	--- (†)	--- (†)	‡ (†)	‡ (†)	‡ (†)	‡ (†)	‡ (†)	‡ (†)	25 (0.7)	75 (0.7)	38 (0.7)	36 (1.0)	32 (0.9)	4 (0.5)
1998	296 (0.9)	284 (1.7)	275 (2.0)	272 (3.3)	23 (3.4)	244 (2.6)	291 (0.6)	46 (2.7)	244 (3.2)	292 (0.6)	48 (3.2)	24 (0.7)	76 (0.7)	36 (0.6)	40 (0.7)	35 (0.8)	6 (0.4)
2000	--- (†)	--- (†)	--- (†)	--- (†)	--- (†)	--- (†)	--- (†)	--- (†)	--- (†)	--- (†)	--- (†)	--- (†)	--- (†)	--- (†)	--- (†)	--- (†)	--- (†)
2002	293 (0.9)	282 (1.6)	275 (2.6)	268 (2.4)	25 (2.6)	245 (2.4)	288 (0.7)	43 (2.5)	247 (2.0)	289 (0.7)	42 (2.1)	26 (0.8)	74 (0.8)	38 (0.6)	36 (0.8)	31 (0.8)	5 (0.3)
2003	--- (†)	--- (†)	--- (†)	--- (†)	--- (†)	--- (†)	--- (†)	--- (†)	--- (†)	--- (†)	--- (†)	--- (†)	--- (†)	--- (†)	--- (†)	--- (†)	--- (†)
2005	292 (1.1)	282 (1.1)	273 (1.8)	266 (2.0)	26 (2.3)	247 (2.4)	288 (0.6)	40 (2.4)	244 (1.8)	289 (0.6)	45 (1.9)	27 (0.8)	73 (0.8)	37 (0.9)	35 (0.7)	31 (0.5)	5 (0.3)
2007	--- (†)	--- (†)	--- (†)	--- (†)	--- (†)	--- (†)	--- (†)	--- (†)	--- (†)	--- (†)	--- (†)	--- (†)	--- (†)	--- (†)	--- (†)	--- (†)	--- (†)
2009	299 (1.1)	286 (0.8)	276 (1.1)	266 (1.0)	33 (1.5)	240 (2.1)	290 (0.7)	50 (2.2)	253 (1.4)	291 (0.7)	38 (1.6)	26 (0.6)	74 (0.6)	36 (0.5)	38 (0.8)	33 (0.7)	5 (0.3)
2011	--- (†)	--- (†)	--- (†)	--- (†)	--- (†)	--- (†)	--- (†)	--- (†)	--- (†)	--- (†)	--- (†)	--- (†)	--- (†)	--- (†)	--- (†)	--- (†)	--- (†)
2013	302 (1.1)	289 (0.9)	280 (0.9)	268 (1.5)	35 (1.9)	237 (1.9)	290 (0.5)	53 (2.0)	252 (1.4)	292 (0.6)	40 (1.5)	25 (0.6)	75 (0.6)	37 (0.6)	38 (0.7)	32 (0.6)	5 (0.3)
2015	298 (1.5)	289 (1.0)	282 (1.2)	266 (1.7)	32 (2.2)	240 (2.0)	289 (0.5)	49 (2.0)	252 (1.8)	291 (0.5)	39 (1.9)	28 (0.5)	72 (0.5)	35 (0.6)	37 (0.6)	31 (0.6)	6 (0.3)
2017	--- (†)	--- (†)	--- (†)	--- (†)	--- (†)	--- (†)	--- (†)	--- (†)	--- (†)	--- (†)	--- (†)	--- (†)	--- (†)	--- (†)	--- (†)	--- (†)	--- (†)
2019[7]	301 (1.1)	288 (0.8)	278 (0.9)	266 (1.3)	35 (1.7)	235 (1.3)	288 (0.6)	53 (1.4)	252 (1.2)	290 (0.5)	38 (1.3)	30 (0.5)	70 (0.5)	33 (0.4)	37 (0.6)	31 (0.5)	6 (0.3)

—Not available.

†Not applicable.

‡Reporting standards not met. Either there are too few cases for a reliable estimate or the coefficient of variation (CV) is 50 percent or greater.

[1] In addition to students with an Individualized Education Program (IEP), also includes students with a 504 plan.

[2] Scale ranges from 0 to 500.

[3] *NAEP Basic* denotes partial mastery of the knowledge and skills that are fundamental for proficient work at a given grade.

[4] *NAEP Proficient* represents solid academic performance. Students reaching this level have demonstrated competency over challenging subject matter.

[5] *NAEP Advanced* signifies superior performance.

[6] Accommodations were not permitted for this assessment.

[7] The nonresponse rate for free or reduced-price lunch was greater than 15 percent but not greater than 50 percent.

NOTE: Includes public, private, Bureau of Indian Education, and Department of Defense Education Activity schools. For 1998 and later years, includes students tested with accommodations (2 to 14 percent of all students, depending on grade level and year); excludes only those students with disabilities and English language learners who were unable to be tested even with accommodations (2 to 6 percent of all students).

SOURCE: U.S. Department of Education, National Center for Education Statistics, National Assessment of Educational Progress (NAEP), 1992, 1994, 1998, 2000, 2002, 2003, 2005, 2007, 2009, 2011, 2013, 2015, 2017, and 2019 Reading Assessments, retrieved October 30, 2020, from the Main NAEP Data Explorer (https://www.nationsreportcard.gov/ndecore/xplore/NDE). (This table was prepared October 2020.)

Table 221.20. Percentage of students at or above selected National Assessment of Educational Progress (NAEP) reading achievement levels, by grade and selected student characteristics: Selected years, 2005 through 2019

[Standard errors appear in parentheses]

Grade and selected student characteristic	2005		2007		2009		2011		2013		2015		2017		2019	
	At or above *NAEP Basic*[1]	At or above *NAEP Proficient*[2]	At or above *NAEP Basic*[1]	At or above *NAEP Proficient*[2]	At or above *NAEP Basic*[1]	At or above *NAEP Proficient*[2]	At or above *NAEP Basic*[1]	At or above *NAEP Proficient*[2]	At or above *NAEP Basic*[1]	At or above *NAEP Proficient*[2]	At or above *NAEP Basic*[1]	At or above *NAEP Proficient*[2]	At or above *NAEP Basic*[1]	At or above *NAEP Proficient*[2]	At or above *NAEP Basic*[1]	At or above *NAEP Proficient*[2]
1	2	3	4	5	6	7	8	9	10	11	12	13	14	15	16	17
4th grade, all students	**64 (0.3)**	**31 (0.2)**	**67 (0.3)**	**33 (0.3)**	**67 (0.3)**	**33 (0.4)**	**67 (0.3)**	**34 (0.4)**	**68 (0.3)**	**35 (0.3)**	**69 (0.4)**	**36 (0.4)**	**68 (0.3)**	**37 (0.3)**	**66 (0.3)**	**35 (0.3)**
Sex																
Male	61 (0.4)	29 (0.3)	64 (0.4)	30 (0.3)	64 (0.3)	30 (0.4)	64 (0.4)	31 (0.4)	65 (0.3)	32 (0.4)	66 (0.5)	33 (0.5)	65 (0.4)	34 (0.4)	63 (0.4)	32 (0.4)
Female	67 (0.3)	34 (0.3)	70 (0.3)	36 (0.4)	70 (0.4)	36 (0.4)	71 (0.4)	37 (0.5)	72 (0.4)	38 (0.4)	72 (0.4)	39 (0.5)	71 (0.4)	39 (0.4)	70 (0.3)	38 (0.3)
Race/ethnicity																
White	76 (0.3)	41 (0.3)	78 (0.3)	43 (0.4)	78 (0.3)	42 (0.4)	78 (0.3)	44 (0.4)	79 (0.3)	46 (0.4)	79 (0.3)	46 (0.5)	78 (0.3)	47 (0.4)	77 (0.3)	45 (0.4)
Black	42 (0.5)	13 (0.3)	46 (0.6)	14 (0.4)	48 (0.8)	16 (0.5)	49 (0.6)	17 (0.5)	50 (0.6)	18 (0.5)	52 (0.6)	18 (0.5)	51 (0.8)	20 (0.5)	48 (0.7)	18 (0.5)
Hispanic	46 (0.7)	16 (0.5)	50 (0.6)	17 (0.6)	49 (0.7)	17 (0.5)	51 (0.8)	18 (0.5)	53 (0.6)	20 (0.6)	55 (1.0)	21 (0.7)	54 (0.6)	23 (0.5)	55 (0.6)	23 (0.4)
Asian/Pacific Islander	73 (0.9)	42 (0.9)	77 (1.0)	46 (1.4)	80 (1.0)	49 (1.3)	80 (1.2)	49 (1.7)	80 (1.0)	51 (1.2)	82 (1.3)	55 (1.8)	82 (0.9)	56 (1.4)	81 (0.8)	55 (1.3)
Asian	— (†)	— (†)	— (†)	— (†)	— (†)	— (†)	81 (1.2)	50 (1.7)	82 (1.0)	53 (1.2)	84 (1.4)	57 (2.0)	84 (0.9)	59 (1.4)	82 (0.8)	57 (1.4)
Pacific Islander	— (†)	— (†)	— (†)	— (†)	— (†)	— (†)	61 (2.4)	28 (3.2)	57 (3.2)	27 (3.0)	60 (3.7)	28 (3.7)	58 (3.7)	27 (3.5)	58 (3.3)	25 (3.8)
American Indian/Alaska Native	48 (1.5)	18 (1.0)	49 (1.4)	18 (1.1)	50 (1.7)	20 (1.4)	47 (1.7)	18 (1.4)	51 (1.6)	21 (1.4)	52 (2.1)	21 (1.9)	48 (2.3)	20 (1.9)	50 (2.3)	19 (1.7)
Two or more races	— (†)	— (†)	— (†)	— (†)	— (†)	— (†)	73 (1.1)	39 (1.6)	73 (1.2)	40 (1.4)	73 (1.4)	40 (1.6)	73 (1.3)	42 (1.3)	72 (1.0)	40 (1.3)
Eligibility for free or reduced-price lunch																
Eligible	46 (0.4)	16 (0.3)	50 (0.4)	17 (0.3)	51 (0.4)	17 (0.3)	52 (0.4)	18 (0.3)	53 (0.4)	20 (0.3)	56 (0.5)	21 (0.4)	54 (0.4)	22 (0.3)	53 (0.4)	21 (0.3)
Not eligible	77 (0.2)	42 (0.3)	79 (0.3)	44 (0.4)	80 (0.3)	45 (0.4)	82 (0.3)	48 (0.5)	83 (0.3)	51 (0.5)	83 (0.3)	52 (0.6)	82 (0.3)	52 (0.4)	81 (0.3)	51 (0.4)
Unknown	77 (1.1)	45 (1.4)	80 (1.3)	46 (1.8)	81 (1.9)	50 (1.9)	82 (1.0)	48 (1.3)	83 (1.6)	51 (2.1)	81 (1.3)	52 (1.8)	80 (1.5)	51 (1.7)	78 (1.2)	47 (1.8)
8th grade, all students	**73 (0.2)**	**31 (0.2)**	**74 (0.2)**	**31 (0.2)**	**75 (0.3)**	**32 (0.4)**	**76 (0.3)**	**34 (0.3)**	**78 (0.3)**	**36 (0.3)**	**76 (0.3)**	**34 (0.3)**	**76 (0.3)**	**36 (0.3)**	**73 (0.3)**	**34 (0.3)**
Sex																
Male	68 (0.3)	26 (0.3)	69 (0.4)	26 (0.3)	71 (0.4)	28 (0.4)	72 (0.4)	29 (0.3)	74 (0.4)	31 (0.4)	72 (0.3)	29 (0.4)	72 (0.4)	31 (0.4)	68 (0.4)	28 (0.4)
Female	78 (0.2)	36 (0.3)	79 (0.3)	36 (0.3)	79 (0.4)	37 (0.5)	80 (0.3)	38 (0.4)	82 (0.3)	42 (0.4)	80 (0.3)	39 (0.5)	81 (0.4)	41 (0.5)	78 (0.4)	39 (0.4)
Race/ethnicity																
White	82 (0.2)	39 (0.3)	84 (0.3)	40 (0.3)	84 (0.2)	41 (0.4)	85 (0.2)	43 (0.4)	86 (0.2)	46 (0.4)	85 (0.2)	44 (0.4)	84 (0.3)	45 (0.4)	82 (0.3)	42 (0.4)
Black	52 (0.6)	12 (0.4)	55 (0.6)	13 (0.4)	57 (0.6)	14 (0.5)	59 (0.7)	15 (0.5)	61 (0.6)	17 (0.5)	58 (0.7)	16 (0.5)	60 (0.6)	18 (0.5)	54 (0.7)	15 (0.4)
Hispanic	56 (0.6)	15 (0.4)	58 (0.5)	15 (0.4)	61 (0.8)	17 (0.6)	64 (0.8)	19 (0.5)	68 (0.7)	22 (0.6)	66 (0.6)	21 (0.5)	67 (0.6)	23 (0.6)	63 (0.7)	22 (0.6)
Asian/Pacific Islander	80 (0.8)	40 (1.2)	80 (1.1)	41 (1.1)	83 (1.1)	45 (1.7)	83 (1.0)	47 (1.4)	86 (0.7)	52 (1.3)	86 (1.0)	52 (1.8)	86 (0.9)	55 (1.5)	85 (0.9)	54 (1.4)
Asian	— (†)	— (†)	— (†)	— (†)	— (†)	— (†)	84 (1.0)	49 (1.5)	87 (0.7)	54 (1.3)	87 (1.0)	54 (1.9)	87 (0.9)	57 (1.5)	87 (0.8)	57 (1.4)
Pacific Islander	— (†)	— (†)	— (†)	— (†)	— (†)	— (†)	63 (2.7)	24 (3.2)	70 (3.5)	27 (3.7)	66 (3.3)	24 (3.0)	65 (3.9)	23 (3.3)	63 (3.6)	25 (3.7)
American Indian/Alaska Native	59 (2.1)	17 (1.7)	56 (1.9)	18 (1.3)	62 (2.0)	21 (1.2)	63 (1.4)	22 (1.7)	62 (1.8)	19 (1.6)	63 (2.2)	22 (1.8)	63 (1.8)	22 (2.1)	59 (2.3)	19 (2.1)
Two or more races	— (†)	— (†)	— (†)	— (†)	— (†)	— (†)	79 (1.7)	39 (1.5)	81 (1.1)	40 (1.4)	79 (1.2)	38 (1.6)	82 (1.2)	42 (1.4)	76 (1.1)	37 (1.3)
Eligibility for free or reduced-price lunch																
Eligible	57 (0.4)	15 (0.3)	58 (0.4)	15 (0.2)	60 (0.5)	16 (0.3)	63 (0.5)	18 (0.3)	66 (0.4)	20 (0.2)	64 (0.4)	20 (0.4)	65 (0.4)	21 (0.3)	60 (0.5)	20 (0.4)
Not eligible	81 (0.3)	39 (0.2)	83 (0.3)	40 (0.4)	85 (0.3)	42 (0.5)	86 (0.3)	45 (0.4)	87 (0.3)	48 (0.4)	87 (0.3)	47 (0.5)	86 (0.3)	48 (0.5)	83 (0.3)	46 (0.4)
Unknown	84 (1.0)	45 (1.3)	86 (1.0)	48 (1.6)	89 (1.3)	51 (1.8)	90 (0.8)	54 (1.4)	92 (0.9)	59 (2.4)	89 (0.9)	53 (1.5)	87 (1.1)	52 (1.8)	84 (1.1)	47 (1.7)
12th grade, all students	**73 (0.8)**	**35 (0.7)**	**— (†)**	**— (†)**	**74 (0.6)**	**38 (0.8)**	**— (†)**	**— (†)**	**75 (0.6)**	**38 (0.7)**	**72 (0.5)**	**37 (0.6)**	**— (†)**	**— (†)**	**— (†)**	**— (†)**
Sex																
Male	67 (0.9)	29 (0.9)	— (†)	— (†)	69 (0.8)	32 (0.9)	— (†)	— (†)	70 (0.7)	33 (0.7)	68 (0.6)	33 (0.7)	— (†)	— (†)	— (†)	— (†)
Female	78 (0.9)	41 (0.9)	— (†)	— (†)	80 (0.6)	43 (1.0)	— (†)	— (†)	79 (0.7)	42 (0.9)	76 (0.8)	42 (0.9)	— (†)	— (†)	— (†)	— (†)
Race/ethnicity																
White	79 (0.8)	43 (0.9)	— (†)	— (†)	81 (0.5)	46 (0.8)	— (†)	— (†)	83 (0.6)	47 (0.8)	79 (0.7)	46 (0.9)	— (†)	— (†)	— (†)	— (†)
Black	54 (1.5)	16 (1.2)	— (†)	— (†)	57 (1.3)	17 (1.2)	— (†)	— (†)	56 (1.2)	16 (0.9)	52 (1.5)	17 (1.0)	— (†)	— (†)	— (†)	— (†)
Hispanic	60 (1.9)	20 (1.3)	— (†)	— (†)	61 (1.1)	22 (1.3)	— (†)	— (†)	64 (1.2)	23 (1.0)	63 (1.1)	25 (1.0)	— (†)	— (†)	— (†)	— (†)
Asian/Pacific Islander	74 (2.3)	36 (2.3)	— (†)	— (†)	81 (1.5)	49 (2.9)	— (†)	— (†)	80 (1.8)	47 (2.5)	79 (1.7)	48 (3.0)	— (†)	— (†)	— (†)	— (†)
Asian	— (†)	— (†)	— (†)	— (†)	— (†)	— (†)	— (†)	— (†)	80 (1.9)	48 (2.6)	80 (1.8)	49 (3.0)	— (†)	— (†)	— (†)	— (†)
Pacific Islander	— (†)	— (†)	— (†)	— (†)	— (†)	— (†)	— (†)	— (†)	75 (8.2)	39 (8.4)	‡ (†)	‡ (†)	— (†)	— (†)	— (†)	— (†)
American Indian/Alaska Native	67 (10.1)	26 (8.6)	— (†)	— (†)	70 (6.4)	29 (5.5)	— (†)	— (†)	65 (5.0)	26 (4.8)	65 (8.6)	28 (6.0)	— (†)	— (†)	— (†)	— (†)
Two or more races	— (†)	— (†)	— (†)	— (†)	— (†)	— (†)	— (†)	— (†)	77 (2.9)	38 (3.4)	79 (3.0)	45 (3.4)	— (†)	— (†)	— (†)	— (†)

—Not available.
†Not applicable.
‡Reporting standards not met (too few cases for a reliable estimate).
[1]*NAEP Basic* denotes partial mastery of the knowledge and skills that are fundamental for proficient work at a given grade.
[2]*NAEP Proficient* represents solid academic performance. Students reaching this level have demonstrated competency over challenging subject matter.
NOTE: Includes public, private, Bureau of Indian Education, and Department of Defense Education Activity schools. Includes students tested with accommodations (2 to 14 percent of all students, depending on grade level and year); excludes only those students with disabilities and English language learners who were unable to be tested even with accommodations (2 to 6 percent of all students). Race categories exclude persons of Hispanic ethnicity. Prior to 2011, separate data for Asian students, Pacific Islander students, and students of Two or more races were not collected.
SOURCE: U.S. Department of Education, National Center for Education Statistics, National Assessment of Educational Progress (NAEP), 2005, 2007, 2009, 2011, 2013, 2015, 2017, and 2019 Reading Assessments, retrieved November 6, 2019, from the Main NAEP Data Explorer (https://nces.ed.gov/nationsreportcard/naepdata/). (This table was prepared November 2019.)

Table 221.32. Average National Assessment of Educational Progress (NAEP) reading scale score and percentage distribution of 4th- and 8th-graders in traditional public, public charter, and private schools, by selected characteristics: 2017

[Standard errors appear in parentheses]

Selected characteristic	Public schools, grade 4			Public schools, grade 8			Private schools, grade 4[1]	Private schools, grade 8[1]
	Total	Traditional public	Public charter	Total	Traditional public	Public charter		
1	2	3	4	5	6	7	8	9
	Average scale score[2]							
All students	**221 (0.2)**	**221 (0.3)**	**222 (1.8)**	**265 (0.3)**	**265 (0.3)**	**266 (1.7)**	**235 (1.1)**	**281 (1.2)**
Sex								
Male	218 (0.3)	218 (0.4)	220 (1.9)	260 (0.3)	260 (0.3)	261 (1.9)	232 (1.4)	277 (1.4)
Female	224 (0.3)	224 (0.3)	223 (2.1)	270 (0.3)	270 (0.4)	271 (1.7)	237 (1.4)	285 (1.4)
Race/ethnicity								
White	231 (0.3)	231 (0.3)	236 (1.9)	274 (0.3)	274 (0.3)	281 (1.7)	238 (1.2)	284 (1.3)
Black	205 (0.5)	205 (0.5)	208 (2.1)	248 (0.5)	248 (0.5)	252 (1.5)	220 (3.3)	265 (2.2)
Hispanic	208 (0.5)	208 (0.5)	216 (4.5)	255 (0.5)	254 (0.5)	262 (2.4)	224 (2.8)	273 (2.0)
Asian	241 (1.0)	241 (1.1)	240 (4.6)	283 (1.0)	283 (1.1)	280 (3.4)	244 (2.2)	289 (2.5)
Pacific Islander	210 (2.7)	210 (2.8)	‡ (†)	254 (2.6)	254 (2.6)	251 (11.4)	‡ (†)	‡ (†)
American Indian/Alaska Native	203 (2.0)	203 (2.1)	‡ (†)	253 (1.3)	252 (1.3)	‡ (†)	‡ (†)	‡ (†)
Two or more races	226 (0.9)	226 (0.9)	231 (5.4)	270 (0.9)	270 (0.9)	276 (4.6)	239 (4.0)	288 (5.4)
English language learner (ELL) status								
ELL	189 (0.9)	188 (0.9)	200 (8.2)	226 (0.8)	225 (0.8)	235 (4.0)	200 (4.9)	‡ (†)
Non-ELL	225 (0.2)	225 (0.3)	224 (1.6)	268 (0.3)	268 (0.3)	269 (1.7)	235 (1.1)	281 (1.2)
Disability status[3]								
Identified as student with disability (SD)	186 (0.5)	186 (0.6)	188 (3.0)	231 (0.5)	231 (0.5)	236 (2.5)	205 (4.8)	260 (5.9)
Not identified as SD	226 (0.2)	226 (0.3)	226 (1.8)	270 (0.3)	270 (0.3)	270 (1.8)	236 (1.2)	282 (1.0)
Percent of students in school eligible for free or reduced-price lunch								
0 to 25 percent eligible	240 (0.6)	240 (0.6)	240 (2.3)	281 (0.5)	281 (0.5)	289 (2.7)	236 (2.5)	283 (1.8)
26 to 50 percent eligible	228 (0.6)	228 (0.6)	232 (2.8)	270 (0.4)	270 (0.5)	275 (4.0)	223 (3.3)	273 (3.4)
51 to 75 percent eligible	218 (0.6)	218 (0.6)	219 (2.9)	261 (0.5)	260 (0.5)	264 (2.3)	‡ (†)	‡ (†)
76 to 100 percent eligible	205 (0.5)	205 (0.5)	207 (3.0)	249 (0.5)	249 (0.5)	253 (1.9)	206 (3.7)	266 (3.8)
School locale								
City	215 (0.5)	215 (0.5)	216 (2.0)	260 (0.5)	260 (0.5)	259 (1.6)	234 (1.7)	280 (1.7)
Suburban	226 (0.4)	226 (0.4)	225 (4.2)	270 (0.4)	270 (0.4)	274 (2.5)	238 (1.7)	286 (1.7)
Town	216 (0.9)	216 (0.9)	218 (5.2)	262 (0.6)	261 (0.5)	283 (6.2)	229 (2.4)	267 (4.2)
Rural	222 (0.7)	221 (0.7)	236 (3.6)	265 (0.6)	265 (0.6)	269 (3.1)	227 (5.6)	277 (2.5)
	Percentage distribution							
All students	**100 (†)**	**100 (†)**	**100 (†)**	**100 (†)**	**100 (†)**	**100 (†)**	**100 (†)**	**100 (†)**
Sex								
Male	51 (0.1)	51 (0.1)	51 (1.0)	51 (0.1)	51 (0.1)	50 (0.8)	49 (1.3)	49 (1.1)
Female	49 (0.1)	49 (0.1)	49 (1.0)	49 (0.1)	49 (0.1)	50 (0.8)	51 (1.3)	51 (1.1)
Race/ethnicity								
White	47 (0.3)	48 (0.3)	34 (2.8)	50 (0.3)	51 (0.3)	30 (2.5)	63 (1.8)	66 (1.9)
Black	15 (0.2)	15 (0.2)	32 (2.7)	15 (0.3)	14 (0.3)	29 (2.5)	12 (1.1)	10 (1.2)
Hispanic	27 (0.3)	27 (0.3)	26 (3.5)	25 (0.3)	25 (0.4)	32 (2.9)	13 (1.3)	12 (1.2)
Asian	5 (0.3)	5 (0.3)	4 (0.7)	6 (0.2)	6 (0.2)	5 (0.6)	7 (0.8)	6 (0.7)
Pacific Islander	# (†)	# (†)	1 (0.2)	# (†)	# (†)	1 (0.2)	# (†)	# (†)
American Indian/Alaska Native	1 (0.1)	1 (0.1)	1 (0.2)	1 (#)	1 (#)	1 (0.2)	# (†)	1 (0.3)
Two or more races	4 (0.1)	4 (0.1)	3 (0.4)	3 (0.1)	3 (0.1)	3 (0.3)	4 (0.5)	4 (0.5)
English language learner (ELL) status								
ELL	12 (0.2)	12 (0.2)	10 (2.4)	6 (0.1)	6 (0.2)	8 (0.9)	3 (0.6)	1 (0.4)
Non-ELL	88 (0.2)	88 (0.2)	90 (2.4)	94 (0.1)	94 (0.2)	92 (0.9)	97 (0.6)	99 (0.4)
Disability status[3]								
Identified as student with disability (SD)	13 (0.1)	13 (0.1)	11 (1.0)	13 (0.1)	13 (0.1)	11 (0.7)	6 (0.8)	6 (0.6)
Not identified as SD	87 (0.1)	87 (0.1)	89 (1.0)	87 (0.1)	87 (0.1)	89 (0.7)	94 (0.8)	94 (0.6)
Percent of students in school eligible for free or reduced-price lunch								
0 to 25 percent eligible	19 (0.7)	20 (0.7)	13 (2.5)	22 (0.8)	22 (0.8)	16 (4.3)	55 (5.2)	67 (5.7)
26 to 50 percent eligible	24 (0.9)	24 (0.9)	20 (5.4)	30 (0.8)	30 (0.9)	24 (4.8)	24 (4.7)	15 (4.5)
51 to 75 percent eligible	24 (0.8)	24 (0.8)	19 (3.8)	24 (0.8)	24 (0.8)	15 (3.0)	6 (2.7)	2 (1.5)
76 to 100 percent eligible	33 (0.8)	33 (0.8)	48 (5.3)	25 (0.7)	24 (0.7)	45 (5.0)	15 (4.2)	16 (4.2)
School locale								
City	30 (0.3)	29 (0.4)	52 (4.5)	29 (0.3)	27 (0.4)	52 (4.1)	42 (1.9)	41 (1.7)
Suburban	40 (0.4)	40 (0.4)	34 (4.2)	40 (0.3)	41 (0.4)	32 (3.9)	42 (2.0)	41 (2.1)
Town	11 (0.3)	11 (0.3)	3 (1.0)	11 (0.4)	12 (0.3)	6 (2.8)	8 (1.0)	8 (1.4)
Rural	19 (0.3)	19 (0.4)	11 (2.4)	19 (0.3)	20 (0.3)	10 (2.2)	9 (1.1)	10 (1.1)

† Not applicable.

Rounds to zero.

‡ Reporting standards not met (too few cases for a reliable estimate).

[1] Results are for private schools overall, including Catholic and other (non-Catholic) private schools. In the 2017 NAEP Nations Report Card, results for private schools overall and for non-Catholic private schools were suppressed because these schools did not meet NAEP statistical and reporting standards requiring a school response rate of at least 70 percent. Response rates for private schools overall were 61 percent at grade 4 and 60 percent at grade 8. (Within the private school sector, response rates for Catholic schools were 89 percent at grade 4 and 86 percent at grade 8, while response rates for non-Catholic private schools were 41 percent at grade 4 and 39 percent at grade 8.) Please interpret these data with caution.

[2] Scale ranges from 0 to 500.

[3] The student with disability (SD) variable used in this table includes students who have a 504 plan, even if they do not have an Individualized Education Plan (IEP).

NOTE: Includes students tested with accommodations (12 percent of all 4th-graders and 11 percent of all 8th-graders); excludes only those students with disabilities and English language learners who were unable to be tested even with accommodations (2 percent of all students at both grades). Race categories exclude persons of Hispanic ethnicity. Detail may not sum to totals because of rounding.

SOURCE: U.S. Department of Education, National Center for Education Statistics, National Assessment of Educational Progress (NAEP), 2017 Reading Assessment, retrieved January 8, 2018, from the Main NAEP Data Explorer (http://nces.ed.gov/nationsreportcard/naepdata/); and unpublished tabulations. (This table was prepared May 2018.)

Table 221.40. Average National Assessment of Educational Progress (NAEP) reading scale score of 4th-grade public school students, by state: Selected years, 1992 through 2019

[Standard errors appear in parentheses]

State	1992[1]	1994[1]	1998	2002	2003	2005	2007	2009	2011	2013	2015	2017	2019
1	2	3	4	5	6	7	8	9	10	11	12	13	14
United States	**215 (1.0)**	**212 (1.1)**	**213 (1.2)**	**217 (0.5)**	**216 (0.3)**	**217 (0.2)**	**220 (0.3)**	**220 (0.3)**	**220 (0.3)**	**221 (0.3)**	**221 (0.4)**	**221 (0.2)**	**219 (0.2)**
Alabama	207 (1.7)	208 (1.5)	211 (1.9)	207 (1.4)	207 (1.7)	208 (1.2)	216 (1.3)	216 (1.2)	220 (1.3)	219 (1.2)	217 (1.4)	216 (1.2)	212 (1.2)
Alaska	— (†)	— (†)	— (†)	— (†)	212 (1.6)	211 (1.4)	214 (1.0)	211 (1.2)	208 (1.1)	209 (1.0)	213 (1.3)	207 (1.2)	204 (1.2)
Arizona	209 (1.2)	206 (1.9)	206 (1.4)	205 (1.5)	209 (1.2)	207 (1.6)	210 (1.6)	210 (1.2)	212 (1.2)	213 (1.4)	215 (1.3)	215 (1.5)	216 (1.3)
Arkansas	211 (1.2)	209 (1.7)	209 (1.6)	213 (1.4)	214 (1.4)	217 (1.1)	217 (1.2)	216 (1.1)	217 (1.0)	219 (0.9)	218 (1.1)	216 (1.2)	215 (1.2)
California[2,3]	202 (2.0)	197 (1.8)	202 (2.5)	206 (2.5)	206 (1.2)	207 (0.7)	209 (1.0)	210 (1.5)	211 (1.8)	213 (1.2)	213 (1.7)	215 (1.3)	216 (1.0)
Colorado	217 (1.1)	213 (1.3)	220 (1.4)	— (†)	224 (1.2)	224 (1.1)	224 (1.1)	226 (1.2)	223 (1.3)	227 (1.0)	224 (1.6)	225 (1.5)	225 (1.1)
Connecticut	222 (1.3)	222 (1.6)	230 (1.6)	229 (1.1)	228 (1.1)	226 (1.0)	227 (1.3)	229 (1.1)	227 (1.3)	230 (0.9)	229 (1.1)	228 (1.2)	224 (1.3)
Delaware[4]	213 (0.6)	206 (1.1)	207 (1.7)	224 (0.6)	224 (0.7)	226 (0.8)	225 (0.7)	226 (0.5)	225 (0.7)	226 (0.8)	224 (0.8)	221 (0.8)	218 (0.9)
District of Columbia	188 (0.8)	179 (0.9)	179 (1.2)	191 (0.9)	188 (0.9)	191 (1.0)	197 (0.9)	202 (1.0)	201 (0.8)	206 (0.9)	212 (0.9)	213 (0.8)	214 (0.8)
Florida	208 (1.2)	205 (1.7)	206 (1.4)	214 (1.4)	218 (1.1)	219 (0.9)	224 (0.8)	226 (1.0)	225 (1.1)	227 (1.1)	227 (1.0)	228 (1.1)	225 (1.1)
Georgia	212 (1.5)	207 (2.4)	209 (1.4)	215 (1.0)	214 (1.3)	214 (1.2)	219 (0.9)	218 (1.1)	221 (1.1)	222 (1.1)	222 (1.2)	220 (1.2)	218 (1.2)
Hawaii	203 (1.7)	201 (1.7)	200 (1.5)	208 (0.9)	208 (1.4)	210 (1.0)	213 (1.1)	211 (1.0)	214 (1.0)	215 (1.0)	215 (1.0)	216 (1.0)	218 (1.1)
Idaho	219 (0.9)	‡ (†)	— (†)	220 (1.1)	218 (1.0)	222 (0.9)	223 (0.8)	221 (0.9)	221 (0.8)	219 (0.9)	222 (1.0)	223 (1.0)	223 (1.2)
Illinois	— (†)	— (†)	‡ (†)	‡ (†)	216 (1.6)	216 (1.2)	219 (1.2)	219 (1.4)	219 (1.1)	219 (1.4)	222 (1.2)	220 (1.2)	218 (1.3)
Indiana	221 (1.3)	220 (1.3)	— (†)	222 (1.4)	220 (1.0)	218 (1.1)	222 (0.9)	223 (1.1)	221 (0.9)	225 (1.0)	227 (1.1)	226 (1.1)	222 (1.2)
Iowa[2,3]	225 (1.1)	223 (1.3)	220 (1.6)	223 (1.1)	223 (1.1)	221 (0.9)	225 (1.1)	221 (1.2)	221 (0.8)	224 (1.1)	224 (1.1)	222 (1.2)	221 (1.1)
Kansas[2,3]	— (†)	— (†)	221 (1.4)	222 (1.4)	220 (1.2)	220 (1.3)	225 (1.1)	224 (1.3)	224 (1.0)	223 (1.3)	221 (1.5)	223 (1.2)	219 (1.2)
Kentucky	213 (1.3)	212 (1.6)	218 (1.5)	219 (1.1)	219 (1.3)	220 (1.1)	222 (1.1)	226 (1.1)	225 (1.0)	224 (1.2)	228 (1.2)	224 (1.1)	221 (1.2)
Louisiana	204 (1.2)	197 (1.3)	200 (1.6)	207 (1.7)	205 (1.4)	209 (1.3)	207 (1.6)	207 (1.1)	210 (1.4)	210 (1.3)	216 (1.5)	212 (1.4)	210 (1.4)
Maine[4]	227 (1.1)	228 (1.3)	225 (1.4)	225 (1.1)	224 (0.9)	225 (0.9)	226 (0.9)	224 (0.9)	222 (0.7)	225 (0.9)	224 (0.9)	221 (1.1)	221 (0.9)
Maryland	211 (1.6)	210 (1.5)	212 (1.6)	217 (1.5)	219 (1.4)	220 (1.3)	225 (1.1)	226 (1.4)	231 (0.9)	232 (1.3)	223 (1.3)	225 (1.3)	220 (1.3)
Massachusetts[2]	226 (0.9)	223 (1.3)	223 (1.4)	234 (1.1)	228 (1.2)	231 (0.9)	236 (1.1)	234 (1.1)	237 (1.0)	232 (1.1)	235 (1.0)	236 (1.1)	231 (1.1)
Michigan	216 (1.5)	‡ (†)	216 (1.5)	219 (1.1)	219 (1.2)	218 (1.5)	220 (1.4)	218 (1.0)	219 (1.2)	217 (1.4)	216 (1.3)	218 (1.5)	218 (1.2)
Minnesota[2,3]	221 (1.2)	218 (1.4)	219 (1.7)	225 (1.1)	223 (1.1)	225 (1.3)	225 (1.1)	223 (1.3)	222 (1.2)	227 (1.2)	223 (1.3)	225 (1.3)	222 (1.1)
Mississippi	199 (1.3)	202 (1.6)	203 (1.3)	203 (1.3)	205 (1.3)	204 (1.3)	208 (1.0)	211 (1.1)	209 (1.2)	209 (0.9)	214 (1.0)	215 (1.2)	219 (1.1)
Missouri	220 (1.2)	217 (1.5)	216 (1.3)	220 (1.3)	222 (1.2)	221 (0.9)	221 (1.1)	224 (1.1)	220 (0.9)	222 (1.0)	223 (1.1)	223 (1.1)	218 (1.2)
Montana[2,3,5]	— (†)	222 (1.4)	225 (1.5)	224 (1.8)	223 (1.2)	225 (1.1)	227 (1.0)	225 (0.8)	225 (0.6)	223 (0.8)	225 (0.8)	222 (0.9)	222 (1.0)
Nebraska[4,5]	221 (1.1)	220 (1.5)	— (†)	222 (1.5)	221 (1.0)	221 (1.2)	223 (1.3)	223 (1.0)	223 (1.0)	223 (1.0)	227 (1.1)	224 (1.2)	222 (1.0)
Nevada	— (†)	— (†)	206 (1.8)	209 (1.2)	207 (1.2)	207 (1.2)	211 (1.2)	211 (1.1)	213 (1.0)	214 (1.1)	214 (1.2)	215 (1.6)	218 (1.1)
New Hampshire[2,4,5]	228 (1.2)	223 (1.5)	226 (1.7)	— (†)	228 (1.0)	227 (0.9)	229 (0.9)	229 (1.0)	230 (0.8)	232 (0.9)	232 (1.0)	229 (1.0)	224 (1.1)
New Jersey[4]	223 (1.4)	219 (1.2)	— (†)	— (†)	225 (1.2)	223 (1.3)	231 (1.2)	229 (0.9)	231 (1.2)	229 (1.3)	229 (1.4)	233 (1.2)	227 (1.3)
New Mexico	211 (1.5)	205 (1.7)	205 (1.4)	208 (1.6)	203 (1.5)	207 (1.3)	212 (1.3)	208 (1.4)	208 (1.0)	206 (1.1)	207 (1.0)	208 (1.1)	208 (1.2)
New York[2,3,4]	215 (1.4)	212 (1.4)	215 (1.6)	222 (1.5)	222 (1.1)	223 (1.0)	224 (1.0)	224 (1.0)	222 (1.1)	224 (1.2)	223 (1.1)	222 (1.3)	220 (1.3)
North Carolina	212 (1.1)	214 (1.5)	213 (1.6)	222 (1.0)	221 (1.0)	217 (1.0)	218 (0.9)	219 (1.1)	221 (1.2)	222 (1.1)	226 (1.1)	224 (1.0)	221 (1.0)
North Dakota[3]	226 (1.1)	225 (1.2)	— (†)	224 (1.0)	222 (0.9)	225 (0.7)	226 (0.9)	226 (0.8)	226 (0.5)	224 (0.5)	225 (0.7)	222 (0.8)	221 (0.8)
Ohio	217 (1.3)	— (†)	— (†)	222 (1.3)	222 (1.2)	223 (1.4)	226 (1.1)	225 (1.1)	224 (1.0)	224 (1.2)	225 (1.2)	225 (1.0)	222 (1.1)
Oklahoma	220 (0.9)	— (†)	219 (1.2)	213 (1.2)	214 (1.2)	214 (1.1)	217 (1.1)	217 (1.1)	215 (1.1)	217 (1.1)	222 (1.1)	217 (1.1)	216 (1.1)
Oregon	— (†)	— (†)	212 (1.8)	220 (1.4)	218 (1.3)	217 (1.4)	215 (1.4)	218 (1.2)	216 (1.1)	219 (1.3)	220 (1.4)	218 (1.4)	218 (1.1)
Pennsylvania[5]	221 (1.3)	215 (1.6)	— (†)	221 (1.2)	219 (1.3)	223 (1.3)	226 (1.0)	224 (1.4)	227 (1.2)	226 (1.3)	227 (1.8)	225 (1.1)	223 (1.2)
Rhode Island[5]	217 (1.8)	220 (1.3)	218 (1.4)	220 (1.2)	216 (1.3)	216 (1.2)	219 (1.0)	223 (1.1)	222 (0.8)	223 (0.9)	225 (0.9)	223 (1.0)	220 (0.9)
South Carolina	210 (1.3)	203 (1.4)	209 (1.4)	214 (1.3)	215 (1.3)	213 (1.3)	214 (1.2)	216 (1.1)	215 (1.2)	214 (1.2)	218 (1.4)	213 (1.2)	216 (1.3)
South Dakota	— (†)	— (†)	— (†)	— (†)	222 (1.2)	222 (0.5)	223 (1.0)	222 (0.6)	220 (0.9)	218 (1.0)	220 (0.9)	222 (1.0)	222 (1.0)
Tennessee[3,5]	212 (1.4)	213 (1.7)	212 (1.4)	214 (1.2)	212 (1.6)	214 (1.4)	216 (1.2)	217 (1.2)	215 (1.1)	220 (1.4)	219 (1.4)	219 (1.1)	219 (1.0)
Texas	213 (1.6)	212 (1.9)	214 (1.9)	217 (1.7)	215 (1.0)	219 (0.8)	220 (0.9)	219 (1.2)	218 (1.5)	217 (1.1)	218 (1.7)	215 (1.1)	216 (1.1)
Utah	220 (1.1)	217 (1.3)	216 (1.2)	222 (1.0)	219 (1.0)	221 (1.0)	221 (1.2)	219 (1.0)	220 (1.0)	223 (1.1)	226 (1.1)	225 (1.1)	225 (1.0)
Vermont	— (†)	— (†)	— (†)	227 (1.1)	226 (0.9)	227 (0.9)	228 (0.8)	229 (0.8)	227 (0.6)	228 (0.6)	230 (0.8)	226 (0.8)	222 (0.8)
Virginia	221 (1.4)	213 (1.5)	217 (1.2)	225 (1.3)	223 (1.5)	226 (0.8)	227 (1.1)	227 (1.2)	226 (1.1)	229 (1.3)	229 (1.7)	228 (1.5)	224 (1.2)
Washington[3]	— (†)	213 1.5	218 (1.4)	224 (1.2)	221 (1.1)	223 (1.1)	224 (1.4)	221 (1.2)	221 (1.1)	225 (1.4)	226 (1.5)	223 (1.4)	220 (1.3)
West Virginia	216 (1.3)	213 (1.1)	216 (1.7)	219 (1.2)	219 (1.0)	215 (0.8)	215 (1.1)	215 (1.0)	214 (0.8)	215 (0.8)	216 (1.2)	217 (1.2)	213 (1.1)
Wisconsin[2,5]	224 (1.0)	224 (1.1)	222 (1.1)	‡ (†)	221 (0.8)	221 (1.0)	223 (1.2)	220 (1.1)	221 (0.8)	221 (1.6)	223 (1.1)	220 (0.9)	220 (1.1)
Wyoming	223 (1.1)	221 (1.2)	218 (1.5)	221 (1.0)	222 (0.8)	223 (0.7)	225 (0.5)	223 (0.7)	224 (0.8)	226 (0.6)	228 (0.7)	227 (0.9)	227 (0.9)
Department of Defense Education Activity (DoDEA)[6]	— (†)	— (†)	220 (0.7)	224 (0.4)	224 (0.5)	226 (0.6)	229 (0.5)	228 (0.5)	229 (0.5)	232 (0.6)	234 (0.7)	234 (0.6)	235 (0.7)

—Not available.
†Not applicable.
‡Reporting standards not met (too few cases for a reliable estimate).
[1]Accommodations were not permitted for this assessment.
[2]Did not meet one or more of the guidelines for school participation in 1998. Data are subject to appreciable nonresponse bias.
[3]Did not meet one or more of the guidelines for school participation in 2002. Data are subject to appreciable nonresponse bias.
[4]Did not meet one or more of the guidelines for school participation in 1992. Data are subject to appreciable nonresponse bias.
[5]Did not meet one or more of the guidelines for school participation in 1994. Data are subject to appreciable nonresponse bias.
[6]Prior to 2005, NAEP divided the DoDEA schools into two jurisdictions, domestic and overseas. In 2005, NAEP began combining the domestic and overseas schools into a single jurisdiction. Data shown in this table for years prior to 2005 were recalculated for comparability.

NOTE: Scale ranges from 0 to 500. State-level data for 2000 are not available. Table does not include private schools, Bureau of Indian Education schools, or (except in the final row) DoDEA schools. For 1998 and later years, includes public school students who were tested with accommodations; excludes only those students with disabilities (SD) and English language learners (ELL) who were unable to be tested even with accommodations. SD and ELL populations, accommodation rates, and exclusion rates vary from state to state.
SOURCE: U.S. Department of Education, National Center for Education Statistics, National Assessment of Educational Progress (NAEP), 1992, 1994, 1998, 2002, 2003, 2005, 2007, 2009, 2011, 2013, 2015, 2017, and 2019 Reading Assessments, retrieved October 30, 2019, from the Main NAEP Data Explorer (https://nces.ed.gov/nationsreportcard/naepdata/). (This table was prepared October 2019.)

Table 221.60. Average National Assessment of Educational Progress (NAEP) reading scale score of 8th-grade public school students, by state: Selected years, 1998 through 2019

[Standard errors appear in parentheses]

State	1998		2002		2003		2005		2007		2009		2011		2013		2015		2017		2019	
1		2		3		4		5		6		7		8		9		10		11		12
United States	**261**	**(0.8)**	**263**	**(0.5)**	**261**	**(0.2)**	**260**	**(0.2)**	**261**	**(0.2)**	**262**	**(0.3)**	**264**	**(0.2)**	**266**	**(0.2)**	**264**	**(0.2)**	**265**	**(0.3)**	**262**	**(0.3)**
Alabama	255	(1.4)	253	(1.3)	253	(1.5)	252	(1.4)	252	(1.0)	255	(1.1)	258	(1.5)	257	(1.2)	259	(1.1)	258	(1.0)	253	(1.4)
Alaska	—	(†)	—	(†)	256	(1.1)	259	(0.9)	259	(1.0)	259	(0.9)	261	(0.9)	261	(0.8)	260	(1.1)	258	(0.8)	252	(1.1)
Arizona	260	(1.1)	257	(1.3)	255	(1.4)	255	(1.0)	255	(1.2)	258	(1.2)	260	(1.2)	260	(1.1)	263	(1.2)	263	(0.9)	259	(1.2)
Arkansas	256	(1.3)	260	(1.1)	258	(1.3)	258	(1.1)	258	(1.0)	258	(1.2)	259	(0.9)	262	(1.1)	259	(1.2)	260	(0.8)	259	(1.1)
California[1,2]	252	(1.6)	250	(1.8)	251	(1.3)	250	(0.6)	251	(0.8)	253	(1.2)	255	(1.0)	262	(1.2)	259	(1.2)	263	(1.2)	259	(1.4)
Colorado	264	(1.0)	—	(†)	268	(1.2)	265	(1.1)	266	(1.0)	266	(0.8)	271	(1.4)	271	(1.1)	268	(1.4)	270	(1.3)	267	(0.9)
Connecticut	270	(1.0)	267	(1.2)	267	(1.1)	264	(1.3)	267	(1.6)	272	(0.9)	275	(0.9)	274	(1.0)	273	(1.1)	273	(0.9)	270	(1.2)
Delaware	254	(1.3)	267	(0.5)	265	(0.7)	266	(0.6)	265	(0.6)	265	(0.7)	266	(0.6)	266	(0.7)	263	(0.8)	263	(0.8)	260	(0.8)
District of Columbia	236	(2.1)	240	(0.9)	239	(0.8)	238	(0.9)	241	(0.7)	242	(0.9)	242	(0.9)	248	(0.9)	248	(1.0)	247	(1.0)	250	(0.9)
Florida	255	(1.4)	261	(1.6)	257	(1.3)	256	(1.2)	260	(1.2)	264	(1.2)	262	(1.0)	266	(1.1)	263	(1.0)	267	(1.1)	263	(1.1)
Georgia	257	(1.4)	258	(1.0)	258	(1.1)	257	(1.3)	259	(1.0)	260	(1.0)	262	(1.1)	265	(1.2)	262	(1.3)	266	(1.1)	262	(1.0)
Hawaii	249	(1.0)	252	(0.9)	251	(0.9)	249	(0.9)	251	(0.8)	255	(0.6)	257	(0.7)	260	(0.8)	257	(0.9)	261	(0.8)	258	(1.0)
Idaho	—	(†)	266	(1.1)	264	(0.9)	264	(1.1)	265	(0.9)	265	(0.9)	268	(0.7)	270	(0.8)	269	(0.9)	270	(0.9)	266	(0.9)
Illinois	‡	(†)	‡	(†)	266	(1.0)	264	(1.0)	263	(1.0)	265	(1.2)	266	(0.8)	267	(1.0)	267	(1.0)	267	(1.1)	265	(1.0)
Indiana	—	(†)	265	(1.3)	265	(1.0)	261	(1.1)	264	(1.1)	266	(1.0)	265	(1.0)	267	(1.2)	268	(1.1)	272	(1.0)	266	(1.3)
Iowa	—	(†)	—	(†)	268	(0.8)	267	(0.9)	267	(0.9)	265	(0.9)	265	(1.0)	269	(0.8)	268	(1.0)	268	(1.1)	262	(1.1)
Kansas[1,2]	268	(1.4)	269	(1.3)	266	(1.5)	267	(1.0)	267	(0.8)	267	(1.1)	267	(1.0)	267	(1.0)	267	(1.2)	267	(1.0)	263	(0.9)
Kentucky	262	(1.4)	265	(1.0)	266	(1.3)	264	(1.1)	262	(1.0)	267	(0.9)	269	(0.8)	270	(0.8)	268	(1.0)	265	(0.8)	263	(1.0)
Louisiana	252	(1.4)	256	(1.5)	253	(1.6)	253	(1.6)	253	(1.1)	253	(1.6)	255	(1.5)	257	(1.0)	255	(1.2)	257	(1.5)	257	(1.4)
Maine	271	(1.2)	270	(0.9)	268	(1.0)	270	(1.0)	270	(0.8)	268	(0.7)	270	(0.8)	269	(0.8)	268	(0.9)	269	(0.9)	265	(0.9)
Maryland[1]	261	(1.8)	263	(1.7)	262	(1.4)	261	(1.2)	265	(1.2)	267	(1.1)	271	(1.2)	274	(1.1)	268	(1.1)	267	(1.0)	264	(1.0)
Massachusetts	269	(1.4)	271	(1.3)	273	(1.0)	274	(1.0)	273	(1.0)	274	(1.2)	275	(1.0)	277	(1.0)	274	(1.1)	278	(1.1)	273	(1.0)
Michigan	—	(†)	265	(1.6)	264	(1.8)	261	(1.2)	260	(1.2)	262	(1.4)	265	(0.9)	266	(1.0)	264	(1.2)	265	(1.1)	263	(1.2)
Minnesota[1]	265	(1.4)	‡	(†)	268	(1.1)	268	(1.2)	268	(0.9)	270	(1.0)	270	(1.0)	271	(1.0)	270	(1.1)	269	(1.0)	264	(1.1)
Mississippi	251	(1.2)	255	(0.9)	255	(1.4)	251	(1.3)	250	(1.1)	251	(1.0)	254	(1.2)	253	(1.0)	252	(1.0)	256	(0.7)	256	(1.0)
Missouri	262	(1.3)	268	(1.0)	267	(1.0)	265	(1.0)	263	(1.0)	267	(1.0)	267	(1.1)	267	(1.1)	267	(1.1)	266	(1.2)	263	(1.2)
Montana[1,2]	271	(1.3)	270	(1.0)	270	(1.0)	269	(0.7)	271	(0.8)	270	(0.6)	273	(0.6)	272	(0.8)	270	(0.8)	267	(0.8)	265	(0.8)
Nebraska	—	(†)	270	(0.9)	266	(0.9)	267	(0.9)	267	(0.9)	267	(0.9)	268	(0.7)	269	(0.8)	269	(0.9)	269	(0.7)	264	(0.9)
Nevada	258	(1.0)	251	(0.8)	252	(0.8)	253	(0.9)	252	(0.8)	254	(0.9)	258	(0.9)	262	(0.7)	259	(0.9)	260	(0.8)	258	(0.9)
New Hampshire	—	(†)	—	(†)	271	(0.9)	270	(1.2)	270	(0.9)	271	(1.0)	272	(0.7)	274	(0.8)	275	(0.9)	275	(0.9)	268	(1.0)
New Jersey	—	(†)	—	(†)	268	(1.2)	269	(1.2)	270	(1.1)	273	(1.3)	275	(1.2)	276	(1.1)	271	(1.0)	275	(1.1)	270	(1.2)
New Mexico	258	(1.2)	254	(1.0)	252	(0.9)	251	(1.0)	251	(0.8)	254	(1.2)	256	(0.9)	256	(0.8)	253	(0.9)	256	(0.9)	252	(1.0)
New York[1,2]	265	(1.5)	264	(1.5)	265	(1.3)	265	(1.0)	264	(1.1)	264	(1.2)	266	(1.1)	266	(1.1)	263	(1.4)	264	(1.0)	262	(1.2)
North Carolina	262	(1.1)	265	(1.1)	262	(1.0)	258	(0.9)	259	(1.1)	260	(1.2)	263	(0.9)	265	(1.1)	261	(1.3)	263	(1.2)	263	(1.1)
North Dakota[2]	—	(†)	268	(0.8)	270	(0.8)	270	(0.6)	268	(0.7)	269	(0.6)	269	(0.7)	268	(0.6)	267	(0.6)	265	(0.8)	263	(0.9)
Ohio	—	(†)	268	(1.6)	267	(1.3)	267	(1.3)	268	(1.2)	269	(1.3)	268	(1.1)	269	(1.0)	266	(1.5)	268	(1.9)	267	(1.2)
Oklahoma	265	(1.2)	262	(0.8)	262	(0.9)	260	(1.1)	260	(0.8)	259	(0.9)	260	(1.1)	262	(0.9)	263	(1.3)	261	(1.0)	258	(0.9)
Oregon[2]	266	(1.5)	268	(1.3)	264	(1.2)	263	(1.1)	266	(0.9)	265	(1.0)	264	(0.9)	268	(0.9)	268	(1.3)	266	(1.2)	264	(1.1)
Pennsylvania	—	(†)	265	(1.0)	264	(1.2)	267	(1.3)	268	(1.2)	271	(0.8)	268	(1.3)	272	(1.0)	269	(1.5)	270	(1.1)	264	(1.1)
Rhode Island	264	(0.9)	262	(0.8)	261	(0.7)	261	(0.7)	258	(0.9)	260	(0.6)	265	(0.7)	267	(0.6)	265	(0.7)	266	(0.8)	262	(0.9)
South Carolina	255	(1.1)	258	(1.1)	258	(1.3)	257	(1.1)	257	(0.9)	257	(1.2)	260	(0.9)	261	(1.0)	260	(1.2)	260	(1.0)	259	(0.9)
South Dakota	—	(†)	—	(†)	270	(0.8)	269	(0.6)	270	(0.7)	270	(0.5)	269	(0.8)	268	(0.8)	267	(1.0)	267	(0.7)	263	(0.9)
Tennessee[2]	258	(1.2)	260	(1.4)	258	(1.2)	259	(0.9)	259	(1.0)	261	(1.1)	259	(1.0)	265	(1.1)	265	(1.4)	262	(1.1)	262	(1.1)
Texas	261	(1.4)	262	(1.4)	259	(1.1)	258	(0.6)	261	(0.9)	260	(1.1)	261	(1.0)	264	(1.1)	261	(1.0)	260	(1.2)	256	(1.2)
Utah	263	(1.0)	263	(1.1)	264	(0.8)	262	(0.8)	262	(1.0)	266	(0.8)	267	(0.8)	270	(0.9)	269	(1.0)	269	(0.9)	267	(1.2)
Vermont	—	(†)	272	(0.9)	271	(0.8)	269	(0.7)	273	(0.8)	272	(0.6)	274	(0.9)	274	(0.7)	274	(0.8)	273	(0.8)	268	(0.8)
Virginia	266	(1.1)	269	(1.0)	268	(1.1)	268	(1.0)	267	(1.1)	266	(1.1)	267	(1.2)	268	(1.3)	267	(1.2)	268	(1.3)	262	(1.3)
Washington[2]	264	(1.2)	268	(1.2)	264	(0.9)	265	(1.3)	265	(0.9)	267	(1.1)	268	(1.0)	272	(1.0)	267	(1.2)	272	(1.4)	266	(1.3)
West Virginia	262	(1.0)	264	(1.0)	260	(1.0)	255	(1.2)	255	(1.0)	255	(0.9)	256	(0.9)	257	(0.9)	260	(0.9)	259	(0.9)	256	(1.0)
Wisconsin[1]	265	(1.8)	‡	(†)	266	(1.3)	266	(1.1)	264	(1.0)	266	(1.0)	267	(0.9)	268	(0.9)	270	(1.1)	269	(1.0)	267	(0.9)
Wyoming	263	(1.3)	265	(0.7)	267	(0.5)	268	(0.7)	266	(0.7)	268	(1.0)	270	(1.0)	271	(0.6)	269	(0.7)	269	(0.7)	265	(0.8)
Department of Defense Education Activity (DoDEA)[3]	269	(1.3)	273	(0.5)	272	(0.6)	271	(0.7)	273	(1.0)	272	(0.7)	272	(0.7)	277	(0.7)	277	(0.7)	280	(0.8)	280	(0.7)

—Not available.

†Not applicable.

‡Reporting standards not met. Participation rates fell below the required standards for reporting.

[1]Did not meet one or more of the guidelines for school participation in 1998. Data are subject to appreciable nonresponse bias.

[2]Did not meet one or more of the guidelines for school participation in 2002. Data are subject to appreciable nonresponse bias.

[3]Prior to 2005, NAEP divided the DoDEA schools into two jurisdictions, domestic and overseas. In 2005, NAEP began combining the domestic and overseas schools into a single jurisdiction. Data shown in this table for years prior to 2005 were recalculated for comparability.

NOTE: Scale ranges from 0 to 500. State-level data for 1992 and 1994 are not available. Table does not include private schools, Bureau of Indian Education schools, or (except in the final row) DoDEA schools. Includes public school students who were tested with accommodations; excludes only those students with disabilities (SD) and English language learners (ELL) who were unable to be tested even with accommodations. SD and ELL populations, accommodation rates, and exclusion rates vary from state to state.

SOURCE: U.S. Department of Education, National Center for Education Statistics, National Assessment of Educational Progress (NAEP), 1998, 2002, 2003, 2005, 2007, 2009, 2011, 2013, 2015, 2017, and 2019 Reading Assessments, retrieved November 3, 2019, from the Main NAEP Data Explorer (https://nces.ed.gov/nationsreportcard/naepdata/). (This table was prepared November 2019.)

Table 221.70. Average National Assessment of Educational Progress (NAEP) reading scale scores of 4th- and 8th-graders in public schools and percentage scoring at or above selected reading achievement levels, by English language learner (ELL) status and state: 2019

[Standard errors appear in parentheses]

State	4th-graders							8th-graders						
	English language learners				Not English language learners			English language learners				Not English language learners		
			Percent			Percent				Percent			Percent	
	Percent of all students assessed	Average scale score[1]	At or above *NAEP Basic*[2]	At or above *NAEP Profi-cient*[3]	Average scale score[1]	At or above *NAEP Basic*[2]	At or above *NAEP Profi-cient*[3]	Percent of all students assessed	Average scale score[1]	At or above *NAEP Basic*[2]	At or above *NAEP Profi-cient*[3]	Average scale score[1]	At or above *NAEP Basic*[2]	At or above *NAEP Profi-cient*[3]
1	2	3	4	5	6	7	8	9	10	11	12	13	14	15
United States	**13 (0.2)**	**191 (0.7)**	**35 (0.9)**	**9 (0.5)**	**224 (0.2)**	**70 (0.3)**	**38 (0.3)**	**7 (0.2)**	**221 (0.9)**	**27 (1.2)**	**3 (0.4)**	**265 (0.3)**	**75 (0.3)**	**35 (0.4)**
Alabama	5 (0.6)	179 (3.8)	24 (5.8)	5 (2.8)	213 (1.2)	59 (1.3)	29 (1.3)	1 (0.3)	‡ (†)	‡ (†)	‡ (†)	254 (1.4)	64 (1.6)	24 (1.5)
Alaska	15 (0.8)	175 (3.5)	29 (3.2)	8 (1.7)	210 (1.3)	58 (1.4)	28 (1.3)	12 (0.9)	206 (2.8)	13 (2.9)	1 (†)	259 (1.0)	70 (1.4)	26 (1.2)
Arizona	8 (0.6)	168 (3.7)	16 (3.5)	4 (2.0)	220 (1.3)	65 (1.6)	34 (1.6)	6 (0.7)	225 (6.6)	28 (8.1)	4 (2.4)	262 (1.2)	72 (1.4)	30 (1.4)
Arkansas	8 (0.8)	188 (3.3)	31 (4.0)	7 (2.3)	217 (1.2)	65 (1.4)	33 (1.6)	6 (0.5)	228 (3.7)	38 (4.8)	4 (2.3)	261 (1.1)	70 (1.2)	31 (1.5)
California	25 (1.1)	189 (1.9)	32 (2.4)	9 (1.6)	226 (1.1)	72 (1.5)	40 (1.5)	15 (1.0)	216 (2.1)	21 (2.9)	2 (0.8)	266 (1.3)	76 (1.4)	35 (1.6)
Colorado	14 (1.0)	187 (2.7)	30 (3.4)	7 (1.5)	231 (1.1)	78 (1.3)	45 (1.6)	8 (0.6)	219 (2.5)	24 (3.8)	2 (1.1)	271 (1.0)	81 (1.1)	41 (1.6)
Connecticut	10 (1.0)	188 (4.1)	32 (3.8)	7 (2.0)	229 (1.1)	74 (1.3)	44 (1.4)	4 (0.4)	220 (4.4)	26 (6.2)	4 (2.8)	272 (1.1)	79 (1.3)	42 (1.4)
Delaware	16 (0.5)	201 (1.9)	46 (3.1)	14 (2.0)	221 (0.9)	65 (1.3)	36 (1.4)	4 (0.3)	213 (3.7)	19 (4.4)	2 (1.5)	262 (0.8)	71 (1.2)	32 (1.2)
District of Columbia	13 (0.5)	196 (2.3)	40 (3.3)	11 (2.2)	217 (0.8)	60 (1.0)	33 (0.9)	6 (0.4)	222 (5.3)	33 (5.6)	8 (3.5)	252 (0.9)	60 (1.3)	24 (1.3)
Florida	10 (0.6)	193 (2.6)	33 (3.2)	6 (1.8)	228 (1.0)	74 (1.3)	41 (1.4)	6 (0.7)	224 (3.5)	33 (4.2)	6 (2.0)	266 (1.0)	75 (1.1)	36 (1.2)
Georgia	11 (1.0)	196 (2.5)	41 (3.5)	11 (2.3)	221 (1.3)	66 (1.6)	35 (1.7)	3 (0.4)	219 (5.1)	24 (6.7)	3 (†)	264 (1.0)	73 (1.2)	33 (1.4)
Hawaii	13 (0.7)	193 (2.3)	37 (3.5)	12 (2.4)	221 (1.3)	66 (1.3)	37 (1.6)	6 (0.4)	219 (4.5)	27 (6.0)	2 (1.3)	261 (1.0)	70 (1.2)	31 (1.3)
Idaho	9 (0.7)	193 (2.8)	36 (3.6)	11 (2.6)	225 (1.1)	72 (1.1)	40 (1.5)	4 (0.3)	219 (4.3)	28 (6.3)	4 (2.7)	268 (0.9)	79 (1.0)	38 (1.3)
Illinois	16 (0.9)	196 (2.3)	42 (3.3)	12 (2.1)	222 (1.4)	69 (1.6)	39 (1.5)	6 (0.6)	218 (3.9)	30 (4.1)	3 (1.4)	268 (1.1)	77 (1.2)	38 (1.4)
Indiana	10 (0.8)	205 (3.1)	51 (4.0)	19 (3.2)	224 (1.2)	69 (1.5)	39 (1.7)	5 (0.5)	250 (4.6)	58 (6.4)	19 (5.3)	267 (1.3)	76 (1.4)	38 (1.5)
Iowa	7 (0.9)	181 (3.8)	23 (4.7)	4 (2.0)	223 (1.1)	71 (1.2)	37 (1.5)	5 (0.5)	225 (4.0)	32 (5.4)	4 (2.5)	264 (1.1)	75 (1.2)	34 (1.5)
Kansas	12 (0.9)	193 (3.0)	39 (3.5)	9 (2.3)	223 (1.2)	70 (1.3)	37 (1.8)	9 (0.6)	231 (2.7)	38 (4.5)	5 (2.2)	266 (1.1)	77 (1.2)	35 (1.5)
Kentucky	5 (0.6)	184 (4.1)	28 (4.9)	7 (2.8)	223 (1.1)	69 (1.3)	36 (1.4)	3 (0.2)	221 (5.5)	32 (7.5)	3 (†)	264 (1.0)	74 (1.1)	34 (1.3)
Louisiana	4 (0.6)	184 (5.6)	29 (6.1)	7 (3.7)	211 (1.4)	56 (1.5)	26 (1.5)	3 (0.4)	‡ (†)	‡ (†)	‡ (†)	258 (1.4)	68 (1.5)	28 (1.6)
Maine	4 (0.5)	194 (4.1)	38 (5.6)	13 (4.3)	222 (1.0)	68 (1.4)	37 (1.2)	3 (0.3)	226 (6.3)	42 (7.7)	7 (4.2)	266 (0.9)	76 (1.1)	36 (1.3)
Maryland	13 (0.7)	192 (2.6)	38 (3.0)	11 (2.5)	224 (1.4)	68 (1.5)	39 (1.4)	5 (0.4)	211 (4.1)	20 (4.9)	1 (†)	267 (1.0)	76 (1.1)	38 (1.3)
Massachusetts	13 (0.8)	196 (2.4)	37 (3.4)	10 (1.8)	236 (1.0)	82 (1.0)	51 (1.5)	6 (0.8)	217 (4.8)	25 (4.7)	3 (†)	276 (1.0)	84 (1.1)	47 (1.4)
Michigan	11 (1.6)	200 (4.1)	43 (4.8)	14 (3.3)	220 (1.2)	67 (1.5)	34 (1.4)	6 (0.9)	234 (5.3)	43 (6.2)	6 (1.8)	264 (1.2)	75 (1.4)	33 (1.6)
Minnesota	13 (0.9)	186 (2.8)	31 (3.2)	6 (2.1)	228 (1.2)	75 (1.4)	43 (1.5)	5 (0.5)	212 (3.5)	16 (4.6)	1 (†)	267 (1.1)	77 (1.3)	36 (1.5)
Mississippi	3 (0.3)	206 (5.0)	49 (6.9)	19 (5.3)	220 (1.2)	66 (1.5)	32 (1.5)	2 (0.2)	‡ (†)	‡ (†)	‡ (†)	257 (1.0)	68 (1.3)	25 (1.3)
Missouri	6 (0.8)	199 (3.9)	42 (5.8)	15 (4.2)	219 (1.2)	65 (1.4)	35 (1.3)	2 (0.3)	‡ (†)	‡ (†)	‡ (†)	264 (1.2)	75 (1.3)	34 (1.6)
Montana	4 (0.5)	181 (6.1)	21 (7.1)	7 (3.8)	223 (1.0)	71 (1.3)	38 (1.4)	2 (0.4)	‡ (†)	‡ (†)	‡ (†)	266 (0.7)	77 (1.1)	35 (1.1)
Nebraska	7 (0.7)	190 (3.3)	29 (5.3)	4 (2.0)	225 (1.0)	72 (1.3)	39 (1.3)	3 (0.3)	218 (4.5)	20 (6.4)	2 (†)	266 (0.8)	76 (1.1)	35 (1.3)
Nevada	20 (0.8)	196 (1.7)	39 (2.4)	9 (1.7)	223 (1.1)	70 (1.4)	36 (1.6)	13 (0.5)	222 (2.1)	29 (3.7)	3 (1.1)	264 (1.0)	75 (1.4)	33 (1.4)
New Hampshire	4 (0.4)	199 (5.7)	43 (6.6)	20 (5.8)	225 (1.1)	72 (1.3)	39 (1.6)	3 (0.3)	‡ (†)	‡ (†)	‡ (†)	269 (1.0)	79 (1.3)	38 (1.3)
New Jersey	7 (1.1)	188 (3.7)	29 (4.9)	6 (2.3)	230 (1.3)	75 (1.6)	45 (1.8)	4 (0.6)	199 (6.4)	14 (4.7)	3 (†)	273 (1.1)	79 (1.1)	45 (1.6)
New Mexico	21 (1.1)	184 (2.0)	28 (2.7)	7 (1.3)	214 (1.2)	60 (1.5)	28 (1.5)	12 (0.6)	214 (2.1)	20 (2.6)	2 (0.8)	257 (1.0)	66 (1.3)	26 (1.3)
New York	9 (0.8)	181 (2.9)	22 (3.6)	4 (1.6)	223 (1.3)	70 (1.4)	37 (1.7)	6 (0.5)	211 (3.6)	17 (4.7)	1 (†)	265 (1.1)	74 (1.1)	35 (1.6)
North Carolina	11 (0.6)	198 (2.3)	41 (3.6)	10 (2.0)	224 (1.1)	70 (1.1)	39 (1.5)	4 (0.3)	210 (4.1)	21 (4.7)	3 (1.7)	265 (1.1)	74 (1.2)	34 (1.4)
North Dakota	4 (0.4)	193 (4.3)	37 (6.0)	13 (4.0)	222 (0.9)	70 (1.1)	35 (1.2)	2 (0.3)	‡ (†)	‡ (†)	‡ (†)	264 (0.9)	76 (1.3)	32 (1.4)
Ohio	2 (0.4)	187 (4.9)	28 (9.4)	2 (†)	223 (1.1)	69 (1.4)	37 (1.2)	2 (0.4)	232 (5.0)	38 (9.5)	6 (4.2)	268 (1.2)	76 (1.4)	39 (1.6)
Oklahoma	11 (1.0)	195 (3.2)	38 (4.5)	9 (2.7)	219 (1.1)	66 (1.5)	31 (1.3)	6 (0.7)	223 (4.5)	35 (5.2)	5 (2.5)	260 (0.9)	74 (1.3)	27 (1.5)
Oregon	11 (0.8)	167 (3.2)	16 (2.5)	2 (1.5)	224 (1.1)	70 (1.5)	38 (1.5)	6 (0.4)	210 (3.6)	15 (4.3)	1 (†)	267 (1.1)	77 (1.3)	36 (1.5)
Pennsylvania	4 (0.5)	182 (5.1)	28 (6.0)	8 (3.7)	225 (1.2)	70 (1.2)	41 (1.4)	3 (0.3)	217 (7.2)	25 (6.5)	5 (†)	266 (1.0)	74 (1.2)	36 (1.4)
Rhode Island	13 (0.6)	185 (2.8)	28 (3.5)	6 (1.7)	225 (1.0)	71 (1.4)	40 (1.5)	7 (0.4)	200 (3.3)	15 (3.0)	2 (†)	267 (0.8)	76 (1.0)	38 (1.2)
South Carolina	5 (0.6)	197 (4.5)	41 (5.7)	16 (4.2)	217 (1.3)	62 (1.4)	33 (1.5)	6 (0.6)	242 (4.0)	51 (6.2)	13 (4.0)	260 (0.9)	70 (1.2)	30 (1.1)
South Dakota	6 (0.4)	196 (4.7)	40 (6.7)	11 (3.6)	224 (1.0)	71 (1.4)	37 (1.5)	3 (0.3)	‡ (†)	‡ (†)	‡ (†)	264 (1.0)	75 (1.2)	33 (1.3)
Tennessee	8 (0.7)	176 (3.2)	22 (3.0)	4 (2.0)	223 (1.0)	69 (1.2)	37 (1.4)	3 (0.3)	219 (4.7)	26 (5.9)	2 (1.5)	264 (1.0)	74 (1.3)	32 (1.2)
Texas	22 (1.5)	196 (1.8)	39 (2.7)	12 (1.4)	222 (1.3)	68 (1.5)	35 (1.5)	15 (1.1)	227 (2.5)	34 (3.5)	4 (1.4)	261 (1.2)	73 (1.6)	29 (1.6)
Utah	11 (0.9)	195 (2.2)	38 (3.2)	10 (2.6)	229 (1.1)	76 (1.2)	44 (1.5)	6 (0.6)	219 (3.9)	26 (4.7)	5 (2.8)	270 (1.0)	80 (1.1)	40 (1.6)
Vermont	3 (0.2)	209 (4.7)	56 (6.9)	23 (6.1)	222 (0.8)	69 (1.1)	38 (1.1)	1 (0.2)	‡ (†)	‡ (†)	‡ (†)	269 (0.8)	77 (1.0)	41 (1.1)
Virginia	11 (1.0)	195 (2.4)	38 (3.7)	9 (2.4)	227 (1.3)	73 (1.5)	42 (1.9)	5 (0.6)	206 (4.2)	15 (4.1)	1 (†)	265 (1.3)	74 (1.4)	35 (1.7)
Washington	14 (1.0)	180 (2.8)	21 (2.9)	5 (1.7)	226 (1.3)	72 (1.4)	40 (1.7)	8 (0.7)	211 (3.0)	20 (3.4)	1 (†)	271 (1.3)	79 (1.2)	42 (1.7)
West Virginia	1 (0.2)	‡ ((†))	‡ (†)	‡ (†)	213 (1.1)	60 (1.3)	30 (1.2)	# (†)	‡ (†)	‡ (†)	‡ (†)	256 (1.0)	67 (1.3)	25 (1.1)
Wisconsin	8 (0.8)	197 (2.3)	40 (4.2)	12 (2.9)	222 (1.1)	68 (1.4)	37 (1.4)	5 (0.4)	230 (3.8)	39 (6.0)	5 (1.9)	269 (1.0)	79 (1.2)	40 (1.4)
Wyoming	4 (0.3)	200 (4.9)	48 (6.8)	13 (6.2)	228 (0.8)	74 (1.1)	42 (1.2)	2 (0.3)	‡ (†)	‡ (†)	‡ (†)	265 (0.8)	76 (1.1)	35 (1.2)
Department of Defense Education Activity (DoDEA)[4]	10 (0.4)	216 (2.2)	63 (3.7)	24 (3.5)	237 (0.7)	85 (0.9)	52 (1.2)	5 (0.4)	254 (4.4)	67 (6.0)	17 (5.4)	282 (0.7)	92 (0.9)	54 (1.3)

†Not applicable.

#Rounds to zero.

‡Reporting standards not met (too few cases for a reliable estimate).

[1] Scale ranges from 0 to 500.

[2] *NAEP Basic* denotes partial mastery of the knowledge and skills that are fundamental for proficient work at a given grade.

[3] *NAEP Proficient* represents solid academic performance. Students reaching this level have demonstrated competency over challenging subject matter.

[4] Includes both domestic and overseas schools.

NOTE: Table does not include private schools, Bureau of Indian Education schools, or (except in the final row) DoDEA schools. The results for English language learners are based on students who were assessed and cannot be generalized to the total population of such students. Although testing accommodations were permitted, some English language learners did not have a sufficient level of English proficiency to participate in the 2019 Reading Assessment.

SOURCE: U.S. Department of Education, National Center for Education Statistics, National Assessment of Educational Progress (NAEP), 2019 Reading Assessment, retrieved November 18, 2019, from the Main NAEP Data Explorer (https://www.nationsreportcard.gov/ndecore/xplore/NDE). (This table was prepared November 2019.)

Table 221.80. Average National Assessment of Educational Progress (NAEP) reading scale scores of 4th- and 8th-grade public school students and percentage attaining selected reading achievement levels, by race/ethnicity and jurisdiction or specific urban district: Selected years, 2009 through 2019

[Standard errors appear in parentheses]

Grade level and jurisdiction or specific urban district	Average reading scale score[1]														Percent of students	
	2009	2011	2013	2015	2017					2019					2019	
	All students	All students	All students	All students	All students	White	Black	Hispanic	Asian	All students	White	Black	Hispanic	Asian	At or above *NAEP Basic*[2]	At or above *NAEP Proficient*[3]
1	2	3	4	5	6	7	8	9	10	11	12	13	14	15	16	17
4th grade																
United States	220 (0.3)	220 (0.3)	221 (0.3)	221 (0.4)	221 (0.2)	231 (0.3)	205 (0.5)	208 (0.5)	241 (1.0)	219 (0.2)	229 (0.2)	203 (0.5)	208 (0.5)	239 (1.0)	65 (0.3)	34 (0.3)
All large cities[4]	210 (0.7)	211 (0.7)	212 (0.7)	214 (0.8)	213 (0.6)	234 (1.2)	203 (0.7)	206 (0.7)	230 (2.2)	212 (0.6)	232 (1.0)	199 (0.7)	205 (0.8)	230 (2.8)	57 (0.7)	27 (0.6)
Selected urban districts																
Albuquerque (NM)	--- (†)	209 (1.6)	207 (1.5)	207 (1.6)	207 (1.6)	229 (3.0)	‡ (†)	201 (1.7)	‡ (†)	208 (1.6)	231 (3.1)	‡ (†)	200 (1.9)	‡ (†)	54 (1.7)	25 (1.8)
Atlanta (GA)	209 (1.5)	212 (1.4)	214 (1.3)	212 (1.6)	214 (1.8)	251 (2.1)	203 (2.0)	204 (4.7)	‡ (†)	214 (1.6)	256 (2.4)	202 (1.9)	206 (4.3)	‡ (†)	56 (1.8)	29 (1.4)
Austin (TX)	220 (1.8)	224 (2.3)	221 (1.6)	220 (1.8)	217 (1.7)	245 (2.7)	198 (4.3)	204 (2.0)	‡ (†)	217 (1.6)	242 (2.1)	‡ (†)	202 (2.2)	‡ (†)	61 (1.8)	34 (1.9)
Baltimore City (MD)	202 (1.7)	200 (1.7)	204 (1.6)	199 (1.7)	197 (1.4)	219 (3.9)	194 (1.5)	198 (3.8)	‡ (†)	193 (2.2)	224 (5.3)	188 (2.3)	194 (4.8)	‡ (†)	36 (2.6)	13 (1.4)
Boston (MA)	215 (1.2)	217 (0.8)	214 (1.1)	219 (1.4)	217 (1.4)	238 (3.0)	209 (2.4)	213 (1.7)	242 (3.6)	214 (1.5)	240 (2.9)	206 (2.2)	205 (2.0)	237 (4.5)	58 (1.8)	27 (1.4)
Charlotte (NC)	225 (1.6)	224 (1.2)	226 (1.6)	226 (1.6)	225 (1.5)	248 (1.9)	215 (2.1)	212 (2.7)	242 (5.9)	225 (1.4)	249 (2.1)	213 (2.0)	212 (2.6)	239 (5.6)	70 (1.6)	39 (2.0)
Chicago (IL)	202 (1.5)	203 (1.3)	206 (1.6)	213 (1.4)	211 (1.4)	239 (4.3)	200 (2.0)	209 (1.6)	236 (5.5)	208 (1.4)	238 (4.5)	199 (2.4)	207 (1.6)	232 (6.1)	53 (1.6)	24 (1.6)
Clark County (NV)	--- (†)	--- (†)	--- (†)	--- (†)	213 (1.1)	228 (2.3)	203 (2.8)	206 (1.5)	234 (4.3)	216 (1.3)	230 (2.0)	199 (3.0)	212 (1.6)	235 (3.6)	62 (1.6)	30 (1.6)
Cleveland (OH)	194 (2.0)	193 (0.9)	190 (1.9)	197 (2.0)	196 (1.8)	213 (3.2)	192 (2.4)	197 (3.6)	‡ (†)	196 (2.1)	214 (3.1)	193 (2.6)	188 (3.0)	‡ (†)	39 (2.2)	13 (1.3)
Dallas (TX)[5]	--- (†)	204 (1.6)	205 (1.4)	204 (1.9)	201 (2.0)	‡ (†)	195 (4.1)	202 (2.3)	‡ (†)	203 (2.1)	‡ (†)	195 (3.5)	201 (2.0)	‡ (†)	46 (2.5)	18 (1.9)
Denver (CO)	--- (†)	--- (†)	--- (†)	--- (†)	214 (1.7)	241 (3.0)	205 (3.3)	201 (1.7)	‡ (†)	217 (1.9)	246 (2.7)	207 (4.3)	202 (2.2)	‡ (†)	59 (2.0)	32 (2.1)
Detroit (MI)	187 (1.9)	191 (2.0)	190 (2.2)	186 (2.0)	182 (1.8)	‡ (†)	181 (1.9)	183 (3.2)	‡ (†)	183 (1.6)	‡ (†)	180 (1.7)	195 (3.2)	‡ (†)	23 (1.5)	7 (0.9)
District of Columbia (DC)	203 (1.2)	201 (1.0)	206 (1.2)	214 (1.0)	213 (0.9)	258 (1.9)	203 (1.3)	202 (2.5)	‡ (†)	214 (0.9)	259 (2.3)	199 (1.3)	214 (2.1)	‡ (†)	57 (1.3)	32 (1.0)
Duval County (FL)	--- (†)	--- (†)	--- (†)	225 (1.5)	226 (1.1)	236 (1.8)	215 (1.7)	226 (2.9)	‡ (†)	222 (1.9)	233 (2.7)	209 (2.4)	226 (4.2)	‡ (†)	67 (2.3)	35 (2.1)
Fort Worth (TX)	--- (†)	--- (†)	--- (†)	--- (†)	206 (1.9)	231 (3.7)	195 (3.6)	204 (2.0)	‡ (†)	204 (1.5)	233 (3.9)	193 (3.4)	202 (1.8)	‡ (†)	48 (1.9)	19 (1.6)
Fresno (CA)	197 (1.7)	194 (2.4)	196 (1.7)	199 (1.6)	203 (1.8)	224 (2.9)	191 (4.0)	200 (1.9)	209 (4.0)	204 (1.7)	223 (3.6)	193 (4.6)	202 (1.9)	209 (3.4)	47 (2.2)	17 (1.7)
Guilford County (NC)	--- (†)	--- (†)	--- (†)	--- (†)	222 (1.3)	241 (1.8)	210 (1.9)	211 (2.8)	226 (4.6)	218 (1.6)	236 (2.5)	206 (2.4)	214 (3.5)	227 (5.0)	65 (2.0)	32 (1.9)
Hillsborough County (FL)	--- (†)	231 (1.7)	228 (1.3)	230 (1.9)	227 (1.4)	237 (2.0)	211 (2.5)	223 (1.9)	‡ (†)	224 (1.7)	236 (2.4)	207 (3.0)	220 (2.3)	‡ (†)	68 (2.0)	38 (2.2)
Houston (TX)	211 (1.7)	213 (1.6)	208 (1.3)	210 (1.9)	205 (1.7)	242 (3.6)	196 (3.5)	203 (1.9)	241 (4.7)	204 (1.5)	233 (4.1)	194 (2.3)	202 (1.7)	‡ (†)	47 (1.8)	19 (1.5)
Jefferson County (KY)	219 (1.8)	223 (1.3)	221 (1.2)	222 (2.0)	221 (1.4)	235 (1.9)	203 (2.0)	215 (3.6)	‡ (†)	214 (1.6)	228 (1.7)	196 (2.6)	202 (4.7)	‡ (†)	58 (1.9)	30 (1.6)
Los Angeles (CA)	197 (1.1)	201 (1.2)	205 (1.6)	204 (1.8)	207 (1.5)	235 (2.7)	196 (4.5)	201 (1.4)	240 (4.2)	205 (1.4)	225 (3.4)	189 (5.6)	201 (1.5)	240 (4.2)	51 (1.6)	20 (1.4)
Miami-Dade (FL)	221 (1.2)	221 (1.5)	223 (1.5)	226 (1.3)	229 (1.2)	246 (3.7)	218 (2.5)	230 (1.5)	‡ (†)	225 (1.1)	239 (3.4)	212 (2.4)	226 (1.3)	‡ (†)	71 (1.3)	38 (1.7)
Milwaukee (WI)	196 (2.0)	195 (1.7)	199 (1.9)	--- (†)	195 (1.6)	218 (3.6)	188 (2.2)	195 (2.9)	207 (4.4)	190 (2.0)	221 (4.3)	180 (2.5)	188 (3.0)	208 (4.1)	36 (2.0)	14 (1.3)
New York City (NY)	217 (1.4)	216 (1.2)	216 (1.4)	214 (1.5)	214 (1.3)	234 (2.4)	207 (2.3)	204 (1.9)	230 (2.1)	212 (1.5)	226 (2.8)	203 (2.3)	203 (2.2)	230 (2.7)	57 (1.6)	27 (1.6)
Philadelphia (PA)	195 (1.8)	199 (1.8)	200 (1.7)	201 (2.2)	197 (2.1)	225 (6.7)	191 (2.2)	186 (3.7)	230 (6.0)	197 (2.2)	225 (4.7)	190 (2.6)	185 (3.0)	225 (5.7)	41 (2.3)	17 (1.9)
San Diego (CA)	213 (2.1)	215 (1.7)	218 (1.6)	216 (2.0)	222 (1.6)	243 (2.7)	208 (4.1)	209 (2.2)	233 (3.1)	223 (1.8)	238 (3.4)	205 (4.7)	212 (2.6)	235 (4.3)	67 (2.0)	37 (2.1)
Shelby County (TN)	--- (†)	--- (†)	--- (†)	--- (†)	203 (1.4)	232 (5.6)	198 (1.6)	206 (3.9)	‡ (†)	205 (1.7)	225 (5.8)	202 (1.9)	205 (2.7)	‡ (†)	49 (2.1)	19 (1.7)
8th grade																
United States	262 (0.3)	264 (0.2)	266 (0.2)	264 (0.2)	265 (0.3)	274 (0.3)	248 (0.5)	255 (0.5)	283 (1.0)	262 (0.3)	271 (0.3)	244 (0.5)	251 (0.6)	284 (1.0)	72 (0.3)	32 (0.4)
All large cities[4]	252 (0.5)	255 (0.5)	258 (0.8)	257 (0.9)	258 (0.7)	276 (1.0)	246 (0.9)	253 (0.7)	274 (2.6)	255 (0.8)	274 (1.0)	241 (0.8)	249 (1.1)	276 (2.7)	64 (0.8)	26 (0.8)
Selected urban districts																
Albuquerque (NM)	--- (†)	254 (1.2)	256 (1.0)	251 (1.2)	255 (1.1)	276 (2.7)	‡ (†)	249 (1.4)	‡ (†)	249 (1.2)	267 (2.7)	‡ (†)	243 (1.6)	‡ (†)	59 (1.8)	22 (1.3)
Atlanta (GA)	250 (1.5)	253 (1.0)	255 (1.0)	252 (1.4)	254 (1.9)	295 (3.1)	246 (2.0)	259 (4.1)	‡ (†)	255 (1.5)	291 (2.5)	247 (1.6)	252 (3.9)	‡ (†)	63 (1.6)	25 (1.5)
Austin (TX)	261 (2.0)	261 (1.5)	261 (1.4)	261 (1.5)	263 (1.7)	286 (2.5)	240 (4.3)	252 (2.0)	‡ (†)	257 (1.5)	280 (2.8)	237 (4.5)	244 (2.0)	‡ (†)	67 (1.8)	30 (1.9)
Baltimore City (MD)	245 (1.7)	246 (1.6)	252 (1.5)	243 (1.7)	243 (1.3)	271 (3.9)	239 (1.3)	243 (5.9)	‡ (†)	241 (1.7)	274 (5.2)	237 (1.7)	233 (8.4)	‡ (†)	50 (2.1)	15 (1.6)
Boston (MA)	257 (1.5)	255 (1.2)	257 (1.0)	258 (1.2)	261 (1.2)	286 (3.1)	251 (2.0)	253 (2.0)	282 (3.5)	257 (1.5)	282 (3.2)	250 (2.1)	246 (2.3)	282 (3.2)	66 (1.6)	30 (1.6)
Charlotte (NC)	259 (1.0)	265 (0.9)	266 (1.2)	263 (1.6)	260 (1.4)	280 (1.9)	248 (2.1)	251 (2.6)	281 (4.4)	261 (1.3)	282 (2.2)	249 (1.9)	254 (2.7)	280 (5.1)	71 (1.8)	32 (1.7)
Chicago (IL)	249 (1.6)	253 (1.1)	253 (1.0)	257 (1.8)	259 (1.3)	283 (3.4)	248 (1.7)	257 (1.7)	292 (4.2)	253 (1.4)	282 (4.0)	246 (2.0)	252 (1.7)	271 (7.7)	64 (1.9)	23 (1.5)
Clark County (NV)	--- (†)	--- (†)	--- (†)	--- (†)	258 (0.8)	271 (1.7)	244 (2.6)	252 (1.1)	275 (3.2)	256 (0.9)	270 (2.1)	241 (3.0)	250 (1.4)	274 (2.9)	66 (1.3)	27 (1.4)
Cleveland (OH)	242 (1.6)	240 (1.7)	239 (1.6)	240 (1.6)	237 (1.8)	248 (3.4)	236 (2.1)	234 (4.8)	‡ (†)	242 (1.9)	254 (3.5)	239 (2.2)	240 (4.1)	‡ (†)	51 (2.5)	13 (1.7)
Dallas (TX)	--- (†)	248 (1.0)	251 (1.3)	250 (1.3)	246 (1.3)	‡ (†)	238 (2.6)	247 (1.4)	‡ (†)	242 (1.2)	‡ (†)	234 (2.8)	242 (1.3)	‡ (†)	51 (1.5)	13 (1.2)
Denver (CO)	--- (†)	--- (†)	--- (†)	--- (†)	258 (1.3)	285 (2.9)	249 (3.8)	250 (1.7)	‡ (†)	257 (1.4)	286 (2.6)	243 (3.8)	246 (1.6)	‡ (†)	64 (1.8)	29 (1.8)
Detroit (MI)	232 (2.4)	237 (1.0)	239 (1.6)	237 (1.2)	235 (1.4)	‡ (†)	233 (1.5)	242 (3.1)	‡ (†)	232 (1.6)	‡ (†)	229 (1.8)	245 (3.0)	‡ (†)	39 (2.3)	6 (1.1)
District of Columbia (DC)	240 (1.5)	237 (1.2)	245 (1.3)	245 (1.4)	246 (1.5)	303 (4.4)	236 (1.6)	237 (4.8)	‡ (†)	251 (1.4)	300 (3.7)	239 (2.0)	247 (3.6)	‡ (†)	58 (1.7)	26 (1.7)
Duval County (FL)	--- (†)	--- (†)	--- (†)	264 (1.4)	263 (1.2)	273 (1.8)	252 (2.0)	258 (3.0)	‡ (†)	258 (1.3)	267 (2.3)	248 (1.6)	256 (3.3)	‡ (†)	67 (2.1)	26 (1.7)
Fort Worth (TX)	--- (†)	--- (†)	--- (†)	--- (†)	248 (1.3)	272 (3.4)	235 (2.5)	249 (1.5)	‡ (†)	243 (1.6)	262 (4.3)	232 (3.0)	243 (1.9)	‡ (†)	52 (1.8)	14 (1.6)
Fresno (CA)	240 (2.4)	238 (1.8)	245 (1.4)	242 (1.9)	244 (1.9)	264 (3.6)	232 (3.7)	241 (2.1)	255 (3.3)	242 (1.9)	253 (3.9)	231 (4.2)	240 (1.9)	256 (3.3)	50 (2.2)	13 (1.7)
Guilford County (NC)	--- (†)	--- (†)	--- (†)	--- (†)	260 (1.3)	278 (2.0)	246 (2.1)	252 (3.2)	258 (5.8)	258 (1.3)	273 (1.9)	244 (1.9)	256 (3.4)	272 (5.7)	68 (1.7)	28 (1.6)
Hillsborough County (FL)	--- (†)	264 (1.5)	267 (1.2)	261 (1.7)	265 (1.3)	275 (1.7)	248 (3.0)	261 (2.1)	284 (6.1)	261 (1.6)	275 (2.4)	247 (3.3)	251 (2.2)	‡ (†)	69 (1.6)	31 (1.7)
Houston (TX)	252 (1.2)	252 (0.9)	252 (1.2)	252 (1.8)	249 (1.0)	276 (3.4)	243 (2.1)	247 (1.4)	‡ (†)	249 (1.5)	276 (4.7)	239 (2.7)	247 (1.7)	‡ (†)	59 (1.9)	18 (1.5)
Jefferson County (KY)	259 (1.0)	260 (1.1)	261 (1.0)	261 (1.8)	261 (1.3)	273 (1.9)	245 (1.7)	256 (4.4)	‡ (†)	258 (1.3)	273 (1.8)	239 (2.2)	261 (4.2)	‡ (†)	66 (1.4)	30 (1.5)
Los Angeles (CA)	244 (1.1)	246 (1.1)	250 (1.4)	251 (1.4)	254 (1.0)	276 (3.1)	249 (3.2)	248 (1.1)	285 (3.1)	248 (1.0)	272 (3.7)	236 (4.8)	244 (1.0)	274 (4.9)	58 (1.5)	18 (1.2)
Miami-Dade (FL)	261 (1.4)	260 (1.4)	259 (1.0)	265 (1.8)	261 (1.2)	272 (4.5)	251 (2.2)	263 (1.3)	‡ (†)	262 (1.2)	276 (3.7)	246 (2.2)	264 (1.4)	‡ (†)	71 (1.5)	32 (1.4)
Milwaukee (WI)	241 (2.0)	238 (1.6)	242 (1.4)	--- (†)	245 (1.4)	265 (5.2)	234 (1.6)	253 (2.8)	252 (7.8)	240 (1.9)	267 (4.8)	228 (2.9)	248 (2.8)	246 (6.3)	50 (2.1)	16 (1.7)
New York City (NY)	252 (1.4)	254 (1.8)	256 (1.2)	258 (1.7)	258 (1.6)	273 (3.3)	246 (2.6)	250 (2.1)	274 (3.8)	254 (1.4)	275 (3.0)	242 (2.7)	249 (1.9)	267 (3.0)	63 (1.5)	26 (1.6)
Philadelphia (PA)	247 (2.5)	247 (1.5)	249 (1.8)	248 (2.0)	248 (1.9)	269 (4.4)	240 (2.1)	242 (3.7)	275 (5.9)	243 (1.6)	260 (4.1)	238 (2.2)	233 (3.1)	266 (6.0)	52 (2.0)	17 (1.8)
San Diego (CA)	254 (2.8)	256 (2.1)	260 (1.5)	262 (2.0)	264 (1.1)	282 (2.4)	239 (4.9)	252 (2.0)	279 (3.0)	266 (1.8)	280 (2.8)	245 (5.4)	254 (2.3)	277 (3.5)	75 (1.7)	36 (2.6)
Shelby County (TN)	--- (†)	--- (†)	--- (†)	--- (†)	248 (1.6)	273 (4.7)	244 (1.9)	251 (4.3)	‡ (†)	249 (1.4)	274 (5.0)	244 (1.5)	254 (3.4)	‡ (†)	58 (1.9)	18 (1.6)

—Not available.

†Not applicable.

‡Reporting standards not met (too few cases for a reliable estimate).

[1] Scale ranges from 0 to 500.

[2] *NAEP Basic* denotes partial mastery of prerequisite knowledge and skills that are fundamental for proficient work at a given grade.

[3] *NAEP Proficient* represents solid academic performance. Students reaching this level have demonstrated competency over challenging subject matter.

[4] Includes public school students from all cities in the nation with populations of 250,000 or more, including the participating districts.

[5] The 2017 4th-grade assessed sample for Dallas was not representative of Hispanic students.

NOTE: Table does not include private schools, Bureau of Indian Education schools, or Department of Defense Education Activity schools. Includes public school students who were tested with accommodations; excludes only those students with disabilities (SD) and English language learners (ELL) who were unable to be tested even with accommodations. SD and ELL populations, accommodation rates, and exclusion rates vary by grade and from district to district. Race categories exclude persons of Hispanic ethnicity. Totals include racial/ethnic groups not shown separately.

SOURCE: U.S. Department of Education, National Center for Education Statistics, National Assessment of Educational Progress (NAEP), 2009, 2011, 2013, 2015, 2017, and 2019 Reading Assessments, retrieved December 4, 2019, from the Main NAEP Data Explorer (https://nces.ed.gov/nationsreportcard/naepdata/). (This table was prepared December 2019.)

Table 221.85. Average National Assessment of Educational Progress (NAEP) reading scale score, by age and selected student characteristics: Selected years, 1971 through 2012

[Standard errors appear in parentheses]

Selected student characteristic	1971	1975	1980	1984	1988	1990	1992	1994	1996	1999	2004[1] Previous format	2004[1] Revised format	2008	2012
1	2	3	4	5	6	7	8	9	10	11	12	13	14	15
9-year-olds														
All students	**208 (1.0)**	**210 (0.7)**	**215 (1.0)**	**211 (0.8)**	**212 (1.1)**	**209 (1.2)**	**211 (0.9)**	**211 (1.2)**	**212 (1.0)**	**212 (1.3)**	**219 (1.1)**	**216 (1.0)**	**220 (0.9)**	**221 (0.8)**
Sex														
Male	201 (1.1)	204 (0.8)	210 (1.1)	207 (1.0)	207 (1.4)	204 (1.7)	206 (1.3)	207 (1.3)	207 (1.4)	209 (1.6)	216 (1.4)	212 (1.1)	216 (1.1)	218 (0.9)
Female	214 (1.0)	216 (0.8)	220 (1.1)	214 (0.9)	216 (1.3)	215 (1.2)	215 (0.9)	215 (1.4)	218 (1.1)	215 (1.5)	221 (1.0)	219 (1.1)	224 (0.9)	223 (0.9)
Gap between female and male score	13 (1.5)	12 (1.1)	10 (1.6)	7 (1.3)	9 (1.9)	11 (2.0)	10 (1.6)	7 (1.9)	11 (1.8)	6 (2.2)	5 (1.8)	8 (1.5)	7 (1.4)	5 (1.3)
Race/ethnicity														
White	214[2] (0.9)	217 (0.7)	221 (0.8)	218 (0.9)	218 (1.4)	217 (1.3)	218 (1.0)	218 (1.3)	220 (1.2)	221 (1.6)	226 (1.1)	224 (0.9)	228 (1.0)	229 (0.8)
Black	170[2] (1.7)	181 (1.2)	189 (1.8)	186 (1.3)	189 (2.4)	182 (2.9)	185 (2.2)	185 (2.3)	191 (2.6)	186 (2.3)	200 (2.2)	197 (1.8)	204 (1.7)	206 (1.9)
Hispanic	[3] (†)	183 (2.2)	190 (2.3)	187 (3.0)	194 (3.5)	189 (2.3)	192 (3.1)	186 (3.9)	195 (3.4)	193 (2.7)	205 (1.7)	199 (1.5)	207 (1.5)	208 (1.5)
Gap between White and Black score	44 (1.9)	35 (1.4)	32 (1.9)	32 (1.6)	29 (2.8)	35 (3.2)	33 (2.4)	33 (2.6)	29 (2.8)	35 (2.8)	26 (2.5)	27 (2.1)	24 (2.0)	23 (2.1)
Gap between White and Hispanic score	† (†)	34 (2.4)	31 (2.4)	31 (3.1)	24 (3.8)	28 (2.6)	26 (3.2)	32 (4.1)	25 (3.6)	28 (3.2)	21 (2.1)	25 (1.8)	21 (1.8)	21 (1.7)
13-year-olds														
All students	**255 (0.9)**	**256 (0.8)**	**258 (0.9)**	**257 (0.6)**	**257 (1.0)**	**257 (0.8)**	**260 (1.2)**	**258 (0.9)**	**258 (1.0)**	**259 (1.0)**	**259 (1.0)**	**257 (1.0)**	**260 (0.8)**	**263 (1.0)**
Sex														
Male	250 (1.0)	250 (0.8)	254 (1.1)	253 (0.7)	252 (1.3)	251 (1.1)	254 (1.7)	251 (1.2)	251 (1.2)	254 (1.3)	254 (1.2)	252 (1.1)	256 (1.0)	259 (1.3)
Female	261 (0.9)	262 (0.9)	263 (0.9)	262 (0.7)	263 (1.0)	263 (1.1)	265 (1.2)	266 (1.2)	264 (1.2)	265 (1.2)	264 (1.3)	262 (1.2)	264 (0.9)	267 (0.9)
Gap between female and male score	11 (1.3)	13 (1.2)	8 (1.4)	9 (1.0)	11 (1.7)	13 (1.6)	11 (2.1)	15 (1.7)	13 (1.7)	12 (1.8)	10 (1.8)	10 (1.6)	8 (1.3)	8 (1.6)
Race/ethnicity														
White	261[2] (0.7)	262 (0.7)	264 (0.7)	263 (0.6)	261 (1.1)	262 (0.9)	266 (1.2)	265 (1.1)	266 (1.0)	267 (1.2)	266 (1.0)	265 (1.0)	268 (1.0)	270 (1.3)
Black	222[2] (1.2)	226 (1.2)	233 (1.5)	236 (1.2)	243 (2.4)	241 (2.2)	238 (2.3)	234 (2.4)	234 (2.6)	238 (2.4)	244 (2.0)	239 (1.9)	247 (1.6)	247 (1.6)
Hispanic	[3] (†)	232 (3.0)	237 (2.0)	240 (2.0)	240 (3.5)	238 (2.3)	239 (3.5)	235 (1.9)	238 (2.9)	244 (2.9)	242 (1.6)	241 (2.1)	242 (1.5)	249 (1.3)
Gap between White and Black score	39 (1.4)	36 (1.4)	32 (1.6)	26 (1.3)	18 (2.6)	21 (2.4)	29 (2.7)	31 (2.7)	32 (2.8)	29 (2.7)	22 (2.3)	25 (2.1)	21 (1.9)	23 (2.1)
Gap between White and Hispanic score	† (†)	30 (3.1)	27 (2.1)	23 (2.1)	21 (3.6)	24 (2.5)	27 (3.7)	30 (2.2)	28 (3.1)	23 (3.1)	24 (1.9)	24 (2.4)	26 (1.8)	21 (1.8)
Parents' highest level of education														
Did not finish high school	— (†)	— (†)	239 (1.1)	240 (1.2)	246 (2.1)	241 (1.8)	239 (2.6)	237 (2.4)	239 (2.8)	238 (3.4)	240 (2.7)	238 (2.3)	239 (1.9)	248 (2.0)
Graduated high school	— (†)	— (†)	253 (0.9)	253 (0.8)	253 (1.2)	251 (0.9)	252 (1.7)	251 (1.4)	251 (1.5)	251 (1.8)	251 (1.6)	249 (1.1)	251 (1.1)	248 (1.7)
Some education after high school	— (†)	— (†)	268 (1.0)	266 (1.1)	265 (1.7)	267 (1.7)	265 (2.7)	266 (1.9)	268 (2.3)	269 (2.4)	264 (2.0)	261 (1.4)	265 (1.1)	264 (1.5)
Graduated college	— (†)	— (†)	273 (0.9)	268 (0.9)	265 (1.6)	267 (1.1)	271 (1.5)	269 (1.2)	269 (1.4)	270 (1.2)	270 (1.0)	266 (1.2)	270 (1.2)	273 (1.3)
17-year-olds														
All students	**285 (1.2)**	**286 (0.8)**	**285 (1.2)**	**289 (0.8)**	**290 (1.0)**	**290 (1.1)**	**290 (1.1)**	**288 (1.3)**	**288 (1.1)**	**288 (1.3)**	**285 (1.2)**	**283 (1.1)**	**286 (0.9)**	**287 (0.9)**
Sex														
Male	279 (1.2)	280 (1.0)	282 (1.3)	284 (0.8)	286 (1.5)	284 (1.6)	284 (1.6)	282 (2.2)	281 (1.3)	281 (1.6)	278 (1.5)	276 (1.4)	280 (1.1)	283 (1.1)
Female	291 (1.3)	291 (1.0)	289 (1.2)	294 (0.9)	294 (1.5)	296 (1.2)	296 (1.1)	295 (1.5)	295 (1.2)	295 (1.4)	292 (1.3)	289 (1.2)	291 (1.0)	291 (1.0)
Gap between female and male score	12 (1.8)	12 (1.4)	7 (1.8)	10 (1.2)	8 (2.1)	12 (2.0)	11 (1.9)	13 (2.7)	15 (1.8)	13 (2.1)	14 (2.0)	14 (1.8)	11 (1.5)	8 (1.5)
Race/ethnicity														
White	291[2] (1.0)	293 (0.6)	293 (0.9)	295 (0.9)	295 (1.2)	297 (1.2)	297 (1.4)	296 (1.5)	295 (1.2)	295 (1.4)	293 (1.1)	289 (1.2)	295 (1.0)	295 (1.0)
Black	239[2] (1.7)	241 (2.0)	243 (1.8)	264 (1.2)	274 (2.4)	267 (2.3)	261 (2.1)	266 (3.9)	266 (2.7)	264 (1.7)	264 (2.7)	262 (1.9)	266 (2.4)	269 (1.6)
Hispanic	[3] (†)	252 (3.6)	261 (2.7)	268 (2.9)	271 (4.3)	275 (3.6)	271 (3.7)	263 (4.9)	265 (4.1)	271 (3.9)	264 (2.9)	267 (2.5)	269 (1.3)	274 (1.5)
Gap between White and Black score	53 (2.0)	52 (2.1)	50 (2.0)	32 (1.5)	20 (2.7)	29 (2.6)	37 (2.5)	30 (4.2)	29 (3.0)	31 (2.3)	29 (2.9)	27 (2.3)	29 (2.6)	26 (1.9)
Gap between White and Hispanic score	† (†)	41 (3.6)	31 (2.9)	27 (3.0)	24 (4.4)	22 (3.8)	26 (3.9)	33 (5.2)	30 (4.2)	24 (4.2)	29 (3.1)	22 (2.8)	26 (1.6)	21 (1.9)
Parents' highest level of education														
Did not finish high school	— (†)	— (†)	262 (1.5)	269 (1.4)	267 (2.0)	270 (2.8)	271 (3.9)	268 (2.7)	267 (3.2)	265 (3.6)	259 (3.4)	259 (2.7)	266 (2.1)	266 (2.1)
Graduated high school	— (†)	— (†)	277 (1.0)	281 (0.8)	282 (1.3)	283 (1.4)	280 (1.6)	276 (1.9)	273 (1.7)	274 (2.1)	274 (1.6)	271 (1.4)	274 (1.4)	270 (1.6)
Some education after high school	— (†)	— (†)	295 (1.2)	298 (0.9)	299 (2.2)	295 (1.9)	293 (1.9)	294 (1.6)	295 (2.2)	295 (1.8)	286 (1.9)	285 (1.5)	288 (1.1)	287 (1.1)
Graduated college	— (†)	— (†)	301 (1.0)	302 (0.9)	300 (1.4)	302 (1.5)	301 (1.7)	300 (1.7)	299 (1.5)	298 (1.3)	298 (1.3)	295 (1.2)	298 (1.1)	300 (1.0)

—Not available.

†Not applicable.

[1] In 2004, two assessments were conducted—one using the same format that was used in previous assessments, and one using a revised assessment format that provides accommodations for students with disabilities and for English language learners. The 2004 data in column 12 are for the format that was used in previous assessment years, while the 2004 data in column 13 are for the revised format. In subsequent years, only the revised format was used.

[2] Data for 1971 include persons of Hispanic ethnicity.

[3] Test scores of Hispanics were not tabulated separately.

NOTE: Scale ranges from 0 to 500. Students scoring 150 (or higher) are able to follow brief written directions and carry out simple, discrete reading tasks. Students scoring 200 are able to understand, combine ideas, and make inferences based on short uncomplicated passages about specific or sequentially related information. Students scoring 250 are able to search for specific information, interrelate ideas, and make generalizations about literature, science, and social studies materials. Students scoring 300 are able to find, understand, summarize, and explain relatively complicated literary and informational material. Includes public and private schools. For assessment years prior to 2004, accommodations were not permitted. For 2004 (revised format) and later years, includes students tested with accommodations; excludes only those students with disabilities and English language learners who were unable to be tested even with accommodations (2 to 5 percent of all students, depending on age and assessment year). Race categories exclude persons of Hispanic ethnicity, except where noted. Totals include other racial/ethnic groups not shown separately.

SOURCE: U.S. Department of Education, National Center for Education Statistics, National Assessment of Educational Progress (NAEP), *NAEP 2012 Trends in Academic Progress*; and 2012 NAEP Long-Term Trend Reading Assessment, retrieved June 27, 2013, from Long-Term Trend NAEP Data Explorer (http://nces.ed.gov/nationsreportcard/naepdata/). (This table was prepared June 2013.)

Table 222.10. Average National Assessment of Educational Progress (NAEP) mathematics scale score, by sex, race/ethnicity, and grade: Selected years, 1990 through 2019

[Standard errors appear in parentheses]

Grade and year	All students	Sex			Race/ethnicity									
		Average mathematics scale score		Gap between female and male score	Average mathematics scale score								Gap between White and Black score	Gap between White and Hispanic score
								Asian/Pacific Islander			American Indian/ Alaska Native	Two or more races[1]		
		Male	Female		White	Black	Hispanic	Total	Asian[1]	Pacific Islander[1]				
1	2	3	4	5	6	7	8	9	10	11	12	13	14	15
Grade 4														
1990[2]	213 (0.9)	214 (1.2)	213 (1.1)	-1 (1.7)	220 (1.0)	188 (1.8)	200 (2.2)	225 (4.1)	— (†)	— (†)	‡ (†)	— (†)	32 (2.0)	20 (2.4)
1992[2]	220 (0.7)	221 (0.8)	219 (1.0)	-2 (1.2)	227 (0.8)	193 (1.4)	202 (1.5)	231 (2.1)	— (†)	— (†)	‡ (†)	— (†)	35 (1.6)	25 (1.7)
1996	224 (1.0)	224 (1.1)	223 (1.1)	# (†)	232 (1.0)	198 (1.6)	207 (1.9)	229 (4.2)	— (†)	— (†)	217 (5.6)	— (†)	34 (1.8)	25 (2.1)
2000	226 (0.9)	227 (1.0)	224 (0.9)	-3 (1.4)	234 (0.8)	203 (1.2)	208 (1.5)	‡ (†)	— (†)	— (†)	208 (3.5)	— (†)	31 (1.5)	27 (1.7)
2003	235 (0.2)	236 (0.3)	233 (0.2)	-3 (0.3)	243 (0.2)	216 (0.4)	222 (0.4)	246 (1.1)	— (†)	— (†)	223 (1.0)	— (†)	27 (0.4)	22 (0.5)
2005	238 (0.1)	239 (0.2)	237 (0.2)	-3 (0.2)	246 (0.1)	220 (0.3)	226 (0.3)	251 (0.7)	— (†)	— (†)	226 (0.9)	— (†)	26 (0.3)	20 (0.3)
2007	240 (0.2)	241 (0.2)	239 (0.2)	-2 (0.3)	248 (0.2)	222 (0.3)	227 (0.3)	253 (0.8)	— (†)	— (†)	228 (0.7)	— (†)	26 (0.4)	21 (0.4)
2009	240 (0.2)	241 (0.3)	239 (0.3)	-2 (0.4)	248 (0.2)	222 (0.3)	227 (0.4)	255 (1.0)	— (†)	— (†)	225 (0.9)	— (†)	26 (0.4)	21 (0.5)
2011	241 (0.2)	241 (0.2)	240 (0.2)	-1 (0.3)	249 (0.2)	224 (0.4)	229 (0.3)	256 (1.0)	257 (1.0)	236 (2.1)	225 (0.9)	245 (0.6)	25 (0.4)	20 (0.4)
2013	242 (0.2)	242 (0.3)	241 (0.2)	-1 (0.4)	250 (0.2)	224 (0.3)	231 (0.4)	258 (0.8)	259 (0.8)	236 (2.0)	227 (1.1)	245 (0.7)	26 (0.4)	19 (0.5)
2015	240 (0.3)	241 (0.3)	239 (0.3)	-2 (0.4)	248 (0.3)	224 (0.4)	230 (0.5)	257 (1.2)	259 (1.2)	231 (2.3)	227 (1.0)	245 (0.8)	24 (0.5)	18 (0.5)
2017	240 (0.2)	241 (0.3)	239 (0.2)	-2 (0.4)	248 (0.2)	223 (0.5)	229 (0.4)	258 (1.1)	260 (1.0)	229 (2.7)	227 (1.3)	245 (0.8)	25 (0.5)	19 (0.5)
2019	241 (0.2)	242 (0.3)	239 (0.2)	-3 (0.4)	249 (0.3)	224 (0.4)	231 (0.3)	260 (1.4)	263 (1.0)	226 (7.9)	227 (1.2)	244 (0.6)	25 (0.5)	18 (0.4)
Grade 8														
1990[2]	263 (1.3)	263 (1.6)	262 (1.3)	-1 (2.1)	270 (1.3)	237 (2.7)	246 (4.3)	275 (5.0)	— (†)	— (†)	‡ (†)	— (†)	33 (3.0)	24 (4.5)
1992[2]	268 (0.9)	268 (1.1)	269 (1.0)	1 (1.5)	277 (1.0)	237 (1.3)	249 (1.2)	290 (5.9)	— (†)	— (†)	‡ (†)	— (†)	40 (1.7)	28 (1.5)
1996	270 (0.9)	271 (1.1)	269 (1.1)	-2 (1.5)	281 (1.1)	240 (1.9)	251 (1.7)	‡ (†)	— (†)	— (†)	‡ (†)	— (†)	41 (2.2)	30 (2.0)
2000	273 (0.8)	274 (0.9)	272 (0.9)	-2 (1.3)	284 (0.8)	244 (1.2)	253 (1.3)	288 (3.5)	— (†)	— (†)	259 (7.5)	— (†)	40 (1.5)	31 (1.6)
2003	278 (0.3)	278 (0.3)	277 (0.3)	-2 (0.4)	288 (0.3)	252 (0.5)	259 (0.6)	291 (1.3)	— (†)	— (†)	263 (1.8)	— (†)	35 (0.6)	29 (0.7)
2005	279 (0.2)	280 (0.2)	278 (0.2)	-2 (0.3)	289 (0.2)	255 (0.4)	262 (0.4)	295 (0.9)	— (†)	— (†)	264 (0.9)	— (†)	34 (0.4)	27 (0.5)
2007	281 (0.3)	282 (0.3)	280 (0.3)	-2 (0.4)	291 (0.3)	260 (0.4)	265 (0.4)	297 (0.9)	— (†)	— (†)	264 (1.2)	— (†)	32 (0.5)	26 (0.5)
2009	283 (0.3)	284 (0.3)	282 (0.4)	-2 (0.5)	293 (0.3)	261 (0.5)	266 (0.6)	301 (1.2)	— (†)	— (†)	266 (1.1)	— (†)	32 (0.5)	26 (0.6)
2011	284 (0.2)	284 (0.3)	283 (0.2)	-1 (0.4)	293 (0.2)	262 (0.5)	270 (0.5)	303 (1.0)	305 (1.1)	269 (2.4)	265 (0.9)	288 (1.3)	31 (0.5)	23 (0.5)
2013	285 (0.3)	285 (0.3)	284 (0.3)	-1 (0.4)	294 (0.3)	263 (0.4)	272 (0.5)	306 (1.1)	309 (1.1)	275 (2.3)	269 (1.2)	288 (1.2)	31 (0.5)	22 (0.5)
2015	282 (0.3)	282 (0.3)	282 (0.4)	# (†)	292 (0.3)	260 (0.5)	270 (0.5)	306 (1.5)	307 (1.5)	276 (2.9)	267 (1.3)	285 (1.1)	32 (0.6)	22 (0.6)
2017	283 (0.3)	283 (0.3)	282 (0.3)	-1 (0.4)	293 (0.3)	260 (0.5)	269 (0.5)	310 (1.5)	312 (1.5)	274 (2.2)	267 (1.4)	287 (1.1)	32 (0.6)	24 (0.6)
2019	282 (0.3)	282 (0.3)	282 (0.3)	# (†)	292 (0.3)	260 (0.4)	268 (0.4)	310 (1.1)	313 (1.0)	266 (2.3)	262 (1.3)	286 (1.0)	32 (0.5)	24 (0.5)
Grade 12														
1990[2]	[3] (†)	[3] (†)	[3] (†)	[3] (†)	[3] (†)	[3] (†)	[3] (†)	[3] (†)	[3] (†)	[3] (†)	[3] (†)	[3] (†)	[3] (†)	[3] (†)
1992[2]	[3] (†)	[3] (†)	[3] (†)	[3] (†)	[3] (†)	[3] (†)	[3] (†)	[3] (†)	[3] (†)	[3] (†)	[3] (†)	[3] (†)	[3] (†)	[3] (†)
1996	[3] (†)	[3] (†)	[3] (†)	[3] (†)	[3] (†)	[3] (†)	[3] (†)	[3] (†)	[3] (†)	[3] (†)	[3] (†)	[3] (†)	[3] (†)	[3] (†)
2000	[3] (†)	[3] (†)	[3] (†)	[3] (†)	[3] (†)	[3] (†)	[3] (†)	[3] (†)	[3] (†)	[3] (†)	[3] (†)	[3] (†)	[3] (†)	[3] (†)
2003	— (†)	— (†)	— (†)	— (†)	— (†)	— (†)	— (†)	— (†)	— (†)	— (†)	— (†)	— (†)	— (†)	— (†)
2005	150 (0.6)	151 (0.7)	149 (0.7)	-3 (1.0)	157 (0.6)	127 (1.1)	133 (1.3)	163 (2.0)	— (†)	— (†)	134 (4.1)	— (†)	31 (1.2)	24 (1.4)
2007	— (†)	— (†)	— (†)	— (†)	— (†)	— (†)	— (†)	— (†)	— (†)	— (†)	— (†)	— (†)	— (†)	— (†)
2009	153 (0.7)	155 (0.9)	152 (0.7)	-3 (1.1)	161 (0.6)	131 (0.8)	138 (0.8)	175 (2.7)	— (†)	— (†)	144 (2.8)	— (†)	30 (1.0)	23 (1.0)
2011	— (†)	— (†)	— (†)	— (†)	— (†)	— (†)	— (†)	— (†)	— (†)	— (†)	— (†)	— (†)	— (†)	— (†)
2013	153 (0.5)	155 (0.6)	152 (0.6)	-3 (0.9)	162 (0.6)	132 (0.8)	141 (0.8)	172 (1.3)	174 (1.3)	151 (2.8)	142 (3.2)	155 (1.7)	30 (1.0)	21 (1.0)
2015	152 (0.5)	153 (0.7)	150 (0.6)	-3 (0.9)	160 (0.6)	130 (1.0)	139 (0.8)	170 (2.0)	171 (1.9)	‡ (†)	138 (2.8)	157 (2.2)	30 (1.2)	22 (1.0)
2017	— (†)	— (†)	— (†)	— (†)	— (†)	— (†)	— (†)	— (†)	— (†)	— (†)	— (†)	— (†)	— (†)	— (†)
2019	— (†)	— (†)	— (†)	— (†)	— (†)	— (†)	— (†)	— (†)	— (†)	— (†)	— (†)	— (†)	— (†)	— (†)

—Not available.
†Not applicable.
#Rounds to zero.
‡Reporting standards not met. Either there are too few cases for a reliable estimate or the coefficient of variation (CV) is 50 percent or greater.
[1]Prior to 2011, separate data for Asian students, Pacific Islander students, and students of Two or more races were not collected.
[2]Accommodations were not permitted for this assessment.
[3]Because of major changes to the framework and content of the grade 12 assessment, scores from 2005 and later assessment years cannot be compared with scores from earlier assessment years. Therefore, this table does not include scores from the earlier grade 12 assessment years (1990, 1992, 1996, and 2000). For data pertaining to scale score comparisons between earlier years, see the *Digest of Education Statistics 2009*, table 138 (https://nces.ed.gov/programs/digest/d09/tables/dt09_138.asp).

NOTE: For the grade 4 and grade 8 assessments, the scale ranges from 0 to 500. For the grade 12 assessment, the scale ranges from 0 to 300. Includes public, private, Bureau of Indian Education, and Department of Defense Education Activity schools. For 1996 and later years, includes students tested with accommodations (3 to 14 percent of all students, depending on grade level and year); excludes only those students with disabilities and English language learners who were unable to be tested even with accommodations (1 to 4 percent of all students). Race categories exclude persons of Hispanic ethnicity.
SOURCE: U.S. Department of Education, National Center for Education Statistics, National Assessment of Educational Progress (NAEP), 1990, 1992, 1996, 2000, 2003, 2005, 2007, 2009, 2011, 2013, 2015, 2017, and 2019 Mathematics Assessments, retrieved November 6, 2019, from the Main NAEP Data Explorer (https://nces.ed.gov/nationsreportcard/naepdata/). (This table was prepared November 2019.)

Table 222.12. Average National Assessment of Educational Progress (NAEP) mathematics scale score and percentage of students attaining NAEP mathematics achievement levels, by selected school and student characteristics and grade: Selected years, 1990 through 2019

[Standard errors appear in parentheses]

Grade and year	Percent of students in school eligible for free or reduced-price lunch					English language learner (ELL) status			Disability status[1]			Percent of all students attaining NAEP mathematics achievement levels					
	Average mathematics scale score[2]					Average mathematics scale score[2]			Average mathematics scale score[2]				At or above *NAEP Basic*[3]				
															At or above *NAEP Proficient*[4]		
	0 to 25 percent eligible (low poverty)	26 to 50 percent eligible	51 to 75 percent eligible	76 to 100 percent eligible (high poverty)	Gap between low-poverty and high-poverty score	ELL	Non-ELL	Gap between non-ELL and ELL score	Identified as student with disability (SD)	Not identified as SD	Gap between non-SD and SD score	Below *NAEP Basic*[3]	Total at or above *NAEP Basic*[3]	At *NAEP Basic*[3]	Total at or above *NAEP Proficient*[4]	At *NAEP Proficient*[4]	At *NAEP Advanced*[5]
1	2	3	4	5	6	7	8	9	10	11	12	13	14	15	16	17	18
Grade 4																	
1990[6]	--- (†)	--- (†)	--- (†)	--- (†)	--- (†)	--- (†)	--- (†)	--- (†)	--- (†)	--- (†)	--- (†)	50 (1.4)	50 (1.4)	37 (1.5)	13 (1.2)	12 (1.1)	1 (0.4)
1992[6]	--- (†)	--- (†)	--- (†)	--- (†)	--- (†)	--- (†)	--- (†)	--- (†)	--- (†)	--- (†)	--- (†)	41 (1.0)	59 (1.0)	41 (1.0)	18 (1.0)	16 (1.0)	2 (0.3)
1996	--- (†)	--- (†)	--- (†)	--- (†)	--- (†)	201 (3.6)	225 (0.9)	24 (3.7)	204 (2.9)	225 (1.1)	22 (3.1)	37 (1.3)	63 (1.3)	43 (1.0)	21 (1.1)	19 (0.9)	2 (0.3)
2000	239 (1.2)	227 (1.2)	216 (1.5)	205 (1.2)	34 (1.7)	199 (2.0)	227 (0.8)	28 (2.1)	198 (2.2)	228 (0.9)	30 (2.4)	35 (1.3)	65 (1.3)	42 (1.1)	24 (1.0)	21 (0.9)	3 (0.3)
2003	247 (0.3)	237 (0.3)	229 (0.4)	216 (0.5)	31 (0.6)	214 (0.6)	237 (0.2)	23 (0.6)	214 (0.4)	237 (0.2)	23 (0.4)	23 (0.3)	77 (0.3)	45 (0.3)	32 (0.3)	29 (0.3)	4 (0.1)
2005	250 (0.3)	240 (0.3)	232 (0.3)	220 (0.3)	30 (0.4)	216 (0.5)	240 (0.1)	24 (0.5)	219 (0.4)	240 (0.2)	22 (0.4)	20 (0.2)	80 (0.2)	44 (0.2)	36 (0.2)	31 (0.2)	5 (0.1)
2007	252 (0.3)	242 (0.3)	234 (0.3)	222 (0.4)	30 (0.5)	217 (0.5)	242 (0.2)	25 (0.5)	220 (0.4)	242 (0.2)	22 (0.4)	18 (0.2)	82 (0.2)	43 (0.3)	39 (0.3)	34 (0.3)	6 (0.1)
2009	254 (0.4)	242 (0.4)	234 (0.4)	223 (0.4)	31 (0.6)	218 (0.6)	242 (0.2)	24 (0.7)	221 (0.5)	242 (0.2)	21 (0.5)	18 (0.3)	82 (0.3)	43 (0.2)	39 (0.3)	33 (0.3)	6 (0.2)
2011	255 (0.4)	245 (0.4)	237 (0.3)	226 (0.3)	29 (0.6)	219 (0.5)	243 (0.2)	24 (0.5)	218 (0.4)	244 (0.2)	26 (0.5)	18 (0.2)	82 (0.2)	42 (0.3)	40 (0.3)	34 (0.3)	7 (0.2)
2013	257 (0.4)	246 (0.4)	238 (0.5)	226 (0.5)	31 (0.6)	219 (0.6)	244 (0.2)	25 (0.6)	218 (0.5)	245 (0.2)	26 (0.5)	17 (0.2)	83 (0.2)	41 (0.3)	42 (0.3)	34 (0.3)	8 (0.2)
2015	257 (0.7)	245 (0.5)	237 (0.5)	226 (0.5)	30 (0.8)	218 (0.7)	243 (0.3)	25 (0.8)	218 (0.5)	244 (0.3)	26 (0.5)	18 (0.3)	82 (0.3)	42 (0.3)	40 (0.4)	33 (0.3)	7 (0.2)
2017[7]	257 (0.6)	245 (0.4)	236 (0.5)	225 (0.5)	32 (0.8)	217 (0.7)	243 (0.2)	26 (0.7)	214 (0.4)	243 (0.2)	29 (0.5)	20 (0.3)	80 (0.3)	39 (0.3)	40 (0.4)	32 (0.3)	8 (0.2)
2019[7]	258 (0.4)	246 (0.4)	238 (0.5)	231 (0.7)	27 (0.8)	220 (0.6)	243 (0.2)	24 (0.6)	214 (0.4)	245 (0.2)	30 (0.5)	19 (0.2)	81 (0.2)	40 (0.3)	41 (0.3)	32 (0.3)	9 (0.2)
Grade 8																	
1990[6]	--- (†)	--- (†)	--- (†)	--- (†)	--- (†)	--- (†)	--- (†)	--- (†)	--- (†)	--- (†)	--- (†)	48 (1.4)	52 (1.4)	37 (1.1)	15 (1.1)	13 (1.0)	2 (0.3)
1992[6]	--- (†)	--- (†)	--- (†)	--- (†)	--- (†)	--- (†)	--- (†)	--- (†)	--- (†)	--- (†)	--- (†)	42 (1.1)	58 (1.1)	37 (0.8)	21 (1.0)	18 (0.8)	3 (0.4)
1996	--- (†)	--- (†)	--- (†)	--- (†)	--- (†)	226 (3.2)	272 (1.0)	46 (3.4)	231 (2.7)	273 (0.9)	42 (2.9)	39 (1.0)	61 (1.0)	38 (0.9)	23 (1.0)	20 (0.9)	4 (0.4)
2000	287 (1.1)	270 (1.4)	260 (1.8)	246 (2.2)	41 (2.4)	234 (2.7)	274 (0.8)	40 (2.8)	230 (2.1)	276 (0.8)	47 (2.3)	37 (0.9)	63 (0.9)	38 (0.7)	26 (0.8)	21 (0.6)	5 (0.4)
2003	291 (0.4)	278 (0.4)	266 (0.7)	251 (0.7)	40 (0.8)	242 (1.0)	279 (0.3)	38 (1.0)	242 (0.6)	282 (0.3)	39 (0.6)	32 (0.3)	68 (0.3)	39 (0.2)	29 (0.3)	23 (0.2)	5 (0.1)
2005	293 (0.4)	280 (0.3)	268 (0.4)	254 (0.6)	38 (0.7)	244 (0.8)	281 (0.2)	37 (0.8)	245 (0.5)	283 (0.2)	38 (0.5)	31 (0.2)	69 (0.2)	39 (0.2)	30 (0.2)	24 (0.2)	6 (0.1)
2007	296 (0.4)	282 (0.4)	271 (0.6)	259 (0.7)	37 (0.8)	246 (0.8)	283 (0.3)	38 (0.8)	246 (0.6)	285 (0.3)	38 (0.7)	29 (0.3)	71 (0.3)	39 (0.2)	32 (0.3)	25 (0.2)	7 (0.2)
2009	298 (0.5)	284 (0.5)	274 (0.7)	260 (0.7)	38 (0.8)	243 (0.9)	285 (0.3)	42 (0.9)	249 (0.5)	287 (0.3)	38 (0.6)	27 (0.3)	73 (0.3)	39 (0.2)	34 (0.3)	26 (0.3)	8 (0.2)
2011	300 (0.5)	287 (0.5)	276 (0.7)	264 (0.7)	36 (0.9)	244 (1.0)	286 (0.2)	42 (1.0)	250 (0.6)	288 (0.2)	38 (0.7)	27 (0.2)	73 (0.2)	39 (0.3)	35 (0.2)	26 (0.2)	8 (0.2)
2013	301 (0.5)	289 (0.5)	277 (0.4)	265 (0.6)	36 (0.8)	246 (0.8)	287 (0.3)	41 (0.8)	249 (0.5)	289 (0.3)	40 (0.6)	26 (0.3)	74 (0.3)	38 (0.3)	35 (0.3)	27 (0.2)	9 (0.2)
2015	301 (0.6)	287 (0.5)	276 (0.7)	264 (0.7)	38 (1.0)	246 (0.8)	284 (0.3)	38 (0.8)	247 (0.5)	287 (0.3)	40 (0.6)	29 (0.3)	71 (0.3)	38 (0.3)	33 (0.3)	25 (0.3)	8 (0.2)
2017[7]	302 (0.7)	287 (0.6)	275 (0.6)	262 (0.5)	39 (0.9)	246 (0.8)	285 (0.3)	40 (0.9)	247 (0.5)	288 (0.3)	41 (0.6)	30 (0.3)	70 (0.3)	36 (0.3)	34 (0.3)	24 (0.3)	10 (0.2)
2019[7]	301 (0.6)	287 (0.5)	276 (0.6)	265 (1.3)	36 (1.4)	243 (0.9)	285 (0.3)	42 (1.0)	247 (0.5)	287 (0.3)	40 (0.5)	31 (0.3)	69 (0.3)	35 (0.3)	34 (0.3)	24 (0.3)	10 (0.2)
Grade 12																	
1990[6]	[8] (†)	[8] (†)	[8] (†)	[8] (†)	[8] (†)	[8] (†)	[8] (†)	[8] (†)	[8] (†)	[8] (†)	[8] (†)	[8] (†)	[8] (†)	[8] (†)	[8] (†)	[8] (†)	[8] (†)
1992[6]	[8] (†)	[8] (†)	[8] (†)	[8] (†)	[8] (†)	[8] (†)	[8] (†)	[8] (†)	[8] (†)	[8] (†)	[8] (†)	[8] (†)	[8] (†)	[8] (†)	[8] (†)	[8] (†)	[8] (†)
1996	[8] (†)	[8] (†)	[8] (†)	[8] (†)	[8] (†)	[8] (†)	[8] (†)	[8] (†)	[8] (†)	[8] (†)	[8] (†)	[8] (†)	[8] (†)	[8] (†)	[8] (†)	[8] (†)	[8] (†)
2000	[8] (†)	[8] (†)	[8] (†)	[8] (†)	[8] (†)	[8] (†)	[8] (†)	[8] (†)	[8] (†)	[8] (†)	[8] (†)	[8] (†)	[8] (†)	[8] (†)	[8] (†)	[8] (†)	[8] (†)
2003	--- (†)	--- (†)	--- (†)	--- (†)	--- (†)	--- (†)	--- (†)	--- (†)	--- (†)	--- (†)	--- (†)	--- (†)	--- (†)	--- (†)	--- (†)	--- (†)	--- (†)
2005	158 (1.0)	147 (1.0)	136 (1.3)	122 (2.7)	36 (2.8)	120 (2.5)	151 (0.6)	31 (2.5)	114 (1.8)	153 (0.6)	39 (1.9)	39 (0.8)	61 (0.8)	38 (0.6)	23 (0.7)	21 (0.6)	2 (0.2)
2007	--- (†)	--- (†)	--- (†)	--- (†)	--- (†)	--- (†)	--- (†)	--- (†)	--- (†)	--- (†)	--- (†)	--- (†)	--- (†)	--- (†)	--- (†)	--- (†)	--- (†)
2009	166 (1.3)	150 (0.7)	140 (1.2)	130 (1.7)	36 (2.1)	117 (1.7)	154 (0.7)	38 (1.9)	120 (1.2)	156 (0.7)	36 (1.4)	36 (0.8)	64 (0.8)	38 (0.5)	26 (0.8)	23 (0.6)	3 (0.3)
2011	--- (†)	--- (†)	--- (†)	--- (†)	--- (†)	--- (†)	--- (†)	--- (†)	--- (†)	--- (†)	--- (†)	--- (†)	--- (†)	--- (†)	--- (†)	--- (†)	--- (†)
2013	169 (1.0)	155 (0.6)	143 (1.0)	134 (1.2)	35 (1.6)	109 (1.7)	155 (0.5)	46 (1.8)	119 (1.0)	157 (0.5)	38 (1.2)	35 (0.7)	65 (0.7)	39 (0.5)	26 (0.6)	23 (0.5)	3 (0.2)
2015	164 (1.2)	154 (1.0)	145 (1.2)	129 (1.4)	36 (1.8)	115 (2.5)	153 (0.6)	37 (2.5)	118 (1.6)	155 (0.5)	37 (1.7)	38 (0.8)	62 (0.8)	37 (0.7)	25 (0.7)	22 (0.6)	3 (0.2)
2017	--- (†)	--- (†)	--- (†)	--- (†)	--- (†)	--- (†)	--- (†)	--- (†)	--- (†)	--- (†)	--- (†)	--- (†)	--- (†)	--- (†)	--- (†)	--- (†)	--- (†)
2019[7]	167 (1.1)	153 (0.7)	143 (1.0)	133 (1.1)	35 (1.6)	111 (1.5)	152 (0.4)	41 (1.5)	119 (1.1)	154 (0.4)	35 (1.2)	40 (0.5)	60 (0.5)	35 (0.5)	24 (0.5)	21 (0.4)	3 (0.2)

—Not available.

†Not applicable.

‡Reporting standards not met. Either there are too few cases for a reliable estimate or the coefficient of variation (CV) is 50 percent or greater.

[1] In addition to students with an Individualized Education Program (IEP), also includes students with a 504 plan.

[2] For the grade 4 and grade 8 assessments, the scale ranges from 0 to 500. For the grade 12 assessment, the scale ranges from 0 to 300.

[3] *NAEP Basic* denotes partial mastery of the knowledge and skills that are fundamental for proficient work at a given grade.

[4] *NAEP Proficient* represents solid academic performance. Students reaching this level have demonstrated competency over challenging subject matter.

[5] *NAEP Advanced* signifies superior performance.

[6] Accommodations were not permitted for this assessment.

[7] The nonresponse rate for free or reduced-price lunch was greater than 15 percent but not greater than 50 percent.

[8] Because of major changes to the framework and content of the grade 12 assessment, results from 2005 and later assessment years cannot be compared with results from earlier assessment years. Therefore, this table does not include results from the earlier grade 12 assessment years (1990, 1992, 1996, and 2000). For data pertaining to comparisons between earlier years, see the Digest of Education Statistics 2009, table 138 (https://nces.ed.gov/programs/digest/d09/tables/dt09_138.asp).

NOTE: Includes public, private, Bureau of Indian Education, and Department of Defense Education Activity schools. For 1996 and later years, includes students tested with accommodations (3 to 14 percent of all students, depending on grade level and year); excludes only those students with disabilities and English language learners who were unable to be tested even with accommodations (1 to 4 percent of all students).

SOURCE: U.S. Department of Education, National Center for Education Statistics, National Assessment of Educational Progress (NAEP), 1990, 1992, 1996, 2000, 2003, 2005, 2007, 2009, 2011, 2013, 2015, 2017, and 2019 Mathematics Assessments, retrieved November 9, 2020, from the Main NAEP Data Explorer (https://www.nationsreportcard.gov/ndecore/xplore/NDE). (This table was prepared November 2020.)

Table 222.20. Percentage of students at or above selected National Assessment of Educational Progress (NAEP) mathematics achievement levels, by grade and selected student characteristics: Selected years, 2005 through 2019

[Standard errors appear in parentheses]

Grade and selected student characteristic	2005		2007		2009		2011		2013		2015		2017		2019	
	At or above *NAEP Basic*[1]	At or above *NAEP Proficient*[2]	At or above *NAEP Basic*[1]	At or above *NAEP Proficient*[2]	At or above *NAEP Basic*[1]	At or above *NAEP Proficient*[2]	At or above *NAEP Basic*[1]	At or above *NAEP Proficient*[2]	At or above *NAEP Basic*[1]	At or above *NAEP Proficient*[2]	At or above *NAEP Basic*[1]	At or above *NAEP Proficient*[2]	At or above *NAEP Basic*[1]	At or above *NAEP Proficient*[2]	At or above *NAEP Basic*[1]	At or above *NAEP Proficient*[2]
1	2	3	4	5	6	7	8	9	10	11	12	13	14	15	16	17
4th grade, all students	**80 (0.2)**	**36 (0.2)**	**82 (0.2)**	**39 (0.3)**	**82 (0.3)**	**39 (0.3)**	**82 (0.2)**	**40 (0.3)**	**83 (0.2)**	**42 (0.3)**	**82 (0.3)**	**40 (0.4)**	**80 (0.3)**	**40 (0.4)**	**81 (0.2)**	**41 (0.3)**
Sex																
Male	81 (0.2)	38 (0.2)	82 (0.2)	41 (0.3)	82 (0.3)	41 (0.4)	83 (0.3)	42 (0.4)	82 (0.3)	43 (0.4)	82 (0.4)	42 (0.5)	80 (0.4)	42 (0.4)	81 (0.3)	44 (0.4)
Female	80 (0.2)	34 (0.3)	82 (0.2)	37 (0.4)	82 (0.3)	37 (0.4)	82 (0.3)	39 (0.4)	83 (0.2)	41 (0.4)	82 (0.3)	38 (0.5)	80 (0.3)	38 (0.4)	80 (0.3)	38 (0.4)
Race/ethnicity																
White	90 (0.2)	47 (0.2)	91 (0.2)	51 (0.4)	91 (0.2)	51 (0.4)	91 (0.2)	52 (0.4)	91 (0.2)	54 (0.4)	90 (0.3)	51 (0.5)	88 (0.3)	51 (0.4)	89 (0.3)	52 (0.4)
Black	60 (0.5)	13 (0.3)	64 (0.6)	15 (0.4)	64 (0.6)	16 (0.5)	66 (0.6)	17 (0.5)	66 (0.6)	18 (0.5)	65 (0.7)	19 (0.6)	63 (0.8)	19 (0.6)	65 (0.7)	20 (0.5)
Hispanic	68 (0.5)	19 (0.3)	70 (0.5)	22 (0.4)	71 (0.7)	22 (0.4)	72 (0.5)	24 (0.5)	73 (0.7)	26 (0.6)	73 (0.6)	26 (0.7)	71 (0.5)	26 (0.6)	73 (0.5)	28 (0.6)
Asian/Pacific Islander	90 (0.5)	55 (1.1)	91 (0.7)	58 (1.3)	92 (0.6)	60 (1.5)	91 (0.6)	62 (1.6)	91 (0.6)	64 (1.2)	91 (0.8)	62 (1.7)	90 (0.8)	64 (1.4)	91 (0.9)	66 (1.4)
Asian	— (†)	— (†)	— (†)	— (†)	— (†)	— (†)	93 (0.5)	64 (1.6)	92 (0.6)	66 (1.2)	93 (0.7)	65 (1.7)	92 (0.7)	67 (1.4)	93 (0.6)	69 (1.2)
Pacific Islander	— (†)	— (†)	— (†)	— (†)	— (†)	— (†)	77 (2.7)	34 (3.2)	77 (3.1)	33 (3.2)	68 (4.0)	30 (2.8)	71 (3.7)	29 (3.5)	64 (5.5)	28 (4.7)
American Indian/Alaska Native	68 (1.5)	21 (1.2)	70 (1.2)	25 (1.1)	66 (1.6)	21 (1.2)	66 (1.2)	22 (1.2)	68 (1.7)	23 (1.4)	69 (1.8)	23 (1.7)	69 (2.0)	24 (1.9)	67 (1.9)	24 (1.8)
Two or more races	— (†)	— (†)	— (†)	— (†)	— (†)	— (†)	87 (0.7)	45 (1.2)	85 (1.0)	46 (1.4)	86 (0.9)	45 (1.3)	85 (0.9)	45 (1.3)	84 (0.9)	44 (1.2)
Eligibility for free or reduced-price lunch																
Eligible	67 (0.3)	19 (0.2)	70 (0.4)	22 (0.3)	70 (0.4)	22 (0.3)	72 (0.3)	24 (0.3)	73 (0.4)	25 (0.4)	72 (0.4)	24 (0.4)	69 (0.4)	25 (0.3)	71 (0.3)	26 (0.4)
Not eligible	90 (0.2)	49 (0.3)	91 (0.2)	53 (0.4)	91 (0.3)	54 (0.4)	92 (0.2)	57 (0.4)	93 (0.2)	59 (0.4)	92 (0.3)	58 (0.6)	91 (0.3)	57 (0.5)	91 (0.2)	58 (0.4)
Unknown	87 (0.7)	45 (1.2)	90 (0.9)	48 (1.5)	88 (1.3)	47 (1.7)	90 (0.8)	52 (1.4)	90 (1.0)	52 (2.2)	89 (1.2)	50 (1.7)	87 (1.1)	49 (1.7)	88 (1.2)	48 (1.7)
8th grade, all students	**69 (0.2)**	**30 (0.2)**	**71 (0.3)**	**32 (0.3)**	**73 (0.3)**	**34 (0.3)**	**73 (0.2)**	**35 (0.2)**	**74 (0.3)**	**35 (0.3)**	**71 (0.3)**	**33 (0.3)**	**70 (0.3)**	**34 (0.3)**	**69 (0.3)**	**34 (0.3)**
Sex																
Male	70 (0.3)	31 (0.3)	72 (0.3)	34 (0.4)	73 (0.3)	36 (0.4)	73 (0.4)	36 (0.3)	74 (0.3)	36 (0.4)	71 (0.4)	34 (0.4)	70 (0.3)	35 (0.4)	68 (0.3)	34 (0.4)
Female	69 (0.3)	28 (0.3)	71 (0.3)	30 (0.3)	72 (0.4)	32 (0.4)	73 (0.2)	34 (0.3)	74 (0.4)	35 (0.4)	72 (0.4)	33 (0.4)	70 (0.3)	33 (0.5)	70 (0.4)	33 (0.4)
Race/ethnicity																
White	80 (0.2)	39 (0.3)	82 (0.3)	42 (0.3)	83 (0.3)	44 (0.4)	84 (0.3)	44 (0.3)	84 (0.2)	45 (0.4)	82 (0.3)	43 (0.4)	80 (0.3)	44 (0.4)	80 (0.3)	44 (0.4)
Black	42 (0.5)	9 (0.3)	47 (0.7)	11 (0.3)	50 (0.6)	12 (0.5)	51 (0.6)	13 (0.4)	52 (0.7)	14 (0.5)	48 (0.9)	13 (0.5)	47 (0.7)	13 (0.5)	47 (0.6)	14 (0.4)
Hispanic	52 (0.6)	13 (0.4)	55 (0.7)	15 (0.4)	57 (0.8)	17 (0.6)	61 (0.7)	20 (0.6)	62 (0.6)	21 (0.5)	60 (0.7)	19 (0.6)	57 (0.7)	20 (0.5)	57 (0.7)	20 (0.5)
Asian/Pacific Islander	81 (0.8)	47 (1.2)	83 (0.8)	50 (1.1)	85 (1.0)	54 (1.8)	86 (1.0)	55 (1.2)	87 (0.8)	60 (1.3)	87 (0.9)	59 (1.7)	87 (0.9)	62 (1.5)	86 (0.8)	62 (1.4)
Asian	— (†)	— (†)	— (†)	— (†)	— (†)	— (†)	88 (0.9)	58 (1.3)	89 (0.8)	63 (1.3)	88 (0.9)	61 (1.7)	88 (0.9)	64 (1.6)	88 (0.8)	64 (1.4)
Pacific Islander	— (†)	— (†)	— (†)	— (†)	— (†)	— (†)	59 (4.7)	22 (1.9)	67 (3.5)	24 (2.9)	63 (4.2)	29 (3.9)	64 (2.8)	25 (3.3)	55 (3.1)	21 (3.6)
American Indian/Alaska Native	53 (1.3)	14 (1.2)	53 (1.8)	16 (1.2)	56 (1.5)	18 (1.3)	55 (1.5)	17 (1.2)	59 (1.7)	21 (1.5)	57 (1.8)	20 (1.7)	56 (1.6)	18 (1.8)	51 (1.6)	15 (1.4)
Two or more races	— (†)	— (†)	— (†)	— (†)	— (†)	— (†)	78 (1.1)	39 (1.7)	76 (1.2)	38 (1.4)	74 (1.5)	36 (1.3)	73 (1.3)	37 (1.4)	73 (1.2)	38 (1.4)
Eligibility for free or reduced-price lunch																
Eligible	51 (0.4)	13 (0.2)	55 (0.5)	15 (0.3)	57 (0.5)	17 (0.3)	59 (0.4)	19 (0.3)	60 (0.4)	20 (0.3)	58 (0.4)	18 (0.3)	55 (0.4)	18 (0.3)	54 (0.4)	18 (0.3)
Not eligible	79 (0.2)	39 (0.3)	81 (0.3)	42 (0.4)	83 (0.3)	45 (0.4)	84 (0.2)	47 (0.4)	86 (0.3)	49 (0.4)	84 (0.3)	48 (0.5)	82 (0.3)	48 (0.4)	82 (0.3)	48 (0.5)
Unknown	79 (1.1)	40 (1.4)	81 (1.7)	43 (1.7)	83 (1.3)	48 (1.9)	85 (0.9)	48 (1.5)	84 (1.3)	50 (2.6)	81 (1.5)	46 (1.9)	83 (1.1)	47 (1.8)	80 (1.2)	45 (1.8)
12th grade, all students	**61 (0.8)**	**23 (0.7)**	**— (†)**	**— (†)**	**64 (0.8)**	**26 (0.8)**	**— (†)**	**— (†)**	**65 (0.7)**	**26 (0.6)**	**62 (0.8)**	**25 (0.7)**	**— (†)**	**— (†)**	**— (†)**	**— (†)**
Sex																
Male	62 (0.9)	25 (1.0)	— (†)	— (†)	65 (0.9)	28 (1.0)	— (†)	— (†)	66 (0.8)	28 (0.8)	63 (1.0)	26 (0.7)	— (†)	— (†)	— (†)	— (†)
Female	60 (1.0)	21 (0.8)	— (†)	— (†)	63 (0.8)	24 (0.8)	— (†)	— (†)	64 (0.9)	24 (0.7)	61 (0.9)	23 (0.7)	— (†)	— (†)	— (†)	— (†)
Race/ethnicity																
White	70 (0.8)	29 (0.8)	— (†)	— (†)	75 (0.7)	33 (0.8)	— (†)	— (†)	75 (0.8)	33 (0.8)	73 (0.9)	32 (0.9)	— (†)	— (†)	— (†)	— (†)
Black	30 (1.7)	6 (0.8)	— (†)	— (†)	37 (1.2)	6 (0.6)	— (†)	— (†)	38 (1.5)	7 (0.6)	36 (1.6)	7 (0.7)	— (†)	— (†)	— (†)	— (†)
Hispanic	40 (2.1)	8 (1.0)	— (†)	— (†)	45 (1.1)	11 (0.8)	— (†)	— (†)	50 (1.3)	12 (0.7)	47 (1.3)	12 (0.7)	— (†)	— (†)	— (†)	— (†)
Asian/Pacific Islander	73 (2.6)	36 (3.0)	— (†)	— (†)	84 (1.9)	52 (3.4)	— (†)	— (†)	81 (1.4)	47 (2.0)	78 (2.1)	46 (2.6)	— (†)	— (†)	— (†)	— (†)
Asian	— (†)	— (†)	— (†)	— (†)	— (†)	— (†)	— (†)	— (†)	83 (1.5)	49 (2.0)	79 (2.0)	47 (2.5)	— (†)	— (†)	— (†)	— (†)
Pacific Islander	— (†)	— (†)	— (†)	— (†)	— (†)	— (†)	— (†)	— (†)	65 (7.3)	16 (6.0)	‡ (†)	‡ (†)	— (†)	— (†)	— (†)	— (†)
American Indian/Alaska Native	42 (8.6)	6 (2.9)	— (†)	— (†)	56 (5.4)	12 (3.3)	— (†)	— (†)	54 (5.8)	12 (4.0)	46 (4.6)	10 (3.3)	— (†)	— (†)	— (†)	— (†)
Two or more races	— (†)	— (†)	— (†)	— (†)	— (†)	— (†)	— (†)	— (†)	67 (3.0)	26 (2.7)	67 (3.2)	31 (3.1)	— (†)	— (†)	— (†)	— (†)

—Not available.
†Not applicable.
‡Reporting standards not met (too few cases for a reliable estimate).
[1]*NAEP Basic* denotes partial mastery of the knowledge and skills that are fundamental for proficient work at a given grade.
[2]*NAEP Proficient* represents solid academic performance. Students reaching this level have demonstrated competency over challenging subject matter.
NOTE: Includes public, private, Bureau of Indian Education, and Department of Defense Education Activity schools. Includes students tested with accommodations (3 to 14 percent of all students, depending on grade level and year); excludes only those students with disabilities and English language learners who were unable to be tested even with accommodations (1 to 4 percent of all students). Race categories exclude persons of Hispanic ethnicity. Prior to 2011, separate data for Asian students, Pacific Islander students, and students of Two or more races were not collected.
SOURCE: U.S. Department of Education, National Center for Education Statistics, National Assessment of Educational Progress (NAEP), 2005, 2007, 2009, 2011, 2013, 2015, 2017, and 2019 Mathematics Assessments, retrieved November 8, 2019, from the Main NAEP Data Explorer (https://nces.ed.gov/nationsreportcard/naepdata/). (This table was prepared November 2019.)

Table 222.32. Average National Assessment of Educational Progress (NAEP) mathematics scale score and percentage distribution of 4th- and 8th-graders in traditional public, public charter, and private schools, by selected characteristics: 2017

[Standard errors appear in parentheses]

Selected characteristic	Public schools, grade 4			Public schools, grade 8			Private schools, grade 4[1]	Private schools, grade 8[1]
	Total	Traditional public	Public charter	Total	Traditional public	Public charter		
1	2	3	4	5	6	7	8	9
	Average scale score[2]							
All students	**239 (0.2)**	**239 (0.2)**	**236 (1.6)**	**282 (0.3)**	**282 (0.3)**	**282 (1.9)**	**246 (0.9)**	**293 (1.3)**
Sex								
Male	240 (0.3)	240 (0.3)	238 (1.6)	282 (0.3)	282 (0.3)	282 (2.1)	248 (1.2)	295 (1.6)
Female	238 (0.2)	238 (0.3)	234 (1.8)	282 (0.3)	282 (0.4)	282 (2.1)	245 (1.2)	291 (1.5)
Race/ethnicity								
White	248 (0.2)	248 (0.2)	250 (1.6)	292 (0.3)	292 (0.3)	299 (2.2)	251 (0.9)	297 (1.4)
Black	223 (0.5)	223 (0.5)	224 (2.0)	260 (0.5)	259 (0.5)	262 (1.7)	226 (2.3)	273 (3.7)
Hispanic	229 (0.4)	229 (0.5)	231 (4.1)	268 (0.5)	268 (0.5)	276 (2.8)	234 (2.1)	281 (2.4)
Asian	260 (1.1)	261 (1.1)	254 (4.8)	312 (1.5)	312 (1.6)	308 (4.8)	258 (2.4)	310 (4.4)
Pacific Islander	228 (2.6)	228 (2.7)	‡ (†)	272 (2.1)	271 (2.3)	293 (6.0)	‡ (†)	‡ (†)
American Indian/Alaska Native	228 (1.3)	228 (1.3)	231 (12.3)	268 (1.5)	268 (1.5)	‡ (†)	‡ (†)	‡ (†)
Two or more races	244 (0.8)	244 (0.8)	239 (3.3)	285 (1.1)	285 (1.3)	294 (6.6)	253 (3.2)	302 (3.7)
English language learner (ELL) status								
ELL	217 (0.7)	216 (0.7)	219 (5.3)	245 (0.8)	245 (0.8)	253 (5.2)	216 (4.3)	‡ (†)
Non-ELL	242 (0.2)	242 (0.3)	238 (1.4)	284 (0.3)	284 (0.3)	284 (1.9)	247 (0.9)	294 (1.3)
Disability status[3]								
Identified as student with disability (SD)	214 (0.4)	214 (0.4)	209 (2.4)	246 (0.4)	246 (0.5)	248 (2.6)	222 (4.0)	263 (5.5)
Not identified as SD	243 (0.3)	243 (0.3)	240 (1.5)	287 (0.3)	287 (0.3)	287 (1.9)	247 (0.9)	296 (1.3)
Percent of students in school eligible for free or reduced-price lunch								
0 to 25 percent eligible	257 (0.6)	257 (0.6)	256 (2.4)	302 (0.7)	302 (0.8)	309 (3.7)	252 (1.9)	295 (2.2)
26 to 50 percent eligible	245 (0.4)	245 (0.4)	243 (1.4)	287 (0.6)	287 (0.5)	291 (4.8)	241 (2.6)	276 (4.9)
51 to 75 percent eligible	236 (0.5)	236 (0.5)	235 (2.4)	275 (0.6)	275 (0.6)	277 (2.2)	‡ (†)	‡ (†)
76 to 100 percent eligible	225 (0.5)	225 (0.5)	223 (2.8)	262 (0.5)	262 (0.6)	265 (2.2)	215 (3.0)	268 (5.4)
School locale								
City	234 (0.5)	234 (0.5)	231 (2.1)	277 (0.5)	277 (0.6)	274 (2.1)	247 (1.5)	292 (1.8)
Suburban	243 (0.4)	243 (0.4)	240 (3.4)	287 (0.4)	287 (0.5)	292 (3.8)	248 (1.7)	296 (1.8)
Town	237 (0.7)	237 (0.7)	231 (5.2)	278 (0.8)	277 (0.7)	295 (4.2)	245 (2.5)	288 (3.5)
Rural	240 (0.6)	240 (0.6)	250 (3.4)	282 (0.6)	282 (0.6)	284 (4.6)	241 (3.1)	288 (5.1)
	Percentage distribution							
All students	**100 (†)**	**100 (†)**	**100 (†)**	**100 (†)**	**100 (†)**	**100 (†)**	**100 (†)**	**100 (†)**
Sex								
Male	51 (0.1)	51 (0.1)	50 (0.8)	51 (0.1)	51 (0.1)	50 (1.0)	49 (1.3)	49 (1.3)
Female	49 (0.1)	49 (0.1)	50 (0.8)	49 (0.1)	49 (0.1)	50 (1.0)	51 (1.3)	51 (1.3)
Race/ethnicity								
White	47 (0.3)	48 (0.3)	33 (2.7)	50 (0.3)	51 (0.3)	32 (2.8)	62 (1.8)	67 (1.8)
Black	15 (0.2)	15 (0.2)	32 (2.9)	15 (0.3)	14 (0.3)	27 (2.4)	10 (1.3)	10 (1.3)
Hispanic	27 (0.3)	27 (0.3)	26 (3.5)	25 (0.3)	25 (0.3)	32 (2.8)	16 (1.4)	13 (1.0)
Asian	5 (0.3)	5 (0.3)	5 (0.9)	5 (0.2)	5 (0.2)	6 (0.8)	7 (0.8)	6 (0.9)
Pacific Islander	# (†)	# (†)	# (†)	# (†)	# (†)	1 (0.1)	# (†)	# (†)
American Indian/Alaska Native	1 (#)	1 (#)	1 (0.3)	1 (#)	1 (#)	# (†)	# (†)	1 (0.3)
Two or more races	4 (0.1)	4 (0.1)	4 (0.6)	3 (0.1)	3 (0.1)	2 (0.5)	5 (0.5)	4 (0.6)
English language learner (ELL) status								
ELL	12 (0.2)	12 (0.2)	11 (2.1)	6 (0.2)	6 (0.2)	8 (1.1)	2 (0.5)	1 (0.4)
Non-ELL	88 (0.2)	88 (0.2)	89 (2.1)	94 (0.2)	94 (0.2)	92 (1.1)	98 (0.5)	99 (0.4)
Disability status[3]								
Identified as student with disability (SD)	13 (0.1)	13 (0.1)	12 (0.8)	13 (0.1)	13 (0.1)	12 (0.7)	5 (0.5)	7 (0.9)
Not identified as SD	87 (0.1)	87 (0.1)	88 (0.8)	87 (0.1)	87 (0.1)	88 (0.7)	95 (0.5)	93 (0.9)
Percent of students in school eligible for free or reduced-price lunch								
0 to 25 percent eligible	19 (0.7)	20 (0.7)	13 (2.5)	22 (0.8)	22 (0.8)	17 (4.5)	55 (5.2)	65 (5.8)
26 to 50 percent eligible	24 (0.9)	24 (0.9)	20 (5.3)	30 (0.8)	30 (0.9)	23 (4.9)	24 (4.7)	17 (4.7)
51 to 75 percent eligible	24 (0.8)	24 (0.8)	18 (3.8)	24 (0.8)	24 (0.8)	15 (2.8)	6 (2.7)	2 (1.5)
76 to 100 percent eligible	33 (0.8)	33 (0.8)	49 (5.5)	25 (0.6)	24 (0.7)	45 (5.0)	15 (4.4)	16 (4.3)
School locale								
City	30 (0.3)	29 (0.4)	53 (4.5)	29 (0.3)	27 (0.4)	53 (4.2)	40 (1.8)	40 (1.6)
Suburban	40 (0.4)	40 (0.4)	34 (4.2)	41 (0.3)	41 (0.5)	32 (3.9)	42 (1.9)	41 (2.2)
Town	11 (0.3)	11 (0.3)	3 (1.0)	11 (0.4)	12 (0.3)	6 (2.9)	8 (1.0)	8 (1.6)
Rural	19 (0.4)	19 (0.4)	11 (2.4)	19 (0.3)	20 (0.3)	10 (2.2)	10 (1.2)	10 (1.1)

† Not applicable.

Rounds to zero.

‡ Reporting standards not met (too few cases for a reliable estimate).

[1] Results are for private schools overall, including Catholic and other (non-Catholic) private schools. In the 2017 NAEP Nations Report Card, results for private schools overall and for non-Catholic private schools were suppressed because these schools did not meet NAEP statistical and reporting standards requiring a school response rate of at least 70 percent. Response rates for private schools overall were 61 percent at grade 4 and 60 percent at grade 8. (Within the private school sector, response rates for Catholic schools were 89 percent at grade 4 and 86 percent at grade 8, while response rates for non-Catholic private schools were 41 percent at grade 4 and 39 percent at grade 8.) Please interpret these data with caution.

[2] Scale ranges from 0 to 500.

[3] The student with disability (SD) variable used in this table includes students who have a 504 plan, even if they do not have an Individualized Education Plan (IEP).

NOTE: Includes students tested with accommodations (12 percent of all 4th-graders and 12 percent of all 8th-graders); excludes only those students with disabilities and English language learners who were unable to be tested even with accommodations (2 percent of all students at both grades). Race categories exclude persons of Hispanic ethnicity. Detail may not sum to totals because of rounding.

SOURCE: U.S. Department of Education, National Center for Education Statistics, National Assessment of Educational Progress (NAEP), 2017 Mathematics Assessment, retrieved January 8, 2018, from the Main NAEP Data Explorer (http://nces.ed.gov/nationsreportcard/naepdata/); and unpublished tabulations. (This table was prepared May 2018.)

Table 222.35. Average National Assessment of Educational Progress (NAEP) mathematics scale score and percentage distribution of 12th-graders, by frequency of experiencing various attitudes in math class and selected student characteristics: 2015

[Standard errors appear in parentheses]

Student characteristic	Math work is engaging and interesting				Math work is challenging				Math work is too easy			
	Never or hardly ever	Sometimes	Often	Always/ almost always	Never or hardly ever	Sometimes	Often	Always/ almost always	Never or hardly ever	Sometimes	Often	Always/ almost always
1	2	3	4	5	6	7	8	9	10	11	12	13
	Average scale score[1]											
All students	**143 (0.9)**	**152 (0.8)**	**162 (0.9)**	**165 (1.7)**	**155 (1.5)**	**153 (0.9)**	**156 (0.9)**	**152 (1.1)**	**154 (0.8)**	**153 (0.9)**	**156 (1.4)**	**158 (1.9)**
Sex												
Male	146 (1.2)	152 (1.1)	163 (1.1)	169 (2.2)	158 (1.8)	156 (1.2)	157 (1.2)	155 (1.8)	157 (1.1)	154 (1.1)	159 (1.4)	161 (2.0)
Female	140 (1.2)	152 (0.8)	162 (1.1)	161 (2.2)	150 (2.4)	150 (1.0)	155 (1.1)	151 (1.3)	153 (1.0)	152 (1.0)	152 (1.7)	152 (2.6)
Race/ethnicity												
White	150 (1.2)	161 (0.9)	173 (1.1)	178 (2.1)	161 (1.9)	162 (1.1)	165 (1.0)	164 (1.3)	162 (1.1)	164 (1.1)	166 (1.4)	164 (2.2)
Black	126 (2.0)	130 (1.6)	135 (1.8)	136 (3.6)	133 (3.6)	130 (1.5)	132 (2.0)	131 (2.4)	135 (2.1)	128 (1.5)	132 (2.4)	135 (3.7)
Hispanic	131 (1.6)	140 (1.4)	145 (1.2)	151 (2.5)	139 (3.5)	142 (1.3)	142 (1.4)	137 (1.8)	140 (1.6)	139 (1.2)	145 (1.7)	146 (3.5)
Asian	158 (3.8)	169 (3.5)	184 (2.1)	184 (4.1)	‡ (†)	173 (3.7)	177 (3.0)	172 (4.7)	178 (2.9)	174 (3.1)	171 (4.4)	‡ (†)
Pacific Islander	‡ (†)	‡ (†)	‡ (†)	‡ (†)	‡ (†)	‡ (†)	‡ (†)	‡ (†)	‡ (†)	‡ (†)	‡ (†)	‡ (†)
American Indian/Alaska Native	‡ (†)	‡ (†)	‡ (†)	‡ (†)	‡ (†)	‡ (†)	‡ (†)	‡ (†)	‡ (†)	‡ (†)	‡ (†)	‡ (†)
Two or more races	149 (4.1)	160 (3.9)	‡ (†)	‡ (†)	‡ (†)	166 (4.4)	159 (3.7)	‡ (†)	159 (3.4)	159 (3.3)	‡ (†)	‡ (†)
Eligibility for free or reduced-price lunch												
Eligible	130 (1.4)	137 (1.1)	144 (1.4)	147 (2.3)	139 (2.4)	140 (1.1)	139 (1.4)	134 (1.4)	137 (1.2)	137 (0.9)	143 (1.5)	144 (2.6)
Not eligible	150 (1.1)	161 (0.9)	172 (1.2)	178 (2.4)	161 (1.9)	161 (1.2)	165 (1.1)	162 (1.4)	161 (1.2)	164 (1.2)	164 (1.6)	166 (2.7)
Unknown	158 (3.7)	166 (2.3)	181 (2.4)	185 (4.5)	‡ (†)	172 (2.6)	170 (2.9)	172 (2.6)	170 (2.1)	169 (3.5)	177 (4.3)	‡ (†)
Highest education level of either parent[2]												
Did not finish high school	128 (1.7)	134 (1.8)	141 (1.9)	136 (5.0)	‡ (†)	135 (1.7)	136 (2.4)	130 (2.1)	135 (1.8)	133 (1.8)	139 (2.1)	‡ (†)
Graduated high school	130 (1.8)	139 (1.7)	146 (2.0)	151 (3.1)	145 (3.9)	141 (1.6)	141 (1.4)	137 (2.4)	140 (1.9)	139 (1.2)	142 (2.2)	148 (3.9)
Some education after high school	141 (1.5)	150 (1.2)	158 (1.6)	159 (2.7)	153 (2.9)	150 (1.4)	152 (1.4)	149 (1.9)	148 (1.6)	150 (1.3)	155 (1.7)	156 (2.8)
Graduated college	153 (1.3)	163 (0.9)	174 (1.1)	180 (2.0)	166 (2.1)	164 (1.2)	167 (1.1)	165 (1.4)	165 (1.0)	165 (1.2)	167 (1.7)	169 (2.4)
	Percentage distribution of students											
All students	**25 (0.5)**	**36 (0.5)**	**28 (0.5)**	**12 (0.4)**	**7 (0.3)**	**35 (0.6)**	**37 (0.6)**	**20 (0.5)**	**31 (0.6)**	**48 (0.5)**	**16 (0.4)**	**6 (0.3)**
Sex												
Male	24 (0.6)	34 (0.6)	30 (0.7)	13 (0.6)	8 (0.4)	37 (0.6)	38 (0.7)	18 (0.6)	26 (0.7)	49 (0.7)	18 (0.5)	7 (0.5)
Female	26 (0.7)	38 (0.8)	26 (0.6)	11 (0.5)	6 (0.4)	34 (0.9)	36 (0.8)	23 (0.7)	35 (0.9)	46 (0.8)	13 (0.6)	5 (0.3)
Race/ethnicity												
White	26 (0.7)	35 (0.7)	28 (0.7)	11 (0.5)	8 (0.5)	35 (0.8)	38 (0.9)	19 (0.7)	33 (0.8)	46 (0.8)	15 (0.5)	6 (0.5)
Black	25 (1.2)	38 (1.3)	24 (1.1)	13 (0.9)	6 (0.7)	38 (1.3)	33 (1.1)	23 (1.0)	30 (1.2)	48 (1.3)	16 (1.0)	6 (0.6)
Hispanic	23 (0.9)	37 (1.0)	28 (0.9)	13 (0.8)	5 (0.5)	36 (1.0)	38 (1.1)	22 (0.9)	27 (1.1)	50 (1.0)	18 (1.1)	5 (0.5)
Asian	13 (1.4)	36 (1.7)	34 (1.9)	17 (1.7)	6 (1.1)	37 (2.2)	35 (2.7)	22 (1.8)	23 (2.4)	51 (2.9)	18 (2.6)	8 (1.4)
Pacific Islander	‡ (†)	‡ (†)	‡ (†)	‡ (†)	‡ (†)	‡ (†)	‡ (†)	‡ (†)	‡ (†)	‡ (†)	‡ (†)	‡ (†)
American Indian/Alaska Native	21 (5.5)	32 (5.3)	39 (6.5)	8 (3.4)	9 (4.3)	23 (4.6)	41 (4.8)	27 (8.0)	25 (4.3)	58 (4.7)	15 (3.2)	2 (1.5)
Two or more races	33 (3.0)	37 (3.1)	21 (2.2)	10 (2.1)	8 (1.7)	33 (3.9)	42 (4.0)	17 (2.6)	36 (4.1)	45 (3.8)	13 (2.8)	6 (1.5)
Eligibility for free or reduced-price lunch												
Eligible	24 (0.8)	36 (0.7)	26 (0.7)	13 (0.6)	6 (0.5)	39 (0.9)	35 (0.9)	20 (0.7)	26 (0.8)	51 (0.7)	17 (0.7)	6 (0.5)
Not eligible	25 (0.7)	36 (0.7)	28 (0.7)	11 (0.5)	8 (0.4)	34 (0.8)	38 (0.8)	20 (0.7)	33 (0.9)	46 (0.9)	15 (0.6)	6 (0.4)
Unknown	23 (1.8)	34 (2.2)	31 (1.7)	12 (1.3)	5 (0.9)	29 (1.5)	44 (1.6)	22 (1.4)	38 (2.0)	43 (1.9)	13 (1.5)	5 (0.8)
Highest education level of either parent[2]												
Did not finish high school	23 (1.5)	37 (1.7)	26 (1.5)	15 (1.4)	5 (0.8)	36 (1.9)	36 (1.8)	23 (1.6)	26 (1.4)	50 (1.7)	19 (1.5)	6 (0.8)
Graduated high school	24 (1.2)	37 (1.3)	27 (1.2)	12 (1.0)	8 (1.0)	38 (1.5)	35 (1.4)	19 (1.1)	26 (1.2)	50 (1.0)	17 (0.9)	7 (0.9)
Some education after high school	25 (1.2)	38 (1.3)	25 (1.2)	12 (0.8)	8 (0.7)	38 (1.0)	36 (1.0)	18 (0.9)	29 (1.1)	47 (1.3)	17 (0.9)	7 (0.7)
Graduated college	24 (0.7)	35 (0.7)	30 (0.8)	12 (0.6)	6 (0.3)	34 (0.7)	38 (0.7)	21 (0.6)	33 (0.9)	46 (0.9)	15 (0.6)	6 (0.3)

†Not applicable.

‡Reporting standards not met (too few cases for a reliable estimate).

[1] Scale ranges from 0 to 300.

[2] Based on student reports. The category of students whose parents have an unknown level of education is not shown, although data for these students is included in table totals.

NOTE: Includes public and private schools. Includes students tested with accommodations (9 percent of all 12th-grade students); excludes only those students with disabilities and English language learners who were unable to be tested even with accommodations (2 percent of all 12th-grade students). Race categories exclude persons of Hispanic ethnicity. Detail may not sum to totals because of rounding.

SOURCE: U.S. Department of Education, National Center for Education Statistics, National Assessment of Educational Progress (NAEP), 2015 Mathematics Assessment, retrieved August 15, 2016, from the Main NAEP Data Explorer (http://nces.ed.gov/nationsreportcard/naepdata/). (This table was prepared August 2016.)

Table 222.40. Average National Assessment of Educational Progress (NAEP) mathematics scale score of high school graduates at grade 12, by highest mathematics course taken in high school and selected student and school characteristics: 2009

[Standard errors appear in parentheses]

Selected student or school characteristic	Algebra I or below[1]		Geometry		Algebra II/ trigonometry		Analysis/ precalculus		Statistics/ probability		Advanced mathematics, other[2]		Calculus	
1	2		3		4		5		6		7		8	
Total[3]	**114**	**(1.1)**	**127**	**(1.0)**	**143**	**(0.6)**	**166**	**(0.9)**	**164**	**(1.8)**	**154**	**(1.3)**	**193**	**(1.2)**
Sex														
Male	117	(1.7)	128	(1.2)	145	(0.8)	169	(1.0)	165	(2.2)	156	(1.5)	197	(1.4)
Female	111	(1.6)	126	(1.1)	142	(0.8)	163	(1.0)	162	(2.0)	153	(1.4)	190	(1.2)
Race/ethnicity														
White	117	(1.6)	133	(1.3)	150	(0.8)	172	(0.9)	169	(1.5)	160	(1.3)	194	(1.1)
Black	104	(2.8)	114	(1.8)	129	(0.9)	147	(1.6)	139	(4.0)	138	(2.1)	170	(2.7)
Hispanic	109	(2.2)	122	(1.0)	136	(0.8)	155	(1.6)	154	(3.2)	142	(2.3)	179	(2.5)
Asian/Pacific Islander	‡	(†)	129	(3.9)	149	(4.1)	170	(2.3)	176	(4.1)	164	(2.9)	203	(1.8)
American Indian/Alaska Native	‡	(†)	‡	(†)	143	(3.8)	‡	(†)	‡	(†)	‡	(†)	‡	(†)
Student with disabilities (SD) status														
SD[4]	103	(1.7)	114	(2.5)	126	(2.1)	166	(5.0)	136	(6.3)	134	(3.5)	197	(3.7)
Non-SD	122	(1.2)	129	(0.9)	144	(0.6)	166	(0.9)	164	(1.7)	156	(1.3)	193	(1.2)
English language learner (ELL) status														
ELL	104	(4.5)	113	(2.8)	121	(2.1)	144	(6.1)	‡	(†)	129	(4.8)	‡	(†)
Non-ELL	114	(1.2)	128	(1.0)	144	(0.6)	166	(0.9)	164	(1.8)	155	(1.3)	193	(1.2)
School type														
Traditional public	114	(1.2)	127	(1.0)	143	(0.7)	166	(0.9)	164	(1.8)	155	(1.4)	193	(1.3)
Public charter	‡	(†)	‡	(†)	137	(10.3)	141	(6.8)	132	(1.6)	‡	(†)	‡	(†)
Private	‡	(†)	123	(3.3)	146	(3.3)	169	(2.7)	168	(3.9)	146	(4.0)	193	(3.3)
Percentage of students eligible for free or reduced-price lunch														
0–25 percent	116	(3.0)	134	(2.0)	151	(1.3)	173	(1.5)	173	(1.5)	162	(1.9)	199	(1.6)
26–50 percent	115	(1.5)	127	(1.4)	144	(1.0)	165	(1.1)	162	(2.9)	154	(1.7)	189	(1.0)
51–75 percent	111	(3.0)	123	(1.8)	136	(1.1)	156	(1.3)	149	(3.6)	146	(3.7)	179	(2.8)
76–100 percent	107	(5.4)	115	(3.1)	126	(2.0)	144	(3.7)	137	(4.1)	131	(2.6)	163	(3.9)
School locale														
City	110	(2.6)	125	(1.7)	140	(1.8)	163	(2.1)	163	(3.3)	151	(3.0)	195	(2.3)
Suburban	112	(2.3)	127	(1.9)	144	(1.0)	169	(1.4)	167	(2.4)	157	(2.0)	195	(2.0)
Town	114	(2.5)	129	(1.9)	144	(1.6)	166	(1.6)	164	(3.1)	152	(3.8)	191	(2.1)
Rural	117	(2.0)	129	(1.4)	145	(1.3)	165	(1.9)	157	(4.9)	155	(2.1)	187	(2.0)

†Not applicable.

‡Reporting standards not met (too few cases for a reliable estimate).

[1] Includes basic math, general math, applied math, pre-algebra, and algebra I.

[2] Includes courses such as actuarial sciences, pure mathematics, discrete math, and advanced functions and modeling.

[3] Includes other racial/ethnic groups not shown separately, as well as students for whom information on race/ethnicity or sex was missing.

[4] SD estimates include both students with an Individualized Education Plan (IEP) and students with a plan under Section 504 of the Rehabilitation Act (a "504 plan"). IEPs are only for students who require specialized instruction, whereas 504 plans apply to students who require accommodations but may not require specialized instruction.

NOTE: Scale ranges from 0 to 300. Includes students tested with accommodations (6 percent of all 12th-graders); excludes only those students with disabilities and English language learners who were unable to be tested even with accommodations (3 percent of all 12th-graders). For a transcript to be included in the analyses, it had to meet three requirements: (1) the graduate received either a standard or honors diploma, (2) the graduate's transcript contained 16 or more Carnegie credits, and (3) the graduate's transcript contained more than 0 Carnegie credits in English courses. Race categories exclude persons of Hispanic ethnicity.

SOURCE: U.S. Department of Education, National Center for Education Statistics, National Assessment of Educational Progress (NAEP), 2009 Mathematics Assessment; and 2009 High School Transcript Study (HSTS). (This table was prepared September 2012.)

Table 222.50. Average National Assessment of Educational Progress (NAEP) mathematics scale score of 4th-grade public school students, by state: Selected years, 1992 through 2019

[Standard errors appear in parentheses]

State	1992[1]	1996[2]	2000	2003	2005	2007	2009	2011	2013	2015	2017	2019
1	2	3	4	5	6	7	8	9	10	11	12	13
United States	**219 (0.8)**	**222 (1.0)**	**224 (1.0)**	**234 (0.2)**	**237 (0.2)**	**239 (0.2)**	**239 (0.2)**	**240 (0.2)**	**241 (0.2)**	**240 (0.3)**	**239 (0.2)**	**240 (0.2)**
Alabama	208 (1.6)	212 (1.2)	217 (1.2)	223 (1.2)	225 (0.9)	229 (1.3)	228 (1.1)	231 (1.0)	233 (1.0)	231 (0.9)	232 (1.0)	230 (1.0)
Alaska[3]	— (†)	224 (1.3)	— (†)	233 (0.8)	236 (1.0)	237 (1.0)	237 (0.9)	236 (0.9)	236 (0.8)	236 (1.1)	230 (0.9)	232 (0.7)
Arizona	215 (1.1)	218 (1.7)	219 (1.3)	229 (1.1)	230 (1.1)	232 (1.0)	230 (1.1)	235 (1.1)	240 (1.2)	238 (1.0)	234 (1.1)	238 (0.8)
Arkansas[3]	210 (0.9)	216 (1.5)	216 (1.1)	229 (0.9)	236 (0.9)	238 (1.1)	238 (0.9)	238 (0.8)	240 (0.9)	235 (0.8)	234 (0.9)	233 (1.0)
California[4]	208 (1.6)	209 (1.8)	213 (1.6)	227 (0.9)	230 (0.6)	230 (0.7)	232 (1.2)	234 (1.4)	234 (1.2)	232 (1.4)	232 (1.2)	235 (0.8)
Colorado	221 (1.0)	226 (1.0)	— (†)	235 (1.0)	239 (1.1)	240 (1.0)	243 (1.0)	244 (0.9)	247 (0.8)	242 (1.0)	241 (1.1)	242 (0.9)
Connecticut	227 (1.1)	232 (1.1)	234 (1.1)	241 (0.8)	242 (0.8)	243 (1.1)	245 (1.0)	242 (1.3)	243 (0.9)	240 (0.9)	239 (1.1)	243 (0.8)
Delaware	218 (0.8)	215 (0.6)	— (†)	236 (0.5)	240 (0.5)	242 (0.4)	239 (0.5)	240 (0.6)	243 (0.7)	239 (0.6)	236 (0.8)	239 (0.7)
District of Columbia	193 (0.5)	187 (1.1)	192 (1.1)	205 (0.7)	211 (0.8)	214 (0.8)	219 (0.7)	222 (0.7)	229 (0.7)	231 (0.6)	231 (0.7)	235 (0.7)
Florida	214 (1.5)	216 (1.2)	— (†)	234 (1.1)	239 (0.7)	242 (0.8)	242 (1.0)	240 (0.8)	242 (0.8)	243 (1.0)	246 (0.7)	246 (0.8)
Georgia	216 (1.2)	215 (1.5)	219 (1.1)	230 (1.0)	234 (1.0)	235 (0.8)	236 (0.9)	238 (0.7)	240 (1.0)	236 (1.2)	236 (1.1)	238 (1.0)
Hawaii	214 (1.3)	215 (1.5)	216 (1.0)	227 (1.0)	230 (0.8)	234 (0.8)	236 (1.1)	239 (0.7)	243 (0.8)	238 (0.9)	238 (0.8)	239 (0.7)
Idaho[4]	222 (1.0)	— (†)	224 (1.4)	235 (0.7)	242 (0.7)	241 (0.7)	241 (0.8)	240 (0.6)	241 (0.9)	239 (0.9)	240 (0.9)	242 (0.9)
Illinois[4]	— (†)	— (†)	223 (1.9)	233 (1.1)	233 (1.0)	237 (1.1)	238 (1.0)	239 (1.1)	239 (1.2)	237 (1.2)	238 (1.0)	237 (1.2)
Indiana[4]	221 (1.0)	229 (1.0)	233 (1.1)	238 (0.9)	240 (0.8)	245 (0.8)	243 (0.9)	244 (1.0)	249 (0.9)	248 (1.1)	247 (1.1)	245 (1.1)
Iowa[3,4]	230 (1.0)	229 (1.1)	231 (1.2)	238 (0.7)	240 (0.7)	243 (0.8)	243 (0.8)	243 (0.8)	246 (0.9)	243 (0.9)	243 (1.1)	241 (1.1)
Kansas[4]	— (†)	— (†)	232 (1.6)	242 (1.0)	246 (1.0)	248 (0.9)	245 (1.0)	246 (0.9)	246 (0.8)	241 (1.0)	241 (0.9)	239 (0.8)
Kentucky	215 (1.0)	220 (1.1)	219 (1.4)	229 (1.1)	231 (0.9)	235 (0.9)	239 (1.1)	241 (0.8)	241 (0.9)	242 (1.1)	239 (0.9)	239 (1.1)
Louisiana	204 (1.5)	209 (1.1)	218 (1.4)	226 (1.0)	230 (0.9)	230 (1.0)	229 (1.0)	231 (1.0)	231 (1.2)	234 (1.1)	229 (1.2)	231 (1.1)
Maine[4]	232 (1.0)	232 (1.0)	230 (1.0)	238 (0.7)	241 (0.8)	242 (0.8)	244 (0.8)	244 (0.7)	246 (0.7)	242 (0.8)	240 (0.9)	241 (1.0)
Maryland	217 (1.3)	221 (1.6)	222 (1.2)	233 (1.3)	238 (1.0)	240 (0.9)	244 (0.9)	247 (0.9)	245 (1.3)	239 (1.0)	241 (1.1)	239 (1.2)
Massachusetts	227 (1.2)	229 (1.3)	233 (1.2)	242 (0.8)	247 (0.8)	252 (0.8)	252 (0.9)	253 (0.8)	253 (1.0)	251 (1.2)	249 (1.0)	247 (1.1)
Michigan[3,4]	220 (1.7)	226 (1.3)	229 (1.6)	236 (0.9)	238 (1.2)	238 (1.3)	236 (1.0)	236 (1.1)	237 (1.1)	236 (1.2)	236 (1.3)	236 (1.2)
Minnesota[4]	228 (0.9)	232 (1.1)	234 (1.3)	242 (0.9)	246 (1.0)	247 (1.0)	249 (1.1)	249 (0.9)	253 (1.1)	250 (1.2)	249 (1.2)	248 (1.0)
Mississippi	202 (1.1)	208 (1.2)	211 (1.1)	223 (1.0)	227 (0.9)	228 (1.0)	227 (1.0)	230 (0.9)	231 (0.7)	234 (0.9)	235 (0.8)	241 (0.8)
Missouri	222 (1.2)	225 (1.1)	228 (1.2)	235 (0.9)	235 (0.9)	239 (0.9)	241 (1.2)	240 (0.9)	240 (0.8)	239 (0.9)	240 (1.1)	238 (1.0)
Montana[3,4]	— (†)	228 (1.2)	228 (1.7)	236 (0.8)	241 (0.8)	244 (0.8)	244 (0.7)	244 (0.6)	244 (0.6)	241 (0.7)	241 (0.8)	241 (0.8)
Nebraska	225 (1.2)	228 (1.2)	225 (1.8)	236 (0.8)	238 (0.9)	238 (1.1)	239 (1.0)	240 (1.0)	243 (1.0)	244 (0.9)	246 (0.9)	244 (0.7)
Nevada[3]	— (†)	218 (1.3)	220 (1.0)	228 (0.8)	230 (0.8)	232 (0.9)	235 (0.9)	237 (0.8)	236 (0.8)	234 (1.1)	232 (1.2)	236 (0.8)
New Hampshire	230 (1.2)	— (†)	— (†)	243 (0.9)	246 (0.8)	249 (0.8)	251 (0.8)	252 (0.6)	253 (0.8)	249 (0.8)	245 (0.9)	245 (0.8)
New Jersey[3]	227 (1.5)	227 (1.5)	— (†)	239 (1.1)	244 (1.1)	249 (1.1)	247 (1.0)	248 (0.9)	247 (1.1)	245 (1.2)	248 (1.3)	246 (1.1)
New Mexico	213 (1.4)	214 (1.8)	213 (1.5)	223 (1.1)	224 (0.8)	228 (0.9)	230 (1.0)	233 (0.8)	233 (0.7)	231 (0.8)	230 (0.8)	231 (0.8)
New York[3,4]	218 (1.2)	223 (1.2)	225 (1.4)	236 (0.9)	238 (0.9)	243 (0.8)	241 (0.7)	238 (0.8)	240 (1.0)	237 (0.9)	236 (1.0)	237 (1.1)
North Carolina	213 (1.1)	224 (1.2)	230 (1.1)	242 (0.8)	241 (0.9)	242 (0.8)	244 (0.8)	245 (0.7)	245 (0.9)	244 (1.0)	241 (1.0)	241 (1.0)
North Dakota	229 (0.8)	231 (1.2)	230 (1.2)	238 (0.7)	243 (0.5)	245 (0.5)	245 (0.6)	245 (0.4)	246 (0.5)	245 (0.5)	244 (0.7)	243 (0.7)
Ohio[4]	219 (1.2)	— (†)	230 (1.5)	238 (1.0)	242 (1.0)	245 (1.0)	244 (1.1)	244 (0.8)	246 (1.1)	244 (1.2)	241 (1.0)	241 (1.0)
Oklahoma	220 (1.0)	— (†)	224 (1.0)	229 (1.0)	234 (1.0)	237 (0.8)	237 (0.9)	237 (0.8)	239 (0.7)	240 (1.0)	237 (0.9)	237 (0.8)
Oregon[4]	— (†)	223 (1.4)	224 (1.8)	236 (0.9)	238 (0.8)	236 (1.0)	238 (0.9)	237 (0.9)	240 (1.3)	238 (1.1)	233 (1.1)	236 (1.0)
Pennsylvania[3]	224 (1.3)	226 (1.2)	— (†)	236 (1.1)	241 (1.2)	244 (0.8)	244 (1.1)	246 (1.1)	244 (1.0)	243 (1.4)	242 (1.0)	244 (1.1)
Rhode Island	215 (1.5)	220 (1.4)	224 (1.1)	230 (1.0)	233 (0.9)	236 (0.9)	239 (0.8)	242 (0.7)	241 (0.8)	238 (0.7)	238 (0.7)	239 (0.8)
South Carolina[3]	212 (1.1)	213 (1.3)	220 (1.4)	236 (0.9)	238 (0.9)	237 (0.8)	236 (0.9)	237 (1.0)	237 (1.0)	237 (1.1)	234 (1.0)	237 (1.1)
South Dakota	— (†)	— (†)	— (†)	237 (0.7)	242 (0.5)	241 (0.7)	242 (0.5)	241 (0.6)	241 (0.5)	240 (0.7)	242 (0.8)	241 (0.7)
Tennessee	211 (1.4)	219 (1.4)	220 (1.4)	228 (1.0)	232 (1.2)	233 (0.9)	232 (1.1)	233 (0.9)	240 (0.9)	241 (1.1)	237 (1.0)	240 (1.0)
Texas	218 (1.2)	229 (1.4)	231 (1.1)	237 (0.9)	242 (0.6)	242 (0.7)	240 (0.7)	241 (1.1)	242 (0.9)	244 (1.3)	241 (1.2)	244 (1.0)
Utah	224 (1.0)	227 (1.2)	227 (1.3)	235 (0.8)	239 (0.8)	239 (0.9)	240 (1.0)	243 (0.8)	243 (0.9)	243 (1.0)	242 (1.0)	244 (1.0)
Vermont[3,4]	— (†)	225 (1.2)	232 (1.6)	242 (0.8)	244 (0.5)	246 (0.5)	248 (0.4)	247 (0.5)	248 (0.6)	243 (0.7)	241 (0.7)	239 (0.7)
Virginia	221 (1.3)	223 (1.4)	230 (1.0)	239 (1.1)	240 (0.9)	244 (0.9)	243 (1.0)	245 (0.8)	246 (1.1)	247 (1.3)	248 (1.0)	247 (1.2)
Washington	— (†)	225 (1.2)	— (†)	238 (1.0)	242 (0.9)	243 (1.0)	242 (0.8)	243 (0.9)	246 (1.1)	245 (1.3)	242 (1.3)	240 (1.2)
West Virginia	215 (1.1)	223 (1.0)	223 (1.3)	231 (0.8)	231 (0.7)	236 (0.9)	233 (0.8)	235 (0.7)	237 (0.8)	235 (0.8)	236 (1.0)	231 (0.9)
Wisconsin	229 (1.1)	231 (1.0)	‡ (†)	237 (0.9)	241 (0.9)	244 (0.9)	244 (0.9)	245 (0.8)	245 (1.0)	243 (1.1)	240 (0.9)	242 (1.1)
Wyoming	225 (0.9)	223 (1.4)	229 (1.1)	241 (0.6)	243 (0.6)	244 (0.5)	242 (0.6)	244 (0.4)	247 (0.4)	247 (0.6)	248 (0.6)	246 (0.7)
Department of Defense Education Activity (DoDEA)[5]	— (†)	224 (0.6)	227 (0.6)	237 (0.4)	239 (0.5)	240 (0.4)	240 (0.5)	241 (0.4)	245 (0.4)	248 (0.5)	249 (0.5)	250 (0.5)

—Not available.
†Not applicable.
‡Reporting standards not met. Participation rates fell below the required standards for reporting.
[1]Accommodations were not permitted for this assessment.
[2]The 1996 data in this table do not include students who were tested with accommodations. Data for students tested with accommodations are not available at the state level for 1996.
[3]Did not meet one or more of the guidelines for school participation in 1996. Data are subject to appreciable nonresponse bias.
[4]Did not meet one or more of the guidelines for school participation in 2000. Data are subject to appreciable nonresponse bias.
[5]Prior to 2005, NAEP divided the DoDEA schools into two jurisdictions, domestic and overseas. In 2005, NAEP began combining the domestic and overseas schools into a single jurisdiction. Data shown in this table for years prior to 2005 were recalculated for comparability.

NOTE: Scale ranges from 0 to 500. State-level data for 1990 are not available. Table does not include private schools, Bureau of Indian Education schools, or (except in the final row) DoDEA schools. For 2000 and later years, includes public school students who were tested with accommodations; excludes only those students with disabilities (SD) and English language learners (ELL) who were unable to be tested even with accommodations. SD and ELL populations, accommodation rates, and exclusion rates vary from state to state.

SOURCE: U.S. Department of Education, National Center for Education Statistics, National Assessment of Educational Progress (NAEP), 1992, 1996, 2000, 2003, 2005, 2007, 2009, 2011, 2013, 2015, 2017, and 2019 Mathematics Assessments, retrieved October 30, 2019, from the Main NAEP Data Explorer (https://nces.ed.gov/nationsreportcard/naepdata/). (This table was prepared November 2019.)

Table 222.60. Average National Assessment of Educational Progress (NAEP) mathematics scale score of 8th-grade public school students, by state: Selected years, 1990 through 2019

[Standard errors appear in parentheses]

State	1990[1]	1992[1]	1996[2]	2000	2003	2005	2007	2009	2011	2013	2015	2017	2019
1	2	3	4	5	6	7	8	9	10	11	12	13	14
United States	**262 (1.4)**	**267 (1.0)**	**271 (1.2)**	**272 (0.9)**	**276 (0.3)**	**278 (0.2)**	**280 (0.3)**	**282 (0.3)**	**283 (0.2)**	**284 (0.2)**	**281 (0.3)**	**282 (0.3)**	**281 (0.3)**
Alabama	253 (1.1)	252 (1.7)	257 (2.1)	264 (1.8)	262 (1.5)	262 (1.5)	266 (1.5)	269 (1.2)	269 (1.4)	269 (1.3)	267 (1.2)	268 (1.3)	269 (1.4)
Alaska[3]	— (†)	— (†)	278 (1.8)	— (†)	279 (0.9)	279 (0.8)	283 (1.1)	283 (1.0)	283 (0.8)	282 (0.9)	280 (1.0)	277 (0.9)	274 (1.1)
Arizona[4]	260 (1.3)	265 (1.3)	268 (1.6)	269 (1.8)	271 (1.2)	274 (1.1)	276 (1.2)	277 (1.4)	279 (1.2)	280 (1.2)	283 (1.4)	282 (1.1)	280 (1.1)
Arkansas[3]	256 (0.9)	256 (1.2)	262 (1.5)	257 (1.5)	266 (1.2)	272 (1.2)	274 (1.1)	276 (1.1)	279 (1.0)	278 (1.1)	275 (1.4)	274 (1.0)	274 (1.2)
California[4]	256 (1.3)	261 (1.7)	263 (1.9)	260 (2.1)	267 (1.2)	269 (0.6)	270 (0.8)	270 (1.3)	273 (1.2)	276 (1.2)	275 (1.3)	277 (1.2)	276 (1.3)
Colorado	267 (0.9)	272 (1.0)	276 (1.1)	— (†)	283 (1.1)	281 (1.2)	286 (0.9)	287 (1.4)	292 (1.1)	290 (1.2)	286 (1.5)	286 (1.4)	285 (1.2)
Connecticut	270 (1.0)	274 (1.1)	280 (1.1)	281 (1.3)	284 (1.2)	281 (1.4)	282 (1.5)	289 (1.0)	287 (1.1)	285 (1.1)	284 (1.2)	284 (0.9)	286 (1.3)
Delaware	261 (0.9)	263 (1.0)	267 (0.9)	— (†)	277 (0.7)	281 (0.6)	283 (0.6)	284 (0.5)	283 (0.7)	282 (0.7)	280 (0.7)	278 (0.7)	277 (0.9)
District of Columbia	231 (0.9)	235 (0.9)	233 (1.3)	235 (1.1)	243 (0.8)	245 (0.9)	248 (0.9)	254 (0.9)	260 (0.7)	265 (0.9)	263 (0.9)	266 (0.9)	269 (0.8)
Florida	255 (1.2)	260 (1.5)	264 (1.8)	— (†)	271 (1.5)	274 (1.1)	277 (1.3)	279 (1.1)	278 (0.8)	281 (0.8)	275 (1.4)	279 (1.1)	279 (1.3)
Georgia	259 (1.3)	259 (1.2)	262 (1.6)	265 (1.2)	270 (1.2)	272 (1.1)	275 (1.0)	278 (0.9)	278 (1.0)	279 (1.2)	279 (1.2)	281 (1.4)	279 (1.0)
Hawaii	251 (0.8)	257 (0.9)	262 (1.0)	262 (1.4)	266 (0.8)	266 (0.7)	269 (0.8)	274 (0.7)	278 (0.7)	281 (0.8)	279 (0.8)	277 (0.8)	275 (1.1)
Idaho[4]	271 (0.8)	275 (0.7)	— (†)	277 (1.0)	280 (0.9)	281 (0.9)	284 (0.9)	287 (0.8)	287 (0.8)	286 (0.7)	284 (0.9)	284 (1.2)	286 (1.0)
Illinois[4]	261 (1.7)	— (†)	— (†)	275 (1.7)	277 (1.2)	278 (1.1)	280 (1.1)	282 (1.2)	283 (1.1)	285 (1.0)	282 (1.3)	282 (1.2)	283 (1.2)
Indiana[4]	267 (1.2)	270 (1.1)	276 (1.4)	281 (1.4)	281 (1.1)	282 (1.0)	285 (1.1)	287 (0.9)	285 (1.0)	288 (1.1)	287 (1.2)	288 (1.3)	286 (1.3)
Iowa[3]	278 (1.1)	283 (1.0)	284 (1.3)	— (†)	284 (0.8)	284 (0.9)	285 (0.9)	284 (1.0)	285 (0.9)	285 (0.9)	286 (1.2)	286 (0.9)	282 (1.0)
Kansas[4]	— (†)	— (†)	— (†)	283 (1.7)	284 (1.3)	284 (1.0)	290 (1.1)	289 (1.0)	290 (0.9)	290 (1.0)	284 (1.3)	285 (1.0)	282 (0.9)
Kentucky	257 (1.2)	262 (1.1)	267 (1.1)	270 (1.3)	274 (1.2)	274 (1.2)	279 (1.1)	279 (1.1)	282 (0.9)	281 (0.9)	278 (0.9)	278 (1.0)	278 (1.1)
Louisiana	246 (1.2)	250 (1.7)	252 (1.6)	259 (1.5)	266 (1.5)	268 (1.4)	272 (1.1)	272 (1.6)	273 (1.2)	273 (0.9)	268 (1.4)	267 (1.3)	272 (1.4)
Maine[4]	— (†)	279 (1.0)	284 (1.3)	281 (1.1)	282 (0.9)	281 (0.8)	286 (0.8)	286 (0.7)	289 (0.8)	289 (0.7)	285 (0.7)	284 (0.9)	282 (0.9)
Maryland[3]	261 (1.4)	265 (1.3)	270 (2.1)	272 (1.7)	278 (1.0)	278 (1.1)	286 (1.2)	288 (1.1)	288 (1.2)	287 (1.1)	283 (1.2)	281 (1.1)	280 (1.1)
Massachusetts	— (†)	273 (1.0)	278 (1.7)	279 (1.5)	287 (0.9)	292 (0.9)	298 (1.3)	299 (1.3)	299 (0.8)	301 (0.9)	297 (1.4)	297 (1.1)	294 (1.2)
Michigan[3,4]	264 (1.2)	267 (1.4)	277 (1.8)	277 (1.9)	276 (2.0)	277 (1.5)	277 (1.4)	278 (1.6)	280 (1.4)	280 (1.3)	278 (1.3)	280 (1.2)	280 (1.3)
Minnesota[4]	275 (0.9)	282 (1.0)	284 (1.3)	287 (1.4)	291 (1.1)	290 (1.2)	292 (1.0)	294 (1.0)	295 (1.0)	295 (1.0)	294 (1.0)	294 (1.5)	291 (1.2)
Mississippi	— (†)	246 (1.2)	250 (1.2)	254 (1.1)	261 (1.1)	262 (1.2)	265 (0.8)	265 (1.2)	269 (1.4)	271 (0.9)	271 (1.1)	271 (0.9)	274 (0.9)
Missouri	— (†)	271 (1.2)	273 (1.4)	271 (1.5)	279 (1.1)	276 (1.3)	281 (1.0)	286 (1.0)	282 (1.1)	283 (1.0)	281 (1.2)	281 (1.1)	281 (1.0)
Montana[3,4]	280 (0.9)	— (†)	283 (1.3)	285 (1.4)	286 (0.8)	286 (0.7)	287 (0.7)	292 (0.9)	293 (0.6)	289 (0.9)	287 (0.8)	286 (0.8)	284 (0.8)
Nebraska	276 (1.0)	278 (1.1)	283 (1.0)	280 (1.2)	282 (0.9)	284 (1.0)	284 (1.0)	284 (1.1)	283 (0.8)	285 (0.9)	286 (0.8)	288 (1.0)	285 (0.9)
Nevada	— (†)	— (†)	‡ (†)	265 (0.8)	268 (0.8)	270 (0.8)	271 (0.8)	274 (0.7)	278 (0.8)	278 (0.7)	275 (0.7)	275 (0.7)	274 (0.8)
New Hampshire	273 (0.9)	278 (1.0)	‡ (†)	— (†)	286 (0.8)	285 (0.8)	288 (0.7)	292 (0.9)	292 (0.7)	296 (0.8)	294 (0.9)	293 (0.8)	287 (0.9)
New Jersey	270 (1.1)	272 (1.6)	‡ (†)	— (†)	281 (1.1)	284 (1.4)	289 (1.2)	293 (1.4)	294 (1.2)	296 (1.1)	293 (1.2)	292 (1.0)	292 (1.5)
New Mexico	256 (0.7)	260 (0.9)	262 (1.2)	259 (1.3)	263 (1.0)	263 (0.9)	268 (0.9)	270 (1.1)	274 (0.8)	273 (0.7)	271 (1.0)	269 (1.0)	269 (0.9)
New York[3,4]	261 (1.4)	266 (2.1)	270 (1.7)	271 (2.2)	280 (1.1)	280 (0.9)	280 (1.2)	283 (1.2)	280 (0.9)	282 (0.9)	280 (1.4)	282 (1.2)	280 (1.3)
North Carolina	250 (1.1)	258 (1.2)	268 (1.4)	276 (1.3)	281 (1.0)	282 (0.9)	284 (1.1)	284 (1.3)	286 (1.0)	286 (1.1)	281 (1.6)	282 (1.2)	284 (1.1)
North Dakota	281 (1.2)	283 (1.1)	284 (0.9)	282 (1.1)	287 (0.8)	287 (0.6)	292 (0.7)	293 (0.7)	292 (0.6)	291 (0.5)	288 (0.7)	288 (0.8)	286 (0.8)
Ohio	264 (1.0)	268 (1.5)	— (†)	281 (1.6)	282 (1.3)	283 (1.1)	285 (1.2)	286 (1.0)	289 (1.0)	290 (1.1)	285 (1.6)	288 (2.0)	286 (1.1)
Oklahoma	263 (1.3)	268 (1.1)	— (†)	270 (1.3)	272 (1.1)	271 (1.0)	275 (0.9)	276 (1.0)	279 (1.0)	276 (1.0)	275 (1.3)	275 (1.1)	276 (1.0)
Oregon[4]	271 (1.0)	— (†)	276 (1.5)	280 (1.5)	281 (1.3)	282 (1.0)	284 (1.1)	285 (1.0)	283 (1.0)	284 (1.1)	283 (1.2)	282 (1.2)	280 (1.2)
Pennsylvania	266 (1.6)	271 (1.5)	— (†)	— (†)	279 (1.1)	281 (1.5)	286 (1.1)	288 (1.3)	286 (1.2)	290 (1.0)	284 (1.5)	286 (1.2)	285 (1.2)
Rhode Island	260 (0.6)	266 (0.7)	269 (0.9)	269 (1.3)	272 (0.7)	272 (0.8)	275 (0.7)	278 (0.8)	283 (0.5)	284 (0.6)	281 (0.7)	277 (0.8)	276 (0.7)
South Carolina[3]	— (†)	261 (1.0)	261 (1.5)	265 (1.5)	277 (1.3)	281 (0.9)	282 (1.0)	280 (1.3)	281 (1.1)	280 (1.1)	276 (1.3)	275 (1.0)	276 (1.0)
South Dakota	— (†)	— (†)	— (†)	— (†)	285 (0.8)	287 (0.6)	288 (0.8)	291 (0.5)	291 (0.5)	287 (0.7)	285 (0.9)	286 (0.7)	287 (1.2)
Tennessee	— (†)	259 (1.4)	263 (1.4)	262 (1.5)	268 (1.8)	271 (1.1)	274 (1.1)	275 (1.4)	274 (1.2)	278 (1.3)	278 (1.8)	279 (1.2)	280 (1.3)
Texas	258 (1.4)	265 (1.3)	270 (1.4)	273 (1.6)	277 (1.1)	281 (0.6)	286 (1.0)	287 (1.3)	290 (0.9)	288 (1.0)	284 (1.2)	282 (1.4)	280 (1.0)
Utah	— (†)	274 (0.7)	277 (1.0)	274 (1.2)	281 (1.0)	279 (0.7)	281 (0.9)	284 (0.9)	283 (0.8)	284 (0.9)	286 (1.1)	287 (0.9)	285 (1.0)
Vermont[3,4]	— (†)	— (†)	279 (1.0)	281 (1.5)	286 (0.8)	287 (0.7)	291 (0.7)	293 (0.6)	294 (0.7)	295 (0.7)	290 (0.7)	288 (0.7)	287 (0.7)
Virginia	264 (1.5)	268 (1.2)	270 (1.6)	275 (1.3)	282 (1.3)	284 (1.1)	288 (1.1)	286 (1.1)	289 (1.1)	288 (1.2)	288 (1.2)	290 (1.5)	287 (1.3)
Washington	— (†)	— (†)	276 (1.3)	— (†)	281 (0.9)	285 (1.0)	285 (1.0)	289 (1.0)	288 (1.0)	290 (1.0)	287 (1.3)	289 (1.4)	286 (1.4)
West Virginia	256 (1.0)	259 (1.0)	265 (1.0)	266 (1.2)	271 (1.2)	269 (1.0)	270 (1.0)	270 (1.0)	273 (0.7)	274 (0.9)	271 (0.9)	273 (0.9)	272 (0.9)
Wisconsin[3]	274 (1.3)	278 (1.5)	283 (1.5)	‡ (†)	284 (1.3)	285 (1.1)	286 (1.1)	288 (0.9)	289 (1.0)	289 (0.9)	289 (1.3)	288 (1.0)	289 (1.1)
Wyoming	272 (0.7)	275 (0.9)	275 (0.9)	276 (1.0)	284 (0.7)	282 (0.7)	287 (0.7)	286 (0.6)	288 (0.6)	288 (0.5)	287 (0.7)	289 (0.7)	286 (0.9)
Department of Defense Education Activity (DoDEA)[5]	— (†)	— (†)	274 (0.9)	277 (1.1)	285 (0.7)	284 (0.7)	285 (0.8)	287 (0.9)	288 (0.8)	290 (0.8)	291 (0.7)	293 (0.7)	292 (0.8)

—Not available.
†Not applicable.
‡Reporting standards not met. Participation rates fell below the required standards for reporting.
[1]Accommodations were not permitted for this assessment.
[2]The 1996 data in this table do not include students who were tested with accommodations. Data for students tested with accommodations are not available at the state level for 1996.
[3]Did not meet one or more of the guidelines for school participation in 1996. Data are subject to appreciable nonresponse bias.
[4]Did not meet one or more of the guidelines for school participation in 2000. Data are subject to appreciable nonresponse bias.
[5]Prior to 2005, NAEP divided the DoDEA schools into two jurisdictions, domestic and overseas. In 2005, NAEP began combining the domestic and overseas schools into a single jurisdiction. Data shown in this table for years prior to 2005 were recalculated for comparability.
NOTE: Scale ranges from 0 to 500. Table does not include private schools, Bureau of Indian Education schools, or (except in the final row) DoDEA schools. For 2000 and later years, includes public school students who were tested with accommodations; excludes only those students with disabilities (SD) and English language learners (ELL) who were unable to be tested even with accommodations. SD and ELL populations, accommodation rates, and exclusion rates vary from state to state.
SOURCE: U.S. Department of Education, National Center for Education Statistics, National Assessment of Educational Progress (NAEP), 1990, 1992, 1996, 2000, 2003, 2005, 2007, 2009, 2011, 2013, 2015, 2017, and 2019 Mathematics Assessments, retrieved October 30, 2019, from the Main NAEP Data Explorer (https://nces.ed.gov/nationsreportcard/naepdata/). (This table was prepared November 2019.)

Table 222.80. Average National Assessment of Educational Progress (NAEP) mathematics scale scores of 4th- and 8th-grade public school students and percentage attaining selected mathematics achievement levels, by race/ethnicity and jurisdiction or specific urban district: Selected years, 2009 through 2019

[Standard errors appear in parentheses]

Grade level and jurisdiction or specific urban district	Average mathematics scale score[1]														Percent of students	
	2009	2011	2013	2015	2017					2019					2019	
	All students	All students	All students	All students	All students	White	Black	Hispanic	Asian	All students	White	Black	Hispanic	Asian	At or above *NAEP Basic*[2]	At or above *NAEP Proficient*[3]
1	2	3	4	5	6	7	8	9	10	11	12	13	14	15	16	17
4th grade																
United States	239 (0.2)	240 (0.2)	241 (0.2)	240 (0.3)	239 (0.2)	248 (0.2)	223 (0.5)	229 (0.4)	260 (1.1)	240 (0.2)	249 (0.3)	224 (0.4)	231 (0.4)	263 (1.0)	80 (0.2)	40 (0.3)
All large cities[4]	231 (0.5)	233 (0.6)	235 (0.7)	234 (0.6)	232 (0.5)	250 (1.3)	220 (0.7)	227 (0.6)	249 (1.8)	235 (0.6)	252 (0.9)	221 (0.7)	230 (0.6)	259 (3.3)	74 (0.6)	34 (0.8)
Selected urban districts																
Albuquerque (NM)	--- (†)	235 (1.3)	235 (1.0)	231 (1.1)	230 (1.3)	250 (2.3)	‡ (†)	224 (1.5)	‡ (†)	230 (1.4)	248 (2.6)	‡ (†)	224 (1.3)	‡ (†)	69 (1.8)	30 (1.7)
Atlanta (GA)	225 (0.8)	228 (0.7)	233 (0.7)	228 (1.2)	231 (1.0)	271 (1.4)	219 (1.1)	224 (2.6)	‡ (†)	232 (1.1)	266 (2.0)	222 (1.3)	227 (3.9)	‡ (†)	69 (1.5)	31 (1.6)
Austin (TX)	240 (1.0)	245 (1.1)	245 (0.9)	246 (1.4)	243 (1.1)	264 (1.7)	229 (3.6)	234 (1.4)	‡ (†)	243 (1.0)	263 (1.7)	229 (3.4)	231 (1.5)	‡ (†)	81 (1.3)	45 (1.7)
Baltimore City (MD)	222 (1.0)	226 (1.1)	223 (1.2)	215 (1.5)	215 (1.2)	232 (4.2)	212 (1.2)	221 (2.7)	‡ (†)	216 (1.3)	244 (4.1)	213 (1.3)	222 (2.9)	‡ (†)	53 (2.0)	15 (1.7)
Boston (MA)	236 (0.7)	237 (0.6)	237 (0.8)	236 (1.3)	233 (0.9)	253 (2.4)	226 (1.5)	228 (1.4)	258 (2.9)	234 (0.9)	258 (2.2)	224 (1.8)	228 (1.1)	257 (2.5)	73 (1.5)	32 (1.2)
Charlotte (NC)	245 (1.3)	247 (1.1)	247 (1.6)	248 (1.3)	244 (1.1)	263 (2.1)	232 (1.6)	237 (1.5)	262 (4.3)	246 (1.0)	264 (2.1)	234 (1.6)	238 (2.4)	266 (3.7)	86 (1.2)	49 (1.8)
Chicago (IL)	222 (1.2)	224 (0.9)	231 (1.3)	232 (1.2)	232 (1.1)	253 (2.0)	222 (2.0)	231 (1.3)	258 (5.2)	232 (1.2)	258 (2.8)	221 (2.0)	232 (1.2)	266 (4.7)	72 (1.7)	31 (1.7)
Clark County (NV)	--- (†)	--- (†)	--- (†)	--- (†)	230 (1.0)	243 (1.6)	214 (2.3)	225 (1.2)	252 (3.7)	235 (1.1)	247 (1.6)	219 (1.9)	231 (1.4)	251 (4.1)	76 (1.5)	33 (1.7)
Cleveland (OH)	213 (1.0)	216 (0.7)	216 (0.9)	219 (1.3)	214 (1.3)	230 (2.7)	210 (1.5)	214 (3.8)	‡ (†)	218 (1.0)	229 (2.4)	214 (1.1)	221 (3.1)	‡ (†)	55 (1.6)	13 (1.0)
Dallas (TX)	--- (†)	233 (1.3)	234 (1.0)	238 (1.3)	234 (1.1)	‡ (†)	223 (2.6)	236 (1.3)	‡ (†)	235 (1.3)	‡ (†)	222 (2.6)	236 (1.3)	‡ (†)	76 (1.8)	32 (2.0)
Denver (CO)	--- (†)	--- (†)	--- (†)	--- (†)	229 (1.5)	257 (2.6)	214 (3.2)	218 (1.4)	‡ (†)	235 (1.3)	265 (2.4)	220 (2.6)	221 (1.7)	‡ (†)	71 (1.6)	35 (1.6)
Detroit (MI)	200 (1.7)	203 (1.4)	204 (1.6)	205 (1.6)	200 (1.7)	‡ (†)	198 (1.7)	204 (3.0)	‡ (†)	205 (1.2)	‡ (†)	203 (1.2)	216 (2.8)	‡ (†)	38 (2.1)	6 (0.8)
District of Columbia (DC)	220 (0.8)	222 (1.0)	229 (0.8)	232 (0.9)	231 (0.9)	274 (2.0)	218 (1.2)	231 (1.9)	‡ (†)	235 (0.7)	274 (1.6)	222 (1.0)	235 (1.9)	‡ (†)	73 (1.4)	36 (1.2)
Duval County (FL)	--- (†)	--- (†)	--- (†)	243 (1.3)	248 (1.2)	259 (1.5)	238 (1.9)	242 (2.8)	‡ (†)	244 (1.5)	254 (2.0)	234 (1.8)	244 (3.3)	‡ (†)	86 (1.7)	45 (2.3)
Fort Worth (TX)	--- (†)	--- (†)	--- (†)	--- (†)	230 (1.1)	254 (3.5)	218 (2.1)	230 (1.4)	‡ (†)	233 (1.0)	253 (2.9)	221 (2.5)	233 (1.2)	‡ (†)	75 (1.6)	29 (1.8)
Fresno (CA)	219 (1.4)	218 (0.9)	220 (1.2)	218 (1.3)	221 (1.2)	238 (3.0)	215 (3.5)	219 (1.4)	225 (2.6)	224 (1.2)	235 (4.2)	213 (3.4)	223 (1.3)	229 (2.9)	65 (1.9)	18 (1.4)
Guilford County (NC)	--- (†)	--- (†)	--- (†)	--- (†)	240 (1.0)	257 (1.7)	227 (1.4)	231 (2.7)	255 (3.9)	236 (1.2)	251 (2.4)	227 (1.6)	227 (2.5)	252 (4.0)	77 (1.6)	35 (2.0)
Hillsborough County (FL)	--- (†)	243 (1.1)	243 (0.9)	244 (1.4)	245 (1.3)	256 (1.4)	227 (2.6)	240 (1.9)	‡ (†)	242 (1.1)	253 (1.6)	229 (2.2)	238 (1.7)	‡ (†)	85 (1.2)	41 (2.2)
Houston (TX)	236 (1.2)	237 (0.8)	236 (1.1)	239 (1.4)	235 (1.1)	263 (2.6)	227 (2.3)	234 (1.2)	‡ (†)	235 (1.1)	264 (3.1)	225 (1.9)	233 (1.1)	266 (6.7)	77 (1.5)	31 (1.7)
Jefferson County (KY)	233 (1.6)	235 (0.9)	234 (1.0)	236 (1.5)	233 (1.2)	247 (1.6)	216 (1.5)	230 (3.2)	‡ (†)	232 (1.4)	243 (1.6)	218 (1.7)	224 (3.3)	‡ (†)	71 (1.7)	33 (1.7)
Los Angeles (CA)	222 (1.2)	223 (0.8)	228 (1.3)	224 (1.4)	223 (1.2)	247 (3.3)	218 (3.7)	217 (1.1)	257 (2.9)	224 (1.2)	242 (2.9)	206 (3.7)	220 (1.2)	‡ (†)	63 (1.8)	20 (1.5)
Miami-Dade (FL)	236 (1.3)	236 (1.0)	237 (1.1)	242 (1.1)	245 (0.7)	259 (2.2)	237 (1.9)	245 (0.9)	‡ (†)	246 (0.8)	258 (2.9)	237 (1.7)	246 (0.9)	‡ (†)	87 (1.0)	47 (1.6)
Milwaukee (WI)	220 (1.5)	220 (1.0)	221 (1.6)	--- (†)	216 (1.0)	240 (2.5)	206 (1.5)	219 (2.1)	229 (3.4)	215 (1.3)	239 (3.1)	206 (1.9)	217 (2.3)	231 (4.0)	52 (2.0)	17 (1.5)
New York City (NY)	237 (1.0)	234 (1.2)	236 (1.1)	231 (1.0)	229 (1.0)	246 (2.3)	220 (2.0)	221 (1.3)	247 (2.2)	231 (1.3)	248 (3.0)	216 (1.9)	220 (1.8)	257 (2.6)	69 (1.4)	32 (1.5)
Philadelphia (PA)	222 (1.4)	225 (1.2)	223 (1.5)	217 (1.9)	214 (1.2)	244 (3.8)	207 (1.6)	207 (2.0)	‡ (†)	217 (1.7)	242 (6.9)	209 (1.9)	209 (2.2)	246 (4.7)	52 (2.4)	18 (2.0)
San Diego (CA)	236 (1.6)	239 (1.3)	241 (1.2)	233 (1.5)	237 (1.3)	254 (2.7)	223 (3.1)	225 (1.6)	254 (3.2)	240 (1.3)	258 (1.8)	218 (4.2)	228 (1.9)	256 (3.2)	79 (1.5)	42 (2.0)
Shelby County (TN)	--- (†)	--- (†)	--- (†)	--- (†)	225 (1.2)	247 (6.9)	221 (1.1)	228 (2.6)	‡ (†)	228 (1.5)	248 (4.2)	225 (1.4)	228 (2.3)	‡ (†)	69 (2.0)	25 (2.1)
8th grade																
United States	282 (0.3)	283 (0.2)	284 (0.2)	281 (0.3)	282 (0.3)	292 (0.3)	260 (0.5)	268 (0.5)	312 (1.5)	281 (0.3)	291 (0.3)	259 (0.4)	268 (0.4)	313 (1.1)	68 (0.3)	33 (0.3)
All large cities[4]	271 (0.7)	274 (0.7)	276 (0.8)	274 (1.0)	274 (0.6)	296 (0.9)	257 (0.8)	267 (0.8)	302 (2.1)	274 (0.8)	296 (1.0)	258 (0.9)	266 (0.9)	310 (3.5)	61 (0.8)	27 (0.7)
Selected urban districts																
Albuquerque (NM)	--- (†)	275 (1.0)	274 (1.2)	271 (1.4)	270 (1.2)	295 (2.8)	‡ (†)	262 (1.4)	‡ (†)	267 (1.1)	288 (2.4)	‡ (†)	260 (1.5)	‡ (†)	54 (1.8)	20 (1.3)
Atlanta (GA)	259 (1.6)	266 (1.3)	267 (1.2)	266 (1.2)	265 (1.4)	314 (2.9)	256 (1.5)	265 (4.2)	‡ (†)	268 (1.2)	312 (2.3)	257 (1.4)	272 (3.9)	‡ (†)	53 (1.6)	21 (1.1)
Austin (TX)	287 (0.9)	287 (1.2)	285 (1.0)	284 (1.3)	283 (1.3)	312 (2.2)	257 (3.9)	269 (1.7)	‡ (†)	282 (1.4)	310 (2.1)	250 (4.1)	266 (1.8)	‡ (†)	66 (1.8)	36 (1.6)
Baltimore City (MD)	257 (1.9)	261 (1.3)	260 (2.0)	255 (1.8)	255 (1.2)	286 (4.8)	251 (1.3)	260 (4.6)	‡ (†)	254 (1.5)	281 (4.3)	250 (1.7)	254 (6.1)	‡ (†)	39 (1.9)	10 (1.1)
Boston (MA)	279 (1.3)	282 (0.9)	283 (1.2)	281 (1.2)	280 (1.3)	314 (3.8)	261 (2.6)	268 (1.8)	323 (3.8)	279 (1.3)	315 (2.6)	263 (2.2)	264 (1.8)	324 (3.5)	61 (1.3)	35 (1.3)
Charlotte (NC)	283 (0.9)	285 (0.8)	289 (1.2)	286 (1.5)	287 (1.6)	316 (1.7)	271 (2.5)	272 (2.7)	318 (6.6)	288 (1.4)	314 (2.0)	273 (2.2)	274 (2.5)	‡ (†)	72 (1.6)	41 (1.5)
Chicago (IL)	264 (1.4)	270 (1.0)	269 (1.0)	275 (2.4)	276 (1.6)	306 (4.4)	259 (1.8)	276 (1.5)	‡ (†)	275 (1.6)	303 (3.0)	264 (2.5)	275 (1.7)	317 (7.7)	62 (1.7)	27 (1.7)
Clark County (NV)	--- (†)	--- (†)	--- (†)	--- (†)	272 (0.9)	289 (2.1)	251 (2.2)	264 (1.3)	299 (3.2)	272 (1.0)	286 (2.3)	252 (2.6)	266 (1.2)	299 (4.2)	59 (1.5)	24 (1.2)
Cleveland (OH)	256 (1.0)	256 (2.1)	253 (1.3)	254 (1.5)	257 (1.5)	269 (3.3)	255 (1.9)	250 (4.4)	‡ (†)	253 (1.4)	272 (3.1)	249 (1.9)	248 (3.9)	‡ (†)	38 (1.9)	8 (1.0)
Dallas (TX)	--- (†)	274 (0.9)	275 (1.0)	271 (1.3)	268 (1.3)	‡ (†)	259 (2.9)	268 (1.4)	‡ (†)	264 (1.3)	‡ (†)	252 (3.1)	265 (1.5)	‡ (†)	52 (2.3)	15 (1.1)
Denver (CO)	--- (†)	--- (†)	--- (†)	--- (†)	272 (1.4)	304 (3.0)	260 (3.4)	262 (1.7)	‡ (†)	275 (1.2)	308 (3.2)	254 (4.0)	263 (1.5)	‡ (†)	62 (1.5)	29 (1.6)
Detroit (MI)	238 (2.7)	246 (1.2)	240 (1.7)	244 (1.7)	246 (1.8)	‡ (†)	245 (1.9)	248 (3.8)	‡ (†)	244 (1.4)	‡ (†)	241 (1.6)	256 (2.8)	‡ (†)	27 (1.8)	5 (0.8)
District of Columbia (DC)	251 (1.3)	255 (0.9)	260 (1.3)	258 (1.3)	262 (1.3)	318 (3.3)	250 (1.6)	262 (4.1)	‡ (†)	269 (1.2)	322 (3.4)	254 (1.7)	268 (2.6)	‡ (†)	53 (1.7)	24 (1.2)
Duval County (FL)	--- (†)	--- (†)	--- (†)	275 (1.0)	275 (1.2)	289 (2.6)	263 (1.6)	272 (3.2)	301 (4.6)	274 (1.3)	287 (2.0)	263 (2.0)	271 (3.2)	‡ (†)	62 (1.7)	25 (1.6)
Fort Worth (TX)	--- (†)	--- (†)	--- (†)	--- (†)	269 (1.2)	294 (3.7)	255 (2.7)	269 (1.3)	‡ (†)	265 (1.3)	296 (3.7)	247 (2.3)	266 (1.6)	‡ (†)	51 (1.9)	18 (1.3)
Fresno (CA)	258 (1.2)	256 (0.9)	260 (1.4)	257 (1.5)	255 (1.6)	278 (4.1)	242 (3.2)	251 (1.9)	268 (3.2)	254 (1.4)	276 (4.0)	243 (4.3)	249 (1.5)	267 (3.3)	39 (1.9)	11 (1.1)
Guilford County (NC)	--- (†)	--- (†)	--- (†)	--- (†)	276 (1.3)	296 (1.9)	262 (2.3)	259 (3.2)	298 (4.9)	280 (1.3)	301 (2.0)	262 (1.9)	276 (3.1)	305 (6.2)	67 (1.6)	33 (1.7)
Hillsborough County (FL)	--- (†)	282 (1.5)	284 (1.1)	276 (1.7)	277 (1.6)	292 (2.1)	257 (3.1)	268 (2.3)	‡ (†)	276 (1.6)	292 (2.2)	257 (3.3)	268 (2.0)	‡ (†)	63 (1.8)	29 (1.8)
Houston (TX)	277 (1.2)	279 (1.0)	280 (1.1)	276 (1.4)	273 (1.0)	315 (3.4)	263 (2.1)	270 (1.2)	‡ (†)	274 (1.1)	315 (3.3)	261 (2.2)	271 (1.1)	‡ (†)	61 (1.7)	25 (1.2)
Jefferson County (KY)	271 (0.9)	274 (1.0)	273 (1.0)	272 (1.7)	271 (1.1)	285 (1.8)	253 (1.6)	269 (3.7)	‡ (†)	273 (1.2)	286 (1.8)	257 (2.0)	268 (3.5)	‡ (†)	61 (1.8)	26 (1.5)
Los Angeles (CA)	258 (1.0)	261 (1.3)	264 (1.5)	263 (1.6)	267 (1.0)	298 (3.0)	254 (3.5)	260 (1.2)	302 (3.7)	261 (1.1)	287 (3.8)	248 (4.5)	255 (1.1)	297 (4.1)	47 (1.4)	16 (1.0)
Miami-Dade (FL)	273 (1.1)	272 (1.1)	274 (1.5)	274 (1.8)	274 (1.3)	294 (4.6)	257 (2.6)	275 (1.2)	‡ (†)	276 (1.2)	295 (2.9)	261 (2.2)	277 (1.3)	‡ (†)	64 (1.6)	27 (1.3)
Milwaukee (WI)	251 (1.5)	254 (1.7)	257 (1.4)	--- (†)	254 (1.4)	277 (3.6)	242 (1.8)	260 (2.6)	272 (5.1)	252 (1.6)	280 (3.7)	242 (2.5)	259 (2.0)	261 (6.6)	40 (2.0)	11 (1.3)
New York City (NY)	273 (1.5)	272 (1.6)	274 (1.1)	275 (2.1)	275 (1.9)	291 (3.8)	256 (2.3)	264 (2.0)	306 (3.5)	273 (1.6)	295 (4.3)	255 (3.0)	260 (1.8)	308 (3.2)	58 (1.7)	27 (1.5)
Philadelphia (PA)	265 (2.0)	265 (2.0)	266 (1.7)	267 (1.9)	260 (1.9)	279 (3.8)	250 (2.3)	253 (3.6)	295 (5.2)	256 (1.7)	282 (4.9)	247 (2.2)	243 (3.2)	292 (4.6)	41 (2.3)	16 (1.5)
San Diego (CA)	280 (2.0)	278 (1.7)	277 (1.4)	280 (1.6)	283 (1.4)	304 (2.5)	258 (5.5)	266 (1.9)	302 (2.8)	283 (1.3)	305 (2.3)	267 (5.0)	262 (2.0)	303 (3.8)	67 (1.5)	35 (1.6)
Shelby County (TN)	--- (†)	--- (†)	--- (†)	--- (†)	257 (1.4)	295 (4.3)	251 (1.6)	260 (4.3)	‡ (†)	265 (1.2)	‡ (†)	261 (1.4)	270 (2.5)	‡ (†)	54 (1.6)	16 (1.4)

—Not available.

†Not applicable.

‡Reporting standards not met.

[1] Scale ranges from 0 to 500.

[2] *NAEP Basic* denotes partial mastery of the knowledge and skills that are fundamental for proficient work at a given grade.

[3] *NAEP Proficient* represents solid academic performance. Students reaching this level have demonstrated competency over challenging subject matter.

[4] Includes public school students from all cities in the nation with populations of 250,000 or more, including the participating districts.

NOTE: Table does not include private schools, Bureau of Indian Education schools, or Department of Defense Education Activity schools. Includes public school students who were tested with accommodations; excludes only those students with disabilities (SD) and English language learners (ELL) who were unable to be tested even with accommodations. SD and ELL populations, accommodation rates, and exclusion rates vary by grade and from district to district. Race categories exclude persons of Hispanic ethnicity. Totals include racial/ethnic groups not shown separately.

SOURCE: U.S. Department of Education, National Center for Education Statistics, National Assessment of Educational Progress (NAEP), 2009, 2011, 2013, 2015, 2017, and 2019 Mathematics Assessments, retrieved November 10, 2019, from the Main NAEP Data Explorer (https://nces.ed.gov/nationsreportcard/naepdata/). (This table was prepared November 2019.)

Table 222.85. Average National Assessment of Educational Progress (NAEP) mathematics scale score, by age and selected student characteristics: Selected years, 1973 through 2012

[Standard errors appear in parentheses]

Selected student characteristic	1973	1978	1982	1986	1990	1992	1994	1996	1999	2004[1] Previous format	2004[1] Revised format	2008	2012
1	2	3	4	5	6	7	8	9	10	11	12	13	14
9-year-olds													
All students	**219 (0.8)**	**219 (0.8)**	**219 (1.1)**	**222 (1.0)**	**230 (0.8)**	**230 (0.8)**	**231 (0.8)**	**231 (0.8)**	**232 (0.8)**	**241 (0.9)**	**239 (0.9)**	**243 (0.8)**	**244 (1.0)**
Sex													
Male	218 (0.7)	217 (0.7)	217 (1.2)	222 (1.1)	229 (0.9)	231 (1.0)	232 (1.0)	233 (1.2)	233 (1.0)	243 (1.1)	239 (1.0)	242 (0.9)	244 (1.2)
Female	220 (1.1)	220 (1.0)	221 (1.2)	222 (1.2)	230 (1.1)	228 (1.0)	230 (0.9)	229 (0.7)	231 (0.9)	240 (1.1)	240 (1.0)	243 (1.0)	244 (1.0)
Gap between female and male score	2 (1.3)	3 (1.3)	4 (1.7)	# (†)	1 (1.4)	-2 (1.4)	-2 (1.4)	-4 (1.4)	-2 (1.3)	-3 (1.5)	1 (1.4)	1 (1.3)	# (†)
Race/ethnicity													
White	225 (1.0)	224 (0.9)	224 (1.1)	227 (1.1)	235 (0.8)	235 (0.8)	237 (1.0)	237 (1.0)	239 (0.9)	247 (0.9)	245 (0.8)	250 (0.8)	252 (1.1)
Black	190 (1.8)	192 (1.1)	195 (1.6)	202 (1.6)	208 (2.2)	208 (2.0)	212 (1.6)	212 (1.4)	211 (1.6)	224 (2.1)	221 (2.1)	224 (1.9)	226 (1.8)
Hispanic	202 (2.4)	203 (2.2)	204 (1.3)	205 (2.1)	214 (2.1)	212 (2.3)	210 (2.3)	215 (1.7)	213 (1.9)	230 (2.0)	229 (2.0)	234 (1.2)	234 (0.9)
Gap between White and Black score	35 (2.1)	32 (1.5)	29 (2.0)	25 (2.0)	27 (2.4)	27 (2.2)	25 (1.8)	25 (1.8)	28 (1.8)	23 (2.2)	24 (2.2)	26 (2.1)	25 (2.1)
Gap between White and Hispanic score	23 (2.6)	21 (2.4)	20 (1.7)	21 (2.3)	21 (2.3)	23 (2.5)	27 (2.5)	22 (2.0)	26 (2.1)	18 (2.2)	16 (2.1)	16 (1.4)	17 (1.5)
13-year-olds													
All students	**266 (1.1)**	**264 (1.1)**	**269 (1.1)**	**269 (1.2)**	**270 (0.9)**	**273 (0.9)**	**274 (1.0)**	**274 (0.8)**	**276 (0.8)**	**281 (1.0)**	**279 (1.0)**	**281 (0.9)**	**285 (1.1)**
Sex													
Male	265 (1.3)	264 (1.3)	269 (1.4)	270 (1.1)	271 (1.2)	274 (1.1)	276 (1.3)	276 (0.9)	277 (0.9)	283 (1.2)	279 (1.0)	284 (1.0)	286 (1.3)
Female	267 (1.1)	265 (1.1)	268 (1.1)	268 (1.5)	270 (0.9)	272 (1.0)	273 (1.0)	272 (1.0)	274 (1.1)	279 (1.0)	278 (1.2)	279 (1.0)	284 (1.1)
Gap between female and male score	2 (1.7)	1 (1.7)	-1 (1.7)	-2 (1.9)	-2 (1.5)	-2 (1.5)	-3 (1.6)	-4 (1.4)	-3 (1.4)	-3 (1.6)	-1 (1.6)	-4 (1.4)	-2 (1.7)
Race/ethnicity													
White	274 (0.9)	272 (0.8)	274 (1.0)	274 (1.3)	276 (1.1)	279 (0.9)	281 (0.9)	281 (0.9)	283 (0.8)	288 (0.9)	287 (0.9)	290 (1.2)	293 (1.1)
Black	228 (1.9)	230 (1.9)	240 (1.6)	249 (2.3)	249 (2.3)	250 (1.9)	252 (3.5)	252 (1.3)	251 (2.6)	262 (1.6)	257 (1.8)	262 (1.2)	264 (1.9)
Hispanic	239 (2.2)	238 (2.0)	252 (1.7)	254 (2.9)	255 (1.8)	259 (1.8)	256 (1.9)	256 (1.6)	259 (1.7)	265 (2.0)	264 (1.5)	268 (1.2)	271 (1.4)
Gap between White and Black score	46 (2.1)	42 (2.1)	34 (1.9)	24 (2.6)	27 (2.6)	29 (2.1)	29 (3.7)	29 (1.6)	32 (2.7)	27 (1.8)	30 (2.1)	28 (1.7)	28 (2.2)
Gap between White and Hispanic score	35 (2.4)	34 (2.1)	22 (1.9)	19 (3.2)	22 (2.1)	20 (2.0)	25 (2.1)	25 (1.9)	24 (1.9)	23 (2.2)	23 (1.8)	23 (1.7)	21 (1.8)
Parents' highest level of education													
Did not finish high school	— (†)	245 (1.2)	251 (1.4)	252 (2.3)	253 (1.8)	256 (1.0)	255 (2.1)	254 (2.4)	256 (2.8)	262 (2.2)	263 (1.9)	268 (1.3)	266 (2.5)
Graduated high school	— (†)	263 (1.0)	263 (0.8)	263 (1.2)	263 (1.2)	263 (1.2)	266 (1.1)	267 (1.1)	264 (1.1)	271 (1.7)	270 (1.3)	272 (1.1)	270 (1.1)
Some education after high school	— (†)	273 (1.2)	275 (0.9)	274 (0.8)	277 (1.0)	278 (1.0)	277 (1.6)	277 (1.4)	279 (0.9)	283 (1.0)	282 (1.4)	285 (1.1)	286 (1.4)
Graduated college	— (†)	284 (1.2)	282 (1.5)	280 (1.4)	280 (1.0)	283 (1.0)	285 (1.2)	283 (1.2)	286 (1.0)	292 (0.9)	289 (1.1)	291 (1.0)	296 (1.3)
17-year-olds													
All students	**304 (1.1)**	**300 (1.0)**	**298 (0.9)**	**302 (0.9)**	**305 (0.9)**	**307 (0.9)**	**306 (1.0)**	**307 (1.2)**	**308 (1.0)**	**307 (0.8)**	**305 (0.7)**	**306 (0.6)**	**306 (0.8)**
Sex													
Male	309 (1.2)	304 (1.0)	301 (1.0)	305 (1.2)	306 (1.1)	309 (1.1)	309 (1.4)	310 (1.3)	310 (1.4)	308 (1.0)	307 (0.9)	309 (0.7)	308 (1.0)
Female	301 (1.1)	297 (1.0)	296 (1.0)	299 (1.0)	303 (1.1)	305 (1.1)	304 (1.1)	305 (1.4)	307 (1.0)	305 (0.9)	304 (0.8)	303 (0.8)	304 (0.8)
Gap between female and male score	-8 (1.6)	-7 (1.4)	-6 (1.4)	-5 (1.5)	-3 (1.5)	-4 (1.5)	-4 (1.8)	-5 (1.9)	-3 (1.7)	-3 (1.4)	-3 (1.2)	-5 (1.1)	-4 (1.3)
Race/ethnicity													
White	310 (1.1)	306 (0.9)	304 (0.9)	308 (1.0)	309 (1.0)	312 (0.8)	312 (1.1)	313 (1.4)	315 (1.1)	313 (0.7)	311 (0.7)	314 (0.7)	314 (1.0)
Black	270 (1.3)	268 (1.3)	272 (1.2)	279 (2.1)	289 (2.8)	286 (2.2)	286 (1.8)	286 (1.7)	283 (1.5)	285 (1.6)	284 (1.4)	287 (1.2)	288 (1.3)
Hispanic	277 (2.2)	276 (2.3)	277 (1.8)	283 (2.9)	284 (2.9)	292 (2.6)	291 (3.7)	292 (2.1)	293 (2.5)	289 (1.8)	292 (1.2)	293 (1.1)	294 (1.1)
Gap between White and Black score	40 (1.7)	38 (1.6)	32 (1.5)	29 (2.3)	21 (3.0)	26 (2.4)	27 (2.1)	27 (2.2)	31 (1.9)	28 (1.8)	27 (1.6)	26 (1.4)	26 (1.6)
Gap between White and Hispanic score	33 (2.5)	30 (2.4)	27 (2.0)	24 (3.0)	26 (3.1)	20 (2.8)	22 (3.9)	21 (2.5)	22 (2.7)	24 (1.9)	19 (1.4)	21 (1.3)	19 (1.5)
Parents' highest level of education													
Did not finish high school	— (†)	280 (1.2)	279 (1.0)	279 (2.3)	285 (2.2)	285 (2.3)	284 (2.4)	281 (2.4)	289 (1.8)	287 (2.4)	287 (1.2)	292 (1.3)	290 (1.4)
Graduated high school	— (†)	294 (0.8)	293 (0.8)	293 (1.0)	294 (0.9)	298 (1.7)	295 (1.1)	297 (2.4)	299 (1.6)	295 (1.1)	294 (0.9)	296 (1.2)	291 (1.1)
Some education after high school	— (†)	305 (0.9)	304 (0.9)	305 (1.2)	308 (1.0)	308 (1.1)	305 (1.3)	307 (1.5)	308 (1.6)	306 (1.1)	305 (0.9)	306 (0.8)	306 (0.9)
Graduated college	— (†)	317 (1.0)	312 (1.0)	314 (1.4)	316 (1.3)	316 (1.0)	318 (1.4)	317 (1.3)	317 (1.2)	317 (0.9)	315 (0.9)	316 (0.7)	317 (0.8)

—Not available.

†Not applicable.

#Rounds to zero.

[1] In 2004, two assessments were conducted—one using the same format that was used in previous assessments, and one using a revised assessment format that provides accommodations for students with disabilities and for English language learners. The 2004 data in column 11 are for the format that was used in previous assessment years, while the 2004 data in column 12 are for the revised format. In subsequent years, only the revised format was used.

NOTE: Scale ranges from 0 to 500. Students scoring 150 (or higher) know some basic addition and subtraction facts. Students scoring 200 have a considerable understanding of two-digit numbers and know some basic multiplication and division facts. Students scoring 250 have an initial understanding of the four basic operations and are developing an ability to analyze simple logical relations. Students scoring 300 can perform reasoning and problem solving involving fractions, decimals, percents, elementary geometry, and simple algebra. Students scoring 350 can perform reasoning and problem solving involving geometry, algebra, and beginning statistics and probability. Includes public and private schools. For assessment years prior to 2004, accommodations were not permitted. For 2004 (revised format) and later years, includes students tested with accommodations; excludes only those students with disabilities and English language learners who were unable to be tested even with accommodations (1 to 4 percent of all students, depending on age and assessment year). Race categories exclude persons of Hispanic ethnicity. Totals include other racial/ethnic groups not shown separately.

SOURCE: U.S. Department of Education, National Center for Education Statistics, National Assessment of Educational Progress (NAEP), *NAEP 2012 Trends in Academic Progress*; and 2012 NAEP Long-Term Trend Mathematics Assessment, retrieved August 29, 2013, from Long-Term Trend NAEP Data Explorer (http://nces.ed.gov/nationsreportcard/naepdata/). (This table was prepared August 2013.)

Table 223.10. Average National Assessment of Educational Progress (NAEP) science scale score, standard deviation, and percentage of students attaining science achievement levels, by grade level, selected student and school characteristics, and percentile: 2009, 2011, and 2015

[Standard errors appear in parentheses]

Selected characteristic, percentile, and achievement level	Grade 4			Grade 8			Grade 12		
	2009	2011	2015	2009	2011	2015	2009	2011	2015
1	2	3	4	5	6	7	8	9	10
	Average science scale score[1]								
All students	**150 (0.3)**	**— (†)**	**154 (0.3)**	**150 (0.3)**	**152 (0.3)**	**154 (0.3)**	**150 (0.8)**	**— (†)**	**150 (0.6)**
Sex									
Male	151 (0.3)	— (†)	154 (0.4)	152 (0.4)	154 (0.3)	155 (0.3)	153 (0.9)	— (†)	153 (0.8)
Female	149 (0.3)	— (†)	154 (0.3)	148 (0.3)	149 (0.3)	152 (0.4)	147 (0.9)	— (†)	148 (0.7)
Gap between male and female score	1 (0.4)	— (†)	1 (0.5)	4 (0.5)	5 (0.5)	3 (0.5)	6 (1.3)	— (†)	5 (1.0)
Race/ethnicity									
White	163 (0.2)	— (†)	166 (0.3)	162 (0.2)	163 (0.2)	166 (0.3)	159 (0.7)	— (†)	160 (0.7)
Black	127 (0.4)	— (†)	133 (0.4)	126 (0.4)	129 (0.5)	132 (0.5)	125 (1.2)	— (†)	125 (1.5)
Hispanic	131 (0.5)	— (†)	139 (0.7)	132 (0.6)	137 (0.5)	140 (0.5)	134 (1.3)	— (†)	136 (1.0)
Asian/Pacific Islander	160 (1.2)	— (†)	167 (1.4)	160 (1.0)	159 (1.3)	164 (0.9)	164 (3.0)	— (†)	166 (2.3)
Asian	— (†)	— (†)	169 (1.4)	— (†)	161 (1.3)	166 (0.9)	— (†)	— (†)	167 (2.3)
Pacific Islander	— (†)	— (†)	143 (2.2)	— (†)	139 (1.9)	138 (2.5)	— (†)	— (†)	‡ (†)
American Indian/Alaska Native	135 (1.3)	— (†)	139 (1.5)	137 (1.4)	141 (1.4)	139 (1.6)	144 (3.7)	— (†)	135 (5.3)
Two or more races[2]	154 (1.1)	— (†)	158 (1.0)	151 (1.2)	156 (1.3)	159 (1.3)	151 (3.7)	— (†)	156 (2.5)
Gap between White and Black score	36 (0.4)	— (†)	33 (0.5)	36 (0.5)	35 (0.6)	34 (0.5)	34 (1.4)	— (†)	36 (1.6)
Gap between White and Hispanic score	32 (0.6)	— (†)	27 (0.7)	30 (0.6)	27 (0.6)	26 (0.6)	25 (1.5)	— (†)	24 (1.2)
English language learner (ELL) status									
ELL	114 (0.8)	— (†)	121 (1.0)	103 (1.0)	106 (1.2)	110 (1.1)	104 (2.4)	— (†)	105 (2.7)
Non-ELL	154 (0.2)	— (†)	158 (0.3)	153 (0.3)	154 (0.2)	157 (0.3)	151 (0.8)	— (†)	152 (0.5)
Gap between ELL and non-ELL score	39 (0.8)	— (†)	36 (1.0)	49 (1.0)	48 (1.3)	46 (1.2)	47 (2.6)	— (†)	47 (2.7)
Disability status[3]									
Identified as student with disability (SD)	129 (0.6)	— (†)	131 (0.6)	123 (0.5)	124 (0.6)	124 (0.6)	121 (1.8)	— (†)	124 (1.8)
Not identified as SD	153 (0.3)	— (†)	157 (0.3)	153 (0.3)	155 (0.3)	158 (0.3)	153 (0.8)	— (†)	153 (0.6)
Gap between SD and non-SD score	23 (0.7)	— (†)	26 (0.7)	31 (0.6)	31 (0.7)	34 (0.7)	31 (2.0)	— (†)	29 (1.9)
Highest education level of either parent									
Did not finish high school	— (†)	— (†)	— (†)	131 (0.6)	132 (0.7)	137 (0.7)	131 (1.4)	— (†)	131 (1.4)
Graduated high school	— (†)	— (†)	— (†)	139 (0.4)	140 (0.4)	142 (0.5)	138 (1.2)	— (†)	136 (1.2)
Some education after high school	— (†)	— (†)	— (†)	152 (0.4)	153 (0.4)	155 (0.5)	147 (0.9)	— (†)	148 (0.9)
Graduated college	— (†)	— (†)	— (†)	161 (0.4)	162 (0.3)	165 (0.3)	161 (0.7)	— (†)	162 (0.7)
Percent of students in school eligible for free or reduced-price lunch									
0–25 percent eligible (low poverty)	167 (0.4)	— (†)	172 (0.6)	165 (0.5)	167 (0.4)	170 (0.6)	163 (1.2)	— (†)	165 (1.1)
26–50 percent eligible	155 (0.5)	— (†)	161 (0.7)	154 (0.5)	157 (0.5)	161 (0.5)	148 (1.1)	— (†)	154 (1.0)
51–75 percent eligible	144 (0.5)	— (†)	151 (0.7)	141 (0.6)	146 (0.5)	150 (0.6)	136 (1.7)	— (†)	143 (1.1)
76–100 percent eligible (high poverty)	126 (0.6)	— (†)	134 (0.6)	124 (0.7)	129 (0.7)	134 (0.8)	124 (2.1)	— (†)	126 (1.7)
Gap between low- and high-poverty score	41 (0.8)	— (†)	38 (0.8)	41 (0.9)	38 (0.8)	36 (1.0)	38 (2.5)	— (†)	39 (2.0)
School locale									
City	142 (0.6)	— (†)	148 (0.6)	142 (0.6)	144 (0.6)	148 (0.6)	146 (1.8)	— (†)	145 (1.2)
Suburban	154 (0.4)	— (†)	157 (0.6)	154 (0.5)	155 (0.5)	158 (0.4)	154 (1.4)	— (†)	153 (1.0)
Town	150 (0.6)	— (†)	153 (0.8)	149 (1.0)	153 (0.7)	154 (0.7)	150 (1.2)	— (†)	150 (2.1)
Rural	155 (0.5)	— (†)	157 (0.7)	154 (0.4)	156 (0.5)	156 (0.6)	150 (1.2)	— (†)	152 (1.3)
Percentile[4]									
10th	104 (0.6)	— (†)	108 (0.6)	103 (0.6)	106 (0.5)	109 (0.6)	104 (1.2)	— (†)	103 (1.0)
25th	128 (0.4)	— (†)	132 (0.4)	128 (0.4)	131 (0.4)	133 (0.5)	126 (0.8)	— (†)	126 (0.9)
50th	153 (0.3)	— (†)	157 (0.4)	153 (0.3)	155 (0.3)	157 (0.4)	151 (1.1)	— (†)	151 (0.6)
75th	175 (0.3)	— (†)	178 (0.3)	175 (0.2)	176 (0.4)	178 (0.4)	174 (1.0)	— (†)	176 (0.6)
90th	192 (0.3)	— (†)	196 (0.4)	192 (0.3)	193 (0.4)	195 (0.3)	194 (1.0)	— (†)	196 (0.6)
	Standard deviation of the science scale score[5]								
All students	35 (0.2)	— (†)	35 (0.2)	35 (0.2)	34 (0.2)	34 (0.2)	35 (0.4)	— (†)	36 (0.4)
	Percent of students attaining science achievement levels								
Achievement level									
Below *Basic*	28 (0.3)	— (†)	24 (0.3)	37 (0.4)	35 (0.3)	32 (0.4)	40 (1.0)	— (†)	40 (0.7)
At or above *Basic*[6]	72 (0.3)	— (†)	76 (0.3)	63 (0.4)	65 (0.3)	68 (0.4)	60 (1.0)	— (†)	60 (0.7)
At or above *Proficient*[7]	34 (0.3)	— (†)	38 (0.4)	30 (0.3)	32 (0.4)	34 (0.4)	21 (0.8)	— (†)	22 (0.6)
At *Advanced*[8]	1 (0.1)	— (†)	1 (0.1)	2 (0.1)	2 (0.1)	2 (0.1)	1 (0.2)	— (†)	2 (0.2)

—Not available.
†Not applicable.
‡Reporting standards not met (too few cases for a reliable estimate).
[1]Scale ranges from 0 to 300 for all three grades, but scores cannot be compared across grades. For example, the average score of 166 for White 4th-graders in 2015 does not denote higher performance than the score of 160 for White 12th-graders.
[2]Prior to 2011, students in the "Two or more races" category were categorized as "Unclassified."
[3]The student with disability (SD) variable used in this table includes students who have a 504 plan, even if they do not have an Individualized Education Plan (IEP).
[4]The percentile represents a specific point on the percentage distribution of all students ranked by their science score from low to high. For example, 10 percent of students scored at or below the 10th percentile score, while 90 percent of students scored above it.
[5]The standard deviation provides an indication of how much the test scores varied. The lower the standard deviation, the closer the scores were clustered around the average score. About two-thirds of the student scores can be expected to fall within the range of one standard deviation above and one standard deviation below the average score. In 2015, for example, the average score for all 4th-graders was 154, and the standard deviation was 35. This means that one would expect about two-thirds of the students to have scores between 189 (one standard deviation above the average) and 119 (one standard deviation below). Standard errors also must be taken into account when making comparisons of these ranges.
[6]*Basic* denotes partial mastery of the knowledge and skills that are fundamental for proficient work.
[7]*Proficient* represents solid academic performance. Students reaching this level have demonstrated competency over challenging subject matter.
[8]*Advanced* signifies superior performance.
NOTE: In 2011, only 8th-grade students were assessed in science. Includes students tested with accommodations (7 to 14 percent of all students, depending on grade level and year); excludes only those students with disabilities and English language learners who were unable to be tested even with accommodations (1 to 3 percent of all students). Race categories exclude persons of Hispanic ethnicity.
SOURCE: U.S. Department of Education, National Center for Education Statistics, National Assessment of Educational Progress (NAEP), 2009, 2011, and 2015 Science Assessments, retrieved January 10, 2017, from the Main NAEP Data Explorer (http://nces.ed.gov/nationsreportcard/naepdata/). (This table was prepared January 2017.)

Table 224.10. Average National Assessment of Educational Progress (NAEP) music and visual arts scale scores of 8th-graders, percentage distribution by frequency of instruction at their school, and percentage participating in selected musical activities in school, by selected characteristics: 2016

[Standard errors appear in parentheses]

Selected characteristic	Average scale score[1]		Percentage distribution of students by school-reported frequency of instruction[2]										Percent of students reporting participation in musical activities in school		
			Music					Visual arts							
	Music[3]	Visual arts[4]	Subject not offered	Less than once a week	Once or twice a week	3 or 4 times a week	Every day	Subject not offered	Less than once a week	Once or twice a week	3 or 4 times a week	Every day	Play in band	Play in orchestra	Sing in chorus or choir
1	2	3	4	5	6	7	8	9	10	11	12	13	14	15	16
All students	**147 (1.0)**	**149 (0.9)**	**8 (1.7)**	**5 (1.4)**	**23 (3.0)**	**19 (3.0)**	**45 (3.4)**	**14 (3.0)**	**7 (1.8)**	**24 (3.1)**	**18 (2.9)**	**37 (3.5)**	**17 (0.8)**	**5 (0.6)**	**16 (1.0)**
Sex															
Male	140 (1.1)	142 (1.1)	7 (1.6)	5 (1.4)	24 (3.2)	19 (3.0)	45 (3.3)	14 (3.0)	7 (1.8)	24 (3.2)	18 (2.8)	37 (3.4)	18 (1.0)	5 (0.7)	8 (0.9)
Female	155 (1.1)	156 (1.0)	9 (1.9)	5 (1.3)	22 (2.8)	19 (3.1)	45 (3.5)	14 (3.0)	7 (1.8)	23 (3.1)	19 (2.9)	37 (3.7)	16 (1.2)	6 (0.7)	24 (1.3)
Race/ethnicity															
White	158 (1.2)	158 (1.1)	8 (2.2)	4 (1.6)	27 (4.2)	19 (4.2)	42 (4.2)	13 (3.9)	8 (2.6)	28 (4.2)	17 (3.5)	34 (4.4)	19 (1.3)	5 (0.9)	19 (1.5)
Black	129 (2.0)	128 (2.0)	9 (3.8)	10 (3.7)	21 (4.2)	16 (4.2)	43 (5.0)	20 (5.5)	7 (2.9)	17 (3.7)	19 (4.5)	37 (4.9)	12 (1.6)	4 (1.0)	16 (1.5)
Hispanic	135 (1.2)	139 (1.3)	9 (2.5)	4 (1.6)	17 (3.0)	17 (3.3)	53 (3.8)	15 (3.5)	5 (1.7)	18 (3.1)	17 (3.3)	44 (3.9)	15 (1.2)	5 (0.8)	10 (1.1)
Asian	163 (2.5)	167 (2.6)	2 (1.2)	4 (2.4)	22 (5.4)	34 (6.2)	38 (6.2)	4 (1.7)	6 (2.5)	26 (5.6)	32 (5.8)	32 (5.5)	17 (2.5)	15 (2.5)	13 (2.3)
Pacific Islander	‡ (†)	‡ (†)	‡ (†)	‡ (†)	‡ (†)	‡ (†)	‡ (†)	‡ (†)	‡ (†)	‡ (†)	‡ (†)	‡ (†)	‡ (†)	‡ (†)	‡ (†)
American Indian/Alaska Native	‡ (†)	‡ (†)	‡ (†)	‡ (†)	‡ (†)	‡ (†)	‡ (†)	‡ (†)	‡ (†)	‡ (†)	‡ (†)	‡ (†)	‡ (†)	‡ (†)	‡ (†)
Two or more races	149 (3.3)	155 (4.5)	4 (2.1)	6 (2.2)	14 (3.0)	20 (4.4)	56 (5.9)	9 (3.2)	3 (1.9)	26 (4.8)	25 (7.0)	37 (6.6)	21 (4.1)	3 (1.9)	24 (3.6)
Free or reduced-price lunch eligibility															
Eligible	134 (1.1)	137 (1.2)	9 (2.1)	5 (1.7)	20 (3.3)	17 (3.2)	48 (4.0)	18 (3.8)	5 (1.6)	18 (3.4)	17 (3.1)	42 (4.5)	15 (1.0)	4 (0.7)	14 (1.2)
Not eligible	160 (1.1)	159 (1.2)	6 (1.8)	4 (1.7)	22 (3.5)	22 (4.3)	47 (4.2)	12 (3.9)	9 (2.8)	24 (4.0)	20 (3.9)	36 (3.8)	19 (1.4)	7 (1.1)	18 (1.5)
Unknown	157 (3.1)	161 (3.7)	13 (8.0)	8 (†)	49 (11.1)	12 (6.3)	17 (7.9)	2 (†)	12 (7.0)	57 (10.0)	16 (7.3)	12 (7.8)	16 (2.7)	4 (0.9)	18 (3.4)
Control of school															
Public	146 (1.0)	148 (0.9)	8 (1.7)	5 (1.4)	20 (3.1)	20 (3.2)	48 (3.6)	15 (3.2)	6 (1.9)	21 (3.4)	19 (3.0)	39 (3.7)	17 (0.9)	6 (0.7)	15 (1.0)
Private	160 (2.6)	164 (3.2)	14 (8.5)	8 (†)	59 (10.8)	8 (4.5)	10 (†)	5 (†)	17 (8.2)	61 (10.2)	11 (5.8)	6 (1.3)	16 (2.9)	3 (0.8)	23 (4.3)
School location															
City	140 (1.9)	145 (1.8)	7 (2.8)	6 (2.8)	25 (4.4)	18 (4.7)	43 (5.1)	13 (3.6)	2 (1.7)	29 (4.1)	19 (4.6)	36 (4.6)	13 (1.1)	6 (0.9)	14 (1.4)
Suburban	153 (1.5)	152 (1.6)	4 (1.7)	3 (1.7)	26 (4.2)	18 (4.2)	49 (5.1)	11 (2.0)	9 (2.9)	21 (3.9)	21 (4.8)	38 (5.3)	16 (1.3)	7 (1.1)	16 (1.3)
Town	143 (4.4)	147 (3.6)	25 (11.3)	4 (0.7)	8 (1.8)	31 (12.1)	32 (9.2)	26 (12.9)	8 (5.2)	19 (9.4)	12 (7.8)	34 (9.0)	22 (5.2)	1 (0.4)	19 (4.2)
Rural	149 (2.1)	148 (2.0)	14 (5.7)	7 (3.6)	18 (4.8)	18 (6.7)	43 (7.6)	17 (8.5)	9 (5.6)	24 (7.8)	13 (5.7)	37 (8.3)	21 (2.0)	2 (0.8)	19 (2.8)
Region															
Northeast	152 (2.3)	160 (1.4)	3 (0.4)	9 (5.4)	61 (11.2)	25 (8.3)	2 (1.1)	8 (1.0)	11 (5.9)	54 (8.8)	22 (6.1)	4 (†)	17 (1.8)	8 (2.8)	24 (2.7)
Midwest	152 (2.2)	148 (2.2)	9 (4.3)	4 (†)	23 (5.1)	27 (8.9)	37 (9.4)	11 (3.6)	11 (5.2)	31 (7.9)	19 (6.3)	29 (8.8)	20 (2.5)	6 (1.3)	20 (3.7)
South	146 (1.6)	146 (1.7)	10 (3.6)	6 (1.9)	15 (4.4)	11 (3.5)	58 (5.8)	16 (6.6)	6 (2.7)	14 (5.2)	12 (4.0)	52 (6.1)	17 (1.3)	5 (0.5)	14 (0.9)
West	143 (1.6)	148 (1.4)	7 (2.3)	2 (0.1)	11 (3.4)	23 (5.2)	57 (5.1)	17 (5.1)	3 (†)	12 (3.0)	27 (6.3)	42 (5.5)	14 (1.2)	5 (0.8)	11 (1.4)
Frequency of instruction[2,5]															
Subject not offered	133 (3.3)	139 (2.6)	† (†)	† (†)	† (†)	† (†)	† (†)	† (†)	† (†)	† (†)	† (†)	† (†)	13 (2.9)	# (†)	13 (3.4)
Less than once a week	145 (5.9)	153 (5.5)	† (†)	† (†)	† (†)	† (†)	† (†)	† (†)	† (†)	† (†)	† (†)	† (†)	14 (2.7)	3 (1.2)	19 (5.0)
Once or twice a week	151 (2.1)	155 (2.5)	† (†)	† (†)	† (†)	† (†)	† (†)	† (†)	† (†)	† (†)	† (†)	† (†)	18 (1.7)	6 (1.7)	20 (2.2)
3 or 4 times a week	152 (3.4)	150 (2.5)	† (†)	† (†)	† (†)	† (†)	† (†)	† (†)	† (†)	† (†)	† (†)	† (†)	18 (3.0)	8 (1.3)	16 (2.0)
Every day	147 (1.7)	149 (1.7)	† (†)	† (†)	† (†)	† (†)	† (†)	† (†)	† (†)	† (†)	† (†)	† (†)	17 (1.2)	5 (0.6)	14 (1.1)

†Not applicable.
#Rounds to zero.
‡Reporting standards not met (too few cases for a reliable estimate).
[1]Scale ranges from 0 to 300 for both music and visual arts.
[2]Based on principals' responses to the following question: "How often does a typical eighth-grade student in your school receive instruction in each of the following subjects?"
[3]Students were asked to analyze, interpret, or critique a piece of music that they listened to or to describe the social, historical, or cultural context of a piece of music.
[4]Students were asked to analyze, describe, or judge works of art and design to show understanding of form, aesthetics, and cultural or historical context.
[5]For columns 2, 14, 15, and 16, refers to music instruction. For column 3, refers to visual arts instruction.

NOTE: Includes students tested with accommodations (10 percent of all 8th-graders for visual arts and 11 percent for music); excludes only those students with disabilities and English language learners who were unable to be tested even with accommodations (2 percent of all 8th-graders both for visual arts and for music). Detail may not sum to totals because of rounding. Race categories exclude persons of Hispanic ethnicity.

SOURCE: U.S. Department of Education, National Center for Education Statistics, National Assessment of Educational Progress (NAEP), 2016 Arts Assessment, retrieved May 11, 2017, from the Main NAEP Data Explorer (http://nces.ed.gov/nationsreportcard/naepdata/). (This table was prepared May 2017.)

Table 224.70. Average National Assessment of Educational Progress (NAEP) technology and engineering literacy (TEL) overall and content area scale scores of 8th-graders and percentage of 8th-graders attaining TEL achievement levels, by selected student and school characteristics: 2018

[Standard errors appear in parentheses]

Selected student or school characteristic	Average scale score[1]				Percent attaining TEL achievement levels[2]					
		Content area				At or above *Basic*[3]				
								At or above *Proficient*[4]		
	Overall TEL score	Technology and society	Design and systems	Information and communication technology	Below *Basic*[3]	Total at or above *Basic*[3]	At *Basic*[3]	Total at or above *Proficient*[4]	At *Proficient*[4]	At *Advanced*[5]
1	2	3	4	5	6	7	8	9	10	11
All students	**152 (0.6)**	**152 (0.7)**	**153 (0.8)**	**153 (0.7)**	**16 (0.6)**	**84 (0.6)**	**38 (0.7)**	**46 (0.8)**	**42 (0.7)**	**5 (0.3)**
Sex										
Male	150 (0.7)	151 (0.7)	152 (0.9)	149 (0.7)	18 (0.7)	82 (0.7)	38 (0.8)	44 (0.9)	40 (0.9)	4 (0.4)
Female	155 (0.8)	154 (0.8)	154 (0.9)	156 (0.9)	14 (0.6)	86 (0.6)	37 (0.8)	49 (1.0)	44 (1.0)	5 (0.4)
Race/ethnicity										
White	163 (0.7)	163 (0.7)	164 (1.0)	162 (0.8)	8 (0.6)	92 (0.6)	33 (0.9)	59 (1.0)	52 (1.0)	7 (0.5)
Black	132 (1.1)	132 (1.1)	131 (1.3)	133 (1.3)	32 (1.4)	68 (1.4)	44 (1.4)	23 (1.3)	23 (1.2)	1 (0.3)
Hispanic	139 (0.8)	139 (0.9)	141 (1.0)	140 (0.9)	24 (0.9)	76 (0.9)	45 (1.0)	31 (1.0)	29 (1.0)	2 (0.3)
Asian	169 (2.0)	167 (2.4)	168 (2.4)	172 (2.7)	8 (1.0)	92 (1.0)	25 (2.7)	66 (2.8)	53 (2.4)	13 (1.4)
Pacific Islander	‡ (†)	‡ (†)	‡ (†)	‡ (†)	‡ (†)	‡ (†)	‡ (†)	‡ (†)	‡ (†)	‡ (†)
American Indian/Alaska Native	133 (6.2)	135 (6.4)	135 (5.7)	131 (5.0)	33 (6.6)	67 (6.6)	38 (4.2)	29 (5.8)	27 (5.6)	2 (†)
Two or more races	157 (1.9)	157 (2.2)	156 (2.7)	157 (2.0)	13 (1.9)	87 (1.9)	34 (2.9)	53 (3.2)	48 (3.3)	5 (1.2)
English language learner (ELL) status										
ELL	106 (1.3)	109 (1.4)	106 (1.8)	106 (1.5)	61 (2.1)	39 (2.1)	34 (2.1)	5 (0.9)	5 (0.9)	# (†)
Non-ELL	155 (0.6)	155 (0.7)	156 (0.8)	156 (0.7)	13 (0.6)	87 (0.6)	38 (0.7)	49 (0.8)	44 (0.7)	5 (0.3)
Disability status[6]										
Identified as student with a disability (SD)	118 (1.1)	120 (1.1)	120 (1.4)	117 (1.3)	48 (1.4)	52 (1.4)	39 (1.5)	13 (1.2)	13 (1.1)	1 (0.2)
Not identified as SD	157 (0.6)	157 (0.6)	158 (0.8)	158 (0.7)	11 (0.5)	89 (0.5)	37 (0.7)	51 (0.8)	46 (0.7)	5 (0.3)
Access to desktop or laptop computer at home										
Yes	156 (0.6)	155 (0.6)	156 (0.8)	156 (0.7)	13 (0.5)	87 (0.5)	37 (0.7)	50 (0.8)	44 (0.7)	5 (0.3)
No	134 (1.1)	134 (1.1)	134 (1.4)	134 (1.0)	31 (1.5)	69 (1.5)	43 (1.5)	26 (1.4)	25 (1.4)	1 (0.4)
Access to Internet at home										
Yes	153 (0.7)	153 (0.6)	154 (0.8)	154 (0.7)	15 (0.6)	85 (0.6)	37 (0.7)	47 (0.8)	42 (0.7)	5 (0.3)
No	127 (2.0)	128 (2.2)	129 (2.9)	126 (2.2)	38 (3.0)	62 (3.0)	41 (3.4)	21 (2.8)	21 (2.9)	1 (†)
Highest education level of either parent[7]										
Did not finish high school	138 (1.3)	138 (1.3)	138 (1.5)	140 (1.5)	24 (1.9)	76 (1.9)	47 (2.3)	29 (1.9)	28 (1.9)	1 (0.4)
Graduated high school	138 (1.0)	138 (1.0)	139 (1.3)	138 (1.0)	26 (1.4)	74 (1.4)	45 (1.6)	29 (1.2)	28 (1.2)	1 (0.4)
Some education after high school	151 (1.1)	151 (1.2)	152 (1.5)	152 (1.2)	14 (0.9)	86 (0.9)	42 (1.4)	44 (1.7)	41 (1.6)	3 (0.7)
Graduated college	163 (0.7)	163 (0.7)	163 (1.0)	163 (0.8)	9 (0.5)	91 (0.5)	32 (0.8)	59 (0.9)	51 (0.9)	7 (0.5)
Percent of students in school eligible for free or reduced-price lunch[8]										
0 to 25 percent eligible	170 (1.4)	169 (1.8)	169 (1.8)	170 (1.7)	6 (0.8)	94 (0.8)	27 (1.7)	67 (2.0)	57 (1.8)	10 (1.2)
26 to 50 percent eligible	157 (1.3)	157 (1.5)	159 (1.7)	157 (1.4)	12 (0.9)	88 (0.9)	37 (1.4)	51 (1.9)	46 (1.5)	5 (0.7)
51 to 75 percent eligible	148 (1.0)	148 (0.9)	148 (1.2)	148 (1.1)	17 (1.1)	83 (1.1)	42 (1.3)	41 (1.5)	39 (1.4)	2 (0.4)
76 to 100 percent eligible	134 (1.2)	135 (1.3)	134 (1.5)	135 (1.4)	30 (1.4)	70 (1.4)	45 (1.2)	26 (1.2)	25 (1.1)	1 (0.3)
School control[9]										
Public	151 (0.7)	151 (0.7)	151 (0.8)	151 (0.7)	17 (0.6)	83 (0.6)	38 (0.7)	45 (0.9)	40 (0.8)	4 (0.3)
Private	‡ (†)	‡ (†)	‡ (†)	‡ (†)	‡ (†)	‡ (†)	‡ (†)	‡ (†)	‡ (†)	‡ (†)
School locale										
City	147 (1.4)	148 (1.3)	148 (1.6)	148 (1.5)	21 (1.2)	79 (1.2)	38 (1.2)	42 (1.8)	37 (1.5)	4 (0.5)
Suburb	156 (0.8)	156 (1.0)	156 (0.9)	157 (0.9)	13 (0.7)	87 (0.7)	36 (1.0)	51 (1.2)	45 (1.1)	6 (0.5)
Town	153 (2.6)	153 (2.3)	156 (2.8)	153 (2.6)	14 (2.4)	86 (2.4)	41 (1.8)	46 (3.1)	42 (2.4)	4 (1.1)
Rural	152 (1.7)	153 (2.0)	153 (2.5)	152 (1.8)	15 (1.2)	85 (1.2)	40 (1.5)	45 (2.1)	41 (1.7)	4 (0.8)

†Not applicable.
#Rounds to zero.
‡Reporting standards not met (too few cases for a reliable estimate) or the standard error could not be accurately determined.
[1]Scale ranges from 0 to 300.
[2]TEL achievement levels are for performance on the TEL assessment overall, rather than performance on any specific content area.
[3]*Basic* denotes partial mastery of the knowledge and skills that are fundamental for proficient work at a given grade.
[4]*Proficient* represents solid academic performance. Students reaching this level have demonstrated competency over challenging subject matter.
[5]*Advanced* signifies superior performance.
[6]In addition to students with an Individualized Education Program (IEP), also includes students with a 504 plan.
[7]These data are based on students' responses to questions about their parents' education level. Data for students whose parents have an unknown level of education are included in table totals, but not shown separately.
[8]Nonresponse rate for this item was greater than 15 percent but not greater than 50 percent.
[9]Bureau of Indian Education and Department of Defense schools are excluded from the Public category but included elsewhere in this table. The Private category includes Catholic and Other private schools.

NOTE: Includes students tested with accommodations (11 percent of all 8th-graders); excludes only those students with disabilities and English language learners who were unable to be tested even with accommodations (2 percent of all 8th-graders). Race categories exclude persons of Hispanic ethnicity. Detail may not sum to totals because of rounding.

SOURCE: U.S. Department of Education, National Center for Education Statistics, National Assessment of Educational Progress (NAEP), 2018 Technology and Engineering Literacy (TEL) Assessment, retrieved February 12, 2019, from the Main NAEP Data Explorer (http://nces.ed.gov/nationsreportcard/naepdata/). (This table was prepared February 2019.)

Table 226.10. Number, percentage distribution, and SAT mean scores of high school seniors taking the SAT, by sex, race/ethnicity, first language learned, and highest level of parental education: 2017, 2018, and 2019

Sex, race/ethnicity, first language learned, and highest level of parental education	2017					2018					2019				
	Seniors who had taken the SAT		Mean score[1]			Seniors who had taken the SAT		Mean score[1]			Seniors who had taken the SAT		Mean score[1]		
	Number (in thousands)	Percentage distribution	Total SAT score	Evidence-based reading and writing (ERW)	Math	Number (in thousands)	Percentage distribution	Total SAT score	Evidence-based reading and writing (ERW)	Math	Number (in thousands)	Percentage distribution	Total SAT score	Evidence-based reading and writing (ERW)	Math
1	2	3	4	5	6	7	8	9	10	11	12	13	14	15	16
All students	**1,715**	**100.0**	**1060**	**533**	**527**	**2,137**	**100.0**	**1068**	**536**	**531**	**2,220**	**100.0**	**1059**	**531**	**528**
Sex															
Male	809	47.2	1070	532	538	1,018	47.7	1076	534	542	1,062	47.8	1066	529	537
Female	906	52.8	1050	534	516	1,117	52.3	1061	539	522	1,157	52.1	1053	534	519
Race/ethnicity															
White	760	44.3	1118	565	553	931	43.6	1123	566	557	948	42.7	1114	562	553
Black	226	13.2	941	479	462	263	12.3	946	483	463	271	12.2	933	476	457
Hispanic	408	23.8	990	500	489	499	23.4	990	501	489	555	25.0	978	495	483
Asian	158	9.2	1181	569	612	218	10.2	1223	588	635	229	10.3	1223	586	637
Pacific Islander	4	0.2	986	498	488	6	0.3	986	498	489	5	#	964	487	478
American Indian/Alaska Native	8	0.5	963	486	477	11	0.5	949	480	469	13	0.6	912	461	451
Two or more races	57	3.3	1103	560	544	77	3.6	1101	558	543	87	3.9	1095	554	540
No response	94	5.5	961	475	485	131	6.1	954	472	481	112	5.1	959	472	487
First language learned															
English only	1,139	66.4	1074	545	530	1,360	63.6	1083	548	535	1,400	63.1	1074	543	530
English and another language	319	18.6	1034	516	518	415	19.4	1056	526	530	440	19.8	1047	521	526
Another language	203	11.8	1049	513	537	247	11.6	1069	521	547	269	12.1	1057	515	543
No response	54	3.2	941	463	479	115	5.4	930	463	467	111	5.0	925	460	465
Highest level of parental education															
No high school diploma	137	8.0	944	472	472	173	8.1	944	473	471	199	8.9	926	464	462
High school diploma	482	28.1	1003	507	497	577	27.0	1005	507	497	608	27.4	989	500	490
Associate's degree	134	7.8	1036	525	511	158	7.4	1039	526	513	160	7.2	1027	519	508
Bachelor's degree	473	27.6	1118	562	556	588	27.5	1129	566	563	621	28.0	1121	561	560
Graduate degree	340	19.8	1177	591	586	443	20.7	1197	599	598	461	20.8	1194	596	598
No response	149	8.7	914	455	460	198	9.3	911	454	457	172	7.7	902	450	452

#Rounds to zero.

[1] Possible scores on each SAT section range from 200 to 800, for a total possible score of 400 to 1600.

NOTE: The SAT was completely redesigned in 2016. The new SAT was first administered in March of 2016. This table reflects 2017, 2018, and 2019 high school graduates who took the new SAT during high school. The data in this table include only test takers from the 2017, 2018, and 2019 graduating classes who took the new SAT. These data do not factor in performance on the old SAT, and the data for 2017 set a new baseline for future year-to-year comparisons. If a student took the new SAT more than once, the most recent score on each section is used, along with the student's most recent responses to the SAT questionnaire. Race categories exclude persons of Hispanic ethnicity. Detail may not sum to totals because of rounding.

SOURCE: College Entrance Examination Board, SAT Suite of Assessments Annual Report: Total Group, 2017, 2018, and 2019, retrieved October 16, 2019, from https://reports.collegeboard.org/pdf/2019-total-group-sat-suite-assessments-annual-report.pdf. (This table was prepared October 2019.)

Table 226.20. SAT mean scores of college-bound seniors, by sex: 1966-67 through 2015-16

School year	SAT[1]									Scholastic Aptitude Test (old scale)					
	Critical reading score			Mathematics score			Writing score[2]			Verbal score			Mathematics score		
	Total	Male	Female	Total	Male	Female	Total	Male	Female	Total	Male	Female	Total	Male	Female
1	2	3	4	5	6	7	8	9	10	11	12	13	14	15	16
1966-67	543	540	545	516	535	495	†	†	†	466	463	468	492	514	467
1967-68	543	541	543	516	533	497	†	†	†	466	464	466	492	512	470
1968-69	540	536	543	517	534	498	†	†	†	463	459	466	493	513	470
1969-70	537	536	538	512	531	493	†	†	†	460	459	461	488	509	465
1970-71	532	531	534	513	529	494	†	†	†	455	454	457	488	507	466
1971-72	530	531	529	509	527	489	†	†	†	453	454	452	484	505	461
1972-73	523	523	521	506	525	489	†	†	†	445	446	443	481	502	460
1973-74	521	524	520	505	524	488	†	†	†	444	447	442	480	501	459
1974-75	512	515	509	498	518	479	†	†	†	434	437	431	472	495	449
1975-76	509	511	508	497	520	475	†	†	†	431	433	430	472	497	446
1976-77	507	509	505	496	520	474	†	†	†	429	431	427	470	497	445
1977-78	507	511	503	494	517	474	†	†	†	429	433	425	468	494	444
1978-79	505	509	501	493	516	473	†	†	†	427	431	423	467	493	443
1979-80	502	506	498	492	515	473	†	†	†	424	428	420	466	491	443
1980-81	502	508	496	492	516	473	†	†	†	424	430	418	466	492	443
1981-82	504	509	499	493	516	473	†	†	†	426	431	421	467	493	443
1982-83	503	508	498	494	516	474	†	†	†	425	430	420	468	493	445
1983-84	504	511	498	497	518	478	†	†	†	426	433	420	471	495	449
1984-85	509	514	503	500	522	480	†	†	†	431	437	425	475	499	452
1985-86	509	515	504	500	523	479	†	†	†	431	437	426	475	501	451
1986-87	507	512	502	501	523	481	†	†	†	430	435	425	476	500	453
1987-88	505	512	499	501	521	483	†	†	†	428	435	422	476	498	455
1988-89	504	510	498	502	523	482	†	†	†	427	434	421	476	500	454
1989-90	500	505	496	501	521	483	†	†	†	424	429	419	476	499	455
1990-91	499	503	495	500	520	482	†	†	†	422	426	418	474	497	453
1991-92	500	504	496	501	521	484	†	†	†	423	428	419	476	499	456
1992-93	500	504	497	503	524	484	†	†	†	424	428	420	478	502	457
1993-94	499	501	497	504	523	487	†	†	†	423	425	421	479	501	460
1994-95	504	505	502	506	525	490	†	†	†	428	429	426	482	503	463
1995-96	505	507	503	508	527	492	†	†	†	—	—	—	—	—	—
1996-97	505	507	503	511	530	494	†	†	†	—	—	—	—	—	—
1997-98	505	509	502	512	531	496	†	†	†	—	—	—	—	—	—
1998-99	505	509	502	511	531	495	†	†	†	—	—	—	—	—	—
1999-2000	505	507	504	514	533	498	†	†	†	†	†	†	†	†	†
2000-01	506	509	502	514	533	498	†	†	†	†	†	†	†	†	†
2001-02	504	507	502	516	534	500	†	†	†	†	†	†	†	†	†
2002-03	507	512	503	519	537	503	†	†	†	†	†	†	†	†	†
2003-04	508	512	504	518	537	501	†	†	†	†	†	†	†	†	†
2004-05	508	513	505	520	538	504	†	†	†	†	†	†	†	†	†
2005-06	503	505	502	518	536	502	497	491	502	†	†	†	†	†	†
2006-07	502	504	502	515	533	499	494	489	500	†	†	†	†	†	†
2007-08	502	504	500	515	533	500	494	488	501	†	†	†	†	†	†
2008-09	501	503	498	515	534	499	493	486	499	†	†	†	†	†	†
2009-10	501	503	498	516	534	500	492	486	498	†	†	†	†	†	†
2010-11	497	500	495	514	531	500	489	482	496	†	†	†	†	†	†
2011-12	496	498	493	514	532	499	488	481	494	†	†	†	†	†	†
2012-13	496	499	494	514	531	499	488	482	493	†	†	†	†	†	†
2013-14	497	499	495	513	530	499	487	481	492	†	†	†	†	†	†
2014-15	495	497	493	511	527	496	484	478	490	†	†	†	†	†	†
2015-16[3]	494	495	493	508	524	494	482	475	487	†	†	†	†	†	†

—Not available.

†Not applicable.

[1] Data for 1966-67 to 1985-86 were converted to the recentered scale by using a formula applied to the original mean and standard deviation. For 1986-87 to 1994-95, individual student scores were converted to the recentered scale and then the mean was recomputed. For 1995-96 to 1998-99, nearly all students received scores on the recentered scale; any score on the original scale was converted to the recentered scale prior to recomputing the mean. From 1999-2000 on, all scores have been reported on the recentered scale.

[2] The SAT writing section was introduced in March 2005.

[3] Data for 2015-16 seniors cannot be compared to data for previous graduating cohorts because the 2015-16 data include testing only through January of the senior year and graduating cohort membership was also calculated differently.

NOTE: Data for 1966-67 through 1970-71 are estimates derived from the test scores of all participants. Data for 1971-72 through 2009-10 are for seniors who took the SAT at any time during their high school years through March of their senior year. Data for 2010-11 through 2014-15 are for seniors who took the SAT at any time during their high school years through June of their senior year. Data for 2015-16 are for seniors who took the SAT at any time during their high school years through the January 2016 administration, which was the final administration prior to a major test redesign; because of the smaller number of test administrations and other differences, the 2015-16 data are not comparable to data for earlier years. For all data years, if a student took the SAT more than once, the most recent score on each section was used. Possible scores on each section of the SAT range from 200 to 800. Prior to 2006, the critical reading section was known as the verbal section. The SAT was formerly known as the Scholastic Assessment Test and the Scholastic Aptitude Test.

SOURCE: College Entrance Examination Board, College-Bound Seniors: Total Group Profile [National] Report, 1966-67 through 2015-16, retrieved January 31, 2017, from https://secure-media.collegeboard.org/digitalServices/pdf/sat/total-group-2016.pdf. (This table was prepared January 2017.)

Table 226.30. Number, percentage distribution, and SAT mean scores of high school seniors taking the SAT, by degree-level goal and intended college major: 2017, 2018, and 2019

Degree-level goal and intended college major	2017					2018					2019				
	Seniors who had taken the SAT		Mean score[1]			Seniors who had taken the SAT		Mean score[1]			Seniors who had taken the SAT		Mean score[1]		
	Number (in thousands)	Percentage distribution	Total SAT score	Evidence-based reading and writing (ERW)	Math	Number (in thousands)	Percentage distribution	Total SAT score	Evidence-based reading and writing (ERW)	Math	Number (in thousands)	Percentage distribution	Total SAT score	Evidence-based reading and writing (ERW)	Math
1	2	3	4	5	6	7	8	9	10	11	12	13	14	15	16
All students	**1,715**	**100.0**	**1060**	**533**	**527**	**2,137**	**100.0**	**1068**	**536**	**531**	**2,220**	**100.0**	**1059**	**531**	**528**
Degree-level goal[2]															
Certificate program	12	0.9	925	466	460	15	1.0	930	468	462	19	1.2	900	453	447
Associate's degree	21	1.6	900	457	444	25	1.6	906	460	446	33	2.1	883	449	434
Bachelor's degree	362	27.4	1038	524	513	430	27.6	1050	530	520	448	28.0	1039	524	515
Master's degree	435	32.9	1104	555	549	508	32.6	1125	564	561	504	31.5	1118	560	558
Doctor's or related degree	305	23.1	1138	573	565	363	23.3	1163	584	579	356	22.2	1157	580	578
Other	9	0.7	918	458	460	11	0.7	923	462	461	12	0.7	903	452	452
Undecided	176	13.3	1064	537	527	206	13.2	1077	542	535	230	14.3	1054	530	524
Intended college major[3]															
Agriculture, agriculture operations, and related sciences	17	1.2	1003	508	495	21	1.2	1000	507	493	25	1.4	977	496	481
Architecture and related services	20	1.4	1056	524	531	25	1.4	1062	527	535	29	1.6	1047	520	527
Area, ethnic, cultural, and gender studies	2	0.1	1084	561	523	2	0.1	1060	547	513	3	0.1	1040	536	504
Biological and biomedical sciences	107	7.3	1132	571	561	136	7.6	1152	579	573	156	8.5	1139	572	566
Business, management, marketing, and related support services	167	11.4	1072	536	537	205	11.5	1087	542	545	222	12.0	1072	534	537
Communication, journalism, and related programs	30	2.1	1071	552	519	35	2.0	1083	557	525	36	2.0	1069	550	519
Computer and information sciences and support services	56	3.8	1143	568	575	72	4.0	1164	576	588	80	4.3	1156	571	585
Construction trades, general	1	0.1	958	479	479	2	0.1	939	469	470	3	0.1	919	459	460
Education	57	3.9	1032	525	507	68	3.8	1037	527	510	72	3.9	1022	519	503
Engineering	156	10.6	1140	560	580	191	10.7	1152	565	587	194	10.6	1139	559	581
Engineering technologies/technicians	24	1.7	1047	516	532	31	1.7	1054	518	536	34	1.8	1041	512	528
English language and literature/letters	15	1.0	1124	591	533	17	0.9	1132	593	539	16	0.9	1119	585	533
Family and consumer sciences/human sciences	4	0.3	969	493	476	5	0.3	966	491	475	6	0.4	953	484	469
Foreign languages and literatures, general	7	0.5	1116	575	541	9	0.5	1116	574	542	10	0.5	1102	566	536
Health professions and related clinical sciences	278	18.9	1045	529	516	333	18.7	1055	533	522	331	18.0	1048	529	518
History, general	11	0.7	1086	562	524	13	0.7	1091	563	527	13	0.7	1090	563	527
Legal studies, general	29	2.0	1084	555	530	35	2.0	1100	562	538	36	1.9	1104	564	540
Liberal arts and sciences, general studies, and humanities	8	0.5	1116	575	541	9	0.5	1136	583	553	9	0.5	1140	584	556
Library science/librarianship	#	#	1118	585	533	#	#	1111	581	530	#	#	1105	577	527
Mathematics and statistics	11	0.7	1228	592	636	14	0.8	1253	603	650	17	0.9	1242	597	646
Mechanic and repair technologies/technicians	3	0.2	937	466	470	5	0.3	938	468	470	7	0.4	916	458	458
Military technologies	7	0.5	986	498	488	8	0.5	982	496	486	7	0.4	984	498	486
Multi/interdisciplinary studies	2	0.2	1160	586	575	4	0.2	1174	591	584	3	0.2	1155	581	574
Natural resources and conservation	8	0.6	1095	558	537	10	0.6	1109	564	545	10	0.6	1104	562	543
Parks, recreation, and leisure studies	13	0.9	966	484	482	15	0.8	965	484	481	13	0.7	960	482	478
Personal and culinary services, general	6	0.4	953	485	468	7	0.4	943	480	463	7	0.4	929	474	456
Philosophy and religious studies	3	0.2	1102	566	535	3	0.2	1118	572	545	3	0.2	1120	572	548
Physical sciences	21	1.5	1186	591	595	26	1.5	1205	599	606	26	1.4	1203	597	606
Precision production	#	#	975	488	486	#	#	962	482	480	#	#	932	466	466
Psychology, general	64	4.4	1055	542	513	74	4.2	1066	548	519	76	4.1	1064	546	518
Public administration and social service professions	6	0.4	996	511	485	8	0.4	1008	517	491	8	0.4	1001	513	488
Security and protective services	55	3.8	973	493	480	66	3.7	978	497	482	68	3.7	975	495	479
Social sciences	27	1.9	1146	588	559	35	2.0	1166	595	571	33	1.8	1164	594	570
Theology and religious vocations	2	0.1	1104	568	535	2	0.1	1101	565	536	2	0.1	1096	561	535
Transportation and materials moving	#	#	1025	513	512	1	0.1	1037	519	518	1	0.1	1019	511	508
Visual and performing arts, general	106	7.2	1046	537	509	126	7.1	1051	539	512	131	7.1	1045	536	510
Other	26	1.8	963	487	476	29	1.6	966	489	477	27	1.5	963	488	476
Undecided	116	7.9	1073	542	531	137	7.7	1087	547	540	127	6.9	1069	538	532

#Rounds to zero.

[1] Possible scores on each SAT section range from 200 to 800, for a total possible score of 400 to 1600.

[2] Includes only those test takers who responded to the question about their degree-level goal.

[3] Includes only those test takers who responded to the question about their intended college major.

NOTE: The SAT was completely redesigned in 2016. The new SAT was first administered in March of 2016. This table reflects 2017, 2018, and 2019 high school graduates who took the new SAT during high school. The data in this table include only test takers from the 2017, 2018, and 2019 graduating classes who took the new SAT. These data do not factor in performance on the old SAT, and the data for 2017 set a new baseline for future year-to-year comparisons. If a student took the new SAT more than once, the most recent score on each section is used, along with the student's most recent responses to the SAT questionnaire. Detail may not sum to totals because of rounding.

SOURCE: College Entrance Examination Board, SAT Suite of Assessments Annual Report: Total Group, 2017, 2018, and 2019, retrieved October 15, 2019, from https://reports.collegeboard.org/pdf/2019-total-group-sat-suite-assessments-annual-report.pdf. (This table was prepared October 2019.)

Table 227.10. Percentage of 9th-grade students participating in various school-sponsored and non-school-sponsored activities, by sex and race/ethnicity: 2009

[Standard errors appear in parentheses]

Sex and race/ethnicity	School-sponsored activities: Math-related[1]	School-sponsored activities: Science-related[1]	School-sponsored activities: At least one of the math- or science-related activities	Non-school-sponsored activities: Music, dance, art, or theater	Non-school-sponsored activities: Organized sports	Non-school-sponsored activities: Religious youth group or instruction	Non-school-sponsored activities: Scouting or other group or club activity	Non-school-sponsored activities: Academic instruction[2]	Non-school-sponsored activities: Math or science camp	Non-school-sponsored activities: Another camp	Non-school-sponsored activities: At least one of the non-school-sponsored activities
1	2	3	4	5	6	7	8	9	10	11	12
Total	**9.8 (0.39)**	**6.4 (0.36)**	**13.4 (0.50)**	**34.6 (0.91)**	**54.9 (0.81)**	**51.4 (0.93)**	**22.8 (0.64)**	**17.7 (0.62)**	**4.1 (0.31)**	**23.8 (0.76)**	**85.7 (0.60)**
Sex											
Male	8.9 (0.44)	6.3 (0.59)	12.6 (0.69)	27.9 (0.93)	59.8 (0.93)	49.5 (1.10)	21.6 (0.87)	17.5 (0.80)	4.1 (0.51)	23.2 (0.92)	86.1 (0.79)
Female	10.7 (0.55)	6.5 (0.45)	14.2 (0.67)	41.3 (1.20)	50.0 (1.10)	53.4 (1.12)	24.1 (0.88)	17.9 (0.80)	4.0 (0.40)	24.4 (0.91)	85.4 (0.75)
Race/ethnicity											
White	8.3 (0.35)	6.4 (0.43)	12.2 (0.46)	36.8 (0.78)	60.5 (0.87)	56.7 (1.04)	24.0 (0.83)	13.2 (0.65)	2.7 (0.26)	30.6 (0.92)	89.7 (0.47)
Black	12.5 (1.54)	5.4 (0.77)	15.3 (1.71)	33.8 (2.90)	49.1 (2.39)	52.3 (2.31)	26.3 (2.02)	32.8 (2.55)	7.4 (1.24)	14.8 (1.79)	84.9 (1.72)
Hispanic	10.5 (0.92)	5.5 (0.72)	13.4 (1.07)	27.5 (1.47)	46.9 (2.46)	39.1 (2.36)	16.6 (1.27)	18.6 (1.20)	3.6 (0.77)	14.5 (1.66)	76.9 (2.28)
Asian	17.3 (2.25)	13.0 (1.93)	22.3 (2.48)	44.4 (3.43)	38.5 (2.87)	38.8 (3.31)	25.8 (2.28)	31.1 (3.49)	15.0 (2.06)	16.2 (2.14)	82.1 (2.76)
Native Hawaiian/Pacific Islander	‡ (†)	‡ (†)	‡ (†)	‡ (†)	‡ (†)	‡ (†)	‡ (†)	‡ (†)	‡ (†)	‡ (†)	‡ (†)
American Indian/Alaska Native	9.1 ! (2.95)	‡ (†)	12.8 ! (3.87)	20.0 ! (6.56)	48.8 (6.60)	42.3 (6.00)	31.6 (6.00)	16.8 (4.36)	‡ (†)	19.1 ! (8.31)	78.9 (5.22)
Two or more races	10.5 (1.19)	7.6 (1.02)	14.2 (1.41)	36.4 (2.49)	55.8 (2.46)	53.6 (2.47)	24.9 (2.13)	15.4 (1.57)	3.4 (0.81)	21.2 (1.60)	86.8 (1.53)
Race/ethnicity by sex											
Male											
White	7.6 (0.45)	6.1 (0.61)	11.5 (0.73)	29.1 (0.95)	63.3 (1.06)	54.5 (1.19)	23.2 (1.12)	14.2 (0.93)	2.8 (0.36)	29.6 (1.22)	89.0 (0.61)
Black	12.2 (1.74)	5.8 (1.10)	15.4 (1.92)	27.4 (2.88)	58.2 (3.15)	49.0 (3.03)	21.0 (2.85)	31.1 (3.11)	7.5 (2.01)	14.6 (2.46)	87.3 (1.95)
Hispanic	9.2 (1.22)	5.5 (1.15)	12.1 (1.50)	22.4 (2.04)	54.4 (2.86)	37.1 (2.92)	15.3 (1.69)	16.9 (1.83)	2.9 ! (0.88)	13.1 (2.11)	78.4 (2.70)
Asian	18.4 (2.96)	11.5 (2.38)	22.8 (3.23)	36.9 (4.02)	42.9 (3.89)	32.8 (5.50)	26.1 (3.78)	31.0 (4.54)	18.4 (3.34)	20.3 (3.47)	78.9 (3.87)
Native Hawaiian/Pacific Islander	‡ (†)	‡ (†)	‡ (†)	‡ (†)	‡ (†)	‡ (†)	‡ (†)	‡ (†)	‡ (†)	‡ (†)	‡ (†)
American Indian/Alaska Native	10.9 ! (4.96)	‡ (†)	‡ (†)	18.8 ! (9.40)	49.9 (9.31)	38.2 (9.74)	31.3 (8.35)	‡ (†)	‡ (†)	‡ (†)	78.4 (6.67)
Two or more races	8.3 (1.37)	9.0 (1.85)	13.4 (2.04)	29.9 (2.96)	59.2 (3.78)	56.9 (3.48)	26.2 (2.99)	16.0 (2.30)	3.4 ! (1.22)	20.4 (2.28)	88.6 (1.82)
Female											
White	9.0 (0.56)	6.7 (0.61)	13.0 (0.71)	44.9 (1.16)	57.5 (1.13)	59.0 (1.17)	24.8 (1.04)	12.1 (0.76)	2.7 (0.34)	31.7 (1.08)	90.4 (0.62)
Black	12.8 (2.14)	5.0 (1.09)	15.2 (2.38)	39.0 (4.64)	41.8 (3.87)	55.0 (3.33)	30.5 (2.59)	34.2 (3.75)	7.3 (1.53)	14.9 (2.58)	83.0 (2.66)
Hispanic	11.9 (1.16)	5.5 (0.76)	14.6 (1.28)	32.9 (2.06)	39.0 (3.27)	41.1 (2.95)	17.9 (1.83)	20.3 (1.85)	4.4 (1.12)	16.0 (2.15)	75.4 (2.71)
Asian	16.1 (2.49)	14.6 (2.92)	21.8 (3.16)	51.8 (4.88)	34.2 (3.19)	44.8 (3.24)	25.6 (3.53)	31.2 (3.72)	11.7 (3.07)	12.2 (2.55)	85.3 (3.16)
Native Hawaiian/Pacific Islander	‡ (†)	‡ (†)	‡ (†)	‡ (†)	‡ (†)	‡ (†)	‡ (†)	‡ (†)	‡ (†)	‡ (†)	‡ (†)
American Indian/Alaska Native	‡ (†)	‡ (†)	‡ (†)	21.4 ! (8.36)	47.4 (9.63)	47.0 (11.74)	32.0 (8.98)	‡ (†)	‡ (†)	‡ (†)	79.5 (8.44)
Two or more races	12.7 (1.71)	6.3 (1.00)	15.0 (1.73)	42.4 (3.39)	52.5 (4.18)	50.4 (3.62)	23.7 (2.95)	14.8 (2.05)	3.4 ! (1.19)	22.0 (2.24)	85.1 (2.47)

†Not applicable.

!Interpret data with caution. The coefficient of variation (CV) for this estimate is between 30 and 50 percent.

‡Reporting standards not met. Either there are too few cases for a reliable estimate or the coefficient of variation (CV) is 50 percent or greater.

[1] Students could indicate that they participated in clubs, competitions, camps, study groups, or tutoring programs.

[2] Academic instruction outside of school such as from a Saturday academy, learning center, personal tutor, or summer school program.

NOTE: Data on school-sponsored activities are based on student responses and are weighted by W1STUDENT. Student reports about school-sponsored activities refer to the period "since the beginning of the last school year," which for most of these students was 8th grade, or the fall of 2008. Data on non-school-sponsored activities are based on parent responses and are weighted by W1PARENT. Parent reports about non-school-sponsored activities refer to the last 12 months. Race categories exclude persons of Hispanic ethnicity.

SOURCE: U.S. Department of Education, National Center for Education Statistics, High School Longitudinal Study of 2009, Base-Year Public-Use Data File. (This table was prepared September 2012.)

Table 227.40. Percentage of elementary and secondary school students who do homework, average time spent doing homework, percentage whose parents check that homework is done, and percentage whose parents help with homework, by frequency and selected characteristics: 2007, 2012, and 2016

[Standard errors appear in parentheses]

Year and selected characteristic	Percent of students who do homework outside of school		Students who do homework outside of school: Average hours spent per week doing homework		Percentage distribution by how frequently they do homework: Less than once per week		1 or 2 days per week		3 or 4 days per week		5 or more days per week		Percent whose parents[1] check that homework is done[2]		Percentage distribution by how frequently their parents[1] help with hor[…]: No help given		Less than once per week		1 or 2 days per week		3 or 4 days per week		5 or mo[…] p[…]
1	2		3		4		5		6		7		8		9		10		11		12		
2007																							
All students	94.4	(0.30)	5.4	(0.06)	3.1	(0.34)	13.1	(0.47)	43.6	(0.62)	40.2	(0.60)	85.4	(0.46)	10.2	(0.41)	20.3	(0.51)	31.7	(0.64)	25.3	(0.59)	12.4
All elementary school students (kindergarten through grade 8)	95.0	(0.37)	4.7	(0.07)	2.1	(0.23)	12.3	(0.56)	46.2	(0.73)	39.4	(0.68)	95.0	(0.34)	4.3	(0.34)	13.1	(0.52)	32.6	(0.77)	32.9	(0.76)	17.0
Sex																							
Male	94.6	(0.51)	4.6	(0.09)	2.1	(0.31)	12.4	(0.71)	47.9	(1.19)	37.6	(1.09)	95.3	(0.47)	4.3	(0.39)	12.9	(0.63)	32.3	(1.02)	32.7	(1.28)	17.8
Female	95.4	(0.53)	4.9	(0.10)	2.1	(0.31)	12.2	(0.96)	44.4	(1.13)	41.3	(1.08)	94.6	(0.48)	4.3	(0.56)	13.4	(0.76)	32.9	(1.17)	33.2	(1.17)	16.1
Race/ethnicity																							
White	94.7	(0.48)	4.4	(0.07)	2.7	(0.36)	13.7	(0.74)	48.3	(1.05)	35.3	(0.99)	94.0	(0.42)	3.8	(0.37)	15.7	(0.74)	34.9	(0.94)	31.3	(0.92)	14.3
Black	95.5	(1.07)	5.6	(0.27)	1.3 !	(0.53)	7.0	(1.19)	44.4	(3.40)	47.2	(3.11)	98.1	(0.63)	3.5	(1.03)	7.4	(1.14)	25.2	(2.22)	38.3	(3.36)	25.5
Hispanic	94.8	(0.85)	4.7	(0.11)	1.3	(0.33)	13.5	(1.39)	40.7	(1.94)	44.4	(1.74)	96.1	(0.70)	7.1	(0.95)	10.3	(0.91)	30.1	(1.79)	34.0	(1.78)	18.6
Asian/Pacific Islander	95.9	(2.14)	5.7	(0.36)	‡	(†)	4.7	(1.35)	40.1	(4.35)	54.3	(4.73)	89.4	(3.22)	3.7 !	(1.35)	15.4	(4.07)	34.7	(4.39)	29.3	(4.03)	17.0
Asian	97.7	(0.97)	5.7	(0.39)	‡	(†)	5.1 !	(1.53)	39.1	(4.31)	54.8	(4.48)	88.5	(3.44)	3.1 !	(1.36)	12.8	(2.84)	37.5	(4.52)	30.7	(4.22)	15.9
Pacific Islander	79.3	(†)	‡	(†)	‡	(†)	‡	(†)	‡	(†)	‡	(†)	‡	(†)	‡	(†)	‡	(†)	‡	(†)	‡	(†)	‡
American Indian/Alaska Native	98.3	(†)	‡	(†)	‡	(†)	‡	(†)	‡	(†)	‡	(†)	‡	(†)	‡	(†)	‡	(†)	‡	(†)	‡	(†)	‡
Other[3]	96.7	(1.24)	4.8	(0.25)	1.2 !	(0.56)	8.5	(1.73)	57.1	(3.81)	33.1	(3.69)	95.1	(1.81)	‡	(†)	12.3	(2.30)	35.5	(3.99)	33.8	(3.81)	16.1
School control																							
Public	95.1	(0.38)	4.7	(0.08)	2.0	(0.25)	12.4	(0.62)	46.1	(0.76)	39.4	(0.73)	95.4	(0.36)	4.4	(0.38)	13.1	(0.55)	32.4	(0.86)	32.9	(0.81)	17.2
Private	94.0	(1.01)	4.8	(0.19)	2.7	(0.63)	11.4	(1.96)	46.7	(2.64)	39.2	(2.46)	91.5	(1.19)	3.6	(0.85)	13.6	(1.48)	34.3	(2.10)	33.5	(2.36)	15.2
Poverty status[4]																							
Poor	94.2	(0.99)	4.7	(0.20)	2.9	(0.72)	16.3	(2.18)	39.0	(2.53)	41.7	(2.21)	97.9	(0.55)	6.1	(1.01)	8.8	(1.29)	28.5	(2.44)	35.2	(2.41)	21.3
Near-poor	93.1	(1.03)	4.7	(0.16)	2.2	(0.49)	13.4	(1.37)	47.0	(1.89)	37.5	(1.91)	95.8	(1.05)	5.2	(0.92)	11.5	(1.13)	31.8	(1.79)	33.3	(1.63)	18.2
Nonpoor	95.9	(0.38)	4.8	(0.08)	1.8	(0.24)	10.7	(0.59)	48.3	(0.94)	39.2	(0.89)	93.7	(0.48)	3.5	(0.32)	15.1	(0.68)	34.2	(0.85)	32.1	(0.79)	15.2
Locale																							
City	95.2	(0.65)	5.1	(0.13)	1.5	(0.31)	9.1	(0.91)	43.4	(1.58)	46.0	(1.43)	95.4	(0.54)	4.8	(0.67)	11.3	(1.02)	29.1	(1.39)	36.0	(1.41)	18.7
Suburban	95.4	(0.51)	4.9	(0.11)	1.9	(0.37)	9.3	(0.71)	46.1	(1.24)	42.7	(1.19)	93.5	(0.67)	4.4	(0.55)	14.5	(0.85)	33.1	(1.05)	30.8	(1.14)	17.1
Town	93.0	(1.50)	4.1	(0.14)	2.7	(0.79)	18.8	(1.98)	46.4	(2.29)	32.2	(2.08)	96.0	(1.04)	3.2	(0.80)	14.2	(1.62)	35.7	(2.68)	31.1	(2.31)	15.7
Rural	95.0	(0.85)	4.2	(0.15)	3.2	(0.69)	19.5	(1.79)	50.6	(1.90)	26.8	(1.63)	96.3	(0.72)	4.1	(0.94)	13.1	(1.30)	35.5	(2.29)	32.8	(2.23)	14.6
All secondary school students (grades 9 through 12)	93.0	(0.55)	6.8	(0.11)	5.4	(0.85)	14.8	(0.96)	38.0	(1.15)	41.9	(1.18)	64.6	(1.21)	23.1	(1.08)	35.9	(1.26)	29.7	(1.19)	8.8	(0.81)	2.5
Sex																							
Male	91.2	(0.80)	6.0	(0.19)	7.4	(1.53)	18.3	(1.59)	38.2	(1.78)	36.0	(1.64)	67.8	(1.88)	24.1	(1.56)	36.9	(1.97)	29.1	(1.84)	8.2	(1.11)	1.8
Female	94.9	(0.79)	7.5	(0.16)	3.3	(0.72)	11.2	(1.10)	37.7	(1.79)	47.9	(1.85)	61.4	(1.78)	22.0	(1.32)	35.0	(1.44)	30.4	(1.35)	9.3	(1.11)	3.3
Race/ethnicity																							
White	94.5	(0.52)	6.8	(0.13)	4.2	(0.58)	12.9	(0.91)	38.6	(1.51)	44.3	(1.42)	57.2	(1.54)	22.5	(1.28)	41.1	(1.36)	27.7	(1.43)	6.3	(0.66)	2.3
Black	91.8	(1.98)	6.3	(0.38)	‡	(†)	20.1	(3.86)	41.0	(4.72)	29.7	(3.43)	83.1	(2.84)	19.5	(2.97)	26.5	(4.77)	34.4	(4.03)	16.7	(4.45)	2.9 !
Hispanic	90.7	(2.11)	6.4	(0.34)	5.9	(1.29)	17.7	(3.55)	36.6	(2.93)	39.9	(3.03)	75.6	(2.71)	26.2	(2.94)	25.8	(2.38)	33.8	(3.49)	11.0	(1.76)	3.3 !
Asian/Pacific Islander	94.2	(4.66)	10.9	(1.22)	‡	(†)	12.2 !	(4.84)	22.3	(6.26)	63.6	(7.16)	65.0	(7.41)	27.1	(7.15)	34.0	(6.73)	27.0	(6.87)	9.2 !	(3.24)	‡
Asian	93.6	(5.45)	10.3	(1.37)	#	(†)	13.8 !	(5.51)	18.5 !	(6.12)	67.7	(7.18)	59.0	(7.69)	26.4	(7.58)	36.1	(7.55)	26.8	(7.61)	7.6 !	(3.11)	‡
Pacific Islander	‡	(†)	‡	(†)	‡	(†)	‡	(†)	‡	(†)	‡	(†)	‡	(†)	‡	(†)	‡	(†)	‡	(†)	‡	(†)	‡
American Indian/Alaska Native	‡	(†)	‡	(†)	‡	(†)	‡	(†)	‡	(†)	‡	(†)	‡	(†)	‡	(†)	‡	(†)	‡	(†)	‡	(†)	‡
Other	86.7	(4.90)	7.2	(0.72)	‡	(†)	9.9	(2.55)	34.1	(4.90)	50.2	(5.29)	64.4	(6.36)	27.2	(6.80)	35.6	(5.57)	27.8	(5.30)	7.9 !	(2.41)	‡
School control																							
Public	92.3	(0.60)	6.5	(0.11)	5.9	(0.96)	15.9	(1.06)	39.7	(1.26)	38.5	(1.17)	66.1	(1.24)	22.8	(1.16)	35.4	(1.29)	30.0	(1.26)	9.1	(0.87)	2.7
Private	98.5	(0.54)	9.3	(0.39)	0.8 !	(0.35)	5.9	(1.34)	24.0	(2.72)	69.4	(2.89)	53.1	(3.98)	25.0	(2.64)	40.1	(3.68)	27.5	(4.07)	6.1	(1.36)	1.4 !
Poverty status[4]																							
Poor	89.5	(2.21)	5.5	(0.32)	‡	(†)	19.2	(3.62)	38.7	(4.32)	33.7	(3.69)	81.0	(3.03)	24.2	(3.80)	24.0	(4.21)	36.1	(3.76)	14.0	(3.21)	1.7 !
Near-poor	89.5	(1.86)	6.4	(0.35)	6.6	(1.58)	20.5	(3.32)	44.2	(3.43)	28.7	(3.10)	70.8	(3.38)	22.9	(2.90)	32.4	(2.97)	28.7	(3.42)	13.0	(2.22)	3.0 !
Nonpoor	94.9	(0.57)	7.2	(0.13)	4.3	(0.54)	12.1	(0.74)	36.1	(1.41)	47.5	(1.34)	58.9	(1.28)	22.8	(1.11)	39.9	(1.29)	28.4	(1.17)	6.3	(0.68)	2.6
Coursework																							
Enrolled in AP classes	96.9	(0.59)	8.5	(0.22)	2.4	(0.70)	7.5	(0.93)	31.9	(1.81)	58.2	(1.97)	56.3	(2.06)	27.4	(1.90)	36.3	(1.69)	28.3	(1.74)	6.0	(0.99)	1.9
Not enrolled in AP classes	90.6	(0.81)	5.7	(0.13)	7.3	(1.31)	19.5	(1.40)	41.9	(1.56)	31.2	(1.42)	70.1	(1.46)	20.2	(1.14)	35.7	(1.70)	30.7	(1.59)	10.5	(1.23)	2.9
Locale																							
City	92.8	(1.01)	6.8	(0.22)	6.3 !	(2.46)	14.1	(1.90)	35.9	(2.32)	43.7	(2.53)	71.5	(1.89)	22.6	(1.88)	33.4	(2.64)	29.3	(2.00)	12.0	(1.80)	2.7
Suburban	93.6	(0.95)	7.5	(0.17)	4.8	(0.86)	11.4	(1.27)	36.5	(1.71)	47.4	(2.07)	58.9	(2.00)	23.6	(1.74)	39.1	(1.79)	27.8	(1.68)	7.5	(1.01)	2.0
Town	89.7	(2.16)	6.4	(0.27)	5.4	(1.48)	13.2	(1.74)	45.9	(3.46)	35.5	(3.17)	64.8	(3.12)	24.3	(2.81)	34.4	(2.96)	27.9	(3.41)	9.3	(1.80)	4.2 !
Rural	93.9	(1.23)	5.6	(0.29)	5.1	(1.20)	22.7	(2.76)	39.6	(3.04)	32.6	(2.79)	65.5	(2.94)	22.1	(2.69)	34.4	(2.71)	34.8	(3.43)	6.2	(1.53)	2.5 !
2012																							
All students	96.0	(0.27)	5.2	(0.05)	5.3	(0.22)	15.3	(0.46)	43.5	(0.58)	35.9	(0.59)	96.6	(0.18)	8.5	(0.24)	22.0	(0.43)	26.5	(0.43)	26.5	(0.52)	16.6
All elementary school students (kindergarten through grade 8)	96.3	(0.29)	4.7	(0.06)	4.1	(0.27)	12.8	(0.50)	46.7	(0.74)	36.3	(0.68)	99.0	(0.12)	3.0	(0.24)	14.5	(0.40)	27.0	(0.54)	33.7	(0.64)	21.9
All secondary school students (grades 9 through 12)	95.1	(0.58)	6.6	(0.10)	8.4	(0.48)	21.8	(0.92)	35.0	(0.91)	34.9	(0.97)	90.4	(0.55)	22.7	(0.70)	41.5	(1.00)	25.3	(0.84)	7.8	(0.63)	2.8
2016																							
All students	94.0	(0.33)	5.4	(0.07)	6.3	(0.36)	15.6	(0.58)	42.3	(0.74)	35.9	(0.61)	96.6	(0.19)	9.2	(0.32)	23.4	(0.51)	26.6	(0.62)	24.8	(0.71)	16.0

[Standard errors appear in parentheses]

Year and selected characteristic	Percent of students who do homework outside of school		Students who do homework outside of school: Average hours spent per week doing homework		Percentage distribution by how frequently they do homework: Less than once per week		1 or 2 days per week		3 or 4 days per week		5 or more days per week		Percent whose parents[1] check that homework is done[2]		Percentage distribution by how frequently their parents[1] help with hor: No help given		Less than once per week		1 or 2 days per week		3 or 4 days per week		5 or mc p
1	2		3		4		5		6		7		8		9		10		11		12		
2007																							
All elementary school students (kindergarten through grade 8)	**95.0**	**(0.42)**	**4.7**	**(0.08)**	**5.4**	**(0.45)**	**14.4**	**(0.68)**	**45.6**	**(0.96)**	**34.6**	**(0.83)**	**99.1**	**(0.12)**	**4.0**	**(0.31)**	**16.6**	**(0.59)**	**26.9**	**(0.79)**	**31.4**	**(0.89)**	**21.0**
Sex																							
Male	94.2	(0.71)	4.5	(0.10)	6.2	(0.67)	14.5	(0.92)	46.2	(1.36)	33.1	(1.19)	99.4	(0.13)	4.2	(0.50)	15.5	(0.76)	26.2	(1.16)	32.2	(1.18)	21.8
Female	95.9	(0.46)	4.8	(0.09)	4.4	(0.59)	14.3	(0.92)	44.9	(1.19)	36.3	(1.14)	98.7	(0.20)	3.9	(0.38)	17.8	(0.97)	27.7	(1.17)	30.5	(1.16)	20.2
Race/ethnicity																							
White	95.4	(0.41)	4.2	(0.09)	6.3	(0.58)	16.2	(0.78)	48.0	(1.14)	29.5	(1.15)	98.9	(0.16)	3.3	(0.42)	19.5	(0.73)	29.5	(0.90)	31.0	(1.00)	16.7
Black	93.6	(1.83)	5.8	(0.33)	4.8	(1.15)	13.4	(2.14)	41.9	(2.62)	39.9	(2.88)	99.6	(0.23)	3.7	(0.91)	10.5	(1.58)	23.1	(2.52)	32.4	(2.63)	30.2
Hispanic	95.4	(0.99)	4.6	(0.12)	4.3	(0.96)	11.7	(1.48)	44.0	(2.09)	40.0	(2.11)	99.4	(0.22)	5.2	(0.87)	14.0	(1.34)	23.7	(1.47)	32.5	(2.03)	24.6
Asian/Pacific Islander	96.5	(0.95)	5.9	(0.30)	‡	(†)	14.4 !	(5.23)	35.0	(3.70)	47.0	(3.48)	99.0	(0.42)	6.6	(1.29)	19.9	(3.13)	25.2	(4.83)	24.3	(2.85)	24.0
Asian	96.3	(1.00)	5.9	(0.31)	‡	(†)	14.8 !	(5.46)	34.4	(3.82)	47.1	(3.70)	99.0	(0.44)	5.9	(1.20)	19.5	(3.27)	25.8	(4.99)	24.9	(2.96)	23.9
Pacific Islander	‡	(†)	‡	(†)	‡	(†)	‡	(†)	‡	(†)	‡	(†)	‡	(†)	‡	(†)	‡	(†)	‡	(†)	‡	(†)	‡
American Indian/Alaska Native	91.5	(6.64)	4.2	(0.49)	‡	(†)	27.3 !	(13.19)	50.3	(11.70)	‡	(†)	‡	(†)	‡	(†)	‡	(†)	‡	(†)	50.8	(11.96)	‡
Two or more races	91.8	(1.87)	4.6	(0.25)	4.4 !	(1.38)	11.3	(1.67)	53.1	(4.21)	31.1	(3.42)	97.7	(0.96)	4.2	(1.21)	13.2	(1.95)	30.4	(3.38)	34.4	(4.86)	17.8
School control																							
Public	95.0	(0.46)	4.5	(0.08)	5.4	(0.51)	14.8	(0.74)	46.1	(1.07)	33.7	(0.88)	99.1	(0.13)	4.2	(0.34)	16.4	(0.65)	26.7	(0.84)	31.6	(0.96)	21.0
Private	94.8	(1.25)	5.6	(0.24)	4.8	(1.24)	10.6	(1.66)	40.8	(2.59)	43.9	(2.57)	99.0	(0.30)	2.1	(0.50)	18.4	(1.73)	28.8	(2.21)	29.1	(2.32)	21.5
Poverty status[4]																							
Poor	92.9	(1.40)	4.5	(0.27)	7.2	(1.32)	16.4	(2.26)	40.3	(2.33)	36.0	(2.29)	99.5	(0.17)	4.9	(0.99)	12.0	(1.63)	25.6	(2.71)	27.9	(2.28)	29.6
Near-poor	94.3	(1.14)	4.6	(0.17)	5.7	(0.87)	15.3	(1.59)	45.9	(2.35)	33.1	(2.17)	99.5	(0.20)	4.9	(0.93)	15.6	(1.29)	26.2	(1.92)	32.1	(2.21)	21.2
Nonpoor	95.9	(0.42)	4.7	(0.08)	4.7	(0.45)	13.5	(0.61)	47.1	(1.02)	34.8	(1.00)	98.8	(0.18)	3.5	(0.37)	18.4	(0.68)	27.6	(0.78)	32.2	(0.95)	18.4
Locale																							
City	93.9	(0.97)	4.9	(0.13)	5.6	(0.77)	13.3	(1.37)	42.0	(1.68)	39.1	(1.51)	99.5	(0.15)	3.6	(0.45)	15.4	(1.19)	26.4	(1.79)	31.6	(1.81)	23.1
Suburban	96.1	(0.52)	4.8	(0.12)	4.0	(0.61)	12.8	(0.85)	46.4	(1.27)	36.9	(1.23)	98.7	(0.22)	4.6	(0.53)	16.6	(0.85)	27.0	(1.06)	30.5	(1.04)	21.2
Town	93.5	(1.29)	3.8	(0.16)	8.2	(1.95)	20.1	(2.16)	46.9	(2.50)	24.8	(2.33)	99.4	(0.30)	4.6	(1.25)	16.1	(2.24)	27.1	(2.28)	32.6	(2.73)	19.6
Rural	95.1	(0.87)	4.1	(0.14)	7.3	(0.92)	18.2	(1.44)	50.1	(2.34)	24.4	(1.99)	99.3	(0.21)	3.1	(0.75)	19.4	(1.43)	27.8	(1.52)	32.7	(2.16)	16.9
All secondary school students (grades 9 through 12)	**91.5**	**(0.72)**	**7.5**	**(0.13)**	**8.7**	**(0.56)**	**18.7**	**(0.85)**	**33.4**	**(0.93)**	**39.2**	**(1.03)**	**89.9**	**(0.61)**	**23.0**	**(0.81)**	**41.4**	**(1.02)**	**25.7**	**(0.96)**	**7.3**	**(0.65)**	**2.6**
Sex																							
Male	88.7	(1.27)	6.4	(0.14)	12.0	(0.97)	22.2	(1.36)	33.9	(1.08)	31.8	(1.51)	91.5	(0.96)	23.2	(1.19)	41.4	(1.25)	25.4	(1.21)	7.4	(0.94)	2.5
Female	94.4	(0.68)	8.5	(0.19)	5.3	(0.68)	15.3	(1.04)	32.9	(1.53)	46.5	(1.51)	88.2	(0.74)	22.8	(1.19)	41.4	(1.46)	26.0	(1.40)	7.2	(0.89)	2.6
Race/ethnicity																							
White	90.6	(1.07)	7.2	(0.13)	9.2	(0.71)	19.6	(1.08)	32.7	(1.09)	38.5	(1.23)	88.4	(0.72)	20.8	(1.08)	49.4	(1.35)	22.2	(1.08)	5.8	(0.74)	1.8
Black	92.7	(1.58)	7.0	(0.33)	9.9	(1.98)	22.1	(2.71)	36.1	(3.35)	31.9	(2.75)	93.5	(2.52)	19.0	(2.76)	33.3	(3.32)	31.7	(3.04)	11.1	(1.81)	4.8
Hispanic	91.2	(1.67)	7.1	(0.33)	8.3	(1.25)	17.8	(1.69)	35.7	(2.39)	38.2	(2.51)	92.0	(0.96)	28.9	(2.20)	28.8	(1.86)	30.3	(2.30)	8.5	(2.01)	3.5
Asian/Pacific Islander	96.4	(2.42)	11.2	(0.81)	1.4 !	(0.65)	7.7	(1.84)	23.2	(3.56)	67.8	(3.85)	84.9	(2.62)	28.6	(3.42)	33.6	(3.58)	27.5	(4.06)	8.9	(1.79)	‡
Asian	96.3	(2.50)	11.4	(0.83)	1.4 !	(0.67)	6.5	(1.42)	22.9	(3.56)	69.2	(3.68)	84.4	(2.69)	29.1	(3.53)	32.3	(3.56)	28.2	(4.14)	9.0	(1.85)	‡
Pacific Islander	‡	(†)	‡	(†)	‡	(†)	‡	(†)	‡	(†)	‡	(†)	‡	(†)	‡	(†)	‡	(†)	‡	(†)	‡	(†)	‡
American Indian/Alaska Native	‡	(†)	‡	(†)	‡	(†)	‡	(†)	‡	(†)	‡	(†)	‡	(†)	‡	(†)	‡	(†)	‡	(†)	‡	(†)	‡
Two or more races	92.6	(2.33)	8.3	(0.83)	6.5	(1.72)	15.9	(2.92)	37.0	(3.92)	40.5	(3.97)	89.8	(2.42)	19.9	(3.41)	50.1	(4.33)	22.2	(4.29)	5.7	(1.59)	‡
School control																							
Public	91.2	(0.74)	7.2	(0.13)	9.3	(0.62)	20.0	(0.92)	34.4	(1.02)	36.3	(1.12)	90.4	(0.64)	23.1	(0.85)	40.6	(1.13)	26.1	(1.04)	7.5	(0.72)	2.7
Private	94.0	(2.44)	9.9	(0.32)	2.4 !	(0.86)	6.5	(1.21)	23.3	(2.22)	67.8	(2.36)	84.6	(1.75)	21.7	(2.01)	49.5	(2.29)	22.0	(2.16)	5.3	(0.97)	1.5 !
Poverty status[4]																							
Poor	85.5	(3.58)	6.2	(0.33)	14.9	(2.45)	23.1	(2.80)	36.7	(3.41)	25.3	(2.88)	91.5	(2.54)	30.0	(2.92)	21.7	(2.49)	29.2	(3.23)	14.4	(3.49)	4.7
Near-poor	90.9	(1.30)	6.7	(0.24)	9.7	(1.44)	22.0	(2.14)	35.1	(2.56)	33.2	(2.49)	93.5	(1.09)	21.7	(2.09)	34.7	(2.22)	33.2	(1.92)	6.7	(1.19)	3.7
Nonpoor	93.0	(0.71)	7.9	(0.13)	7.0	(0.53)	16.8	(0.84)	32.2	(0.93)	43.9	(1.07)	88.4	(0.59)	21.9	(0.87)	47.6	(1.13)	22.7	(1.16)	6.0	(0.57)	1.8
Coursework																							
Enrolled in AP classes	96.9	(0.62)	9.4	(0.24)	4.5	(0.58)	13.0	(1.08)	30.3	(1.38)	52.2	(1.57)	86.7	(0.87)	28.7	(1.25)	42.7	(1.51)	21.8	(1.44)	5.8	(0.86)	1.0
Not enrolled in AP classes	88.1	(1.04)	6.1	(0.12)	11.5	(0.81)	22.7	(1.15)	35.5	(1.23)	30.3	(1.32)	92.1	(0.80)	19.1	(1.05)	40.5	(1.47)	28.4	(1.22)	8.3	(0.86)	3.7
Locale																							
City	91.6	(1.25)	7.8	(0.27)	8.7	(1.14)	17.2	(1.59)	32.7	(1.73)	41.4	(2.14)	91.3	(0.91)	22.8	(1.90)	38.0	(1.93)	27.9	(1.90)	8.6	(1.28)	2.7
Suburban	93.6	(1.11)	7.9	(0.17)	6.1	(0.73)	16.7	(1.38)	33.7	(1.47)	43.5	(1.37)	89.3	(1.07)	22.6	(1.20)	43.3	(1.53)	24.2	(1.37)	7.2	(1.04)	2.7
Town	85.7	(3.15)	6.1	(0.33)	11.9	(1.96)	26.3	(3.48)	31.7	(3.10)	30.1	(3.68)	91.5	(2.01)	24.6	(3.42)	41.8	(3.83)	24.1	(2.90)	6.6	(1.79)	3.0 !
Rural	87.8	(2.02)	6.1	(0.22)	14.6	(1.83)	24.3	(1.98)	34.8	(1.97)	26.3	(1.83)	88.3	(1.15)	23.7	(2.04)	41.9	(2.19)	26.9	(2.22)	5.4	(1.15)	2.1 !

†Not applicable.

#Rounds to zero.

!Interpret data with caution. The coefficient of variation (CV) for this estimate is between 30 and 50 percent.

‡Reporting standards not met. Either there are too few cases for a reliable estimate or the coefficient of variation (CV) is 50 percent or greater.

[1] Refers to one or more parent or other household adult.

[2] The 2007 and 2016 questionnaire items differed. In 2007, parents responded "yes" or "no" to an item asking whether they check that homework is done. In 2016, parents responded to a multiple-choice question asking how often they check that homework is done, and the 2016 estimates include all parents who "rarely," "sometimes," or "always" check. Therefore, the 2007 and 2016 estimates are not comparable.

[3] Includes children of Two or more races as well as those for whom "Other race" was reported. "Other race" was not included on the 2012 and 2016 questionnaires.

[4] Poor children are those whose family incomes were below the Census Bureau's poverty threshold in the year prior to data collection; near-poor children are those whose family incomes ranged from the poverty threshold to 199 percent of the poverty threshold; and nonpoor children are those whose family incomes were at or above 200 percent of the poverty threshold. The poverty threshold is a dollar amount that varies depending on a family's size and composition and is updated annually to account for inflation. In 2015, for example, the poverty threshold for a family of four with two children was $24,257. Survey respondents are asked to select the range within which their income falls, rather than giving the exact amount of their income; therefore, the measure of poverty status is an approximation.

NOTE: While National Household Education Surveys Program (NHES) administrations prior to 2012 were administered via telephone with an interviewer, NHES:2012 and NHES:2016 used self-administered paper-and-pencil questionnaires that were mailed to respondents. Measurable differences between estimates for years prior to 2012 and estimates for later years could reflect actual changes in the population, or the changes could be due to the mode change from telephone to mail. Includes children enrolled in kindergarten through grade 12 and ungraded students. Excludes homeschooled students. Data based on responses of the parent most knowledgeable about the student's education. Race categories exclude persons of Hispanic ethnicity. Detail may not sum to totals because of rounding.

SOURCE: U.S. Department of Education, National Center for Education Statistics, Parent and Family Involvement in Education Survey of the National Household Education Surveys Program (PFI-NHES:2007, 2012, and 2016). (This table was prepared May 2018.)

Table 227.50. Average National Assessment of Educational Progress (NAEP) reading and mathematics scale scores of 4th-, 8th-, and 12th-graders and percentage absent from school, by selected characteristics and number of days absent in the last month: 2019

[Standard errors appear in parentheses]

Grade level and days absent from school in the last month	All students	Sex		Race/ethnicity							Eligibility for free or reduced-price lunch (public school students only)			Control of school		
		Male	Female	White	Black	Hispanic	Asian	Pacific Islander	American Indian/ Alaska Native	Two or more races	Eligible	Not eligible	Unknown	Public	Catholic	Other private
1	2	3	4	5	6	7	8	9	10	11	12	13	14	15	16	17
	Average mathematics scale score[1]															
4th-graders	**241 (0.2)**	**242 (0.3)**	**239 (0.2)**	**249 (0.3)**	**224 (0.4)**	**231 (0.3)**	**263 (1.0)**	**226 (7.9)**	**227 (1.2)**	**244 (0.6)**	**229 (0.2)**	**253 (0.3)**	**247 (1.2)**	**240 (0.2)**	**246 (1.3)**	**‡ (†)**
0 days	248 (0.3)	250 (0.4)	245 (0.3)	254 (0.4)	232 (0.5)	239 (0.5)	269 (1.0)	236 (9.2)	235 (2.3)	251 (0.8)	236 (0.3)	258 (0.3)	252 (1.3)	247 (0.3)	249 (1.6)	‡ (†)
1-2 days	241 (0.3)	243 (0.5)	240 (0.4)	250 (0.4)	225 (0.5)	232 (0.6)	260 (1.6)	238 (4.2)	231 (2.2)	245 (1.3)	231 (0.4)	253 (0.5)	247 (1.5)	241 (0.3)	246 (1.9)	‡ (†)
3-4 days	234 (0.4)	234 (0.6)	233 (0.5)	243 (0.5)	221 (0.9)	226 (0.7)	253 (2.1)	232 (5.5)	226 (2.9)	235 (2.2)	225 (0.5)	246 (0.6)	241 (2.7)	233 (0.4)	242 (2.8)	‡ (†)
5 or more days	223 (0.5)	223 (0.7)	223 (0.8)	234 (0.8)	209 (0.7)	215 (0.9)	242 (3.4)	195 (22.9)	214 (2.8)	228 (2.2)	215 (0.6)	238 (0.8)	233 (5.1)	222 (0.5)	237 (3.4)	‡ (†)
5-10 days	229 (0.6)	230 (0.7)	229 (0.9)	241 (0.8)	213 (1.1)	220 (1.3)	250 (4.8)	220 (6.2)	218 (4.0)	232 (2.6)	220 (0.7)	244 (0.7)	243 (3.1)	228 (0.6)	241 (4.6)	‡ (†)
More than 10 days	213 (0.8)	212 (1.4)	214 (1.0)	221 (1.4)	205 (0.9)	208 (1.4)	234 (5.1)	180 (34.8)	208 (4.1)	219 (3.2)	207 (0.8)	226 (1.6)	219 (10.8)	212 (0.7)	‡ (†)	‡ (†)
8th-graders	**282 (0.3)**	**282 (0.3)**	**282 (0.3)**	**292 (0.3)**	**260 (0.4)**	**268 (0.4)**	**313 (1.0)**	**266 (2.3)**	**262 (1.3)**	**286 (1.0)**	**266 (0.3)**	**296 (0.3)**	**294 (1.6)**	**281 (0.3)**	**293 (1.6)**	**‡ (†)**
0 days	290 (0.4)	290 (0.5)	290 (0.5)	298 (0.4)	267 (0.6)	275 (0.7)	318 (1.2)	274 (5.6)	266 (2.7)	294 (1.4)	274 (0.5)	302 (0.4)	299 (1.8)	289 (0.4)	297 (1.9)	‡ (†)
1-2 days	283 (0.3)	282 (0.4)	283 (0.5)	293 (0.5)	261 (0.8)	269 (0.5)	311 (2.1)	268 (5.6)	267 (2.2)	288 (1.6)	267 (0.4)	296 (0.5)	296 (1.9)	281 (0.3)	293 (1.9)	‡ (†)
3-4 days	271 (0.5)	271 (0.7)	270 (0.7)	283 (0.6)	252 (0.9)	259 (1.0)	298 (3.3)	254 (6.9)	260 (3.0)	275 (2.0)	259 (0.5)	285 (0.8)	281 (3.0)	270 (0.5)	288 (4.3)	‡ (†)
5 or more days	260 (0.8)	259 (1.2)	262 (1.0)	273 (1.1)	243 (1.3)	251 (1.3)	282 (5.7)	247 (7.6)	253 (6.6)	265 (3.1)	250 (0.8)	277 (1.2)	274 (6.2)	260 (0.7)	276 (4.7)	‡ (†)
5-10 days	265 (0.8)	265 (1.1)	266 (1.2)	277 (1.2)	247 (1.4)	257 (1.6)	290 (6.4)	259 (8.7)	262 (8.7)	270 (3.8)	255 (1.0)	282 (1.1)	282 (5.6)	265 (0.8)	‡ (†)	‡ (†)
More than 10 days	246 (1.4)	244 (2.1)	248 (1.6)	259 (2.3)	233 (2.7)	238 (2.0)	264 (7.3)	‡ (†)	232 (4.4)	252 (6.4)	239 (1.2)	262 (2.5)	251 (16.3)	245 (1.1)	‡ (†)	‡ (†)
12th-graders	**150 (0.4)**	**152 (0.6)**	**149 (0.4)**	**159 (0.5)**	**128 (0.7)**	**138 (0.5)**	**175 (1.5)**	**135 (5.9)**	**136 (1.9)**	**157 (1.9)**	**136 (0.4)**	**160 (0.5)**	**161 (1.9)**	**149 (0.4)**	**‡ (†)**	**‡ (†)**
0 days	155 (0.5)	156 (0.7)	153 (0.7)	163 (0.8)	133 (1.1)	143 (0.7)	177 (1.9)	‡ (†)	138 (3.6)	161 (3.5)	140 (0.6)	163 (0.7)	164 (2.5)	154 (0.5)	‡ (†)	‡ (†)
1-2 days	153 (0.5)	154 (0.8)	151 (0.6)	162 (0.7)	130 (1.0)	138 (0.9)	178 (2.5)	‡ (†)	140 (3.4)	161 (2.4)	137 (0.6)	162 (0.7)	163 (2.3)	152 (0.5)	‡ (†)	‡ (†)
3-4 days	144 (0.8)	146 (1.2)	143 (1.1)	154 (1.1)	122 (1.7)	133 (1.1)	166 (3.7)	‡ (†)	130 (4.3)	151 (4.8)	132 (1.0)	155 (1.1)	153 (4.4)	143 (0.8)	‡ (†)	‡ (†)
5 or more days	137 (1.0)	137 (1.4)	137 (1.2)	146 (1.6)	120 (1.6)	126 (1.3)	169 (5.9)	‡ (†)	‡ (†)	137 (5.3)	126 (1.2)	148 (1.5)	150 (4.6)	136 (1.1)	‡ (†)	‡ (†)
5-10 days	141 (1.2)	141 (1.8)	141 (1.4)	150 (1.6)	123 (2.0)	130 (1.5)	178 (6.7)	‡ (†)	‡ (†)	‡ (†)	129 (1.3)	152 (1.5)	151 (5.2)	140 (1.2)	‡ (†)	‡ (†)
More than 10 days	127 (1.9)	128 (2.8)	126 (2.6)	134 (3.3)	114 (3.3)	118 (2.3)	‡ (†)	‡ (†)	‡ (†)	‡ (†)	117 (2.4)	137 (2.9)	‡ (†)	126 (2.0)	‡ (†)	‡ (†)
	Average reading scale score[2]															
4th-graders	**220 (0.2)**	**217 (0.3)**	**224 (0.2)**	**230 (0.2)**	**204 (0.5)**	**209 (0.5)**	**239 (1.0)**	**212 (2.0)**	**204 (1.7)**	**226 (0.8)**	**207 (0.3)**	**235 (0.3)**	**232 (1.1)**	**219 (0.2)**	**235 (1.6)**	**‡ (†)**
0 days	228 (0.3)	225 (0.4)	231 (0.4)	235 (0.3)	212 (0.7)	217 (0.7)	246 (1.1)	225 (3.4)	214 (2.1)	232 (1.2)	214 (0.4)	240 (0.3)	238 (1.4)	227 (0.3)	239 (1.6)	‡ (†)
1-2 days	222 (0.4)	219 (0.5)	226 (0.4)	232 (0.4)	205 (0.8)	211 (0.8)	239 (1.7)	218 (4.5)	210 (2.5)	227 (1.4)	210 (0.6)	236 (0.5)	232 (1.7)	221 (0.4)	236 (2.5)	‡ (†)
3-4 days	215 (0.5)	212 (0.7)	219 (0.6)	226 (0.7)	200 (1.2)	206 (1.1)	229 (3.2)	200 (6.4)	205 (3.0)	222 (2.1)	205 (0.7)	229 (0.8)	230 (3.0)	214 (0.5)	231 (5.3)	‡ (†)
5 or more days	199 (0.7)	194 (0.9)	204 (0.8)	212 (0.9)	185 (0.9)	188 (1.3)	216 (3.9)	196 (6.0)	192 (3.8)	207 (2.6)	189 (0.8)	217 (1.1)	214 (3.2)	197 (0.7)	225 (3.8)	‡ (†)
5-10 days	208 (0.9)	203 (1.2)	213 (1.0)	220 (1.2)	193 (1.3)	197 (1.9)	223 (4.8)	203 (6.3)	201 (5.2)	213 (3.1)	197 (1.0)	224 (1.3)	219 (3.9)	207 (0.9)	232 (4.4)	‡ (†)
More than 10 days	185 (1.1)	181 (1.4)	191 (1.3)	196 (1.5)	176 (1.5)	177 (1.9)	207 (6.5)	183 (7.2)	176 (4.4)	198 (3.8)	178 (1.1)	202 (1.9)	204 (6.7)	184 (1.1)	‡ (†)	‡ (†)
8th-graders	**263 (0.3)**	**258 (0.3)**	**269 (0.3)**	**272 (0.3)**	**244 (0.5)**	**252 (0.6)**	**284 (0.9)**	**252 (2.3)**	**248 (1.6)**	**267 (0.9)**	**250 (0.4)**	**275 (0.3)**	**276 (1.0)**	**262 (0.3)**	**278 (1.3)**	**‡ (†)**
0 days	268 (0.4)	263 (0.5)	274 (0.5)	276 (0.3)	250 (0.7)	256 (0.9)	288 (1.1)	262 (3.8)	257 (2.3)	271 (1.7)	254 (0.5)	279 (0.4)	279 (1.5)	267 (0.4)	281 (1.9)	‡ (†)
1-2 days	264 (0.4)	259 (0.5)	270 (0.5)	273 (0.4)	245 (0.7)	254 (0.6)	281 (1.7)	253 (5.3)	251 (2.7)	271 (1.4)	251 (0.5)	276 (0.5)	276 (1.3)	263 (0.4)	278 (1.6)	‡ (†)
3-4 days	256 (0.6)	250 (0.9)	262 (0.7)	267 (0.6)	239 (1.2)	246 (1.2)	277 (3.8)	244 (6.2)	242 (3.5)	260 (2.7)	245 (0.9)	268 (0.8)	272 (3.0)	255 (0.7)	277 (2.6)	‡ (†)
5 or more days	243 (0.8)	236 (1.2)	251 (1.0)	255 (0.9)	230 (1.1)	235 (1.9)	256 (4.1)	233 (5.0)	234 (3.7)	243 (5.1)	234 (1.0)	257 (1.1)	265 (4.7)	242 (0.8)	267 (5.3)	‡ (†)
5-10 days	249 (0.8)	242 (1.3)	256 (1.2)	260 (1.1)	235 (1.2)	241 (1.9)	265 (4.4)	237 (5.7)	240 (3.9)	250 (5.1)	240 (1.0)	261 (1.2)	272 (4.8)	248 (0.8)	‡ (†)	‡ (†)
More than 10 days	226 (1.6)	221 (2.5)	234 (2.4)	238 (2.1)	217 (2.4)	219 (3.3)	237 (8.5)	‡ (†)	214 (7.6)	225 (10.2)	220 (1.9)	241 (2.6)	242 (12.5)	225 (1.6)	‡ (†)	‡ (†)
12th-graders	**285 (0.5)**	**279 (0.7)**	**292 (0.6)**	**295 (0.6)**	**263 (1.0)**	**274 (0.7)**	**299 (1.7)**	**278 (5.2)**	**272 (2.4)**	**295 (2.1)**	**271 (0.6)**	**294 (0.7)**	**299 (1.9)**	**284 (0.6)**	**‡ (†)**	**‡ (†)**
0 days	290 (0.7)	284 (0.8)	296 (0.9)	298 (0.8)	267 (1.8)	278 (1.0)	302 (2.3)	‡ (†)	273 (5.1)	303 (3.8)	276 (1.0)	297 (0.9)	300 (2.4)	288 (0.7)	‡ (†)	‡ (†)
1-2 days	288 (0.7)	281 (0.9)	294 (0.8)	297 (0.9)	266 (1.4)	276 (0.9)	302 (2.3)	‡ (†)	281 (4.3)	293 (2.9)	274 (0.8)	296 (0.9)	303 (2.3)	286 (0.7)	‡ (†)	‡ (†)
3-4 days	280 (0.9)	274 (1.3)	286 (1.0)	292 (1.2)	260 (1.8)	268 (1.2)	297 (4.0)	‡ (†)	270 (5.3)	295 (5.2)	266 (1.0)	291 (1.3)	297 (3.4)	279 (0.9)	‡ (†)	‡ (†)
5 or more days	272 (1.2)	263 (1.8)	279 (1.4)	280 (1.7)	256 (2.6)	265 (1.6)	283 (5.0)	‡ (†)	‡ (†)	283 (7.3)	262 (1.4)	281 (1.9)	287 (5.9)	270 (1.3)	‡ (†)	‡ (†)
5-10 days	276 (1.3)	269 (2.0)	283 (1.5)	285 (1.8)	259 (2.9)	269 (1.9)	288 (5.6)	‡ (†)	‡ (†)	‡ (†)	266 (1.6)	285 (2.1)	291 (6.5)	275 (1.3)	‡ (†)	‡ (†)
More than 10 days	256 (2.7)	245 (3.5)	266 (3.4)	261 (3.9)	242 (5.8)	254 (3.0)	‡ (†)	‡ (†)	‡ (†)	‡ (†)	248 (2.9)	265 (3.9)	‡ (†)	255 (2.7)	‡ (†)	‡ (†)
	Percent of students absent[3]															
4th-graders	**100 (†)**	**100 (†)**	**100 (†)**	**100 (†)**	**100 (†)**	**100 (†)**	**100 (†)**	**100 (†)**	**100 (†)**	**100 (†)**	**100 (†)**	**100 (†)**	**100 (†)**	**100 (†)**	**100 (†)**	**100 (†)**
0 days	44 (0.2)	44 (0.3)	43 (0.3)	45 (0.3)	40 (0.4)	41 (0.6)	59 (0.9)	35 (3.2)	38 (2.0)	44 (1.1)	39 (0.3)	49 (0.4)	49 (1.3)	43 (0.2)	48 (1.6)	‡ (†)
1-2 days	32 (0.2)	30 (0.3)	33 (0.3)	33 (0.3)	31 (0.4)	32 (0.6)	24 (0.7)	26 (3.4)	28 (2.2)	32 (1.0)	32 (0.3)	32 (0.3)	29 (1.0)	32 (0.2)	31 (1.4)	‡ (†)
3-4 days	13 (0.2)	13 (0.3)	14 (0.2)	13 (0.2)	15 (0.4)	14 (0.4)	8 (0.7)	18 (3.2)	18 (1.8)	14 (0.9)	15 (0.3)	12 (0.2)	13 (0.9)	14 (0.2)	13 (1.1)	‡ (†)
5 or more days	11 (0.2)	12 (0.2)	10 (0.2)	9 (0.2)	14 (0.3)	13 (0.3)	9 (0.6)	21 (3.8)	17 (1.6)	10 (0.7)	14 (0.2)	8 (0.2)	9 (1.0)	11 (0.2)	8 (0.8)	‡ (†)
5-10 days	7 (0.1)	7 (0.2)	6 (0.1)	6 (0.1)	8 (0.2)	7 (0.2)	5 (0.5)	14 (3.6)	11 (1.1)	6 (0.5)	8 (0.1)	5 (0.2)	6 (0.7)	7 (0.1)	6 (0.7)	‡ (†)
More than 10 days	4 (0.1)	5 (0.1)	4 (0.1)	3 (0.1)	7 (0.2)	6 (0.2)	4 (0.3)	7 (1.3)	6 (0.9)	4 (0.4)	6 (0.2)	3 (0.1)	3 (0.6)	5 (0.1)	2 (0.4)	‡ (†)
8th-graders	**100 (†)**	**100 (†)**	**100 (†)**	**100 (†)**	**100 (†)**	**100 (†)**	**100 (†)**	**100 (†)**	**100 (†)**	**100 (†)**	**100 (†)**	**100 (†)**	**100 (†)**	**100 (†)**	**100 (†)**	**100 (†)**
0 days	41 (0.3)	43 (0.4)	40 (0.3)	41 (0.3)	39 (0.6)	40 (0.6)	59 (1.5)	40 (3.8)	32 (1.7)	41 (1.3)	37 (0.4)	45 (0.4)	47 (1.4)	41 (0.3)	43 (1.3)	‡ (†)
1-2 days	38 (0.2)	37 (0.3)	39 (0.3)	40 (0.3)	35 (0.6)	38 (0.5)	29 (1.2)	34 (3.7)	40 (1.5)	36 (1.1)	37 (0.3)	39 (0.3)	37 (1.3)	38 (0.2)	40 (1.3)	‡ (†)
3-4 days	14 (0.2)	13 (0.2)	14 (0.2)	13 (0.2)	17 (0.5)	15 (0.4)	8 (0.7)	16 (2.6)	18 (1.2)	15 (1.0)	16 (0.2)	12 (0.2)	12 (0.8)	14 (0.2)	12 (0.8)	‡ (†)
5 or more days	7 (0.1)	7 (0.2)	7 (0.2)	6 (0.1)	9 (0.3)	8 (0.3)	4 (0.5)	10 (1.4)	10 (1.0)	8 (0.7)	9 (0.2)	5 (0.1)	4 (0.5)	7 (0.1)	5 (0.7)	‡ (†)
5-10 days	5 (0.1)	5 (0.1)	5 (0.2)	5 (0.1)	6 (0.3)	6 (0.3)	3 (0.4)	7 (1.3)	8 (0.8)	6 (0.5)	7 (0.2)	4 (0.1)	3 (0.4)	5 (0.1)	4 (0.6)	‡ (†)
More than 10 days	2 (0.1)	2 (0.1)	2 (0.1)	1 (0.1)	3 (0.2)	2 (0.1)	1 (0.2)	3 (0.5)	2 (0.4)	2 (0.4)	3 (0.1)	1 (0.1)	1 (0.3)	2 (0.1)	1 (0.2)	‡ (†)
12th-graders	**100 (†)**	**100 (†)**	**100 (†)**	**100 (†)**	**100 (†)**	**100 (†)**	**100 (†)**	**100 (†)**	**100 (†)**	**100 (†)**	**100 (†)**	**100 (†)**	**100 (†)**	**100 (†)**	**100 (†)**	**100 (†)**
0 days	34 (0.4)	37 (0.5)	31 (0.5)	34 (0.5)	33 (0.7)	33 (0.8)	47 (1.5)	‡ (†)	28 (3.0)	31 (1.7)	31 (0.5)	36 (0.5)	39 (2.8)	34 (0.3)	‡ (†)	‡ (†)
1-2 days	41 (0.4)	39 (0.5)	42 (0.5)	43 (0.5)	37 (0.7)	39 (0.7)	35 (1.2)	‡ (†)	35 (2.9)	42 (2.2)	39 (0.5)	42 (0.5)	39 (2.2)	41 (0.3)	‡ (†)	‡ (†)
3-4 days	17 (0.3)	16 (0.4)	18 (0.4)	16 (0.4)	19 (0.7)	18 (0.5)	12 (1.0)	‡ (†)	22 (2.7)	17 (1.7)	19 (0.4)	15 (0.4)	17 (1.6)	17 (0.3)	‡ (†)	‡ (†)
5 or more days	9 (0.2)	8 (0.3)	9 (0.3)	8 (0.3)	10 (0.5)	10 (0.4)	6 (0.7)	‡ (†)	15 (2.1)	10 (1.2)	11 (0.4)	7 (0.2)	5 (0.6)	9 (0.2)	‡ (†)	‡ (†)
5-10 days	7 (0.2)	6 (0.2)	7 (0.3)	6 (0.2)	8 (0.4)	7 (0.4)	5 (0.6)	‡ (†)	12 (1.9)	8 (1.1)	8 (0.3)	6 (0.2)	4 (0.5)	7 (0.2)	‡ (†)	‡ (†)
More than 10 days	2 (0.1)	2 (0.1)	2 (0.1)	2 (0.1)	2 (0.3)	3 (0.2)	2 (0.3)	‡ (†)	3 (0.9)	2 (0.7)	3 (0.2)	2 (0.1)	1 (0.3)	2 (0.1)	‡ (†)	‡ (†)

†Not applicable.

‡Reporting standards not met (too few cases for a reliable estimate).

[1] For grades 4 and 8, the mathematics scale ranges from 0 to 500. For grade 12, the mathematics scale ranges from 0 to 300.

[2] Reading scale ranges from 0 to 500.

[3] Data on percent of students absent are based on the Reading Assessment.

NOTE: Includes public, private, Bureau of Indian Education, and Department of Defense Education Activity schools. Includes students tested with accommodations (9 to 14 percent of all students, depending on assessment and grade level); excludes only those students with disabilities and English language learners who were unable to be tested even with accommodations (1 or 2 percent of all students). Race categories exclude persons of Hispanic ethnicity. Detail may not sum to totals because of rounding.

SOURCE: U.S. Department of Education, National Center for Education Statistics, National Assessment of Educational Progress (NAEP), 2019 Mathematics and Reading Assessments, retrieved November 4, 2020, from the Main NAEP Data Explorer (https://www.nationsreportcard.gov/ndecore/xplore/NDE). (This table was prepared November 2020.)

Table 228.10. School-associated violent deaths of all persons, homicides and suicides of youth ages 5-18 at school, and total homicides and suicides of youth ages 5-18, by type of violent death: 1992-93 through 2017-18

Year	School-associated violent deaths[1] of all persons (includes students, staff, and other nonstudents)						Homicides of youth ages 5-18		Suicides of youth ages 5-18	
	Total	Homicides	Suicides	Legal inter-ventions	Unintentional firearm-related deaths	Undetermined violent deaths[2]	Homicides at school[3]	Total homicides	Suicides at school[3]	Total suicides[4]
1	2	3	4	5	6	7	8	9	10	11
1992-93	57	47	10	0	0	0	34	3,003	6	1,657
1993-94	48	38	10	0	0	0	29	3,253	7	1,779
1994-95	48	39	8	0	1	0	28	3,001	7	1,704
1995-96	53	46	6	1	0	0	32	2,791	6	1,691
1996-97	48	45	2	1	0	0	28	2,430	1	1,584
1997-98	57	47	9	1	0	0	34	2,231	6	1,681
1998-99	47	38	6	2	1	0	33	1,923	4	1,480
1999-2000	37[5]	26[5]	11[5]	0[5]	0[5]	0[5]	14[5]	1,694	8[5]	1,420
2000-01	34[5]	26[5]	7[5]	1[5]	0[5]	0[5]	14[5]	1,636	6[5]	1,451
2001-02	36[5]	27[5]	8[5]	1[5]	0[5]	0[5]	16[5]	1,593	5[5]	1,343
2002-03	36[5]	25[5]	11[5]	0[5]	0[5]	0[5]	18[5]	1,658	10[5]	1,264
2003-04	45[5]	37[5]	7[5]	1[5]	0[5]	0[5]	23[5]	1,620	5[5]	1,411
2004-05	52[5]	40[5]	10[5]	2[5]	0[5]	0[5]	22[5]	1,720	8[5]	1,484
2005-06	44[5]	37[5]	6[5]	1[5]	0[5]	0[5]	21[5]	1,859	3[5]	1,311
2006-07	63[5]	48[5]	13[5]	2[5]	0[5]	0[5]	32[5]	1,906	9[5]	1,243
2007-08	48[5]	39[5]	7[5]	2[5]	0[5]	0[5]	21[5]	1,858	5[5]	1,256
2008-09	44[5]	29[5]	15[5]	0[5]	0[5]	0[5]	18[5]	1,720	7[5]	1,425
2009-10	35[5]	27[5]	5[5]	3[5]	0[5]	0[5]	19[5]	1,551	2[5]	1,441
2010-11	32[5]	26[5]	6[5]	0[5]	0[5]	0[5]	11[5]	1,436	3[5]	1,559
2011-12	45[5]	26[5]	14[5]	5[5]	0[5]	0[5]	15[5]	1,360	5[5]	1,541
2012-13	53[5]	41[5]	11[5]	1[5]	0[5]	0[5]	31[5]	1,310	6[5]	1,608
2013-14	48[5]	26[5]	20[5]	1[5]	0[5]	1[5]	12[5]	1,160	8[5]	1,638
2014-15	47[5]	28[5]	17[5]	2[5]	0[5]	0[5]	20[5]	1,273	9[5]	1,882
2015-16	38[5]	30[5]	7[5]	1[5]	0[5]	0[5]	18[5]	1,478	3[5]	1,941
2016-17	42[5]	28[5]	13[5]	1[5]	0[5]	0[5]	18[5]	1,587	6[5]	2,186
2017-18	56[5]	46[5]	9[5]	1[5]	0[5]	0[5]	35[5]	1,502	8[5]	2,408

[1] A school-associated violent death is defined as "a homicide, suicide, or legal intervention (involving a law enforcement officer), in which the fatal injury occurred on the campus of a functioning elementary or secondary school in the United States," while the victim was on the way to or from regular sessions at school, or while the victim was attending or traveling to or from an official school-sponsored event.

[2] Violent deaths for which the manner was undetermined; that is, the information pointing to one manner of death was no more compelling than the information pointing to one or more other competing manners of death when all available information was considered.

[3] "At school" includes on the property of a functioning elementary or secondary school, on the way to or from regular sessions at school, and while attending or traveling to or from a school-sponsored event.

[4] Excludes self-inflicted deaths among 5- to 9-year-olds. The number of self-inflicted deaths among 5- to 9-year-olds was generally less than 7 per year during the period covered by this table.

[5] Data from 1999-2000 onward are subject to change until law enforcement reports have been obtained and interviews with school and law enforcement officials have been completed. The details learned during the interviews can occasionally change the classification of a case.

NOTE: All data are reported for the school year, defined as July 1 through June 30.

SOURCE: Centers for Disease Control and Prevention (CDC), 1992-2018 School-Associated Violent Death Surveillance System (SAVD-SS) (partially funded by the U.S. Department of Education, Office of Safe and Healthy Students), previously unpublished tabulation; and CDC, National Center for Health Statistics, 1992-2018 National Vital Statistics System (NVSS), previously unpublished tabulation prepared by CDC's National Center for Injury Prevention and Control. (This table was prepared November 2020.)

Table 228.20. Number of nonfatal victimizations against students ages 12-18 and rate of victimization per 1,000 students, by type of victimization and location: 1992 through 2019

[Standard errors appear in parentheses]

Location and year	Number of nonfatal victimizations				Rate of victimization per 1,000 students			
			Violent				Violent	
	Total	Theft	All violent	Violent excluding simple assault[1]	Total	Theft	All violent	Violent excluding simple assault[1]
1	2	3	4	5	6	7	8	9
At school[2]								
1992	4,281,200 (225,600)	2,679,400 (147,660)	1,601,800 (121,630)	197,600 (35,430)	181.5 (7.99)	113.6 (5.64)	67.9 (4.77)	8.4 (1.48)
1993	4,692,800 (321,220)	2,477,100 (121,200)	2,215,700 (194,520)	535,500 (76,050)	193.5 (11.02)	102.1 (4.61)	91.4 (7.23)	22.1 (3.02)
1994	4,721,000 (271,730)	2,474,100 (121,260)	2,246,900 (165,530)	459,100 (58,110)	187.7 (9.04)	98.4 (4.46)	89.3 (5.95)	18.3 (2.24)
1995	4,400,700 (267,610)	2,468,400 (120,690)	1,932,200 (152,670)	294,500 (42,890)	172.2 (8.82)	96.6 (4.37)	75.6 (5.44)	11.5 (1.64)
1996	4,130,400 (281,640)	2,205,200 (107,650)	1,925,300 (166,690)	371,900 (54,150)	158.4 (9.17)	84.5 (3.88)	73.8 (5.81)	14.3 (2.01)
1997	3,610,900 (282,430)	1,975,000 (111,830)	1,635,900 (164,530)	376,200 (60,990)	136.6 (9.25)	74.7 (3.95)	61.9 (5.74)	14.2 (2.24)
1998	3,247,300 (254,250)	1,635,100 (104,210)	1,612,200 (155,840)	314,500 (49,770)	121.3 (8.27)	61.1 (3.69)	60.2 (5.34)	11.7 (1.80)
1999	3,152,400 (258,560)	1,752,200 (104,970)	1,400,200 (148,230)	281,100 (50,060)	117.0 (8.43)	65.1 (3.69)	52.0 (5.11)	10.4 (1.81)
2000	2,301,000 (211,140)	1,331,500 (95,940)	969,500 (115,680)	214,200 (40,980)	84.9 (7.00)	49.1 (3.34)	35.8 (4.02)	7.9 (1.48)
2001	2,521,300 (202,890)	1,348,500 (93,240)	1,172,700 (120,560)	259,400 (44,110)	92.3 (6.67)	49.4 (3.23)	42.9 (4.14)	9.5 (1.58)
2002	2,082,600 (212,520)	1,088,800 (77,110)	993,800 (126,210)	173,500 (37,300)	75.4 (6.96)	39.4 (2.69)	36.0 (4.29)	6.3 (1.32)
2003	2,308,800 (210,930)	1,270,500 (88,550)	1,038,300 (121,490)	188,400 (38,240)	87.4 (7.16)	48.1 (3.18)	39.3 (4.32)	7.1 (1.42)
2004	1,762,200 (154,390)	1,065,400 (75,160)	696,800 (83,090)	107,300 (25,110)	67.2 (5.40)	40.6 (2.76)	26.6 (3.03)	4.1 (0.95)
2005	1,678,600 (169,040)	875,900 (70,140)	802,600 (102,360)	140,300 (32,400)	63.2 (5.85)	33.0 (2.56)	30.2 (3.66)	5.3 (1.20)
2006[3]	1,799,900 (170,490)	859,000 (68,730)	940,900 (109,880)	249,900 (45,670)	67.5 (5.86)	32.2 (2.52)	35.3 (3.90)	9.4 (1.68)
2007	1,801,200 (188,450)	896,700 (66,230)	904,400 (114,320)	116,100 (25,430)	67.8 (6.40)	33.7 (2.41)	34.0 (4.02)	4.4 (0.94)
2008	1,435,500 (161,330)	648,000 (61,170)	787,500 (108,480)	128,700 (34,370)	54.3 (5.67)	24.5 (2.26)	29.8 (3.91)	4.9 (1.28)
2009	1,322,800 (168,370)	594,500 (54,480)	728,300 (111,550)	233,700 (51,610)	51.0 (6.00)	22.9 (2.05)	28.1 (4.08)	9.0 (1.94)
2010	892,000 (124,260)	469,800 (45,300)	422,300 (73,310)	155,000 (36,500)	34.9 (4.55)	18.4 (1.75)	16.5 (2.75)	6.1 (1.40)
2011	1,246,200 (139,940)	647,700 (61,500)	598,600 (84,090)	89,500 (23,360)	49.3 (5.11)	25.6 (2.36)	23.7 (3.16)	3.5 (0.91)
2012	1,364,900 (133,810)	615,600 (51,440)	749,200 (90,250)	89,000 (23,850)	52.4 (4.78)	23.6 (1.93)	28.8 (3.31)	3.4 (0.91)
2013	1,420,900 (176,390)	454,900 (43,390)	966,000 (134,140)	125,500 (32,110)	55.0 (6.24)	17.6 (1.65)	37.4 (4.84)	4.9 (1.22)
2014	850,100 (109,100)	363,700 (39,120)	486,400 (74,790)	93,800 (25,550)	33.0 (4.00)	14.1 (1.50)	18.9 (2.79)	3.6 (0.98)
2015	841,100 (112,860)	309,100 (36,480)	531,900 (82,870)	99,000 (27,740)	32.9 (4.17)	12.1 (1.41)	20.8 (3.11)	3.9 (1.07)
2016[4]	--- (†)	--- (†)	--- (†)	--- (†)	--- (†)	--- (†)	--- (†)	--- (†)
2017	827,000 (91,040)	306,500 (31,360)	520,500 (67,030)	110,600 (24,960)	32.7 (3.41)	12.1 (1.23)	20.6 (2.55)	4.4 (0.97)
2018	836,100 (99,530)	225,600 (26,450)	610,500 (80,190)	152,400 (31,550)	32.9 (3.69)	8.9 (1.03)	24.0 (3.01)	6.0 (1.22)
2019	764,600 (92,230)	239,400 (28,190)	525,300 (71,680)	125,600 (28,220)	30.0 (3.42)	9.4 (1.10)	20.6 (2.69)	4.9 (1.09)
Away from school								
1992	4,084,100 (218,910)	1,857,600 (118,610)	2,226,500 (149,210)	1,025,100 (92,600)	173.1 (7.81)	78.7 (4.66)	94.4 (5.70)	43.5 (3.72)
1993	3,835,900 (280,790)	1,731,100 (96,700)	2,104,800 (187,960)	1,004,300 (114,870)	158.2 (9.90)	71.4 (3.75)	86.8 (7.01)	41.4 (4.47)
1994	4,147,100 (249,260)	1,713,900 (96,250)	2,433,200 (174,580)	1,074,900 (101,370)	164.9 (8.44)	68.1 (3.61)	96.7 (6.24)	42.7 (3.80)
1995	3,626,600 (234,640)	1,604,800 (92,000)	2,021,800 (157,470)	829,700 (85,830)	141.9 (7.91)	62.8 (3.41)	79.1 (5.59)	32.5 (3.19)
1996	3,483,200 (250,620)	1,572,700 (87,830)	1,910,600 (165,810)	870,000 (96,510)	133.5 (8.32)	60.3 (3.22)	73.3 (5.79)	33.4 (3.50)
1997	3,717,600 (288,080)	1,710,700 (101,810)	2,006,900 (189,180)	853,300 (105,660)	140.7 (9.41)	64.7 (3.62)	75.9 (6.51)	32.3 (3.79)
1998	3,047,800 (243,270)	1,408,000 (94,900)	1,639,800 (157,700)	684,900 (85,520)	113.8 (7.96)	52.6 (3.38)	61.3 (5.40)	25.6 (3.04)
1999	2,713,800 (233,350)	1,129,200 (79,770)	1,584,500 (161,350)	675,400 (90,150)	100.8 (7.71)	41.9 (2.85)	58.8 (5.53)	25.1 (3.20)
2000	2,303,600 (211,310)	1,228,900 (90,770)	1,074,800 (124,280)	402,100 (62,950)	85.0 (7.01)	45.3 (3.17)	39.6 (4.30)	14.8 (2.24)
2001	1,780,300 (160,090)	961,400 (74,230)	819,000 (94,590)	314,800 (50,070)	65.2 (5.39)	35.2 (2.60)	30.0 (3.30)	11.5 (1.79)
2002	1,619,500 (178,050)	820,100 (64,530)	799,400 (108,260)	341,200 (59,590)	58.6 (5.92)	29.7 (2.27)	28.9 (3.71)	12.4 (2.09)
2003	1,824,100 (179,240)	780,900 (64,210)	1,043,200 (121,880)	412,800 (64,660)	69.1 (6.19)	29.6 (2.34)	39.5 (4.33)	15.6 (2.37)
2004	1,371,800 (130,480)	718,000 (59,070)	653,700 (79,660)	272,500 (45,080)	52.3 (4.63)	27.4 (2.19)	24.9 (2.91)	10.4 (1.68)
2005	1,429,000 (151,460)	637,700 (57,740)	791,300 (101,380)	257,100 (47,950)	53.8 (5.29)	24.0 (2.12)	29.8 (3.63)	9.7 (1.77)
2006[3]	1,413,100 (144,660)	714,200 (61,900)	698,900 (89,980)	263,600 (47,280)	53.0 (5.04)	26.8 (2.27)	26.2 (3.22)	9.9 (1.73)
2007	1,371,700 (154,740)	614,300 (52,740)	757,400 (100,440)	337,700 (55,630)	51.6 (5.34)	23.1 (1.94)	28.5 (3.55)	12.7 (2.01)
2008	1,132,600 (137,840)	498,500 (52,350)	634,100 (94,160)	258,600 (52,980)	42.8 (4.90)	18.9 (1.94)	24.0 (3.42)	9.8 (1.96)
2009	857,200 (124,770)	484,200 (48,320)	372,900 (70,660)	176,800 (42,890)	33.1 (4.54)	18.7 (1.83)	14.4 (2.63)	6.8 (1.62)
2010	689,900 (103,620)	378,800 (40,200)	311,200 (59,190)	167,300 (38,460)	27.0 (3.83)	14.8 (1.55)	12.2 (2.24)	6.5 (1.47)
2011	966,100 (117,200)	541,900 (55,160)	424,300 (66,350)	137,600 (31,000)	38.2 (4.33)	21.4 (2.13)	16.8 (2.52)	5.4 (1.20)
2012	991,200 (108,370)	470,800 (44,070)	520,400 (71,280)	169,900 (35,260)	38.0 (3.93)	18.1 (1.66)	20.0 (2.64)	6.5 (1.33)
2013	778,500 (115,110)	403,000 (40,470)	375,500 (68,800)	151,200 (36,490)	30.1 (4.19)	15.6 (1.54)	14.5 (2.56)	5.8 (1.38)
2014	621,300 (88,190)	288,900 (34,370)	332,400 (58,000)	165,000 (36,650)	24.1 (3.27)	11.2 (1.32)	12.9 (2.18)	6.4 (1.40)
2015	545,100 (84,230)	263,100 (33,310)	281,900 (54,370)	110,900 (29,800)	21.3 (3.16)	10.3 (1.29)	11.0 (2.07)	4.3 (1.15)
2016[4]	--- (†)	--- (†)	--- (†)	--- (†)	--- (†)	--- (†)	--- (†)	--- (†)
2017	503,800 (65,600)	188,600 (24,340)	315,200 (48,350)	145,300 (29,570)	19.9 (2.49)	7.4 (0.96)	12.4 (1.86)	5.7 (1.15)
2018	410,200 (61,150)	158,800 (21,960)	251,400 (43,970)	117,500 (26,620)	16.1 (2.32)	6.3 (0.86)	9.9 (1.68)	4.6 (1.03)
2019	509,300 (70,210)	160,500 (22,740)	348,800 (54,620)	138,000 (29,960)	20.0 (2.64)	6.3 (0.89)	13.7 (2.07)	5.4 (1.16)

—Not available.

†Not applicable.

[1] In previous versions of the table, "violent excluding simple assault" was labeled as "serious violent" victimization.

[2] "At school" includes in the school building, on school property, on a school bus, and going to or from school.

[3] Every 10 years, the survey sample is redesigned to reflect changes in the population. Due to the sample redesign and other methodological changes implemented in 2006, use caution when comparing 2006 estimates to other years.

[4] Every 10 years, the survey sample is redesigned to reflect changes in the population. Due to a sample increase and redesign in 2016, victimization estimates among youth in 2016 were not comparable to estimates for other years.

NOTE: "All violent" victimization includes the crimes of rape, sexual assault, robbery, aggravated assault, and simple assault. "Theft" includes attempted and completed purse-snatching, completed pickpocketing, and all attempted and completed thefts, with the exception of motor vehicle thefts. Theft does not include robbery, which involves the threat or use of force and is classified as a violent crime. "Total victimization" includes theft and violent crimes. Data in this table are from the National Crime Victimization Survey (NCVS); due to differences in time coverage and administration between the NCVS and the School Crime Supplement (SCS) to the NCVS, data in this table cannot be compared with data in tables that are based on the SCS. Detail may not sum to totals because of rounding.

SOURCE: U.S. Department of Justice, Bureau of Justice Statistics, National Crime Victimization Survey (NCVS), 1992 through 2019. (This table was prepared November 2020.)

Table 228.25. Number of nonfatal victimizations against students ages 12-18 and rate of victimization per 1,000 students, by type of victimization, location, and selected student characteristics: 2019

[Standard errors appear in parentheses]

Location and student characteristic	Number of nonfatal victimizations								Rate of victimization per 1,000 students							
					Violent								Violent			
	Total		Theft		All violent		Violent excluding simple assault[1]		Total		Theft		All violent		Violent excluding simple assault[1]	
1	2		3		4		5		6		7		8		9	
At school[2]																
Total	**764,600**	**(92,230)**	**239,400**	**(28,190)**	**525,300**	**(71,680)**	**125,600**	**(28,220)**	**30.0**	**(3.42)**	**9.4**	**(1.10)**	**20.6**	**(2.69)**	**4.9**	**(1.09)**
Sex																
Male	522,400	(71,420)	142,800	(21,350)	379,700	(57,770)	113,500	(26,480)	39.8	(5.09)	10.9	(1.61)	28.9	(4.17)	8.7	(1.97)
Female	242,200	(43,020)	96,600	(17,350)	145,600	(31,000)	12,000 !	(6,920)	19.5	(3.33)	7.8	(1.39)	11.7	(2.43)	1.0 !	(0.56)
Age																
12-14	450,100	(64,670)	118,200	(19,310)	331,900	(52,870)	34,400	(12,730)	35.8	(4.83)	9.4	(1.52)	26.4	(4.00)	2.7	(1.00)
15-18	314,500	(51,030)	121,200	(19,570)	193,300	(37,170)	91,200	(23,080)	24.3	(3.75)	9.3	(1.50)	14.9	(2.77)	7.0	(1.75)
Race/ethnicity[3]																
White	410,900	(60,870)	132,300	(20,510)	278,500	(47,120)	33,300 !	(12,490)	31.1	(4.35)	10.0	(1.54)	21.1	(3.41)	2.5 !	(0.94)
Black	91,600	(23,150)	27,500	(8,990)	64,200	(18,570)	2,900 !	(3,170)	26.8	(6.47)	8.0	(2.61)	18.8	(5.25)	0.9 !	(0.93)
Hispanic	208,100	(38,980)	64,200	(13,990)	143,900	(30,760)	79,300 !	(21,160)	32.9	(5.82)	10.1	(2.19)	22.7	(4.65)	12.5 !	(3.25)
Other	54,100	(16,720)	15,400 !	(6,680)	38,700	(13,660)	10,100 !	(6,260)	21.1	(6.30)	6.0 !	(2.60)	15.1	(5.19)	3.9 !	(2.42)
Urbanicity[4]																
Urban	316,800	(51,270)	99,700	(17,640)	217,100	(40,070)	23,600 !	(10,200)	41.1	(6.21)	12.9	(2.26)	28.2	(4.93)	3.1 !	(1.31)
Suburban	331,600	(52,840)	101,100	(17,780)	230,500	(41,660)	82,200 !	(21,640)	23.1	(3.52)	7.1	(1.23)	16.1	(2.81)	5.7 !	(1.49)
Rural	116,200	(26,870)	38,600	(10,730)	77,600	(20,880)	19,700 !	(9,180)	33.3	(7.30)	11.1	(3.05)	22.3	(5.76)	5.7 !	(2.60)
Household income[5]																
Less than $25,000	118,600	(27,220)	39,000	(10,780)	79,700	(21,220)	1,000 !	(1,790)	32.7	(7.11)	10.7	(2.95)	22.0	(5.62)	0.3 !	(0.49)
$25,000 to 49,999	156,500	(32,450)	33,000	(9,890)	123,500	(27,920)	14,700 !	(7,740)	25.7	(5.09)	5.4	(1.62)	20.3	(4.41)	2.4 !	(1.26)
$50,000 to 99,999	212,800	(39,550)	79,800	(15,680)	133,000	(29,270)	37,200 !	(13,350)	26.1	(4.61)	9.8	(1.91)	16.3	(3.46)	4.6 !	(1.62)
$100,000 or more	276,800	(46,930)	87,700	(16,490)	189,100	(36,650)	72,700 !	(20,050)	36.2	(5.76)	11.5	(2.13)	24.7	(4.57)	9.5 !	(2.56)
Away from school																
Total	**509,300**	**(70,210)**	**160,500**	**(22,740)**	**348,800**	**(54,620)**	**138,000**	**(29,960)**	**20.0**	**(2.64)**	**6.3**	**(0.89)**	**13.7**	**(2.07)**	**5.4**	**(1.16)**
Sex																
Male	205,900	(38,720)	99,100	(17,580)	106,900	(25,490)	44,900	(14,940)	15.7	(2.85)	7.6	(1.33)	8.1	(1.90)	3.4	(1.13)
Female	303,400	(49,830)	61,500	(13,680)	241,900	(42,980)	93,200	(23,390)	24.4	(3.83)	5.0	(1.10)	19.5	(3.33)	7.5	(1.85)
Age																
12-14	149,200	(31,490)	61,900	(13,730)	87,300	(22,460)	25,200	(10,590)	11.9	(2.44)	4.9	(1.09)	6.9	(1.75)	2.0	(0.84)
15-18	360,100	(55,780)	98,600	(17,540)	261,500	(45,210)	112,900	(26,380)	27.8	(4.08)	7.6	(1.34)	20.2	(3.35)	8.7	(1.99)
Race/ethnicity[3]																
White	332,800	(52,960)	78,500	(15,550)	254,300	(44,410)	91,500	(23,120)	25.2	(3.82)	5.9	(1.17)	19.2	(3.23)	6.9	(1.72)
Black	47,600	(15,480)	20,100	(7,670)	27,500 !	(11,140)	12,600 !	(7,100)	13.9	(4.41)	5.9	(2.23)	8.0 !	(3.21)	3.7 !	(2.06)
Hispanic	69,300	(19,470)	35,400	(10,260)	33,900	(12,630)	19,700 !	(9,170)	10.9	(3.00)	5.6	(1.61)	5.4	(1.97)	3.1 !	(1.44)
Other	59,600	(17,740)	26,500	(8,830)	33,100 !	(12,450)	14,300 !	(7,630)	23.3	(6.66)	10.3	(3.42)	12.9 !	(4.75)	5.6 !	(2.94)
Urbanicity[4]																
Urban	141,000	(30,370)	73,600	(15,030)	67,400	(19,140)	23,500 !	(10,180)	18.3	(3.79)	9.5	(1.93)	8.7	(2.43)	3.1 !	(1.31)
Suburban	278,900	(47,170)	44,100	(11,500)	234,800	(42,160)	98,500	(24,210)	19.5	(3.16)	3.1	(0.80)	16.4	(2.84)	6.9	(1.66)
Rural	89,400	(22,790)	42,900	(11,330)	46,500	(15,270)	16,000 !	(8,140)	25.6	(6.26)	12.3	(3.22)	13.4	(4.27)	4.6 !	(2.31)
Household income[5]																
Less than $25,000	111,100	(26,120)	55,700	(12,990)	55,400	(16,970)	15,800 !	(8,080)	30.6	(6.84)	15.4	(3.54)	15.3	(4.54)	4.4 !	(2.20)
$25,000 to 49,999	130,600	(28,930)	43,800	(11,460)	86,800	(22,380)	69,600	(19,520)	21.5	(4.56)	7.2	(1.87)	14.3	(3.57)	11.4	(3.13)
$50,000 to 99,999	97,100	(24,010)	30,900	(9,560)	66,200	(18,930)	31,300	(12,030)	11.9	(2.86)	3.8	(1.17)	8.1	(2.27)	3.8	(1.46)
$100,000 or more	170,400	(34,280)	30,100	(9,420)	140,400	(30,280)	21,400 !	(9,620)	22.3	(4.29)	3.9	(1.23)	18.3	(3.81)	2.8 !	(1.25)

! Interpret data with caution. Estimate based on 10 or fewer sample cases, or the coefficient of variation (CV) is greater than 50 percent.

[1] In previous versions of the table, "violent excluding simple assault" was labeled as "serious violent" victimization.

[2] "At school" includes in the school building, on school property, on a school bus, and going to or from school.

[3] Race categories exclude persons of Hispanic ethnicity. "Other" includes Asian, Pacific Islander, American Indian/Alaska Native, and Two or more races.

[4] Refers to the Standard Metropolitan Statistical Area (MSA) status of the respondent's household as defined by the U.S. Census Bureau. Categories include "central city of an MSA (Urban)," "in MSA but not in central city (Suburban)," and "not MSA (Rural)."

[5] Income data for 2019 were imputed. For more information, see *Criminal Victimization, 2019*, available at https://www.bjs.gov/content/pub/pdf/cv19.pdf.

NOTE: "All violent" victimization includes the crimes of rape, sexual assault, robbery, aggravated assault, and simple assault. "Theft" includes attempted and completed purse-snatching, completed pickpocketing, and all attempted and completed thefts, with the exception of motor vehicle thefts. Theft does not include robbery, which involves the threat or use of force and is classified as a violent crime. "Total victimization" includes theft and violent crimes. Data in this table are from the National Crime Victimization Survey (NCVS) and are reported in accordance with Bureau of Justice Statistics standards. Detail may not sum to totals because of rounding. The population size for students ages 12-18 was 25,528,100 in 2019.

SOURCE: U.S. Department of Justice, Bureau of Justice Statistics, National Crime Victimization Survey (NCVS), 2019. (This table was prepared November 2020.)

Table 228.30. Percentage of students ages 12-18 who reported criminal victimization at school during the previous 6 months, by type of victimization and selected student and school characteristics: Selected years, 1995 through 2019

[Standard errors appear in parentheses]

Type of victimization and student or school characteristic	1995		2001		2003		2005		2007		2009		2011		2013		2015		2017		2019	
1	2		3		4		5		6		7		8		9		10		11		12	
Total	**9.1**	**(0.33)**	**5.5**	**(0.31)**	**5.1**	**(0.24)**	**4.3**	**(0.31)**	**4.3**	**(0.29)**	**3.9**	**(0.28)**	**3.5**	**(0.28)**	**3.0**	**(0.25)**	**2.7**	**(0.25)**	**2.2**	**(0.22)**	**2.5**	**(0.24)**
Sex																						
Male	9.6	(0.44)	6.1	(0.41)	5.3	(0.33)	4.6	(0.43)	4.5	(0.43)	4.6	(0.40)	3.7	(0.35)	3.2	(0.40)	2.6	(0.35)	2.6	(0.34)	3.1	(0.39)
Female	8.5	(0.45)	4.9	(0.39)	4.8	(0.36)	3.9	(0.38)	3.9	(0.38)	3.2	(0.35)	3.4	(0.38)	2.8	(0.34)	2.8	(0.38)	1.8	(0.28)	1.9	(0.28)
Race/ethnicity[1]																						
White	9.4	(0.36)	5.7	(0.40)	5.4	(0.32)	4.6	(0.36)	4.2	(0.38)	3.9	(0.37)	3.6	(0.35)	3.0	(0.32)	2.9	(0.36)	2.2	(0.27)	2.5	(0.32)
Black	9.6	(1.02)	6.1	(0.78)	5.1	(0.78)	3.9	(0.80)	4.3	(0.83)	4.4	(0.74)	4.6	(0.89)	3.2	(0.71)	2.2 !	(0.77)	2.6	(0.52)	3.0 !	(0.97)
Hispanic	7.1	(0.96)	4.6	(0.64)	3.9	(0.50)	3.9	(0.70)	3.6	(0.54)	3.9	(0.75)	2.9	(0.47)	3.2	(0.46)	2.3	(0.47)	2.0	(0.45)	1.8	(0.38)
Asian/Pacific Islander	8.3	(1.63)	3.7	(1.08)	3.2	(0.93)	1.4 !	(0.64)	3.4 !	(1.33)	‡	(†)	2.3 !	(1.13)	2.4 !	(0.99)	‡	(†)	2.1 !	(1.02)	‡	(†)
Asian	---	(†)	---	(†)	3.3 !	(1.00)	1.5 !	(0.69)	3.6 !	(1.38)	‡	(†)	2.5 !	(1.23)	2.6 !	(1.08)	‡	(†)	2.1 !	(1.05)	‡	(†)
Pacific Islander	---	(†)	---	(†)	‡	(†)	‡	(†)	‡	(†)	‡	(†)	‡	(†)	‡	(†)	‡	(†)	‡	(†)	‡	(†)
American Indian/Alaska Native	9.6 !	(3.27)	‡	(†)	‡	(†)	‡	(†)	‡	(†)	‡	(†)	‡	(†)	‡	(†)	‡	(†)	11.1 !	(4.80)	‡	(†)
Two or more races	---	(†)	---	(†)	9.8	(2.85)	‡	(†)	10.1	(2.59)	‡	(†)	4.9 !	(1.77)	3.0 !	(1.46)	6.5 !	(2.24)	‡	(†)	6.5 !	(2.17)
Grade																						
6th	8.8	(0.92)	5.9	(0.90)	3.8	(0.77)	4.6	(0.83)	3.9	(0.86)	3.7	(0.91)	3.8	(0.85)	4.1	(0.92)	3.1	(0.79)	3.1	(0.75)	3.1	(0.93)
7th	10.6	(0.79)	5.8	(0.67)	6.3	(0.74)	5.4	(0.71)	4.7	(0.69)	3.4	(0.70)	3.1	(0.61)	2.5	(0.51)	3.4	(0.70)	2.6	(0.60)	2.9	(0.62)
8th	10.1	(0.76)	4.3	(0.61)	5.2	(0.65)	3.6	(0.63)	4.4	(0.63)	3.8	(0.78)	3.8	(0.67)	2.3	(0.52)	2.3	(0.57)	1.8	(0.51)	2.1	(0.54)
9th	11.4	(0.86)	7.9	(0.81)	6.3	(0.70)	4.7	(0.69)	5.3	(0.75)	5.3	(0.85)	5.1	(0.83)	4.1	(0.76)	3.0	(0.62)	2.7	(0.67)	2.6	(0.57)
10th	8.7	(0.73)	6.5	(0.77)	4.7	(0.63)	4.3	(0.71)	4.4	(0.67)	4.2	(0.79)	3.0	(0.58)	3.3	(0.57)	1.6	(0.47)	2.7	(0.49)	3.3	(0.76)
11th	7.0	(0.72)	4.8	(0.62)	5.0	(0.69)	3.6	(0.51)	4.0	(0.75)	4.7	(0.88)	3.1	(0.65)	3.3	(0.65)	4.4	(1.04)	1.4	(0.40)	2.4	(0.66)
12th	5.8	(0.73)	2.9	(0.52)	3.6	(0.71)	3.7	(0.85)	2.7	(0.70)	2.0	(0.52)	2.9	(0.68)	2.0 !	(0.67)	1.3 !	(0.45)	1.4	(0.41)	1.1 !	(0.34)
School locale[2]																						
City	---	(†)	---	(†)	---	(†)	---	(†)	---	(†)	---	(†)	---	(†)	---	(†)	3.1	(0.45)	2.5	(0.44)	3.3	(0.51)
Suburban	---	(†)	---	(†)	---	(†)	---	(†)	---	(†)	---	(†)	---	(†)	---	(†)	3.2	(0.47)	1.9	(0.30)	2.1	(0.31)
Town	---	(†)	---	(†)	---	(†)	---	(†)	---	(†)	---	(†)	---	(†)	---	(†)	1.3 !	(0.43)	2.3	(0.66)	2.8 !	(0.86)
Rural	---	(†)	---	(†)	---	(†)	---	(†)	---	(†)	---	(†)	---	(†)	---	(†)	2.2	(0.47)	2.0	(0.46)	2.4	(0.52)
Control of school[2,3]																						
Public	9.3	(0.37)	5.7	(0.34)	5.1	(0.26)	4.4	(0.32)	4.5	(0.32)	4.1	(0.30)	3.7	(0.29)	3.1	(0.27)	2.8	(0.27)	2.2	(0.24)	2.7	(0.26)
Private	6.2	(0.89)	3.4	(0.72)	4.9	(0.79)	2.7	(0.77)	1.1 !	(0.50)	1.8 !	(0.76)	1.9 !	(0.68)	2.8 !	(0.89)	‡	(†)	‡	(†)	‡	(†)
Theft	**7.0**	**(0.28)**	**4.2**	**(0.24)**	**4.0**	**(0.20)**	**3.1**	**(0.27)**	**3.0**	**(0.23)**	**2.8**	**(0.23)**	**2.6**	**(0.23)**	**1.9**	**(0.20)**	**1.9**	**(0.22)**	**1.5**	**(0.17)**	**1.5**	**(0.19)**
Sex																						
Male	7.0	(0.37)	4.5	(0.34)	3.9	(0.27)	3.1	(0.34)	3.0	(0.34)	3.4	(0.36)	2.6	(0.29)	2.0	(0.30)	1.7	(0.26)	1.6	(0.27)	1.6	(0.29)
Female	7.0	(0.41)	3.8	(0.33)	4.1	(0.31)	3.2	(0.36)	3.0	(0.32)	2.1	(0.28)	2.6	(0.33)	1.8	(0.28)	2.0	(0.34)	1.3	(0.24)	1.4	(0.24)
Race/ethnicity[1]																						
White	7.3	(0.32)	4.1	(0.31)	4.3	(0.28)	3.4	(0.32)	3.1	(0.29)	2.9	(0.31)	2.5	(0.28)	1.6	(0.22)	2.0	(0.28)	1.3	(0.20)	1.6	(0.26)
Black	6.9	(0.87)	5.0	(0.68)	3.8	(0.64)	2.7	(0.66)	3.1	(0.70)	2.5	(0.61)	3.7	(0.78)	2.7	(0.67)	1.3 !	(0.63)	1.8	(0.51)	1.7 !	(0.60)
Hispanic	5.7	(0.79)	3.7	(0.69)	3.0	(0.41)	3.1	(0.64)	2.2	(0.47)	3.0	(0.63)	2.0	(0.41)	1.8	(0.39)	1.6	(0.39)	1.4	(0.36)	1.2	(0.32)
Asian/Pacific Islander	6.4	(1.47)	3.5	(1.03)	3.2	(0.93)	‡	(†)	3.0 !	(1.27)	‡	(†)	2.3 !	(1.13)	2.4 !	(0.99)	‡	(†)	2.1 !	(1.02)	‡	(†)
Asian	---	(†)	---	(†)	3.3 !	(1.00)	‡	(†)	3.2 !	(1.32)	‡	(†)	2.5 !	(1.23)	2.6 !	(1.08)	‡	(†)	2.1 !	(1.05)	‡	(†)
Pacific Islander	---	(†)	---	(†)	‡	(†)	‡	(†)	‡	(†)	‡	(†)	‡	(†)	‡	(†)	‡	(†)	‡	(†)	‡	(†)
American Indian/Alaska Native	7.2 !	(3.04)	‡	(†)	‡	(†)	‡	(†)	‡	(†)	‡	(†)	‡	(†)	‡	(†)	‡	(†)	7.2 !	(3.37)	‡	(†)
Two or more races	---	(†)	---	(†)	8.3 !	(2.72)	‡	(†)	5.3 !	(2.01)	‡	(†)	3.7 !	(1.56)	‡	(†)	4.3 !	(1.80)	‡	(†)	‡	(†)
Grade																						
6th	5.4	(0.66)	4.0	(0.70)	2.2	(0.63)	2.8	(0.75)	2.6	(0.75)	1.3 !	(0.52)	2.7	(0.70)	1.4 !	(0.57)	1.6 !	(0.65)	1.0 !	(0.42)	1.4 !	(0.63)
7th	8.1	(0.72)	3.4	(0.51)	4.8	(0.67)	2.9	(0.50)	2.7	(0.54)	2.1	(0.57)	1.9	(0.44)	1.4	(0.38)	1.6 !	(0.54)	1.3 !	(0.39)	1.5 !	(0.47)
8th	7.8	(0.72)	3.3	(0.50)	4.1	(0.57)	2.4	(0.53)	2.5	(0.54)	2.0	(0.55)	2.0	(0.48)	1.0 !	(0.33)	1.8	(0.50)	1.1 !	(0.41)	1.1 !	(0.43)
9th	8.8	(0.76)	6.2	(0.76)	5.2	(0.63)	3.7	(0.61)	4.6	(0.70)	4.9	(0.80)	4.4	(0.78)	2.7	(0.58)	2.1	(0.52)	2.4	(0.60)	1.7	(0.46)
10th	7.6	(0.70)	5.7	(0.72)	3.7	(0.59)	3.8	(0.66)	3.6	(0.63)	3.5	(0.72)	2.1	(0.50)	2.6	(0.48)	1.4 !	(0.43)	2.1	(0.39)	2.1	(0.57)
11th	5.4	(0.66)	3.8	(0.57)	4.1	(0.64)	2.8	(0.45)	2.6	(0.61)	3.3	(0.74)	2.7	(0.58)	2.3	(0.50)	3.4	(0.85)	1.1 !	(0.36)	1.7 !	(0.54)
12th	4.5	(0.67)	2.3	(0.45)	3.1	(0.68)	3.4	(0.84)	1.9	(0.55)	1.5	(0.44)	2.4	(0.62)	1.6 !	(0.62)	1.0 !	(0.40)	1.2 !	(0.42)	0.9 !	(0.31)
School locale[2]																						
City	---	(†)	---	(†)	---	(†)	---	(†)	---	(†)	---	(†)	---	(†)	---	(†)	2.3	(0.41)	1.6	(0.33)	2.0	(0.40)
Suburban	---	(†)	---	(†)	---	(†)	---	(†)	---	(†)	---	(†)	---	(†)	---	(†)	1.8	(0.38)	1.4	(0.27)	1.1	(0.25)
Town	---	(†)	---	(†)	---	(†)	---	(†)	---	(†)	---	(†)	---	(†)	---	(†)	1.1 !	(0.37)	1.0 !	(0.46)	1.9 !	(0.79)
Rural	---	(†)	---	(†)	---	(†)	---	(†)	---	(†)	---	(†)	---	(†)	---	(†)	1.6	(0.41)	1.4	(0.38)	1.5	(0.44)
Control of school[2,3]																						
Public	7.2	(0.31)	4.4	(0.26)	4.0	(0.22)	3.3	(0.28)	3.2	(0.25)	2.9	(0.25)	2.7	(0.24)	1.9	(0.21)	1.9	(0.23)	1.5	(0.20)	1.7	(0.21)
Private	4.9	(0.73)	2.4	(0.67)	4.0	(0.77)	1.3 !	(0.48)	1.1 !	(0.50)	‡	(†)	1.2 !	(0.52)	2.0 !	(0.76)	‡	(†)	‡	(†)	‡	(†)
All violent	**2.5**	**(0.19)**	**1.8**	**(0.19)**	**1.3**	**(0.15)**	**1.2**	**(0.15)**	**1.6**	**(0.18)**	**1.4**	**(0.17)**	**1.1**	**(0.15)**	**1.2**	**(0.15)**	**0.9**	**(0.15)**	**0.7**	**(0.12)**	**1.1**	**(0.15)**
Sex																						
Male	3.0	(0.26)	2.1	(0.26)	1.7	(0.23)	1.6	(0.25)	1.7	(0.26)	1.6	(0.25)	1.2	(0.21)	1.3	(0.23)	1.0	(0.21)	1.0	(0.20)	1.6	(0.28)
Female	2.0	(0.22)	1.4	(0.24)	0.9	(0.16)	0.8	(0.15)	1.4	(0.23)	1.1	(0.21)	0.9	(0.17)	1.1	(0.23)	0.9	(0.19)	0.5	(0.14)	0.5	(0.14)
Race/ethnicity[1]																						
White	2.5	(0.21)	2.0	(0.24)	1.4	(0.17)	1.3	(0.21)	1.5	(0.22)	1.2	(0.21)	1.2	(0.17)	1.5	(0.24)	1.0	(0.22)	0.9	(0.19)	1.1	(0.21)
Black	3.0	(0.57)	1.3 !	(0.40)	1.5	(0.41)	1.3 !	(0.47)	1.6 !	(0.50)	2.3	(0.62)	1.1 !	(0.42)	‡	(†)	0.9 !	(0.44)	0.8 !	(0.31)	1.4 !	(0.67)
Hispanic	2.0	(0.47)	1.5	(0.41)	1.1	(0.28)	0.9	(0.24)	1.4	(0.42)	1.3 !	(0.40)	1.0	(0.28)	1.5	(0.26)	0.6 !	(0.23)	0.5 !	(0.23)	0.6 !	(0.20)
Asian/Pacific Islander	2.2 !	(0.98)	‡	(†)	‡	(†)	‡	(†)	‡	(†)	‡	(†)	‡	(†)	‡	(†)	‡	(†)	‡	(†)	‡	(†)
Asian	---	(†)	---	(†)	‡	(†)	‡	(†)	‡	(†)	‡	(†)	‡	(†)	‡	(†)	‡	(†)	‡	(†)	‡	(†)
Pacific Islander	---	(†)	---	(†)	‡	(†)	‡	(†)	‡	(†)	‡	(†)	‡	(†)	‡	(†)	‡	(†)	‡	(†)	‡	(†)
American Indian/Alaska Native	‡	(†)	‡	(†)	‡	(†)	‡	(†)	‡	(†)	‡	(†)	‡	(†)	‡	(†)	‡	(†)	‡	(†)	‡	(†)
Two or more races	---	(†)	---	(†)	‡	(†)	‡	(†)	5.3 !	(1.90)	‡	(†)	‡	(†)	‡	(†)	3.6 !	(1.64)	‡	(†)	3.2 !	(1.46)

[Standard errors appear in parentheses]

Type of victimization and student or school characteristic	1995		2001		2003		2005		2007		2009		2011		2013		2015		2017		2019	
1	2		3		4		5		6		7		8		9		10		11		12	
Grade																						
6th	4.3	(0.68)	2.6	(0.66)	1.9	(0.53)	1.9	(0.55)	1.5 !	(0.54)	2.6 !	(0.83)	1.3 !	(0.49)	2.7	(0.73)	1.6 !	(0.65)	2.1	(0.60)	1.7 !	(0.70)
7th	3.1	(0.50)	2.6	(0.46)	1.7	(0.43)	2.6	(0.53)	2.4	(0.50)	1.2 !	(0.42)	1.2 !	(0.41)	1.2 !	(0.38)	1.9	(0.47)	1.4 !	(0.45)	1.7	(0.49)
8th	2.7	(0.39)	1.3	(0.34)	1.4	(0.34)	1.4	(0.39)	2.1	(0.47)	2.0	(0.60)	2.1	(0.50)	1.4	(0.42)	0.6 !	(0.30)	0.7 !	(0.29)	1.0 !	(0.34)
9th	2.9	(0.47)	2.4	(0.46)	1.5	(0.31)	1.0	(0.29)	1.2 !	(0.37)	0.9 !	(0.37)	1.1 !	(0.35)	1.4 !	(0.44)	0.8 !	(0.34)	‡	(†)	1.1 !	(0.37)
10th	1.8	(0.35)	1.2	(0.31)	1.3	(0.36)	0.5 !	(0.24)	1.2 !	(0.39)	1.0 !	(0.37)	0.9 !	(0.34)	1.0 !	(0.35)	‡	(†)	0.7 !	(0.32)	1.2 !	(0.58)
11th	1.6	(0.35)	1.6	(0.39)	0.9 !	(0.32)	0.7 !	(0.31)	1.5	(0.46)	1.5 !	(0.51)	‡	(†)	1.0 !	(0.43)	1.3 !	(0.49)	‡	(†)	0.8 !	(0.34)
12th	1.6	(0.36)	0.9 !	(0.31)	0.5 !	(0.26)	‡	(†)	0.8 !	(0.35)	‡	(†)	‡	(†)	‡	(†)	‡	(†)	‡	(†)	‡	(†)
School locale[2]																						
City	---	(†)	---	(†)	---	(†)	---	(†)	---	(†)	---	(†)	---	(†)	---	(†)	0.8 !	(0.23)	1.0	(0.24)	1.3	(0.38)
Suburban	---	(†)	---	(†)	---	(†)	---	(†)	---	(†)	---	(†)	---	(†)	---	(†)	1.5	(0.30)	0.5 !	(0.17)	1.0	(0.20)
Town	---	(†)	---	(†)	---	(†)	---	(†)	---	(†)	---	(†)	---	(†)	---	(†)	‡	(†)	1.3 !	(0.48)	1.2 !	(0.45)
Rural	---	(†)	---	(†)	---	(†)	---	(†)	---	(†)	---	(†)	---	(†)	---	(†)	0.6 !	(0.24)	0.5 !	(0.25)	1.2 !	(0.37)
Control of school[2,3]																						
Public	2.6	(0.19)	1.8	(0.20)	1.4	(0.15)	1.2	(0.15)	1.7	(0.20)	1.4	(0.19)	1.1	(0.15)	1.2	(0.16)	1.0	(0.16)	0.8	(0.13)	1.2	(0.17)
Private	1.6	(0.44)	1.0 !	(0.32)	0.9 !	(0.39)	1.4 !	(0.60)	‡	(†)	‡	(†)	‡	(†)	‡	(†)	‡	(†)	‡	(†)	‡	(†)
Violent excluding simple assault[4]	**0.5**	**(0.08)**	**0.4**	**(0.08)**	**0.2**	**(0.05)**	**0.3**	**(0.07)**	**0.4**	**(0.08)**	**0.3**	**(0.09)**	**0.1 !**	**(0.05)**	**0.2 !**	**(0.07)**	**0.2 !**	**(0.07)**	**0.2 !**	**(0.06)**	**0.3**	**(0.08)**
Sex																						
Male	0.7	(0.12)	0.5	(0.11)	0.3 !	(0.09)	0.3 !	(0.10)	0.5 !	(0.14)	0.6	(0.16)	0.2 !	(0.08)	0.2 !	(0.10)	0.2 !	(0.12)	0.2 !	(0.10)	0.4 !	(0.14)
Female	0.3	(0.08)	0.4 !	(0.12)	‡	(†)	0.3	(0.07)	0.2 !	(0.08)	‡	(†)	‡	(†)	0.2 !	(0.10)	‡	(†)	0.2 !	(0.08)	‡	(†)
Race/ethnicity[1]																						
White	0.5	(0.08)	0.4	(0.08)	0.2 !	(0.07)	0.3 !	(0.09)	0.2 !	(0.08)	0.3 !	(0.10)	0.2 !	(0.07)	0.2 !	(0.09)	0.3 !	(0.10)	0.3 !	(0.11)	0.2 !	(0.10)
Black	0.8 !	(0.28)	0.5 !	(0.25)	‡	(†)	‡	(†)	‡	(†)	‡	(†)	‡	(†)	‡	(†)	‡	(†)	‡	(†)	‡	(†)
Hispanic	0.4 !	(0.18)	0.8 !	(0.33)	0.4 !	(0.18)	0.4 !	(0.16)	0.8 !	(0.32)	‡	(†)	‡	(†)	0.4 !	(0.17)	‡	(†)	‡	(†)	‡	(†)
Asian/Pacific Islander	‡	(†)	‡	(†)	‡	(†)	‡	(†)	‡	(†)	‡	(†)	‡	(†)	‡	(†)	‡	(†)	‡	(†)	‡	(†)
Asian	---	(†)	---	(†)	‡	(†)	‡	(†)	‡	(†)	‡	(†)	‡	(†)	‡	(†)	‡	(†)	‡	(†)	‡	(†)
Pacific Islander	---	(†)	---	(†)	‡	(†)	‡	(†)	‡	(†)	‡	(†)	‡	(†)	‡	(†)	‡	(†)	‡	(†)	‡	(†)
American Indian/Alaska Native	‡	(†)	‡	(†)	‡	(†)	‡	(†)	‡	(†)	‡	(†)	‡	(†)	‡	(†)	‡	(†)	‡	(†)	‡	(†)
Two or more races	---	(†)	---	(†)	‡	(†)	‡	(†)	‡	(†)	‡	(†)	‡	(†)	‡	(†)	‡	(†)	‡	(†)	‡	(†)
Grade																						
6th	1.2 !	(0.38)	‡	(†)	‡	(†)	‡	(†)	‡	(†)	‡	(†)	‡	(†)	0.8 !	(0.42)	‡	(†)	‡	(†)	‡	(†)
7th	0.5 !	(0.19)	0.6 !	(0.24)	‡	(†)	‡	(†)	0.4 !	(0.20)	‡	(†)	0.5 !	(0.23)	‡	(†)	‡	(†)	‡	(†)	‡	(†)
8th	0.6 !	(0.19)	0.3 !	(0.14)	‡	(†)	‡	(†)	‡	(†)	‡	(†)	#	(†)	‡	(†)	‡	(†)	‡	(†)	‡	(†)
9th	0.5 !	(0.19)	0.8 !	(0.31)	0.6 !	(0.21)	‡	(†)	‡	(†)	‡	(†)	‡	(†)	‡	(†)	‡	(†)	‡	(†)	‡	(†)
10th	0.2 !	(0.11)	0.4 !	(0.18)	‡	(†)	‡	(†)	‡	(†)	‡	(†)	#	(†)	‡	(†)	‡	(†)	‡	(†)	‡	(†)
11th	0.3 !	(0.16)	‡	(†)	‡	(†)	‡	(†)	0.6 !	(0.27)	‡	(†)	#	(†)	‡	(†)	‡	(†)	‡	(†)	‡	(†)
12th	‡	(†)	‡	(†)	‡	(†)	‡	(†)	‡	(†)	‡	(†)	#	(†)	‡	(†)	‡	(†)	‡	(†)	‡	(†)
School locale[2]																						
City	---	(†)	---	(†)	---	(†)	---	(†)	---	(†)	---	(†)	---	(†)	---	(†)	‡	(†)	‡	(†)	0.3 !	(0.15)
Suburban	---	(†)	---	(†)	---	(†)	---	(†)	---	(†)	---	(†)	---	(†)	---	(†)	0.5 !	(0.19)	‡	(†)	‡	(†)
Town	---	(†)	---	(†)	---	(†)	---	(†)	---	(†)	---	(†)	---	(†)	---	(†)	‡	(†)	‡	(†)	‡	(†)
Rural	---	(†)	---	(†)	---	(†)	---	(†)	---	(†)	---	(†)	---	(†)	---	(†)	‡	(†)	‡	(†)	‡	(†)
Control of school[2,3]																						
Public	0.5	(0.08)	0.5	(0.09)	0.2	(0.06)	0.3	(0.06)	0.4	(0.09)	0.4	(0.10)	0.1 !	(0.06)	0.2 !	(0.08)	0.2 !	(0.08)	0.2 !	(0.06)	0.3 !	(0.08)
Private	‡	(†)	‡	(†)	‡	(†)	‡	(†)	‡	(†)	‡	(†)	#	(†)	‡	(†)	‡	(†)	‡	(†)	‡	(†)

---Not available.

†Not applicable.

#Rounds to zero.

!Interpret data with caution. The coefficient of variation (CV) for this estimate is between 30 and 50 percent.

‡Reporting standards not met. Either there are too few cases for a reliable estimate or the coefficient of variation (CV) is 50 percent or greater.

[1] Race categories exclude persons of Hispanic ethnicity. Prior to 2003, separate data for Asian students, Pacific Islander students, and students of Two or more races were not collected.

[2] Excludes students with missing information about the school characteristic.

[3] Data for 2013 and prior years were based on school information provided by the respondent. Beginning in 2015, data were based on school information collected in the Common Core of Data and the Private School Universe Survey, which was appended to the School Crime Supplement data file; therefore, these data may not be entirely comparable with figures for earlier years.

[4] In previous versions of this table, "violent excluding simple assault" was labeled as "serious violent" victimization. This category includes all types of violent victimization with the exception of simple assault.

NOTE: "Total victimization" includes theft and violent victimization. A single student could report more than one type of victimization. In the total victimization section, students who reported both theft and violent victimization are counted only once. "Theft" includes attempted and completed purse-snatching, completed pickpocketing, and all attempted and completed thefts, with the exception of motor vehicle thefts. Theft does not include robbery, which involves the threat or use of force and is classified as a violent crime. "All violent" victimization includes the crimes of rape, sexual assault, robbery, aggravated assault, and simple assault. "At school" includes in the school building, on school property, on a school bus, and, from 2001 onward, going to and from school. Some data have been revised from previously published figures.

SOURCE: U.S. Department of Justice, Bureau of Justice Statistics, School Crime Supplement (SCS) to the National Crime Victimization Survey, 1995 through 2019. (This table was prepared October 2020.)

Table 228.40. Percentage of students in grades 9-12 who reported being threatened or injured with a weapon on school property at least one time during the previous 12 months, by selected student characteristics: Selected years, 1993 through 2019

[Standard errors appear in parentheses]

Student characteristic	1993	1999	2001	2003	2005	2007	2009	2011	2013	2015	2017	2019
1	2	3	4	5	6	7	8	9	10	11	12	13
Total	**7.3 (0.44)**	**7.7 (0.42)**	**8.9 (0.55)**	**9.2 (0.75)**	**7.9 (0.35)**	**7.8 (0.44)**	**7.7 (0.37)**	**7.4 (0.31)**	**6.9 (0.38)**	**6.0 (0.38)**	**6.0 (0.33)**	**7.4 (0.50)**
Sex												
Male	9.2 (0.64)	9.5 (0.80)	11.5 (0.66)	11.6 (0.96)	9.7 (0.42)	10.2 (0.59)	9.6 (0.59)	9.5 (0.39)	7.7 (0.54)	7.0 (0.50)	7.8 (0.39)	8.0 (0.58)
Female	5.4 (0.40)	5.8 (0.64)	6.5 (0.52)	6.5 (0.61)	6.1 (0.41)	5.4 (0.41)	5.5 (0.37)	5.2 (0.37)	6.1 (0.40)	4.6 (0.42)	4.1 (0.46)	6.5 (0.61)
Race/ethnicity												
White	6.3 (0.58)	6.6 (0.35)	8.5 (0.66)	7.8 (0.77)	7.2 (0.46)	6.9 (0.52)	6.4 (0.43)	6.1 (0.35)	5.8 (0.32)	4.9 (0.50)	5.0 (0.51)	7.1 (0.60)
Black	11.2 (0.95)	7.6 (0.85)	9.3 (0.71)	10.9 (0.80)	8.1 (0.69)	9.7 (0.86)	9.4 (0.80)	8.9 (0.64)	8.4 (0.82)	7.9 (1.10)	7.8 (0.66)	8.8 (1.02)
Hispanic	8.6 (0.83)	9.8 (1.09)	8.9 (1.05)	9.4 (1.23)	9.8 (0.86)	8.7 (0.60)	9.1 (0.61)	9.2 (0.81)	8.5 (0.73)	6.6 (0.65)	6.1 (0.45)	6.9 (0.78)
Asian[1]	--- (†)	7.7 (1.05)	11.3 (2.73)	11.5 (2.66)	4.6 (1.10)	7.6 ! (2.29)	5.5 (0.91)	7.0 (0.99)	5.3 (1.41)	3.6 ! (1.40)	4.3 (0.89)	3.2 (0.87)
Pacific Islander[1]	--- (†)	15.6 (4.46)	24.8 (7.16)	16.3 (4.31)	14.5 ! (4.93)	8.1 ! (2.45)	12.5 (3.11)	11.3 (3.23)	8.7 ! (2.71)	20.5 ! (7.28)	7.0 ! (2.33)	12.3 ! (5.76)
American Indian/ Alaska Native	11.7 (2.50)	13.2 ! (5.45)	15.2 ! (4.57)	22.1 (4.79)	9.8 (2.67)	5.9 (1.24)	16.5 (2.68)	8.2 (1.52)	18.5 (5.24)	8.2 ! (2.69)	13.7 (3.57)	12.6 (3.77)
Two or more races[1]	--- (†)	9.3 (1.22)	10.3 (2.33)	18.7 (3.11)	10.7 (2.33)	13.3 (2.25)	9.2 (1.50)	9.9 (1.35)	7.7 (2.11)	8.0 (1.82)	8.0 (1.23)	11.4 (2.00)
Sexual identity[2]												
Heterosexual	--- (†)	--- (†)	--- (†)	--- (†)	--- (†)	--- (†)	--- (†)	--- (†)	--- (†)	5.1 (0.36)	5.4 (0.30)	6.3 (0.43)
Gay, lesbian, or bisexual	--- (†)	--- (†)	--- (†)	--- (†)	--- (†)	--- (†)	--- (†)	--- (†)	--- (†)	10.0 (1.19)	9.4 (1.08)	11.9 (1.44)
Not sure	--- (†)	--- (†)	--- (†)	--- (†)	--- (†)	--- (†)	--- (†)	--- (†)	--- (†)	12.6 (2.03)	11.1 (1.84)	12.9 (2.19)
Grade												
9th	9.4 (0.92)	10.5 (0.95)	12.7 (0.89)	12.1 (1.25)	10.5 (0.63)	9.2 (0.69)	8.7 (0.53)	8.3 (0.63)	8.5 (0.75)	7.2 (0.51)	6.8 (0.60)	8.1 (0.66)
10th	7.3 (0.59)	8.2 (0.92)	9.1 (0.75)	9.2 (1.02)	8.8 (0.72)	8.4 (0.51)	8.4 (0.72)	7.7 (0.58)	7.0 (0.67)	6.2 (0.57)	6.8 (0.60)	8.0 (0.84)
11th	7.3 (0.64)	6.1 (0.46)	6.9 (0.65)	7.3 (0.69)	5.5 (0.43)	6.8 (0.57)	7.9 (0.60)	7.3 (0.61)	6.8 (0.60)	5.5 (0.68)	5.1 (0.57)	7.1 (0.73)
12th	5.5 (0.62)	5.1 (0.79)	5.3 (0.52)	6.3 (0.92)	5.8 (0.52)	6.3 (0.64)	5.2 (0.53)	5.9 (0.45)	4.9 (0.61)	4.4 (0.69)	4.6 (0.52)	5.9 (0.82)

—Not available.

†Not applicable.

!Interpret data with caution. The coefficient of variation (CV) for this estimate is between 30 and 50 percent.

[1] Before 1999, Asian students and Pacific Islander students were not categorized separately, and students could not be classified as Two or more races. Because the response categories changed in 1999, caution should be used in comparing data on race from 1993 with data from later years.

[2] Students were asked which of the following–"heterosexual (straight)," "gay or lesbian," "bisexual," or "not sure"–best described them.

NOTE: Survey respondents were asked about being threatened or injured "with a weapon such as a gun, knife, or club on school property." "On school property" was not defined for respondents. Race categories exclude persons of Hispanic ethnicity.

SOURCE: Centers for Disease Control and Prevention, Division of Adolescent and School Health, Youth Risk Behavior Surveillance System (YRBSS), 1993 through 2019. (This table was prepared September 2020.)

Table 228.50. Percentage of public school students in grades 9-12 who reported being threatened or injured with a weapon on school property at least one time during the previous 12 months, by state or jurisdiction: Selected years, 2003 through 2017

[Standard errors appear in parentheses]

State or jurisdiction	2003		2005		2007		2009		2011		2013		2015		2017	
1	2		3		4		5		6		7		8		9	
United States[1]	**9.2**	**(0.75)**	**7.9**	**(0.35)**	**7.8**	**(0.44)**	**7.7**	**(0.37)**	**7.4**	**(0.31)**	**6.9**	**(0.38)**	**6.0**	**(0.38)**	**6.0**	**(0.33)**
Alabama	7.2	(0.91)	10.6	(0.86)	—	(†)	10.4	(1.56)	7.6	(1.20)	9.9	(1.17)	8.8	(0.92)	—	(†)
Alaska	8.1	(1.01)	—	(†)	7.7	(0.88)	7.3	(0.90)	5.6	(0.70)	—	(†)	—	(†)	—	(†)
Arizona	9.7	(1.10)	10.7	(0.55)	11.2	(0.79)	9.3	(0.92)	10.4	(0.74)	9.1	(1.32)	7.5	(0.97)	7.9	(1.05)
Arkansas	—	(†)	9.6	(1.06)	9.1	(1.03)	11.9	(1.38)	6.3	(0.85)	10.9	(1.14)	10.6	(0.66)	11.7	(1.00)
California	—	(†)	—	(†)	—	(†)	—	(†)	—	(†)	—	(†)	5.2	(0.72)	5.0	(0.81)
Colorado	—	(†)	7.6	(0.75)	—	(†)	8.0	(0.74)	6.7	(0.80)	—	(†)	—	(†)	5.8	(0.47)
Connecticut	—	(†)	9.1	(0.91)	7.7	(0.59)	7.0	(0.62)	6.8	(0.71)	7.1	(0.74)	6.7	(0.71)	7.1	(0.82)
Delaware	7.7	(0.60)	6.2	(0.63)	5.6	(0.50)	7.8	(0.63)	6.4	(0.62)	5.6	(0.46)	6.2	(0.90)	6.0	(0.62)
District of Columbia	12.7	(1.42)	12.1	(0.78)	11.3	(0.98)	—	(†)	8.7	(0.92)	8.5	(0.30)	7.6	(0.27)	9.8	(0.37)
Florida	8.4	(0.44)	7.9	(0.45)	8.6	(0.57)	8.2	(0.39)	7.2	(0.31)	7.1	(0.37)	7.4	(0.42)	8.4	(0.48)
Georgia	8.2	(0.75)	8.3	(2.08)	8.1	(0.81)	8.2	(0.83)	11.7	(2.08)	7.2	(0.81)	—	(†)	—	(†)
Hawaii	—	(†)	6.8	(0.87)	6.4	(1.10)	7.7	(1.03)	6.3	(0.62)	—	(†)	—	(†)	—	(†)
Idaho	9.4	(0.82)	8.3	(0.59)	10.2	(1.07)	7.9	(0.62)	7.3	(0.99)	5.8	(0.59)	6.1	(0.48)	6.2	(0.61)
Illinois	—	(†)	—	(†)	7.8	(0.69)	8.8	(0.86)	7.6	(0.48)	8.5	(0.82)	6.6	(0.80)	7.5	(0.49)
Indiana	6.7	(0.91)	8.8	(0.96)	9.6	(0.68)	6.5	(0.66)	6.8	(1.14)	—	(†)	6.6	(1.02)	—	(†)
Iowa	—	(†)	7.8	(1.02)	7.1	(0.86)	—	(†)	6.3	(0.85)	—	(†)	—	(†)	8.2	(1.26)
Kansas	—	(†)	7.4	(0.82)	8.6	(1.12)	6.2	(0.62)	5.6	(0.68)	5.3	(0.65)	—	(†)	5.8	(0.60)
Kentucky	5.2	(0.72)	8.0	(0.75)	8.3	(0.53)	7.9	(1.00)	7.4	(0.98)	5.4	(0.57)	7.2	(0.87)	7.1	(0.83)
Louisiana	—	(†)	—	(†)	—	(†)	9.5	(1.29)	8.7	(1.18)	10.5	(0.99)	—	(†)	12.8	(1.75)
Maine	8.5	(0.78)	7.1	(0.68)	6.8	(0.84)	7.7	(0.32)	6.8	(0.26)	5.3	(0.29)	5.2	(0.36)	5.5	(0.39)
Maryland	—	(†)	11.7	(1.30)	9.6	(0.86)	9.1	(0.75)	8.4	(0.67)	9.4	(0.22)	7.3	(0.17)	7.8	(0.18)
Massachusetts	6.3	(0.54)	5.4	(0.44)	5.3	(0.47)	7.0	(0.58)	6.8	(0.67)	4.4	(0.38)	4.1	(0.46)	4.8	(0.62)
Michigan	9.7	(0.57)	8.6	(0.81)	8.1	(0.77)	9.4	(0.63)	6.8	(0.50)	6.7	(0.52)	6.6	(0.67)	6.5	(0.55)
Minnesota	—	(†)	—	(†)	—	(†)	—	(†)	—	(†)	—	(†)	—	(†)	—	(†)
Mississippi	6.6	(0.82)	—	(†)	8.3	(0.59)	8.0	(0.69)	7.5	(0.63)	8.8	(0.78)	10.1	(0.98)	—	(†)
Missouri	7.5	(0.93)	9.1	(1.19)	9.3	(1.03)	7.8	(0.76)	—	(†)	—	(†)	—	(†)	—	(†)
Montana	7.1	(0.46)	8.0	(0.64)	7.0	(0.51)	7.4	(0.99)	7.5	(0.53)	6.3	(0.40)	5.5	(0.48)	7.0	(0.60)
Nebraska	8.8	(0.80)	9.7	(0.68)	—	(†)	—	(†)	6.4	(0.54)	6.4	(0.57)	7.1	(0.83)	7.1	(1.07)
Nevada	6.0	(0.65)	8.1	(0.96)	7.8	(0.70)	10.7	(0.84)	—	(†)	6.4	(0.80)	6.9	(0.79)	8.1	(0.84)
New Hampshire	7.5	(0.98)	8.6	(0.91)	7.3	(0.69)	—	(†)	—	(†)	—	(†)	—	(†)	6.7	(0.29)
New Jersey	—	(†)	8.0	(1.07)	—	(†)	6.6	(0.75)	5.7	(0.51)	6.2	(0.81)	—	(†)	—	(†)
New Mexico	—	(†)	10.4	(0.96)	10.1	(0.68)	—	(†)	—	(†)	—	(†)	—	(†)	—	(†)
New York	7.2	(0.44)	7.2	(0.47)	7.3	(0.57)	7.5	(0.55)	7.3	(0.60)	7.3	(0.61)	8.4	(0.68)	8.0	(1.00)
North Carolina	7.2	(0.74)	7.9	(0.92)	6.6	(0.62)	6.8	(0.61)	9.1	(0.95)	6.9	(0.45)	4.9	(0.69)	6.9	(0.73)
North Dakota	5.9	(0.89)	6.6	(0.58)	5.2	(0.59)	—	(†)	—	(†)	—	(†)	—	(†)	—	(†)
Ohio[2]	7.7	(1.30)	8.2	(0.67)	8.3	(0.77)	—	(†)	—	(†)	—	(†)	—	(†)	—	(†)
Oklahoma	7.4	(1.10)	6.0	(0.65)	7.0	(0.72)	5.8	(0.66)	5.7	(0.88)	4.6	(0.53)	5.1	(0.78)	4.8	(0.77)
Oregon	—	(†)	—	(†)	—	(†)	—	(†)	—	(†)	—	(†)	—	(†)	—	(†)
Pennsylvania	—	(†)	—	(†)	—	(†)	5.6	(0.73)	—	(†)	—	(†)	5.0	(0.47)	5.4	(0.49)
Rhode Island	8.2	(0.84)	8.7	(0.87)	8.3	(0.42)	6.5	(0.65)	—	(†)	6.4	(0.51)	—	(†)	—	(†)
South Carolina	—	(†)	10.1	(0.93)	9.8	(0.85)	8.8	(1.48)	9.2	(0.92)	6.5	(0.83)	5.3	(0.73)	9.4	(1.16)
South Dakota[3]	6.5	(0.71)	8.1	(1.04)	5.9	(0.87)	6.8	(0.87)	6.1	(0.77)	5.0	(0.69)	7.3	(1.10)	—	(†)
Tennessee	8.4	(1.17)	7.4	(0.79)	7.3	(0.76)	7.0	(0.71)	5.8	(0.52)	9.3	(0.73)	10.2	(1.04)	6.5	(0.74)
Texas	—	(†)	9.3	(0.84)	8.7	(0.52)	7.2	(0.52)	6.8	(0.40)	7.1	(0.62)	—	(†)	7.4	(0.96)
Utah	7.3	(1.44)	9.8	(1.32)	11.4	(1.92)	7.7	(0.88)	7.0	(0.98)	5.5	(0.59)	—	(†)	7.0	(0.75)
Vermont[4]	7.3	(0.20)	6.3	(0.46)	6.2	(0.56)	6.0	(0.30)	5.5	(0.37)	6.4	(0.43)	5.3	(0.16)	4.8	(0.15)
Virginia	—	(†)	—	(†)	—	(†)	—	(†)	7.0	(0.86)	6.1	(0.43)	6.4	(0.62)	6.4	(0.69)
Washington	—	(†)	—	(†)	—	(†)	—	(†)	—	(†)	—	(†)	—	(†)	—	(†)
West Virginia	8.5	(1.26)	8.0	(0.78)	9.7	(0.77)	9.2	(0.77)	6.6	(0.93)	5.6	(0.51)	6.9	(0.58)	6.5	(1.07)
Wisconsin	5.5	(0.70)	7.6	(0.73)	5.6	(0.66)	6.7	(0.75)	5.1	(0.48)	4.3	(0.64)	—	(†)	6.9	(1.30)
Wyoming	9.7	(1.00)	7.8	(0.67)	8.3	(0.67)	9.4	(0.58)	7.3	(0.58)	6.8	(0.47)	6.6	(0.74)	—	(†)
Puerto Rico	—	(†)	6.3	(0.62)	—	(†)	—	(†)	4.9	(0.93)	4.1	(0.54)	4.7	(0.70)	7.5 !	(2.33)

—Not available.

†Not applicable.

!Interpret data with caution. The coefficient of variation (CV) for this estimate is between 30 and 50 percent.

[1] U.S. total data are representative of all public and private school students in grades 9-12 in the 50 states and the District of Columbia. U.S. total data for all years were collected through a separate national survey (rather than being aggregated from state-level data) and include both public and private schools.

[2] Ohio data for 2003 through 2013 include both public and private schools.

[3] South Dakota data for 2003 through 2015 include both public and private schools.

[4] Vermont data for 2013 include both public and private schools.

NOTE: Survey respondents were asked about being threatened or injured "with a weapon such as a gun, knife, or club on school property." "On school property" was not defined for respondents. For the U.S. total, data for all years include both public and private schools. State-level data include public schools only, except where otherwise noted. For specific states, a given year's data may be unavailable (1) because the state did not participate in the survey that year; (2) because the state omitted this particular survey item from the state-level questionnaire; or (3) because the state had an overall response rate of less than 60 percent (the overall response rate is the school response rate multiplied by the student response rate).

SOURCE: Centers for Disease Control and Prevention, Division of Adolescent and School Health, Youth Risk Behavior Surveillance System (YRBSS), 2003 through 2017. (This table was prepared July 2018.)

Table 228.70. Number and percentage of public school teachers who reported that they were threatened with injury or physically attacked by a student from school during the previous 12 months, by selected teacher characteristics: Selected years, 1993-94 through 2015-16

[Standard errors appear in parentheses]

Year	Total	Sex: Male	Sex: Female	Race/ethnicity: White	Race/ethnicity: Black	Race/ethnicity: Hispanic	Race/ethnicity: Other[2]	Instructional level[1]: Elementary	Instructional level[1]: Secondary
1	2	3	4	5	6	7	8	9	10
	Number of teachers								
Threatened with injury									
1993-94	326,800 (7,040)	111,200 (3,830)	215,600 (5,380)	281,300 (6,220)	23,400 (1,360)	15,100 (1,770)	6,900 (650)	128,000 (4,450)	198,800 (5,150)
1999-2000	287,400 (7,060)	89,600 (3,680)	197,800 (5,370)	237,100 (5,630)	27,200 (2,170)	16,300 (1,940)	6,700 (840)	138,000 (5,480)	149,300 (4,360)
2003-04	242,100 (7,840)	75,300 (3,640)	166,800 (6,840)	189,800 (6,310)	31,900 (3,120)	11,800 (1,760)	8,600 (1,170)	108,800 (6,990)	133,300 (4,970)
2007-08	276,600 (10,570)	85,200 (5,800)	191,500 (8,220)	223,200 (8,760)	27,600 (3,000)	17,400 (3,230)	8,400 (1,580)	123,800 (7,670)	152,800 (7,090)
2011-12	338,400 (17,290)	79,800 (5,400)	258,600 (15,480)	266,800 (13,430)	33,400 (4,400)	26,600 (4,660)	11,600 (2,200)	184,000 (13,400)	154,400 (7,750)
2015-16	327,900 (7,840)	80,700 (3,630)	247,200 (6,490)	262,800 (7,210)	26,200 (1,900)	24,400 (1,790)	14,600 (1,380)	182,100 (6,370)	145,800 (5,050)
Physically attacked									
1993-94	112,400 (3,730)	28,700 (1,780)	83,700 (3,710)	96,300 (3,720)	7,600 (860)	5,900 (1,270)	2,600 (430)	71,600 (3,120)	40,700 (1,850)
1999-2000	125,000 (4,630)	29,100 (2,010)	95,900 (4,230)	103,100 (3,590)	11,000 (1,550)	8,400 (1,640)	2,500 (450)	94,400 (4,180)	30,600 (2,240)
2003-04	121,400 (7,180)	21,700 (2,420)	99,700 (6,100)	95,500 (5,450)	14,800 (2,320)	6,400 (1,820)	4,700 (1,050)	85,100 (6,380)	36,300 (3,310)
2007-08	146,400 (8,200)	33,400 (4,750)	113,000 (6,250)	124,100 (6,990)	11,600 (2,330)	7,800 (1,990)	2,800 ! (1,230)	109,100 (7,340)	37,300 (3,090)
2011-12	197,400 (11,730)	29,500 (3,310)	167,900 (11,200)	160,700 (10,890)	18,000 (3,590)	11,300 (2,890)	7,400 (1,940)	153,800 (10,100)	43,600 (4,380)
2015-16	192,500 (6,040)	30,200 (1,850)	162,300 (5,430)	155,600 (5,460)	12,700 (1,370)	14,200 (1,430)	10,000 (1,210)	153,700 (5,640)	38,800 (2,230)
	Percent of teachers								
Threatened with injury									
1993-94	12.8 (0.26)	16.0 (0.44)	11.5 (0.28)	12.7 (0.28)	12.4 (0.64)	13.9 (1.42)	14.5 (1.14)	9.6 (0.35)	16.2 (0.30)
1999-2000	9.6 (0.22)	11.9 (0.44)	8.8 (0.23)	9.4 (0.22)	11.9 (0.91)	9.7 (1.12)	9.1 (1.12)	8.6 (0.34)	10.7 (0.29)
2003-04	7.4 (0.24)	9.3 (0.43)	6.8 (0.28)	7.0 (0.24)	12.4 (1.03)	5.8 (0.90)	9.6 (1.24)	6.3 (0.39)	8.7 (0.29)
2007-08	8.1 (0.30)	10.4 (0.68)	7.4 (0.31)	7.9 (0.30)	11.5 (0.99)	7.3 (1.34)	8.7 (1.54)	7.2 (0.43)	9.1 (0.41)
2011-12	10.0 (0.48)	10.0 (0.56)	10.0 (0.57)	9.6 (0.47)	14.5 (1.84)	10.1 (1.70)	9.9 (1.69)	10.7 (0.76)	9.3 (0.38)
2015-16	9.8 (0.21)	10.4 (0.42)	9.6 (0.22)	9.8 (0.24)	11.7 (0.74)	8.4 (0.57)	10.3 (0.91)	10.8 (0.30)	8.8 (0.26)
Physically attacked									
1993-94	4.4 (0.14)	4.1 (0.24)	4.5 (0.20)	4.3 (0.17)	4.0 (0.43)	5.4 (1.09)	5.4 (0.82)	5.4 (0.22)	3.3 (0.15)
1999-2000	4.2 (0.15)	3.9 (0.25)	4.3 (0.18)	4.1 (0.14)	4.8 (0.63)	5.0 (0.92)	3.4 (0.59)	5.9 (0.26)	2.2 (0.15)
2003-04	3.7 (0.22)	2.7 (0.29)	4.1 (0.25)	3.5 (0.21)	5.8 (0.84)	3.2 (0.93)	5.3 (1.16)	5.0 (0.37)	2.4 (0.21)
2007-08	4.3 (0.24)	4.1 (0.57)	4.4 (0.24)	4.4 (0.25)	4.9 (0.95)	3.3 (0.79)	3.0 ! (1.09)	6.3 (0.44)	2.2 (0.18)
2011-12	5.8 (0.33)	3.7 (0.39)	6.5 (0.41)	5.8 (0.38)	7.8 (1.52)	4.3 (1.05)	6.3 (1.53)	8.9 (0.57)	2.6 (0.24)
2015-16	5.7 (0.17)	3.9 (0.24)	6.3 (0.19)	5.8 (0.19)	5.7 (0.58)	4.9 (0.47)	7.1 (0.83)	9.1 (0.28)	2.3 (0.13)

!Interpret data with caution. The coefficient of variation (CV) for this estimate is between 30 and 50 percent.

[1] Instructional level divides teachers into elementary or secondary based on a combination of grades taught, main teaching assignment, and structure of teachers' class(es), rather than the level of school in which teachers taught. Teachers with only ungraded classes were classified based on their main teaching assignment and the structure of their class(es). Among teachers with regularly graded classes, elementary teachers generally include those teaching prekindergarten through grade 6 and those teaching multiple grades, with a preponderance of grades taught being kindergarten through grade 6. In general, secondary teachers include those teaching any of grades 7 through 12 and those teaching multiple grades, with a preponderance of grades taught being grades 7 through 12 and usually with no grade taught being lower than grade 5.

[2] Includes American Indian/Alaska Native, Asian, and Pacific Islander; for 2003-04 and later years, also includes Two or more races.

NOTE: Teachers who taught only prekindergarten students are excluded. Includes teachers in both traditional public schools and public charter schools. Race categories exclude persons of Hispanic ethnicity. Detail may not sum to totals because of rounding. Some data have been revised from previously published figures.

SOURCE: U.S. Department of Education, National Center for Education Statistics, Schools and Staffing Survey (SASS), "Public School Teacher Data File," 1993-94, 1999-2000, 2003-04, 2007-08, and 2011-12; "Charter School Teacher Data File," 1999-2000; and National Teacher and Principal Survey (NTPS), "Public School Teacher Data File," 2015-16. (This table was prepared September 2020.)

Table 229.10. Percentage of public schools recording incidents of crime at school, percentage reporting incidents of crime at school to police, and number of incidents recorded or reported, by type of crime: Selected years, 1999-2000 through 2017-18

[Standard errors appear in parentheses]

Type of crime recorded or reported to police	Percent of schools												2015-16				2017-18			
	1999-2000		2003-04		2005-06		2007-08		2009-10		2013-14[1]		Percent of schools		Number of incidents		Percent of schools		Number of incidents	
1	2		3		4		5		6		7		8		9		10		11	
Recorded incidents																				
Total	**86.4**	**(1.23)**	**88.5**	**(0.85)**	**85.7**	**(1.07)**	**85.5**	**(0.87)**	**85.0**	**(1.07)**	---	(†)	**78.9**	**(1.28)**	**1,381,200**	**(42,660)**	**79.8**	**(1.23)**	**1,438,500**	**(54,530)**
Violent incidents	**71.4**	**(1.37)**	**81.4**	**(1.05)**	**77.7**	**(1.11)**	**75.5**	**(1.09)**	**73.8**	**(1.07)**	**65.0**	**(1.46)**	**68.9**	**(1.30)**	**864,900**	**(42,950)**	**70.7**	**(1.38)**	**962,300**	**(45,850)**
Serious violent incidents	19.7	(0.98)	18.3	(0.99)	17.1	(0.91)	17.2	(1.06)	16.4	(0.94)	13.1	(1.00)	15.5	(0.93)	40,800	(3,460)	21.3	(0.98)	54,400	(7,770)
Rape or attempted rape	0.7	(0.10)	0.8	(0.17)	0.3	(0.07)	0.8	(0.17)	0.5	(0.10)	0.2 !	(0.10)	0.9	(0.19)	1,100	(190)	0.9	(0.16)	1,100	(200)
Sexual assault other than rape[2]	2.5	(0.33)	3.0	(0.32)	2.8	(0.24)	2.5	(0.33)	2.3	(0.34)	1.7	(0.37)	3.4	(0.38)	6,100	(1,360)	5.2	(0.46)	7,100	(590)
Physical attack or fight with a weapon	5.2	(0.60)	4.0	(0.46)	3.0	(0.38)	3.0	(0.33)	3.9	(0.48)	1.8	(0.34)	2.6	(0.38)	5,300	(1,280)	3.0	(0.42)	10,500	(2,850)
Threat of physical attack with a weapon	11.1	(0.70)	8.6	(0.71)	8.8	(0.66)	9.3	(0.77)	7.7	(0.72)	8.7	(0.78)	8.5	(0.79)	18,300	(2,420)	13.2	(0.86)	26,700	(4,460)
Robbery with a weapon	0.5 !	(0.15)	0.6	(0.15)	0.4	(0.12)	0.4 !	(0.14)	0.2	(0.05)	‡	(†)	0.5 !	(0.16)	600	(160)	0.4	(0.10)	500	(140)
Robbery without a weapon	5.3	(0.56)	6.3	(0.60)	6.4	(0.59)	5.2	(0.56)	4.4	(0.49)	2.5	(0.42)	2.7	(0.36)	9,500	(1,440)	3.5	(0.39)	8,500	(1,050)
Physical attack or fight without a weapon	63.7	(1.52)	76.7	(1.21)	74.3	(1.20)	72.7	(1.07)	70.5	(1.11)	57.5	(1.43)	64.9	(1.28)	567,000	(36,780)	65.7	(1.39)	597,300	(34,030)
Threat of physical attack without a weapon	52.2	(1.47)	53.0	(1.34)	52.2	(1.27)	47.8	(1.19)	46.4	(1.33)	47.1	(1.50)	39.4	(1.48)	257,000	(15,630)	41.4	(1.38)	310,700	(18,050)
Theft/larceny[3]	**45.6**	**(1.37)**	**46.0**	**(1.29)**	**46.0**	**(1.07)**	**47.3**	**(1.29)**	**44.1**	**(1.31)**	---	(†)	**38.7**	**(1.29)**	**166,000**	**(5,190)**	**33.4**	**(1.31)**	**132,500**	**(6,130)**
Other incidents[4]	**72.7**	**(1.30)**	**64.0**	**(1.27)**	**68.2**	**(1.07)**	**67.4**	**(1.13)**	**68.1**	**(1.12)**	---	(†)	**58.5**	**(1.68)**	**350,400**	**(10,710)**	**59.8**	**(1.18)**	**343,700**	**(9,270)**
Possession of a firearm/explosive device	5.5	(0.44)	6.1	(0.49)	7.2	(0.60)	4.7	(0.38)	4.7	(0.52)	---	(†)	4.0	(0.50)	10,500 !	(3,220)	3.3	(0.37)	3,600	(390)
Possession of a knife or sharp object	42.6	(1.28)	---	(†)	42.8	(1.23)	40.6	(1.10)	39.7	(1.06)	---	(†)	38.4	(1.26)	70,600	(3,210)	38.2	(1.12)	69,100	(2,220)
Distribution of illegal drugs[5]	12.3	(0.50)	12.9	(0.55)	---	(†)	---	(†)	---	(†)	---	(†)	---	(†)	---	(†)	---	(†)	---	(†)
Possession or use of alcohol or illegal drugs[5]	26.6	(0.72)	29.3	(0.87)	---	(†)	---	(†)	---	(†)	---	(†)	---	(†)	---	(†)	---	(†)	---	(†)
Distribution, possession, or use of illegal drugs[6]	---	(†)	---	(†)	25.9	(0.68)	23.2	(0.68)	24.6	(0.57)	---	(†)	24.9	(0.85)	112,100	(4,250)	24.9	(0.69)	120,300	(4,480)
Inappropriate distribution, possession, or use of prescription drugs[7]	---	(†)	---	(†)	---	(†)	---	(†)	12.1	(0.47)	---	(†)	9.5	(0.55)	20,100	(1,580)	9.7	(0.46)	21,100	(1,350)
Distribution, possession, or use of alcohol[6]	---	(†)	---	(†)	16.2	(0.68)	14.9	(0.57)	14.1	(0.50)	---	(†)	13.3	(0.50)	29,900	(1,620)	13.4	(0.45)	29,000	(1,420)
Sexual harassment	36.3	(1.26)	---	(†)	---	(†)	---	(†)	---	(†)	---	(†)	---	(†)	---	(†)	---	(†)	---	(†)
Vandalism	51.4	(1.61)	51.4	(1.17)	50.5	(1.17)	49.3	(1.16)	45.8	(1.12)	---	(†)	33.4	(1.25)	107,200	(7,040)	33.1	(1.10)	100,600	(5,720)
Reported incidents to police																				
Total	**62.5**	**(1.37)**	**65.2**	**(1.35)**	**60.9**	**(1.15)**	**62.0**	**(1.24)**	**60.0**	**(1.58)**	---	(†)	**47.4**	**(1.54)**	**448,900**	**(13,330)**	**46.9**	**(1.04)**	**422,800**	**(12,650)**
Violent incidents	**36.0**	**(1.26)**	**43.6**	**(1.15)**	**37.7**	**(1.09)**	**37.8**	**(1.16)**	**39.9**	**(1.13)**	---	(†)	**32.7**	**(1.13)**	**195,600**	**(9,620)**	**32.5**	**(1.08)**	**192,100**	**(8,050)**
Serious violent incidents	14.8	(0.82)	13.3	(0.88)	12.6	(0.70)	12.6	(0.86)	10.4	(0.62)	---	(†)	10.0	(0.68)	20,000	(1,700)	14.9	(0.86)	26,100	(1,680)
Rape or attempted rape	0.6	(0.10)	0.8	(0.17)	0.3	(0.07)	0.8	(0.17)	0.5	(0.10)	---	(†)	0.7	(0.14)	900	(160)	0.8	(0.16)	1,000	(190)
Sexual assault other than rape[2]	2.3	(0.34)	2.6	(0.28)	2.6	(0.26)	2.1	(0.29)	1.4	(0.20)	---	(†)	2.7	(0.28)	3,600	(490)	4.3	(0.42)	5,600	(440)
Physical attack or fight with a weapon	3.9	(0.50)	2.8	(0.38)	2.2	(0.27)	2.1	(0.27)	2.2	(0.32)	---	(†)	1.3	(0.24)	2,500 !	(830)	1.5	(0.23)	2,400	(390)
Threat of physical attack with a weapon	8.5	(0.59)	6.0	(0.55)	5.9	(0.49)	5.7	(0.59)	4.5	(0.43)	---	(†)	5.3	(0.53)	7,500	(770)	9.0	(0.67)	12,400	(1,290)
Robbery with a weapon	0.3 !	(0.09)	0.6	(0.15)	0.4	(0.12)	0.4 !	(0.14)	0.2	(0.05)	---	(†)	0.3 !	(0.13)	400 !	(140)	0.3	(0.08)	400	(90)
Robbery without a weapon	3.4	(0.41)	4.2	(0.51)	4.9	(0.48)	4.1	(0.42)	3.5	(0.40)	---	(†)	1.9	(0.28)	5,000	(690)	2.4	(0.33)	4,300	(560)
Physical attack or fight without a weapon	25.8	(0.91)	35.6	(0.98)	29.2	(1.00)	28.2	(0.90)	34.3	(0.90)	---	(†)	25.1	(1.03)	121,500	(8,560)	21.7	(0.70)	107,600	(5,570)
Threat of physical attack without a weapon	18.9	(0.94)	21.0	(0.82)	19.7	(0.69)	19.5	(0.76)	15.2	(0.79)	---	(†)	12.9	(0.65)	54,200	(3,680)	14.3	(0.63)	58,400	(4,090)
Theft/larceny[3]	**28.5**	**(1.04)**	**30.5**	**(1.17)**	**27.9**	**(0.97)**	**31.0**	**(1.12)**	**25.4**	**(1.01)**	---	(†)	**18.1**	**(0.80)**	**71,600**	**(3,280)**	**14.9**	**(0.75)**	**53,900**	**(2,780)**
Other incidents[4]	**52.0**	**(1.14)**	**50.0**	**(1.18)**	**50.6**	**(1.00)**	**48.7**	**(1.17)**	**46.3**	**(1.23)**	---	(†)	**33.5**	**(1.15)**	**181,700**	**(5,500)**	**35.1**	**(0.86)**	**176,900**	**(5,210)**
Possession of a firearm/explosive device	4.5	(0.41)	4.9	(0.44)	5.5	(0.51)	3.6	(0.32)	3.1	(0.39)	---	(†)	1.9	(0.29)	7,500 !	(2,760)	2.1	(0.30)	2,300	(320)
Possession of a knife or sharp object	23.0	(0.84)	---	(†)	25.0	(1.00)	23.3	(0.69)	20.0	(0.88)	---	(†)	15.8	(0.66)	27,700	(1,330)	18.0	(0.68)	30,500	(1,260)
Distribution of illegal drugs[5]	11.4	(0.48)	12.4	(0.57)	---	(†)	---	(†)	---	(†)	---	(†)	---	(†)	---	(†)	---	(†)	---	(†)
Possession or use of alcohol or illegal drugs[5]	22.2	(0.67)	26.0	(0.76)	---	(†)	---	(†)	---	(†)	---	(†)	---	(†)	---	(†)	---	(†)	---	(†)
Distribution, possession, or use of illegal drugs[6]	---	(†)	---	(†)	22.8	(0.62)	20.7	(0.60)	21.4	(0.57)	---	(†)	19.9	(0.71)	82,200	(3,300)	19.9	(0.52)	84,800	(3,380)
Inappropriate distribution, possession, or use of prescription drugs[7]	---	(†)	---	(†)	---	(†)	---	(†)	9.6	(0.42)	---	(†)	7.4	(0.56)	15,100	(1,270)	7.1	(0.36)	15,100	(960)
Distribution, possession, or use of alcohol[6]	---	(†)	---	(†)	11.6	(0.61)	10.6	(0.55)	10.0	(0.41)	---	(†)	8.6	(0.41)	17,800	(1,330)	8.0	(0.39)	16,900	(950)
Sexual harassment	14.7	(0.78)	---	(†)	---	(†)	---	(†)	---	(†)	---	(†)	---	(†)	---	(†)	---	(†)	---	(†)
Vandalism	32.7	(1.10)	34.3	(1.06)	31.9	(1.02)	30.8	(1.18)	26.8	(1.09)	---	(†)	12.9	(0.86)	31,600	(2,370)	12.0	(0.66)	27,300	(2,220)

—Not available.

†Not applicable.

!Interpret data with caution. The coefficient of variation (CV) for this estimate is between 30 and 50 percent.

‡Reporting standards not met. Either there are too few cases for a reliable estimate or the coefficient of variation (CV) is 50 percent or greater.

[1] Data for 2013-14 were collected using the Fast Response Survey System (FRSS), while data for all other years were collected using the School Survey on Crime and Safety (SSOCS). The 2013-14 FRSS survey was designed to allow comparisons with SSOCS data. However, all respondents to the 2013-14 survey could choose either to complete the survey on paper (and mail it back) or to complete the survey online, whereas all respondents to SSOCS had only the option of completing a paper survey prior to 2017-18, when SSOCS experimented with offering an online option to some respondents. The 2013-14 FRSS survey also relied on a smaller sample than SSOCS. The FRSS survey's smaller sample size and difference in survey administration may have impacted the 2013-14 results.

[2] Prior to 2015-16, the wording of the survey item was "sexual battery other than rape."

[3] Theft/larceny is taking things worth over $10 without personal confrontation.

[4] Caution should be used when making direct comparisons of "Other incidents" between years because the survey questions about alcohol and drugs changed, as outlined in footnotes 5, 6, and 7, and because sexual harassment was only included in 1999-2000.

[5] The survey items "Distribution of illegal drugs" and "Possession or use of alcohol or illegal drugs" appear only on the 1999-2000 and 2003-04 questionnaires. Different alcohol- and drug-related survey items were used on the SSOCS questionnaires for later years.

[6] The survey items "Distribution, possession, or use of illegal drugs" and "Distribution, possession, or use of alcohol" appear only on the SSOCS questionnaires for 2005-06 and later years.

[7] The survey item "Inappropriate distribution, possession, or use of prescription drugs" appears only on the SSOCS questionnaires for 2009-10 and later years.

NOTE: Responses were provided by the principal or the person most knowledgeable about crime and safety issues at the school. "At school" was defined to include activities that happen in school buildings, on school grounds, on school buses, and at places that hold school-sponsored events or activities. Respondents were instructed to include incidents that occurred before, during, and after normal school hours or when school activities or events were in session. Detail may not sum to totals because of rounding and because schools that recorded or reported more than one type of crime incident were counted only once in the total percentage of schools recording or reporting incidents.

SOURCE: U.S. Department of Education, National Center for Education Statistics, 1999-2000, 2003-04, 2005-06, 2007-08, 2009-10, 2015-16, and 2017-18 School Survey on Crime and Safety (SSOCS), 2000, 2004, 2006, 2008, 2010, 2016, and 2018; and Fast Response Survey System (FRSS), "School Safety and Discipline: 2013-14," FRSS 106, 2014. (This table was prepared July 2019.)

Table 229.20. Rate of crime incidents at school per 1,000 students recorded by public schools and reported to police by public schools, by school level, percentage of students eligible for free or reduced-price lunch, and type of crime: Selected years, 1999–2000 through 2017–18

[Standard errors appear in parentheses]

Type of crime recorded or reported to police	Rate of crime incidents at school per 1,000 students[1]																							
													2017–18											
															School level[2]						Percent of students e			
	1999-2000		2003-04		2005-06		2007-08		2009-10		2015-16		Total		Primary		Middle		High school		0 to 25		26	
1	2		3		4		5		6		7		8		9		10		11		12			
Incidents recorded																								
Total	**48.5**	**(2.52)**	**45.7**	**(1.65)**	**45.8**	**(0.96)**	**42.7**	**(1.34)**	**39.6**	**(1.04)**	**28.0**	**(0.90)**	**29.3**	**(1.18)**	**22.5**	**(1.93)**	**42.4**	**(1.32)**	**33.6**	**(1.06)**	**13.6**	**(0.67)**	**25.3**	**(**
Violent incidents	**31.5**	**(2.24)**	**33.3**	**(1.55)**	**31.2**	**(0.82)**	**27.9**	**(1.28)**	**25.0**	**(0.91)**	**17.5**	**(0.89)**	**19.6**	**(0.98)**	**18.3**	**(1.67)**	**29.6**	**(1.07)**	**16.0**	**(0.69)**	**7.0**	**(0.46)**	**15.2**	**(**
Serious violent incidents	1.3	(0.15)	1.2	(0.10)	1.2	(0.14)	1.2	(0.14)	1.1	(0.12)	0.8	(0.07)	1.1	(0.16)	0.9	(0.24)	1.7	(0.25)	1.1	(0.09)	0.6	(0.08)	1.0	(
Rape or attempted rape	#	(†)	#	(†)	#	(†)	#	(†)	#	(†)	#	(†)	#	(†)	‡	(†)	#	(†)	#	(†)	‡	(†)	#	
Sexual assault other than rape[3]	0.1	(0.02)	0.1	(0.01)	0.1	(0.01)	0.1	(0.01)	0.1	(0.01)	0.1	(0.03)	0.1	(0.01)	0.1 !	(0.02)	0.2	(0.03)	0.3	(0.03)	0.1	(0.02)	0.1	(
Physical attack or fight with a weapon	0.3	(0.05)	0.3	(0.05)	0.1	(0.03)	0.3	(0.08)	0.3	(0.08)	0.1	(0.03)	0.2	(0.06)	0.1 !	(0.06)	0.5 !	(0.24)	0.1 !	(0.05)	‡	(†)	0.1 !	(
Threat of physical attack with a weapon	0.5	(0.04)	0.4	(0.05)	0.5	(0.14)	0.4	(0.05)	0.4	(0.06)	0.4	(0.05)	0.5	(0.09)	0.6 !	(0.18)	0.7	(0.06)	0.4	(0.04)	0.3	(0.05)	0.5	(
Robbery with a weapon	‡	(†)	#	(†)	#	(†)	#	(†)	#	(†)	#	(†)	#	(†)	‡	(†)	#	(†)	#	(†)	‡	(†)	#	
Robbery without a weapon	0.4	(0.07)	0.3	(0.04)	0.5	(0.05)	0.4	(0.07)	0.3	(0.04)	0.2	(0.03)	0.2	(0.02)	0.1 !	(0.04)	0.3	(0.04)	0.3	(0.04)	0.1	(0.03)	0.2	(
Physical attack or fight without a weapon	17.3	(1.29)	20.0	(0.82)	18.8	(0.55)	17.0	(0.94)	15.3	(0.58)	11.5	(0.75)	12.2	(0.71)	11.8	(1.26)	18.4	(0.89)	9.3	(0.41)	3.9	(0.32)	8.9	(
Threat of physical attack without a weapon	12.9	(1.13)	12.1	(1.01)	11.1	(0.43)	9.7	(0.62)	8.6	(0.47)	5.2	(0.33)	6.3	(0.38)	5.7	(0.70)	9.5	(0.54)	5.6	(0.41)	2.5	(0.23)	5.3	(
Theft/larceny[4]	**4.7**	**(0.20)**	**4.3**	**(0.15)**	**5.1**	**(0.13)**	**5.6**	**(0.20)**	**5.5**	**(0.18)**	**3.4**	**(0.11)**	**2.7**	**(0.13)**	**1.2**	**(0.17)**	**4.2**	**(0.29)**	**4.3**	**(0.19)**	**1.8**	**(0.15)**	**2.9**	**(**
Other incidents[5]	**12.3**	**(0.45)**	**8.1**	**(0.20)**	**9.6**	**(0.24)**	**9.2**	**(0.23)**	**9.2**	**(0.23)**	**7.1**	**(0.22)**	**7.0**	**(0.20)**	**3.0**	**(0.24)**	**8.6**	**(0.28)**	**13.3**	**(0.52)**	**4.8**	**(0.30)**	**7.2**	**(**
Possession of a firearm/explosive device	0.2	(0.05)	0.2	(0.01)	0.3	(0.04)	0.1	(0.01)	0.1	(0.01)	0.2 !	(0.06)	0.1	(0.01)	#	(†)	0.1	(0.02)	0.1	(0.02)	#	(†)	#	
Possession of a knife or sharp object	1.8	(0.09)	0.6	(0.03)	1.9	(0.05)	1.6	(0.05)	1.5	(0.05)	1.4	(0.07)	1.4	(0.05)	1.0	(0.07)	1.9	(0.08)	1.7	(0.08)	0.7	(0.06)	1.5	(
Distribution of illegal drugs[6]	0.6	(0.03)	0.7	(0.03)	---	(†)	---	(†)	---	(†)	---	(†)	---	(†)	---	(†)	---	(†)	---	(†)	---	(†)	---	
Possession or use of alcohol or illegal drugs[6]	2.5	(0.10)	2.8	(0.09)	---	(†)	---	(†)	---	(†)	---	(†)	---	(†)	---	(†)	---	(†)	---	(†)	---	(†)	---	
Distribution, possession, or use of illegal drugs[7]	---	(†)	---	(†)	2.4	(0.09)	2.2	(0.08)	2.4	(0.10)	2.3	(0.09)	2.4	(0.09)	0.2	(0.05)	2.7	(0.14)	6.6	(0.28)	1.7	(0.14)	2.6	(
Inappropriate distribution, possession, or use of prescription drugs[8]	---	(†)	---	(†)	---	(†)	---	(†)	0.6	(0.04)	0.4	(0.03)	0.4	(0.03)	#	(†)	0.5	(0.04)	1.1	(0.10)	0.4	(0.05)	0.4	(
Distribution, possession, or use of alcohol[7]	---	(†)	---	(†)	1.0	(0.05)	0.8	(0.03)	0.9	(0.04)	0.6	(0.03)	0.6	(0.03)	#	(†)	0.8	(0.06)	1.5	(0.07)	0.6	(0.07)	0.8	(
Sexual harassment	2.7	(0.13)	---	(†)	---	(†)	---	(†)	---	(†)	---	(†)	---	(†)	---	(†)	---	(†)	---	(†)	---	(†)	---	
Vandalism	4.5	(0.29)	3.8	(0.14)	4.0	(0.15)	4.4	(0.19)	3.6	(0.15)	2.2	(0.14)	2.0	(0.12)	1.7	(0.19)	2.7	(0.13)	2.2	(0.20)	1.3	(0.15)	1.8	(
Incidents reported to police																								
Total	**14.1**	**(0.44)**	**16.4**	**(0.49)**	**16.0**	**(0.44)**	**14.7**	**(0.44)**	**14.6**	**(0.41)**	**9.1**	**(0.27)**	**8.6**	**(0.27)**	**1.8**	**(0.21)**	**12.9**	**(0.70)**	**18.2**	**(0.59)**	**5.6**	**(0.41)**	**10.0**	**(**
Violent incidents	**5.5**	**(0.30)**	**8.3**	**(0.38)**	**7.4**	**(0.28)**	**6.3**	**(0.28)**	**6.4**	**(0.28)**	**4.0**	**(0.20)**	**3.9**	**(0.17)**	**0.9**	**(0.12)**	**7.0**	**(0.50)**	**7.4**	**(0.43)**	**1.9**	**(0.16)**	**4.6**	**(**
Serious violent incidents	0.7	(0.06)	0.7	(0.05)	0.7	(0.05)	0.6	(0.05)	0.5	(0.05)	0.4	(0.04)	0.5	(0.03)	0.3	(0.06)	0.9	(0.07)	0.8	(0.04)	0.3	(0.05)	0.6	(
Rape or attempted rape	#	(†)	#	(†)	#	(†)	#	(†)	#	(†)	#	(†)	#	(†)	‡	(†)	#	(†)	#	(†)	‡	(†)	#	
Sexual assault other than rape[3]	0.1	(0.01)	0.1	(0.01)	0.1	(0.01)	0.1	(0.01)	#	(†)	0.1	(0.01)	0.1	(0.01)	#	(†)	0.2	(0.03)	0.2	(0.02)	0.1	(0.02)	0.1	(
Physical attack or fight with a weapon	0.1	(0.01)	0.1	(0.03)	0.1	(0.01)	0.1	(0.03)	0.1	(0.02)	0.1 !	(0.02)	#	(†)	‡	(†)	0.1	(0.03)	0.1	(0.01)	#	(†)	#	
Threat of physical attack with a weapon	0.3	(0.03)	0.2	(0.03)	0.2	(0.02)	0.2	(0.02)	0.2	(0.02)	0.2	(0.02)	0.3	(0.03)	0.2	(0.05)	0.4	(0.03)	0.3	(0.03)	0.2	(0.03)	0.3	(
Robbery with a weapon	#	(†)	#	(†)	#	(†)	#	(†)	#	(†)	#	(†)	#	(†)	‡	(†)	#	(†)	#	(†)	‡	(†)	#	
Robbery without a weapon	0.2	(0.04)	0.2	(0.02)	0.3	(0.04)	0.2	(0.03)	0.2	(0.02)	0.1	(0.01)	0.1	(0.01)	#	(†)	0.1	(0.04)	0.1	(0.02)	0.1 !	(0.03)	0.1	(
Physical attack or fight without a weapon	3.0	(0.12)	5.3	(0.26)	4.3	(0.20)	3.6	(0.15)	4.1	(0.25)	2.5	(0.18)	2.2	(0.12)	0.3	(0.06)	3.7	(0.34)	4.6	(0.30)	1.0	(0.10)	2.4	(
Threat of physical attack without a weapon	1.8	(0.21)	2.3	(0.21)	2.4	(0.12)	2.1	(0.16)	1.8	(0.11)	1.1	(0.07)	1.2	(0.08)	0.3	(0.07)	2.4	(0.29)	2.0	(0.23)	0.6	(0.08)	1.6	(
Theft/larceny[4]	**2.3**	**(0.12)**	**2.4**	**(0.10)**	**2.5**	**(0.09)**	**2.8**	**(0.14)**	**2.6**	**(0.09)**	**1.5**	**(0.07)**	**1.1**	**(0.06)**	**0.1**	**(0.03)**	**1.5**	**(0.16)**	**2.5**	**(0.14)**	**0.9**	**(0.11)**	**1.4**	**(**
Other incidents[5]	**6.3**	**(0.18)**	**5.6**	**(0.15)**	**6.1**	**(0.19)**	**5.6**	**(0.17)**	**5.5**	**(0.17)**	**3.7**	**(0.11)**	**3.6**	**(0.11)**	**0.8**	**(0.10)**	**4.4**	**(0.25)**	**8.3**	**(0.25)**	**2.8**	**(0.22)**	**4.0**	**(**
Possession of a firearm/explosive device	0.1	(0.01)	0.1	(0.01)	0.2	(0.04)	0.1	(0.01)	0.1	(0.01)	0.2 !	(0.06)	#	(†)	#	(†)	#	(†)	0.1	(0.02)	#	(†)	#	
Possession of a knife or sharp object	1.0	(0.05)	0.5	(0.03)	1.1	(0.04)	0.9	(0.03)	0.8	(0.04)	0.6	(0.03)	0.6	(0.03)	0.3	(0.04)	0.9	(0.08)	1.0	(0.05)	0.3	(0.04)	0.6	(
Distribution of illegal drugs[6]	0.5	(0.03)	0.7	(0.03)	---	(†)	---	(†)	---	(†)	---	(†)	---	(†)	---	(†)	---	(†)	---	(†)	---	(†)	---	
Possession or use of alcohol or illegal drugs[6]	1.9	(0.07)	2.3	(0.08)	---	(†)	---	(†)	---	(†)	---	(†)	---	(†)	---	(†)	---	(†)	---	(†)	---	(†)	---	
Distribution, possession, or use of illegal drugs[7]	---	(†)	---	(†)	2.1	(0.09)	2.0	(0.08)	2.0	(0.07)	1.7	(0.07)	1.7	(0.07)	0.1 !	(0.05)	1.8	(0.12)	4.7	(0.21)	1.3	(0.12)	2.0	(
Inappropriate distribution, possession, or use of prescription drugs[8]	---	(†)	---	(†)	---	(†)	---	(†)	0.5	(0.04)	0.3	(0.03)	0.3	(0.02)	#	(†)	0.4	(0.04)	0.8	(0.05)	0.3	(0.04)	0.3	(
Distribution, possession, or use of alcohol[7]	---	(†)	---	(†)	0.7	(0.05)	0.6	(0.02)	0.6	(0.03)	0.4	(0.03)	0.3	(0.02)	#	(†)	0.5	(0.05)	0.9	(0.05)	0.3	(0.03)	0.5	(
Sexual harassment	0.7	(0.05)	---	(†)	---	(†)	---	(†)	---	(†)	---	(†)	---	(†)	---	(†)	---	(†)	---	(†)	---	(†)	---	
Vandalism	2.0	(0.13)	2.0	(0.09)	1.9	(0.09)	2.1	(0.12)	1.6	(0.09)	0.6	(0.05)	0.6	(0.04)	0.3	(0.06)	0.7	(0.08)	0.9	(0.09)	0.5	(0.09)	0.6	(

—Not available.

†Not applicable.

#Rounds to zero.

!Interpret data with caution. The coefficient of variation (CV) for this estimate is between 30 and 50 percent.

‡Reporting standards not met. Either there are too few cases for a reliable estimate or the coefficient of variation (CV) is 50 percent or greater.

[1] The number of incidents of crime at school per 1,000 students enrolled.

[2] Primary schools are defined as schools in which the lowest grade is not higher than grade 3 and the highest grade is not higher than grade 8. Middle schools are defined as schools in which the lowest grade is not lower than grade 4 and the highest grade is not higher than grade 9. High schools are defined as schools in which the lowest grade is not lower than grade 9. Combined schools—which are included in the totals but not shown separately—include all other combinations of grades, including K–12 schools.

[3] Prior to 2015-16, the wording of the survey item was "sexual battery other than rape."

[4] Theft/larceny is taking things worth over $10 without personal confrontation.

[5] Caution should be used when making direct comparisons of "Other incidents" between years because the survey questions about alcohol and drugs changed, as outlined in footnotes 6, 7, and 8, and because sexual harassment was only included in 1999-2000.

[6] The survey items "Distribution of illegal drugs" and "Possession or use of alcohol or illegal drugs" appear only on the 1999-2000 and 2003-04 questionnaires. Different alcohol- and drug-related survey items were used on the SSOCS questionnaires for later years.

[7] The survey items "Distribution, possession, or use of illegal drugs" and "Distribution, possession, or use of alcohol" appear only on the SSOCS questionnaires for 2005-06 and later years.

[8] The survey item "Inappropriate distribution, possession, or use of prescription drugs" appears only on the SSOCS questionnaires for 2009-10 and later years.

NOTE: Responses were provided by the principal or the person most knowledgeable about crime and safety issues at the school. "At school" was defined to include activities that happen in school buildings, on school grounds, on school buses, and at places that hold school-sponsored events or activities. Respondents were instructed to include incidents that occurred before, during, and after normal school hours or when school activities or events were in session. Detail may not sum to totals because of rounding and because schools that recorded or reported more than one type of crime incident were counted only once in the total percentage of schools recording or reporting incidents.

SOURCE: U.S. Department of Education, National Center for Education Statistics, 1999-2000, 2003-04, 2005–06, 2007–08, 2009–10, 2015-16, and 2017-18 School Survey on Crime and Safety (SSOCS), 2000, 2004, 2006, 2008, 2010, 2016, and 2018. (This table was prepared July 2019.)

Table 229.30. Percentage of public schools recording incidents of crime at school, number of incidents, and rate per 1,000 students, by type of crime and selected school characteristics: 2017-18

[Standard errors appear in parentheses]

School characteristic	Total number of schools		Violent incidents: All violent[1]: Percent of schools recording		Number of incidents		Rate per 1,000 students		Serious violent[2]: Percent of schools recording		Number of incidents		Rate per 1,000 students		Theft/larceny[3]: Percent of schools recording		Number of incidents		Rate per 1,000 students		Other: Percent of schools recording		
1	2		3		4		5		6		7		8		9		10		11		12		
Total	**82,300**	**(350)**	**70.7**	**(1.38)**	**962,300**	**(45,850)**	**19.6**	**(0.98)**	**21.3**	**(0.98)**	**54,400**	**(7,770)**	**1.1**	**(0.16)**	**33.4**	**(1.31)**	**132,500**	**(6,130)**	**2.7**	**(0.13)**	**59.8**	**(1.18)**	**343,7**
School level[5]																							
Primary	48,300	(290)	59.1	(2.17)	441,700	(38,950)	18.3	(1.67)	13.9	(1.55)	21,200	(5,660)	0.9	(0.24)	19.5	(1.73)	29,500	(4,100)	1.2	(0.17)	46.3	(2.10)	72,0
Middle	15,100	(60)	89.8	(1.02)	287,800	(11,470)	29.6	(1.07)	32.5	(1.52)	16,700	(2,410)	1.7	(0.25)	52.0	(1.83)	41,200	(2,850)	4.2	(0.29)	78.2	(1.77)	83,8
High school	12,600	(40)	90.4	(1.12)	205,200	(8,830)	16.0	(0.69)	35.5	(1.69)	14,300	(1,090)	1.1	(0.09)	63.3	(1.27)	55,000	(2,560)	4.3	(0.19)	87.1	(1.24)	170,4
Combined	6,300	(180)	74.4	(4.95)	27,600	(3,690)	11.1	(1.40)	22.9	(5.23)	2,200	(550)	0.9	(0.22)	36.0	(4.99)	6,800	(1,220)	2.7	(0.48)	64.3	(5.35)	17,4
Enrollment size																							
Less than 300	16,800	(310)	53.1	(3.36)	74,000	(9,980)	20.3	(2.83)	13.7	(2.38)	4,500	(1,060)	1.2	(0.29)	19.9	(3.61)	9,500	(2,360)	2.6	(0.63)	44.3	(3.43)	27,0
300 to 499	24,900	(120)	69.2	(2.44)	242,400	(31,230)	22.7	(2.97)	17.9	(1.46)	15,800 !	(5,100)	1.5 !	(0.48)	27.7	(1.96)	24,700	(3,190)	2.3	(0.30)	55.2	(2.00)	58,9
500 to 999	31,700	(70)	75.0	(1.86)	430,300	(28,770)	19.9	(1.32)	22.0	(1.60)	18,200	(2,090)	0.8	(0.10)	35.3	(2.06)	45,400	(3,600)	2.1	(0.16)	63.2	(1.70)	110,0
1,000 or more	8,900	(20)	92.7	(1.43)	215,600	(10,170)	16.3	(0.80)	42.8	(2.04)	15,900	(2,610)	1.2	(0.20)	68.9	(1.64)	52,900	(3,230)	4.0	(0.24)	90.4	(1.61)	147,8
Locale																							
City	22,500	(170)	75.0	(2.22)	377,600	(32,520)	26.2	(2.26)	23.1	(1.79)	14,300	(1,280)	1.0	(0.09)	35.6	(2.58)	44,500	(3,960)	3.1	(0.26)	63.9	(2.38)	113,0
Suburban	27,300	(150)	67.7	(2.24)	299,800	(18,780)	14.9	(0.98)	21.5	(1.52)	20,000	(3,830)	1.0	(0.19)	31.5	(1.74)	45,700	(3,390)	2.3	(0.17)	54.4	(2.15)	117,9
Town	10,500	(150)	72.0	(2.95)	118,400	(12,100)	21.1	(2.18)	20.4	(2.18)	5,800	(740)	1.0	(0.13)	43.8	(2.99)	18,200	(1,570)	3.2	(0.27)	65.0	(2.77)	47,1
Rural	22,000	(210)	69.3	(2.79)	166,500	(23,340)	18.3	(2.55)	19.5	(2.00)	14,300 !	(4,730)	1.6 !	(0.52)	28.7	(2.54)	24,100	(2,340)	2.6	(0.25)	59.8	(2.93)	65,7
Percent minority enrollment[6]																							
0 to 25 percent	29,800	(930)	66.8	(2.47)	193,000	(13,430)	12.6	(0.84)	19.3	(1.44)	15,200	(1,800)	1.0	(0.12)	32.2	(2.10)	36,700	(2,740)	2.4	(0.18)	59.2	(2.42)	102,2
26 to 50 percent	18,000	(870)	69.5	(2.30)	203,200	(26,580)	18.3	(2.24)	20.9	(2.16)	13,200 !	(4,780)	1.2 !	(0.43)	32.4	(2.17)	29,300	(2,950)	2.6	(0.24)	60.3	(2.58)	75,4
51 to 75 percent	12,500	(850)	75.1	(3.90)	210,100	(24,470)	24.7	(2.78)	21.9	(2.68)	7,800	(1,240)	0.9	(0.14)	40.2	(3.61)	28,200	(2,720)	3.3	(0.34)	64.8	(3.88)	63,1
76 to 100 percent	22,000	(800)	74.4	(1.93)	356,000	(32,450)	25.1	(2.16)	24.0	(1.87)	18,200	(2,870)	1.3	(0.20)	32.2	(2.34)	38,200	(3,820)	2.7	(0.26)	57.3	(2.06)	103,0
Percent of students eligible for free or reduced-price lunch																							
0 to 25 percent	15,000	(610)	57.6	(3.14)	72,400	(4,810)	7.0	(0.46)	17.5	(2.20)	6,100	(820)	0.6	(0.08)	27.3	(2.04)	18,900	(1,610)	1.8	(0.15)	48.6	(2.91)	49,4
26 to 50 percent	19,600	(870)	71.5	(2.74)	180,700	(16,090)	15.2	(1.20)	21.8	(1.50)	11,600	(1,710)	1.0	(0.14)	38.0	(1.95)	35,100	(3,040)	2.9	(0.23)	60.9	(2.74)	85,2
51 to 75 percent	20,600	(950)	74.7	(3.07)	256,500	(21,600)	22.0	(1.76)	20.2	(1.93)	10,400	(1,360)	0.9	(0.10)	38.1	(2.63)	35,400	(3,100)	3.0	(0.24)	67.2	(2.85)	92,5
76 to 100 percent	27,100	(880)	74.3	(2.11)	452,700	(41,400)	29.6	(2.79)	23.9	(1.86)	26,300	(7,130)	1.7	(0.47)	30.0	(2.30)	43,100	(4,750)	2.8	(0.32)	59.6	(2.23)	116,5

!Interpret data with caution. The coefficient of variation (CV) for this estimate is between 30 and 50 percent.

[1] "All violent" incidents include "serious violent" incidents (see footnote 2) as well as physical attack or fight without a weapon and threat of physical attack without a weapon.

[2] "Serious violent" incidents include rape, sexual assault other than rape, physical attack or fight with a weapon, threat of physical attack with a weapon, and robbery with or without a weapon.

[3] Theft/larceny is taking things worth over $10 without personal confrontation.

[4] "Other incidents" include possession of a firearm or explosive device; possession of a knife or sharp object; distribution, possession, or use of illegal drugs or alcohol; inappropriate distribution, possession, or use of prescription drugs; and vandalism.

[5] Primary schools are defined as schools in which the lowest grade is not higher than grade 3 and the highest grade is not higher than grade 8. Middle schools are defined as schools in which the lowest grade is not lower than grade 4 and the highest grade is not higher than grade 9. High schools are defined as schools in which the lowest grade is not lower than grade 9. Combined schools include all other combinations of grades, including K-12 schools.

[6] Percent combined enrollment of Black, Hispanic, Asian, Pacific Islander, and American Indian/Alaska Native students, and students of Two or more races.

NOTE: Responses were provided by the principal or the person most knowledgeable about crime and safety issues at the school. "At school" was defined to include activities that happen in school buildings, on school grounds, on school buses, and at places that hold school-sponsored events or activities. Respondents were instructed to include incidents that occurred before, during, or after normal school hours or when school activities or events were in session. Detail may not sum to totals because of rounding.

SOURCE: U.S. Department of Education, National Center for Education Statistics, 2017-18 School Survey on Crime and Safety (SSOCS), 2018. (This table was prepared August 2019.)

Table 229.40. Percentage of public schools reporting incidents of crime at school to the police, number of incidents, and rate per 1,000 students, by type of crime and selected school characteristics: 2017-18

[Standard errors appear in parentheses]

School characteristic	Total number of schools	Violent incidents						Theft/larceny[3]			Other incid	
		All violent[1]			Serious violent[2]							
		Percent of schools reporting to police	Number of incidents	Rate per 1,000 students	Percent of schools reporting to police	Number of incidents	Rate per 1,000 students	Percent of schools reporting to police	Number of incidents	Rate per 1,000 students	Percent of schools reporting to police	Nur i
1	2	3	4	5	6	7	8	9	10	11	12	
Total	**82,300 (350)**	**32.5 (1.08)**	**192,100 (8,050)**	**3.9 (0.17)**	**14.9 (0.86)**	**26,100 (1,680)**	**0.5 (0.03)**	**14.9 (0.75)**	**53,900 (2,780)**	**1.1 (0.06)**	**35.1 (0.86)**	**176,900 (**
School level[5]												
Primary	48,300 (290)	15.7 (1.43)	22,100 (2,950)	0.9 (0.12)	7.3 (1.25)	6,300 (1,410)	0.3 (0.06)	4.4 (0.91)	3,600 (800)	0.1 (0.03)	17.9 (1.33)	18,900
Middle	15,100 (60)	54.0 (1.75)	67,700 (5,010)	7.0 (0.50)	25.1 (1.50)	8,300 (660)	0.9 (0.07)	24.2 (1.48)	14,800 (1,610)	1.5 (0.16)	53.1 (1.92)	42,700
High school	12,600 (40)	66.9 (1.82)	94,300 (5,530)	7.4 (0.43)	30.8 (1.59)	9,900 (560)	0.8 (0.04)	41.8 (1.40)	32,600 (1,830)	2.5 (0.14)	74.8 (1.41)	106,700
Combined	6,300 (180)	40.6 (5.84)	8,000 (1,770)	3.2 (0.69)	16.4 (3.88)	1,600 (480)	0.6 ! (0.19)	19.1 (3.90)	3,000 ! (960)	1.2 ! (0.38)	44.8 (5.23)	8,600
Enrollment size												
Less than 300	16,800 (310)	19.8 (2.82)	13,800 (3,100)	3.8 (0.84)	8.6 (1.92)	2,200 (590)	0.6 (0.17)	8.8 (2.52)	3,400 ! (1,250)	0.9 ! (0.34)	23.1 (2.68)	8,200
300 to 499	24,900 (120)	24.7 (1.72)	26,800 (3,490)	2.5 (0.33)	10.9 (1.12)	4,800 (780)	0.5 (0.07)	9.7 (1.24)	6,000 (1,020)	0.6 (0.10)	28.1 (1.58)	20,600
500 to 999	31,700 (70)	34.6 (1.62)	64,600 (4,250)	3.0 (0.19)	15.3 (1.49)	10,000 (1,010)	0.5 (0.05)	13.3 (1.00)	13,800 (1,480)	0.6 (0.07)	35.6 (1.56)	55,100
1,000 or more	8,900 (20)	70.6 (1.74)	86,800 (5,640)	6.6 (0.44)	36.0 (1.68)	9,100 (610)	0.7 (0.05)	46.7 (1.46)	30,800 (2,110)	2.3 (0.16)	75.6 (1.82)	93,000
Locale												
City	22,500 (170)	32.2 (1.89)	64,400 (5,390)	4.5 (0.35)	15.8 (1.71)	7,900 (810)	0.5 (0.06)	17.5 (1.70)	19,500 (2,140)	1.4 (0.14)	37.6 (2.08)	54,000
Suburban	27,300 (150)	32.0 (1.49)	69,000 (4,440)	3.4 (0.24)	15.3 (1.30)	9,500 (1,080)	0.5 (0.05)	13.5 (0.77)	19,400 (1,540)	1.0 (0.07)	30.9 (1.74)	66,800
Town	10,500 (150)	39.4 (2.40)	31,200 (3,610)	5.6 (0.62)	14.9 (1.66)	3,300 (410)	0.6 (0.07)	19.1 (1.99)	7,000 (760)	1.2 (0.14)	43.0 (2.70)	26,000
Rural	22,000 (210)	29.9 (2.49)	27,400 (1,980)	3.0 (0.21)	13.4 (1.75)	5,400 (790)	0.6 (0.09)	11.8 (1.31)	8,000 (1,080)	0.9 (0.12)	34.1 (2.23)	30,100
Percent minority enrollment[6]												
0 to 25 percent	29,800 (930)	33.5 (2.11)	50,200 (3,000)	3.3 (0.22)	13.5 (1.13)	8,400 (930)	0.5 (0.06)	14.8 (1.12)	16,200 (1,410)	1.1 (0.09)	35.2 (1.80)	53,200
26 to 50 percent	18,000 (870)	31.5 (2.21)	36,900 (3,210)	3.3 (0.29)	13.6 (1.66)	4,900 (690)	0.4 (0.06)	15.9 (1.47)	11,800 (1,360)	1.1 (0.12)	34.2 (2.08)	38,300
51 to 75 percent	12,500 (850)	31.0 (2.44)	40,200 (4,230)	4.7 (0.55)	14.7 (1.96)	4,400 (680)	0.5 (0.08)	16.7 (1.73)	13,300 (1,560)	1.6 (0.19)	38.0 (2.98)	34,100
76 to 100 percent	22,000 (800)	32.7 (2.16)	64,800 (5,990)	4.6 (0.42)	17.9 (1.71)	8,300 (750)	0.6 (0.05)	13.1 (1.53)	12,600 (1,790)	0.9 (0.12)	34.2 (1.98)	51,300
Percent of students eligible for free or reduced-price lunch												
0 to 25 percent	15,000 (610)	27.4 (1.95)	20,000 (1,690)	1.9 (0.16)	11.1 (1.19)	3,500 (500)	0.3 (0.05)	14.0 (1.49)	9,700 (1,200)	0.9 (0.11)	27.5 (1.83)	28,500
26 to 50 percent	19,600 (870)	36.4 (2.15)	54,200 (4,160)	4.6 (0.39)	15.6 (1.38)	7,200 (900)	0.6 (0.08)	17.5 (1.44)	16,800 (1,800)	1.4 (0.15)	37.3 (2.04)	47,500
51 to 75 percent	20,600 (950)	35.9 (2.38)	50,700 (5,070)	4.4 (0.40)	15.8 (1.68)	6,100 (720)	0.5 (0.05)	15.0 (1.77)	13,200 (1,550)	1.1 (0.13)	40.0 (2.59)	47,900
76 to 100 percent	27,100 (880)	29.8 (1.87)	67,200 (6,500)	4.4 (0.42)	15.7 (1.38)	9,300 (890)	0.6 (0.06)	13.3 (1.64)	14,100 (1,760)	0.9 (0.11)	34.0 (1.90)	53,000

!Interpret data with caution. The coefficient of variation (CV) for this estimate is between 30 and 50 percent.

[1] "All violent" incidents include "serious violent" incidents (see footnote 2) as well as physical attack or fight without a weapon and threat of physical attack without a weapon.

[2] "Serious violent" incidents include rape, sexual assault other than rape, physical attack or fight with a weapon, threat of physical attack with a weapon, and robbery with or without a weapon.

[3] Theft/larceny is taking things worth over $10 without personal confrontation.

[4] "Other incidents" include possession of a firearm or explosive device; possession of a knife or sharp object; distribution, possession, or use of illegal drugs or alcohol; inappropriate distribution, possession, or use of prescription drugs; and vandalism.

[5] Primary schools are defined as schools in which the lowest grade is not higher than grade 3 and the highest grade is not higher than grade 8. Middle schools are defined as schools in which the lowest grade is not lower than grade 4 and the highest grade is not higher than grade 9. High schools are defined as schools in which the lowest grade is not lower than grade 9. Combined schools include all other combinations of grades, including K-12 schools.

[6] Percent combined enrollment of Black, Hispanic, Asian, Pacific Islander, and American Indian/Alaska Native students, and students of Two or more races.

NOTE: Responses were provided by the principal or the person most knowledgeable about crime and safety issues at the school. "At school" was defined to include activities that happen in school buildings, on school grounds, on school buses, and at places that hold school-sponsored events or activities. Respondents were instructed to include incidents that occurred before, during, or after normal school hours or when school activities or events were in session. Detail may not sum to totals because of rounding.

SOURCE: U.S. Department of Education, National Center for Education Statistics, 2017–18 School Survey on Crime and Safety (SSOCS), 2018. (This table was prepared August 2019.)

Table 229.50. Percentage distribution of public schools, by number of violent incidents of crime at school recorded and reported to the police and selected school characteristics: 2017-18

[Standard errors appear in parentheses]

School characteristic	Number of violent incidents recorded							Number of violent incidents reported to the police					
	None	1-2 incidents	3-5 incidents	6-9 incidents	10-14 incidents	15-19 incidents	20 or more incidents	None	1-2 incidents	3-5 incidents	6-9 incidents	10-14 incidents	15-19 incidents
1	2	3	4	5	6	7	8	9	10	11	12	13	14
Total	**29.3 (1.38)**	**13.0 (0.92)**	**15.5 (0.77)**	**11.3 (0.66)**	**9.2 (0.66)**	**5.1 (0.40)**	**16.5 (0.78)**	**67.5 (1.08)**	**15.1 (1.04)**	**7.4 (0.63)**	**3.6 (0.27)**	**2.3 (0.26)**	**1.4 (0.16)**
School level[1]													
Primary	40.9 (2.17)	11.7 (1.33)	14.8 (1.19)	9.1 (1.17)	7.5 (1.06)	3.3 (0.65)	12.7 (1.26)	84.3 (1.43)	10.3 (1.13)	3.9 (0.82)	0.8 ! (0.32)	‡ (†)	‡ (†)
Middle	10.2 (1.02)	9.7 (0.97)	15.4 (1.15)	15.7 (1.22)	11.4 (0.86)	9.8 (0.92)	27.8 (1.01)	46.0 (1.75)	22.0 (1.31)	13.1 (1.02)	6.6 (0.77)	3.9 (0.57)	3.1 (0.51)
High school	9.6 (1.12)	12.1 (1.37)	17.7 (1.52)	15.7 (1.39)	13.9 (1.24)	7.5 (0.80)	23.5 (1.25)	33.1 (1.82)	20.3 (1.58)	14.1 (1.17)	10.3 (1.03)	7.9 (0.94)	4.5 (0.62)
Combined	25.6 (4.95)	33.4 (4.61)	17.3 (3.55)	9.7 ! (3.13)	6.7 ! (2.86)	‡ (†)	4.6 ! (1.90)	59.4 (5.84)	25.2 (4.98)	7.7 (1.90)	4.1 ! (1.94)	‡ (†)	‡ (†)
Enrollment size													
Less than 300	46.9 (3.36)	18.1 (2.53)	14.3 (2.31)	10.0 (2.15)	3.7 ! (1.21)	1.3 ! (0.61)	5.8 (1.59)	80.2 (2.82)	14.2 (2.78)	3.3 (0.89)	1.3 ! (0.63)	‡ (†)	‡ (†)
300 to 499	30.8 (2.44)	13.9 (1.54)	19.4 (1.80)	10.3 (1.38)	9.3 (1.31)	4.1 (0.74)	12.2 (1.60)	75.3 (1.72)	12.9 (1.63)	6.8 (1.19)	2.2 (0.57)	1.1 ! (0.53)	‡ (†)
500 to 999	25.0 (1.86)	11.8 (1.13)	14.3 (1.19)	11.9 (1.07)	10.8 (1.21)	6.4 (0.94)	19.8 (1.34)	65.4 (1.62)	16.8 (1.32)	8.1 (1.05)	3.8 (0.47)	2.5 (0.42)	1.6 (0.29)
1,000 or more	7.3 (1.43)	5.6 (1.10)	11.5 (1.55)	14.7 (1.46)	13.2 (0.98)	10.5 (1.07)	37.2 (1.72)	29.4 (1.74)	16.8 (1.39)	14.6 (1.16)	10.9 (1.12)	9.0 (1.08)	5.5 (0.78)
Locale													
City	25.0 (2.22)	10.2 (1.50)	13.7 (1.97)	12.0 (2.00)	10.2 (1.45)	5.5 (1.10)	23.3 (1.83)	67.8 (1.89)	14.1 (1.83)	7.3 (1.08)	3.0 (0.46)	2.4 (0.59)	1.7 (0.38)
Suburban	32.3 (2.24)	11.9 (1.14)	14.3 (1.34)	9.5 (1.07)	9.7 (1.22)	6.0 (0.94)	16.3 (1.61)	68.0 (1.49)	14.5 (1.38)	6.6 (0.73)	4.2 (0.65)	2.5 (0.42)	1.4 (0.23)
Town	28.0 (2.95)	6.7 (1.63)	14.7 (2.46)	14.7 (2.30)	11.9 (2.32)	7.4 (1.45)	16.6 (1.65)	60.6 (2.40)	14.1 (2.10)	11.5 (2.11)	5.0 (0.88)	3.2 (0.65)	2.4 ! (0.84)
Rural	30.7 (2.79)	20.4 (2.14)	19.3 (1.89)	11.3 (1.60)	6.2 (1.09)	2.5 (0.56)	9.6 (1.48)	70.1 (2.49)	17.4 (2.38)	6.6 (1.03)	2.8 (0.60)	1.6 (0.40)	0.7 (0.19)
Percent minority enrollment[2]													
0 to 25 percent	33.2 (2.47)	16.4 (1.68)	17.3 (1.46)	11.7 (1.01)	8.6 (1.09)	4.0 (0.61)	8.9 (1.16)	66.5 (2.11)	16.6 (1.63)	8.7 (1.08)	3.4 (0.43)	2.6 (0.36)	0.9 (0.19)
26 to 50 percent	30.5 (2.30)	14.3 (2.32)	15.1 (1.65)	12.5 (1.54)	6.8 (1.15)	6.5 (1.12)	14.3 (1.58)	68.5 (2.21)	14.9 (1.91)	6.5 (0.90)	3.8 (0.62)	2.0 (0.42)	2.3 (0.57)
51 to 75 percent	24.9 (3.90)	9.1 (2.09)	16.6 (2.71)	10.7 (1.84)	7.8 (1.88)	6.5 (1.42)	24.4 (2.70)	69.0 (2.44)	12.7 (1.77)	6.5 (1.21)	3.7 (1.01)	1.9 (0.42)	1.6 (0.40)
76 to 100 percent	25.6 (1.93)	9.7 (1.51)	13.0 (1.81)	10.3 (1.63)	12.6 (1.59)	4.7 (0.93)	24.1 (1.86)	67.3 (2.16)	14.6 (1.79)	7.0 (1.20)	3.6 (0.66)	2.4 (0.68)	1.3 ! (0.40)
Percent of students eligible for free or reduced-price lunch													
0 to 25 percent	42.4 (3.14)	16.4 (2.50)	13.4 (1.79)	10.3 (1.44)	8.6 (1.41)	4.1 (1.00)	4.8 (0.72)	72.6 (1.95)	14.6 (1.93)	5.8 (1.03)	3.6 (0.75)	1.4 (0.32)	1.0 (0.24)
26 to 50 percent	28.5 (2.74)	15.5 (1.87)	16.9 (1.65)	10.9 (1.27)	8.1 (1.24)	6.5 (0.84)	13.5 (1.67)	63.6 (2.15)	16.1 (1.77)	7.6 (0.94)	3.6 (0.61)	3.7 (0.61)	2.3 (0.56)
51 to 75 percent	25.3 (3.07)	11.8 (1.86)	17.8 (1.76)	12.5 (1.33)	9.3 (1.52)	4.5 (0.75)	18.8 (1.57)	64.1 (2.38)	15.9 (1.87)	10.1 (1.55)	3.5 (0.54)	2.7 (0.75)	1.2 (0.23)
76 to 100 percent	25.7 (2.11)	10.3 (1.33)	14.0 (1.81)	11.3 (1.60)	10.1 (1.47)	5.1 (0.87)	23.4 (1.79)	70.2 (1.87)	14.1 (1.76)	6.2 (0.91)	3.6 (0.64)	1.5 (0.30)	1.2 (0.30)

†Not applicable.

!Interpret data with caution. The coefficient of variation (CV) for this estimate is between 30 and 50 percent.

‡Reporting standards not met. Either there are too few cases for a reliable estimate or the coefficient of variation (CV) is 50 percent or greater.

[1] Primary schools are defined as schools in which the lowest grade is not higher than grade 3 and the highest grade is not higher than grade 8. Middle schools are defined as schools in which the lowest grade is not lower than grade 4 and the highest grade is not higher than grade 9. High schools are defined as schools in which the lowest grade is not lower than grade 9. Combined schools include all other combinations of grades, including K-12 schools.

[2] Percent combined enrollment of Black, Hispanic, Asian, Pacific Islander, and American Indian/Alaska Native students, and students of Two or more races.

NOTE: "Violent incidents" include rape, sexual assault other than rape, physical attack or fight with or without a weapon, threat of physical attack with or without a weapon, and robbery with or without a weapon. Responses were provided by the principal or the person most knowledgeable about crime and safety issues at the school. "At school" was defined to include activities that happen in school buildings, on school grounds, on school buses, and at places that hold school-sponsored events or activities. Respondents were instructed to include incidents that occurred before, during, or after normal school hours or when school activities or events were in session. Detail may not sum to totals because of rounding.

SOURCE: U.S. Department of Education, National Center for Education Statistics, 2017-18 School Survey on Crime and Safety (SSOCS), 2018. (This table was prepared August 2019.)

Table 229.60. Percentage distribution of public schools, by number of serious violent incidents of crime at school recorded and reported to the police and selected school characteristics: 2017-18

[Standard errors appear in parentheses]

School characteristic	Number of serious violent incidents recorded												Number of serious violent incidents reported to the police											
	None		1 incident		2 incidents		3-5 incidents		6-9 incidents		10 or more incidents		None		1 incident		2 incidents		3-5 incidents		6-9 incidents		10 or more incidents	
1	2		3		4		5		6		7		8		9		10		11		12		13	
Total	**78.7**	**(0.98)**	**10.0**	**(0.74)**	**4.7**	**(0.48)**	**4.4**	**(0.44)**	**1.2**	**(0.20)**	**1.0**	**(0.27)**	**85.1**	**(0.86)**	**7.8**	**(0.59)**	**3.7**	**(0.36)**	**2.5**	**(0.28)**	**0.7**	**(0.14)**	**0.2**	**(0.05)**
School level[1]																								
Primary	86.1	(1.55)	6.7	(1.09)	3.2	(0.74)	2.6	(0.71)	0.8 !	(0.34)	‡	(†)	92.7	(1.25)	4.3	(0.85)	1.9 !	(0.57)	0.9 !	(0.34)	‡	(†)	‡	(†)
Middle	67.5	(1.52)	14.1	(1.31)	8.1	(0.78)	6.6	(0.70)	1.4	(0.34)	2.2	(0.43)	74.9	(1.50)	12.5	(1.28)	7.0	(0.81)	4.2	(0.66)	0.7 !	(0.22)	0.7 !	(0.25)
High school	64.5	(1.69)	14.6	(1.32)	7.3	(0.77)	8.7	(0.92)	3.0	(0.41)	1.8	(0.46)	69.2	(1.59)	14.0	(1.34)	7.0	(0.82)	6.7	(0.80)	2.7	(0.40)	0.3 !	(0.15)
Combined	77.1	(5.23)	16.5	(4.90)	2.8 !	(1.23)	‡	(†)	‡	(†)	‡	(†)	83.6	(3.88)	10.7 !	(3.22)	3.6 !	(1.46)	‡	(†)	‡	(†)	‡	(†)
Enrollment size																								
Less than 300	86.3	(2.38)	9.7	(2.08)	‡	(†)	1.6 !	(0.63)	‡	(†)	‡	(†)	91.4	(1.92)	6.2	(1.63)	‡	(†)	‡	(†)	‡	(†)	‡	(†)
300 to 499	82.1	(1.46)	9.0	(1.25)	3.7	(0.74)	3.5	(0.85)	0.6 !	(0.32)	1.0 !	(0.49)	89.1	(1.12)	6.4	(1.02)	2.8	(0.62)	1.3 !	(0.52)	‡	(†)	‡	(†)
500 to 999	78.0	(1.60)	9.4	(0.99)	5.9	(0.86)	5.0	(0.65)	0.9 !	(0.32)	0.8 !	(0.34)	84.7	(1.49)	7.9	(0.89)	4.2	(0.67)	2.5	(0.47)	0.5 !	(0.21)	‡	(†)
1,000 or more	57.2	(2.04)	15.7	(1.58)	10.1	(1.28)	9.6	(1.10)	4.0	(0.57)	3.4	(0.65)	64.0	(1.68)	13.9	(1.38)	9.5	(1.20)	8.1	(0.87)	3.5	(0.54)	1.0 !	(0.32)
Locale																								
City	76.9	(1.79)	11.6	(1.80)	4.8	(0.86)	4.5	(0.88)	1.1	(0.29)	1.1	(0.24)	84.2	(1.71)	8.4	(1.55)	4.3	(0.82)	1.8	(0.39)	0.9 !	(0.28)	0.5 !	(0.17)
Suburban	78.5	(1.52)	9.4	(1.07)	4.7	(0.72)	4.7	(0.61)	1.4	(0.35)	1.3 !	(0.66)	84.7	(1.30)	8.1	(1.05)	3.1	(0.35)	2.8	(0.46)	1.1 !	(0.33)	0.1 !	(0.07)
Town	79.6	(2.18)	8.3	(1.49)	4.6	(1.28)	5.6	(1.34)	1.4 !	(0.61)	‡	(†)	85.1	(1.66)	7.3	(1.36)	3.7 !	(1.12)	3.3	(0.96)	0.6 !	(0.25)	‡	(†)
Rural	80.5	(2.00)	9.9	(1.27)	4.6	(1.11)	3.2	(0.64)	‡	(†)	‡	(†)	86.6	(1.75)	7.0	(1.05)	4.0	(1.03)	2.3	(0.66)	‡	(†)	‡	(†)
Percent minority enrollment[2]																								
0 to 25 percent	80.7	(1.44)	9.6	(1.04)	3.8	(0.69)	4.2	(0.66)	1.0	(0.28)	0.7 !	(0.30)	86.5	(1.13)	6.9	(0.75)	3.5	(0.59)	2.3	(0.39)	0.8 !	(0.37)	‡	(†)
26 to 50 percent	79.1	(2.16)	11.5	(1.58)	4.1	(0.82)	3.8 !	(1.19)	‡	(†)	1.2 !	(0.56)	86.4	(1.66)	7.9	(1.22)	2.3	(0.51)	3.0	(0.66)	0.3 !	(0.16)	‡	(†)
51 to 75 percent	78.1	(2.68)	8.0	(2.16)	6.8	(1.44)	4.7	(1.19)	1.4 !	(0.69)	1.0 !	(0.35)	85.3	(1.96)	5.8	(1.12)	5.1	(0.95)	2.6 !	(0.92)	0.9 !	(0.27)	‡	(†)
76 to 100 percent	76.0	(1.87)	10.5	(1.74)	5.2	(0.96)	4.9	(0.82)	2.0 !	(0.66)	1.4 !	(0.43)	82.1	(1.71)	10.0	(1.68)	4.4	(0.77)	2.2	(0.50)	0.7	(0.18)	0.5 !	(0.17)
Percent of students eligible for free or reduced-price lunch																								
0 to 25 percent	82.5	(2.20)	8.8	(1.30)	3.6	(0.83)	4.0	(0.95)	1.0 !	(0.39)	0.2 !	(0.12)	88.9	(1.19)	6.1	(1.02)	2.2	(0.36)	2.2	(0.58)	‡	(†)	‡	(†)
26 to 50 percent	78.2	(1.50)	10.7	(1.51)	4.5	(0.75)	4.9	(0.76)	0.8	(0.23)	1.0 !	(0.47)	84.4	(1.38)	7.3	(1.07)	4.0	(0.60)	3.1	(0.55)	1.1 !	(0.48)	‡	(†)
51 to 75 percent	79.8	(1.93)	10.1	(1.40)	4.9	(0.89)	3.6	(0.68)	0.8 !	(0.37)	0.7 !	(0.26)	84.2	(1.68)	8.8	(1.19)	4.3	(0.81)	2.2	(0.50)	0.4 !	(0.13)	‡	(†)
76 to 100 percent	76.1	(1.86)	10.2	(1.30)	5.3	(0.91)	4.8	(0.89)	1.9	(0.54)	1.8	(0.51)	84.3	(1.38)	8.3	(1.14)	4.0	(0.65)	2.4	(0.63)	0.7	(0.17)	0.3 !	(0.13)

†Not applicable.

!Interpret data with caution. The coefficient of variation (CV) for this estimate is between 30 and 50 percent.

‡Reporting standards not met. Either there are too few cases for a reliable estimate or the coefficient of variation (CV) is 50 percent or greater.

[1] Primary schools are defined as schools in which the lowest grade is not higher than grade 3 and the highest grade is not higher than grade 8. Middle schools are defined as schools in which the lowest grade is not lower than grade 4 and the highest grade is not higher than grade 9. High schools are defined as schools in which the lowest grade is not lower than grade 9. Combined schools include all other combinations of grades, including K-12 schools.

[2] Percent combined enrollment of Black, Hispanic, Asian, Pacific Islander, and American Indian/Alaska Native students, and students of Two or more races.

NOTE: "Serious violent" incidents include rape, sexual assault other than rape, physical attack or fight with a weapon, threat of physical attack with a weapon, and robbery with or without a weapon. Responses were provided by the principal or the person most knowledgeable about crime and safety issues at the school. "At school" was defined to include activities that happen in school buildings, on school grounds, on school buses, and at places that hold school-sponsored events or activities. Respondents were instructed to include incidents that occurred before, during, or after normal school hours or when school activities or events were in session. Detail may not sum to totals because of rounding.

SOURCE: U.S. Department of Education, National Center for Education Statistics, 2017–18 School Survey on Crime and Safety (SSOCS), 2018. (This table was prepared August 2019.)

Table 230.10. Percentage of public schools reporting selected discipline problems that occurred at school, by frequency and selected school characteristics: Selected years, 1999-2000 through 2017-18

[Standard errors appear in parentheses]

Year and school characteristic	Happens at least once a week[1]														Happens at all[2]			
	Student racial/ethnic tensions[3]		Student bullying[4]		Student sexual harassment of other students		Student harassment of other students based on sexual orientation or gender identity[5]		Student verbal abuse of teachers		Widespread disorder in classrooms		Student acts of disrespect for teachers other than verbal abuse		Gang activities		Cult or extremist group activities	
1	2		3		4		5		6		7		8		9		10	
All schools																		
1999-2000	3.4	(0.41)	29.3	(1.21)	---	(†)	---	(†)	12.5	(0.69)	3.1	(0.44)	---	(†)	18.7	(0.85)	6.7	(0.46)
2003-04	2.1	(0.28)	26.8	(1.09)	4.0	(0.40)	---	(†)	10.7	(0.80)	2.8	(0.39)	---	(†)	16.7	(0.78)	3.4	(0.35)
2005-06	2.8	(0.31)	24.5	(1.14)	3.5	(0.40)	---	(†)	9.5	(0.61)	2.3	(0.24)	---	(†)	16.9	(0.76)	3.7	(0.41)
2007-08	3.7	(0.49)	25.3	(1.11)	3.0	(0.39)	---	(†)	6.0	(0.48)	4.0	(0.45)	10.5	(0.71)	19.8	(0.88)	2.6	(0.36)
2009-10	2.8	(0.39)	23.1	(1.12)	3.2	(0.55)	2.5	(0.41)	4.8	(0.49)	2.5	(0.37)	8.6	(0.67)	16.4	(0.84)	1.7	(0.31)
2013-14[6]	1.4	(0.31)	15.7	(1.12)	1.4	(0.26)	0.8	(0.19)	5.1	(0.54)	2.3	(0.45)	8.6	(0.74)	---	(†)	---	(†)
2015-16	1.7	(0.33)	11.9	(0.79)	1.0	(0.19)	0.6	(0.13)	4.8	(0.51)	2.3	(0.38)	10.3	(0.80)	10.4	(0.62)	---	(†)
2017-18																		
All schools	**2.8**	**(0.42)**	**13.6**	**(0.72)**	**1.4**	**(0.27)**	**1.0**	**(0.19)**	**6.0**	**(0.53)**	**3.1**	**(0.41)**	**11.8**	**(0.72)**	**11.0**	**(0.66)**	**---**	**(†)**
School level[7]																		
Primary	1.9	(0.51)	8.7	(0.94)	‡	(†)	‡	(†)	4.6	(0.83)	2.6	(0.62)	10.1	(1.02)	4.9	(0.85)	---	(†)
Middle	4.9	(0.68)	27.9	(1.51)	3.3	(0.58)	2.6	(0.47)	10.3	(0.89)	5.5	(0.79)	17.3	(1.18)	19.0	(1.19)	---	(†)
High school	4.5	(0.69)	15.8	(1.25)	2.8	(0.49)	2.3	(0.49)	7.1	(0.81)	2.6	(0.60)	13.1	(1.25)	27.9	(1.20)	---	(†)
Combined	‡	(†)	12.3	(3.17)	‡	(†)	‡	(†)	4.3 !	(1.98)	‡	(†)	8.2 !	(2.67)	4.5 !	(1.46)	---	(†)
Enrollment size																		
Less than 300	‡	(†)	9.6	(1.89)	‡	(†)	‡	(†)	3.0 !	(1.04)	1.5 !	(0.64)	4.9	(1.29)	3.3	(0.56)	---	(†)
300 to 499	3.4	(0.76)	11.3	(1.26)	1.2 !	(0.41)	0.6 !	(0.23)	5.9	(1.18)	4.3	(0.97)	14.4	(1.60)	6.6	(1.19)	---	(†)
500 to 999	2.3	(0.45)	15.6	(1.20)	0.9	(0.25)	0.8	(0.18)	6.8	(0.87)	2.7	(0.51)	12.1	(1.09)	12.3	(1.15)	---	(†)
1,000 or more	5.9	(0.89)	20.7	(1.67)	3.3	(0.56)	2.2	(0.45)	9.5	(1.29)	3.9	(0.71)	16.2	(1.48)	33.4	(1.61)	---	(†)
Locale																		
City	3.1	(0.69)	13.4	(1.11)	0.9	(0.24)	0.6 !	(0.18)	8.9	(1.32)	3.9	(0.74)	14.9	(1.64)	17.8	(1.37)	---	(†)
Suburban	3.7	(0.79)	13.0	(1.51)	1.4	(0.36)	0.7	(0.18)	5.3	(0.74)	2.7	(0.64)	10.5	(1.23)	10.1	(0.89)	---	(†)
Town	2.6 !	(0.85)	17.9	(2.35)	2.4 !	(0.73)	1.8 !	(0.57)	6.6	(1.80)	4.8 !	(1.63)	14.8	(2.16)	10.0	(1.20)	---	(†)
Rural	1.4 !	(0.60)	12.5	(1.53)	1.5 !	(0.62)	1.3 !	(0.60)	3.7	(0.90)	1.8 !	(0.66)	8.7	(1.44)	5.7	(0.84)	---	(†)
Percent minority enrollment[8]																		
0 to 25 percent	1.7	(0.40)	13.0	(1.10)	1.5 !	(0.49)	1.5 !	(0.45)	2.3	(0.44)	1.5 !	(0.46)	7.8	(1.10)	2.7	(0.48)	---	(†)
26 to 50 percent	2.4	(0.57)	11.7	(1.48)	1.3	(0.29)	0.7 !	(0.24)	5.2	(1.17)	3.6	(0.98)	10.1	(1.50)	9.8	(1.13)	---	(†)
51 to 75 percent	5.1	(1.52)	16.5	(2.45)	2.3 !	(0.82)	0.9 !	(0.37)	10.1	(1.91)	4.2 !	(1.38)	18.9	(2.45)	17.8	(1.62)	---	(†)
76 to 100 percent	3.3	(0.85)	14.3	(1.50)	0.8	(0.25)	0.6 !	(0.23)	9.5	(1.23)	4.1	(0.77)	14.5	(1.47)	19.3	(1.52)	---	(†)
Percent of students eligible for free or reduced-price lunch																		
0 to 25 percent	1.5	(0.36)	8.5	(0.97)	1.5 !	(0.49)	1.2	(0.32)	1.4	(0.36)	1.1 !	(0.44)	5.8	(1.43)	3.2	(0.54)	---	(†)
26 to 50 percent	3.5	(0.76)	13.8	(1.45)	1.9	(0.55)	1.1	(0.28)	3.0	(0.71)	2.5 !	(0.77)	8.1	(1.07)	7.5	(0.79)	---	(†)
51 to 75 percent	2.2	(0.61)	14.5	(1.63)	0.4 !	(0.15)	‡	(†)	7.1	(0.98)	3.3	(0.83)	13.8	(1.35)	12.2	(1.39)	---	(†)
76 to 100 percent	3.5	(0.93)	15.6	(1.52)	1.7 !	(0.63)	0.7 !	(0.24)	10.0	(1.25)	4.4	(0.82)	16.2	(1.73)	16.9	(1.43)	---	(†)
Prevalence of violent incidents[9] at school during school year																		
No violent incidents	‡	(†)	4.2	(1.06)	‡	(†)	‡	(†)	‡	(†)	‡	(†)	3.0 !	(0.95)	2.6	(0.65)	---	(†)
Any violent incidents	3.9	(0.61)	17.5	(0.93)	1.7	(0.29)	1.4	(0.26)	8.2	(0.74)	3.9	(0.50)	15.4	(0.98)	14.5	(0.86)	---	(†)

---Not available.

†Not applicable.

!Interpret data with caution. The coefficient of variation (CV) for this estimate is between 30 and 50 percent.

‡Reporting standards not met. Either there are too few cases for a reliable estimate or the coefficient of variation (CV) is 50 percent or greater.

[1] Includes schools that reported the problem happens either at least once a week or daily.

[2] Includes schools that reported the problem happens at all at their school during the school year. In the 1999-2000 survey administration, the questionnaire specified "undesirable" gang activities and "undesirable" cult or extremist group activities. As of 2013-14, the questionnaires have no longer asked about cult or extremist group activities.

[3] Prior to the 2007-08 survey administration, the questionnaire wording was "student racial tensions."

[4] The 2015-16 and 2017-18 questionnaires defined bullying as "any unwanted aggressive behavior(s) by another youth or group of youths who are not siblings or current dating partners that involves an observed or perceived power imbalance and is repeated multiple times or is highly likely to be repeated." The term was not defined for respondents in previous survey administrations.

[5] Prior to 2015-16, the questionnaire asked about "student harassment of other students based on sexual orientation or gender identity (i.e., lesbian, gay, bisexual, transgender, questioning)" in one single item. The 2015-16 and 2017-18 questionnaires had one item asking about "student harassment of other students based on sexual orientation," followed by a separate item asking about "student harassment of other students based on gender identity." For 2015-16 and 2017-18, schools are included in this column if they responded "daily" or "at least once a week" to either or both of these items; each school is counted only once, even if it indicated daily/weekly frequency for both items. The 2015-16 and 2017-18 questionnaires provided definitions for sexual orientation—"one's emotional or physical attraction to the same and/or opposite sex"—and gender identity—"one's inner sense of one's own gender, which may or may not match the sex assigned at birth." These terms were not defined for respondents in previous survey administrations.

[6] Data for 2013-14 were collected using the Fast Response Survey System (FRSS), while data for all other years were collected using the School Survey on Crime and Safety (SSOCS). The 2013-14 FRSS survey was designed to allow comparisons with SSOCS data. However, all respondents to the 2013-14 survey could choose either to complete the survey on paper (and mail it back) or to complete the survey online, whereas all respondents to SSOCS had only the option of completing a paper survey prior to 2017-18, when SSOCS experimented with offering an online option to some respondents. The 2013-14 FRSS survey also relied on a smaller sample than SSOCS. The FRSS survey's smaller sample size and difference in survey administration may have impacted the 2013-14 results.

[7] Primary schools are defined as schools in which the lowest grade is not higher than grade 3 and the highest grade is not higher than grade 8. Middle schools are defined as schools in which the lowest grade is not lower than grade 4 and the highest grade is not higher than grade 9. High schools are defined as schools in which the lowest grade is not lower than grade 9. Combined schools include all other combinations of grades, including K-12 schools.

[8] Percent combined enrollment of Black, Hispanic, Asian, Pacific Islander, and American Indian/Alaska Native students, and students of Two or more races.

[9] "Violent incidents" include rape or attempted rape, sexual assault other than rape, physical attack or fight with or without a weapon, threat of physical attack or fight with or without a weapon, and robbery with or without a weapon. Respondents were instructed to include violent incidents that occurred before, during, or after normal school hours or when school activities or events were in session.

NOTE: Responses were provided by the principal or the person most knowledgeable about crime and safety issues at the school. "At school" was defined for respondents to include activities that happen in school buildings, on school grounds, on school buses, and at places that hold school-sponsored events or activities. Respondents were instructed to respond only for those times that were during normal school hours or when school activities or events were in session, unless the survey specified otherwise.

SOURCE: U.S. Department of Education, National Center for Education Statistics, 1999-2000, 2003-04, 2005-06, 2007-08, 2009-10, 2015-16, and 2017-18 School Survey on Crime and Safety (SSOCS), 2000, 2004, 2006, 2008, 2010, 2016, and 2018; and Fast Response Survey System (FRSS), "School Safety and Discipline: 2013-14," FRSS 106, 2014. (This table was prepared July 2019.)

Table 230.20. Percentage of students ages 12-18 who reported that gangs were present at school during the school year, by selected student and school characteristics: Selected years, 2001 through 2019

[Standard errors appear in parentheses]

Student or school characteristic	2001[1]		2003[1]		2005[1]		2007		2009		2011		2013		2015		2017		2019[2]	
1		2		3		4		5		6		7		8		9		10		11
Total	**20.3**	**(0.72)**	**21.0**	**(0.71)**	**24.2**	**(0.93)**	**23.2**	**(0.80)**	**20.4**	**(0.85)**	**17.5**	**(0.71)**	**12.4**	**(0.62)**	**10.7**	**(0.60)**	**8.6**	**(0.48)**	**9.0**	**(0.52)**
Sex																				
Male	21.5	(0.87)	22.4	(0.95)	25.3	(1.07)	25.1	(1.07)	20.9	(1.12)	17.5	(0.95)	12.9	(0.85)	10.9	(0.79)	7.9	(0.62)	9.5	(0.71)
Female	18.9	(0.90)	19.6	(0.80)	22.9	(1.09)	21.3	(0.87)	19.9	(1.03)	17.5	(0.88)	12.0	(0.73)	10.4	(0.82)	9.3	(0.73)	8.5	(0.64)
Race/ethnicity[3]																				
White	15.5	(0.73)	14.2	(0.59)	16.7	(0.83)	16.0	(0.70)	14.1	(0.79)	11.1	(0.67)	7.4	(0.63)	7.4	(0.56)	5.3	(0.50)	6.3	(0.50)
Black	28.8	(1.92)	29.7	(2.15)	37.5	(2.42)	37.5	(2.28)	31.4	(2.62)	32.7	(2.23)	18.6	(1.72)	17.1	(1.85)	16.6	(1.75)	14.7	(2.08)
Hispanic	32.3	(1.84)	37.3	(1.73)	38.9	(2.69)	36.1	(2.04)	33.0	(2.20)	26.4	(1.55)	20.1	(1.34)	15.3	(1.45)	12.3	(1.13)	12.5	(1.23)
Asian/Pacific Islander	23.3	(2.38)	21.8	(3.04)	21.3	(2.59)	18.1	(2.58)	16.9	(3.14)	10.1	(2.09)	9.8	(1.85)	5.0 !	(1.58)	2.4 !	(0.96)	5.3	(1.34)
Asian	---	(†)	21.2	(3.03)	20.3	(2.61)	17.4	(2.72)	17.2	(3.21)	9.9	(2.24)	9.4	(1.85)	4.1 !	(1.47)	2.0 !	(0.89)	4.5	(1.33)
Pacific Islander	---	(†)	‡	(†)	‡	(†)	‡	(†)	‡	(†)	‡	(†)	‡	(†)	‡	(†)	‡	(†)	‡	(†)
American Indian/Alaska Native	13.2 !	(4.49)	24.8 !	(10.51)	‡	(†)	17.2 !	(6.52)	‡	(†)	‡	(†)	18.3 !	(9.01)	‡	(†)	‡	(†)	15.8 !	(7.12)
Two or more races	---	(†)	22.3	(3.65)	23.6	(4.85)	28.3	(4.52)	18.0	(5.18)	10.3	(2.58)	13.3	(3.10)	13.5	(3.77)	9.7	(2.65)	9.1	(2.38)
Grade																				
6th	11.3	(1.29)	10.9	(1.28)	12.1	(1.41)	15.3	(1.99)	11.0	(1.76)	8.2	(1.20)	5.0	(1.15)	5.7	(1.13)	4.8	(1.10)	5.8	(1.30)
7th	15.8	(1.09)	16.4	(1.15)	17.3	(1.21)	17.4	(1.28)	14.8	(1.70)	10.2	(1.08)	7.7	(0.96)	6.8	(0.95)	5.4	(0.82)	5.5	(0.82)
8th	17.4	(1.23)	17.9	(1.29)	19.1	(1.79)	20.6	(1.68)	15.9	(1.60)	11.3	(1.02)	7.8	(0.96)	7.2	(1.00)	6.6	(0.96)	5.9	(0.86)
9th	24.3	(1.27)	26.2	(1.45)	28.3	(1.59)	28.0	(1.51)	24.9	(2.01)	21.7	(1.47)	13.9	(1.43)	13.3	(1.42)	10.9	(1.15)	11.6	(1.44)
10th	23.8	(1.49)	26.6	(1.39)	32.6	(1.89)	28.1	(1.73)	27.7	(1.75)	23.0	(1.63)	17.7	(1.46)	13.3	(1.27)	11.4	(1.16)	12.1	(1.21)
11th	24.2	(1.56)	23.5	(1.67)	28.0	(1.89)	25.9	(1.61)	22.6	(1.53)	23.2	(1.74)	17.1	(1.65)	13.3	(1.74)	9.7	(1.15)	9.9	(1.25)
12th	21.2	(1.55)	22.4	(1.52)	27.9	(2.16)	24.4	(1.69)	21.9	(2.02)	21.3	(1.82)	14.6	(1.58)	13.1	(1.58)	9.8	(1.28)	11.0	(1.37)
School locale[4]																				
City	---	(†)	---	(†)	---	(†)	---	(†)	---	(†)	---	(†)	---	(†)	15.4	(1.33)	12.3	(1.06)	13.5	(1.22)
Suburban	---	(†)	---	(†)	---	(†)	---	(†)	---	(†)	---	(†)	---	(†)	11.0	(0.77)	7.4	(0.65)	7.9	(0.76)
Town	---	(†)	---	(†)	---	(†)	---	(†)	---	(†)	---	(†)	---	(†)	8.3	(1.51)	9.1	(1.74)	8.9	(1.76)
Rural	---	(†)	---	(†)	---	(†)	---	(†)	---	(†)	---	(†)	---	(†)	4.9	(1.08)	5.6	(0.74)	6.0	(0.84)
Control of school[4,5]																				
Public	21.7	(0.78)	22.6	(0.78)	25.8	(1.01)	24.9	(0.87)	22.0	(0.89)	18.9	(0.77)	13.3	(0.67)	11.4	(0.65)	9.2	(0.52)	9.8	(0.57)
Private	5.0	(1.06)	3.9	(0.82)	4.2	(0.94)	5.2	(1.14)	2.3 !	(0.82)	1.9 !	(0.69)	2.3 !	(0.94)	2.0 !	(0.86)	‡	(†)	‡	(†)

—Not available.

†Not applicable.

!Interpret data with caution. The coefficient of variation (CV) for this estimate is between 30 and 50 percent.

‡Reporting standards not met. Either there are too few cases for a reliable estimate or the coefficient of variation (CV) is 50 percent or greater.

1 In 2005 and prior years, the period covered by the survey question was "during the last 6 months," but this was changed to "during this school year" beginning in 2007. Cognitive testing suggested that modifications to the reference period would not have a substantial impact on the survey responses.

2 The 2019 survey included a split sample design to test alternate introductions for the section assessing the presence of gangs at school. Approximately 60 percent of the sample received the version of the questionnaire that was consistent with prior years, where the section introduction included the definition "All gangs, whether or not they are involved in violent or illegal activity, are included." The remaining 40 percent of the sample received the alternate questionnaire, which excluded the definition. Estimates in this table include all respondents, regardless of which version of the questionnaire they received. For more information about the 2019 survey collection and experiment, see *Methodology Report: Split-Half Administration of the 2019 School Crime Supplement to the National Crime Victimization Survey* (NCES 2021-016).

3 Race categories exclude persons of Hispanic ethnicity. In 2001, separate data for Asian students, Pacific Islander students, and students of Two or more races were not collected.

4 Excludes students with missing information about the school characteristic.

5 Data for 2013 and prior years were based on school information provided by the respondent. Beginning in 2015, data were based on school information collected in the Common Core of Data and the Private School Universe Survey, which was appended to the School Crime Supplement data file; therefore, these data may not be entirely comparable with figures for earlier years.

NOTE: "At school" includes in the school building, on school property, on a school bus, and going to and from school. Some data have been revised from previously published figures.

SOURCE: U.S. Department of Justice, Bureau of Justice Statistics, School Crime Supplement (SCS) to the National Crime Victimization Survey, 1995 through 2019. (This table was prepared October 2020.)

Table 230.20a. Percentage of students ages 12-18 who reported that gangs were present at school during the school year, by grade, control of school, and urbanicity: Selected years, 2001 through 2017

[Standard errors appear in parentheses]

Year and urbanicity[1]	Total		Grade														Control of school			
			6th grade		7th grade		8th grade		9th grade		10th grade		11th grade		12th grade		Public		Private	
1	2		3		4		5		6		7		8		9		10		11	
2001[2]																				
Total	**20.3**	**(0.72)**	**11.3**	**(1.29)**	**15.8**	**(1.09)**	**17.4**	**(1.23)**	**24.3**	**(1.27)**	**23.8**	**(1.49)**	**24.2**	**(1.56)**	**21.2**	**(1.55)**	**21.7**	**(0.78)**	**5.0**	**(1.06)**
Urban	29.2	(1.24)	15.2	(2.45)	23.9	(2.53)	24.5	(2.70)	35.4	(2.78)	33.6	(3.08)	34.2	(3.18)	34.2	(3.23)	32.2	(1.35)	5.1	(1.41)
Suburban	18.4	(0.72)	9.1	(1.53)	13.8	(1.17)	16.6	(1.51)	20.9	(1.48)	22.5	(1.58)	22.9	(1.71)	18.8	(1.82)	19.6	(0.80)	4.3 !	(1.46)
Rural	13.3	(1.72)	11.2	(2.80)	8.9	(1.87)	10.1	(2.24)	18.9	(3.03)	14.5	(3.05)	15.8	(3.86)	11.6 !	(4.53)	13.8	(1.81)	‡	(†)
2003[2]																				
Total	**21.0**	**(0.71)**	**10.9**	**(1.28)**	**16.4**	**(1.15)**	**17.9**	**(1.29)**	**26.2**	**(1.45)**	**26.6**	**(1.39)**	**23.5**	**(1.67)**	**22.4**	**(1.52)**	**22.6**	**(0.78)**	**3.9**	**(0.82)**
Urban	31.0	(1.34)	21.6	(3.42)	25.6	(2.33)	25.3	(2.62)	38.3	(3.25)	35.6	(2.86)	34.6	(2.81)	35.1	(2.76)	33.8	(1.51)	6.0	(1.63)
Suburban	18.5	(0.84)	7.6	(1.26)	13.3	(1.29)	16.3	(1.66)	24.3	(1.58)	24.3	(1.74)	20.5	(2.34)	19.6	(1.94)	20.1	(0.92)	2.4 !	(0.78)
Rural	12.5	(1.86)	‡	(†)	9.5	(2.58)	10.9	(3.26)	13.8	(3.00)	18.7	(3.66)	15.4	(3.64)	13.3	(3.60)	12.9	(2.04)	‡	(†)
2005[2]																				
Total	**24.2**	**(0.93)**	**12.1**	**(1.41)**	**17.3**	**(1.21)**	**19.1**	**(1.79)**	**28.3**	**(1.59)**	**32.6**	**(1.89)**	**28.0**	**(1.89)**	**27.9**	**(2.16)**	**25.8**	**(1.01)**	**4.2**	**(0.94)**
Urban	36.2	(2.00)	19.9	(3.11)	24.2	(2.64)	30.5	(3.81)	40.3	(3.70)	50.6	(3.79)	44.3	(3.89)	39.5	(3.73)	39.1	(2.12)	7.7	(2.26)
Suburban	20.8	(0.93)	8.9	(1.52)	14.9	(1.46)	14.6	(2.01)	24.8	(1.92)	27.9	(2.37)	25.5	(2.21)	25.1	(2.60)	22.3	(1.01)	3.0 !	(1.02)
Rural	16.4	(2.53)	8.3 !	(3.29)	15.2	(3.46)	14.7	(4.22)	21.0	(4.00)	22.0	(3.61)	13.3 !	(4.36)	15.8 !	(5.82)	17.2	(2.67)	‡	(†)
2007																				
Total	**23.2**	**(0.80)**	**15.3**	**(1.99)**	**17.4**	**(1.28)**	**20.6**	**(1.68)**	**28.0**	**(1.51)**	**28.1**	**(1.73)**	**25.9**	**(1.61)**	**24.4**	**(1.69)**	**24.9**	**(0.87)**	**5.2**	**(1.14)**
Urban	32.3	(1.49)	17.8	(3.45)	24.1	(2.96)	25.9	(2.90)	41.1	(3.40)	38.6	(3.36)	34.7	(3.05)	38.4	(4.01)	35.6	(1.61)	7.3	(2.07)
Suburban	21.0	(0.97)	14.0	(2.40)	15.4	(1.67)	19.6	(2.23)	23.1	(1.78)	26.6	(2.01)	23.6	(2.22)	22.4	(2.26)	22.7	(1.05)	2.8 !	(1.09)
Rural	15.5	(2.78)	15.6 !	(6.21)	13.1	(2.79)	14.7	(4.26)	21.7	(4.43)	15.2	(3.39)	18.7	(3.98)	7.6 !	(2.90)	15.6	(2.91)	11.8 !	(5.84)
2009																				
Total	**20.4**	**(0.85)**	**11.0**	**(1.76)**	**14.8**	**(1.70)**	**15.9**	**(1.60)**	**24.9**	**(2.01)**	**27.7**	**(1.75)**	**22.6**	**(1.53)**	**21.9**	**(2.02)**	**22.0**	**(0.89)**	**2.3 !**	**(0.82)**
Urban	30.7	(1.86)	14.5	(4.13)	21.0	(3.37)	24.4	(3.24)	34.2	(4.01)	44.8	(3.41)	34.9	(4.08)	36.0	(4.32)	33.7	(1.94)	4.1 !	(1.83)
Suburban	16.6	(0.80)	9.7	(1.90)	11.2	(1.89)	11.8	(1.73)	22.4	(2.10)	21.0	(2.07)	19.4	(1.88)	17.6	(2.29)	18.1	(0.85)	‡	(†)
Rural	16.0	(3.08)	8.3 !	(3.11)	16.5	(4.19)	14.2 !	(4.41)	18.8	(5.04)	19.6	(5.02)	13.4	(3.50)	17.3 !	(5.37)	16.2	(3.18)	‡	(†)
2011																				
Total	**17.5**	**(0.71)**	**8.2**	**(1.20)**	**10.2**	**(1.08)**	**11.3**	**(1.02)**	**21.7**	**(1.47)**	**23.0**	**(1.63)**	**23.2**	**(1.74)**	**21.3**	**(1.82)**	**18.9**	**(0.77)**	**1.9 !**	**(0.69)**
Urban	22.8	(1.34)	5.4 !	(1.98)	11.7	(2.02)	16.2	(2.29)	27.5	(3.12)	31.1	(3.13)	28.1	(3.17)	32.9	(3.88)	25.7	(1.47)	‡	(†)
Suburban	16.1	(0.97)	8.6	(1.79)	9.3	(1.37)	9.0	(1.22)	18.9	(1.79)	21.5	(2.10)	23.7	(2.46)	18.5	(2.27)	17.1	(1.01)	2.9 !	(1.20)
Rural	12.1	(2.42)	11.1	(2.97)	10.1	(2.64)	9.6 !	(2.89)	19.3	(4.99)	13.9	(4.02)	10.6 !	(3.69)	9.2 !	(3.04)	12.5	(2.49)	‡	(†)
2013																				
Total	**12.4**	**(0.62)**	**5.0**	**(1.15)**	**7.7**	**(0.96)**	**7.8**	**(0.96)**	**13.9**	**(1.43)**	**17.7**	**(1.46)**	**17.1**	**(1.65)**	**14.6**	**(1.58)**	**13.3**	**(0.67)**	**2.3 !**	**(0.94)**
Urban	18.3	(1.23)	9.6	(2.75)	12.0	(2.44)	13.2	(2.30)	19.6	(2.53)	24.8	(2.86)	26.7	(3.21)	18.2	(3.07)	19.9	(1.35)	4.6 !	(2.08)
Suburban	10.8	(0.76)	3.0 !	(1.25)	6.6	(1.14)	6.3	(1.19)	12.2	(1.95)	15.4	(1.91)	15.1	(2.00)	14.1	(2.06)	11.7	(0.82)	‡	(†)
Rural	6.8	(1.44)	‡	(†)	4.2 !	(1.88)	‡	(†)	8.0 !	(3.19)	11.3	(3.37)	8.1 !	(3.32)	9.0 !	(3.56)	6.8	(1.47)	‡	(†)
2015																				
Total	**10.7**	**(0.60)**	**5.7**	**(1.13)**	**6.8**	**(0.95)**	**7.2**	**(1.00)**	**13.3**	**(1.42)**	**13.3**	**(1.27)**	**13.3**	**(1.74)**	**13.1**	**(1.58)**	**11.3**	**(0.64)**	**2.4 !**	**(0.90)**
Urban	15.3	(1.22)	6.4 !	(2.02)	9.0	(2.10)	10.9	(2.21)	19.5	(3.12)	19.8	(2.48)	21.9	(3.69)	17.3	(3.12)	16.4	(1.31)	4.4 !	(1.89)
Suburban	10.2	(0.75)	6.0	(1.46)	5.8	(1.11)	6.3	(1.37)	13.4	(1.93)	12.1	(1.82)	12.1	(2.02)	13.3	(2.07)	10.7	(0.80)	‡	(†)
Rural	3.9	(0.90)	‡	(†)	5.5 !	(1.96)	3.2 !	(1.60)	4.5 !	(1.80)	5.3 !	(2.63)	‡	(†)	‡	(†)	4.1	(0.93)	‡	(†)
2017																				
Total	**8.6**	**(0.48)**	**4.8**	**(1.10)**	**5.4**	**(0.82)**	**6.6**	**(0.96)**	**10.9**	**(1.15)**	**11.4**	**(1.16)**	**9.7**	**(1.15)**	**9.8**	**(1.28)**	**9.2**	**(0.53)**	**1.6 !**	**(0.79)**
Urban	11.3	(1.06)	5.2 !	(2.36)	5.8	(1.55)	10.1	(2.31)	13.2	(2.49)	14.9	(2.80)	14.2	(2.95)	12.9	(2.72)	12.0	(1.14)	‡	(†)
Suburban	7.6	(0.56)	3.7	(0.97)	5.1	(1.00)	5.2	(1.06)	10.1	(1.55)	10.6	(1.59)	8.5	(1.21)	8.5	(1.39)	8.2	(0.61)	‡	(†)
Rural	6.6	(1.56)	7.5 !	(3.34)	5.9 !	(2.42)	4.7 !	(2.19)	9.3	(2.46)	6.3 !	(2.26)	5.2 !	(2.24)	7.5 !	(2.79)	6.7	(1.62)	‡	(†)

†Not applicable.

!Interpret data with caution. The coefficient of variation (CV) for this estimate is between 30 and 50 percent.

‡Reporting standards not met. Either there are too few cases for a reliable estimate or the coefficient of variation (CV) is 50 percent or greater.

[1] "Urbanicity" refers to the Standard Metropolitan Statistical Area (MSA) status of the respondent's household as defined by the U.S. Census Bureau. Categories include "central city of an MSA (Urban)," "in MSA but not in central city (Suburban)," and "not MSA (Rural)."

[2] In 2005 and prior years, the period covered by the survey question was "during the last 6 months," whereas the period was "during this school year" beginning in 2007. Cognitive testing showed that estimates for earlier years are comparable to those for 2007 and later years.

NOTE: All gangs, whether or not they are involved in violent or illegal activity, are included. "At school" includes in the school building, on school property, on a school bus, and going to and from school. Some data have been revised from previously published figures.

SOURCE: U.S. Department of Justice, Bureau of Justice Statistics, School Crime Supplement (SCS) to the National Crime Victimization Survey, 2001 through 2017. (This table was prepared September 2018.)

Table 230.30. Percentage of students ages 12-18 who reported being called hate-related words and seeing hate-related graffiti at school during the school year, by selected student and school characteristics: Selected years, 1999 through 2019

[Standard errors appear in parentheses]

Student or school characteristic	1999[1]		2001[1]		2003[1]		2005[1]		2007		2009		2011		2013		2015		2017		2019	
1	2		3		4		5		6		7		8		9		10		11		12	
Hate-related words																						
Total	**13.3**	**(0.53)**	**12.3**	**(0.47)**	**11.8**	**(0.47)**	**11.2**	**(0.50)**	**9.7**	**(0.43)**	**8.7**	**(0.52)**	**9.1**	**(0.48)**	**6.6**	**(0.40)**	**7.2**	**(0.43)**	**6.4**	**(0.34)**	**6.7**	**(0.40)**
Sex																						
Male	12.4	(0.66)	12.9	(0.65)	12.1	(0.61)	11.7	(0.68)	9.9	(0.61)	8.5	(0.62)	9.0	(0.60)	6.6	(0.51)	7.8	(0.58)	6.0	(0.41)	6.0	(0.57)
Female	14.4	(0.71)	11.8	(0.52)	11.4	(0.64)	10.7	(0.64)	9.6	(0.57)	8.9	(0.72)	9.1	(0.68)	6.7	(0.53)	6.7	(0.61)	6.9	(0.50)	7.5	(0.56)
Race/ethnicity[2]																						
White	12.6	(0.68)	12.0	(0.58)	11.0	(0.57)	10.4	(0.60)	8.9	(0.50)	7.2	(0.59)	8.3	(0.60)	5.3	(0.43)	6.3	(0.60)	6.1	(0.48)	5.6	(0.46)
Black	16.6	(1.17)	14.1	(1.10)	14.3	(1.13)	15.0	(1.49)	11.4	(1.35)	11.1	(1.35)	10.7	(1.30)	7.8	(1.20)	9.4	(1.07)	7.4	(1.03)	8.6	(1.31)
Hispanic	12.1	(1.08)	11.1	(1.15)	11.4	(0.96)	10.5	(1.15)	10.6	(1.18)	11.2	(1.13)	9.8	(0.98)	7.4	(0.84)	6.5	(0.78)	6.3	(0.74)	6.5	(0.80)
Asian/Pacific Islander	13.9	(1.98)	13.0	(2.07)	11.4	(2.06)	10.7	(2.45)	10.5	(1.91)	10.9	(2.61)	9.6	(1.92)	9.8	(2.02)	11.2	(2.28)	4.7	(1.21)	7.7	(1.49)
Asian	---	(†)	---	(†)	11.4	(2.17)	11.0	(2.57)	11.1	(1.97)	10.7	(2.81)	9.0	(2.00)	10.3	(2.19)	10.8	(2.39)	4.8	(1.24)	7.2	(1.62)
Pacific Islander	---	(†)	---	(†)	‡	(†)	‡	(†)	‡	(†)	‡	(†)	‡	(†)	‡	(†)	‡	(†)	‡	(†)	‡	(†)
American Indian/Alaska Native	28.5	(6.62)	17.4 !	(7.96)	18.6 !	(5.92)	‡	(†)	‡	(†)	‡	(†)	‡	(†)	‡	(†)	‡	(†)	‡	(†)	‡	(†)
Two or more races	---	(†)	---	(†)	19.4	(4.92)	10.6 !	(3.79)	11.7	(3.34)	9.8 !	(3.24)	11.1	(2.89)	13.5	(3.19)	8.5	(2.34)	11.4	(2.50)	16.5	(2.76)
Grade																						
6th	13.1	(1.36)	12.2	(1.26)	11.9	(1.32)	11.1	(1.58)	12.1	(1.54)	8.3	(1.39)	9.0	(1.43)	6.7	(1.33)	10.1	(1.58)	6.7	(1.20)	7.7	(1.28)
7th	15.8	(1.14)	14.2	(1.13)	12.5	(1.05)	13.1	(1.16)	10.7	(1.02)	9.6	(1.22)	9.9	(1.02)	7.5	(0.89)	7.0	(1.03)	7.3	(0.95)	8.1	(1.09)
8th	16.1	(1.00)	13.0	(1.07)	12.9	(0.92)	11.2	(1.04)	11.0	(1.19)	10.9	(1.22)	8.4	(0.94)	7.4	(1.01)	9.2	(1.11)	7.0	(0.89)	8.6	(1.09)
9th	13.3	(0.91)	12.2	(1.00)	13.5	(1.24)	12.8	(1.12)	10.9	(1.08)	8.0	(1.09)	10.2	(1.10)	6.6	(0.94)	7.4	(0.89)	8.2	(1.07)	6.7	(1.04)
10th	11.9	(1.10)	13.2	(0.95)	11.7	(1.13)	10.9	(1.04)	9.0	(0.99)	9.7	(1.18)	9.6	(1.14)	6.4	(0.97)	6.5	(0.94)	6.3	(0.86)	5.3	(0.85)
11th	10.6	(1.04)	12.7	(1.13)	8.3	(0.97)	9.0	(1.17)	8.6	(1.01)	8.4	(1.14)	8.7	(1.01)	7.5	(1.01)	6.0	(0.97)	4.7	(0.90)	6.8	(1.01)
12th	11.8	(1.27)	8.0	(0.88)	10.9	(1.27)	9.7	(1.35)	6.0	(0.98)	5.8	(0.96)	7.5	(1.01)	4.1	(0.78)	5.4	(0.99)	4.6	(0.82)	4.2	(0.73)
School locale[3]																						
City	---	(†)	---	(†)	---	(†)	---	(†)	---	(†)	---	(†)	---	(†)	---	(†)	7.4	(0.69)	6.7	(0.67)	7.9	(0.84)
Suburban	---	(†)	---	(†)	---	(†)	---	(†)	---	(†)	---	(†)	---	(†)	---	(†)	8.2	(0.64)	5.9	(0.58)	6.5	(0.64)
Town	---	(†)	---	(†)	---	(†)	---	(†)	---	(†)	---	(†)	---	(†)	---	(†)	5.5	(1.15)	7.5	(1.05)	5.8	(1.14)
Rural	---	(†)	---	(†)	---	(†)	---	(†)	---	(†)	---	(†)	---	(†)	---	(†)	6.3	(0.93)	6.7	(0.86)	6.8	(0.80)
Control of school[3,4]																						
Public	13.9	(0.56)	12.7	(0.51)	11.9	(0.49)	11.6	(0.53)	10.1	(0.46)	8.9	(0.54)	9.3	(0.50)	6.6	(0.41)	7.5	(0.44)	6.7	(0.39)	7.1	(0.45)
Private	8.2	(1.05)	8.2	(1.13)	9.8	(1.14)	6.8	(1.18)	6.1	(1.25)	6.6	(1.62)	6.9	(1.29)	6.7	(1.41)	3.4 !	(1.18)	3.3	(0.95)	2.5 !	(0.93)
Hate-related graffiti																						
Total	**36.6**	**(0.95)**	**36.0**	**(0.76)**	**36.9**	**(0.83)**	**38.4**	**(0.83)**	**35.0**	**(0.89)**	**29.2**	**(0.96)**	**28.4**	**(0.88)**	**24.6**	**(0.88)**	**27.2**	**(0.98)**	**23.2**	**(0.83)**	**22.6**	**(0.72)**
Sex																						
Male	34.0	(1.06)	35.4	(0.91)	35.6	(0.97)	37.7	(1.10)	34.5	(1.12)	29.0	(1.26)	28.6	(1.11)	24.1	(1.11)	26.3	(1.20)	22.6	(1.11)	22.0	(0.90)
Female	39.3	(1.14)	36.6	(0.94)	38.2	(1.07)	39.1	(0.93)	35.5	(1.11)	29.3	(1.09)	28.1	(1.07)	25.1	(1.05)	28.1	(1.25)	23.8	(0.99)	23.1	(1.09)
Race/ethnicity[2]																						
White	36.8	(1.21)	36.5	(0.96)	35.8	(0.86)	38.5	(0.96)	35.6	(1.05)	28.3	(1.10)	28.2	(1.19)	23.7	(1.20)	28.6	(1.42)	24.0	(1.09)	22.9	(1.04)
Black	38.0	(1.74)	34.0	(1.56)	38.7	(1.99)	37.9	(2.29)	33.7	(2.37)	29.0	(2.44)	28.1	(1.90)	26.3	(2.10)	24.9	(1.92)	24.8	(1.94)	21.7	(2.16)
Hispanic	35.8	(1.48)	35.6	(1.88)	40.9	(2.24)	38.0	(1.78)	34.9	(1.79)	32.2	(1.61)	29.1	(1.33)	25.6	(1.52)	26.7	(1.48)	21.0	(1.48)	23.2	(1.34)
Asian/Pacific Islander	30.9	(2.49)	33.5	(3.23)	27.7	(3.58)	34.5	(3.64)	28.5	(3.05)	29.9	(3.56)	29.8	(4.35)	20.8	(3.07)	19.5	(2.37)	15.2	(2.71)	17.0	(2.43)
Asian	---	(†)	---	(†)	26.8	(3.68)	34.7	(3.76)	28.2	(3.01)	31.2	(3.59)	29.9	(4.56)	20.8	(3.22)	17.5	(2.62)	14.6	(2.64)	16.8	(2.56)
Pacific Islander	---	(†)	---	(†)	‡	(†)	‡	(†)	‡	(†)	‡	(†)	‡	(†)	‡	(†)	‡	(†)	‡	(†)	‡	(†)
American Indian/Alaska Native	47.1	(7.97)	31.5	(5.28)	35.9 !	(13.33)	‡	(†)	27.3	(7.87)	‡	(†)	16.8 !	(6.61)	22.0 !	(8.04)	‡	(†)	27.8 !	(11.39)	30.6 !	(11.02)
Two or more races	---	(†)	---	(†)	40.8	(4.91)	47.7	(5.81)	41.9	(4.25)	30.3	(5.19)	27.4	(4.27)	31.1	(4.39)	29.1	(4.24)	35.0	(4.39)	24.4	(3.63)
Grade																						
6th	30.7	(1.84)	35.2	(1.90)	36.1	(1.85)	34.0	(2.24)	35.6	(2.31)	28.1	(2.26)	25.9	(2.13)	21.9	(1.77)	30.0	(2.36)	20.6	(2.32)	20.3	(1.90)
7th	35.1	(1.42)	35.5	(1.38)	37.6	(1.43)	37.0	(1.63)	32.4	(1.52)	27.9	(1.88)	26.0	(1.70)	21.7	(1.49)	24.7	(1.77)	21.2	(1.51)	22.5	(1.61)
8th	35.9	(1.53)	37.2	(1.40)	35.1	(1.51)	35.7	(1.61)	33.5	(1.80)	30.8	(1.80)	25.9	(1.55)	24.0	(1.80)	27.2	(2.05)	22.4	(1.68)	22.3	(1.63)
9th	39.5	(1.56)	36.1	(1.56)	37.6	(1.52)	41.6	(1.64)	34.6	(1.77)	28.1	(1.83)	28.7	(1.69)	27.2	(1.74)	28.2	(1.88)	25.2	(1.49)	25.2	(1.84)
10th	39.3	(1.78)	36.8	(1.53)	41.4	(1.67)	40.7	(1.83)	36.5	(1.69)	31.0	(2.03)	33.3	(1.78)	26.0	(1.58)	28.6	(1.85)	27.0	(1.93)	23.7	(1.73)
11th	37.3	(1.75)	36.5	(1.76)	37.2	(1.76)	40.2	(1.70)	35.4	(1.81)	27.4	(2.01)	32.1	(1.70)	25.8	(2.03)	26.2	(1.72)	22.6	(1.74)	22.0	(1.57)
12th	35.8	(2.04)	33.5	(1.81)	32.6	(1.80)	37.8	(2.34)	37.7	(2.03)	30.4	(2.00)	25.7	(1.51)	24.2	(1.91)	26.1	(1.97)	22.2	(1.79)	20.6	(1.65)
School locale[3]																						
City	---	(†)	---	(†)	---	(†)	---	(†)	---	(†)	---	(†)	---	(†)	---	(†)	27.9	(1.44)	24.3	(1.55)	24.3	(1.32)
Suburban	---	(†)	---	(†)	---	(†)	---	(†)	---	(†)	---	(†)	---	(†)	---	(†)	27.9	(1.21)	23.0	(1.26)	22.4	(1.08)
Town	---	(†)	---	(†)	---	(†)	---	(†)	---	(†)	---	(†)	---	(†)	---	(†)	35.6	(3.76)	28.9	(2.58)	22.3	(2.38)
Rural	---	(†)	---	(†)	---	(†)	---	(†)	---	(†)	---	(†)	---	(†)	---	(†)	22.3	(1.96)	21.4	(1.44)	24.1	(1.63)
Control of school[3,4]																						
Public	38.3	(0.98)	37.8	(0.81)	38.5	(0.90)	40.0	(0.87)	36.5	(0.93)	30.7	(1.01)	29.7	(0.95)	25.6	(0.94)	28.6	(1.05)	25.1	(0.91)	24.2	(0.79)
Private	20.8	(1.86)	17.3	(1.38)	19.8	(1.74)	18.6	(1.97)	18.5	(2.07)	11.8	(1.93)	13.4	(1.56)	12.6	(1.74)	13.9	(2.19)	4.1	(0.92)	8.6	(1.54)

—Not available.

†Not applicable.

!Interpret data with caution. The coefficient of variation (CV) for this estimate is between 30 and 50 percent.

‡Reporting standards not met. Either there are too few cases for a reliable estimate or the coefficient of variation (CV) is 50 percent or greater.

[1] In 2005 and prior years, the period covered by the survey question was "during the last 6 months," but this was changed to "during this school year" beginning in 2007. Cognitive testing suggested that modifications to the reference period would not have a substantial impact on the survey responses.

[2] Race categories exclude persons of Hispanic ethnicity. Prior to 2003, separate data for Asian students, Pacific Islander students, and students of Two or more races were not collected.

[3] Excludes students with missing information about the school characteristic.

[4] Data for 2013 and prior years were based on school information provided by the respondent. Beginning in 2015, data were based on school information collected in the Common Core of Data and the Private School Universe Survey, which was appended to the School Crime Supplement data file; therefore, these data may not be entirely comparable with figures for earlier years.

NOTE: "At school" includes in the school building, on school property, on a school bus, and, from 2001 onward, going to and from school. "Hate-related" refers to derogatory terms used by others in reference to students' personal characteristics. Some data have been revised from previously published figures.

SOURCE: U.S. Department of Justice, Bureau of Justice Statistics, School Crime Supplement (SCS) to the National Crime Victimization Survey, 1999 through 2019. (This table was prepared October 2020.)

Table 230.35. Percentage of students ages 12-18 who reported being called hate-related words at school, by type of hate-related word and selected student and school characteristics: 2019

[Standard errors appear in parentheses]

Student or school characteristic	Total, any hate-related words[1]		Type of hate-related word (specific characteristic targeted)											
			Race		Ethnicity		Religion		Disability		Gender		Sexual orientation	
1		2		3		4		5		6		7		8
Total	**6.7**	**(0.40)**	**3.3**	**(0.29)**	**1.7**	**(0.21)**	**0.5**	**(0.12)**	**0.8**	**(0.13)**	**1.3**	**(0.19)**	**1.3**	**(0.19)**
Sex														
Male	6.0	(0.57)	3.1	(0.42)	1.5	(0.28)	0.4	(0.11)	1.0	(0.22)	0.2 !	(0.09)	0.9	(0.21)
Female	7.5	(0.56)	3.4	(0.40)	1.9	(0.29)	0.7	(0.19)	0.6	(0.16)	2.4	(0.35)	1.7	(0.29)
Race/ethnicity														
White	5.6	(0.46)	1.8	(0.27)	0.5	(0.13)	0.6	(0.18)	0.9	(0.16)	1.3	(0.24)	1.3	(0.28)
Black	8.6	(1.31)	5.3	(1.01)	2.3 !	(0.77)	0.3 !	(0.14)	‡	(†)	1.0 !	(0.42)	‡	(†)
Hispanic	6.5	(0.80)	3.6	(0.58)	3.1	(0.54)	‡	(†)	0.7 !	(0.24)	1.0	(0.30)	1.4	(0.33)
Asian/Pacific Islander	7.7	(1.49)	6.5	(1.46)	4.3	(1.27)	‡	(†)	‡	(†)	‡	(†)	‡	(†)
Asian	7.2	(1.62)	6.4	(1.49)	4.5	(1.33)	‡	(†)	‡	(†)	‡	(†)	‡	(†)
Pacific Islander	‡	(†)	‡	(†)	‡	(†)	‡	(†)	‡	(†)	‡	(†)	‡	(†)
American Indian/Alaska Native	‡	(†)	‡	(†)	‡	(†)	‡	(†)	‡	(†)	‡	(†)	‡	(†)
Two or more races	16.5	(2.76)	9.0	(2.42)	2.0 !	(0.96)	‡	(†)	‡	(†)	4.9 !	(2.21)	‡	(†)
Grade														
6th	7.7	(1.28)	3.2	(0.94)	2.2 !	(0.78)	‡	(†)	1.4 !	(0.56)	1.5 !	(0.64)	‡	(†)
7th	8.1	(1.09)	3.8	(0.77)	1.7	(0.47)	0.6 !	(0.26)	0.9 !	(0.34)	1.7 !	(0.57)	1.4	(0.38)
8th	8.6	(1.09)	3.7	(0.66)	1.7	(0.47)	‡	(†)	1.2 !	(0.43)	1.8	(0.52)	2.0 !	(0.65)
9th	6.7	(1.04)	3.2	(0.65)	1.9	(0.48)	‡	(†)	‡	(†)	1.1 !	(0.38)	1.5 !	(0.53)
10th	5.3	(0.85)	2.4	(0.60)	0.7 !	(0.25)	‡	(†)	0.6 !	(0.23)	1.6	(0.45)	1.6 !	(0.49)
11th	6.8	(1.01)	4.2	(0.77)	2.2 !	(0.68)	0.5 !	(0.26)	‡	(†)	0.7 !	(0.33)	1.1 !	(0.43)
12th	4.2	(0.73)	2.5	(0.69)	1.6 !	(0.53)	1.1 !	(0.44)	‡	(†)	‡	(†)	‡	(†)
School locale[2]														
City	7.9	(0.84)	4.2	(0.59)	2.3	(0.38)	0.6 !	(0.21)	0.6 !	(0.23)	1.1	(0.31)	2.1	(0.49)
Suburban	6.5	(0.64)	3.4	(0.45)	1.5	(0.33)	0.6 !	(0.22)	0.6	(0.18)	1.4	(0.29)	0.9	(0.23)
Town	5.8	(1.14)	2.7 !	(0.93)	1.9 !	(0.77)	0.4 !	(0.19)	‡	(†)	1.3 !	(0.64)	0.8 !	(0.34)
Rural	6.8	(0.80)	2.6	(0.50)	1.1 !	(0.33)	0.6 !	(0.26)	1.3	(0.35)	1.4	(0.38)	1.1	(0.33)
Control of school[2]														
Public	7.1	(0.45)	3.6	(0.33)	1.8	(0.23)	0.6	(0.12)	0.8	(0.15)	1.3	(0.20)	1.4	(0.21)
Private	2.5 !	(0.93)	‡	(†)	‡	(†)	‡	(†)	‡	(†)	‡	(†)	‡	(†)

†Not applicable.

!Interpret data with caution. The coefficient of variation (CV) for this estimate is between 30 and 50 percent.

‡Reporting standards not met. Either there are too few cases for a reliable estimate or the coefficient of variation (CV) is 50 percent or greater.

[1] Students who reported being called hate-related words were asked which specific characteristics these words were related to. If a student reported being called more than one type of hate-related word--e.g., a derogatory term related to race as well as a derogatory term related to sexual orientation--the student was counted only once in the total percentage of students who were called any hate-related words.

[2] Excludes students with missing information about the school characteristic.

NOTE: "At school" includes in the school building, on school property, on a school bus, and going to and from school. "Hate-related" refers to derogatory terms used by others in reference to students' personal characteristics. Race categories exclude persons of Hispanic ethnicity.

SOURCE: U.S. Department of Justice, Bureau of Justice Statistics, School Crime Supplement (SCS) to the National Crime Victimization Survey, 2019. (This table was prepared October 2020.)

Table 230.40. Percentage of students ages 12-18 who reported being bullied at school during the school year, by selected student and school characteristics: Selected years, 2005 through 2019

[Standard errors appear in parentheses]

Student or school characteristic	2005[1]		2007		2009		2011		2013		2015[2]		2017		2019[3]	
1	2		3		4		5		6		7		8		9	
Total	**28.5**	**(0.70)**	**31.7**	**(0.74)**	**28.0**	**(0.83)**	**27.8**	**(0.76)**	**21.5**	**(0.66)**	**20.8**	**(0.99)**	**20.2**	**(0.71)**	**22.2**	**(0.85)**
Sex																
Male	27.5	(0.90)	30.3	(0.96)	26.6	(1.04)	24.5	(0.91)	19.5	(0.81)	18.8	(1.31)	16.7	(0.87)	19.1	(1.04)
Female	29.7	(0.85)	33.2	(0.99)	29.5	(1.08)	31.4	(0.99)	23.7	(0.98)	22.8	(1.39)	23.8	(1.01)	25.5	(1.18)
Race/ethnicity																
White	30.3	(0.85)	34.1	(0.97)	29.3	(1.03)	31.5	(1.07)	23.7	(0.93)	21.6	(1.43)	22.8	(1.02)	24.6	(1.16)
Black	29.2	(2.23)	30.4	(2.18)	29.1	(2.29)	27.2	(1.97)	20.3	(1.81)	24.7	(3.29)	22.9	(1.98)	22.2	(2.48)
Hispanic	22.3	(1.29)	27.3	(1.53)	25.5	(1.71)	21.9	(1.07)	19.2	(1.30)	17.2	(1.58)	15.7	(1.12)	18.0	(1.32)
Asian/Pacific Islander	20.8	(2.61)	17.2	(2.47)	17.8	(2.79)	13.8	(2.48)	9.3	(1.67)	19.4	(4.45)	7.3	(1.54)	13.7	(2.67)
Asian	20.9	2.7	18.1	(2.60)	17.3	(3.01)	14.9	(2.70)	9.2	(1.67)	15.6	(4.02)	7.3	(1.56)	13.5	(2.71)
Pacific Islander	‡	(†)	‡	(†)	‡	(†)	‡	(†)	‡	(†)	‡	(†)	‡	(†)	‡	(†)
American Indian/Alaska Native	‡	(†)	29.8	(7.40)	‡	(†)	21.1 !	(6.72)	24.3 !	(9.87)	‡	(†)	27.2	(5.93)	‡	(†)
Two or more races	34.6	(4.44)	38.2	(3.95)	27.3	(5.56)	26.9	(4.30)	27.6	(4.50)	17.7	(3.96)	23.2	(3.03)	37.1	(5.96)
Grade																
6th	37.0	(2.06)	42.7	(2.23)	39.4	(2.60)	37.0	(2.17)	27.8	(2.31)	31.0	(3.53)	29.5	(2.79)	28.1	(2.68)
7th	35.1	(1.70)	35.6	(1.78)	33.1	(1.87)	30.3	(1.64)	26.4	(1.65)	25.1	(2.48)	24.4	(1.60)	28.0	(2.36)
8th	31.3	(1.60)	36.9	(1.84)	31.7	(1.85)	30.7	(1.68)	21.7	(1.42)	22.2	(2.41)	25.3	(1.69)	26.7	(2.14)
9th	28.3	(1.59)	30.6	(1.72)	28.0	(1.90)	26.5	(1.66)	23.0	(1.42)	19.0	(2.11)	19.3	(1.52)	18.9	(1.95)
10th	25.1	(1.42)	27.7	(1.44)	26.6	(1.71)	28.0	(1.56)	19.5	(1.48)	21.2	(2.13)	18.9	(1.67)	18.7	(1.72)
11th	23.5	(1.62)	28.5	(1.48)	21.1	(1.69)	23.8	(1.72)	20.0	(1.50)	15.8	(2.24)	14.7	(1.45)	21.7	(2.08)
12th	20.8	(1.83)	23.0	(1.60)	20.4	(1.63)	22.0	(1.34)	14.1	(1.51)	14.9	(2.18)	12.2	(1.34)	15.8	(1.90)
School locale[4]																
City	---	(†)	---	(†)	---	(†)	---	(†)	---	(†)	21.3	(1.73)	19.9	(1.35)	22.4	(1.80)
Suburban	---	(†)	---	(†)	---	(†)	---	(†)	---	(†)	21.3	(1.55)	18.1	(0.90)	20.5	(1.18)
Town	---	(†)	---	(†)	---	(†)	---	(†)	---	(†)	20.3	(3.00)	26.9	(1.75)	21.7	(2.37)
Rural	---	(†)	---	(†)	---	(†)	---	(†)	---	(†)	20.0	(2.53)	23.8	(1.56)	27.7	(1.89)
Control of school[4,5]																
Public	29.0	(0.74)	32.0	(0.76)	28.8	(0.88)	28.4	(0.82)	21.5	(0.67)	21.3	(1.05)	21.1	(0.76)	22.7	(0.90)
Private	23.3	(2.16)	29.1	(2.10)	18.9	(2.16)	21.5	(1.91)	22.4	(2.71)	15.3	(3.43)	15.0	(2.47)	21.7	(3.86)

---Not available.

†Not applicable.

!Interpret data with caution. The coefficient of variation (CV) for this estimate is between 30 and 50 percent.

‡Reporting standards not met. Either there are too few cases for a reliable estimate or the coefficient of variation (CV) is 50 percent or greater.

[1] In 2005 and prior years, the period covered by the survey question was "during the last 6 months," but this was changed to "during this school year" beginning in 2007. Cognitive testing suggested that modifications to the reference period would not have a substantial impact on the survey responses.

[2] The 2015 survey included a split sample design to compare two versions of an updated questionnaire on bullying that would provide data on repetition and power imbalance aligned with the Centers for Disease Control and Prevention's uniform definition of bullying. Half the sample received version 1, and the other half received version 2. Estimates in this table are based on the 50 percent of the sample who received version 1 of the questionnaire. For more information, see Split-Half Administration of the 2015 School Crime Supplement to the National Crime Victimization Survey Methodology Report (NCES 2017-004).

[3] The 2019 survey included a split sample design to compare two versions of an updated questionnaire on bullying. Approximately 60 percent of the sample received version 1, which was consistent with prior years; the remaining 40 percent received version 2, which included changes such as removing the word "bullying." Estimates in this table are based on the 60 percent of the sample who received version 1 of the questionnaire. For more information, see Methodology Report: Split-Half Administration of the 2019 School Crime Supplement to the National Crime Victimization Survey (NCES 2021-016).

[4] Excludes students with missing information about the school characteristic.

[5] Data for 2013 and prior years were based on school information provided by the respondent. Beginning in 2015, data were based on school information collected in the Common Core of Data and the Private School Universe Survey, which was appended to the School Crime Supplement data file; therefore, these data may not be entirely comparable with figures for earlier years.

NOTE: "At school" includes in the school building, on school property, on a school bus, and going to and from school. Race categories exclude persons of Hispanic ethnicity. Some data have been revised from previously published figures.

SOURCE: U.S. Department of Justice, Bureau of Justice Statistics, School Crime Supplement (SCS) to the National Crime Victimization Survey, selected years, 2005 through 2019. (This table was prepared December 2020.)

Table 230.50. Percentage of students ages 12-18 who reported being bullied at school during the school year and, among bullied students, percentage who reported being bullied in various locations, by selected student and school characteristics: 2019

[Standard errors appear in parentheses]

Student or school characteristic	Total bullied at school	Among students who were bullied, percent by location[1]							
		Inside classroom	In hallway or stairwell	In bathroom or locker room	In cafeteria	Somewhere else in school building	Outside on school grounds	On the way to or from school[2]	Online or by text
1	2	3	4	5	6	7	8	9	10
Total	**22.2 (0.85)**	**46.7 (2.25)**	**38.9 (2.04)**	**10.9 (1.28)**	**25.7 (1.88)**	**3.0 (0.69)**	**20.2 (1.94)**	**9.9 (1.17)**	**15.8 (1.59)**
Sex									
Male	19.1 (1.04)	47.5 (3.28)	33.6 (3.01)	12.5 (1.88)	25.9 (2.55)	2.4 ! (0.88)	21.3 (2.68)	9.8 (1.63)	7.6 (1.49)
Female	25.5 (1.18)	46.1 (2.80)	43.1 (2.74)	9.7 (1.66)	25.6 (2.68)	3.4 ! (1.11)	19.2 (2.37)	10.0 (1.62)	22.4 (2.37)
Race/ethnicity									
White	24.6 (1.16)	45.7 (2.83)	41.3 (2.68)	12.1 (1.71)	28.5 (2.54)	3.1 (0.91)	20.8 (2.44)	9.5 (1.43)	17.2 (2.27)
Black	22.2 (2.48)	50.4 (6.33)	34.8 (6.02)	5.1 ! (2.45)	16.8 (4.29)	‡ (†)	18.0 (4.89)	10.2 (3.06)	9.6 ! (3.84)
Hispanic	18.0 (1.32)	47.0 (4.46)	37.6 (4.12)	11.7 (3.36)	24.3 (3.74)	‡ (†)	18.5 (3.51)	11.1 (2.85)	16.6 (3.82)
Asian/Pacific Islander	13.7 (2.67)	‡ (†)	‡ (†)	‡ (†)	‡ (†)	‡ (†)	‡ (†)	‡ (†)	‡ (†)
Asian	13.5 (2.71)	‡ (†)	‡ (†)	‡ (†)	‡ (†)	‡ (†)	‡ (†)	‡ (†)	‡ (†)
Pacific Islander	‡ (†)	‡ (†)	‡ (†)	‡ (†)	‡ (†)	‡ (†)	‡ (†)	‡ (†)	‡ (†)
American Indian/Alaska Native	‡ (†)	‡ (†)	‡ (†)	‡ (†)	‡ (†)	‡ (†)	‡ (†)	‡ (†)	‡ (†)
Two or more races	37.1 (5.96)	41.7 (10.73)	37.3 (7.31)	‡ (†)	30.0 (8.69)	‡ (†)	29.6 ! (9.80)	‡ (†)	12.1 ! (5.37)
Grade									
6th	28.1 (2.68)	56.6 (6.96)	27.5 (5.95)	6.3 ! (2.49)	17.1 (4.50)	‡ (†)	17.8 (4.44)	12.2 ! (3.95)	‡ (†)
7th	28.0 (2.36)	42.9 (5.39)	47.1 (5.44)	11.4 (2.97)	30.9 (4.09)	‡ (†)	28.9 (4.18)	13.9 (2.83)	10.0 (2.59)
8th	26.7 (2.14)	45.3 (3.93)	37.4 (4.63)	9.4 (2.54)	26.7 (3.73)	3.4 ! (1.72)	22.2 (3.64)	8.5 (2.26)	22.7 (3.69)
9th	18.9 (1.95)	38.8 (5.12)	42.4 (5.34)	9.9 ! (2.97)	28.1 (5.01)	3.5 ! (1.75)	15.8 (4.00)	8.1 ! (2.59)	9.7 ! (3.20)
10th	18.7 (1.72)	49.5 (5.65)	37.2 (4.84)	17.6 (3.82)	25.0 (5.02)	‡ (†)	13.6 (3.94)	6.9 ! (2.23)	20.4 (5.13)
11th	21.7 (2.08)	47.6 (5.39)	36.8 (5.20)	10.5 (2.96)	22.3 (4.20)	‡ (†)	16.7 (4.99)	5.1 ! (2.13)	21.6 (3.91)
12th	15.8 (1.90)	52.0 (7.07)	39.2 (6.75)	11.5 ! (4.77)	26.1 (6.75)	‡ (†)	22.4 (6.45)	16.0 ! (4.94)	21.5 (5.32)
School locale[3]									
City	22.4 (1.80)	47.5 (3.56)	36.8 (3.72)	7.5 (1.70)	22.1 (3.11)	2.7 ! (1.34)	20.3 (2.90)	9.9 (2.45)	12.4 (2.44)
Suburban	20.5 (1.18)	44.5 (3.38)	39.1 (3.15)	10.4 (2.31)	26.0 (3.23)	2.7 ! (1.07)	18.6 (2.90)	8.6 (1.66)	18.0 (2.94)
Town	21.7 (2.37)	51.6 (7.42)	43.9 (6.47)	14.7 ! (5.21)	21.9 (5.43)	‡ (†)	26.3 (6.07)	11.3 ! (4.38)	18.2 (5.28)
Rural	27.7 (1.89)	46.5 (4.54)	37.4 (4.27)	12.5 (2.31)	30.0 (3.75)	3.1 ! (1.27)	19.4 (3.60)	10.7 (2.46)	15.9 (2.84)
Control of school[3]									
Public	22.7 (0.90)	47.3 (2.35)	39.1 (2.12)	10.9 (1.37)	25.3 (2.04)	3.0 (0.73)	20.1 (2.01)	9.9 (1.23)	15.2 (1.69)
Private	21.7 (3.86)	35.3 (8.56)	28.3 (7.05)	‡ (†)	30.7 (6.44)	‡ (†)	18.3 ! (6.20)	8.7 ! (4.05)	27.3 (7.98)

†Not applicable.

!Interpret data with caution. The coefficient of variation (CV) for this estimate is between 30 and 50 percent.

‡Reporting standards not met. Either there are too few cases for a reliable estimate or the coefficient of variation (CV) is 50 percent or greater.

1 Includes only students who indicated the location of bullying. Excludes students who indicated that they were bullied but did not answer the question about where the bullying occurred.

2 Examples provided to the respondent include on a school bus or at a bus stop.

3 Excludes students with missing information about the school characteristic.

NOTE: The 2019 survey included a split sample design to compare two versions of an updated questionnaire on bullying. Approximately 60 percent of the sample received version 1, which was consistent with prior years; the remaining 40 percent received version 2, which included changes such as removing the word "bullying." Estimates in this table are based on the 60 percent of the sample who received version 1 of the questionnaire. For more information, see Methodology Report: Split-Half Administration of the 2019 School Crime Supplement to the National Crime Victimization Survey (NCES 2021-016). "At school" includes in the school building, on school property, on a school bus, and going to and from school. Students who reported being bullied at school were also asked whether the bullying occurred "online or by text." Location totals may sum to more than 100 percent because students could have been bullied in more than one location. Race categories exclude persons of Hispanic ethnicity.

SOURCE: U.S. Department of Justice, Bureau of Justice Statistics, School Crime Supplement (SCS) to the National Crime Victimization Survey, 2019. (This table was prepared December 2020.)

Table 230.52. Among students ages 12-18 who reported being bullied at school during the school year, percentage reporting that bullying had varying degrees of negative effect on various aspects of their life, by aspect of life affected and selected student and school characteristics: 2017

[Standard errors appear in parentheses]

Degree of negative effect and student or school characteristic	School work		Relationships with friends or family		Feeling about oneself		Physical health	
1	2		3		4		5	
Percentage distribution of bullied students, by degree of negative effect reported								
Total	**100.0**	**(†)**	**100.0**	**(†)**	**100.0**	**(†)**	**100.0**	**(†)**
Not at all	59.2	(1.62)	67.7	(1.62)	60.5	(1.66)	77.8	(1.32)
Not very much	21.4	(1.36)	13.6	(1.13)	12.7	(1.15)	8.4	(0.79)
Somewhat	14.9	(1.30)	14.3	(1.38)	17.2	(1.16)	10.6	(1.11)
A lot	4.5	(0.67)	4.3	(0.72)	9.5	(1.03)	3.1	(0.57)
Percent of bullied students reporting a somewhat negative effect or a lot of negative effect								
Total	**19.4**	**(1.41)**	**18.6**	**(1.52)**	**26.8**	**(1.55)**	**13.7**	**(1.18)**
Sex								
Male	18.2	(1.90)	12.7	(1.61)	21.0	(2.17)	9.7	(1.65)
Female	20.3	(1.74)	22.9	(2.26)	30.9	(1.97)	16.7	(1.71)
Race/ethnicity								
White	18.1	(1.63)	20.3	(1.86)	29.2	(2.12)	15.1	(1.49)
Black	20.3	(4.53)	14.8	(3.32)	23.9	(4.15)	14.5	(3.43)
Hispanic	21.5	(2.92)	15.2	(2.89)	20.7	(2.44)	8.6	(1.84)
Asian/Pacific Islander	26.2 !	(8.99)	34.9	(10.15)	40.9	(10.42)	23.3 !	(9.03)
Asian	‡	(†)	‡	(†)	‡	(†)	‡	(†)
Pacific Islander	‡	(†)	‡	(†)	‡	(†)	‡	(†)
American Indian/Alaska Native	‡	(†)	‡	(†)	‡	(†)	‡	(†)
Two or more races	13.5 !	(5.64)	13.8 !	(5.39)	20.7	(5.68)	10.3 !	(4.63)
Grade								
6th	25.4	(4.73)	19.5	(3.73)	23.8	(4.40)	21.3	(4.82)
7th	20.1	(3.05)	16.8	(3.56)	24.4	(3.11)	13.9	(3.23)
8th	14.7	(2.56)	17.6	(3.13)	30.1	(3.37)	11.7	(2.02)
9th	20.0	(3.54)	18.2	(3.57)	27.6	(4.30)	14.7	(3.35)
10th	18.8	(3.55)	20.8	(3.75)	22.2	(3.21)	17.0	(3.33)
11th	22.9	(4.41)	19.3	(4.12)	35.2	(5.19)	7.6 !	(2.32)
12th	16.5	(3.94)	20.0	(4.83)	23.6	(4.70)	7.6 !	(2.74)
Urbanicity[1]								
Urban	24.9	(3.03)	19.7	(2.72)	26.9	(2.73)	15.6	(2.48)
Suburban	18.0	(1.74)	17.2	(1.77)	26.7	(1.99)	12.7	(1.39)
Rural	15.5	(3.07)	21.4	(3.97)	26.8	(3.94)	13.8	(3.39)
Control of school								
Public	19.4	(1.45)	19.2	(1.59)	26.2	(1.53)	13.5	(1.18)
Private	21.1	(6.24)	10.3 !	(4.09)	36.1	(7.84)	16.4 !	(5.54)

†Not applicable.

!Interpret data with caution. The coefficient of variation (CV) for this estimate is between 30 and 50 percent.

‡Reporting standards not met. Either there are too few cases for a reliable estimate or the coefficient of variation (CV) is 50 percent or greater.

[1] Refers to the Standard Metropolitan Statistical Area (MSA) status of the respondent's household as defined by the U.S. Census Bureau. Categories include "central city of an MSA (Urban)," "in MSA but not in central city (Suburban)," and "not MSA (Rural)."

NOTE: "At school" includes in the school building, on school property, on a school bus, and going to and from school. Race categories exclude persons of Hispanic ethnicity. Detail may not sum to totals because of rounding.

SOURCE: U.S. Department of Justice, Bureau of Justice Statistics, School Crime Supplement (SCS) to the National Crime Victimization Survey, 2017. (This table was prepared October 2018.)

Table 230.53. Among students ages 12-18 who reported being bullied at school during the school year, percentage reporting that bullying was related to specific characteristics, by type of characteristic related to bullying and other selected student and school characteristics: 2017

[Standard errors appear in parentheses]

Student or school characteristic	Percentage distribution of bullied students, by whether bullying was related to specific characteristics[1]						Percent of bullied students reporting that bullying was related to characteristic													
	Total		No, not related to any listed characteristic		Yes, related to at least one listed characteristic		Race		Ethnicity		Religion		Disability		Gender		Sexual orientation		Physical appearance	
1	2		3		4		5		6		7		8		9		10		11	
Total	**100.0**	**(†)**	**57.5**	**1.8**	**42.5**	**1.8**	**9.5**	**(1.05)**	**7.3**	**(0.83)**	**4.5**	**(0.79)**	**7.3**	**(0.90)**	**7.5**	**(0.86)**	**3.6**	**(0.60)**	**29.7**	**(1.41)**
Sex																				
Male	100.0	(†)	59.9	(2.79)	40.1	(2.79)	11.1	(1.73)	8.8	(1.43)	6.0	(1.23)	7.4	(1.17)	2.6 !	(0.85)	2.7	(0.78)	26.2	(2.01)
Female	100.0	(†)	55.8	(2.17)	44.2	(2.17)	8.3	(1.25)	6.2	(1.03)	3.4	(0.74)	7.2	(1.29)	11.1	(1.37)	4.3	(0.91)	32.1	(2.08)
Race/ethnicity																				
White	100.0	(†)	60.2	(2.17)	39.8	(2.17)	5.5	(0.94)	3.2	(0.78)	4.4	(1.01)	8.0	(1.22)	8.2	(1.23)	4.1	(0.83)	28.9	(1.94)
Black	100.0	(†)	55.1	(5.64)	44.9	(5.64)	11.6	(3.31)	6.3 !	(2.36)	‡	(†)	10.2	(3.01)	7.5 !	(2.63)	3.8 !	(1.74)	32.3	(4.70)
Hispanic	100.0	(†)	52.3	(3.34)	47.7	(3.34)	17.1	(2.83)	15.9	(2.51)	4.3 !	(1.41)	3.0 !	(1.16)	6.6 !	(1.97)	‡	(†)	30.8	(2.99)
Asian/Pacific Islander	100.0	(†)	37.6	(9.47)	62.4	(9.47)	‡	(†)	39.8	(10.62)	24.0 !	(9.22)	‡	(†)	‡	(†)	‡	(†)	‡	(†)
Asian	‡	(†)	‡	(†)	‡	(†)	‡	(†)	‡	(†)	‡	(†)	‡	(†)	‡	(†)	‡	(†)	‡	(†)
Pacific Islander	‡	(†)	‡	(†)	‡	(†)	‡	(†)	‡	(†)	‡	(†)	‡	(†)	‡	(†)	‡	(†)	‡	(†)
American Indian/Alaska Native	‡	(†)	‡	(†)	‡	(†)	‡	(†)	‡	(†)	‡	(†)	‡	(†)	‡	(†)	‡	(†)	‡	(†)
Two or more races	100.0	(†)	59.6	(6.93)	40.4	(6.93)	20.7 !	(6.98)	16.6	(4.86)	‡	(†)	9.9 !	(4.75)	‡	(†)	‡	(†)	33.1	(6.06)
Grade																				
6th	100.0	(†)	55.2	(5.44)	44.8	(5.44)	8.6 !	(2.91)	5.4 !	(2.30)	2.2 !	(1.00)	10.4	(2.98)	7.3 !	(2.83)	‡	(†)	32.5	(5.25)
7th	100.0	(†)	60.3	(3.17)	39.7	(3.17)	11.4	(2.41)	7.7	(1.95)	6.3 !	(2.32)	7.4	(1.77)	5.5 !	(1.65)	2.9 !	(1.24)	28.3	(2.80)
8th	100.0	(†)	61.9	(3.28)	38.1	(3.28)	7.8	(1.93)	4.7 !	(1.45)	6.4	(1.80)	5.2	(1.34)	5.3	(1.59)	2.3 !	(0.91)	22.7	(2.84)
9th	100.0	(†)	53.3	(4.58)	46.7	(4.58)	11.9	(2.72)	8.7	(2.55)	4.2 !	(1.95)	7.2 !	(2.51)	9.1	(2.64)	4.4 !	(1.77)	30.7	(4.01)
10th	100.0	(†)	52.9	(4.16)	47.1	(4.16)	7.4	(2.00)	9.8	(2.38)	4.6 !	(1.71)	6.3	(1.73)	11.5	(2.87)	4.9 !	(1.91)	34.2	(4.11)
11th	100.0	(†)	53.9	(5.11)	46.1	(5.11)	9.8 !	(3.13)	6.0 !	(1.89)	‡	(†)	10.9 !	(3.33)	7.6 !	(3.18)	5.7 !	(2.38)	35.6	(4.83)
12th	100.0	(†)	63.8	(5.64)	36.2	(5.64)	10.0 !	(3.16)	10.3 !	(3.44)	‡	(†)	5.0 !	(1.88)	8.1 !	(2.87)	‡	(†)	28.3	(5.61)
Urbanicity[2]																				
Urban	100.0	(†)	51.6	(3.61)	48.4	(3.61)	11.3	(1.76)	11.3	(1.93)	6.1	(1.70)	7.6	(1.85)	8.8	(1.99)	5.2	(1.44)	33.7	(3.12)
Suburban	100.0	(†)	57.2	(2.35)	42.8	(2.35)	9.5	(1.47)	7.2	(1.27)	4.8	(1.05)	7.9	(1.23)	7.1	(1.18)	2.8	(0.65)	29.9	(1.85)
Rural	100.0	(†)	67.2	(3.43)	32.8	(3.43)	7.1 !	(2.32)	1.5 !	(0.70)	1.5 !	(0.66)	5.1 !	(1.94)	6.7	(1.91)	3.8 !	(1.57)	22.9	(2.93)
Control of school																				
Public	100.0	(†)	58.0	(1.75)	42.0	(1.75)	9.8	(1.11)	7.5	(0.88)	4.7	(0.82)	7.4	(0.92)	7.9	(0.91)	3.8	(0.63)	28.9	(1.42)
Private	100.0	(†)	49.8	(6.89)	50.2	(6.89)	‡	(†)	‡	(†)	‡	(†)	‡	(†)	‡	(†)	‡	(†)	41.9	(6.91)

†Not applicable.

!Interpret data with caution. The coefficient of variation (CV) for this estimate is between 30 and 50 percent.

‡Reporting standards not met. Either there are too few cases for a reliable estimate or the coefficient of variation (CV) is 50 percent or greater.

[1] Students who reported being bullied were asked whether the bullying was related to specific characteristics; for each characteristic, students could select "Yes" or "No." Students could select "Yes" for multiple characteristics. The seven characteristics that appeared on the questionnaire are shown in columns 5-11. Includes only students who answered the question about characteristics related to bullying; excludes students who reported being bullied but did not answer this question.

[2] Refers to the Standard Metropolitan Statistical Area (MSA) status of the respondent's household as defined by the U.S. Census Bureau. Categories include "central city of an MSA (Urban)," "in MSA but not in central city (Suburban)," and "not MSA (Rural)."

NOTE: "At school" includes in the school building, on school property, on a school bus, and going to and from school. Race categories exclude persons of Hispanic ethnicity. Detail may not sum to totals because of rounding.

SOURCE: U.S. Department of Justice, Bureau of Justice Statistics, School Crime Supplement (SCS) to the National Crime Victimization Survey, 2017. (This table was prepared October 2018.)

Table 230.55. Percentage of students in grades 9–12 who reported having been electronically bullied during the previous 12 months, by selected student characteristics: Selected years, 2011 through 2019

[Standard errors appear in parentheses]

Student characteristic	2011		2013		2015		2017		2019	
1	2		3		4		5		6	
Total	**16.2**	**(0.45)**	**14.8**	**(0.54)**	**15.5**	**(0.53)**	**14.9**	**(0.61)**	**15.7**	**(0.56)**
Sex										
Male	10.8	(0.60)	8.5	(0.45)	9.7	(0.68)	9.9	(0.37)	10.9	(0.69)
Female	22.1	(0.60)	21.0	(0.91)	21.7	(0.82)	19.7	(1.20)	20.4	(0.76)
Race/ethnicity										
White	18.6	(0.73)	16.9	(0.84)	18.4	(0.78)	17.3	(0.88)	18.6	(0.76)
Black	8.9	(0.68)	8.7	(0.78)	8.6	(0.97)	10.9	(1.01)	8.6	(0.65)
Hispanic	13.6	(0.80)	12.8	(0.98)	12.4	(0.97)	12.3	(0.40)	12.7	(0.84)
Asian	14.4	(2.45)	12.9	(1.70)	13.9	(2.42)	10.0	(1.49)	12.1	(1.16)
Pacific Islander	19.6	(5.25)	15.7	(3.46)	11.8 !	(4.27)	15.0	(2.75)	19.0 !	(6.58)
American Indian/Alaska Native	16.2	(1.56)	18.0	(4.38)	18.7	(3.67)	13.2	(3.79)	21.3 !	(6.78)
Two or more races	21.0	(2.16)	18.9	(1.94)	20.4	(2.43)	16.0	(2.21)	19.2	(2.00)
Sexual identity[1]										
Heterosexual	---	(†)	---	(†)	14.2	(0.56)	13.3	(0.49)	14.1	(0.60)
Gay, lesbian, or bisexual	---	(†)	---	(†)	28.0	(2.06)	27.1	(2.04)	26.6	(1.67)
Not sure	---	(†)	---	(†)	22.5	(2.36)	22.0	(2.73)	19.4	(2.09)
Grade										
9th	15.5	(0.78)	16.1	(1.00)	16.5	(1.00)	16.7	(0.67)	16.5	(0.85)
10th	18.1	(0.90)	14.5	(1.00)	16.6	(0.96)	14.8	(0.75)	16.0	(0.86)
11th	16.0	(1.19)	14.9	(0.98)	14.7	(1.17)	14.2	(1.20)	14.4	(0.97)
12th	15.0	(0.89)	13.5	(0.67)	14.3	(0.85)	13.5	(1.10)	15.4	(0.98)

---Not available.

†Not applicable.

!Interpret data with caution. The coefficient of variation (CV) for this estimate is between 30 and 50 percent.

[1] Students were asked which of the following--"heterosexual (straight)," "gay or lesbian," "bisexual," or "not sure"--best described them.

NOTE: Electronic bullying includes "being bullied through e-mail, chat rooms, instant messaging, websites, or texting" for 2011 through 2015, and "being bullied through texting, Instagram, Facebook, or other social media" for 2017 and 2019. Race categories exclude persons of Hispanic ethnicity.

SOURCE: Centers for Disease Control and Prevention, Division of Adolescent and School Health, Youth Risk Behavior Surveillance System (YRBSS), 2011 through 2019. (This table was prepared September 2020.)

Table 230.60. Among students ages 12-18 who reported being bullied at school during the school year, percentage reporting various frequencies of bullying and the notification of an adult at school, by selected student and school characteristics: 2019

[Standard errors appear in parentheses]

Student or school characteristic	Frequency of bullying: 1 day in the school year: Total[2]		Once in the day		Two to ten times in the day		2 days in the school year		3 to 10 days in the school year		More than 10 days in the school year		Adult at school was notified[1]	
1	2		3		4		5		6		7		8	
Total	**32.3**	**(2.28)**	**22.5**	**(1.96)**	**6.3**	**(1.05)**	**19.9**	**(1.61)**	**28.7**	**(2.05)**	**19.0**	**(1.62)**	**45.7**	**(1.86)**
Sex														
Male	34.4	(3.08)	23.2	(2.51)	6.0	(1.36)	18.7	(2.48)	29.7	(2.98)	17.2	(2.29)	44.9	(3.56)
Female	30.6	(2.72)	21.9	(2.35)	6.6	(1.49)	20.9	(2.17)	28.0	(2.72)	20.5	(2.22)	46.3	(2.45)
Race/ethnicity														
White	28.9	(2.66)	21.7	(2.38)	4.4	(1.08)	18.2	(2.13)	32.9	(2.59)	20.0	(2.08)	46.7	(2.69)
Black	40.4	(5.89)	25.6	(5.51)	10.4 !	(4.07)	27.5	(5.23)	19.0	(4.96)	13.1 !	(4.37)	61.2	(6.39)
Hispanic	34.9	(4.05)	20.9	(3.34)	7.8 !	(2.40)	18.8	(3.06)	25.7	(4.42)	20.6	(3.78)	34.7	(3.81)
Asian/Pacific Islander	‡	(†)	‡	(†)	‡	(†)	‡	(†)	‡	(†)	‡	(†)	‡	(†)
Asian	‡	(†)	‡	(†)	‡	(†)	‡	(†)	‡	(†)	‡	(†)	‡	(†)
Pacific Islander	‡	(†)	‡	(†)	‡	(†)	‡	(†)	‡	(†)	‡	(†)	‡	(†)
American Indian/Alaska Native	‡	(†)	‡	(†)	‡	(†)	‡	(†)	‡	(†)	‡	(†)	‡	(†)
Two or more races	46.2	(7.97)	40.3	(9.30)	‡	(†)	13.9 !	(5.99)	21.3 !	(7.52)	18.6 !	(7.09)	47.2	(11.37)
Grade														
6th	32.5	(6.33)	29.2	(6.13)	‡	(†)	21.1	(5.03)	39.2	(6.61)	7.2 !	(2.66)	53.4	(6.50)
7th	28.6	(4.59)	18.2	(3.74)	7.1 !	(2.43)	23.9	(4.21)	28.1	(4.48)	19.5	(3.59)	57.3	(4.98)
8th	33.3	(4.67)	22.0	(4.06)	7.8 !	(2.79)	16.8	(3.80)	21.8	(3.59)	28.1	(3.71)	49.1	(4.25)
9th	40.6	(5.76)	28.4	(5.16)	9.8 !	(3.23)	18.0	(4.75)	24.0	(4.75)	17.4	(4.43)	38.6	(5.49)
10th	30.7	(5.44)	23.6	(4.75)	‡	(†)	18.2	(4.53)	33.4	(5.61)	17.6	(4.37)	40.4	(4.91)
11th	29.3	(5.15)	18.8	(4.53)	7.5 !	(2.69)	21.7	(4.31)	32.3	(5.72)	16.7	(3.88)	44.0	(6.59)
12th	31.7	(5.57)	19.6	(4.19)	7.4 !	(3.42)	20.1	(5.42)	27.8	(6.44)	20.4	(5.34)	27.9	(5.18)
School locale[3]														
City	32.8	(4.02)	21.4	(2.89)	6.8 !	(2.13)	19.5	(3.21)	27.1	(3.38)	20.6	(2.96)	47.4	(3.63)
Suburban	32.9	(3.66)	22.7	(3.05)	6.4	(1.68)	21.8	(2.83)	29.4	(2.96)	15.9	(2.51)	41.8	(3.38)
Town	24.7	(5.82)	16.4	(4.84)	7.0 !	(3.33)	18.5 !	(6.21)	34.5	(7.62)	22.2	(5.17)	49.0	(6.46)
Rural	34.4	(3.65)	26.8	(3.64)	5.5 !	(1.82)	16.4	(3.33)	29.1	(3.70)	20.1	(3.44)	46.4	(3.85)
Control of school[3]														
Public	32.0	(2.31)	22.6	(2.02)	6.1	(1.04)	18.9	(1.72)	30.1	(2.15)	19.0	(1.67)	45.1	(1.95)
Private	40.0	(8.69)	26.9	(7.84)	‡	(†)	27.8 !	(8.85)	14.3 !	(5.92)	17.8 !	(5.65)	47.2	(10.41)
Total indicating adult at school notified,[1] by frequency of bullying	**35.3**	**(3.74)**	**34.4**	**(4.37)**	**38.3**	**(7.48)**	**42.6**	**(4.69)**	**50.6**	**(3.75)**	**60.1**	**(4.55)**	**†**	**(†)**
Males indicating adult notified	29.4	(4.98)	32.1	(6.16)	‡	(†)	49.8	(7.78)	52.2	(5.91)	59.7	(7.67)	†	(†)
Females indicating adult notified	40.7	(5.21)	36.4	(6.19)	‡	(†)	37.4	(6.20)	49.3	(4.73)	60.4	(5.86)	†	(†)

†Not applicable.

!Interpret data with caution. The coefficient of variation (CV) for this estimate is between 30 and 50 percent.

‡Reporting standards not met. Either there are too few cases for a reliable estimate or the coefficient of variation (CV) is 50 percent or greater.

[1] Teacher or other adult at school notified.

[2] Includes students who reported being bullied 1 day in the school year but did not report how many times in the day the bullying occurred. No students reported being bullied more than ten times in the day.

[3] Excludes students with missing information about the school characteristic.

NOTE: The 2019 survey included a split sample design to compare two versions of an updated questionnaire on bullying. Approximately 60 percent of the sample received version 1, which was consistent with prior years; the remaining 40 percent received version 2, which included changes such as removing the word "bullying." Estimates in this table are based on the 60 percent of the sample who received version 1 of the questionnaire. For more information, see Methodology Report: Split-Half Administration of the 2019 School Crime Supplement to the National Crime Victimization Survey (NCES 2021-016). "At school" includes in the school building, on school property, on a school bus, and going to and from school. Race categories exclude persons of Hispanic ethnicity. Detail may not sum to totals because of rounding.

SOURCE: U.S. Department of Justice, Bureau of Justice Statistics, School Crime Supplement (SCS) to the National Crime Victimization Survey, 2019. (This table was prepared December 2020.)

Table 230.62. Percentage of public school students in grades 9-12 who reported having been bullied on school property or electronically bullied during the previous 12 months, by state or jurisdiction: Selected years, 2009 through 2017

[Standard errors appear in parentheses]

State or jurisdiction	Bullied on school property[1]					Electronically bullied[2]				
	2009	2011	2013	2015	2017	2009	2011	2013	2015	2017
1	2	3	4	5	6	7	8	9	10	11
United States[3]	**19.9 (0.58)**	**20.1 (0.68)**	**19.6 (0.55)**	**20.2 (0.70)**	**19.0 (0.71)**	**— (†)**	**16.2 (0.45)**	**14.8 (0.54)**	**15.5 (0.53)**	**14.9 (0.61)**
Alabama	19.3 (1.45)	14.1 (1.22)	20.8 (1.28)	19.0 (1.13)	— (†)	— (†)	12.3 (1.64)	13.5 (0.95)	13.5 (0.91)	— (†)
Alaska	20.7 (1.29)	23.0 (1.32)	20.7 (1.35)	22.8 (1.27)	23.3 (1.44)	— (†)	15.3 (1.04)	14.7 (1.10)	17.7 (1.05)	19.8 (1.38)
Arizona	— (†)	— (†)	— (†)	— (†)	19.2 (1.40)	— (†)	— (†)	— (†)	— (†)	15.2 (1.25)
Arkansas	— (†)	21.9 (1.74)	25.0 (1.51)	22.9 (1.38)	26.7 (1.57)	— (†)	16.7 (1.48)	17.6 (1.05)	18.2 (1.29)	19.7 (1.02)
California	— (†)	— (†)	— (†)	18.5 (1.61)	17.9 (1.39)	— (†)	— (†)	— (†)	13.5 (1.87)	13.6 (0.96)
Colorado	18.8 (1.60)	19.3 (1.33)	— (†)	— (†)	18.0 (1.02)	— (†)	14.4 (1.09)	— (†)	— (†)	14.5 (0.89)
Connecticut	— (†)	21.6 (1.09)	21.9 (0.96)	18.6 (0.86)	18.9 (1.08)	— (†)	16.3 (0.81)	17.5 (1.23)	13.9 (0.78)	15.8 (1.02)
Delaware	15.9 (1.11)	16.5 (1.03)	18.5 (0.96)	16.4 (0.99)	14.1 (0.80)	— (†)	— (†)	13.4 (0.78)	11.7 (0.69)	10.1 (0.82)
District of Columbia	— (†)	— (†)	10.9 (0.35)	12.1 (0.34)	11.5 (0.40)	— (†)	— (†)	7.9 (0.29)	7.9 (0.27)	8.9 (0.34)
Florida	13.4 (0.51)	14.0 (0.54)	15.7 (0.50)	15.0 (0.49)	14.3 (0.53)	— (†)	12.4 (0.53)	12.3 (0.54)	11.6 (0.35)	11.6 (0.48)
Georgia	— (†)	19.1 (1.66)	19.5 (1.36)	— (†)	— (†)	— (†)	13.6 (1.09)	13.9 (0.93)	— (†)	— (†)
Hawaii	— (†)	20.3 (1.29)	18.7 (1.00)	18.6 (1.00)	18.4 (0.69)	— (†)	14.9 (0.80)	15.6 (0.98)	14.7 (0.73)	14.6 (0.48)
Idaho	22.3 (1.03)	22.8 (1.76)	25.4 (1.12)	26.0 (1.05)	25.8 (1.19)	— (†)	17.0 (1.18)	18.8 (1.18)	21.1 (1.18)	20.3 (1.16)
Illinois	19.6 (1.46)	19.3 (1.31)	22.2 (1.00)	19.6 (1.06)	21.4 (1.29)	— (†)	16.0 (1.38)	16.9 (0.77)	15.3 (1.05)	17.3 (1.04)
Indiana	22.8 (1.69)	25.0 (1.38)	— (†)	18.7 (1.31)	— (†)	— (†)	18.7 (1.15)	— (†)	15.7 (0.91)	— (†)
Iowa	— (†)	22.5 (1.47)	— (†)	— (†)	23.3 (1.25)	— (†)	16.8 (0.97)	— (†)	— (†)	18.0 (1.61)
Kansas	18.5 (1.21)	20.5 (1.31)	22.1 (1.57)	— (†)	19.8 (1.25)	— (†)	15.5 (0.88)	16.9 (0.97)	— (†)	15.8 (0.77)
Kentucky	20.8 (1.30)	18.9 (1.24)	21.4 (1.41)	22.1 (1.40)	21.2 (1.17)	— (†)	17.4 (1.14)	13.2 (1.06)	17.0 (1.35)	18.2 (1.16)
Louisiana	15.9 (1.88)	19.2 (1.40)	24.2 (1.64)	— (†)	23.8 (1.75)	— (†)	18.0 (1.53)	16.9 (1.91)	— (†)	21.3 (1.66)
Maine	22.4 (0.49)	22.4 (0.43)	24.2 (0.66)	23.2 (0.64)	21.8 (0.88)	— (†)	19.7 (0.55)	20.6 (0.61)	18.9 (0.59)	17.8 (0.52)
Maryland	20.9 (0.96)	21.2 (1.28)	19.6 (0.25)	17.7 (0.23)	18.2 (0.26)	— (†)	14.2 (0.78)	14.0 (0.22)	13.8 (0.18)	14.1 (0.20)
Massachusetts	19.4 (0.89)	18.1 (1.04)	16.6 (0.98)	15.6 (0.84)	14.6 (0.92)	— (†)	— (†)	13.8 (0.79)	13.0 (0.76)	13.6 (0.77)
Michigan	24.0 (1.77)	22.7 (1.40)	25.3 (1.47)	25.6 (1.45)	22.8 (1.62)	— (†)	18.0 (0.91)	18.8 (1.20)	18.9 (1.14)	19.6 (1.20)
Minnesota	— (†)	— (†)	— (†)	— (†)	— (†)	— (†)	— (†)	— (†)	— (†)	— (†)
Mississippi	16.0 (1.04)	15.6 (1.32)	19.2 (0.93)	19.5 (1.12)	— (†)	— (†)	12.5 (0.93)	11.9 (0.74)	15.5 (1.25)	— (†)
Missouri	22.8 (1.74)	— (†)	25.2 (1.72)	21.4 (1.65)	23.3 (1.90)	— (†)	— (†)	— (†)	16.6 (1.18)	19.4 (1.29)
Montana	23.1 (1.32)	26.0 (1.06)	26.3 (0.68)	25.3 (1.00)	21.6 (0.90)	— (†)	19.2 (0.92)	18.1 (0.62)	18.5 (0.67)	17.6 (0.67)
Nebraska	— (†)	22.9 (0.85)	20.8 (1.10)	26.3 (1.28)	22.4 (1.64)	— (†)	15.8 (0.81)	15.7 (0.91)	18.9 (1.27)	17.5 (1.48)
Nevada	— (†)	— (†)	19.7 (1.09)	18.6 (0.95)	16.1 (0.82)	— (†)	— (†)	15.0 (1.28)	14.6 (0.87)	13.0 (0.89)
New Hampshire	22.1 (1.53)	25.3 (1.21)	22.8 (1.05)	22.1 (0.46)	21.4 (0.53)	— (†)	21.6 (1.27)	18.1 (1.02)	18.6 (0.43)	19.0 (0.46)
New Jersey	20.7 (1.44)	20.0 (1.57)	21.3 (1.12)	— (†)	— (†)	— (†)	15.6 (1.65)	14.8 (1.25)	— (†)	— (†)
New Mexico	19.5 (0.80)	18.7 (0.72)	18.2 (0.95)	18.4 (0.62)	18.7 (0.66)	— (†)	13.2 (0.66)	13.1 (0.67)	13.7 (0.54)	14.0 (0.56)
New York	18.2 (1.01)	17.7 (0.66)	19.7 (1.43)	20.6 (0.81)	21.7 (1.08)	— (†)	16.2 (0.68)	15.3 (0.89)	15.7 (0.75)	17.6 (0.71)
North Carolina	16.6 (1.00)	20.5 (1.34)	19.2 (0.94)	15.6 (1.65)	18.7 (1.13)	— (†)	15.7 (0.83)	12.5 (1.11)	12.1 (1.46)	13.9 (1.05)
North Dakota	21.1 (1.29)	24.9 (1.24)	25.4 (1.28)	24.0 (1.11)	24.3 (1.25)	— (†)	17.4 (1.15)	17.1 (0.82)	15.9 (0.78)	18.8 (0.92)
Ohio[4]	— (†)	22.7 (1.83)	20.8 (1.40)	— (†)	— (†)	— (†)	14.7 (1.08)	15.1 (1.31)	— (†)	— (†)
Oklahoma	17.5 (1.25)	16.7 (1.27)	18.6 (1.08)	20.4 (1.43)	21.3 (1.51)	— (†)	15.6 (1.21)	14.3 (1.33)	14.5 (1.14)	16.1 (1.23)
Oregon	— (†)	— (†)	— (†)	— (†)	— (†)	— (†)	— (†)	— (†)	— (†)	— (†)
Pennsylvania	19.2 (1.18)	— (†)	— (†)	19.9 (1.08)	21.7 (1.24)	— (†)	— (†)	— (†)	14.3 (0.97)	17.3 (0.86)
Rhode Island	16.3 (0.85)	19.1 (1.74)	18.1 (1.00)	15.5 (0.91)	17.3 (2.60)	— (†)	15.3 (1.14)	14.3 (1.11)	12.4 (1.03)	14.2 (1.51)
South Carolina	15.1 (1.53)	18.3 (1.36)	20.2 (1.33)	19.8 (1.23)	21.5 (1.13)	— (†)	15.6 (1.44)	13.8 (1.00)	14.1 (1.33)	13.6 (0.99)
South Dakota[5]	— (†)	26.7 (1.25)	24.3 (2.05)	21.6 (2.38)	— (†)	— (†)	19.6 (0.94)	17.8 (1.05)	18.4 (1.57)	— (†)
Tennessee	17.3 (1.24)	17.5 (0.88)	21.1 (1.22)	24.1 (0.71)	20.3 (1.11)	— (†)	13.9 (0.69)	15.5 (0.94)	15.3 (0.54)	15.6 (1.18)
Texas	18.7 (1.06)	16.5 (0.73)	19.1 (1.06)	— (†)	18.9 (0.98)	— (†)	13.0 (0.66)	13.8 (1.04)	— (†)	14.7 (1.07)
Utah	18.8 (1.05)	21.7 (0.97)	21.8 (0.99)	— (†)	19.4 (1.18)	— (†)	16.6 (1.12)	16.9 (0.87)	— (†)	18.0 (1.52)
Vermont[6]	— (†)	— (†)	— (†)	— (†)	— (†)	— (†)	15.2 (0.54)	18.0 (0.32)	16.5 (0.26)	15.9 (0.25)
Virginia	— (†)	20.3 (1.37)	21.9 (0.87)	19.5 (1.00)	15.7 (0.81)	— (†)	14.8 (1.49)	14.5 (0.61)	13.8 (0.67)	12.6 (0.70)
Washington	— (†)	— (†)	— (†)	— (†)	— (†)	— (†)	— (†)	— (†)	— (†)	— (†)
West Virginia	23.5 (1.33)	18.6 (1.71)	22.1 (1.72)	24.4 (1.18)	23.7 (1.66)	— (†)	15.5 (1.18)	17.2 (0.89)	20.2 (1.62)	19.3 (1.53)
Wisconsin	22.5 (1.28)	24.0 (1.35)	22.7 (1.23)	— (†)	24.3 (1.39)	— (†)	16.6 (0.74)	17.6 (0.86)	— (†)	18.3 (1.10)
Wyoming	24.4 (0.93)	25.0 (0.98)	23.3 (0.82)	23.8 (1.06)	— (†)	— (†)	18.7 (0.80)	16.1 (0.71)	17.5 (0.94)	— (†)
Puerto Rico	— (†)	12.7 (1.10)	10.6 (0.72)	10.0 (1.05)	17.1 (3.00)	— (†)	8.0 (0.79)	6.7 (0.80)	6.7 (0.97)	13.2 (3.01)

—Not available.

†Not applicable.

[1] Bullying was defined for respondents as "when one or more students tease, threaten, spread rumors about, hit, shove, or hurt another student over and over again." "On school property" was not defined for survey respondents.

[2] Includes "being bullied through e-mail, chat rooms, instant messaging, websites, or texting" for 2011 through 2015, and "being bullied through texting, Instagram, Facebook, or other social media" for 2017. Data on electronic bullying were not collected in 2009.

[3] U.S. total data are representative of all public and private school students in grades 9-12 in the 50 states and the District of Columbia. U.S. total data for all years were collected through a separate national survey (rather than being aggregated from state-level data) and include both public and private schools.

[4] Ohio data for 2009 through 2013 include both public and private schools.

[5] South Dakota data for 2009 through 2015 include both public and private schools.

[6] Vermont data for 2013 include both public and private schools.

NOTE: For the U.S. total, data for all years include both public and private schools. State-level data include public schools only, except where otherwise noted. For specific states, a given year's data may be unavailable (1) because the state did not participate in the survey that year; (2) because the state omitted this particular survey item from the state-level questionnaire; or (3) because the state had an overall response rate of less than 60 percent (the overall response rate is the school response rate multiplied by the student response rate).

SOURCE: Centers for Disease Control and Prevention, Division of Adolescent and School Health, Youth Risk Behavior Surveillance System (YRBSS), 2009 through 2017. (This table was prepared July 2018.)

Table 230.65. Percentage of public schools reporting selected types of cyberbullying problems occurring at school or away from school at least once a week, by selected school characteristics: 2017-18

[Standard errors appear in parentheses]

School characteristic	Cyberbullying among students		School environment is affected by cyberbullying		Staff resources are used to deal with cyberbullying	
1		2		3		4
All public schools	**14.9**	**(0.59)**	**8.8**	**(0.50)**	**8.1**	**(0.40)**
School level[1]						
Primary	4.5	(0.81)	2.3	(0.58)	2.0	(0.51)
Middle	33.1	(1.65)	21.2	(1.28)	19.5	(1.32)
High school	30.2	(1.21)	18.0	(1.19)	18.9	(1.27)
Combined	20.2	(3.60)	10.2	(2.87)	5.3 !	(2.00)
Enrollment size						
Less than 300	10.9	(1.94)	5.8	(1.51)	4.4	(1.27)
300 to 499	10.9	(1.22)	6.2	(0.88)	4.6	(0.71)
500 to 999	15.5	(0.97)	9.1	(0.74)	9.5	(0.81)
1,000 or more	31.6	(1.67)	20.5	(1.40)	19.9	(1.32)
Locale						
City	12.7	(1.18)	7.4	(0.68)	7.4	(0.82)
Suburban	14.1	(1.06)	9.0	(0.91)	8.7	(0.81)
Town	20.2	(1.90)	10.3	(1.62)	9.4	(1.14)
Rural	15.8	(1.60)	9.3	(1.35)	7.4	(1.10)
Percent minority enrollment[2]						
0 to 25 percent	17.4	(1.20)	10.2	(1.01)	8.8	(0.86)
26 to 50 percent	14.2	(1.35)	8.7	(1.05)	8.1	(1.05)
51 to 75 percent	18.2	(2.04)	10.7	(1.60)	9.6	(1.31)
76 to 100 percent	10.2	(1.07)	5.8	(0.75)	6.1	(0.66)
Percent of students eligible for free or reduced-price lunch						
0 to 25 percent	12.9	(1.50)	6.8	(1.12)	7.2	(1.06)
26 to 50 percent	18.4	(1.44)	11.2	(1.13)	9.7	(0.98)
51 to 75 percent	16.5	(1.60)	10.1	(1.25)	8.1	(0.98)
76 to 100 percent	12.2	(1.22)	7.1	(0.84)	7.3	(0.82)
Prevalence of violent incidents[3] at school during school year						
No violent incidents	3.4	(0.88)	2.4 !	(0.81)	2.4 !	(0.79)
Any violent incidents	19.7	(0.83)	11.4	(0.64)	10.4	(0.51)

!Interpret data with caution. The coefficient of variation (CV) for this estimate is between 30 and 50 percent.

[1] Primary schools are defined as schools in which the lowest grade is not higher than grade 3 and the highest grade is not higher than grade 8. Middle schools are defined as schools in which the lowest grade is not lower than grade 4 and the highest grade is not higher than grade 9. High schools are defined as schools in which the lowest grade is not lower than grade 9. Combined schools include all other combinations of grades, including K–12 schools.

[2] Percent combined enrollment of Black, Hispanic, Asian, Pacific Islander, and American Indian/Alaska Native students, and students of Two or more races.

[3] "Violent incidents" include rape or attempted rape, sexual assault other than rape, physical attack or fight with or without a weapon, threat of physical attack or fight with or without a weapon, and robbery with or without a weapon. Respondents were instructed to include violent incidents that occurred before, during, or after normal school hours or when school activities or events were in session.

NOTE: Includes schools reporting that cyberbullying happens either "daily" or "at least once a week." "Cyberbullying" was defined for respondents as occurring "when willful and repeated harm is inflicted through the use of computers, cell phones, or other electronic devices." Responses were provided by the principal or the person most knowledgeable about crime and safety issues at the school. Respondents were instructed to include cyberbullying "problems that can occur anywhere (both at your school and away from school)."

SOURCE: U.S. Department of Education, National Center for Education Statistics, 2017-18 School Survey on Crime and Safety (SSOCS), 2018. (This table was prepared July 2019.)

Table 230.70. Percentage of students ages 12-18 who reported being afraid of attack or harm, by location and selected student and school characteristics: Selected years, 1995 through 2019

[Standard errors appear in parentheses]

Student or school characteristic	1995[1]		1999[1]		2001[1]		2003[1]		2005[1]		2007		2009		2011		2013		2015		2017		2019	
1	2		3		4		5		6		7		8		9		10		11		12		13	
At school																								
Total	**11.8**	**(0.40)**	**7.4**	**(0.37)**	**6.4**	**(0.31)**	**6.1**	**(0.31)**	**6.4**	**(0.39)**	**5.3**	**(0.33)**	**4.2**	**(0.33)**	**3.7**	**(0.28)**	**3.5**	**(0.33)**	**3.3**	**(0.31)**	**4.2**	**(0.32)**	**4.8**	**(0.33)**
Sex																								
Male	10.9	(0.51)	6.5	(0.44)	6.4	(0.38)	5.4	(0.34)	6.1	(0.56)	4.6	(0.42)	3.7	(0.38)	3.7	(0.41)	3.1	(0.38)	2.6	(0.34)	3.4	(0.38)	4.6	(0.44)
Female	12.9	(0.58)	8.3	(0.54)	6.4	(0.43)	7.0	(0.48)	6.7	(0.47)	6.0	(0.45)	4.8	(0.51)	3.8	(0.36)	4.0	(0.48)	4.1	(0.50)	5.1	(0.47)	5.1	(0.47)
Race/ethnicity[2]																								
White	8.2	(0.36)	5.0	(0.32)	4.9	(0.35)	4.2	(0.35)	4.6	(0.39)	4.2	(0.37)	3.3	(0.35)	3.0	(0.31)	2.6	(0.33)	2.8	(0.34)	3.6	(0.40)	3.4	(0.35)
Black	20.9	(1.36)	13.6	(1.30)	9.0	(0.88)	10.7	(1.23)	9.3	(1.19)	8.6	(1.18)	7.0	(1.12)	4.9	(1.03)	4.6	(0.85)	3.4	(0.76)	6.9	(1.06)	7.4	(1.18)
Hispanic	21.1	(1.30)	11.8	(1.20)	10.7	(1.08)	9.6	(0.75)	10.3	(1.16)	7.1	(0.88)	4.9	(0.89)	4.8	(0.59)	4.9	(0.78)	4.8	(0.72)	3.9	(0.50)	6.7	(0.86)
Asian/Pacific Islander	16.5	(1.88)	6.2	(0.98)	6.4	(1.22)	6.3	(1.79)	6.1 !	(1.99)	2.2 !	(1.00)	5.7 !	(2.16)	4.3 !	(1.45)	3.2 !	(1.04)	2.6 !	(1.13)	4.0 !	(1.36)	1.6 !	(0.61)
Asian	---	(†)	---	(†)	---	(†)	6.4	(1.76)	6.2 !	(2.10)	2.3 !	(1.05)	5.9 !	(2.25)	4.2 !	(1.52)	3.1 !	(1.09)	2.7 !	(1.19)	3.9 !	(1.38)	1.4 !	(0.62)
Pacific Islander	---	(†)	---	(†)	---	(†)	‡	(†)	‡	(†)	‡	(†)	‡	(†)	‡	(†)	‡	(†)	‡	(†)	‡	(†)	‡	(†)
American Indian/ Alaska Native	‡	(†)	‡	(†)	‡	(†)	‡	(†)	‡	(†)	‡	(†)	‡	(†)	‡	(†)	‡	(†)	‡	(†)	14.1	(3.88)	‡	(†)
Two or more races	---	(†)	---	(†)	---	(†)	‡	(†)	5.0 !	(2.18)	2.7 !	(1.28)	‡	(†)	4.3 !	(1.59)	3.9 !	(1.76)	‡	(†)	3.5 !	(1.63)	8.8	(2.48)
Grade																								
6th	14.5	(1.15)	10.9	(1.39)	10.7	(1.27)	10.0	(1.35)	9.5	(1.14)	9.9	(1.33)	6.4	(1.20)	5.6	(1.08)	4.7	(1.01)	4.6	(1.11)	4.3	(0.81)	8.0	(1.51)
7th	15.4	(1.03)	9.5	(0.79)	9.3	(0.96)	8.2	(0.87)	9.1	(1.04)	6.7	(0.86)	6.2	(1.06)	4.5	(0.69)	4.3	(0.69)	4.2	(0.74)	4.9	(0.84)	6.1	(0.90)
8th	13.1	(0.84)	8.2	(0.74)	7.6	(0.69)	6.3	(0.68)	7.1	(0.95)	4.6	(0.71)	3.5	(0.75)	4.6	(0.71)	3.3	(0.78)	4.1	(0.73)	4.4	(0.76)	4.6	(0.72)
9th	11.7	(0.82)	7.1	(0.75)	5.6	(0.63)	6.3	(0.61)	5.9	(0.71)	5.5	(0.87)	4.6	(0.75)	4.2	(0.66)	3.4	(0.71)	3.9	(0.75)	5.6	(0.89)	4.4	(0.79)
10th	11.0	(0.83)	7.1	(0.77)	5.1	(0.72)	4.5	(0.68)	5.5	(0.89)	5.2	(0.87)	4.6	(0.79)	3.9	(0.63)	4.4	(0.75)	2.1	(0.56)	5.1	(0.92)	4.1	(0.75)
11th	8.9	(0.81)	4.9	(0.68)	4.8	(0.65)	4.8	(0.66)	4.6	(0.73)	3.1	(0.63)	3.3	(0.74)	1.8	(0.48)	2.6	(0.55)	2.6	(0.65)	3.2	(0.68)	4.4	(0.80)
12th	7.9	(0.95)	4.8	(0.89)	2.9	(0.55)	3.7	(0.54)	3.3	(0.69)	3.1	(0.65)	1.9 !	(0.57)	2.2	(0.57)	2.0	(0.56)	2.0 !	(0.61)	1.9	(0.48)	3.4	(0.71)
School locale[3]																								
City	---	(†)	---	(†)	---	(†)	---	(†)	---	(†)	---	(†)	---	(†)	---	(†)	---	(†)	3.6	(0.57)	6.0	(0.73)	6.5	(0.72)
Suburban	---	(†)	---	(†)	---	(†)	---	(†)	---	(†)	---	(†)	---	(†)	---	(†)	---	(†)	3.5	(0.52)	3.6	(0.44)	4.7	(0.57)
Town	---	(†)	---	(†)	---	(†)	---	(†)	---	(†)	---	(†)	---	(†)	---	(†)	---	(†)	4.4	(0.94)	3.1	(0.79)	4.4	(0.85)
Rural	---	(†)	---	(†)	---	(†)	---	(†)	---	(†)	---	(†)	---	(†)	---	(†)	---	(†)	2.0	(0.46)	3.5	(0.64)	3.4	(0.64)
Control of school[3,4]																								
Public	12.3	(0.43)	7.8	(0.38)	6.6	(0.33)	6.4	(0.34)	6.6	(0.42)	5.5	(0.34)	4.4	(0.35)	3.9	(0.30)	3.5	(0.35)	3.5	(0.33)	4.4	(0.36)	5.0	(0.35)
Private	7.4	(1.01)	3.6	(0.81)	4.6	(0.93)	3.0	(0.75)	3.8	(0.82)	2.5 !	(0.89)	1.9 !	(0.74)	1.5 !	(0.64)	2.6 !	(0.83)	‡	(†)	‡	(†)	2.9 !	(1.10)
Away from school																								
Total	**---**	**(†)**	**5.7**	**(0.32)**	**4.7**	**(0.29)**	**5.4**	**(0.29)**	**5.2**	**(0.33)**	**3.5**	**(0.29)**	**3.3**	**(0.32)**	**2.4**	**(0.23)**	**2.7**	**(0.35)**	**2.2**	**(0.29)**	**2.7**	**(0.26)**	**2.7**	**(0.27)**
Sex																								
Male	---	(†)	4.1	(0.34)	3.7	(0.32)	4.0	(0.30)	4.6	(0.42)	2.4	(0.31)	2.5	(0.34)	2.0	(0.27)	2.4	(0.40)	1.2	(0.25)	2.1	(0.33)	2.4	(0.35)
Female	---	(†)	7.4	(0.50)	5.7	(0.42)	6.8	(0.48)	5.8	(0.48)	4.5	(0.40)	4.1	(0.51)	2.7	(0.30)	3.0	(0.44)	3.3	(0.48)	3.4	(0.42)	3.1	(0.40)
Race/ethnicity[2]																								
White	---	(†)	4.3	(0.32)	3.7	(0.30)	3.8	(0.32)	4.2	(0.40)	2.5	(0.28)	2.2	(0.28)	1.6	(0.24)	1.6	(0.30)	1.7	(0.30)	2.3	(0.32)	1.9	(0.26)
Black	---	(†)	8.8	(1.02)	6.4	(0.89)	10.1	(1.14)	7.4	(0.96)	4.9	(0.73)	5.7	(1.10)	3.5	(0.86)	3.6	(0.78)	2.7 !	(0.82)	4.1	(1.04)	3.8	(0.89)
Hispanic	---	(†)	9.0	(1.04)	6.6	(0.76)	7.5	(0.80)	6.2	(0.84)	5.9	(0.80)	3.9	(0.70)	3.3	(0.50)	4.5	(0.86)	3.4	(0.61)	2.8	(0.45)	4.0	(0.78)
Asian/Pacific Islander	---	(†)	5.5	(1.12)	6.6	(1.46)	4.9	(1.28)	6.6 !	(2.66)	‡	(†)	7.4 !	(2.44)	3.9 !	(1.23)	2.6 !	(0.94)	‡	(†)	2.1 !	(1.04)	‡	(†)
Asian	---	(†)	‡	(†)	‡	(†)	4.9	(1.31)	7.1 !	(2.86)	‡	(†)	7.1 !	(2.50)	3.2 !	(1.15)	2.9 !	(1.03)	‡	(†)	2.1 !	(1.06)	‡	(†)
Pacific Islander	---	(†)	‡	(†)	‡	(†)	‡	(†)	‡	(†)	‡	(†)	‡	(†)	‡	(†)	‡	(†)	‡	(†)	‡	(†)	‡	(†)
American Indian/ Alaska Native	---	(†)	‡	(†)	7.7 !	(3.67)	‡	(†)	‡	(†)	‡	(†)	‡	(†)	‡	(†)	‡	(†)	‡	(†)	‡	(†)	‡	(†)
Two or more races	---	(†)	‡	(†)	‡	(†)	‡	(†)	‡	(†)	‡	(†)	‡	(†)	‡	(†)	4.4 !	(1.96)	‡	(†)	4.5 !	(1.75)	4.3 !	(1.92)
Grade																								
6th	---	(†)	7.9	(1.12)	6.4	(1.16)	6.8	(1.01)	5.6	(0.99)	5.9	(1.20)	3.3	(0.89)	3.0	(0.86)	3.9	(0.88)	2.8 !	(0.96)	2.3	(0.69)	3.0	(0.75)
7th	---	(†)	6.1	(0.73)	5.5	(0.80)	6.7	(0.81)	7.5	(0.89)	3.0	(0.55)	4.0	(0.78)	2.7	(0.58)	2.2	(0.54)	2.2	(0.54)	3.0	(0.73)	2.6	(0.58)
8th	---	(†)	5.6	(0.67)	4.5	(0.61)	5.4	(0.71)	5.0	(0.72)	3.6	(0.65)	3.3	(0.72)	2.1	(0.43)	2.4 !	(0.80)	2.9	(0.68)	2.7	(0.57)	3.0	(0.62)
9th	---	(†)	4.6	(0.63)	4.5	(0.63)	4.3	(0.55)	3.8	(0.61)	4.0	(0.75)	2.6	(0.62)	3.5	(0.65)	2.8	(0.59)	2.5	(0.58)	3.1	(0.63)	2.9	(0.64)
10th	---	(†)	4.8	(0.63)	4.2	(0.64)	5.4	(0.68)	4.7	(0.66)	3.0	(0.60)	5.5	(0.96)	1.7	(0.46)	4.4	(0.83)	1.2 !	(0.41)	2.9	(0.71)	1.8	(0.53)
11th	---	(†)	5.9	(0.72)	4.7	(0.62)	4.7	(0.69)	4.2	(0.74)	2.3	(0.56)	2.2	(0.56)	2.9	(0.70)	2.2	(0.47)	2.0 !	(0.64)	3.6	(0.79)	3.0	(0.58)
12th	---	(†)	6.1	(0.87)	3.3	(0.63)	5.0	(0.73)	5.4	(0.98)	3.2	(0.61)	2.1	(0.63)	1.0 !	(0.37)	1.3 !	(0.46)	2.1	(0.63)	1.1 !	(0.35)	3.0	(0.66)
School locale[3]																								
City	---	(†)	---	(†)	---	(†)	---	(†)	---	(†)	---	(†)	---	(†)	---	(†)	---	(†)	2.6	(0.49)	3.1	(0.50)	2.8	(0.57)
Suburban	---	(†)	---	(†)	---	(†)	---	(†)	---	(†)	---	(†)	---	(†)	---	(†)	---	(†)	2.6	(0.46)	2.4	(0.42)	3.1	(0.50)
Town	---	(†)	---	(†)	---	(†)	---	(†)	---	(†)	---	(†)	---	(†)	---	(†)	---	(†)	1.6 !	(0.56)	2.5	(0.73)	2.5 !	(0.74)
Rural	---	(†)	---	(†)	---	(†)	---	(†)	---	(†)	---	(†)	---	(†)	---	(†)	---	(†)	1.2 !	(0.47)	2.5	(0.60)	2.4	(0.54)
Control of school[3,4]																								
Public	---	(†)	5.8	(0.33)	4.6	(0.30)	5.5	(0.31)	5.2	(0.34)	3.6	(0.30)	3.5	(0.33)	2.4	(0.23)	2.7	(0.36)	2.2	(0.30)	2.6	(0.28)	2.8	(0.29)
Private	---	(†)	5.0	(0.93)	5.2	(1.09)	4.8	(0.92)	4.9	(1.41)	2.1 !	(0.72)	1.8 !	(0.71)	1.6 !	(0.68)	2.0 !	(0.70)	2.3 !	(1.00)	‡	(†)	2.1 !	(0.77)

—Not available.

†Not applicable.

!Interpret data with caution. The coefficient of variation (CV) for this estimate is between 30 and 50 percent.

‡Reporting standards not met. Either there are too few cases for a reliable estimate or the coefficient of variation (CV) is 50 percent or greater.

[1] In 2005 and prior years, the period covered by the survey question was "during the last 6 months," but this was changed to "during this school year" beginning in 2007. Cognitive testing suggested that modifications to the reference period would not have a substantial impact on the survey responses.

[2] Race categories exclude persons of Hispanic ethnicity. Prior to 2003, separate data for Asian students, Pacific Islander students, and students of Two or more races were not collected.

[3] Excludes students with missing information about the school characteristic.

[4] Data for 2013 and prior years were based on school information provided by the respondent. Beginning in 2015, data were based on school information collected in the Common Core of Data and the Private School Universe Survey, which was appended to the School Crime Supplement data file; therefore, these data may not be entirely comparable with figures for earlier years.

NOTE: "At school" includes in the school building, on school property, on a school bus, and, from 2001 onward, going to and from school. Students were asked if they were "never," "almost never," "sometimes," or "most of the time" afraid that someone would attack or harm them at school or away from school. Students who responded "sometimes" or "most of the time" were considered afraid. For the 2001 survey only, the wording was changed from "attack or harm" to "attack or threaten to attack." Some data have been revised from previously reported figures.

SOURCE: U.S. Department of Justice, Bureau of Justice Statistics, School Crime Supplement (SCS) to the National Crime Victimization Survey, 1995 through 2019. (This table was prepared October 2020.)

Table 230.80. Percentage of students ages 12-18 who reported avoiding one or more places in school or avoiding school activities or classes because of fear of attack or harm, by selected student and school characteristics: Selected years, 1995 through 2019

[Standard errors appear in parentheses]

Type of avoidance and student or school characteristic	1995[1]	1999[1]	2001[1]	2003[1]	2005[1]	2007	2009	2011	2013	2015	2017	2019
1	2	3	4	5	6	7	8	9	10	11	12	13
Total, any avoidance[2]	**--- (†)**	**6.9 (0.34)**	**6.1 (0.32)**	**5.0 (0.30)**	**5.5 (0.32)**	**7.2 (0.36)**	**5.0 (0.35)**	**5.5 (0.34)**	**4.7 (0.31)**	**4.9 (0.37)**	**6.1 (0.39)**	**6.3 (0.35)**
Avoided one or more places in school[3]												
Total	8.7 (0.30)	4.7 (0.29)	4.7 (0.27)	4.0 (0.27)	4.5 (0.28)	5.8 (0.31)	4.0 (0.32)	4.7 (0.30)	3.7 (0.27)	3.9 (0.32)	4.9 (0.34)	5.0 (0.32)
Entrance to the school	2.1 (0.15)	1.1 (0.14)	1.3 (0.11)	1.2 (0.12)	1.0 (0.14)	1.5 (0.15)	0.9 (0.15)	0.9 (0.13)	0.8 (0.14)	0.9 (0.14)	0.9 (0.13)	0.9 (0.12)
Hallways or stairs in school	4.3 (0.21)	2.1 (0.17)	2.1 (0.18)	1.7 (0.17)	2.1 (0.21)	2.6 (0.21)	2.2 (0.23)	2.5 (0.21)	1.7 (0.18)	1.7 (0.20)	2.2 (0.24)	2.1 (0.22)
Parts of the school cafeteria	2.5 (0.19)	1.3 (0.15)	1.4 (0.16)	1.2 (0.13)	1.8 (0.16)	1.9 (0.19)	1.1 (0.17)	1.8 (0.18)	1.4 (0.19)	1.2 (0.19)	2.3 (0.27)	2.2 (0.22)
Any school restrooms	4.5 (0.22)	2.2 (0.19)	2.2 (0.19)	2.1 (0.16)	2.1 (0.20)	2.6 (0.24)	1.4 (0.19)	1.7 (0.19)	1.3 (0.16)	1.5 (0.21)	2.2 (0.25)	2.4 (0.21)
Other places inside the school building	2.5 (0.18)	1.4 (0.17)	1.4 (0.14)	1.3 (0.14)	1.4 (0.18)	1.5 (0.17)	1.0 (0.16)	1.1 (0.15)	0.8 (0.13)	0.8 (0.13)	1.1 (0.18)	1.0 (0.15)
Sex												
Male	8.9 (0.43)	4.7 (0.35)	4.8 (0.40)	3.9 (0.34)	4.9 (0.46)	6.1 (0.47)	3.9 (0.45)	3.9 (0.42)	3.4 (0.34)	3.4 (0.41)	4.1 (0.40)	4.9 (0.43)
Female	8.6 (0.46)	4.6 (0.40)	4.7 (0.35)	4.1 (0.37)	4.1 (0.40)	5.5 (0.41)	4.0 (0.42)	5.5 (0.40)	3.9 (0.43)	4.4 (0.45)	5.7 (0.51)	5.2 (0.45)
Race/ethnicity[4]												
White	7.1 (0.33)	3.8 (0.29)	3.9 (0.29)	3.1 (0.27)	3.6 (0.30)	5.3 (0.36)	3.3 (0.38)	4.4 (0.38)	3.0 (0.34)	3.8 (0.43)	4.5 (0.49)	4.4 (0.40)
Black	12.2 (1.04)	6.8 (0.92)	6.6 (0.74)	5.1 (0.79)	7.2 (0.98)	8.3 (1.02)	6.1 (1.04)	4.5 (0.80)	3.3 (0.79)	3.9 (0.80)	6.5 (1.10)	6.7 (1.04)
Hispanic	13.0 (0.98)	6.2 (0.73)	5.6 (0.72)	6.3 (0.70)	6.0 (0.80)	6.8 (0.82)	4.8 (0.86)	6.0 (0.68)	4.9 (0.63)	4.2 (0.68)	5.0 (0.72)	4.7 (0.58)
Asian/Pacific Islander	12.8 (1.87)	4.7 (0.92)	7.0 (1.35)	4.6 (1.14)	3.2 ! (1.06)	1.8 ! (0.88)	3.5 ! (1.47)	2.5 ! (0.99)	4.0 ! (1.25)	3.7 ! (1.28)	3.5 ! (1.28)	4.9 ! (1.48)
Asian	--- (†)	--- (†)	--- (†)	3.9 (1.04)	2.5 ! (0.88)	‡ (†)	3.7 ! (1.53)	2.7 ! (1.06)	3.8 ! (1.26)	3.7 ! (1.33)	3.6 ! (1.30)	4.4 ! (1.40)
Pacific Islander	--- (†)	--- (†)	--- (†)	‡ (†)	‡ (†)	‡ (†)	‡ (†)	‡ (†)	‡ (†)	‡ (†)	‡ (†)	‡ (†)
American Indian/Alaska Native	‡ (†)	10.0 ! (4.47)	‡ (†)	‡ (†)	‡ (†)	‡ (†)	‡ (†)	‡ (†)	12.2 ! (4.95)	‡ (†)	‡ (†)	‡ (†)
Two or more races	--- (†)	--- (†)	--- (†)	5.7 ! (2.52)	‡ (†)	4.7 ! (1.65)	‡ (†)	3.7 ! (1.31)	4.5 ! (1.87)	‡ (†)	6.6 ! (2.08)	10.7 (2.67)
Grade												
6th	11.8 (1.01)	6.0 (0.93)	6.9 (0.93)	5.6 (0.94)	7.9 (1.27)	7.8 (1.20)	7.1 (1.13)	6.9 (0.99)	4.4 (0.92)	6.2 (1.15)	7.0 (1.29)	4.6 (0.97)
7th	11.9 (0.90)	6.1 (0.72)	6.3 (0.80)	5.7 (0.73)	5.8 (0.93)	7.5 (0.86)	5.5 (0.86)	5.1 (0.76)	4.6 (0.72)	5.4 (0.88)	6.6 (0.93)	5.1 (0.75)
8th	8.9 (0.77)	5.6 (0.71)	5.2 (0.63)	4.7 (0.64)	4.5 (0.67)	5.9 (0.84)	4.8 (0.93)	5.2 (0.75)	2.7 (0.62)	4.0 (0.80)	3.6 (0.65)	5.9 (0.85)
9th	9.6 (0.71)	5.3 (0.63)	5.0 (0.61)	5.1 (0.62)	5.2 (0.78)	6.7 (0.81)	4.5 (0.89)	3.7 (0.67)	5.1 (0.78)	4.0 (0.71)	6.8 (1.04)	6.6 (1.06)
10th	7.8 (0.76)	4.8 (0.61)	4.3 (0.64)	3.1 (0.55)	4.2 (0.65)	5.5 (0.80)	4.2 (0.88)	5.4 (0.72)	4.0 (0.72)	2.8 (0.53)	4.3 (0.84)	4.9 (0.83)
11th	6.9 (0.64)	2.5 (0.46)	2.8 (0.43)	2.5 (0.53)	3.3 (0.58)	4.2 (0.70)	1.2 ! (0.44)	3.6 (0.65)	2.5 (0.61)	2.2 (0.56)	4.3 (0.83)	5.0 (0.92)
12th	4.1 (0.74)	2.4 (0.51)	3.0 (0.65)	1.2 ! (0.42)	1.3 ! (0.41)	3.2 (0.71)	1.6 ! (0.50)	3.7 (0.71)	2.3 (0.62)	3.3 (0.81)	2.6 (0.59)	2.8 (0.65)
School locale[5]												
City	--- (†)	--- (†)	--- (†)	--- (†)	--- (†)	--- (†)	--- (†)	--- (†)	--- (†)	4.9 (0.66)	6.5 (0.87)	5.9 (0.69)
Suburban	--- (†)	--- (†)	--- (†)	--- (†)	--- (†)	--- (†)	--- (†)	--- (†)	--- (†)	4.1 (0.51)	4.1 (0.53)	5.0 (0.49)
Town	--- (†)	--- (†)	--- (†)	--- (†)	--- (†)	--- (†)	--- (†)	--- (†)	--- (†)	3.4 (0.94)	5.0 (0.88)	5.0 (1.17)
Rural	--- (†)	--- (†)	--- (†)	--- (†)	--- (†)	--- (†)	--- (†)	--- (†)	--- (†)	2.1 (0.46)	3.7 (0.57)	4.1 (0.55)
School control[5,6]												
Public	9.4 (0.33)	5.0 (0.31)	5.0 (0.29)	4.2 (0.29)	4.8 (0.30)	6.2 (0.35)	4.2 (0.34)	4.9 (0.32)	3.9 (0.29)	4.0 (0.33)	5.0 (0.38)	5.3 (0.34)
Private	2.2 (0.47)	1.6 (0.45)	2.0 ! (0.70)	1.5 ! (0.49)	1.4 ! (0.55)	1.4 ! (0.54)	1.8 ! (0.73)	2.1 ! (0.70)	1.0 ! (0.49)	‡ (†)	‡ (†)	1.6 ! (0.78)
Avoided school activities or classes[7]												
Total	--- (†)	3.2 (0.22)	2.3 (0.19)	1.9 (0.18)	2.1 (0.23)	2.6 (0.23)	2.1 (0.25)	2.0 (0.20)	2.0 (0.21)	2.1 (0.24)	2.4 (0.24)	2.7 (0.25)
Any activities[8]	1.7 (0.15)	0.9 (0.10)	1.1 (0.12)	1.0 (0.11)	1.0 (0.16)	1.8 (0.20)	1.3 (0.20)	1.2 (0.16)	1.0 (0.13)	1.3 (0.18)	1.3 (0.17)	1.6 (0.19)
Any classes	--- (†)	0.6 (0.09)	0.6 (0.09)	0.6 (0.11)	0.7 (0.13)	0.7 (0.12)	0.6 (0.13)	0.7 (0.10)	0.5 (0.10)	0.6 (0.11)	0.8 (0.12)	1.0 (0.15)
Stayed home from school	--- (†)	2.3 (0.19)	1.1 (0.13)	0.8 (0.11)	0.7 (0.11)	0.8 (0.13)	0.6 (0.14)	0.8 (0.12)	0.9 (0.13)	0.8 (0.14)	1.2 (0.16)	1.4 (0.19)

—Not available.

†Not applicable.

!Interpret data with caution. The coefficient of variation (CV) for this estimate is between 30 and 50 percent.

‡Reporting standards not met. Either there are too few cases for a reliable estimate or the coefficient of variation (CV) is 50 percent or greater.

[1] In 2005 and prior years, the period covered by the survey question was "during the last 6 months," but this was changed to "during this school year" beginning in 2007. Cognitive testing suggested that modifications to the reference period would not have a substantial impact on the survey responses.

[2] In the total for any avoidance, students who reported both avoiding one or more places in school and avoiding school activities or classes were counted only once.

[3] Students who reported avoiding multiple places in school were counted only once in the total for students avoiding one or more places.

[4] Race categories exclude persons of Hispanic ethnicity. Prior to 2003, separate data for Asian students, Pacific Islander students, and students of Two or more races were not collected.

[5] Excludes students with missing information about the school characteristic.

[6] Data for 2013 and prior years were based on school information provided by the respondent. Beginning in 2015, data were based on school information collected in the Common Core of Data and the Private School Universe Survey, which was appended to the School Crime Supplement data file; therefore, these data may not be entirely comparable with figures for earlier years.

[7] Students who reported more than one type of avoidance of school activities or classes—e.g., reported that they avoided "any activities" and also reported that they stayed home from school—were counted only once in the total for avoiding activities or classes.

[8] Before 2007, students were asked whether they avoided "any extracurricular activities." Starting in 2007, the survey wording was changed to "any activities."

NOTE: Students were asked whether they avoided places or activities because they thought that someone might attack or harm them. For the 2001 survey only, the wording was changed from "attack or harm" to "attack or threaten to attack." Some data have been revised from previously published figures.

SOURCE: U.S. Department of Justice, Bureau of Justice Statistics, School Crime Supplement (SCS) to the National Crime Victimization Survey, 1995 through 2019. (This table was prepared October 2020.)

Table 231.10. Percentage of students in grades 9-12 who reported having been in a physical fight at least one time during the previous 12 months, by location and selected student characteristics: Selected years, 1993 through 2019

[Standard errors appear in parentheses]

Location and student characteristic	1993	1999	2001	2003	2005	2007	2009	2011	2013	2015	2017	2019
1	2	3	4	5	6	7	8	9	10	11	12	13
Anywhere (including on school property)[1]												
Total	**41.8 (0.99)**	**35.7 (1.17)**	**33.2 (0.71)**	**33.0 (0.99)**	**35.9 (0.77)**	**35.5 (0.77)**	**31.5 (0.70)**	**32.8 (0.65)**	**24.7 (0.74)**	**22.6 (0.87)**	**23.6 (0.97)**	**21.9 (0.81)**
Sex												
Male	51.2 (1.05)	44.0 (1.27)	43.1 (0.84)	40.5 (1.32)	43.4 (1.01)	44.4 (0.89)	39.3 (1.20)	40.7 (0.74)	30.2 (1.10)	28.4 (1.04)	30.0 (1.14)	28.3 (1.23)
Female	31.7 (1.19)	27.3 (1.70)	23.9 (0.95)	25.1 (0.85)	28.1 (0.94)	26.5 (0.99)	22.9 (0.74)	24.4 (0.92)	19.2 (0.72)	16.5 (1.04)	17.2 (1.01)	15.3 (1.01)
Race/ethnicity												
White	40.3 (1.13)	33.1 (1.45)	32.2 (0.95)	30.5 (1.11)	33.1 (0.88)	31.7 (0.96)	27.8 (0.88)	29.4 (0.74)	20.9 (0.70)	20.1 (1.13)	20.8 (0.82)	19.8 (0.97)
Black	49.5 (1.82)	41.4 (3.12)	36.5 (1.60)	39.7 (1.23)	43.1 (1.74)	44.7 (1.33)	41.1 (1.71)	39.1 (1.52)	34.7 (1.67)	32.4 (2.11)	33.2 (2.49)	30.2 (1.77)
Hispanic	43.2 (1.58)	39.9 (1.65)	35.8 (0.91)	36.1 (0.98)	41.0 (1.64)	40.4 (1.25)	36.2 (0.95)	36.8 (1.44)	28.4 (1.15)	23.0 (1.10)	25.7 (1.85)	22.6 (1.12)
Asian[2]	--- (†)	22.7 (2.71)	22.3 (2.73)	25.9 (2.99)	21.6 (2.43)	24.3 (3.50)	18.9 (1.72)	18.4 (1.87)	16.1 (1.87)	14.7 (1.12)	11.0 (1.61)	12.0 (1.87)
Pacific Islander[2]	--- (†)	50.7 (3.42)	51.7 (6.25)	30.0 (5.21)	34.4 (5.58)	42.6 (7.74)	32.6 (3.50)	43.0 (5.14)	22.0 (4.95)	29.2 (7.98)	22.6 (2.47)	18.2 (4.85)
American Indian/Alaska Native	49.8 (4.79)	48.7 (6.78)	49.2 (6.58)	46.6 (6.53)	44.2 (3.40)	36.0 (1.49)	42.4 (5.23)	42.4 (2.12)	32.1 (7.39)	29.9 (5.07)	34.7 (6.36)	40.2 (6.85)
Two or more races[2]	--- (†)	40.2 (2.76)	39.6 (2.85)	38.2 (3.64)	46.9 (4.16)	47.8 (3.30)	34.2 (3.51)	45.0 (2.60)	28.5 (2.31)	27.6 (2.58)	25.5 (2.30)	28.7 (2.43)
Sexual identity[3]												
Heterosexual	--- (†)	--- (†)	--- (†)	--- (†)	--- (†)	--- (†)	--- (†)	--- (†)	--- (†)	21.7 (0.78)	23.2 (0.95)	21.4 (0.87)
Gay, lesbian, or bisexual	--- (†)	--- (†)	--- (†)	--- (†)	--- (†)	--- (†)	--- (†)	--- (†)	--- (†)	28.4 (2.34)	27.9 (1.66)	23.9 (1.68)
Not sure	--- (†)	--- (†)	--- (†)	--- (†)	--- (†)	--- (†)	--- (†)	--- (†)	--- (†)	34.5 (4.44)	19.8 (2.83)	21.1 (2.59)
Grade												
9th	50.4 (1.54)	41.1 (1.96)	39.5 (1.27)	38.6 (1.38)	43.5 (1.15)	40.9 (1.16)	37.0 (1.21)	37.7 (1.11)	28.3 (1.17)	27.9 (1.51)	28.3 (1.53)	25.8 (1.51)
10th	42.2 (1.45)	37.7 (2.11)	34.7 (1.37)	33.5 (1.20)	36.6 (1.09)	36.2 (1.34)	33.5 (1.19)	35.3 (1.35)	26.4 (1.42)	23.4 (1.46)	26.2 (1.14)	23.3 (1.07)
11th	40.5 (1.52)	31.3 (1.55)	29.1 (1.10)	30.9 (1.38)	31.6 (1.44)	34.8 (1.36)	28.6 (0.93)	29.7 (1.14)	24.0 (1.04)	20.5 (1.23)	20.4 (0.91)	20.0 (1.01)
12th	34.8 (1.56)	30.4 (1.91)	26.5 (1.01)	26.5 (1.08)	29.1 (1.26)	28.0 (1.42)	24.9 (0.99)	26.9 (0.95)	18.8 (1.19)	17.4 (1.23)	17.8 (1.52)	17.6 (1.08)
On school property[4]												
Total	**16.2 (0.59)**	**14.2 (0.62)**	**12.5 (0.49)**	**12.8 (0.76)**	**13.6 (0.56)**	**12.4 (0.48)**	**11.1 (0.54)**	**12.0 (0.39)**	**8.1 (0.35)**	**7.8 (0.54)**	**8.5 (0.53)**	**8.0 (0.50)**
Sex												
Male	23.5 (0.71)	18.5 (0.66)	18.0 (0.74)	17.1 (0.92)	18.2 (0.93)	16.3 (0.60)	15.1 (1.05)	16.0 (0.58)	10.7 (0.55)	10.3 (0.79)	11.6 (0.62)	11.4 (0.72)
Female	8.6 (0.73)	9.8 (0.95)	7.2 (0.47)	8.0 (0.70)	8.8 (0.52)	8.5 (0.62)	6.7 (0.42)	7.8 (0.43)	5.6 (0.38)	5.0 (0.45)	5.6 (0.54)	4.4 (0.45)
Race/ethnicity												
White	15.0 (0.68)	12.3 (0.86)	11.2 (0.60)	10.0 (0.73)	11.6 (0.66)	10.2 (0.56)	8.6 (0.58)	9.9 (0.51)	6.4 (0.45)	5.6 (0.35)	6.5 (0.64)	6.4 (0.51)
Black	22.0 (1.39)	18.7 (1.51)	16.8 (1.26)	17.1 (1.30)	16.9 (1.39)	17.6 (1.10)	17.4 (0.99)	16.4 (0.89)	12.8 (0.84)	12.6 (1.96)	15.3 (1.45)	15.5 (1.06)
Hispanic	17.9 (1.75)	15.7 (0.91)	14.1 (0.89)	16.7 (1.14)	18.3 (1.62)	15.5 (0.81)	13.5 (0.82)	14.4 (0.79)	9.4 (0.44)	8.9 (0.87)	9.4 (0.90)	7.8 (0.68)
Asian[2]	--- (†)	10.4 (0.95)	10.8 (1.92)	13.1 (2.26)	5.9 (1.53)	8.5 (1.99)	7.7 (1.09)	6.2 (1.06)	5.5 (1.39)	6.3 (1.63)	3.7 (1.00)	4.9 (1.47)
Pacific Islander[2]	--- (†)	25.3 (4.60)	29.1 (7.63)	22.2 (4.82)	24.5 (5.60)	9.6 ! (3.47)	14.8 (2.37)	20.9 (4.41)	7.1 ! (2.58)	20.9 ! (7.11)	14.2 (3.58)	9.1 ! (3.38)
American Indian/Alaska Native	18.6 (2.74)	16.2 ! (5.23)	18.2 (4.41)	24.2 (5.03)	22.0 (3.16)	15.0 (1.12)	20.7 (3.73)	12.0 (1.77)	10.7 (3.13)	13.2 (3.54)	8.6 ! (3.74)	18.9 ! (5.70)
Two or more races[2]	--- (†)	16.9 (2.40)	14.7 (1.97)	20.2 (3.83)	15.8 (2.61)	19.6 (2.39)	12.4 (2.19)	16.6 (1.41)	10.0 (1.04)	9.3 (1.49)	9.2 (1.36)	11.0 (1.76)
Sexual identity[3]												
Heterosexual	--- (†)	--- (†)	--- (†)	--- (†)	--- (†)	--- (†)	--- (†)	--- (†)	--- (†)	7.1 (0.51)	8.3 (0.56)	7.8 (0.51)
Gay, lesbian, or bisexual	--- (†)	--- (†)	--- (†)	--- (†)	--- (†)	--- (†)	--- (†)	--- (†)	--- (†)	11.2 (1.22)	9.6 (1.16)	8.2 (1.00)
Not sure	--- (†)	--- (†)	--- (†)	--- (†)	--- (†)	--- (†)	--- (†)	--- (†)	--- (†)	14.6 (2.38)	11.8 (2.25)	9.6 (1.99)
Grade												
9th	23.1 (1.55)	18.6 (1.02)	17.3 (0.77)	18.0 (1.24)	18.9 (0.93)	17.0 (0.67)	14.9 (0.98)	16.2 (0.77)	10.9 (0.78)	11.6 (0.82)	12.3 (1.05)	11.0 (0.87)
10th	17.2 (1.07)	17.2 (1.23)	13.5 (0.88)	12.8 (0.89)	14.4 (1.08)	11.7 (0.86)	12.1 (0.83)	12.8 (0.86)	8.3 (0.61)	7.3 (0.76)	9.6 (0.74)	8.3 (0.60)
11th	13.8 (1.27)	10.8 (1.01)	9.4 (0.71)	10.4 (0.89)	10.4 (0.75)	11.0 (0.73)	9.5 (0.63)	9.2 (0.55)	7.5 (0.53)	6.5 (0.83)	6.0 (0.66)	6.4 (0.73)
12th	11.4 (0.66)	8.1 (1.00)	7.5 (0.56)	7.3 (0.70)	8.5 (0.70)	8.6 (0.62)	6.6 (0.59)	8.8 (0.69)	4.9 (0.63)	4.5 (0.51)	5.0 (0.61)	5.8 (0.70)

---Not available.

†Not applicable.

!Interpret data with caution. The coefficient of variation (CV) for this estimate is between 30 and 50 percent.

[1] The term "anywhere" is not used in the Youth Risk Behavior Survey (YRBS) questionnaire; students were simply asked how many times in the past 12 months they had been in a physical fight.

[2] Before 1999, Asian students and Pacific Islander students were not categorized separately, and students could not be classified as Two or more races. Because the response categories changed in 1999, caution should be used in comparing data on race from 1993 with data from later years.

[3] Students were asked which of the following—"heterosexual (straight)," "gay or lesbian," "bisexual," or "not sure"—best described them.

[4] In the question asking students about physical fights at school, "on school property" was not defined for respondents.

NOTE: Race categories exclude persons of Hispanic ethnicity.

SOURCE: Centers for Disease Control and Prevention, Division of Adolescent and School Health, Youth Risk Behavior Surveillance System (YRBSS), 1993 through 2019. (This table was prepared September 2020.)

Table 231.20. Percentage distribution of students in grades 9-12, by number of times they reported having been in a physical fight anywhere or on school property during the previous 12 months and selected student characteristics: 2019

[Standard errors appear in parentheses]

Student characteristic	Anywhere (including on school property)[1]								On school property[2]							
	0 times		1 to 3 times		4 to 11 times		12 or more times		0 times		1 to 3 times		4 to 11 times		12 or more times	
1	2		3		4		5		6		7		8		9	
Total	**78.1**	**(0.81)**	**17.2**	**(0.68)**	**3.2**	**(0.24)**	**1.4**	**(0.17)**	**92.0**	**(0.50)**	**6.9**	**(0.39)**	**0.5**	**(0.11)**	**0.6**	**(0.15)**
Sex																
Male	71.7	(1.23)	21.3	(1.00)	4.6	(0.39)	2.3	(0.29)	88.6	(0.72)	9.8	(0.60)	0.8	(0.17)	0.8	(0.22)
Female	84.7	(1.01)	13.0	(0.89)	1.8	(0.27)	0.4	(0.09)	95.6	(0.45)	3.9	(0.33)	0.2 !	(0.06)	0.3 !	(0.13)
Race/ethnicity																
White	80.2	(0.97)	16.3	(0.86)	2.6	(0.30)	0.8	(0.14)	93.6	(0.51)	5.9	(0.46)	0.3	(0.08)	0.2 !	(0.07)
Black	69.8	(1.77)	21.3	(1.66)	5.9	(0.88)	3.0	(0.78)	84.5	(1.06)	13.3	(0.80)	1.0	(0.25)	1.1 !	(0.43)
Hispanic	77.4	(1.12)	17.3	(1.15)	3.4	(0.47)	1.8	(0.38)	92.2	(0.68)	6.1	(0.47)	0.7 !	(0.26)	1.0 !	(0.39)
Asian	88.0	(1.87)	10.8	(1.72)	‡	(†)	‡	(†)	95.1	(1.47)	4.4 !	(1.35)	‡	(†)	‡	(†)
Pacific Islander	81.8	(4.85)	12.2	(3.20)	‡	(†)	‡	(†)	90.9	(3.38)	9.1 !	(3.38)	‡	(†)	‡	(†)
American Indian/Alaska Native	59.8	(6.85)	30.4	(5.62)	7.6 !	(2.96)	‡	(†)	81.1	(5.70)	15.8 !	(5.05)	‡	(†)	‡	(†)
Two or more races	71.3	(2.43)	22.6	(2.27)	4.3	(0.95)	1.8 !	(0.68)	89.0	(1.76)	9.5	(1.75)	1.0 !	(0.50)	‡	(†)
Sexual identity[3]																
Heterosexual	78.6	(0.87)	17.1	(0.74)	3.0	(0.25)	1.2	(0.16)	92.2	(0.51)	6.9	(0.44)	0.5	(0.11)	0.4 !	(0.11)
Gay, lesbian, or bisexual	76.1	(1.68)	18.1	(1.41)	4.2	(0.82)	1.6 !	(0.56)	91.8	(1.00)	6.6	(0.80)	0.8	(0.22)	‡	(†)
Not sure	78.9	(2.59)	15.3	(2.08)	3.7	(1.02)	2.2 !	(0.89)	90.4	(1.99)	6.2	(1.11)	0.8 !	(0.40)	‡	(†)
Grade																
9th	74.2	(1.51)	20.2	(1.25)	4.0	(0.52)	1.5	(0.41)	89.0	(0.87)	9.8	(0.83)	0.8	(0.20)	0.4 !	(0.18)
10th	76.7	(1.07)	18.8	(0.88)	3.1	(0.40)	1.3	(0.31)	91.7	(0.60)	7.5	(0.54)	0.4 !	(0.12)	0.5 !	(0.24)
11th	80.0	(1.01)	15.2	(0.89)	3.5	(0.34)	1.3	(0.25)	93.6	(0.73)	5.4	(0.67)	0.7 !	(0.23)	0.3 !	(0.11)
12th	82.4	(1.08)	14.3	(0.87)	2.3	(0.43)	1.1	(0.29)	94.2	(0.70)	4.8	(0.57)	0.3 !	(0.11)	0.7 !	(0.27)

†Not applicable.

!Interpret data with caution. The coefficient of variation (CV) for this estimate is between 30 and 50 percent.

‡Reporting standards not met. Either there are too few cases for a reliable estimate or the coefficient of variation (CV) is 50 percent or greater.

[1] The term "anywhere" is not used in the Youth Risk Behavior Survey (YRBS) questionnaire; students were simply asked how many times in the past 12 months they had been in a physical fight.

[2] In the question asking students about physical fights at school, "on school property" was not defined for respondents.

[3] Students were asked which of the following--"heterosexual (straight)," "gay or lesbian," "bisexual," or "not sure"--best described them.

NOTE: Race categories exclude persons of Hispanic ethnicity. Detail may not sum to totals because of rounding and the suppression of cells that do not meet National Center for Education Statistics reporting standards.

SOURCE: Centers for Disease Control and Prevention, Division of Adolescent and School Health, Youth Risk Behavior Surveillance System (YRBSS), 2019. (This table was prepared September 2020.)

Table 231.40. Percentage of students in grades 9-12 who reported carrying a weapon at least 1 day during the previous 30 days, by location and selected student characteristics: Selected years, 1993 through 2019

[Standard errors appear in parentheses]

Location and student characteristic	1993		1999		2001		2003		2005		2007		2009		2011		2013		2015		2017		2019	
1	2		3		4		5		6		7		8		9		10		11		12		13	
Anywhere (including on school property)[1]																								
Total	**22.1**	**(1.18)**	**17.3**	**(0.97)**	**17.4**	**(0.99)**	**17.1**	**(0.90)**	**18.5**	**(0.80)**	**18.0**	**(0.87)**	**17.5**	**(0.73)**	**16.6**	**(0.65)**	**17.9**	**(0.73)**	**16.2**	**(0.91)**	**15.7**	**(1.26)**	**13.2**	**(0.65)**
Sex																								
Male	34.3	(1.68)	28.6	(1.71)	29.3	(1.67)	26.9	(1.31)	29.8	(1.35)	28.5	(1.41)	27.1	(1.45)	25.9	(1.07)	28.1	(1.31)	24.3	(1.27)	24.2	(1.67)	19.5	(0.92)
Female	9.2	(0.85)	6.0	(0.56)	6.2	(0.41)	6.7	(0.60)	7.1	(0.43)	7.5	(0.66)	7.1	(0.38)	6.8	(0.41)	7.9	(0.56)	7.5	(0.79)	7.4	(0.85)	6.7	(0.48)
Race/ethnicity																								
White	20.6	(1.43)	16.4	(1.36)	17.9	(1.30)	16.7	(0.95)	18.7	(1.13)	18.2	(1.28)	18.6	(1.16)	17.0	(1.05)	20.8	(0.90)	18.1	(1.37)	18.1	(1.78)	15.0	(0.96)
Black	28.5	(1.24)	17.2	(2.68)	15.2	(1.23)	17.3	(1.77)	16.4	(0.81)	17.2	(1.05)	14.4	(1.33)	14.2	(0.85)	12.5	(0.96)	12.4	(1.37)	10.8	(1.13)	9.4	(0.96)
Hispanic	24.4	(1.35)	18.7	(1.35)	16.5	(0.78)	16.5	(1.31)	19.0	(1.10)	18.5	(1.21)	17.2	(0.94)	16.2	(0.82)	15.5	(0.95)	13.7	(1.16)	12.7	(1.09)	11.7	(1.13)
Asian[2]	---	(†)	13.0	(2.01)	10.6	(2.10)	11.6	(2.67)	7.0	(1.70)	7.8	(1.41)	8.4	(1.28)	9.1	(1.57)	8.7	(1.79)	7.1	(1.33)	5.6	(1.10)	5.2	(0.81)
Pacific Islander[2]	---	(†)	25.3	(5.02)	17.4	(4.35)	16.3 !	(6.37)	20.0 !	(6.52)	25.5	(4.35)	20.3	(3.40)	20.7	(5.00)	12.6 !	(3.98)	26.3	(7.87)	18.2	(5.25)	10.0 !	(4.77)
American Indian/Alaska Native	34.2	(8.08)	21.8	(5.68)	31.2	(5.52)	29.3	(4.58)	25.6	(3.79)	20.6	(3.02)	20.7	(3.40)	27.6	(2.41)	17.8	(4.01)	22.4	(4.01)	21.3	(4.50)	27.3	(6.56)
Two or more races[2]	---	(†)	22.2	(3.34)	25.2	(3.41)	29.8	(5.03)	26.7	(3.11)	19.0	(2.46)	17.9	(1.61)	23.7	(2.58)	18.8	(2.09)	20.8	(2.52)	16.1	(2.95)	17.5	(2.38)
Sexual identity[3]																								
Heterosexual	---	(†)	---	(†)	---	(†)	---	(†)	---	(†)	---	(†)	---	(†)	---	(†)	---	(†)	16.0	(0.96)	15.6	(1.13)	12.7	(0.66)
Gay, lesbian, or bisexual	---	(†)	---	(†)	---	(†)	---	(†)	---	(†)	---	(†)	---	(†)	---	(†)	---	(†)	18.9	(2.07)	16.2	(1.49)	13.9	(1.64)
Not sure	---	(†)	---	(†)	---	(†)	---	(†)	---	(†)	---	(†)	---	(†)	---	(†)	---	(†)	14.7	(3.00)	17.4	(3.25)	12.9	(2.46)
Grade																								
9th	25.5	(1.42)	17.6	(1.58)	19.8	(1.44)	18.0	(1.81)	19.9	(1.21)	20.1	(1.41)	18.0	(0.87)	17.3	(1.07)	17.5	(0.99)	16.1	(1.11)	15.3	(1.66)	12.5	(0.78)
10th	21.4	(1.11)	18.7	(1.31)	16.7	(1.11)	15.9	(1.14)	19.4	(1.19)	18.8	(1.21)	18.4	(1.51)	16.6	(0.89)	17.8	(1.09)	16.3	(1.49)	15.3	(1.14)	12.2	(0.95)
11th	21.5	(1.66)	16.1	(1.31)	16.8	(1.26)	18.2	(1.21)	17.1	(1.13)	16.7	(1.08)	16.2	(0.93)	16.2	(0.84)	17.9	(1.43)	16.0	(1.19)	16.8	(1.56)	12.9	(1.10)
12th	19.9	(1.46)	15.9	(1.44)	15.1	(1.28)	15.5	(1.06)	16.9	(0.95)	15.5	(1.28)	16.6	(0.85)	15.8	(0.90)	18.3	(1.17)	15.8	(1.26)	14.6	(1.32)	14.9	(1.24)
On school property[4]																								
Total	**11.8**	**(0.73)**	**6.9**	**(0.60)**	**6.4**	**(0.52)**	**6.1**	**(0.57)**	**6.5**	**(0.46)**	**5.9**	**(0.37)**	**5.6**	**(0.32)**	**5.4**	**(0.35)**	**5.2**	**(0.44)**	**4.1**	**(0.29)**	**3.8**	**(0.45)**	**2.8**	**(0.34)**
Sex																								
Male	17.9	(0.96)	11.0	(1.07)	10.2	(0.88)	8.9	(0.74)	10.2	(0.83)	9.0	(0.65)	8.0	(0.52)	8.2	(0.59)	7.6	(0.70)	5.9	(0.45)	5.6	(0.64)	3.7	(0.39)
Female	5.1	(0.65)	2.8	(0.38)	2.9	(0.27)	3.1	(0.50)	2.6	(0.30)	2.7	(0.33)	2.9	(0.24)	2.3	(0.19)	3.0	(0.40)	2.0	(0.28)	1.9	(0.29)	1.7	(0.38)
Race/ethnicity																								
White	10.9	(0.86)	6.4	(0.87)	6.1	(0.62)	5.5	(0.57)	6.1	(0.66)	5.3	(0.55)	5.6	(0.44)	5.1	(0.40)	5.7	(0.65)	3.7	(0.42)	3.8	(0.63)	2.1	(0.33)
Black	15.0	(0.85)	5.0	(0.50)	6.3	(0.92)	6.9	(0.96)	5.1	(0.66)	6.0	(0.46)	5.3	(0.74)	4.6	(0.67)	3.9	(0.42)	3.4	(0.69)	3.6	(0.72)	4.2	(0.94)
Hispanic	13.3	(1.09)	7.9	(0.73)	6.4	(0.53)	6.0	(0.56)	8.2	(0.91)	7.3	(0.82)	5.8	(0.58)	5.8	(0.70)	4.7	(0.61)	4.5	(0.57)	3.5	(0.39)	3.1	(0.55)
Asian[2]	---	(†)	6.5	(1.44)	7.2	(2.05)	6.6 !	(2.44)	2.8 !	(1.24)	4.1	(1.01)	3.6	(0.84)	4.3 !	(1.66)	3.8	(1.13)	2.3 !	(0.78)	2.2 !	(0.89)	1.3 !	(0.47)
Pacific Islander[2]	---	(†)	9.3	(2.66)	10.0 !	(3.05)	4.9 !	(2.05)	15.4 !	(6.10)	9.5 !	(3.40)	9.8	(2.33)	10.9 !	(3.73)	4.0 !	(1.95)	15.0 !	(6.42)	2.7 !	(1.36)	‡	(†)
American Indian/Alaska Native	17.6 !	(5.70)	11.6 !	(5.13)	16.4	(4.02)	12.9	(3.40)	7.2	(1.60)	7.7	(2.08)	4.2 !	(1.50)	7.5	(1.62)	7.0 !	(3.22)	10.5	(2.48)	6.3 !	(2.66)	10.8 !	(3.78)
Two or more races[2]	---	(†)	11.4	(2.76)	13.2	(3.61)	13.3 !	(4.10)	11.9	(2.99)	5.0	(1.11)	5.8	(1.35)	7.5	(1.87)	6.3	(1.58)	5.7	(1.54)	4.1	(1.11)	3.3	(0.71)
Sexual identity[3]																								
Heterosexual	---	(†)	---	(†)	---	(†)	---	(†)	---	(†)	---	(†)	---	(†)	---	(†)	---	(†)	3.7	(0.31)	3.4	(0.37)	2.1	(0.26)
Gay, lesbian, or bisexual	---	(†)	---	(†)	---	(†)	---	(†)	---	(†)	---	(†)	---	(†)	---	(†)	---	(†)	6.2	(1.18)	5.9	(1.38)	4.3	(1.07)
Not sure	---	(†)	---	(†)	---	(†)	---	(†)	---	(†)	---	(†)	---	(†)	---	(†)	---	(†)	7.1	(1.88)	4.9	(1.09)	6.9 !	(2.20)
Grade																								
9th	12.6	(0.73)	7.2	(1.07)	6.7	(0.66)	5.3	(1.13)	6.4	(0.75)	6.0	(0.59)	4.9	(0.46)	4.8	(0.50)	4.8	(0.69)	3.4	(0.31)	2.5	(0.46)	2.0	(0.38)
10th	11.5	(0.97)	6.6	(0.83)	6.7	(0.60)	6.0	(0.53)	6.9	(0.70)	5.8	(0.61)	6.1	(0.57)	6.1	(0.72)	4.8	(0.58)	4.1	(0.54)	3.2	(0.56)	2.2	(0.49)
11th	11.9	(1.41)	7.0	(0.60)	6.1	(0.74)	6.6	(0.80)	5.9	(0.71)	5.5	(0.68)	5.2	(0.44)	4.7	(0.44)	5.9	(1.19)	4.8	(0.50)	5.0	(0.59)	3.3	(0.45)
12th	10.8	(0.83)	6.2	(0.78)	6.1	(0.71)	6.4	(0.64)	6.7	(0.64)	6.0	(0.58)	6.0	(0.57)	5.6	(0.51)	5.3	(0.88)	3.6	(0.56)	4.2	(0.59)	3.3	(0.60)

—Not available.

†Not applicable.

!Interpret data with caution. The coefficient of variation (CV) for this estimate is between 30 and 50 percent.

‡Reporting standards not met. Either there are too few cases for a reliable estimate or the coefficient of variation (CV) is 50 percent or greater.

[1] The term "anywhere" is not used in the Youth Risk Behavior Survey (YRBS) questionnaire; students were simply asked how many days they carried a weapon during the past 30 days.

[2] Before 1999, Asian students and Pacific Islander students were not categorized separately, and students could not be classified as Two or more races. Because the response categories changed in 1999, caution should be used in comparing data on race from 1993 with data from later years.

[3] Students were asked which of the following—"heterosexual (straight)," "gay or lesbian," "bisexual," or "not sure"—best described them.

[4] In the question asking students about carrying a weapon at school, "on school property" was not defined for respondents.

NOTE: Respondents were asked about carrying "a weapon such as a gun, knife, or club." Race categories exclude persons of Hispanic ethnicity.

SOURCE: Centers for Disease Control and Prevention, Division of Adolescent and School Health, Youth Risk Behavior Surveillance System (YRBSS), 1993 through 2019. (This table was prepared September 2020.)

Table 231.50. Percentage distribution of students in grades 9-12, by number of days they reported carrying a weapon anywhere or on school property during the previous 30 days and selected student characteristics: 2019

[Standard errors appear in parentheses]

Student characteristic	Anywhere (including on school property)[1]								On school property[2]							
	0 days		1 day		2 to 5 days		6 or more days		0 days		1 day		2 to 5 days		6 or more days	
1	2		3		4		5		6		7		8		9	
Total	**86.8**	**(0.65)**	**2.7**	**(0.17)**	**4.6**	**(0.29)**	**5.8**	**(0.46)**	**97.2**	**(0.34)**	**0.7**	**(0.14)**	**0.7**	**(0.12)**	**1.4**	**(0.19)**
Sex																
Male	80.5	(0.92)	3.7	(0.28)	6.6	(0.42)	9.2	(0.78)	96.3	(0.39)	0.7	(0.14)	1.1	(0.23)	1.9	(0.26)
Female	93.3	(0.48)	1.7	(0.25)	2.5	(0.27)	2.4	(0.27)	98.3	(0.38)	0.6 !	(0.18)	0.2	(0.05)	0.8	(0.24)
Race/ethnicity																
White	85.0	(0.96)	3.0	(0.24)	5.2	(0.38)	6.9	(0.71)	97.9	(0.33)	0.4	(0.10)	0.5 !	(0.17)	1.2	(0.20)
Black	90.6	(0.96)	2.0	(0.39)	3.0	(0.48)	4.3	(0.70)	95.8	(0.94)	1.2 !	(0.40)	1.1 !	(0.35)	1.9 !	(0.64)
Hispanic	88.3	(1.13)	2.7	(0.31)	4.2	(0.52)	4.8	(0.63)	96.9	(0.55)	0.8	(0.22)	0.8 !	(0.24)	1.5	(0.36)
Asian	94.8	(0.80)	1.1	(0.30)	2.6	(0.53)	1.5 !	(0.71)	98.7	(0.47)	‡	(†)	0.9 !	(0.43)	‡	(†)
Pacific Islander	90.0	(4.95)	‡	(†)	‡	(†)	‡	(†)	98.2	(1.04)	‡	(†)	‡	(†)	‡	(†)
American Indian/Alaska Native	72.7	(6.40)	3.2 !	(1.59)	‡	(†)	20.0	(5.07)	89.2	(3.81)	4.0 !	(1.88)	‡	(†)	‡	(†)
Two or more races	82.5	(2.38)	3.9	(1.02)	6.0	(1.47)	7.7	(1.22)	96.7	(0.71)	‡	(†)	‡	(†)	2.1 !	(0.70)
Sexual identity[3]																
Heterosexual	87.3	(0.66)	2.6	(0.18)	4.4	(0.30)	5.6	(0.49)	97.9	(0.26)	0.5	(0.10)	0.6	(0.12)	1.0	(0.15)
Gay, lesbian, or bisexual	86.1	(1.64)	3.5	(0.63)	5.4	(0.92)	5.0	(0.95)	95.7	(1.07)	1.5 !	(0.54)	0.8 !	(0.31)	2.0 !	(0.63)
Not sure	87.1	(2.46)	3.3 !	(1.10)	4.0 !	(1.33)	5.6	(1.66)	93.1	(2.20)	1.1 !	(0.51)	1.7 !	(0.62)	4.1 !	(1.83)
Grade																
9th	87.5	(0.78)	3.1	(0.37)	4.6	(0.53)	4.8	(0.66)	98.0	(0.38)	0.5 !	(0.15)	0.8 !	(0.29)	0.7 !	(0.22)
10th	87.8	(0.95)	2.4	(0.38)	4.6	(0.56)	5.2	(0.61)	97.8	(0.49)	0.6	(0.15)	0.5	(0.15)	1.1	(0.32)
11th	87.1	(1.09)	2.8	(0.53)	3.8	(0.41)	6.3	(0.81)	96.7	(0.45)	0.8	(0.22)	0.7	(0.19)	1.9	(0.34)
12th	85.1	(1.23)	2.5	(0.36)	5.4	(0.65)	7.0	(0.85)	96.7	(0.60)	0.8 !	(0.33)	0.7	(0.18)	1.9	(0.34)

†Not applicable.

!Interpret data with caution. The coefficient of variation (CV) for this estimate is between 30 and 50 percent.

‡Reporting standards not met. Either there are too few cases for a reliable estimate or the coefficient of variation (CV) is 50 percent or greater.

[1] The term "anywhere" is not used in the Youth Risk Behavior Survey (YRBS) questionnaire; students were simply asked how many days they carried a weapon during the past 30 days.

[2] In the question asking students about carrying a weapon at school, "on school property" was not defined for respondents.

[3] Students were asked which of the following--"heterosexual (straight)," "gay or lesbian," "bisexual," or "not sure"--best described them.

NOTE: Respondents were asked about carrying "a weapon such as a gun, knife, or club." Race categories exclude persons of Hispanic ethnicity. Detail may not sum to totals because of rounding and the suppression of cells that do not meet National Center for Education Statistics reporting standards.

SOURCE: Centers for Disease Control and Prevention, Division of Adolescent and School Health, Youth Risk Behavior Surveillance System (YRBSS), 2019. (This table was prepared September 2020.)

Table 231.60. Percentage of public school students in grades 9-12 who reported carrying a weapon at least 1 day during the previous 30 days, by location and state or jurisdiction: Selected years, 2005 through 2017

[Standard errors appear in parentheses]

State or jurisdiction	Anywhere (including on school property)[1]							On school property[2]						
	2005	2007	2009	2011	2013	2015	2017	2005	2007	2009	2011	2013	2015	2017
1	2	3	4	5	6	7	8	9	10	11	12	13	14	15
United States[3]	**18.5 (0.80)**	**18.0 (0.87)**	**17.5 (0.73)**	**16.6 (0.65)**	**17.9 (0.73)**	**16.2 (0.91)**	**15.7 (1.26)**	**6.5 (0.46)**	**5.9 (0.37)**	**5.6 (0.32)**	**5.4 (0.35)**	**5.2 (0.44)**	**4.1 (0.29)**	**3.8 (0.45)**
Alabama	21.0 (1.72)	— (†)	22.9 (2.27)	21.5 (1.54)	23.1 (1.55)	22.5 (1.91)	— (†)	8.4 (1.44)	— (†)	8.7 (1.42)	8.2 (1.02)	5.5 (0.56)	5.6 (1.15)	— (†)
Alaska	— (†)	24.4 (1.61)	20.0 (1.30)	19.0 (1.19)	19.2 (1.31)	— (†)	— (†)	— (†)	8.4 (1.07)	7.8 (0.83)	5.7 (0.72)	6.1 (0.80)	8.2 (0.87)	10.2 (1.01)
Arizona	20.6 (0.84)	20.5 (0.91)	19.9 (1.25)	17.5 (1.17)	17.5 (1.17)	18.0 (1.28)	15.6 (1.83)	7.4 (0.53)	7.0 (0.75)	6.5 (0.64)	5.7 (0.59)	4.8 (0.86)	4.5 (0.93)	3.5 (0.54)
Arkansas	25.9 (1.15)	20.7 (1.36)	22.9 (1.82)	21.1 (1.76)	27.1 (1.76)	21.0 (1.40)	22.2 (2.57)	10.5 (1.10)	6.8 (0.85)	8.4 (1.02)	6.5 (0.95)	9.1 (1.10)	5.4 (0.90)	6.3 (0.77)
California	— (†)	— (†)	— (†)	— (†)	— (†)	8.9 (1.25)	— (†)	— (†)	— (†)	— (†)	— (†)	— (†)	2.8 (0.50)	4.7 (0.87)
Colorado	17.0 (1.57)	— (†)	16.7 (1.27)	15.5 (1.31)	— (†)	— (†)	— (†)	5.4 (0.81)	— (†)	5.5 (0.90)	5.5 (0.69)	— (†)	— (†)	4.9 (0.62)
Connecticut	16.3 (1.30)	17.2 (1.72)	12.4 (0.89)	— (†)	— (†)	— (†)	— (†)	6.4 (0.83)	5.5 (1.03)	3.9 (0.45)	6.6 (0.67)	6.6 (0.82)	6.2 (0.59)	5.4 (0.55)
Delaware	16.6 (1.04)	17.1 (1.00)	18.5 (0.92)	13.5 (0.88)	14.4 (0.80)	13.0 (0.91)	13.5 (0.97)	5.7 (0.54)	5.4 (0.55)	5.1 (0.59)	5.2 (0.57)	3.1 (0.34)	4.0 (0.54)	3.1 (0.42)
District of Columbia	17.2 (1.11)	21.3 (1.45)	— (†)	18.9 (1.34)	20.0 (0.47)	18.1 (0.40)	18.8 (0.48)	6.7 (0.60)	7.4 (0.76)	— (†)	5.5 (0.88)	— (†)	— (†)	— (†)
Florida	15.2 (0.68)	18.0 (0.93)	17.3 (0.60)	15.6 (0.76)	15.7 (0.67)	15.4 (0.92)	14.2 (0.64)	4.7 (0.41)	5.6 (0.41)	4.7 (0.35)	— (†)	— (†)	— (†)	3.2 (0.26)
Georgia	22.1 (1.99)	19.5 (0.96)	18.8 (1.11)	22.8 (2.25)	18.5 (1.51)	— (†)	— (†)	7.5 (1.50)	5.3 (0.48)	6.0 (0.90)	8.6 (1.80)	4.2 (0.66)	— (†)	— (†)
Hawaii	13.3 (1.03)	14.8 (1.56)	15.9 (2.06)	13.9 (0.81)	10.5 (0.87)	10.7 (0.58)	11.9 (0.79)	4.9 (0.72)	3.7 (0.92)	4.7 (0.63)	4.2 (0.45)	— (†)	— (†)	— (†)
Idaho	23.9 (1.45)	23.6 (1.35)	21.8 (1.15)	22.8 (1.30)	27.1 (1.31)	28.2 (1.52)	29.6 (1.36)	— (†)	8.9 (0.96)	6.7 (0.59)	6.3 (0.78)	6.5 (0.92)	6.8 (1.02)	9.8 (1.31)
Illinois	— (†)	14.3 (1.01)	16.0 (1.04)	12.6 (0.91)	15.8 (1.22)	15.4 (1.41)	14.0 (1.04)	— (†)	3.7 (0.67)	4.8 (0.59)	3.9 (0.53)	4.7 (0.57)	4.3 (0.51)	3.7 (0.68)
Indiana	19.2 (1.25)	20.9 (0.80)	18.1 (1.58)	17.0 (1.46)	— (†)	19.6 (1.84)	— (†)	5.8 (0.71)	6.9 (0.64)	5.7 (0.80)	3.7 (0.46)	— (†)	5.6 (1.13)	— (†)
Iowa	15.7 (1.49)	12.8 (1.13)	— (†)	15.8 (1.26)	— (†)	— (†)	18.1 (2.15)	4.3 (0.70)	4.4 (0.61)	— (†)	4.5 (0.76)	— (†)	— (†)	4.2 (0.62)
Kansas	16.2 (1.37)	18.4 (1.19)	16.0 (1.26)	— (†)	16.1 (0.87)	— (†)	16.9 (1.12)	4.9 (0.85)	5.7 (0.75)	5.1 (0.65)	5.2 (0.72)	— (†)	— (†)	— (†)
Kentucky	23.1 (1.49)	24.4 (1.08)	21.7 (1.72)	22.8 (1.72)	20.7 (1.35)	23.1 (1.62)	20.5 (1.68)	6.8 (0.72)	8.0 (0.59)	6.5 (0.77)	7.4 (1.25)	6.4 (0.73)	6.5 (1.03)	4.9 (0.87)
Louisiana	— (†)	— (†)	19.6 (1.73)	22.2 (0.98)	22.8 (2.78)	— (†)	22.8 (2.05)	— (†)	— (†)	5.8 (1.12)	4.2 (1.01)	7.0 (1.37)	— (†)	5.7 (0.83)
Maine	18.3 (2.00)	15.0 (1.47)	— (†)	— (†)	— (†)	— (†)	— (†)	5.9 (1.03)	4.9 (0.70)	— (†)	8.0 (0.45)	7.1 (0.46)	5.8 (0.37)	5.3 (0.39)
Maryland	19.1 (1.59)	19.3 (1.51)	16.6 (1.19)	15.9 (1.10)	15.8 (0.27)	14.9 (0.24)	— (†)	6.9 (0.88)	5.9 (0.81)	4.6 (0.58)	5.3 (0.55)	4.8 (0.13)	4.3 (0.14)	7.4 (0.21)
Massachusetts	15.2 (0.88)	14.9 (0.88)	12.8 (1.00)	12.3 (0.95)	11.6 (0.83)	12.6 (1.20)	11.1 (0.75)	5.8 (0.59)	5.0 (0.48)	4.4 (0.58)	3.7 (0.46)	3.1 (0.50)	3.2 (0.38)	2.7 (0.24)
Michigan	15.8 (1.49)	17.9 (1.30)	16.6 (0.69)	15.7 (0.94)	15.5 (1.06)	16.6 (1.50)	17.5 (1.21)	4.7 (0.54)	5.0 (0.66)	5.4 (0.33)	3.5 (0.37)	3.8 (0.35)	3.6 (0.60)	4.1 (0.86)
Minnesota	— (†)	— (†)	— (†)	— (†)	— (†)	— (†)	— (†)	— (†)	— (†)	— (†)	— (†)	— (†)	— (†)	— (†)
Mississippi	— (†)	17.3 (1.33)	17.2 (1.02)	18.0 (1.39)	19.1 (1.56)	21.0 (1.50)	— (†)	— (†)	4.8 (0.60)	4.5 (0.48)	4.2 (0.76)	4.1 (0.66)	5.2 (0.51)	— (†)
Missouri	19.4 (1.79)	18.6 (1.48)	16.0 (1.44)	— (†)	22.2 (1.93)	22.1 (1.72)	19.8 (1.65)	7.3 (0.99)	4.6 (0.83)	5.3 (1.02)	— (†)	— (†)	5.9 (0.68)	4.2 (0.92)
Montana	21.4 (1.20)	22.1 (0.76)	23.0 (1.07)	23.5 (0.96)	25.7 (0.84)	26.4 (0.94)	25.2 (0.82)	10.2 (0.89)	9.7 (0.57)	7.9 (0.67)	9.3 (0.69)	9.9 (0.58)	10.6 (0.80)	8.5 (0.62)
Nebraska	17.9 (0.89)	— (†)	— (†)	18.6 (0.90)	— (†)	— (†)	— (†)	4.8 (0.48)	— (†)	— (†)	3.8 (0.45)	— (†)	8.1 (0.95)	5.4 (1.00)
Nevada	18.4 (1.32)	14.5 (1.08)	19.1 (1.08)	— (†)	16.0 (1.50)	18.3 (1.53)	— (†)	6.8 (0.91)	4.7 (0.61)	6.2 (0.62)	— (†)	3.3 (0.64)	3.7 (0.59)	4.8 (0.61)
New Hampshire	16.2 (1.26)	18.1 (1.46)	— (†)	14.5 (1.04)	— (†)	— (†)	16.0 (0.46)	6.5 (0.93)	5.8 (0.61)	8.8 (1.00)	— (†)	— (†)	— (†)	3.6 (0.21)
New Jersey	10.5 (0.95)	— (†)	9.6 (0.81)	9.6 (1.17)	10.2 (1.08)	— (†)	— (†)	3.1 (0.53)	— (†)	3.1 (0.45)	— (†)	2.7 (0.34)	— (†)	— (†)
New Mexico	24.5 (1.44)	27.5 (1.20)	27.4 (0.90)	22.8 (0.93)	22.2 (0.88)	22.5 (0.82)	24.2 (0.96)	8.0 (0.29)	9.3 (0.66)	8.1 (0.59)	6.5 (0.51)	5.4 (0.42)	4.6 (0.33)	5.8 (0.52)
New York	14.3 (0.74)	14.2 (0.76)	13.9 (0.98)	12.6 (0.76)	12.8 (0.82)	13.0 (0.96)	11.6 (0.84)	5.2 (0.42)	4.7 (0.41)	4.8 (0.64)	4.2 (0.32)	4.0 (0.38)	4.5 (0.51)	3.4 (0.39)
North Carolina	21.5 (1.35)	21.2 (1.19)	19.6 (0.95)	20.8 (1.24)	20.6 (1.34)	19.3 (1.33)	18.4 (1.27)	6.4 (0.77)	6.8 (0.94)	4.7 (0.57)	6.1 (0.64)	4.5 (0.67)	3.9 (0.54)	3.4 (0.44)
North Dakota	— (†)	— (†)	— (†)	— (†)	— (†)	— (†)	— (†)	6.0 (0.74)	5.0 (0.57)	5.4 (0.64)	5.7 (0.73)	6.4 (0.75)	5.2 (0.49)	5.9 (0.75)
Ohio[4]	15.2 (1.27)	16.6 (1.42)	— (†)	16.4 (1.37)	14.2 (1.61)	— (†)	— (†)	4.4 (0.63)	4.1 (0.51)	— (†)	— (†)	— (†)	— (†)	— (†)
Oklahoma	18.9 (1.38)	22.3 (1.65)	19.0 (1.44)	19.4 (1.86)	19.9 (1.41)	19.5 (1.66)	20.4 (1.55)	7.0 (0.77)	9.0 (1.43)	5.6 (0.79)	6.1 (1.14)	6.0 (0.77)	4.8 (0.80)	6.4 (0.79)
Oregon	— (†)	— (†)	— (†)	— (†)	— (†)	— (†)	— (†)	— (†)	— (†)	— (†)	— (†)	— (†)	— (†)	— (†)
Pennsylvania	— (†)	— (†)	14.8 (1.28)	— (†)	— (†)	17.4 (1.27)	17.4 (1.14)	— (†)	— (†)	3.3 (0.47)	— (†)	— (†)	2.0 (0.44)	2.2 (0.30)
Rhode Island	12.4 (0.90)	12.0 (0.74)	10.4 (0.50)	11.2 (0.82)	— (†)	— (†)	— (†)	4.9 (0.41)	4.9 (0.63)	4.0 (0.33)	4.0 (0.39)	5.0 (0.78)	4.8 (0.80)	5.1 (1.01)
South Carolina	20.5 (1.42)	19.8 (1.69)	20.4 (2.22)	23.4 (1.86)	21.2 (1.25)	20.5 (1.88)	18.3 (1.32)	6.7 (0.82)	4.8 (0.79)	4.6 (0.67)	6.3 (0.89)	3.7 (0.48)	2.9 (0.46)	3.9 (0.65)
South Dakota[5]	— (†)	— (†)	— (†)	— (†)	— (†)	— (†)	— (†)	8.3 (0.72)	6.3 (0.80)	9.2 (0.76)	5.7 (0.52)	6.8 (0.87)	7.1 (1.29)	— (†)
Tennessee	24.1 (1.58)	22.6 (1.41)	20.5 (1.64)	21.1 (1.34)	19.2 (1.70)	— (†)	18.5 (1.45)	8.1 (0.92)	5.6 (0.70)	5.1 (0.70)	5.2 (0.80)	5.4 (0.79)	— (†)	— (†)
Texas	19.3 (0.93)	18.8 (0.71)	18.2 (0.89)	17.6 (0.73)	18.4 (1.33)	— (†)	16.5 (1.23)	7.9 (0.63)	6.8 (0.55)	6.4 (0.76)	4.9 (0.45)	5.6 (0.68)	— (†)	— (†)
Utah	17.7 (1.70)	17.1 (1.38)	16.0 (1.40)	16.8 (1.48)	17.2 (1.19)	— (†)	24.0 (1.86)	7.0 (1.03)	7.5 (1.00)	4.6 (0.63)	5.9 (1.01)	5.0 (0.57)	— (†)	7.1 (0.70)
Vermont[6]	— (†)	— (†)	— (†)	— (†)	— (†)	— (†)	— (†)	9.1 (0.90)	9.6 (1.05)	9.0 (0.61)	9.1 (0.73)	10.4 (1.28)	7.7 (0.19)	6.9 (0.18)
Virginia	— (†)	— (†)	— (†)	20.4 (1.26)	15.8 (0.69)	15.0 (0.75)	— (†)	— (†)	— (†)	— (†)	5.7 (0.64)	— (†)	2.6 (0.44)	3.8 (0.38)
Washington	— (†)	— (†)	— (†)	— (†)	— (†)	— (†)	— (†)	— (†)	— (†)	— (†)	— (†)	— (†)	— (†)	— (†)
West Virginia	22.3 (1.32)	21.3 (1.52)	24.4 (1.05)	20.7 (1.64)	24.3 (2.16)	26.1 (1.57)	23.9 (1.63)	8.5 (1.00)	6.9 (0.89)	6.5 (0.72)	5.5 (0.75)	5.5 (0.99)	6.5 (0.87)	4.8 (0.79)
Wisconsin	15.8 (1.19)	12.7 (0.76)	10.9 (0.81)	10.4 (0.66)	14.4 (1.32)	— (†)	— (†)	3.9 (0.54)	3.6 (0.49)	3.4 (0.50)	3.1 (0.41)	3.2 (0.52)	— (†)	5.2 (0.74)
Wyoming	28.0 (1.17)	26.8 (1.28)	26.0 (1.04)	27.1 (1.19)	28.8 (0.95)	29.6 (1.33)	— (†)	10.0 (0.71)	11.4 (0.76)	11.5 (0.81)	10.5 (0.71)	9.9 (0.62)	10.7 (0.82)	— (†)
Puerto Rico	8.9 (0.80)	— (†)	— (†)	10.0 (1.19)	8.9 (0.62)	7.1 (0.90)	9.4 (2.18)	3.7 (0.49)	— (†)	— (†)	4.4 (0.58)	2.8 (0.44)	2.8 (0.42)	5.5! (1.80)

—Not available.

†Not applicable.

!Interpret data with caution. The coefficient of variation (CV) for this estimate is between 30 and 50 percent.

[1] The term "anywhere" is not used in the Youth Risk Behavior Survey (YRBS) questionnaire; students were simply asked how many days they carried a weapon during the past 30 days.

[2] In the question asking students about carrying a weapon at school, "on school property" was not defined for survey respondents.

[3] U.S. total data are representative of all public and private school students in grades 9-12 in the 50 states and the District of Columbia. U.S. total data for all years were collected through a separate national survey (rather than being aggregated from state-level data) and include both public and private schools.

[4] Ohio data for 2005 through 2013 include both public and private schools.

[5] South Dakota data for 2005 through 2015 include both public and private schools.

[6] Vermont data for 2013 include both public and private schools.

NOTE: Respondents were asked about carrying "a weapon such as a gun, knife, or club." For the U.S. total, data for all years include both public and private schools. State-level data include public schools only, except where otherwise noted. For specific states, a given year's data may be unavailable (1) because the state did not participate in the survey that year; (2) because the state omitted this particular survey item from the state-level questionnaire; or (3) because the state had an overall response rate of less than 60 percent (the overall response rate is the school response rate multiplied by the student response rate).

SOURCE: Centers for Disease Control and Prevention, Division of Adolescent and School Health, Youth Risk Behavior Surveillance System (YRBSS), 2005 through 2017. (This table was prepared July 2018.)

Table 231.65. Total number of public school students who brought firearms to or possessed firearms at school and number of students who did this per 100,000 students enrolled, by state or jurisdiction: 2009-10 through 2018-19

State or jurisdiction	Total number of students who brought firearms to or possessed firearms at school										Number of students who did this per 100,000 students enrolled									
	2009-10	2010-11	2011-12	2012-13	2013-14	2014-15	2015-16	2016-17	2017-18	2018-19	2009-10	2010-11	2011-12	2012-13	2013-14	2014-15	2015-16	2016-17	2017-18	2018-19
1	2	3	4	5	6	7	8	9	10	11	12	13	14	15	16	17	18	19	20	21
United States	**2,660**	**2,534**	**2,687**	**2,936**	**3,048**	**2,888**	**3,186**	**3,272**	**3,482**	**2,939**	**5.4**	**5.1**	**5.4**	**5.9**	**6.1**	**5.7**	**6.3**	**6.5**	**6.9**	**5.8**
Alabama	52	39	12	91	97	67	100	70	40	40	6.9	5.2	1.6	12.2	13.0	9.0	13.4	9.4	5.4	5.4
Alaska	8	3	6	5	4	4	7	7	10	8	6.1	2.3	4.6	3.8	3.1	3.0	5.3	5.3	7.5	6.1
Arizona	33	33	43	39	34	36	29	79	41	27	3.1	3.1	4.0	3.6	3.1	3.2	2.6	7.0	3.7	2.4
Arkansas	97	114	105	115	113	123	112	142	148	126	20.2	23.6	21.7	23.7	23.1	25.1	22.8	28.8	29.8	25.4
California	375	238	157	323	316	321	380	346	376	310	6.0	3.8	2.5	5.1	5.0	5.1	6.0	5.5	6.0	4.9
Colorado	47	65	67	42	45	22	27	30	48	51	5.6	7.7	7.8	4.9	5.1	2.5	3.0	3.3	5.3	5.6
Connecticut	35	40	42	45	24	36	41	40	22	23	6.2	7.1	7.6	8.2	4.4	6.6	7.6	7.5	4.1	4.4
Delaware	8	6	2	3	7	3	7	3	6	8	6.3	4.6	1.6	2.3	5.3	2.2	5.2	2.2	4.4	5.8
District of Columbia	7	6	49	0	72	19	13	11	14	11	10.1	8.4	66.3	0.0	92.1	23.5	15.5	12.8	16.0	12.4
Florida	104	113	105	96	120	134	146	131	172	181	3.9	4.3	3.9	3.6	4.4	4.9	5.2	4.7	6.1	6.4
Georgia	169	180	141	179	134	122	185	204	203	167	10.1	10.7	8.4	10.5	7.8	7.0	10.5	11.6	11.5	9.4
Hawaii	8	2	1	1	0	0	34	25	26	21	4.4	1.1	0.5	0.5	0.0	0.0	18.7	13.8	14.4	11.6
Idaho	25	0	17	5	7	6	9	8	7	2	9.0	0.0	6.1	1.8	2.4	2.1	3.1	2.7	2.3	0.6
Illinois	22	7	7	5	5	184	177	189	190	57[1]	1.0	0.3	0.3	0.2	0.2	9.0	8.7	9.3	9.5	2.9[1]
Indiana	50	33	48	49	51	56	81	67	74	72	4.8	3.2	4.6	4.7	4.9	5.4	7.7	6.4	7.0	6.8
Iowa	5	2	3	4	3	3	1	36	38	58	1.0	0.4	0.6	0.8	0.6	0.6	0.2	7.1	7.4	11.3
Kansas	89	40	30	48	40	35	35	51	42	50	18.8	8.3	6.2	9.8	8.1	7.0	7.1	10.3	8.4	10.0
Kentucky	22	19	23	36	45	50	52	58	45	34	3.2	2.8	3.4	5.3	6.6	7.3	7.6	8.5	6.6	5.0
Louisiana	198	188	162	194	214	143	178	170	179	148	28.7	27.0	23.0	27.3	30.1	19.9	24.8	23.7	25.0	20.8
Maine	2	2	4	2	0	1	0	3	6	8	1.1	1.1	2.1	1.1	0.0	0.5	0.0	1.7	3.3	4.4
Maryland	9	12	12	11	7	8	9	14	15	12	1.1	1.4	1.4	1.3	0.8	0.9	1.0	1.6	1.7	1.3
Massachusetts	77	93	67	108	91	96	60	25	22	25	8.0	9.7	7.0	11.3	9.5	10.0	6.2	2.6	2.3	2.6
Michigan	48	110	110	114	70	50	58	44	134	85	2.9	6.9	7.0	7.3	4.5	3.3	3.8	2.9	8.8	5.7
Minnesota	25	29	14	21	32	26	30	28	33	18	3.0	3.5	1.7	2.5	3.8	3.0	3.5	3.2	3.7	2.0
Mississippi	71	32	32	39	49	18	24	38	18	9	14.4	6.5	6.5	7.9	9.9	3.7	4.9	7.9	3.8	1.9
Missouri	12	9	4	8	5	9	8	9	9	4	1.3	1.0	0.4	0.9	0.5	1.0	0.9	1.0	1.0	0.4
Montana	23	17	32	15	16	13	16	9	12	9	16.2	12.0	22.5	10.5	11.1	9.0	11.0	6.1	8.0	6.0
Nebraska	8	14	11	17	16	17	10	12	19	23	2.7	4.7	3.7	5.6	5.2	5.4	3.2	3.8	5.9	7.0
Nevada	19	20	23	25	26	12	9	28	28	28	4.4	4.6	5.2	5.6	5.8	2.6	1.9	5.9	5.8	5.7
New Hampshire	4	10	19	17	22	13	9	8	16	5	2.0	5.1	9.9	9.0	11.8	7.0	4.9	4.4	8.9	2.8
New Jersey	6	5	6	9	5	7	3	7	8	6	0.4	0.4	0.4	0.7	0.4	0.5	0.2	0.5	0.6	0.4
New Mexico	82	65	53	52	59	25	78	70	58	39	24.5	19.2	15.7	15.4	17.4	7.3	23.2	20.8	17.3	11.7
New York	73[2]	103[2]	253	180	238	247	184	137	277	265	2.6[2]	3.8[2]	9.4	6.6	8.7	9.0	6.8	5.0	10.2	9.8
North Carolina	40	72	67	75	98	84	115	100	124	117	2.7	4.8	4.4	4.9	6.4	5.4	7.4	6.5	8.0	7.5
North Dakota	5	15	14	8	15	4	11	4	18	9	5.3	15.6	14.3	7.9	14.4	3.8	10.1	3.6	16.1	7.9
Ohio	103	91	75	71	102	88	83	81	70	58	5.8	5.2	4.3	4.1	5.9	5.1	4.8	4.7	4.1	3.4
Oklahoma	49	17	25	32	23	29	38	29	41	33	7.5	2.6	3.8	4.8	3.4	4.2	5.5	4.2	5.9	4.7
Oregon	43	43	59	47	37	42	30	38	51	43	7.4	7.5	10.4	8.0	6.2	7.0	4.9	6.3	8.4	7.1
Pennsylvania	52	24	22	34	24	46	18	24	27	22	2.9	1.3	1.2	1.9	1.4	2.6	1.0	1.4	1.6	1.3
Rhode Island	3	8	2	0	2	0	5	9	0	5	2.1	5.6	1.4	0.0	1.4	0.0	3.5	6.3	0.0	3.5
South Carolina	35	10	38	74	108	76	91	102	117	90	4.8	1.4	5.2	10.1	14.5	10.0	11.9	13.2	15.0	11.5
South Dakota	12	6	10	13	5	1	10	9	16	10	9.7	4.8	7.8	10.0	3.8	0.8	7.4	6.6	11.6	7.2
Tennessee	115	42[1]	75[1]	64[1]	57[1]	57[1]	121	127	128	99	11.8	4.3[1]	7.5[1]	6.4[1]	5.7[1]	5.7[1]	12.1	12.7	12.8	9.8
Texas	108	397	397	397	95	104	107	146	195	182	2.2	8.0	7.9	7.8	1.8	2.0	2.0	2.7	3.6	3.3
Utah	35	‡	‡	‡	101	---	---	---	47	117	6.1	‡	‡	‡	16.1	---	---	---	7.0	17.3
Vermont	2	9	4	3	11	4	5	5	5	1	2.2	9.3	4.4	3.3	12.4	4.6	5.7	5.7	5.7	1.1
Virginia	59	57	52	50	45	54	53	65	73	51	4.7	4.6	4.1	4.0	3.5	4.2	4.1	5.1	5.7	4.0
Washington	134	33	127	100	91	97	42	125	156	111	12.9	3.2	12.1	9.5	8.6	9.0	3.9	11.3	14.0	9.9
West Virginia	9	7	12	1	211	220	281	229	19	13	3.2	2.5	4.2	0.4	75.1	78.5	101.3	83.6	7.0	4.9
Wisconsin	31	40	39	47	43	63	51	57	55	41	3.6	4.6	4.5	5.4	4.9	7.2	5.9	6.6	6.4	4.8
Wyoming	12	14	9	22	13	13	13	23	4	7	13.6	15.7	10.0	24.0	14.0	13.8	13.7	24.4	4.2	7.4
Bureau of Indian Education	0	---	---	---	---	---	---	1	1	1	0.0	---	---	---	---	---	---	2.2	2.2	2.3
DoDEA[3]	---	---	---	---	---	---	---	---	---	---	---	---	---	---	---	---	---	---	---	---
Other jurisdictions																				
American Samoa	---	---	---	---	---	---	---	---	---	---	---	---	---	---	---	---	---	---	---	---
Guam	---	---	---	---	0	0	0	0	0	1	---	---	---	---	0.0	0.0	0.0	0.0	0.0	3.4
Northern Marianas	---	---	---	---	---	---	---	---	---	---	---	---	---	---	---	---	---	---	---	---
Puerto Rico	7	24	16	10	4	0	2	12	7	10	1.4	5.1	3.5	2.3	0.9	0.0	0.5	3.3	2.0	3.3
U.S. Virgin Islands	0	---	---	---	---	---	0	0	0	0	0.0	---	---	---	---	---	0.0	0.0	0.0	0.0

—Not available.

‡Reporting standards not met (suppressed due to data quality concerns).

[1] Due to data quality concerns, totals exclude students reported under the "other" firearm type category.

[2] Data for New York City Public Schools were not reported.

[3] DoDEA = Department of Defense Education Activity. Includes both domestic and overseas schools.

NOTE: Unless otherwise noted, data represent the sum of student counts for all firearm type categories (handguns, rifles/shotguns, other firearms, and multiple types of firearms).

SOURCE: U.S. Department of Education, National Center for Education Statistics, EDFacts file 086, Data Group 596, extracted September 30, 2020, from the EDFacts Data Warehouse (internal U.S. Department of Education source); and Common Core of Data (CCD), "State Nonfiscal Survey of Public Elementary and Secondary Education," 2009-10 through 2018-19. (This table was prepared October 2020.)

Table 231.70. Percentage of students ages 12-18 who reported having access to a loaded gun, without adult permission, at school or away from school during the school year, by selected student and school characteristics: Selected years, 2007 through 2019

[Standard errors appear in parentheses]

Student or school characteristic	2007		2009		2011		2013		2015		2017		2019	
1	2		3		4		5		6		7		8	
Total	**6.7**	**(0.40)**	**5.5**	**(0.47)**	**4.7**	**(0.43)**	**3.7**	**(0.38)**	**4.2**	**(0.48)**	**3.4**	**(0.29)**	**4.1**	**(0.42)**
Sex														
Male	8.4	(0.56)	7.6	(0.72)	5.6	(0.59)	3.9	(0.56)	5.3	(0.63)	4.0	(0.43)	5.1	(0.75)
Female	5.0	(0.47)	3.4	(0.44)	3.6	(0.44)	3.4	(0.35)	3.1	(0.50)	2.7	(0.33)	3.2	(0.36)
Race/ethnicity														
White	7.7	(0.55)	6.4	(0.60)	5.3	(0.50)	4.2	(0.45)	5.2	(0.67)	4.2	(0.41)	4.6	(0.62)
Black	6.2	(0.98)	3.9	(0.92)	4.1	(0.86)	3.4	(0.78)	3.3	(0.79)	4.1	(0.82)	3.1	(0.84)
Hispanic	4.8	(0.79)	4.9	(0.90)	4.1	(0.89)	3.0	(0.71)	2.8	(0.65)	1.7	(0.40)	3.6	(0.64)
Asian/Pacific Islander	‡	(†)	‡	(†)	‡	(†)	‡	(†)	‡	(†)	‡	(†)	2.4 !	(0.86)
Asian	‡	(†)	‡	(†)	‡	(†)	‡	(†)	‡	(†)	‡	(†)	1.2 !	(0.58)
Pacific Islander	‡	(†)	‡	(†)	‡	(†)	‡	(†)	‡	(†)	‡	(†)	‡	(†)
American Indian/ Alaska Native	‡	(†)	‡	(†)	‡	(†)	‡	(†)	‡	(†)	9.6 !	(4.35)	‡	(†)
Two or more races	9.7	(2.67)	5.2 !	(2.44)	‡	(†)	4.5 !	(2.03)	5.9 !	(2.27)	3.4 !	(1.69)	9.0 !	(3.38)
Grade														
6th	2.4	(0.64)	0.8 !	(0.40)	2.0 !	(0.89)	‡	(†)	1.7 !	(0.65)	‡	(†)	‡	(†)
7th	2.6	(0.56)	3.6	(0.84)	3.0	(0.63)	2.0	(0.50)	3.0	(0.66)	1.1 !	(0.33)	2.7	(0.73)
8th	3.2	(0.63)	3.2	(0.63)	2.9	(0.60)	2.4	(0.62)	2.6	(0.58)	2.2	(0.49)	2.6	(0.63)
9th	6.8	(0.98)	4.4	(0.80)	4.0	(0.75)	3.3	(0.80)	3.3	(0.72)	3.5	(0.81)	4.6	(0.85)
10th	9.2	(1.13)	7.3	(1.02)	5.3	(0.70)	4.7	(0.80)	4.7	(1.07)	4.0	(0.81)	5.1	(0.88)
11th	9.9	(1.00)	7.6	(1.16)	6.4	(1.06)	5.9	(0.99)	6.4	(1.10)	4.8	(0.82)	5.0	(1.00)
12th	12.3	(1.33)	9.8	(1.44)	8.2	(1.06)	5.8	(0.99)	7.3	(1.08)	5.8	(0.88)	6.8	(1.05)
School locale[1]														
City	---	(†)	---	(†)	---	(†)	---	(†)	3.2	(0.67)	2.6	(0.44)	3.3	(0.58)
Suburban	---	(†)	---	(†)	---	(†)	---	(†)	5.0	(0.90)	3.2	(0.42)	3.1	(0.41)
Town	---	(†)	---	(†)	---	(†)	---	(†)	5.6	(1.21)	5.5	(1.28)	8.8	(2.25)
Rural	---	(†)	---	(†)	---	(†)	---	(†)	3.9	(0.80)	4.4	(0.63)	5.2	(0.75)
Control of school[1,2]														
Public	6.9	(0.44)	5.8	(0.49)	4.8	(0.42)	3.7	(0.40)	4.4	(0.53)	3.6	(0.31)	4.4	(0.47)
Private	4.5	(0.88)	2.3 !	(0.83)	3.2 !	(0.98)	3.6	(1.01)	2.7 !	(0.80)	2.3 !	(0.81)	1.3 !	(0.58)

—Not available.

†Not applicable.

!Interpret data with caution. The coefficient of variation (CV) for this estimate is between 30 and 50 percent.

‡Reporting standards not met. Either there are too few cases for a reliable estimate or the coefficient of variation (CV) is 50 percent or greater.

[1] Excludes students with missing information about the school characteristic.

[2] Data for 2013 and prior years were based on school information provided by the respondent. Beginning in 2015, data were based on school information collected in the Common Core of Data and the Private School Universe Survey, which was appended to the School Crime Supplement data file; therefore, these data may not be entirely comparable with figures for earlier years.

NOTE: Race categories exclude persons of Hispanic ethnicity.

SOURCE: U.S. Department of Justice, Bureau of Justice Statistics, School Crime Supplement (SCS) to the National Crime Victimization Survey, 2007 through 2019. (This table was prepared October 2020.)

Table 232.10. Percentage of students in grades 9-12 who reported using alcohol at least 1 day during the previous 30 days, by location and selected student characteristics: Selected years, 1993 through 2019

[Standard errors appear in parentheses]

Location and student characteristic	1993		1999		2001		2003		2005		2007		2009		2011		2013		2015		2017		2019	
1	2		3		4		5		6		7		8		9		10		11		12		13	
Anywhere (including on school property)[1]																								
Total	**48.0**	**(1.06)**	**50.0**	**(1.30)**	**47.1**	**(1.11)**	**44.9**	**(1.21)**	**43.3**	**(1.38)**	**44.7**	**(1.15)**	**41.8**	**(0.80)**	**38.7**	**(0.75)**	**34.9**	**(1.08)**	**32.8**	**(1.18)**	**29.8**	**(1.27)**	**29.2**	**(0.96)**
Sex																								
Male	50.1	(1.23)	52.3	(1.47)	49.2	(1.42)	43.8	(1.31)	43.8	(1.40)	44.7	(1.39)	40.8	(1.11)	39.5	(0.93)	34.4	(1.30)	32.2	(0.89)	27.6	(1.24)	26.4	(1.03)
Female	45.9	(1.32)	47.7	(1.45)	45.0	(1.11)	45.8	(1.29)	42.8	(1.56)	44.6	(1.42)	42.9	(0.85)	37.9	(0.91)	35.5	(1.39)	33.5	(1.89)	31.8	(1.57)	31.9	(1.16)
Race/ethnicity																								
White	49.9	(1.26)	52.5	(1.62)	50.4	(1.12)	47.1	(1.51)	46.4	(1.84)	47.3	(1.67)	44.7	(1.16)	40.3	(0.97)	36.3	(1.63)	35.2	(2.00)	32.4	(1.73)	34.2	(1.26)
Black	42.5	(1.82)	39.9	(4.07)	32.7	(2.33)	37.4	(1.67)	31.2	(1.05)	34.5	(1.65)	33.4	(1.45)	30.5	(1.40)	29.6	(1.65)	23.8	(2.82)	20.8	(2.27)	16.8	(1.78)
Hispanic	50.8	(2.82)	52.8	(2.41)	49.2	(1.52)	45.6	(1.39)	46.8	(1.39)	47.6	(1.80)	42.9	(1.43)	42.3	(1.38)	37.5	(2.11)	34.4	(1.28)	31.3	(1.53)	28.4	(1.17)
Asian[2]	---	(†)	25.7	(2.24)	28.4	(3.22)	27.5	(3.47)	21.5	(1.98)	25.4	(2.17)	18.3	(1.60)	25.6	(2.90)	21.7	(1.80)	13.1	(1.83)	12.2	(1.74)	13.9	(1.98)
Pacific Islander[2]	---	(†)	60.8	(5.11)	52.3	(8.54)	40.0	(7.04)	38.7	(8.43)	48.8	(6.58)	34.8	(4.36)	38.4	(6.40)	26.8	(5.84)	36.9	(10.62)	18.7	(3.17)	42.1	(8.62)
American Indian/Alaska Native	45.3	(7.18)	49.4	(6.43)	51.4	(3.97)	51.9	(5.29)	57.4	(4.13)	34.5	(1.77)	42.8	(5.43)	44.9	(2.26)	33.4	(5.13)	46.0	(8.12)	31.8	(8.15)	32.6	(5.43)
Two or more races[2]	---	(†)	51.1	(3.98)	45.4	(4.11)	47.1	(3.59)	39.0	(3.59)	46.2	(2.89)	44.3	(2.42)	36.9	(3.08)	36.1	(2.87)	39.6	(2.68)	32.7	(2.50)	26.0	(2.39)
Sexual identity[3]																								
Heterosexual	---	(†)	---	(†)	---	(†)	---	(†)	---	(†)	---	(†)	---	(†)	---	(†)	---	(†)	32.1	(1.30)	29.7	(1.02)	28.8	(1.00)
Gay, lesbian, or bisexual	---	(†)	---	(†)	---	(†)	---	(†)	---	(†)	---	(†)	---	(†)	---	(†)	---	(†)	40.5	(2.07)	37.4	(2.39)	33.9	(2.11)
Not sure	---	(†)	---	(†)	---	(†)	---	(†)	---	(†)	---	(†)	---	(†)	---	(†)	---	(†)	34.6	(2.81)	21.5	(2.77)	25.3	(2.80)
Grade																								
9th	40.5	(1.79)	40.6	(2.17)	41.1	(1.82)	36.2	(1.43)	36.2	(1.23)	35.7	(1.15)	31.5	(1.28)	29.8	(1.35)	24.4	(1.13)	23.4	(1.28)	18.8	(1.23)	19.0	(1.41)
10th	44.0	(2.00)	49.7	(1.89)	45.2	(1.29)	43.5	(1.66)	42.0	(1.95)	41.8	(1.68)	40.6	(1.42)	35.7	(1.37)	30.9	(1.84)	29.0	(2.49)	27.0	(1.60)	26.7	(1.60)
11th	49.7	(1.73)	50.9	(1.98)	49.3	(1.70)	47.0	(2.08)	46.0	(1.98)	49.0	(1.83)	45.7	(2.05)	42.7	(1.28)	39.2	(1.52)	38.0	(1.68)	34.4	(1.68)	32.3	(1.25)
12th	56.4	(1.35)	61.7	(2.25)	55.2	(1.53)	55.9	(1.65)	50.8	(2.12)	54.9	(2.09)	51.7	(1.37)	48.4	(1.29)	46.8	(1.85)	42.4	(2.00)	40.8	(1.92)	39.9	(1.45)
On school property[4]																								
Total	**5.2**	**(0.39)**	**4.9**	**(0.39)**	**4.9**	**(0.28)**	**5.2**	**(0.46)**	**4.3**	**(0.30)**	**4.1**	**(0.32)**	**4.5**	**(0.29)**	**5.1**	**(0.33)**	**---**	**(†)**	**---**	**(†)**	**---**	**(†)**	**---**	**(†)**
Sex																								
Male	6.2	(0.39)	6.1	(0.54)	6.1	(0.43)	6.0	(0.61)	5.3	(0.39)	4.6	(0.35)	5.3	(0.41)	5.4	(0.43)	---	(†)	---	(†)	---	(†)	---	(†)
Female	4.2	(0.54)	3.6	(0.39)	3.8	(0.39)	4.2	(0.41)	3.3	(0.32)	3.6	(0.37)	3.6	(0.34)	4.7	(0.35)	---	(†)	---	(†)	---	(†)	---	(†)
Race/ethnicity																								
White	4.6	(0.44)	4.8	(0.55)	4.2	(0.26)	3.9	(0.45)	3.8	(0.38)	3.2	(0.35)	3.3	(0.27)	4.0	(0.38)	---	(†)	---	(†)	---	(†)	---	(†)
Black	6.9	(0.98)	4.3	(0.52)	5.3	(0.65)	5.8	(0.80)	3.2	(0.45)	3.4	(0.63)	5.4	(0.59)	5.1	(0.50)	---	(†)	---	(†)	---	(†)	---	(†)
Hispanic	6.8	(0.84)	7.0	(0.88)	7.0	(0.71)	7.6	(1.08)	7.7	(1.04)	7.5	(0.86)	6.9	(0.70)	7.3	(0.68)	---	(†)	---	(†)	---	(†)	---	(†)
Asian[2]	---	(†)	2.0	(0.42)	6.8	(1.42)	5.6	(1.55)	1.3 !	(0.62)	4.4	(1.17)	2.9	(0.65)	3.5 !	(1.21)	---	(†)	---	(†)	---	(†)	---	(†)
Pacific Islander[2]	---	(†)	6.7	(1.59)	12.4	(3.50)	8.5 !	(3.29)	‡	(†)	‡	(†)	10.0	(2.34)	8.3 !	(3.61)	---	(†)	---	(†)	---	(†)	---	(†)
American Indian/Alaska Native	6.7 !	(3.06)	‡	(†)	8.2	(1.69)	7.1 !	(2.61)	6.2 !	(2.05)	5.0	(0.89)	4.3 !	(1.58)	20.9	(4.15)	---	(†)	---	(†)	---	(†)	---	(†)
Two or more races[2]	---	(†)	5.2	(1.09)	7.0 !	(2.36)	13.3	(2.93)	3.5	(1.02)	5.4	(1.25)	6.7	(1.37)	5.8	(1.32)	---	(†)	---	(†)	---	(†)	---	(†)
Grade																								
9th	5.2	(0.38)	4.4	(0.60)	5.3	(0.47)	5.1	(0.69)	3.7	(0.48)	3.4	(0.43)	4.4	(0.37)	5.4	(0.56)	---	(†)	---	(†)	---	(†)	---	(†)
10th	4.7	(0.43)	5.0	(0.67)	5.1	(0.45)	5.6	(0.60)	4.5	(0.45)	4.1	(0.50)	4.8	(0.46)	4.4	(0.51)	---	(†)	---	(†)	---	(†)	---	(†)
11th	5.2	(0.80)	4.7	(0.57)	4.7	(0.45)	5.0	(0.57)	4.0	(0.47)	4.2	(0.54)	4.6	(0.44)	5.2	(0.56)	---	(†)	---	(†)	---	(†)	---	(†)
12th	5.5	(0.64)	5.0	(0.89)	4.3	(0.44)	4.5	(0.68)	4.8	(0.57)	4.8	(0.55)	4.1	(0.44)	5.1	(0.48)	---	(†)	---	(†)	---	(†)	---	(†)

---Not available.

†Not applicable.

!Interpret data with caution. The coefficient of variation (CV) for this estimate is between 30 and 50 percent.

‡Reporting standards not met. The coefficient of variation (CV) for this estimate is 50 percent or greater.

[1] The term "anywhere" is not used in the Youth Risk Behavior Survey (YRBS) questionnaire; students were simply asked how many days during the previous 30 days they had at least one drink of alcohol.

[2] Before 1999, Asian students and Pacific Islander students were not categorized separately, and students could not be classified as Two or more races. Because the response categories changed in 1999, caution should be used in comparing data on race from 1993 with data from later years.

[3] Students were asked which of the following--"heterosexual (straight)," "gay or lesbian," "bisexual," or "not sure"--best described them.

[4] In the question about drinking alcohol at school, "on school property" was not defined for respondents. Data on alcohol use at school were not collected from 2013 onward.

NOTE: Race categories exclude persons of Hispanic ethnicity.

SOURCE: Centers for Disease Control and Prevention, Division of Adolescent and School Health, Youth Risk Behavior Surveillance System (YRBSS), 1993 through 2019. (This table was prepared September 2020.)

Table 232.20. Percentage distribution of students in grades 9-12, by number of days they reported using alcohol anywhere during the previous 30 days and selected student characteristics: Selected years, 2013 through 2019

[Standard errors appear in parentheses]

Year and student characteristic	0 days		1 or 2 days		3 to 29 days		All 30 days	
1	2		3		4		5	
2013								
Total	**65.1**	**(1.08)**	**17.3**	**(0.56)**	**16.9**	**(0.78)**	**0.8**	**(0.12)**
Sex								
Male	65.6	(1.30)	15.7	(0.75)	17.4	(0.90)	1.2	(0.19)
Female	64.5	(1.39)	18.8	(0.98)	16.3	(0.88)	0.3	(0.09)
Race/ethnicity								
White	63.7	(1.63)	17.6	(0.87)	18.0	(1.11)	0.6	(0.13)
Black	70.4	(1.65)	15.5	(0.90)	13.6	(1.46)	0.6	(0.16)
Hispanic	62.5	(2.11)	18.0	(1.30)	18.3	(1.27)	1.2	(0.35)
Asian	78.3	(1.80)	14.8	(2.26)	6.3	(1.27)	‡	(†)
Pacific Islander	73.2	(5.84)	18.2	(4.71)	7.5	(2.24)	‡	(†)
American Indian/Alaska Native	66.6	(5.13)	14.8	(4.41)	17.4 !	(5.62)	‡	(†)
Two or more races	63.9	(2.87)	18.7	(1.71)	16.4	(2.12)	1.0 !	(0.42)
Grade								
9th	75.6	(1.13)	13.6	(0.89)	10.0	(0.85)	0.7	(0.22)
10th	69.1	(1.84)	15.9	(1.17)	14.5	(1.22)	0.6	(0.16)
11th	60.8	(1.52)	18.6	(1.01)	19.7	(1.26)	0.9	(0.23)
12th	53.2	(1.85)	21.5	(0.93)	24.6	(1.31)	0.7	(0.17)
2015								
Total	**67.2**	**(1.18)**	**17.6**	**(0.67)**	**14.5**	**(0.85)**	**0.7**	**(0.12)**
Sex								
Male	67.8	(0.89)	16.1	(0.76)	15.1	(0.87)	1.0	(0.23)
Female	66.5	(1.89)	19.3	(1.09)	13.9	(1.12)	0.3	(0.13)
Race/ethnicity								
White	64.8	(2.00)	18.5	(0.83)	16.2	(1.40)	0.5	(0.11)
Black	76.2	(2.82)	14.4	(1.82)	8.6	(1.24)	‡	(†)
Hispanic	65.6	(1.28)	18.9	(1.25)	14.4	(0.76)	1.1	(0.25)
Asian	86.9	(1.83)	7.1	(1.48)	4.9	(0.88)	‡	(†)
Pacific Islander	63.1	(10.62)	22.1 !	(8.78)	13.5 !	(5.64)	‡	(†)
American Indian/Alaska Native	54.0	(8.12)	16.3 !	(5.91)	29.3 !	(8.96)	‡	(†)
Two or more races	60.4	(2.68)	20.2	(2.17)	19.0	(2.32)	‡	(†)
Sexual identity[1]								
Heterosexual	67.9	(1.30)	17.5	(0.74)	13.9	(0.99)	0.6	(0.11)
Gay, lesbian, or bisexual	59.5	(2.07)	21.7	(1.84)	18.1	(1.54)	‡	(†)
Not sure	65.4	(2.81)	14.6	(2.03)	16.6	(2.32)	3.4 !	(1.16)
Grade								
9th	76.6	(1.28)	14.2	(1.20)	8.5	(0.98)	0.6	(0.16)
10th	71.0	(2.49)	16.0	(1.53)	12.2	(1.25)	0.8	(0.21)
11th	62.0	(1.68)	19.9	(1.49)	17.8	(1.39)	0.3 !	(0.12)
12th	57.6	(2.00)	21.0	(1.22)	20.4	(1.49)	0.9	(0.26)
2017								
Total	**70.2**	**(1.27)**	**16.4**	**(0.66)**	**12.8**	**(0.74)**	**0.6**	**(0.10)**
Sex								
Male	72.4	(1.24)	14.6	(0.73)	12.0	(0.77)	0.9	(0.17)
Female	68.2	(1.57)	18.1	(0.94)	13.5	(0.94)	0.3	(0.08)
Race/ethnicity								
White	67.6	(1.73)	16.9	(0.90)	15.0	(0.96)	0.5	(0.17)
Black	79.2	(2.27)	13.8	(1.45)	6.5	(0.94)	0.6	(0.21)
Hispanic	68.7	(1.53)	17.5	(0.85)	13.2	(1.09)	0.6	(0.18)
Asian	87.8	(1.74)	8.2	(1.44)	2.9 !	(0.97)	‡	(†)
Pacific Islander	81.3	(3.17)	9.5	(2.45)	9.0 !	(3.20)	‡	(†)
American Indian/Alaska Native	68.2	(8.15)	14.6	(3.29)	‡	(†)	‡	(†)
Two or more races	67.3	(2.50)	20.5	(2.37)	11.5	(1.66)	‡	(†)
Sexual identity[1]								
Heterosexual	70.3	(1.02)	16.6	(0.58)	12.7	(0.64)	0.4	(0.09)
Gay, lesbian, or bisexual	62.6	(2.39)	18.9	(1.63)	17.6	(1.49)	0.8 !	(0.25)
Not sure	78.5	(2.77)	11.7	(1.64)	6.5	(1.15)	3.4 !	(1.59)
Grade								
9th	81.2	(1.23)	11.6	(0.69)	7.0	(0.83)	0.1 !	(0.06)
10th	73.0	(1.60)	15.2	(0.92)	11.3	(0.93)	0.6 !	(0.26)
11th	65.6	(1.68)	18.5	(1.07)	15.4	(1.15)	0.5 !	(0.20)
12th	59.2	(1.92)	21.3	(1.15)	18.5	(1.35)	1.1 !	(0.33)
2019								
Total	**70.8**	**(0.96)**	**16.0**	**(0.58)**	**12.6**	**(0.55)**	**0.6**	**(0.11)**
Sex								
Male	73.6	(1.03)	13.4	(0.55)	12.2	(0.66)	0.8	(0.15)
Female	68.1	(1.16)	18.7	(0.87)	12.8	(0.66)	0.4 !	(0.12)
Race/ethnicity								
White	65.8	(1.25)	17.9	(0.74)	16.0	(0.81)	0.3	(0.09)
Black	83.2	(1.78)	9.9	(1.09)	6.1	(1.07)	0.8 !	(0.28)
Hispanic	71.6	(1.17)	16.5	(1.01)	10.7	(0.57)	1.2	(0.33)

[Standard errors appear in parentheses]

Year and student characteristic	0 days		1 or 2 days		3 to 29 days		All 30 days	
1		2		3		4		5
Asian	86.1	(2.01)	9.4	(1.51)	4.2	(1.08)	‡	(†)
Pacific Islander	57.9	(9.09)	29.1 !	(9.30)	‡	(†)	‡	(†)
American Indian/Alaska Native	67.4	(5.35)	17.7	(4.49)	11.5	(3.24)	3.4 !	(1.63)
Two or more races	74.0	(2.39)	13.3	(1.89)	12.7	(1.57)	‡	(†)
Sexual identity[1]								
Heterosexual	71.2	(1.00)	15.7	(0.65)	12.6	(0.58)	0.5	(0.10)
Gay, lesbian, or bisexual	66.1	(2.11)	19.0	(1.65)	13.9	(1.36)	‡	(†)
Not sure	74.7	(2.80)	13.9	(1.97)	8.6	(1.68)	2.7 !	(1.09)
Grade								
9th	81.0	(1.41)	11.0	(1.00)	7.5	(0.74)	0.5 !	(0.20)
10th	73.3	(1.60)	15.8	(0.96)	10.4	(0.85)	0.6 !	(0.23)
11th	67.7	(1.25)	18.4	(1.04)	13.4	(0.79)	0.5	(0.15)
12th	60.1	(1.45)	19.5	(0.93)	19.8	(1.19)	0.6 !	(0.23)

†Not applicable.

!Interpret data with caution. The coefficient of variation (CV) for this estimate is between 30 and 50 percent.

‡Reporting standards not met. Either there are too few cases for a reliable estimate or the coefficient of variation (CV) is 50 percent or greater.

[1] Students were asked which of the following--"heterosexual (straight)," "gay or lesbian," "bisexual," or "not sure"--best described them.

NOTE: The term "anywhere" is not used in the Youth Risk Behavior Survey (YRBS) questionnaire; students were simply asked how many days during the previous 30 days they had at least one drink of alcohol. Race categories exclude persons of Hispanic ethnicity. Detail may not sum to totals because of rounding and the suppression of cells that do not meet National Center for Education Statistics reporting standards.

SOURCE: Centers for Disease Control and Prevention, Division of Adolescent and School Health, Youth Risk Behavior Surveillance System (YRBSS), 2013 through 2019. (This table was prepared September 2020.)

Table 232.30. Percentage of public school students in grades 9-12 who reported using alcohol at least 1 day during the previous 30 days, by location and state or jurisdiction: Selected years, 2005 through 2017

[Standard errors appear in parentheses]

State or jurisdiction	Anywhere (including on school property)[1]							On school property[2]						
	2005	2007	2009	2011	2013	2015	2017	2005	2007	2009	2011	2013	2015	2017
1	2	3	4	5	6	7	8	9	10	11	12	13	14	15
United States[3]	**43.3 (1.38)**	**44.7 (1.15)**	**41.8 (0.80)**	**38.7 (0.75)**	**34.9 (1.08)**	**32.8 (1.18)**	**29.8 (1.27)**	**4.3 (0.30)**	**4.1 (0.32)**	**4.5 (0.29)**	**5.1 (0.33)**	**— (†)**	**— (†)**	**— (†)**
Alabama	39.4 (2.55)	— (†)	39.5 (2.22)	35.6 (1.99)	35.0 (2.45)	30.7 (1.70)	— (†)	4.5 (0.59)	— (†)	5.4 (0.76)	5.7 (1.08)	— (†)	— (†)	— (†)
Alaska	— (†)	39.7 (2.11)	33.2 (1.66)	28.6 (1.95)	22.5 (1.69)	22.0 (1.21)	22.8 (1.90)	— (†)	4.1 (0.58)	3.0 (0.48)	3.4 (0.52)	— (†)	— (†)	— (†)
Arizona	47.1 (1.73)	45.6 (1.73)	44.5 (1.67)	43.8 (1.47)	36.0 (2.25)	34.8 (2.65)	33.2 (1.90)	7.5 (0.88)	6.0 (0.54)	5.9 (0.61)	6.2 (0.55)	— (†)	— (†)	— (†)
Arkansas	43.1 (1.99)	42.2 (1.75)	39.7 (1.91)	33.9 (1.81)	36.3 (1.97)	27.6 (1.58)	25.7 (2.69)	5.2 (0.62)	5.1 (0.65)	6.1 (0.89)	4.2 (0.68)	— (†)	— (†)	— (†)
California	— (†)	— (†)	— (†)	— (†)	— (†)	28.9 (2.61)	30.0 (2.69)	— (†)	— (†)	— (†)	— (†)	— (†)	— (†)	— (†)
Colorado	47.4 (4.42)	— (†)	40.8 (2.44)	36.4 (2.29)	— (†)	— (†)	26.2 (1.74)	5.9 (1.08)	— (†)	4.1 (0.61)	5.3 (0.87)	— (†)	— (†)	— (†)
Connecticut	45.3 (2.16)	46.0 (2.13)	43.5 (2.22)	41.5 (1.90)	36.7 (2.02)	30.2 (1.50)	30.4 (1.54)	6.6 (0.71)	5.6 (0.99)	5.0 (0.47)	4.6 (0.61)	— (†)	— (†)	— (†)
Delaware	43.1 (1.16)	45.2 (1.40)	43.7 (1.65)	40.4 (1.55)	36.3 (1.34)	31.4 (1.95)	28.7 (1.39)	5.5 (0.66)	4.5 (0.48)	5.0 (0.73)	5.0 (0.50)	— (†)	— (†)	— (†)
District of Columbia	23.1 (1.40)	32.6 (1.47)	— (†)	32.8 (1.89)	31.4 (0.58)	20.2 (0.43)	20.5 (0.51)	4.6 (0.55)	6.1 (0.92)	— (†)	6.8 (0.91)	— (†)	— (†)	— (†)
Florida	39.7 (1.43)	42.3 (1.30)	40.5 (1.03)	37.0 (0.98)	34.9 (0.87)	33.0 (0.96)	27.0 (0.74)	4.5 (0.30)	5.3 (0.31)	4.9 (0.26)	5.1 (0.29)	— (†)	— (†)	— (†)
Georgia	39.9 (2.12)	37.7 (1.52)	34.3 (1.65)	34.6 (1.93)	27.9 (2.04)	— (†)	— (†)	4.3 (0.67)	4.4 (0.58)	4.2 (0.48)	5.4 (0.80)	— (†)	— (†)	— (†)
Hawaii	34.8 (2.05)	29.1 (2.93)	37.8 (3.02)	29.1 (1.64)	25.2 (1.75)	25.2 (1.02)	24.5 (1.18)	8.8 (0.93)	6.0 (0.93)	7.9 (1.31)	5.0 (0.42)	— (†)	— (†)	— (†)
Idaho	39.8 (2.62)	42.5 (2.73)	34.2 (1.97)	36.2 (2.28)	28.3 (2.23)	28.3 (2.21)	26.5 (1.83)	4.3 (0.69)	6.2 (0.81)	3.5 (0.53)	4.1 (0.50)	— (†)	— (†)	— (†)
Illinois	— (†)	43.7 (2.72)	39.8 (1.91)	37.8 (1.87)	36.6 (2.41)	30.7 (2.07)	27.4 (2.07)	— (†)	5.5 (0.75)	4.4 (0.64)	3.3 (0.40)	— (†)	— (†)	— (†)
Indiana	41.4 (2.12)	43.9 (2.24)	38.5 (2.13)	33.5 (1.65)	— (†)	30.5 (2.19)	— (†)	3.4 (0.64)	4.1 (0.47)	3.5 (0.52)	2.0 (0.36)	— (†)	— (†)	— (†)
Iowa	43.8 (2.56)	41.0 (2.36)	— (†)	37.1 (2.58)	— (†)	— (†)	27.6 (1.73)	4.6 (0.89)	3.4 (0.78)	— (†)	2.3 (0.41)	— (†)	— (†)	— (†)
Kansas	43.9 (1.74)	42.4 (1.69)	38.7 (1.93)	32.6 (1.53)	27.6 (1.02)	— (†)	29.9 (1.42)	5.1 (0.74)	4.8 (0.66)	3.2 (0.55)	2.9 (0.45)	— (†)	— (†)	— (†)
Kentucky	37.4 (1.77)	40.6 (1.25)	37.8 (1.30)	34.6 (1.56)	30.4 (1.37)	28.5 (1.70)	26.6 (1.80)	3.5 (0.37)	4.7 (0.47)	5.2 (0.87)	4.1 (0.53)	— (†)	— (†)	— (†)
Louisiana	— (†)	— (†)	47.5 (2.80)	44.4 (2.00)	38.6 (2.75)	— (†)	34.0 (3.00)	— (†)	— (†)	5.6 (1.33)	6.0 (1.36)	— (†)	— (†)	— (†)
Maine	43.0 (2.15)	39.3 (2.29)	32.2 (0.66)	28.7 (0.69)	26.6 (0.90)	24.0 (0.69)	22.0 (0.68)	3.9 (0.44)	5.6 (0.89)	4.0 (0.23)	3.1 (0.21)	— (†)	— (†)	— (†)
Maryland	39.8 (2.17)	42.9 (3.13)	37.0 (1.44)	34.8 (1.98)	31.2 (0.45)	26.1 (0.41)	25.5 (0.39)	3.2 (0.42)	6.2 (1.10)	4.8 (0.67)	5.4 (0.63)	— (†)	— (†)	— (†)
Massachusetts	47.8 (1.36)	46.2 (1.57)	43.6 (1.28)	40.1 (1.54)	35.6 (1.14)	33.9 (1.48)	31.4 (2.04)	4.2 (0.32)	4.7 (0.45)	3.8 (0.48)	3.6 (0.44)	— (†)	— (†)	— (†)
Michigan	38.1 (1.73)	42.8 (1.70)	37.0 (1.28)	30.6 (1.64)	28.3 (1.81)	25.9 (1.81)	29.6 (2.54)	3.6 (0.46)	3.6 (0.51)	3.7 (0.40)	2.7 (0.37)	— (†)	— (†)	— (†)
Minnesota	— (†)	— (†)	— (†)	— (†)	— (†)	— (†)	— (†)	— (†)	— (†)	— (†)	— (†)	— (†)	— (†)	— (†)
Mississippi	— (†)	40.6 (1.57)	39.2 (1.43)	36.2 (2.07)	32.9 (2.09)	31.5 (1.67)	— (†)	— (†)	5.1 (0.71)	4.3 (0.45)	4.6 (0.67)	— (†)	— (†)	— (†)
Missouri	40.8 (2.04)	44.4 (2.35)	39.3 (2.71)	— (†)	35.6 (1.33)	34.5 (2.09)	32.0 (2.31)	3.3 (0.57)	3.4 (0.74)	3.0 (0.55)	— (†)	— (†)	— (†)	— (†)
Montana	48.6 (1.50)	46.5 (1.39)	42.8 (1.81)	38.3 (1.08)	37.1 (1.20)	34.2 (1.03)	33.1 (1.06)	6.4 (0.73)	5.7 (0.47)	5.1 (0.69)	3.5 (0.35)	— (†)	— (†)	— (†)
Nebraska	42.9 (1.27)	— (†)	— (†)	26.6 (1.24)	22.1 (1.46)	22.7 (1.65)	24.4 (1.63)	3.6 (0.42)	— (†)	— (†)	3.0 (0.41)	— (†)	— (†)	— (†)
Nevada	41.4 (1.73)	37.0 (1.52)	38.6 (1.66)	— (†)	34.0 (2.11)	33.5 (2.29)	25.8 (1.37)	6.8 (0.92)	4.4 (0.58)	4.4 (0.52)	— (†)	— (†)	— (†)	— (†)
New Hampshire	44.0 (2.31)	44.8 (1.83)	39.3 (2.18)	38.4 (1.83)	32.9 (1.71)	30.0 (0.88)	29.6 (0.79)	— (†)	5.1 (0.73)	4.3 (0.68)	5.6 (0.70)	— (†)	— (†)	— (†)
New Jersey	46.5 (2.65)	— (†)	45.2 (2.21)	42.9 (2.46)	39.3 (1.92)	— (†)	— (†)	3.7 (0.42)	— (†)	— (†)	— (†)	— (†)	— (†)	— (†)
New Mexico	42.3 (1.93)	43.2 (1.07)	40.5 (1.41)	36.9 (1.40)	28.9 (1.25)	26.1 (0.89)	26.3 (1.49)	7.6 (0.87)	8.7 (1.35)	8.0 (0.90)	6.4 (0.54)	— (†)	— (†)	— (†)
New York	43.4 (1.47)	43.7 (1.41)	41.4 (1.38)	38.4 (1.96)	32.5 (1.36)	29.7 (1.80)	27.1 (1.52)	4.1 (0.45)	5.1 (0.58)	— (†)	— (†)	— (†)	— (†)	— (†)
North Carolina	42.3 (2.16)	37.7 (1.36)	35.0 (2.43)	34.3 (1.41)	32.2 (1.27)	29.2 (1.63)	26.5 (1.54)	5.4 (0.74)	4.7 (0.65)	4.1 (0.57)	5.5 (0.77)	— (†)	— (†)	— (†)
North Dakota	49.0 (1.89)	46.1 (1.82)	43.3 (1.79)	38.8 (1.67)	35.3 (1.59)	30.8 (1.58)	29.1 (1.67)	3.6 (0.52)	4.4 (0.65)	4.2 (0.53)	3.1 (0.51)	— (†)	— (†)	— (†)
Ohio[4]	42.4 (1.96)	45.7 (1.70)	— (†)	38.0 (2.94)	29.5 (2.21)	— (†)	— (†)	3.2 (0.59)	3.2 (0.50)	— (†)	— (†)	— (†)	— (†)	— (†)
Oklahoma	40.5 (1.62)	43.1 (1.88)	39.0 (1.97)	38.3 (1.75)	33.4 (1.91)	27.3 (1.95)	31.6 (1.75)	3.8 (0.49)	5.0 (0.59)	3.9 (0.55)	2.6 (0.65)	— (†)	— (†)	— (†)
Oregon	— (†)	— (†)	— (†)	— (†)	— (†)	— (†)	— (†)	— (†)	— (†)	— (†)	— (†)	— (†)	— (†)	— (†)
Pennsylvania	— (†)	— (†)	38.4 (2.10)	— (†)	— (†)	30.6 (1.61)	31.1 (1.28)	— (†)	— (†)	2.8 (0.50)	— (†)	— (†)	— (†)	— (†)
Rhode Island	42.7 (1.15)	42.9 (1.76)	34.0 (2.01)	34.0 (1.25)	30.9 (1.78)	26.2 (1.92)	23.2 (1.50)	5.3 (0.66)	4.8 (0.54)	3.2 (0.50)	— (†)	— (†)	— (†)	— (†)
South Carolina	43.2 (1.64)	36.8 (2.31)	35.2 (2.80)	39.7 (1.72)	28.9 (1.34)	24.6 (1.57)	25.4 (2.04)	6.0 (0.96)	4.7 (0.73)	3.6 (0.79)	5.9 (0.90)	— (†)	— (†)	— (†)
South Dakota[5]	46.6 (2.12)	44.5 (1.80)	40.1 (1.54)	39.3 (2.14)	30.8 (1.45)	28.0 (2.53)	— (†)	4.0 (0.70)	3.6 (0.92)	— (†)	— (†)	— (†)	— (†)	— (†)
Tennessee	41.8 (1.90)	36.7 (1.90)	33.5 (1.71)	33.3 (1.39)	28.4 (1.35)	— (†)	25.9 (1.32)	3.7 (0.66)	4.1 (0.54)	3.0 (0.38)	3.2 (0.34)	— (†)	— (†)	— (†)
Texas	47.3 (1.93)	48.3 (1.64)	44.8 (1.25)	39.7 (1.15)	36.1 (1.75)	— (†)	26.8 (1.36)	5.7 (0.56)	4.9 (0.57)	4.7 (0.36)	3.9 (0.35)	— (†)	— (†)	— (†)
Utah	15.8 (1.92)	17.0 (1.88)	18.2 (2.72)	15.1 (1.54)	11.0 (0.90)	— (†)	10.6 (1.40)	2.1 (0.39)	4.7 ! (1.69)	2.7 (0.45)	2.7 (0.54)	— (†)	— (†)	— (†)
Vermont[6]	41.8 (1.53)	42.6 (1.04)	39.0 (1.57)	35.3 (1.10)	— (†)	30.0 (0.33)	33.0 (0.34)	4.8 (0.54)	4.6 (0.40)	3.3 (0.28)	3.3 (0.50)	— (†)	— (†)	— (†)
Virginia	— (†)	— (†)	— (†)	30.5 (2.49)	27.3 (1.22)	23.4 (1.20)	24.5 (1.11)	— (†)	— (†)	— (†)	3.3 (0.59)	— (†)	— (†)	— (†)
Washington	— (†)	— (†)	— (†)	— (†)	— (†)	— (†)	— (†)	— (†)	— (†)	— (†)	— (†)	— (†)	— (†)	— (†)
West Virginia	41.5 (1.41)	43.5 (1.45)	40.4 (1.10)	34.3 (2.40)	37.1 (2.04)	31.1 (1.45)	27.9 (1.41)	6.4 (1.08)	5.5 (0.89)	5.7 (0.61)	4.2 (0.67)	— (†)	— (†)	— (†)
Wisconsin	49.2 (1.51)	48.9 (1.56)	41.3 (1.83)	39.2 (1.35)	32.7 (1.21)	— (†)	30.4 (1.52)	— (†)	— (†)	— (†)	— (†)	— (†)	— (†)	— (†)
Wyoming	45.4 (1.47)	42.4 (1.22)	41.7 (1.36)	36.1 (1.34)	34.4 (1.14)	31.0 (1.48)	— (†)	6.2 (0.56)	6.9 (0.63)	6.4 (0.50)	5.1 (0.48)	— (†)	— (†)	— (†)
Puerto Rico	39.0 (1.71)	— (†)	— (†)	30.4 (2.37)	25.5 (2.03)	21.2 (1.45)	23.8 (1.49)	4.4 (0.49)	— (†)	— (†)	3.9 (0.85)	— (†)	— (†)	— (†)

—Not available.

†Not applicable.

! Interpret data with caution. The coefficient of variation (CV) for this estimate is between 30 and 50 percent.

[1] The term "anywhere" is not used in the Youth Risk Behavior Survey (YRBS) questionnaire; students were simply asked how many days during the previous 30 days they had at least one drink of alcohol.

[2] In the question about drinking alcohol at school, "on school property" was not defined for survey respondents. Data on alcohol use at school were not collected from 2013 onward.

[3] U.S. total data are representative of all public and private school students in grades 9-12 in the 50 states and the District of Columbia. U.S. total data for all years were collected through a separate national survey (rather than being aggregated from state-level data) and include both public and private schools.

[4] Ohio data for 2005 through 2013 include both public and private schools.

[5] South Dakota data for 2005 through 2015 include both public and private schools.

[6] Vermont data for 2013 include both public and private schools.

NOTE: For the U.S. total, data for all years include both public and private schools. State-level data include public schools only, except where otherwise noted. For specific states, a given year's data may be unavailable (1) because the state did not participate in the survey that year; (2) because the state omitted this particular survey item from the state-level questionnaire; or (3) because the state had an overall response rate of less than 60 percent (the overall response rate is the school response rate multiplied by the student response rate).

SOURCE: Centers for Disease Control and Prevention, Division of Adolescent and School Health, Youth Risk Behavior Surveillance System (YRBSS), 2005 through 2017. (This table was prepared June 2018.)

Table 232.40. Percentage of students in grades 9-12 who reported using marijuana at least one time during the previous 30 days, by location and selected student characteristics: Selected years, 1993 through 2019

[Standard errors appear in parentheses]

Location and student characteristic	1993	1999	2001	2003	2005	2007	2009	2011	2013	2015	2017	2019
1	2	3	4	5	6	7	8	9	10	11	12	13
Anywhere (including on school property)[1]												
Total	**17.7 (1.22)**	**26.7 (1.30)**	**23.9 (0.77)**	**22.4 (1.09)**	**20.2 (0.84)**	**19.7 (0.97)**	**20.8 (0.70)**	**23.1 (0.80)**	**23.4 (1.08)**	**21.7 (1.22)**	**19.8 (0.84)**	**21.7 (0.94)**
Sex												
Male	20.6 (1.61)	30.8 (1.92)	27.9 (0.81)	25.1 (1.25)	22.1 (0.98)	22.4 (1.02)	23.4 (0.80)	25.9 (1.01)	25.0 (1.14)	23.2 (1.46)	20.0 (0.89)	22.5 (0.95)
Female	14.6 (1.02)	22.6 (0.96)	20.0 (0.87)	19.3 (0.96)	18.2 (0.99)	17.0 (1.13)	17.9 (0.87)	20.1 (0.95)	21.9 (1.28)	20.1 (1.33)	19.6 (1.14)	20.8 (1.07)
Race/ethnicity												
White	17.3 (1.41)	26.4 (1.59)	24.4 (1.04)	21.7 (1.20)	20.3 (1.11)	19.9 (1.28)	20.7 (0.93)	21.7 (1.09)	20.4 (1.36)	19.9 (1.67)	17.7 (1.12)	22.1 (1.16)
Black	18.6 (1.84)	26.4 (3.49)	21.8 (2.12)	23.9 (1.58)	20.4 (1.11)	21.5 (1.64)	22.2 (1.44)	25.1 (1.35)	28.9 (1.30)	27.1 (1.57)	25.3 (1.24)	21.7 (1.33)
Hispanic	19.4 (1.33)	28.2 (2.29)	24.6 (0.81)	23.8 (1.16)	23.0 (1.22)	18.5 (1.41)	21.6 (1.04)	24.4 (1.27)	27.6 (1.50)	24.5 (1.49)	23.4 (1.85)	22.4 (1.04)
Asian[2]	--- (†)	13.5 (2.04)	10.9 (2.12)	9.5 (2.21)	6.7 (1.64)	9.4 (1.63)	7.5 (1.40)	13.6 (3.75)	16.4 (2.99)	8.2 (1.58)	7.3 (1.79)	8.5 (1.53)
Pacific Islander[2]	--- (†)	33.8 (4.11)	21.9 (4.07)	28.1 (6.47)	12.4 ! (3.87)	28.7 (6.14)	24.8 (5.50)	31.1 (7.08)	23.4 ! (7.35)	17.4 (4.88)	16.1 (4.08)	14.3 ! (4.70)
American Indian/Alaska Native	17.4 (4.77)	36.2 (6.55)	36.4 (5.48)	32.8 (5.29)	30.3 (4.36)	27.4 (3.50)	31.6 (5.26)	47.4 (3.20)	35.5 (6.37)	26.9 (5.20)	29.7 (6.30)	33.8 (6.55)
Two or more races[2]	--- (†)	29.1 (4.00)	31.8 (3.22)	28.3 (5.57)	16.9 (2.43)	20.5 (2.73)	21.7 (2.33)	26.8 (2.10)	28.8 (2.55)	23.5 (2.18)	20.3 (2.27)	27.8 (2.13)
Sexual identity[3]												
Heterosexual	--- (†)	--- (†)	--- (†)	--- (†)	--- (†)	--- (†)	--- (†)	--- (†)	--- (†)	20.7 (1.29)	19.1 (0.83)	20.9 (0.99)
Gay, lesbian, or bisexual	--- (†)	--- (†)	--- (†)	--- (†)	--- (†)	--- (†)	--- (†)	--- (†)	--- (†)	32.0 (1.64)	30.6 (1.68)	31.1 (1.89)
Not sure	--- (†)	--- (†)	--- (†)	--- (†)	--- (†)	--- (†)	--- (†)	--- (†)	--- (†)	26.0 (2.28)	18.9 (2.76)	19.5 (2.61)
Grade												
9th	13.2 (1.10)	21.7 (1.84)	19.4 (1.25)	18.5 (1.52)	17.4 (1.16)	14.7 (1.02)	15.5 (0.97)	18.0 (1.11)	17.7 (1.13)	15.2 (0.98)	13.1 (1.07)	14.6 (0.93)
10th	16.5 (1.79)	27.8 (2.21)	24.8 (1.12)	22.0 (1.47)	20.2 (1.27)	19.3 (1.12)	21.1 (1.11)	21.6 (1.15)	23.5 (1.89)	20.0 (1.87)	18.7 (0.93)	19.8 (1.26)
11th	18.4 (1.77)	26.7 (2.47)	25.8 (1.33)	24.1 (1.56)	21.0 (1.24)	21.4 (1.49)	23.2 (1.52)	25.5 (1.44)	25.5 (1.37)	24.8 (1.27)	22.6 (1.23)	24.9 (1.66)
12th	22.0 (1.40)	31.5 (2.81)	26.9 (1.77)	25.8 (1.19)	22.8 (1.23)	25.1 (1.96)	24.6 (1.49)	28.0 (1.08)	27.7 (1.58)	27.6 (1.93)	25.7 (1.43)	28.3 (1.59)
On school property[4]												
Total	**5.6 (0.65)**	**7.2 (0.73)**	**5.4 (0.37)**	**5.8 (0.68)**	**4.5 (0.32)**	**4.5 (0.46)**	**4.6 (0.35)**	**5.9 (0.39)**	**--- (†)**	**--- (†)**	**--- (†)**	**--- (†)**
Sex												
Male	7.8 (0.83)	10.1 (1.30)	8.0 (0.54)	7.6 (0.88)	6.0 (0.44)	5.9 (0.61)	6.3 (0.54)	7.5 (0.56)	--- (†)	--- (†)	--- (†)	--- (†)
Female	3.3 (0.48)	4.4 (0.40)	2.9 (0.28)	3.7 (0.48)	3.0 (0.31)	3.0 (0.39)	2.8 (0.32)	4.1 (0.32)	--- (†)	--- (†)	--- (†)	--- (†)
Race/ethnicity												
White	5.0 (0.72)	6.5 (0.84)	4.8 (0.45)	4.5 (0.66)	3.8 (0.41)	4.0 (0.63)	3.8 (0.38)	4.5 (0.42)	--- (†)	--- (†)	--- (†)	--- (†)
Black	7.3 (1.23)	7.2 (1.10)	6.1 (0.60)	6.6 (0.89)	4.9 (0.65)	5.0 (0.73)	5.6 (0.64)	6.7 (0.77)	--- (†)	--- (†)	--- (†)	--- (†)
Hispanic	7.5 (1.10)	10.7 (1.21)	7.4 (0.58)	8.2 (0.72)	7.7 (0.76)	5.4 (0.80)	6.5 (0.76)	7.7 (0.54)	--- (†)	--- (†)	--- (†)	--- (†)
Asian[2]	--- (†)	4.3 (0.71)	4.7 ! (1.56)	4.3 ! (1.38)	‡ (†)	2.7 ! (1.06)	2.0 (0.54)	4.5 (1.34)	--- (†)	--- (†)	--- (†)	--- (†)
Pacific Islander[2]	--- (†)	11.0 (3.21)	6.4 ! (2.46)	9.1 ! (3.17)	‡ (†)	13.4 ! (5.38)	9.0 (2.40)	12.5 ! (4.94)	--- (†)	--- (†)	--- (†)	--- (†)
American Indian/Alaska Native	‡ (†)	‡ (†)	21.5 ! (6.55)	11.4 ! (4.42)	9.2 (1.85)	8.2 (2.30)	2.9 ! (1.25)	20.9 (4.05)	--- (†)	--- (†)	--- (†)	--- (†)
Two or more races[2]	--- (†)	7.8 (1.81)	5.2 (1.24)	11.4 ! (5.49)	3.6 (0.91)	3.6 ! (1.08)	5.4 (1.34)	8.1 (1.79)	--- (†)	--- (†)	--- (†)	--- (†)
Grade												
9th	4.4 (0.40)	6.6 (0.97)	5.5 (0.62)	6.6 (1.03)	5.0 (0.59)	4.0 (0.52)	4.3 (0.38)	5.4 (0.65)	--- (†)	--- (†)	--- (†)	--- (†)
10th	6.5 (0.94)	7.6 (1.14)	5.8 (0.51)	5.2 (0.70)	4.6 (0.54)	4.8 (0.60)	4.6 (0.50)	6.2 (0.63)	--- (†)	--- (†)	--- (†)	--- (†)
11th	6.5 (1.07)	7.0 (0.72)	5.1 (0.48)	5.6 (0.71)	4.1 (0.49)	4.1 (0.73)	5.0 (0.55)	6.2 (0.70)	--- (†)	--- (†)	--- (†)	--- (†)
12th	5.1 (0.78)	7.3 (1.14)	4.9 (0.71)	5.0 (0.75)	4.1 (0.45)	5.1 (0.73)	4.6 (0.49)	5.4 (0.39)	--- (†)	--- (†)	--- (†)	--- (†)

—Not available.

†Not applicable.

!Interpret data with caution. The coefficient of variation (CV) for this estimate is between 30 and 50 percent.

‡Reporting standards not met. The coefficient of variation (CV) for this estimate is 50 percent or greater.

[1] The term "anywhere" is not used in the Youth Risk Behavior Survey (YRBS) questionnaire; students were simply asked how many times during the previous 30 days they had used marijuana.

[2] Before 1999, Asian students and Pacific Islander students were not categorized separately, and students could not be classified as Two or more races. Because the response categories changed in 1999, caution should be used in comparing data on race from 1993 with data from later years.

[3] Students were asked which of the following—"heterosexual (straight)," "gay or lesbian," "bisexual," or "not sure"—best described them.

[4] In the question about using marijuana at school, "on school property" was not defined for respondents. Data on marijuana use at school were not collected from 2013 onward.

NOTE: Estimates in this table do not include the use of synthetic marijuana (also called K2, Spice, fake weed, King Kong, Yucatan Fire, Skunk, or Moon Rocks). Race categories exclude persons of Hispanic ethnicity.

SOURCE: Centers for Disease Control and Prevention, Division of Adolescent and School Health, Youth Risk Behavior Surveillance System (YRBSS), 1993 through 2019. (This table was prepared September 2020.)

Table 232.50. Percentage distribution of students in grades 9-12, by number of times they reported using marijuana anywhere during the previous 30 days and selected student characteristics: Selected years, 2013 through 2019

[Standard errors appear in parentheses]

Year and student characteristic	0 times		1 or 2 times		3 to 39 times		40 or more times	
1		2		3		4		5
2013								
Total	**76.6**	**(1.08)**	**7.1**	**(0.42)**	**11.3**	**(0.68)**	**5.0**	**(0.39)**
Sex								
Male	75.0	(1.14)	6.5	(0.42)	12.0	(0.72)	6.5	(0.53)
Female	78.1	(1.28)	7.8	(0.59)	10.7	(0.77)	3.4	(0.36)
Race/ethnicity								
White	79.6	(1.36)	6.3	(0.63)	9.7	(0.75)	4.4	(0.42)
Black	71.1	(1.30)	8.2	(0.52)	14.3	(0.90)	6.3	(0.71)
Hispanic	72.4	(1.50)	8.6	(0.52)	13.4	(1.22)	5.6	(0.70)
Asian	83.6	(2.99)	4.1	(1.02)	7.6	(1.32)	4.7 !	(2.03)
Pacific Islander	76.6	(7.35)	4.9 !	(2.31)	17.1 !	(5.82)	‡	(†)
American Indian/Alaska Native	64.5	(6.37)	8.8 !	(2.70)	18.9	(4.54)	7.9 !	(2.77)
Two or more races	71.2	(2.55)	9.7	(1.36)	12.4	(1.45)	6.7	(1.29)
Grade								
9th	82.3	(1.13)	6.3	(0.59)	8.6	(0.70)	2.8	(0.38)
10th	76.5	(1.89)	7.2	(0.65)	11.3	(1.35)	5.0	(0.81)
11th	74.5	(1.37)	7.6	(0.68)	12.0	(0.85)	6.0	(0.56)
12th	72.3	(1.58)	7.6	(0.68)	13.8	(1.00)	6.4	(0.63)
2015								
Total	**78.3**	**(1.22)**	**7.0**	**(0.37)**	**10.4**	**(0.81)**	**4.2**	**(0.40)**
Sex								
Male	76.8	(1.46)	6.4	(0.47)	11.4	(0.91)	5.5	(0.61)
Female	79.9	(1.33)	7.6	(0.44)	9.6	(0.87)	2.9	(0.31)
Race/ethnicity								
White	80.1	(1.67)	6.9	(0.45)	9.6	(1.20)	3.5	(0.44)
Black	72.9	(1.57)	8.3	(1.14)	13.7	(1.06)	5.1	(0.99)
Hispanic	75.5	(1.49)	7.7	(0.64)	11.4	(0.84)	5.3	(0.62)
Asian	91.8	(1.58)	2.6 !	(0.87)	4.1	(0.87)	1.5 !	(0.72)
Pacific Islander	82.6	(4.88)	‡	(†)	5.5 !	(2.03)	‡	(†)
American Indian/Alaska Native	73.1	(5.20)	6.3 !	(2.47)	12.1 !	(3.74)	‡	(†)
Two or more races	76.5	(2.18)	6.0	(1.08)	12.1	(1.58)	5.4	(1.10)
Sexual identity[1]								
Heterosexual	79.3	(1.29)	6.7	(0.41)	10.0	(0.87)	4.0	(0.40)
Gay, lesbian, or bisexual	68.0	(1.64)	10.3	(1.31)	15.7	(1.28)	6.0	(1.00)
Not sure	74.0	(2.28)	6.7	(1.50)	11.4	(1.56)	7.8	(1.44)
Grade								
9th	84.8	(0.98)	5.5	(0.56)	7.3	(0.56)	2.4	(0.34)
10th	80.0	(1.87)	6.1	(0.73)	10.0	(1.18)	3.9	(0.59)
11th	75.2	(1.27)	7.7	(0.55)	12.9	(1.13)	4.3	(0.55)
12th	72.4	(1.93)	8.9	(0.61)	12.2	(1.33)	6.4	(0.82)
2017								
Total	**80.2**	**(0.84)**	**6.7**	**(0.33)**	**9.1**	**(0.52)**	**3.9**	**(0.34)**
Sex								
Male	80.0	(0.89)	6.3	(0.45)	8.9	(0.48)	4.7	(0.45)
Female	80.4	(1.14)	7.1	(0.45)	9.3	(0.73)	3.1	(0.44)
Race/ethnicity								
White	82.3	(1.12)	6.1	(0.51)	8.1	(0.62)	3.5	(0.46)
Black	74.7	(1.24)	7.6	(0.81)	12.4	(1.04)	5.3	(0.66)
Hispanic	76.6	(1.85)	8.6	(0.42)	10.8	(1.39)	4.0	(0.51)
Asian	92.7	(1.79)	2.3	(0.68)	3.5	(0.98)	‡	(†)
Pacific Islander	83.9	(4.08)	7.1 !	(2.46)	6.3 !	(2.64)	‡	(†)
American Indian/Alaska Native	70.3	(6.30)	3.0 !	(1.34)	12.7 !	(4.28)	14.1 !	(5.10)
Two or more races	79.7	(2.27)	6.9	(1.14)	8.7	(1.41)	4.7	(1.17)
Sexual identity[1]								
Heterosexual	80.9	(0.83)	6.6	(0.36)	9.0	(0.50)	3.5	(0.35)
Gay, lesbian, or bisexual	69.4	(1.68)	9.6	(1.39)	13.8	(1.12)	7.3	(1.12)
Not sure	81.1	(2.76)	5.5	(1.37)	7.6	(1.52)	5.8 !	(2.00)
Grade								
9th	86.9	(1.07)	5.2	(0.43)	5.7	(0.65)	2.1	(0.37)
10th	81.3	(0.93)	6.7	(0.50)	9.0	(0.76)	3.0	(0.41)
11th	77.4	(1.23)	7.3	(0.46)	10.9	(0.90)	4.4	(0.45)
12th	74.3	(1.43)	8.0	(0.70)	11.5	(1.03)	6.2	(0.73)
2019								
Total	**78.3**	**(0.94)**	**8.0**	**(0.33)**	**9.9**	**(0.53)**	**3.9**	**(0.44)**
Sex								
Male	77.5	(0.95)	7.4	(0.46)	10.2	(0.67)	4.9	(0.53)
Female	79.2	(1.07)	8.5	(0.46)	9.4	(0.61)	2.9	(0.44)
Race/ethnicity								
White	77.9	(1.16)	8.1	(0.51)	9.8	(0.57)	4.2	(0.66)
Black	78.3	(1.33)	8.0	(0.82)	10.1	(0.89)	3.6	(0.66)
Hispanic	77.6	(1.04)	8.3	(0.60)	10.8	(0.80)	3.3	(0.50)

[Standard errors appear in parentheses]

Year and student characteristic	0 times		1 or 2 times		3 to 39 times		40 or more times	
1		2		3		4		5
Asian	91.5	(1.53)	3.5	(0.68)	2.9	(0.80)	2.1 !	(0.84)
Pacific Islander	85.7	(4.70)	5.3 !	(2.31)	‡	(†)	‡	(†)
American Indian/Alaska Native	66.2	(6.55)	‡	(†)	15.0 !	(4.99)	11.0 !	(4.25)
Two or more races	72.2	(2.13)	9.2	(1.32)	12.5	(1.56)	6.1	(1.10)
Sexual identity[1]								
Heterosexual	79.1	(0.99)	7.6	(0.43)	9.6	(0.55)	3.7	(0.43)
Gay, lesbian, or bisexual	68.9	(1.89)	11.0	(1.00)	13.7	(1.08)	6.4	(1.07)
Not sure	80.5	(2.61)	7.8	(1.86)	7.8	(1.57)	3.9 !	(1.27)
Grade								
9th	85.4	(0.93)	7.3	(0.71)	5.7	(0.55)	1.6	(0.35)
10th	80.2	(1.26)	7.7	(0.70)	9.0	(0.75)	3.0	(0.39)
11th	75.1	(1.66)	8.2	(0.60)	11.9	(0.94)	4.7	(0.84)
12th	71.7	(1.59)	8.7	(0.71)	13.3	(1.06)	6.3	(0.92)

†Not applicable.

!Interpret data with caution. The coefficient of variation (CV) for this estimate is between 30 and 50 percent.

‡Reporting standards not met. Either there are too few cases for a reliable estimate or the coefficient of variation (CV) is 50 percent or greater.

[1] Students were asked which of the following--"heterosexual (straight)," "gay or lesbian," "bisexual," or "not sure"--best described them.

NOTE: The term "anywhere" is not used in the Youth Risk Behavior Survey (YRBS) questionnaire; students were simply asked how many times during the previous 30 days they had used marijuana. Estimates in this table do not include the use of synthetic marijuana (also called K2, Spice, fake weed, King Kong, Yucatan Fire, Skunk, or Moon Rocks). Race categories exclude persons of Hispanic ethnicity. Detail may not sum to totals because of rounding and the suppression of cells that do not meet National Center for Education Statistics reporting standards.

SOURCE: Centers for Disease Control and Prevention, Division of Adolescent and School Health, Youth Risk Behavior Surveillance System (YRBSS), 2013 through 2019. (This table was prepared September 2020.)

Table 232.60. Percentage of public school students in grades 9-12 who reported using marijuana at least one time during the previous 30 days, by location and state or jurisdiction: Selected years, 2005 through 2017

[Standard errors appear in parentheses]

State or jurisdiction	Anywhere (including on school property)[1]							On school property[2]						
	2005	2007	2009	2011	2013	2015	2017	2005	2007	2009	2011	2013	2015	2017
1	2	3	4	5	6	7	8	9	10	11	12	13	14	15
United States[3]	**20.2 (0.84)**	**19.7 (0.97)**	**20.8 (0.70)**	**23.1 (0.80)**	**23.4 (1.08)**	**21.7 (1.22)**	**19.8 (0.84)**	**4.5 (0.32)**	**4.5 (0.46)**	**4.6 (0.35)**	**5.9 (0.39)**	**— (†)**	**— (†)**	**— (†)**
Alabama	18.5 (1.49)	— (†)	16.2 (1.28)	20.8 (1.62)	19.2 (1.46)	17.3 (1.08)	— (†)	3.5 (0.80)	— (†)	4.6 (0.81)	4.0 (0.68)	— (†)	— (†)	— (†)
Alaska	— (†)	20.5 (1.47)	22.7 (1.65)	21.2 (1.68)	19.7 (1.35)	19.0 (1.15)	21.5 (1.42)	— (†)	5.9 (0.70)	5.9 (0.69)	4.3 (0.59)	— (†)	— (†)	— (†)
Arizona	20.0 (1.08)	22.0 (1.38)	23.7 (1.90)	22.9 (1.59)	23.5 (1.75)	23.3 (1.98)	19.5 (2.00)	5.1 (0.63)	6.1 (0.68)	6.4 (0.74)	5.6 (0.75)	— (†)	— (†)	— (†)
Arkansas	18.9 (1.70)	16.4 (1.08)	17.8 (1.24)	16.8 (1.72)	19.0 (0.98)	17.8 (0.95)	14.7 (1.49)	4.1 (0.61)	2.8 (0.50)	4.5 (1.02)	3.9 (0.78)	— (†)	— (†)	— (†)
California	— (†)	— (†)	— (†)	— (†)	— (†)	22.9 (2.19)	21.8 (1.92)	— (†)	— (†)	— (†)	— (†)	— (†)	— (†)	— (†)
Colorado	22.7 (2.99)	— (†)	24.8 (2.22)	22.0 (1.16)	— (†)	— (†)	19.6 (1.78)	6.0 (0.88)	— (†)	6.1 (0.89)	6.0 (0.77)	— (†)	— (†)	— (†)
Connecticut	23.1 (1.37)	23.2 (1.35)	21.8 (1.52)	24.2 (1.44)	26.1 (1.44)	20.4 (1.41)	20.4 (1.16)	5.1 (0.49)	5.9 (0.77)	6.2 (0.76)	5.2 (0.68)	— (†)	— (†)	— (†)
Delaware	22.8 (1.12)	25.1 (1.03)	25.8 (1.30)	27.6 (1.37)	25.6 (1.17)	23.3 (1.61)	26.1 (1.38)	5.6 (0.57)	5.4 (0.53)	5.6 (0.71)	6.1 (0.65)	— (†)	— (†)	— (†)
District of Columbia	14.5 (1.08)	20.8 (1.33)	— (†)	26.1 (1.29)	32.2 (0.58)	28.7 (0.48)	33.0 (0.58)	4.8 (0.62)	5.8 (0.66)	— (†)	7.9 (0.91)	— (†)	— (†)	— (†)
Florida	16.8 (0.86)	18.9 (0.88)	21.4 (0.72)	22.5 (0.86)	22.0 (0.81)	21.5 (0.79)	20.2 (0.70)	4.0 (0.31)	4.7 (0.40)	5.2 (0.39)	6.3 (0.39)	— (†)	— (†)	— (†)
Georgia	18.9 (1.59)	19.6 (0.96)	18.3 (1.02)	21.2 (1.23)	20.3 (1.64)	— (†)	— (†)	3.3 (0.58)	3.6 (0.58)	3.4 (0.62)	5.6 (0.70)	— (†)	— (†)	— (†)
Hawaii	17.2 (1.73)	15.7 (1.78)	22.1 (2.03)	22.0 (1.32)	18.9 (1.54)	19.4 (0.98)	18.1 (1.07)	7.2 (1.14)	5.7 (0.85)	8.3 (1.86)	7.6 (0.67)	— (†)	— (†)	— (†)
Idaho	17.1 (1.32)	17.9 (1.73)	13.7 (1.07)	18.8 (1.76)	15.3 (1.10)	17.1 (1.55)	16.2 (1.43)	3.9 (0.61)	4.7 (0.80)	3.0 (0.44)	4.9 (0.73)	— (†)	— (†)	— (†)
Illinois	— (†)	20.3 (1.38)	21.0 (1.53)	23.1 (1.59)	24.0 (1.70)	18.7 (1.47)	20.8 (1.90)	— (†)	4.2 (0.76)	5.0 (0.77)	4.7 (0.50)	— (†)	— (†)	— (†)
Indiana	18.9 (1.38)	18.9 (1.19)	20.9 (1.83)	20.0 (1.13)	— (†)	16.4 (1.17)	— (†)	3.4 (0.57)	4.1 (0.45)	4.4 (0.62)	3.3 (0.66)	— (†)	— (†)	— (†)
Iowa	15.6 (1.74)	11.5 (1.53)	— (†)	14.6 (1.99)	— (†)	— (†)	13.2 (1.80)	2.7 (0.64)	2.5 (0.66)	— (†)	3.4 (0.88)	— (†)	— (†)	— (†)
Kansas	15.6 (1.46)	15.3 (0.93)	14.7 (1.19)	16.8 (0.87)	14.3 (1.19)	— (†)	13.5 (0.87)	3.2 (0.51)	3.8 (0.53)	2.7 (0.35)	2.9 (0.53)	— (†)	— (†)	— (†)
Kentucky	15.8 (1.19)	16.4 (1.07)	16.1 (1.15)	19.2 (1.47)	17.7 (1.50)	17.2 (1.34)	15.8 (1.41)	3.2 (0.45)	3.9 (0.44)	3.1 (0.54)	4.2 (0.65)	— (†)	— (†)	— (†)
Louisiana	— (†)	— (†)	16.3 (1.29)	16.8 (1.02)	17.5 (1.38)	— (†)	18.8 (2.00)	— (†)	— (†)	3.6 (0.89)	4.1 (0.59)	— (†)	— (†)	— (†)
Maine	22.2 (2.13)	22.0 (1.55)	20.5 (0.57)	21.2 (0.72)	21.3 (0.89)	19.9 (0.58)	18.8 (0.74)	4.6 (0.72)	5.2 (0.65)	— (†)	— (†)	— (†)	— (†)	— (†)
Maryland	18.5 (2.25)	19.4 (1.91)	21.9 (1.57)	23.2 (1.51)	19.8 (0.36)	18.8 (0.32)	18.4 (0.34)	3.7 (0.82)	4.7 (1.13)	5.0 (0.65)	5.7 (0.70)	— (†)	— (†)	— (†)
Massachusetts	26.2 (1.22)	24.6 (1.43)	27.1 (1.24)	27.9 (1.31)	24.8 (0.92)	24.5 (1.42)	24.1 (1.40)	5.3 (0.54)	4.8 (0.44)	5.9 (0.79)	6.3 (0.51)	— (†)	— (†)	— (†)
Michigan	18.8 (1.29)	18.0 (1.10)	20.7 (0.91)	18.6 (1.15)	18.2 (0.73)	19.3 (1.51)	23.7 (2.42)	3.7 (0.50)	4.0 (0.57)	4.8 (0.59)	3.3 (0.44)	— (†)	— (†)	— (†)
Minnesota	— (†)	— (†)	— (†)	— (†)	— (†)	— (†)	— (†)	— (†)	— (†)	— (†)	— (†)	— (†)	— (†)	— (†)
Mississippi	— (†)	16.7 (1.02)	17.7 (1.21)	17.5 (1.18)	17.7 (1.28)	19.7 (1.24)	— (†)	— (†)	2.7 (0.35)	2.5 (0.46)	3.2 (0.58)	— (†)	— (†)	— (†)
Missouri	18.1 (2.23)	19.0 (1.23)	20.6 (2.02)	— (†)	20.5 (1.69)	16.3 (1.34)	19.9 (1.54)	4.0 (0.82)	3.6 (0.63)	3.4 (0.48)	— (†)	— (†)	— (†)	— (†)
Montana	22.3 (1.43)	21.0 (1.44)	23.1 (1.58)	21.2 (1.50)	21.0 (1.18)	19.5 (1.10)	19.8 (0.95)	6.1 (0.70)	5.0 (0.49)	5.8 (0.67)	5.5 (0.59)	— (†)	— (†)	— (†)
Nebraska	17.5 (1.05)	— (†)	— (†)	12.7 (1.06)	11.7 (1.10)	13.7 (1.60)	13.4 (1.36)	3.1 (0.41)	— (†)	— (†)	2.7 (0.43)	— (†)	— (†)	— (†)
Nevada	17.3 (1.34)	15.5 (1.07)	20.0 (1.36)	— (†)	18.7 (1.57)	19.3 (1.50)	17.9 (1.44)	5.7 (0.81)	3.6 (0.55)	4.9 (0.53)	— (†)	— (†)	— (†)	— (†)
New Hampshire	25.9 (1.69)	22.9 (1.39)	25.6 (1.86)	28.4 (1.82)	24.4 (1.36)	22.2 (0.76)	23.1 (0.68)	— (†)	4.7 (0.64)	6.8 (0.78)	7.3 (0.87)	— (†)	— (†)	— (†)
New Jersey	19.9 (2.18)	— (†)	20.3 (1.53)	21.1 (1.33)	21.0 (1.20)	— (†)	— (†)	3.4 (0.67)	— (†)	— (†)	— (†)	— (†)	— (†)	— (†)
New Mexico	26.2 (2.00)	25.0 (2.07)	28.0 (1.52)	27.6 (1.58)	27.8 (1.70)	25.3 (0.88)	27.3 (1.68)	8.4 (0.98)	7.9 (0.86)	9.7 (1.06)	9.7 (0.84)	— (†)	— (†)	— (†)
New York	18.3 (1.13)	18.6 (0.78)	20.9 (1.32)	20.6 (1.07)	21.4 (1.04)	19.3 (1.23)	18.4 (0.93)	3.6 (0.41)	4.1 (0.44)	— (†)	— (†)	— (†)	— (†)	— (†)
North Carolina	21.4 (1.61)	19.1 (1.27)	19.8 (1.67)	24.2 (1.25)	23.2 (1.83)	22.3 (1.15)	19.3 (1.53)	4.1 (0.65)	4.3 (0.54)	4.0 (0.63)	5.2 (0.91)	— (†)	— (†)	— (†)
North Dakota	15.5 (1.62)	14.8 (1.18)	16.9 (1.55)	15.3 (1.52)	15.9 (1.26)	15.2 (1.12)	15.5 (1.12)	4.0 (0.71)	2.7 (0.43)	3.8 (0.59)	3.4 (0.45)	— (†)	— (†)	— (†)
Ohio[4]	20.9 (1.79)	17.7 (1.50)	— (†)	23.6 (1.95)	20.7 (2.30)	— (†)	— (†)	4.3 (0.62)	3.7 (0.67)	— (†)	— (†)	— (†)	— (†)	— (†)
Oklahoma	18.7 (1.12)	15.9 (1.37)	17.2 (2.04)	19.1 (1.90)	16.3 (1.57)	17.5 (1.79)	15.9 (1.74)	3.0 (0.38)	2.6 (0.40)	2.9 (0.70)	2.4 (0.58)	— (†)	— (†)	— (†)
Oregon	— (†)	— (†)	— (†)	— (†)	— (†)	— (†)	— (†)	— (†)	— (†)	— (†)	— (†)	— (†)	— (†)	— (†)
Pennsylvania	— (†)	— (†)	19.3 (1.43)	— (†)	— (†)	18.2 (1.17)	17.7 (1.18)	— (†)	— (†)	3.5 (0.58)	— (†)	— (†)	— (†)	— (†)
Rhode Island	25.0 (1.16)	23.2 (1.85)	26.3 (1.33)	26.3 (1.35)	23.9 (1.92)	23.6 (0.73)	23.3 (1.21)	7.2 (0.65)	6.5 (0.93)	5.1 (0.60)	— (†)	— (†)	— (†)	— (†)
South Carolina	19.0 (1.24)	18.6 (1.44)	20.4 (1.56)	24.1 (1.99)	19.7 (1.22)	17.8 (1.70)	18.6 (1.38)	4.6 (0.64)	3.3 (0.52)	3.7 (0.63)	5.2 (0.75)	— (†)	— (†)	— (†)
South Dakota[5]	16.8 (1.87)	17.7 (3.72)	15.2 (1.36)	17.8 (3.57)	16.1 (3.01)	12.4 (2.21)	— (†)	2.9 (0.73)	5.0 ! (2.41)	2.9 (0.49)	— (†)	— (†)	— (†)	— (†)
Tennessee	19.5 (1.38)	19.4 (1.29)	20.1 (1.31)	20.6 (0.96)	21.4 (1.70)	— (†)	18.1 (0.95)	3.5 (0.67)	4.1 (0.60)	3.8 (0.65)	3.6 (0.40)	— (†)	— (†)	— (†)
Texas	21.7 (0.99)	19.3 (1.01)	19.5 (0.71)	20.8 (1.30)	20.5 (1.26)	— (†)	17.0 (1.24)	3.8 (0.52)	3.6 (0.30)	4.6 (0.51)	4.8 (0.47)	— (†)	— (†)	— (†)
Utah	7.6 (1.18)	8.7 (2.00)	10.0 (1.53)	9.6 (1.26)	7.6 (0.79)	— (†)	8.1 (0.89)	1.7 (0.42)	3.8 ! (1.24)	2.5 (0.48)	4.0 (0.72)	— (†)	— (†)	— (†)
Vermont[6]	25.3 (1.59)	24.1 (0.88)	24.6 (1.14)	24.4 (1.43)	25.7 (0.83)	22.4 (0.29)	23.5 (0.30)	7.0 (0.80)	6.3 (0.63)	6.3 (0.57)	6.0 (0.84)	— (†)	— (†)	— (†)
Virginia	— (†)	— (†)	— (†)	18.0 (1.79)	17.9 (0.85)	16.2 (0.96)	16.5 (0.92)	— (†)	— (†)	— (†)	3.5 (0.70)	— (†)	— (†)	— (†)
Washington	— (†)	— (†)	— (†)	— (†)	— (†)	— (†)	— (†)	— (†)	— (†)	— (†)	— (†)	— (†)	— (†)	— (†)
West Virginia	19.6 (1.70)	23.5 (1.05)	20.3 (1.73)	19.7 (1.61)	18.9 (1.39)	16.5 (1.65)	18.5 (1.60)	4.9 (0.85)	5.8 (0.97)	3.9 (0.37)	3.0 (0.45)	— (†)	— (†)	— (†)
Wisconsin	15.9 (1.07)	20.3 (1.30)	18.9 (1.64)	21.6 (1.78)	17.3 (1.12)	— (†)	16.0 (1.60)	— (†)	— (†)	— (†)	— (†)	— (†)	— (†)	— (†)
Wyoming	17.8 (1.05)	14.4 (0.79)	16.9 (0.91)	18.5 (1.23)	17.8 (0.81)	18.3 (1.55)	— (†)	4.0 (0.43)	4.7 (0.52)	5.3 (0.45)	4.7 (0.44)	— (†)	— (†)	— (†)
Puerto Rico	6.8 (0.66)	— (†)	— (†)	4.6 (0.71)	4.8 (0.55)	6.0 (0.54)	7.9 (0.84)	2.5 (0.37)	— (†)	— (†)	1.6 (0.36)	— (†)	— (†)	— (†)

—Not available.

†Not applicable.

!Interpret data with caution. The coefficient of variation (CV) for this estimate is between 30 and 50 percent.

[1] The term "anywhere" is not used in the Youth Risk Behavior Survey (YRBS) questionnaire; students were simply asked how many times during the previous 30 days they had used marijuana.

[2] In the question about using marijuana at school, "on school property" was not defined for survey respondents. Data on marijuana use at school were not collected from 2013 onward.

[3] U.S. total data are representative of all public and private school students in grades 9-12 in the 50 states and the District of Columbia. U.S. total data for all years were collected through a separate national survey (rather than being aggregated from state-level data) and include both public and private schools.

[4] Ohio data for 2005 through 2013 include both public and private schools.

[5] South Dakota data for 2005 through 2015 include both public and private schools.

[6] Vermont data for 2013 include both public and private schools.

NOTE: For the U.S. total, data for all years include both public and private schools. State-level data include public schools only, except where otherwise noted. For specific states, a given year's data may be unavailable (1) because the state did not participate in the survey that year; (2) because the state omitted this particular survey item from the state-level questionnaire; or (3) because the state had an overall response rate of less than 60 percent (the overall response rate is the school response rate multiplied by the student response rate).

SOURCE: Centers for Disease Control and Prevention, Division of Adolescent and School Health, Youth Risk Behavior Surveillance System (YRBSS), 2005 through 2017. (This table was prepared July 2018.)

Table 232.70. Percentage of students in grades 9-12 who reported that illegal drugs were made available to them on school property during the previous 12 months, by selected student characteristics: Selected years, 1993 through 2019

[Standard errors appear in parentheses]

Student characteristic	1993	1999	2001	2003	2005	2007	2009	2011	2013	2015	2017	2019
1	2	3	4	5	6	7	8	9	10	11	12	13
Total	**24.0 (1.33)**	**30.2 (1.23)**	**28.5 (1.01)**	**28.7 (1.95)**	**25.4 (1.05)**	**22.3 (1.04)**	**22.7 (1.04)**	**25.6 (0.99)**	**22.1 (0.96)**	**21.7 (1.18)**	**19.8 (0.78)**	**21.8 (0.77)**
Sex												
Male	28.5 (1.50)	34.7 (1.69)	34.6 (1.20)	31.9 (2.07)	28.8 (1.23)	25.7 (1.15)	25.9 (1.36)	29.2 (1.10)	24.5 (1.21)	24.2 (1.29)	20.9 (0.77)	22.8 (0.97)
Female	19.1 (1.31)	25.7 (1.26)	22.7 (1.03)	25.0 (1.92)	21.8 (1.03)	18.7 (1.16)	19.3 (1.01)	21.7 (1.17)	19.7 (0.89)	19.1 (1.29)	18.7 (0.98)	20.8 (0.92)
Race/ethnicity												
White	24.1 (1.69)	28.8 (1.50)	28.3 (1.31)	27.5 (2.68)	23.6 (1.32)	20.8 (1.23)	19.8 (1.13)	22.7 (0.96)	20.4 (1.11)	19.8 (1.66)	17.7 (1.04)	19.8 (0.96)
Black	17.5 (1.49)	25.3 (2.03)	21.9 (1.72)	23.1 (1.42)	23.9 (2.22)	19.2 (1.36)	22.2 (1.42)	22.8 (1.82)	18.6 (1.11)	20.6 (2.54)	18.9 (1.45)	21.5 (1.17)
Hispanic	34.1 (1.58)	36.9 (2.10)	34.2 (1.17)	36.5 (1.91)	33.5 (1.18)	29.1 (1.94)	31.2 (1.53)	33.2 (1.70)	27.4 (1.42)	27.2 (1.25)	25.4 (1.22)	26.7 (1.08)
Asian[1]	--- (†)	25.7 (2.65)	25.7 (2.92)	22.5 (3.71)	15.9 (2.68)	21.0 (2.78)	18.3 (2.03)	23.3 (2.46)	22.6 (2.57)	15.3 (2.42)	17.7 (1.63)	14.5 (2.17)
Pacific Islander[1]	--- (†)	46.9 (4.33)	50.2 (5.73)	34.7 (6.19)	41.3 (5.75)	38.5 (5.45)	27.6 (5.10)	38.9 (5.01)	27.7 (3.68)	30.1 ! (9.25)	25.7 (4.57)	17.0 ! (7.86)
American Indian/Alaska Native	20.9 (4.55)	30.6 (5.90)	34.5 (5.15)	31.3 (5.64)	24.4 (3.57)	25.1 (2.04)	34.0 (4.81)	40.5 (2.80)	25.5 (4.10)	19.8 (3.87)	17.1 (3.42)	24.2 (5.02)
Two or more races[1]	--- (†)	36.0 (2.72)	34.5 (3.22)	36.6 (3.99)	31.6 (3.13)	24.6 (3.55)	26.9 (2.62)	33.3 (2.79)	26.4 (2.67)	24.7 (2.45)	19.2 (2.56)	27.8 (2.18)
Sexual identity[2]												
Heterosexual	--- (†)	--- (†)	--- (†)	--- (†)	--- (†)	--- (†)	--- (†)	--- (†)	--- (†)	20.8 (1.24)	18.9 (0.65)	20.8 (0.76)
Gay, lesbian, or bisexual	--- (†)	--- (†)	--- (†)	--- (†)	--- (†)	--- (†)	--- (†)	--- (†)	--- (†)	29.3 (2.03)	28.2 (2.00)	30.3 (1.93)
Not sure	--- (†)	--- (†)	--- (†)	--- (†)	--- (†)	--- (†)	--- (†)	--- (†)	--- (†)	28.4 (3.03)	19.6 (2.65)	23.6 (2.21)
Grade												
9th	21.8 (1.24)	27.6 (2.51)	29.0 (1.59)	29.5 (2.39)	24.0 (1.21)	21.2 (1.23)	22.0 (1.32)	23.7 (1.22)	22.4 (1.15)	21.6 (1.28)	18.9 (1.18)	21.6 (1.13)
10th	23.7 (1.86)	32.1 (1.94)	29.0 (1.39)	29.2 (2.02)	27.5 (1.68)	25.3 (1.29)	23.7 (1.11)	27.8 (1.21)	23.2 (1.54)	21.9 (1.96)	20.3 (1.32)	23.7 (1.16)
11th	27.5 (1.61)	31.1 (2.16)	28.7 (1.39)	29.9 (2.33)	24.9 (1.03)	22.8 (1.42)	24.3 (1.44)	27.0 (1.51)	23.2 (1.32)	22.7 (1.42)	20.0 (1.15)	22.0 (1.11)
12th	23.0 (1.82)	30.5 (1.11)	26.9 (1.30)	24.9 (2.24)	24.9 (1.40)	19.6 (1.26)	20.6 (1.21)	23.8 (1.13)	18.8 (1.11)	20.3 (1.41)	19.6 (1.04)	19.6 (1.35)

—Not available.

†Not applicable.

!Interpret data with caution. The coefficient of variation (CV) for this estimate is between 30 and 50 percent.

[1] Before 1999, Asian students and Pacific Islander students were not categorized separately, and students could not be classified as Two or more races. Because the response categories changed in 1999, caution should be used in comparing data on race from 1993 with data from later years.

[2] Students were asked which of the following--"heterosexual (straight)," "gay or lesbian," "bisexual," or "not sure"--best described them.

NOTE: Students were asked if anyone offered, sold, or gave them an illegal drug on school property during the previous 12 months. "On school property" was not defined for respondents. Race categories exclude persons of Hispanic ethnicity.

SOURCE: Centers for Disease Control and Prevention, Division of Adolescent and School Health, Youth Risk Behavior Surveillance System (YRBSS), 1993 through 2019. (This table was prepared September 2020.)

Table 232.80. Percentage of public school students in grades 9-12 who reported that illegal drugs were made available to them on school property during the previous 12 months, by state or jurisdiction: Selected years, 2003 through 2017

[Standard errors appear in parentheses]

State or jurisdiction	2003		2005		2007		2009		2011		2013		2015		2017	
1	2		3		4		5		6		7		8		9	
United States[1]	**28.7**	**(1.95)**	**25.4**	**(1.05)**	**22.3**	**(1.04)**	**22.7**	**(1.04)**	**25.6**	**(0.99)**	**22.1**	**(0.96)**	**21.7**	**(1.18)**	**19.8**	**(0.78)**
Alabama	26.0	(1.78)	26.2	(1.90)	—	(†)	27.6	(1.30)	20.3	(1.32)	25.3	(1.11)	24.8	(1.68)	—	(†)
Alaska	28.4	(1.24)	—	(†)	25.1	(1.36)	24.8	(1.25)	23.2	(0.98)	—	(†)	—	(†)	—	(†)
Arizona	28.6	(1.23)	38.7	(1.18)	37.1	(1.45)	34.6	(1.43)	34.6	(1.55)	31.3	(1.46)	29.3	(1.35)	29.1	(1.67)
Arkansas	—	(†)	29.2	(1.35)	28.1	(1.28)	31.4	(1.56)	26.1	(1.30)	27.4	(1.28)	27.1	(1.57)	30.7	(4.82)
California	—	(†)	—	(†)	—	(†)	—	(†)	—	(†)	—	(†)	26.1	(1.83)	27.0	(1.48)
Colorado	—	(†)	21.2	(1.81)	—	(†)	22.7	(1.52)	17.2	(1.28)	—	(†)	—	(†)	18.0	(0.82)
Connecticut	—	(†)	31.5	(0.90)	30.5	(1.52)	28.9	(1.25)	27.8	(1.43)	27.1	(0.85)	28.5	(1.32)	28.6	(1.39)
Delaware	27.9	(0.90)	26.1	(1.05)	22.9	(0.99)	20.9	(0.87)	23.1	(1.20)	19.1	(0.83)	15.6	(0.84)	16.8	(1.07)
District of Columbia	30.2	(1.46)	20.3	(1.18)	25.7	(1.20)	—	(†)	22.6	(1.53)	—	(†)	—	(†)	—	(†)
Florida	25.7	(0.81)	23.2	(0.85)	19.0	(0.80)	21.8	(0.72)	22.9	(0.84)	20.0	(0.64)	18.4	(0.69)	17.0	(0.67)
Georgia	33.3	(1.00)	30.7	(1.25)	32.0	(1.23)	32.9	(1.22)	32.1	(1.34)	26.5	(1.32)	—	(†)	—	(†)
Hawaii	—	(†)	32.7	(1.74)	36.2	(2.46)	36.1	(1.51)	31.7	(1.48)	31.2	(0.99)	25.4	(0.98)	—	(†)
Idaho	19.6	(1.26)	24.8	(1.52)	25.1	(1.63)	22.7	(1.39)	24.4	(1.56)	22.1	(1.31)	21.5	(1.39)	22.2	(1.19)
Illinois	—	(†)	—	(†)	21.2	(1.18)	27.5	(1.97)	27.3	(1.46)	27.2	(1.06)	25.6	(1.55)	25.3	(1.70)
Indiana	28.3	(1.55)	28.9	(1.33)	20.5	(1.02)	25.5	(1.24)	28.3	(1.33)	—	(†)	22.5	(1.13)	—	(†)
Iowa	—	(†)	15.5	(1.37)	10.1	(1.08)	—	(†)	11.9	(1.16)	—	(†)	—	(†)	22.1	(1.99)
Kansas	—	(†)	16.7	(1.27)	15.0	(1.24)	15.1	(0.78)	24.9	(1.19)	19.4	(1.06)	—	(†)	18.0	(0.99)
Kentucky	30.4	(1.51)	19.8	(1.23)	27.0	(1.11)	25.6	(1.49)	24.4	(1.40)	20.6	(1.15)	20.9	(1.27)	22.4	(1.23)
Louisiana	—	(†)	—	(†)	—	(†)	22.8	(1.66)	25.1	(1.82)	—	(†)	—	(†)	28.5	(1.86)
Maine	32.6	(1.73)	33.5	(1.89)	29.1	(1.67)	21.2	(0.51)	21.7	(0.80)	18.4	(0.87)	14.7	(0.56)	14.0	(0.68)
Maryland	—	(†)	28.9	(2.04)	27.4	(1.46)	29.3	(1.35)	30.4	(1.99)	29.1	(0.37)	26.2	(0.28)	23.6	(0.30)
Massachusetts	31.9	(1.08)	29.9	(1.09)	27.3	(1.06)	26.1	(1.34)	27.1	(1.04)	23.0	(0.90)	20.3	(0.87)	20.1	(0.95)
Michigan	31.3	(1.50)	28.8	(1.37)	29.1	(1.07)	29.5	(0.90)	25.4	(0.90)	23.8	(0.94)	25.4	(1.75)	26.0	(1.84)
Minnesota	—	(†)	—	(†)	—	(†)	—	(†)	—	(†)	—	(†)	—	(†)	—	(†)
Mississippi	22.3	(1.31)	—	(†)	15.6	(1.53)	18.0	(1.07)	15.9	(0.89)	12.1	(1.00)	23.7	(1.40)	—	(†)
Missouri	21.6	(2.09)	18.2	(1.92)	17.8	(1.49)	17.3	(1.32)	—	(†)	—	(†)	—	(†)	—	(†)
Montana	26.9	(1.23)	25.3	(1.09)	24.9	(0.83)	20.7	(1.10)	25.2	(0.93)	22.8	(0.71)	21.7	(0.77)	21.7	(0.72)
Nebraska	23.3	(1.04)	22.0	(0.82)	—	(†)	—	(†)	20.3	(1.01)	19.2	(1.15)	19.9	(1.57)	18.5	(1.40)
Nevada	34.5	(1.30)	32.6	(1.53)	28.8	(1.39)	35.6	(1.30)	—	(†)	31.2	(1.90)	29.8	(1.50)	29.8	(0.95)
New Hampshire	28.2	(1.87)	26.9	(1.40)	22.5	(1.25)	22.1	(1.44)	23.2	(1.44)	20.1	(1.03)	16.6	(0.48)	16.3	(0.43)
New Jersey	—	(†)	32.6	(1.32)	—	(†)	32.2	(1.38)	27.3	(1.41)	30.7	(1.70)	—	(†)	—	(†)
New Mexico	—	(†)	33.5	(1.37)	31.3	(1.39)	30.9	(1.54)	34.5	(1.24)	32.8	(1.04)	27.5	(0.82)	26.2	(0.94)
New York	23.0	(0.97)	23.7	(0.76)	26.6	(1.09)	24.0	(1.05)	—	(†)	—	(†)	—	(†)	—	(†)
North Carolina	31.9	(1.74)	27.4	(1.66)	28.5	(1.37)	30.2	(1.51)	29.8	(1.87)	23.6	(1.61)	24.5	(1.67)	21.9	(1.02)
North Dakota	21.3	(1.07)	19.6	(1.10)	18.7	(1.05)	19.5	(1.16)	20.8	(1.03)	14.1	(0.79)	18.2	(0.91)	12.1	(0.91)
Ohio[2]	31.1	(1.68)	30.9	(1.88)	26.7	(1.26)	—	(†)	24.3	(1.70)	19.9	(1.41)	—	(†)	—	(†)
Oklahoma	22.2	(1.23)	18.4	(1.49)	19.1	(1.12)	16.8	(1.50)	17.2	(1.36)	14.0	(1.07)	15.0	(1.12)	22.5	(1.42)
Oregon	—	(†)	—	(†)	—	(†)	—	(†)	—	(†)	—	(†)	—	(†)	—	(†)
Pennsylvania	—	(†)	—	(†)	—	(†)	16.1	(1.07)	—	(†)	—	(†)	19.4	(1.04)	17.9	(0.88)
Rhode Island	26.0	(1.26)	24.1	(1.11)	25.3	(1.33)	25.2	(1.52)	22.4	(0.95)	22.6	(1.16)	—	(†)	—	(†)
South Carolina	—	(†)	29.1	(1.45)	26.6	(1.58)	27.6	(1.74)	29.3	(1.83)	24.5	(1.43)	22.8	(1.36)	26.0	(1.55)
South Dakota[3]	22.1	(1.25)	20.9	(2.30)	21.1	(1.98)	17.7	(0.64)	16.0	(1.81)	15.4	(1.70)	19.0	(1.88)	—	(†)
Tennessee	24.3	(2.25)	26.6	(1.21)	21.6	(1.35)	18.8	(1.06)	16.6	(0.88)	24.8	(1.57)	—	(†)	23.7	(1.38)
Texas	—	(†)	30.7	(1.73)	26.5	(0.83)	25.9	(1.25)	29.4	(1.34)	26.4	(1.24)	—	(†)	26.7	(1.24)
Utah	24.7	(2.04)	20.6	(1.36)	23.2	(1.83)	19.7	(1.52)	21.4	(1.55)	20.0	(1.57)	—	(†)	25.9	(2.89)
Vermont[4]	29.4	(1.67)	23.1	(1.59)	22.0	(0.99)	21.1	(1.21)	17.6	(1.51)	—	(†)	18.1	(0.27)	15.2	(0.25)
Virginia	—	(†)	—	(†)	—	(†)	—	(†)	24.0	(1.67)	—	(†)	15.6	(0.75)	15.5	(0.76)
Washington	—	(†)	—	(†)	—	(†)	—	(†)	—	(†)	—	(†)	—	(†)	—	(†)
West Virginia	26.5	(2.06)	24.8	(1.36)	28.6	(2.76)	28.0	(1.27)	17.3	(1.04)	17.1	(1.16)	25.9	(1.49)	24.0	(1.57)
Wisconsin	26.3	(1.18)	21.7	(1.18)	22.7	(1.34)	20.5	(1.03)	20.9	(1.29)	18.3	(1.01)	—	(†)	18.4	(1.01)
Wyoming	18.1	(0.99)	22.7	(0.97)	24.7	(1.08)	23.7	(0.93)	25.2	(0.97)	20.2	(0.74)	22.0	(1.46)	—	(†)
Puerto Rico	—	(†)	18.3	(0.89)	—	(†)	—	(†)	18.7	(1.65)	18.3	(1.06)	18.6	(1.32)	22.8	(2.21)

—Not available.

†Not applicable.

[1] U.S. total data are representative of all public and private school students in grades 9-12 in the 50 states and the District of Columbia. U.S. total data for all years were collected through a separate national survey (rather than being aggregated from state-level data) and include both public and private schools.

[2] Ohio data for 2003 through 2013 include both public and private schools.

[3] South Dakota data for 2003 through 2015 include both public and private schools.

[4] Vermont data for 2013 include both public and private schools.

NOTE: "On school property" was not defined for survey respondents. For the U.S. total, data for all years include both public and private schools. State-level data include public schools only, except where otherwise noted. For three states, data for one or more years include both public and private schools: Ohio (2003 through 2013), South Dakota (2003 through 2015), and Vermont (2013 only). For specific states, a given year's data may be unavailable (1) because the state did not participate in the survey that year; (2) because the state omitted this particular survey item from the state-level questionnaire; or (3) because the state had an overall response rate of less than 60 percent (the overall response rate is the school response rate multiplied by the student response rate).

SOURCE: Centers for Disease Control and Prevention, Division of Adolescent and School Health, Youth Risk Behavior Surveillance System (YRBSS), 2003 through 2017. (This table was prepared June 2018.)

Table 232.95. Percentage of 12- to 17-year-olds reporting use of illicit drugs, alcohol, and cigarettes during the past 30 days and the past year, by substance used, sex, and race/ethnicity: Selected years, 1985 through 2018

[Standard errors appear in parentheses]

Year, sex, and race/ethnicity	Percent reporting use during past 30 days										Percent reporting use during past year									
	Illicit drugs										Illicit drugs									
	Any[1]		Marijuana[2]		Cocaine[3]		Alcohol		Cigarettes		Any[1]		Marijuana[2]		Cocaine[3]		Alcohol		Cigarettes	
1	2		3		4		5		6		7		8		9		10		11	
1985	13.2	(---)	10.2	(---)	1.5	(---)	41.2	(---)	29.4	(---)	20.7	(---)	16.7	(---)	3.4	(---)	52.7	(---)	29.9	(---)
1990	7.1	(---)	4.4	(---)	0.6	(---)	32.5	(---)	22.4	(---)	14.1	(---)	9.6	(---)	1.9	(---)	41.8	(---)	26.2	(---)
1995	10.9	(---)	8.2	(---)	0.8	(---)	21.1	(---)	20.2	(---)	18.0	(---)	14.2	(---)	1.7	(---)	35.1	(---)	26.6	(---)
1999	9.8	(0.23)	7.2	(0.20)	0.5	(0.06)	16.5	(0.30)	14.9	(0.31)	19.8	(0.32)	14.2	(0.29)	1.6	(0.10)	34.1	(0.41)	23.4	(0.37)
2000	9.7	(0.24)	7.2	(0.21)	0.6	(0.07)	16.4	(0.29)	13.4	(0.28)	18.6	(0.31)	13.4	(0.27)	1.7	(0.12)	33.0	(0.39)	20.8	(0.34)
2001	10.8	(0.26)	8.0	(0.24)	0.4	(0.06)	17.3	(0.33)	13.0	(0.28)	20.8	(0.36)	15.2	(0.32)	1.5	(0.10)	33.9	(0.39)	20.0	(0.35)
2002	11.6	(0.29)	8.2	(0.24)	0.6	(0.07)	17.6	(0.32)	13.0	(0.30)	22.2	(0.38)	15.8	(0.32)	2.1	(0.13)	34.6	(0.42)	20.3	(0.35)
2003	11.2	(0.27)	7.9	(0.24)	0.6	(0.06)	17.7	(0.33)	12.2	(0.29)	21.8	(0.36)	15.0	(0.31)	1.8	(0.11)	34.3	(0.42)	19.0	(0.36)
2004	10.6	(0.27)	7.6	(0.23)	0.5	(0.06)	17.6	(0.32)	11.9	(0.30)	21.0	(0.34)	14.5	(0.31)	1.6	(0.11)	33.9	(0.41)	18.4	(0.35)
2005	9.9	(0.25)	6.8	(0.22)	0.6	(0.06)	16.5	(0.32)	10.8	(0.28)	19.9	(0.35)	13.3	(0.30)	1.7	(0.11)	33.3	(0.41)	17.3	(0.36)
2006	9.8	(0.27)	6.7	(0.21)	0.4	(0.05)	16.6	(0.32)	10.4	(0.26)	19.6	(0.37)	13.2	(0.31)	1.6	(0.11)	32.9	(0.42)	17.0	(0.35)
2007	9.5	(0.27)	6.7	(0.22)	0.4	(0.05)	15.9	(0.34)	9.8	(0.26)	18.7	(0.35)	12.5	(0.30)	1.5	(0.11)	31.8	(0.42)	15.7	(0.34)
2008	9.3	(0.24)	6.7	(0.22)	0.4	(0.05)	14.6	(0.31)	9.1	(0.24)	19.0	(0.35)	13.0	(0.29)	1.2	(0.10)	30.8	(0.40)	15.0	(0.31)
2009	10.0	(0.27)	7.3	(0.24)	0.3	(0.05)	14.7	(0.32)	8.9	(0.26)	19.5	(0.36)	13.6	(0.31)	1.0	(0.09)	30.3	(0.42)	15.0	(0.33)
2010	10.1	(0.29)	7.4	(0.25)	0.2	(0.05)	13.6	(0.33)	8.4	(0.26)	19.5	(0.38)	14.0	(0.34)	1.0	(0.09)	28.7	(0.43)	14.2	(0.34)
2011	10.1	(0.27)	7.9	(0.24)	0.3	(0.05)	13.3	(0.31)	7.8	(0.24)	19.0	(0.37)	14.2	(0.33)	0.9	(0.08)	27.8	(0.43)	13.2	(0.31)
2012	9.5	(0.25)	7.2	(0.22)	0.1 !	(0.03)	12.9	(0.31)	6.6	(0.22)	17.9	(0.33)	13.5	(0.30)	0.7	(0.08)	26.3	(0.42)	11.8	(0.29)
2013	8.8	(0.25)	7.1	(0.23)	0.2	(0.04)	11.6	(0.29)	5.6	(0.20)	17.2	(0.35)	13.4	(0.31)	0.5	(0.06)	24.6	(0.40)	10.3	(0.27)
2014	9.4	(0.30)	7.4	(0.27)	0.2	(0.04)	11.5	(0.33)	4.9	(0.21)	17.4	(0.38)	13.1	(0.33)	0.7	(0.09)	24.0	(0.42)	8.9	(0.29)
2015	8.8	(0.27)	7.0	(0.24)	0.2	(0.05)	9.6	(0.29)	4.2	(0.20)	17.5	(0.37)	12.6	(0.32)	0.6	(0.08)	22.7	(0.42)	8.1	(0.27)
2016	7.9	(0.26)	6.5	(0.24)	0.1 !	(0.03)	9.2	(0.30)	3.4	(0.18)	15.8	(0.35)	12.0	(0.31)	0.5	(0.07)	21.6	(0.42)	7.2	(0.26)
2017	7.9	(0.26)	6.5	(0.24)	0.1 !	(0.03)	9.9	(0.30)	3.2	(0.17)	16.3	(0.37)	12.4	(0.33)	0.5	(0.06)	21.9	(0.43)	6.3	(0.24)
Sex																				
Male	7.7	(0.35)	6.3	(0.32)	0.1 !	(0.03)	8.8	(0.39)	3.4	(0.25)	15.7	(0.48)	12.0	(0.44)	0.5	(0.09)	20.0	(0.57)	6.4	(0.34)
Female	8.1	(0.40)	6.6	(0.37)	0.1 !	(0.04)	11.0	(0.46)	2.9	(0.23)	16.9	(0.56)	12.8	(0.48)	0.5	(0.09)	23.9	(0.62)	6.2	(0.34)
Race/ethnicity																				
White	8.5	(0.37)	7.1	(0.33)	0.2	(0.05)	11.9	(0.43)	4.2	(0.26)	16.8	(0.49)	13.2	(0.44)	0.6	(0.09)	25.7	(0.62)	7.9	(0.36)
Black	8.2	(0.76)	6.3	(0.71)	‡	(†)	6.0	(0.66)	1.2	(0.29)	16.8	(1.00)	12.1	(0.87)	‡	(†)	13.0	(0.89)	3.0	(0.44)
Hispanic	6.8	(0.49)	5.7	(0.47)	‡	(†)	8.6	(0.60)	2.2	(0.31)	16.6	(0.82)	12.2	(0.73)	0.5	(0.14)	20.9	(0.89)	5.2	(0.47)
Asian	3.0	(0.81)	2.1	(0.60)	‡	(†)	5.8	(1.13)	1.9 !	(0.60)	6.9	(1.16)	3.9	(0.86)	‡	(†)	11.1	(1.49)	2.9	(0.78)
Pacific Islander	‡	(†)	‡	(†)	‡	(†)	‡	(†)	‡	(†)	‡	(†)	‡	(†)	‡	(†)	‡	(†)	‡	(†)
American Indian/Alaska Native	15.0	(3.41)	14.6	(3.41)	‡	(†)	7.8 !	(2.71)	6.4	(1.82)	27.8	(4.38)	25.1	(4.42)	‡	(†)	21.3	(3.97)	12.2	(3.18)
Two or more races	10.8	(1.30)	9.4	(1.25)	‡	(†)	10.8	(1.45)	3.5	(0.73)	18.0	(1.68)	14.1	(1.52)	0.9 !	(0.42)	24	(1.95)	7.0	(1.05)
2018	8.0	(0.27)	6.7	(0.25)	#	(†)	9.0	(0.29)	2.7	(0.16)	16.7	(0.37)	12.5	(0.33)	0.4	(0.07)	20.8	(0.42)	5.5	(0.23)
Sex																				
Male	8.1	(0.37)	6.9	(0.35)	#	(†)	8.4	(0.39)	2.8	(0.22)	16.1	(0.50)	12.1	(0.45)	0.4	(0.09)	19.5	(0.53)	5.5	(0.31)
Female	8.0	(0.38)	6.4	(0.35)	0.1 !	(0.04)	9.6	(0.41)	2.6	(0.23)	17.3	(0.54)	12.8	(0.48)	0.5	(0.11)	22.2	(0.61)	5.5	(0.32)
Race/ethnicity																				
White	8.2	(0.37)	6.8	(0.34)	0.1 !	(0.03)	11.2	(0.44)	3.7	(0.26)	16.6	(0.49)	12.6	(0.44)	0.5	(0.11)	24.1	(0.61)	7.1	(0.35)
Black	8.5	(0.73)	7.5	(0.71)	‡	(†)	5.1	(0.57)	1.1	(0.27)	17.9	(1.02)	14.0	(0.95)	‡	(†)	14.5	(0.92)	2.5	(0.41)
Hispanic	8.1	(0.63)	6.5	(0.56)	‡	(†)	7.4	(0.61)	1.7	(0.28)	17.4	(0.86)	12.6	(0.77)	0.6 !	(0.18)	19.8	(0.88)	4.5	(0.46)
Asian	4.0	(0.93)	2.9	(0.83)	‡	(†)	4.4	(0.97)	‡	(†)	8.6	(1.44)	5.3	(1.09)	‡	(†)	11.0	(1.47)	‡	(†)
Pacific Islander	‡	(†)	‡	(†)	‡	(†)	‡	(†)	‡	(†)	‡	(†)	‡	(†)	‡	(†)	‡	(†)	‡	(†)
American Indian/Alaska Native	11.9	(3.00)	9.4	(2.69)	‡	(†)	5.0 !	(1.93)	4.8 !	(1.62)	18.1	(3.34)	13.6	(3.03)	‡	(†)	12.0	(2.85)	7.0	(2.01)
Two or more races	9.4	(1.35)	8.1	(1.28)	‡	(†)	10.0	(1.47)	2.7 !	(0.83)	21.2	(2.07)	16.2	(1.90)	‡	(†)	23.2	(1.91)	6.0	(1.12)

---Not available.

†Not applicable.

#Rounds to zero.

!Interpret data with caution. The coefficient of variation (CV) for this estimate is between 30 and 50 percent.

‡Reporting standards not met. Either there are too few cases for a reliable estimate or the coefficient of variation (CV) is 50 percent or greater.

[1] Includes other illegal drug use not shown separately--specifically, the use of heroin, hallucinogens, and inhalants, as well as the nonmedical use of prescription-type pain relievers, tranquilizers, stimulants, and sedatives.

[2] Includes hashish.

[3] Includes all the different forms of cocaine, such as powder, "crack," free base, and coca paste.

NOTE: Data for 1999 and later years were gathered using Computer Assisted Interviewing (CAI) and may not be directly comparable to previous years. Because of survey improvements in 2002, the 2002 data constitute a new baseline for tracking trends. In addition, the questionnaire underwent a partial redesign in 2015, and new baselines were started for estimates that were affected by the questionnaire changes. Valid trend comparisons can be made from 1985 through 1995, from 1999 through 2001, and--for most estimates in this table--from 2002 through 2018. For estimates of any illicit drug use (columns 2 and 7), the 2015 data constitute a new baseline for tracking trends; comparisons can be made from 2015 to 2018. Race categories exclude persons of Hispanic ethnicity.

SOURCE: U.S. Department of Health and Human Services, Substance Abuse and Mental Health Services Administration, National Household Survey on Drug Abuse: Main Findings, selected years, 1985 through 2001, and National Survey on Drug Use and Health, 2002 through 2018. Retrieved September 13, 2019, from https://www.samhsa.gov/data/sites/default/files/cbhsq-reports/NSDUHDetailedTabs2018R2/NSDUHDetTabsAppB2018.htm. (This table was prepared September 2019.)

Table 233.10. Number and percentage of public schools that took a serious disciplinary action in response to specific offenses, number and percentage distribution of serious actions taken, and number of students involved in specific offenses, by type of offense and type of action: Selected years, 1999-2000 through 2017–18

[Standard errors appear in parentheses]

Type of offense and type of serious disciplinary action	1999-2000[1]		2003-04		2005-06		2007-08		2009-10[2]		2015-16[2]		2017-18[2]	
1	2		3		4		5		6		7		8	
Number of schools taking at least one action														
Total, in response to any listed offense[3]	---	(†)	36,800	(960)	40,000	(990)	38,500	(1,010)	32,300	(940)	31,100	(900)	28,700	(1,010)
Physical fights or attacks	29,000	(840)	25,800	(780)	26,300	(880)	26,100	(740)	24,000	(770)	22,500	(900)	20,500	(860)
Insubordination	15,000	(640)	17,400	(690)	17,700	(700)	17,800	(800)	---	(†)	---	(†)	---	(†)
Distribution, possession, or use of alcohol	---	(†)	7,400	(400)	8,500	(380)	8,100	(400)	7,600	(320)	6,700	(340)	6,700	(270)
Distribution, possession, or use of illegal drugs	---	(†)	17,000	(470)	17,400	(490)	16,000	(470)	16,100	(400)	15,600	(500)	14,400	(430)
Use or possession of firearm or explosive device	---	(†)	3,200	(320)	3,800	(290)	2,300	(220)	2,500	(340)	1,700	(240)	1,400	(160)
Use or possession of weapon other than firearm or explosive device[4]	---	(†)	13,500	(690)	16,100	(760)	12,700	(650)	11,200	(650)	8,700	(510)	9,100	(610)
Percent of schools taking at least one action														
Total, in response to any listed offense[3]	---	(†)	45.7	(1.15)	48.1	(1.17)	46.4	(1.16)	39.1	(1.14)	37.2	(1.06)	34.9	(1.27)
Physical fights or attacks	35.4	(1.02)	32.0	(0.94)	31.6	(1.00)	31.5	(0.89)	29.0	(0.94)	26.9	(1.06)	24.9	(1.07)
Insubordination	18.3	(0.79)	21.6	(0.85)	21.2	(0.84)	21.4	(0.95)	---	(†)	---	(†)	---	(†)
Distribution, possession, or use of alcohol	---	(†)	9.2	(0.50)	10.2	(0.47)	9.8	(0.48)	9.2	(0.39)	8.1	(0.40)	8.1	(0.33)
Distribution, possession, or use of illegal drugs	---	(†)	21.2	(0.58)	20.8	(0.61)	19.3	(0.53)	19.5	(0.48)	18.6	(0.59)	17.5	(0.53)
Use or possession of firearm or explosive device	---	(†)	3.9	(0.40)	4.5	(0.35)	2.8	(0.26)	3.0	(0.41)	2.0	(0.29)	1.7	(0.19)
Use or possession of weapon other than firearm or explosive device[4]	---	(†)	16.8	(0.84)	19.4	(0.91)	15.3	(0.77)	13.5	(0.78)	10.4	(0.61)	11.1	(0.76)
Number of actions taken in response to offenses														
Total, in response to any listed offense	---	(†)	655,700	(29,160)	842,400	(46,080)	767,900	(44,010)	433,800	(22,880)	305,700	(11,500)	291,100	(12,730)
Physical fights or attacks	332,500	(27,420)	273,500	(14,450)	328,900	(16,880)	271,800	(15,180)	265,100	(22,170)	178,000	(10,890)	170,400	(10,380)
Insubordination	253,500	(27,720)	220,400	(16,990)	312,900	(34,200)	327,100	(38,470)	---	(†)	---	(†)	---	(†)
Distribution, possession, or use of alcohol	---	(†)	25,500	(1,600)	30,500	(1,910)	28,400	(1,470)	28,700	(1,920)	18,400	(1,180)	19,100	(990)
Distribution, possession, or use of illegal drugs	---	(†)	91,100	(3,410)	108,300	(4,930)	98,700	(5,780)	105,400	(4,070)	83,800	(3,670)	76,700	(2,910)
Use or possession of firearm or explosive device	---	(†)	9,900 !	(4,300)	14,500	(2,740)	5,200	(910)	5,800	(1,360)	4,100 !	(1,240)	2,500	(550)
Use or possession of weapon other than firearm or explosive device[4]	---	(†)	35,400	(1,470)	47,300	(2,100)	36,800	(2,630)	28,800	(1,580)	21,300	(1,430)	22,400	(1,590)
Percentage distribution of actions taken														
Total, in response to any listed offense	---	(†)	100.0	(†)	100.0	(†)	100.0	(†)	100.0	(†)	100.0	(†)	100.0	(†)
Out-of-school suspensions lasting 5 days or more	---	(†)	74.2	(1.60)	74.2	(1.98)	76.0	(1.63)	73.9	(1.79)	71.7	(1.32)	72.6	(1.18)
Removal with no services for remainder of school year	---	(†)	4.8	(0.72)	5.4	(0.77)	5.4	(1.06)	6.1	(0.86)	4.3	(0.49)	5.1	(0.60)
Transfer to specialized schools	---	(†)	21.0	(1.49)	20.4	(1.77)	18.7	(1.38)	20.0	(1.36)	23.9	(1.18)	22.3	(1.11)
Physical fights or attacks	100.0	(†)	100.0	(†)	100.0	(†)	100.0	(†)	100.0	(†)	100.0	(†)	100.0	(†)
Out-of-school suspensions lasting 5 days or more	85.1	(1.78)	80.8	(1.67)	80.8	(1.58)	78.7	(1.40)	81.2	(2.18)	79.4	(1.60)	79.6	(1.38)
Removal with no services for remainder of school year	9.0	(1.64)	3.6	(0.76)	4.1	(0.71)	4.4	(0.72)	5.0	(1.22)	2.9	(0.53)	4.5	(0.81)
Transfer to specialized schools	5.9	(0.59)	15.5	(1.59)	15.1	(1.40)	16.9	(1.19)	13.9	(1.57)	17.7	(1.50)	15.9	(1.27)
Insubordination	100.0	(†)	100.0	(†)	100.0	(†)	100.0	(†)	---	(†)	---	(†)	---	(†)
Out-of-school suspensions lasting 5 days or more	81.6	(3.27)	78.1	(2.54)	76.0	(4.24)	82.2	(3.14)	---	(†)	---	(†)	---	(†)
Removal with no services for remainder of school year	15.0	(3.16)	3.1 !	(1.53)	4.1 !	(1.57)	‡	(†)	---	(†)	---	(†)	---	(†)
Transfer to specialized schools	3.4	(0.76)	18.8	(2.41)	19.9	(3.62)	13.1	(2.29)	---	(†)	---	(†)	---	(†)
Distribution, possession, or use of alcohol	---	(†)	100.0	(†)	100.0	(†)	100.0	(†)	100.0	(†)	100.0	(†)	100.0	(†)
Out-of-school suspensions lasting 5 days or more	---	(†)	70.8	(2.91)	77.0	(2.07)	73.9	(2.56)	74.3	(2.23)	67.7	(2.94)	73.1	(2.39)
Removal with no services for remainder of school year	---	(†)	5.5	(1.56)	4.5	(0.80)	4.5	(1.00)	4.0	(0.92)	3.7	(0.89)	1.8 !	(0.56)
Transfer to specialized schools	---	(†)	23.7	(2.82)	18.5	(2.01)	21.6	(1.97)	21.7	(2.27)	28.6	(3.00)	25.1	(2.31)
Distribution, possession, or use of illegal drugs	---	(†)	100.0	(†)	100.0	(†)	100.0	(†)	100.0	(†)	100.0	(†)	100.0	(†)
Out-of-school suspensions lasting 5 days or more	---	(†)	53.4	(2.27)	55.6	(1.96)	55.4	(2.05)	59.6	(1.70)	58.8	(2.07)	60.4	(1.93)
Removal with no services for remainder of school year	---	(†)	10.1	(0.91)	10.2	(0.90)	9.1	(1.10)	8.0	(0.94)	6.9	(0.96)	5.8	(0.68)
Transfer to specialized schools	---	(†)	36.4	(2.23)	34.2	(2.02)	35.5	(1.84)	32.4	(1.57)	34.3	(2.08)	33.8	(1.87)
Use or possession of firearm or explosive device	---	(†)	100.0	(†)	100.0	(†)	100.0	(†)	100.0	(†)	100.0	(†)	100.0	(†)
Out-of-school suspensions lasting 5 days or more	---	(†)	66.6 !	(25.42)	67.9	(7.07)	52.9	(5.94)	55.5	(9.64)	66.3	(14.94)	34.1	(4.28)
Removal with no services for remainder of school year	---	(†)	‡	(†)	10.9	(2.89)	18.3	(5.18)	22.2	(4.96)	8.3 !	(3.69)	20.5 !	(7.09)
Transfer to specialized schools	---	(†)	‡	(†)	21.2	(5.59)	28.8	(3.96)	22.3 !	(7.91)	25.3 !	(12.63)	45.4	(7.40)
Use or possession of weapon other than firearm or explosive device[4]	---	(†)	100.0	(†)	100.0	(†)	100.0	(†)	100.0	(†)	100.0	(†)	100.0	(†)
Out-of-school suspensions lasting 5 days or more	---	(†)	57.2	(2.20)	60.0	(1.89)	60.3	(2.24)	62.2	(2.44)	63.0	(2.47)	64.5	(2.23)
Removal with no services for remainder of school year	---	(†)	7.7	(0.81)	10.8	(1.09)	7.8	(1.29)	8.8	(1.31)	6.2	(1.46)	8.9	(1.93)
Transfer to specialized schools	---	(†)	35.1	(2.04)	29.2	(1.83)	31.9	(1.75)	29.0	(2.32)	30.9	(2.56)	26.5	(1.78)
Number of students involved in offenses[5]														
Total, all listed offenses	---	(†)	3,912,500	(162,670)	3,919,500	(129,350)	4,783,700	(324,130)	1,057,200	(31,810)	826,300	(37,980)	854,500	(31,770)
Physical fights or attacks	766,900	(50,410)	1,108,600	(46,250)	1,026,100	(35,050)	987,900	(42,620)	820,100	(27,890)	633,300	(37,820)	667,700	(30,140)
Insubordination	1,104,200	(69,490)	2,558,500	(131,830)	2,606,700	(107,660)	3,589,300	(319,390)	---	(†)	---	(†)	---	(†)
Distribution, possession, or use of alcohol	---	(†)	44,100	(2,290)	49,900	(2,750)	38,700	(1,690)	42,200	(2,450)	30,200	(1,670)	32,400	(2,300)
Distribution, possession, or use of illegal drugs	---	(†)	118,900	(4,590)	119,400	(4,350)	106,300	(4,240)	125,700	(5,540)	119,200	(6,310)	112,900	(4,310)
Use or possession of firearm or explosive device	---	(†)	‡	(†)	55,700	(16,540)	13,400 !	(4,270)	27,100 !	(11,180)	9,900 !	(3,090)	5,100 !	(2,490)
Use or possession of weapon other than firearm or explosive device[4]	---	(†)	57,500	(4,260)	61,700	(2,540)	48,100	(3,430)	42,100	(2,220)	33,800	(2,420)	36,300	(2,250)

—Not available.

†Not applicable.

!Interpret data with caution. The coefficient of variation (CV) for this estimate is between 30 and 50 percent.

‡Reporting standards not met. The coefficient of variation (CV) for this estimate is 50 percent or greater.

[1] In the 1999-2000 questionnaire, only two items are the same as in questionnaires for later years: the item on physical attacks or fights and the item on insubordination. There are no comparable 1999-2000 data for serious disciplinary actions taken in response to the other specific offenses listed in this table, nor for total actions taken in response to all the listed offenses.

[2] Totals for 2009-10, 2015-16, and 2017-18 are not comparable to totals for earlier years, because the 2009-10, 2015-16, and 2017-18 questionnaires did not include an item on insubordination.

[3] Schools that took serious disciplinary actions in response to more than one type of offense were counted only once in the total.

[4] Prior to 2005-06, the questionnaire wording was simply "a weapon other than a firearm" (instead of "a weapon other than a firearm or explosive device").

[5] Includes all students involved in committing the listed offenses regardless of the disciplinary action taken. If more than one student was involved in a single incident, each student was counted separately. If one student was involved in multiple incidents, that student was counted more than once; for example, a student involved in two separate incidents would be counted twice.

NOTE: Serious disciplinary actions include out-of-school suspensions lasting 5 or more days, but less than the remainder of the school year; removals with no continuing services for at least the remainder of the school year; and transfers to specialized schools for disciplinary reasons. Responses were provided by the principal or the person most knowledgeable about crime and safety issues at the school. Detail may not sum to totals because of rounding and because schools that reported serious disciplinary actions in response to more than one type of offense were counted only once in the total number or percentage of schools.

SOURCE: U.S. Department of Education, National Center for Education Statistics, 1999-2000, 2003-04, 2005-06, 2007-08, 2009-10, 2015-16, and 2017-18 School Survey on Crime and Safety (SSOCS), 2000, 2004, 2006, 2008, 2010, 2016, and 2018. (This table was prepared July 2019.)

Table 233.12. Percentage of public schools that took a serious disciplinary action in response to specific offenses, by type of offense and selected school characteristics: 2017-18

[Standard errors appear in parentheses]

School characteristic	Total, at least one action[1]		Type of offense: Physical attacks or fights		Distribution, possession, or use of alcohol		Distribution, possession, or use of illegal drugs		Use or possession of a firearm or explosive device		Use or possession of a weapon other than a firearm or explosive device	
1	2		3		4		5		6		7	
Total	**34.9**	**(1.27)**	**24.9**	**(1.07)**	**8.1**	**(0.33)**	**17.5**	**(0.53)**	**1.7**	**(0.19)**	**11.1**	**(0.76)**
School level[2]												
Primary	16.9	(1.74)	12.6	(1.47)	0.7 !	(0.35)	2.6	(0.59)	‡	(†)	5.0	(0.97)
Middle	57.7	(1.60)	41.4	(1.39)	12.8	(0.90)	31.3	(1.63)	2.4	(0.50)	21.0	(1.43)
High school	75.5	(1.65)	53.8	(1.64)	31.0	(1.28)	57.7	(1.46)	6.5	(0.76)	24.0	(1.42)
Combined	36.7	(5.54)	21.8	(4.31)	7.6	(1.95)	18.8	(3.68)	‡	(†)	7.6 !	(3.17)
Enrollment size												
Less than 300	24.6	(3.69)	16.5	(2.70)	3.0	(0.88)	6.7	(1.47)	‡	(†)	5.6	(1.62)
300 to 499	27.4	(2.13)	17.3	(1.51)	3.3	(0.43)	10.7	(1.11)	0.8 !	(0.36)	8.2	(1.39)
500 to 999	35.2	(1.51)	26.9	(1.69)	7.9	(0.66)	16.9	(0.83)	1.4	(0.30)	11.3	(1.09)
1,000 or more	74.0	(1.50)	54.8	(1.76)	31.9	(1.56)	59.3	(1.67)	7.3	(0.92)	28.7	(1.55)
Locale												
City	35.2	(1.94)	26.0	(1.86)	6.2	(0.71)	15.3	(1.03)	2.2	(0.45)	11.4	(1.37)
Suburban	30.5	(1.34)	22.7	(1.39)	8.3	(0.66)	17.7	(0.75)	1.4	(0.22)	10.7	(0.92)
Town	39.4	(2.31)	27.9	(2.39)	11.0	(1.12)	20.8	(1.55)	2.3	(0.53)	11.3	(1.75)
Rural	37.8	(3.22)	25.0	(2.42)	8.5	(0.90)	18.1	(1.38)	1.2	(0.36)	11.1	(1.51)
Percent minority enrollment[3]												
0 to 25 percent	33.1	(2.16)	22.9	(1.76)	9.4	(0.76)	17.5	(1.22)	1.3	(0.31)	9.2	(1.03)
26 to 50 percent	36.1	(2.39)	24.4	(2.10)	9.0	(0.97)	19.2	(1.31)	0.9	(0.23)	10.1	(1.30)
51 to 75 percent	33.6	(2.53)	25.1	(1.92)	8.3	(0.97)	18.1	(1.70)	3.5	(0.82)	13.9	(1.95)
76 to 100 percent	36.9	(2.34)	27.8	(2.20)	5.4	(0.83)	15.9	(1.19)	1.7	(0.31)	12.9	(1.54)
Percent of students eligible for free or reduced-price lunch												
0 to 25 percent	22.7	(1.92)	14.5	(1.71)	8.3	(1.12)	13.3	(1.08)	0.7	(0.20)	5.5	(0.61)
26 to 50 percent	37.6	(2.66)	26.1	(2.17)	11.6	(0.99)	20.8	(1.61)	1.6	(0.31)	10.7	(1.46)
51 to 75 percent	39.4	(2.31)	28.9	(2.07)	9.3	(0.99)	20.9	(1.63)	1.9	(0.42)	14.4	(1.64)
76 to 100 percent	36.1	(2.27)	26.6	(1.81)	4.6	(0.64)	14.9	(1.21)	2.1	(0.41)	11.9	(1.36)

†Not applicable.

!Interpret data with caution. The coefficient of variation (CV) for this estimate is between 30 and 50 percent.

‡Reporting standards not met. Either there are too few cases for a reliable estimate or the coefficient of variation (CV) is 50 percent or greater.

[1] Schools that took serious disciplinary actions in response to more than one type of offense were counted only once in the total.

[2] Primary schools are defined as schools in which the lowest grade is not higher than grade 3 and the highest grade is not higher than grade 8. Middle schools are defined as schools in which the lowest grade is not lower than grade 4 and the highest grade is not higher than grade 9. High schools are defined as schools in which the lowest grade is not lower than grade 9. Combined schools include all other combinations of grades, including K–12 schools.

[3] Percent combined enrollment of Black, Hispanic, Asian, Pacific Islander, and American Indian/Alaska Native students, and students of Two or more races.

NOTE: Serious disciplinary actions include out-of-school suspensions lasting 5 or more days, but less than the remainder of the school year; removals with no continuing services for at least the remainder of the school year; and transfers to specialized schools for disciplinary reasons. Percentages of schools taking such actions are based on all public schools, rather than only those at which offenses occurred. Responses were provided by the principal or the person most knowledgeable about crime and safety issues at the school.

SOURCE: U.S. Department of Education, National Center for Education Statistics, 2017-18 School Survey on Crime and Safety (SSOCS), 2018. (This table was prepared July 2019.)

Table 233.25. Number and percentage of fall 2009 ninth-graders who were ever suspended or expelled through spring 2012, by when student was suspended or expelled and selected student characteristics: 2013

[Standard errors appear in parentheses]

Selected student characteristic	Number of fall 2009 ninth-graders: Total, all students[1]		Number of fall 2009 ninth-graders: Total, ever suspended or expelled		Percentage distribution of fall 2009 ninth-graders: All students		Percentage distribution of fall 2009 ninth-graders: Ever suspended or expelled		Percent ever suspended or expelled: Total		When suspended or expelled: Only before fall of 2009		When suspended or expelled: Only between fall 2009 and spring 2012		When suspended or expelled: Both before fall 2009 and between fall 2009 and spring 2012	
1	2		3		4		5		6		7		8		9	
Total, all students	**3,776,000**	**(38,600)**	**734,000**	**(35,400)**	**100.0**	**(†)**	**100.0**	**(†)**	**19.4**	**(0.91)**	**7.2**	**(0.72)**	**6.6**	**(0.54)**	**5.7**	**(0.65)**
High school completion status in 2013																
Less than high school completion	213,000	(26,600)	116,000	(18,500)	5.8	(0.72)	16.7	(2.52)	54.5	(5.05)	13.8	(3.76)	17.5	(3.69)	23.2	(4.45)
High school completion	3,456,000	(44,300)	578,000	(31,600)	94.2	(0.72)	83.3	(2.52)	16.7	(0.88)	6.6	(0.74)	5.8	(0.46)	4.4	(0.63)
Sex																
Male	1,906,000	(20,000)	498,000	(26,200)	50.5	(0.42)	67.8	(2.34)	26.1	(1.35)	8.9	(1.22)	8.5	(0.88)	8.7	(1.20)
Female	1,869,000	(29,100)	236,000	(22,200)	49.5	(0.42)	32.2	(2.34)	12.6	(1.17)	5.5	(0.89)	4.6	(0.62)	2.6	(0.55)
Race/ethnicity																
White	2,001,000	(39,400)	288,000	(19,400)	53.0	(1.00)	39.3	(2.37)	14.4	(0.93)	4.3	(0.51)	6.7	(0.65)	3.4	(0.38)
Black	478,000	(25,400)	170,000	(18,300)	12.7	(0.68)	23.2	(2.63)	35.6	(3.42)	14.8	(2.47)	6.9	(1.60)	13.9	(3.17)
Hispanic	819,000	(39,200)	175,000	(29,700)	21.7	(0.96)	23.8	(3.66)	21.3	(3.21)	10.1	(2.77)	7.0	(1.38)	4.3	(0.95)
Asian	129,000	(9,800)	‡	(†)	3.4	(0.26)	1.1 !	(0.42)	6.4 !	(2.38)	‡	(†)	1.2 !	(0.54)	‡	(†)
Pacific Islander	15,000	(5,400)	‡	(†)	0.4 !	(0.14)	‡	(†)	‡	(†)	‡	(†)	‡	(†)	‡	(†)
American Indian/Alaska Native	30,000	(8,100)	‡	(†)	0.8	(0.21)	1.6 !	(0.66)	40.6 !	(14.16)	‡	(†)	‡	(†)	‡	(†)
Two or more races	304,000	(20,700)	78,000	(14,100)	8.1	(0.54)	10.6	(1.84)	25.6	(4.07)	6.7	(1.84)	5.8 !	(1.76)	13.1 !	(4.09)
Highest education of parents in 2012																
High school completion or less	1,456,000	(67,800)	398,000	(38,100)	38.6	(1.76)	54.2	(3.91)	27.3	(1.92)	10.6	(1.55)	8.6	(1.00)	8.1	(1.57)
Some college	745,000	(35,200)	152,000	(19,800)	19.7	(0.92)	20.8	(2.76)	20.5	(2.20)	7.1	(1.62)	6.6	(1.20)	6.8	(1.30)
Bachelor's degree	881,000	(41,200)	118,000	(12,300)	23.3	(1.06)	16.0	(1.71)	13.4	(1.20)	4.3	(0.84)	5.8	(0.99)	3.3	(0.72)
Master's or higher degree	693,000	(37,700)	66,000	(10,500)	18.4	(0.98)	9.0	(1.44)	9.5	(1.41)	3.9	(0.94)	3.1	(0.57)	2.5 !	(0.80)
Socioeconomic status of parents in 2012[2]																
Lowest two fifths	1,391,000	(62,200)	400,000	(35,300)	36.8	(1.60)	54.5	(3.39)	28.8	(1.88)	10.7	(1.57)	8.8	(1.00)	9.3	(1.62)
Middle two fifths	1,381,000	(44,500)	241,000	(19,800)	36.6	(1.14)	32.8	(2.68)	17.4	(1.41)	6.6	(1.02)	6.0	(0.88)	4.8	(0.76)
Highest fifth	1,004,000	(45,700)	93,000	(12,400)	26.6	(1.18)	12.7	(1.74)	9.3	(1.10)	3.2	(0.69)	4.2	(0.66)	1.9 !	(0.59)
Cumulative high school grade point average																
0.00-1.99	601,000	(42,500)	279,000	(27,500)	16.7	(1.15)	40.2	(3.50)	46.4	(3.31)	11.3	(1.82)	13.7	(2.06)	21.4	(3.44)
2.00-2.49	655,000	(43,100)	186,000	(23,200)	18.2	(1.11)	26.9	(3.22)	28.5	(2.49)	12.5	(2.73)	9.6	(1.65)	6.4	(1.11)
2.50-2.99	752,000	(37,400)	136,000	(15,300)	20.9	(1.01)	19.6	(2.02)	18.1	(1.99)	7.0	(1.30)	7.3	(1.22)	3.7	(0.76)
3.00-3.49	845,000	(33,800)	72,000	(11,800)	23.5	(0.98)	10.3	(1.56)	8.5	(1.33)	4.7	(1.11)	3.0	(0.57)	‡	(†)
3.50 or higher	743,000	(29,900)	21,000	(4,500)	20.7	(0.78)	3.0	(0.65)	2.8	(0.60)	1.0 !	(0.33)	1.5	(0.45)	‡	(†)
School engagement in 2009[3]																
Low	794,000	(43,700)	222,000	(22,200)	21.8	(1.12)	31.9	(2.77)	28.0	(2.40)	9.1	(1.46)	7.8	(1.34)	11.1	(1.71)
Middle	1,923,000	(43,900)	395,000	(26,200)	52.8	(1.16)	56.6	(2.99)	20.5	(1.34)	8.2	(1.25)	7.6	(0.82)	4.7	(0.77)
High	922,000	(34,200)	81,000	(14,400)	25.3	(0.94)	11.6	(1.97)	8.8	(1.50)	3.5	(0.85)	2.4	(0.49)	2.8 !	(1.21)
Sense of school belonging in 2009[4]																
Low	854,000	(40,600)	243,000	(24,200)	23.7	(1.13)	35.4	(3.07)	28.5	(2.22)	9.6	(1.54)	9.2	(1.04)	9.7	(1.57)
Middle	1,850,000	(46,700)	304,000	(28,000)	51.2	(1.12)	44.2	(3.57)	16.4	(1.36)	5.8	(0.73)	6.4	(0.78)	4.2	(0.69)
High	907,000	(40,600)	140,000	(21,600)	25.1	(1.08)	20.4	(3.03)	15.5	(2.13)	7.4	(2.14)	3.6	(0.71)	4.5	(1.30)

†Not applicable.

!Interpret data with caution. The coefficient of variation (CV) for this estimate is between 30 and 50 percent.

‡Reporting standards not met. Either there are too few cases for a reliable estimate or the coefficient of variation (CV) is 50 percent or greater.

[1] The total includes all students whose parents provided a response about their child's suspension and expulsion status both on the base-year (2009) questionnaire and on the first follow-up (2012) questionnaire.

[2] Socioeconomic status (SES) was measured by a composite score on parental education and occupations, and family income.

[3] A school engagement scale was constructed based on students' responses to questions about how frequently they went to class without homework done, without pencil or paper, without books, or late. Students' school engagement is considered low if they were in the bottom quarter of the scale distribution, middle if they were in the middle two quarters, and high if they were in the highest quarter.

[4] A school belonging scale was constructed based on the extent to which students agreed or disagreed that they felt safe at school, that they felt proud of being part of the school, that there were always teachers or other adults at school they could talk to if they had a problem, that school was often a waste of time, and that getting good grades was important to them. Students' sense of school belonging is considered low if they were in the bottom quarter of the scale distribution, middle if they were in the middle two quarters, and high if they were in the highest quarter.

NOTE: Estimates weighted by W2W1PAR. Race categories exclude persons of Hispanic ethnicity. Detail may not sum to totals because of rounding and survey item nonresponse.

SOURCE: U.S. Department of Education, National Center for Education Statistics, High School Longitudinal Study of 2009 (HSLS:2009), 2013 Update and High School Transcripts Public-Use Data File. (This table was prepared October 2015.)

Table 233.27. Number of students receiving selected disciplinary actions in public elementary and secondary schools, by type of disciplinary action, disability status, sex, and race/ethnicity: 2013-14

Disability status, sex, and race/ethnicity	Corporal punishment[1]	One or more in-school suspension[2]	Out-of-school suspensions[3]			Expulsions[4]				Referral to law enforcement[5]	School-related arrest[6]
			Total	Only one	More than one	Total[7]: All expulsions	Total[7]: Under zero-tolerance policies[8]	With educational services	Without educational services		
1	2	3	4	5	6	7	8	9	10	11	12
All students											
Total	**106,055**	**2,710,924**	**2,635,743**	**1,560,486**	**1,075,257**	**111,215**	**16,035**	**66,133**	**45,082**	**177,127**	**60,170**
Sex											
Male	84,738	1,847,655	1,860,002	1,076,965	783,037	82,787	12,603	49,666	33,121	126,841	43,188
Female	21,317	863,269	775,741	483,521	292,220	28,428	3,432	16,467	11,961	50,286	16,982
Race/ethnicity[9]											
White	53,069	1,036,590	843,381	538,782	304,599	49,144	8,400	27,495	21,649	72,310	19,736
Black	40,023	861,194	1,042,991	557,430	485,561	33,557	3,628	20,852	12,705	49,584	20,562
Hispanic	7,680	618,734	554,498	345,240	209,258	18,271	2,761	11,904	6,367	41,319	14,891
Asian	210	26,984	26,499	19,454	7,045	790	164	504	286	2,155	865
Pacific Islander	62	6,213	8,784	5,796	2,988	241	39	128	113	427	452
American Indian/Alaska Native	2,033	34,494	35,756	21,941	13,815	1,944	291	1,026	918	3,671	892
Two or more races	1,505	74,697	78,469	46,539	31,930	4,613	558	2,425	2,188	4,871	1,657
Race/ethnicity by sex[9]											
Male											
White	44,319	747,574	636,731	398,754	237,977	37,340	6,596	21,059	16,281	53,564	14,686
Black	29,840	545,505	684,082	352,849	331,233	23,724	2,789	14,907	8,817	33,728	13,939
Hispanic	6,211	417,223	397,077	240,248	156,829	14,168	2,241	9,316	4,852	29,591	10,964
Asian	174	20,315	20,907	15,164	5,743	665	141	428	237	1,700	646
Pacific Islander	46	4,159	6,212	3,948	2,264	167	27	92	75	304	326
American Indian/Alaska Native	1,654	23,017	24,585	14,720	9,865	1,343	218	708	635	2,532	620
Two or more races	1,221	50,323	55,457	32,164	23,293	3,224	434	1,696	1,528	3,309	1,129
Female											
White	8,750	289,016	206,650	140,028	66,622	11,804	1,804	6,436	5,368	18,746	5,050
Black	10,183	315,689	358,909	204,581	154,328	9,833	839	5,945	3,888	15,856	6,623
Hispanic	1,469	201,511	157,421	104,992	52,429	4,103	520	2,588	1,515	11,728	3,927
Asian	36	6,669	5,592	4,290	1,302	125	23	76	49	455	219
Pacific Islander	16	2,054	2,572	1,848	724	74	12	36	38	123	126
American Indian/Alaska Native	379	11,477	11,171	7,221	3,950	601	73	318	283	1,139	272
Two or more races	284	24,374	23,012	14,375	8,637	1,389	124	729	660	1,562	528
Students with disabilities											
Total	**16,064**	**568,234**	**644,605**	**341,752**	**302,864**	**26,852**	**3,449**	**18,147**	**8,776**	**47,360**	**15,800**
Sex											
Male	13,728	438,222	510,705	265,562	245,147	21,916	2,936	14,892	7,075	37,598	12,526
Female	2,336	130,012	133,900	76,190	57,717	4,936	513	3,255	1,701	9,762	3,274
Race/ethnicity[9]											
White	7,897	221,833	225,340	127,904	97,436	11,992	1,815	7,359	4,634	18,959	5,275
Black	5,144	164,118	226,463	107,793	118,680	6,873	718	5,241	1,657	13,767	5,147
Hispanic	899	104,682	115,358	63,481	51,878	3,829	526	2,870	998	9,290	3,397
Asian	13	2,860	3,684	2,304	1,380	106	23	67	39	315	101
Pacific Islander	8	968	1,544	781	763	28	4	17	11	70	101
American Indian/Alaska Native	441	6,870	8,107	4,560	3,547	383	59	210	173	809	201
Two or more races	189	14,885	19,268	9,915	9,353	986	110	584	408	1,360	463
Race/ethnicity by sex[9]											
Male											
White	6,872	176,082	185,110	103,299	81,811	9,865	1,544	6,077	3,789	15,374	4,281
Black	4,278	122,415	172,309	79,759	92,553	5,485	602	4,218	1,283	10,681	3,940
Hispanic	755	80,396	92,359	49,611	42,749	3,210	469	2,430	811	7,427	2,764
Asian	11	2,340	3,129	1,943	1,186	88	21	58	30	266	86
Pacific Islander	6	803	1,288	641	647	22	4	13	9	51	81
American Indian/Alaska Native	362	5,288	6,464	3,567	2,897	309	44	173	136	646	160
Two or more races	171	11,359	15,337	7,757	7,580	781	95	463	321	1,040	336
Female											
White	1,025	45,751	40,230	24,605	15,625	2,127	271	1,282	845	3,585	994
Black	866	41,703	54,154	28,034	26,127	1,388	116	1,023	374	3,086	1,207
Hispanic	144	24,286	22,999	13,870	9,129	619	57	440	187	1,863	633
Asian	1-3	520	555	361	194	18	1-3	9	9	49	15
Pacific Islander	1-3	165	256	140	116	6	0	4	1-3	19	20
American Indian/Alaska Native	79	1,582	1,643	993	650	74	15	37	37	163	41
Two or more races	18	3,526	3,931	2,158	1,773	205	15	121	87	320	127

[1] Corporal punishment is paddling, spanking, or other forms of physical punishment imposed on a student.

[2] An in-school suspension is an instance in which a student is temporarily removed from his or her regular classroom(s) for at least half a day but remains under the direct supervision of school personnel.

[3] An out-of-school suspension is an instance in which a student is temporarily removed from his or her regular school for disciplinary purposes for at least half a day (but less than the remainder of the school year) to another setting (e.g., home or behavior center). Data on out-of-school suspensions by race/ethnicity exclude Connecticut Pacific Islander students pending further data quality review.

[4] Expulsions are actions taken by a local education agency that result in the removal of a student from his or her regular school for disciplinary purposes for the remainder of the school year or longer in accordance with local education agency policy. Expulsions also include removals resulting from violations of the Gun Free Schools Act that are modified to less than 365 days.

[5] Referral to law enforcement is an action by which a student is reported to any law enforcement agency or official, including a school police unit, for an incident that occurs on school grounds, during school-related events, or while taking school transportation, regardless of whether official action is taken. Excludes Hawaii data pending further data quality review.

[6] A school-related arrest is an arrest of a student for any activity conducted on school grounds, during off-campus school activities (including while taking school

transportation), or due to a referral by any school official.

[7] Totals include expulsions with and without educational services.

[8] Includes all expulsions under zero-tolerance policies, including expulsions with and without educational services. A zero-tolerance policy results in mandatory expulsion of any student who commits one or more specified offenses (for example, offenses involving guns, other weapons, violence, or similar factors, or combinations of these factors). A policy is considered "zero tolerance" even if there are some exceptions to the mandatory aspect of the expulsion, such as allowing the chief administering officer of a local education agency to modify the expulsion on a case-by-case basis.

[9] Data by race/ethnicity exclude data for students with disabilities served only under Section 504 (not receiving services under IDEA).

NOTE: Student counts between 1 and 3 are displayed as 1-3 to protect student privacy. Detail may not sum to totals because of privacy protection routines applied to the data. Race categories exclude persons of Hispanic ethnicity.

SOURCE: U.S. Department of Education, Office for Civil Rights, Civil Rights Data Collection, "2013-14 Discipline Estimations by Discipline Type." (This table was prepared January 2018.)

Table 233.28. Percentage of students receiving selected disciplinary actions in public elementary and secondary schools, by type of disciplinary action, disability status, sex, and race/ethnicity: 2013-14

Disability status, sex, and race/ethnicity	Corporal punishment[1]	One or more in-school suspension[2]	Out-of-school suspensions[3]			Expulsions[4]				Referral to law enforcement[5]	School-related arrest[6]
						Total[7]					
			Total	Only one	More than one	All expulsions	Under zero-tolerance policies[8]	With educational services	Without educational services		
1	2	3	4	5	6	7	8	9	10	11	12
All students											
Total	**0.21**	**5.43**	**5.28**	**3.13**	**2.15**	**0.22**	**0.03**	**0.13**	**0.09**	**0.36**	**0.12**
Sex											
Male	0.33	7.20	7.25	4.20	3.05	0.32	0.05	0.19	0.13	0.50	0.17
Female	0.09	3.56	3.20	1.99	1.20	0.12	0.01	0.07	0.05	0.21	0.07
Race/ethnicity[9]											
White	0.22	4.22	3.43	2.19	1.24	0.20	0.03	0.11	0.09	0.29	0.08
Black	0.53	11.30	13.68	7.31	6.37	0.44	0.05	0.27	0.17	0.65	0.27
Hispanic	0.06	5.07	4.54	2.83	1.71	0.15	0.02	0.10	0.05	0.34	0.12
Asian	0.01	1.13	1.11	0.82	0.30	0.03	0.01	0.02	0.01	0.09	0.04
Pacific Islander	0.03	3.18	4.53	2.99	1.54	0.12	0.02	0.07	0.06	0.31	0.23
American Indian/Alaska Native	0.38	6.51	6.74	4.14	2.61	0.37	0.05	0.19	0.17	0.69	0.17
Two or more races	0.10	5.01	5.26	3.12	2.14	0.31	0.04	0.16	0.15	0.33	0.11
Race/ethnicity by sex[9]											
Male											
White	0.35	5.92	5.04	3.16	1.88	0.30	0.05	0.17	0.13	0.42	0.12
Black	0.77	14.04	17.61	9.08	8.53	0.61	0.07	0.38	0.23	0.87	0.36
Hispanic	0.10	6.68	6.36	3.85	2.51	0.23	0.04	0.15	0.08	0.47	0.18
Asian	0.01	1.68	1.73	1.25	0.47	0.05	0.01	0.04	0.02	0.14	0.05
Pacific Islander	0.05	4.14	6.22	3.95	2.27	0.17	0.03	0.09	0.07	0.44	0.32
American Indian/Alaska Native	0.61	8.48	9.05	5.42	3.63	0.49	0.08	0.26	0.23	0.93	0.23
Two or more races	0.16	6.68	7.37	4.27	3.09	0.43	0.06	0.23	0.20	0.45	0.15
Female											
White	0.07	2.42	1.73	1.17	0.56	0.10	0.02	0.05	0.04	0.16	0.04
Black	0.27	8.45	9.60	5.47	4.13	0.26	0.02	0.16	0.10	0.42	0.18
Hispanic	0.02	3.38	2.64	1.76	0.88	0.07	0.01	0.04	0.03	0.20	0.07
Asian	#	0.57	0.48	0.37	0.11	0.01	#	0.01	#	0.04	0.02
Pacific Islander	0.02	2.17	2.73	1.96	0.77	0.08	0.01	0.04	0.04	0.19	0.13
American Indian/Alaska Native	0.15	4.44	4.32	2.79	1.53	0.23	0.03	0.12	0.11	0.44	0.11
Two or more races	0.04	3.30	3.12	1.95	1.17	0.19	0.02	0.10	0.09	0.21	0.07
Students with disabilities											
Total	**0.26**	**9.30**	**10.55**	**5.59**	**4.96**	**0.44**	**0.06**	**0.30**	**0.14**	**0.78**	**0.26**
Sex											
Male	0.34	10.77	12.55	6.53	6.02	0.54	0.07	0.37	0.17	0.93	0.31
Female	0.11	6.37	6.56	3.74	2.83	0.24	0.03	0.16	0.08	0.48	0.16
Race/ethnicity[9]											
White	0.25	7.07	7.18	4.08	3.11	0.38	0.06	0.23	0.15	0.60	0.17
Black	0.45	14.48	19.99	9.51	10.47	0.61	0.06	0.46	0.15	1.22	0.45
Hispanic	0.06	7.44	8.20	4.51	3.69	0.27	0.04	0.20	0.07	0.66	0.24
Asian	0.01	1.97	2.53	1.58	0.95	0.07	0.02	0.05	0.03	0.22	0.07
Pacific Islander	0.04	4.79	7.64	3.87	3.78	0.14	0.02	0.08	0.05	0.58	0.50
American Indian/Alaska Native	0.52	8.05	9.50	5.34	4.16	0.45	0.07	0.25	0.20	0.95	0.24
Two or more races	0.10	8.20	10.62	5.46	5.15	0.54	0.06	0.32	0.22	0.76	0.26
Race/ethnicity by sex[9]											
Male											
White	0.33	8.45	8.88	4.96	3.93	0.47	0.07	0.29	0.18	0.74	0.21
Black	0.56	16.10	22.67	10.49	12.17	0.72	0.08	0.55	0.17	1.41	0.52
Hispanic	0.08	8.59	9.87	5.30	4.57	0.34	0.05	0.26	0.09	0.79	0.30
Asian	0.01	2.36	3.16	1.96	1.20	0.09	0.02	0.06	0.03	0.28	0.09
Pacific Islander	0.04	5.80	9.30	4.63	4.67	0.16	0.03	0.09	0.06	0.63	0.58
American Indian/Alaska Native	0.65	9.47	11.57	6.39	5.19	0.55	0.08	0.31	0.24	1.16	0.29
Two or more races	0.14	9.40	12.69	6.42	6.27	0.65	0.08	0.38	0.27	0.87	0.28
Female											
White	0.10	4.34	3.82	2.34	1.48	0.20	0.03	0.12	0.08	0.34	0.09
Black	0.23	11.19	14.53	7.52	7.01	0.37	0.03	0.27	0.10	0.83	0.32
Hispanic	0.03	5.15	4.88	2.94	1.94	0.13	0.01	0.09	0.04	0.40	0.13
Asian	0.00-0.01	1.12	1.20	0.78	0.42	0.04	0.00-0.01	0.02	0.02	0.11	0.03
Pacific Islander	0.02-0.05	2.60	4.03	2.20	1.82	0.09	0.00	0.06	0.02-0.05	0.49	0.31
American Indian/Alaska Native	0.27	5.37	5.58	3.37	2.21	0.25	0.05	0.13	0.13	0.55	0.14
Two or more races	0.03	5.82	6.49	3.56	2.93	0.34	0.02	0.20	0.14	0.53	0.21

#Rounds to zero.

[1] Corporal punishment is paddling, spanking, or other forms of physical punishment imposed on a student.

[2] An in-school suspension is an instance in which a student is temporarily removed from his or her regular classroom(s) for at least half a day but remains under the direct supervision of school personnel.

[3] An out-of-school suspension is an instance in which a student is temporarily removed from his or her regular school for disciplinary purposes for at least half a day (but less than the remainder of the school year) to another setting (e.g., home or behavior center). Data on out-of-school suspensions by race/ethnicity exclude Connecticut Pacific Islander students pending further data quality review.

[4] Expulsions are actions taken by a local education agency that result in the removal of a student from his or her regular school for disciplinary purposes for the remainder of the school year or longer in accordance with local education agency policy. Expulsions also include removals resulting from violations of the Gun Free Schools Act that are modified to less than 365 days.

[5] Referral to law enforcement is an action by which a student is reported to any law enforcement agency or official, including a school police unit, for an incident that occurs on school grounds, during school-related events, or while taking school transportation, regardless of whether official action is taken. Excludes Hawaii data pending further data quality review.

6 A school-related arrest is an arrest of a student for any activity conducted on school grounds, during off-campus school activities (including while taking school transportation), or due to a referral by any school official.

7 Totals include expulsions with and without educational services.

8 Includes all expulsions under zero-tolerance policies, including expulsions with and without educational services. A zero-tolerance policy results in mandatory expulsion of any student who commits one or more specified offenses (for example, offenses involving guns, other weapons, violence, or similar factors, or combinations of these factors). A policy is considered "zero tolerance" even if there are some exceptions to the mandatory aspect of the expulsion, such as allowing the chief administering officer of a local education agency to modify the expulsion on a case-by-case basis.

9 Data by race/ethnicity exclude data for students with disabilities served only under Section 504 (not receiving services under IDEA).

NOTE: The percentage of students receiving a disciplinary action is calculated by dividing the cumulative number of students receiving that type of disciplinary action for the entire 2013-14 school year by the student enrollment based on a count of students taken on a single day between September 27 and December 31. Percentages based on disciplinary action counts of between 1 and 3 students are displayed as ranges to protect student privacy. Race categories exclude persons of Hispanic ethnicity.

SOURCE: U.S. Department of Education, Office for Civil Rights, Civil Rights Data Collection, "2013-14 Discipline Estimations by Discipline Type" and "2013-14 Estimations for Enrollment." (This table was prepared January 2018.)

Table 233.30. Number of students suspended and expelled from public elementary and secondary schools, by sex, race/ethnicity, and state: 2013-14

State	Number receiving out-of-school suspensions[1]										Number expelled[2]									
	Total	Sex		Race/ethnicity[3]							Total	Sex		Race/ethnicity[3]						
		Male	Female	White	Black	Hispanic	Asian	Pacific Islander[4]	American Indian/ Alaska Native	Two or more races		Male	Female	White	Black	Hispanic	Asian	Pacific Islander	American Indian/ Alaska Native	Two or more races
1	2	3	4	5	6	7	8	9	10	11	12	13	14	15	16	17	18	19	20	21
United States	**2,635,743**	**1,860,002**	**775,741**	**843,381**	**1,042,991**	**554,498**	**26,499**	**8,784**	**35,756**	**78,469**	**111,215**	**82,787**	**28,428**	**49,144**	**33,557**	**18,271**	**790**	**241**	**1,944**	**4,613**
Alabama	59,129	40,077	19,052	18,841	37,614	1,214	156	28	251	727	1,379	1,053	326	387	892	26	0	1-3	1-3	61
Alaska	6,526	4,832	1,694	2,152	385	408	163	206	2,591	534	108	89	19	32	9	14	0	1-3	37	12
Arizona	57,055	42,110	14,945	17,268	6,410	26,296	471	201	4,670	1,187	434	327	107	157	39	191	1-3	4	22	13
Arkansas	33,585	23,608	9,977	13,216	17,134	2,029	103	84	148	381	846	625	221	492	224	54	5	1-3	14	9
California	249,111	184,217	64,894	49,660	42,997	133,414	7,978	2,097	3,001	6,944	8,741	6,999	1,742	1,938	1,346	4,643	241	58	109	249
Colorado	38,673	28,197	10,476	14,869	4,530	16,743	363	72	450	1,463	1,306	1,066	240	508	167	519	15	7	25	46
Connecticut	21,523	14,721	6,802	6,059	6,253	7,427	206	([4])	94	421	1,222	1,006	216	499	340	301	9	0	4	20
Delaware	11,459	7,537	3,922	2,759	6,494	1,109	79	9	54	212	115	84	31	40	61	11	0	0	0	1-3
District of Columbia	9,471	5,898	3,573	61	8,783	474	17	9	7	46	112	67	45	1-3	103	5	0	0	1-3	0
Florida	136,931	98,570	38,361	39,427	60,625	31,078	697	102	411	4,123	155	120	35	51	64	30	0	0	1-3	7
Georgia	126,549	87,764	38,785	25,592	85,137	10,198	779	129	168	3,610	2,768	2,058	710	787	1,669	147	12	17	7	100
Hawaii	6,497	4,650	1,847	633	173	534	1,217	3,299	45	412	8	6	1-3	0	0	1-3	1-3	1-3	0	0
Idaho	7,445	5,695	1,750	5,161	114	1,623	48	30	193	139	168	135	33	100	4	49	1-3	0	9	1-3
Illinois	139,521	94,651	44,870	28,808	76,744	26,887	797	87	279	3,477	2,682	1,898	784	1,058	1,210	228	20	0	11	114
Indiana	69,891	49,417	20,474	32,584	24,674	6,385	284	20	150	4,472	5,229	3,660	1,569	2,743	1,505	546	19	5	16	235
Iowa	12,980	9,466	3,514	7,637	2,930	1,430	120	23	85	711	180	157	23	131	24	18	1-3	0	0	4
Kansas	19,861	14,509	5,352	9,059	4,982	3,948	160	29	326	1,244	787	604	183	417	121	146	6	1-3	17	65
Kentucky	33,336	24,335	9,001	21,906	8,849	1,088	89	20	49	1,131	353	276	77	280	42	14	0	0	1-3	12
Louisiana	59,380	40,200	19,180	14,995	37,069	1,407	194	26	315	663	4,397	3,230	1,167	991	2,937	55	7	1-3	24	41
Maine	6,015	4,458	1,557	5,151	374	135	33	4	39	76	189	148	41	164	8	4	0	0	0	7
Maryland	45,772	31,425	14,347	9,858	28,189	4,039	403	33	150	1,561	786	574	212	73	618	41	1-3	1-3	4	14
Massachusetts	40,494	28,701	11,793	15,272	8,537	13,138	724	22	135	1,571	327	254	73	173	47	65	1-3	0	1-3	26
Michigan	114,844	79,742	35,102	47,847	54,346	6,671	785	53	939	3,491	2,239	1,686	553	1,226	764	142	18	0	14	58
Minnesota	28,258	20,140	8,118	11,981	10,139	2,780	603	20	1,439	1,060	840	642	198	495	177	67	14	0	31	45
Mississippi	47,813	32,503	15,310	10,746	36,188	630	88	9	67	50	1,418	1,071	347	331	1,062	10	6	0	1-3	6
Missouri	51,905	36,657	15,248	25,991	21,765	2,036	271	56	227	1,205	3,124	2,111	1,013	2,274	478	235	1-3	8	18	101
Montana	5,276	3,810	1,466	2,901	63	154	14	7	2,022	67	204	141	63	84	1-3	6	0	0	89	18
Nebraska	13,056	9,391	3,665	6,015	3,288	2,464	130	14	416	671	918	674	244	350	279	187	12	0	29	53
Nevada	20,845	14,921	5,924	5,611	4,820	8,062	390	197	309	1,088	1,898	1,428	470	347	547	793	36	14	15	95
New Hampshire	9,105	6,689	2,416	6,647	658	1,197	122	16	41	124	34	26	8	33	0	0	0	0	0	0
New Jersey	59,240	40,780	18,460	14,334	25,635	16,959	1,019	39	67	606	200	157	43	82	74	36	1-3	0	0	5
New Mexico	21,060	14,173	6,887	3,977	659	13,769	113	11	2,033	455	1,955	1,380	575	295	80	1,400	13	0	99	60
New York	88,032	61,285	26,747	33,087	34,424	15,224	1,142	71	633	1,616	2,490	1,868	622	1,360	633	343	21	0	20	54
North Carolina	101,924	72,183	29,741	28,901	52,807	11,012	495	81	2,510	3,899	870	655	215	247	449	91	4	1-3	20	42
North Dakota	2,304	1,661	643	1,232	180	89	11	1-3	749	6	93	71	22	28	21	6	0	0	38	0
Ohio	125,976	88,165	37,811	59,601	50,817	5,298	488	51	177	7,094	31,059	22,594	8,465	19,501	7,698	1,025	94	27	59	1,709
Oklahoma	38,622	27,667	10,955	15,186	10,549	5,804	155	87	4,627	1,960	7,318	5,150	2,168	2,528	2,288	987	15	13	881	589
Oregon	23,282	17,479	5,803	13,785	1,244	5,420	271	164	593	1,369	1,159	906	253	714	35	267	9	9	41	65
Pennsylvania	97,711	67,221	30,490	35,376	44,221	12,341	762	55	125	3,515	1,899	1,420	479	991	493	294	7	1-3	6	81
Rhode Island	8,777	6,227	2,550	3,551	1,395	2,984	121	9	123	392	61	40	21	32	4	17	0	0	1-3	6
South Carolina	76,755	52,380	24,375	23,713	46,387	3,232	207	51	226	1,903	2,851	2,176	675	883	1,775	80	10	0	16	63
South Dakota	3,634	2,620	1,014	1,971	250	233	32	1-3	983	104	36	28	8	15	4	1-3	0	1-3	14	0
Tennessee	66,130	45,490	20,640	22,676	38,759	3,258	298	29	96	663	4,245	3,200	1,045	1,595	2,299	221	15	4	4	50
Texas	246,474	173,302	73,172	35,826	76,431	118,651	1,728	233	832	3,689	7,821	6,093	1,728	1,693	1,890	3,669	57	7	68	125
Utah	10,711	8,222	2,489	6,257	350	3,061	127	234	372	231	148	120	28	85	4	43	7	1-3	5	1-3
Vermont	3,257	2,379	878	2,770	121	40	12	1-3	63	50	44	33	11	39	5	0	0	0	0	0
Virginia	72,448	51,235	21,213	24,401	37,324	5,649	668	71	189	2,817	819	634	185	314	310	119	11	1-3	6	45
Washington	48,972	36,844	12,128	23,513	5,056	11,989	1,091	660	1,388	3,839	3,496	2,726	770	1,580	266	1,001	82	49	125	281
West Virginia	20,724	15,070	5,654	18,154	1,773	171	20	4	14	315	491	403	88	431	43	6	1-3	0	1-3	4
Wisconsin	34,494	24,495	9,999	14,234	14,280	3,860	241	22	709	1,030	1,088	825	263	494	444	98	7	0	23	14
Wyoming	2,910	2,233	677	2,129	65	456	14	4	176	55	105	93	12	74	1-3	18	0	0	8	1-3

[1] An out-of-school suspension is an instance in which a student is temporarily removed from his or her regular school for disciplinary purposes for at least half a day (but less than the remainder of the school year) to another setting (e.g., home or behavior center).

[2] Expulsions are actions taken by a local education agency that result in the removal of a student from his or her regular school for disciplinary purposes, with or without the continuation of educational services, for the remainder of the school year or longer in accordance with local education agency policy. Expulsions also include removals resulting from violations of the Gun Free Schools Act that are modified to less than 365 days.

[3] Data by race/ethnicity exclude students with disabilities served only under Section 504 (not receiving services under IDEA).

[4] Connecticut Pacific Islander data are suppressed and excluded from the Pacific Islander U.S. total pending further data quality review.

NOTE: Student counts between 1 and 3 are displayed as 1-3 to protect student privacy. Detail may not sum to totals because of privacy protection routines applied to the data. Race categories exclude persons of Hispanic ethnicity.

SOURCE: U.S. Department of Education, Office for Civil Rights, Civil Rights Data Collection, "2013-14 Discipline Estimations by Discipline Type." (This table was prepared January 2018.)

Table 233.40. Percentage of students suspended and expelled from public elementary and secondary schools, by sex, race/ethnicity, and state: 2013-14

State	Percent receiving out-of-school suspensions[1]										Percent expelled[2]									
	Total	Sex		Race/ethnicity[3]							Total	Sex		Race/ethnicity[3]						
		Male	Female	White	Black	Hispanic	Asian	Pacific Islander[4]	American Indian/ Alaska Native	Two or more races		Male	Female	White	Black	Hispanic	Asian	Pacific Islander	American Indian/ Alaska Native	Two or more races
1	2	3	4	5	6	7	8	9	10	11	12	13	14	15	16	17	18	19	20	21
United States	**5.28**	**7.25**	**3.20**	**3.43**	**13.68**	**4.54**	**1.11**	**4.53**	**6.74**	**5.26**	**0.22**	**0.32**	**0.12**	**0.20**	**0.44**	**0.15**	**0.03**	**0.12**	**0.37**	**0.31**
Alabama	7.98	10.50	5.30	4.51	15.25	2.97	1.58	4.03	3.87	5.90	0.19	0.28	0.09	0.09	0.36	0.06	0.00	0.14-0.43	0.02-0.05	0.49
Alaska	5.06	7.24	2.72	3.47	8.81	4.80	2.03	6.49	8.48	4.82	0.08	0.13	0.03	0.05	0.21	0.16	0.00	0.03-0.09	0.12	0.11
Arizona	5.18	7.45	2.78	3.90	11.54	5.50	1.54	4.81	8.90	5.02	0.04	0.06	0.02	0.04	0.07	0.04	0.00-0.01	0.10	0.04	0.05
Arkansas	7.00	9.63	4.25	4.47	17.87	3.82	1.45	3.11	4.83	4.34	0.18	0.25	0.09	0.17	0.23	0.10	0.07	0.04-0.11	0.46	0.10
California	3.99	5.74	2.14	3.25	11.24	4.03	1.18	4.80	7.11	3.43	0.14	0.22	0.06	0.13	0.35	0.14	0.04	0.13	0.26	0.12
Colorado	4.41	6.27	2.45	3.13	11.04	5.84	1.35	3.64	6.80	4.87	0.15	0.24	0.06	0.11	0.41	0.18	0.06	0.35	0.38	0.15
Connecticut	3.94	5.23	2.57	1.99	9.02	6.61	0.82	(4)	6.23	3.31	0.22	0.36	0.08	0.16	0.49	0.27	0.04	0.00	0.26	0.16
Delaware	8.48	10.72	6.05	4.43	15.64	5.83	1.68	6.08	9.18	6.25	0.09	0.12	0.05	0.06	0.15	0.06	0.00	0.00	0.00	0.03-0.09
District of Columbia	12.44	15.52	9.37	0.90	15.98	4.26	1.52	10.00	9.86	3.83	0.15	0.18	0.12	0.01-0.04	0.19	0.04	0.00	0.00	1.41-4.23	0.00
Florida	5.04	7.06	2.90	3.67	9.89	3.86	1.00	2.92	4.65	4.91	0.01	0.01	#	#	0.01	#	0.00	0.00	0.01-0.03	0.01
Georgia	7.29	9.86	4.59	3.52	13.38	4.46	1.28	6.53	4.57	6.71	0.16	0.23	0.08	0.11	0.26	0.06	0.02	0.86	0.19	0.19
Hawaii	3.47	4.76	2.06	2.54	4.53	2.96	2.05	5.58	6.16	2.22	#	0.01	#	0.00	0.00	0.01-0.02	0.00-0.01	0.00-0.01	0.00	0.00
Idaho	2.57	3.82	1.25	2.37	3.61	3.43	1.27	2.38	4.66	2.33	0.06	0.09	0.02	0.05	0.13	0.10	0.03-0.08	0.00	0.22	0.02-0.05
Illinois	6.83	9.02	4.51	2.88	21.91	5.45	0.87	3.56	4.57	5.78	0.13	0.18	0.08	0.11	0.35	0.05	0.02	0.00	0.18	0.19
Indiana	6.79	9.35	4.09	4.50	20.58	6.21	1.44	2.78	5.93	10.00	0.51	0.69	0.31	0.38	1.26	0.53	0.10	0.70	0.63	0.53
Iowa	2.60	3.68	1.45	1.96	11.03	2.99	1.08	2.57	4.27	4.66	0.04	0.06	0.01	0.03	0.09	0.04	0.01-0.03	0.00	0.00	0.03
Kansas	4.04	5.73	2.24	2.82	14.03	4.40	1.22	3.41	6.21	5.51	0.16	0.24	0.08	0.13	0.34	0.16	0.05	0.12-0.35	0.32	0.29
Kentucky	4.87	6.91	2.71	4.08	12.21	3.08	0.90	3.12	5.67	5.82	0.05	0.08	0.02	0.05	0.06	0.04	0.00	0.00	0.12-0.35	0.06
Louisiana	8.38	11.08	5.54	4.70	12.61	4.22	1.83	5.68	6.44	5.90	0.62	0.89	0.34	0.31	1.00	0.17	0.07	0.22-0.66	0.49	0.36
Maine	3.45	4.96	1.84	3.36	6.62	4.56	1.26	2.08	3.51	2.75	0.11	0.16	0.05	0.11	0.14	0.14	0.00	0.00	0.00	0.25
Maryland	5.19	6.95	3.34	2.89	9.26	3.34	0.76	2.69	5.86	4.56	0.09	0.13	0.05	0.02	0.20	0.03	0.00-0.01	0.08-0.24	0.16	0.04
Massachusetts	4.28	5.92	2.55	2.61	10.46	8.60	1.26	2.13	5.94	5.34	0.03	0.05	0.02	0.03	0.06	0.04	0.00-0.01	0.00	0.04-0.13	0.09
Michigan	7.34	9.91	4.62	4.51	19.23	6.60	1.69	3.22	7.96	7.48	0.14	0.21	0.07	0.12	0.27	0.14	0.04	0.00	0.12	0.12
Minnesota	3.30	4.57	1.95	2.00	12.29	4.04	1.11	2.69	9.50	4.00	0.10	0.15	0.05	0.08	0.21	0.10	0.03	0.00	0.20	0.17
Mississippi	9.67	12.83	6.35	4.77	14.80	4.08	1.76	3.85	6.03	3.77	0.29	0.42	0.14	0.15	0.43	0.06	0.12	0.00	0.09-0.27	0.45
Missouri	5.74	7.86	3.48	3.87	17.02	4.38	1.62	2.90	5.96	5.33	0.35	0.45	0.23	0.34	0.37	0.51	0.01-0.02	0.41	0.47	0.45
Montana	3.66	5.12	2.10	2.54	4.44	2.85	1.14	1.99	11.84	2.26	0.14	0.19	0.09	0.07	0.07-0.21	0.11	0.00	0.00	0.52	0.61
Nebraska	4.27	5.95	2.48	2.88	16.20	4.68	1.83	3.26	9.23	6.82	0.30	0.43	0.17	0.17	1.37	0.35	0.17	0.00	0.64	0.54
Nevada	4.60	6.38	2.70	3.52	10.87	4.42	1.55	3.33	6.47	4.41	0.42	0.61	0.21	0.22	1.23	0.43	0.14	0.24	0.31	0.38
New Hampshire	4.88	6.95	2.67	4.29	19.21	14.21	2.22	7.51	7.30	3.71	0.02	0.03	0.01	0.02	0.00	0.00	0.00	0.00	0.00	0.00
New Jersey	4.44	5.95	2.84	2.21	12.79	5.59	0.80	1.26	3.70	3.10	0.01	0.02	0.01	0.01	0.04	0.01	#	0.00	0.00	0.03
New Mexico	6.25	8.20	4.19	4.82	10.22	6.78	2.83	2.52	6.03	8.55	0.58	0.80	0.35	0.36	1.24	0.69	0.33	0.00	0.29	1.13
New York	3.22	4.36	2.01	2.68	7.05	2.29	0.49	1.20	4.00	4.23	0.09	0.13	0.05	0.11	0.13	0.05	0.01	0.00	0.13	0.14
North Carolina	6.67	9.19	4.00	3.77	13.42	4.92	1.17	4.68	11.57	7.01	0.06	0.08	0.03	0.03	0.11	0.04	0.01	0.06-0.17	0.09	0.08
North Dakota	2.21	3.09	1.27	1.49	5.21	2.50	0.74	0.31-0.93	8.13	0.50	0.09	0.13	0.04	0.03	0.61	0.17	0.00	0.00	0.41	0.00
Ohio	7.14	9.71	4.42	4.68	18.70	6.79	1.47	3.47	7.73	9.24	1.76	2.49	0.99	1.53	2.83	1.31	0.28	1.84	2.58	2.23
Oklahoma	5.64	7.86	3.29	4.33	16.99	5.75	1.22	4.22	4.42	4.29	1.07	1.46	0.65	0.72	3.68	0.98	0.12	0.63	0.84	1.29
Oregon	4.12	6.03	2.11	3.86	9.24	4.46	1.22	4.18	6.45	4.52	0.20	0.31	0.09	0.20	0.26	0.22	0.04	0.23	0.45	0.21
Pennsylvania	5.62	7.52	3.61	3.01	17.13	7.53	1.28	4.23	4.43	7.30	0.11	0.16	0.06	0.08	0.19	0.18	0.01	0.08-0.23	0.21	0.17
Rhode Island	6.24	8.57	3.75	4.28	12.41	9.29	2.93	4.69	9.33	6.95	0.04	0.06	0.03	0.04	0.04	0.05	0.00	0.00	0.08-0.23	0.11
South Carolina	10.29	13.68	6.72	6.17	17.88	5.88	1.94	5.43	9.22	8.56	0.38	0.57	0.19	0.23	0.68	0.15	0.09	0.00	0.65	0.28
South Dakota	2.70	3.77	1.55	1.93	7.03	3.95	1.43	0.76-2.27	6.20	2.88	0.03	0.04	0.01	0.01	0.11	0.02-0.05	0.00	0.76-2.27	0.09	0.00
Tennessee	6.70	8.97	4.30	3.55	17.10	4.22	1.69	2.87	5.19	4.52	0.43	0.63	0.22	0.25	1.01	0.29	0.08	0.40	0.22	0.34
Texas	4.77	6.53	2.91	2.49	12.14	4.57	0.91	3.60	4.38	3.51	0.15	0.23	0.07	0.12	0.30	0.14	0.03	0.11	0.36	0.12
Utah	1.70	2.53	0.82	1.32	4.29	3.00	1.19	2.52	5.17	1.72	0.02	0.04	0.01	0.02	0.05	0.04	0.07	0.01-0.03	0.07	0.01-0.02
Vermont	3.88	5.48	2.17	3.79	6.59	3.49	0.68	0.90-2.70	12.60	2.83	0.05	0.08	0.03	0.05	0.27	0.00	0.00	0.00	0.00	0.00
Virginia	5.68	7.80	3.43	3.74	12.72	3.40	0.82	3.81	4.65	4.95	0.06	0.10	0.03	0.05	0.11	0.07	0.01	0.05-0.16	0.15	0.08
Washington	4.58	6.68	2.34	3.89	10.52	5.35	1.44	6.42	9.31	5.34	0.33	0.49	0.15	0.26	0.55	0.45	0.11	0.48	0.84	0.39
West Virginia	7.30	10.27	4.12	7.11	13.60	4.35	1.04	3.60	4.53	5.72	0.17	0.27	0.06	0.17	0.33	0.15	0.05-0.16	0.00	0.32-0.97	0.07
Wisconsin	3.96	5.46	2.36	2.27	17.03	4.22	0.76	3.01	6.53	4.82	0.12	0.18	0.06	0.08	0.53	0.11	0.02	0.00	0.21	0.07
Wyoming	3.12	4.61	1.51	2.92	6.05	3.79	1.69	3.17	5.18	3.03	0.11	0.19	0.03	0.10	0.09-0.28	0.15	0.00	0.00	0.24	0.06-0.17

#Rounds to zero.

[1] An out-of-school suspension is an instance in which a student is temporarily removed from his or her regular school for disciplinary purposes for at least half a day (but less than the remainder of the school year) to another setting (e.g., home or behavior center).

[2] Expulsions are actions taken by a local education agency that result in the removal of a student from his or her regular school for disciplinary purposes, with or without the continuation of educational services, for the remainder of the school year or longer in accordance with local education agency policy. Expulsions also include removals resulting from violations of the Gun Free Schools Act that are modified to less than 365 days.

[3] Data by race/ethnicity exclude students with disabilities served only under Section 504 (not receiving services under IDEA).

[4] Connecticut Pacific Islander data are suppressed and excluded from the Pacific Islander U.S. total pending further data quality review.

NOTE: The percentage of students receiving a disciplinary action is calculated by dividing the cumulative number of students receiving that type of disciplinary action for the entire 2013-14 school year by the student enrollment based on a count of students taken on a single day between September 27 and December 31. Percentages based on suspension or expulsion counts of between 1 and 3 students are displayed as ranges to protect student privacy. Race categories exclude persons of Hispanic ethnicity.

SOURCE: U.S. Department of Education, Office for Civil Rights, Civil Rights Data Collection, "2013-14 Discipline Estimations by Discipline Type" and "2013-14 Estimations for Enrollment." (This table was prepared January 2018.)

Table 233.45. Number of discipline incidents resulting in removal of a student from a regular education program for at least an entire school day and rate of incidents per 100,000 students, by discipline reason and state: 2014-15

State	Number of discipline incidents					Rate of discipline incidents per 100,000 students				
	Total	Alcohol	Illicit drug	Violent incident[1]	Weapons possession	Total	Alcohol	Illicit drug	Violent incident[1]	Weapons possession
1	2	3	4	5	6	7	8	9	10	11
United States[2]	**1,297,163**	**22,498[4]**	**195,186[4]**	**1,017,143**	**62,336**	**2,583**	**45[4]**	**389[4]**	**2,025**	**124**
Alabama	40,561	527	5,774	32,683	1,577	5,451	71	776	4,392	212
Alaska	3,578	138	717	2,495	228	2,728	105	547	1,902	174
Arizona[3]	30,217	851	3,915	24,536	915	2,718	77	352	2,207	82
Arkansas	23,099	499	2,116	19,685	799	4,705	102	431	4,010	163
California	251,483	([4])	42,828[4]	196,643	12,012	3,984	([4])	678[4]	3,115	190
Colorado	65,725	1,082	6,773	57,104	766	7,393	122	762	6,423	86
Connecticut	24,336	365	1,390	21,490	1,091	4,484	67	256	3,960	201
Delaware	613	67	335	50	161	457	50	250	37	120
District of Columbia	5,924	20	282	5,259	363	7,317	25	348	6,496	448
Florida	16,125	1,071	10,252	3,261	1,541	585	39	372	118	56
Georgia	69,897	844	10,917	55,452	2,684	4,007	48	626	3,179	154
Hawaii	2,195	175	678	1,066	276	1,204	96	372	584	151
Idaho	842	78	460	195	109	289	27	158	67	37
Illinois	42,915	969	6,358	32,438	3,150	2,093	47	310	1,582	154
Indiana	41,358	1,215	3,182	35,344	1,617	3,953	116	304	3,378	155
Iowa[3]	12,533	277	1,945	9,546	765	2,480	55	385	1,889	151
Kansas	12,026	253	2,246	8,839	688	2,418	51	452	1,777	138
Kentucky[3]	51,619	811	10,997	39,414	397	7,496	118	1,597	5,723	58
Louisiana	47,145	341	4,924	40,631	1,249	6,577	48	687	5,668	174
Maine	1,899	114	735	979	71	1,041	62	403	537	39
Maryland	32,094	416	2,620	27,452	1,606	3,670	48	300	3,139	184
Massachusetts	21,254	503	2,686	16,775	1,290	2,224	53	281	1,755	135
Michigan[3]	11,476	212	1,292	9,141	831	746	14	84	594	54
Minnesota[3]	20,647	496	3,572	15,525	1,054	2,409	58	417	1,811	123
Mississippi	17,432	334	757	15,812	529	3,551	68	154	3,221	108
Missouri	21,891	1,040	6,800	12,665	1,386	2,385	113	741	1,380	151
Montana	4,530	141	917	3,253	219	3,134	98	634	2,251	152
Nebraska	9,176	212	1,156	7,389	419	2,935	68	370	2,363	134
Nevada	11,009	420	2,161	7,820	608	2,397	91	471	1,703	132
New Hampshire	4,829	141	797	3,583	308	2,615	76	432	1,940	167
New Jersey	11,679	339	2,162	8,357	821	834	24	154	597	59
New Mexico	11,435	293	2,338	8,249	555	3,360	86	687	2,424	163
New York	18,932	1,171	4,838	7,772	5,151	691	43	176	284	188
North Carolina	69,415	837	11,451	54,373	2,754	4,482	54	739	3,510	178
North Dakota	1,314	52	370	830	62	1,233	49	347	779	58
Ohio	80,159	1,063	8,835	67,255	3,006	4,647	62	512	3,899	174
Oklahoma	14,632	456	2,181	10,824	1,171	2,125	66	317	1,572	170
Oregon	15,004	465	2,899	11,079	561	2,495	77	482	1,842	93
Pennsylvania	36,436	628	2,927	30,536	2,345	2,090	36	168	1,752	135
Rhode Island	12,715	66	701	11,771	177	8,957	46	494	8,292	125
South Carolina	21,051	401	1,392	18,941	317	2,783	53	184	2,504	42
South Dakota[3]	3,351	102	912	2,107	230	2,519	77	686	1,584	173
Tennessee	32,686	514	2,213	29,691	268	3,283	52	222	2,983	27
Texas	2,405	48	1,364	565	428	46	1	26	11	8
Utah	5,010	146	1,230	3,285	349	788	23	194	517	55
Vermont	—	—	—	—	—	—	—	—	—	—
Virginia	20,772	797	1,692	16,343	1,940	1,622	62	132	1,276	152
Washington[3]	20,098	944	5,024	11,951	2,179	1,872	88	468	1,113	203
West Virginia	3,438	48	599	2,738	53	1,226	17	214	977	19
Wisconsin	17,552	512	2,468	13,582	990	2,014	59	283	1,559	114
Wyoming	651	4	8	369	270	692	4	9	392	287

—Not available.

[1] Includes violent incidents with and without physical injury.

[2] U.S. totals exclude Vermont data, which were not reported.

[3] This state did not report state-level counts of discipline incidents, but did report school-level counts. The sums of the school-level counts are displayed in place of the unreported state-level counts.

[4] California reported alcohol incidents in the illicit drug category.

SOURCE: U.S. Department of Education, National Center for Education Statistics, ED*Facts* file 030, Data Group 523, extracted August 1, 2016, from the ED*Facts* Data Warehouse (internal U.S. Department of Education source); Common Core of Data (CCD), "State Nonfiscal Survey of Public Elementary and Secondary Education," 2014-15. (This table was prepared August 2016.)

Table 233.50. Percentage of public schools with various safety and security measures: Selected years, 1999-2000 through 2017-18

[Standard errors appear in parentheses]

School safety and security measures	1999-2000		2003-04		2005-06		2007-08		2009-10		2013-14[1]		2015-16		2017-18	
1		2		3		4		5		6		7		8		9
Controlled access during school hours																
Buildings (e.g., locked or monitored doors, loading docks)[2]	74.6	(1.35)	83.0	(1.04)	84.9	(0.89)	89.5	(0.80)	91.7	(0.80)	93.3	(0.95)	94.1	(0.64)	95.4	(0.52)
Grounds (e.g., locked or monitored gates)	33.7	(1.26)	36.2	(1.08)	41.1	(1.25)	42.6	(1.41)	46.0	(1.26)	42.7	(1.53)	49.9	(1.53)	50.8	(1.38)
Visitors required to sign or check in and wear badges[3]	96.6	(0.54)	98.3	(0.40)	97.6	(0.42)	98.7	(0.37)	99.3	(0.27)	98.6	(0.49)	93.5	(0.69)	94.6	(0.65)
Classrooms equipped with locks so that doors can be locked from inside	---	(†)	---	(†)	---	(†)	---	(†)	---	(†)	---	(†)	66.7	(1.34)	64.8	(1.01)
Student dress, IDs, and school supplies																
Required students to wear uniforms	11.8	(0.82)	13.8	(0.85)	13.8	(0.78)	17.5	(0.70)	18.9	(1.02)	20.4	(1.27)	21.5	(1.36)	19.8	(0.87)
Enforced a strict dress code	47.4	(1.50)	55.1	(1.24)	55.3	(1.18)	54.8	(1.20)	56.9	(1.56)	58.5	(1.60)	53.1	(1.22)	48.8	(1.32)
Required students to wear badges or picture IDs	3.9	(0.32)	6.4	(0.64)	6.2	(0.47)	7.6	(0.60)	6.9	(0.57)	8.9	(0.81)	7.0	(0.53)	9.2	(0.60)
Required faculty and staff to wear badges or picture IDs	25.4	(1.39)	48.0	(1.21)	47.9	(1.12)	58.3	(1.37)	62.9	(1.14)	68.0	(1.65)	67.9	(1.36)	69.9	(1.18)
Required clear book bags or banned book bags on school grounds	5.9	(0.50)	6.2	(0.63)	6.4	(0.43)	6.0	(0.48)	5.5	(0.53)	6.3	(0.81)	3.9	(0.44)	3.5	(0.42)
Provided school lockers to students	46.5	(1.07)	49.5	(1.24)	50.5	(1.08)	48.9	(1.17)	52.1	(1.10)	49.9	(1.35)	50.4	(1.24)	49.0	(1.25)
Drug testing																
Students participating in athletics or other extracurricular activities[4]	---	(†)	4.3	(0.44)	5.0	(0.46)	6.6	(0.53)	6.2	(0.51)	6.7	(0.61)	7.7	(0.57)	8.9	(0.57)
Athletes	---	(†)	4.2	(0.44)	5.0	(0.46)	6.4	(0.48)	6.0	(0.52)	6.6	(0.59)	7.2	(0.55)	---	(†)
Students in extracurricular activities (other than athletes)	---	(†)	2.6	(0.37)	3.4	(0.32)	4.5	(0.51)	4.6	(0.47)	4.3	(0.47)	6.0	(0.53)	---	(†)
Any other students	---	(†)	---	(†)	3.0	(0.34)	3.0	(0.42)	3.0	(0.26)	3.5	(0.44)	---	(†)	---	(†)
Metal detectors, dogs, and sweeps																
Random metal detector checks on students	7.2	(0.54)	5.6	(0.55)	4.9	(0.40)	5.3	(0.37)	5.2	(0.42)	4.2	(0.48)	4.5	(0.48)	4.9	(0.49)
Metal detector checks on students every day[5]	0.9	(0.16)	1.1	(0.16)	1.1	(0.18)	1.3	(0.20)	1.4	(0.24)	2.0	(0.40)	1.8	(0.32)	2.2	(0.35)
Random sweeps (e.g., locker checks, dog sniffs) for contraband (e.g., drugs or weapons)[6]	25.3	(0.77)	26.6	(0.73)	28.0	(0.89)	26.3	(0.77)	27.7	(0.86)	28.2	(1.02)	28.2	(0.89)	27.4	(0.88)
Random dog sniffs to check for drugs	20.6	(0.75)	21.3	(0.77)	23.0	(0.79)	21.5	(0.59)	22.9	(0.71)	24.1	(0.97)	24.6	(0.85)	---	(†)
Random sweeps (not including dog sniffs) for contraband	11.8	(0.54)	12.8	(0.58)	13.1	(0.76)	11.4	(0.71)	12.1	(0.68)	11.4	(0.86)	11.9	(0.78)	---	(†)
Communication systems and technology																
Provided telephones in most classrooms	44.6	(1.80)	60.8	(1.48)	66.9	(1.30)	71.6	(1.16)	74.0	(1.13)	78.7	(1.34)	79.3	(1.14)	---	(†)
Provided electronic notification system for schoolwide emergency	---	(†)	---	(†)	---	(†)	43.2	(1.26)	63.1	(1.40)	81.6	(1.12)	73.0	(1.35)	71.6	(1.17)
Provided structured anonymous threat reporting system[7]	---	(†)	---	(†)	---	(†)	31.2	(1.22)	35.9	(1.19)	46.5	(1.63)	43.9	(1.58)	49.3	(1.32)
Had silent alarms directly connected to law enforcement	---	(†)	---	(†)	---	(†)	---	(†)	---	(†)	---	(†)	27.1	(1.23)	29.1	(1.15)
Used security cameras to monitor the school	19.4	(0.88)	36.0	(1.28)	42.8	(1.29)	55.0	(1.37)	61.1	(1.16)	75.1	(1.31)	80.6	(0.96)	83.5	(1.09)
Provided two-way radios to any staff	---	(†)	71.2	(1.18)	70.9	(1.22)	73.1	(1.15)	73.3	(1.33)	74.2	(1.42)	73.3	(1.22)	77.8	(1.06)
Limited access to social networking sites from school computers	---	(†)	---	(†)	---	(†)	---	(†)	93.4	(0.59)	91.9	(0.80)	89.1	(0.88)	---	(†)
Prohibited non-academic use of cell phones or smartphones during school hours[8]	---	(†)	---	(†)	---	(†)	---	(†)	90.9	(0.67)	75.9	(1.07)	65.8	(1.36)	70.3	(1.30)

---Not available.

†Not applicable.

[1] Data for 2013-14 were collected using the Fast Response Survey System (FRSS), while data for all other years were collected using the School Survey on Crime and Safety (SSOCS). The 2013-14 FRSS survey was designed to allow comparisons with SSOCS data. However, all respondents to the 2013-14 survey could choose either to complete the survey on paper (and mail it back) or to complete the survey online, whereas all respondents to SSOCS had only the option of completing a paper survey prior to 2017-18, when SSOCS experimented with offering an online option to some respondents. The 2013-14 FRSS survey also relied on a smaller sample than SSOCS. The FRSS survey's smaller sample size and difference in survey administration may have impacted the 2013-14 results.

[2] Prior to 2017-18, the examples of controlled access to buildings included only "locked or monitored doors" and did not include loading docks.

[3] Prior to 2015-16, the questionnaire asked only if visitors were required "to sign or check in" and did not include the requirement to wear badges.

[4] In the 2017-18 questionnaire, a single item asked about drug testing "for students participating in athletics or other extracurricular activities." Prior to 2017-18, the questionnaire included one item about testing for athletes, followed by a separate item about testing for students in other extracurricular activities. For years prior to 2017-18, schools are included in this row if they answered "yes" to either or both of these items; each school is counted only once in this row, even if it answered "yes" to both items.

[5] The wording of this item was revised in 2015-16. Prior to 2015-16, the item asked whether students were required "to pass through metal detectors each day."

[6] The 2017-18 questionnaire included only a single item about random sweeps for contraband, and it provided locker checks and dog sniffs as examples of types of sweeps. Prior to 2017-18, the questionnaire included one item about dog sniffs for drugs, followed by a separate item about sweeps not including dog sniffs. For years prior to 2017-18, schools are included in this row if they answered "yes" to either or both of these items; each school is counted only once in this row, even if it answered "yes" to both items.

[7] For example, a system for reporting threats through online submission, telephone hotline, or written submission via drop box.

[8] Prior to 2017-18, the questionnaire asked about prohibiting the "use of cell phones and text messaging devices during school hours." It did not refer to "non-academic" use or "smartphones."

NOTE: Responses were provided by the principal or the person most knowledgeable about crime and safety issues at the school.

SOURCE: U.S. Department of Education, National Center for Education Statistics, 1999–2000, 2003–04, 2005–06, 2007–08, 2009–10, 2015–16, and 2017–18 School Survey on Crime and Safety (SSOCS), 2000, 2004, 2006, 2008, 2010, 2016, and 2018; and Fast Response Survey System (FRSS), "School Safety and Discipline: 2013-14," FRSS 106, 2014. (This table was prepared August 2019.)

Table 233.60. Percentage of public schools with various safety and security measures, by selected school characteristics: 2017-18

[Standard errors appear in parentheses]

School characteristic	Total schools		Percent of schools with safety and security measures										
			Controlled access		Student dress, IDs, and school supplies					Metal detectors and sweeps			
	Number	Percentage distribution	School buildings[1]	School grounds[2]	School uniforms required	Strict dress code enforced	Student badges or picture IDs required	Faculty/staff badges or picture IDs required	Book bags must be clear or are banned	Random metal detector checks on students	Daily metal detector checks on students	Random sweeps for contraband[3]	Used secu camera monitor sch
1	2	3	4	5	6	7	8	9	10	11	12	13	
Total	**82,300 (350)**	**100.0 (†)**	**95.4 (0.52)**	**50.8 (1.38)**	**19.8 (0.87)**	**48.8 (1.32)**	**9.2 (0.60)**	**69.9 (1.18)**	**3.5 (0.42)**	**4.9 (0.49)**	**2.2 (0.35)**	**27.4 (0.88)**	**83.5 (1.**
School level[4]													
Primary	48,300 (290)	58.7 (0.20)	97.5 (0.65)	55.2 (2.10)	22.9 (1.44)	42.6 (1.98)	6.0 (0.89)	75.6 (1.71)	1.8 ! (0.59)	1.5 ! (0.48)	‡ (†)	7.6 (1.12)	77.9 (1.7
Middle	15,100 (60)	18.4 (0.10)	94.7 (0.70)	45.2 (1.63)	18.0 (1.16)	61.6 (1.86)	13.2 (1.08)	69.3 (1.59)	8.0 (0.92)	7.0 (0.84)	2.5 (0.48)	49.8 (1.72)	91.5 (0.8
High school	12,600 (40)	15.3 (0.08)	91.4 (0.91)	46.3 (1.47)	10.4 (1.13)	55.9 (1.94)	17.6 (1.06)	63.5 (1.96)	5.4 (0.80)	13.2 (1.25)	7.3 (0.87)	65.2 (1.71)	93.6 (0.9
Combined	6,300 (180)	7.7 (0.20)	89.1 (3.66)	39.4 (4.68)	18.8 (3.06)	51.4 (5.35)	7.6 ! (2.50)	39.8 (5.08)	‡ (†)	8.8 ! (3.18)	‡ (†)	49.3 (5.94)	86.6 (4.1
Enrollment size													
Less than 300	16,800 (310)	20.4 (0.31)	93.6 (1.63)	48.2 (4.27)	15.8 (2.70)	41.3 (3.63)	4.3 (1.10)	49.5 (3.62)	‡ (†)	4.6 (1.15)	1.9 (0.50)	27.5 (2.65)	79.1 (3.4
300 to 499	24,900 (120)	30.3 (0.15)	95.4 (0.94)	47.8 (2.58)	19.8 (1.41)	47.3 (2.33)	7.5 (1.21)	72.2 (2.06)	3.0 (0.60)	3.4 (0.81)	2.3 (0.67)	19.8 (1.43)	84.1 (1.8
500 to 999	31,700 (70)	38.5 (0.17)	97.0 (0.57)	52.3 (1.80)	23.3 (1.71)	52.2 (1.86)	10.2 (1.15)	77.4 (1.69)	3.9 (0.58)	4.5 (0.76)	1.7 (0.46)	25.5 (1.21)	82.9 (1.5
1,000 or more	8,900 (20)	10.8 (0.04)	92.8 (0.99)	58.6 (1.84)	14.6 (1.46)	55.1 (1.96)	20.2 (1.77)	75.0 (1.63)	5.1 (1.11)	10.9 (1.22)	4.0 (0.64)	55.0 (1.81)	91.9 (1.3
Locale													
City	22,500 (170)	27.3 (0.20)	95.6 (0.90)	61.7 (2.62)	39.8 (2.22)	57.9 (2.51)	11.6 (1.44)	66.4 (1.93)	4.7 (0.73)	8.4 (0.98)	6.0 (1.06)	18.6 (1.22)	77.9 (2.5
Suburban	27,300 (150)	33.2 (0.16)	96.4 (0.72)	49.4 (2.38)	17.9 (1.56)	47.1 (2.02)	10.4 (0.92)	83.1 (1.60)	2.5 (0.65)	3.5 (0.73)	0.9 (0.25)	21.2 (0.96)	82.6 (1.7
Town	10,500 (150)	12.8 (0.16)	94.4 (1.20)	46.2 (3.74)	11.1 (2.28)	48.9 (3.50)	8.8 (1.70)	70.8 (3.25)	3.9 (1.03)	2.6 (0.65)	‡ (†)	37.9 (2.59)	87.8 (2.4
Rural	22,000 (210)	26.7 (0.20)	94.5 (1.24)	43.5 (2.78)	5.8 (1.03)	41.6 (2.92)	5.6 (0.93)	56.4 (2.55)	3.3 (0.74)	4.1 (0.90)	0.6 ! (0.28)	38.9 (2.61)	88.1 (2.1
Percent minority enrollment[5]													
0 to 25 percent	29,800 (930)	36.2 (1.10)	95.8 (0.97)	35.5 (1.84)	2.4 (0.66)	35.7 (1.78)	4.0 (0.76)	71.0 (2.26)	3.1 (0.60)	2.9 (0.69)	‡ (†)	35.2 (2.00)	88.7 (1.6
26 to 50 percent	18,000 (870)	21.9 (1.07)	96.3 (0.75)	52.8 (2.91)	11.2 (1.82)	48.7 (3.18)	7.5 (1.45)	76.5 (2.54)	2.7 (0.63)	1.6 (0.41)	‡ (†)	25.7 (1.93)	87.7 (1.9
51 to 75 percent	12,500 (850)	15.1 (1.02)	94.4 (1.05)	56.7 (2.88)	20.4 (2.61)	52.1 (3.10)	12.5 (2.00)	69.7 (3.58)	2.2 ! (0.66)	4.7 (0.96)	1.6 ! (0.65)	22.6 (2.25)	81.0 (3.1
76 to 100 percent	22,000 (800)	26.8 (0.99)	94.7 (1.07)	66.4 (2.49)	49.9 (2.75)	64.7 (2.54)	16.0 (1.70)	63.0 (2.43)	5.5 (0.98)	10.4 (1.40)	6.4 (1.05)	20.8 (1.54)	74.2 (2.4
Percent of students eligible for free or reduced-price lunch													
0 to 25 percent	15,000 (610)	18.2 (0.73)	94.3 (1.73)	38.9 (2.90)	3.4 ! (1.38)	32.3 (2.69)	4.8 (0.95)	78.5 (2.68)	1.5 ! (0.45)	0.5 ! (0.19)	‡ (†)	21.3 (1.75)	82.4 (2.2
26 to 50 percent	19,600 (870)	23.8 (1.05)	95.8 (0.93)	43.7 (2.71)	7.0 (1.14)	42.5 (2.29)	6.5 (1.27)	71.1 (2.33)	3.4 (0.68)	2.1 (0.43)	‡ (†)	35.3 (2.32)	88.9 (1.9
51 to 75 percent	20,600 (950)	25.1 (1.13)	96.1 (0.91)	46.2 (2.59)	13.2 (1.63)	51.6 (3.03)	9.5 (1.32)	70.1 (2.50)	2.1 (0.41)	5.6 (1.14)	1.7 ! (0.75)	30.5 (2.08)	86.1 (2.0
76 to 100 percent	27,100 (880)	32.9 (1.09)	95.1 (0.88)	66.0 (2.51)	43.1 (2.58)	60.4 (2.50)	13.5 (1.19)	63.9 (2.09)	5.8 (1.14)	8.7 (1.08)	5.0 (0.81)	22.6 (1.47)	78.1 (1.

†Not applicable.

!Interpret data with caution. The coefficient of variation (CV) for this estimate is between 30 and 50 percent.

‡Reporting standards not met. Either there are too few cases for a reliable estimate or the coefficient of variation (CV) is 50 percent or greater.

[1] Access to buildings is controlled during school hours (e.g., by locked or monitored doors, loading docks).

[2] Access to grounds is controlled during school hours (e.g., by locked or monitored gates).

[3] Examples of random sweeps include locker checks and dog sniffs. Examples of contraband include drugs and weapons.

[4] Primary schools are defined as schools in which the lowest grade is not higher than grade 3 and the highest grade is not higher than grade 8. Middle schools are defined as schools in which the lowest grade is not lower than grade 4 and the highest grade is not higher than grade 9. High schools are defined as schools in which the lowest grade is not lower than grade 9. Combined schools include all other combinations of grades, including K–12 schools.

[5] Percent combined enrollment of Black, Hispanic, Asian, Pacific Islander, and American Indian/Alaska Native students, and students of Two or more races.

NOTE: Responses were provided by the principal or the person most knowledgeable about crime and safety issues at the school. Detail may not sum to totals because of rounding.

SOURCE: U.S. Department of Education, National Center for Education Statistics, 2017–18 School Survey on Crime and Safety (SSOCS), 2018. (This table was prepared August 2019.)

Table 233.65. Percentage of public schools with a written plan for procedures to be performed in selected scenarios and percentage that have drilled students on the use of selected emergency procedures, by selected school characteristics: Selected years, 2003–04 through 2017–18

[Standard errors appear in parentheses]

Year and school characteristic	Percent with a written plan that describes procedures to be performed in selected scenarios																		Percent that have drilled students during the current school year on the use of selected emergency procedures					
	Active shooter[1]		Natural disasters[2]		Hostages		Bomb threats or incidents		Chemical, biological, or radiological threats or incidents[3]		Suicide threat or incident		Pandemic flu		Pandemic disease		Post-crisis reunification of students with their families		Evacuation[4]		Lockdown[5]		Shelter-in-place[6]	
1	2		3		4		5		6		7		8		9		10		11		12		13	
2003–04	78.5	(1.17)	96.0	(0.52)	73.5	(1.12)	94.0	(0.71)	69.2	(1.15)	---	(†)	---	(†)	---	(†)	---	(†)	---	(†)	---	(†)	---	(†)
2005–06	79.3	(1.31)	95.0	(0.65)	73.1	(1.12)	94.5	(0.65)	70.5	(1.04)	---	(†)	---	(†)	---	(†)	---	(†)	---	(†)	---	(†)	---	(†)
2007–08	83.0	(1.31)	95.8	(0.48)	71.3	(1.26)	93.8	(0.65)	71.5	(1.16)	74.1	(1.33)	36.1	(1.10)	---	(†)	---	(†)	---	(†)	---	(†)	---	(†)
2009–10	84.3	(1.10)	95.1	(0.54)	74.3	(1.20)	93.5	(0.66)	71.1	(1.28)	74.9	(1.30)	69.4	(1.34)	---	(†)	---	(†)	---	(†)	---	(†)	---	(†)
2015–16																								
All public schools	**92.4**	**(0.78)**	**96.1**	**(0.57)**	**60.5**	**(1.30)**	**94.1**	**(0.87)**	**73.1**	**(1.26)**	**84.6**	**(1.11)**	**51.0**	**(1.49)**	**---**	**(†)**	**86.3**	**(1.09)**	**91.5**	**(1.02)**	**94.6**	**(0.78)**	**75.9**	**(1.12)**
School level[7]																								
Primary	91.2	(1.22)	96.4	(0.86)	57.1	(2.07)	92.5	(1.36)	71.4	(1.84)	80.7	(1.76)	50.9	(2.26)	---	(†)	87.2	(1.39)	91.2	(1.60)	95.5	(0.95)	75.2	(1.56)
Middle	94.0	(0.94)	96.3	(0.79)	62.6	(1.73)	96.5	(0.87)	75.2	(1.78)	89.4	(1.06)	49.5	(1.91)	---	(†)	84.1	(1.49)	93.2	(0.96)	95.5	(0.86)	79.0	(1.91)
High school	95.3	(1.07)	95.5	(0.79)	67.3	(1.79)	97.3	(0.76)	77.2	(1.74)	91.3	(1.03)	50.9	(1.96)	---	(†)	87.2	(1.49)	91.5	(1.23)	94.1	(1.05)	80.8	(1.57)
Combined	91.6	(3.24)	93.5	(2.99)	68.4	(5.96)	94.5	(2.76)	73.1	(5.24)	89.8	(3.57)	55.2	(6.23)	---	(†)	82.6	(4.49)	89.8	(3.33)	86.2	(5.17)	63.0	(6.55)
Enrollment size																								
Less than 300	89.0	(2.48)	93.1	(1.82)	58.7	(3.55)	88.9	(2.74)	70.4	(2.97)	79.2	(2.94)	43.8	(3.73)	---	(†)	81.7	(2.76)	87.7	(2.93)	89.9	(2.47)	68.2	(3.47)
300 to 499	94.3	(1.28)	96.5	(1.01)	59.7	(2.97)	94.8	(1.31)	72.3	(3.05)	85.1	(2.16)	52.4	(3.44)	---	(†)	85.9	(2.14)	90.2	(2.13)	94.9	(1.51)	77.1	(2.23)
500 to 999	91.5	(1.39)	97.6	(0.74)	60.5	(2.18)	95.3	(1.06)	73.6	(1.90)	84.8	(1.54)	53.5	(2.05)	---	(†)	87.9	(1.57)	94.5	(1.04)	96.6	(0.78)	78.1	(1.70)
1,000 or more	96.9	(0.76)	95.3	(0.99)	67.1	(2.40)	98.9	(0.37)	79.6	(1.95)	93.8	(0.88)	52.7	(2.40)	---	(†)	90.7	(1.44)	92.3	(1.30)	96.8	(0.78)	80.2	(1.92)
Locale																								
City	91.3	(1.76)	96.6	(1.03)	63.3	(2.93)	93.6	(1.83)	74.9	(2.27)	85.4	(2.72)	50.5	(2.68)	---	(†)	90.0	(1.82)	94.0	(1.37)	95.9	(1.26)	80.5	(2.27)
Suburban	92.3	(1.25)	95.5	(1.00)	57.3	(2.56)	94.9	(1.29)	71.2	(2.22)	85.8	(1.53)	52.0	(2.42)	---	(†)	85.1	(1.82)	91.0	(1.46)	96.7	(0.89)	79.1	(1.72)
Town	94.4	(1.92)	96.6	(1.48)	54.5	(3.87)	96.2	(1.55)	75.2	(3.43)	82.0	(3.47)	48.0	(3.94)	---	(†)	84.2	(3.11)	91.7	(2.20)	97.6	(0.83)	66.8	(3.71)
Rural	92.6	(1.71)	95.9	(1.23)	64.7	(2.84)	92.8	(1.79)	72.7	(2.45)	83.6	(2.38)	51.6	(2.87)	---	(†)	84.9	(2.17)	89.5	(1.60)	89.5	(1.85)	71.7	(2.63)
Percent minority enrollment[8]																								
0 to 25 percent	93.7	(1.14)	96.3	(0.89)	58.4	(2.12)	94.1	(1.36)	71.8	(2.08)	86.3	(1.71)	52.7	(2.20)	---	(†)	85.4	(1.82)	89.2	(1.62)	93.3	(1.34)	75.9	(2.46)
26 to 50 percent	93.6	(1.63)	96.0	(1.48)	57.5	(3.36)	92.7	(2.16)	71.9	(2.82)	81.7	(2.61)	52.0	(3.30)	---	(†)	86.0	(2.26)	92.0	(2.22)	98.1	(0.54)	76.7	(2.73)
51 to 75 percent	92.9	(1.98)	96.9	(0.99)	64.7	(3.80)	96.5	(1.62)	75.2	(3.18)	82.8	(3.00)	47.7	(3.72)	---	(†)	88.1	(1.97)	93.3	(1.75)	94.7	(1.93)	79.6	(3.12)
76 to 100 percent	89.2	(2.09)	95.1	(1.11)	63.6	(3.07)	93.8	(1.50)	74.8	(2.73)	85.7	(2.41)	49.6	(2.87)	---	(†)	86.6	(2.30)	93.5	(1.68)	93.8	(1.65)	72.8	(2.64)
Percent of students eligible for free or reduced-price lunch																								
0 to 25 percent	96.1	(1.30)	96.0	(1.38)	53.0	(3.49)	95.0	(1.60)	70.6	(3.64)	87.4	(2.37)	52.9	(4.16)	---	(†)	85.0	(2.91)	91.5	(1.96)	95.8	(1.97)	79.4	(2.60)
26 to 50 percent	93.4	(1.45)	96.2	(1.04)	63.8	(2.73)	93.8	(1.80)	76.4	(2.37)	86.6	(2.26)	56.8	(2.82)	---	(†)	87.3	(1.92)	89.5	(1.95)	95.3	(1.17)	77.5	(2.48)
51 to 75 percent	92.2	(1.49)	95.8	(1.16)	60.8	(2.56)	94.4	(1.33)	71.4	(2.18)	80.8	(2.06)	48.2	(2.27)	---	(†)	86.5	(1.69)	92.0	(1.72)	94.6	(1.31)	74.5	(2.67)
76 to 100 percent	89.3	(2.04)	96.2	(1.02)	61.5	(3.07)	93.7	(1.47)	73.1	(2.81)	84.9	(2.59)	46.7	(3.35)	---	(†)	85.8	(2.35)	93.1	(1.50)	93.4	(1.48)	73.6	(2.36)
2017–18																								
All public schools	**92.4**	**(0.73)**	**94.0**	**(0.57)**	**48.0**	**(1.38)**	**91.3**	**(0.72)**	**69.7**	**(1.44)**	**85.4**	**(1.06)**	**---**	**(†)**	**45.7**	**(1.34)**	**85.0**	**(0.89)**	**92.8**	**(0.71)**	**95.7**	**(0.53)**	**82.6**	**(1.14)**
School level[7]																								
Primary	92.5	(1.16)	95.0	(0.80)	46.2	(1.99)	89.7	(1.12)	70.1	(2.17)	82.8	(1.78)	---	(†)	45.0	(1.83)	86.2	(1.38)	92.8	(1.13)	96.5	(0.71)	83.4	(1.57)
Middle	92.5	(0.96)	94.0	(0.79)	49.4	(1.50)	93.7	(0.78)	69.6	(1.37)	89.1	(1.06)	---	(†)	44.9	(1.74)	84.7	(1.36)	92.6	(0.89)	96.9	(0.56)	83.2	(1.17)
High school	93.0	(1.02)	92.5	(0.96)	51.4	(1.62)	94.7	(0.84)	71.9	(1.63)	92.1	(1.18)	---	(†)	50.1	(1.93)	83.5	(1.33)	94.0	(0.73)	95.6	(0.75)	83.8	(1.27)
Combined	90.6	(3.43)	89.7	(3.29)	50.9	(5.81)	90.5	(3.59)	62.7	(5.94)	82.6	(4.39)	---	(†)	44.7	(5.68)	79.3	(4.16)	90.6	(3.50)	86.8	(4.00)	72.8	(4.55)
Enrollment size																								
Less than 300	88.3	(2.41)	93.6	(1.64)	43.2	(4.15)	92.3	(1.87)	66.3	(3.92)	79.0	(2.93)	---	(†)	37.6	(3.65)	79.7	(3.16)	93.0	(1.99)	93.6	(1.72)	79.5	(3.45)
300 to 499	92.3	(1.42)	94.3	(1.14)	48.6	(2.42)	88.9	(1.60)	68.9	(2.41)	83.9	(1.80)	---	(†)	47.5	(2.51)	85.4	(1.52)	92.9	(1.24)	95.3	(1.08)	82.0	(1.87)
500 to 999	94.3	(0.87)	93.8	(0.89)	49.9	(2.17)	91.3	(1.11)	71.2	(1.41)	87.4	(1.27)	---	(†)	47.7	(2.02)	86.8	(1.37)	92.0	(1.15)	96.2	(0.73)	84.0	(1.49)
1,000 or more	94.1	(1.08)	95.0	(0.82)	48.3	(2.13)	96.2	(0.60)	73.2	(1.94)	94.5	(0.86)	---	(†)	49.3	(2.14)	87.6	(1.33)	95.0	(0.82)	98.7	(0.42)	85.3	(1.68)
Locale																								
City	91.7	(1.56)	93.4	(0.95)	45.2	(2.11)	89.8	(1.48)	68.4	(2.52)	86.4	(1.95)	---	(†)	44.6	(2.09)	85.3	(2.02)	94.2	(1.37)	96.3	(1.17)	84.0	(1.79)
Suburban	93.3	(1.02)	92.7	(1.06)	45.3	(2.04)	91.8	(1.09)	69.9	(1.97)	86.6	(1.41)	---	(†)	46.1	(2.59)	84.9	(1.33)	93.9	(1.06)	97.0	(0.83)	86.6	(1.45)
Town	92.5	(1.69)	97.7	(0.94)	53.0	(3.26)	91.4	(1.94)	70.5	(3.28)	83.9	(2.66)	---	(†)	45.1	(4.00)	85.3	(2.15)	91.2	(2.27)	94.0	(1.76)	82.4	(2.11)
Rural	92.1	(1.61)	94.7	(1.27)	51.7	(2.94)	92.1	(1.36)	70.4	(2.72)	83.6	(2.09)	---	(†)	46.7	(2.40)	84.6	(2.28)	90.8	(1.53)	94.2	(1.12)	76.4	(2.74)
Percent minority enrollment[8]																								
0 to 25 percent	93.5	(1.24)	94.5	(1.05)	50.0	(2.62)	93.4	(1.08)	71.1	(2.52)	86.0	(1.51)	---	(†)	45.8	(2.15)	84.4	(1.63)	91.7	(1.02)	95.6	(0.71)	83.7	(1.91)
26 to 50 percent	93.5	(1.28)	94.4	(1.34)	49.2	(3.08)	91.7	(1.61)	72.9	(2.70)	86.3	(2.10)	---	(†)	49.9	(2.78)	88.7	(1.61)	93.7	(1.80)	96.7	(0.97)	83.3	(2.23)
51 to 75 percent	91.4	(1.85)	95.1	(1.39)	43.5	(3.81)	88.3	(1.96)	65.9	(3.25)	83.9	(2.63)	---	(†)	39.6	(3.34)	85.0	(2.53)	92.1	(2.22)	95.4	(2.14)	80.2	(2.58)
76 to 100 percent	90.7	(1.29)	92.5	(1.27)	46.7	(2.32)	89.7	(1.68)	67.4	(2.58)	84.7	(2.15)	---	(†)	45.7	(2.51)	82.7	(2.11)	93.9	(1.33)	95.0	(1.26)	81.9	(2.19)
Percent of students eligible for free or reduced-price lunch																								
0 to 25 percent	92.1	(1.84)	93.5	(1.26)	50.9	(3.09)	90.2	(2.04)	72.3	(2.60)	87.9	(2.08)	---	(†)	45.7	(3.05)	84.4	(2.13)	94.9	(1.02)	96.4	(1.18)	87.2	(2.15)
26 to 50 percent	93.4	(1.33)	94.0	(1.37)	46.0	(2.58)	94.0	(1.12)	75.0	(2.60)	86.3	(2.10)	---	(†)	48.4	(3.46)	86.6	(1.55)	91.1	(1.66)	95.7	(0.81)	83.0	(2.14)
51 to 75 percent	92.6	(1.52)	94.5	(1.29)	46.3	(2.63)	92.1	(1.32)	68.1	(3.15)	85.2	(2.07)	---	(†)	44.2	(2.75)	86.1	(1.82)	92.4	(1.47)	95.6	(1.30)	81.3	(2.10)
76 to 100 percent	91.8	(1.13)	94.0	(0.83)	49.0	(2.55)	89.3	(1.52)	65.7	(2.29)	83.6	(1.96)	---	(†)	45.0	(2.47)	83.3	(1.79)	93.1	(1.18)	95.3	(1.21)	80.8	(2.15)

—Not available.

†Not applicable.

[1] Prior to 2015-16, this scenario was described in the questionnaire as "shootings."

[2] For example, earthquakes or tornadoes.

[3] For example, release of mustard gas, anthrax, smallpox, or radioactive materials.

[4] Defined for respondents as "a procedure that requires all students and staff to leave the building. While evacuating to the school's field makes sense for a fire drill that only lasts a few minutes, it may not be an appropriate location for a longer period of time. The evacuation plan should encompass relocation procedures and include backup buildings to serve as emergency shelters, such as nearby community centers, religious institutions, businesses, or other schools. Evacuation also includes 'reverse evacuation,' a procedure for schools to return students to the building quickly if an incident occurs while students are outside."

[5] Defined for respondents as "a procedure that involves occupants of a school building being directed to remain confined to a room or area within a building with specific procedures to follow. A lockdown may be used when a crisis occurs outside of the school and an evacuation would be dangerous. A lockdown may also be called for when there is a crisis inside and movement within the school will put students in jeopardy. All exterior doors are locked and students and staff stay in their classrooms."

[6] Defined for respondents as "a procedure similar to a lockdown in that the occupants are to remain on the premises; however, shelter-in-place is designed to use a facility and its indoor atmosphere to temporarily separate people from a hazardous outdoor environment. Everyone would be brought indoors and building personnel would close all windows and doors and shut down the heating, ventilation, and air conditioning system (HVAC). This would create a neutral pressure in the building, meaning the contaminated air would not be drawn into the building."

[7] Primary schools are defined as schools in which the lowest grade is not higher than grade 3 and the highest grade is not higher than grade 8. Middle schools are defined as schools in which the lowest grade is not lower than grade 4 and the highest grade is not higher than grade 9. High schools are defined as schools in which the lowest grade is not lower than grade 9. Combined schools include all other combinations of grades, including K–12 schools.

[8] Percent combined enrollment of Black, Hispanic, Asian, Pacific Islander, and American Indian/Alaska Native students, and students of Two or more races.

NOTE: Responses were provided by the principal or the person most knowledgeable about crime and safety issues at the school.

SOURCE: U.S. Department of Education, National Center for Education Statistics, 2003–04, 2005–06, 2007–08, 2009–10, 2015-16, and 2017-18 School Survey on Crime and Safety (SSOCS), 2004, 2006, 2008, 2010, 2016, and 2018. (This table was prepared August 2019.)

Table 233.67a. Percentage of public schools providing training for classroom teachers or aides in specific safety and discipline topics, by safety and discipline training topic: Selected years, 2003-04 through 2015-16

[Standard errors appear in parentheses]

Safety and discipline training topic	2003-04		2005-06		2007-08		2009-10		2013-14[1]		2015-16	
1		2		3		4		5		6		7
Classroom management for teachers	72.3	(1.14)	80.7	(1.03)	81.5	(1.20)	79.7	(1.07)	77.7	(1.34)	83.8	(1.23)
Safety procedures	87.8	(0.92)	90.7	(0.61)	88.7	(1.01)	88.2	(0.76)	94.8	(0.73)	93.4	(0.87)
Schoolwide discipline policies and practices related to												
Bullying[2,3]	—	(†)	—	(†)	—	(†)	—	(†)	89.1	(1.09)	—	(†)
Cyberbullying[4]	—	(†)	—	(†)	—	(†)	—	(†)	—	(†)	67.5	(1.24)
Bullying[3] other than cyberbullying[4]	—	(†)	—	(†)	—	(†)	—	(†)	—	(†)	78.7	(1.11)
Violence,[5] alcohol, and/or drug use[6]	67.5	(1.15)	72.1	(1.32)	65.6	(1.31)	—	(†)	—	(†)	—	(†)
Violence[5,7]	—	(†)	—	(†)	—	(†)	61.9	(1.26)	66.7	(1.47)	68.8	(1.40)
Alcohol and/or drug use[7]	—	(†)	—	(†)	—	(†)	44.4	(1.36)	46.5	(1.34)	41.6	(1.21)
Recognizing												
Early warning signs of students likely to exhibit violent behavior	44.8	(1.31)	50.8	(1.27)	47.9	(1.37)	45.7	(1.02)	48.1	(1.42)	47.8	(1.45)
Physical, social, and verbal bullying[3] behaviors	—	(†)	—	(†)	—	(†)	—	(†)	78.8	(1.26)	75.5	(1.21)
Signs of students using/abusing alcohol and/or drugs	39.9	(1.27)	46.4	(1.08)	36.1	(1.45)	34.7	(1.34)	34.3	(1.38)	29.7	(1.08)
Intervention and referral strategies for students with signs of mental health disorders[8]	—	(†)	—	(†)	—	(†)	—	(†)	—	(†)	53.4	(1.50)
Positive behavioral intervention strategies	76.2	(1.12)	83.0	(1.03)	79.0	(1.09)	79.4	(1.00)	81.0	(1.22)	82.1	(0.91)
Crisis prevention and intervention	—	(†)	—	(†)	—	(†)	66.6	(1.25)	74.3	(1.32)	71.2	(1.11)

—Not available.

†Not applicable.

[1] Data for 2013-14 were collected using the Fast Response Survey System (FRSS), while data for all other years were collected using the School Survey on Crime and Safety (SSOCS). The 2013-14 FRSS survey was designed to allow comparisons with SSOCS data. However, respondents to the 2013-14 survey could choose either to complete the survey on paper (and mail it back) or to complete the survey online, whereas respondents to SSOCS did not have the option of completing the survey online. The 2013-14 survey also relied on a smaller sample. The smaller sample size and difference in survey administration may have impacted the 2013-14 results.

[2] In 2013-14, a single item on the questionnaire asked about training in policies and practices "related to bullying" and did not specifically include "cyberbullying."

[3] In survey years prior to 2015-16, bullying was not defined for respondents. The 2015-16 questionnaire defined bullying as "any unwanted aggressive behavior(s) by another youth or group of youths who are not siblings or current dating partners that involves an observed or perceived power imbalance and is repeated multiple times or is highly likely to be repeated."

[4] The 2015-16 questionnaire included one item on cyberbullying and a separate item on "bullying other than cyberbullying." The questionnaire defined cyberbullying as occurring "when willful and repeated harm is inflicted through the use of computers, cell phones, or other electronic devices."

[5] In all survey years included in this table, the questionnaire defined violence as "actual, attempted, or threatened fight or assault."

[6] In 2007-08 and earlier survey years, a single item on the questionnaire asked about "violence, alcohol, and/or drug use."

[7] In 2009-10 and later years, the questionnaire included one item that asked about violence and a separate item that asked about alcohol and/or drug use.

[8] This item, which was included only on the 2015-16 questionnaire, provided the following examples of mental health disorders: depression, mood disorders, and ADHD. The questionnaire defined mental health disorders as "collectively, all diagnosable mental health disorders or health conditions that are characterized by alterations in thinking, mood, or behavior (or some combination thereof) associated with distress and/or impaired functioning."

NOTE: Responses were provided by the principal or the person most knowledgeable about crime and safety issues at the school.

SOURCE: U.S. Department of Education, National Center for Education Statistics, 2003-04, 2005-06, 2007-08, 2009-10, and 2015-16 School Survey on Crime and Safety (SSOCS), 2004, 2006, 2008, 2010, and 2016; and Fast Response Survey System (FRSS), "School Safety and Discipline: 2013-14," FRSS 106, 2014. (This table was prepared September 2017.)

Table 233.67b. Percentage of public schools providing training for classroom teachers or aides in specific safety and discipline topics, by safety and discipline training topic and selected school characteristics: 2017-18

[Standard errors appear in parentheses]

School characteristic	Safety and discipline training topic												
			Schoolwide discipline policies and practices related to				Recognizing				Intervention and referral strategies for students displaying signs of mental health disorders[4]	Positive behavioral intervention strategies	Cr prevent … a … intervent
	Classroom management for teachers	Safety procedures	Cyberbullying[1]	Bullying[2] other than cyberbullying	Violence[3]	Alcohol and/or drug use	Early warning signs of student violent behavior	Physical, social, and verbal bullying[2] behaviors	Signs of self-harm or suicidal tendencies	Signs of students using/abusing alcohol and/or drugs			
1	2	3	4	5	6	7	8	9	10	11	12	13	
Total	**86.8 (0.94)**	**94.8 (0.64)**	**70.1 (1.48)**	**82.5 (1.20)**	**74.7 (1.08)**	**48.3 (1.26)**	**52.1 (1.25)**	**76.1 (1.17)**	**66.9 (0.98)**	**38.5 (1.43)**	**59.6 (1.39)**	**84.3 (0.98)**	**73.4 (1.(**
School level[5]													
Primary	87.7 (1.28)	94.9 (0.84)	67.4 (2.20)	83.5 (1.66)	73.4 (1.63)	41.7 (1.97)	51.1 (1.89)	76.4 (1.51)	63.0 (1.46)	32.4 (2.05)	58.6 (1.86)	89.0 (1.31)	73.7 (1.
Middle	86.4 (0.94)	96.2 (0.59)	77.0 (1.20)	84.6 (1.07)	76.4 (1.29)	53.4 (1.45)	50.1 (1.50)	79.1 (1.28)	74.6 (1.45)	42.1 (1.59)	62.8 (1.53)	82.8 (1.36)	73.9 (1.
High school	85.0 (1.31)	95.5 (0.89)	74.1 (1.45)	80.4 (1.26)	77.5 (1.47)	64.3 (1.54)	58.5 (1.71)	75.3 (1.36)	76.3 (1.64)	53.4 (1.86)	63.1 (1.77)	76.1 (1.75)	74.3 (1.
Combined	83.8 (3.85)	88.4 (3.82)	66.4 (5.66)	73.8 (4.70)	74.3 (4.79)	54.3 (5.56)	51.2 (5.79)	68.4 (5.09)	59.0 (5.79)	46.8 (6.03)	52.2 (6.14)	68.1 (5.14)	68.5 (4.
Enrollment size													
Less than 300	81.7 (2.87)	92.5 (2.12)	68.4 (3.58)	80.8 (3.05)	73.8 (2.98)	53.3 (3.99)	49.1 (3.70)	73.2 (3.04)	67.0 (3.19)	44.5 (4.15)	55.7 (3.68)	80.4 (3.06)	73.5 (3.
300 to 499	84.3 (1.65)	93.4 (1.38)	65.6 (2.49)	79.7 (1.94)	71.2 (2.21)	40.7 (2.45)	51.9 (2.09)	75.4 (2.17)	62.1 (2.21)	30.8 (2.22)	57.0 (2.43)	84.7 (1.68)	69.9 (2.
500 to 999	90.4 (1.03)	96.3 (0.65)	72.3 (1.67)	84.8 (1.26)	76.8 (1.53)	46.8 (1.67)	53.1 (1.88)	77.6 (1.43)	67.7 (1.42)	37.0 (1.64)	61.4 (1.67)	86.5 (1.08)	75.3 (1.
1,000 or more	90.7 (1.00)	97.6 (0.57)	78.1 (1.95)	84.9 (1.33)	78.4 (1.77)	65.5 (1.71)	54.3 (1.48)	78.3 (1.72)	77.1 (1.51)	54.1 (1.96)	67.3 (1.84)	83.0 (1.46)	76.6 (1.
Locale													
City	94.0 (1.03)	95.6 (1.12)	75.7 (2.58)	86.4 (1.93)	81.8 (1.78)	49.3 (2.39)	54.7 (2.48)	80.1 (2.33)	71.2 (2.26)	40.4 (2.56)	64.5 (2.83)	92.1 (1.10)	76.5 (1.
Suburban	85.4 (1.58)	95.3 (0.88)	70.9 (2.07)	84.4 (1.62)	74.0 (2.00)	48.5 (2.46)	52.6 (2.22)	79.3 (1.83)	67.0 (1.76)	38.2 (1.90)	61.3 (2.30)	85.3 (1.53)	73.9 (1.
Town	85.2 (2.45)	94.0 (1.64)	69.6 (2.95)	82.4 (2.78)	71.8 (2.91)	46.0 (3.03)	54.7 (2.99)	74.8 (3.13)	67.5 (3.23)	37.9 (3.35)	60.4 (2.97)	84.2 (2.15)	74.8 (3.
Rural	81.8 (2.24)	93.6 (1.40)	63.7 (3.20)	76.0 (2.57)	69.5 (2.36)	48.0 (2.67)	47.5 (2.74)	68.7 (2.64)	62.0 (2.67)	37.3 (2.90)	52.0 (3.09)	75.1 (2.35)	69.2 (2.
Percent minority enrollment[6]													
0 to 25 percent	80.7 (2.05)	94.0 (1.17)	64.3 (2.38)	77.3 (2.08)	69.5 (2.34)	45.1 (2.17)	50.3 (1.86)	70.6 (2.31)	63.5 (2.21)	37.5 (2.36)	56.2 (2.37)	76.2 (2.17)	70.6 (2.
26 to 50 percent	89.4 (1.96)	97.3 (0.80)	71.9 (3.00)	86.7 (2.02)	79.2 (1.77)	49.5 (2.88)	53.0 (3.15)	80.4 (2.43)	68.2 (2.56)	35.5 (2.52)	59.4 (3.62)	88.7 (1.41)	79.4 (2.
51 to 75 percent	90.0 (2.18)	96.1 (1.55)	71.3 (2.84)	84.3 (2.65)	75.4 (2.91)	43.8 (2.93)	53.3 (3.52)	78.0 (2.82)	69.5 (2.95)	37.8 (3.82)	62.5 (3.26)	88.4 (1.75)	75.3 (2.
76 to 100 percent	90.9 (1.61)	93.0 (1.29)	75.9 (2.72)	84.9 (2.26)	77.6 (1.87)	54.1 (2.38)	53.0 (2.70)	78.9 (2.34)	68.9 (2.21)	42.7 (2.27)	62.6 (2.72)	89.3 (1.57)	71.4 (2.
Percent of students eligible for free or reduced-price lunch													
0 to 25 percent	81.1 (2.40)	94.5 (1.41)	66.9 (2.97)	80.4 (2.53)	69.7 (3.36)	42.0 (2.99)	47.5 (2.82)	72.7 (2.99)	63.0 (2.95)	34.6 (2.64)	58.2 (2.90)	81.1 (2.28)	69.9 (2.
26 to 50 percent	84.2 (1.97)	95.0 (1.13)	68.0 (2.66)	82.3 (2.01)	73.5 (2.42)	45.6 (2.37)	49.2 (2.63)	76.4 (2.50)	67.8 (2.62)	38.4 (2.10)	59.0 (2.49)	79.1 (2.46)	73.2 (2.
51 to 75 percent	86.7 (1.84)	94.4 (1.43)	68.8 (2.35)	82.1 (2.21)	73.4 (2.96)	46.9 (2.42)	51.1 (3.10)	75.4 (2.73)	65.9 (2.50)	34.4 (2.47)	54.8 (2.93)	83.9 (2.18)	74.2 (2.
76 to 100 percent	91.8 (1.23)	95.0 (0.92)	74.5 (2.29)	84.0 (1.92)	79.2 (1.77)	54.8 (2.19)	57.4 (2.25)	78.3 (1.93)	69.2 (1.82)	43.8 (2.59)	64.3 (2.15)	90.2 (1.20)	75.0 (1.

[1] The questionnaire defined cyberbullying as "bullying that occurs when willful and repeated harm is inflicted through the use of computers, cell phones, or other electronic devices."

[2] The questionnaire defined bullying as "any unwanted aggressive behavior(s) by another youth or group of youths that involves an observed or perceived power imbalance and is repeated multiple times or is highly likely to be repeated. Bullying occurs among youth who are not siblings or current dating partners."

[3] The questionnaire defined violence as "actual, attempted, or threatened fight or assault."

[4] This item on the questionnaire provided the following examples of mental health disorders: depression, mood disorders, and ADHD. The questionnaire defined mental health disorders as "collectively, all diagnosable mental health disorders or health conditions that are characterized by alterations in thinking, mood, or behavior (or some combination thereof) associated with distress and/or impaired functioning."

[5] Primary schools are defined as schools in which the lowest grade is not higher than grade 3 and the highest grade is not higher than grade 8. Middle schools are defined as schools in which the lowest grade is not lower than grade 4 and the highest grade is not higher than grade 9. High schools are defined as schools in which the lowest grade is not lower than grade 9. Combined schools include all other combinations of grades, including K–12 schools.

[6] Percent combined enrollment of Black, Hispanic, Asian, Pacific Islander, and American Indian/Alaska Native students, and students of Two or more races.

NOTE: Includes trainings provided by the school or school district. Responses were provided by the principal or the person most knowledgeable about crime and safety issues at the school.

SOURCE: U.S. Department of Education, National Center for Education Statistics, 2017-18 School Survey on Crime and Safety (SSOCS), 2018. (This table was prepared August 2019.)

Table 233.70. Percentage of public schools with security staff present at least once a week, and percentage with security staff routinely carrying a firearm, by selected school characteristics: 2005–06 through 2017-18

[Standard errors appear in parentheses]

School characteristic	Percent with one or more security staff[1]												Percent with any security staff routinely carrying a firearm[2]						Percent with sworn law enforcement officers routinely carrying a firearm[2]			
	2005–06		2007–08		2009–10		2013-14[3]		2015-16		2017-18		2005–06		2007–08		2009–10		2015-16		2017–18	
1	2		3		4		5		6		7		8		9		10		11		12	
All public schools	**41.7**	**(1.28)**	**46.3**	**(1.29)**	**42.8**	**(1.07)**	**43.0**	**(1.48)**	**56.5**	**(1.29)**	**61.4**	**(1.27)**	**30.7**	**(1.10)**	**34.1**	**(1.11)**	**28.0**	**(0.97)**	**42.9**	**(1.50)**	**46.7**	**(1.06)**
School level[4]																						
Primary	26.2	(1.87)	33.1	(2.04)	27.7	(1.50)	28.6	(2.15)	45.4	(1.95)	51.4	(2.00)	15.7	(1.55)	20.1	(1.68)	12.5	(1.25)	30.6	(2.35)	36.0	(1.68)
Middle	63.7	(1.30)	65.5	(1.59)	66.4	(1.45)	63.3	(2.15)	73.4	(1.65)	80.0	(1.32)	51.8	(1.32)	54.2	(1.92)	51.0	(1.84)	60.0	(1.52)	67.6	(1.68)
High school/combined	62.9	(2.65)	65.5	(2.02)	62.8	(1.74)	64.1	(2.44)	71.3	(2.19)	72.3	(1.67)	51.8	(2.39)	54.9	(1.90)	50.1	(1.80)	60.7	(1.96)	57.1	(1.78)
High school	75.2	(1.66)	79.6	(1.47)	76.4	(1.45)	---	(†)	81.0	(1.40)	84.3	(1.11)	64.0	(1.71)	67.5	(1.51)	63.3	(1.75)	70.9	(1.55)	72.0	(1.55)
Combined	43.5	(5.25)	39.9	(5.59)	36.6	(4.89)	---	(†)	51.2	(5.86)	48.4	(4.86)	32.4	(4.50)	32.1	(4.89)	24.6	(4.26)	39.7	(5.34)	27.5	(4.17)
Enrollment size																						
Less than 300	22.7	(2.65)	27.6	(2.55)	25.6	(2.91)	21.7	(3.05)	34.8	(3.61)	44.7	(3.28)	16.2	(2.17)	16.1	(2.39)	13.5	(2.16)	26.8	(3.38)	34.4	(3.30)
300 to 499	29.8	(2.29)	36.1	(2.66)	33.5	(2.26)	35.4	(2.90)	49.9	(2.66)	51.5	(2.49)	20.5	(1.83)	26.7	(2.37)	19.8	(1.84)	37.8	(2.70)	36.0	(2.06)
500 to 999	50.5	(1.90)	52.7	(1.99)	47.3	(1.60)	50.6	(2.37)	64.6	(1.99)	69.0	(1.62)	36.9	(1.67)	39.5	(1.98)	30.3	(1.42)	46.0	(2.16)	52.4	(1.77)
1,000 or more	86.9	(1.39)	90.6	(1.59)	90.0	(1.37)	87.2	(2.27)	91.4	(1.73)	94.3	(0.97)	70.3	(1.67)	73.5	(1.62)	74.6	(1.75)	80.5	(1.65)	79.4	(1.63)
Locale																						
City	49.1	(2.57)	57.3	(3.05)	50.9	(2.51)	45.5	(3.13)	61.9	(2.87)	63.3	(2.48)	30.5	(1.73)	33.1	(2.32)	27.6	(1.98)	36.0	(2.89)	36.0	(1.76)
Suburban	42.7	(1.67)	45.4	(2.08)	45.4	(1.90)	47.7	(2.70)	57.9	(2.30)	63.3	(1.78)	32.2	(1.51)	33.7	(1.94)	29.6	(1.45)	44.6	(2.28)	51.0	(1.89)
Town	44.4	(3.86)	51.1	(3.50)	39.0	(3.11)	48.0	(4.08)	62.0	(3.55)	68.9	(3.46)	38.1	(3.62)	45.0	(3.54)	31.6	(2.81)	56.5	(3.56)	59.4	(3.82)
Rural	33.8	(1.87)	36.0	(1.98)	35.2	(2.20)	35.5	(2.33)	46.7	(2.54)	53.7	(3.02)	27.1	(1.84)	30.5	(2.05)	25.3	(1.78)	41.3	(2.48)	46.1	(2.58)
Percent minority enrollment[5]																						
0 to 25 percent	34.9	(1.53)	40.7	(1.55)	35.0	(1.98)	---	(†)	51.1	(2.36)	58.3	(2.34)	27.6	(1.33)	34.3	(1.54)	25.9	(1.56)	45.6	(2.31)	52.5	(2.06)
26 to 50 percent	42.4	(2.64)	44.9	(3.16)	42.8	(2.21)	---	(†)	51.6	(2.83)	59.2	(2.81)	36.7	(2.29)	38.2	(3.01)	32.1	(2.25)	43.3	(3.04)	47.4	(2.81)
51 to 75 percent	47.5	(4.20)	44.8	(4.35)	49.5	(3.17)	---	(†)	62.9	(3.61)	61.5	(4.04)	34.3	(3.12)	31.7	(3.07)	33.4	(2.97)	47.3	(3.29)	48.1	(3.87)
76 to 100 percent	53.9	(3.12)	62.3	(3.14)	54.5	(2.89)	---	(†)	64.5	(2.88)	67.4	(2.36)	28.5	(2.53)	31.6	(2.56)	26.1	(2.00)	35.8	(2.79)	37.4	(2.05)
Percent of students eligible for free or reduced-price lunch[6]																						
0 to 25 percent	37.9	(2.14)	46.5	(2.33)	39.2	(2.44)	41.6	(3.81)	52.9	(3.77)	53.6	(2.69)	30.3	(1.95)	34.8	(2.12)	27.2	(1.93)	42.5	(3.25)	44.1	(2.78)
26 to 50 percent	42.1	(2.08)	40.8	(2.52)	40.0	(1.68)	39.6	(3.10)	50.8	(2.89)	64.7	(2.69)	33.8	(1.78)	35.2	(2.02)	30.3	(1.59)	41.3	(2.61)	55.4	(2.95)
51 to 75 percent	39.3	(2.21)	46.1	(2.83)	42.3	(2.60)	44.4	(2.71)	58.7	(2.47)	61.6	(2.96)	31.8	(2.05)	35.8	(2.77)	27.4	(2.07)	49.0	(2.76)	51.3	(2.89)
76 to 100 percent	49.8	(2.73)	55.0	(3.68)	49.8	(2.76)	45.8	(3.24)	62.2	(2.62)	63.4	(2.01)	25.6	(2.17)	29.7	(2.68)	26.8	(2.32)	38.9	(3.04)	38.2	(1.79)

—Not available.

†Not applicable.

[1] Security staff include security guards, security personnel, School Resource Officers (SROs), and sworn law enforcement officers who are not SROs. "Security guards" and "security personnel" do not include law enforcement. SROs include all career law enforcement officers with arrest authority who have specialized training and are assigned to work in collaboration with school organizations.

[2] Prior to 2015-16, the School Survey on Crime and Safety (SSOCS) questionnaire asked respondents whether any of the security guards, security personnel, or sworn law enforcement officers at their school routinely carried a firearm. In 2015-16 and 2017-18, the SSOCS questionnaire asked respondents only whether any of the sworn law enforcement officers (including SROs) at their school routinely carried a firearm; therefore, direct comparisons with earlier years should be avoided. Data on security staff routinely carrying a firearm were not collected in the 2013-14 Fast Response Survey System (FRSS).

[3] Data for 2013-14 were collected using the Fast Response Survey System (FRSS), while data for all other years were collected using the School Survey on Crime and Safety (SSOCS). The 2013-14 FRSS survey was designed to allow comparisons with SSOCS data. However, all respondents to the 2013-14 survey could choose either to complete the survey on paper (and mail it back) or to complete the survey online, whereas all respondents to SSOCS had only the option of completing a paper survey prior to 2017-18, when SSOCS experimented with offering an online option to some respondents. The 2013-14 FRSS survey also relied on a smaller sample than SSOCS. The FRSS survey's smaller sample size and difference in survey administration may have impacted the 2013-14 results.

[4] Primary schools are defined as schools in which the lowest grade is not higher than grade 3 and the highest grade is not higher than grade 8. Middle schools are defined as schools in which the lowest grade is not lower than grade 4 and the highest grade is not higher than grade 9. High schools are defined as schools in which the lowest grade is not lower than grade 9. Combined schools include all other combinations of grades, including K–12 schools. Separate data on high schools and combined schools are not available for 2013–14.

[5] Percent combined enrollment of Black, Hispanic, Asian, Pacific Islander, and American Indian/Alaska Native students, and students of Two or more races.

[6] Because the 2013-14 survey did not collect data on the percentage of students eligible for free or reduced-price lunch, the classification of schools by the percentage of eligible students was computed based on data obtained from the Common Core of Data.

NOTE: Responses were provided by the principal or the person most knowledgeable about crime and safety issues at the school.

SOURCE: U.S. Department of Education, National Center for Education Statistics, 2005–06, 2007–08, 2009–10, 2015-16, and 2017-18 School Survey on Crime and Safety (SSOCS), 2006, 2008, 2010, 2016, and 2018; Fast Response Survey System (FRSS), "School Safety and Discipline: 2013-14," FRSS 106, 2014; and Common Core of Data (CCD), "Public Elementary/Secondary School Universe Survey," 2013-14. (This table was prepared August 2019.)

Table 233.70a. Percentage of public schools with security staff present at least once a week, by full-time or part-time status and selected school characteristics: 2005-06 through 2015-16

[Standard errors appear in parentheses]

School characteristic	Full-time					Part-time only				
	2005-06	2007-08	2009-10	2013-14[1]	2015-16	2005-06	2007-08	2009-10	2013-14[1]	2015-16
1	2	3	4	5	6	7	8	9	10	11
All public schools	**27.0 (0.88)**	**30.4 (0.98)**	**28.7 (0.97)**	**23.7 (1.10)**	**33.6 (1.31)**	**14.6 (1.06)**	**15.9 (0.89)**	**14.1 (0.66)**	**19.3 (1.18)**	**22.9 (1.17)**
School level[2]										
Primary	12.5 (1.32)	17.8 (1.37)	15.7 (1.43)	10.4 (1.46)	19.9 (1.74)	13.7 (1.59)	15.3 (1.31)	12.1 (0.89)	18.2 (1.73)	25.5 (1.83)
Middle	44.5 (1.17)	44.9 (1.55)	45.8 (1.39)	36.9 (2.21)	49.9 (2.00)	19.2 (1.18)	20.7 (1.17)	20.6 (1.32)	26.4 (2.17)	23.5 (1.80)
High school/combined	49.6 (2.22)	51.9 (1.98)	49.0 (1.58)	48.1 (2.25)	55.6 (1.88)	13.4 (1.76)	13.5 (1.73)	13.9 (1.68)	16.1 (1.98)	15.7 (1.44)
High school	64.0 (1.53)	66.1 (1.48)	62.0 (1.56)	— (†)	67.4 (1.60)	11.2 (1.14)	13.5 (1.42)	14.5 (1.50)	— (†)	13.6 (1.17)
Combined	26.8 (4.44)	26.2 (4.79)	24.0 (4.49)	— (†)	31.0 (4.67)	16.7 (4.13)	13.6 ! (4.15)	12.7 (3.56)	— (†)	20.2 (3.39)
Enrollment size										
Less than 300	10.8 (1.58)	15.1 (2.09)	15.1 (2.29)	6.8 (1.72)	18.2 (3.09)	11.9 (2.07)	12.5 (2.07)	10.5 (2.20)	14.9 (2.81)	16.6 (2.72)
300 to 499	16.7 (1.93)	19.4 (1.84)	18.0 (1.96)	15.4 (2.12)	25.0 (2.45)	13.0 (1.64)	16.8 (2.05)	15.5 (1.76)	20.0 (2.28)	24.9 (2.39)
500 to 999	31.0 (1.27)	34.0 (1.52)	31.2 (1.34)	26.4 (1.79)	35.5 (1.96)	19.5 (1.62)	18.8 (1.53)	16.1 (1.08)	24.2 (1.91)	29.1 (1.87)
1,000 or more	77.3 (1.61)	79.5 (1.65)	79.3 (1.82)	77.5 (2.66)	83.4 (2.02)	9.7 (1.40)	11.1 (1.83)	10.7 (1.50)	9.8 (2.06)	8.0 (1.49)
Locale										
City	37.7 (2.04)	45.3 (2.24)	39.7 (2.19)	35.0 (2.71)	43.8 (2.87)	11.4 (1.59)	12.0 (1.97)	11.2 (1.69)	10.4 (2.13)	18.1 (2.77)
Suburban	27.1 (1.41)	30.0 (1.64)	31.3 (1.58)	26.2 (1.97)	33.4 (1.95)	15.6 (1.44)	15.4 (1.59)	14.1 (1.50)	21.5 (2.23)	24.6 (2.15)
Town	26.3 (2.88)	26.9 (2.32)	21.2 (2.15)	18.4 (2.63)	34.5 (3.31)	18.1 (2.90)	24.2 (2.75)	17.8 (2.39)	29.6 (3.88)	27.4 (3.69)
Rural	18.6 (1.39)	20.2 (1.67)	20.5 (1.83)	15.3 (1.42)	23.0 (2.04)	15.2 (1.87)	15.7 (1.70)	14.7 (1.51)	20.2 (2.26)	23.7 (2.46)
Percent combined enrollment of Black, Hispanic, Asian, Pacific Islander, and American Indian/Alaska Native students, and students of Two or more races										
Less than 5 percent	12.4 (1.60)	16.9 (2.70)	13.6 (2.41)	8.7 ! (2.72)	20.1 (3.87)	16.0 (1.81)	18.7 (2.56)	16.8 (2.51)	26.9 (5.40)	24.6 (5.31)
5 percent to less than 20 percent	23.9 (1.73)	23.1 (1.63)	19.9 (2.26)	13.7 (1.66)	27.3 (2.20)	15.0 (1.98)	19.9 (1.93)	16.6 (1.71)	21.2 (2.41)	27.0 (2.24)
20 percent to less than 50 percent	28.3 (1.94)	29.1 (2.21)	27.8 (1.69)	25.3 (2.28)	27.3 (1.82)	13.3 (1.75)	15.5 (1.93)	14.1 (1.50)	21.5 (2.48)	22.7 (2.31)
50 percent or more	37.3 (1.91)	43.8 (2.16)	41.3 (2.09)	33.3 (2.09)	43.3 (2.37)	14.0 (1.81)	11.6 (1.68)	11.2 (1.33)	14.6 (1.73)	20.4 (2.08)
Percent of students eligible for free or reduced-price lunch[3]										
0 to 25 percent	24.9 (1.70)	29.7 (2.01)	27.9 (2.17)	21.0 (2.20)	30.4 (2.74)	13.0 (1.33)	16.8 (1.52)	11.3 (1.21)	20.6 (3.01)	22.6 (2.80)
26 to 50 percent	26.4 (1.63)	24.2 (2.01)	21.5 (1.52)	17.7 (1.87)	26.6 (2.00)	15.7 (2.01)	16.6 (1.65)	18.5 (1.37)	21.8 (2.64)	24.2 (2.55)
51 to 75 percent	25.7 (1.85)	29.7 (2.34)	29.0 (2.04)	24.3 (2.00)	34.3 (2.38)	13.7 (1.90)	16.4 (2.34)	13.3 (1.45)	20.2 (2.38)	24.4 (2.15)
76 to 100 percent	33.0 (2.49)	42.1 (3.17)	37.6 (2.66)	31.3 (2.86)	41.8 (3.02)	16.8 (2.07)	12.9 (2.17)	12.2 (1.84)	14.6 (2.37)	20.4 (2.70)

—Not available.

†Not applicable.

!Interpret data with caution. The coefficient of variation (CV) for this estimate is between 30 and 50 percent.

[1] Data for 2013-14 were collected using the Fast Response Survey System (FRSS), while data for all other years were collected using the School Survey on Crime and Safety (SSOCS). The 2013-14 FRSS survey was designed to allow comparisons with SSOCS data. However, respondents to the 2013-14 survey could choose either to complete the survey on paper (and mail it back) or to complete the survey online, whereas respondents to SSOCS did not have the option of completing the survey online. The 2013-14 survey also relied on a smaller sample. The smaller sample size and difference in survey administration may have impacted the 2013-14 results.

[2] Primary schools are defined as schools in which the lowest grade is not higher than grade 3 and the highest grade is not higher than grade 8. Middle schools are defined as schools in which the lowest grade is not lower than grade 4 and the highest grade is not higher than grade 9. High schools are defined as schools in which the lowest grade is not lower than grade 9 and the highest grade is not higher than grade 12. Combined schools include all other combinations of grades, including K-12 schools. Separate data on high schools and combined schools are not available for 2013-14.

[3] Because the 2013-14 survey did not collect data on the percentage of students eligible for free or reduced-price lunch, the classification of schools by the percentage of eligible students was computed based on data obtained from the Common Core of Data.

NOTE: Security staff include security guards, security personnel, School Resource Officers (SROs), and sworn law enforcement officers who are not SROs. "Security guards" and "security personnel" do not include law enforcement. SROs include all career law enforcement officers with arrest authority who have specialized training and are assigned to work in collaboration with school organizations. Responses were provided by the principal or the person most knowledgeable about crime and safety issues at the school.

SOURCE: U.S. Department of Education, National Center for Education Statistics, 2005-06, 2007-08, 2009-10, and 2015-16 School Survey on Crime and Safety (SSOCS), 2006, 2008, 2010, and 2016; Fast Response Survey System (FRSS), "School Safety and Discipline: 2013-14," FRSS 106, 2014; and Common Core of Data (CCD), "Public Elementary/Secondary School Universe Survey," 2013-14. (This table was prepared September 2017.)

Table 233.70b. Percentage of public schools with security staff present at school at least once a week, by type of security staff, school level, and selected school characteristics: 2005-06, 2015-16, and 2017-18

[Standard errors appear in parentheses]

School level and characteristic	Any security staff[1]			Sworn law enforcement officers: Any sworn law enforcement officers, including School Resource Officers (SROs)[2]			At least one officer who is an SRO			At least one officer who is not an SRO			Security personn e
	2005–06	2015–16	2017–18	2005–06	2015–16	2017–18	2005–06	2015–16	2017–18	2005–06	2015–16	2017–18	2005–0
1	2	3	4	5	6	7	8	9	10	11	12	13	1
All public schools[3]	**41.7 (1.28)**	**56.5 (1.29)**	**61.4 (1.27)**	**36.3 (1.13)**	**47.7 (1.45)**	**51.2 (1.15)**	**32.4 (1.07)**	**42.0 (1.27)**	**44.8 (1.17)**	**9.3 (0.69)**	**10.9 (0.90)**	**13.2 (0.74)**	**19.3 (0.9**
Enrollment size													
Less than 300	22.7 (2.65)	34.8 (3.61)	44.7 (3.28)	20.0 (2.32)	28.8 (3.38)	38.2 (3.54)	16.4 (1.88)	23.6 (3.12)	31.8 (3.12)	5.9 (1.55)	8.3 (2.02)	12.4 (2.19)	7.4 (1.8
300 to 499	29.8 (2.29)	49.9 (2.66)	51.5 (2.49)	25.4 (2.04)	42.0 (2.81)	40.8 (2.26)	21.7 (1.91)	36.2 (2.74)	35.9 (2.01)	7.0 (1.06)	10.4 (1.83)	10.6 (1.47)	11.3 (1.6
500 to 999	50.5 (1.90)	64.6 (1.99)	69.0 (1.62)	43.9 (1.74)	53.3 (2.22)	57.6 (1.87)	40.3 (1.70)	47.4 (2.06)	49.7 (1.69)	9.9 (0.93)	11.5 (1.22)	14.6 (1.24)	21.9 (1.6
1,000 or more	86.9 (1.39)	91.4 (1.73)	94.3 (0.97)	77.3 (1.51)	83.6 (1.58)	82.1 (1.54)	70.4 (1.71)	77.1 (1.58)	77.3 (1.57)	20.8 (1.57)	15.9 (2.17)	17.3 (1.12)	57.9 (1.9
Locale													
City	49.1 (2.57)	61.9 (2.87)	63.3 (2.48)	39.4 (2.22)	44.5 (2.97)	44.3 (2.18)	34.0 (2.13)	39.0 (2.50)	39.5 (2.18)	13.4 (1.49)	10.7 (1.76)	11.1 (1.37)	33.3 (2.2
Suburban	42.7 (1.67)	57.9 (2.30)	63.3 (1.78)	37.9 (1.69)	49.1 (2.39)	53.3 (1.81)	34.6 (1.78)	43.6 (2.34)	47.0 (1.75)	9.2 (1.02)	12.4 (1.69)	14.5 (1.32)	18.6 (1.2
Town	44.4 (3.86)	62.0 (3.55)	68.9 (3.46)	42.0 (3.64)	58.3 (3.67)	64.5 (3.56)	39.0 (3.78)	49.0 (3.84)	56.4 (3.75)	7.6 (2.20)	15.7 (2.90)	16.1 (2.48)	15.3 (2.7
Rural	33.8 (1.87)	46.7 (2.54)	53.7 (3.02)	30.5 (1.77)	44.3 (2.65)	49.3 (2.77)	26.7 (1.56)	39.7 (2.73)	42.0 (2.50)	6.6 (1.17)	7.1 (1.22)	12.5 (1.75)	10.1 (1.2
Percent minority enrollment[4]													
0 to 25 percent	34.9 (1.53)	51.1 (2.36)	58.3 (2.34)	31.7 (1.46)	48.8 (2.23)	55.2 (2.34)	28.4 (1.45)	42.9 (2.16)	47.4 (2.42)	6.4 (0.69)	10.6 (1.34)	15.3 (1.62)	11.1 (0.9
26 to 50 percent	42.4 (2.64)	51.6 (2.83)	59.2 (2.81)	36.9 (2.54)	46.2 (2.90)	50.4 (2.85)	34.6 (2.55)	42.0 (2.65)	44.5 (2.70)	8.8 (1.70)	9.4 (1.90)	12.4 (1.81)	20.8 (2.2
51 to 75 percent	47.5 (4.20)	62.9 (3.61)	61.5 (4.04)	42.7 (4.35)	52.1 (3.67)	51.2 (3.79)	38.7 (4.09)	45.8 (3.57)	47.1 (3.58)	13.0 (2.54)	11.4 (2.33)	9.8 (1.78)	25.4 (2.6
76 to 100 percent	53.9 (3.12)	64.5 (2.88)	67.4 (2.36)	41.7 (2.54)	44.7 (3.09)	46.5 (2.50)	34.4 (2.32)	38.2 (3.11)	40.3 (2.57)	15.6 (1.84)	12.3 (1.52)	13.0 (1.31)	36.8 (2.7
Percent of students eligible for free or reduced-price lunch													
0 to 25 percent	37.9 (2.14)	52.9 (3.77)	53.6 (2.69)	33.0 (2.13)	47.4 (3.59)	45.2 (2.76)	30.4 (2.23)	43.9 (3.48)	39.3 (2.40)	6.6 (0.71)	10.6 (1.87)	11.8 (1.90)	16.1 (1.2
26 to 50 percent	42.1 (2.08)	50.8 (2.89)	64.7 (2.69)	38.7 (2.07)	45.4 (2.71)	59.2 (2.91)	34.5 (1.87)	41.4 (2.84)	50.6 (2.76)	8.9 (1.14)	9.5 (1.34)	16.9 (1.85)	16.4 (1.2
51 to 75 percent	39.3 (2.21)	58.7 (2.47)	61.6 (2.96)	34.9 (2.03)	53.5 (2.63)	54.7 (2.94)	31.7 (2.06)	45.6 (2.46)	47.7 (3.05)	8.9 (1.21)	11.9 (1.67)	13.6 (1.54)	17.9 (1.8
76 to 100 percent	49.8 (2.73)	62.2 (2.62)	63.4 (2.01)	39.8 (2.34)	44.6 (3.18)	46.1 (2.11)	33.1 (1.91)	37.9 (2.87)	41.5 (2.34)	14.4 (1.79)	11.6 (1.68)	11.1 (1.28)	30.0 (2.6
Percent of students who are Limited English Proficient (LEP)													
0 to 5 percent	39.9 (1.52)	55.5 (2.13)	60.9 (1.92)	35.1 (1.31)	49.1 (2.13)	53.3 (1.82)	31.4 (1.28)	43.6 (2.09)	46.6 (1.77)	8.9 (0.70)	10.1 (1.00)	14.0 (1.04)	16.6 (1.0
6 to 20 percent	44.0 (2.14)	56.6 (3.08)	66.0 (2.29)	39.2 (2.13)	49.1 (3.27)	57.2 (2.28)	35.5 (2.29)	43.6 (3.13)	49.9 (2.11)	8.0 (1.18)	13.5 (1.88)	15.2 (1.96)	21.3 (1.8
21 to 100 percent	46.2 (3.87)	59.2 (3.32)	57.4 (2.86)	37.6 (3.40)	42.1 (4.07)	38.6 (2.55)	32.1 (3.50)	35.5 (3.71)	34.2 (2.39)	13.2 (2.06)	9.9 (2.41)	9.0 (1.68)	29.0 (3.3
All primary schools[5]	**26.2 (1.87)**	**45.4 (1.95)**	**51.4 (2.00)**	**21.0 (1.68)**	**35.8 (2.32)**	**40.1 (1.69)**	**18.5 (1.56)**	**30.4 (1.99)**	**33.7 (1.73)**	**4.9 (0.84)**	**9.0 (1.36)**	**11.3 (1.14)**	**11.1 (1.2**
Enrollment size													
Less than 300	15.7 (3.28)	30.7 (4.96)	43.5 (5.67)	14.4 (3.13)	24.9 (4.93)	38.3 (5.72)	12.1 (2.87)	18.9 (4.42)	31.7 (5.42)	3.3! (1.61)	8.1! (3.06)	14.3 (3.81)	‡ (
300 to 499	22.8 (2.77)	44.1 (3.33)	44.9 (3.35)	18.0 (2.42)	35.3 (3.75)	33.2 (2.79)	14.6 (2.21)	30.5 (3.60)	28.8 (2.52)	4.9 (1.22)	10.0 (2.33)	9.4 (1.95)	10.4 (2.0
500 to 999	34.2 (2.73)	53.7 (2.99)	58.9 (2.50)	26.9 (2.56)	41.8 (3.29)	46.5 (2.86)	25.3 (2.49)	36.5 (3.01)	38.0 (2.64)	6.0 (1.25)	8.6 (1.78)	12.0 (1.74)	15.0 (2.0
1,000 or more	66.7 (8.90)	‡ (†)	‡ (†)	46.2 (9.37)	‡ (†)	‡ (†)	39.1 (9.15)	‡ (†)	‡ (†)	‡ (†)	‡ (†)	‡ (†)	38.3 (9.3
Locale													
City	33.0 (3.74)	48.7 (4.24)	50.3 (3.74)	22.0 (3.05)	29.4 (4.48)	30.7 (3.20)	18.3 (2.92)	23.8 (3.58)	26.5 (3.19)	6.6 (1.76)	7.4! (2.83)	8.1 (2.03)	22.7 (3.1
Suburban	25.7 (2.39)	43.7 (3.56)	49.5 (2.61)	22.0 (2.38)	35.9 (3.64)	39.4 (2.52)	20.3 (2.42)	31.5 (3.47)	33.6 (2.52)	5.3 (1.34)	10.7 (2.37)	11.9 (2.07)	7.6 (1.3
Town	26.7 (6.36)	55.4 (5.96)	59.5 (6.09)	25.4 (5.95)	52.0 (6.24)	54.5 (6.05)	23.3 (5.75)	40.7 (6.01)	46.4 (5.93)	‡ (†)	16.8! (5.18)	13.7 (4.09)	‡ (
Rural	19.3 (2.93)	39.0 (4.51)	51.7 (4.97)	17.1 (2.92)	35.8 (4.71)	46.6 (4.56)	14.6 (2.58)	32.2 (4.76)	37.1 (4.24)	3.5! (1.60)	4.7! (1.94)	13.3 (3.32)	4.6! (1.6
Percent minority enrollment[4]													
0 to 25 percent	20.5 (2.21)	40.2 (4.01)	51.5 (3.45)	18.3 (2.08)	38.0 (3.92)	48.5 (3.52)	15.7 (1.97)	33.5 (3.77)	40.0 (3.92)	4.1! (1.23)	7.5 (1.95)	15.0 (2.77)	4.6! (1.4
26 to 50 percent	20.5 (3.77)	36.4 (4.22)	46.6 (3.79)	13.2 (3.16)	32.9 (4.39)	37.2 (3.77)	13.2 (3.16)	28.2 (4.16)	31.4 (3.60)	‡ (†)	9.2 (2.68)	10.8 (2.78)	11.6 (2.9
51 to 75 percent	27.8 (5.57)	51.6 (5.14)	44.7 (5.61)	22.6 (5.51)	43.4 (5.42)	36.8 (4.65)	20.7 (5.38)	35.8 (5.30)	33.1 (4.63)	5.5! (2.62)	11.9! (3.73)	8.2! (2.61)	11.0 (3.2
76 to 100 percent	40.9 (4.13)	55.0 (4.44)	58.4 (3.51)	30.2 (3.18)	30.5 (4.51)	34.9 (3.38)	25.2 (3.10)	25.0 (4.42)	28.8 (3.40)	9.6 (2.32)	8.9 (2.19)	9.2 (1.75)	25.5 (3.5
Percent of students eligible for free or reduced-price lunch													
0 to 25 percent	20.9 (3.02)	33.8 (5.61)	39.8 (3.97)	16.3 (2.95)	30.0 (5.40)	32.5 (4.10)	14.5 (2.88)	29.4 (5.40)	26.7 (3.66)	3.1! (1.12)	5.9! (2.37)	10.3 (2.83)	7.7 (1.7
26 to 50 percent	22.1 (3.04)	39.8 (3.99)	55.3 (4.86)	19.6 (2.89)	34.9 (3.97)	49.0 (5.29)	16.7 (2.61)	32.3 (3.99)	39.8 (5.32)	3.9! (1.57)	6.8 (1.93)	16.9 (3.12)	5.0! (1.6
51 to 75 percent	22.4 (3.13)	48.2 (4.00)	52.5 (4.55)	18.0 (3.08)	42.9 (4.38)	45.7 (4.53)	17.6 (3.03)	33.6 (3.78)	37.9 (4.39)	2.8! (1.09)	12.5 (2.83)	12.5 (2.92)	9.5 (2.1
76 to 100 percent	40.6 (3.26)	54.1 (3.67)	54.3 (2.72)	30.9 (2.79)	33.6 (4.40)	35.7 (2.70)	25.7 (2.52)	26.7 (3.86)	31.4 (3.06)	10.2 (2.22)	9.6 (2.49)	8.1 (1.58)	22.9 (3.2
Percent of students who are Limited English Proficient (LEP)													
0 to 5 percent	22.6 (2.24)	42.8 (3.28)	50.4 (3.55)	17.7 (1.81)	36.3 (3.47)	42.0 (3.35)	15.2 (1.57)	31.0 (3.46)	35.2 (3.26)	4.4 (1.02)	8.4 (1.79)	12.3 (1.85)	8.2 (1.4
6 to 20 percent	28.0 (3.21)	41.2 (4.47)	54.7 (3.59)	23.3 (3.01)	35.0 (4.55)	46.4 (3.62)	20.8 (3.09)	30.5 (4.24)	39.2 (3.16)	4.6! (1.68)	11.5 (2.80)	13.7 (2.69)	11.5 (2.7
21 to 100 percent	35.9 (4.32)	54.0 (3.94)	49.7 (3.49)	28.9 (4.10)	35.4 (4.65)	30.6 (2.89)	26.3 (4.08)	29.4 (4.19)	25.8 (2.69)	7.0! (2.18)	7.7! (2.51)	7.2 (2.02)	20.0 (3.0
All secondary schools[6]	**68.7 (0.98)**	**76.8 (1.23)**	**82.0 (0.75)**	**62.8 (1.05)**	**69.8 (1.32)**	**73.8 (1.04)**	**57.0 (1.12)**	**62.9 (1.34)**	**67.3 (1.21)**	**15.2 (0.88)**	**15.0 (1.08)**	**17.4 (0.92)**	**34.0 (0.9**
Enrollment size													
Less than 300	37.9 (3.26)	45.4 (4.63)	55.7 (2.36)	33.6 (3.01)	41.1 (4.98)	48.7 (2.99)	27.0 (2.93)	35.0 (4.55)	39.1 (3.24)	10.0 (1.85)	12.9 (3.29)	15.2 (2.50)	13.1 (2.5
300 to 499	53.8 (3.28)	65.6 (3.31)	76.7 (2.37)	50.0 (3.34)	59.4 (3.62)	68.9 (2.59)	46.2 (3.30)	52.1 (3.86)	60.8 (2.60)	11.5 (2.08)	11.3 (1.91)	17.6 (2.17)	15.4 (2.3
500 to 999	74.6 (1.67)	84.7 (1.40)	86.6 (1.10)	68.1 (1.65)	74.9 (1.56)	78.2 (1.69)	62.5 (1.79)	67.7 (1.73)	73.0 (1.90)	13.7 (1.28)	16.8 (1.50)	16.7 (1.38)	32.8 (2.0
1,000 or more	90.7 (0.86)	96.5 (0.82)	96.6 (0.61)	83.2 (1.27)	90.9 (1.16)	87.6 (1.08)	76.6 (1.46)	84.3 (1.47)	82.3 (1.22)	23.0 (1.49)	16.6 (1.74)	19.6 (1.11)	61.4 (1.7
Locale													
City	86.2 (1.89)	86.8 (2.11)	87.9 (1.63)	78.2 (2.39)	75.4 (2.37)	74.3 (2.13)	69.9 (2.72)	69.4 (2.80)	67.6 (2.47)	25.8 (1.95)	18.7 (2.37)	17.6 (1.75)	56.5 (2.7
Suburban	72.5 (1.70)	84.0 (1.43)	87.4 (1.17)	65.6 (2.06)	74.5 (1.83)	77.7 (1.50)	59.3 (2.12)	66.6 (2.32)	70.7 (1.56)	15.1 (1.14)	15.9 (1.71)	18.5 (1.56)	37.3 (1.7
Town	63.7 (3.30)	66.8 (3.69)	80.3 (2.68)	59.5 (3.21)	64.8 (3.81)	76.1 (2.89)	56.3 (3.40)	57.9 (3.88)	69.3 (3.32)	9.4 (1.88)	12.5 (2.28)	17.5 (2.48)	23.1 (2.5
Rural	53.1 (2.34)	63.6 (2.51)	69.4 (2.27)	49.2 (2.18)	61.0 (2.60)	66.2 (2.23)	45.0 (2.17)	54.7 (2.61)	60.7 (2.31)	9.8 (1.55)	11.7 (1.96)	15.4 (1.83)	17.9 (1.6
Percent minority enrollment[4]													
0 to 25 percent	59.3 (1.49)	69.8 (2.05)	75.0 (1.63)	54.4 (1.56)	66.3 (2.24)	70.6 (1.79)	50.1 (1.71)	58.0 (2.07)	63.3 (1.79)	10.1 (0.99)	15.7 (1.75)	17.6 (1.29)	23.3 (1.2
26 to 50 percent	72.5 (2.54)	76.3 (2.59)	83.8 (1.90)	69.3 (2.64)	69.5 (2.40)	75.3 (2.43)	64.8 (2.95)	66.8 (2.72)	69.6 (2.66)	13.6 (1.58)	9.3 (1.65)	14.3 (2.30)	30.6 (2.5
51 to 75 percent	83.3 (2.52)	83.9 (2.47)	88.2 (2.40)	78.5 (2.72)	74.2 (3.05)	79.5 (3.20)	72.6 (2.95)	69.1 (3.21)	74.1 (3.37)	23.4 (2.71)	12.1 (1.78)	14.1 (2.13)	49.0 (3.6
76 to 100 percent	84.5 (2.73)	84.4 (2.47)	87.7 (1.82)	69.6 (3.62)	72.9 (3.07)	73.9 (2.51)	57.4 (3.27)	63.6 (3.62)	67.0 (2.47)	29.2 (3.18)	21.1 (2.57)	22.2 (2.05)	64.7 (3.1

[Standard errors appear in parentheses]

School level and characteristic	Any security staff[1]			Sworn law enforcement officers									Securit personr e
				Any sworn law enforcement officers, including School Resource Officers (SROs)[2]			At least one officer who is an SRO			At least one officer who is not an SRO			
	2005–06	2015–16	2017–18	2005–06	2015–16	2017–18	2005–06	2015–16	2017–18	2005–06	2015–16	2017–18	2005–0
1	2	3	4	5	6	7	8	9	10	11	12	13	1
Percent of students eligible for free or reduced-price lunch													
0 to 25 percent	62.8 (1.83)	81.1 (2.11)	80.5 (2.40)	56.6 (1.91)	73.2 (2.34)	70.8 (2.66)	52.3 (2.05)	64.3 (2.79)	64.1 (2.40)	11.8 (1.11)	18.7 (2.26)	15.9 (1.93)	28.9 (1.6
26 to 50 percent	71.9 (2.19)	71.1 (2.59)	79.5 (1.85)	67.6 (2.20)	65.5 (2.57)	74.5 (1.91)	62.7 (2.36)	59.9 (2.73)	67.0 (2.30)	14.2 (1.55)	12.5 (1.62)	17.3 (1.49)	33.9 (1.9
51 to 75 percent	68.9 (2.57)	77.4 (2.52)	81.1 (2.16)	63.9 (2.58)	71.5 (2.44)	75.1 (2.49)	56.6 (2.45)	64.5 (2.60)	68.6 (2.57)	17.0 (1.89)	13.3 (1.77)	17.0 (1.82)	32.0 (2.1
76 to 100 percent	77.0 (3.78)	80.3 (2.67)	86.8 (1.80)	65.6 (3.93)	70.5 (3.33)	73.9 (2.43)	56.6 (3.99)	63.9 (3.53)	68.6 (2.45)	24.7 (3.57)	17.5 (2.55)	18.9 (2.03)	54.1 (3.7
Percent of students who are Limited English Proficient (LEP)													
0 to 5 percent	64.3 (1.26)	72.7 (1.56)	79.0 (0.89)	59.1 (1.26)	66.6 (1.62)	72.4 (1.16)	54.1 (1.37)	60.4 (1.45)	65.3 (1.37)	13.5 (1.01)	12.9 (1.03)	17.4 (1.10)	29.0 (1.1
6 to 20 percent	80.7 (2.28)	84.5 (2.19)	88.5 (1.70)	74.6 (2.38)	77.2 (2.59)	80.6 (2.12)	67.9 (2.48)	69.0 (2.81)	73.5 (2.25)	16.5 (1.89)	19.1 (2.07)	18.3 (1.96)	45.1 (2.3
21 to 100 percent	79.0 (4.06)	84.7 (3.85)	84.0 (3.07)	66.8 (4.13)	72.5 (4.02)	68.1 (3.84)	57.1 (4.67)	64.6 (4.79)	65.3 (3.70)	27.2 (3.41)	18.3 (3.94)	15.5 (2.16)	52.7 (4.2

†Not applicable.

!Interpret data with caution. The coefficient of variation (CV) for this estimate is between 30 and 50 percent.

‡Reporting standards not met. Either there are too few cases for a reliable estimate or the coefficient of variation (CV) is 50 percent or greater.

1 Under "Any security staff," schools that reported having more than one type of security staff were counted only once.

2 School Resource Officers (SROs) include all career sworn law enforcement officers with arrest authority who have specialized training and are assigned to work in collaboration with school organizations. Under "Any sworn law enforcement officers," schools that reported having both SROs and other sworn law enforcement officers were counted only once.

3 Includes combined schools, which are not shown separately. Combined schools have any combination of grades (including K-12) that is not defined specifically as primary, middle, or high school.

4 Percent combined enrollment of Black, Hispanic, Asian, Pacific Islander, and American Indian/Alaska Native students, and students of Two or more races.

5 Primary schools are defined as schools in which the lowest grade is not higher than grade 3 and the highest grade is not higher than grade 8.

6 Secondary schools include both middle and high schools. Middle schools are defined as schools in which the lowest grade is not lower than grade 4 and the highest grade is not higher than grade 9. High schools are defined as schools in which the lowest grade is not lower than grade 9.

NOTE: Responses were provided by the principal or the person most knowledgeable about crime and safety issues at the school. "At school" was defined to include activities happening in school buildings, on school grounds, on school buses, and at places that hold school-sponsored events or activities.

SOURCE: U.S. Department of Education, National Center for Education Statistics, 2005–06, 2015–16, and 2017–18 School Survey on Crime and Safety (SSOCS), 2006, 2016, and 2018. (This table was prepared July 2019.)

Table 233.72. Among public schools with any sworn law enforcement officers present at school at least once a week, percentage with officers present at specific times and percentage with any officers present for all instructional hours every day, by school level, times present, and selected school characteristics: 2015-16

[Standard errors appear in parentheses]

School characteristic	Among primary schools[1] with sworn law enforcement officers present, percent reporting that officers were					Among secondary schools[2] with sworn law enforcement officers present, percent reporting that officers were				
	Present at specific times at least once a week[3]					Present at specific times at least once a week[3]				
	At any time during school hours	While students were arriving or leaving	At selected school activities[4]	When school/school activities were not occurring	Present for all instructional hours every day[3]	At any time during school hours	While students were arriving or leaving	At selected school activities[4]	When school/school activities were not occurring	Present for all instructional hours every day[3]
1	2	3	4	5	6	7	8	9	10	11
Total	**84.8 (2.52)**	**66.9 (3.80)**	**60.2 (4.00)**	**37.1 (3.63)**	**13.4 (2.43)**	**96.5 (0.65)**	**88.3 (1.23)**	**86.8 (1.39)**	**45.2 (1.77)**	**45.8 (1.85)**
Enrollment size										
Less than 300	‡ (†)	‡ (†)	‡ (†)	‡ (†)	‡ (†)	93.0 (2.92)	83.0 (6.24)	84.6 (4.60)	59.3 (6.30)	38.8 (7.42)
300 to 499	89.5 (3.94)	67.8 (7.39)	64.4 (6.74)	39.2 (6.11)	10.9 ! (4.35)	94.9 (2.46)	81.6 (3.97)	79.9 (4.49)	39.1 (3.95)	30.9 (4.02)
500 to 999	80.3 (4.16)	69.7 (4.89)	64.0 (4.84)	39.6 (4.66)	18.2 (3.69)	96.3 (0.94)	87.9 (1.42)	85.2 (1.42)	39.8 (2.28)	41.2 (2.29)
1,000 or more	‡ (†)	‡ (†)	‡ (†)	‡ (†)	‡ (†)	99.2 (0.45)	94.8 (0.92)	94.0 (1.31)	50.4 (2.12)	63.3 (2.15)
Locale										
City	81.2 (5.80)	66.1 (6.96)	57.2 (7.67)	23.1 ! (7.79)	9.8 ! (4.70)	97.8 (1.00)	88.9 (2.03)	85.0 (2.73)	47.3 (2.99)	55.0 (3.36)
Suburban	87.0 (4.31)	70.7 (5.72)	58.1 (5.96)	44.6 (5.80)	11.8 ! (3.87)	96.7 (0.91)	91.1 (1.42)	85.9 (1.69)	39.5 (2.41)	47.4 (2.21)
Town	85.0 (6.81)	78.4 (8.84)	71.8 (8.44)	37.0 (8.71)	32.8 (7.97)	96.3 (1.64)	89.4 (2.56)	90.1 (2.48)	45.6 (4.63)	37.6 (3.50)
Rural	85.3 (4.54)	54.0 (7.29)	58.2 (8.30)	40.6 (8.13)	‡ (†)	95.2 (1.93)	83.4 (2.86)	87.9 (2.90)	50.1 (4.62)	39.5 (4.46)
Percent combined enrollment of Black, Hispanic, Asian, Pacific Islander, and American Indian/Alaska Native students, and students of Two or more races										
Less than 5 percent	‡ (†)	‡ (†)	‡ (†)	‡ (†)	‡ (†)	96.9 (1.83)	80.4 (6.83)	87.8 (5.48)	47.1 (9.43)	40.8 (7.50)
5 to less than 20 percent	82.9 (6.02)	60.2 (7.48)	62.5 (6.97)	36.5 (7.27)	18.7 (4.93)	96.7 (1.48)	85.2 (2.42)	85.1 (2.47)	46.7 (3.64)	32.3 (3.58)
20 to less than 50 percent	88.1 (5.79)	74.1 (7.00)	46.3 (7.62)	42.1 (7.69)	10.4 ! (4.23)	96.3 (1.51)	91.9 (1.61)	88.9 (2.19)	41.1 (3.11)	48.7 (3.23)
50 percent or more	85.1 (4.17)	69.2 (5.16)	65.7 (5.38)	37.4 (5.79)	12.9 (3.67)	96.5 (0.94)	89.2 (2.14)	86.5 (1.78)	46.7 (2.37)	53.9 (2.60)
Percent of students eligible for free or reduced-price lunch										
0 to 25 percent	‡ (†)	‡ (†)	‡ (†)	‡ (†)	‡ (†)	96.2 (2.01)	86.4 (2.90)	82.3 (4.35)	40.2 (4.31)	33.8 (3.25)
26 to 50 percent	83.7 (6.12)	67.2 (7.88)	64.2 (5.83)	42.6 (6.61)	14.6 ! (4.85)	96.3 (1.22)	85.4 (2.09)	84.4 (2.12)	38.1 (3.01)	42.8 (3.31)
51 to 75 percent	84.5 (5.00)	67.0 (6.46)	66.0 (7.80)	37.7 (6.79)	14.4 (4.26)	96.1 (1.17)	90.3 (2.30)	91.2 (1.42)	51.2 (3.58)	47.1 (3.43)
76 to 100 percent	88.0 (5.17)	72.1 (7.21)	61.7 (6.39)	34.4 (6.72)	14.7 ! (4.62)	97.6 (1.15)	90.4 (3.04)	87.6 (2.56)	49.8 (3.44)	57.0 (4.02)
Percent of students who are Limited English Proficient (LEP)										
0 to 5 percent	85.3 (4.02)	62.8 (5.59)	57.3 (5.52)	28.5 (4.76)	12.5 ! (3.84)	96.4 (0.84)	86.9 (1.75)	86.5 (1.74)	44.9 (2.34)	41.8 (2.27)
6 to 20 percent	77.5 (6.33)	70.9 (5.71)	62.1 (7.39)	42.6 (7.26)	11.9 ! (5.20)	96.9 (1.31)	90.4 (1.66)	88.4 (2.07)	45.2 (3.04)	51.3 (3.01)
21 to 100 percent	90.8 (4.09)	70.6 (6.31)	63.6 (6.76)	47.1 (7.66)	16.2 ! (5.12)	96.7 (1.97)	91.3 (2.22)	85.3 (3.66)	47.2 (5.01)	57.2 (4.62)

†Not applicable.

!Interpret data with caution. The coefficient of variation (CV) for this estimate is between 30 and 50 percent.

‡Reporting standards not met. Either there are too few cases for a reliable estimate or the coefficient of variation (CV) is 50 percent or greater.

[1] Primary schools are defined as schools in which the lowest grade is not higher than grade 3 and the highest grade is not higher than grade 8.

[2] Secondary schools include both middle and high schools as well as combined schools. Middle schools are defined as schools in which the lowest grade is not lower than grade 4 and the highest grade is not higher than grade 9. High schools are defined as schools in which the lowest grade is not lower than grade 9 and the highest grade is not higher than grade 12. Combined schools have any combination of grades (including K-12) that is not defined specifically as primary, middle, or high school.

[3] Schools could answer "yes" to more than one question about the presence of officers at various times. Schools indicating the presence of officers at multiple times are included in each applicable column. For example, a school that indicated officers were present at any time during school hours at least once a week and also indicated officers were present for all instructional hours every day would be shown in both of these columns.

[4] The questionnaire provided the following examples of selected school activities: athletic and social events, open houses, and science fairs.

NOTE: Sworn law enforcement officers include School Resource Officers as well as other sworn law enforcement officers who are not School Resource Officers. School Resource Officers are sworn law enforcement officers with arrest authority who have specialized training and are assigned to work in collaboration with school organizations. Responses were provided by the principal or the person most knowledgeable about crime and safety issues at the school. "At school" was defined to include activities happening in school buildings, on school grounds, on school buses, and at places that hold school-sponsored events or activities.

SOURCE: U.S. Department of Education, National Center for Education Statistics, 2015-16 School Survey on Crime and Safety (SSOCS), 2016. (This table was prepared September 2017.)

Table 233.74a. Among public schools with any sworn law enforcement officers present at school at least once a week, percentage with any officers who routinely carry or wear specific items, by school level, type of item, and selected school characteristics: 2015-16

[Standard errors appear in parentheses]

School characteristic	Among primary schools[1] with sworn law enforcement officers present, percent with officers who routinely								Among secondary schools[2] with sworn law enforcement officers present, percent with officers who routinely							
	Carry a stun gun[3]		Carry chemical aerosol sprays[4]		Carry a firearm		Wear a body camera		Carry a stun gun[3]		Carry chemical aerosol sprays[4]		Carry a firearm		Wear a body camera	
1	2		3		4		5		6		7		8		9	
Total	**63.5**	**(3.53)**	**58.7**	**(3.57)**	**85.6**	**(2.39)**	**13.4**	**(2.51)**	**70.4**	**(1.96)**	**72.1**	**(1.73)**	**93.3**	**(0.76)**	**18.6**	**(1.03)**
Enrollment size																
Less than 300	‡	(†)	‡	(†)	‡	(†)	‡	(†)	76.6	(8.32)	61.0	(7.41)	91.4	(3.60)	14.0	(3.93)
300 to 499	58.5	(7.25)	64.3	(6.32)	91.1	(3.66)	14.8 !	(5.05)	63.0	(5.05)	67.6	(4.06)	88.3	(3.14)	14.7	(2.73)
500 to 999	64.3	(4.92)	50.6	(4.12)	77.8	(3.97)	13.5	(3.44)	69.2	(2.65)	73.5	(2.21)	94.0	(1.12)	21.2	(2.16)
1,000 or more	‡	(†)	‡	(†)	‡	(†)	‡	(†)	74.1	(2.37)	77.4	(2.21)	96.1	(0.84)	19.4	(2.07)
Locale																
City	48.1	(7.65)	42.5	(7.68)	73.1	(7.03)	‡	(†)	66.6	(3.24)	70.0	(2.87)	86.8	(2.21)	18.4	(2.24)
Suburban	70.9	(5.40)	59.8	(5.19)	85.9	(4.77)	9.1 !	(3.09)	69.6	(2.61)	76.1	(2.32)	95.2	(1.11)	13.1	(1.50)
Town	76.6	(7.48)	70.6	(8.94)	97.0	(3.02)	25.0 !	(8.33)	81.0	(2.57)	77.3	(3.67)	96.9	(1.30)	29.2	(3.69)
Rural	59.4	(7.49)	65.4	(6.22)	90.1	(4.03)	20.2	(5.73)	68.9	(4.49)	66.3	(3.71)	95.2	(1.76)	19.4	(2.53)
Percent combined enrollment of Black, Hispanic, Asian, Pacific Islander, and American Indian/ Alaska Native students, and students of Two or more races																
Less than 5 percent	‡	(†)	‡	(†)	‡	(†)	‡	(†)	67.2	(8.30)	56.8	(7.41)	95.2	(3.15)	15.7 !	(5.35)
5 to less than 20 percent	68.2	(6.89)	66.1	(7.59)	89.7	(4.71)	16.6 !	(5.82)	72.6	(3.68)	72.9	(3.09)	94.4	(1.74)	19.2	(2.18)
20 to less than 50 percent	72.8	(7.11)	62.4	(7.52)	92.2	(4.61)	16.9 !	(7.30)	74.8	(3.15)	76.7	(3.18)	97.0	(0.93)	21.4	(2.75)
50 percent or more	57.2	(5.46)	51.5	(5.29)	79.3	(3.62)	9.9 !	(3.26)	66.5	(2.80)	71.2	(2.53)	89.7	(1.49)	16.9	(1.68)
Percent of students eligible for free or reduced-price lunch																
0 to 25 percent	‡	(†)	‡	(†)	‡	(†)	‡	(†)	69.4	(3.79)	73.5	(2.95)	95.0	(1.50)	17.2	(3.32)
26 to 50 percent	62.4	(7.82)	63.9	(7.31)	85.1	(5.87)	17.2 !	(5.95)	76.0	(3.02)	72.4	(3.43)	95.2	(1.48)	20.1	(2.69)
51 to 75 percent	67.2	(5.90)	59.0	(7.00)	88.5	(4.03)	24.7	(6.36)	69.6	(3.02)	74.5	(2.64)	94.0	(1.66)	20.3	(2.20)
76 to 100 percent	63.0	(5.84)	55.4	(5.38)	85.5	(4.42)	‡	(†)	65.6	(3.86)	67.6	(3.63)	88.7	(2.39)	15.8	(2.37)
Percent of students who are Limited English Proficient (LEP)																
0 to 5 percent	64.5	(6.62)	62.3	(6.07)	84.5	(4.16)	10.3 !	(3.11)	69.8	(2.46)	71.2	(2.21)	93.8	(0.93)	15.8	(1.36)
6 to 20 percent	64.1	(6.36)	52.8	(5.27)	92.7	(3.56)	18.5 !	(5.60)	72.8	(2.83)	73.9	(3.11)	93.3	(1.86)	21.0	(2.18)
21 to 100 percent	61.3	(6.94)	57.7	(6.86)	80.9	(4.99)	14.3 !	(5.43)	68.4	(4.90)	73.6	(4.90)	89.9	(3.00)	30.8	(5.54)

†Not applicable.

!Interpret data with caution. The coefficient of variation (CV) for this estimate is between 30 and 50 percent.

‡Reporting standards not met. Either there are too few cases for a reliable estimate or the coefficient of variation (CV) is 50 percent or greater.

[1] Primary schools are defined as schools in which the lowest grade is not higher than grade 3 and the highest grade is not higher than grade 8.

[2] Secondary schools include both middle and high schools as well as combined schools. Middle schools are defined as schools in which the lowest grade is not lower than grade 4 and the highest grade is not higher than grade 9. High schools are defined as schools in which the lowest grade is not lower than grade 9 and the highest grade is not higher than grade 12. Combined schools have any combination of grades (including K-12) that is not defined specifically as primary, middle, or high school.

[3] The questionnaire cited a Taser gun as an example of a stun gun.

[4] The questionnaire provided the following examples of chemical aerosol sprays: Mace and pepper spray.

NOTE: Sworn law enforcement officers include School Resource Officers as well as other sworn law enforcement officers who are not School Resource Officers. School Resource Officers are sworn law enforcement officers with arrest authority who have specialized training and are assigned to work in collaboration with school organizations. Responses were provided by the principal or the person most knowledgeable about crime and safety issues at the school. "At school" was defined to include activities happening in school buildings, on school grounds, on school buses, and at places that hold school-sponsored events or activities.

SOURCE: U.S. Department of Education, National Center for Education Statistics, 2015-16 School Survey on Crime and Safety (SSOCS), 2016. (This table was prepared September 2017.)

Table 233.74b. Among public schools with any sworn law enforcement officers present at school at least once a week, percentage with officers participating in selected activities, by type of activity, school level, and selected school characteristics: 2015-16

[Standard errors appear in parentheses]

School level and characteristic	Among schools with sworn law enforcement officers present, percent with officers participating in activity									
	Motor vehicle traffic control	Security enforcement and patrol	Maintaining school discipline	Coordinating with local police and emergency team(s)	Identifying problems in the school and proactively seeking solutions	Training teachers and staff in school safety or crime prevention	Mentoring students	Teaching a law-related education course or training students[1]	Recording or reporting discipline problems to school authorities	Providing information to school authorities about legal definitions[2]
1	2	3	4	5	6	7	8	9	10	11
All primary schools[3] with sworn law enforcement officers present	**58.6 (3.96)**	**67.4 (3.20)**	**43.3 (3.51)**	**73.3 (2.68)**	**63.6 (3.18)**	**45.4 (4.07)**	**59.5 (3.30)**	**31.0 (3.21)**	**50.1 (3.58)**	**48.8 (3.35)**
Enrollment size										
Less than 300	‡ (†)	‡ (†)	‡ (†)	‡ (†)	‡ (†)	‡ (†)	‡ (†)	‡ (†)	‡ (†)	‡ (†)
300 to 499	53.7 (7.13)	68.6 (5.64)	43.8 (6.87)	72.5 (5.83)	66.6 (6.45)	47.2 (7.40)	62.1 (6.02)	31.1 (6.45)	55.3 (6.33)	55.0 (6.71)
500 to 999	63.1 (5.67)	68.3 (4.52)	48.9 (4.96)	79.1 (3.70)	63.0 (4.61)	44.1 (4.65)	58.3 (4.72)	29.7 (4.40)	51.7 (5.29)	50.0 (4.14)
1,000 or more	‡ (†)	‡ (†)	‡ (†)	‡ (†)	‡ (†)	‡ (†)	‡ (†)	‡ (†)	‡ (†)	‡ (†)
Locale										
City	49.0 (7.11)	54.1 (6.55)	34.8 (6.31)	54.1 (6.84)	60.1 (7.64)	32.0 (7.84)	60.8 (6.88)	29.7 (6.63)	48.2 (8.34)	36.4 (8.47)
Suburban	67.8 (6.21)	71.9 (5.94)	41.7 (5.82)	84.0 (3.85)	64.8 (4.98)	54.0 (5.86)	55.6 (5.48)	36.1 (5.74)	45.7 (5.80)	48.9 (5.90)
Town	70.6 (9.61)	75.4 (7.59)	50.2 (9.58)	82.0 (8.45)	67.6 (9.59)	44.2 (9.50)	44.8 (10.28)	17.4 ! (7.52)	55.0 (8.71)	56.8 (9.57)
Rural	46.4 (8.45)	69.2 (6.95)	49.6 (7.40)	71.3 (7.21)	62.6 (7.07)	47.4 (6.46)	74.2 (7.15)	34.6 (7.08)	55.3 (6.12)	56.0 (6.18)
Percent combined enrollment of Black, Hispanic, Asian, Pacific Islander, and American Indian/Alaska Native students, and students of Two or more races										
Less than 5 percent	‡ (†)	‡ (†)	‡ (†)	‡ (†)	‡ (†)	‡ (†)	‡ (†)	‡ (†)	‡ (†)	‡ (†)
5 to less than 20 percent	49.7 (7.66)	65.1 (6.23)	34.6 (6.93)	80.4 (5.96)	68.7 (6.03)	47.9 (6.89)	54.0 (6.99)	32.5 (6.42)	57.8 (6.48)	55.3 (7.31)
20 to less than 50 percent	65.3 (8.32)	73.1 (7.26)	47.1 (7.22)	74.0 (6.95)	62.1 (8.21)	51.0 (8.17)	58.9 (8.63)	24.7 (6.18)	45.0 (7.74)	46.1 (7.90)
50 percent or more	61.7 (5.14)	65.6 (5.30)	45.3 (4.73)	71.1 (5.18)	64.3 (5.05)	43.5 (6.36)	63.0 (6.26)	34.0 (5.19)	48.1 (5.06)	47.1 (5.57)
Percent of students eligible for free or reduced-price lunch										
0 to 25 percent	‡ (†)	‡ (†)	‡ (†)	‡ (†)	‡ (†)	‡ (†)	‡ (†)	‡ (†)	‡ (†)	‡ (†)
26 to 50 percent	65.5 (8.25)	64.3 (6.41)	38.3 (7.29)	66.2 (7.34)	61.5 (6.54)	46.7 (7.45)	58.4 (6.79)	23.5 (5.76)	50.8 (7.72)	57.2 (7.63)
51 to 75 percent	59.3 (7.10)	74.5 (5.62)	52.2 (6.18)	81.6 (5.38)	63.2 (6.53)	47.2 (6.72)	63.4 (4.98)	44.3 (7.45)	45.3 (6.64)	50.5 (6.72)
76 to 100 percent	56.9 (6.35)	67.4 (6.30)	47.6 (5.06)	64.6 (6.43)	69.9 (5.70)	37.2 (7.41)	63.0 (7.26)	27.2 (7.33)	55.7 (5.83)	46.2 (6.92)
Percent of students who are Limited English Proficient (LEP)										
0 to 5 percent	57.4 (5.29)	63.5 (5.06)	42.5 (5.53)	71.5 (4.76)	61.6 (5.66)	46.3 (6.17)	54.1 (4.97)	23.3 (4.33)	50.2 (4.86)	47.2 (5.22)
6 to 20 percent	65.5 (7.88)	73.7 (7.71)	36.8 (5.21)	82.0 (5.26)	62.5 (7.01)	50.1 (6.20)	64.6 (7.43)	42.5 (6.62)	48.3 (8.27)	43.8 (8.17)
21 to 100 percent	54.1 (7.58)	68.6 (5.63)	50.7 (6.40)	68.4 (6.39)	68.2 (6.73)	39.3 (7.36)	64.1 (8.37)	34.0 (7.01)	51.8 (6.74)	56.4 (7.15)
All secondary schools[4] with sworn law enforcement officers present	**74.7 (1.48)**	**87.8 (1.24)**	**63.3 (1.58)**	**93.0 (0.88)**	**80.9 (1.15)**	**57.1 (1.72)**	**68.3 (1.71)**	**37.3 (1.70)**	**79.0 (1.42)**	**81.5 (1.35)**
Enrollment size										
Less than 300	76.7 (7.00)	89.1 (5.97)	53.4 (7.93)	95.8 (2.33)	72.7 (6.83)	51.7 (7.13)	55.0 (7.65)	30.6 (6.19)	71.8 (6.56)	69.1 (5.55)
300 to 499	63.2 (4.13)	75.1 (4.00)	58.0 (4.68)	83.2 (3.53)	70.2 (4.42)	54.5 (3.90)	55.7 (4.95)	33.8 (4.14)	70.4 (4.97)	72.9 (3.22)
500 to 999	76.4 (1.93)	88.2 (1.40)	64.9 (2.34)	93.4 (1.16)	81.0 (1.91)	57.2 (2.39)	70.8 (2.27)	40.2 (2.83)	78.8 (2.29)	81.9 (2.01)
1,000 or more	78.7 (2.40)	94.4 (0.95)	68.5 (2.07)	97.2 (0.59)	90.5 (1.17)	60.7 (2.41)	77.8 (1.97)	38.4 (2.43)	87.1 (1.68)	90.8 (1.45)
Locale										
City	66.5 (3.56)	88.3 (2.07)	65.9 (2.98)	91.7 (1.47)	80.4 (2.41)	50.1 (3.50)	66.9 (3.29)	30.8 (3.16)	82.4 (2.21)	81.7 (2.77)
Suburban	75.5 (2.46)	86.9 (1.91)	65.0 (2.08)	94.9 (1.16)	83.6 (2.07)	59.7 (2.78)	71.4 (2.18)	42.0 (2.34)	81.4 (2.19)	83.5 (1.77)
Town	79.7 (3.40)	93.5 (2.50)	60.7 (4.52)	94.4 (1.65)	80.6 (3.22)	60.3 (4.72)	66.1 (4.58)	34.8 (4.41)	76.4 (4.40)	83.0 (3.12)
Rural	78.9 (3.13)	85.1 (3.02)	60.3 (4.14)	91.1 (2.53)	78.2 (3.44)	58.9 (4.00)	67.1 (4.78)	39.4 (3.84)	74.1 (3.95)	77.7 (3.36)
Percent combined enrollment of Black, Hispanic, Asian, Pacific Islander, and American Indian/Alaska Native students, and students of Two or more races										
Less than 5 percent	73.7 (7.61)	82.7 (8.13)	68.8 (9.13)	85.3 (6.09)	79.8 (6.70)	51.5 (9.18)	67.9 (8.74)	42.8 (7.96)	71.3 (8.91)	74.7 (9.08)
5 to less than 20 percent	77.6 (2.74)	86.2 (2.11)	57.7 (3.38)	94.4 (1.37)	77.9 (3.14)	67.3 (3.04)	64.9 (3.66)	43.5 (3.26)	75.0 (3.79)	79.7 (2.98)
20 to less than 50 percent	81.2 (2.35)	90.5 (1.78)	62.8 (3.30)	94.9 (1.69)	85.1 (2.40)	61.4 (2.77)	75.0 (2.81)	42.2 (3.18)	80.9 (2.98)	85.1 (1.54)
50 percent or more	68.5 (3.03)	87.9 (2.07)	66.6 (2.77)	92.1 (1.30)	80.3 (2.00)	48.2 (2.80)	66.1 (2.50)	28.9 (2.28)	81.6 (1.69)	81.3 (1.80)
Percent of students eligible for free or reduced-price lunch										
0 to 25 percent	76.9 (3.05)	82.6 (3.20)	51.8 (3.54)	90.9 (2.56)	82.6 (2.26)	63.1 (3.25)	66.2 (2.90)	51.6 (3.96)	75.8 (3.98)	78.1 (3.86)
26 to 50 percent	75.1 (2.79)	86.8 (2.12)	64.8 (2.81)	93.5 (1.55)	82.3 (2.10)	62.7 (3.20)	72.5 (2.52)	36.9 (2.96)	82.7 (1.83)	85.9 (2.49)
51 to 75 percent	76.0 (2.55)	90.8 (2.08)	65.1 (3.48)	93.2 (1.39)	80.9 (2.60)	55.8 (3.68)	69.7 (3.21)	36.1 (3.06)	74.4 (2.84)	79.1 (2.46)
76 to 100 percent	70.9 (3.52)	89.2 (3.18)	68.5 (4.10)	93.7 (1.62)	77.9 (3.39)	47.6 (3.88)	63.0 (3.95)	28.2 (4.23)	83.0 (2.75)	82.0 (2.88)
Percent of students who are Limited English Proficient (LEP)										
0 to 5 percent	74.7 (1.82)	85.7 (1.83)	61.7 (2.38)	92.7 (1.31)	80.3 (1.83)	58.9 (2.08)	67.0 (2.34)	40.0 (2.14)	76.9 (2.02)	80.7 (1.91)
6 to 20 percent	75.3 (2.79)	91.0 (1.63)	66.7 (3.02)	92.9 (1.48)	82.8 (2.29)	56.4 (3.62)	74.0 (2.61)	31.4 (2.94)	81.4 (2.35)	84.8 (2.22)
21 to 100 percent	73.4 (5.72)	92.9 (2.28)	65.6 (5.76)	94.8 (1.95)	80.3 (4.60)	47.9 (5.19)	61.9 (5.41)	35.2 (5.09)	85.6 (3.45)	78.1 (4.95)

†Not applicable.

!Interpret data with caution. The coefficient of variation (CV) for this estimate is between 30 and 50 percent.

‡Reporting standards not met. Either there are too few cases for a reliable estimate or the coefficient of variation (CV) is 50 percent or greater.

[1] The questionnaire provided the following examples of courses or training: drug-related education, criminal law, or crime prevention courses.

[2] The questionnaire provided the following example of providing information about legal definitions for recording or reporting purposes: defining assault for school authorities.

[3] Primary schools are defined as schools in which the lowest grade is not higher than grade 3 and the highest grade is not higher than grade 8.

[4] Secondary schools include both middle and high schools as well as combined schools. Middle schools are defined as schools in which the lowest grade is not lower than grade 4 and the highest grade is not higher than grade 9. High schools are defined as schools in which the lowest grade is not lower than grade 9 and the highest grade is not higher than grade 12. Combined schools have any combination of grades (including K-12) that is not defined specifically as primary, middle, or high school.

NOTE: Sworn law enforcement officers include School Resource Officers as well as other sworn law enforcement officers who are not School Resource Officers. School Resource Officers are sworn law enforcement officers with arrest authority who have specialized training and are assigned to work in collaboration with school organizations. Responses were provided by the principal or the person most knowledgeable about crime and safety issues at the school. "At school" was defined to include activities happening in school buildings, on school grounds, on school buses, and at places that hold school-sponsored events or activities.

SOURCE: U.S. Department of Education, National Center for Education Statistics, 2015-16 School Survey on Crime and Safety (SSOCS), 2016. (This table was prepared September 2017.)

Table 233.74c. Among public schools with any sworn law enforcement officers present at school at least once a week, percentage with formalized policies or written documents defining the roles of officers at school, by school level, specific areas for which officers' role is defined, and selected school characteristics: 2015-16

[Standard errors appear in parentheses]

School characteristic	Among primary schools[1] with sworn law enforcement officers present						Among secondary schools[2] with sworn law enforcement officers present					
	Percent with any formalized policies or documents defining officers' roles at school[3]	Among schools with any formalized policies or documents, percent with policies or documents defining officers' role in specific area					Percent with any formalized policies or documents defining officers' roles at school[3]	Among schools with any formalized policies or documents, percent with policies or documents defining officers' role in specific area				
		Student discipline	Use of physical restraints[4]	Use of firearms	Making arrests on school grounds	Reporting criminal offenses to a law enforcement agency		Student discipline	Use of physical restraints[4]	Use of firearms	Making arrests on school grounds	Reporting criminal offenses to a law enforcement agency
1	2	3	4	5	6	7	8	9	10	11	12	13
Total	**50.9 (3.64)**	**56.4 (6.01)**	**38.3 (5.69)**	**31.7 (5.15)**	**47.9 (6.00)**	**52.6 (5.49)**	**69.6 (1.80)**	**58.7 (1.83)**	**48.7 (1.95)**	**44.8 (2.26)**	**63.0 (1.77)**	**71.1 (1.67)**
Enrollment size												
Less than 300	‡ (†)	‡ (†)	‡ (†)	‡ (†)	‡ (†)	‡ (†)	42.8 (7.77)	‡ (†)	‡ (†)	‡ (†)	‡ (†)	‡ (†)
300 to 499	47.2 (6.65)	53.0 (9.71)	41.3 (9.47)	35.6 (8.52)	53.0 (10.13)	48.1 (9.50)	54.5 (4.39)	43.7 (6.03)	36.8 (5.48)	39.5 (5.72)	56.5 (5.25)	68.9 (5.25)
500 to 999	56.4 (5.02)	62.2 (6.20)	38.4 (6.16)	30.4 (5.95)	46.5 (6.60)	52.4 (6.10)	75.6 (2.25)	59.3 (2.90)	45.4 (3.27)	40.6 (3.47)	60.3 (3.13)	68.3 (2.69)
1,000 or more	‡ (†)	‡ (†)	‡ (†)	‡ (†)	‡ (†)	‡ (†)	81.3 (2.11)	62.3 (2.76)	54.1 (2.48)	48.4 (2.64)	67.0 (2.41)	75.0 (2.14)
Locale												
City	55.0 (6.96)	‡ (†)	‡ (†)	‡ (†)	‡ (†)	‡ (†)	75.7 (3.17)	68.7 (3.54)	63.2 (3.73)	53.4 (3.95)	70.9 (3.07)	78.2 (2.71)
Suburban	49.2 (6.62)	57.0 (7.78)	41.0 (7.76)	38.4 (7.79)	54.9 (8.52)	60.8 (7.99)	76.1 (2.11)	56.1 (2.56)	43.5 (2.79)	41.9 (3.23)	59.0 (2.89)	68.1 (2.77)
Town	62.8 (9.99)	‡ (†)	‡ (†)	‡ (†)	‡ (†)	‡ (†)	68.8 (4.30)	48.6 (5.05)	36.7 (4.49)	36.3 (4.27)	57.1 (5.09)	62.0 (4.57)
Rural	40.5 (6.94)	‡ (†)	‡ (†)	‡ (†)	‡ (†)	‡ (†)	55.8 (4.09)	57.2 (4.22)	46.8 (4.64)	44.2 (4.54)	63.6 (4.37)	73.1 (3.35)
Percent combined enrollment of Black, Hispanic, Asian, Pacific Islander, and American Indian/Alaska Native students, and students of Two or more races												
Less than 5 percent	‡ (†)	‡ (†)	‡ (†)	‡ (†)	‡ (†)	‡ (†)	48.3 (8.55)	45.0 (9.59)	49.6 (10.15)	31.8 (9.38)	61.6 (9.73)	70.9 (9.09)
5 to less than 20 percent	48.2 (5.75)	‡ (†)	‡ (†)	‡ (†)	‡ (†)	‡ (†)	58.7 (3.20)	47.1 (3.67)	35.3 (3.22)	37.8 (3.75)	51.4 (4.22)	64.7 (3.05)
20 to less than 50 percent	54.0 (9.30)	‡ (†)	‡ (†)	‡ (†)	‡ (†)	‡ (†)	77.7 (2.92)	61.1 (2.78)	49.4 (3.30)	46.7 (3.06)	65.6 (3.28)	73.6 (2.96)
50 percent or more	53.7 (5.69)	55.2 (8.35)	38.3 (8.51)	30.6 (7.73)	51.3 (8.86)	53.9 (8.68)	75.1 (2.72)	64.8 (2.54)	55.3 (3.03)	48.6 (3.19)	67.6 (2.03)	72.7 (2.14)
Percent of students eligible for free or reduced-price lunch												
0 to 25 percent	‡ (†)	‡ (†)	‡ (†)	‡ (†)	‡ (†)	‡ (†)	71.1 (3.14)	53.0 (4.07)	34.2 (3.40)	38.5 (4.61)	53.4 (4.98)	68.3 (3.88)
26 to 50 percent	51.7 (8.33)	‡ (†)	‡ (†)	‡ (†)	‡ (†)	‡ (†)	69.9 (2.66)	51.4 (3.73)	41.8 (3.50)	38.2 (3.42)	54.8 (4.23)	64.0 (3.53)
51 to 75 percent	54.9 (7.25)	34.0 ! (11.40)	18.1 ! (8.54)	19.5 ! (8.40)	34.5 (8.84)	40.6 (9.43)	64.3 (3.13)	60.6 (3.38)	51.2 (3.68)	47.4 (3.92)	68.9 (3.10)	73.4 (3.46)
76 to 100 percent	54.1 (6.85)	‡ (†)	‡ (†)	‡ (†)	‡ (†)	‡ (†)	74.8 (4.60)	69.1 (3.52)	64.2 (4.09)	53.8 (4.51)	72.7 (3.40)	78.3 (2.80)
Percent of students who are Limited English Proficient (LEP)												
0 to 5 percent	47.4 (4.38)	55.8 (8.88)	38.3 (7.93)	27.2 (7.51)	41.4 (8.34)	51.1 (7.58)	64.5 (2.08)	57.0 (2.38)	46.6 (2.58)	44.8 (2.77)	62.1 (2.46)	72.4 (2.11)
6 to 20 percent	57.6 (8.21)	48.2 (9.12)	42.3 (9.12)	43.3 (9.02)	48.4 (9.14)	50.9 (8.76)	79.7 (2.74)	60.0 (3.90)	49.3 (3.03)	42.7 (2.64)	63.1 (3.13)	67.7 (3.12)
21 to 100 percent	50.7 (7.14)	‡ (†)	‡ (†)	‡ (†)	‡ (†)	‡ (†)	76.4 (4.54)	64.6 (6.75)	58.6 (6.62)	49.9 (6.48)	67.9 (5.80)	72.5 (5.08)
Officers routinely carry or wear specific items												
Carry a stun gun[5]	53.4 (4.74)	54.9 (7.14)	39.8 (6.40)	33.2 (6.46)	47.2 (7.53)	58.3 (6.84)	70.7 (2.05)	56.3 (2.32)	47.5 (2.46)	43.4 (2.68)	61.5 (2.29)	69.3 (2.03)
Carry chemical aerosol sprays[6]	52.0 (4.92)	56.5 (7.18)	40.3 (6.40)	35.9 (6.82)	49.9 (7.30)	56.4 (7.40)	71.8 (2.15)	59.0 (2.14)	50.5 (2.32)	47.6 (2.50)	64.9 (2.27)	71.9 (2.13)
Carry a firearm	52.8 (3.90)	55.7 (6.20)	37.4 (5.71)	34.5 (5.39)	49.5 (6.09)	52.5 (5.84)	70.1 (1.69)	58.3 (1.96)	48.9 (2.03)	46.4 (2.27)	63.3 (1.81)	71.0 (1.72)
Wear a body camera	‡ (†)	‡ (†)	‡ (†)	‡ (†)	‡ (†)	‡ (†)	77.8 (3.42)	60.0 (4.28)	48.9 (4.50)	46.6 (5.05)	65.5 (4.09)	70.9 (4.08)

†Not applicable.

!Interpret data with caution. The coefficient of variation (CV) for this estimate is between 30 and 50 percent.

‡Reporting standards not met (too few cases for a reliable estimate).

[1] Primary schools are defined as schools in which the lowest grade is not higher than grade 3 and the highest grade is not higher than grade 8.

[2] Secondary schools include both middle and high schools as well as combined schools. Middle schools are defined as schools in which the lowest grade is not lower than grade 4 and the highest grade is not higher than grade 9. High schools are defined as schools in which the lowest grade is not lower than grade 9 and the highest grade is not higher than grade 12. Combined schools have any combination of grades (including K-12) that is not defined specifically as primary, middle, or high school.

[3] The questionnaire asked, "did your school or school district have any formalized policies or written documents (e.g., Memorandum of Use, Memorandum of Agreement) that outlined the roles, responsibilities, and expectations of sworn law enforcement officers (including School Resource Officers) at school?"

[4] The questionnaire provided the following examples of use of physical restraints: handcuffs, Tasers, Mace, pepper spray, or other physical or chemical restraints.

[5] The questionnaire cited a Taser gun as an example of a stun gun.

[6] The questionnaire provided the following examples of chemical aerosol sprays: Mace and pepper spray.

NOTE: Sworn law enforcement officers include School Resource Officers as well as other sworn law enforcement officers who are not School Resource Officers. School Resource Officers are sworn law enforcement officers with arrest authority who have specialized training and are assigned to work in collaboration with school organizations. Responses were provided by the principal or the person most knowledgeable about crime and safety issues at the school. "At school" was defined to include activities happening in school buildings, on school grounds, on school buses, and at places that hold school-sponsored events or activities.

SOURCE: U.S. Department of Education, National Center for Education Statistics, 2015-16 School Survey on Crime and Safety (SSOCS), 2016. (This table was prepared September 2017.)

Table 233.80. Percentage of students ages 12-18 who reported various security measures at school: Selected years, 1999 through 2017

[Standard errors appear in parentheses]

Year	Total, at least one of the listed security measures	Metal detectors	Locker checks	One or more security cameras to monitor the school	Security guards and/or assigned police officers	Other school staff or other adults supervising the hallway	A requirement that students wear badges or picture identification	A written code of student conduct	Locked entrance or exit doors during the day	A requirement that visitors sign in and wear visitor badges or stickers[1]
1	2	3	4	5	6	7	8	9	10	11
1999	— (†)	9.1 (0.51)	54.6 (0.84)	— (†)	54.4 (1.37)	85.8 (0.54)	— (†)	— (†)	38.9 (1.00)	— (†)
2001	99.7 (0.07)	8.8 (0.61)	54.0 (0.93)	39.1 (1.14)	63.8 (1.25)	88.6 (0.45)	21.2 (0.99)	95.5 (0.33)	49.1 (1.13)	— (†)
2003	99.5 (0.10)	10.2 (0.84)	53.3 (0.92)	48.1 (1.17)	69.8 (0.91)	90.8 (0.39)	22.6 (1.11)	95.6 (0.35)	53.0 (1.16)	— (†)
2005	99.6 (0.10)	10.7 (0.74)	53.2 (0.90)	57.9 (1.35)	68.3 (1.13)	90.1 (0.42)	24.9 (1.20)	95.5 (0.36)	54.3 (1.06)	— (†)
2007	99.8 (0.06)	10.1 (0.51)	53.6 (0.95)	66.0 (0.99)	68.8 (0.98)	90.0 (0.50)	24.3 (1.00)	95.9 (0.29)	60.9 (1.07)	— (†)
2009	99.3 (0.10)	10.6 (0.76)	53.8 (1.17)	70.0 (1.05)	68.1 (1.05)	90.6 (0.46)	23.4 (1.14)	95.6 (0.39)	64.3 (1.27)	— (†)
2011	99.6 (0.08)	11.2 (0.64)	53.0 (0.99)	76.7 (0.83)	69.8 (1.01)	88.9 (0.46)	24.8 (1.02)	95.7 (0.30)	64.5 (1.02)	— (†)
2013	99.6 (0.07)	11.0 (0.72)	52.0 (1.13)	76.7 (1.06)	70.4 (1.04)	90.5 (0.51)	26.2 (1.02)	95.9 (0.30)	75.8 (1.10)	— (†)
2015	99.8 (0.06)	12.3 (0.74)	52.9 (1.25)	82.5 (0.85)	69.5 (1.07)	89.5 (0.55)	23.9 (1.06)	95.7 (0.38)	78.2 (0.97)	90.2 (0.62)
2017	99.4 (0.10)	10.4 (0.57)	47.8 (1.03)	83.8 (0.76)	70.9 (1.06)	88.2 (0.58)	24.4 (0.99)	94.7 (0.40)	78.8 (0.85)	90.4 (0.53)

—Not available.

†Not applicable.

[1] Prior to 2015, the question asked simply whether the school had "A requirement that visitors sign in." As of 2015, the question has also included the requirement that visitors wear badges or stickers. Data for years prior to 2015 have been omitted because the change in questionnaire wording may affect comparability of the data over time.

NOTE: "At school" includes in the school building, on school property, on a school bus, and, from 2001 onward, going to and from school. Some data have been revised from previously published figures.

SOURCE: U.S. Department of Justice, Bureau of Justice Statistics, School Crime Supplement (SCS) to the National Crime Victimization Survey, 1999 through 2017. (This table was prepared September 2018.)

Table 234.10. Age range for compulsory school attendance and special education services, and policies on year-round schools and kindergarten programs, by state: Selected years, 2000 through 2018

State	Compulsory attendance							Compulsory special education services, 2004[1]	Year-round schools, 2008		Kindergarten programs, 2018		
											School districts required to offer		
	2000	2002	2004	2006	2010	2015	2017		Has policy on year-round schools	Has districts with year-round schools	Program	Full-day program	Attendance required
1	2	3	4	5	6	7	8	9	10	11	12	13	14
Alabama	7 to 16	7 to 16	7 to 16[2]	7 to 16	7 to 17	6 to 17[3]	6 to 17[3]	6 to 21		Yes	X	X	
Alaska	7 to 16	7 to 16	7 to 16[2]	7 to 16	7 to 16	7 to 16[2]	7 to 16[2]	3 to 22		Yes			
Arizona	6 to 16[2]	6 to 16[2]	6 to 16[2]	6 to 16[2]	6 to 16[2]	6 to 16[2]	6 to 16[2]	3 to 21	—	—	X		
Arkansas	5 to 17[2,3]	5 to 17[2,3]	5 to 17[2,3]	5 to 17[2,3]	5 to 17[2,3]	5 to 18	5 to 18	5 to 21	X	Yes	X	X	X
California	6 to 18[2]	6 to 18	6 to 18	6 to 18	6 to 18	6 to 18	6 to 18	Birth to 21[4]	X	Yes	X		
Colorado	—	—	7 to 16	7 to 16	6 to 17	6 to 17	6 to 17	3 to 21		Yes	X		
Connecticut	7 to 16	7 to 18[2]	7 to 18[2]	5 to 18[3]	5 to 18[3]	5 to 18[3]	5 to 18[3]	3 to 21		—	X		X
Delaware	5 to 16	5 to 16	5 to 16[2]	5 to 16	5 to 16	5 to 16	5 to 16	Birth to 20		Yes	X	X	X
District of Columbia	—	5 to 18	5 to 18	5 to 18	5 to 18	5 to 18	5 to 18	—	—	—	X	X	X
Florida	6 to 16[5]	6 to 16[5]	6 to 16[5]	6 to 16[5]	6 to 16[5]	6 to 16	6 to 16	3 to 21	X	Yes	X		
Georgia	6 to 16	6 to 16	6 to 16	6 to 16	6 to 16	6 to 16	6 to 16	Birth to 21[6]		Yes	X		
Hawaii	6 to 18	6 to 18	6 to 18	6 to 18	6 to 18	5 to 18	5 to 18	Birth to 19		([7])	X	X	X
Idaho	7 to 16	7 to 16	7 to 16	7 to 16	7 to 16	7 to 16	7 to 16	3 to 21		Yes			
Illinois	7 to 16	7 to 16	7 to 17	7 to 17	7 to 17	6 to 17	6 to 17	3 to 21	X	Yes	X	([8])	
Indiana	7 to 16	7 to 16	7 to 16	7 to 18[2]	7 to 18[2]	7 to 18	7 to 18	3 to 22		Yes	X		
Iowa	6 to 16[2]	6 to 16[2]	6 to 16	6 to 16	6 to 16	6 to 16[9]	6 to 16[9]	Birth to 21	X	Yes	X		([10])
Kansas	7 to 18[2]	7 to 18[2]	7 to 18[2]	7 to 18[2]	7 to 18[2]	7 to 18	7 to 18	3 to 21[11]		—	X		
Kentucky	6 to 16	6 to 16	6 to 16[2]	6 to 16	6 to 16	6 to 18[12]	6 to 18	Birth to 21		Yes	X		
Louisiana	7 to 17	7 to 17	7 to 17[2]	7 to 18[2]	7 to 18[2]	7 to 18	7 to 18	3 to 21[13]		Yes	X	X	X[14]
Maine	7 to 17	7 to 17	7 to 17[2]	7 to 17[2]	7 to 17[2]	7 to 17	7 to 17	5 to 19[13,15]		—	X		([10])
Maryland	5 to 16	5 to 16	5 to 16	5 to 16	5 to 16[3]	5 to 17	5 to 18	Birth to 21	X	—	X	X	X
Massachusetts	6 to 16	6 to 16	6 to 16	6 to 16[2]	6 to 16[2]	6 to 16	6 to 16[16]	3 to 21[6]	([17])	—	X		([10])
Michigan	6 to 16	6 to 16	6 to 16	6 to 16	6 to 18	6 to 18	6 to 18	Birth to 25	X	Yes			
Minnesota	7 to 18[2]	7 to 16	7 to 16	7 to 16[2]	7 to 16[2]	7 to 17	7 to 17	Birth to 21	X	Yes			
Mississippi	6 to 17	6 to 17	6 to 16	6 to 16	6 to 17	6 to 17	6 to 17	Birth to 20		—	X	X	([10])
Missouri	7 to 16	7 to 16	7 to 16	7 to 16	7 to 17	7 to 17[2,3]	7 to 17[2,3]	Birth to 20		Yes[18]	X		
Montana	7 to 16[2]	7 to 16[2]	7 to 16[2]	7 to 16[2]	7 to 16[2]	7 to 16[2]	7 to 16[2]	3 to 18[13]		—	X	([8])	
Nebraska	7 to 16	7 to 16	7 to 16	6 to 18	6 to 18	6 to 18	6 to 18	Birth to 20		Yes	X		
Nevada	7 to 17	7 to 17	7 to 17	7 to 17	7 to 18[2]	7 to 18	7 to 18	Birth to 21[4]		Yes	X		X[14]
New Hampshire	6 to 16	6 to 16	6 to 16	6 to 16	6 to 18	6 to 18	6 to 18	3 to 21		—			
New Jersey	6 to 16	6 to 16	6 to 16	6 to 16	6 to 16	6 to 16	6 to 16	5 to 21		—		([19])	([19])
New Mexico	5 to 18	5 to 18	5 to 18[2]	5 to 18[2]	5 to 18[2]	5 to 18	5 to 18	3 to 21	X	Yes	X		X
New York	6 to 16[2]	6 to 16	6 to 16	6 to 16[20]	6 to 16[20]	6 to 16[20]	6 to 16[20]	Birth to 20		—		([20])	([20])
North Carolina	7 to 16	7 to 16	7 to 16	7 to 16	7 to 16	7 to 16	7 to 16	5 to 20	X	Yes	X	X	
North Dakota	7 to 16	7 to 16	7 to 16	7 to 16	7 to 16	7 to 16	7 to 16	3 to 21		No	X		
Ohio	6 to 18	6 to 18	6 to 18	6 to 18	6 to 18	6 to 18	6 to 18	3 to 21	X	—	X		X
Oklahoma	5 to 18	5 to 18	5 to 18	5 to 18	5 to 18	5 to 18	5 to 18	Birth to 21[13]		Yes	X	X	X
Oregon	7 to 18	7 to 18	7 to 18[2]	7 to 18	7 to 18	7 to 18	6 to 18	3 to 20		Yes	X		
Pennsylvania	8 to 17	8 to 17	8 to 17[2]	8 to 17[2]	8 to 17[2]	8 to 17	8 to 17	6 to 21	X[18]	—[18]			
Rhode Island	6 to 16	6 to 16	6 to 16	6 to 16	6 to 16	6 to 18[2]	5 to 18[2]	3 to 21		—	X	X	X
South Carolina	5 to 16	5 to 16	5 to 16	5 to 17[3]	5 to 17[3]	5 to 17	5 to 17	3 to 21[21]		—	X	X	X
South Dakota	6 to 16	6 to 16	6 to 16	6 to 16	6 to 18[2]	6 to 18[2]	6 to 18[2]	Birth to 21	X	—	X		X[22]
Tennessee	6 to 17	6 to 17	6 to 17	6 to 17[3]	6 to 17[3]	6 to 18	6 to 18	3 to 21[4]	X	Yes	X	X	X
Texas	6 to 18	6 to 18	6 to 18	6 to 18	6 to 18	6 to 18	6 to 19	3 to 21	X	Yes	X		
Utah	6 to 18	6 to 18	6 to 18	6 to 18	6 to 18	6 to 18	6 to 18	3 to 22		Yes	X		
Vermont	7 to 16	6 to 16	6 to 16	6 to 16[2]	6 to 16[2]	6 to 16[2]	6 to 16[2]	3 to 21		—[18]	X		
Virginia	5 to 18	5 to 18	5 to 18	5 to 18[2]	5 to 18[2,3]	5 to 18	5 to 18	2 to 21	X	Yes	X		X
Washington	8 to 17[2]	8 to 17[2]	8 to 16[2]	8 to 18	8 to 18	8 to 18	8 to 18	3 to 21[21]		Yes	X	X	
West Virginia	6 to 16	6 to 16	6 to 16	6 to 16	6 to 17	6 to 17	6 to 17	5 to 21[23]	X	Yes	X	X	X
Wisconsin	6 to 18	6 to 18	6 to 18	6 to 18	6 to 18	6 to 18	6 to 18	3 to 21		Yes	X		X[24]
Wyoming	6 to 16[2]	6 to 16[2]	7 to 16[2]	7 to 16[2]	7 to 16[2]	7 to 16[2]	7 to 16[2]	3 to 21		—	X	([25])	([10])

—Not available.
X Denotes that the state has a policy. A blank denotes that the state does not have a policy.
[1]Most states have a provision whereby education is provided up to a certain age or completion of secondary school, whichever comes first.
[2]Child may be exempted from compulsory attendance if he/she meets state requirements for early withdrawal with or without meeting conditions for a diploma or equivalency.
[3]Parent/guardian may delay child's entry until a later age per state law/regulation.
[4]Student may continue in the program if 22nd birthday falls before the end of the school year.
[5]Attendance is compulsory until age 18 for Manatee County students, unless they earn a high school diploma prior to reaching their 18th birthday.
[6]Through age 21 or until child graduates with a high school or special education diploma or equivalent.
[7]Some schools operate on a multitrack system; the schools are open year round, but different cohorts start and end at different times.
[8]District must offer either a half-day or full-day program.
[9]Children enrolled in preschool programs (who must be 4 years old on or before September 15) are considered to be of compulsory school attendance age.
[10]Not specified in statute, rules, or regulations.
[11]To be determined by rules and regulations adopted by the state board.
[12]All districts adopted a policy to raise the upper compulsory school age from 16 to 18. The policy took effect for most districts in the 2015-16 school year.
[13]Children from birth through age 2 are eligible for additional services.
[14]Attendance is required unless the student otherwise satisfactorily passes an academic readiness screening upon enrollment in grade 1.
[15]Must be age 5 before October 15 and not age 20 before start of school year.
[16]Each school committee is permitted to establish its own minimum age for school attendance, provided that it is not older than the mandatory minimum age established by the state.
[17]Policies about year-round schools are decided locally.
[18]State did not participate in 2008 online survey. Data are from 2006.
[19]Abbott Districts are required to offer full-day kindergarten and students are required to attend.
[20]Local boards of education can require school attendance until age 17 unless employed. In Syracuse, New York City, Rochester, Utica, Buffalo, Cohoes, Watervliet, and Yonkers, districts are required to offer full-day kindergarten and children are required to attend full-day kindergarten.
[21]Student may complete school year if 21st birthday occurs while attending school.
[22]All children must attend kindergarten before age 7.
[23]Children with severe disabilities may begin receiving services at age 3.
[24]Children must attend in districts that offer kindergarten.
[25]School districts must establish and maintain relationships with a district that offers full-day kindergarten.
NOTE: The Education of the Handicapped Act (EHA) Amendments of 1986 make it mandatory for all states receiving EHA funds to serve all 3- to 18-year-old disabled children.
SOURCE: Council of Chief State School Officers, *Key State Education Policies on PK–12 Education*, 2000, 2002, 2004, 2006, and 2008; Education Commission of the States (ECS), ECS StateNotes, *Compulsory School Age Requirements*, retrieved August 9, 2010, from http://www.ecs.org/clearinghouse/86/62/8662.pdf; ECS StateNotes, *Special Education: State Special Education Definitions, Ages Served*, retrieved August 9, 2010, from http://www.ecs.org/clearinghouse/52/29/5229.pdf; ECS StateNotes, *Compulsory School Age Requirements*, retrieved May 19, 2015, from http://www.ecs.org/clearinghouse/01/18/68/11868.pdf; ECS StateNotes, *Age Requirements for Free and Compulsory Education*, retrieved July 2, 2018, from https://www.ecs.org/age-requirements-for-free-and-compulsory-education/; ESC StateNotes, *Does the state require the district to offer kindergarten and if so, full day or half day? What exemptions exist for districts?*, retrieved July 2, 2018, from http://ecs.force.com/mbdata/MBQuest2RTanw?rep=KK3Q1805; ESC StateNotes, *Does the state require children to attend kindergarten?*, retrieved July 2, 2018, from http://ecs.force.com/mbdata/MBQuest2RTanw?rep=KK3Q1804; and supplemental information retrieved from various state websites. (This table was prepared July 2018.)

Table 234.20. Minimum amount of instructional time per year and policies on textbooks, by state: Selected years, 2000 through 2020

State	Minimum amount of instructional time per year						Policies on textbooks, 2014		
	In days					In hours	Textbook selection level		Free textbooks provided to students
	2000	2006	2011	2014	2020	2020	State	Local education agency	
1	2	3	4	5	6	7	8	9	10
Alabama	175	175	180	180[1]	180[1]	1,080	X		X
Alaska	180	180	170[2]	180[3]	180[1]	740 (K-3); 900 (4-12)		X	X
Arizona	—	180	180[1]	180[1]	180[1]	712 (1-3); 890 (4-8); 720 (9-12)		X	X[4]
Arkansas	178	178	178[2]	178[3]	178	†		X[5]	X
California	175	180	180/175[6]	180/175[6]	180[7]	600 (K); 840 (1-3); 900 (4-8); 1,080 (9-12)	X[8]		X
Colorado	[9]	160	160	160	160	450/900 (K); 990 (1-5); 1,080 (6-12)		X	
Connecticut	180	180	180	180	180	450/900 (K); 900 (1-12)		X	X
Delaware	[9]	†	†	†	†	1,060 (K-11); 1,032 (12)		X	X
District of Columbia	180[10]	180	178	180	180	†			X
Florida	180	180	180	180	180[1]	720 (K-3); 900 (4-12)	X		X
Georgia	180[10]	180	180	180	180[1]	†	X		X
Hawaii	184	179	180[11]	180[11]	180[2,11]	1,080[11]	X		X[12]
Idaho	180	†	†	†	†	450[3] (K); 810[3] (1-3); 900[3] (4-8); 990[3] (9-12)	X		X
Illinois	180[13]	176	176	180[3]	185	†		X	[4]
Indiana	180	180	180	180	180	†		X	
Iowa	180	180	180	180	180	1,080		X	
Kansas	186	186 (K-11); 181 (12)	186 (K-11); 181 (12)	186 (K-11); 181 (12)	186 (1-11); 181 (12)	465 (K); 1,116 (1-11); 1,086 (12)		X	
Kentucky	175	175	175[2]	170[2]	170[3]	1,062	X		X[15]
Louisiana	175	177	177[2]	177[2,16]	177[1]	1,062	X		X
Maine	175	175	175[2]	175[2]	180[16]	†		X	X
Maryland	180	180	180	180	180	1,080; 1,170 (High)		X	X
Massachusetts	180	180	180	180	180[16]	425 (K); 900 (1-5); 990 (6-12)		X	X
Michigan	180	†	165	175	180	1,098		X	X[17]
Minnesota	[9]	[9]	†	†	165 (1-11)	425/850 (K); 935 (1-6); 1,020 (7-12)		X	X
Mississippi	180	180	180	180	180	†	X		X
Missouri	174	174	174/142[18]	174/142[18]	†	522 (K); 1,044 (1-12)		X	X
Montana	180	90 (K); 180 (K-12)	†	†	†	360/720 (K); 720 (1-3); 1,080[16] (4-12)		X	X
Nebraska	[9]	†	†	†	†	400 (K); 1,032 (1-8); 1,080 (9-12)		X	X
Nevada	180	180	180	180	180	†	X		X[12]
New Hampshire	180	180	180	180	180[1,16]	450 (K); 945 (Elementary); 990 (Middle); 990 (High)		X	X
New Jersey	180	180	180	180	180	†		X	X
New Mexico	180	180	180	†	†	450/990 (K); 990 (1-6); 1,080 (7-12)	X		X
New York	180[10]	180	180	180	180	450/900 (K); 900 (1-6); 990 (7-12)		X	X
North Carolina	180	180	180	185	185[1]	1,025	X		X
North Dakota	173	173	175[2]	175[2]	†	481.25/962.5[3] (K); 962.5[3] (1-5); 1,050[3] (6-12)		X	X[17]
Ohio	182	182	182[3]	†	†	450/910 (K); 910 (1-6); 1,001 (7-12)		X	X
Oklahoma	180	180	180[3]	180	180[1]	1,080[3]	X		X
Oregon	[9]	†	†	†	†	450/900 (K); 900 (1-8); 990 (9-11); 966 (12)	X		X
Pennsylvania	180	180	180	180	180[1]	450 (K); 900 (1-6); 990 (7-12)		X	X
Rhode Island	180	180	180	180	180[1]	1,080		X	X[17]
South Carolina	180	180	180[2]	180[2]	180[3]	†	X		
South Dakota	—	†	†	†	†	437.5 (K); 875 (1–5); 962.5[16] (6-12)		X	X
Tennessee	180	180	180[2]	180[2]	180[3]	†	X		X
Texas	187	180	180	180	†	1,260	X		X
Utah	180	180	180	180	180	990	X	[19]	

See notes at end of table.

Table 234.20. Minimum amount of instructional time per year and policies on textbooks, by state: Selected years, 2000 through 2020—Continued

State	Minimum amount of instructional time per year						Policies on textbooks, 2014		
	In days					In hours	Textbook selection level		Free textbooks provided to students
	2000	2006	2011	2014	2020	2020	State	Local education agency	
1	2	3	4	5	6	7	8	9	10
Vermont	175	175	175	175	175[3]	†		X	X
Virginia	180	180	180	180	180[1]	540 (K); 990 (1-12)	X		X
Washington	180[13]	180	180	180	180[20]	450 (K); 1,000 (1-8); 1,080 (9-12)		X	[21]
West Virginia	180	180	180	180	180	†	X		X
Wisconsin	180	180	180	†	†	437 (K); 1,050 (1-6); 1,137 (7-12)		X	
Wyoming	175	175	180	175	175	450 (K); 900 (1-5); 1,050 (6-8); 1,100 (9-12)		X	X

—Not available.
†Not applicable.
X Denotes that the state has a policy. A blank denotes that the state does not have a policy.
[1]Or an equivalent number of hours or minutes of instruction per year.
[2]Does not include time for in-service or staff development or parent-teacher conferences.
[3]Includes time for in-service or staff development or parent-teacher conferences. No more than 22 hours of staff development can be counted toward Idaho's instructional time requirement, and no more than 30 hours of staff development can be counted toward Oklahoma's requirement.
[4]Fees permitted at the high school level for nonrequired or supplementary textbooks.
[5]State Department of Education prepares a list of suggestions, but the districts choose.
[6]Through 2014–15, districts were allowed to shorten the 180-day instructional year to 175 days without fiscal penalty.
[7]Select districts are required to have 175 days.
[8]Statewide textbook adoption is only at the elementary level. Adoption practices have been suspended until the 2015–16 school year.
[9]No statewide policy; varies by district.
[10]1996 data.
[11]Does not apply to charter and multitrack schools.
[12]Fees for lost or damaged books permitted.
[13]1998 data.
[14]Fees permitted, but if 5 percent or more of the voters in a district petition the school board, a majority of the district's voters may decide to furnish free textbooks to students.
[15]Fees permitted for students in grades 9–12, but students who qualify for free or reduced-price lunch are exempted.
[16]Instructional time for graduating seniors may be reduced.
[17]Refundable or security deposits permitted.
[18]174 days required for a 5-day week; 142 days required for a 4-day week.
[19]Local districts may select textbooks not on the state recommended list provided the textbooks meet specific criteria and the selection is based on recommendations by the district's curriculum materials review committee.
[20]180 half-days for kindergarten.
[21]A district may provide free textbooks to students when, in its judgment, the best interests of the district will be served.
NOTE: Minimum number of instructional days refers to the actual number of days that pupils have contact with a teacher. Some states allow for different types of school calendars by setting instructional time in both days and hours, while others use only days or only hours. For states in which the number of days or hours varies by grade, the relevant grade(s) appear in parentheses. For states that specify minimum hours both for part-day kindergarten and for full-day kindergarten, a slash separates the part-day hours from the full-day hours.
SOURCE: Council of Chief State School Officers, *Key State Education Policies on PK–12 Education*, 2000 and 2006; Education Commission of the States, StateNotes, *Number of Instructional Days/Hours in the School Year* (August 2011 and October 2014 revisions), retrieved September 22, 2011, from http://www.ecs.org/clearinghouse/95/05/9505.pdf and May 9, 2015, from http://www.ecs.org/clearinghouse/01/15/05/11505.pdf; *State Textbook Adoption* (September 2013 edition), retrieved May 19, 2015, from http://www.ecs.org/clearinghouse/01/09/23/10923.pdf; *Instructional Time: What's the State's Requirement of Minimum Number of Days or Hours/Minutes in a School Year?*, retrieved May 20, 2020, from https://www.ecs.org/50-state-comparison-instructional-time-policies/; and supplemental information retrieved from various state websites. (This table was prepared May 2020.)

Table 235.10. Revenues for public elementary and secondary schools, by source of funds: Selected years, 1919–20 through 2016–17

School year	Revenues (in thousands)							Revenues per pupil						
				Local (including intermediate sources below the state level)							Local (including intermediate sources below the state level)			
	Total	Federal	State	Total	Property taxes	Other public revenue	Private[1]	Total	Federal	State	Total	Property taxes	Other public revenue	Private[1]
1	2	3	4	5	6	7	8	9	10	11	12	13	14	15
							Current dollars							
1919–20	$970,121	$2,475	$160,085	$807,561	—	—	—	$45	#	$7	$37	—	—	—
1929–30	2,088,557	7,334	353,670	1,727,553	—	—	—	81	#	14	67	—	—	—
1939–40	2,260,527	39,810	684,354	1,536,363	—	—	—	89	$2	27	60	—	—	—
1949–50	5,437,044	155,848	2,165,689	3,115,507	—	—	—	217	6	86	124	—	—	—
1959–60	14,746,618	651,639	5,768,047	8,326,932	—	—	—	419	19	164	237	—	—	—
1969–70	40,266,922	3,219,557	16,062,776	20,984,589	—	—	—	884	71	353	461	—	—	—
1979–80	96,881,164	9,503,537	45,348,814	42,028,813	—	—	—	2,326	228	1,089	1,009	—	—	—
1989–90	208,547,573	12,700,784	98,238,633	97,608,157	$74,867,627	$17,084,494	$5,656,036	5,144	313	2,423	2,408	$1,847	$421	$140
1994–95	273,149,449	18,582,157	127,729,576	126,837,717	97,978,129	21,560,162	7,299,425	6,192	421	2,896	2,875	2,221	489	165
1996–97	305,065,192	20,081,287	146,435,584	138,548,321	106,545,881	24,288,693	7,713,747	6,688	440	3,211	3,038	2,336	533	169
1997–98	325,925,708	22,201,965	157,645,372	146,078,370	111,184,150	26,676,244	8,217,977	7,066	481	3,418	3,167	2,410	578	178
1998–99	347,377,993	24,521,817	169,298,232	153,557,944	119,483,487	25,348,879	8,725,578	7,464	527	3,638	3,300	2,567	545	187
1999–2000	372,943,802	27,097,866	184,613,352	161,232,584	124,735,516	27,628,923	8,868,145	7,959	578	3,940	3,441	2,662	590	189
2000–01	401,356,120	29,100,183	199,583,097	172,672,840	132,575,925	30,889,273	9,207,643	8,503	616	4,228	3,658	2,809	654	195
2001–02	419,501,976	33,144,633	206,541,793	179,815,551	141,095,685	28,924,825	9,795,041	8,800	695	4,333	3,772	2,960	607	205
2002–03	440,111,653	37,515,909	214,277,407	188,318,337	148,511,786	29,579,240	10,227,310	9,134	779	4,447	3,908	3,082	614	212
2003–04	462,026,099	41,923,435	217,384,191	202,718,474	160,602,055	31,651,489	10,464,930	9,518	864	4,478	4,176	3,309	652	216
2004–05	487,753,525	44,809,532	228,553,579	214,390,414	167,909,883	35,433,486	11,047,044	9,996	918	4,684	4,394	3,441	726	226
2005–06	520,621,788	47,553,778	242,151,076	230,916,934	178,279,408	41,111,066	11,526,460	10,600	968	4,930	4,702	3,630	837	235
2006–07	555,710,762	47,150,608	263,608,741	244,951,413	188,287,298	44,806,422	11,857,694	11,281	957	5,351	4,972	3,822	910	241
2007–08	584,683,686	47,788,467	282,622,523	254,272,697	196,521,569	45,314,965	12,436,163	11,879	971	5,742	5,166	3,993	921	253
2008–09	592,422,033	56,670,261	276,525,603	259,226,169	205,821,844	41,195,313	12,209,012	12,032	1,151	5,616	5,265	4,180	837	248
2009–10	596,390,664	75,997,858	258,863,973	261,528,833	210,837,095	38,771,186	11,920,551	12,089	1,540	5,247	5,301	4,274	786	242
2010–11	604,228,585	75,549,471	266,786,402	261,892,711	211,649,523	38,558,755	11,684,433	12,218	1,528	5,395	5,296	4,280	780	236
2011–12	597,885,111	60,921,462	269,043,077	267,920,572	215,830,316	40,290,007	11,800,249	12,075	1,230	5,434	5,411	4,359	814	238
2012–13	603,769,917	55,860,888	273,215,485	274,693,545	221,970,384	41,129,568	11,593,592	12,137	1,123	5,492	5,522	4,462	827	233
2013–14	623,649,738	54,505,981	288,637,122	280,506,635	227,019,185	41,943,022	11,544,428	12,469	1,090	5,771	5,608	4,539	839	231
2014–15	647,679,130	55,002,853	301,529,692	291,146,585	235,870,943	43,978,246	11,297,396	12,884	1,094	5,998	5,792	4,692	875	225
2015–16	677,218,527	55,975,104	317,660,406	303,583,016	246,997,299	45,057,328	11,528,389	13,451	1,112	6,310	6,030	4,906	895	229
2016–17	705,267,398	57,310,693	331,322,010	316,634,696	258,159,622	46,809,893	11,665,181	13,962	1,135	6,559	6,268	5,111	927	231
							Constant 2018–19 dollars[2]							
1919–20	$12,892,256	$32,891	$2,127,422	$10,731,942	—	—	—	$597	$2	$99	$497	—	—	—
1929–30	30,902,883	108,516	5,233,002	25,561,365	—	—	—	1,203	4	204	995	—	—	—
1939–40	40,967,381	721,474	12,402,502	27,843,405	—	—	—	1,611	28	488	1,095	—	—	—
1949–50	58,144,207	1,666,652	23,160,061	33,317,495	—	—	—	2,315	66	922	1,327	—	—	—
1959–60	127,109,092	5,616,830	49,717,923	71,774,339	—	—	—	3,613	160	1,413	2,040	—	—	—
1969–70	269,975,455	21,585,990	107,695,226	140,694,239	—	—	—	5,927	474	2,364	3,089	—	—	—
1979–80	316,062,739	31,004,107	147,944,861	137,113,771	—	—	—	7,588	744	3,552	3,292	—	—	—
1989–90	415,975,009	25,333,350	195,949,612	194,692,047	$149,333,130	$34,077,226	$11,281,692	10,260	625	4,833	4,802	$3,683	$841	$278
1994–95	459,949,037	31,289,996	215,080,409	213,578,631	164,982,745	36,304,580	12,291,306	10,427	709	4,876	4,842	3,740	823	279
1996–97	486,213,727	32,005,609	233,389,429	220,818,689	169,813,113	38,711,385	12,294,191	10,660	702	5,117	4,841	3,723	849	270
1997–98	510,359,413	34,765,536	246,853,187	228,740,690	174,100,649	41,771,703	12,868,337	11,064	754	5,352	4,959	3,774	906	279
1998–99	534,694,665	37,744,720	260,588,935	236,361,011	183,912,580	39,017,758	13,430,672	11,489	811	5,599	5,079	3,952	838	289
1999–2000	557,939,718	40,539,555	276,189,391	241,210,772	186,609,613	41,334,038	13,267,121	11,907	865	5,894	5,148	3,983	882	283
2000–01	580,555,718	42,092,986	288,694,012	249,768,721	191,769,123	44,680,878	13,318,719	12,299	892	6,116	5,291	4,063	947	282
2001–02	596,246,894	47,109,157	293,562,151	255,575,586	200,542,235	41,111,456	13,921,895	12,507	988	6,158	5,361	4,207	862	292
2002–03	612,088,421	52,175,518	298,007,832	261,905,070	206,543,826	41,137,540	14,223,704	12,703	1,083	6,185	5,436	4,287	854	295
2003–04	628,809,546	57,057,071	295,856,131	275,896,344	218,576,624	43,077,131	14,242,589	12,954	1,175	6,095	5,684	4,503	887	293
2004–05	644,431,482	59,203,412	301,970,389	283,257,681	221,846,505	46,815,559	14,595,616	13,207	1,213	6,188	5,805	4,546	959	299

See notes at end of table.

Table 235.10. Revenues for public elementary and secondary schools, by source of funds: Selected years, 1919–20 through 2016–17—Continued

School year	Revenues (in thousands)							Revenues per pupil						
				Local (including intermediate sources below the state level)							Local (including intermediate sources below the state level)			
	Total	Federal	State	Total	Property taxes	Other public revenue	Private[1]	Total	Federal	State	Total	Property taxes	Other public revenue	Private[1]
1	2	3	4	5	6	7	8	9	10	11	12	13	14	15
2005–06	662,623,819	60,524,294	308,198,916	293,900,609	226,905,951	52,324,301	14,670,356	13,492	1,232	6,275	5,984	4,620	1,065	299
2006–07	689,453,964	58,498,370	327,051,595	303,903,999	233,602,501	55,590,007	14,711,491	13,996	1,187	6,639	6,169	4,742	1,128	299
2007–08	699,481,666	57,171,351	338,113,202	304,197,114	235,107,012	54,212,197	14,877,905	14,211	1,162	6,869	6,180	4,777	1,101	302
2008–09	698,979,509	66,863,400	326,263,575	305,852,534	242,842,507	48,605,011	14,405,016	14,197	1,358	6,627	6,212	4,932	987	293
2009–10	696,918,683	88,808,109	302,498,262	305,612,312	246,375,941	45,306,484	13,929,887	14,127	1,800	6,132	6,195	4,994	918	282
2010–11	692,178,940	86,546,307	305,619,320	300,013,313	242,456,821	44,171,294	13,385,197	13,997	1,750	6,180	6,067	4,903	893	271
2011–12	665,415,008	67,802,416	299,430,941	298,181,651	240,207,908	44,840,680	13,133,063	13,439	1,369	6,047	6,022	4,851	906	265
2012–13	660,965,107	61,152,596	299,097,217	300,715,294	242,997,662	45,025,777	12,691,855	13,287	1,229	6,012	6,045	4,885	905	255
2013–14	672,227,138	58,751,568	311,119,679	302,355,891	244,702,191	45,210,053	12,443,648	13,440	1,175	6,220	6,045	4,892	904	249
2014–15	693,081,279	58,858,539	322,666,850	311,555,890	252,405,439	47,061,110	12,089,340	13,787	1,171	6,419	6,198	5,021	936	240
2015–16	719,837,253	59,497,730	337,651,416	322,688,107	262,541,337	47,892,877	12,253,894	14,298	1,182	6,707	6,409	5,215	951	243
2016–17	736,110,640	59,817,043	345,811,613	330,481,984	269,449,637	48,857,016	12,175,331	14,573	1,184	6,846	6,543	5,334	967	241
	Percentage distribution													
1919–20	100.0	0.3	16.5	83.2	—	—	—	100.0	0.3	16.5	83.2	—	—	—
1929–30	100.0	0.4	16.9	82.7	—	—	—	100.0	0.4	16.9	82.7	—	—	—
1939–40	100.0	1.8	30.3	68.0	—	—	—	100.0	1.8	30.3	68.0	—	—	—
1949–50	100.0	2.9	39.8	57.3	—	—	—	100.0	2.9	39.8	57.3	—	—	—
1959–60	100.0	4.4	39.1	56.5	—	—	—	100.0	4.4	39.1	56.5	—	—	—
1969–70	100.0	8.0	39.9	52.1	—	—	—	100.0	8.0	39.9	52.1	—	—	—
1979–80	100.0	9.8	46.8	43.4	—	—	—	100.0	9.8	46.8	43.4	—	—	—
1989–90	100.0	6.1	47.1	46.8	35.9	8.2	2.7	100.0	6.1	47.1	46.8	35.9	8.2	2.7
1994–95	100.0	6.8	46.8	46.4	35.9	7.9	2.7	100.0	6.8	46.8	46.4	35.9	7.9	2.7
1996–97	100.0	6.6	48.0	45.4	34.9	8.0	2.5	100.0	6.6	48.0	45.4	34.9	8.0	2.5
1997–98	100.0	6.8	48.4	44.8	34.1	8.2	2.5	100.0	6.8	48.4	44.8	34.1	8.2	2.5
1998–99	100.0	7.1	48.7	44.2	34.4	7.3	2.5	100.0	7.1	48.7	44.2	34.4	7.3	2.5
1999–2000	100.0	7.3	49.5	43.2	33.4	7.4	2.4	100.0	7.3	49.5	43.2	33.4	7.4	2.4
2000–01	100.0	7.3	49.7	43.0	33.0	7.7	2.3	100.0	7.3	49.7	43.0	33.0	7.7	2.3
2001–02	100.0	7.9	49.2	42.9	33.6	6.9	2.3	100.0	7.9	49.2	42.9	33.6	6.9	2.3
2002–03	100.0	8.5	48.7	42.8	33.7	6.7	2.3	100.0	8.5	48.7	42.8	33.7	6.7	2.3
2003–04	100.0	9.1	47.1	43.9	34.8	6.9	2.3	100.0	9.1	47.1	43.9	34.8	6.9	2.3
2004–05	100.0	9.2	46.9	44.0	34.4	7.3	2.3	100.0	9.2	46.9	44.0	34.4	7.3	2.3
2005–06	100.0	9.1	46.5	44.4	34.2	7.9	2.2	100.0	9.1	46.5	44.4	34.2	7.9	2.2
2006–07	100.0	8.5	47.4	44.1	33.9	8.1	2.1	100.0	8.5	47.4	44.1	33.9	8.1	2.1
2007–08	100.0	8.2	48.3	43.5	33.6	7.8	2.1	100.0	8.2	48.3	43.5	33.6	7.8	2.1
2008–09	100.0	9.6	46.7	43.8	34.7	7.0	2.1	100.0	9.6	46.7	43.8	34.7	7.0	2.1
2009–10	100.0	12.7	43.4	43.9	35.4	6.5	2.0	100.0	12.7	43.4	43.9	35.4	6.5	2.0
2010–11	100.0	12.5	44.2	43.3	35.0	6.4	1.9	100.0	12.5	44.2	43.3	35.0	6.4	1.9
2011–12	100.0	10.2	45.0	44.8	36.1	6.7	2.0	100.0	10.2	45.0	44.8	36.1	6.7	2.0
2012–13	100.0	9.3	45.3	45.5	36.8	6.8	1.9	100.0	9.3	45.3	45.5	36.8	6.8	1.9
2013–14	100.0	8.7	46.3	45.0	36.4	6.7	1.9	100.0	8.7	46.3	45.0	36.4	6.7	1.9
2014–15	100.0	8.5	46.6	45.0	36.4	6.8	1.7	100.0	8.5	46.6	45.0	36.4	6.8	1.7
2015–16	100.0	8.3	46.9	44.8	36.5	6.7	1.7	100.0	8.3	46.9	44.8	36.5	6.7	1.7
2016–17	100.0	8.1	47.0	44.9	36.6	6.6	1.7	100.0	8.1	47.0	44.9	36.6	6.6	1.7

—Not available.
#Rounds to zero.
[1]Includes revenues from gifts, and tuition and fees from patrons.
[2]Constant dollars based on the Consumer Price Index, prepared by the Bureau of Labor Statistics, U.S. Department of Labor, adjusted to a school-year basis.

NOTE: Beginning in 1989–90, revenues for state education agencies were excluded and new survey collection procedures were initiated; data may not be entirely comparable with figures for earlier years. Detail may not sum to totals because of rounding.
SOURCE: U.S. Department of Education, National Center for Education Statistics, *Biennial Survey of Education in the United States*, 1919–20 through 1949–50; *Statistics of State School Systems*, 1959–60 and 1969–70; *Revenues and Expenditures for Public Elementary and Secondary Education, 1979–80*; and Common Core of Data (CCD), "National Public Education Financial Survey," 1989–90 through 2016–17. (This table was prepared August 2019.)

Table 235.20. Revenues for public elementary and secondary schools, by source of funds and state or jurisdiction: 2016–17

[In current dollars]

State or jurisdiction	Total (in thousands)	Federal			State		Local (including intermediate sources below the state level)					
									Property taxes		Private[2]	
		Amount (in thousands)	Per pupil	Percent of total	Amount (in thousands)	Percent of total	Amount (in thousands)[1]	Percent of total	Amount (in thousands)	Percent of total	Amount (in thousands)	Percent of total
1	2	3	4	5	6	7	8	9	10	11	12	13
United States	**$705,267,398**	**$57,310,693**	**$1,135**	**8.1**	**$331,322,010**	**47.0**	**$316,634,696**	**44.9**	**$258,159,622**	**36.6**	**$11,665,181**	**1.7**
Alabama	7,889,120	863,637	1,159	10.9	4,350,890	55.2	2,674,593	33.9	1,223,602	15.5	325,777	4.1
Alaska	2,508,281	354,045	2,667	14.1	1,600,510	63.8	553,726	22.1	319,889	12.8	18,951	0.8
Arizona	10,259,496	1,326,469	1,191	12.9	4,778,454	46.6	4,154,572	40.5	3,182,393	31.0	248,513	2.4
Arkansas	5,619,332	625,993	1,269	11.1	2,950,895	52.5	2,042,443	36.3	1,782,061	31.7	158,048	2.8
California	88,108,864	7,455,046	1,182	8.5	50,841,072	57.7	29,812,746	33.8	24,101,208	27.4	394,460	0.4
Colorado	10,600,561	706,162	780	6.7	4,602,299	43.4	5,292,101	49.9	4,287,369	40.4	393,355	3.7
Connecticut	11,583,918	503,812	941	4.3	4,494,453	38.8	6,585,653	56.9	6,431,528	55.5	92,242	0.8
Delaware	2,729,986	188,717	1,385	6.9	1,323,678	48.5	1,217,591	44.6	646,622	23.7	17,771	0.7
District of Columbia	2,526,099	237,820	2,770	9.4	†	†	2,288,279	90.6	767,117	30.4	11,358	0.4
Florida	28,808,723	3,288,570	1,167	11.4	11,346,675	39.4	14,173,479	49.2	11,738,747	40.7	935,775	3.2
Georgia	20,443,717	1,925,205	1,091	9.4	9,439,804	46.2	9,078,707	44.4	6,020,224	29.4	474,428	2.3
Hawaii	2,844,167	252,145	1,389	8.9	2,534,177	89.1	57,844	2.0	0	0.0	28,852	1.0
Idaho	2,575,178	252,533	850	9.8	1,706,894	66.3	615,751	23.9	517,769	20.1	35,395	1.4
Illinois	35,480,443	2,312,325	1,141	6.5	13,710,764	38.6	19,457,354	54.8	17,082,907	48.1	480,875	1.4
Indiana	11,952,546	974,150	928	8.2	7,087,311	59.3	3,891,085	32.6	3,005,433	25.1	342,023	2.9
Iowa	6,904,458	497,385	976	7.2	3,732,324	54.1	2,674,750	38.7	2,187,985	31.7	145,240	2.1
Kansas	6,344,151	537,797	1,088	8.5	4,031,070	63.5	1,775,284	28.0	1,103,725	17.4	152,835	2.4
Kentucky	7,782,860	912,224	1,334	11.7	4,229,780	54.3	2,640,856	33.9	1,975,137	25.4	85,541	1.1
Louisiana	8,949,726	1,168,690	1,632	13.1	3,903,101	43.6	3,877,936	43.3	1,689,558	18.9	50,474	0.6
Maine	2,820,246	195,168	1,081	6.9	1,093,382	38.8	1,531,696	54.3	1,457,658	51.7	36,636	1.3
Maryland	15,045,717	851,860	961	5.7	6,625,703	44.0	7,568,154	50.3	3,703,439	24.6	115,109	0.8
Massachusetts	18,423,533	929,798	964	5.0	6,999,777	38.0	10,493,958	57.0	9,766,156	53.0	273,640	1.5
Michigan	20,163,387	1,734,557	1,135	8.6	12,224,090	60.6	6,204,741	30.8	5,289,166	26.2	273,047	1.4
Minnesota	13,242,082	743,953	850	5.6	8,762,296	66.2	3,735,833	28.2	2,449,514	18.5	350,318	2.6
Mississippi	4,753,225	672,881	1,393	14.2	2,415,769	50.8	1,664,576	35.0	1,393,467	29.3	110,153	2.3
Missouri	11,485,402	1,003,289	1,096	8.7	3,749,129	32.6	6,732,984	58.6	5,286,304	46.0	349,579	3.0
Montana	1,841,286	225,892	1,543	12.3	867,286	47.1	748,107	40.6	476,318	25.9	62,801	3.4
Nebraska	4,470,153	349,144	1,094	7.8	1,450,774	32.5	2,670,235	59.7	2,369,879	53.0	161,587	3.6
Nevada	4,919,401	444,730	939	9.0	1,780,380	36.2	2,694,292	54.8	1,201,302	24.4	28,596	0.6
New Hampshire	3,132,306	173,816	961	5.5	1,007,310	32.2	1,951,180	62.3	1,859,886	59.4	46,040	1.5
New Jersey	30,368,383	1,269,661	900	4.2	12,920,845	42.5	16,177,878	53.3	15,304,628	50.4	581,364	1.9
New Mexico	4,023,795	589,017	1,752	14.6	2,726,305	67.8	708,473	17.6	572,792	14.2	54,087	1.3
New York	69,228,226	3,657,578	1,373	5.3	28,253,045	40.8	37,317,603	53.9	34,657,273	50.1	305,467	0.4
North Carolina	14,481,275	1,641,260	1,059	11.3	9,057,842	62.5	3,782,173	26.1	3,290,986	22.7	166,817	1.2
North Dakota	1,757,100	163,446	1,490	9.3	1,014,779	57.8	578,875	32.9	423,505	24.1	69,564	4.0
Ohio	24,762,785	1,949,822	1,140	7.9	10,538,278	42.6	12,274,685	49.6	10,070,121	40.7	642,876	2.6
Oklahoma	6,361,194	726,159	1,046	11.4	3,007,742	47.3	2,627,292	41.3	2,007,824	31.6	281,400	4.4
Oregon	7,689,411	550,627	951	7.2	4,018,900	52.3	3,119,884	40.6	2,524,905	32.8	137,680	1.8
Pennsylvania	31,353,132	2,152,130	1,246	6.9	12,104,094	38.6	17,096,908	54.5	13,601,256	43.4	385,862	1.2
Rhode Island	2,561,477	192,929	1,357	7.5	1,087,361	42.5	1,281,187	50.0	1,242,366	48.5	25,406	1.0
South Carolina	9,992,973	913,225	1,184	9.1	4,867,687	48.7	4,212,060	42.2	3,195,782	32.0	245,374	2.5
South Dakota	1,580,004	205,299	1,506	13.0	540,408	34.2	834,297	52.8	716,885	45.4	44,816	2.8
Tennessee	10,077,253	1,161,636	1,160	11.5	4,629,304	45.9	4,286,312	42.5	2,008,470	19.9	438,170	4.3
Texas	60,006,975	6,298,581	1,175	10.5	23,339,969	38.9	30,368,425	50.6	27,675,817	46.1	1,022,545	1.7
Utah	5,757,609	459,308	696	8.0	3,183,265	55.3	2,115,036	36.7	1,598,326	27.8	241,408	4.2
Vermont	1,742,206	113,778	1,287	6.5	1,560,743	89.6	67,685	3.9	2,385	0.1	21,859	1.3
Virginia	16,611,639	1,131,683	879	6.8	6,565,661	39.5	8,914,296	53.7	5,399,824	32.5	241,647	1.5
Washington	15,654,623	1,071,035	972	6.8	9,846,364	62.9	4,737,224	30.3	4,056,493	25.9	299,337	1.9
West Virginia	3,526,416	404,295	1,476	11.5	1,917,056	54.4	1,205,066	34.2	1,115,409	31.6	19,618	0.6
Wisconsin	11,591,278	832,985	964	7.2	5,360,746	46.2	5,397,548	46.6	4,891,353	42.2	224,031	1.9
Wyoming	1,931,277	118,429	1,258	6.1	1,141,567	59.1	671,281	34.8	486,856	25.2	16,436	0.9
Other jurisdictions												
American Samoa	73,876	62,906	—	85.2	10,738	14.5	232	0.3	0	0.0	14	#
Guam	332,552	60,166	1,956	18.1	0	0.0	272,386	81.9	0	0.0	147	#
Northern Marianas	87,683	39,503	—	45.1	47,227	53.9	953	1.1	0	0.0	711	0.8
Puerto Rico	2,819,791	935,887	2,563	33.2	1,883,850	66.8	55	#	0	0.0	55	#
U.S. Virgin Islands	193,314	26,259	1,990	13.6	0	0.0	167,056	86.4	0	0.0	5	#

—Not available.
†Not applicable.
#Rounds to zero.
[1]Includes other categories of revenue not separately shown.
[2]Includes revenues from gifts, and tuition and fees from patrons.

NOTE: Excludes revenues for state education agencies. Detail may not sum to totals because of rounding.
SOURCE: U.S. Department of Education, National Center for Education Statistics, Common Core of Data (CCD), "National Public Education Financial Survey," 2016–17. (This table was prepared August 2019.)

Table 235.40. Public elementary and secondary revenues and expenditures, by locale, source of revenue, and purpose of expenditure: 2016–17

Source of revenue and purpose of expenditure	Total	City, large	City, midsize	City, small	Suburban, large	Suburban, midsize	Suburban, small	Town, fringe	Town, distant	Town, remote	Rural, fringe	Rural, distant	Rural, remote
1	2	3	4	5	6	7	8	9	10	11	12	13	14
Revenue amounts (in millions of current dollars)													
Total revenue[1]	$708,834	$135,044	$50,112	$48,905	$266,735	$23,599	$13,138	$16,533	$33,777	$19,814	$51,673	$35,081	$14,423
Federal	56,838	13,752	5,051	4,236	16,072	1,650	945	1,225	3,155	2,278	4,020	2,854	1,600
Title I	14,602	4,392	1,289	1,098	3,597	401	214	272	812	531	916	715	366
Child Nutrition Act	16,553	3,849	1,396	1,235	4,850	520	272	366	992	556	1,231	914	371
Children with disabilities (IDEA)	11,473	1,983	991	880	4,192	369	230	249	615	362	883	525	194
Impact aid	1,363	122	78	64	165	27	8	67	45	232	139	89	329
Bilingual education	338	93	37	30	122	8	6	6	11	7	13	4	2
Indian education	98	11	3	4	7	2	3	2	9	17	5	9	27
Math, science, and professional development	1,470	338	134	114	369	44	30	32	97	67	105	91	49
Safe and drug-free schools	70	16	4	6	16	2	#	2	5	5	9	3	2
Vocational and technical education	556	119	46	42	169	17	12	12	36	24	47	23	10
Other and unclassified	10,313	2,828	1,074	762	2,588	260	171	219	533	477	671	481	249
State	331,912	59,083	25,082	24,371	115,524	11,817	6,493	8,828	18,350	10,340	25,694	19,058	7,271
Special education programs	20,889	4,365	1,619	1,421	8,132	650	304	445	921	505	1,418	815	293
Compensatory and basic skills	5,282	824	407	476	1,910	263	79	99	281	130	418	286	110
Bilingual education	1,185	108	67	68	784	36	10	6	32	12	47	10	4
Gifted and talented	1,193	42	100	53	749	19	10	11	34	9	131	28	7
Vocational education	1,241	47	82	85	497	49	27	22	93	56	159	91	33
Other[2]	302,122	53,698	22,808	22,267	103,451	10,800	6,063	8,245	16,989	9,628	23,521	17,829	6,823
Local[1]	320,084	62,209	19,978	20,299	135,139	10,132	5,700	6,480	12,272	7,196	21,960	13,168	5,553
Property tax[3]	203,125	29,852	12,357	13,070	92,794	5,741	3,998	4,635	8,490	5,242	13,839	9,126	3,983
Parent government contribution[3]	57,983	21,085	3,298	2,732	21,882	2,565	557	389	871	190	3,126	986	301
Private[4]	13,905	1,519	862	809	5,897	486	263	361	727	443	1,276	892	369
Other[5]	45,071	9,753	3,461	3,688	14,565	1,340	883	1,095	2,184	1,320	3,718	2,163	900
Percentage distribution of revenue													
Total revenue	100.0	100.0	100.0	100.0	100.0	100.0	100.0	100.0	100.0	100.0	100.0	100.0	100.0
Federal	8.0	10.2	10.1	8.7	6.0	7.0	7.2	7.4	9.3	11.5	7.8	8.1	11.1
State	46.8	43.8	50.1	49.8	43.3	50.1	49.4	53.4	54.3	52.2	49.7	54.3	50.4
Local	45.2	46.1	39.9	41.5	50.7	42.9	43.4	39.2	36.3	36.3	42.5	37.5	38.5
Expenditure amounts (in millions of current dollars)													
Total expenditures	$725,239	$138,911	$51,060	$50,310	$272,398	$23,958	$13,265	$17,379	$34,861	$20,411	$52,621	$35,254	$14,811
Current expenditures for schools	609,072	113,540	42,997	42,147	229,779	20,522	11,486	14,338	29,453	17,223	44,769	30,367	12,451
Instruction	368,949	70,341	25,043	25,301	140,942	12,287	6,878	8,656	17,563	10,110	26,782	17,917	7,128
Student support[6]	35,605	5,372	2,848	2,705	14,707	1,255	734	798	1,623	1,008	2,550	1,462	542
Instructional staff support services[7]	28,706	5,189	2,605	2,239	10,614	1,032	530	614	1,372	802	1,953	1,225	531
General and school administration	46,120	7,784	3,252	3,110	16,823	1,497	880	1,165	2,471	1,483	3,581	2,814	1,260
Operation and maintenance	56,489	11,066	3,861	3,858	20,662	1,936	1,059	1,343	2,728	1,702	4,126	2,866	1,283
Student transportation	25,523	4,363	1,627	1,509	9,529	849	498	642	1,262	667	2,275	1,672	630
Food services	23,723	4,481	1,761	1,691	7,762	811	439	580	1,393	821	1,920	1,450	612
Other	23,957	4,943	1,999	1,734	8,739	855	469	539	1,041	629	1,583	961	464
Other current expenditures	33,921	9,361	2,568	2,215	11,967	858	424	617	1,231	671	2,064	1,328	615
Interest on school debt	18,271	4,076	1,270	1,209	7,021	508	324	500	755	388	1,328	690	202
Capital outlay	63,975	11,935	4,225	4,738	23,632	2,070	1,030	1,924	3,421	2,128	4,459	2,869	1,543
Percentage distribution of current expenditures for schools													
All current expenditures for schools	100.0	100.0	100.0	100.0	100.0	100.0	100.0	100.0	100.0	100.0	100.0	100.0	100.0
Instruction	60.6	62.0	58.2	60.0	61.3	59.9	59.9	60.4	59.6	58.7	59.8	59.0	57.3
Support services	10.6	9.3	12.7	11.7	11.0	11.1	11.0	9.8	10.2	10.5	10.1	8.8	8.6
General and school administration	7.6	6.9	7.6	7.4	7.3	7.3	7.7	8.1	8.4	8.6	8.0	9.3	10.1
Operation and maintenance	9.3	9.7	9.0	9.2	9.0	9.4	9.2	9.4	9.3	9.9	9.2	9.4	10.3
Student transportation	4.2	3.8	3.8	3.6	4.1	4.1	4.3	4.5	4.3	3.9	5.1	5.5	5.1
Food service and other	7.8	8.3	8.7	8.1	7.2	8.1	7.9	7.8	8.3	8.4	7.8	7.9	8.6
Per student amounts (in current dollars)													
Current expenditure per student	$12,089	$12,980	$11,648	$11,869	$12,397	$11,550	$11,698	$11,523	$11,083	$10,801	$11,301	$11,336	$12,954
Instruction expenditure per student	7,323	8,041	6,784	7,125	7,604	6,915	7,005	6,957	6,609	6,340	6,760	6,689	7,416

#Rounds to zero.

[1]Excludes revenues from other in-state school systems.

[2]Includes general formula assistance, staff improvement programs, school lunch programs, capital outlay and debt service programs, transportation programs, all other revenues from state sources, state payments on behalf of the local education agency, Census state NCES local revenue, and unspecified state revenue.

[3]Property tax and parent government contributions are determined on the basis of independence or dependence of the local school system and are mutually exclusive.

[4]Includes tuition fees, transportation fees, textbook sales and rentals, school lunch revenues, district activity receipts, other student fees, and private contributions.

[5]Includes revenues from other taxes, rents and royalties, sales and services, interest earnings, and other local revenues.

[6]Includes expenditures for guidance, health, attendance, social work, student accounting, counseling, student appraisal, information, record maintenance, placement services, and medical, dental, nursing, psychological, and speech pathology services.

[7]Includes expenditures for curriculum development, staff training, supervision of instruction service improvements, academic assessment, and media, library, and instruction-related technology services.

NOTE: Detail may not sum to totals because of rounding.

SOURCE: U.S. Department of Education, National Center for Education Statistics, Common Core of Data (CCD), "School District Finance Survey (F33), Fiscal year 2017"; and Education Demographic and Geographic Estimates (EDGE) program, "Public Local Education Agency Geocode File," 2016–17. (This table was prepared April 2020.)

Table 236.10. Summary of expenditures for public elementary and secondary education and other related programs, by purpose: Selected years, 1919–20 through 2016–17

School year	Total expenditures	Current expenditures for public elementary and secondary education							Current expenditures for other programs[1]	Capital outlay[2]	Interest on school debt
		Total	Administration	Instruction	Plant operation	Plant maintenance	Fixed charges	Other school services[3]			
1	2	3	4	5	6	7	8	9	10	11	12
	Amounts in thousands of current dollars										
1919–20	$1,036,151	$861,120	$36,752	$632,556	$115,707	$30,432	$9,286	$36,387	$3,277	$153,543	$18,212
1929–30	2,316,790	1,843,552	78,680	1,317,727	216,072	78,810	50,270	101,993	9,825	370,878	92,536
1939–40	2,344,049	1,941,799	91,571	1,403,285	194,365	73,321	50,116	129,141	13,367	257,974	130,909
1949–50	5,837,643	4,687,274	220,050	3,112,340	427,587	214,164	261,469	451,663	35,614	1,014,176	100,578
1959–60	15,613,254	12,329,388	528,408	8,350,738	1,085,036	422,586	909,323	1,033,297	132,566	2,661,786	489,514
1969–70	40,683,429	34,217,773	1,606,646	23,270,158	2,537,257	974,941	3,266,920	2,561,856	635,803	4,659,072	1,170,782
1979–80	95,961,561	86,984,142	4,263,757	53,257,937	9,744,785	(4)	11,793,934	7,923,729	597,585	6,506,167	1,873,666
1989–90	212,769,564	188,229,359	16,346,991[5]	113,550,405[5]	20,261,415[5]	(4)	—	38,070,548[5]	2,982,543	17,781,342	3,776,321
1999–2000	381,838,155	323,888,508	25,079,298[5]	199,968,138[5]	31,190,295[5]	(4)	—	67,650,776[5]	5,457,015	43,357,186	9,135,445
2000–01	410,811,185	348,360,841	26,689,182[5]	214,333,003[5]	34,034,158[5]	(4)	—	73,304,498[5]	6,063,700	46,220,704	10,165,940
2006–07	562,194,807	476,814,206	36,213,814[5]	290,678,482[5]	46,828,916[5]	(4)	—	103,092,995[5]	7,804,253	62,863,465	14,712,882
2007–08	597,313,726	506,884,219	38,203,341[5]	308,238,664[5]	49,362,661[5]	(4)	—	111,079,554[5]	8,307,720	66,426,299	15,695,488
2008–09	610,326,007	518,922,842	38,811,325[5]	316,075,710[5]	50,559,027[5]	(4)	—	113,476,779[5]	8,463,793	65,890,367	17,049,004
2009–10	607,018,292	524,715,242	38,972,700[5]	321,213,401[5]	50,023,919[5]	(4)	—	114,505,223[5]	8,355,761	56,714,992	17,232,297
2010–11	604,355,852	527,291,339	39,154,833[5]	322,536,983[5]	50,214,709[5]	(4)	—	115,384,813[5]	8,161,474	50,968,815	17,934,224
2011–12	601,993,584	527,207,246	39,491,926[5]	320,994,474[5]	49,834,165[5]	(4)	—	116,886,681[5]	8,188,640	48,793,436	17,804,262
2012–13	606,813,352	535,795,823	40,349,598[5]	325,682,380[5]	50,674,499[5]	(4)	—	119,089,346[5]	8,031,416	45,720,570	17,265,542
2013–14	625,018,277	553,501,209	41,538,042[5]	336,426,927[5]	53,051,141[5]	(4)	—	122,485,100[5]	7,926,285	46,438,323	17,152,459
2014–15	651,135,383	575,331,825	43,328,198[5]	349,453,258[5]	54,200,172[5]	(4)	—	128,350,197[5]	7,713,966	50,610,125	17,479,466
2015–16	677,605,095	596,201,554	45,252,877[5]	363,106,915[5]	55,045,039[5]	(4)	—	132,796,722[5]	7,913,839	55,989,128	17,500,574
2016–17	707,601,350	619,164,572	46,874,132[5]	376,069,486[5]	57,433,468[5]	(4)	—	138,787,485[5]	8,660,874	61,441,963	18,333,942
	Amounts in thousands of constant 2018–19 dollars[6]										
1919–20	$13,769,750	$11,443,706	$488,409	$8,406,244	$1,537,668	$404,421	$123,405	$483,559	$43,549	$2,040,483	$242,025
1929–30	34,279,884	27,277,720	1,164,172	19,497,463	3,197,063	1,166,095	743,809	1,509,117	145,373	5,487,616	1,369,189
1939–40	42,481,045	35,191,095	1,659,535	25,431,641	3,522,464	1,328,792	908,249	2,340,414	242,249	4,675,246	2,372,455
1949–50	62,428,247	50,126,093	2,353,233	33,283,627	4,572,651	2,290,288	2,796,172	4,830,122	380,859	10,845,684	1,075,590
1959–60	134,579,097	106,273,677	4,554,635	71,979,536	9,352,513	3,642,498	7,837,948	8,906,547	1,142,658	22,943,376	4,219,386
1969–70	272,767,987	229,418,086	10,771,993	156,018,170	17,011,410	6,536,634	21,903,542	17,176,337	4,262,834	31,237,428	7,849,679
1979–80	313,062,649	283,774,937	13,909,977	173,747,391	31,791,148	(4)	38,476,242	25,850,180	1,949,547	21,225,560	6,112,602
1989–90	424,396,314	375,447,713	32,606,180[5]	226,490,915[5]	40,414,003[5]	(4)	—	75,936,614[5]	5,949,066	35,467,178	7,532,359
1999–2000	571,246,047	484,550,921	37,519,692[5]	299,160,801[5]	46,662,001[5]	(4)	—	101,208,425[5]	8,163,926	64,864,187	13,667,013
2000–01	594,232,331	503,898,830	38,605,508[5]	310,029,533[5]	49,229,909[5]	(4)	—	106,033,877[5]	8,771,053	66,857,568	14,704,882
2006–07	697,498,527	591,569,332	44,929,412[5]	360,636,225[5]	58,099,255[5]	(4)	—	127,904,440[5]	9,682,507	77,992,848	18,253,840
2007–08	714,591,514	606,406,895	45,704,263[5]	368,758,868[5]	59,054,626[5]	(4)	—	132,889,139[5]	9,938,874	79,468,573	18,777,172
2008–09	720,103,826	612,260,201	45,792,222[5]	372,927,461[5]	59,652,954[5]	(4)	—	133,887,565[5]	9,986,155	77,741,904	20,115,566
2009–10	709,337,711	613,161,603	45,541,965[5]	375,357,351[5]	58,455,985[5]	(4)	—	133,806,302[5]	9,764,214	66,274,909	20,136,985
2010–11	692,324,731	604,042,855	44,854,135[5]	369,484,848[5]	57,523,866[5]	(4)	—	132,180,006[5]	9,349,442	58,387,738	20,544,696
2011–12	669,987,525	586,754,223	43,952,458[5]	357,250,142[5]	55,462,831[5]	(4)	—	130,088,792[5]	9,113,530	54,304,555	19,815,217
2012–13	664,296,846	586,551,819	44,171,920[5]	356,534,307[5]	55,474,900[5]	(4)	—	130,370,693[5]	8,792,233	50,051,685	18,901,109
2013–14	673,702,276	596,614,592	44,773,528[5]	362,631,933[5]	57,183,406[5]	(4)	—	132,025,724[5]	8,543,681	50,055,503	18,488,500
2014–15	696,779,814	615,662,446	46,365,494[5]	373,949,847[5]	57,999,590[5]	(4)	—	137,347,514[5]	8,254,713	54,157,883	18,704,773
2015–16	720,248,149	633,721,719	48,100,732[5]	385,957,965[5]	58,509,134[5]	(4)	—	141,153,887[5]	8,411,873	59,512,637	18,601,920
2016–17	738,546,661	646,242,305	48,924,064[5]	392,516,017[5]	59,945,188[5]	(4)	—	144,857,035[5]	9,039,637	64,128,985	19,135,734
	Percentage distribution										
1919–20	100.0	83.1	3.5	61.0	11.2	2.9	0.9	3.5	0.3	14.8	1.8
1929–30	100.0	79.6	3.4	56.9	9.3	3.4	2.2	4.4	0.4	16.0	4.0
1939–40	100.0	82.8	3.9	59.9	8.3	3.1	2.1	5.5	0.6	11.0	5.6
1949–50	100.0	80.3	3.8	53.3	7.3	3.7	4.5	7.7	0.6	17.4	1.7
1959–60	100.0	79.0	3.4	53.5	6.9	2.7	5.8	6.6	0.8	17.0	3.1
1969–70	100.0	84.1	3.9	57.2	6.2	2.4	8.0	6.3	1.6	11.5	2.9
1979–80	100.0	90.6	4.4	55.5	10.2	(4)	12.3	8.3	0.6	6.8	2.0
1989–90	100.0	88.5	7.7[5]	53.4[5]	9.5[5]	(4)	—	17.9[5]	1.4	8.4	1.8
1999–2000	100.0	84.8	6.6[5]	52.4[5]	8.2[5]	(4)	—	17.7[5]	1.4	11.4	2.4
2000–01	100.0	84.8	6.5[5]	52.2[5]	8.3[5]	(4)	—	17.8[5]	1.5	11.3	2.5
2006–07	100.0	84.8	6.4[5]	51.7[5]	8.3[5]	(4)	—	18.3[5]	1.4	11.2	2.6
2007–08	100.0	84.9	6.4[5]	51.6[5]	8.3[5]	(4)	—	18.6[5]	1.4	11.1	2.6
2008–09	100.0	85.0	6.4[5]	51.8[5]	8.3[5]	(4)	—	18.6[5]	1.4	10.8	2.8
2009–10	100.0	86.4	6.4[5]	52.9[5]	8.2[5]	(4)	—	18.9[5]	1.4	9.3	2.8
2010–11	100.0	87.2	6.5[5]	53.4[5]	8.3[5]	(4)	—	19.1[5]	1.4	8.4	3.0
2011–12	100.0	87.6	6.6[5]	53.3[5]	8.3[5]	(4)	—	19.4[5]	1.4	8.1	3.0
2012–13	100.0	88.3	6.6[5]	53.7[5]	8.4[5]	(4)	—	19.6[5]	1.3	7.5	2.8
2013–14	100.0	88.6	6.6[5]	53.8[5]	8.5[5]	(4)	—	19.6[5]	1.3	7.4	2.7
2014–15	100.0	88.4	6.7[5]	53.7[5]	8.3[5]	(4)	—	19.7[5]	1.2	7.8	2.7
2015–16	100.0	88.0	6.7[5]	53.6[5]	8.1[5]	(4)	—	19.6[5]	1.2	8.3	2.6
2016–17	100.0	87.5	6.6[5]	53.1[5]	8.1[5]	(4)	—	19.6[5]	1.2	8.7	2.6

—Not available.
[1]Includes expenditures for summer schools, adult education, community colleges, and community services.
[2]Prior to 1969–70, excludes capital outlay by state and local school housing authorities.
[3]Prior to 1959–60, items included under "other school services" were listed under "auxiliary services," a more comprehensive classification that also included community services.
[4]Plant operation also includes plant maintenance.
[5]Data not comparable to figures prior to 1989–90.
[6]Constant dollars based on the Consumer Price Index, prepared by the Bureau of Labor Statistics, U.S. Department of Labor, adjusted to a school-year basis.

NOTE: Beginning in 1959–60, includes Alaska and Hawaii. Beginning in 1989–90, state administration expenditures were excluded from both "total" and "current" expenditures. Beginning in 1989–90, extensive changes were made in the data collection procedures. Detail may not sum to totals because of rounding. Some data have been revised from previously published figures.
SOURCE: U.S. Department of Education, National Center for Education Statistics, *Biennial Survey of Education in the United States*, 1919–20 through 1949–50; *Statistics of State School Systems*, 1959–60 and 1969–70; *Revenues and Expenditures for Public Elementary and Secondary Education, 1979–80*; and Common Core of Data (CCD), "National Public Education Financial Survey," 1989–90 through 2016–17. (This table was prepared August 2019.)

Table 236.15. Current expenditures and current expenditures per pupil in public elementary and secondary schools: 1989–90 through 2029–30

School year	Current expenditures in unadjusted dollars[1]			Current expenditures in constant 2018–19 dollars[2]					
				Total current expenditures		Per pupil in fall enrollment		Per pupil in average daily attendance (ADA)	
	Total, in billions	Per pupil in fall enrollment	Per pupil in average daily attendance (ADA)	In billions	Annual percentage change	Per pupil enrolled	Annual percentage change	Per pupil in ADA	Annual percentage change
1	2	3	4	5	6	7	8	9	10
1989–90	$188.2	$4,643	$4,980	$375.4	3.8	$9,261	2.9	$9,933	2.3
1990–91	202.0	4,902	5,258	382.1	1.8	9,271	0.1	9,944	0.1
1991–92	211.2	5,023	5,421	387.0	1.3	9,205	-0.7	9,934	-0.1
1992–93	220.9	5,160	5,584	392.6	1.4	9,169	-0.4	9,922	-0.1
1993–94	231.5	5,327	5,767	401.1	2.1	9,227	0.6	9,990	0.7
1994–95	243.9	5,529	5,989	410.7	2.4	9,310	0.9	10,085	0.9
1995–96	255.1	5,689	6,147	418.2	1.8	9,326	0.2	10,076	-0.1
1996–97	270.2	5,923	6,393	430.6	3.0	9,441	1.2	10,189	1.1
1997–98	285.5	6,189	6,676	447.0	3.8	9,691	2.7	10,453	2.6
1998–99	302.9	6,508	7,013	466.2	4.3	10,017	3.4	10,795	3.3
1999–2000	323.9	6,912	7,394	484.6	3.9	10,341	3.2	11,061	2.5
2000–01	348.4	7,380	7,904	503.9	4.0	10,675	3.2	11,433	3.4
2001–02	368.4	7,727	8,259	523.6	3.9	10,983	2.9	11,738	2.7
2002–03	387.6	8,044	8,610	539.0	3.0	11,188	1.9	11,974	2.0
2003–04	403.4	8,310	8,900	549.0	1.8	11,310	1.1	12,112	1.2
2004–05	425.0	8,711	9,316	561.6	2.3	11,509	1.8	12,309	1.6
2005–06	449.1	9,145	9,778	571.6	1.8	11,639	1.1	12,445	1.1
2006–07	476.8	9,679	10,336	591.6	3.5	12,009	3.2	12,823	3.0
2007–08	506.9	10,298	10,982	606.4	2.5	12,320	2.6	13,138	2.5
2008–09	518.9	10,540	11,239	612.3	1.0	12,435	0.9	13,260	0.9
2009–10	524.7	10,636	11,427	613.2	0.1	12,429	-0.1	13,353	0.7
2010–11	527.3	10,663	11,433	604.0	-1.5	12,215	-1.7	13,098	-1.9
2011–12	527.2	10,648	11,362	586.8	-2.9	11,850	-3.0	12,645	-3.5
2012–13	535.8	10,771	11,509	586.6	#	11,791	-0.5	12,599	-0.4
2013–14	553.5	11,066	11,819	596.6	1.7	11,928	1.2	12,740	1.1
2014–15	575.3	11,445	12,224	615.7	3.2	12,247	2.7	13,081	2.7
2015–16	596.2	11,842	12,619	633.7	2.9	12,587	2.8	13,413	2.5
2016–17	619.2	12,258	13,094	646.2	2.0	12,794	1.6	13,667	1.9
2017–18[3]	643.8	12,700	13,590	657.1	1.7	12,970	1.4	13,870	1.5
2018–19[3]	669.6	13,220	14,140	669.6	1.9	13,220	1.9	14,140	1.9
2019–20[3]	691.8	13,660	14,610	678.4	1.3	13,400	1.3	14,330	1.3
2020–21[3]	709.2	14,000	14,980	684.1	0.8	13,500	0.8	14,450	0.8
2021–22[3]	731.5	14,440	15,450	690.1	0.9	13,630	0.9	14,570	0.9
2022–23[3]	757.1	14,930	15,970	696.9	1.0	13,740	0.8	14,700	0.8
2023–24[3]	783.4	15,430	16,500	703.6	1.0	13,860	0.9	14,820	0.9
2024–25[3]	810.9	15,980	17,090	711.2	1.1	14,010	1.1	14,990	1.1
2025–26[3]	838.8	16,540	17,690	718.5	1.0	14,170	1.1	15,160	1.1
2026–27[3]	867.2	17,110	18,310	725.7	1.0	14,320	1.1	15,320	1.1
2027–28[3]	898.4	17,710	18,940	734.8	1.3	14,480	1.1	15,490	1.1
2028–29[3]	932.7	18,330	19,610	746.0	1.5	14,660	1.2	15,680	1.2
2029–30[3]	959.0	18,780	20,090	754.6	1.2	14,780	0.8	15,810	0.8

#Rounds to zero.
[1]Unadjusted (or "current") dollars have not been adjusted to compensate for inflation.
[2]Constant dollars based on the Consumer Price Index, prepared by the Bureau of Labor Statistics, U.S. Department of Labor, adjusted to a school-year basis.
[3]Projected.
NOTE: Current expenditures include instruction, support services, food services, and enterprise operations. Some data have been revised from previously published figures.

SOURCE: U.S. Department of Education, National Center for Education Statistics, Common Core of Data (CCD), "National Public Education Financial Survey," 1989–90 through 2016–17; National Elementary and Secondary Enrollment Projection Model, 1972 through 2029; and Public Elementary and Secondary Education Current Expenditure Projection Model, 1973–74 through 2029–30. (This table was prepared December 2019.)

Table 236.20. Total expenditures for public elementary and secondary education and other related programs, by function and subfunction: Selected years, 1990–91 through 2016–17

Function and subfunction	Expenditures (in thousands of current dollars)								Percentage distribution of current expenditures for public schools							
	1990–91	2000–01	2006–07	2010–11	2013–14	2014–15	2015–16	2016–17	1990–91	2000–01	2006–07	2010–11	2013–14	2014–15	2015–16	2016–17
1	2	3	4	5	6	7	8	9	10	11	12	13	14	15	16	17
Total expenditures	**$229,429,715**	**$410,811,185**	**$562,194,807**	**$604,355,852**	**$625,018,277**	**$651,135,383**	**$677,605,095**	**$707,601,350**	†	†	†	†	†	†	†	†
Current expenditures for public schools	202,037,752	348,360,841	476,814,206	527,291,339	553,501,209	575,331,825	596,201,554	619,164,572	100.00	100.00	100.00	100.00	100.00	100.00	100.00	100.00
Salaries	132,730,931[1]	224,305,806	288,146,674	311,541,792	318,705,822	328,252,700	339,731,757	349,913,306	65.70	64.39	60.43	59.08	57.58	57.05	56.98	56.51
Employee benefits	33,954,456[1]	57,976,490	95,308,994	111,750,200	123,655,529	130,868,877	136,788,690	145,381,103	16.81	16.64	19.99	21.19	22.34	22.75	22.94	23.48
Purchased services	16,380,643[1]	31,778,754	46,266,516	53,498,786	58,171,703	61,118,818	64,572,861	66,905,790	8.11	9.12	9.70	10.15	10.51	10.62	10.83	10.81
Tuition	1,192,505[1]	2,458,366	3,951,411	4,988,203	5,296,241	5,572,087	5,743,719	6,135,308	0.59	0.71	0.83	0.95	0.96	0.97	0.96	0.99
Supplies	14,805,956[1]	28,262,078	38,378,936	40,417,163	42,895,737	43,793,547	43,774,032	44,771,753	7.33	8.11	8.05	7.67	7.75	7.61	7.34	7.23
Other	2,973,261[1]	3,579,347	4,761,675	5,095,195	4,776,178	5,725,796	5,590,495	6,057,312	1.47	1.03	1.00	0.97	0.86	1.00	0.94	0.98
Instruction	122,223,362	214,333,003	290,678,482	322,536,983	336,426,927	349,453,258	363,106,915	376,069,486	60.50	61.53	60.96	61.17	60.78	60.74	60.90	60.74
Salaries	90,742,284	154,512,089	196,900,968	212,998,609	217,274,753	223,044,251	230,477,780	236,792,085	44.91	44.35	41.30	40.39	39.25	38.77	38.66	38.24
Employee benefits	22,347,524	39,522,678	64,153,369	75,248,811	83,946,609	88,840,559	92,808,865	98,321,490	11.06	11.35	13.45	14.27	15.17	15.44	15.57	15.88
Purchased services	2,722,639	6,430,708	10,997,609	14,694,620	15,177,204	16,559,278	18,048,424	18,476,414	1.35	1.85	2.31	2.79	2.74	2.88	3.03	2.98
Tuition	1,192,505	2,458,366	3,951,411	4,988,203	5,296,241	5,572,087	5,743,719	6,135,308	0.59	0.71	0.83	0.95	0.96	0.97	0.96	0.99
Supplies	4,584,754	10,377,554	13,359,899	13,135,284	13,344,523	14,060,733	14,602,677	14,900,908	2.27	2.98	2.80	2.49	2.41	2.44	2.45	2.41
Textbooks	—	—	2,779,800	2,324,846	2,321,424	2,438,331	2,540,299	2,636,445	—	—	0.58	0.44	0.42	0.42	0.43	0.43
Other	633,656	1,031,608	1,315,226	1,471,457	1,387,596	1,376,350	1,425,450	1,443,281	0.31	0.30	0.28	0.28	0.25	0.24	0.24	0.23
Student support[2]	8,926,010	17,292,756	25,207,881	29,368,646	30,754,056	32,363,375	34,013,896	35,946,038	4.42	4.96	5.29	5.57	5.56	5.63	5.71	5.81
Salaries	6,565,965	12,354,464	16,868,875	19,367,865	19,823,136	20,658,101	21,598,398	22,550,036	3.25	3.55	3.54	3.67	3.58	3.59	3.62	3.64
Employee benefits	1,660,082	3,036,037	5,352,820	6,533,691	7,315,689	7,872,711	8,360,099	9,135,154	0.82	0.87	1.12	1.24	1.32	1.37	1.40	1.48
Purchased services	455,996	1,328,600	2,141,301	2,583,714	2,850,087	3,024,871	3,202,463	3,390,784	0.23	0.38	0.45	0.49	0.51	0.53	0.54	0.55
Supplies	191,482	421,838	521,050	521,729	564,419	599,269	628,105	645,129	0.09	0.12	0.11	0.10	0.10	0.10	0.11	0.10
Other	52,485	151,817	323,835	361,647	200,727	208,422	224,831	224,936	0.03	0.04	0.07	0.07	0.04	0.04	0.04	0.04
Instructional staff services[3]	8,467,142	15,926,856	23,156,534	24,893,140	25,354,104	26,953,637	28,015,976	29,169,348	4.19	4.57	4.86	4.72	4.58	4.68	4.70	4.71
Salaries	5,560,129	9,790,767	13,753,355	14,490,521	14,685,427	15,490,102	16,082,881	16,712,372	2.75	2.81	2.88	2.75	2.65	2.69	2.70	2.70
Employee benefits	1,408,217	2,356,440	4,225,114	4,933,118	5,234,451	5,640,401	5,899,056	6,354,157	0.70	0.68	0.89	0.94	0.95	0.98	0.99	1.03
Purchased services	622,487	2,003,598	3,071,613	3,438,979	3,444,243	3,659,324	3,942,599	3,966,323	0.31	0.58	0.64	0.65	0.62	0.64	0.66	0.64
Supplies	776,863	1,566,954	1,894,927	1,810,950	1,786,877	1,950,698	1,875,189	1,920,987	0.38	0.45	0.40	0.34	0.32	0.34	0.31	0.31
Other	99,445	209,097	211,525	219,573	203,106	213,112	216,251	215,509	0.05	0.06	0.04	0.04	0.04	0.04	0.04	0.03
General administration	5,791,253	7,108,291	9,338,308	10,494,526	11,117,393	11,535,748	12,052,726	12,305,191	2.87	2.04	1.96	1.99	2.01	2.01	2.02	1.99
Salaries	2,603,562	3,351,554	4,024,030	4,401,697	4,622,952	4,746,838	4,883,367	5,074,357	1.29	0.96	0.84	0.83	0.84	0.83	0.82	0.82
Employee benefits	777,381	1,000,698	1,560,360	1,856,221	1,915,512	2,036,756	2,089,102	2,243,394	0.38	0.29	0.33	0.35	0.35	0.35	0.35	0.36
Purchased services	1,482,427	2,099,032	2,902,431	3,236,857	3,585,418	3,735,708	4,037,348	3,903,190	0.73	0.60	0.61	0.61	0.65	0.65	0.68	0.63
Supplies	172,898	206,137	227,885	228,417	237,184	249,401	265,647	276,833	0.09	0.06	0.05	0.04	0.04	0.04	0.04	0.04
Other	754,985	450,870	623,601	771,334	756,327	767,045	777,262	807,418	0.37	0.13	0.13	0.15	0.14	0.13	0.13	0.13
School administration	11,695,344	19,580,890	26,875,507	28,660,307	30,420,650	31,792,450	33,200,151	34,568,941	5.79	5.62	5.64	5.44	5.50	5.53	5.57	5.58
Salaries	8,935,903	14,817,213	19,209,872	20,191,545	21,132,933	21,921,938	22,759,806	23,536,654	4.42	4.25	4.03	3.83	3.82	3.81	3.82	3.80
Employee benefits	2,257,783	3,689,689	6,092,292	6,972,708	7,718,180	8,194,129	8,633,567	9,222,994	1.12	1.06	1.28	1.32	1.39	1.42	1.45	1.49
Purchased services	247,750	611,638	947,665	931,765	973,307	1,067,751	1,159,015	1,145,693	0.12	0.18	0.20	0.18	0.18	0.19	0.19	0.19
Supplies	189,711	369,257	481,794	426,864	435,766	443,385	475,970	485,616	0.09	0.11	0.10	0.08	0.08	0.08	0.08	0.08
Other	64,197	93,093	143,884	137,426	160,463	165,248	171,794	177,984	0.03	0.03	0.03	0.03	0.03	0.03	0.03	0.03
Operation and maintenance	21,290,655	34,034,158	46,828,916	50,214,709	53,051,141	54,200,172	55,045,039	57,433,468	10.54	9.77	9.82	9.52	9.58	9.42	9.23	9.28
Salaries	8,849,559	13,461,242	16,837,148	17,604,634	17,846,272	18,205,576	18,735,694	19,288,241	4.38	3.86	3.53	3.34	3.22	3.16	3.14	3.12
Employee benefits	2,633,075	3,778,520	6,276,703	7,195,927	7,694,270	8,024,419	8,293,750	8,794,259	1.30	1.08	1.32	1.36	1.39	1.39	1.39	1.42
Purchased services	5,721,125	9,642,217	12,650,704	13,351,922	15,022,138	15,514,037	15,895,748	16,881,488	2.83	2.77	2.65	2.53	2.71	2.70	2.67	2.73
Supplies	3,761,738	6,871,845	10,648,015	11,638,187	12,078,609	12,047,041	11,728,040	12,075,145	1.86	1.97	2.23	2.21	2.18	2.09	1.97	1.95
Other	325,157	280,334	416,345	424,039	409,852	409,098	391,807	394,335	0.16	0.08	0.09	0.08	0.07	0.07	0.07	0.06
Student transportation	8,678,954	14,052,654	19,979,068	22,370,807	23,845,036	23,961,692	24,325,727	25,350,286	4.30	4.03	4.19	4.24	4.31	4.16	4.08	4.09
Salaries	3,285,127	5,406,092	7,080,752	7,527,611	7,683,616	7,897,110	8,198,056	8,513,080	1.63	1.55	1.49	1.43	1.39	1.37	1.38	1.37
Employee benefits	892,985	1,592,127	2,719,742	3,124,937	3,296,150	3,412,883	3,599,805	3,808,782	0.44	0.46	0.57	0.59	0.60	0.59	0.60	0.62
Purchased services	3,345,232	5,767,462	8,085,392	9,153,621	9,926,270	10,063,360	10,392,864	10,819,968	1.66	1.66	1.70	1.74	1.79	1.75	1.74	1.75
Supplies	961,447	1,159,350	1,937,360	2,370,182	2,695,508	2,356,982	1,886,842	1,955,427	0.48	0.33	0.41	0.45	0.49	0.41	0.32	0.32
Other	194,163	127,623	155,822	194,456	243,492	231,357	248,160	253,029	0.10	0.04	0.03	0.04	0.04	0.04	0.04	0.04

See notes at end of table.

Table 236.20. Total expenditures for public elementary and secondary education and other related programs, by function and subfunction: Selected years, 1990–91 through 2016–17—Continued

Function and subfunction	Expenditures (in thousands of current dollars)								Percentage distribution of current expenditures for public schools							
	1990–91	2000–01	2006–07	2010–11	2013–14	2014–15	2015–16	2016–17	1990–91	2000–01	2006–07	2010–11	2013–14	2014–15	2015–16	2016–17
1	2	3	4	5	6	7	8	9	10	11	12	13	14	15	16	17
Other support services[4]	5,587,837	11,439,134	15,514,445	17,246,807	19,034,045	20,885,114	21,595,016	22,981,403	2.77	3.28	3.25	3.27	3.44	3.63	3.62	3.71
Salaries	2,900,394	5,521,381	7,140,671	8,139,084	8,618,767	9,104,041	9,565,073	9,879,480	1.44	1.58	1.50	1.54	1.56	1.58	1.60	1.60
Employee benefits	980,859	1,594,540	2,658,808	3,295,052	3,694,720	3,912,721	4,061,850	4,313,953	0.49	0.46	0.56	0.62	0.67	0.68	0.68	0.70
Purchased services	798,922	2,783,176	3,664,598	3,876,650	4,671,337	4,853,416	5,120,351	5,442,999	0.40	0.80	0.77	0.74	0.84	0.84	0.86	0.88
Supplies	294,527	626,889	874,764	876,293	1,097,951	1,163,493	1,241,221	1,337,399	0.15	0.18	0.18	0.17	0.20	0.20	0.21	0.22
Other	613,135	913,148	1,175,605	1,059,728	951,270	1,851,443	1,606,520	2,007,572	0.30	0.26	0.25	0.20	0.17	0.32	0.27	0.32
Food services	8,430,490	13,816,635	18,150,488	20,394,768	22,342,085	23,064,706	23,643,250	24,095,216	4.17	3.97	3.81	3.87	4.04	4.01	3.97	3.89
Salaries	—	4,966,092	6,092,744	6,482,085	6,699,499	6,873,015	7,098,376	7,215,563	—	1.43	1.28	1.23	1.21	1.19	1.19	1.17
Employee benefits	—	1,381,923	2,186,495	2,492,673	2,731,484	2,818,033	2,923,479	3,055,407	—	0.40	0.46	0.47	0.49	0.49	0.49	0.49
Purchased services	—	923,091	1,558,949	2,058,018	2,335,017	2,460,967	2,566,875	2,671,160	—	0.26	0.33	0.39	0.42	0.43	0.43	0.43
Supplies	—	6,420,201	8,123,362	9,118,886	10,333,931	10,628,481	10,753,015	10,843,608	—	1.84	1.70	1.73	1.87	1.85	1.80	1.75
Other	—	125,327	188,937	243,105	242,155	284,209	301,505	309,478	—	0.04	0.04	0.05	0.04	0.05	0.05	0.05
Enterprise operations[5]	946,705	776,463	1,084,578	1,110,646	1,155,773	1,121,673	1,202,858	1,245,194	0.47	0.22	0.23	0.21	0.21	0.19	0.20	0.20
Salaries	—	124,913	238,259	338,141	318,467	311,727	332,327	351,440	—	0.04	0.05	0.06	0.06	0.05	0.06	0.06
Employee benefits	—	23,837	83,290	97,063	108,464	116,266	119,116	131,513	—	0.01	0.02	0.02	0.02	0.02	0.02	0.02
Purchased services	—	189,230	246,253	172,641	186,682	180,106	207,176	207,769	—	0.05	0.05	0.03	0.03	0.03	0.03	0.03
Supplies	—	242,052	309,881	290,372	320,969	294,064	317,326	330,702	—	0.07	0.06	0.06	0.06	0.05	0.05	0.05
Other	—	196,430	206,895	212,430	221,191	219,510	226,914	223,771	—	0.06	0.04	0.04	0.04	0.04	0.04	0.04
Current expenditures for other programs	3,295,717	6,063,700	7,804,253	8,161,474	7,926,285	7,713,966	7,913,839	8,660,874	†	†	†	†	†	†	†	†
Community services	964,370	2,426,189	3,105,955	3,269,802	3,187,692	3,279,485	3,426,859	3,576,730	†	†	†	†	†	†	†	†
Private school programs	527,609	1,026,695	1,445,984	1,427,539	1,431,807	1,590,684	1,662,359	1,674,995	†	†	†	†	†	†	†	†
Adult education	1,365,523	1,838,265	2,047,409	2,013,156	1,804,646	1,815,963	1,946,215	2,039,281	†	†	†	†	†	†	†	†
Community colleges	5,356	351	31,352	34,045	30,906	28,238	29,113	10,659	†	†	†	†	†	†	†	†
Other	432,858	772,200	1,173,552	1,416,931	1,471,234	999,597	849,293	1,359,209	†	†	†	†	†	†	†	†
Capital outlay[6]	19,771,478	46,220,704	62,863,465	50,968,815	46,438,323	50,610,125	55,989,128	61,441,963	†	†	†	†	†	†	†	†
Public schools	19,655,496	46,078,494	62,763,411	50,888,951	46,297,257	50,448,404	55,841,211	61,280,584	†	†	†	†	†	†	†	†
Other current expenditures	115,982	142,210	100,054	79,864	141,066	161,722	147,917	161,379	†	†	†	†	†	†	†	†
Interest on school debt	4,324,768	10,165,940	14,712,882	17,934,224	17,152,459	17,479,466	17,500,574	18,333,942	†	†	†	†	†	†	†	†

—Not available.
†Not applicable.
[1]Includes estimated data for subfunctions of food services and enterprise operations.
[2]Includes expenditures for guidance, health, attendance, and speech pathology services.
[3]Includes expenditures for curriculum development, staff training, libraries, and media and computer centers.
[4]Includes business support services concerned with paying, transporting, exchanging, and maintaining goods and services for local education agencies; central support services, including planning, research, evaluation, information, staff, and data processing services; and other support services.
[5]Includes expenditures for operations funded by sales of products or services (e.g., school bookstore or computer time). Includes very small amounts for direct program support made by state education agencies for local school districts.
[6]Includes expenditures for property and for buildings and alterations completed by school district staff or contractors.
NOTE: Excludes expenditures for state education agencies. Detail may not sum to totals because of rounding. Some data have been revised from previously published figures.
SOURCE: U.S. Department of Education, National Center for Education Statistics, Common Core of Data (CCD), "National Public Education Financial Survey," 1990–91 through 2016–17. (This table was prepared August 2019.)

Table 236.25. Current expenditures for public elementary and secondary education, by state or jurisdiction: Selected years, 1969–70 through 2016–17

[In thousands of current dollars]

State or jurisdiction	1969–70	1979–80	1989–90	1999–2000	2004–05	2006–07	2007–08	2008–09	2009–10	2010–11	2011–12	2012–13	2013–14	2014–15	2015–16	2016–17
1	2	3	4	5	6	7	8	9	10	11	12	13	14	15	16	17
United States	**$34,217,773**	**$86,984,142**	**$188,229,359**	**$323,888,508**	**$425,047,565**	**$476,814,206**	**$506,884,219**	**$518,922,842**	**$524,715,242**	**$527,291,339**	**$527,207,246**	**$535,795,823**	**$553,501,209**	**$575,331,825**	**$596,201,554**	**$619,164,572**
Alabama	422,730	1,146,713	2,275,233	4,176,082	5,164,406	6,245,031	6,832,439	6,683,843	6,670,517	6,592,925	6,386,517	6,532,358	6,742,829	6,806,467	6,885,677	7,097,472
Alaska	81,374	377,947	828,051	1,183,499	1,442,269	1,634,316	1,918,375	2,007,319	2,084,019	2,201,270	2,292,205	2,395,354	2,418,000	2,648,552	2,319,662	2,367,707
Arizona	281,941	949,753	2,258,660	4,288,739	6,579,957	7,815,720	8,403,221	8,726,755	8,482,552	8,340,211	7,976,089	8,164,529	8,187,607	8,370,884	8,551,673	8,966,684
Arkansas	235,083	666,949	1,404,545	2,380,331	3,546,999	3,997,701	4,156,368	4,240,839	4,459,910	4,578,136	4,606,995	4,637,169	4,778,074	4,813,321	4,872,214	4,936,465
California	3,831,595	9,172,158	21,485,782	38,129,479	50,918,654	57,352,599	61,570,555	60,080,929	58,248,662	57,526,835	57,975,189	58,323,458	61,050,894	65,953,946	72,003,129	76,663,731
Colorado	369,218	1,243,049	2,451,833	4,401,010	5,994,440	6,579,053	7,338,766	7,187,267	7,429,302	7,409,462	7,341,585	7,506,978	7,924,319	8,260,461	8,648,369	8,913,931
Connecticut	588,710	1,227,892	3,444,520	5,402,836	7,080,396	7,855,459	8,336,789	8,708,294	8,853,337	9,094,036	9,344,999	9,543,010	10,050,439	10,321,511	10,551,327	10,664,567
Delaware	108,747	269,108	520,953	937,630	1,299,349	1,437,707	1,489,594	1,518,786	1,549,812	1,613,304	1,751,143	1,761,559	1,816,383	1,860,732	1,941,408	2,029,229
District of Columbia	141,138	298,448	639,983	780,192	1,067,500	1,130,006	1,282,437	1,352,905	1,451,870	1,482,202	1,466,888	1,557,117	1,605,030	1,668,528	1,778,057	1,936,852
Florida	961,273	2,766,468	8,228,531	13,885,988	19,042,877	22,887,024	24,224,114	23,328,028	23,349,314	23,870,090	22,732,752	23,214,634	24,363,817	25,123,548	25,621,239	26,404,135
Georgia	599,371	1,608,028	4,505,962	9,158,624	12,528,856	14,828,715	16,030,039	15,976,945	15,730,409	15,527,907	15,623,633	15,536,733	15,921,673	16,530,506	17,283,295	18,126,272
Hawaii	141,324	351,889	700,012	1,213,695	1,648,086	2,045,198	2,122,779	2,225,438	2,136,144	2,141,561	2,187,480	2,178,284	2,316,586	2,344,496	2,502,117	2,600,074
Idaho	103,107	313,927	627,794	1,302,817	1,618,215	1,777,491	1,891,505	1,957,740	1,961,857	1,881,746	1,854,556	1,925,676	1,949,963	2,015,654	2,107,693	2,245,167
Illinois	1,896,067	4,579,355	8,125,493	14,462,773	18,658,428	20,326,591	21,874,484	23,495,271	24,695,773	24,554,467	25,012,915	25,783,911	27,289,963	28,545,089	29,253,457	31,449,028
Indiana	809,105	1,851,292	4,074,578	7,110,930	9,108,931	9,497,077	9,281,709	9,680,895	9,921,243	9,687,949	9,978,491	9,811,166	9,841,337	9,970,350	10,140,639	10,309,827
Iowa	527,086	1,186,659	2,004,742	3,264,336	3,808,200	4,231,932	4,499,236	4,731,463	4,794,308	4,855,871	4,971,944	5,143,771	5,354,843	5,526,877	5,663,444	5,840,808
Kansas	362,593	830,133	1,848,302	2,971,814	3,718,153	4,339,477	4,633,517	4,806,603	4,731,676	4,741,372	4,871,381	4,895,863	5,083,374	5,136,532	5,065,968	5,154,894
Kentucky	353,265	1,054,459	2,134,011	3,837,794	4,812,591	5,424,621	5,822,550	5,886,890	6,091,814	6,211,453	6,360,799	6,354,306	6,375,119	6,583,287	6,750,052	6,897,155
Louisiana	503,217	1,303,902	2,838,283	4,391,189	5,554,766	6,040,368	6,814,455	7,276,651	7,393,452	7,522,098	7,544,782	7,492,539	7,721,469	7,960,448	8,027,058	8,150,463
Maine	155,907	385,492	1,048,195	1,604,438	2,056,266	2,258,764	2,308,071	2,350,447	2,370,085	2,377,878	2,330,842	2,357,739	2,441,064	2,538,313	2,579,299	2,641,420
Maryland	721,794	1,783,056	3,894,644	6,545,135	8,682,586	10,210,303	11,211,176	11,591,965	11,883,677	11,885,333	11,850,634	12,108,546	12,314,446	12,620,036	12,774,063	13,233,589
Massachusetts	907,341	2,638,734	4,760,390	8,564,039	11,357,857	12,383,447	13,182,987	13,937,097	13,356,373	13,962,366	14,151,659	14,627,898	15,183,018	15,723,617	16,374,676	17,089,142
Michigan	1,799,945	4,642,847	8,025,621	13,994,294	16,353,921	17,013,259	17,053,521	17,217,584	17,227,515	16,786,444	16,485,178	16,354,807	16,493,575	16,849,135	16,977,163	17,206,122
Minnesota	781,243	1,786,768	3,474,398	6,140,442	7,310,284	8,060,410	8,426,264	9,182,281	8,927,288	8,944,867	9,053,021	9,354,376	9,723,759	10,222,017	10,687,048	11,056,128
Mississippi	262,760	756,018	1,472,710	2,510,376	3,243,888	3,692,358	3,898,401	3,967,232	3,990,876	3,887,981	3,972,787	4,006,798	4,071,006	4,145,632	4,234,977	4,229,767
Missouri	642,030	1,504,988	3,288,738	5,655,531	7,115,207	7,957,705	8,526,641	8,827,224	8,923,448	8,691,887	8,719,925	8,905,756	9,125,949	9,390,061	9,545,816	9,776,478
Montana	127,176	358,118	641,345	994,770	1,193,182	1,320,112	1,392,449	1,436,062	1,498,252	1,518,818	1,504,531	1,523,696	1,576,937	1,601,097	1,652,848	1,688,944
Nebraska	231,612	581,615	1,233,431	1,926,500	2,512,914	2,825,608	2,970,323	3,053,575	3,213,646	3,345,530	3,462,575	3,563,939	3,654,376	3,805,871	3,911,805	4,041,479
Nevada	87,273	281,901	712,898	1,875,467	2,722,264	3,311,471	3,515,004	3,606,035	3,592,994	3,676,997	3,574,233	3,577,346	3,738,777	3,880,472	4,092,457	4,320,504
New Hampshire	101,370	295,400	821,671	1,418,503	2,021,144	2,246,692	2,399,330	2,490,623	2,576,956	2,637,911	2,643,256	2,655,077	2,720,225	2,764,233	2,833,893	2,886,649
New Jersey	1,343,564	3,638,533	8,119,336	13,327,645	19,669,576	22,448,262	24,357,079	23,446,911	24,261,392	23,639,281	24,391,278	25,417,320	25,733,921	25,993,208	26,825,114	27,622,861
New Mexico	183,736	515,451	1,020,148	1,890,274	2,554,638	2,904,474	3,057,061	3,186,252	3,217,328	3,127,463	3,039,461	3,099,308	3,189,842	3,309,622	3,343,152	3,345,338
New York	4,111,839	8,760,500	18,090,978	28,433,240	38,866,853	43,679,908	46,443,426	48,635,363	50,251,461	51,574,134	52,460,494	52,938,586	55,080,662	56,862,010	59,161,439	60,905,055
North Carolina	676,193	1,880,862	4,342,826	7,713,293	9,835,550	11,248,336	11,482,912	12,598,382	12,200,362	12,322,555	12,303,426	12,666,607	12,685,461	13,210,839	13,466,942	13,943,070
North Dakota	97,895	228,483	459,391	638,946	832,157	838,221	886,317	928,528	1,000,095	1,049,772	1,098,090	1,174,364	1,287,133	1,373,266	1,451,309	1,510,292
Ohio	1,639,805	3,836,576	7,994,379	12,974,575	17,167,866	18,251,361	18,892,374	19,387,318	19,801,670	19,988,921	19,701,810	19,506,123	19,714,149	20,231,423	20,484,182	21,494,254
Oklahoma	339,105	1,055,844	1,905,332	3,382,581	4,161,024	4,750,536	4,932,913	5,082,062	5,192,124	5,036,031	5,170,978	5,329,897	5,451,048	5,560,047	5,606,044	5,496,402
Oregon	403,844	1,126,812	2,297,944	3,896,287	4,458,028	5,039,632	5,409,630	5,529,831	5,401,667	5,430,888	5,389,273	5,395,742	5,647,470	5,969,321	6,238,574	6,514,334
Pennsylvania	1,912,644	4,584,320	9,496,788	14,120,112	18,711,100	20,404,304	21,157,430	21,831,816	22,733,518	23,485,203	23,190,198	23,712,931	24,264,551	25,109,991	26,045,127	27,263,106
Rhode Island	145,443	362,046	801,908	1,393,143	1,825,900	2,039,633	2,134,609	2,139,317	2,136,582	2,149,366	2,167,450	2,121,403	2,182,976	2,242,486	2,283,927	2,362,463
South Carolina	367,689	997,984	2,322,618	4,087,355	5,312,739	6,023,043	6,453,817	6,626,763	6,566,165	6,465,486	6,619,072	6,950,410	7,163,995	7,437,182	7,727,135	8,035,426
South Dakota	109,375	238,332	447,074	737,998	916,563	977,006	1,037,875	1,080,054	1,115,861	1,126,503	1,100,100	1,125,929	1,182,721	1,211,080	1,253,268	1,379,026
Tennessee	473,226	1,319,303	2,790,808	4,931,734	6,446,691	6,975,099	7,540,306	7,768,063	7,894,661	8,225,374	8,345,584	8,531,675	8,606,624	8,736,367	8,886,994	9,260,615
Texas	1,518,181	4,997,689	12,763,954	25,098,703	31,919,107	36,105,784	39,033,235	40,688,181	42,621,886	42,864,291	41,067,619	42,066,035	44,330,579	47,527,971	49,577,688	51,033,537
Utah	179,981	518,251	1,130,135	2,102,655	2,627,022	2,987,810	3,444,936	3,638,775	3,635,085	3,704,133	3,779,760	3,944,736	4,094,074	4,290,876	4,539,291	4,754,714
Vermont	78,921	189,811	546,901	870,198	1,177,478	1,300,149	1,356,165	1,413,329	1,432,683	1,424,507	1,497,093	1,549,228	1,602,256	1,638,720	1,671,433	1,722,621
Virginia	704,677	1,881,519	4,621,071	7,757,598	10,705,162	12,465,858	13,125,666	13,505,290	13,193,633	12,968,457	13,403,576	13,868,587	13,955,249	14,384,705	14,677,698	15,296,646
Washington	699,984	1,825,782	3,550,819	6,399,885	7,870,979	8,752,007	9,331,539	9,940,325	9,832,913	10,040,312	10,040,607	10,216,676	10,911,929	11,470,245	12,483,668	13,188,097
West Virginia	249,404	678,386	1,316,637	2,086,937	2,527,767	2,742,344	2,841,962	2,998,657	3,328,177	3,388,294	3,275,246	3,188,181	3,194,770	3,226,918	3,169,684	3,216,323
Wisconsin	777,288	1,908,523	3,929,920	6,852,178	8,435,359	9,029,660	9,366,134	9,696,228	9,966,244	10,333,016	9,704,932	9,758,650	9,920,370	10,054,346	10,122,041	10,340,697
Wyoming	69,584	226,067	509,084	683,918	863,423	1,124,564	1,191,736	1,268,407	1,334,655	1,398,444	1,432,216	1,439,041	1,466,579	1,509,532	1,556,321	1,555,016
Other jurisdictions																
American Samoa	—	—	21,838	42,395	58,163	57,093	63,105	65,436	70,305	75,355	80,105	65,039	71,709	63,693	58,675	65,490
Guam	16,652	—	101,130	—	—	219,881	229,243	235,711	235,639	266,952	290,575	279,077	286,844	293,713	298,708	298,340
Northern Marianas	—	—	20,476	49,832	58,400	55,048	51,241	62,787	62,210	84,657	68,775	61,029	62,502	65,304	75,562	87,920
Puerto Rico	—	—	1,045,407	2,086,414	2,865,945	3,268,200	3,433,229	3,502,757	3,464,044	3,519,547	3,351,423	3,676,880	3,510,706	3,247,136	2,970,386	2,789,459
U.S. Virgin Islands	—	—	128,065	135,174	137,793	157,446	196,533	201,326	220,234	204,932	183,333	161,955	175,022	158,652	160,559	171,521

—Not available.

NOTE: *Current expenditures include instruction, support services, food services, and enterprise operations. Beginning in* 1989–90, expenditures for state administration are excluded. Data are not adjusted for changes in the purchasing power of the dollar due to inflation. Detail may not sum to totals because of rounding. Some data have been revised from previously published figures.

SOURCE: U.S. Department of Education, National Center for Education Statistics, *Statistics of State School Systems, 1969–70*; *Revenues and Expenditures for Public Elementary and Secondary Education, 1979–80*; and Common Core of Data (CCD), "National Public Education Financial Survey," 1989–90 through 2016–17. (This table was prepared August 2019.)

Table 236.30. Total expenditures for public elementary and secondary education and other related programs, by function and state or jurisdiction: 2016–17

[In thousands of current dollars]

State or jurisdiction	Total expenditures															
		Current expenditures for elementary and secondary programs														
				Support services												
	Total	Elementary/ secondary current expendi- tures, total	Instruction	Support services, total	Student support[4]	Instructional staff[5]	General adminis- tration	School adminis- tration	Operation and maintenance	Student transpor- tation	Other support services	Food services	Enterprise operations[3]	Current expenditures for other programs[1]	Capital outlay[2]	Interest on school debt
1	2	3	4	5	6	7	8	9	10	11	12	13	14	15	16	17
United States	**$707,601,350**	**$619,164,572**	**$376,069,486**	**$217,754,675**	**$35,946,038**	**$29,169,348**	**$12,305,191**	**$34,568,941**	**$57,433,468**	**$25,350,286**	**$22,981,403**	**$24,095,216**	**$1,245,194**	**$8,660,874**	**$61,441,963**	**$18,333,942**
Alabama	8,030,225	7,097,472	4,049,192	2,563,159	446,175	298,519	182,443	442,733	660,054	366,671	166,563	485,121	0	122,765	637,471	172,517
Alaska	2,582,582	2,367,707	1,266,042	1,013,894	183,607	196,525	33,856	144,766	283,842	80,673	90,624	76,820	10,952	7,959	169,582	37,334
Arizona	10,530,826	8,966,684	4,828,965	3,669,286	687,666	434,553	173,941	502,905	1,098,094	371,832	400,295	467,132	1,301	92,293	1,220,401	251,447
Arkansas	5,622,673	4,936,465	2,769,224	1,898,530	266,940	415,124	124,843	258,857	500,434	181,436	150,896	263,084	5,627	30,111	529,540	126,558
California	87,968,218	76,663,731	45,442,062	28,155,354	4,598,429	4,880,880	753,775	5,082,339	7,573,197	1,679,133	3,587,603	2,878,381	187,935	924,523	7,470,798	2,909,165
Colorado	10,632,736	8,913,931	4,989,814	3,570,698	502,458	513,143	144,538	679,279	814,583	265,301	651,397	305,496	47,923	77,653	1,183,120	458,032
Connecticut	11,573,665	10,664,567	6,722,928	3,614,923	684,769	335,452	239,206	624,118	915,695	537,460	278,224	234,506	92,211	146,121	641,349	121,628
Delaware	2,247,039	2,029,229	1,269,553	691,907	90,650	37,248	31,895	128,691	216,676	100,560	86,188	67,769	0	53,793	141,956	22,062
District of Columbia	2,625,829	1,936,852	1,039,933	826,686	86,016	97,241	141,543	134,950	190,735	117,259	58,942	69,429	804	39,350	510,487	139,140
Florida	29,875,971	26,404,135	16,305,281	8,782,010	1,161,081	1,660,734	242,525	1,470,634	2,548,825	1,017,779	680,431	1,316,843	0	566,061	2,292,633	613,143
Georgia	20,344,480	18,126,272	11,061,068	6,035,059	943,009	941,356	231,190	1,144,159	1,361,543	847,547	566,256	977,222	52,922	33,899	1,959,953	224,356
Hawaii	2,778,688	2,600,074	1,520,054	949,131	244,802	87,772	13,048	186,738	289,131	63,216	64,424	130,889	0	16,960	161,655	0
Idaho	2,560,406	2,245,167	1,323,118	811,616	125,438	130,399	56,390	129,058	212,304	97,989	60,038	109,263	1,170	4,852	251,888	58,499
Illinois	34,588,140	31,449,028	19,603,947	11,068,443	2,214,977	1,134,511	1,182,158	1,638,178	2,440,415	1,334,997	1,123,207	776,639	0	162,530	2,018,535	958,047
Indiana	11,866,554	10,309,827	5,939,926	3,872,427	537,800	414,873	212,946	671,823	1,161,592	623,109	250,283	497,474	0	167,568	1,095,237	293,922
Iowa	6,809,987	5,840,808	3,524,206	2,050,887	341,231	364,865	148,834	330,146	484,172	205,084	176,556	258,951	6,764	38,180	813,457	117,542
Kansas	6,279,467	5,154,894	3,074,527	1,836,380	328,022	212,934	138,347	299,424	503,876	209,520	144,257	243,986	0	4,285	877,514	242,774
Kentucky	7,878,382	6,897,155	3,954,611	2,472,297	336,798	384,692	155,583	401,723	614,507	393,211	185,782	451,699	18,548	77,289	721,214	182,724
Louisiana	8,983,530	8,150,463	4,551,129	3,169,566	495,861	406,228	211,453	523,649	822,880	465,492	244,002	429,670	99	28,511	690,293	114,263
Maine	2,838,337	2,641,420	1,545,474	989,537	180,995	149,247	89,805	139,360	265,690	129,800	34,641	106,085	324	27,954	123,321	45,642
Maryland	14,669,628	13,233,589	8,432,187	4,424,391	595,713	610,473	128,514	893,341	1,116,465	691,807	388,078	377,011	0	39,956	1,237,379	158,705
Massachusetts	17,909,571	17,089,142	10,912,548	5,698,222	1,270,086	788,946	275,981	731,675	1,437,462	776,589	417,483	478,372	0	76,127	507,504	236,798
Michigan	19,612,463	17,206,122	9,875,810	6,695,573	1,360,804	871,777	386,016	960,612	1,510,634	720,147	885,583	634,739	0	290,037	1,393,502	722,803
Minnesota	14,127,456	11,056,128	7,153,109	3,388,197	323,867	565,322	415,002	444,288	746,716	625,079	267,924	467,516	47,304	513,373	2,160,797	397,158
Mississippi	4,673,532	4,229,767	2,400,216	1,570,271	224,419	196,756	142,223	257,398	433,815	202,096	113,565	259,057	223	29,715	360,550	53,501
Missouri	11,189,561	9,776,478	5,767,922	3,552,049	441,238	447,079	362,602	573,398	977,605	505,638	244,489	456,507	0	259,729	841,235	312,118
Montana	1,908,339	1,688,944	991,332	619,787	115,746	59,838	53,622	94,081	169,682	79,292	47,525	75,187	2,638	10,712	185,247	23,436
Nebraska	4,844,039	4,041,479	2,616,805	1,150,951	154,575	129,927	118,339	191,203	345,168	119,441	92,298	168,307	105,416	2,062	704,266	96,233
Nevada	4,987,380	4,320,504	2,554,828	1,597,247	237,070	238,700	69,977	317,085	400,038	169,077	165,299	168,244	185	25,125	477,784	163,967
New Hampshire	3,082,887	2,886,649	1,839,343	977,914	222,126	94,964	103,951	160,992	231,303	127,292	37,285	69,392	0	6,427	144,183	45,629
New Jersey	29,839,108	27,622,861	16,589,382	10,140,298	2,858,018	864,829	563,247	1,369,401	2,686,395	1,139,284	659,124	617,300	275,881	248,666	1,301,715	665,866
New Mexico	3,901,217	3,345,338	1,914,568	1,268,925	337,928	91,409	79,625	198,495	349,245	103,752	108,472	159,640	2,205	1,959	553,767	152
New York	67,194,754	60,905,055	42,389,679	17,303,620	1,950,611	1,567,910	984,799	2,332,684	5,600,964	3,073,409	1,793,244	1,211,757	0	2,236,181	2,588,199	1,465,319
North Carolina	15,389,536	13,943,070	8,718,633	4,488,163	758,525	479,501	241,840	826,515	1,146,436	568,542	466,805	736,274	0	65,366	1,359,657	21,444
North Dakota	1,824,684	1,510,292	906,313	491,975	60,781	51,919	65,204	78,090	129,557	60,165	46,259	70,245	41,759	11,520	270,221	32,651
Ohio	24,503,675	21,494,254	12,703,608	8,083,921	1,454,986	856,705	674,296	1,188,192	1,840,935	1,020,880	1,047,926	705,533	1,192	468,613	1,921,438	619,370
Oklahoma	6,228,822	5,496,402	3,072,797	2,004,138	374,211	221,748	164,623	306,275	576,296	173,226	187,759	363,634	55,833	28,946	637,138	66,337
Oregon	7,731,996	6,514,334	3,807,508	2,478,957	494,587	262,616	91,127	415,589	516,505	286,763	411,770	224,745	3,123	32,995	827,259	357,408
Pennsylvania	30,765,985	27,263,106	16,871,795	9,385,807	1,538,734	976,882	823,115	1,214,207	2,495,880	1,297,216	1,039,772	889,644	115,861	568,044	1,992,715	942,120
Rhode Island	2,591,928	2,362,463	1,428,107	869,618	248,744	90,506	35,431	112,808	183,344	102,335	96,450	64,216	522	57,258	132,829	39,378
South Carolina	9,721,717	8,035,426	4,455,636	3,147,018	619,625	497,997	78,239	520,441	788,674	303,877	338,165	412,078	20,694	61,891	1,286,658	337,743
South Dakota	1,571,670	1,379,026	816,490	484,102	76,803	48,890	46,268	66,995	143,576	49,059	52,510	71,486	6,948	7,171	152,374	33,099
Tennessee	10,418,228	9,260,615	5,652,110	3,091,904	416,268	546,464	192,701	560,592	767,734	347,912	260,232	516,601	0	82,703	849,531	225,379
Texas	64,601,315	51,033,537	29,431,662	18,755,366	2,515,067	2,622,675	750,018	2,926,014	5,379,370	1,485,564	3,076,659	2,846,509	0	349,734	9,830,252	3,387,792
Utah	5,813,157	4,754,714	3,019,473	1,485,927	185,373	190,712	53,508	312,558	432,719	140,222	170,835	238,818	10,496	10,557	929,100	118,786

See notes at end of table.

Table 236.30. Total expenditures for public elementary and secondary education and other related programs, by function and state or jurisdiction: 2016–17—Continued

[In thousands of current dollars]

State or jurisdiction	Total expenditures															
		Current expenditures for elementary and secondary programs												Current expenditures for other programs[1]	Capital outlay[2]	Interest on school debt
				Support services												
	Total	Elementary/secondary current expenditures, total	Instruction	Support services, total	Student support[4]	Instructional staff[5]	General administration	School administration	Operation and maintenance	Student transportation	Other support services	Food services	Enterprise operations[3]			
1	2	3	4	5	6	7	8	9	10	11	12	13	14	15	16	17
Vermont	1,797,465	1,722,621	1,107,391	570,073	133,216	71,370	36,224	108,604	128,666	56,760	35,234	43,217	1,940	10,448	55,204	9,193
Virginia	16,798,809	15,296,646	9,313,749	5,390,585	774,800	1,013,488	247,977	897,282	1,365,285	787,814	303,939	588,958	3,354	77,176	1,328,791	96,197
Washington	16,007,632	13,188,097	7,646,339	5,018,087	967,929	854,897	225,675	800,156	1,118,968	493,731	556,730	401,398	122,273	50,814	2,329,122	439,599
West Virginia	3,487,741	3,216,323	1,842,144	1,167,027	166,921	127,203	55,147	172,428	346,891	238,828	59,608	207,152	0	46,028	210,863	14,527
Wisconsin	11,876,059	10,340,697	6,136,689	3,824,345	516,870	545,466	298,849	521,086	958,276	438,470	545,329	379,585	78	363,949	1,011,285	160,128
Wyoming	1,913,258	1,555,016	920,260	588,428	93,676	86,084	32,731	82,920	150,621	77,950	64,448	45,637	691	4,935	350,996	2,312
Other jurisdictions																
American Samoa	76,797	65,490	31,446	14,110	35	7,235	891	4,188	0	531	1,231	19,934	0	1,800	9,507	0
Guam	361,502	298,340	142,210	136,084	28,008	16,535	4,802	18,225	38,523	7,948	22,043	20,046	0	0	50,806	12,356
Northern Marianas	92,633	87,920	41,483	33,459	6,742	8,246	1,727	4,276	7,083	1,443	3,942	12,977	0	2,993	1,720	0
Puerto Rico	2,891,749	2,789,459	1,128,669	1,262,150	317,681	166,391	79,112	121,196	407,424	93,059	77,287	398,641	0	67,690	34,600	0
U.S. Virgin Islands	172,940	171,521	100,419	59,708	14,841	4,219	8,199	9,465	6,854	7,536	8,592	11,236	158	1,303	116	0

[1]Includes expenditures for adult education, community colleges, private school programs funded by local and state education agencies, and community services.
[2]Includes expenditures for property and for buildings and alterations completed by school district staff or contractors.
[3]Includes expenditures for operations funded by sales of products or services (e.g., school bookstore or computer time). Also includes small amounts for direct program support made by state education agencies for local school districts.
[4]Includes expenditures for guidance, health, attendance, and speech pathology services.
[5]Includes expenditures for curriculum development, staff training, libraries, and media and computer centers.
NOTE: Excludes expenditures for state education agencies. Detail may not sum to totals because of rounding.
SOURCE: U.S. Department of Education, National Center for Education Statistics, Common Core of Data (CCD), "National Public Education Financial Survey," 2016–17. (This table was prepared August 2019.)

Table 236.50. Expenditures for instruction in public elementary and secondary schools, by subfunction and state or jurisdiction: 2015–16 and 2016–17

State or jurisdiction	In thousands of current dollars											
	2015–16						2016–17					
	Total	Salaries	Employee benefits	Purchased services[2]	Supplies	Tuition and other	Total	Salaries	Employee benefits	Purchased services[2]	Supplies	Tuition and other
1	2	3	4	5	6	7	8	9	10	11	12	13
United States	**$363,106,915**	**$230,477,780**	**$92,808,865**	**$18,048,424**	**$14,602,677**	**$7,169,169**	**$376,069,486**	**$236,792,085**	**$98,321,490**	**$18,476,414**	**$14,900,908**	**$7,578,589**
Alabama	3,919,656	2,477,404	965,949	169,353	285,000	21,950	4,049,192	2,582,189	996,372	177,983	270,097	22,552
Alaska	1,251,726	711,182	414,485	58,577	56,348	11,134	1,266,042	721,744	414,054	61,383	57,179	11,682
Arizona	4,596,134	3,126,187	934,003	309,608	194,855	31,482	4,828,965	3,260,105	972,152	338,868	221,550	36,290
Arkansas	2,734,078	1,846,357	524,988	126,960	197,711	38,062	2,769,224	1,876,614	530,842	124,196	201,653	35,919
California	42,606,846	27,148,052	10,154,297	2,228,377	2,185,023	891,098	45,442,062	28,385,595	11,385,176	2,364,304	2,359,697	947,290
Colorado	4,872,737	3,348,613	953,906	133,253	304,275	132,690	4,989,814	3,421,045	1,004,243	135,159	298,385	130,982
Connecticut	6,654,475	3,909,375	1,885,230	220,157	112,589	527,124	6,722,928	3,963,987	1,899,984	217,458	103,922	537,577
Delaware	1,217,984	732,116	382,812	13,611	55,002	34,444	1,269,553	758,279	419,882	17,908	51,864	21,620
District of Columbia	985,046	687,092	139,236	42,456	24,852	91,410	1,039,933	709,164	167,435	48,003	22,171	93,159
Florida	15,763,102	9,227,638	2,794,944	3,131,946	487,810	120,763	16,305,281	9,375,840	2,907,840	3,366,298	529,449	125,854
Georgia	10,690,729	6,932,398	2,674,848	399,785	625,381	58,319	11,061,068	7,297,731	2,824,024	258,060	620,321	60,934
Hawaii	1,466,292	948,100	381,962	55,103	71,682	9,444	1,520,054	955,344	420,171	53,923	80,064	10,552
Idaho	1,249,823	854,488	300,346	45,711	47,744	1,533	1,323,118	902,280	316,921	50,903	51,567	1,448
Illinois	18,155,294	10,057,461	6,270,188	1,024,980	444,020	358,645	19,603,947	10,142,329	7,673,293	1,007,196	423,696	357,434
Indiana	5,829,338	3,622,089	1,891,038	104,080	202,779	9,352	5,939,926	3,687,499	1,911,384	113,159	218,550	9,334
Iowa	3,431,757	2,414,681	786,969	90,387	104,827	34,894	3,524,206	2,487,050	812,850	81,752	106,932	35,622
Kansas	3,027,649	2,153,182	624,906	89,900	135,838	23,823	3,074,527	2,173,096	633,067	94,200	147,246	26,919
Kentucky	3,909,722	2,653,544	1,049,594	61,715	130,899	13,970	3,954,611	2,678,619	1,061,769	63,738	136,607	13,878
Louisiana	4,518,231	2,781,019	1,326,846	144,108	206,561	59,697	4,551,129	2,786,077	1,331,231	152,312	215,036	66,472
Maine	1,516,283	964,407	394,300	39,953	36,233	81,389	1,545,474	993,471	386,470	42,733	35,655	87,145
Maryland	8,028,897	5,029,476	2,283,910	250,071	187,431	278,008	8,432,187	5,256,375	2,387,876	299,548	198,799	289,589
Massachusetts	10,492,714	6,656,111	2,641,926	95,886	277,803	820,988	10,912,548	6,823,131	2,863,534	99,994	273,503	852,386
Michigan	9,766,683	5,176,562	3,368,889	947,726	254,201	19,306	9,875,810	5,203,188	3,414,023	976,162	261,915	20,522
Minnesota	6,949,478	4,641,312	1,642,237	367,612	207,138	91,179	7,153,109	4,835,058	1,613,811	378,176	224,881	101,184
Mississippi	2,414,582	1,667,459	552,238	72,636	102,866	19,384	2,400,216	1,658,005	549,816	70,947	100,228	21,220
Missouri	5,651,864	3,890,461	1,178,624	191,790	358,768	32,221	5,767,922	3,973,411	1,213,296	185,357	365,050	30,808
Montana	970,897	643,783	195,581	58,266	68,008	5,259	991,332	660,424	201,945	59,733	63,835	5,395
Nebraska	2,486,681	1,637,339	583,658	131,445	112,253	21,987	2,616,805	1,679,453	660,061	134,212	119,991	23,089
Nevada	2,398,324	1,565,794	640,137	47,619	140,144	4,631	2,554,828	1,648,455	669,525	48,597	182,143	6,108
New Hampshire	1,804,284	1,070,727	499,636	48,479	35,651	149,791	1,839,343	1,085,209	510,293	50,275	35,204	158,362
New Jersey	16,132,662	9,674,517	4,594,280	636,802	455,518	771,545	16,589,382	9,803,635	4,888,507	660,988	443,100	793,153
New Mexico	1,902,034	1,284,541	443,881	67,436	105,846	331	1,914,568	1,282,898	450,510	74,019	106,860	280
New York	41,924,498	24,955,914	13,224,238	2,330,671	729,050	684,624	42,389,679	25,538,666	13,445,451	1,947,701	752,814	705,047
North Carolina	8,395,193	5,810,078	1,895,980	284,479	404,208	449	8,718,633	5,972,552	2,014,735	295,971	435,369	6
North Dakota	869,633	590,288	221,357	23,072	28,732	6,183	906,313	616,846	231,438	22,323	29,926	5,780
Ohio	11,954,341	7,526,394	2,775,349	725,767	459,953	466,877	12,703,608	7,852,213	2,868,220	934,872	475,638	572,665
Oklahoma	3,125,438	2,163,799	696,168	59,181	193,959	12,330	3,072,797	2,124,218	695,511	58,739	182,005	12,324
Oregon	3,650,480	2,144,702	1,138,171	130,150	197,142	40,315	3,807,508	2,239,094	1,186,291	139,382	202,781	39,959
Pennsylvania	16,083,136	9,192,617	5,305,250	783,388	474,936	326,944	16,871,795	9,396,615	5,724,229	833,924	541,482	375,546
Rhode Island	1,393,738	870,708	420,972	11,913	23,693	66,453	1,428,107	892,529	433,087	14,093	23,157	65,241
South Carolina	4,294,386	2,842,958	1,027,856	174,223	225,632	23,717	4,455,636	2,922,021	1,075,491	192,972	240,425	24,728
South Dakota	730,833	492,308	148,723	28,656	48,482	12,665	816,490	552,513	162,846	32,537	54,046	14,549
Tennessee	5,465,563	3,665,541	1,205,593	127,147	454,033	13,249	5,652,110	3,791,470	1,258,410	126,009	461,240	14,980
Texas	28,970,556	22,035,575	3,664,960	1,003,668	1,928,691	337,661	29,431,662	22,537,224	3,794,495	1,058,061	1,687,197	354,685
Utah	2,868,057	1,748,837	810,108	101,254	192,319	15,539	3,019,473	1,831,170	846,311	105,540	217,834	18,617
Vermont	1,061,379	599,678	291,342	61,557	21,518	87,283	1,107,391	613,350	317,302	58,196	20,116	98,428
Virginia	8,944,628	6,054,755	2,366,965	188,634	321,229	13,045	9,313,749	6,256,908	2,499,818	206,591	342,165	8,266
Washington	7,211,513	4,685,619	1,732,671	445,329	284,788	63,107	7,646,339	5,000,463	1,826,380	471,563	283,814	64,118
West Virginia	1,824,705	1,122,269	526,003	39,033	131,236	6,164	1,842,144	1,104,748	558,286	38,753	132,865	7,492
Wisconsin	6,018,974	3,856,289	1,623,439	90,922	225,236	223,087	6,136,689	3,898,231	1,631,245	100,318	248,504	258,391
Wyoming	923,865	585,983	257,877	33,597	42,785	3,623	920,260	583,957	259,585	31,325	42,383	3,010
Other jurisdictions												
American Samoa	29,612	21,780	4,591	450	985	1,806	31,446	22,500	4,691	1,230	1,193	1,831
Guam	143,897	105,474	36,814	166	1,441	1	142,210	104,755	36,469	479	507	0
Northern Marianas	36,419	25,031	4,666	3,424	2,054	1,244	41,483	24,861	6,288	3,828	4,502	2,004
Puerto Rico	1,194,926	886,323	240,157	51,266	16,900	280	1,128,669	836,793	225,101	53,047	13,402	326
U.S. Virgin Islands	94,624	63,079	26,493	2,136	2,915	0	100,419	66,997	28,139	2,249	3,034	0

See notes at end of table.

Table 236.50. Expenditures for instruction in public elementary and secondary schools, by subfunction and state or jurisdiction: 2015–16 and 2016–17—Continued

State or jurisdiction	In thousands of constant 2018–19 dollars[1]											
	2015–16						2016–17					
	Total	Salaries	Employee benefits	Purchased services[2]	Supplies	Tuition and other	Total	Salaries	Employee benefits	Purchased services[2]	Supplies	Tuition and other
1	14	15	16	17	18	19	20	21	22	23	24	25
United States	**$385,957,965**	**$244,982,211**	**$98,649,514**	**$19,184,248**	**$15,521,653**	**$7,620,340**	**$392,516,017**	**$247,147,640**	**$102,621,354**	**$19,284,438**	**$15,552,565**	**$7,910,021**
Alabama	4,166,328	2,633,312	1,026,738	180,011	302,936	23,332	4,226,274	2,695,115	1,039,946	185,766	281,909	23,538
Alaska	1,330,499	755,938	440,569	62,263	59,894	11,835	1,321,409	753,308	432,161	64,068	59,679	12,192
Arizona	4,885,378	3,322,924	992,781	329,092	207,118	33,463	5,040,149	3,402,678	1,014,667	353,687	231,239	37,877
Arkansas	2,906,139	1,962,552	558,027	134,950	210,153	40,457	2,890,329	1,958,683	554,057	129,627	210,472	37,490
California	45,288,181	28,856,533	10,793,328	2,368,613	2,322,530	947,176	47,429,366	29,626,973	11,883,080	2,467,702	2,462,893	988,718
Colorado	5,179,389	3,559,348	1,013,937	141,639	323,424	141,040	5,208,032	3,570,657	1,048,161	141,070	311,434	136,710
Connecticut	7,073,254	4,155,400	2,003,871	234,012	119,675	560,297	7,016,939	4,137,343	1,983,075	226,968	108,466	561,087
Delaware	1,294,634	778,189	406,903	14,467	58,463	36,611	1,325,074	791,440	438,244	18,691	54,132	22,565
District of Columbia	1,047,037	730,332	147,999	45,128	26,416	97,163	1,085,412	740,178	174,758	50,103	23,141	97,233
Florida	16,755,105	9,808,352	2,970,836	3,329,046	518,508	128,363	17,018,355	9,785,871	3,035,008	3,513,516	552,603	131,358
Georgia	11,363,519	7,368,667	2,843,181	424,944	664,737	61,989	11,544,799	7,616,880	2,947,526	269,346	647,449	63,598
Hawaii	1,558,568	1,007,766	405,999	58,571	76,194	10,039	1,586,530	997,124	438,546	56,281	83,565	11,014
Idaho	1,328,476	908,263	319,248	48,588	50,748	1,630	1,380,982	941,739	330,781	53,129	53,822	1,511
Illinois	19,297,843	10,690,398	6,664,784	1,089,484	471,963	381,215	20,461,280	10,585,880	8,008,866	1,051,243	442,225	373,065
Indiana	6,196,190	3,850,034	2,010,045	110,630	215,540	9,941	6,199,695	3,848,764	1,994,974	118,108	228,107	9,742
Iowa	3,647,724	2,566,641	836,495	96,075	111,424	37,090	3,678,329	2,595,816	848,398	85,327	111,608	37,180
Kansas	3,218,185	2,288,686	664,233	95,557	144,386	25,322	3,208,984	2,268,131	660,753	98,319	153,685	28,096
Kentucky	4,155,769	2,820,536	1,115,648	65,599	139,137	14,849	4,127,557	2,795,762	1,108,203	66,526	142,581	14,485
Louisiana	4,802,572	2,956,034	1,410,347	153,177	219,560	63,454	4,750,162	2,907,920	1,389,450	158,973	224,440	69,378
Maine	1,611,705	1,025,099	419,114	42,467	38,514	86,511	1,613,062	1,036,918	403,372	44,602	37,214	90,956
Maryland	8,534,171	5,345,991	2,427,641	265,808	199,227	295,504	8,800,949	5,486,250	2,492,304	312,649	207,493	302,253
Massachusetts	11,153,042	7,074,993	2,808,188	101,920	295,286	872,654	11,389,783	7,121,525	2,988,764	104,367	285,464	889,663
Michigan	10,381,320	5,502,333	3,580,900	1,007,369	270,198	20,521	10,307,706	5,430,738	3,563,327	1,018,852	273,369	21,419
Minnesota	7,386,822	4,933,399	1,745,586	390,747	220,174	96,917	7,465,934	5,046,508	1,684,387	394,714	234,715	105,609
Mississippi	2,566,537	1,772,396	586,991	77,207	109,339	20,604	2,505,184	1,730,514	573,861	74,050	104,611	22,148
Missouri	6,007,548	4,135,296	1,252,797	203,860	381,346	34,249	6,020,168	4,147,178	1,266,357	193,463	381,015	32,155
Montana	1,031,997	684,298	207,889	61,932	72,288	5,590	1,034,685	689,306	210,776	62,345	66,626	5,631
Nebraska	2,643,173	1,740,380	620,388	139,717	119,317	23,370	2,731,245	1,752,900	688,928	140,081	125,238	24,099
Nevada	2,549,256	1,664,333	680,422	50,615	148,963	4,922	2,666,558	1,720,546	698,805	50,723	190,109	6,375
New Hampshire	1,917,832	1,138,110	531,079	51,530	37,894	159,218	1,919,782	1,132,668	532,609	52,474	36,743	165,287
New Jersey	17,147,923	10,283,354	4,883,407	676,877	484,185	820,100	17,314,880	10,232,374	5,102,294	689,894	462,478	827,840
New Mexico	2,021,733	1,365,379	471,815	71,680	112,507	352	1,998,297	1,339,003	470,212	77,256	111,533	293
New York	44,562,891	26,526,440	14,056,466	2,477,345	774,931	727,709	44,243,493	26,655,540	14,033,456	2,032,879	785,737	735,881
North Carolina	8,923,519	6,175,718	2,015,298	302,382	429,645	477	9,099,922	6,233,748	2,102,845	308,915	454,408	6
North Dakota	924,360	627,436	235,288	24,524	30,541	6,572	945,948	643,823	241,559	23,299	31,235	6,033
Ohio	12,706,652	8,000,045	2,950,007	771,441	488,899	496,259	13,259,171	8,195,612	2,993,655	975,756	496,439	597,710
Oklahoma	3,322,128	2,299,971	739,980	62,906	206,165	13,106	3,207,179	2,217,116	725,927	61,307	189,965	12,863
Oregon	3,880,212	2,279,673	1,209,798	138,340	209,548	42,852	3,974,021	2,337,015	1,238,171	145,478	211,650	41,707
Pennsylvania	17,095,280	9,771,127	5,639,120	832,689	504,825	347,520	17,609,644	9,807,554	5,974,565	870,393	565,162	391,970
Rhode Island	1,481,449	925,503	447,465	12,662	25,184	70,635	1,490,562	931,562	452,027	14,710	24,170	68,094
South Carolina	4,564,641	3,021,871	1,092,541	185,188	239,832	25,209	4,650,493	3,049,809	1,122,525	201,411	250,939	25,809
South Dakota	776,826	523,289	158,082	30,459	51,533	13,462	852,197	576,676	169,968	33,960	56,410	15,185
Tennessee	5,809,522	3,896,221	1,281,463	135,149	482,606	14,083	5,899,292	3,957,281	1,313,444	131,520	481,412	15,635
Texas	30,793,731	23,422,318	3,895,603	1,066,831	2,050,068	358,911	30,718,788	23,522,838	3,960,438	1,104,332	1,760,983	370,196
Utah	3,048,549	1,858,895	861,090	107,626	204,422	16,517	3,151,523	1,911,252	883,323	110,156	227,361	19,431
Vermont	1,128,174	637,417	309,677	65,431	22,873	92,776	1,155,820	640,173	331,178	60,741	20,996	102,732
Virginia	9,507,532	6,435,793	2,515,923	200,505	341,445	13,866	9,721,064	6,530,540	2,609,142	215,626	357,129	8,627
Washington	7,665,348	4,980,495	1,841,711	473,354	302,710	67,078	7,980,734	5,219,147	1,906,253	492,186	296,226	66,922
West Virginia	1,939,537	1,192,896	559,105	41,489	139,495	6,552	1,922,706	1,153,062	582,702	40,447	138,676	7,820
Wisconsin	6,397,760	4,098,973	1,725,605	96,644	239,411	237,126	6,405,063	4,068,711	1,702,584	104,705	259,372	269,691
Wyoming	982,005	622,861	274,106	35,711	45,477	3,851	960,506	609,495	270,937	32,695	44,236	3,142
Other jurisdictions												
American Samoa	31,476	23,151	4,880	479	1,047	1,919	32,821	23,484	4,896	1,284	1,245	1,912
Guam	152,952	112,112	39,131	176	1,532	2	148,429	109,336	38,063	500	529	0
Northern Marianas	38,711	26,607	4,959	3,639	2,183	1,322	43,297	25,948	6,563	3,995	4,699	2,091
Puerto Rico	1,270,125	942,101	255,271	54,492	17,963	297	1,178,028	873,388	234,945	55,367	13,988	340
U.S. Virgin Islands	100,578	67,049	28,161	2,270	3,098	0	104,811	69,927	29,369	2,348	3,167	0

[1]Constant dollars based on the Consumer Price Index (CPI), prepared by the Bureau of Labor Statistics, U.S. Department of Labor, adjusted to a school-year basis. The CPI does not account for differences in inflation rates from state to state. For more information about adjusting for differences in the cost of living from state to state, see the American Community Survey Comparable Wage Index for Teachers (ACS-CWIFT) at https://nces.ed.gov/programs/edge/Docs/EDGE_ACS_CWIFT2015_FILEDOC.pdf.

[2]Includes purchased professional services of teachers or others who provide instruction for students.

NOTE: Excludes expenditures for state education agencies. Detail may not sum to totals because of rounding. Some data have been revised from previously published figures.

SOURCE: U.S. Department of Education, National Center for Education Statistics, Common Core of Data (CCD), "National Public Education Financial Survey," 2015–16 and 2016–17. (This table was prepared November 2019.)

Table 236.55. Total and current expenditures per pupil in public elementary and secondary schools: Selected years, 1919–20 through 2016–17

School year	Expenditure per pupil in average daily attendance				Expenditure per pupil in fall enrollment[1]				
	Unadjusted dollars[2]		Constant 2018–19 dollars[3]		Unadjusted dollars[2]		Constant 2018–19 dollars[3]		
	Total expenditure[4]	Current expenditure	Total expenditure[4]	Current expenditure	Total expenditure[4]	Current expenditure	Total expenditure[4]	Current expenditure	Annual percent change in current expenditure
1	2	3	4	5	6	7	8	9	10
1919–20	$64	$53	$850	$709	$48	$40	$636	$530	—
1929–30	108	87	1,605	1,283	90	72	1,329	1,062	—
1931–32	97	81	1,702	1,424	82	69	1,441	1,206	—
1933–34	76	67	1,458	1,291	65	57	1,239	1,097	—
1935–36	88	74	1,621	1,369	74	63	1,371	1,158	—
1937–38	100	84	1,763	1,483	86	72	1,513	1,273	—
1939–40	106	88	1,916	1,597	92	76	1,661	1,384	—
1941–42	110	98	1,787	1,597	94	84	1,530	1,367	—
1943–44	125	117	1,812	1,700	105	99	1,527	1,433	—
1945–46	146	136	2,025	1,894	124	116	1,725	1,613	—
1947–48	205	181	2,227	1,973	179	158	1,945	1,723	—
1949–50	260	210	2,784	2,249	231	187	2,471	1,996	—
1951–52	314	246	3,030	2,371	275	215	2,653	2,076	—
1953–54	351	265	3,305	2,494	312	236	2,939	2,218	—
1955–56	387	294	3,646	2,772	354	269	3,333	2,534	—
1957–58	447	341	3,968	3,025	408	311	3,619	2,759	—
1959–60	471	375	4,060	3,234	440	350	3,793	3,021	—
1961–62	517	419	4,357	3,530	485	393	4,089	3,313	—
1963–64	559	460	4,588	3,780	520	428	4,270	3,518	—
1965–66	654	538	5,190	4,268	607	499	4,818	3,962	—
1967–68	786	658	5,857	4,903	732	612	5,448	4,560	—
1969–70	955	816	6,403	5,471	879	751	5,895	5,037	—
1970–71	1,049	911	6,691	5,809	970	842	6,186	5,370	6.6
1971–72	1,128	990	6,941	6,091	1,034	908	6,366	5,587	4.0
1972–73	1,211	1,077	7,162	6,371	1,117	993	6,607	5,877	5.2
1973–74	1,364	1,207	7,409	6,558	1,244	1,101	6,756	5,979	1.7
1974–75	1,545	1,365	7,554	6,673	1,423	1,257	6,959	6,147	2.8
1975–76	1,697	1,504	7,751	6,867	1,563	1,385	7,137	6,323	2.9
1976–77	1,816	1,638	7,838	7,066	1,674	1,509	7,222	6,512	3.0
1977–78	2,002	1,823	8,097	7,371	1,842	1,677	7,447	6,779	4.1
1978–79	2,210	2,020	8,171	7,470	2,029	1,855	7,504	6,860	1.2
1979–80	2,491	2,272	8,125	7,411	2,290	2,088	7,470	6,813	-0.7
1980–81	2,742[5]	2,502	8,018[5]	7,314	2,529[5]	2,307	7,395[5]	6,746	-1.0
1981–82	2,973[5]	2,726	8,002[5]	7,336	2,754[5]	2,525	7,413[5]	6,795	0.7
1982–83	3,203[5]	2,955	8,266[5]	7,626	2,966[5]	2,736	7,654[5]	7,061	3.9
1983–84	3,471[5]	3,173	8,638[5]	7,896	3,216[5]	2,940	8,002[5]	7,315	3.6
1984–85	3,722[5]	3,470	8,912[5]	8,310	3,456[5]	3,222	8,275[5]	7,716	5.5
1985–86	4,020[5]	3,756	9,356[5]	8,741	3,724[5]	3,479	8,668[5]	8,098	5.0
1986–87	4,308[5]	3,970	9,809[5]	9,040	3,995[5]	3,682	9,096[5]	8,383	3.5
1987–88	4,654[5]	4,240	10,175[5]	9,270	4,310[5]	3,927	9,423[5]	8,585	2.4
1988–89	5,108	4,645	10,674	9,707	4,737	4,307	9,899	9,001	4.8
1989–90	5,547	4,980	11,064	9,933	5,172	4,643	10,316	9,261	2.9
1990–91	5,882	5,258	11,124	9,944	5,484	4,902	10,371	9,271	0.1
1991–92	6,072	5,421	11,127	9,934	5,626	5,023	10,310	9,205	-0.7
1992–93	6,279	5,584	11,158	9,922	5,802	5,160	10,311	9,169	-0.4
1993–94	6,489	5,767	11,240	9,990	5,994	5,327	10,382	9,227	0.6
1994–95	6,723	5,989	11,320	10,085	6,206	5,529	10,450	9,310	0.9
1995–96	6,959	6,147	11,408	10,076	6,441	5,689	10,559	9,326	0.2
1996–97	7,297	6,393	11,630	10,189	6,761	5,923	10,776	9,441	1.2
1997–98	7,701	6,676	12,058	10,453	7,139	6,189	11,179	9,691	2.7
1998–99	8,115	7,013	12,492	10,795	7,531	6,508	11,592	10,017	3.4
1999–2000	8,589	7,394	12,849	11,061	8,030	6,912	12,013	10,341	3.2
2000–01	9,180	7,904	13,278	11,433	8,572	7,380	12,399	10,675	3.2
2001–02	9,611	8,259	13,661	11,738	8,993	7,727	12,782	10,983	2.9
2002–03	9,950	8,610	13,838	11,974	9,296	8,044	12,929	11,188	1.9
2003–04	10,308	8,900	14,029	12,112	9,625	8,310	13,100	11,310	1.1
2004–05	10,779	9,316	14,241	12,309	10,078	8,711	13,316	11,509	1.8
2005–06	11,338	9,778	14,430	12,445	10,603	9,145	13,495	11,639	1.1
2006–07	12,015	10,336	14,907	12,823	11,252	9,679	13,960	12,009	3.2
2007–08	12,759	10,982	15,264	13,138	11,965	10,298	14,314	12,320	2.6
2008–09	13,033	11,239	15,377	13,260	12,222	10,540	14,421	12,435	0.9
2009–10	13,035	11,427	15,232	13,353	12,133	10,636	14,178	12,429	-0.1
2010–11	12,926	11,433	14,807	13,098	12,054	10,663	13,809	12,215	-1.7
2011–12	12,796	11,362	14,241	12,645	11,991	10,648	13,346	11,850	-3.0
2012–13	12,859	11,509	14,077	12,599	12,033	10,771	13,173	11,791	-0.5
2013–14	13,174	11,819	14,201	12,740	12,335	11,066	13,296	11,928	1.2
2014–15	13,668	12,224	14,626	13,081	12,796	11,445	13,693	12,247	2.7
2015–16	14,171	12,619	15,063	13,413	13,299	11,842	14,136	12,587	2.8
2016–17	14,778	13,094	15,424	13,667	13,834	12,258	14,439	12,794	1.6

—Not available.
[1]Data for 1919–20 to 1953–54 are based on school-year enrollment.
[2]Unadjusted (or "current") dollars have not been adjusted to compensate for inflation.
[3]Constant dollars based on the Consumer Price Index, prepared by the Bureau of Labor Statistics, U.S. Department of Labor, adjusted to a school-year basis.
[4]Excludes "Other current expenditures," such as community services, private school programs, adult education, and other programs not allocable to expenditures per student at public schools.
[5]Estimated.

NOTE: Beginning in 1980–81, state administration expenditures are excluded from both "total" and "current" expenditures. Current expenditures include instruction, support services, food services, and enterprise operations. Total expenditures include current expenditures, capital outlay, and interest on debt. Beginning in 1988–89, extensive changes were made in the data collection procedures. Some data have been revised from previously published figures.

SOURCE: U.S. Department of Education, National Center for Education Statistics, *Biennial Survey of Education in the United States*, 1919–20 through 1955–56; *Statistics of State School Systems*, 1957–58 through 1969–70; *Revenues and Expenditures for Public Elementary and Secondary Education*, 1970–71 through 1986–87; and Common Core of Data (CCD), "National Public Education Financial Survey," 1987–88 through 2016–17. (This table was prepared August 2019.)

Table 236.60. Total and current expenditures per pupil in fall enrollment in public elementary and secondary schools, by function and subfunction: Selected years, 1990–91 through 2016–17

Function and subfunction	Expenditures per pupil in current dollars									Expenditures per pupil in constant 2018–19 dollars[1]								
	1990–91	2000–01	2006–07	2010–11	2012–13	2013–14	2014–15	2015–16	2016–17	1990–91	2000–01	2006–07	2010–11	2012–13	2013–14	2014–15	2015–16	2016–17
1	2	3	4	5	6	7	8	9	10	11	12	13	14	15	16	17	18	19
Total expenditures	**$5,484**	**$8,572**	**$11,252**	**$12,054**	**$12,033**	**$12,335**	**$12,796**	**$13,299**	**$13,834**	**$10,371**	**$12,399**	**$13,960**	**$13,809**	**$13,173**	**$13,296**	**$13,693**	**$14,136**	**$14,439**
Current expenditures for public schools	4,902	7,380	9,679	10,663	10,771	11,066	11,445	11,842	12,258	9,271	10,675	12,009	12,215	11,791	11,928	12,247	12,587	12,794
Salaries	3,220[2]	4,752	5,849	6,300	6,265	6,372	6,530	6,748	6,927	6,090[2]	6,874	7,257	7,217	6,858	6,868	6,987	7,173	7,230
Employee benefits	824[2]	1,228	1,935	2,260	2,372	2,472	2,603	2,717	2,878	1,558[2]	1,777	2,400	2,589	2,596	2,665	2,786	2,888	3,004
Purchased services	397[2]	673	939	1,082	1,121	1,163	1,216	1,283	1,325	752[2]	974	1,165	1,239	1,228	1,254	1,301	1,363	1,382
Tuition	29[2]	52	80	101	102	106	111	114	121	55[2]	75	100	116	112	114	119	121	127
Supplies	359[2]	599	779	817	817	858	871	869	886	679[2]	866	967	936	895	924	932	924	925
Other	72[2]	76	97	103	93	95	114	111	120	136[2]	110	120	118	102	103	122	118	125
Instruction	2,965	4,541	5,901	6,522	6,547	6,726	6,951	7,212	7,445	5,608	6,568	7,321	7,471	7,167	7,250	7,439	7,666	7,771
Salaries	2,202	3,273	3,997	4,307	4,273	4,344	4,437	4,578	4,688	4,164	4,735	4,959	4,934	4,678	4,682	4,748	4,866	4,893
Employee benefits	542	837	1,302	1,522	1,598	1,678	1,767	1,843	1,946	1,025	1,211	1,616	1,743	1,750	1,809	1,891	1,959	2,032
Purchased services	66	136	223	297	297	303	329	358	366	125	197	277	340	325	327	352	381	382
Tuition	29	52	80	101	102	106	111	114	121	55	75	100	116	112	114	119	121	127
Supplies	111	220	271	266	250	267	280	290	295	210	318	336	304	273	288	299	308	308
Textbooks	—	—	—	47	43	46	49	50	52	—	—	—	54	47	50	52	54	54
Other	15	22	27	30	27	28	27	28	29	29	32	33	34	30	30	29	30	30
Student support[3]	217	366	512	594	601	615	644	676	712	410	530	635	680	658	663	689	718	743
Salaries	159	262	342	392	389	396	411	429	446	301	379	425	449	425	427	440	456	466
Employee benefits	40	64	109	132	142	146	157	166	181	76	93	135	151	155	158	168	177	189
Purchased services	11	28	43	52	56	57	60	64	67	21	41	54	60	61	61	64	68	70
Supplies	5	9	11	11	11	11	12	12	13	9	13	13	12	12	12	13	13	13
Other	1	3	7	7	4	4	4	4	4	2	5	8	8	4	4	4	5	5
Instructional staff services[4]	205	337	470	503	501	507	536	556	577	389	488	583	577	549	546	574	591	603
Salaries	135	207	279	293	291	294	308	319	331	255	300	346	336	319	316	330	340	345
Employee benefits	34	50	86	100	102	105	112	117	126	65	72	106	114	112	113	120	125	131
Purchased services	15	42	62	70	70	69	73	78	79	29	61	77	80	77	74	78	83	82
Supplies	19	33	38	37	33	36	39	37	38	36	48	48	42	37	39	42	40	40
Other	2	4	4	4	4	4	4	4	4	5	6	5	5	5	4	5	5	4
General administration	141	151	190	212	218	222	229	239	244	266	218	235	243	238	240	246	254	254
Salaries	63	71	82	89	90	92	94	97	100	119	103	101	102	98	100	101	103	105
Employee benefits	19	21	32	38	39	38	41	41	44	36	31	39	43	43	41	43	44	46
Purchased services	36	44	59	65	69	72	74	80	77	68	64	73	75	76	77	80	85	81
Supplies	4	4	5	5	5	5	5	5	5	8	6	6	5	5	5	5	6	6
Other	18	10	13	16	14	15	15	15	16	35	14	16	18	16	16	16	16	17
School administration	284	415	546	580	593	608	632	659	684	537	600	677	664	650	656	677	701	714
Salaries	217	314	390	408	414	423	436	452	466	410	454	484	468	453	455	467	481	486
Employee benefits	55	78	124	141	149	154	163	171	183	104	113	153	162	163	166	174	182	191
Purchased services	6	13	19	19	19	19	21	23	23	11	19	24	22	21	21	23	24	24
Supplies	5	8	10	9	9	9	9	9	10	9	11	12	10	10	9	9	10	10
Other	2	2	3	3	3	3	3	3	4	3	3	4	3	3	3	4	4	4
Operation and maintenance	517	721	951	1,015	1,019	1,061	1,078	1,093	1,137	977	1,043	1,179	1,163	1,115	1,143	1,154	1,162	1,187
Salaries	215	285	342	356	351	357	362	372	382	406	413	424	408	384	385	388	396	399
Employee benefits	64	80	127	146	150	154	160	165	174	121	116	158	167	164	166	171	175	182
Purchased services	139	204	257	270	282	300	309	316	334	263	295	319	309	308	324	330	336	349
Supplies	91	146	216	235	228	241	240	233	239	173	211	268	270	250	260	256	248	250
Other	8	6	8	9	7	8	8	8	8	15	9	10	10	8	9	9	8	8

See notes at end of table.

Table 236.60. Total and current expenditures per pupil in fall enrollment in public elementary and secondary schools, by function and subfunction: Selected years, 1990–91 through 2016–17—Continued

Function and subfunction	Expenditures per pupil in current dollars									Expenditures per pupil in constant 2018–19 dollars[1]								
	1990–91	2000–01	2006–07	2010–11	2012–13	2013–14	2014–15	2015–16	2016–17	1990–91	2000–01	2006–07	2010–11	2012–13	2013–14	2014–15	2015–16	2016–17
1	2	3	4	5	6	7	8	9	10	11	12	13	14	15	16	17	18	19
Student transportation	211	298	406	452	467	477	477	483	502	398	431	503	518	511	514	510	514	524
Salaries	80	115	144	152	151	154	157	163	169	151	166	178	174	166	166	168	173	176
Employee benefits	22	34	55	63	65	66	68	72	75	41	49	68	72	72	71	73	76	79
Purchased services	81	122	164	185	193	198	200	206	214	153	177	204	212	211	214	214	219	224
Supplies	23	25	39	48	53	54	47	37	39	44	36	49	55	58	58	50	40	40
Other	5	3	3	4	5	5	5	5	5	9	4	4	5	5	5	5	5	5
Other support services[5]	136	242	315	349	363	381	415	429	455	256	351	391	400	397	410	445	456	475
Salaries	70	117	145	165	167	172	181	190	196	133	169	180	189	183	186	194	202	204
Employee benefits	24	34	54	67	70	74	78	81	85	45	49	67	76	77	80	83	86	89
Purchased services	19	59	74	78	87	93	97	102	108	37	85	92	90	95	101	103	108	112
Supplies	7	13	18	18	19	22	23	25	26	14	19	22	20	21	24	25	26	28
Other	15	19	24	21	19	19	37	32	40	28	28	30	25	21	21	39	34	41
Food services	205	293	368	412	439	447	459	470	477	387	423	457	472	481	481	491	499	498
Salaries	—	105	124	131	133	134	137	141	143	—	152	153	150	145	144	146	150	149
Employee benefits	—	29	44	50	52	55	56	58	60	—	42	55	58	57	59	60	62	63
Purchased services	—	20	32	42	46	47	49	51	53	—	28	39	48	50	50	52	54	55
Supplies	—	136	165	184	203	207	211	214	215	—	197	205	211	223	223	226	227	224
Other	—	3	4	5	5	5	6	6	6	—	4	5	6	5	5	6	6	6
Enterprise operations[6]	23	16	22	22	22	23	22	24	25	43	24	27	26	24	25	24	25	26
Salaries	—	3	5	7	6	6	6	7	7	—	4	6	8	7	7	7	7	7
Employee benefits	—	1	2	2	2	2	2	2	3	—	1	2	2	2	2	2	3	3
Purchased services	—	4	5	3	4	4	4	4	4	—	6	6	4	4	4	4	4	4
Supplies	—	5	6	6	6	6	6	6	7	—	7	8	7	7	7	6	7	7
Other	—	4	4	4	4	4	4	5	4	—	6	5	5	5	5	5	5	5
Capital outlay[7]	477	976	1,274	1,029	916	926	1,004	1,109	1,213	902	1,412	1,581	1,179	1,003	998	1,074	1,179	1,266
Interest on school debt	105	215	299	363	347	343	348	348	363	198	312	371	415	380	370	372	369	379

—Not available.
[1]Constant dollars based on the Consumer Price Index, prepared by the Bureau of Labor Statistics, U.S. Department of Labor, adjusted to a school-year basis.
[2]Includes estimated data for subfunctions of food services and enterprise operations.
[3]Includes expenditures for guidance, health, attendance, and speech pathology services.
[4]Includes expenditures for curriculum development, staff training, libraries, and media and computer centers.
[5]Includes business support services concerned with paying, transporting, exchanging, and maintaining goods and services for local education agencies; central support services, including planning, research, evaluation, information, staff, and data processing services; and other support services.
[6]Includes expenditures for operations funded by sales of products or services (e.g., school bookstore or computer time).
[7]Includes expenditures for property and for buildings and alterations completed by school district staff or contractors.
NOTE: Excludes expenditures for state education agencies. Detail may not sum to totals because of rounding. Some data have been revised from previously published figures.
SOURCE: U.S. Department of Education, National Center for Education Statistics, Common Core of Data (CCD), "National Public Education Financial Survey," 1990–91 through 2016–17. (This table was prepared August 2019.)

Table 236.65. Current expenditure per pupil in fall enrollment in public elementary and secondary schools, by state or jurisdiction: Selected years, 1969–70 through 2016–17

State or jurisdiction	Unadjusted dollars[1]														
	1969–70	1979–80	1989–90	1999–2000	2006–07	2007–08	2008–09	2009–10	2010–11	2011–12	2012–13	2013–14	2014–15	2015–16	2016–17
1	2	3	4	5	6	7	8	9	10	11	12	13	14	15	16
United States	**$751**	**$2,088**	**$4,643**	**$6,912**	**$9,679**	**$10,298**	**$10,540**	**$10,636**	**$10,663**	**$10,648**	**$10,771**	**$11,066**	**$11,445**	**$11,842**	**$12,258**
Alabama	512	1,520	3,144	5,638	8,398	9,197	8,964	8,907	8,726	8,577	8,773	9,036	9,146	9,258	9,528
Alaska	1,059	4,267	7,577	8,806	12,324	14,641	15,363	15,829	16,663	17,475	18,217	18,466	20,191	17,510	17,838
Arizona	674	1,865	3,717	5,030	7,316	7,727	8,022	7,870	7,782	7,383	7,495	7,427	7,590	7,772	8,053
Arkansas	511	1,472	3,229	5,277	8,391	8,677	8,854	9,281	9,496	9,536	9,538	9,752	9,805	9,900	10,004
California	833	2,227	4,502	6,314	8,952	9,706	9,503	9,300	9,146	9,220	9,258	9,671	10,449	11,420	12,151
Colorado	686	2,258	4,357	6,215	8,286	9,152	8,782	8,926	8,786	8,594	8,693	9,036	9,292	9,619	9,849
Connecticut	911	2,167	7,463	9,753	13,659	14,610	15,353	15,698	16,224	16,855	17,321	18,401	19,020	19,615	19,929
Delaware	833	2,587	5,326	8,310	11,760	12,153	12,109	12,222	12,467	13,580	13,653	13,793	13,882	14,397	14,892
District of Columbia	947	2,811	7,872	10,107	15,511	16,353	19,698	20,910	20,793	19,847	20,451	20,537	20,610	21,161	22,561
Florida	683	1,834	4,597	5,831	8,567	9,084	8,867	8,863	9,030	8,520	8,623	8,955	9,113	9,176	9,374
Georgia	539	1,491	4,000	6,437	9,102	9,718	9,649	9,432	9,259	9,272	9,121	9,236	9,476	9,835	10,274
Hawaii	792	2,086	4,130	6,530	11,316	11,800	12,400	11,855	11,924	11,973	11,790	12,400	12,855	13,748	14,322
Idaho	573	1,548	2,921	5,315	6,648	6,951	7,118	7,100	6,821	6,626	6,761	6,577	6,929	7,211	7,554
Illinois	816	2,241	4,521	7,133	9,596	10,353	11,097	11,739	11,742	12,011	12,443	13,213	13,935	14,327	15,517
Indiana	661	1,708	4,270	7,192	9,080	8,867	9,254	9,479	9,251	9,588	9,421	9,396	9,529	9,688	9,823
Iowa	798	2,164	4,190	6,564	8,791	9,520	9,704	9,748	9,795	10,027	10,291	10,647	10,938	11,148	11,456
Kansas	699	1,963	4,290	6,294	9,243	9,894	10,204	9,972	9,802	10,021	10,011	10,240	10,329	10,216	10,428
Kentucky	502	1,557	3,384	5,921	7,941	8,740	8,786	8,957	9,228	9,327	9,274	9,411	9,560	9,831	10,083
Louisiana	589	1,629	3,625	5,804	8,937	10,006	10,625	10,701	10,799	10,726	10,539	10,853	11,106	11,169	11,379
Maine	649	1,692	4,903	7,667	11,644	11,761	12,183	12,525	12,576	12,335	12,694	13,267	13,976	14,202	14,633
Maryland	809	2,293	5,573	7,731	11,989	13,257	13,737	14,007	13,946	13,875	14,086	14,217	14,431	14,523	14,933
Massachusetts	791	2,548	5,766	8,816	12,784	13,690	14,534	13,956	14,612	14,844	15,321	15,886	16,450	16,986	17,718
Michigan	841	2,495	5,090	8,110	9,876	10,075	10,373	10,447	10,577	10,477	10,515	10,649	10,956	11,051	11,256
Minnesota	855	2,296	4,698	7,190	9,589	10,060	10,983	10,665	10,674	10,781	11,065	11,427	11,924	12,364	12,635
Mississippi	457	1,568	2,934	5,014	7,459	7,890	8,064	8,104	7,926	8,097	8,117	8,265	8,445	8,692	8,755
Missouri	596	1,724	4,071	6,187	8,848	9,532	9,617	9,721	9,461	9,514	9,702	9,938	10,231	10,385	10,684
Montana	728	2,264	4,240	6,314	9,191	9,786	10,120	10,565	10,719	10,569	10,662	10,941	11,078	11,374	11,538
Nebraska	700	2,025	4,553	6,683	10,068	10,565	10,846	11,339	11,704	11,492	11,743	11,877	12,174	12,379	12,662
Nevada	706	1,908	3,816	5,760	7,796	8,187	8,321	8,376	8,411	8,130	8,026	8,275	8,451	8,753	9,120
New Hampshire	666	1,732	4,786	6,860	11,036	11,951	12,583	13,072	13,548	13,774	14,050	14,601	14,969	15,535	15,958
New Jersey	924	2,825	7,546	10,337	16,163	17,620	16,973	17,379	16,855	17,982	18,523	18,780	18,559	19,041	19,585
New Mexico	665	1,870	3,446	5,825	8,849	9,291	9,648	9,621	9,250	9,013	9,164	9,403	9,724	9,959	9,949
New York	1,194	2,950	7,051	9,846	15,546	16,794	17,746	18,167	18,857	19,396	19,529	20,156	20,744	22,231	22,861
North Carolina	570	1,635	4,018	6,045	7,878	7,798	8,463	8,225	8,267	8,160	8,342	8,287	8,529	8,717	8,995
North Dakota	662	1,941	3,899	5,667	8,671	9,324	9,802	10,519	10,898	11,246	11,615	12,383	12,884	13,358	13,767
Ohio	677	1,894	4,531	7,065	9,937	10,340	10,669	11,224	11,395	11,323	11,276	11,434	11,730	11,933	12,569
Oklahoma	554	1,810	3,293	5,395	7,430	7,683	7,878	7,929	7,631	7,763	7,914	7,995	8,075	8,091	7,921
Oregon	843	2,412	4,864	7,149	8,958	9,565	9,611	9,268	9,516	9,485	9,572	9,959	10,457	10,823	11,252
Pennsylvania	815	2,328	5,737	7,772	10,905	11,741	12,299	12,729	13,096	13,091	13,445	13,824	14,405	15,165	15,782
Rhode Island	807	2,340	5,908	8,904	13,453	14,459	14,719	14,723	14,948	15,172	14,889	15,372	15,797	16,082	16,620
South Carolina	567	1,597	3,769	6,130	8,507	9,060	9,228	9,080	8,908	9,102	9,444	9,608	9,831	10,120	10,419
South Dakota	656	1,781	3,511	5,632	8,064	8,535	8,543	9,020	8,931	8,593	8,630	9,036	9,103	9,335	10,117
Tennessee	531	1,523	3,405	5,383	7,129	7,820	7,992	8,117	8,330	8,348	8,588	8,662	8,776	8,876	9,246
Texas	551	1,740	3,835	6,288	7,850	8,350	8,562	8,788	8,685	8,213	8,285	8,602	9,081	9,352	9,520
Utah	595	1,556	2,577	4,378	5,709	5,978	6,612	6,452	6,440	6,312	6,432	6,546	6,751	7,006	7,206
Vermont	790	1,930	5,770	8,323	13,629	14,421	15,096	15,666	14,707	16,651	17,286	18,066	18,769	19,023	19,480
Virginia	654	1,824	4,690	6,841	10,214	10,664	10,928	10,594	10,363	10,656	10,960	10,955	11,235	11,435	11,885
Washington	853	2,387	4,382	6,376	8,524	9,058	9,585	9,497	9,619	9,604	9,714	10,305	10,684	11,484	11,971
West Virginia	621	1,749	4,020	7,152	9,727	10,059	10,606	11,774	11,978	11,579	11,264	11,371	11,512	11,424	11,745
Wisconsin	793	2,225	5,020	7,806	10,372	10,791	11,183	11,507	11,947	11,233	11,186	11,345	11,538	11,664	11,962
Wyoming	805	2,369	5,239	7,425	13,266	13,856	14,628	15,232	15,815	15,988	15,815	15,903	16,047	16,431	16,513
Other jurisdictions															
American Samoa	—	—	1,781	2,739	3,481	—	—	—	—	—	—	—	—	—	—
Guam	766	—	3,817	—	—	—	—	—	8,443	9,300	8,949	8,585	9,431	9,692	9,700
Northern Marianas	—	—	3,356	5,120	4,707	4,535	5,753	5,676	7,623	6,246	5,733	5,875	—	—	—
Puerto Rico	—	—	1,605	3,404	6,006	6,520	6,955	7,021	7,429	7,403	8,460	8,281	7,902	7,821	7,639
U.S. Virgin Islands	—	—	6,043	6,478	9,669	12,358	12,768	14,215	13,226	11,669	10,661	11,705	11,141	11,631	13,000

See notes at end of table.

Table 236.65. Current expenditure per pupil in fall enrollment in public elementary and secondary schools, by state or jurisdiction: Selected years, 1969–70 through 2016–17—Continued

State or jurisdiction	Constant 2018–19 dollars[2]														
	1969–70	1979–80	1989–90	1999–2000	2006–07	2007–08	2008–09	2009–10	2010–11	2011–12	2012–13	2013–14	2014–15	2015–16	2016–17
1	17	18	19	20	21	22	23	24	25	26	27	28	29	30	31
United States	**$5,037**	**$6,813**	**$9,261**	**$10,341**	**$12,009**	**$12,320**	**$12,435**	**$12,429**	**$12,215**	**$11,850**	**$11,791**	**$11,928**	**$12,247**	**$12,587**	**$12,794**
Alabama	3,430	4,960	6,271	8,434	10,419	11,002	10,576	10,409	9,996	9,546	9,604	9,740	9,788	9,840	9,944
Alaska	7,101	13,921	15,114	13,175	15,291	17,515	18,126	18,497	19,089	19,449	19,943	19,904	21,606	18,612	18,618
Arizona	4,522	6,084	7,415	7,525	9,077	9,245	9,465	9,197	8,915	8,217	8,205	8,005	8,122	8,261	8,405
Arkansas	3,426	4,802	6,441	7,895	10,411	10,381	10,447	10,845	10,878	10,613	10,442	10,511	10,492	10,523	10,442
California	5,587	7,264	8,981	9,446	11,106	11,612	11,212	10,867	10,478	10,262	10,136	10,425	11,181	12,139	12,683
Colorado	4,600	7,366	8,690	9,298	10,280	10,949	10,361	10,430	10,065	9,565	9,517	9,740	9,943	10,224	10,280
Connecticut	6,106	7,070	14,885	14,590	16,947	17,478	18,115	18,344	18,585	18,759	18,962	19,834	20,353	20,849	20,801
Delaware	5,588	8,439	10,624	12,432	14,590	14,539	14,287	14,283	14,282	15,114	14,946	14,868	14,855	15,303	15,543
District of Columbia	6,349	9,172	15,701	15,120	19,245	19,564	23,241	24,435	23,819	22,088	22,388	22,137	22,055	22,493	23,548
Florida	4,577	5,984	9,170	8,723	10,629	10,867	10,461	10,357	10,345	9,482	9,440	9,652	9,752	9,753	9,784
Georgia	3,612	4,864	7,978	9,630	11,293	11,626	11,385	11,022	10,607	10,319	9,985	9,955	10,140	10,454	10,723
Hawaii	5,310	6,807	8,238	9,769	14,040	14,117	14,630	13,853	13,660	13,325	12,907	13,366	13,756	14,613	14,948
Idaho	3,843	5,051	5,826	7,951	8,248	8,316	8,398	8,297	7,814	7,375	7,401	7,089	7,415	7,665	7,885
Illinois	5,469	7,312	9,017	10,671	11,905	12,386	13,093	13,717	13,451	13,368	13,622	14,242	14,912	15,229	16,196
Indiana	4,433	5,572	8,518	10,760	11,265	10,608	10,918	11,077	10,598	10,671	10,314	10,128	10,197	10,297	10,253
Iowa	5,351	7,060	8,357	9,820	10,907	11,389	11,450	11,391	11,220	11,159	11,266	11,476	11,704	11,850	11,957
Kansas	4,685	6,404	8,556	9,416	11,467	11,837	12,039	11,653	11,229	11,153	10,959	11,037	11,053	10,859	10,884
Kentucky	3,366	5,080	6,749	8,858	9,852	10,456	10,366	10,467	10,571	10,380	10,153	10,144	10,230	10,450	10,524
Louisiana	3,952	5,314	7,230	8,683	11,088	11,971	12,536	12,505	12,371	11,938	11,538	11,698	11,884	11,872	11,876
Maine	4,352	5,520	9,780	11,471	14,446	14,070	14,374	14,636	14,407	13,728	13,896	14,300	14,956	15,096	15,273
Maryland	5,425	7,480	11,117	11,566	14,874	15,860	16,208	16,368	15,976	15,442	15,420	15,325	15,443	15,436	15,586
Massachusetts	5,301	8,312	11,501	13,189	15,861	16,378	17,149	16,308	16,739	16,520	16,772	17,124	17,603	18,055	18,493
Michigan	5,642	8,141	10,152	12,132	12,253	12,053	12,238	12,208	12,117	11,660	11,511	11,478	11,724	11,747	11,748
Minnesota	5,731	7,492	9,371	10,756	11,897	12,036	12,958	12,463	12,227	11,998	12,113	12,317	12,760	13,142	13,188
Mississippi	3,062	5,117	5,851	7,501	9,254	9,439	9,515	9,470	9,080	9,012	8,886	8,908	9,037	9,240	9,137
Missouri	3,996	5,625	8,119	9,256	10,977	11,404	11,347	11,359	10,838	10,588	10,621	10,712	10,948	11,038	11,151
Montana	4,878	7,385	8,457	9,446	11,404	11,708	11,941	12,346	12,279	11,763	11,672	11,793	11,854	12,090	12,043
Nebraska	4,692	6,605	9,081	9,998	12,491	12,639	12,797	13,250	13,408	12,790	12,855	12,802	13,027	13,158	13,215
Nevada	4,732	6,225	7,611	8,617	9,672	9,794	9,818	9,788	9,636	9,048	8,787	8,919	9,043	9,304	9,519
New Hampshire	4,466	5,651	9,546	10,263	13,692	14,297	14,846	15,275	15,520	15,330	15,381	15,738	16,018	16,512	16,656
New Jersey	6,194	9,217	15,051	15,465	20,053	21,080	20,026	20,308	19,308	20,013	20,278	20,243	19,860	20,239	20,441
New Mexico	4,459	6,102	6,873	8,715	10,979	11,115	11,384	11,242	10,596	10,031	10,032	10,135	10,405	10,586	10,384
New York	8,008	9,625	14,064	14,730	19,288	20,092	20,938	21,229	21,602	21,587	21,379	21,726	22,198	23,630	23,861
North Carolina	3,824	5,335	8,015	9,044	9,774	9,329	9,985	9,611	9,470	9,081	9,132	8,932	9,127	9,265	9,389
North Dakota	4,441	6,334	7,777	8,478	10,758	11,155	11,565	12,292	12,485	12,516	12,715	13,347	13,787	14,199	14,369
Ohio	4,536	6,180	9,037	10,569	12,328	12,370	12,588	13,115	13,054	12,602	12,344	12,325	12,552	12,684	13,118
Oklahoma	3,713	5,904	6,569	8,071	9,218	9,191	9,295	9,266	8,742	8,640	8,664	8,617	8,642	8,600	8,267
Oregon	5,654	7,870	9,703	10,695	11,114	11,443	11,339	10,830	10,901	10,556	10,479	10,734	11,190	11,504	11,744
Pennsylvania	5,466	7,596	11,444	11,628	13,530	14,047	14,512	14,874	15,002	14,570	14,719	14,901	15,415	16,120	16,472
Rhode Island	5,409	7,635	11,785	13,321	16,691	17,298	17,367	17,205	17,123	16,886	16,299	16,570	16,904	17,095	17,346
South Carolina	3,803	5,211	7,519	9,171	10,554	10,839	10,888	10,611	10,204	10,130	10,338	10,356	10,520	10,757	10,874
South Dakota	4,399	5,809	7,003	8,426	10,005	10,210	10,079	10,540	10,231	9,564	9,447	9,740	9,741	9,923	10,560
Tennessee	3,559	4,969	6,791	8,053	8,845	9,355	9,430	9,486	9,543	9,291	9,401	9,337	9,391	9,435	9,651
Texas	3,695	5,676	7,649	9,407	9,739	9,989	10,102	10,269	9,949	9,140	9,069	9,272	9,718	9,940	9,936
Utah	3,991	5,077	5,140	6,550	7,083	7,152	7,802	7,540	7,377	7,025	7,042	7,056	7,224	7,447	7,521
Vermont	5,294	6,297	11,510	12,451	16,909	17,253	17,811	18,307	16,848	18,532	18,923	19,473	20,084	20,220	20,332
Virginia	4,388	5,951	9,354	10,234	12,672	12,758	12,894	12,380	11,871	11,859	11,998	11,809	12,022	12,155	12,405
Washington	5,720	7,787	8,741	9,539	10,575	10,836	11,310	11,098	11,019	10,689	10,635	11,107	11,432	12,207	12,494
West Virginia	4,166	5,704	8,018	10,699	12,068	12,034	12,514	13,759	13,721	12,886	12,331	12,257	12,319	12,143	12,258
Wisconsin	5,317	7,258	10,012	11,679	12,868	12,910	13,195	13,447	13,686	12,502	12,245	12,229	12,347	12,398	12,486
Wyoming	5,397	7,729	10,450	11,109	16,459	16,576	17,259	17,800	18,117	17,794	17,313	17,142	17,172	17,465	17,235
Other jurisdictions															
American Samoa	—	—	3,553	4,098	4,319	—	—	—	—	—	—	—	—	—	—
Guam	5,139	—	7,614	—	—	—	—	—	9,672	10,351	9,796	9,253	10,092	10,302	10,124
Northern Marianas	—	—	6,694	7,660	5,840	5,425	6,788	6,632	8,733	6,952	6,276	6,333	—	—	—
Puerto Rico	—	—	3,202	5,092	7,452	7,800	8,206	8,204	8,511	8,239	9,262	8,926	8,455	8,313	7,973
U.S. Virgin Islands	—	—	12,053	9,692	11,996	14,785	15,065	16,611	15,151	12,987	11,670	12,617	11,921	12,362	13,568

—Not available.
[1]Unadjusted (or "current") dollars have not been adjusted to compensate for inflation.
[2]Constant dollars based on the Consumer Price Index (CPI), prepared by the Bureau of Labor Statistics, U.S. Department of Labor, adjusted to a school-year basis. The CPI does not account for differences in inflation rates from state to state.

NOTE: Current expenditures include instruction, support services, food services, and enterprise operations. Expenditures for state administration are excluded in all years except 1969–70 and 1979–80. Beginning in 1989–90, extensive changes were made in the data collection procedures. Some data have been revised from previously published figures.
SOURCE: U.S. Department of Education, National Center for Education Statistics, *Statistics of State School Systems*, 1969–70; *Revenues and Expenditures for Public Elementary and Secondary Schools, 1979–80*; and Common Core of Data (CCD), "National Public Education Financial Survey," 1989–90 through through 2016–17. (This table was prepared August 2019.)

Table 236.70. Current expenditure per pupil in average daily attendance in public elementary and secondary schools, by state or jurisdiction: Selected years, 1969–70 through 2016–17

State or jurisdiction	Unadjusted dollars[1]														
	1969–70	1979–80	1989–90	1999–2000	2006–07	2007–08	2008–09	2009–10	2010–11	2011–12	2012–13	2013–14	2014–15	2015–16	2016–17
1	2	3	4	5	6	7	8	9	10	11	12	13	14	15	16
United States	**$816**	**$2,272**	**$4,980**	**$7,394**	**$10,336**	**$10,982**	**$11,239**	**$11,427**	**$11,433**	**$11,362**	**$11,509**	**$11,819**	**$12,224**	**$12,619**	**$13,094**
Alabama	544	1,612	3,327	5,758	8,743	9,345	9,385	9,554	9,296	8,927	9,486	9,543	9,690	9,870	10,161
Alaska	1,123	4,728	8,431	9,668	13,508	16,002	16,822	17,350	18,352	19,134	19,982	20,254	22,161	19,242	19,550
Arizona	720	1,971	4,053	5,478	8,038	8,630	8,732	8,756	8,646	8,224	8,388	8,278	8,426	8,572	8,867
Arkansas	568	1,574	3,485	5,628	9,152	9,460	9,651	10,237	10,332	10,397	9,853	10,622	10,756	10,837	10,968
California	867	2,268	4,391	6,401	9,029	9,673	9,439	9,680	9,540	9,608	9,686	10,094	10,924	11,937	12,730
Colorado	738	2,421	4,720	6,702	9,110	9,977	9,611	9,747	9,709	9,415	9,572	9,924	10,349	10,619	10,946
Connecticut	951	2,420	7,837	10,122	14,143	15,063	15,840	16,133	16,932	17,472	17,859	19,029	19,731	20,380	20,731
Delaware	900	2,861	5,799	8,809	12,612	12,789	12,753	12,928	13,228	14,253	14,129	14,203	14,556	15,150	15,824
District of Columbia	1,018	3,259	8,955	11,935	18,285	20,807	19,766	21,283	21,304	20,399	20,333	21,629	21,362	22,340	23,632
Florida	732	1,889	4,997	6,383	9,055	9,711	9,452	9,363	9,394	8,825	8,925	9,189	9,295	9,337	9,571
Georgia	588	1,625	4,275	6,903	9,615	10,263	10,178	9,855	9,577	9,492	9,437	9,529	9,809	10,185	10,722
Hawaii	841	2,322	4,448	7,090	12,364	12,774	13,397	12,887	12,603	12,735	12,585	13,219	13,849	14,728	15,325
Idaho	603	1,659	3,078	5,644	7,074	7,402	7,567	7,481	7,155	7,041	7,273	7,215	7,409	7,642	8,024
Illinois	909	2,587	5,118	8,084	10,816	11,624	12,489	13,083	13,180	13,459	13,808	14,682	15,473	15,909	17,332
Indiana	728	1,882	4,606	7,652	9,727	9,569	9,946	10,160	9,924	10,220	10,037	10,078	10,202	10,368	10,472
Iowa	844	2,326	4,453	6,925	8,789	9,128	10,482	10,524	10,565	10,748	10,915	11,359	11,698	11,846	12,167
Kansas	771	2,173	4,752	6,962	10,280	11,065	11,485	10,859	10,700	10,712	10,789	11,180	11,106	10,815	11,159
Kentucky	545	1,701	3,745	6,784	9,303	9,940	10,054	10,376	10,469	10,700	10,269	10,248	10,659	10,912	11,193
Louisiana	648	1,792	3,903	6,256	9,650	10,797	11,410	11,492	11,500	11,352	11,118	11,415	11,697	11,775	12,051
Maine	692	1,824	5,373	8,247	12,628	13,177	13,558	14,090	14,406	14,000	14,347	14,926	15,839	16,060	16,103
Maryland	918	2,598	6,275	8,273	12,836	14,122	14,612	14,937	14,876	14,746	15,010	15,109	15,403	15,478	15,982
Massachusetts	859	2,819	6,237	9,375	13,263	14,373	15,249	14,632	15,334	15,607	16,111	16,646	17,311	18,026	18,853
Michigan	904	2,640	5,546	8,886	10,932	11,155	11,493	11,661	11,560	11,462	11,495	11,678	12,048	12,243	12,448
Minnesota	904	2,387	4,971	7,499	10,185	10,663	11,602	11,366	11,368	11,424	11,754	12,140	12,707	13,169	13,496
Mississippi	501	1,664	3,094	5,356	7,988	8,448	8,610	8,670	8,436	8,623	8,685	8,926	9,129	9,380	9,467
Missouri	709	1,936	4,507	6,764	9,266	10,007	10,341	10,468	10,348	10,370	10,555	10,764	11,079	11,233	11,527
Montana	782	2,476	4,736	6,990	10,244	10,541	10,881	11,463	11,599	11,290	11,493	11,840	11,999	12,379	12,489
Nebraska	736	2,150	4,842	7,360	10,711	11,217	11,457	11,920	12,324	12,114	12,374	12,502	12,825	13,700	14,062
Nevada	769	2,088	4,117	6,148	8,372	8,891	8,865	8,869	9,035	8,677	8,525	8,734	8,939	9,233	9,620
New Hampshire	723	1,916	5,304	7,082	11,347	12,280	12,912	13,424	13,964	14,215	14,463	15,013	15,380	15,934	16,360
New Jersey	1,016	3,191	8,139	10,903	16,650	18,174	17,466	18,060	17,654	18,197	19,020	19,282	19,296	20,055	20,735
New Mexico	707	2,034	3,515	5,835	8,876	9,377	9,727	9,716	9,356	9,069	9,230	9,546	9,891	9,954	9,978
New York	1,327	3,462	8,062	10,957	17,182	18,423	19,373	19,965	20,517	20,881	21,172	22,048	22,771	23,678	24,480
North Carolina	612	1,754	4,290	6,505	8,373	8,415	9,167	8,930	8,943	8,828	9,041	8,948	9,245	9,347	9,708
North Dakota	690	1,920	4,189	6,078	9,203	9,637	10,113	10,976	11,356	11,643	12,090	12,952	13,552	14,002	14,443
Ohio	730	2,075	5,045	7,816	10,792	11,374	11,905	12,307	12,484	12,271	12,284	12,447	12,285	12,488	13,019
Oklahoma	604	1,926	3,508	5,770	7,968	8,270	8,423	8,511	8,165	8,281	8,450	8,526	8,633	8,624	8,469
Oregon	925	2,692	5,474	8,129	9,762	10,487	10,673	10,476	10,497	10,386	10,370	10,739	11,356	11,856	12,320
Pennsylvania	882	2,535	6,228	8,380	11,995	12,493	12,989	13,678	14,072	13,973	14,378	14,789	15,405	15,997	16,828
Rhode Island	891	2,601	6,368	9,646	14,674	15,843	16,211	16,243	16,346	16,498	16,187	16,702	17,151	17,332	17,929
South Carolina	613	1,752	4,082	6,545	9,226	9,823	10,007	9,887	9,735	9,823	10,200	10,408	10,670	10,910	11,306
South Dakota	690	1,908	3,731	6,037	8,506	9,047	9,457	9,683	9,431	9,095	9,138	9,539	9,637	9,897	10,905
Tennessee	566	1,635	3,664	5,837	7,843	8,459	8,676	8,810	9,146	9,235	9,370	9,431	9,549	9,719	10,106
Texas	624	1,916	4,150	6,771	8,484	9,029	9,260	9,528	9,418	8,862	8,951	9,273	9,789	10,067	10,264
Utah	626	1,657	2,764	4,692	6,116	6,841	7,081	6,877	6,851	6,787	7,023	7,156	7,375	7,659	7,892
Vermont	807	1,997	6,227	8,799	14,219	15,089	16,073	16,586	16,661	17,575	18,372	19,032	19,793	20,196	20,929
Virginia	708	1,970	4,672	6,491	10,913	11,410	11,696	11,383	11,123	11,385	11,748	11,716	11,810	12,022	12,535
Washington	915	2,568	4,702	6,914	9,233	9,846	10,423	10,242	10,402	10,413	10,553	11,199	11,648	12,533	13,099
West Virginia	670	1,920	4,360	7,637	10,080	10,605	11,122	12,378	12,505	11,982	11,665	11,800	12,414	12,299	12,649
Wisconsin	883	2,477	5,524	8,299	10,813	11,370	11,773	12,194	12,515	11,750	11,768	11,963	12,227	12,312	12,716
Wyoming	856	2,527	5,577	7,944	14,219	14,936	15,658	16,535	17,126	17,228	17,135	17,165	17,445	17,796	17,950
Other jurisdictions															
American Samoa	—	—	1,908	2,807	3,909	4,309	4,468	4,881	4,877	5,154	4,870	5,504	5,120	5,235	5,817
Guam	820	—	4,234	—	7,450	8,084	8,264	8,393	9,280	10,112	9,431	9,914	10,120	9,983	9,939
Northern Marianas	—	—	3,007	5,720	5,356	5,162	6,397	6,284	8,495	7,068	6,381	6,548	6,921	8,127	9,529
Puerto Rico	—	—	1,750	3,859	6,152	6,937	7,329	7,426	8,560	7,798	8,701	8,822	8,025	8,124	7,697
U.S. Virgin Islands	—	—	6,767	7,238	10,548	12,358	12,768	14,215	13,014	11,669	10,661	14,372	14,849	15,805	16,117

See notes at end of table.

Table 236.70. Current expenditure per pupil in average daily attendance in public elementary and secondary schools, by state or jurisdiction: Selected years, 1969–70 through 2016–17—Continued

State or jurisdiction	Constant 2018–19 dollars[2]														
	1969–70	1979–80	1989–90	1999–2000	2006–07	2007–08	2008–09	2009–10	2010–11	2011–12	2012–13	2013–14	2014–15	2015–16	2016–17
1	17	18	19	20	21	22	23	24	25	26	27	28	29	30	31
United States	**$5,471**	**$7,411**	**$9,933**	**$11,061**	**$12,823**	**$13,138**	**$13,260**	**$13,353**	**$13,098**	**$12,645**	**$12,599**	**$12,740**	**$13,081**	**$13,413**	**$13,667**
Alabama	3,647	5,258	6,636	8,615	10,847	11,179	11,073	11,164	10,649	9,935	10,385	10,286	10,369	10,491	10,605
Alaska	7,526	15,423	16,817	14,464	16,759	19,144	19,847	20,274	21,023	21,295	21,875	21,832	23,714	20,453	20,405
Arizona	4,828	6,430	8,085	8,196	9,972	10,325	10,303	10,232	9,904	9,153	9,182	8,923	9,017	9,111	9,255
Arkansas	3,806	5,136	6,951	8,419	11,355	11,318	11,387	11,962	11,835	11,571	10,786	11,450	11,510	11,519	11,448
California	5,814	7,398	8,758	9,575	11,202	11,572	11,137	11,312	10,929	10,693	10,603	10,880	11,690	12,688	13,287
Colorado	4,947	7,898	9,415	10,026	11,303	11,936	11,339	11,390	11,122	10,479	10,479	10,697	11,075	11,287	11,424
Connecticut	6,378	7,895	15,632	15,143	17,547	18,021	18,689	18,852	19,396	19,446	19,551	20,511	21,115	21,662	21,637
Delaware	6,035	9,334	11,566	13,178	15,648	15,300	15,047	15,107	15,154	15,863	15,468	15,309	15,576	16,104	16,516
District of Columbia	6,827	10,632	17,862	17,855	22,686	24,892	23,321	24,871	24,405	22,703	22,260	23,314	22,859	23,746	24,665
Florida	4,910	6,163	9,968	9,549	11,235	11,618	11,152	10,942	10,761	9,822	9,771	9,905	9,947	9,925	9,989
Georgia	3,942	5,302	8,526	10,328	11,929	12,278	12,009	11,516	10,971	10,564	10,331	10,271	10,496	10,826	11,191
Hawaii	5,635	7,574	8,873	10,607	15,340	15,282	15,806	15,059	14,437	14,174	13,777	14,249	14,819	15,654	15,995
Idaho	4,045	5,413	6,139	8,444	8,776	8,856	8,928	8,742	8,196	7,837	7,962	7,777	7,928	8,123	8,374
Illinois	6,098	8,438	10,208	12,094	13,419	13,906	14,735	15,289	15,098	14,980	15,116	15,825	16,557	16,910	18,090
Indiana	4,881	6,141	9,188	11,448	12,068	11,448	11,735	11,873	11,368	11,375	10,988	10,863	10,917	11,021	10,930
Iowa	5,660	7,590	8,882	10,360	10,904	10,920	12,367	12,297	12,103	11,962	11,949	12,243	12,518	12,592	12,699
Kansas	5,169	7,089	9,478	10,416	12,754	13,238	13,551	12,689	12,257	11,922	11,811	12,051	11,884	11,496	11,647
Kentucky	3,655	5,550	7,470	10,150	11,542	11,892	11,862	12,125	11,993	11,909	11,242	11,046	11,406	11,598	11,683
Louisiana	4,345	5,846	7,786	9,359	11,973	12,917	13,462	13,429	13,174	12,634	12,171	12,304	12,517	12,516	12,578
Maine	4,643	5,949	10,717	12,337	15,667	15,764	15,997	16,465	16,502	15,582	15,706	16,089	16,949	17,071	16,807
Maryland	6,157	8,475	12,517	12,377	15,925	16,895	17,240	17,455	17,041	16,411	16,432	16,286	16,483	16,452	16,681
Massachusetts	5,760	9,198	12,441	14,025	16,455	17,195	17,992	17,099	17,566	17,370	17,637	17,943	18,524	19,161	19,678
Michigan	6,061	8,614	11,063	13,294	13,563	13,345	13,560	13,627	13,243	12,756	12,584	12,588	12,893	13,014	12,993
Minnesota	6,058	7,787	9,914	11,219	12,636	12,757	13,689	13,282	13,023	12,715	12,868	13,086	13,597	13,997	14,087
Mississippi	3,358	5,428	6,171	8,012	9,910	10,107	10,158	10,131	9,664	9,597	9,508	9,621	9,769	9,970	9,881
Missouri	4,751	6,317	8,990	10,119	11,496	11,971	12,201	12,232	11,854	11,541	11,555	11,602	11,856	11,940	12,031
Montana	5,242	8,079	9,447	10,457	12,709	12,610	12,838	13,395	13,287	12,565	12,581	12,762	12,840	13,158	13,035
Nebraska	4,937	7,014	9,657	11,010	13,289	13,419	13,517	13,930	14,118	13,482	13,546	13,476	13,724	14,562	14,677
Nevada	5,159	6,813	8,212	9,197	10,387	10,636	10,459	10,365	10,350	9,657	9,332	9,414	9,566	9,814	10,041
New Hampshire	4,848	6,250	10,580	10,596	14,078	14,691	15,235	15,687	15,996	15,821	15,834	16,182	16,458	16,937	17,076
New Jersey	6,813	10,411	16,235	16,311	20,657	21,742	20,608	21,104	20,224	20,253	20,822	20,784	20,649	21,317	21,642
New Mexico	4,740	6,635	7,011	8,729	11,012	11,218	11,477	11,353	10,718	10,093	10,105	10,290	10,584	10,581	10,414
New York	8,895	11,295	16,080	16,392	21,317	22,040	22,857	23,331	23,503	23,240	23,178	23,766	24,368	25,168	25,551
North Carolina	4,105	5,723	8,557	9,732	10,389	10,067	10,816	10,436	10,245	9,826	9,898	9,645	9,894	9,936	10,133
North Dakota	4,623	6,265	8,356	9,093	11,418	11,529	11,932	12,826	13,009	12,959	13,235	13,960	14,502	14,883	15,075
Ohio	4,894	6,768	10,062	11,694	13,389	13,607	14,046	14,381	14,301	13,657	13,448	13,416	13,146	13,273	13,588
Oklahoma	4,053	6,285	6,997	8,632	9,886	9,894	9,938	9,946	9,354	9,217	9,250	9,190	9,238	9,167	8,839
Oregon	6,200	8,782	10,919	12,161	12,111	12,546	12,593	12,241	12,025	11,559	11,352	11,576	12,152	12,602	12,859
Pennsylvania	5,912	8,269	12,423	12,537	14,882	14,946	15,325	15,984	16,120	15,551	15,740	15,941	16,485	17,004	17,564
Rhode Island	5,975	8,485	12,701	14,431	18,206	18,953	19,127	18,981	18,725	18,361	17,720	18,002	18,354	18,422	18,713
South Carolina	4,107	5,716	8,142	9,792	11,447	11,752	11,807	11,553	11,152	10,932	11,166	11,219	11,418	11,596	11,800
South Dakota	4,625	6,224	7,442	9,031	10,553	10,823	11,158	11,315	10,804	10,123	10,003	10,282	10,312	10,520	11,382
Tennessee	3,795	5,335	7,308	8,733	9,731	10,119	10,237	10,295	10,477	10,278	10,258	10,166	10,219	10,330	10,548
Texas	4,185	6,250	8,279	10,130	10,525	10,802	10,926	11,134	10,789	9,863	9,799	9,995	10,475	10,700	10,713
Utah	4,199	5,405	5,513	7,020	7,588	8,184	8,355	8,036	7,848	7,554	7,688	7,714	7,892	8,141	8,237
Vermont	5,412	6,515	12,420	13,164	17,641	18,051	18,964	19,382	19,086	19,560	20,112	20,515	21,181	21,467	21,845
Virginia	4,746	6,427	9,318	9,711	13,539	13,651	13,800	13,301	12,742	12,671	12,861	12,629	12,638	12,778	13,083
Washington	6,137	8,378	9,379	10,343	11,456	11,779	12,297	11,968	11,917	11,589	11,552	12,071	12,464	13,321	13,672
West Virginia	4,492	6,265	8,698	11,425	12,507	12,687	13,122	14,465	14,325	13,335	12,770	12,719	13,284	13,073	13,202
Wisconsin	5,918	8,080	11,018	12,415	13,415	13,602	13,891	14,250	14,337	13,077	12,883	12,895	13,084	13,087	13,272
Wyoming	5,739	8,243	11,125	11,885	17,641	17,869	18,475	19,322	19,619	19,174	18,758	18,502	18,668	18,916	18,735
Other jurisdictions															
American Samoa	—	—	3,805	4,200	4,850	5,155	5,271	5,704	5,587	5,737	5,331	5,933	5,479	5,565	6,071
Guam	5,496	—	8,446	—	9,243	9,671	9,751	9,808	10,631	11,254	10,325	10,687	10,830	10,611	10,374
Northern Marianas	—	—	5,998	8,557	6,646	6,175	7,548	7,343	9,732	7,866	6,986	7,058	7,406	8,638	9,945
Puerto Rico	—	—	3,490	5,773	7,632	8,300	8,647	8,678	9,806	8,678	9,526	9,509	8,588	8,635	8,033
U.S. Virgin Islands	—	—	13,498	10,828	13,086	14,785	15,065	16,611	14,908	12,987	11,670	15,491	15,890	16,799	16,822

—Not available.
[1]Unadjusted (or "current") dollars have not been adjusted to compensate for inflation.
[2]Constant dollars based on the Consumer Price Index (CPI), prepared by the Bureau of Labor Statistics, U.S. Department of Labor, adjusted to a school-year basis. The CPI does not account for differences in inflation rates from state to state.
NOTE: Current expenditures include instruction, support services, food services, and enterprise operations. Expenditures for state administration are excluded in all years except 1969–70 and 1979–80. Beginning in 1989–90, extensive changes were made in the data collection procedures. There are discrepancies in average daily attendance reporting practices from state to state. Some data have been revised from previously published figures.
SOURCE: U.S. Department of Education, National Center for Education Statistics, *Statistics of State School Systems, 1969–70*; *Revenues and Expenditures for Public Elementary and Secondary Education, 1979–80*; and Common Core of Data (CCD), "National Public Education Financial Survey," 1989–90 through 2016–17. (This table was prepared August 2019.)

Table 236.75. Total and current expenditures per pupil in fall enrollment in public elementary and secondary schools, by function and state or jurisdiction: 2016–17

State or jurisdiction	Current expenditures, capital expenditures, and interest on school debt per pupil														
		Current expenditures													
				Support services											
	Total[1]	Total	Instruction	Total	Student support[4]	Instructional staff[5]	General adminis-tration	School adminis-tration	Operation and maintenance	Student transpor-tation	Other support services	Food services	Enterprise operations[3]	Capital outlay[2]	Interest on school debt
1	2	3	4	5	6	7	8	9	10	11	12	13	14	15	16
United States	**$13,834**	**$12,258**	**$7,445**	**$4,311**	**$712**	**$577**	**$244**	**$684**	**$1,137**	**$502**	**$455**	**$477**	**$25**	**$1,213**	**$363**
Alabama	10,615	9,528	5,436	3,441	599	401	245	594	886	492	224	651	0	856	232
Alaska	19,396	17,838	9,538	7,638	1,383	1,481	255	1,091	2,138	608	683	579	83	1,277	281
Arizona	9,374	8,053	4,337	3,295	618	390	156	452	986	334	360	420	1	1,095	226
Arkansas	11,332	10,004	5,612	3,847	541	841	253	525	1,014	368	306	533	11	1,072	256
California	13,796	12,151	7,203	4,463	729	774	119	806	1,200	266	569	456	30	1,184	461
Colorado	11,662	9,849	5,513	3,945	555	567	160	751	900	293	720	338	53	1,306	506
Connecticut	21,354	19,929	12,563	6,755	1,280	627	447	1,166	1,711	1,004	520	438	172	1,197	227
Delaware	16,096	14,892	9,317	5,078	665	273	234	944	1,590	738	633	497	0	1,042	162
District of Columbia	30,115	22,561	12,113	9,629	1,002	1,133	1,649	1,572	2,222	1,366	687	809	9	5,934	1,621
Florida	10,405	9,374	5,789	3,118	412	590	86	522	905	361	242	467	0	813	218
Georgia	11,512	10,274	6,269	3,421	534	534	131	648	772	480	321	554	30	1,111	127
Hawaii	15,210	14,322	8,373	5,228	1,348	483	72	1,029	1,593	348	355	721	0	889	0
Idaho	8,599	7,554	4,452	2,731	422	439	190	434	714	330	202	368	4	847	197
Illinois	16,985	15,517	9,673	5,461	1,093	560	583	808	1,204	659	554	383	0	995	473
Indiana	11,145	9,823	5,660	3,690	512	395	203	640	1,107	594	238	474	0	1,042	280
Iowa	13,282	11,456	6,912	4,023	669	716	292	648	950	402	346	508	13	1,595	231
Kansas	12,694	10,428	6,219	3,715	664	431	280	606	1,019	424	292	494	0	1,775	491
Kentucky	11,404	10,083	5,781	3,614	492	562	227	587	898	575	272	660	27	1,054	267
Louisiana	12,502	11,379	6,354	4,425	692	567	295	731	1,149	650	341	600	0	964	160
Maine	15,568	14,633	8,562	5,482	1,003	827	498	772	1,472	719	192	588	2	682	253
Maryland	16,508	14,933	9,515	4,992	672	689	145	1,008	1,260	781	438	425	0	1,396	179
Massachusetts	18,490	17,718	11,314	5,908	1,317	818	286	759	1,490	805	433	496	0	526	246
Michigan	12,639	11,256	6,460	4,380	890	570	253	628	988	471	579	415	0	910	473
Minnesota	15,554	12,635	8,175	3,872	370	646	474	508	853	714	306	534	54	2,465	454
Mississippi	9,611	8,755	4,968	3,250	464	407	294	533	898	418	235	536	0	746	111
Missouri	11,943	10,684	6,303	3,882	482	489	396	627	1,068	553	267	499	0	917	341
Montana	12,964	11,538	6,773	4,234	791	409	366	643	1,159	542	325	514	18	1,265	160
Nebraska	15,169	12,662	8,198	3,606	484	407	371	599	1,081	374	289	527	330	2,206	301
Nevada	10,475	9,120	5,393	3,372	500	504	148	669	844	357	349	355	0	1,009	346
New Hampshire	17,006	15,958	10,168	5,406	1,228	525	575	890	1,279	704	206	384	0	796	252
New Jersey	20,980	19,585	11,762	7,190	2,026	613	399	971	1,905	808	467	438	196	923	472
New Mexico	11,596	9,949	5,694	3,774	1,005	272	237	590	1,039	309	323	475	7	1,647	0
New York	24,377	22,861	15,911	6,495	732	589	370	876	2,102	1,154	673	455	0	967	550
North Carolina	9,886	8,995	5,625	2,895	489	309	156	533	740	367	301	475	0	877	14
North Dakota	16,526	13,767	8,261	4,484	554	473	594	712	1,181	548	422	640	381	2,462	298
Ohio	14,028	12,569	7,428	4,727	851	501	394	695	1,076	597	613	413	1	1,097	362
Oklahoma	8,935	7,921	4,428	2,888	539	320	237	441	831	250	271	524	80	918	96
Oregon	13,298	11,252	6,577	4,282	854	454	157	718	892	495	711	388	5	1,429	617
Pennsylvania	17,479	15,782	9,767	5,433	891	565	476	703	1,445	751	602	515	67	1,152	545
Rhode Island	17,345	16,620	10,046	6,118	1,750	637	249	794	1,290	720	679	452	4	449	277
South Carolina	12,525	10,419	5,777	4,080	803	646	101	675	1,023	394	438	534	27	1,668	438
South Dakota	11,478	10,117	5,990	3,552	563	359	339	492	1,053	360	385	524	51	1,118	243
Tennessee	10,318	9,246	5,643	3,087	416	546	192	560	767	347	260	516	0	847	225
Texas	11,985	9,520	5,490	3,499	469	489	140	546	1,003	277	574	531	0	1,833	632
Utah	8,794	7,206	4,576	2,252	281	289	81	474	656	213	259	362	16	1,408	180
Vermont	20,207	19,480	12,523	6,447	1,506	807	410	1,228	1,455	642	398	489	22	623	104
Virginia	12,992	11,885	7,237	4,188	602	787	193	697	1,061	612	236	458	3	1,032	75
Washington	14,483	11,971	6,940	4,555	879	776	205	726	1,016	448	505	364	111	2,114	399
West Virginia	12,566	11,745	6,727	4,261	610	464	201	630	1,267	872	218	756	0	768	53
Wisconsin	13,315	11,962	7,099	4,424	598	631	346	603	1,109	507	631	439	0	1,167	185
Wyoming	20,264	16,513	9,772	6,249	995	914	348	881	1,599	828	684	485	7	3,727	25
Other jurisdictions															
American Samoa	—	—	—	—	—	—	—	—	—	—	—	—	—	—	—
Guam	11,753	9,700	4,624	4,424	911	538	156	593	1,252	258	717	652	0	1,652	402
Northern Marianas	—	—	—	—	—	—	—	—	—	—	—	—	—	—	—
Puerto Rico	7,731	7,639	3,091	3,456	870	456	217	332	1,116	255	212	1,092	0	93	0
U.S. Virgin Islands	13,009	13,000	7,611	4,525	1,125	320	621	717	519	571	651	852	12	9	0

—Not available.
[1]Excludes "Other current expenditures," such as community services, private school programs, adult education, and other programs not allocable to expenditures per pupil in public schools.
[2]Includes expenditures for property and for buildings and alterations completed by school district staff or contractors.
[3]Includes expenditures for operations funded by sales of products or services (e.g., school bookstore or computer time).
[4]Includes expenditures for guidance, health, attendance, and speech pathology services.
[5]Includes expenditures for curriculum development, staff training, libraries, and media and computer centers.
NOTE: Excludes expenditures for state education agencies. "0" indicates none or less than $0.50. Detail may not sum to totals because of rounding.
SOURCE: U.S. Department of Education, National Center for Education Statistics, Common Core of Data (CCD), "National Public Education Financial Survey," 2016–17. (This table was prepared August 2019.)

Table 236.90. Students transported at public expense and current expenditures for transportation: Selected years, 1929-30 through 2016-17

School year	Average daily attendance, all students	Students transported at public expense		Expenditures for transportation (in unadjusted dollars)[1]		Expenditures for transportation (in constant 2018-19 dollars)[2]	
		Number	Percent of total	Total[3] (in thousands)	Average per student transported	Total[3] (in thousands)	Average per student transported
1	2	3	4	5	6	7	8
1929-30	21,265,000	1,902,826	8.9	$54,823	$29	$811,177	$426
1931-32	22,245,000	2,419,173	10.9	58,078	24	1,020,275	422
1933-34	22,458,000	2,794,724	12.4	53,908	19	1,031,051	369
1935-36	22,299,000	3,250,658	14.6	62,653	19	1,154,708	355
1937-38	22,298,000	3,769,242	16.9	75,637	20	1,337,273	355
1939-40	22,042,000	4,144,161	18.8	83,283	20	1,509,332	364
1941-42	21,031,000	4,503,081	21.4	92,922	21	1,509,375	335
1943-44	19,603,000	4,512,412	23.0	107,754	24	1,566,177	347
1945-46	19,849,000	5,056,966	25.5	129,756	26	1,801,504	356
1947-48	20,910,000	5,854,041	28.0	176,265	30	1,915,978	327
1949-50	22,284,000	6,947,384	31.2	214,504	31	2,293,924	330
1951-52	23,257,000	7,697,130	33.1	268,827	35	2,590,468	337
1953-54	25,643,871	8,411,719	32.8	307,437	37	2,895,432	344
1955-56	27,740,149	9,695,819	35.0	353,972	37	3,334,813	344
1957-58	29,722,275	10,861,689	36.5	416,491	38	3,693,671	340
1959-60	32,477,440	12,225,142	37.6	486,338	40	4,192,011	343
1961-62	34,682,340	13,222,667	38.1	576,361	44	4,856,404	367
1963-64	37,405,058	14,475,778	38.7	673,845	47	5,533,473	382
1965-66	39,154,497	15,536,567	39.7	787,358	51	6,249,611	402
1967-68	40,827,965	17,130,873	42.0	981,006	57	7,305,852	426
1969-70	41,934,376	18,198,577	43.4	1,218,557	67	8,169,993	449
1971-72	42,254,272	19,474,355	46.1	1,507,830	77	9,280,318	477
1973-74	41,438,054	21,347,039	51.5	1,858,141	87	10,093,462	473
1975-76	41,269,720	21,772,483	52.8	2,377,313	109	10,856,816	499
1977-78	40,079,590	21,800,000[4]	54.4	2,731,041	125[4]	11,043,464	507[4]
1979-80	38,288,911	21,713,515	56.7	3,833,145	177	12,505,158	576
1980-81	37,703,744	22,272,000[4]	59.1	4,408,000[4]	198[4]	12,887,796[4]	579[4]
1981-82	37,094,652	22,246,000[4]	60.0	4,793,000[4]	215[4]	12,899,153[4]	580[4]
1982-83	36,635,868	22,199,000[4]	60.6	5,000,000[4]	225[4]	12,902,089[4]	581[4]
1983-84	36,362,978	22,031,000[4]	60.6	5,284,000[4]	240[4]	13,148,248[4]	597[4]
1984-85	36,404,261	22,320,000[4]	61.3	5,722,000[4]	256[4]	13,701,811[4]	614[4]
1985-86	36,523,103	22,041,000[4]	60.3	6,123,000[4]	278[4]	14,251,082[4]	647[4]
1986-87	36,863,867	22,397,000[4]	60.8	6,551,000[4]	292[4]	14,916,065[4]	666[4]
1987-88	37,050,707	22,158,000[4]	59.8	6,888,000[4]	311[4]	15,059,391[4]	680[4]
1988-89	37,268,072	22,635,000[4]	60.7	7,550,000[4]	334[4]	15,778,050[4]	697[4]
1989-90	37,799,296	22,459,000[4]	59.4	8,030,990	358[4]	16,018,845	713[4]
1990-91	38,426,543	22,000,000[4]	57.3	8,678,954	394[4]	16,413,909	746[4]
1991-92	38,960,783	23,165,000[4]	59.5	8,769,754	379[4]	16,070,691	694[4]
1992-93	39,570,462	23,439,000[4]	59.2	9,252,300	395[4]	16,441,407	701[4]
1993-94	40,146,393	23,858,000[4]	59.4	9,627,155	404[4]	16,675,560	699[4]
1994-95	40,720,763	23,693,000[4]	58.2	9,889,034	417[4]	16,651,879	703[4]
1995-96	41,501,596	24,155,000[4]	58.2	10,396,426	430[4]	17,042,601	706[4]
1996-97	42,262,004	24,090,000[4]	57.0	10,989,809	456[4]	17,515,587	727[4]
1997-98	42,765,774	24,342,000[4]	56.9	11,465,658	471[4]	17,953,805	738[4]
1998-99	43,186,715	24,898,000[4]	57.7	12,224,454	491[4]	18,816,248	756[4]
1999-2000	43,806,726	24,951,000[4]	57.0	13,007,625	521[4]	19,459,958	780[4]
2000-01	44,075,930	24,471,000[4]	55.5	14,052,654	574[4]	20,326,957	831[4]
2001-02	44,604,592	24,529,000[5]	55.0	14,799,365	603[5]	21,034,646	858[5]
2002-03	45,017,360	24,621,000[5]	54.7	15,648,821	636[5]	21,763,709	884[5]
2003-04	45,325,731	25,159,000[5]	55.5	16,348,784	650[5]	22,250,412	884[5]
2004-05	45,625,458	25,318,000[5]	55.5	17,459,659	690[5]	23,068,114	911[5]
2005-06	45,931,617	25,252,000[5]	55.0	18,850,234	746[5]	23,991,723	950[5]
2006-07	46,132,663	25,285,000[5]	54.8	19,979,068	790[5]	24,787,441	980[5]
2007-08	46,155,880	25,221,000[4]	54.6	21,536,978	854[4]	25,765,592	1,022[4]
2008-09	46,173,477	---	---	21,679,876	860[4]	25,579,381	1,015[4]
2009-10	45,919,206	---	---	21,819,304	870[4]	25,497,181	1,017[4]
2010-11	46,118,737	---	---	22,370,807	888[4]	25,627,059	1,018[4]
2011-12	46,400,465	---	---	22,926,700	905[4]	25,516,223	1,007[4]
2012-13	46,553,754	---	---	23,237,941	914[4]	25,439,273	1,001[4]
2013-14	46,829,716	---	---	23,845,036	933[4]	25,702,376	1,005[4]
2014-15	47,064,337	---	---	23,961,692	932[4]	25,641,401	998[4]
2015-16	47,248,060	---	---	24,325,727	943[4]	25,856,594	1,002[4]
2016-17	47,285,848	---	---	25,350,286	982[4]	26,458,922	1,025[4]

—Not available.

[1] Unadjusted (or "current") dollars have not been adjusted to compensate for inflation.

[2] Constant dollars based on the Consumer Price Index, prepared by the Bureau of Labor Statistics, U.S. Department of Labor, adjusted to a school-year basis.

[3] Excludes capital outlay for years through 1979-80 and for 1989-90 to the latest year. From 1980-81 to 1988-89, total transportation figures include capital outlay.

[4] Estimate based on data appearing in January issues of *School Bus Fleet*.

[5] Estimate based on data reported by *School Transportation News*.

SOURCE: U.S. Department of Education, National Center for Education Statistics, Statistics of State School Systems, 1929-30 through 1975-76; Revenues and Expenditures for Public Elementary and Secondary Education, 1977-78 and 1979-80; Common Core of Data (CCD), "National Public Education Financial Survey," 1987-88 through 2016-17; Bobit Publishing Co., School Bus Fleet, "School Transportation: 2000-2001 School Year" and "2010 Fact Book"; School Transportation News, "K-12 Enrollment/Transportation Data," 2001-02 through 2007-08; and unpublished data. (This table was prepared February 2020.)

Table 302.10. Recent high school completers and their enrollment in college, by sex and level of institution: 1960 through 2018

[Standard errors appear in parentheses]

Year	Number of high school completers[1] (in thousands)			Percent of recent high school completers[1] enrolled in college[2]								
				Total			Males			Females		
	Total	Males	Females	Total	2-year college	4-year college or university	Total	2-year college	4-year college or university	Total	2-year college	4-year college or university
1	2	3	4	5	6	7	8	9	10	11	12	13
1960	1,679 (44.5)	756 (32.3)	923 (30.1)	45.1 (2.16)	— (†)	— (†)	54.0 (3.23)	— (†)	— (†)	37.9 (2.85)	— (†)	— (†)
1961	1,763 (46.7)	790 (33.7)	973 (31.8)	48.0 (2.12)	— (†)	— (†)	56.3 (3.14)	— (†)	— (†)	41.3 (2.81)	— (†)	— (†)
1962	1,838 (44.3)	872 (32.0)	966 (30.4)	49.0 (2.08)	— (†)	— (†)	55.0 (3.00)	— (†)	— (†)	43.5 (2.84)	— (†)	— (†)
1963	1,741 (44.9)	794 (32.6)	947 (30.5)	45.0 (2.12)	— (†)	— (†)	52.3 (3.16)	— (†)	— (†)	39.0 (2.82)	— (†)	— (†)
1964	2,145 (43.6)	997 (32.3)	1,148 (28.9)	48.3 (1.92)	— (†)	— (†)	57.2 (2.79)	— (†)	— (†)	40.7 (2.58)	— (†)	— (†)
1965	2,659 (48.5)	1,254 (35.7)	1,405 (32.5)	50.9 (1.73)	— (†)	— (†)	57.3 (2.49)	— (†)	— (†)	45.3 (2.37)	— (†)	— (†)
1966	2,612 (45.7)	1,207 (34.4)	1,405 (29.5)	50.1 (1.74)	— (†)	— (†)	58.7 (2.53)	— (†)	— (†)	42.7 (2.35)	— (†)	— (†)
1967	2,525 (38.5)	1,142 (28.9)	1,383 (24.7)	51.9 (1.44)	— (†)	— (†)	57.6 (2.12)	— (†)	— (†)	47.2 (1.95)	— (†)	— (†)
1968	2,606 (38.0)	1,184 (28.7)	1,422 (24.2)	55.4 (1.41)	— (†)	— (†)	63.2 (2.04)	— (†)	— (†)	48.9 (1.93)	— (†)	— (†)
1969	2,842 (36.6)	1,352 (27.3)	1,490 (24.2)	53.3 (1.36)	— (†)	— (†)	60.1 (1.93)	— (†)	— (†)	47.2 (1.88)	— (†)	— (†)
1970	2,758 (38.1)	1,343 (26.6)	1,415 (27.3)	51.7 (1.38)	— (†)	— (†)	55.2 (1.97)	— (†)	— (†)	48.5 (1.93)	— (†)	— (†)
1971	2,875 (38.7)	1,371 (27.1)	1,504 (27.6)	53.5 (1.35)	— (†)	— (†)	57.6 (1.94)	— (†)	— (†)	49.8 (1.87)	— (†)	— (†)
1972	2,964 (38.5)	1,423 (27.5)	1,542 (26.9)	49.2 (1.33)	— (†)	— (†)	52.7 (1.92)	— (†)	— (†)	46.0 (1.84)	— (†)	— (†)
1973	3,058 (37.7)	1,460 (28.0)	1,599 (25.0)	46.6 (1.31)	14.9 (0.94)	31.6 (1.22)	50.0 (1.90)	14.6 (1.34)	35.4 (1.82)	43.4 (1.80)	15.2 (1.30)	28.2 (1.63)
1974	3,101 (39.3)	1,491 (28.2)	1,611 (27.3)	47.6 (1.30)	15.2 (0.94)	32.4 (1.22)	49.4 (1.88)	16.6 (1.40)	32.8 (1.77)	45.9 (1.80)	13.9 (1.25)	32.0 (1.69)
1975	3,185 (39.3)	1,513 (27.8)	1,672 (27.7)	50.7 (1.29)	18.2 (0.99)	32.6 (1.21)	52.6 (1.86)	19.0 (1.47)	33.6 (1.76)	49.0 (1.78)	17.4 (1.35)	31.6 (1.65)
1976	2,986 (40.5)	1,451 (29.4)	1,535 (27.8)	48.8 (1.33)	15.6 (0.96)	33.3 (1.25)	47.2 (1.90)	14.5 (1.34)	32.7 (1.79)	50.3 (1.85)	16.6 (1.38)	33.8 (1.75)
1977	3,141 (41.0)	1,483 (29.8)	1,659 (27.9)	50.6 (1.30)	17.5 (0.98)	33.1 (1.22)	52.1 (1.88)	17.2 (1.42)	35.0 (1.80)	49.3 (1.78)	17.8 (1.36)	31.5 (1.66)
1978	3,163 (40.0)	1,485 (29.4)	1,677 (26.8)	50.1 (1.29)	17.0 (0.97)	33.1 (1.22)	51.1 (1.88)	15.6 (1.37)	35.5 (1.80)	49.3 (1.77)	18.3 (1.37)	31.0 (1.64)
1979	3,160 (40.3)	1,475 (29.4)	1,685 (27.4)	49.3 (1.29)	17.5 (0.98)	31.8 (1.20)	50.4 (1.89)	16.9 (1.42)	33.5 (1.79)	48.4 (1.77)	18.1 (1.36)	30.3 (1.63)
1980	3,088 (39.6)	1,498 (28.5)	1,589 (27.5)	49.3 (1.31)	19.4 (1.03)	29.9 (1.20)	46.7 (1.87)	17.1 (1.41)	29.7 (1.71)	51.8 (1.82)	21.6 (1.50)	30.2 (1.67)
1981	3,056 (42.4)	1,491 (30.6)	1,565 (29.3)	53.9 (1.31)	20.5 (1.06)	33.5 (1.24)	54.8 (1.87)	20.9 (1.53)	33.9 (1.78)	53.1 (1.83)	20.1 (1.47)	33.0 (1.73)
1982	3,100 (41.0)	1,509 (29.4)	1,592 (28.6)	50.6 (1.38)	19.1 (1.09)	31.5 (1.28)	49.1 (1.98)	17.5 (1.50)	31.6 (1.84)	52.0 (1.93)	20.6 (1.56)	31.4 (1.79)
1983	2,963 (42.2)	1,389 (30.8)	1,573 (28.6)	52.7 (1.41)	19.2 (1.11)	33.5 (1.33)	51.9 (2.06)	20.2 (1.66)	31.7 (1.92)	53.4 (1.93)	18.4 (1.50)	35.1 (1.85)
1984	3,012 (37.0)	1,429 (29.1)	1,584 (22.2)	55.2 (1.39)	19.4 (1.11)	35.8 (1.34)	56.0 (2.02)	17.7 (1.55)	38.4 (1.98)	54.5 (1.92)	21.0 (1.57)	33.5 (1.82)
1985	2,668 (40.7)	1,287 (29.1)	1,381 (28.3)	57.7 (1.47)	19.6 (1.18)	38.1 (1.45)	58.6 (2.11)	19.9 (1.71)	38.8 (2.09)	56.8 (2.05)	19.3 (1.63)	37.5 (2.00)
1986	2,786 (39.2)	1,332 (28.9)	1,454 (26.4)	53.8 (1.45)	19.2 (1.15)	34.5 (1.39)	55.8 (2.09)	21.3 (1.73)	34.5 (2.00)	51.9 (2.02)	17.3 (1.53)	34.6 (1.92)
1987	2,647 (41.5)	1,278 (30.2)	1,369 (28.4)	56.8 (1.48)	18.9 (1.17)	37.9 (1.45)	58.3 (2.12)	17.3 (1.63)	41.0 (2.12)	55.3 (2.07)	20.3 (1.67)	35.0 (1.98)
1988	2,673 (47.7)	1,334 (34.6)	1,339 (32.8)	58.9 (1.60)	21.9 (1.34)	37.1 (1.57)	57.1 (2.27)	21.3 (1.88)	35.8 (2.20)	60.7 (2.24)	22.4 (1.91)	38.3 (2.23)
1989	2,450 (44.8)	1,204 (31.7)	1,246 (31.7)	59.6 (1.58)	20.7 (1.30)	38.9 (1.57)	57.6 (2.27)	18.3 (1.77)	39.3 (2.24)	61.6 (2.19)	23.1 (1.90)	38.5 (2.20)
1990	2,362 (43.0)	1,173 (30.6)	1,189 (30.2)	60.1 (1.60)	20.1 (1.31)	40.0 (1.61)	58.0 (2.29)	19.6 (1.85)	38.4 (2.26)	62.2 (2.24)	20.6 (1.87)	41.6 (2.28)
1991	2,276 (41.1)	1,140 (29.0)	1,136 (29.0)	62.5 (1.62)	24.9 (1.44)	37.7 (1.62)	57.9 (2.33)	22.9 (1.98)	35.0 (2.25)	67.1 (2.22)	26.8 (2.09)	40.3 (2.32)
1992	2,397 (40.5)	1,216 (29.1)	1,180 (28.1)	61.9 (1.58)	23.0 (1.37)	38.9 (1.59)	60.0 (2.24)	22.1 (1.89)	37.8 (2.21)	63.8 (2.23)	23.9 (1.98)	40.0 (2.27)
1993	2,342 (41.4)	1,120 (30.6)	1,223 (27.7)	62.6 (1.59)	22.8 (1.38)	39.8 (1.61)	59.9 (2.33)	22.9 (2.00)	37.0 (2.30)	65.2 (2.17)	22.8 (1.91)	42.4 (2.25)
1994	2,517 (41.1)	1,244 (30.1)	1,273 (27.9)	61.9 (1.54)	21.0 (1.29)	40.9 (1.56)	60.6 (2.21)	23.0 (1.90)	37.5 (2.19)	63.2 (2.15)	19.1 (1.75)	44.1 (2.22)
1995	2,599 (41.0)	1,238 (30.0)	1,361 (27.7)	61.9 (1.41)	21.5 (1.19)	40.4 (1.43)	62.6 (2.04)	25.3 (1.83)	37.4 (2.04)	61.3 (1.96)	18.1 (1.55)	43.2 (1.99)
1996	2,660 (40.5)	1,297 (29.5)	1,363 (27.7)	65.0 (1.42)	23.1 (1.26)	41.9 (1.47)	60.1 (2.09)	21.5 (1.76)	38.5 (2.08)	69.7 (1.91)	24.6 (1.79)	45.1 (2.07)
1997	2,769 (41.8)	1,354 (31.0)	1,415 (27.9)	67.0 (1.37)	22.8 (1.23)	44.3 (1.45)	63.6 (2.01)	21.4 (1.71)	42.2 (2.06)	70.3 (1.87)	24.1 (1.75)	46.2 (2.04)
1998	2,810 (43.9)	1,452 (31.0)	1,358 (31.0)	65.6 (1.38)	24.4 (1.25)	41.3 (1.43)	62.4 (1.96)	24.4 (1.73)	38.0 (1.96)	69.1 (1.93)	24.3 (1.79)	44.8 (2.08)
1999	2,897 (41.5)	1,474 (29.9)	1,423 (28.8)	62.9 (1.38)	21.0 (1.16)	41.9 (1.41)	61.4 (1.95)	21.0 (1.63)	40.5 (1.97)	64.4 (1.95)	21.1 (1.66)	43.3 (2.02)
2000	2,756 (45.3)	1,251 (33.6)	1,505 (29.7)	63.3 (1.41)	21.4 (1.20)	41.9 (1.45)	59.9 (2.13)	23.1 (1.83)	36.8 (2.10)	66.2 (1.88)	20.0 (1.59)	46.2 (1.98)
2001	2,549 (44.1)	1,277 (32.0)	1,273 (30.3)	61.8 (1.41)	19.6 (1.15)	42.1 (1.43)	60.1 (2.00)	18.6 (1.59)	41.4 (2.01)	63.5 (1.97)	20.6 (1.66)	42.8 (2.02)
2002	2,796 (42.7)	1,412 (31.3)	1,384 (29.0)	65.2 (1.31)	21.6 (1.14)	43.6 (1.37)	62.1 (1.88)	20.4 (1.57)	41.7 (1.92)	68.4 (1.82)	22.8 (1.65)	45.6 (1.95)
2003	2,677 (42.2)	1,306 (29.9)	1,372 (29.7)	63.9 (1.35)	21.5 (1.16)	42.5 (1.39)	61.2 (1.97)	21.9 (1.67)	39.3 (1.97)	66.5 (1.86)	21.0 (1.61)	45.5 (1.96)
2004	2,752 (40.0)	1,327 (29.1)	1,425 (27.3)	66.7 (1.31)	22.4 (1.16)	44.2 (1.38)	61.4 (1.95)	21.8 (1.65)	39.6 (1.96)	71.5 (1.74)	23.1 (1.63)	48.5 (1.93)
2005	2,675 (40.8)	1,262 (31.5)	1,414 (24.9)	68.6 (1.31)	24.0 (1.21)	44.6 (1.40)	66.5 (1.94)	24.7 (1.77)	41.8 (2.03)	70.4 (1.77)	23.4 (1.64)	47.0 (1.94)
2006	2,692 (44.6)	1,328 (32.7)	1,363 (30.1)	66.0 (1.33)	24.7 (1.21)	41.3 (1.39)	65.8 (1.90)	24.9 (1.73)	40.9 (1.97)	66.1 (1.87)	24.5 (1.70)	41.7 (1.95)
2007	2,955 (42.6)	1,511 (30.0)	1,444 (30.3)	67.2 (1.26)	24.1 (1.15)	43.1 (1.33)	66.1 (1.78)	22.7 (1.57)	43.4 (1.86)	68.3 (1.79)	25.5 (1.67)	42.8 (1.90)
2008	3,151 (42.8)	1,640 (29.6)	1,511 (30.9)	68.6 (1.21)	27.7 (1.16)	40.9 (1.28)	65.9 (1.71)	24.9 (1.56)	41.0 (1.77)	71.6 (1.69)	30.6 (1.73)	40.9 (1.85)
2009	2,937 (45.0)	1,407 (32.8)	1,531 (30.6)	70.1 (1.23)	27.7 (1.21)	42.4 (1.33)	66.0 (1.84)	25.1 (1.69)	40.9 (1.91)	73.8 (1.64)	30.1 (1.71)	43.8 (1.85)
2010	3,160 (91.8)	1,679 (64.6)	1,482 (58.4)	68.1 (1.49)	26.7 (1.52)	41.4 (1.61)	62.8 (1.88)	28.5 (2.03)	34.3 (1.97)	74.0 (2.31)	24.6 (2.32)	49.5 (2.59)
2011	3,079 (88.3)	1,611 (60.6)	1,468 (58.4)	68.2 (1.45)	25.9 (1.49)	42.3 (1.44)	64.7 (2.16)	24.7 (1.79)	40.0 (2.10)	72.2 (1.98)	27.3 (2.17)	44.9 (2.37)
2012	3,203 (96.2)	1,622 (70.1)	1,581 (54.0)	66.2 (1.59)	28.8 (1.57)	37.5 (1.60)	61.3 (2.17)	26.9 (2.20)	34.4 (2.15)	71.3 (2.11)	30.7 (2.09)	40.6 (2.21)
2013	2,977 (84.4)	1,524 (62.9)	1,453 (57.0)	65.9 (1.58)	23.8 (1.44)	42.1 (1.76)	63.5 (2.20)	24.5 (2.14)	39.0 (2.48)	68.4 (2.17)	23.0 (2.15)	45.3 (2.21)
2014	2,868 (78.5)	1,423 (58.1)	1,445 (57.5)	68.4 (1.67)	24.6 (1.56)	43.7 (1.81)	64.0 (2.32)	21.2 (2.07)	42.8 (2.69)	72.6 (2.50)	28.0 (2.35)	44.6 (2.57)
2015	2,965 (87.5)	1,448 (64.6)	1,516 (56.6)	69.2 (1.54)	25.2 (1.48)	44.0 (1.61)	65.8 (2.27)	24.3 (2.00)	41.5 (2.27)	72.5 (2.18)	26.2 (2.08)	46.4 (2.42)
2016	3,137 (102.3)	1,517 (70.6)	1,620 (66.7)	69.8 (1.64)	23.7 (1.56)	46.0 (1.85)	67.5 (2.12)	25.3 (2.26)	42.2 (2.47)	71.9 (2.40)	22.3 (1.99)	49.6 (2.46)
2017	2,870 (95.9)	1,345 (60.2)	1,525 (71.3)	66.7 (1.68)	22.6 (1.50)	44.2 (1.83)	61.1 (2.57)	23.9 (2.36)	37.2 (2.32)	71.7 (2.29)	21.4 (2.09)	50.3 (2.70)
2018	3,212 (94.6)	1,614 (61.2)	1,598 (69.9)	69.1 (1.62)	25.5 (1.54)	43.6 (1.76)	66.9 (2.22)	24.9 (1.92)	42.0 (2.23)	71.4 (2.32)	26.1 (2.19)	45.2 (2.75)

—Not available.

†Not applicable.

[1]Individuals ages 16 to 24 who graduated from high school or completed a GED or other high school equivalency credential.

[2]Enrollment in college as of October of each year for individuals ages 16 to 24 who had completed high school earlier in the calendar year.

NOTE: Data are based on sample surveys of the civilian noninstitutionalized population. High school completion data in this table differ from figures appearing in other tables because of varying survey procedures and coverage. Prior to 2010, standard errors were computed using generalized variance function methodology rather than the more precise replicate weight methodology used in later years. Detail may not sum to totals because of rounding.

SOURCE: American College Testing Program, unpublished tabulations, derived from statistics collected by the Census Bureau, 1960 through 1969. U.S. Department of Commerce, Census Bureau, Current Population Survey (CPS), October, 1970 through 2018. (This table was prepared August 2019.)

Table 302.20. Percentage of recent high school completers enrolled in college, by race/ethnicity: 1960 through 2018

[Standard errors appear in parentheses]

Year	Percent of recent high school completers[1] enrolled in college[2] (annual data)					3-year moving averages[3]							
						Percent of recent high school completers[1] enrolled in college[2]					Difference between percent enrolled		
	Total	White	Black	Hispanic	Asian[4]	Total	White	Black	Hispanic	Asian[4]	White-Black	White-Hispanic	White-Asian[4]
1	2	3	4	5	6	7	8	9	10	11	12	13	14
1960[5]	45.1 (2.16)	45.8 (2.24)	— (†)	— (†)	— (†)	46.6 (1.52)	47.7 (1.58)	— (†)	— (†)	— (†)	— (†)	— (†)	— (†)
1961[5]	48.0 (2.12)	49.5 (2.22)	— (†)	— (†)	— (†)	47.4 (1.22)	48.7 (1.28)	— (†)	— (†)	— (†)	— (†)	— (†)	— (†)
1962[5]	49.0 (2.08)	50.6 (2.19)	— (†)	— (†)	— (†)	47.4 (1.22)	48.6 (1.27)	— (†)	— (†)	— (†)	— (†)	— (†)	— (†)
1963[5]	45.0 (2.12)	45.6 (2.21)	— (†)	— (†)	— (†)	47.5 (1.18)	48.5 (1.23)	— (†)	— (†)	— (†)	— (†)	— (†)	— (†)
1964[5]	48.3 (1.92)	49.2 (2.01)	— (†)	— (†)	— (†)	48.5 (1.10)	49.2 (1.15)	— (†)	— (†)	— (†)	— (†)	— (†)	— (†)
1965[5]	50.9 (1.73)	51.7 (1.81)	— (†)	— (†)	— (†)	49.9 (1.03)	51.0 (1.08)	— (†)	— (†)	— (†)	— (†)	— (†)	— (†)
1966[5]	50.1 (1.74)	51.7 (1.82)	— (†)	— (†)	— (†)	51.0 (1.01)	52.1 (1.06)	— (†)	— (†)	— (†)	— (†)	— (†)	— (†)
1967[5]	51.9 (1.44)	53.0 (1.52)	— (†)	— (†)	— (†)	52.5 (0.82)	53.8 (0.87)	— (†)	— (†)	— (†)	— (†)	— (†)	— (†)
1968[5]	55.4 (1.41)	56.6 (1.50)	— (†)	— (†)	— (†)	53.6 (0.81)	55.0 (0.86)	— (†)	— (†)	— (†)	— (†)	— (†)	— (†)
1969[5]	53.3 (1.36)	55.2 (1.43)	— (†)	— (†)	— (†)	53.5 (0.80)	54.6 (0.85)	— (†)	— (†)	— (†)	— (†)	— (†)	— (†)
1970[5]	51.7 (1.38)	52.0 (1.46)	— (†)	— (†)	— (†)	52.9 (0.79)	53.8 (0.83)	— (†)	— (†)	— (†)	— (†)	— (†)	— (†)
1971[5]	53.5 (1.35)	54.0 (1.42)	— (†)	— (†)	— (†)	51.5 (0.78)	51.9 (0.83)	— (†)	— (†)	— (†)	— (†)	— (†)	— (†)
1972	49.2 (1.33)	49.7 (1.45)	44.6 (4.74)	45.0 (12.85)	— (†)	49.7 (0.77)	50.5 (0.83)	38.4 (3.26)	49.9 (8.76)	— (†)	12.1 (3.36)	‡ (†)	— (†)
1973	46.6 (1.31)	47.8 (1.43)	32.5 (4.40)	54.1 (11.89)	— (†)	47.8 (0.76)	48.2 (0.83)	41.4 (2.68)	48.8 (7.04)	— (†)	6.8! (2.81)	‡ (†)	— (†)
1974	47.6 (1.30)	47.2 (1.42)	47.2 (4.69)	46.9 (11.79)	— (†)	48.3 (0.75)	48.7 (0.82)	40.5 (2.69)	53.1 (6.72)	— (†)	8.3! (2.82)	‡ (†)	— (†)
1975	50.7 (1.29)	51.1 (1.40)	41.7 (4.81)	58.0 (11.14)	— (†)	49.1 (0.75)	49.1 (0.82)	44.5 (2.78)	52.7 (6.44)	— (†)	‡ (†)	‡ (†)	— (†)
1976	48.8 (1.33)	48.8 (1.45)	44.4 (4.94)	52.7 (10.52)	— (†)	50.1 (0.75)	50.3 (0.82)	45.3 (2.78)	53.6 (6.18)	— (†)	‡ (†)	‡ (†)	— (†)
1977	50.6 (1.30)	50.8 (1.42)	49.5 (4.70)	50.8 (10.43)	— (†)	49.9 (0.75)	50.1 (0.83)	46.8 (2.73)	48.8 (6.18)	— (†)	‡ (†)	‡ (†)	— (†)
1978	50.1 (1.29)	50.5 (1.42)	46.4 (4.55)	42.0 (11.06)	— (†)	50.0 (0.75)	50.4 (0.82)	47.5 (2.69)	46.1 (6.14)	— (†)	‡ (†)	‡ (†)	— (†)
1979	49.3 (1.29)	49.9 (1.42)	46.7 (4.73)	45.0 (10.37)	— (†)	49.6 (0.75)	50.1 (0.82)	45.2 (2.65)	46.3 (6.32)	— (†)	‡ (†)	‡ (†)	— (†)
1980	49.3 (1.31)	49.8 (1.44)	42.7 (4.48)	52.3 (11.39)	— (†)	50.8 (0.75)	51.5 (0.83)	44.0 (2.64)	49.6 (6.25)	— (†)	7.5! (2.76)	‡ (†)	— (†)
1981	53.9 (1.31)	54.9 (1.45)	42.7 (4.48)	52.1 (10.73)	— (†)	51.3 (0.76)	52.4 (0.84)	40.3 (2.53)	48.7 (6.13)	— (†)	12.2 (2.66)	‡ (†)	— (†)
1982	50.6 (1.38)	52.7 (1.54)	35.8 (4.39)	43.2 (10.37)	— (†)	52.4 (0.80)	54.2 (0.90)	38.8 (2.61)	49.4 (6.44)	— (†)	15.4 (2.76)	‡ (†)	— (†)
1983	52.7 (1.41)	55.0 (1.57)	38.2 (4.41)	54.2 (11.69)	— (†)	52.8 (0.81)	55.5 (0.90)	38.0 (2.50)	46.7 (6.16)	— (†)	17.5 (2.66)	‡ (†)	— (†)
1984	55.2 (1.39)	59.0 (1.57)	39.8 (4.21)	44.3 (10.00)	— (†)	55.1 (0.82)	57.9 (0.92)	39.9 (2.58)	49.3 (6.38)	— (†)	18.0 (2.74)	‡ (†)	— (†)
1985	57.7 (1.47)	60.1 (1.64)	42.2 (4.86)	51.0 (9.79)	— (†)	55.5 (0.83)	58.6 (0.93)	39.5 (2.59)	46.1 (5.20)	— (†)	19.1 (2.75)	12.5! (5.28)	— (†)
1986	53.8 (1.45)	56.8 (1.64)	36.9 (4.44)	44.0 (8.88)	— (†)	56.1 (0.85)	58.5 (0.96)	43.5 (2.75)	42.3 (5.21)	— (†)	15.0 (2.91)	16.2! (5.30)	— (†)
1987	56.8 (1.48)	58.6 (1.68)	52.2 (4.90)	33.5 (8.28)	— (†)	56.5 (0.85)	58.8 (0.96)	44.2 (2.69)	45.0 (5.06)	— (†)	14.6 (2.86)	13.8! (5.15)	— (†)
1988	58.9 (1.60)	61.1 (1.82)	44.4 (4.98)	57.1 (9.60)	— (†)	58.4 (0.94)	60.1 (1.07)	49.7 (3.02)	48.5 (5.67)	— (†)	10.4! (3.20)	11.6! (5.77)	— (†)
1989	59.6 (1.58)	60.7 (1.79)	53.4 (5.07)	55.1 (9.21)	81.1 (10.23)	59.5 (0.90)	61.6 (1.02)	48.0 (2.87)	52.7 (5.54)	81.4 (6.36)	13.6 (3.04)	‡ (†)	-19.8! (6.44)
1990	60.1 (1.60)	63.0 (1.80)	46.8 (5.08)	42.7 (10.82)	81.7 (8.12)	60.7 (0.92)	63.0 (1.04)	48.9 (2.97)	52.5 (5.70)	81.4 (6.36)	14.0 (3.14)	‡ (†)	-18.5! (6.44)
1991	62.5 (1.62)	65.4 (1.82)	46.4 (5.24)	57.2 (9.57)	78.9 (9.04)	61.5 (0.92)	64.2 (1.05)	47.2 (2.93)	52.6 (5.52)	80.6 (5.21)	17.0 (3.11)	11.7! (5.62)	-16.3! (5.31)
1992	61.9 (1.58)	64.3 (1.84)	48.2 (4.91)	55.0 (8.50)	81.7 (7.00)	62.3 (0.92)	64.2 (1.06)	50.0 (2.97)	58.2 (5.04)	80.9 (4.58)	14.2 (3.16)	‡ (†)	-16.7 (4.70)
1993	62.6 (1.59)	62.9 (1.86)	55.6 (5.27)	62.2 (8.21)	86.2 (6.63)	62.1 (0.91)	63.9 (1.04)	51.3 (2.96)	55.7 (4.97)	82.5 (4.30)	12.6 (3.14)	‡ (†)	-18.6 (4.42)
1994	61.9 (1.54)	64.5 (1.74)	50.8 (5.20)	49.1 (9.00)	78.3 (8.55)	62.1 (0.89)	64.0 (1.03)	52.4 (2.97)	55.0 (4.63)	82.2 (4.25)	11.5 (3.14)	‡ (†)	-18.2 (4.37)
1995	61.9 (1.41)	64.3 (1.65)	51.2 (4.22)	53.7 (4.94)	83.0 (6.94)	63.0 (0.81)	65.4 (0.94)	52.9 (2.40)	51.6 (3.19)	82.7 (4.47)	12.5 (2.58)	13.8 (3.33)	-17.3 (4.57)
1996	65.0 (1.42)	67.4 (1.66)	56.0 (4.03)	50.8 (5.79)	85.3 (5.21)	64.7 (0.82)	66.6 (0.97)	55.4 (2.41)	57.6 (2.96)	82.7 (3.59)	11.3 (2.60)	9.0! (3.11)	-16.0 (3.72)
1997	67.0 (1.37)	68.2 (1.64)	58.5 (4.11)	65.6 (4.52)	80.5 (6.09)	65.9 (0.80)	68.1 (0.94)	58.8 (2.35)	55.3 (2.93)	83.0 (3.49)	9.3 (2.53)	12.8 (3.08)	-15.0 (3.62)
1998	65.6 (1.38)	68.5 (1.61)	61.9 (4.04)	47.4 (4.92)	85.5 (5.71)	65.2 (0.80)	67.7 (0.94)	59.8 (2.31)	51.9 (2.79)	83.8 (3.28)	7.9! (2.49)	15.7 (2.94)	-16.1 (3.41)
1999	62.9 (1.38)	66.3 (1.63)	58.9 (3.85)	42.3 (4.76)	78.3 (5.73)	64.0 (0.80)	66.8 (0.94)	58.6 (2.31)	47.4 (2.84)	81.1 (3.40)	8.3! (2.50)	19.5 (2.99)	-14.3 (3.53)
2000	63.3 (1.41)	65.7 (1.66)	54.9 (4.10)	52.9 (5.03)	81.0 (6.29)	62.7 (0.82)	65.4 (0.96)	56.4 (2.33)	48.6 (2.96)	81.3 (3.44)	9.1 (2.52)	16.9 (3.11)	-15.8 (3.57)
2001	61.8 (1.41)	64.3 (1.63)	55.0 (3.96)	51.7 (5.33)	73.8 (8.71)	63.5 (0.78)	66.3 (0.92)	56.4 (2.26)	52.8 (2.78)	78.4 (3.87)	10.0 (2.44)	13.5 (2.93)	-12.0! (3.97)
2002	65.2 (1.31)	69.1 (1.55)	59.4 (3.90)	53.6 (4.46)	63.7 (6.51)	63.7 (0.78)	66.5 (0.92)	57.3 (2.33)	54.8 (2.75)	71.9 (4.05)	9.3 (2.50)	11.7 (2.90)	‡ (†)
2003[6]	63.9 (1.35)	66.2 (1.61)	57.5 (4.25)	58.6 (4.61)	84.1 (5.10)	65.3 (0.77)	68.0 (0.91)	59.9 (2.29)	57.7 (2.66)	74.2 (3.51)	8.1! (2.46)	10.3 (2.81)	‡ (†)
2004[6]	66.7 (1.31)	68.8 (1.57)	62.5 (3.77)	61.8 (4.76)	75.6 (6.13)	66.4 (0.77)	69.4 (0.91)	58.8 (2.34)	57.7 (2.60)	81.6 (3.37)	10.6 (2.51)	11.7 (2.75)	-12.2 (3.49)
2005[6]	68.6 (1.31)	73.2 (1.52)	55.7 (4.15)	54.0 (4.18)	86.7 (5.99)	67.1 (0.76)	70.2 (0.90)	58.2 (2.35)	57.5 (2.52)	80.9 (3.64)	12.0 (2.52)	12.6 (2.67)	-10.7! (3.75)
2006[6]	66.0 (1.33)	68.5 (1.60)	55.5 (4.33)	57.9 (4.18)	82.3 (5.32)	67.2 (0.75)	70.4 (0.89)	55.6 (2.35)	58.5 (2.43)	85.1 (3.64)	14.7 (2.51)	11.9 (2.59)	-14.7 (3.74)
2007[6]	67.2 (1.26)	69.5 (1.49)	55.7 (3.78)	64.0 (4.22)	88.8 (6.26)	67.3 (0.73)	70.0 (0.87)	55.7 (2.27)	62.0 (2.33)	85.8 (3.45)	14.3 (2.43)	8.0! (2.48)	-15.8 (3.56)
2008[6]	68.6 (1.21)	71.7 (1.44)	55.7 (3.78)	63.9 (3.72)	88.4 (5.08)	68.6 (0.71)	70.8 (0.86)	60.3 (2.15)	62.3 (2.25)	90.1 (3.01)	10.5 (2.31)	8.6 (2.41)	-19.2 (3.13)
2009[6]	70.1 (1.23)	71.3 (1.53)	69.5 (3.51)	59.3 (3.80)	92.1 (3.90)	68.9 (0.70)	71.2 (0.86)	62.4 (2.09)	60.9 (2.14)	88.1 (2.85)	8.8 (2.26)	10.3 (2.31)	-16.9 (2.98)
2010[6]	68.1 (1.49)	70.5 (1.68)	62.0 (4.81)	59.7 (4.18)	84.7 (5.27)	68.8 (0.71)	70.1 (0.90)	66.1 (2.01)	62.3 (2.01)	87.4 (2.78)	‡ (†)	7.8 (2.21)	-17.3 (2.92)
2011[6]	68.2 (1.45)	68.3 (1.86)	67.1 (4.01)	66.6 (3.50)	86.1 (4.25)	67.5 (0.89)	68.2 (1.03)	62.1 (2.86)	66.1 (2.17)	83.9 (2.79)	6.1! (3.04)	‡ (†)	-15.7 (2.97)
2012[6]	66.2 (1.59)	65.7 (1.94)	56.4 (4.84)	70.3 (3.22)	81.5 (5.15)	66.8 (0.94)	67.6 (1.12)	60.5 (2.64)	65.9 (1.99)	82.3 (3.59)	7.1! (2.87)	‡ (†)	-14.7 (3.76)
2013[6]	65.9 (1.58)	68.8 (1.90)	56.7 (5.59)	59.8 (3.62)	80.1 (6.52)	66.8 (0.98)	67.4 (1.26)	60.7 (3.09)	65.5 (2.06)	83.6 (3.20)	6.7! (3.34)	‡ (†)	-16.2 (3.44)
2014[6]	68.4 (1.67)	67.7 (2.25)	70.2 (4.56)	65.2 (4.08)	90.9 (3.91)	67.8 (1.00)	69.3 (1.17)	60.6 (3.40)	64.7 (2.16)	84.2 (3.16)	8.8! (3.59)	‡ (†)	-14.9 (3.37)
2015[6]	69.2 (1.54)	71.3 (1.74)	55.6 (5.69)	68.9 (3.64)	83.2 (4.65)	69.1 (1.07)	69.6 (1.32)	60.8 (3.41)	69.0 (2.05)	88.5 (2.48)	8.8! (3.66)	‡ (†)	-18.9 (2.81)
2016[6]	69.8 (1.64)	69.7 (2.34)	57.3 (6.11)	72.0 (3.24)	91.9 (3.65)	68.6 (1.02)	70.1 (1.28)	57.5 (3.44)	67.6 (2.20)	85.7 (2.60)	12.6 (3.67)	‡ (†)	-15.7 (2.90)
2017[6]	66.7 (1.68)	69.1 (2.09)	59.4 (4.79)	61.0 (3.98)	82.7 (5.20)	68.6 (1.00)	69.9 (1.23)	60.7 (2.86)	66.5 (2.19)	82.0 (2.96)	9.2! (3.11)	‡ (†)	-12.1 (3.20)
2018[6]	69.1 (1.62)	70.9 (1.93)	64.5 (4.37)	65.4 (3.59)	73.6 (5.64)	68.0 (1.19)	70.0 (1.42)	62.1 (3.22)	63.4 (2.58)	77.9 (3.74)	7.9! (3.52)	6.6! (2.95)	‡ (†)

—Not available.
†Not applicable.
!Interpret data with caution. The coefficient of variation (CV) for this estimate is between 30 and 50 percent.
‡Reporting standards not met. The coefficient of variation (CV) for this estimate is 50 percent or greater.
[1]Individuals ages 16 to 24 who graduated from high school or completed a GED or other high school equivalency credential.
[2]Enrollment in college as of October of each year for individuals ages 16 to 24 who had completed high school earlier in the calendar year.
[3]A 3-year moving average is a weighted average of the year indicated, the year immediately preceding, and the year immediately following. For the first and final years of available data, a 2-year moving average is used: The moving average for 1960 reflects an average of 1960 and 1961; for Black and Hispanic data, the moving average for 1972 reflects an average of 1972 and 1973; for Asian data, the moving average for 2003 reflects an average of 2003 and 2004; and the moving average for 2018 reflects an average of 2017 and 2018. Moving averages are used to produce more stable estimates.
[4]Prior to 2003, Asian data include Pacific Islanders.
[5]Prior to 1972, White data include persons of Hispanic ethnicity.
[6]After 2002, White, Black, and Asian data exclude persons of Two or more races.
NOTE: Data are based on sample surveys of the civilian noninstitutionalized population. Includes enrollment in 2-year colleges and in 4-year colleges and universities. Race categories exclude persons of Hispanic ethnicity except where otherwise noted. Total includes persons of other racial/ethnic groups not separately shown. Prior to 2010, standard errors were computed using generalized variance function methodology rather than the more precise replicate weight methodology used in later years. Some data have been revised from previously published figures.
SOURCE: American College Testing Program, unpublished tabulations, derived from statistics collected by the Census Bureau, 1960 through 1969. U.S. Department of Commerce, Census Bureau, Current Population Survey (CPS), October, 1970 through 2018. (This table was prepared August 2019.)

Table 302.40. Number of high schools with 12th-graders and percentage of high school graduates attending 4-year colleges, by selected high school characteristics: Selected years, 1998–99 through 2011–12

[Standard errors appear in parentheses]

Selected high school characteristic	Number of high schools with 12th-graders				Graduation rate of 12th-graders in 2010–11[1]	Percent of graduates attending 4-year colleges			
	1998–99	2002–03	2006–07	2010–11		1998–99 graduates attending in 1999–2000	2002–03 graduates attending in 2003–04	2006–07 graduates attending in 2007–08	2010–11 graduates attending in 2011–12
1	2	3	4	5	6	7	8	9	10
Public high schools	**20,000 (230)**	**22,500 (400)**	**24,100 (540)**	**23,300 (330)**	**88.7 (0.90)**	**35.4 (0.43)**	**35.0 (0.61)**	**39.5 (0.91)**	**39.4 (0.59)**
Percent of students who are Black, Hispanic, Asian, Pacific Islander, American Indian/Alaska Native, or of Two or more races									
Less than 5 percent	6,400 (170)	6,100 (220)	5,200 (270)	3,600 (140)	94.7 (1.19)	41.3 (0.67)	42.6 (0.96)	46.8 (1.54)	43.9 (1.40)
5 to 19 percent	4,800 (180)	5,200 (270)	5,400 (320)	5,700 (310)	92.4 (2.55)	36.6 (0.88)	38.0 (1.77)	48.4 (2.06)	44.9 (1.02)
20 to 49 percent	4,000 (170)	4,700 (180)	6,200 (440)	5,900 (270)	91.2 (1.14)	32.5 (0.92)	34.1 (1.27)	35.0 (1.89)	39.6 (1.31)
50 percent or more	4,800 (150)	6,500 (280)	7,300 (430)	8,100 (320)	81.7 (1.58)	28.7 (0.89)	25.8 (1.43)	30.8 (2.00)	33.0 (1.17)
Percent of students approved for free or reduced-price lunch									
School does not participate	2,400 (130)	2,400 (230)	2,800 (320)	1,900 (250)	72.8 (7.11)	30.0 (1.75)	23.2 (2.26)	25.4 (4.12)	27.6 (5.24)
0 to 25 percent	8,600 (180)	6,800 (230)	6,700 (360)	5,100 (220)	93.3 (1.02)	42.6 (0.67)	46.9 (0.78)	52.1 (1.63)	50.7 (1.42)
26 to 50 percent	4,800 (160)	6,700 (220)	7,300 (350)	6,800 (230)	92.8 (0.91)	33.4 (0.81)	36.7 (1.08)	41.5 (1.44)	42.5 (1.00)
51 to 75 percent	2,300 (140)	4,000 (270)	4,100 (290)	5,100 (260)	90.3 (1.06)	29.1 (1.57)	27.3 (1.58)	33.2 (1.91)	35.8 (1.35)
76 to 100 percent	2,000 (100)	2,600 (260)	3,300 (360)	4,300 (230)	82.3 (1.93)	22.2 (1.35)	20.7 (2.79)	26.0 (2.93)	29.1 (1.66)
School locale									
City	— (†)	4,500 (240)	4,800 (300)	5,100 (220)	81.3 (3.11)	— (†)	32.5 (1.61)	36.1 (2.73)	38.6 (1.53)
Suburb	— (†)	4,800 (200)	5,400 (360)	4,800 (160)	86.1 (1.50)	— (†)	40.3 (1.11)	41.2 (2.35)	42.2 (1.42)
Town	— (†)	3,700 (200)	3,900 (310)	3,300 (260)	89.9 (2.21)	— (†)	31.1 (1.65)	35.2 (2.28)	35.3 (1.76)
Rural	— (†)	9,500 (390)	10,000 (460)	10,100 (260)	93.4 (0.67)	— (†)	35.2 (1.28)	41.9 (1.47)	39.8 (0.88)
Private high schools	**7,600 (240)**	**8,200 (260)**	**8,900 (280)**	**8,900 (310)**	**92.4 (1.34)**	**55.6 (1.74)**	**56.2 (1.77)**	**66.5 (1.57)**	**64.3 (2.10)**
Percent of students who are Black, Hispanic, Asian, Pacific Islander, American Indian/Alaska Native, or of Two or more races									
Less than 5 percent	2,700 (150)	2,500 (180)	2,100 (160)	1,600 (190)	96.1 (1.72)	53.3 (2.85)	54.4 (3.31)	68.2 (3.81)	58.0 (6.31)
5 to 19 percent	2,500 (130)	2,900 (170)	3,500 (200)	3,100 (230)	95.1 (1.90)	63.6 (2.37)	64.2 (2.71)	70.3 (2.24)	67.9 (3.40)
20 to 49 percent	1,400 (100)	1,700 (140)	2,000 (190)	2,200 (200)	90.4 (2.33)	55.3 (3.29)	56.7 (3.70)	58.7 (3.39)	69.4 (3.89)
50 percent or more	1,000 (110)	1,100 (140)	1,400 (130)	1,900 (190)	87.1 (3.49)	41.6 (5.34)	38.3 (4.52)	65.3 (3.37)	57.6 (5.18)
Percent of students approved for free or reduced-price lunch									
School does not participate	6,700 (230)	7,100 (250)	7,300 (280)	7,400 (280)	93.3 (1.27)	57.0 (1.74)	56.2 (2.00)	68.3 (1.77)	66.5 (2.29)
0 to 25 percent	700 (70)	600 (80)	700 (100)	600 (80)	96.8 (2.45)	53.8 (5.69)	66.2 (4.35)	73.2 (4.64)	74.6 (5.23)
26 to 100 percent	‡ (†)	400 (80)	1,000 (130)	900 (140)	83.0 (5.65)	‡ (†)	38.9 (6.70)	46.7 (6.86)	37.8 (8.06)
School locale									
City	— (†)	— (†)	3,100 (170)	‡ (†)	‡ (†)	— (†)	— (†)	71.8 (2.62)	‡ (†)
Suburb	— (†)	— (†)	2,800 (180)	‡ (†)	‡ (†)	— (†)	— (†)	67.0 (2.99)	‡ (†)
Town	— (†)	— (†)	1,000 (150)	‡ (†)	‡ (†)	— (†)	— (†)	63.8 (5.02)	‡ (†)
Rural	— (†)	— (†)	2,000 (190)	‡ (†)	‡ (†)	— (†)	— (†)	58.9 (3.54)	‡ (†)

—Not available.
†Not applicable.
‡Reporting standards not met. Data may be suppressed because the response rate is under 50 percent, there are too few cases for a reliable estimate, or the coefficient of variation (CV) is 50 percent or greater.
[1]The 12th-grade graduation rate is the number of students who graduated from grade 12 with a diploma during the 2010–11 school year divided by 12th-grade enrollment in October 2010.

NOTE: Data are based on a sample survey and may not be strictly comparable with data reported elsewhere. Includes all schools, including combined schools, with students enrolled in the 12th grade. Some data have been revised from previously published figures. Detail may not sum to totals because of rounding.
SOURCE: U.S. Department of Education, National Center for Education Statistics, Schools and Staffing Survey (SASS), "Public School Teacher Data File" and "Private School Teacher Data File," 1999–2000, 2003–04, 2007–08, and 2011–12; and "Charter School Teacher Data File," 1999–2000. (This table was prepared April 2014.)

Table 302.43. Percentage distribution of fall 2009 ninth-graders who had completed high school, by postsecondary enrollment status in fall 2013, and selected measures of their high school achievement and selected student characteristics: 2013

[Standard errors appear in parentheses]

Selected student characteristic	All students who had completed high school		Students not enrolled in a postsecondary institution		Students enrolled in a postsecondary institution: Total enrolled in a postsecondary institution		Enrolled in a degree or certificate program: Total, all programs		Occupational certificate program[1]		Associate's degree program		Bachelor's degree program		Taking classes only, not enrolled in program	
1	2		3		4		5		6		7		8		9	
	Percentage distribution															
Total	**100.0**	**(†)**	**25.5**	**(0.85)**	**74.5**	**(0.85)**	**60.1**	**(0.88)**	**3.3**	**(0.27)**	**25.0**	**(0.60)**	**31.8**	**(0.85)**	**14.5**	**(0.56)**
Sex																
Male	100.0	(†)	30.0	(1.22)	70.0	(1.22)	56.6	(1.32)	3.4	(0.41)	23.1	(0.84)	30.1	(1.07)	13.4	(0.76)
Female	100.0	(†)	21.0	(0.92)	79.0	(0.92)	63.5	(0.96)	3.3	(0.34)	26.8	(0.80)	33.4	(0.97)	15.5	(0.77)
Race/ethnicity																
White	100.0	(†)	23.4	(0.81)	76.6	(0.81)	65.1	(0.83)	3.1	(0.33)	23.3	(0.75)	38.7	(1.01)	11.6	(0.54)
Black	100.0	(†)	28.8	(2.11)	71.2	(2.11)	52.9	(2.73)	3.3	(0.78)	25.9	(1.93)	23.8	(2.37)	18.3	(1.97)
Hispanic	100.0	(†)	30.0	(2.36)	70.0	(2.36)	51.5	(2.07)	4.1	(0.74)	29.1	(1.74)	18.3	(1.38)	18.4	(1.59)
Asian	100.0	(†)	10.2	(2.38)	89.8	(2.38)	73.6	(2.74)	0.9 !	(0.37)	22.5	(2.46)	50.1	(3.57)	16.2	(2.21)
Pacific Islander	100.0	(†)	‡	(†)	80.2	(10.01)	39.9 !	(13.24)	‡	(†)	‡	(†)	17.7 !	(7.74)	40.3 !	(15.26)
American Indian/Alaska Native	100.0	(†)	27.5	(7.09)	72.5	(7.09)	60.6	(6.79)	16.1 !	(7.64)	22.0 !	(7.58)	22.5 !	(10.09)	11.9 !	(5.06)
Two or more races	100.0	(†)	28.8	(2.52)	71.2	(2.52)	56.4	(2.44)	3.2 !	(1.08)	25.2	(1.97)	28.0	(2.18)	14.8	(1.89)
Socioeconomic status (SES)[2]																
Low SES	100.0	(†)	41.1	(1.89)	58.9	(1.89)	40.8	(2.11)	5.3	(0.80)	23.1	(1.57)	12.3	(1.39)	18.2	(1.68)
Middle SES	100.0	(†)	26.7	(1.00)	73.3	(1.00)	58.4	(1.04)	3.4	(0.36)	27.4	(0.79)	27.6	(0.92)	14.9	(0.67)
High SES	100.0	(†)	8.4	(0.67)	91.6	(0.67)	81.5	(1.01)	1.4	(0.36)	19.8	(0.98)	60.4	(1.36)	10.1	(0.82)
Highest mathematics course completed in high school																
Algebra I or below	100.0	(†)	56.2	(3.79)	43.8	(3.79)	28.7	(3.01)	9.5	(1.93)	15.5	(2.23)	3.7 !	(1.33)	15.0	(2.67)
Geometry	100.0	(†)	53.5	(3.39)	46.5	(3.39)	30.5	(2.57)	5.0	(1.17)	21.5	(2.58)	4.0	(0.87)	16.0	(2.34)
Algebra II/trigonometry	100.0	(†)	31.2	(1.39)	68.8	(1.39)	52.2	(1.37)	4.6	(0.69)	29.7	(1.31)	17.9	(1.23)	16.6	(1.05)
Other math[3]	100.0	(†)	25.5	(1.77)	74.5	(1.77)	60.3	(1.82)	3.2	(0.48)	29.7	(1.58)	27.5	(1.54)	14.2	(1.18)
Precalculus	100.0	(†)	11.7	(1.07)	88.3	(1.07)	72.8	(1.28)	1.5	(0.31)	24.7	(1.15)	46.6	(1.47)	15.5	(0.96)
Calculus[4]	100.0	(†)	5.1	(0.89)	94.9	(0.89)	86.7	(1.44)	0.6 !	(0.26)	16.4	(1.34)	69.8	(1.72)	8.2	(1.04)
Ever took dual enrollment course(s) in high school	100.0	(†)	9.3	(0.93)	90.7	(0.93)	79.9	(1.27)	1.8	(0.39)	29.2	(1.33)	48.9	(1.44)	10.8	(0.96)
As 9th-grader, expected to complete																
High school or less	100.0	(†)	47.0	(2.49)	53.0	(2.49)	36.4	(2.29)	4.8	(1.24)	21.7	(1.83)	9.9	(2.15)	16.6	(2.00)
Some college	100.0	(†)	33.0	(2.66)	67.0	(2.66)	49.9	(3.28)	7.1	(1.17)	29.0	(2.89)	13.8	(1.82)	17.1	(2.33)
Bachelor's or graduate/professional degree	100.0	(†)	17.1	(0.75)	82.9	(0.75)	69.7	(0.90)	2.3	(0.28)	25.9	(0.75)	41.6	(0.94)	13.1	(0.60)
Bachelor's degree	100.0	(†)	41.7	(1.92)	58.3	(1.92)	41.5	(1.84)	5.7	(0.83)	24.5	(1.53)	11.4	(1.39)	16.8	(1.38)
Graduate or professional degree	100.0	(†)	20.2	(1.23)	79.8	(1.23)	65.8	(1.72)	2.1	(0.41)	26.6	(1.46)	37.1	(1.72)	14.0	(1.40)
Don't know	100.0	(†)	15.8	(0.89)	84.2	(0.89)	71.4	(1.02)	2.3	(0.35)	25.5	(0.93)	43.5	(1.22)	12.8	(0.72)
As of spring of 11th grade, had taken the following at least once																
PSAT or PLAN	100.0	(†)	18.5	(0.81)	81.5	(0.81)	68.1	(0.91)	2.4	(0.27)	24.3	(0.74)	41.4	(0.99)	13.4	(0.66)
SAT or ACT	100.0	(†)	19.0	(1.12)	81.0	(1.12)	68.0	(1.27)	3.3	(0.47)	21.8	(0.94)	42.9	(1.34)	13.0	(0.86)
Any Advanced Placement (AP) test	100.0	(†)	15.8	(1.24)	84.2	(1.24)	71.0	(1.42)	3.1	(0.71)	21.8	(1.22)	46.1	(1.60)	13.2	(1.13)
Any International Baccalaureate(IB) test	100.0	(†)	18.8	(3.72)	81.2	(3.72)	63.9	(5.05)	‡	(†)	21.1	(5.01)	31.2	(5.85)	17.3	(3.95)
As 11th-grader, thought would qualify for this type of financial aid																
Aid based on financial need	100.0	(†)	26.8	(1.03)	73.2	(1.03)	57.2	(1.13)	3.6	(0.35)	28.2	(0.97)	25.4	(0.90)	16.0	(0.91)
Aid based on academic achievement such as good grades or college admission test scores	100.0	(†)	17.0	(0.73)	83.0	(0.73)	69.3	(0.97)	2.3	(0.28)	25.4	(0.81)	41.6	(0.94)	13.7	(0.69)
Aid through an athletic scholarship	100.0	(†)	23.3	(1.57)	76.7	(1.57)	62.0	(1.84)	2.8	(0.58)	26.9	(1.66)	32.4	(1.67)	14.7	(1.29)
Federal or state loans	100.0	(†)	24.0	(1.09)	76.0	(1.09)	60.4	(1.14)	3.8	(0.43)	27.4	(0.98)	29.3	(0.97)	15.6	(0.90)
Private loans	100.0	(†)	21.9	(1.25)	78.1	(1.25)	64.0	(1.42)	3.0	(0.50)	26.3	(1.35)	34.7	(1.40)	14.2	(1.04)
Completed a Free Application for Federal Student Aid (FAFSA)	100.0	(†)	11.1	(0.62)	88.9	(0.62)	74.8	(0.84)	3.4	(0.35)	30.4	(0.72)	41.0	(1.01)	14.0	(0.66)
For students who did not complete a FAFSA, did not do so because student or family																
Did not want to take on debt	100.0	(†)	47.2	(3.04)	52.8	(3.04)	38.4	(2.95)	4.8 !	(1.47)	15.6	(1.90)	18.0	(2.02)	14.4	(2.18)
Can afford without financial aid	100.0	(†)	31.3	(2.35)	68.7	(2.35)	55.0	(2.72)	2.6 !	(0.94)	21.6	(2.01)	30.7	(2.64)	13.8	(1.96)
Thought may be ineligible or not qualify	100.0	(†)	32.9	(2.67)	67.1	(2.67)	53.2	(2.57)	2.8 !	(0.92)	20.6	(2.05)	29.8	(2.26)	13.9	(1.82)
Thought would not qualify because																
Other family member didn't qualify	100.0	(†)	33.1	(6.16)	66.9	(6.16)	52.5	(5.61)	‡	(†)	22.6	(3.88)	28.3	(4.88)	14.4	(4.25)
Concerns about credit score	100.0	(†)	64.6	(7.70)	35.4	(7.70)	21.1	(5.01)	‡	(†)	17.2	(4.90)	‡	(†)	14.3 !	(6.15)
Family income too high	100.0	(†)	16.4	(2.42)	83.6	(2.42)	69.9	(2.79)	1.6 !	(0.64)	24.5	(2.66)	43.8	(2.85)	13.6	(2.09)

[Standard errors appear in parentheses]

Selected student characteristic	All students who had completed high school	Students not enrolled in a postsecondary institution	Students enrolled in a postsecondary institution: Total enrolled in a postsecondary institution	Enrolled in a degree or certificate program: Total, all programs	Occupational certificate program[1]	Associate's degree program	Bachelor's degree program	Taking classes only, not enrolled in program
1	2	3	4	5	6	7	8	9
Grades or test scores too low	100.0 (†)	60.7 (5.31)	39.3 (5.31)	22.7 (4.18)	‡ (†)	15.1 (3.96)	5.0 ! (2.04)	16.5 (3.55)
Part-time postsecondary enrollment	100.0 (†)	70.2 (5.94)	29.8 (5.94)	13.2 ! (4.69)	‡ (†)	10.6 ! (4.62)	‡ (†)	16.6 (4.91)
Did not have enough information about how to complete a FAFSA	100.0 (†)	56.2 (3.42)	43.8 (3.42)	29.3 (2.90)	4.5 (1.30)	18.2 (2.58)	6.7 (1.28)	14.5 (2.55)
Thought FAFSA forms too much work or too time-consuming	100.0 (†)	43.2 (4.83)	56.8 (4.83)	42.2 (4.67)	‡ (†)	18.6 (4.42)	19.5 (2.79)	14.7 (3.23)
Did not know you could complete a FAFSA	100.0 (†)	59.5 (4.12)	40.5 (4.12)	24.1 (3.29)	4.9 ! (1.86)	14.0 (2.44)	5.2 (1.45)	16.3 (3.32)
Not planning to continue education after high school	100.0 (†)	93.4 (1.89)	6.6 (1.89)	3.2 ! (0.97)	‡ (†)	1.8 ! (0.81)	‡ (†)	3.4 ! (1.61)
			Selected measures of high school achievement					
Total number of credits earned in high school[5]	25.8 (0.12)	23.9 (0.21)	26.4 (0.13)	26.6 (0.14)	24.2 (0.54)	26.1 (0.18)	27.3 (0.20)	25.6 (0.28)
Overall GPA earned in high school[6]	2.8 (0.01)	2.3 (0.02)	3.0 (0.01)	3.0 (0.01)	2.4 (0.06)	2.8 (0.02)	3.3 (0.01)	2.6 (0.03)
Average SAT/ACT score (standardized to SAT)[7]	988 (6.5)	854 (10.4)	1008 (6.4)	1023 (5.9)	811 (29.7)	936 (7.3)	1083 (6.4)	922 (14.1)

†Not applicable.

!Interpret data with caution. The coefficient of variation (CV) for this estimate is between 30 and 50 percent.

‡Reporting standards not met. Either there are too few cases for a reliable estimate or the coefficient of variation (CV) is 50 percent or greater.

[1] A certificate or diploma program at a school that provides occupational training. Such a program usually takes 2 years or less to complete and often leads to a license, such as cosmetology.

[2] SES was measured by a composite score based on parental education and occupations, family income, and school urbanicity in the student's 11th-grade year. The weighted SES distribution (weighted by W2STUDENT) was divided into five equal groups. Low SES corresponds to the lowest one-fifth of the population, and high SES corresponds to the highest one-fifth of the population. The three fifths in the middle were combined to form the middle SES category.

[3] Includes integrated math, algebra III, probability and statistics, and non-calculus Advanced Placement (AP) or International Baccalaureate (IB) courses.

[4] Includes AP/IB calculus.

[5] Ranges from 0 to 59.

[6] Includes all courses and ranges from 0 to 4.

[7] The average applies to all students who took the SAT or ACT. For those who took the SAT, the combined critical reading and mathematics score was used. For those who took the ACT, scores were converted to the equivalent of the SAT combined score. Scale ranges from 400 to 1600.

NOTE: Includes students who completed high school by September 2013. Estimates weighted by W3W1W2STUTR. Race categories exclude persons of Hispanic ethnicity. Detail may not sum to totals because of rounding.

SOURCE: U.S. Department of Education, National Center for Education Statistics, High School Longitudinal Study of 2009 (HSLS:09), Base-Year, First Follow-up, 2013 Update, and High School Transcripts Restricted-Use Data File. (This table was prepared January 2016.)

Table 302.50. Estimated rate of 2011–12 high school graduates attending degree-granting postsecondary institutions, by state: 2012

State	Number of graduates from high schools located in the state			Number of fall 2012 first-time freshmen graduating from high school in the previous 12 months		Estimated rate of high school graduates going to college	
	Total[1]	Public, 2011–12	Private, 2012–13	State residents enrolled in institutions in any state[2]	State residents enrolled in institutions in their home state[3]	In any state	In their home state
1	2	3	4	5	6	7	8
United States	**3,457,955**	**3,149,185**	**308,770**	**2,132,264[4]**	**1,729,792**	**61.7**	**50.0**
Alabama	50,164	45,394	4,770	29,728	26,567	59.3	53.0
Alaska	8,189	7,989	200	3,732	2,413	45.6	29.5
Arizona	66,218	63,208	3,010	35,181	31,132	53.1	47.0
Arkansas	30,019	28,419	1,600	20,185	18,244	67.2	60.8
California	451,364	418,664	32,700	263,843	231,215	58.5	51.2
Colorado	52,607	50,087	2,520	31,139	23,268	59.2	44.2
Connecticut	44,751	38,681	6,070	31,662	17,396	70.8	38.9
Delaware	10,037	8,247	1,790	6,500	4,632	64.8	46.1
District of Columbia[5]	5,680	3,860	1,820	2,463	450	43.4	7.9
Florida	171,404	151,964	19,440	107,716	94,985	62.8	55.4
Georgia	99,952	90,582	9,370	66,494	55,399	66.5	55.4
Hawaii	13,970	11,360	2,610	9,040	6,091	64.7	43.6
Idaho	18,238	17,568	670	8,782	6,179	48.2	33.9
Illinois	153,605	139,575	14,030	92,394	63,610	60.2	41.4
Indiana	70,767	65,667	5,100	44,612	38,812	63.0	54.8
Iowa	41,550	33,230	2,400	23,488	20,340	56.5	49.0
Kansas	34,078	31,898	2,180	22,239	19,058	65.3	55.9
Kentucky	47,442	42,642	4,800	29,830	26,624	62.9	56.1
Louisiana	44,575	36,675	7,900	28,831	26,024	64.7	58.4
Maine	16,103	13,473	2,630	8,681	5,829	53.9	36.2
Maryland	67,781	58,811	8,970	41,033	25,773	60.5	38.0
Massachusetts	76,177	65,157	11,020	53,836	36,132	70.7	47.4
Michigan	115,256	105,446	9,810	70,843	63,296	61.5	54.9
Minnesota	61,891	57,501	4,390	43,264	30,237	69.9	48.9
Mississippi	29,748	26,158	3,590	23,436	21,752	78.8	73.1
Missouri	69,053	61,313	7,740	42,762	35,648	61.9	51.6
Montana	10,140	9,750	390	5,907	4,598	58.3	45.3
Nebraska	22,844	20,464	2,380	14,750	11,969	64.6	52.4
Nevada	22,731	21,891	840	12,288	9,310	54.1	41.0
New Hampshire	16,886	14,426	2,460	10,418	5,618	61.7	33.3
New Jersey	106,919	93,819	13,100	72,631	41,204	67.9	38.5
New Mexico	21,375	20,315	1,060	14,831	12,903	69.4	60.4
New York	209,216	180,806	28,410	146,458	117,960	70.0	56.4
North Carolina	101,097	93,977	7,120	62,531	55,578	61.9	55.0
North Dakota	7,322	6,942	380	4,751	3,527	64.9	48.2
Ohio	135,885	123,135	12,750	81,428	69,039	59.9	50.8
Oklahoma	39,295	37,305	1,990	22,667	20,207	57.7	51.4
Oregon	37,301	34,261	3,040	17,509	13,343	46.9	35.8
Pennsylvania	146,493	131,733	14,760	87,075	70,625	59.4	48.2
Rhode Island	11,501	9,751	1,750	7,715	5,056	67.1	44.0
South Carolina	44,452	41,442	3,010	29,023	26,154	65.3	58.8
South Dakota	8,456	8,196	260	5,825	4,443	68.9	52.5
Tennessee	67,964	62,454	5,510	41,027	34,318	60.4	50.5
Texas	306,591	292,531	14,060	176,871	156,566	57.7	51.1
Utah	32,757	31,157	1,600	16,650	15,101	50.8	46.1
Vermont	7,789	6,859	930	4,142	2,040	53.2	26.2
Virginia	89,866	83,336	6,530	58,035	47,582	64.6	52.9
Washington	71,165	65,205	5,960	34,168	25,854	48.0	36.3
West Virginia	18,383	17,603	780	10,241	9,110	55.7	49.6
Wisconsin	71,225	62,705	8,520	41,715	33,972	58.6	47.7
Wyoming	5,603	5,553	50	3,170	2,426	56.6	43.3

[1]Total includes public high school graduates for 2011–12 and private high school graduates for 2012–13. Data on private high school graduates are not available for 2011–12.

[2]All U.S. resident students living in a particular state when admitted to an institution in any state. Students may be enrolled in any state.

[3]Students who attend institutions in their home state. Total includes 183 students attending U.S. Service Academies in their home state, not shown separately.

[4]U.S. total includes some U.S. residents whose home state is unknown.

[5]A percentage of the private high school graduates are not residents of the District of Columbia.

NOTE: Degree-granting institutions grant associate's or higher degrees and participate in Title IV federal financial aid programs. Detail may not sum to totals because of rounding.

SOURCE: U.S. Department of Education, National Center for Education Statistics, Common Core of Data (CCD), "NCES Common Core of Data State Dropout and Completion Data File," 2011–12; Private School Universe Survey (PSS), 2013–14; and Integrated Postsecondary Education Data System (IPEDS), Spring 2013, Fall Enrollment component. (This table was prepared January 2016.)

Table 302.60. Percentage of 18- to 24-year-olds enrolled in college, by level of institution and sex and race/ethnicity of student: 1970 through 2018

[Standard errors appear in parentheses]

Year	Total, all students	Level of institution		Sex		Race/ethnicity							Race/ethnicity, by sex					
													White		Black		Hispanic	
		2-year college	4-year college or university	Male	Female	White	Black	Hispanic	Asian[1]	Pacific Islander	American Indian/ Alaska Native	Two or more races	Male	Female	Male	Female	Male	Female
1	2	3	4	5	6	7	8	9	10	11	12	13	14	15	16	17	18	19
1970[2]	25.7 (0.42)	— (†)	— (†)	32.1 (0.67)	20.3 (0.53)	27.1 (0.46)	15.5 (1.18)	— (†)	— (†)	— (†)	— (†)	— (†)	— (†)	— (†)	— (†)	— (†)	— (†)	— (†)
1971[2]	26.2 (0.42)	— (†)	— (†)	32.5 (0.65)	20.8 (0.53)	27.2 (0.45)	18.2 (1.22)	— (†)	— (†)	— (†)	— (†)	— (†)	— (†)	— (†)	— (†)	— (†)	— (†)	— (†)
1972	25.5 (0.40)	— (†)	— (†)	30.2 (0.62)	21.2 (0.52)	27.2 (0.46)	18.3 (1.20)	13.4 (2.42)	— (†)	— (†)	— (†)	— (†)	32.3 (0.69)	22.5 (0.60)	21.1 (1.87)	15.9 (1.55)	15.1 (3.77)	12.0 (3.13)
1973	24.0 (0.39)	6.9 (0.23)	17.1 (0.34)	27.7 (0.59)	20.5 (0.51)	25.5 (0.44)	15.9 (1.11)	16.1 (2.66)	— (†)	— (†)	— (†)	— (†)	29.6 (0.67)	21.8 (0.58)	18.7 (1.75)	13.5 (1.42)	16.7 (3.88)	15.5 (3.66)
1974	24.6 (0.39)	7.6 (0.24)	17.0 (0.34)	27.7 (0.59)	21.7 (0.52)	25.8 (0.44)	17.6 (1.17)	18.0 (2.57)	— (†)	— (†)	— (†)	— (†)	28.9 (0.66)	22.9 (0.59)	19.8 (1.82)	15.9 (1.51)	19.7 (3.85)	16.5 (3.44)
1975	26.3 (0.39)	9.0 (0.26)	17.3 (0.34)	29.0 (0.58)	23.7 (0.53)	27.4 (0.44)	20.4 (1.21)	20.4 (2.75)	— (†)	— (†)	— (†)	— (†)	30.7 (0.66)	24.3 (0.60)	19.9 (1.78)	20.8 (1.65)	21.4 (4.10)	19.5 (3.71)
1976	26.7 (0.39)	6.4 (0.22)	20.2 (0.36)	28.2 (0.57)	25.2 (0.53)	27.6 (0.44)	22.5 (1.23)	20.0 (2.64)	— (†)	— (†)	— (†)	— (†)	29.3 (0.64)	26.1 (0.61)	22.0 (1.82)	22.9 (1.68)	21.3 (4.02)	18.8 (3.48)
1977	26.1 (0.39)	6.8 (0.22)	19.4 (0.35)	28.1 (0.57)	24.3 (0.52)	27.2 (0.44)	21.1 (1.19)	17.2 (2.45)	— (†)	— (†)	— (†)	— (†)	29.4 (0.64)	25.1 (0.60)	20.3 (1.74)	21.9 (1.63)	18.3 (3.66)	16.3 (3.28)
1978	25.3 (0.38)	6.6 (0.22)	18.7 (0.34)	27.1 (0.56)	23.6 (0.52)	26.5 (0.43)	20.1 (1.16)	15.2 (2.28)	— (†)	— (†)	— (†)	— (†)	28.4 (0.63)	24.6 (0.59)	19.7 (1.72)	20.4 (1.57)	16.1 (3.42)	14.3 (3.05)
1979	25.0 (0.38)	6.3 (0.21)	18.7 (0.34)	25.9 (0.55)	24.2 (0.52)	26.3 (0.43)	19.8 (1.14)	16.7 (2.31)	— (†)	— (†)	— (†)	— (†)	27.1 (0.62)	25.5 (0.60)	19.1 (1.69)	20.3 (1.55)	18.3 (3.47)	15.2 (3.08)
1980	25.7 (0.38)	7.1 (0.22)	18.6 (0.34)	26.4 (0.55)	25.0 (0.52)	27.3 (0.44)	19.4 (1.13)	16.1 (2.15)	— (†)	— (†)	— (†)	— (†)	28.4 (0.63)	26.3 (0.60)	17.5 (1.62)	20.9 (1.57)	15.9 (3.05)	16.2 (3.04)
1981	26.1 (0.38)	7.5 (0.22)	18.6 (0.33)	27.1 (0.54)	25.2 (0.52)	27.7 (0.43)	19.9 (1.10)	16.6 (2.14)	— (†)	— (†)	— (†)	— (†)	28.7 (0.62)	26.6 (0.60)	18.9 (1.60)	20.7 (1.52)	16.6 (3.08)	16.7 (2.97)
1982	26.6 (0.40)	7.7 (0.24)	18.9 (0.35)	27.2 (0.58)	26.0 (0.56)	28.1 (0.46)	19.9 (1.16)	16.8 (2.30)	— (†)	— (†)	— (†)	— (†)	28.9 (0.67)	27.4 (0.64)	18.7 (1.66)	21.0 (1.61)	14.9 (3.19)	18.6 (3.29)
1983	26.2 (0.40)	7.4 (0.24)	18.8 (0.36)	27.3 (0.58)	25.1 (0.55)	27.9 (0.47)	19.2 (1.14)	17.3 (2.31)	— (†)	— (†)	— (†)	— (†)	29.4 (0.67)	26.5 (0.64)	18.1 (1.63)	20.1 (1.59)	15.6 (3.21)	18.8 (3.31)
1984	27.1 (0.41)	7.3 (0.24)	19.8 (0.37)	28.6 (0.59)	25.6 (0.56)	28.9 (0.48)	20.3 (1.16)	17.9 (2.35)	— (†)	— (†)	— (†)	— (†)	30.8 (0.69)	27.1 (0.66)	20.3 (1.70)	20.3 (1.60)	16.1 (3.27)	19.6 (3.35)
1985	27.8 (0.42)	7.4 (0.24)	20.4 (0.38)	28.4 (0.60)	27.2 (0.58)	30.0 (0.49)	19.6 (1.17)	16.9 (1.85)	— (†)	— (†)	— (†)	— (†)	30.9 (0.71)	29.2 (0.68)	20.2 (1.74)	19.1 (1.58)	14.9 (2.46)	18.9 (2.75)
1986	27.9 (0.42)	7.6 (0.25)	20.3 (0.38)	28.2 (0.61)	27.6 (0.59)	29.7 (0.50)	21.9 (1.23)	17.6 (1.77)	— (†)	— (†)	— (†)	— (†)	30.6 (0.73)	28.8 (0.69)	20.0 (1.75)	23.4 (1.72)	16.7 (2.37)	18.7 (2.65)
1987	29.6 (0.44)	8.1 (0.26)	21.5 (0.39)	30.6 (0.63)	28.7 (0.60)	31.9 (0.52)	22.8 (1.26)	17.5 (1.74)	— (†)	— (†)	— (†)	— (†)	33.0 (0.75)	30.8 (0.72)	22.6 (1.86)	22.9 (1.72)	18.5 (2.47)	16.5 (2.44)
1988	30.3 (0.48)	8.8 (0.30)	21.5 (0.43)	30.2 (0.69)	30.4 (0.67)	33.2 (0.58)	21.2 (1.35)	17.0 (1.90)	— (†)	— (†)	— (†)	— (†)	33.4 (0.83)	33.0 (0.80)	18.5 (1.90)	23.5 (1.91)	16.5 (2.60)	17.6 (2.77)
1989	30.9 (0.46)	8.0 (0.27)	22.9 (0.42)	30.2 (0.66)	31.6 (0.65)	34.2 (0.56)	23.4 (1.32)	16.1 (1.66)	46.1 (3.77)	— (†)	15.7! (5.13)	— (†)	34.1 (0.80)	34.4 (0.79)	19.7 (1.82)	26.7 (1.89)	14.6 (2.23)	17.6 (2.47)
1990	32.0 (0.47)	8.7 (0.28)	23.3 (0.43)	32.3 (0.68)	31.8 (0.66)	35.1 (0.57)	25.4 (1.37)	15.8 (1.67)	56.9 (3.56)	— (†)	15.8! (5.07)	— (†)	35.5 (0.82)	34.7 (0.80)	26.0 (2.03)	24.8 (1.85)	15.3 (2.31)	16.4 (2.42)
1991	33.3 (0.48)	9.7 (0.30)	23.6 (0.43)	32.8 (0.68)	33.6 (0.67)	36.8 (0.58)	23.5 (1.34)	17.9 (1.72)	57.1 (3.19)	— (†)	15.9! (5.45)	— (†)	36.5 (0.83)	37.0 (0.82)	23.2 (1.95)	23.8 (1.84)	14.0 (2.15)	22.2 (2.70)
1992	34.4 (0.49)	9.9 (0.31)	24.4 (0.44)	32.7 (0.68)	36.0 (0.69)	37.3 (0.59)	25.2 (1.36)	21.3 (1.87)	58.4 (3.27)	— (†)	18.5! (6.17)	— (†)	36.2 (0.83)	38.3 (0.83)	21.3 (1.87)	28.8 (1.96)	17.8 (2.47)	24.7 (2.80)
1993	34.0 (0.49)	9.8 (0.30)	24.2 (0.44)	33.6 (0.69)	34.4 (0.68)	36.8 (0.59)	24.5 (1.35)	21.7 (1.88)	61.2 (3.26)	— (†)	18.9 (5.65)	— (†)	36.5 (0.84)	37.1 (0.83)	22.9 (1.92)	26.0 (1.90)	19.7 (2.59)	23.7 (2.71)
1994	34.6 (0.48)	9.1 (0.29)	25.5 (0.44)	33.1 (0.67)	36.0 (0.68)	38.1 (0.59)	27.7 (1.38)	18.8 (1.58)	62.7 (3.31)	— (†)	29.4 (6.65)	— (†)	37.0 (0.84)	39.2 (0.84)	25.6 (1.95)	29.5 (1.94)	16.5 (2.04)	21.5 (2.44)
1995	34.3 (0.45)	8.9 (0.27)	25.4 (0.41)	33.1 (0.63)	35.5 (0.63)	37.9 (0.55)	27.5 (1.18)	20.7 (1.13)	54.6 (3.11)	— (†)	27.6 (6.16)	— (†)	37.0 (0.78)	38.8 (0.78)	26.0 (1.72)	28.7 (1.63)	18.7 (1.50)	23.0 (1.72)
1996	35.5 (0.47)	9.5 (0.29)	26.1 (0.43)	34.1 (0.66)	37.0 (0.67)	39.5 (0.59)	27.4 (1.23)	20.1 (1.18)	53.9 (2.47)	— (†)	30.3 (5.24)	— (†)	38.3 (0.83)	40.6 (0.84)	25.7 (1.77)	28.8 (1.70)	16.5 (1.52)	24.0 (1.81)
1997	36.8 (0.47)	9.9 (0.29)	27.0 (0.43)	35.0 (0.66)	38.7 (0.67)	40.6 (0.59)	29.8 (1.25)	22.4 (1.21)	55.1 (2.60)	— (†)	27.1 (4.62)	— (†)	39.3 (0.82)	41.8 (0.84)	25.4 (1.75)	33.7 (1.77)	19.2 (1.56)	26.1 (1.88)
1998	36.5 (0.46)	10.2 (0.29)	26.3 (0.42)	34.5 (0.65)	38.6 (0.66)	40.6 (0.59)	29.8 (1.24)	20.4 (1.11)	60.4 (2.49)	— (†)	20.3 (4.90)	— (†)	39.4 (0.82)	41.9 (0.84)	26.1 (1.76)	32.9 (1.73)	16.4 (1.41)	24.9 (1.73)
1999	35.6 (0.46)	9.1 (0.27)	26.5 (0.42)	34.1 (0.64)	37.0 (0.65)	39.4 (0.58)	30.4 (1.24)	18.7 (1.08)	55.7 (2.42)	— (†)	19.5 (4.70)	— (†)	38.3 (0.81)	40.6 (0.82)	28.9 (1.81)	31.6 (1.69)	15.8 (1.41)	21.9 (1.65)
2000	35.5 (0.45)	9.4 (0.27)	26.0 (0.41)	32.6 (0.62)	38.4 (0.65)	38.7 (0.57)	30.5 (1.21)	21.7 (1.12)	55.9 (2.42)	— (†)	15.9 (4.30)	— (†)	36.2 (0.79)	41.3 (0.81)	25.1 (1.67)	35.2 (1.72)	18.5 (1.45)	25.4 (1.71)
2001	36.3 (0.43)	9.8 (0.26)	26.6 (0.39)	33.6 (0.59)	39.0 (0.61)	39.5 (0.54)	31.4 (1.15)	21.7 (1.04)	61.3 (2.23)	— (†)	23.3 (4.07)	— (†)	37.2 (0.75)	41.9 (0.77)	26.7 (1.62)	35.5 (1.62)	17.4 (1.35)	26.1 (1.58)
2002	36.7 (0.43)	9.7 (0.26)	27.0 (0.39)	33.7 (0.59)	39.7 (0.61)	40.9 (0.55)	31.9 (1.18)	19.9 (0.94)	60.9 (2.10)	— (†)	23.6 (3.96)	— (†)	38.9 (0.77)	42.8 (0.78)	26.3 (1.63)	36.9 (1.68)	16.2 (1.17)	24.4 (1.51)
2003[3]	37.8 (0.43)	10.2 (0.27)	27.7 (0.39)	34.3 (0.59)	41.3 (0.61)	41.6 (0.55)	32.3 (1.20)	23.5 (1.02)	61.2 (2.27)	43.3 (9.97)	17.7 (4.45)	41.6 (3.58)	38.5 (0.77)	44.5 (0.78)	28.2 (1.68)	36.0 (1.69)	18.3 (1.27)	29.4 (1.60)
2004[3]	38.0 (0.42)	9.4 (0.25)	28.6 (0.39)	34.7 (0.59)	41.2 (0.61)	41.7 (0.55)	31.8 (1.18)	24.7 (1.02)	60.6 (2.24)	55.8 (8.99)	24.4 (4.52)	36.8 (3.44)	38.4 (0.76)	45.0 (0.78)	26.5 (1.63)	36.6 (1.67)	21.7 (1.33)	28.2 (1.56)
2005[3]	38.9 (0.43)	9.6 (0.26)	29.2 (0.40)	35.3 (0.59)	42.5 (0.61)	42.8 (0.55)	33.1 (1.18)	24.8 (1.02)	61.0 (2.26)	50.6 (10.95)	27.8 (4.88)	41.8 (3.48)	39.4 (0.76)	46.1 (0.79)	28.2 (1.64)	37.6 (1.69)	20.7 (1.31)	29.5 (1.58)
2006[3]	37.3 (0.42)	9.6 (0.25)	27.8 (0.39)	34.1 (0.58)	40.6 (0.60)	41.0 (0.54)	32.6 (1.16)	23.6 (0.99)	58.3 (2.28)	39.1 (8.36)	26.2 (5.18)	38.5 (3.51)	37.9 (0.75)	44.1 (0.78)	28.1 (1.60)	36.9 (1.65)	20.0 (1.29)	27.6 (1.52)
2007[3]	38.8 (0.42)	10.9 (0.27)	27.9 (0.39)	35.5 (0.58)	42.1 (0.60)	42.6 (0.54)	33.1 (1.15)	26.6 (1.02)	57.2 (2.28)	37.1 (9.07)	24.7 (4.63)	39.2 (3.48)	39.6 (0.76)	45.7 (0.78)	32.2 (1.63)	34.0 (1.61)	20.7 (1.29)	33.0 (1.57)
2008[3]	39.6 (0.42)	11.8 (0.28)	27.8 (0.38)	37.0 (0.58)	42.3 (0.60)	44.2 (0.54)	32.1 (1.13)	25.8 (1.01)	59.3 (2.32)	27.3! (8.92)	21.9 (4.22)	45.7 (3.55)	41.7 (0.76)	46.9 (0.78)	29.7 (1.61)	34.2 (1.59)	23.0 (1.35)	28.9 (1.50)
2009[3]	41.3 (0.42)	11.7 (0.27)	29.6 (0.39)	38.4 (0.59)	44.2 (0.60)	45.0 (0.55)	37.7 (1.17)	27.5 (1.01)	65.2 (2.17)	33.4 (7.45)	29.8 (5.10)	39.3 (3.32)	42.3 (0.76)	47.7 (0.78)	33.2 (1.64)	41.9 (1.64)	24.2 (1.35)	31.0 (1.50)
2010[3]	41.2 (0.57)	12.9 (0.36)	28.2 (0.53)	38.3 (0.78)	44.1 (0.84)	43.3 (0.81)	38.4 (1.66)	31.9 (1.15)	63.6 (2.70)	36.0 (8.36)	41.4 (6.60)	38.3 (4.38)	40.6 (1.00)	46.1 (1.17)	35.2 (2.13)	41.4 (2.16)	27.9 (1.57)	36.1 (1.60)
2011[3]	42.0 (0.59)	12.0 (0.35)	30.0 (0.58)	39.1 (0.80)	44.9 (0.80)	44.7 (0.77)	37.1 (1.53)	34.8 (1.20)	60.1 (2.45)	37.8 (7.93)	23.5 (5.30)	38.8 (3.60)	42.4 (0.96)	47.1 (1.08)	34.0 (2.29)	39.9 (1.90)	31.0 (1.63)	39.4 (1.58)
2012[3]	41.0 (0.62)	12.7 (0.38)	28.3 (0.58)	37.6 (0.79)	44.5 (0.86)	42.1 (0.83)	36.4 (1.62)	37.5 (1.18)	59.8 (2.61)	50.3 (9.60)	27.8 (4.43)	39.4 (3.64)	38.3 (1.06)	46.0 (1.08)	33.9 (2.04)	38.7 (2.33)	33.5 (1.58)	41.7 (1.73)
2013[3]	39.9 (0.63)	11.6 (0.36)	28.3 (0.57)	36.6 (0.85)	43.3 (0.80)	41.6 (0.90)	34.2 (1.58)	33.8 (1.24)	62.3 (2.62)	32.9 (8.26)	31.8 (5.58)	44.7 (3.99)	38.1 (1.11)	45.3 (1.11)	30.6 (2.13)	37.6 (2.18)	29.1 (1.72)	38.8 (1.58)
2014[3]	40.0 (0.65)	10.6 (0.40)	29.4 (0.61)	37.3 (0.89)	42.8 (0.79)	42.2 (0.87)	32.6 (1.48)	34.7 (1.21)	65.2 (2.27)	41.0 (11.29)	35.4 (4.63)	31.6 (3.20)	40.2 (1.28)	44.2 (0.99)	28.5 (1.95)	36.6 (2.04)	30.3 (1.65)	39.4 (1.70)
2015[3]	40.5 (0.70)	10.6 (0.35)	29.9 (0.69)	37.8 (0.91)	43.2 (0.93)	41.8 (0.88)	34.9 (1.54)	36.6 (1.31)	62.6 (2.65)	24.1! (7.29)	23.0 (4.45)	38.3 (3.86)	39.1 (1.16)	44.5 (1.10)	34.1 (2.21)	35.7 (2.17)	32.8 (1.76)	40.5 (1.91)
2016[3]	41.2 (0.71)	10.1 (0.36)	31.1 (0.64)	38.6 (0.83)	43.9 (0.91)	42.1 (0.88)	36.2 (1.69)	39.2 (1.28)	57.6 (2.17)	20.7! (8.02)	18.6 (3.72)	42.3 (3.64)	39.8 (1.09)	44.5 (1.12)	33.0 (2.18)	39.4 (2.51)	34.9 (1.67)	43.6 (1.76)
2017[3]	40.4 (0.66)	10.0 (0.37)	30.4 (0.64)	36.8 (0.84)	44.0 (0.91)	41.0 (0.76)	36.5 (1.71)	36.2 (1.50)	64.7 (2.49)	32.6! (10.94)	20.1 (4.47)	41.5 (3.66)	37.8 (1.05)	44.4 (1.12)	33.1 (2.45)	39.6 (2.18)	31.1 (1.82)	41.4 (2.02)
2018[3]	40.9 (0.68)	9.9 (0.37)	31.0 (0.64)	37.6 (0.90)	44.3 (0.80)	42.3 (0.86)	37.2 (1.58)	35.9 (1.25)	59.0 (3.20)	23.8! (8.62)	24.2 (5.60)	44.3 (3.86)	39.1 (1.08)	45.4 (1.08)	33.3 (1.86)	40.9 (2.43)	31.6 (1.59)	40.4 (1.80)

—Not available.
†Not applicable.
!Interpret data with caution. The coefficient of variation (CV) for this estimate is between 30 and 50 percent.
[1]Prior to 2003, Asian data include Pacific Islanders.
[2]Prior to 1972, White and Black data include persons of Hispanic ethnicity.
[3]After 2002, data for individual race categories exclude persons of Two or more races. In 2002 and earlier years, the questionnaire did not include the "Two or more races" category, and each respondent could select only one race category.

NOTE: Data are based on sample surveys of the civilian noninstitutionalized population. Totals include other racial/ethnic groups not separately shown. Race categories exclude persons of Hispanic ethnicity except where otherwise noted. Prior to 2010, standard errors were computed using generalized variance function methodology rather than the more precise replicate weight methodology used in later years.
SOURCE: U.S. Department of Commerce, Census Bureau, Current Population Survey (CPS), October, 1970 through 2018. (This table was prepared August 2019.)

Table 302.62. Percentage of 18- to 24-year-olds enrolled in college and percentage distribution of those enrolled, by sex, race/ethnicity, and selected racial/ethnic subgroups: 2010 and 2018

[Standard errors appear in parentheses]

Race/ethnicity	2010 Total		2010 Male		2010 Female		2018 Total		2018 Male		2018 Female	
1	2		3		4		5		6		7	
	Percent of 18- to 24-year-olds enrolled											
Total[1]	**42.9**	**(0.11)**	**38.6**	**(0.16)**	**47.5**	**(0.15)**	**42.5**	**(0.13)**	**38.4**	**(0.16)**	**46.8**	**(0.18)**
White	46.9	(0.15)	43.0	(0.20)	51.0	(0.20)	44.1	(0.16)	40.2	(0.24)	48.3	(0.23)
Black	36.6	(0.33)	30.6	(0.43)	42.7	(0.48)	37.0	(0.39)	32.0	(0.44)	42.1	(0.60)
Hispanic	31.1	(0.31)	26.4	(0.38)	36.3	(0.39)	36.7	(0.27)	32.1	(0.32)	41.6	(0.42)
Cuban	45.8	(1.57)	41.2	(2.14)	50.3	(2.10)	47.6	(1.57)	43.1	(1.95)	53.0	(2.12)
Dominican	40.0	(1.64)	33.3	(2.06)	46.7	(2.22)	38.5	(1.21)	32.9	(1.86)	44.0	(2.01)
Mexican	27.9	(0.35)	23.8	(0.44)	32.6	(0.45)	35.3	(0.34)	30.7	(0.44)	40.1	(0.51)
Puerto Rican	34.2	(0.83)	28.6	(1.13)	39.8	(1.32)	34.4	(0.97)	30.7	(1.22)	38.5	(1.37)
Spaniard	50.9	(2.16)	50.5	(3.33)	51.4	(3.07)	47.6	(2.18)	40.0	(3.49)	56.0	(3.05)
Central American[2]	26.3	(0.85)	21.6	(0.89)	32.6	(1.51)	31.7	(0.77)	26.6	(0.90)	37.4	(1.22)
Costa Rican	59.6	(4.52)	58.1	(6.62)	61.5	(6.82)	52.8	(6.00)	51.4	(7.22)	55.0	(9.64)
Guatemalan	17.3	(1.28)	13.5	(1.34)	24.7	(2.67)	26.9	(1.32)	22.5	(1.70)	33.1	(2.08)
Honduran	20.2	(1.75)	13.9	(1.86)	30.1	(3.31)	27.5	(1.97)	22.8	(2.67)	32.4	(2.72)
Nicaraguan	40.9	(2.82)	37.7	(3.97)	44.4	(4.03)	43.3	(3.55)	37.0	(4.73)	48.6	(5.05)
Panamanian	48.0	(3.86)	47.0	(5.65)	49.0	(5.96)	46.2	(4.66)	41.1	(6.13)	50.7	(7.01)
Salvadoran	27.7	(1.27)	24.3	(1.61)	31.6	(1.95)	31.8	(1.22)	26.6	(1.58)	37.4	(1.75)
South American	50.5	(1.20)	44.8	(1.65)	56.5	(1.65)	52.1	(0.99)	49.6	(1.48)	54.5	(1.56)
Chilean	54.6	(5.50)	53.9	(7.73)	55.2	(7.33)	65.5	(4.89)	62.2	(8.12)	68.0	(7.30)
Colombian	53.0	(2.35)	50.7	(3.16)	55.4	(3.16)	50.3	(1.55)	50.5	(2.20)	50.0	(2.46)
Ecuadorian	40.3	(2.96)	30.9	(3.25)	52.2	(4.19)	54.1	(2.47)	51.0	(3.29)	57.3	(3.81)
Peruvian	53.6	(2.87)	47.9	(3.89)	58.9	(3.51)	55.8	(2.61)	48.5	(4.10)	62.2	(3.22)
Venezuelan	54.9	(4.32)	46.8	(6.02)	63.8	(5.68)	46.7	(3.13)	44.3	(4.20)	49.2	(4.00)
Other South American	52.6	(2.97)	47.0	(5.01)	57.6	(3.84)	49.2	(3.41)	48.0	(4.11)	50.3	(4.92)
Other Hispanic	38.6	(1.42)	33.7	(2.03)	43.8	(2.17)	43.5	(1.38)	38.2	(1.85)	48.9	(1.85)
Asian	66.0	(0.55)	65.3	(0.71)	66.7	(0.75)	66.2	(0.59)	65.4	(0.78)	67.0	(0.72)
Chinese[3]	74.0	(0.95)	74.0	(1.22)	74.1	(1.11)	73.8	(0.92)	74.8	(1.12)	72.9	(1.37)
Filipino	57.8	(1.38)	54.5	(1.60)	61.4	(2.21)	56.3	(1.42)	54.9	(1.94)	57.9	(1.72)
Japanese	72.0	(2.95)	70.0	(3.92)	74.1	(3.93)	67.8	(3.07)	67.1	(4.32)	68.6	(4.47)
Korean	72.3	(1.43)	71.3	(2.00)	73.2	(1.86)	64.1	(1.37)	62.5	(2.11)	65.8	(2.21)
South Asian[4]	67.1	(1.16)	68.9	(1.61)	65.0	(1.67)	69.3	(1.10)	69.3	(1.31)	69.3	(1.51)
Asian Indian	68.6	(1.30)	71.5	(1.80)	65.4	(1.79)	70.8	(1.17)	70.0	(1.43)	71.8	(1.80)
Bangladeshi	58.3	(5.63)	57.7	(8.07)	58.9	(7.06)	60.5	(5.18)	62.2	(6.50)	59.0	(6.65)
Bhutanese	---	(†)	---	(†)	---	(†)	‡	(†)	‡	(†)	‡	(†)
Nepalese	---	(†)	---	(†)	---	(†)	58.1	(5.45)	63.2	(7.15)	52.2	(7.98)
Pakistani	61.7	(3.00)	58.9	(4.44)	64.6	(4.11)	70.3	(2.77)	71.5	(3.70)	69.0	(3.35)
Southeast Asian	58.3	(1.17)	57.0	(1.55)	59.5	(1.56)	59.1	(1.19)	55.1	(1.70)	62.9	(1.65)
Burmese	---	(†)	---	(†)	---	(†)	33.9	(4.95)	30.8	(6.31)	36.5	(7.00)
Cambodian	38.1	(3.02)	38.2	(4.77)	38.0	(4.55)	44.4	(4.11)	48.8	(5.17)	38.6	(6.52)
Hmong	39.7	(3.18)	36.3	(3.56)	42.9	(4.49)	47.3	(2.88)	39.4	(3.19)	56.5	(4.28)
Laotian	44.9	(4.40)	38.5	(5.46)	52.3	(5.63)	43.1	(6.10)	26.0	(6.57)	56.3	(7.78)
Thai	63.3	(5.72)	61.1	(9.35)	65.1	(6.55)	54.6	(5.02)	52.0	(8.62)	56.8	(6.57)
Vietnamese	68.2	(1.35)	68.4	(1.81)	68.1	(2.02)	66.9	(1.11)	63.7	(2.06)	69.9	(1.69)
Other Southeast Asian[5]	74.5	(5.03)	62.7	(7.82)	89.4	(5.17)	77.1	(4.84)	73.3	(6.23)	80.9	(6.53)
Other Asian	58.7	(2.01)	56.3	(2.69)	61.0	(3.03)	63.7	(2.33)	63.6	(3.35)	63.9	(3.43)
Pacific Islander	39.1	(2.21)	34.9	(3.44)	43.5	(2.97)	28.9	(2.87)	23.9	(3.41)	34.1	(4.53)
American Indian/Alaska Native	28.7	(1.17)	24.5	(1.76)	32.9	(1.56)	29.2	(1.35)	24.8	(1.69)	33.6	(1.89)
Two or more races	44.7	(0.81)	40.1	(1.06)	49.3	(1.03)	42.1	(0.70)	37.9	(1.00)	46.5	(0.94)
White and Black	37.2	(1.57)	30.9	(2.16)	42.9	(1.96)	35.5	(1.05)	31.8	(1.72)	39.2	(1.58)
White and Asian	58.5	(1.42)	54.2	(1.82)	62.9	(2.07)	55.5	(1.18)	52.9	(1.41)	58.3	(1.69)
White and American Indian/ Alaska Native	36.5	(1.62)	31.4	(2.13)	42.6	(2.47)	34.3	(1.66)	29.8	(1.95)	39.2	(2.33)
Other Two or more races	45.3	(1.65)	42.4	(1.88)	48.3	(2.21)	43.6	(1.51)	36.1	(1.85)	51.4	(2.03)
	Percentage distribution of those enrolled											
Total[1]	**100.0**	**(†)**	**46.0**	**(0.14)**	**54.0**	**(0.14)**	**100.0**	**(†)**	**46.4**	**(0.13)**	**53.6**	**(0.13)**
White	100.0	(†)	46.6	(0.15)	53.4	(0.15)	100.0	(†)	46.8	(0.19)	53.2	(0.19)
Black	100.0	(†)	41.5	(0.49)	58.5	(0.49)	100.0	(†)	43.7	(0.51)	56.3	(0.51)
Hispanic	100.0	(†)	45.2	(0.38)	54.8	(0.38)	100.0	(†)	45.1	(0.37)	54.9	(0.37)
Cuban	100.0	(†)	44.2	(2.06)	55.8	(2.06)	100.0	(†)	49.2	(1.89)	50.8	(1.89)
Dominican	100.0	(†)	41.6	(2.34)	58.4	(2.34)	100.0	(†)	43.0	(2.40)	57.0	(2.40)
Mexican	100.0	(†)	45.6	(0.49)	54.4	(0.49)	100.0	(†)	44.7	(0.53)	55.3	(0.53)
Puerto Rican	100.0	(†)	41.9	(1.48)	58.1	(1.48)	100.0	(†)	46.5	(1.31)	53.5	(1.31)
Spaniard	100.0	(†)	49.9	(3.16)	50.1	(3.16)	100.0	(†)	44.2	(3.65)	55.8	(3.65)
Central American[2]	100.0	(†)	47.8	(1.60)	52.2	(1.60)	100.0	(†)	44.9	(1.41)	55.1	(1.41)
Costa Rican	100.0	(†)	52.4	(6.41)	47.6	(6.41)	100.0	(†)	59.9	(9.26)	40.1	(9.26)
Guatemalan	100.0	(†)	51.2	(3.97)	48.8	(3.97)	100.0	(†)	49.7	(2.81)	50.3	(2.81)
Honduran	100.0	(†)	41.9	(4.74)	58.1	(4.74)	100.0	(†)	43.1	(4.33)	56.9	(4.33)
Nicaraguan	100.0	(†)	47.4	(4.05)	52.6	(4.05)	100.0	(†)	39.4	(4.90)	60.6	(4.90)
Panamanian	100.0	(†)	49.7	(6.23)	50.3	(6.23)	100.0	(†)	41.7	(6.22)	58.3	(6.22)
Salvadoran	100.0	(†)	47.3	(2.59)	52.7	(2.59)	100.0	(†)	43.2	(2.20)	56.8	(2.20)

[Standard errors appear in parentheses]

Race/ethnicity	2010						2018					
	Total		Male		Female		Total		Male		Female	
1		2		3		4		5		6		7
South American	100.0	(†)	45.2	(1.72)	54.8	(1.72)	100.0	(†)	47.2	(1.53)	52.8	(1.53)
Chilean	100.0	(†)	45.7	(7.45)	54.3	(7.45)	100.0	(†)	41.5	(6.68)	58.5	(6.68)
Colombian	100.0	(†)	48.9	(2.73)	51.1	(2.73)	100.0	(†)	51.0	(2.50)	49.0	(2.50)
Ecuadorian	100.0	(†)	42.8	(3.87)	57.2	(3.87)	100.0	(†)	48.4	(3.46)	51.6	(3.46)
Peruvian	100.0	(†)	43.3	(3.57)	56.7	(3.57)	100.0	(†)	40.5	(3.34)	59.5	(3.34)
Venezuelan	100.0	(†)	44.7	(5.19)	55.3	(5.19)	100.0	(†)	48.2	(3.73)	51.8	(3.73)
Other South American	100.0	(†)	42.2	(4.98)	57.8	(4.98)	100.0	(†)	47.5	(4.67)	52.5	(4.67)
Other Hispanic	100.0	(†)	45.4	(2.58)	54.6	(2.58)	100.0	(†)	43.9	(1.90)	56.1	(1.90)
Asian	100.0	(†)	50.3	(0.43)	49.7	(0.43)	100.0	(†)	50.4	(0.50)	49.6	(0.50)
Chinese[3]	100.0	(†)	51.8	(1.13)	48.2	(1.13)	100.0	(†)	49.6	(1.03)	50.4	(1.03)
Filipino	100.0	(†)	48.9	(1.81)	51.1	(1.81)	100.0	(†)	50.6	(1.54)	49.4	(1.54)
Japanese	100.0	(†)	48.7	(3.42)	51.3	(3.42)	100.0	(†)	49.9	(4.00)	50.1	(4.00)
Korean	100.0	(†)	46.0	(1.91)	54.0	(1.91)	100.0	(†)	49.3	(2.00)	50.7	(2.00)
South Asian[4]	100.0	(†)	54.2	(1.35)	45.8	(1.35)	100.0	(†)	54.8	(1.30)	45.2	(1.30)
Asian Indian	100.0	(†)	55.4	(1.48)	44.6	(1.48)	100.0	(†)	54.6	(1.45)	45.4	(1.45)
Bangladeshi	100.0	(†)	50.1	(7.72)	49.9	(7.72)	100.0	(†)	49.1	(5.23)	50.9	(5.23)
Bhutanese	---	(†)	---	(†)	---	(†)	100.0	(†)	‡	(†)	‡	(†)
Nepalese	---	(†)	---	(†)	---	(†)	100.0	(†)	58.4	(5.74)	41.6	(5.74)
Pakistani	100.0	(†)	47.5	(3.54)	52.5	(3.54)	100.0	(†)	55.2	(2.98)	44.8	(2.98)
Southeast Asian	100.0	(†)	48.5	(1.23)	51.5	(1.23)	100.0	(†)	45.5	(1.46)	54.5	(1.46)
Burmese	---	(†)	---	(†)	---	(†)	100.0	(†)	41.9	(7.13)	58.1	(7.13)
Cambodian	100.0	(†)	47.7	(5.75)	52.3	(5.75)	100.0	(†)	62.7	(5.76)	37.3	(5.76)
Hmong	100.0	(†)	44.8	(3.95)	55.2	(3.95)	100.0	(†)	44.9	(3.99)	55.1	(3.99)
Laotian	100.0	(†)	45.8	(5.45)	54.2	(5.45)	100.0	(†)	26.3	(7.35)	73.7	(7.35)
Thai	100.0	(†)	43.3	(7.35)	56.7	(7.35)	100.0	(†)	43.3	(7.94)	56.7	(7.94)
Vietnamese	100.0	(†)	50.0	(1.50)	50.0	(1.50)	100.0	(†)	45.5	(1.60)	54.5	(1.60)
Other Southeast Asian[5]	100.0	(†)	46.8	(8.62)	53.2	(8.62)	100.0	(†)	46.9	(7.34)	53.1	(7.34)
Other Asian	100.0	(†)	47.7	(2.74)	52.3	(2.74)	100.0	(†)	49.9	(3.13)	50.1	(3.13)
Pacific Islander	100.0	(†)	45.8	(3.84)	54.2	(3.84)	100.0	(†)	42.3	(5.58)	57.7	(5.58)
American Indian/Alaska Native	100.0	(†)	43.4	(2.28)	56.6	(2.28)	100.0	(†)	42.5	(2.29)	57.5	(2.29)
Two or more races	100.0	(†)	45.4	(1.01)	54.6	(1.01)	100.0	(†)	45.7	(0.93)	54.3	(0.93)
White and Black	100.0	(†)	39.3	(2.37)	60.7	(2.37)	100.0	(†)	44.3	(2.00)	55.7	(2.00)
White and Asian	100.0	(†)	47.8	(1.77)	52.2	(1.77)	100.0	(†)	49.7	(1.67)	50.3	(1.67)
White and American Indian/ Alaska Native	100.0	(†)	46.4	(2.43)	53.6	(2.43)	100.0	(†)	45.0	(2.18)	55.0	(2.18)
Other Two or more races	100.0	(†)	46.9	(1.94)	53.1	(1.94)	100.0	(†)	41.9	(1.84)	58.1	(1.84)

---Not available.

†Not applicable.

‡Reporting standards not met (too few cases for a reliable estimate).

1 Total includes other racial/ethnic groups not shown separately.

2 Includes other Central American subgroups not shown separately.

3 Includes Taiwanese.

4 In addition to the subgroups shown, also includes Sri Lankan.

5 Consists of Indonesian and Malaysian.

NOTE: Data are based on sample surveys of the entire population in the given age range residing within the United States, including both noninstitutionalized persons (e.g., those living in households, college housing, or military housing located within the United States) and institutionalized persons (e.g., those living in prisons, nursing facilities, or other healthcare facilities). Enrollment data in this table may differ from data in tables based on the Current Population Survey (CPS) because of differences in survey design and target populations. Race categories exclude persons of Hispanic ethnicity. Detail may not sum to totals because of rounding.

SOURCE: U.S. Department of Commerce, Census Bureau, American Community Survey (ACS), 2010 and 2018. (This table was prepared April 2020.)

Table 303.10. Total fall enrollment in degree-granting postsecondary institutions, by attendance status, sex of student, and control of institution: Selected years, 1947 through 2029

Year	Total enrollment	Attendance status			Sex of student			Control of institution			
		Full-time	Part-time	Percent part-time	Male	Female	Percent female	Public	Private		
									Total	Nonprofit	For-profit
1	2	3	4	5	6	7	8	9	10	11	12
1947[1]	2,338,226	—	—	—	1,659,249	678,977	29.0	1,152,377	1,185,849	—	—
1948[1]	2,403,396	—	—	—	1,709,367	694,029	28.9	1,185,588	1,217,808	—	—
1949[1]	2,444,900	—	—	—	1,721,572	723,328	29.6	1,207,151	1,237,749	—	—
1950[1]	2,281,298	—	—	—	1,560,392	720,906	31.6	1,139,699	1,141,599	—	—
1951[1]	2,101,962	—	—	—	1,390,740	711,222	33.8	1,037,938	1,064,024	—	—
1952[1]	2,134,242	—	—	—	1,380,357	753,885	35.3	1,101,240	1,033,002	—	—
1953[1]	2,231,054	—	—	—	1,422,598	808,456	36.2	1,185,876	1,045,178	—	—
1954[1]	2,446,693	—	—	—	1,563,382	883,311	36.1	1,353,531	1,093,162	—	—
1955[1]	2,653,034	—	—	—	1,733,184	919,850	34.7	1,476,282	1,176,752	—	—
1956[1]	2,918,212	—	—	—	1,911,458	1,006,754	34.5	1,656,402	1,261,810	—	—
1957	3,323,783	—	—	—	2,170,765	1,153,018	34.7	1,972,673	1,351,110	—	—
1959	3,639,847	2,421,016	1,218,831[2]	33.5	2,332,617	1,307,230	35.9	2,180,982	1,458,865	—	—
1961	4,145,065	2,785,133	1,359,932[2]	32.8	2,585,821	1,559,244	37.6	2,561,447	1,583,618	—	—
1963	4,779,609	3,183,833	1,595,776[2]	33.4	2,961,540	1,818,069	38.0	3,081,279	1,698,330	—	—
1964	5,280,020	3,573,238	1,706,782[2]	32.3	3,248,713	2,031,307	38.5	3,467,708	1,812,312	—	—
1965	5,920,864	4,095,728	1,825,136[2]	30.8	3,630,020	2,290,844	38.7	3,969,596	1,951,268	—	—
1966	6,389,872	4,438,606	1,951,266[2]	30.5	3,856,216	2,533,656	39.7	4,348,917	2,040,955	—	—
1967	6,911,748	4,793,128	2,118,620[2]	30.7	4,132,800	2,778,948	40.2	4,816,028	2,095,720	2,074,041	21,679
1968	7,513,091	5,210,155	2,302,936	30.7	4,477,649	3,035,442	40.4	5,430,652	2,082,439	2,061,211	21,228
1969	8,004,660	5,498,883	2,505,777	31.3	4,746,201	3,258,459	40.7	5,896,868	2,107,792	2,087,653	20,139
1970	8,580,887	5,816,290	2,764,597	32.2	5,043,642	3,537,245	41.2	6,428,134	2,152,753	2,134,420	18,333
1971	8,948,644	6,077,232	2,871,412	32.1	5,207,004	3,741,640	41.8	6,804,309	2,144,335	2,121,913	22,422
1972	9,214,860	6,072,389	3,142,471	34.1	5,238,757	3,976,103	43.1	7,070,635	2,144,225	2,123,245	20,980
1973	9,602,123	6,189,493	3,412,630	35.5	5,371,052	4,231,071	44.1	7,419,516	2,182,607	2,148,784	33,823
1974	10,223,729	6,370,273	3,853,456	37.7	5,622,429	4,601,300	45.0	7,988,500	2,235,229	2,200,963	34,266
1975	11,184,859	6,841,334	4,343,525	38.8	6,148,997	5,035,862	45.0	8,834,508	2,350,351	2,311,448	38,903
1976	11,012,137	6,717,058	4,295,079	39.0	5,810,828	5,201,309	47.2	8,653,477	2,358,660	2,314,298	44,362
1977	11,285,787	6,792,925	4,492,862	39.8	5,789,016	5,496,771	48.7	8,846,993	2,438,794	2,386,652	52,142
1978	11,260,092	6,667,657	4,592,435	40.8	5,640,998	5,619,094	49.9	8,785,893	2,474,199	2,408,331	65,868
1979	11,569,899	6,794,039	4,775,860	41.3	5,682,877	5,887,022	50.9	9,036,822	2,533,077	2,461,773	71,304
1980	12,096,895	7,097,958	4,998,937	41.3	5,874,374	6,222,521	51.4	9,457,394	2,639,501	2,527,787	111,714[3]
1981	12,371,672	7,181,250	5,190,422	42.0	5,975,056	6,396,616	51.7	9,647,032	2,724,640	2,572,405	152,235[3]
1982	12,425,780	7,220,618	5,205,162	41.9	6,031,384	6,394,396	51.5	9,696,087	2,729,693	2,552,739	176,954[3]
1983	12,464,661	7,261,050	5,203,611	41.7	6,023,725	6,440,936	51.7	9,682,734	2,781,927	2,589,187	192,740
1984	12,241,940	7,098,388	5,143,552	42.0	5,863,574	6,378,366	52.1	9,477,370	2,764,570	2,574,419	190,151
1985	12,247,055	7,075,221	5,171,834	42.2	5,818,450	6,428,605	52.5	9,479,273	2,767,782	2,571,791	195,991
1986	12,503,511	7,119,550	5,383,961	43.1	5,884,515	6,618,996	52.9	9,713,893	2,789,618	2,572,479	217,139[4]
1987	12,766,642	7,231,085	5,535,557	43.4	5,932,056	6,834,586	53.5	9,973,254	2,793,388	2,602,350	191,038[4]
1988	13,055,337	7,436,768	5,618,569	43.0	6,001,896	7,053,441	54.0	10,161,388	2,893,949	2,673,567	220,382
1989	13,538,560	7,660,950	5,877,610	43.4	6,190,015	7,348,545	54.3	10,577,963	2,960,597	2,731,174	229,423
1990	13,818,637	7,820,985	5,997,652	43.4	6,283,909	7,534,728	54.5	10,844,717	2,973,920	2,760,227	213,693
1991	14,358,953	8,115,329	6,243,624	43.5	6,501,844	7,857,109	54.7	11,309,563	3,049,390	2,819,041	230,349
1992	14,487,359	8,162,118	6,325,241	43.7	6,523,989	7,963,370	55.0	11,384,567	3,102,792	2,872,523	230,269
1993	14,304,803	8,127,618	6,177,185	43.2	6,427,450	7,877,353	55.1	11,189,088	3,115,715	2,888,897	226,818
1994	14,278,790	8,137,776	6,141,014	43.0	6,371,898	7,906,892	55.4	11,133,680	3,145,110	2,910,107	235,003
1995	14,261,781	8,128,802	6,132,979	43.0	6,342,539	7,919,242	55.5	11,092,374	3,169,407	2,929,044	240,363
1996	14,367,520	8,302,953	6,064,567	42.2	6,352,825	8,014,695	55.8	11,120,499	3,247,021	2,942,556	304,465
1997	14,502,334	8,438,062	6,064,272	41.8	6,396,028	8,106,306	55.9	11,196,119	3,306,215	2,977,614	328,601
1998	14,506,967	8,563,338	5,943,629	41.0	6,369,265	8,137,702	56.1	11,137,769	3,369,198	3,004,925	364,273
1999	14,849,691	8,803,139	6,046,552	40.7	6,515,164	8,334,527	56.1	11,375,739	3,473,952	3,055,029	418,923
2000	15,312,289	9,009,600	6,302,689	41.2	6,721,769	8,590,520	56.1	11,752,786	3,559,503	3,109,419	450,084
2001	15,927,987	9,447,502	6,480,485	40.7	6,960,815	8,967,172	56.3	12,233,156	3,694,831	3,167,330	527,501
2002	16,611,711	9,946,359	6,665,352	40.1	7,202,116	9,409,595	56.6	12,751,993	3,859,718	3,265,476	594,242
2003	16,911,481	10,326,133	6,585,348	38.9	7,260,264	9,651,217	57.1	12,858,698	4,052,783	3,341,048	711,735
2004	17,272,044	10,610,177	6,661,867	38.6	7,387,262	9,884,782	57.2	12,980,112	4,291,932	3,411,685	880,247
2005	17,487,475	10,797,011	6,690,464	38.3	7,455,925	10,031,550	57.4	13,021,834	4,465,641	3,454,692	1,010,949
2006	17,754,230	10,957,538	6,796,692	38.3	7,572,265	10,181,965	57.3	13,175,350	4,578,880	3,512,929	1,065,951
2007	18,258,138	11,270,929	6,987,209	38.3	7,819,938	10,438,200	57.2	13,500,894	4,757,244	3,571,395	1,185,849
2008	19,081,686	11,734,636	7,347,050	38.5	8,177,714	10,903,972	57.1	13,970,862	5,110,824	3,660,827	1,449,997
2009	20,313,594	12,605,355	7,708,239	37.9	8,732,953	11,580,641	57.0	14,810,768	5,502,826	3,767,672	1,735,154
2010	21,019,438	13,087,182	7,932,256	37.7	9,045,759	11,973,679	57.0	15,142,171	5,877,267	3,854,482	2,022,785
2011	21,010,590	13,002,531	8,008,059	38.1	9,034,256	11,976,334	57.0	15,116,303	5,894,287	3,926,819	1,967,468
2012	20,644,478	12,734,404	7,910,074	38.3	8,919,006	11,725,472	56.8	14,884,667	5,759,811	3,951,388	1,808,423
2013	20,376,677	12,596,610	7,780,067	38.2	8,861,197	11,515,480	56.5	14,746,848	5,629,829	3,971,390	1,658,439
2014	20,209,092	12,454,464	7,754,628	38.4	8,797,530	11,411,562	56.5	14,654,660	5,554,432	3,997,249	1,557,183

See notes at end of table.

Table 303.10. Total fall enrollment in degree-granting postsecondary institutions, by attendance status, sex of student, and control of institution: Selected years, 1947 through 2029—Continued

Year	Total enrollment	Attendance status			Sex of student			Control of institution			
									Private		
		Full-time	Part-time	Percent part-time	Male	Female	Percent female	Public	Total	Nonprofit	For-profit
1	2	3	4	5	6	7	8	9	10	11	12
2015	19,988,204	12,287,512	7,700,692	38.5	8,723,819	11,264,385	56.4	14,572,843	5,415,361	4,065,891	1,349,470
2016	19,846,904	12,125,314	7,721,590	38.9	8,638,422	11,208,482	56.5	14,585,840	5,261,064	4,078,956	1,182,108
2017	19,778,151	12,076,141	7,702,010	38.9	8,571,314	11,206,837	56.7	14,571,739	5,206,412	4,108,489	1,097,923
2018	19,645,918	11,991,721	7,654,197	39.0	8,442,662	11,203,256	57.0	14,529,264	5,116,654	4,134,244	982,410
2019[5]	19,720,000	12,025,000	7,695,000	39.0	8,470,000	11,250,000	57.0	14,586,000	5,135,000	—	—
2020[5]	19,744,000	12,022,000	7,722,000	39.1	8,476,000	11,268,000	57.1	14,605,000	5,139,000	—	—
2021[5]	19,778,000	12,021,000	7,757,000	39.2	8,487,000	11,292,000	57.1	14,633,000	5,145,000	—	—
2022[5]	19,813,000	12,027,000	7,786,000	39.3	8,498,000	11,315,000	57.1	14,661,000	5,152,000	—	—
2023[5]	19,862,000	12,045,000	7,817,000	39.4	8,515,000	11,346,000	57.1	14,698,000	5,163,000	—	—
2024[5]	19,926,000	12,078,000	7,848,000	39.4	8,544,000	11,382,000	57.1	14,747,000	5,179,000	—	—
2025[5]	19,993,000	12,120,000	7,873,000	39.4	8,574,000	11,419,000	57.1	14,796,000	5,197,000	—	—
2026[5]	20,070,000	12,165,000	7,905,000	39.4	8,608,000	11,463,000	57.1	14,854,000	5,217,000	—	—
2027[5]	20,099,000	12,169,000	7,930,000	39.5	8,621,000	11,478,000	57.1	14,877,000	5,222,000	—	—
2028[5]	20,110,000	12,159,000	7,951,000	39.5	8,627,000	11,483,000	57.1	14,887,000	5,223,000	—	—
2029[5]	20,115,000	12,144,000	7,971,000	39.6	8,630,000	11,485,000	57.1	14,893,000	5,222,000	—	—

—Not available.
[1]Degree-credit enrollment only.
[2]Includes part-time resident students and all extension students (students attending courses at sites separate from the primary reporting campus). In later years, part-time student enrollment was collected as a distinct category.
[3]Large increases are due to the addition of schools accredited by the Accrediting Commission of Career Schools and Colleges of Technology.
[4]Because of imputation techniques, data are not consistent with figures for other years.
[5]Projected.
NOTE: Data through 1995 are for institutions of higher education, while later data are for degree-granting institutions. Degree-granting institutions grant associate's or higher degrees and participate in Title IV federal financial aid programs. The degree-granting classification is very similar to the earlier higher education classification, but it includes more 2-year colleges and excludes a few higher education institutions that did not grant degrees. Some data have been revised from previously published figures.
SOURCE: U.S. Department of Education, National Center for Education Statistics, *Biennial Survey of Education in the United States; Opening Fall Enrollment in Higher Education*, 1963 through 1965; Higher Education General Information Survey (HEGIS), "Fall Enrollment in Colleges and Universities" surveys, 1966 through 1985; Integrated Postsecondary Education Data System (IPEDS), "Fall Enrollment Survey" (IPEDS-EF:86-99); IPEDS Spring 2001 through Spring 2019, Fall Enrollment component; and Enrollment in Degree-Granting Institutions Projection Model, 2000 through 2029. (This table was prepared December 2019.)

Table 303.20. Total fall enrollment in all postsecondary institutions participating in Title IV aid programs and annual percentage change in enrollment, by degree-granting status and control of institution: 1995 through 2018

Year	All Title IV institutions[1]				Degree-granting institutions[2]					Non-degree-granting institutions[3]			
			Private				Private					Private	
	Total	Public	Nonprofit	For-profit	Total	Public	Total	Nonprofit	For-profit	Total	Public	Nonprofit	For-profit
1	2	3	4	5	6	7	8	9	10	11	12	13	14
	Enrollment												
1995	14,836,338	11,312,491	2,977,794	546,053	14,261,781	11,092,374	3,169,407	2,929,044	240,363	574,557	220,117	48,750	305,690
1996	14,809,897	11,312,775	2,976,850	520,272	14,367,520	11,120,499	3,247,021	2,942,556	304,465	442,377	192,276	34,294	215,807
1997	14,900,416	11,370,755	3,012,106	517,555	14,502,334	11,196,119	3,306,215	2,977,614	328,601	398,082	174,636	34,492	188,954
1998	14,923,839	11,330,811	3,040,251	552,777	14,506,967	11,137,769	3,369,198	3,004,925	364,273	416,872	193,042	35,326	188,504
1999	15,262,888	11,556,731	3,088,233	617,924	14,849,691	11,375,739	3,473,952	3,055,029	418,923	413,197	180,992	33,204	199,001
2000	15,701,409	11,891,450	3,137,108	672,851	15,312,289	11,752,786	3,559,503	3,109,419	450,084	389,120	138,664	27,689	222,767
2001	16,334,134	12,370,079	3,198,354	765,701	15,927,987	12,233,156	3,694,831	3,167,330	527,501	406,147	136,923	31,024	238,200
2002	17,035,027	12,883,071	3,299,094	852,862	16,611,711	12,751,993	3,859,718	3,265,476	594,242	423,316	131,078	33,618	258,620
2003	17,330,775	12,965,502	3,372,647	992,626	16,911,481	12,858,698	4,052,783	3,341,048	711,735	419,294	106,804	31,599	280,891
2004	17,710,798	13,081,358	3,440,559	1,188,881	17,272,044	12,980,112	4,291,932	3,411,685	880,247	438,754	101,246	28,874	308,634
2005	17,921,804	13,115,177	3,484,013	1,322,614	17,487,475	13,021,834	4,465,641	3,454,692	1,010,949	434,329	93,343	29,321	311,665
2006	18,198,370	13,276,881	3,543,064	1,378,425	17,754,230	13,175,350	4,578,880	3,512,929	1,065,951	444,140	101,531	30,135	312,474
2007	18,677,469	13,603,772	3,595,466	1,478,231	18,258,138	13,500,894	4,757,244	3,571,395	1,185,849	419,331	102,878	24,071	292,382
2008	19,553,784	14,090,863	3,684,190	1,778,731	19,081,686	13,970,862	5,110,824	3,660,827	1,449,997	472,098	120,001	23,363	328,734
2009	20,853,423	14,936,402	3,793,751	2,123,270	20,313,594	14,810,768	5,502,826	3,767,672	1,735,154	539,829	125,634	26,079	388,116
2010	21,591,742	15,279,455	3,881,630	2,430,657	21,019,438	15,142,171	5,877,267	3,854,482	2,022,785	572,304	137,284	27,148	407,872
2011	21,573,798	15,251,185	3,954,173	2,368,440	21,010,590	15,116,303	5,894,287	3,926,819	1,967,468	563,208	134,882	27,354	400,972
2012	21,148,181	15,000,302	3,973,422	2,174,457	20,644,478	14,884,667	5,759,811	3,951,388	1,808,423	503,703	115,635	22,034	366,034
2013	20,848,050	14,856,309	3,990,858	2,000,883	20,376,677	14,746,848	5,629,829	3,971,390	1,658,439	471,373	109,461	19,468	342,444
2014	20,664,180	14,764,741	4,016,240	1,883,199	20,209,092	14,654,660	5,554,432	3,997,249	1,557,183	455,088	110,081	18,991	326,016
2015	20,400,164	14,682,321	4,088,450	1,629,393	19,988,204	14,572,843	5,415,361	4,065,891	1,349,470	411,960	109,478	22,559	279,923
2016	20,230,012	14,695,538	4,097,022	1,437,452	19,846,904	14,585,840	5,261,064	4,078,956	1,182,108	383,108	109,698	18,066	255,344
2017	20,151,151	14,681,145	4,125,316	1,344,690	19,778,151	14,571,739	5,206,412	4,108,489	1,097,923	373,000	109,406	16,827	246,767
2018	20,008,434	14,639,681	4,147,604	1,221,149	19,645,918	14,529,264	5,116,654	4,134,244	982,410	362,516	110,417	13,360	238,739
	Annual percentage change												
1995 to 1996	-0.2	#	#	-4.7	0.7	0.3	2.4	0.5	26.7	-23.0	-12.6	-29.7	-29.4
1996 to 1997	0.6	0.5	1.2	-0.5	0.9	0.7	1.8	1.2	7.9	-10.0	-9.2	0.6	-12.4
1997 to 1998	0.2	-0.4	0.9	6.8	#	-0.5	1.9	0.9	10.9	4.7	10.5	2.4	-0.2
1998 to 1999	2.3	2.0	1.6	11.8	2.4	2.1	3.1	1.7	15.0	-0.9	-6.2	-6.0	5.6
1999 to 2000	2.9	2.9	1.6	8.9	3.1	3.3	2.5	1.8	7.4	-5.8	-23.4	-16.6	11.9
2000 to 2001	4.0	4.0	2.0	13.8	4.0	4.1	3.8	1.9	17.2	4.4	-1.3	12.0	6.9
2001 to 2002	4.3	4.1	3.1	11.4	4.3	4.2	4.5	3.1	12.7	4.2	-4.3	8.4	8.6
2002 to 2003	1.7	0.6	2.2	16.4	1.8	0.8	5.0	2.3	19.8	-1.0	-18.5	-6.0	8.6
2003 to 2004	2.2	0.9	2.0	19.8	2.1	0.9	5.9	2.1	23.7	4.6	-5.2	-8.6	9.9
2004 to 2005	1.2	0.3	1.3	11.2	1.2	0.3	4.0	1.3	14.8	-1.0	-7.8	1.5	1.0
2005 to 2006	1.5	1.2	1.7	4.2	1.5	1.2	2.5	1.7	5.4	2.3	8.8	2.8	0.3
2006 to 2007	2.6	2.5	1.5	7.2	2.8	2.5	3.9	1.7	11.2	-5.6	1.3	-20.1	-6.4
2007 to 2008	4.7	3.6	2.5	20.3	4.5	3.5	7.4	2.5	22.3	12.6	16.6	-2.9	12.4
2008 to 2009	6.6	6.0	3.0	19.4	6.5	6.0	7.7	2.9	19.7	14.3	4.7	11.6	18.1
2009 to 2010	3.5	2.3	2.3	14.5	3.5	2.2	6.8	2.3	16.6	6.0	9.3	4.1	5.1
2010 to 2011	-0.1	-0.2	1.9	-2.6	#	-0.2	0.3	1.9	-2.7	-1.6	-1.7	0.8	-1.7
2011 to 2012	-2.0	-1.6	0.5	-8.2	-1.7	-1.5	-2.3	0.6	-8.1	-10.6	-14.3	-19.4	-8.7
2012 to 2013	-1.4	-1.0	0.4	-8.0	-1.3	-0.9	-2.3	0.5	-8.3	-6.4	-5.3	-11.6	-6.4
2013 to 2014	-0.9	-0.6	0.6	-5.9	-0.8	-0.6	-1.3	0.7	-6.1	-3.5	0.6	-2.5	-4.8
2014 to 2015	-1.3	-0.6	1.8	-13.5	-1.1	-0.6	-2.5	1.7	-13.3	-9.5	-0.5	18.8	-14.1
2015 to 2016	-0.8	0.1	0.2	-11.8	-0.7	0.1	-2.8	0.3	-12.4	-7.0	0.2	-19.9	-8.8
2016 to 2017	-0.4	-0.1	0.7	-6.5	-0.3	-0.1	-1.0	0.7	-7.1	-2.6	-0.3	-6.9	-3.4
2017 to 2018	-0.7	-0.3	0.5	-9.2	-0.7	-0.3	-1.7	0.6	-10.5	-2.8	0.9	-20.6	-3.3

#Rounds to zero.
[1]Includes degree-granting and non-degree-granting institutions.
[2]Data for 1995 are for institutions of higher education, while later data are for degree-granting institutions. Degree-granting institutions grant associate's or higher degrees and participate in Title IV federal financial aid programs. The degree-granting classification is very similar to the earlier higher education classification, but it includes more 2-year colleges and excludes a few higher education institutions that did not grant degrees.
[3]Data are for institutions that did not offer accredited 4-year or 2-year programs, but were participating in Title IV federal financial aid programs. Includes some institutions transitioning to higher level program offerings, though still classified at a lower level.
NOTE: Some data have been revised from previously published figures.
SOURCE: U.S. Department of Education, National Center for Education Statistics, Integrated Postsecondary Education Data System (IPEDS), "Fall Enrollment Survey" (IPEDS-EF:95–99); and IPEDS Spring 2001 through Spring 2019, Fall Enrollment component. (This table was prepared November 2019.)

Table 303.25. Total fall enrollment in degree-granting postsecondary institutions, by control and level of institution: 1970 through 2018

Year	All institutions			Public institutions			Private institutions								
							All private institutions			Nonprofit			For-profit		
	Total	4-year	2-year	Total	4-year	2-year	Total	4-year	2-year	Total	4-year	2-year	Total	4-year	2-year
1	2	3	4	5	6	7	8	9	10	11	12	13	14	15	16
1970	8,580,887	6,261,502	2,319,385	6,428,134	4,232,722	2,195,412	2,152,753	2,028,780	123,973	2,134,420	2,021,121	113,299	18,333	7,659	10,674
1971	8,948,644	6,369,355	2,579,289	6,804,309	4,346,990	2,457,319	2,144,335	2,022,365	121,970	2,121,913	2,011,682	110,231	22,422	10,683	11,739
1972	9,214,860	6,458,674	2,756,186	7,070,635	4,429,696	2,640,939	2,144,225	2,028,978	115,247	2,123,245	2,019,380	103,865	20,980	9,598	11,382
1973	9,602,123	6,590,023	3,012,100	7,419,516	4,529,895	2,889,621	2,182,607	2,060,128	122,479	2,148,784	2,045,804	102,980	33,823	14,324	19,499
1974	10,223,729	6,819,735	3,403,994	7,988,500	4,703,018	3,285,482	2,235,229	2,116,717	118,512	2,200,963	2,098,599	102,364	34,266	18,118	16,148
1975	11,184,859	7,214,740	3,970,119	8,834,508	4,998,142	3,836,366	2,350,351	2,216,598	133,753	2,311,448	2,198,451	112,997	38,903	18,147	20,756
1976	11,012,137	7,128,816	3,883,321	8,653,477	4,901,691	3,751,786	2,358,660	2,227,125	131,535	2,314,298	2,206,457	107,841	44,362	20,668	23,694
1977	11,285,787	7,242,845	4,042,942	8,846,993	4,945,224	3,901,769	2,438,794	2,297,621	141,173	2,386,652	2,277,072	109,580	52,142	20,549	31,593
1978	11,260,092	7,231,625	4,028,467	8,785,893	4,912,203	3,873,690	2,474,199	2,319,422	154,777	2,408,331	2,299,132	109,199	65,868	20,290	45,578
1979	11,569,899	7,353,233	4,216,666	9,036,822	4,980,012	4,056,810	2,533,077	2,373,221	159,856	2,461,773	2,351,364	110,409	71,304	21,857	49,447
1980	12,096,895	7,570,608	4,526,287	9,457,394	5,128,612	4,328,782	2,639,501	2,441,996	197,505[1]	2,527,787	2,413,693	114,094	111,714	28,303	83,411[1]
1981	12,371,672	7,655,461	4,716,211	9,647,032	5,166,324	4,480,708	2,724,640	2,489,137	235,503[1]	2,572,405	2,453,239	119,166	152,235	35,898	116,337[1]
1982	12,425,780	7,654,074	4,771,706	9,696,087	5,176,434	4,519,653	2,729,693	2,477,640	252,053[1]	2,552,739	2,437,763	114,976	176,954	39,877	137,077[1]
1983	12,464,661	7,741,195	4,723,466	9,682,734	5,223,404	4,459,330	2,781,927	2,517,791	264,136	2,589,187	2,472,894	116,293	192,740	44,897	147,843
1984	12,241,940	7,711,167	4,530,773	9,477,370	5,198,273	4,279,097	2,764,570	2,512,894	251,676	2,574,419	2,466,172	108,247	190,151	46,722	143,429
1985	12,247,055	7,715,978	4,531,077	9,479,273	5,209,540	4,269,733	2,767,782	2,506,438	261,344	2,571,791	2,463,000	108,791	195,991	43,438	152,553
1986	12,503,511	7,823,963	4,679,548	9,713,893	5,300,202	4,413,691	2,789,618	2,523,761	265,857[2]	2,572,479	2,470,981	101,498	217,139	52,780	164,359[2]
1987	12,766,642	7,990,420	4,776,222	9,973,254	5,432,200	4,541,054	2,793,388	2,558,220	235,168[2]	2,602,350	2,512,248	90,102	191,038	45,972	145,066[2]
1988	13,055,337	8,180,182	4,875,155	10,161,388	5,545,901	4,615,487	2,893,949	2,634,281	259,668	—	—	—	—	—	—
1989	13,538,560	8,387,671	5,150,889	10,577,963	5,694,303	4,883,660	2,960,597	2,693,368	267,229	—	—	—	—	—	—
1990	13,818,637	8,578,554	5,240,083	10,844,717	5,848,242	4,996,475	2,973,920	2,730,312	243,608	2,760,227	2,671,069	89,158	213,693	59,243	154,450
1991	14,358,953	8,707,053	5,651,900	11,309,563	5,904,748	5,404,815	3,049,390	2,802,305	247,085	2,819,041	2,729,752	89,289	230,349	72,553	157,796
1992	14,487,359	8,764,969	5,722,390	11,384,567	5,900,012	5,484,555	3,102,792	2,864,957	237,835	2,872,523	2,789,235	83,288	230,269	75,722	154,547
1993	14,304,803	8,738,936	5,565,867	11,189,088	5,851,760	5,337,328	3,115,715	2,887,176	228,539	2,888,897	2,802,540	86,357	226,818	84,636	142,182
1994	14,278,790	8,749,080	5,529,710	11,133,680	5,825,213	5,308,467	3,145,110	2,923,867	221,243	2,910,107	2,824,500	85,607	235,003	99,367	135,636
1995	14,261,781	8,769,252	5,492,529	11,092,374	5,814,545	5,277,829	3,169,407	2,954,707	214,700	2,929,044	2,853,890	75,154	240,363	100,817	139,546
1996	14,367,520	8,804,193	5,563,327	11,120,499	5,806,036	5,314,463	3,247,021	2,998,157	248,864	2,942,556	2,867,181	75,375	304,465	130,976	173,489
1997	14,502,334	8,896,765	5,605,569	11,196,119	5,835,433	5,360,686	3,306,215	3,061,332	244,883	2,977,614	2,905,820	71,794	328,601	155,512	173,089
1998	14,506,967	9,017,653	5,489,314	11,137,769	5,891,806	5,245,963	3,369,198	3,125,847	243,351	3,004,925	2,939,055	65,870	364,273	186,792	177,481
1999	14,849,691	9,196,160	5,653,531	11,375,739	5,977,678	5,398,061	3,473,952	3,218,482	255,470	3,055,029	2,991,728	63,301	418,923	226,754	192,169
2000	15,312,289	9,363,858	5,948,431	11,752,786	6,055,398	5,697,388	3,559,503	3,308,460	251,043	3,109,419	3,050,575	58,844	450,084	257,885	192,199
2001	15,927,987	9,677,408	6,250,579	12,233,156	6,236,455	5,996,701	3,694,831	3,440,953	253,878	3,167,330	3,119,781	47,549	527,501	321,172	206,329
2002	16,611,711	10,082,332	6,529,379	12,751,993	6,481,613	6,270,380	3,859,718	3,600,719	258,999	3,265,476	3,218,389	47,087	594,242	382,330	211,912
2003	16,911,481	10,417,247	6,494,234	12,858,698	6,649,441	6,209,257	4,052,783	3,767,806	284,977	3,341,048	3,297,180	43,868	711,735	470,626	241,109
2004	17,272,044	10,726,181	6,545,863	12,980,112	6,736,536	6,243,576	4,291,932	3,989,645	302,287	3,411,685	3,369,435	42,250	880,247	620,210	260,037
2005	17,487,475	10,999,420	6,488,055	13,021,834	6,837,605	6,184,229	4,465,641	4,161,815	303,826	3,454,692	3,411,170	43,522	1,010,949	750,645	260,304
2006	17,754,230	11,240,678	6,513,552	13,175,350	6,955,221	6,220,129	4,578,880	4,285,457	293,423	3,512,929	3,473,773	39,156	1,065,951	811,684	254,267
2007	18,258,138	11,628,893	6,629,245	13,500,894	7,164,759	6,336,135	4,757,244	4,464,134	293,110	3,571,395	3,537,903	33,492	1,185,849	926,231	259,618
2008	19,081,686	12,110,487	6,971,199	13,970,862	7,330,682	6,640,180	5,110,824	4,779,805	331,019	3,660,827	3,625,469	35,358	1,449,997	1,154,336	295,661
2009	20,313,594	12,791,012	7,522,582	14,810,768	7,709,198	7,101,570	5,502,826	5,081,814	421,012	3,767,672	3,732,900	34,772	1,735,154	1,348,914	386,240
2010	21,019,438	13,335,841	7,683,597	15,142,171	7,924,108	7,218,063	5,877,267	5,411,733	465,534	3,854,482	3,821,799	32,683	2,022,785	1,589,934	432,851
2011	21,010,590	13,499,440	7,511,150	15,116,303	8,048,145	7,068,158	5,894,287	5,451,295	442,992	3,926,819	3,886,964	39,855	1,967,468	1,564,331	403,137
2012	20,644,478	13,476,638	7,167,840	14,884,667	8,092,602	6,792,065	5,759,811	5,384,036	375,775	3,951,388	3,913,690	37,698	1,808,423	1,470,346	338,077
2013	20,376,677	13,406,033	6,970,644	14,746,848	8,120,437	6,626,411	5,629,829	5,285,596	344,233	3,971,390	3,939,199	32,191	1,658,439	1,346,397	312,042
2014	20,209,092	13,494,414	6,714,678	14,654,660	8,257,108	6,397,552	5,554,432	5,237,306	317,126	3,997,249	3,966,873	30,376	1,557,183	1,270,433	286,750
2015	19,988,204	13,488,743	6,499,461	14,572,843	8,348,539	6,224,304	5,415,361	5,140,204	275,157	4,065,891	4,015,882	50,009	1,349,470	1,124,322	225,148
2016	19,846,904	13,754,486	6,092,418	14,585,840	8,742,931	5,842,909	5,261,064	5,011,555	249,509	4,078,956	4,028,401	50,555	1,182,108	983,154	198,954
2017	19,778,151	13,825,380	5,952,771	14,571,739	8,854,279	5,717,460	5,206,412	4,971,101	235,311	4,108,489	4,060,094	48,395	1,097,923	911,007	186,916
2018	19,645,918	13,900,710	5,745,208	14,529,264	8,982,560	5,546,704	5,116,654	4,918,150	198,504	4,134,244	4,089,090	45,154	982,410	829,060	153,350

—Not available.

[1]Large increases are due to the addition of schools accredited by the Accrediting Commission of Career Schools and Colleges of Technology.

[2]Because of imputation techniques, data are not consistent with figures for other years.

NOTE: Data through 1995 are for institutions of higher education, while later data are for degree-granting institutions. Degree-granting institutions grant associate's or higher degrees and participate in Title IV federal financial aid programs. The degree-granting classification is very similar to the earlier higher education classification, but it includes more 2-year colleges and excludes a few higher education institutions that did not grant degrees. Some data have been revised from previously published figures.

SOURCE: U.S. Department of Education, National Center for Education Statistics, Higher Education General Information Survey (HEGIS), "Fall Enrollment in Institutions of Higher Education" surveys, 1970 through 1985; Integrated Postsecondary Education Data System (IPEDS), "Fall Enrollment Survey" (IPEDS-EF:86–99); and IPEDS Spring 2001 through Spring 2019, Fall Enrollment component. (This table was prepared November 2019.)

Table 303.30. Total fall enrollment in degree-granting postsecondary institutions, by level and control of institution, attendance status, and sex of student: Selected years, 1970 through 2029

Level and control of institution, attendance status, and sex of student	Actual													
	1970	1975	1980[1]	1985	1990	1995	2000	2005	2010	2014	2015	2016	2017	2018
1	2	3	4	5	6	7	8	9	10	11	12	13	14	15
Total	**8,580,887**	**11,184,859**	**12,096,895**	**12,247,055**	**13,818,637**	**14,261,781**	**15,312,289**	**17,487,475**	**21,019,438**	**20,209,092**	**19,988,204**	**19,846,904**	**19,778,151**	**19,645,918**
Full-time	5,816,290	6,841,334	7,097,958	7,075,221	7,820,985	8,128,802	9,009,600	10,797,011	13,087,182	12,454,464	12,287,512	12,125,314	12,076,141	11,991,721
Males	3,504,095	3,926,753	3,689,244	3,607,720	3,807,752	3,807,392	4,111,093	4,803,388	5,838,383	5,619,778	5,558,447	5,472,798	5,423,955	5,338,934
Females	2,312,195	2,914,581	3,408,714	3,467,501	4,013,233	4,321,410	4,898,507	5,993,623	7,248,799	6,834,686	6,729,065	6,652,516	6,652,186	6,652,787
Part-time	2,764,597	4,343,525	4,998,937	5,171,834	5,997,652	6,132,979	6,302,689	6,690,464	7,932,256	7,754,628	7,700,692	7,721,590	7,702,010	7,654,197
Males	1,539,547	2,222,244	2,185,130	2,210,730	2,476,157	2,535,147	2,610,676	2,652,537	3,207,376	3,177,752	3,165,372	3,165,624	3,147,359	3,103,728
Females	1,225,050	2,121,281	2,813,807	2,961,104	3,521,495	3,597,832	3,692,013	4,037,927	4,724,880	4,576,876	4,535,320	4,555,966	4,554,651	4,550,469
4-year	**6,261,502**	**7,214,740**	**7,570,608**	**7,715,978**	**8,578,554**	**8,769,252**	**9,363,858**	**10,999,420**	**13,335,841**	**13,494,414**	**13,488,743**	**13,754,486**	**13,825,380**	**13,900,710**
Full-time	4,587,379	5,080,256	5,344,163	5,384,614	5,937,023	6,151,755	6,792,551	8,150,209	9,721,803	9,793,357	9,776,828	9,815,967	9,848,817	9,880,953
Males	2,732,796	2,891,192	2,809,528	2,781,412	2,926,360	2,929,177	3,115,252	3,649,622	4,355,153	4,419,130	4,414,743	4,414,959	4,410,360	4,385,208
Females	1,854,583	2,189,064	2,534,635	2,603,202	3,010,663	3,222,578	3,677,299	4,500,587	5,366,650	5,374,227	5,362,085	5,401,008	5,438,457	5,495,745
Part-time	1,674,123	2,134,484	2,226,445	2,331,364	2,641,531	2,617,497	2,571,307	2,849,211	3,614,038	3,701,057	3,711,915	3,938,519	3,976,563	4,019,757
Males	936,189	1,092,461	1,017,813	1,034,804	1,124,780	1,084,753	1,047,917	1,125,935	1,424,721	1,484,380	1,491,001	1,586,069	1,594,427	1,605,785
Females	737,934	1,042,023	1,208,632	1,296,560	1,516,751	1,532,744	1,523,390	1,723,276	2,189,317	2,216,677	2,220,914	2,352,450	2,382,136	2,413,972
Public 4-year	4,232,722	4,998,142	5,128,612	5,209,540	5,848,242	5,814,545	6,055,398	6,837,605	7,924,108	8,257,108	8,348,539	8,742,931	8,854,279	8,982,560
Full-time	3,086,491	3,469,821	3,592,193	3,623,341	4,033,654	4,084,711	4,371,218	5,021,745	5,811,214	6,011,908	6,081,177	6,236,018	6,309,569	6,336,978
Males	1,813,584	1,947,823	1,873,397	1,863,689	1,982,369	1,951,140	2,008,618	2,295,456	2,707,307	2,806,792	2,833,998	2,894,232	2,911,441	2,895,088
Females	1,272,907	1,521,998	1,718,796	1,759,652	2,051,285	2,133,571	2,362,600	2,726,289	3,103,907	3,205,116	3,247,179	3,341,786	3,398,128	3,441,890
Part-time	1,146,231	1,528,321	1,536,419	1,586,199	1,814,588	1,729,834	1,684,180	1,815,860	2,112,894	2,245,200	2,267,362	2,506,913	2,544,710	2,645,582
Males	609,422	760,469	685,051	693,115	764,248	720,402	683,100	724,375	860,968	941,104	955,658	1,065,112	1,077,611	1,110,660
Females	536,809	767,852	851,368	893,084	1,050,340	1,009,432	1,001,080	1,091,485	1,251,926	1,304,096	1,311,704	1,441,801	1,467,099	1,534,922
Private 4-year	2,028,780	2,216,598	2,441,996	2,506,438	2,730,312	2,954,707	3,308,460	4,161,815	5,411,733	5,237,306	5,140,204	5,011,555	4,971,101	4,918,150
Full-time	1,500,888	1,610,435	1,751,970	1,761,273	1,903,369	2,067,044	2,421,333	3,128,464	3,910,589	3,781,449	3,695,651	3,579,949	3,539,248	3,543,975
Males	919,212	943,369	936,131	917,723	943,991	978,037	1,106,634	1,354,166	1,647,846	1,612,338	1,580,745	1,520,727	1,498,919	1,490,120
Females	581,676	667,066	815,839	843,550	959,378	1,089,007	1,314,699	1,774,298	2,262,743	2,169,111	2,114,906	2,059,222	2,040,329	2,053,855
Part-time	527,892	606,163	690,026	745,165	826,943	887,663	887,127	1,033,351	1,501,144	1,455,857	1,444,553	1,431,606	1,431,853	1,374,175
Males	326,767	331,992	332,762	341,689	360,532	364,351	364,817	401,560	563,753	543,276	535,343	520,957	516,816	495,125
Females	201,125	274,171	357,264	403,476	466,411	523,312	522,310	631,791	937,391	912,581	909,210	910,649	915,037	879,050
Nonprofit 4-year	2,021,121	2,198,451	2,413,693	2,463,000	2,671,069	2,853,890	3,050,575	3,411,170	3,821,799	3,966,873	4,015,882	4,028,401	4,060,094	4,089,090
Full-time	1,494,625	1,596,074	1,733,014	1,727,707	1,859,124	1,989,457	2,226,028	2,534,793	2,864,640	2,981,188	3,009,240	3,019,342	3,040,980	3,088,150
Males	914,020	930,842	921,253	894,080	915,100	931,956	996,113	1,109,075	1,259,638	1,313,286	1,320,947	1,318,323	1,318,131	1,328,444
Females	580,605	665,232	811,761	833,627	944,024	1,057,501	1,229,915	1,425,718	1,605,002	1,667,902	1,688,293	1,701,019	1,722,849	1,759,706
Part-time	526,496	602,377	680,679	735,293	811,945	864,433	824,547	876,377	957,159	985,685	1,006,642	1,009,059	1,019,114	1,000,940
Males	325,693	329,662	327,986	336,168	352,106	351,874	332,814	339,572	366,735	379,513	385,942	385,008	389,975	382,813
Females	200,803	272,715	352,693	399,125	459,839	512,559	491,733	536,805	590,424	606,172	620,700	624,051	629,139	618,127
For-profit 4-year	7,659	18,147	28,303	43,438	59,243	100,817	257,885	750,645	1,589,934	1,270,433	1,124,322	983,154	911,007	829,060
2-year	**2,319,385**	**3,970,119**	**4,526,287**	**4,531,077**	**5,240,083**	**5,492,529**	**5,948,431**	**6,488,055**	**7,683,597**	**6,714,678**	**6,499,461**	**6,092,418**	**5,952,771**	**5,745,208**
Full-time	1,228,911	1,761,078	1,753,795	1,690,607	1,883,962	1,977,047	2,217,049	2,646,802	3,365,379	2,661,107	2,510,684	2,309,347	2,227,324	2,110,768
Males	771,299	1,035,561	879,716	826,308	881,392	878,215	995,841	1,153,766	1,483,230	1,200,648	1,143,704	1,057,839	1,013,595	953,726
Females	457,612	725,517	874,079	864,299	1,002,570	1,098,832	1,221,208	1,493,036	1,882,149	1,460,459	1,366,980	1,251,508	1,213,729	1,157,042
Part-time	1,090,474	2,209,041	2,772,492	2,840,470	3,356,121	3,515,482	3,731,382	3,841,253	4,318,218	4,053,571	3,988,777	3,783,071	3,725,447	3,634,440
Males	603,358	1,129,783	1,167,317	1,175,926	1,351,377	1,450,394	1,562,759	1,526,602	1,782,655	1,693,372	1,674,371	1,579,555	1,552,932	1,497,943
Females	487,116	1,079,258	1,605,175	1,664,544	2,004,744	2,065,088	2,168,623	2,314,651	2,535,563	2,360,199	2,314,406	2,203,516	2,172,515	2,136,497
Public 2-year	2,195,412	3,836,366	4,328,782	4,269,733	4,996,475	5,277,829	5,697,388	6,184,229	7,218,063	6,397,552	6,224,304	5,842,909	5,717,460	5,546,704
Full-time	1,129,165	1,662,621	1,595,493	1,496,905	1,716,843	1,840,590	2,000,008	2,387,016	2,950,024	2,385,023	2,272,769	2,091,361	2,016,905	1,931,842
Males	720,440	988,701	811,871	742,673	810,664	818,605	891,282	1,055,029	1,340,820	1,107,410	1,062,633	983,567	945,990	892,853
Females	408,725	673,920	783,622	754,232	906,179	1,021,985	1,108,726	1,331,987	1,609,204	1,277,613	1,210,136	1,107,794	1,070,915	1,038,989
Part-time	1,066,247	2,173,745	2,733,289	2,772,828	3,279,632	3,437,239	3,697,380	3,797,213	4,268,039	4,012,529	3,951,535	3,751,548	3,700,555	3,614,862
Males	589,439	1,107,680	1,152,268	1,138,011	1,317,730	1,417,488	1,549,407	1,514,363	1,769,737	1,683,249	1,665,373	1,571,824	1,546,504	1,492,870
Females	476,808	1,066,065	1,581,021	1,634,817	1,961,902	2,019,751	2,147,973	2,282,850	2,498,302	2,329,280	2,286,162	2,179,724	2,154,051	2,121,992
Private 2-year	123,973	133,753	197,505	261,344	243,608	214,700	251,043	303,826	465,534	317,126	275,157	249,509	235,311	198,504
Full-time	99,746	98,457	158,302	193,702	167,119	136,457	217,041	259,786	415,355	276,084	237,915	217,986	210,419	178,926
Males	50,859	46,860	67,845	83,635	70,728	59,610	104,559	98,737	142,410	93,238	81,071	74,272	67,605	60,873
Females	48,887	51,597	90,457	110,067	96,391	76,847	112,482	161,049	272,945	182,846	156,844	143,714	142,814	118,053
Part-time	24,227	35,296	39,203	67,642	76,489	78,243	34,002	44,040	50,179	41,042	37,242	31,523	24,892	19,578
Males	13,919	22,103	15,049	37,915	33,647	32,906	13,352	12,239	12,918	10,123	8,998	7,731	6,428	5,073
Females	10,308	13,193	24,154	29,727	42,842	45,337	20,650	31,801	37,261	30,919	28,244	23,792	18,464	14,505
Nonprofit 2-year	113,299	112,997	114,094	108,791	89,158	75,154	58,844	43,522	32,683	30,376	50,009	50,555	48,395	45,154
Full-time	91,514	82,158	83,009	76,547	62,003	54,033	46,670	28,939	23,127	22,789	36,027	39,513	41,091	37,980
Males	46,030	40,548	34,968	30,878	25,946	23,265	21,950	12,086	9,944	9,074	11,972	11,950	10,794	9,397
Females	45,484	41,610	48,041	45,669	36,057	30,768	24,720	16,853	13,183	13,715	24,055	27,563	30,297	28,583
Part-time	21,785	30,839	31,085	32,244	27,155	21,121	12,174	14,583	9,556	7,587	13,982	11,042	7,304	7,174
Males	12,097	18,929	11,445	10,786	7,970	6,080	4,499	3,566	2,585	2,198	2,707	2,547	1,925	1,863
Females	9,688	11,910	19,640	21,458	19,185	15,041	7,675	11,017	6,971	5,389	11,275	8,495	5,379	5,311
For-profit 2-year	10,674	20,756	83,411	152,553	154,450	139,546	192,199	260,304	432,851	286,750	225,148	198,954	186,916	153,350

See notes at end of table.

Table 303.30. Total fall enrollment in degree-granting postsecondary institutions, by level and control of institution, attendance status, and sex of student: Selected years, 1970 through 2029—Continued

Level and control of institution, attendance status, and sex of student	Projected										
	2019	2020	2021	2022	2023	2024	2025	2026	2027	2028	2029
1	16	17	18	19	20	21	22	23	24	25	26
Total	**19,720,000**	**19,744,000**	**19,778,000**	**19,813,000**	**19,862,000**	**19,926,000**	**19,993,000**	**20,070,000**	**20,099,000**	**20,110,000**	**20,115,000**
Full-time	12,025,000	12,022,000	12,021,000	12,027,000	12,045,000	12,078,000	12,120,000	12,165,000	12,169,000	12,159,000	12,144,000
Males	5,350,000	5,345,000	5,343,000	5,343,000	5,347,000	5,361,000	5,381,000	5,400,000	5,403,000	5,400,000	5,395,000
Females	6,676,000	6,677,000	6,678,000	6,685,000	6,698,000	6,716,000	6,740,000	6,765,000	6,767,000	6,759,000	6,748,000
Part-time	7,695,000	7,722,000	7,757,000	7,786,000	7,817,000	7,848,000	7,873,000	7,905,000	7,930,000	7,951,000	7,971,000
Males	3,121,000	3,131,000	3,143,000	3,155,000	3,169,000	3,182,000	3,193,000	3,207,000	3,219,000	3,226,000	3,235,000
Females	4,574,000	4,591,000	4,614,000	4,631,000	4,648,000	4,666,000	4,680,000	4,698,000	4,711,000	4,724,000	4,736,000
4-year	**13,950,000**	**13,961,000**	**13,979,000**	**13,999,000**	**14,030,000**	**14,074,000**	**14,122,000**	**14,175,000**	**14,192,000**	**14,194,000**	**14,192,000**
Full-time	9,909,000	9,906,000	9,905,000	9,910,000	9,925,000	9,952,000	9,987,000	10,024,000	10,027,000	10,019,000	10,006,000
Males	4,394,000	4,390,000	4,389,000	4,388,000	4,392,000	4,404,000	4,420,000	4,436,000	4,438,000	4,436,000	4,431,000
Females	5,515,000	5,516,000	5,517,000	5,522,000	5,533,000	5,548,000	5,567,000	5,588,000	5,590,000	5,583,000	5,575,000
Part-time	4,041,000	4,055,000	4,074,000	4,089,000	4,105,000	4,122,000	4,134,000	4,152,000	4,165,000	4,175,000	4,186,000
Males	1,615,000	1,620,000	1,626,000	1,632,000	1,639,000	1,646,000	1,652,000	1,659,000	1,665,000	1,669,000	1,674,000
Females	2,427,000	2,436,000	2,447,000	2,457,000	2,466,000	2,475,000	2,483,000	2,492,000	2,499,000	2,506,000	2,513,000
Public 4-year	9,014,000	9,022,000	9,033,000	9,046,000	9,066,000	9,095,000	9,126,000	9,161,000	9,171,000	9,173,000	9,172,000
Full-time	6,355,000	6,353,000	6,352,000	6,355,000	6,365,000	6,382,000	6,405,000	6,428,000	6,430,000	6,425,000	6,417,000
Males	2,901,000	2,898,000	2,897,000	2,897,000	2,899,000	2,907,000	2,918,000	2,928,000	2,930,000	2,928,000	2,926,000
Females	3,454,000	3,454,000	3,455,000	3,458,000	3,465,000	3,475,000	3,487,000	3,500,000	3,501,000	3,497,000	3,491,000
Part-time	2,660,000	2,669,000	2,681,000	2,691,000	2,702,000	2,713,000	2,721,000	2,732,000	2,741,000	2,748,000	2,755,000
Males	1,117,000	1,120,000	1,125,000	1,129,000	1,134,000	1,139,000	1,143,000	1,148,000	1,152,000	1,155,000	1,158,000
Females	1,543,000	1,549,000	1,556,000	1,562,000	1,568,000	1,574,000	1,579,000	1,585,000	1,589,000	1,594,000	1,598,000
Private 4-year	4,935,000	4,940,000	4,946,000	4,953,000	4,964,000	4,979,000	4,996,000	5,015,000	5,021,000	5,021,000	5,020,000
Full-time	3,554,000	3,553,000	3,553,000	3,555,000	3,560,000	3,570,000	3,582,000	3,596,000	3,597,000	3,594,000	3,589,000
Males	1,493,000	1,492,000	1,491,000	1,491,000	1,492,000	1,496,000	1,502,000	1,507,000	1,508,000	1,507,000	1,506,000
Females	2,061,000	2,061,000	2,062,000	2,064,000	2,068,000	2,073,000	2,081,000	2,088,000	2,089,000	2,087,000	2,083,000
Part-time	1,381,000	1,386,000	1,393,000	1,398,000	1,403,000	1,409,000	1,413,000	1,419,000	1,424,000	1,427,000	1,431,000
Males	498,000	499,000	501,000	503,000	505,000	508,000	509,000	512,000	513,000	515,000	516,000
Females	884,000	887,000	891,000	895,000	898,000	901,000	904,000	908,000	910,000	913,000	915,000
Nonprofit 4-year	—	—	—	—	—	—	—	—	—	—	—
Full-time	—	—	—	—	—	—	—	—	—	—	—
Males	—	—	—	—	—	—	—	—	—	—	—
Females	—	—	—	—	—	—	—	—	—	—	—
Part-time	—	—	—	—	—	—	—	—	—	—	—
Males	—	—	—	—	—	—	—	—	—	—	—
Females	—	—	—	—	—	—	—	—	—	—	—
For-profit 4-year	—	—	—	—	—	—	—	—	—	—	—
2-year	**5,770,000**	**5,783,000**	**5,799,000**	**5,814,000**	**5,832,000**	**5,853,000**	**5,872,000**	**5,895,000**	**5,907,000**	**5,915,000**	**5,922,000**
Full-time	2,117,000	2,116,000	2,116,000	2,117,000	2,120,000	2,126,000	2,133,000	2,141,000	2,142,000	2,140,000	2,137,000
Males	956,000	955,000	955,000	954,000	955,000	958,000	961,000	965,000	965,000	965,000	964,000
Females	1,161,000	1,161,000	1,161,000	1,163,000	1,165,000	1,168,000	1,172,000	1,176,000	1,177,000	1,175,000	1,174,000
Part-time	3,654,000	3,667,000	3,683,000	3,697,000	3,712,000	3,727,000	3,738,000	3,754,000	3,765,000	3,775,000	3,785,000
Males	1,506,000	1,511,000	1,517,000	1,523,000	1,529,000	1,536,000	1,541,000	1,548,000	1,553,000	1,557,000	1,561,000
Females	2,148,000	2,156,000	2,166,000	2,174,000	2,183,000	2,191,000	2,197,000	2,206,000	2,212,000	2,218,000	2,224,000
Public 2-year	5,571,000	5,584,000	5,600,000	5,614,000	5,632,000	5,652,000	5,670,000	5,693,000	5,705,000	5,714,000	5,721,000
Full-time	1,937,000	1,937,000	1,937,000	1,937,000	1,940,000	1,946,000	1,952,000	1,960,000	1,960,000	1,959,000	1,956,000
Males	895,000	894,000	894,000	893,000	894,000	897,000	900,000	903,000	904,000	903,000	902,000
Females	1,043,000	1,043,000	1,043,000	1,044,000	1,046,000	1,049,000	1,053,000	1,056,000	1,057,000	1,056,000	1,054,000
Part-time	3,634,000	3,647,000	3,663,000	3,677,000	3,692,000	3,707,000	3,718,000	3,734,000	3,745,000	3,755,000	3,765,000
Males	1,501,000	1,506,000	1,512,000	1,518,000	1,524,000	1,531,000	1,536,000	1,543,000	1,548,000	1,552,000	1,556,000
Females	2,133,000	2,141,000	2,151,000	2,159,000	2,168,000	2,176,000	2,182,000	2,191,000	2,197,000	2,203,000	2,209,000
Private 2-year	199,000	199,000	199,000	199,000	200,000	200,000	201,000	202,000	202,000	202,000	202,000
Full-time	179,000	179,000	179,000	180,000	180,000	180,000	181,000	182,000	182,000	182,000	181,000
Males	61,000	61,000	61,000	61,000	61,000	61,000	61,000	62,000	62,000	62,000	62,000
Females	118,000	118,000	119,000	119,000	119,000	119,000	120,000	120,000	120,000	120,000	120,000
Part-time	20,000	20,000	20,000	20,000	20,000	20,000	20,000	20,000	20,000	20,000	20,000
Males	5,000	5,000	5,000	5,000	5,000	5,000	5,000	5,000	5,000	5,000	5,000
Females	15,000	15,000	15,000	15,000	15,000	15,000	15,000	15,000	15,000	15,000	15,000
Nonprofit 2-year	—	—	—	—	—	—	—	—	—	—	—
Full-time	—	—	—	—	—	—	—	—	—	—	—
Males	—	—	—	—	—	—	—	—	—	—	—
Females	—	—	—	—	—	—	—	—	—	—	—
Part-time	—	—	—	—	—	—	—	—	—	—	—
Males	—	—	—	—	—	—	—	—	—	—	—
Females	—	—	—	—	—	—	—	—	—	—	—
For-profit 2-year	—	—	—	—	—	—	—	—	—	—	—

—Not available.

[1]Large increase in private 2-year institutions in 1980 is due to the addition of schools accredited by the Accrediting Commission of Career Schools and Colleges of Technology.

NOTE: Data through 1995 are for institutions of higher education, while later data are for degree-granting institutions. Degree-granting institutions grant associate's or higher degrees and participate in Title IV federal financial aid programs. The degree-granting classification is very similar to the earlier higher education classification, but it includes more 2-year colleges and excludes a few higher education institutions that did not grant degrees. Some data have been revised from previously published figures.

SOURCE: U.S. Department of Education, National Center for Education Statistics, Higher Education General Information Survey (HEGIS), "Fall Enrollment in Colleges and Universities" surveys, 1970 through 1985; Integrated Postsecondary Education Data System (IPEDS), "Fall Enrollment Survey" (IPEDS-EF:90–99); IPEDS Spring 2001 through Spring 2019, Fall Enrollment component; and Enrollment in Degree-Granting Institutions Projection Model, 2000 through 2029. (This table was prepared December 2019.)

Table 303.40. Total fall enrollment in degree-granting postsecondary institutions, by attendance status, sex, and age of student: Selected years, 1970 through 2029

[In thousands]

Attendance status, sex, and age																Projected			
	1970	1980	1990	2000	2005	2009	2010	2011	2012	2013	2014	2015	2016	2017	2018	2019	2020	2021	2029
1	2	3	4	5	6	7	8	9	10	11	12	13	14	15	16	17	18	19	20
All students	**8,581**	**12,097**	**13,819**	**15,312**	**17,487**	**20,314**	**21,019**	**21,011**	**20,644**	**20,377**	**20,209**	**19,988**	**19,847**	**19,778**	**19,646**	**19,720**	**19,744**	**19,778**	**20,115**
14 to 17 years old	263	257	153	131	187	215	202	221	242	256	239	214	214	210	206	204	205	207	204
18 and 19 years old	2,579	2,852	2,777	3,258	3,444	4,009	4,057	3,956	3,782	3,720	3,720	3,732	3,738	3,782	3,768	4,091	4,029	3,996	4,025
20 and 21 years old	1,885	2,395	2,593	3,005	3,563	3,916	4,103	4,269	4,235	4,183	4,163	4,148	4,204	4,160	4,142	4,467	4,519	4,537	4,517
22 to 24 years old	1,469	1,947	2,202	2,600	3,114	3,571	3,759	3,793	3,951	3,964	3,910	3,785	3,736	3,691	3,666	3,551	3,540	3,547	3,619
25 to 29 years old	1,091	1,843	2,083	2,044	2,469	3,082	3,254	3,272	3,155	3,050	3,084	3,165	3,192	3,226	3,194	3,058	3,033	2,996	2,957
30 to 34 years old	527	1,227	1,384	1,333	1,438	1,735	1,805	1,788	1,684	1,606	1,586	1,600	1,589	1,587	1,562	1,565	1,597	1,632	1,625
35 years old and over	767	1,577	2,627	2,942	3,272	3,785	3,840	3,712	3,597	3,597	3,507	3,344	3,174	3,123	3,107	2,785	2,821	2,864	3,166
Males	**5,044**	**5,874**	**6,284**	**6,722**	**7,456**	**8,733**	**9,046**	**9,034**	**8,919**	**8,861**	**8,798**	**8,724**	**8,638**	**8,571**	**8,443**	**8,470**	**8,476**	**8,487**	**8,630**
14 to 17 years old	125	106	66	58	68	103	94	104	119	125	117	94	83	75	77	81	81	82	81
18 and 19 years old	1,355	1,368	1,298	1,464	1,523	1,795	1,820	1,782	1,707	1,661	1,673	1,684	1,688	1,686	1,654	1,815	1,784	1,769	1,786
20 and 21 years old	1,064	1,219	1,259	1,411	1,658	1,866	1,948	1,985	1,960	1,955	1,960	1,954	1,945	1,915	1,889	2,025	2,048	2,055	2,044
22 to 24 years old	1,004	1,075	1,129	1,222	1,410	1,599	1,723	1,769	1,864	1,846	1,789	1,746	1,739	1,690	1,653	1,613	1,606	1,608	1,639
25 to 29 years old	796	983	1,024	908	1,057	1,378	1,410	1,404	1,353	1,356	1,379	1,382	1,366	1,385	1,378	1,299	1,291	1,276	1,251
30 to 34 years old	333	564	605	581	591	707	731	700	661	634	643	655	670	667	662	623	636	651	652
35 years old and over	366	559	902	1,077	1,149	1,285	1,320	1,290	1,255	1,283	1,237	1,208	1,148	1,154	1,131	1,015	1,030	1,047	1,177
Females	**3,537**	**6,223**	**7,535**	**8,591**	**10,032**	**11,581**	**11,974**	**11,976**	**11,725**	**11,515**	**11,412**	**11,264**	**11,208**	**11,207**	**11,203**	**11,250**	**11,268**	**11,292**	**11,485**
14 to 17 years old	137	151	87	73	119	113	108	116	123	131	121	120	131	135	130	123	124	125	123
18 and 19 years old	1,224	1,484	1,479	1,794	1,920	2,214	2,237	2,173	2,074	2,059	2,047	2,049	2,050	2,096	2,115	2,276	2,244	2,227	2,239
20 and 21 years old	821	1,177	1,334	1,593	1,905	2,050	2,155	2,284	2,276	2,228	2,203	2,194	2,259	2,245	2,253	2,442	2,470	2,482	2,473
22 to 24 years old	464	871	1,073	1,378	1,704	1,972	2,036	2,024	2,087	2,118	2,122	2,038	1,997	2,001	2,014	1,937	1,934	1,939	1,980
25 to 29 years old	296	859	1,059	1,136	1,413	1,704	1,844	1,868	1,802	1,694	1,706	1,783	1,826	1,841	1,816	1,759	1,743	1,720	1,706
30 to 34 years old	194	663	779	752	847	1,028	1,074	1,088	1,022	972	943	945	919	920	899	943	961	981	973
35 years old and over	401	1,018	1,725	1,865	2,123	2,500	2,520	2,422	2,341	2,314	2,270	2,136	2,026	1,969	1,976	1,770	1,791	1,816	1,990
Full-time	**5,816**	**7,098**	**7,821**	**9,010**	**10,797**	**12,605**	**13,087**	**13,003**	**12,734**	**12,597**	**12,454**	**12,288**	**12,125**	**12,076**	**11,992**	**12,025**	**12,022**	**12,021**	**12,144**
14 to 17 years old	246	231	134	121	152	179	170	185	207	210	200	182	186	183	179	178	179	181	178
18 and 19 years old	2,374	2,544	2,471	2,823	3,026	3,481	3,496	3,351	3,226	3,199	3,174	3,188	3,161	3,242	3,238	3,390	3,339	3,313	3,337
20 and 21 years old	1,649	2,007	2,137	2,452	2,976	3,241	3,364	3,427	3,386	3,327	3,326	3,290	3,365	3,332	3,361	3,419	3,460	3,471	3,455
22 to 24 years old	904	1,181	1,405	1,714	2,122	2,511	2,585	2,580	2,603	2,650	2,597	2,568	2,502	2,433	2,374	2,244	2,238	2,243	2,290
25 to 29 years old	426	641	791	886	1,174	1,506	1,605	1,600	1,555	1,528	1,525	1,519	1,478	1,480	1,453	1,385	1,375	1,358	1,339
30 to 34 years old	113	272	383	418	547	657	745	763	711	664	626	601	583	570	563	564	575	588	586
35 years old and over	104	221	500	596	800	1,030	1,122	1,096	1,047	1,018	1,005	941	852	835	824	844	855	868	959
Males	**3,504**	**3,689**	**3,808**	**4,111**	**4,803**	**5,632**	**5,838**	**5,793**	**5,708**	**5,682**	**5,620**	**5,558**	**5,473**	**5,424**	**5,339**	**5,350**	**5,345**	**5,343**	**5,395**
14 to 17 years old	121	95	55	51	53	77	71	85	102	106	100	81	71	65	66	68	69	69	69
18 and 19 years old	1,261	1,219	1,171	1,252	1,339	1,570	1,574	1,510	1,461	1,423	1,402	1,414	1,416	1,435	1,407	1,458	1,433	1,422	1,436
20 and 21 years old	955	1,046	1,035	1,156	1,398	1,536	1,586	1,586	1,537	1,542	1,549	1,546	1,552	1,536	1,546	1,564	1,582	1,587	1,579
22 to 24 years old	686	717	768	834	982	1,169	1,215	1,217	1,254	1,270	1,236	1,208	1,173	1,129	1,099	1,032	1,028	1,030	1,050
25 to 29 years old	346	391	433	410	506	661	715	727	728	734	732	709	689	693	683	672	667	660	647
30 to 34 years old	77	142	171	186	225	279	301	299	278	257	242	251	253	256	244	249	255	261	261
35 years old and over	58	80	174	222	300	341	376	369	349	351	360	349	320	310	293	306	310	315	354
Females	**2,312**	**3,409**	**4,013**	**4,899**	**5,994**	**6,973**	**7,249**	**7,210**	**7,026**	**6,914**	**6,835**	**6,729**	**6,653**	**6,652**	**6,653**	**6,676**	**6,677**	**6,678**	**6,748**
14 to 17 years old	125	136	78	70	98	102	99	100	105	104	101	101	115	118	113	110	111	111	110
18 and 19 years old	1,113	1,325	1,300	1,571	1,687	1,911	1,922	1,842	1,765	1,776	1,773	1,774	1,745	1,807	1,831	1,932	1,906	1,891	1,901
20 and 21 years old	693	961	1,101	1,296	1,578	1,705	1,778	1,840	1,849	1,785	1,777	1,744	1,813	1,795	1,815	1,855	1,878	1,885	1,876
22 to 24 years old	218	464	638	880	1,140	1,343	1,370	1,364	1,349	1,380	1,362	1,359	1,329	1,305	1,275	1,212	1,210	1,213	1,240
25 to 29 years old	80	250	358	476	668	845	891	873	827	794	793	810	789	788	769	714	707	698	692
30 to 34 years old	37	130	212	232	322	378	444	464	433	408	384	350	330	314	318	314	320	327	325
35 years old and over	46	141	326	374	500	690	746	727	698	667	645	592	532	526	531	538	545	552	605
Part-time	**2,765**	**4,999**	**5,998**	**6,303**	**6,690**	**7,708**	**7,932**	**8,008**	**7,910**	**7,780**	**7,755**	**7,701**	**7,722**	**7,702**	**7,654**	**7,695**	**7,722**	**7,757**	**7,971**
14 to 17 years old	16	26	19	10	36	36	32	36	35	47	38	32	28	27	27	26	26	26	26
18 and 19 years old	205	308	306	435	417	528	561	604	556	521	546	545	577	540	531	700	690	683	688
20 and 21 years old	236	388	456	553	586	675	738	842	850	855	836	858	839	828	781	1,048	1,058	1,065	1,062
22 to 24 years old	564	765	796	886	992	1,059	1,174	1,212	1,348	1,314	1,313	1,217	1,235	1,257	1,292	1,306	1,302	1,304	1,330
25 to 29 years old	665	1,202	1,291	1,158	1,296	1,576	1,648	1,672	1,600	1,522	1,560	1,646	1,715	1,745	1,741	1,672	1,659	1,638	1,618
30 to 34 years old	414	954	1,001	915	891	1,079	1,060	1,025	973	942	960	1,000	1,006	1,016	999	1,002	1,022	1,044	1,040
35 years old and over	663	1,356	2,127	2,345	2,472	2,754	2,718	2,616	2,550	2,579	2,502	2,404	2,322	2,288	2,283	1,941	1,966	1,996	2,207
Males	**1,540**	**2,185**	**2,476**	**2,611**	**2,653**	**3,101**	**3,207**	**3,241**	**3,211**	**3,179**	**3,178**	**3,165**	**3,166**	**3,147**	**3,104**	**3,121**	**3,131**	**3,143**	**3,235**
14 to 17 years old	4	12	11	7	15	25	23	20	17	20	18	13	12	10	10	12	12	12	12
18 and 19 years old	94	149	127	212	184	226	245	273	246	239	271	270	272	251	247	357	351	347	351
20 and 21 years old	108	172	224	255	260	330	362	398	423	413	411	408	393	378	342	461	466	468	465
22 to 24 years old	318	359	361	388	428	430	508	552	610	576	553	538	566	561	554	581	578	578	589
25 to 29 years old	450	592	591	498	551	718	695	677	625	622	646	673	677	692	695	627	623	616	604
30 to 34 years old	257	422	435	395	365	428	430	401	383	377	401	405	417	410	418	373	381	390	391
35 years old and over	309	479	728	855	850	944	944	921	906	932	877	859	829	845	838	710	720	732	822
Females	**1,225**	**2,814**	**3,521**	**3,692**	**4,038**	**4,607**	**4,725**	**4,767**	**4,699**	**4,601**	**4,577**	**4,535**	**4,556**	**4,555**	**4,550**	**4,574**	**4,591**	**4,614**	**4,736**
14 to 17 years old	12	14	9	3	21	11	9	16	18	27	20	19	16	17	16	14	14	14	14
18 and 19 years old	112	159	179	223	233	303	316	332	310	283	274	275	305	289	284	343	339	336	338
20 and 21 years old	128	216	233	298	327	345	377	444	427	443	425	450	446	450	439	587	592	598	597
22 to 24 years old	246	407	435	497	564	629	666	660	738	738	760	679	668	696	738	725	724	725	741
25 to 29 years old	216	609	700	660	745	859	953	995	975	900	913	973	1,037	1,053	1,047	1,045	1,036	1,022	1,014
30 to 34 years old	158	532	567	520	526	651	630	624	589	565	559	595	589	606	581	629	641	654	649
35 years old and over	354	876	1,399	1,491	1,623	1,810	1,774	1,695	1,643	1,647	1,625	1,544	1,493	1,443	1,445	1,232	1,247	1,264	1,385

NOTE: Distributions by age are estimates based on samples of the civilian noninstitutionalized population from the U.S. Census Bureau's Current Population Survey. Data through 1995 are for institutions of higher education, while later data are for degree-granting institutions. Degree-granting institutions grant associate's or higher degrees and participate in Title IV federal financial aid programs. The degree-granting classification is very similar to the earlier higher education classification, but it includes more 2-year colleges and excludes a few higher education institutions that did not grant degrees. Some data have been revised from previously published figures. Detail may not sum to totals because of rounding.

SOURCE: U.S. Department of Education, National Center for Education Statistics, Higher Education General Information Survey (HEGIS), "Fall Enrollment in Colleges and Universities" surveys, 1970 and 1980; Integrated Postsecondary Education Data System (IPEDS), "Fall Enrollment Survey" (IPEDS-EF:90–99); IPEDS Spring 2001 through Spring 2019, Fall Enrollment component; and Enrollment in Degree-Granting Institutions Projection Model, 2000 through 2029. U.S. Department of Commerce, Census Bureau, Current Population Survey (CPS), October, selected years, 1970 through 2018. (This table was prepared April 2020.)

Table 303.45. Total fall enrollment in degree-granting postsecondary institutions, by level of enrollment, sex, attendance status, and age of student: 2013, 2015, and 2017

Attendance status and age of student	Fall 2013	Fall 2015			Fall 2017								
	All levels	All levels			All levels			Undergraduate			Postbaccalaureate		
	Total	Total	Males	Females	Total	Males	Females	Total	Males	Females	Total	Males	Females
1	2	3	4	5	6	7	8	9	10	11	12	13	14
All students	**20,376,677**	**19,988,204**	**8,723,819**	**11,264,385**	**19,778,151**	**8,571,314**	**11,206,837**	**16,773,036**	**7,351,259**	**9,421,777**	**3,005,115**	**1,220,055**	**1,785,060**
Under 18	878,766	1,053,854	435,452	618,402	1,233,155	506,387	726,768	1,233,021	506,327	726,694	134	60	74
18 and 19	4,265,916	4,341,382	1,954,795	2,386,587	4,446,105	1,994,211	2,451,894	4,445,215	1,993,914	2,451,301	890	297	593
20 and 21	4,086,686	4,078,990	1,849,082	2,229,908	4,096,336	1,844,738	2,251,598	4,059,944	1,831,887	2,228,057	36,392	12,851	23,541
22 to 24	3,431,880	3,324,891	1,540,990	1,783,901	3,204,527	1,471,011	1,733,516	2,541,944	1,208,478	1,333,466	662,583	262,533	400,050
25 to 29	2,856,287	2,778,912	1,227,002	1,551,910	2,694,183	1,167,840	1,526,343	1,732,765	752,678	980,087	961,418	415,162	546,256
30 to 34	1,641,631	1,511,847	644,424	867,423	1,421,657	597,664	823,993	946,325	389,598	556,727	475,332	208,066	267,266
35 to 39	1,033,809	973,402	384,395	589,007	933,343	366,653	566,690	634,889	246,082	388,807	298,454	120,571	177,883
40 to 49	1,346,668	1,190,153	428,681	761,472	1,090,103	389,284	700,819	727,226	260,318	466,908	362,877	128,966	233,911
50 to 64	717,355	627,528	214,632	412,896	560,173	192,051	368,122	372,091	128,351	243,740	188,082	63,700	124,382
65 and over	66,202	66,683	28,234	38,449	67,094	28,537	38,557	53,541	22,728	30,813	13,553	5,809	7,744
Age unknown	51,477	40,562	16,132	24,430	31,475	12,938	18,537	26,075	10,898	15,177	5,400	2,040	3,360
Full-time	12,596,610	12,287,512	5,558,447	6,729,065	12,076,141	5,423,955	6,652,186	10,371,863	4,683,715	5,688,148	1,704,278	740,240	964,038
Under 18	185,285	206,770	83,135	123,635	220,590	86,108	134,482	220,547	86,084	134,463	43	24	19
18 and 19	3,549,171	3,612,294	1,612,557	1,999,737	3,695,990	1,644,606	2,051,384	3,695,241	1,644,373	2,050,868	749	233	516
20 and 21	3,245,703	3,241,515	1,470,848	1,770,667	3,267,198	1,475,104	1,792,094	3,234,340	1,463,343	1,770,997	32,858	11,761	21,097
22 to 24	2,240,365	2,156,073	1,033,642	1,122,431	2,068,425	983,041	1,085,384	1,538,218	768,645	769,573	530,207	214,396	315,811
25 to 29	1,497,997	1,442,151	681,881	760,270	1,372,010	636,740	735,270	761,468	353,742	407,726	610,542	282,998	327,544
30 to 34	724,235	649,695	296,410	353,285	591,317	266,301	325,016	361,865	156,078	205,787	229,452	110,223	119,229
35 to 39	408,932	368,319	151,776	216,543	338,499	138,827	199,672	221,791	87,570	134,221	116,708	51,257	65,451
40 to 49	483,716	403,959	151,610	252,349	350,409	129,668	220,741	229,041	83,394	145,647	121,368	46,274	75,094
50 to 64	226,402	177,157	64,530	112,627	148,671	53,859	94,812	91,788	33,175	58,613	56,883	20,684	36,199
65 and over	9,105	10,556	4,747	5,809	8,951	3,941	5,010	5,161	2,318	2,843	3,790	1,623	2,167
Age unknown	25,699	19,023	7,311	11,712	14,081	5,760	8,321	12,403	4,993	7,410	1,678	767	911
Part-time	7,780,067	7,700,692	3,165,372	4,535,320	7,702,010	3,147,359	4,554,651	6,401,173	2,667,544	3,733,629	1,300,837	479,815	821,022
Under 18	693,481	847,084	352,317	494,767	1,012,565	420,279	592,286	1,012,474	420,243	592,231	91	36	55
18 and 19	716,745	729,088	342,238	386,850	750,115	349,605	400,510	749,974	349,541	400,433	141	64	77
20 and 21	840,983	837,475	378,234	459,241	829,138	369,634	459,504	825,604	368,544	457,060	3,534	1,090	2,444
22 to 24	1,191,515	1,168,818	507,348	661,470	1,136,102	487,970	648,132	1,003,726	439,833	563,893	132,376	48,137	84,239
25 to 29	1,358,290	1,336,761	545,121	791,640	1,322,173	531,100	791,073	971,297	398,936	572,361	350,876	132,164	218,712
30 to 34	917,396	862,152	348,014	514,138	830,340	331,363	498,977	584,460	233,520	350,940	245,880	97,843	148,037
35 to 39	624,877	605,083	232,619	372,464	594,844	227,826	367,018	413,098	158,512	254,586	181,746	69,314	112,432
40 to 49	862,952	786,194	277,071	509,123	739,694	259,616	480,078	498,185	176,924	321,261	241,509	82,692	158,817
50 to 64	490,953	450,371	150,102	300,269	411,502	138,192	273,310	280,303	95,176	185,127	131,199	43,016	88,183
65 and over	57,097	56,127	23,487	32,640	58,143	24,596	33,547	48,380	20,410	27,970	9,763	4,186	5,577
Age unknown	25,778	21,539	8,821	12,718	17,394	7,178	10,216	13,672	5,905	7,767	3,722	1,273	2,449
	Percentage distribution of students with known age[1]												
All students	**100.0**	**100.0**	**100.0**	**100.0**	**100.0**	**100.0**	**100.0**	**100.0**	**100.0**	**100.0**	**100.0**	**100.0**	**100.0**
Under 18	4.3	5.3	5.0	5.5	6.2	5.9	6.5	7.4	6.9	7.7	#	#	#
18 and 19	21.0	21.8	22.4	21.2	22.5	23.3	21.9	26.5	27.2	26.1	#	#	#
20 and 21	20.1	20.4	21.2	19.8	20.7	21.6	20.1	24.2	25.0	23.7	1.2	1.1	1.3
22 to 24	16.9	16.7	17.7	15.9	16.2	17.2	15.5	15.2	16.5	14.2	22.1	21.6	22.5
25 to 29	14.1	13.9	14.1	13.8	13.6	13.6	13.6	10.3	10.3	10.4	32.1	34.1	30.7
30 to 34	8.1	7.6	7.4	7.7	7.2	7.0	7.4	5.7	5.3	5.9	15.8	17.1	15.0
35 to 39	5.1	4.9	4.4	5.2	4.7	4.3	5.1	3.8	3.4	4.1	9.9	9.9	10.0
40 to 49	6.6	6.0	4.9	6.8	5.5	4.5	6.3	4.3	3.5	5.0	12.1	10.6	13.1
50 to 64	3.5	3.1	2.5	3.7	2.8	2.2	3.3	2.2	1.7	2.6	6.3	5.2	7.0
65 and over	0.3	0.3	0.3	0.3	0.3	0.3	0.3	0.3	0.3	0.3	0.5	0.5	0.4
Full-time	100.0	100.0	100.0	100.0	100.0	100.0	100.0	100.0	100.0	100.0	100.0	100.0	100.0
Under 18	1.5	1.7	1.5	1.8	1.8	1.6	2.0	2.1	1.8	2.4	#	#	#
18 and 19	28.2	29.4	29.0	29.8	30.6	30.4	30.9	35.7	35.1	36.1	#	#	0.1
20 and 21	25.8	26.4	26.5	26.4	27.1	27.2	27.0	31.2	31.3	31.2	1.9	1.6	2.2
22 to 24	17.8	17.6	18.6	16.7	17.1	18.1	16.3	14.8	16.4	13.5	31.1	29.0	32.8
25 to 29	11.9	11.8	12.3	11.3	11.4	11.8	11.1	7.4	7.6	7.2	35.9	38.3	34.0
30 to 34	5.8	5.3	5.3	5.3	4.9	4.9	4.9	3.5	3.3	3.6	13.5	14.9	12.4
35 to 39	3.3	3.0	2.7	3.2	2.8	2.6	3.0	2.1	1.9	2.4	6.9	6.9	6.8
40 to 49	3.8	3.3	2.7	3.8	2.9	2.4	3.3	2.2	1.8	2.6	7.1	6.3	7.8
50 to 64	1.8	1.4	1.2	1.7	1.2	1.0	1.4	0.9	0.7	1.0	3.3	2.8	3.8
65 and over	0.1	0.1	0.1	0.1	0.1	0.1	0.1	#	#	0.1	0.2	0.2	0.2
Part-time	100.0	100.0	100.0	100.0	100.0	100.0	100.0	100.0	100.0	100.0	100.0	100.0	100.0
Under 18	8.9	11.0	11.2	10.9	13.2	13.4	13.0	15.9	15.8	15.9	#	#	#
18 and 19	9.2	9.5	10.8	8.6	9.8	11.1	8.8	11.7	13.1	10.7	#	#	#
20 and 21	10.8	10.9	12.0	10.2	10.8	11.8	10.1	12.9	13.8	12.3	0.3	0.2	0.3
22 to 24	15.4	15.2	16.1	14.6	14.8	15.5	14.3	15.7	16.5	15.1	10.2	10.1	10.3
25 to 29	17.5	17.4	17.3	17.5	17.2	16.9	17.4	15.2	15.0	15.4	27.1	27.6	26.7
30 to 34	11.8	11.2	11.0	11.4	10.8	10.6	11.0	9.2	8.8	9.4	19.0	20.4	18.1
35 to 39	8.1	7.9	7.4	8.2	7.7	7.3	8.1	6.5	6.0	6.8	14.0	14.5	13.7
40 to 49	11.1	10.2	8.8	11.3	9.6	8.3	10.6	7.8	6.6	8.6	18.6	17.3	19.4
50 to 64	6.3	5.9	4.8	6.6	5.4	4.4	6.0	4.4	3.6	5.0	10.1	9.0	10.8
65 and over	0.7	0.7	0.7	0.7	0.8	0.8	0.7	0.8	0.8	0.8	0.8	0.9	0.7

#Rounds to zero.
[1]Percentage distributions exclude students whose age is unknown.
NOTE: Degree-granting institutions grant associate's or higher degrees and participate in Title IV federal financial aid programs. Detail may not sum to totals because of rounding.

Some data have been revised from previously published figures.
SOURCE: U.S. Department of Education, National Center for Education Statistics, Integrated Postsecondary Education Data System (IPEDS), Spring 2014, 2016, and 2018, Fall Enrollment component. (This table was prepared September 2019.)

Table 303.50. Total fall enrollment in degree-granting postsecondary institutions, by level of enrollment, control and level of institution, attendance status, and age of student: 2017

Attendance status and age of student	Undergraduate										Postbaccalaureate			
		Public			Private nonprofit			Private for-profit						
	Total	Total	4-year	2-year	Total	4-year	2-year	Total	4-year	2-year	Total	Public	Private nonprofit	Private for-profit
1	2	3	4	5	6	7	8	9	10	11	12	13	14	15
All students	**16,773,036**	**13,112,594**	**7,395,134**	**5,717,460**	**2,819,080**	**2,770,685**	**48,395**	**841,362**	**654,446**	**186,916**	**3,005,115**	**1,459,145**	**1,289,409**	**256,561**
Under 18	1,233,021	1,132,042	379,252	752,790	96,410	95,753	657	4,569	3,457	1,112	134	40	92	2
18 and 19	4,445,215	3,526,795	2,172,927	1,353,868	859,865	852,685	7,180	58,555	36,666	21,889	890	449	413	28
20 and 21	4,059,944	3,132,168	2,171,402	960,766	847,338	841,906	5,432	80,438	54,061	26,377	36,392	19,785	16,146	461
22 to 24	2,541,944	2,063,145	1,293,776	769,369	362,913	355,868	7,045	115,886	82,912	32,974	662,583	358,913	290,793	12,877
25 to 29	1,732,765	1,339,447	630,619	708,828	209,967	200,300	9,667	183,351	143,343	40,008	961,418	492,261	422,550	46,607
30 to 34	946,325	674,873	283,074	391,799	134,710	128,665	6,045	136,742	113,202	23,540	475,332	234,815	195,546	44,971
35 to 39	634,889	432,454	172,682	259,772	103,114	98,923	4,191	99,321	83,715	15,606	298,454	134,762	121,331	42,361
40 to 49	727,226	487,302	185,390	301,912	128,754	123,608	5,146	111,170	94,363	16,807	362,877	146,499	150,493	65,885
50 to 64	372,091	262,585	88,723	173,862	62,440	59,712	2,728	47,066	39,662	7,404	188,082	66,177	81,872	40,033
65 and over	53,541	47,310	13,167	34,143	4,421	4,206	215	1,810	1,464	346	13,553	5,014	5,734	2,805
Age unknown	26,075	14,473	4,122	10,351	9,148	9,059	89	2,454	1,601	853	5,400	430	4,439	531
Full-time	10,371,863	7,515,398	5,498,493	2,016,905	2,300,518	2,259,427	41,091	555,947	386,619	169,328	1,704,278	811,076	781,553	111,649
Under 18	220,547	185,310	103,906	81,404	33,098	32,834	264	2,139	1,052	1,087	43	18	24	1
18 and 19	3,695,241	2,812,605	1,983,407	829,198	830,043	823,231	6,812	52,593	31,590	21,003	749	404	327	18
20 and 21	3,234,340	2,354,762	1,921,413	433,349	813,857	809,134	4,723	65,721	41,211	24,510	32,858	18,007	14,515	336
22 to 24	1,538,218	1,161,147	924,814	236,333	293,846	288,032	5,814	83,225	53,388	29,837	530,207	285,663	236,769	7,775
25 to 29	761,468	515,303	320,680	194,623	124,840	116,701	8,139	121,325	85,420	35,905	610,542	302,408	285,291	22,843
30 to 34	361,865	208,220	112,487	95,733	69,373	64,304	5,069	84,272	63,342	20,930	229,452	106,932	103,218	19,302
35 to 39	221,791	114,346	57,303	57,043	49,018	45,528	3,490	58,427	44,532	13,895	116,708	46,004	52,918	17,786
40 to 49	229,041	109,944	51,973	57,971	57,059	52,763	4,296	62,038	47,218	14,820	121,368	37,424	57,399	26,545
50 to 64	91,788	44,149	18,726	25,423	23,781	21,524	2,257	23,858	17,620	6,238	56,883	13,387	27,886	15,610
65 and over	5,161	3,273	1,022	2,251	953	775	178	935	632	303	3,790	745	1,903	1,142
Age unknown	12,403	6,339	2,762	3,577	4,650	4,601	49	1,414	614	800	1,678	84	1,303	291
Part-time	6,401,173	5,597,196	1,896,641	3,700,555	518,562	511,258	7,304	285,415	267,827	17,588	1,300,837	648,069	507,856	144,912
Under 18	1,012,474	946,732	275,346	671,386	63,312	62,919	393	2,430	2,405	25	91	22	68	1
18 and 19	749,974	714,190	189,520	524,670	29,822	29,454	368	5,962	5,076	886	141	45	86	10
20 and 21	825,604	777,406	249,989	527,417	33,481	32,772	709	14,717	12,850	1,867	3,534	1,778	1,631	125
22 to 24	1,003,726	901,998	368,962	533,036	69,067	67,836	1,231	32,661	29,524	3,137	132,376	73,250	54,024	5,102
25 to 29	971,297	824,144	309,939	514,205	85,127	83,599	1,528	62,026	57,923	4,103	350,876	189,853	137,259	23,764
30 to 34	584,460	466,653	170,587	296,066	65,337	64,361	976	52,470	49,860	2,610	245,880	127,883	92,328	25,669
35 to 39	413,098	318,108	115,379	202,729	54,096	53,395	701	40,894	39,183	1,711	181,746	88,758	68,413	24,575
40 to 49	498,185	377,358	133,417	243,941	71,695	70,845	850	49,132	47,145	1,987	241,509	109,075	93,094	39,340
50 to 64	280,303	218,436	69,997	148,439	38,659	38,188	471	23,208	22,042	1,166	131,199	52,790	53,986	24,423
65 and over	48,380	44,037	12,145	31,892	3,468	3,431	37	875	832	43	9,763	4,269	3,831	1,663
Age unknown	13,672	8,134	1,360	6,774	4,498	4,458	40	1,040	987	53	3,722	346	3,136	240
	Percentage distribution of students with known age[1]													
All students	**100.0**	**100.0**	**100.0**	**100.0**	**100.0**	**100.0**	**100.0**	**100.0**	**100.0**	**100.0**	**100.0**	**100.0**	**100.0**	**100.0**
Under 18	7.4	8.6	5.1	13.2	3.4	3.5	1.4	0.5	0.5	0.6	#	#	#	#
18 and 19	26.5	26.9	29.4	23.7	30.6	30.9	14.9	7.0	5.6	11.8	#	#	#	#
20 and 21	24.2	23.9	29.4	16.8	30.2	30.5	11.2	9.6	8.3	14.2	1.2	1.4	1.3	0.2
22 to 24	15.2	15.8	17.5	13.5	12.9	12.9	14.6	13.8	12.7	17.7	22.1	24.6	22.6	5.0
25 to 29	10.3	10.2	8.5	12.4	7.5	7.3	20.0	21.9	22.0	21.5	32.1	33.7	32.9	18.2
30 to 34	5.7	5.2	3.8	6.9	4.8	4.7	12.5	16.3	17.3	12.7	15.8	16.1	15.2	17.6
35 to 39	3.8	3.3	2.3	4.6	3.7	3.6	8.7	11.8	12.8	8.4	9.9	9.2	9.4	16.5
40 to 49	4.3	3.7	2.5	5.3	4.6	4.5	10.7	13.3	14.5	9.0	12.1	10.0	11.7	25.7
50 to 64	2.2	2.0	1.2	3.0	2.2	2.2	5.6	5.6	6.1	4.0	6.3	4.5	6.4	15.6
65 and over	0.3	0.4	0.2	0.6	0.2	0.2	0.4	0.2	0.2	0.2	0.5	0.3	0.4	1.1
Full-time	100.0	100.0	100.0	100.0	100.0	100.0	100.0	100.0	100.0	100.0	100.0	100.0	100.0	100.0
Under 18	2.1	2.5	1.9	4.0	1.4	1.5	0.6	0.4	0.3	0.6	#	#	#	#
18 and 19	35.7	37.5	36.1	41.2	36.2	36.5	16.6	9.5	8.2	12.5	#	#	#	#
20 and 21	31.2	31.4	35.0	21.5	35.4	35.9	11.5	11.9	10.7	14.5	1.9	2.2	1.9	0.3
22 to 24	14.8	15.5	16.8	11.7	12.8	12.8	14.2	15.0	13.8	17.7	31.1	35.2	30.3	7.0
25 to 29	7.4	6.9	5.8	9.7	5.4	5.2	19.8	21.9	22.1	21.3	35.9	37.3	36.6	20.5
30 to 34	3.5	2.8	2.0	4.8	3.0	2.9	12.4	15.2	16.4	12.4	13.5	13.2	13.2	17.3
35 to 39	2.1	1.5	1.0	2.8	2.1	2.0	8.5	10.5	11.5	8.2	6.9	5.7	6.8	16.0
40 to 49	2.2	1.5	0.9	2.9	2.5	2.3	10.5	11.2	12.2	8.8	7.1	4.6	7.4	23.8
50 to 64	0.9	0.6	0.3	1.3	1.0	1.0	5.5	4.3	4.6	3.7	3.3	1.7	3.6	14.0
65 and over	#	#	#	0.1	#	#	0.4	0.2	0.2	0.2	0.2	0.1	0.2	1.0
Part-time	100.0	100.0	100.0	100.0	100.0	100.0	100.0	100.0	100.0	100.0	100.0	100.0	100.0	100.0
Under 18	15.9	16.9	14.5	18.2	12.3	12.4	5.4	0.9	0.9	0.1	#	#	#	#
18 and 19	11.7	12.8	10.0	14.2	5.8	5.8	5.1	2.1	1.9	5.1	#	#	#	#
20 and 21	12.9	13.9	13.2	14.3	6.5	6.5	9.8	5.2	4.8	10.6	0.3	0.3	0.3	0.1
22 to 24	15.7	16.1	19.5	14.4	13.4	13.4	16.9	11.5	11.1	17.9	10.2	11.3	10.7	3.5
25 to 29	15.2	14.7	16.4	13.9	16.6	16.5	21.0	21.8	21.7	23.4	27.1	29.3	27.2	16.4
30 to 34	9.2	8.3	9.0	8.0	12.7	12.7	13.4	18.5	18.7	14.9	19.0	19.7	18.3	17.7
35 to 39	6.5	5.7	6.1	5.5	10.5	10.5	9.7	14.4	14.7	9.8	14.0	13.7	13.6	17.0
40 to 49	7.8	6.8	7.0	6.6	13.9	14.0	11.7	17.3	17.7	11.3	18.6	16.8	18.4	27.2
50 to 64	4.4	3.9	3.7	4.0	7.5	7.5	6.5	8.2	8.3	6.6	10.1	8.2	10.7	16.9
65 and over	0.8	0.8	0.6	0.9	0.7	0.7	0.5	0.3	0.3	0.2	0.8	0.7	0.8	1.1

#Rounds to zero.
[1]Percentage distributions exclude students whose age is unknown.
NOTE: Degree-granting institutions grant associate's or higher degrees and participate in Title IV federal financial aid programs. Detail may not sum to totals because of rounding. Some data have been revised from previously published figures.

SOURCE: U.S. Department of Education, National Center for Education Statistics, Integrated Postsecondary Education Data System (IPEDS), Spring 2018, Fall Enrollment component. (This table was prepared September 2019.)

Table 303.55. Total fall enrollment in degree-granting postsecondary institutions, by control and level of institution, attendance status, and age of student: 2017

Attendance status and age of student	All institutions			Public institutions			Private (nonprofit and for-profit) institutions						
								Nonprofit institutions			For-profit institutions		
	Total	4-year	2-year	Total	4-year	2-year	Total	Total	4-year	2-year	Total	4-year	2-year
1	2	3	4	5	6	7	8	9	10	11	12	13	14
All students	**19,778,151**	**13,825,380**	**5,952,771**	**14,571,739**	**8,854,279**	**5,717,460**	**5,206,412**	**4,108,489**	**4,060,094**	**48,395**	**1,097,923**	**911,007**	**186,916**
Under 18	1,233,155	478,596	754,559	1,132,082	379,292	752,790	101,073	96,502	95,845	657	4,571	3,459	1,112
18 and 19	4,446,105	3,063,168	1,382,937	3,527,244	2,173,376	1,353,868	918,861	860,278	853,098	7,180	58,583	36,694	21,889
20 and 21	4,096,336	3,103,761	992,575	3,151,953	2,191,187	960,766	944,383	863,484	858,052	5,432	80,899	54,522	26,377
22 to 24	3,204,527	2,395,139	809,388	2,422,058	1,652,689	769,369	782,469	653,706	646,661	7,045	128,763	95,789	32,974
25 to 29	2,694,183	1,935,680	758,503	1,831,708	1,122,880	708,828	862,475	632,517	622,850	9,667	229,958	189,950	40,008
30 to 34	1,421,657	1,000,273	421,384	909,688	517,889	391,799	511,969	330,256	324,211	6,045	181,713	158,173	23,540
35 to 39	933,343	653,774	279,569	567,216	307,444	259,772	366,127	224,445	220,254	4,191	141,682	126,076	15,606
40 to 49	1,090,103	766,238	323,865	633,801	331,889	301,912	456,302	279,247	274,101	5,146	177,055	160,248	16,807
50 to 64	560,173	376,179	183,994	328,762	154,900	173,862	231,411	144,312	141,584	2,728	87,099	79,695	7,404
65 and over	67,094	32,390	34,704	52,324	18,181	34,143	14,770	10,155	9,940	215	4,615	4,269	346
Age unknown	31,475	20,182	11,293	14,903	4,552	10,351	16,572	13,587	13,498	89	2,985	2,132	853
Full-time	12,076,141	9,848,817	2,227,324	8,326,474	6,309,569	2,016,905	3,749,667	3,082,071	3,040,980	41,091	667,596	498,268	169,328
Under 18	220,590	137,835	82,755	185,328	103,924	81,404	35,262	33,122	32,858	264	2,140	1,053	1,087
18 and 19	3,695,990	2,838,977	857,013	2,813,009	1,983,811	829,198	882,981	830,370	823,558	6,812	52,611	31,608	21,003
20 and 21	3,267,198	2,804,616	462,582	2,372,769	1,939,420	433,349	894,429	828,372	823,649	4,723	66,057	41,547	24,510
22 to 24	2,068,425	1,796,441	271,984	1,446,810	1,210,477	236,333	621,615	530,615	524,801	5,814	91,000	61,163	29,837
25 to 29	1,372,010	1,133,343	238,667	817,711	623,088	194,623	554,299	410,131	401,992	8,139	144,168	108,263	35,905
30 to 34	591,317	469,585	121,732	315,152	219,419	95,733	276,165	172,591	167,522	5,069	103,574	82,644	20,930
35 to 39	338,499	264,071	74,428	160,350	103,307	57,043	178,149	101,936	98,446	3,490	76,213	62,318	13,895
40 to 49	350,409	273,322	77,087	147,368	89,397	57,971	203,041	114,458	110,162	4,296	88,583	73,763	14,820
50 to 64	148,671	114,753	33,918	57,536	32,113	25,423	91,135	51,667	49,410	2,257	39,468	33,230	6,238
65 and over	8,951	6,219	2,732	4,018	1,767	2,251	4,933	2,856	2,678	178	2,077	1,774	303
Age unknown	14,081	9,655	4,426	6,423	2,846	3,577	7,658	5,953	5,904	49	1,705	905	800
Part-time	7,702,010	3,976,563	3,725,447	6,245,265	2,544,710	3,700,555	1,456,745	1,026,418	1,019,114	7,304	430,327	412,739	17,588
Under 18	1,012,565	340,761	671,804	946,754	275,368	671,386	65,811	63,380	62,987	393	2,431	2,406	25
18 and 19	750,115	224,191	525,924	714,235	189,565	524,670	35,880	29,908	29,540	368	5,972	5,086	886
20 and 21	829,138	299,145	529,993	779,184	251,767	527,417	49,954	35,112	34,403	709	14,842	12,975	1,867
22 to 24	1,136,102	598,698	537,404	975,248	442,212	533,036	160,854	123,091	121,860	1,231	37,763	34,626	3,137
25 to 29	1,322,173	802,337	519,836	1,013,997	499,792	514,205	308,176	222,386	220,858	1,528	85,790	81,687	4,103
30 to 34	830,340	530,688	299,652	594,536	298,470	296,066	235,804	157,665	156,689	976	78,139	75,529	2,610
35 to 39	594,844	389,703	205,141	406,866	204,137	202,729	187,978	122,509	121,808	701	65,469	63,758	1,711
40 to 49	739,694	492,916	246,778	486,433	242,492	243,941	253,261	164,789	163,939	850	88,472	86,485	1,987
50 to 64	411,502	261,426	150,076	271,226	122,787	148,439	140,276	92,645	92,174	471	47,631	46,465	1,166
65 and over	58,143	26,171	31,972	48,306	16,414	31,892	9,837	7,299	7,262	37	2,538	2,495	43
Age unknown	17,394	10,527	6,867	8,480	1,706	6,774	8,914	7,634	7,594	40	1,280	1,227	53
	Percentage distribution of students with known age[1]												
All students	**100.0**	**100.0**	**100.0**	**100.0**	**100.0**	**100.0**	**100.0**	**100.0**	**100.0**	**100.0**	**100.0**	**100.0**	**100.0**
Under 18	6.2	3.5	12.7	7.8	4.3	13.2	1.9	2.4	2.4	1.4	0.4	0.4	0.6
18 and 19	22.5	22.2	23.3	24.2	24.6	23.7	17.7	21.0	21.1	14.9	5.4	4.0	11.8
20 and 21	20.7	22.5	16.7	21.7	24.8	16.8	18.2	21.1	21.2	11.2	7.4	6.0	14.2
22 to 24	16.2	17.3	13.6	16.6	18.7	13.5	15.1	16.0	16.0	14.6	11.8	10.5	17.7
25 to 29	13.6	14.0	12.8	12.6	12.7	12.4	16.6	15.4	15.4	20.0	21.0	20.9	21.5
30 to 34	7.2	7.2	7.1	6.2	5.9	6.9	9.9	8.1	8.0	12.5	16.6	17.4	12.7
35 to 39	4.7	4.7	4.7	3.9	3.5	4.6	7.1	5.5	5.4	8.7	12.9	13.9	8.4
40 to 49	5.5	5.6	5.5	4.4	3.8	5.3	8.8	6.8	6.8	10.7	16.2	17.6	9.0
50 to 64	2.8	2.7	3.1	2.3	1.8	3.0	4.5	3.5	3.5	5.6	8.0	8.8	4.0
65 and over	0.3	0.2	0.6	0.4	0.2	0.6	0.3	0.2	0.2	0.4	0.4	0.5	0.2
Full-time	100.0	100.0	100.0	100.0	100.0	100.0	100.0	100.0	100.0	100.0	100.0	100.0	100.0
Under 18	1.8	1.4	3.7	2.2	1.6	4.0	0.9	1.1	1.1	0.6	0.3	0.2	0.6
18 and 19	30.6	28.9	38.6	33.8	31.5	41.2	23.6	27.0	27.1	16.6	7.9	6.4	12.5
20 and 21	27.1	28.5	20.8	28.5	30.8	21.5	23.9	26.9	27.1	11.5	9.9	8.4	14.5
22 to 24	17.1	18.3	12.2	17.4	19.2	11.7	16.6	17.2	17.3	14.2	13.7	12.3	17.7
25 to 29	11.4	11.5	10.7	9.8	9.9	9.7	14.8	13.3	13.2	19.8	21.7	21.8	21.3
30 to 34	4.9	4.8	5.5	3.8	3.5	4.8	7.4	5.6	5.5	12.4	15.6	16.6	12.4
35 to 39	2.8	2.7	3.3	1.9	1.6	2.8	4.8	3.3	3.2	8.5	11.4	12.5	8.2
40 to 49	2.9	2.8	3.5	1.8	1.4	2.9	5.4	3.7	3.6	10.5	13.3	14.8	8.8
50 to 64	1.2	1.2	1.5	0.7	0.5	1.3	2.4	1.7	1.6	5.5	5.9	6.7	3.7
65 and over	0.1	0.1	0.1	#	#	0.1	0.1	0.1	0.1	0.4	0.3	0.4	0.2
Part-time	100.0	100.0	100.0	100.0	100.0	100.0	100.0	100.0	100.0	100.0	100.0	100.0	100.0
Under 18	13.2	8.6	18.1	15.2	10.8	18.2	4.5	6.2	6.2	5.4	0.6	0.6	0.1
18 and 19	9.8	5.7	14.1	11.5	7.5	14.2	2.5	2.9	2.9	5.1	1.4	1.2	5.1
20 and 21	10.8	7.5	14.3	12.5	9.9	14.3	3.5	3.4	3.4	9.8	3.5	3.2	10.6
22 to 24	14.8	15.1	14.5	15.6	17.4	14.4	11.1	12.1	12.0	16.9	8.8	8.4	17.9
25 to 29	17.2	20.2	14.0	16.3	19.7	13.9	21.3	21.8	21.8	21.0	20.0	19.9	23.4
30 to 34	10.8	13.4	8.1	9.5	11.7	8.0	16.3	15.5	15.5	13.4	18.2	18.4	14.9
35 to 39	7.7	9.8	5.5	6.5	8.0	5.5	13.0	12.0	12.0	9.7	15.3	15.5	9.8
40 to 49	9.6	12.4	6.6	7.8	9.5	6.6	17.5	16.2	16.2	11.7	20.6	21.0	11.3
50 to 64	5.4	6.6	4.0	4.3	4.8	4.0	9.7	9.1	9.1	6.5	11.1	11.3	6.6
65 and over	0.8	0.7	0.9	0.8	0.6	0.9	0.7	0.7	0.7	0.5	0.6	0.6	0.2

#Rounds to zero.
[1]Percentage distributions exclude students whose age is unknown.
NOTE: Degree-granting institutions grant associate's or higher degrees and participate in Title IV federal financial aid programs. Detail may not sum to totals because of rounding. Some data have been revised from previously published figures.

SOURCE: U.S. Department of Education, National Center for Education Statistics, Integrated Postsecondary Education Data System (IPEDS), Spring 2018, Fall Enrollment component. (This table was prepared September 2019.)

Table 303.60. Total fall enrollment in degree-granting postsecondary institutions, by level of enrollment, sex of student, level and control of institution, and attendance status of student: 2018

Level and control of institution and attendance status of student	Total			Undergraduate			Postbaccalaureate		
	Total	Males	Females	Total	Males	Females	Total	Males	Females
1	2	3	4	5	6	7	8	9	10
Total	**19,645,918**	**8,442,662**	**11,203,256**	**16,610,235**	**7,225,999**	**9,384,236**	**3,035,683**	**1,216,663**	**1,819,020**
Full-time	11,991,721	5,338,934	6,652,787	10,267,135	4,602,752	5,664,383	1,724,586	736,182	988,404
Part-time	7,654,197	3,103,728	4,550,469	6,343,100	2,623,247	3,719,853	1,311,097	480,481	830,616
4-year	**13,900,710**	**5,990,993**	**7,909,717**	**10,865,027**	**4,774,330**	**6,090,697**	**3,035,683**	**1,216,663**	**1,819,020**
Full-time	9,880,953	4,385,208	5,495,745	8,156,367	3,649,026	4,507,341	1,724,586	736,182	988,404
Part-time	4,019,757	1,605,785	2,413,972	2,708,660	1,125,304	1,583,356	1,311,097	480,481	830,616
2-year	**5,745,208**	**2,451,669**	**3,293,539**	**5,745,208**	**2,451,669**	**3,293,539**	†	†	†
Full-time	2,110,768	953,726	1,157,042	2,110,768	953,726	1,157,042	†	†	†
Part-time	3,634,440	1,497,943	2,136,497	3,634,440	1,497,943	2,136,497	†	†	†
Public	**14,529,264**	**6,391,471**	**8,137,793**	**13,049,326**	**5,774,848**	**7,274,478**	**1,479,938**	**616,623**	**863,315**
Full-time	8,268,820	3,787,941	4,480,879	7,451,638	3,427,581	4,024,057	817,182	360,360	456,822
Part-time	6,260,444	2,603,530	3,656,914	5,597,688	2,347,267	3,250,421	662,756	256,263	406,493
Public 4-year	8,982,560	4,005,748	4,976,812	7,502,622	3,389,125	4,113,497	1,479,938	616,623	863,315
Full-time	6,336,978	2,895,088	3,441,890	5,519,796	2,534,728	2,985,068	817,182	360,360	456,822
Part-time	2,645,582	1,110,660	1,534,922	1,982,826	854,397	1,128,429	662,756	256,263	406,493
Public 2-year	5,546,704	2,385,723	3,160,981	5,546,704	2,385,723	3,160,981	†	†	†
Full-time	1,931,842	892,853	1,038,989	1,931,842	892,853	1,038,989	†	†	†
Part-time	3,614,862	1,492,870	2,121,992	3,614,862	1,492,870	2,121,992	†	†	†
Private	**5,116,654**	**2,051,191**	**3,065,463**	**3,560,909**	**1,451,151**	**2,109,758**	**1,555,745**	**600,040**	**955,705**
Full-time	3,722,901	1,550,993	2,171,908	2,815,497	1,175,171	1,640,326	907,404	375,822	531,582
Part-time	1,393,753	500,198	893,555	745,412	275,980	469,432	648,341	224,218	424,123
Private 4-year	4,918,150	1,985,245	2,932,905	3,362,405	1,385,205	1,977,200	1,555,745	600,040	955,705
Full-time	3,543,975	1,490,120	2,053,855	2,636,571	1,114,298	1,522,273	907,404	375,822	531,582
Part-time	1,374,175	495,125	879,050	725,834	270,907	454,927	648,341	224,218	424,123
Private 2-year	198,504	65,946	132,558	198,504	65,946	132,558	†	†	†
Full-time	178,926	60,873	118,053	178,926	60,873	118,053	†	†	†
Part-time	19,578	5,073	14,505	19,578	5,073	14,505	†	†	†
Nonprofit	4,134,244	1,722,517	2,411,727	2,821,653	1,191,128	1,630,525	1,312,591	531,389	781,202
Full-time	3,126,130	1,337,841	1,788,289	2,321,433	995,083	1,326,350	804,697	342,758	461,939
Part-time	1,008,114	384,676	623,438	500,220	196,045	304,175	507,894	188,631	319,263
Nonprofit 4-year	4,089,090	1,711,257	2,377,833	2,776,499	1,179,868	1,596,631	1,312,591	531,389	781,202
Full-time	3,088,150	1,328,444	1,759,706	2,283,453	985,686	1,297,767	804,697	342,758	461,939
Part-time	1,000,940	382,813	618,127	493,046	194,182	298,864	507,894	188,631	319,263
Nonprofit 2-year	45,154	11,260	33,894	45,154	11,260	33,894	†	†	†
Full-time	37,980	9,397	28,583	37,980	9,397	28,583	†	†	†
Part-time	7,174	1,863	5,311	7,174	1,863	5,311	†	†	†
For-profit	982,410	328,674	653,736	739,256	260,023	479,233	243,154	68,651	174,503
Full-time	596,771	213,152	383,619	494,064	180,088	313,976	102,707	33,064	69,643
Part-time	385,639	115,522	270,117	245,192	79,935	165,257	140,447	35,587	104,860
For-profit 4-year	829,060	273,988	555,072	585,906	205,337	380,569	243,154	68,651	174,503
Full-time	455,825	161,676	294,149	353,118	128,612	224,506	102,707	33,064	69,643
Part-time	373,235	112,312	260,923	232,788	76,725	156,063	140,447	35,587	104,860
For-profit 2-year	153,350	54,686	98,664	153,350	54,686	98,664	†	†	†
Full-time	140,946	51,476	89,470	140,946	51,476	89,470	†	†	†
Part-time	12,404	3,210	9,194	12,404	3,210	9,194	†	†	†

†Not applicable.

NOTE: Degree-granting institutions grant associate's or higher degrees and participate in Title IV federal financial aid programs.

SOURCE: U.S. Department of Education, National Center for Education Statistics, Integrated Postsecondary Education Data System (IPEDS), Spring 2019, Fall Enrollment component. (This table was prepared September 2019.)

Table 303.70. Total undergraduate fall enrollment in degree-granting postsecondary institutions, by attendance status, sex of student, and control and level of institution: Selected years, 1970 through 2029

Level and year	Total	Full-time	Part-time	Males	Females	Males		Females		Public	Private		
						Full-time	Part-time	Full-time	Part-time		Total	Nonprofit	For-profit
1	2	3	4	5	6	7	8	9	10	11	12	13	14
Total, all levels													
1970	7,368,644	5,280,064	2,088,580	4,249,702	3,118,942	3,096,371	1,153,331	2,183,693	935,249	5,620,255	1,748,389	1,730,133	18,256
1975	9,679,455	6,168,396	3,511,059	5,257,005	4,422,450	3,459,328	1,797,677	2,709,068	1,713,382	7,826,032	1,853,423	1,814,844	38,579
1980	10,475,055	6,361,744	4,113,311	5,000,177	5,474,878	3,226,857	1,773,320	3,134,887	2,339,991	8,441,955	2,033,100	1,926,703	106,397
1985	10,596,674	6,319,592	4,277,082	4,962,080	5,634,594	3,156,446	1,805,634	3,163,146	2,471,448	8,477,125	2,119,549	1,928,996	190,553
1986	10,797,975	6,352,073	4,445,902	5,017,505	5,780,470	3,146,330	1,871,175	3,205,743	2,574,727	8,660,716	2,137,259	1,928,294	208,965
1987	11,046,235	6,462,549	4,583,686	5,068,457	5,977,778	3,163,676	1,904,781	3,298,873	2,678,905	8,918,589	2,127,646	1,939,942	187,704
1988	11,316,548	6,642,428	4,674,120	5,137,644	6,178,904	3,206,442	1,931,202	3,435,986	2,742,918	9,103,146	2,213,402	—	—
1989	11,742,531	6,840,696	4,901,835	5,310,990	6,431,541	3,278,647	2,032,343	3,562,049	2,869,492	9,487,742	2,254,789	—	—
1990	11,959,106	6,976,030	4,983,076	5,379,759	6,579,347	3,336,535	2,043,224	3,639,495	2,939,852	9,709,596	2,249,510	2,043,407	206,103
1991	12,439,287	7,221,412	5,217,875	5,571,003	6,868,284	3,435,526	2,135,477	3,785,886	3,082,398	10,147,957	2,291,330	2,072,354	218,976
1992	12,537,700	7,244,442	5,293,258	5,582,936	6,954,764	3,424,739	2,158,197	3,819,703	3,135,061	10,216,297	2,321,403	2,101,721	219,682
1993	12,323,959	7,179,482	5,144,477	5,483,682	6,840,277	3,381,997	2,101,685	3,797,485	3,042,792	10,011,787	2,312,172	2,099,197	212,975
1994	12,262,608	7,168,706	5,093,902	5,422,113	6,840,495	3,341,591	2,080,522	3,827,115	3,013,380	9,945,128	2,317,480	2,100,465	217,015
1995	12,231,719	7,145,268	5,086,451	5,401,130	6,830,589	3,296,610	2,104,520	3,848,658	2,981,931	9,903,626	2,328,093	2,104,693	223,400
1996	12,326,948	7,298,839	5,028,109	5,420,672	6,906,276	3,339,108	2,081,564	3,959,731	2,946,545	9,935,283	2,391,665	2,112,318	279,347
1997	12,450,587	7,418,598	5,031,989	5,468,532	6,982,055	3,379,597	2,088,935	4,039,001	2,943,054	10,007,479	2,443,108	2,139,824	303,284
1998	12,436,937	7,538,711	4,898,226	5,446,133	6,990,804	3,428,161	2,017,972	4,110,550	2,880,254	9,950,212	2,486,725	2,152,655	334,070
1999	12,739,445	7,753,548	4,985,897	5,584,234	7,155,211	3,524,586	2,059,648	4,228,962	2,926,249	10,174,228	2,565,217	2,185,290	379,927
2000	13,155,393	7,922,926	5,232,467	5,778,268	7,377,125	3,588,246	2,190,022	4,334,680	3,042,445	10,539,322	2,616,071	2,213,180	402,891
2001	13,715,610	8,327,640	5,387,970	6,004,431	7,711,179	3,768,630	2,235,801	4,559,010	3,152,169	10,985,871	2,729,739	2,257,718	472,021
2002	14,257,077	8,734,252	5,522,825	6,192,390	8,064,687	3,934,168	2,258,222	4,800,084	3,264,603	11,432,855	2,824,222	2,306,091	518,131
2003	14,480,364	9,045,253	5,435,111	6,227,372	8,252,992	4,048,682	2,178,690	4,996,571	3,256,421	11,523,103	2,957,261	2,346,673	610,588
2004	14,780,630	9,284,336	5,496,294	6,340,048	8,440,582	4,140,628	2,199,420	5,143,708	3,296,874	11,650,580	3,130,050	2,389,366	740,684
2005	14,963,964	9,446,430	5,517,534	6,408,871	8,555,093	4,200,863	2,208,008	5,245,567	3,309,526	11,697,730	3,266,234	2,418,368	847,866
2006	15,179,591	9,571,349	5,608,242	6,511,198	8,668,393	4,264,722	2,246,476	5,306,627	3,361,766	11,842,625	3,336,966	2,448,250	888,716
2007	15,613,540	9,841,973	5,771,567	6,731,561	8,881,979	4,397,402	2,334,159	5,444,571	3,437,408	12,147,744	3,465,796	2,470,463	995,333
2008	16,344,592	10,244,174	6,100,418	7,055,640	9,288,952	4,570,913	2,484,727	5,673,261	3,615,691	12,589,947	3,754,645	2,535,789	1,218,856
2009	17,464,179	11,038,275	6,425,904	7,563,176	9,901,003	4,942,120	2,621,056	6,096,155	3,804,848	13,386,375	4,077,804	2,595,171	1,482,633
2010	18,082,427	11,457,040	6,625,387	7,836,282	10,246,145	5,118,975	2,717,307	6,338,065	3,908,080	13,703,000	4,379,427	2,652,993	1,726,434
2011	18,077,303	11,365,175	6,712,128	7,822,992	10,254,311	5,070,553	2,752,439	6,294,622	3,959,689	13,694,899	4,382,404	2,718,923	1,663,481
2012	17,735,638	11,097,092	6,638,546	7,714,938	10,020,700	4,984,389	2,730,549	6,112,703	3,907,997	13,478,100	4,257,538	2,744,400	1,513,138
2013	17,476,304	10,939,276	6,537,028	7,660,140	9,816,164	4,950,210	2,709,930	5,989,066	3,827,098	13,348,292	4,128,012	2,755,463	1,372,549
2014	17,294,136	10,784,392	6,509,744	7,586,299	9,707,837	4,877,531	2,708,768	5,906,861	3,800,976	13,244,533	4,049,603	2,772,065	1,277,538
2015	17,046,673	10,603,030	6,443,643	7,502,254	9,544,419	4,809,098	2,693,156	5,793,932	3,750,487	13,150,823	3,895,850	2,822,122	1,073,728
2016	16,874,649	10,430,068	6,444,581	7,416,859	9,457,790	4,725,510	2,691,349	5,704,558	3,753,232	13,143,979	3,730,670	2,813,742	916,928
2017	16,773,036	10,371,863	6,401,173	7,351,259	9,421,777	4,683,715	2,667,544	5,688,148	3,733,629	13,112,594	3,660,442	2,819,080	841,362
2018	16,610,235	10,267,135	6,343,100	7,225,999	9,384,236	4,602,752	2,623,247	5,664,383	3,719,853	13,049,326	3,560,909	2,821,653	739,256
2019[1]	16,673,000	10,296,000	6,377,000	7,250,000	9,423,000	4,612,000	2,638,000	5,684,000	3,739,000	13,100,000	3,573,000	—	—
2020[1]	16,692,000	10,293,000	6,399,000	7,254,000	9,438,000	4,608,000	2,646,000	5,685,000	3,753,000	13,118,000	3,575,000	—	—
2021[1]	16,721,000	10,292,000	6,428,000	7,263,000	9,457,000	4,606,000	2,657,000	5,686,000	3,771,000	13,142,000	3,578,000	—	—
2022[1]	16,750,000	10,297,000	6,452,000	7,273,000	9,477,000	4,606,000	2,667,000	5,692,000	3,785,000	13,167,000	3,582,000	—	—
2023[1]	16,790,000	10,312,000	6,478,000	7,288,000	9,503,000	4,610,000	2,678,000	5,703,000	3,800,000	13,201,000	3,590,000	—	—
2024[1]	16,845,000	10,341,000	6,504,000	7,312,000	9,533,000	4,622,000	2,690,000	5,718,000	3,814,000	13,244,000	3,600,000	—	—
2025[1]	16,901,000	10,377,000	6,524,000	7,338,000	9,564,000	4,639,000	2,699,000	5,738,000	3,826,000	13,289,000	3,613,000	—	—
2026[1]	16,967,000	10,415,000	6,551,000	7,367,000	9,600,000	4,656,000	2,711,000	5,760,000	3,841,000	13,340,000	3,626,000	—	—
2027[1]	16,991,000	10,419,000	6,572,000	7,378,000	9,613,000	4,658,000	2,720,000	5,761,000	3,851,000	13,361,000	3,630,000	—	—
2028[1]	16,999,000	10,410,000	6,589,000	7,383,000	9,616,000	4,656,000	2,727,000	5,755,000	3,862,000	13,370,000	3,629,000	—	—
2029[1]	17,003,000	10,397,000	6,606,000	7,385,000	9,618,000	4,651,000	2,734,000	5,746,000	3,872,000	13,375,000	3,628,000	—	—
2-year institutions[2]													
1970	2,318,956	1,228,909	1,090,047	1,374,426	944,530	771,298	603,128	457,611	486,919	2,194,983	123,973	113,299	10,674
1975	3,965,726	1,761,009	2,204,717	2,163,604	1,802,122	1,035,531	1,128,073	725,478	1,076,644	3,831,973	133,753	112,997	20,756
1980	4,525,097	1,753,637	2,771,460	2,046,642	2,478,455	879,619	1,167,023	874,018	1,604,437	4,327,592	197,505	114,094	83,411
1985	4,531,077	1,690,607	2,840,470	2,002,234	2,528,843	826,308	1,175,926	864,299	1,664,544	4,269,733	261,344	108,791	152,553
1986	4,679,548	1,696,261	2,983,287	2,060,932	2,618,616	824,551	1,236,381	871,710	1,746,906	4,413,691	265,857	101,498	164,359
1987	4,776,222	1,708,669	3,067,553	2,072,823	2,703,399	820,167	1,252,656	888,502	1,814,897	4,541,054	235,168	90,102	145,066
1988	4,875,155	1,743,592	3,131,563	2,089,689	2,785,466	818,593	1,271,096	924,999	1,860,467	4,615,487	259,668	—	—
1989	5,150,889	1,855,701	3,295,188	2,216,800	2,934,089	869,688	1,347,112	986,013	1,948,076	4,883,660	267,229	—	—
1990	5,240,083	1,883,962	3,356,121	2,232,769	3,007,314	881,392	1,351,377	1,002,570	2,004,744	4,996,475	243,608	89,158	154,450
1991	5,651,900	2,074,530	3,577,370	2,401,910	3,249,990	961,397	1,440,513	1,113,133	2,136,857	5,404,815	247,085	89,289	157,796
1992	5,722,349	2,080,005	3,642,344	2,413,266	3,309,083	951,816	1,461,450	1,128,189	2,180,894	5,484,514	237,835	83,288	154,547
1993	5,565,561	2,043,319	3,522,242	2,345,396	3,220,165	928,216	1,417,180	1,115,103	2,105,062	5,337,022	228,539	86,357	142,182
1994	5,529,609	2,031,713	3,497,896	2,323,161	3,206,448	911,589	1,411,572	1,120,124	2,086,324	5,308,366	221,243	85,607	135,636
1995	5,492,098	1,977,046	3,515,052	2,328,500	3,163,598	878,215	1,450,285	1,098,831	2,064,767	5,277,398	214,700	75,154	139,546
1996	5,562,780	2,072,215	3,490,565	2,358,792	3,203,988	916,452	1,442,340	1,155,763	2,048,225	5,314,038	248,742	75,253	173,489
1997	5,605,569	2,095,171	3,510,398	2,389,711	3,215,858	931,394	1,458,317	1,163,777	2,052,081	5,360,686	244,883	71,794	173,089
1998	5,489,314	2,085,906	3,403,408	2,333,334	3,155,980	936,421	1,396,913	1,149,485	2,006,495	5,245,963	243,351	65,870	177,481
1999	5,653,256	2,167,242	3,486,014	2,413,322	3,239,934	979,203	1,434,119	1,188,039	2,051,895	5,397,786	255,470	63,301	192,169
2000	5,948,104	2,217,044	3,731,060	2,558,520	3,389,584	995,839	1,562,681	1,221,205	2,168,379	5,697,061	251,043	58,844	192,199
2001	6,250,529	2,374,490	3,876,039	2,675,193	3,575,336	1,066,281	1,608,912	1,308,209	2,267,127	5,996,651	253,878	47,549	206,329
2002	6,529,198	2,556,032	3,973,166	2,753,405	3,775,793	1,135,669	1,617,736	1,420,363	2,355,430	6,270,199	258,999	47,087	211,912
2003	6,493,862	2,650,337	3,843,525	2,689,928	3,803,934	1,162,555	1,527,373	1,487,782	2,316,152	6,208,885	284,977	43,868	241,109
2004	6,545,570	2,683,489	3,862,081	2,697,507	3,848,063	1,166,554	1,530,953	1,516,935	2,331,128	6,243,344	302,226	42,250	259,976
2005	6,487,826	2,646,763	3,841,063	2,680,299	3,807,527	1,153,759	1,526,540	1,493,004	2,314,523	6,184,000	303,826	43,522	260,304
2006	6,513,303	2,643,162	3,870,141	2,701,970	3,811,333	1,159,733	1,542,237	1,483,429	2,327,904	6,219,880	293,423	39,156	254,267
2007	6,628,936	2,694,608	3,934,328	2,775,166	3,853,770	1,191,058	1,584,108	1,503,550	2,350,220	6,335,826	293,110	33,492	259,618
2008	6,970,947	2,832,412	4,138,535	2,935,799	4,035,148	1,250,063	1,685,736	1,582,349	2,452,799	6,639,928	331,019	35,358	295,661
2009	7,522,581	3,243,952	4,278,629	3,197,338	4,325,243	1,446,372	1,750,966	1,797,580	2,527,663	7,101,569	421,012	34,772	386,240

See notes at end of table.

Table 303.70. Total undergraduate fall enrollment in degree-granting postsecondary institutions, by attendance status, sex of student, and control and level of institution: Selected years, 1970 through 2029—Continued

Level and year	Total	Full-time	Part-time	Males	Females	Males		Females		Public	Private		
						Full-time	Part-time	Full-time	Part-time		Total	Nonprofit	For-profit
1	2	3	4	5	6	7	8	9	10	11	12	13	14
2010	7,683,597	3,365,379	4,318,218	3,265,885	4,417,712	1,483,230	1,782,655	1,882,149	2,535,563	7,218,063	465,534	32,683	432,851
2011	7,511,150	3,170,207	4,340,943	3,175,803	4,335,347	1,391,183	1,784,620	1,779,024	2,556,323	7,068,158	442,992	39,855	403,137
2012	7,167,840	2,941,797	4,226,043	3,046,093	4,121,747	1,305,657	1,740,436	1,636,140	2,485,607	6,792,065	375,775	37,698	338,077
2013	6,970,644	2,836,274	4,134,370	2,998,440	3,972,204	1,279,794	1,718,646	1,556,480	2,415,724	6,626,411	344,233	32,191	312,042
2014	6,714,678	2,661,107	4,053,571	2,894,020	3,820,658	1,200,648	1,693,372	1,460,459	2,360,199	6,397,552	317,126	30,376	286,750
2015	6,499,461	2,510,684	3,988,777	2,818,075	3,681,386	1,143,704	1,674,371	1,366,980	2,314,406	6,224,304	275,157	50,009	225,148
2016	6,092,418	2,309,347	3,783,071	2,637,394	3,455,024	1,057,839	1,579,555	1,251,508	2,203,516	5,842,909	249,509	50,555	198,954
2017	5,952,771	2,227,324	3,725,447	2,566,527	3,386,244	1,013,595	1,552,932	1,213,729	2,172,515	5,717,460	235,311	48,395	186,916
2018	5,745,208	2,110,768	3,634,440	2,451,669	3,293,539	953,726	1,497,943	1,157,042	2,136,497	5,546,704	198,504	45,154	153,350
2019[1]	5,770,000	2,117,000	3,654,000	2,462,000	3,309,000	956,000	1,506,000	1,161,000	2,148,000	5,571,000	199,000	—	—
2020[1]	5,783,000	2,116,000	3,667,000	2,466,000	3,317,000	955,000	1,511,000	1,161,000	2,156,000	5,584,000	199,000	—	—
2021[1]	5,799,000	2,116,000	3,683,000	2,472,000	3,328,000	955,000	1,517,000	1,161,000	2,166,000	5,600,000	199,000	—	—
2022[1]	5,814,000	2,117,000	3,697,000	2,477,000	3,337,000	954,000	1,523,000	1,163,000	2,174,000	5,614,000	199,000	—	—
2023[1]	5,832,000	2,120,000	3,712,000	2,484,000	3,347,000	955,000	1,529,000	1,165,000	2,183,000	5,632,000	200,000	—	—
2024[1]	5,853,000	2,126,000	3,727,000	2,494,000	3,359,000	958,000	1,536,000	1,168,000	2,191,000	5,652,000	200,000	—	—
2025[1]	5,872,000	2,133,000	3,738,000	2,502,000	3,369,000	961,000	1,541,000	1,172,000	2,197,000	5,670,000	201,000	—	—
2026[1]	5,895,000	2,141,000	3,754,000	2,513,000	3,382,000	965,000	1,548,000	1,176,000	2,206,000	5,693,000	202,000	—	—
2027[1]	5,907,000	2,142,000	3,765,000	2,519,000	3,389,000	965,000	1,553,000	1,177,000	2,212,000	5,705,000	202,000	—	—
2028[1]	5,915,000	2,140,000	3,775,000	2,522,000	3,394,000	965,000	1,557,000	1,175,000	2,218,000	5,714,000	202,000	—	—
2029[1]	5,922,000	2,137,000	3,785,000	2,525,000	3,397,000	964,000	1,561,000	1,174,000	2,224,000	5,721,000	202,000	—	—
4-year institutions													
1970	5,049,688	4,051,155	998,533	2,875,276	2,174,412	2,325,073	550,203	1,726,082	448,330	3,425,272	1,624,416	1,616,834	7,582
1975	5,713,729	4,407,387	1,306,342	3,093,401	2,620,328	2,423,797	669,604	1,983,590	636,738	3,994,059	1,719,670	1,701,847	17,823
1980	5,949,958	4,608,107	1,341,851	2,953,535	2,996,423	2,347,238	606,297	2,260,869	735,554	4,114,363	1,835,595	1,812,609	22,986
1985	6,065,597	4,628,985	1,436,612	2,959,846	3,105,751	2,330,138	629,708	2,298,847	806,904	4,207,392	1,858,205	1,820,205	38,000
1986	6,118,427	4,655,812	1,462,615	2,956,573	3,161,854	2,321,779	634,794	2,334,033	827,821	4,247,025	1,871,402	1,826,796	44,606
1987	6,270,013	4,753,880	1,516,133	2,995,634	3,274,379	2,343,509	652,125	2,410,371	864,008	4,377,535	1,892,478	1,849,840	42,638
1988	6,441,393	4,898,836	1,542,557	3,047,955	3,393,438	2,387,849	660,106	2,510,987	882,451	4,487,659	1,953,734	—	—
1989	6,591,642	4,984,995	1,606,647	3,094,190	3,497,452	2,408,959	685,231	2,576,036	921,416	4,604,082	1,987,560	—	—
1990	6,719,023	5,092,068	1,626,955	3,146,990	3,572,033	2,455,143	691,847	2,636,925	935,108	4,713,121	2,005,902	1,954,249	51,653
1991	6,787,387	5,146,882	1,640,505	3,169,093	3,618,294	2,474,129	694,964	2,672,753	945,541	4,743,142	2,044,245	1,983,065	61,180
1992	6,815,351	5,164,437	1,650,914	3,169,670	3,645,681	2,472,923	696,747	2,691,514	954,167	4,731,783	2,083,568	2,018,433	65,135
1993	6,758,398	5,136,163	1,622,235	3,138,286	3,620,112	2,453,781	684,505	2,682,382	937,730	4,674,765	2,083,633	2,012,840	70,793
1994	6,732,999	5,136,993	1,596,006	3,098,952	3,634,047	2,430,002	668,950	2,706,991	927,056	4,636,762	2,096,237	2,014,858	81,379
1995	6,739,621	5,168,222	1,571,399	3,072,630	3,666,991	2,418,395	654,235	2,749,827	917,164	4,626,228	2,113,393	2,029,539	83,854
1996	6,764,168	5,226,624	1,537,544	3,061,880	3,702,288	2,422,656	639,224	2,803,968	898,320	4,621,245	2,142,923	2,037,065	105,858
1997	6,845,018	5,323,427	1,521,591	3,078,821	3,766,197	2,448,203	630,618	2,875,224	890,973	4,646,793	2,198,225	2,068,030	130,195
1998	6,947,623	5,452,805	1,494,818	3,112,799	3,834,824	2,491,740	621,059	2,961,065	873,759	4,704,249	2,243,374	2,086,785	156,589
1999	7,086,189	5,586,306	1,499,883	3,170,912	3,915,277	2,545,383	625,529	3,040,923	874,354	4,776,442	2,309,747	2,121,989	187,758
2000	7,207,289	5,705,882	1,501,407	3,219,748	3,987,541	2,592,407	627,341	3,113,475	874,066	4,842,261	2,365,028	2,154,336	210,692
2001	7,465,081	5,953,150	1,511,931	3,329,238	4,135,843	2,702,349	626,889	3,250,801	885,042	4,989,220	2,475,861	2,210,169	265,692
2002	7,727,879	6,178,220	1,549,659	3,438,985	4,288,894	2,798,499	640,486	3,379,721	909,173	5,162,656	2,565,223	2,259,004	306,219
2003	7,986,502	6,394,916	1,591,586	3,537,444	4,449,058	2,886,127	651,317	3,508,789	940,269	5,314,218	2,672,284	2,302,805	369,479
2004	8,235,060	6,600,847	1,634,213	3,642,541	4,592,519	2,974,074	668,467	3,626,773	965,746	5,407,236	2,827,824	2,347,116	480,708
2005	8,476,138	6,799,667	1,676,471	3,728,572	4,747,566	3,047,104	681,468	3,752,563	995,003	5,513,730	2,962,408	2,374,846	587,562
2006	8,666,288	6,928,187	1,738,101	3,809,228	4,857,060	3,104,989	704,239	3,823,198	1,033,862	5,622,745	3,043,543	2,409,094	634,449
2007	8,984,604	7,147,365	1,837,239	3,956,395	5,028,209	3,206,344	750,051	3,941,021	1,087,188	5,811,918	3,172,686	2,436,971	735,715
2008	9,373,645	7,411,762	1,961,883	4,119,841	5,253,804	3,320,850	798,991	4,090,912	1,162,892	5,950,019	3,423,626	2,500,431	923,195
2009	9,941,598	7,794,323	2,147,275	4,365,838	5,575,760	3,495,748	870,090	4,298,575	1,277,185	6,284,806	3,656,792	2,560,399	1,096,393
2010	10,398,830	8,091,661	2,307,169	4,570,397	5,828,433	3,635,745	934,652	4,455,916	1,372,517	6,484,937	3,913,893	2,620,310	1,293,583
2011	10,566,153	8,194,968	2,371,185	4,647,189	5,918,964	3,679,370	967,819	4,515,598	1,403,366	6,626,741	3,939,412	2,679,068	1,260,344
2012	10,567,798	8,155,295	2,412,503	4,668,845	5,898,953	3,678,732	990,113	4,476,563	1,422,390	6,686,035	3,881,763	2,706,702	1,175,061
2013	10,505,660	8,103,002	2,402,658	4,661,700	5,843,960	3,670,416	991,284	4,432,586	1,411,374	6,721,881	3,783,779	2,723,272	1,060,507
2014	10,579,458	8,123,285	2,456,173	4,692,279	5,887,179	3,676,883	1,015,396	4,446,402	1,440,777	6,846,981	3,732,477	2,741,689	990,788
2015	10,547,212	8,092,346	2,454,866	4,684,179	5,863,033	3,665,394	1,018,785	4,426,952	1,436,081	6,926,519	3,620,693	2,772,113	848,580
2016	10,782,231	8,120,721	2,661,510	4,779,465	6,002,766	3,667,671	1,111,794	4,453,050	1,549,716	7,301,070	3,481,161	2,763,187	717,974
2017	10,820,265	8,144,539	2,675,726	4,784,732	6,035,533	3,670,120	1,114,612	4,474,419	1,561,114	7,395,134	3,425,131	2,770,685	654,446
2018	10,865,027	8,156,367	2,708,660	4,774,330	6,090,697	3,649,026	1,125,304	4,507,341	1,583,356	7,502,622	3,362,405	2,776,499	585,906
2019[1]	10,902,000	8,179,000	2,723,000	4,788,000	6,114,000	3,656,000	1,131,000	4,523,000	1,592,000	7,528,000	3,374,000	—	—
2020[1]	10,910,000	8,177,000	2,733,000	4,788,000	6,121,000	3,653,000	1,135,000	4,524,000	1,598,000	7,534,000	3,376,000	—	—
2021[1]	10,921,000	8,177,000	2,745,000	4,792,000	6,130,000	3,652,000	1,140,000	4,525,000	1,605,000	7,543,000	3,379,000	—	—
2022[1]	10,936,000	8,180,000	2,755,000	4,795,000	6,140,000	3,652,000	1,144,000	4,529,000	1,611,000	7,553,000	3,383,000	—	—
2023[1]	10,958,000	8,192,000	2,766,000	4,803,000	6,155,000	3,654,000	1,149,000	4,538,000	1,617,000	7,569,000	3,390,000	—	—
2024[1]	10,992,000	8,215,000	2,777,000	4,818,000	6,174,000	3,664,000	1,154,000	4,550,000	1,624,000	7,592,000	3,400,000	—	—
2025[1]	11,030,000	8,244,000	2,786,000	4,835,000	6,194,000	3,678,000	1,158,000	4,566,000	1,628,000	7,618,000	3,412,000	—	—
2026[1]	11,072,000	8,274,000	2,798,000	4,854,000	6,218,000	3,691,000	1,163,000	4,583,000	1,635,000	7,647,000	3,425,000	—	—
2027[1]	11,083,000	8,277,000	2,806,000	4,860,000	6,224,000	3,693,000	1,167,000	4,584,000	1,639,000	7,656,000	3,428,000	—	—
2028[1]	11,084,000	8,270,000	2,814,000	4,861,000	6,223,000	3,691,000	1,170,000	4,579,000	1,644,000	7,656,000	3,428,000	—	—
2029[1]	11,080,000	8,260,000	2,821,000	4,860,000	6,220,000	3,687,000	1,173,000	4,572,000	1,648,000	7,654,000	3,426,000	—	—

—Not available.
[1]Projected.
[2]Beginning in 1980, 2-year institutions include schools accredited by the Accrediting Commission of Career Schools and Colleges of Technology.
NOTE: Data through 1995 are for institutions of higher education, while later data are for degree-granting institutions. Degree-granting institutions grant associate's or higher degrees and participate in Title IV federal financial aid programs. The degree-granting classification is very similar to the earlier higher education classification, but it includes more 2-year colleges and excludes a few higher education institutions that did not grant degrees. Some data have been revised from previously published figures.
SOURCE: U.S. Department of Education, National Center for Education Statistics, Higher Education General Information Survey (HEGIS), "Fall Enrollment in Colleges and Universities" surveys, 1970 through 1985; Integrated Postsecondary Education Data System (IPEDS), "Fall Enrollment Survey" (IPEDS-EF:86–99); IPEDS Spring 2001 through Spring 2019, Fall Enrollment component; and Enrollment in Degree-Granting Institutions Projection Model, 2000 through 2029. (This table was prepared December 2019.)

Table 303.80. Total postbaccalaureate fall enrollment in degree-granting postsecondary institutions, by attendance status, sex of student, and control of institution: 1970 through 2029

Year	Total	Full-time	Part-time	Males	Females	Males		Females		Public	Private		
						Full-time	Part-time	Full-time	Part-time		Total	Nonprofit	For-profit
1	2	3	4	5	6	7	8	9	10	11	12	13	14
1970	1,212,243	536,226	676,017	793,940	418,303	407,724	386,216	128,502	289,801	807,879	404,364	404,287	77
1971	1,204,390	564,236	640,154	789,131	415,259	428,167	360,964	136,069	279,190	796,516	407,874	407,804	70
1972	1,272,421	583,299	689,122	810,164	462,257	436,533	373,631	146,766	315,491	848,031	424,390	424,278	112
1973	1,342,452	610,935	731,517	833,453	508,999	444,219	389,234	166,716	342,283	897,104	445,348	445,205	143
1974	1,425,001	643,927	781,074	856,847	568,154	454,706	402,141	189,221	378,933	956,770	468,231	467,950	281
1975	1,505,404	672,938	832,466	891,992	613,412	467,425	424,567	205,513	407,899	1,008,476	496,928	496,604	324
1976	1,577,546	683,825	893,721	904,551	672,995	459,286	445,265	224,539	448,456	1,033,115	544,431	541,064	3,367
1977	1,569,084	698,902	870,182	891,819	677,265	462,038	429,781	236,864	440,401	1,004,013	565,071	561,384	3,687
1978	1,575,693	704,831	870,862	879,931	695,762	458,865	421,066	245,966	449,796	998,608	577,085	573,563	3,522
1979	1,571,922	714,624	857,298	862,754	709,168	456,197	406,557	258,427	450,741	989,991	581,931	578,425	3,506
1980	1,621,840	736,214	885,626	874,197	747,643	462,387	411,810	273,827	473,816	1,015,439	606,401	601,084	5,317
1981	1,617,150	732,182	884,968	866,785	750,365	452,364	414,421	279,818	470,547	998,669	618,481	613,557	4,924
1982	1,600,718	736,813	863,905	860,890	739,828	453,519	407,371	283,294	456,534	983,014	617,704	613,350	4,354
1983	1,618,666	747,016	871,650	865,425	753,241	455,540	409,885	291,476	461,765	985,616	633,050	628,111	4,939
1984	1,623,869	750,735	873,134	856,761	767,108	452,579	404,182	298,156	468,952	983,879	639,990	634,109	5,881
1985	1,650,381	755,629	894,752	856,370	794,011	451,274	405,096	304,355	489,656	1,002,148	648,233	642,795	5,438
1986	1,705,536	767,477	938,059	867,010	838,526	452,717	414,293	314,760	523,766	1,053,177	652,359	644,185	8,174
1987	1,720,407	768,536	951,871	863,599	856,808	447,212	416,387	321,324	535,484	1,054,665	665,742	662,408	3,334
1988	1,738,789	794,340	944,449	864,252	874,537	455,337	408,915	339,003	535,534	1,058,242	680,547	—	—
1989	1,796,029	820,254	975,775	879,025	917,004	461,596	417,429	358,658	558,346	1,090,221	705,808	—	—
1990	1,859,531	844,955	1,014,576	904,150	955,381	471,217	432,933	373,738	581,643	1,135,121	724,410	716,820	7,590
1991	1,919,666	893,917	1,025,749	930,841	988,825	493,849	436,992	400,068	588,757	1,161,606	758,060	746,687	11,373
1992	1,949,659	917,676	1,031,983	941,053	1,008,606	502,166	438,887	415,510	593,096	1,168,270	781,389	770,802	10,587
1993	1,980,844	948,136	1,032,708	943,768	1,037,076	508,574	435,194	439,562	597,514	1,177,301	803,543	789,700	13,843
1994	2,016,182	969,070	1,047,112	949,785	1,066,397	513,592	436,193	455,478	610,919	1,188,552	827,630	809,642	17,988
1995	2,030,062	983,534	1,046,528	941,409	1,088,653	510,782	430,627	472,752	615,901	1,188,748	841,314	824,351	16,963
1996	2,040,572	1,004,114	1,036,458	932,153	1,108,419	512,100	420,053	492,014	616,405	1,185,216	855,356	830,238	25,118
1997	2,051,747	1,019,464	1,032,283	927,496	1,124,251	510,845	416,651	508,619	615,632	1,188,640	863,107	837,790	25,317
1998	2,070,030	1,024,627	1,045,403	923,132	1,146,898	505,492	417,640	519,135	627,763	1,187,557	882,473	852,270	30,203
1999	2,110,246	1,049,591	1,060,655	930,930	1,179,316	508,930	422,000	540,661	638,655	1,201,511	908,735	869,739	38,996
2000	2,156,896	1,086,674	1,070,222	943,501	1,213,395	522,847	420,654	563,827	649,568	1,213,464	943,432	896,239	47,193
2001	2,212,377	1,119,862	1,092,515	956,384	1,255,993	531,260	425,124	588,602	667,391	1,247,285	965,092	909,612	55,480
2002	2,354,634	1,212,107	1,142,527	1,009,726	1,344,908	566,930	442,796	645,177	699,731	1,319,138	1,035,496	959,385	76,111
2003	2,431,117	1,280,880	1,150,237	1,032,892	1,398,225	589,190	443,702	691,690	706,535	1,335,595	1,095,522	994,375	101,147
2004	2,491,414	1,325,841	1,165,573	1,047,214	1,444,200	598,727	448,487	727,114	717,086	1,329,532	1,161,882	1,022,319	139,563
2005	2,523,511	1,350,581	1,172,930	1,047,054	1,476,457	602,525	444,529	748,056	728,401	1,324,104	1,199,407	1,036,324	163,083
2006	2,574,639	1,386,189	1,188,450	1,061,067	1,513,572	614,706	446,361	771,483	742,089	1,332,725	1,241,914	1,064,679	177,235
2007	2,644,598	1,428,956	1,215,642	1,088,377	1,556,221	632,619	455,758	796,337	759,884	1,353,150	1,291,448	1,100,932	190,516
2008	2,737,094	1,490,462	1,246,632	1,122,074	1,615,020	656,213	465,861	834,249	780,771	1,380,915	1,356,179	1,125,038	231,141
2009	2,849,415	1,567,080	1,282,335	1,169,777	1,679,638	689,977	479,800	877,103	802,535	1,424,393	1,425,022	1,172,501	252,521
2010	2,937,011	1,630,142	1,306,869	1,209,477	1,727,534	719,408	490,069	910,734	816,800	1,439,171	1,497,840	1,201,489	296,351
2011	2,933,287	1,637,356	1,295,931	1,211,264	1,722,023	722,265	488,999	915,091	806,932	1,421,404	1,511,883	1,207,896	303,987
2012	2,908,840	1,637,312	1,271,528	1,204,068	1,704,772	724,017	480,051	913,295	791,477	1,406,567	1,502,273	1,206,988	295,285
2013	2,900,373	1,657,334	1,243,039	1,201,057	1,699,316	732,112	468,945	925,222	774,094	1,398,556	1,501,817	1,215,927	285,890
2014	2,914,956	1,670,072	1,244,884	1,211,231	1,703,725	742,247	468,984	927,825	775,900	1,410,127	1,504,829	1,225,184	279,645
2015	2,941,531	1,684,482	1,257,049	1,221,565	1,719,966	749,349	472,216	935,133	784,833	1,422,020	1,519,511	1,243,769	275,742
2016	2,972,255	1,695,246	1,277,009	1,221,563	1,750,692	747,288	474,275	947,958	802,734	1,441,861	1,530,394	1,265,214	265,180
2017	3,005,115	1,704,278	1,300,837	1,220,055	1,785,060	740,240	479,815	964,038	821,022	1,459,145	1,545,970	1,289,409	256,561
2018	3,035,683	1,724,586	1,311,097	1,216,663	1,819,020	736,182	480,481	988,404	830,616	1,479,938	1,555,745	1,312,591	243,154
2019[1]	3,048,000	1,729,000	1,318,000	1,221,000	1,827,000	738,000	483,000	992,000	835,000	1,486,000	1,562,000	—	—
2020[1]	3,052,000	1,729,000	1,323,000	1,222,000	1,830,000	737,000	485,000	992,000	838,000	1,488,000	1,564,000	—	—
2021[1]	3,058,000	1,729,000	1,329,000	1,223,000	1,834,000	737,000	487,000	992,000	842,000	1,491,000	1,567,000	—	—
2022[1]	3,064,000	1,730,000	1,334,000	1,225,000	1,838,000	737,000	488,000	993,000	845,000	1,494,000	1,570,000	—	—
2023[1]	3,071,000	1,732,000	1,339,000	1,228,000	1,844,000	737,000	491,000	995,000	849,000	1,498,000	1,574,000	—	—
2024[1]	3,081,000	1,737,000	1,344,000	1,232,000	1,850,000	739,000	493,000	998,000	852,000	1,503,000	1,579,000	—	—
2025[1]	3,092,000	1,743,000	1,349,000	1,236,000	1,856,000	742,000	494,000	1,001,000	854,000	1,508,000	1,584,000	—	—
2026[1]	3,104,000	1,750,000	1,354,000	1,241,000	1,863,000	745,000	497,000	1,005,000	858,000	1,514,000	1,590,000	—	—
2027[1]	3,109,000	1,750,000	1,358,000	1,243,000	1,865,000	745,000	498,000	1,005,000	860,000	1,516,000	1,593,000	—	—
2028[1]	3,111,000	1,749,000	1,362,000	1,244,000	1,866,000	745,000	499,000	1,004,000	862,000	1,517,000	1,594,000	—	—
2029[1]	3,112,000	1,747,000	1,365,000	1,245,000	1,867,000	744,000	501,000	1,003,000	865,000	1,518,000	1,594,000	—	—

—Not available.

[1]Projected.

NOTE: Data include unclassified graduate students. Data through 1995 are for institutions of higher education, while later data are for degree-granting institutions. Degree-granting institutions grant associate's or higher degrees and participate in Title IV federal financial aid programs. The degree-granting classification is very similar to the earlier higher education classification, but it includes more 2-year colleges and excludes a few higher education institutions that did not grant degrees. Some data have been revised from previously published figures.

SOURCE: U.S. Department of Education, National Center for Education Statistics, Higher Education General Information Survey (HEGIS), "Fall Enrollment in Colleges and Universities" surveys, 1970 through 1985; Integrated Postsecondary Education Data System (IPEDS), "Fall Enrollment Survey" (IPEDS-EF:86–99); IPEDS Spring 2001 through Spring 2019, Fall Enrollment component; and Enrollment in Degree-Granting Institutions Projection Model, 2000 through 2029. (This table was prepared December 2019.)

Table 303.90. Fall enrollment and number of degree-granting postsecondary institutions, by control and religious affiliation of institution: Selected years, 1980 through 2018

Control and religious affiliation of institution	Total enrollment						Enrollment, fall 2018					Number of institutions[1]				
								Full-time		Part-time						
	Fall 1980	Fall 1990	Fall 2000	Fall 2010	Fall 2016	Fall 2017	Total	Males	Females	Males	Females	Fall 1980	Fall 1990	Fall 2000	Fall 2010	Fall 2018
1	2	3	4	5	6	7	8	9	10	11	12	13	14	15	16	17
All institutions	**12,096,895**	**13,818,637**	**15,312,289**	**21,019,438**	**19,846,904**	**19,778,151**	**19,645,918**	**5,338,934**	**6,652,787**	**3,103,728**	**4,550,469**	**3,226**	**3,501**	**4,056**	**4,589**	**4,034**
Public institutions	9,457,394	10,844,717	11,752,786	15,142,171	14,585,840	14,571,739	14,529,264	3,787,941	4,480,879	2,603,530	3,656,914	1,493	1,548	1,676	1,652	1,634
Federal	50,989	50,669	16,917	21,610	19,804	20,265	20,379	12,657	5,978	592	1,152	12	17	12	14	14
State	([2])	7,181,380	9,548,090	12,364,881	12,089,310	12,103,707	12,104,962	3,361,325	4,002,394	1,964,287	2,776,956	([2])	978	1,355	1,331	1,320
Local	([2])	3,508,941	2,078,090	2,542,044	2,276,473	2,246,845	2,206,015	364,309	412,242	604,092	825,372	([2])	523	277	261	258
Other public	9,406,405	103,727	109,689	213,636	200,253	200,922	197,908	49,650	60,265	34,559	53,434	1,481	30	32	46	42
Private institutions	2,639,501	2,973,920	3,559,503	5,877,267	5,261,064	5,206,412	5,116,654	1,550,993	2,171,908	500,198	893,555	1,733	1,953	2,380	2,937	2,400
Independent nonprofit	1,521,614	1,474,818	1,577,242	1,994,900	2,190,233	2,222,677	2,246,622	743,384	968,932	205,119	329,187	795	709	729	736	785
For-profit	111,714	213,693	450,084	2,022,785	1,182,108	1,097,923	982,410	213,152	383,619	115,522	270,117	164	322	724	1,310	736
Religiously affiliated[3]	1,006,173	1,285,409	1,532,177	1,859,582	1,888,723	1,885,812	1,887,622	594,457	819,357	179,557	294,251	774	922	927	891	879
Advent Christian Church	143	—	—	—	—	—	—	—	—	—	—	1	—	—	—	—
African Methodist Episcopal Zion Church	1,091	88	34	1,536	1,547	1,462	1,484	740	685	33	26	3	1	1	3	3
African Methodist Episcopal	4,541	3,220	5,980	2,674	5,379	5,887	5,633	1,594	1,586	1,180	1,273	6	5	6	5	6
American Baptist	6,131	10,800	15,410	15,120	12,801	12,500	12,622	3,784	5,099	1,274	2,465	11	15	17	18	18
American Evangelical Lutheran Church	—	—	743	1,340	1,295	1,394	1,443	684	678	33	48	—	—	1	1	1
American Lutheran and Lutheran Church in America	3,092	—	1,460	—	—	—	—	—	—	—	—	3	—	1	—	—
American Lutheran	21,608	—	—	—	—	—	—	—	—	—	—	13	—	—	—	—
Assemblies of God Church	7,814	8,307	14,272	15,806	17,780	19,240	20,792	6,032	8,198	2,878	3,684	10	11	14	16	13
Baptist	38,231	99,510	107,610	174,538	111,744	111,124	113,415	34,111	47,269	14,590	17,445	33	69	68	69	63
Brethren Church	3,925	958	2,088	8,506	9,135	8,627	8,656	2,694	3,320	1,455	1,187	3	3	3	3	2
Brethren in Christ Church	1,301	2,239	2,797	—	—	—	—	—	—	—	—	1	1	1	—	—
Christian and Missionary Alliance Church	1,705	2,519	5,278	6,455	6,094	6,122	6,351	1,791	2,313	969	1,278	3	4	4	4	4
Christian Church (Disciples of Christ)	14,913	30,397	35,984	52,839	47,970	46,260	49,521	14,599	21,603	5,615	7,704	12	18	16	18	19
Christian Churches and Churches of Christ	1,342	2,263	7,277	10,074	10,061	9,970	10,050	3,641	3,432	1,433	1,544	7	8	18	18	17
Christian Methodist Episcopal	2,486	2,174	1,502	4,817	4,207	4,053	3,824	1,890	1,789	57	88	4	4	1	3	3
Christian Reformed Church	5,408	4,488	5,999	5,625	5,710	5,714	5,630	2,465	2,560	325	280	3	2	3	3	3
Church of Christ (Scientist)	2,773	2,557	—	—	—	—	—	—	—	—	—	6	8	—	—	—
Church of God of Prophecy	—	249	—	—	—	—	—	—	—	—	—	—	1	—	—	—
Church of God	6,082	5,627	12,540	16,731	17,768	16,962	16,422	4,653	7,543	1,932	2,294	9	9	7	7	9
Church of New Jerusalem	170	—	—	—	—	—	—	—	—	—	—	1	—	—	—	—
Church of the Brethren	8,482	4,463	4,187	6,154	6,484	6,401	6,255	2,594	3,076	226	359	6	5	4	5	6
Church of the Nazarene	11,716	10,779	16,661	21,144	22,572	23,267	23,353	6,528	10,358	2,136	4,331	10	9	12	10	10
Churches of Christ	9,343	14,611	30,140	35,538	36,299	36,131	35,453	11,200	15,690	3,126	5,437	9	19	19	17	18
Cumberland Presbyterian	594	746	1,112	4,652	6,142	6,007	5,615	1,694	2,010	738	1,173	2	2	2	2	2
Episcopal Church, Reformed	67	—	—	—	1,242	1,286	1,179	66	318	113	682	1	—	—	—	2
Evangelical Christian	—	—	—	—	77,375	76,654	83,835	18,652	27,140	15,932	22,111	—	—	—	—	4
Evangelical Congregational Church	80	88	148	153	120	111	151	28	11	82	30	1	1	1	1	1
Evangelical Covenant Church of America	1,401	1,035	2,387	3,233	3,122	3,011	2,981	755	1,211	362	653	1	1	1	1	2
Evangelical Free Church of America	833	2,355	4,022	2,926	2,391	2,409	1,998	629	368	630	371	1	2	3	2	2
Evangelical Lutheran Church	743	49,210	49,085	56,162	49,863	49,960	52,138	20,241	26,905	1,785	3,207	3	33	34	33	27
Free Methodist	5,543	5,902	7,323	12,270	11,324	10,965	10,721	2,880	5,913	545	1,383	5	3	4	5	5
Free Will Baptist Church	1,132	1,177	2,378	528	713	704	733	286	255	103	89	4	3	4	3	3
Friends United Meeting	1,109	—	—	—	—	—	—	—	—	—	—	1	—	—	—	—
Friends	5,157	5,844	10,898	13,876	11,636	11,368	11,070	4,140	4,886	821	1,223	5	6	8	7	7
General Baptist	—	—	—	—	1,469	1,303	1,419	332	353	338	396	—	—	—	—	1

See notes at end of table.

Table 303.90. Fall enrollment and number of degree-granting postsecondary institutions, by control and religious affiliation of institution: Selected years, 1980 through 2018—Continued

Control and religious affiliation of institution	Total enrollment						Enrollment, fall 2018					Number of institutions[1]				
								Full-time		Part-time						
	Fall 1980	Fall 1990	Fall 2000	Fall 2010	Fall 2016	Fall 2017	Total	Males	Females	Males	Females	Fall 1980	Fall 1990	Fall 2000	Fall 2010	Fall 2018
1	2	3	4	5	6	7	8	9	10	11	12	13	14	15	16	17
General Conference Mennonite Church	820	1,243	1,059	—	—	—	—	—	—	—	—	2	2	1	—	—
Greek Orthodox	204	148	132	220	195	170	341	202	110	19	10	1	1	1	1	1
Interdenominational	1,254	11,103	9,788	33,778	41,113	41,175	40,777	12,111	17,164	5,587	5,915	4	17	14	31	34
Jewish	5,738	12,217	14,182	12,755	13,846	14,066	14,221	10,290	2,561	416	954	24	63	62	36	34
Latter-Day Saints	39,172	42,274	44,680	53,514	84,046	91,403	82,012	25,584	27,048	12,322	17,058	4	4	4	4	4
Lutheran Church—Missouri Synod	11,727	13,827	18,866	28,255	36,542	36,243	35,715	7,970	14,710	4,403	8,632	15	14	13	12	11
Lutheran Church in America	23,877	5,796	4,322	8,240	8,708	8,181	6,004	2,218	3,175	182	429	20	5	2	3	2
Mennonite Brethren Church	1,344	1,864	2,390	4,136	4,291	4,875	5,005	1,124	2,400	446	1,035	3	3	3	3	2
Mennonite Church	4,008	2,859	3,553	4,263	4,131	3,886	3,704	1,271	1,639	209	585	6	5	5	6	6
Missionary Church Inc	487	699	1,647	2,152	1,639	1,513	1,513	435	667	109	302	1	1	1	1	1
Moravian Church	2,434	2,511	2,939	3,095	3,513	3,430	3,356	808	1,754	147	647	2	2	2	2	2
Multiple Protestant denominations	5,526	211	4,690	5,350	4,758	4,766	4,663	967	1,555	1,213	928	8	1	7	6	6
Nondenominational	—	—	—	—	—	—	1,364	547	800	7	10	—	—	—	—	2
North American Baptist	155	—	124	120	207	229	306	48	20	167	71	1	—	1	1	1
Original Free Will Baptist	—	—	—	3,855	3,430	3,451	3,208	591	819	541	1,257	—	—	—	1	1
Pentacostal Holiness Church	767	566	976	1,272	1,684	1,623	1,518	712	598	91	117	3	3	2	3	2
Presbyterian	—	—	—	—	2,965	3,079	3,295	1,076	1,622	176	421	—	—	—	—	4
Presbyterian USA	47,144	77,700	78,950	85,719	82,215	80,862	80,706	29,177	38,490	4,029	9,010	57	70	64	58	56
Presbyterian Church in America	—	1,877	4,499	2,071	1,611	1,585	1,567	665	588	163	151	—	1	5	2	2
Protestant Episcopal	5,396	4,559	5,479	5,006	3,687	3,719	3,535	1,577	1,645	152	161	12	9	12	11	8
Protestant, other	4,072	38,136	30,116	13,450	19,342	19,238	18,950	5,467	7,378	2,651	3,454	11	44	34	23	25
Reformed Church in America	2,713	5,525	6,002	6,555	6,205	6,125	5,992	2,222	3,006	269	495	4	4	5	5	5
Reformed Presbyterian Church	2,014	1,556	2,355	2,982	2,585	2,393	2,325	1,019	825	257	224	4	2	2	3	3
Reorganized Latter-Day Saints Church	4,274	4,793	3,390	—	—	—	—	—	—	—	—	2	1	2	—	—
Roman Catholic	422,842	530,585	636,336	751,091	720,808	711,801	707,105	217,382	323,277	56,043	110,403	229	239	239	237	227
Russian Orthodox	47	38	106	60	75	89	90	68	6	15	1	1	1	1	1	1
Seventh-Day Adventists	19,168	15,771	19,223	25,430	23,914	23,602	23,315	7,320	10,979	1,831	3,185	11	11	13	14	13
Southern Baptist	85,281	49,493	54,275	49,936	55,308	60,043	65,762	21,888	22,887	8,800	12,187	54	29	32	22	22
Undenominational	—	6,758	23,573	27,748	35,365	36,006	35,983	8,006	12,426	6,009	9,542	—	14	16	16	20
Unitarian Universalist	87	82	132	166	181	178	164	24	76	17	47	2	2	2	2	2
United Brethren Church	545	601	938	1,260	1,295	1,321	1,302	426	698	75	103	1	1	1	1	1
United Church of Christ	14,169	20,175	23,709	20,537	15,641	15,324	15,336	5,042	6,529	1,229	2,536	16	18	18	17	14
United Methodist	127,099	148,851	171,109	206,744	200,792	200,217	199,759	72,248	95,922	11,556	20,033	91	96	100	96	94
Wesleyan Church	3,583	5,311	11,128	20,670	19,240	18,608	18,339	4,765	10,225	1,040	2,309	5	4	4	6	8
Wisconsin Evangelical Lutheran Synod	808	931	1,660	1,677	2,051	2,095	2,220	823	887	215	295	1	3	2	2	2
Other religiously affiliated	462	5,743	2,534	4,778	5,097	5,624	5,426	1,681	2,302	460	983	1	9	4	11	12

—Not available.

[1]Counts of institutions in this table may be lower than reported in other tables because counts in this table include only institutions reporting separate enrollment data.

[2]Included under "Other public."

[3]Religious affiliation as reported by institution.

NOTE: Data for 1980 and 1990 are for institutions of higher education, while later data are for degree-granting institutions. Degree-granting institutions grant associate's or higher degrees and participate in Title IV federal financial aid programs. The degree-granting classification is very similar to the earlier higher education classification, but it includes more 2-year colleges and excludes a few higher education institutions that did not grant degrees. Some data have been revised from previously published figures.

SOURCE: U.S. Department of Education, National Center for Education Statistics, Higher Education General Information Survey (HEGIS), "Fall Enrollment in Institutions of Higher Education" and "Institutional Characteristics" surveys, 1980; Integrated Postsecondary Education Data System (IPEDS), "Fall Enrollment Survey" (IPEDS-EF:90) and "Institutional Characteristics Survey" (IPEDS-IC:90); and IPEDS Spring 2001 through Spring 2019, Fall Enrollment component. (This table was prepared February 2020.)

Table 304.10. Total fall enrollment in degree-granting postsecondary institutions, by state or jurisdiction: Selected years, 1970 through 2018

State or jurisdiction	1970	1980	1990	2000	2010	2013	2015	2016	2017	2018	Percent change, 2013 to 2018
1	2	3	4	5	6	7	8	9	10	11	12
United States	**8,580,887**	**12,096,895**	**13,818,637**	**15,312,289**	**21,019,438**	**20,376,677**	**19,988,204**	**19,846,904**	**19,778,151**	**19,645,918**	**-3.6**
Alabama	103,936	164,306	218,589	233,962	327,606	305,817	302,959	304,052	306,817	304,182	-0.5
Alaska	9,471	21,296	29,833	27,953	34,799	34,890	31,373	28,436	26,905	25,692	-26.4
Arizona	109,619	202,716	264,148	342,490	793,871	693,714	650,422	608,086	591,122	581,982	-16.1
Arkansas	52,039	77,347	90,425	115,172	175,848	172,432	168,402	167,235	163,963	159,738	-7.4
California	1,257,245	1,791,088	1,808,740	2,256,708	2,714,699	2,641,331	2,687,410	2,700,445	2,724,446	2,712,420	2.7
Colorado	123,395	162,916	227,131	263,872	369,450	358,330	348,159	352,255	360,236	360,537	0.6
Connecticut	124,700	159,632	168,604	161,243	199,384	201,028	199,666	198,010	197,534	197,480	-1.8
Delaware	25,260	32,939	42,004	43,897	55,258	59,615	60,392	61,139	60,338	60,700	1.8
District of Columbia	77,158	86,675	79,551	72,689	91,992	89,257	93,972	93,040	95,999	97,776	9.5
Florida	235,525	411,891	588,086	707,684	1,124,778	1,125,872	1,083,570	1,075,527	1,073,338	1,068,063	-5.1
Georgia	126,511	184,159	251,786	346,204	568,916	533,425	530,711	533,073	538,124	543,443	1.9
Hawaii	36,562	49,009	56,436	60,182	78,073	76,434	69,332	65,843	64,125	61,855	-19.1
Idaho	34,567	43,018	51,881	65,594	85,201	109,044	121,109	123,796	131,803	123,487	13.2
Illinois	452,146	645,288	729,246	743,918	906,845	842,888	802,211	777,720	757,001	738,448	-12.4
Indiana	192,668	247,253	284,832	314,334	459,493	444,409	426,364	419,284	398,802	388,348	-12.6
Iowa	108,902	140,449	170,515	188,974	381,867	339,738	275,106	266,513	260,801	254,058	-25.2
Kansas	102,485	136,605	163,733	179,968	214,849	215,855	219,994	215,832	213,997	212,737	-1.4
Kentucky	98,591	143,066	177,852	188,341	291,104	273,073	255,722	255,062	258,498	262,961	-3.7
Louisiana	120,728	160,058	186,840	223,800	263,676	251,935	245,305	239,278	241,567	241,401	-4.2
Maine	34,134	43,264	57,186	58,473	72,406	72,412	71,719	72,116	71,811	71,773	-0.9
Maryland	149,607	225,180	259,700	273,745	377,967	363,699	364,225	366,809	364,178	361,442	-0.6
Massachusetts	303,809	418,415	417,833	421,142	507,753	513,964	510,512	505,722	503,539	499,769	-2.8
Michigan	392,726	520,131	569,803	567,631	697,765	643,575	601,462	583,034	558,072	541,096	-15.9
Minnesota	160,788	206,691	253,789	293,445	465,449	441,637	430,466	422,793	412,966	408,783	-7.4
Mississippi	73,967	102,364	122,883	137,389	179,995	173,084	174,183	172,588	171,824	169,360	-2.2
Missouri	183,930	233,378	289,899	321,348	444,750	438,446	409,999	401,098	385,483	374,424	-14.6
Montana	30,062	35,177	35,876	42,240	53,282	52,777	50,799	50,918	50,642	49,363	-6.5
Nebraska	66,915	89,488	112,831	112,117	144,692	137,943	136,091	136,098	135,710	134,938	-2.2
Nevada	13,669	40,455	61,728	87,893	129,360	116,738	116,101	116,030	117,574	117,798	0.9
New Hampshire	29,400	46,794	59,510	61,718	75,539	92,440	123,508	133,159	149,184	160,743	73.9
New Jersey	216,121	321,610	324,286	335,945	444,092	436,939	423,759	421,386	419,037	414,416	-5.2
New Mexico	44,461	58,629	85,500	110,739	162,552	153,455	138,248	134,607	129,595	123,297	-19.7
New York	806,479	992,349	1,048,286	1,043,395	1,305,151	1,305,121	1,285,406	1,273,634	1,260,557	1,250,287	-4.2
North Carolina	171,925	287,537	352,138	404,652	585,792	575,020	562,442	561,415	564,111	563,710	-2.0
North Dakota	31,495	34,069	37,878	40,248	56,903	55,030	53,834	54,203	53,749	53,286	-3.2
Ohio	376,267	488,938	557,690	549,553	745,115	696,912	664,623	658,043	649,586	644,962	-7.5
Oklahoma	110,155	160,295	173,221	178,016	230,560	220,897	211,117	208,333	202,150	195,943	-11.3
Oregon	122,177	157,458	165,741	183,065	251,708	251,087	240,649	236,851	229,988	228,140	-9.1
Pennsylvania	411,044	507,716	604,060	609,521	804,640	765,581	736,163	725,682	717,025	700,329	-8.5
Rhode Island	45,898	66,869	78,273	75,450	85,110	83,460	82,292	83,348	82,765	80,868	-3.1
South Carolina	69,518	132,476	159,302	185,931	257,064	257,844	249,655	246,563	246,416	240,533	-6.7
South Dakota	30,639	32,761	34,208	43,221	58,360	55,129	53,664	53,683	53,620	53,365	-3.2
Tennessee	135,103	204,841	226,238	263,910	351,762	338,197	323,869	321,752	323,157	322,115	-4.8
Texas	442,225	701,391	901,437	1,033,973	1,535,864	1,541,279	1,579,614	1,605,498	1,630,520	1,643,542	6.6
Utah	81,687	92,159	121,303	163,776	255,653	261,897	292,995	311,450	331,996	359,772	37.4
Vermont	22,209	30,628	36,398	35,489	45,572	43,536	43,865	44,719	43,855	42,914	-1.4
Virginia	151,915	280,504	353,442	381,893	577,922	583,755	569,752	557,444	554,120	552,041	-5.4
Washington	183,544	303,603	263,384	320,840	388,116	363,377	364,844	366,547	367,943	367,056	1.0
West Virginia	63,153	81,973	84,790	87,888	152,431	157,952	150,897	146,608	142,966	140,103	-11.3
Wisconsin	202,058	269,086	299,774	307,179	384,181	362,379	350,255	341,717	340,301	336,409	-7.2
Wyoming	15,220	21,147	31,326	30,004	38,298	37,031	34,205	33,365	33,014	32,510	-12.2
U.S. Service Academies[1]	17,079	49,808	48,692	13,475	15,925	14,997	14,812	15,065	15,281	15,523	3.5
Other jurisdictions	**67,237**	**137,749**	**164,618**	**194,633**	**264,240**	**254,543**	**247,886**	**241,896**	**192,717**	**212,565**	**-16.5**
American Samoa	0	976	1,219	297	2,193	1,488	1,285	1,253	1,095	1,037	-30.3
Federated States of Micronesia	0	224	975	1,576	2,699	2,446	2,215	2,090	2,022	1,931	-21.1
Guam	2,719	3,217	4,741	5,215	6,188	6,518	6,395	6,084	6,027	5,888	-9.7
Marshall Islands	0	0	0	328	869	1,000	995	978	1,032	1,119	11.9
Northern Marianas	0	0	661	1,078	1,137	1,109	1,157	1,038	1,216	1,194	7.7
Palau	0	0	491	581	694	646	627	587	532	497	-23.1
Puerto Rico	63,073	131,184	154,065	183,290	247,727	239,015	232,891	227,496	178,623	198,915	-16.8
U.S. Virgin Islands	1,445	2,148	2,466	2,268	2,733	2,321	2,321	2,370	2,170	1,984	-14.5

[1]Data for 2000 and later years reflect a substantial reduction in the number of Department of Defense institutions included in the IPEDS survey.

NOTE: Data through 1990 are for institutions of higher education, while later data are for degree-granting institutions. Degree-granting institutions grant associate's or higher degrees and participate in Title IV federal financial aid programs. The degree-granting classification is very similar to the earlier higher education classification, but it includes more 2-year colleges and excludes a few higher education institutions that did not grant degrees. Some data have been revised from previously published figures.

SOURCE: U.S. Department of Education, National Center for Education Statistics, Higher Education General Information Survey (HEGIS), "Fall Enrollment in Colleges and Universities" surveys, 1970 and 1980; Integrated Postsecondary Education Data System (IPEDS), "Fall Enrollment Survey" (IPEDS-EF:90); and IPEDS Spring 2001 through Spring 2019, Fall Enrollment component. (This table was prepared January 2020.)

Table 304.15. Total fall enrollment in public degree-granting postsecondary institutions, by state or jurisdiction: Selected years, 1970 through 2018

State or jurisdiction	1970	1980	1990	2000	2010	2013	2015	2016	2017	2018	Percent change, 2013 to 2018
1	2	3	4	5	6	7	8	9	10	11	12
United States	**6,428,134**	**9,457,394**	**10,844,717**	**11,752,786**	**15,142,171**	**14,746,848**	**14,572,843**	**14,585,840**	**14,571,739**	**14,529,264**	**-1.5**
Alabama	87,884	143,674	195,939	207,435	267,083	248,296	247,450	251,038	254,071	255,087	2.7
Alaska	8,563	20,561	27,792	26,559	32,303	31,600	28,429	27,352	25,850	24,649	-22.0
Arizona	107,315	194,034	248,213	284,522	366,976	354,485	360,976	361,400	366,787	367,198	3.6
Arkansas	43,599	66,068	78,645	101,775	155,780	153,898	150,165	149,298	146,578	142,382	-7.5
California	1,123,529	1,599,838	1,594,710	1,927,771	2,223,163	2,151,521	2,202,258	2,228,592	2,257,256	2,250,219	4.6
Colorado	108,562	145,598	200,653	217,897	269,433	271,223	265,828	272,668	278,909	279,495	3.0
Connecticut	73,391	97,788	109,556	101,027	127,194	123,093	119,766	117,345	116,090	114,529	-7.0
Delaware	21,151	28,325	34,252	34,194	39,935	40,992	40,611	41,816	42,321	42,601	3.9
District of Columbia	12,194	13,900	11,990	5,499	5,840	5,347	5,118	4,587	4,529	4,500	-15.8
Florida	189,450	334,349	489,081	556,912	790,027	795,860	794,390	797,048	798,045	800,451	0.6
Georgia	101,900	140,158	196,413	271,755	436,047	413,706	417,860	422,159	428,586	435,744	5.3
Hawaii	32,963	43,269	45,728	44,579	60,090	58,941	55,756	53,418	51,674	51,063	-13.4
Idaho	27,072	34,491	41,315	53,751	64,204	75,910	72,339	74,667	75,792	77,133	1.6
Illinois	315,634	491,274	551,333	534,155	585,515	546,483	509,104	492,578	478,042	465,229	-14.9
Indiana	136,739	189,224	223,953	240,023	337,705	335,923	321,501	319,581	301,562	296,229	-11.8
Iowa	68,390	97,454	117,834	135,008	177,781	168,644	171,005	171,075	170,262	199,231	18.1
Kansas	88,215	121,987	149,117	159,976	185,623	184,075	179,532	180,170	179,624	179,600	-2.4
Kentucky	77,240	114,884	147,095	151,973	229,725	218,472	205,908	205,431	202,266	199,748	-8.6
Louisiana	101,127	136,703	158,290	189,213	224,811	215,701	212,098	208,254	210,166	210,696	-2.3
Maine	25,405	31,878	41,500	40,662	50,903	49,602	47,408	47,763	46,999	48,332	-2.6
Maryland	118,988	195,051	220,783	223,797	309,779	301,565	303,849	306,892	303,614	301,959	0.1
Massachusetts	116,127	183,765	186,035	183,248	224,542	228,253	222,243	218,465	213,388	207,767	-9.0
Michigan	339,625	454,147	487,359	467,861	562,448	527,745	501,411	492,771	478,735	466,806	-11.5
Minnesota	130,567	162,379	199,211	218,617	276,176	266,440	256,187	253,239	249,385	245,164	-8.0
Mississippi	64,968	90,661	109,038	125,355	161,493	154,366	155,334	153,082	152,392	150,583	-2.5
Missouri	132,540	165,179	200,093	201,509	256,030	254,650	248,516	244,921	237,454	232,040	-8.9
Montana	27,287	31,178	31,865	37,387	48,231	47,851	45,935	46,262	46,002	44,925	-6.1
Nebraska	51,454	73,509	94,614	88,531	107,979	101,893	100,030	101,032	101,038	100,594	-1.3
Nevada	13,576	40,280	61,242	83,120	113,103	102,538	104,418	106,196	107,864	108,658	6.0
New Hampshire	15,979	24,119	32,163	35,870	44,077	42,711	42,628	41,170	39,761	38,735	-9.3
New Jersey	145,373	247,028	261,601	266,921	358,256	352,822	339,722	337,099	334,597	329,037	-6.7
New Mexico	40,795	55,077	83,403	101,450	150,844	144,381	131,343	129,038	125,381	120,293	-16.7
New York	449,437	563,251	616,884	583,417	723,500	720,948	709,243	700,875	697,458	690,097	-4.3
North Carolina	123,761	228,154	285,405	329,422	475,064	460,125	448,055	450,080	454,998	456,128	-0.9
North Dakota	30,192	31,709	34,690	36,014	48,904	48,718	48,191	47,964	47,574	46,531	-4.5
Ohio	281,099	381,765	427,613	411,161	547,551	520,039	501,677	501,146	497,409	495,612	-4.7
Oklahoma	91,438	137,188	151,073	153,699	197,641	187,078	179,008	177,629	174,239	170,979	-8.6
Oregon	108,483	140,102	144,427	154,756	208,001	208,317	197,948	197,819	192,402	191,943	-7.9
Pennsylvania	232,982	292,499	343,478	339,229	432,923	419,856	408,522	406,346	401,045	392,771	-6.5
Rhode Island	25,527	35,052	42,350	38,458	43,224	42,786	41,320	41,369	41,018	40,082	-6.3
South Carolina	47,101	107,683	131,134	155,519	205,080	207,717	202,487	200,295	200,622	196,525	-5.4
South Dakota	23,936	24,328	26,596	34,857	44,569	44,272	44,254	44,305	44,630	43,871	-0.9
Tennessee	98,897	156,835	175,049	202,530	242,486	229,302	223,411	221,288	223,179	225,281	-1.8
Texas	365,522	613,552	802,314	896,534	1,334,110	1,349,490	1,388,266	1,423,205	1,448,398	1,468,587	8.8
Utah	49,588	59,598	86,108	123,046	179,061	168,311	170,689	175,308	180,034	183,949	9.3
Vermont	12,536	17,984	20,910	20,021	27,524	25,852	25,383	25,736	25,300	25,197	-2.5
Virginia	123,279	246,500	291,286	313,780	409,004	405,915	394,210	389,446	389,251	384,879	-5.2
Washington	162,718	276,028	227,632	273,928	330,853	310,192	313,964	315,356	318,336	319,377	3.0
West Virginia	51,363	71,228	74,108	76,136	96,104	90,780	86,342	85,099	83,898	81,605	-10.1
Wisconsin	170,374	235,179	253,529	249,737	301,259	287,619	282,250	278,300	279,097	277,178	-3.6
Wyoming	15,220	21,121	30,623	28,715	36,292	35,547	33,693	32,802	32,550	32,472	-8.7
U.S. Service Academies[1]	17,079	49,808	48,692	13,475	15,925	14,997	14,812	15,065	15,281	15,523	3.5
Other jurisdictions	**46,680**	**60,692**	**66,244**	**84,464**	**83,719**	**78,136**	**80,129**	**81,479**	**37,419**	**72,399**	**-7.3**
American Samoa	0	976	1,219	297	2,193	1,488	1,285	1,253	1,095	1,037	-30.3
Federated States of Micronesia	0	224	975	1,576	2,699	2,446	2,215	2,090	2,022	1,931	-21.1
Guam	2,719	3,217	4,741	5,215	6,103	6,439	6,325	6,017	5,972	5,826	-9.5
Marshall Islands	0	0	0	328	869	1,000	995	978	1,032	1,119	11.9
Northern Marianas	0	0	661	1,078	1,137	1,109	1,157	1,038	1,216	1,194	7.7
Palau	0	0	491	581	694	646	627	587	532	497	-23.1
Puerto Rico	42,516	54,127	55,691	73,121	67,291	62,687	65,204	67,146	23,380	58,811	-6.2
U.S. Virgin Islands	1,445	2,148	2,466	2,268	2,733	2,321	2,321	2,370	2,170	1,984	-14.5

[1]Data for 2000 and later years reflect a substantial reduction in the number of Department of Defense institutions included in the IPEDS survey.

NOTE: Data through 1990 are for institutions of higher education, while later data are for degree-granting institutions. Degree-granting institutions grant associate's or higher degrees and participate in Title IV federal financial aid programs. The degree-granting classification is very similar to the earlier higher education classification, but it includes more 2-year colleges and excludes a few higher education institutions that did not grant degrees. Some data have been revised from previously published figures.

SOURCE: U.S. Department of Education, National Center for Education Statistics, Higher Education General Information Survey (HEGIS), "Fall Enrollment in Colleges and Universities" surveys, 1970 and 1980; Integrated Postsecondary Education Data System (IPEDS), "Fall Enrollment Survey" (IPEDS-EF:90); and IPEDS Spring 2001 through Spring 2019, Fall Enrollment component. (This table was prepared January 2020.)

Table 304.20. Total fall enrollment in private degree-granting postsecondary institutions, by state or jurisdiction: Selected years, 1970 through 2018

State or jurisdiction	1970	1980	1990	2000	2010	2013	2015	2016	2017	2018	Percent change, 2013 to 2018
1	2	3	4	5	6	7	8	9	10	11	12
United States	**2,152,753**	**2,639,501**	**2,973,920**	**3,559,503**	**5,877,267**	**5,629,829**	**5,415,361**	**5,261,064**	**5,206,412**	**5,116,654**	**-9.1**
Alabama	16,052	20,632	22,650	26,527	60,523	57,521	55,509	53,014	52,746	49,095	-14.6
Alaska	908	735	2,041	1,394	2,496	3,290	2,944	1,084	1,055	1,043	-68.3
Arizona	2,304	8,682	15,935	57,968	426,895	339,229	289,446	246,686	224,335	214,784	-36.7
Arkansas	8,440	11,279	11,780	13,397	20,068	18,534	18,237	17,937	17,385	17,356	-6.4
California	133,716	191,250	214,030	328,937	491,536	489,810	485,152	471,853	467,190	462,201	-5.6
Colorado	14,833	17,318	26,478	45,975	100,017	87,107	82,331	79,587	81,327	81,042	-7.0
Connecticut	51,309	61,844	59,048	60,216	72,190	77,935	79,900	80,665	81,444	82,951	6.4
Delaware	4,109	4,614	7,752	9,703	15,323	18,623	19,781	19,323	18,017	18,099	-2.8
District of Columbia	64,964	72,775	67,561	67,190	86,152	83,910	88,854	88,453	91,470	93,276	11.2
Florida	46,075	77,542	99,005	150,772	334,751	330,012	289,180	278,479	275,293	267,612	-18.9
Georgia	24,611	44,001	55,373	74,449	132,869	119,719	112,851	110,914	109,538	107,699	-10.0
Hawaii	3,599	5,740	10,708	15,603	17,983	17,493	13,576	12,425	12,451	10,792	-38.3
Idaho	7,495	8,527	10,566	11,843	20,997	33,134	48,770	49,129	56,011	46,354	39.9
Illinois	136,512	154,014	177,913	209,763	321,330	296,405	293,107	285,142	278,959	273,219	-7.8
Indiana	55,929	58,029	60,879	74,311	121,788	108,486	104,863	99,703	97,240	92,119	-15.1
Iowa	40,512	42,995	52,681	53,966	204,086	171,094	104,101	95,438	90,539	54,827	-68.0
Kansas	14,270	14,618	14,616	19,992	29,226	31,780	40,462	35,662	34,373	33,137	4.3
Kentucky	21,351	28,182	30,757	36,368	61,379	54,601	49,814	49,631	56,232	63,213	15.8
Louisiana	19,601	23,355	28,550	34,587	38,865	36,234	33,207	31,024	31,401	30,705	-15.3
Maine	8,729	11,386	15,686	17,811	21,503	22,810	24,311	24,353	24,812	23,441	2.8
Maryland	30,619	30,129	38,917	49,948	68,188	62,134	60,376	59,917	60,564	59,483	-4.3
Massachusetts	187,682	234,650	231,798	237,894	283,211	285,711	288,269	287,257	290,151	292,002	2.2
Michigan	53,101	65,984	82,444	99,770	135,317	115,830	100,051	90,263	79,337	74,290	-35.9
Minnesota	30,221	44,312	54,578	74,828	189,273	175,197	174,279	169,554	163,581	163,619	-6.6
Mississippi	8,999	11,703	13,845	12,034	18,502	18,718	18,849	19,506	19,432	18,777	0.3
Missouri	51,390	68,199	89,806	119,839	188,720	183,796	161,483	156,177	148,029	142,384	-22.5
Montana	2,775	3,999	4,011	4,853	5,051	4,926	4,864	4,656	4,640	4,438	-9.9
Nebraska	15,461	15,979	18,217	23,586	36,713	36,050	36,061	35,066	34,672	34,344	-4.7
Nevada	93	175	486	4,773	16,257	14,200	11,683	9,834	9,710	9,140	-35.6
New Hampshire	13,421	22,675	27,347	25,848	31,462	49,729	80,880	91,989	109,423	122,008	145.3
New Jersey	70,748	74,582	62,685	69,024	85,836	84,117	84,037	84,287	84,440	85,379	1.5
New Mexico	3,666	3,552	2,097	9,289	11,708	9,074	6,905	5,569	4,214	3,004	-66.9
New York	357,042	429,098	431,402	459,978	581,651	584,173	576,163	572,759	563,099	560,190	-4.1
North Carolina	48,164	59,383	66,733	75,230	110,728	114,895	114,387	111,335	109,113	107,582	-6.4
North Dakota	1,303	2,360	3,188	4,234	7,999	6,312	5,643	6,239	6,175	6,755	7.0
Ohio	95,168	107,173	130,077	138,392	197,564	176,873	162,946	156,897	152,177	149,350	-15.6
Oklahoma	18,717	23,107	22,148	24,317	32,919	33,819	32,109	30,704	27,911	24,964	-26.2
Oregon	13,694	17,356	21,314	28,309	43,707	42,770	42,701	39,032	37,586	36,197	-15.4
Pennsylvania	178,062	215,217	260,582	270,292	371,717	345,725	327,641	319,336	315,980	307,558	-11.0
Rhode Island	20,371	31,817	35,923	36,992	41,886	40,674	40,972	41,979	41,747	40,786	0.3
South Carolina	22,417	24,793	28,168	30,412	51,984	50,127	47,168	46,268	45,794	44,008	-12.2
South Dakota	6,703	8,433	7,612	8,364	13,791	10,857	9,410	9,378	8,990	9,494	-12.6
Tennessee	36,206	48,006	51,189	61,380	109,276	108,895	100,458	100,464	99,978	96,834	-11.1
Texas	76,703	87,839	99,123	137,439	201,754	191,789	191,348	182,293	182,122	174,955	-8.8
Utah	32,099	32,561	35,195	40,730	76,592	93,586	122,306	136,142	151,962	175,823	87.9
Vermont	9,673	12,644	15,488	15,468	18,048	17,684	18,482	18,983	18,555	17,717	0.2
Virginia	28,636	34,004	62,156	68,113	168,918	177,840	175,542	167,998	164,869	167,162	-6.0
Washington	20,826	27,575	35,752	46,912	57,263	53,185	50,880	51,191	49,607	47,679	-10.4
West Virginia	11,790	10,745	10,682	11,752	56,327	67,172	64,555	61,509	59,068	58,498	-12.9
Wisconsin	31,684	33,907	46,245	57,442	82,922	74,760	68,005	63,417	61,204	59,231	-20.8
Wyoming	0	26	703	1,289	2,006	1,484	512	563	464	38	-97.4
Other jurisdictions	**20,557**	**77,057**	**98,374**	**110,169**	**180,521**	**176,407**	**167,757**	**160,417**	**155,298**	**140,166**	**-20.5**
American Samoa	0	0	0	0	0	0	0	0	0	0	†
Federated States of Micronesia	0	0	0	0	0	0	0	0	0	0	†
Guam	0	0	0	0	85	79	70	67	55	62	-21.5
Marshall Islands	0	0	0	0	0	0	0	0	0	0	†
Northern Marianas	0	0	0	0	0	0	0	0	0	0	†
Palau	0	0	0	0	0	0	0	0	0	0	†
Puerto Rico	20,557	77,057	98,374	110,169	180,436	176,328	167,687	160,350	155,243	140,104	-20.5
U.S. Virgin Islands	0	0	0	0	0	0	0	0	0	0	†

†Not applicable.

NOTE: Data through 1990 are for institutions of higher education, while later data are for degree-granting institutions. Degree-granting institutions grant associate's or higher degrees and participate in Title IV federal financial aid programs. The degree-granting classification is very similar to the earlier higher education classification, but it includes more 2-year colleges and excludes a few higher education institutions that did not grant degrees. Some data have been revised from previously published figures.

SOURCE: U.S. Department of Education, National Center for Education Statistics, Higher Education General Information Survey (HEGIS), "Fall Enrollment in Colleges and Universities" surveys, 1970 and 1980; Integrated Postsecondary Education Data System (IPEDS), "Fall Enrollment Survey" (IPEDS-EF:90); and IPEDS Spring 2001 through Spring 2019, Fall Enrollment component. (This table was prepared January 2020.)

Table 304.30. Total fall enrollment in degree-granting postsecondary institutions, by attendance status, sex, and state or jurisdiction: 2017 and 2018

State or jurisdiction	2017					2018					Percent change, 2017 to 2018
	Total	Full-time		Part-time		Total	Full-time		Part-time		
		Males	Females	Males	Females		Males	Females	Males	Females	
1	2	3	4	5	6	7	8	9	10	11	12
United States	**19,778,151**	**5,423,955**	**6,652,186**	**3,147,359**	**4,554,651**	**19,645,918**	**5,338,934**	**6,652,787**	**3,103,728**	**4,550,469**	**-0.7**
Alabama	306,817	91,970	118,873	39,522	56,452	304,182	89,797	116,948	39,958	57,479	-0.9
Alaska	26,905	5,485	6,705	5,409	9,306	25,692	5,126	6,323	5,057	9,186	-4.5
Arizona	591,122	141,786	196,426	94,483	158,427	581,982	135,977	188,169	94,537	163,299	-1.5
Arkansas	163,963	44,881	58,757	23,301	37,024	159,738	43,198	57,698	22,762	36,080	-2.6
California	2,724,446	665,176	827,351	558,940	672,979	2,712,420	660,564	832,468	550,771	668,617	-0.4
Colorado	360,236	95,560	109,193	64,269	91,214	360,537	94,850	111,629	63,371	90,687	0.1
Connecticut	197,534	58,447	70,992	25,363	42,732	197,480	57,954	71,751	24,775	43,000	#
Delaware	60,338	15,918	21,376	7,965	15,079	60,700	15,831	21,559	7,881	15,429	0.6
District of Columbia	95,999	25,965	38,178	12,279	19,577	97,776	26,073	38,737	12,474	20,492	1.9
Florida	1,073,338	265,282	350,453	182,876	274,727	1,068,063	262,973	353,235	179,316	272,539	-0.5
Georgia	538,124	144,116	194,896	75,723	123,389	543,443	142,719	196,570	79,369	124,785	1.0
Hawaii	64,125	15,659	21,771	10,376	16,319	61,855	14,533	20,926	10,065	16,331	-3.5
Idaho	131,803	27,695	32,239	29,016	42,853	123,487	27,904	33,060	24,625	37,898	-6.3
Illinois	757,001	201,572	236,661	123,667	195,101	738,448	195,385	234,805	118,461	189,797	-2.5
Indiana	398,802	121,301	142,262	57,892	77,347	388,348	118,999	140,588	54,526	74,235	-2.6
Iowa	260,801	73,441	79,614	41,604	66,142	254,058	71,910	78,623	40,862	62,663	-2.6
Kansas	213,997	59,690	64,184	37,923	52,200	212,737	58,189	63,617	37,830	53,101	-0.6
Kentucky	258,498	66,423	89,574	43,704	58,797	262,961	69,016	90,575	44,286	59,084	1.7
Louisiana	241,567	66,556	94,299	29,315	51,397	241,401	66,364	96,614	28,291	50,132	-0.1
Maine	71,811	19,554	24,020	9,644	18,593	71,773	19,187	23,873	10,053	18,660	-0.1
Maryland	364,178	87,111	101,730	74,525	100,812	361,442	85,352	100,876	73,751	101,463	-0.8
Massachusetts	503,539	161,201	192,140	57,461	92,737	499,769	159,187	191,879	57,138	91,565	-0.7
Michigan	558,072	157,306	176,811	95,601	128,354	541,096	153,053	175,363	90,558	122,122	-3.0
Minnesota	412,966	94,227	125,640	66,074	127,025	408,783	92,241	126,186	64,338	126,018	-1.0
Mississippi	171,824	53,131	75,552	15,386	27,755	169,360	50,286	72,829	16,464	29,781	-1.4
Missouri	385,483	105,974	129,656	59,274	90,579	374,424	100,863	125,363	58,730	89,468	-2.9
Montana	50,642	17,412	17,980	5,869	9,381	49,363	16,635	17,498	5,953	9,277	-2.5
Nebraska	135,710	40,242	47,157	19,992	28,319	134,938	38,980	46,347	20,289	29,322	-0.6
Nevada	117,574	26,886	36,078	22,872	31,738	117,798	26,965	36,032	22,807	31,994	0.2
New Hampshire	149,184	29,337	38,914	28,460	52,473	160,743	30,576	42,121	30,624	57,422	7.7
New Jersey	419,037	131,377	143,515	59,872	84,273	414,416	130,541	143,158	58,234	82,483	-1.1
New Mexico	129,595	28,211	35,831	25,972	39,581	123,297	26,026	33,859	24,685	38,727	-4.9
New York	1,260,557	404,510	491,234	146,069	218,744	1,250,287	400,139	491,531	143,092	215,525	-0.8
North Carolina	564,111	156,448	203,139	77,753	126,771	563,710	154,504	201,933	78,070	129,203	-0.1
North Dakota	53,749	18,770	18,292	7,514	9,173	53,286	18,235	18,126	7,489	9,436	-0.9
Ohio	649,586	192,545	219,991	94,259	142,791	644,962	188,767	218,435	92,003	145,757	-0.7
Oklahoma	202,150	60,390	70,764	27,760	43,236	195,943	56,725	69,359	27,009	42,850	-3.1
Oregon	229,988	64,634	78,304	38,827	48,223	228,140	62,439	77,280	39,104	49,317	-0.8
Pennsylvania	717,025	242,852	279,962	72,050	122,161	700,329	234,273	275,567	70,105	120,384	-2.3
Rhode Island	82,765	27,742	34,659	7,682	12,682	80,868	27,453	34,120	7,272	12,023	-2.3
South Carolina	246,416	74,108	97,010	26,901	48,397	240,533	72,906	95,054	25,475	47,098	-2.4
South Dakota	53,620	16,230	16,728	7,984	12,678	53,365	15,905	16,707	8,070	12,683	-0.5
Tennessee	323,157	100,053	130,691	35,515	56,898	322,115	97,314	130,278	35,830	58,693	-0.3
Texas	1,630,520	387,457	465,124	318,908	459,031	1,643,542	384,004	467,710	319,572	472,256	0.8
Utah	331,996	103,614	138,924	43,149	46,309	359,772	111,363	156,848	42,809	48,752	8.4
Vermont	43,855	15,396	16,407	4,724	7,328	42,914	14,973	16,316	4,534	7,091	-2.1
Virginia	554,120	153,150	188,204	86,804	125,962	552,041	152,793	191,686	84,284	123,278	-0.4
Washington	367,943	115,274	138,436	49,054	65,179	367,056	113,364	138,830	49,513	65,349	-0.2
West Virginia	142,966	34,777	39,523	36,928	31,738	140,103	32,257	37,948	37,348	32,550	-2.0
Wisconsin	340,301	96,750	112,774	54,071	76,706	336,409	94,452	112,491	52,641	76,825	-1.1
Wyoming	33,014	8,931	9,364	6,760	7,959	32,510	8,332	9,267	6,650	8,261	-1.5
U.S. Service Academies	15,281	11,432	3,828	18	3	15,523	11,482	4,022	17	2	1.6
Other jurisdictions	**192,717**	**62,759**	**86,060**	**17,998**	**25,900**	**212,565**	**69,481**	**98,503**	**18,092**	**26,489**	**10.3**
American Samoa	1,095	205	410	164	316	1,037	195	418	124	300	-5.3
Federated States of Micronesia	2,022	639	815	257	311	1,931	634	781	234	282	-4.5
Guam	6,027	1,695	2,237	886	1,209	5,888	1,651	2,174	896	1,167	-2.3
Marshall Islands	1,032	331	336	196	169	1,119	380	360	191	188	8.4
Northern Marianas	1,216	354	559	124	179	1,194	349	578	104	163	-1.8
Palau	532	164	188	74	106	497	117	150	72	158	-6.6
Puerto Rico	178,623	58,889	80,635	16,067	23,032	198,915	65,722	93,171	16,272	23,750	11.4
U.S. Virgin Islands	2,170	482	880	230	578	1,984	433	871	199	481	-8.6

#Rounds to zero.
NOTE: Degree-granting institutions grant associate's or higher degrees and participate in Title IV federal financial aid programs. Some data have been revised from previously published figures.

SOURCE: U.S. Department of Education, National Center for Education Statistics, Integrated Postsecondary Education Data System (IPEDS), Spring 2018 and Spring 2019, Fall Enrollment component. (This table was prepared January 2020.)

Table 304.35. Total fall enrollment in public degree-granting postsecondary institutions, by attendance status, sex, and state or jurisdiction: 2017 and 2018

State or jurisdiction	2017					2018					Percent change, 2017 to 2018
	Total	Full-time		Part-time		Total	Full-time		Part-time		
		Males	Females	Males	Females		Males	Females	Males	Females	
1	2	3	4	5	6	7	8	9	10	11	12
United States	**14,571,739**	**3,857,431**	**4,469,043**	**2,624,115**	**3,621,150**	**14,529,264**	**3,787,941**	**4,480,879**	**2,603,530**	**3,656,914**	**-0.3**
Alabama	254,071	74,203	96,246	32,969	50,653	255,087	72,952	97,147	33,201	51,787	0.4
Alaska	25,850	5,289	6,133	5,306	9,122	24,649	4,936	5,735	4,953	9,025	-4.6
Arizona	366,787	90,375	98,218	75,047	103,147	367,198	87,940	98,735	74,940	105,583	0.1
Arkansas	146,578	38,360	50,741	22,134	35,343	142,382	36,664	49,735	21,565	34,418	-2.9
California	2,257,256	515,912	604,857	521,696	614,791	2,250,219	514,188	611,606	514,775	609,650	-0.3
Colorado	278,909	74,706	78,038	54,672	71,493	279,495	74,548	78,844	54,141	71,962	0.2
Connecticut	116,090	32,653	36,476	18,798	28,163	114,529	32,028	36,521	18,281	27,699	-1.3
Delaware	42,321	12,727	17,222	4,488	7,884	42,601	12,787	17,560	4,363	7,891	0.7
District of Columbia	4,529	1,050	1,206	830	1,443	4,500	1,036	1,197	848	1,419	-0.6
Florida	798,045	181,640	227,474	155,578	233,353	800,451	180,635	231,016	154,014	234,786	0.3
Georgia	428,586	115,084	146,935	66,216	100,351	435,744	113,576	149,155	70,018	102,995	1.7
Hawaii	51,674	12,080	15,581	9,201	14,812	51,063	11,482	15,453	9,089	15,039	-1.2
Idaho	75,792	18,453	20,740	14,690	21,909	77,133	18,142	21,085	14,870	23,036	1.8
Illinois	478,042	122,250	129,588	96,430	129,774	465,229	117,478	127,488	93,360	126,903	-2.7
Indiana	301,562	87,402	96,787	51,562	65,811	296,229	86,116	97,242	48,548	64,323	-1.8
Iowa	170,262	51,117	50,326	30,347	38,472	199,231	51,927	55,569	36,783	54,952	17.0
Kansas	179,624	49,741	53,637	31,783	44,463	179,600	48,500	53,240	32,132	45,728	#
Kentucky	202,266	53,145	68,233	34,491	46,397	199,748	50,979	67,572	34,719	46,478	-1.2
Louisiana	210,166	57,512	77,279	27,768	47,607	210,696	57,368	80,314	26,701	46,313	0.3
Maine	46,999	12,283	13,326	7,845	13,545	48,332	12,010	13,446	8,281	14,595	2.8
Maryland	303,614	70,748	79,761	66,368	86,737	301,959	69,549	79,629	65,438	87,343	-0.5
Massachusetts	213,388	59,644	64,619	34,182	54,943	207,767	57,016	62,954	33,684	54,113	-2.6
Michigan	478,735	133,968	150,110	83,964	110,693	466,806	130,309	149,192	80,258	107,047	-2.5
Minnesota	249,385	66,561	73,545	45,331	63,948	245,164	64,864	73,047	44,292	62,961	-1.7
Mississippi	152,392	48,624	67,625	13,279	22,864	150,583	45,900	65,448	14,356	24,879	-1.2
Missouri	237,454	66,014	78,906	36,840	55,694	232,040	62,660	76,836	36,225	56,319	-2.3
Montana	46,002	15,834	15,819	5,648	8,701	44,925	15,115	15,466	5,725	8,619	-2.3
Nebraska	101,038	29,570	31,906	17,199	22,363	100,594	29,278	32,112	16,645	22,559	-0.4
Nevada	107,864	23,908	30,673	22,445	30,838	108,658	24,258	30,972	22,387	31,041	0.7
New Hampshire	39,761	12,907	15,160	4,447	7,247	38,735	12,685	14,851	4,375	6,824	-2.6
New Jersey	334,597	99,889	110,370	52,439	71,899	329,037	98,373	109,706	51,043	69,915	-1.7
New Mexico	125,381	27,136	33,469	25,757	39,019	120,293	25,212	32,061	24,566	38,454	-4.1
New York	697,458	215,895	248,886	95,192	137,485	690,097	211,638	247,145	94,227	137,087	-1.1
North Carolina	454,998	118,312	152,809	71,274	112,603	456,128	116,740	152,933	71,619	114,836	0.2
North Dakota	47,574	16,888	15,366	7,034	8,286	46,531	16,257	15,063	6,870	8,341	-2.2
Ohio	497,409	140,321	154,805	82,121	120,162	495,612	136,593	153,336	80,742	124,941	-0.4
Oklahoma	174,239	48,788	58,315	26,081	41,055	170,979	46,536	58,025	25,510	40,908	-1.9
Oregon	192,402	53,364	58,990	36,471	43,577	191,943	51,780	58,291	36,950	44,922	-0.2
Pennsylvania	401,045	132,642	142,412	49,588	76,403	392,771	127,742	139,774	48,664	76,591	-2.1
Rhode Island	41,018	10,563	14,628	5,775	10,052	40,082	10,631	14,810	5,397	9,244	-2.3
South Carolina	200,622	59,898	74,953	24,044	41,727	196,525	59,162	74,160	22,698	40,505	-2.0
South Dakota	44,630	14,203	13,525	6,747	10,155	43,871	13,736	13,481	6,576	10,078	-1.7
Tennessee	223,179	67,470	83,070	28,797	43,842	225,281	65,732	83,417	29,616	46,516	0.9
Texas	1,448,398	326,263	380,891	303,811	437,433	1,468,587	324,380	388,301	305,072	450,834	1.4
Utah	180,034	48,153	48,276	40,039	43,566	183,949	48,712	49,749	39,868	45,620	2.2
Vermont	25,300	7,565	9,503	2,667	5,565	25,197	7,475	9,642	2,629	5,451	-0.4
Virginia	389,251	109,603	127,095	64,099	88,454	384,879	108,617	127,274	62,198	86,790	-1.1
Washington	318,336	99,257	113,978	45,683	59,418	319,377	97,946	115,019	46,438	59,974	0.3
West Virginia	83,898	28,669	32,107	8,648	14,474	81,605	26,750	31,242	8,776	14,837	-2.7
Wisconsin	279,097	78,858	85,271	49,516	65,452	277,178	77,222	84,999	48,437	66,520	-0.7
Wyoming	32,550	8,502	9,329	6,760	7,959	32,472	8,299	9,262	6,650	8,261	-0.2
U.S. Service Academies	15,281	11,432	3,828	18	3	15,523	11,482	4,022	17	2	1.6
Other jurisdictions	**37,419**	**14,488**	**15,921**	**3,145**	**3,865**	**72,399**	**26,338**	**34,587**	**5,004**	**6,470**	**93.5**
American Samoa	1,095	205	410	164	316	1,037	195	418	124	300	-5.3
Federated States of Micronesia	2,022	639	815	257	311	1,931	634	781	234	282	-4.5
Guam	5,972	1,673	2,217	880	1,202	5,826	1,628	2,150	888	1,160	-2.4
Marshall Islands	1,032	331	336	196	169	1,119	380	360	191	188	8.4
Northern Marianas	1,216	354	559	124	179	1,194	349	578	104	163	-1.8
Palau	532	164	188	74	106	497	117	150	72	158	-6.6
Puerto Rico	23,380	10,640	10,516	1,220	1,004	58,811	22,602	29,279	3,192	3,738	151.5
U.S. Virgin Islands	2,170	482	880	230	578	1,984	433	871	199	481	-8.6

#Rounds to zero.
NOTE: Degree-granting institutions grant associate's or higher degrees and participate in Title IV federal financial aid programs. Some data have been revised from previously published figures.

SOURCE: U.S. Department of Education, National Center for Education Statistics, Integrated Postsecondary Education Data System (IPEDS), Spring 2018 and Spring 2019, Fall Enrollment component. (This table was prepared January 2020.)

Table 304.60. Total fall enrollment in degree-granting postsecondary institutions, by control and level of institution and state or jurisdiction: 2017 and 2018

State or jurisdiction	2017						2018					
	Public 4-year	Public 2-year	Private 4-year		Private 2-year		Public 4-year	Public 2-year	Private 4-year		Private 2-year	
			Nonprofit	For-profit	Nonprofit	For-profit			Nonprofit	For-profit	Nonprofit	For-profit
1	2	3	4	5	6	7	8	9	10	11	12	13
United States	**8,854,279**	**5,717,460**	**4,060,094**	**911,007**	**48,395**	**186,916**	**8,982,560**	**5,546,704**	**4,089,090**	**829,060**	**45,154**	**153,350**
Alabama	173,335	80,736	26,144	24,841	†	1,761	174,857	80,230	26,261	22,728	†	106
Alaska	25,850	†	551	†	74	430	24,649	†	547	†	81	415
Arizona	180,262	186,525	9,935	203,877	†	10,523	188,360	178,838	10,923	194,257	†	9,604
Arkansas	100,055	46,523	15,713	323	1,296	53	98,718	43,664	15,606	368	1,326	56
California	1,014,651	1,242,605	307,742	131,822	1,497	26,129	1,016,497	1,233,722	310,313	127,229	1,260	23,399
Colorado	212,011	66,898	33,730	39,861	351	7,385	238,952	40,543	33,750	38,775	130	8,387
Connecticut	66,710	49,380	72,360	9,084	†	†	66,620	47,909	73,023	9,928	†	†
Delaware	42,321	†	17,554	320	143	†	42,601	†	17,630	351	118	†
District of Columbia	4,529	†	81,099	9,984	†	387	4,500	†	81,391	11,537	†	348
Florida	770,419	27,626	184,960	50,603	20,146	19,584	777,268	23,183	179,885	50,822	20,444	16,461
Georgia	314,455	114,131	77,092	24,084	1,763	6,599	318,412	117,332	79,170	21,258	1,931	5,340
Hawaii	27,535	24,139	10,159	1,670	†	622	27,336	23,727	9,695	406	†	691
Idaho	52,432	23,360	55,503	79	†	429	53,392	23,741	45,926	†	†	428
Illinois	184,631	293,411	214,829	59,655	421	4,054	181,814	283,415	213,041	56,854	411	2,913
Indiana	226,076	75,486	89,435	4,403	548	2,854	224,223	72,006	88,384	668	415	2,652
Iowa	80,020	90,242	52,882	37,550	†	107	109,809	89,422	51,467	3,284	†	76
Kansas	100,731	78,893	23,177	10,154	†	1,042	100,937	78,663	23,312	9,015	†	810
Kentucky	124,710	77,556	47,958	7,272	†	1,002	122,074	77,674	55,504	6,726	†	983
Louisiana	143,905	66,261	25,955	56	481	4,909	145,708	64,988	26,826	75	492	3,312
Maine	30,040	16,959	23,226	1,096	242	248	31,720	16,612	23,173	†	61	207
Maryland	184,495	119,119	54,644	3,511	†	2,409	186,212	115,747	55,012	3,181	†	1,290
Massachusetts	125,770	87,618	286,926	1,914	1,093	218	124,447	83,320	288,720	1,937	1,212	133
Michigan	327,750	150,985	76,782	1,411	†	1,144	322,932	143,874	72,631	411	†	1,248
Minnesota	132,119	117,266	70,563	92,658	90	270	128,746	116,418	71,084	92,204	106	225
Mississippi	80,730	71,662	17,576	359	†	1,497	78,558	72,025	17,576	508	†	693
Missouri	148,708	88,746	139,805	4,929	173	3,122	146,372	85,668	138,235	2,885	183	1,081
Montana	38,116	7,886	4,228	†	375	37	36,977	7,948	4,090	†	305	43
Nebraska	60,740	40,298	33,668	903	32	69	60,365	40,229	34,176	107	15	46
Nevada	97,144	10,720	3,994	1,862	272	3,582	108,658	†	4,136	1,836	97	3,071
New Hampshire	27,308	12,453	109,300	†	123	†	26,950	11,785	121,896	†	112	†
New Jersey	187,735	146,862	73,693	6,894	†	3,853	189,539	139,498	74,254	6,891	159	4,075
New Mexico	58,353	67,028	1,590	1,283	†	1,341	55,908	64,385	1,498	519	†	987
New York	400,971	296,487	521,931	27,702	2,696	10,770	403,935	286,162	519,645	27,680	2,705	10,160
North Carolina	232,872	222,126	96,497	8,875	624	3,117	237,460	218,668	96,528	8,335	594	2,125
North Dakota	40,368	7,206	5,648	527	†	†	39,204	7,327	6,140	615	†	†
Ohio	326,478	170,931	135,357	6,092	1,419	9,309	334,004	161,608	134,139	4,904	1,164	9,143
Oklahoma	117,916	56,323	23,338	1,464	581	2,528	116,267	54,712	21,971	1,088	578	1,327
Oregon	104,604	87,798	34,573	2,209	34	770	103,375	88,568	33,764	1,621	45	767
Pennsylvania	277,538	123,507	288,384	8,544	6,053	12,999	271,256	121,515	289,345	4,083	4,692	9,438
Rhode Island	26,260	14,758	41,747	†	†	†	25,543	14,539	40,786	†	†	†
South Carolina	114,569	86,053	33,375	7,883	790	3,746	115,686	80,839	36,081	4,308	869	2,750
South Dakota	37,897	6,733	7,060	1,930	†	†	37,034	6,837	7,405	2,089	†	†
Tennessee	136,810	86,369	83,777	7,698	682	7,821	137,180	88,101	83,265	7,510	709	5,350
Texas	737,555	710,843	140,806	18,175	1,921	21,220	785,517	683,070	140,143	17,501	1,610	15,701
Utah	150,414	29,620	145,565	3,862	2,045	490	154,793	29,156	169,648	3,699	1,996	480
Vermont	19,796	5,504	18,411	144	†	†	19,819	5,378	17,644	73	†	†
Virginia	219,882	169,369	132,378	28,278	578	3,635	220,817	164,062	136,722	26,840	393	3,207
Washington	282,316	36,020	41,472	5,044	1,388	1,703	286,838	32,539	41,326	4,110	941	1,302
West Virginia	67,191	16,707	8,583	47,715	†	2,770	65,121	16,484	8,368	47,815	†	2,315
Wisconsin	189,518	89,579	58,419	2,407	†	378	186,627	90,551	57,035	2,029	†	167
Wyoming	12,397	20,153	†	†	464	†	12,450	20,022	†	†	†	38
U.S. Service Academies	15,281	†	†	†	†	†	15,523	†	†	†	†	†
Other jurisdictions	**29,524**	**7,895**	**118,239**	**18,879**	**358**	**17,822**	**65,951**	**6,448**	**108,807**	**17,989**	**127**	**13,243**
American Samoa	1,095	†	†	†	†	†	1,037	†	†	†	†	†
Federated States of Micronesia	†	2,022	†	†	†	†	†	1,931	†	†	†	†
Guam	3,917	2,055	55	†	†	†	3,744	2,082	62	†	†	†
Marshall Islands	†	1,032	†	†	†	†	1,119	†	†	†	†	†
Northern Marianas	1,216	†	†	†	†	†	1,194	†	†	†	†	†
Palau	†	532	†	†	†	†	†	497	†	†	†	†
Puerto Rico	21,126	2,254	118,184	18,879	358	17,822	56,873	1,938	108,745	17,989	127	13,243
U.S. Virgin Islands	2,170	†	†	†	†	†	1,984	†	†	†	†	†

†Not applicable.
NOTE: Degree-granting institutions grant associate's or higher degrees and participate in Title IV federal financial aid programs. Some data have been revised from previously published figures.

SOURCE: U.S. Department of Education, National Center for Education Statistics, Integrated Postsecondary Education Data System (IPEDS), Spring 2018 and Spring 2019, Fall Enrollment component. (This table was prepared January 2020.)

Table 304.70. Total fall enrollment in degree-granting postsecondary institutions, by level of enrollment and state or jurisdiction: Selected years, 2000 through 2018

State or jurisdiction	Undergraduate						Postbaccalaureate					
	2000	2010	2015	2016	2017	2018	2000	2010	2015	2016	2017	2018
1	2	3	4	5	6	7	8	9	10	11	12	13
United States	**13,155,393**	**18,082,427**	**17,046,673**	**16,874,649**	**16,773,036**	**16,610,235**	**2,156,896**	**2,937,011**	**2,941,531**	**2,972,255**	**3,005,115**	**3,035,683**
Alabama	201,389	282,128	257,649	258,008	259,558	255,394	32,573	45,478	45,310	46,044	47,259	48,788
Alaska	26,222	31,925	28,818	25,987	24,607	23,501	1,731	2,874	2,555	2,449	2,298	2,191
Arizona	299,529	672,083	541,853	510,367	492,906	483,016	42,961	121,788	108,569	97,719	98,216	98,966
Arkansas	104,580	156,970	148,630	145,875	142,923	139,236	10,592	18,878	19,772	21,360	21,040	20,502
California	2,012,213	2,444,496	2,415,506	2,416,526	2,425,729	2,410,234	244,495	270,203	271,904	283,919	298,717	302,186
Colorado	220,059	312,099	289,534	293,223	299,805	299,642	43,813	57,351	58,625	59,032	60,431	60,895
Connecticut	127,715	163,291	162,925	160,651	160,568	160,539	33,528	36,093	36,741	37,359	36,966	36,941
Delaware	37,930	45,848	47,981	49,047	49,068	49,479	5,967	9,410	12,411	12,092	11,270	11,221
District of Columbia	40,703	50,330	50,556	48,948	50,565	52,097	31,986	41,662	43,416	44,092	45,434	45,679
Florida	623,071	993,545	956,598	947,837	946,179	943,811	84,613	131,233	126,972	127,690	127,159	124,252
Georgia	296,980	499,187	456,792	457,293	459,860	463,223	49,224	69,729	73,919	75,780	78,264	80,220
Hawaii	51,783	68,244	61,367	58,328	56,968	55,359	8,399	9,829	7,965	7,515	7,157	6,496
Idaho	58,644	76,998	113,245	115,259	123,597	115,045	6,950	8,203	7,864	8,537	8,206	8,442
Illinois	623,018	748,921	650,597	626,068	604,972	586,599	120,900	157,924	151,614	151,652	152,029	151,849
Indiana	273,198	404,033	369,200	360,576	339,666	328,359	41,136	55,460	57,164	58,708	59,136	59,989
Iowa	165,360	339,036	237,013	229,452	224,190	218,069	23,614	42,831	38,093	37,061	36,611	35,989
Kansas	156,385	188,326	191,680	187,934	186,155	184,614	23,583	26,523	28,314	27,898	27,842	28,123
Kentucky	164,183	256,447	219,870	216,868	215,826	212,915	24,158	34,657	35,852	38,194	42,672	50,046
Louisiana	191,517	230,370	214,594	209,521	210,336	208,000	32,283	33,306	30,711	29,757	31,231	33,401
Maine	50,728	63,599	62,252	62,456	61,919	62,061	7,745	8,807	9,467	9,660	9,892	9,712
Maryland	221,952	305,358	294,032	295,200	291,328	288,623	51,793	72,609	70,193	71,609	72,850	72,819
Massachusetts	320,012	377,241	374,979	367,735	363,084	357,121	101,130	130,512	135,533	137,987	140,455	142,648
Michigan	480,618	605,990	517,079	500,050	476,469	460,778	87,013	91,775	84,383	82,984	81,603	80,318
Minnesota	254,632	346,864	311,536	303,941	297,523	293,289	38,813	118,585	118,930	118,852	115,443	115,494
Mississippi	123,299	159,262	153,551	151,467	151,476	149,453	14,090	20,733	20,632	21,121	20,348	19,907
Missouri	266,802	367,032	331,955	324,162	310,398	298,364	54,546	77,718	78,044	76,936	75,085	76,060
Montana	38,481	48,446	46,067	45,714	45,207	43,807	3,759	4,836	4,732	5,204	5,435	5,556
Nebraska	96,759	121,430	110,313	110,332	109,964	109,313	15,358	23,262	25,778	25,766	25,746	25,625
Nevada	79,053	116,743	104,845	104,809	105,916	105,999	8,840	12,617	11,256	11,221	11,658	11,799
New Hampshire	51,990	62,442	96,588	104,321	119,473	130,099	9,728	13,097	26,920	28,838	29,711	30,644
New Jersey	284,785	380,060	360,074	357,479	355,613	351,139	51,160	64,032	63,685	63,907	63,424	63,277
New Mexico	96,377	147,976	124,385	120,692	116,055	110,178	14,362	14,576	13,863	13,915	13,540	13,119
New York	839,423	1,059,332	1,048,058	1,033,325	1,017,621	1,004,822	203,972	245,819	237,348	240,309	242,936	245,465
North Carolina	358,912	516,254	490,350	488,859	490,174	488,740	45,740	69,538	72,092	72,556	73,937	74,970
North Dakota	36,899	50,003	46,568	46,669	46,064	45,573	3,349	6,900	7,266	7,534	7,685	7,713
Ohio	469,999	650,546	574,217	567,491	560,808	556,548	79,554	94,569	90,406	90,552	88,778	88,414
Oklahoma	157,021	204,217	185,545	182,743	177,238	171,164	20,995	26,343	25,572	25,590	24,912	24,779
Oregon	160,805	221,825	206,895	204,626	198,266	196,274	22,260	29,883	33,754	32,225	31,722	31,866
Pennsylvania	506,948	664,384	598,510	584,400	573,388	555,690	102,573	140,256	137,653	141,282	143,637	144,639
Rhode Island	65,067	73,974	71,972	72,496	71,400	69,394	10,383	11,136	10,320	10,852	11,365	11,474
South Carolina	161,699	231,375	223,671	220,218	219,943	213,787	24,232	25,689	25,984	26,345	26,473	26,746
South Dakota	37,497	50,605	46,901	46,726	46,809	46,241	5,724	7,755	6,763	6,957	6,811	7,124
Tennessee	230,376	302,248	277,409	274,666	275,340	273,722	33,534	49,514	46,460	47,086	47,817	48,393
Texas	905,649	1,360,528	1,390,972	1,412,148	1,437,389	1,450,560	128,324	175,336	188,642	193,350	193,131	192,982
Utah	149,954	231,721	259,006	272,520	287,130	308,768	13,822	23,932	33,989	38,930	44,866	51,004
Vermont	30,809	38,608	37,298	37,784	37,233	36,469	4,680	6,964	6,567	6,935	6,622	6,445
Virginia	325,395	486,820	474,525	462,335	457,665	451,558	56,498	91,102	95,227	95,109	96,455	100,483
Washington	290,292	351,863	328,355	329,698	331,252	329,799	30,548	36,253	36,489	36,849	36,691	37,257
West Virginia	76,556	128,335	127,619	123,779	121,053	118,682	11,332	24,096	23,278	22,829	21,913	21,421
Wisconsin	271,839	341,698	310,350	302,211	300,692	297,526	35,340	42,483	39,905	39,506	39,609	38,883
Wyoming	26,811	35,466	31,602	30,787	30,408	30,058	3,193	2,832	2,603	2,578	2,606	2,452
U.S. Service Academies	13,475	15,905	14,786	15,042	15,260	15,504	0	20	26	23	21	19
Other jurisdictions	**174,410**	**234,281**	**218,927**	**212,157**	**166,387**	**183,959**	**20,223**	**29,959**	**28,959**	**29,739**	**26,330**	**28,606**
American Samoa	297	2,193	1,285	1,253	1,095	1,037	0	0	0	0	0	0
Federated States of Micronesia	1,576	2,699	2,215	2,090	2,022	1,931	0	0	0	0	0	0
Guam	4,746	5,857	6,095	5,768	5,689	5,562	469	331	300	316	338	326
Marshall Islands	328	869	995	978	1,032	1,119	0	0	0	0	0	0
Northern Marianas	1,078	1,137	1,157	1,038	1,216	1,194	0	0	0	0	0	0
Palau	581	694	627	587	532	497	0	0	0	0	0	0
Puerto Rico	163,690	218,312	204,415	198,331	152,903	170,882	19,600	29,415	28,476	29,165	25,720	28,033
U.S. Virgin Islands	2,114	2,520	2,138	2,112	1,898	1,737	154	213	183	258	272	247

NOTE: Degree-granting institutions grant associate's or higher degrees and participate in Title IV federal financial aid programs. Some data have been revised from previously published figures.

SOURCE: U.S. Department of Education, National Center for Education Statistics, Integrated Postsecondary Education Data System (IPEDS), selected years, Spring 2001 through Spring 2019, Fall Enrollment component. (This table was prepared January 2020.)

Table 304.80. Total fall enrollment in degree-granting postsecondary institutions, by control of institution, level of enrollment, level of institution, and state or jurisdiction: 2018

State or jurisdiction	Public				Private							
	Undergraduate			Post-baccalaureate	Undergraduate					Postbaccalaureate		
	Total	4-year	2-year		Total	Nonprofit 4-year	For-profit 4-year	Nonprofit 2-year	For-profit 2-year	Total	Nonprofit 4-year	For-profit 4-year
1	2	3	4	5	6	7	8	9	10	11	12	13
United States	**13,049,326**	**7,502,622**	**5,546,704**	**1,479,938**	**3,560,909**	**2,776,499**	**585,906**	**45,154**	**153,350**	**1,555,745**	**1,312,591**	**243,154**
Alabama	217,610	137,380	80,230	37,477	37,784	21,155	16,523	†	106	11,311	5,106	6,205
Alaska	22,659	22,659	†	1,990	842	346	†	81	415	201	201	†
Arizona	331,864	153,026	178,838	35,334	151,152	5,496	136,052	†	9,604	63,632	5,427	58,205
Arkansas	124,058	80,394	43,664	18,324	15,178	13,504	292	1,326	56	2,178	2,102	76
California	2,131,013	897,291	1,233,722	119,206	279,221	167,358	87,204	1,260	23,399	182,980	142,955	40,025
Colorado	240,200	199,657	40,543	39,295	59,442	20,933	29,992	130	8,387	21,600	12,817	8,783
Connecticut	101,145	53,236	47,909	13,384	59,394	50,262	9,132	†	†	23,557	22,761	796
Delaware	38,059	38,059	†	4,542	11,420	11,010	292	118	†	6,679	6,620	59
District of Columbia	3,867	3,867	†	633	48,230	40,395	7,487	†	348	45,046	40,996	4,050
Florida	730,278	707,095	23,183	70,173	213,533	130,141	46,487	20,444	16,461	54,079	49,744	4,335
Georgia	383,200	265,868	117,332	52,544	80,023	57,441	15,311	1,931	5,340	27,676	21,729	5,947
Hawaii	45,731	22,004	23,727	5,332	9,628	8,624	313	†	691	1,164	1,071	93
Idaho	69,427	45,686	23,741	7,706	45,618	45,190	†	†	428	736	736	†
Illinois	416,652	133,237	283,415	48,577	169,947	127,625	38,998	411	2,913	103,272	85,416	17,856
Indiana	254,093	182,087	72,006	42,136	74,266	70,602	597	415	2,652	17,853	17,782	71
Iowa	176,979	87,557	89,422	22,252	41,090	38,244	2,770	†	76	13,737	13,223	514
Kansas	157,337	78,674	78,663	22,263	27,277	18,804	7,663	†	810	5,860	4,508	1,352
Kentucky	176,907	99,233	77,674	22,841	36,008	29,190	5,835	†	983	27,205	26,314	891
Louisiana	184,973	119,985	64,988	25,723	23,027	19,148	75	492	3,312	7,678	7,678	†
Maine	44,050	27,438	16,612	4,282	18,011	17,743	†	61	207	5,430	5,430	†
Maryland	259,256	143,509	115,747	42,703	29,367	25,512	2,565	†	1,290	30,116	29,500	616
Massachusetts	180,511	97,191	83,320	27,256	176,610	173,512	1,753	1,212	133	115,392	115,208	184
Michigan	402,635	258,761	143,874	64,171	58,143	56,503	392	†	1,248	16,147	16,128	19
Minnesota	220,809	104,391	116,418	24,355	72,480	49,757	22,392	106	225	91,139	21,327	69,812
Mississippi	136,456	64,431	72,025	14,127	12,997	11,862	442	†	693	5,780	5,714	66
Missouri	206,021	120,353	85,668	26,019	92,343	88,415	2,664	183	1,081	50,041	49,820	221
Montana	39,639	31,691	7,948	5,286	4,168	3,820	†	305	43	270	270	†
Nebraska	86,113	45,884	40,229	14,481	23,200	23,032	107	15	46	11,144	11,144	†
Nevada	99,950	99,950	†	8,708	6,049	1,118	1,763	97	3,071	3,091	3,018	73
New Hampshire	34,762	22,977	11,785	3,973	95,337	95,225	†	112	†	26,671	26,671	†
New Jersey	290,369	150,871	139,498	38,668	60,770	50,006	6,530	159	4,075	24,609	24,248	361
New Mexico	107,982	43,597	64,385	12,311	2,196	736	473	†	987	808	762	46
New York	620,840	334,678	286,162	69,257	383,982	346,439	24,678	2,705	10,160	176,208	173,206	3,002
North Carolina	409,025	190,357	218,668	47,103	79,715	69,937	7,059	594	2,125	27,867	26,591	1,276
North Dakota	40,348	33,021	7,327	6,183	5,225	4,612	613	†	†	1,530	1,528	2
Ohio	435,996	274,388	161,608	59,616	120,552	105,503	4,742	1,164	9,143	28,798	28,636	162
Oklahoma	150,793	96,081	54,712	20,186	20,371	17,378	1,088	578	1,327	4,593	4,593	†
Oregon	173,373	84,805	88,568	18,570	22,901	20,723	1,366	45	767	13,296	13,041	255
Pennsylvania	342,616	221,101	121,515	50,155	213,074	195,317	3,627	4,692	9,438	94,484	94,028	456
Rhode Island	36,001	21,462	14,539	4,081	33,393	33,393	†	†	†	7,393	7,393	†
South Carolina	175,543	94,704	80,839	20,982	38,244	31,696	2,929	869	2,750	5,764	4,385	1,379
South Dakota	38,327	31,490	6,837	5,544	7,914	6,069	1,845	†	†	1,580	1,336	244
Tennessee	200,939	112,838	88,101	24,342	72,783	60,524	6,200	709	5,350	24,051	22,741	1,310
Texas	1,317,560	634,490	683,070	151,027	133,000	99,810	15,879	1,610	15,701	41,955	40,333	1,622
Utah	170,354	141,198	29,156	13,595	138,414	133,169	2,769	1,996	480	37,409	36,479	930
Vermont	22,521	17,143	5,378	2,676	13,948	13,875	73	†	†	3,769	3,769	†
Virginia	338,130	174,068	164,062	46,749	113,428	86,041	23,787	393	3,207	53,734	50,681	3,053
Washington	293,919	261,380	32,539	25,458	35,880	29,694	3,943	941	1,302	11,799	11,632	167
West Virginia	70,170	53,686	16,484	11,435	48,512	6,983	39,214	†	2,315	9,986	1,385	8,601
Wisconsin	252,742	162,191	90,551	24,436	44,784	42,627	1,990	†	167	14,447	14,408	39
Wyoming	30,020	9,998	20,022	2,452	38	†	†	†	38	†	†	†
U.S. Service Academies	15,504	15,504	†	19	†	†	†	†	†	†	†	†
Other jurisdictions	**65,719**	**59,271**	**6,448**	**6,680**	**118,240**	**89,148**	**15,722**	**127**	**13,243**	**21,926**	**19,659**	**2,267**
American Samoa	1,037	1,037	†	†	†	†	†	†	†	†	†	†
Federated States of Micronesia	1,931	†	1,931	†	†	†	†	†	†	†	†	†
Guam	5,503	3,421	2,082	323	59	59	†	†	†	3	3	†
Marshall Islands	1,119	1,119	†	†	†	†	†	†	†	†	†	†
Northern Marianas	1,194	1,194	†	†	†	†	†	†	†	†	†	†
Palau	497	†	497	†	†	†	†	†	†	†	†	†
Puerto Rico	52,701	50,763	1,938	6,110	118,181	89,089	15,722	127	13,243	21,923	19,656	2,267

State or jurisdiction	Public				Private							
	Undergraduate			Post-baccalaureate	Undergraduate					Postbaccalaureate		
	Total	4-year	2-year		Total	Nonprofit 4-year	For-profit 4-year	Nonprofit 2-year	For-profit 2-year	Total	Nonprofit 4-year	For-profit 4-year
1	2	3	4	5	6	7	8	9	10	11	12	13
U.S. Virgin Islands	1,737	1,737	†	247	†	†	†	†	†	†	†	†

†Not applicable.

NOTE: Degree-granting institutions grant associate's or higher degrees and participate in Title IV federal financial aid programs.

SOURCE: U.S. Department of Education, National Center for Education Statistics, Integrated Postsecondary Education Data System (IPEDS), Spring 2019, Fall Enrollment component. (This table was prepared January 2020.)

Table 305.10. Total fall enrollment of first-time degree/certificate-seeking students in degree-granting postsecondary institutions, by attendance status, sex of student, and level and control of institution: 1960 through 2029

Year	Total	Full-time	Part-time	Males			Females			4-year		2-year	
				Total	Full-time	Part-time	Total	Full-time	Part-time	Public	Private	Public	Private
1	2	3	4	5	6	7	8	9	10	11	12	13	14
1960[1]	923,069	—	—	539,512	—	—	383,557	—	—	395,884[2]	313,209[2]	181,860[2]	32,116[2]
1961[1]	1,018,361	—	—	591,913	—	—	426,448	—	—	438,135[2]	336,449[2]	210,101[2]	33,676[2]
1962[1]	1,030,554	—	—	598,099	—	—	432,455	—	—	445,191[2]	324,923[2]	224,537[2]	35,903[2]
1963[1]	1,046,424	—	—	604,282	—	—	442,142	—	—	—	—	—	—
1964[1]	1,224,840	—	—	701,524	—	—	523,316	—	—	539,251[2]	363,348[2]	275,413[2]	46,828[2]
1965[1]	1,441,822	—	—	829,215	—	—	612,607	—	—	642,233[2]	398,792[2]	347,788[2]	53,009[2]
1966	1,554,337	—	—	889,516	—	—	664,821	—	—	626,472[2]	382,889[2]	478,459[2]	66,517[2]
1967	1,640,936	1,335,512	305,424	931,127	761,299	169,828	709,809	574,213	135,596	644,525	368,300	561,488	66,623
1968	1,892,849	1,470,653	422,196	1,082,367	847,005	235,362	810,482	623,648	186,834	724,377	378,052	718,562	71,858
1969	1,967,104	1,525,290	441,814	1,118,269	876,280	241,989	848,835	649,010	199,825	699,167	391,508	814,132	62,297
1970	2,063,397	1,587,072	476,325	1,151,960	896,281	255,679	911,437	690,791	220,646	717,449	395,886	890,703	59,359
1971	2,119,018	1,606,036	512,982	1,170,518	895,715	274,803	948,500	710,321	238,179	704,052	384,695	971,295	58,976
1972	2,152,778	1,574,197	578,581	1,157,501	858,254	299,247	995,277	715,943	279,334	680,337	380,982	1,036,616	54,843
1973	2,226,041	1,607,269	618,772	1,182,173	867,314	314,859	1,043,868	739,955	303,913	698,777	378,994	1,089,182	59,088
1974	2,365,761	1,673,333	692,428	1,243,790	896,077	347,713	1,121,971	777,256	344,715	745,637	386,391	1,175,759	57,974
1975	2,515,155	1,763,296	751,859	1,327,935	942,198	385,737	1,187,220	821,098	366,122	771,725	395,440	1,283,523	64,467
1976	2,347,014	1,662,333	684,681	1,170,326	854,597	315,729	1,176,688	807,736	368,952	717,373	413,961	1,152,944	62,736
1977	2,394,426	1,680,916	713,510	1,155,856	839,848	316,008	1,238,570	841,068	397,502	737,497	404,631	1,185,648	66,650
1978	2,389,627	1,650,848	738,779	1,141,777	817,294	324,483	1,247,850	833,554	414,296	736,703	406,669	1,173,544	72,711
1979	2,502,896	1,706,732	796,164	1,179,846	840,315	339,531	1,323,050	866,417	456,633	760,119	415,126	1,253,854	73,797
1980	2,587,644	1,749,928	837,716	1,218,961	862,458	356,503	1,368,683	887,470	481,213	765,395	417,937	1,313,591	90,721[3]
1981	2,595,421	1,737,714	857,707	1,217,680	851,833	365,847	1,377,741	885,881	491,860	754,007	419,257	1,318,436	103,721[3]
1982	2,505,466	1,688,620	816,846	1,199,237	837,223	362,014	1,306,229	851,397	454,832	730,775	404,252	1,254,193	116,246[3]
1983	2,443,703	1,678,071	765,632	1,159,049	824,609	334,440	1,284,654	853,462	431,192	728,244	403,882	1,189,869	121,708
1984	2,356,898	1,613,185	743,713	1,112,303	786,099	326,204	1,244,595	827,086	417,509	713,790	402,959	1,130,311	109,838
1985	2,292,222	1,602,038	690,184	1,075,736	774,858	300,878	1,216,486	827,180	389,306	717,199	398,556	1,060,275	116,192
1986	2,219,208	1,589,451	629,757	1,046,527	768,856	277,671	1,172,681	820,595	352,086	719,974	391,673	990,973	116,588
1987	2,246,359	1,626,719	619,640	1,046,615	779,226	267,389	1,199,744	847,493	352,251	757,833	405,113	979,820	103,593
1988	2,378,803	1,698,927	679,876	1,100,026	807,319	292,707	1,278,777	891,608	387,169	783,358	425,907	1,048,914	120,624
1989	2,341,035	1,656,594	684,441	1,094,750	791,295	303,455	1,246,285	865,299	380,986	762,217	413,836	1,048,529	116,453
1990	2,256,624	1,617,118	639,506	1,045,191	771,372	273,819	1,211,433	845,746	365,687	727,264	400,120	1,041,097	88,143
1991	2,277,920	1,652,983	624,937	1,068,433	798,043	270,390	1,209,487	854,940	354,547	717,697	392,904	1,070,048	97,271
1992	2,184,113	1,603,737	580,376	1,013,058	760,290	252,768	1,171,055	843,447	327,608	697,393	408,306	993,074	85,340
1993	2,160,710	1,608,274	552,436	1,007,647	762,240	245,407	1,153,063	846,034	307,029	702,273	410,688	973,545	74,204
1994	2,133,205	1,603,106	530,099	984,558	751,081	233,477	1,148,647	852,025	296,622	709,042	405,917	952,468	65,778
1995	2,168,831	1,646,812	522,019	1,001,052	767,185	233,867	1,167,779	879,627	288,152	731,836	419,025	954,595	63,375
1996	2,274,319	1,739,852	534,467	1,046,662	805,982	240,680	1,227,657	933,870	293,787	741,164	427,442	989,536	116,177
1997	2,219,255	1,733,512	485,743	1,026,058	806,054	220,004	1,193,197	927,458	265,739	755,362	442,397	923,954	97,542
1998	2,212,593	1,775,412	437,181	1,022,656	825,577	197,079	1,189,937	949,835	240,102	792,772	460,948	858,417	100,456
1999	2,357,590	1,849,741	507,849	1,094,539	865,545	228,994	1,263,051	984,196	278,855	819,503	474,223	955,499	108,365
2000	2,427,551	1,918,093	509,458	1,123,948	894,432	229,516	1,303,603	1,023,661	279,942	842,228	498,532	952,175	134,616
2001	2,497,078	1,989,179	507,899	1,152,837	926,393	226,444	1,344,241	1,062,786	281,455	866,619	508,030	988,726	133,703
2002	2,570,611	2,053,065	517,546	1,170,609	945,938	224,671	1,400,002	1,107,127	292,875	886,297	517,621	1,037,267	129,426
2003	2,591,754	2,102,394	489,360	1,175,856	965,075	210,781	1,415,898	1,137,319	278,579	918,602	537,726	1,004,428	130,998
2004	2,630,243	2,147,546	482,697	1,190,268	981,591	208,677	1,439,975	1,165,955	274,020	925,249	562,485	1,009,082	133,427
2005	2,657,338	2,189,884	467,454	1,200,055	995,610	204,445	1,457,283	1,194,274	263,009	953,903	606,712	977,224	119,499
2006	2,707,205	2,220,184	487,021	1,228,703	1,015,786	212,917	1,478,502	1,204,398	274,104	990,077	598,266	1,013,419	105,443
2007	2,777,168	2,295,518	481,650	1,268,137	1,053,375	214,762	1,509,031	1,242,143	266,888	1,023,789	633,772	1,016,636	102,971
2008	3,022,736	2,425,987	596,749	1,388,441	1,114,724	273,717	1,634,295	1,311,263	323,032	1,053,829	672,372	1,186,640	109,895
2009	3,156,882	2,534,440	622,442	1,464,424	1,177,119	287,305	1,692,458	1,357,321	335,137	1,090,980	658,808	1,275,974	131,120
2010	3,156,727	2,533,636	623,091	1,461,016	1,171,090	289,926	1,695,711	1,362,546	333,165	1,110,601	674,573	1,238,491	133,062
2011	3,091,496	2,479,155	612,341	1,424,140	1,140,843	283,297	1,667,356	1,338,312	329,044	1,131,091	656,864	1,195,083	108,458
2012	2,994,187	2,408,063	586,124	1,387,316	1,115,266	272,050	1,606,871	1,292,797	314,074	1,128,344	642,716	1,137,927	85,200
2013	2,985,366	2,415,969	569,397	1,383,852	1,117,525	266,327	1,601,514	1,298,444	303,070	1,144,102	633,184	1,126,978	81,102
2014	2,925,998	2,383,328	542,670	1,355,164	1,100,005	255,159	1,570,834	1,283,323	287,511	1,170,639	612,162	1,070,625	72,572
2015	2,882,949	2,368,283	514,666	1,338,853	1,096,976	241,877	1,544,096	1,271,307	272,789	1,190,206	599,242	1,031,117	62,384
2016	2,882,991	2,369,021	513,970	1,333,598	1,093,968	239,630	1,549,393	1,275,053	274,340	1,259,214	581,098	981,029	61,650
2017	2,883,001	2,377,999	505,002	1,326,237	1,091,909	234,328	1,556,764	1,286,090	270,674	1,285,500	588,395	954,930	54,176
2018	2,885,818	2,392,319	493,499	1,317,522	1,093,233	224,289	1,568,296	1,299,086	269,210	1,309,453	595,543	934,085	46,737
2019[4]	2,895,000	—	—	1,320,000	—	—	1,575,000	—	—	—	—	—	—
2020[4]	2,898,000	—	—	1,321,000	—	—	1,577,000	—	—	—	—	—	—
2021[4]	2,903,000	—	—	1,323,000	—	—	1,581,000	—	—	—	—	—	—
2022[4]	2,908,000	—	—	1,325,000	—	—	1,584,000	—	—	—	—	—	—
2023[4]	2,915,000	—	—	1,327,000	—	—	1,588,000	—	—	—	—	—	—
2024[4]	2,925,000	—	—	1,332,000	—	—	1,593,000	—	—	—	—	—	—
2025[4]	2,935,000	—	—	1,336,000	—	—	1,598,000	—	—	—	—	—	—
2026[4]	2,946,000	—	—	1,342,000	—	—	1,604,000	—	—	—	—	—	—
2027[4]	2,950,000	—	—	1,344,000	—	—	1,606,000	—	—	—	—	—	—
2028[4]	2,952,000	—	—	1,345,000	—	—	1,607,000	—	—	—	—	—	—
2029[4]	2,952,000	—	—	1,345,000	—	—	1,607,000	—	—	—	—	—	—

—Not available.

[1]Excludes first-time degree/certificate-seeking students in occupational programs not creditable towards a bachelor's degree.

[2]Data for 2-year branches of 4-year college systems are aggregated with the 4-year institutions.

[3]Large increases are due to the addition of schools accredited by the Accrediting Commission of Career Schools and Colleges of Technology.

[4]Projected.

NOTE: Data through 1995 are for institutions of higher education, while later data are for degree-granting institutions. Degree-granting institutions grant associate's or higher degrees and participate in Title IV federal financial aid programs. The degree-granting classification is very similar to the earlier higher education classification, but it includes more 2-year colleges and excludes a few higher education institutions that did not grant degrees. Alaska and Hawaii are included in all years. Some data have been revised from previously published figures.

SOURCE: U.S. Department of Education, National Center for Education Statistics, *Biennial Survey of Education in the United States*; *Opening Fall Enrollment in Higher Education*, 1963 through 1965; Higher Education General Information Survey (HEGIS), "Fall Enrollment in Colleges and Universities" surveys, 1966 through 1985; Integrated Postsecondary Education Data System (IPEDS), "Fall Enrollment Survey" (IPEDS-EF:86–99); IPEDS Spring 2001 through Spring 2019, Fall Enrollment component; and First-Time Freshmen Projection Model, 1980 through 2029. (This table was prepared December 2019.)

Table 305.20. Total fall enrollment of first-time degree/certificate-seeking students in degree-granting postsecondary institutions, by attendance status, sex of student, control of institution, and state or jurisdiction: Selected years, 2000 through 2018

State or jurisdiction	Total, fall 2000	Total, fall 2010	Total, fall 2015	Total, fall 2016	Total, fall 2017	Fall 2018								
							Full-time			Part-time				
						Total	Total	Males	Females	Total	Males	Females	Public	Private
1	2	3	4	5	6	7	8	9	10	11	12	13	14	15
United States	**2,427,551**	**3,156,727**	**2,882,949**	**2,882,991**	**2,883,001**	**2,885,818**	**2,392,319**	**1,093,233**	**1,299,086**	**493,499**	**224,289**	**269,210**	**2,243,538**	**642,280**
Alabama	43,411	52,990	50,151	50,108	50,263	48,346	43,016	18,863	24,153	5,330	2,441	2,889	43,501	4,845
Alaska	2,432	5,400	3,849	3,049	3,234	2,931	2,227	969	1,258	704	279	425	2,623	308
Arizona	46,646	76,832	67,751	65,784	62,440	61,748	44,007	20,329	23,678	17,741	7,594	10,147	51,814	9,934
Arkansas	22,695	29,321	27,388	27,276	26,779	26,567	24,053	10,782	13,271	2,514	1,104	1,410	22,902	3,665
California	246,128	402,832	383,920	394,845	390,289	387,767	277,907	127,275	150,632	109,860	57,322	52,538	344,117	43,650
Colorado	43,201	54,594	43,349	43,832	45,436	45,827	37,808	17,957	19,851	8,019	3,468	4,551	38,288	7,539
Connecticut	24,212	32,719	31,398	31,741	31,804	31,656	27,105	12,308	14,797	4,551	1,953	2,598	19,037	12,619
Delaware	7,636	8,947	9,352	9,727	10,051	9,879	8,469	3,572	4,897	1,410	535	875	8,731	1,148
District of Columbia	9,150	10,747	11,075	9,012	10,617	10,506	9,453	3,501	5,952	1,053	362	691	617	9,889
Florida	109,931	176,040	157,687	158,956	160,114	161,033	123,638	52,844	70,794	37,395	15,818	21,577	119,415	41,618
Georgia	67,616	100,140	86,071	84,932	85,737	87,518	72,456	31,274	41,182	15,062	6,526	8,536	71,495	16,023
Hawaii	8,931	10,740	8,851	8,398	8,691	8,645	7,104	2,720	4,384	1,541	653	888	6,952	1,693
Idaho	10,669	12,668	14,179	14,520	15,450	14,874	12,754	5,481	7,273	2,120	934	1,186	9,781	5,093
Illinois	107,592	114,467	95,852	93,994	92,736	92,486	78,563	37,344	41,219	13,923	6,343	7,580	63,451	29,035
Indiana	59,320	82,406	66,876	64,028	62,696	64,865	57,172	26,689	30,483	7,693	3,603	4,090	48,430	16,435
Iowa	39,564	47,257	37,851	38,130	38,056	35,591	31,645	16,084	15,561	3,946	1,551	2,395	27,103	8,488
Kansas	31,424	33,544	32,268	32,597	32,379	30,960	26,786	13,364	13,422	4,174	1,889	2,285	26,804	4,156
Kentucky	34,140	43,735	37,623	36,378	37,257	38,634	33,950	14,585	19,365	4,684	2,067	2,617	31,356	7,278
Louisiana	45,383	43,144	40,740	40,261	39,782	40,876	36,527	15,419	21,108	4,349	1,804	2,545	35,184	5,692
Maine	9,231	12,203	11,357	11,727	11,597	11,665	10,586	5,044	5,542	1,079	431	648	7,742	3,923
Maryland	35,552	51,104	44,767	47,084	44,436	44,708	35,180	16,491	18,689	9,528	4,104	5,424	37,992	6,716
Massachusetts	66,044	76,857	73,189	72,432	73,366	71,899	64,620	29,717	34,903	7,279	3,058	4,221	33,584	38,315
Michigan	84,998	101,063	89,224	86,314	83,041	81,937	66,626	31,214	35,412	15,311	7,110	8,201	72,113	9,824
Minnesota	63,893	55,723	45,323	45,102	44,752	44,218	38,424	18,361	20,063	5,794	2,553	3,241	33,153	11,065
Mississippi	30,356	37,034	31,185	32,088	31,145	31,041	29,399	12,860	16,539	1,642	744	898	29,084	1,957
Missouri	48,639	64,381	54,660	53,824	52,028	50,900	45,079	20,360	24,719	5,821	2,662	3,159	37,792	13,108
Montana	7,771	9,959	8,749	8,959	8,770	8,511	7,333	3,764	3,569	1,178	535	643	7,657	854
Nebraska	19,027	19,284	18,092	18,423	17,883	18,258	16,612	8,016	8,596	1,646	751	895	14,797	3,461
Nevada	10,490	18,572	15,917	16,112	17,169	18,143	13,744	5,917	7,827	4,399	2,124	2,275	17,118	1,025
New Hampshire	13,143	13,613	17,097	15,728	18,388	20,398	12,826	5,796	7,030	7,572	2,581	4,991	7,802	12,596
New Jersey	52,233	71,296	65,232	65,178	65,109	65,246	57,771	28,056	29,715	7,475	3,385	4,090	53,495	11,751
New Mexico	15,261	22,353	18,045	19,085	18,282	16,654	13,345	5,959	7,386	3,309	1,352	1,957	16,275	379
New York	168,181	197,849	187,059	185,714	187,805	188,267	179,943	84,480	95,463	8,324	3,807	4,517	112,664	75,603
North Carolina	69,343	92,627	88,995	88,547	88,204	88,920	72,867	32,378	40,489	16,053	6,825	9,228	69,228	19,692
North Dakota	8,929	9,073	8,606	8,709	8,874	8,368	8,065	4,281	3,784	303	142	161	7,294	1,074
Ohio	98,823	123,063	100,029	101,393	99,542	107,591	89,106	42,131	46,975	18,485	7,233	11,252	81,991	25,600
Oklahoma	35,094	39,107	36,371	36,266	35,306	33,781	27,445	12,534	14,911	6,336	2,550	3,786	29,494	4,287
Oregon	26,946	35,442	30,765	31,324	32,002	32,046	25,631	11,540	14,091	6,415	3,043	3,372	27,330	4,716
Pennsylvania	125,578	144,184	126,933	125,063	122,264	118,558	106,220	49,337	56,883	12,338	5,088	7,250	69,744	48,814
Rhode Island	13,789	15,698	15,004	14,942	14,602	14,959	14,048	6,582	7,466	911	410	501	7,312	7,647
South Carolina	32,353	47,535	46,080	45,173	46,455	46,053	40,907	18,085	22,822	5,146	2,114	3,032	37,044	9,009
South Dakota	8,597	10,074	8,473	8,316	8,673	8,646	7,993	4,120	3,873	653	247	406	7,200	1,446
Tennessee	43,327	59,279	56,498	56,605	58,398	57,576	53,566	23,075	30,491	4,010	1,479	2,531	42,336	15,240
Texas	181,813	228,503	234,131	235,197	242,984	244,190	181,812	82,378	99,434	62,378	28,385	33,993	214,139	30,051
Utah	24,953	35,126	31,884	32,141	34,851	40,979	35,656	14,149	21,507	5,323	2,566	2,757	26,457	14,522
Vermont	6,810	8,242	7,202	7,474	7,393	7,249	6,626	3,215	3,411	623	209	414	4,343	2,906
Virginia	52,661	83,166	80,362	79,020	79,374	79,615	67,268	30,815	36,453	12,347	5,537	6,810	63,076	16,539
Washington	36,287	41,124	46,370	47,853	48,447	48,363	42,488	19,083	23,405	5,875	2,506	3,369	40,371	7,992
West Virginia	15,659	23,020	18,866	18,874	18,077	17,106	15,050	6,875	8,175	2,056	1,179	877	13,428	3,678
Wisconsin	53,662	61,249	50,978	51,423	50,654	50,357	42,953	20,180	22,773	7,404	3,139	4,265	41,000	9,357
Wyoming	4,209	6,042	5,210	5,227	5,173	4,828	4,411	2,084	2,327	417	194	223	4,803	25
U.S. Service Academies	3,818	4,359	4,065	4,106	4,146	4,079	4,079	2,996	1,083	0	0	0	4,079	†
Other jurisdictions	**39,609**	**52,222**	**43,746**	**48,706**	**31,606**	**37,759**	**35,795**	**15,956**	**19,839**	**1,964**	**867**	**1,097**	**13,813**	**23,946**
American Samoa	297	657	382	392	381	309	253	92	161	56	20	36	309	0
Federated States of Micronesia	786	653	708	760	647	698	607	289	318	91	39	52	698	0
Guam	770	1,043	1,101	985	1,275	1,093	792	318	474	301	132	169	1,077	16
Marshall Islands	199	240	327	303	279	336	292	144	148	44	23	21	336	0
Northern Marianas	333	360	290	305	336	343	297	121	176	46	25	21	343	0
Palau	147	114	200	148	165	121	111	53	58	10	4	6	121	0
Puerto Rico	36,773	48,672	40,347	45,468	28,215	34,539	33,149	14,841	18,308	1,390	612	778	10,609	23,930
U.S. Virgin Islands	304	483	391	345	308	320	294	98	196	26	12	14	320	0

†Not applicable.

NOTE: Degree-granting institutions grant associate's or higher degrees and participate in Title IV federal financial aid programs. Some data have been revised from previously published figures.

SOURCE: U.S. Department of Education, National Center for Education Statistics, Integrated Postsecondary Education Data System (IPEDS), Spring 2001 through Spring 2019, Fall Enrollment component. (This table was prepared December 2019.)

Table 305.30. Number and percentage of degree-granting postsecondary institutions with first-year undergraduates using various selection criteria for admission, by control and level of institution: Selected years, 2000-01 through 2019-20

Selection criteria	All institutions			Public institutions			Private institutions								
										Nonprofit			For-profit		
	Total	4-year	2-year	Total	4-year	2-year	Total	4-year	2-year	Total	4-year	2-year	Total	4-year	2-year
1	2	3	4	5	6	7	8	9	10	11	12	13	14	15	16
	Number of institutions with first-year undergraduates														
2000-01	3,717	2,034	1,683	1,647	580	1,067	2,070	1,454	616	1,383	1,247	136	687	207	480
2010-11	4,209	2,487	1,722	1,614	637	977	2,595	1,850	745	1,321	1,238	83	1,274	612	662
2015-16	4,147	2,584	1,563	1,578	669	909	2,569	1,915	654	1,400	1,298	102	1,169	617	552
2019-20	3,596	2,300	1,296	1,585	732	853	2,011	1,568	443	1,375	1,286	89	636	282	354
	Percent of institutions														
Open admissions															
2000-01	40.2	12.9	73.2	63.8	12.1	91.9	21.4	13.3	40.7	14.0	11.7	34.6	36.5	22.7	42.5
2010-11	47.2	22.5	82.9	65.6	17.6	96.9	35.8	24.2	64.6	15.4	13.0	51.8	56.9	46.9	66.2
2015-16	51.0	27.5	89.8	64.3	19.0	97.7	42.8	30.4	78.9	18.4	15.1	60.8	71.9	62.7	82.2
2019-20	48.7	24.3	92.1	65.0	25.8	98.6	35.9	23.5	79.7	17.3	14.2	61.8	76.1	66.0	84.2
Some admission requirements[1]															
2000-01	58.4	85.8	25.1	35.4	87.4	7.1	76.6	85.2	56.3	84.5	86.8	63.2	60.7	75.4	54.4
2010-11	52.1	76.6	16.8	34.4	82.4	3.1	63.2	74.6	34.8	84.4	86.8	48.2	41.1	49.8	33.1
2015-16	48.3	71.9	9.3	35.4	81.0	1.9	56.3	68.8	19.7	80.5	84.1	35.3	27.3	36.6	16.8
2019-20	50.5	74.6	7.9	33.8	71.4	1.4	63.7	76.0	20.3	82.6	85.7	38.2	23.0	31.9	15.8
Secondary grades															
2000-01	34.6	58.7	5.5	23.9	63.4	2.4	43.0	56.7	10.7	60.1	64.1	23.5	8.7	12.6	7.1
2010-11	33.3	54.2	3.2	27.8	67.8	1.7	36.7	49.5	5.1	66.0	68.7	26.5	6.4	10.6	2.4
2015-16	35.4	55.3	2.4	30.4	69.8	1.3	38.5	50.2	4.0	64.9	68.8	14.7	6.8	11.2	2.0
2019-20	39.9	61.0	2.5	29.9	63.5	1.1	47.8	59.9	5.2	64.9	68.2	18.0	10.8	22.0	2.0
Secondary class rank															
2000-01	13.7	24.3	1.0	10.9	30.3	0.3	16.0	21.9	2.3	23.2	25.1	5.9	1.6	2.4	1.3
2010-11	8.4	13.9	0.4	9.2	22.9	0.3	7.8	10.8	0.5	15.0	15.8	3.6	0.4	0.7	0.2
2015-16	6.0	9.5	0.3	7.8	18.2	0.1	4.9	6.4	0.6	8.8	9.3	2.0	0.3	0.3	0.4
2019-20	4.7	7.2	0.3	6.1	13.1	0.0	3.7	4.5	0.9	5.2	5.4	3.4	0.3	0.4	0.3
Secondary school record															
2000-01	45.8	70.3	16.2	29.4	72.9	5.8	58.7	69.2	34.1	73.2	75.5	52.2	29.5	30.9	29.0
2010-11	45.9	70.1	10.8	33.0	78.8	3.1	53.9	67.1	20.9	77.1	79.4	42.2	29.8	42.3	18.3
2015-16	44.0	65.9	7.8	34.0	77.9	1.8	50.1	61.7	16.2	71.7	75.4	24.5	24.3	32.9	14.7
2019-20	45.3	67.5	5.9	32.6	69.0	1.4	55.3	66.8	14.7	72.4	75.5	27.0	18.4	27.0	11.6
College preparatory program															
2000-01	15.5	27.3	1.2	16.2	44.0	1.1	14.9	20.7	1.3	22.1	24.1	4.4	0.4	0.5	0.4
2010-11	14.7	24.4	0.6	18.3	45.4	0.7	12.4	17.1	0.5	24.0	25.4	2.4	0.3	0.3	0.3
2015-16	14.7	23.3	0.5	19.3	44.4	0.8	12.0	16.0	0.2	21.9	23.6	1.0	0.0	0.0	0.0
2019-20	17.0	26.1	0.8	18.7	39.8	0.6	15.7	19.8	1.4	23.0	24.1	6.7	0.0	0.0	0.0
Recommendations															
2000-01	20.4	34.4	3.5	2.7	7.4	0.2	34.4	45.1	9.3	46.6	49.2	22.8	10.0	20.8	5.4
2010-11	18.1	29.2	2.1	3.3	8.3	0.1	27.2	36.3	4.7	51.6	53.3	25.3	2.0	2.0	2.1
2015-16	17.9	27.8	1.7	4.5	10.5	0.1	26.2	33.8	3.8	46.1	48.6	13.7	2.4	2.8	2.0
2019-20	18.4	27.4	2.2	4.2	9.2	0.0	29.5	36.0	6.5	41.5	42.8	22.5	3.5	4.6	2.5
Demonstration of competencies[2]															
2000-01	8.0	12.1	3.0	2.2	5.0	0.7	12.7	15.0	7.1	12.1	12.7	7.4	13.7	29.0	7.1
2010-11	5.8	8.0	2.5	1.8	4.6	0.0	8.2	9.2	5.8	8.9	8.8	9.6	7.6	10.1	5.3
2015-16	4.1	5.7	1.3	1.6	3.9	0.0	5.6	6.4	3.2	7.6	7.8	5.9	3.1	3.4	2.7
2019-20	4.2	5.9	1.2	1.4	3.0	0.0	6.4	7.2	3.4	7.2	7.2	7.9	4.6	7.4	2.3
Test scores[3]															
2000-01	47.2	72.5	16.7	33.2	83.4	5.8	58.5	68.2	35.6	70.3	73.4	41.9	34.6	36.7	33.8
2010-11	37.6	55.1	12.2	30.5	74.1	2.0	42.0	48.6	25.5	63.5	66.0	26.5	19.6	13.4	25.4
2015-16	34.3	51.0	6.7	32.4	74.7	1.3	35.5	42.7	14.2	56.5	58.9	25.5	10.3	8.6	12.1
2019-20	32.9	48.4	5.4	29.2	61.9	1.2	35.8	42.1	13.5	46.3	48.3	18.0	13.1	13.8	12.4
TOEFL[4]															
2000-01	43.4	71.2	9.9	30.2	77.4	4.6	54.0	68.7	19.2	66.2	70.1	30.9	29.3	60.4	15.8
2010-11	38.7	61.9	5.1	29.9	71.6	2.7	44.2	58.6	8.3	66.3	69.1	25.3	21.2	37.4	6.2
2015-16	35.7	55.7	2.8	30.1	69.2	1.3	39.2	50.9	4.7	59.6	63.5	10.8	14.6	24.5	3.6
2019-20	35.6	54.7	1.6	27.9	59.0	1.2	41.6	52.7	2.5	58.7	62.0	11.2	4.7	10.3	0.3
No admission requirements, only recommendations for admission															
2000-01	1.4	1.2	1.7	0.8	0.5	0.9	1.9	1.5	2.9	1.5	1.4	2.2	2.8	1.9	3.1
2010-11	0.6	0.9	0.3	0.0	0.0	0.0	1.0	1.2	0.7	0.2	0.2	0.0	2.0	3.3	0.8
2015-16	0.7	0.6	0.8	0.3	0.0	0.4	0.9	0.8	1.4	1.1	0.8	3.9	0.8	0.6	0.9
2019-20	0.8	1.2	0.0	1.3	2.7	0.0	0.3	0.4	0.0	0.1	0.1	0.0	0.9	2.1	0.0

[1] Many institutions have more than one admission requirement.

[2] Formal demonstration of competencies (e.g., portfolios, certificates of mastery, assessment instruments).

[3] Includes SAT, ACT, or other admission tests.

[4] Test of English as a Foreign Language.

NOTE: Data in this table represent the 50 states and the District of Columbia. Degree-granting institutions grant associate's or higher degrees and participate in Title IV federal financial aid programs. Excludes institutions not enrolling any first-time degree/certificate-seeking undergraduates. The three admission categories reported in this table sum to 100%: (1) Open admissions, (2) Some admission requirements, and (3) No admission requirements, only recommendations for admissions. Some data have been revised from previously published figures. Detail may not sum to totals because of rounding.

SOURCE: U.S. Department of Education, National Center for Education Statistics, Integrated Postsecondary Education Data System (IPEDS), Fall 2000 and Fall 2010, Institutional Characteristics component; and Winter 2015-16 and 2019-20, Admissions component. (This table was prepared September 2020.)

Table 305.40. Acceptance rates; number of applications, admissions, and enrollees; and enrollees' SAT and ACT scores for degree-granting postsecondary institutions with first-year undergraduates, by control and level of institution: 2018–19

Acceptance rates, applications, admissions, enrollees, and SAT and ACT scores	All institutions			Public institutions			Private institutions								
										Nonprofit			For-profit		
	Total	4-year	2-year	Total	4-year	2-year	Total	4-year	2-year	Total	4-year	2-year	Total	4-year	2-year
1	2	3	4	5	6	7	8	9	10	11	12	13	14	15	16
Number of institutions reporting application data[1]	3,608	2,296	1,312	1,589	724	865	2,019	1,572	447	1,359	1,280	79	660	292	368
Percentage distribution of institutions by their acceptance of applications	100.0	100.0	100.0	100.0	100.0	100.0	100.0	100.0	100.0	100.0	100.0	100.0	100.0	100.0	100.0
No application criteria	49.3	25.0	92.0	65.3	25.6	98.6	36.8	24.7	79.2	17.4	14.5	64.6	76.5	69.2	82.3
90.0 percent or more accepted	8.0	11.1	2.6	4.5	9.9	0.0	10.7	11.6	7.6	11.8	12.0	7.6	8.6	9.9	7.6
75.0 to 89.9 percent accepted	12.9	19.2	2.0	12.1	26.4	0.1	13.6	15.9	5.6	17.7	18.2	10.1	5.2	5.8	4.6
50.0 to 74.9 percent accepted	20.2	30.3	2.6	13.2	27.6	1.0	25.8	31.6	5.6	35.4	36.8	12.7	6.1	8.6	4.1
25.0 to 49.9 percent accepted	7.0	10.7	0.7	4.2	8.8	0.2	9.3	11.5	1.6	12.6	13.1	3.8	2.6	4.5	1.1
10.0 to 24.9 percent accepted	1.9	2.8	0.2	0.7	1.5	0.0	2.8	3.4	0.4	3.6	3.8	1.3	1.1	2.1	0.3
Less than 10.0 percent accepted	0.6	0.9	0.0	0.1	0.1	0.0	1.0	1.3	0.0	1.5	1.6	0.0	0.0	0.0	0.0
Number of applications (in thousands)	11,273	11,210	63	6,350	6,326	24	4,922	4,884	39	4,834	4,810	24	89	74	15
Percentage distribution of admissions by institutions' acceptance of applications	100.0	100.0	100.0	100.0	100.0	100.0	100.0	100.0	100.0	100.0	100.0	100.0	100.0	100.0	100.0
No application criteria	†	†	†	†	†	†	†	†	†	†	†	†	†	†	†
90.0 percent or more accepted	4.4	4.4	10.6	5.4	5.4	0.0	3.2	3.1	17.3	3.0	3.0	1.2	12.4	6.2	42.4
75.0 to 89.9 percent accepted	20.5	20.6	13.1	24.6	24.7	4.9	15.3	15.3	18.3	15.4	15.4	13.1	10.2	6.8	26.5
50.0 to 74.9 percent accepted	37.4	37.3	46.8	37.8	37.5	91.6	36.9	37.0	18.5	36.3	36.5	14.4	65.0	73.2	24.8
25.0 to 49.9 percent accepted	22.7	22.8	2.7	25.9	26.0	3.5	18.6	18.7	2.2	18.7	18.8	0.8	12.0	13.6	4.4
10.0 to 24.9 percent accepted	10.3	10.2	26.8	6.1	6.1	0.0	15.7	15.5	43.8	16.0	15.8	70.4	0.4	0.1	1.8
Less than 10.0 percent accepted	4.6	4.7	0.0	0.3	0.3	0.0	10.3	10.4	0.0	10.5	10.6	0.0	0.0	0.0	0.0
Number of admissions (in thousands)	6,262	6,225	37	3,806	3,790	16	2,457	2,435	21	2,395	2,385	9	62	50	12
Percentage distribution of admissions by institutions' acceptance of applications	100.0	100.0	100.0	100.0	100.0	100.0	100.0	100.0	100.0	100.0	100.0	100.0	100.0	100.0	100.0
No application criteria	†	†	†	†	†	†	†	†	†	†	†	†	†	†	†
90.0 percent or more accepted	7.5	7.4	17.1	8.4	8.5	0.0	6.0	5.8	29.6	5.7	5.8	3.1	16.9	8.8	49.6
75.0 to 89.9 percent accepted	30.1	30.2	18.2	33.5	33.7	5.9	24.8	24.8	27.2	25.1	25.1	27.9	11.8	8.2	26.6
50.0 to 74.9 percent accepted	42.6	42.6	51.7	39.4	39.2	92.1	47.7	47.9	22.0	47.3	47.4	23.1	64.0	74.5	21.2
25.0 to 49.9 percent accepted	15.9	16.0	1.8	16.8	16.9	2.0	14.6	14.7	1.6	14.8	14.9	0.8	7.1	8.4	2.1
10.0 to 24.9 percent accepted	3.2	3.2	11.3	1.8	1.8	0.0	5.4	5.3	19.7	5.6	5.4	45.1	0.1	#	0.5
Less than 10.0 percent accepted	0.6	0.6	0.0	#	#	0.0	1.5	1.5	0.0	1.5	1.5	0.0	0.0	0.0	0.0
Number of enrollees (in thousands)	1,625	1,610	15	1,090	1,084	7	535	526	9	514	512	3	21	15	6
Percentage distribution of admissions by institutions' acceptance of applications	100.0	100.0	100.0	100.0	100.0	100.0	100.0	100.0	100.0	100.0	100.0	100.0	100.0	100.0	100.0
No application criteria	†	†	†	†	†	†	†	†	†	†	†	†	†	†	†
90.0 percent or more accepted	8.4	8.3	20.0	9.1	9.1	0.0	7.0	6.5	35.3	6.2	6.2	6.1	26.7	17.8	49.4
75.0 to 89.9 percent accepted	29.5	29.6	21.4	33.9	34.0	8.0	20.7	20.5	31.6	21.0	20.8	45.0	13.2	8.5	25.1
50.0 to 74.9 percent accepted	40.1	40.0	52.1	38.5	38.1	88.3	43.5	43.8	24.5	43.2	43.3	28.1	50.2	61.0	22.7
25.0 to 49.9 percent accepted	15.6	15.7	2.6	15.6	15.7	3.7	15.5	15.7	1.8	15.7	15.8	1.8	9.6	12.6	1.8
10.0 to 24.9 percent accepted	4.9	4.9	3.9	2.9	2.9	0.0	9.1	9.1	6.9	9.5	9.4	19.0	0.4	0.1	1.0
Less than 10.0 percent accepted	1.5	1.5	0.0	0.1	0.1	0.0	4.3	4.3	0.0	4.4	4.5	0.0	0.0	0.0	0.0
SAT scores of enrollees															
Evidence-based reading and writing (ERW), 25th percentile[2]	517	517	461	511	512	454	520	520	473	520	521	473	474	474	—
ERW, 75th percentile[2]	613	614	564	607	607	563	618	618	565	618	618	565	583	583	—
Mathematics, 25th percentile[2]	511	511	451	505	506	439	514	514	471	514	515	471	478	478	—
Mathematics, 75th percentile[2]	610	610	563	604	605	551	613	613	583	613	613	583	591	591	—
ACT scores of enrollees															
Composite, 25th percentile[2]	20.6	20.7	15.8	20.1	20.2	15.3	20.9	20.9	16.3	20.9	20.9	16.3	18.8	18.8	—
Composite, 75th percentile[2]	26.0	26.0	20.6	25.6	25.6	21.1	26.2	26.2	20.0	26.2	26.3	20.0	25.2	25.2	—
English, 25th percentile[2]	19.7	19.8	13.0	19.1	19.2	13.6	20.1	20.1	12.2	20.1	20.1	12.2	18.0	18.0	—
English, 75th percentile[2]	26.3	26.4	19.3	25.8	25.8	20.4	26.6	26.7	17.8	26.7	26.7	17.8	24.0	24.0	—
Mathematics, 25th percentile[2]	19.4	19.4	14.6	19.1	19.1	15.4	19.5	19.6	13.4	19.5	19.6	13.4	19.5	19.5	—
Mathematics, 75th percentile[2]	25.4	25.4	19.4	25.2	25.2	20.9	25.5	25.6	17.4	25.5	25.6	17.4	23.5	23.5	—

—Not available.
†Not applicable.
#Rounds to zero.
[1]The total on this table differs slightly from other counts of institutions with first-year undergraduates because approximately 1.0 percent of these institutions did not report application information.
[2]Data are only for institutions that require test scores for admission. Relatively few 2-year institutions require test scores for admission. The SAT evidence-based reading and writing (ERW) and mathematics scales range from 200 to 800. The ACT composite, English, and mathematics scales range from 1 to 36.

NOTE: Degree-granting institutions grant associate's or higher degrees and participate in Title IV federal financial aid programs. Excludes institutions not enrolling any first-time degree/certificate-seeking undergraduates. Detail may not sum to totals because of rounding.
SOURCE: U.S. Department of Education, National Center for Education Statistics, Integrated Postsecondary Education Data System (IPEDS), Winter 2018–19, Admissions component. (This table was prepared November 2019.)

Table 313.10. Fall enrollment, degrees conferred, and expenditures in degree-granting historically Black colleges and universities, by institution: 2017, 2018, and 2017–18

Institution	State	Level and control[1]	Total enrollment, fall 2018[2]	Enrollment, fall 2018		Full-time-equivalent enrollment, fall 2018	Degrees conferred, 2017–18				Total expenditures, 2017–18 (in thousands of current dollars)[4]
				Total	Black enrollment		Associate's	Bachelor's	Master's	Doctor's[3]	
1	2	3	4	5	6	7	8	9	10	11	12
Total	**†**	**†**	**298,134**	**291,767**	**223,163**	**251,390**	**5,465**	**32,639**	**7,697**	**2,518**	**$7,966,186**
Alabama A&M University[5]	AL	1	6,001	6,106	5,701	5,726	0	507	332	8	148,803
Alabama State University	AL	1	4,760	4,413	4,067	4,118	0	650	144	32	148,377
Bishop State Community College	AL	2	3,233	2,860	1,796	1,907	275	†	†	†	32,081
Gadsden State Community College	AL	2	4,979	4,736	850	3,117	642	†	†	†	50,921
H. Councill Trenholm State Technical College	AL	2	1,845	1,855	1,267	1,181	178	†	†	†	21,972
J.F. Drake State Community and Technical College	AL	2	752	831	432	486	64	†	†	†	10,863
Lawson State Community College	AL	2	3,248	3,274	2,653	2,192	316	†	†	†	50,318
Miles College	AL	3	1,650	1,550	1,470	1,501	0	295	0	0	30,916
Oakwood University	AL	3	1,711	1,636	1,391	1,555	4	306	5	0	54,786
Selma University	AL	3	324	317	308	264	13	20	4	0	4,007
Shelton State Community College	AL	2	4,607	4,350	1,667	2,771	535	†	†	†	42,421
Stillman College	AL	3	677	797	750	714	0	72	0	0	14,207
Talladega College	AL	3	782	1,212	1,042	1,138	0	128	0	0	14,708
Tuskegee University[5]	AL	3	3,289	3,026	2,771	2,953	0	423	86	67	122,619
Arkansas Baptist College	AR	3	593	525	472	486	41	30	0	0	14,820
Philander Smith College	AR	3	891	1,000	935	973	0	89	0	0	21,513
Shorter College	AR	4	521	569	323	425	30	†	†	†	5,409
University of Arkansas at Pine Bluff[5]	AR	1	2,612	2,579	2,318	2,405	9	377	34	1	80,292
Delaware State University[5]	DE	1	4,352	4,586	3,235	4,247	0	613	101	21	143,128
Howard University	DC	3	9,392	9,139	7,676	8,747	0	1,232	313	504	791,820
University of the District of Columbia[5]	DC	1	4,247	4,244	2,735	2,967	172	338	114	0	158,530
Bethune-Cookman University	FL	3	4,143	3,773	3,408	3,673	0	508	63	0	97,091
Edward Waters College	FL	3	3,443	2,906	1,803	1,703	0	121	0	0	24,685
Florida A&M University[5]	FL	1	9,913	10,021	8,254	9,151	40	1,258	303	340	290,819
Florida Memorial University	FL	3	1,250	1,189	874	1,126	0	214	25	0	35,256
Albany State University	GA	1	6,615	6,371	4,822	5,168	648	481	138	0	113,575
Clark Atlanta University	GA	3	3,992	3,911	3,673	3,732	0	411	233	30	98,282
Fort Valley State University[5]	GA	1	2,752	2,776	2,537	2,522	0	334	112	0	78,548
Interdenominational Theological Center	GA	3	295	293	288	182	0	0	38	28	7,546
Morehouse College	GA	3	2,202	2,206	2,106	2,170	0	398	0	0	87,802
Morehouse School of Medicine	GA	3	520	542	415	528	0	0	46	83	165,187
Paine College	GA	3	426	469	442	447	0	74	0	0	13,830
Savannah State University	GA	1	4,429	4,077	3,297	3,698	41	548	69	0	102,918
Spelman College	GA	3	2,137	2,171	2,107	2,142	0	446	0	0	99,659
Kentucky State University[5]	KY	1	1,926	1,778	963	1,389	52	222	57	6	67,996
Simmons College of Kentucky	KY	3	216	210	202	178	16	10	0	0	3,273
Dillard University	LA	3	1,290	1,309	1,272	1,257	0	220	0	0	45,815
Grambling State University	LA	1	5,191	5,205	4,758	4,511	1	551	215	10	91,270
Southern University and A&M College[5]	LA	1	6,118	6,693	6,191	5,851	0	736	297	14	138,156
Southern University at New Orleans	LA	1	2,546	2,356	2,202	1,949	17	296	167	0	39,063
Southern University at Shreveport	LA	2	3,088	2,651	2,419	1,894	207	†	†	†	31,499
Xavier University of Louisiana	LA	3	3,044	3,231	2,408	3,139	0	299	32	165	115,404
Bowie State University	MD	1	6,148	6,320	5,278	5,441	0	781	245	8	121,201
Coppin State University	MD	1	2,893	2,738	2,211	2,219	0	399	74	6	89,373
Morgan State University	MD	1	7,747	7,712	6,141	7,168	0	1,153	268	54	244,280
University of Maryland, Eastern Shore[5]	MD	1	3,490	3,193	2,181	2,908	0	482	52	100	118,011
Alcorn State University[5]	MS	1	3,716	3,658	3,345	3,257	16	450	151	0	89,836
Coahoma Community College	MS	2	1,954	1,895	1,777	1,540	287	†	†	†	34,137
Hinds Community College, Utica Campus	MS	2	688	646	621	615	114	0	0	0	—
Jackson State University	MS	1	8,558	7,250	6,504	6,203	0	1,109	374	75	192,155
Mississippi Valley State University	MS	1	2,385	2,285	2,191	1,888	0	302	109	0	51,506
Rust College	MS	3	860	846	820	794	5	110	0	0	17,107
Tougaloo College	MS	3	809	736	719	716	0	130	7	0	24,780
Harris-Stowe State University	MO	1	1,442	1,716	1,488	1,526	0	176	0	0	35,290
Lincoln University[5]	MO	1	2,619	2,478	1,191	2,029	72	289	48	0	52,840
Bennett College	NC	3	493	534	488	491	0	72	0	0	15,621
Elizabeth City State University	NC	1	1,411	1,677	1,213	1,530	0	245	17	0	62,244
Fayetteville State University	NC	1	6,226	6,318	3,871	5,189	0	1,004	160	8	122,105
Johnson C. Smith University	NC	3	1,483	1,565	1,448	1,525	0	206	37	0	43,393
Livingstone College	NC	3	1,150	1,148	1,083	1,143	10	157	0	0	30,461
North Carolina A&T State University[5]	NC	1	11,877	12,142	9,724	11,111	0	1,662	423	57	288,219
North Carolina Central University	NC	1	8,097	8,207	6,248	7,204	0	1,026	467	134	208,311
Saint Augustine's College	NC	3	974	767	711	757	0	121	0	0	30,191
Shaw University	NC	3	1,660	1,411	1,054	1,349	0	179	28	0	42,219
Winston-Salem State University	NC	1	5,098	5,190	3,897	4,719	0	999	99	40	141,832
Central State University	OH	1	1,784	2,099	1,943	2,057	0	211	0	0	60,652
Wilberforce University	OH	3	627	672	662	612	0	66	7	0	15,479
Langston University[5]	OK	1	2,219	2,119	1,645	1,945	13	242	62	14	59,768
Cheyney University of Pennsylvania	PA	1	755	466	392	446	0	152	24	0	27,338
Lincoln University	PA	1	2,266	2,376	2,121	2,241	0	260	126	0	58,979

See notes at end of table.

Table 313.10. Fall enrollment, degrees conferred, and expenditures in degree-granting historically Black colleges and universities, by institution: 2017, 2018, and 2017–18—Continued

Institution	State	Level and control[1]	Total enrollment, fall 2018[2]	Enrollment, fall 2018		Full-time-equivalent enrollment, fall 2018	Degrees conferred, 2017–18				Total expenditures, 2017–18 (in thousands of current dollars)[4]
				Total	Black enrollment		Associate's	Bachelor's	Master's	Doctor's[3]	
1	2	3	4	5	6	7	8	9	10	11	12
Allen University	SC	3	590	743	724	709	0	59	0	0	15,485
Benedict College	SC	3	2,090	2,165	2,032	2,134	0	248	0	0	50,115
Claflin University	SC	3	2,129	2,172	2,022	2,101	0	310	32	0	51,419
Clinton College	SC	3	170	193	183	193	9	11	0	0	4,192
Denmark Technical College	SC	2	523	489	397	329	52	†	†	†	10,393
Morris College	SC	3	747	649	635	639	0	117	0	0	18,485
South Carolina State University[5]	SC	1	2,942	3,022	2,858	2,638	0	310	83	11	88,257
Voorhees College	SC	3	475	491	471	484	0	65	0	0	13,348
American Baptist College	TN	3	115	123	121	108	2	32	0	0	4,266
Fisk University	TN	3	701	780	690	762	0	132	9	0	28,687
Lane College	TN	3	1,420	1,232	1,207	1,203	0	171	0	0	24,731
Le Moyne-Owen College	TN	3	863	885	865	810	0	106	0	0	15,806
Meharry Medical College	TN	3	826	828	682	828	0	0	57	159	147,926
Tennessee State University[5]	TN	1	8,177	7,774	5,341	6,474	67	1,085	374	74	197,131
Huston-Tillotson University	TX	3	1,102	1,119	719	1,068	33	210	4	0	21,401
Jarvis Christian College	TX	3	909	964	791	939	11	77	0	0	18,224
Paul Quinn College	TX	3	519	550	438	532	0	41	0	0	11,410
Prairie View A&M University[5]	TX	1	9,219	9,516	7,932	8,844	0	1,104	393	13	245,322
Saint Philip's College	TX	2	12,050	11,590	1,103	4,925	1,242	†	†	†	80,787
Southwestern Christian College	TX	3	159	87	81	83	25	2	0	0	4,473
Texas College	TX	3	983	1,042	864	1,032	21	84	0	0	16,206
Texas Southern University	TX	1	10,237	9,732	7,624	8,689	0	974	360	312	212,216
Wiley College	TX	3	1,323	1,003	821	926	1	224	0	0	25,289
Hampton University	VA	3	4,618	4,321	4,043	4,156	3	594	150	91	183,386
Norfolk State University	VA	1	5,305	5,204	4,456	4,781	2	729	213	12	158,619
Virginia State University[5]	VA	1	4,713	4,385	3,123	4,193	0	731	126	13	145,558
Virginia Union University	VA	3	1,674	1,552	1,490	1,459	0	204	92	16	37,953
Virginia University of Lynchburg	VA	3	307	298	292	274	35	12	5	12	4,370
Bluefield State College	WV	1	1,379	1,275	95	1,102	113	226	0	0	21,039
West Virginia State University[5]	WV	1	3,879	3,692	314	2,498	0	370	32	0	46,809
University of the Virgin Islands[5]	VI	1	2,170	1,984	1,482	1,571	31	221	61	0	75,370

—Not available.

†Not applicable.

[1]1 = 4-year public; 2 = 2-year public; 3 = 4-year private nonprofit; and 4 = 2-year private nonprofit.

[2]Total fall 2017 enrollment includes enrollment at Concordia College in Alabama. This institution closed in 2018 and therefore does not appear in this table.

[3]Includes Ph.D., Ed.D., and comparable degrees at the doctoral level, as well as such degrees as M.D., D.D.S., and law degrees that were classified as first-professional degrees prior to 2010–11.

[4]Includes private and some public institutions reporting total expenses and deductions under Financial Accounting Standards Board (FASB) reporting standards and public institutions reporting total expenses and deductions under Governmental Accounting Standards Board (GASB) 34/35 reporting standards.

[5]Land-grant institution.

NOTE: Degree-granting institutions grant associate's or higher degrees and participate in Title IV federal financial aid programs. Excludes historically Black colleges and universities that are not participating in Title IV programs. Historically Black colleges and universities are degree-granting institutions established prior to 1964 with the principal mission of educating Black Americans. Federal regulations, 20 U.S. Code, Section 1061 (2), allow for certain exceptions to the founding date. Totals include persons of other racial/ethnic groups not separately identified. Detail may not sum to totals because of rounding.

SOURCE: U.S. Department of Education, National Center for Education Statistics, Integrated Postsecondary Education Data System (IPEDS), Fall 2018, Completions component; Spring 2018 and Spring 2019, Fall Enrollment component; and Spring 2019, Finance component. (This table was prepared November 2019.)

Table 313.20. Fall enrollment in degree-granting historically Black colleges and universities, by sex of student and level and control of institution: Selected years, 1976 through 2018

Year	Total enrollment	Males	Females	4-year	2-year	Public			Private		
						Total	4-year	2-year	Total	4-year	2-year
1	2	3	4	5	6	7	8	9	10	11	12
						All students					
1976	222,613	104,669	117,944	206,676	15,937	156,836	143,528	13,308	65,777	63,148	2,629
1980	233,557	106,387	127,170	218,009	15,548	168,217	155,085	13,132	65,340	62,924	2,416
1982	228,371	104,897	123,474	212,017	16,354	165,871	151,472	14,399	62,500	60,545	1,955
1984	227,519	102,823	124,696	212,844	14,675	164,116	151,289	12,827	63,403	61,555	1,848
1986	223,275	97,523	125,752	207,231	16,044	162,048	147,631	14,417	61,227	59,600	1,627
1988	239,755	100,561	139,194	223,250	16,505	173,672	158,606	15,066	66,083	64,644	1,439
1990	257,152	105,157	151,995	240,497	16,655	187,046	171,969	15,077	70,106	68,528	1,578
1992	279,541	114,622	164,919	261,089	18,452	204,966	188,143	16,823	74,575	72,946	1,629
1993	282,856	116,397	166,459	262,430	20,426	208,197	189,032	19,165	74,659	73,398	1,261
1994	280,071	114,006	166,065	259,997	20,074	206,520	187,735	18,785	73,551	72,262	1,289
1995	278,725	112,637	166,088	259,409	19,316	204,726	186,278	18,448	73,999	73,131	868
1996	273,018	109,498	163,520	253,654	19,364	200,569	182,063	18,506	72,449	71,591	858
1997	269,167	106,865	162,302	248,860	20,307	194,674	175,297	19,377	74,493	73,563	930
1998	273,472	108,752	164,720	248,931	24,541	198,603	174,776	23,827	74,869	74,155	714
1999	274,321	108,301	166,020	249,156	25,165	199,826	175,364	24,462	74,495	73,792	703
2000	275,680	108,164	167,516	250,710	24,970	199,725	175,404	24,321	75,955	75,306	649
2001	289,985	112,874	177,111	260,547	29,438	210,083	181,346	28,737	79,902	79,201	701
2002	299,041	115,466	183,575	269,020	30,021	218,433	189,183	29,250	80,608	79,837	771
2003	306,727	117,795	188,932	274,326	32,401	228,096	196,077	32,019	78,631	78,249	382
2004	308,939	118,129	190,810	276,136	32,803	231,179	198,810	32,369	77,760	77,326	434
2005	311,768	120,023	191,745	272,666	39,102	235,875	197,200	38,675	75,893	75,466	427
2006	308,774	118,865	189,909	272,770	36,004	234,505	198,676	35,829	74,269	74,094	175
2007	306,742	118,672	188,070	270,554	36,188	234,034	197,939	36,095	72,708	72,615	93
2008	313,491	121,874	191,617	274,568	38,923	235,824	197,025	38,799	77,667	77,543	124
2009	322,860	125,728	197,132	280,133	42,727	246,595	204,016	42,579	76,265	76,117	148
2010	326,614	127,437	199,177	283,099	43,515	249,146	205,774	43,372	77,468	77,325	143
2011	323,648	126,160	197,488	281,150	42,498	246,685	204,363	42,322	76,963	76,787	176
2012	312,438	121,719	190,719	273,033	39,405	237,782	198,568	39,214	74,656	74,465	191
2013	303,191	119,299	183,892	264,454	38,737	230,325	191,918	38,407	72,866	72,536	330
2014	294,316	115,837	178,479	256,936	37,380	222,876	185,899	36,977	71,440	71,037	403
2015	293,304	115,818	177,486	256,295	37,009	221,276	184,503	36,773	72,028	71,792	236
2016	292,083	114,705	177,378	254,839	37,244	220,292	183,494	36,798	71,791	71,345	446
2017	298,134	115,316	182,818	260,646	37,488	225,181	188,214	36,967	72,953	72,432	521
2018	291,767	110,853	180,914	256,021	35,746	220,910	185,733	35,177	70,857	70,288	569
						Black students					
1976	190,305	84,492	105,813	179,848	10,457	129,770	121,851	7,919	60,535	57,997	2,538
1980	190,989	81,818	109,171	181,237	9,752	131,661	124,236	7,425	59,328	57,001	2,327
1982	182,639	78,874	103,765	171,942	10,697	126,368	117,562	8,806	56,271	54,380	1,891
1984	180,803	76,819	103,984	171,401	9,402	124,445	116,845	7,600	56,358	54,556	1,802
1986	178,628	74,276	104,352	167,971	10,657	123,555	114,502	9,053	55,073	53,469	1,604
1988	194,151	78,268	115,883	183,402	10,749	133,786	124,438	9,348	60,365	58,964	1,401
1990	208,682	82,897	125,785	198,237	10,445	144,204	134,924	9,280	64,478	63,313	1,165
1992	228,963	91,949	137,014	217,614	11,349	159,585	149,754	9,831	69,378	67,860	1,518
1993	231,198	93,110	138,088	219,431	11,767	161,444	150,867	10,577	69,754	68,564	1,190
1994	230,162	91,908	138,254	218,565	11,597	161,098	150,682	10,416	69,064	67,883	1,181
1995	229,418	91,132	138,286	218,379	11,039	159,925	149,661	10,264	69,493	68,718	775
1996	224,201	88,306	135,895	213,309	10,892	156,851	146,753	10,098	67,350	66,556	794
1997	222,331	86,641	135,690	210,741	11,590	153,039	142,326	10,713	69,292	68,415	877
1998	223,745	87,163	136,582	211,822	11,923	154,244	142,985	11,259	69,501	68,837	664
1999	226,592	87,987	138,605	213,779	12,813	156,292	144,166	12,126	70,300	69,613	687
2000	227,239	87,319	139,920	215,172	12,067	156,706	145,277	11,429	70,533	69,895	638
2001	238,638	90,718	147,920	224,417	14,221	164,354	150,831	13,523	74,284	73,586	698
2002	247,292	93,538	153,754	231,834	15,458	172,203	157,507	14,696	75,089	74,327	762
2003	253,257	95,703	157,554	236,753	16,504	180,104	163,977	16,127	73,153	72,776	377
2004	257,545	96,750	160,795	241,030	16,515	184,708	168,619	16,089	72,837	72,411	426
2005	256,584	96,891	159,693	238,030	18,554	186,047	167,916	18,131	70,537	70,114	423
2006	255,144	96,507	158,637	238,440	16,704	185,894	169,365	16,529	69,250	69,075	175
2007	253,241	96,214	157,027	236,571	16,670	185,170	168,592	16,578	68,071	67,979	92
2008	258,402	98,633	159,769	240,132	18,270	186,446	168,299	18,147	71,956	71,833	123
2009	264,092	100,590	163,502	243,956	20,136	194,088	174,099	19,989	70,004	69,857	147
2010	265,908	101,605	164,303	245,158	20,750	193,840	173,233	20,607	72,068	71,925	143
2011	263,435	100,526	162,909	242,881	20,554	192,042	171,664	20,378	71,393	71,217	176
2012	251,527	96,079	155,448	232,897	18,630	183,018	164,578	18,440	68,509	68,319	190
2013	241,485	92,491	148,994	223,491	17,994	175,308	157,640	17,668	66,177	65,851	326
2014	231,889	88,469	143,420	214,631	17,258	167,246	150,383	16,863	64,643	64,248	395
2015	228,062	86,857	141,205	211,698	16,364	163,508	147,376	16,132	64,554	64,322	232
2016	223,512	84,153	139,359	207,379	16,133	160,053	144,176	15,877	63,459	63,203	256
2017	226,847	83,917	142,930	210,664	16,183	162,703	146,804	15,899	64,144	63,860	284
2018	223,163	81,055	142,108	207,858	15,305	160,871	145,889	14,982	62,292	61,969	323

NOTE: Historically Black colleges and universities are degree-granting institutions established prior to 1964 with the principal mission of educating Black Americans. Federal regulations, 20 U.S. Code, Section 1061 (2), allow for certain exceptions to the founding date. Data through 1995 are for institutions of higher education, while later data are for degree-granting institutions. Degree-granting institutions grant associate's or higher degrees and participate in Title IV federal financial aid programs. The degree-granting classification is very similar to the earlier higher education classification, but it includes more 2-year colleges and excludes a few higher education institutions that did not grant degrees. Some data have been revised from previously published figures.

SOURCE: U.S. Department of Education, National Center for Education Statistics, Higher Education General Information Survey (HEGIS), "Fall Enrollment in Colleges and Universities," 1976 through 1985 surveys; Integrated Postsecondary Education Data System (IPEDS), "Fall Enrollment Survey" (IPEDS-EF:86–99); and IPEDS Spring 2001 through Spring 2019, Fall Enrollment component. (This table was prepared November 2019.)

Table 313.30. Selected statistics on degree-granting historically Black colleges and universities, by control and level of institution: Selected years, 1990 through 2018

Selected statistics	Total	Public			Private		
		Total	4-year	2-year	Total	4-year	2-year
1	2	3	4	5	6	7	8
Number of institutions, fall 2017	**101**	**51**	**40**	**11**	**50**	**49**	**1**
Fall enrollment							
Total enrollment, fall 1990	257,152	187,046	171,969	15,077	70,106	68,528	1,578
Males	105,157	76,541	70,220	6,321	28,616	28,054	562
Males, Black	82,897	57,255	54,041	3,214	25,642	25,198	444
Females	151,995	110,505	101,749	8,756	41,490	40,474	1,016
Females, Black	125,785	86,949	80,883	6,066	38,836	38,115	721
Total enrollment, fall 2000	275,680	199,725	175,404	24,321	75,955	75,306	649
Males	108,164	78,186	68,322	9,864	29,978	29,771	207
Males, Black	87,319	60,029	56,017	4,012	27,290	27,085	205
Females	167,516	121,539	107,082	14,457	45,977	45,535	442
Females, Black	139,920	96,677	89,260	7,417	43,243	42,810	433
Total enrollment, fall 2010	326,614	249,146	205,774	43,372	77,468	77,325	143
Males	127,437	95,883	78,528	17,355	31,554	31,482	72
Males, Black	101,605	72,629	65,512	7,117	28,976	28,904	72
Females	199,177	153,263	127,246	26,017	45,914	45,843	71
Females, Black	164,303	121,211	107,721	13,490	43,092	43,021	71
Total enrollment, fall 2018	291,767	220,910	185,733	35,177	70,857	70,288	569
Males	110,853	83,015	68,415	14,600	27,838	27,530	308
Males, Black	81,055	57,283	51,863	5,420	23,772	23,634	138
Females	180,914	137,895	117,318	20,577	43,019	42,758	261
Females, Black	142,108	103,588	94,026	9,562	38,520	38,335	185
Full-time enrollment, fall 2018	227,415	163,126	149,356	13,770	64,289	63,958	331
Males	87,026	62,050	55,954	6,096	24,976	24,806	170
Females	140,389	101,076	93,402	7,674	39,313	39,152	161
Part-time enrollment, fall 2018	64,352	57,784	36,377	21,407	6,568	6,330	238
Males	23,827	20,965	12,461	8,504	2,862	2,724	138
Females	40,525	36,819	23,916	12,903	3,706	3,606	100
Degrees conferred, 2017–18							
Associate's	5,465	5,206	1,294	3,912	259	229	30
Males	1,909	1,794	320	1,474	115	106	9
Males, Black	716	619	135	484	97	88	9
Females	3,556	3,412	974	2,438	144	123	21
Females, Black	1,658	1,523	456	1,067	135	114	21
Bachelor's	32,639	23,603	23,603	†	9,036	9,036	†
Males	11,952	8,715	8,715	†	3,237	3,237	†
Males, Black	9,083	6,292	6,292	†	2,791	2,791	†
Females	20,687	14,888	14,888	†	5,799	5,799	†
Females, Black	17,193	11,924	11,924	†	5,269	5,269	†
Master's	7,697	6,424	6,424	†	1,273	1,273	†
Males	2,449	2,011	2,011	†	438	438	†
Males, Black	1,591	1,261	1,261	†	330	330	†
Females	5,248	4,413	4,413	†	835	835	†
Females, Black	3,836	3,153	3,153	†	683	683	†
Doctor's[1]	2,518	1,363	1,363	†	1,155	1,155	†
Males	975	538	538	†	437	437	†
Males, Black	519	256	256	†	263	263	†
Females	1,543	825	825	†	718	718	†
Females, Black	1,036	535	535	†	501	501	†
Financial statistics, 2017–18[2]	In thousands of current dollars						
Total revenue	$8,673,522	$5,408,362	$5,039,982	$368,380	$3,265,159	$3,258,836	$6,323
Student tuition and fees	1,939,022	1,008,241	966,772	41,469	930,781	926,978	3,803
Federal government[3]	2,007,472	1,290,761	1,162,948	127,813	716,711	715,530	1,180
State governments	1,989,311	1,892,318	1,763,450	128,868	96,993	96,993	0
Local governments	115,050	79,745	35,774	43,971	35,305	34,848	457
Private gifts and grants[4]	478,947	203,192	190,642	12,550	275,755	275,427	328
Investment return (gain or loss)	455,325	62,397	61,683	714	392,928	392,928	0
Auxiliary (essentially self-supporting) enterprises	977,002	613,770	607,247	6,523	363,232	362,678	554
Hospitals and other sources	711,392	257,938	251,467	6,472	453,454	453,454	0
Total expenditures	7,966,186	5,181,127	4,815,735	365,392	2,785,059	2,779,649	5,409
Instruction	2,301,598	1,589,122	1,442,240	146,882	712,476	710,741	1,735
Research	487,564	326,112	326,112	0	161,452	161,452	0
Academic support	662,825	462,427	431,000	31,427	200,398	199,976	423
Institutional support	1,416,307	757,939	693,358	64,581	658,369	656,278	2,090
Auxiliary (essentially self-supporting) enterprises	1,121,950	802,029	795,308	6,721	319,921	318,958	963
Other expenditures	1,975,941	1,243,498	1,127,717	115,781	732,443	732,245	198

†Not applicable.
[1]Includes Ph.D., Ed.D., and comparable degrees at the doctoral level, as well as such degrees as M.D., D.D.S., and law degrees that were classified as first-professional degrees prior to 2010–11.
[2]Totals (column 2) of public and private institutions together are approximate because reporting is based on two different survey forms with different accounting concepts. Included are data reported by public institutions using the Governmental Accounting Standards Board (GASB) form as well as data reported by private and some public institutions using the Financial Accounting Standards Board (FASB) form.
[3]Includes independent operations.
[4]Includes contributions from affiliated entities.
NOTE: Degree-granting institutions grant associate's or higher degrees and participate in Title IV federal financial aid programs. Historically Black colleges and universities are degree-granting institutions established prior to 1964 with the principal mission of educating Black Americans. Federal regulations, 20 U.S. Code, Section 1061 (2), allow for certain exceptions to the founding date. Federal, state, and local governments revenue includes appropriations, grants, and contracts. Totals include persons of other racial/ethnic groups not separately identified. Detail may not sum to totals because of rounding.
SOURCE: U.S. Department of Education, National Center for Education Statistics, Integrated Postsecondary Education Data System (IPEDS), "Fall Enrollment Survey" (IPEDS-EF:90); IPEDS Spring 2001, Spring 2011, and Spring 2019, Fall Enrollment component; IPEDS Spring 2019, Finance component; and IPEDS Fall 2018, Finance component; and IPEDS Fall 2018, Completions component. (This table was prepared November 2019.)

Table 315.10. Number of faculty in degree-granting postsecondary institutions, by employment status, sex, control, and level of institution: Selected years, fall 1970 through fall 2018

Year	Total	Employment status			Sex			Control				Level	
									Private				
		Full-time	Part-time	Percent full-time	Males	Females	Percent female	Public	Total	Nonprofit	For-profit	4-year	2-year
1	2	3	4	5	6	7	8	9	10	11	12	13	14
1970	474,000	369,000	104,000	77.8	—	—	—	314,000	160,000	—	—	382,000	92,000
1971[1]	492,000	379,000	113,000	77.0	—	—	—	333,000	159,000	—	—	387,000	105,000
1972	500,000	380,000	120,000	76.0	—	—	—	343,000	157,000	—	—	384,000	116,000
1973[1]	527,000	389,000	138,000	73.8	—	—	—	365,000	162,000	—	—	401,000	126,000
1974[1]	567,000	406,000	161,000	71.6	—	—	—	397,000	170,000	—	—	427,000	140,000
1975[1]	628,000	440,000	188,000	70.1	—	—	—	443,000	185,000	—	—	467,000	161,000
1976	633,000	434,000	199,000	68.6	—	—	—	449,000	184,000	—	—	467,000	166,000
1977	678,000	448,000	230,000	66.1	—	—	—	492,000	186,000	—	—	485,000	193,000
1979[1]	675,000	445,000	230,000	65.9	—	—	—	488,000	187,000	—	—	494,000	182,000
1980[1]	686,000	450,000	236,000	65.6	—	—	—	495,000	191,000	—	—	494,000	192,000
1981	705,000	461,000	244,000	65.4	—	—	—	509,000	196,000	—	—	493,000	212,000
1982[1]	710,000	462,000	248,000	65.1	—	—	—	506,000	204,000	—	—	493,000	217,000
1983	724,000	471,000	254,000	65.1	—	—	—	512,000	212,000	—	—	504,000	220,000
1984[1]	717,000	462,000	255,000	64.4	—	—	—	505,000	212,000	—	—	504,000	213,000
1985[1]	715,000	459,000	256,000	64.2	—	—	—	503,000	212,000	—	—	504,000	211,000
1986[1]	722,000	459,000	263,000	63.6	—	—	—	510,000	212,000	—	—	506,000	216,000
1987[2]	793,070	523,420	269,650	66.0	529,413	263,657	33.2	552,749	240,321	—	—	547,505	245,565
1989[2]	824,220	524,426	299,794	63.6	534,254	289,966	35.2	577,298	246,922	—	—	583,700	240,520
1991[2]	826,252	535,623	290,629	64.8	525,599	300,653	36.4	580,908	245,344	236,066	9,278	591,269	234,983
1993[2]	915,474	545,706	369,768	59.6	561,123	354,351	38.7	650,434	265,040	254,130	10,910	625,969	289,505
1995[2]	931,706	550,822	380,884	59.1	562,893	368,813	39.6	656,833	274,873	260,900	13,973	647,059	284,647
1997[2]	989,813	568,719	421,094	57.5	587,420	402,393	40.7	694,560	295,253	271,257	23,996	682,650	307,163
1999[2]	1,037,529	593,375	444,154	57.2	608,007	429,522	41.4	718,585	318,944	288,663	30,281	719,256	318,273
2001[2]	1,113,183	617,868	495,315	55.5	644,514	468,669	42.1	771,124	342,059	306,487	35,572	764,172	349,011
2003[2]	1,173,593	630,092	543,501	53.7	663,723	509,870	43.4	791,766	381,827	330,097	51,730	814,289	359,304
2005[2]	1,290,426	675,624	614,802	52.4	714,453	575,973	44.6	841,188	449,238	361,523	87,715	916,996	373,430
2007[2]	1,371,587	703,757	667,830	51.3	744,047	627,540	45.8	876,526	495,061	386,688	108,373	992,385	379,202
2009[2]	1,439,074	729,152	709,922	50.7	761,002	678,072	47.1	913,788	525,286	408,382	116,904	1,038,349	400,725
2011[2]	1,524,469	762,114	762,355	50.0	789,567	734,902	48.2	954,159	570,310	432,630	137,680	1,115,642	408,827
2013[2]	1,545,381	791,378	754,003	51.2	791,971	753,410	48.8	968,734	576,647	449,072	127,575	1,151,638	393,743
2015[2]	1,552,256	807,109	745,147	52.0	789,405	762,851	49.1	970,991	581,265	472,638	108,627	1,180,545	371,711
2016[2]	1,546,081	813,978	732,103	52.6	783,495	762,586	49.3	974,239	571,842	476,872	94,970	1,196,657	349,424
2017[2]	1,545,653	822,513	723,140	53.2	778,873	766,780	49.6	972,689	572,964	486,761	86,203	1,209,143	336,510
2018[2]	1,542,613	832,119	710,494	53.9	771,594	771,019	50.0	980,835	561,778	491,014	70,764	1,216,524	326,089

—Not available.

[1]Estimated on the basis of enrollment. For methodological details on estimates, see National Center for Education Statistics, *Projections of Education Statistics to 2000*.

[2]Because of revised survey methods, data are not directly comparable with figures for years prior to 1987.

NOTE: Includes faculty members with the title of professor, associate professor, assistant professor, instructor, lecturer, assisting professor, adjunct professor, or interim professor (or the equivalent). Excluded are graduate students with titles such as graduate or teaching fellow who assist senior faculty. Data through 1995 are for institutions of higher education, while later data are for degree-granting institutions. Degree-granting institutions grant associate's or higher degrees and participate in Title IV federal financial aid programs. The degree-granting classification is very similar to the earlier higher education classification, but it includes more 2-year colleges and excludes a few higher education institutions that did not grant degrees. Beginning in 2007, includes institutions with fewer than 15 full-time employees; these institutions did not report staff data prior to 2007. Some data have been revised from previously published figures. Detail may not sum to totals because of rounding.

SOURCE: U.S. Department of Education, National Center for Education Statistics, Higher Education General Information Survey (HEGIS), *Employees in Institutions of Higher Education*, 1970 and 1972, and "Staff Survey" 1976; *Projections of Education Statistics to 2000*; Integrated Postsecondary Education Data System (IPEDS), "Fall Staff Survey" (IPEDS-S:87–99); IPEDS Winter 2001–02 through Winter 2011–12, Human Resources component, Fall Staff section; IPEDS Spring 2014 and Spring 2016 through Spring 2019, Human Resources component, Fall Staff section; and U.S. Equal Employment Opportunity Commission, Higher Education Staff Information Survey (EEO-6), 1977, 1981, and 1983. (This table was prepared November 2019.)

Table 315.20. Full-time faculty in degree-granting postsecondary institutions, by race/ethnicity, sex, and academic rank: Fall 2015, fall 2017, and fall 2018

Year, sex, and academic rank	Total	White	Black, Hispanic, Asian, Pacific Islander, American Indian/Alaska Native, and Two or more races									Race/ ethnicity unknown	Non-resident alien[2]
			Total	Percent[1]	Black	Hispanic	Asian/Pacific Islander			American Indian/ Alaska Native	Two or more races		
							Total	Asian	Pacific Islander				
1	2	3	4	5	6	7	8	9	10	11	12	13	14
2015[3]													
Total	**807,109**	**575,752**	**167,372**	**22.5**	**44,106**	**35,811**	**77,456**	**76,298**	**1,158**	**3,530**	**6,469**	**22,359**	**41,626**
Professors	182,388	147,095	31,171	17.5	6,731	5,957	16,938	16,734	204	599	946	2,486	1,636
Associate professors	158,082	116,754	35,132	23.1	9,090	6,978	17,285	17,067	218	608	1,171	3,070	3,126
Assistant professors	173,409	115,226	40,251	25.9	10,874	7,634	19,432	19,132	300	639	1,672	6,577	11,355
Instructors	99,915	73,052	21,673	22.9	7,264	6,890	5,696	5,467	229	862	961	3,563	1,627
Lecturers	40,894	30,488	7,635	20.0	2,074	2,367	2,690	2,653	37	142	362	1,256	1,515
Other faculty	152,421	93,137	31,510	25.3	8,073	5,985	15,415	15,245	170	680	1,357	5,407	22,367
2017[3]													
Total	**822,513**	**574,364**	**179,251**	**23.8**	**45,461**	**39,190**	**83,516**	**82,316**	**1,200**	**3,477**	**7,607**	**23,467**	**45,431**
Professors	184,428	145,927	33,971	18.9	6,936	6,535	18,817	18,624	193	633	1,050	2,714	1,816
Associate professors	157,975	115,065	36,527	24.1	9,157	7,253	18,269	18,033	236	573	1,275	3,308	3,075
Assistant professors	179,051	115,830	43,727	27.4	11,507	8,571	20,993	20,713	280	631	2,025	6,876	12,618
Instructors	98,673	70,967	22,469	24.0	7,048	7,431	6,019	5,787	232	851	1,120	3,378	1,859
Lecturers	43,222	32,031	8,121	20.2	1,994	2,708	2,760	2,722	38	160	499	1,493	1,577
Other faculty	159,164	94,544	34,436	26.7	8,819	6,692	16,658	16,437	221	629	1,638	5,698	24,486
Males	441,472	307,287	92,804	23.2	19,432	19,732	48,424	47,835	589	1,693	3,523	12,422	28,959
Professors	123,867	97,492	23,146	19.2	4,127	4,115	13,895	13,767	128	381	628	1,874	1,355
Associate professors	86,222	62,422	19,927	24.2	4,300	3,908	10,808	10,694	114	269	642	1,937	1,936
Assistant professors	86,236	54,432	20,503	27.4	4,345	4,111	10,905	10,772	133	295	847	3,556	7,745
Instructors	42,843	31,031	9,348	23.2	2,577	3,298	2,554	2,455	99	429	490	1,472	992
Lecturers	19,219	14,396	3,318	18.7	847	1,154	1,061	1,043	18	60	196	699	806
Other faculty	83,085	47,514	16,562	25.8	3,236	3,146	9,201	9,104	97	259	720	2,884	16,125
Females	381,041	267,077	86,447	24.5	26,029	19,458	35,092	34,481	611	1,784	4,084	11,045	16,472
Professors	60,561	48,435	10,825	18.3	2,809	2,420	4,922	4,857	65	252	422	840	461
Associate professors	71,753	52,643	16,600	24.0	4,857	3,345	7,461	7,339	122	304	633	1,371	1,139
Assistant professors	92,815	61,398	23,224	27.4	7,162	4,460	10,088	9,941	147	336	1,178	3,320	4,873
Instructors	55,830	39,936	13,121	24.7	4,471	4,133	3,465	3,332	133	422	630	1,906	867
Lecturers	24,003	17,635	4,803	21.4	1,147	1,554	1,699	1,679	20	100	303	794	771
Other faculty	76,079	47,030	17,874	27.5	5,583	3,546	7,457	7,333	124	370	918	2,814	8,361
2018[3]													
Total	**832,119**	**572,586**	**184,941**	**24.4**	**45,748**	**41,403**	**86,035**	**84,806**	**1,229**	**3,413**	**8,342**	**25,180**	**49,412**
Professors	185,758	145,207	35,404	19.6	7,005	6,826	19,729	19,529	200	606	1,238	3,107	2,040
Associate professors	159,135	114,804	37,463	24.6	9,196	7,684	18,696	18,451	245	578	1,309	3,686	3,182
Assistant professors	181,239	115,381	44,822	28.0	11,628	8,913	21,408	21,137	271	663	2,210	7,591	13,445
Instructors	98,798	70,171	23,327	24.9	7,225	7,885	6,165	5,885	280	786	1,266	3,480	1,820
Lecturers	44,969	32,808	8,790	21.1	2,120	2,986	2,975	2,936	39	162	547	1,594	1,777
Other faculty	162,220	94,215	35,135	27.2	8,574	7,109	17,062	16,868	194	618	1,772	5,722	27,148
Males	443,589	304,009	94,801	23.8	19,351	20,621	49,507	48,872	635	1,617	3,705	13,352	31,427
Professors	123,569	96,178	23,736	19.8	4,091	4,222	14,401	14,271	130	351	671	2,109	1,546
Associate professors	86,082	61,665	20,259	24.7	4,282	4,117	10,963	10,831	132	279	618	2,171	1,987
Assistant professors	86,493	53,673	20,748	27.9	4,334	4,227	10,987	10,851	136	295	905	3,798	8,274
Instructors	42,923	30,679	9,642	23.9	2,616	3,497	2,624	2,501	123	384	521	1,605	997
Lecturers	19,891	14,637	3,577	19.6	904	1,247	1,164	1,147	17	56	206	772	905
Other faculty	84,631	47,177	16,839	26.3	3,124	3,311	9,368	9,271	97	252	784	2,897	17,718
Females	388,530	268,577	90,140	25.1	26,397	20,782	36,528	35,934	594	1,796	4,637	11,828	17,985
Professors	62,189	49,029	11,668	19.2	2,914	2,604	5,328	5,258	70	255	567	998	494
Associate professors	73,053	53,139	17,204	24.5	4,914	3,567	7,733	7,620	113	299	691	1,515	1,195
Assistant professors	94,746	61,708	24,074	28.1	7,294	4,686	10,421	10,286	135	368	1,305	3,793	5,171
Instructors	55,875	39,492	13,685	25.7	4,609	4,388	3,541	3,384	157	402	745	1,875	823
Lecturers	25,078	18,171	5,213	22.3	1,216	1,739	1,811	1,789	22	106	341	822	872
Other faculty	77,589	47,038	18,296	28.0	5,450	3,798	7,694	7,597	97	366	988	2,825	9,430

[1]Combined total of faculty who were Black, Hispanic, Asian, Pacific Islander, American Indian/Alaska Native, and of Two or more races as a percentage of total faculty, excluding race/ethnicity unknown and nonresident alien.
[2]Race/ethnicity not collected.
[3]Only instructional faculty were classified by academic rank. Primarily research and primarily public service faculty, as well as faculty without ranks, appear under "other faculty."

NOTE: Degree-granting institutions grant associate's or higher degrees and participate in Title IV federal financial aid programs. Race categories exclude persons of Hispanic ethnicity. Some data have been revised from previously published figures.
SOURCE: U.S. Department of Education, National Center for Education Statistics, Integrated Postsecondary Education Data System (IPEDS), Spring 2016 through Spring 2019 Human Resources component, Fall Staff section. (This table was prepared November 2019.)

Table 316.10. Average salary of full-time instructional faculty on 9-month contracts in degree-granting postsecondary institutions, by academic rank, control and level of institution, and sex: Selected years, 1970–71 through 2018–19

Sex and academic year	All faculty	Academic rank						Public institutions			Private institutions		
		Professor	Associate professor	Assistant professor	Instructor	Lecturer	No rank	Total	4-year	2-year	Total	4-year	2-year
1	2	3	4	5	6	7	8	9	10	11	12	13	14
	Current dollars												
Total													
1970–71	$12,710	$17,958	$13,563	$11,176	$9,360	$11,196	$12,333	$12,953	$13,121	$12,644	$11,619	$11,824	$8,664
1975–76	16,659	22,649	17,065	13,986	13,672	12,906	15,196	16,942	17,400	15,820	15,921	16,116	10,901
1980–81	23,302	30,753	23,214	18,901	15,178	17,301	22,334	23,745	24,373	22,177	22,093	22,325	15,065
1982–83	27,196	35,540	26,921	22,056	17,601	20,072	25,557	27,488	28,293	25,567	26,393	26,691	16,595
1984–85	30,447	39,743	29,945	24,668	20,230	22,334	27,683	30,646	31,764	27,864	29,910	30,247	18,510
1985–86	32,392	42,268	31,787	26,277	20,918	23,770	29,088	32,750	34,033	29,590	31,402	31,732	19,436
1987–88	35,897	47,040	35,231	29,110	22,728	25,977	31,532	36,231	37,840	32,209	35,049	35,346	21,867
1989–90	40,133	52,810	39,392	32,689	25,030	28,990	34,559	40,416	42,365	35,516	39,464	39,817	24,601
1990–91	42,165	55,540	41,414	34,434	26,332	30,097	36,395	42,317	44,510	37,055	41,788	42,224	24,088
1991–92	43,851	57,433	42,929	35,745	30,916	30,456	37,783	43,641	45,638	38,959	44,376	44,793	25,673
1992–93	44,714	58,788	43,945	36,625	28,499	30,543	37,771	44,197	46,515	38,935	45,985	46,427	26,105
1993–94	46,364	60,649	45,278	37,630	28,828	32,729	40,584	45,920	48,019	41,040	47,465	47,880	28,435
1994–95	47,811	62,709	46,713	38,756	29,665	33,198	41,227	47,432	49,738	42,101	48,741	49,379	25,613
1995–96	49,309	64,540	47,966	39,696	30,344	34,136	42,996	48,837	51,172	43,295	50,466	50,819	31,915
1996–97	50,829	66,659	49,307	40,687	31,193	34,962	44,200	50,303	52,718	44,584	52,112	52,443	32,628
1997–98	52,335	68,731	50,828	41,830	32,449	35,484	45,268	51,638	54,114	45,919	54,039	54,379	33,592
1998–99	54,097	71,322	52,576	43,348	33,819	36,819	46,250	53,319	55,948	47,285	55,981	56,284	34,821
1999–2000	55,888	74,410	54,524	44,978	34,918	38,194	47,389	55,011	57,950	48,240	58,013	58,323	35,925
2001–02	59,742	80,792	58,724	48,796	46,959	41,798	46,569	58,524	62,013	50,837	62,818	63,088	33,139
2002–03	61,330	83,466	60,471	50,552	48,304	42,622	46,338	60,014	63,486	52,330	64,533	64,814	34,826
2003–04	62,579	85,333	61,746	51,798	49,065	43,648	47,725	60,874	64,340	53,076	66,666	66,932	36,322
2004–05	64,234	88,158	63,558	53,308	49,730	44,514	48,942	62,346	66,053	53,932	68,755	68,995	37,329
2005–06	66,172	91,208	65,714	55,106	50,883	45,896	50,425	64,158	67,951	55,405	71,016	71,263	38,549
2006–07	68,479	94,649	68,056	57,079	53,272	47,306	52,180	66,443	70,287	57,459	73,358	73,575	41,138
2007–08	71,101	98,595	70,830	59,293	55,356	49,389	54,377	68,988	72,852	59,672	76,169	76,378	43,402
2008–09	73,587	102,336	73,445	61,544	56,918	51,316	56,408	71,236	75,244	61,432	79,191	79,454	43,542
2009–10	74,620	103,682	74,125	62,245	57,791	52,185	56,803	72,178	76,147	62,264	80,379	80,597	44,748
2010–11	75,481	104,961	75,107	63,136	58,003	52,584	56,549	72,715	76,857	62,359	81,897	82,098	45,146
2011–12	76,567	107,090	76,177	64,011	58,350	53,359	56,898	73,496	77,843	62,553	83,540	83,701	47,805
2012–13	77,278	108,074	77,029	64,673	57,674	53,072	58,752	73,877	78,012	62,907	84,932	85,096	44,978
2013–14	78,733	109,998	78,693	66,093	58,240	54,566	59,161	75,491	79,897	63,714	86,178	86,390	44,598
2014–15	80,157	112,825	80,335	67,589	59,208	55,335	58,305	76,811	81,372	64,116	87,605	88,212	38,168
2015–16	82,224	115,539	82,147	69,378	60,911	57,306	60,341	78,869	83,389	66,018	89,867	90,309	31,296
2016–17	84,737	119,159	84,244	71,748	63,613	58,770	61,785	81,392	85,803	67,664	92,458	92,642	53,017
2017–18	86,870	122,069	86,130	73,474	65,176	60,816	62,748	83,433	87,900	68,723	94,819	94,941	57,030
2018–19	88,703	124,671	87,841	75,102	67,789	62,542	63,153	85,148	89,641	70,404	96,962	97,115	54,452
Males													
1975–76	17,414	22,902	17,209	14,174	14,430	13,579	15,761	17,661	18,121	16,339	16,784	16,946	11,378
1980–81	24,499	31,082	23,451	19,227	15,545	18,281	23,170	24,873	25,509	22,965	23,493	23,669	16,075
1982–83	28,664	35,956	27,262	22,586	18,160	21,225	26,541	28,851	29,661	26,524	28,159	28,380	17,346
1984–85	32,182	40,269	30,392	25,330	21,159	23,557	28,670	32,240	33,344	28,891	32,028	32,278	19,460
1985–86	34,294	42,833	32,273	27,094	21,693	25,238	30,267	34,528	35,786	30,758	33,656	33,900	20,412
1987–88	38,112	47,735	35,823	30,086	23,645	27,652	32,747	38,314	39,898	33,477	37,603	37,817	22,641
1989–90	42,763	53,650	40,131	33,781	25,933	31,162	35,980	42,959	44,834	37,081	42,312	42,595	25,218
1990–91	45,065	56,549	42,239	35,636	27,388	32,398	38,036	45,084	47,168	38,787	45,019	45,319	25,937
1991–92	46,848	58,494	43,814	36,969	33,359	32,843	39,422	46,483	48,401	40,811	47,733	48,042	26,825
1992–93	47,866	59,972	44,855	37,842	29,583	32,512	39,365	47,175	49,392	40,725	49,518	49,837	27,402
1993–94	49,579	61,857	46,229	38,794	29,815	34,796	42,251	48,956	50,989	42,938	51,076	51,397	30,783
1994–95	51,228	64,046	47,705	39,923	30,528	35,082	43,103	50,629	52,874	44,020	52,653	53,036	29,639
1995–96	52,814	65,949	49,037	40,858	30,940	36,135	44,624	52,163	54,448	45,209	54,364	54,649	33,301
1996–97	54,465	68,214	50,457	41,864	31,738	36,932	45,688	53,737	56,162	46,393	56,185	56,453	34,736
1997–98	56,115	70,468	52,041	43,017	33,070	37,481	46,822	55,191	57,744	47,690	58,293	58,576	36,157
1998–99	58,048	73,260	53,830	44,650	34,741	38,976	47,610	57,038	59,805	48,961	60,392	60,641	38,040
1999–2000	60,084	76,478	55,939	46,414	35,854	40,202	48,788	58,984	62,030	50,033	62,631	62,905	38,636
2001–02	64,320	83,356	60,300	50,518	48,844	44,519	48,049	62,835	66,577	52,360	67,871	68,100	33,395
2002–03	66,126	86,191	62,226	52,441	50,272	45,469	47,412	64,564	68,322	53,962	69,726	69,976	34,291
2003–04	67,485	88,262	63,466	53,649	50,985	46,214	48,973	65,476	69,248	54,623	72,021	72,250	35,604
2004–05	69,337	91,290	65,394	55,215	51,380	46,929	50,102	67,130	71,145	55,398	74,318	74,540	34,970
2005–06	71,569	94,733	67,654	57,099	52,519	48,256	51,811	69,191	73,353	56,858	76,941	77,143	38,215
2006–07	74,050	98,348	70,077	59,090	55,051	49,487	53,701	71,659	75,890	58,960	79,428	79,599	41,196
2007–08	76,957	102,605	72,943	61,374	57,134	51,795	56,170	74,394	78,671	61,189	82,734	82,903	42,995
2008–09	79,718	106,743	75,633	63,710	58,812	53,935	58,404	76,897	81,394	62,868	86,033	86,231	43,871
2009–10	80,881	108,225	76,400	64,451	59,793	54,947	58,647	77,948	82,423	63,697	87,382	87,546	44,500
2010–11	81,873	109,656	77,429	65,391	59,851	55,457	58,392	78,609	83,279	63,745	89,000	89,160	44,542
2011–12	83,150	112,066	78,560	66,303	60,066	56,367	58,807	79,544	84,444	63,918	90,840	90,976	45,250
2012–13	83,979	113,311	79,423	67,085	59,350	55,759	61,086	80,016	84,700	64,282	92,385	92,530	42,906
2013–14	85,545	115,466	81,178	68,492	59,777	57,218	61,511	81,703	86,646	65,076	93,898	94,065	44,277
2014–15	87,199	118,573	82,954	70,260	60,707	58,441	60,310	83,291	88,393	65,513	95,455	96,041	37,389
2015–16	89,361	121,535	84,781	72,272	62,390	60,428	62,468	85,367	90,464	67,352	98,016	98,466	30,050
2016–17	92,068	125,303	86,943	74,929	65,282	61,466	64,456	88,083	93,062	68,943	100,859	101,034	51,866
2017–18	94,444	128,467	88,936	76,816	67,177	63,623	65,005	90,319	95,363	69,908	103,606	103,694	61,840
2018–19	96,369	131,403	90,721	78,575	69,903	65,504	64,992	92,098	97,208	71,606	105,915	106,072	52,171

See notes at end of table.

Table 316.10. Average salary of full-time instructional faculty on 9-month contracts in degree-granting postsecondary institutions, by academic rank, control and level of institution, and sex: Selected years, 1970–71 through 2018–19—Continued

Sex and academic year	All faculty	Academic rank						Public institutions			Private institutions		
		Professor	Associate professor	Assistant professor	Instructor	Lecturer	No rank	Total	4-year	2-year	Total	4-year	2-year
1	2	3	4	5	6	7	8	9	10	11	12	13	14
Females													
1975–76	14,308	20,308	16,364	13,522	12,572	11,901	14,094	14,762	14,758	14,769	13,030	13,231	10,201
1980–81	19,996	27,959	22,295	18,302	14,854	16,168	20,843	20,673	20,608	20,778	18,073	18,326	13,892
1982–83	23,261	32,221	25,738	21,130	17,102	18,830	23,855	23,892	23,876	23,917	21,451	21,785	15,845
1984–85	25,941	35,824	28,517	23,575	19,362	21,004	26,050	26,566	26,813	26,172	24,186	24,560	17,575
1985–86	27,576	38,252	30,300	24,966	20,237	22,273	27,171	28,299	28,680	27,693	25,523	25,889	18,504
1987–88	30,499	42,371	33,528	27,600	21,962	24,370	29,605	31,215	31,820	30,228	28,621	28,946	21,215
1989–90	34,183	47,663	37,469	31,090	24,320	26,995	32,528	34,796	35,704	33,307	32,650	33,010	24,002
1990–91	35,881	49,728	39,329	32,724	25,534	28,111	34,179	36,459	37,573	34,720	34,359	34,898	22,585
1991–92	37,534	51,621	40,766	34,063	28,873	28,550	35,622	37,800	38,634	36,517	36,828	37,309	24,683
1992–93	38,385	52,755	41,861	35,032	27,700	28,922	35,792	38,356	39,470	36,710	38,460	38,987	25,068
1993–94	40,058	54,746	43,178	36,169	28,136	31,048	38,474	40,118	41,031	38,707	39,902	40,378	26,142
1994–95	41,369	56,555	44,626	37,352	29,072	31,677	38,967	41,548	42,663	39,812	40,908	41,815	22,851
1995–96	42,871	58,318	45,803	38,345	29,940	32,584	41,085	42,871	43,986	41,086	42,871	43,236	30,671
1996–97	44,325	60,160	47,101	39,350	30,819	33,415	42,474	44,306	45,402	42,531	44,374	44,726	30,661
1997–98	45,775	61,965	48,597	40,504	32,011	33,918	43,491	45,648	46,709	43,943	46,106	46,466	30,995
1998–99	47,421	64,236	50,347	41,894	33,152	35,115	44,723	47,247	48,355	45,457	47,874	48,204	31,524
1999–2000	48,997	67,079	52,091	43,367	34,228	36,607	45,865	48,714	50,168	46,340	49,737	50,052	32,951
2001–02	52,662	72,542	56,186	46,824	45,262	39,538	45,003	52,123	53,895	49,290	54,149	54,434	32,921
2002–03	54,105	75,028	57,716	48,380	46,573	40,265	45,251	53,435	55,121	50,717	55,881	56,158	35,296
2003–04	55,378	76,652	59,095	49,689	47,404	41,536	46,519	54,408	56,117	51,591	57,921	58,192	36,896
2004–05	56,926	79,160	60,809	51,154	48,351	42,455	47,860	55,780	57,714	52,566	59,919	60,143	39,291
2005–06	58,665	81,514	62,860	52,901	49,533	43,934	49,172	57,462	59,437	54,082	61,830	62,092	38,786
2006–07	60,926	84,857	65,131	54,909	51,828	45,505	50,814	59,677	61,713	56,121	64,194	64,428	41,099
2007–08	63,357	88,340	67,823	57,102	53,929	47,410	52,809	62,138	64,223	58,346	66,538	66,755	43,670
2008–09	65,662	91,528	70,393	59,291	55,431	49,184	54,663	64,230	66,391	60,195	69,375	69,668	43,344
2009–10	66,647	92,830	71,017	59,997	56,239	49,957	55,206	65,139	67,276	61,047	70,507	70,746	44,892
2010–11	67,473	94,041	72,003	60,888	56,566	50,270	54,985	65,632	67,935	61,193	72,091	72,306	45,518
2011–12	68,468	95,845	73,057	61,763	57,013	50,994	55,299	66,368	68,897	61,417	73,629	73,788	49,382
2012–13	69,124	96,563	73,966	62,321	56,361	50,963	56,777	66,703	69,083	61,774	74,987	75,149	46,407
2013–14	70,589	98,374	75,592	63,782	57,043	52,497	57,196	68,335	71,059	62,597	76,127	76,358	44,789
2014–15	71,792	100,783	77,115	65,009	58,020	52,901	56,616	69,384	72,288	62,971	77,504	78,089	38,841
2015–16	73,850	103,364	78,977	66,603	59,726	54,825	58,562	71,493	74,378	64,924	79,549	79,959	32,495
2016–17	76,199	106,881	81,037	68,701	62,277	56,601	59,568	73,826	76,696	66,616	81,976	82,146	53,866
2017–18	78,153	109,605	82,814	70,316	63,595	58,575	60,902	75,716	78,689	67,755	84,065	84,201	54,319
2018–19	79,995	111,945	84,488	71,856	66,103	60,188	61,616	77,450	80,437	69,425	86,179	86,311	56,267
	Constant 2018–19 dollars[1]												
Total													
1970–71	$81,030	$114,489	$86,474	$71,253	$59,673	$71,381	$78,631	$82,585	$83,656	$80,612	$74,074	$75,386	$55,238
1975–76	76,077	103,435	77,934	63,872	62,440	58,939	69,398	77,372	79,463	72,246	72,708	73,601	49,782
1980–81	68,129	89,913	67,871	55,261	44,376	50,583	65,299	69,424	71,260	64,840	64,594	65,272	44,046
1982–83	70,177	91,708	69,467	56,914	45,418	51,794	65,948	70,931	73,008	65,974	68,105	68,874	42,822
1984–85	72,908	95,168	71,706	59,070	48,442	53,481	66,289	73,384	76,062	66,723	71,622	72,429	44,324
1985–86	75,391	98,377	73,983	61,159	48,686	55,324	67,701	76,225	79,211	68,870	73,087	73,855	45,237
1987–88	78,483	102,845	77,026	63,644	49,690	56,793	68,940	79,213	82,730	70,419	76,628	77,278	47,808
1989–90	80,050	105,336	78,573	65,203	49,926	57,825	68,931	80,615	84,502	70,842	78,715	79,421	49,070
1990–91	79,745	105,039	78,323	65,123	49,800	56,921	68,832	80,032	84,179	70,079	79,031	79,856	45,556
1991–92	80,358	105,246	78,668	65,504	56,654	55,810	69,238	79,973	83,632	71,393	81,319	82,083	47,046
1992–93	79,457	104,466	78,090	65,083	50,643	54,275	67,119	78,538	82,657	69,188	81,715	82,502	46,389
1993–94	80,310	105,053	78,427	65,181	49,934	56,690	70,297	79,540	83,176	71,086	82,216	82,934	49,253
1994–95	80,508	105,593	78,659	65,260	49,951	55,901	69,421	79,869	83,752	70,893	82,073	83,148	43,129
1995–96	80,832	105,799	78,629	65,073	49,743	55,958	70,482	80,058	83,886	70,973	82,728	83,307	52,318
1996–97	81,012	106,242	78,586	64,847	49,716	55,722	70,447	80,173	84,022	71,058	83,056	83,584	52,003
1997–98	81,950	107,625	79,590	65,500	50,811	55,564	70,884	80,858	84,737	71,904	84,619	85,151	52,600
1998–99	83,267	109,781	80,926	66,723	52,055	56,672	71,190	82,070	86,116	72,782	86,168	86,634	53,597
1999–2000	83,611	111,321	81,570	67,290	52,239	57,140	70,896	82,299	86,695	72,170	86,790	87,254	53,745
2001–02	84,912	114,831	83,466	69,354	66,744	59,409	66,189	83,181	88,140	72,256	89,284	89,669	47,101
2002–03	85,295	116,081	84,100	70,306	67,179	59,277	64,445	83,465	88,294	72,779	89,750	90,141	48,434
2003–04	85,169	116,137	84,035	70,496	66,776	59,404	64,953	82,849	87,566	72,236	90,731	91,093	49,433
2004–05	84,868	116,477	83,974	70,432	65,704	58,813	64,663	82,372	87,270	71,256	90,841	91,158	49,320
2005–06	84,221	116,085	83,638	70,136	64,761	58,414	64,178	81,658	86,485	70,517	90,386	90,701	49,063
2006–07	84,960	117,428	84,436	70,817	66,093	58,691	64,738	82,434	87,202	71,287	91,013	91,282	51,039
2007–08	85,061	117,953	84,737	70,934	66,225	59,086	65,053	82,533	87,156	71,388	91,124	91,374	51,924
2008–09	86,823	120,743	86,656	72,613	67,155	60,547	66,554	84,050	88,778	72,482	93,435	93,745	51,373
2009–10	87,198	121,158	86,619	72,737	67,532	60,982	66,378	84,345	88,982	72,760	93,928	94,182	52,291
2010–11	86,468	120,239	86,040	72,326	66,446	60,238	64,780	83,299	88,044	71,436	93,818	94,048	51,717
2011–12	85,215	119,186	84,781	71,241	64,941	59,386	63,325	81,797	86,635	69,618	92,976	93,155	53,205
2012–13	84,599	118,311	84,326	70,799	63,137	58,100	64,318	80,875	85,402	68,866	92,978	93,158	49,239
2013–14	84,866	118,566	84,822	71,241	62,777	58,816	63,769	81,372	86,121	68,677	92,891	93,119	48,072
2014–15	85,776	120,735	85,967	72,327	63,358	59,214	62,393	82,195	87,076	68,611	93,746	94,396	40,844
2015–16	87,399	122,811	87,317	73,744	64,744	60,912	64,138	83,832	88,636	70,172	95,523	95,992	33,265
2016–17	88,443	124,370	87,928	74,886	66,395	61,340	64,487	84,952	89,556	70,624	96,501	96,693	55,336
2017–18	88,670	124,599	87,915	74,996	66,526	62,077	64,049	85,162	89,721	70,147	96,784	96,909	58,212
2018–19	88,703	124,671	87,841	75,102	67,789	62,542	63,153	85,148	89,641	70,404	96,962	97,115	54,452

See notes at end of table.

Table 316.10. Average salary of full-time instructional faculty on 9-month contracts in degree-granting postsecondary institutions, by academic rank, control and level of institution, and sex: Selected years, 1970–71 through 2018–19—Continued

Sex and academic year	All faculty	Academic rank						Public institutions			Private institutions		
		Professor	Associate professor	Assistant professor	Instructor	Lecturer	No rank	Total	4-year	2-year	Total	4-year	2-year
1	2	3	4	5	6	7	8	9	10	11	12	13	14
Males													
1975–76	79,525	104,589	78,589	64,732	65,899	62,013	71,977	80,656	82,754	74,620	76,651	77,388	51,960
1980–81	71,628	90,875	68,564	56,215	45,449	53,449	67,743	72,722	74,581	67,143	68,687	69,202	46,999
1982–83	73,965	92,781	70,347	58,281	46,860	54,769	68,487	74,448	76,538	68,443	72,662	73,232	44,760
1984–85	77,063	96,428	72,776	60,655	50,667	56,409	68,653	77,201	79,845	69,182	76,694	77,292	46,599
1985–86	79,818	99,692	75,114	63,060	50,490	58,741	70,445	80,363	83,291	71,588	78,333	78,901	47,508
1987–88	83,324	104,363	78,321	65,779	51,695	60,457	71,595	83,767	87,230	73,192	82,212	82,680	49,501
1989–90	85,297	107,012	80,046	67,380	51,726	62,156	71,767	85,687	89,428	73,964	84,398	84,960	50,301
1990–91	85,229	106,947	79,883	67,395	51,798	61,272	71,935	85,265	89,205	73,355	85,142	85,709	49,052
1991–92	85,850	107,190	80,290	67,745	61,131	60,186	72,241	85,181	88,696	74,787	87,471	88,037	49,157
1992–93	85,057	106,571	79,709	67,245	52,569	57,774	69,952	83,830	87,771	72,368	87,994	88,561	48,693
1993–94	85,877	107,144	80,075	67,196	51,644	60,271	73,184	84,798	88,320	74,374	88,471	89,027	53,321
1994–95	86,262	107,846	80,329	67,225	51,405	59,074	72,581	85,253	89,032	74,124	88,661	89,306	49,909
1995–96	86,577	108,109	80,386	66,977	50,720	59,235	73,152	85,509	89,256	74,110	89,117	89,585	54,590
1996–97	86,806	108,720	80,418	66,723	50,584	58,862	72,818	85,646	89,511	73,941	89,548	89,974	55,362
1997–98	87,870	110,344	81,490	67,359	51,784	58,691	73,317	86,423	90,420	74,677	91,280	91,724	56,618
1998–99	89,349	112,765	82,856	68,726	53,475	59,992	73,283	87,795	92,054	75,363	92,957	93,340	58,553
1999–2000	89,888	114,414	83,687	69,437	53,639	60,144	72,989	88,242	92,800	74,852	93,699	94,108	57,801
2001–02	91,420	118,475	85,705	71,802	69,422	63,276	68,294	89,308	94,627	74,421	96,466	96,791	47,465
2002–03	91,966	119,871	86,541	72,932	69,916	63,236	65,939	89,793	95,019	75,048	96,971	97,320	47,690
2003–04	91,845	120,123	86,377	73,015	69,389	62,896	66,652	89,111	94,245	74,341	98,020	98,330	48,457
2004–05	91,610	120,614	86,400	72,952	67,884	62,004	66,196	88,694	93,999	73,193	98,191	98,485	46,203
2005–06	91,090	120,572	86,107	72,673	66,844	61,418	65,943	88,063	93,361	72,366	97,927	98,184	48,639
2006–07	91,871	122,018	86,943	73,311	68,300	61,397	66,625	88,905	94,155	73,150	98,543	98,756	51,111
2007–08	92,066	122,751	87,265	73,425	68,351	61,964	67,198	89,001	94,117	73,203	98,978	99,180	51,437
2008–09	94,057	125,942	89,236	75,169	69,391	63,636	68,909	90,728	96,034	74,176	101,508	101,741	51,762
2009–10	94,515	126,468	89,278	75,315	69,871	64,209	68,532	91,086	96,316	74,434	102,111	102,303	52,001
2010–11	93,790	125,618	88,699	74,909	68,563	63,529	66,891	90,051	95,401	73,024	101,955	102,138	51,026
2011–12	92,542	124,723	87,433	73,792	66,850	62,733	65,449	88,529	93,982	71,138	101,100	101,251	50,361
2012–13	91,934	124,045	86,946	73,440	64,972	61,041	66,872	87,596	92,723	70,372	101,136	101,295	46,971
2013–14	92,209	124,460	87,501	73,827	64,433	61,675	66,302	88,067	93,395	70,145	101,212	101,392	47,725
2014–15	93,311	126,884	88,769	75,185	64,963	62,538	64,537	89,129	94,590	70,105	102,146	102,773	40,010
2015–16	94,984	129,184	90,116	76,821	66,316	64,230	66,399	90,740	96,157	71,590	104,185	104,662	31,941
2016–17	96,094	130,783	90,746	78,205	68,137	64,154	67,274	91,935	97,132	71,958	105,270	105,452	54,134
2017–18	96,401	131,129	90,779	78,408	68,569	64,941	66,352	92,191	97,339	71,357	105,753	105,843	63,121
2018–19	96,369	131,403	90,721	78,575	69,903	65,504	64,992	92,098	97,208	71,606	105,915	106,072	52,171
Females													
1975–76	65,340	92,743	74,731	61,752	57,413	54,348	64,365	67,418	67,400	67,447	59,508	60,423	46,584
1980–81	58,463	81,745	65,185	53,510	43,429	47,271	60,939	60,442	60,252	60,749	52,841	53,580	40,616
1982–83	60,023	83,144	66,415	54,524	44,130	48,589	61,556	61,651	61,610	61,716	55,353	56,214	40,887
1984–85	62,118	85,784	68,286	56,452	46,364	50,296	62,379	63,615	64,206	62,671	57,915	58,811	42,085
1985–86	64,182	89,030	70,522	58,108	47,101	51,840	63,240	65,865	66,752	64,455	59,404	60,256	43,067
1987–88	66,681	92,637	73,303	60,343	48,016	53,281	64,726	68,246	69,569	66,088	62,575	63,285	46,383
1989–90	68,182	95,069	74,736	62,012	48,509	53,846	64,882	69,406	71,217	66,435	65,124	65,843	47,875
1990–91	67,858	94,048	74,381	61,889	48,291	53,165	64,640	68,953	71,060	65,664	64,980	66,000	42,714
1991–92	68,781	94,596	74,704	62,421	52,910	52,318	65,278	69,269	70,797	66,918	67,487	68,369	45,232
1992–93	68,210	93,747	74,387	62,253	49,224	51,395	63,602	68,158	70,138	65,234	68,344	69,280	44,546
1993–94	69,387	94,828	74,790	62,649	48,736	53,780	66,642	69,489	71,070	67,046	69,116	69,940	45,281
1994–95	69,661	95,231	75,145	62,896	48,954	53,339	65,615	69,961	71,839	67,038	68,884	70,411	38,479
1995–96	70,277	95,599	75,084	62,859	49,080	53,414	67,349	70,277	72,105	67,352	70,278	70,876	50,279
1996–97	70,645	95,883	75,070	62,716	49,120	53,257	67,696	70,614	72,362	67,786	70,723	71,285	48,868
1997–98	71,678	97,029	76,098	63,424	50,126	53,111	68,101	71,479	73,140	68,810	72,197	72,761	48,535
1998–99	72,991	98,874	77,496	64,484	51,029	54,050	68,838	72,724	74,429	69,968	73,690	74,197	48,522
1999–2000	73,301	100,353	77,930	64,879	51,206	54,766	68,616	72,878	75,053	69,327	74,409	74,880	49,296
2001–02	74,849	103,105	79,859	66,552	64,331	56,195	63,963	74,083	76,603	70,056	76,963	77,369	46,791
2002–03	75,246	104,346	80,270	67,284	64,772	55,999	62,933	74,315	76,660	70,535	77,717	78,103	49,089
2003–04	75,368	104,322	80,428	67,626	64,516	56,530	63,312	74,048	76,375	70,215	78,830	79,198	50,215
2004–05	75,212	104,588	80,342	67,586	63,882	56,093	63,233	73,698	76,253	69,452	79,166	79,462	51,912
2005–06	74,666	103,747	80,005	67,330	63,044	55,917	62,584	73,135	75,648	68,834	78,695	79,028	49,365
2006–07	75,589	105,280	80,806	68,124	64,301	56,457	63,043	74,040	76,565	69,628	79,643	79,933	50,991
2007–08	75,796	105,685	81,139	68,314	64,518	56,718	63,178	74,338	76,832	69,802	79,602	79,862	52,245
2008–09	77,472	107,991	83,054	69,955	65,401	58,031	64,495	75,783	78,333	71,023	81,853	82,199	51,140
2009–10	77,881	108,478	82,987	70,110	65,719	58,378	64,511	76,119	78,616	71,337	82,391	82,671	52,459
2010–11	77,295	107,730	82,484	69,751	64,799	57,588	62,988	75,185	77,824	70,100	82,584	82,830	52,144
2011–12	76,202	106,671	81,308	68,739	63,453	56,754	61,545	73,864	76,679	68,354	81,945	82,122	54,960
2012–13	75,672	105,710	80,973	68,225	61,700	55,791	62,156	73,022	75,627	67,626	82,090	82,268	50,803
2013–14	76,088	106,036	81,480	68,751	61,486	56,586	61,651	73,658	76,594	67,472	82,056	82,305	48,278
2014–15	76,825	107,848	82,521	69,566	62,088	56,609	60,584	74,248	77,355	67,385	82,937	83,563	41,564
2015–16	78,497	109,869	83,948	70,795	63,485	58,275	62,247	75,992	79,059	69,010	84,555	84,991	34,540
2016–17	79,532	111,555	84,581	71,706	65,000	59,076	62,173	77,055	80,050	69,529	85,561	85,739	56,221
2017–18	79,773	111,876	84,530	71,774	64,913	59,789	62,164	77,285	80,319	69,159	85,807	85,946	55,445
2018–19	79,995	111,945	84,488	71,856	66,103	60,188	61,616	77,450	80,437	69,425	86,179	86,311	56,267

[1]Constant dollars based on the Consumer Price Index, prepared by the Bureau of Labor Statistics, U.S. Department of Labor, adjusted to an academic-year basis.
NOTE: Data exclude instructional faculty at medical schools. Data through 1995–96 are for institutions of higher education, while later data are for degree-granting institutions. Degree-granting institutions grant associate's or higher degrees and participate in Title IV federal financial aid programs. Data for 1987–88 and later years include imputations for nonrespondent institutions. Some data have been revised from previously published figures.

SOURCE: U.S. Department of Education, National Center for Education Statistics, Higher Education General Information Survey (HEGIS), "Faculty Salaries, Tenure, and Fringe Benefits" surveys, 1970–71 through 1985–86; Integrated Postsecondary Education Data System (IPEDS), "Salaries, Tenure, and Fringe Benefits of Full-Time Instructional Faculty Survey" (IPEDS-SA:87–99); and IPEDS, Winter 2001–02 through Winter 2011–12 and Spring 2013 through Spring 2019, Human Resources component, Salaries section. (This table was prepared November 2019.)

Table 316.20. Average salary of full-time instructional faculty on 9-month contracts in degree-granting postsecondary institutions, by academic rank, sex, and control and level of institution: Selected years, 1999–2000 through 2018–19

Academic year, control and level of institution	Constant 2018–19 dollars[1]	Current dollars												
		All faculty			Academic rank									
					Professor			Associate professor						
	All faculty, total	Total	Males	Females	Total	Males	Females	Total	Males	Females	Assistant professor	Instructor	Lecturer	No academic rank
1	2	3	4	5	6	7	8	9	10	11	12	13	14	15
1999–2000														
All institutions	$83,611	$55,888	$60,084	$48,997	$74,410	$76,478	$67,079	$54,524	$55,939	$52,091	$44,978	$34,918	$38,194	$47,389
Public	82,299	55,011	58,984	48,714	72,475	74,501	65,568	54,641	55,992	52,305	45,285	35,007	37,403	47,990
4-year	86,695	57,950	62,030	50,168	75,204	76,530	69,619	55,681	56,776	53,599	45,822	33,528	37,261	40,579
Doctoral[2]	93,133	62,253	66,882	52,287	81,182	82,445	74,653	57,744	58,999	55,156	48,190	33,345	38,883	39,350
Master's[3]	78,951	52,773	55,565	48,235	66,588	67,128	64,863	53,048	53,686	51,977	43,396	33,214	34,448	43,052
Other 4-year	71,611	47,867	49,829	44,577	60,360	60,748	59,052	49,567	50,133	48,548	42,306	35,754	36,088	38,330
2-year	72,170	48,240	50,033	46,340	57,806	59,441	55,501	48,056	49,425	46,711	41,984	37,634	40,061	48,233
Nonprofit	87,027	58,172	62,788	49,881	78,512	80,557	70,609	54,300	55,836	51,687	44,423	34,670	40,761	41,415
4-year	87,406	58,425	63,028	50,117	78,604	80,622	70,774	54,388	55,898	51,809	44,502	34,813	40,783	41,761
Doctoral[2]	107,525	71,873	77,214	59,586	95,182	96,768	87,342	62,503	63,951	59,536	52,134	39,721	42,693	45,887
Master's[3]	74,610	49,871	52,642	45,718	62,539	63,603	59,353	50,176	51,470	48,165	41,447	33,991	37,923	44,153
Other 4-year	69,979	46,776	48,847	43,544	60,200	60,757	58,364	46,822	47,135	46,365	38,775	31,574	33,058	35,120
2-year	56,226	37,583	39,933	34,733	39,454	38,431	40,571	36,349	37,342	35,608	31,818	27,696	25,965	40,373
For-profit	44,198	29,543	30,023	28,942	45,505	44,248	49,693	48,469	53,548	43,389	33,043	29,894	‡	27,958
2009–10														
All institutions	87,198	74,620	80,881	66,647	103,682	108,225	92,830	74,125	76,400	71,017	62,245	57,791	52,185	56,803
Public	84,345	72,178	77,948	65,139	99,208	103,746	88,815	73,379	75,687	70,256	62,160	59,310	50,228	55,864
4-year	88,982	76,147	82,423	67,276	103,948	107,191	95,048	75,251	77,282	72,298	63,442	46,028	50,104	54,005
Doctoral[2]	95,647	81,850	89,186	70,307	113,063	115,829	103,793	78,539	80,830	74,963	66,902	44,406	50,313	53,135
Master's[3]	79,746	68,243	71,574	64,239	87,917	88,929	85,883	70,332	71,340	69,036	59,396	44,422	49,746	55,765
Other 4-year	71,519	61,202	63,678	58,349	76,448	79,143	72,073	65,003	66,297	63,338	55,055	54,050	49,432	54,487
2-year	72,760	62,264	63,697	61,047	72,377	74,423	70,429	60,632	61,565	59,852	54,161	65,503	53,548	56,239
Nonprofit	94,171	80,587	87,600	70,676	112,146	116,401	101,119	75,565	77,764	72,502	62,395	47,842	57,508	62,242
4-year	94,347	80,738	87,720	70,834	112,252	116,472	101,290	75,664	77,827	72,642	62,465	47,885	57,520	62,542
Doctoral[2]	111,574	95,480	104,514	80,888	134,776	138,354	123,283	85,864	88,699	81,499	71,973	53,825	58,932	66,634
Master's[3]	76,863	65,776	68,776	62,128	82,516	84,062	79,452	66,524	67,508	65,309	55,469	45,305	53,637	60,591
Other 4-year	75,506	64,614	67,178	61,326	84,869	85,528	83,480	64,747	64,949	64,478	53,130	42,145	52,422	52,775
2-year	53,440	45,731	44,417	46,529	53,063	55,046	51,310	45,768	45,863	45,717	42,706	46,010	32,393	43,562
For-profit	64,087	54,842	56,689	52,925	79,574	81,765	75,817	71,376	72,429	70,199	66,027	41,742	‡	53,705
2017–18														
All institutions	88,670	86,870	94,444	78,153	122,069	128,467	109,605	86,130	88,936	82,814	73,474	65,176	60,816	62,748
Public	85,162	83,433	90,319	75,716	115,675	121,960	103,855	85,030	87,868	81,670	73,503	66,561	58,433	60,605
4-year	89,721	87,900	95,363	78,689	122,122	126,856	111,746	87,498	89,986	84,359	75,507	58,699	58,372	61,519
Doctoral[2]	96,259	94,305	102,935	82,930	132,004	136,342	121,379	91,828	94,614	88,200	79,942	53,367	59,479	60,723
Master's[3]	76,795	75,236	78,724	71,382	96,212	97,611	93,833	78,316	79,301	77,145	67,252	49,820	55,529	58,318
Other 4-year	70,607	69,173	70,967	67,421	80,794	83,274	77,490	70,240	71,706	68,646	61,212	74,216	52,801	62,706
2-year	70,147	68,723	69,908	67,755	79,170	80,694	77,865	67,430	68,273	66,795	60,343	72,741	60,610	60,167
Nonprofit	97,168	95,195	103,979	84,411	134,378	140,602	121,408	88,307	91,064	85,057	73,531	58,117	68,198	75,680
4-year	97,257	95,282	104,059	84,492	134,437	140,638	121,497	88,323	91,076	85,075	73,566	58,237	68,205	75,824
Doctoral[2]	113,020	110,726	122,121	95,349	160,179	166,375	144,995	99,148	102,838	94,590	84,103	63,983	69,754	81,783
Master's[3]	76,138	74,593	77,835	71,075	92,484	93,658	90,537	74,409	75,698	72,958	63,298	53,927	62,123	75,222
Other 4-year	76,563	75,008	77,176	72,641	98,505	98,427	98,635	75,740	75,898	75,568	61,552	48,098	63,604	59,277
2-year	58,221	57,039	54,468	58,676	70,019	71,602	68,984	72,127	71,674	72,362	54,995	50,491	62,508	52,523
For-profit	57,318	56,155	59,043	53,543	70,020	69,939	70,218	65,084	62,200	67,616	53,762	49,334	‡	57,206
2018–19														
All institutions	88,703	88,703	96,369	79,995	124,671	131,403	111,945	87,841	90,721	84,488	75,102	67,789	62,542	63,153
Public	85,148	85,148	92,098	77,450	117,969	124,480	106,060	86,469	89,441	83,006	75,061	69,162	59,871	61,467
4-year	89,641	89,641	97,208	80,437	124,169	129,276	113,465	89,025	91,662	85,753	77,107	60,529	59,834	61,870
Doctoral[2]	95,942	95,942	104,629	84,700	134,213	138,903	123,296	93,266	96,135	89,578	81,563	54,719	60,750	62,179
Master's[3]	76,321	76,321	79,871	72,439	97,246	98,841	94,604	79,107	80,215	77,829	68,215	50,896	56,853	56,557
Other 4-year	70,858	70,858	72,706	69,088	81,276	84,316	77,514	72,126	73,849	70,335	62,406	77,157	54,627	62,577
2-year	70,404	70,404	71,606	69,425	80,480	81,994	79,180	68,067	68,680	67,611	60,956	75,441	61,278	61,275
Nonprofit	97,338	97,338	106,353	86,474	137,539	144,262	123,986	90,503	93,211	87,354	75,213	60,132	70,481	76,366
4-year	97,447	97,447	106,459	86,570	137,587	144,299	124,045	90,523	93,226	87,376	75,251	60,374	70,501	76,569
Doctoral[2]	112,794	112,794	124,378	97,525	163,299	169,943	147,610	101,284	104,875	96,946	86,034	66,825	72,311	81,379
Master's[3]	75,367	75,367	78,459	72,054	92,990	94,243	90,993	75,515	76,821	74,049	64,279	54,067	63,482	76,307
Other 4-year	76,487	76,487	78,890	73,936	100,460	100,635	100,182	77,412	77,643	77,162	62,770	49,352	64,320	61,071
2-year	57,120	57,120	54,179	59,181	77,990	75,217	80,234	76,058	73,806	76,991	57,190	46,528	59,064	54,550
For-profit	53,692	53,692	53,816	53,553	82,216	84,096	79,253	72,399	71,922	72,834	65,524	61,083	82,871	44,335

‡Reporting standards not met (too few cases).
[1]Constant dollars based on the Consumer Price Index, prepared by the Bureau of Labor Statistics, U.S. Department of Labor, adjusted to an academic-year basis.
[2]Institutions that awarded 20 or more doctor's degrees during the previous academic year.
[3]Institutions that awarded 20 or more master's degrees, but less than 20 doctor's degrees, during the previous academic year. This definition differs from the definition of master's institutions that is used in some *Digest* tables that present postsecondary finance data.

NOTE: Data exclude instructional faculty at medical schools. Degree-granting institutions grant associate's or higher degrees and participate in Title IV federal financial aid programs. Some data have been revised from previously published figures.
SOURCE: U.S. Department of Education, National Center for Education Statistics, Integrated Postsecondary Education Data System (IPEDS), "Salaries, Tenure, and Fringe Benefits of Full-Time Instructional Faculty Survey" (IPEDS-SA:99); and IPEDS, Winter 2009–10, Spring 2018, and Spring 2019, Human Resources component, Salaries section. (This table was prepared November 2019.)

Table 316.30. Average salary of full-time instructional faculty on 9-month contracts in degree-granting postsecondary institutions, by control and level of institution and state or jurisdiction: 2018–19

[In current dollars]

State or jurisdiction	All institutions	Public institutions						Nonprofit institutions						For-profit institutions
		Total	4-year institutions				2-year	Total	4-year institutions				2-year	
			Total	Doctoral[1]	Master's[2]	Other			Total	Doctoral[1]	Master's[2]	Other		
1	2	3	4	5	6	7	8	9	10	11	12	13	14	15
United States	**$88,703**	**$85,148**	**$89,641**	**$95,942**	**$76,321**	**$70,858**	**$70,404**	**$97,338**	**$97,447**	**$112,794**	**$75,367**	**$76,487**	**$57,120**	**$53,692**
Alabama	73,892	76,153	82,523	87,030	67,788	†	56,046	59,473	59,473	64,032	51,251	56,563	†	66,321
Alaska	81,258	82,350	82,350	85,871	80,408	†	†	54,804	54,776	†	54,776	†	55,106	†
Arizona	86,878	87,562	91,434	92,499	84,373	51,429	75,774	76,004	76,004	†	76,004	†	†	69,139
Arkansas	63,583	64,092	69,771	75,132	58,079	62,110	46,908	60,731	60,760	66,175	64,630	56,901	56,927	†
California	109,371	107,450	113,518	124,260	89,765	100,951	96,416	116,271	116,271	125,713	86,593	107,407	†	78,026
Colorado	85,512	84,218	86,808	94,760	63,813	64,189	58,228	93,307	93,307	95,360	88,867	†	†	52,575
Connecticut	107,248	94,380	99,571	110,044	88,482	†	76,987	119,082	119,082	126,266	92,376	87,925	†	93,049
Delaware	105,103	105,831	105,831	112,746	†	70,754	†	73,575	76,679	†	76,679	†	60,714	‡
District of Columbia	115,372	83,712	83,712	143,504	76,695	†	†	117,754	117,754	118,087	76,837	†	†	72,060
Florida	82,728	81,901	82,351	96,182	80,302	60,767	60,530	85,314	85,314	97,046	76,818	66,449	†	47,728
Georgia	78,218	76,684	78,017	83,759	62,325	58,983	48,700	83,669	83,897	105,122	71,417	63,259	74,961	53,257
Hawaii	92,066	93,852	101,893	104,939	†	80,566	76,092	79,474	79,474	†	76,438	113,483	†	†
Idaho	69,774	70,205	73,572	75,293	†	55,921	56,131	64,536	64,536	58,681	†	69,499	†	†
Illinois	93,330	85,996	89,931	92,948	75,549	†	78,928	102,805	102,853	120,598	72,204	65,738	52,817	61,339
Indiana	84,101	83,888	89,052	95,646	68,852	53,069	50,839	84,523	84,523	96,083	66,668	70,168	†	†
Iowa	78,834	85,361	95,342	95,342	†	†	62,148	67,766	67,766	74,069	61,064	69,618	†	47,400
Kansas	70,493	73,337	80,161	85,028	64,394	†	56,420	52,935	52,935	55,198	56,614	46,651	†	†
Kentucky	68,514	70,156	76,008	77,858	57,088	†	52,135	62,129	62,129	66,242	55,072	67,632	†	†
Louisiana	70,111	65,833	71,292	80,203	58,696	53,091	45,262	88,344	88,344	94,979	60,053	52,146	†	†
Maine	80,266	74,073	78,653	83,844	63,879	64,458	58,663	88,465	88,653	69,418	57,518	101,547	59,714	†
Maryland	85,635	84,622	89,415	91,922	77,518	†	75,021	88,980	88,980	102,224	74,276	71,745	†	68,722
Massachusetts	112,141	89,950	97,295	104,909	84,239	†	66,164	122,612	122,616	135,715	97,377	96,010	‡	†
Michigan	94,098	97,490	99,824	102,466	81,216	81,876	82,986	71,706	71,706	92,595	70,347	66,607	†	†
Minnesota	83,875	86,259	93,541	107,095	81,131	66,067	72,612	78,517	78,558	77,051	70,483	82,719	39,147	†
Mississippi	62,811	62,897	70,387	73,043	57,060	†	52,000	61,895	61,895	66,812	73,842	44,588	†	66,406
Missouri	77,741	71,761	75,769	84,393	63,142	†	59,229	87,487	87,487	102,883	66,113	57,372	†	70,587
Montana	67,356	70,891	73,818	79,165	62,103	55,955	50,541	48,185	52,829	†	54,770	51,540	19,102	†
Nebraska	78,724	80,878	85,080	91,660	67,015	†	62,348	71,423	71,423	88,428	60,138	58,369	†	†
Nevada	86,920	86,936	86,936	94,254	†	73,064	†	78,922	78,922	‡	75,153	†	†	†
New Hampshire	99,666	91,918	97,833	107,879	81,376	86,524	67,223	110,282	110,282	151,186	73,577	75,882	†	†
New Jersey	109,290	105,646	113,212	114,387	107,508	†	77,802	118,043	118,043	133,590	86,989	75,976	†	47,838
New Mexico	68,015	67,968	73,692	79,724	63,697	50,155	54,281	69,321	69,321	†	69,321	†	†	‡
New York	100,116	89,939	94,158	109,000	87,074	76,926	80,591	110,324	110,401	120,468	83,498	91,751	74,311	32,266
North Carolina	80,384	76,047	87,134	90,736	73,652	74,259	52,332	91,946	92,261	114,336	62,777	66,258	42,156	69,724
North Dakota	70,099	71,372	73,066	80,997	60,300	53,745	58,228	58,573	58,573	65,711	†	52,476	†	†
Ohio	82,517	85,652	89,711	92,721	60,947	71,151	67,227	76,009	76,033	82,760	67,807	73,841	38,750	52,935
Oklahoma	69,602	68,926	73,417	80,692	62,644	49,601	49,942	72,641	72,641	84,449	61,677	39,807	†	47,743
Oregon	81,965	82,613	86,583	90,928	67,682	68,618	74,108	79,690	79,690	81,513	59,044	82,408	†	†
Pennsylvania	94,446	91,562	95,507	103,726	88,122	76,231	66,538	97,395	97,783	111,061	73,930	87,191	58,185	65,139
Rhode Island	101,815	82,037	87,541	94,465	73,070	†	62,179	115,224	115,224	143,426	93,540	†	†	†
South Carolina	70,530	72,922	82,126	95,713	69,639	62,144	50,093	61,262	61,370	67,269	62,679	56,839	54,598	85,949
South Dakota	66,146	67,919	70,116	71,599	70,130	51,717	58,490	57,038	57,038	†	58,371	47,743	†	†
Tennessee	79,423	74,886	81,011	83,488	71,093	†	54,383	89,209	89,209	108,571	67,216	51,752	†	62,658
Texas	82,383	80,147	87,608	92,277	70,029	59,898	62,140	93,080	93,171	106,557	71,423	58,708	38,602	41,630
Utah	78,986	78,672	80,572	93,980	71,013	62,928	59,680	84,893	84,893	114,059	76,370	†	†	‡
Vermont	82,642	83,320	83,320	92,534	60,336	57,874	†	82,019	82,019	†	84,976	55,726	†	†
Virginia	85,083	87,337	92,550	96,225	72,864	76,232	64,269	77,580	77,580	86,742	58,179	66,823	†	52,885
Washington	84,110	84,946	86,387	103,758	85,600	65,680	64,400	81,044	81,044	87,552	66,500	79,105	†	83,252
West Virginia	66,772	68,500	71,462	79,844	59,915	57,514	49,589	52,397	52,397	56,711	49,888	51,193	†	†
Wisconsin	79,637	81,433	82,140	90,995	63,582	95,928	79,600	72,322	72,322	79,641	67,029	67,740	†	†
Wyoming	76,182	76,182	90,173	90,173	†	†	59,268	†	†	†	†	†	†	†
U.S. Service Academies	109,778	109,778	109,778	†	†	109,778	†	†	†	†	†	†	†	†
Other jurisdictions	**60,987**	**64,575**	**68,770**	**70,847**	**76,258**	**55,570**	**31,877**	**53,066**	**53,066**	**60,481**	**50,584**	**37,846**	**†**	**25,857**
American Samoa	29,068	29,068	29,068	†	†	29,068	†	†	†	†	†	†	†	†
Federated States of Micronesia	25,272	25,272	†	†	†	†	25,272	†	†	†	†	†	†	†
Guam	66,511	66,511	69,979	†	69,979	†	57,347	†	†	†	†	†	†	†
Marshall Islands	†	†	†	†	†	†	†	†	†	†	†	†	†	†
Northern Marianas	51,249	51,249	51,249	†	†	51,249	†	†	†	†	†	†	†	†
Palau	20,492	20,492	†	†	†	†	20,492	†	†	†	†	†	†	†
Puerto Rico	62,761	68,400	70,311	70,847	79,149	59,601	26,460	53,066	53,066	60,481	50,584	37,846	†	25,857
U.S. Virgin Islands	71,002	71,002	71,002	†	71,002	†	†	†	†	†	†	†	†	†

†Not applicable.
‡Reporting standards not met (too few cases).
[1]Institutions that awarded 20 or more doctor's degrees during the previous academic year.
[2]Institutions that awarded 20 or more master's degrees, but less than 20 doctor's degrees, during the previous academic year. This definition differs from the definition of master's institutions that is used in some *Digest* tables that present postsecondary finance data.

NOTE: Data exclude instructional faculty at medical schools. Degree-granting institutions grant associate's or higher degrees and participate in Title IV federal financial aid programs. Data include imputations for nonrespondent institutions.
SOURCE: U.S. Department of Education, National Center for Education Statistics, Integrated Postsecondary Education Data System (IPEDS), Spring 2019, Human Resources component, Salaries section. (This table was prepared November 2019.)

Table 316.50. Average salary of full-time instructional faculty on 9-month contracts in 4-year degree-granting postsecondary institutions, by control and classification of institution, academic rank of faculty, and state or jurisdiction: 2018–19

[In current dollars]

State or jurisdiction	Public doctoral[1]			Public master's[2]			Nonprofit doctoral[1]			Nonprofit master's[2]		
	Professor	Associate professor	Assistant professor	Professor	Associate professor	Assistant professor	Professor	Associate professor	Assistant professor	Professor	Associate professor	Assistant professor
1	2	3	4	5	6	7	8	9	10	11	12	13
United States	**$134,213**	**$93,266**	**$81,563**	**$97,246**	**$79,107**	**$68,215**	**$163,299**	**$101,284**	**$86,034**	**$92,990**	**$75,515**	**$64,279**
Alabama	129,750	90,765	76,975	86,003	71,112	61,776	101,006	73,957	43,630	56,331	54,653	47,333
Alaska	105,822	87,480	73,678	103,252	85,404	69,466	†	†	†	66,703	54,168	47,985
Arizona	133,813	97,421	82,188	151,796	97,068	75,853	†	†	†	111,636	73,181	69,390
Arkansas	108,093	80,003	71,898	73,755	65,397	56,673	80,697	67,932	60,202	72,755	65,253	58,805
California	165,791	112,818	95,132	110,072	94,554	83,845	174,220	110,813	94,711	103,941	83,724	71,910
Colorado	127,627	95,433	85,068	82,461	67,849	61,549	135,739	99,919	81,711	118,742	88,746	70,507
Connecticut	150,560	102,214	82,889	103,734	83,742	69,843	190,700	99,116	89,948	123,581	99,133	80,452
Delaware	152,773	104,784	90,995	†	†	†	†	†	†	96,922	79,494	71,504
District of Columbia	164,016	125,544	100,439	104,672	75,415	62,622	171,141	109,987	92,214	88,364	77,221	72,547
Florida	134,226	94,696	83,881	113,039	88,358	70,224	132,585	93,721	78,223	99,003	82,558	68,448
Georgia	117,492	84,748	74,968	77,078	63,318	58,577	148,156	94,825	82,132	80,827	62,670	56,005
Hawaii	134,748	99,617	87,964	†	†	†	†	†	†	91,545	79,176	73,324
Idaho	98,097	78,886	71,918	†	†	†	66,436	58,161	52,460	†	†	†
Illinois	128,284	90,100	84,185	98,001	78,465	69,196	185,577	106,316	94,023	86,676	73,579	62,376
Indiana	133,964	93,902	81,862	88,585	73,216	65,818	143,362	93,238	76,156	83,561	69,580	56,680
Iowa	130,245	91,946	81,117	†	†	†	89,991	73,681	59,603	72,497	61,294	55,582
Kansas	115,255	82,198	70,886	78,994	67,937	61,103	68,002	54,060	51,286	65,117	60,699	52,080
Kentucky	107,575	77,915	68,460	70,258	61,946	51,697	79,507	65,348	55,613	64,390	55,801	50,840
Louisiana	113,129	78,869	75,292	76,937	62,823	57,263	134,310	84,670	90,386	68,830	58,399	56,034
Maine	108,777	86,779	69,464	78,160	65,284	53,303	94,505	77,861	64,276	67,245	58,671	53,035
Maryland	130,926	94,503	80,256	93,166	76,577	69,919	157,104	109,428	95,845	85,558	72,006	64,409
Massachusetts	145,572	107,333	90,632	101,791	80,494	68,225	194,058	116,725	102,673	125,001	93,769	78,981
Michigan	138,714	96,301	84,281	97,578	82,814	74,118	114,007	91,123	76,845	80,814	70,599	62,441
Minnesota	138,384	98,468	88,672	97,654	81,574	69,308	101,476	77,541	65,099	80,487	67,721	61,061
Mississippi	101,987	79,369	70,520	69,118	63,313	55,108	84,834	67,390	58,465	98,568	69,051	60,494
Missouri	111,473	79,785	72,994	79,329	65,921	58,259	148,326	93,357	80,099	83,333	68,473	58,723
Montana	97,127	75,365	69,075	74,738	67,695	58,247	†	†	†	66,750	53,402	50,413
Nebraska	121,964	89,440	87,131	83,027	66,927	55,434	119,865	88,131	70,997	67,259	62,013	55,416
Nevada	133,361	97,595	82,420	†	†	†	†	†	‡	‡	‡	‡
New Hampshire	134,951	106,519	86,399	97,126	79,873	67,190	198,177	123,727	101,527	93,536	74,055	67,738
New Jersey	158,393	109,725	88,230	127,843	102,044	83,936	198,777	107,817	95,243	107,717	93,139	70,235
New Mexico	104,648	76,441	73,215	81,828	67,610	58,114	†	†	†	‡	58,998	46,909
New York	141,102	102,036	86,544	112,097	87,609	74,193	171,248	109,522	90,310	102,383	82,539	72,534
North Carolina	128,728	87,984	80,004	93,500	76,295	69,005	166,605	99,825	81,087	74,556	64,891	58,856
North Dakota	107,334	82,124	71,451	79,182	64,981	54,512	69,443	74,154	60,961	†	†	†
Ohio	126,030	91,074	80,913	75,607	63,092	53,948	113,899	82,155	74,264	80,497	67,710	58,600
Oklahoma	110,488	80,704	75,205	81,090	65,596	57,881	103,407	78,411	77,347	72,406	60,687	55,267
Oregon	128,787	96,026	84,047	84,789	69,433	55,846	104,454	81,888	67,037	68,635	58,908	53,005
Pennsylvania	145,409	100,169	81,737	112,206	91,293	72,296	161,783	99,770	87,384	92,401	74,425	64,417
Rhode Island	123,929	92,025	85,831	83,318	73,013	63,047	186,408	124,143	101,455	120,777	90,287	77,002
South Carolina	135,110	95,422	87,370	88,520	72,603	63,222	71,675	66,449	62,810	77,883	64,073	55,568
South Dakota	96,468	77,456	71,796	92,669	72,601	65,556	†	†	†	69,357	58,622	55,430
Tennessee	114,699	83,983	72,556	88,115	72,159	64,245	152,613	95,727	81,279	83,606	67,963	58,015
Texas	135,495	93,713	80,710	92,342	77,284	67,511	148,198	99,258	89,140	87,593	73,988	62,810
Utah	126,152	90,798	81,633	91,653	74,575	67,092	156,795	110,530	76,368	88,971	74,151	66,622
Vermont	122,428	96,557	79,789	70,181	56,615	49,204	†	†	†	108,411	78,386	72,830
Virginia	135,195	94,081	80,299	89,489	74,613	66,064	116,740	85,324	67,565	74,914	57,604	53,189
Washington	138,980	101,663	93,164	109,446	92,466	80,557	116,109	87,935	71,750	82,048	68,045	64,389
West Virginia	102,535	80,001	69,932	71,043	62,592	55,614	67,748	58,829	53,661	59,860	54,836	46,324
Wisconsin	120,677	82,397	79,570	74,079	63,894	64,445	108,493	82,935	73,888	81,867	67,962	59,741
Wyoming	123,387	86,994	81,558	†	†	†	†	†	†	†	†	†
U.S. Service Academies	†	†	†	†	†	†	†	†	†	†	†	†
Other jurisdictions	**83,092**	**70,144**	**54,303**	**85,605**	**73,054**	**58,787**	**78,036**	**60,374**	**51,444**	**71,747**	**60,408**	**48,338**
American Samoa	†	†	†	†	†	†	†	†	†	†	†	†
Federated States of Micronesia	†	†	†	†	†	†	†	†	†	†	†	†
Guam	†	†	†	92,939	74,686	56,253	†	†	†	†	†	†
Marshall Islands	†	†	†	†	†	†	†	†	†	†	†	†
Northern Marianas	†	†	†	†	†	†	†	†	†	†	†	†
Palau	†	†	†	†	†	†	†	†	†	†	†	†
Puerto Rico	83,092	70,144	54,303	84,388	72,112	56,700	78,036	60,374	51,444	71,747	60,408	48,338
U.S. Virgin Islands	†	†	†	93,336	73,742	63,835	†	†	†	†	†	†

†Not applicable.
‡Reporting standards not met (too few cases).
[1]Institutions that awarded 20 or more doctor's degrees during the previous academic year.
[2]Institutions that awarded 20 or more master's degrees, but less than 20 doctor's degrees, during the previous academic year. This definition differs from the definition of master's institutions that is used in some *Digest* tables that present postsecondary finance data.

NOTE: Data exclude instructional faculty at medical schools. Degree-granting institutions grant associate's or higher degrees and participate in Title IV federal financial aid programs. Data include imputations for nonrespondent institutions.
SOURCE: U.S. Department of Education, National Center for Education Statistics, Integrated Postsecondary Education Data System (IPEDS), Spring 2019, Human Resources component, Salaries section. (This table was prepared November 2019.)

Table 316.80. Percentage of degree-granting postsecondary institutions with a tenure system and percentage of full-time faculty with tenure at these institutions, by control and level of institution and selected characteristics of faculty: Selected years, 1993–94 through 2018–19

Selected characteristic and academic year	All institutions	Public institutions						Nonprofit institutions						For-profit institutions
		Total	4-year institutions				2-year	Total	4-year institutions				2-year	
			Total	Doctoral[1]	Master's[2]	Other			Total	Doctoral[1]	Master's[2]	Other		
1	2	3	4	5	6	7	8	9	10	11	12	13	14	15
Percent of institutions with a tenure system														
1993–94	62.6	73.6	92.6	100.0	98.3	76.4	62.1	62.0	66.3	90.5	76.5	58.3	26.1	7.8
1999–2000	55.0	72.8	94.6	100.0	95.5	86.3	60.3	59.0	63.4	81.2	72.6	54.9	14.0	4.0
2003–04	52.7	71.3	90.9	100.0	98.0	70.9	59.4	57.9	61.2	86.6	71.6	49.5	14.4	3.6
2005–06	50.9	71.5	90.9	99.5	98.0	71.6	59.4	56.5	59.8	85.1	67.1	49.2	11.5	2.0
2007–08	49.5	70.7	91.0	100.0	98.6	70.1	57.4	57.5	60.2	81.3	64.2	45.4	13.0	1.4
2009–10	47.8	71.2	90.9	99.6	98.5	71.3	57.7	57.1	59.5	80.6	64.4	44.6	12.9	1.5
2011–12	45.3	71.6	90.8	99.6	98.5	70.5	57.8	55.6	58.6	79.5	64.0	42.7	8.0	1.3
2013–14	49.3	74.6	95.8	99.6	98.1	86.6	58.9	59.7	61.8	79.6	63.2	49.0	12.5	1.2
2015–16	51.9	74.8	95.2	99.6	97.6	85.7	58.9	57.7	60.6	79.8	60.8	47.0	7.5	1.3
2016–17	54.4	74.6	94.6	99.6	97.2	85.0	58.0	58.8	61.5	79.3	61.1	48.8	9.2	1.5
2017–18	55.1	74.7	94.6	99.6	96.8	86.2	57.7	58.3	60.6	80.2	59.4	46.9	7.8	1.6
2018–19	57.4	74.3	93.6	99.3	97.5	82.4	57.5	58.8	60.8	78.7	58.2	49.0	8.8	1.3
Faculty with tenure at institutions with a tenure system														
Percent of all full-time faculty[3]														
1993–94	56.2	58.9	56.3	54.5	60.5	51.1	69.9	49.5	49.5	47.6	51.8	50.4	47.9	33.8
1999–2000	53.7	55.9	53.2	50.4	59.1	54.7	67.7	48.2	48.1	43.4	52.3	53.5	59.7	77.4
2003–04	50.4	53.0	50.2	48.9	52.9	51.2	65.2	44.6	44.6	40.1	48.7	51.9	47.7	69.2
2005–06	49.6	51.5	48.7	47.2	52.3	49.1	64.1	45.1	45.1	40.7	49.1	52.5	45.2	69.3
2007–08	48.8	50.5	47.8	45.9	52.7	49.5	63.6	44.7	44.7	41.0	50.5	53.1	41.3	51.3
2009–10	48.7	50.6	47.8	45.7	53.6	51.3	64.1	44.3	44.3	40.4	50.5	54.1	38.5	51.0
2011–12	48.5	50.7	48.0	45.8	54.3	53.4	64.7	43.7	43.7	39.7	50.7	54.3	31.4	31.0
2013–14	48.3	50.4	47.3	44.9	55.4	52.2	67.2	43.8	43.8	39.5	51.7	55.9	31.5	19.8
2015–16	47.2	49.3	46.6	44.2	54.7	53.5	65.0	42.8	42.8	38.6	51.6	55.6	33.9	17.0
2016–17	46.4	48.2	45.8	43.3	53.4	56.9	63.6	42.4	42.4	38.3	51.1	55.4	32.2	17.2
2017–18	45.5	47.3	44.8	42.3	52.7	56.1	63.2	41.8	41.8	37.9	50.7	55.0	27.2	17.6
2018–19	45.1	46.9	44.5	42.2	52.8	54.7	62.8	41.4	41.4	37.6	50.0	55.2	28.9	12.8
Percent of full-time instructional faculty only														
2017–18														
Total	48.0	49.7	47.4	45.5	52.9	56.1	63.2	44.4	44.4	41.2	50.7	55.0	27.2	17.6
Male	54.0	55.5	54.2	52.8	58.8	59.4	65.5	50.8	50.9	48.2	56.4	60.5	32.9	20.1
Female	40.8	42.8	39.1	35.9	46.4	52.8	61.3	36.4	36.5	32.0	44.7	49.0	24.0	15.3
Professor	89.6	90.7	90.7	88.9	98.2	96.2	90.6	87.5	87.5	85.0	92.7	95.9	60.9	70.7
Male	90.1	91.3	91.3	89.8	98.1	96.5	91.6	87.9	87.9	85.9	92.7	95.9	77.8	74.5
Female	88.5	89.5	89.4	86.5	98.3	95.7	89.8	86.6	86.6	82.7	92.8	95.9	50.0	65.7
Associate professor	75.0	78.3	78.5	75.5	89.6	86.4	75.1	68.6	68.6	62.5	77.7	87.6	52.7	41.5
Male	75.5	79.1	79.2	76.4	89.8	86.3	77.4	68.6	68.6	63.0	77.7	86.7	71.4	37.5
Female	74.3	77.3	77.8	74.3	89.4	86.5	73.3	68.6	68.7	61.8	77.8	88.6	46.3	45.5
Assistant professor	5.1	6.5	3.5	1.3	8.3	21.8	43.9	2.5	2.5	1.7	5.4	2.8	†	†
Male	5.0	6.3	3.5	1.3	8.6	22.7	47.0	2.6	2.6	1.7	5.7	3.3	†	†
Female	5.2	6.8	3.6	1.4	8.0	21.0	41.7	2.4	2.4	1.6	5.2	2.4	†	†
Instructor	25.6	31.4	9.6	0.6	1.5	45.3	55.5	0.3	0.3	0.2	0.4	1.1	†	3.6
Lecturer	1.7	2.2	1.6	1.0	3.2	5.7	28.2	0.2	0.2	0.1	‡	1.7	†	†
No academic rank	28.4	35.6	21.3	1.2	6.9	56.5	65.3	4.8	4.6	2.1	21.0	1.5	41.4	†
2018–19														
Total	47.5	49.2	47.0	45.2	53.0	54.7	62.8	43.9	43.9	40.8	50.0	55.2	28.9	12.8
Male	53.5	55.0	53.7	52.5	58.7	57.6	65.3	50.4	50.5	47.9	55.7	60.9	30.1	14.8
Female	40.5	42.5	38.9	35.9	46.8	51.9	60.8	36.0	36.0	31.8	44.0	49.2	28.1	10.8
Professor	89.4	90.5	90.5	88.8	98.3	95.1	90.0	87.3	87.3	84.7	92.4	96.5	60.9	61.0
Male	90.1	91.2	91.2	89.8	98.4	95.4	91.2	87.8	87.8	85.8	92.5	96.6	75.0	70.6
Female	88.0	89.0	89.0	86.3	98.2	94.6	89.0	86.1	86.1	82.2	92.1	96.2	53.3	48.0
Associate professor	74.5	77.8	78.0	75.2	89.5	84.7	74.7	68.2	68.2	62.1	77.8	88.0	56.9	49.1
Male	75.3	78.8	78.9	76.4	89.6	85.4	76.8	68.4	68.4	62.8	78.4	86.7	66.7	42.3
Female	73.6	76.5	76.9	73.6	89.3	83.9	73.0	68.0	68.0	61.2	77.2	89.5	53.5	55.6
Assistant professor	4.9	6.3	3.3	1.3	7.8	21.3	44.8	2.3	2.3	1.5	4.9	3.3	†	†
Male	4.7	6.0	3.2	1.2	7.9	22.5	47.6	2.4	2.4	1.6	5.0	3.9	†	†
Female	5.0	6.6	3.4	1.4	7.7	20.2	42.7	2.2	2.2	1.4	4.9	2.8	†	†
Instructor	24.9	30.7	9.1	0.6	2.4	41.5	54.6	0.3	0.3	0.1	0.4	1.5	†	2.3
Lecturer	1.7	2.2	1.6	1.0	3.7	5.6	28.9	0.1	0.1	0.1	‡	1.1	†	†
No academic rank	28.3	35.4	21.0	1.2	3.6	56.6	68.2	4.5	4.3	1.6	24.2	1.5	48.3	†

†Not applicable.
‡Reporting standards not met (too few cases).
[1]Institutions that awarded 20 or more doctor's degrees during the previous academic year.
[2]Institutions that awarded 20 or more master's degrees, but less than 20 doctor's degrees, during the previous academic year.
[3]Includes instructional, research, and public service faculty.

NOTE: Degree-granting institutions grant associate's or higher degrees and participate in Title IV federal financial aid programs. Data include imputations for nonrespondent institutions. Some data have been revised from previously published figures.
SOURCE: U.S. Department of Education, National Center for Education Statistics, Integrated Postsecondary Education Data System (IPEDS), "Fall Staff Survey" (IPEDS-S:93–99); and IPEDS Winter 2003–04 through Winter 2011–12 and Spring 2014 through Spring 2019, Human Resources component, Fall Staff section. (This table was prepared November 2019.)

Table 318.10. Degrees conferred by postsecondary institutions, by level of degree and sex of student: Selected years, 1869–70 through 2029–30

Year	Associate's degrees				Bachelor's degrees				Master's degrees				Doctor's degrees[1]			
	Total	Males	Females	Percent female	Total	Males	Females	Percent female	Total	Males	Females	Percent female	Total	Males	Females	Percent female
1	2	3	4	5	6	7	8	9	10	11	12	13	14	15	16	17
1869–70	—	—	—	—	9,371[2]	7,993[2]	1,378[2]	14.7	0	0	0	—	1	1	0	0.0
1879–80	—	—	—	—	12,896[2]	10,411[2]	2,485[2]	19.3	879	868	11	1.3	54	51	3	5.6
1889–90	—	—	—	—	15,539[2]	12,857[2]	2,682[2]	17.3	1,015	821	194	19.1	149	147	2	1.3
1899–1900	—	—	—	—	27,410[2]	22,173[2]	5,237[2]	19.1	1,583	1,280	303	19.1	382	359	23	6.0
1909–10	—	—	—	—	37,199[2]	28,762[2]	8,437[2]	22.7	2,113	1,555	558	26.4	443	399	44	9.9
1919–20	—	—	—	—	48,622[2]	31,980[2]	16,642[2]	34.2	4,279	2,985	1,294	30.2	615	522	93	15.1
1929–30	—	—	—	—	122,484[2]	73,615[2]	48,869[2]	39.9	14,969	8,925	6,044	40.4	2,299	1,946	353	15.4
1939–40	—	—	—	—	186,500[2]	109,546[2]	76,954[2]	41.3	26,731	16,508	10,223	38.2	3,290	2,861	429	13.0
1949–50	—	—	—	—	432,058[2]	328,841[2]	103,217[2]	23.9	58,183	41,220	16,963	29.2	6,420	5,804	616	9.6
1959–60	—	—	—	—	392,440[2]	254,063[2]	138,377[2]	35.3	74,435	50,898	23,537	31.6	9,829	8,801	1,028	10.5
1969–70	206,023	117,432	88,591	43.0	792,316	451,097	341,219	43.1	213,589	130,799	82,790	38.8	59,486	53,792	5,694	9.6
1979–80	400,910	183,737	217,173	54.2	929,417	473,611	455,806	49.0	305,196	156,882	148,314	48.6	95,631	69,526	26,105	27.3
1980–81	416,377	188,638	227,739	54.7	935,140	469,883	465,257	49.8	302,637	152,979	149,658	49.5	98,016	69,567	28,449	29.0
1981–82	434,526	196,944	237,582	54.7	952,998	473,364	479,634	50.3	302,447	151,349	151,098	50.0	97,838	68,630	29,208	29.9
1982–83	449,620	203,991	245,629	54.6	969,510	479,140	490,370	50.6	296,415	150,092	146,323	49.4	99,335	67,757	31,578	31.8
1983–84	452,240	202,704	249,536	55.2	974,309	482,319	491,990	50.5	291,141	149,268	141,873	48.7	100,799	67,769	33,030	32.8
1984–85	454,712	202,932	251,780	55.4	979,477	482,528	496,949	50.7	293,472	149,276	144,196	49.1	100,785	66,269	34,516	34.2
1985–86	446,047	196,166	249,881	56.0	987,823	485,923	501,900	50.8	295,850	149,373	146,477	49.5	100,280	65,215	35,065	35.0
1986–87	436,304	190,839	245,465	56.3	991,264	480,782	510,482	51.5	296,530	147,063	149,467	50.4	98,477	62,790	35,687	36.2
1987–88	435,085	190,047	245,038	56.3	994,829	477,203	517,626	52.0	305,783	150,243	155,540	50.9	99,139	63,019	36,120	36.4
1988–89	436,764	186,316	250,448	57.3	1,018,755	483,346	535,409	52.6	316,626	153,993	162,633	51.4	100,571	63,055	37,516	37.3
1989–90	455,102	191,195	263,907	58.0	1,051,344	491,696	559,648	53.2	330,152	158,052	172,100	52.1	103,508	63,963	39,545	38.2
1990–91	481,720	198,634	283,086	58.8	1,094,538	504,045	590,493	53.9	342,863	160,842	182,021	53.1	105,547	64,242	41,305	39.1
1991–92	504,231	207,481	296,750	58.9	1,136,553	520,811	615,742	54.2	358,089	165,867	192,222	53.7	109,554	66,603	42,951	39.2
1992–93	514,756	211,964	302,792	58.8	1,165,178	532,881	632,297	54.3	375,032	173,354	201,678	53.8	112,072	67,130	44,942	40.1
1993–94	530,632	215,261	315,371	59.4	1,169,275	532,422	636,853	54.5	393,037	180,571	212,466	54.1	112,636	66,773	45,863	40.7
1994–95	539,691	218,352	321,339	59.5	1,160,134	526,131	634,003	54.6	403,609	183,043	220,566	54.6	114,266	67,324	46,942	41.1
1995–96	555,216	219,514	335,702	60.5	1,164,792	522,454	642,338	55.1	412,180	183,481	228,699	55.5	115,507	67,189	48,318	41.8
1996–97	571,226	223,948	347,278	60.8	1,172,879	520,515	652,364	55.6	425,260	185,270	239,990	56.4	118,747	68,387	50,360	42.4
1997–98	558,555	217,613	340,942	61.0	1,184,406	519,956	664,450	56.1	436,037	188,718	247,319	56.7	118,735	67,232	51,503	43.4
1998–99	564,984	220,508	344,476	61.0	1,202,239	519,961	682,278	56.8	446,038	190,230	255,808	57.4	116,700	65,340	51,360	44.0
1999–2000	564,933	224,721	340,212	60.2	1,237,875	530,367	707,508	57.2	463,185	196,129	267,056	57.7	118,736	64,930	53,806	45.3
2000–01	578,865	231,645	347,220	60.0	1,244,171	531,840	712,331	57.3	473,502	197,770	275,732	58.2	119,585	64,171	55,414	46.3
2001–02	595,133	238,109	357,024	60.0	1,291,900	549,816	742,084	57.4	487,313	202,604	284,709	58.4	119,663	62,731	56,932	47.6
2002–03	634,016	253,451	380,565	60.0	1,348,811	573,258	775,553	57.5	518,699	215,172	303,527	58.5	121,579	62,730	58,849	48.4
2003–04	665,301	260,033	405,268	60.9	1,399,542	595,425	804,117	57.5	564,272	233,056	331,216	58.7	126,087	63,981	62,106	49.3
2004–05	696,660	267,536	429,124	61.6	1,439,264	613,000	826,264	57.4	580,151	237,155	342,996	59.1	134,387	67,257	67,130	50.0
2005–06	713,315	270,139	443,176	62.1	1,485,104	630,502	854,602	57.5	599,862	241,701	358,161	59.7	138,056	68,912	69,144	50.1
2006–07	727,616	275,034	452,582	62.2	1,524,729	649,816	874,913	57.4	610,703	242,213	368,490	60.3	144,694	71,311	73,383	50.7
2007–08	750,166	282,695	467,471	62.3	1,563,734	668,184	895,550	57.3	630,844	250,203	380,641	60.3	149,190	73,340	75,850	50.8
2008–09	787,243	298,066	489,177	62.1	1,601,399	685,422	915,977	57.2	662,082	263,515	398,567	60.2	154,564	75,674	78,890	51.0
2009–10	848,856	322,747	526,109	62.0	1,649,919	706,660	943,259	57.2	693,313	275,317	417,996	60.3	158,590	76,610	81,980	51.7
2010–11	943,506	361,408	582,098	61.7	1,716,053	734,159	981,894	57.2	730,922	291,680	439,242	60.1	163,827	79,672	84,155	51.4
2011–12	1,021,718	393,479	628,239	61.5	1,792,163	765,772	1,026,391	57.3	755,967	302,484	453,483	60.0	170,217	82,670	87,547	51.4
2012–13	1,007,427	389,195	618,232	61.4	1,840,381	787,408	1,052,973	57.2	751,718	301,552	450,166	59.9	175,026	85,080	89,946	51.4
2013–14	1,005,155	391,474	613,681	61.1	1,870,150	801,905	1,068,245	57.1	754,582	302,846	451,736	59.9	177,587	85,585	92,002	51.8
2014–15	1,014,341	396,782	617,559	60.9	1,894,969	812,693	1,082,276	57.1	758,804	306,615	452,189	59.6	178,548	84,922	93,626	52.4
2015–16	1,008,228	392,084	616,144	61.1	1,920,750	821,746	1,099,004	57.2	785,757	320,574	465,183	59.2	178,134	84,240	93,894	52.7
2016–17	1,005,687	394,147	611,540	60.8	1,956,114	836,021	1,120,093	57.3	804,542	326,857	477,685	59.4	181,357	84,649	96,708	53.3
2017–18	1,011,487	398,600	612,887	60.6	1,980,644	844,960	1,135,684	57.3	820,102	326,870	493,232	60.1	184,074	85,568	98,506	53.5
2018–19[3]	977,000	381,000	596,000	61.0	1,989,000	843,000	1,146,000	57.6	829,000	326,000	502,000	60.6	186,000	85,000	100,000	54.1
2019–20[3]	981,000	382,000	599,000	61.0	1,996,000	846,000	1,151,000	57.6	832,000	327,000	505,000	60.7	186,000	86,000	101,000	54.1
2020–21[3]	983,000	383,000	600,000	61.1	1,998,000	846,000	1,152,000	57.7	833,000	327,000	506,000	60.7	187,000	86,000	101,000	54.1
2021–22[3]	986,000	384,000	602,000	61.1	2,000,000	846,000	1,154,000	57.7	835,000	328,000	507,000	60.7	187,000	86,000	101,000	54.1
2022–23[3]	989,000	385,000	604,000	61.1	2,002,000	847,000	1,156,000	57.7	836,000	328,000	508,000	60.7	187,000	86,000	101,000	54.2
2023–24[3]	992,000	386,000	606,000	61.1	2,007,000	848,000	1,158,000	57.7	838,000	329,000	509,000	60.7	188,000	86,000	102,000	54.2
2024–25[3]	995,000	387,000	608,000	61.1	2,013,000	851,000	1,162,000	57.7	841,000	330,000	511,000	60.7	188,000	86,000	102,000	54.2
2025–26[3]	998,000	389,000	610,000	61.1	2,020,000	854,000	1,166,000	57.7	844,000	331,000	513,000	60.7	189,000	87,000	102,000	54.2
2026–27[3]	1,002,000	390,000	612,000	61.1	2,027,000	857,000	1,170,000	57.7	847,000	333,000	514,000	60.7	190,000	87,000	103,000	54.2
2027–28[3]	1,005,000	391,000	613,000	61.1	2,030,000	858,000	1,171,000	57.7	849,000	333,000	515,000	60.7	190,000	87,000	103,000	54.2
2028–29[3]	1,006,000	392,000	614,000	61.1	2,030,000	858,000	1,171,000	57.7	849,000	333,000	516,000	60.7	190,000	87,000	103,000	54.2
2029–30[3]	1,007,000	392,000	615,000	61.1	2,029,000	858,000	1,171,000	57.7	849,000	334,000	516,000	60.7	190,000	87,000	103,000	54.2

—Not available.
[1]Includes Ph.D., Ed.D., and comparable degrees at the doctoral level. Includes most degrees that were classified as first-professional prior to 2010–11, such as M.D., D.D.S., and law degrees.
[2]Includes some degrees classified as master's or doctor's degrees in later years.
[3]Projected.
NOTE: Data through 1994–95 are for institutions of higher education, while later data are for degree-granting institutions. Degree-granting institutions grant associate's or higher degrees and participate in Title IV federal financial aid programs. Some data have been revised from previously published figures. Detail may not sum to totals because of rounding.
SOURCE: U.S. Department of Education, National Center for Education Statistics, *Earned Degrees Conferred*, 1869–70 through 1964–65; Higher Education General Information Survey (HEGIS), "Degrees and Other Formal Awards Conferred" surveys, 1965–66 through 1985–86; Integrated Postsecondary Education Data System (IPEDS), "Completions Survey" (IPEDS-C:87–99); IPEDS Fall 2000 through Fall 2018, Completions component; and Degrees Conferred Projection Model, 1980–81 through 2029–30. (This table was prepared December 2019.)

Table 318.20. Bachelor's, master's, and doctor's degrees conferred by postsecondary institutions, by field of study: Selected years, 1970–71 through 2017–18

[Standard errors appear in parentheses]

Degree and year	Number of degrees conferred								Percentage distribution of degrees conferred							
	Total degrees	Humanities[1]	Social and behavioral sciences[2]	Natural sciences and mathematics[3]	Computer sciences and engineering[4]	Education	Business	Other fields[5]	Total degrees	Humanities[1]	Social and behavioral sciences[2]	Natural sciences and mathematics[3]	Computer sciences and engineering[4]	Education	Business	Other fields[5]
1	2	3	4	5	6	7	8	9	10	11	12	13	14	15	16	17
Bachelor's degrees																
1970–71	839,730	143,549	193,511	81,916	52,570	176,307	115,396	76,481	100.0	17.1	23.0	9.8	6.3	21.0	13.7	9.1
1975–76	925,746	150,736	176,674	91,596	52,328	154,437	143,171	156,804	100.0	16.3	19.1	9.9	5.7	16.7	15.5	16.9
1980–81	935,140	134,139	141,581	78,092	90,476	108,074	200,521	182,257	100.0	14.3	15.1	8.4	9.7	11.6	21.4	19.5
1985–86	987,823	132,891	134,468	76,228	139,459	87,147	236,700	180,930	100.0	13.5	13.6	7.7	14.1	8.8	24.0	18.3
1990–91	1,094,538	172,485	183,762	70,209	104,910	110,807	249,165	203,200	100.0	15.8	16.8	6.4	9.6	10.1	22.8	18.6
1995–96	1,164,792	193,404	199,895	93,443	102,503	105,384	226,623	243,540	100.0	16.6	17.2	8.0	8.8	9.0	19.5	20.9
2000–01	1,244,171	214,107	201,681	89,772	117,011	105,458	263,515	252,627	100.0	17.2	16.2	7.2	9.4	8.5	21.2	20.3
2005–06	1,485,104	261,666	249,600	105,883	129,108	107,235	318,043	313,569	100.0	17.6	16.8	7.1	8.7	7.2	21.4	21.1
2010–11	1,716,053	288,446	278,075	131,871	136,163	104,008	365,133	412,357	100.0	16.8	16.2	7.7	7.9	6.1	21.3	24.0
2014–15	1,894,969	280,956	284,544	161,800	174,691	91,596	363,741	537,641	100.0	14.8	15.0	8.5	9.2	4.8	19.2	28.4
2015–16	1,920,750	274,513	278,658	167,055	188,350	87,221	371,690	553,263	100.0	14.3	14.5	8.7	9.8	4.5	19.4	28.8
2016–17	1,956,114	270,931	275,956	172,115	205,206	85,130	381,109	565,667	100.0	13.9	14.1	8.8	10.5	4.4	19.5	28.9
2017–18	1,980,644	268,554	276,399	175,461	220,281	82,621	386,201	571,127	100.0	13.6	14.0	8.9	11.1	4.2	19.5	28.8
Master's degrees																
1970–71	235,564	34,510	22,256	17,152	18,535	87,666	26,490	28,955	100.0	14.6	9.4	7.3	7.9	37.2	11.2	12.3
1975–76	317,477	37,079	26,120	15,742	19,403	126,061	42,592	50,480	100.0	11.7	8.2	5.0	6.1	39.7	13.4	15.9
1980–81	302,637	35,130	22,168	13,579	21,434	96,713	57,888	55,725	100.0	11.6	7.3	4.5	7.1	32.0	19.1	18.4
1985–86	295,850	34,834	20,409	14,055	30,216	74,816	66,676	54,844	100.0	11.8	6.9	4.8	10.2	25.3	22.5	18.5
1990–91	342,863	35,984	23,582	13,664	34,774	87,352	78,255	69,252	100.0	10.5	6.9	4.0	10.1	25.5	22.8	20.2
1995–96	412,180	40,795	30,164	16,154	39,422	104,936	93,554	87,155	100.0	9.9	7.3	3.9	9.6	25.5	22.7	21.1
2000–01	473,502	40,625	30,330	15,360	44,098	127,829	115,602	99,658	100.0	8.6	6.4	3.2	9.3	27.0	24.4	21.0
2005–06	599,862	49,590	37,143	19,575	50,581	174,622	146,396	121,955	100.0	8.3	6.2	3.3	8.4	29.1	24.4	20.3
2010–11	730,922	57,160	46,147	23,576	62,695	185,127	187,178	169,039	100.0	7.8	6.3	3.2	8.6	25.3	25.6	23.1
2014–15	758,804	59,181	47,305	29,344	82,916	146,581	185,236	208,241	100.0	7.8	6.2	3.9	10.9	19.3	24.4	27.4
2015–16	785,757	59,067	47,506	31,299	97,843	145,792	186,835	217,415	100.0	7.5	6.0	4.0	12.5	18.6	23.8	27.7
2016–17	804,542	57,895	47,543	32,500	106,782	145,624	187,412	226,786	100.0	7.2	5.9	4.0	13.3	18.1	23.3	28.2
2017–18	820,102	59,088	47,725	34,819	105,436	146,367	192,184	234,483	100.0	7.2	5.8	4.2	12.9	17.8	23.4	28.6
Doctor's degrees[6]																
1970–71	64,998	4,402	5,804	9,126	3,816	6,041	774	35,035	100.0	6.8	8.9	14.0	5.9	9.3	1.2	53.9
1975–76	91,007	5,461	7,314	7,591	3,118	7,202	906	59,415	100.0	6.0	8.0	8.3	3.4	7.9	1.0	65.3
1980–81	98,016	4,827	6,698	7,473	2,860	7,279	808	68,071	100.0	4.9	6.8	7.6	2.9	7.4	0.8	69.4
1985–86	100,280	4,648	6,548	7,668	3,800	6,610	923	70,083	100.0	4.6	6.5	7.6	3.8	6.6	0.9	69.9
1990–91	105,547	4,858	6,944	9,378	6,006	6,189	1,185	70,987	100.0	4.6	6.6	8.9	5.7	5.9	1.1	67.3
1995–96	115,507	6,356	7,901	10,997	7,223	6,246	1,366	75,418	100.0	5.5	6.8	9.5	6.3	5.4	1.2	65.3
2000–01	119,585	6,466	9,021	10,190	6,315	6,284	1,180	80,129	100.0	5.4	7.5	8.5	5.3	5.3	1.0	67.0
2005–06	138,056	6,628	8,835	12,097	8,734	7,584	1,711	92,467	100.0	4.8	6.4	8.8	6.3	5.5	1.2	67.0
2010–11	163,827	8,359	10,241	14,574	10,013	9,642	2,286	108,712	100.0	5.1	6.3	8.9	6.1	5.9	1.4	66.4
2014–15	178,548	8,391	11,411	15,677	12,360	11,772	3,116	115,821	100.0	4.7	6.4	8.8	6.9	6.6	1.7	64.9
2015–16	178,134	8,324	11,246	15,851	12,387	11,838	3,325	115,163	100.0	4.7	6.3	8.9	7.0	6.6	1.9	64.6
2016–17	181,357	8,120	11,408	16,039	12,505	12,692	3,328	117,265	100.0	4.5	6.3	8.8	6.9	7.0	1.8	64.7
2017–18	184,074	8,336	10,951	16,413	13,046	12,780	3,338	119,210	100.0	4.5	5.9	8.9	7.1	6.9	1.8	64.8

[1]Includes degrees in Area, ethnic, cultural, gender, and group studies; English language and literature/letters; Foreign languages, literatures, and linguistics; Liberal arts and sciences, general studies, and humanities; Multi/interdisciplinary studies; Philosophy and religious studies; Theology and religious vocations; and Visual and performing arts.
[2]Includes Psychology; Social sciences; and History.
[3]Includes Biological and biomedical sciences; Mathematics and statistics; and Physical sciences and science technologies.
[4]Includes Computer and information sciences; Engineering; and Engineering technologies.
[5]Includes Agriculture and natural resources; Architecture and related services; Communication, journalism, and related programs; Communications technologies; Family and consumer sciences/human sciences; Health professions and related programs; Homeland security, law enforcement, and firefighting; Legal professions and studies; Library science; Military technologies and applied sciences; Parks, recreation, leisure, and fitness studies; Precision production; Public administration and social services; Transportation and materials moving; and Not classified by field of study.
[6]Includes Ph.D., Ed.D., and comparable degrees at the doctoral level. Includes most degrees that were classified as first-professional prior to 2010–11, such as M.D., D.D.S., and law degrees.

NOTE: Data are for postsecondary institutions participating in Title IV federal financial aid programs. Data in this table are based on the 2010 Classification of Instructional Programs. The figures for earlier years have been reclassified when necessary to make them conform to the new taxonomy. To facilitate trend comparisons, certain aggregations have been made of the degree fields as reported in the Integrated Postsecondary Education Data System (IPEDS): "Agriculture and natural resources" includes Agriculture, agriculture operations, and related sciences and Natural resources and conservation; "Business" includes Business, management, marketing, and related support services and Personal and culinary services; and "Engineering technologies" includes Engineering technologies and engineering-related fields, Construction trades, and Mechanic and repair technologies/technicians. Detail may not sum to totals because of rounding. Some data have been revised from previously published figures.
SOURCE: U.S. Department of Education, National Center for Education Statistics, Higher Education General Information Survey (HEGIS), "Degrees and Other Formal Awards Conferred" surveys, 1970–71 through 1985–86; Integrated Postsecondary Education Data System (IPEDS), "Completions Survey" (IPEDS-C:91–96); and IPEDS Fall 2001 through Fall 2018, Completions component. (This table was prepared Februray 2020.)

Table 318.30. Bachelor's, master's, and doctor's degrees conferred by postsecondary institutions, by sex of student and discipline division: 2017–18

Discipline division	Bachelor's degrees			Master's degrees			Doctor's degrees[1]		
	Total	Males	Females	Total	Males	Females	Total	Males	Females
1	2	3	4	5	6	7	8	9	10
All fields, total	**1,980,644**	**844,960**	**1,135,684**	**820,102**	**326,870**	**493,232**	**184,074**	**85,568**	**98,506**
Agriculture and natural resources	39,314	18,202	21,112	6,967	2,997	3,970	1,496	798	698
Agriculture, agriculture operations, and related sciences	20,215	9,003	11,212	2,856	1,247	1,609	886	488	398
Agriculture, general	2,194	1,096	1,098	301	120	181	14	11	3
Agricultural business and management, general	1,124	745	379	66	40	26	1	0	1
Agribusiness/agricultural business operations	2,195	1,362	833	43	21	22	0	0	0
Agricultural economics	1,531	1,046	485	336	175	161	131	80	51
Farm/farm and ranch management	171	129	42	6	5	1	0	0	0
Agricultural/farm supplies retailing and wholesaling	1	0	1	0	0	0	0	0	0
Agricultural business technology	36	20	16	2	1	1	0	0	0
Agricultural business and management, other	81	42	39	8	2	6	0	0	0
Agricultural mechanization, general	336	310	26	1	0	1	0	0	0
Agricultural mechanics and equipment/machine technology	0	0	0	0	0	0	0	0	0
Agricultural production operations, general	81	43	38	7	3	4	0	0	0
Animal/livestock husbandry and production	193	54	139	1	0	1	0	0	0
Aquaculture	58	39	19	41	26	15	12	8	4
Crop production	75	61	14	0	0	0	0	0	0
Dairy husbandry and production	2	0	2	0	0	0	0	0	0
Horse husbandry/equine science and management	159	9	150	7	0	7	0	0	0
Agroecology and sustainable agriculture	211	108	103	73	25	48	13	7	6
Viticulture and enology	132	67	65	0	0	0	0	0	0
Agricultural and food products processing	103	56	47	0	0	0	0	0	0
Animal training	23	5	18	0	0	0	0	0	0
Equestrian/equine studies	302	14	288	0	0	0	0	0	0
Agricultural and domestic animal services, other	1	0	1	0	0	0	0	0	0
Applied horticulture/horticultural operations, general	87	33	54	7	5	2	5	3	2
Ornamental horticulture	28	16	12	6	4	2	6	4	2
Landscaping and groundskeeping	132	96	36	2	0	2	0	0	0
Plant nursery operations and management	2	1	1	0	0	0	0	0	0
Turf and turfgrass management	94	90	4	4	4	0	0	0	0
Floriculture/floristry operations and management	1	1	0	0	0	0	0	0	0
Applied horticulture/horticultural business services, other	32	22	10	0	0	0	0	0	0
International agriculture	54	16	38	54	14	40	0	0	0
Agricultural and extension education services	67	29	38	94	23	71	15	8	7
Agricultural communication/journalism	422	72	350	27	4	23	0	0	0
Agricultural public services, other	53	22	31	5	1	4	0	0	0
Animal sciences, general	5,890	1,184	4,706	414	137	277	166	82	84
Agricultural animal breeding	0	0	0	4	0	4	1	0	1
Animal health	2	1	1	1	0	1	0	0	0
Animal nutrition	0	0	0	0	0	0	3	0	3
Dairy science	153	60	93	33	9	24	5	2	3
Livestock management	3	1	2	2	0	2	0	0	0
Poultry science	103	46	57	17	10	7	17	8	9
Animal sciences, other	79	11	68	4	1	3	0	0	0
Food science	1,318	388	930	451	139	312	140	55	85
Food technology and processing	13	5	8	10	5	5	7	3	4
Food science and technology, other	74	42	32	29	13	16	0	0	0
Plant sciences, general	531	327	204	87	58	29	46	29	17
Agronomy and crop science	704	485	219	276	173	103	110	72	38
Horticultural science	485	251	234	137	68	69	38	25	13
Agricultural and horticultural plant breeding	6	3	3	25	15	10	28	22	6
Plant protection and integrated pest management	109	90	19	28	21	7	7	3	4
Range science and management	110	62	48	37	18	19	14	8	6
Plant sciences, other	32	21	11	61	30	31	42	24	18
Soil science and agronomy, general	190	132	58	91	53	38	55	31	24
Soil chemistry and physics	38	33	5	1	1	0	0	0	0
Soil sciences, other	38	18	20	8	4	4	4	2	2
Agriculture, agriculture operations, and related sciences, other	356	239	117	49	19	30	6	1	5
Natural resources and conservation	19,099	9,199	9,900	4,111	1,750	2,361	610	310	300
Natural resources/conservation, general	1,377	660	717	581	238	343	100	51	49
Environmental studies	6,532	2,752	3,780	1,199	492	707	110	45	65
Environmental science	6,697	3,166	3,531	899	375	524	168	91	77
Natural resources conservation and research, other	130	67	63	79	38	41	25	11	14
Natural resources management and policy	695	399	296	497	191	306	25	11	14
Natural resource economics	73	41	32	8	3	5	1	0	1
Water, wetlands, and marine resources management	77	39	38	171	61	110	1	1	0
Land use planning and management/development	66	54	12	44	20	24	1	1	0
Natural resource recreation and tourism	53	33	20	62	29	33	1	0	1
Natural resources law enforcement and protective services	31	25	6	0	0	0	0	0	0
Natural resources management and policy, other	253	154	99	25	9	16	0	0	0
Fishing and fisheries sciences and management	357	196	161	41	19	22	17	10	7
Forestry, general	521	373	148	136	75	61	39	24	15
Forest sciences and biology	192	157	35	122	70	52	50	24	26
Forest management/forest resources management	166	136	30	36	21	15	5	4	1
Urban forestry	20	5	15	13	8	5	4	2	2
Wood science and wood products/pulp and paper technology	78	58	20	12	9	3	9	4	5
Forest resources production and management	5	4	1	8	4	4	8	6	2
Forest technology/technician	0	0	0	0	0	0	0	0	0
Forestry, other	76	53	23	6	4	2	8	5	3
Wildlife, fish, and wildlands science and management	1,564	741	823	157	80	77	36	20	16
Natural resources and conservation, other	136	86	50	15	4	11	2	0	2

See notes at end of table.

Table 318.30. Bachelor's, master's, and doctor's degrees conferred by postsecondary institutions, by sex of student and discipline division: 2017–18—Continued

Discipline division	Bachelor's degrees			Master's degrees			Doctor's degrees[1]		
	Total	Males	Females	Total	Males	Females	Total	Males	Females
1	2	3	4	5	6	7	8	9	10
Architecture and related services	8,464	4,474	3,990	7,317	3,516	3,801	250	136	114
Architecture	4,511	2,422	2,089	2,609	1,385	1,224	117	70	47
City/urban, community and regional planning	825	492	333	1,667	733	934	101	52	49
Environmental design/architecture	521	288	233	91	31	60	11	5	6
Interior architecture	425	38	387	144	20	124	0	0	0
Landscape architecture	720	394	326	524	194	330	3	1	2
Architectural history and criticism, general	80	38	42	28	11	17	2	0	2
Architectural technology/technician	128	77	51	9	4	5	0	0	0
Architectural and building sciences/technology	986	575	411	1,907	917	990	16	8	8
Real estate development	60	49	11	292	203	89	0	0	0
Architecture and related services, other	208	101	107	46	18	28	0	0	0
Area, ethnic, cultural, gender, and group studies	7,717	2,118	5,599	1,673	565	1,108	335	116	219
African studies	94	18	76	44	17	27	14	5	9
American/United States studies/civilization	958	368	590	220	60	160	88	40	48
Asian studies/civilization	679	294	385	84	40	44	0	0	0
East Asian studies	281	115	166	165	69	96	25	9	16
Russian, Central European, East European and Eurasian studies	41	16	25	29	11	18	0	0	0
European studies/civilization	48	14	34	19	12	7	0	0	0
Latin American studies	305	101	204	168	65	103	3	0	3
Near and Middle Eastern studies	143	50	93	159	75	84	33	17	16
Pacific Area/Pacific Rim studies	17	8	9	2	0	2	0	0	0
Russian studies	70	31	39	39	21	18	0	0	0
Scandinavian studies	11	7	4	4	2	2	1	0	1
South Asian studies	4	2	2	10	4	6	4	3	1
Southeast Asian studies	0	0	0	6	4	2	0	0	0
Western European studies	8	2	6	33	18	15	0	0	0
Canadian studies	1	0	1	4	4	0	0	0	0
Slavic studies	5	1	4	5	3	2	3	1	2
Ural-Altaic and Central Asian studies	6	3	3	4	4	0	2	0	2
Regional studies (U.S., Canadian, foreign)	16	7	9	14	5	9	3	1	2
Chinese studies	45	23	22	9	4	5	0	0	0
French studies	49	10	39	16	4	12	8	2	6
German studies	43	19	24	6	2	4	7	3	4
Italian studies	32	8	24	17	3	14	2	0	2
Japanese studies	57	26	31	4	3	1	0	0	0
Korean studies	0	0	0	0	0	0	0	0	0
Spanish and Iberian studies	19	5	14	0	0	0	0	0	0
Irish studies	0	0	0	4	0	4	0	0	0
Latin American and Caribbean studies	37	14	23	14	2	12	0	0	0
Area studies, other	612	202	410	51	19	32	8	5	3
Ethnic studies	181	45	136	7	0	7	5	1	4
African-American/Black studies	677	210	467	72	25	47	39	12	27
American Indian/Native American studies	212	80	132	69	24	45	10	2	8
Hispanic-American, Puerto Rican, and Mexican-American/Chicano studies	420	94	326	41	11	30	13	6	7
Asian-American studies	82	34	48	8	2	6	0	0	0
Women's studies	1,459	100	1,359	187	20	167	21	2	19
Gay/lesbian studies	7	0	7	0	0	0	0	0	0
Folklore studies	10	2	8	19	4	15	7	0	7
Disability studies	32	3	29	36	3	33	7	0	7
Deaf studies	236	36	200	4	1	3	0	0	0
Ethnic, cultural minority, gender, and group studies, other	820	170	650	100	24	76	32	7	25
Biological and biomedical sciences	118,663	44,852	73,811	17,180	7,028	10,152	8,222	3,829	4,393
Biology/biological sciences, general	73,983	26,686	47,297	3,579	1,409	2,170	1,036	485	551
Biomedical sciences, general	4,460	1,749	2,711	2,532	1,111	1,421	628	287	341
Biochemistry	8,861	4,287	4,574	321	160	161	521	274	247
Biophysics	167	109	58	26	17	9	102	67	35
Molecular biology	841	353	488	193	88	105	162	66	96
Molecular biochemistry	398	202	196	95	37	58	59	32	27
Molecular biophysics	0	0	0	1	0	1	14	14	0
Structural biology	0	0	0	0	0	0	0	0	0
Radiation biology/radiobiology	5	0	5	10	9	1	6	4	2
Biochemistry and molecular biology	1,051	482	569	125	49	76	147	66	81
Biochemistry, biophysics and molecular biology, other	219	95	124	22	12	10	34	14	20
Botany/plant biology	231	111	120	93	47	46	109	59	50
Plant pathology/phytopathology	17	5	12	68	35	33	81	42	39
Plant physiology	0	0	0	5	2	3	9	5	4
Plant molecular biology	0	0	0	2	2	0	13	7	6
Botany/plant biology, other	30	13	17	8	4	4	9	4	5
Cell/cellular biology and histology	371	180	191	45	15	30	136	55	81
Anatomy	482	169	313	235	107	128	38	14	24
Developmental biology and embryology	48	18	30	5	2	3	47	21	26
Cell/cellular and molecular biology	2,773	1,184	1,589	192	86	106	420	207	213
Cell biology and anatomy	15	9	6	34	12	22	35	22	13
Cell/cellular biology and anatomical sciences, other	100	33	67	144	64	80	115	59	56
Microbiology, general	2,024	874	1,150	177	61	116	198	82	116
Medical microbiology and bacteriology	398	152	246	205	68	137	131	52	79
Virology	0	0	0	1	1	0	13	7	6
Parasitology	0	0	0	0	0	0	0	0	0
Immunology	0	0	0	90	36	54	143	68	75
Microbiology and immunology	137	61	76	74	26	48	75	33	42
Microbiological sciences and immunology, other	131	56	75	38	16	22	62	26	36
Zoology/animal biology	1,568	471	1,097	87	38	49	87	35	52
Entomology	98	41	57	137	65	72	112	64	48
Animal physiology	124	46	78	30	15	15	19	11	8
Animal behavior and ethology	146	22	124	29	3	26	9	3	6

See notes at end of table.

Table 318.30. Bachelor's, master's, and doctor's degrees conferred by postsecondary institutions, by sex of student and discipline division: 2017–18—Continued

Discipline division	Bachelor's degrees			Master's degrees			Doctor's degrees[1]		
	Total	Males	Females	Total	Males	Females	Total	Males	Females
1	2	3	4	5	6	7	8	9	10
Wildlife biology	450	163	287	9	5	4	3	1	2
Zoology/animal biology, other	2	1	1	14	5	9	7	4	3
Genetics, general	359	107	252	58	24	34	138	53	85
Molecular genetics	212	62	150	16	6	10	83	40	43
Animal genetics	36	9	27	0	0	0	18	5	13
Plant genetics	6	3	3	4	3	1	15	8	7
Human/medical genetics	0	0	0	184	33	151	89	35	54
Genome sciences/genomics	7	2	5	11	3	8	31	13	18
Genetics, other	0	0	0	1	0	1	19	12	7
Physiology, general	1,593	637	956	812	387	425	146	79	67
Molecular physiology	0	0	0	0	0	0	37	16	21
Cell physiology	3	0	3	25	10	15	29	11	18
Endocrinology	0	0	0	2	0	2	9	2	7
Reproductive biology	0	0	0	25	7	18	3	0	3
Cardiovascular science	0	0	0	7	2	5	7	6	1
Exercise physiology	3,879	1,658	2,221	531	219	312	86	51	35
Vision science/physiological optics	97	17	80	40	12	28	16	7	9
Pathology/experimental pathology	22	3	19	105	39	66	176	77	99
Oncology and cancer biology	0	0	0	25	6	19	130	70	60
Physiology, pathology, and related sciences, other	59	14	45	20	5	15	7	6	1
Pharmacology	78	39	39	226	115	111	210	100	110
Molecular pharmacology	0	0	0	5	1	4	57	27	30
Neuropharmacology	0	0	0	32	19	13	0	0	0
Toxicology	63	18	45	55	21	34	71	28	43
Molecular toxicology	0	0	0	0	0	0	1	1	0
Environmental toxicology	22	8	14	46	19	27	41	16	25
Pharmacology and toxicology	68	31	37	102	36	66	55	22	33
Pharmacology and toxicology, other	0	0	0	0	0	0	0	0	0
Biometry/biometrics	31	18	13	34	20	14	11	6	5
Biostatistics	30	8	22	718	284	434	206	98	108
Bioinformatics	284	163	121	420	221	199	119	81	38
Computational biology	40	20	20	30	17	13	49	28	21
Biomathematics, bioinformatics, and computational biology, other	38	11	27	65	42	23	22	16	6
Biotechnology	844	399	445	1,344	557	787	15	9	6
Ecology	715	280	435	159	65	94	172	78	94
Marine biology and biological oceanography	1,357	418	939	244	63	181	75	33	42
Evolutionary biology	103	29	74	22	9	13	33	18	15
Aquatic biology/limnology	91	52	39	9	4	5	0	0	0
Environmental biology	337	140	197	42	14	28	16	8	8
Population biology	0	0	0	8	3	5	8	3	5
Conservation biology	141	49	92	91	29	62	12	6	6
Systematic biology/biological systematics	0	0	0	4	1	3	11	7	4
Epidemiology	23	5	18	1,400	399	1,001	359	95	264
Ecology and evolutionary biology	452	164	288	57	21	36	94	48	46
Ecology, evolution, systematics and population biology, other	194	83	111	26	14	12	41	22	19
Molecular medicine	0	0	0	16	3	13	34	16	18
Neuroscience	6,191	2,110	4,081	243	95	148	618	272	346
Neurobiology and anatomy	834	327	507	11	2	9	54	17	37
Neurobiology and behavior	139	40	99	33	10	23	15	10	5
Neurobiology and neurosciences, other	44	11	33	0	0	0	5	4	1
Biological and biomedical sciences, other	1,141	345	796	1,246	581	665	199	79	120
Business, management, marketing, and personal and culinary services	386,201	204,839	181,362	192,184	99,860	92,324	3,338	1,926	1,412
Business, management, marketing, and related support services	385,400	204,563	180,837	192,154	99,855	92,299	3,338	1,926	1,412
Business/commerce, general	25,128	13,342	11,786	9,402	5,576	3,826	249	149	100
Business administration and management, general	138,905	74,085	64,820	106,000	58,051	47,949	2,003	1,217	786
Purchasing, procurement/acquisitions and contracts management	655	388	267	409	211	198	3	3	0
Logistics, materials, and supply chain management	5,494	3,679	1,815	959	638	321	2	1	1
Office management and supervision	430	175	255	62	31	31	0	0	0
Operations management and supervision	3,005	1,940	1,065	544	326	218	9	5	4
Nonprofit/public/organizational management	386	112	274	1,860	553	1,307	5	3	2
Customer service management	57	18	39	2	0	2	0	0	0
E-commerce/electronic commerce	99	42	57	41	26	15	0	0	0
Transportation/mobility management	167	108	59	147	117	30	4	4	0
Research and development management	8	5	3	164	60	104	0	0	0
Project management	601	361	240	1,018	555	463	8	4	4
Retail management	306	49	257	97	3	94	0	0	0
Organizational leadership	3,946	1,900	2,046	5,605	2,437	3,168	366	177	189
Business administration, management and operations, other	8,466	3,984	4,482	5,704	2,778	2,926	48	22	26
Accounting	50,128	24,316	25,812	19,637	8,737	10,900	36	16	20
Accounting technology/technician and bookkeeping	200	115	85	0	0	0	0	0	0
Auditing	31	10	21	126	53	73	0	0	0
Accounting and finance	818	477	341	868	370	498	0	0	0
Accounting and business/management	968	415	553	400	195	205	0	0	0
Accounting and related services, other	142	79	63	207	91	116	2	1	1
Administrative assistant and secretarial science, general	57	21	36	0	0	0	0	0	0
Executive assistant/executive secretary	0	0	0	0	0	0	0	0	0
Business/office automation/technology/data entry	29	9	20	0	0	0	0	0	0
General office occupations and clerical services	0	0	0	0	0	0	0	0	0
Parts, warehousing, and inventory management operations	0	0	0	0	0	0	0	0	0
Traffic, customs, and transportation clerk/technician	47	31	16	0	0	0	0	0	0
Business operations support and secretarial services, other	0	0	0	0	0	0	0	0	0
Business/corporate communications	937	324	613	72	18	54	0	0	0
Business/managerial economics	5,535	3,632	1,903	250	155	95	53	33	20
Entrepreneurship/entrepreneurial studies	2,600	1,664	936	680	357	323	11	7	4
Franchising and franchise operations	2	1	1	0	0	0	0	0	0
Small business administration/management	165	82	83	9	6	3	0	0	0

See notes at end of table.

Table 318.30. Bachelor's, master's, and doctor's degrees conferred by postsecondary institutions, by sex of student and discipline division: 2017–18—Continued

Discipline division	Bachelor's degrees			Master's degrees			Doctor's degrees[1]		
	Total	Males	Females	Total	Males	Females	Total	Males	Females
1	2	3	4	5	6	7	8	9	10
Entrepreneurial and small business operations, other	91	54	37	92	29	63	1	0	1
Finance, general	39,479	27,985	11,494	5,648	3,429	2,219	33	22	11
Banking and financial support services	494	316	178	34	15	19	0	0	0
Financial planning and services	480	335	145	222	134	88	12	7	5
International finance	3	1	2	26	16	10	0	0	0
Investments and securities	64	54	10	149	100	49	0	0	0
Public finance	16	12	4	12	9	3	0	0	0
Finance and financial management services, other	198	136	62	128	81	47	0	0	0
Hospitality administration/management, general	7,522	2,233	5,289	544	168	376	29	13	16
Tourism and travel services management	684	198	486	108	38	70	2	1	1
Hotel/motel administration/management	1,677	543	1,134	106	41	65	7	3	4
Restaurant/food services management	738	296	442	1	1	0	0	0	0
Resort management	258	104	154	0	0	0	0	0	0
Meeting and event planning	618	51	567	6	3	3	0	0	0
Casino management	0	0	0	0	0	0	0	0	0
Hotel, motel, and restaurant management	48	20	28	0	0	0	0	0	0
Hospitality administration/management, other	383	142	241	72	33	39	1	0	1
Human resources management/personnel administration, general	6,850	1,862	4,988	4,700	1,181	3,519	44	18	26
Labor and industrial relations	974	448	526	728	246	482	8	6	2
Organizational behavior studies	2,276	966	1,310	1,292	482	810	153	71	82
Labor studies	53	21	32	17	9	8	0	0	0
Human resources development	724	139	585	978	249	729	34	18	16
Human resources management and services, other	349	69	280	1,128	392	736	0	0	0
International business/trade/commerce	5,698	2,694	3,004	1,960	1,047	913	29	13	16
Management information systems, general	8,335	6,006	2,329	1,760	1,171	589	28	16	12
Information resources management	236	159	77	668	486	182	29	21	8
Knowledge management	43	23	20	199	106	93	0	0	0
Management information systems and services, other	141	73	68	164	99	65	0	0	0
Management science, general	3,556	2,119	1,437	4,689	2,615	2,074	46	31	15
Business statistics	412	249	163	1,143	631	512	0	0	0
Actuarial science	1,440	852	588	550	319	231	0	0	0
Management sciences and quantitative methods, other	708	452	256	2,902	1,605	1,297	9	6	3
Marketing/marketing management, general	37,010	17,036	19,974	1,969	679	1,290	32	15	17
Marketing research	28	13	15	140	64	76	2	1	1
International marketing	206	49	157	493	206	287	2	1	1
Marketing, other	755	370	385	277	80	197	4	0	4
Real estate	977	735	242	1,039	764	275	0	0	0
Taxation	9	8	1	1,619	807	812	0	0	0
Insurance	1,138	738	400	115	58	57	0	0	0
Sales, distribution, and marketing operations, general	1,549	829	720	557	151	406	3	1	2
Merchandising and buying operations	0	0	0	7	0	7	0	0	0
Retailing and retail operations	387	87	300	3	0	3	0	0	0
Selling skills and sales operations	341	225	116	0	0	0	0	0	0
General merchandising/sales/related marketing operations, other	94	24	70	3	2	1	0	0	0
Fashion merchandising	2,649	156	2,493	67	6	61	0	0	0
Apparel and accessories marketing operations	40	6	34	50	5	45	0	0	0
Tourism and travel services marketing operations	29	11	18	0	0	0	0	0	0
Tourism promotion operations	1	1	0	0	0	0	0	0	0
Vehicle and vehicle parts and accessories marketing operations	68	55	13	0	0	0	0	0	0
Business and personal/financial services marketing operations	0	0	0	0	0	0	0	0	0
Special products marketing operations	202	83	119	14	5	9	0	0	0
Hospitality and recreation marketing operations	78	65	13	0	0	0	0	0	0
Specialized merchandising/sales/related marketing operations, other	133	41	92	52	23	29	0	0	0
Construction management	2,274	2,056	218	425	308	117	6	6	0
Telecommunications management	0	0	0	24	16	8	0	0	0
Business/management/marketing/related support services, other	3,572	1,999	1,573	1,011	602	409	25	14	11
Personal and culinary services	801	276	525	30	5	25	0	0	0
Funeral service and mortuary science, general	137	42	95	0	0	0	0	0	0
Funeral direction/service	44	16	28	0	0	0	0	0	0
Cosmetology/cosmetologist, general	0	0	0	0	0	0	0	0	0
Cooking and related culinary arts, general	0	0	0	0	0	0	0	0	0
Baking and pastry arts/baker/pastry chef	79	11	68	0	0	0	0	0	0
Culinary arts/chef training	324	114	210	0	0	0	0	0	0
Restaurant, culinary, and catering management/manager	111	57	54	0	0	0	0	0	0
Food service, waiter/waitress, and dining room management	0	0	0	0	0	0	0	0	0
Culinary science/culinology	57	24	33	0	0	0	0	0	0
Culinary arts and related services, other	49	12	37	30	5	25	0	0	0
Personal and culinary services, other	0	0	0	0	0	0	0	0	0
Communication and communications technologies	96,521	34,187	62,334	10,772	3,187	7,585	666	252	414
Communication, journalism, and related programs	92,290	31,811	60,479	10,243	2,923	7,320	666	252	414
Communication, general	9,540	3,045	6,495	994	291	703	71	16	55
Speech communication and rhetoric	32,804	11,421	21,383	1,812	564	1,248	303	109	194
Mass communication/media studies	9,218	3,331	5,887	932	272	660	139	61	78
Communication and media studies, other	1,707	591	1,116	547	155	392	48	23	25
Journalism	11,049	3,574	7,475	1,095	332	763	39	14	25
Broadcast journalism	815	365	450	24	8	16	0	0	0
Photojournalism	101	23	78	18	7	11	0	0	0
Journalism, other	738	195	543	456	109	347	0	0	0
Radio and television	4,618	2,459	2,159	150	54	96	13	6	7
Digital communication and media/multimedia	4,186	1,805	2,381	1,226	439	787	30	17	13
Radio, television, and digital communication, other	871	469	402	15	7	8	0	0	0
Public relations, advertising, and applied communication	2,397	578	1,819	394	85	309	0	0	0
Organizational communication, general	1,478	442	1,036	319	78	241	0	0	0
Public relations/image management	4,971	977	3,994	561	137	424	0	0	0
Advertising	4,451	1,443	3,008	213	46	167	6	0	6

See notes at end of table.

Table 318.30. Bachelor's, master's, and doctor's degrees conferred by postsecondary institutions, by sex of student and discipline division: 2017–18—Continued

Discipline division	Bachelor's degrees			Master's degrees			Doctor's degrees[1]		
	Total	Males	Females	Total	Males	Females	Total	Males	Females
1	2	3	4	5	6	7	8	9	10
Political communication	80	26	54	43	17	26	0	0	0
Health communication	128	22	106	163	22	141	4	1	3
Sports communication	258	184	74	57	34	23	0	0	0
International and intercultural communication	115	35	80	141	35	106	0	0	0
Technical and scientific communication	48	24	24	24	7	17	8	3	5
Public relations, advertising and applied communication, other	1,558	349	1,209	244	71	173	0	0	0
Publishing	13	3	10	203	19	184	0	0	0
Communication, journalism, and related programs, other	1,146	450	696	612	134	478	5	2	3
Communications technologies/technicians and support services	4,231	2,376	1,855	529	264	265	0	0	0
Communications technology/technician	281	234	47	17	8	9	0	0	0
Photographic and film/video technology/technician and assistant	70	43	27	0	0	0	0	0	0
Radio and television broadcasting technology/technician	372	196	176	75	32	43	0	0	0
Recording arts technology/technician	438	361	77	54	35	19	0	0	0
Audiovisual communications technologies/technicians, other	161	144	17	0	0	0	0	0	0
Graphic communications, general	422	156	266	33	8	25	0	0	0
Printing management	92	25	67	0	0	0	0	0	0
Prepress/desktop publishing and digital imaging design	55	21	34	0	0	0	0	0	0
Animation/interactive technology/video graphics/special effects	2,081	1,081	1,000	341	174	167	0	0	0
Graphic and printing equipment operator, general production	17	7	10	0	0	0	0	0	0
Printing press operator	14	7	7	0	0	0	0	0	0
Graphic communications, other	110	44	66	0	0	0	0	0	0
Communications technologies/technicians and support services, other	118	57	61	9	7	2	0	0	0
Computer and information sciences and support services	79,598	63,704	15,894	46,468	31,397	15,071	2,017	1,580	437
Computer and information sciences, general	20,707	17,024	3,683	11,217	7,948	3,269	648	508	140
Artificial intelligence	11	11	0	204	152	52	31	25	6
Information technology	10,054	8,022	2,032	4,988	2,940	2,048	57	43	14
Informatics	1,268	909	359	498	273	225	24	14	10
Computer and information sciences, other	529	418	111	222	133	89	12	6	6
Computer programming/programmer, general	918	796	122	40	29	11	5	5	0
Computer programming, specific applications	386	334	52	31	29	2	0	0	0
Computer programming, vendor/product certification	27	21	6	0	0	0	0	0	0
Computer programming, other	44	40	4	38	24	14	0	0	0
Data processing and data processing technology/technician	136	110	26	11	8	3	0	0	0
Information science/studies	8,047	6,030	2,017	6,856	4,177	2,679	164	89	75
Computer systems analysis/analyst	1,070	847	223	692	438	254	2	2	0
Data entry/microcomputer applications, general	0	0	0	20	12	8	0	0	0
Computer science	26,313	21,497	4,816	12,483	8,885	3,598	1,003	835	168
Web page, digital/multimedia and information resources design	1,217	549	668	556	231	325	0	0	0
Data modeling/warehousing and database administration	130	94	36	766	460	306	0	0	0
Computer graphics	721	390	331	285	124	161	0	0	0
Modeling, virtual environments and simulation	346	287	59	141	101	40	0	0	0
Computer software and media applications, other	262	180	82	194	130	64	1	1	0
Computer systems networking and telecommunications	1,352	1,139	213	726	528	198	3	1	2
Network and system administration/administrator	392	357	35	66	35	31	0	0	0
System, networking, and LAN/WAN management/manager	194	171	23	26	19	7	0	0	0
Computer and information systems security/information assurance	3,813	3,204	609	4,926	3,780	1,146	43	35	8
Web/multimedia management and webmaster	145	98	47	5	2	3	0	0	0
Information technology project management	555	449	106	397	236	161	1	1	0
Computer support specialist	5	5	0	0	0	0	0	0	0
Computer/information tech. services admin. and management, other	771	591	180	813	537	276	0	0	0
Computer and information sciences and support services, other	185	131	54	267	166	101	23	15	8
Education	82,621	15,167	67,454	146,367	32,871	113,496	12,780	4,112	8,668
Education, general	3,611	590	3,021	20,231	4,372	15,859	2,565	747	1,818
Bilingual and multilingual education	147	7	140	322	56	266	10	2	8
Multicultural education	2	0	2	100	21	79	13	4	9
Indian/Native American education	0	0	0	0	0	0	0	0	0
Bilingual, multilingual, and multicultural education, other	0	0	0	85	7	78	3	0	3
Curriculum and instruction	31	8	23	14,713	2,666	12,047	1,374	322	1,052
Educational leadership and administration, general	316	13	303	18,500	6,031	12,469	4,677	1,720	2,957
Administration of special education	0	0	0	66	6	60	11	2	9
Adult and continuing education administration	0	0	0	369	96	273	48	14	34
Educational, instructional, and curriculum supervision	36	5	31	1,281	319	962	103	25	78
Higher education/higher education administration	0	0	0	3,133	961	2,172	643	231	412
Community college education	0	0	0	62	17	45	191	78	113
Elementary and middle school administration/principalship	120	7	113	732	299	433	12	2	10
Secondary school administration/principalship	2	0	2	293	140	153	3	3	0
Urban education and leadership	79	26	53	384	97	287	77	21	56
Superintendency and educational system administration	0	0	0	462	177	285	135	38	97
Educational administration and supervision, other	0	0	0	1,247	374	873	397	135	262
Educational/instructional technology	62	27	35	5,176	1,404	3,772	177	69	108
Educational evaluation and research	0	0	0	96	37	59	144	44	100
Educational statistics and research methods	0	0	0	94	39	55	45	17	28
Educational assessment, testing, and measurement	0	0	0	64	5	59	12	3	9
Learning sciences	370	50	320	99	21	78	10	3	7
Educational assessment, evaluation, and research, other	14	1	13	128	37	91	30	7	23
International and comparative education	47	8	39	313	39	274	11	5	6
Social and philosophical foundations of education	20	2	18	333	89	244	130	48	82
Special education and teaching, general	6,197	656	5,541	11,666	1,884	9,782	197	47	150
Education/teaching of individuals with hearing impairments/deafness	76	2	74	132	7	125	6	3	3
Education/teaching of the gifted and talented	0	0	0	312	35	277	1	0	1
Education/teaching of individuals with emotional disturbances	33	3	30	80	18	62	11	1	10
Education/teaching of individuals with mental retardation	112	16	96	44	8	36	3	2	1
Education/teaching of individuals with multiple disabilities	111	8	103	263	44	219	0	0	0
Education/teaching of individuals with orthopedic/physical health impairments	2	0	2	0	0	0	4	0	4
Education/teaching of individuals with vision impairments/blindness	8	2	6	126	20	106	0	0	0

See notes at end of table.

Table 318.30. Bachelor's, master's, and doctor's degrees conferred by postsecondary institutions, by sex of student and discipline division: 2017–18—Continued

Discipline division	Bachelor's degrees			Master's degrees			Doctor's degrees[1]		
	Total	Males	Females	Total	Males	Females	Total	Males	Females
1	2	3	4	5	6	7	8	9	10
Education/teaching of individuals with specific learning disabilities	151	11	140	272	31	241	0	0	0
Education/teaching of individuals with speech/language impairments	143	8	135	301	10	291	0	0	0
Education/teaching of individuals with autism	6	0	6	1,071	103	968	0	0	0
Education/teaching of individuals who are developmentally delayed	20	1	19	171	23	148	0	0	0
Education/teaching of individuals in early childhood special educ. programs	589	34	555	1,051	39	1,012	0	0	0
Education/teaching of individuals in elementary special educ. programs	450	32	418	980	122	858	0	0	0
Education/teaching of individuals in jr. high/middle school special educ. programs	39	4	35	42	9	33	0	0	0
Education/teaching of individuals in secondary special educ. programs	21	2	19	481	129	352	0	0	0
Special education and teaching, other	373	26	347	674	126	548	15	1	14
Counselor education/school counseling and guidance services	3	0	3	11,033	1,893	9,140	323	78	245
College student counseling and personnel services	0	0	0	1,148	299	849	57	18	39
Student counseling and personnel services, other	0	0	0	235	42	193	5	2	3
Adult and continuing education and teaching	28	9	19	976	289	687	113	42	71
Elementary education and teaching	27,484	2,230	25,254	7,619	906	6,713	23	5	18
Junior high/intermediate/middle school education and teaching	2,147	571	1,576	682	180	502	0	0	0
Secondary education and teaching	3,055	1,213	1,842	5,298	2,019	3,279	15	5	10
Teacher education, multiple levels	1,405	176	1,229	3,994	977	3,017	6	2	4
Montessori teacher education	4	0	4	201	12	189	0	0	0
Waldorf/Steiner teacher education	0	0	0	0	0	0	0	0	0
Kindergarten/preschool education and teaching	904	39	865	201	12	189	10	2	8
Early childhood education and teaching	12,179	458	11,721	3,029	115	2,914	17	0	17
Teacher education and prof. dev., specific levels and methods, other	162	22	140	3,522	824	2,698	94	27	67
Agricultural teacher education	645	190	455	245	60	185	32	8	24
Art teacher education	879	92	787	639	113	526	32	5	27
Business teacher education	144	69	75	68	31	37	0	0	0
Driver and safety teacher education	0	0	0	23	17	6	0	0	0
English/language arts teacher education	1,717	351	1,366	727	184	543	16	7	9
Foreign language teacher education	73	11	62	192	38	154	9	4	5
Health teacher education	1,134	316	818	297	87	210	26	4	22
Family and consumer sciences/home economics teacher education	239	18	221	71	1	70	1	0	1
Technology teacher education/industrial arts teacher education	259	214	45	353	156	197	4	3	1
Sales and marketing operations/marketing and dist. teacher educ.	13	7	6	0	0	0	0	0	0
Mathematics teacher education	1,382	387	995	1,418	421	997	51	25	26
Music teacher education	3,122	1,272	1,850	1,078	428	650	87	48	39
Physical education teaching and coaching	6,537	3,617	2,920	1,574	932	642	40	24	16
Reading teacher education	25	1	24	5,437	280	5,157	102	15	87
Science teacher education/general science teacher education	423	151	272	828	272	556	59	23	36
Social science teacher education	396	224	172	119	69	50	0	0	0
Social studies teacher education	1,028	622	406	417	241	176	2	1	1
Technical teacher education	157	66	91	139	62	77	39	10	29
Trade and industrial teacher education	501	286	215	193	86	107	19	6	13
Computer teacher education	62	8	54	135	48	87	0	0	0
Biology teacher education	288	99	189	283	73	210	1	1	0
Chemistry teacher education	74	34	40	83	35	48	0	0	0
Drama and dance teacher education	108	11	97	66	8	58	0	0	0
French language teacher education	19	5	14	19	5	14	0	0	0
German language teacher education	4	0	4	1	0	1	0	0	0
Health occupations teacher education	4	0	4	159	10	149	43	2	41
History teacher education	469	263	206	82	43	39	0	0	0
Physics teacher education	36	23	13	54	32	22	2	0	2
Spanish language teacher education	208	42	166	142	41	101	0	0	0
Speech teacher education	13	5	8	30	5	25	7	1	6
Geography teacher education	0	0	0	1	0	1	0	0	0
Latin teacher education	2	1	1	4	3	1	0	0	0
School librarian/library media specialist	0	0	0	253	20	233	0	0	0
Psychology teacher education	4	0	4	0	0	0	0	0	0
Earth science teacher education	29	11	18	51	21	30	2	1	1
Environmental education	1	0	1	80	18	62	1	1	0
Teacher education and prof. dev., specific subject areas, other	163	52	111	1,389	307	1,082	42	10	32
Teaching English as a second/foreign language/ESL language instructor	283	55	228	3,427	681	2,746	38	15	23
Teaching English or French as a second or foreign language, other	13	5	8	17	2	15	0	0	0
Teacher assistant/aide	4	1	3	0	0	0	0	0	0
Adult literacy tutor/instructor	0	0	0	16	1	15	0	0	0
Education, other	1,604	391	1,213	2,370	554	1,816	404	123	281
Engineering and engineering technologies	140,683	111,171	29,512	58,968	43,627	15,341	11,029	8,331	2,698
Engineering	121,956	94,847	27,109	51,721	38,496	13,225	10,817	8,180	2,637
Engineering, general	2,673	2,025	648	2,730	2,068	662	443	340	103
Pre-engineering	27	22	5	0	0	0	0	0	0
Aerospace, aeronautical and astronautical engineering	4,132	3,557	575	1,620	1,351	269	348	306	42
Agricultural engineering	1,170	712	458	207	124	83	153	94	59
Architectural engineering	660	433	227	148	99	49	9	5	4
Bioengineering and biomedical engineering	7,416	4,009	3,407	2,831	1,604	1,227	1,091	653	438
Ceramic sciences and engineering	81	49	32	16	14	2	14	12	2
Chemical engineering	11,384	7,443	3,941	1,875	1,196	679	986	688	298
Chemical and biomolecular engineering	158	95	63	43	30	13	24	18	6
Chemical engineering, other	0	0	0	2	2	0	0	0	0
Civil engineering, general	13,836	10,305	3,531	5,336	3,791	1,545	1,027	726	301
Geotechnical and geoenvironmental engineering	0	0	0	2	2	0	0	0	0
Structural engineering	160	120	40	250	172	78	8	6	2
Transportation and highway engineering	9	9	0	97	67	30	11	7	4
Water resources engineering	16	10	6	56	32	24	6	1	5
Civil engineering, other	18	14	4	55	41	14	4	4	0
Computer engineering, general	8,266	7,225	1,041	2,826	2,106	720	376	295	81
Computer hardware engineering	0	0	0	43	33	10	0	0	0
Computer software engineering	1,309	1,122	187	1,698	1,128	570	7	5	2
Computer engineering, other	25	23	2	78	63	15	5	4	1
Electrical and electronics engineering	16,694	14,296	2,398	11,144	8,526	2,618	2,295	1,896	399

See notes at end of table.

Table 318.30. Bachelor's, master's, and doctor's degrees conferred by postsecondary institutions, by sex of student and discipline division: 2017–18—Continued

Discipline division	Bachelor's degrees			Master's degrees			Doctor's degrees[1]		
	Total	Males	Females	Total	Males	Females	Total	Males	Females
1	2	3	4	5	6	7	8	9	10
Laser and optical engineering	63	44	19	41	35	6	17	15	2
Telecommunications engineering	5	5	0	201	137	64	2	2	0
Electrical, electronics and communications engineering, other	139	116	23	128	101	27	13	10	3
Engineering mechanics	119	96	23	99	87	12	80	65	15
Engineering physics/applied physics	676	545	131	106	78	28	90	67	23
Engineering science	553	374	179	321	227	94	114	85	29
Environmental/environmental health engineering	1,578	822	756	945	501	444	165	85	80
Materials engineering	1,522	1,050	472	1,162	837	325	708	512	196
Mechanical engineering	35,182	30,150	5,032	8,150	7,019	1,131	1,586	1,346	240
Metallurgical engineering	162	107	55	35	23	12	20	16	4
Mining and mineral engineering	253	217	36	99	77	22	20	18	2
Naval architecture and marine engineering	453	392	61	35	29	6	7	6	1
Nuclear engineering	535	451	84	247	211	36	181	154	27
Ocean engineering	194	138	56	70	53	17	16	13	3
Petroleum engineering	2,151	1,786	365	515	429	86	134	108	26
Systems engineering	755	529	226	1,808	1,331	477	108	73	35
Textile sciences and engineering	254	68	186	80	28	52	25	11	14
Polymer/plastics engineering	164	123	41	106	70	36	61	44	17
Construction engineering	521	443	78	331	244	87	1	1	0
Forest engineering	39	35	4	0	0	0	0	0	0
Industrial engineering	5,538	3,703	1,835	3,235	2,458	777	330	246	84
Manufacturing engineering	484	411	73	331	258	73	13	12	1
Operations research	466	277	189	774	461	313	81	60	21
Surveying engineering	43	39	4	6	5	1	2	1	1
Geological/geophysical engineering	275	172	103	137	102	35	18	15	3
Paper science and engineering	23	22	1	10	7	3	6	4	2
Electromechanical engineering	35	30	5	0	0	0	3	3	0
Mechatronics, robotics, and automation engineering	271	234	37	272	227	45	30	26	4
Biochemical engineering	107	50	57	13	9	4	0	0	0
Engineering chemistry	5	3	2	0	0	0	0	0	0
Biological/biosystems engineering	363	184	179	21	13	8	16	10	6
Engineering, other	994	762	232	1,386	990	396	163	112	51
Engineering technologies/construction trades/mechanics and repairers	18,727	16,324	2,403	7,247	5,131	2,116	212	151	61
Engineering technologies and engineering-related fields	18,228	15,861	2,367	7,246	5,131	2,115	212	151	61
Engineering technology, general	1,520	1,376	144	331	221	110	12	8	4
Architectural engineering technology/technician	331	272	59	18	9	9	0	0	0
Civil engineering technology/technician	527	461	66	0	0	0	0	0	0
Electrical/electronic/communications eng. technology/technician	1,368	1,247	121	16	14	2	0	0	0
Laser and optical technology/technician	0	0	0	0	0	0	0	0	0
Telecommunications technology/technician	51	44	7	186	141	45	0	0	0
Electrical/electronic eng. technologies/technicians, other	199	175	24	13	10	3	0	0	0
Biomedical technology/technician	55	44	11	5	4	1	3	0	3
Electromechanical technology/electromechanical eng. technology	141	132	9	6	6	0	0	0	0
Instrumentation technology/technician	35	34	1	0	0	0	0	0	0
Robotics technology/technician	34	32	2	12	9	3	0	0	0
Automation engineer technology/technician	128	119	9	0	0	0	0	0	0
Electromechanical/instrumentation and maintenance technol./tech.	15	11	4	0	0	0	0	0	0
Heating, ventilation, air conditioning and refrig. eng. technol./tech.	1	1	0	0	0	0	0	0	0
Energy management and systems technology/technician	116	96	20	102	87	15	0	0	0
Solar energy technology/technician	0	0	0	15	11	4	0	0	0
Water quality/wastewater treatment management/recycling technol./tech.	1	1	0	0	0	0	0	0	0
Environmental engineering technology/environmental technology	135	92	43	83	41	42	0	0	0
Hazardous materials management and waste technology/technician	1	1	0	0	0	0	0	0	0
Environmental control technologies/technicians, other	6	3	3	25	17	8	0	0	0
Plastics and polymer engineering technology/technician	106	89	17	5	5	0	0	0	0
Industrial technology/technician	1,754	1,554	200	379	260	119	15	13	2
Manufacturing engineering technology/technician	676	617	59	86	70	16	0	0	0
Welding engineering technology/technician	19	18	1	0	0	0	0	0	0
Industrial production technologies/technicians, other	250	212	38	7	2	5	0	0	0
Occupational safety and health technology/technician	1,576	1,290	286	592	443	149	4	4	0
Quality control technology/technician	5	4	1	62	34	28	0	0	0
Industrial safety technology/technician	196	157	39	20	17	3	0	0	0
Quality control and safety technologies/technicians, other	36	35	1	11	3	8	0	0	0
Aeronautical/aerospace engineering technology/technician	204	174	30	43	36	7	0	0	0
Automotive engineering technology/technician	365	343	22	97	94	3	2	1	1
Mechanical engineering/mechanical technology/technician	1,954	1,810	144	17	7	10	0	0	0
Mechanical engineering related technologies/technicians, other	256	240	16	0	0	0	0	0	0
Mining technology/technician	1	1	0	0	0	0	0	0	0
Petroleum technology/technician	61	53	8	0	0	0	0	0	0
Mining and petroleum technologies/technicians, other	0	0	0	0	0	0	0	0	0
Construction engineering technology/technician	2,148	1,936	212	181	133	48	1	1	0
Surveying technology/surveying	170	155	15	7	6	1	7	5	2
Hydraulics and fluid power technology/technician	0	0	0	0	0	0	0	0	0
Engineering-related technologies, other	12	9	3	0	0	0	0	0	0
Computer engineering technology/technician	588	537	51	0	0	0	0	0	0
Computer technology/computer systems technology	245	218	27	354	257	97	1	0	1
Computer hardware technology/technician	0	0	0	0	0	0	0	0	0
Computer software technology/technician	57	46	11	0	0	0	2	2	0
Computer engineering technologies/technicians, other	42	40	2	0	0	0	0	0	0
Drafting and design technologies/technicians, general	114	51	63	58	10	48	0	0	0
CAD/CADD drafting and/or design technology/technician	169	130	39	62	40	22	1	0	1
Architectural drafting and architectural CAD/CADD	25	20	5	34	21	13	0	0	0
Civil drafting and civil engineering CAD/CADD	4	3	1	0	0	0	0	0	0
Mechanical drafting and mechanical drafting CAD/CADD	30	21	9	0	0	0	0	0	0
Drafting/design engineering technologies/technicians, other	25	21	4	0	0	0	0	0	0
Nuclear engineering technology/technician	175	162	13	1	1	0	0	0	0

See notes at end of table.

Table 318.30. Bachelor's, master's, and doctor's degrees conferred by postsecondary institutions, by sex of student and discipline division: 2017–18—Continued

Discipline division	Bachelor's degrees			Master's degrees			Doctor's degrees[1]		
	Total	Males	Females	Total	Males	Females	Total	Males	Females
1	2	3	4	5	6	7	8	9	10
Engineering/industrial management	1,100	862	238	4,014	2,855	1,159	134	100	34
Engineering design	2	1	1	77	43	34	2	2	0
Packaging science	390	223	167	38	23	15	2	0	2
Engineering-related fields, other	117	80	37	18	11	7	11	4	7
Nanotechnology	21	13	8	63	49	14	15	11	4
Engineering tech. and engineering-related fields, other	671	595	76	208	141	67	0	0	0
Construction trades	151	130	21	0	0	0	0	0	0
Construction trades, general	0	0	0	0	0	0	0	0	0
Mason/masonry	0	0	0	0	0	0	0	0	0
Electrician	0	0	0	0	0	0	0	0	0
Building/property maintenance	0	0	0	0	0	0	0	0	0
Building/construction site management/manager	151	130	21	0	0	0	0	0	0
Building construction technology	0	0	0	0	0	0	0	0	0
Building/construction finishing, mgmt., and inspection, other	0	0	0	0	0	0	0	0	0
Construction trades, other	0	0	0	0	0	0	0	0	0
Mechanic and repair technologies/technicians	348	333	15	1	0	1	0	0	0
Communications systems installation and repair technology	0	0	0	0	0	0	0	0	0
Industrial electronics technology/technician	3	3	0	0	0	0	0	0	0
Heating, air conditioning, ventilation and refrig. main. technician	0	0	0	0	0	0	0	0	0
Heavy equipment maintenance technology/technician	20	20	0	0	0	0	0	0	0
Autobody/collision and repair technology/technician	0	0	0	0	0	0	0	0	0
Automobile/automotive mechanics technology/technician	43	42	1	0	0	0	0	0	0
Diesel mechanics technology/technician	39	36	3	0	0	0	0	0	0
Airframe mechanics and aircraft maintenance technology/technician	36	31	5	0	0	0	0	0	0
Aircraft powerplant technology/technician	117	115	2	1	0	1	0	0	0
Avionics maintenance technology/technician	88	84	4	0	0	0	0	0	0
Vehicle maintenance and repair technologies, other	2	2	0	0	0	0	0	0	0
English language and literature/letters	40,002	11,680	28,322	8,300	2,640	5,660	1,295	512	783
English language and literature, general	32,098	9,139	22,959	4,367	1,283	3,084	1,107	445	662
Writing, general	590	153	437	66	9	57	0	0	0
Creative writing	2,829	874	1,955	2,994	1,091	1,903	16	8	8
Professional, technical, business, and scientific writing	657	212	445	317	91	226	30	14	16
Rhetoric and composition	2,612	895	1,717	153	47	106	107	33	74
Rhetoric and composition/writing studies, other	241	119	122	128	47	81	4	1	3
General literature	244	60	184	20	10	10	0	0	0
American literature (United States)	16	7	9	8	0	8	0	0	0
English literature (British and Commonwealth)	179	52	127	84	22	62	7	4	3
Children's and adolescent literature	1	0	1	15	0	15	0	0	0
Literature, other	9	1	8	5	0	5	0	0	0
English language and literature/letters, other	526	168	358	143	40	103	24	7	17
Family and consumer sciences/human sciences	24,349	2,947	21,402	3,308	467	2,841	274	63	211
Work and family studies	0	0	0	0	0	0	0	0	0
Family and consumer sciences/human sciences, general	3,484	413	3,071	542	121	421	50	17	33
Business family and consumer sciences/human sciences	162	64	98	13	8	5	2	0	2
Family and consumer sciences/human sciences communication	14	2	12	0	0	0	0	0	0
Consumer merchandising/retailing management	177	30	147	26	4	22	1	0	1
Family and consumer sciences/human sciences business services, other	9	1	8	0	0	0	0	0	0
Family resource management studies, general	886	263	623	236	49	187	1	1	0
Consumer economics	144	64	80	0	0	0	0	0	0
Consumer services and advocacy	23	4	19	0	0	0	0	0	0
Family and consumer economics and related services, other	308	28	280	5	1	4	14	6	8
Foods, nutrition, and wellness studies, general	2,379	458	1,921	571	68	503	31	6	25
Human nutrition	396	86	310	412	55	357	13	4	9
Food service systems administration/management	783	273	510	4	1	3	0	0	0
Foods, nutrition, and related services, other	30	11	19	44	7	37	0	0	0
Housing and human environments, general	98	29	69	37	14	23	6	3	3
Facilities planning and management	46	43	3	3	3	0	0	0	0
Housing and human environments, other	2	0	2	0	0	0	0	0	0
Human development and family studies, general	8,499	684	7,815	622	55	567	108	19	89
Adult development and aging	6	2	4	90	9	81	2	0	2
Family systems	514	53	461	33	1	32	6	2	4
Child development	1,569	57	1,512	187	12	175	9	2	7
Family and community services	1,098	122	976	232	26	206	10	1	9
Child care and support services management	445	20	425	75	2	73	0	0	0
Child care provider/assistant	36	0	36	2	0	2	0	0	0
Developmental services worker	0	0	0	0	0	0	0	0	0
Human development, family studies, and related services, other	580	33	547	48	9	39	7	1	6
Apparel and textiles, general	2,092	158	1,934	42	7	35	12	0	12
Apparel and textile manufacture	98	9	89	2	0	2	0	0	0
Textile science	4	0	4	0	0	0	1	0	1
Apparel and textile marketing management	388	33	355	66	10	56	1	1	0
Fashion and fabric consultant	31	1	30	0	0	0	0	0	0
Apparel and textiles, other	14	2	12	7	1	6	0	0	0
Family and consumer sciences/human sciences, other	34	4	30	9	4	5	0	0	0
Foreign languages, literatures, and linguistics	16,958	5,288	11,670	3,261	1,084	2,177	1,213	507	706
Foreign languages and literatures, general	1,627	511	1,116	243	85	158	28	9	19
Linguistics	2,040	619	1,421	543	188	355	243	92	151
Language interpretation and translation	39	7	32	227	49	178	5	3	2
Comparative literature	671	219	452	159	61	98	151	61	90
Applied linguistics	35	8	27	88	25	63	0	0	0
Linguistic/comparative/related language studies and serv., other	230	75	155	27	13	14	14	3	11
African languages, literatures, and linguistics	2	1	1	4	2	2	0	0	0
East Asian languages, literatures, and linguistics, general	152	62	90	88	33	55	36	14	22

See notes at end of table.

Table 318.30. Bachelor's, master's, and doctor's degrees conferred by postsecondary institutions, by sex of student and discipline division: 2017–18—Continued

Discipline division	Bachelor's degrees			Master's degrees			Doctor's degrees[1]		
	Total	Males	Females	Total	Males	Females	Total	Males	Females
1	2	3	4	5	6	7	8	9	10
Chinese language and literature	466	221	245	46	8	38	11	4	7
Japanese language and literature	560	262	298	20	7	13	6	2	4
Korean language and literature	55	21	34	6	2	4	2	0	2
East Asian languages, literatures, and linguistics, other	60	33	27	17	7	10	24	10	14
Slavic languages, literatures, and linguistics, general	35	12	23	44	20	24	20	7	13
Russian language and literature	296	157	139	10	2	8	3	2	1
Polish language and literature	3	0	3	0	0	0	0	0	0
Germanic languages, literatures, and linguistics, general	63	30	33	23	12	11	21	10	11
German language and literature	697	343	354	77	29	48	42	21	21
Scandinavian languages, literatures, and linguistics	14	5	9	2	0	2	4	2	2
Danish language and literature	0	0	0	0	0	0	0	0	0
Dutch/Flemish language and literature	0	0	0	0	0	0	0	0	0
Norwegian language and literature	6	3	3	0	0	0	0	0	0
Swedish language and literature	0	0	0	0	0	0	0	0	0
Germanic languages, literatures, and linguistics, other	13	6	7	0	0	0	0	0	0
Modern Greek language and literature	0	0	0	0	0	0	0	0	0
South Asian languages, literatures, and linguistics, general	2	2	0	1	0	1	2	2	0
Sanskrit and classical Indian languages, literatures, and linguistics	0	0	0	0	0	0	0	0	0
Iranian languages, literatures, and linguistics	6	4	2	0	0	0	0	0	0
Romance languages, literatures, and linguistics, general	130	42	88	74	22	52	39	12	27
French language and literature	1,438	348	1,090	277	76	201	86	21	65
Italian language and literature	145	47	98	36	12	24	22	7	15
Portuguese language and literature	28	13	15	9	3	6	6	3	3
Spanish language and literature	6,011	1,554	4,457	731	217	514	209	91	118
Hispanic and Latin American languages, lit., and linguistics, general	138	35	103	23	11	12	16	9	7
Romance languages, literatures, and linguistics, other	45	8	37	51	19	32	39	22	17
American Indian/Native American languages, literatures, and linguistics	2	0	2	10	4	6	0	0	0
Middle/Near Eastern and Semitic languages, lit., and linguistics, general	16	9	7	22	11	11	26	16	10
Arabic language and literature	153	67	86	6	4	2	2	1	1
Hebrew language and literature	4	2	2	10	4	6	4	2	2
Ancient Near Eastern and biblical languages, lit., and linguistics	16	7	9	19	13	6	6	6	0
Middle/Near Eastern and Semitic languages, lit., and linguistics, other	43	23	20	33	18	15	27	17	10
Classics and classical languages, lit., and linguistics, general	818	346	472	189	85	104	90	46	44
Ancient/classical Greek language and literature	18	6	12	1	1	0	0	0	0
Latin language and literature	47	19	28	18	9	9	1	1	0
Classics and classical languages, lit., and linguistics, other	23	14	9	14	9	5	0	0	0
Celtic languages, literatures, and linguistics	0	0	0	2	0	2	0	0	0
Filipino/Tagalog language and literature	8	6	2	0	0	0	0	0	0
Turkish language and literature	0	0	0	0	0	0	0	0	0
Uralic languages, literatures, and linguistics	1	1	0	0	0	0	0	0	0
American sign language (ASL)	156	19	137	25	7	18	0	0	0
Linguistics of ASL and other sign languages	0	0	0	13	2	11	1	0	1
Sign language interpretation and translation	419	48	371	40	7	33	5	1	4
American sign language, other	3	0	3	0	0	0	0	0	0
Foreign languages, literatures, and linguistics, other	224	73	151	33	7	26	22	10	12
Health professions and related programs	244,909	38,022	206,887	125,216	22,768	102,448	80,305	32,494	47,811
Health and wellness, general	15,559	3,702	11,857	919	266	653	265	103	162
Chiropractic	0	0	0	0	0	0	2,503	1,436	1,067
Communication sciences and disorders, general	4,748	228	4,520	1,740	90	1,650	38	10	28
Audiology/audiologist	205	11	194	141	13	128	698	84	614
Speech-language pathology/pathologist	1,379	42	1,337	3,896	173	3,723	44	3	41
Audiology/audiologist and speech-language pathology/pathologist	4,611	201	4,410	2,682	121	2,561	234	40	194
Communication disorders sciences and services, other	78	2	76	89	3	86	8	3	5
Dentistry	0	0	0	0	0	0	6,441	3,258	3,183
Dental clinical sciences, general	0	0	0	306	151	155	11	6	5
Advanced general dentistry	0	0	0	28	19	9	0	0	0
Oral biology and oral maxillofacial pathology	0	0	0	120	66	54	19	9	10
Dental public health and education	0	0	0	7	1	6	5	3	2
Dental materials	0	0	0	0	0	0	0	0	0
Endodontics/endodontology	0	0	0	35	25	10	1	1	0
Oral/maxillofacial surgery	0	0	0	0	0	0	0	0	0
Orthodontics/orthodontology	0	0	0	103	52	51	0	0	0
Pediatric dentistry/pedodontics	0	0	0	27	6	21	0	0	0
Periodontics/periodontology	0	0	0	31	18	13	1	0	1
Prosthodontics/prosthodontology	0	0	0	26	18	8	4	2	2
Advanced/graduate dentistry and oral sciences, other	0	0	0	79	35	44	9	2	7
Dental assisting/assistant	3	0	3	0	0	0	0	0	0
Dental hygiene/hygienist	2,410	100	2,310	92	4	88	0	0	0
Dental laboratory technology/technician	6	0	6	0	0	0	0	0	0
Dental services and allied professions, other	14	0	14	7	2	5	0	0	0
Health/health care administration/management	11,963	2,427	9,536	10,067	2,808	7,259	225	73	152
Hospital and health care facilities administration/management	2,440	319	2,121	1,397	381	1,016	2	0	2
Health unit manager/ward supervisor	0	0	0	1	0	1	0	0	0
Medical office management/administration	3	0	3	0	0	0	0	0	0
Health information/medical records administration/administrator	1,508	267	1,241	495	142	353	0	0	0
Health information/medical records technology/technician	60	20	40	47	16	31	0	0	0
Medical office assistant/specialist	5	0	5	0	0	0	0	0	0
Medical/health management and clinical assistant/specialist	69	8	61	2	0	2	0	0	0
Medical staff services technology/technician	0	0	0	0	0	0	0	0	0
Long term care administration/management	145	13	132	9	1	8	0	0	0
Clinical research coordinator	9	1	8	93	21	72	0	0	0
Health and medical administrative services, other	748	120	628	272	79	193	8	3	5
Medical/clinical assistant	9	0	9	35	8	27	0	0	0
Occupational therapist assistant	9	2	7	30	4	26	0	0	0
Pharmacy technician/assistant	0	0	0	0	0	0	0	0	0
Physical therapy technician/assistant	45	14	31	0	0	0	0	0	0
Veterinary/animal health technology/technician and vet. assistant	441	33	408	0	0	0	0	0	0

See notes at end of table.

Table 318.30. Bachelor's, master's, and doctor's degrees conferred by postsecondary institutions, by sex of student and discipline division: 2017–18—Continued

Discipline division	Bachelor's degrees			Master's degrees			Doctor's degrees[1]		
	Total	Males	Females	Total	Males	Females	Total	Males	Females
1	2	3	4	5	6	7	8	9	10
Anesthesiologist assistant	0	0	0	207	104	103	0	0	0
Emergency care attendant (EMT ambulance)	2	1	1	0	0	0	0	0	0
Pathology/pathologist assistant	12	5	7	77	19	58	0	0	0
Respiratory therapy technician/assistant	17	3	14	0	0	0	0	0	0
Radiologist assistant	0	0	0	4	2	2	0	0	0
Speech-language pathology assistant	21	1	20	0	0	0	0	0	0
Allied health and medical assisting services, other	297	75	222	136	34	102	0	0	0
Cardiovascular technology/technologist	98	26	72	23	15	8	0	0	0
Electrocardiograph technology/technician	0	0	0	0	0	0	0	0	0
Electroneurodiagnostic/electroencephalographic technology/technologist	6	1	5	0	0	0	0	0	0
Emergency medical technology/technician (EMT paramedic)	299	208	91	13	6	7	0	0	0
Nuclear medical technology/technologist	255	74	181	10	5	5	0	0	0
Perfusion technology/perfusionist	8	6	2	74	35	39	0	0	0
Medical radiologic technology/science radiation therapist	1,195	236	959	83	36	47	1	0	1
Respiratory care therapy/therapist	1,332	391	941	70	27	43	0	0	0
Surgical technology/technologist	20	5	15	0	0	0	0	0	0
Diagnostic medical sonography/sonographer and ultrasound technician	752	95	657	9	1	8	0	0	0
Radiologic technology/science radiographer	1,441	356	1,085	85	35	50	1	1	0
Physician assistant	580	155	425	8,527	2,253	6,274	16	10	6
Athletic training/trainer	3,958	1,432	2,526	991	385	606	80	32	48
Gene/genetic therapy	14	10	4	0	0	0	1	1	0
Cardiopulmonary technology/technologist	19	2	17	0	0	0	0	0	0
Radiation protection/health physics technician	16	4	12	6	4	2	0	0	0
Polysomnography	3	2	1	0	0	0	0	0	0
Magnetic resonance imaging (MRI) technology/technician	38	13	25	6	3	3	0	0	0
Allied health diagnostic/intervention/treatment professions, other	549	150	399	55	19	36	73	14	59
Blood bank technology specialist	0	0	0	13	1	12	0	0	0
Cytotechnology/cytotechnologist	32	14	18	11	6	5	0	0	0
Hematology technology/technician	0	0	0	5	2	3	0	0	0
Clinical/medical laboratory technician	187	54	133	0	0	0	0	0	0
Clinical laboratory science/medical technology/technologist	2,924	749	2,175	260	68	192	0	0	0
Histologic technology/histotechnologist	20	2	18	5	1	4	0	0	0
Histologic technician	11	4	7	0	0	0	0	0	0
Cytogenetics/genetics/clinical genetics technology/technologist	37	15	22	14	5	9	0	0	0
Clinical/medical laboratory science and allied professions, other	536	136	400	110	27	83	7	5	2
Pre-dentistry studies	17	6	11	0	0	0	0	0	0
Pre-medicine/pre-medical studies	917	345	572	63	26	37	0	0	0
Pre-pharmacy studies	27	12	15	0	0	0	0	0	0
Pre-veterinary studies	440	60	380	1	0	1	0	0	0
Pre-nursing studies	19	1	18	0	0	0	0	0	0
Pre-occupational therapy studies	69	5	64	0	0	0	0	0	0
Pre-optometry studies	2	1	1	0	0	0	0	0	0
Pre-physical therapy studies	259	107	152	0	0	0	0	0	0
Health/medical preparatory programs, other	1,774	495	1,279	230	103	127	0	0	0
Medicine	0	0	0	0	0	0	19,142	10,049	9,093
Medical scientist	0	0	0	584	276	308	38	15	23
Substance abuse/addiction counseling	461	99	362	420	114	306	2	1	1
Psychiatric/mental health services technician	269	50	219	0	0	0	3	0	3
Clinical/medical social work	200	32	168	962	137	825	9	2	7
Community health services/liaison/counseling	1,628	297	1,331	215	36	179	9	0	9
Marriage and family therapy/counseling	39	8	31	2,751	429	2,322	137	34	103
Clinical pastoral counseling/patient counseling	0	0	0	109	39	70	6	1	5
Psychoanalysis and psychotherapy	0	0	0	10	4	6	6	2	4
Mental health counseling/counselor	12	2	10	5,545	917	4,628	25	4	21
Genetic counseling/counselor	0	0	0	172	13	159	0	0	0
Mental and social health services and allied professions, other	451	60	391	1,688	331	1,357	30	4	26
Optometry	0	0	0	0	0	0	1,623	531	1,092
Ophthalmic technician/technologist	2	1	1	0	0	0	0	0	0
Orthoptics/orthoptist	0	0	0	0	0	0	0	0	0
Ophthalmic/optometric support services/allied professions, other	6	1	5	22	6	16	6	3	3
Osteopathic medicine/osteopathy	0	0	0	0	0	0	6,392	3,611	2,781
Pharmacy	834	311	523	3	2	1	14,926	5,629	9,297
Pharmacy admin. and pharmacy policy and regulatory affairs	0	0	0	483	152	331	17	7	10
Pharmaceutics and drug design	131	53	78	151	63	88	197	109	88
Medicinal and pharmaceutical chemistry	19	11	8	54	24	30	94	51	43
Natural products chemistry and pharmacognosy	0	0	0	0	0	0	4	2	2
Clinical and industrial drug development	37	4	33	130	47	83	5	3	2
Pharmacoeconomics/pharmaceutical economics	0	0	0	57	25	32	39	19	20
Clinical, hospital, and managed care pharmacy	0	0	0	12	6	6	0	0	0
Industrial and physical pharmacy and cosmetic sciences	10	0	10	60	24	36	0	0	0
Pharmaceutical sciences	1,007	374	633	254	110	144	175	96	79
Pharmaceutical marketing and management	63	33	30	12	4	8	0	0	0
Pharmacy, pharmaceutical sciences, and administration, other	634	226	408	237	60	177	26	13	13
Podiatric medicine/podiatry	0	0	0	0	0	0	543	341	202
Public health, general	6,656	1,274	5,382	10,059	2,480	7,579	479	136	343
Environmental health	307	134	173	624	211	413	104	42	62
Health/medical physics	46	23	23	133	92	41	44	33	11
Occupational health and industrial hygiene	184	140	44	56	34	22	3	2	1
Public health education and promotion	3,032	599	2,433	938	130	808	57	5	52
Community health and preventive medicine	1,802	322	1,480	258	54	204	19	1	18
Maternal and child health	34	0	34	104	3	101	15	1	14
International public health/international health	160	37	123	490	109	381	21	7	14
Health services administration	1,198	179	1,019	1,015	355	660	16	5	11
Behavioral aspects of health	307	59	248	68	8	60	28	9	19
Public health, other	1,424	323	1,101	931	216	715	103	27	76
Art therapy/therapist	210	3	207	448	24	424	8	1	7
Dance therapy/therapist	0	0	0	60	2	58	0	0	0

See notes at end of table.

Table 318.30. Bachelor's, master's, and doctor's degrees conferred by postsecondary institutions, by sex of student and discipline division: 2017–18—Continued

Discipline division	Bachelor's degrees			Master's degrees			Doctor's degrees[1]		
	Total	Males	Females	Total	Males	Females	Total	Males	Females
1	2	3	4	5	6	7	8	9	10
Music therapy/therapist	456	67	389	137	28	109	1	0	1
Occupational therapy/therapist	835	61	774	6,871	743	6,128	895	76	819
Orthotist/prosthetist	8	4	4	238	117	121	0	0	0
Physical therapy/therapist	286	87	199	59	17	42	11,872	4,406	7,466
Therapeutic recreation/recreational therapy	838	102	736	64	10	54	0	0	0
Vocational rehabilitation counseling/counselor	320	57	263	904	175	729	29	10	19
Kinesiotherapy/kinesiotherapist	98	42	56	44	18	26	0	0	0
Assistive/augmentative technology and rehabilitation engineering	0	0	0	67	8	59	2	0	2
Animal-assisted therapy	36	2	34	0	0	0	0	0	0
Rehabilitation science	899	152	747	152	43	109	68	27	41
Rehabilitation and therapeutic professions, other	603	144	459	275	57	218	41	8	33
Veterinary medicine	0	0	0	0	0	0	3,169	632	2,537
Veterinary sciences/veterinary clinical sciences, general	28	6	22	178	42	136	74	26	48
Veterinary physiology	0	0	0	0	0	0	2	1	1
Veterinary microbiology and immunobiology	40	12	28	3	0	3	9	6	3
Veterinary pathology and pathobiology	0	0	0	14	3	11	56	26	30
Large animal/food animal/equine surgery and medicine	0	0	0	1	0	1	1	0	1
Small/companion animal surgery and medicine	0	0	0	5	1	4	0	0	0
Comparative and laboratory animal medicine	0	0	0	44	8	36	0	0	0
Veterinary preventive medicine epidemiology/public health	0	0	0	18	7	11	0	0	0
Veterinary infectious diseases	0	0	0	15	3	12	7	3	4
Medical illustration/medical illustrator	44	5	39	38	4	34	0	0	0
Medical informatics	166	44	122	1,079	391	688	46	20	26
Medical illustration and informatics, other	0	0	0	38	10	28	0	0	0
Dietetics/dietitian	2,712	341	2,371	497	44	453	3	1	2
Clinical nutrition/nutritionist	201	21	180	599	76	523	9	2	7
Dietetic technician	0	0	0	0	0	0	0	0	0
Dietitian assistant	111	32	79	0	0	0	0	0	0
Dietetics and clinical nutrition services, other	222	41	181	135	12	123	19	3	16
Bioethics/medical ethics	29	9	20	369	130	239	41	13	28
Alternative and complementary medicine and medical systems, general	134	19	115	12	1	11	0	0	0
Acupuncture and oriental medicine	28	8	20	1,227	329	898	542	174	368
Traditional Chinese medicine and Chinese herbology	0	0	0	164	43	121	23	7	16
Naturopathic medicine/naturopathy	0	0	0	0	0	0	322	70	252
Ayurvedic medicine/Ayurveda	0	0	0	21	5	16	0	0	0
Holistic health	180	28	152	35	4	31	0	0	0
Alternative and complementary medicine and medical systems, other	54	6	48	29	1	28	0	0	0
Direct entry midwifery	23	0	23	15	0	15	0	0	0
Alternative and complementary medical support services, other	0	0	0	69	3	66	0	0	0
Massage therapy/therapeutic massage	31	5	26	0	0	0	0	0	0
Asian bodywork therapy	0	0	0	0	0	0	0	0	0
Somatic bodywork and related therapeutic services, other	0	0	0	0	0	0	0	0	0
Movement therapy and movement education	55	19	36	28	2	26	3	2	1
Yoga teacher training/Yoga therapy	2	1	1	24	2	22	0	0	0
Herbalism/herbalist	10	2	8	9	0	9	0	0	0
Energy and biologically based therapies, other	0	0	0	0	0	0	0	0	0
Registered nursing/registered nurse	139,952	17,459	122,493	16,620	1,932	14,688	1,011	122	889
Nursing administration	796	96	700	7,131	745	6,386	318	35	283
Adult health nurse/nursing	275	46	229	1,427	193	1,234	48	3	45
Nurse anesthetist	0	0	0	1,328	568	760	496	205	291
Family practice nurse/nursing	288	34	254	12,723	1,592	11,131	513	63	450
Maternal/child health and neonatal nurse/nursing	0	0	0	179	7	172	10	2	8
Nurse midwife/nursing midwifery	0	0	0	438	1	437	4	0	4
Nursing science	1,234	141	1,093	1,623	167	1,456	882	89	793
Pediatric nurse/nursing	0	0	0	419	15	404	12	2	10
Psychiatric/mental health nurse/nursing	0	0	0	359	78	281	36	3	33
Public health/community nurse/nursing	435	44	391	279	20	259	4	2	2
Perioperative/operating room and surgical nurse/nursing	0	0	0	136	10	126	0	0	0
Clinical nurse specialist	13	2	11	376	39	337	35	5	30
Critical care nursing	0	0	0	414	80	334	11	1	10
Occupational and environmental health nursing	0	0	0	36	9	27	9	1	8
Emergency room/trauma nursing	0	0	0	22	7	15	0	0	0
Nursing education	22	1	21	1,610	124	1,486	115	8	107
Nursing practice	786	84	702	307	40	267	4,131	485	3,646
Palliative care nursing	0	0	0	5	1	4	2	0	2
Clinical nurse leader	66	4	62	418	48	370	0	0	0
Geriatric nurse/nursing	0	0	0	294	36	258	3	0	3
Women's health nurse/nursing	0	0	0	163	0	163	0	0	0
Reg. nursing, nursing admin., nursing research and clinical nursing, other	1,969	250	1,719	1,512	178	1,334	278	23	255
Licensed practical/vocational nurse training	0	0	0	0	0	0	0	0	0
Practical nursing, vocational nursing and nursing assistants, other	7	3	4	0	0	0	0	0	0
Health professions and related clinical sciences, other	4,784	1,119	3,665	941	259	682	107	37	70
Homeland security, law enforcement, firefighting and related prot. services	58,114	30,481	27,633	10,293	5,276	5,017	150	58	92
Corrections	414	175	239	7	3	4	0	0	0
Criminal justice/law enforcement administration	15,629	8,059	7,570	2,495	1,252	1,243	40	18	22
Criminal justice/safety studies	30,513	15,293	15,220	3,216	1,336	1,880	78	28	50
Forensic science and technology	1,551	431	1,120	549	140	409	3	0	3
Criminal justice/police science	2,925	1,603	1,322	50	9	41	6	3	3
Security and loss prevention services	4	2	2	32	17	15	0	0	0
Juvenile corrections	24	9	15	10	4	6	2	0	2
Criminalistics and criminal science	174	41	133	12	3	9	1	0	1
Securities services administration/management	474	366	108	174	134	40	0	0	0
Corrections administration	113	61	52	6	4	2	0	0	0
Law enforcement investigation and interviewing	0	0	0	59	26	33	0	0	0
Cyber/computer forensics and counterterrorism	362	285	77	513	328	185	0	0	0
Financial forensics and fraud investigation	109	40	69	152	52	100	0	0	0

See notes at end of table.

Table 318.30. Bachelor's, master's, and doctor's degrees conferred by postsecondary institutions, by sex of student and discipline division: 2017–18—Continued

Discipline division	Bachelor's degrees			Master's degrees			Doctor's degrees[1]		
	Total	Males	Females	Total	Males	Females	Total	Males	Females
1	2	3	4	5	6	7	8	9	10
Law enforcement intelligence analysis	18	8	10	10	3	7	0	0	0
Critical incident response/special police operations	0	0	0	0	0	0	0	0	0
Protective services operations	1	1	0	0	0	0	0	0	0
Corrections and criminal justice, other	1,371	613	758	424	176	248	0	0	0
Fire prevention and safety technology/technician	170	151	19	9	7	2	0	0	0
Fire services administration	859	813	46	65	41	24	3	0	3
Fire science/firefighting	363	326	37	6	5	1	0	0	0
Fire/arson investigation and prevention	55	36	19	0	0	0	0	0	0
Fire protection, other	40	33	7	17	17	0	0	0	0
Homeland security	972	715	257	757	530	227	4	3	1
Crisis/emergency/disaster management	956	734	222	768	519	249	9	3	6
Critical infrastructure protection	96	74	22	415	304	111	0	0	0
Terrorism and counterterrorism operations	4	3	1	15	11	4	0	0	0
Homeland security, other	91	69	22	19	11	8	0	0	0
Homeland sec., law enforcement, firefighting and related prot. serv., other	826	540	286	513	344	169	4	3	1
Legal professions and studies	4,239	1,340	2,899	9,177	4,110	5,067	34,544	17,383	17,161
Pre-law studies	231	109	122	36	16	20	0	0	0
Legal studies, general	2,098	742	1,356	264	96	168	9	1	8
Law	0	0	0	0	0	0	34,128	17,161	16,967
Advanced legal research/studies, general	69	31	38	2,241	990	1,251	228	125	103
Programs for foreign lawyers	0	0	0	1,757	794	963	9	3	6
American/U.S. law/legal studies/jurisprudence	88	29	59	474	209	265	20	13	7
Banking, corporate, finance, and securities law	0	0	0	271	125	146	0	0	0
Comparative law	0	0	0	49	29	20	0	0	0
Energy, environment, and natural resources law	16	12	4	198	103	95	2	2	0
Health law	0	0	0	292	84	208	2	0	2
International law and legal studies	1	0	1	486	207	279	9	6	3
International business, trade, and tax law	0	0	0	256	123	133	0	0	0
Tax law/taxation	0	0	0	795	485	310	1	0	1
Intellectual property law	0	0	0	111	45	66	0	0	0
Legal research and advanced professional studies, other	0	0	0	895	403	492	29	23	6
Legal administrative assistant/secretary	10	3	7	11	8	3	0	0	0
Legal assistant/paralegal	1,271	261	1,010	99	16	83	0	0	0
Court reporting/court reporter	4	0	4	0	0	0	0	0	0
Legal support services, other	5	1	4	6	4	2	0	0	0
Legal professions and studies, other	446	152	294	936	373	563	107	49	58
Liberal arts and sciences, general studies and humanities	44,262	15,966	28,296	2,473	880	1,593	93	35	58
Liberal arts and sciences/liberal studies	24,179	7,786	16,393	1,514	580	934	19	7	12
General studies	14,268	5,930	8,338	179	59	120	2	0	2
Humanities/humanistic studies	1,804	610	1,194	487	162	325	65	27	38
Liberal arts and sciences, general studies and humanities, other	4,011	1,640	2,371	293	79	214	7	1	6
Library science	81	7	74	4,953	856	4,097	54	16	38
Library and information science	81	7	74	4,665	814	3,851	54	16	38
Children and youth library services	0	0	0	18	1	17	0	0	0
Archives/archival administration	0	0	0	144	25	119	0	0	0
Library science, other	0	0	0	126	16	110	0	0	0
Mathematics and statistics	25,256	14,541	10,715	10,443	5,959	4,484	2,010	1,448	562
Mathematics, general	17,944	10,225	7,719	2,707	1,684	1,023	1,176	909	267
Analysis and functional analysis	4	3	1	0	0	0	0	0	0
Topology and foundations	0	0	0	0	0	0	1	1	0
Mathematics, other	349	189	160	30	15	15	18	9	9
Applied mathematics, general	2,494	1,561	933	1,040	634	406	241	167	74
Computational mathematics	205	143	62	9	5	4	28	19	9
Computational and applied mathematics	261	160	101	229	127	102	15	8	7
Financial mathematics	361	216	145	2,886	1,589	1,297	18	14	4
Mathematical biology	34	12	22	0	0	0	0	0	0
Applied mathematics, other	210	127	83	8	4	4	11	10	1
Statistics, general	2,560	1,417	1,143	3,181	1,695	1,486	456	279	177
Mathematical statistics and probability	216	118	98	168	92	76	14	11	3
Mathematics and statistics	116	77	39	86	52	34	1	0	1
Statistics, other	196	126	70	58	37	21	4	1	3
Mathematics and statistics, other	306	167	139	41	25	16	27	20	7
Military technologies and applied sciences	655	533	122	355	265	90	0	0	0
Intelligence, general	360	294	66	58	30	28	0	0	0
Strategic intelligence	4	3	1	44	30	14	0	0	0
Signal/geospatial intelligence	13	8	5	2	2	0	0	0	0
Cyber/electronic operations and warfare	93	76	17	236	190	46	0	0	0
Intelligence, command control and information operations, other	0	0	0	0	0	0	0	0	0
Military applied sciences, other	73	68	5	0	0	0	0	0	0
Aerospace ground equipment technology	3	3	0	0	0	0	0	0	0
Air and space operations technology	24	19	5	0	0	0	0	0	0
Military systems and maintenance technology, other	0	0	0	0	0	0	0	0	0
Military technologies and applied sciences, other	85	62	23	15	13	2	0	0	0
Multi/interdisciplinary studies	51,909	17,573	34,336	10,175	3,677	6,498	850	345	505
Multi/interdisciplinary studies, general	5,175	1,998	3,177	141	55	86	3	1	2
Biological and physical sciences	2,207	866	1,341	450	185	265	68	33	35
Peace studies and conflict resolution	483	157	326	457	151	306	27	13	14
Systems science and theory	339	208	131	225	115	110	17	9	8
Mathematics and computer science	663	514	149	118	75	43	15	13	2
Biopsychology	147	33	114	3	1	2	3	0	3
Gerontology	287	29	258	485	87	398	24	4	20
Historic preservation and conservation	86	16	70	199	54	145	1	0	1

See notes at end of table.

Table 318.30. Bachelor's, master's, and doctor's degrees conferred by postsecondary institutions, by sex of student and discipline division: 2017–18—Continued

Discipline division	Bachelor's degrees			Master's degrees			Doctor's degrees[1]		
	Total	Males	Females	Total	Males	Females	Total	Males	Females
1	2	3	4	5	6	7	8	9	10
Cultural resource management and policy analysis	0	0	0	37	12	25	0	0	0
Historic preservation and conservation, other	2	1	1	12	4	8	0	0	0
Medieval and renaissance studies	15	8	7	27	7	20	10	5	5
Museology/museum studies	20	6	14	579	85	494	0	0	0
Science, technology and society	824	423	401	132	49	83	24	11	13
Accounting and computer science	8	3	5	5	2	3	0	0	0
Behavioral sciences	3,190	613	2,577	327	61	266	31	8	23
Natural sciences	554	193	361	58	20	38	13	6	7
Nutrition sciences	3,380	574	2,806	1,219	150	1,069	186	38	148
International/global studies	5,810	2,031	3,779	1,141	567	574	2	0	2
Holocaust and related studies	9	3	6	34	15	19	0	0	0
Ancient studies/civilization	89	36	53	5	3	2	16	6	10
Classical, ancient Mediterranean/Near Eastern studies/archaeology	71	26	45	4	2	2	2	0	2
Intercultural/multicultural and diversity studies	158	27	131	117	43	74	4	4	0
Cognitive science	1,575	611	964	109	46	63	36	22	14
Cultural studies/critical theory and analysis	124	40	84	46	12	34	4	1	3
Human biology	1,015	256	759	0	0	0	0	0	0
Dispute resolution	0	0	0	299	96	203	35	16	19
Maritime studies	10	3	7	5	4	1	0	0	0
Computational science	47	33	14	510	364	146	25	20	5
Human computer interaction	603	496	107	402	191	211	11	5	6
Marine sciences	118	38	80	79	29	50	19	7	12
Sustainability studies	510	211	299	788	295	493	9	5	4
Multi/interdisciplinary studies, other	24,390	8,120	16,270	2,162	897	1,265	265	118	147
Parks, recreation, leisure, and fitness studies	53,883	27,558	26,325	9,005	5,104	3,901	298	157	141
Parks, recreation and leisure studies	2,937	1,318	1,619	173	73	100	14	3	11
Parks, recreation and leisure facilities management	3,133	1,416	1,717	404	197	207	22	13	9
Golf course operation and grounds management	7	6	1	0	0	0	0	0	0
Parks, recreation and leisure facilities management, other	6	6	0	0	0	0	0	0	0
Health and physical education/fitness, general	10,475	5,123	5,352	1,150	635	515	33	13	20
Sport and fitness administration/management	10,248	7,472	2,776	4,390	2,775	1,615	32	15	17
Kinesiology and exercise science	25,376	11,245	14,131	2,580	1,279	1,301	160	97	63
Physical fitness technician	104	67	37	15	7	8	0	0	0
Sports studies	199	145	54	87	42	45	5	5	0
Health and physical education/fitness, other	1,091	579	512	153	77	76	25	5	20
Outdoor education	143	86	57	35	10	25	0	0	0
Parks, recreation, leisure, and fitness studies, other	164	95	69	18	9	9	7	6	1
Philosophy and religious studies	9,603	5,935	3,668	1,692	1,110	582	768	532	236
Philosophy and religious studies, general	109	80	29	7	6	1	27	16	11
Philosophy	5,644	3,756	1,888	713	529	184	458	341	117
Logic	3	2	1	4	2	2	9	7	2
Ethics	49	11	38	50	23	27	0	0	0
Applied and professional ethics	16	8	8	18	10	8	0	0	0
Philosophy, other	235	134	101	8	5	3	0	0	0
Religion/religious studies	2,779	1,536	1,243	470	272	198	243	147	96
Buddhist studies	0	0	0	4	2	2	1	1	0
Christian studies	303	204	99	204	141	63	0	0	0
Hindu studies	0	0	0	0	0	0	0	0	0
Islamic studies	8	4	4	17	9	8	1	1	0
Jewish/Judaic studies	213	50	163	89	34	55	11	9	2
Religion/religious studies, other	67	30	37	41	22	19	8	6	2
Philosophy and religious studies, other	177	120	57	67	55	12	10	4	6
Physical sciences and science technologies	31,542	18,938	12,604	7,196	4,492	2,704	6,181	4,074	2,107
Physical sciences	31,003	18,628	12,375	7,131	4,470	2,661	6,178	4,073	2,105
Physical sciences	274	143	131	49	30	19	21	14	7
Astronomy	323	210	113	90	63	27	120	71	49
Astrophysics	209	134	75	27	19	8	60	43	17
Planetary astronomy and science	13	6	7	12	6	6	22	9	13
Astronomy and astrophysics, other	46	33	13	16	7	9	9	6	3
Atmospheric sciences and meteorology, general	502	328	174	219	133	86	154	94	60
Atmospheric chemistry and climatology	9	5	4	0	0	0	0	0	0
Atmospheric physics and dynamics	0	0	0	1	0	1	1	1	0
Meteorology	184	124	60	16	12	4	17	12	5
Atmospheric sciences and meteorology, other	19	11	8	2	2	0	2	1	1
Chemistry, general	14,040	6,999	7,041	2,256	1,246	1,010	2,809	1,712	1,097
Analytical chemistry	11	2	9	28	16	12	5	3	2
Inorganic chemistry	0	0	0	1	0	1	1	0	1
Organic chemistry	0	0	0	0	0	0	11	8	3
Physical chemistry	0	0	0	0	0	0	3	3	0
Polymer chemistry	1	1	0	63	38	25	52	38	14
Chemical physics	32	23	9	6	4	2	17	11	6
Environmental chemistry	7	5	2	3	1	2	9	3	6
Forensic chemistry	171	33	138	6	2	4	0	0	0
Theoretical chemistry	7	4	3	0	0	0	2	2	0
Chemistry, other	468	217	251	25	9	16	42	24	18
Geology/earth science, general	5,699	3,537	2,162	1,306	748	558	462	258	204
Geochemistry	23	17	6	5	3	2	8	5	3
Geophysics and seismology	175	110	65	99	60	39	70	38	32
Paleontology	16	12	4	4	3	1	0	0	0
Hydrology and water resources science	32	20	12	85	42	43	22	11	11
Geochemistry and petrology	0	0	0	0	0	0	0	0	0
Oceanography, chemical and physical	181	75	106	153	67	86	111	49	62
Geological and earth sciences/geosciences, other	576	333	243	161	106	55	86	53	33
Physics, general	7,211	5,712	1,499	1,886	1,441	445	1,734	1,365	369
Atomic/molecular physics	2	0	2	11	7	4	8	7	1

See notes at end of table.

Table 318.30. Bachelor's, master's, and doctor's degrees conferred by postsecondary institutions, by sex of student and discipline division: 2017–18—Continued

Discipline division	Bachelor's degrees			Master's degrees			Doctor's degrees[1]		
	Total	Males	Females	Total	Males	Females	Total	Males	Females
1	2	3	4	5	6	7	8	9	10
Elementary particle physics	0	0	0	0	0	0	2	2	0
Nuclear physics	1	0	1	1	1	0	1	1	0
Optics/optical sciences	52	36	16	97	81	16	55	38	17
Condensed matter and materials physics	3	2	1	3	2	1	6	6	0
Acoustics	15	12	3	32	26	6	9	7	2
Theoretical and mathematical physics	14	12	2	0	0	0	1	1	0
Physics, other	217	176	41	119	96	23	63	50	13
Materials science	163	98	65	234	159	75	149	100	49
Materials chemistry	4	3	1	7	3	4	8	5	3
Materials sciences, other	0	0	0	3	2	1	5	4	1
Physical sciences, other	303	195	108	105	35	70	21	18	3
Science technologies/technicians	539	310	229	65	22	43	3	1	2
Science technologies/technicians, general	47	44	3	7	0	7	0	0	0
Biology technician/biotechnology laboratory technician	43	19	24	0	0	0	3	1	2
Nuclear/nuclear power technology/technician	16	13	3	0	0	0	0	0	0
Nuclear and industrial radiologic technologies/technicians, other	0	0	0	0	0	0	0	0	0
Chemical technology/technician	0	0	0	0	0	0	0	0	0
Physical science technologies/technicians, other	0	0	0	0	0	0	0	0	0
Science technologies/technicians, other	433	234	199	58	22	36	0	0	0
Precision production	45	19	26	11	5	6	0	0	0
Tool and die technology/technician	0	0	0	0	0	0	0	0	0
Welding technology/welder	2	2	0	0	0	0	0	0	0
Furniture design and manufacturing	43	17	26	11	5	6	0	0	0
Psychology	116,432	24,578	91,854	27,841	5,526	22,315	6,275	1,649	4,626
Psychology, general	103,801	21,944	81,857	6,306	1,521	4,785	1,735	515	1,220
Cognitive psychology and psycholinguistics	150	36	114	26	5	21	19	7	12
Comparative psychology	0	0	0	14	3	11	0	0	0
Developmental and child psychology	552	51	501	313	26	287	44	6	38
Experimental psychology	1,920	468	1,452	274	94	180	192	84	108
Personality psychology	12	3	9	8	2	6	6	1	5
Physiological psychology/psychobiology	1,191	325	866	42	11	31	16	7	9
Social psychology	1,039	225	814	36	11	25	43	19	24
Psychometrics and quantitative psychology	1	1	0	18	2	16	7	1	6
Psychopharmacology	0	0	0	43	15	28	0	0	0
Research and experimental psychology, other	4,432	940	3,492	195	67	128	192	76	116
Clinical psychology	206	30	176	2,388	431	1,957	2,202	476	1,726
Community psychology	368	72	296	218	34	184	50	9	41
Counseling psychology	422	69	353	8,054	1,470	6,584	400	101	299
Industrial and organizational psychology	168	37	131	1,360	417	943	174	60	114
School psychology	1	0	1	1,811	261	1,550	353	68	285
Educational psychology	113	9	104	1,255	219	1,036	347	100	247
Clinical child psychology	0	0	0	21	1	20	25	5	20
Environmental psychology	0	0	0	9	5	4	1	0	1
Geropsychology	0	0	0	2	0	2	1	0	1
Health/medical psychology	98	18	80	8	3	5	30	7	23
Family psychology	15	2	13	65	11	54	0	0	0
Forensic psychology	583	107	476	775	116	659	94	15	79
Applied psychology	842	160	682	415	107	308	33	12	21
Applied behavior analysis	220	39	181	1,869	237	1,632	97	25	72
Clinical, counseling and applied psychology, other	58	13	45	299	59	240	42	11	31
Psychology, other	240	29	211	2,017	398	1,619	172	44	128
Public administration and social service professions	35,629	6,127	29,502	46,294	10,692	35,602	1,157	399	758
Human services, general	6,938	952	5,986	1,299	176	1,123	48	7	41
Community organization and advocacy	1,688	345	1,343	311	98	213	6	2	4
Public administration	3,093	1,548	1,545	12,173	5,095	7,078	300	153	147
Public policy analysis, general	1,678	718	960	2,693	1,184	1,509	199	83	116
Education policy analysis	0	0	0	63	13	50	11	4	7
Health policy analysis	81	13	68	85	26	59	18	4	14
International policy analysis	14	2	12	12	7	5	4	2	2
Public policy analysis, other	0	0	0	80	26	54	8	4	4
Social work	21,698	2,456	19,242	29,127	3,949	25,178	520	121	399
Youth services/administration	88	13	75	92	12	80	0	0	0
Social work, other	33	4	29	111	17	94	0	0	0
Public administration and social service professions, other	318	76	242	248	89	159	43	19	24
Social sciences and history	159,967	79,628	80,339	19,884	9,832	10,052	4,676	2,475	2,201
Social sciences	136,585	65,758	70,827	16,612	8,062	8,550	3,765	1,983	1,782
Social sciences, general	6,486	2,435	4,051	637	210	427	22	10	12
Research methodology and quantitative methods	0	0	0	54	29	25	2	2	0
Anthropology	8,227	2,221	6,006	1,094	325	769	519	175	344
Physical and biological anthropology	31	7	24	29	4	25	3	1	2
Medical anthropology	67	13	54	7	2	5	1	0	1
Cultural anthropology	43	14	29	14	2	12	10	2	8
Anthropology, other	60	13	47	36	10	26	7	0	7
Archeology	167	58	109	47	14	33	33	11	22
Criminology	7,677	3,472	4,205	721	236	485	54	22	32
Demography and population studies	0	0	0	47	20	27	20	6	14
Economics, general	29,275	20,389	8,886	1,713	1,058	655	770	521	249
Applied economics	326	205	121	309	182	127	31	18	13
Econometrics and quantitative economics	4,669	2,936	1,733	1,625	982	643	369	266	103
Development economics and international development	293	65	228	302	108	194	18	11	7
International economics	397	152	245	39	21	18	2	1	1
Economics, other	367	231	136	110	69	41	5	2	3
Geography	3,723	2,278	1,445	617	354	263	229	122	107
Geographic information science and cartography	588	438	150	563	341	222	19	14	5

See notes at end of table.

Table 318.30. Bachelor's, master's, and doctor's degrees conferred by postsecondary institutions, by sex of student and discipline division: 2017–18—Continued

Discipline division	Bachelor's degrees			Master's degrees			Doctor's degrees[1]		
	Total	Males	Females	Total	Males	Females	Total	Males	Females
1	2	3	4	5	6	7	8	9	10
Geography, other	156	87	69	60	37	23	5	4	1
International relations and affairs	8,392	3,282	5,110	4,134	2,062	2,072	77	39	38
National security policy studies	74	62	12	194	129	65	0	0	0
International relations and national security studies, other	117	67	50	175	95	80	1	1	0
Political science and government, general	33,845	17,762	16,083	1,567	836	731	774	459	315
American government and politics (United States)	148	95	53	178	117	61	0	0	0
Political economy	214	115	99	10	3	7	0	0	0
Political science and government, other	761	401	360	99	60	39	15	6	9
Sociology	27,294	7,780	19,514	1,411	501	910	687	253	434
Urban studies/affairs	951	414	537	345	136	209	47	24	23
Sociology and anthropology	443	104	339	2	0	2	0	0	0
Rural sociology	28	8	20	0	0	0	0	0	0
Social sciences, other	1,766	654	1,112	473	119	354	45	13	32
History	23,382	13,870	9,512	3,272	1,770	1,502	911	492	419
History, general	22,752	13,526	9,226	2,913	1,553	1,360	856	468	388
American history (United States)	50	30	20	57	30	27	1	1	0
European history	21	16	5	0	0	0	0	0	0
History and philosophy of science and technology	100	47	53	30	15	15	27	10	17
Public/applied history	50	21	29	93	33	60	4	1	3
Asian history	1	1	0	0	0	0	0	0	0
Military history	71	62	9	108	95	13	0	0	0
History, other	337	167	170	71	44	27	23	12	11
Theology and religious vocations	9,521	6,601	2,920	13,828	9,023	4,805	2,023	1,476	547
Bible/biblical studies	1,984	1,315	669	725	506	219	39	36	3
Missions/missionary studies and missiology	579	215	364	398	238	160	100	84	16
Religious education	764	361	403	550	239	311	63	44	19
Religious/sacred music	276	144	132	77	43	34	13	8	5
Theology/theological studies	976	667	309	3,972	2,585	1,387	430	321	109
Divinity/ministry	406	304	102	5,236	3,654	1,582	501	365	136
Pre-theology/pre-ministerial studies	169	142	27	10	10	0	0	0	0
Rabbinical studies	3	3	0	96	58	38	9	9	0
Talmudic studies	2,269	2,213	56	502	501	1	26	26	0
Theological and ministerial studies, other	415	249	166	689	417	272	339	253	86
Pastoral studies/counseling	471	327	144	603	267	336	187	127	60
Youth ministry	469	274	195	42	18	24	0	0	0
Urban ministry	16	7	9	38	18	20	26	14	12
Women's ministry	7	0	7	4	0	4	0	0	0
Lay ministry	168	86	82	119	60	59	10	7	3
Pastoral counseling and specialized ministries, other	173	91	82	164	65	99	19	16	3
Theology and religious vocations, other	376	203	173	603	344	259	261	166	95
Transportation and materials moving	4,924	4,282	642	815	657	158	16	13	3
Aeronautics/aviation/aerospace science and technology, general	2,596	2,264	332	556	472	84	11	8	3
Airline/commercial/professional pilot and flight crew	708	643	65	0	0	0	0	0	0
Aviation/airway management and operations	880	728	152	224	156	68	5	5	0
Air traffic controller	89	74	15	0	0	0	0	0	0
Flight instructor	10	9	1	0	0	0	0	0	0
Air transportation, other	36	34	2	29	23	6	0	0	0
Marine science/merchant marine officer	602	528	74	0	0	0	0	0	0
Transportation and materials moving, other	3	2	1	6	6	0	0	0	0
Visual and performing arts	88,582	34,202	54,380	17,686	7,399	10,287	1,759	852	907
Visual and performing arts, general	1,538	539	999	134	46	88	13	8	5
Digital arts	1,445	769	676	238	137	101	3	3	0
Crafts/craft design, folk art and artisanry	118	30	88	22	8	14	0	0	0
Dance, general	2,269	258	2,011	226	42	184	10	1	9
Ballet	49	7	42	0	0	0	0	0	0
Dance, other	56	2	54	0	0	0	3	0	3
Design and visual communications, general	2,786	861	1,925	390	141	249	4	2	2
Commercial and advertising art	988	339	649	39	12	27	0	0	0
Industrial and product design	1,656	917	739	224	108	116	0	0	0
Commercial photography	138	37	101	3	0	3	0	0	0
Fashion/apparel design	1,870	186	1,684	153	20	133	1	0	1
Interior design	2,433	234	2,199	299	46	253	0	0	0
Graphic design	4,488	1,520	2,968	165	48	117	0	0	0
Illustration	1,891	530	1,361	159	53	106	0	0	0
Game and interactive media design	1,231	894	337	121	69	52	3	3	0
Design and applied arts, other	715	251	464	278	99	179	3	0	3
Drama and dramatics/theatre arts, general	8,464	3,041	5,423	997	396	601	76	29	47
Technical theatre/theatre design and technology	541	194	347	176	67	109	0	0	0
Playwriting and screenwriting	313	154	159	354	159	195	0	0	0
Theatre literature, history and criticism	36	9	27	7	3	4	9	5	4
Acting	998	363	635	189	89	100	0	0	0
Directing and theatrical production	117	33	84	84	42	42	0	0	0
Musical theatre	592	214	378	18	5	13	0	0	0
Costume design	19	4	15	5	0	5	0	0	0
Dramatic/theatre arts and stagecraft, other	597	252	345	66	28	38	4	0	4
Film/cinema/video studies	3,600	1,997	1,603	560	294	266	30	14	16
Cinematography and film/video production	4,583	2,717	1,866	1,056	545	511	6	4	2
Photography	1,252	409	843	259	114	145	0	0	0
Documentary production	12	7	5	46	22	24	0	0	0
Film/video and photographic arts, other	897	507	390	56	14	42	5	4	1
Art/art studies, general	10,413	3,078	7,335	713	248	465	3	0	3
Fine/studio arts, general	8,943	2,575	6,368	1,394	522	872	0	0	0
Art history, criticism and conservation	2,269	339	1,930	849	128	721	200	46	154
Drawing	260	75	185	25	7	18	0	0	0

See notes at end of table.

Table 318.30. Bachelor's, master's, and doctor's degrees conferred by postsecondary institutions, by sex of student and discipline division: 2017–18—Continued

Discipline division	Bachelor's degrees			Master's degrees			Doctor's degrees[1]		
	Total	Males	Females	Total	Males	Females	Total	Males	Females
1	2	3	4	5	6	7	8	9	10
Intermedia/multimedia	773	411	362	41	22	19	1	1	0
Painting	578	160	418	142	46	96	0	0	0
Sculpture	191	58	133	50	19	31	0	0	0
Printmaking	121	30	91	33	10	23	0	0	0
Ceramic arts and ceramics	99	30	69	46	18	28	0	0	0
Fiber, textile and weaving arts	153	12	141	43	3	40	0	0	0
Metal and jewelry arts	109	21	88	56	7	49	0	0	0
Fine arts and art studies, other	579	189	390	287	85	202	4	0	4
Music, general	7,318	3,917	3,401	1,830	955	875	580	313	267
Music history, literature, and theory	118	66	52	42	23	19	9	4	5
Music performance, general	4,031	2,168	1,863	2,195	1,129	1,066	469	226	243
Music theory and composition	564	427	137	324	216	108	70	52	18
Musicology and ethnomusicology	59	35	24	75	32	43	48	22	26
Conducting	5	3	2	184	133	51	35	23	12
Keyboard instruments	159	58	101	262	86	176	46	22	24
Voice and opera	294	90	204	294	81	213	17	7	10
Jazz/jazz studies	330	278	52	183	155	28	22	22	0
Stringed instruments	189	81	108	247	96	151	13	10	3
Music pedagogy	66	27	39	92	39	53	12	5	7
Music technology	640	529	111	120	100	20	3	2	1
Brass instruments	35	32	3	50	43	7	1	1	0
Woodwind instruments	47	22	25	71	36	35	8	1	7
Percussion instruments	12	9	3	16	11	5	0	0	0
Music, other	1,163	739	424	265	157	108	21	15	6
Arts, entertainment, and media management, general	486	213	273	299	61	238	0	0	0
Fine and studio arts management	624	154	470	576	94	482	7	1	6
Music management	1,531	824	707	49	21	28	0	0	0
Theatre/theatre arts management	173	41	132	49	16	33	0	0	0
Arts, entertainment, and media management, other	130	64	66	229	127	102	0	0	0
Visual and performing arts, other	428	172	256	231	66	165	20	6	14
Not classified by field of study	0	0	0	0	0	0	0	0	0

[1]Includes Ph.D., Ed.D., and comparable degrees at the doctoral level. Includes most degrees that were classified as first-professional prior to 2010–11, such as M.D., D.D.S., and law degrees.
NOTE: Data are for postsecondary institutions participating in Title IV federal financial aid programs. Aggregations by field of study derived from the Classification of Instructional Programs developed by the National Center for Education Statistics.

SOURCE: U.S. Department of Education, National Center for Education Statistics, Integrated Postsecondary Education Data System (IPEDS), Fall 2018, Completions component. (This table was prepared September 2019.)

Table 318.40. Degrees/certificates conferred by postsecondary institutions, by control of institution and level of degree/certificate: 1970–71 through 2017–18

Year	Public institutions					Private institutions: Total					Private institutions: Nonprofit					Private institutions: For-profit				
	Certificates below the associate's	Associate's degrees	Bachelor's degrees	Master's degrees	Doctor's degrees[1]	Certificates below the associate's	Associate's degrees	Bachelor's degrees	Master's degrees	Doctor's degrees[1]	Certificates below the associate's	Associate's degrees	Bachelor's degrees	Master's degrees	Doctor's degrees[1]	Certificates below the associate's	Associate's degrees	Bachelor's degrees	Master's degrees	Doctor's degrees[1]
1	2	3	4	5	6	7	8	9	10	11	12	13	14	15	16	17	18	19	20	21
1970–71	—	215,645	557,996	151,603	36,927	—	36,666	281,734	83,961	28,071	—	—	—	—	—	—	—	—	—	—
1971–72	—	255,218	599,615	167,075	40,297	—	36,796	287,658	90,126	30,909	—	—	—	—	—	—	—	—	—	—
1972–73	—	278,132	630,899	174,405	44,229	—	38,042	291,463	94,249	35,283	—	—	—	—	—	—	—	—	—	—
1973–74	—	303,188	651,544	184,632	45,018	—	40,736	294,232	97,442	37,573	—	—	—	—	—	—	—	—	—	—
1974–75	—	318,474	634,785	193,804	45,788	—	41,697	288,148	103,741	39,116	—	—	—	—	—	—	—	—	—	—
1975–76	—	345,006	635,161	206,298	47,517	—	46,448	290,585	111,179	43,490	—	—	—	—	—	—	—	—	—	—
1976–77	—	355,650	630,463	208,901	47,573	—	50,727	289,086	114,124	44,157	—	—	—	—	—	—	—	—	—	—
1977–78	—	358,874	627,903	202,099	47,553	—	53,372	293,301	115,888	44,792	—	—	—	—	—	—	—	—	—	—
1978–79	—	346,808	621,666	192,016	48,602	—	55,894	299,724	115,670	46,369	—	—	—	—	—	—	—	—	—	—
1979–80	—	344,536	624,084	187,499	48,550	—	56,374	305,333	117,697	47,081	—	—	—	—	—	—	—	—	—	—
1980–81	—	352,391	626,452	184,384	50,023	—	63,986[2]	308,688	118,253	47,993	—	—	—	—	—	—	—	—	—	—
1981–82	—	366,732	636,475	182,295	50,500	—	67,794[2]	316,523	120,152	47,338	—	—	—	—	—	—	—	—	—	—
1982–83	—	377,817	646,317	176,246	50,943	—	71,803[2]	323,193	120,169	48,392	—	—	—	—	—	—	—	—	—	—
1983–84	—	379,249	646,013	170,693	50,727	—	72,991	328,296	120,448	50,072	—	—	—	—	—	—	—	—	—	—
1984–85	—	377,625	652,246	170,000	51,489	—	77,087	327,231	123,472	49,296	—	—	—	—	—	—	—	—	—	—
1985–86	—	369,052	658,586	169,903	51,001	—	76,995	329,237	125,947	49,279	—	—	—	—	—	—	—	—	—	—
1986–87	—	358,811	659,260	167,797	51,216	—	77,493	332,004	128,733	47,261	—	—	—	—	—	—	—	—	—	—
1987–88	—	354,180	658,491	173,778	51,641	—	80,905	336,338	132,005	47,498	—	—	—	—	—	—	—	—	—	—
1988–89	—	357,001	675,675	179,109	51,963	—	79,763	343,080	137,517	48,608	—	—	—	—	—	—	—	—	—	—
1989–90	—	375,635	700,015	186,104	53,451	—	79,467	351,329	144,048	50,057	—	42,497	344,569	142,681	49,655	—	36,970	6,760	1,367	402
1990–91	—	398,055	724,062	193,057	55,235	—	83,665	370,476	149,806	50,312	—	45,821	360,634	146,161	49,841	—	37,844	9,842	3,645	471
1991–92	—	420,265	759,475	203,398	56,186	—	83,966	377,078	154,691	53,368	—	45,700	370,718	153,291	52,830	—	38,266	6,360	1,400	538
1992–93	—	430,321	785,112	213,843	57,020	—	84,435	380,066	161,189	55,052	—	47,713	373,346	159,562	54,399	—	36,722	6,720	1,627	653
1993–94	—	444,373	789,148	221,428	58,366	—	86,259	380,127	171,609	54,270	—	48,493	371,561	168,718	53,502	—	37,766	8,566	2,891	768
1994–95	—	451,539	776,670	224,152	58,788	—	88,152	383,464	179,457	55,478	—	48,643	373,454	176,485	54,675	—	39,509	10,010	2,972	803
1995–96	307,358	454,291	774,070	227,179	59,398	313,311	100,925	390,722	185,001	56,109	34,259	50,678	379,916	181,142	55,506	279,052	50,247	10,806	3,859	603
1996–97	326,687	465,494	776,677	233,237	61,081	272,237	105,732	396,202	192,023	57,666	35,560	49,168	384,086	186,963	56,864	236,677	56,564	12,116	5,060	802
1997–98	305,910	455,084	784,296	235,922	60,948	246,571	103,471	400,110	200,115	57,787	32,166	47,625	386,455	194,048	57,089	214,405	55,846	13,655	6,067	698
1998–99	304,294	452,616	792,392	238,954	60,028	251,589	112,368	409,847	207,084	56,672	29,402	47,757	394,749	198,481	55,663	222,187	64,611	15,098	8,603	1,009
1999–2000	294,912	448,446	810,855	243,157	60,655	263,217	116,487	427,020	220,028	58,081	28,580	46,337	406,958	209,720	56,972	234,637	70,150	20,062	10,308	1,109
2000–01	309,624	456,487	812,438	246,054	60,820	242,879	122,378	431,733	227,448	58,765	29,336	45,711	408,701	215,815	57,722	213,543	76,667	23,032	11,633	1,043
2001–02	319,291	471,660	841,180	249,820	61,061	264,957	123,473	450,720	237,493	58,602	32,904	45,761	424,322	223,229	57,707	232,053	77,712	26,398	14,264	895
2002–03	355,727	498,279	875,596	265,643	61,611	290,698	135,737	473,215	253,056	59,968	36,926	46,183	442,060	238,069	58,894	253,772	89,554	31,155	14,987	1,074
2003–04	364,053	524,875	905,718	285,138	64,205	323,734	140,426	493,824	279,134	61,882	35,316	45,759	451,518	250,894	60,447	288,418	94,667	42,306	28,240	1,435
2004–05	370,683	547,519	932,443	291,505	67,511	340,190	149,141	506,821	288,646	66,876	35,968	45,344	457,963	253,564	65,278	304,222	103,797	48,858	35,082	1,598
2005–06	370,570	557,366	955,370	293,535	70,036	344,220	155,949	529,734	306,327	68,020	35,909	46,459	467,697	261,203	66,066	308,311	109,490	62,037	45,124	1,954
2006–07	389,244	566,219	975,903	292,073	73,087	339,071	161,397	548,826	318,630	71,607	34,195	43,790	478,053	267,694	69,241	304,876	117,607	70,773	50,936	2,366
2007–08	399,741	578,661	996,769	300,019	75,551	348,613	171,505	566,965	330,825	73,639	33,915	45,014	491,016	275,971	70,473	314,698	126,491	75,949	54,854	3,166
2008–09	428,849	596,391	1,020,521	308,215	77,270	375,771	190,852	580,878	353,867	77,294	31,939	46,930	496,353	290,401	73,583	343,832	143,922	84,525	63,466	3,711
2009–10	472,428	640,265	1,049,179	322,389	78,805	463,291	208,591	600,740	370,924	79,785	35,652	46,673	503,264	300,053	75,172	427,639	161,918	97,476	70,871	4,613
2010–11	519,711	696,884	1,088,722	339,420	82,013	510,766	246,622	627,331	391,502	81,814	36,534	51,967	512,821	313,317	76,595	474,232	194,655	114,510	78,185	5,219
2011–12	525,264	756,484	1,131,885	349,349	84,730	463,797	265,234	660,278	406,618	85,487	32,856	54,347	526,022	325,175	79,498	430,941	210,887	134,256	81,443	5,989
2012–13	545,446	772,978	1,163,616	346,751	86,411	421,768	234,449	676,765	404,967	88,615	30,913	55,651	535,958	327,013	81,543	390,855	178,798	140,807	77,954	7,072
2013–14	576,468	794,925	1,186,742	346,238	88,911	392,810	210,230	683,408	408,344	88,676	30,738	53,127	544,253	333,539	80,894	362,072	157,103	139,155	74,805	7,782
2014–15	602,904	822,218	1,209,464	351,216	90,252	358,242	192,123	685,505	407,588	88,296	46,090	58,613	553,543	336,181	80,093	312,152	133,510	131,962	71,407	8,203
2015–16	615,137	848,081	1,240,423	364,619	90,030	324,154	160,147	680,327	421,138	88,104	40,010	56,595	560,834	350,790	80,067	284,144	103,552	119,493	70,348	8,037
2016–17	631,076	861,970	1,275,610	374,160	91,532	314,947	143,717	680,504	430,382	89,825	35,281	56,487	566,607	360,437	81,550	279,666	87,230	113,897	69,945	8,275
2017–18	671,880	885,870	1,310,988	383,929	92,855	282,858	125,617	669,656	436,173	91,219	25,789	56,187	571,155	372,086	83,888	257,069	69,430	98,501	64,087	7,331

—Not available.

[1]Includes Ph.D., Ed.D., and comparable degrees at the doctoral level. Includes most degrees that were classified as first-professional prior to 2010–11, such as M.D., D.D.S., and law degrees.

[2]Part of the increase is due to the addition of schools accredited by the Accrediting Commission of Career Schools and Colleges of Technology.

NOTE: Data are for postsecondary institutions participating in Title IV federal financial aid programs. Some data have been revised from previously published figures.

SOURCE: U.S. Department of Education, National Center for Education Statistics, Higher Education General Information Survey (HEGIS), "Degrees and Other Formal Awards Conferred" surveys, 1970–71 through 1985–86; Integrated Postsecondary Education Data System (IPEDS), "Completions Survey" (IPEDS-C:87–99); and IPEDS Fall 2000 through Fall 2018, Completions component. (This table was prepared November 2019.)

Table 318.50. Degrees conferred by postsecondary institutions, by control of institution, level of degree, and field of study: 2017–18

Field of study	All institutions				Public institutions				Private nonprofit institutions				Private for-profit institutions			
	Associate's degrees	Bachelor's degrees	Master's degrees	Doctor's degrees[1]	Associate's degrees	Bachelor's degrees	Master's degrees	Doctor's degrees[1]	Associate's degrees	Bachelor's degrees	Master's degrees	Doctor's degrees[1]	Associate's degrees	Bachelor's degrees	Master's degrees	Doctor's degrees[1]
1	2	3	4	5	6	7	8	9	10	11	12	13	14	15	16	17
All fields, total	**1,011,487**	**1,980,644**	**820,102**	**184,074**	**885,870**	**1,310,988**	**383,929**	**92,855**	**56,187**	**571,155**	**372,086**	**83,888**	**69,430**	**98,501**	**64,087**	**7,331**
Agriculture and natural resources	8,076	39,314	6,967	1,496	7,799	32,962	5,392	1,378	267	5,708	1,475	118	10	644	100	0
Architecture and related services	539	8,464	7,317	250	511	6,024	4,339	180	27	2,360	2,945	70	1	80	33	0
Area, ethnic, cultural, gender, and group studies	559	7,717	1,673	335	549	5,280	989	204	10	2,437	684	131	0	0	0	0
Biological and biomedical sciences	6,390	118,663	17,180	8,222	6,272	82,654	9,642	5,499	115	35,710	7,514	2,723	3	299	24	0
Business	117,782	386,201	192,184	3,338	94,654	238,673	75,163	1,111	9,494	116,498	96,141	936	13,634	31,030	20,880	1,291
Communication, journalism, and related programs	7,785	92,290	10,243	666	7,658	67,292	4,290	530	71	24,226	5,672	136	56	772	281	0
Communications technologies	4,197	4,231	529	0	3,495	1,606	43	0	77	1,555	342	0	625	1,070	144	0
Computer and information sciences	31,479	79,598	46,468	2,017	26,080	52,555	24,150	1,308	1,588	20,156	19,825	624	3,811	6,887	2,493	85
Construction trades	5,277	151	0	0	4,574	151	0	0	204	0	0	0	499	0	0	0
Education	16,182	82,621	146,367	12,780	14,783	56,931	72,924	6,278	617	22,924	63,055	5,141	782	2,766	10,388	1,361
Engineering	6,408	121,956	51,721	10,817	6,276	96,656	34,574	7,904	31	25,188	17,110	2,913	101	112	37	0
Engineering technologies and engineering-related fields[2]	26,745	18,228	7,246	212	23,740	14,591	3,583	89	1,307	1,986	3,112	123	1,698	1,651	551	0
English language and literature/letters	3,133	40,002	8,300	1,295	3,027	27,549	4,713	958	8	11,907	3,467	337	98	546	120	0
Family and consumer sciences/human sciences	8,854	24,349	3,308	274	8,336	19,618	2,155	233	264	4,121	964	36	254	610	189	5
Foreign languages, literatures, and linguistics	2,607	16,958	3,261	1,213	2,594	12,292	2,277	800	13	4,636	984	413	0	30	0	0
Health professions and related programs	181,056	244,909	125,216	80,305	126,226	135,750	48,713	38,652	21,742	79,069	57,688	38,712	33,088	30,090	18,815	2,941
Homeland security, law enforcement, and firefighting	35,276	58,114	10,293	150	30,139	36,634	4,714	96	1,347	13,929	3,884	20	3,790	7,551	1,695	34
Legal professions and studies	6,237	4,239	9,177	34,544	4,623	2,582	2,472	12,953	449	1,311	6,616	21,093	1,165	346	89	498
Liberal arts and sciences, general studies, and humanities	397,926	44,262	2,473	93	386,151	31,309	1,283	36	10,281	12,771	1,148	47	1,494	182	42	10
Library science	156	81	4,953	54	156	54	4,171	49	0	0	782	5	0	27	0	0
Mathematics and statistics	4,135	25,256	10,443	2,010	4,129	17,390	6,078	1,504	6	7,845	4,365	506	0	21	0	0
Mechanic and repair technologies/technicians	21,295	348	1	0	14,715	198	0	0	2,161	150	1	0	4,419	0	0	0
Military technologies and applied sciences	1,226	655	355	0	1,180	175	57	0	0	392	290	0	46	88	8	0
Multi/interdisciplinary studies	31,068	51,909	10,175	850	30,155	37,041	5,461	570	433	11,545	4,271	280	480	3,323	443	0
Parks, recreation, leisure, and fitness studies	5,095	53,883	9,005	298	4,636	39,994	5,854	254	193	13,214	3,000	40	266	675	151	4
Philosophy and religious studies	1,049	9,603	1,692	768	371	4,287	527	292	678	5,268	1,165	476	0	48	0	0
Physical sciences and science technologies	10,116	31,542	7,196	6,181	10,042	22,820	5,324	4,479	74	8,722	1,872	1,702	0	0	0	0
Precision production	5,333	45	11	0	4,823	1	0	0	179	44	11	0	331	0	0	0
Psychology	12,489	116,432	27,841	6,275	12,095	81,526	9,250	2,577	383	33,420	14,873	2,856	11	1,486	3,718	842
Public administration and social services	7,136	35,629	46,294	1,157	5,516	23,902	27,763	573	1,198	9,344	16,825	352	422	2,383	1,706	232
Social sciences and history	23,683	159,967	19,884	4,676	23,570	110,767	10,409	3,063	86	48,395	8,978	1,594	27	805	497	19
Social sciences	21,545	136,585	16,612	3,765	21,495	94,879	8,313	2,486	50	41,148	8,012	1,260	0	558	287	19
History	2,138	23,382	3,272	911	2,075	15,888	2,096	577	36	7,247	966	334	27	247	210	0
Theology and religious vocations	1,435	9,521	13,828	2,023	0	0	0	0	1,435	9,256	13,668	2,014	0	265	160	9
Transportation and materials moving	1,610	4,924	815	16	1,147	2,802	151	1	412	2,118	664	15	51	4	0	0
Visual and performing arts	19,153	88,582	17,686	1,759	15,848	48,922	7,468	1,284	1,037	34,950	8,695	475	2,268	4,710	1,523	0

[1]Includes Ph.D., Ed.D., and comparable degrees at the doctoral level, as well as such degrees as M.D., D.D.S., and law degrees that were classified as first-professional degrees prior to 2010–11.

[2]Excludes "Construction trades" and "Mechanic and repair technologies/technicians," which are listed separately.

NOTE: Data are for degree-granting postsecondary institutions, which are institutions that grant associate's or higher degrees and participate in Title IV federal financial aid programs. To facilitate trend comparisons, certain aggregations have been made of the degree fields as reported in the Integrated Postsecondary Education Data System (IPEDS): "Agriculture and natural resources" includes Agriculture, agriculture operations, and related sciences and Natural resources and conservation; and "Business" includes Business, management, marketing, and related support services and Personal and culinary services.

SOURCE: U.S. Department of Education, National Center for Education Statistics, Integrated Postsecondary Education Data System (IPEDS), Fall 2018, Completions component. (This table was prepared February 2020.)

Table 318.60. Number of postsecondary institutions conferring degrees, by control of institution, level of degree, and field of study: 2017–18

Field of study	All institutions				Public institutions				Private nonprofit institutions				Private for-profit institutions			
	Associate's degrees	Bachelor's degrees	Master's degrees	Doctor's degrees[1]	Associate's degrees	Bachelor's degrees	Master's degrees	Doctor's degrees[1]	Associate's degrees	Bachelor's degrees	Master's degrees	Doctor's degrees[1]	Associate's degrees	Bachelor's degrees	Master's degrees	Doctor's degrees[1]
1	2	3	4	5	6	7	8	9	10	11	12	13	14	15	16	17
All fields, total	**2,457**	**2,335**	**1,884**	**1,011**	**1,242**	**712**	**557**	**364**	**635**	**1,326**	**1,151**	**599**	**580**	**297**	**176**	**48**
Agriculture and natural resources	515	799	241	106	490	355	184	95	23	438	56	11	2	6	1	0
Architecture and related services	75	198	160	41	70	120	105	30	4	74	53	11	1	4	2	0
Area, ethnic, cultural, gender, and group studies	75	475	150	60	70	241	102	39	5	234	48	21	0	0	0	0
Biological and biomedical sciences	307	1,378	522	268	289	544	351	183	17	829	170	85	1	5	1	0
Business	1,598	1,791	1,238	212	1,085	635	458	111	260	954	658	89	253	202	122	12
Communication, journalism, and related programs	309	1,186	361	78	286	472	228	61	16	688	129	17	7	26	4	0
Communications technologies	304	153	22	0	282	55	7	0	7	77	13	0	15	21	2	0
Computer and information sciences	1,177	1,352	553	176	920	554	315	120	86	669	182	52	171	129	56	4
Construction trades	357	6	0	0	326	6	0	0	13	0	0	0	18	0	0	0
Education	694	1,244	1,162	449	615	491	477	249	62	732	636	188	17	21	49	12
Engineering	405	566	337	219	382	304	224	158	16	254	110	61	7	8	3	0
Engineering technologies and engineering-related fields[2]	920	344	182	25	834	241	122	14	37	77	56	11	49	26	4	0
English language and literature/letters	213	1,329	499	151	204	521	324	104	6	801	174	47	3	7	1	0
Family and consumer sciences/human sciences	499	355	166	52	476	207	114	39	16	139	48	12	7	9	4	1
Foreign languages, literatures, and linguistics	201	871	226	99	196	398	165	67	5	472	61	32	0	1	0	0
Health professions and related programs	1,700	1,514	1,116	601	1,055	582	430	268	237	751	582	303	408	181	104	30
Homeland security, law enforcement, and firefighting	1,072	958	334	34	869	384	187	27	98	448	125	4	105	126	22	3
Legal professions and studies	520	246	173	213	384	92	71	87	42	121	97	119	94	33	5	7
Liberal arts and sciences, general studies, and humanities	1,390	896	165	18	1,092	382	89	7	290	508	74	10	8	6	2	1
Library science	29	6	63	10	29	5	51	8	0	0	12	2	0	1	0	0
Mathematics and statistics	230	1,200	356	179	226	507	264	128	4	692	92	51	0	1	0	0
Mechanic and repair technologies/technicians	696	18	1	0	628	11	0	0	20	7	1	0	48	0	0	0
Military technologies and applied sciences	11	20	12	0	8	6	3	0	0	10	7	0	3	4	2	0
Multi/interdisciplinary studies	414	1,009	405	133	383	418	230	94	27	569	170	39	4	22	5	0
Parks, recreation, leisure, and fitness studies	329	883	317	53	302	359	219	45	15	516	97	7	12	8	1	1
Philosophy and religious studies	96	892	229	117	74	314	93	58	22	577	136	59	0	1	0	0
Physical sciences and science technologies	377	1,112	329	221	365	490	244	155	12	622	85	66	0	0	0	0
Precision production	410	6	2	0	389	1	0	0	9	5	2	0	12	0	0	0
Psychology	260	1,455	698	324	233	547	348	168	26	885	337	147	1	23	13	9
Public administration and social services	356	810	557	135	309	380	322	88	33	409	205	45	14	21	30	2
Social sciences and history	298	1,366	469	194	278	535	317	137	19	816	147	56	1	15	5	1
Social sciences	276	1,277	403	183	262	520	268	128	14	744	130	54	0	13	5	1
History	179	1,230	345	142	170	498	270	98	8	727	74	44	1	5	1	0
Theology and religious vocations	121	417	367	158	0	0	0	0	121	416	366	154	0	1	1	4
Transportation and materials moving	107	89	15	4	92	56	8	1	10	31	7	3	5	2	0	0
Visual and performing arts	719	1,399	472	113	603	505	262	75	54	832	200	38	62	62	10	0

[1]Includes Ph.D., Ed.D., and comparable degrees at the doctoral level, as well as such degrees as M.D., D.D.S., and law degrees that were classified as first-professional degrees prior to 2010–11.
[2]Excludes "Construction trades" and "Mechanic and repair technologies/technicians," which are listed separately.
NOTE: Data are for degree-granting postsecondary institutions, which are institutions that grant associate's or higher degrees and participate in Title IV federal financial aid programs. To facilitate trend comparisons, certain aggregations have been made of the degree fields as reported in the Integrated Postsecondary Education Data System (IPEDS): "Agriculture and natural resources" includes Agriculture, agriculture operations, and related sciences and Natural resources and conservation; and "Business" includes Business, management, marketing, and related support services and Personal and culinary services.
SOURCE: U.S. Department of Education, National Center for Education Statistics, Integrated Postsecondary Education Data System (IPEDS), Fall 2018, Completions component. (This table was prepared February 2020.)

Table 319.10. Degrees conferred by postsecondary institutions, by control of institution, level of degree, and state or jurisdiction: 2017–18

State or jurisdiction	Public				Private nonprofit				Private for-profit			
	Associate's degrees	Bachelor's degrees	Master's degrees	Doctor's degrees[1]	Associate's degrees	Bachelor's degrees	Master's degrees	Doctor's degrees[1]	Associate's degrees	Bachelor's degrees	Master's degrees	Doctor's degrees[1]
1	2	3	4	5	6	7	8	9	10	11	12	13
United States	**885,870**	**1,310,988**	**383,929**	**92,855**	**56,187**	**571,155**	**372,086**	**83,888**	**69,430**	**98,501**	**64,087**	**7,331**
Alabama	9,914	25,353	10,175	1,965	234	3,786	925	682	2,152	3,359	2,019	16
Alaska	1,172	1,876	561	57	11	47	67	4	38	0	0	0
Arizona	19,383	31,505	9,986	2,106	189	827	630	852	8,192	24,863	16,319	667
Arkansas	8,628	13,667	5,495	951	391	2,534	526	87	42	14	21	0
California	159,087	160,876	32,775	7,167	1,980	40,715	38,768	9,976	9,822	15,221	8,939	2,569
Colorado	10,341	26,788	9,006	1,934	411	4,133	3,742	603	2,599	4,628	1,941	388
Connecticut	5,237	11,497	3,421	730	843	10,502	7,801	1,469	204	828	189	0
Delaware	1,979	4,828	1,039	334	129	2,522	3,222	163	13	35	20	0
District of Columbia	172	338	114	64	218	8,684	11,744	3,340	268	587	949	0
Florida	74,651	75,432	19,009	5,130	12,409	22,365	13,685	3,948	5,971	7,048	2,059	194
Georgia	16,581	39,776	12,184	2,695	869	10,318	5,028	1,939	1,429	2,443	2,526	233
Hawaii	3,823	4,693	1,035	513	407	1,577	498	0	23	188	52	0
Idaho	3,581	6,648	1,860	362	1,676	5,664	195	23	127	0	0	0
Illinois	34,422	32,948	13,142	3,123	942	31,243	25,153	5,439	2,419	11,419	5,230	245
Indiana	11,185	33,171	10,336	2,723	1,521	14,491	5,524	1,295	440	102	37	0
Iowa	12,805	17,079	5,365	1,601	337	9,609	2,734	1,349	213	597	133	0
Kansas	9,564	15,922	5,662	1,481	296	3,736	1,412	190	834	648	454	0
Kentucky	10,383	19,086	5,665	1,735	294	4,609	4,598	567	1,162	566	308	93
Louisiana	5,782	19,031	5,557	1,553	270	3,466	2,037	853	500	0	0	0
Maine	2,487	4,388	845	140	111	3,185	1,380	529	97	0	0	0
Maryland	16,780	28,253	11,840	2,141	3	6,062	8,825	932	182	255	236	0
Massachusetts	11,251	21,932	6,436	841	1,222	39,614	34,721	7,618	172	232	91	0
Michigan	24,338	48,140	17,205	4,626	2,248	12,394	4,353	1,163	189	176	69	0
Minnesota	15,279	21,555	5,466	1,736	674	10,955	5,777	1,108	1,270	4,641	13,870	2,337
Mississippi	13,576	13,482	3,415	1,113	58	2,306	1,713	277	85	8	18	0
Missouri	12,351	23,039	7,401	1,760	2,925	17,801	13,170	3,310	498	402	87	0
Montana	2,056	5,101	1,226	437	132	788	82	0	10	0	0	0
Nebraska	4,478	9,089	3,017	794	170	5,270	2,626	869	55	15	0	0
Nevada	5,558	8,589	1,818	536	64	499	316	504	511	341	59	0
New Hampshire	2,109	5,377	1,124	168	2,081	11,821	8,413	296	0	0	0	0
New Jersey	21,280	33,368	9,950	2,291	325	10,208	7,243	969	1,561	795	159	0
New Mexico	9,661	8,558	2,935	671	0	166	276	0	228	161	36	0
New York	52,244	66,533	18,763	3,177	6,932	70,921	54,804	11,640	6,484	3,654	1,488	1
North Carolina	31,738	40,484	11,955	2,744	908	14,838	6,422	2,310	852	631	432	0
North Dakota	1,983	5,844	1,381	500	171	728	388	122	164	8	0	0
Ohio	24,778	49,982	15,929	4,513	3,131	21,166	8,201	1,548	2,487	513	112	3
Oklahoma	10,201	17,424	5,314	1,350	183	3,892	1,538	270	395	46	0	0
Oregon	13,825	18,431	4,613	1,071	34	5,257	3,510	1,151	381	17	70	0
Pennsylvania	17,157	48,815	13,117	3,442	3,335	42,405	26,281	7,078	3,214	609	172	0
Rhode Island	1,944	4,781	831	275	1,586	7,528	2,348	487	0	0	0	0
South Carolina	9,966	19,759	4,992	1,563	316	6,247	1,083	180	305	311	235	140
South Dakota	2,039	4,702	1,301	447	66	1,042	440	3	145	247	9	4
Tennessee	11,997	22,544	5,589	1,959	785	12,382	5,736	1,976	1,076	449	257	172
Texas	88,326	112,806	43,154	8,702	1,593	20,903	11,158	2,524	4,367	1,958	714	36
Utah	12,035	16,584	4,088	863	1,306	23,907	12,424	224	642	346	117	195
Vermont	873	3,380	479	228	154	3,190	1,988	147	55	60	0	0
Virginia	18,331	37,866	11,712	3,409	1,610	17,223	11,051	2,046	3,571	3,620	1,762	37
Washington	30,385	26,990	6,555	2,007	119	6,954	3,466	737	489	278	68	1
West Virginia	3,485	9,345	2,770	1,015	110	1,472	374	116	2,930	6,131	2,809	0
Wisconsin	11,794	27,731	5,816	1,850	408	9,203	3,690	975	507	51	21	0
Wyoming	2,875	2,127	501	262	0	0	0	0	60	0	0	0
U.S. Service Academies	0	3,475	4	0	†	†	†	†	†	†	†	†
Other jurisdictions	**2,501**	**7,966**	**948**	**510**	**3,489**	**10,972**	**3,994**	**714**	**2,844**	**2,028**	**577**	**109**
American Samoa	215	10	0	0	0	0	0	0	0	0	0	0
Federated States of Micronesia	284	0	0	0	0	0	0	0	0	0	0	0
Guam	283	485	110	0	7	13	0	0	0	0	0	0
Marshall Islands	118	0	0	0	0	0	0	0	0	0	0	0
Northern Marianas	195	47	0	0	0	0	0	0	0	0	0	0
Palau	114	0	0	0	0	0	0	0	0	0	0	0
Puerto Rico	1,261	7,203	777	510	3,482	10,959	3,994	714	2,844	2,028	577	109
U.S. Virgin Islands	31	221	61	0	0	0	0	0	0	0	0	0

†Not applicable.
[1]Includes Ph.D., Ed.D., and comparable degrees at the doctoral level. Includes most degrees classified as first-professional prior to 2010–11, such as M.D., D.D.S., and law degrees.

NOTE: Data are for postsecondary institutions participating in Title IV federal financial aid programs.
SOURCE: U.S. Department of Education, National Center for Education Statistics, Integrated Postsecondary Education Data System (IPEDS), Fall 2018, Completions component. (This table was prepared May 2020.)

Table 319.20. Degrees conferred by postsecondary institutions, by level of degree and state or jurisdiction: 2015–16 through 2017–18

State or jurisdiction	2015–16				2016–17				2017–18			
	Associate's degrees	Bachelor's degrees	Master's degrees	Doctor's degrees[1]	Associate's degrees	Bachelor's degrees	Master's degrees	Doctor's degrees[1]	Associate's degrees	Bachelor's degrees	Master's degrees	Doctor's degrees[1]
1	2	3	4	5	6	7	8	9	10	11	12	13
United States	**1,008,228**	**1,920,750**	**785,757**	**178,134**	**1,005,687**	**1,956,114**	**804,542**	**181,357**	**1,011,487**	**1,980,644**	**820,102**	**184,074**
Alabama	12,882	31,123	12,074	2,432	13,042	31,912	12,753	2,585	12,300	32,498	13,119	2,663
Alaska	1,372	1,957	670	53	1,353	2,006	633	59	1,221	1,923	628	61
Arizona	33,564	56,625	27,353	3,607	30,019	56,385	26,274	3,565	27,764	57,195	26,935	3,625
Arkansas	8,767	16,019	5,277	1,041	8,600	16,107	6,149	1,022	9,061	16,215	6,042	1,038
California	143,571	203,797	77,468	18,820	151,343	211,947	79,142	19,336	170,889	216,812	80,482	19,712
Colorado	14,027	33,580	14,934	2,969	13,523	34,590	14,812	2,899	13,351	35,549	14,689	2,925
Connecticut	7,320	22,721	10,829	2,052	6,908	23,365	11,391	2,234	6,284	22,827	11,411	2,199
Delaware	2,064	6,988	3,903	418	2,091	6,873	3,938	418	2,121	7,385	4,281	497
District of Columbia	603	9,337	11,512	3,496	727	9,519	12,059	3,443	658	9,609	12,807	3,404
Florida	93,341	101,876	33,785	9,098	92,755	103,726	34,928	9,274	93,031	104,845	34,753	9,272
Georgia	19,815	50,827	18,557	4,751	19,342	51,997	18,956	4,863	18,879	52,537	19,738	4,867
Hawaii	4,571	6,922	1,917	527	4,452	6,812	1,733	537	4,253	6,458	1,585	513
Idaho	5,588	11,424	1,860	413	5,310	11,759	1,916	372	5,384	12,312	2,055	385
Illinois	40,410	75,716	42,129	8,860	39,728	76,093	43,774	8,866	37,783	75,610	43,525	8,807
Indiana	14,703	47,614	14,841	3,609	14,436	47,964	15,648	3,905	13,146	47,764	15,897	4,018
Iowa	15,639	27,761	8,341	2,721	15,189	27,702	8,315	2,851	13,355	27,285	8,232	2,950
Kansas	11,008	20,249	7,480	1,578	10,692	20,092	7,627	1,634	10,694	20,306	7,528	1,671
Kentucky	12,276	23,221	9,503	2,143	12,350	23,752	9,702	2,164	11,839	24,261	10,571	2,395
Louisiana	7,396	22,602	7,508	2,554	6,931	22,542	7,367	2,471	6,552	22,497	7,594	2,406
Maine	3,103	7,652	2,237	571	2,864	7,688	2,231	670	2,695	7,573	2,225	669
Maryland	17,003	33,883	18,829	2,821	16,877	34,150	19,505	2,840	16,965	34,570	20,901	3,073
Massachusetts	13,776	61,053	38,391	8,475	13,367	61,712	39,039	8,253	12,645	61,778	41,248	8,459
Michigan	29,787	60,305	21,675	5,576	28,283	61,341	22,060	5,640	26,775	60,710	21,627	5,789
Minnesota	19,526	36,588	23,884	5,433	17,927	36,795	24,465	5,346	17,223	37,151	25,113	5,181
Mississippi	13,759	14,702	5,029	1,344	13,497	15,219	5,176	1,421	13,719	15,796	5,146	1,390
Missouri	18,305	41,447	22,162	4,700	17,278	41,207	22,670	5,077	15,774	41,242	20,658	5,070
Montana	2,339	6,011	1,196	430	2,244	5,994	1,211	489	2,198	5,889	1,308	437
Nebraska	5,144	14,301	5,506	1,699	5,067	14,133	5,972	1,607	4,703	14,374	5,643	1,663
Nevada	6,097	8,638	2,229	1,016	6,169	8,944	2,187	1,091	6,133	9,429	2,193	1,040
New Hampshire	3,076	12,527	6,960	468	3,699	14,869	7,634	432	4,190	17,198	9,537	464
New Jersey	23,845	42,464	16,970	2,987	23,421	43,720	17,079	3,147	23,166	44,371	17,352	3,260
New Mexico	9,435	9,183	3,212	656	10,457	9,207	3,308	651	9,889	8,885	3,247	671
New York	66,966	139,136	71,571	14,668	65,436	139,738	73,163	14,292	65,660	141,108	75,055	14,818
North Carolina	32,108	53,537	18,162	4,607	33,887	54,947	18,662	5,138	33,498	55,953	18,809	5,054
North Dakota	2,222	6,298	1,625	569	2,349	6,427	1,682	554	2,318	6,580	1,769	622
Ohio	31,494	70,052	24,213	6,046	31,374	71,631	24,922	6,013	30,396	71,661	24,242	6,064
Oklahoma	12,027	21,024	6,576	1,662	11,561	21,297	6,735	1,713	10,779	21,362	6,852	1,620
Oregon	12,955	22,614	10,024	1,973	13,161	23,400	9,093	2,123	14,240	23,705	8,193	2,222
Pennsylvania	25,877	92,353	36,940	10,077	24,398	92,757	38,079	10,426	23,706	91,829	39,570	10,520
Rhode Island	3,291	11,989	2,676	716	3,353	12,180	2,942	744	3,530	12,309	3,179	762
South Carolina	11,517	25,107	6,068	1,892	11,259	25,831	6,193	1,825	10,587	26,317	6,310	1,883
South Dakota	2,236	6,040	1,538	437	2,319	6,068	1,563	395	2,250	5,991	1,750	454
Tennessee	13,225	35,255	11,841	3,670	13,538	35,801	12,180	3,981	13,858	35,375	11,582	4,107
Texas	86,838	126,128	52,585	10,978	91,644	130,818	53,047	11,072	94,286	135,667	55,026	11,262
Utah	13,367	34,118	11,081	1,263	13,778	36,862	13,354	1,277	13,983	40,837	16,629	1,282
Vermont	1,176	6,222	2,251	347	1,056	6,428	2,486	352	1,082	6,630	2,467	375
Virginia	25,123	58,642	24,665	5,258	24,187	58,563	24,658	5,455	23,512	58,709	24,525	5,492
Washington	30,591	33,598	9,750	2,591	30,217	34,218	10,090	2,642	30,993	34,222	10,089	2,745
West Virginia	6,479	16,519	6,244	1,160	6,456	16,344	6,330	1,233	6,525	16,948	5,953	1,131
Wisconsin	13,854	37,493	9,298	2,686	13,008	37,075	9,229	2,728	12,709	36,985	9,527	2,825
Wyoming	2,770	2,164	425	216	2,765	2,207	475	232	2,935	2,127	501	262
U.S. Service Academies	0	3,348	3	0	0	3,400	5	0	0	3,475	4	0
Other jurisdictions	**9,635**	**21,422**	**5,642**	**1,476**	**8,979**	**17,080**	**5,424**	**1,143**	**8,834**	**20,966**	**5,519**	**1,333**
American Samoa	216	17	0	0	220	8	0	0	215	10	0	0
Federated States of Micronesia	281	0	0	0	241	0	0	0	284	0	0	0
Guam	253	470	112	0	263	456	121	0	290	498	110	0
Marshall Islands	86	0	0	0	103	0	0	0	118	0	0	0
Northern Marianas	120	34	0	0	140	30	0	0	195	47	0	0
Palau	63	0	0	0	102	0	0	0	114	0	0	0
Puerto Rico	8,572	20,684	5,486	1,476	7,874	16,358	5,255	1,143	7,587	20,190	5,348	1,333
U.S. Virgin Islands	44	217	44	0	36	228	48	0	31	221	61	0

[1]Includes Ph.D., Ed.D., and comparable degrees at the doctoral level. Includes most degrees classified as first-professional prior to 2010–11, such as M.D., D.D.S., and law degrees.

NOTE: Data are for postsecondary institutions participating in Title IV federal financial aid programs. Some data have been revised from previously published figures.

SOURCE: U.S. Department of Education, National Center for Education Statistics, Integrated Postsecondary Education Data System (IPEDS), Fall 2016 through Fall 2018, Completions component. (This table was prepared May 2020.)

Table 319.30. Bachelor's degrees conferred by postsecondary institutions, by field of study and state or jurisdiction: 2018-19

State or jurisdiction	Total	Humanities[1]	Psychology	Social sciences and history	Natural sciences and mathematics[2]	Computer sciences	Engineering[3]	Education	Business[4]	Health professions and related programs	Other fields[5]
1	2	3	4	5	6	7	8	9	10	11	12
United States	**2,012,854**	**269,934**	**116,536**	**160,628**	**178,485**	**88,633**	**146,307**	**83,946**	**390,564**	**251,355**	**326,466**
Alabama	33,068	2,712	1,428	1,450	2,675	936	3,554	1,989	8,048	4,025	6,251
Alaska	1,922	298	95	113	194	44	222	87	332	219	318
Arizona	60,301	6,680	1,893	2,896	3,731	2,424	3,144	3,055	15,147	10,644	10,687
Arkansas	16,746	2,096	837	960	1,385	474	920	1,188	3,390	2,321	3,175
California	219,511	35,237	16,122	26,416	22,358	8,442	15,561	5,541	38,591	16,839	34,404
Colorado	36,814	3,800	1,947	2,906	3,782	1,913	3,086	733	8,097	4,660	5,890
Connecticut	23,785	3,448	1,758	2,565	2,271	536	1,452	557	4,515	3,071	3,612
Delaware	7,274	646	340	602	459	239	511	478	1,514	1,214	1,271
District of Columbia	10,220	1,120	487	2,800	666	372	413	67	2,112	935	1,248
Florida	108,197	13,074	7,156	7,382	8,574	4,188	6,390	4,362	23,955	15,406	17,710
Georgia	54,036	6,774	3,377	3,859	5,087	3,150	3,884	2,682	11,087	5,569	8,567
Hawaii	6,365	890	366	564	588	182	297	291	1,426	603	1,158
Idaho	12,955	2,005	538	593	1,005	461	933	813	2,229	2,144	2,234
Illinois	72,735	9,292	3,799	4,784	5,933	3,206	4,799	3,175	12,039	14,845	10,863
Indiana	51,271	5,398	2,380	2,539	3,617	2,548	5,133	2,802	10,102	8,166	8,586
Iowa	24,153	2,742	1,172	1,337	2,030	774	2,527	1,678	5,044	1,812	5,037
Kansas	20,359	2,402	920	1,118	1,436	651	1,603	1,622	4,830	2,472	3,305
Kentucky	24,522	2,939	1,309	1,366	1,828	637	1,612	1,792	4,209	3,493	5,337
Louisiana	23,093	3,197	1,278	1,423	2,099	568	2,217	1,415	4,419	3,173	3,304
Maine	7,337	1,038	391	817	783	177	511	361	911	1,199	1,149
Maryland	34,586	3,568	2,178	3,515	3,181	4,818	1,935	1,010	5,781	3,211	5,389
Massachusetts	61,699	8,645	3,984	6,988	6,634	3,542	4,976	1,547	11,207	6,454	7,722
Michigan	59,782	6,092	2,971	3,597	5,324	2,639	6,163	2,093	12,580	7,588	10,735
Minnesota	37,024	4,328	2,434	2,573	3,821	1,801	1,718	2,268	6,766	6,317	4,998
Mississippi	16,608	2,375	867	690	1,461	275	1,177	1,213	3,223	2,046	3,281
Missouri	40,610	4,925	2,351	2,082	3,164	1,670	2,501	2,669	8,563	5,730	6,955
Montana	6,242	662	260	457	722	148	920	513	901	677	982
Nebraska	14,445	1,411	700	669	1,191	596	619	1,240	3,505	1,679	2,835
Nevada	9,702	884	623	802	869	221	651	452	1,997	1,737	1,466
New Hampshire	19,005	2,644	1,617	1,427	1,002	873	587	384	4,806	2,744	2,921
New Jersey	44,690	6,921	3,431	3,640	4,297	2,470	2,993	1,191	8,891	4,174	6,682
New Mexico	8,560	1,550	578	463	714	198	893	584	1,225	1,237	1,118
New York	143,790	24,728	10,627	15,027	12,954	7,283	8,719	4,206	25,649	14,183	20,414
North Carolina	56,892	6,248	3,422	4,741	5,946	2,378	3,717	2,540	10,143	5,926	11,831
North Dakota	6,623	571	295	211	425	175	720	613	1,165	906	1,542
Ohio	72,250	7,532	3,294	4,566	5,930	1,893	6,966	4,185	14,202	12,053	11,629
Oklahoma	21,574	3,126	1,028	965	1,690	665	2,117	1,279	4,620	2,129	3,955
Oregon	24,107	3,593	1,392	2,949	2,275	1,123	1,663	762	3,704	2,286	4,360
Pennsylvania	91,190	10,858	4,829	7,234	9,117	4,489	7,702	3,568	17,834	12,420	13,139
Rhode Island	12,345	1,477	653	908	1,051	453	633	380	3,169	1,220	2,401
South Carolina	26,761	2,923	1,505	1,968	3,070	834	1,751	1,642	6,149	2,673	4,246
South Dakota	6,170	472	191	325	469	274	525	661	841	1,314	1,098
Tennessee	34,960	5,986	1,787	2,421	2,403	819	2,112	1,668	6,501	4,131	7,132
Texas	141,280	24,727	7,248	8,736	12,367	5,035	11,859	1,409	26,994	17,502	25,403
Utah	46,121	3,397	1,395	2,237	2,356	3,452	1,744	4,529	8,988	13,474	4,549
Vermont	6,481	1,154	339	736	692	398	322	203	852	463	1,322
Virginia	59,752	10,720	3,972	6,020	5,205	3,162	3,836	1,710	10,934	5,520	8,673
Washington	35,690	5,449	2,233	3,625	4,042	2,550	2,473	1,602	5,842	2,903	4,971
West Virginia	16,841	2,705	738	1,059	925	828	1,092	583	3,474	1,429	4,008
Wisconsin	36,626	3,926	1,842	2,605	4,021	1,469	2,944	2,372	7,386	4,233	5,828
Wyoming	2,228	171	119	169	277	41	306	182	336	186	441
U.S. Service Academies	3,556	378	40	733	389	139	1,204	0	339	0	334
Other jurisdictions	**21,217**	**1,260**	**1,204**	**643**	**2,358**	**788**	**1,141**	**1,238**	**3,948**	**5,349**	**3,288**
American Samoa	14	0	0	0	0	0	0	14	0	0	0
Guam	522	70	22	20	43	22	0	48	137	32	128
Marshall Islands	13	0	0	0	0	0	0	13	0	0	0
Northern Marianas	44	0	0	0	0	0	0	24	20	0	0
Puerto Rico	20,417	1,186	1,172	618	2,271	757	1,141	1,125	3,718	5,297	3,132
U.S. Virgin Islands	207	4	10	5	44	9	0	14	73	20	28

[1] Includes degrees in area, ethnic, cultural, gender, and group studies; English language and literature/letters; foreign languages, literatures, and linguistics; liberal arts and sciences, general studies and humanities; multi/interdisciplinary studies; philosophy and religious studies; theology and religious vocations; and visual and performing arts.

[2] Includes biological and biomedical sciences; physical sciences; science technologies/technicians; and mathematics and statistics.

[3] Includes engineering; engineering technologies/technicians; mechanic and repair technologies/technicians; and construction trades.

[4] Includes business, management, marketing, and related support services; and personal and culinary services.

[5] Includes agriculture, agricultural operations, and related sciences; natural resources and conservation; architecture and related services; communication, journalism, and related programs; communications technologies/technicians and support services; family and consumer services/human sciences; homeland security, law enforcement, and firefighting; legal professions and studies; library science; military technologies and applied sciences; parks, recreation, leisure, and fitness studies; precision production; public administration and social service professions; and transportation and materials moving.

NOTE: Data are for postsecondary institutions participating in Title IV federal financial aid programs. This table includes only those jurisdictions with 4-year institutions.

SOURCE: U.S. Department of Education, National Center for Education Statistics, Integrated Postsecondary Education Data System (IPEDS), Fall 2019, Completions component. (This table was prepared July 2020.)

Table 319.40. Master's degrees conferred by postsecondary institutions, by field of study and state or jurisdiction: 2018-19

State or jurisdiction	Total	Humanities[1]	Psychology	Social sciences and history	Natural sciences and mathematics[2]	Computer sciences	Engineering[3]	Education	Business[4]	Health professions and related programs	Other fields[5]
1	2	3	4	5	6	7	8	9	10	11	12
United States	**833,706**	**57,952**	**29,135**	**20,301**	**36,591**	**45,667**	**55,922**	**146,432**	**197,089**	**131,569**	**113,048**
Alabama	13,418	397	324	214	455	239	1,051	2,257	3,393	2,876	2,212
Alaska	605	47	11	7	33	4	57	203	83	28	132
Arizona	29,583	805	1,451	483	620	929	1,364	8,486	6,641	5,914	2,890
Arkansas	5,766	221	26	52	146	263	309	2,441	583	743	982
California	83,342	6,839	5,194	1,963	3,549	4,190	8,018	14,181	17,112	9,971	12,325
Colorado	15,447	969	903	426	691	919	1,211	2,072	4,212	2,193	1,851
Connecticut	11,322	949	434	305	817	269	673	1,683	2,896	1,720	1,576
Delaware	3,480	85	14	65	174	496	104	547	1,184	443	368
District of Columbia	13,226	1,014	204	1,628	1,030	562	402	625	3,128	1,725	2,908
Florida	34,375	2,066	1,163	518	1,576	1,458	2,327	3,284	10,362	6,740	4,881
Georgia	20,136	1,428	380	373	886	1,976	1,263	3,345	4,081	4,093	2,311
Hawaii	1,312	130	84	50	74	18	34	275	254	97	296
Idaho	2,008	116	17	60	90	28	119	545	328	294	411
Illinois	42,953	2,883	1,554	925	1,843	2,905	2,761	5,389	10,667	7,934	6,092
Indiana	18,865	1,798	437	233	559	571	1,354	2,951	4,981	3,471	2,510
Iowa	5,865	458	80	48	213	593	312	1,216	1,345	901	699
Kansas	7,570	531	230	120	256	144	367	2,391	1,777	636	1,118
Kentucky	12,207	605	598	132	281	2,142	379	3,164	1,444	1,821	1,641
Louisiana	8,645	434	146	154	728	139	215	1,284	2,577	1,462	1,506
Maine	2,195	149	19	24	43	8	30	452	340	607	523
Maryland	21,045	1,407	200	1,203	1,256	2,584	1,482	2,790	5,524	2,746	1,853
Massachusetts	42,146	2,888	1,097	1,444	2,096	2,617	3,696	6,031	10,987	5,232	6,058
Michigan	20,919	1,292	544	309	1,122	722	3,065	2,531	5,249	2,807	3,278
Minnesota	26,203	778	2,276	254	494	665	553	5,938	4,311	8,118	2,816
Mississippi	5,216	175	70	70	520	59	178	1,661	1,182	641	660
Missouri	19,721	1,224	475	347	554	808	1,030	3,436	5,766	3,442	2,639
Montana	1,309	109	44	45	100	15	66	324	145	258	203
Nebraska	5,390	283	71	249	223	314	109	1,511	1,230	848	552
Nevada	2,296	118	32	52	89	60	108	714	396	379	348
New Hampshire	9,465	706	568	325	65	487	255	931	3,975	1,210	943
New Jersey	17,236	1,578	600	268	1,124	1,520	1,672	3,006	3,582	1,626	2,260
New Mexico	3,341	280	47	84	164	115	353	791	592	492	423
New York	76,229	7,364	2,044	2,418	3,927	5,507	4,717	12,980	15,334	9,738	12,200
North Carolina	19,722	1,746	219	513	1,107	1,048	1,525	2,607	5,255	2,905	2,797
North Dakota	1,876	53	79	34	70	22	103	516	292	416	291
Ohio	24,153	1,653	836	573	1,584	750	1,978	3,460	5,324	4,882	3,113
Oklahoma	6,671	818	368	105	233	184	510	1,079	1,618	772	984
Oregon	8,152	613	210	114	353	171	483	3,108	903	1,273	924
Pennsylvania	39,367	2,355	1,394	762	1,727	2,229	3,170	6,572	8,917	7,233	5,008
Rhode Island	3,328	308	79	103	195	187	160	374	925	465	532
South Carolina	6,516	350	142	74	333	125	460	1,513	1,481	1,068	970
South Dakota	2,024	81	52	16	92	110	166	586	443	241	237
Tennessee	11,974	862	358	163	540	278	415	2,453	2,974	2,424	1,507
Texas	54,215	3,598	1,807	1,226	2,393	3,193	4,290	9,268	14,468	7,204	6,768
Utah	19,343	283	179	98	232	1,400	412	5,151	6,770	4,054	764
Vermont	2,335	547	57	228	75	99	40	347	492	173	277
Virginia	24,971	2,859	1,118	567	850	1,200	1,047	5,041	5,691	3,724	2,874
Washington	10,282	688	374	138	514	840	667	1,833	2,046	1,267	1,915
West Virginia	5,937	450	126	372	129	229	204	900	1,597	557	1,373
Wisconsin	9,518	514	392	341	329	269	620	2,089	2,151	1,658	1,155
Wyoming	484	48	8	26	37	7	36	100	81	47	94
U.S. Service Academies	2	0	0	0	0	0	2	0	0	0	0
Other jurisdictions	**5,857**	**291**	**394**	**81**	**234**	**87**	**218**	**920**	**1,523**	**1,453**	**656**
American Samoa	0	0	0	0	0	0	0	0	0	0	0
Guam	118	8	5	0	6	0	0	63	6	0	30
Marshall Islands	0	0	0	0	0	0	0	0	0	0	0
Northern Marianas	0	0	0	0	0	0	0	0	0	0	0
Puerto Rico	5,708	283	388	81	228	87	218	851	1,512	1,453	607
U.S. Virgin Islands	31	0	1	0	0	0	0	6	5	0	19

[1] Includes degrees in area, ethnic, cultural, gender, and group studies; English language and literature/letters; foreign languages, literatures, and linguistics; liberal arts and sciences, general studies and humanities; multi/interdisciplinary studies; philosophy and religious studies; theology and religious vocations; and visual and performing arts.

[2] Includes biological and biomedical sciences; physical sciences; science technologies/technicians; and mathematics and statistics.

[3] Includes engineering; engineering technologies/technicians; mechanic and repair technologies/technicians; and construction trades.

[4] Includes business, management, marketing, and related support services; and personal and culinary services.

[5] Includes agriculture, agricultural operations, and related sciences; natural resources and conservation; architecture and related services; communication, journalism, and related programs; communications technologies/technicians and support services; family and consumer services/human sciences; homeland security, law enforcement, and firefighting; legal professions and studies; library science; military technologies and applied sciences; parks, recreation, leisure, and fitness studies; precision production; public administration and social service professions; and transportation and materials moving.

NOTE: Data are for postsecondary institutions participating in Title IV federal financial aid programs. This table includes only those jurisdictions with 4-year institutions.

SOURCE: U.S. Department of Education, National Center for Education Statistics, Integrated Postsecondary Education Data System (IPEDS), Fall 2019, Completions component. (This table was prepared July 2020.)

Table 320.10. Certificates below the associate's degree level conferred by postsecondary institutions, by length of curriculum, sex of student, institution level and control, and field of study: 2017–18

Field of study	Less-than-1-year certificates: Total	Sex: Males	Sex: Females	Institution level: Non-degree-granting (less-than-2-year)[1]	Institution level: Degree-granting (2-year and 4-year)	Institution control: Public	Institution control: Nonprofit	Institution control: For-profit	1- to less-than-4-year certificates: Total	Sex: Males	Sex: Females	Institution level: Non-degree-granting (less-than-2-year)[1]	Institution level: Degree-granting (2-year and 4-year)	Institution control: Public	Institution control: Nonprofit	Institution control: For-profit
1	2	3	4	5	6	7	8	9	10	11	12	13	14	15	16	17
Total	**518,424**	**247,426**	**270,998**	**97,192**	**421,232**	**406,906**	**9,378**	**102,140**	**436,314**	**172,758**	**263,556**	**139,093**	**297,221**	**264,974**	**16,411**	**154,929**
Agriculture and natural resources	4,777	2,844	1,933	84	4,693	4,597	41	139	2,628	1,693	935	142	2,486	2,412	95	121
Agriculture, agriculture operations, and related sciences	3,635	2,209	1,426	84	3,551	3,531	28	76	2,388	1,524	864	141	2,247	2,178	89	121
Natural resources and conservation	1,142	635	507	0	1,142	1,066	13	63	240	169	71	1	239	234	6	0
Architecture and related services	259	166	93	0	259	245	14	0	97	58	39	0	97	96	0	1
Area, ethnic, cultural, gender, and group studies	862	185	677	0	862	857	5	0	101	25	76	0	101	75	26	0
Biological and biomedical sciences	593	203	390	9	584	575	9	9	213	74	139	100	113	177	36	0
Business, management, marketing, and support services	70,106	26,734	43,372	2,051	68,055	63,437	958	5,711	21,589	6,631	14,958	1,971	19,618	19,492	820	1,277
Accounting and related services	11,782	3,459	8,323	408	11,374	11,046	136	600	4,939	1,249	3,690	506	4,433	4,540	294	105
Business/commerce, general	2,788	1,183	1,605	0	2,788	2,786	1	1	1,604	761	843	0	1,604	1,581	1	22
Business administration, management, and operations	22,387	9,379	13,008	49	22,338	20,537	131	1,719	5,430	1,952	3,478	89	5,341	5,369	22	39
Management information systems and services	607	424	183	28	579	474	133	0	121	88	33	39	82	113	0	8
Business operations support and assistant services	9,004	2,834	6,170	1,053	7,951	8,013	7	984	4,831	865	3,966	1,260	3,571	3,690	186	955
Business and management, other	23,538	9,455	14,083	513	23,025	20,581	550	2,407	4,664	1,716	2,948	77	4,587	4,199	317	148
Communication, journalism, and related programs	3,960	1,829	2,131	909	3,051	2,561	46	1,353	1,022	557	465	518	504	592	16	414
Communications technologies	3,286	2,188	1,098	502	2,784	2,591	4	691	2,600	1,893	707	1,224	1,376	1,479	26	1,095
Computer and information sciences and support services	31,968	24,305	7,663	2,243	29,725	27,459	420	4,089	9,500	7,492	2,008	2,100	7,400	8,107	146	1,247
Construction trades	14,576	13,715	861	2,437	12,139	12,637	526	1,413	12,626	12,037	589	3,737	8,889	9,668	566	2,392
Education	8,855	890	7,965	48	8,807	7,919	430	506	3,863	499	3,364	58	3,805	2,834	772	257
Engineering	1,057	833	224	192	865	907	4	146	396	330	66	170	226	368	28	0
Engineering technologies and engineering-related fields[2]	22,883	19,687	3,196	1,960	20,923	20,857	98	1,928	13,491	11,963	1,528	2,009	11,482	10,340	459	2,692
English language and literature/letters	962	299	663	239	723	713	142	107	450	166	284	78	372	136	35	279
Family and consumer sciences/human sciences	18,456	1,224	17,232	932	17,524	18,256	64	136	4,044	172	3,872	366	3,678	3,989	41	14
Foreign languages, literatures, and linguistics	2,104	454	1,650	8	2,096	1,939	164	1	674	136	538	2	672	664	10	0
Health professions and related programs	144,958	29,424	115,534	34,099	110,859	103,317	2,778	38,863	138,699	18,785	119,914	45,424	93,275	64,347	8,113	66,239
Dental assisting	5,896	461	5,435	1,617	4,279	1,433	268	4,195	9,970	820	9,150	3,590	6,380	4,027	213	5,730
Emergency medical technician (EMT paramedic)	18,423	11,400	7,023	1,213	17,210	17,980	99	344	5,814	4,279	1,535	428	5,386	5,480	121	213
Clinical/medical lab science	9,775	1,341	8,434	2,477	7,298	6,943	226	2,606	1,787	422	1,365	238	1,549	632	463	692
Medical assisting	10,651	738	9,913	4,849	5,802	2,791	12	7,848	37,767	2,979	34,788	14,530	23,237	6,319	1,876	29,572
Pharmacy assisting	2,626	535	2,091	1,177	1,449	1,276	42	1,308	3,934	822	3,112	1,253	2,681	1,476	200	2,258
Other allied health assisting	7,287	2,463	4,824	1,416	5,871	5,316	1	1,970	2,002	197	1,805	567	1,435	1,122	164	716
Nursing and patient care assistant	40,599	4,917	35,682	8,015	32,584	35,819	524	4,256	892	122	770	304	588	453	0	439
Practical nursing	5,135	647	4,488	526	4,609	4,770	7	358	40,597	4,155	36,442	13,585	27,012	27,996	1,040	11,561
Nursing, registered nurse and other	1,384	178	1,206	0	1,384	1,378	6	0	2,287	295	1,992	1,448	839	816	1,273	198
Health sciences, other	43,182	6,744	36,438	12,809	30,373	25,611	1,593	15,978	33,649	4,694	28,955	9,481	24,168	16,026	2,763	14,860
Homeland security, law enforcement, and firefighting	34,156	25,542	8,614	2,036	32,120	32,952	467	737	7,531	4,959	2,572	488	7,043	6,848	72	611
Criminal justice and corrections	20,714	13,547	7,167	1,058	19,656	19,752	359	603	6,401	3,959	2,442	432	5,969	5,768	22	611
Fire control and safety	12,508	11,457	1,051	932	11,576	12,491	4	13	997	908	89	56	941	997	0	0
Homeland security and related protective services, other	934	538	396	46	888	709	104	121	133	92	41	0	133	83	50	0
Legal professions and studies	1,943	379	1,564	23	1,920	1,428	242	273	2,368	399	1,969	236	2,132	1,968	203	197
Liberal arts and sciences, general studies, and humanities	3,883	1,416	2,467	0	3,883	3,881	2	0	65,701	26,091	39,610	0	65,701	65,616	85	0
Library science	216	48	168	0	216	216	0	0	44	9	35	0	44	40	4	0
Mathematics and statistics	270	203	67	0	270	262	8	0	67	48	19	0	67	57	10	0
Mechanic and repair technologies/technicians	39,191	37,024	2,167	3,637	35,554	36,715	294	2,182	45,047	42,831	2,216	17,574	27,473	24,082	1,071	19,894
Military technologies and applied sciences	47	40	7	0	47	33	0	14	10	9	1	7	3	7	3	0
Multi/interdisciplinary studies	2,423	939	1,484	0	2,423	2,126	89	208	1,683	878	805	0	1,683	1,680	3	0

See notes at end of table.

Table 320.10. Certificates below the associate's degree level conferred by postsecondary institutions, by length of curriculum, sex of student, institution level and control, and field of study: 2017–18—Continued

Field of study	Less-than-1-year certificates								1- to less-than-4-year certificates							
		Sex		Institution level		Institution control				Sex		Institution level		Institution control		
	Total	Males	Females	Non-degree-granting (less-than-2-year)[1]	Degree-granting (2-year and 4-year)	Public	Nonprofit	For-profit	Total	Males	Females	Non-degree-granting (less-than-2-year)[1]	Degree-granting (2-year and 4-year)	Public	Nonprofit	For-profit
1	2	3	4	5	6	7	8	9	10	11	12	13	14	15	16	17
Parks, recreation, leisure, and fitness studies studies	1,756	838	918	414	1,342	1,333	0	423	422	224	198	83	339	271	15	136
Personal and culinary services	42,209	5,342	36,867	31,388	10,821	11,346	373	30,490	67,528	10,561	56,967	55,068	12,460	13,357	745	53,426
Philosophy and religious studies	100	52	48	0	100	68	32	0	48	21	27	0	48	18	30	0
Physical sciences and science technologies	1,535	787	748	56	1,479	1,535	0	0	1,243	790	453	27	1,216	1,216	0	27
Physical sciences	276	166	110	0	276	276	0	0	28	19	9	0	28	28	0	0
Science technologies/technicians	1,259	621	638	56	1,203	1,259	0	0	1,215	771	444	27	1,188	1,188	0	27
Precision production	30,505	28,476	2,029	4,408	26,097	26,478	353	3,674	18,660	17,482	1,178	6,101	12,559	14,357	1,130	3,173
Psychology	201	27	174	0	201	178	23	0	95	26	69	0	95	93	2	0
Public administration and social services	2,233	436	1,797	0	2,233	1,820	48	365	810	126	684	0	810	728	39	43
Social sciences and history	1,588	742	846	3	1,585	1,496	92	0	496	263	233	0	496	395	101	0
Social sciences	1,538	728	810	3	1,535	1,447	91	0	485	257	228	0	485	384	101	0
History	50	14	36	0	50	49	1	0	11	6	5	0	11	11	0	0
Theology and religious vocations	260	125	135	0	260	0	252	8	895	363	532	320	575	0	895	0
Transportation and materials moving	18,741	16,612	2,129	8,546	10,195	9,618	737	8,386	1,063	978	85	346	717	695	20	348
Visual and performing arts	7,505	3,418	4,087	968	6,537	6,554	663	288	10,610	4,189	6,421	944	9,666	8,770	794	1,046
Fine and studio arts	862	281	581	618	244	241	525	96	6,187	2,273	3,914	79	6,108	6,081	34	72
Music and dance	377	234	143	0	377	312	7	58	427	230	197	89	338	140	129	158
Visual and performing arts, other[3]	6,266	2,903	3,363	350	5,916	6,001	131	134	3,996	1,686	2,310	776	3,220	2,549	631	816

[1]Non-degree-granting institutions do not offer accredited 4-year or 2-year programs for degrees at the associate's or higher level, but they may include institutions offering programs 2 years or longer in duration for lower level awards.
[2]Excludes "Construction trades" and "Mechanic and repair technologies/technicians," which are listed separately.
[3]Includes design and applied arts, drama and theatre arts, film and photographic arts, and all other arts not included under "Fine and studio arts" or "Music and dance."

NOTE: Data are for postsecondary institutions participating in Title IV federal financial aid programs. Degree-granting institutions grant degrees at the associate's or higher level, while non-degree-granting institutions grant only awards below that level.
SOURCE: U.S. Department of Education, National Center for Education Statistics, Integrated Postsecondary Education Data System (IPEDS), Fall 2018, Completions component. (This table was prepared May 2020.)

Table 320.20. Certificates below the associate's degree level conferred by postsecondary institutions, by race/ethnicity and sex of student: 1998–99 through 2017–18

Year and sex	Number of certificates conferred to U.S. citizens, permanent residents, and nonresident aliens								Percentage distribution of certificates conferred to U.S. citizens and permanent residents						
	Total	White	Black	Hispanic	Asian/ Pacific Islander	American Indian/ Alaska Native	Two or more races	Non-resident alien	Total	White	Black	Hispanic	Asian/ Pacific Islander	American Indian/ Alaska Native	Two or more races
1	2	3	4	5	6	7	8	9	10	11	12	13	14	15	16
Total															
1998–99	555,883	345,359	92,800	76,833	27,920	7,510	—	5,461	100.0	62.7	16.9	14.0	5.1	1.4	—
1999–2000	558,129	337,546	97,329	81,132	29,361	6,966	—	5,795	100.0	61.1	17.6	14.7	5.3	1.3	—
2000–01	552,503	333,478	99,397	78,528	28,123	6,598	—	6,379	100.0	61.1	18.2	14.4	5.1	1.2	—
2001–02	584,248	352,559	106,647	83,950	27,490	7,430	—	6,172	100.0	61.0	18.4	14.5	4.8	1.3	—
2002–03	646,425	382,289	120,582	95,499	32,981	8,117	—	6,957	100.0	59.8	18.9	14.9	5.2	1.3	—
2003–04	687,787	402,989	129,891	107,216	32,819	8,375	—	6,497	100.0	59.2	19.1	15.7	4.8	1.2	—
2004–05	710,873	415,670	133,601	114,089	32,783	8,150	—	6,580	100.0	59.0	19.0	16.2	4.7	1.2	—
2005–06	714,790	411,919	135,387	118,728	33,848	8,393	—	6,515	100.0	58.2	19.1	16.8	4.8	1.2	—
2006–07	728,315	420,199	139,796	119,375	32,963	8,781	—	7,201	100.0	58.3	19.4	16.6	4.6	1.2	—
2007–08	748,354	429,670	144,982	122,406	35,791	8,548	—	6,957	100.0	58.0	19.6	16.5	4.8	1.2	—
2008–09	804,620	450,562	161,487	138,301	37,941	9,485	—	6,844	100.0	56.5	20.2	17.3	4.8	1.2	—
2009–10	935,719	511,186	191,657	172,015	41,407	12,003	—	7,451	100.0	55.1	20.6	18.5	4.5	1.3	—
2010–11	1,030,477	557,595	207,693	187,433	44,294	11,204	14,999	7,259	100.0	54.5	20.3	18.3	4.3	1.1	1.5
2011–12	989,061	535,621	190,253	187,014	43,048	10,638	14,140	8,347	100.0	54.6	19.4	19.1	4.4	1.1	1.4
2012–13	967,214	524,000	177,006	186,248	44,196	10,824	17,642	7,298	100.0	54.6	18.4	19.4	4.6	1.1	1.8
2013–14	969,278	523,015	177,860	185,677	43,800	10,817	19,971	8,138	100.0	54.4	18.5	19.3	4.6	1.1	2.1
2014–15	961,146	512,077	174,828	187,943	44,707	11,084	21,681	8,826	100.0	53.8	18.4	19.7	4.7	1.2	2.3
2015–16	939,291	496,717	162,367	192,977	43,923	10,558	23,222	9,527	100.0	53.4	17.5	20.8	4.7	1.1	2.5
2016–17	946,023	493,302	159,209	202,731	44,886	10,911	24,710	10,274	100.0	52.7	17.0	21.7	4.8	1.2	2.6
2017–18	954,738	495,461	150,779	212,099	47,088	10,998	26,882	11,431	100.0	52.5	16.0	22.5	5.0	1.2	2.8
Males															
1998–99	219,872	144,735	29,875	27,719	11,742	3,061	—	2,740	100.0	66.7	13.8	12.8	5.4	1.4	—
1999–2000	226,110	143,634	33,792	30,337	13,082	2,862	—	2,403	100.0	64.2	15.1	13.6	5.8	1.3	—
2000–01	223,951	143,144	34,381	28,685	12,072	2,719	—	2,950	100.0	64.8	15.6	13.0	5.5	1.2	—
2001–02	235,275	152,226	36,482	29,749	10,938	3,226	—	2,654	100.0	65.4	15.7	12.8	4.7	1.4	—
2002–03	254,238	161,001	40,080	33,925	12,930	3,506	—	2,796	100.0	64.0	15.9	13.5	5.1	1.4	—
2003–04	257,138	161,684	40,809	36,157	12,713	3,135	—	2,640	100.0	63.5	16.0	14.2	5.0	1.2	—
2004–05	259,261	161,126	41,644	38,297	12,448	3,068	—	2,678	100.0	62.8	16.2	14.9	4.9	1.2	—
2005–06	259,413	158,719	41,847	40,682	12,575	3,214	—	2,376	100.0	61.7	16.3	15.8	4.9	1.3	—
2006–07	269,470	164,856	44,862	40,932	12,621	3,524	—	2,675	100.0	61.8	16.8	15.3	4.7	1.3	—
2007–08	283,102	172,438	48,013	43,076	13,460	3,431	—	2,684	100.0	61.5	17.1	15.4	4.8	1.2	—
2008–09	302,449	179,813	53,879	47,860	14,427	3,856	—	2,614	100.0	60.0	18.0	16.0	4.8	1.3	—
2009–10	355,381	205,404	65,487	60,771	15,940	5,067	—	2,712	100.0	58.2	18.6	17.2	4.5	1.4	—
2010–11	391,676	223,755	71,867	66,514	16,944	4,760	4,884	2,952	100.0	57.6	18.5	17.1	4.4	1.2	1.3
2011–12	374,086	213,833	65,224	65,838	16,180	4,507	4,952	3,552	100.0	57.7	17.6	17.8	4.4	1.2	1.3
2012–13	375,928	215,432	61,668	67,377	17,352	4,446	6,511	3,142	100.0	57.8	16.5	18.1	4.7	1.2	1.7
2013–14	390,795	223,180	65,595	68,821	17,280	4,731	7,781	3,407	100.0	57.6	16.9	17.8	4.5	1.2	2.0
2014–15	394,707	222,413	64,574	72,020	18,132	4,848	8,836	3,884	100.0	56.9	16.5	18.4	4.6	1.2	2.3
2015–16	396,834	223,269	60,835	76,483	17,667	4,613	9,622	4,345	100.0	56.9	15.5	19.5	4.5	1.2	2.5
2016–17	405,430	225,423	60,124	81,767	18,034	4,969	10,307	4,806	100.0	56.3	15.0	20.4	4.5	1.2	2.6
2017–18	420,184	231,999	58,064	88,597	19,832	4,987	11,436	5,269	100.0	55.9	14.0	21.4	4.8	1.2	2.8
Females															
1998–99	336,011	200,624	62,925	49,114	16,178	4,449	—	2,721	100.0	60.2	18.9	14.7	4.9	1.3	—
1999–2000	332,019	193,912	63,537	50,795	16,279	4,104	—	3,392	100.0	59.0	19.3	15.5	5.0	1.2	—
2000–01	328,552	190,334	65,016	49,843	16,051	3,879	—	3,429	100.0	58.5	20.0	15.3	4.9	1.2	—
2001–02	348,973	200,333	70,165	54,201	16,552	4,204	—	3,518	100.0	58.0	20.3	15.7	4.8	1.2	—
2002–03	392,187	221,288	80,502	61,574	20,051	4,611	—	4,161	100.0	57.0	20.7	15.9	5.2	1.2	—
2003–04	430,649	241,305	89,082	71,059	20,106	5,240	—	3,857	100.0	56.5	20.9	16.6	4.7	1.2	—
2004–05	451,612	254,544	91,957	75,792	20,335	5,082	—	3,902	100.0	56.9	20.5	16.9	4.5	1.1	—
2005–06	455,377	253,200	93,540	78,046	21,273	5,179	—	4,139	100.0	56.1	20.7	17.3	4.7	1.1	—
2006–07	458,845	255,343	94,934	78,443	20,342	5,257	—	4,526	100.0	56.2	20.9	17.3	4.5	1.2	—
2007–08	465,252	257,232	96,969	79,330	22,331	5,117	—	4,273	100.0	55.8	21.0	17.2	4.8	1.1	—
2008–09	502,171	270,749	107,608	90,441	23,514	5,629	—	4,230	100.0	54.4	21.6	18.2	4.7	1.1	—
2009–10	580,338	305,782	126,170	111,244	25,467	6,936	—	4,739	100.0	53.1	21.9	19.3	4.4	1.2	—
2010–11	638,801	333,840	135,826	120,919	27,350	6,444	10,115	4,307	100.0	52.6	21.4	19.1	4.3	1.0	1.6
2011–12	614,975	321,788	125,029	121,176	26,868	6,131	9,188	4,795	100.0	52.7	20.5	19.9	4.4	1.0	1.5
2012–13	591,286	308,568	115,338	118,871	26,844	6,378	11,131	4,156	100.0	52.6	19.6	20.2	4.6	1.1	1.9
2013–14	578,483	299,835	112,265	116,856	26,520	6,086	12,190	4,731	100.0	52.3	19.6	20.4	4.6	1.1	2.1
2014–15	566,439	289,664	110,254	115,923	26,575	6,236	12,845	4,942	100.0	51.6	19.6	20.6	4.7	1.1	2.3
2015–16	542,457	273,448	101,532	116,494	26,256	5,945	13,600	5,182	100.0	50.9	18.9	21.7	4.9	1.1	2.5
2016–17	540,593	267,879	99,085	120,964	26,852	5,942	14,403	5,468	100.0	50.1	18.5	22.6	5.0	1.1	2.7
2017–18	534,554	263,462	92,715	123,502	27,256	6,011	15,446	6,162	100.0	49.9	17.5	23.4	5.2	1.1	2.9

—Not available.
NOTE: Includes less-than-1-year awards and 1- to less-than-4-year awards (excluding associate's degrees) conferred by postsecondary institutions participating in Title IV federal financial aid programs. Race categories exclude persons of Hispanic ethnicity. Reported racial/ethnic distributions of students by level of degree, field of degree, and sex were used to estimate race/ethnicity for students whose race/ethnicity was not reported. Some data have been revised from previously published figures. Detail may not sum to totals because of rounding.
SOURCE: U.S. Department of Education, National Center for Education Statistics, Integrated Postsecondary Education Data System (IPEDS), "Completions Survey" (IPEDS-C:99); and IPEDS Fall 2000 through Fall 2018, Completions component. (This table was prepared October 2019.)

Table 321.10. Associate's degrees conferred by postsecondary institutions, by sex of student and discipline division: 2007–08 through 2017–18

Discipline division	2007–08	2008–09	2009–10	2010–11	2011–12	2012–13	2013–14	2014–15	2015–16	2016–17	2017–18 Total	2017–18 Males	2017–18 Females
1	2	3	4	5	6	7	8	9	10	11	12	13	14
Total	**750,166**	**787,243**	**848,856**	**943,506**	**1,021,718**	**1,007,427**	**1,005,155**	**1,014,341**	**1,008,228**	**1,005,687**	**1,011,487**	**398,600**	**612,887**
Agriculture and natural resources	5,738	5,724	5,852	6,430	7,068	6,826	7,057	7,693	7,858	8,208	8,076	4,834	3,242
Agriculture, agriculture operations, and related sciences	4,554	4,525	4,615	4,925	5,400	5,227	5,420	5,975	6,158	6,439	6,306	3,659	2,647
Natural resources and conservation	1,184	1,199	1,237	1,505	1,668	1,599	1,637	1,718	1,700	1,769	1,770	1,175	595
Architecture and related services	568	605	553	569	593	468	425	491	478	503	539	358	181
Area, ethnic, cultural, gender, and group studies	169	174	199	209	194	271	363	382	419	420	559	230	329
Biological and biomedical sciences	2,200	2,337	2,664	3,276	3,834	4,185	4,557	4,883	5,266	5,550	6,390	2,072	4,318
Business	121,221	127,882	133,265	139,994	143,390	134,114	129,957	132,374	128,259	122,252	117,782	47,418	70,364
Business, management, marketing, and support services	104,631	111,524	116,798	121,735	123,014	114,842	113,056	113,681	110,036	108,376	105,751	43,015	62,736
Accounting and related services	15,963	16,707	17,925	20,180	20,270	18,061	17,400	16,080	14,790	13,760	13,013	3,798	9,215
Business/commerce, general	12,496	13,100	14,553	15,083	17,301	17,211	17,372	18,235	18,087	18,293	17,060	7,491	9,569
Business administration, management, and operations	47,910	52,938	46,086	46,253	45,879	49,816	50,121	52,668	52,758	53,930	55,382	25,198	30,184
Management information systems and services	1,232	1,103	1,221	1,244	1,164	1,085	1,176	987	935	953	920	646	274
Business operations support and assistant services	7,838	7,550	7,399	8,259	8,977	7,986	7,331	6,570	5,871	5,141	4,617	473	4,144
Business and management, other	19,192	20,126	29,614	30,716	29,423	20,683	19,656	19,141	17,595	16,299	14,759	5,409	9,350
Personal and culinary services	16,590	16,358	16,467	18,259	20,376	19,272	16,901	18,693	18,223	13,876	12,031	4,403	7,628
Communication, journalism, and related programs	2,620	2,722	2,841	3,051	3,495	4,299	4,970	6,034	6,759	7,379	7,785	3,269	4,516
Communications technologies	4,268	4,805	4,418	4,209	5,004	5,028	4,713	4,628	4,569	4,307	4,197	2,782	1,415
Computer and information sciences and support services	28,298	29,912	32,351	37,689	41,250	38,954	37,646	36,420	30,571	31,171	31,479	25,236	6,243
Construction trades	4,309	4,252	4,684	5,402	5,750	5,038	4,837	4,643	4,699	5,308	5,277	4,968	309
Education	13,111	14,123	17,346	20,460	20,762	18,744	17,605	17,178	17,032	16,603	16,182	1,843	14,339
Engineering	2,279	2,170	2,508	2,825	3,382	3,732	4,306	4,875	5,278	5,915	6,408	5,334	1,074
Engineering technologies and engineering-related fields[1]	29,359	30,441	31,883	35,519	36,642	33,752	31,792	31,958	27,243	27,021	26,745	22,899	3,846
English language and literature/letters	1,402	1,534	1,658	2,019	2,137	2,089	2,082	2,324	2,551	2,870	3,133	1,049	2,084
Family and consumer sciences/human sciences	8,614	9,035	9,515	8,532	9,506	8,996	8,669	8,750	8,930	8,871	8,854	400	8,454
Foreign languages, literatures, and linguistics	1,258	1,630	1,683	1,888	1,980	2,131	2,284	2,102	2,208	2,363	2,607	625	1,982
Health professions and related programs	155,794	165,015	177,321	202,920	219,491	214,040	208,885	200,018	191,442	186,312	181,056	29,483	151,573
Dental assisting	6,642	6,574	7,063	7,498	7,790	7,823	7,988	7,762	7,584	7,397	7,073	361	6,712
Emergency medical technician (EMT paramedic)	2,140	2,270	2,413	2,895	3,352	3,520	3,521	3,456	3,380	3,453	3,410	2,306	1,104
Clinical/medical lab science	2,316	2,538	2,621	2,811	3,240	3,387	3,517	3,143	3,186	3,062	3,051	722	2,329
Medical and other health assisting	24,291	25,858	29,776	39,277	46,950	41,921	39,126	36,813	34,749	32,297	28,723	4,611	24,112
Nursing and patient care assistant	329	385	1	33	36	35	38	50	52	56	100	11	89
Practical nursing	1,417	1,299	1,973	2,069	2,366	2,361	2,230	1,858	1,404	1,420	1,105	99	1,006
Nursing, registered nurse and other	73,398	77,922	81,281	83,023	84,569	86,380	86,435	82,953	78,577	77,083	77,674	11,217	66,457
Health sciences, other	45,261	48,169	52,193	65,314	71,188	68,613	66,030	63,983	62,510	61,544	59,920	10,156	49,764
Homeland security, law enforcement, and firefighting	29,485	33,012	37,154	44,922	51,318	48,460	45,771	43,041	39,930	37,362	35,276	19,997	15,279
Criminal justice and corrections	25,471	28,998	32,648	40,022	45,971	42,785	40,297	37,820	35,122	32,589	30,463	15,713	14,750
Fire control and safety	3,949	3,947	4,307	4,603	4,779	4,910	4,649	4,525	4,241	4,191	4,287	3,916	371
Homeland security and related protective services, other	65	67	199	297	568	765	825	696	567	582	526	368	158
Legal professions and studies	9,464	9,062	9,999	11,619	12,315	11,862	10,502	9,095	8,017	6,904	6,237	1,011	5,226
Liberal arts and sciences, general studies, and humanities	253,990	263,947	284,954	306,674	336,938	344,171	353,946	367,852	381,202	386,746	397,926	151,028	246,898
Library science	117	116	112	160	159	181	194	170	146	158	156	21	135
Mathematics and statistics	855	933	1,051	1,644	1,529	1,801	2,148	2,697	3,027	3,454	4,135	2,880	1,255
Mechanic and repair technologies/technicians	15,518	16,059	16,326	19,969	20,715	20,487	20,100	19,984	20,543	20,821	21,295	19,846	1,449
Military technologies and applied sciences	851	721	668	856	986	1,002	1,084	1,229	1,047	1,093	1,226	946	280
Multi/interdisciplinary studies	16,247	15,472	17,279	23,729	27,263	27,407	28,167	29,139	30,482	30,780	31,068	13,002	18,066
Parks, recreation, leisure, and fitness studies	1,345	1,587	2,006	2,366	3,123	3,455	4,383	4,669	4,771	5,037	5,095	2,758	2,337
Philosophy and religious studies	458	193	256	283	308	326	435	697	814	1,002	1,049	640	409
Physical sciences and science technologies	3,394	3,650	4,141	5,078	5,827	6,376	6,916	7,568	8,484	9,223	10,116	5,927	4,189
Physical sciences	1,979	2,196	2,378	3,148	3,652	4,083	4,518	5,040	5,528	5,838	6,688	3,908	2,780
Science technologies/technicians	1,415	1,454	1,763	1,930	2,175	2,293	2,398	2,528	2,956	3,385	3,428	2,019	1,409
Precision production	1,967	2,127	2,794	3,254	3,320	3,345	3,903	4,382	4,794	5,251	5,333	4,967	366
Psychology	2,411	3,957	6,582	3,866	4,717	6,122	7,604	8,780	10,603	11,283	12,489	2,921	9,568
Public administration and social services	4,194	4,177	4,522	7,472	9,222	8,788	8,914	8,436	7,988	7,591	7,136	1,003	6,133
Social sciences and history	7,812	9,157	10,649	12,772	14,132	15,668	16,554	17,916	20,056	21,392	23,683	8,849	14,834
Social sciences	7,358	8,670	10,108	12,072	13,321	14,749	15,473	16,631	18,451	19,636	21,545	7,516	14,029
History	454	487	541	700	811	919	1,081	1,285	1,605	1,756	2,138	1,333	805
Theology and religious vocations	582	676	613	758	839	881	944	1,135	1,089	1,546	1,435	786	649
Transportation and materials moving	1,550	1,430	1,444	1,698	2,098	2,119	2,102	1,810	1,497	1,547	1,610	1,394	216
Visual and performing arts	18,704	18,606	19,565	21,394	22,431	22,309	21,340	20,988	20,176	19,444	19,153	7,824	11,329
Fine and studio arts	1,706	2,019	2,277	2,414	2,339	2,541	2,699	2,866	3,082	3,315	3,766	1,260	2,506
Music and dance	1,317	1,152	1,335	1,356	1,683	1,743	1,715	1,886	1,989	1,993	2,313	1,456	857
Visual and performing arts, other[2]	15,681	15,435	15,953	17,624	18,409	18,025	16,926	16,236	15,105	14,136	13,074	5,108	7,966
Not classified by field of study	14	0	0	0	0	0	0	0	0	0	0	0	0

[1]Excludes "Construction trades" and "Mechanic and repair technologies/technicians," which are listed separately.
[2]Includes design and applied arts, drama and theatre arts, film and photographic arts, and all other arts not included under "Fine and studio arts" or "Music and dance."
NOTE: Data are for postsecondary institutions participating in Title IV federal financial aid programs. Some data have been revised from previously published figures.

SOURCE: U.S. Department of Education, National Center for Education Statistics, Integrated Postsecondary Education Data System (IPEDS), Fall 2008 through Fall 2018, Completions component. (This table was prepared August 2019.)

Table 321.20. Associate's degrees conferred by postsecondary institutions, by race/ethnicity and sex of student: Selected years, 1976–77 through 2017–18

Year and sex	Number of degrees conferred to U.S. citizens, permanent residents, and nonresident aliens								Percentage distribution of degrees conferred to U.S. citizens and permanent residents						
	Total	White	Black	Hispanic	Asian/ Pacific Islander	American Indian/ Alaska Native	Two or more races[1]	Non-resident alien	Total	White	Black	Hispanic	Asian/ Pacific Islander	American Indian/ Alaska Native	Two or more races[1]
1	2	3	4	5	6	7	8	9	10	11	12	13	14	15	16
Total															
1976–77[2]	404,956	342,290	33,159	16,636	7,044	2,498	—	3,329	100.0	85.2	8.3	4.1	1.8	0.6	—
1980–81[3]	410,174	339,167	35,330	17,800	8,650	2,584	—	6,643	100.0	84.0	8.8	4.4	2.1	0.6	—
1990–91	481,720	391,264	38,835	25,540	15,257	3,871	—	6,953	100.0	82.4	8.2	5.4	3.2	0.8	—
1999–2000	564,933	408,822	60,208	51,563	27,778	6,474	—	10,088	100.0	73.7	10.9	9.3	5.0	1.2	—
2000–01	578,865	411,075	63,855	57,288	28,463	6,623	—	11,561	100.0	72.5	11.3	10.1	5.0	1.2	—
2003–04	665,301	456,047	81,183	72,270	33,149	8,119	—	14,533	100.0	70.1	12.5	11.1	5.1	1.2	—
2004–05	696,660	475,513	86,402	78,557	33,669	8,435	—	14,084	100.0	69.7	12.7	11.5	4.9	1.2	—
2005–06	713,315	485,481	89,813	80,870	35,215	8,555	—	13,381	100.0	69.4	12.8	11.6	5.0	1.2	—
2006–07	727,616	491,333	91,440	85,275	37,243	8,579	—	13,746	100.0	68.8	12.8	11.9	5.2	1.2	—
2007–08	750,166	501,467	95,566	91,289	38,848	8,827	—	14,169	100.0	68.1	13.0	12.4	5.3	1.2	—
2008–09	787,243	521,834	101,631	98,408	41,364	8,823	—	15,183	100.0	67.6	13.2	12.7	5.4	1.1	—
2009–10	848,856	552,376	113,867	112,403	44,026	10,101	—	16,083	100.0	66.3	13.7	13.5	5.3	1.2	—
2010–11	943,506	604,745	129,044	126,297	45,489	10,180	11,126	16,625	100.0	65.2	13.9	13.6	4.9	1.1	1.2
2011–12	1,021,718	635,755	142,512	151,807	48,861	10,738	14,858	17,187	100.0	63.3	14.2	15.1	4.9	1.1	1.5
2012–13	1,007,427	617,308	135,892	157,989	49,474	10,546	19,383	16,835	100.0	62.3	13.7	15.9	5.0	1.1	2.0
2013–14	1,005,155	601,959	134,621	168,106	50,368	10,338	22,695	17,068	100.0	60.9	13.6	17.0	5.1	1.0	2.3
2014–15	1,014,341	590,616	137,920	180,598	51,767	9,996	25,505	17,939	100.0	59.3	13.8	18.1	5.2	1.0	2.6
2015–16	1,008,228	566,622	134,012	196,044	53,753	9,490	28,933	19,374	100.0	57.3	13.6	19.8	5.4	1.0	2.9
2016–17	1,005,687	551,057	129,880	209,159	55,814	9,265	29,603	20,909	100.0	56.0	13.2	21.2	5.7	0.9	3.0
2017–18	1,011,487	536,256	125,517	225,462	58,952	9,285	32,971	23,044	100.0	54.3	12.7	22.8	6.0	0.9	3.3
Males															
1976–77[2]	209,672	178,236	15,330	9,105	3,630	1,216	—	2,155	100.0	85.9	7.4	4.4	1.7	0.6	—
1980–81[3]	183,819	151,242	14,290	8,327	4,557	1,108	—	4,295	100.0	84.2	8.0	4.6	2.5	0.6	—
1990–91	198,634	161,858	14,143	10,738	7,164	1,439	—	3,292	100.0	82.9	7.2	5.5	3.7	0.7	—
1999–2000	224,721	164,317	20,968	20,947	12,009	2,222	—	4,258	100.0	74.5	9.5	9.5	5.4	1.0	—
2000–01	231,645	166,322	22,147	23,350	12,339	2,294	—	5,193	100.0	73.4	9.8	10.3	5.4	1.0	—
2003–04	260,033	183,819	25,961	27,828	13,907	2,740	—	5,778	100.0	72.3	10.2	10.9	5.5	1.1	—
2004–05	267,536	188,569	27,151	29,658	13,802	2,774	—	5,582	100.0	72.0	10.4	11.3	5.3	1.1	—
2005–06	270,139	190,174	27,618	30,043	14,227	2,777	—	5,300	100.0	71.8	10.4	11.3	5.4	1.0	—
2006–07	275,034	191,487	28,251	31,609	15,502	2,872	—	5,313	100.0	71.0	10.5	11.7	5.7	1.1	—
2007–08	282,695	194,354	29,984	33,852	15,941	2,989	—	5,575	100.0	70.1	10.8	12.2	5.8	1.1	—
2008–09	298,066	202,670	32,004	36,919	17,305	3,075	—	6,093	100.0	69.4	11.0	12.6	5.9	1.1	—
2009–10	322,747	215,977	36,148	42,210	18,268	3,555	—	6,589	100.0	68.3	11.4	13.4	5.8	1.1	—
2010–11	361,408	238,012	41,649	47,911	19,085	3,727	4,197	6,827	100.0	67.1	11.7	13.5	5.4	1.1	1.2
2011–12	393,479	251,964	46,377	57,926	20,537	3,924	5,569	7,182	100.0	65.2	12.0	15.0	5.3	1.0	1.4
2012–13	389,195	243,868	45,458	60,536	21,223	3,638	7,434	7,038	100.0	63.8	11.9	15.8	5.6	1.0	1.9
2013–14	391,474	239,289	45,868	64,658	21,824	3,682	8,969	7,184	100.0	62.3	11.9	16.8	5.7	1.0	2.3
2014–15	396,782	236,381	47,393	69,291	22,377	3,590	9,997	7,753	100.0	60.8	12.2	17.8	5.8	0.9	2.6
2015–16	392,084	226,142	44,777	74,531	23,426	3,335	11,251	8,622	100.0	59.0	11.7	19.4	6.1	0.9	2.9
2016–17	394,147	223,637	43,170	78,470	24,459	3,370	11,678	9,363	100.0	58.1	11.2	20.4	6.4	0.9	3.0
2017–18	398,600	219,372	41,820	84,868	25,736	3,366	12,958	10,480	100.0	56.5	10.8	21.9	6.6	0.9	3.3
Females															
1976–77[2]	195,284	164,054	17,829	7,531	3,414	1,282	—	1,174	100.0	84.5	9.2	3.9	1.8	0.7	—
1980–81[3]	226,355	187,925	21,040	9,473	4,093	1,476	—	2,348	100.0	83.9	9.4	4.2	1.8	0.7	—
1990–91	283,086	229,406	24,692	14,802	8,093	2,432	—	3,661	100.0	82.1	8.8	5.3	2.9	0.9	—
1999–2000	340,212	244,505	39,240	30,616	15,769	4,252	—	5,830	100.0	73.1	11.7	9.2	4.7	1.3	—
2000–01	347,220	244,753	41,708	33,938	16,124	4,329	—	6,368	100.0	71.8	12.2	10.0	4.7	1.3	—
2003–04	405,268	272,228	55,222	44,442	19,242	5,379	—	8,755	100.0	68.7	13.9	11.2	4.9	1.4	—
2004–05	429,124	286,944	59,251	48,899	19,867	5,661	—	8,502	100.0	68.2	14.1	11.6	4.7	1.3	—
2005–06	443,176	295,307	62,195	50,827	20,988	5,778	—	8,081	100.0	67.9	14.3	11.7	4.8	1.3	—
2006–07	452,582	299,846	63,189	53,666	21,741	5,707	—	8,433	100.0	67.5	14.2	12.1	4.9	1.3	—
2007–08	467,471	307,113	65,582	57,437	22,907	5,838	—	8,594	100.0	66.9	14.3	12.5	5.0	1.3	—
2008–09	489,177	319,164	69,627	61,489	24,059	5,748	—	9,090	100.0	66.5	14.5	12.8	5.0	1.2	—
2009–10	526,109	336,399	77,719	70,193	25,758	6,546	—	9,494	100.0	65.1	15.0	13.6	5.0	1.3	—
2010–11	582,098	366,733	87,395	78,386	26,404	6,453	6,929	9,798	100.0	64.1	15.3	13.7	4.6	1.1	1.2
2011–12	628,239	383,791	96,135	93,881	28,324	6,814	9,289	10,005	100.0	62.1	15.5	15.2	4.6	1.1	1.5
2012–13	618,232	373,440	90,434	97,453	28,251	6,908	11,949	9,797	100.0	61.4	14.9	16.0	4.6	1.1	2.0
2013–14	613,681	362,670	88,753	103,448	28,544	6,656	13,726	9,884	100.0	60.1	14.7	17.1	4.7	1.1	2.3
2014–15	617,559	354,235	90,527	111,307	29,390	6,406	15,508	10,186	100.0	58.3	14.9	18.3	4.8	1.1	2.6
2015–16	616,144	340,480	89,235	121,513	30,327	6,155	17,682	10,752	100.0	56.2	14.7	20.1	5.0	1.0	2.9
2016–17	611,540	327,420	86,710	130,689	31,355	5,895	17,925	11,546	100.0	54.6	14.5	21.8	5.2	1.0	3.0
2017–18	612,887	316,884	83,697	140,594	33,216	5,919	20,013	12,564	100.0	52.8	13.9	23.4	5.5	1.0	3.3

—Not available.
[1]For years prior to 2010–11, the survey did not yet include the "Two or more races" category, and each student could be counted in only one race category.
[2]Excludes 1,170 males and 251 females whose racial/ethnic group was not available.
[3]Excludes 4,819 males and 1,384 females whose racial/ethnic group was not available.
NOTE: Data are for postsecondary institutions participating in Title IV federal financial aid programs. Race categories exclude persons of Hispanic ethnicity. For 1989–90 and later years, reported racial/ethnic distributions of students by level of degree, field of degree, and sex were used to estimate race/ethnicity for students whose race/ethnicity was not reported. Detail may not sum to totals because of rounding. Some data have been revised from previously published figures.
SOURCE: U.S. Department of Education, National Center for Education Statistics, Higher Education General Information Survey (HEGIS), "Degrees and Other Formal Awards Conferred" surveys, 1976–77 and 1980–81; Integrated Postsecondary Education Data System (IPEDS), "Completions Survey" (IPEDS-C:90–99); and IPEDS Fall 2000 through Fall 2018, Completions component. (This table was prepared October 2019.)

Table 321.30. Associate's degrees conferred by postsecondary institutions, by race/ethnicity and field of study: 2016–17 and 2017–18

Field of study	2016–17										2017–18									
					Asian/Pacific Islander										Asian/Pacific Islander					
	Total	White	Black	Hispanic	Total	Asian	Pacific Islander	American Indian/ Alaska Native	Two or more races	Non-resident alien	Total	White	Black	Hispanic	Total	Asian	Pacific Islander	American Indian/ Alaska Native	Two or more races	Non-resident alien
1	2	3	4	5	6	7	8	9	10	11	12	13	14	15	16	17	18	19	20	21
All fields, total	**1,005,687**	**551,057**	**129,880**	**209,159**	**55,814**	**52,633**	**3,181**	**9,265**	**29,603**	**20,909**	**1,011,487**	**536,256**	**125,517**	**225,462**	**58,952**	**55,840**	**3,112**	**9,285**	**32,971**	**23,044**
Agriculture and natural resources	8,208	7,189	127	524	65	56	9	107	153	43	8,076	6,988	126	578	73	61	12	108	158	45
Architecture and related services	503	195	26	211	31	31	0	1	17	22	539	204	24	222	56	55	1	6	9	18
Area, ethnic, cultural, gender, and group studies	420	115	47	118	30	19	11	66	37	7	559	122	67	177	38	28	10	81	67	7
Biological and biomedical sciences	5,550	2,213	473	1,783	682	670	12	66	194	139	6,390	2,401	501	2,173	842	811	31	80	225	168
Business	122,252	61,949	18,952	23,190	8,966	8,539	427	1,205	3,430	4,560	117,782	58,058	17,186	23,443	9,190	8,805	385	1,243	3,618	5,044
Communication, journalism, and related programs	7,379	3,036	857	2,433	541	519	22	39	276	197	7,785	3,073	764	2,781	573	546	27	27	365	202
Communications technologies	4,307	2,385	662	780	169	161	8	31	154	126	4,197	2,207	627	884	177	170	7	31	162	109
Computer and information sciences	31,171	18,464	4,038	4,279	2,390	2,281	109	269	947	784	31,479	18,014	3,971	4,521	2,640	2,542	98	277	981	1,075
Construction trades	5,308	3,660	519	507	275	230	45	125	198	24	5,277	3,889	367	530	197	175	22	99	171	24
Education	16,603	9,254	2,444	3,582	400	359	41	365	397	161	16,182	8,677	2,298	3,885	396	366	30	335	408	183
Engineering	5,915	3,162	407	1,204	589	582	7	48	152	353	6,408	3,323	476	1,304	651	635	16	35	191	428
Engineering technologies and engineering-related fields[1]	27,021	18,689	2,688	3,296	1,001	920	81	257	645	445	26,745	18,479	2,422	3,448	1,097	1,031	66	254	660	385
English language and literature/letters	2,870	1,154	200	1,110	219	214	5	12	124	51	3,133	1,197	190	1,345	208	201	7	15	137	41
Family and consumer sciences/human sciences	8,871	3,767	1,499	2,791	411	392	19	93	187	123	8,854	3,606	1,351	3,035	431	410	21	99	193	139
Foreign languages, literatures, and linguistics	2,363	1,026	106	991	92	88	4	10	84	54	2,607	1,079	106	1,164	108	105	3	14	100	36
Health professions and related programs	186,312	115,554	27,392	26,827	9,130	8,536	594	1,760	4,487	1,162	181,056	109,919	26,293	27,809	9,265	8,649	616	1,641	4,905	1,224
Homeland security, law enforcement, and firefighting	37,362	18,629	5,476	10,837	1,060	924	136	314	881	165	35,276	16,992	4,725	10,991	1,039	932	107	355	957	217
Legal professions and studies	6,904	4,023	1,072	1,350	160	141	19	64	175	60	6,237	3,376	958	1,290	275	257	18	47	182	109
Liberal arts and sciences, general studies, and humanities	386,746	208,757	49,492	85,562	18,684	17,555	1,129	3,145	12,277	8,829	397,926	208,180	49,958	93,087	19,665	18,510	1,155	3,228	14,064	9,744
Library science	158	109	10	25	7	7	0	2	5	0	156	107	7	25	10	10	0	5	2	0
Mathematics and statistics	3,454	1,221	108	1,149	629	615	14	15	121	211	4,135	1,312	119	1,456	798	788	10	23	167	260
Mechanic and repair technologies/technicians	20,821	13,817	1,828	3,469	700	608	92	268	522	217	21,295	13,856	1,659	3,878	787	692	95	278	623	214
Military technologies and applied sciences	1,093	702	144	141	50	43	7	11	45	0	1,226	756	166	211	58	52	6	9	26	0
Multi/interdisciplinary studies	30,780	13,961	2,416	8,875	3,643	3,567	76	153	1,096	636	31,068	12,859	2,206	9,947	3,973	3,884	89	173	1,239	671
Parks, recreation, leisure, and fitness studies	5,037	2,242	489	1,606	394	366	28	38	188	80	5,095	1,928	489	1,852	462	438	24	53	214	97
Philosophy and religious studies	1,002	719	78	123	31	29	2	4	23	24	1,049	720	59	176	31	28	3	2	23	38
Physical sciences and science technologies	9,223	4,226	942	2,136	1,036	1,011	25	73	312	498	10,116	4,314	1,014	2,613	1,208	1,185	23	84	371	512
Precision production	5,251	3,970	256	663	140	125	15	81	129	12	5,333	4,013	238	674	169	164	5	73	149	17
Psychology	11,283	3,758	864	5,085	891	844	47	117	445	123	12,489	3,928	924	5,938	937	908	29	106	494	162
Public administration and social services	7,591	3,420	2,206	1,475	121	99	22	140	191	38	7,136	2,991	2,238	1,410	133	111	22	139	193	32
Social sciences and history	21,392	7,467	1,715	8,635	1,973	1,870	103	209	913	480	23,683	7,902	1,868	9,914	2,120	1,996	124	221	1,033	625
Social sciences	19,636	6,586	1,661	7,983	1,894	1,795	99	199	841	472	21,545	6,923	1,807	9,050	2,017	1,897	120	198	937	613
History	1,756	881	54	652	79	75	4	10	72	8	2,138	979	61	864	103	99	4	23	96	12
Theology and religious vocations	1,546	1,071	288	98	29	27	2	16	29	15	1,435	976	271	96	20	15	5	8	34	30
Transportation and materials moving	1,547	948	116	230	107	91	16	10	51	85	1,610	1,014	110	236	86	78	8	14	49	101
Visual and performing arts	19,444	10,205	1,943	4,074	1,168	1,114	54	151	718	1,185	19,153	9,796	1,739	4,369	1,239	1,202	37	122	801	1,087
Other and not classified	0	0	0	0	0	0	0	0	0	0	0	0	0	0	0	0	0	0	0	0

[1]Excludes "Construction trades" and "Mechanic and repair technologies/technicians," which are listed separately.

NOTE: Data are for postsecondary institutions participating in Title IV federal financial aid programs. Race categories exclude persons of Hispanic ethnicity. Reported racial/ethnic distributions of students by level of degree, field of degree, and sex were used to estimate race/ethnicity for students whose race/ethnicity was not reported. To facilitate trend comparisons, certain aggregations have been made of the degree fields as reported in the Integrated Postsecondary Education Data System (IPEDS): "Agriculture and natural resources" includes Agriculture, agriculture operations, and related sciences and Natural resources and conservation; and "Business" includes Business management, marketing, and related support services and Personal and culinary services. Some data have been revised from previously published figures.

SOURCE: U.S. Department of Education, National Center for Education Statistics, Integrated Postsecondary Education Data System (IPEDS), Fall 2017 and Fall 2018, Completions component. (This table was prepared October 2019.)

Table 322.10. Bachelor's degrees conferred by postsecondary institutions, by field of study: Selected years, 1970–71 through 2017–18

Field of study	1970–71	1975–76	1980–81	1985–86	1990–91	1995–96	2000–01	2005–06	2007–08	2009–10	2010–11	2011–12	2012–13	2013–14	2014–15	2015–16	2016–17	2017–18
1	2	3	4	5	6	7	8	9	10	11	12	13	14	15	16	17	18	19
Total	**839,730**	**925,746**	**935,140**	**987,823**	**1,094,538**	**1,164,792**	**1,244,171**	**1,485,104**	**1,563,734**	**1,649,919**	**1,716,053**	**1,792,163**	**1,840,381**	**1,870,150**	**1,894,969**	**1,920,750**	**1,956,114**	**1,980,644**
Agriculture and natural resources	12,672	19,402	21,886	16,823	13,124	21,425	23,370	23,052	24,125	26,343	28,630	30,972	33,592	35,125	36,278	36,995	37,734	39,314
Architecture and related services	5,570	9,146	9,455	9,119	9,781	8,352	8,480	9,515	9,809	10,051	9,831	9,727	9,757	9,149	9,090	8,825	8,579	8,464
Area, ethnic, cultural, gender, and group studies	2,579	3,577	2,887	3,021	4,776	5,633	6,160	7,878	8,453	8,620	8,955	9,228	8,850	8,275	7,783	7,840	7,720	7,717
Biological and biomedical sciences	35,705	54,154	43,078	38,395	39,482	61,014	60,576	70,602	79,869	86,391	89,984	95,850	100,397	104,657	109,904	113,794	116,768	118,663
Business	115,396	143,171	200,521	236,700	249,165	226,623	263,515	318,043	335,495	358,119	365,133	367,235	360,887	358,132	363,741	371,690	381,109	386,201
Communication, journalism, and related programs	10,324	20,045	29,428	41,666	51,650	47,320	58,013	73,658	76,400	81,280	83,231	83,771	84,818	87,612	90,658	92,551	93,794	92,290
Communications technologies	478	1,237	1,854	1,479	1,397	853	1,178	2,987	4,654	4,782	4,858	4,983	4,987	4,991	5,135	4,824	4,615	4,231
Computer and information sciences	2,388	5,652	15,121	42,337	25,159	24,506	44,142	47,702	38,523	39,593	43,066	47,406	50,961	55,271	59,586	64,402	71,416	79,598
Education	176,307	154,437	108,074	87,147	110,807	105,384	105,458	107,235	102,849	101,287	104,008	105,656	104,698	98,838	91,596	87,221	85,130	82,621
Engineering	45,034	38,733	63,642	77,391	62,448	62,168	58,209	66,841	68,404	72,657	76,356	81,371	85,987	92,169	97,852	106,789	115,671	121,956
Engineering technologies	5,148	7,943	11,713	19,731	17,303	15,829	14,660	14,565	15,278	16,078	16,741	17,283	17,010	16,807	17,253	17,159	18,119	18,727
English language and literature/letters	63,914	41,452	31,922	34,083	51,064	49,928	50,569	55,094	55,001	53,229	52,754	53,765	52,401	50,464	45,851	42,797	41,314	40,002
Family and consumer sciences/human sciences	11,167	17,409	18,370	13,847	13,920	14,353	16,421	20,775	21,880	21,832	22,438	23,441	23,930	24,689	24,584	25,389	25,080	24,349
Foreign languages, literatures, and linguistics	20,988	17,068	11,638	11,550	13,937	14,832	16,128	19,393	20,976	21,507	21,705	21,756	21,647	20,332	19,493	18,436	17,643	16,958
Health professions and related programs	25,223	53,885	63,665	65,309	59,875	86,087	75,933	91,973	111,548	129,623	143,463	163,675	181,149	198,777	216,228	228,907	237,979	244,909
Homeland security, law enforcement, and firefighting	2,045	12,507	13,707	12,704	16,806	24,810	25,211	35,319	40,297	43,613	47,600	54,091	60,264	62,416	62,723	61,159	59,553	58,114
Legal professions and studies	545	531	776	1,223	1,827	2,123	1,991	3,302	3,771	3,886	4,429	4,595	4,425	4,513	4,420	4,243	4,272	4,239
Liberal arts and sciences, general studies, and humanities	7,481	18,855	21,643	21,336	30,526	33,997	37,962	44,898	46,882	46,963	46,717	46,961	46,790	45,281	43,649	43,669	44,103	44,262
Library science	1,013	843	375	155	90	58	52	76	68	85	96	95	102	127	99	85	99	81
Mathematics and statistics	24,801	15,984	11,078	16,122	14,393	12,713	11,171	14,760	15,169	16,029	17,182	18,841	20,449	20,987	21,854	22,778	24,075	25,256
Military technologies and applied sciences	357	952	42	255	183	7	21	33	39	56	64	86	105	185	276	358	469	655
Multi/interdisciplinary studies	6,324	13,709	12,986	13,754	17,774	26,885	26,478	30,583	34,172	37,717	42,473	45,717	47,658	48,392	47,556	48,833	49,631	51,909
Parks, recreation, leisure, and fitness studies	1,621	5,182	5,729	4,623	4,315	12,974	17,948	25,489	29,908	33,332	35,934	38,998	42,628	46,047	49,008	50,912	53,292	53,883
Philosophy and religious studies	8,149	8,447	6,776	6,396	7,423	7,541	8,717	11,980	12,259	12,503	12,830	12,645	12,792	11,999	11,071	10,155	9,711	9,603
Physical sciences and science technologies	21,410	21,458	23,936	21,711	16,334	19,716	18,025	20,521	22,164	23,381	24,705	26,664	28,053	29,307	30,042	30,483	31,272	31,542
Precision production	0	0	0	2	2	12	31	55	33	29	43	37	36	37	48	51	32	45
Psychology	38,187	50,278	41,068	40,628	58,655	73,416	73,645	88,132	92,562	97,215	100,906	109,099	114,446	117,312	117,573	117,447	116,859	116,432
Public administration and social services	5,466	15,440	16,707	11,887	14,350	19,849	19,447	21,986	23,523	25,421	26,799	29,695	31,950	33,483	34,364	34,433	35,461	35,629
Social sciences and history	155,324	126,396	100,513	93,840	125,107	126,479	128,036	161,468	167,321	172,782	177,169	178,534	177,767	173,132	166,971	161,211	159,097	159,967
Theology and religious vocations	3,720	5,490	5,808	5,510	4,799	5,292	6,945	8,548	8,992	8,719	9,073	9,304	9,385	9,642	9,713	9,804	9,518	9,521
Transportation and materials moving	0	225	263	1,838	2,622	3,561	3,748	5,349	5,202	4,998	4,941	4,876	4,661	4,588	4,730	4,531	4,708	4,924
Visual and performing arts	30,394	42,138	40,479	37,241	42,186	49,296	61,148	83,292	87,731	91,798	93,939	95,806	97,799	97,414	95,840	92,979	91,291	88,582
Not classified by field of study	0	0	0	0	13,258	1,756	783	0	377	0	0	0	0	0	0	0	0	0

NOTE: Data are for postsecondary institutions participating in Title IV federal financial aid programs. The new Classification of Instructional Programs was initiated in 2009–10. The figures for earlier years have been reclassified when necessary to make them conform to the new taxonomy. To facilitate trend comparisons, certain aggregations have been made of the degree fields as reported in the Integrated Postsecondary Education Data System (IPEDS): "Agriculture and natural resources" includes Agriculture, agriculture operations, and related sciences and Natural resources and conservation; "Business" includes Business, management, marketing, and related support services and Personal and culinary services; and "Engineering technologies" includes Engineering technologies and engineering-related fields, Construction trades, and Mechanic and repair technologies/technicians. Some data have been revised from previously published figures.

SOURCE: U.S. Department of Education, National Center for Education Statistics, Higher Education General Information Survey (HEGIS), "Degrees and Other Formal Awards Conferred" surveys, 1970–71 through 1985–86; Integrated Postsecondary Education Data System (IPEDS), "Completions Survey" (IPEDS-C:91–99); and IPEDS Fall 2000 through Fall 2018, Completions component. (This table was prepared November 2019.)

Table 322.20. Bachelor's degrees conferred by postsecondary institutions, by race/ethnicity and sex of student: Selected years, 1976–77 through 2017–18

Year and sex	Number of degrees conferred to U.S. citizens, permanent residents, and nonresident aliens								Percentage distribution of degrees conferred to U.S. citizens and permanent residents						
	Total	White	Black	Hispanic	Asian/ Pacific Islander	American Indian/ Alaska Native	Two or more races[1]	Non-resident alien	Total	White	Black	Hispanic	Asian/ Pacific Islander	American Indian/ Alaska Native	Two or more races[1]
1	2	3	4	5	6	7	8	9	10	11	12	13	14	15	16
Total															
1976–77[2]	917,900	807,688	58,636	18,743	13,793	3,326	—	15,714	100.0	89.5	6.5	2.1	1.5	0.4	—
1980–81[3]	934,800	807,319	60,673	21,832	18,794	3,593	—	22,589	100.0	88.5	6.7	2.4	2.1	0.4	—
1990–91	1,094,538	914,093	66,375	37,342	42,529	4,583	—	29,616	100.0	85.8	6.2	3.5	4.0	0.4	—
1999–2000	1,237,875	929,102	108,018	75,063	77,909	8,717	—	39,066	100.0	77.5	9.0	6.3	6.5	0.7	—
2000–01	1,244,171	927,357	111,307	77,745	78,902	9,049	—	39,811	100.0	77.0	9.2	6.5	6.6	0.8	—
2003–04	1,399,542	1,026,114	131,241	94,644	92,073	10,638	—	44,832	100.0	75.7	9.7	7.0	6.8	0.8	—
2004–05	1,439,264	1,049,141	136,122	101,124	97,209	10,307	—	45,361	100.0	75.3	9.8	7.3	7.0	0.7	—
2005–06	1,485,104	1,075,471	142,405	107,575	102,371	10,938	—	46,344	100.0	74.7	9.9	7.5	7.1	0.8	—
2006–07	1,524,729	1,100,308	146,767	114,962	105,287	11,463	—	45,942	100.0	74.4	9.9	7.8	7.1	0.8	—
2007–08	1,563,734	1,123,246	152,627	122,770	109,177	11,509	—	44,405	100.0	73.9	10.0	8.1	7.2	0.8	—
2008–09	1,601,399	1,144,628	156,603	129,473	112,581	12,221	—	45,893	100.0	73.6	10.1	8.3	7.2	0.8	—
2009–10	1,649,919	1,167,322	164,789	140,426	117,391	12,405	—	47,586	100.0	72.9	10.3	8.8	7.3	0.8	—
2010–11	1,716,053	1,182,690	172,731	154,450	121,118	11,935	20,589	52,540	100.0	71.1	10.4	9.3	7.3	0.7	1.2
2011–12	1,792,163	1,212,417	185,916	169,736	126,177	11,498	27,234	59,185	100.0	70.0	10.7	9.8	7.3	0.7	1.6
2012–13	1,840,381	1,221,908	191,233	186,677	130,129	11,432	34,128	64,874	100.0	68.8	10.8	10.5	7.3	0.6	1.9
2013–14	1,870,150	1,218,998	191,437	202,425	131,662	10,784	45,422	69,422	100.0	67.7	10.6	11.2	7.3	0.6	2.5
2014–15	1,894,969	1,210,071	192,829	218,098	133,916	10,202	54,215	75,638	100.0	66.5	10.6	12.0	7.4	0.6	3.0
2015–16	1,920,750	1,197,323	194,408	235,190	138,257	9,735	61,584	84,253	100.0	65.2	10.6	12.8	7.5	0.5	3.4
2016–17	1,956,114	1,195,977	196,338	252,203	144,093	9,589	66,532	91,382	100.0	64.1	10.5	13.5	7.7	0.5	3.6
2017–18	1,980,644	1,189,619	195,014	267,065	150,999	9,157	70,553	98,237	100.0	63.2	10.4	14.2	8.0	0.5	3.7
Males															
1976–77[2]	494,424	438,161	25,147	10,318	7,638	1,804	—	11,356	100.0	90.7	5.2	2.1	1.6	0.4	—
1980–81[3]	469,625	406,173	24,511	10,810	10,107	1,700	—	16,324	100.0	89.6	5.4	2.4	2.2	0.4	—
1990–91	504,045	421,290	24,800	16,598	21,203	1,938	—	18,216	100.0	86.7	5.1	3.4	4.4	0.4	—
1999–2000	530,367	402,954	37,029	30,304	35,853	3,463	—	20,764	100.0	79.1	7.3	5.9	7.0	0.7	—
2000–01	531,840	401,780	38,103	31,368	35,865	3,700	—	21,024	100.0	78.7	7.5	6.1	7.0	0.7	—
2003–04	595,425	445,483	43,851	37,288	41,360	4,244	—	23,199	100.0	77.9	7.7	6.5	7.2	0.7	—
2004–05	613,000	456,592	45,810	39,490	43,711	4,143	—	23,254	100.0	77.4	7.8	6.7	7.4	0.7	—
2005–06	630,502	467,397	48,073	41,805	45,803	4,202	—	23,222	100.0	77.0	7.9	6.9	7.5	0.7	—
2006–07	649,816	480,747	49,715	44,761	47,577	4,508	—	22,508	100.0	76.6	7.9	7.1	7.6	0.7	—
2007–08	668,184	492,360	52,298	47,797	49,535	4,523	—	21,671	100.0	76.2	8.1	7.4	7.7	0.7	—
2008–09	685,422	503,396	53,465	50,596	50,773	4,849	—	22,343	100.0	75.9	8.1	7.6	7.7	0.7	—
2009–10	706,660	513,711	56,136	55,139	53,365	4,879	—	23,430	100.0	75.2	8.2	8.1	7.8	0.7	—
2010–11	734,159	519,992	59,015	60,869	55,321	4,798	8,028	26,136	100.0	73.4	8.3	8.6	7.8	0.7	1.1
2011–12	765,772	532,463	63,736	67,083	57,521	4,476	10,945	29,548	100.0	72.3	8.7	9.1	7.8	0.6	1.5
2012–13	787,408	535,358	67,351	74,067	59,806	4,611	13,834	32,381	100.0	70.9	8.9	9.8	7.9	0.6	1.8
2013–14	801,905	536,009	68,290	80,312	59,844	4,171	18,137	35,142	100.0	69.9	8.9	10.5	7.8	0.5	2.4
2014–15	812,693	530,418	69,316	86,881	61,080	4,061	22,245	38,692	100.0	68.5	9.0	11.2	7.9	0.5	2.9
2015–16	821,746	522,834	69,847	92,989	63,182	3,822	25,157	43,915	100.0	67.2	9.0	12.0	8.1	0.5	3.2
2016–17	836,021	521,359	70,568	99,344	65,405	3,731	27,089	48,525	100.0	66.2	9.0	12.6	8.3	0.5	3.4
2017–18	844,960	516,621	70,316	104,926	68,196	3,506	28,868	52,527	100.0	65.2	8.9	13.2	8.6	0.4	3.6
Females															
1976–77[2]	423,476	369,527	33,489	8,425	6,155	1,522	—	4,358	100.0	88.2	8.0	2.0	1.5	0.4	—
1980–81[3]	465,175	401,146	36,162	11,022	8,687	1,893	—	6,265	100.0	87.4	7.9	2.4	1.9	0.4	—
1990–91	590,493	492,803	41,575	20,744	21,326	2,645	—	11,400	100.0	85.1	7.2	3.6	3.7	0.5	—
1999–2000	707,508	526,148	70,989	44,759	42,056	5,254	—	18,302	100.0	76.3	10.3	6.5	6.1	0.8	—
2000–01	712,331	525,577	73,204	46,377	43,037	5,349	—	18,787	100.0	75.8	10.6	6.7	6.2	0.8	—
2003–04	804,117	580,631	87,390	57,356	50,713	6,394	—	21,633	100.0	74.2	11.2	7.3	6.5	0.8	—
2004–05	826,264	592,549	90,312	61,634	53,498	6,164	—	22,107	100.0	73.7	11.2	7.7	6.7	0.8	—
2005–06	854,602	608,074	94,332	65,770	56,568	6,736	—	23,122	100.0	73.1	11.3	7.9	6.8	0.8	—
2006–07	874,913	619,561	97,052	70,201	57,710	6,955	—	23,434	100.0	72.8	11.4	8.2	6.8	0.8	—
2007–08	895,550	630,886	100,329	74,973	59,642	6,986	—	22,734	100.0	72.3	11.5	8.6	6.8	0.8	—
2008–09	915,977	641,232	103,138	78,877	61,808	7,372	—	23,550	100.0	71.9	11.6	8.8	6.9	0.8	—
2009–10	943,259	653,611	108,653	85,287	64,026	7,526	—	24,156	100.0	71.1	11.8	9.3	7.0	0.8	—
2010–11	981,894	662,698	113,716	93,581	65,797	7,137	12,561	26,404	100.0	69.4	11.9	9.8	6.9	0.7	1.3
2011–12	1,026,391	679,954	122,180	102,653	68,656	7,022	16,289	29,637	100.0	68.2	12.3	10.3	6.9	0.7	1.6
2012–13	1,052,973	686,550	123,882	112,610	70,323	6,821	20,294	32,493	100.0	67.3	12.1	11.0	6.9	0.7	2.0
2013–14	1,068,245	682,989	123,147	122,113	71,818	6,613	27,285	34,280	100.0	66.1	11.9	11.8	6.9	0.6	2.6
2014–15	1,082,276	679,653	123,513	131,217	72,836	6,141	31,970	36,946	100.0	65.0	11.8	12.6	7.0	0.6	3.1
2015–16	1,099,004	674,489	124,561	142,201	75,075	5,913	36,427	40,338	100.0	63.7	11.8	13.4	7.1	0.6	3.4
2016–17	1,120,093	674,618	125,770	152,859	78,688	5,858	39,443	42,857	100.0	62.6	11.7	14.2	7.3	0.5	3.7
2017–18	1,135,684	672,998	124,698	162,139	82,803	5,651	41,685	45,710	100.0	61.7	11.4	14.9	7.6	0.5	3.8

—Not available.
[1]For years prior to 2010–11, the survey did not yet include the "Two or more races" category, and each student could be counted in only one race category.
[2]Excludes 1,121 males and 528 females whose racial/ethnic group was not available.
[3]Excludes 258 males and 82 females whose racial/ethnic group was not available.
NOTE: Data are for postsecondary institutions participating in Title IV federal financial aid programs. Race categories exclude persons of Hispanic ethnicity. For 1989–90 and later years, reported racial/ethnic distributions of students by level of degree, field of degree, and sex were used to estimate race/ethnicity for students whose race/ethnicity was not reported. Detail may not sum to totals because of rounding. Some data have been revised from previously published figures.
SOURCE: U.S. Department of Education, National Center for Education Statistics, Higher Education General Information Survey (HEGIS), "Degrees and Other Formal Awards Conferred" surveys, 1976–77 and 1980–81; Integrated Postsecondary Education Data System (IPEDS), "Completions Survey" (IPEDS-C:90–99); and IPEDS Fall 2000 through Fall 2018, Completions component. (This table was prepared October 2019.)

Table 322.30. Bachelor's degrees conferred by postsecondary institutions, by race/ethnicity and field of study: 2016–17 and 2017–18

Field of study	2016–17 Total	2016–17 White	2016–17 Black	2016–17 Hispanic	2016–17 Asian/Pacific Islander Total	2016–17 Asian/Pacific Islander Asian	2016–17 Asian/Pacific Islander Pacific Islander	2016–17 American Indian/ Alaska Native	2016–17 Two or more races	2016–17 Non-resident alien	2017–18 Total	2017–18 White	2017–18 Black	2017–18 Hispanic	2017–18 Asian/Pacific Islander Total	2017–18 Asian/Pacific Islander Asian	2017–18 Asian/Pacific Islander Pacific Islander	2017–18 American Indian/ Alaska Native	2017–18 Two or more races	2017–18 Non-resident alien
1	2	3	4	5	6	7	8	9	10	11	12	13	14	15	16	17	18	19	20	21
All fields, total	**1,956,114**	**1,195,977**	**196,338**	**252,203**	**144,093**	**139,541**	**4,552**	**9,589**	**66,532**	**91,382**	**1,980,644**	**1,189,619**	**195,014**	**267,065**	**150,999**	**146,648**	**4,351**	**9,157**	**70,553**	**98,237**
Agriculture and natural resources	37,734	29,586	1,180	3,196	1,383	1,317	66	250	1,235	904	39,314	30,377	1,201	3,481	1,479	1,412	67	273	1,445	1,058
Architecture and related services	8,579	4,631	466	1,356	744	721	23	23	271	1,088	8,464	4,520	439	1,296	693	684	9	23	320	1,173
Area, ethnic, cultural, gender, and group studies	7,720	3,169	1,145	1,701	700	662	38	163	519	323	7,717	3,118	1,143	1,739	643	621	22	187	516	371
Biological and biomedical sciences	116,768	66,728	9,335	14,138	17,923	17,691	232	455	4,688	3,501	118,663	66,377	9,313	15,416	18,286	18,048	238	448	5,019	3,804
Business	381,109	228,592	38,206	45,607	28,037	27,090	947	1,792	10,579	28,296	386,201	229,344	37,425	48,804	28,579	27,724	855	1,748	11,573	28,728
Communication, journalism, and related programs	93,794	58,712	11,155	12,502	3,806	3,621	185	297	3,778	3,544	92,290	57,024	10,781	12,823	3,936	3,766	170	298	3,797	3,631
Communications technologies	4,615	2,586	626	647	278	259	19	24	200	254	4,231	2,352	575	573	295	283	12	22	171	243
Computer and information sciences	71,416	39,485	6,391	7,234	10,426	10,239	187	268	2,470	5,142	79,598	42,080	6,862	8,084	12,609	12,444	165	262	2,905	6,796
Construction trades	153	103	1	43	1	1	0	0	2	3	151	98	2	41	3	2	1	0	0	7
Education	85,130	64,694	6,289	8,280	2,273	2,135	138	552	2,143	899	82,621	61,794	6,130	8,642	2,350	2,221	129	501	2,210	994
Engineering	115,671	70,006	4,505	11,875	13,368	13,207	161	301	3,820	11,796	121,956	72,484	4,836	12,777	14,080	13,909	171	360	4,138	13,281
Engineering technologies and engineering-related fields[1]	17,667	11,766	1,522	1,709	778	749	29	119	440	1,333	18,228	11,959	1,536	1,833	836	795	41	118	485	1,461
English language and literature/letters	41,314	28,421	3,260	5,353	1,803	1,740	63	185	1,718	574	40,002	27,105	3,210	5,538	1,718	1,659	59	156	1,720	555
Family and consumer sciences/human sciences	25,080	15,306	3,221	3,620	1,388	1,338	50	133	891	521	24,349	14,536	3,088	3,676	1,472	1,414	58	116	901	560
Foreign languages, literatures, and linguistics	17,643	10,274	859	4,074	1,071	1,051	20	48	781	536	16,958	9,788	813	3,849	1,063	1,043	20	40	772	633
Health professions and related programs	237,979	155,642	27,359	26,378	18,289	17,532	757	1,199	6,457	2,655	244,909	158,507	27,908	28,279	19,136	18,346	790	1,162	7,095	2,822
Homeland security, law enforcement, and firefighting	59,553	31,286	11,539	12,161	1,696	1,465	231	440	1,828	603	58,114	30,316	11,036	12,122	1,719	1,504	215	370	1,845	706
Legal professions and studies	4,272	2,387	659	779	201	194	7	39	155	52	4,239	2,341	669	746	220	209	11	30	169	64
Liberal arts and sciences, general studies, and humanities	44,103	26,946	6,684	6,131	1,605	1,463	142	360	1,550	827	44,262	25,942	6,943	6,622	1,665	1,549	116	365	1,750	975
Library science	99	80	7	4	1	0	1	2	5	0	81	65	5	8	0	0	0	0	3	0
Mathematics and statistics	24,075	13,190	1,022	2,321	2,620	2,598	22	59	772	4,091	25,256	13,294	1,059	2,506	3,116	3,075	41	63	816	4,402
Mechanic and repair technologies/technicians	299	213	25	25	11	11	0	4	9	12	348	262	18	23	10	10	0	8	14	13
Military technologies and applied sciences	469	351	39	40	14	12	2	4	14	7	655	486	44	59	17	16	1	5	32	12
Multi/interdisciplinary studies	49,631	28,160	6,391	7,944	3,404	3,281	123	269	1,990	1,473	51,909	28,627	6,570	8,744	3,777	3,663	114	267	2,141	1,783
Parks, recreation, leisure, and fitness studies	53,292	34,485	6,219	6,582	2,557	2,434	123	323	2,072	1,054	53,883	33,899	6,524	7,171	2,845	2,720	125	253	2,122	1,069
Philosophy and religious studies	9,711	6,454	791	1,124	571	554	17	40	421	310	9,603	6,278	729	1,227	590	570	20	40	420	319
Physical sciences and science technologies	31,272	20,449	1,653	3,119	2,934	2,901	33	126	1,200	1,791	31,542	20,007	1,688	3,419	3,004	2,947	57	143	1,322	1,959
Precision production	32	24	1	2	4	3	1	0	0	1	45	30	0	2	4	4	0	0	3	6
Psychology	116,859	65,183	14,809	20,787	7,814	7,520	294	633	4,585	3,048	116,432	63,253	14,382	22,435	7,782	7,547	235	563	4,757	3,260
Public administration and social services	35,461	19,015	7,662	5,824	1,106	1,003	103	287	1,140	427	35,629	18,783	7,516	6,185	1,243	1,129	114	282	1,174	446
Social sciences and history	159,097	90,382	15,206	25,064	11,177	10,861	316	728	6,372	10,168	159,967	89,641	14,880	26,056	11,566	11,240	326	616	6,471	10,737
Social sciences	135,043	72,594	13,902	22,119	10,420	10,139	281	591	5,537	9,880	136,585	72,584	13,630	22,958	10,829	10,535	294	513	5,665	10,406
History	24,054	17,788	1,304	2,945	757	722	35	137	835	288	23,382	17,057	1,250	3,098	737	705	32	103	806	331
Theology and religious vocations	9,518	7,488	806	561	240	223	17	45	161	217	9,521	7,511	713	574	263	245	18	32	216	212
Transportation and materials moving	4,708	3,304	280	355	205	187	18	25	201	338	4,924	3,355	294	441	253	237	16	32	147	402
Visual and performing arts	91,291	56,879	7,025	11,667	5,665	5,478	187	396	4,065	5,594	88,582	54,066	6,682	11,874	5,747	5,612	135	374	4,084	5,755
Other and not classified	0	0	0	0	0	0	0	0	0	0	0	0	0	0	0	0	0	0	0	0

[1]Excludes "Construction trades" and "Mechanic and repair technologies/technicians," which are listed separately.

NOTE: *Data are for postsecondary institutions participating in Title IV federal financial aid programs. Race categories exclude persons of Hispanic ethnicity.* Reported racial/ethnic distributions of students by level of degree, field of degree, and sex were used to estimate race/ethnicity for students whose race/ethnicity was not reported. To facilitate trend comparisons, certain aggregations have been made of the degree fields as reported in the Integrated Postsecondary Education Data System (IPEDS): "Agriculture and natural resources" includes Agriculture, agriculture operations, and related sciences and Natural *resources and conservation; and "Business" includes Business management, marketing, and related support services and* Personal and culinary services. Some data have been revised from previously published figures.

SOURCE: U.S. Department of Education, National Center for Education Statistics, Integrated Postsecondary Education Data System (IPEDS), Fall 2017 and Fall 2018, Completions component. (This table was prepared October 2019.)

Table 322.40. Bachelor's degrees conferred to males by postsecondary institutions, by race/ethnicity and field of study: 2017-18 and 2018-19

Field of study	2017-18										2018-19							
	Total	White	Black	Hispanic	Asian/Pacific Islander: Total	Asian/Pacific Islander: Asian	Asian/Pacific Islander: Pacific Islander	American Indian/ Alaska Native	Two or more races	Non-resident alien	Total	White	Black	Hispanic	Asian/Pacific Islander: Total	Asian/Pacific Islander: Asian	Asian/Pacific Islander: Pacific Islander	American Indian/ Alaska Native
1	2	3	4	5	6	7	8	9	10	11	12	13	14	15	16	17	18	19
All fields, total	**844,979**	**516,614**	**70,327**	**104,919**	**68,196**	**66,283**	**1,913**	**3,505**	**28,900**	**52,518**	**857,545**	**516,342**	**70,811**	**111,468**	**70,925**	**68,988**	**1,937**	**3,419**
Agriculture and natural resources[1]	18,204	14,646	514	1,364	538	509	29	124	542	476	18,208	14,517	487	1,500	513	491	22	117
Architecture and related services	4,474	2,474	251	744	296	290	6	12	146	551	4,569	2,377	275	793	354	347	7	17
Area, ethnic, cultural, gender, and group studies	2,118	849	304	411	204	201	3	73	131	146	2,060	772	333	419	224	215	9	49
Biological and biomedical sciences	44,851	25,635	2,709	5,789	7,221	7,141	80	176	1,869	1,452	44,624	25,096	2,781	6,016	7,251	7,157	94	165
Business[2]	204,865	128,556	16,535	23,868	13,853	13,410	443	759	5,982	15,312	208,098	129,570	16,379	25,460	14,212	13,724	488	768
Communication, journalism, and related programs	31,810	19,655	4,075	4,355	1,252	1,193	59	95	1,258	1,120	32,704	20,153	4,229	4,500	1,357	1,298	59	103
Communications technologies	2,376	1,331	354	340	139	132	7	10	76	126	2,544	1,409	435	353	120	109	11	8
Computer and information sciences	63,703	35,285	5,054	6,584	9,403	9,265	138	197	2,246	4,934	70,319	37,749	5,693	7,523	10,848	10,692	156	204
Construction trades	130	92	2	28	3	2	1	0	0	5	184	115	8	40	3	2	1	0
Education	15,166	11,086	1,469	1,404	449	416	33	100	445	213	15,069	11,053	1,338	1,463	455	427	28	94
Engineering	94,845	57,399	3,560	9,784	10,230	10,092	138	272	3,015	10,585	97,849	58,059	3,700	10,917	10,795	10,666	129	237
Engineering technologies and engineering-related fields[3]	15,862	10,535	1,278	1,549	686	651	35	97	422	1,295	16,561	10,948	1,294	1,721	759	729	30	71
English language and literature/letters	11,680	7,948	894	1,630	499	481	18	50	471	188	11,273	7,649	856	1,627	460	443	17	52
Family and consumer sciences/human sciences	2,948	1,596	440	405	253	242	11	13	123	118	2,833	1,457	408	454	228	217	11	17
Foreign languages, literatures, and linguistics	5,287	3,227	206	1,072	345	336	9	12	235	190	5,119	3,074	209	1,021	321	314	7	21
Health professions and related programs	38,018	22,436	4,119	4,835	4,338	4,155	183	189	1,266	835	39,433	23,145	4,173	5,391	4,393	4,210	183	203
Homeland security, law enforcement, and firefighting	30,482	17,821	4,567	5,592	1,013	896	117	187	870	432	29,148	16,570	4,344	5,746	982	881	101	191
Legal professions and studies	1,341	780	180	214	82	78	4	6	55	24	1,315	732	200	225	65	61	4	8
Liberal arts and sciences, general studies, and humanities	15,966	9,695	2,669	1,898	607	552	55	125	579	393	15,905	9,699	2,515	1,992	592	553	39	115
Library science	7	5	0	1	0	0	0	0	1	0	12	11	0	1	0	0	0	0
Mathematics and statistics	14,539	7,800	552	1,442	1,858	1,831	27	31	470	2,386	15,037	7,929	524	1,544	1,897	1,884	13	27
Mechanic and repair technologies/technicians	333	250	18	22	9	9	0	7	14	13	292	203	19	38	11	11	0	4
Military technologies and applied sciences	533	398	31	51	16	15	1	3	27	7	608	440	56	66	11	9	2	3
Multi/interdisciplinary studies	17,605	10,063	2,203	2,484	1,337	1,291	46	101	690	727	18,653	10,344	2,101	2,794	1,624	1,564	60	101
Parks, recreation, leisure, and fitness studies	27,562	16,972	3,644	3,622	1,477	1,410	67	127	1,079	641	26,984	16,173	3,697	3,790	1,452	1,381	71	127
Philosophy and religious studies	5,935	3,973	422	753	336	323	13	27	248	176	5,799	3,798	394	761	338	311	27	28
Physical sciences and science technologies	18,938	12,557	736	2,065	1,571	1,543	28	74	757	1,178	18,498	11,886	755	2,191	1,532	1,500	32	80
Precision production	19	14	0	1	1	1	0	0	1	2	23	13	1	1	3	3	0	1
Psychology	24,579	13,156	2,870	4,669	1,963	1,896	67	138	1,009	774	24,313	12,651	2,888	4,728	2,043	1,976	67	125
Public administration and social services	6,127	3,316	1,139	1,011	278	256	22	37	235	111	6,094	3,213	1,189	1,063	268	244	24	38
Social sciences and history	79,623	48,266	5,923	11,128	5,537	5,363	174	257	2,893	5,619	78,596	47,030	5,802	11,402	5,452	5,307	145	258
Social sciences	65,753	37,905	5,299	9,328	5,124	4,968	156	192	2,476	5,429	64,765	36,804	5,179	9,545	5,091	4,962	129	193
History	13,870	10,361	624	1,800	413	395	18	65	417	190	13,831	10,226	623	1,857	361	345	16	65
Theology and religious vocations	6,601	5,469	357	324	156	140	16	23	117	155	6,464	5,372	346	317	152	139	13	23
Transportation and materials moving	4,282	2,960	247	369	221	207	14	27	128	330	4,435	3,055	270	449	185	170	15	19
Visual and performing arts	34,170	20,369	3,005	5,111	2,025	1,956	69	156	1,500	2,004	33,922	20,080	3,112	5,162	2,025	1,953	72	145
Other and not classified	0	0	0	0	0	0	0	0	0	0	0	0	0	0	0	0	0	0

[1] Includes Agriculture, agriculture operations, and related sciences; and Natural resources and conservation.

[2] Includes Business, management, marketing, and related support services; and Personal and culinary services.

[3] Excludes "Construction trades" and "Mechanic and repair technologies/technicians," which are listed separately.

NOTE: Data in this table represent the 50 states and the District of Columbia. Data are for postsecondary institutions participating in Title IV federal financial aid programs. Race categories exclude persons of Hispanic ethnicity. Reported racial/ethnic distributions of students by level of degree, field of study, and sex were used to estimate race/ethnicity for students whose race/ethnicity was not reported. To facilitate trend comparisons, certain aggregations have been made of the degree fields as reported in the Integrated Postsecondary Education Data System (IPEDS). Some data have been revised from previously published figures.

SOURCE: U.S. Department of Education, National Center for Education Statistics, Integrated Postsecondary Education Data System (IPEDS), Fall 2018 and Fall 2019, Completions component. (This table was prepared June 2020.)

Table 323.10. Master's degrees conferred by postsecondary institutions, by field of study: Selected years, 1970–71 through 2017–18

Field of study	1970–71	1975–76	1980–81	1985–86	1990–91	1995–96	2000–01	2005–06	2007–08	2009–10	2010–11	2011–12	2012–13	2013–14	2014–15	2015–16	2016–17	2017–18
1	2	3	4	5	6	7	8	9	10	11	12	13	14	15	16	17	18	19
Total	**235,564**	**317,477**	**302,637**	**295,850**	**342,863**	**412,180**	**473,502**	**599,862**	**630,844**	**693,313**	**730,922**	**755,967**	**751,718**	**754,582**	**758,804**	**785,757**	**804,542**	**820,102**
Agriculture and natural resources	2,457	3,340	4,003	3,801	3,295	4,551	4,272	4,653	4,682	5,215	5,766	6,390	6,336	6,544	6,426	6,702	6,843	6,967
Architecture and related services	1,705	3,215	3,153	3,260	3,490	3,993	4,302	5,743	6,059	7,280	7,788	8,448	8,095	8,048	8,006	7,991	7,883	7,317
Area, ethnic, cultural, gender, and group studies	1,032	993	802	915	1,233	1,652	1,555	2,080	1,778	1,775	1,913	1,947	1,897	1,844	1,847	1,767	1,717	1,673
Biological and biomedical sciences	5,625	6,457	5,766	5,064	4,834	6,593	7,017	8,783	9,691	10,730	11,324	12,419	13,300	13,964	14,655	15,717	16,282	17,180
Business	26,490	42,592	57,888	66,676	78,255	93,554	115,602	146,396	155,804	177,748	187,178	191,606	188,617	189,364	185,236	186,835	187,412	192,184
Communication, journalism, and related programs	1,770	2,961	2,896	3,500	4,123	5,080	5,218	7,106	6,916	7,630	8,302	9,005	8,760	9,353	9,581	9,676	10,119	10,243
Communications technologies	86	165	209	308	204	481	427	521	631	463	502	497	577	577	554	491	539	529
Computer and information sciences	1,588	2,603	4,218	8,070	9,324	10,579	16,911	17,195	17,096	17,955	19,516	20,925	22,782	24,514	31,475	40,130	46,553	46,468
Education	87,666	126,061	96,713	74,816	87,352	104,936	127,829	174,622	175,880	182,165	185,127	179,047	164,652	154,655	146,581	145,792	145,624	146,367
Engineering	16,813	16,472	16,893	21,529	24,454	26,789	25,174	30,845	31,559	35,133	38,664	40,323	40,420	42,376	46,117	51,646	52,826	51,721
Engineering technologies	134	328	323	617	996	2,054	2,013	2,541	2,884	4,258	4,515	4,793	4,908	4,967	5,324	6,067	7,403	7,247
English language and literature/letters	10,441	8,599	5,742	5,335	6,784	7,657	6,763	8,845	9,142	9,202	9,475	9,938	9,755	9,294	8,928	8,581	8,244	8,300
Family and consumer sciences/human sciences	1,452	2,179	2,570	2,011	1,541	1,712	1,838	1,983	2,199	2,592	2,918	3,155	3,255	3,082	3,148	3,228	3,295	3,308
Foreign languages, literatures, and linguistics	5,480	4,432	2,934	2,690	3,049	3,443	3,035	3,539	3,564	3,756	3,727	3,827	3,708	3,482	3,566	3,407	3,271	3,261
Health professions and related programs	5,330	12,164	16,176	18,603	21,354	33,920	43,623	51,492	58,147	69,112	75,571	84,355	90,933	97,416	103,052	110,350	119,242	125,216
Homeland security, law enforcement, and firefighting	194	1,197	1,538	1,074	1,108	1,812	2,514	4,277	5,779	6,717	7,433	8,420	8,868	9,310	9,643	9,775	10,209	10,293
Legal professions and studies	955	1,442	1,832	1,924	2,057	2,751	3,829	4,453	4,823	5,767	6,475	6,614	7,013	7,654	7,924	8,181	8,674	9,177
Liberal arts and sciences, general studies, and humanities	885	2,633	2,375	1,586	2,213	2,778	3,193	3,702	3,797	3,822	3,997	3,792	3,264	3,002	2,794	2,598	2,485	2,473
Library science	7,001	8,037	4,859	3,564	4,763	5,099	4,727	6,448	7,169	7,448	7,729	7,443	6,983	5,840	5,259	4,926	4,843	4,953
Mathematics and statistics	5,191	3,857	2,567	3,131	3,549	3,651	3,209	4,729	4,993	5,639	5,866	6,246	6,957	7,273	7,589	8,451	9,082	10,443
Military technologies and applied sciences	2	0	43	83	0	136	0	0	0	0	0	29	32	29	71	152	274	355
Multi/interdisciplinary studies	924	1,283	2,356	2,869	2,079	2,713	3,413	4,396	5,166	5,947	6,762	7,746	7,953	8,120	8,100	8,554	9,264	10,175
Parks, recreation, leisure, and fitness studies	218	571	643	570	483	1,684	2,354	3,994	4,443	5,617	6,546	7,047	7,139	7,609	7,654	8,268	8,651	9,005
Philosophy and religious studies	1,326	1,358	1,231	1,193	1,471	1,363	1,386	1,739	1,879	2,045	1,839	2,003	1,934	2,095	1,912	1,756	1,704	1,692
Physical sciences and science technologies	6,336	5,428	5,246	5,860	5,281	5,910	5,134	6,063	6,058	6,066	6,386	6,911	7,014	6,984	7,100	7,131	7,136	7,196
Precision production	0	0	0	0	0	8	2	9	3	10	5	11	9	15	4	10	14	11
Psychology	5,717	10,167	10,223	9,845	11,349	15,152	16,539	19,775	21,420	23,763	25,062	27,052	27,787	27,926	26,772	27,645	27,539	27,841
Public administration and social services	7,785	15,209	17,803	15,692	17,905	24,229	25,268	30,492	32,962	35,740	38,614	41,737	43,591	44,508	45,948	46,754	45,361	46,294
Social sciences and history	16,539	15,953	11,945	10,564	12,233	15,012	13,791	17,368	18,496	20,234	21,085	21,891	21,591	21,497	20,533	19,861	20,004	19,884
Theology and religious vocations	7,747	8,964	11,061	11,826	10,498	10,909	9,876	11,758	12,578	12,848	13,170	13,341	14,275	14,128	14,278	14,352	13,694	13,828
Transportation and materials moving	0	0	0	454	406	919	756	784	992	1,074	1,390	1,702	1,444	1,243	971	911	839	815
Visual and performing arts	6,675	8,817	8,629	8,420	8,657	10,280	11,404	13,531	14,170	15,562	16,277	17,307	17,869	17,869	17,756	18,052	17,516	17,686
Not classified by field of study	0	0	0	0	8,523	780	528	0	84	0	0	0	0	0	0	0	0	0

NOTE: Data are for postsecondary institutions participating in Title IV federal financial aid programs. The new Classification of Instructional Programs was initiated in 2009–10. The figures for earlier years have been reclassified when necessary to make them conform to the new taxonomy. To facilitate trend comparisons, certain aggregations have been made of the degree fields as reported in the Integrated Postsecondary Education Data System (IPEDS): "Agriculture and natural resources" includes Agriculture, agriculture operations, and related sciences and Natural resources and conservation; "Business" includes Business, management, marketing, and related support services and Personal and culinary services; and "Engineering technologies" includes Engineering technologies and engineering-related fields, Construction trades, and Mechanic and repair technologies/technicians. Some data have been revised from previously published figures.

SOURCE: U.S. Department of Education, National Center for Education Statistics, Higher Education General Information Survey (HEGIS), "Degrees and Other Formal Awards Conferred" surveys, 1970–71 through 1985–86; Integrated Postsecondary Education Data System (IPEDS), "Completions Survey" (IPEDS-C:91–99); and IPEDS Fall 2000 through Fall 2018, Completions component. (This table was prepared November 2019.)

Table 323.20. Master's degrees conferred by postsecondary institutions, by race/ethnicity and sex of student: Selected years, 1976–77 through 2017–18

Year and sex	Number of degrees conferred to U.S. citizens, permanent residents, and nonresident aliens								Percentage distribution of degrees conferred to U.S. citizens and permanent residents						
	Total	White	Black	Hispanic	Asian/ Pacific Islander	American Indian/ Alaska Native	Two or more races[1]	Non-resident alien	Total	White	Black	Hispanic	Asian/ Pacific Islander	American Indian/ Alaska Native	Two or more races[1]
1	2	3	4	5	6	7	8	9	10	11	12	13	14	15	16
Total															
1976–77[2]	322,463	271,402	21,252	6,136	5,127	1,018	—	17,528	100.0	89.0	7.0	2.0	1.7	0.3	—
1980–81[3]	301,081	247,475	17,436	6,534	6,348	1,044	—	22,244	100.0	88.8	6.3	2.3	2.3	0.4	—
1990–91	342,863	265,927	17,023	8,981	11,869	1,189	—	37,874	100.0	87.2	5.6	2.9	3.9	0.4	—
1999–2000	463,185	324,990	36,606	19,379	23,523	2,263	—	56,424	100.0	79.9	9.0	4.8	5.8	0.6	—
2000–01	473,502	324,211	38,853	21,661	24,544	2,496	—	61,737	100.0	78.7	9.4	5.3	6.0	0.6	—
2003–04	564,272	373,448	51,402	29,806	31,202	3,206	—	75,208	100.0	76.4	10.5	6.1	6.4	0.7	—
2004–05	580,151	383,246	55,330	31,639	33,042	3,310	—	73,584	100.0	75.7	10.9	6.2	6.5	0.7	—
2005–06	599,862	397,519	59,822	32,578	34,302	3,519	—	72,122	100.0	75.3	11.3	6.2	6.5	0.7	—
2006–07	610,703	403,623	63,439	34,962	36,420	3,590	—	68,669	100.0	74.5	11.7	6.5	6.7	0.7	—
2007–08	630,844	413,348	65,912	36,899	37,743	3,775	—	73,167	100.0	74.1	11.8	6.6	6.8	0.7	—
2008–09	662,082	427,713	70,772	39,567	40,510	3,777	—	79,743	100.0	73.4	12.2	6.8	7.0	0.6	—
2009–10	693,313	445,158	76,472	43,603	42,520	3,965	—	81,595	100.0	72.8	12.5	7.1	7.0	0.6	—
2010–11	730,922	462,922	80,742	46,823	43,482	3,946	6,597	86,410	100.0	71.8	12.5	7.3	6.7	0.6	1.0
2011–12	755,967	470,822	86,007	50,994	45,379	3,681	9,823	89,261	100.0	70.6	12.9	7.6	6.8	0.6	1.5
2012–13	751,718	455,896	87,989	52,991	44,906	3,693	11,794	94,449	100.0	69.4	13.4	8.1	6.8	0.6	1.8
2013–14	754,582	444,771	88,606	55,962	44,533	3,512	13,417	103,781	100.0	68.3	13.6	8.6	6.8	0.5	2.1
2014–15	758,804	433,096	87,288	58,752	44,489	3,410	14,628	117,141	100.0	67.5	13.6	9.2	6.9	0.5	2.3
2015–16	785,757	431,885	88,786	63,060	45,921	3,538	16,589	135,978	100.0	66.5	13.7	9.7	7.1	0.5	2.6
2016–17	804,542	433,638	89,577	67,026	47,810	3,397	17,674	145,420	100.0	65.8	13.6	10.2	7.3	0.5	2.7
2017–18	820,102	439,051	91,273	72,470	50,091	3,318	18,850	145,049	100.0	65.0	13.5	10.7	7.4	0.5	2.8
Males															
1976–77[2]	172,703	144,042	7,970	3,328	3,128	565	—	13,670	100.0	90.6	5.0	2.1	2.0	0.4	—
1980–81[3]	151,602	120,927	6,418	3,155	3,830	507	—	16,765	100.0	89.7	4.8	2.3	2.8	0.4	—
1990–91	160,842	117,993	6,201	4,017	6,765	495	—	25,371	100.0	87.1	4.6	3.0	5.0	0.4	—
1999–2000	196,129	131,221	11,642	7,738	11,299	845	—	33,384	100.0	80.6	7.2	4.8	6.9	0.5	—
2000–01	197,770	128,516	11,878	8,371	11,561	925	—	36,519	100.0	79.7	7.4	5.2	7.2	0.6	—
2003–04	233,056	146,369	15,027	10,929	14,551	1,137	—	45,043	100.0	77.9	8.0	5.8	7.7	0.6	—
2004–05	237,155	150,076	16,136	11,501	15,238	1,167	—	43,037	100.0	77.3	8.3	5.9	7.8	0.6	—
2005–06	241,701	153,696	17,388	11,738	16,037	1,253	—	41,589	100.0	76.8	8.7	5.9	8.0	0.6	—
2006–07	242,213	154,250	18,340	12,471	16,689	1,275	—	39,188	100.0	76.0	9.0	6.1	8.2	0.6	—
2007–08	250,203	157,622	18,759	13,166	17,480	1,294	—	41,882	100.0	75.7	9.0	6.3	8.4	0.6	—
2008–09	263,515	162,863	20,146	14,314	18,865	1,349	—	45,978	100.0	74.9	9.3	6.6	8.7	0.6	—
2009–10	275,317	170,243	22,121	15,554	19,423	1,419	—	46,557	100.0	74.4	9.7	6.8	8.5	0.6	—
2010–11	291,680	177,786	23,746	17,183	19,918	1,409	2,540	49,098	100.0	73.3	9.8	7.1	8.2	0.6	1.0
2011–12	302,484	183,222	25,284	18,633	20,751	1,298	3,518	49,778	100.0	72.5	10.0	7.4	8.2	0.5	1.4
2012–13	301,552	177,208	26,417	19,441	20,456	1,280	4,472	52,278	100.0	71.1	10.6	7.8	8.2	0.5	1.8
2013–14	302,846	173,303	26,608	20,565	19,955	1,219	4,890	56,306	100.0	70.3	10.8	8.3	8.1	0.5	2.0
2014–15	306,615	168,151	26,295	21,384	19,577	1,223	5,438	64,547	100.0	69.5	10.9	8.8	8.1	0.5	2.2
2015–16	320,574	166,161	27,024	22,749	20,071	1,229	6,129	77,211	100.0	68.3	11.1	9.3	8.2	0.5	2.5
2016–17	326,857	164,734	26,978	23,749	20,693	1,151	6,453	83,099	100.0	67.6	11.1	9.7	8.5	0.5	2.6
2017–18	326,870	164,714	27,552	25,255	21,273	1,076	6,658	80,342	100.0	66.8	11.2	10.2	8.6	0.4	2.7
Females															
1976–77[2]	149,760	127,360	13,282	2,808	1,999	453	—	3,858	100.0	87.3	9.1	1.9	1.4	0.3	—
1980–81[3]	149,479	126,548	11,018	3,379	2,518	537	—	5,479	100.0	87.9	7.7	2.3	1.7	0.4	—
1990–91	182,021	147,934	10,822	4,964	5,104	694	—	12,503	100.0	87.3	6.4	2.9	3.0	0.4	—
1999–2000	267,056	193,769	24,964	11,641	12,224	1,418	—	23,040	100.0	79.4	10.2	4.8	5.0	0.6	—
2000–01	275,732	195,695	26,975	13,290	12,983	1,571	—	25,218	100.0	78.1	10.8	5.3	5.2	0.6	—
2003–04	331,216	227,079	36,375	18,877	16,651	2,069	—	30,165	100.0	75.4	12.1	6.3	5.5	0.7	—
2004–05	342,996	233,170	39,194	20,138	17,804	2,143	—	30,547	100.0	74.6	12.5	6.4	5.7	0.7	—
2005–06	358,161	243,823	42,434	20,840	18,265	2,266	—	30,533	100.0	74.4	13.0	6.4	5.6	0.7	—
2006–07	368,490	249,373	45,099	22,491	19,731	2,315	—	29,481	100.0	73.6	13.3	6.6	5.8	0.7	—
2007–08	380,641	255,726	47,153	23,733	20,263	2,481	—	31,285	100.0	73.2	13.5	6.8	5.8	0.7	—
2008–09	398,567	264,850	50,626	25,253	21,645	2,428	—	33,765	100.0	72.6	13.9	6.9	5.9	0.7	—
2009–10	417,996	274,915	54,351	28,049	23,097	2,546	—	35,038	100.0	71.8	14.2	7.3	6.0	0.7	—
2010–11	439,242	285,136	56,996	29,640	23,564	2,537	4,057	37,312	100.0	70.9	14.2	7.4	5.9	0.6	1.0
2011–12	453,483	287,600	60,723	32,361	24,628	2,383	6,305	39,483	100.0	69.5	14.7	7.8	5.9	0.6	1.5
2012–13	450,166	278,688	61,572	33,550	24,450	2,413	7,322	42,171	100.0	68.3	15.1	8.2	6.0	0.6	1.8
2013–14	451,736	271,468	61,998	35,397	24,578	2,293	8,527	47,475	100.0	67.2	15.3	8.8	6.1	0.6	2.1
2014–15	452,189	264,945	60,993	37,368	24,912	2,187	9,190	52,594	100.0	66.3	15.3	9.4	6.2	0.5	2.3
2015–16	465,183	265,724	61,762	40,311	25,850	2,309	10,460	58,767	100.0	65.4	15.2	9.9	6.4	0.6	2.6
2016–17	477,685	268,904	62,599	43,277	27,117	2,246	11,221	62,321	100.0	64.7	15.1	10.4	6.5	0.5	2.7
2017–18	493,232	274,337	63,721	47,215	28,818	2,242	12,192	64,707	100.0	64.0	14.9	11.0	6.7	0.5	2.8

—Not available.

[1]For years prior to 2010–11, the survey did not yet include the "Two or more races" category, and each student could be counted in only one race category.

[2]Excludes 387 males and 175 females whose racial/ethnic group was not available.

[3]Excludes 1,377 males and 179 females whose racial/ethnic group was not available.

NOTE: Data are for postsecondary institutions participating in Title IV federal financial aid programs. Race categories exclude persons of Hispanic ethnicity. For 1989–90 and later years, reported racial/ethnic distributions of students by level of degree, field of degree, and sex were used to estimate race/ethnicity for students whose race/ethnicity was not reported. Detail may not sum to totals because of rounding. Some data have been revised from previously published figures.

SOURCE: U.S. Department of Education, National Center for Education Statistics, Higher Education General Information Survey (HEGIS), "Degrees and Other Formal Awards Conferred" surveys, 1976–77 and 1980–81; Integrated Postsecondary Education Data System (IPEDS), "Completions Survey" (IPEDS-C:90–99); and IPEDS Fall 2000 through Fall 2018, Completions component. (This table was prepared October 2019.)

Table 323.30. Master's degrees conferred by postsecondary institutions, by race/ethnicity and field of study: 2016–17 and 2017–18

Field of study	2016–17										2017–18									
					Asian/Pacific Islander										Asian/Pacific Islander					
	Total	White	Black	Hispanic	Total	Asian	Pacific Islander	American Indian/ Alaska Native	Two or more races	Non-resident alien	Total	White	Black	Hispanic	Total	Asian	Pacific Islander	American Indian/ Alaska Native	Two or more races	Non-resident alien
1	2	3	4	5	6	7	8	9	10	11	12	13	14	15	16	17	18	19	20	21
All fields, total	**804,542**	**433,638**	**89,577**	**67,026**	**47,810**	**46,225**	**1,585**	**3,397**	**17,674**	**145,420**	**820,102**	**439,051**	**91,273**	**72,470**	**50,091**	**48,480**	**1,611**	**3,318**	**18,850**	**145,049**
Agriculture and natural resources	6,843	4,615	245	392	221	214	7	34	185	1,151	6,967	4,651	249	420	235	225	10	39	185	1,188
Architecture and related services	7,883	3,630	332	700	443	435	8	25	169	2,584	7,317	3,236	338	639	430	421	9	18	179	2,477
Area, ethnic, cultural, gender, and group studies	1,717	765	165	222	129	121	8	69	64	303	1,673	715	172	255	81	80	1	67	74	309
Biological and biomedical sciences	16,282	8,504	1,198	1,287	2,162	2,146	16	43	495	2,593	17,180	8,865	1,336	1,410	2,352	2,334	18	33	514	2,670
Business	187,412	94,277	25,669	15,354	13,874	13,409	465	737	3,752	33,749	192,184	96,470	25,642	16,292	14,455	14,008	447	745	4,088	34,492
Communication, journalism, and related programs	10,119	5,116	1,349	939	380	370	10	38	304	1,993	10,243	5,039	1,438	1,028	336	325	11	32	314	2,056
Communications technologies	539	197	27	29	33	33	0	3	8	242	529	159	33	38	31	29	2	2	7	259
Computer and information sciences	46,553	8,664	2,345	1,275	3,587	3,538	49	78	531	30,073	46,468	9,411	2,601	1,492	3,484	3,441	43	53	609	28,818
Construction trades	0	0	0	0	0	0	0	0	0	0	0	0	0	0	0	0	0	0	0	0
Education	145,624	101,795	15,955	15,098	4,562	4,291	271	709	3,069	4,436	146,367	101,246	15,958	16,223	4,870	4,573	297	687	3,238	4,145
Engineering	52,826	14,861	1,147	2,137	3,740	3,701	39	67	697	30,177	51,721	15,186	1,142	2,253	3,727	3,698	29	64	767	28,582
Engineering technologies and engineering-related fields[1]	7,403	2,324	394	253	296	290	6	28	82	4,026	7,246	2,418	384	330	313	309	4	16	91	3,694
English language and literature/ letters	8,244	6,107	484	699	276	270	6	57	270	351	8,300	6,020	581	709	257	253	4	47	310	376
Family and consumer sciences/ human sciences	3,295	2,025	498	318	129	116	13	15	82	228	3,308	2,018	488	326	133	127	6	14	88	241
Foreign languages, literatures, and linguistics	3,271	1,547	81	532	96	96	0	9	95	911	3,261	1,540	75	569	131	127	4	6	68	872
Health professions and related programs	119,242	76,101	15,905	9,725	9,627	9,313	314	588	2,831	4,465	125,216	78,737	16,508	10,946	10,596	10,240	356	596	3,043	4,790
Homeland security, law enforcement, and firefighting	10,209	5,728	2,438	1,160	293	252	41	65	286	239	10,293	5,773	2,412	1,200	308	265	43	69	321	210
Legal professions and studies	8,674	2,083	699	494	326	320	6	61	92	4,919	9,177	2,208	753	574	315	306	9	81	139	5,107
Liberal arts and sciences, general studies, and humanities	2,485	1,668	287	257	63	59	4	25	62	123	2,473	1,585	316	232	73	71	2	30	81	156
Library science	4,843	3,824	256	389	131	125	6	24	146	73	4,953	3,881	240	446	133	128	5	18	154	81
Mathematics and statistics	9,082	2,777	187	309	663	658	5	5	132	5,009	10,443	2,965	188	363	720	716	4	4	124	6,079
Mechanic and repair technologies/ technicians	0	0	0	0	0	0	0	0	0	0	1	1	0	0	0	0	0	0	0	0
Military technologies and applied sciences	274	158	67	15	5	5	0	0	3	26	355	198	75	29	16	15	1	3	9	25
Multi/interdisciplinary studies	9,264	5,158	902	811	516	506	10	45	297	1,535	10,175	5,495	934	928	647	631	16	41	294	1,836
Parks, recreation, leisure, and fitness studies	8,651	5,824	1,183	691	202	179	23	31	287	433	9,005	5,974	1,242	747	205	185	20	45	279	513
Philosophy and religious studies	1,704	1,148	116	144	80	79	1	4	40	172	1,692	1,144	130	141	77	74	3	6	44	150
Physical sciences and science technologies	7,136	3,855	186	394	380	374	6	14	159	2,148	7,196	3,879	197	443	414	406	8	11	193	2,059
Precision production	14	4	0	0	1	1	0	0	0	9	11	4	0	1	2	2	0	0	0	4
Psychology	27,539	16,974	3,788	3,461	1,199	1,108	91	150	897	1,070	27,841	16,707	3,907	3,777	1,286	1,206	80	145	928	1,091
Public administration and social services	45,361	24,289	8,755	6,203	1,892	1,781	111	285	1,295	2,642	46,294	24,602	9,023	6,621	1,842	1,738	104	289	1,366	2,551
Social sciences and history	20,004	10,942	1,430	1,713	892	872	20	74	546	4,407	19,884	10,588	1,456	1,820	844	826	18	60	566	4,550
Social sciences	16,569	8,205	1,312	1,447	827	808	19	63	446	4,269	16,612	8,012	1,313	1,544	786	771	15	50	484	4,423
History	3,435	2,737	118	266	65	64	1	11	100	138	3,272	2,576	143	276	58	55	3	10	82	127
Theology and religious vocations	13,694	8,774	2,237	691	708	685	23	54	243	987	13,828	8,624	2,215	766	808	778	30	45	271	1,099
Transportation and materials moving	839	547	98	43	35	33	2	4	43	69	815	507	71	72	35	33	2	6	32	92
Visual and performing arts	17,516	9,357	1,154	1,291	869	845	24	56	512	4,277	17,686	9,205	1,169	1,380	935	910	25	46	474	4,477
Other and not classified	0	0	0	0	0	0	0	0	0	0	0	0	0	0	0	0	0	0	0	0

[1]Excludes "Construction trades" and "Mechanic and repair technologies/technicians," which are listed separately.

NOTE: Data are for postsecondary institutions participating in Title IV federal financial aid programs. Race categories exclude persons of Hispanic ethnicity. Reported racial/ethnic distributions of students by level of degree, field of degree, and sex were used to estimate race/ethnicity for students whose race/ethnicity was not reported. To facilitate trend comparisons, certain aggregations have been made of the degree fields as reported in the Integrated Postsecondary Education Data System (IPEDS): "Agriculture and natural resources" includes Agriculture, agriculture operations, and related sciences and Natural resources and conservation; and "Business" includes Business management, marketing, and related support services and Personal and culinary services. Some data have been revised from previously published figures.

SOURCE: U.S. Department of Education, National Center for Education Statistics, Integrated Postsecondary Education Data System (IPEDS), Fall 2017 and Fall 2018, Completions component. (This table was prepared October 2019.)

Table 324.10. Doctor's degrees conferred by postsecondary institutions, by field of study: Selected years, 1970–71 through 2017–18

Field of study	1970–71	1975–76	1980–81	1985–86	1990–91	1995–96	2000–01	2005–06	2007–08	2009–10	2010–11	2011–12	2012–13	2013–14	2014–15	2015–16	2016–17	2017–18
1	2	3	4	5	6	7	8	9	10	11	12	13	14	15	16	17	18	19
Total	**64,998**	**91,007**	**98,016**	**100,280**	**105,547**	**115,507**	**119,585**	**138,056**	**149,190**	**158,590**	**163,827**	**170,217**	**175,026**	**177,587**	**178,548**	**178,134**	**181,357**	**184,074**
Agriculture and natural resources	1,086	928	1,067	1,158	1,185	1,259	1,127	1,194	1,261	1,149	1,246	1,333	1,411	1,407	1,561	1,526	1,561	1,496
Architecture and related services	36	82	93	73	135	141	153	201	199	210	205	255	247	247	272	245	291	250
Area, ethnic, cultural, gender, and group studies	143	186	161	156	159	183	216	226	270	253	278	302	291	336	312	323	349	335
Biological and biomedical sciences	3,603	3,347	3,640	3,405	4,152	5,250	5,225	6,162	7,398	7,672	7,693	7,935	7,939	8,302	8,053	7,939	8,087	8,222
Business	774	906	808	923	1,185	1,366	1,180	1,711	2,084	2,249	2,286	2,538	2,828	3,039	3,116	3,325	3,328	3,338
Communication, journalism, and related programs	145	196	171	212	259	338	368	461	489	570	577	563	612	611	644	629	615	666
Communications technologies	0	8	11	6	13	7	2	3	7	3	1	4	0	3	0	4	0	0
Computer and information sciences	128	244	252	344	676	869	768	1,416	1,697	1,599	1,588	1,698	1,834	1,982	1,998	1,989	1,982	2,017
Education	6,041	7,202	7,279	6,610	6,189	6,246	6,284	7,584	8,496	9,237	9,642	10,118	10,572	10,929	11,772	11,838	12,692	12,780
Engineering	3,687	2,872	2,598	3,444	5,316	6,304	5,485	7,243	7,929	7,706	8,369	8,722	9,356	10,010	10,239	10,265	10,371	10,817
Engineering technologies	1	2	10	12	14	50	62	75	55	67	56	134	111	107	123	133	152	212
English language and literature/letters	1,554	1,514	1,040	895	1,056	1,395	1,330	1,254	1,262	1,334	1,344	1,427	1,377	1,393	1,418	1,402	1,347	1,295
Family and consumer sciences/human sciences	123	178	247	307	229	375	354	340	323	296	320	325	351	335	335	374	317	274
Foreign languages, literatures, and linguistics	1,084	1,245	931	768	889	1,020	1,078	1,074	1,078	1,091	1,158	1,231	1,304	1,230	1,243	1,278	1,168	1,213
Health professions and related programs	15,988	25,267	29,595	31,922	29,842	32,678	39,019	45,677	51,655	57,750	60,221	62,097	64,192	67,447	71,004	73,687	77,693	80,305
Homeland security, law enforcement, and firefighting	1	9	21	21	28	38	44	80	88	106	131	117	147	152	193	205	177	150
Legal professions and studies	17,441	32,369	36,391	35,898	38,035	39,919	38,190	43,569	43,699	44,627	44,853	46,836	47,246	44,169	40,329	37,034	35,123	34,544
Liberal arts and sciences, general studies, and humanities	32	162	121	90	70	75	102	84	76	96	95	93	98	90	96	105	95	93
Library science	39	71	71	62	56	53	58	44	64	64	50	60	50	52	44	54	42	54
Mathematics and statistics	1,199	856	728	742	978	1,158	997	1,293	1,360	1,596	1,586	1,669	1,823	1,863	1,801	1,855	1,925	2,010
Multi/interdisciplinary studies	101	156	236	352	306	549	512	600	660	631	660	727	730	769	840	849	854	850
Parks, recreation, leisure, and fitness studies	2	15	42	39	28	104	177	194	228	266	257	288	295	317	311	331	319	298
Philosophy and religious studies	555	556	411	480	464	550	600	578	635	667	804	778	794	698	762	750	741	768
Physical sciences and science technologies	4,324	3,388	3,105	3,521	4,248	4,589	3,968	4,642	4,995	5,065	5,295	5,370	5,514	5,806	5,823	6,057	6,027	6,181
Psychology	2,144	3,157	3,576	3,593	3,932	4,141	5,091	4,921	5,296	5,540	5,851	5,936	6,326	6,634	6,583	6,540	6,702	6,275
Public administration and social services	174	292	362	382	430	499	574	704	760	838	851	890	979	1,047	1,123	1,066	1,116	1,157
Social sciences and history	3,660	4,157	3,122	2,955	3,012	3,760	3,930	3,914	4,058	4,238	4,390	4,597	4,610	4,724	4,828	4,706	4,706	4,676
Theology and religious vocations	312	1,022	1,273	1,185	1,076	1,517	1,461	1,429	1,615	2,071	2,374	2,446	2,174	2,103	1,927	1,808	1,792	2,023
Transportation and materials moving	0	0	0	3	0	0	0	0	0	0	0	0	1	7	5	8	11	16
Visual and performing arts	621	620	654	722	838	1,067	1,167	1,383	1,453	1,599	1,646	1,728	1,814	1,778	1,793	1,809	1,774	1,759
Not classified by field of study	0	0	0	0	747	7	63	0	0	0	0	0	0	0	0	0	0	0

NOTE: Data are for postsecondary institutions participating in Title IV federal financial aid programs. Includes Ph.D., Ed.D., and comparable degrees at the doctoral level, as well as such degrees as M.D., D.D.S., and law degrees that were classified as first-professional degrees prior to 2010–11. The new Classification of Instructional Programs was initiated in 2009–10. The figures for earlier years have been reclassified when necessary to make them conform to the new taxonomy. To facilitate trend comparisons, certain aggregations have been made of the degree fields as reported in the Integrated Postsecondary Education Data System (IPEDS): "Agriculture and natural resources" includes Agriculture, agriculture operations, and related sciences and Natural resources and conservation; "Business" includes Business, management, marketing, and related support services and Personal and culinary services; and "Engineering technologies" includes Engineering technologies and engineering-related fields, Construction trades, and Mechanic and repair technologies/technicians. Some data have been revised from previously published figures.

SOURCE: U.S. Department of Education, National Center for Education Statistics, Higher Education General Information Survey (HEGIS), "Degrees and Other Formal Awards Conferred" surveys, 1970–71 through 1985–86; Integrated Postsecondary Education Data System (IPEDS), "Completions Survey" (IPEDS-C:91–99); and IPEDS Fall 2000 through Fall 2018, Completions component. (This table was prepared November 2019.)

Table 324.20. Doctor's degrees conferred by postsecondary institutions, by race/ethnicity and sex of student: Selected years, 1976–77 through 2017–18

Year and sex	Number of degrees conferred[1] to U.S. citizens, permanent residents, and nonresident aliens								Percentage distribution of degrees conferred[1] to U.S. citizens and permanent residents						
	Total	White	Black	Hispanic	Asian/ Pacific Islander	American Indian/ Alaska Native	Two or more races[2]	Non-resident alien	Total	White	Black	Hispanic	Asian/ Pacific Islander	American Indian/ Alaska Native	Two or more races[2]
1	2	3	4	5	6	7	8	9	10	11	12	13	14	15	16
Total															
1976–77[3]	91,218	79,932	3,575	1,533	1,674	240	—	4,264	100.0	91.9	4.1	1.8	1.9	0.3	—
1980–81[4]	97,281	84,200	3,893	1,924	2,267	312	—	4,685	100.0	90.9	4.2	2.1	2.4	0.3	—
1990–91	105,547	81,791	4,429	3,210	5,120	356	—	10,641	100.0	86.2	4.7	3.4	5.4	0.4	—
1999–2000	118,736	82,984	7,078	5,042	10,682	708	—	12,242	100.0	77.9	6.6	4.7	10.0	0.7	—
2000–01	119,585	82,321	7,035	5,204	11,587	705	—	12,733	100.0	77.0	6.6	4.9	10.8	0.7	—
2003–04	126,087	84,695	8,089	5,795	12,371	771	—	14,366	100.0	75.8	7.2	5.2	11.1	0.7	—
2004–05	134,387	89,763	8,527	6,115	13,176	788	—	16,018	100.0	75.8	7.2	5.2	11.1	0.7	—
2005–06	138,056	91,050	8,523	6,202	13,686	929	—	17,666	100.0	75.6	7.1	5.2	11.4	0.8	—
2006–07	144,694	94,225	9,371	6,576	14,727	917	—	18,878	100.0	74.9	7.4	5.2	11.7	0.7	—
2007–08	149,190	97,701	9,451	6,933	15,170	932	—	19,003	100.0	75.0	7.3	5.3	11.7	0.7	—
2008–09	154,564	101,400	10,188	7,497	15,840	978	—	18,661	100.0	74.6	7.5	5.5	11.7	0.7	—
2009–10	158,590	104,419	10,413	8,085	16,560	952	—	18,161	100.0	74.4	7.4	5.8	11.8	0.7	—
2010–11	163,827	105,990	10,934	8,662	17,078	947	1,251	18,965	100.0	73.2	7.5	6.0	11.8	0.7	0.9
2011–12	170,217	109,365	11,794	9,223	17,896	915	1,571	19,453	100.0	72.5	7.8	6.1	11.9	0.6	1.0
2012–13	175,026	110,759	12,085	10,108	18,406	900	2,440	20,328	100.0	71.6	7.8	6.5	11.9	0.6	1.6
2013–14	177,587	110,157	12,621	10,665	19,118	861	2,966	21,199	100.0	70.4	8.1	6.8	12.2	0.6	1.9
2014–15	178,548	108,914	13,272	11,263	19,186	884	3,670	21,359	100.0	69.3	8.4	7.2	12.2	0.6	2.3
2015–16	178,134	107,235	13,377	11,781	19,614	811	3,782	21,534	100.0	68.5	8.5	7.5	12.5	0.5	2.4
2016–17	181,357	107,444	14,070	12,493	20,345	747	4,166	22,092	100.0	67.5	8.8	7.8	12.8	0.5	2.6
2017–18	184,074	107,415	14,241	13,253	20,762	707	4,497	23,199	100.0	66.8	8.9	8.2	12.9	0.4	2.8
Males															
1976–77[3]	71,709	62,977	2,338	1,216	1,311	182	—	3,685	100.0	92.6	3.4	1.8	1.9	0.3	—
1980–81[4]	68,853	59,574	2,206	1,338	1,589	223	—	3,923	100.0	91.8	3.4	2.1	2.4	0.3	—
1990–91	64,242	48,812	1,991	1,835	3,038	196	—	8,370	100.0	87.4	3.6	3.3	5.4	0.4	—
1999–2000	64,930	45,308	2,762	2,602	5,467	333	—	8,458	100.0	80.2	4.9	4.6	9.7	0.6	—
2000–01	64,171	44,131	2,655	2,564	5,759	346	—	8,716	100.0	79.6	4.8	4.6	10.4	0.6	—
2003–04	63,981	43,014	2,888	2,731	5,620	357	—	9,371	100.0	78.8	5.3	5.0	10.3	0.7	—
2004–05	67,257	44,749	2,904	2,863	5,913	370	—	10,458	100.0	78.8	5.1	5.0	10.4	0.7	—
2005–06	68,912	45,476	2,949	2,850	5,977	429	—	11,231	100.0	78.8	5.1	4.9	10.4	0.7	—
2006–07	71,311	46,215	3,223	3,037	6,449	421	—	11,966	100.0	77.9	5.4	5.1	10.9	0.7	—
2007–08	73,340	48,118	3,291	3,139	6,516	447	—	11,829	100.0	78.2	5.4	5.1	10.6	0.7	—
2008–09	75,674	49,880	3,531	3,388	6,914	460	—	11,501	100.0	77.7	5.5	5.3	10.8	0.7	—
2009–10	76,610	50,707	3,609	3,642	7,184	430	—	11,038	100.0	77.3	5.5	5.6	11.0	0.7	—
2010–11	79,672	51,688	3,838	3,990	7,545	454	557	11,600	100.0	75.9	5.6	5.9	11.1	0.7	0.8
2011–12	82,670	53,488	4,121	4,218	7,792	418	701	11,932	100.0	75.6	5.8	6.0	11.0	0.6	1.0
2012–13	85,080	54,196	4,310	4,473	8,190	400	1,085	12,426	100.0	74.6	5.9	6.2	11.3	0.6	1.5
2013–14	85,585	53,374	4,510	4,788	8,270	365	1,297	12,981	100.0	73.5	6.2	6.6	11.4	0.5	1.8
2014–15	84,922	52,069	4,464	5,011	8,330	410	1,678	12,960	100.0	72.4	6.2	7.0	11.6	0.6	2.3
2015–16	84,240	50,694	4,564	5,122	8,632	371	1,718	13,139	100.0	71.3	6.4	7.2	12.1	0.5	2.4
2016–17	84,649	50,002	4,794	5,421	8,906	307	1,780	13,439	100.0	70.2	6.7	7.6	12.5	0.4	2.5
2017–18	85,568	49,649	4,957	5,856	9,004	309	1,869	13,924	100.0	69.3	6.9	8.2	12.6	0.4	2.6
Females															
1976–77[3]	19,509	16,955	1,237	317	363	58	—	579	100.0	89.6	6.5	1.7	1.9	0.3	—
1980–81[4]	28,428	24,626	1,687	586	678	89	—	762	100.0	89.0	6.1	2.1	2.5	0.3	—
1990–91	41,305	32,979	2,438	1,375	2,082	160	—	2,271	100.0	84.5	6.2	3.5	5.3	0.4	—
1999–2000	53,806	37,676	4,316	2,440	5,215	375	—	3,784	100.0	75.3	8.6	4.9	10.4	0.7	—
2000–01	55,414	38,190	4,380	2,640	5,828	359	—	4,017	100.0	74.3	8.5	5.1	11.3	0.7	—
2003–04	62,106	41,681	5,201	3,064	6,751	414	—	4,995	100.0	73.0	9.1	5.4	11.8	0.7	—
2004–05	67,130	45,014	5,623	3,252	7,263	418	—	5,560	100.0	73.1	9.1	5.3	11.8	0.7	—
2005–06	69,144	45,574	5,574	3,352	7,709	500	—	6,435	100.0	72.7	8.9	5.3	12.3	0.8	—
2006–07	73,383	48,010	6,148	3,539	8,278	496	—	6,912	100.0	72.2	9.2	5.3	12.5	0.7	—
2007–08	75,850	49,583	6,160	3,794	8,654	485	—	7,174	100.0	72.2	9.0	5.5	12.6	0.7	—
2008–09	78,890	51,520	6,657	4,109	8,926	518	—	7,160	100.0	71.8	9.3	5.7	12.4	0.7	—
2009–10	81,980	53,712	6,804	4,443	9,376	522	—	7,123	100.0	71.8	9.1	5.9	12.5	0.7	—
2010–11	84,155	54,302	7,096	4,672	9,533	493	694	7,365	100.0	70.7	9.2	6.1	12.4	0.6	0.9
2011–12	87,547	55,877	7,673	5,005	10,104	497	870	7,521	100.0	69.8	9.6	6.3	12.6	0.6	1.1
2012–13	89,946	56,563	7,775	5,635	10,216	500	1,355	7,902	100.0	68.9	9.5	6.9	12.5	0.6	1.7
2013–14	92,002	56,783	8,111	5,877	10,848	496	1,669	8,218	100.0	67.8	9.7	7.0	12.9	0.6	2.0
2014–15	93,626	56,845	8,808	6,252	10,856	474	1,992	8,399	100.0	66.7	10.3	7.3	12.7	0.6	2.3
2015–16	93,894	56,541	8,813	6,659	10,982	440	2,064	8,395	100.0	66.1	10.3	7.8	12.8	0.5	2.4
2016–17	96,708	57,442	9,276	7,072	11,439	440	2,386	8,653	100.0	65.2	10.5	8.0	13.0	0.5	2.7
2017–18	98,506	57,766	9,284	7,397	11,758	398	2,628	9,275	100.0	64.7	10.4	8.3	13.2	0.4	2.9

—Not available.

[1]Includes Ph.D., Ed.D., and comparable degrees at the doctoral level, as well as such degrees as M.D., D.D.S., and law degrees that were classified as first-professional degrees prior to 2010–11.

[2]For years prior to 2010–11, the survey did not yet include the "Two or more races" category, and each student could be counted in only one race category.

[3]Excludes 500 males and 12 females whose racial/ethnic group was not available.

[4]Excludes 714 males and 21 females whose racial/ethnic group was not available.

NOTE: Data are for postsecondary institutions participating in Title IV federal financial aid programs. Race categories exclude persons of Hispanic ethnicity. For 1989–90 and later years, reported racial/ethnic distributions of students by level of degree, field of degree, and sex were used to estimate race/ethnicity for students whose race/ethnicity was not reported. Detail may not sum to totals because of rounding. Some data have been revised from previously published figures.

SOURCE: U.S. Department of Education, National Center for Education Statistics, Higher Education General Information Survey (HEGIS), "Degrees and Other Formal Awards Conferred" surveys, 1976–77 and 1980–81; Integrated Postsecondary Education Data System (IPEDS), "Completions Survey" (IPEDS-C:90–99); and IPEDS Fall 2000 through Fall 2018, Completions component. (This table was prepared October 2019.)

Table 324.25. Doctor's degrees conferred by postsecondary institutions, by race/ethnicity and field of study: 2016–17 and 2017–18

Field of study	2016–17										2017–18									
					Asian/Pacific Islander										Asian/Pacific Islander					
	Total	White	Black	Hispanic	Total	Asian	Pacific Islander	American Indian/ Alaska Native	Two or more races	Non-resident alien	Total	White	Black	Hispanic	Total	Asian	Pacific Islander	American Indian/ Alaska Native	Two or more races	Non-resident alien
1	2	3	4	5	6	7	8	9	10	11	12	13	14	15	16	17	18	19	20	21
All fields, total	**181,357**	**107,444**	**14,070**	**12,493**	**20,345**	**20,017**	**328**	**747**	**4,166**	**22,092**	**184,074**	**107,415**	**14,241**	**13,253**	**20,762**	**20,447**	**315**	**707**	**4,497**	**23,199**
Agriculture and natural resources	1,561	722	49	56	51	51	0	3	20	660	1,496	726	49	52	45	43	2	5	20	599
Architecture and related services	291	103	7	15	36	33	3	1	9	120	250	81	14	13	25	24	1	1	9	107
Area, ethnic, cultural, gender, and group studies	349	153	58	42	18	18	0	4	9	65	335	139	55	35	28	26	2	13	12	53
Biological and biomedical sciences	8,087	4,246	303	467	769	758	11	25	210	2,067	8,222	4,427	322	479	733	727	6	13	179	2,069
Business	3,328	1,411	721	206	238	231	7	14	43	695	3,338	1,467	726	148	217	206	11	11	64	705
Communication, journalism, and related programs	615	357	49	30	35	35	0	2	12	130	666	385	34	19	28	27	1	3	13	184
Communications technologies	0	0	0	0	0	0	0	0	0	0	0	0	0	0	0	0	0	0	0	0
Computer and information sciences	1,982	617	85	54	116	115	1	2	19	1,089	2,017	572	76	58	122	122	0	4	27	1,158
Construction trades	0	0	0	0	0	0	0	0	0	0	0	0	0	0	0	0	0	0	0	0
Education	12,692	7,582	2,639	1,009	444	407	37	90	219	709	12,780	7,582	2,491	1,156	462	431	31	79	260	750
Engineering	10,371	3,076	187	319	749	744	5	12	117	5,911	10,817	3,190	179	303	720	720	0	11	143	6,271
Engineering technologies and engineering-related fields[1]	152	65	13	6	11	11	0	0	0	57	212	92	33	7	20	20	0	0	3	57
English language and literature/ letters	1,347	994	54	97	49	47	2	10	32	111	1,295	946	65	74	64	63	1	7	25	114
Family and consumer sciences/ human sciences	317	172	30	18	21	21	0	1	5	70	274	141	25	15	16	16	0	0	6	71
Foreign languages, literatures, and linguistics	1,168	604	12	121	50	50	0	4	13	364	1,213	565	20	147	49	48	1	3	21	408
Health professions and related programs	77,693	49,286	5,031	4,851	13,715	13,536	179	260	1,949	2,601	80,305	50,069	5,345	5,322	14,325	14,146	179	274	2,186	2,784
Homeland security, law enforcement, and firefighting	177	107	30	16	2	2	0	1	0	21	150	88	20	16	5	4	1	1	3	17
Legal professions and studies	35,123	23,319	3,006	3,730	2,594	2,537	57	231	1,022	1,221	34,544	22,601	3,073	3,946	2,385	2,333	52	198	1,007	1,334
Liberal arts and sciences, general studies, and humanities	95	74	3	5	4	3	1	1	3	5	93	67	3	4	4	4	0	1	2	12
Library science	42	21	4	3	4	3	1	0	0	10	54	27	4	2	6	6	0	0	1	14
Mathematics and statistics	1,925	739	22	50	138	138	0	3	30	943	2,010	753	35	62	124	122	2	1	32	1,003
Mechanic and repair technologies/ technicians	0	0	0	0	0	0	0	0	0	0	0	0	0	0	0	0	0	0	0	0
Military technologies and applied sciences	0	0	0	0	0	0	0	0	0	0	0	0	0	0	0	0	0	0	0	0
Multi/interdisciplinary studies	854	462	82	40	44	44	0	5	20	201	850	462	79	51	49	47	2	4	12	193
Parks, recreation, leisure, and fitness studies	319	208	20	11	6	6	0	1	7	66	298	189	21	7	10	10	0	1	8	62
Philosophy and religious studies	741	509	42	29	31	31	0	2	18	110	768	526	57	28	23	23	0	2	12	120
Physical sciences and science technologies	6,027	2,910	110	227	327	326	1	14	85	2,354	6,181	2,910	120	226	367	359	8	9	109	2,440
Precision production	0	0	0	0	0	0	0	0	0	0	0	0	0	0	0	0	0	0	0	0
Psychology	6,702	4,525	623	597	388	373	15	25	162	382	6,275	4,231	515	576	386	380	6	30	166	371
Public administration and social services	1,116	575	238	67	54	54	0	5	26	151	1,157	596	223	75	42	40	2	9	30	182
Social sciences and history	4,706	2,564	238	259	215	211	4	19	88	1,323	4,676	2,472	218	259	247	243	4	17	96	1,367
Social sciences	3,781	1,909	197	184	189	185	4	13	71	1,218	3,765	1,827	170	190	221	218	3	15	85	1,257
History	925	655	41	75	26	26	0	6	17	105	911	645	48	69	26	25	1	2	11	110
Theology and religious vocations	1,792	950	364	71	143	140	3	4	12	248	2,023	1,070	385	90	148	146	2	6	22	302
Transportation and materials moving	11	7	0	0	0	0	0	0	0	4	16	9	0	0	2	2	0	0	0	5
Visual and performing arts	1,774	1,086	50	97	93	92	1	8	36	404	1,759	1,032	54	83	110	109	1	4	29	447
Other and not classified	0	0	0	0	0	0	0	0	0	0	0	0	0	0	0	0	0	0	0	0

[1]Excludes "Construction trades" and "Mechanic and repair technologies/technicians," which are listed separately.

NOTE: Data are for postsecondary institutions participating in Title IV federal financial aid programs. Race categories exclude persons of Hispanic ethnicity. Reported racial/ethnic distributions of students by level of degree, field of degree, and sex were used to estimate race/ethnicity for students whose race/ethnicity was not reported. To facilitate trend comparisons, certain aggregations have been made of the degree fields as reported in the Integrated Postsecondary Education Data System (IPEDS): "Agriculture and natural resources" includes Agriculture, agriculture operations, and related sciences and Natural resources and conservation; and "Business" includes Business management, marketing, and related support services and Personal and culinary services. Some data have been revised from previously published figures.

SOURCE: U.S. Department of Education, National Center for Education Statistics, Integrated Postsecondary Education Data System (IPEDS), Fall 2017 and Fall 2018, Completions component. (This table was prepared October 2019.)

Table 324.40. Number of postsecondary institutions conferring doctor's degrees in dentistry, medicine, and law, and number of such degrees conferred, by sex of student: Selected years, 1949–50 through 2017–18

Year	Dentistry (D.D.S. or D.M.D.)				Medicine (M.D.)				Law (LL.B. or J.D.)			
	Number of institutions conferring degrees	Number of degrees conferred			Number of institutions conferring degrees	Number of degrees conferred			Number of institutions conferring degrees	Number of degrees conferred		
		Total	Males	Females		Total	Males	Females		Total	Males	Females
1	2	3	4	5	6	7	8	9	10	11	12	13
1949–50	40	2,579	2,561	18	72	5,612	5,028	584	—	—	—	—
1951–52	41	2,918	2,895	23	72	6,201	5,871	330	—	—	—	—
1953–54	42	3,102	3,063	39	73	6,712	6,377	335	—	—	—	—
1955–56	42	3,009	2,975	34	73	6,810	6,464	346	131	8,262	7,974	288
1957–58	43	3,065	3,031	34	75	6,816	6,469	347	131	9,394	9,122	272
1959–60	45	3,247	3,221	26	79	7,032	6,645	387	134	9,240	9,010	230
1961–62	46	3,183	3,166	17	81	7,138	6,749	389	134	9,364	9,091	273
1963–64	46	3,180	3,168	12	82	7,303	6,878	425	133	10,679	10,372	307
1964–65	46	3,108	3,086	22	81	7,304	6,832	472	137	11,583	11,216	367
1965–66	47	3,178	3,146	32	84	7,673	7,170	503	136	13,246	12,776	470
1967–68	48	3,422	3,375	47	85	7,944	7,318	626	138	16,454	15,805	649
1968–69	—	3,408	3,376	32	—	8,025	7,415	610	—	17,053	16,373	680
1969–70	48	3,718	3,684	34	86	8,314	7,615	699	145	14,916	14,115	801
1970–71	48	3,745	3,703	42	89	8,919	8,110	809	147	17,421	16,181	1,240
1971–72	48	3,862	3,819	43	92	9,253	8,423	830	147	21,764	20,266	1,498
1972–73	51	4,047	3,992	55	97	10,307	9,388	919	152	27,205	25,037	2,168
1973–74	52	4,440	4,355	85	99	11,356	10,093	1,263	151	29,326	25,986	3,340
1974–75	52	4,773	4,627	146	104	12,447	10,818	1,629	154	29,296	24,881	4,415
1975–76	56	5,425	5,187	238	107	13,426	11,252	2,174	166	32,293	26,085	6,208
1976–77	57	5,138	4,764	374	109	13,461	10,891	2,570	169	34,104	26,447	7,657
1977–78	57	5,189	4,623	566	109	14,279	11,210	3,069	169	34,402	25,457	8,945
1978–79	58	5,434	4,794	640	109	14,786	11,381	3,405	175	35,206	25,180	10,026
1979–80	58	5,258	4,558	700	112	14,902	11,416	3,486	179	35,647	24,893	10,754
1980–81	58	5,460	4,672	788	116	15,505	11,672	3,833	176	36,331	24,563	11,768
1981–82	59	5,282	4,467	815	119	15,814	11,867	3,947	180	35,991	23,965	12,026
1982–83	59	5,585	4,631	954	118	15,484	11,350	4,134	177	36,853	23,550	13,303
1983–84	60	5,353	4,302	1,051	119	15,813	11,359	4,454	179	37,012	23,382	13,630
1984–85	59	5,339	4,233	1,106	120	16,041	11,167	4,874	181	37,491	23,070	14,421
1985–86	59	5,046	3,907	1,139	120	15,938	11,022	4,916	181	35,844	21,874	13,970
1986–87	58	4,741	3,603	1,138	121	15,428	10,431	4,997	179	36,056	21,561	14,495
1987–88	57	4,477	3,300	1,177	122	15,358	10,278	5,080	180	35,397	21,067	14,330
1988–89	58	4,265	3,124	1,141	124	15,460	10,310	5,150	182	35,634	21,069	14,565
1989–90	57	4,100	2,834	1,266	124	15,075	9,923	5,152	182	36,485	21,079	15,406
1990–91	55	3,699	2,510	1,189	121	15,043	9,629	5,414	179	37,945	21,643	16,302
1991–92	52	3,593	2,431	1,162	120	15,243	9,796	5,447	177	38,848	22,260	16,588
1992–93	55	3,605	2,383	1,222	122	15,531	9,679	5,852	184	40,302	23,182	17,120
1993–94	53	3,787	2,330	1,457	121	15,368	9,544	5,824	185	40,044	22,826	17,218
1994–95	53	3,897	2,480	1,417	119	15,537	9,507	6,030	183	39,349	22,592	16,757
1995–96	53	3,697	2,374	1,323	119	15,341	9,061	6,280	183	39,828	22,508	17,320
1996–97	52	3,784	2,387	1,397	118	15,571	9,121	6,450	184	40,079	22,548	17,531
1997–98	53	4,032	2,490	1,542	117	15,424	9,006	6,418	185	39,331	21,876	17,455
1998–99	53	4,143	2,673	1,470	118	15,566	8,972	6,594	185	38,297	21,102	17,195
1999–2000	54	4,250	2,547	1,703	118	15,286	8,761	6,525	190	38,152	20,638	17,514
2000–01	54	4,391	2,696	1,695	118	15,403	8,728	6,675	192	37,904	19,981	17,923
2001–02	53	4,239	2,608	1,631	118	15,237	8,469	6,768	192	38,981	20,254	18,727
2002–03	53	4,345	2,654	1,691	118	15,034	8,221	6,813	194	39,067	19,916	19,151
2003–04	53	4,335	2,532	1,803	118	15,442	8,273	7,169	195	40,209	20,332	19,877
2004–05	53	4,454	2,505	1,949	120	15,461	8,151	7,310	198	43,423	22,297	21,126
2005–06	54	4,389	2,435	1,954	119	15,455	7,900	7,555	197	43,440	22,597	20,843
2006–07	55	4,596	2,548	2,048	120	15,730	7,987	7,743	200	43,485	22,777	20,708
2007–08	55	4,795	2,661	2,134	120	15,646	7,935	7,711	201	43,588	23,110	20,478
2008–09	55	4,918	2,637	2,281	120	15,987	8,164	7,823	203	44,045	23,860	20,185
2009–10	55	5,062	2,745	2,317	120	16,356	8,468	7,888	205	44,346	23,384	20,962
2010–11	55	5,071	2,764	2,307	120	16,863	8,701	8,162	206	44,421	23,481	20,940
2011–12	55	5,109	2,748	2,361	120	16,927	8,809	8,118	207	46,445	24,576	21,869
2012–13	56	5,219	2,707	2,512	122	17,264	8,976	8,288	209	46,811	25,087	21,724
2013–14	57	5,407	2,839	2,568	124	17,604	9,232	8,372	210	43,772	23,278	20,494
2014–15	60	5,816	3,030	2,786	127	18,302	9,558	8,744	212	40,024	20,810	19,214
2015–16	61	5,951	3,032	2,919	128	18,409	9,852	8,557	214	36,798	18,935	17,863
2016–17	63	6,388	3,328	3,060	131	18,698	9,834	8,864	214	34,894	17,579	17,315
2017–18	63	6,441	3,258	3,183	133	19,142	10,049	9,093	211	34,128	17,161	16,967

—Not available.

NOTE: Data are for postsecondary institutions participating in Title IV federal financial aid programs. Some data have been revised from previously published figures.

SOURCE: U.S. Department of Education, National Center for Education Statistics, *Earned Degrees Conferred*, 1949–50 through 1964–65; Higher Education General Information Survey (HEGIS), "Degrees and Other Formal Awards Conferred" surveys, 1965–66 through 1985–86; Integrated Postsecondary Education Data System (IPEDS), "Completions Survey" (IPEDS-C:87–99); and IPEDS Fall 2000 through Fall 2018, Completions component. (This table was prepared April 2020.)

Table 324.50. Degrees conferred by postsecondary institutions in selected professional fields, by sex of student, control of institution, and field of study: Selected years, 1985-86 through 2018-19

Control of institution and field of study	1985-86	1990-91	1995-96	2000-01	2005-06	2009-10	2010-11	2011-12	2012-13	2013-14	2014-15	2015-16	2016-17			2017-18			2018-19		
													Total	Males	Females	Total	Males	Females	Total	Males	Females
1	2	3	4	5	6	7	8	9	10	11	12	13	14	15	16	17	18	19	20	21	22
Total, all institutions	**73,910**	**71,948**	**76,734**	**79,707**	**87,655**	**94,582**	**96,129**	**99,161**	**100,852**	**99,524**	**97,957**	**95,140**	**94,789**	**46,715**	**48,074**	**94,860**	**46,712**	**48,148**	**95,681**	**45,985**	**49,696**
Dentistry (D.D.S. or D.M.D.)	5,046	3,699	3,697	4,391	4,389	5,062	5,071	5,109	5,219	5,407	5,816	5,951	6,388	3,328	3,060	6,267	3,164	3,103	6,321	3,118	3,203
Medicine (M.D.)	15,938	15,043	15,341	15,403	15,455	16,356	16,863	16,927	17,264	17,604	18,302	18,409	18,698	9,834	8,864	19,142	10,049	9,093	19,423	10,069	9,354
Optometry (O.D.)	1,029	1,115	1,231	1,289	1,198	1,335	1,322	1,361	1,521	1,523	1,511	1,631	1,630	547	1,083	1,623	531	1,092	1,685	526	1,159
Osteopathic medicine (D.O.)	1,547	1,459	1,895	2,450	2,718	3,890	4,141	4,336	4,691	4,991	5,355	5,466	6,046	3,287	2,759	6,392	3,611	2,781	6,700	3,699	3,001
Pharmacy (Pharm.D.)	903	1,244	2,555	6,324	9,292	11,873	12,271	12,943	13,374	13,921	14,310	14,734	14,855	5,659	9,196	14,929	5,631	9,298	14,875	5,592	9,283
Podiatry (Pod.D. or D.P.) or podiatric medicine (D.P.M.)	612	589	650	528	347	491	543	535	471	567	574	544	601	364	237	543	341	202	579	352	227
Veterinary medicine (D.V.M.)	2,270	2,032	2,109	2,248	2,370	2,478	2,564	2,616	2,610	2,686	2,815	2,859	2,991	596	2,395	3,169	632	2,537	3,231	624	2,607
Chiropractic (D.C. or D.C.M.)	3,395	2,640	3,379	3,796	2,564	2,601	2,694	2,496	2,219	2,420	2,544	2,417	2,521	1,463	1,058	2,503	1,436	1,067	2,608	1,475	1,133
Law (LL.B. or J.D.)	35,844	37,945	39,828	37,904	43,440	44,346	44,421	46,445	46,811	43,772	40,024	36,798	34,894	17,579	17,315	34,128	17,161	16,967	34,133	16,512	17,621
Theology (M. Div., M.H.L./Rav., B.D., or Ord.)	7,283	5,695	5,879	5,026	5,666	5,825	5,981	6,094	6,399	6,339	6,300	5,950	5,830	3,977	1,853	5,842	4,086	1,756	5,774	3,951	1,823
Other[1]	43	487	170	348	216	325	258	299	273	294	406	381	335	81	254	322	70	252	352	67	285
Total, public institutions	**29,568**	**29,554**	**29,882**	**32,633**	**36,269**	**38,132**	**39,071**	**39,776**	**39,774**	**40,375**	**40,145**	**39,643**	**39,650**	**19,059**	**20,591**	**39,899**	**19,068**	**20,831**	**40,586**	**19,007**	**21,579**
Dentistry (D.D.S. or D.M.D.)	2,827	2,308	2,198	2,477	2,669	2,984	3,008	3,053	2,972	3,187	3,336	3,307	3,402	1,749	1,653	3,441	1,718	1,723	3,426	1,704	1,722
Medicine (M.D.)	9,991	9,364	9,370	9,408	9,650	10,043	10,577	10,626	10,654	11,075	11,653	11,696	11,899	6,398	5,501	12,238	6,557	5,681	12,482	6,555	5,927
Optometry (O.D.)	441	477	499	497	462	507	515	508	520	514	513	527	504	163	341	536	187	349	551	166	385
Osteopathic medicine (D.O.)	486	493	528	562	585	817	856	841	854	1,025	1,054	1,102	1,090	588	502	1,111	624	487	1,201	655	546
Pharmacy (Pharm.D.)	473	808	1,557	3,876	5,523	6,587	6,888	6,919	6,897	6,933	7,057	7,198	7,345	2,803	4,542	7,223	2,735	4,488	7,428	2,912	4,516
Podiatry (Pod.D. or D.P.) or podiatric medicine (D.P.M.)	0	0	0	84	65	85	87	204	105	202	186	158	197	117	80	191	116	75	193	123	70
Veterinary medicine (D.V.M.)	1,931	1,814	1,889	2,017	2,048	2,048	2,134	2,168	2,184	2,251	2,332	2,391	2,490	507	1,983	2,511	497	2,014	2,571	503	2,068
Chiropractic (D.C. or D.C.M.)	0	0	0	0	0	0	0	0	0	0	0	0	0	0	0	0	0	0	0	0	0
Law (LL.B. or J.D.)	13,419	14,290	13,841	13,712	15,267	15,061	15,006	15,457	15,588	15,188	14,014	13,264	12,723	6,734	5,989	12,648	6,634	6,014	12,734	6,389	6,345
Theology (M. Div., M.H.L./Rav., B.D., or Ord.)	0	0	0	0	0	0	0	0	0	0	0	0	0	0	0	0	0	0	0	0	0
Other[1]	0	0	0	0	0	0	0	0	0	0	0	0	0	0	0	0	0	0	0	0	0
Total, private institutions	**44,342**	**42,394**	**46,852**	**47,074**	**51,386**	**56,450**	**57,058**	**59,385**	**61,078**	**59,149**	**57,812**	**55,497**	**55,139**	**27,656**	**27,483**	**54,961**	**27,644**	**27,317**	**55,095**	**26,978**	**28,117**
Dentistry (D.D.S. or D.M.D.)	2,219	1,391	1,499	1,914	1,720	2,078	2,063	2,056	2,247	2,220	2,480	2,644	2,986	1,579	1,407	2,826	1,446	1,380	2,895	1,414	1,481
Medicine (M.D.)	5,947	5,679	5,971	5,995	5,805	6,313	6,286	6,301	6,610	6,529	6,649	6,713	6,799	3,436	3,363	6,904	3,492	3,412	6,941	3,514	3,427
Optometry (O.D.)	588	638	732	792	736	828	807	853	1,001	1,009	998	1,104	1,126	384	742	1,087	344	743	1,134	360	774
Osteopathic medicine (D.O.)	1,061	966	1,367	1,888	2,133	3,073	3,285	3,495	3,837	3,966	4,301	4,364	4,956	2,699	2,257	5,281	2,987	2,294	5,499	3,044	2,455
Pharmacy (Pharm.D.)	430	436	998	2,448	3,769	5,286	5,383	6,024	6,477	6,988	7,253	7,536	7,510	2,856	4,654	7,706	2,896	4,810	7,447	2,680	4,767
Podiatry (Pod.D. or D.P.) or podiatric medicine (D.P.M.)	612	589	650	444	282	406	456	331	366	365	388	386	404	247	157	352	225	127	386	229	157
Veterinary medicine (D.V.M.)	339	218	220	231	322	430	430	448	426	435	483	468	501	89	412	658	135	523	660	121	539
Chiropractic (D.C. or D.C.M.)	3,395	2,640	3,379	3,796	2,564	2,601	2,694	2,496	2,219	2,420	2,544	2,417	2,521	1,463	1,058	2,503	1,436	1,067	2,608	1,475	1,133
Law (LL.B. or J.D.)	22,425	23,655	25,987	24,192	28,173	29,285	29,415	30,988	31,223	28,584	26,010	23,534	22,171	10,845	11,326	21,480	10,527	10,953	21,399	10,123	11,276
Theology (M. Div., M.H.L./Rav., B.D., or Ord.)	7,283	5,695	5,879	5,026	5,666	5,825	5,981	6,094	6,399	6,339	6,300	5,950	5,830	3,977	1,853	5,842	4,086	1,756	5,774	3,951	1,823
Other[1]	43	487	170	348	216	325	258	299	273	294	406	381	335	81	254	322	70	252	352	67	285

[1] Includes naturopathic medicine and degrees that were not classified by field of study by the reporting institution.

NOTE: Data in this table represent the 50 states and the District of Columbia. Data are for postsecondary institutions participating in Title IV federal financial aid programs. Includes degrees that require at least 6 years of college work for completion (including at least 2 years of preprofessional training). Data in this table are based on the 2010 Classification of Instructional Programs. Some data have been revised from previously published figures.

SOURCE: U.S. Department of Education, National Center for Education Statistics, Higher Education General Information Survey (HEGIS), "Degrees and Other Formal Awards Conferred," 1985-86; Integrated Postsecondary Education Data System (IPEDS), "Completions Survey" (IPEDS-C:91-99); and IPEDS Fall 2000 through Fall 2019, Completions component. (This table was prepared July 2020.)

Table 324.55. Degrees conferred by postsecondary institutions in selected professional fields, by race/ethnicity and field of study: 2016-17 and 2017-18

Field of study	2016-17										2017-18									
					Asian/Pacific Islander										Asian/Pacific Islander					
	Total	White	Black	His-panic	Total	Asian	Pacific Islander	American Indian/ Alaska Native	Two or more races	Non-resi-dent alien	Total	White	Black	His-panic	Total	Asian	Pacific Islander	American Indian/ Alaska Native	Two or more races	Non-resi-dent alien
1	2	3	4	5	6	7	8	9	10	11	12	13	14	15	16	17	18	19	20	21
All fields, total	**94,789**	**59,679**	**7,257**	**7,428**	**14,620**	**14,435**	**185**	**408**	**2,467**	**2,930**	**95,034**	**58,917**	**7,406**	**7,852**	**14,760**	**14,601**	**159**	**373**	**2,633**	**3,093**
Dentistry (D.D.S. or D.M.D.)	6,388	3,446	300	505	1,477	1,463	14	17	161	482	6,441	3,445	289	503	1,543	1,536	7	24	160	477
Medicine (M.D.)	18,698	11,229	1,156	1,437	4,128	4,102	26	57	484	207	19,142	11,392	1,208	1,491	4,235	4,209	26	45	524	247
Optometry (O.D.)	1,630	910	45	76	407	404	3	7	50	135	1,623	881	43	69	431	429	2	8	50	141
Osteopathic medicine (D.O.)	6,046	4,071	182	248	1,250	1,236	14	14	206	75	6,392	4,179	172	318	1,373	1,360	13	24	251	75
Pharmacy (Pharm.D.)	14,855	8,178	1,238	781	3,873	3,837	36	36	350	399	14,929	7,964	1,320	839	3,939	3,908	31	35	409	423
Podiatry (Pod.D. or D.P.) or podiatric medicine (D.P.M.)	601	366	34	30	144	142	2	0	15	12	543	319	25	32	141	139	2	4	15	7
Veterinary medicine (D.V.M.)	2,991	2,454	81	184	161	161	0	14	79	18	3,169	2,638	84	195	144	144	0	10	83	15
Chiropractic (D.C. or D.C.M.)	2,521	1,872	113	183	187	176	11	14	39	113	2,503	1,799	136	201	178	171	7	21	46	122
Law (LL.B. or J.D.)	34,894	23,376	2,939	3,682	2,580	2,526	54	226	983	1,108	34,128	22,531	2,999	3,882	2,357	2,307	50	182	974	1,203
Theology (M.Div., M.H.L./Rav., B.D., or Ord.)	5,830	3,566	1,146	275	383	373	10	22	81	357	5,842	3,542	1,119	301	386	373	13	18	107	369
Other[1]	335	211	23	27	30	15	15	1	19	24	322	227	11	21	33	25	8	2	14	14

[1] Includes naturopathic medicine and degrees that were not classified by field of study by the reporting institution.

NOTE: Data are for postsecondary institutions participating in Title IV federal financial aid programs. Includes degrees that require at least 6 years of college work for completion (including at least 2 years of preprofessional training). Race categories exclude persons of Hispanic ethnicity. Reported racial/ethnic distributions of students by level of degree, field of degree, and sex were used to estimate race/ethnicity for students whose race/ethnicity was not reported. Some data have been revised from previously published figures.

SOURCE: U.S. Department of Education, National Center for Education Statistics, Integrated Postsecondary Education Data System (IPEDS), Fall 2017 and Fall 2018, Completions component. (This table was prepared April 2020.)

Table 324.80. Statistical profile of persons receiving doctor's degrees, by field of study and selected characteristics: 2016-17 and 2017-18

Selected characteristic	All fields, 2016-17	Field of study, 2017-18								
		All fields	Educa-tion	Engineer-ing	Human-ities	Life sciences[1]	Physical sciences and earth sciences	Mathemat-ics and computer sciences	Social sciences and psychol-ogy	Other fields
1	2	3	4	5	6	7	8	9	10	11
Number of doctor's degrees conferred	54,664	55,195	4,834	10,183	5,145	12,780	6,335	4,030	8,899	2,989
Sex (percent)[2]										
Male	53.3	54.0	30.9	75.9	49.9	44.3	66.5	75.5	40.9	48.6
Female	46.6	46.0	69.0	24.1	50.0	55.7	33.4	24.4	59.1	51.3
Race/ethnicity (percent)[3]										
White	69.5	70.5	67.3	67.1	76.3	69.4	77.1	70.9	69.4	67.0
Black	6.7	6.9	14.5	4.0	4.9	6.5	2.7	3.7	7.8	12.7
Hispanic	7.1	7.3	7.5	6.6	8.4	7.3	5.9	5.4	8.8	4.6
Asian	9.8	9.3	5.1	16.1	4.9	11.0	9.4	13.3	7.1	9.3
American Indian/Alaska Native	0.3	0.3	0.6	0.2	0.3	0.2	0.2	0.2	0.5	0.2
Two or more races	2.8	3.1	2.9	3.1	2.7	3.2	2.7	3.3	3.8	2.7
Other and unknown[4]	3.7	2.5	2.2	3.0	2.5	2.3	2.0	3.2	2.6	3.4
Citizenship (percent)										
U.S. citizen/permanent resident	65.5	64.1	83.4	41.4	80.7	70.7	59.5	43.2	75.3	58.5
Temporary visa holder	29.9	31.9	12.7	54.8	14.3	26.3	37.5	52.9	19.9	34.5
Unknown	4.7	4.0	3.9	3.8	5.0	2.9	3.0	4.0	4.8	7.1
Median age at doctorate (years)	31.6	31.4	38.2	29.9	34.3	30.9	29.5	30.2	32.3	34.7
Percent with bachelor's degree in same field as doctorate	54.7	56.4	23.9	77.9	54.2	51.3	70.0	64.1	52.1	36.0
Median time lapse to doctorate (years)										
Since bachelor's degree completion	8.8	8.6	14.7	7.3	11.0	8.2	7.0	7.6	9.3	11.2
Since starting graduate school	7.5	7.3	11.9	6.7	9.4	6.8	6.3	6.8	7.8	9.2
Postdoctoral plans (percent)[5]										
Definite postdoctoral study[6]	25.8	26.3	6.4	22.4	12.1	38.9	39.1	24.0	28.9	6.9
Fellowship or research associateship	24.3	24.7	5.7	21.4	11.2	36.6	38.0	23.1	26.1	6.4
Other[7]	1.5	1.5	0.7	1.0	0.8	2.3	1.1	0.9	2.8	0.5
Definite postdoctoral employment[8]	40.2	41.9	64.6	43.1	47.1	26.5	27.9	51.0	44.9	69.8
Academe[9]	19.4	18.8	36.6	6.9	35.2	10.9	5.6	16.6	25.1	53.2
Government	3.1	3.0	3.1	3.4	1.4	2.7	2.0	2.2	4.8	3.5
Industry, business	13.2	14.7	4.1	30.5	3.2	9.3	18.3	30.1	8.9	7.8
Nonprofit organization	2.5	2.6	5.0	1.4	4.0	2.6	0.9	1.2	3.7	2.8
Other and unknown[10]	2.0	2.8	15.8	0.9	3.3	0.9	1.1	0.8	2.3	2.5
Seeking employment or study	30.3	28.8	26.2	32.3	37.6	29.0	30.8	23.4	24.0	21.3
Other and unknown[11]	3.6	3.1	2.9	2.2	3.3	5.6	2.2	1.6	2.2	2.1
Primary work activity after doctorate (percent)[12]										
Research and development	41.6	44.1	12.6	74.2	8.9	46.0	67.6	65.1	36.1	37.9
Teaching	32.9	31.6	42.7	9.0	71.0	25.5	16.2	22.8	34.8	44.4
Management or administration	10.4	10.2	32.7	3.9	9.7	8.7	3.1	2.4	8.3	9.7
Professional services	10.0	13.8	11.7	12.4	10.1	19.0	12.3	9.5	20.4	7.9
Other	5.1	0.4	0.2	0.5	0.3	0.8	0.7	0.2	0.3	0.1
Location after doctorate (percent)[13]										
New England	8.1	8.7	4.1	8.6	9.0	10.8	9.9	7.7	8.9	6.4
Middle Atlantic	12.3	12.5	11.0	10.1	16.7	12.4	11.7	14.1	13.5	13.0
East North Central	11.8	11.3	14.1	10.9	12.0	10.5	9.9	10.8	11.6	13.7
West North Central	4.9	4.9	6.9	3.4	5.1	6.4	3.3	3.1	5.1	6.0
South Atlantic	14.7	15.8	20.1	12.4	15.5	18.2	13.1	11.9	17.9	15.8
East South Central	3.4	3.5	7.6	2.5	4.4	3.9	1.9	1.9	2.6	4.5
West South Central	6.8	7.2	10.6	7.2	7.8	6.3	6.4	5.2	7.1	9.0
Mountain	5.6	5.8	8.3	6.2	4.7	5.2	7.1	3.6	5.5	5.5
Pacific and insular	20.6	19.4	10.3	28.4	13.1	17.8	24.5	29.1	14.7	10.5
Foreign	11.1	10.2	6.6	9.8	11.1	7.5	11.9	12.0	12.5	14.6
Region unknown	#	#	#	0.1	0.1	#	#	0.0	0.1	0.1

#Rounds to zero.

[1] Includes agricultural sciences and natural resources; biological and biomedical sciences; and health sciences.

[2] Distribution based on respondents reporting sex data.

[3] Distribution based on U.S. citizens and permanent residents.

[4] Includes Pacific Islanders and persons whose race was not reported.

[5] Percentages are based on only those doctorate recipients who responded to questions about postgraduation plans.

[6] Excludes doctorate recipients who indicated plans for another full-time degree program. Percentages are based on doctorate recipients reporting other definite

postgraduation plans for study.

[7] Includes respondents who indicated definite postgraduation study plans for traineeship, internship/clinical residency, or other study.

[8] Percentages are based on only those doctorate recipients who indicated definite postgraduation plans for employment and who indicated the sector of employment.

[9] Includes 2-year, 4-year, and foreign colleges and universities, and medical schools.

[10] "Other" is mainly composed of elementary and secondary schools.

[11] Includes doctorate recipients who indicated that they did not plan to work or study, those who indicated some other type of postgraduation plans, and those who indicated definite plans for another full-time degree program.

[12] Percentages are based on only those doctorate recipients who indicated definite postgraduation plans for employment and who indicated their primary work activity.

[13] Percentages are based on only those doctorate recipients who indicated definite postgraduation plans and type of plans.

NOTE: The above classification of degrees by field differs somewhat from that in most publications by the National Center for Education Statistics (NCES). One major difference is that history is included under humanities rather than social sciences. Includes Ph.D., Ed.D., and comparable degrees at the doctoral level. Includes only graduates of research programs, which typically require the preparation and defense of a dissertation based on original research, or the planning and execution of an original project demonstrating substantial artistic or scholarly achievement. Excludes nonresearch professional practice doctor's degrees (e.g., M.D., D.D.S., and J.D.) that are conferred upon completion of a program providing the knowledge and skills for the recognition, credential, or license required for professional practice in such fields as health and theology. The number of doctor's degrees in this table differs from that reported in the NCES Integrated Postsecondary Education Data System (IPEDS), which includes both research and nonresearch degrees. Race categories exclude persons of Hispanic ethnicity. Detail may not sum to totals because of rounding.

SOURCE: Doctorate Recipients From U.S. Universities: 2017 and 2018, Survey of Earned Doctorates, National Science Foundation, National Institutes of Health, U.S. Department of Education, National Endowment for the Humanities, U.S. Department of Agriculture, and the National Aeronautics and Space Administration. (This table was prepared June 2020.)

Table 324.90. Doctor's degrees conferred by the 60 institutions conferring the most doctor's degrees, by rank order: 2008-09 through 2017-18

Institution	Rank order	Total, 2008-09 to 2017-18	2008-09	2009-10	2010-11	2011-12	2012-13	2013-14	2014-15	2015-16	2016-17	2017-18
1	2	3	4	5	6	7	8	9	10	11	12	13
United States, all institutions	†	**1,721,924**	**154,564**	**158,590**	**163,827**	**170,217**	**175,026**	**177,587**	**178,548**	**178,134**	**181,357**	**184,074**
Total, 60 institutions conferring most doctorates	†	**634,572**	**59,732**	**60,529**	**62,328**	**63,253**	**64,760**	**64,826**	**64,434**	**63,971**	**65,197**	**65,542**
University of Florida	1	20,040	2,028	2,127	2,127	1,954	1,964	1,994	1,914	1,941	2,008	1,983
Nova Southeastern University	2	17,962	1,732	1,806	1,699	1,800	1,729	1,739	1,802	1,804	1,974	1,877
University of Minnesota, Twin Cities	3	17,139	1,594	1,618	1,692	1,680	1,826	1,794	1,761	1,822	1,686	1,666
Ohio State University, Main Campus	4	16,329	1,617	1,596	1,658	1,628	1,661	1,604	1,693	1,609	1,601	1,662
University of Southern California	5	15,823	1,571	1,459	1,474	1,518	1,554	1,481	1,538	1,593	1,803	1,832
University of Michigan, Ann Arbor	6	15,712	1,576	1,534	1,550	1,566	1,647	1,636	1,606	1,526	1,515	1,556
Harvard University	7	14,865	1,418	1,401	1,450	1,474	1,464	1,535	1,534	1,512	1,528	1,549
New York University	8	14,735	1,419	1,444	1,413	1,481	1,494	1,507	1,484	1,548	1,496	1,449
University of Wisconsin, Madison	9	14,525	1,430	1,355	1,417	1,514	1,440	1,497	1,502	1,458	1,432	1,480
University of California, Los Angeles	10	13,717	1,382	1,358	1,330	1,326	1,393	1,432	1,384	1,373	1,418	1,321
Rutgers University, New Brunswick[2]	11	13,609	1,382	1,401	1,424	1,430	1,495	1,265	1,253	1,247	1,322	1,390
University of Texas at Austin	12	13,480	1,379	1,382	1,309	1,372	1,351	1,378	1,379	1,386	1,284	1,260
Texas A&M University, College Station[3]	13	13,460	1,107	1,206	1,256	1,324	1,344	1,443	1,488	1,423	1,443	1,426
Columbia University in the City of New York	14	13,339	1,281	1,295	1,291	1,329	1,382	1,397	1,287	1,289	1,331	1,457
University of Washington, Seattle Campus	15	12,980	1,176	1,224	1,251	1,273	1,329	1,328	1,395	1,296	1,337	1,371
University of California, Berkeley	16	12,409	1,216	1,245	1,292	1,264	1,304	1,288	1,165	1,211	1,182	1,242
University of Pennsylvania	17	12,204	1,190	1,212	1,212	1,189	1,207	1,244	1,244	1,200	1,283	1,223
University of North Carolina at Chapel Hill	18	11,960	1,101	1,155	1,172	1,179	1,203	1,229	1,219	1,245	1,249	1,208
Temple University	19	11,603	1,169	1,144	1,246	1,154	1,191	1,146	1,115	1,138	1,183	1,117
Boston University	20	11,344	1,179	1,097	1,111	1,177	1,175	1,107	1,116	1,216	1,066	1,100
University of Illinois at Urbana-Champaign	21	11,076	1,081	1,066	1,106	1,210	1,159	1,118	1,134	1,015	1,095	1,092
University of Tennessee, Knoxville[4]	22	10,943	994	1,024	1,002	1,110	1,104	1,054	1,141	1,197	1,150	1,167
University of Pittsburgh, Pittsburgh Campus	23	10,649	1,022	944	1,113	1,059	1,086	1,135	1,090	1,087	1,073	1,040
George Washington University	24	10,580	1,011	1,005	974	1,050	1,071	1,091	959	1,105	1,165	1,149
Michigan State University	25	10,552	876	921	951	962	993	1,172	1,204	1,152	1,185	1,136
Stanford University	26	10,042	920	978	1,053	1,019	1,052	1,003	961	1,032	1,023	1,001
University of Illinois at Chicago	27	9,763	851	965	914	912	974	969	990	1,051	1,062	1,075
University at Buffalo	28	9,737	964	919	948	913	992	957	1,028	967	946	1,103
Capella University	29	9,640	700	841	819	810	889	1,189	1,159	1,260	1,191	782
Georgetown University	30	9,601	967	950	936	934	973	955	975	968	983	960
University of Iowa	31	9,502	937	920	949	948	1,045	1,000	943	902	922	936
Northwestern University	32	9,452	872	891	927	898	1,009	986	983	969	946	971
University of California, Davis	33	9,397	894	891	927	1,002	1,009	901	978	888	919	988
Duke University	34	9,360	718	820	887	1,010	1,100	1,140	801	862	1,021	1,001
Purdue University, Main Campus	35	9,324	882	845	924	880	926	965	973	959	992	978
University of Georgia	36	9,202	897	854	889	903	901	948	892	967	967	984
Walden University	37	9,038	344	503	619	682	805	1,038	964	1,233	1,300	1,550
University of Arizona	38	8,781	824	824	813	850	854	870	939	907	936	964
University of Virginia, Main Campus	39	8,745	907	861	933	904	908	919	891	797	809	816
University of Kansas	40	8,721	766	819	856	821	870	847	953	889	938	962
University of Maryland, Baltimore	41	8,537	775	835	875	900	889	875	889	797	828	874
University of Miami	42	8,314	758	860	803	911	874	815	886	799	755	853
University of Kentucky	43	8,287	719	734	783	888	864	870	808	863	892	866
University of Houston	44	7,984	786	757	831	798	796	755	779	811	809	862
Western Michigan University-Thomas M. Cooley Law School	45	7,948	981	955	1,039	1,080	1,143	871	688	462	352	377
Wayne State University	46	7,934	772	717	856	807	777	807	810	767	795	826
Cornell University[5]	47	7,855	785	779	782	775	771	781	765	778	804	835
Indiana University-Purdue University, Indianapolis	48	7,760	687	751	755	771	755	772	810	805	826	828
Florida State University	49	7,613	680	683	818	850	736	813	817	716	746	754
Washington University in St. Louis	50	7,605	760	737	805	783	806	771	751	694	791	707
Pennsylvania State University, Main Campus	51	7,604	703	718	736	755	800	761	775	755	809	792
A.T. Still University of Health Sciences	52	7,460	730	815	810	755	732	671	674	701	763	809
University of Connecticut	53	7,415	687	746	720	773	720	762	760	745	802	700
Indiana University, Bloomington	54	7,368	729	718	693	748	771	761	793	728	712	715
Lake Erie College of Osteopathic Medicine	55	7,314	499	484	595	632	720	789	817	891	933	954
Yale University	56	7,304	685	752	686	712	758	743	762	710	709	787
University of South Carolina, Columbia	57	7,300	703	643	703	674	748	719	751	748	761	850
Virginia Commonwealth University	58	7,239	622	687	730	748	758	749	714	718	743	770
University of Utah	59	7,222	684	632	723	718	726	711	767	715	790	756
University of Missouri, Columbia	60	7,169	613	626	671	666	743	729	781	724	813	803

†Not applicable.

[1] Institutions are ranked by the total number of doctor's degrees conferred during the 10-year period from July 1, 2008, to June 30, 2018.

[2] Includes degrees conferred by the University of Medicine and Dentistry of New Jersey, which merged with Rutgers University in 2013-14.

[3] Includes law degrees conferred by Texas Wesleyan University, which was acquired by Texas A&M in 2013, as well as degrees in all fields from Texas A&M Health Sciences Center.

[4] Includes degrees conferred by the University of Tennessee Health Sciences Center, which in 2014-15 began reporting separately from the University of Tennessee, Knoxville.

[5] Includes degrees conferred by the Endowed and Statutory Colleges.

NOTE: Includes Ph.D., Ed.D., and comparable degrees at the doctoral level, as well as such degrees as M.D., D.D.S., and law degrees that were classified as first-professional degrees prior to 2010-11. Some data have been revised from previously published figures.

SOURCE: U.S. Department of Education, National Center for Education Statistics, Integrated Postsecondary Education Data System (IPEDS), Fall 2009 through Fall 2018, Completions component. (This table was prepared May 2020.)

Table 325.35. Degrees in computer and information sciences conferred by postsecondary institutions, by level of degree and sex of student: 1970-71 through 2017-18

Year	Bachelor's degrees					Master's degrees			Doctor's degrees		
	Total										
	Number	Annual percent change	Males	Females	Females as a percent of total	Total	Males	Females	Total	Males	Females
1	2	3	4	5	6	7	8	9	10	11	12
1970-71	2,388	†	2,064	324	13.6	1,588	1,424	164	128	125	3
1971-72	3,402	42.5	2,941	461	13.6	1,977	1,752	225	167	155	12
1972-73	4,304	26.5	3,664	640	14.9	2,113	1,888	225	196	181	15
1973-74	4,756	10.5	3,976	780	16.4	2,276	1,983	293	198	189	9
1974-75	5,033	5.8	4,080	953	18.9	2,299	1,961	338	213	199	14
1975-76	5,652	12.3	4,534	1,118	19.8	2,603	2,226	377	244	221	23
1976-77	6,407	13.4	4,876	1,531	23.9	2,798	2,332	466	216	197	19
1977-78	7,201	12.4	5,349	1,852	25.7	3,038	2,471	567	196	181	15
1978-79	8,719	21.1	6,272	2,447	28.1	3,055	2,480	575	236	206	30
1979-80	11,154	27.9	7,782	3,372	30.2	3,647	2,883	764	240	213	27
1980-81	15,121	35.6	10,202	4,919	32.5	4,218	3,247	971	252	227	25
1981-82	20,267	34.0	13,218	7,049	34.8	4,935	3,625	1,310	251	230	21
1982-83	24,565	21.2	15,641	8,924	36.3	5,321	3,813	1,508	262	228	34
1983-84	32,439	32.1	20,416	12,023	37.1	6,190	4,379	1,811	251	225	26
1984-85	39,121	20.6	24,737	14,384	36.8	7,101	5,064	2,037	248	223	25
1985-86	42,337	8.2	27,208	15,129	35.7	8,070	5,658	2,412	344	299	45
1986-87	39,767	-6.1	25,962	13,805	34.7	8,481	5,985	2,496	374	322	52
1987-88	34,651	-12.9	23,414	11,237	32.4	9,197	6,726	2,471	428	380	48
1988-89	30,560	-11.8	21,143	9,417	30.8	9,414	6,775	2,639	551	466	85
1989-90	27,347	-10.5	19,159	8,188	29.9	9,677	6,960	2,717	627	534	93
1990-91	25,159	-8.0	17,771	7,388	29.4	9,324	6,563	2,761	676	584	92
1991-92	24,821	-1.3	17,685	7,136	28.7	9,655	6,980	2,675	772	669	103
1992-93	24,519	-1.2	17,606	6,913	28.2	10,353	7,557	2,796	805	689	116
1993-94	24,527	#	17,528	6,999	28.5	10,568	7,836	2,732	810	685	125
1994-95	24,737	0.9	17,684	7,053	28.5	10,595	7,805	2,790	887	726	161
1995-96	24,506	-0.9	17,757	6,749	27.5	10,579	7,729	2,850	869	743	126
1996-97	25,422	3.7	18,527	6,895	27.1	10,513	7,526	2,987	857	721	136
1997-98	27,829	9.5	20,372	7,457	26.8	11,765	8,343	3,422	858	718	140
1998-99	30,552	9.8	22,289	8,263	27.0	12,843	8,866	3,977	806	656	150
1999-2000	37,788	23.7	27,185	10,603	28.1	14,990	9,978	5,012	779	648	131
2000-01	44,142	16.8	31,923	12,219	27.7	16,911	11,195	5,716	768	632	136
2001-02	50,365	14.1	36,462	13,903	27.6	17,173	11,447	5,726	752	581	171
2002-03	57,433	14.0	41,950	15,483	27.0	19,509	13,267	6,242	816	648	168
2003-04	59,488	3.6	44,585	14,903	25.1	20,143	13,868	6,275	909	709	200
2004-05	54,111	-9.0	42,125	11,986	22.2	18,416	13,136	5,280	1,119	905	214
2005-06	47,702	-11.8	37,905	9,797	20.5	17,195	12,579	4,616	1,416	1,109	307
2006-07	42,164	-11.6	34,338	7,826	18.6	16,232	11,985	4,247	1,595	1,267	328
2007-08	38,523	-8.6	31,731	6,792	17.6	17,096	12,516	4,580	1,697	1,322	375
2008-09	37,992	-1.4	31,213	6,779	17.8	17,907	13,063	4,844	1,580	1,226	354
2009-10	39,593	4.2	32,414	7,179	18.1	17,955	13,019	4,936	1,599	1,250	349
2010-11	43,066	8.8	35,477	7,589	17.6	19,516	14,010	5,506	1,588	1,267	321
2011-12	47,406	10.1	38,796	8,610	18.2	20,925	15,132	5,793	1,698	1,332	366
2012-13	50,961	7.5	41,874	9,087	17.8	22,782	16,539	6,243	1,834	1,480	354
2013-14	55,271	8.5	45,320	9,951	18.0	24,514	17,472	7,042	1,982	1,566	416
2014-15	59,586	7.8	48,844	10,742	18.0	31,475	21,893	9,582	1,998	1,548	450
2015-16	64,402	8.1	52,330	12,072	18.7	40,130	27,788	12,342	1,989	1,591	398
2016-17	71,416	10.9	57,763	13,653	19.1	46,553	32,172	14,381	1,982	1,538	444
2017-18	79,598	11.5	63,704	15,894	20.0	46,468	31,397	15,071	2,017	1,580	437
Percent change											
2007-08 to 2012-13	32.3	†	32.0	33.8	†	33.3	32.1	36.3	8.1	12.0	-5.6
2012-13 to 2017-18	56.2	†	52.1	74.9	†	104.0	89.8	141.4	10.0	6.8	23.4

†Not applicable.

#Rounds to zero.

NOTE: Data are for postsecondary institutions participating in Title IV federal financial aid programs. Some data have been revised from previously published figures.

SOURCE: U.S. Department of Education, National Center for Education Statistics, Higher Education General Information Survey (HEGIS), "Degrees and Other Formal Awards Conferred" surveys, 1970-71 through 1985-86; Integrated Postsecondary Education Data System (IPEDS), "Completions Survey" (IPEDS-C:87-99); and IPEDS Fall 2000 through Fall 2018, Completions component. (This table was prepared September 2019.)

Table 325.45. Degrees in engineering and engineering technologies conferred by postsecondary institutions, by level of degree and sex of student: Selected years, 1949-50 through 2017-18

Year	Bachelor's degrees					Master's degrees			Doctor's degrees		
	Total										
	Number	Annual percent change	Males	Females	Females as a percent of total	Total	Males	Females	Total	Males	Females
1	2	3	4	5	6	7	8	9	10	11	12
1949-50	52,246	†	52,071	175	0.3	4,496	4,481	15	417	416	1
1959-60	37,679	†	37,537	142	0.4	7,159	7,133	26	786	783	3
1969-70	44,479	†	44,149	330	0.7	15,593	15,421	172	3,681	3,657	24
1970-71	50,182	12.8	49,775	407	0.8	16,947	16,734	213	3,688	3,663	25
1971-72	51,258	2.1	50,726	532	1.0	17,299	17,009	290	3,708	3,685	23
1972-73	51,384	0.2	50,766	618	1.2	16,988	16,694	294	3,513	3,459	54
1973-74	50,412	-1.9	49,611	801	1.6	15,851	15,470	381	3,374	3,318	56
1974-75	47,131	-6.5	46,105	1,026	2.2	15,837	15,426	411	3,181	3,113	68
1975-76	46,676	-1.0	45,184	1,492	3.2	16,800	16,174	626	2,874	2,805	69
1976-77	49,482	6.0	47,238	2,244	4.5	16,659	15,891	768	2,622	2,547	75
1977-78	56,150	13.5	52,353	3,797	6.8	16,887	15,940	947	2,483	2,424	59
1978-79	62,898	12.0	57,603	5,295	8.4	16,012	14,971	1,041	2,545	2,459	86
1979-80	69,387	10.3	62,877	6,510	9.4	16,765	15,535	1,230	2,546	2,447	99
1980-81	75,355	8.6	67,573	7,782	10.3	17,216	15,761	1,455	2,608	2,499	109
1981-82	80,632	7.0	71,305	9,327	11.6	18,475	16,747	1,728	2,676	2,532	144
1982-83	89,811	11.4	78,673	11,138	12.4	19,949	18,038	1,911	2,871	2,742	129
1983-84	95,295	6.1	82,841	12,454	13.1	21,197	18,916	2,281	3,032	2,864	168
1984-85	97,099	1.9	83,991	13,108	13.5	22,124	19,688	2,436	3,269	3,055	214
1985-86	97,122	#	84,050	13,072	13.5	22,146	19,545	2,601	3,456	3,220	236
1986-87	93,560	-3.7	80,543	13,017	13.9	23,101	20,137	2,964	3,854	3,585	269
1987-88	89,406	-4.4	76,886	12,520	14.0	23,839	20,815	3,024	4,237	3,941	296
1988-89	85,982	-3.8	74,020	11,962	13.9	25,066	21,731	3,335	4,572	4,160	412
1989-90	82,480	-4.1	70,859	11,621	14.1	25,294	21,753	3,541	5,030	4,576	454
1990-91	79,751	-3.3	68,482	11,269	14.1	25,450	21,780	3,670	5,330	4,834	496
1991-92	78,036	-2.2	67,086	10,950	14.0	26,373	22,397	3,976	5,499	4,967	532
1992-93	78,619	0.7	67,214	11,405	14.5	29,103	24,721	4,382	5,870	5,300	570
1993-94	78,580	#	66,867	11,713	14.9	30,102	25,394	4,708	5,954	5,288	666
1994-95	78,483	-0.1	66,157	12,326	15.7	29,949	25,028	4,921	6,108	5,378	730
1995-96	77,997	-0.6	65,362	12,635	16.2	28,843	23,840	5,003	6,354	5,559	795
1996-97	75,659	-3.0	62,994	12,665	16.7	27,016	22,047	4,969	6,166	5,408	758
1997-98	74,557	-1.5	61,880	12,677	17.0	27,244	21,800	5,444	5,966	5,230	736
1998-99	72,796	-2.4	59,859	12,937	17.8	26,689	21,348	5,341	5,413	4,643	770
1999-2000	73,323	0.7	59,668	13,655	18.6	26,648	21,047	5,601	5,367	4,539	828
2000-01	72,869	-0.6	59,489	13,380	18.4	27,187	21,341	5,846	5,547	4,630	917
2001-02	74,588	2.4	60,417	14,171	19.0	26,987	21,212	5,775	5,181	4,285	896
2002-03	77,231	3.5	62,821	14,410	18.7	30,583	24,097	6,486	5,252	4,353	899
2003-04	78,079	1.1	63,401	14,678	18.8	35,053	27,561	7,492	5,859	4,821	1,038
2004-05	79,544	1.9	65,033	14,511	18.2	34,988	27,049	7,939	6,467	5,263	1,204
2005-06	81,406	2.3	66,866	14,540	17.9	33,386	25,565	7,821	7,318	5,848	1,470
2006-07	81,868	0.6	68,093	13,775	16.8	31,990	24,747	7,243	7,928	6,285	1,643
2007-08	83,682	2.2	69,604	14,078	16.8	34,443	26,477	7,966	7,984	6,269	1,715
2008-09	84,404	0.9	70,504	13,900	16.5	38,008	29,458	8,550	7,803	6,123	1,680
2009-10	88,735	5.1	73,838	14,897	16.8	39,391	30,554	8,837	7,773	5,986	1,787
2010-11	93,097	4.9	77,080	16,017	17.2	43,179	33,372	9,807	8,425	6,548	1,877
2011-12	98,654	6.0	81,364	17,290	17.5	45,116	34,712	10,404	8,856	6,838	2,018
2012-13	102,997	4.4	84,645	18,352	17.8	45,328	34,496	10,832	9,467	7,305	2,162
2013-14	108,976	5.8	88,941	20,035	18.4	47,343	35,791	11,552	10,117	7,820	2,297
2014-15	115,105	5.6	93,541	21,564	18.7	51,441	38,453	12,988	10,362	7,958	2,404
2015-16	123,948	7.7	99,568	24,380	19.7	57,713	43,198	14,515	10,398	7,960	2,438
2016-17	133,790	7.9	106,559	27,231	20.4	60,229	45,206	15,023	10,523	8,027	2,496
2017-18	140,683	5.2	111,171	29,512	21.0	58,968	43,627	15,341	11,029	8,331	2,698
Percent change											
2007-08 to 2012-13	23.1	†	21.6	30.4	†	31.6	30.3	36.0	18.6	16.5	26.1
2012-13 to 2017-18	36.6	†	31.3	60.8	†	30.1	26.5	41.6	16.5	14.0	24.8

†Not applicable.

#Rounds to zero.

NOTE: Data are for postsecondary institutions participating in Title IV federal financial aid programs. Includes degrees in engineering, engineering-related technologies, mechanic and repair technologies, and construction trades for 1969-70 and later years. Degrees in engineering include degrees in all areas of engineering--for example, chemical, civil, electrical, and mechanical engineering--as well as degrees in general engineering. Some data have been revised from previously published figures.

SOURCE: U.S. Department of Education, National Center for Education Statistics, Earned Degrees Conferred, 1949-50 and 1959-60; Higher Education General Information Survey (HEGIS), "Degrees and Other Formal Awards Conferred" surveys, 1969-70 through 1985-86; Integrated Postsecondary Education Data System (IPEDS), "Completions

Table 326.10. Graduation rate from first institution attended for first-time, full-time bachelor's degree-seeking students at 4-year postsecondary institutions, by race/ethnicity, time to completion, sex, control of institution, and percentage of applications accepted: Selected cohort entry years, 1996 through 2013

Time to completion, sex, control of institution, cohort entry year, and percentage of applications accepted	Total	White	Black	Hispanic	Asian/Pacific Islander			American Indian/Alaska Native	Two or more races	Non-resident alien[1]
					Total	Asian	Pacific Islander			
1	2	3	4	5	6	7	8	9	10	11
Graduating within 4 years after entry, males and females										
All 4-year institutions										
1996 entry cohort	33.7	36.3	19.5	22.8	37.5	---	---	18.8	---	41.7
2000 entry cohort	36.1	38.9	21.2	25.8	40.9	---	---	21.0	---	41.9
2002 entry cohort	36.6	39.6	20.5	26.6	43.0	---	---	20.6	---	39.1
2003 entry cohort	37.0	40.2	20.2	26.7	43.9	---	---	20.6	---	39.4
2004 entry cohort	38.0	41.3	20.5	27.9	45.0	---	---	21.8	---	43.7
2005 entry cohort	38.3	41.8	20.2	28.2	45.1	45.5	22.2	21.8	44.1	44.0
2006 entry cohort	39.1	42.7	20.6	29.3	46.0	46.4	24.2	21.9	46.6	44.1
2007 entry cohort	39.4	43.3	20.8	29.8	46.2	46.7	25.9	23.0	49.1	44.6
2008 entry cohort	39.8	43.7	21.4	30.4	47.1	47.7	26.7	23.0	46.5	46.4
2009 entry cohort	39.9	44.2	20.6	30.7	48.8	49.5	26.7	24.0	41.0	49.1
2010 entry cohort	40.7	45.4	21.2	31.7	49.6	50.2	31.0	22.7	39.6	50.1
2011 entry cohort	41.6	46.4	21.6	32.5	50.1	50.7	31.0	21.6	38.3	50.8
2012 entry cohort	43.7	48.3	23.8	34.1	52.0	52.6	31.6	24.5	39.3	51.9
2013 entry cohort	45.3	49.8	25.7	35.7	53.5	54.0	33.8	26.2	40.9	52.7
Public institutions										
1996 entry cohort	26.0	28.3	15.0	15.8	28.5	---	---	14.5	---	30.9
2000 entry cohort	29.0	31.4	17.9	18.9	33.7	---	---	16.5	---	32.7
2002 entry cohort	29.9	32.4	17.0	20.2	35.8	---	---	16.1	---	33.5
2003 entry cohort	30.7	33.5	16.5	20.7	37.5	---	---	17.0	---	33.8
2004 entry cohort	31.4	34.2	16.4	21.5	38.0	---	---	17.2	---	34.4
2005 entry cohort	32.0	35.1	16.8	22.4	38.7	39.1	16.9	17.9	28.7	33.5
2006 entry cohort	32.9	36.1	17.2	23.1	40.0	40.4	18.6	17.9	30.5	33.9
2007 entry cohort	33.5	36.9	17.4	24.0	39.8	40.2	21.3	19.5	35.9	34.4
2008 entry cohort	34.4	37.9	18.6	24.8	41.1	41.6	22.1	19.1	35.2	38.0
2009 entry cohort	34.9	38.5	18.1	25.5	42.9	43.5	23.7	19.8	31.9	41.3
2010 entry cohort	35.8	39.7	18.5	26.4	43.5	44.0	28.6	17.9	32.6	43.5
2011 entry cohort	36.9	41.2	18.9	27.3	44.6	44.9	31.1	18.7	32.8	45.0
2012 entry cohort	38.8	43.2	20.6	28.9	46.5	46.9	31.0	20.4	34.1	46.8
2013 entry cohort	40.7	45.1	22.7	30.7	48.3	48.7	31.7	22.7	35.9	47.6
Nonprofit institutions										
1996 entry cohort	48.6	51.3	29.3	39.9	57.9	---	---	33.7	---	50.4
2000 entry cohort	50.3	53.5	28.2	42.9	58.8	---	---	36.0	---	50.3
2002 entry cohort	51.5	54.5	29.3	44.4	61.9	---	---	36.9	---	55.4
2003 entry cohort	51.6	54.7	29.8	44.0	61.5	---	---	34.4	---	55.3
2004 entry cohort	52.6	55.5	30.6	46.2	62.8	---	---	39.0	---	57.4
2005 entry cohort	52.2	55.4	29.2	45.1	62.3	62.8	34.9	35.2	59.9	57.4
2006 entry cohort	52.9	56.2	29.7	47.4	62.8	63.5	37.2	38.3	62.1	56.8
2007 entry cohort	52.9	56.5	29.6	46.8	63.6	64.3	40.4	37.0	62.6	56.9
2008 entry cohort	52.8	56.4	29.7	47.2	63.4	63.9	44.8	37.0	59.3	57.2
2009 entry cohort	53.1	57.1	29.1	47.2	64.4	65.1	41.5	39.6	56.8	59.4
2010 entry cohort	53.6	58.0	29.2	48.2	64.9	65.7	40.0	37.7	55.8	58.9
2011 entry cohort	54.4	58.5	30.5	49.9	65.3	66.0	39.1	34.0	54.0	59.0
2012 entry cohort	55.3	59.4	32.0	50.1	66.7	67.6	37.5	37.9	53.4	59.1
2013 entry cohort	56.4	60.3	33.8	51.1	67.4	68.2	42.4	38.0	53.1	59.9
For-profit institutions										
1996 entry cohort	21.8	26.3	14.8	20.1	24.6	---	---	16.5	---	33.8
2000 entry cohort	23.9	28.2	19.6	26.3	40.6	---	---	26.8	---	34.5
2002 entry cohort	14.7	17.8	10.3	19.2	29.2	---	---	11.2	---	3.4
2003 entry cohort	14.8	18.2	10.4	19.5	25.5	---	---	8.4	---	4.7
2004 entry cohort	20.6	27.3	13.3	20.7	31.4	---	---	9.4	---	10.6
2005 entry cohort	20.0	27.9	11.0	19.6	31.7	33.8	15.4	15.2	24.7	15.4
2006 entry cohort	22.8	32.5	12.7	23.0	30.1	32.4	9.4	13.0	27.6	22.4
2007 entry cohort	22.5	32.6	11.7	22.7	32.0	36.3	7.2	12.6	27.2	24.4
2008 entry cohort	17.5	26.5	9.5	20.8	30.6	34.8	8.3	12.8	30.0	19.7
2009 entry cohort	13.9	21.3	7.6	18.1	29.2	35.1	7.0	10.2	17.1	20.9
2010 entry cohort	17.6	25.8	11.5	20.1	35.1	38.9	14.6	13.3	24.7	24.1
2011 entry cohort	14.5	16.9	7.9	17.5	27.8	33.3	12.0	6.6	19.3	31.6
2012 entry cohort	19.4	21.1	13.2	21.1	30.3	36.3	12.4	10.1	22.4	32.9
2013 entry cohort	19.4	20.6	13.6	21.9	31.0	35.8	14.1	11.3	27.7	40.2
Graduating within 4 years after entry, males										
All 4-year institutions										
1996 entry cohort	28.5	30.6	13.9	19.0	32.2	---	---	15.1	---	38.6
2000 entry cohort	31.1	33.4	15.3	21.7	35.6	---	---	17.1	---	39.2
2002 entry cohort	31.4	33.9	14.8	21.9	37.5	---	---	17.3	---	36.8

Time to completion, sex, control of institution, cohort entry year, and percentage of applications accepted	Total	White	Black	His-panic	Asian/Pacific Islander			American Indian/ Alaska Native	Two or more races	Non-resident alien[1]
					Total	Asian	Pacific Islander			
1	2	3	4	5	6	7	8	9	10	11
2003 entry cohort	32.2	34.8	14.7	22.5	39.0	---	---	17.7	---	37.7
2004 entry cohort	33.0	35.7	15.1	23.3	39.9	---	---	18.9	---	39.7
2005 entry cohort	33.5	36.4	15.0	24.2	39.9	40.2	19.6	18.8	40.2	40.1
2006 entry cohort	34.3	37.2	15.7	24.9	41.2	41.6	21.6	17.6	43.2	39.6
2007 entry cohort	34.5	37.7	15.6	25.5	41.1	41.5	24.3	18.6	44.7	39.3
2008 entry cohort	34.8	38.1	16.2	25.7	42.1	42.5	25.0	18.9	40.7	41.0
2009 entry cohort	34.7	38.2	16.0	25.7	43.8	44.4	24.3	20.6	36.4	43.0
2010 entry cohort	35.6	39.6	16.5	26.8	44.4	44.9	26.5	18.5	34.3	43.8
2011 entry cohort	36.5	40.7	16.5	27.6	44.8	45.3	26.4	18.6	33.3	43.8
2012 entry cohort	38.2	42.2	18.1	28.6	46.9	47.4	28.6	20.0	33.9	44.6
2013 entry cohort	39.7	43.7	19.8	30.2	47.8	48.4	28.1	23.1	35.4	45.9
Public institutions										
1996 entry cohort	20.8	22.6	9.9	12.5	23.4	---	---	10.9	---	28.6
2000 entry cohort	23.6	25.5	11.7	14.5	27.8	---	---	11.9	---	30.3
2002 entry cohort	24.6	26.6	11.0	15.8	30.4	---	---	12.8	---	30.4
2003 entry cohort	25.7	27.9	10.9	16.4	32.5	---	---	14.1	---	30.8
2004 entry cohort	26.2	28.5	11.2	16.9	32.9	---	---	14.5	---	30.1
2005 entry cohort	27.1	29.6	11.7	18.3	33.5	33.8	14.1	15.0	26.4	29.8
2006 entry cohort	27.9	30.4	12.1	18.8	34.9	35.2	15.4	13.8	29.2	29.7
2007 entry cohort	28.3	31.1	12.1	19.5	34.8	35.0	19.2	14.7	34.0	29.4
2008 entry cohort	29.3	32.1	13.3	20.0	36.1	36.5	18.7	15.4	30.7	33.1
2009 entry cohort	29.5	32.4	13.2	20.3	37.9	38.4	21.0	16.0	27.6	35.2
2010 entry cohort	30.5	33.7	13.4	21.4	38.7	39.1	23.6	13.8	27.2	37.0
2011 entry cohort	31.6	35.2	13.7	22.1	39.3	39.6	25.7	15.1	28.1	38.1
2012 entry cohort	33.2	36.9	14.9	23.1	41.3	41.7	27.7	16.4	28.7	39.6
2013 entry cohort	35.0	38.7	16.8	25.1	42.8	43.2	25.3	19.7	30.1	40.8
Nonprofit institutions										
1996 entry cohort	43.6	46.2	22.1	35.0	53.5	---	---	28.9	---	47.0
2000 entry cohort	46.0	48.9	22.3	38.2	56.1	---	---	33.2	---	48.0
2002 entry cohort	46.5	49.4	22.9	38.9	57.7	---	---	32.1	---	50.9
2003 entry cohort	47.0	49.8	23.1	39.9	58.6	---	---	30.7	---	51.3
2004 entry cohort	47.8	50.6	23.2	41.2	59.0	---	---	35.4	---	53.2
2005 entry cohort	47.5	50.5	22.6	40.7	58.8	59.3	29.4	30.8	55.7	52.7
2006 entry cohort	48.2	51.2	23.4	42.4	60.2	60.8	34.5	34.2	58.4	52.2
2007 entry cohort	47.9	51.5	23.0	42.3	60.0	60.5	37.7	32.2	57.8	51.4
2008 entry cohort	47.7	51.3	23.0	42.4	59.5	59.9	43.5	31.5	53.9	51.8
2009 entry cohort	47.8	51.5	22.9	42.0	60.7	61.4	37.3	36.3	52.7	53.9
2010 entry cohort	48.4	52.5	23.1	43.0	60.4	61.2	35.3	32.7	51.2	53.3
2011 entry cohort	49.2	53.3	23.7	45.1	61.6	62.4	32.7	30.6	48.5	52.4
2012 entry cohort	49.9	54.1	24.7	45.2	63.2	64.2	33.4	31.9	48.0	52.3
2013 entry cohort	50.9	55.0	26.1	46.2	63.6	64.4	36.7	33.4	47.8	53.4
For-profit institutions										
1996 entry cohort	22.3	25.5	16.1	23.0	27.7	---	---	25.6	---	33.1
2000 entry cohort	28.2	32.1	20.9	30.2	42.6	---	---	27.7	---	35.1
2002 entry cohort	17.8	21.3	12.2	20.2	33.2	---	---	17.6	---	4.0
2003 entry cohort	17.4	20.9	11.8	20.8	28.1	---	---	11.1	---	6.4
2004 entry cohort	23.5	30.5	15.0	21.6	36.6	---	---	12.1	---	10.7
2005 entry cohort	23.6	31.4	12.0	22.2	32.2	33.2	24.0	20.8	25.2	16.7
2006 entry cohort	27.8	37.2	16.6	26.0	33.7	35.2	17.2	14.7	30.1	23.7
2007 entry cohort	28.4	39.3	15.3	25.7	35.8	38.3	14.1	19.0	25.8	26.9
2008 entry cohort	20.7	30.5	11.1	21.9	34.0	35.8	16.4	12.4	27.8	14.9
2009 entry cohort	17.0	25.4	10.4	19.2	32.1	36.2	7.1	12.2	23.8	15.1
2010 entry cohort	21.8	32.4	13.6	22.3	38.4	41.1	18.5	16.3	30.0	17.9
2011 entry cohort	17.1	21.8	9.5	19.2	28.6	32.3	14.5	7.5	22.9	28.5
2012 entry cohort	21.2	24.1	14.0	22.8	32.3	36.7	16.1	11.7	24.7	26.2
2013 entry cohort	22.1	24.9	15.2	22.9	30.1	33.2	14.7	16.4	33.9	37.9
Graduating within 4 years after entry, females										
All 4-year institutions										
1996 entry cohort	38.0	41.1	23.2	25.8	42.2	---	---	21.7	---	45.8
2000 entry cohort	40.1	43.4	25.1	28.9	45.6	---	---	24.0	---	45.3
2002 entry cohort	40.8	44.2	24.4	30.1	47.8	---	---	23.1	---	41.4
2003 entry cohort	41.0	44.8	23.9	29.8	48.1	---	---	22.8	---	41.1
2004 entry cohort	42.2	45.9	24.2	31.4	49.4	---	---	24.0	---	48.1
2005 entry cohort	42.2	46.4	23.7	31.3	49.6	50.1	24.2	24.1	47.3	48.4
2006 entry cohort	43.1	47.4	23.9	32.5	50.2	50.8	26.2	25.2	49.1	49.3
2007 entry cohort	43.5	48.1	24.3	33.1	50.7	51.3	27.1	26.3	52.2	50.8
2008 entry cohort	44.0	48.6	24.9	33.9	51.6	52.4	27.8	26.0	50.6	52.5
2009 entry cohort	44.2	49.4	23.9	34.4	53.3	54.1	28.7	26.7	44.5	56.0
2010 entry cohort	45.1	50.5	24.8	35.5	54.3	54.9	34.7	25.9	43.7	57.5
2011 entry cohort	45.9	51.3	25.2	36.1	54.9	55.5	34.8	24.0	42.1	59.4
2012 entry cohort	48.4	53.5	28.0	38.3	56.8	57.5	34.2	27.9	43.5	61.0
2013 entry cohort	49.9	55.0	30.0	39.8	58.4	59.0	38.5	28.6	45.1	61.2
Public institutions										
1996 entry cohort	30.3	33.3	18.3	18.4	33.2	---	---	17.3	---	34.1
2000 entry cohort	33.5	36.3	22.0	22.2	39.2	---	---	19.9	---	36.2
2002 entry cohort	34.4	37.3	21.0	23.5	40.8	---	---	18.5	---	37.1
2003 entry cohort	35.0	38.3	20.2	23.9	42.0	---	---	19.2	---	37.2
2004 entry cohort	35.7	39.2	19.9	24.9	42.6	---	---	19.3	---	39.6
2005 entry cohort	36.2	39.9	20.2	25.5	43.5	43.9	19.0	20.1	30.7	37.7
2006 entry cohort	37.2	41.1	20.6	26.4	44.7	45.1	21.3	21.1	31.5	39.1
2007 entry cohort	37.8	42.0	21.0	27.5	44.6	45.1	22.9	23.2	37.5	40.8
2008 entry cohort	38.8	43.1	22.2	28.5	45.8	46.4	24.5	21.9	38.7	44.0
2009 entry cohort	39.5	44.0	21.6	29.4	47.7	48.3	26.2	22.8	35.4	49.0
2010 entry cohort	40.3	45.1	22.0	30.3	48.2	48.6	33.1	21.2	36.9	51.9

Time to completion, sex, control of institution, cohort entry year, and percentage of applications accepted	Total	White	Black	Hispanic	Asian/Pacific Islander: Total	Asian/Pacific Islander: Asian	Asian/Pacific Islander: Pacific Islander	American Indian/Alaska Native	Two or more races	Non-resident alien[1]
1	2	3	4	5	6	7	8	9	10	11
2011 entry cohort	41.4	46.6	22.5	31.2	49.7	50.0	35.9	21.4	36.4	54.6
2012 entry cohort	43.6	48.8	24.5	33.3	51.6	52.0	34.1	23.7	38.2	56.9
2013 entry cohort	45.5	50.7	26.7	35.0	53.6	54.0	37.4	25.1	40.4	56.9
Nonprofit institutions										
1996 entry cohort	52.6	55.5	34.2	43.5	61.6	---	---	37.5	---	54.4
2000 entry cohort	53.6	57.2	32.2	46.2	60.9	---	---	38.1	---	53.2
2002 entry cohort	55.3	58.5	33.9	48.1	65.0	---	---	40.4	---	60.2
2003 entry cohort	55.3	58.6	34.4	46.7	63.7	---	---	37.0	---	59.7
2004 entry cohort	56.4	59.4	35.9	49.6	65.6	---	---	41.5	---	61.9
2005 entry cohort	55.9	59.2	34.1	48.1	64.9	65.5	38.6	38.5	63.1	62.7
2006 entry cohort	56.7	60.1	34.4	50.8	64.9	65.7	39.2	40.9	64.4	61.8
2007 entry cohort	56.8	60.6	34.6	49.8	66.4	67.2	42.0	40.7	65.6	62.9
2008 entry cohort	56.8	60.5	34.8	50.5	66.5	67.1	45.6	41.0	62.5	63.0
2009 entry cohort	57.3	61.5	33.9	51.0	67.3	67.9	45.1	42.3	59.4	65.2
2010 entry cohort	57.8	62.4	34.1	51.7	68.3	69.1	43.6	41.2	59.0	64.9
2011 entry cohort	58.6	62.6	35.9	53.3	68.1	68.8	44.0	36.7	57.8	66.1
2012 entry cohort	59.7	63.7	38.0	53.6	69.4	70.3	40.8	42.3	57.2	66.7
2013 entry cohort	60.8	64.6	40.1	54.6	70.1	70.9	46.6	41.5	56.9	67.0
For-profit institutions										
1996 entry cohort	21.1	27.5	13.7	16.1	20.3	---	---	9.6	---	34.6
2000 entry cohort	19.0	22.9	18.4	21.7	36.8	---	---	25.6	---	33.6
2002 entry cohort	11.9	14.3	9.0	18.1	23.6	---	---	6.0	---	3.1
2003 entry cohort	12.8	15.9	9.5	18.3	22.8	---	---	6.7	---	3.7
2004 entry cohort	17.8	23.8	12.2	19.9	25.0	---	---	7.4	---	10.5
2005 entry cohort	16.9	24.1	10.4	17.3	30.9	34.6	5.9	11.4	24.0	14.4
2006 entry cohort	18.1	26.7	10.1	20.3	26.2	29.3	3.7	11.8	24.1	21.3
2007 entry cohort	17.0	24.3	9.4	19.9	28.5	34.2	3.6	8.1	29.4	22.3
2008 entry cohort	14.7	22.3	8.6	19.8	27.4	33.6	4.9	13.1	33.0	23.7
2009 entry cohort	11.3	17.4	5.7	17.0	26.6	34.0	7.0	8.5	11.7	25.8
2010 entry cohort	13.4	18.6	9.4	17.8	31.3	36.1	12.0	10.9	17.6	29.5
2011 entry cohort	12.3	13.2	6.7	16.2	27.1	34.4	10.4	6.0	14.5	34.2
2012 entry cohort	17.4	17.9	12.4	19.6	28.1	35.8	9.4	8.7	18.6	39.0
2013 entry cohort	16.9	16.7	12.1	21.0	31.9	38.6	13.8	7.4	20.7	42.2
Graduating within 5 years after entry, males and females										
All 4-year institutions										
1996 entry cohort	50.2	53.3	33.3	38.9	56.4	---	---	33.3	---	54.3
2000 entry cohort	52.6	55.7	36.0	42.4	60.1	---	---	35.1	---	55.2
2002 entry cohort	52.6	56.0	34.4	42.7	61.3	---	---	34.0	---	51.0
2003 entry cohort	53.2	56.9	34.2	43.0	62.1	---	---	33.7	---	52.1
2004 entry cohort	54.1	57.7	34.5	44.0	62.9	---	---	34.7	---	57.2
2005 entry cohort	54.2	58.0	34.2	44.6	63.2	63.6	40.6	34.7	58.6	58.1
2006 entry cohort	54.9	58.7	34.9	45.8	64.4	64.9	41.7	35.6	61.8	59.0
2007 entry cohort	55.1	59.1	35.4	46.4	64.2	64.7	42.7	36.3	63.9	58.9
2008 entry cohort	55.4	59.5	35.7	47.1	65.1	65.7	43.7	36.3	60.6	60.9
2009 entry cohort	55.3	59.7	34.3	47.6	67.0	67.7	42.2	36.9	54.8	64.0
2010 entry cohort	55.8	60.4	34.7	48.8	67.4	68.1	46.5	34.6	55.2	65.4
2011 entry cohort	56.6	61.1	35.4	49.4	68.2	68.9	44.3	33.9	53.1	66.2
2012 entry cohort	58.7	62.8	37.9	51.4	69.8	70.5	45.6	36.2	53.9	67.2
2013 entry cohort	59.9	63.8	40.2	52.6	70.9	71.5	49.0	37.5	55.6	68.2
Public institutions										
1996 entry cohort	45.9	49.0	30.5	34.1	51.3	---	---	30.0	---	46.5
2000 entry cohort	49.1	51.9	34.6	38.0	56.8	---	---	31.9	---	49.8
2002 entry cohort	49.4	52.3	33.1	38.9	57.8	---	---	30.9	---	50.6
2003 entry cohort	50.3	53.6	32.4	39.5	59.0	---	---	31.6	---	51.4
2004 entry cohort	50.7	54.1	32.2	40.2	59.3	---	---	31.6	---	51.9
2005 entry cohort	51.1	54.7	32.6	41.4	59.9	60.2	39.1	32.5	47.6	51.3
2006 entry cohort	51.9	55.5	33.5	42.2	61.6	62.0	41.3	32.9	50.1	51.9
2007 entry cohort	52.3	56.0	34.1	43.3	61.0	61.4	41.4	34.5	55.0	51.9
2008 entry cohort	53.1	56.7	35.1	44.4	62.1	62.6	41.8	34.1	52.1	55.1
2009 entry cohort	53.4	57.2	34.2	45.4	64.3	64.9	42.7	34.1	48.8	59.0
2010 entry cohort	54.0	57.8	34.5	46.6	64.6	65.1	47.4	31.4	51.0	61.5
2011 entry cohort	55.0	59.0	35.5	47.3	65.6	66.1	47.5	32.9	50.4	63.1
2012 entry cohort	56.7	60.6	37.2	49.1	67.3	67.8	47.8	34.2	51.4	64.7
2013 entry cohort	58.1	61.8	39.8	50.4	68.7	69.1	49.3	35.7	53.1	65.7
Nonprofit institutions										
1996 entry cohort	59.2	61.8	40.2	51.4	68.7	---	---	45.2	---	60.4
2000 entry cohort	60.8	63.8	39.9	55.0	69.9	---	---	46.9	---	60.4
2002 entry cohort	61.8	64.8	40.1	56.0	72.0	---	---	46.9	---	65.3
2003 entry cohort	62.3	65.2	41.2	56.1	72.0	---	---	44.4	---	65.6
2004 entry cohort	63.0	65.8	41.8	57.8	73.1	---	---	47.9	---	67.9
2005 entry cohort	62.6	65.6	40.5	56.6	73.1	73.6	49.4	44.0	71.5	67.9
2006 entry cohort	63.2	66.1	41.2	59.0	73.5	74.2	47.4	48.8	74.5	68.6
2007 entry cohort	63.2	66.4	41.3	58.4	74.2	74.8	53.6	45.9	74.1	68.2
2008 entry cohort	63.2	66.4	41.3	58.6	74.3	74.7	57.6	46.6	70.7	68.8
2009 entry cohort	63.3	66.8	39.7	58.6	75.1	75.8	51.5	49.5	67.1	71.2
2010 entry cohort	63.7	67.6	39.8	59.5	75.4	76.2	50.8	47.4	66.2	71.2
2011 entry cohort	64.3	67.8	41.2	60.4	76.3	77.0	49.4	43.9	64.1	71.3
2012 entry cohort	65.0	68.6	42.3	60.7	77.2	78.1	49.0	46.1	63.0	71.2
2013 entry cohort	65.9	69.3	44.1	61.7	77.7	78.4	54.9	46.6	63.1	72.1
For-profit institutions										
1996 entry cohort	25.4	30.1	17.8	23.1	27.3	---	---	19.8	---	51.6
2000 entry cohort	28.5	33.2	25.8	30.5	43.4	---	---	28.3	---	42.6
2002 entry cohort	18.0	21.3	13.2	22.7	32.2	---	---	12.7	---	6.0

Time to completion, sex, control of institution, cohort entry year, and percentage of applications accepted	Total	White	Black	Hispanic	Asian/Pacific Islander: Total	Asian/Pacific Islander: Asian	Asian/Pacific Islander: Pacific Islander	American Indian/ Alaska Native	Two or more races	Non-resident alien[1]
1	2	3	4	5	6	7	8	9	10	11
2003 entry cohort	20.2	23.6	15.6	24.4	30.4	---	---	11.4	---	10.0
2004 entry cohort	25.9	32.9	19.1	25.8	36.5	---	---	15.5	---	17.7
2005 entry cohort	25.5	33.3	15.8	26.0	38.2	40.2	23.1	18.9	27.3	24.1
2006 entry cohort	28.0	37.2	17.8	29.8	38.0	40.2	18.7	16.8	30.5	30.3
2007 entry cohort	27.8	37.5	16.7	29.1	39.0	43.2	14.4	16.2	31.0	34.6
2008 entry cohort	23.0	31.8	14.8	27.7	37.4	40.9	18.8	16.9	34.6	33.3
2009 entry cohort	19.5	26.5	12.3	24.9	36.9	43.1	14.1	14.7	20.9	35.4
2010 entry cohort	22.2	30.4	14.8	26.3	41.9	45.9	20.2	16.7	27.7	38.4
2011 entry cohort	19.0	21.8	11.4	23.6	34.4	40.7	16.1	9.5	21.5	44.8
2012 entry cohort	23.8	25.7	16.6	25.9	37.0	44.6	14.3	13.1	24.7	47.2
2013 entry cohort	23.9	25.1	17.3	26.7	39.3	44.7	20.2	13.4	31.8	53.4
Graduating within 5 years after entry, males										
All 4-year institutions										
1996 entry cohort	46.2	49.2	27.0	34.4	51.8	---	---	31.2	---	51.5
2000 entry cohort	49.0	52.0	29.8	37.8	56.5	---	---	31.6	---	53.0
2002 entry cohort	49.0	52.4	28.3	37.7	57.5	---	---	31.0	---	49.6
2003 entry cohort	49.9	53.5	28.5	38.6	58.6	---	---	31.1	---	50.9
2004 entry cohort	50.6	54.2	28.8	39.3	59.3	---	---	31.9	---	53.5
2005 entry cohort	50.9	54.7	28.8	40.7	59.4	59.7	39.0	33.1	55.6	54.2
2006 entry cohort	51.6	55.2	29.8	41.4	61.1	61.5	39.7	31.8	59.3	54.5
2007 entry cohort	51.6	55.5	29.8	42.2	60.4	60.7	42.3	32.6	60.5	53.9
2008 entry cohort	51.6	55.6	30.1	42.3	61.4	61.8	42.8	32.9	56.1	55.5
2009 entry cohort	51.5	55.8	29.1	42.8	63.3	63.9	41.7	33.5	50.8	58.0
2010 entry cohort	52.1	56.7	29.3	44.0	63.5	64.1	43.8	30.5	51.4	59.3
2011 entry cohort	52.9	57.5	29.8	44.7	64.1	64.8	39.8	31.7	48.9	60.0
2012 entry cohort	54.7	59.0	31.6	46.0	66.1	66.7	43.7	32.1	49.8	61.1
2013 entry cohort	55.9	60.0	33.7	47.6	66.9	67.5	44.6	34.6	51.5	62.4
Public institutions										
1996 entry cohort	41.6	44.6	24.0	29.4	46.4	---	---	27.7	---	44.1
2000 entry cohort	44.9	47.7	27.4	32.6	52.1	---	---	27.6	---	47.2
2002 entry cohort	45.4	48.4	26.2	33.8	53.7	---	---	27.6	---	47.2
2003 entry cohort	46.7	50.0	26.3	34.7	55.1	---	---	28.7	---	48.2
2004 entry cohort	47.0	50.4	26.3	35.2	55.4	---	---	28.6	---	47.2
2005 entry cohort	47.8	51.3	26.9	37.2	56.0	56.3	37.1	31.2	44.9	46.9
2006 entry cohort	48.4	51.8	27.8	37.4	57.7	58.0	38.8	29.0	48.5	47.0
2007 entry cohort	48.6	52.2	28.1	38.6	56.9	57.2	40.8	30.2	53.7	46.8
2008 entry cohort	49.1	52.7	29.1	39.0	58.1	58.5	39.1	31.2	47.3	50.3
2009 entry cohort	49.5	53.1	28.3	40.2	60.4	60.9	41.6	30.1	45.0	53.2
2010 entry cohort	50.2	53.9	28.7	41.4	60.8	61.2	43.8	27.3	47.1	55.2
2011 entry cohort	51.1	55.2	29.4	42.1	61.4	61.9	41.5	30.2	46.4	56.8
2012 entry cohort	52.7	56.8	30.9	43.2	63.4	63.9	44.9	29.8	47.5	59.0
2013 entry cohort	54.1	57.9	33.1	44.9	64.5	65.0	44.5	33.2	48.9	60.1
Nonprofit institutions										
1996 entry cohort	55.8	58.5	34.0	47.4	65.9	---	---	42.9	---	57.7
2000 entry cohort	58.5	61.3	35.1	51.7	69.9	---	---	45.9	---	58.9
2002 entry cohort	58.8	61.8	34.7	51.6	70.1	---	---	44.0	---	62.2
2003 entry cohort	59.3	62.3	35.0	53.2	70.7	---	---	41.5	---	62.2
2004 entry cohort	60.1	62.9	35.6	54.0	71.2	---	---	46.0	---	64.4
2005 entry cohort	59.5	62.5	34.7	53.3	70.6	71.0	45.2	40.4	69.3	63.9
2006 entry cohort	60.2	63.2	35.6	55.4	72.1	72.9	44.6	45.7	72.8	64.4
2007 entry cohort	59.7	63.2	34.9	55.1	71.5	72.0	51.2	42.5	70.9	63.1
2008 entry cohort	59.6	63.2	35.0	54.8	72.1	72.5	56.9	41.7	68.6	63.1
2009 entry cohort	59.6	63.3	34.2	54.6	72.4	73.1	49.4	47.5	63.5	65.4
2010 entry cohort	60.0	64.1	33.9	55.7	72.3	73.1	48.7	42.8	63.3	65.7
2011 entry cohort	60.5	64.5	34.7	56.6	73.6	74.5	44.8	41.7	59.9	65.5
2012 entry cohort	61.1	65.2	35.5	56.7	74.9	75.7	47.4	42.4	59.4	65.0
2013 entry cohort	61.8	65.8	37.1	57.7	75.1	75.9	49.6	41.1	59.1	66.2
For-profit institutions										
1996 entry cohort	25.6	29.2	18.1	25.4	29.9	---	---	30.8	---	51.0
2000 entry cohort	32.1	36.5	25.3	33.9	45.0	---	---	27.7	---	42.1
2002 entry cohort	21.0	24.7	14.9	23.7	35.5	---	---	18.5	---	6.2
2003 entry cohort	22.6	26.3	16.0	24.9	32.0	---	---	16.0	---	10.2
2004 entry cohort	27.8	35.1	19.1	25.9	41.6	---	---	15.0	---	16.8
2005 entry cohort	28.7	36.4	16.4	27.4	38.1	38.7	33.3	23.8	28.5	24.9
2006 entry cohort	32.5	41.5	20.9	32.0	40.8	42.1	25.9	18.2	34.0	32.4
2007 entry cohort	32.7	43.3	19.5	30.7	41.8	44.2	21.1	23.1	27.7	34.8
2008 entry cohort	25.1	34.9	14.7	27.4	40.6	42.2	25.4	14.7	31.1	26.7
2009 entry cohort	21.4	29.7	13.7	24.7	38.9	42.9	14.1	14.8	27.2	26.4
2010 entry cohort	25.4	35.9	16.2	27.2	44.8	47.7	23.5	17.6	32.4	31.2
2011 entry cohort	20.4	25.2	11.8	24.5	34.3	39.0	16.9	9.0	24.0	37.7
2012 entry cohort	24.4	27.4	16.5	26.5	38.3	43.8	18.3	13.6	26.0	37.0
2013 entry cohort	25.9	28.7	18.0	27.0	39.0	42.9	20.0	18.5	37.4	49.1
Graduating within 5 years after entry, females										
All 4-year institutions										
1996 entry cohort	53.6	56.8	37.5	42.4	60.5	---	---	34.9	---	57.9
2000 entry cohort	55.6	58.8	40.1	45.9	63.4	---	---	37.8	---	58.0
2002 entry cohort	55.6	59.0	38.6	46.4	64.6	---	---	36.1	---	52.6
2003 entry cohort	55.9	59.7	38.0	46.2	65.1	---	---	35.8	---	53.5
2004 entry cohort	56.9	60.7	38.3	47.6	66.0	---	---	36.8	---	61.4
2005 entry cohort	56.8	60.8	37.8	47.5	66.5	66.9	41.9	35.9	61.2	62.4
2006 entry cohort	57.6	61.7	38.4	49.0	67.4	68.0	43.2	38.5	63.7	64.2
2007 entry cohort	58.1	62.2	39.3	49.6	67.7	68.4	42.9	39.0	66.3	64.9
2008 entry cohort	58.5	62.8	39.6	50.8	68.4	69.2	44.4	38.8	63.7	66.9

Time to completion, sex, control of institution, cohort entry year, and percentage of applications accepted	Total	White	Black	His-panic	Asian/Pacific Islander Total	Asian	Pacific Islander	American Indian/ Alaska Native	Two or more races	Non-resident alien[1]
1	2	3	4	5	6	7	8	9	10	11
2009 entry cohort	58.4	63.1	37.9	51.3	70.3	71.2	42.6	39.6	57.8	70.8
2010 entry cohort	58.9	63.7	38.7	52.4	70.9	71.6	48.7	37.8	58.0	72.5
2011 entry cohort	59.7	64.2	39.5	52.9	71.8	72.6	48.0	35.7	56.4	73.8
2012 entry cohort	62.0	66.1	42.5	55.4	73.2	74.0	47.2	39.5	57.1	74.8
2013 entry cohort	63.2	67.0	45.0	56.5	74.4	75.1	52.6	39.8	58.7	75.3
Public institutions										
1996 entry cohort	49.5	52.7	34.8	37.8	56.0	---	---	31.8	---	50.0
2000 entry cohort	52.7	55.5	39.3	42.1	61.0	---	---	35.1	---	53.5
2002 entry cohort	52.6	55.6	37.8	42.8	61.5	---	---	33.3	---	54.6
2003 entry cohort	53.3	56.8	36.5	43.1	62.6	---	---	33.9	---	55.0
2004 entry cohort	53.8	57.4	36.2	44.0	62.9	---	---	34.0	---	57.6
2005 entry cohort	53.9	57.7	36.3	44.5	63.4	63.7	40.5	33.5	50.0	56.5
2006 entry cohort	54.9	58.7	37.2	45.7	65.2	65.6	43.3	36.0	51.3	58.0
2007 entry cohort	55.5	59.4	38.1	46.8	64.8	65.3	41.9	37.7	56.0	58.3
2008 entry cohort	56.5	60.3	39.1	48.4	65.9	66.6	43.7	36.2	55.7	61.0
2009 entry cohort	56.9	60.8	38.3	49.3	68.0	68.7	43.8	37.2	51.9	66.3
2010 entry cohort	57.3	61.4	38.5	50.6	68.3	68.8	50.7	34.6	54.0	69.5
2011 entry cohort	58.2	62.4	39.6	51.2	69.7	70.2	52.8	35.0	53.4	71.8
2012 entry cohort	60.0	64.0	41.6	53.5	71.1	71.6	50.5	37.6	54.5	72.6
2013 entry cohort	61.5	65.3	44.4	54.6	72.6	73.1	53.6	37.7	56.3	73.2
Nonprofit institutions										
1996 entry cohort	61.8	64.5	44.5	54.3	71.0	---	---	47.0	---	63.7
2000 entry cohort	62.7	65.8	43.2	57.4	70.0	---	---	47.7	---	62.3
2002 entry cohort	64.2	67.1	43.9	59.0	73.4	---	---	49.0	---	68.7
2003 entry cohort	64.6	67.5	45.5	58.0	73.0	---	---	46.5	---	69.3
2004 entry cohort	65.4	68.0	46.3	60.4	74.6	---	---	49.3	---	71.6
2005 entry cohort	65.1	68.0	44.8	58.8	75.0	75.5	52.3	46.7	73.1	72.4
2006 entry cohort	65.7	68.5	45.4	61.5	74.5	75.2	49.5	50.8	75.5	73.3
2007 entry cohort	65.9	68.9	46.2	60.7	76.2	76.9	55.1	48.5	76.2	73.7
2008 entry cohort	66.0	69.0	46.1	61.3	76.0	76.5	58.0	50.1	72.0	74.7
2009 entry cohort	66.3	69.7	44.0	61.5	77.2	77.9	53.4	51.1	69.4	77.2
2010 entry cohort	66.7	70.4	44.5	62.1	77.8	78.6	52.4	50.6	68.2	77.2
2011 entry cohort	67.3	70.6	46.3	63.1	78.3	79.0	53.0	45.7	67.0	77.5
2012 entry cohort	68.1	71.4	47.8	63.5	79.0	79.9	50.3	48.8	65.6	78.1
2013 entry cohort	69.2	72.2	50.0	64.5	79.6	80.3	58.8	50.8	65.9	78.4
For-profit institutions										
1996 entry cohort	25.1	31.4	17.6	20.0	23.7	---	---	11.5	---	52.2
2000 entry cohort	24.5	28.6	26.1	26.4	40.4	---	---	29.1	---	43.3
2002 entry cohort	15.3	17.8	12.1	21.7	27.5	---	---	8.1	---	5.8
2003 entry cohort	18.3	21.4	15.3	23.9	28.8	---	---	8.5	---	9.9
2004 entry cohort	24.2	30.5	19.1	25.6	30.3	---	---	15.8	---	18.3
2005 entry cohort	22.6	29.9	15.5	24.7	38.3	42.3	11.8	15.5	26.0	23.5
2006 entry cohort	23.8	31.8	15.8	27.8	35.1	38.1	13.6	15.8	25.9	28.5
2007 entry cohort	23.2	30.4	14.9	27.5	36.3	42.2	10.9	11.4	35.8	34.4
2008 entry cohort	21.2	28.6	14.9	27.9	34.4	39.5	16.0	18.7	39.6	38.9
2009 entry cohort	17.8	23.5	11.4	25.2	35.2	43.3	14.1	14.6	15.7	42.9
2010 entry cohort	19.1	24.4	13.5	25.5	38.6	43.7	17.9	16.0	21.3	44.6
2011 entry cohort	17.7	19.1	11.1	22.8	34.4	42.6	15.6	9.8	18.0	50.7
2012 entry cohort	23.1	23.8	16.7	25.4	35.6	45.5	11.1	12.7	22.7	56.5
2013 entry cohort	22.1	21.9	16.7	26.4	39.6	46.7	20.3	9.5	25.2	57.2
Graduating within 6 years after entry, males and females										
All 4-year institutions										
1996 entry cohort	55.4	58.1	38.9	45.7	63.4	---	---	38.0	---	58.0
2000 entry cohort	57.6	60.2	42.1	49.1	66.7	---	---	40.2	---	59.6
2002 entry cohort	57.4	60.4	40.2	49.0	67.2	---	---	38.4	---	55.4
2003 entry cohort	57.8	61.1	39.5	49.1	68.1	---	---	38.7	---	56.1
2004 entry cohort	58.4	61.6	39.6	50.2	68.7	---	---	39.4	---	61.6
2005 entry cohort	58.6	62.0	39.5	51.0	69.2	69.6	48.3	39.3	64.2	62.6
2006 entry cohort	59.2	62.5	40.2	51.9	70.1	70.6	48.5	40.2	66.6	63.6
2007 entry cohort	59.4	62.9	40.7	52.5	70.0	70.5	49.5	40.6	67.8	63.9
2008 entry cohort	59.6	63.2	40.9	53.5	70.6	71.2	49.9	41.0	65.2	65.7
2009 entry cohort	59.4	63.3	39.5	53.6	72.3	73.0	48.5	41.2	59.2	68.8
2010 entry cohort	59.7	63.7	39.3	54.3	72.8	73.5	50.9	38.5	59.4	70.0
2011 entry cohort	60.4	64.4	39.8	55.0	73.4	74.1	48.8	37.7	57.1	71.0
2012 entry cohort	62.4	65.9	42.4	56.7	74.7	75.5	49.0	40.6	57.7	71.5
2013 entry cohort[2]	63.4	66.6	44.3	57.8	75.5	76.1	53.3	40.8	59.3	72.2
Open admissions	28.6	32.4	19.5	26.2	34.7	36.6	24.1	14.6	27.9	46.7
90 percent or more accepted	51.8	56.3	34.0	42.6	51.0	52.3	34.1	30.5	46.0	52.3
75.0 to 89.9 percent accepted	59.1	62.7	40.1	52.1	64.6	65.3	53.0	42.2	51.9	64.0
50.0 to 74.9 percent accepted	64.5	68.5	47.2	57.4	72.4	72.9	54.7	43.4	59.3	70.6
25.0 to 49.9 percent accepted	73.6	77.6	51.5	69.4	81.8	81.9	70.2	57.9	73.8	77.9
Less than 25.0 percent accepted	89.1	90.5	70.8	86.7	94.4	94.5	81.2	77.1	91.1	90.8
Public institutions										
1996 entry cohort	51.7	54.3	36.8	42.1	59.5	---	---	35.3	---	51.3
2000 entry cohort	54.8	57.1	40.8	46.0	64.1	---	---	37.5	---	54.6
2002 entry cohort	55.0	57.6	39.6	46.5	64.7	---	---	35.8	---	55.7
2003 entry cohort	55.8	58.7	38.6	47.0	65.9	---	---	37.2	---	56.4
2004 entry cohort	56.1	59.0	38.5	47.9	66.3	---	---	37.0	---	57.2
2005 entry cohort	56.6	59.6	38.8	48.9	67.0	67.2	49.7	37.8	55.7	57.3
2006 entry cohort	57.2	60.3	39.7	49.5	68.2	68.5	49.1	38.2	57.0	57.7
2007 entry cohort	57.7	60.7	40.3	50.7	68.0	68.3	49.8	39.5	60.6	58.2
2008 entry cohort	58.5	61.4	41.2	52.3	68.9	69.4	49.2	39.7	59.0	61.0
2009 entry cohort	58.6	61.6	40.4	52.8	70.7	71.2	49.9	39.1	54.4	64.9

Time to completion, sex, control of institution, cohort entry year, and percentage of applications accepted	Total	White	Black	His-panic	Asian/Pacific Islander			American Indian/ Alaska Native	Two or more races	Non-resident alien[1]
					Total	Asian	Pacific Islander			
1	2	3	4	5	6	7	8	9	10	11
2010 entry cohort	58.9	62.0	40.3	53.6	71.1	71.7	52.5	36.3	56.3	67.1
2011 entry cohort	59.7	63.0	40.9	54.2	71.8	72.3	52.9	37.5	55.3	68.5
2012 entry cohort	61.2	64.3	42.8	55.6	73.1	73.6	51.7	39.5	56.0	69.7
2013 entry cohort[2]	62.4	65.3	44.7	56.8	74.0	74.5	54.4	39.7	57.4	70.3
Open admissions	29.5	32.5	20.3	24.8	31.4	32.6	19.4	15.0	21.8	43.6
90 percent or more accepted	51.3	56.4	33.3	39.9	49.0	49.9	36.5	28.5	44.7	50.6
75.0 to 89.9 percent accepted	57.6	61.0	38.9	50.7	63.4	64.2	48.9	42.0	50.8	63.8
50.0 to 74.9 percent accepted	64.9	68.7	49.2	57.2	72.9	73.3	54.9	42.8	59.6	72.2
25.0 to 49.9 percent accepted	71.4	75.7	47.9	67.4	80.5	80.6	74.8	58.7	72.6	74.1
Less than 25.0 percent accepted	86.2	88.9	58.1	81.1	92.1	92.2	85.1	77.8	90.2	88.5
Nonprofit institutions										
1996 entry cohort	63.1	65.7	44.6	55.7	73.5	---	---	48.1	---	63.4
2000 entry cohort	64.5	67.0	45.9	59.0	75.2	---	---	50.9	---	64.5
2002 entry cohort	64.8	67.5	44.6	59.6	75.7	---	---	49.8	---	68.4
2003 entry cohort	65.1	67.8	45.0	59.4	76.0	---	---	47.6	---	69.3
2004 entry cohort	65.5	67.9	45.0	60.6	76.2	---	---	50.8	---	71.3
2005 entry cohort	65.2	67.8	43.9	60.4	76.5	77.0	52.6	46.5	75.2	71.0
2006 entry cohort	65.5	68.1	44.5	62.0	76.8	77.5	52.6	51.3	77.5	71.9
2007 entry cohort	65.3	68.3	44.5	60.9	77.0	77.5	57.6	47.9	76.8	71.5
2008 entry cohort	65.4	68.3	44.6	61.5	76.9	77.3	60.5	48.7	73.2	72.2
2009 entry cohort	65.6	68.8	43.5	61.2	77.9	78.5	55.6	52.0	69.6	74.8
2010 entry cohort	65.9	69.4	42.9	61.9	78.4	79.2	54.6	49.3	68.5	74.7
2011 entry cohort	66.5	69.7	44.0	62.8	79.1	79.8	52.6	46.1	66.4	75.2
2012 entry cohort	67.2	70.6	44.8	63.1	79.9	80.8	52.2	48.4	65.4	74.4
2013 entry cohort[2]	67.9	71.0	46.7	63.9	80.3	81.0	58.2	48.5	65.4	75.2
Open admissions	30.0	38.9	21.5	21.7	43.6	42.7	50.0	16.5	22.2	38.2
90 percent or more accepted	53.1	56.2	35.3	50.6	56.4	59.0	25.6	39.1	48.9	57.3
75.0 to 89.9 percent accepted	64.4	68.3	45.5	57.7	68.1	68.4	62.9	44.2	56.7	64.8
50.0 to 74.9 percent accepted	63.8	68.2	42.7	58.7	70.9	71.6	55.7	45.3	58.6	67.1
25.0 to 49.9 percent accepted	76.8	79.8	57.1	75.2	85.4	85.9	62.5	57.0	75.6	80.7
Less than 25.0 percent accepted	90.1	90.9	75.2	89.4	95.8	95.9	76.3	77.0	91.4	91.6
For-profit institutions										
1996 entry cohort	28.0	33.2	19.2	24.6	28.9	---	---	23.1	---	54.0
2000 entry cohort	31.3	36.8	27.9	33.3	45.9	---	---	29.3	---	46.4
2002 entry cohort	22.8	25.9	17.0	27.6	35.7	---	---	17.2	---	12.5
2003 entry cohort	23.5	27.3	18.3	26.8	33.3	---	---	13.9	---	11.8
2004 entry cohort	28.6	35.5	21.4	29.0	38.8	---	---	19.0	---	21.8
2005 entry cohort	29.1	36.2	19.8	30.2	42.3	44.3	27.3	22.3	27.8	28.4
2006 entry cohort	31.5	40.3	21.1	33.7	42.5	44.4	25.2	18.8	32.4	35.5
2007 entry cohort	31.9	40.0	22.4	35.0	43.2	47.0	21.2	19.6	32.5	41.1
2008 entry cohort	26.4	34.5	18.7	31.6	41.1	44.1	25.3	19.8	35.4	41.3
2009 entry cohort	22.7	29.3	15.5	28.7	40.0	45.3	20.4	16.7	26.7	42.2
2010 entry cohort	24.1	31.3	15.7	28.8	43.7	47.8	21.7	17.1	28.8	42.9
2011 entry cohort	20.8	23.5	13.4	26.2	37.1	43.6	18.4	11.0	22.7	49.0
2012 entry cohort	25.4	27.1	17.7	27.7	39.0	46.6	16.2	14.6	25.9	53.2
2013 entry cohort	26.3	27.6	19.0	29.6	41.6	47.1	22.2	14.9	33.4	58.2
Graduating within 6 years after entry, males										
All 4-year institutions										
1996 entry cohort	52.0	54.8	32.8	41.3	59.5	---	---	36.2	---	55.4
2000 entry cohort	54.3	57.1	35.6	44.6	62.9	---	---	37.0	---	56.8
2002 entry cohort	54.4	57.5	34.0	44.2	64.1	---	---	35.3	---	54.0
2003 entry cohort	55.1	58.4	34.1	44.9	65.1	---	---	36.7	---	55.0
2004 entry cohort	55.6	58.9	34.3	45.7	65.7	---	---	37.5	---	58.5
2005 entry cohort	56.0	59.4	34.2	47.2	66.3	66.6	48.6	37.9	61.3	59.2
2006 entry cohort	56.5	59.8	35.2	47.8	67.4	67.8	46.4	37.2	64.5	60.1
2007 entry cohort	56.5	60.0	35.3	48.6	66.7	67.1	50.0	37.3	64.9	59.8
2008 entry cohort	56.5	60.1	35.3	48.9	67.6	68.0	49.9	38.6	61.7	61.7
2009 entry cohort	56.2	60.0	34.3	49.2	69.2	69.8	48.8	38.2	55.9	64.2
2010 entry cohort	56.5	60.6	33.9	50.0	69.5	70.1	49.5	34.7	56.2	65.4
2011 entry cohort	57.3	61.4	34.1	50.7	70.0	70.7	44.6	36.0	53.6	66.3
2012 entry cohort	59.0	62.7	36.2	51.9	71.7	72.4	47.8	36.6	53.9	66.5
2013 entry cohort[2]	59.9	63.4	38.0	53.3	72.3	72.9	49.4	37.9	55.6	67.6
Open admissions	28.1	31.9	17.6	26.9	35.3	37.0	24.4	17.3	29.0	43.4
90 percent or more accepted	47.3	51.9	29.4	37.1	45.3	46.4	28.8	26.5	41.4	47.5
75.0 to 89.9 percent accepted	55.5	59.0	35.1	47.7	60.9	61.5	50.8	38.2	48.6	60.7
50.0 to 74.9 percent accepted	60.8	65.0	40.7	52.5	69.3	69.9	48.6	40.2	55.5	66.2
25.0 to 49.9 percent accepted	70.1	74.8	43.5	64.1	78.3	78.5	64.1	52.8	69.6	74.2
Less than 25.0 percent accepted	87.9	89.8	67.2	85.0	92.9	93.0	87.5	76.8	88.7	87.9
Public institutions										
1996 entry cohort	48.1	50.8	30.3	37.5	55.2	---	---	33.1	---	48.8
2000 entry cohort	51.4	53.9	34.1	41.1	60.0	---	---	33.6	---	52.1
2002 entry cohort	51.9	54.6	33.0	41.5	61.3	---	---	32.3	---	52.6
2003 entry cohort	52.9	55.9	32.9	42.4	62.7	---	---	35.0	---	53.5
2004 entry cohort	53.2	56.2	32.9	43.1	63.0	---	---	34.9	---	53.1
2005 entry cohort	53.9	57.0	33.3	44.9	64.0	64.2	50.9	36.8	52.7	53.3
2006 entry cohort	54.4	57.4	34.2	45.0	65.1	65.4	47.2	35.3	56.1	53.7
2007 entry cohort	54.6	57.7	34.7	46.3	64.4	64.7	49.5	35.8	59.4	54.1
2008 entry cohort	55.2	58.2	35.4	47.3	65.6	65.9	47.7	37.9	54.9	57.4
2009 entry cohort	55.3	58.3	34.8	48.1	67.4	67.8	50.0	35.6	51.4	60.5
2010 entry cohort	55.7	58.9	34.7	49.0	67.8	68.2	49.9	32.5	53.0	62.3
2011 entry cohort	56.6	59.9	35.0	49.5	68.2	68.7	47.2	35.7	52.3	63.6
2012 entry cohort	57.9	61.2	36.8	50.3	69.9	70.4	49.5	35.0	52.5	65.1

Time to completion, sex, control of institution, cohort entry year, and percentage of applications accepted	Total	White	Black	Hispanic	Asian/Pacific Islander: Total	Asian/Pacific Islander: Asian	Asian/Pacific Islander: Pacific Islander	American Indian/ Alaska Native	Two or more races	Non-resident alien[1]
1	2	3	4	5	6	7	8	9	10	11
2013 entry cohort[2]	59.0	62.1	38.4	52.0	70.7	71.2	50.1	37.3	53.7	66.0
Open admissions	26.5	29.0	16.8	23.1	27.5	29.2	10.3	15.7	18.3	42.3
90 percent or more accepted	47.1	52.4	28.1	34.9	44.0	44.6	32.4	27.0	39.6	47.0
75.0 to 89.9 percent accepted	54.2	57.5	33.6	46.6	60.2	61.0	46.3	38.0	47.5	59.6
50.0 to 74.9 percent accepted	61.7	65.5	42.9	52.5	69.9	70.3	50.2	40.7	55.8	68.2
25.0 to 49.9 percent accepted	68.0	72.8	40.8	61.8	76.9	77.0	67.9	55.2	68.9	71.2
Less than 25.0 percent accepted	84.7	87.8	57.0	78.2	90.0	90.0	87.5	80.0	86.5	85.0
Nonprofit institutions										
1996 entry cohort	60.4	63.0	38.9	52.1	71.5	---	---	46.7	---	60.9
2000 entry cohort	61.7	64.4	39.3	55.3	73.1	---	---	50.1	---	61.7
2002 entry cohort	62.1	65.0	38.4	55.5	74.0	---	---	46.6	---	65.3
2003 entry cohort	62.5	65.3	38.9	56.7	74.2	---	---	45.4	---	65.8
2004 entry cohort	63.0	65.7	39.3	57.1	74.5	---	---	49.5	---	68.3
2005 entry cohort	62.5	65.3	38.2	57.2	74.6	75.1	49.2	42.8	73.5	67.4
2006 entry cohort	62.9	65.6	39.2	58.7	75.6	76.3	49.1	48.6	76.2	68.8
2007 entry cohort	62.3	65.6	38.2	58.0	74.9	75.3	58.1	44.5	74.3	67.3
2008 entry cohort	62.3	65.6	38.3	57.8	75.0	75.3	60.7	44.4	72.2	68.0
2009 entry cohort	62.2	65.6	37.5	57.6	75.7	76.3	54.3	50.0	66.8	70.3
2010 entry cohort	62.6	66.3	37.0	58.5	75.8	76.5	53.6	45.3	65.8	70.6
2011 entry cohort	63.1	66.7	37.5	59.3	76.9	77.7	48.3	44.0	62.7	71.1
2012 entry cohort	63.6	67.4	38.2	59.4	77.9	78.8	50.9	45.5	61.8	69.2
2013 entry cohort[2]	64.1	67.6	39.7	60.1	78.2	79.0	53.6	43.0	61.7	70.5
Open admissions	30.1	40.2	17.2	24.7	47.7	47.4	50.0	18.4	18.6	33.8
90 percent or more accepted	47.6	50.6	31.6	44.6	50.0	53.0	17.6	24.5	45.9	49.8
75.0 to 89.9 percent accepted	60.8	64.6	41.3	53.3	63.7	63.6	63.9	40.8	53.2	62.8
50.0 to 74.9 percent accepted	59.0	64.0	36.4	53.1	67.2	68.2	47.4	39.2	54.7	61.7
25.0 to 49.9 percent accepted	73.5	77.6	47.3	70.7	82.9	83.4	56.9	50.3	70.9	76.6
Less than 25.0 percent accepted	89.0	90.4	70.7	88.0	94.8	94.8	87.5	76.0	89.4	89.0
For-profit institutions										
1996 entry cohort	28.0	32.3	19.4	26.7	31.7	---	---	30.8	---	53.0
2000 entry cohort	34.2	38.8	28.1	36.0	47.3	---	---	29.4	---	45.6
2002 entry cohort	24.7	28.2	17.4	26.8	38.6	---	---	23.5	---	11.7
2003 entry cohort	25.7	29.3	18.5	26.9	35.0	---	---	18.8	---	12.1
2004 entry cohort	30.3	37.2	21.5	29.0	43.6	---	---	18.6	---	23.7
2005 entry cohort	31.6	38.8	19.5	30.4	42.5	43.3	36.0	27.7	28.5	29.4
2006 entry cohort	35.4	43.9	23.5	35.4	44.0	45.5	27.6	19.6	34.6	37.4
2007 entry cohort	35.7	44.9	23.3	36.0	43.7	45.9	23.9	27.2	28.9	41.4
2008 entry cohort	27.8	37.0	17.8	30.6	43.0	44.4	29.9	18.8	31.8	33.4
2009 entry cohort	23.9	32.1	16.0	27.4	40.9	44.9	16.5	16.4	28.7	33.2
2010 entry cohort	26.8	36.8	17.1	29.1	46.7	49.3	27.2	18.6	33.7	35.0
2011 entry cohort	21.7	26.6	12.9	26.6	36.7	41.3	19.4	10.6	24.8	42.9
2012 entry cohort	25.6	28.5	17.0	28.0	40.1	45.3	21.5	14.8	26.7	43.6
2013 entry cohort	27.6	30.2	19.4	29.3	40.8	44.8	21.3	19.9	38.5	53.5
Graduating within 6 years after entry, females										
All 4-year institutions										
1996 entry cohort	58.2	60.9	43.0	49.1	66.8	---	---	39.5	---	61.5
2000 entry cohort	60.2	62.8	46.4	52.4	70.1	---	---	42.7	---	63.1
2002 entry cohort	59.9	62.8	44.3	52.6	70.0	---	---	40.8	---	56.9
2003 entry cohort	60.0	63.3	43.2	52.2	70.7	---	---	40.2	---	57.3
2004 entry cohort	60.7	63.9	43.3	53.5	71.3	---	---	40.9	---	65.0
2005 entry cohort	60.8	64.2	43.0	53.8	71.8	72.2	48.1	40.3	66.7	66.6
2006 entry cohort	61.4	64.9	43.6	54.9	72.6	73.1	50.2	42.5	68.1	67.6
2007 entry cohort	61.9	65.4	44.5	55.5	73.0	73.6	49.1	43.1	69.9	68.7
2008 entry cohort	62.3	65.9	44.7	57.0	73.4	74.1	50.0	42.8	67.7	70.2
2009 entry cohort	62.1	66.1	43.2	57.0	75.1	75.9	48.2	43.6	61.7	74.0
2010 entry cohort	62.3	66.4	43.3	57.7	75.9	76.6	52.1	41.4	61.9	75.4
2011 entry cohort	63.0	66.9	43.9	58.2	76.4	77.2	52.1	38.9	59.8	76.7
2012 entry cohort	65.3	68.6	46.9	60.4	77.5	78.3	50.1	43.8	60.7	77.8
2013 entry cohort[2]	66.3	69.4	48.9	61.2	78.2	78.9	56.5	43.1	62.1	77.9
Open admissions	29.1	32.9	21.4	25.7	34.1	36.2	23.9	12.5	26.8	52.2
90 percent or more accepted	55.7	60.2	38.0	46.9	56.0	57.4	37.8	33.8	49.5	61.9
75.0 to 89.9 percent accepted	62.0	65.8	43.7	55.3	67.7	68.5	54.9	45.1	54.3	69.3
50.0 to 74.9 percent accepted	67.6	71.4	52.0	61.0	75.3	75.7	60.0	45.9	62.1	76.3
25.0 to 49.9 percent accepted	76.3	79.8	56.7	73.2	84.7	84.8	74.4	62.0	76.6	81.4
Less than 25.0 percent accepted	90.4	91.2	73.9	88.2	95.7	95.8	75.6	77.4	93.1	93.8
Public institutions										
1996 entry cohort	54.7	57.4	41.0	45.7	63.5	---	---	37.0	---	54.9
2000 entry cohort	57.7	59.9	45.2	49.7	67.9	---	---	40.5	---	58.1
2002 entry cohort	57.7	60.1	43.9	50.2	67.8	---	---	38.4	---	59.2
2003 entry cohort	58.2	61.0	42.4	50.4	68.8	---	---	38.9	---	59.7
2004 entry cohort	58.6	61.5	42.3	51.5	69.2	---	---	38.5	---	62.3
2005 entry cohort	58.8	61.8	42.4	51.9	69.7	70.0	48.7	38.5	58.4	62.0
2006 entry cohort	59.6	62.7	43.3	52.9	71.1	71.5	50.7	40.5	57.8	62.6
2007 entry cohort	60.3	63.3	44.1	54.1	71.3	71.8	49.9	42.3	61.5	63.4
2008 entry cohort	61.2	64.3	45.1	56.1	72.0	72.6	50.3	41.0	62.1	65.3
2009 entry cohort	61.4	64.5	44.2	56.4	73.8	74.5	49.8	41.8	56.9	70.3
2010 entry cohort	61.7	64.9	44.2	57.2	74.4	75.0	54.8	39.3	58.9	73.2
2011 entry cohort	62.4	65.7	45.0	57.8	75.3	75.8	57.9	39.0	57.5	75.2
2012 entry cohort	64.0	67.1	46.9	59.7	76.2	76.8	53.7	43.1	58.7	76.2
2013 entry cohort[2]	65.2	68.1	49.0	60.4	77.1	77.6	58.2	41.6	60.3	76.2
Open admissions	32.0	35.4	23.2	26.4	34.8	35.7	26.3	14.4	24.7	47.1

Time to completion, sex, control of institution, cohort entry year, and percentage of applications accepted	Total	White	Black	Hispanic	Asian/Pacific Islander			American Indian/Alaska Native	Two or more races	Non-resident alien[1]
					Total	Asian	Pacific Islander			
1	2	3	4	5	6	7	8	9	10	11
90 percent or more accepted	55.0	60.0	37.6	44.1	53.8	55.0	39.2	29.6	48.9	58.8
75.0 to 89.9 percent accepted	60.4	64.0	42.7	53.8	66.3	67.2	51.4	45.0	53.2	70.8
50.0 to 74.9 percent accepted	67.7	71.5	53.4	60.7	75.9	76.2	59.4	44.5	62.4	77.7
25.0 to 49.9 percent accepted	74.1	78.3	52.3	71.5	83.7	83.8	80.0	61.6	75.5	77.1
Less than 25.0 percent accepted	87.9	90.6	59.1	83.4	94.2	94.3	82.6	75.0	93.8	92.6
Nonprofit institutions										
1996 entry cohort	65.4	67.9	48.4	58.3	75.0	---	---	49.2	---	66.4
2000 entry cohort	66.7	69.1	50.4	61.7	76.7	---	---	51.5	---	67.8
2002 entry cohort	66.9	69.5	49.0	62.3	76.9	---	---	52.1	---	71.7
2003 entry cohort	67.2	69.8	49.2	61.3	77.3	---	---	49.3	---	73.2
2004 entry cohort	67.4	69.7	49.2	63.0	77.6	---	---	51.7	---	74.5
2005 entry cohort	67.3	69.8	48.1	62.6	77.9	78.4	54.9	49.2	76.5	75.1
2006 entry cohort	67.6	70.1	48.5	64.2	77.7	78.4	55.1	53.0	78.3	75.4
2007 entry cohort	67.7	70.5	49.2	62.9	78.6	79.3	57.3	50.6	78.4	76.0
2008 entry cohort	67.9	70.5	49.3	64.1	78.4	78.9	60.4	51.8	73.9	76.6
2009 entry cohort	68.3	71.4	48.2	63.8	79.6	80.2	56.7	53.5	71.4	79.4
2010 entry cohort	68.5	71.8	47.5	64.3	80.4	81.3	55.4	52.1	70.3	79.2
2011 entry cohort	69.2	72.2	49.0	65.3	80.7	81.4	56.0	47.8	69.0	79.7
2012 entry cohort	70.1	73.1	50.3	65.7	81.5	82.4	53.1	50.6	67.9	80.3
2013 entry cohort[2]	71.0	73.7	52.5	66.6	81.8	82.5	61.6	52.7	68.1	80.4
Open admissions	29.9	36.9	25.9	19.5	39.8	38.3	50.0	15.1	24.8	45.8
90 percent or more accepted	57.5	60.7	38.9	54.5	60.7	63.0	31.8	52.6	50.8	68.2
75.0 to 89.9 percent accepted	67.0	71.0	48.5	60.3	70.9	71.4	62.2	46.0	59.1	67.6
50.0 to 74.9 percent accepted	67.7	71.6	48.5	62.5	73.5	74.0	62.5	50.4	61.6	73.6
25.0 to 49.9 percent accepted	79.4	81.6	63.5	78.3	87.2	87.6	66.0	62.2	78.3	84.5
Less than 25.0 percent accepted	91.2	91.4	79.0	90.8	96.6	96.7	68.2	77.8	92.9	94.2
For-profit institutions										
1996 entry cohort	27.9	34.5	19.0	21.9	24.9	---	---	17.3	---	55.1
2000 entry cohort	27.9	34.0	27.7	30.0	43.2	---	---	29.1	---	47.5
2002 entry cohort	21.1	23.6	16.7	28.4	31.7	---	---	12.1	---	13.0
2003 entry cohort	21.8	25.6	18.2	26.7	31.6	---	---	10.8	---	11.6
2004 entry cohort	26.9	33.6	21.3	28.9	33.1	---	---	19.3	---	20.4
2005 entry cohort	26.9	33.3	20.0	30.0	42.1	45.8	17.6	18.7	26.9	27.7
2006 entry cohort	28.0	35.8	19.5	32.1	40.8	43.3	23.5	18.2	29.3	33.9
2007 entry cohort	28.4	33.8	21.8	34.1	42.8	48.1	19.7	14.3	37.6	40.8
2008 entry cohort	25.3	31.9	19.3	32.5	39.4	43.8	23.5	20.6	40.6	48.0
2009 entry cohort	21.7	26.6	15.2	29.8	39.3	45.8	22.2	16.9	25.1	49.7
2010 entry cohort	21.5	25.4	14.3	28.6	40.3	45.9	17.9	16.0	22.1	49.8
2011 entry cohort	20.1	21.1	13.8	25.9	37.4	46.0	17.7	11.2	19.8	54.0
2012 entry cohort	25.2	25.6	18.5	27.3	37.8	48.3	12.0	14.5	24.6	62.0
2013 entry cohort	25.1	25.3	18.6	29.9	42.5	49.7	22.8	11.1	27.4	62.4

---Not available.

[1] Race/ethnicity not collected.

[2] Includes institutions that did not report admissions data, which are not shown separately.

NOTE: Data in this table represent the 50 states and the District of Columbia. Data are for 4-year degree-granting postsecondary institutions participating in Title IV federal financial aid programs. Graduation rates refer to students receiving bachelor's degrees from their initial institutions of attendance only. Totals include data for persons whose race/ethnicity was not reported. Race categories exclude persons of Hispanic ethnicity. Some data have been revised from previously published figures.

SOURCE: U.S. Department of Education, National Center for Education Statistics, Integrated Postsecondary Education Data System (IPEDS), Spring 2002 through Spring 2013 and Winter 2013-14 through Winter 2019-20, Graduation Rates component; and IPEDS Fall 2013, Institutional Characteristics component. (This table was prepared August 2020.)

Table 326.20. Graduation rate from first institution attended within 150 percent of normal time for first-time, full-time degree/certificate-seeking students at 2-year postsecondary institutions, by race/ethnicity, sex, and control of institution: Selected cohort entry years, 2000 through 2016

Sex, control of institution, and cohort entry year	Percent graduating with a certificate or associate's degree within 150 percent of normal time									
	Total	White	Black	Hispanic	Asian/Pacific Islander			American Indian/ Alaska Native	Two or more races	Non-resident alien[1]
					Total	Asian	Pacific Islander			
1	2	3	4	5	6	7	8	9	10	11
Males and females										
All 2-year institutions										
2000 entry cohort	30.5	31.5	26.1	30.1	33.3	---	---	29.3	---	25.5
2005 entry cohort	27.6	28.7	22.8	25.7	31.5	---	---	24.9	---	32.2
2008 entry cohort	31.2	30.1	27.6	35.1	34.3	35.2	24.1	25.7	33.3	33.7
2009 entry cohort	30.9	30.1	26.4	36.3	35.1	36.0	25.0	25.7	30.5	34.6
2010 entry cohort	29.4	29.4	23.7	33.8	35.4	35.1	37.9	23.9	25.9	36.2
2011 entry cohort	27.9	29.0	20.2	29.9	33.6	33.7	32.1	22.5	24.5	34.5
2012 entry cohort	29.0	30.5	22.1	29.8	35.7	35.8	34.4	24.4	24.4	35.8
2013 entry cohort	30.3	32.2	23.0	30.1	36.1	36.2	34.2	26.8	25.1	35.0
2014 entry cohort	31.6	33.5	25.3	30.9	37.3	37.5	34.5	28.1	26.2	35.6
2015 entry cohort	32.3	34.6	27.6	30.3	37.8	38.3	30.0	29.1	26.7	34.7
2016 entry cohort	33.5	36.0	28.5	31.6	39.6	40.1	32.1	27.1	28.1	36.5
Public institutions										
2000 entry cohort	23.6	25.7	17.8	16.8	25.5	---	---	19.6	---	23.2
2005 entry cohort	20.6	23.0	12.1	15.6	25.8	---	---	18.3	---	29.9
2008 entry cohort	20.2	22.8	11.8	15.8	26.2	27.2	15.2	15.4	17.0	30.5
2009 entry cohort	19.8	22.5	11.3	15.9	26.1	27.3	11.9	15.9	18.5	32.6
2010 entry cohort	19.5	22.5	10.8	16.2	26.7	27.6	15.7	15.0	17.4	32.6
2011 entry cohort	20.0	23.4	9.8	17.5	27.2	28.1	14.0	14.4	17.6	31.0
2012 entry cohort	21.9	25.5	11.7	19.1	30.2	30.7	22.1	15.5	18.4	32.9
2013 entry cohort	23.6	27.4	13.3	20.7	31.0	31.6	19.9	17.3	19.6	31.9
2014 entry cohort	25.1	28.9	14.6	22.1	32.5	33.1	22.8	19.3	20.7	33.3
2015 entry cohort	27.0	30.8	16.2	24.0	34.7	35.5	19.5	20.4	22.5	33.2
2016 entry cohort	28.2	32.4	17.7	24.8	36.3	37.0	23.5	20.0	23.3	34.9
Nonprofit institutions										
2000 entry cohort	50.1	49.6	37.5	56.3	61.4	---	---	62.1	---	43.1
2005 entry cohort	48.3	52.4	41.6	47.3	41.6	---	---	14.8	---	51.7
2008 entry cohort	56.6	59.7	53.4	62.4	52.9	53.9	‡	25.0	55.8	59.5
2009 entry cohort	62.3	66.0	59.7	68.3	57.9	57.7	‡	30.4	66.5	50.0
2010 entry cohort	53.4	55.9	50.9	61.9	51.7	52.2	‡	18.2	39.5	52.5
2011 entry cohort	51.2	56.3	46.5	57.5	47.0	48.0	35.7	21.6	45.6	51.5
2012 entry cohort	56.5	63.1	47.3	60.4	61.6	60.2	68.9	44.6	51.9	65.1
2013 entry cohort	59.6	65.8	50.4	64.1	72.9	75.3	65.3	52.2	53.8	70.6
2014 entry cohort	62.2	67.2	57.3	65.6	80.2	81.8	74.8	48.6	55.4	68.8
2015 entry cohort	62.3	65.7	59.5	63.0	70.9	73.3	62.0	46.4	56.4	68.2
2016 entry cohort	58.7	63.7	54.1	67.6	67.0	77.5	36.8	27.4	49.0	70.7
For-profit institutions										
2000 entry cohort	59.1	63.1	47.6	60.3	64.4	---	---	60.3	---	55.4
2005 entry cohort	57.8	62.9	48.2	61.5	66.0	---	---	55.9	---	57.7
2008 entry cohort	61.7	64.1	52.6	67.9	69.9	70.2	66.2	60.3	57.4	62.0
2009 entry cohort	62.7	65.1	52.9	68.4	70.8	71.6	64.0	60.7	59.9	61.7
2010 entry cohort	62.8	65.8	53.3	68.3	72.3	73.4	68.8	61.2	58.9	69.7
2011 entry cohort	58.4	62.5	48.4	62.2	65.9	66.4	63.6	55.5	56.8	69.6
2012 entry cohort	60.0	63.0	48.9	68.7	70.5	71.4	65.0	60.7	55.9	66.1
2013 entry cohort	59.8	63.9	47.6	66.2	68.9	68.9	68.5	60.6	57.4	70.3
2014 entry cohort	61.0	64.2	48.2	69.2	70.4	70.8	67.6	61.8	59.2	62.7
2015 entry cohort	60.8	65.0	51.1	64.9	67.6	68.3	63.7	62.9	55.9	59.2
2016 entry cohort	61.2	65.2	49.1	67.4	71.0	72.4	63.2	60.9	60.2	70.3
Males										
All 2-year institutions										
2000 entry cohort	28.7	30.0	23.1	27.9	30.1	---	---	28.3	---	22.9
2005 entry cohort	25.4	27.2	18.6	21.8	28.5	---	---	23.5	---	29.4
2008 entry cohort	27.4	27.7	22.7	29.1	30.3	30.9	23.8	23.0	28.8	30.5
2009 entry cohort	27.2	27.8	22.1	30.0	30.9	31.7	21.6	23.6	24.6	31.5
2010 entry cohort	26.2	27.5	19.5	27.7	31.5	31.5	31.8	21.4	22.3	33.2
2011 entry cohort	25.3	27.5	16.8	25.7	29.8	29.9	28.7	20.6	21.7	31.7
2012 entry cohort	26.6	29.2	18.8	25.0	31.8	31.8	31.0	22.7	22.9	32.5
2013 entry cohort	27.5	30.5	19.1	25.3	31.7	31.9	29.5	23.9	22.8	31.2
2014 entry cohort	28.7	31.9	20.8	26.3	32.7	32.9	28.9	23.3	23.2	31.7
2015 entry cohort	29.6	33.1	21.9	26.6	34.6	35.2	25.4	27.3	23.7	30.9
2016 entry cohort	30.9	34.9	22.9	27.6	36.0	36.5	27.7	26.0	25.7	33.6
Public institutions										
2000 entry cohort	22.2	24.2	16.5	15.4	22.6	---	---	19.3	---	20.4
2005 entry cohort	19.9	22.2	12.0	14.6	23.5	---	---	18.8	---	27.4
2008 entry cohort	19.6	22.1	12.0	14.9	24.3	25.1	15.2	15.2	16.7	28.1
2009 entry cohort	19.3	22.0	11.4	14.8	24.4	25.4	12.4	16.0	16.8	29.9

Sex, control of institution, and cohort entry year	Percent graduating with a certificate or associate's degree within 150 percent of normal time									
	Total	White	Black	His-panic	Asian/Pacific Islander			Ameri-can Indian/ Alaska Native	Two or more races	Non-resident alien[1]
					Total	Asian	Pacific Islander			
1	2	3	4	5	6	7	8	9	10	11
2010 entry cohort	19.0	21.9	10.7	15.1	24.7	25.4	14.8	14.1	16.2	30.1
2011 entry cohort	19.5	23.0	9.8	16.4	24.6	25.4	12.9	14.2	16.3	28.2
2012 entry cohort	21.4	25.1	11.4	17.6	27.8	28.2	21.4	15.6	17.4	29.7
2013 entry cohort	22.9	26.9	13.0	19.0	27.9	28.4	18.6	16.7	18.9	27.9
2014 entry cohort	24.4	28.7	14.4	20.2	29.2	29.7	19.2	17.7	19.5	29.1
2015 entry cohort	26.1	30.5	15.7	21.8	32.1	32.9	18.0	21.0	20.9	29.5
2016 entry cohort	27.2	32.1	16.6	22.4	33.2	33.8	20.7	19.2	21.9	32.1
Nonprofit institutions										
2000 entry cohort	49.5	49.3	31.7	54.3	62.5	---	---	64.5	---	42.6
2005 entry cohort	44.5	49.2	38.7	42.9	43.7	---	---	10.4	---	47.7
2008 entry cohort	49.8	53.8	47.3	49.4	45.4	46.3	‡	14.6	46.7	52.1
2009 entry cohort	53.6	57.5	51.0	58.2	47.4	47.7	‡	22.4	56.1	45.1
2010 entry cohort	46.2	49.4	42.5	52.1	47.6	48.8	‡	19.8	27.0	44.0
2011 entry cohort	45.7	52.0	38.0	48.9	41.1	42.8	‡	19.2	42.0	50.3
2012 entry cohort	57.4	65.5	42.7	58.3	56.8	55.2	68.3	46.3	44.8	67.2
2013 entry cohort	56.3	64.8	39.7	58.5	71.5	73.8	60.5	43.7	51.8	67.6
2014 entry cohort	56.2	63.9	42.5	60.9	79.3	79.6	78.1	29.8	48.5	62.4
2015 entry cohort	54.7	56.6	49.9	59.3	69.5	73.0	40.9	23.2	48.2	59.2
2016 entry cohort	54.9	60.2	49.2	63.1	70.5	79.6	19.2	29.4	40.7	65.1
For-profit institutions										
2000 entry cohort	59.3	63.7	45.6	58.2	63.1	---	---	55.9	---	55.0
2005 entry cohort	57.8	64.9	43.3	57.6	66.3	---	---	56.2	---	56.3
2008 entry cohort	58.9	63.9	48.2	63.1	67.7	68.1	65.1	54.6	58.2	54.6
2009 entry cohort	59.6	63.7	49.3	63.8	67.7	68.7	59.2	59.4	55.2	59.9
2010 entry cohort	60.8	66.0	49.5	63.3	71.2	72.8	65.3	59.1	57.2	66.4
2011 entry cohort	57.7	63.3	45.6	59.9	65.9	65.6	67.1	53.6	56.0	67.7
2012 entry cohort	57.7	61.7	46.7	63.9	67.2	68.3	61.9	57.4	56.6	60.6
2013 entry cohort	57.1	61.8	44.5	62.9	67.3	67.4	67.0	56.6	54.5	69.0
2014 entry cohort	58.2	62.8	46.0	65.2	66.6	66.7	66.0	55.4	57.5	62.9
2015 entry cohort	59.5	64.0	49.8	62.6	66.6	67.6	61.1	61.3	52.5	53.8
2016 entry cohort	61.1	66.1	47.6	65.8	71.9	73.6	61.8	61.5	60.5	74.5
Females										
All 2-year institutions										
2000 entry cohort	32.1	33.0	28.1	31.8	36.3	---	---	30.0	---	28.3
2005 entry cohort	29.5	30.1	25.4	28.6	34.7	---	---	26.0	---	34.8
2008 entry cohort	34.4	32.3	30.9	39.4	38.3	39.6	24.3	27.9	36.2	36.7
2009 entry cohort	34.1	32.3	29.4	40.9	39.3	40.3	28.0	27.3	35.0	37.6
2010 entry cohort	32.1	31.1	26.7	38.2	39.4	38.9	43.2	26.0	28.9	39.1
2011 entry cohort	30.0	30.5	22.6	33.1	37.6	37.9	35.3	24.0	26.8	37.3
2012 entry cohort	31.2	31.7	24.6	33.6	39.8	40.0	37.5	25.8	25.8	39.4
2013 entry cohort	32.8	33.7	26.0	33.8	40.6	40.8	38.5	29.2	27.1	39.3
2014 entry cohort	34.1	35.0	28.6	34.6	42.2	42.4	39.6	31.9	28.7	40.2
2015 entry cohort	34.7	36.2	31.8	33.3	41.2	41.7	34.4	30.5	29.3	39.4
2016 entry cohort	35.8	37.1	32.4	34.9	43.5	44.1	35.5	28.0	30.2	39.9
Public institutions										
2000 entry cohort	24.8	27.1	18.8	17.9	28.4	---	---	19.9	---	26.2
2005 entry cohort	21.3	23.9	12.1	16.3	28.3	---	---	17.9	---	32.2
2008 entry cohort	20.7	23.5	11.7	16.5	28.3	29.6	15.2	15.6	17.3	32.9
2009 entry cohort	20.2	23.0	11.2	16.8	28.0	29.5	11.4	15.8	20.0	35.4
2010 entry cohort	20.1	23.0	10.8	17.2	29.0	30.0	16.8	15.7	18.6	35.1
2011 entry cohort	20.4	23.8	9.7	18.4	30.3	31.3	15.3	14.6	18.7	33.9
2012 entry cohort	22.5	25.8	11.8	20.3	32.9	33.7	22.8	15.4	19.2	36.4
2013 entry cohort	24.4	27.9	13.5	22.2	34.5	35.3	21.4	17.8	20.2	36.5
2014 entry cohort	25.8	29.2	14.7	23.8	36.4	37.0	26.6	20.8	21.9	38.4
2015 entry cohort	27.8	31.1	16.7	26.0	37.6	38.5	21.2	19.8	24.0	37.8
2016 entry cohort	29.2	32.7	18.7	27.0	39.8	40.6	25.9	20.7	24.7	38.2
Nonprofit institutions										
2000 entry cohort	50.7	50.0	43.1	58.3	60.1	---	---	60.2	---	43.8
2005 entry cohort	51.3	54.9	44.9	49.6	40.1	---	---	18.0	---	55.2
2008 entry cohort	59.9	63.2	55.8	67.7	56.8	57.7	‡	31.5	58.3	66.8
2009 entry cohort	66.6	70.8	63.4	72.5	63.2	62.7	‡	34.5	70.3	54.5
2010 entry cohort	57.5	60.0	54.8	66.4	54.5	54.5	‡	17.3	45.5	58.7
2011 entry cohort	54.1	59.2	50.2	60.8	50.0	50.6	‡	23.6	47.7	52.7
2012 entry cohort	56.1	61.2	49.2	61.3	64.1	62.9	69.2	43.6	55.0	63.6
2013 entry cohort	60.8	66.4	53.5	66.3	73.7	76.3	66.9	56.3	54.7	73.3
2014 entry cohort	63.6	68.2	59.9	66.9	80.6	83.0	73.6	55.4	57.7	74.8
2015 entry cohort	63.7	67.4	60.8	63.9	71.5	73.5	66.1	51.0	58.1	79.4
2016 entry cohort	59.4	64.4	54.7	69.0	65.5	76.5	40.5	26.8	50.7	74.8
For-profit institutions										
2000 entry cohort	58.9	62.6	48.6	61.8	65.3	---	---	63.8	---	55.7
2005 entry cohort	57.8	61.5	50.0	63.3	65.9	---	---	55.8	---	58.6
2008 entry cohort	63.2	64.2	54.7	70.3	71.2	71.4	67.3	64.0	57.1	67.6
2009 entry cohort	64.4	66.0	54.7	70.7	72.7	73.4	66.9	61.5	61.9	62.8
2010 entry cohort	63.8	65.7	55.0	70.7	73.1	73.7	71.0	62.5	59.8	72.7
2011 entry cohort	58.8	62.0	49.7	63.4	65.9	66.9	61.4	56.6	57.1	71.4
2012 entry cohort	61.3	63.9	50.1	71.0	72.5	73.4	67.4	62.7	55.4	72.7
2013 entry cohort	61.4	65.2	49.3	67.7	69.8	69.8	69.6	63.1	58.9	71.9
2014 entry cohort	62.6	65.2	49.4	71.3	72.8	73.4	68.8	65.6	60.1	62.4
2015 entry cohort	61.8	65.9	51.8	66.3	68.4	68.9	65.7	64.1	58.2	67.0
2016 entry cohort	61.3	64.4	50.0	68.3	70.4	71.5	64.0	60.5	60.0	66.5

---Not available.

‡Reporting standards not met (too few cases).

[1] Race/ethnicity not collected.

NOTE: Data in this table represent the 50 states and the District of Columbia. Data are for 2-year degree-granting postsecondary institutions participating in Title IV federal financial aid programs. Graduation rates refer to students receiving associate's degrees or certificates from their initial institutions of attendance only. Totals include data for persons whose race/ethnicity was not reported. Race categories exclude persons of Hispanic ethnicity. Some data have been revised from previously published figures.

SOURCE: U.S. Department of Education, National Center for Education Statistics, Integrated Postsecondary Education Data System (IPEDS), Spring 2004 through Spring 2013 and Winter 2013-14 through Winter 2019-20, Graduation Rates component. (This table was prepared August 2020.)

Table 326.30. Retention of first-time degree-seeking undergraduates at degree-granting postsecondary institutions, by attendance status, level and control of institution, and percentage of applications accepted: Selected years, 2006 to 2018

Attendance status, level, control, and percent of applications accepted	First-time degree-seekers (adjusted entry cohort),[1] by entry year							Students from adjusted cohort returning in the following year							Percent of first-time undergraduates retained						
	2006	2009	2013	2014	2015	2016	2017	2007	2010	2014	2015	2016	2017	2018	2006 to 2007	2009 to 2010	2013 to 2014	2014 to 2015	2015 to 2016	2016 to 2017	2017 to 2018
1	2	3	4	5	6	7	8	9	10	11	12	13	14	15	16	17	18	19	20	21	22
Full-time students																					
All institutions	**2,170,504**	**2,371,220**	**2,222,085**	**2,211,406**	**2,180,675**	**2,177,194**	**2,180,170**	**1,541,201**	**1,705,242**	**1,642,567**	**1,647,295**	**1,640,963**	**1,643,904**	**1,648,776**	**71.0**	**71.9**	**73.9**	**74.5**	**75.3**	**75.5**	**75.6**
Public institutions	1,522,928	1,732,822	1,646,902	1,639,875	1,619,768	1,620,387	1,624,433	1,071,986	1,222,688	1,193,200	1,200,374	1,198,609	1,203,750	1,206,993	70.4	70.6	72.5	73.2	74.0	74.3	74.3
Nonprofit institutions	466,078	478,755	483,617	489,834	491,898	491,742	505,768	368,783	381,364	392,080	396,659	399,434	399,354	409,821	79.1	79.7	81.1	81.0	81.2	81.2	81.0
For-profit institutions	181,498	159,643	91,566	81,697	69,009	65,065	49,969	100,432	101,190	57,287	50,262	42,920	40,800	31,962	55.3	63.4	62.6	61.5	62.2	62.7	64.0
4-year institutions	1,457,745	1,452,575	1,483,526	1,501,582	1,524,088	1,534,945	1,553,162	1,114,923	1,146,534	1,194,097	1,212,464	1,231,920	1,242,850	1,257,978	76.5	78.9	80.5	80.7	80.8	81.0	81.0
Public institutions	911,509	936,840	978,041	995,110	1,018,253	1,028,968	1,041,749	711,200	745,703	790,227	807,687	825,885	836,675	846,079	78.0	79.6	80.8	81.2	81.1	81.3	81.2
Open admissions	61,832	45,458	34,706	31,477	26,888	26,839	27,498	38,383	28,675	21,547	19,618	16,689	16,671	17,278	62.1	63.1	62.1	62.3	62.1	62.1	62.8
90.0 percent or more accepted	68,835	63,453	55,188	60,160	71,117	69,603	82,664	49,274	46,280	40,116	43,559	51,533	50,537	60,453	71.6	72.9	72.7	72.4	72.5	72.6	73.1
75.0 to 89.9 percent accepted	244,177	212,573	261,763	281,422	317,658	288,854	306,567	185,457	163,639	203,517	221,245	251,113	228,127	241,826	76.0	77.0	77.7	78.6	79.1	79.0	78.9
50.0 to 74.9 percent accepted	417,093	462,554	461,551	456,622	435,275	468,321	433,808	336,365	376,021	381,607	376,587	357,438	383,791	354,792	80.6	81.3	82.7	82.5	82.1	82.0	81.8
25.0 to 49.9 percent accepted	103,118	131,241	147,849	145,622	150,981	156,438	167,075	88,908	112,209	127,595	128,568	133,668	139,838	148,465	86.2	85.5	86.3	88.3	88.5	89.4	88.9
Less than 25.0 percent accepted	7,716	14,326	15,315	14,947	15,563	15,951	22,740	7,048	13,649	14,651	14,336	14,959	15,330	21,999	91.3	95.3	95.7	95.9	96.1	96.1	96.7
Information not available	8,738	7,235	1,669	4,860	771	2,962	1,397	5,765	5,230	1,194	3,774	485	2,381	1,266	66.0	72.3	71.5	77.7	62.9	80.4	90.6
Nonprofit institutions	457,505	470,795	476,437	476,823	481,241	484,334	495,026	363,459	376,668	387,685	388,745	392,330	394,415	402,106	79.4	80.0	81.4	81.5	81.5	81.4	81.2
Open admissions	26,565	22,613	12,549	11,792	13,289	13,378	12,117	16,019	14,349	7,653	7,414	8,499	8,795	7,873	60.3	63.5	61.0	62.9	64.0	65.7	65.0
90.0 percent or more accepted	13,632	15,135	22,841	22,225	28,503	23,596	33,038	9,543	10,953	16,881	16,188	20,247	16,897	23,971	70.0	72.4	73.9	72.8	71.0	71.6	72.6
75.0 to 89.9 percent accepted	102,358	80,301	86,040	94,830	80,940	91,372	92,986	78,424	62,196	68,481	74,984	63,872	71,328	72,983	76.6	77.5	79.6	79.1	78.9	78.1	78.5
50.0 to 74.9 percent accepted	190,079	218,072	207,431	199,677	199,442	203,979	201,207	148,681	170,232	162,937	157,866	157,181	162,016	158,256	78.2	78.1	78.5	79.1	78.8	79.4	78.7
25.0 to 49.9 percent accepted	93,560	98,312	98,202	95,164	102,823	98,053	95,878	81,880	84,941	85,484	82,511	89,426	84,421	82,935	87.5	86.4	87.0	86.7	87.0	86.1	86.5
Less than 25.0 percent accepted	26,696	32,980	45,222	48,076	54,573	51,642	55,035	25,639	31,790	43,522	46,054	51,699	49,508	53,162	96.0	96.4	96.2	95.8	94.7	95.9	96.6
Information not available	4,615	3,382	4,152	5,059	1,671	2,314	4,765	3,273	2,207	2,727	3,728	1,406	1,450	2,926	70.9	65.3	65.7	73.7	84.1	62.7	61.4
For-profit institutions	88,731	44,940	29,048	29,649	24,594	21,643	16,387	40,264	24,163	16,185	16,032	13,705	11,760	9,793	45.4	53.8	55.7	54.1	55.7	54.3	59.8
Open admissions	45,240	16,826	19,206	21,732	16,511	13,943	10,036	18,720	9,260	10,053	10,827	8,270	6,706	5,490	41.4	55.0	52.3	49.8	50.1	48.1	54.7
90.0 percent or more accepted	6,285	3,722	717	591	770	1,108	803	3,454	1,311	509	308	472	559	560	55.0	35.2	71.0	52.1	61.3	50.5	69.7
75.0 to 89.9 percent accepted	3,703	3,224	2,920	5,265	3,253	1,174	2,874	2,081	1,549	1,865	3,459	2,159	885	1,839	56.2	48.0	63.9	65.7	66.4	75.4	64.0
50.0 to 74.9 percent accepted	12,845	12,061	3,690	1,489	3,000	4,577	2,344	6,536	6,839	2,472	994	1,973	3,108	1,642	50.9	56.7	67.0	66.8	65.8	67.9	70.1
25.0 to 49.9 percent accepted	18,142	6,098	419	463	1,020	672	300	8,036	3,423	293	353	802	363	240	44.3	56.1	69.9	76.2	78.6	54.0	80.0
Less than 25.0 percent accepted	0	3	0	0	8	1	0	0	2	0	0	8	1	0	†	66.7	†	†	100.0	100.0	†
Information not available	2,516	3,006	2,096	109	32	168	30	1,437	1,779	993	91	21	138	22	57.1	59.2	47.4	83.5	65.6	82.1	73.3
2-year institutions	712,759	918,645	738,559	709,824	656,587	642,249	627,008	426,278	558,708	448,470	434,831	409,043	401,054	390,798	59.8	60.8	60.7	61.3	62.3	62.4	62.3
Public institutions	611,419	795,982	668,861	644,765	601,515	591,419	582,684	360,786	476,985	402,973	392,687	372,724	367,075	360,914	59.0	59.9	60.2	60.9	62.0	62.1	61.9
Nonprofit institutions	8,573	7,960	7,180	13,011	10,657	7,408	10,742	5,324	4,696	4,395	7,914	7,104	4,939	7,715	62.1	59.0	61.2	60.8	66.7	66.7	71.8
For-profit institutions	92,767	114,703	62,518	52,048	44,415	43,422	33,582	60,168	77,027	41,102	34,230	29,215	29,040	22,169	64.9	67.2	65.7	65.8	65.8	66.9	66.0
Part-time students																					
All institutions	**461,574**	**545,635**	**490,124**	**470,772**	**429,109**	**411,269**	**404,081**	**190,547**	**229,566**	**213,235**	**205,366**	**192,527**	**186,683**	**182,838**	**41.3**	**42.1**	**43.5**	**43.6**	**44.9**	**45.4**	**45.2**
Public institutions	417,314	497,453	461,943	445,495	404,279	390,075	380,256	170,682	209,164	202,243	195,147	181,993	177,878	172,830	40.9	42.0	43.8	43.8	45.0	45.6	45.5
Nonprofit institutions	14,618	10,359	9,340	8,885	10,446	8,825	13,902	7,027	4,892	3,883	3,681	4,951	3,893	5,968	48.1	47.2	41.6	41.4	47.4	44.1	42.9
For-profit institutions	29,642	37,823	18,841	16,392	14,384	12,369	9,923	12,838	15,510	7,109	6,538	5,583	4,912	4,040	43.3	41.0	37.7	39.9	38.8	39.7	40.7
4-year institutions	81,423	72,046	49,304	46,606	48,716	46,515	50,441	37,988	32,344	22,269	21,818	23,845	22,669	24,771	46.7	44.9	45.2	46.8	48.9	48.7	49.1
Public institutions	47,377	33,327	26,473	25,833	28,096	29,746	29,470	23,337	16,944	13,862	13,917	15,374	16,029	16,158	49.3	50.8	52.4	53.9	54.7	53.9	54.8
Open admissions	19,247	8,356	5,250	4,605	4,412	5,403	4,176	8,004	3,586	2,098	1,791	1,873	2,136	1,654	41.6	42.9	40.0	38.9	42.5	39.5	39.6
90.0 percent or more accepted	3,745	4,004	2,098	1,951	2,931	2,326	2,509	1,909	1,959	1,063	880	1,382	1,013	1,089	51.0	48.9	50.7	45.1	47.2	43.6	43.4
75.0 to 89.9 percent accepted	8,969	6,493	7,424	6,663	8,722	9,007	9,649	4,196	3,268	3,964	3,591	4,972	4,925	5,324	46.8	50.3	53.4	53.9	57.0	54.7	55.2
50.0 to 74.9 percent accepted	11,599	11,254	9,042	10,343	9,815	10,729	10,891	6,766	6,053	5,065	6,107	5,654	6,458	6,630	58.3	53.8	56.0	59.0	57.6	60.2	60.9
25.0 to 49.9 percent accepted	3,373	3,046	2,553	2,040	2,112	2,103	2,177	2,223	1,982	1,617	1,395	1,433	1,392	1,413	65.9	65.1	63.3	68.4	67.9	66.2	64.9
Less than 25.0 percent accepted	65	44	51	58	48	65	58	50	35	33	49	38	57	44	76.9	79.5	64.7	84.5	79.2	87.7	75.9
Information not available	379	130	55	173	56	113	10	189	61	22	104	22	48	4	49.9	46.9	40.0	60.1	39.3	42.5	40.0

See notes at end of table.

Table 326.30. Retention of first-time degree-seeking undergraduates at degree-granting postsecondary institutions, by attendance status, level and control of institution, and percentage of applications accepted: Selected years, 2006 to 2018—Continued

Attendance status, level, control, and percent of applications accepted	First-time degree-seekers (adjusted entry cohort),[1] by entry year							Students from adjusted cohort returning in the following year								Percent of first-time undergraduates retained						
	2006	2009	2013	2014	2015	2016	2017	2007	2010	2014	2015	2016	2017	2018	2006 to 2007	2009 to 2010	2013 to 2014	2014 to 2015	2015 to 2016	2016 to 2017	2017 to 2018
1	2	3	4	5	6	7	8	9	10	11	12	13	14	15	16	17	18	19	20	21	22
Nonprofit institutions	12,861	9,599	8,501	8,093	9,686	7,962	13,356	6,054	4,491	3,448	3,322	4,612	3,553	5,758	47.1	46.8	40.6	41.0	47.6	44.6	43.1
Open admissions	5,419	3,821	2,434	1,450	1,540	1,583	1,757	2,558	1,693	848	486	673	660	758	47.2	44.3	34.8	33.5	43.7	41.7	43.1
90.0 percent or more accepted	523	393	1,159	494	3,769	1,990	911	237	199	468	204	1,882	887	566	45.3	50.6	40.4	41.3	49.9	44.6	62.1
75.0 to 89.9 percent accepted	2,459	1,164	1,332	1,903	874	938	4,522	1,047	550	622	811	422	465	1,967	42.6	47.3	46.7	42.6	48.3	49.6	43.5
50.0 to 74.9 percent accepted	3,131	3,256	1,515	2,231	1,812	2,358	1,985	1,406	1,531	701	928	839	1,018	871	44.9	47.0	46.3	41.6	46.3	43.2	43.9
25.0 to 49.9 percent accepted	853	715	606	815	866	587	1,030	452	366	305	394	381	263	430	53.0	51.2	50.3	48.3	44.0	44.8	41.7
Less than 25.0 percent accepted	112	93	115	136	640	458	99	86	78	101	123	302	238	84	76.8	83.9	87.8	90.4	47.2	52.0	84.8
Information not available	364	157	1,340	1,064	185	48	3,052	268	74	403	376	113	22	1,082	73.6	47.1	30.1	35.3	61.1	45.8	35.5
For-profit institutions	21,185	29,120	14,330	12,680	10,934	8,807	7,615	8,597	10,909	4,959	4,579	3,859	3,087	2,855	40.6	37.5	34.6	36.1	35.3	35.1	37.5
Open admissions	10,514	10,926	10,395	10,089	8,822	6,384	5,667	4,121	4,299	3,751	3,863	3,183	2,388	2,227	39.2	39.3	36.1	38.3	36.1	37.4	39.3
90.0 percent or more accepted	2,212	1,372	126	123	246	453	204	639	375	59	30	85	115	47	28.9	27.3	46.8	24.4	34.6	25.4	23.0
75.0 to 89.9 percent accepted	2,838	3,151	1,232	1,794	1,027	109	1,065	1,342	1,093	353	492	259	29	382	47.3	34.7	28.7	27.4	25.2	26.6	35.9
50.0 to 74.9 percent accepted	2,774	4,591	2,471	586	753	812	668	1,134	2,249	756	158	282	328	196	40.9	49.0	30.6	27.0	37.5	40.4	29.3
25.0 to 49.9 percent accepted	2,033	1,099	73	9	81	1,043	6	627	342	25	2	45	227	3	30.8	31.1	34.2	22.2	55.6	21.8	50.0
Less than 25.0 percent accepted	0	0	0	0	0	0	0	0	0	0	0	0	0	0	†	†	†	†	†	†	†
Information not available	814	7,981	33	79	5	6	5	734	2,551	15	34	5	0	0	90.2	32.0	45.5	43.0	100.0	0.0	0.0
2-year institutions	380,151	473,589	440,820	424,166	380,393	364,754	353,640	152,559	197,222	190,966	183,548	168,682	164,014	158,067	40.1	41.6	43.3	43.3	44.3	45.0	44.7
Public institutions	369,937	464,126	435,470	419,662	376,183	360,329	350,786	147,345	192,220	188,381	181,230	166,619	161,849	156,672	39.8	41.4	43.3	43.2	44.3	44.9	44.7
Nonprofit institutions	1,757	760	839	792	760	863	546	973	401	435	359	339	340	210	55.4	52.8	51.8	45.3	44.6	39.4	38.5
For-profit institutions	8,457	8,703	4,511	3,712	3,450	3,562	2,308	4,241	4,601	2,150	1,959	1,724	1,825	1,185	50.1	52.9	47.7	52.8	50.0	51.2	51.3

†Not applicable.

[1]Adjusted entry cohort counts exclude students who died or were totally and permanently disabled, served in the armed forces (including those called to active duty), served with a foreign aid service of the federal government (e.g., Peace Corps), or served on official church missions. For 4-year institutions, the adjusted entry cohort is based on first-time bachelor's degree-seeking students.

NOTE: Returning students data for 2-year institutions include returning students, plus students who completed their program. Some data have been revised from previously published figures.

SOURCE: U.S. Department of Education, National Center for Education Statistics, Integrated Postsecondary Education Data System (IPEDS), Spring 2008 through Spring 2018, Fall Enrollment component; and IPEDS Fall 2006 through Fall 2017, Institutional Characteristics component. (This table was prepared October 2019.)

Table 326.40. Percentage distribution of first-time postsecondary students starting at 2- and 4-year institutions during the 2003-04 academic year, by highest degree attained, enrollment status, and selected characteristics: Spring 2009

[Standard errors appear in parentheses]

Selected characteristic	Students starting at 2-year institutions: Highest degree attained: Total, any degree[1]	Certificate	Associate's	Bachelor's[2]	No degree, still enrolled	No degree, not enrolled	Students starting at 4-year institutions: Highest degree attained: Total, any degree[1]	Certificate	Associate's	Bachelor's[2]	No degree, still enrolled	No de not enr
1	2	3	4	5	6	7	8	9	10	11	12	
Total	**35.1 (0.86)**	**9.5 (0.68)**	**15.0 (0.63)**	**10.6 (0.63)**	**18.5 (0.98)**	**46.4 (1.01)**	**64.2 (1.18)**	**1.7 (0.24)**	**4.6 (0.49)**	**58.0 (1.34)**	**12.2 (0.60)**	**23.6**
Sex												
Male	33.3 (1.54)	9.4 (1.19)	13.7 (1.00)	10.3 (0.79)	19.1 (1.64)	47.6 (1.54)	61.4 (1.40)	1.2 (0.29)	5.1 (0.72)	55.1 (1.54)	13.9 (0.86)	24.8
Female	36.5 (1.18)	9.6 (0.90)	16.0 (0.92)	10.9 (0.83)	18.1 (0.93)	45.4 (1.37)	66.5 (1.45)	2.1 (0.34)	4.2 (0.51)	60.2 (1.58)	10.9 (0.71)	22.6
Age when first enrolled												
18 years old or younger	39.4 (1.63)	6.1 (0.78)	15.5 (1.24)	17.9 (1.36)	20.6 (1.70)	40.0 (1.58)	69.1 (1.27)	1.6 (0.29)	3.7 (0.45)	63.8 (1.41)	11.2 (0.76)	19.8
19 years old	37.7 (2.04)	8.9 (2.01)	16.2 (1.46)	12.6 (1.21)	17.7 (1.57)	44.6 (1.75)	65.1 (1.43)	1.0 (0.24)	4.2 (0.63)	59.9 (1.51)	12.3 (0.92)	22.6
20 to 23 years old	29.1 (1.94)	10.3 (1.38)	14.6 (1.68)	4.1 (0.69)	21.9 (1.92)	49.0 (2.10)	41.9 (3.78)	4.1 ! (1.62)	8.4 (1.74)	29.4 (3.71)	17.8 (2.91)	40.3
24 to 29 years old	28.8 (4.04)	15.6 (3.98)	10.8 (1.98)	2.5 (0.74)	17.2 (2.62)	53.9 (4.05)	32.7 (5.77)	‡ (†)	9.4 ! (4.28)	20.4 (5.06)	18.8 (4.87)	48.6
30 years old or over	31.7 (2.43)	14.4 (2.08)	15.0 (1.89)	‡ (†)	10.4 (1.97)	57.9 (2.65)	33.7 (7.09)	3.9 ! (1.84)	13.4 ! (5.05)	16.4 ! (6.14)	14.8 (3.97)	51.4
Race/ethnicity												
White	38.9 (1.16)	9.8 (1.0)	16.6 (0.82)	12.5 (0.85)	16.2 (1.21)	44.9 (1.31)	68.9 (1.04)	1.5 (0.31)	4.8 (0.54)	62.6 (1.31)	9.8 (0.58)	21.4
Black	28.1 (2.60)	11.3 (1.66)	11.4 (2.12)	5.3 (1.10)	22.0 (2.04)	50.0 (2.79)	46.9 (3.16)	2.2 ! (0.91)	4.2 ! (1.48)	40.5 (3.03)	19.6 (2.21)	33.6
Hispanic	28.3 (2.18)	8.2 (1.67)	12.7 (1.51)	7.4 (1.10)	18.8 (2.03)	52.9 (2.58)	48.8 (3.24)	2.2 ! (0.83)	5.1 (1.39)	41.5 (2.96)	18.6 (2.36)	32.5
Asian/Pacific Islander	38.3 (4.50)	6.5 ! (2.29)	14.6 (2.91)	17.2 (3.50)	29.0 (4.58)	32.7 (3.51)	72.8 (3.21)	1.4 ! (0.67)	2.1 ! (0.94)	69.3 (3.22)	11.9 (2.23)	15.2
American Indian/Alaska Native	32.1 (9.62)	‡ (†)	‡ (†)	‡ (†)	28.4 ! (10.89)	39.6 (10.68)	51.5 (9.53)	‡ (†)	‡ (†)	39.3 (9.11)	19.3 ! (8.63)	29.3 !
Two or more races	33.9 (5.51)	9.0 ! (3.65)	14.6 ! (4.39)	10.3 (2.87)	21.4 (4.98)	44.7 (5.50)	57.1 (5.42)	‡ (†)	4.0 ! (1.83)	50.4 (5.57)	19.2 (4.71)	23.6
Highest education level of parents												
High school diploma or less	32.0 (1.42)	11.0 (1.30)	14.3 (1.05)	6.7 (0.72)	17.1 (1.18)	50.9 (1.51)	49.9 (2.12)	2.9 (0.83)	6.6 (0.97)	40.4 (2.01)	15.4 (1.33)	34.7
Some college/vocational	38.3 (2.24)	9.6 (1.48)	17.6 (1.17)	11.1 (1.07)	18.0 (1.70)	43.8 (2.06)	59.1 (1.90)	2.3 ! (0.76)	7.0 (1.08)	49.8 (2.11)	13.4 (1.24)	27.5
Bachelor's degree	39.4 (1.91)	8.2 (1.60)	14.1 (1.87)	17.2 (1.74)	20.6 (2.09)	40.0 (2.53)	70.1 (1.60)	1.2 (0.28)	3.4 (0.58)	65.6 (1.62)	11.0 (0.87)	18.9
Advanced (higher than bachelor's) degree	37.2 (3.03)	6.2 (1.70)	13.7 (1.81)	17.2 (2.09)	22.4 (2.56)	40.4 (3.74)	75.8 (1.44)	0.6 ! (0.24)	2.1 (0.39)	73.1 (1.51)	9.2 (0.78)	15.0
Dependency status when first enrolled												
Dependent	39.4 (1.26)	7.5 (0.76)	16.7 (0.85)	15.2 (0.88)	19.6 (1.19)	41.0 (1.15)	68.3 (1.06)	1.4 (0.22)	4.2 (0.45)	62.7 (1.22)	11.6 (0.63)	20.1
Independent	28.3 (1.44)	12.8 (1.26)	12.3 (1.13)	3.3 (0.60)	16.8 (1.42)	54.9 (1.75)	31.4 (3.08)	3.7 (1.10)	7.5 (1.92)	20.2 (2.84)	17.3 (2.61)	51.3
Dependent student family income in 2002												
Less than $25,000	34.6 (2.35)	8.4 (1.48)	14.5 (1.54)	11.7 (1.73)	18.0 (1.91)	47.4 (2.43)	52.7 (2.28)	2.8 ! (1.09)	5.0 (1.00)	44.9 (2.40)	15.9 (1.63)	31.4
$25,000 to $44,999	36.0 (2.12)	7.3 (1.36)	16.4 (1.75)	12.3 (1.60)	19.0 (2.24)	45.0 (2.67)	62.7 (2.31)	1.9 (0.53)	5.4 (1.03)	55.3 (2.50)	13.1 (1.69)	24.2
$45,000 to $69,999	41.3 (2.13)	7.1 (1.29)	17.6 (1.59)	16.6 (1.58)	22.0 (1.92)	36.7 (1.86)	67.1 (1.94)	1.5 (0.34)	5.1 (0.77)	60.6 (2.00)	12.8 (1.27)	20.1
$70,000 to $99,999	43.1 (3.50)	7.6 ! (3.67)	16.3 (2.58)	19.1 (2.14)	18.4 (2.75)	38.5 (2.76)	71.9 (1.64)	0.9 ! (0.30)	4.4 (0.88)	66.7 (1.85)	9.4 (0.83)	18.7
$100,000 or more	45.0 (3.56)	6.6 (1.77)	19.6 (3.74)	18.8 (2.40)	20.5 (3.25)	34.4 (3.61)	80.0 (1.30)	0.7 ! (0.29)	1.9 (0.37)	77.5 (1.38)	8.5 (0.94)	11.4
Timing of postsecondary enrollment												
Delayed entry	29.1 (1.25)	11.0 (1.11)	13.2 (1.02)	4.9 (0.63)	17.2 (1.26)	53.7 (1.44)	36.6 (2.80)	3.8 (1.01)	7.9 (1.54)	24.9 (2.53)	17.8 (2.06)	45.6
Did not delay entry[3]	41.0 (1.36)	7.8 (0.86)	17.0 (0.99)	16.2 (1.00)	20.1 (1.44)	38.8 (1.16)	69.2 (1.05)	1.3 (0.21)	4.0 (0.40)	64.0 (1.17)	11.1 (0.61)	19.6
Intensity of enrollment through 2009												
Always full-time	44.9 (1.66)	11.4 (1.50)	18.0 (1.42)	15.5 (1.11)	10.1 (0.87)	44.9 (1.65)	73.7 (1.15)	1.2 (0.26)	3.8 (0.55)	68.7 (1.41)	6.7 (0.46)	19.6
Always part-time	13.9 (2.80)	8.4 ! (2.79)	5.5 (1.12)	‡ (†)	13.3 (1.79)	72.8 (2.68)	12.5 ! (4.93)	‡ (†)	‡ (†)	‡ (†)	13.8 ! (4.23)	73.6
Mixed	36.6 (1.32)	8.7 (0.83)	16.6 (1.10)	11.4 (0.99)	26.1 (1.34)	37.2 (1.69)	48.3 (1.59)	2.7 (0.47)	6.1 (0.72)	39.5 (1.60)	23.3 (1.39)	28.4
Remedial course taken in 2003-04												
No	35.4 (0.95)	10.0 (0.84)	14.5 (0.81)	10.9 (0.78)	17.6 (0.99)	47.0 (1.21)	65.2 (1.23)	1.8 (0.28)	4.4 (0.53)	59.0 (1.43)	11.5 (0.62)	23.4
Yes	34.3 (2.10)	8.3 (1.62)	16.2 (1.37)	9.8 (0.98)	21.0 (1.70)	44.7 (1.92)	59.6 (1.98)	1.2 (0.32)	5.4 (0.92)	53.0 (2.13)	15.7 (1.44)	24.6
Highest degree expected in 2003-04												
No degree or certificate	‡ (†)	‡ (†)	‡ (†)	# (†)	‡ (†)	87.3 (4.75)	‡ (†)	‡ (†)	‡ (†)	‡ (†)	‡ (†)	‡
Certificate	44.8 (5.47)	42.8 (5.28)	‡ (†)	‡ (†)	6.9 (2.02)	48.3 (5.60)	41.2 ! (18.43)	‡ (†)	‡ (†)	‡ (†)	‡ (†)	‡
Associate's degree	34.6 (2.38)	13.9 (2.05)	19.3 (1.86)	1.4 ! (0.49)	12.3 (1.69)	53.1 (2.80)	43.7 (8.43)	16.2 ! (5.50)	21.3 ! (7.06)	6.1 ! (2.93)	12.8 ! (5.09)	43.5
Bachelor's degree[4]	32.7 (1.81)	8.0 (1.49)	15.4 (1.02)	9.3 (1.03)	18.1 (1.50)	49.3 (1.60)	55.2 (2.02)	2.2 (0.52)	6.8 (1.02)	46.2 (2.07)	15.1 (1.37)	29.7
Master's degree[4]	38.2 (1.72)	7.0 (1.32)	14.8 (1.21)	16.4 (1.19)	22.7 (1.63)	39.1 (1.66)	66.7 (1.42)	1.0 (0.25)	4.1 (0.62)	61.7 (1.42)	11.2 (0.77)	22.1
Doctoral/first-professional degree[4]	34.7 (2.30)	4.8 (0.93)	13.8 (2.02)	16.0 (1.65)	22.4 (2.54)	42.9 (3.25)	70.6 (1.57)	1.3 (0.36)	1.9 (0.36)	67.4 (1.69)	11.0 (0.95)	18.3
Work intensity (including work-study) in 2003-04												
Did not work	34.7 (1.79)	11.2 (1.57)	15.8 (1.20)	7.7 (0.85)	19.9 (1.80)	45.3 (2.16)	69.9 (1.35)	0.8 (0.18)	3.4 (0.55)	65.8 (1.47)	10.9 (0.92)	19.1
Worked part time	39.9 (2.08)	7.9 (1.20)	17.4 (1.00)	14.6 (1.04)	17.2 (1.28)	42.8 (1.70)	66.2 (1.42)	1.7 (0.31)	5.2 (0.69)	59.3 (1.44)	12.1 (0.85)	21.7
Worked full time	28.6 (1.96)	10.6 (1.63)	10.9 (1.08)	7.2 (0.94)	19.3 (1.53)	52.1 (2.10)	40.1 (2.93)	4.1 (1.22)	5.9 (1.20)	30.1 (2.60)	16.5 (1.77)	43.4
Control of first institution												
Public	34.4 (0.95)	8.5 (0.68)	14.4 (0.61)	11.6 (0.68)	19.6 (1.03)	46.0 (1.00)	64.8 (1.22)	1.6 (0.23)	3.8 (0.45)	59.5 (1.32)	12.9 (0.73)	22.2
Private, nonprofit	46.2 (8.52)	13.3 ! (6.56)	21.5 ! (6.76)	11.3 ! (4.99)	10.4 ! (3.32)	43.4 (8.28)	69.9 (1.45)	1.5 (0.37)	3.8 (0.95)	64.6 (1.89)	11.1 (1.02)	19.0
Private, for-profit	39.5 (3.70)	19.6 (4.78)	19.5 (3.51)	‡ (†)	9.6 (2.61)	50.9 (4.64)	33.9 (4.37)	‡ (†)	14.6 (3.45)	15.7 (3.78)	11.3 (2.44)	54.8
Income quartile in 2003-04[5]												
Lowest quartile	30.6 (1.45)	9.4 (1.27)	13.0 (1.14)	8.3 (0.84)	18.4 (1.46)	51.0 (1.78)	49.5 (1.91)	2.7 (0.73)	4.6 (0.74)	42.2 (2.15)	16.2 (1.37)	34.3
Second quartile	37.1 (1.58)	10.5 (1.56)	15.8 (1.26)	10.8 (0.97)	19.7 (1.58)	43.2 (1.86)	60.5 (2.04)	2.4 (0.51)	6.5 (1.10)	51.6 (2.20)	13.5 (1.16)	26.0

[Standard errors appear in parentheses]

Selected characteristic	Students starting at 2-year institutions						Students starting at 4-year institutions					
	Highest degree attained						Highest degree attained					
	Total, any degree[1]	Certificate	Associate's	Bachelor's[2]	No degree, still enrolled	No degree, not enrolled	Total, any degree[1]	Certificate	Associate's	Bachelor's[2]	No degree, still enrolled	No degree, not enrolled
1	2	3	4	5	6	7	8	9	10	11	12	13
Third quartile	36.3 (2.51)	9.6 (1.71)	15.0 (1.35)	11.6 (1.53)	18.7 (1.64)	45.0 (2.18)	67.2 (1.58)	1.3 (0.31)	4.9 (0.80)	61.0 (1.85)	11.2 (0.88)	21.6 (1.55)
Highest quartile	38.6 (2.51)	8.1 (1.49)	17.3 (1.96)	13.2 (1.65)	16.5 (2.30)	45.0 (3.20)	76.8 (1.37)	0.6 ! (0.25)	2.4 (0.46)	73.8 (1.42)	8.7 (0.80)	14.4 (1.18)

†Not applicable.

#Rounds to zero.

!Interpret data with caution. The coefficient of variation (CV) for this estimate is between 30 and 50 percent.

‡Reporting standards not met. Either there are too few cases for a reliable estimate or the coefficient of variation (CV) is 50 percent or greater.

1 Includes a small percentage of students who had attained a degree and were still enrolled. Includes recipients of degrees not shown separately.

2 Includes a small percentage of students who had attained an advanced degree.

3 Includes students with a standard high school diploma who enrolled in postsecondary education in the same year as their graduation.

4 Students starting at 2-year institutions include students whose goal was to transfer to a 4-year institution.

5 Indicates the income quartile of the student, based on the student's total income in 2002 for independent students or the parents' total income in 2002 for dependent students. Income quartiles were determined separately for dependent and independent students based on percentile rankings and then combined into one variable.

NOTE: Race categories exclude persons of Hispanic ethnicity. Detail may not sum to totals because of rounding.

SOURCE: U.S. Department of Education, National Center for Education Statistics, 2004/09 Beginning Postsecondary Students Longitudinal Study (BPS:04/09). (This table was prepared November 2011.)

Table 326.50. Number and percentage distribution of first-time postsecondary students starting at 2- and 4-year institutions during the 2011-12 academic year, by attainment and enrollment status and selected characteristics: Spring 2014

[Standard errors appear in parentheses]

Selected characteristic	Total				Students starting at 2-year institutions				Students starting at 4-year institutions			
	Number (in thousands)	Percentage distribution	Percent who attained any degree or were still enrolled	Percent with no degree and not enrolled	Number (in thousands)	Percentage distribution	Percent who attained any degree or were still enrolled	Percent with no degree and not enrolled	Number (in thousands)	Percentage distribution	Percent who attained any degree or were still enrolled	Perce[nt with] no [degree and not enrolled]
1	2	3	4	5	6	7	8	9	10	11	12	
Total	**4,073 (254.9)**	**100.0 (†)**	**69.8 (0.99)**	**30.2 (0.99)**	**1,832 (170.4)**	**100.0 (†)**	**56.9 (1.52)**	**43.1 (1.52)**	**2,241 (87.5)**	**100.0 (†)**	**80.2 (0.56)**	**19.8**
Sex												
Male	1,839 (127.8)	45.2 (0.61)	66.3 (1.54)	33.7 (1.54)	859 (82.8)	46.9 (0.96)	53.6 (2.04)	46.4 (2.04)	980 (50.3)	43.7 (0.84)	77.5 (1.09)	22.5
Female	2,234 (131.7)	54.8 (0.61)	72.6 (0.82)	27.4 (0.82)	972 (91.9)	53.1 (0.96)	59.9 (1.59)	40.1 (1.59)	1,261 (43.9)	56.3 (0.84)	82.4 (0.93)	17.6
Age when first enrolled												
19 years old or younger	3,103 (169.8)	76.2 (0.85)	75.9 (0.61)	24.1 (0.61)	1,201 (88.8)	65.6 (1.69)	61.5 (1.37)	38.5 (1.37)	1,902 (84.0)	84.9 (0.60)	85.0 (0.63)	15.0
20 to 23 years old	406 (37.7)	10.0 (0.44)	50.2 (3.38)	49.8 (3.38)	262 (34.0)	14.3 (0.76)	48.6 (2.99)	51.4 (2.99)	144 (9.4)	6.4 (0.39)	53.1 (5.48)	46.9
24 to 29 years old	252 (33.6)	6.2 (0.47)	47.6 (2.53)	52.4 (2.53)	173 (30.5)	9.4 (0.84)	47.6 (3.09)	52.4 (3.09)	79 (7.0)	3.5 (0.28)	47.5 (4.32)	52.5
30 years old or over	312 (27.2)	7.7 (0.35)	51.7 (3.08)	48.3 (3.08)	196 (28.1)	10.7 (0.71)	48.3 (3.23)	51.7 (3.23)	116 (7.7)	5.2 (0.43)	57.4 (4.36)	42.6
Race/ethnicity												
White	2,306 (159.0)	56.6 (0.74)	72.2 (0.95)	27.8 (0.95)	949 (99.4)	51.8 (1.16)	57.7 (1.65)	42.3 (1.65)	1,357 (64.2)	60.5 (0.89)	82.4 (0.75)	17.6
Black	564 (28.7)	13.9 (0.61)	59.6 (1.96)	40.4 (1.96)	258 (24.2)	14.1 (0.76)	48.0 (2.84)	52.0 (2.84)	307 (15.4)	13.7 (0.83)	69.4 (1.74)	30.6
Hispanic	765 (51.2)	18.8 (0.53)	67.3 (1.74)	32.7 (1.74)	453 (43.0)	24.7 (0.88)	59.4 (2.16)	40.6 (2.16)	312 (14.5)	13.9 (0.57)	78.6 (1.71)	21.4
Asian	234 (23.1)	5.7 (0.29)	80.9 (2.94)	19.1 (2.94)	81 (12.9)	4.4 (0.41)	64.6 (5.97)	35.4 (5.97)	153 (13.6)	6.8 (0.44)	89.6 (2.14)	10.4
Pacific Islander	16 (2.5)	0.4 (0.06)	72.4 (6.51)	27.6 (6.51)	7 (1.8)	0.4 (0.09)	64.2 (12.71)	35.8 ! (12.71)	9 (1.7)	0.4 (0.07)	79.4 (7.95)	20.6 !
American Indian/Alaska Native	38 (7.2)	0.9 (0.14)	54.9 (6.97)	45.1 (6.97)	20 (4.6)	1.1 (0.23)	47.1 (9.84)	52.9 (9.84)	18 (4.9)	0.8 (0.19)	63.8 (8.70)	36.2
Two or more races	149 (12.2)	3.7 (0.20)	68.6 (2.62)	31.4 (2.62)	64 (6.8)	3.5 (0.32)	57.0 (4.65)	43.0 (4.65)	86 (7.8)	3.8 (0.26)	77.2 (3.03)	22.8
Highest education level of parents												
Do not know	155 (18.0)	3.8 (0.26)	55.7 (3.45)	44.3 (3.45)	99 (14.8)	5.4 (0.45)	52.4 (4.73)	47.6 (4.73)	56 (5.7)	2.5 (0.22)	61.5 (7.12)	38.5
High school diploma or less	1,222 (85.4)	30.0 (0.56)	59.0 (2.01)	41.0 (2.01)	714 (74.7)	39.0 (0.92)	52.5 (2.10)	47.5 (2.10)	508 (18.3)	22.7 (0.73)	68.1 (2.08)	31.9
Some college/vocational	1,082 (71.5)	26.6 (0.51)	67.9 (1.59)	32.1 (1.59)	558 (47.4)	30.5 (0.87)	59.2 (2.29)	40.8 (2.29)	524 (27.7)	23.4 (0.66)	77.1 (1.37)	22.9
Bachelor's or higher degree	1,614 (93.8)	39.6 (0.66)	80.6 (0.80)	19.4 (0.80)	461 (44.2)	25.2 (0.83)	62.1 (2.07)	37.9 (2.07)	1,153 (53.2)	51.4 (0.74)	87.9 (0.82)	12.1
Dependency status when first enrolled												
Dependent	3,160 (185.4)	77.6 (0.69)	75.1 (0.67)	24.9 (0.67)	1,248 (97.2)	68.2 (1.46)	61.2 (1.42)	38.8 (1.42)	1,911 (91.7)	85.3 (0.90)	84.2 (0.66)	15.8
Independent with no dependents	416 (41.4)	10.2 (0.49)	54.0 (3.29)	46.0 (3.29)	265 (43.4)	14.5 (1.09)	49.0 (2.96)	51.0 (2.96)	151 (9.4)	6.7 (0.54)	63.0 (4.53)	37.0
Independent, married, and with dependents	178 (22.8)	4.4 (0.34)	51.5 (3.59)	48.5 (3.59)	121 (20.4)	6.6 (0.60)	48.0 (3.88)	52.0 (3.88)	57 (5.3)	2.5 (0.21)	58.9 (5.76)	41.1
Independent, not married, and with dependents	319 (21.0)	7.8 (0.36)	47.6 (2.55)	52.4 (2.55)	197 (21.1)	10.8 (0.63)	46.3 (3.07)	53.7 (3.07)	122 (8.0)	5.5 (0.44)	49.8 (3.62)	50.2
Income quarter in 2012[1]												
Lowest quarter	990 (55.4)	24.3 (0.57)	61.8 (1.33)	38.2 (1.33)	527 (43.4)	28.8 (1.04)	54.8 (2.05)	45.2 (2.05)	463 (18.4)	20.7 (0.64)	69.7 (1.60)	30.3
Second quarter	1,006 (77.6)	24.7 (0.52)	67.1 (1.41)	32.9 (1.41)	513 (45.7)	28.0 (0.74)	58.2 (2.26)	41.8 (2.26)	493 (35.0)	22.0 (0.80)	76.4 (1.31)	23.6
Third quarter	1,031 (65.4)	25.3 (0.51)	71.0 (1.06)	29.0 (1.06)	466 (52.6)	25.5 (0.92)	58.0 (1.87)	42.0 (1.87)	565 (17.8)	25.2 (0.67)	81.7 (1.31)	18.3
Highest quarter	1,046 (70.4)	25.7 (0.50)	78.7 (1.90)	21.3 (1.90)	325 (41.0)	17.8 (0.85)	57.0 (3.21)	43.0 (3.21)	720 (33.3)	32.1 (0.63)	88.5 (1.02)	11.5
Disability in 2012[2]												
With a disability	472 (31.9)	11.6 (0.38)	55.1 (2.93)	44.9 (2.93)	233 (28.8)	12.7 (0.69)	42.0 (3.85)	58.0 (3.85)	240 (10.5)	10.7 (0.54)	67.9 (2.36)	32.1
Without a disability	3,600 (228.2)	88.4 (0.38)	71.7 (0.86)	28.3 (0.86)	1,599 (145.5)	87.3 (0.69)	59.1 (1.38)	40.9 (1.38)	2,001 (85.9)	89.3 (0.54)	81.7 (0.61)	18.3
High school completion type												
High school diploma	3,664 (228.5)	90.0 (0.38)	71.7 (0.96)	28.3 (0.96)	1,571 (136.4)	85.8 (0.85)	58.3 (1.53)	41.7 (1.53)	2,093 (95.2)	93.4 (0.68)	81.8 (0.57)	18.2
GED or equivalent	274 (18.6)	6.7 (0.32)	46.7 (2.40)	53.3 (2.40)	177 (22.5)	9.7 (0.56)	46.3 (2.81)	53.7 (2.81)	97 (9.5)	4.3 (0.53)	47.5 (3.71)	52.5
Other type or no completion[3]	134 (17.0)	3.3 (0.26)	63.4 (4.23)	36.6 (4.23)	83 (17.2)	4.5 (0.56)	54.5 (5.16)	45.5 (5.16)	51 (4.9)	2.3 (0.25)	78.0 (5.07)	22.0
Highest level of high school mathematics[4]												
Less than algebra II	575 (58.7)	15.3 (0.68)	54.9 (2.22)	45.1 (2.22)	395 (53.1)	24.2 (1.25)	49.6 (2.79)	50.4 (2.79)	180 (10.7)	8.5 (0.41)	66.6 (2.37)	33.4
Algebra II/trigonometry	1,408 (87.4)	37.4 (0.55)	67.1 (1.49)	32.9 (1.49)	726 (65.1)	44.4 (1.03)	57.5 (1.74)	42.5 (1.74)	682 (26.7)	32.1 (0.65)	77.3 (1.46)	22.7
Precalculus/calculus or higher	1,778 (95.2)	47.3 (0.72)	79.8 (0.72)	20.2 (0.72)	515 (36.8)	31.5 (1.19)	65.1 (1.64)	34.9 (1.64)	1,263 (62.7)	59.4 (0.76)	85.9 (0.82)	14.1
Earned any college-level credits in high school[4]												
No	1,535 (105.7)	40.8 (0.64)	61.3 (1.13)	38.7 (1.13)	926 (95.4)	56.6 (1.15)	55.4 (1.40)	44.6 (1.40)	609 (18.4)	28.7 (1.01)	70.5 (1.31)	29.5
Yes	2,226 (132.1)	59.2 (0.64)	78.1 (0.91)	21.9 (0.91)	710 (54.7)	43.4 (1.15)	61.4 (2.11)	38.6 (2.11)	1,516 (81.5)	71.3 (1.01)	85.9 (0.66)	14.1
High school GPA[4,5]												
0.5 to 1.9	201 (16.8)	5.3 (0.26)	51.6 (2.85)	48.4 (2.85)	143 (13.4)	8.8 (0.56)	51.1 (3.61)	48.9 (3.61)	58 (6.2)	2.7 (0.24)	53.1 (4.59)	46.9
2.0 to 2.4	670 (54.2)	17.8 (0.52)	60.4 (1.54)	39.6 (1.54)	427 (42.6)	26.1 (0.88)	56.2 (2.04)	43.8 (2.04)	243 (15.7)	11.4 (0.45)	67.8 (2.36)	32.2
2.5 to 2.9	536 (40.5)	14.3 (0.40)	66.9 (1.83)	33.1 (1.83)	260 (27.8)	15.9 (0.60)	58.0 (2.41)	42.0 (2.41)	276 (16.9)	13.0 (0.50)	75.4 (2.13)	24.6
3.0 to 3.4	1,434 (80.1)	38.1 (0.59)	74.1 (1.20)	25.9 (1.20)	562 (56.6)	34.4 (0.88)	59.6 (2.46)	40.4 (2.46)	871 (27.4)	41.0 (0.86)	83.5 (1.00)	16.5
3.5 to 4.0	920 (57.1)	24.5 (0.49)	81.5 (0.96)	18.5 (0.96)	243 (21.3)	14.9 (0.81)	61.4 (2.58)	38.6 (2.58)	677 (40.3)	31.9 (0.76)	88.7 (0.75)	11.3
Took the SAT or ACT exam[4,6]												
No	636 (65.1)	16.9 (0.76)	54.5 (1.47)	45.5 (1.47)	498 (60.6)	30.5 (1.23)	55.1 (1.68)	44.9 (1.68)	137 (10.0)	6.5 (0.40)	52.4 (3.36)	47.6
Yes	3,125 (172.0)	83.1 (0.76)	74.7 (0.83)	25.3 (0.83)	1,138 (89.4)	69.5 (1.23)	59.2 (1.77)	40.8 (1.77)	1,988 (85.6)	93.5 (0.40)	83.5 (0.54)	16.5
Lowest quarter SAT (400 to 850)	729 (36.0)	19.4 (0.59)	62.4 (1.83)	37.6 (1.83)	429 (36.3)	26.2 (0.90)	56.6 (2.06)	43.4 (2.06)	300 (11.1)	14.1 (0.81)	70.6 (2.02)	29.4
Second quarter SAT (860 to 990)	793 (47.3)	21.1 (0.48)	72.0 (1.58)	28.0 (1.58)	317 (29.0)	19.4 (0.72)	61.7 (3.02)	38.3 (3.02)	476 (22.2)	22.4 (0.62)	78.9 (1.26)	21.1
Third quarter SAT (1000 to 1140)	801 (50.5)	21.3 (0.48)	78.1 (1.23)	21.9 (1.23)	249 (20.4)	15.2 (0.81)	60.7 (3.18)	39.3 (3.18)	553 (34.7)	26.0 (0.75)	85.9 (1.19)	14.1
Highest quarter SAT (1150 or higher)	802 (53.3)	21.3 (0.49)	85.1 (1.03)	14.9 (1.03)	143 (17.1)	8.7 (0.63)	59.1 (3.62)	40.9 (3.62)	659 (40.3)	31.0 (0.79)	90.7 (0.70)	9.3
Control of first institution												
Public	2,952 (191.9)	72.5 (0.38)	67.7 (1.16)	32.3 (1.16)	1,636 (161.1)	89.3 (0.60)	55.9 (1.39)	44.1 (1.39)	1,316 (34.7)	58.7 (0.94)	82.3 (0.85)	17.7
Private, nonprofit	691 (40.3)	17.0 (0.34)	87.1 (0.98)	12.9 (0.98)	27 (4.9)	1.5 (0.31)	67.7 (6.12)	32.3 (6.12)	664 (41.8)	29.6 (0.78)	87.9 (0.86)	12.1

[Standard errors appear in parentheses]

Selected characteristic	Total				Students starting at 2-year institutions				Students starting at 4-year institutions			
	Number (in thousands)	Percentage distribution	Percent who attained any degree or were still enrolled	Percent with no degree and not enrolled	Number (in thousands)	Percentage distribution	Percent who attained any degree or were still enrolled	Percent with no degree and not enrolled	Number (in thousands)	Percentage distribution	Percent who attained any degree or were still enrolled	Percent wit no degre and nc enrolle
1	2	3	4	5	6	7	8	9	10	11	12	1
Private, for-profit	430 (27.9)	10.5 (0.25)	56.0 (2.68)	44.0 (2.68)	168 (13.3)	9.2 (0.42)	64.9 (4.54)	35.1 (4.54)	261 (16.4)	11.7 (0.39)	50.3 (2.33)	49.7 (2.33
Intensity of enrollment through 2014[7]												
Always full-time	2,402 (112.4)	59.0 (1.03)	76.4 (0.84)	23.6 (0.84)	761 (59.1)	41.5 (1.07)	61.1 (2.03)	38.9 (2.03)	1,642 (57.2)	73.3 (0.70)	83.5 (0.56)	16.5 (0.56
Part-time for some or all semesters.	1,670 (145.7)	41.0 (1.03)	60.2 (1.25)	39.8 (1.25)	1,071 (114.8)	58.5 (1.07)	54.0 (1.57)	46.0 (1.57)	599 (34.8)	26.7 (0.70)	71.4 (1.51)	28.6 (1.51
Remedial course taken												
No	3,141 (224.4)	77.1 (0.77)	71.8 (1.07)	28.2 (1.07)	1,242 (130.8)	67.8 (1.09)	56.8 (1.82)	43.2 (1.82)	1,899 (97.0)	84.7 (1.08)	81.6 (0.61)	18.4 (0.61
Yes	931 (37.3)	22.9 (0.77)	62.9 (1.38)	37.1 (1.38)	589 (44.1)	32.2 (1.09)	57.3 (1.60)	42.7 (1.60)	342 (15.1)	15.3 (1.08)	72.6 (1.64)	27.4 (1.64
Work intensity while enrolled in 2011-12												
Did not work	2,542 (146.3)	62.4 (0.65)	70.4 (1.04)	29.6 (1.04)	1,058 (100.5)	57.8 (0.91)	56.1 (1.73)	43.9 (1.73)	1,483 (50.6)	66.2 (0.78)	80.7 (0.72)	19.3 (0.72
Worked less than 20 hours per week	424 (23.7)	10.4 (0.33)	84.1 (1.38)	15.9 (1.38)	119 (11.4)	6.5 (0.46)	70.0 (3.94)	30.0 (3.94)	305 (16.4)	13.6 (0.46)	89.6 (1.72)	10.4 (1.72
Worked at least 20 hours per week	1,106 (93.0)	27.2 (0.70)	62.7 (1.59)	37.3 (1.59)	654 (66.2)	35.7 (0.85)	55.9 (1.84)	44.1 (1.84)	453 (30.0)	20.2 (0.70)	72.5 (1.79)	27.5 (1.79
Declared a major during first year[8]												
No	513 (40.8)	12.8 (0.44)	75.0 (1.46)	25.0 (1.46)	183 (19.1)	10.3 (0.63)	57.1 (2.96)	42.9 (2.96)	330 (25.6)	14.8 (0.65)	84.9 (1.19)	15.1 (1.19
Yes	3,486 (220.1)	87.2 (0.44)	69.2 (1.05)	30.8 (1.05)	1,592 (149.2)	89.7 (0.63)	57.0 (1.56)	43.0 (1.56)	1,894 (74.0)	85.2 (0.65)	79.5 (0.65)	20.5 (0.65
Number of transfers through 2014												
Zero	3,332 (232.0)	81.8 (0.69)	65.9 (1.16)	34.1 (1.16)	1,475 (157.6)	80.6 (1.22)	49.5 (1.51)	50.5 (1.51)	1,856 (77.3)	82.8 (0.59)	78.9 (0.65)	21.1 (0.65
One or more	741 (30.5)	18.2 (0.69)	87.3 (0.93)	12.7 (0.93)	356 (19.8)	19.4 (1.22)	87.9 (1.26)	12.1 (1.26)	385 (17.4)	17.2 (0.59)	86.7 (1.30)	13.3 (1.30
Number of stopouts through 2014[9]												
Zero	3,369 (210.6)	82.7 (0.44)	69.0 (1.16)	31.0 (1.16)	1,429 (135.3)	78.0 (0.74)	52.6 (1.68)	47.4 (1.68)	1,940 (78.4)	86.6 (0.55)	81.1 (0.61)	18.9 (0.61
One or more	704 (49.1)	17.3 (0.44)	73.3 (1.17)	26.7 (1.17)	403 (38.8)	22.0 (0.74)	72.2 (1.96)	27.8 (1.96)	301 (16.3)	13.4 (0.55)	74.8 (1.89)	25.2 (1.89
Took out loans in 2011-12[10]												
No	2,240 (145.0)	55.0 (0.55)	66.0 (1.24)	34.0 (1.24)	1,362 (108.6)	74.3 (1.31)	56.1 (1.53)	43.9 (1.53)	878 (41.6)	39.2 (0.71)	81.3 (1.12)	18.7 (1.12
Yes	1,833 (114.3)	45.0 (0.55)	74.4 (0.97)	25.6 (0.97)	470 (65.6)	25.7 (1.31)	59.4 (2.49)	40.6 (2.49)	1,363 (51.6)	60.8 (0.71)	79.5 (0.64)	20.5 (0.64
Up to $4,499	460 (45.9)	11.3 (0.49)	60.7 (2.30)	39.3 (2.30)	210 (39.2)	11.5 (1.10)	52.2 (2.48)	47.8 (2.48)	250 (11.5)	11.1 (0.42)	67.9 (2.55)	32.1 (2.55
$4,500 to $6,009	479 (33.0)	11.8 (0.31)	78.1 (1.15)	21.9 (1.15)	97 (9.6)	5.3 (0.29)	57.9 (3.65)	42.1 (3.65)	382 (25.4)	17.0 (0.61)	83.2 (1.21)	16.8 (1.21
$6,010 to $9,500	430 (23.9)	10.6 (0.37)	72.3 (1.45)	27.7 (1.45)	110 (17.7)	6.0 (0.51)	64.2 (4.39)	35.8 (4.39)	319 (11.6)	14.2 (0.58)	75.1 (1.33)	24.9 (1.33
$9,501 or more	464 (21.8)	11.4 (0.34)	86.0 (0.84)	14.0 (0.84)	52 (6.1)	2.9 (0.28)	81.4 (4.47)	18.6 (4.47)	412 (18.6)	18.4 (0.43)	86.6 (0.97)	13.4 (0.97

†Not applicable.

!Interpret data with caution. The coefficient of variation (CV) for this estimate is between 30 and 50 percent.

[1] Income quarters were computed separately for dependent and independent students. Quarters for independent students were based on the students' total family income, while quarters for dependent students were based on their parents' income.

[2] Indicates whether student has a long-lasting condition such as deafness or serious difficulty hearing; blindness or serious difficulty seeing; serious difficulty concentrating, remembering, or making decisions; or a long-term impairment that substantially limits one or more basic physical activities such as walking, climbing stairs, reaching, lifting, or carrying.

[3] Includes students who attended a foreign high school, were home schooled, or received a completion certificate, as well as those without a high school diploma, certificate, or equivalency.

[4] Survey questions regarding highest level of high school mathematics, college credits earned during high school, high school GPA, and SAT scores were restricted to respondents less than 30 years old.

[5] A grade point average (GPA) of 4.0 corresponds to an A, a GPA of 3.0 corresponds to a B, a GPA of 2.0 corresponds to a C, and a GPA of 1.0 corresponds to a D.

[6] Test score quarters are based on the SAT combined critical reading and mathematics score; scale ranges from 400 to 1600. ACT scores for students who only took the ACT exam were converted to SAT scores using a concordance table from the following source: Dorans, N. (1999). Correspondences Between ACT and SAT I Scores (College Board Report No. 99-1). New York: College Entrance Examination Board.

[7] Full-time enrollment may vary by school. Full-time undergraduate students are typically enrolled for at least 12 semester or quarter hours per term or at least 24 clock hours per week.

[8] The question regarding declaration of a major was restricted to students enrolled in a degree program.

[9] A stopout is a break in enrollment of 5 or more consecutive months.

[10] Includes amount of all loans received in 2011-12, including federal Direct PLUS Loans to parents of undergraduate students.

NOTE: Race categories exclude persons of Hispanic ethnicity. Detail may not sum to totals because of rounding.

SOURCE: U.S. Department of Education, National Center for Education Statistics, 2012/14 Beginning Postsecondary Students Longitudinal Study (BPS:12/14). (This table was prepared February 2017.)

Table 329.10 On-campus crimes, arrests, and referrals for disciplinary action at degree-granting postsecondary institutions, by location of incident, control and level of institution, and type of incident: Selected years, 2001 through 2017

Control and level of institution and type of incident	Number of incidents															
	Total, in residence halls and at other locations													2017		
	2001	2005	2006	2007	2008	2009	2010	2011	2012	2013	2014	2015	2016	Total	In residence halls	At other locations
1	2	3	4	5	6	7	8	9	10	11	12	13	14	15	16	17
All institutions																
Selected crimes against persons and property	41,596	42,710	44,492	41,829	40,296	34,054	32,097	30,407	29,766	27,236	26,818	27,532	28,376	28,873	14,671	14,202
Murder[1]	17	11	8	44	12	16	15	16	12	23	11	28	15	21	2	19
Negligent manslaughter[2]	2	2	0	3	3	0	1	1	1	0	2	2	2	3	1	2
Sex offenses—forcible[3]	2,201	2,674	2,670	2,694	2,639	2,544	2,927	3,375	4,015	4,977	6,751	8,022	8,931	10,398	7,517	2,881
Rape	—	—	—	—	—	—	—	—	—	—	4,431	5,119	5,853	6,521	5,386	1,135
Fondling	—	—	—	—	—	—	—	—	—	—	2,320	2,903	3,078	3,877	2,131	1,746
Sex offenses—nonforcible[4]	461	42	43	40	35	65	33	46	46	45	53	63	60	80	57	23
Robbery[5]	1,663	1,551	1,547	1,561	1,576	1,409	1,392	1,285	1,368	1,317	1,041	1,044	1,097	1,040	230	810
Aggravated assault[6]	2,947	2,656	2,817	2,604	2,495	2,327	2,221	2,239	2,423	2,044	2,048	2,258	2,181	2,216	699	1,517
Burglary[7]	26,904	29,256	31,260	29,488	28,737	23,083	21,335	19,472	18,183	15,232	13,419	12,320	11,965	11,053	5,810	5,243
Motor vehicle theft[8]	6,221	5,531	5,231	4,619	4,104	3,977	3,441	3,334	3,013	2,971	2,890	3,218	3,528	3,450	26	3,424
Arson[9]	1,180	987	916	776	695	633	732	639	705	627	603	577	597	612	329	283
Weapons-, drug-, and liquor-related arrests and referrals																
Arrests[10]	40,348	49,024	50,187	50,558	50,639	50,066	51,519	54,285	52,325	46,975	44,531	40,299	39,018	37,626	18,527	19,099
Illegal weapons possession	1,073	1,316	1,316	1,318	1,190	1,077	1,112	1,023	1,023	1,018	990	1,183	1,200	1,245	317	928
Drug law violations	11,854	13,707	13,952	14,135	15,146	15,871	18,589	20,729	21,212	19,799	19,172	19,431	19,239	19,568	9,441	10,127
Liquor law violations	27,421	34,001	34,919	35,105	34,303	33,118	31,818	32,533	30,090	26,158	24,369	19,685	18,579	16,813	8,769	8,044
Referrals for disciplinary action[10]	155,201	202,816	218,040	216,600	217,526	220,987	230,269	249,694	251,402	244,985	253,315	241,687	229,589	216,379	198,302	18,077
Illegal weapons possession	1,277	1,882	1,871	1,658	1,455	1,275	1,314	1,282	1,404	1,410	1,425	1,425	1,405	1,309	923	386
Drug law violations	23,900	25,356	27,251	28,476	32,469	36,344	42,022	51,562	53,959	53,439	56,575	56,037	55,768	58,079	49,700	8,379
Liquor law violations	130,024	175,578	188,918	186,466	183,602	183,368	186,933	196,850	196,039	190,136	195,315	184,225	172,416	156,991	147,679	9,312
Public 4-year																
Selected crimes against persons and property	18,710	19,582	20,648	19,579	18,695	15,975	15,503	14,675	14,510	13,127	13,346	13,592	14,189	14,814	7,138	7,676
Murder[1]	9	4	5	42	9	8	9	10	7	10	3	13	8	12	1	11
Negligent manslaughter[2]	2	1	0	2	1	0	0	1	1	0	1	1	2	3	1	2
Sex offenses—forcible[3]	1,245	1,398	1,400	1,425	1,317	1,214	1,461	1,638	1,973	2,264	3,211	3,960	4,421	5,252	3,674	1,578
Rape	—	—	—	—	—	—	—	—	—	—	2,118	2,541	2,945	3,379	2,728	651
Fondling	—	—	—	—	—	—	—	—	—	—	1,093	1,419	1,476	1,873	946	927
Sex offenses—nonforcible[4]	207	25	15	23	12	40	15	17	17	18	28	37	30	63	49	14
Robbery[5]	584	696	680	722	750	647	662	612	657	635	550	580	590	525	125	400
Aggravated assault[6]	1,434	1,280	1,338	1,258	1,182	1,134	1,076	1,076	1,200	1,000	1,016	1,144	1,153	1,139	394	745
Burglary[7]	11,520	12,935	14,027	13,371	12,970	10,708	10,219	9,373	8,821	7,258	6,678	5,782	5,599	5,429	2,688	2,741
Motor vehicle theft[8]	3,072	2,667	2,662	2,266	2,027	1,824	1,604	1,592	1,406	1,537	1,500	1,770	2,049	2,036	8	2,028
Arson[9]	637	576	521	470	427	400	457	356	428	405	359	305	337	355	198	157
Weapons-, drug-, and liquor-related arrests and referrals																
Arrests[10]	31,077	38,051	39,900	39,570	40,607	40,780	41,992	44,891	43,155	38,073	36,249	32,717	31,606	30,062	14,455	15,607
Illegal weapons possession	692	878	859	825	759	659	669	629	621	637	619	721	759	813	226	587
Drug law violations	9,125	10,606	10,850	10,693	11,714	12,186	14,362	16,323	16,792	15,571	15,119	15,509	15,545	15,610	7,624	7,986
Liquor law violations	21,260	26,567	28,191	28,052	28,134	27,935	26,961	27,939	25,742	21,865	20,511	16,487	15,302	13,639	6,605	7,034
Referrals for disciplinary action[10]	79,152	100,211	107,289	106,148	104,585	108,756	116,029	129,667	132,363	127,155	134,310	127,315	119,009	112,112	102,052	10,060
Illegal weapons possession	678	1,097	972	867	792	669	664	610	644	604	646	569	602	530	388	142
Drug law violations	13,179	13,020	13,798	14,458	16,656	18,260	21,451	27,339	28,880	28,259	30,376	30,599	29,759	31,990	26,769	5,221
Liquor law violations	65,295	86,094	92,519	90,823	87,137	89,827	93,914	101,718	102,839	98,292	103,288	96,147	88,648	79,592	74,895	4,697
Nonprofit 4-year																
Selected crimes against persons and property	14,844	15,574	16,864	15,452	14,892	11,964	11,202	10,740	10,790	10,290	9,995	10,460	11,062	10,954	6,748	4,206
Murder[1]	5	5	3	2	1	6	5	3	2	5	5	2	4	6	0	6
Negligent manslaughter[2]	0	1	0	1	0	0	0	0	0	0	0	1	0	0	0	0
Sex offenses—forcible[3]	820	1,088	1,080	1,065	1,083	1,102	1,225	1,431	1,741	2,379	3,105	3,510	3,961	4,497	3,580	917
Rape	—	—	—	—	—	—	—	—	—	—	2,152	2,366	2,704	2,876	2,469	407
Fondling	—	—	—	—	—	—	—	—	—	—	953	1,144	1,257	1,621	1,111	510
Sex offenses—nonforcible[4]	113	6	10	8	16	11	8	13	10	12	7	15	11	8	6	2
Robbery[5]	649	500	502	460	437	366	319	320	386	373	263	280	330	352	90	262
Aggravated assault[6]	882	744	834	768	754	661	641	631	667	681	655	727	673	756	249	507
Burglary[7]	10,471	11,657	13,051	11,941	11,551	8,810	8,138	7,421	7,046	5,999	5,020	4,894	5,035	4,284	2,695	1,589
Motor vehicle theft[8]	1,471	1,248	1,077	984	859	834	641	704	711	667	754	821	836	847	7	840
Arson[9]	433	325	307	223	191	174	225	217	227	174	186	210	212	204	121	83
Weapons-, drug-, and liquor-related arrests and referrals																
Arrests[10]	6,329	7,406	6,134	6,732	6,112	5,777	5,459	5,444	5,477	5,642	4,950	4,583	4,505	4,216	2,423	1,793
Illegal weapons possession	167	150	146	178	158	148	137	129	127	131	129	168	195	188	61	127
Drug law violations	1,628	1,691	1,650	1,804	1,883	2,080	2,248	2,425	2,415	2,503	2,258	2,237	2,199	2,281	1,298	983
Liquor law violations	4,534	5,565	4,338	4,750	4,071	3,549	3,074	2,890	2,935	3,008	2,563	2,178	2,111	1,747	1,064	683
Referrals for disciplinary action[10]	71,293	96,646	103,484	103,254	105,289	103,457	104,939	110,607	110,268	109,298	110,150	105,567	102,444	95,840	89,287	6,553
Illegal weapons possession	443	590	622	545	457	358	393	417	498	535	481	569	573	535	428	107
Drug law violations	9,688	11,208	12,114	12,685	14,157	15,845	17,841	21,240	22,168	22,116	23,000	22,180	22,931	22,867	20,645	2,222
Liquor law violations	61,162	84,848	90,748	90,024	90,675	87,254	86,705	88,950	87,602	86,647	86,669	82,818	78,940	72,438	68,214	4,224

See notes at end of table.

Table 329.10 On-campus crimes, arrests, and referrals for disciplinary action at degree-granting postsecondary institutions, by location of incident, control and level of institution, and type of incident: Selected years, 2001 through 2017—Continued

Control and level of institution and type of incident	Number of incidents: Total, in residence halls and at other locations: 2001	2005	2006	2007	2008	2009	2010	2011	2012	2013	2014	2015	2016	2017: Total	2017: In residence halls	2017: At other locations
1	2	3	4	5	6	7	8	9	10	11	12	13	14	15	16	17
For-profit 4-year																
Selected crimes against persons and property	505	829	641	612	574	525	561	446	364	511	442	295	293	317	130	187
Murder[1]	0	0	0	0	0	0	0	1	0	1	0	0	0	0	0	0
Negligent manslaughter[2]	0	0	0	0	0	0	0	0	0	0	0	0	0	0	0	0
Sex offenses—forcible[3]	4	4	12	12	9	9	22	26	18	18	43	34	32	56	42	14
Rape	—	—	—	—	—	—	—	—	—	—	26	11	18	33	28	5
Fondling	—	—	—	—	—	—	—	—	—	—	17	23	14	23	14	9
Sex offenses—nonforcible[4]	13	1	0	2	0	1	1	0	3	2	2	0	1	0	0	0
Robbery[5]	64	43	25	31	38	86	70	74	51	86	52	24	26	23	1	22
Aggravated assault[6]	23	59	31	31	63	43	51	36	43	58	33	27	41	32	3	29
Burglary[7]	347	607	489	446	385	299	350	249	195	276	251	162	126	147	72	75
Motor vehicle theft[8]	52	110	78	89	79	85	65	58	53	68	59	47	64	56	11	45
Arson[9]	2	5	6	1	0	2	2	2	1	2	2	1	3	3	1	2
Weapons-, drug-, and liquor-related arrests and referrals																
Arrests[10]	11	28	52	28	40	54	165	152	126	74	117	102	116	132	57	75
Illegal weapons possession	2	2	5	3	8	6	13	11	10	12	9	14	11	7	0	7
Drug law violations	4	16	14	16	14	22	66	41	49	48	68	78	83	114	54	60
Liquor law violations	5	10	33	9	18	26	86	100	67	14	40	10	22	11	3	8
Referrals for disciplinary action[10]	316	529	513	519	566	882	760	718	668	1,161	935	804	747	1,035	883	152
Illegal weapons possession	11	42	13	11	13	23	9	16	23	18	16	11	8	12	10	2
Drug law violations	92	128	138	132	159	231	221	233	254	537	403	330	298	334	241	93
Liquor law violations	213	359	362	376	394	628	530	469	391	606	516	463	441	689	632	57
Public 2-year																
Selected crimes against persons and property	6,817	5,981	5,669	5,381	5,464	4,984	4,396	4,141	3,749	3,075	2,845	3,014	2,660	2,643	628	2,015
Murder[1]	2	2	0	0	2	2	1	2	3	7	3	13	3	2	1	1
Negligent manslaughter[2]	0	0	0	0	0	0	1	0	0	0	1	0	0	0	0	0
Sex offenses—forcible[3]	118	175	167	181	210	205	210	262	263	303	385	495	492	575	209	366
Rape	—	—	—	—	—	—	—	—	—	—	132	197	176	222	153	69
Fondling	—	—	—	—	—	—	—	—	—	—	253	298	316	353	56	297
Sex offenses—nonforcible[4]	119	10	16	7	7	12	8	16	13	11	16	11	18	9	2	7
Robbery[5]	245	248	284	279	285	251	298	262	244	197	148	149	138	129	14	115
Aggravated assault[6]	545	501	546	462	401	431	409	406	437	278	305	335	281	261	52	209
Burglary[7]	4,132	3,541	3,261	3,202	3,430	2,920	2,398	2,235	1,964	1,583	1,383	1,411	1,135	1,147	342	805
Motor vehicle theft[8]	1,552	1,428	1,319	1,174	1,059	1,109	1,028	899	776	651	548	541	549	471	0	471
Arson[9]	104	76	76	76	70	54	43	59	49	45	56	59	44	49	8	41
Weapons-, drug-, and liquor-related arrests and referrals																
Arrests[10]	2,660	3,416	3,993	4,124	3,764	3,335	3,811	3,723	3,464	3,060	3,121	2,840	2,701	3,146	1,571	1,575
Illegal weapons possession	198	278	300	304	258	256	282	248	253	230	220	268	215	227	27	200
Drug law violations	989	1,326	1,378	1,563	1,490	1,507	1,866	1,892	1,885	1,588	1,671	1,568	1,373	1,505	447	1,058
Liquor law violations	1,473	1,812	2,315	2,257	2,016	1,572	1,663	1,583	1,326	1,242	1,230	1,004	1,113	1,414	1,097	317
Referrals for disciplinary action[10]	3,529	4,688	5,897	5,987	6,425	7,241	8,017	8,174	7,586	6,845	7,240	7,292	6,868	6,816	5,555	1,261
Illegal weapons possession	127	133	238	218	183	210	242	228	224	243	269	271	214	220	89	131
Drug law violations	761	819	908	1,006	1,302	1,745	2,336	2,573	2,468	2,304	2,548	2,626	2,575	2,661	1,853	808
Liquor law violations	2,641	3,736	4,751	4,763	4,940	5,286	5,439	5,373	4,894	4,298	4,423	4,395	4,079	3,935	3,613	322
Nonprofit 2-year																
Selected crimes against persons and property	248	314	250	258	272	147	120	148	107	66	64	53	57	60	25	35
Murder[1]	1	0	0	0	0	0	0	0	0	0	0	0	0	0	0	0
Negligent manslaughter[2]	0	0	0	0	1	0	0	0	0	0	0	0	0	0	0	0
Sex offenses—forcible[3]	2	8	3	9	16	8	7	11	8	4	3	11	16	13	12	1
Rape	—	—	—	—	—	—	—	—	—	—	2	1	8	9	8	1
Fondling	—	—	—	—	—	—	—	—	—	—	1	10	8	4	4	0
Sex offenses—nonforcible[4]	2	0	1	0	0	0	0	0	0	2	0	0	0	0	0	0
Robbery[5]	54	9	7	2	13	9	5	1	2	3	0	2	5	2	0	2
Aggravated assault[6]	23	22	35	52	66	5	9	53	46	13	27	7	8	12	1	11
Burglary[7]	142	266	187	178	160	120	95	74	47	41	29	27	24	20	11	9
Motor vehicle theft[8]	23	7	14	14	9	4	2	7	4	3	5	4	3	12	0	12
Arson[9]	1	2	3	3	7	1	2	2	0	0	0	2	1	1	1	0
Weapons-, drug-, and liquor-related arrests and referrals																
Arrests[10]	108	76	67	59	93	58	49	52	52	66	39	32	56	47	18	29
Illegal weapons possession	1	5	3	4	3	4	6	5	5	5	5	9	12	9	2	7
Drug law violations	21	32	34	27	33	35	18	34	31	49	28	20	21	37	16	21
Liquor law violations	86	39	30	28	57	19	25	13	16	12	6	3	23	1	0	1
Referrals for disciplinary action[10]	624	514	537	519	413	348	377	360	300	320	448	546	420	488	462	26
Illegal weapons possession	2	12	19	10	6	7	4	1	6	7	11	2	3	7	7	0
Drug law violations	91	47	74	73	85	100	105	109	103	129	155	214	163	185	165	20
Liquor law violations	531	455	444	436	322	241	268	250	191	184	282	330	254	296	290	6

See notes at end of table.

Table 329.10 On-campus crimes, arrests, and referrals for disciplinary action at degree-granting postsecondary institutions, by location of incident, control and level of institution, and type of incident: Selected years, 2001 through 2017—Continued

Control and level of institution and type of incident	Number of incidents															
	Total, in residence halls and at other locations													2017		
	2001	2005	2006	2007	2008	2009	2010	2011	2012	2013	2014	2015	2016	Total	In residence halls	At other locations
1	2	3	4	5	6	7	8	9	10	11	12	13	14	15	16	17
For-profit 2-year																
Selected crimes against persons and property	472	430	420	547	399	459	315	257	246	167	126	118	115	85	2	83
Murder[1]	0	0	0	0	0	0	0	0	0	0	0	0	0	1	0	1
Negligent manslaughter[2]	0	0	0	0	1	0	0	0	0	0	0	0	0	0	0	0
Sex offenses—forcible[3]	12	1	8	2	4	6	2	7	12	9	4	12	9	5	0	5
Rape	—	—	—	—	—	—	—	—	—	—	1	3	2	2	0	2
Fondling	—	—	—	—	—	—	—	—	—	—	3	9	7	3	0	3
Sex offenses—nonforcible[4]	7	0	1	0	0	1	1	0	3	0	0	0	0	0	0	0
Robbery[5]	67	55	49	67	53	50	38	16	28	23	28	9	8	9	0	9
Aggravated assault[6]	40	50	33	33	29	53	35	37	30	14	12	18	25	16	0	16
Burglary[7]	292	250	245	350	241	226	135	120	110	75	58	44	46	26	2	24
Motor vehicle theft[8]	51	71	81	92	71	121	101	74	63	45	24	35	27	28	0	28
Arson[9]	3	3	3	3	0	2	3	3	0	1	0	0	0	0	0	0
Weapons-, drug-, and liquor-related arrests and referrals																
Arrests[10]	163	47	41	45	23	62	43	23	51	60	55	25	34	23	3	20
Illegal weapons possession	13	3	3	4	4	4	5	1	7	3	8	3	8	1	1	0
Drug law violations	87	36	26	32	12	41	29	14	40	40	28	19	18	21	2	19
Liquor law violations	63	8	12	9	7	17	9	8	4	17	19	3	8	1	0	1
Referrals for disciplinary action[10]	287	228	320	173	248	303	147	168	217	206	232	163	101	88	63	25
Illegal weapons possession	16	8	7	7	4	8	2	10	9	3	2	3	5	5	1	4
Drug law violations	89	134	219	122	110	163	68	68	86	94	93	88	42	42	27	15
Liquor law violations	182	86	94	44	134	132	77	90	122	109	137	72	54	41	35	6

—Not available.

[1]Excludes suicides, fetal deaths, traffic fatalities, accidental deaths, and justifiable homicide (such as the killing of a felon by a law enforcement officer in the line of duty).

[2]Killing of another person through gross negligence (excludes traffic fatalities).

[3]Any sexual act directed against another person forcibly and/or against that person's will.

[4]Includes only statutory rape or incest.

[5]Taking or attempting to take anything of value using actual or threatened force or violence.

[6]Attack upon a person for the purpose of inflicting severe or aggravated bodily injury.

[7]Unlawful entry of a structure to commit a felony or theft.

[8]Theft or attempted theft of a motor vehicle.

[9]Willful or malicious burning or attempt to burn a dwelling house, public building, motor vehicle, or personal property of another.

[10]If an individual is both arrested and referred to college officials for disciplinary action for a single offense, only the arrest is counted.

NOTE: Data are for degree-granting institutions, which are institutions that grant associate's or higher degrees and participate in Title IV federal financial aid programs. Some institutions that report Clery data—specifically, non-degree-granting institutions and institutions outside of the 50 states and the District of Columbia—are excluded from this table. Crimes, arrests, and referrals include incidents involving students, staff, and on-campus guests. Excludes off-campus crimes and arrests even if they involve college students or staff. Some data have been revised from previously published figures.

SOURCE: U.S. Department of Education, Office of Postsecondary Education, Campus Safety and Security Reporting System, 2001 through 2017; and National Center for Education Statistics, Integrated Postsecondary Education Data System (IPEDS), Fall 2002 through Fall 2017, Institutional Characteristics component. (This table was prepared September 2019.)

Table 329.20 On-campus crimes, arrests, and referrals for disciplinary action per 10,000 full-time-equivalent (FTE) students at degree-granting postsecondary institutions, by whether institution has residence halls, control and level of institution, and type of incident: Selected years, 2001 through 2017

Control and level of institution and type of incident	Number of incidents per 10,000 FTE students[1]															
	Total, institutions with and without residence halls													2017		
	2001	2005	2006	2007	2008	2009	2010	2011	2012	2013	2014	2015	2016	Total	Institutions with residence halls	Institutions without residence halls
1	2	3	4	5	6	7	8	9	10	11	12	13	14	15	16	17
All institutions																
Selected crimes against persons and property	35.619	32.864	33.350	30.559	28.993	22.955	20.869	20.027	19.983	18.461	18.069	18.694	19.258	19.605	25.065	6.211
Murder[2]	0.015	0.008	0.006	0.032	0.009	0.011	0.010	0.011	0.008	0.016	0.007	0.019	0.010	0.014	0.018	0.005
Negligent manslaughter[3]	0.002	0.002	0.000	0.002	0.002	0.000	0.001	0.001	0.001	0.000	0.001	0.001	0.001	0.002	0.003	0.000
Sex offenses—forcible[4]	1.885	2.058	2.001	1.968	1.899	1.715	1.903	2.223	2.695	3.374	4.549	5.447	6.061	7.060	9.529	1.006
Rape	—	—	—	—	—	—	—	—	—	—	2.985	3.476	3.972	4.428	6.157	0.185
Fondling	—	—	—	—	—	—	—	—	—	—	1.563	1.971	2.089	2.633	3.371	0.821
Sex offenses—nonforcible[5]	0.395	0.032	0.032	0.029	0.025	0.044	0.021	0.030	0.031	0.031	0.036	0.043	0.041	0.054	0.068	0.021
Robbery[6]	1.424	1.193	1.160	1.140	1.134	0.950	0.905	0.846	0.918	0.893	0.701	0.709	0.745	0.706	0.820	0.427
Aggravated assault[7]	2.524	2.044	2.112	1.902	1.795	1.569	1.444	1.475	1.627	1.385	1.380	1.533	1.480	1.505	1.788	0.809
Burglary[8]	23.038	22.511	23.432	21.543	20.676	15.559	13.872	12.825	12.207	10.325	9.041	8.365	8.120	7.505	9.621	2.314
Motor vehicle theft[9]	5.327	4.256	3.921	3.375	2.953	2.681	2.237	2.196	2.023	2.014	1.947	2.185	2.394	2.343	2.682	1.510
Arson[10]	1.010	0.759	0.687	0.567	0.500	0.427	0.476	0.421	0.473	0.425	0.406	0.392	0.405	0.416	0.536	0.120
Weapons-, drug-, and liquor-related arrests and referrals																
Arrests[11]	34.550	37.722	37.619	36.936	36.435	33.748	33.497	35.755	35.127	31.841	30.004	27.362	26.481	25.549	34.570	3.419
Illegal weapons possession	0.919	1.013	0.986	0.963	0.856	0.726	0.723	0.674	0.687	0.690	0.667	0.803	0.814	0.845	0.995	0.478
Drug law violations	10.151	10.547	10.458	10.327	10.898	10.698	12.086	13.653	14.240	13.420	12.917	13.193	13.057	13.287	17.764	2.305
Liquor law violations	23.481	26.163	26.175	25.647	24.681	22.324	20.687	21.428	20.200	17.730	16.419	13.366	12.609	11.416	15.811	0.635
Referrals for disciplinary action[11]	132.899	156.060	163.438	158.241	156.511	148.959	149.716	164.460	168.772	166.056	170.675	164.100	155.818	146.925	205.702	2.741
Illegal weapons possession	1.093	1.448	1.402	1.211	1.047	0.859	0.854	0.844	0.943	0.956	0.960	0.968	0.954	0.889	1.141	0.270
Drug law violations	20.466	19.511	20.427	20.804	23.362	24.498	27.322	33.961	36.224	36.222	38.118	38.048	37.849	39.437	54.950	1.381
Liquor law violations	111.340	135.101	141.609	136.226	132.103	123.602	121.540	129.654	131.606	128.878	131.597	125.084	117.016	106.600	149.610	1.090
Public 4-year																
Selected crimes against persons and property	36.191	34.295	35.531	32.846	30.535	24.898	23.448	21.958	21.669	19.553	19.545	19.655	19.811	20.411	21.899	7.014
Murder[2]	0.017	0.007	0.009	0.070	0.015	0.012	0.014	0.015	0.010	0.015	0.004	0.019	0.011	0.017	0.017	0.014
Negligent manslaughter[3]	0.004	0.002	0.000	0.003	0.002	0.000	0.000	0.001	0.001	0.000	0.001	0.001	0.003	0.004	0.005	0.000
Sex offenses—forcible[4]	2.408	2.448	2.409	2.391	2.151	1.892	2.210	2.451	2.946	3.372	4.702	5.726	6.173	7.236	7.916	1.116
Rape	—	—	—	—	—	—	—	—	—	—	3.102	3.674	4.112	4.656	5.158	0.138
Fondling	—	—	—	—	—	—	—	—	—	—	1.601	2.052	2.061	2.581	2.759	0.978
Sex offenses—nonforcible[5]	0.400	0.044	0.026	0.039	0.020	0.062	0.023	0.025	0.025	0.027	0.041	0.054	0.042	0.087	0.093	0.028
Robbery[6]	1.130	1.219	1.170	1.211	1.225	1.008	1.001	0.916	0.981	0.946	0.805	0.839	0.824	0.723	0.761	0.386
Aggravated assault[7]	2.774	2.242	2.302	2.110	1.931	1.767	1.627	1.610	1.792	1.490	1.488	1.654	1.610	1.569	1.673	0.634
Burglary[8]	22.283	22.654	24.138	22.432	21.184	16.689	15.456	14.025	13.173	10.811	9.780	8.361	7.817	7.480	7.999	2.811
Motor vehicle theft[9]	5.942	4.671	4.581	3.802	3.311	2.843	2.426	2.382	2.100	2.289	2.197	2.560	2.861	2.805	2.913	1.833
Arson[10]	1.232	1.009	0.897	0.788	0.697	0.623	0.691	0.533	0.639	0.603	0.526	0.441	0.471	0.489	0.522	0.193
Weapons-, drug-, and liquor-related arrests and referrals																
Arrests[11]	60.113	66.641	68.660	66.384	66.324	63.558	63.512	67.169	64.447	56.711	53.086	47.311	44.128	41.420	45.437	5.264
Illegal weapons possession	1.339	1.538	1.478	1.384	1.240	1.027	1.012	0.941	0.927	0.949	0.907	1.043	1.060	1.120	1.180	0.579
Drug law violations	17.651	18.575	18.671	17.939	19.133	18.993	21.722	24.424	25.077	23.194	22.142	22.427	21.704	21.508	23.554	3.087
Liquor law violations	41.123	46.529	48.511	47.061	45.952	43.539	40.778	41.804	38.443	32.569	30.038	23.842	21.365	18.792	20.702	1.598
Referrals for disciplinary action[11]	153.104	175.506	184.622	178.077	170.820	169.503	175.490	194.017	197.669	189.403	196.696	184.108	166.160	154.470	171.440	1.722
Illegal weapons possession	1.311	1.921	1.673	1.455	1.294	1.043	1.004	0.913	0.962	0.900	0.946	0.823	0.841	0.730	0.779	0.289
Drug law violations	25.492	22.803	23.744	24.255	27.204	28.459	32.444	40.907	43.129	42.093	44.485	44.249	41.549	44.076	48.877	0.868
Liquor law violations	126.301	150.782	159.206	152.367	142.322	140.001	142.042	152.198	153.578	146.410	151.264	139.036	123.770	109.663	121.784	0.565
Nonprofit 4-year																
Selected crimes against persons and property	57.358	54.165	57.679	52.036	49.337	38.613	35.193	33.154	33.198	31.205	30.156	31.148	32.667	32.071	34.431	9.294
Murder[2]	0.019	0.017	0.010	0.007	0.003	0.019	0.016	0.009	0.006	0.015	0.015	0.006	0.012	0.018	0.019	0.000
Negligent manslaughter[3]	0.000	0.003	0.000	0.003	0.000	0.000	0.000	0.000	0.000	0.000	0.000	0.003	0.000	0.000	0.000	0.000
Sex offenses—forcible[4]	3.169	3.784	3.694	3.586	3.588	3.557	3.848	4.417	5.357	7.214	9.368	10.452	11.697	13.166	14.404	1.216
Rape	—	—	—	—	—	—	—	—	—	—	6.493	7.046	7.985	8.420	9.267	0.250
Fondling	—	—	—	—	—	—	—	—	—	—	2.875	3.407	3.712	4.746	5.138	0.967
Sex offenses—nonforcible[5]	0.437	0.021	0.034	0.027	0.053	0.036	0.025	0.040	0.031	0.036	0.021	0.045	0.032	0.023	0.026	0.000
Robbery[6]	2.508	1.739	1.717	1.549	1.448	1.181	1.002	0.988	1.188	1.131	0.793	0.834	0.975	1.031	1.063	0.717
Aggravated assault[7]	3.408	2.588	2.853	2.586	2.498	2.133	2.014	1.948	2.052	2.065	1.976	2.165	1.987	2.213	2.120	3.119
Burglary[8]	40.460	40.542	44.638	40.212	38.269	28.434	25.567	22.908	21.679	18.192	15.146	14.573	14.869	12.543	13.555	2.776
Motor vehicle theft[9]	5.684	4.340	3.684	3.314	2.846	2.692	2.014	2.173	2.188	2.023	2.275	2.445	2.469	2.480	2.591	1.403
Arson[10]	1.673	1.130	1.050	0.751	0.633	0.562	0.707	0.670	0.698	0.528	0.561	0.625	0.626	0.597	0.653	0.062

See notes at end of table.

Table 329.20 On-campus crimes, arrests, and referrals for disciplinary action per 10,000 full-time-equivalent (FTE) students at degree-granting postsecondary institutions, by whether institution has residence halls, control and level of institution, and type of incident: Selected years, 2001 through 2017—Continued

Control and level of institution and type of incident	Number of incidents per 10,000 FTE students[1] — Total, institutions with and without residence halls: 2001	2005	2006	2007	2008	2009	2010	2011	2012	2013	2014	2015	2016	2017: Total	2017: Institutions with residence halls	2017: Institutions without residence halls
1	2	3	4	5	6	7	8	9	10	11	12	13	14	15	16	17
Weapons-, drug-, and liquor-related arrests and referrals																
Arrests[11]	24.456	25.758	20.980	22.670	20.249	18.645	17.150	16.805	16.851	17.110	14.935	13.647	13.304	12.344	13.477	1.403
Illegal weapons possession	0.645	0.522	0.499	0.599	0.523	0.478	0.430	0.398	0.391	0.397	0.389	0.500	0.576	0.550	0.598	0.094
Drug law violations	6.291	5.881	5.643	6.075	6.238	6.713	7.062	7.486	7.430	7.590	6.813	6.661	6.494	6.678	7.251	1.154
Liquor law violations	17.520	19.355	14.837	15.996	13.487	11.454	9.657	8.921	9.030	9.122	7.733	6.486	6.234	5.115	5.629	0.156
Referrals for disciplinary action[11]	275.480	336.127	353.943	347.714	348.824	333.904	329.679	341.437	339.263	331.451	332.331	314.359	302.523	280.603	308.611	10.261
Illegal weapons possession	1.712	2.052	2.127	1.835	1.514	1.155	1.235	1.287	1.532	1.622	1.451	1.694	1.692	1.566	1.725	0.031
Drug law violations	37.435	38.981	41.433	42.718	46.902	51.139	56.050	65.567	68.205	67.068	69.393	66.048	67.717	66.951	73.680	1.996
Liquor law violations	236.333	295.095	310.383	303.161	300.408	281.609	272.395	274.583	269.526	262.761	261.487	246.617	233.115	212.086	233.205	8.234
For-profit 4-year																
Selected crimes against persons and property	19.109	17.049	9.552	8.092	10.334	7.513	6.499	6.003	5.531	8.553	5.763	4.371	4.489	5.277	19.368	2.561
Murder[2]	0.000	0.000	0.000	0.000	0.000	0.000	0.000	0.013	0.000	0.017	0.000	0.000	0.000	0.000	0.000	0.000
Negligent manslaughter[3]	0.000	0.000	0.000	0.000	0.000	0.000	0.000	0.000	0.000	0.000	0.000	0.000	0.000	0.000	0.000	0.000
Sex offenses—forcible[4]	0.151	0.082	0.179	0.159	0.162	0.129	0.255	0.350	0.274	0.301	0.561	0.504	0.490	0.932	5.151	0.119
Rape	—	—	—	—	—	—	—	—	—	—	0.339	0.163	0.276	0.549	3.194	0.040
Fondling	—	—	—	—	—	—	—	—	—	—	0.222	0.341	0.215	0.383	1.957	0.079
Sex offenses—nonforcible[5]	0.492	0.021	0.000	0.026	0.000	0.014	0.012	0.000	0.046	0.033	0.026	0.000	0.015	0.000	0.000	0.000
Robbery[6]	2.422	0.884	0.373	0.410	0.684	1.231	0.811	0.996	0.775	1.440	0.678	0.356	0.398	0.383	0.515	0.357
Aggravated assault[7]	0.870	1.213	0.462	0.410	1.134	0.615	0.591	0.485	0.653	0.971	0.430	0.400	0.628	0.533	1.030	0.437
Burglary[8]	13.130	12.484	7.287	5.897	6.931	4.279	4.055	3.351	2.963	4.620	3.273	2.401	1.931	2.447	9.993	0.993
Motor vehicle theft[9]	1.968	2.262	1.162	1.177	1.422	1.216	0.753	0.781	0.805	1.138	0.769	0.696	0.981	0.932	2.369	0.655
Arson[10]	0.076	0.103	0.089	0.013	0.000	0.029	0.023	0.027	0.015	0.033	0.026	0.015	0.046	0.050	0.309	0.000
Weapons-, drug-, and liquor-related arrests and referrals																
Arrests[11]	0.416	0.576	0.775	0.370	0.720	0.773	1.911	2.046	1.915	1.239	1.526	1.511	1.777	2.197	11.847	0.338
Illegal weapons possession	0.076	0.041	0.075	0.040	0.144	0.086	0.151	0.148	0.152	0.201	0.117	0.207	0.169	0.117	0.309	0.079
Drug law violations	0.151	0.329	0.209	0.212	0.252	0.315	0.765	0.552	0.745	0.803	0.887	1.156	1.272	1.898	10.508	0.238
Liquor law violations	0.189	0.206	0.492	0.119	0.324	0.372	0.996	1.346	1.018	0.234	0.522	0.148	0.337	0.183	1.030	0.020
Referrals for disciplinary action[11]	11.957	10.880	7.645	6.862	10.190	12.623	8.804	9.663	10.150	19.433	12.191	11.914	11.446	17.230	103.125	0.675
Illegal weapons possession	0.416	0.864	0.194	0.145	0.234	0.329	0.104	0.215	0.349	0.301	0.209	0.163	0.123	0.200	1.030	0.040
Drug law violations	3.481	2.632	2.056	1.745	2.863	3.306	2.560	3.136	3.860	8.989	5.255	4.890	4.566	5.560	31.525	0.556
Liquor law violations	8.060	7.383	5.394	4.971	7.093	8.988	6.140	6.312	5.941	10.143	6.728	6.861	6.757	11.470	70.570	0.079
Public 2-year																
Selected crimes against persons and property	19.867	16.389	15.430	14.365	13.990	11.745	10.195	9.998	9.379	7.912	7.682	8.415	7.973	8.155	14.371	6.374
Murder[2]	0.006	0.005	0.000	0.000	0.005	0.005	0.002	0.005	0.008	0.018	0.008	0.036	0.009	0.006	0.014	0.004
Negligent manslaughter[3]	0.000	0.000	0.000	0.000	0.000	0.000	0.002	0.000	0.000	0.000	0.003	0.000	0.000	0.000	0.000	0.000
Sex offenses—forcible[4]	0.344	0.480	0.455	0.483	0.538	0.483	0.487	0.633	0.658	0.780	1.040	1.382	1.475	1.774	3.852	1.179
Rape	—	—	—	—	—	—	—	—	—	—	0.356	0.550	0.528	0.685	2.300	0.222
Fondling	—	—	—	—	—	—	—	—	—	—	0.683	0.832	0.947	1.089	1.552	0.957
Sex offenses—nonforcible[5]	0.347	0.027	0.044	0.019	0.018	0.028	0.019	0.039	0.033	0.028	0.043	0.031	0.054	0.028	0.028	0.028
Robbery[6]	0.714	0.680	0.773	0.745	0.730	0.591	0.691	0.633	0.610	0.507	0.400	0.416	0.414	0.398	0.374	0.405
Aggravated assault[7]	1.588	1.373	1.486	1.233	1.027	1.016	0.949	0.980	1.093	0.715	0.824	0.935	0.842	0.805	1.497	0.607
Burglary[8]	12.042	9.703	8.876	8.548	8.782	6.881	5.561	5.396	4.914	4.073	3.734	3.940	3.402	3.539	7.372	2.441
Motor vehicle theft[9]	4.523	3.913	3.590	3.134	2.712	2.613	2.384	2.171	1.941	1.675	1.480	1.511	1.645	1.453	1.039	1.572
Arson[10]	0.303	0.208	0.207	0.203	0.179	0.127	0.100	0.142	0.123	0.116	0.151	0.165	0.132	0.151	0.194	0.139
Weapons-, drug-, and liquor-related arrests and referrals																
Arrests[11]	7.752	9.360	10.868	11.009	9.638	7.859	8.838	8.989	8.666	7.874	8.427	7.930	8.095	9.706	30.030	3.886
Illegal weapons possession	0.577	0.762	0.817	0.812	0.661	0.603	0.654	0.599	0.633	0.592	0.594	0.748	0.644	0.700	1.025	0.607
Drug law violations	2.882	3.633	3.751	4.172	3.815	3.551	4.328	4.568	4.716	4.086	4.512	4.378	4.115	4.643	11.460	2.691
Liquor law violations	4.293	4.965	6.301	6.025	5.162	3.704	3.857	3.822	3.317	3.196	3.321	2.803	3.336	4.363	17.544	0.587
Referrals for disciplinary action[11]	10.284	12.846	16.051	15.983	16.451	17.063	18.592	19.735	18.979	17.613	19.549	20.360	20.585	21.030	85.420	2.588
Illegal weapons possession	0.370	0.364	0.648	0.582	0.469	0.495	0.561	0.550	0.560	0.625	0.726	0.757	0.641	0.679	1.815	0.353
Drug law violations	2.218	2.244	2.471	2.686	3.334	4.112	5.417	6.212	6.174	5.928	6.880	7.332	7.718	8.210	31.139	1.643
Liquor law violations	7.697	10.237	12.932	12.715	12.649	12.456	12.614	12.972	12.244	11.059	11.942	12.271	12.226	12.141	52.466	0.591

See notes at end of table.

Table 329.20 On-campus crimes, arrests, and referrals for disciplinary action per 10,000 full-time-equivalent (FTE) students at degree-granting postsecondary institutions, by whether institution has residence halls, control and level of institution, and type of incident: Selected years, 2001 through 2017—Continued

Control and level of institution and type of incident	Number of incidents per 10,000 FTE students[1]															
	Total, institutions with and without residence halls													2017		
	2001	2005	2006	2007	2008	2009	2010	2011	2012	2013	2014	2015	2016	Total	Institutions with residence halls	Institutions without residence halls
1	2	3	4	5	6	7	8	9	10	11	12	13	14	15	16	17
Nonprofit 2-year																
Selected crimes against persons and property	63.955	91.263	81.948	103.794	99.274	55.883	48.448	45.531	35.148	26.993	27.354	20.036	21.920	14.389	37.843	8.423
Murder[2]	0.258	0.000	0.000	0.000	0.000	0.000	0.000	0.000	0.000	0.000	0.000	0.000	0.000	0.000	0.000	0.000
Negligent manslaughter[3]	0.000	0.000	0.000	0.000	0.365	0.000	0.000	0.000	0.000	0.000	0.000	0.000	0.000	0.000	0.000	0.000
Sex offenses—forcible[4]	0.516	2.325	0.983	3.621	5.840	3.041	2.826	3.384	2.628	1.636	1.282	4.158	6.153	3.118	14.191	0.301
Rape	—	—	—	—	—	—	—	—	—	—	0.855	0.378	3.076	2.158	9.461	0.301
Fondling	—	—	—	—	—	—	—	—	—	—	0.427	3.780	3.076	0.959	4.730	0.000
Sex offenses—nonforcible[5]	0.516	0.000	0.328	0.000	0.000	0.000	0.000	0.000	0.000	0.818	0.000	0.000	0.000	0.000	0.000	0.000
Robbery[6]	13.926	2.616	2.295	0.805	4.745	3.421	2.019	0.308	0.657	1.227	0.000	0.756	1.923	0.480	0.000	0.602
Aggravated assault[7]	5.931	6.394	11.473	20.920	24.088	1.901	3.634	16.305	15.110	5.317	11.540	2.646	3.076	2.878	4.730	2.407
Burglary[8]	36.620	77.312	61.297	71.610	58.396	45.619	38.354	22.766	15.439	16.768	12.395	10.207	9.229	4.796	16.556	1.805
Motor vehicle theft[9]	5.931	2.035	4.589	5.632	3.285	1.521	0.807	2.154	1.314	1.227	2.137	1.512	1.154	2.878	1.183	3.309
Arson[10]	0.258	0.581	0.983	1.207	2.555	0.380	0.807	0.615	0.000	0.000	0.000	0.756	0.385	0.240	1.183	0.000
Weapons-, drug-, and liquor-related arrests and referrals																
Arrests[11]	27.852	22.089	21.962	23.736	33.943	22.049	19.783	15.998	17.081	26.993	16.669	12.097	21.535	11.271	37.843	4.512
Illegal weapons possession	0.258	1.453	0.983	1.609	1.095	1.521	2.422	1.538	1.642	2.045	2.137	3.402	4.615	2.158	8.278	0.602
Drug law violations	5.416	9.301	11.145	10.862	12.044	13.305	7.267	10.460	10.183	20.040	11.967	7.561	8.076	8.873	28.382	3.911
Liquor law violations	22.178	11.335	9.834	11.264	20.804	7.223	10.093	3.999	5.256	4.908	2.564	1.134	8.845	0.240	1.183	0.000
Referrals for disciplinary action[11]	160.920	149.393	176.025	208.794	150.735	132.294	152.206	110.752	98.545	130.874	191.478	206.404	161.514	117.029	570.009	1.805
Illegal weapons possession	0.516	3.488	6.228	4.023	2.190	2.661	1.615	0.308	1.971	2.863	4.701	0.756	1.154	1.679	8.278	0.000
Drug law violations	23.468	13.660	24.257	29.368	31.023	38.016	42.392	33.533	33.834	52.759	66.248	80.898	62.683	44.366	212.867	1.504
Liquor law violations	136.937	132.244	145.540	175.403	117.523	91.618	108.200	76.911	62.740	75.253	120.528	124.750	97.677	70.985	348.865	0.301
For-profit 2-year																
Selected crimes against persons and property	25.385	17.851	18.237	23.731	14.825	13.033	8.167	7.503	9.325	7.141	6.140	6.867	6.736	4.993	7.426	4.871
Murder[2]	0.000	0.000	0.000	0.000	0.000	0.000	0.000	0.000	0.000	0.000	0.000	0.000	0.000	0.059	1.238	0.000
Negligent manslaughter[3]	0.000	0.000	0.000	0.000	0.037	0.000	0.000	0.000	0.000	0.000	0.000	0.000	0.000	0.000	0.000	0.000
Sex offenses—forcible[4]	0.645	0.042	0.347	0.087	0.149	0.170	0.052	0.204	0.455	0.385	0.195	0.698	0.527	0.294	0.000	0.308
Rape	—	—	—	—	—	—	—	—	—	—	0.049	0.175	0.117	0.117	0.000	0.123
Fondling	—	—	—	—	—	—	—	—	—	—	0.146	0.524	0.410	0.176	0.000	0.185
Sex offenses—nonforcible[5]	0.376	0.000	0.043	0.000	0.000	0.028	0.026	0.000	0.114	0.000	0.000	0.000	0.000	0.000	0.000	0.000
Robbery[6]	3.603	2.283	2.128	2.907	1.969	1.420	0.985	0.467	1.061	0.983	1.364	0.524	0.469	0.529	0.000	0.555
Aggravated assault[7]	2.151	2.076	1.433	1.432	1.078	1.505	0.907	1.080	1.137	0.599	0.585	1.048	1.464	0.940	0.000	0.987
Burglary[8]	15.704	10.378	10.638	15.185	8.954	6.417	3.500	3.503	4.170	3.207	2.826	2.561	2.695	1.527	3.713	1.418
Motor vehicle theft[9]	2.743	2.947	3.517	3.991	2.638	3.436	2.619	2.160	2.388	1.924	1.170	2.037	1.582	1.645	2.475	1.603
Arson[10]	0.161	0.125	0.130	0.130	0.000	0.057	0.078	0.088	0.000	0.043	0.000	0.000	0.000	0.000	0.000	0.000
Weapons-, drug-, and liquor-related arrests and referrals																
Arrests[11]	8.766	1.951	1.780	1.952	0.855	1.760	1.115	0.671	1.933	2.565	2.680	1.455	1.992	1.351	3.713	1.233
Illegal weapons possession	0.699	0.125	0.130	0.174	0.149	0.114	0.130	0.029	0.265	0.128	0.390	0.175	0.469	0.059	1.238	0.000
Drug law violations	4.679	1.495	1.129	1.388	0.446	1.164	0.752	0.409	1.516	1.710	1.364	1.106	1.054	1.233	2.475	1.172
Liquor law violations	3.388	0.332	0.521	0.390	0.260	0.483	0.233	0.234	0.152	0.727	0.926	0.175	0.469	0.059	0.000	0.062
Referrals for disciplinary action[11]	15.435	9.465	13.894	7.506	9.215	8.603	3.811	4.905	8.225	8.808	11.305	9.486	5.916	5.169	80.446	1.418
Illegal weapons possession	0.861	0.332	0.304	0.304	0.149	0.227	0.052	0.292	0.341	0.128	0.097	0.175	0.293	0.294	3.713	0.123
Drug law violations	4.787	5.563	9.509	5.293	4.087	4.628	1.763	1.985	3.260	4.019	4.532	5.122	2.460	2.467	33.416	0.925
Liquor law violations	9.788	3.570	4.082	1.909	4.979	3.748	1.996	2.627	4.624	4.661	6.676	4.190	3.163	2.408	43.317	0.370

—Not available.

[1]Although crimes, arrests, and referrals include incidents involving students, staff, and campus guests, they are expressed as a ratio to FTE students because comprehensive FTE counts of all these groups are not available.

[2]Excludes suicides, fetal deaths, traffic fatalities, accidental deaths, and justifiable homicide (such as the killing of a felon by a law enforcement officer in the line of duty).

[3]Killing of another person through gross negligence (excludes traffic fatalities).

[4]Any sexual act directed against another person forcibly and/or against that person's will.

[5]Includes only statutory rape or incest.

[6]Taking or attempting to take anything of value using actual or threatened force or violence.

[7]Attack upon a person for the purpose of inflicting severe or aggravated bodily injury.

[8]Unlawful entry of a structure to commit a felony or theft.

[9]Theft or attempted theft of a motor vehicle.

[10]Willful or malicious burning or attempt to burn a dwelling house, public building, motor vehicle, or personal property of another.

[11]If an individual is both arrested and referred to college officials for disciplinary action for a single offense, only the arrest is counted.

NOTE: Data are for degree-granting institutions, which are institutions that grant associate's or higher degrees and participate in Title IV federal financial aid programs. Some institutions that report Clery data—specifically, non-degree-granting institutions and institutions outside of the 50 states and the District of Columbia—are excluded from this table. Crimes, arrests, and referrals include incidents involving students, staff, and on-campus guests. Excludes off-campus crimes and arrests even if they involve college students or staff. Detail may not sum to totals because of rounding. Some data have been revised from previously published figures.

SOURCE: U.S. Department of Education, Office of Postsecondary Education, Campus Safety and Security Reporting System, 2001 through 2017; and National Center for Education Statistics, Integrated Postsecondary Education Data System (IPEDS), Spring 2002 through Spring 2018; and National Center for Education Statistics, Integrated Postsecondary Education Data System (IPEDS), Spring 2001 through Spring 2018, Fall Enrollment component. (This table was prepared September 2019.)

Table 329.30. On-campus hate crimes at degree-granting postsecondary institutions, by level and control of institution, type of crime, and category of bias motivating the crime: Selected years, 2010 through 2017

Type of crime and category of bias motivating the crime[1]	Total, 2010	Total, 2012	Total, 2013	Total, 2014	Total, 2015	2016							2017						
							4-year			2-year				4-year			2-year		
						Total	Public	Non-profit	For-profit	Public	Non-profit	For-profit	Total	Public	Non-profit	For-profit	Public	Non-profit	For-profit
1	2	3	4	5	6	7	8	9	10	11	12	13	14	15	16	17	18	19	20
All on-campus hate crimes	**928**	**784**	**778**	**794**	**859**	**1,072**	**483**	**395**	**7**	**183**	**0**	**4**	**958**	**416**	**405**	**1**	**136**	**0**	**0**
Murder[2]	0	0	0	0	0	0	0	0	0	0	0	0	1	1	0	0	0	0	0
Sex offenses—forcible[3]	7	4	7	4	7	8	1	1	0	6	0	0	6	1	3	0	2	0	0
Race	0	1	2	1	0	1	1	0	0	0	0	0	0	0	0	0	0	0	0
Ethnicity	0	0	0	0	0	0	0	0	0	0	0	0	0	0	0	0	0	0	0
Religion	0	0	0	0	1	0	0	0	0	0	0	0	0	0	0	0	0	0	0
Sexual orientation	4	2	1	1	3	1	0	1	0	0	0	0	0	0	0	0	0	0	0
Gender	3	1	4	2	1	5	0	0	0	5	0	0	4	1	1	0	2	0	0
Gender identity	—	—	—	0	2	1	0	0	0	1	0	0	2	0	2	0	0	0	0
Disability	0	0	0	0	0	0	0	0	0	0	0	0	0	0	0	0	0	0	0
Sex offenses—nonforcible[4]	0	0	0	0	0	0	0	0	0	0	0	0	0	0	0	0	0	0	0
Robbery[5]	2	5	1	2	3	2	1	0	0	1	0	0	2	1	1	0	0	0	0
Aggravated assault[6]	17	14	7	18	18	35	26	2	0	7	0	0	15	6	3	0	6	0	0
Race	6	6	5	5	5	8	5	0	0	3	0	0	6	2	3	0	1	0	0
Ethnicity	1	0	1	4	4	15	14	0	0	1	0	0	5	1	0	0	4	0	0
Religion	1	1	0	1	0	1	1	0	0	0	0	0	1	1	0	0	0	0	0
Sexual orientation	9	5	1	7	7	8	6	1	0	1	0	0	2	2	0	0	0	0	0
Gender	0	1	0	1	1	1	0	0	0	1	0	0	0	0	0	0	0	0	0
Gender identity	—	—	—	0	1	2	0	1	0	1	0	0	0	0	0	0	0	0	0
Disability	0	1	0	0	0	0	0	0	0	0	0	0	1	0	0	0	1	0	0
Burglary[7]	11	5	4	28	4	6	0	4	0	2	0	0	3	0	2	0	1	0	0
Race	7	0	1	24	0	1	0	1	0	0	0	0	1	0	1	0	0	0	0
Ethnicity	0	0	0	0	0	0	0	0	0	0	0	0	1	0	0	0	1	0	0
Religion	0	1	1	3	0	0	0	0	0	0	0	0	0	0	0	0	0	0	0
Sexual orientation	2	0	0	1	0	2	0	2	0	0	0	0	0	0	0	0	0	0	0
Gender	1	4	2	0	0	3	0	1	0	2	0	0	1	0	1	0	0	0	0
Gender identity	—	—	—	0	4	0	0	0	0	0	0	0	0	0	0	0	0	0	0
Disability	1	0	0	0	0	0	0	0	0	0	0	0	0	0	0	0	0	0	0
Motor vehicle theft[8]	0	0	0	0	1	0	0	0	0	0	0	0	1	0	1	0	0	0	0
Arson[9]	0	0	0	1	2	2	2	0	0	0	0	0	1	1	0	0	0	0	0
Simple assault[10]	67	79	91	63	80	98	64	26	0	7	0	1	83	41	23	0	19	0	0
Race	25	36	36	14	36	42	27	13	0	2	0	0	40	18	15	0	7	0	0
Ethnicity	5	5	5	11	9	14	10	2	0	2	0	0	8	3	1	0	4	0	0
Religion	4	9	6	2	9	12	9	2	0	1	0	0	9	7	2	0	0	0	0
Sexual orientation	23	21	27	23	18	16	9	5	0	2	0	0	18	9	3	0	6	0	0
Gender	9	5	17	9	2	11	8	2	0	0	0	1	3	1	0	0	2	0	0
Gender identity	—	—	—	3	5	2	1	1	0	0	0	0	5	3	2	0	0	0	0
Disability	1	3	0	1	1	1	0	1	0	0	0	0	0	0	0	0	0	0	0
Larceny[11]	9	9	15	17	25	33	3	16	3	10	0	1	24	4	19	0	1	0	0
Race	1	2	5	5	1	12	1	5	3	2	0	1	6	1	5	0	0	0	0
Ethnicity	3	2	2	1	0	4	0	0	0	4	0	0	3	2	1	0	0	0	0
Religion	1	2	3	3	19	5	2	3	0	0	0	0	1	0	1	0	0	0	0
Sexual orientation	1	3	3	1	1	5	0	5	0	0	0	0	6	1	4	0	1	0	0
Gender	3	0	2	7	3	3	0	0	0	3	0	0	7	0	7	0	0	0	0
Gender identity	—	—	—	0	1	3	0	2	0	1	0	0	1	0	1	0	0	0	0
Disability	0	0	0	0	0	1	0	1	0	0	0	0	0	0	0	0	0	0	0
Intimidation[12]	260	265	296	339	355	425	183	169	1	70	0	2	385	191	147	0	47	0	0
Race	79	120	111	111	141	170	81	62	0	27	0	0	172	92	63	0	17	0	0
Ethnicity	17	22	49	32	37	48	19	22	0	7	0	0	45	20	19	0	6	0	0
Religion	38	28	25	35	48	67	35	22	0	10	0	0	48	26	18	0	4	0	0
Sexual orientation	87	70	68	78	77	83	32	35	1	14	0	1	66	29	25	0	12	0	0
Gender	37	21	37	63	34	28	9	16	0	3	0	0	26	11	12	0	3	0	0
Gender identity	—	—	—	13	11	20	4	11	0	4	0	1	19	9	6	0	4	0	0
Disability	2	4	6	7	7	9	3	1	0	5	0	0	9	4	4	0	1	0	0
Destruction, damage, and vandalism[13]	555	403	357	322	364	463	203	177	3	80	0	0	437	170	206	1	60	0	0
Race	257	186	147	116	151	175	82	56	1	36	0	0	186	80	78	0	28	0	0
Ethnicity	43	34	38	29	25	30	17	11	0	2	0	0	33	16	15	0	2	0	0
Religion	103	70	48	67	108	134	54	51	0	29	0	0	111	34	59	1	17	0	0
Sexual orientation	135	104	108	89	61	67	33	27	2	5	0	0	61	30	21	0	10	0	0
Gender	17	9	14	13	10	35	14	15	0	6	0	0	22	5	16	0	1	0	0
Gender identity	—	—	—	6	8	22	3	17	0	2	0	0	24	5	17	0	2	0	0
Disability	0	0	2	2	1	0	0	0	0	0	0	0	0	0	0	0	0	0	0

—Not available.

[1]Bias categories correspond to characteristics against which the bias is directed (i.e., race, ethnicity, religion, sexual orientation, gender, gender identity, or disability).

[2]Excludes suicides, fetal deaths, traffic fatalities, accidental deaths, and justifiable homicide (such as the killing of a felon by a law enforcement officer in the line of duty).

[3]Any sexual act directed against another person forcibly and/or against that person's will.

[4]Includes only statutory rape or incest.

[5]Taking or attempting to take anything of value using actual or threatened force or violence.

[6]Attack upon a person for the purpose of inflicting severe or aggravated bodily injury.

[7]Unlawful entry of a structure to commit a felony or theft.

[8]Theft or attempted theft of a motor vehicle.

[9]Willful or malicious burning or attempt to burn a dwelling house, public building, motor vehicle, or personal property of another.

[10]A physical attack by one person upon another where neither the offender displays a weapon, nor the victim suffers obvious severe or aggravated bodily injury involving apparent broken bones, loss of teeth, possible internal injury, severe laceration, or loss of consciousness.

[11]The unlawful taking, carrying, leading, or riding away of property from the possession of another.

[12]Placing another person in reasonable fear of bodily harm through the use of threatening words and/or other conduct, but without displaying a weapon or subjecting the victim to actual physical attack.

[13]Willfully or maliciously destroying, damaging, defacing, or otherwise injuring real or personal property without the consent of the owner or the person having custody or control of it.

NOTE: Data are for degree-granting institutions, which are institutions that grant associate's or higher degrees and participate in Title IV federal financial aid programs. Some institutions that report Clery data—specifically, non-degree-granting institutions and institutions outside of the 50 states and the District of Columbia—are excluded from this table. A hate crime is a criminal offense that is motivated, in whole or in part, by the perpetrator's bias against a group of people based on their race, ethnicity, religion, sexual orientation, gender, gender identity, or disability. Includes on-campus incidents involving students, staff, and on-campus guests. Excludes off-campus crimes and arrests even if they involve college students or staff. Some data have been revised from previously published figures.

SOURCE: U.S. Department of Education, Office of Postsecondary Education, Campus Safety and Security Reporting System, 2010 through 2017. (This table was prepared September 2019.)

Table 330.10. Average undergraduate tuition and fees and room and board rates charged for full-time students in degree-granting postsecondary institutions, by level and control of institution: Selected years, 1963–64 through 2018–19

Year and control of institution	Constant 2018–19 dollars[1]												Current dollars											
	Total tuition, fees, room, and board			Tuition and required fees[2]			Dormitory rooms			Board[3]			Total tuition, fees, room, and board			Tuition and required fees[2]			Dormitory rooms			Board[3]		
	All institutions	4-year	2-year	All institutions	4-year	2-year	All institutions	4-year	2-year	All institutions	4-year	2-year	All institutions	4-year	2-year	All institutions	4-year	2-year	All institutions	4-year	2-year	All institutions	4-year	2-year
1	2	3	4	5	6	7	8	9	10	11	12	13	14	15	16	17	18	19	20	21	22	23	24	25
All institutions																								
1963–64	$10,248	$10,561	$6,368	$4,174	$4,538	$1,406	$2,319	$2,288	$1,717	$3,756	$3,736	$3,244	$1,248	$1,286	$775	$508	$553	$171	$282	$279	$209	$457	$455	$395
1968–69	10,357	10,973	7,477	4,234	4,852	1,778	2,558	2,557	2,321	3,565	3,564	3,378	1,459	1,545	1,053	596	683	250	360	360	327	502	502	476
1969–70	10,460	11,227	7,304	4,325	5,062	1,659	2,610	2,627	2,326	3,524	3,537	3,319	1,560	1,674	1,089	645	755	247	389	392	347	526	528	495
1970–71	10,537	11,376	7,143	4,387	5,188	1,590	2,670	2,690	2,355	3,480	3,498	3,197	1,653	1,784	1,120	688	814	249	419	422	369	546	549	501
1971–72	10,651	11,556	7,212	4,455	5,326	1,544	2,738	2,760	2,406	3,458	3,470	3,262	1,730	1,878	1,172	724	865	251	445	448	391	562	564	530
1972–73	10,853	12,015	7,549	4,493	5,623	1,697	2,886	2,913	2,454	3,474	3,479	3,398	1,834	2,031	1,276	759	950	287	488	492	415	587	588	574
1973–74	10,337	11,392	7,379	4,322	5,348	1,784	2,691	2,715	2,334	3,324	3,329	3,260	1,903	2,097	1,358	796	985	328	495	500	430	612	613	600
1974–75	9,698	10,693	7,000	3,958	4,930	1,602	2,582	2,605	2,250	3,158	3,158	3,148	1,983	2,187	1,432	809	1,008	328	528	533	460	646	646	644
1975–76	9,605	10,754	6,729	3,786	4,901	1,357	2,598	2,631	2,165	3,221	3,222	3,207	2,103	2,355	1,473	829	1,073	297	569	576	474	705	706	702
1976–77	9,818	11,120	6,895	3,987	5,258	1,491	2,604	2,636	2,169	3,227	3,226	3,235	2,275	2,577	1,598	924	1,218	346	603	611	503	748	748	750
1977–78	9,748	11,019	6,888	3,981	5,222	1,529	2,609	2,644	2,122	3,158	3,153	3,237	2,411	2,725	1,703	984	1,291	378	645	654	525	781	780	801
1978–79	9,564	10,786	6,759	3,966	5,164	1,519	2,544	2,572	2,126	3,054	3,050	3,114	2,587	2,917	1,828	1,073	1,397	411	688	696	575	826	825	842
1979–80	9,164	10,332	6,458	3,794	4,936	1,471	2,450	2,477	2,049	2,920	2,919	2,938	2,809	3,167	1,979	1,163	1,513	451	751	759	628	895	895	900
1980–81	9,067	10,231	6,520	3,768	4,908	1,538	2,445	2,473	2,060	2,855	2,850	2,923	3,101	3,499	2,230	1,289	1,679	526	836	846	705	976	975	1,000
1981–82	9,391	10,633	6,663	3,920	5,133	1,587	2,556	2,587	2,133	2,914	2,912	2,943	3,489	3,951	2,476	1,457	1,907	590	950	961	793	1,083	1,082	1,094
1982–83	10,003	11,369	7,002	4,195	5,520	1,741	2,745	2,781	2,254	3,064	3,067	3,007	3,877	4,406	2,713	1,626	2,139	675	1,064	1,078	873	1,187	1,189	1,165
1983–84	10,369	11,812	7,103	4,436	5,832	1,817	2,849	2,892	2,280	3,084	3,089	3,006	4,167	4,747	2,854	1,783	2,344	730	1,145	1,162	916	1,239	1,242	1,208
1984–85	10,926	12,357	7,613	4,754	6,148	1,966	3,034	3,070	2,533	3,138	3,139	3,114	4,563	5,160	3,179	1,985	2,567	821	1,267	1,282	1,058	1,310	1,311	1,301
1985–86[4]	11,369	12,811	7,836	5,076	6,481	2,068	3,115	3,153	2,576	3,178	3,177	3,192	4,885	5,504	3,367	2,181	2,784	888	1,338	1,355	1,107	1,365	1,365	1,372
1986–87	11,853	13,580	7,503	5,264	6,927	2,043	3,198	3,248	2,355	3,390	3,405	3,106	5,206	5,964	3,295	2,312	3,042	897	1,405	1,427	1,034	1,489	1,495	1,364
1987–88	12,013	13,713	7,134	5,374	6,998	1,769	3,252	3,315	2,224	3,386	3,400	3,141	5,494	6,272	3,263	2,458	3,201	809	1,488	1,516	1,017	1,549	1,555	1,437
1988–89	12,264	14,055	7,467	5,554	7,256	2,047	3,291	3,362	2,267	3,420	3,437	3,153	5,869	6,725	3,573	2,658	3,472	979	1,575	1,609	1,085	1,636	1,644	1,509
1989–90	12,381	14,384	7,390	5,663	7,580	1,950	3,267	3,340	2,204	3,451	3,464	3,236	6,207	7,212	3,705	2,839	3,800	978	1,638	1,675	1,105	1,730	1,737	1,622
1990–91	12,410	14,376	7,433	5,704	7,582	2,057	3,297	3,370	2,236	3,408	3,425	3,140	6,562	7,602	3,930	3,016	4,009	1,087	1,743	1,782	1,182	1,802	1,811	1,660
1991–92	12,969	15,096	7,499	6,021	8,036	2,179	3,434	3,520	2,218	3,514	3,539	3,101	7,077	8,238	4,092	3,286	4,385	1,189	1,874	1,921	1,210	1,918	1,931	1,692
1992–93	13,243	15,562	7,477	6,250	8,444	2,267	3,445	3,538	2,204	3,548	3,580	3,006	7,452	8,758	4,207	3,517	4,752	1,276	1,939	1,991	1,240	1,996	2,015	1,692
1993–94	13,738	16,103	7,706	6,629	8,867	2,423	3,563	3,656	2,308	3,546	3,580	2,976	7,931	9,296	4,449	3,827	5,119	1,399	2,057	2,111	1,332	2,047	2,067	1,718
1994–95	13,985	16,381	7,802	6,810	9,078	2,505	3,612	3,704	2,351	3,563	3,599	2,946	8,306	9,728	4,633	4,044	5,391	1,488	2,145	2,200	1,396	2,116	2,138	1,750
1995–96	14,426	16,934	7,745	7,111	9,485	2,495	3,711	3,800	2,414	3,604	3,649	2,836	8,800	10,330	4,725	4,338	5,786	1,522	2,264	2,318	1,473	2,199	2,226	1,730
1996–97	14,672	17,278	7,802	7,274	9,752	2,459	3,770	3,860	2,427	3,628	3,667	2,916	9,206	10,841	4,895	4,564	6,118	1,543	2,365	2,422	1,522	2,276	2,301	1,830
1997–98	15,013	17,659	8,130	7,445	9,944	2,653	3,827	3,926	2,502	3,740	3,789	2,975	9,588	11,277	5,192	4,755	6,351	1,695	2,444	2,507	1,598	2,389	2,419	1,900
1998–99	15,509	18,299	8,144	7,716	10,348	2,656	3,936	4,041	2,487	3,857	3,910	3,001	10,076	11,888	5,291	5,013	6,723	1,725	2,557	2,626	1,616	2,506	2,540	1,950
1999–2000	15,604	18,475	8,108	7,812	10,533	2,585	4,018	4,115	2,650	3,774	3,827	2,873	10,430	12,349	5,420	5,222	7,040	1,728	2,686	2,751	1,771	2,523	2,558	1,920
2000–01	15,651	18,692	7,907	7,778	10,663	2,456	4,081	4,184	2,576	3,791	3,845	2,875	10,820	12,922	5,466	5,377	7,372	1,698	2,821	2,893	1,781	2,621	2,658	1,987
2001–02	16,175	19,386	8,127	8,025	11,066	2,558	4,237	4,349	2,627	3,912	3,970	2,942	11,380	13,639	5,718	5,646	7,786	1,800	2,981	3,060	1,848	2,753	2,793	2,070
2002–03	16,708	20,081	8,695	8,348	11,555	2,647	4,421	4,538	2,889	3,939	3,988	3,160	12,014	14,439	6,252	6,002	8,309	1,903	3,179	3,263	2,077	2,832	2,867	2,272
2003–04	17,629	21,103	9,125	8,993	12,288	2,959	4,572	4,693	3,005	4,064	4,122	3,161	12,953	15,505	6,705	6,608	9,029	2,174	3,359	3,448	2,208	2,986	3,028	2,322
2004–05	18,224	21,813	9,374	9,410	12,824	3,089	4,719	4,838	3,110	4,095	4,151	3,176	13,793	16,510	7,095	7,122	9,706	2,338	3,572	3,662	2,354	3,100	3,142	2,404
2005–06	18,625	22,211	9,209	9,675	13,082	3,076	4,849	4,970	3,068	4,101	4,159	3,065	14,634	17,451	7,236	7,601	10,279	2,417	3,810	3,905	2,411	3,222	3,268	2,408
2006–07	19,212	22,918	9,264	10,041	13,561	3,097	4,986	5,107	3,136	4,186	4,250	3,031	15,486	18,473	7,467	8,093	10,931	2,496	4,019	4,116	2,528	3,374	3,426	2,443
2007–08	19,413	23,166	9,137	10,145	13,704	3,010	5,041	5,164	3,151	4,228	4,298	2,975	16,227	19,364	7,637	8,480	11,455	2,516	4,213	4,317	2,634	3,534	3,593	2,487
2008–09	20,111	24,024	9,697	10,492	14,212	3,088	5,246	5,377	3,282	4,374	4,435	3,327	17,045	20,361	8,219	8,892	12,046	2,617	4,446	4,557	2,782	3,707	3,759	2,820
2009–10	20,625	24,687	9,981	10,674	14,495	3,416	5,443	5,591	3,498	4,507	4,601	3,066	17,650	21,126	8,541	9,135	12,404	2,923	4,658	4,785	2,994	3,857	3,937	2,624
2010–11	21,165	25,287	10,159	10,969	14,830	3,505	5,588	5,751	3,521	4,608	4,706	3,133	18,475	22,074	8,868	9,575	12,945	3,060	4,878	5,020	3,074	4,023	4,108	2,734
2011–12	21,593	25,610	10,402	11,328	15,105	3,611	5,659	5,814	3,563	4,605	4,691	3,229	19,401	23,011	9,347	10,179	13,572	3,244	5,085	5,224	3,201	4,138	4,215	2,901
2012–13	22,150	26,132	10,480	11,693	15,435	3,636	5,797	5,948	3,657	4,659	4,749	3,187	20,233	23,871	9,573	10,681	14,099	3,322	5,296	5,433	3,340	4,256	4,338	2,911
2013–14	22,630	26,625	10,662	11,935	15,697	3,632	5,950	6,094	3,817	4,745	4,834	3,213	20,995	24,701	9,891	11,073	14,563	3,369	5,520	5,654	3,541	4,402	4,484	2,981
2014–15	23,252	27,190	10,864	12,293	16,005	3,627	6,120	6,261	3,911	4,840	4,924	3,327	21,729	25,409	10,153	11,487	14,957	3,389	5,719	5,850	3,655	4,523	4,602	3,109
2015–16	23,851	27,777	11,062	12,608	16,309	3,626	6,287	6,423	4,091	4,955	5,046	3,345	22,439	26,132	10,407	11,862	15,343	3,412	5,915	6,043	3,849	4,662	4,747	3,147
2016–17	24,101	27,755	11,061	12,753	16,190	3,673	6,374	6,503	4,104	4,974	5,062	3,285	23,091	26,592	10,597	12,219	15,512	3,519	6,107	6,231	3,932	4,766	4,850	3,147
2017–18	24,327	27,923	10,925	12,874	16,253	3,611	6,452	6,585	4,008	5,001	5,085	3,307	23,833	27,357	10,704	12,613	15,923	3,537	6,321	6,451	3,926	4,899	4,982	3,240
2018–19	24,623	28,123	11,389	13,016	16,318	3,564	6,542	6,675	4,123	5,065	5,131	3,702	24,623	28,123	11,389	13,016	16,318	3,564	6,542	6,675	4,123	5,065	5,131	3,702

See notes at end of table.

Table 330.10. Average undergraduate tuition and fees and room and board rates charged for full-time students in degree-granting postsecondary institutions, by level and control of institution: Selected years, 1963–64 through 2018–19—Continued

Year and control of institution	Constant 2018–19 dollars[1]												Current dollars											
	Total tuition, fees, room, and board			Tuition and required fees[2]			Dormitory rooms			Board[3]			Total tuition, fees, room, and board			Tuition and required fees[2]			Dormitory rooms			Board[3]		
	All institutions	4-year	2-year	All institutions	4-year	2-year	All institutions	4-year	2-year	All institutions	4-year	2-year	All institutions	4-year	2-year	All institutions	4-year	2-year	All institutions	4-year	2-year	All institutions	4-year	2-year
1	2	3	4	5	6	7	8	9	10	11	12	13	14	15	16	17	18	19	20	21	22	23	24	25
Public institutions																								
1963–64	7,493	7,626	5,173	1,922	1,998	797	2,051	2,081	1,412	3,520	3,546	2,964	912	929	630	234	243	97	250	253	172	429	432	361
1968–69	7,893	8,116	6,270	2,095	2,279	1,207	2,372	2,393	1,974	3,426	3,443	3,089	1,112	1,143	883	295	321	170	334	337	278	482	485	435
1969–70	8,023	8,300	6,376	2,166	2,403	1,193	2,453	2,476	2,065	3,404	3,421	3,118	1,197	1,238	951	323	358	178	366	369	308	508	510	465
1970–71	8,135	8,453	6,363	2,238	2,510	1,192	2,533	2,557	2,155	3,364	3,386	3,016	1,276	1,326	998	351	394	187	397	401	338	528	531	473
1971–72	8,290	8,646	6,604	2,314	2,633	1,182	2,620	2,645	2,253	3,356	3,368	3,170	1,347	1,405	1,073	376	428	192	426	430	366	545	547	515
1972–73	8,593	9,191	7,082	2,408	2,974	1,379	2,789	2,818	2,355	3,396	3,399	3,349	1,452	1,553	1,197	407	503	233	471	476	398	574	575	566
1973–74	8,229	8,670	6,920	2,379	2,790	1,488	2,599	2,626	2,222	3,251	3,254	3,210	1,515	1,596	1,274	438	514	274	479	483	409	598	599	591
1974–75	7,634	8,052	6,548	2,113	2,506	1,355	2,470	2,500	2,073	3,051	3,046	3,120	1,561	1,647	1,339	432	512	277	505	511	424	624	623	638
1975–76	7,594	8,127	6,330	1,977	2,476	1,119	2,481	2,520	2,019	3,136	3,131	3,192	1,663	1,780	1,386	433	542	245	543	552	442	687	686	699
1976–77	7,720	8,350	6,432	2,065	2,661	1,223	2,514	2,554	2,006	3,141	3,136	3,203	1,789	1,935	1,491	479	617	283	582	592	465	728	727	742
1977–78	7,633	8,240	6,428	2,069	2,647	1,239	2,511	2,552	1,965	3,053	3,040	3,224	1,888	2,038	1,590	512	655	306	621	631	486	755	752	797
1978–79	7,371	7,930	6,252	2,007	2,543	1,210	2,421	2,455	1,948	2,943	2,932	3,094	1,994	2,145	1,691	543	688	327	655	664	527	796	793	837
1979–80	7,063	7,593	5,942	1,903	2,406	1,158	2,333	2,366	1,872	2,827	2,821	2,913	2,165	2,327	1,822	583	738	355	715	725	574	867	865	893
1980–81	6,939	7,457	5,927	1,856	2,350	1,144	2,335	2,371	1,876	2,748	2,736	2,907	2,373	2,550	2,027	635	804	391	799	811	642	940	936	994
1981–82	7,166	7,726	5,985	1,921	2,448	1,169	2,448	2,491	1,893	2,798	2,788	2,923	2,663	2,871	2,224	714	909	434	909	925	703	1,039	1,036	1,086
1982–83	7,599	8,247	6,166	2,060	2,662	1,221	2,607	2,659	1,948	2,932	2,927	2,997	2,945	3,196	2,390	798	1,031	473	1,010	1,030	755	1,136	1,134	1,162
1983–84	7,853	8,542	6,305	2,218	2,856	1,314	2,705	2,761	1,992	2,930	2,925	2,999	3,156	3,433	2,534	891	1,148	528	1,087	1,110	801	1,178	1,175	1,205
1984–85	8,161	8,816	6,722	2,325	2,940	1,398	2,864	2,914	2,205	2,973	2,962	3,119	3,408	3,682	2,807	971	1,228	584	1,196	1,217	921	1,241	1,237	1,302
1985–86[4]	8,312	8,981	6,938	2,432	3,067	1,492	2,890	2,940	2,234	2,991	2,974	3,212	3,571	3,859	2,981	1,045	1,318	641	1,242	1,263	960	1,285	1,278	1,380
1986–87	8,664	9,421	6,805	2,519	3,219	1,504	2,962	3,012	2,229	3,183	3,191	3,073	3,805	4,138	2,989	1,106	1,414	660	1,301	1,323	979	1,398	1,401	1,349
1987–88	8,854	9,627	6,702	2,664	3,361	1,543	3,013	3,082	2,061	3,178	3,184	3,098	4,050	4,403	3,066	1,218	1,537	706	1,378	1,410	943	1,454	1,456	1,417
1988–89	8,932	9,777	6,651	2,685	3,440	1,526	3,044	3,126	2,016	3,203	3,210	3,110	4,274	4,678	3,183	1,285	1,646	730	1,457	1,496	965	1,533	1,536	1,488
1989–90	8,983	9,924	6,581	2,705	3,550	1,508	3,018	3,106	1,919	3,260	3,268	3,154	4,504	4,975	3,299	1,356	1,780	756	1,513	1,557	962	1,635	1,638	1,581
1990–91	8,996	9,915	6,558	2,750	3,571	1,559	3,049	3,133	1,985	3,198	3,211	3,014	4,757	5,243	3,467	1,454	1,888	824	1,612	1,657	1,050	1,691	1,698	1,594
1991–92	9,416	10,433	6,639	2,983	3,879	1,716	3,172	3,270	1,969	3,261	3,283	2,954	5,138	5,693	3,623	1,628	2,117	936	1,731	1,785	1,074	1,780	1,792	1,612
1992–93	9,558	10,697	6,751	3,166	4,174	1,822	3,121	3,228	1,965	3,271	3,295	2,963	5,379	6,020	3,799	1,782	2,349	1,025	1,756	1,816	1,106	1,841	1,854	1,668
1993–94	9,863	11,025	6,921	3,364	4,394	1,948	3,244	3,350	2,061	3,256	3,282	2,912	5,694	6,365	3,996	1,942	2,537	1,125	1,873	1,934	1,190	1,880	1,895	1,681
1994–95	10,044	11,232	6,966	3,464	4,514	2,008	3,299	3,406	2,074	3,282	3,312	2,883	5,965	6,670	4,137	2,057	2,681	1,192	1,959	2,023	1,232	1,949	1,967	1,712
1995–96	10,255	11,498	6,912	3,572	4,668	2,032	3,373	3,477	2,125	3,311	3,353	2,755	6,256	7,014	4,217	2,179	2,848	1,239	2,057	2,121	1,297	2,020	2,045	1,681
1996–97	10,407	11,689	7,019	3,620	4,761	2,033	3,423	3,528	2,134	3,364	3,400	2,851	6,530	7,334	4,404	2,271	2,987	1,276	2,148	2,214	1,339	2,111	2,133	1,789
1997–98	10,669	12,016	7,061	3,696	4,869	2,058	3,484	3,602	2,193	3,488	3,544	2,810	6,813	7,673	4,509	2,360	3,110	1,314	2,225	2,301	1,401	2,228	2,263	1,795
1998–99	10,939	12,355	7,087	3,741	4,970	2,042	3,586	3,708	2,232	3,613	3,677	2,813	7,107	8,027	4,604	2,430	3,229	1,327	2,330	2,409	1,450	2,347	2,389	1,828
1999–2000	10,933	12,378	7,076	3,745	5,010	2,016	3,650	3,769	2,317	3,537	3,600	2,743	7,308	8,274	4,730	2,504	3,349	1,348	2,440	2,519	1,549	2,364	2,406	1,834
2000–01	10,973	12,517	7,000	3,706	5,063	1,928	3,716	3,839	2,315	3,552	3,614	2,757	7,586	8,653	4,839	2,562	3,501	1,333	2,569	2,654	1,600	2,455	2,499	1,906
2001–02	11,401	13,071	7,302	3,838	5,309	1,961	3,870	4,003	2,448	3,693	3,759	2,893	8,022	9,196	5,137	2,700	3,735	1,380	2,723	2,816	1,722	2,598	2,645	2,036
2002–03	11,824	13,612	7,790	4,037	5,627	2,063	4,075	4,212	2,717	3,712	3,772	3,010	8,502	9,787	5,601	2,903	4,046	1,483	2,930	3,029	1,954	2,669	2,712	2,164
2003–04	12,585	14,527	8,182	4,517	6,242	2,316	4,227	4,372	2,843	3,841	3,914	3,023	9,247	10,674	6,012	3,319	4,587	1,702	3,106	3,212	2,089	2,822	2,876	2,221
2004–05	13,033	15,096	8,423	4,795	6,641	2,443	4,366	4,517	2,872	3,873	3,938	3,108	9,864	11,426	6,375	3,629	5,027	1,849	3,304	3,418	2,174	2,931	2,981	2,353
2005–06	13,306	15,411	8,262	4,930	6,810	2,463	4,512	4,664	2,865	3,863	3,937	2,935	10,454	12,108	6,492	3,874	5,351	1,935	3,545	3,664	2,251	3,035	3,093	2,306
2006–07	13,711	15,880	8,456	5,089	7,030	2,503	4,661	4,812	2,988	3,961	4,038	2,965	11,051	12,799	6,815	4,102	5,666	2,017	3,757	3,878	2,408	3,192	3,255	2,390
2007–08	13,842	16,066	8,347	5,130	7,110	2,463	4,727	4,883	2,997	3,986	4,072	2,888	11,570	13,429	6,977	4,288	5,943	2,058	3,951	4,082	2,505	3,332	3,404	2,414
2008–09	14,405	16,768	8,906	5,323	7,447	2,520	4,943	5,110	3,143	4,138	4,211	3,244	12,209	14,212	7,549	4,512	6,312	2,136	4,190	4,331	2,664	3,507	3,569	2,749
2009–10	14,980	17,570	9,007	5,566	7,849	2,668	5,143	5,334	3,335	4,271	4,388	3,004	12,819	15,036	7,708	4,763	6,717	2,283	4,401	4,564	2,854	3,655	3,755	2,571
2010–11	15,540	18,237	9,255	5,814	8,170	2,796	5,322	5,535	3,385	4,405	4,532	3,073	13,566	15,919	8,079	5,075	7,132	2,441	4,646	4,832	2,955	3,845	3,956	2,683
2011–12	15,980	18,683	9,590	6,192	8,585	2,951	5,397	5,599	3,450	4,392	4,499	3,189	14,359	16,787	8,617	5,563	7,713	2,651	4,849	5,031	3,100	3,946	4,042	2,866
2012–13	16,444	19,130	9,773	6,457	8,835	3,056	5,541	5,738	3,555	4,446	4,557	3,162	15,021	17,475	8,927	5,899	8,070	2,792	5,062	5,241	3,247	4,061	4,163	2,888
2013–14	16,846	19,509	10,006	6,597	8,959	3,105	5,717	5,906	3,716	4,532	4,644	3,185	15,628	18,100	9,283	6,120	8,312	2,881	5,304	5,479	3,448	4,205	4,308	2,955
2014–15	17,323	19,938	10,257	6,817	9,142	3,162	5,890	6,075	3,808	4,616	4,721	3,287	16,188	18,632	9,585	6,370	8,543	2,955	5,504	5,677	3,559	4,313	4,412	3,072
2015–16	17,821	20,413	10,538	7,028	9,331	3,229	6,043	6,219	3,995	4,750	4,863	3,314	16,766	19,204	9,914	6,612	8,778	3,038	5,686	5,850	3,759	4,469	4,576	3,118
2016–17	17,992	20,341	10,531	7,116	9,189	3,294	6,115	6,281	3,990	4,761	4,870	3,247	17,238	19,488	10,090	6,818	8,804	3,156	5,859	6,018	3,823	4,562	4,666	3,111
2017–18	18,163	20,464	10,493	7,198	9,223	3,309	6,186	6,356	3,914	4,780	4,885	3,271	17,794	20,049	10,280	7,051	9,036	3,242	6,060	6,227	3,834	4,682	4,785	3,204
2018–19	18,383	20,598	10,950	7,250	9,212	3,313	6,290	6,459	4,055	4,843	4,927	3,581	18,383	20,598	10,950	7,250	9,212	3,313	6,290	6,459	4,055	4,843	4,927	3,581

See notes at end of table.

Table 330.10. Average undergraduate tuition and fees and room and board rates charged for full-time students in degree-granting postsecondary institutions, by level and control of institution: Selected years, 1963–64 through 2018–19—Continued

Year and control of institution	Constant 2018–19 dollars[1]												Current dollars											
	Total tuition, fees, room, and board			Tuition and required fees[2]			Dormitory rooms			Board[3]			Total tuition, fees, room, and board			Tuition and required fees[2]			Dormitory rooms			Board[3]		
	All institutions	4-year	2-year	All institutions	4-year	2-year	All institutions	4-year	2-year	All institutions	4-year	2-year	All institutions	4-year	2-year	All institutions	4-year	2-year	All institutions	4-year	2-year	All institutions	4-year	2-year
1	2	3	4	5	6	7	8	9	10	11	12	13	14	15	16	17	18	19	20	21	22	23	24	25
Private nonprofit and for-profit institutions																								
1963–64	14,904	14,861	10,782	8,310	8,300	5,272	2,595	2,568	2,004	3,999	3,993	3,506	1,815	1,810	1,313	1,012	1,011	642	316	313	244	487	486	427
1968–69	16,481	16,731	13,321	9,821	10,063	6,788	2,869	2,872	2,776	3,792	3,795	3,756	2,321	2,356	1,876	1,383	1,417	956	404	405	391	534	534	529
1969–70	16,946	17,156	13,362	10,278	10,472	6,933	2,911	2,920	2,769	3,757	3,764	3,661	2,527	2,559	1,993	1,533	1,562	1,034	434	436	413	560	561	546
1970–71	17,399	17,561	13,408	10,736	10,879	7,070	2,948	2,959	2,767	3,715	3,724	3,570	2,729	2,754	2,103	1,684	1,706	1,109	462	464	434	583	584	560
1971–72	17,863	17,963	13,454	11,202	11,276	7,213	2,988	3,002	2,763	3,673	3,685	3,477	2,902	2,919	2,186	1,820	1,832	1,172	486	488	449	597	599	565
1972–73	17,963	18,289	13,448	11,229	11,527	7,224	3,094	3,116	2,704	3,640	3,646	3,520	3,036	3,091	2,273	1,898	1,948	1,221	523	527	457	615	616	595
1973–74	17,178	17,501	13,091	10,804	11,106	7,078	2,890	2,906	2,624	3,484	3,489	3,390	3,162	3,222	2,410	1,989	2,045	1,303	532	535	483	641	642	624
1974–75	16,568	16,647	12,670	10,352	10,418	6,685	2,826	2,830	2,758	3,389	3,398	3,227	3,388	3,404	2,591	2,117	2,130	1,367	578	579	564	693	695	660
1975–76	16,643	16,754	12,381	10,376	10,464	6,517	2,856	2,871	2,612	3,410	3,420	3,252	3,644	3,669	2,711	2,272	2,291	1,427	625	629	572	747	749	712
1976–77	16,855	17,161	12,820	10,644	10,935	6,870	2,800	2,811	2,621	3,411	3,415	3,329	3,906	3,977	2,971	2,467	2,534	1,592	649	651	607	790	791	772
1977–78	16,815	17,145	12,729	10,609	10,919	6,896	2,823	2,839	2,553	3,382	3,387	3,279	4,158	4,240	3,148	2,624	2,700	1,706	698	702	631	836	838	811
1978–79	16,691	17,043	12,532	10,602	10,936	6,769	2,802	2,814	2,589	3,287	3,292	3,174	4,514	4,609	3,389	2,867	2,958	1,831	758	761	700	889	890	858
1979–80	16,026	16,353	12,238	10,211	10,521	6,726	2,699	2,711	2,500	3,116	3,121	3,012	4,912	5,013	3,751	3,130	3,225	2,062	827	831	766	955	957	923
1980–81	15,993	16,354	12,580	10,227	10,575	7,055	2,683	2,691	2,548	3,083	3,088	2,978	5,470	5,594	4,303	3,498	3,617	2,413	918	921	871	1,054	1,056	1,019
1981–82	16,593	17,035	12,774	10,637	11,070	7,010	2,792	2,795	2,752	3,163	3,170	3,012	6,166	6,330	4,746	3,953	4,113	2,605	1,038	1,039	1,022	1,175	1,178	1,119
1982–83	17,856	18,388	13,842	11,454	11,970	7,762	3,048	3,049	3,038	3,354	3,369	3,042	6,920	7,126	5,364	4,439	4,639	3,008	1,181	1,181	1,177	1,300	1,306	1,179
1983–84	18,683	19,308	13,862	12,070	12,673	7,711	3,179	3,183	3,118	3,434	3,452	3,034	7,508	7,759	5,571	4,851	5,093	3,099	1,278	1,279	1,253	1,380	1,387	1,219
1984–85	19,641	20,236	14,854	12,726	13,304	8,345	3,414	3,415	3,410	3,500	3,517	3,099	8,202	8,451	6,203	5,315	5,556	3,485	1,426	1,426	1,424	1,462	1,469	1,294
1985–86[4]	20,678	21,478	15,156	13,473	14,245	8,546	3,616	3,623	3,491	3,590	3,610	3,119	8,885	9,228	6,512	5,789	6,121	3,672	1,553	1,557	1,500	1,542	1,551	1,340
1986–87	22,032	22,859	14,535	14,380	15,161	8,387	3,776	3,810	2,882	3,875	3,888	3,265	9,676	10,039	6,384	6,316	6,658	3,684	1,658	1,673	1,266	1,702	1,708	1,434
1987–88	22,982	23,305	15,475	15,279	15,558	9,097	3,821	3,848	3,018	3,882	3,898	3,360	10,512	10,659	7,078	6,988	7,116	4,161	1,748	1,760	1,380	1,775	1,783	1,537
1988–89	23,384	23,979	16,649	15,592	16,137	10,068	3,864	3,894	3,218	3,928	3,948	3,363	11,189	11,474	7,967	7,461	7,722	4,817	1,849	1,863	1,540	1,880	1,889	1,609
1989–90	23,972	24,502	17,294	16,251	16,748	10,365	3,836	3,859	3,317	3,885	3,895	3,612	12,018	12,284	8,670	8,147	8,396	5,196	1,923	1,935	1,663	1,948	1,953	1,811
1990–91	24,415	25,035	17,593	16,590	17,177	10,534	3,902	3,929	3,298	3,923	3,928	3,761	12,910	13,237	9,302	8,772	9,083	5,570	2,063	2,077	1,744	2,074	2,077	1,989
1991–92	25,458	26,127	17,652	17,261	17,884	10,545	4,071	4,106	3,277	4,126	4,136	3,830	13,892	14,258	9,632	9,419	9,759	5,754	2,221	2,241	1,788	2,252	2,257	2,090
1992–93	26,004	26,672	17,598	17,666	18,292	10,767	4,172	4,197	3,501	4,165	4,183	3,331	14,634	15,009	9,903	9,942	10,294	6,059	2,348	2,362	1,970	2,344	2,354	1,875
1993–94	26,840	27,547	18,025	18,312	18,971	11,034	4,313	4,341	3,580	4,216	4,235	3,412	15,496	15,904	10,406	10,572	10,952	6,370	2,490	2,506	2,067	2,434	2,445	1,970
1994–95	27,290	27,956	18,810	18,709	19,332	11,643	4,357	4,380	3,761	4,224	4,243	3,406	16,207	16,602	11,170	11,111	11,481	6,914	2,587	2,601	2,233	2,509	2,520	2,023
1995–96	28,209	28,870	18,956	19,449	20,070	11,630	4,488	4,510	3,887	4,272	4,290	3,439	17,208	17,612	11,563	11,864	12,243	7,094	2,738	2,751	2,371	2,606	2,617	2,098
1996–97	28,750	29,393	19,053	19,919	20,530	11,533	4,586	4,604	4,044	4,245	4,259	3,476	18,039	18,442	11,954	12,498	12,881	7,236	2,878	2,889	2,537	2,663	2,672	2,181
1997–98	28,994	29,861	20,233	20,044	20,895	11,688	4,625	4,642	4,185	4,325	4,324	4,360	18,516	19,070	12,921	12,801	13,344	7,464	2,954	2,964	2,672	2,762	2,761	2,785
1998–99	29,812	30,675	20,501	20,669	21,507	12,088	4,732	4,758	3,973	4,411	4,410	4,440	19,368	19,929	13,319	13,428	13,973	7,854	3,075	3,091	2,581	2,865	2,865	2,884
1999–2000	30,240	31,023	21,012	21,094	21,866	12,305	4,841	4,850	4,589	4,304	4,308	4,118	20,213	20,737	14,045	14,100	14,616	8,225	3,236	3,242	3,067	2,877	2,879	2,753
2000–01	30,916	31,614	21,563	21,698	22,378	13,115	4,892	4,907	4,348	4,326	4,330	4,100	21,373	21,856	14,907	15,000	15,470	9,067	3,382	3,392	3,006	2,991	2,993	2,834
2001–02	31,857	32,542	22,493	22,375	23,041	14,322	5,070	5,083	4,429	4,412	4,419	3,742	22,413	22,896	15,825	15,742	16,211	10,076	3,567	3,576	3,116	3,104	3,109	2,633
2002–03	32,461	33,082	24,690	22,784	23,401	14,813	5,218	5,235	4,495	4,458	4,447	5,382	23,340	23,787	17,753	16,383	16,826	10,651	3,752	3,764	3,232	3,206	3,197	3,870
2003–04	33,513	34,120	26,619	23,565	24,175	15,713	5,369	5,379	4,873	4,578	4,565	6,032	24,624	25,070	19,558	17,315	17,763	11,545	3,945	3,952	3,581	3,364	3,354	4,432
2004–05	34,110	34,695	26,817	23,985	24,580	16,016	5,520	5,513	5,913	4,604	4,602	4,888	25,817	26,260	20,297	18,154	18,604	12,122	4,178	4,173	4,475	3,485	3,483	3,700
2005–06	34,247	34,788	27,242	24,007	24,554	15,846	5,600	5,605	5,312	4,640	4,629	6,085	26,908	27,333	21,404	18,862	19,292	12,450	4,400	4,404	4,173	3,645	3,637	4,781
2006–07	35,285	35,879	25,166	24,871	25,454	15,766	5,715	5,723	5,145	4,698	4,702	4,255	28,440	28,919	20,284	20,047	20,517	12,708	4,606	4,613	4,147	3,787	3,790	3,430
2007–08	35,613	36,160	25,944	25,090	25,634	15,705	5,746	5,751	5,364	4,776	4,775	4,874	29,768	30,226	21,686	20,972	21,427	13,128	4,803	4,808	4,484	3,992	3,992	4,074
2008–09	36,298	36,850	26,810	25,456	26,004	16,007	5,929	5,936	5,372	4,913	4,909	5,431	30,764	31,232	22,723	21,575	22,040	13,567	5,025	5,031	4,553	4,164	4,161	4,603
2009–10	36,624	37,215	28,587	25,432	26,023	17,368	6,132	6,133	6,089	5,059	5,059	5,130	31,341	31,847	24,463	21,764	22,269	14,862	5,248	5,248	5,211	4,329	4,329	4,390
2010–11	36,515	37,250	26,464	25,250	25,978	15,680	6,189	6,197	5,658	5,075	5,075	5,127	31,875	32,517	23,101	22,042	22,677	13,687	5,403	5,410	4,939	4,430	4,430	4,475
2011–12	36,792	37,481	26,271	25,431	26,114	15,538	6,257	6,263	5,752	5,104	5,104	4,980	33,058	33,677	23,605	22,850	23,464	13,961	5,622	5,627	5,169	4,586	4,586	4,475
2012–13	37,750	38,394	25,567	26,212	26,846	15,490	6,383	6,390	5,723	5,155	5,158	4,354	34,483	35,071	23,355	23,943	24,523	14,149	5,831	5,837	5,228	4,709	4,712	3,977
2013–14	38,799	39,450	25,730	27,066	27,709	15,274	6,490	6,496	5,916	5,243	5,245	4,539	35,995	36,599	23,870	25,110	25,707	14,170	6,021	6,026	5,489	4,864	4,866	4,211
2014–15	40,045	40,651	26,032	28,017	28,613	15,261	6,657	6,665	5,892	5,371	5,373	4,879	37,422	37,988	24,327	26,182	26,739	14,261	6,221	6,228	5,506	5,019	5,021	4,560
2015–16	41,472	42,021	25,909	29,163	29,700	15,442	6,863	6,871	6,023	5,445	5,450	4,444	39,016	39,534	24,375	27,436	27,942	14,528	6,457	6,464	5,666	5,123	5,128	4,181
2016–17	42,712	43,279	25,976	30,211	30,765	15,227	7,003	7,011	6,209	5,499	5,503	4,540	40,922	41,465	24,888	28,945	29,476	14,589	6,710	6,717	5,949	5,268	5,273	4,350
2017–18	43,557	44,025	26,126	30,902	31,359	15,203	7,106	7,113	6,182	5,550	5,553	4,742	42,673	43,131	25,596	30,274	30,723	14,894	6,961	6,968	6,057	5,437	5,440	4,645
2018–19	44,306	44,662	28,627	31,519	31,875	15,727	7,171	7,179	5,967	5,616	5,608	6,933	44,306	44,662	28,627	31,519	31,875	15,727	7,171	7,179	5,967	5,616	5,608	6,933

See notes at end of table.

Table 330.10. Average undergraduate tuition and fees and room and board rates charged for full-time students in degree-granting postsecondary institutions, by level and control of institution: Selected years, 1963–64 through 2018–19—Continued

Year and control of institution	Constant 2018–19 dollars[1]												Current dollars											
	Total tuition, fees, room, and board			Tuition and required fees[2]			Dormitory rooms			Board[3]			Total tuition, fees, room, and board			Tuition and required fees[2]			Dormitory rooms			Board[3]		
	All institutions	4-year	2-year	All institutions	4-year	2-year	All institutions	4-year	2-year	All institutions	4-year	2-year	All institutions	4-year	2-year	All institutions	4-year	2-year	All institutions	4-year	2-year	All institutions	4-year	2-year
1	2	3	4	5	6	7	8	9	10	11	12	13	14	15	16	17	18	19	20	21	22	23	24	25
Nonprofit																								
1999–2000	31,401	31,763	17,486	22,307	22,637	10,312	4,793	4,818	3,164	4,301	4,308	4,010	20,989	21,231	11,688	14,911	15,131	6,893	3,204	3,221	2,115	2,875	2,879	2,680
2000–01	31,727	32,068	16,948	22,559	22,871	10,079	4,842	4,868	2,905	4,326	4,330	3,964	21,934	22,170	11,717	15,596	15,811	6,968	3,347	3,365	2,008	2,991	2,993	2,740
2001–02	32,804	33,056	18,435	23,367	23,599	11,550	5,025	5,038	3,275	4,412	4,419	3,610	23,080	23,257	12,970	16,440	16,604	8,126	3,536	3,544	2,304	3,104	3,109	2,540
2002–03	33,763	33,998	20,085	24,142	24,363	12,387	5,177	5,189	3,680	4,443	4,447	4,018	24,276	24,446	14,442	17,359	17,517	8,907	3,723	3,731	2,646	3,195	3,197	2,889
2003–04	34,957	35,185	21,190	25,081	25,293	13,047	5,317	5,328	3,884	4,558	4,565	4,259	25,685	25,853	15,569	18,429	18,584	9,587	3,907	3,915	2,853	3,349	3,354	3,129
2004–05	35,783	36,010	21,016	25,762	25,965	13,093	5,434	5,443	3,870	4,588	4,602	4,053	27,083	27,255	15,906	19,498	19,652	9,910	4,113	4,119	2,929	3,472	3,483	3,067
2005–06	36,299	36,518	20,783	26,178	26,387	13,132	5,492	5,502	3,839	4,629	4,629	3,811	28,520	28,692	16,329	20,568	20,732	10,318	4,315	4,323	3,017	3,637	3,637	2,994
2006–07	37,425	37,618	21,937	27,097	27,287	13,568	5,623	5,629	4,436	4,705	4,702	3,933	30,166	30,321	17,682	21,841	21,994	10,936	4,532	4,537	3,576	3,793	3,790	3,170
2007–08	38,188	38,343	22,559	27,757	27,909	14,103	5,653	5,659	4,541	4,779	4,775	3,915	31,921	32,050	18,857	23,201	23,329	11,789	4,725	4,730	3,796	3,994	3,992	3,272
2008–09	39,685	39,833	23,906	28,910	29,069	14,869	5,848	5,854	4,589	4,926	4,909	4,448	33,635	33,761	20,261	24,503	24,638	12,602	4,957	4,962	3,889	4,175	4,161	3,770
2009–10	40,806	40,949	24,254	29,676	29,839	14,766	6,046	6,051	4,810	5,084	5,059	4,678	34,920	35,042	20,756	25,396	25,535	12,636	5,173	5,178	4,116	4,351	4,329	4,004
2010–11	41,588	41,717	23,016	30,290	30,451	14,512	6,184	6,191	4,559	5,114	5,075	3,945	36,304	36,416	20,092	26,441	26,581	12,668	5,398	5,404	3,980	4,464	4,430	3,444
2011–12	41,964	42,108	25,515	30,543	30,735	15,668	6,263	6,269	4,765	5,158	5,104	5,083	37,705	37,835	22,926	27,443	27,616	14,078	5,628	5,633	4,281	4,634	4,586	4,567
2012–13	42,881	43,022	24,246	31,272	31,466	15,090	6,391	6,397	4,822	5,217	5,158	4,333	39,171	39,299	22,148	28,566	28,743	13,785	5,838	5,844	4,405	4,766	4,712	3,958
2013–14	43,802	43,903	24,793	31,983	32,146	15,093	6,507	6,512	5,166	5,312	5,245	4,533	40,636	40,731	23,001	29,671	29,823	14,003	6,037	6,042	4,793	4,928	4,866	4,206
2014–15	44,911	45,012	25,235	32,789	32,947	15,295	6,687	6,692	5,391	5,434	5,373	4,550	41,969	42,063	23,582	30,641	30,789	14,293	6,249	6,254	5,038	5,078	5,021	4,252
2015–16	45,787	45,921	25,882	33,386	33,565	15,651	6,900	6,905	5,718	5,502	5,450	4,513	43,077	43,202	24,349	31,409	31,578	14,724	6,491	6,497	5,379	5,176	5,128	4,246
2016–17	46,496	46,654	26,373	33,977	34,148	15,970	6,997	7,003	5,860	5,522	5,503	4,543	44,548	44,699	25,268	32,553	32,717	15,301	6,704	6,709	5,615	5,291	5,273	4,352
2017–18	46,961	47,100	27,079	34,294	34,448	16,116	7,095	7,099	6,141	5,572	5,553	4,823	46,008	46,144	26,530	33,598	33,748	15,789	6,951	6,955	6,016	5,459	5,440	4,725
2018–19	47,419	47,541	27,962	34,621	34,758	16,629	7,173	7,174	6,686	5,625	5,608	4,647	47,419	47,541	27,962	34,621	34,758	16,629	7,173	7,174	6,686	5,625	5,608	4,647
For-profit																								
1999–2000	24,123	24,756	23,538	13,026	12,957	13,114	6,353	6,929	5,852	4,744	4,870	4,572	16,124	16,547	15,734	8,707	8,661	8,766	4,247	4,631	3,912	3,171	3,255	3,056
2000–01	25,585	26,355	24,679	14,743	15,059	14,386	6,519	7,175	5,720	4,323	4,121	4,573	17,688	18,220	17,061	10,192	10,411	9,945	4,507	4,960	3,955	2,988	2,849	3,161
2001–02	26,403	28,103	24,101	15,435	15,733	15,108	6,580	7,670	5,087	4,388	4,700	3,905	18,576	19,772	16,956	10,860	11,069	10,629	4,629	5,396	3,579	3,087	3,307	2,748
2002–03	27,390	27,870	26,987	15,729	15,864	15,478	6,367	7,487	4,909	5,293	4,518	6,600	19,694	20,039	19,404	11,310	11,407	11,129	4,578	5,384	3,530	3,806	3,249	4,746
2003–04	29,699	29,782	30,446	16,711	16,874	16,364	6,930	7,831	5,433	6,058	5,077	8,650	21,822	21,883	22,371	12,278	12,398	12,024	5,092	5,754	3,992	4,451	3,730	6,355
2004–05	30,518	30,937	29,533	17,223	17,437	16,657	7,472	7,746	6,803	5,823	5,753	6,072	23,098	23,415	22,353	13,036	13,197	12,607	5,655	5,863	5,149	4,407	4,355	4,596
2005–06	29,983	29,560	32,672	16,847	16,946	16,493	7,745	8,253	6,079	5,390	4,361	10,100	23,557	23,225	25,670	13,237	13,315	12,959	6,085	6,485	4,776	4,235	3,426	7,935
2006–07	29,785	30,659	26,365	17,713	18,105	16,234	7,698	8,235	5,541	4,374	4,319	4,591	24,007	24,712	21,251	14,277	14,593	13,084	6,205	6,638	4,466	3,525	3,481	3,701
2007–08	29,605	30,007	28,143	17,238	17,519	15,989	7,711	8,112	5,863	4,656	4,376	6,291	24,746	25,083	23,524	14,409	14,643	13,365	6,445	6,781	4,901	3,892	3,658	5,258
2008–09	28,683	28,833	29,081	16,888	17,022	16,201	7,330	7,600	5,805	4,466	4,211	7,075	24,311	24,437	24,648	14,313	14,427	13,731	6,212	6,441	4,920	3,785	3,569	5,997
2009–10	28,184	27,911	30,351	16,394	16,090	17,682	7,294	7,400	6,641	4,496	4,421	6,027	24,118	23,885	25,973	14,029	13,769	15,132	6,242	6,332	5,683	3,847	3,783	5,158
2010–11	26,327	26,204	29,540	15,739	15,725	15,800	6,254	6,276	6,102	4,334	4,203	7,638	22,982	22,875	25,787	13,739	13,727	13,792	5,460	5,479	5,327	3,783	3,669	6,668
2011–12	25,567	25,512	26,138	15,304	15,261	15,519	6,186	6,178	6,262	4,077	4,074	4,357	22,972	22,923	23,486	13,751	13,712	13,944	5,558	5,551	5,627	3,663	3,660	3,915
2012–13	25,360	25,276	26,291	15,075	14,988	15,558	6,284	6,291	6,206	4,001	3,996	4,527	23,165	23,088	24,016	13,770	13,691	14,212	5,740	5,747	5,669	3,655	3,651	4,135
2013–14	24,939	24,842	26,242	14,863	14,782	15,302	6,255	6,246	6,349	3,820	3,813	4,591	23,137	23,047	24,346	13,789	13,714	14,196	5,803	5,795	5,891	3,544	3,538	4,260
2014–15	25,011	24,908	27,426	14,951	14,901	15,255	6,202	6,204	6,185	3,858	3,803	5,986	23,373	23,277	25,629	13,972	13,924	14,256	5,796	5,798	5,780	3,605	3,554	5,594
2015–16	25,273	25,215	25,840	15,086	15,041	15,388	6,217	6,209	6,301	3,970	3,965	4,151	23,777	23,722	24,310	14,193	14,150	14,477	5,849	5,842	5,928	3,735	3,731	3,905
2016–17	26,543	26,648	26,121	15,050	15,053	15,028	7,190	7,302	6,563	4,304	4,293	4,530	25,431	25,531	25,027	14,419	14,423	14,399	6,889	6,996	6,288	4,123	4,113	4,340
2017–18	26,797	26,951	25,584	14,973	14,982	14,908	7,418	7,565	6,229	4,406	4,404	4,447	26,253	26,404	25,065	14,669	14,677	14,606	7,268	7,411	6,102	4,317	4,315	4,357
2018–19	27,040	26,575	30,052	14,780	14,715	15,360	7,118	7,410	5,305	5,143	4,450	9,387	27,040	26,575	30,052	14,780	14,715	15,360	7,118	7,410	5,305	5,143	4,450	9,387

[1]Constant dollars based on the Consumer Price Index, prepared by the Bureau of Labor Statistics, U.S. Department of Labor, adjusted to an academic-year basis.

[2]For public institutions, in-state tuition and required fees are used.

[3]Data for 1986–87 and later years reflect a basis of 20 meals per week, while data for earlier years are for meals served 7 days a week (the number of meals per day was not specified). Because of this revision in data collection and tabulation procedures, data are not entirely comparable with figures for previous years. In particular, data on board rates are somewhat higher than in earlier years because they reflect the basis of 20 meals per week rather than meals served 7 days a week. Since many institutions serve fewer than 3 meals each day, the 1986-87 and later data reflect a more accurate accounting of total board costs.

[4]Room and board data are estimated.

NOTE: Data are for the entire academic year and are average charges for full-time students. Tuition and fees were weighted by the number of full-time-equivalent undergraduates, but were not adjusted to reflect student residency. Room and board are based on full-time students. Data through 1995-96 are for institutions of higher education, while later data are for degree-granting institutions. Degree-granting institutions grant associate's or higher degrees and participate in Title IV federal financial aid programs. The degree-granting classification is very similar to the earlier higher education classification, but it includes more 2-year colleges and excludes a few higher education institutions that did not grant degrees. Some data have been revised from previously published figures. Detail may not sum to totals because of rounding.

SOURCE: U.S. Department of Education, National Center for Education Statistics, *Projections of Education Statistics to 1986–87*; Higher Education General Information Survey (HEGIS), "Institutional Characteristics of Colleges and Universities" surveys, 1969–70 through 1985–86; "Fall Enrollment in Institutions of Higher Education" surveys, 1963 through 1985; Integrated Postsecondary Education Data System (IPEDS), "Fall Enrollment Survey" (IPEDS-EF:86–99) and "Institutional Characteristics Survey" (IPEDS-IC:86–99); IPEDS Spring 2001 through Spring 2019, Fall Enrollment component; and IPEDS Fall 2000 through Fall 2018, Institutional Characteristics component. (This table was prepared December 2019.)

Table 330.20. Average undergraduate tuition and fees and room and board rates charged for full-time students in degree-granting postsecondary institutions, by control and level of institution and state or jurisdiction: 2017–18 and 2018–19

[In current dollars]

State or jurisdiction	Public 4-year, In-state, 2017–18, Total	Public 4-year, In-state, 2017–18, Tuition and required fees	Public 4-year, In-state, 2018–19, Total	Public 4-year, In-state, 2018–19, Tuition and required fees	Public 4-year, In-state, 2018–19, Room	Public 4-year, In-state, 2018–19, Board	Public 4-year, Out-of-state tuition and required fees, 2018–19	Private 4-year, 2017–18, Total	Private 4-year, 2017–18, Tuition and required fees	Private 4-year, 2018–19, Total	Private 4-year, 2018–19, Tuition and required fees	Private 4-year, 2018–19, Room	Private 4-year, 2018–19, Board	Public 2-year, tuition and required fees, In-state, 2017–18	Public 2-year, tuition and required fees, In-state, 2018–19	Public 2-year, tuition and required fees, Out-of-state, 2018–19
1	2	3	4	5	6	7	8	9	10	11	12	13	14	15	16	17
United States	**$20,049**	**$9,036**	**$20,598**	**$9,212**	**$6,459**	**$4,927**	**$26,382**	**$43,131**	**$30,723**	**$44,662**	**$31,875**	**$7,179**	**$5,608**	**$3,242**	**$3,313**	**$7,917**
Alabama	19,673	9,827	19,982	10,138	5,543	4,301	25,782	26,165	16,321	26,195	16,119	5,005	5,071	4,403	4,770	9,612
Alaska	18,373	7,221	19,563	8,396	6,226	4,941	24,454	26,887	19,360	26,788	19,315	3,720	3,753	†	†	†
Arizona	22,629	10,557	23,105	10,666	7,199	5,240	26,383	22,939	13,487	22,419	12,711	5,330	4,378	2,152	2,161	8,516
Arkansas	17,479	8,187	17,977	8,391	5,310	4,276	20,825	30,828	22,610	31,564	23,179	4,255	4,130	3,292	3,291	4,698
California	22,075	8,014	22,664	8,118	8,147	6,399	31,423	47,411	33,485	49,860	35,524	7,976	6,360	1,268	1,271	7,849
Colorado	21,514	9,540	21,867	9,394	6,323	6,149	30,140	35,152	22,873	36,285	23,560	7,482	5,243	3,638	3,655	7,967
Connecticut	25,182	12,355	26,203	12,959	7,254	5,990	33,709	54,819	40,410	56,549	41,807	8,527	6,215	4,312	4,434	13,202
Delaware	22,371	9,999	23,447	10,607	7,661	5,179	30,405	26,928	15,096	26,709	14,758	6,032	5,920	†	†	†
District of Columbia	†	5,756	†	5,888	†	†	12,416	57,611	41,775	59,233	43,143	10,844	5,246	†	†	†
Florida	14,896	4,455	15,059	4,443	6,173	4,443	18,456	37,275	25,471	38,438	26,317	6,918	5,203	2,506	2,506	9,111
Georgia	17,705	7,206	18,003	7,319	6,346	4,337	22,751	40,377	27,777	41,520	28,839	6,955	5,726	2,901	2,916	8,038
Hawaii	21,201	9,709	21,865	9,952	6,046	5,868	31,581	28,858	16,447	29,781	17,098	5,870	6,813	3,080	3,140	8,277
Idaho	15,455	7,247	16,134	7,586	4,061	4,487	23,850	13,488	5,833	13,157	6,139	2,436	4,583	3,282	3,345	7,971
Illinois	25,089	13,971	25,469	14,259	6,087	5,122	28,522	44,943	32,389	46,552	33,454	7,530	5,568	3,891	3,966	11,480
Indiana	19,297	9,038	19,755	9,225	5,553	4,977	29,092	43,764	32,338	45,382	33,402	6,204	5,775	4,255	4,368	8,402
Iowa	18,427	8,767	20,122	9,966	5,709	4,448	24,521	37,379	27,991	43,364	33,821	4,687	4,855	4,923	5,137	6,449
Kansas	17,963	8,737	18,618	8,941	5,062	4,616	23,302	30,262	21,339	31,701	22,571	4,406	4,723	3,384	3,435	4,491
Kentucky	20,745	10,365	21,313	10,674	6,038	4,601	25,430	35,948	26,719	37,081	27,648	4,661	4,773	4,106	4,274	14,418
Louisiana	18,834	9,164	19,206	9,358	5,704	4,144	22,208	49,452	36,715	51,025	37,830	7,315	5,880	4,093	4,143	8,034
Maine	19,500	9,664	20,195	9,930	5,119	5,146	27,735	49,994	37,043	52,527	38,972	6,772	6,783	3,698	3,753	6,614
Maryland	21,176	9,288	21,895	9,521	7,057	5,317	26,883	55,685	41,859	57,222	43,141	8,180	5,901	4,090	4,225	9,990
Massachusetts	25,229	12,778	26,787	13,286	8,337	5,164	30,966	59,540	44,362	61,747	46,016	9,177	6,555	4,991	5,192	10,606
Michigan	22,665	12,435	23,376	12,888	5,262	5,226	35,844	36,660	26,961	38,074	27,936	5,096	5,043	3,469	3,582	6,372
Minnesota	20,420	11,226	20,860	11,381	5,194	4,286	22,780	42,716	32,416	43,677	33,212	5,616	4,850	5,381	5,389	5,947
Mississippi	17,718	7,980	18,391	8,340	5,887	4,164	19,942	25,774	17,625	26,352	17,953	4,352	4,046	3,183	3,262	5,709
Missouri	18,106	8,387	18,121	8,554	5,612	3,956	19,914	34,617	24,608	35,803	25,417	6,021	4,366	3,271	3,358	6,558
Montana	15,800	6,783	16,604	6,972	4,481	5,150	24,481	33,739	24,953	34,988	25,918	4,291	4,779	3,631	3,756	8,394
Nebraska	18,449	8,188	19,551	8,467	6,239	4,845	21,516	34,650	23,711	34,626	25,075	5,502	4,049	3,212	3,174	3,985
Nevada	16,810	5,920	17,503	5,845	6,039	5,619	21,125	36,163	23,261	38,130	24,423	6,711	6,996	3,075	†	†
New Hampshire	27,570	15,949	28,145	16,329	7,258	4,558	29,447	47,030	33,322	46,952	33,364	8,690	4,898	7,337	7,599	16,429
New Jersey	26,542	13,633	27,481	13,963	8,343	5,175	28,669	50,321	36,589	51,045	37,329	7,963	5,753	4,536	4,715	8,257
New Mexico	15,788	6,711	16,256	6,902	4,764	4,590	18,350	33,620	23,865	40,206	30,137	5,645	4,424	1,667	1,705	6,698
New York	22,343	7,938	23,053	8,184	9,746	5,123	22,083	53,658	39,006	55,741	40,527	9,115	6,098	5,229	5,367	9,197
North Carolina	17,343	7,354	17,302	7,174	5,766	4,362	22,968	44,058	32,149	46,268	33,990	6,350	5,928	2,499	2,504	8,655
North Dakota	15,998	7,687	16,668	8,091	3,733	4,844	15,565	22,511	15,256	22,856	15,206	3,099	4,551	4,700	4,895	9,293
Ohio	21,674	10,026	22,153	10,068	6,597	5,488	24,454	42,252	31,240	44,035	32,597	5,942	5,496	3,672	4,082	7,300
Oklahoma	16,263	7,623	16,732	7,866	4,738	4,128	21,526	35,542	26,240	37,447	27,694	4,872	4,882	3,875	4,112	9,393
Oregon	22,710	10,363	22,585	10,286	7,204	5,095	30,929	50,617	38,674	53,036	40,597	6,536	5,903	4,487	4,709	8,779
Pennsylvania	25,795	14,534	26,287	14,812	6,893	4,582	28,527	53,258	40,086	55,248	41,703	7,434	6,111	5,171	5,284	14,111
Rhode Island	24,280	12,239	24,827	12,576	7,666	4,585	29,998	54,877	40,361	57,176	42,108	8,981	6,088	4,564	4,564	12,156
South Carolina	22,132	12,579	23,113	13,013	6,241	3,859	32,174	34,423	24,932	35,174	25,621	4,811	4,743	4,502	4,728	9,874
South Dakota	16,421	8,540	16,847	8,772	3,917	4,159	12,465	32,157	24,219	31,359	23,252	4,002	4,105	6,027	6,170	5,839
Tennessee	18,951	9,574	19,713	9,789	5,205	4,719	26,068	37,162	26,939	38,571	28,080	5,885	4,607	4,148	4,287	16,582
Texas	18,271	8,645	18,779	8,678	5,553	4,548	25,031	43,868	32,484	46,268	34,476	6,580	5,213	2,209	2,259	5,920
Utah	14,174	6,557	14,389	6,731	3,554	4,104	21,557	15,377	7,536	15,804	7,852	4,002	3,950	3,781	3,843	12,206
Vermont	27,782	16,103	28,681	16,604	7,646	4,431	39,947	56,172	42,637	58,137	44,068	7,683	6,387	6,414	7,120	14,090
Virginia	23,427	12,637	24,492	13,413	6,242	4,838	34,890	33,662	23,018	34,470	23,380	5,890	5,199	5,118	5,241	11,455
Washington	18,323	6,830	19,272	7,036	6,517	5,719	29,228	48,518	36,807	50,873	38,754	6,381	5,739	4,078	4,169	5,691
West Virginia	17,803	7,619	18,461	8,016	5,603	4,842	21,996	21,321	12,361	21,892	12,513	4,505	4,874	4,077	4,276	9,834
Wisconsin	16,544	8,475	17,172	8,697	5,407	3,068	25,063	43,332	33,156	45,269	34,424	6,183	4,663	4,337	4,411	6,408
Wyoming	14,486	4,443	14,639	4,596	4,493	5,550	14,268	†	†	†	†	†	†	3,142	3,219	7,752

†Not applicable.

NOTE: Data are for the entire academic year and are average charges for full-time students. In-state tuition and fees were weighted by the number of full-time-equivalent undergraduates, but were not adjusted to reflect the number of students who were state residents. Out-of-state tuition and fees were weighted by the number of first-time freshmen attending the institution in fall 2018 from out of state. Institutional room and board rates are weighted by the number of full-time students. Degree-granting institutions grant associate's or higher degrees and participate in Title IV federal financial aid programs. Some data have been revised from previously published figures. Detail may not sum to totals because of rounding.

SOURCE: U.S. Department of Education, National Center for Education Statistics, Integrated Postsecondary Education Data System (IPEDS), Fall 2017 and Fall 2018, Institutional Characteristics component; and Spring 2018 and Spring 2019, Fall Enrollment component. (This table was prepared December 2019.)

Table 330.30. Average undergraduate tuition, fees, room, and board charges for full-time students in degree-granting postsecondary institutions, by percentile of charges and control and level of institution: Selected years, 2000–01 through 2018–19

Control and level of institution, and year	Current dollars										Constant 2018–19 dollars[1]				
	Tuition, fees, room, and board					Tuition and required fees					Tuition and required fees				
	10th percentile	25th percentile	Median (50th percentile)	75th percentile	90th percentile	10th percentile	25th percentile	Median (50th percentile)	75th percentile	90th percentile	10th percentile	25th percentile	Median (50th percentile)	75th percentile	90th percentile
1	2	3	4	5	6	7	8	9	10	11	12	13	14	15	16
Public institutions[2]															
2000–01	$5,741	$6,880	$8,279	$9,617	$11,384	$612	$1,480	$2,403	$3,444	$4,583	$885	$2,141	$3,476	$4,982	$6,629
2005–06	7,700	9,623	11,348	13,543	16,264	990	2,070	3,329	5,322	6,972	1,260	2,635	4,237	6,774	8,874
2010–11	9,889	12,856	15,234	17,860	21,593	1,230	2,626	4,632	7,115	9,420	1,409	3,008	5,306	8,151	10,791
2015–16	13,215	15,947	18,648	21,735	25,180	1,632	3,456	6,452	9,326	11,948	1,735	3,673	6,858	9,913	12,700
2017–18	13,965	16,749	19,922	23,093	26,927	1,632	3,724	6,897	9,952	12,700	1,666	3,801	7,040	10,158	12,963
2018–19	14,111	17,281	20,554	23,755	27,960	1,696	3,843	7,140	10,308	13,110	1,696	3,843	7,140	10,308	13,110
Public 4-year[2]															
2000–01	6,503	7,347	8,468	9,816	11,611	2,118	2,520	3,314	4,094	5,085	3,064	3,645	4,794	5,922	7,355
2005–06	8,863	10,219	11,596	13,830	16,443	3,094	3,822	5,084	6,458	8,097	3,938	4,864	6,471	8,219	10,305
2010–11	12,048	13,604	15,823	18,419	22,191	4,336	5,091	6,779	8,689	11,029	4,967	5,832	7,766	9,954	12,634
2015–16	14,733	16,559	19,217	21,979	25,658	5,360	6,691	8,256	10,509	13,431	5,697	7,112	8,776	11,170	14,276
2017–18	15,663	17,461	20,369	23,274	27,283	4,343	6,958	8,738	10,974	14,018	4,433	7,102	8,919	11,201	14,308
2018–19	15,852	18,068	20,864	24,108	28,095	4,200	7,120	8,938	11,261	14,184	4,200	7,120	8,938	11,261	14,184
Public 2-year[2]															
2000–01	3,321	3,804	4,627	5,750	6,871	310	724	1,387	1,799	2,460	448	1,047	2,006	2,602	3,558
2005–06	4,380	4,822	6,234	7,567	8,993	691	1,109	1,920	2,589	3,100	879	1,411	2,444	3,295	3,946
2010–11	5,347	6,327	7,339	9,370	11,312	700	1,412	2,537	3,315	3,840	802	1,618	2,906	3,798	4,399
2015–16	6,474	7,503	9,337	11,854	14,978	1,182	1,514	3,077	4,115	5,032	1,256	1,609	3,271	4,374	5,349
2017–18	6,896	8,355	9,787	12,587	15,400	1,244	1,632	3,304	4,394	5,190	1,270	1,666	3,372	4,485	5,298
2018–19	7,076	8,386	10,389	12,900	15,680	1,220	1,661	3,375	4,530	5,300	1,220	1,661	3,375	4,530	5,300
Private nonprofit institutions															
2000–01	13,514	17,552	22,493	27,430	32,659	7,800	11,730	15,540	19,600	24,532	11,283	16,967	22,478	28,351	35,485
2005–06	18,243	23,258	29,497	35,918	41,707	9,981	15,375	21,070	26,265	31,690	12,703	19,569	26,817	33,429	40,334
2010–11	23,143	29,884	38,063	47,061	52,235	11,930	19,625	26,920	34,536	40,082	13,667	22,482	30,838	39,563	45,916
2015–16	25,903	36,436	45,951	57,465	63,209	11,900	23,162	32,250	42,270	48,190	12,649	24,620	34,280	44,930	51,223
2017–18	28,232	39,206	49,182	61,550	67,643	12,300	24,695	34,440	45,548	51,992	12,555	25,207	35,154	46,492	53,069
2018–19	28,314	40,449	50,968	63,838	70,091	12,132	25,122	35,160	47,280	53,425	12,132	25,122	35,160	47,280	53,425
Nonprofit 4-year															
2000–01	13,972	17,714	22,554	27,476	32,659	8,450	11,920	15,746	19,730	24,532	12,223	17,242	22,776	28,539	35,485
2005–06	18,350	23,322	29,598	36,028	41,774	10,300	15,560	21,190	26,500	31,690	13,109	19,804	26,970	33,728	40,334
2010–11	23,548	30,042	38,129	47,061	52,235	12,220	19,854	27,100	34,580	40,082	13,999	22,744	31,045	39,613	45,916
2015–16	26,315	36,537	46,094	57,465	63,209	12,240	23,748	32,400	42,288	48,190	13,010	25,243	34,439	44,949	51,223
2017–18	28,370	39,206	49,464	61,550	67,643	12,360	25,025	34,600	45,620	52,002	12,616	25,544	35,317	46,565	53,080
2018–19	28,581	40,457	51,028	63,838	70,091	12,306	25,390	35,350	47,290	53,430	12,306	25,390	35,350	47,290	53,430
Nonprofit 2-year															
2000–01	6,850	6,850	9,995	14,209	20,240	2,430	4,825	7,250	8,266	11,100	3,515	6,979	10,487	11,957	16,056
2005–06	8,030	15,680	16,830	20,829	28,643	4,218	8,640	9,940	12,270	14,472	5,368	10,997	12,651	15,617	18,419
2010–11	10,393	19,718	21,186	27,386	30,758	3,840	9,730	12,000	14,640	18,965	4,399	11,146	13,747	16,771	21,726
2015–16	22,582	23,059	25,696	31,405	53,387	4,904	10,800	14,110	17,346	22,060	5,213	11,480	14,998	18,438	23,448
2017–18	14,587	26,265	29,227	33,546	59,560	4,904	9,867	15,022	18,450	23,670	5,006	10,071	15,333	18,832	24,161
2018–19	16,334	26,181	29,520	34,694	65,073	4,593	10,439	14,539	18,971	28,432	4,593	10,439	14,539	18,971	28,432
Private for-profit institutions															
2000–01	13,396	15,778	19,403	21,400	21,845	6,900	8,202	9,644	12,090	14,600	9,981	11,864	13,950	17,488	21,119
2005–06	17,278	19,098	25,589	26,499	31,903	7,632	10,011	12,450	14,335	17,740	9,714	12,742	15,846	18,245	22,579
2010–11	16,097	16,097	17,484	26,175	31,639	10,194	10,194	13,520	15,750	18,048	11,678	11,678	15,488	18,043	20,675
2015–16	17,407	17,407	26,028	26,405	35,377	10,575	11,003	13,320	17,132	19,286	11,241	11,695	14,158	18,210	20,500
2017–18	25,281	26,226	26,226	27,253	37,319	10,935	11,330	13,794	17,002	21,331	11,162	11,565	14,080	17,354	21,773
2018–19	26,278	26,302	26,302	27,274	35,986	9,552	9,552	13,380	17,076	24,030	9,552	9,552	13,380	17,076	24,030
For-profit 4-year															
2000–01	13,396	15,818	20,417	21,400	21,400	7,206	8,305	9,675	12,800	15,090	10,423	12,013	13,995	18,515	21,827
2005–06	17,383	19,098	25,589	26,499	31,903	7,632	10,418	12,900	14,450	17,735	9,714	13,260	16,419	18,391	22,572
2010–11	16,097	16,097	17,484	26,175	31,639	10,194	10,194	13,560	16,500	18,048	11,678	11,678	15,534	18,902	20,675
2015–16	17,407	17,407	26,028	26,405	35,377	10,607	11,003	12,975	17,132	19,459	11,275	11,695	13,792	18,210	20,684
2017–18	25,281	26,226	26,226	27,253	37,319	10,935	11,330	13,516	17,002	23,204	11,162	11,565	13,796	17,354	23,685
2018–19	26,278	26,302	26,302	27,274	39,253	9,552	9,552	13,354	17,076	24,109	9,552	9,552	13,354	17,076	24,109
For-profit 2-year															
2000–01	15,778	15,778	19,403	21,845	21,845	6,025	7,365	9,644	12,000	14,255	8,715	10,653	13,950	17,358	20,620
2005–06	13,010	18,281	43,425	43,425	43,425	7,870	9,285	11,550	14,196	19,425	10,017	11,818	14,700	18,068	24,723
2010–11	23,687	23,687	25,161	25,161	25,161	10,075	12,049	13,418	15,263	17,918	11,541	13,803	15,371	17,485	20,526
2015–16	25,732	25,732	25,732	25,732	25,732	10,510	12,678	13,975	15,760	18,048	11,171	13,476	14,854	16,752	19,184
2017–18	27,356	27,356	27,356	27,356	27,356	10,880	11,580	14,220	15,743	17,614	11,105	11,820	14,515	16,069	17,979
2018–19	30,718	30,718	30,718	30,718	30,718	11,156	12,945	14,843	16,207	18,060	11,156	12,945	14,843	16,207	18,060

[1]Constant dollars based on the Consumer Price Index, prepared by the Bureau of Labor Statistics, U.S. Department of Labor, adjusted to an academic-year basis.

[2]Average undergraduate tuition and fees are based on in-state students only.

NOTE: Data are for the entire academic year and are average charges for full-time students. Student charges were weighted by the number of full-time-equivalent undergraduates, but were not adjusted to reflect student residency. Degree-granting institutions grant associate's or higher degrees and participate in Title IV federal financial aid programs. Some data have been revised from previously published figures.

SOURCE: U.S. Department of Education, National Center for Education Statistics, Integrated Postsecondary Education Data System (IPEDS), Fall 2000 through Fall 2018, Institutional Characteristics component; and Spring 2001 through Spring 2019, Fall Enrollment component. (This table was prepared December 2019.)

Table 330.40. Average total cost of attendance for first-time, full-time undergraduate students in degree-granting postsecondary institutions, by control and level of institution, living arrangement, and component of student costs: Selected years, 2010–11 through 2018–19

Level of institution, living arrangement, and component of student costs	2010–11				2015–16				2016–17				2017–18				2018–19			
	All insti-tutions	Public, in-state	Private		All insti-tutions	Public, in-state	Private		All insti-tutions	Public, in-state	Private		All insti-tutions	Public, in-state	Private		All insti-tutions	Public, in-state	Private	
			Non-profit	For-profit			Non-profit	For-profit			Non-profit	For-profit			Non-profit	For-profit			Non-profit	For-profit
1	2	3	4	5	6	7	8	9	10	11	12	13	14	15	16	17	18	19	20	21
	Current dollars																			
4-year institutions																				
Average total cost, by living arrangement																				
On campus	$27,589	$20,035	$39,676	$31,897	$31,652	$23,113	$47,300	$31,546	$32,575	$23,765	$48,827	$32,416	$33,495	$24,351	$50,387	$32,876	$34,346	$24,869	$51,874	$33,219
Off campus, living with family	20,084	12,554	31,689	22,268	22,243	13,907	37,479	21,831	22,748	14,102	38,733	22,096	23,363	14,387	39,996	22,589	23,874	14,589	41,100	22,733
Off campus, not living with family	29,142	21,324	40,033	31,000	31,543	23,416	47,105	29,609	32,165	23,813	48,435	29,680	33,137	24,356	50,370	30,405	33,903	24,925	51,728	30,217
Component of student costs																				
Tuition and required fees	14,596	7,163	26,637	15,191	16,896	8,520	32,312	16,154	17,442	8,776	33,487	16,810	18,000	9,014	34,658	17,207	18,510	9,216	35,769	17,262
Books and supplies	1,223	1,196	1,221	1,522	1,255	1,267	1,241	1,149	1,263	1,277	1,247	1,101	1,269	1,281	1,257	1,102	1,272	1,283	1,258	1,148
Room, board, and other expenses																				
On campus																				
Room and board	8,912	8,497	9,455	9,304	10,526	10,078	11,186	9,669	10,826	10,369	11,497	10,005	11,174	10,720	11,851	10,032	11,486	11,011	12,194	10,244
Other	2,858	3,179	2,363	5,879	2,976	3,248	2,561	4,574	3,045	3,343	2,596	4,500	3,052	3,335	2,621	4,534	3,078	3,359	2,652	4,565
Off campus, living with family																				
Other	4,265	4,195	3,832	5,554	4,092	4,120	3,926	4,528	4,043	4,049	3,999	4,185	4,095	4,091	4,080	4,280	4,093	4,089	4,073	4,324
Off campus, not living with family																				
Room and board	8,802	8,942	8,202	8,866	9,144	9,658	8,778	7,587	9,269	9,799	8,838	7,339	9,593	10,073	9,231	7,694	9,823	10,366	9,387	7,718
Other	4,521	4,022	3,974	5,421	4,248	3,971	4,773	4,719	4,192	3,960	4,863	4,430	4,275	3,987	5,224	4,402	4,299	4,059	5,314	4,090
2-year institutions																				
Average total cost, by living arrangement																				
On campus	13,777	12,336	25,763	29,179	15,096	14,345	31,749	27,776	15,448	14,677	31,828	28,711	15,687	14,972	32,339	29,499	16,153	15,420	33,227	29,958
Off campus, living with family	8,964	7,843	18,931	19,350	9,303	8,838	22,655	20,144	9,482	8,997	22,945	20,078	9,596	9,169	23,453	20,208	9,805	9,369	23,951	20,652
Off campus, not living with family	16,389	15,153	27,458	27,366	17,405	16,911	30,901	28,663	17,804	17,310	32,068	28,282	18,162	17,710	31,996	29,206	18,722	18,256	32,935	30,072
Component of student costs																				
Tuition and required fees	3,850	2,748	13,832	13,954	3,893	3,425	17,137	14,779	4,031	3,542	17,429	14,667	4,066	3,637	17,876	14,648	4,177	3,737	18,387	15,021
Books and supplies	1,302	1,295	1,153	1,407	1,444	1,451	1,144	1,291	1,456	1,465	1,127	1,265	1,483	1,489	1,106	1,349	1,516	1,524	1,020	1,339
Room, board, and other expenses																				
On campus																				
Room and board	5,654	5,351	7,806	9,961	6,697	6,406	10,359	8,883	6,880	6,551	10,688	9,682	7,046	6,713	10,837	9,920	7,240	6,889	11,272	9,970
Other	2,971	2,941	2,973	3,857	3,062	3,062	3,108	2,822	3,081	3,119	2,585	3,096	3,092	3,132	2,520	3,582	3,220	3,270	2,548	3,628
Off campus, living with family																				
Other	3,812	3,799	3,947	3,989	3,966	3,962	4,374	4,073	3,995	3,990	4,389	4,146	4,047	4,042	4,471	4,211	4,113	4,107	4,544	4,292
Off campus, not living with family																				
Room and board	7,478	7,412	7,999	7,889	8,200	8,200	8,212	8,195	8,405	8,424	8,864	7,970	8,647	8,652	8,595	8,534	8,955	8,958	9,066	8,867
Other	3,759	3,698	4,475	4,117	3,868	3,834	4,408	4,397	3,913	3,879	4,650	4,380	3,967	3,931	4,418	4,675	4,074	4,036	4,463	4,845
	Constant 2018–19 dollars[1]																			
4-year institutions																				
Average total cost, by living arrangement																				
On campus	$31,605	$22,951	$45,451	$36,539	$33,644	$24,568	$50,276	$33,532	$34,000	$24,804	$50,962	$33,834	$34,189	$24,855	$51,432	$33,557	$34,346	$24,869	$51,874	$33,219
Off campus, living with family	23,007	14,382	36,302	25,509	23,643	14,783	39,838	23,205	23,743	14,719	40,427	23,063	23,848	14,685	40,824	23,057	23,874	14,589	41,100	22,733
Off campus, not living with family	33,384	24,427	45,860	35,512	33,528	24,889	50,069	31,472	33,572	24,854	50,553	30,978	33,823	24,860	51,414	31,035	33,903	24,925	51,728	30,217
Tuition and required fees	16,721	8,206	30,514	17,403	17,959	9,056	34,345	17,171	18,205	9,160	34,951	17,546	18,373	9,201	35,377	17,563	18,510	9,216	35,769	17,262
2-year institutions																				
Average total cost, by living arrangement																				
On campus	15,782	14,131	29,513	33,426	16,046	15,247	33,747	29,524	16,124	15,319	33,220	29,967	16,012	15,283	33,010	30,110	16,153	15,420	33,227	29,958
Off campus, living with family	10,268	8,984	21,686	22,167	9,888	9,394	24,081	21,411	9,897	9,391	23,948	20,956	9,794	9,359	23,939	20,627	9,805	9,369	23,951	20,652
Off campus, not living with family	18,774	17,359	31,455	31,349	18,500	17,975	32,846	30,467	18,583	18,067	33,471	29,519	18,538	18,077	32,659	29,811	18,722	18,256	32,935	30,072
Tuition and required fees	4,410	3,148	15,845	15,985	4,138	3,641	18,216	15,709	4,207	3,697	18,191	15,309	4,150	3,713	18,247	14,952	4,177	3,737	18,387	15,021

[1]Constant dollars based on the Consumer Price Index, prepared by the Bureau of Labor Statistics, U.S. Department of Labor, adjusted to an academic-year basis.

NOTE: Excludes students who previously attended another postsecondary institution or who began their studies on a part-time basis. Tuition and fees at public institutions are the lower of either in-district or in-state tuition and fees. Data illustrating the average total cost of attendance for all students are weighted by the number of students at the institution receiving Title IV aid. Detail may not sum to totals because of rounding. Some data have been revised from previously published figures.

SOURCE: U.S. Department of Education, National Center for Education Statistics, Integrated Postsecondary Education Data System (IPEDS), Spring 2011 and Winter 2015–16 through Winter 2018–19, Student Financial Aid component; and Fall 2010 through Fall 2018, Institutional Characteristics component. (This table was prepared December 2019.)

Table 330.50. Average and percentiles of graduate tuition and required fees in degree-granting postsecondary institutions, by control of institution: 1989–90 through 2018–19

Year	Average: Total	Average: Public institutions[1]	Average: Private institutions: Total	Average: Private institutions: Nonprofit	Average: Private institutions: For-profit	Percentiles: Public institutions[1]: 25th percentile	Percentiles: Public institutions[1]: Median (50th percentile)	Percentiles: Public institutions[1]: 75th percentile	Percentiles: Nonprofit institutions: 25th percentile	Percentiles: Nonprofit institutions: Median (50th percentile)	Percentiles: Nonprofit institutions: 75th percentile
1	2	3	4	5	6	7	8	9	10	11	12
					Current dollars						
1989–90	$4,135	$1,999	$7,881	—	—	—	—	—	—	—	—
1990–91	4,488	2,206	8,507	—	—	—	—	—	—	—	—
1991–92	5,116	2,524	9,592	—	—	—	—	—	—	—	—
1992–93	5,475	2,791	10,008	—	—	—	—	—	—	—	—
1993–94	5,973	3,050	10,790	—	—	—	—	—	—	—	—
1994–95	6,247	3,250	11,338	—	—	—	—	—	—	—	—
1995–96	6,741	3,449	12,083	—	—	—	—	—	—	—	—
1996–97	7,111	3,607	12,537	—	—	—	—	—	—	—	—
1997–98	7,246	3,744	12,774	—	—	—	—	—	—	—	—
1998–99	7,685	3,897	13,299	—	—	—	—	—	—	—	—
1999–2000	8,069	4,042	13,821	$14,123	$9,611	$2,640	$3,637	$5,163	$7,998	$12,870	$20,487
2000–01	8,429	4,243	14,420	14,457	13,229	2,931	3,822	5,347	8,276	13,200	21,369
2001–02	8,857	4,496	15,165	15,232	13,414	3,226	4,119	5,596	8,583	14,157	22,054
2002–03	9,226	4,842	14,983	15,676	9,644	3,395	4,452	5,927	8,690	14,140	22,700
2003–04	10,312	5,544	16,209	16,807	12,542	3,795	5,103	7,063	9,072	15,030	25,600
2004–05	11,004	6,080	16,751	17,551	13,133	4,236	5,663	7,616	9,300	16,060	26,140
2005–06	11,621	6,493	17,244	18,171	13,432	4,608	6,209	7,977	9,745	16,222	26,958
2006–07	12,312	6,894	18,109	19,034	14,421	4,909	6,594	8,341	10,346	17,057	29,118
2007–08	13,001	7,415	18,876	19,896	14,709	5,176	6,990	9,288	10,705	17,647	30,247
2008–09	13,652	7,999	19,245	20,509	14,414	5,612	7,376	9,912	11,340	18,465	30,514
2009–10	14,542	8,763	20,078	21,317	14,512	6,074	7,983	10,658	12,290	19,460	31,730
2010–11	15,017	9,238	20,397	21,993	13,811	6,550	8,788	10,937	12,510	19,586	33,215
2011–12	15,845	9,978	21,230	22,899	14,285	7,506	9,440	11,954	12,936	20,625	34,680
2012–13	16,407	10,408	21,907	23,642	14,418	7,706	9,900	12,590	12,960	21,352	36,820
2013–14	16,948	10,725	22,617	24,482	14,209	7,791	10,242	12,779	13,590	22,018	36,720
2014–15	17,385	10,979	23,263	25,168	14,264	7,914	10,428	12,829	13,868	22,170	38,948
2015–16	17,871	11,306	23,917	25,826	14,432	8,242	10,769	13,193	13,878	22,570	40,670
2016–17	18,417	11,617	24,713	26,555	14,778	8,500	11,097	13,509	13,826	22,913	42,305
2017–18	18,949	11,929	25,446	27,356	14,304	8,778	11,201	13,982	14,460	23,542	43,848
2018–19	19,314	12,171	25,929	27,776	14,208	8,875	11,495	14,331	13,990	23,138	44,667
					Constant 2018–19 dollars[2]						
1989–90	$8,248	$3,987	$15,720	—	—	—	—	—	—	—	—
1990–91	8,488	4,172	16,089	—	—	—	—	—	—	—	—
1991–92	9,375	4,625	17,577	—	—	—	—	—	—	—	—
1992–93	9,729	4,960	17,784	—	—	—	—	—	—	—	—
1993–94	10,346	5,283	18,690	—	—	—	—	—	—	—	—
1994–95	10,519	5,473	19,092	—	—	—	—	—	—	—	—
1995–96	11,050	5,654	19,807	—	—	—	—	—	—	—	—
1996–97	11,334	5,749	19,982	—	—	—	—	—	—	—	—
1997–98	11,346	5,863	20,003	—	—	—	—	—	—	—	—
1998–99	11,828	5,998	20,470	—	—	—	—	—	—	—	—
1999–2000	12,072	6,047	20,676	$21,129	$14,379	$3,950	$5,441	$7,724	$11,965	$19,254	$30,649
2000–01	12,193	6,138	20,858	20,911	19,135	4,240	5,528	7,734	11,971	19,094	30,910
2001–02	12,589	6,390	21,555	21,650	19,065	4,585	5,854	7,954	12,199	20,122	31,346
2002–03	12,831	6,733	20,837	21,802	13,413	4,722	6,192	8,243	12,086	19,665	31,570
2003–04	14,034	7,545	22,060	22,874	17,070	5,165	6,945	9,613	12,347	20,456	34,841
2004–05	14,539	8,033	22,132	23,189	17,352	5,597	7,482	10,062	12,287	21,219	34,537
2005–06	14,791	8,264	21,947	23,127	17,096	5,865	7,903	10,153	12,403	20,647	34,311
2006–07	15,275	8,553	22,467	23,615	17,892	6,090	8,181	10,348	12,836	21,162	36,126
2007–08	15,554	8,871	22,582	23,802	17,597	6,192	8,362	11,112	12,807	21,112	36,186
2008–09	16,108	9,437	22,707	24,198	17,007	6,621	8,703	11,695	13,380	21,786	36,002
2009–10	16,993	10,240	23,463	24,910	16,959	7,098	9,329	12,455	14,362	22,740	37,078
2010–11	17,203	10,583	23,366	25,195	15,821	7,503	10,067	12,529	14,331	22,437	38,050
2011–12	17,634	11,105	23,628	25,485	15,899	8,354	10,506	13,304	14,397	22,955	38,597
2012–13	17,962	11,394	23,982	25,882	15,784	8,436	10,838	13,783	14,188	23,375	40,308
2013–14	18,269	11,560	24,379	26,389	15,316	8,398	11,040	13,774	14,649	23,733	39,580
2014–15	18,603	11,749	24,894	26,932	15,264	8,469	11,159	13,728	14,840	23,724	41,678
2015–16	18,996	12,018	25,422	27,451	15,340	8,761	11,447	14,023	14,751	23,990	43,229
2016–17	19,222	12,125	25,794	27,717	15,425	8,872	11,582	14,100	14,431	23,915	44,155
2017–18	19,342	12,176	25,973	27,922	14,600	8,960	11,433	14,272	14,760	24,030	44,757
2018–19	19,314	12,171	25,929	27,776	14,208	8,875	11,495	14,331	13,990	23,138	44,667

—Not available.

[1]Data are based on in-state tuition only.

[2]Constant dollars based on the Consumer Price Index, prepared by the Bureau of Labor Statistics, U.S. Department of Labor, adjusted to an academic-year basis.

NOTE: Average graduate student tuition weighted by fall full-time-equivalent graduate enrollment. Excludes doctoral students in professional practice programs. Data through 1995–96 are for institutions of higher education, while later data are for degree-granting institutions. Degree-granting institutions grant associate's or higher degrees and participate in Title IV federal financial aid programs. The degree-granting classification is very similar to the earlier higher education classification, but it includes more 2-year colleges and excludes a few higher education institutions that did not grant degrees. Some data have been revised from previously published figures.

SOURCE: U.S. Department of Education, National Center for Education Statistics, Integrated Postsecondary Education Data System (IPEDS), "Fall Enrollment Survey" (IPEDS-EF:89–99), "Completions Survey" (IPEDS-C:90–99), and "Institutional Characteristics Survey" (IPEDS-IC:89–99); IPEDS Fall 2000 through Fall 2018, Institutional Characteristics component; and IPEDS Spring 2001 through Spring 2019, Fall Enrollment component. (This table was prepared December 2019.)

Table 331.10. Percentage of undergraduates receiving financial aid, by type and source of aid and selected student characteristics: 2015–16

[Standard errors appear in parentheses]

Selected student characteristic	Number of undergraduates[1] (in thousands)	Any aid			Grants			Loans			Work study
		Total[2]	Federal[3]	Nonfederal	Total	Federal	Nonfederal	Total[4]	Federal[4]	Nonfederal	Total[5]
1	2	3	4	5	6	7	8	9	10	11	12
All undergraduates	19,308	72.2 (0.22)	55.9 (0.14)	49.0 (0.31)	63.1 (0.23)	41.2 (0.11)	46.1 (0.33)	38.7 (0.11)	36.7 (0.09)	5.9 (0.11)	5.2 (0.14)
Sex											
Male	8,406	69.1 (0.38)	52.0 (0.33)	47.8 (0.41)	58.9 (0.36)	37.4 (0.31)	44.9 (0.42)	35.4 (0.27)	33.2 (0.25)	5.7 (0.17)	4.8 (0.18)
Female	10,903	74.6 (0.28)	59.0 (0.24)	49.9 (0.39)	66.3 (0.31)	44.1 (0.24)	47.1 (0.41)	41.3 (0.23)	39.3 (0.21)	6.0 (0.17)	5.5 (0.18)
Race/ethnicity											
White	10,276	71.2 (0.42)	53.5 (0.41)	49.3 (0.41)	60.0 (0.40)	34.3 (0.32)	46.0 (0.43)	40.2 (0.37)	37.8 (0.36)	7.1 (0.18)	5.6 (0.17)
Black	3,006	80.0 (0.62)	70.6 (0.71)	45.9 (0.73)	72.4 (0.68)	60.1 (0.70)	43.4 (0.74)	50.8 (0.76)	49.4 (0.76)	4.2 (0.24)	5.2 (0.34)
Hispanic	3,723	71.4 (0.66)	55.6 (0.65)	49.4 (0.75)	65.5 (0.65)	47.1 (0.60)	47.2 (0.76)	30.7 (0.62)	28.9 (0.60)	4.3 (0.26)	4.4 (0.41)
Asian	1,399	62.0 (1.09)	40.5 (1.05)	49.9 (1.11)	56.6 (1.12)	32.1 (1.06)	47.6 (1.09)	23.3 (0.85)	20.9 (0.81)	4.7 (0.41)	5.4 (0.41)
Pacific Islander	83	69.1 (3.97)	54.2 (3.95)	49.8 (4.53)	60.5 (4.50)	42.7 (3.98)	48.1 (4.50)	31.8 (3.49)	30.9 (3.44)	3.1 (0.83)	2.8 ! (1.26)
American Indian/Alaska Native	160	76.7 (3.02)	62.5 (3.34)	44.1 (3.07)	70.8 (2.93)	56.1 (3.16)	42.6 (3.00)	30.9 (2.66)	29.5 (2.64)	2.6 (0.68)	3.3 ! (1.15)
Two or more races	661	76.8 (1.50)	59.9 (1.78)	53.6 (1.46)	67.9 (1.46)	45.9 (1.59)	51.2 (1.40)	42.6 (1.59)	39.9 (1.56)	6.1 (0.65)	4.7 (0.62)
Age											
15 to 23	11,368	74.7 (0.32)	56.4 (0.26)	56.6 (0.41)	65.8 (0.33)	37.6 (0.22)	53.5 (0.43)	40.5 (0.22)	38.1 (0.22)	7.5 (0.15)	7.6 (0.19)
24 to 29	3,536	69.9 (0.63)	58.6 (0.62)	38.5 (0.60)	61.6 (0.66)	50.6 (0.61)	35.9 (0.64)	37.4 (0.53)	35.6 (0.54)	4.0 (0.24)	2.5 (0.24)
30 or older	4,404	67.4 (0.54)	52.7 (0.61)	37.8 (0.64)	57.3 (0.53)	43.0 (0.54)	35.3 (0.65)	35.2 (0.50)	33.9 (0.49)	3.1 (0.19)	1.3 (0.13)
Marital status											
Not married[6]	16,098	73.5 (0.26)	57.0 (0.17)	51.4 (0.34)	64.8 (0.27)	41.2 (0.15)	48.4 (0.36)	40.2 (0.16)	38.0 (0.15)	6.4 (0.13)	6.0 (0.16)
Married	2,940	64.7 (0.67)	49.7 (0.68)	36.8 (0.76)	53.4 (0.69)	39.6 (0.59)	34.4 (0.78)	30.2 (0.53)	28.8 (0.53)	3.0 (0.22)	1.2 (0.18)
Separated	270	75.0 (2.10)	63.6 (2.29)	38.1 (1.90)	68.8 (2.18)	59.1 (2.19)	35.9 (1.87)	41.5 (2.08)	40.6 (2.05)	3.3 (0.75)	2.0 (0.49)
Attendance status[7]											
Full-time, full-year	7,239	86.4 (0.26)	69.8 (0.33)	66.9 (0.40)	76.7 (0.31)	46.3 (0.30)	63.8 (0.41)	54.7 (0.33)	52.5 (0.34)	9.2 (0.21)	10.5 (0.26)
Part-time or part-year	12,069	63.6 (0.33)	47.6 (0.26)	38.2 (0.40)	54.9 (0.33)	38.2 (0.23)	35.5 (0.41)	29.2 (0.23)	27.1 (0.21)	3.9 (0.13)	2.0 (0.15)
Dependency status and family income											
Dependent	9,772	76.9 (0.35)	58.9 (0.28)	59.2 (0.43)	67.1 (0.35)	37.3 (0.24)	56.0 (0.45)	43.2 (0.25)	40.7 (0.24)	8.2 (0.17)	8.3 (0.21)
Less than $20,000	1,713	87.5 (0.72)	80.3 (0.72)	60.9 (0.93)	86.9 (0.75)	79.5 (0.74)	59.2 (0.93)	40.1 (0.83)	38.3 (0.81)	4.1 (0.31)	9.5 (0.50)
$20,000–$39,999	1,644	84.6 (0.75)	76.3 (0.80)	62.4 (0.98)	83.0 (0.76)	74.4 (0.81)	60.8 (0.99)	42.1 (0.81)	40.7 (0.79)	5.3 (0.42)	10.9 (0.56)
$40,000–$59,999	1,281	81.4 (0.96)	68.3 (1.04)	65.1 (1.02)	75.5 (1.00)	56.8 (0.98)	61.8 (1.03)	48.1 (1.11)	45.9 (1.09)	8.2 (0.52)	10.7 (0.65)
$60,000–$79,999	1,157	72.7 (0.98)	50.3 (1.00)	58.4 (1.09)	60.1 (1.03)	19.8 (0.78)	54.9 (1.08)	44.5 (0.92)	42.3 (0.93)	8.6 (0.54)	8.1 (0.52)
$80,000–$99,999	946	69.9 (1.20)	46.3 (1.03)	56.7 (1.26)	53.7 (1.29)	4.9 (0.51)	53.0 (1.28)	45.4 (1.02)	43.1 (0.99)	10.3 (0.67)	8.2 (0.71)
$100,000 or more	3,032	68.6 (0.72)	40.5 (0.57)	55.0 (0.70)	50.7 (0.68)	1.9 (0.17)	50.4 (0.69)	42.2 (0.56)	38.6 (0.54)	11.2 (0.38)	5.3 (0.29)
Independent	9,536	67.3 (0.34)	52.9 (0.31)	38.5 (0.47)	58.9 (0.34)	45.2 (0.29)	36.0 (0.48)	34.2 (0.26)	32.5 (0.24)	3.5 (0.14)	2.0 (0.14)
Less than $10,000	2,909	69.8 (0.64)	56.0 (0.72)	41.0 (0.76)	66.3 (0.69)	53.8 (0.72)	38.7 (0.77)	35.0 (0.58)	33.2 (0.55)	3.6 (0.23)	3.7 (0.26)
$10,000–$19,999	1,783	74.6 (0.86)	64.7 (0.94)	39.9 (0.89)	70.1 (0.90)	61.6 (0.91)	36.8 (0.87)	41.0 (0.79)	38.9 (0.75)	4.3 (0.34)	2.2 (0.24)
$20,000–$29,999	1,372	72.7 (0.96)	58.5 (1.06)	40.6 (1.08)	63.4 (0.96)	48.8 (0.98)	38.2 (1.10)	37.4 (1.04)	36.3 (1.01)	3.1 (0.31)	1.7 (0.21)
$30,000–$49,999	1,467	65.8 (1.00)	53.0 (1.09)	35.3 (1.04)	53.0 (1.02)	40.0 (1.01)	32.8 (1.03)	33.6 (0.81)	32.3 (0.80)	3.2 (0.29)	1.0 (0.24)
$50,000 or more	2,005	54.5 (0.90)	34.1 (0.82)	34.6 (0.85)	39.5 (0.82)	19.7 (0.61)	32.2 (0.86)	25.1 (0.69)	23.2 (0.69)	3.2 (0.33)	0.4 (0.09)
Housing status[8]											
School-owned	2,756	86.8 (0.49)	65.7 (0.63)	76.5 (0.61)	78.6 (0.60)	37.1 (0.62)	73.5 (0.67)	59.5 (0.63)	56.8 (0.64)	12.2 (0.51)	17.1 (0.57)
Off-campus, not with parents	9,926	70.0 (0.39)	54.6 (0.41)	43.4 (0.43)	60.3 (0.36)	42.5 (0.36)	40.3 (0.45)	37.3 (0.36)	35.2 (0.35)	5.0 (0.15)	3.2 (0.15)
With parents	4,749	66.0 (0.57)	49.8 (0.54)	44.3 (0.68)	58.9 (0.58)	39.4 (0.48)	42.0 (0.68)	26.0 (0.52)	24.2 (0.50)	3.9 (0.22)	2.7 (0.24)

! Interpret data with caution. The coefficient of variation (CV) for this estimate is between 30 and 50 percent.
[1]Numbers of undergraduates may not equal figures reported in other tables, since these data are based on a sample survey of students who enrolled at any time during the school year. Includes all postsecondary institutions.
[2]Includes students who reported they were awarded aid, but did not specify the source or type of aid.
[3]Includes Department of Veterans Affairs and Department of Defense benefits.
[4]Includes Parent Loans for Undergraduate Students (PLUS).
[5]Details on federal and nonfederal work-study participants are not available.
[6]Includes students who were single, divorced, or widowed.
[7]Full-time, full-year includes students enrolled full time for 9 or more months. Part-time or part-year includes students enrolled part time for 9 or more months and students enrolled less than 9 months either part time or full time.
[8]Excludes students attending more than one institution.
NOTE: Detail may not sum to totals because of rounding and because some students receive multiple types of aid and aid from different sources. Data include undergraduates in degree-granting and non-degree-granting institutions. Data exclude students attending institutions in Puerto Rico. Race categories exclude persons of Hispanic ethnicity.
SOURCE: U.S. Department of Education, National Center for Education Statistics, 2015-16 National Postsecondary Student Aid Study (NPSAS:16). (This table was prepared June 2018.)

Table 331.20. Full-time, first-time degree/certificate-seeking undergraduate students enrolled in degree-granting postsecondary institutions, by participation and average amount awarded in financial aid programs, and control and level of institution: 2000–01 through 2017–18

Control and level of institution, and year	Number enrolled	Number awarded financial aid	Percent awarded aid	Percent of enrolled students awarded aid				Average award for students in aid programs[1]							
								Current dollars				Constant 2018–19 dollars[2]			
				Federal grants	State/local grants	Institutional grants	Student loans[3]	Federal grants	State/local grants	Institutional grants	Student loans[3]	Federal grants	State/local grants	Institutional grants	Student loans[3]
1	2	3	4	5	6	7	8	9	10	11	12	13	14	15	16
All institutions															
2000–01	1,976,600	1,390,527	70.3	31.6	31.2	31.1	40.1	$2,486	$2,039	$4,740	$3,764	$3,597	$2,949	$6,856	$5,445
2001–02	2,050,016	1,481,592	72.3	33.3	32.5	31.5	40.7	2,739	2,057	4,918	3,970	3,893	2,924	6,990	5,643
2002–03	2,135,613	1,553,024	72.7	34.1	30.9	31.5	41.4	2,947	2,189	5,267	4,331	4,099	3,044	7,325	6,023
2003–04	2,178,517	1,610,967	73.9	34.6	31.2	31.9	43.1	2,934	2,226	5,648	4,193	3,993	3,030	7,687	5,707
2004–05	2,260,590	1,689,910	74.8	35.2	31.3	31.7	44.0	2,939	2,343	5,958	4,463	3,883	3,096	7,872	5,896
2005–06	2,309,543	1,731,315	75.0	33.7	30.8	32.7	44.6	2,959	2,441	6,213	4,831	3,766	3,107	7,908	6,149
2006–07	2,426,599	1,766,783	72.8	32.1	30.0	32.2	43.5	3,131	2,526	6,598	5,018	3,885	3,134	8,186	6,226
2007–08	2,528,579	1,911,296	75.6	35.4	30.6	33.6	45.5	3,381	2,586	6,808	6,008	4,045	3,094	8,145	7,187
2008–09	2,542,748	1,974,063	77.6	36.4	31.7	34.6	46.6	3,927	2,706	7,518	6,723	4,633	3,193	8,871	7,932
2009–10	2,855,241	2,323,706	81.4	46.2	28.6	33.3	51.2	4,693	2,771	7,693	7,019	5,485	3,238	8,990	8,202
2010–11	2,648,101	2,179,582	82.3	47.8	31.0	35.8	50.1	4,758	2,843	8,393	6,624	5,451	3,257	9,615	7,588
2011–12	2,571,120	2,140,556	83.3	47.6	30.8	37.9	51.2	4,424	2,912	8,767	6,641	4,924	3,241	9,757	7,391
2012–13	2,510,994	2,077,909	82.8	45.5	31.2	39.8	49.4	4,452	3,051	9,223	6,896	4,874	3,340	10,096	7,549
2013–14	2,505,306	2,077,487	82.9	45.3	32.2	41.4	47.3	4,533	3,101	9,603	7,015	4,886	3,342	10,351	7,562
2014–15	2,471,045	2,062,252	83.5	44.5	32.9	42.8	47.0	4,599	3,214	10,066	6,925	4,922	3,439	10,772	7,410
2015–16	2,458,068	2,031,557	82.6	42.6	32.3	44.3	45.6	4,682	3,375	10,353	6,989	4,977	3,587	11,004	7,429
2016–17	2,491,341	2,063,481	82.8	42.3	31.8	44.7	46.1	4,700	3,463	10,772	7,080	4,906	3,615	11,243	7,389
2017–18	2,463,084	2,057,247	83.5	42.6	33.6	46.6	44.4	4,926	3,684	11,236	7,082	5,028	3,760	11,469	7,228
Public															
2000–01	1,333,236	872,109	65.4	30.0	33.5	22.7	30.7	2,408	1,707	2,275	3,050	3,483	2,469	3,290	4,412
2005–06	1,510,268	1,066,041	70.6	31.1	34.8	25.1	34.2	2,926	2,226	3,162	3,866	3,724	2,834	4,024	4,921
2010–11	1,802,335	1,421,369	78.9	46.0	35.9	27.2	40.2	4,765	2,676	4,160	5,780	5,459	3,066	4,766	6,621
2013–14	1,752,745	1,410,234	80.5	44.9	37.3	32.4	39.8	4,518	2,961	4,950	6,213	4,870	3,191	5,336	6,696
2014–15	1,743,119	1,412,510	81.0	44.2	38.1	34.3	39.6	4,592	3,080	5,165	6,243	4,914	3,296	5,527	6,680
2015–16	1,747,471	1,399,831	80.1	42.2	37.2	35.6	38.1	4,636	3,238	5,322	6,316	4,928	3,441	5,657	6,713
2016–17	1,752,934	1,407,452	80.3	41.6	37.2	37.2	38.2	4,641	3,332	5,498	6,440	4,844	3,478	5,738	6,721
2017–18	1,766,003	1,438,174	81.4	42.8	38.9	38.9	37.2	4,907	3,558	5,550	6,483	5,008	3,632	5,665	6,617
4-year															
2000–01	804,793	573,430	71.3	26.6	36.5	29.6	40.7	2,569	2,068	2,616	3,212	3,716	2,991	3,784	4,646
2005–06	906,948	695,017	76.6	26.6	36.8	34.2	44.4	3,071	2,752	3,573	4,166	3,908	3,503	4,548	5,302
2010–11	1,039,126	858,424	82.6	38.9	38.2	39.6	51.5	4,983	3,469	4,634	6,127	5,709	3,974	5,309	7,019
2013–14	1,076,356	892,192	82.9	37.9	37.4	45.4	49.5	4,597	3,724	5,435	6,658	4,955	4,015	5,858	7,177
2014–15	1,095,363	915,024	83.5	37.5	37.6	47.2	49.5	4,669	3,842	5,651	6,694	4,997	4,111	6,047	7,163
2015–16	1,144,409	948,342	82.9	36.8	36.8	47.2	47.2	4,707	3,905	5,812	6,710	5,003	4,151	6,178	7,132
2016–17	1,161,684	965,117	83.1	36.4	36.5	48.9	47.1	4,723	3,996	5,995	6,837	4,930	4,170	6,258	7,136
2017–18	1,183,447	994,201	84.0	37.9	38.3	50.3	46.0	4,958	4,250	6,091	6,862	5,060	4,338	6,218	7,004
2-year															
2000–01	528,443	298,679	56.5	35.2	28.8	12.1	15.3	2,222	1,009	1,004	2,396	3,215	1,460	1,452	3,465
2005–06	603,320	371,024	61.5	38.0	31.9	11.3	16.1	2,774	1,314	1,297	2,812	3,530	1,673	1,651	3,580
2010–11	763,209	562,945	73.8	55.7	32.8	10.3	15.3	4,557	1,418	1,677	4,802	5,221	1,625	1,921	5,501
2013–14	676,389	518,042	76.6	56.0	37.1	11.8	17.5	4,432	1,736	1,983	4,772	4,778	1,871	2,137	5,144
2014–15	647,756	497,486	76.8	55.6	39.0	12.4	18.2	4,504	1,839	2,031	4,595	4,820	1,968	2,174	4,917
2015–16	603,062	451,489	74.9	52.4	38.0	13.5	20.7	4,542	2,010	2,066	4,610	4,828	2,137	2,196	4,900
2016–17	591,250	442,335	74.8	51.9	38.6	14.1	20.7	4,527	2,098	2,112	4,667	4,725	2,190	2,204	4,871
2017–18	582,556	443,973	76.2	53.0	40.0	15.9	19.4	4,832	2,211	2,064	4,656	4,932	2,257	2,107	4,753
Private nonprofit															
2000–01	439,369	363,044	82.6	28.4	31.8	68.1	57.7	2,879	2,998	7,368	4,019	4,164	4,336	10,657	5,814
2005–06	471,069	401,908	85.3	26.5	31.3	73.8	59.8	3,426	3,117	9,932	5,270	4,361	3,967	12,641	6,707
2010–11	517,831	462,840	89.4	36.4	27.7	78.4	64.3	5,076	3,556	14,324	7,296	5,815	4,073	16,409	8,358
2013–14	513,574	458,526	89.3	33.7	26.1	81.1	61.1	4,738	3,760	16,832	8,064	5,107	4,053	18,143	8,692
2014–15	535,142	479,437	89.6	35.0	24.9	78.3	60.1	4,763	3,839	17,705	7,940	5,097	4,108	18,946	8,496
2015–16	540,835	484,705	89.6	35.2	23.8	78.7	61.0	4,998	4,013	18,452	7,925	5,312	4,266	19,613	8,424
2016–17	569,122	511,634	89.9	36.9	22.6	75.7	62.3	5,097	4,125	19,299	8,010	5,320	4,305	20,143	8,360
2017–18	550,431	496,948	90.3	35.8	23.8	79.2	60.6	5,215	4,369	20,626	8,100	5,323	4,460	21,053	8,268

See notes at end of table.

Table 331.20. Full-time, first-time degree/certificate-seeking undergraduate students enrolled in degree-granting postsecondary institutions, by participation and average amount awarded in financial aid programs, and control and level of institution: 2000–01 through 2017–18—Continued

Control and level of institution, and year	Number enrolled	Number awarded financial aid	Percent awarded aid	Percent of enrolled students awarded aid				Average award for students in aid programs[1]							
								Current dollars				Constant 2018–19 dollars[2]			
				Federal grants	State/local grants	Institutional grants	Student loans[3]	Federal grants	State/local grants	Institutional grants	Student loans[3]	Federal grants	State/local grants	Institutional grants	Student loans[3]
1	2	3	4	5	6	7	8	9	10	11	12	13	14	15	16
4-year															
2000–01	419,499	347,638	82.9	27.4	32.2	70.1	58.1	2,930	3,001	7,458	4,000	4,239	4,342	10,788	5,786
2005–06	460,832	393,429	85.4	26.0	31.2	74.6	59.8	3,437	3,121	10,002	5,264	4,375	3,972	12,731	6,700
2010–11	504,715	451,012	89.4	35.4	27.7	79.6	64.3	5,105	3,574	14,414	7,305	5,848	4,094	16,513	8,368
2013–14	504,584	450,228	89.2	33.1	26.1	81.6	61.0	4,758	3,762	16,966	8,069	5,129	4,055	18,288	8,697
2014–15	503,662	450,897	89.5	32.6	25.9	82.3	60.9	4,830	3,838	17,835	7,994	5,169	4,107	19,086	8,554
2015–16	505,549	451,276	89.3	31.9	25.0	82.1	59.2	4,931	4,017	18,826	8,002	5,241	4,270	20,011	8,505
2016–17	508,494	454,979	89.5	31.5	24.9	82.2	59.4	4,929	4,125	19,774	8,179	5,144	4,305	20,638	8,537
2017–18	516,571	464,446	89.9	32.6	24.9	83.0	58.8	5,146	4,373	20,885	8,187	5,253	4,464	21,318	8,357
2-year															
2000–01	19,870	15,406	77.5	49.2	23.9	25.7	49.5	2,269	2,892	2,168	4,509	3,283	4,183	3,135	6,522
2005–06	10,237	8,479	82.8	51.6	36.1	38.5	55.9	3,176	2,974	3,799	5,531	4,043	3,785	4,835	7,040
2010–11	13,116	11,828	90.2	73.3	26.8	29.8	64.3	4,553	2,835	5,059	6,944	5,215	3,248	5,796	7,955
2013–14	8,990	8,298	92.3	70.6	27.3	49.5	65.5	4,216	3,618	4,346	7,818	4,544	3,899	4,685	8,427
2014–15	31,480	28,540	90.7	74.3	8.4	14.4	48.4	4,288	3,881	5,768	6,855	4,588	4,153	6,172	7,336
2015–16	35,286	33,429	94.7	81.8	7.2	30.0	85.8	5,374	3,810	3,770	7,171	5,712	4,049	4,007	7,622
2016–17	60,628	56,655	93.4	81.7	3.7	21.1	86.9	5,641	4,145	3,778	7,041	5,888	4,326	3,943	7,349
2017–18	33,860	32,502	96.0	84.1	6.3	20.0	88.5	5,624	4,130	4,235	7,220	5,740	4,215	4,323	7,369
Private for-profit															
2000–01	203,995	155,374	76.2	49.3	15.2	6.2	63.5	2,312	2,494	1,540	5,517	3,345	3,607	2,227	7,981
2005–06	328,206	263,366	80.2	55.6	11.4	8.8	70.4	2,725	2,796	1,423	6,454	3,468	3,558	1,811	8,214
2010–11	327,935	295,373	90.1	75.7	9.0	15.5	82.0	4,494	3,028	1,884	8,064	5,148	3,469	2,158	9,238
2013–14	238,987	208,727	87.3	72.8	8.2	21.5	73.3	4,394	3,278	2,489	8,336	4,737	3,534	2,683	8,986
2014–15	192,784	170,305	88.3	73.1	8.6	20.7	76.6	4,421	3,571	3,193	7,906	4,730	3,821	3,416	8,460
2015–16	169,762	147,021	86.6	69.9	8.7	25.3	74.4	4,460	3,841	2,860	8,096	4,741	4,083	3,039	8,606
2016–17	169,285	144,395	85.3	67.9	7.6	18.9	73.6	4,354	3,490	3,319	7,871	4,544	3,642	3,464	8,215
2017–18	146,650	122,125	83.3	65.4	7.2	17.0	69.1	4,484	3,333	3,915	7,614	4,577	3,402	3,997	7,771
4-year															
2000–01	81,075	51,739	63.8	36.1	11.9	8.3	57.7	2,295	2,889	1,616	5,749	3,320	4,178	2,337	8,315
2005–06	157,705	116,237	73.7	46.8	8.9	10.9	67.2	2,490	2,945	1,641	7,046	3,170	3,748	2,089	8,968
2010–11	112,706	102,000	90.5	73.6	11.3	23.6	82.9	4,733	2,950	2,805	8,561	5,422	3,379	3,213	9,808
2013–14	90,264	80,686	89.4	72.5	10.5	34.5	78.1	4,624	3,021	3,065	8,581	4,984	3,256	3,304	9,250
2014–15	81,791	73,040	89.3	71.9	9.8	30.9	75.7	4,677	3,262	4,137	8,237	5,005	3,491	4,427	8,814
2015–16	59,269	51,636	87.1	65.5	10.9	38.5	73.4	4,641	3,715	4,128	8,413	4,933	3,949	4,388	8,942
2016–17	57,680	49,045	85.0	63.6	9.9	31.8	71.5	4,646	3,609	4,690	8,331	4,849	3,767	4,895	8,695
2017–18	52,371	43,342	82.8	62.2	9.1	30.6	65.1	4,888	3,822	4,880	8,330	4,989	3,901	4,981	8,502
2-year															
2000–01	122,920	103,635	84.3	58.0	17.3	4.8	67.3	2,319	2,314	1,453	5,387	3,355	3,347	2,101	7,792
2005–06	170,501	147,129	86.3	63.6	13.7	6.8	73.4	2,885	2,706	1,098	5,951	3,672	3,444	1,398	7,575
2010–11	215,229	193,373	89.8	76.8	7.8	11.3	81.5	4,374	3,088	875	7,799	5,011	3,538	1,002	8,934
2013–14	148,723	128,041	86.1	73.0	6.7	13.6	70.3	4,256	3,523	1,602	8,171	4,587	3,798	1,727	8,808
2014–15	110,993	97,265	87.6	74.0	7.8	13.1	77.2	4,237	3,856	1,556	7,667	4,534	4,126	1,666	8,205
2015–16	110,493	95,385	86.3	72.3	7.5	18.3	75.0	4,373	3,940	1,425	7,930	4,648	4,188	1,515	8,429
2016–17	111,605	95,350	85.4	70.1	6.4	12.2	74.6	4,217	3,394	1,464	7,643	4,401	3,542	1,528	7,978
2017–18	94,279	78,783	83.6	67.2	6.1	9.5	71.3	4,276	2,930	2,187	7,251	4,365	2,991	2,232	7,401

[1]Average amounts for students participating in indicated programs.
[2]Constant dollars based on the Consumer Price Index, prepared by the Bureau of Labor Statistics, U.S. Department of Labor, adjusted to an academic-year basis.
[3]Includes only loans made directly to students. Does not include Parent Loans for Undergraduate Students (PLUS) and other loans made directly to parents.

NOTE: Degree-granting institutions grant associate's or higher degrees and participate in Title IV federal financial aid programs. Data through 2009–10 are for students receiving aid, while later data are for students awarded aid. Students were counted as receiving aid only if they were awarded and accepted aid and their aid was also disbursed. Some data have been revised from previously published figures.
SOURCE: U.S. Department of Education, National Center for Education Statistics, Integrated Postsecondary Education Data System (IPEDS), Spring 2002 through Spring 2011 and Winter 2011–12 through Winter 2018–19, Student Financial Aid component. (This table was prepared December 2019.)

Table 331.30. Average amount of grant and scholarship aid and average net price for first-time, full-time degree/certificate-seeking students awarded Title IV aid, by control and level of institution and income level: Selected years, 2009–10 through 2017–18

Level of institution and income level	2009–10[1]				2015–16				2016–17				2017–18			
	All institutions	Public	Private		All institutions	Public	Private		All institutions	Public	Private		All institutions	Public	Private	
			Nonprofit	For-profit			Nonprofit	For-profit			Nonprofit	For-profit			Nonprofit	For-profit
1	2	3	4	5	6	7	8	9	10	11	12	13	14	15	16	17
	Current dollars															
4-year institutions																
Grant and scholarship aid[2]																
All income levels	$9,050	$5,980	$15,560	$4,420	$11,810	$7,190	$20,890	$5,920	$12,260	$7,370	$21,800	$6,170	$13,100	$7,930	$23,190	$6,510
$0 to $30,000	10,290	9,080	17,460	5,110	13,100	10,360	21,890	6,060	13,650	10,700	22,780	6,540	14,350	11,190	24,070	6,700
$30,001 to $48,000	11,170	8,330	18,710	4,530	13,980	9,810	24,570	6,460	14,460	10,130	25,720	6,020	15,280	10,630	27,130	6,970
$48,001 to $75,000	9,140	4,910	16,810	2,430	12,250	6,720	23,190	5,550	12,790	7,090	24,220	5,310	13,730	7,540	25,810	5,690
$75,001 to $110,000	7,150	2,270	14,650	1,220	10,080	3,440	20,740	4,880	10,550	3,710	21,720	4,950	11,450	4,020	23,230	5,140
$110,001 or more	6,300	1,590	11,560	1,020	9,210	2,150	17,270	4,250	9,660	2,280	18,220	5,210	10,340	2,430	19,360	5,770
Net price[3]																
All income levels	15,900	11,070	21,780	22,590	17,660	13,080	25,680	21,750	18,020	13,440	26,200	21,370	18,120	13,460	26,440	21,650
$0 to $30,000	12,570	7,720	15,970	21,770	12,690	9,170	19,450	20,720	12,660	9,260	19,610	20,080	12,730	9,300	19,860	20,660
$30,001 to $48,000	13,110	9,260	17,200	23,590	13,720	10,710	19,810	22,490	13,820	10,910	19,970	21,770	13,870	10,900	20,210	22,290
$48,001 to $75,000	16,610	13,290	20,270	26,710	17,430	14,560	22,500	24,800	17,560	14,660	22,740	25,290	17,670	14,770	22,780	24,990
$75,001 to $110,000	19,860	16,410	23,900	29,830	21,540	18,570	26,040	27,380	21,790	18,790	26,450	27,090	22,020	19,050	26,540	27,080
$110,001 or more	24,080	17,880	30,210	32,910	26,880	20,960	33,490	30,160	27,320	21,390	34,120	29,180	27,890	21,850	34,690	29,930
2-year institutions																
Grant and scholarship aid[2]																
All income levels	4,460	4,540	5,180	4,090	5,080	5,090	7,070	4,250	5,110	5,150	6,750	4,170	5,470	5,520	7,580	4,300
$0 to $30,000	5,250	5,450	5,540	4,590	6,010	6,140	6,770	4,650	6,020	6,200	6,450	4,540	6,410	6,600	7,260	4,680
$30,001 to $48,000	4,380	4,520	5,080	3,670	5,500	5,530	8,130	4,130	5,530	5,600	7,280	4,140	5,910	5,980	8,670	4,180
$48,001 to $75,000	2,240	2,250	4,150	1,960	3,330	3,290	7,850	2,790	3,480	3,430	7,730	2,940	3,700	3,670	8,310	3,040
$75,001 to $110,000	800	750	3,240	830	1,210	1,090	9,210	1,130	1,380	1,260	8,750	1,260	1,470	1,360	8,790	1,340
$110,001 or more	610	600	2,940	470	680	540	7,610	720	1,070	940	8,370	790	920	710	10,480	930
Net price[3]																
All income levels	8,930	6,290	16,270	18,360	8,500	7,050	18,180	20,640	8,800	7,200	18,830	21,110	8,670	7,060	18,400	21,180
$0 to $30,000	8,560	5,380	16,500	18,240	7,900	5,900	17,720	20,680	8,250	6,060	18,410	21,260	8,050	5,810	17,970	21,400
$30,001 to $48,000	8,720	6,330	16,620	19,070	7,640	6,610	19,480	20,990	7,920	6,680	20,160	21,430	7,690	6,550	19,600	21,500
$48,001 to $75,000	10,690	8,810	18,650	21,290	9,730	8,960	20,460	22,510	9,840	9,000	20,760	22,220	9,780	8,980	20,680	22,470
$75,001 to $110,000	12,230	10,630	20,760	23,020	12,200	11,430	22,840	24,290	12,360	11,530	21,890	24,000	12,430	11,580	23,060	24,090
$110,001 or more	12,760	10,820	20,930	24,620	13,030	12,110	27,890	25,100	12,890	11,910	29,390	25,340	13,380	12,380	29,730	24,830
	Constant 2018–19 dollars[4]															
4-year institutions																
Grant and scholarship aid[2]																
All income levels	$10,570	$6,980	$18,180	$5,160	$12,560	$7,640	$22,210	$6,290	$12,800	$7,700	$22,750	$6,440	$13,370	$8,100	$23,670	$6,650
$0 to $30,000	12,030	10,610	20,400	5,970	13,920	11,010	23,270	6,440	14,250	11,170	23,780	6,820	14,650	11,430	24,560	6,840
$30,001 to $48,000	13,050	9,740	21,870	5,290	14,860	10,420	26,110	6,860	15,090	10,570	26,850	6,280	15,600	10,850	27,690	7,120
$48,001 to $75,000	10,680	5,740	19,650	2,840	13,020	7,150	24,650	5,900	13,340	7,400	25,280	5,540	14,010	7,700	26,350	5,810
$75,001 to $110,000	8,360	2,650	17,120	1,420	10,710	3,660	22,050	5,190	11,010	3,870	22,670	5,170	11,690	4,110	23,710	5,240
$110,001 or more	7,360	1,860	13,510	1,190	9,790	2,280	18,350	4,520	10,080	2,380	19,010	5,440	10,560	2,480	19,760	5,890
Net price[3]																
All income levels	18,580	12,940	25,450	26,400	18,770	13,900	27,290	23,110	18,810	14,020	27,340	22,300	18,500	13,740	26,990	22,100
$0 to $30,000	14,690	9,020	18,670	25,440	13,480	9,750	20,680	22,030	13,210	9,670	20,470	20,960	12,990	9,500	20,270	21,090
$30,001 to $48,000	15,320	10,820	20,100	27,570	14,580	11,380	21,060	23,900	14,430	11,390	20,850	22,720	14,160	11,120	20,630	22,750
$48,001 to $75,000	19,410	15,530	23,680	31,210	18,520	15,480	23,920	26,360	18,320	15,300	23,740	26,390	18,040	15,080	23,250	25,500
$75,001 to $110,000	23,200	19,170	27,930	34,850	22,890	19,740	27,680	29,100	22,740	19,610	27,600	28,270	22,470	19,440	27,090	27,640
$110,001 or more	28,140	20,890	35,300	38,460	28,570	22,280	35,600	32,060	28,520	22,320	35,610	30,460	28,470	22,310	35,410	30,550

See notes at end of table.

Table 331.30. Average amount of grant and scholarship aid and average net price for first-time, full-time degree/certificate-seeking students awarded Title IV aid, by control and level of institution and income level: Selected years, 2009–10 through 2017–18—Continued

Level of institution and income level	2009–10[1]				2015–16				2016–17				2017–18			
	All institutions	Public	Private Nonprofit	Private For-profit	All institutions	Public	Private Nonprofit	Private For-profit	All institutions	Public	Private Nonprofit	Private For-profit	All institutions	Public	Private Nonprofit	Private For-profit
1	2	3	4	5	6	7	8	9	10	11	12	13	14	15	16	17
2-year institutions																
Grant and scholarship aid[2]																
All income levels	5,210	5,300	6,060	4,780	5,400	5,410	7,510	4,520	5,330	5,370	7,050	4,350	5,580	5,630	7,730	4,390
$0 to $30,000	6,130	6,370	6,480	5,370	6,390	6,520	7,200	4,940	6,280	6,470	6,730	4,740	6,540	6,740	7,410	4,780
$30,001 to $48,000	5,120	5,290	5,930	4,280	5,840	5,880	8,640	4,390	5,780	5,850	7,600	4,320	6,030	6,110	8,850	4,260
$48,001 to $75,000	2,620	2,630	4,860	2,290	3,540	3,500	8,340	2,960	3,630	3,590	8,070	3,060	3,770	3,740	8,480	3,110
$75,001 to $110,000	930	880	3,780	970	1,290	1,160	9,790	1,200	1,440	1,310	9,130	1,310	1,500	1,390	8,970	1,370
$110,001 or more	720	700	3,440	550	730	570	8,090	770	1,120	980	8,740	820	940	730	10,700	950
Net price[3]																
All income levels	10,430	7,350	19,020	21,450	9,030	7,500	19,330	21,930	9,190	7,520	19,660	22,030	8,850	7,200	18,780	21,620
$0 to $30,000	10,010	6,290	19,280	21,310	8,390	6,280	18,840	21,980	8,610	6,330	19,220	22,190	8,220	5,930	18,340	21,840
$30,001 to $48,000	10,190	7,400	19,430	22,280	8,120	7,030	20,700	22,310	8,270	6,980	21,040	22,370	7,850	6,690	20,010	21,950
$48,001 to $75,000	12,490	10,300	21,790	24,880	10,340	9,530	21,750	23,930	10,270	9,390	21,670	23,190	9,980	9,160	21,100	22,940
$75,001 to $110,000	14,290	12,420	24,260	26,900	12,970	12,150	24,280	25,810	12,900	12,030	22,840	25,050	12,690	11,820	23,540	24,590
$110,001 or more	14,920	12,640	24,460	28,770	13,850	12,870	29,640	26,680	13,450	12,430	30,670	26,450	13,650	12,640	30,350	25,350

[1]Data for 2009–10 are for students receiving aid, while later data are for students awarded aid. Students were counted as receiving aid only if they were awarded and accepted aid and their aid was also disbursed.
[2]Grant and scholarship aid consists of federal Title IV grants, as well as other grant or scholarship aid from the federal government, state or local governments, or institutional sources. Title IV grants include Federal Pell Grants, Federal Supplemental Educational Opportunity Grants (FSEOGs), Academic Competitiveness Grants (ACGs), National Science and Mathematics Access to Retain Talent Grants (National SMART Grants), and Teacher Education Assistance for College and Higher Education (TEACH) Grants. The average amount of grant and scholarship aid by income level was calculated based on all students who were awarded any type of Title IV aid, even those students who were awarded zero Title IV aid in the form of grants and were awarded Title IV aid only in the form of work-study aid or loan aid.
[3]Net price is the total cost of attendance minus grant and scholarship aid from the federal government, state or local governments, or institutional sources. However, average net price by income level was calculated based on all students who were awarded any type of Title IV aid, even those who were awarded zero Title IV aid in the form of grants and were awarded Title IV aid only in the form of work-study aid or loan aid.
[4]Constant dollars based on the Consumer Price Index, prepared by the Bureau of Labor Statistics, U.S. Department of Labor, adjusted to an academic-year basis.
NOTE: Excludes students who previously attended another postsecondary institution or who began their studies on a part-time basis. Includes only first-time, full-time students who paid the in-state or in-district tuition rate (if they attended public institutions) and who were awarded Title IV aid. Excludes the approximately 17 percent of students who were not awarded any Title IV aid. Title IV aid includes grant aid, work-study aid, and loan aid. Data are weighted by the number of students at the institution who were awarded Title IV aid. Totals include students for whom income data were not available. Some data have been revised from previously published figures.
SOURCE: U.S. Department of Education, National Center for Education Statistics, Integrated Postsecondary Education Data System (IPEDS), Spring 2011 and Winter 2016–17 through Winter 2018–19, Student Financial Aid component. (This table was prepared December 2019.)

Table 331.35. Percentage of full-time, full-year undergraduates receiving financial aid, and average annual amount received, by type and source of aid and selected student characteristics: Selected years, 1999–2000 through 2015–16

[Standard errors appear in parentheses. Amounts in constant 2018–19 dollars]

Year and selected student characteristic	Number enrolled[1] (in thousands)	Any aid						Grants				Loans[2]	
		Percent receiving			Average amount			Percent receiving		Average amount		Percent receiving	Average amount
		Total[3]	Federal[4]	Nonfederal	Total[3]	Federal[4]	Nonfederal	Total	Pell	Total	Pell		
1	2	3	4	5	6	7	8	9	10	11	12	13	14
1999–2000													
Total	**6,145 (—)**	**71.9 (0.59)**	**56.7 (0.44)**	**52.3 (0.67)**	**$12,670 (149)**	**$8,930 (87)**	**$7,720 (142)**	**58.5 (0.60)**	**28.3 (0.43)**	**$7,630 (121)**	**$3,420 (22)**	**45.6 (0.44)**	**$9,020 (88)**
Sex													
Male	2,687 (—)	69.1 (0.74)	53.9 (0.65)	49.7 (0.79)	12,640 (230)	9,040 (127)	7,760 (221)	53.9 (0.83)	24.5 (0.59)	7,600 (185)	3,350 (32)	43.8 (0.67)	9,210 (154)
Female	3,458 (—)	74.0 (0.73)	59.0 (0.62)	54.3 (0.86)	12,690 (170)	8,840 (100)	7,700 (144)	62.1 (0.75)	31.3 (0.61)	7,650 (127)	3,460 (30)	46.9 (0.64)	8,880 (110)
Race/ethnicity													
White	4,335 (—)	69.9 (0.73)	53.1 (0.59)	52.2 (0.73)	12,800 (200)	8,980 (111)	8,010 (183)	55.2 (0.70)	21.5 (0.53)	7,680 (154)	3,230 (32)	45.3 (0.61)	9,240 (120)
Black	675 (—)	88.0 (1.16)	78.6 (1.49)	54.7 (2.09)	12,430 (431)	9,290 (257)	6,630 (376)	76.2 (1.24)	55.7 (1.38)	7,160 (225)	3,670 (50)	59.2 (2.36)	8,230 (285)
Hispanic	500 (—)	77.1 (1.41)	65.6 (1.84)	53.1 (2.20)	11,580 (452)	8,380 (315)	6,450 (353)	66.7 (1.76)	45.4 (2.10)	6,920 (279)	3,570 (57)	42.7 (1.99)	8,840 (289)
Asian	372 (—)	60.3 (1.65)	47.8 (1.79)	47.9 (1.55)	13,300 (842)	8,750 (327)	8,010 (771)	53.0 (1.67)	31.7 (1.62)	8,830 (695)	3,730 (92)	33.0 (2.03)	8,480 (316)
Pacific Islander	41 (—)	62.3 (6.39)	56.0 (5.70)	48.8 (5.63)	13,070 (1,217)	7,860 (671)	7,660 (1,141)	53.1 (6.29)	31.9 (5.85)	7,840 (902)	3,360 (281)	40.7 (5.58)	9,220 (1,282)
American Indian/Alaska Native	42 (—)	81.5 (4.72)	75.0 (5.05)	61.7 (6.64)	13,050 (1,114)	8,180 (821)	7,290 (1,026)	78.7 (4.73)	50.8 (7.04)	8,000 (723)	3,790 (188)	44.6 (7.94)	8,340 (819)
Two or more races	93 (—)	75.6 (3.00)	60.6 (3.36)	57.1 (3.44)	13,330 (710)	8,560 (433)	8,560 (595)	62.0 (3.22)	34.2 (3.30)	9,030 (642)	3,580 (194)	43.8 (2.76)	8,780 (395)
Other	86 (—)	61.9 (3.54)	45.2 (3.64)	46.9 (4.04)	12,050 (1,092)	7,990 (507)	8,210 (1,084)	51.4 (4.32)	26.0 (3.70)	8,320 (878)	3,250 (243)	29.8 (4.02)	8,840 (928)
Dependency status and family income													
Dependent	4,612 (—)	70.2 (0.65)	53.4 (0.52)	53.7 (0.75)	13,110 (177)	8,590 (100)	8,600 (178)	56.2 (0.70)	21.1 (0.52)	8,330 (147)	3,180 (28)	45.6 (0.50)	8,920 (111)
Low-income[5]	990 (—)	85.4 (0.90)	78.1 (1.03)	65.2 (1.43)	13,420 (239)	8,610 (132)	7,270 (209)	82.3 (0.94)	70.4 (1.12)	8,570 (162)	3,630 (30)	50.5 (1.27)	7,530 (153)
Middle-income[5]	2,383 (—)	70.6 (0.85)	53.4 (0.79)	54.7 (1.01)	13,260 (268)	8,200 (120)	9,100 (263)	54.3 (1.00)	11.6 (0.47)	8,270 (250)	2,030 (52)	49.8 (0.80)	8,790 (128)
High-income[5]	1,238 (—)	57.3 (1.10)	33.7 (0.77)	42.6 (1.07)	12,410 (242)	9,720 (277)	9,010 (196)	38.8 (1.08)	‡ (†)	8,090 (194)	‡ (†)	33.5 (0.72)	10,970 (286)
Independent	1,533 (—)	76.9 (0.88)	66.8 (0.80)	48.1 (1.11)	11,450 (208)	9,750 (137)	4,760 (151)	65.5 (0.84)	50.0 (0.72)	5,810 (119)	3,730 (35)	45.6 (1.17)	9,310 (111)
2003–04													
Total	**7,562 (—)**	**75.3 (0.62)**	**60.3 (0.49)**	**54.9 (0.63)**	**$13,290 (127)**	**$9,540 (82)**	**$7,740 (161)**	**62.2 (0.58)**	**31.4 (0.31)**	**$7,720 (137)**	**$4,140 (24)**	**48.6 (0.42)**	**$9,520 (98)**
Sex													
Male	3,340 (—)	72.8 (0.89)	57.2 (0.83)	53.8 (0.78)	13,440 (167)	9,700 (112)	7,860 (177)	58.6 (0.82)	28.0 (0.62)	7,690 (155)	4,050 (37)	46.8 (0.77)	9,860 (138)
Female	4,222 (—)	77.3 (0.56)	62.7 (0.51)	55.8 (0.70)	13,170 (146)	9,420 (87)	7,650 (183)	65.0 (0.61)	34.2 (0.46)	7,740 (151)	4,210 (28)	50.0 (0.45)	9,280 (100)
Race/ethnicity													
White	5,137 (—)	73.3 (0.86)	56.3 (0.79)	55.2 (0.81)	13,240 (161)	9,510 (94)	7,880 (175)	59.0 (0.79)	23.9 (0.54)	7,540 (160)	3,940 (30)	48.4 (0.68)	9,710 (104)
Black	895 (—)	88.7 (0.90)	81.3 (1.08)	55.5 (1.68)	13,840 (298)	10,130 (202)	7,280 (270)	79.0 (1.27)	61.5 (1.64)	7,900 (249)	4,410 (38)	59.2 (1.90)	9,030 (243)
Hispanic	718 (—)	78.8 (1.09)	67.8 (1.21)	55.0 (1.32)	12,870 (280)	9,160 (174)	7,150 (278)	68.1 (1.15)	46.7 (1.17)	7,850 (200)	4,340 (61)	46.3 (1.19)	9,180 (244)
Asian	459 (—)	65.1 (1.55)	51.4 (1.46)	50.6 (1.70)	13,550 (332)	8,770 (243)	8,530 (285)	54.5 (1.74)	30.6 (1.40)	9,350 (279)	4,390 (78)	35.7 (1.28)	8,920 (317)
Pacific Islander	34 (—)	71.1 (5.10)	61.5 (4.79)	46.2 (4.95)	12,940 (1,267)	9,230 (944)	7,620 (1,235)	53.0 (5.12)	28.1 (4.85)	7,930 (834)	4,410 (310)	45.0 (5.02)	10,000 (1,149)
American Indian/Alaska Native	59 (—)	81.1 (5.18)	66.2 (6.31)	64.5 (4.42)	12,290 (849)	9,350 (493)	5,860 (1,017)	73.8 (5.79)	43.4 (4.64)	7,390 (800)	3,970 (211)	46.5 (5.70)	8,660 (572)
Two or more races	156 (—)	77.1 (2.12)	61.6 (2.12)	55.9 (2.11)	13,530 (552)	9,900 (388)	7,750 (475)	63.8 (2.18)	31.5 (2.39)	7,610 (403)	4,140 (120)	49.3 (2.34)	10,080 (524)
Other	104 (—)	72.2 (2.56)	56.6 (2.71)	53.2 (2.58)	12,340 (671)	9,280 (447)	6,870 (612)	61.7 (2.89)	35.5 (2.94)	7,090 (429)	4,230 (147)	42.9 (2.65)	9,390 (592)
Dependency status and family income													
Dependent	5,574 (—)	73.3 (0.79)	56.3 (0.68)	57.2 (0.74)	13,740 (158)	9,140 (87)	8,600 (177)	59.6 (0.74)	23.6 (0.39)	8,340 (170)	3,900 (28)	47.5 (0.62)	9,670 (110)
Low-income[5]	1,250 (—)	87.9 (0.70)	77.8 (0.80)	66.6 (1.00)	14,620 (277)	9,790 (129)	7,850 (265)	84.8 (0.80)	70.8 (0.92)	9,590 (225)	4,600 (26)	51.0 (0.91)	7,900 (178)
Middle-income[5]	2,886 (—)	72.7 (1.01)	55.4 (0.89)	58.0 (0.97)	13,450 (187)	8,560 (113)	8,690 (196)	57.2 (0.88)	14.8 (0.42)	7,690 (193)	2,440 (37)	50.4 (0.80)	9,680 (134)
High-income[5]	1,438 (—)	61.6 (0.98)	39.3 (0.82)	47.4 (0.91)	13,340 (232)	9,690 (164)	9,310 (231)	42.5 (1.02)	‡ (†)	7,930 (229)	‡ (†)	38.8 (0.83)	11,670 (204)
Independent	1,988 (—)	80.9 (0.77)	71.5 (0.79)	48.5 (0.91)	12,120 (143)	10,400 (122)	4,890 (135)	69.4 (0.79)	53.5 (0.82)	6,230 (92)	4,450 (33)	51.6 (0.85)	9,140 (122)

See notes at end of table.

Table 331.35. Percentage of full-time, full-year undergraduates receiving financial aid, and average annual amount received, by type and source of aid and selected student characteristics: Selected years, 1999–2000 through 2015–16—Continued

[Standard errors appear in parentheses. Amounts in constant 2018–19 dollars]

Year and selected student characteristic	Number enrolled[1] (in thousands)	Any aid: Percent receiving: Total[3]	Any aid: Percent receiving: Federal[4]	Any aid: Percent receiving: Nonfederal	Any aid: Average amount: Total[3]	Any aid: Average amount: Federal[4]	Any aid: Average amount: Nonfederal	Grants: Percent receiving: Total	Grants: Percent receiving: Pell	Grants: Average amount: Total	Grants: Average amount: Pell	Loans[2]: Percent receiving	Loans[2]: Average amount
1	2	3	4	5	6	7	8	9	10	11	12	13	14
2007–08													
Total	**7,527 (—)**	**80.1 (0.28)**	**63.9 (0.31)**	**63.7 (0.36)**	**$15,540 (118)**	**$9,780 (61)**	**$9,730 (106)**	**64.6 (0.37)**	**32.7 (0.29)**	**$8,670 (85)**	**$3,890 (17)**	**54.8 (0.32)**	**$11,390 (92)**
Sex													
Male	3,277 (—)	77.1 (0.44)	60.0 (0.47)	61.8 (0.49)	15,650 (170)	9,930 (110)	9,890 (131)	60.8 (0.54)	27.7 (0.42)	8,740 (113)	3,840 (26)	52.1 (0.56)	11,610 (140)
Female	4,249 (—)	82.4 (0.36)	66.9 (0.42)	65.2 (0.47)	15,450 (138)	9,670 (67)	9,610 (134)	67.6 (0.47)	36.6 (0.41)	8,630 (101)	3,910 (25)	56.9 (0.43)	11,220 (103)
Race/ethnicity													
White	4,983 (—)	78.1 (0.39)	59.6 (0.44)	63.2 (0.46)	15,540 (150)	9,670 (84)	10,080 (136)	61.1 (0.51)	24.1 (0.37)	8,560 (109)	3,700 (25)	54.0 (0.45)	11,700 (117)
Black	899 (—)	92.1 (0.58)	83.9 (0.86)	67.8 (0.85)	16,220 (199)	10,730 (133)	8,750 (194)	79.6 (0.92)	61.5 (1.06)	8,500 (169)	4,140 (45)	70.3 (0.84)	10,640 (179)
Hispanic	844 (—)	84.3 (0.71)	71.8 (0.88)	65.8 (0.91)	14,760 (233)	9,360 (129)	8,690 (215)	72.0 (0.85)	50.5 (1.02)	8,400 (146)	4,000 (40)	52.0 (0.92)	11,160 (247)
Asian	489 (—)	69.5 (1.35)	53.7 (1.33)	57.6 (1.47)	15,240 (341)	8,940 (216)	10,070 (301)	57.0 (1.61)	32.2 (1.21)	10,580 (288)	4,120 (52)	38.6 (1.29)	10,430 (297)
Pacific Islander	45 (—)	81.4 (3.79)	67.3 (4.93)	64.1 (4.44)	16,220 (1,073)	10,750 (853)	9,320 (878)	69.0 (4.14)	36.1 (4.59)	7,530 (622)	3,770 (252)	53.8 (4.44)	13,360 (833)
American Indian/Alaska Native	50 (—)	85.9 (3.32)	71.3 (3.81)	61.8 (4.53)	13,130 (940)	9,210 (623)	7,630 (772)	76.3 (3.20)	48.3 (4.15)	8,010 (715)	3,930 (201)	48.7 (4.70)	9,690 (716)
Two or more races	199 (—)	83.4 (1.31)	68.1 (1.72)	67.1 (2.01)	16,570 (471)	10,300 (277)	10,150 (419)	67.9 (1.66)	37.6 (1.87)	9,890 (401)	3,990 (104)	59.1 (1.92)	10,710 (409)
Other	17 (—)	79.8 (5.18)	72.9 (5.30)	50.9 (6.42)	14,990 (1,484)	9,440 (711)	9,990 (1,393)	67.3 (5.59)	51.9 (5.87)	9,040 (1,330)	3,770 (285)	54.7 (5.64)	8,780 (888)
Dependency status and family income													
Dependent	5,675 (—)	78.0 (0.34)	59.5 (0.37)	65.1 (0.40)	16,030 (144)	9,450 (77)	10,590 (123)	62.7 (0.44)	25.2 (0.27)	9,500 (104)	3,810 (20)	51.9 (0.38)	11,630 (116)
Low-income[5]	1,203 (—)	92.3 (0.49)	85.9 (0.59)	74.9 (0.62)	16,530 (190)	9,930 (94)	8,970 (156)	89.2 (0.57)	80.9 (0.66)	10,660 (133)	4,460 (19)	56.7 (0.75)	9,000 (170)
Middle-income[5]	2,825 (—)	79.3 (0.41)	59.4 (0.50)	67.1 (0.48)	15,940 (175)	8,870 (102)	11,000 (159)	61.6 (0.50)	16.1 (0.33)	9,030 (139)	2,410 (33)	56.0 (0.50)	11,640 (132)
High-income[5]	1,647 (—)	65.5 (0.66)	40.3 (0.65)	54.4 (0.76)	15,710 (250)	10,170 (226)	11,370 (194)	45.2 (0.84)	‡ (†)	8,930 (178)	‡ (†)	41.4 (0.68)	14,240 (241)
Independent	1,851 (—)	86.4 (0.47)	77.4 (0.59)	59.6 (0.74)	14,170 (143)	10,550 (92)	6,840 (122)	70.5 (0.64)	55.8 (0.64)	6,420 (84)	4,000 (31)	63.6 (0.74)	10,780 (118)
2011–12													
Total	**8,864 (—)**	**84.4 (0.36)**	**72.8 (0.51)**	**56.9 (0.46)**	**$17,260 (118)**	**$12,040 (84)**	**$10,200 (123)**	**72.4 (0.41)**	**47.1 (0.50)**	**$10,280 (102)**	**$4,920 (18)**	**56.7 (0.53)**	**$11,230 (83)**
Sex													
Male	3,868 (—)	82.3 (0.50)	70.1 (0.65)	56.2 (0.61)	17,480 (187)	12,240 (121)	10,350 (193)	68.9 (0.58)	42.9 (0.60)	10,480 (166)	4,900 (27)	53.9 (0.70)	11,330 (125)
Female	4,996 (—)	86.0 (0.42)	74.9 (0.60)	57.5 (0.53)	17,090 (149)	11,900 (97)	10,080 (157)	75.1 (0.46)	50.4 (0.62)	10,130 (122)	4,940 (24)	58.8 (0.58)	11,170 (105)
Race/ethnicity[6]													
White	5,369 (—)	82.6 (0.45)	68.5 (0.63)	57.0 (0.50)	17,120 (162)	11,980 (113)	10,420 (154)	68.8 (0.50)	37.8 (0.57)	10,090 (128)	4,720 (27)	56.4 (0.67)	11,450 (110)
Black	1,209 (—)	94.0 (0.54)	90.7 (0.70)	52.8 (1.24)	17,940 (286)	13,230 (174)	9,200 (334)	84.6 (0.72)	73.5 (1.07)	9,570 (213)	5,160 (29)	71.9 (1.12)	11,120 (185)
Hispanic	1,274 (—)	88.3 (0.74)	79.1 (0.91)	60.4 (1.12)	16,400 (345)	11,340 (174)	9,130 (355)	79.9 (0.84)	62.7 (0.94)	10,330 (298)	5,110 (38)	51.2 (1.09)	10,520 (200)
Asian	603 (—)	71.4 (1.77)	58.5 (1.82)	56.4 (1.60)	18,060 (596)	10,600 (276)	11,900 (570)	63.3 (1.71)	40.8 (1.60)	13,070 (494)	5,070 (71)	38.4 (1.59)	10,560 (445)
Pacific Islander	42 (—)	82.1 (3.87)	71.5 (5.20)	55.0 (4.22)	19,830 (1,846)	13,260 (970)	12,360 (2,082)	67.3 (4.42)	44.6 (4.76)	13,310 (1,897)	5,360 (164)	50.7 (5.38)	11,970 (1,303)
American Indian/Alaska Native	67 (—)	93.0 (2.55)	86.4 (2.44)	57.1 (3.82)	16,420 (1,104)	11,110 (572)	9,940 (1,257)	85.4 (3.24)	69.5 (3.37)	10,410 (874)	4,960 (186)	62.3 (3.60)	8,910 (676)
Two or more races	301 (—)	85.8 (1.46)	76.3 (1.76)	59.6 (2.14)	18,990 (606)	12,790 (328)	10,950 (638)	73.1 (1.71)	49.4 (1.94)	11,210 (463)	5,060 (93)	59.3 (2.06)	12,120 (393)
Age													
15 to 23	6,650 (—)	82.7 (0.39)	68.6 (0.54)	62.4 (0.46)	18,020 (140)	11,640 (101)	11,090 (138)	70.9 (0.43)	39.7 (0.44)	11,510 (124)	4,890 (21)	54.0 (0.53)	11,470 (110)
24 to 29	1,048 (—)	87.5 (0.76)	83.1 (0.91)	43.4 (1.01)	15,710 (268)	13,100 (183)	6,620 (395)	76.7 (0.95)	68.6 (1.11)	7,290 (224)	4,990 (41)	61.9 (1.20)	10,800 (137)
30 or over	1,165 (—)	91.1 (0.72)	87.2 (0.80)	37.8 (1.14)	14,650 (233)	12,940 (161)	5,470 (261)	77.0 (0.90)	70.3 (1.01)	6,460 (139)	4,970 (40)	67.3 (1.08)	10,530 (136)
Marital status													
Not married[7]	7,920 (—)	84.0 (0.37)	71.6 (0.53)	59.1 (0.47)	17,680 (123)	12,030 (88)	10,520 (128)	72.5 (0.41)	45.3 (0.50)	10,700 (108)	4,940 (19)	56.4 (0.54)	11,360 (90)
Married	828 (—)	86.9 (0.90)	80.6 (1.06)	38.4 (1.18)	13,790 (283)	12,010 (198)	5,980 (373)	69.5 (1.15)	59.5 (1.28)	6,670 (208)	4,780 (52)	57.3 (1.16)	10,310 (187)
Separated	117 (—)	97.2 (1.02)	95.9 (1.25)	37.5 (2.73)	14,610 (576)	12,650 (398)	5,530 (909)	88.6 (2.00)	85.0 (2.35)	6,690 (338)	5,160 (82)	71.4 (2.68)	9,960 (350)
Dependency status and family income													
Dependent	6,141 (—)	82.3 (0.39)	67.7 (0.56)	63.3 (0.46)	18,310 (147)	11,690 (106)	11,300 (139)	69.9 (0.43)	37.0 (0.43)	11,770 (131)	4,830 (22)	54.3 (0.55)	11,620 (117)
Low-income[5]	1,361 (—)	94.2 (0.58)	90.6 (0.73)	67.9 (0.94)	18,510 (250)	11,720 (130)	10,040 (298)	93.6 (0.61)	89.2 (0.76)	12,650 (228)	5,800 (17)	56.1 (0.89)	8,960 (147)
Middle-income[5]	3,045 (—)	83.2 (0.50)	69.0 (0.68)	65.8 (0.64)	18,360 (204)	11,250 (124)	11,420 (190)	70.1 (0.59)	34.6 (0.55)	11,420 (180)	3,710 (34)	58.2 (0.70)	11,530 (142)
High-income[5]	1,735 (—)	71.3 (0.73)	47.4 (0.89)	55.4 (0.81)	18,020 (334)	12,780 (281)	12,260 (310)	50.9 (0.83)	0.4 (0.07)	11,330 (301)	3,680 (469)	46.1 (0.92)	14,370 (269)
Independent	2,723 (—)	89.2 (0.54)	84.3 (0.64)	42.5 (0.80)	15,070 (184)	12,680 (116)	6,480 (247)	78.1 (0.67)	70.0 (0.79)	7,260 (131)	5,040 (28)	62.0 (0.86)	10,470 (99)

See notes at end of table.

Table 331.35. Percentage of full-time, full-year undergraduates receiving financial aid, and average annual amount received, by type and source of aid and selected student characteristics: Selected years, 1999–2000 through 2015–16—Continued

[Standard errors appear in parentheses. Amounts in constant 2018–19 dollars]

Year and selected student characteristic	Number enrolled[1] (in thousands)	Any aid: Percent receiving: Total[3]	Any aid: Percent receiving: Federal[4]	Any aid: Percent receiving: Nonfederal	Any aid: Average amount: Total[3]	Any aid: Average amount: Federal[4]	Any aid: Average amount: Nonfederal	Grants: Percent receiving: Total	Grants: Percent receiving: Pell	Grants: Average amount: Total	Grants: Average amount: Pell	Loans[2]: Percent receiving	Loans[2]: Average amount
1	2	3	4	5	6	7	8	9	10	11	12	13	14
Housing status													
School-owned	2,219 (—)	88.2 (0.50)	72.9 (0.66)	76.3 (0.59)	24,720 (279)	13,730 (179)	15,440 (277)	78.1 (0.59)	35.9 (0.67)	16,020 (286)	4,870 (40)	65.9 (0.75)	12,690 (156)
Off-campus, not with parents	3,222 (—)	84.4 (0.63)	74.6 (0.73)	48.9 (0.73)	15,000 (188)	12,000 (125)	7,590 (192)	71.6 (0.63)	53.0 (0.77)	8,000 (137)	4,940 (30)	56.1 (0.74)	10,940 (138)
With parents	2,502 (—)	82.7 (0.69)	72.0 (0.85)	52.0 (0.86)	13,780 (186)	10,630 (109)	7,180 (215)	71.2 (0.73)	52.1 (0.87)	8,170 (157)	4,970 (35)	49.4 (0.88)	10,210 (147)
Attended more than one institution	921 (—)	79.9 (0.74)	68.2 (0.94)	51.5 (0.87)	15,540 (249)	11,880 (159)	8,380 (263)	64.9 (0.90)	40.0 (0.86)	8,700 (203)	4,780 (44)	56.3 (1.00)	10,570 (163)
2015–16													
Total	**7,239 (—)**	**86.4 (0.26)**	**69.8 (0.33)**	**66.9 (0.40)**	**$19,360 (112)**	**$12,530 (62)**	**$11,940 (129)**	**76.7 (0.31)**	**44.0 (0.31)**	**$12,060 (98)**	**$4,980 (16)**	**54.7 (0.33)**	**$11,850 (80)**
Sex													
Male	3,202 (—)	84.2 (0.45)	66.7 (0.56)	65.4 (0.62)	19,730 (181)	12,990 (126)	12,150 (198)	73.3 (0.52)	40.0 (0.58)	12,230 (169)	4,900 (26)	52.0 (0.51)	11,980 (141)
Female	4,037 (—)	88.3 (0.31)	72.3 (0.41)	68.1 (0.51)	19,080 (163)	12,190 (91)	11,790 (166)	79.3 (0.40)	47.2 (0.46)	11,930 (131)	5,030 (22)	56.8 (0.49)	11,750 (117)
Race/ethnicity[6]													
White	4,171 (—)	85.7 (0.42)	66.7 (0.54)	67.6 (0.52)	19,540 (161)	12,510 (95)	12,430 (184)	73.8 (0.48)	34.0 (0.49)	11,920 (132)	4,810 (27)	56.0 (0.52)	12,350 (114)
Black	935 (—)	95.5 (0.42)	88.3 (0.60)	65.9 (1.23)	20,570 (402)	14,060 (230)	10,970 (396)	88.0 (0.66)	71.8 (0.88)	11,890 (305)	5,120 (36)	70.9 (1.08)	11,370 (239)
Hispanic	1,168 (—)	89.0 (0.65)	76.2 (0.81)	67.9 (0.84)	17,920 (349)	11,680 (187)	10,360 (355)	82.4 (0.74)	59.8 (0.90)	11,580 (283)	5,070 (37)	50.1 (0.90)	10,710 (216)
Asian	618 (—)	71.3 (1.30)	49.5 (1.45)	61.1 (1.37)	19,140 (499)	11,080 (293)	13,380 (549)	65.9 (1.35)	36.4 (1.35)	14,440 (449)	5,250 (65)	31.2 (1.26)	11,160 (476)
Pacific Islander	22 (—)	90.1 (3.86)	76.0 (5.62)	71.7 (5.83)	18,300 (1,628)	12,930 (1,248)	9,300 (1,536)	83.5 (4.79)	58.5 (6.28)	10,730 (1,366)	5,250 (229)	52.9 (7.06)	12,820 (1,545)
American Indian/Alaska Native	49 (—)	92.2 (2.28)	77.4 (3.78)	64.5 (4.46)	15,740 (1,546)	10,140 (653)	10,330 (1,789)	87.5 (2.76)	61.6 (4.57)	11,220 (1,534)	4,880 (182)	37.7 (4.26)	9,400 (608)
Two or more races	277 (—)	88.6 (1.39)	70.3 (2.07)	68.5 (1.60)	19,610 (640)	12,930 (459)	12,100 (633)	79.1 (1.59)	48.0 (1.84)	12,460 (516)	5,040 (86)	53.7 (1.95)	11,650 (465)
Age													
15 to 23	5,835 (—)	85.6 (0.28)	66.3 (0.37)	70.5 (0.39)	19,850 (132)	11,800 (65)	13,000 (141)	75.9 (0.34)	38.4 (0.33)	13,200 (119)	4,940 (20)	53.0 (0.37)	12,090 (96)
24 to 29	722 (—)	89.4 (0.73)	84.0 (0.84)	53.6 (1.25)	18,010 (284)	14,820 (207)	6,820 (266)	80.7 (0.86)	69.5 (1.00)	8,140 (172)	5,030 (47)	60.4 (1.01)	11,030 (183)
30 or over	682 (—)	90.7 (0.76)	84.4 (0.90)	50.4 (1.67)	16,780 (245)	15,030 (227)	5,030 (198)	78.9 (1.02)	65.1 (1.07)	6,880 (110)	5,110 (41)	62.3 (1.15)	10,940 (140)
Marital status													
Not married[7]	6,684 (—)	86.4 (0.26)	69.1 (0.34)	68.4 (0.39)	19,570 (117)	12,300 (64)	12,310 (130)	76.9 (0.31)	42.9 (0.32)	12,450 (102)	4,970 (18)	54.8 (0.34)	11,930 (87)
Married	506 (—)	86.6 (1.04)	77.8 (1.25)	48.9 (1.55)	16,750 (324)	14,950 (268)	5,870 (312)	72.4 (1.36)	56.1 (1.34)	7,050 (177)	4,910 (59)	52.0 (1.45)	10,860 (221)
Separated	48 (—)	91.4 (2.46)	87.2 (2.90)	53.2 (4.31)	17,580 (783)	15,240 (653)	5,200 (802)	87.2 (2.79)	80.9 (3.27)	8,000 (470)	5,510 (89)	67.9 (3.86)	10,740 (487)
Dependency status and family income													
Dependent	5,352 (—)	86.7 (0.30)	68.0 (0.37)	71.9 (0.41)	20,100 (135)	11,710 (68)	13,160 (145)	76.5 (0.35)	38.0 (0.35)	13,360 (123)	4,890 (23)	54.8 (0.39)	12,190 (100)
Low-income[5]	1,043 (—)	96.2 (0.40)	91.3 (0.62)	76.7 (0.92)	20,310 (308)	11,970 (158)	11,240 (301)	95.9 (0.41)	90.2 (0.65)	14,370 (261)	5,900 (16)	55.4 (0.95)	9,480 (217)
Middle-income[5]	2,691 (—)	88.2 (0.41)	71.8 (0.51)	74.5 (0.52)	19,930 (193)	11,140 (117)	12,890 (189)	78.9 (0.51)	40.5 (0.59)	12,910 (172)	4,010 (32)	58.4 (0.55)	11,720 (149)
High-income[5]	1,619 (—)	78.0 (0.71)	46.8 (0.77)	64.5 (0.79)	20,230 (306)	12,840 (226)	15,150 (325)	60.0 (0.79)	# (†)	13,300 (299)	‡ (†)	48.6 (0.75)	15,100 (285)
Independent	1,887 (—)	85.7 (0.53)	74.8 (0.63)	52.8 (0.97)	17,250 (196)	14,650 (146)	7,240 (206)	77.2 (0.62)	61.2 (0.68)	8,390 (134)	5,130 (29)	54.1 (0.74)	10,870 (106)
Housing status													
School-owned	2,089 (—)	90.4 (0.45)	69.5 (0.65)	81.2 (0.54)	26,380 (276)	13,840 (159)	17,520 (288)	82.4 (0.57)	35.9 (0.66)	17,590 (256)	4,970 (44)	63.6 (0.71)	13,380 (201)
Off-campus, not with parents	2,794 (—)	85.5 (0.47)	71.3 (0.61)	60.1 (0.72)	17,350 (167)	13,070 (120)	9,180 (167)	74.5 (0.57)	48.3 (0.66)	9,550 (120)	5,020 (25)	55.2 (0.60)	11,450 (115)
With parents	1,502 (—)	83.6 (0.64)	66.4 (0.85)	63.1 (0.93)	13,390 (232)	9,610 (158)	7,640 (183)	75.4 (0.74)	47.8 (0.84)	8,980 (165)	4,960 (38)	39.7 (0.96)	10,010 (225)
Attended more than one institution	855 (—)	84.7 (0.71)	71.6 (0.99)	60.9 (1.07)	18,060 (287)	12,440 (172)	10,490 (404)	72.2 (1.03)	43.4 (1.28)	10,730 (294)	4,870 (43)	57.5 (1.07)	11,170 (182)

—Not available.
†Not applicable.
#Rounds to zero.
‡Reporting standards not met. Either there are too few cases for a reliable estimate or the coefficient of variation (CV) is 50 percent or greater.
[1]Numbers of undergraduates may not equal figures reported in other tables, since these data are based on a sample survey of students who enrolled at any time during the academic year.
[2]Includes Parent Loans for Undergraduate Students (PLUS).
[3]Includes students who reported they were awarded aid but did not specify the source or type of aid as well as students who specified work study, vocational rehabilitation and training, and military education assistance, which are not separately shown.
[4]Includes Department of Veterans Affairs and Department of Defense benefits.
[5]Low-income students have family incomes below the 25th percentile, middle-income students have family incomes from the 25th to the 75th percentile, and high-income students have family incomes above the 75th percentile.
[6]The 2012 and 2016 questionnaires did not offer students the option of choosing an "Other" race category.
[7]Includes students who were single, divorced, or widowed.

NOTE: Full-time, full-year undergraduates are those who were enrolled full time for 9 or more months at one or more institutions. Data include undergraduates in degree-granting and non-degree-granting institutions. Constant dollars based on the Consumer Price Index, prepared by the Bureau of Labor Statistics, U.S. Department of Labor, adjusted to an academic-year basis. Detail may not sum to totals because of rounding and because some students receive multiple types of aid and aid from different sources. Data exclude Puerto Rico. Race categories exclude persons of Hispanic ethnicity. Some data have been revised from previously published figures.

SOURCE: U.S. Department of Education, National Center for Education Statistics, 1999–2000, 2003–04, 2007–08, 2011–12, and 2015–16 National Postsecondary Student Aid Study (NPSAS:2000, NPSAS:04, NPSAS:08, NPSAS:12, and NPSAS:16). (This table was prepared October 2019.)

Table 331.40. Average amount of financial aid awarded to full-time, full-year undergraduates, by type and source of aid and selected student characteristics: 2015–16

[In current dollars. Standard errors appear in parentheses]

Selected student characteristic	Any aid			Grants			Loans			Work study
	Total[1]	Federal[2]	Nonfederal	Total	Federal	Nonfederal	Total[3]	Federal[3]	Nonfederal	Total[4]
1	2	3	4	5	6	7	8	9	10	11
All full-time, full-year undergraduates	**$18,210 (105)**	**$11,790 (58)**	**$11,240 (121)**	**$11,340 (92)**	**$6,190 (57)**	**$10,220 (114)**	**$11,140 (75)**	**$9,810 (48)**	**$10,200 (238)**	**$2,430 (30)**
Sex										
Male	18,560 (170)	12,220 (118)	11,430 (187)	11,510 (159)	7,040 (103)	10,440 (182)	11,270 (133)	9,910 (106)	10,460 (341)	2,450 (51)
Female	17,950 (153)	11,470 (85)	11,090 (156)	11,220 (123)	5,590 (67)	10,050 (151)	11,050 (110)	9,740 (85)	10,010 (326)	2,420 (43)
Race/ethnicity										
White	18,380 (152)	11,770 (89)	11,690 (173)	11,220 (125)	6,370 (86)	10,390 (152)	11,620 (107)	9,900 (73)	10,770 (292)	2,360 (35)
Black	19,350 (378)	13,230 (217)	10,320 (373)	11,180 (287)	5,960 (105)	9,880 (373)	10,700 (225)	10,080 (200)	8,790 (838)	2,450 (98)
Hispanic	16,860 (328)	10,990 (176)	9,750 (334)	10,890 (266)	5,950 (101)	9,100 (327)	10,080 (203)	9,250 (186)	8,630 (697)	2,620 (86)
Asian	18,010 (470)	10,420 (276)	12,580 (517)	13,590 (423)	6,080 (177)	11,900 (481)	10,500 (448)	9,300 (406)	10,120 (992)	2,540 (104)
Pacific Islander	17,220 (1,532)	12,160 (1,174)	8,750 (1,445)	10,090 (1,285)	5,940 (527)	7,990 (1,426)	12,060 (1,454)	10,810 (1,276)	‡ (†)	‡ (†)
American Indian/Alaska Native	14,810 (1,455)	9,540 (614)	9,720 (1,683)	10,560 (1,443)	6,210 (490)	9,420 (1,713)	8,840 (572)	8,450 (544)	‡ (†)	‡ (†)
Two or more races	18,450 (602)	12,170 (432)	11,390 (596)	11,730 (486)	6,630 (315)	10,450 (558)	10,960 (437)	10,060 (393)	8,590 (876)	2,590 (200)
Age										
15 to 23 years old	18,680 (124)	11,100 (61)	12,230 (132)	12,420 (112)	5,330 (51)	11,180 (124)	11,370 (91)	9,860 (57)	10,260 (251)	2,380 (30)
24 to 29 years old	16,950 (267)	13,940 (195)	6,410 (250)	7,660 (162)	8,030 (189)	5,410 (209)	10,370 (172)	9,510 (112)	10,050 (804)	2,780 (149)
30 years old or over	15,780 (231)	14,140 (213)	4,730 (187)	6,470 (104)	8,250 (230)	3,940 (159)	10,290 (132)	9,720 (120)	9,410 (598)	3,430 (257)
Marital status										
Not married[5]	18,410 (110)	11,570 (60)	11,580 (122)	11,710 (96)	5,810 (56)	10,550 (115)	11,220 (82)	9,830 (51)	10,210 (243)	2,420 (30)
Married	15,760 (305)	14,070 (252)	5,520 (294)	6,630 (167)	9,550 (293)	4,640 (256)	10,220 (208)	9,470 (150)	10,350 (911)	2,730 (214)
Separated	16,540 (737)	14,340 (615)	4,890 (754)	7,520 (442)	6,970 (428)	4,450 (757)	10,110 (458)	9,900 (435)	‡ (†)	‡ (†)
Dependency status and family income										
Dependent	18,910 (127)	11,010 (64)	12,380 (137)	12,570 (116)	5,190 (54)	11,300 (128)	11,470 (94)	9,910 (59)	10,240 (250)	2,360 (30)
Less than $20,000	19,080 (352)	11,200 (175)	10,620 (354)	13,570 (306)	5,930 (37)	10,270 (356)	8,810 (235)	8,430 (227)	6,820 (629)	2,460 (83)
$20,000–$39,999	19,360 (369)	11,090 (181)	10,850 (321)	13,420 (281)	5,400 (57)	10,390 (310)	9,160 (224)	8,520 (195)	6,320 (572)	2,510 (80)
$40,000–$59,999	19,210 (396)	10,270 (199)	11,720 (380)	12,130 (333)	3,690 (85)	10,910 (371)	10,390 (245)	9,140 (214)	8,590 (676)	2,470 (89)
$60,000–$79,999	17,730 (413)	9,700 (259)	12,380 (367)	11,360 (338)	2,740 (157)	11,350 (349)	11,150 (317)	9,600 (266)	9,580 (772)	2,250 (101)
$80,000–$99,999	18,810 (481)	11,010 (331)	12,960 (439)	11,440 (429)	6,870 (1,075)	11,320 (430)	12,900 (388)	10,600 (354)	11,270 (671)	2,240 (119)
$100,000 or more	18,910 (266)	11,800 (177)	14,080 (282)	12,420 (261)	13,760 (1,299)	12,440 (264)	13,850 (228)	11,530 (174)	12,030 (394)	2,180 (55)
Independent	16,230 (184)	13,780 (137)	6,810 (194)	7,890 (126)	7,890 (135)	6,010 (189)	10,220 (99)	9,520 (72)	9,970 (526)	2,900 (110)
Less than $10,000	17,120 (307)	13,850 (220)	8,120 (310)	9,630 (230)	7,430 (164)	7,430 (297)	10,100 (167)	9,470 (132)	10,190 (1,082)	2,890 (139)
$10,000–$19,999	15,570 (364)	13,180 (274)	5,780 (318)	7,220 (190)	6,510 (212)	5,110 (278)	9,870 (193)	9,310 (165)	8,220 (677)	2,580 (206)
$20,000–$29,999	16,520 (553)	14,180 (388)	6,120 (585)	6,810 (368)	8,440 (428)	5,320 (557)	10,400 (339)	9,700 (225)	10,690 (1,706)	3,440 (560)
$30,000–$49,999	15,780 (377)	14,210 (331)	5,140 (322)	6,290 (157)	9,770 (390)	4,000 (257)	10,420 (265)	9,580 (199)	10,320 (1,104)	2,850 (256)
$50,000 or more	14,670 (431)	13,710 (414)	6,190 (432)	5,340 (255)	10,760 (704)	4,910 (331)	10,860 (374)	9,850 (222)	10,930 (1,337)	‡ (†)
Housing status										
School-owned	24,820 (260)	13,020 (149)	16,480 (271)	16,550 (241)	5,780 (109)	15,050 (260)	12,590 (189)	10,690 (147)	11,120 (449)	2,300 (38)
Off-campus, not with parents	16,320 (157)	12,290 (113)	8,640 (157)	8,980 (113)	6,810 (98)	7,620 (146)	10,770 (108)	9,610 (89)	10,320 (372)	2,740 (75)
With parents	12,600 (219)	9,040 (148)	7,190 (172)	8,440 (155)	5,260 (81)	6,710 (166)	9,420 (212)	8,670 (202)	7,860 (442)	2,450 (96)
Attended more than one institution	17,000 (270)	11,710 (162)	9,870 (380)	10,100 (277)	6,450 (168)	9,020 (383)	10,510 (171)	9,480 (150)	9,010 (443)	2,290 (71)

†Not applicable.
‡Reporting standards not met. Either there are too few cases for a reliable estimate or the coefficient of variation (CV) is 50 percent or greater.
[1]Includes students who reported they were awarded aid, but did not specify the source or type of aid.
[2]Includes Department of Veterans Affairs and Department of Defense benefits.
[3]Includes Parent Loans for Undergraduate Students (PLUS).
[4]Details on federal and nonfederal work-study participants are not available.
[5]Includes students who were single, divorced, or widowed.
NOTE: Aid averages are for those students who received the specified type of aid. Detail may not sum to totals because of rounding and because some students receive multiple types of aid and aid from different sources. Full-time, full-year undergraduates were enrolled full time for 9 or more months at one or more institutions. Data include undergraduates in degree-granting and non-degree-granting institutions. Data exclude Puerto Rico. Race categories exclude persons of Hispanic ethnicity.
SOURCE: U.S. Department of Education, National Center for Education Statistics, 2015–16 National Postsecondary Student Aid Study (NPSAS:16). (This table was prepared June 2018.)

Table 331.45. Average amount of financial aid awarded to part-time or part-year undergraduates, by type and source of aid and selected student characteristics: 2015-16

[In current dollars. Standard errors appear in parentheses]

Selected student characteristic	Any aid			Grants			Loans			Work study
	Total[1]	Federal[2]	Nonfederal	Total	Federal	Nonfederal	Total[3]	Federal[3]	Nonfederal	Total[4]
1	2	3	4	5	6	7	8	9	10	11
All part-time or part-year undergraduates	**$7,550 (81)**	**$7,000 (62)**	**$3,830 (79)**	**$4,210 (54)**	**$3,860 (57)**	**$3,420 (77)**	**$7,030 (67)**	**$6,700 (56)**	**$6,030 (234)**	**$2,370 (85)**
Sex										
Male	7,610 (124)	7,300 (131)	3,820 (92)	4,170 (65)	4,600 (132)	3,430 (86)	6,990 (113)	6,660 (94)	6,050 (342)	2,320 (106)
Female	7,500 (98)	6,810 (63)	3,840 (99)	4,250 (69)	3,410 (32)	3,410 (99)	7,050 (83)	6,720 (68)	6,030 (279)	2,410 (102)
Race/ethnicity										
White	7,570 (122)	7,040 (97)	4,080 (124)	4,140 (84)	4,040 (97)	3,580 (118)	6,980 (91)	6,560 (76)	6,250 (310)	2,290 (102)
Black	8,480 (155)	7,680 (137)	3,740 (143)	4,310 (97)	3,670 (76)	3,450 (145)	7,100 (125)	6,910 (128)	5,280 (309)	2,210 (182)
Hispanic	6,430 (133)	6,110 (118)	3,060 (103)	3,960 (81)	3,630 (70)	2,760 (97)	6,820 (142)	6,620 (138)	5,320 (384)	2,560 (172)
Asian	7,860 (348)	6,880 (278)	4,850 (284)	5,320 (242)	4,020 (152)	4,370 (271)	8,390 (439)	7,730 (430)	7,790 (1,157)	2,850 (182)
Pacific Islander	8,610 (1,095)	8,800 (1,285)	2,910 (586)	4,050 (477)	6,220 (1,551)	2,800 (602)	7,290 (698)	7,260 (704)	‡ (†)	‡ (†)
American Indian/ Alaska Native	6,400 (408)	6,170 (408)	2,920 (436)	3,680 (284)	3,540 (252)	2,750 (451)	6,000 (568)	6,040 (600)	‡ (†)	‡ (†)
Two or more races	8,430 (314)	7,530 (249)	4,220 (364)	4,620 (256)	4,060 (219)	3,860 (363)	6,920 (255)	6,670 (221)	6,430 (1,047)	2,190 (512)
Age										
15 to 23	7,800 (127)	6,220 (87)	4,960 (126)	5,180 (94)	3,450 (48)	4,500 (121)	6,950 (140)	6,400 (118)	6,440 (335)	2,200 (77)
24 to 29	7,670 (126)	7,670 (129)	2,840 (85)	3,560 (63)	4,250 (125)	2,420 (83)	7,170 (84)	6,980 (80)	5,660 (317)	2,520 (171)
30 or older	7,070 (98)	7,570 (98)	2,590 (67)	3,260 (49)	4,080 (80)	2,280 (64)	7,020 (83)	6,870 (81)	5,320 (358)	3,060 (264)
Marital status										
Not married[5]	7,670 (97)	6,840 (70)	4,130 (94)	4,450 (64)	3,670 (58)	3,690 (90)	7,010 (85)	6,630 (69)	6,210 (262)	2,320 (77)
Married	6,980 (109)	7,520 (115)	2,630 (76)	3,220 (63)	4,580 (122)	2,350 (76)	7,110 (104)	7,000 (95)	5,110 (345)	2,890 (384)
Separated	8,130 (366)	8,320 (339)	2,710 (332)	3,740 (205)	4,630 (308)	2,450 (355)	6,860 (234)	6,670 (232)	4,210 (804)	‡ (†)
Dependency status and family income										
Dependent	8,040 (148)	6,140 (96)	5,240 (145)	5,450 (110)	3,360 (38)	4,770 (137)	7,040 (165)	6,450 (137)	6,430 (374)	2,210 (77)
Less than $20,000	7,540 (182)	5,740 (127)	4,120 (180)	5,420 (132)	3,630 (50)	3,860 (173)	5,870 (199)	5,620 (197)	5,720 (585)	2,260 (141)
$20,000-$39,999	8,130 (257)	6,090 (201)	4,660 (184)	5,710 (152)	3,550 (57)	4,440 (188)	6,390 (316)	6,200 (340)	4,640 (611)	2,570 (143)
$40,000-$59,999	7,400 (291)	5,560 (226)	4,410 (250)	4,690 (194)	2,300 (65)	4,240 (254)	6,360 (295)	6,260 (312)	3,950 (535)	2,090 (162)
$60,000-$79,999	6,740 (311)	5,890 (258)	4,440 (264)	3,960 (232)	2,020 (226)	3,980 (253)	6,680 (326)	6,180 (277)	5,460 (566)	1,940 (229)
$80,000-$99,999	8,130 (513)	6,490 (413)	6,010 (503)	5,280 (490)	2,910 ! (1,170)	5,200 (488)	7,560 (423)	6,600 (398)	7,490 (963)	2,170 (277)
$100,000 or more	9,850 (456)	7,910 (399)	7,830 (421)	6,920 (361)	10,480 (1,751)	6,930 (367)	8,950 (445)	7,600 (389)	8,330 (853)	1,810 (175)
Independent	7,250 (76)	7,500 (79)	2,820 (58)	3,480 (40)	4,110 (81)	2,450 (57)	7,020 (52)	6,840 (47)	5,640 (248)	2,640 (149)
Less than $10,000	7,800 (134)	7,740 (116)	3,150 (136)	4,100 (88)	4,140 (98)	2,760 (130)	6,880 (96)	6,650 (92)	5,950 (423)	2,300 (156)
$10,000-$19,999	7,300 (143)	7,010 (145)	2,650 (96)	3,530 (67)	3,500 (92)	2,200 (87)	6,750 (132)	6,560 (125)	5,630 (308)	2,860 (213)
$20,000-$29,999	7,110 (191)	7,400 (183)	2,470 (112)	3,090 (70)	4,080 (171)	2,100 (94)	6,930 (159)	6,690 (132)	5,770 (764)	3,100 (335)
$30,000-$49,999	7,290 (196)	7,610 (216)	2,670 (112)	3,290 (84)	4,670 (220)	2,370 (109)	7,190 (144)	7,050 (142)	5,300 (461)	3,010 (536)
$50,000 or more	6,440 (148)	7,770 (179)	2,890 (100)	2,760 (86)	4,880 (226)	2,590 (96)	7,550 (152)	7,490 (150)	5,350 (442)	‡ (†)
Housing status										
School-owned	13,740 (558)	9,340 (330)	8,670 (485)	8,870 (442)	4,110 (163)	8,010 (480)	8,660 (350)	7,780 (314)	7,590 (833)	1,880 (136)
Off-campus, not with parents	7,350 (99)	7,250 (94)	3,300 (67)	3,730 (43)	3,960 (83)	2,850 (58)	7,040 (73)	6,750 (63)	6,010 (297)	2,500 (117)
With parents	5,910 (97)	5,340 (89)	3,260 (99)	4,020 (76)	3,370 (51)	3,000 (101)	6,020 (129)	5,810 (133)	4,920 (295)	2,780 (175)
Attended more than one institution	8,680 (178)	7,980 (157)	4,020 (157)	4,430 (103)	4,370 (152)	3,570 (158)	7,280 (177)	6,940 (177)	6,840 (419)	1,940 (156)

†Not applicable.

‡Reporting standards not met. Either there are too few cases for a reliable estimate or the coefficient of variation (CV) is 50 percent or greater.

[1] Includes students who reported they were awarded aid but did not specify the source or type of aid.

[2] Includes Department of Veterans Affairs and Department of Defense benefits.

[3] Includes Parent Loans for Undergraduate Students (PLUS).

[4] Details on federal and nonfederal work-study participants are not available.

[5] Includes students who were single, divorced, or widowed.

NOTE: Aid averages are for those students who received the specified type of aid. Detail may not sum to totals because of rounding and because some students receive multiple types of aid and aid from different sources. Part-time or part-year undergraduates include students enrolled part time for 9 or more months and students enrolled less than 9 months either part time or full time. Data include undergraduates in degree-granting and non-degree-granting institutions. Data exclude students attending institutions in Puerto Rico. Race categories exclude persons of Hispanic ethnicity.

SOURCE: U.S. Department of Education, National Center for Education Statistics, 2015-16 National Postsecondary Student Aid Study (NPSAS:16). (This table was prepared June 2018.)

Table 331.50. Aid status and sources of aid for full-time and part-time undergraduates, by control and level of institution: 2011–12 and 2015–16

[Standard errors appear in parentheses]

Control and level of institution	Number of undergraduates[1] (in thousands)	Aid status (percent of students)											
		Nonaided		Any aid[2,3]		Source of aid: Federal[3]		State		Institutional		Other[2]	
1	2	3		4		5		6		7		8	
2011–12													
Full-time, full-year student[4]													
All institutions	**8,864**	**15.6**	**(0.36)**	**84.4**	**(0.36)**	**72.8**	**(0.51)**	**26.5**	**(0.48)**	**31.0**	**(0.45)**	**28.1**	**(0.36)**
Public	5,997	19.6	(0.47)	80.4	(0.47)	68.4	(0.61)	30.2	(0.64)	22.0	(0.52)	24.3	(0.36)
4-year doctoral	2,893	16.1	(0.46)	83.9	(0.46)	70.9	(0.47)	31.2	(0.69)	32.2	(0.90)	28.1	(0.49)
Other 4-year	969	16.5	(0.93)	83.5	(0.93)	72.7	(1.34)	31.3	(1.36)	21.6	(1.32)	27.5	(0.90)
2-year	2,104	25.5	(1.03)	74.5	(1.03)	63.0	(1.24)	28.3	(1.31)	8.3	(0.54)	17.8	(0.57)
Less-than-2-year	31	28.4	(4.50)	71.6	(4.50)	67.8	(4.72)	18.2 !	(6.85)	‡	(†)	18.9	(4.08)
Private, nonprofit	1,875	8.4	(0.55)	91.6	(0.55)	76.1	(0.75)	25.3	(0.87)	73.7	(0.97)	39.6	(0.96)
4-year doctoral	990	9.6	(0.84)	90.4	(0.84)	74.3	(0.94)	23.3	(1.29)	74.5	(1.29)	38.9	(1.50)
Other 4-year	849	6.9	(0.68)	93.1	(0.68)	78.0	(1.20)	28.0	(1.24)	74.3	(1.38)	40.5	(1.08)
Less-than-4-year	36	9.8 !	(4.12)	90.2	(4.12)	78.1	(5.04)	19.5 !	(7.60)	34.5 !	(11.90)	38.4	(4.24)
Private, for-profit	992	5.2	(0.46)	94.8	(0.46)	93.1	(0.51)	6.9	(0.70)	4.8	(0.72)	29.2	(0.89)
2-year and above	859	5.4	(0.53)	94.6	(0.53)	92.8	(0.59)	7.5	(0.78)	5.4	(0.83)	30.7	(0.96)
Less-than-2-year	133	4.1	(0.75)	95.9	(0.75)	95.2	(0.79)	‡	(†)	‡	(†)	19.3	(2.30)
Part-time or part-year students[5]													
All institutions	**14,192**	**37.9**	**(1.05)**	**62.1**	**(1.05)**	**51.1**	**(1.10)**	**14.6**	**(0.51)**	**7.3**	**(0.27)**	**16.4**	**(0.34)**
Public	10,929	44.0	(1.18)	56.0	(1.18)	44.5	(1.22)	16.7	(0.63)	5.6	(0.24)	13.4	(0.36)
4-year doctoral	1,875	33.9	(1.04)	66.1	(1.04)	53.4	(0.81)	15.1	(0.61)	13.4	(0.87)	20.7	(0.73)
Other 4-year	1,477	40.5	(1.46)	59.5	(1.46)	49.7	(1.66)	12.0	(0.74)	6.8	(0.80)	16.9	(0.94)
2-year	7,521	47.3	(1.36)	52.7	(1.36)	41.2	(1.39)	18.0	(0.87)	3.5	(0.25)	10.9	(0.39)
Less-than-2-year	56	29.8	(4.21)	70.2	(4.21)	60.3	(4.47)	19.7	(5.84)	3.1 !	(1.37)	9.2	(2.44)
Private, nonprofit	1,135	22.6	(1.47)	77.4	(1.47)	61.0	(1.61)	13.5	(1.28)	30.2	(1.95)	28.7	(1.58)
4-year doctoral	557	24.0	(1.87)	76.0	(1.87)	57.9	(2.12)	9.5	(1.49)	30.1	(2.15)	28.1	(2.61)
Other 4-year	527	20.8	(2.42)	79.2	(2.42)	64.0	(2.54)	18.6	(2.12)	32.3	(3.36)	30.2	(2.14)
Less-than-4-year	51	25.7	(4.47)	74.3	(4.47)	64.3	(3.22)	‡	(†)	‡	(†)	18.2	(4.18)
Private, for-profit	2,128	14.6	(1.02)	85.4	(1.02)	79.7	(0.83)	4.2	(0.52)	3.7	(0.71)	25.3	(1.09)
2-year and above	1,790	14.7	(1.20)	85.3	(1.20)	78.8	(0.97)	4.2	(0.49)	3.6	(0.68)	27.0	(1.22)
Less-than-2-year	337	14.1	(1.39)	85.9	(1.39)	84.6	(1.40)	‡	(†)	‡	(†)	16.3	(1.71)
2015–16													
Full-time, full-year students[4]													
All institutions	**7,239**	**13.6**	**(0.26)**	**86.4**	**(0.26)**	**69.8**	**(0.33)**	**29.7**	**(0.44)**	**42.8**	**(0.45)**	**28.6**	**(0.36)**
Public	5,023	16.0	(0.34)	84.0	(0.34)	67.7	(0.42)	34.1	(0.55)	32.7	(0.58)	25.8	(0.43)
4-year doctoral	2,849	13.3	(0.38)	86.7	(0.38)	69.4	(0.48)	34.0	(0.61)	42.8	(0.66)	29.0	(0.54)
Other 4-year	765	14.7	(0.78)	85.3	(0.78)	72.6	(0.98)	36.0	(1.61)	29.5	(1.76)	27.5	(1.39)
2-year	1,391	22.2	(0.79)	77.8	(0.79)	61.6	(0.85)	33.4	(1.07)	14.0	(1.22)	18.6	(0.77)
Less-than-2-year	19	18.0 !	(6.98)	82.0	(6.98)	67.0	(8.01)	12.5	(2.54)	23.1 !	(10.82)	9.2 !	(3.31)
Private, nonprofit	1,735	8.3	(0.48)	91.7	(0.48)	70.3	(0.61)	22.6	(0.73)	75.1	(0.82)	37.8	(0.81)
4-year doctoral	1,011	9.0	(0.62)	91.0	(0.62)	67.5	(0.89)	21.4	(0.99)	78.1	(1.07)	39.7	(1.07)
Other 4-year	684	7.1	(0.72)	92.9	(0.72)	73.7	(0.89)	25.1	(1.06)	73.7	(1.46)	36.3	(1.08)
Less-than-4-year	40	13.1	(2.20)	86.9	(2.20)	81.7	(3.76)	‡	(†)	22.3 !	(11.17)	14.0 !	(6.88)
Private, for-profit	481	7.1	(0.59)	92.9	(0.59)	89.4	(0.71)	9.5	(1.01)	30.8	(3.37)	24.3	(0.91)
2-year and above	382	6.4	(0.65)	93.6	(0.65)	89.7	(0.77)	10.2	(1.15)	36.4	(3.98)	26.8	(1.14)
Less-than-2-year	99	9.5	(1.36)	90.5	(1.36)	88.6	(1.74)	7.2	(1.84)	9.1	(2.52)	14.6	(1.55)
Part-time or part-year students[5]													
All institutions	**12,069**	**36.4**	**(0.33)**	**63.6**	**(0.33)**	**47.6**	**(0.26)**	**18.0**	**(0.34)**	**13.9**	**(0.31)**	**17.0**	**(0.30)**
Public	9,468	41.5	(0.39)	58.5	(0.39)	42.0	(0.30)	20.1	(0.43)	9.8	(0.27)	14.9	(0.31)
4-year doctoral	1,825	27.6	(0.74)	72.4	(0.74)	55.5	(0.71)	20.7	(0.80)	24.6	(0.75)	22.2	(0.68)
Other 4-year	1,346	39.7	(1.33)	60.3	(1.33)	44.8	(1.25)	16.9	(0.94)	12.2	(0.93)	18.2	(0.81)
2-year	6,249	45.9	(0.54)	54.1	(0.54)	37.5	(0.38)	20.7	(0.62)	4.9	(0.29)	12.1	(0.40)
Less-than-2-year	48	33.3	(7.04)	66.7	(7.04)	38.4	(2.59)	10.8	(2.31)	23.0	(5.88)	10.8	(3.21)
Private, nonprofit	1,220	21.0	(0.82)	79.0	(0.82)	58.0	(1.03)	12.5	(0.76)	32.6	(1.28)	29.2	(1.19)
4-year doctoral	622	19.9	(1.27)	80.1	(1.27)	53.5	(1.58)	11.9	(0.97)	33.9	(1.89)	34.3	(1.80)
Other 4-year	540	22.1	(0.94)	77.9	(0.94)	61.6	(1.13)	12.8	(1.03)	33.5	(1.81)	24.2	(1.38)
Less-than-4-year	58	21.8	(4.07)	78.2	(4.07)	73.2	(4.47)	15.5 !	(7.70)	10.4	(2.15)	21.4	(5.96)
Private, for-profit	1,381	15.5	(0.48)	84.5	(0.48)	77.0	(0.59)	8.4	(0.75)	25.5	(1.30)	21.2	(0.78)
2-year and above	1,140	14.5	(0.54)	85.5	(0.54)	77.5	(0.67)	9.1	(0.88)	28.9	(1.52)	22.2	(0.70)
Less-than-2-year	240	20.3	(1.47)	79.7	(1.47)	74.6	(1.55)	5.4	(1.18)	9.4	(2.57)	16.5	(3.08)

†Not applicable.

!Interpret data with caution. The coefficient of variation (CV) for this estimate is between 30 and 50 percent.

‡Reporting standards not met. The coefficient of variation (CV) for this estimate is 50 percent or greater.

[1]Numbers of undergraduates may not equal figures reported in other tables, since these data are based on a sample survey of students who enrolled at any time during the academic year.

[2]Includes students who reported that they were awarded aid but did not specify the source of the aid.

[3]Includes Department of Veterans Affairs and Department of Defense benefits.

[4]Full-time, full-year undergraduates are those who were enrolled full time for 9 or more months at one or more institutions.

[5]Part-time or part-year undergraduates include those who were enrolled part time for 9 or more months and those who were enrolled for less than 9 months either part time or full time.

NOTE: Data exclude students whose attendance status was not reported. Data include undergraduates in degree-granting and non-degree-granting institutions. Detail may not sum to totals because of rounding and because some students received multiple types of aid and aid from different sources. Data exclude Puerto Rico.

SOURCE: U.S. Department of Education, National Center for Education Statistics, 2011–12 and 2015–16 National Postsecondary Student Aid Study (NPSAS:12 and NPSAS:16). (This table was prepared July 2018.)

Table 331.60. Percentage of full-time, full-year undergraduates receiving financial aid, by type and source of aid and control and level of institution: Selected years, 1992–93 through 2015–16

[Standard errors appear in parentheses]

Control and level of institution	Any aid			Grants			Loans			Work study[1]	
	Total[2]	Federal[3]	Nonfederal	Total	Federal	Nonfederal	Total[4]	Federal[4]	Nonfederal	Total	Federal
1	2	3	4	5	6	7	8	9	10	11	12
1992–93, all institutions	**58.2 (0.50)**	**45.0 (0.50)**	**37.9 (0.58)**	**48.3 (0.51)**	**28.6 (0.47)**	**34.9 (0.51)**	**34.0 (0.61)**	**33.1 (0.61)**	**2.7 (0.22)**	**10.3 (0.38)**	**6.8 (0.30)**
Public	52.4 (0.67)	39.8 (0.60)	32.7 (0.69)	42.8 (0.58)	27.4 (0.50)	29.6 (0.64)	27.1 (0.57)	26.3 (0.54)	2.0 (0.27)	6.8 (0.36)	4.2 (0.23)
4-year doctoral	54.0 (0.94)	39.1 (0.80)	34.7 (0.82)	42.2 (0.80)	23.6 (0.65)	31.2 (0.79)	33.1 (0.86)	32.3 (0.86)	2.4 (0.29)	7.1 (0.50)	4.3 (0.34)
Other 4-year	56.5 (1.07)	45.4 (1.19)	36.7 (1.27)	45.4 (1.29)	31.1 (1.24)	32.4 (1.32)	34.4 (0.98)	33.4 (0.93)	2.8 (0.69)	9.7 (0.77)	5.6 (0.57)
2-year	47.2 (1.93)	36.0 (1.70)	27.0 (1.62)	41.9 (1.68)	29.9 (1.43)	25.7 (1.65)	12.7 (1.23)	12.3 (1.17)	0.7 ! (0.28)	4.1 (0.79)	3.0 (0.54)
Less-than-2-year	35.4 (3.60)	31.6 (4.08)	15.7 (4.47)	30.3 (2.53)	26.6 (2.91)	13.3 ! (4.75)	3.0 ! (1.30)	3.0 ! (1.30)	‡ (†)	‡ (†)	‡ (†)
Private, nonprofit	69.5 (1.38)	52.3 (1.42)	58.9 (1.49)	62.0 (1.36)	25.8 (1.59)	55.9 (1.47)	47.6 (1.33)	45.9 (1.40)	5.1 (0.47)	22.5 (1.10)	16.1 (1.00)
4-year doctoral	63.5 (1.65)	44.3 (1.37)	54.7 (1.76)	56.0 (1.61)	17.0 (0.97)	52.7 (1.68)	41.7 (1.27)	39.8 (1.27)	6.1 (0.74)	18.9 (1.33)	13.2 (1.40)
Other 4-year	75.4 (1.91)	59.4 (2.08)	64.3 (2.46)	68.4 (2.11)	33.0 (2.79)	60.6 (2.81)	53.8 (1.88)	52.4 (1.99)	4.3 (0.80)	27.7 (1.75)	20.1 (1.58)
Less-than-4-year	70.7 (3.80)	59.5 (4.15)	44.4 (6.26)	56.6 (4.50)	40.9 (3.70)	39.2 (6.82)	43.5 (5.33)	41.7 (5.08)	2.8 ! (1.17)	4.1 ! (1.90)	2.3 ! (1.00)
Private, for-profit	77.0 (2.18)	72.0 (2.17)	16.8 (2.32)	56.2 (1.75)	49.9 (1.71)	13.6 (2.41)	55.4 (4.82)	55.1 (4.79)	2.2 ! (0.91)	1.9 ! (0.78)	0.7 ! (0.25)
2-year and above	82.2 (4.50)	76.5 (4.35)	24.1 (4.65)	50.3 (4.06)	40.5 (2.52)	21.0 (5.02)	68.5 (5.41)	68.5 (5.41)	‡ (†)	3.6 ! (1.62)	1.4 ! (0.54)
Less-than-2-year	73.2 (2.46)	68.8 (2.64)	11.5 (2.49)	60.4 (2.46)	56.7 (2.31)	8.3 ! (2.53)	46.0 (5.63)	45.4 (5.56)	1.5 ! (0.53)	‡ (†)	0.2 ! (0.09)
1999–2000, all institutions	**71.9 (0.59)**	**56.7 (0.44)**	**52.3 (0.67)**	**58.5 (0.60)**	**29.0 (0.44)**	**49.0 (0.69)**	**45.6 (0.44)**	**44.5 (0.41)**	**6.8 (0.31)**	**11.6 (0.46)**	**8.9 (0.36)**
Public	66.9 (0.73)	51.6 (0.51)	46.4 (0.86)	52.8 (0.68)	29.3 (0.43)	43.0 (0.81)	37.9 (0.50)	36.9 (0.46)	4.4 (0.30)	7.5 (0.47)	5.6 (0.38)
4-year doctoral	71.1 (0.79)	54.4 (0.68)	49.7 (0.77)	53.3 (0.87)	25.1 (0.74)	45.6 (0.68)	49.0 (0.73)	47.9 (0.69)	5.6 (0.41)	8.7 (0.51)	6.1 (0.42)
Other 4-year	75.7 (1.29)	63.0 (1.43)	50.6 (2.13)	57.5 (1.38)	33.7 (1.53)	46.6 (2.10)	51.5 (1.66)	50.7 (1.66)	4.7 (0.45)	11.0 (1.33)	8.1 (1.12)
2-year	55.7 (1.47)	40.5 (1.08)	39.5 (1.51)	49.2 (1.34)	31.9 (0.97)	37.3 (1.49)	14.9 (0.75)	13.9 (0.62)	2.5 (0.40)	3.8 (0.69)	3.5 (0.68)
Less-than-2-year	58.4 (6.03)	45.0 (6.96)	35.0 (5.14)	48.4 (7.50)	39.7 (7.40)	26.4 (6.54)	4.7 ! (2.14)	4.7 ! (2.13)	‡ (†)	‡ (†)	# (†)
Private, nonprofit	84.0 (0.77)	67.3 (0.75)	73.5 (1.37)	74.9 (1.13)	24.2 (1.24)	71.1 (1.42)	62.6 (0.83)	61.2 (0.83)	14.2 (0.89)	25.8 (1.27)	19.8 (0.88)
4-year doctoral	79.0 (1.03)	62.7 (1.22)	71.0 (1.27)	70.4 (1.19)	20.6 (1.22)	68.2 (1.33)	60.0 (1.16)	58.4 (1.19)	16.0 (1.08)	25.7 (1.16)	21.7 (1.05)
Other 4-year	88.7 (1.08)	72.2 (1.31)	76.3 (2.29)	78.9 (1.63)	26.3 (1.80)	74.1 (2.28)	67.4 (1.41)	66.0 (1.45)	13.4 (1.20)	26.7 (2.24)	19.0 (1.55)
Less-than-4-year	77.2 (4.01)	53.3 (2.88)	64.0 (5.11)	72.7 (4.37)	37.0 (3.48)	62.5 (5.62)	27.4 (2.59)	27.3 (2.60)	3.1 (0.62)	13.7 (2.56)	10.0 (2.71)
Private, for-profit	89.9 (1.11)	87.0 (1.39)	33.4 (3.08)	63.5 (2.14)	52.9 (2.59)	26.6 (2.83)	82.7 (1.49)	82.0 (1.50)	7.8 (1.62)	2.2 ! (0.87)	1.9 ! (0.86)
2-year and above	88.6 (1.50)	85.7 (1.77)	37.5 (4.17)	60.8 (2.81)	47.3 (3.29)	32.6 (3.88)	82.9 (2.19)	82.2 (2.19)	6.9 (2.04)	2.9 ! (1.17)	2.5 ! (1.15)
Less-than-2-year	93.7 (1.32)	91.1 (1.88)	20.8 (2.75)	71.9 (2.96)	69.8 (2.97)	8.6 (2.27)	81.9 (3.65)	81.5 (3.64)	10.4 (1.93)	‡ (†)	‡ (0.18)
2007–08, all institutions	**80.1 (0.28)**	**63.9 (0.31)**	**63.7 (0.36)**	**64.6 (0.37)**	**33.1 (0.29)**	**53.6 (0.41)**	**54.8 (0.32)**	**51.0 (0.32)**	**20.5 (0.31)**	**13.8 (0.29)**	**10.6 (0.23)**
Public	75.4 (0.33)	58.7 (0.36)	58.0 (0.39)	59.2 (0.38)	32.3 (0.29)	49.6 (0.40)	46.2 (0.34)	42.7 (0.33)	14.2 (0.25)	9.5 (0.25)	7.1 (0.22)
4-year doctoral	77.8 (0.40)	59.6 (0.48)	62.8 (0.49)	59.9 (0.55)	27.8 (0.38)	53.8 (0.53)	54.7 (0.50)	50.8 (0.50)	17.4 (0.38)	10.2 (0.35)	7.6 (0.32)
Other 4-year	82.5 (0.59)	67.6 (0.68)	62.7 (0.80)	63.2 (0.81)	35.2 (0.66)	52.7 (0.85)	57.5 (0.72)	54.4 (0.72)	16.4 (0.61)	11.5 (0.60)	8.7 (0.45)
2-year	66.9 (0.69)	51.4 (0.73)	47.5 (0.79)	55.5 (0.63)	37.3 (0.65)	41.3 (0.76)	25.5 (0.59)	22.3 (0.57)	7.8 (0.37)	7.1 (0.36)	5.5 (0.29)
Less-than-2-year	69.1 (3.87)	58.6 (3.84)	33.0 (4.74)	56.6 (3.58)	50.0 (3.97)	16.1 (2.88)	26.5 (4.79)	23.6 (4.33)	10.7 (2.75)	# (†)	# (†)
Private, nonprofit	89.5 (0.57)	71.2 (0.62)	83.2 (0.79)	80.9 (0.85)	27.4 (0.67)	77.5 (1.02)	68.1 (0.66)	64.3 (0.61)	30.4 (0.74)	32.2 (1.08)	25.0 (0.86)
4-year doctoral	85.5 (0.93)	67.1 (1.12)	79.4 (1.11)	76.5 (1.18)	23.6 (0.82)	73.6 (1.38)	64.2 (1.21)	60.0 (1.22)	29.7 (1.02)	30.3 (1.10)	24.5 (1.04)
Other 4-year	93.6 (0.74)	75.1 (1.12)	87.5 (1.06)	85.8 (1.11)	31.0 (1.18)	82.1 (1.40)	72.3 (1.18)	68.8 (1.21)	31.2 (1.06)	34.7 (1.88)	26.0 (1.45)
Less-than-4-year	92.0 (2.79)	84.4 (3.65)	61.8 (10.16)	61.3 (4.96)	45.3 (5.77)	48.2 (9.77)	60.2 (7.26)	56.8 (7.31)	26.0 ! (7.94)	5.8 (1.50)	4.7 ! (1.63)
Private, for-profit	92.6 (0.70)	84.6 (1.24)	59.8 (1.60)	65.5 (1.48)	53.0 (1.50)	25.8 (1.66)	86.5 (1.19)	81.2 (1.29)	43.1 (1.67)	1.8 (0.29)	1.6 (0.28)
2-year and above	92.4 (0.79)	84.2 (1.41)	61.7 (1.82)	64.7 (1.69)	50.7 (1.70)	27.8 (1.90)	86.4 (1.36)	81.3 (1.46)	44.1 (1.92)	2.0 (0.34)	1.8 (0.33)
Less-than-2-year	93.6 (0.82)	87.4 (1.74)	47.6 (2.52)	70.8 (2.12)	67.6 (2.14)	13.5 (2.33)	87.2 (1.70)	80.7 (2.44)	36.9 (1.61)	0.7 ! (0.27)	‡ (†)
2011–12, all institutions	**84.4 (0.36)**	**72.8 (0.51)**	**56.9 (0.46)**	**72.4 (0.41)**	**47.4 (0.50)**	**52.6 (0.45)**	**56.7 (0.53)**	**55.5 (0.54)**	**9.2 (0.22)**	**11.9 (0.25)**	**10.5 (0.24)**
Public	80.4 (0.47)	68.4 (0.61)	53.3 (0.58)	67.3 (0.49)	46.1 (0.59)	49.7 (0.56)	48.5 (0.57)	47.4 (0.57)	6.3 (0.19)	6.9 (0.24)	6.2 (0.23)
4-year doctoral	83.9 (0.46)	70.9 (0.47)	61.2 (0.63)	67.8 (0.51)	41.1 (0.40)	56.8 (0.61)	61.6 (0.44)	60.4 (0.43)	8.6 (0.31)	8.3 (0.37)	7.4 (0.37)
Other 4-year	83.5 (0.93)	72.7 (1.34)	54.1 (1.23)	69.2 (0.99)	48.3 (1.10)	50.1 (1.32)	55.5 (1.49)	54.3 (1.51)	7.4 (0.60)	9.3 (0.70)	8.6 (0.61)
2-year	74.5 (1.03)	63.0 (1.24)	42.5 (1.14)	65.7 (1.09)	51.6 (1.30)	40.2 (1.15)	27.5 (0.99)	26.6 (1.00)	2.7 (0.24)	3.9 (0.28)	3.4 (0.28)
Less-than-2-year	71.6 (4.50)	67.8 (4.72)	33.5 (5.54)	68.6 (4.05)	63.7 (4.54)	27.2 (3.90)	20.5 (5.20)	20.2 (5.20)	‡ (†)	1.0 ! (0.46)	‡ (†)
Private, nonprofit	91.6 (0.55)	76.1 (0.75)	83.1 (0.77)	85.4 (0.77)	37.6 (0.65)	80.3 (0.85)	68.4 (0.90)	66.7 (0.88)	15.3 (0.65)	33.1 (0.85)	29.2 (0.81)
4-year doctoral	90.4 (0.84)	74.3 (0.94)	82.9 (1.13)	84.2 (1.17)	34.9 (0.80)	80.4 (1.21)	66.7 (1.08)	65.3 (1.05)	15.0 (0.92)	33.2 (1.27)	30.0 (1.26)
Other 4-year	93.1 (0.68)	78.0 (1.20)	84.2 (0.98)	87.2 (0.92)	40.3 (1.10)	81.3 (1.15)	70.7 (1.41)	68.7 (1.44)	15.8 (0.91)	33.9 (1.22)	29.1 (1.14)
Less-than-4-year	90.2 (4.12)	78.1 (5.04)	60.2 (7.07)	77.8 (6.09)	48.5 (6.54)	51.1 (8.78)	61.2 (5.71)	59.0 (7.42)	12.2 (2.62)	‡ (†)	‡ (†)
Private, for-profit	94.8 (0.46)	93.1 (0.51)	29.3 (1.05)	78.6 (0.76)	73.9 (0.82)	17.4 (0.94)	84.1 (0.85)	83.4 (0.89)	14.8 (0.75)	1.9 (0.21)	1.8 (0.20)
2-year and above	94.6 (0.53)	92.8 (0.59)	30.7 (1.16)	77.4 (0.86)	72.2 (0.92)	18.9 (1.05)	84.2 (0.85)	83.4 (0.89)	15.0 (0.82)	2.2 (0.24)	2.1 (0.23)
Less-than-2-year	95.9 (0.75)	95.2 (0.79)	20.3 (2.64)	86.2 (1.54)	85.4 (1.63)	7.5 (1.82)	83.8 (3.56)	83.0 (3.52)	13.5 (1.58)	‡ (†)	‡ (†)

See notes at end of table.

Table 331.60. Percentage of full-time, full-year undergraduates receiving financial aid, by type and source of aid and control and level of institution: Selected years, 1992–93 through 2015–16—Continued

[Standard errors appear in parentheses]

Control and level of institution	Any aid			Grants			Loans			Work study[1]	
	Total[2]	Federal[3]	Nonfederal	Total	Federal	Nonfederal	Total[4]	Federal[4]	Nonfederal	Total	Federal
1	2	3	4	5	6	7	8	9	10	11	12
2015–16, all institutions	**86.4 (0.26)**	**69.8 (0.33)**	**66.9 (0.40)**	**76.7 (0.31)**	**44.7 (0.31)**	**63.8 (0.41)**	**54.7 (0.33)**	**52.5 (0.34)**	**9.2 (0.21)**	**10.5 (0.26)**	**9.1 (0.25)**
Public	84.0 (0.34)	67.7 (0.42)	63.4 (0.49)	72.5 (0.40)	44.9 (0.39)	60.1 (0.49)	48.5 (0.41)	46.7 (0.41)	6.9 (0.21)	6.6 (0.25)	5.8 (0.24)
4-year doctoral	86.7 (0.38)	69.4 (0.48)	69.8 (0.53)	73.7 (0.47)	41.8 (0.39)	65.8 (0.54)	59.7 (0.43)	57.5 (0.44)	9.1 (0.31)	8.3 (0.36)	7.1 (0.35)
Other 4-year	85.3 (0.78)	72.6 (0.98)	63.3 (1.45)	71.8 (1.18)	45.9 (1.27)	59.6 (1.42)	53.2 (1.29)	51.2 (1.29)	8.3 (0.65)	5.4 (0.68)	5.2 (0.67)
2-year	77.8 (0.79)	61.6 (0.85)	50.6 (1.11)	70.3 (0.86)	50.4 (0.79)	48.9 (1.10)	23.4 (0.62)	22.6 (0.62)	1.9 (0.21)	3.8 (0.44)	3.4 (0.41)
Less-than-2-year	82.0 (6.98)	67.0 (8.01)	36.3 (10.64)	72.2 (7.51)	56.0 (7.26)	34.6 ! (11.07)	25.1 (6.39)	25.1 (6.39)	‡ (†)	‡ (†)	‡ (†)
Private, nonprofit	91.7 (0.48)	70.3 (0.61)	83.1 (0.70)	87.1 (0.59)	36.4 (0.52)	81.1 (0.76)	65.9 (0.61)	62.5 (0.60)	15.9 (0.64)	24.4 (0.82)	21.0 (0.75)
4-year doctoral	91.0 (0.62)	67.5 (0.89)	85.6 (0.84)	87.1 (0.66)	32.9 (0.62)	84.0 (0.88)	62.9 (0.85)	59.3 (0.81)	16.7 (0.87)	23.7 (1.05)	21.3 (1.03)
Other 4-year	92.9 (0.72)	73.7 (0.89)	82.2 (1.20)	87.6 (1.03)	39.3 (0.84)	80.0 (1.37)	69.8 (0.93)	66.7 (0.95)	15.1 (0.95)	26.8 (1.35)	21.7 (1.22)
Less-than-4-year	86.9 (2.20)	81.7 (3.76)	37.5 (10.42)	78.4 (3.61)	72.4 (4.87)	29.3 ! (9.48)	72.9 (5.85)	71.1 (5.79)	8.7 (2.22)	‡ (†)	‡ (†)
Private, for-profit	92.9 (0.59)	89.4 (0.71)	45.4 (2.86)	82.9 (0.97)	72.2 (0.84)	39.9 (3.14)	78.1 (0.77)	76.8 (0.81)	8.9 (0.59)	1.5 (0.23)	1.5 (0.23)
2-year and above	93.6 (0.65)	89.7 (0.77)	50.9 (3.34)	83.5 (1.10)	70.7 (0.97)	45.6 (3.68)	78.4 (0.75)	77.4 (0.79)	9.1 (0.69)	1.6 (0.28)	1.5 (0.28)
Less-than-2-year	90.5 (1.36)	88.6 (1.74)	24.4 (2.72)	80.6 (2.11)	78.0 (2.12)	18.0 (2.87)	76.9 (2.54)	74.7 (2.62)	8.1 (0.94)	‡ (†)	‡ (†)

† Not applicable.
# Rounds to zero.
! Interpret data with caution. The coefficient of variation (CV) for this estimate is between 30 and 50 percent.
‡ Reporting standards not met. The coefficient of variation (CV) for this estimate is 50 percent or greater.
[1] Details on nonfederal work-study participants are not available.
[2] Includes students who reported they were awarded aid, but did not specify the source or type of aid.
[3] Includes Department of Veterans Affairs and Department of Defense benefits.
[4] Includes Parent Loans for Undergraduate Students (PLUS).
NOTE: Full-time, full-year undergraduates were enrolled full time for 9 or more months at one or more institutions. Data include undergraduates in degree-granting and non-degree-granting institutions. Detail may not sum to totals because of rounding and because some students receive multiple types of aid and aid from different sources. Data exclude Puerto Rico.
SOURCE: U.S. Department of Education, National Center for Education Statistics, 1992–93, 1999–2000, 2007–08, 2011–12, and 2015–16 National Postsecondary Student Aid Study (NPSAS:93, NPSAS:2000, NPSAS:08, NPSAS:12, and NPSAS:16). (This table was prepared June 2018.)

Table 331.70. Average amount of financial aid awarded to full-time, full-year undergraduates, by type and source of aid and control and level of institution: Selected years, 1992–93 through 2015–16

[Standard errors appear in parentheses]

Control and level of institution	Any aid			Grants			Loans			Work study[1]	
	Total[2]	Federal[3]	Nonfederal	Total[4]	Federal	Nonfederal	Total[5]	Federal[5]	Nonfederal	Total	Federal
1	2	3	4	5	6	7	8	9	10	11	12
	Current dollars										
1992–93, all institutions	**$5,600 (80)**	**$4,320 (54)**	**$3,390 (85)**	**$3,520 (63)**	**$2,000 (17)**	**$3,250 (85)**	**$3,860 (59)**	**$3,750 (54)**	**$2,640 (133)**	**$1,360 (34)**	**$1,280 (38)**
Public	4,030 (39)	3,740 (40)	1,860 (34)	2,420 (28)	1,900 (18)	1,740 (34)	3,350 (42)	3,290 (40)	2,020 (133)	1,380 (48)	1,350 (52)
4-year doctoral	4,720 (60)	4,390 (49)	2,330 (55)	2,750 (45)	1,970 (26)	2,230 (55)	3,660 (46)	3,590 (43)	2,150 (142)	1,440 (57)	1,360 (55)
Other 4-year	4,240 (92)	3,850 (68)	1,710 (47)	2,430 (48)	1,960 (26)	1,530 (52)	3,200 (65)	3,120 (71)	2,150 (198)	1,240 (59)	1,260 (69)
2-year	2,720 (88)	2,640 (87)	1,170 (84)	1,940 (59)	1,760 (42)	1,120 (88)	2,500 (125)	2,530 (112)	‡ (†)	1,500 (179)	1,490 (155)
Less-than-2-year	2,250 (198)	1,950 (192)	1,100! (476)	1,930 (154)	1,760 (60)	880 (154)	3,310 (472)	3,120 (621)	‡ (†)	‡ (†)	‡ (†)
Private nonprofit	9,040 (184)	5,280 (94)	5,880 (206)	6,010 (183)	2,320 (39)	5,600 (171)	4,360 (86)	4,140 (67)	3,350 (274)	1,320 (44)	1,230 (48)
4-year doctoral	10,160 (250)	5,650 (147)	7,060 (225)	6,940 (201)	2,420 (74)	6,590 (200)	4,910 (140)	4,560 (106)	3,750 (411)	1,520 (64)	1,360 (79)
Other 4-year	8,460 (253)	5,120 (130)	5,100 (276)	5,500 (275)	2,290 (56)	4,970 (233)	4,000 (115)	3,880 (103)	2,750 (272)	1,190 (48)	1,140 (51)
Less-than-4-year	4,910 (507)	3,980 (258)	2,490 (434)	2,890 (431)	2,140 (149)	1,940 (427)	3,520 (260)	3,410 (257)	‡ (†)	‡ (†)	‡ (†)
Private for-profit	5,460 (321)	5,130 (301)	2,590 (377)	2,290 (116)	1,950 (47)	2,320 (452)	4,910 (276)	4,840 (254)	2,410 (373)	‡ (†)	‡ (†)
2-year and above	6,670 (296)	6,130 (251)	2,820 (528)	2,780 (265)	2,060 (93)	2,670 (582)	5,590 (291)	5,480 (260)	‡ (†)	‡ (†)	‡ (†)
Less-than-2-year	4,480 (425)	4,330 (416)	2,240 (533)	2,010 (95)	1,890 (68)	1,680 (532)	4,180 (383)	4,150 (372)	‡ (†)	‡ (†)	‡ (†)
1995–96, all institutions	**$6,880 (159)**	**$5,250 (61)**	**$4,000 (163)**	**$3,990 (138)**	**$2,000 (23)**	**$3,710 (162)**	**$4,830 (61)**	**$4,770 (58)**	**$2,790 (232)**	**$1,410 (40)**	**$1,350 (37)**
Public	5,160 (105)	4,670 (77)	2,410 (74)	2,740 (68)	1,920 (23)	2,110 (74)	4,390 (87)	4,370 (81)	2,440 (476)	1,390 (63)	1,350 (63)
4-year doctoral	6,230 (124)	5,490 (122)	3,050 (82)	3,250 (107)	1,920 (35)	2,790 (105)	4,910 (149)	4,850 (140)	2,750 (500)	1,330 (100)	1,290 (89)
Other 4-year	5,440 (235)	4,790 (166)	2,170 (81)	2,720 (81)	1,970 (25)	1,870 (60)	4,100 (139)	4,090 (137)	‡ (†)	1,450 (56)	1,380 (58)
2-year	3,130 (162)	3,110 (101)	1,530 (213)	2,020 (106)	1,900 (53)	1,100 (140)	3,140 (120)	3,210 (137)	‡ (†)	1,430 (254)	1,410 (234)
Less-than-2-year	2,440! (887)	2,040 (267)	2,120! (897)	2,190 (485)	1,650 (127)	2,360! (882)	2,870 (441)	2,870 (441)	‡ (†)	‡ (†)	‡ (†)
Private nonprofit	10,870 (388)	6,470 (137)	6,740 (331)	6,640 (312)	2,280 (75)	6,230 (305)	5,600 (128)	5,470 (126)	3,210 (328)	1,430 (52)	1,350 (45)
4-year doctoral	13,130 (727)	7,160 (176)	8,720 (735)	8,370 (674)	2,350 (63)	8,000 (641)	6,260 (188)	6,120 (160)	3,610 (933)	1,660 (84)	1,550 (63)
Other 4-year	10,220 (453)	6,310 (179)	6,040 (357)	6,090 (349)	2,280 (106)	5,590 (345)	5,340 (162)	5,220 (160)	3,300 (417)	1,320 (40)	1,250 (39)
Less-than-4-year	5,310 (229)	4,150 (229)	3,050 (201)	3,230 (364)	2,060 (159)	2,780 (340)	4,520 (189)	4,480 (181)	‡ (†)	1,260 (81)	1,210 (241)
Private for-profit	6,150 (137)	5,540 (162)	3,010 (188)	2,470 (123)	1,940 (30)	2,350 (211)	4,940 (237)	4,920 (212)	2,300 (210)	‡ (†)	‡ (†)
2-year and above	6,850 (235)	6,110 (310)	3,340 (157)	2,880 (264)	2,010 (40)	2,860 (148)	5,330 (164)	5,250 (200)	‡ (†)	‡ (†)	‡ (†)
Less-than-2-year	5,520 (337)	5,020 (318)	2,700 (284)	2,120 (67)	1,880 (43)	1,520 (264)	4,550 (525)	4,570 (443)	2,080 (160)	‡ (†)	‡ (†)
1999–2000, all institutions	**$8,470 (100)**	**$5,970 (58)**	**$5,160 (95)**	**$5,100 (81)**	**$2,520 (19)**	**$4,590 (92)**	**$6,030 (59)**	**$5,430 (51)**	**$4,870 (155)**	**$1,680 (37)**	**$1,570 (39)**
Public	6,140 (90)	5,260 (60)	2,990 (61)	3,520 (55)	2,490 (22)	2,630 (53)	5,180 (72)	4,870 (55)	3,820 (194)	1,720 (56)	1,630 (69)
4-year doctoral	7,410 (84)	6,180 (65)	3,840 (85)	4,170 (77)	2,530 (33)	3,480 (80)	5,620 (81)	5,300 (68)	3,850 (209)	1,780 (45)	1,680 (42)
Other 4-year	6,190 (175)	5,280 (136)	2,690 (105)	3,270 (91)	2,430 (28)	2,290 (83)	4,770 (179)	4,520 (147)	3,540 (426)	1,670 (148)	1,580 (194)
2-year	3,990 (135)	3,670 (96)	1,860 (96)	2,800 (91)	2,490 (45)	1,560 (80)	4,190 (198)	3,750 (122)	4,090 (841)	1,650 (118)	1,580 (105)
Less-than-2-year	3,490 (383)	3,050 (387)	1,900 (296)	2,930 (234)	2,410 (167)	1,750 (357)	5,090 (950)	5,040 (975)	‡ (†)	‡ (†)	‡ (†)
Private nonprofit	14,050 (307)	7,280 (104)	9,390 (238)	8,710 (235)	2,660 (52)	8,280 (218)	7,460 (117)	6,300 (93)	5,750 (211)	1,620 (41)	1,500 (33)
4-year doctoral	16,060 (359)	7,890 (149)	10,910 (326)	10,140 (302)	2,860 (81)	9,600 (283)	8,240 (156)	6,700 (131)	6,430 (237)	1,810 (51)	1,700 (51)
Other 4-year	12,930 (424)	6,930 (162)	8,480 (318)	7,880 (317)	2,530 (70)	7,490 (291)	6,910 (166)	6,020 (149)	5,070 (312)	1,490 (69)	1,330 (47)
Less-than-4-year	7,700 (780)	5,540 (645)	4,680 (485)	5,070 (459)	2,640 (196)	4,340 (550)	6,010 (186)	5,380 (176)	5,590 (1,440)	950 (96)	850 (63)
Private for-profit	8,730 (285)	7,440 (240)	4,120 (296)	3,380 (144)	2,490 (77)	3,110 (285)	6,590 (285)	6,070 (266)	5,970 (474)	‡ (†)	‡ (†)
2-year and above	9,430 (381)	7,920 (315)	4,190 (375)	3,730 (197)	2,550 (109)	3,240 (321)	7,030 (367)	6,530 (345)	6,620 (663)	‡ (†)	‡ (†)
Less-than-2-year	6,730 (354)	6,080 (330)	3,700 (556)	2,490 (64)	2,370 (63)	1,570 (385)	5,240 (355)	4,670 (319)	4,660 (800)	‡ (†)	‡ (†)
2003–04, all institutions	**$9,760 (93)**	**$7,010 (60)**	**$5,690 (118)**	**$5,670 (101)**	**$3,230 (22)**	**$4,930 (125)**	**$7,000 (72)**	**$6,060 (57)**	**$6,100 (138)**	**$1,940 (36)**	**$1,790 (37)**
Public	7,400 (95)	6,260 (90)	3,620 (45)	4,230 (45)	3,190 (31)	3,110 (45)	6,060 (72)	5,520 (64)	5,100 (114)	2,020 (45)	1,860 (51)
4-year doctoral	8,970 (109)	7,360 (99)	4,500 (70)	4,890 (64)	3,220 (39)	3,930 (63)	6,760 (100)	6,150 (81)	5,510 (160)	2,070 (64)	1,900 (66)
Other 4-year	7,870 (183)	6,440 (146)	3,560 (84)	4,230 (118)	3,150 (64)	2,900 (91)	5,870 (127)	5,280 (112)	5,260 (227)	1,930 (86)	1,820 (100)
2-year	4,690 (130)	4,420 (143)	2,140 (84)	3,330 (64)	3,180 (45)	1,810 (86)	4,170 (146)	3,850 (147)	3,700 (207)	2,010 (100)	1,830 (109)
Less-than-2-year	4,770 (389)	4,490 (368)	2,920 (250)	3,180 (206)	2,800 (157)	2,500 (243)	5,260 (621)	4,740 (402)	4,230 (802)	2,460! (1,180)	‡ (†)
Private nonprofit	16,250 (258)	8,480 (127)	10,270 (234)	9,620 (261)	3,390 (49)	8,860 (250)	8,800 (178)	7,040 (135)	7,430 (273)	1,810 (52)	1,670 (51)
4-year doctoral	17,650 (367)	9,000 (204)	11,590 (383)	10,660 (465)	3,460 (101)	9,950 (466)	9,790 (272)	7,600 (190)	8,220 (333)	2,120 (78)	1,980 (75)
Other 4-year	15,650 (352)	8,260 (161)	9,580 (303)	9,130 (295)	3,340 (57)	8,280 (283)	8,270 (219)	6,740 (161)	6,920 (391)	1,620 (56)	1,470 (52)
Less-than-4-year	8,910 (647)	6,240 (375)	5,160 (534)	5,720 (547)	3,560 (333)	4,600 (607)	6,200 (584)	5,630 (470)	4,460 (774)	1,570! (549)	1,580! (557)
Private for-profit	10,480 (328)	8,550 (222)	5,070 (285)	4,300 (167)	3,230 (72)	3,880 (317)	7,640 (267)	6,580 (190)	5,730 (525)	2,660 (275)	2,730 (328)
2-year and above	11,380 (433)	9,100 (297)	5,330 (349)	4,660 (222)	3,370 (101)	4,030 (369)	8,140 (351)	6,950 (253)	6,050 (657)	2,780 (308)	2,890 (361)
Less-than-2-year	7,810 (139)	6,890 (93)	3,980 (157)	3,210 (102)	2,850 (58)	3,010 (185)	6,050 (140)	5,350 (112)	4,560 (205)	1,760 (129)	1,570 (108)

See notes at end of table.

Table 331.70. Average amount of financial aid awarded to full-time, full-year undergraduates, by type and source of aid and control and level of institution: Selected years, 1992–93 through 2015–16—Continued

[Standard errors appear in parentheses]

Control and level of institution	Any aid			Grants			Loans			Work study[1]	
	Total[2]	Federal[3]	Nonfederal	Total[4]	Federal	Nonfederal	Total[5]	Federal[5]	Nonfederal	Total	Federal
1	2	3	4	5	6	7	8	9	10	11	12
2007–08, all institutions	**$12,990 (98)**	**$8,170 (51)**	**$8,130 (89)**	**$7,250 (71)**	**$3,680 (19)**	**$6,470 (79)**	**$9,520 (77)**	**$7,080 (56)**	**$7,800 (112)**	**$2,270 (26)**	**$2,160 (30)**
Public	9,680 (62)	7,250 (51)	5,240 (50)	5,420 (40)	3,670 (18)	4,080 (43)	7,990 (60)	6,470 (58)	6,520 (108)	2,430 (37)	2,360 (44)
4-year doctoral	11,670 (96)	8,320 (82)	6,550 (83)	6,410 (71)	3,780 (33)	5,170 (67)	8,870 (90)	7,100 (83)	7,130 (156)	2,440 (42)	2,290 (46)
Other 4-year	10,040 (136)	7,430 (110)	5,200 (95)	5,420 (88)	3,690 (32)	4,040 (99)	7,690 (123)	6,240 (95)	6,300 (204)	2,280 (69)	2,110 (81)
2-year	5,750 (68)	5,160 (63)	2,510 (45)	3,750 (44)	3,530 (29)	1,860 (35)	5,450 (91)	4,600 (73)	4,670 (150)	2,560 (107)	2,760 (122)
Less-than-2-year	6,210 (528)	5,200 (441)	3,750 (477)	3,610 (212)	3,320 (153)	2,390 (351)	6,910 (500)	5,550 (387)	4,920 (284)	‡ (†)	‡ (†)
Private nonprofit	21,640 (307)	10,020 (158)	14,700 (221)	12,470 (186)	4,090 (51)	11,570 (176)	12,320 (207)	8,350 (164)	9,930 (224)	2,090 (35)	1,930 (35)
4-year doctoral	22,880 (388)	10,380 (192)	15,850 (289)	13,170 (250)	4,280 (82)	12,320 (231)	13,420 (253)	8,840 (213)	11,140 (351)	2,230 (52)	2,080 (55)
Other 4-year	20,620 (447)	9,720 (224)	13,710 (341)	11,880 (268)	3,920 (60)	10,940 (263)	11,330 (313)	7,920 (223)	8,750 (263)	1,970 (40)	1,780 (43)
Less-than-4-year	12,530 (1,097)	8,340 (1,134)	7,270 (1,107)	6,970 (1,588)	4,710 (935)	4,440 (1,230)	11,310 (613)	8,000 (1,208)	8,740 (1,011)	‡ (†)	‡ (†)
Private for-profit	12,890 (294)	9,160 (176)	6,990 (269)	4,050 (96)	3,200 (60)	3,720 (201)	10,260 (233)	7,040 (133)	7,340 (307)	3,650 (392)	3,840 (385)
2-year and above	13,270 (340)	9,270 (203)	7,220 (303)	4,130 (113)	3,180 (73)	3,810 (216)	10,600 (269)	7,140 (153)	7,610 (350)	3,760 (402)	3,940 (386)
Less-than-2-year	10,540 (234)	8,510 (188)	5,100 (250)	3,590 (86)	3,270 (52)	2,470 (381)	8,150 (215)	6,380 (166)	5,320 (212)	‡ (†)	‡ (†)
2011–12, all institutions	**$15,510 (106)**	**$10,820 (75)**	**$9,160 (110)**	**$9,230 (92)**	**$4,580 (20)**	**$8,590 (115)**	**$10,090 (75)**	**$9,160 (69)**	**$6,980 (187)**	**$2,250 (48)**	**$2,180 (37)**
Public	11,420 (93)	9,400 (71)	5,170 (75)	6,610 (62)	4,560 (22)	4,730 (75)	8,860 (87)	8,300 (81)	5,790 (237)	2,330 (60)	2,290 (60)
4-year doctoral	14,130 (125)	11,000 (106)	6,610 (108)	7,880 (101)	4,610 (27)	6,070 (112)	9,750 (112)	9,040 (109)	6,400 (289)	2,410 (80)	2,320 (79)
Other 4-year	11,730 (229)	9,800 (150)	4,920 (170)	6,440 (133)	4,650 (49)	4,410 (155)	8,790 (186)	8,210 (152)	5,630 (483)	2,020 (106)	2,050 (112)
2-year	7,120 (117)	6,740 (91)	2,480 (76)	4,910 (76)	4,460 (41)	2,320 (74)	6,200 (78)	6,060 (79)	3,380 (208)	2,460 (130)	2,460 (146)
Less-than-2-year	7,300 (989)	6,360 (1,018)	2,740 (813)	5,050 (458)	4,510 (464)	2,170! (676)	7,260 (950)	7,060 (939)	‡ (†)	‡ (†)	‡ (†)
Private nonprofit	27,250 (300)	13,300 (217)	17,870 (265)	17,780 (264)	4,710 (46)	16,720 (266)	12,550 (200)	10,930 (190)	8,460 (437)	2,150 (67)	2,050 (44)
4-year doctoral	29,080 (456)	13,700 (355)	19,410 (383)	19,380 (410)	4,690 (81)	18,260 (396)	13,120 (356)	11,420 (330)	8,700 (728)	2,280 (65)	2,220 (60)
Other 4-year	25,630 (384)	12,870 (216)	16,400 (355)	16,370 (336)	4,720 (46)	15,210 (348)	11,960 (167)	10,430 (172)	8,200 (385)	1,980 (130)	1,830 (69)
Less-than-4-year	16,190 (2,359)	12,830 (1,038)	7,610! (2,474)	7,410 (1,336)	4,870 (140)	6,670! (2,156)	11,600 (1,621)	10,330 (1,239)	8,170! (3,055)	2,750 (478)	2,790 (508)
Private for-profit	15,070 (214)	13,300 (173)	6,480 (205)	5,270 (85)	4,520 (49)	4,600 (257)	10,610 (139)	9,440 (107)	7,170 (211)	3,690 (272)	3,760 (291)
2-year and above	15,520 (219)	13,660 (181)	6,530 (218)	5,310 (85)	4,500 (40)	4,580 (267)	10,960 (151)	9,740 (117)	7,350 (222)	3,750 (281)	3,830 (299)
Less-than-2-year	12,170 (633)	10,990 (483)	5,960 (551)	5,050 (268)	4,670 (230)	4,880 (532)	8,370 (313)	7,510 (211)	5,810 (675)	‡ (†)	‡ (†)
2015–16, all institutions	**$18,210 (105)**	**$11,790 (58)**	**$11,240 (121)**	**$11,340 (92)**	**$4,880 (22)**	**$10,220 (114)**	**$11,140 (75)**	**$9,810 (48)**	**$10,200 (238)**	**$2,430 (30)**	**$2,340 (31)**
Public	13,420 (88)	10,330 (59)	6,740 (83)	8,050 (74)	4,840 (22)	6,100 (77)	9,750 (66)	8,920 (53)	8,160 (222)	2,550 (52)	2,430 (50)
4-year doctoral	16,060 (95)	11,870 (81)	8,140 (96)	9,380 (90)	4,890 (28)	7,390 (90)	10,580 (82)	9,650 (63)	8,510 (268)	2,500 (55)	2,400 (55)
Other 4-year	12,820 (215)	9,610 (135)	6,270 (221)	7,570 (199)	4,750 (82)	5,470 (213)	9,250 (182)	8,270 (143)	8,260 (572)	2,470 (139)	2,410 (135)
2-year	7,820 (135)	7,300 (97)	3,130 (172)	5,520 (120)	4,800 (39)	2,990 (179)	6,080 (104)	5,920 (90)	4,490 (460)	2,820 (195)	2,620 (164)
Less-than-2-year	7,230 (637)	7,110 (655)	3,200! (971)	4,690 (480)	4,130 (250)	3,120! (1,031)	7,630 (1,281)	7,630 (1,281)	‡ (†)	‡ (†)	‡ (†)
Private nonprofit	30,920 (310)	14,380 (130)	21,950 (316)	20,610 (265)	5,120 (71)	19,840 (287)	13,870 (193)	11,380 (98)	12,720 (440)	2,330 (35)	2,250 (40)
4-year doctoral	32,620 (442)	14,630 (173)	23,150 (444)	22,010 (380)	5,170 (122)	20,810 (404)	14,800 (255)	11,950 (137)	13,290 (604)	2,450 (52)	2,380 (58)
Other 4-year	29,450 (460)	14,150 (210)	20,610 (449)	19,360 (416)	5,070 (57)	18,700 (426)	12,960 (250)	10,830 (133)	12,100 (604)	2,180 (51)	2,070 (58)
Less-than-4-year	13,150 (897)	12,550 (571)	3,130! (1,333)	5,600 (469)	5,020 (121)	2,600! (994)	8,470 (624)	8,230 (577)	‡ (†)	‡ (†)	‡ (†)
Private for-profit	18,310 (376)	15,960 (330)	6,030 (415)	6,240 (147)	4,730 (55)	4,420 (316)	11,880 (222)	10,850 (191)	10,560 (653)	3,160 (395)	3,160 (407)
2-year and above	19,750 (471)	17,140 (412)	6,130 (462)	6,500 (173)	4,780 (59)	4,510 (349)	12,700 (263)	11,550 (219)	11,210 (742)	3,410 (400)	3,410 (409)
Less-than-2-year	12,580 (470)	11,380 (414)	5,290 (687)	5,190 (258)	4,550 (121)	3,510 (803)	8,680 (359)	8,090 (355)	7,750 (1,036)	‡ (†)	‡ (†)
	Constant 2018–19 dollars[6]										
All institutions											
1992–93	$9,960 (142)	$7,680 (96)	$6,0200 (150)	$6,260 (111)	$3,550 (30)	$5,770 (151)	$6,870 (104)	$6,670 (96)	$4,690 (236)	$2,4200 (61)	$2,2700 (68)
1995–96	11,270 (261)	8,600 (100)	6,5600 (267)	6,540 (226)	3,280 (38)	6,080 (266)	7,920 (100)	7,820 (95)	4,570 (381)	2,3100 (66)	2,2100 (60)
1999–2000	12,670 (149)	8,930 (87)	7,7200 (142)	7,630 (121)	3,770 (28)	6,870 (138)	9,020 (88)	8,120 (76)	7,290 (231)	2,5100 (55)	2,3400 (59)
2003–04	13,290 (127)	9,540 (82)	7,7400 (161)	7,720 (137)	4,390 (31)	6,720 (170)	9,520 (98)	8,250 (77)	8,300 (188)	2,6300 (48)	2,4300 (51)
2007–08	15,540 (118)	9,780 (61)	9,7300 (106)	8,670 (85)	4,400 (22)	7,740 (95)	11,390 (92)	8,470 (67)	9,330 (134)	2,7100 (31)	2,5800 (36)
2011–12	17,260 (118)	12,040 (84)	10,2000 (123)	10,280 (102)	5,090 (22)	9,560 (128)	11,230 (83)	10,190 (77)	7,770 (208)	2,5000 (53)	2,4200 (41)
2015–16	19,360 (112)	12,530 (62)	11,9400 (129)	12,060 (98)	5,190 (23)	10,860 (122)	11,850 (80)	10,430 (51)	10,840 (253)	2,5900 (32)	2,4900 (33)

†Not applicable.
!Interpret data with caution. The coefficient of variation (CV) for this estimate is between 30 and 50 percent.
‡Reporting standards not met. Either there are too few cases for a reliable estimate or the coefficient of variation (CV) is 50 percent or greater.
[1]Details on nonfederal work-study participants are not available.
[2]Includes students who reported that they were awarded aid but did not specify the source or type of aid.
[3]Includes Department of Veterans Affairs and Department of Defense benefits.
[4]Indicates all grants, scholarships, or tuition waivers received from federal, state, institutional, or private sources, including employers.
[5]Includes Parent Loans for Undergraduate Students (PLUS).
[6]Constant dollars based on the Consumer Price Index, prepared by the Bureau of Labor Statistics, U.S. Department of Labor, adjusted to a school-year basis.
NOTE: Aid averages are for those students who received the specified type of aid. Full-time, full-year students were enrolled full time for 9 or more months from July 1 through June 30. Data exclude Puerto Rico.
SOURCE: U.S. Department of Education, National Center for Education Statistics, 1992–93, 1995–96, 1999–2000, 2003–04, 2007–08, 2011–12, and 2015–16 National Postsecondary Student Aid Study (NPSAS:93, NPSAS:96, NPSAS:2000, NPSAS:04, NPSAS:08, NPSAS:12, and NPSAS:16). (This table was prepared October 2019.)

Table 331.90. Percentage of full-time and part-time undergraduates receiving federal aid, by aid program and control and level of institution: 2011–12 and 2015–16

[Standard errors appear in parentheses]

Control and level of institution	Number of undergraduates[1] (in thousands)	Percent receiving federal aid: Any federal aid		Selected Title IV programs[2]: Any Title IV aid		Pell		SEOG[3]		CWS[4]		Perkins[5]		Stafford[6]		PLUS[7]	
1	2	3		4		5		6		7		8		9		10	
2011–12																	
Full-time, full-year students																	
All institutions	**8,864**	**72.8**	**(0.51)**	**71.4**	**(0.54)**	**47.1**	**(0.50)**	**9.0**	**(0.24)**	**10.5**	**(0.24)**	**4.2**	**(0.18)**	**55.1**	**(0.54)**	**9.1**	**(0.23)**
Public	5,997	68.4	(0.61)	67.1	(0.64)	45.8	(0.59)	6.6	(0.26)	6.2	(0.23)	2.7	(0.15)	47.1	(0.57)	7.1	(0.28)
4-year doctoral	2,893	70.9	(0.47)	70.1	(0.48)	40.8	(0.39)	7.1	(0.39)	7.4	(0.37)	4.3	(0.30)	60.0	(0.43)	11.4	(0.45)
Other 4-year	969	72.7	(1.34)	71.4	(1.43)	48.1	(1.07)	6.5	(0.52)	8.6	(0.61)	2.8	(0.35)	54.0	(1.53)	8.1	(0.67)
2-year	2,104	63.0	(1.24)	61.0	(1.29)	51.4	(1.30)	5.9	(0.40)	3.4	(0.28)	0.3	(0.06)	26.5	(0.99)	1.0	(0.11)
Less-than-2-year	31	67.8	(4.72)	66.4	(5.20)	62.4	(5.04)	‡	(†)	‡	(†)	#	(†)	19.7	(4.83)	‡	(†)
Private, nonprofit	1,875	76.1	(0.75)	74.9	(0.75)	37.2	(0.64)	12.2	(0.60)	29.2	(0.81)	10.6	(0.61)	66.0	(0.90)	16.5	(0.67)
4-year doctoral	990	74.3	(0.94)	73.4	(0.96)	34.5	(0.77)	11.0	(0.89)	30.0	(1.26)	13.3	(0.97)	64.4	(1.08)	16.7	(1.10)
Other 4-year	849	78.0	(1.20)	76.7	(1.17)	39.8	(1.11)	13.6	(0.74)	29.1	(1.14)	8.0	(0.69)	68.2	(1.48)	16.2	(0.76)
Less-than-4-year	36	78.1	(5.04)	74.6	(5.35)	48.5	(6.54)	13.1 !	(5.38)	‡	(†)	‡	(†)	59.0	(7.42)	13.9	(3.36)
Private, for-profit	992	93.1	(0.51)	90.4	(0.52)	73.8	(0.81)	17.8	(0.87)	1.8	(0.20)	1.4	(0.23)	83.2	(0.90)	7.1	(0.44)
2-year and above	859	92.8	(0.59)	89.7	(0.59)	72.1	(0.91)	15.7	(0.81)	2.1	(0.23)	1.6	(0.27)	83.3	(0.91)	7.3	(0.48)
Less-than-2-year	133	95.2	(0.79)	95.1	(0.80)	85.0	(1.46)	31.4	(4.40)	‡	(†)	‡	(†)	82.9	(3.51)	5.9	(0.77)
Part-time or part-year students																	
All institutions	**14,192**	**51.1**	**(1.10)**	**48.4**	**(1.09)**	**37.6**	**(0.85)**	**4.4**	**(0.19)**	**2.0**	**(0.12)**	**0.9**	**(0.08)**	**30.7**	**(0.44)**	**1.6**	**(0.10)**
Public	10,929	44.5	(1.22)	42.4	(1.13)	33.4	(0.89)	2.6	(0.14)	1.6	(0.11)	0.5	(0.05)	22.1	(0.43)	1.0	(0.08)
Private, nonprofit	1,135	61.0	(1.61)	56.5	(1.99)	34.8	(1.51)	6.8	(0.66)	7.1	(0.76)	1.9	(0.30)	49.5	(1.57)	4.3	(0.51)
Private, for-profit	2,128	79.7	(0.83)	75.2	(1.16)	60.5	(1.09)	12.8	(0.83)	0.9	(0.14)	2.0	(0.47)	65.3	(0.47)	3.4	(0.32)
2015–16																	
Full-time, full-year students																	
All institutions	**7,239**	**69.8**	**(0.33)**	**68.4**	**(0.34)**	**44.0**	**(0.31)**	**10.4**	**(0.22)**	**9.1**	**(0.25)**	**4.3**	**(0.17)**	**52.0**	**(0.34)**	**9.3**	**(0.18)**
Public	5,023	67.7	(0.42)	66.3	(0.42)	44.3	(0.38)	8.6	(0.25)	5.8	(0.24)	3.3	(0.18)	46.3	(0.40)	7.8	(0.18)
4-year doctoral	2,849	69.4	(0.48)	68.3	(0.48)	41.3	(0.38)	9.4	(0.35)	7.1	(0.35)	4.9	(0.29)	56.9	(0.44)	11.5	(0.28)
Other 4-year	765	72.6	(0.98)	70.9	(1.05)	45.0	(1.20)	7.2	(0.54)	5.2	(0.67)	2.7	(0.49)	50.4	(1.25)	7.3	(0.49)
2-year	1,391	61.6	(0.85)	59.5	(0.86)	50.0	(0.80)	8.0	(0.51)	3.4	(0.41)	0.5	(0.08)	22.6	(0.62)	0.6	(0.10)
Less-than-2-year	19	67.0	(8.01)	64.4	(8.15)	56.0	(7.26)	3.0 !	(1.20)	‡	(†)	‡	(†)	25.1	(6.39)	‡	(†)
Private, nonprofit	1,735	70.3	(0.61)	69.6	(0.59)	35.5	(0.52)	13.9	(0.46)	21.0	(0.75)	8.2	(0.52)	61.9	(0.63)	14.0	(0.43)
4-year doctoral	1,011	67.5	(0.89)	66.8	(0.88)	31.9	(0.61)	13.2	(0.49)	21.3	(1.03)	9.0	(0.71)	58.6	(0.82)	14.2	(0.63)
Other 4-year	684	73.7	(0.89)	73.0	(0.86)	38.7	(0.81)	15.3	(0.82)	21.7	(1.22)	7.4	(0.76)	66.3	(1.00)	14.2	(0.55)
Less-than-4-year	40	81.7	(3.76)	81.0	(3.83)	72.2	(4.88)	‡	(†)	‡	(†)	‡	(†)	70.7	(5.65)	‡	(†)
Private, for-profit	481	89.4	(0.71)	86.7	(0.68)	71.9	(0.85)	15.6	(0.95)	1.5	(0.23)	0.7	(0.16)	76.5	(0.79)	8.0	(0.59)
2-year and above	382	89.7	(0.77)	86.3	(0.74)	70.4	(0.97)	16.2	(0.81)	1.5	(0.28)	0.8	(0.21)	77.2	(0.79)	7.8	(0.48)
Less-than-2-year	99	88.6	(1.74)	88.2	(1.76)	77.5	(2.19)	13.2	(3.37)	1.1 !	(0.54)	‡	(†)	73.9	(2.40)	8.8	(2.05)
Part-time or part-year students																	
All institutions	**12,069**	**47.6**	**(0.26)**	**45.4**	**(0.24)**	**35.5**	**(0.20)**	**5.9**	**(0.16)**	**1.8**	**(0.15)**	**0.8**	**(0.07)**	**27.0**	**(0.21)**	**1.4**	**(0.08)**
Public	9,468	42.0	(0.30)	40.0	(0.28)	31.4	(0.24)	4.4	(0.16)	1.5	(0.16)	0.6	(0.05)	19.8	(0.21)	0.9	(0.07)
4-year doctoral	1,825	55.5	(0.71)	53.5	(0.73)	34.1	(0.72)	5.5	(0.37)	2.2	(0.26)	2.5	(0.26)	43.4	(0.67)	3.6	(0.32)
Other 4-year	1,346	44.8	(1.25)	42.8	(1.12)	32.9	(0.99)	3.5	(0.42)	1.1	(0.24)	0.4	(0.08)	21.9	(0.75)	1.0	(0.19)
2-year	6,249	37.5	(0.38)	35.5	(0.35)	30.3	(0.30)	4.3	(0.19)	1.4	(0.24)	#	(†)	12.6	(0.15)	0.1	(0.02)
Less-than-2-year	48	38.4	(2.59)	35.2	(2.52)	30.0	(2.05)	1.9 !	(0.61)	‡	(†)	‡	(†)	12.4	(2.70)	‡	(†)
Private, nonprofit	1,220	58.0	(1.03)	55.9	(1.03)	37.7	(0.93)	8.0	(0.69)	4.7	(0.63)	2.7	(0.50)	46.7	(0.93)	3.7	(0.40)
4-year doctoral	622	53.5	(1.58)	51.4	(1.55)	32.5	(1.37)	6.5	(0.77)	4.8	(0.98)	3.5	(0.89)	44.7	(1.34)	3.4	(0.52)
Other 4-year	540	61.6	(1.13)	59.5	(1.16)	41.7	(1.18)	9.5	(1.14)	4.9	(0.79)	2.0	(0.46)	48.5	(1.12)	3.9	(0.63)
Less-than-4-year	58	73.2	(4.47)	70.2	(4.96)	56.2	(5.18)	9.0 !	(3.71)	1.1 !	(0.47)	‡	(†)	52.7	(4.60)	3.7 !	(1.39)
Private, for-profit	1,381	77.0	(0.59)	73.5	(0.53)	61.5	(0.57)	14.6	(0.76)	0.9	(0.11)	0.8	(0.19)	58.4	(0.53)	3.0	(0.28)
2-year and above	1,140	77.5	(0.67)	73.6	(0.60)	61.4	(0.60)	15.6	(0.87)	1.0	(0.12)	0.9	(0.22)	59.2	(0.47)	2.9	(0.31)
Less-than-2-year	240	74.6	(1.55)	73.1	(1.41)	61.8	(1.63)	9.9	(1.60)	0.7 !	(0.32)	‡	(†)	54.6	(2.11)	3.5	(0.63)

†Not applicable.
#Rounds to zero.
!Interpret data with caution. The coefficient of variation (CV) for this estimate is between 30 and 50 percent.
‡Reporting standards not met. The coefficient of variation (CV) for this estimate is 50 percent or greater.
[1]Numbers of undergraduates may not equal figures reported in other tables, since these data are based on a sample survey of students who enrolled at any point during the year.
[2]Refers to Title IV of the Higher Education Act.
[3]Supplemental Educational Opportunity Grants.
[4]College Work Study. Prior to October 17, 1986, private for-profit institutions were prohibited by law from spending CWS funds for on-campus work. Includes persons who participated in the program but had no earnings.
[5]Formerly National Direct Student Loans (NDSL).
[6]Formerly Guaranteed Student Loans (GSL).
[7]Parent Loans for Undergraduate Students.
NOTE: Full-time, full-year undergraduates are those who were enrolled full time for 9 or more months. Part-time or part-year undergraduates include those who were enrolled part time for 9 or more months and those who were enrolled for less than 9 months either part time or full time. Excludes students whose attendance status was not reported. Detail may not sum to totals because of rounding and because some students receive multiple types of aid and aid from different sources. Data exclude students attending institutions in Puerto Rico.
SOURCE: U.S. Department of Education, National Center for Education Statistics, 2011–12 and 2015–16 National Postsecondary Student Aid Study (NPSAS:12 and NPSAS:16). (This table was prepared June 2018.)

Table 331.95. Percentage of undergraduate degree/certificate completers who ever received loans and average cumulative amount borrowed, by degree level, selected student characteristics, and institution control: Selected years, 1999–2000 through 2015–16

[Standard errors appear in parentheses]

Degree level, selected student characteristic, and institution control	1999–2000: Loans to students: Total loans to students	1999–2000: Loans to students: Federal loan to students	1999–2000: Parent PLUS Loans[1]	2011–12: Loans to students: Total loans to students	2011–12: Loans to students: Federal loans to students	2011–12: Loans to students: Nonfederal loans	2011–12: Parent PLUS Loans[1]	2015–16: Loans to students: Total loans to students	2015–16: Loans to students: Federal loan to students	2015–16: Loans to students: Nonfederal loans	2015–16: Parent PLUS Loans[1]
1	2	3	4	5	6	7	8	9	10	11	12
	Percent of completers who ever received loans										
Total, all completers	**52.5 (0.75)**	**50.5 (0.74)**	**7.2 (0.27)**	**61.6 (0.62)**	**58.6 (0.62)**	**24.8 (0.50)**	**10.5 (0.40)**	**61.8 (0.55)**	**59.7 (0.56)**	**10.4 (0.27)**	**10.3 (0.24)**
Certificate below associate's level	**43.5 (2.64)**	**39.6 (2.57)**	**3.3 (0.55)**	**66.3 (1.71)**	**63.8 (1.79)**	**23.4 (1.25)**	**7.9 (0.83)**	**67.7 (1.76)**	**65.9 (1.88)**	**9.2 (0.71)**	**7.2 (0.65)**
Sex											
Male	39.3 (3.48)	35.9 (3.55)	3.4 (0.81)	58.0 (2.93)	55.9 (3.00)	21.5 (2.01)	8.7 (1.67)	57.4 (3.21)	55.9 (3.25)	7.7 (0.86)	8.4 (1.25)
Female	46.7 (3.12)	42.5 (2.95)	3.3 (0.68)	70.0 (1.90)	67.2 (1.96)	24.2 (1.50)	7.6 (0.93)	73.6 (1.75)	71.6 (1.87)	10.0 (0.93)	6.6 (0.76)
Institution control											
Public	27.1 (2.64)	22.2 (2.26)	0.9! (0.39)	36.2 (3.17)	31.8 (3.18)	10.5 (1.81)	1.8! (0.74)	44.6 (2.43)	43.0 (2.47)	4.3 (0.96)	3.4 (0.82)
Private nonprofit	53.2 (7.86)	49.8 (7.91)	9.8! (3.05)	76.1 (5.06)	73.3 (5.80)	23.1 (4.84)	‡ (†)	80.1 (3.50)	76.4 (4.97)	11.9 (2.42)	6.4! (2.07)
Private for-profit	86.3 (1.60)	85.0 (1.75)	8.5 (1.33)	85.9 (1.73)	84.6 (1.92)	32.2 (1.64)	12.0 (1.27)	87.5 (1.58)	85.7 (1.89)	13.3 (1.11)	11.0 (0.98)
Associate's degree	**38.9 (1.59)**	**36.9 (1.65)**	**4.3 (0.54)**	**49.8 (1.09)**	**46.1 (1.03)**	**18.7 (0.83)**	**5.0 (0.44)**	**48.1 (1.04)**	**46.2 (1.04)**	**5.8 (0.46)**	**5.1 (0.42)**
Sex											
Male	37.9 (2.76)	36.0 (2.82)	5.8 (1.28)	46.2 (1.75)	42.1 (1.73)	18.6 (1.05)	6.0 (0.75)	41.9 (1.48)	39.8 (1.46)	5.3 (0.72)	5.4 (0.72)
Female	39.4 (2.04)	37.4 (2.11)	3.5 (0.80)	52.3 (1.41)	48.9 (1.29)	18.9 (1.13)	4.3 (0.47)	52.5 (1.25)	50.8 (1.28)	6.1 (0.58)	4.9 (0.49)
Race/ethnicity											
White	39.5 (2.04)	37.4 (2.03)	4.5 (0.76)	49.2 (1.52)	45.7 (1.54)	19.8 (1.11)	5.0 (0.54)	50.2 (1.60)	48.4 (1.63)	6.4 (0.66)	6.1 (0.67)
Black	44.5 (4.38)	42.3 (4.26)	2.8! (1.06)	66.2 (2.62)	60.8 (2.67)	22.1 (2.06)	3.2 (0.93)	66.7 (2.41)	65.6 (2.48)	5.4 (1.03)	4.2 (0.72)
Hispanic	41.3 (5.26)	39.5 (5.00)	7.2! (2.98)	44.6 (2.34)	40.7 (2.28)	15.8 (1.60)	5.9 (1.18)	35.4 (1.89)	34.0 (1.86)	3.6 (0.70)	4.1 (0.73)
Asian	16.9! (5.79)	16.3! (5.73)	‡ (†)	26.1 (4.11)	23.0 (3.93)	9.9 (2.87)	6.1! (2.18)	26.7 (3.28)	22.1 (3.07)	6.2! (1.95)	2.5! (0.88)
Pacific Islander	‡ (†)	‡ (†)	‡ (†)	‡ (†)	‡ (†)	‡ (†)	‡ (†)	47.3 (11.14)	41.7 (11.28)	‡ (†)	‡ (†)
American Indian/Alaska Native	‡ (†)	‡ (†)	‡ (†)	64.6 (11.14)	64.6 (11.14)	‡ (†)	‡ (†)	67.2 (10.02)	63.3 (10.20)	19.0! (8.22)	‡ (†)
Two or more races	‡ (†)	‡ (†)	‡ (†)	52.1 (6.13)	51.5 (5.97)	21.9 (5.24)	6.2! (2.47)	47.1 (5.10)	45.5 (5.18)	6.4! (2.55)	4.6! (1.95)
Other[2]	‡ (†)	‡ (†)	‡ (†)	† (†)	† (†)	† (†)	† (†)	† (†)	† (†)	† (†)	† (†)
Dependency status											
Dependent	36.7 (2.91)	35.6 (2.89)	8.9 (1.38)	41.3 (1.57)	38.6 (1.54)	16.2 (1.10)	7.9 (0.79)	34.9 (1.57)	33.2 (1.50)	4.4 (0.51)	5.3 (0.59)
Independent	40.1 (1.87)	37.6 (2.04)	1.7 (0.50)	54.7 (1.39)	50.4 (1.34)	20.2 (1.01)	3.3 (0.48)	55.4 (1.29)	53.4 (1.35)	6.5 (0.65)	5.0 (0.59)
Institution control											
Public	32.6 (1.66)	30.6 (1.69)	1.9 (0.48)	42.1 (1.28)	38.1 (1.17)	14.9 (0.87)	3.2 (0.40)	40.9 (1.15)	38.8 (1.15)	4.8 (0.49)	3.9 (0.47)
Private nonprofit	45.7 (5.92)	43.0 (5.63)	11.1! (3.83)	86.9 (5.23)	84.8 (6.80)	43.2 (6.75)	12.5! (4.28)	83.9 (3.01)	83.1 (3.26)	11.9 (3.49)	9.0 (1.99)
Private for-profit	92.5 (1.29)	91.6 (1.20)	22.4 (3.49)	88.3 (1.77)	86.4 (1.87)	37.2 (1.93)	14.1 (1.63)	88.3 (1.16)	87.8 (1.15)	10.6 (0.86)	12.4 (1.02)
Bachelor's degree	**62.2 (0.70)**	**61.0 (0.70)**	**10.2 (0.40)**	**69.0 (0.75)**	**66.3 (0.72)**	**29.8 (0.79)**	**15.5 (0.68)**	**68.9 (0.62)**	**66.7 (0.64)**	**13.8 (0.33)**	**14.6 (0.36)**
Sex											
Male	61.4 (1.00)	60.2 (1.01)	10.6 (0.56)	67.0 (1.39)	63.9 (1.37)	29.4 (1.20)	15.1 (1.00)	65.7 (0.85)	63.3 (0.86)	13.3 (0.53)	14.8 (0.57)
Female	62.8 (0.94)	61.6 (0.92)	9.8 (0.54)	70.5 (0.94)	68.2 (0.92)	30.1 (1.04)	15.9 (0.92)	71.4 (0.71)	69.3 (0.75)	14.2 (0.44)	14.4 (0.46)
Race/ethnicity											
White	60.7 (0.87)	59.5 (0.85)	10.2 (0.45)	67.5 (0.94)	64.8 (0.92)	30.2 (1.03)	16.0 (0.87)	69.4 (0.69)	67.1 (0.70)	15.5 (0.45)	15.7 (0.44)
Black	80.5 (1.81)	80.0 (1.82)	13.9 (1.66)	84.2 (1.78)	82.0 (1.92)	33.2 (2.37)	16.9 (1.83)	84.9 (1.17)	83.8 (1.20)	10.6 (1.03)	16.7 (1.23)
Hispanic	68.7 (1.86)	67.1 (2.00)	11.7 (1.69)	71.9 (2.42)	69.2 (2.32)	30.0 (2.08)	15.1 (1.82)	66.6 (1.57)	64.7 (1.59)	10.2 (0.80)	11.8 (0.94)
Asian	50.2 (2.43)	49.0 (2.55)	4.3 (0.85)	47.2 (3.22)	42.7 (3.02)	20.5 (2.49)	7.8 (1.70)	45.1 (2.04)	41.4 (1.98)	10.6 (1.02)	8.7 (1.19)
Pacific Islander	66.7 (6.35)	66.7 (6.35)	19.1 (5.45)	‡ (†)	‡ (†)	‡ (†)	‡ (†)	89.4 (4.56)	80.7 (8.09)	18.3! (8.05)	14.1! (5.77)
American Indian/Alaska Native	75.2 (6.58)	71.8 (6.80)	3.8! (1.73)	61.5 (11.92)	60.2 (12.04)	19.5! (8.06)	‡ (†)	76.1 (5.87)	69.9 (6.68)	14.4 (4.23)	6.9! (2.22)
Two or more races	55.0 (5.12)	52.7 (5.48)	7.6 (1.95)	81.0 (3.68)	78.7 (3.94)	31.7 (4.43)	21.0 (4.63)	72.9 (2.35)	70.1 (2.60)	17.5 (2.58)	17.1 (2.01)
Other[2]	53.5 (6.22)	53.1 (6.19)	6.3! (2.25)	† (†)	† (†)	† (†)	† (†)	† (†)	† (†)	† (†)	† (†)
Dependency status											
Dependent	59.2 (0.95)	58.0 (0.92)	14.4 (0.63)	64.9 (1.09)	61.6 (1.06)	29.8 (1.02)	21.0 (0.96)	65.9 (0.69)	63.4 (0.70)	15.9 (0.43)	18.9 (0.54)
Independent	65.9 (0.92)	64.8 (0.94)	4.9 (0.34)	74.1 (1.16)	72.2 (1.13)	29.7 (1.19)	8.6 (0.76)	72.6 (0.92)	70.6 (0.97)	11.3 (0.52)	9.3 (0.50)
Institution control											
Public	60.0 (0.80)	58.8 (0.81)	8.3 (0.42)	64.1 (0.89)	61.2 (0.86)	25.9 (0.84)	13.5 (0.69)	66.4 (0.68)	64.1 (0.66)	11.7 (0.40)	13.7 (0.45)
Private nonprofit	66.2 (1.16)	65.2 (1.17)	14.1 (0.93)	73.5 (1.72)	70.7 (1.74)	34.6 (1.83)	21.5 (1.75)	69.2 (0.94)	66.7 (0.96)	17.9 (0.75)	17.0 (0.66)
Private for-profit	77.2 (4.41)	77.0 (4.45)	10.8! (3.55)	87.2 (1.62)	86.3 (1.59)	40.5 (1.76)	10.9 (1.17)	86.5 (1.95)	85.3 (2.43)	15.1 (1.16)	12.7 (1.63)

See notes at end of table.

Table 331.95. Percentage of undergraduate degree/certificate completers who ever received loans and average cumulative amount borrowed, by degree level, selected student characteristics, and institution control: Selected years, 1999–2000 through 2015–16—Continued

[Standard errors appear in parentheses]

Degree level, selected student characteristic, and institution control	1999–2000			2011–12				2015–16			
	Loans to students			Loans to students				Loans to students			
	Total loans to students	Federal loan to students	Parent PLUS Loans[1]	Total loans to students	Federal loans to students	Nonfederal loans	Parent PLUS Loans[1]	Total loans to students	Federal loan to students	Nonfederal loans	Parent PLUS Loans[1]
1	2	3	4	5	6	7	8	9	10	11	12
	Average cumulative loan amount for students with loans (current dollars)[3]										
Total, all completers	**$14,260 (186)**	**$13,540 (162)**	**$12,630 (443)**	**$23,050 (285)**	**$19,510 (208)**	**$11,210 (450)**	**$22,990 (1,197)**	**$24,480 (336)**	**$22,520 (305)**	**$16,160 (439)**	**$27,170 (676)**
Certificate below associate's level	**7,790 (418)**	**7,150 (330)**	**6,850 (1,081)**	**13,280 (374)**	**11,380 (343)**	**6,630 (526)**	**8,900 (612)**	**15,520 (502)**	**14,280 (413)**	**12,080 (1,649)**	**12,920 (1,158)**
Sex											
Male	8,110 (533)	7,550 (544)	8,290 (2,316)	13,370 (743)	10,970 (629)	7,540 (1,314)	10,080 (1,199)	15,380 (1,091)	13,760 (891)	14,630 (3,942)	16,320 (2,136)
Female	7,590 (492)	6,900 (373)	5,720 (941)	13,250 (393)	11,520 (357)	6,280 (510)	8,300 (775)	15,590 (476)	14,520 (423)	10,950 (1,549)	10,450 (1,172)
Institution control											
Public	7,640 (819)	7,540 (623)	‡ (†)	12,420 (1,151)	11,030 (1,095)	9,410 (2,241)	‡ (†)	16,400 (1,080)	15,550 (946)	‡ (†)	‡ (†)
Private nonprofit	11,240 (2,280)	9,880 (1,828)	9,680 (2,443)	15,820 (2,721)	11,850 (1,463)	14,530! (6,937)	‡ (†)	17,110 (2,536)	15,840 (1,951)	13,520! (6,105)	17,470! (6,447)
Private for-profit	7,470 (323)	6,540 (287)	6,260 (1,604)	13,320 (345)	11,430 (329)	5,510 (338)	9,180 (650)	14,880 (434)	13,480 (326)	11,040 (1,616)	11,110 (943)
Associate's degree	**9,490 (334)**	**8,840 (339)**	**7,630 (1,046)**	**17,160 (359)**	**15,130 (305)**	**8,370 (413)**	**14,830 (1,095)**	**18,550 (408)**	**18,060 (392)**	**9,950 (1,136)**	**12,980 (1,148)**
Sex											
Male	9,320 (698)	8,590 (663)	7,860 (2,013)	15,950 (536)	13,930 (418)	8,090 (561)	16,000 (1,696)	17,010 (652)	16,150 (552)	13,220 (2,547)	13,500 (1,712)
Female	9,570 (436)	8,970 (384)	7,430 (803)	17,900 (535)	15,850 (447)	8,570 (621)	13,690 (1,445)	19,420 (492)	19,110 (485)	7,970 (792)	12,580 (1,338)
Race/ethnicity											
White	9,590 (480)	8,910 (433)	8,510 (1,285)	17,110 (485)	14,630 (377)	8,810 (577)	15,400 (1,429)	17,760 (533)	17,100 (486)	10,210 (1,837)	13,350 (1,638)
Black	9,500 (771)	8,590 (659)	‡ (†)	19,280 (922)	17,580 (783)	9,380 (1,321)	15,050 (4,419)	22,300 (834)	21,930 (792)	9,020 (2,182)	11,310 (1,748)
Hispanic	8,840 (2,037)	9,090 (2,124)	‡ (†)	15,170 (912)	14,020 (786)	6,650 (667)	12,220 (1,572)	15,970 (904)	15,590 (928)	9,770 (1,659)	12,440 (1,563)
Asian	‡ (†)	‡ (†)	‡ (†)	13,580 (1,965)	13,400 (1,786)	4,640 (902)	‡ (†)	16,830 (1,772)	17,720 (1,981)	9,340 (2,170)	‡ (†)
Pacific Islander	‡ (†)	‡ (†)	‡ (†)	‡ (†)	‡ (†)	‡ (†)	‡ (†)	‡ (†)	‡ (†)	‡ (†)	‡ (†)
American Indian/Alaska Native	‡ (†)	‡ (†)	‡ (†)	22,330 (3,730)	22,100 (3,720)	‡ (†)	‡ (†)	18,230 (3,431)	17,830 (3,110)	‡ (†)	‡ (†)
Two or more races	‡ (†)	‡ (†)	‡ (†)	17,570 (1,740)	15,260 (1,453)	5,920 (1,367)	‡ (†)	21,790 (2,159)	20,940 (2,134)	‡ (†)	‡ (†)
Other[2]	‡ (†)	‡ (†)	‡ (†)	† (†)	† (†)	† (†)	† (†)	† (†)	† (†)	† (†)	† (†)
Dependency status											
Dependent	8,280 (530)	7,400 (452)	8,830 (1,306)	13,240 (512)	11,200 (391)	7,090 (618)	15,520 (1,739)	12,140 (438)	11,660 (440)	8,340 (1,100)	15,470 (1,677)
Independent	10,120 (479)	9,630 (459)	‡ (†)	18,860 (471)	16,860 (420)	8,960 (534)	13,880 (1,419)	20,780 (474)	20,250 (448)	10,550 (1,504)	11,510 (1,381)
Institution control											
Public	8,060 (431)	7,360 (398)	‡ (†)	13,970 (349)	12,300 (315)	8,080 (538)	12,070 (1,154)	15,640 (511)	15,230 (494)	10,110 (1,639)	11,600 (1,490)
Private nonprofit	11,850 (1,035)	11,950 (999)	‡ (†)	25,310 (2,076)	20,420 (1,564)	10,790 (2,742)	‡ (†)	24,830 (1,159)	23,890 (1,239)	8,180 (2,395)	14,950 (2,567)
Private for-profit	13,440 (685)	12,540 (672)	9,550 (1,804)	24,680 (624)	21,550 (537)	8,550 (486)	17,590 (1,854)	26,420 (512)	25,340 (537)	10,220 (718)	15,740 (1,994)
Bachelor's degree	**17,480 (204)**	**16,530 (180)**	**14,350 (548)**	**29,380 (456)**	**24,400 (295)**	**13,760 (704)**	**27,350 (1,613)**	**29,910 (402)**	**27,050 (384)**	**18,700 (432)**	**32,600 (796)**
Sex											
Male	17,470 (247)	16,530 (232)	14,730 (784)	29,030 (666)	23,740 (451)	14,630 (1,044)	29,780 (3,015)	28,920 (477)	26,120 (429)	18,760 (800)	33,790 (1,296)
Female	17,490 (256)	16,530 (230)	14,050 (627)	29,650 (551)	24,890 (378)	13,090 (857)	25,530 (1,602)	30,610 (451)	27,710 (420)	18,650 (641)	31,660 (967)
Race/ethnicity											
White	17,370 (211)	16,390 (195)	14,720 (591)	29,060 (579)	23,690 (354)	14,050 (766)	27,450 (2,033)	30,090 (346)	26,460 (325)	20,040 (595)	34,370 (1,088)
Black	19,510 (793)	18,760 (718)	10,880 (1,006)	33,020 (1,066)	29,200 (842)	11,620 (1,662)	24,490 (4,344)	34,000 (877)	32,370 (809)	16,450 (1,555)	24,800 (2,009)
Hispanic	17,450 (821)	16,270 (626)	13,810 (1,693)	29,520 (1,584)	23,710 (825)	16,050 (2,820)	26,470 (3,900)	26,820 (774)	25,420 (725)	13,900 (1,028)	29,440 (2,070)
Asian	14,540 (619)	13,990 (545)	20,260 (4,188)	23,130 (1,259)	20,740 (1,041)	10,070 (2,255)	‡ (†)	25,450 (1,094)	22,770 (882)	19,250 (2,191)	34,080 (3,962)
Pacific Islander	18,380 (1,787)	16,850 (1,222)	‡ (†)	‡ (†)	‡ (†)	‡ (†)	‡ (†)	26,520 (3,981)	27,690 (3,236)	‡ (†)	‡ (†)
American Indian/Alaska Native	18,770 (1,553)	18,290 (1,646)	‡ (†)	‡ (†)	‡ (†)	‡ (†)	‡ (†)	26,380 (2,659)	25,550 (2,696)	‡ (†)	‡ (†)
Two or more races	17,720 (1,352)	16,470 (1,229)	‡ (†)	28,050 (1,731)	23,950 (1,427)	12,250 (2,067)	‡ (†)	29,680 (1,097)	27,280 (940)	14,490 (1,605)	40,070 (3,890)
Other[2]	16,210 (1,378)	15,250 (1,361)	‡ (†)	† (†)	† (†)	† (†)	† (†)	† (†)	† (†)	† (†)	† (†)
Dependency status											
Dependent	16,910 (221)	15,620 (177)	15,680 (671)	26,070 (575)	20,370 (285)	14,700 (917)	28,410 (1,566)	26,760 (282)	22,450 (199)	21,340 (575)	36,790 (1,047)
Independent	18,110 (320)	17,540 (300)	9,490 (802)	33,040 (637)	28,740 (481)	12,570 (905)	24,060 (4,374)	33,340 (649)	32,010 (587)	14,230 (634)	22,420 (1,257)
Institution control											
Public	16,210 (233)	15,700 (213)	11,600 (550)	25,640 (454)	22,030 (336)	11,400 (621)	20,460 (1,080)	26,930 (278)	25,000 (235)	15,770 (611)	27,530 (990)
Private nonprofit	19,620 (373)	17,810 (313)	17,950 (810)	32,310 (1,181)	24,610 (594)	18,370 (1,698)	37,130 (3,739)	31,890 (453)	26,670 (331)	23,840 (766)	41,940 (1,853)
Private for-profit	24,040 (1,204)	23,170 (1,160)	‡ (†)	40,040 (798)	34,880 (612)	11,870 (911)	25,650 (2,506)	41,320 (1,592)	39,150 (1,303)	15,460 (1,060)	31,890 (2,316)

See notes at end of table.

Table 331.95. Percentage of undergraduate degree/certificate completers who ever received loans and average cumulative amount borrowed, by degree level, selected student characteristics, and institution control: Selected years, 1999–2000 through 2015–16—Continued

[Standard errors appear in parentheses]

Degree level, selected student characteristic, and institution control	1999–2000: Loans to students: Total loans to students	1999–2000: Loans to students: Federal loan to students	1999–2000: Parent PLUS Loans[1]	2011–12: Loans to students: Total loans to students	2011–12: Loans to students: Federal loans to students	2011–12: Loans to students: Nonfederal loans	2011–12: Parent PLUS Loans[1]	2015–16: Loans to students: Total loans to students	2015–16: Loans to students: Federal loan to students	2015–16: Loans to students: Nonfederal loans	2015–16: Parent PLUS Loans[1]
1	2	3	4	5	6	7	8	9	10	11	12
	Average cumulative loan amount for students with loans (constant 2018–19 dollars)[3,4]										
Total, all completers	**$21,330 (279)**	**$20,250 (243)**	**$18,890 (662)**	**$25,660 (317)**	**$21,710 (231)**	**$12,480 (500)**	**$25,590 (1,332)**	**$26,020 (357)**	**$23,940 (324)**	**$17,180 (467)**	**$28,880 (718)**
Certificate below associate's level	**11,660 (626)**	**10,700 (494)**	**10,250 (1,617)**	**14,780 (416)**	**12,660 (382)**	**7,380 (586)**	**9,900 (681)**	**16,500 (533)**	**15,180 (439)**	**12,840 (1,753)**	**13,740 (1,231)**
Sex											
Male	12,130 (797)	11,300 (814)	12,410 (3,465)	14,880 (827)	12,210 (700)	8,390 (1,462)	11,220 (1,335)	16,340 (1,160)	14,630 (948)	15,550 (4,190)	17,350 (2,271)
Female	11,360 (737)	10,330 (558)	8,560 (1,408)	14,740 (437)	12,830 (397)	6,990 (567)	9,230 (863)	16,570 (506)	15,430 (449)	11,640 (1,647)	11,110 (1,246)
Institution control											
Public	11,430 (1,225)	11,280 (932)	‡ (†)	13,820 (1,281)	12,280 (1,219)	10,470 (2,494)	‡ (†)	17,430 (1,148)	16,530 (1,005)	‡ (†)	‡ (†)
Private nonprofit	16,810 (3,410)	14,780 (2,734)	14,490 (3,655)	17,610 (3,029)	13,190 (1,629)	16,170! (7,721)	‡ (†)	18,190 (2,695)	16,830 (2,073)	14,370! (6,490)	18,570! (6,852)
Private for-profit	11,180 (484)	9,790 (429)	9,360 (2,399)	14,830 (384)	12,720 (366)	6,130 (376)	10,220 (723)	15,820 (461)	14,320 (346)	11,740 (1,717)	11,810 (1,002)
Associate's degree	**14,190 (500)**	**13,230 (507)**	**11,420 (1,564)**	**19,100 (400)**	**16,840 (340)**	**9,320 (459)**	**16,510 (1,219)**	**19,720 (434)**	**19,200 (416)**	**10,570 (1,207)**	**13,800 (1,220)**
Sex											
Male	13,940 (1,044)	12,850 (993)	11,760 (3,011)	17,750 (597)	15,500 (466)	9,000 (624)	17,800 (1,887)	18,080 (693)	17,170 (587)	14,050 (2,708)	14,350 (1,820)
Female	14,320 (653)	13,420 (575)	11,120 (1,201)	19,930 (595)	17,640 (497)	9,540 (691)	15,230 (1,609)	20,640 (523)	20,320 (516)	8,470 (842)	13,370 (1,422)
Race/ethnicity											
White	14,340 (717)	13,320 (649)	12,730 (1,922)	19,050 (540)	16,280 (420)	9,800 (642)	17,140 (1,591)	18,880 (567)	18,170 (516)	10,860 (1,952)	14,190 (1,741)
Black	14,210 (1,153)	12,850 (986)	‡ (†)	21,460 (1,026)	19,560 (871)	10,440 (1,470)	16,750 (4,918)	23,710 (887)	23,310 (841)	9,580 (2,319)	12,020 (1,858)
Hispanic	13,230 (3,047)	13,590 (3,178)	‡ (†)	16,880 (1,015)	15,600 (875)	7,400 (743)	13,600 (1,750)	16,980 (961)	16,570 (987)	10,380 (1,763)	13,230 (1,662)
Asian	‡ (†)	‡ (†)	‡ (†)	15,110 (2,187)	14,920 (1,987)	5,160 (1,003)	‡ (†)	17,890 (1,883)	18,830 (2,105)	9,930 (2,307)	‡ (†)
Pacific Islander	‡ (†)	‡ (†)	‡ (†)	‡ (†)	‡ (†)	‡ (†)	‡ (†)	‡ (†)	‡ (†)	‡ (†)	‡ (†)
American Indian/Alaska Native	‡ (†)	‡ (†)	‡ (†)	22,330 (3,730)	22,100 (3,720)	‡ (†)	‡ (†)	19,370 (3,647)	18,950 (3,306)	‡ (†)	‡ (†)
Two or more races	‡ (†)	‡ (†)	‡ (†)	19,560 (1,937)	16,980 (1,617)	6,590 (1,521)	‡ (†)	23,170 (2,295)	22,260 (2,269)	‡ (†)	‡ (†)
Other[2]	‡ (†)	‡ (†)	‡ (†)	† (†)	† (†)	† (†)	† (†)	† (†)	† (†)	† (†)	† (†)
Dependency status											
Dependent	12,390 (793)	11,070 (676)	13,200 (1,954)	14,740 (570)	12,460 (436)	7,900 (688)	17,280 (1,936)	12,900 (466)	12,390 (468)	8,870 (1,169)	16,440 (1,783)
Independent	15,130 (716)	14,400 (687)	‡ (†)	20,990 (525)	18,760 (468)	9,970 (594)	15,450 (1,579)	22,090 (504)	21,530 (476)	11,210 (1,599)	12,230 (1,468)
Institution control											
Public	12,060 (645)	11,020 (596)	‡ (†)	15,550 (388)	13,690 (351)	8,990 (599)	13,440 (1,285)	16,620 (544)	16,190 (525)	10,740 (1,743)	12,330 (1,584)
Private nonprofit	17,720 (1,548)	17,880 (1,495)	‡ (†)	28,170 (2,311)	22,730 (1,741)	12,010 (3,052)	‡ (†)	26,390 (1,232)	25,400 (1,317)	8,690 (2,546)	15,900 (2,728)
Private for-profit	20,110 (1,025)	18,770 (1,006)	14,290 (2,698)	27,470 (695)	23,980 (598)	9,510 (540)	19,580 (2,064)	28,080 (544)	26,940 (571)	10,860 (763)	16,730 (2,120)
Bachelor's degree	**26,150 (305)**	**24,730 (270)**	**21,470 (820)**	**32,700 (508)**	**27,160 (329)**	**15,310 (784)**	**30,440 (1,796)**	**31,790 (427)**	**28,760 (408)**	**19,870 (459)**	**34,650 (846)**
Sex											
Male	26,130 (370)	24,730 (347)	22,040 (1,173)	32,310 (741)	26,420 (502)	16,280 (1,162)	33,140 (3,355)	30,740 (507)	27,760 (456)	19,940 (851)	35,920 (1,377)
Female	26,160 (383)	24,740 (344)	21,010 (938)	33,000 (614)	27,710 (421)	14,560 (954)	28,410 (1,783)	32,540 (479)	29,450 (446)	19,820 (682)	33,650 (1,028)
Race/ethnicity											
White	25,990 (316)	24,530 (291)	22,020 (885)	32,350 (644)	26,370 (394)	15,640 (852)	30,550 (2,262)	31,980 (367)	28,120 (346)	21,300 (633)	36,530 (1,156)
Black	29,190 (1,187)	28,060 (1,075)	16,270 (1,505)	36,740 (1,186)	32,490 (937)	12,940 (1,849)	27,260 (4,835)	36,140 (932)	34,400 (860)	17,490 (1,653)	26,370 (2,136)
Hispanic	26,100 (1,228)	24,340 (936)	20,670 (2,533)	32,850 (1,763)	26,380 (918)	17,860 (3,139)	29,460 (4,340)	28,510 (823)	27,020 (771)	14,770 (1,092)	31,290 (2,200)
Asian	21,750 (926)	20,930 (815)	30,310 (6,266)	25,750 (1,401)	23,080 (1,159)	11,210 (2,509)	‡ (†)	27,050 (1,163)	24,200 (938)	20,460 (2,328)	36,230 (4,211)
Pacific Islander	27,490 (2,673)	25,210 (1,828)	‡ (†)	‡ (†)	‡ (†)	‡ (†)	‡ (†)	28,180 (4,231)	29,430 (3,440)	‡ (†)	‡ (†)
American Indian/Alaska Native	28,080 (2,324)	27,360 (2,463)	‡ (†)	‡ (†)	‡ (†)	‡ (†)	‡ (†)	28,040 (2,826)	27,160 (2,866)	‡ (†)	‡ (†)
Two or more races	26,500 (2,022)	24,650 (1,838)	‡ (†)	31,220 (1,926)	26,650 (1,588)	13,630 (2,301)	‡ (†)	31,540 (1,166)	29,000 (999)	15,400 (1,706)	42,590 (4,135)
Other[2]	24,250 (2,061)	22,820 (2,037)	‡ (†)	† (†)	† (†)	† (†)	† (†)	† (†)	† (†)	† (†)	† (†)
Dependency status											
Dependent	25,300 (330)	23,370 (265)	23,470 (1,004)	29,020 (640)	22,670 (318)	16,360 (1,021)	31,620 (1,743)	28,440 (300)	23,860 (212)	22,680 (611)	39,110 (1,113)
Independent	27,100 (479)	26,240 (449)	14,200 (1,200)	36,770 (709)	31,990 (535)	13,990 (1,007)	26,780 (4,868)	35,440 (690)	34,020 (624)	15,130 (674)	23,840 (1,336)
Institution control											
Public	24,250 (348)	23,490 (318)	17,350 (822)	28,540 (505)	24,520 (374)	12,690 (691)	22,770 (1,202)	28,620 (296)	26,570 (250)	16,760 (649)	29,260 (1,052)
Private nonprofit	29,350 (558)	26,650 (468)	26,850 (1,211)	35,960 (1,315)	27,390 (661)	20,440 (1,890)	41,320 (4,161)	33,900 (482)	28,350 (352)	25,340 (815)	44,580 (1,970)
Private for-profit	35,960 (1,801)	34,660 (1,736)	‡ (†)	44,560 (888)	38,820 (681)	13,210 (1,014)	28,550 (2,789)	43,920 (1,692)	41,610 (1,386)	16,440 (1,127)	33,900 (2,462)

†Not applicable.
!Interpret data with caution. The coefficient of variation (CV) for this estimate is between 30 and 50 percent.
‡Reporting standards not met. Either there are too few cases for a reliable estimate or the coefficient of variation (CV) is 50 percent or greater.
[1]Parent PLUS Loans are taken out by parents of dependent students and are used toward the students' undergraduate education. Parent PLUS Loans were available through both the William D. Ford Federal Direct Loan Program and the Federal Family Education Loan Program (FFELP) until FFELP was discontinued in 2010. Since then, Parent PLUS Loans have been referred to as Direct PLUS Loans.
[2]The 2012 and 2016 questionnaires did not offer students the option of choosing an "Other" race category.
[3]Average loan amounts were calculated only for students who took out each type of loan (or whose parents took out a PLUS Loan on their behalf).
[4]Constant dollars based on the Consumer Price Index, prepared by the Bureau of Labor Statistics, U.S. Department of Labor, adjusted to a school-year basis.
NOTE: Race categories exclude persons of Hispanic ethnicity. Data exclude students attending institutions in Puerto Rico.
SOURCE: U.S. Department of Education, National Center for Education Statistics, 1999–2000, 2011–12, and 2015–16 National Postsecondary Student Aid Study (NPSAS:2000, NPSAS:12, and NPSAS:16). (This table was prepared September 2019.)

Table 332.10. Amount borrowed, aid status, and sources of aid for full-time, full-year postbaccalaureate students, by level of study and control and level of institution: Selected years, 1992–93 through 2015–16

[Standard errors appear in parentheses]

Level of study, control and level of institution	Cumulative borrowing for undergraduate and graduate education[1]: Percent who borrowed		Average amount for those who borrowed: Current dollars		Average amount for those who borrowed: Constant 2018–19 dollars[2]		Aid status (percent of students): Nonaided		Any aid[3]		Source of aid: Federal[4]		State		Institutional		Employer	
1	2		3		4		5		6		7		8		9		10	
1992–93, all institutions	**—**	**(†)**	**—**	**(†)**	**—**	**(†)**	**30.7**	**(1.43)**	**69.3**	**(1.43)**	**44.3**	**(1.42)**	**6.9**	**(0.64)**	**40.6**	**(2.02)**	**5.3**	**(0.59)**
Master's degree	—	(†)	—	(†)	—	(†)	35.5	(2.54)	64.5	(2.54)	33.8	(1.91)	5.8	(0.79)	42.4	(2.97)	8.3	(1.01)
Public	—	(†)	—	(†)	—	(†)	32.7	(2.40)	67.3	(2.40)	33.9	(2.04)	7.8	(1.10)	44.1	(2.68)	7.6	(1.24)
4-year doctoral	—	(†)	—	(†)	—	(†)	32.4	(2.59)	67.6	(2.59)	32.4	(2.23)	6.7	(0.96)	46.4	(3.19)	7.7	(1.28)
Other 4-year	—	(†)	—	(†)	—	(†)	34.6	(4.38)	65.4	(4.38)	42.5	(5.30)	14.4	(4.13)	30.5	(3.67)	6.8!	(2.66)
Private	—	(†)	—	(†)	—	(†)	39.2	(4.74)	60.8	(4.74)	33.7	(3.62)	3.2	(0.89)	40.2	(6.34)	9.4	(1.88)
4-year doctoral	—	(†)	—	(†)	—	(†)	37.4	(4.70)	62.6	(4.70)	34.2	(4.09)	2.9!	(1.00)	42.9	(6.75)	8.9	(1.88)
Other 4-year	—	(†)	—	(†)	—	(†)	50.5	(10.60)	49.5	(10.60)	30.5	(7.06)	‡	(†)	22.8!	(9.39)	‡	(†)
Doctor's degree	—	(†)	—	(†)	—	(†)	30.1	(2.32)	69.9	(2.32)	28.3	(2.14)	4.4	(0.71)	51.6	(2.70)	3.0	(0.79)
Public	—	(†)	—	(†)	—	(†)	29.9	(2.99)	70.1	(2.99)	22.3	(2.26)	6.5	(1.14)	55.5	(3.01)	3.9	(1.00)
Private	—	(†)	—	(†)	—	(†)	30.4	(3.27)	69.6	(3.27)	37.8	(3.54)	‡	(†)	45.5	(3.52)	‡	(†)
First-professional	—	(†)	—	(†)	—	(†)	22.6	(0.96)	77.4	(0.96)	68.2	(1.54)	9.9	(1.34)	37.0	(1.81)	2.3	(0.52)
Public	—	(†)	—	(†)	—	(†)	20.4	(1.02)	79.6	(1.02)	72.5	(1.29)	13.4	(1.75)	37.7	(1.67)	2.3	(0.59)
Private	—	(†)	—	(†)	—	(†)	24.6	(1.66)	75.4	(1.66)	64.2	(2.42)	6.8	(1.19)	36.4	(3.29)	2.3!	(0.70)
Other graduate	—	(†)	—	(†)	—	(†)	38.3	(6.82)	61.7	(6.82)	42.1	(4.26)	6.6	(1.81)	23.0	(4.05)	6.0!	(2.98)
1999–2000, all institutions	**69.4**	**(0.74)**	**$41,920**	**(863)**	**$62,720**	**(1,291)**	**18.3**	**(0.66)**	**81.7**	**(0.66)**	**52.5**	**(0.76)**	**6.0**	**(0.60)**	**49.7**	**(1.03)**	**6.0**	**(0.57)**
Master's degree	68.3	(1.12)	31,930	(1,097)	47,770	(1,642)	20.6	(1.15)	79.4	(1.15)	50.6	(1.23)	5.1	(0.66)	45.4	(1.61)	9.2	(1.03)
Public	63.2	(1.60)	28,070	(1,079)	42,000	(1,614)	22.3	(1.52)	77.7	(1.52)	44.8	(1.82)	7.3	(1.14)	49.8	(2.16)	7.0	(1.04)
4-year doctoral	62.5	(1.56)	27,510	(1,234)	41,160	(1,846)	20.2	(1.46)	79.8	(1.46)	43.3	(1.71)	7.0	(1.31)	54.3	(2.02)	7.3	(1.20)
Other 4-year	70.9	(6.04)	31,920	(2,822)	47,750	(4,222)	29.9	(5.08)	70.1	(5.08)	54.7	(6.88)	10.2!	(3.32)	27.4	(6.85)	5.1!	(1.79)
Private	74.4	(1.55)	35,890	(1,855)	53,700	(2,775)	18.6	(1.59)	81.4	(1.59)	57.8	(1.88)	2.5	(0.63)	40.2	(2.63)	11.8	(1.89)
4-year doctoral	73.3	(1.76)	38,420	(2,521)	57,480	(3,772)	17.1	(1.93)	82.9	(1.93)	58.3	(2.36)	2.9!	(0.90)	50.5	(3.22)	8.3	(1.31)
Other[5]	76.9	(3.74)	30,770	(1,850)	46,030	(2,768)	21.8	(2.75)	78.2	(2.75)	56.6	(4.41)	‡	(†)	18.1	(3.91)	19.1	(5.24)
Doctor's degree	56.8	(1.95)	38,990	(3,421)	58,330	(5,118)	12.0	(1.38)	88.0	(1.38)	29.6	(2.80)	2.6	(0.54)	77.4	(1.65)	5.4	(0.64)
Public	54.5	(1.92)	33,600	(1,564)	50,260	(2,340)	11.4	(1.38)	88.6	(1.38)	26.1	(1.86)	3.2	(0.75)	80.0	(1.59)	7.3	(0.88)
Private	60.5	(3.62)	46,680	(7,288)	69,830	(10,904)	13.0	(2.80)	87.0	(2.80)	35.2	(6.26)	‡	(†)	73.2	(3.22)	2.3	(0.55)
First-professional	85.1	(1.14)	60,860	(1,713)	91,040	(2,563)	13.4	(1.18)	86.6	(1.18)	77.1	(1.29)	9.9	(1.65)	41.4	(2.40)	1.7!	(0.53)
Public	86.8	(1.70)	52,790	(1,954)	78,980	(2,923)	13.8	(1.82)	86.2	(1.82)	78.3	(2.13)	12.7	(2.57)	38.9	(2.84)	1.8!	(0.87)
Private	83.6	(1.63)	67,820	(3,213)	101,460	(4,807)	13.1	(1.49)	86.9	(1.49)	76.1	(1.84)	7.5	(2.11)	43.4	(3.65)	1.7!	(0.66)
Other graduate	57.5	(3.81)	27,840	(2,036)	41,640	(3,046)	39.3	(3.68)	60.7	(3.68)	44.9	(3.72)	8.1	(2.37)	25.3	(3.22)	2.8!	(1.20)
2007–08, all institutions	**71.3**	**(1.04)**	**$55,110**	**(993)**	**$65,930**	**(1,188)**	**13.1**	**(0.80)**	**86.9**	**(0.80)**	**56.6**	**(1.18)**	**3.8**	**(0.28)**	**43.9**	**(1.17)**	**11.6**	**(0.93)**
Master's degree	71.8	(1.77)	43,250	(1,374)	51,750	(1,644)	15.6	(1.34)	84.4	(1.34)	55.5	(1.93)	2.9	(0.40)	35.5	(1.48)	16.3	(1.76)
Public	66.5	(1.79)	37,770	(1,473)	45,190	(1,762)	13.3	(1.27)	86.7	(1.27)	50.7	(1.91)	4.1	(0.83)	52.2	(2.40)	13.4	(1.49)
4-year doctoral	65.1	(1.95)	38,450	(1,644)	46,000	(1,967)	12.1	(1.34)	87.9	(1.34)	50.1	(2.07)	4.2	(0.93)	56.0	(2.62)	14.5	(1.68)
Other 4-year	77.1	(4.81)	33,440	(2,285)	40,010	(2,734)	22.7	(3.92)	77.3	(3.92)	55.6	(5.96)	‡	(†)	23.5	(4.89)	5.1!	(1.92)
Private	75.5	(2.58)	46,590	(1,974)	55,730	(2,361)	17.2	(1.96)	82.8	(1.96)	58.8	(2.81)	2.0	(0.35)	24.0	(1.59)	18.3	(2.79)
4-year doctoral	71.4	(1.85)	46,510	(1,654)	55,640	(1,979)	19.1	(1.45)	80.9	(1.45)	55.1	(1.51)	2.4	(0.50)	36.0	(2.46)	14.4	(1.17)
Other[5]	80.8	(5.13)	46,670	(3,671)	55,840	(4,392)	14.8	(3.91)	85.2	(3.91)	63.6	(5.96)	1.6	(0.43)	8.4	(1.44)	23.4	(6.23)
Doctor's degree	59.8	(1.73)	55,200	(2,108)	66,040	(2,522)	7.1	(0.88)	92.9	(0.88)	38.4	(2.18)	2.9	(0.41)	70.7	(3.03)	7.9	(0.79)
Public	52.3	(2.17)	44,190	(1,604)	52,870	(1,919)	7.9	(1.48)	92.1	(1.48)	29.7	(1.80)	3.6	(0.65)	81.1	(1.89)	7.7	(0.93)
Private	67.8	(2.41)	64,120	(3,123)	76,720	(3,737)	6.2	(1.08)	93.8	(1.08)	47.6	(3.43)	2.2!	(0.65)	59.8	(5.02)	8.0	(1.36)
First-professional	84.9	(1.29)	81,400	(1,782)	97,380	(2,131)	11.5	(1.12)	88.5	(1.12)	81.7	(1.35)	7.5	(0.83)	35.7	(1.89)	4.6	(0.75)
Public	84.4	(1.96)	73,230	(2,717)	87,600	(3,251)	11.5	(1.65)	88.5	(1.65)	81.8	(2.12)	10.6	(1.46)	34.0	(2.67)	4.9	(1.44)
Private	85.4	(1.57)	87,800	(2,183)	105,040	(2,612)	11.5	(1.46)	88.5	(1.46)	81.5	(1.67)	5.1	(0.85)	37.0	(2.56)	4.4	(0.72)
Other graduate	62.4	(6.48)	43,740	(3,904)	52,330	(4,671)	30.8	(6.54)	69.2	(6.54)	51.0	(6.62)	‡	(†)	25.5	(5.78)	6.2!	(2.33)
2011–12, all institutions	**73.3**	**(0.90)**	**$74,710**	**(996)**	**$83,150**	**(1,109)**	**13.9**	**(0.77)**	**86.1**	**(0.77)**	**62.3**	**(0.93)**	**2.4**	**(0.34)**	**42.2**	**(1.19)**	**10.2**	**(0.48)**
Master's degree	73.5	(1.45)	58,590	(1,142)	65,210	(1,271)	17.4	(1.28)	82.6	(1.28)	63.0	(1.44)	1.8	(0.35)	35.1	(1.53)	8.8	(0.70)
Public	71.8	(2.24)	50,200	(1,816)	55,870	(2,021)	16.2	(1.84)	83.8	(1.84)	58.2	(2.41)	3.7	(0.80)	45.6	(2.35)	10.3	(1.17)
4-year doctoral	70.7	(2.41)	50,620	(2,015)	56,330	(2,242)	16.3	(2.03)	83.7	(2.03)	57.0	(2.60)	4.0	(0.89)	47.1	(2.56)	10.8	(1.28)
Other 4-year	82.2	(3.71)	46,900	(2,538)	52,190	(2,825)	15.4	(4.13)	84.6	(4.13)	69.5	(5.18)	‡	(†)	31.2	(3.46)	5.9	(1.68)
Private	74.8	(1.95)	64,510	(1,456)	71,790	(1,620)	18.2	(1.80)	81.8	(1.80)	66.5	(2.13)	0.4!	(0.19)	27.5	(2.09)	7.8	(0.88)
4-year doctoral	70.1	(2.41)	67,130	(2,165)	74,710	(2,410)	19.6	(2.06)	80.4	(2.06)	59.5	(2.45)	‡	(†)	35.2	(2.96)	7.8	(1.23)
Other[5]	81.8	(3.20)	61,140	(1,816)	68,040	(2,021)	16.1	(3.09)	83.9	(3.09)	77.0	(3.66)	‡	(†)	15.9	(2.70)	7.6	(1.04)
Doctor's degree—research/scholarship	50.5	(1.42)	65,090	(2,343)	72,450	(2,608)	6.6	(0.73)	93.4	(0.73)	27.8	(1.19)	1.5!	(0.49)	79.8	(1.27)	24.0	(1.25)
Public	47.9	(2.23)	55,500	(2,291)	61,770	(2,550)	5.9	(1.04)	94.1	(1.04)	24.2	(1.41)	2.1!	(0.78)	87.2	(1.59)	27.0	(1.93)
Private	54.0	(1.86)	76,180	(4,351)	84,790	(4,843)	7.5	(1.07)	92.5	(1.07)	32.3	(2.30)	‡	(†)	70.1	(2.28)	20.1	(1.06)
Doctor's degree—professional practice and other[6]	88.3	(0.90)	110,570	(1,848)	123,050	(2,056)	9.3	(0.88)	90.7	(0.88)	84.4	(1.03)	4.5	(0.96)	35.1	(1.66)	4.4	(0.51)
Public	88.3	(1.00)	102,220	(2,726)	113,770	(3,034)	8.9	(1.09)	91.1	(1.09)	84.4	(1.31)	8.1	(2.27)	40.6	(2.51)	5.4	(0.82)
Private	88.3	(1.28)	116,000	(2,490)	129,100	(2,771)	9.6	(1.22)	90.4	(1.22)	84.4	(1.50)	2.2	(0.53)	31.5	(2.19)	3.7	(0.62)
Other graduate	74.9	(6.28)	57,540	(5,456)	64,040	(6,072)	29.1	(6.46)	70.9	(6.46)	61.4	(7.24)	‡	(†)	16.9	(4.78)	5.5!	(2.47)

See notes at end of table.

Table 332.10. Amount borrowed, aid status, and sources of aid for full-time, full-year postbaccalaureate students, by level of study and control and level of institution: Selected years, 1992–93 through 2015–16—Continued

[Standard errors appear in parentheses]

Level of study, control and level of institution	Cumulative borrowing for undergraduate and graduate education[1]			Aid status (percent of students)					
		Average amount for those who borrowed				Source of aid			
	Percent who borrowed	Current dollars	Constant 2018–19 dollars[2]	Nonaided	Any aid[3]	Federal[4]	State	Institutional	Employer
1	2	3	4	5	6	7	8	9	10
2015–16, all institutions	**68.3 (0.93)**	**$80,750 (2,158)**	**$85,830 (2,294)**	**17.0 (0.82)**	**83.0 (0.82)**	**54.0 (0.89)**	**3.3 (0.52)**	**46.6 (1.25)**	**6.9 (0.54)**
Master's degree	66.6 (1.45)	59,100 (1,608)	62,820 (1,709)	20.0 (1.17)	80.0 (1.17)	51.9 (1.48)	3.1 (0.46)	41.6 (1.62)	9.0 (0.75)
Public	63.7 (2.22)	49,450 (2,109)	52,570 (2,242)	21.6 (1.77)	78.4 (1.77)	45.0 (2.10)	5.5 (0.93)	44.4 (2.17)	6.6 (0.89)
4-year doctoral	63.1 (2.34)	49,950 (2,287)	53,090 (2,431)	21.2 (1.86)	78.8 (1.86)	44.2 (2.23)	5.4 (1.00)	46.2 (2.28)	6.6 (0.96)
Other 4-year	71.7 (3.46)	44,240 (2,997)	47,030 (3,186)	25.9 (3.22)	74.1 (3.22)	54.7 (3.65)	5.8! (1.82)	23.6 (4.31)	6.3! (2.28)
Private	69.1 (1.74)	66,890 (2,295)	71,100 (2,439)	18.5 (1.52)	81.5 (1.52)	57.9 (1.98)	1.0! (0.35)	39.1 (2.52)	11.1 (1.14)
4-year doctoral	65.3 (2.35)	67,870 (3,010)	72,140 (3,199)	20.4 (1.97)	79.6 (1.97)	54.3 (2.57)	1.2! (0.48)	39.7 (3.06)	9.2 (1.44)
Other[5]	78.4 (2.23)	64,910 (2,838)	68,990 (3,016)	14.0 (1.56)	86.0 (1.56)	66.7 (2.52)	0.7! (0.28)	37.7 (4.15)	15.8 (1.46)
Doctor's degree—research/scholarship	52.5 (2.13)	74,510 (3,435)	79,200 (3,652)	9.9 (1.05)	90.1 (1.05)	27.9 (1.94)	1.2 (0.31)	71.9 (1.93)	6.2 (0.78)
Public	46.6 (2.93)	61,200 (4,167)	65,050 (4,429)	10.9 (1.82)	89.1 (1.82)	18.3 (2.49)	1.5 (0.44)	78.7 (2.56)	5.0 (0.90)
Private	58.2 (3.11)	84,910 (5,368)	90,250 (5,706)	8.8 (1.18)	91.2 (1.18)	37.3 (2.86)	0.9! (0.40)	65.2 (3.08)	7.4 (1.24)
Doctor's degree—professional practice and other[6]	80.3 (1.56)	121,940 (6,425)	129,610 (6,830)	14.0 (1.48)	86.0 (1.48)	73.0 (1.54)	4.6! (1.57)	45.9 (2.17)	2.3 (0.68)
Public	79.8 (2.45)	99,450 (3,685)	105,710 (3,917)	15.9 (2.29)	84.1 (2.29)	71.8 (2.26)	4.5 (1.06)	48.6 (3.18)	2.2! (0.84)
Private	80.7 (2.02)	138,370 (11,011)	147,070 (11,704)	12.6 (2.00)	87.4 (2.00)	74.0 (2.11)	‡ (†)	43.9 (2.93)	2.5! (1.04)
Other graduate	70.9 (4.84)	80,210 (8,667)	85,250 (9,213)	20.7 (3.95)	79.3 (3.95)	54.0 (5.41)	‡ (†)	28.2 (5.29)	10.7 (3.09)

—Not available.
†Not applicable.
!Interpret data with caution. The coefficient of variation (CV) for this estimate is between 30 and 50 percent.
‡Reporting standards not met. Either there are too few cases for a reliable estimate or the coefficient of variation (CV) is 50 percent or greater.
[1]Includes all loans ever taken out for both graduate and undergraduate education. Does not include Parent Loans for Undergraduate Students (PLUS) or loans from families and friends.
[2]Constant dollars based on the Consumer Price Index, prepared by the Bureau of Labor Statistics, U.S. Department of Labor, adjusted to a school-year basis.
[3]Includes students who reported they were awarded aid but did not specify the source of aid.
[4]Includes Department of Veterans Affairs and Department of Defense benefits.
[5]Includes nonprofit 4-year nondoctoral institutions and for-profit 2-year-and-above institutions.
[6]Professional practice doctor's degrees include most degrees that were classified as first-professional degrees prior to 2010–11 (such as M.D., D.D.S., and J.D.). "Other" doctor's degrees are those that are neither research/scholarship degrees nor professional practice degrees.
NOTE: Full-time, full-year students are those who were enrolled full time for 9 or more months. Excludes students whose attendance status was not reported. Total includes some students whose level of study or control of institution was unknown. Detail may not sum to totals because of rounding and because some students receive multiple types of aid and aid from different sources. Data exclude students attending institutions in Puerto Rico.
SOURCE: U.S. Department of Education, National Center for Education Statistics, 1992–93, 1999–2000, 2007–08, 2011–12, and 2015–16 National Postsecondary Student Aid Study (NPSAS:93, NPSAS:2000, NPSAS:08, NPSAS:12, and NPSAS:16). (This table was prepared October 2019.)

Table 332.45. Percentage of graduate degree completers with student loan debt and average cumulative amount owed, by level of education funded and graduate degree type, institution control, and degree program: Selected years, 1999–2000 through 2015–16

[Standard errors appear in parentheses]

Graduate degree type, institution control, and degree program	Loans for graduate education only					Total loans (for undergraduate and graduate education)				
	1999–2000	2003–04	2007–08	2011–12	2015–16	1999–2000	2003–04	2007–08	2011–12	2015–16
1	2	3	4	5	6	7	8	9	10	11
Total	**44.6 (1.06)**	**54.6 (1.77)**	**54.6 (1.18)**	**58.6 (1.25)**	**54.2 (1.05)**	**51.3 (1.00)**	**60.9 (1.72)**	**62.9 (1.15)**	**64.1 (1.23)**	**60.5 (1.08)**
Graduate degree type and institution control[1]										
Postbaccalaureate certificate	35.8 (5.12)	46.3 (7.43)	49.5 (5.02)	39.4 (4.66)	47.6 (4.18)	49.2 (4.72)	53.0 (7.02)	64.1 (4.68)	44.5 (4.53)	55.1 (3.88)
Public	33.4 (6.29)	30.1 (5.25)	45.1 (7.45)	35.5 (6.04)	39.0 (5.78)	51.2 (5.62)	39.9 (6.22)	64.5 (6.95)	41.5 (5.84)	48.7 (5.49)
Private nonprofit	32.8 (9.10)	70.3 (9.55)	54.7 (6.47)	48.0 (7.97)	53.5 (5.99)	40.4 (9.55)	73.1 (9.13)	63.8 (5.82)	50.5 (8.06)	57.8 (6.03)
Private for-profit	‡ (†)	‡ (†)	‡ (†)	‡ (†)	72.5 (4.88)	‡ (†)	‡ (†)	‡ (†)	‡ (†)	78.1 (3.99)
Master's	39.9 (1.30)	52.0 (2.10)	53.8 (1.47)	59.0 (1.50)	52.8 (1.23)	47.2 (1.19)	59.4 (2.03)	62.7 (1.45)	65.2 (1.48)	60.0 (1.28)
Public	35.6 (1.53)	41.6 (2.20)	48.4 (1.79)	53.0 (2.19)	49.1 (1.87)	43.7 (1.57)	50.0 (2.28)	59.1 (1.87)	62.1 (2.14)	57.3 (2.04)
Private nonprofit	44.1 (2.65)	60.8 (3.13)	55.2 (1.69)	60.8 (2.29)	53.0 (1.82)	50.9 (2.46)	67.6 (2.85)	63.3 (1.84)	64.6 (2.38)	59.8 (1.74)
Private for-profit	60.4 (11.61)	76.7 (10.88)	80.3 (6.41)	74.9 (4.97)	67.5 (3.18)	61.6 (10.98)	77.2 (10.76)	83.5 (6.34)	78.6 (4.86)	71.3 (2.74)
Doctor's, research	38.8 (2.92)	45.3 (2.14)	43.1 (2.54)	40.7 (2.33)	43.6 (3.45)	43.6 (3.04)	50.5 (2.28)	49.3 (2.77)	47.5 (2.44)	48.2 (3.51)
Public	34.6 (3.35)	39.6 (2.52)	38.5 (3.12)	35.3 (2.73)	32.7 (3.96)	39.5 (3.52)	45.7 (2.82)	45.0 (3.73)	42.1 (3.04)	36.7 (4.16)
Private nonprofit	46.0 (6.55)	54.5 (4.19)	51.2 (3.39)	39.9 (3.38)	46.8 (6.14)	50.9 (6.29)	58.3 (4.13)	57.2 (3.22)	48.7 (3.30)	54.2 (6.01)
Private for-profit	‡ (†)	‡ (†)	‡ (†)	95.1 (3.45)	75.8 (6.27)	‡ (†)	‡ (†)	‡ (†)	95.1 (3.45)	76.2 (6.26)
Doctor's, professional[2]	79.4 (2.82)	84.8 (2.39)	83.8 (2.09)	84.6 (1.60)	73.5 (2.43)	81.2 (2.77)	84.8 (2.39)	84.9 (1.97)	84.9 (1.65)	74.5 (2.39)
Public	83.6 (4.65)	87.2 (2.82)	82.8 (3.61)	85.9 (2.72)	74.1 (4.18)	84.7 (4.59)	87.2 (2.82)	84.3 (3.28)	85.9 (2.72)	75.9 (4.07)
Private nonprofit	76.7 (4.06)	82.8 (4.21)	84.5 (2.42)	84.2 (2.25)	71.3 (3.40)	79.0 (3.95)	82.8 (4.21)	85.4 (2.34)	84.7 (2.31)	71.9 (3.42)
Private for-profit	‡ (†)	‡ (†)	‡ (†)	94.1 (5.12)	89.5 (1.95)	‡ (†)	‡ (†)	‡ (†)	94.1 (5.12)	90.2 (1.82)
Graduate degree program										
Postbaccalaureate certificate	35.8 (5.12)	46.3 (7.43)	49.5 (5.02)	39.4 (4.66)	47.6 (4.18)	49.2 (4.72)	53.0 (7.02)	64.1 (4.68)	44.5 (4.53)	55.1 (3.88)
Master of business administration (M.B.A.)	35.7 (2.70)	49.2 (5.05)	54.2 (3.45)	49.4 (4.63)	43.8 (3.41)	41.0 (2.78)	54.8 (4.67)	60.6 (3.29)	57.0 (4.78)	51.0 (3.34)
Master of education (any)	35.7 (2.86)	49.1 (3.14)	55.5 (3.46)	59.7 (3.55)	51.2 (2.83)	45.6 (2.86)	60.2 (3.24)	68.4 (3.13)	67.3 (3.64)	61.9 (3.21)
Other master of arts (M.A.) except in education	46.8 (4.97)	57.7 (5.07)	60.4 (4.04)	62.1 (3.53)	51.9 (4.81)	55.6 (5.09)	62.6 (5.04)	66.6 (3.76)	69.5 (3.50)	58.5 (4.42)
Other master of science (M.S.) except in education	35.9 (2.89)	40.0 (3.85)	45.8 (2.88)	53.6 (2.47)	49.5 (2.42)	41.9 (2.58)	47.1 (4.12)	53.9 (2.83)	59.3 (2.56)	56.1 (2.33)
Theology (M.Div., M.H.L., or B.D.)	‡ (†)	‡ (†)	‡ (†)	‡ (†)	‡ (†)	‡ (†)	‡ (†)	‡ (†)	‡ (†)	‡ (†)
Other master's degree[3]	52.5 (4.06)	69.3 (4.70)	56.3 (2.65)	71.8 (2.61)	65.0 (2.65)	58.4 (3.85)	74.5 (4.33)	62.2 (2.69)	75.0 (2.55)	70.2 (2.53)
Ph.D. except in education	36.3 (3.02)	33.5 (2.01)	31.9 (2.89)	31.6 (2.22)	38.5 (3.41)	43.6 (3.37)	40.3 (2.12)	40.2 (3.52)	40.3 (2.63)	44.7 (3.55)
Education (any doctorate)	33.4 (6.36)	49.7 (4.81)	58.0 (5.68)	72.3 (3.46)	61.4 (6.82)	33.4 (6.36)	51.9 (4.75)	61.4 (5.44)	73.3 (3.33)	63.0 (6.74)
Medicine (M.D. or D.O.)	86.4 (7.18)	91.8 (3.02)	78.3 (4.73)	84.3 (4.12)	80.3 (4.38)	86.4 (7.18)	91.8 (3.02)	79.6 (4.81)	84.3 (4.12)	81.0 (4.34)
Other health science professional practice doctorate[4]	79.1 (6.47)	88.3 (4.13)	86.7 (5.64)	89.5 (3.54)	73.6 (6.22)	80.9 (6.47)	88.3 (4.13)	88.6 (4.54)	89.5 (3.54)	74.6 (5.94)
Law (LL.B. or J.D.)	82.4 (2.69)	86.8 (3.05)	87.3 (2.50)	85.6 (2.46)	68.8 (5.84)	84.6 (2.52)	86.8 (3.05)	87.3 (2.50)	86.3 (2.54)	68.8 (5.84)
Other doctorate (non-Ph.D.)[5]	49.0 (7.64)	66.7 (4.99)	59.6 (4.47)	66.0 (4.09)	65.5 (7.35)	51.5 (7.46)	70.5 (4.56)	62.6 (4.47)	66.7 (4.15)	66.3 (7.42)
	Average cumulative amount owed (current dollars)									
Total	**$33,290 ($1,197)**	**$39,460 ($1,440)**	**$43,680 ($1,014)**	**$59,420 ($1,257)**	**$70,980 ($2,155)**	**$37,890 ($1,168)**	**$45,600 ($1,516)**	**$51,730 ($1,001)**	**$73,130 ($1,339)**	**$82,810 ($2,127)**
Graduate degree type and institution control[1]										
Postbaccalaureate certificate	21,400 (3,254)	20,900 (4,492)	31,370 (3,171)	44,240 (5,085)	54,090 (7,671)	25,550 (2,679)	29,920 (4,291)	38,640 (3,633)	60,790 (5,338)	66,550 (7,946)
Public	‡ (†)	10,310 (1,716)	32,070 (5,333)	40,370 (6,120)	43,270 (8,478)	22,760 (3,112)	19,060 (2,980)	38,680 (4,797)	57,050 (6,204)	50,130 (8,080)
Private nonprofit	‡ (†)	26,880 (5,250)	30,280 (3,870)	48,610 (8,683)	65,680 (18,039)	‡ (†)	37,770 (4,980)	38,220 (6,019)	67,960 (10,010)	80,010 (19,084)
Private for-profit	‡ (†)	‡ (†)	‡ (†)	‡ (†)	61,300 (6,394)	‡ (†)	‡ (†)	‡ (†)	‡ (†)	95,500 (8,527)
Master's	23,540 (967)	29,060 (1,145)	34,330 (1,091)	45,070 (1,252)	50,290 (1,635)	29,390 (1,109)	35,240 (1,327)	43,860 (1,168)	60,000 (1,472)	64,770 (1,688)
Public	19,720 (1,058)	24,750 (997)	31,110 (1,096)	35,620 (1,644)	42,330 (2,369)	25,570 (1,099)	31,440 (1,294)	38,750 (1,328)	49,100 (2,182)	53,470 (2,397)
Private nonprofit	27,330 (1,795)	32,280 (1,729)	38,020 (1,373)	50,740 (1,994)	56,350 (2,664)	32,730 (2,087)	37,700 (2,166)	46,790 (1,606)	64,660 (2,168)	70,590 (2,702)
Private for-profit	29,670 (3,676)	‡ (†)	33,870 (6,033)	49,510 (4,434)	62,010 (3,347)	40,920 (6,394)	‡ (†)	54,120 (6,093)	71,900 (3,704)	88,680 (4,064)
Doctor's, research	34,650 (3,721)	52,030 (3,051)	62,730 (3,664)	77,580 (2,757)	101,490 (6,346)	37,330 (3,925)	56,210 (3,211)	65,210 (3,443)	80,330 (3,289)	106,430 (6,551)
Public	28,730 (2,788)	44,450 (2,668)	51,180 (3,468)	60,440 (3,593)	84,820 (9,384)	31,740 (3,044)	48,430 (3,004)	54,020 (3,277)	63,230 (3,982)	90,510 (8,614)
Private nonprofit	42,770 (9,509)	61,310 (5,721)	78,810 (7,053)	84,410 (5,554)	89,430 (13,755)	45,330 (9,646)	66,550 (6,411)	81,360 (6,631)	85,400 (5,396)	92,370 (13,680)
Private for-profit	‡ (†)	‡ (†)	‡ (†)	125,930 (7,663)	144,890 (7,544)	‡ (†)	‡ (†)	‡ (†)	140,330 (7,749)	157,260 (8,520)
Doctor's, professional[2]	61,930 (2,712)	78,850 (3,858)	91,470 (2,901)	132,610 (3,070)	171,670 (9,386)	68,480 (2,993)	90,630 (4,157)	102,600 (3,184)	150,140 (3,645)	183,200 (10,316)
Public	53,470 (2,875)	66,740 (3,001)	81,450 (4,652)	114,580 (3,922)	130,750 (8,468)	60,830 (3,175)	78,030 (3,182)	91,860 (5,142)	130,210 (4,118)	140,070 (9,564)
Private nonprofit	68,930 (4,244)	89,820 (5,753)	97,530 (4,114)	142,550 (4,118)	205,050 (16,330)	74,680 (4,574)	102,330 (6,075)	109,070 (4,637)	160,200 (5,015)	217,830 (18,532)
Private for-profit	‡ (†)	‡ (†)	‡ (†)	175,900 (18,040)	167,380 (5,860)	‡ (†)	‡ (†)	‡ (†)	184,690 (21,607)	186,790 (5,877)

See notes at end of table.

Table 332.45. Percentage of graduate degree completers with student loan debt and average cumulative amount owed, by level of education funded and graduate degree type, institution control, and degree program: Selected years, 1999–2000 through 2015–16—Continued

[Standard errors appear in parentheses]

Graduate degree type, institution control, and degree program	Loans for graduate education only					Total loans (for undergraduate and graduate education)				
	1999–2000	2003–04	2007–08	2011–12	2015–16	1999–2000	2003–04	2007–08	2011–12	2015–16
1	2	3	4	5	6	7	8	9	10	11
Graduate degree program										
Postbaccalaureate certificate	21,400 (3,254)	20,900 (4,492)	31,370 (3,171)	44,240 (5,085)	54,090 (7,671)	25,550 (2,679)	29,920 (4,291)	38,640 (3,633)	60,790 (5,338)	66,550 (7,946)
Master of business administration (M.B.A.)	27,930 (2,856)	36,090 (4,254)	36,420 (3,676)	40,860 (2,884)	50,150 (3,784)	33,060 (2,437)	42,720 (4,543)	47,500 (3,012)	51,430 (3,819)	65,090 (4,175)
Master of education (any)	17,990 (1,244)	25,940 (1,449)	29,920 (1,705)	41,600 (2,509)	41,750 (3,419)	22,470 (1,627)	31,780 (1,934)	39,340 (2,543)	58,720 (3,718)	54,180 (3,409)
Other master of arts (M.A.) except in education	22,900 (1,985)	28,180 (3,721)	35,960 (3,199)	48,850 (3,553)	52,920 (5,165)	30,730 (2,913)	37,420 (3,923)	47,960 (4,166)	66,340 (5,564)	71,470 (5,044)
Other master of science (M.S.) except in education	23,000 (1,621)	29,810 (2,963)	33,610 (2,053)	45,450 (2,668)	47,950 (3,020)	31,320 (2,421)	35,150 (3,103)	42,910 (2,414)	60,900 (3,011)	61,200 (2,954)
Theology (M.Div., M.H.L., or B.D.)	‡ (†)	‡ (†)	‡ (†)	‡ (†)	‡ (†)	‡ (†)	‡ (†)	‡ (†)	‡ (†)	‡ (†)
Other master's degree[3]	26,820 (1,654)	27,150 (1,823)	40,690 (1,878)	48,960 (2,320)	57,340 (3,589)	32,950 (2,182)	32,840 (2,536)	48,820 (2,086)	62,490 (2,566)	73,730 (3,643)
Ph.D. except in education	33,870 (4,154)	41,860 (2,962)	47,950 (2,850)	66,450 (3,268)	96,750 (7,789)	33,740 (4,219)	45,080 (2,767)	49,180 (2,931)	65,070 (3,456)	97,000 (7,873)
Education (any doctorate)	‡ (†)	48,210 (9,267)	58,550 (7,140)	80,940 (6,008)	101,730 (12,692)	‡ (†)	51,590 (8,728)	60,980 (7,025)	93,820 (7,235)	109,880 (13,724)
Medicine (M.D. or D.O.)	78,660 (4,069)	108,110 (8,209)	128,260 (7,373)	166,330 (7,790)	223,060 (24,919)	87,020 (4,317)	118,690 (7,793)	135,510 (7,906)	182,610 (8,001)	241,560 (30,768)
Other health science professional practice doctorate[4]	72,470 (6,419)	79,020 (9,754)	91,750 (8,221)	133,510 (7,024)	190,310 (16,900)	80,590 (6,322)	94,870 (10,227)	108,280 (9,453)	157,690 (7,895)	198,760 (16,398)
Law (LL.B. or J.D.)	51,760 (2,207)	71,320 (3,936)	82,770 (2,640)	126,570 (5,041)	129,290 (10,279)	57,490 (2,541)	82,080 (4,463)	94,350 (3,166)	140,420 (5,883)	142,870 (10,786)
Other doctorate (non-Ph.D.)[5]	36,800 (6,987)	64,060 (5,041)	81,350 (7,115)	104,950 (5,885)	115,510 (12,106)	44,970 (6,843)	71,140 (6,520)	88,870 (7,019)	119,170 (6,600)	129,840 (11,534)
	Average cumulative amount owed (constant 2018–19 dollars)[6]									
Total	**$49,800 ($1,791)**	**$53,710 ($1,960)**	**$52,250 ($1,213)**	**$66,130 ($1,399)**	**$75,440 ($2,291)**	**$56,680 ($1,748)**	**$62,060 ($2,064)**	**$61,880 ($1,197)**	**$81,390 ($1,490)**	**$88,020 ($2,261)**
Graduate degree type and institution control[1]										
Postbaccalaureate certificate	32,020 (4,868)	28,450 (6,113)	37,530 (3,794)	49,240 (5,659)	57,490 (8,154)	38,220 (4,007)	40,720 (5,841)	46,230 (4,346)	67,650 (5,940)	70,740 (8,446)
Public	‡ (†)	14,030 (2,336)	38,370 (6,380)	44,930 (6,811)	45,990 (9,012)	34,050 (4,656)	25,940 (4,056)	46,280 (5,739)	63,490 (6,904)	53,290 (8,588)
Private nonprofit	‡ (†)	36,580 (7,145)	36,220 (4,630)	54,100 (9,664)	69,810 (19,174)	‡ (†)	51,410 (6,777)	45,720 (7,200)	75,640 (11,141)	85,040 (20,284)
Private for-profit	‡ (†)	‡ (†)	‡ (†)	‡ (†)	65,160 (6,797)	‡ (†)	‡ (†)	‡ (†)	‡ (†)	101,510 (9,064)
Master's	35,220 (1,447)	39,550 (1,559)	41,070 (1,306)	50,160 (1,393)	53,450 (1,738)	43,970 (1,659)	47,970 (1,806)	52,470 (1,397)	66,780 (1,638)	68,840 (1,794)
Public	29,500 (1,583)	33,690 (1,357)	37,220 (1,311)	39,650 (1,830)	45,000 (2,518)	38,260 (1,644)	42,790 (1,761)	46,360 (1,589)	54,650 (2,428)	56,840 (2,548)
Private nonprofit	40,880 (2,685)	43,940 (2,353)	45,490 (1,643)	56,470 (2,219)	59,900 (2,832)	48,970 (3,123)	51,310 (2,948)	55,970 (1,922)	71,960 (2,413)	75,030 (2,872)
Private for-profit	44,390 (5,499)	‡ (†)	40,520 (7,218)	55,100 (4,935)	65,910 (3,558)	61,220 (9,565)	‡ (†)	64,750 (7,290)	80,020 (4,123)	94,260 (4,319)
Doctor's, research	51,830 (5,566)	70,810 (4,152)	75,050 (4,383)	86,340 (3,069)	107,870 (6,746)	55,850 (5,872)	76,500 (4,370)	78,020 (4,119)	89,400 (3,660)	113,130 (6,963)
Public	42,980 (4,171)	60,500 (3,632)	61,230 (4,149)	67,260 (3,999)	90,150 (9,974)	47,490 (4,554)	65,920 (4,088)	64,620 (3,920)	70,370 (4,432)	96,200 (9,156)
Private nonprofit	63,980 (14,226)	83,440 (7,786)	94,290 (8,438)	93,950 (6,181)	95,060 (14,620)	67,810 (14,431)	90,580 (8,725)	97,340 (7,933)	95,040 (6,005)	98,180 (14,541)
Private for-profit	‡ (†)	‡ (†)	‡ (†)	140,150 (8,528)	154,010 (8,019)	‡ (†)	‡ (†)	‡ (†)	156,170 (8,624)	167,150 (9,056)
Doctor's, professional[2]	92,640 (4,058)	107,310 (5,251)	109,430 (3,470)	147,580 (3,417)	182,470 (9,977)	102,450 (4,477)	123,350 (5,657)	122,750 (3,809)	167,090 (4,057)	194,730 (10,966)
Public	79,990 (4,301)	90,830 (4,084)	97,440 (5,566)	127,520 (4,365)	138,980 (9,001)	91,000 (4,749)	106,190 (4,330)	109,890 (6,152)	144,910 (4,583)	148,880 (10,166)
Private nonprofit	103,130 (6,349)	122,240 (7,830)	116,680 (4,922)	158,650 (4,583)	217,950 (17,357)	111,720 (6,843)	139,270 (8,268)	130,490 (5,547)	178,300 (5,582)	231,530 (19,698)
Private for-profit	‡ (†)	‡ (†)	‡ (†)	195,760 (20,078)	177,910 (6,228)	‡ (†)	‡ (†)	‡ (†)	205,550 (24,048)	198,540 (6,247)
Graduate degree program										
Postbaccalaureate certificate	32,020 (4,868)	28,450 (6,113)	37,530 (3,794)	49,240 (5,659)	57,490 (8,154)	38,220 (4,007)	40,720 (5,841)	46,230 (4,346)	67,650 (5,940)	70,740 (8,446)
Master of business administration (M.B.A.)	41,790 (4,273)	49,120 (5,790)	43,570 (4,397)	45,480 (3,209)	53,300 (4,022)	49,450 (3,646)	58,140 (6,183)	56,830 (3,604)	57,240 (4,250)	69,180 (4,438)
Master of education (any)	26,920 (1,861)	35,300 (1,972)	35,790 (2,039)	46,300 (2,792)	44,380 (3,635)	33,610 (2,433)	43,260 (2,632)	47,060 (3,042)	65,350 (4,138)	57,590 (3,624)
Other master of arts (M.A.) except in education	34,270 (2,970)	38,350 (5,064)	43,020 (3,827)	54,370 (3,954)	56,250 (5,490)	45,980 (4,358)	50,930 (5,339)	57,370 (4,984)	73,830 (6,193)	75,970 (5,362)
Other master of science (M.S.) except in education	34,420 (2,425)	40,570 (4,033)	40,210 (2,457)	50,590 (2,969)	50,970 (3,210)	46,860 (3,622)	47,830 (4,223)	51,330 (2,888)	67,780 (3,351)	65,050 (3,140)
Theology (M.Div., M.H.L., or B.D.)	‡ (†)	‡ (†)	‡ (†)	‡ (†)	‡ (†)	‡ (†)	‡ (†)	‡ (†)	‡ (†)	‡ (†)
Other master's degree[3]	40,120 (2,474)	36,950 (2,480)	48,680 (2,247)	54,490 (2,582)	60,950 (3,815)	49,290 (3,265)	44,690 (3,452)	58,400 (2,495)	69,550 (2,856)	78,370 (3,873)
Ph.D. except in education	50,660 (6,214)	56,970 (4,031)	57,360 (3,409)	73,950 (3,637)	102,840 (8,279)	50,480 (6,311)	61,350 (3,765)	58,840 (3,507)	72,420 (3,847)	103,110 (8,368)
Education (any doctorate)	‡ (†)	65,620 (12,612)	70,050 (8,542)	90,080 (6,686)	108,130 (13,491)	‡ (†)	70,210 (11,879)	72,960 (8,404)	104,410 (8,052)	116,800 (14,588)
Medicine (M.D. or D.O.)	117,680 (6,088)	147,130 (11,173)	153,450 (8,820)	185,110 (8,669)	237,090 (26,487)	130,190 (6,459)	161,530 (10,606)	162,120 (9,458)	203,230 (8,905)	256,760 (32,704)
Other health science professional practice doctorate[4]	108,410 (9,603)	107,550 (13,275)	109,760 (9,835)	148,590 (7,817)	202,290 (17,964)	120,570 (9,457)	129,120 (13,919)	129,540 (11,309)	175,500 (8,787)	211,270 (17,430)
Law (LL.B. or J.D.)	77,440 (3,301)	97,060 (5,357)	99,020 (3,158)	140,870 (5,610)	137,430 (10,926)	86,010 (3,801)	111,720 (6,073)	112,880 (3,788)	156,280 (6,547)	151,860 (11,465)
Other doctorate (non-Ph.D.)[5]	55,050 (10,454)	87,180 (6,860)	97,320 (8,512)	116,800 (6,549)	122,780 (12,867)	67,270 (10,237)	96,820 (8,873)	106,320 (8,397)	132,630 (7,345)	138,000 (12,260)

†Not applicable.
‡Reporting standards not met. Either there are too few cases for a reliable estimate or the coefficient of variation (CV) is 50 percent or greater.
[1]Individuals who attended more than one institution for graduate studies are included in the subtotals by degree type but excluded from the detail by control of institution.
[2]Includes chiropractic, dentistry, law, medicine, optometry, pharmacy, podiatry, and veterinary medicine.
[3]Includes public administration or policy, social work, fine arts, public health, and other.
[4]Includes chiropractic, dentistry, optometry, pharmacy, podiatry, and veterinary medicine.
[5]Includes science or engineering, psychology, business or public administration, fine arts, theology, and other. Estimates for 2011–12 and 2015–16 also include "other professional practice doctoral degrees," which were not reported as a separate category in previous years.
[6]Constant dollars based on the Consumer Price Index, prepared by the Bureau of Labor Statistics, U.S. Department of Labor, adjusted to a school-year basis.

NOTE: Data refer to students who completed graduate degrees in the academic years indicated. Data are based on the principal balance (excluding interest) as of June 30th of the survey year (e.g., the 2015–16 data are based on the principal balance as of June 30, 2016). Average amounts owed were calculated only for graduate degree completers who had outstanding loans at the level of education indicated. Data include federal and private student loans, but exclude Parent PLUS loans. Direct Subsidized Loans for graduate students were discontinued after academic year 2011–12.

SOURCE: U.S. Department of Education, National Center for Education Statistics, 1999–2000, 2003–04, 2007–08, 2011–12, and 2015–16 National Postsecondary Student Aid Study (NPSAS:2000, NPSAS:04, NPSAS:08, NPSAS:12, and NPSAS:16). (This table was prepared October 2019.)

Table 332.50. Number of postsecondary students who entered the student loan repayment phase, number of students who defaulted within a 3-year period, and 3-year student loan cohort default rate, by level and control of institution: Fiscal years 2010 through 2016

Fiscal year, number of students, and default rate	All institutions				Less-than-2-year institutions				2-year institutions				4-year institutions			
			Private				Private				Private				Private	
	Total[1]	Public	Nonprofit	For-profit	Total	Public	Non-profit	For-profit	Total	Public	Non-profit	For-profit	Total	Public	Nonprofit	For-profit
1	2	3	4	5	6	7	8	9	10	11	12	13	14	15	16	17
Fiscal year 2010																
Number of students																
Entering repayment phase in given fiscal year[2]	4,082,570	1,922,773	879,269	1,270,965	178,904	7,963	5,020	165,921	950,143	599,467	16,217	334,459	2,943,960	1,315,343	858,032	770,585
Defaulting by end of second following fiscal year[3]	600,545	250,661	72,347	277,088	37,223	1,315	1,097	34,811	199,922	125,764	2,305	71,853	362,951	123,582	68,945	170,424
3-year cohort default rate[4]	14.7	13.0	8.2	21.8	20.8	16.5	21.8	20.9	21.0	20.9	14.2	21.4	12.3	9.3	8.0	22.1
Fiscal year 2011																
Number of students																
Entering repayment phase in given fiscal year[2]	4,732,793	2,252,334	969,156	1,500,812	202,526	8,750	6,567	187,209	1,174,583	767,073	16,861	390,649	3,345,193	1,476,511	945,728	922,954
Defaulting by end of second following fiscal year[3]	650,727	292,012	70,186	288,126	41,526	1,196	1,644	38,686	237,571	158,104	2,026	77,441	371,227	132,712	66,516	171,999
3-year cohort default rate[4]	13.7	12.9	7.2	19.1	20.5	13.6	25.0	20.6	20.2	20.6	12.0	19.8	11.1	8.9	7.0	18.6
Fiscal year 2012																
Number of students																
Entering repayment phase in given fiscal year[2]	5,143,918	2,563,157	1,083,328	1,486,162	209,036	10,151	10,336	188,549	1,301,109	905,058	42,274	353,777	3,622,502	1,647,948	1,030,718	943,836
Defaulting by end of second following fiscal year[3]	610,956	301,453	73,747	235,384	36,952	1,241	2,318	33,393	242,471	173,628	6,193	62,650	331,161	126,584	65,236	139,341
3-year cohort default rate[4]	11.8	11.7	6.8	15.8	17.7	12.2	22.4	17.7	18.6	19.1	14.6	17.7	9.1	7.6	6.3	14.7
Fiscal year 2013																
Number of students																
Entering repayment phase in given fiscal year[2]	5,211,531	2,691,995	1,118,051	1,387,815	197,189	10,823	10,649	175,717	1,301,834	948,515	42,974	310,345	3,698,838	1,732,657	1,064,428	901,753
Defaulting by end of second following fiscal year[3]	593,182	305,516	78,659	208,570	33,327	1,414	2,194	29,719	234,986	176,206	6,593	52,187	324,432	127,896	69,872	126,664
3-year cohort default rate[4]	11.3	11.3	7.0	15.0	16.9	13.0	20.6	16.9	18.1	18.5	15.3	16.8	8.8	7.3	6.5	14.0
Fiscal year 2014																
Number of students																
Entering repayment phase in given fiscal year[2]	5,047,954	2,678,811	1,108,120	1,250,242	180,437	10,775	8,312	161,350	1,220,298	921,537	39,336	259,425	3,636,438	1,746,499	1,060,472	829,467
Defaulting by end of second following fiscal year[3]	580,671	303,389	82,867	194,027	30,604	1,491	1,654	27,459	221,748	169,325	6,958	45,465	327,931	132,573	74,255	121,103
3-year cohort default rate[4]	11.5	11.3	7.4	15.5	17.0	13.8	19.8	17.0	18.2	18.3	17.6	17.5	9.0	7.5	7.0	14.6
Fiscal year 2015																
Number of students																
Entering repayment phase in given fiscal year[2]	4,900,932	2,616,327	1,106,590	1,167,289	177,886	9,838	10,198	157,850	1,123,770	852,423	33,070	238,277	3,588,550	1,754,066	1,063,322	771,162
Defaulting by end of second following fiscal year[3]	531,653	269,876	78,706	182,686	31,687	1,152	2,247	28,288	191,872	142,775	5,541	43,556	307,709	125,949	70,918	110,842
3-year cohort default rate[4]	10.8	10.3	7.1	15.6	17.8	11.7	22.0	17.9	17.1	16.7	16.7	18.2	8.6	7.1	6.6	14.3
Fiscal year 2016																
Number of students																
Entering repayment phase in given fiscal year[2]	4,533,276	2,467,803	1,069,593	985,335	163,168	9,277	7,778	146,113	981,825	730,146	29,332	222,347	3,377,738	1,728,380	1,032,483	616,875
Defaulting by end of second following fiscal year[3]	458,687	236,948	71,515	149,892	28,259	1,184	1,296	25,779	160,644	116,647	4,471	39,526	269,452	119,117	65,748	84,587
3-year cohort default rate[4]	10.1	9.6	6.6	15.2	17.3	12.7	16.6	17.6	16.4	15.9	15.2	17.7	8.0	6.8	6.3	13.7

[1] Includes borrowers from foreign and unclassified schools, which account for less than 1 percent of borrowers and are not included elsewhere.

[2] The repayment phase is the period when student loans must be repaid; it generally begins 6 months after a student leaves an institution. Students who enter the repayment phase during a particular federal fiscal year (October 1 through September 30) make up the cohort for that fiscal year. For example, members of the fiscal year (FY) 2016 cohort entered the repayment phase any time from October 1, 2015, through September 30, 2016.

[3] Borrowers are considered to be in default if they make no payments for 360 days after missing a regularly scheduled payment.

[4] The 3-year cohort default rate is the percentage of borrowers entering repayment during the specified fiscal year and defaulting by the end of the second fiscal year that follows. For example, the 3-year cohort default rate for FY 2010 is the percentage of borrowers who entered repayment during FY 2010 (any time from October 1, 2009, through September 30, 2010) and who defaulted by the end of FY 2012 (September 30, 2012). For purposes of computing default rates, if an individual or entity affiliated with the institution makes a payment to prevent a borrower's default on a loan, the borrower is still considered in default.

NOTE: Data are for certain loans under the Federal Family Education Loan (FFEL) Program and the William D. Ford Federal Direct Loan Program (commonly referred to as the Direct Loan Program). Includes Federal Stafford Loans. Does not include PLUS loans, Federal Insured Student Loans (FISLs), or Federal Perkins Loans. For more details, see https://ifap.ed.gov/DefaultManagement/guide/attachments/CDRGuideCh2Pt1CDRCalculation.pdf. The default rates shown in this table for the FY 2010, FY 2011, and FY 2012 cohorts are no longer available online; therefore, no source for these default rates can be provided.

SOURCE: U.S. Department of Education, Office of Federal Student Aid, Direct Loan and Federal Family Education Loan Programs, Cohort Default Rate Database; retrieved April 7, 2020, from https://www2.ed.gov/offices/OSFAP/defaultmanagement/schooltyperates.pdf. (This table was prepared April 2020.)

Table 333.10. Revenues of public degree-granting postsecondary institutions, by source of revenue and level of institution: Selected years, 2007–08 through 2017–18

Level of institution and year	Total revenues	Operating revenue							
		Tuition and fees[1,2]	Grants and contracts			Sales and services of auxiliary enterprises[1]	Sales and services of hospitals	Independent operations	Other operating revenues[3]
			Federal[2]	State	Local and private				
1	2	3	4	5	6	7	8	9	10
	In thousands of current dollars								
All levels									
2007–08	$273,070,439	$48,068,614	$25,499,038	$7,831,049	$8,699,401	$20,487,684	$25,183,379	$1,174,836	$14,085,890
2010–11	324,473,342	60,268,927	29,821,416	7,019,420	10,110,953	23,605,640	30,998,993	1,330,334	15,758,118
2014–15	346,812,800	73,476,374	27,290,446	7,409,069	12,460,665	26,583,777	41,582,927	1,508,778	19,489,191
2015–16	364,349,979	76,603,554	27,677,857	7,779,950	12,979,361	27,585,281	45,956,104	1,537,639	20,825,325
2016–17	390,508,373	79,244,979	28,267,575	8,017,761	13,812,044	28,421,678	50,089,201	1,635,853	21,535,947
2017–18	408,855,251	81,300,494	29,529,310	8,804,327	14,187,478	28,987,897	53,558,528	1,805,852	22,699,302
4-year									
2007–08	223,530,092	40,083,063	23,500,633	5,715,188	8,106,887	18,507,688	25,183,379	1,174,836	13,112,536
2010–11	266,688,058	51,046,786	27,656,656	5,480,573	9,543,780	21,506,767	30,998,993	1,330,334	14,830,150
2014–15	290,239,686	64,152,076	25,570,548	5,578,550	11,912,198	24,830,846	41,582,927	1,508,778	18,615,218
2015–16	308,813,202	67,533,647	26,106,025	6,007,791	12,472,377	25,984,815	45,956,104	1,537,639	19,950,465
2016–17	335,175,388	70,090,665	26,800,717	6,142,106	13,304,532	26,896,786	50,089,201	1,635,853	20,640,711
2017–18	353,195,723	72,453,183	27,988,187	6,415,440	13,623,951	27,557,917	53,558,528	1,805,852	21,794,537
2-year									
2007–08	49,540,347	7,985,551	1,998,404	2,115,861	592,513	1,979,996	0	0	973,353
2010–11	57,785,284	9,222,142	2,164,760	1,538,848	567,174	2,098,872	0	0	927,968
2014–15	56,573,114	9,324,298	1,719,898	1,830,518	548,467	1,752,931	0	0	873,974
2015–16	55,536,777	9,069,907	1,571,832	1,772,158	506,984	1,600,466	0	0	874,859
2016–17	55,332,985	9,154,315	1,466,858	1,875,655	507,512	1,524,892	0	0	895,236
2017–18	55,659,527	8,847,312	1,541,123	2,388,887	563,527	1,429,979	0	0	904,764
	Percentage distribution								
All levels									
2007–08	100.00	17.60	9.34	2.87	3.19	7.50	9.22	0.43	5.16
2010–11	100.00	18.57	9.19	2.16	3.12	7.28	9.55	0.41	4.86
2014–15	100.00	21.19	7.87	2.14	3.59	7.67	11.99	0.44	5.62
2015–16	100.00	21.02	7.60	2.14	3.56	7.57	12.61	0.42	5.72
2016–17	100.00	20.29	7.24	2.05	3.54	7.28	12.83	0.42	5.51
2017–18	100.00	19.88	7.22	2.15	3.47	7.09	13.10	0.44	5.55
4-year									
2007–08	100.00	17.93	10.51	2.56	3.63	8.28	11.27	0.53	5.87
2010–11	100.00	19.14	10.37	2.06	3.58	8.06	11.62	0.50	5.56
2014–15	100.00	22.10	8.81	1.92	4.10	8.56	14.33	0.52	6.41
2015–16	100.00	21.87	8.45	1.95	4.04	8.41	14.88	0.50	6.46
2016–17	100.00	20.91	8.00	1.83	3.97	8.02	14.94	0.49	6.16
2017–18	100.00	20.51	7.92	1.82	3.86	7.80	15.16	0.51	6.17
2-year									
2007–08	100.00	16.12	4.03	4.27	1.20	4.00	0.00	0.00	1.96
2010–11	100.00	15.96	3.75	2.66	0.98	3.63	0.00	0.00	1.61
2014–15	100.00	16.48	3.04	3.24	0.97	3.10	0.00	0.00	1.54
2015–16	100.00	16.33	2.83	3.19	0.91	2.88	0.00	0.00	1.58
2016–17	100.00	16.54	2.65	3.39	0.92	2.76	0.00	0.00	1.62
2017–18	100.00	15.90	2.77	4.29	1.01	2.57	0.00	0.00	1.63
	Revenue per full-time-equivalent student in constant 2018–19 dollars[4]								
All levels									
2007–08	$32,846	$5,782	$3,067	$942	$1,046	$2,464	$3,029	$141	$1,694
2010–11	33,049	6,139	3,037	715	1,030	2,404	3,157	135	1,605
2014–15	34,223	7,251	2,693	731	1,230	2,623	4,103	149	1,923
2015–16	35,897	7,547	2,727	767	1,279	2,718	4,528	151	2,052
2016–17	37,771	7,665	2,734	775	1,336	2,749	4,845	158	2,083
2017–18	38,686	7,693	2,794	833	1,342	2,743	5,068	171	2,148
4-year									
2007–08	43,719	7,840	4,596	1,118	1,586	3,620	4,925	230	2,565
2010–11	45,104	8,633	4,678	927	1,614	3,637	5,243	225	2,508
2014–15	44,150	9,758	3,890	849	1,812	3,777	6,325	230	2,832
2015–16	46,137	10,090	3,900	898	1,863	3,882	6,866	230	2,981
2016–17	47,462	9,925	3,795	870	1,884	3,809	7,093	232	2,923
2017–18	48,321	9,912	3,829	878	1,864	3,770	7,327	247	2,982
2-year									
2007–08	15,478	2,495	624	661	185	619	0	0	304
2010–11	14,797	2,361	554	394	145	537	0	0	238
2014–15	15,891	2,619	483	514	154	492	0	0	246
2015–16	16,067	2,624	455	513	147	463	0	0	253
2016–17	16,885	2,793	448	572	155	465	0	0	273
2017–18	17,077	2,714	473	733	173	439	0	0	278

See notes at end of table.

Table 333.10. Revenues of public degree-granting postsecondary institutions, by source of revenue and level of institution: Selected years, 2007–08 through 2017–18—Continued

Level of institution and year	Nonoperating revenue									Other revenues and additions			
	Appropriations			Nonoperating grants									
	Federal	State	Local	Federal	State	Local	Gifts	Investment return (gain or loss)	Other non-operating revenues	Capital appro-priations	Capital grants and gifts	Additions to per-manent endow-ments	Other
1	11	12	13	14	15	16	17	18	19	20	21	22	23
	In thousands of current dollars												
All levels													
2007–08	$1,849,775	$68,394,962	$9,302,794	$10,045,255	$1,925,994	$177,116	$6,053,147	$5,278,656	$2,234,287	$7,575,827	$3,092,817	$1,151,300	$4,958,618
2010–11	1,946,965	63,063,322	10,023,157	24,231,846	3,404,970	228,055	6,287,358	14,215,863	6,888,955	5,645,126	3,745,699	965,007	4,913,217
2014–15	1,779,758	65,172,431	11,248,036	21,590,392	4,406,434	291,197	8,087,953	1,342,180	5,155,201	6,295,695	3,709,702	1,012,258	6,920,335
2015–16	1,666,978	67,145,689	12,213,323	20,477,681	4,861,395	417,856	8,490,640	3,926,734	5,417,126	6,467,364	3,781,347	1,130,058	7,408,716
2016–17	1,923,743	68,641,049	12,958,544	19,697,011	5,163,737	432,922	8,264,805	15,042,298	8,072,507	6,575,388	3,665,778	1,189,554	7,855,999
2017–18	2,036,103	72,891,268	13,401,408	20,903,792	5,645,582	382,323	9,099,000	16,923,007	7,408,113	6,335,749	4,010,781	1,360,786	7,584,152
4-year													
2007–08	1,776,452	53,268,648	436,856	5,194,645	1,217,818	103,824	5,781,369	4,430,479	1,773,078	5,635,746	2,764,505	1,138,323	4,624,141
2010–11	1,853,109	49,025,814	507,010	11,812,776	2,320,005	130,451	6,061,629	13,781,509	6,061,802	3,884,591	3,249,844	943,748	4,661,730
2014–15	1,675,671	51,089,552	587,588	11,329,817	2,866,382	158,091	7,767,802	1,194,597	4,464,354	4,632,561	3,383,607	998,211	6,340,310
2015–16	1,617,876	53,067,153	1,051,753	11,522,288	3,008,676	205,597	8,207,812	3,771,368	4,666,805	4,742,620	3,482,369	1,117,698	6,802,323
2016–17	1,884,327	54,721,859	1,400,806	11,399,315	3,227,298	243,196	7,995,012	14,811,646	7,230,940	4,994,288	3,307,489	1,176,695	7,181,945
2017–18	1,984,446	58,513,022	1,708,949	12,507,190	4,024,166	234,277	8,786,344	16,581,753	6,643,024	4,708,911	3,686,661	1,347,758	7,271,628
2-year													
2007–08	73,324	15,126,314	8,865,938	4,850,610	708,176	73,292	271,778	848,177	461,209	1,940,082	328,312	12,978	334,477
2010–11	93,856	14,037,508	9,516,147	12,419,069	1,084,965	97,604	225,730	434,353	827,153	1,760,535	495,855	21,258	251,487
2014–15	104,087	14,082,879	10,660,448	10,260,575	1,540,052	133,106	320,151	147,583	690,846	1,663,135	326,095	14,047	580,025
2015–16	49,102	14,078,537	11,161,570	8,955,393	1,852,719	212,259	282,827	155,366	750,321	1,724,744	298,979	12,361	606,393
2016–17	39,417	13,919,190	11,557,739	8,297,696	1,936,438	189,726	269,793	230,652	841,567	1,581,100	358,288	12,859	674,054
2017–18	51,656	14,378,246	11,692,459	8,396,602	1,621,417	148,046	312,656	341,254	765,089	1,626,839	324,120	13,028	312,524
	Percentage distribution												
All levels													
2007–08	0.68	25.05	3.41	3.68	0.71	0.06	2.22	1.93	0.82	2.77	1.13	0.42	1.82
2010–11	0.60	19.44	3.09	7.47	1.05	0.07	1.94	4.38	2.12	1.74	1.15	0.30	1.51
2014–15	0.51	18.79	3.24	6.23	1.27	0.08	2.33	0.39	1.49	1.82	1.07	0.29	2.00
2015–16	0.46	18.43	3.35	5.62	1.33	0.11	2.33	1.08	1.49	1.78	1.04	0.31	2.03
2016–17	0.49	17.58	3.32	5.04	1.32	0.11	2.12	3.85	2.07	1.68	0.94	0.30	2.01
2017–18	0.50	17.83	3.28	5.11	1.38	0.09	2.23	4.14	1.81	1.55	0.98	0.33	1.85
4-year													
2007–08	0.79	23.83	0.20	2.32	0.54	0.05	2.59	1.98	0.79	2.52	1.24	0.51	2.07
2010–11	0.69	18.38	0.19	4.43	0.87	0.05	2.27	5.17	2.27	1.46	1.22	0.35	1.75
2014–15	0.58	17.60	0.20	3.90	0.99	0.05	2.68	0.41	1.54	1.60	1.17	0.34	2.18
2015–16	0.52	17.18	0.34	3.73	0.97	0.07	2.66	1.22	1.51	1.54	1.13	0.36	2.20
2016–17	0.56	16.33	0.42	3.40	0.96	0.07	2.39	4.42	2.16	1.49	0.99	0.35	2.14
2017–18	0.56	16.57	0.48	3.54	1.14	0.07	2.49	4.69	1.88	1.33	1.04	0.38	2.06
2-year													
2007–08	0.15	30.53	17.90	9.79	1.43	0.15	0.55	1.71	0.93	3.92	0.66	0.03	0.68
2010–11	0.16	24.29	16.47	21.49	1.88	0.17	0.39	0.75	1.43	3.05	0.86	0.04	0.44
2014–15	0.18	24.89	18.84	18.14	2.72	0.24	0.57	0.26	1.22	2.94	0.58	0.02	1.03
2015–16	0.09	25.35	20.10	16.13	3.34	0.38	0.51	0.28	1.35	3.11	0.54	0.02	1.09
2016–17	0.07	25.16	20.89	15.00	3.50	0.34	0.49	0.42	1.52	2.86	0.65	0.02	1.22
2017–18	0.09	25.83	21.01	15.09	2.91	0.27	0.56	0.61	1.37	2.92	0.58	0.02	0.56
	Revenue per full-time-equivalent student in constant 2018–19 dollars[4]												
All levels													
2007–08	$222	$8,227	$1,119	$1,208	$232	$21	$728	$635	$269	$911	$372	$138	$596
2010–11	198	6,423	1,021	2,468	347	23	640	1,448	702	575	382	98	500
2014–15	176	6,431	1,110	2,131	435	29	798	132	509	621	366	100	683
2015–16	164	6,615	1,203	2,018	479	41	837	387	534	637	373	111	730
2016–17	186	6,639	1,253	1,905	499	42	799	1,455	781	636	355	115	760
2017–18	193	6,897	1,268	1,978	534	36	861	1,601	701	599	379	129	718
4-year													
2007–08	347	10,418	85	1,016	238	20	1,131	867	347	1,102	541	223	904
2010–11	313	8,292	86	1,998	392	22	1,025	2,331	1,025	657	550	160	788
2014–15	255	7,771	89	1,723	436	24	1,182	182	679	705	515	152	964
2015–16	242	7,928	157	1,721	450	31	1,226	563	697	709	520	167	1,016
2016–17	267	7,749	198	1,614	457	34	1,132	2,097	1,024	707	468	167	1,017
2017–18	271	8,005	234	1,711	551	32	1,202	2,269	909	644	504	184	995
2-year													
2007–08	23	4,726	2,770	1,515	221	23	85	265	144	606	103	4	105
2010–11	24	3,594	2,437	3,180	278	25	58	111	212	451	127	5	64
2014–15	29	3,956	2,995	2,882	433	37	90	41	194	467	92	4	163
2015–16	14	4,073	3,229	2,591	536	61	82	45	217	499	86	4	175
2016–17	12	4,248	3,527	2,532	591	58	82	70	257	482	109	4	206
2017–18	16	4,411	3,587	2,576	497	45	96	105	235	499	99	4	96

[1]After deducting discounts and allowances.
[2]Public institutions typically report Pell grants as revenues from federal grants and as allowances that reduce revenues from tuition and fees.
[3]Includes sales and services of educational activities.
[4]Constant dollars based on the Consumer Price Index, prepared by the Bureau of Labor Statistics, U.S. Department of Labor, adjusted to a school-year basis.
NOTE: Degree-granting institutions grant associate's or higher degrees and participate in Title IV federal financial aid programs. Includes data for public institutions reporting data according to either Governmental Accounting Standards Board (GASB) or Financial Accounting Standards Board (FASB) guidance. Data in this table pertain to institutions' fiscal years that end in the academic year noted. Some data have been revised from previously published figures. Detail may not sum to totals because of rounding.
SOURCE: U.S. Department of Education, National Center for Education Statistics, Integrated Postsecondary Education Data System (IPEDS), Spring 2008 through Spring 2018, Fall Enrollment component; and Spring 2009 through Spring 2019, Finance component. (This table was prepared December 2019.)

Table 333.20. Revenues of public degree-granting postsecondary institutions, by source of revenue and state or jurisdiction: 2017–18

[In thousands of current dollars]

State or jurisdiction	Total revenues	Operating revenue: Total	Tuition and fees[1,2]	Federal grants and contracts[2]	State, local, and private grants and contracts	Sales and services of auxiliary enterprises[1]	Sales and services of hospitals	Independent operations and other[3]	Nonoperating revenue: Total[4]	State appropriations	Local appropriations	Other revenues and additions
1	2	3	4	5	6	7	8	9	10	11	12	13
United States	**$408,855,251**	**$240,873,187**	**$81,300,494**	**$29,529,310**	**$22,991,804**	**$28,987,897**	**$53,558,528**	**$24,505,154**	**$148,690,596**	**$72,891,268**	**$13,401,408**	**$19,291,468**
Alabama	8,716,819	6,217,058	1,989,264	714,569	271,299	572,120	2,280,790	389,016	2,234,559	1,404,166	2,917	265,202
Alaska	855,302	380,903	135,131	122,752	63,130	39,222	0	20,668	419,453	325,302	13,986	54,946
Arizona	7,078,915	3,974,707	2,435,757	571,274	293,523	454,067	0	220,086	3,010,510	745,394	890,883	93,697
Arkansas	4,396,924	2,981,845	626,140	228,792	202,433	320,765	1,231,064	372,652	1,305,929	764,581	34,966	109,150
California	63,233,502	36,323,599	8,024,339	3,701,170	4,007,661	2,448,689	12,064,599	6,077,142	24,418,114	11,563,516	4,048,931	2,491,789
Colorado	7,889,190	6,542,222	2,393,366	1,068,569	820,575	647,436	1,035,850	576,425	1,006,648	44,306	100,434	340,321
Connecticut	3,923,056	2,129,856	766,751	176,905	98,656	321,640	439,491	326,413	1,402,990	1,124,904	0	390,211
Delaware	1,425,523	962,176	525,959	137,165	83,272	162,662	0	53,117	451,405	236,699	0	11,942
District of Columbia	159,987	57,169	33,759	13,829	5,969	417	0	3,194	91,169	80,000	0	11,649
Florida	13,472,403	6,136,343	2,509,411	1,177,619	1,350,949	919,685	0	178,679	6,728,937	4,195,023	0	607,122
Georgia	9,246,194	5,337,378	2,271,578	938,347	666,834	925,084	236,420	299,115	3,567,264	2,442,075	737	341,551
Hawaii	1,846,509	793,277	259,446	305,248	90,435	100,246	0	37,901	846,279	485,153	0	206,954
Idaho	1,387,428	704,885	366,495	133,117	49,038	105,163	0	51,072	637,327	431,993	31,430	45,216
Illinois	14,459,180	6,236,993	2,458,427	798,550	386,482	859,753	835,807	897,975	8,147,020	2,282,662	1,164,980	75,167
Indiana	7,385,602	4,661,601	2,451,011	600,871	317,358	812,256	0	480,105	2,508,441	1,566,933	8,802	215,561
Iowa	7,081,669	5,121,444	1,407,655	501,295	162,970	597,416	2,040,227	411,881	1,391,815	806,471	153,442	568,411
Kansas	3,854,195	2,269,389	978,546	317,642	213,591	471,928	0	287,683	1,428,852	735,972	307,814	155,953
Kentucky	6,453,223	4,573,365	1,111,410	438,287	250,934	396,679	1,893,750	482,305	1,613,590	879,606	25,389	266,269
Louisiana	4,392,001	2,805,547	1,206,100	298,239	755,312	405,966	18,785	121,145	1,365,564	780,591	0	220,890
Maine	922,920	507,618	249,040	60,202	54,950	83,935	0	59,492	392,066	276,659	0	23,236
Maryland	7,395,279	4,198,607	1,777,871	774,498	464,032	742,916	0	439,291	2,745,123	1,754,397	415,121	451,548
Massachusetts	5,639,240	3,496,215	1,508,549	404,013	290,572	582,469	0	710,612	1,924,525	1,461,553	0	218,500
Michigan	18,552,490	12,897,848	4,376,569	1,592,860	605,115	1,230,407	4,438,744	654,152	5,215,134	1,851,003	573,630	439,508
Minnesota	5,794,811	3,158,962	1,353,065	456,774	486,453	677,439	0	185,232	2,428,356	1,395,343	0	207,493
Mississippi	4,627,187	2,962,437	738,965	350,505	223,880	370,549	1,097,356	181,182	1,478,340	900,717	73,997	186,410
Missouri	5,451,878	3,579,142	1,157,516	220,362	188,370	839,160	1,014,469	159,264	1,734,982	866,474	162,976	137,755
Montana	1,144,329	731,595	314,429	173,512	43,844	106,763	0	93,047	358,538	231,921	11,098	54,195
Nebraska	2,869,951	1,523,962	502,317	275,053	215,889	376,305	22,333	132,064	1,197,775	706,512	179,912	148,215
Nevada	1,913,800	927,392	431,319	168,216	73,255	97,199	0	157,402	853,065	610,647	0	133,344
New Hampshire	1,072,058	768,862	392,934	67,823	55,871	220,407	0	31,827	265,463	127,475	0	37,732
New Jersey	8,681,858	5,023,918	2,440,064	561,548	391,964	563,624	782,023	284,695	3,391,225	1,731,245	213,900	266,714
New Mexico	3,822,225	2,338,552	318,233	382,522	143,447	97,433	1,222,291	174,626	1,383,717	743,941	273,450	99,956
New York	18,270,637	9,154,681	2,784,447	766,020	1,362,005	719,850	3,255,196	267,163	8,435,340	5,163,444	1,032,349	680,616
North Carolina	12,279,465	5,465,160	2,056,200	992,922	309,430	1,845,806	0	260,802	6,253,077	3,916,624	250,200	561,228
North Dakota	1,183,443	746,007	330,578	140,754	59,170	108,926	0	106,579	415,376	311,308	4,707	22,060
Ohio	15,013,059	10,613,391	3,727,381	682,204	630,381	1,230,740	3,980,411	362,274	3,975,751	2,108,298	203,217	423,917
Oklahoma	4,555,584	2,965,434	1,011,723	322,787	304,899	551,231	98,766	676,028	1,407,262	702,760	64,797	182,888
Oregon	7,573,819	5,516,113	1,335,342	701,629	393,511	584,029	2,278,051	223,552	1,838,945	848,629	273,572	218,760
Pennsylvania	16,181,115	12,971,027	4,518,170	1,376,998	714,326	1,111,380	4,240,139	1,010,016	3,098,216	1,301,307	118,653	111,872
Rhode Island	887,305	548,547	306,552	71,040	31,503	109,630	0	29,822	251,985	175,942	0	86,773
South Carolina	4,994,148	3,532,139	1,681,901	422,744	493,918	541,823	0	391,752	1,324,853	649,971	75,821	137,155
South Dakota	937,110	556,120	263,673	95,715	62,603	76,735	0	57,394	299,443	201,270	0	81,548
Tennessee	4,845,600	2,383,086	1,170,821	278,557	322,859	377,189	0	233,660	2,262,071	1,310,889	0	200,444
Texas	44,583,655	18,772,861	6,038,734	2,185,617	2,697,356	1,660,613	3,013,706	3,176,834	19,780,081	6,163,142	2,189,620	6,030,712
Utah	7,261,544	5,346,507	884,630	509,073	178,024	279,888	2,209,201	1,285,691	1,568,327	942,253	0	346,710
Vermont	926,655	755,131	412,792	124,364	70,731	113,130	0	34,114	166,880	73,329	0	4,643
Virginia	11,710,707	7,705,123	2,971,140	917,166	285,935	1,477,155	1,672,286	381,440	3,508,504	1,806,299	4,104	497,080
Washington	10,679,623	7,621,928	2,072,003	1,295,707	946,454	807,479	2,008,317	491,968	2,673,494	1,528,779	0	384,202
West Virginia	1,920,743	1,290,117	635,377	134,673	220,911	243,556	0	55,601	589,591	362,646	833	41,036
Wisconsin	6,791,863	3,999,110	1,460,158	648,199	513,835	494,859	0	882,058	2,601,182	1,338,784	446,893	191,572
Wyoming	923,839	349,451	100,831	75,636	62,982	62,378	0	47,625	450,921	303,171	47,847	123,467
U.S. Service Academies	2,189,686	256,386	26,625	55,377	2,910	41,700	148,455	-18,680	1,845,125	129,186	0	88,175
Other jurisdictions	**1,540,141**	**418,746**	**95,182**	**162,720**	**42,012**	**9,249**	**68,198**	**41,384**	**1,113,295**	**781,855**	**45,961**	**8,099**
American Samoa	16,947	9,196	1,128	5,625	0	334	0	2,109	7,750	2,028	0	0
Federated States of Micronesia	19,865	11,385	1,061	2,627	4,889	1,711	0	1,095	8,480	0	0	0
Guam	146,093	63,431	16,538	31,078	2,382	2,798	0	10,636	82,515	30,491	21,722	147
Marshall Islands	15,180	7,226	625	4,326	0	894	0	1,380	7,335	3,120	0	620
Northern Marianas	20,180	11,097	2,454	8,396	0	225	0	22	9,082	5,634	0	0
Palau	9,437	4,406	2,255	1,599	0	170	0	383	5,031	2,411	0	0
Puerto Rico	1,237,067	272,288	57,590	87,820	31,505	1,615	68,198	25,561	962,439	738,172	2,119	2,340
U.S. Virgin Islands	75,372	39,717	13,532	21,249	3,235	1,503	0	198	30,663	0	22,120	4,992

[1]After deducting discounts and allowances.

[2]Public institutions typically report Pell grants as revenues from federal grants and as allowances that reduce revenues from tuition and fees.

[3]Includes sales and services of educational activities.

[4]Includes other categories not separately shown.

NOTE: Degree-granting institutions grant associate's or higher degrees and participate in Title IV federal financial aid programs. Includes data for public institutions reporting data according to either Governmental Accounting Standards Board (GASB) or Financial Accounting Standards Board (FASB) guidance. Data in this table pertain to institutions' fiscal years that end in the academic year noted. Detail may not sum to totals because of rounding.

SOURCE: U.S. Department of Education, National Center for Education Statistics, Integrated Postsecondary Education Data System (IPEDS), Spring 2019, Finance component. (This table was prepared December 2019.)

Table 333.30. Appropriations from state and local governments for public degree-granting postsecondary institutions, by state or jurisdiction: Selected years, 1990-91 through 2017-18

[In thousands of current dollars]

State or jurisdiction	State appropriations						Local appropriations					
	1990-91	2000-01	2010-11	2015-16	2016-17	2017-18	1990-91	2000-01	2010-11	2015-16	2016-17	2017-18
1	2	3	4	5	6	7	8	9	10	11	12	13
United States	**$35,898,653**	**$56,268,990**	**$63,063,322**	**$67,145,689**	**$68,641,049**	**$72,891,268**	**$3,159,789**	**$5,582,287**	**$10,023,157**	**$12,213,323**	**$12,958,544**	**$13,401,408**
Alabama	708,191	991,302	1,281,923	1,343,704	1,397,897	1,404,166	6,796	4,829	1,204	1,951	3,005	2,917
Alaska	168,395	190,650	346,644	359,284	333,895	325,302	260	10,340	9,681	11,769	12,356	13,986
Arizona	591,656	903,196	1,006,196	713,709	739,905	745,394	149,337	310,762	746,962	860,992	874,897	890,883
Arkansas	315,372	583,794	753,573	737,815	758,090	764,581	216	9,496	30,375	33,607	34,099	34,966
California	5,313,052	7,891,669	9,367,909	9,898,949	10,085,262	11,563,516	771,160	1,764,717	2,490,057	3,643,602	3,975,545	4,048,931
Colorado	423,710	655,037	33,667	35,124	37,332	44,306	22,400	36,840	82,141	114,979	96,273	100,434
Connecticut	363,427	664,356	1,018,015	1,235,326	1,185,582	1,124,904	0	0	0	0	0	0
Delaware	115,729	193,695	214,445	236,036	243,897	236,699	0	0	0	0	0	0
District of Columbia	0	3,019	66,420	71,942	77,671	80,000	73,495	46,933	0	0	0	0
Florida	1,638,218	2,656,376	3,243,232	3,773,040	4,040,225	4,195,023	1,850	2	0	0	0	0
Georgia	915,303	1,826,961	1,938,523	2,141,041	2,267,964	2,442,075	25,705	21,615	23	23	138	737
Hawaii	304,131	395,884	359,077	441,373	471,453	485,153	0	0	0	0	0	0
Idaho	177,918	290,746	312,809	385,878	419,837	431,993	6,161	11,148	13,398	29,171	30,247	31,430
Illinois	1,296,895	1,760,300	1,789,707	664,824	1,108,209	2,282,662	284,635	520,136	1,001,566	1,082,455	1,142,872	1,164,980
Indiana	886,124	1,257,919	1,431,488	1,521,652	1,527,994	1,566,933	1,507	6,190	7,951	8,501	4,514	8,802
Iowa	544,945	813,805	731,485	847,265	828,453	806,471	21,624	36,129	107,022	140,233	147,960	153,442
Kansas	437,413	664,201	741,285	737,012	734,734	735,972	87,026	160,873	228,630	285,420	296,897	307,814
Kentucky	617,915	939,047	971,263	914,783	885,900	879,606	4,682	14,930	18,261	23,717	24,906	25,389
Louisiana	566,798	834,643	1,018,696	826,723	776,872	780,591	1,462	517	0	0	0	0
Maine	174,737	212,144	252,786	263,476	277,049	276,659	0	0	0	0	0	0
Maryland	724,223	999,723	1,392,864	1,660,524	1,719,050	1,754,397	117,913	185,034	319,337	372,794	393,599	415,121
Massachusetts	471,368	1,038,998	1,034,211	1,333,373	1,421,967	1,461,553	0	0	0	0	0	0
Michigan	1,326,884	1,991,098	1,713,747	1,711,176	1,798,264	1,851,003	159,202	288,112	551,945	555,497	559,346	573,630
Minnesota	744,381	1,174,797	1,206,301	1,322,366	1,306,661	1,395,343	2,040	0	0	0	0	0
Mississippi	365,574	758,242	868,311	1,015,214	965,054	900,717	25,670	38,167	58,179	67,068	69,843	73,997
Missouri	563,430	945,746	904,594	926,656	895,680	866,474	38,097	101,562	148,970	152,019	157,277	162,976
Montana	110,199	137,341	173,250	243,656	243,809	231,921	3,310	4,069	8,151	9,893	10,799	11,098
Nebraska	318,482	514,235	621,957	708,412	721,691	706,512	36,569	19,892	120,979	160,297	170,110	179,912
Nevada	161,581	333,117	539,712	532,599	560,702	610,647	0	0	0	0	0	0
New Hampshire	71,226	96,157	131,878	123,500	124,775	127,475	6	0	7	0	0	0
New Jersey	854,989	1,246,554	1,495,505	1,546,464	1,589,958	1,731,245	145,010	172,667	211,638	206,836	210,672	213,900
New Mexico	307,083	538,822	724,046	795,942	752,122	743,941	34,364	60,183	120,930	146,242	264,227	273,450
New York	2,313,128	4,461,671	4,247,113	5,079,139	4,899,793	5,163,444	372,650	431,415	762,484	980,353	976,477	1,032,349
North Carolina	1,351,111	2,221,600	3,434,423	3,682,530	3,805,619	3,916,624	62,785	113,448	196,168	240,152	242,273	250,200
North Dakota	129,986	188,047	268,488	352,578	336,141	311,308	9	21	2,459	4,961	5,424	4,707
Ohio	1,360,141	1,922,571	1,888,347	2,039,078	2,107,699	2,108,298	63,899	101,647	163,891	190,092	178,479	203,217
Oklahoma	473,898	754,540	924,623	796,238	750,534	702,760	12,822	28,367	49,857	61,889	63,604	64,797
Oregon	377,476	640,347	537,918	778,527	676,660	848,629	118,499	106,436	206,762	242,332	265,502	273,572
Pennsylvania	962,121	1,331,544	1,401,316	1,287,045	1,294,264	1,301,307	62,794	94,338	117,967	114,862	119,756	118,653
Rhode Island	113,614	157,137	137,071	164,729	172,599	175,942	0	0	0	0	0	0
South Carolina	578,794	853,139	480,329	582,745	648,894	649,971	18,670	36,060	62,799	67,954	71,292	75,821
South Dakota	81,859	129,680	157,444	199,367	194,881	201,270	0	0	0	0	0	0
Tennessee	663,536	969,316	1,250,509	1,163,475	1,252,490	1,310,889	1,779	3,824	5,327	6,216	6,254	0
Texas	2,627,916	4,236,852	5,179,075	5,900,536	5,908,211	6,163,142	210,934	439,342	1,377,390	1,920,271	2,064,832	2,189,620
Utah	304,738	531,975	661,823	869,969	904,721	942,253	0	0	0	0	0	0
Vermont	40,997	53,605	72,466	68,719	69,724	73,329	4	0	0	0	0	0
Virginia	886,208	1,395,308	1,534,717	1,717,775	1,815,144	1,806,299	973	1,570	3,737	3,750	3,815	4,104
Washington	828,700	1,200,392	1,329,108	1,284,204	1,440,334	1,528,779	2,470	0	0	0	0	0
West Virginia	263,269	382,269	395,050	375,295	374,378	362,646	574	503	316	603	601	833
Wisconsin	841,192	1,186,415	1,151,462	1,303,319	1,308,309	1,338,784	197,712	379,648	757,773	420,273	435,592	446,893
Wyoming	120,623	149,009	326,523	372,838	349,444	303,171	12,721	20,525	38,818	52,552	45,062	47,847
U.S. Service Academies	0	0	0	58,744	33,258	129,186	0	0	0	0	0	0
Other jurisdictions	**337,393**	**709,473**	**883,692**	**981,347**	**490,701**	**781,855**	**12,724**	**20,612**	**46,944**	**48,314**	**38,726**	**45,961**
American Samoa	0	0	0	3,000	3,000	2,028	0	0	0	0	0	0
Federated States of Micronesia	0	40	0	0	0	0	0	3,327	0	0	0	0
Guam	28,283	29,122	31,936	29,679	26,134	30,491	10,028	12,826	15,700	18,742	18,321	21,722
Marshall Islands	0	1,924	2,000	2,753	2,971	3,120	0	0	0	0	0	0
Northern Marianas	0	9,055	4,385	4,787	5,376	5,634	0	0	0	0	0	0
Palau	644	2,345	2,039	2,411	2,411	2,411	0	0	0	0	0	0
Puerto Rico	277,295	647,623	843,332	938,717	450,809	738,172	2,375	4,459	1,824	2,755	0	2,119
U.S. Virgin Islands	31,170	19,365	0	0	0	0	320	0	29,420	26,817	20,405	22,120

NOTE: Data for 1990-91 are for institutions of higher education, while later data are for degree-granting institutions. Degree-granting institutions grant associate's or higher degrees and participate in Title IV federal financial aid programs. The degree-granting classification is very similar to the earlier higher education classification, but it includes more 2-year colleges and excludes a few higher education institutions that did not grant degrees. Includes data for public institutions reporting data according to either

Governmental Accounting Standards Board (GASB) or Financial Accounting Standards Board (FASB) guidance. Data in this table pertain to institutions' fiscal years that end in the academic year noted. Some data have been revised from previously published figures. Detail may not sum to totals because of rounding.

SOURCE: U.S. Department of Education, National Center for Education Statistics, Integrated Postsecondary Education Data System (IPEDS), "Finance Survey" (IPEDS-F:FY91); and Spring 2002 through Spring 2019, Finance component. (This table was prepared December 2019.)

Table 333.40. Total revenue of private nonprofit degree-granting postsecondary institutions, by source of funds and level of institution: Selected years, 1999–2000 through 2017–18

Level of institution and year	Total	Student tuition and fees (net of allowances)[1]	Federal appropriations, grants, and contracts[1,2]	State and local appropriations, grants, and contracts	Private gifts, grants, and contracts: Total	Private gifts, grants, and contracts: Private grants and contracts	Private gifts, grants, and contracts: Private gifts and contributions from affiliated entities	Investment return (gain or loss)	Educational activities	Auxiliary enterprises (net of allowances)	Hospitals	Other
1	2	3	4	5	6	7	8	9	10	11	12	13
	In thousands of current dollars											
All levels												
1999–2000	$120,625,806	$29,651,812	$12,191,827	$1,697,979	$16,488,984	—	—	$37,763,518	$2,865,606	$8,317,607	$7,208,600	$4,439,874
2004–05	140,150,716	41,394,424	19,699,204	1,957,921	16,738,916	—	—	30,431,521	3,595,559	10,823,963	10,377,808	5,131,401
2006–07	182,377,987	47,482,331	20,193,722	2,164,167	20,194,264	—	—	55,907,577	4,104,373	12,291,765	12,636,904	7,402,884
2007–08	139,261,907	50,741,273	20,204,251	2,386,121	20,991,920	—	—	6,261,553	4,848,435	12,930,918	13,298,642	7,598,794
2008–09	69,064,340	53,698,893	21,026,721	2,391,238	17,670,642	—	—	-64,204,943	4,787,360	13,579,506	14,790,231	5,324,691
2009–10	168,688,480	56,386,895	22,913,755	2,193,062	18,019,300	$4,189,574	$13,829,726	28,427,192	4,821,683	14,080,329	16,541,461	5,304,802
2010–11	207,132,349	60,069,691	24,319,663	2,165,584	22,096,853	4,379,206	17,717,647	53,574,169	4,979,595	14,797,601	17,521,091	7,608,102
2011–12	161,843,203	63,010,873	24,147,131	1,964,921	21,619,470	4,446,517	17,172,953	4,538,153	5,082,873	15,500,185	18,658,649	7,320,948
2012–13	202,042,331	65,562,231	23,710,290	1,939,417	22,335,345	4,834,258	17,501,087	38,532,782	5,530,428	15,969,232	19,011,711	9,450,894
2013–14	228,806,876	67,681,378	23,640,029	1,971,815	25,842,976	5,152,784	20,690,192	57,147,772	6,280,766	16,407,013	20,667,484	9,167,642
2014–15	200,395,534	70,181,110	24,186,839	2,113,187	26,932,309	5,520,105	21,412,204	21,274,906	6,702,519	16,883,478	23,880,282	8,240,906
2015–16	182,571,838	72,100,188	23,471,268	2,162,083	28,622,642	5,819,574	22,803,069	-2,735,211	7,042,281	17,608,294	24,107,516	10,192,778
2016–17	242,602,673	73,966,392	25,244,371	2,103,049	28,864,670	6,197,207	22,667,463	48,838,957	7,516,359	18,004,385	26,744,919	11,319,571
2017–18	248,465,960	75,871,170	26,440,108	2,165,914	30,668,285	6,574,834	24,093,451	45,451,443	7,991,521	18,326,993	29,399,644	12,150,882
4-year												
1999–2000	119,708,625	29,257,523	12,133,829	1,673,707	16,346,616	—	—	37,698,219	2,837,784	8,261,507	7,208,600	4,290,841
2004–05	139,528,763	41,045,608	19,622,002	1,931,021	16,671,017	—	—	30,408,545	3,581,869	10,784,161	10,377,808	5,106,733
2006–07	181,850,660	47,211,942	20,137,197	2,143,146	20,144,883	—	—	55,857,135	4,096,086	12,253,089	12,636,904	7,370,278
2007–08	138,760,610	50,436,622	20,143,562	2,361,744	20,938,758	—	—	6,273,767	4,837,355	12,892,828	13,298,642	7,577,331
2008–09	68,617,705	53,399,912	20,967,794	2,370,169	17,624,319	—	—	-64,172,755	4,781,845	13,542,690	14,790,231	5,313,500
2009–10	168,169,216	56,087,965	22,843,520	2,179,050	17,968,453	4,185,607	13,782,846	28,406,397	4,814,283	14,044,652	16,541,461	5,283,434
2010–11	206,473,105	59,603,541	24,260,568	2,150,124	22,057,300	4,376,381	17,680,919	53,557,782	4,975,158	14,762,888	17,521,091	7,584,652
2011–12	161,246,877	62,571,879	24,098,863	1,953,307	21,580,612	4,444,004	17,136,608	4,532,992	5,079,866	15,471,860	18,658,649	7,298,849
2012–13	201,526,648	65,213,804	23,664,427	1,925,893	22,293,530	4,831,951	17,461,579	38,519,232	5,527,564	15,939,735	19,011,711	9,430,753
2013–14	228,233,305	67,325,986	23,578,760	1,959,405	25,792,211	5,149,819	20,642,392	57,105,397	6,278,456	16,376,022	20,667,484	9,149,584
2014–15	199,546,338	69,519,464	24,127,099	2,102,335	26,895,138	5,518,411	21,376,727	21,267,202	6,696,900	16,840,357	23,880,282	8,217,562
2015–16	181,729,580	71,425,134	23,427,914	2,155,610	28,581,387	5,816,843	22,764,544	-2,736,188	7,037,367	17,562,236	24,107,516	10,168,604
2016–17	241,772,907	73,307,606	25,206,303	2,097,462	28,824,410	6,194,800	22,629,610	48,824,390	7,511,347	17,964,144	26,744,919	11,292,325
2017–18	247,644,652	75,218,369	26,404,744	2,159,775	30,615,084	6,572,718	24,042,366	45,435,307	7,986,306	18,290,555	29,399,644	12,134,868
2-year												
1999–2000	917,181	394,289	57,998	24,272	142,368	—	—	65,299	27,822	56,100	0	149,033
2004–05	621,953	348,815	77,202	26,900	67,899	—	—	22,976	13,690	39,802	0	24,668
2006–07	527,327	270,389	56,525	21,021	49,381	—	—	50,442	8,288	38,675	0	32,606
2007–08	501,297	304,651	60,689	24,377	53,162	—	—	-12,214	11,080	38,091	0	21,462
2008–09	446,635	298,981	58,927	21,069	46,323	—	—	-32,187	5,515	36,816	0	11,191
2009–10	519,264	298,930	70,235	14,012	50,847	3,967	46,880	20,795	7,400	35,677	0	21,368
2010–11	659,244	466,149	59,095	15,460	39,553	2,825	36,727	16,388	4,437	34,712	0	23,450
2011–12	596,326	438,994	48,269	11,614	38,858	2,513	36,345	5,161	3,007	28,325	0	22,099
2012–13	515,683	348,427	45,863	13,524	41,815	2,307	39,508	13,550	2,865	29,498	0	20,140
2013–14	573,571	355,392	61,269	12,409	50,766	2,965	47,800	42,376	2,311	30,991	0	18,058
2014–15	849,197	661,646	59,740	10,852	37,171	1,694	35,477	7,704	5,619	43,121	0	23,344
2015–16	842,258	675,053	43,354	6,473	41,256	2,731	38,525	976	4,913	46,058	0	24,174
2016–17	829,766	658,786	38,068	5,587	40,260	2,407	37,853	14,567	5,012	40,241	0	27,245
2017–18	821,309	652,801	35,364	6,139	53,201	2,116	51,085	16,135	5,216	36,438	0	16,014
	Percentage distribution											
All levels												
1999–2000	100.00	24.58	10.11	1.41	13.67	—	—	31.31	2.38	6.90	5.98	3.68
2004–05	100.00	29.54	14.06	1.40	11.94	—	—	21.71	2.57	7.72	7.40	3.66
2006–07	100.00	26.04	11.07	1.19	11.07	—	—	30.65	2.25	6.74	6.93	4.06
2007–08	100.00	36.44	14.51	1.71	15.07	—	—	4.50	3.48	9.29	9.55	5.46
2008–09	100.00	77.75	30.45	3.46	25.59	—	—	-92.96	6.93	19.66	21.42	7.71
2009–10	100.00	33.43	13.58	1.30	10.68	2.48	8.20	16.85	2.86	8.35	9.81	3.14
2010–11	100.00	29.00	11.74	1.05	10.67	2.11	8.55	25.86	2.40	7.14	8.46	3.67
2011–12	100.00	38.93	14.92	1.21	13.36	2.75	10.61	2.80	3.14	9.58	11.53	4.52
2012–13	100.00	32.45	11.74	0.96	11.05	2.39	8.66	19.07	2.74	7.90	9.41	4.68
2013–14	100.00	29.58	10.33	0.86	11.29	2.25	9.04	24.98	2.75	7.17	9.03	4.01
2014–15	100.00	35.02	12.07	1.05	13.44	2.75	10.68	10.62	3.34	8.43	11.92	4.11
2015–16	100.00	39.49	12.86	1.18	15.68	3.19	12.49	-1.50	3.86	9.64	13.20	5.58
2016–17	100.00	30.49	10.41	0.87	11.90	2.55	9.34	20.13	3.10	7.42	11.02	4.67
2017–18	100.00	30.54	10.64	0.87	12.34	2.65	9.70	18.29	3.22	7.38	11.83	4.89
4-year												
1999–2000	100.00	24.44	10.14	1.40	13.66	—	—	31.49	2.37	6.90	6.02	3.58
2004–05	100.00	29.42	14.06	1.38	11.95	—	—	21.79	2.57	7.73	7.44	3.66
2006–07	100.00	25.96	11.07	1.18	11.08	—	—	30.72	2.25	6.74	6.95	4.05
2007–08	100.00	36.35	14.52	1.70	15.09	—	—	4.52	3.49	9.29	9.58	5.46
2008–09	100.00	77.82	30.56	3.45	25.68	—	—	-93.52	6.97	19.74	21.55	7.74
2009–10	100.00	33.35	13.58	1.30	10.68	2.49	8.20	16.89	2.86	8.35	9.84	3.14
2010–11	100.00	28.87	11.75	1.04	10.68	2.12	8.56	25.94	2.41	7.15	8.49	3.67
2011–12	100.00	38.81	14.95	1.21	13.38	2.76	10.63	2.81	3.15	9.60	11.57	4.53
2012–13	100.00	32.36	11.74	0.96	11.06	2.40	8.66	19.11	2.74	7.91	9.43	4.68
2013–14	100.00	29.50	10.33	0.86	11.30	2.26	9.04	25.02	2.75	7.18	9.06	4.01
2014–15	100.00	34.84	12.09	1.05	13.48	2.77	10.71	10.66	3.36	8.44	11.97	4.12
2015–16	100.00	39.30	12.89	1.19	15.73	3.20	12.53	-1.51	3.87	9.66	13.27	5.60
2016–17	100.00	30.32	10.43	0.87	11.92	2.56	9.36	20.19	3.11	7.43	11.06	4.67
2017–18	100.00	30.37	10.66	0.87	12.36	2.65	9.71	18.35	3.22	7.39	11.87	4.90

See notes at end of table.

Table 333.40. Total revenue of private nonprofit degree-granting postsecondary institutions, by source of funds and level of institution: Selected years, 1999–2000 through 2017–18—Continued

Level of institution and year	Total	Student tuition and fees (net of allowances)[1]	Federal appropri-ations, grants, and contracts[1,2]	State and local appropri-ations, grants, and contracts	Private gifts, grants, and contracts: Total	Private gifts, grants, and contracts: Private grants and contracts	Private gifts, grants, and contracts: Private gifts and contribu-tions from affiliated entities	Investment return (gain or loss)	Educational activities	Auxiliary enterprises (net of allowances)	Hospitals	Other
1	2	3	4	5	6	7	8	9	10	11	12	13
2-year												
1999–2000	100.00	42.99	6.32	2.65	15.52	—	—	7.12	3.03	6.12	0.00	16.25
2004–05	100.00	56.08	12.41	4.33	10.92	—	—	3.69	2.20	6.40	0.00	3.97
2006–07	100.00	51.28	10.72	3.99	9.36	—	—	9.57	1.57	7.33	0.00	6.18
2007–08	100.00	60.77	12.11	4.86	10.60	—	—	-2.44	2.21	7.60	0.00	4.28
2008–09	100.00	66.94	13.19	4.72	10.37	—	—	-7.21	1.23	8.24	0.00	2.51
2009–10	100.00	57.57	13.53	2.70	9.79	0.76	9.03	4.00	1.43	6.87	0.00	4.12
2010–11	100.00	70.71	8.96	2.35	6.00	0.43	5.57	2.49	0.67	5.27	0.00	3.56
2011–12	100.00	73.62	8.09	1.95	6.52	0.42	6.09	0.87	0.50	4.75	0.00	3.71
2012–13	100.00	67.57	8.89	2.62	8.11	0.45	7.66	2.63	0.56	5.72	0.00	3.91
2013–14	100.00	61.96	10.68	2.16	8.85	0.52	8.33	7.39	0.40	5.40	0.00	3.15
2014–15	100.00	77.91	7.03	1.28	4.38	0.20	4.18	0.91	0.66	5.08	0.00	2.75
2015–16	100.00	80.15	5.15	0.77	4.90	0.32	4.57	0.12	0.58	5.47	0.00	2.87
2016–17	100.00	79.39	4.59	0.67	4.85	0.29	4.56	1.76	0.60	4.85	0.00	3.28
2017–18	100.00	79.48	4.31	0.75	6.48	0.26	6.22	1.96	0.64	4.44	0.00	1.95
	Revenue per full-time-equivalent student in constant 2018–19 dollars[3]											
All levels												
1999–2000	$71,078	$17,472	$7,184	$1,001	$9,716	—	—	$22,252	$1,689	$4,901	$4,248	$2,616
2004–05	64,531	19,060	9,070	902	7,707	—	—	14,012	1,656	4,984	4,778	2,363
2006–07	76,404	19,892	8,460	907	8,460	—	—	23,422	1,719	5,149	5,294	3,101
2007–08	54,878	19,995	7,962	940	8,272	—	—	2,467	1,911	5,096	5,241	2,994
2008–09	26,446	20,562	8,051	916	6,766	—	—	-24,585	1,833	5,200	5,663	2,039
2009–10	62,281	20,818	8,460	810	6,653	$1,547	$5,106	10,496	1,780	5,199	6,107	1,959
2010–11	72,235	20,949	8,481	755	7,706	1,527	6,179	18,683	1,737	5,160	6,110	2,653
2011–12	54,360	21,164	8,111	660	7,262	1,494	5,768	1,524	1,707	5,206	6,267	2,459
2012–13	65,994	21,415	7,745	633	7,295	1,579	5,716	12,586	1,806	5,216	6,210	3,087
2013–14	73,483	21,736	7,592	633	8,300	1,655	6,645	18,353	2,017	5,269	6,637	2,944
2014–15	62,958	22,049	7,599	664	8,461	1,734	6,727	6,684	2,106	5,304	7,502	2,589
2015–16	56,531	22,325	7,268	669	8,863	1,802	7,061	-847	2,181	5,452	7,465	3,156
2016–17	73,251	22,333	7,622	635	8,715	1,871	6,844	14,746	2,269	5,436	8,075	3,418
2017–18	73,205	22,354	7,790	638	9,036	1,937	7,099	13,391	2,355	5,400	8,662	3,580
4-year												
1999–2000	72,049	17,609	7,303	1,007	9,839	—	—	22,689	1,708	4,972	4,339	2,583
2004–05	65,025	19,129	9,145	900	7,769	—	—	14,171	1,669	5,026	4,836	2,380
2006–07	76,844	19,950	8,509	906	8,513	—	—	23,603	1,731	5,178	5,340	3,114
2007–08	55,171	20,054	8,009	939	8,325	—	—	2,494	1,923	5,126	5,288	3,013
2008–09	26,498	20,621	8,097	915	6,806	—	—	-24,781	1,847	5,230	5,712	2,052
2009–10	62,599	20,878	8,503	811	6,689	1,558	5,131	10,574	1,792	5,228	6,157	1,967
2010–11	72,778	21,009	8,551	758	7,775	1,543	6,232	18,878	1,754	5,204	6,176	2,673
2011–12	54,697	21,225	8,175	663	7,320	1,507	5,813	1,538	1,723	5,248	6,329	2,476
2012–13	66,380	21,481	7,795	634	7,343	1,592	5,752	12,688	1,821	5,250	6,262	3,106
2013–14	73,891	21,797	7,634	634	8,350	1,667	6,683	18,488	2,033	5,302	6,691	2,962
2014–15	63,531	22,133	7,681	669	8,563	1,757	6,806	6,771	2,132	5,362	7,603	2,616
2015–16	56,953	22,384	7,342	676	8,957	1,823	7,134	-858	2,205	5,504	7,555	3,187
2016–17	73,891	22,404	7,704	641	8,809	1,893	6,916	14,922	2,296	5,490	8,174	3,451
2017–18	73,841	22,428	7,873	644	9,129	1,960	7,169	13,548	2,381	5,454	8,766	3,618
2-year												
1999–2000	25,762	11,075	1,629	682	3,999	—	—	1,834	781	1,576	0	4,186
2004–05	23,864	13,384	2,962	1,032	2,605	—	—	882	525	1,527	0	947
2006–07	25,706	13,181	2,755	1,025	2,407	—	—	2,459	404	1,885	0	1,589
2007–08	22,216	13,501	2,690	1,080	2,356	—	—	-541	491	1,688	0	951
2008–09	20,292	13,584	2,677	957	2,105	—	—	-1,462	251	1,673	0	508
2009–10	23,531	13,546	3,183	635	2,304	180	2,124	942	335	1,617	0	968
2010–11	21,651	15,310	1,941	508	1,299	93	1,206	538	146	1,140	0	770
2011–12	20,391	15,011	1,651	397	1,329	86	1,243	176	103	969	0	756
2012–13	20,140	13,608	1,791	528	1,633	90	1,543	529	112	1,152	0	787
2013–14	22,970	14,233	2,454	497	2,033	119	1,914	1,697	93	1,241	0	723
2014–15	20,198	15,737	1,421	258	884	40	844	183	134	1,026	0	555
2015–16	21,767	17,446	1,120	167	1,066	71	996	25	127	1,190	0	625
2016–17	20,801	16,514	954	140	1,009	60	949	365	126	1,009	0	683
2017–18	20,355	16,179	876	152	1,319	52	1,266	400	129	903	0	397

—Not available.
[1]Private institutions typically report Pell grants as revenues from tuition and fees rather than as revenues from federal grants.
[2]Includes independent operations.
[3]Constant dollars based on the Consumer Price Index, prepared by the Bureau of Labor Statistics, U.S. Department of Labor, adjusted to a school-year basis.
NOTE: Degree-granting institutions grant associate's or higher degrees and participate in Title IV federal financial aid programs. Data in this table pertain to institutions' fiscal years that end in the academic year noted. Some data have been revised from previously published figures. Detail may not sum to totals because of rounding.
SOURCE: U.S. Department of Education, National Center for Education Statistics, Integrated Postsecondary Education Data System (IPEDS), "Fall Enrollment Survey" (IPEDS-EF:99); Spring 2001 through Spring 2007, Enrollment component; Spring 2008 through Spring 2018, Fall Enrollment component; and Spring 2001 through Spring 2019, Finance component. (This table was prepared December 2019.)

Table 333.50. Total revenue of private nonprofit degree-granting postsecondary institutions, by source of funds and classification of institution: 2017–18

Classification of institution	Total	Student tuition and fees (net of allowances)[1]	Federal appropriations, grants, and contracts[1,2]	State appropriations, grants, and contracts	Local appropriations, grants, and contracts	Private grants and contracts	Private gifts and contributions from affiliated entities	Investment return (gain or loss)	Educational activities	Auxiliary enterprises (net of allowances)	Hospitals	Other
1	2	3	4	5	6	7	8	9	10	11	12	13
	In thousands of current dollars											
Total	**$248,465,960**	**$75,871,170**	**$26,440,108**	**$1,676,697**	**$489,217**	**$6,574,834**	**$24,093,451**	**$45,451,443**	**$7,991,521**	**$18,326,993**	**$29,399,644**	**$12,150,882**
4-year	247,644,652	75,218,369	26,404,744	1,671,850	487,925	6,572,718	24,042,366	45,435,307	7,986,306	18,290,555	29,399,644	12,134,868
Research university, very high[3]	127,519,521	19,589,241	20,165,663	858,374	226,256	4,337,374	11,619,637	30,437,749	5,994,725	5,427,298	20,368,962	8,494,243
Research university, high[4]	17,828,061	7,265,595	1,361,977	126,482	29,551	333,538	2,196,512	2,751,321	892,017	1,645,394	502,711	722,962
Doctoral/research[5]	11,115,848	7,304,558	294,560	105,899	3,535	52,501	725,714	960,244	53,624	1,262,889	0	352,324
Master's[6]	34,970,904	22,545,043	852,411	261,910	8,968	155,239	2,602,695	2,627,314	166,748	4,781,855	13,773	954,946
Baccalaureate[7]	27,564,073	10,398,318	635,604	103,155	4,319	259,275	4,374,179	6,651,087	161,084	4,286,562	0	690,490
Special-focus institutions[8]	28,646,245	8,115,613	3,094,529	216,031	215,297	1,434,791	2,523,629	2,007,593	718,108	886,556	8,514,198	919,902
Arts, music, or design	2,916,192	1,806,906	36,917	13,611	5,135	27,569	334,008	275,785	18,030	322,001	0	76,230
Business and management	726,431	438,264	27,161	10,049	0	3,542	60,632	82,235	5,471	91,229	0	7,848
Engineering and other technology-related	318,482	180,748	2,971	1,086	0	1,483	41,776	54,054	1,443	28,918	0	6,003
Faith related	2,228,694	631,585	46,384	2,290	311	55,994	739,305	437,937	12,151	175,748	0	126,990
Law	472,683	335,577	8,943	2,614	422	4,393	33,424	60,914	558	14,733	0	11,104
Medical schools and centers and other heath professions schools	21,262,589	4,366,610	2,811,524	180,905	199,975	1,334,393	1,241,892	1,061,734	668,261	217,274	8,514,198	665,823
Tribal colleges[9]	90,269	7,683	72,413	1,242	242	1,199	958	443	697	978	0	4,413
Other special focus	630,905	348,240	88,214	4,233	9,213	6,218	71,634	34,491	11,496	35,674	0	21,491
2-year	821,309	652,801	35,364	4,847	1,292	2,116	51,085	16,135	5,216	36,438	0	16,014
Associate's colleges	804,017	651,623	23,238	3,684	717	906	50,485	16,100	5,142	36,162	0	15,959
Tribal colleges[9]	17,292	1,178	12,126	1,163	575	1,210	600	35	73	276	0	55
	Percentage distribution											
Total	**100.00**	**30.54**	**10.64**	**0.67**	**0.20**	**2.65**	**9.70**	**18.29**	**3.22**	**7.38**	**11.83**	**4.89**
4-year	100.00	30.37	10.66	0.68	0.20	2.65	9.71	18.35	3.22	7.39	11.87	4.90
Research university, very high[3]	100.00	15.36	15.81	0.67	0.18	3.40	9.11	23.87	4.70	4.26	15.97	6.66
Research university, high[4]	100.00	40.75	7.64	0.71	0.17	1.87	12.32	15.43	5.00	9.23	2.82	4.06
Doctoral/research[5]	100.00	65.71	2.65	0.95	0.03	0.47	6.53	8.64	0.48	11.36	0.00	3.17
Master's[6]	100.00	64.47	2.44	0.75	0.03	0.44	7.44	7.51	0.48	13.67	0.04	2.73
Baccalaureate[7]	100.00	37.72	2.31	0.37	0.02	0.94	15.87	24.13	0.58	15.55	0.00	2.51
Special-focus institutions[8]	100.00	28.33	10.80	0.75	0.75	5.01	8.81	7.01	2.51	3.09	29.72	3.21
Arts, music, or design	100.00	61.96	1.27	0.47	0.18	0.95	11.45	9.46	0.62	11.04	0.00	2.61
Business and management	100.00	60.33	3.74	1.38	0.00	0.49	8.35	11.32	0.75	12.56	0.00	1.08
Engineering and other technology-related	100.00	56.75	0.93	0.34	0.00	0.47	13.12	16.97	0.45	9.08	0.00	1.88
Faith related	100.00	28.34	2.08	0.10	0.01	2.51	33.17	19.65	0.55	7.89	0.00	5.70
Law	100.00	70.99	1.89	0.55	0.09	0.93	7.07	12.89	0.12	3.12	0.00	2.35
Medical schools and centers and other heath professions schools	100.00	20.54	13.22	0.85	0.94	6.28	5.84	4.99	3.14	1.02	40.04	3.13
Tribal colleges[9]	100.00	8.51	80.22	1.38	0.27	1.33	1.06	0.49	0.77	1.08	0.00	4.89
Other special focus	100.00	55.20	13.98	0.67	1.46	0.99	11.35	5.47	1.82	5.65	0.00	3.41
2-year	100.00	79.48	4.31	0.59	0.16	0.26	6.22	1.96	0.64	4.44	0.00	1.95
Associate's colleges	100.00	81.05	2.89	0.46	0.09	0.11	6.28	2.00	0.64	4.50	0.00	1.98
Tribal colleges[9]	100.00	6.81	70.13	6.73	3.33	7.00	3.47	0.20	0.42	1.60	0.00	0.32
	Revenue per full-time-equivalent student in current dollars											
Total	**$71,719**	**$21,900**	**$7,632**	**$484**	**$141**	**$1,898**	**$6,954**	**$13,119**	**$2,307**	**$5,290**	**$8,486**	**$3,507**
4-year	72,342	21,973	7,713	488	143	1,920	7,023	13,273	2,333	5,343	8,588	3,545
Research university, very high[3]	221,773	34,068	35,071	1,493	393	7,543	20,208	52,935	10,426	9,439	35,424	14,773
Research university, high[4]	61,028	24,871	4,662	433	101	1,142	7,519	9,418	3,054	5,632	1,721	2,475
Doctoral/research[5]	31,512	20,708	835	300	10	149	2,057	2,722	152	3,580	0	999
Master's[6]	27,217	17,546	663	204	7	121	2,026	2,045	130	3,722	11	743
Baccalaureate[7]	46,210	17,432	1,066	173	7	435	7,333	11,150	270	7,186	0	1,158
Special-focus institutions[8]	88,963	25,204	9,610	671	669	4,456	7,837	6,235	2,230	2,753	26,441	2,857
Arts, music, or design	49,511	30,678	627	231	87	468	5,671	4,682	306	5,467	0	1,294
Business and management	30,453	18,373	1,139	421	0	148	2,542	3,447	229	3,824	0	329
Engineering and other technology-related	26,022	14,768	243	89	0	121	3,413	4,417	118	2,363	0	490
Faith related	32,957	9,340	686	34	5	828	10,932	6,476	180	2,599	0	1,878
Law	46,224	32,816	875	256	41	430	3,269	5,957	55	1,441	0	1,086
Medical schools and centers and other heath professions schools	159,165	32,687	21,046	1,354	1,497	9,989	9,296	7,948	5,002	1,626	63,735	4,984
Tribal colleges[9]	43,841	3,731	35,169	603	118	582	465	215	339	475	0	2,143
Other special focus	46,696	25,775	6,529	313	682	460	5,302	2,553	851	2,640	0	1,591
2-year	19,942	15,850	859	118	31	51	1,240	392	127	885	0	389
Associate's colleges	19,712	15,975	570	90	18	22	1,238	395	126	887	0	391
Tribal colleges[9]	43,667	2,974	30,622	2,937	1,452	3,055	1,515	88	185	698	0	140

[1]Private institutions typically report Pell grants as revenues from tuition and fees rather than as revenues from federal grants.
[2]Includes independent operations.
[3]Research universities with a very high level of research activity.
[4]Research universities with a high level of research activity.
[5]Institutions that award at least 20 research/scholarship doctor's degrees per year, but did not have high levels of research activity.
[6]Institutions that award at least 50 master's and fewer than 20 doctor's degrees per year.
[7]Institutions that primarily emphasize undergraduate education. In addition to institutions that primarily award bachelor's degrees, also includes institutions classified as 4-year in the IPEDS system, but classified as 2-year baccalaureate/associate's colleges in the Carnegie Classification system because they primarily award associate's degrees.
[8]Four-year institutions that award degrees primarily in single fields of study, such as medicine, business, fine arts, theology, and engineering.
[9]Tribally controlled colleges, which are located on reservations and are members of the American Indian Higher Education Consortium.

NOTE: Relative levels of research activity for research universities were determined by an analysis of research and development expenditures, science and engineering research staffing, and doctor's degrees conferred, by field. Further information on the Carnegie 2015 classification system used in this table may be obtained from https://carnegieclassifications.iu.edu/downloads/CCIHE2015-FactsFigures.pdf. Degree-granting institutions grant associate's or higher degrees and participate in Title IV federal financial aid programs. Data in this table pertain to institutions' fiscal years that end in the academic year noted. Detail may not sum to totals because of rounding.

SOURCE: U.S. Department of Education, National Center for Education Statistics, Integrated Postsecondary Education Data System (IPEDS), Spring 2018, Fall Enrollment component; and Spring 2019, Finance component. (This table was prepared December 2019.)

Table 333.55. Total revenue of private for-profit degree-granting postsecondary institutions, by source of funds and level of institution: Selected years, 1999–2000 through 2017–18

Level of institution and year	Total	Student tuition and fees (net of allowances)[1]	Federal appropriations, grants, and contracts[1]	State and local appropriations, grants, and contracts	Private gifts, grants, and contracts	Investment return (gain or loss)	Educational activities	Auxiliary enterprises (net of allowances)	Other
1	2	3	4	5	6	7	8	9	10
	In thousands of current dollars								
All levels									
1999–2000	$4,321,985	$3,721,032	$198,923	$71,904	$2,151	$18,537	$70,672	$156,613	$82,153
2010–11	28,285,216	25,157,459	1,583,370	157,290	31,272	32,551	402,206	542,622	378,447
2013–14	22,645,566	20,481,607	941,363	77,986	12,206	43,032	256,321	482,439	350,611
2014–15	19,665,772	17,705,922	848,223	53,217	15,935	45,317	224,389	434,253	338,516
2015–16	17,049,389	15,493,140	712,642	46,680	14,901	27,484	176,339	312,166	266,036
2016–17	15,778,912	14,427,696	520,794	40,206	12,588	41,453	203,365	247,202	285,609
2017–18	13,233,730	12,374,965	228,157	21,357	12,175	58,806	159,937	147,597	230,737
4-year									
1999–2000	2,381,042	2,050,136	103,865	39,460	1,109	10,340	33,764	102,103	40,266
2010–11	21,690,069	19,483,895	1,113,186	118,054	29,118	28,671	346,786	405,604	164,755
2013–14	17,832,352	16,188,360	709,409	51,830	10,232	36,012	222,841	395,509	218,160
2014–15	15,845,578	14,281,696	626,082	37,570	14,474	37,530	198,393	371,131	278,702
2015–16	13,575,294	12,376,301	519,399	32,097	13,708	21,959	151,174	255,030	205,627
2016–17	12,733,999	11,692,675	368,141	27,872	11,586	34,559	180,112	210,935	208,120
2017–18	10,779,287	10,190,630	111,302	12,118	11,521	51,759	138,034	121,056	142,867
2-year									
1999–2000	1,940,943	1,670,896	95,058	32,444	1,042	8,197	36,908	54,510	41,888
2010–11	6,595,147	5,673,564	470,183	39,236	2,154	3,880	55,420	137,018	213,692
2013–14	4,813,214	4,293,247	231,954	26,157	1,975	7,021	33,480	86,930	132,450
2014–15	3,820,194	3,424,226	222,141	15,647	1,461	7,787	25,996	63,122	59,814
2015–16	3,474,095	3,116,840	193,243	14,583	1,193	5,525	25,166	57,136	60,409
2016–17	3,044,913	2,735,021	152,652	12,334	1,002	6,894	23,253	36,266	77,490
2017–18	2,454,442	2,184,335	116,855	9,240	654	7,047	21,903	26,540	87,869
	Percentage distribution								
All levels									
1999–2000	100.00	86.10	4.60	1.66	0.05	0.43	1.64	3.62	1.90
2010–11	100.00	88.94	5.60	0.56	0.11	0.12	1.42	1.92	1.34
2013–14	100.00	90.44	4.16	0.34	0.05	0.19	1.13	2.13	1.55
2014–15	100.00	90.03	4.31	0.27	0.08	0.23	1.14	2.21	1.72
2015–16	100.00	90.87	4.18	0.27	0.09	0.16	1.03	1.83	1.56
2016–17	100.00	91.44	3.30	0.25	0.08	0.26	1.29	1.57	1.81
2017–18	100.00	93.51	1.72	0.16	0.09	0.44	1.21	1.12	1.74
4-year									
1999–2000	100.00	86.10	4.36	1.66	0.05	0.43	1.42	4.29	1.69
2010–11	100.00	89.83	5.13	0.54	0.13	0.13	1.60	1.87	0.76
2013–14	100.00	90.78	3.98	0.29	0.06	0.20	1.25	2.22	1.22
2014–15	100.00	90.13	3.95	0.24	0.09	0.24	1.25	2.34	1.76
2015–16	100.00	91.17	3.83	0.24	0.10	0.16	1.11	1.88	1.51
2016–17	100.00	91.82	2.89	0.22	0.09	0.27	1.41	1.66	1.63
2017–18	100.00	94.54	1.03	0.11	0.11	0.48	1.28	1.12	1.33
2-year									
1999–2000	100.00	86.09	4.90	1.67	0.05	0.42	1.90	2.81	2.16
2010–11	100.00	86.03	7.13	0.59	0.03	0.06	0.84	2.08	3.24
2013–14	100.00	89.20	4.82	0.54	0.04	0.15	0.70	1.81	2.75
2014–15	100.00	89.63	5.81	0.41	0.04	0.20	0.68	1.65	1.57
2015–16	100.00	89.72	5.56	0.42	0.03	0.16	0.72	1.64	1.74
2016–17	100.00	89.82	5.01	0.41	0.03	0.23	0.76	1.19	2.54
2017–18	100.00	89.00	4.76	0.38	0.03	0.29	0.89	1.08	3.58
	Revenue per full-time-equivalent student in constant 2018–19 dollars[2]								
All levels									
1999–2000	$16,811	$14,474	$774	$280	$8	$72	$275	$609	$320
2010–11	19,595	17,428	1,097	109	22	23	279	376	262
2013–14	23,017	20,818	957	79	12	44	261	490	356
2014–15	17,803	16,029	768	48	14	41	203	393	306
2015–16	18,326	16,653	766	50	16	30	190	336	286
2016–17	18,387	16,813	607	47	15	48	237	288	333
2017–18	17,989	16,821	310	29	17	80	217	201	314
4-year									
1999–2000	17,063	14,691	744	283	8	74	242	732	289
2010–11	19,755	17,746	1,014	108	27	26	316	369	150
2013–14	24,661	22,387	981	72	14	50	308	547	302
2014–15	17,807	16,049	704	42	16	42	223	417	313
2015–16	18,265	16,652	699	43	18	30	203	343	277
2016–17	18,364	16,863	531	40	17	50	260	304	300
2017–18	18,167	17,174	188	20	19	87	233	204	241
2-year									
1999–2000	16,513	14,215	809	276	9	70	314	464	356
2010–11	19,087	16,420	1,361	114	6	11	160	397	618
2013–14	18,460	16,465	890	100	8	27	128	333	508
2014–15	17,786	15,943	1,034	73	7	36	121	294	278
2015–16	18,568	16,658	1,033	78	6	30	134	305	323
2016–17	18,484	16,602	927	75	6	42	141	220	470
2017–18	17,247	15,349	821	65	5	50	154	186	617

[1]Private institutions typically report Pell grants as revenues from tuition and fees rather than as revenues from federal grants.

[2]Constant dollars based on the Consumer Price Index, prepared by the Bureau of Labor Statistics, U.S. Department of Labor, adjusted to a school-year basis.

NOTE: Degree-granting institutions grant associate's or higher degrees and participate in Title IV federal financial aid programs. Data in this table pertain to institutions' fiscal years that end in the academic year noted. Some data have been revised from previously published figures. Detail may not sum to totals because of rounding.

SOURCE: U.S. Department of Education, National Center for Education Statistics, Integrated Postsecondary Education Data System (IPEDS), "Fall Enrollment Survey" (IPEDS-EF:99); Spring 2011 through Spring 2018, Fall Enrollment component; and selected years, Spring 2001 through Spring 2019, Finance component. (This table was prepared December 2019.)

Table 333.90. Endowment funds of the 120 degree-granting postsecondary institutions with the largest endowments, by rank order: Fiscal year 2018

Institution	Fiscal year (FY) 2018			
	Rank order, end of FY[1]	Market value of endowment		
		Beginning of FY (in thousands)	End of FY (in thousands)	Percent change[2]
1	2	3	4	5
United States (all institutions)	†	**$597,008,695**	**$648,043,073**	**8.5**
120 institutions with the largest amounts	†	**442,307,601**	**482,184,763**	**9.0**
Harvard University (MA)	1	37,096,474	39,233,736	5.8
University of Texas System Office	2	25,947,842	30,597,370	17.9
Yale University (CT)	3	27,216,639	29,444,936	8.2
Stanford University (CA)	4	24,784,943	26,464,912	6.8
Princeton University (NJ)	5	23,353,233	25,438,281	8.9
Massachusetts Institute of Technology	6	14,832,483	16,400,027	10.6
University of Pennsylvania	7	12,213,207	13,777,441	12.8
Texas A & M University, College Station	8	10,812,432	12,688,651	17.4
University of Michigan, Ann Arbor	9	10,777,563	11,733,013	8.9
University of Notre Dame (IN)	10	9,684,936	11,065,058	14.3
Columbia University in the City of New York (NY)	11	9,996,596	10,869,245	8.7
University of California System Admin Central Office	12	9,837,900	10,828,968	10.1
Duke University (NC)	13	7,911,175	8,524,846	7.8
Northwestern University (IL)	14	7,947,574	8,386,918	5.5
Emory University (GA)	15	7,613,022	7,985,467	4.9
Washington University in St Louis (MO)	16	7,214,958	7,687,392	6.5
University of Chicago (IL)	17	6,617,076	7,009,012	5.9
Cornell University (NY)	18	6,516,445	6,871,481	5.4
University of Virginia, Main Campus	19	6,308,922	6,856,258	8.7
Rice University (TX)	20	5,835,568	6,228,857	6.7
University of Southern California	21	5,130,520	5,544,267	8.1
Dartmouth College (NH)	22	4,956,494	5,494,203	10.8
Ohio State University, Main Campus	23	4,233,106	5,189,801	22.6
Vanderbilt University (TN)	24	4,136,465	4,608,461	11.4
University of Wisconsin, Madison	25	3,759,387	4,243,440	12.9
New York University	26	4,076,048	4,222,210	3.6
Johns Hopkins University (MD)	27	3,744,751	4,190,520	11.9
University of Pittsburgh, Pittsburgh Campus (PA)	28	3,921,014	4,174,775	6.5
University of Texas at Austin	29	3,678,480	4,039,907	9.8
Brown University (RI)	30	3,245,531	3,603,848	11.0
University of Washington, Seattle Campus	31	3,239,135	3,534,519	9.1
University of Minnesota, Twin Cities	32	3,290,771	3,500,753	6.4
University of North Carolina at Chapel Hill	33	2,947,111	3,307,663	12.2
Michigan State University	34	3,084,973	3,306,597	7.2
California Institute of Technology	35	2,641,050	2,907,002	10.1
Pennsylvania State University, Main Campus	36	2,615,568	2,891,684	10.6
Williams College (MA)	37	2,383,500	2,626,267	10.2
Boston College (MA)	38	2,334,883	2,515,667	7.7
University of Richmond (VA)	39	2,373,506	2,511,584	5.8
Amherst College (MA)	40	2,248,141	2,377,537	5.8
Purdue University, Main Campus (IN)	41	2,347,515	2,336,955	-0.4
Pomona College (CA)	42	2,165,208	2,273,707	5.0
University of Rochester (NY)	43	2,121,390	2,257,357	6.4
Boston University (MA)	44	1,957,021	2,179,287	11.4
University of California, Los Angeles	45	1,961,228	2,125,752	8.4
Swarthmore College (PA)	46	1,955,532	2,115,768	8.2
Wellesley College (MA)	47	1,930,752	2,105,212	9.0
Georgia Institute of Technology, Main Campus	48	1,985,802	2,091,110	5.3
University of California, Berkeley	49	1,909,978	1,999,056	4.7
Grinnell College (IA)	50	1,871,046	1,991,605	6.4
Brigham Young University, Provo (UT)	51	1,720,824	1,974,414	14.7
Virginia Commonwealth University	52	1,843,001	1,951,337	5.9
Case Western Reserve University (OH)	53	1,798,790	1,886,761	4.9
Smith College (MA)	54	1,767,466	1,875,093	6.1
Carnegie Mellon University (PA)	55	1,718,583	1,872,191	8.9
Tufts University (MA)	56	1,738,706	1,845,956	6.2
George Washington University (DC)	57	1,729,147	1,798,810	4.0
Georgetown University (DC)	58	1,661,745	1,769,557	6.5
University of Kansas	59	1,634,789	1,765,780	8.0
Bowdoin College (ME)	61	1,455,909	1,628,165	11.8
Southern Methodist University (TX)	62	1,505,303	1,619,232	7.6
Washington and Lee University (VA)	63	1,547,135	1,603,114	3.6
Texas Christian University	64	1,471,789	1,595,949	8.4
University of Illinois at Urbana-Champaign	65	1,534,717	1,578,169	2.8
University of Iowa	66	1,387,001	1,500,456	8.2
Liberty University (VA)	67	1,290,703	1,432,964	11.0
University of California, San Francisco	68	1,106,873	1,432,799	29.4
University of Delaware	69	1,364,057	1,413,197	3.6
Tulane University of Louisiana	70	1,297,740	1,383,967	6.6
University of Cincinnati, Main Campus (OH)	71	1,280,295	1,364,778	6.6
Lehigh University (PA)	72	1,278,120	1,353,116	5.9
Syracuse University (NY)	73	1,258,728	1,338,287	6.3
University of Kentucky	74	1,268,396	1,334,530	5.2
Wake Forest University (NC)	75	1,205,323	1,329,255	10.3
Baylor University (TX)	76	1,231,712	1,310,781	6.4
Trinity University (TX)	77	1,200,924	1,299,405	8.2
North Carolina State University at Raleigh	78	1,122,932	1,293,743	15.2
Soka University of America (CA)	79	1,239,053	1,275,811	3.0
University of Georgia	80	1,151,904	1,274,343	10.6
Saint Louis University (MO)	81	1,149,590	1,226,095	6.7
University of Texas Southwestern Medical Center	82	1,115,840	1,199,509	7.5
Berea College (KY)	83	1,150,360	1,192,078	3.6
University of Arkansas	84	996,019	1,185,715	19.0
Indiana University, Purdue University, Indianapolis	85	1,087,532	1,177,984	8.3
Baylor College of Medicine (TX)	86	1,133,559	1,171,285	3.3
Indiana University, Bloomington	87	1,081,730	1,154,032	6.7
Virginia Polytechnic Institute and State U	88	987,600	1,136,900	15.1
Princeton Theological Seminary (NJ)	89	1,076,534	1,129,412	4.9
Middlebury College (VT)	90	1,073,976	1,124,144	4.7
University of Tulsa (OK)	91	1,053,445	1,114,621	5.8
Juilliard School (NY)	92	1,046,080	1,106,640	5.8
Vassar College (NY)	93	1,002,570	1,082,831	8.0
Wesleyan University (CT)	94	967,177	1,065,219	10.1
University of Utah	95	1,006,446	1,051,841	4.5
Brandeis University (MA)	96	976,887	1,046,386	7.1
Washington State University	97	975,177	1,024,301	5.0
University of Miami (FL)	98	948,579	1,021,508	7.7
University of Nebraska, Lincoln	99	958,039	1,021,199	6.6
Massachusetts College of Pharmacy and Health Sciences	100	847,845	1,020,134	20.3
Iowa State University	101	910,356	1,017,089	11.7
Rutgers University, New Brunswick (NJ)	102	985,463	1,015,059	3.0
Hamilton College (NY)	103	954,714	1,012,841	6.1
University of Missouri, Columbia	104	922,077	1,003,025	8.8
Berry College (GA)	105	968,546	985,124	1.7
Santa Clara University (CA)	106	905,858	979,248	8.1
University of Arizona	107	843,529	959,632	13.8
Oberlin College (OH)	108	879,535	947,149	7.7
Rochester Institute of Technology (NY)	109	847,211	938,162	10.7
College of William and Mary (VA)	110	874,081	935,544	7.0
Thomas Jefferson University (PA)	111	841,741	932,897	10.8
Medical College of Wisconsin	112	875,817	930,961	6.3
Colgate University (NY)	113	881,303	923,604	4.8
University of Oregon	114	828,459	912,512	10.1
Pepperdine University (CA)	115	860,333	904,142	5.1
Bryn Mawr College (PA)	116	852,743	897,236	5.2
Carleton College (MN)	117	828,168	878,494	6.1
Lafayette College (PA)	118	833,069	870,742	4.5
Bucknell University (PA)	119	800,765	851,309	6.3

Institution	Fiscal year (FY) 2018				Institution	Fiscal year (FY) 2018			
	Rank order, end of FY[1]	Market value of endowment				Rank order, end of FY[1]	Market value of endowment		
		Beginning of FY (in thousands)	End of FY (in thousands)	Percent change[2]			Beginning of FY (in thousands)	End of FY (in thousands)	Percent change[2]
1	2	3	4	5	1	2	3	4	5
University of Florida	60	1,605,037	1,727,400	7.6	Denison University (OH)	120	797,249	850,416	6.7

†Not applicable.

[1] Institutions ranked by size of endowment at end of 2018 fiscal year.

[2] Change in market value of endowment. Includes growth from gifts and returns on investments, as well as reductions from expenditures and withdrawals. In addition to individual degree-granting institution campuses, table includes two state university systems (University of Texas System Office and University of California System Admin Central Office).

NOTE: Degree-granting institutions grant associate's or higher degrees and participate in Title IV federal financial aid programs.

SOURCE: U.S. Department of Education, National Center for Education Statistics, Integrated Postsecondary Education Data System (IPEDS), Spring 2019, Finance component. (This table was prepared January 2020.)

Table 334.10. Total expenditures of public degree-granting postsecondary institutions, by purpose of expenditure and level of institution: 2009–10 through 2017–18

Level of institution and year	Total	Instruction		Research	Public service	Academic support	Student services	Institutional support	Auxiliary enterprises[1]	Net grant aid to students[2]	Hospitals	Independent operations	Other
		Total[3]	Salaries and wages										
1	2	3	4	5	6	7	8	9	10	11	12	13	14
						In thousands of current dollars							
All levels													
2009–10	$281,390,445	$89,237,995	$51,808,563	$32,270,072	$12,980,154	$22,788,482	$15,661,212	$27,554,886	$25,981,203	$15,494,246	$28,484,978	$1,310,925	$9,626,291
2010–11	296,862,854	93,090,749	53,586,472	33,866,656	13,426,331	23,441,698	16,276,833	29,051,411	27,649,838	17,487,275	29,980,642	1,233,264	11,358,158
2011–12	305,537,590	95,093,836	54,341,187	34,282,999	13,567,337	24,712,457	17,019,195	29,512,479	28,475,340	16,611,881	33,063,066	1,297,507	11,901,492
2012–13	311,421,148	97,716,338	55,555,358	34,634,474	13,495,216	25,725,240	17,679,256	30,850,117	29,002,556	16,227,767	34,208,788	1,320,284	10,561,112
2013–14	323,893,053	101,281,681	57,591,057	34,407,750	13,906,406	27,038,128	18,668,134	32,398,315	30,031,093	15,978,858	36,965,327	1,512,402	11,704,959
2014–15	335,630,086	105,240,912	59,348,073	35,189,410	14,105,428	28,349,420	19,545,937	33,290,396	31,011,138	15,881,788	39,887,678	1,603,180	11,524,799
2015–16	354,775,570	108,299,168	61,715,250	36,125,887	14,756,434	29,627,129	20,278,907	34,475,739	31,449,402	15,518,286	45,053,249	1,688,715	17,502,653
2016–17	371,705,042	111,838,548	63,829,915	37,352,788	15,588,815	31,088,231	21,200,127	35,967,658	33,203,335	15,370,320	49,002,994	1,712,683	19,379,543
2017–18	384,971,839	112,541,721	65,056,485	38,644,659	15,852,432	32,028,659	21,784,611	35,665,052	33,938,680	16,152,444	51,588,949	1,751,610	25,023,022
4-year													
2009–10	230,212,346	67,643,385	39,032,863	32,246,034	12,071,239	18,517,775	10,439,050	19,637,465	23,267,303	9,103,655	28,484,978	1,310,925	7,490,538
2010–11	242,591,219	70,524,278	40,420,752	33,842,288	12,497,023	19,037,101	10,918,171	20,760,495	24,856,936	10,088,873	29,980,642	1,233,264	8,852,149
2011–12	251,518,494	72,456,621	41,334,687	34,259,475	12,635,035	20,246,241	11,548,269	21,042,773	25,720,831	9,737,295	33,063,066	1,297,507	9,511,380
2012–13	257,550,418	74,836,904	42,537,154	34,613,057	12,608,770	21,150,882	12,114,278	22,151,644	26,335,976	9,823,162	34,208,788	1,320,284	8,386,673
2013–14	269,871,401	78,181,765	44,567,486	34,381,434	13,042,105	22,291,975	12,983,254	23,519,705	27,469,515	9,914,507	36,965,327	1,512,402	9,609,411
2014–15	281,198,453	81,857,112	46,260,575	35,166,043	13,257,351	23,504,976	13,595,835	24,290,848	28,543,769	10,057,062	39,887,678	1,603,180	9,434,598
2015–16	301,270,243	85,962,887	48,769,505	36,100,447	13,954,900	24,946,937	14,449,291	25,621,839	29,213,644	10,403,387	45,053,249	1,688,715	13,874,946
2016–17	317,579,534	89,338,819	50,967,703	37,324,213	14,748,258	26,371,904	15,226,010	26,688,763	31,028,018	10,631,345	49,002,994	1,712,683	15,506,527
2017–18	331,147,172	90,341,563	52,367,162	38,615,952	14,982,606	27,343,769	15,734,637	26,981,641	31,830,062	11,285,805	51,588,949	1,751,610	20,690,580
2-year													
2009–10	51,178,098	21,594,609	12,775,700	24,038	908,915	4,270,708	5,222,163	7,917,422	2,713,901	6,390,591	0	0	2,135,752
2010–11	54,271,635	22,566,471	13,165,721	24,368	929,308	4,404,597	5,358,662	8,290,916	2,792,902	7,398,402	0	0	2,506,009
2011–12	54,019,096	22,637,215	13,006,500	23,525	932,302	4,466,216	5,470,926	8,469,706	2,754,509	6,874,585	0	0	2,390,112
2012–13	53,870,729	22,879,434	13,018,204	21,417	886,446	4,574,358	5,564,978	8,698,474	2,666,580	6,404,605	0	0	2,174,439
2013–14	54,021,651	23,099,916	13,023,571	26,316	864,300	4,746,153	5,684,879	8,878,610	2,561,577	6,064,351	0	0	2,095,548
2014–15	54,431,633	23,383,800	13,087,499	23,367	848,077	4,844,444	5,950,102	8,999,548	2,467,368	5,824,726	0	0	2,090,201
2015–16	53,505,327	22,336,281	12,945,745	25,440	801,533	4,680,192	5,829,616	8,853,900	2,235,758	5,114,899	0	0	3,627,707
2016–17	54,125,509	22,499,729	12,862,211	28,574	840,557	4,716,327	5,974,117	9,278,896	2,175,317	4,738,975	0	0	3,873,016
2017–18	53,824,666	22,200,158	12,689,323	28,707	869,826	4,684,890	6,049,974	8,683,412	2,108,618	4,866,639	0	0	4,332,442
						Percentage distribution							
All levels													
2009–10	100.00	31.71	18.41	11.47	4.61	8.10	5.57	9.79	9.23	5.51	10.12	0.47	3.42
2010–11	100.00	31.36	18.05	11.41	4.52	7.90	5.48	9.79	9.31	5.89	10.10	0.42	3.83
2011–12	100.00	31.12	17.79	11.22	4.44	8.09	5.57	9.66	9.32	5.44	10.82	0.42	3.90
2012–13	100.00	31.38	17.84	11.12	4.33	8.26	5.68	9.91	9.31	5.21	10.98	0.42	3.39
2013–14	100.00	31.27	17.78	10.62	4.29	8.35	5.76	10.00	9.27	4.93	11.41	0.47	3.61
2014–15	100.00	31.36	17.68	10.48	4.20	8.45	5.82	9.92	9.24	4.73	11.88	0.48	3.43
2015–16	100.00	30.53	17.40	10.18	4.16	8.35	5.72	9.72	8.86	4.37	12.70	0.48	4.93
2016–17	100.00	30.09	17.17	10.05	4.19	8.36	5.70	9.68	8.93	4.14	13.18	0.46	5.21
2017–18	100.00	29.23	16.90	10.04	4.12	8.32	5.66	9.26	8.82	4.20	13.40	0.45	6.50
4-year													
2009–10	100.00	29.38	16.96	14.01	5.24	8.04	4.53	8.53	10.11	3.95	12.37	0.57	3.25
2010–11	100.00	29.07	16.66	13.95	5.15	7.85	4.50	8.56	10.25	4.16	12.36	0.51	3.65
2011–12	100.00	28.81	16.43	13.62	5.02	8.05	4.59	8.37	10.23	3.87	13.15	0.52	3.78
2012–13	100.00	29.06	16.52	13.44	4.90	8.21	4.70	8.60	10.23	3.81	13.28	0.51	3.26
2013–14	100.00	28.97	16.51	12.74	4.83	8.26	4.81	8.72	10.18	3.67	13.70	0.56	3.56
2014–15	100.00	29.11	16.45	12.51	4.71	8.36	4.83	8.64	10.15	3.58	14.18	0.57	3.36
2015–16	100.00	28.53	16.19	11.98	4.63	8.28	4.80	8.50	9.70	3.45	14.95	0.56	4.61
2016–17	100.00	28.13	16.05	11.75	4.64	8.30	4.79	8.40	9.77	3.35	15.43	0.54	4.88
2017–18	100.00	27.28	15.81	11.66	4.52	8.26	4.75	8.15	9.61	3.41	15.58	0.53	6.25

See notes at end of table.

Table 334.10. Total expenditures of public degree-granting postsecondary institutions, by purpose of expenditure and level of institution: 2009–10 through 2017–18—Continued

Level of institution and year	Total	Instruction		Research	Public service	Academic support	Student services	Institutional support	Auxiliary enterprises[1]	Net grant aid to students[2]	Hospitals	Independent operations	Other
		Total[3]	Salaries and wages										
1	2	3	4	5	6	7	8	9	10	11	12	13	14
2-year													
2009–10	100.00	42.20	24.96	0.05	1.78	8.34	10.20	15.47	5.30	12.49	0.00	0.00	4.17
2010–11	100.00	41.58	24.26	0.04	1.71	8.12	9.87	15.28	5.15	13.63	0.00	0.00	4.62
2011–12	100.00	41.91	24.08	0.04	1.73	8.27	10.13	15.68	5.10	12.73	0.00	0.00	4.42
2012–13	100.00	42.47	24.17	0.04	1.65	8.49	10.33	16.15	4.95	11.89	0.00	0.00	4.04
2013–14	100.00	42.76	24.11	0.05	1.60	8.79	10.52	16.44	4.74	11.23	0.00	0.00	3.88
2014–15	100.00	42.96	24.04	0.04	1.56	8.90	10.93	16.53	4.53	10.70	0.00	0.00	3.84
2015–16	100.00	41.75	24.20	0.05	1.50	8.75	10.90	16.55	4.18	9.56	0.00	0.00	6.78
2016–17	100.00	41.57	23.76	0.05	1.55	8.71	11.04	17.14	4.02	8.76	0.00	0.00	7.16
2017–18	100.00	41.25	23.58	0.05	1.62	8.70	11.24	16.13	3.92	9.04	0.00	0.00	8.05
	Expenditure per full-time-equivalent student in constant 2018–19 dollars[4]												
All levels													
2009–10	$30,598	$9,704	$5,634	$3,509	$1,411	$2,478	$1,703	$2,996	$2,825	$1,685	$3,097	$143	$1,047
2010–11	30,863	9,678	5,571	3,521	1,396	2,437	1,692	3,020	2,875	1,818	3,117	128	1,181
2011–12	31,041	9,661	5,521	3,483	1,378	2,511	1,729	2,998	2,893	1,688	3,359	132	1,209
2012–13	31,620	9,922	5,641	3,517	1,370	2,612	1,795	3,132	2,945	1,648	3,473	134	1,072
2013–14	32,634	10,205	5,803	3,467	1,401	2,724	1,881	3,264	3,026	1,610	3,725	152	1,179
2014–15	33,806	10,600	5,978	3,544	1,421	2,855	1,969	3,353	3,124	1,600	4,018	161	1,161
2015–16	35,678	10,891	6,206	3,633	1,484	2,979	2,039	3,467	3,163	1,561	4,531	170	1,760
2016–17	36,697	11,041	6,302	3,688	1,539	3,069	2,093	3,551	3,278	1,517	4,838	169	1,913
2017–18	37,181	10,869	6,283	3,732	1,531	3,093	2,104	3,445	3,278	1,560	4,982	169	2,417
4-year													
2009–10	41,692	12,251	7,069	5,840	2,186	3,354	1,891	3,556	4,214	1,649	5,159	237	1,357
2010–11	41,879	12,175	6,978	5,842	2,157	3,286	1,885	3,584	4,291	1,742	5,176	213	1,528
2011–12	41,568	11,975	6,831	5,662	2,088	3,346	1,909	3,478	4,251	1,609	5,464	214	1,572
2012–13	41,683	12,112	6,884	5,602	2,041	3,423	1,961	3,585	4,262	1,590	5,536	214	1,357
2013–14	42,835	12,409	7,074	5,457	2,070	3,538	2,061	3,733	4,360	1,574	5,867	240	1,525
2014–15	43,661	12,710	7,183	5,460	2,058	3,650	2,111	3,772	4,432	1,562	6,193	249	1,465
2015–16	45,943	13,109	7,437	5,505	2,128	3,804	2,203	3,907	4,455	1,586	6,871	258	2,116
2016–17	45,903	12,913	7,367	5,395	2,132	3,812	2,201	3,858	4,485	1,537	7,083	248	2,241
2017–18	46,244	12,616	7,313	5,393	2,092	3,818	2,197	3,768	4,445	1,576	7,204	245	2,889
2-year													
2009–10	13,927	5,876	3,477	7	247	1,162	1,421	2,155	739	1,739	0	0	581
2010–11	14,185	5,898	3,441	6	243	1,151	1,401	2,167	730	1,934	0	0	655
2011–12	14,244	5,969	3,430	6	246	1,178	1,443	2,233	726	1,813	0	0	630
2012–13	14,679	6,234	3,547	6	242	1,246	1,516	2,370	727	1,745	0	0	592
2013–14	14,904	6,373	3,593	7	238	1,309	1,568	2,449	707	1,673	0	0	578
2014–15	15,607	6,705	3,752	7	243	1,389	1,706	2,580	707	1,670	0	0	599
2015–16	15,800	6,596	3,823	8	237	1,382	1,722	2,615	660	1,510	0	0	1,071
2016–17	16,859	7,008	4,006	9	262	1,469	1,861	2,890	678	1,476	0	0	1,206
2017–18	16,856	6,952	3,974	9	272	1,467	1,895	2,719	660	1,524	0	0	1,357

[1]Essentially self-supporting operations of institutions that furnish a service to students, faculty, or staff, such as residence halls and food services.
[2]Scholarship and fellowship expenses, net of discounts and allowances. Excludes the amount of discounts and allowances that were recorded as a reduction to revenues from tuition and fees and from auxiliary enterprises, such as room, board, and books.
[3]Includes other categories not separately shown.
[4]Constant dollars based on the Consumer Price Index, prepared by the Bureau of Labor Statistics, U.S. Department of Labor, adjusted to a school-year basis.

NOTE: Degree-granting institutions grant associate's or higher degrees and participate in Title IV federal financial aid programs. Includes data for public institutions reporting data according to either the Governmental Accounting Standards Board (GASB) or the Financial Accounting Standards Board (FASB) guidance. Data in this table pertain to institutions' fiscal years that end in the academic year noted. Some data have been revised from previously published figures. Detail may not sum to totals because of rounding.
SOURCE: U.S. Department of Education, National Center for Education Statistics, Integrated Postsecondary Education Data System (IPEDS), Spring 2010 through Spring 2018, Fall Enrollment component; and Spring 2011 through Spring 2019, Finance component. (This table was prepared December 2019.)

Table 334.20. Total expenditures of public degree-granting postsecondary institutions, by level of institution, purpose of expenditure, and state or jurisdiction: 2014–15 through 2017–18

[In thousands of current dollars]

State or jurisdiction	Total, 2014–15	Total, 2015–16	Total, 2016–17			2017–18					
			All institutions	4-year institutions	2-year institutions	All institutions		4-year institutions		2-year institutions	
						Total[1]	Instruction	Total[1]	Instruction	Total[1]	Instruction
1	2	3	4	5	6	7	8	9	10	11	12
United States	**$335,630,086**	**$354,775,570**	**$371,705,042**	**$317,579,534**	**$54,125,509**	**$384,971,839**	**$112,541,721**	**$331,147,172**	**$90,341,563**	**$53,824,666**	**$22,200,158**
Alabama	6,961,128	7,306,483	7,785,726	7,028,015	757,711	8,208,437	1,940,080	7,445,895	1,620,897	762,541	319,182
Alaska	850,928	868,913	839,381	839,381	0	804,290	250,159	804,290	250,159	0	0
Arizona	5,931,197	6,296,207	6,507,273	5,130,163	1,377,110	6,834,890	2,290,487	5,438,363	1,766,297	1,396,527	524,190
Arkansas	3,800,707	3,934,428	4,106,519	3,647,177	459,342	4,264,757	959,029	3,801,104	771,493	463,653	187,536
California	50,652,807	55,642,923	57,844,991	45,542,517	12,302,474	61,868,678	15,879,303	49,392,235	11,433,986	12,476,443	4,445,317
Colorado	6,109,407	6,587,748	7,781,063	7,265,477	515,585	8,445,117	2,504,779	8,053,205	2,348,433	391,913	156,346
Connecticut	3,496,698	3,662,471	3,798,052	3,277,990	520,062	3,908,139	1,169,712	3,390,801	954,605	517,338	215,107
Delaware	1,190,562	1,247,600	1,264,208	1,264,208	0	1,335,450	592,062	1,335,450	592,062	0	0
District of Columbia	139,524	147,290	141,861	141,861	0	158,530	43,712	158,530	43,712	0	0
Florida	11,511,020	11,822,548	12,415,119	12,232,102	183,017	13,163,072	4,257,666	12,972,157	4,184,349	190,915	73,318
Georgia	7,826,896	8,050,634	8,496,265	7,570,386	925,880	8,958,011	2,593,283	8,021,957	2,209,630	936,054	383,653
Hawaii	1,664,624	1,816,736	1,847,752	1,575,966	271,786	1,821,603	631,700	1,532,735	480,771	288,868	150,930
Idaho	1,203,133	1,255,012	1,306,952	1,093,158	213,794	1,359,948	500,405	1,138,288	412,685	221,660	87,720
Illinois	12,195,375	12,355,733	12,961,076	9,604,390	3,356,686	13,280,125	4,574,301	9,788,570	3,169,674	3,491,555	1,404,626
Indiana	6,372,728	6,563,583	6,805,880	6,263,480	542,399	6,949,227	2,853,632	6,414,537	2,616,663	534,691	236,969
Iowa	5,261,496	5,512,712	5,789,532	4,842,637	946,894	6,383,620	1,316,608	5,431,567	898,782	952,054	417,827
Kansas	3,451,776	3,436,560	3,498,812	2,748,778	750,035	3,709,971	1,303,424	2,940,791	1,002,698	769,180	300,726
Kentucky	5,547,286	5,873,502	6,113,027	5,541,058	571,969	6,166,575	1,343,745	5,603,907	1,117,207	562,668	226,537
Louisiana	3,910,077	3,883,693	4,108,399	3,624,253	484,147	4,133,564	1,339,865	3,680,115	1,162,909	453,449	176,955
Maine	864,068	849,532	869,566	738,682	130,885	894,187	286,390	765,817	222,965	128,370	63,424
Maryland	6,343,340	6,502,220	6,724,452	5,287,563	1,436,889	6,958,575	2,101,528	5,516,612	1,502,509	1,441,963	599,018
Massachusetts	4,758,073	5,170,474	5,246,452	4,334,984	911,468	5,411,839	1,838,525	4,500,608	1,450,023	911,231	388,502
Michigan	14,627,268	15,327,986	16,259,165	14,803,153	1,456,011	17,589,767	4,445,796	16,122,686	3,816,280	1,467,081	629,516
Minnesota	5,215,646	5,303,793	5,927,210	4,738,233	1,188,977	5,952,483	1,761,270	4,780,542	1,243,585	1,171,941	517,685
Mississippi	4,171,973	4,451,207	4,623,103	3,675,243	947,861	4,603,388	1,130,522	3,669,367	771,027	934,021	359,495
Missouri	4,904,991	5,010,347	5,175,185	4,420,785	754,400	5,202,013	1,530,046	4,452,878	1,199,662	749,134	330,384
Montana	1,022,708	1,046,082	1,101,301	987,966	113,334	1,101,233	329,145	989,266	288,907	111,967	40,239
Nebraska	2,398,348	2,450,500	2,574,085	2,146,023	428,062	2,643,655	869,695	2,196,035	671,570	447,620	198,125
Nevada	1,544,133	1,621,662	1,701,829	1,633,648	68,181	1,794,822	773,264	1,794,822	773,264	0	0
New Hampshire	973,796	997,737	989,727	842,941	146,786	1,010,063	319,221	862,491	268,420	147,572	50,801
New Jersey	7,266,925	7,473,275	7,999,108	6,680,061	1,319,047	8,645,442	2,655,631	7,270,427	2,114,350	1,375,015	541,281
New Mexico	3,454,803	3,523,749	3,786,755	3,176,827	609,928	4,134,037	838,375	3,452,140	589,589	681,897	248,785
New York	16,791,853	17,785,235	18,073,969	14,594,521	3,479,447	18,562,136	6,362,628	15,107,942	4,683,210	3,454,194	1,679,419
North Carolina	10,484,190	10,499,040	11,144,591	8,942,833	2,201,758	11,479,183	3,692,580	9,218,460	2,713,475	2,260,722	979,105
North Dakota	1,150,777	1,192,090	1,194,445	1,090,829	103,616	1,164,255	431,205	1,064,138	390,326	100,117	40,879
Ohio	12,534,515	13,257,601	14,314,104	12,875,624	1,438,480	12,433,497	3,634,154	11,475,674	3,117,620	957,822	516,534
Oklahoma	4,158,353	4,335,312	4,364,905	3,884,702	480,203	4,411,735	1,349,828	3,941,232	1,159,165	470,503	190,663
Oregon	5,843,944	7,025,969	6,949,056	5,723,589	1,225,467	7,231,394	1,662,681	6,036,895	1,187,740	1,194,499	474,941
Pennsylvania	13,046,794	13,752,080	14,340,017	13,147,338	1,192,679	14,773,798	3,867,582	13,564,163	3,344,515	1,209,635	523,067
Rhode Island	737,640	775,112	792,218	667,893	124,325	827,466	281,000	698,103	213,295	129,363	67,705
South Carolina	4,352,405	4,459,393	4,646,259	3,827,382	818,877	4,899,684	1,795,711	4,082,571	1,431,884	817,113	363,827
South Dakota	784,051	827,198	841,747	754,648	87,099	851,429	299,830	769,171	258,931	82,258	40,899
Tennessee	4,172,603	4,320,721	4,503,298	3,836,474	666,824	4,595,946	1,848,382	3,877,564	1,549,342	718,382	299,040
Texas	31,050,594	33,792,807	35,461,725	30,311,913	5,149,812	36,447,523	10,628,437	31,430,227	8,546,091	5,017,296	2,082,347
Utah	5,349,506	5,700,948	6,189,020	5,971,621	217,399	6,483,500	1,140,874	6,278,272	1,044,534	205,228	96,341
Vermont	854,406	865,326	896,401	862,131	34,270	905,945	277,083	873,832	267,204	32,112	9,879
Virginia	9,540,486	9,896,996	10,253,120	9,125,778	1,127,342	10,796,512	3,256,187	9,659,568	2,720,015	1,136,944	536,172
Washington	8,588,560	9,171,287	10,229,088	9,808,391	420,697	10,220,427	3,085,099	9,829,859	2,919,746	390,568	165,354
West Virginia	1,819,173	1,874,851	1,889,691	1,752,931	136,760	1,866,864	616,135	1,733,190	563,086	133,674	53,050
Wisconsin	6,285,882	6,566,464	6,598,862	5,367,016	1,231,846	6,538,284	2,230,861	5,293,472	1,523,866	1,244,812	706,995
Wyoming	798,626	878,588	877,311	579,425	297,886	819,916	274,028	527,813	174,282	292,104	99,746
U.S. Service Academies	1,662,286	1,805,213	1,755,387	1,755,387	0	1,966,837	584,072	1,966,837	584,072	0	0
Other jurisdictions	**1,638,670**	**1,693,441**	**987,460**	**891,071**	**96,389**	**1,798,094**	**645,709**	**1,723,072**	**618,519**	**75,022**	**27,190**
American Samoa	13,690	13,952	14,337	14,337	0	15,470	3,783	15,470	3,783	0	0
Federated States of Micronesia	18,324	20,070	20,331	0	20,331	19,435	7,227	0	0	19,435	7,227
Guam	116,302	129,640	127,294	88,902	38,392	132,066	32,586	99,617	22,487	32,449	10,099
Marshall Islands	11,382	13,731	15,022	0	15,022	15,008	2,240	15,008	2,240	0	0
Northern Marianas	19,048	16,502	17,443	17,443	0	18,358	3,968	18,358	3,968	0	0
Palau	10,209	9,425	9,621	0	9,621	8,861	3,085	0	0	8,861	3,085
Puerto Rico	1,362,861	1,406,463	701,403	688,381	13,022	1,513,526	579,668	1,499,249	572,889	14,277	6,779
U.S. Virgin Islands	86,855	83,659	82,008	82,008	0	75,370	13,152	75,370	13,152	0	0

[1]Includes other categories not separately shown.

NOTE: Degree-granting institutions grant associate's or higher degrees and participate in Title IV federal financial aid programs. Includes data for public institutions reporting data according to either the Governmental Accounting Standards Board (GASB) or the Financial Accounting Standards Board (FASB) guidance. Data in this table pertain to institutions' fiscal years that end in the academic year noted. Some data have been revised from previously published figures. Detail may not sum to totals because of rounding.

SOURCE: U.S. Department of Education, National Center for Education Statistics, Integrated Postsecondary Education Data System (IPEDS), Spring 2016 through Spring 2019, Finance component. (This table was prepared December 2019.)

Table 334.30. Total expenditures of private nonprofit degree-granting postsecondary institutions, by purpose and level of institution: Selected years, 1999–2000 through 2017–18

Level of institution and year	Total	Instruction	Research	Public service	Academic support	Student services	Institutional support	Auxiliary enterprises[1]	Net grant aid to students[2]	Hospitals	Independent operations	Other
1	2	3	4	5	6	7	8	9	10	11	12	13
	In thousands of current dollars											
All levels												
1999–2000	$80,613,037	$26,012,599	$8,381,926	$1,446,958	$6,510,951	$5,688,499	$10,585,850	$8,300,021	$1,180,882	$7,355,110	$2,753,679	$2,396,563
2004–05	110,394,127	36,258,473	12,812,857	2,000,437	9,342,064	8,191,737	14,690,328	10,944,342	1,069,591	9,180,775	4,223,779	1,679,741
2005–06	116,821,175	38,451,724	13,242,851	1,937,149	10,225,476	8,925,987	15,668,595	11,790,104	707,411	9,645,428	4,203,523	2,022,926
2006–07	124,558,591	41,224,316	13,704,450	2,036,662	10,881,954	9,591,801	16,831,560	12,449,053	728,200	10,400,055	4,680,393	2,030,146
2007–08	133,501,778	44,227,021	14,474,152	2,182,525	11,883,707	10,361,344	18,366,446	13,317,944	720,764	10,752,821	4,887,609	2,327,446
2008–09	141,363,564	46,456,178	15,264,804	2,298,520	12,585,948	11,016,097	19,403,346	13,713,701	754,752	11,930,840	5,158,480	2,780,898
2009–10	145,115,244	47,566,210	16,221,823	2,090,243	12,953,023	11,422,737	19,438,608	13,890,396	826,379	13,174,405	5,154,851	2,376,569
2010–11	152,501,429	49,759,574	17,362,082	2,255,075	13,601,137	12,198,263	20,214,683	14,460,084	759,683	14,239,347	5,376,016	2,275,486
2011–12	159,831,378	52,163,647	17,483,157	2,333,298	14,215,689	12,881,102	21,175,119	14,948,315	845,525	15,474,737	5,450,038	2,860,752
2012–13	165,515,671	54,296,267	17,597,379	2,317,116	14,924,886	13,692,561	21,766,760	15,349,949	844,435	16,726,819	5,437,783	2,561,716
2013–14	172,529,736	56,711,775	17,736,647	2,459,956	15,454,493	14,555,421	22,623,170	15,984,991	867,482	17,377,766	5,693,990	3,064,047
2014–15	181,419,541	58,769,788	18,310,027	2,636,019	15,557,155	15,421,897	23,845,927	16,358,009	887,495	20,529,450	6,063,555	3,040,219
2015–16	188,689,819	60,227,646	18,386,969	2,730,335	16,011,794	16,061,062	24,829,855	16,723,913	914,001	21,267,887	6,192,792	5,343,565
2016–17	197,171,304	62,161,805	21,059,795	2,890,409	16,261,179	16,868,202	25,517,409	17,224,876	942,542	24,090,294	5,810,625	4,344,168
2017–18	206,778,042	63,489,832	21,872,856	3,090,888	17,843,700	17,560,444	26,471,439	17,824,434	986,591	26,740,972	6,294,985	4,601,901
4-year												
1999–2000	79,699,659	25,744,199	8,376,568	1,438,544	6,476,338	5,590,978	10,398,914	8,228,409	1,162,570	7,355,110	2,752,019	2,176,011
2004–05	109,789,731	36,051,084	12,812,326	1,993,767	9,307,600	8,101,214	14,516,197	10,899,456	1,051,216	9,180,775	4,223,779	1,652,317
2005–06	116,250,621	38,235,791	13,242,277	1,927,434	10,185,584	8,854,613	15,525,499	11,745,356	698,715	9,645,428	4,203,523	1,986,402
2006–07	124,062,344	41,057,423	13,703,502	2,028,438	10,850,196	9,523,002	16,694,195	12,412,575	714,459	10,400,055	4,680,393	1,998,105
2007–08	132,965,591	44,041,854	14,473,179	2,176,544	11,847,284	10,284,649	18,218,103	13,280,036	711,180	10,752,821	4,887,609	2,292,334
2008–09	140,866,945	46,289,898	15,264,459	2,294,909	12,544,436	10,947,638	19,261,017	13,676,329	747,586	11,930,840	5,158,480	2,751,352
2009–10	144,624,598	47,400,673	16,221,238	2,085,201	12,910,113	11,353,608	19,303,251	13,855,994	819,196	13,174,405	5,154,851	2,346,068
2010–11	151,878,613	49,550,398	17,361,796	2,252,726	13,547,801	12,111,973	20,048,321	14,430,101	758,318	14,239,347	5,376,016	2,201,817
2011–12	159,245,924	51,959,761	17,482,484	2,331,249	14,164,326	12,795,619	21,024,665	14,924,702	843,453	15,474,737	5,450,038	2,794,891
2012–13	165,015,452	54,115,153	17,597,050	2,315,345	14,885,715	13,624,969	21,628,217	15,323,444	839,753	16,726,819	5,437,783	2,521,204
2013–14	171,974,051	56,513,597	17,736,254	2,458,223	15,405,771	14,462,852	22,499,365	15,953,094	863,119	17,377,766	5,693,990	3,010,020
2014–15	180,583,663	58,497,366	18,309,351	2,633,736	15,460,861	15,226,681	23,669,210	16,323,295	883,309	20,529,450	6,063,555	2,986,850
2015–16	187,829,392	59,962,885	18,386,002	2,728,006	15,907,072	15,846,653	24,654,441	16,684,252	910,455	21,267,887	6,192,792	5,288,945
2016–17	196,311,110	61,907,159	21,058,634	2,889,051	16,157,576	16,652,370	25,330,274	17,187,656	941,362	24,090,294	5,810,625	4,286,108
2017–18	205,992,273	63,268,589	21,872,111	3,089,523	17,745,371	17,345,090	26,293,205	17,794,013	985,036	26,740,972	6,294,985	4,563,379
2-year												
1999–2000	913,378	268,400	5,358	8,415	34,612	97,521	186,936	71,612	18,311	0	1,660	220,553
2004–05	604,395	207,389	532	6,670	34,464	90,523	174,131	44,886	18,375	0	0	27,425
2005–06	570,554	215,934	574	9,715	39,893	71,374	143,096	44,748	8,696	0	0	36,524
2006–07	496,247	166,893	947	8,224	31,758	68,799	137,366	36,478	13,741	0	0	32,041
2007–08	536,187	185,167	973	5,982	36,423	76,696	148,343	37,908	9,584	0	0	35,112
2008–09	496,620	166,280	345	3,612	41,511	68,459	142,330	37,372	7,165	0	0	29,546
2009–10	490,645	165,538	585	5,041	42,909	69,129	135,357	34,402	7,183	0	0	30,502
2010–11	622,815	209,176	285	2,349	53,336	86,290	166,362	29,983	1,365	0	0	73,669
2011–12	585,454	203,885	673	2,049	51,363	85,483	150,455	23,613	2,072	0	0	65,861
2012–13	500,218	181,113	329	1,771	39,171	67,591	138,543	26,505	4,682	0	0	40,512
2013–14	555,685	198,178	393	1,732	48,722	92,569	123,804	31,897	4,364	0	0	54,027
2014–15	835,878	272,422	677	2,283	96,294	195,216	176,718	34,714	4,186	0	0	53,369
2015–16	860,427	264,761	967	2,329	104,722	214,409	175,414	39,660	3,546	0	0	54,620
2016–17	860,194	254,647	1,160	1,358	103,603	215,833	187,135	37,219	1,180	0	0	58,060
2017–18	785,770	221,244	745	1,366	98,329	215,354	178,234	30,421	1,555	0	0	38,522
	Percentage distribution											
All levels												
1999–2000	100.00	32.27	10.40	1.79	8.08	7.06	13.13	10.30	1.46	9.12	3.42	2.97
2004–05	100.00	32.84	11.61	1.81	8.46	7.42	13.31	9.91	0.97	8.32	3.83	1.52
2005–06	100.00	32.92	11.34	1.66	8.75	7.64	13.41	10.09	0.61	8.26	3.60	1.73
2006–07	100.00	33.10	11.00	1.64	8.74	7.70	13.51	9.99	0.58	8.35	3.76	1.63
2007–08	100.00	33.13	10.84	1.63	8.90	7.76	13.76	9.98	0.54	8.05	3.66	1.74
2008–09	100.00	32.86	10.80	1.63	8.90	7.79	13.73	9.70	0.53	8.44	3.65	1.97
2009–10	100.00	32.78	11.18	1.44	8.93	7.87	13.40	9.57	0.57	9.08	3.55	1.64
2010–11	100.00	32.63	11.38	1.48	8.92	8.00	13.26	9.48	0.50	9.34	3.53	1.49
2011–12	100.00	32.64	10.94	1.46	8.89	8.06	13.25	9.35	0.53	9.68	3.41	1.79
2012–13	100.00	32.80	10.63	1.40	9.02	8.27	13.15	9.27	0.51	10.11	3.29	1.55
2013–14	100.00	32.87	10.28	1.43	8.96	8.44	13.11	9.27	0.50	10.07	3.30	1.78
2014–15	100.00	32.39	10.09	1.45	8.58	8.50	13.14	9.02	0.49	11.32	3.34	1.68
2015–16	100.00	31.92	9.74	1.45	8.49	8.51	13.16	8.86	0.48	11.27	3.28	2.83
2016–17	100.00	31.53	10.68	1.47	8.25	8.56	12.94	8.74	0.48	12.22	2.95	2.20
2017–18	100.00	30.70	10.58	1.49	8.63	8.49	12.80	8.62	0.48	12.93	3.04	2.23
4-year												
1999–2000	100.00	32.30	10.51	1.80	8.13	7.02	13.05	10.32	1.46	9.23	3.45	2.73
2004–05	100.00	32.84	11.67	1.82	8.48	7.38	13.22	9.93	0.96	8.36	3.85	1.50
2005–06	100.00	32.89	11.39	1.66	8.76	7.62	13.36	10.10	0.60	8.30	3.62	1.71
2006–07	100.00	33.09	11.05	1.64	8.75	7.68	13.46	10.01	0.58	8.38	3.77	1.61
2007–08	100.00	33.12	10.88	1.64	8.91	7.73	13.70	9.99	0.53	8.09	3.68	1.72
2008–09	100.00	32.86	10.84	1.63	8.91	7.77	13.67	9.71	0.53	8.47	3.66	1.95
2009–10	100.00	32.77	11.22	1.44	8.93	7.85	13.35	9.58	0.57	9.11	3.56	1.62
2010–11	100.00	32.63	11.43	1.48	8.92	7.97	13.20	9.50	0.50	9.38	3.54	1.45
2011–12	100.00	32.63	10.98	1.46	8.89	8.04	13.20	9.37	0.53	9.72	3.42	1.76
2012–13	100.00	32.79	10.66	1.40	9.02	8.26	13.11	9.29	0.51	10.14	3.30	1.53
2013–14	100.00	32.86	10.31	1.43	8.96	8.41	13.08	9.28	0.50	10.10	3.31	1.75
2014–15	100.00	32.39	10.14	1.46	8.56	8.43	13.11	9.04	0.49	11.37	3.36	1.65
2015–16	100.00	31.92	9.79	1.45	8.47	8.44	13.13	8.88	0.48	11.32	3.30	2.82
2016–17	100.00	31.54	10.73	1.47	8.23	8.48	12.90	8.76	0.48	12.27	2.96	2.18
2017–18	100.00	30.71	10.62	1.50	8.61	8.42	12.76	8.64	0.48	12.98	3.06	2.22

See notes at end of table.

Table 334.30. Total expenditures of private nonprofit degree-granting postsecondary institutions, by purpose and level of institution: Selected years, 1999–2000 through 2017–18—Continued

Level of institution and year	Total	Instruction	Research	Public service	Academic support	Student services	Institutional support	Auxiliary enterprises[1]	Net grant aid to students[2]	Hospitals	Independent operations	Other
1	2	3	4	5	6	7	8	9	10	11	12	13
2-year												
1999–2000	100.00	29.39	0.59	0.92	3.79	10.68	20.47	7.84	2.00	0.00	0.18	24.15
2004–05	100.00	34.31	0.09	1.10	5.70	14.98	28.81	7.43	3.04	0.00	0.00	4.54
2005–06	100.00	37.85	0.10	1.70	6.99	12.51	25.08	7.84	1.52	0.00	0.00	6.40
2006–07	100.00	33.63	0.19	1.66	6.40	13.86	27.68	7.35	2.77	0.00	0.00	6.46
2007–08	100.00	34.53	0.18	1.12	6.79	14.30	27.67	7.07	1.79	0.00	0.00	6.55
2008–09	100.00	33.48	0.07	0.73	8.36	13.78	28.66	7.53	1.44	0.00	0.00	5.95
2009–10	100.00	33.74	0.12	1.03	8.75	14.09	27.59	7.01	1.46	0.00	0.00	6.22
2010–11	100.00	33.59	0.05	0.38	8.56	13.85	26.71	4.81	0.22	0.00	0.00	11.83
2011–12	100.00	34.83	0.11	0.35	8.77	14.60	25.70	4.03	0.35	0.00	0.00	11.25
2012–13	100.00	36.21	0.07	0.35	7.83	13.51	27.70	5.30	0.94	0.00	0.00	8.10
2013–14	100.00	35.66	0.07	0.31	8.77	16.66	22.28	5.74	0.79	0.00	0.00	9.72
2014–15	100.00	32.59	0.08	0.27	11.52	23.35	21.14	4.15	0.50	0.00	0.00	6.38
2015–16	100.00	30.77	0.11	0.27	12.17	24.92	20.39	4.61	0.41	0.00	0.00	6.35
2016–17	100.00	29.60	0.13	0.16	12.04	25.09	21.75	4.33	0.14	0.00	0.00	6.75
2017–18	100.00	28.16	0.09	0.17	12.51	27.41	22.68	3.87	0.20	0.00	0.00	4.90
	Expenditure per full-time-equivalent student in constant 2018–19 dollars[3]											
All levels												
1999–2000	$47,501	$15,328	$4,939	$853	$3,837	$3,352	$6,238	$4,891	$696	$4,334	$1,623	$1,412
2004–05	50,830	16,695	5,900	921	4,301	3,772	6,764	5,039	492	4,227	1,945	773
2005–06	51,110	16,823	5,794	848	4,474	3,905	6,855	5,158	309	4,220	1,839	885
2006–07	52,182	17,270	5,741	853	4,559	4,018	7,051	5,215	305	4,357	1,961	850
2007–08	52,608	17,428	5,704	860	4,683	4,083	7,238	5,248	284	4,237	1,926	917
2008–09	54,130	17,789	5,845	880	4,819	4,218	7,430	5,251	289	4,568	1,975	1,065
2009–10	53,578	17,562	5,989	772	4,782	4,217	7,177	5,128	305	4,864	1,903	877
2010–11	53,183	17,353	6,055	786	4,743	4,254	7,050	5,043	265	4,966	1,875	794
2011–12	53,685	17,521	5,872	784	4,775	4,327	7,112	5,021	284	5,198	1,831	961
2012–13	54,063	17,735	5,748	757	4,875	4,472	7,110	5,014	276	5,464	1,776	837
2013–14	55,409	18,213	5,696	790	4,963	4,675	7,266	5,134	279	5,581	1,829	984
2014–15	56,997	18,464	5,752	828	4,888	4,845	7,492	5,139	279	6,450	1,905	955
2015–16	58,426	18,649	5,693	845	4,958	4,973	7,688	5,178	283	6,585	1,918	1,655
2016–17	59,534	18,769	6,359	873	4,910	5,093	7,705	5,201	285	7,274	1,754	1,312
2017–18	60,923	18,706	6,444	911	5,257	5,174	7,799	5,252	291	7,879	1,855	1,356
4-year												
1999–2000	47,969	15,495	5,042	866	3,898	3,365	6,259	4,952	700	4,427	1,656	1,310
2004–05	51,166	16,801	5,971	929	4,338	3,775	6,765	5,080	490	4,279	1,968	770
2005–06	51,413	16,910	5,857	852	4,505	3,916	6,866	5,195	309	4,266	1,859	879
2006–07	52,424	17,349	5,791	857	4,585	4,024	7,054	5,245	302	4,395	1,978	844
2007–08	52,867	17,511	5,755	865	4,710	4,089	7,244	5,280	283	4,275	1,943	911
2008–09	54,398	17,876	5,895	886	4,844	4,228	7,438	5,281	289	4,607	1,992	1,062
2009–10	53,835	17,644	6,038	776	4,806	4,226	7,185	5,158	305	4,904	1,919	873
2010–11	53,534	17,466	6,120	794	4,775	4,269	7,067	5,086	267	5,019	1,895	776
2011–12	54,019	17,626	5,930	791	4,805	4,340	7,132	5,063	286	5,249	1,849	948
2012–13	54,354	17,825	5,796	763	4,903	4,488	7,124	5,047	277	5,510	1,791	830
2013–14	55,677	18,296	5,742	796	4,988	4,682	7,284	5,165	279	5,626	1,843	974
2014–15	57,493	18,624	5,829	839	4,922	4,848	7,536	5,197	281	6,536	1,930	951
2015–16	58,865	18,792	5,762	855	4,985	4,966	7,727	5,229	285	6,665	1,941	1,658
2016–17	59,997	18,920	6,436	883	4,938	5,089	7,741	5,253	288	7,363	1,776	1,310
2017–18	61,421	18,865	6,522	921	5,291	5,172	7,840	5,306	294	7,973	1,877	1,361
2-year												
1999–2000	25,655	7,539	150	236	972	2,739	5,251	2,011	514	0	47	6,195
2004–05	23,190	7,957	20	256	1,322	3,473	6,681	1,722	705	0	0	1,052
2005–06	23,215	8,786	23	395	1,623	2,904	5,822	1,821	354	0	0	1,486
2006–07	24,191	8,136	46	401	1,548	3,354	6,696	1,778	670	0	0	1,562
2007–08	23,762	8,206	43	265	1,614	3,399	6,574	1,680	425	0	0	1,556
2008–09	22,563	7,555	16	164	1,886	3,110	6,467	1,698	326	0	0	1,342
2009–10	22,234	7,501	27	228	1,944	3,133	6,134	1,559	325	0	0	1,382
2010–11	20,455	6,870	9	77	1,752	2,834	5,464	985	45	0	0	2,419
2011–12	20,019	6,972	23	70	1,756	2,923	5,145	807	71	0	0	2,252
2012–13	19,536	7,074	13	69	1,530	2,640	5,411	1,035	183	0	0	1,582
2013–14	22,254	7,937	16	69	1,951	3,707	4,958	1,277	175	0	0	2,164
2014–15	19,881	6,479	16	54	2,290	4,643	4,203	826	100	0	0	1,269
2015–16	22,236	6,842	25	60	2,706	5,541	4,533	1,025	92	0	0	1,412
2016–17	21,563	6,383	29	34	2,597	5,410	4,691	933	30	0	0	1,455
2017–18	19,474	5,483	18	34	2,437	5,337	4,417	754	39	0	0	955

[1]Essentially self-supporting operations of institutions that furnish a service to students, faculty, or staff, such as residence halls and food services.

[2]Excludes allowances that were recorded as a reduction to revenues from tuition and fees and from auxiliary enterprises, such as room, board, and books; also excludes agency transactions, such as student awards made from contributed funds or grant funds. These exclusions account for the majority of total student grants.

[3]Constant dollars based on the Consumer Price Index, prepared by the Bureau of Labor Statistics, U.S. Department of Labor, adjusted to a school-year basis.

NOTE: Degree-granting institutions grant associate's or higher degrees and participate in Title IV federal financial aid programs. Data in this table pertain to institutions' fiscal years that end in the academic year noted. Some data have been revised from previously published figures. Detail may not sum to totals because of rounding.

SOURCE: U.S. Department of Education, National Center for Education Statistics, Integrated Postsecondary Education Data System (IPEDS), "Fall Enrollment Survey" (IPEDS-EF:99); Spring 2005 through Spring 2007, Enrollment component; Spring 2008 through Spring 2018, Fall Enrollment component; and Spring 2001 through Spring 2019, Finance component. (This table was prepared December 2019.)

Table 334.40. Total expenditures of private nonprofit degree-granting postsecondary institutions, by purpose and classification of institution: 2017–18

Classification of institution	Total	Instruction	Research	Public service	Academic support	Student services	Institutional support	Auxiliary enterprises[1]	Net grant aid to students[2]	Hospitals	Independent operations	Other
1	2	3	4	5	6	7	8	9	10	11	12	13
	In thousands of current dollars											
Total	**$206,778,042**	**$63,489,832**	**$21,872,856**	**$3,090,888**	**$17,843,700**	**$17,560,444**	**$26,471,439**	**$17,824,434**	**$986,591**	**$26,740,972**	**$6,294,985**	**$4,601,901**
4-year	205,992,273	63,268,589	21,872,111	3,089,523	17,745,371	17,345,090	26,293,205	17,794,013	985,036	26,740,972	6,294,985	4,563,379
Research university, very high[3]	101,260,896	29,581,680	17,638,396	1,094,333	7,563,986	4,053,799	8,959,755	6,545,325	685,271	17,680,570	4,239,227	3,218,555
Research university, high[4]	15,062,942	5,063,970	1,408,749	259,422	2,420,869	1,264,753	2,164,286	1,792,043	34,484	499,279	82,486	72,600
Doctoral/research[5]	9,676,253	3,859,881	178,397	118,602	1,032,995	1,536,102	1,686,602	1,197,216	7,002	0	33,388	26,067
Master's[6]	31,610,369	11,872,385	254,173	234,696	3,206,398	5,493,979	6,044,947	3,894,197	114,820	28,873	124,800	341,100
Baccalaureate[7]	22,030,214	7,750,332	215,145	184,662	2,003,276	3,761,583	4,198,525	3,533,439	75,007	0	46,614	261,630
Special-focus institutions[8]	26,351,599	5,140,341	2,177,251	1,197,807	1,517,846	1,234,874	3,239,090	831,792	68,452	8,532,249	1,768,470	643,426
Arts, music, or design	2,471,665	999,416	1,091	27,551	312,765	257,447	510,317	272,625	4,626	0	48,636	37,190
Business and management	605,790	155,921	2,276	965	72,852	107,557	181,779	75,047	635	0	0	8,759
Engineering and other technology-related	259,879	111,205	3,775	0	22,563	45,229	52,512	19,028	4,081	0	0	1,487
Faith related	1,928,756	601,819	6,900	64,080	203,568	187,516	512,868	185,618	43,131	0	14,019	109,239
Law	492,177	201,053	3,342	9,373	77,201	64,758	120,779	13,437	1,394	0	0	840
Medical schools and centers and other heath professions schools	19,893,768	2,842,277	2,151,002	987,097	775,697	484,958	1,709,264	222,768	13,087	8,532,249	1,705,796	469,575
Tribal colleges[9]	88,983	24,300	2,383	6,157	5,420	13,099	21,532	1,534	742	0	0	13,817
Other special focus	610,581	204,350	6,482	102,586	47,780	74,313	130,041	41,734	757	0	19	2,520
2-year	785,770	221,244	745	1,366	98,329	215,354	178,234	30,421	1,555	0	0	38,522
Associate's colleges	770,539	217,993	19	1,060	95,733	213,901	174,135	30,072	322	0	0	37,305
Tribal colleges[9]	15,231	3,251	726	306	2,596	1,454	4,099	349	1,233	0	0	1,217
	Percentage distribution											
Total	**100.00**	**30.70**	**10.58**	**1.49**	**8.63**	**8.49**	**12.80**	**8.62**	**0.48**	**12.93**	**3.04**	**2.23**
4-year	100.00	30.71	10.62	1.50	8.61	8.42	12.76	8.64	0.48	12.98	3.06	2.22
Research university, very high[3]	100.00	29.21	17.42	1.08	7.47	4.00	8.85	6.46	0.68	17.46	4.19	3.18
Research university, high[4]	100.00	33.62	9.35	1.72	16.07	8.40	14.37	11.90	0.23	3.31	0.55	0.48
Doctoral/research[5]	100.00	39.89	1.84	1.23	10.68	15.87	17.43	12.37	0.07	0.00	0.35	0.27
Master's[6]	100.00	37.56	0.80	0.74	10.14	17.38	19.12	12.32	0.36	0.09	0.39	1.08
Baccalaureate[7]	100.00	35.18	0.98	0.84	9.09	17.07	19.06	16.04	0.34	0.00	0.21	1.19
Special-focus institutions[8]	100.00	19.51	8.26	4.55	5.76	4.69	12.29	3.16	0.26	32.38	6.71	2.44
Arts, music, or design	100.00	40.43	0.04	1.11	12.65	10.42	20.65	11.03	0.19	0.00	1.97	1.50
Business and management	100.00	25.74	0.38	0.16	12.03	17.75	30.01	12.39	0.10	0.00	0.00	1.45
Engineering and other technology-related	100.00	42.79	1.45	0.00	8.68	17.40	20.21	7.32	1.57	0.00	0.00	0.57
Faith related	100.00	31.20	0.36	3.32	10.55	9.72	26.59	9.62	2.24	0.00	0.73	5.66
Law	100.00	40.85	0.68	1.90	15.69	13.16	24.54	2.73	0.28	0.00	0.00	0.17
Medical schools and centers and other heath professions schools	100.00	14.29	10.81	4.96	3.90	2.44	8.59	1.12	0.07	42.89	8.57	2.36
Tribal colleges[9]	100.00	27.31	2.68	6.92	6.09	14.72	24.20	1.72	0.83	0.00	0.00	15.53
Other special focus	100.00	33.47	1.06	16.80	7.83	12.17	21.30	6.84	0.12	0.00	#	0.41
2-year	100.00	28.16	0.09	0.17	12.51	27.41	22.68	3.87	0.20	0.00	0.00	4.90
Associate's colleges	100.00	28.29	#	0.14	12.42	27.76	22.60	3.90	0.04	0.00	0.00	4.84
Tribal colleges[9]	100.00	21.34	4.77	2.01	17.05	9.54	26.91	2.29	8.10	0.00	0.00	7.99

See notes at end of table.

Table 334.40. Total expenditures of private nonprofit degree-granting postsecondary institutions, by purpose and classification of institution: 2017–18—Continued

Classification of institution	Total	Instruction	Research	Public service	Academic support	Student services	Institutional support	Auxiliary enterprises[1]	Net grant aid to students[2]	Hospitals	Independent operations	Other
1	2	3	4	5	6	7	8	9	10	11	12	13
	Expenditure per full-time-equivalent student in current dollars											
Total	**$59,686**	**$18,326**	**$6,314**	**$892**	**$5,151**	**$5,069**	**$7,641**	**$5,145**	**$285**	**$7,719**	**$1,817**	**$1,328**
4-year	60,174	18,482	6,389	903	5,184	5,067	7,681	5,198	288	7,812	1,839	1,333
Research university, very high[3]	176,106	51,446	30,676	1,903	13,155	7,050	15,582	11,383	1,192	30,749	7,373	5,597
Research university, high[4]	51,563	17,335	4,822	888	8,287	4,329	7,409	6,134	118	1,709	282	249
Doctoral/research[5]	27,431	10,942	506	336	2,928	4,355	4,781	3,394	20	0	95	74
Master's[6]	24,602	9,240	198	183	2,495	4,276	4,705	3,031	89	22	97	265
Baccalaureate[7]	36,932	12,993	361	310	3,358	6,306	7,039	5,924	126	0	78	439
Special-focus institutions[8]	81,837	15,964	6,762	3,720	4,714	3,835	10,059	2,583	213	26,498	5,492	1,998
Arts, music, or design	41,964	16,968	19	468	5,310	4,371	8,664	4,629	79	0	826	631
Business and management	25,396	6,536	95	40	3,054	4,509	7,620	3,146	27	0	0	367
Engineering and other technology-related	21,234	9,086	308	0	1,844	3,695	4,291	1,555	333	0	0	121
Faith related	28,521	8,899	102	948	3,010	2,773	7,584	2,745	638	0	207	1,615
Law	48,130	19,661	327	917	7,550	6,333	11,811	1,314	136	0	0	82
Medical schools and centers and other heath professions schools	148,919	21,276	16,102	7,389	5,807	3,630	12,795	1,668	98	63,870	12,769	3,515
Tribal colleges[9]	43,217	11,802	1,157	2,990	2,632	6,362	10,458	745	360	0	0	6,710
Other special focus	45,191	15,125	480	7,593	3,536	5,500	9,625	3,089	56	0	1	187
2-year	19,079	5,372	18	33	2,387	5,229	4,328	739	38	0	0	935
Associate's colleges	18,890	5,344	#	26	2,347	5,244	4,269	737	8	0	0	915
Tribal colleges[9]	38,461	8,209	1,834	772	6,557	3,671	10,351	880	3,114	0	0	3,073

#Rounds to zero.
[1]Essentially self-supporting operations of institutions that furnish a service to students, faculty, or staff, such as residence halls and food services.
[2]Excludes allowances that were recorded as a reduction to revenues from tuition and fees and from auxiliary enterprises, such as room, board, and books; also excludes agency transactions, such as student awards made from contributed funds or grant funds. These exclusions account for the majority of total student grants.
[3]Research universities with a very high level of research activity.
[4]Research universities with a high level of research activity.
[5]Institutions that award at least 20 research/scholarship doctor's degrees per year, but did not have high levels of research activity.
[6]Institutions that award at least 50 master's and fewer than 20 doctor's degrees per year.
[7]Institutions that primarily emphasize undergraduate education. In addition to institutions that primarily award bachelor's degrees, also includes institutions classified as 4-year in the IPEDS system, but classified as 2-year baccalaureate/associate's colleges in the Carnegie Classification system because they primarily award associate's degrees.
[8]Four-year institutions that award degrees primarily in single fields of study, such as medicine, business, fine arts, theology, and engineering.
[9]Tribally controlled colleges, which are located on reservations and are members of the American Indian Higher Education Consortium.
NOTE: Relative levels of research activity for research universities were determined by an analysis of research and development expenditures, science and engineering research staffing, and doctor's degrees conferred, by field. Further information on the Carnegie 2015 classification system used in this table may be obtained from https://carnegieclassifications.iu.edu/downloads/CCIHE2015-FactsFigures.pdf. Degree-granting institutions grant associate's or higher degrees and participate in Title IV federal financial aid programs. Data in this table pertain to institutions' fiscal years that end in the academic year noted. Detail may not sum to totals because of rounding.
SOURCE: U.S. Department of Education, National Center for Education Statistics, Integrated Postsecondary Education Data System (IPEDS), Spring 2018, Fall Enrollment component; and Spring 2019, Finance component. (This table was prepared December 2019.)

Table 334.50. Total expenditures of private for-profit degree-granting postsecondary institutions, by purpose and level of institution: Selected years, 1999–2000 through 2017–18

Year and level of institution	Total	Instruction	Research and public service	Academic support, student services, and institutional support	Auxiliary enterprises[1]	Net grant aid to students[2]	Other[3]
1	2	3	4	5	6	7	8
	In thousands of current dollars						
All levels							
1999–2000	$3,846,246	$1,171,732	$24,738	$2,041,594	$144,305	$26,278	$437,599
2004–05	8,830,792	2,313,895	7,583	5,693,200	269,883	54,819	491,411
2005–06	10,208,845	2,586,870	8,445	6,575,800	276,108	66,569	695,053
2006–07	12,165,629	2,883,207	6,087	7,776,210	332,887	67,090	1,100,148
2007–08	13,939,251	3,273,627	9,695	9,299,306	421,714	82,072	852,837
2008–09	16,375,034	3,876,258	9,939	11,069,416	396,715	44,440	978,267
2009–10	19,973,034	4,759,300	13,257	13,230,271	466,040	120,032	1,384,134
2010–11	22,632,244	5,656,167	19,327	14,853,799	486,433	87,151	1,529,368
2011–12	22,713,683	5,538,070	42,657	15,111,978	489,409	54,579	1,476,991
2012–13	21,923,722	5,467,671	27,729	14,294,090	467,973	53,555	1,612,705
2013–14	20,644,593	5,536,025	16,447	13,103,182	472,204	36,569	1,480,166
2014–15	18,441,030	4,917,479	20,028	11,624,796	504,091	35,524	1,339,112
2015–16	16,000,640	4,248,320	17,453	10,081,942	399,110	25,277	1,228,537
2016–17	14,698,133	3,923,606	17,027	9,196,550	318,897	26,649	1,215,403
2017–18	12,165,398	3,304,987	19,403	7,712,011	232,192	15,417	881,389
4-year							
1999–2000	2,022,622	595,976	4,393	1,104,001	92,071	11,805	214,377
2004–05	5,989,792	1,430,196	3,513	4,110,514	180,036	38,639	226,894
2005–06	7,218,830	1,680,603	4,065	4,986,009	178,587	54,291	315,276
2006–07	8,850,759	1,856,614	4,303	5,925,855	228,624	56,930	778,433
2007–08	10,422,080	2,184,872	7,682	7,312,117	312,834	71,324	533,252
2008–09	12,409,748	2,585,133	7,629	8,893,714	276,211	33,417	613,644
2009–10	15,286,893	3,268,070	10,726	10,732,002	337,499	72,082	866,514
2010–11	17,141,926	3,925,347	15,582	12,031,073	343,319	74,921	751,684
2011–12	17,407,585	3,928,903	37,912	12,153,860	349,405	51,818	885,687
2012–13	16,759,402	3,939,227	24,432	11,377,216	359,987	46,446	1,012,095
2013–14	16,017,246	4,078,270	15,190	10,545,883	371,018	32,306	974,579
2014–15	14,628,734	3,729,921	17,904	9,617,433	334,087	33,089	896,300
2015–16	12,564,815	3,199,028	15,489	8,199,419	323,247	22,834	804,796
2016–17	11,680,961	2,995,663	15,090	7,592,227	261,821	24,039	792,122
2017–18	9,748,366	2,539,652	18,026	6,418,623	175,954	13,803	582,308
2-year							
1999–2000	1,823,624	575,756	20,345	937,593	52,234	14,473	223,223
2004–05	2,840,999	883,699	4,070	1,582,687	89,846	16,181	264,517
2005–06	2,990,015	906,267	4,381	1,589,791	97,521	12,278	379,777
2006–07	3,314,870	1,026,592	1,784	1,850,355	104,264	10,160	321,715
2007–08	3,517,171	1,088,755	2,014	1,987,189	108,880	10,747	319,586
2008–09	3,965,287	1,291,124	2,310	2,175,703	120,504	11,023	364,623
2009–10	4,686,142	1,491,230	2,531	2,498,269	128,542	47,950	517,619
2010–11	5,490,318	1,730,820	3,744	2,822,726	143,113	12,230	777,685
2011–12	5,306,098	1,609,167	4,745	2,958,118	140,004	2,761	591,304
2012–13	5,164,320	1,528,444	3,297	2,916,874	107,986	7,109	600,609
2013–14	4,627,347	1,457,755	1,257	2,557,299	101,186	4,263	505,588
2014–15	3,812,297	1,187,558	2,124	2,007,363	170,004	2,435	442,812
2015–16	3,435,825	1,049,292	1,964	1,882,523	75,863	2,443	423,740
2016–17	3,017,172	927,944	1,937	1,604,323	57,076	2,610	423,281
2017–18	2,417,033	765,335	1,377	1,293,388	56,238	1,615	299,080
	Percentage distribution						
All levels							
1999–2000	100.00	30.46	0.64	53.08	3.75	0.68	11.38
2004–05	100.00	26.20	0.09	64.47	3.06	0.62	5.56
2005–06	100.00	25.34	0.08	64.41	2.70	0.65	6.81
2006–07	100.00	23.70	0.05	63.92	2.74	0.55	9.04
2007–08	100.00	23.48	0.07	66.71	3.03	0.59	6.12
2008–09	100.00	23.67	0.06	67.60	2.42	0.27	5.97
2009–10	100.00	23.83	0.07	66.24	2.33	0.60	6.93
2010–11	100.00	24.99	0.09	65.63	2.15	0.39	6.76
2011–12	100.00	24.38	0.19	66.53	2.15	0.24	6.50
2012–13	100.00	24.94	0.13	65.20	2.13	0.24	7.36
2013–14	100.00	26.82	0.08	63.47	2.29	0.18	7.17
2014–15	100.00	26.67	0.11	63.04	2.73	0.19	7.26
2015–16	100.00	26.55	0.11	63.01	2.49	0.16	7.68
2016–17	100.00	26.69	0.12	62.57	2.17	0.18	8.27
2017–18	100.00	27.17	0.16	63.39	1.91	0.13	7.25
4-year							
1999–2000	100.00	29.47	0.22	54.58	4.55	0.58	10.60
2004–05	100.00	23.88	0.06	68.63	3.01	0.65	3.79
2005–06	100.00	23.28	0.06	69.07	2.47	0.75	4.37
2006–07	100.00	20.98	0.05	66.95	2.58	0.64	8.80
2007–08	100.00	20.96	0.07	70.16	3.00	0.68	5.12
2008–09	100.00	20.83	0.06	71.67	2.23	0.27	4.94
2009–10	100.00	21.38	0.07	70.20	2.21	0.47	5.67
2010–11	100.00	22.90	0.09	70.19	2.00	0.44	4.39
2011–12	100.00	22.57	0.22	69.82	2.01	0.30	5.09
2012–13	100.00	23.50	0.15	67.89	2.15	0.28	6.04

See notes at end of table.

Table 334.50. Total expenditures of private for-profit degree-granting postsecondary institutions, by purpose and level of institution: Selected years, 1999–2000 through 2017–18—Continued

Year and level of institution	Total	Instruction	Research and public service	Academic support, student services, and institutional support	Auxiliary enterprises[1]	Net grant aid to students[2]	Other[3]
1	2	3	4	5	6	7	8
2013–14	100.00	25.46	0.09	65.84	2.32	0.20	6.08
2014–15	100.00	25.50	0.12	65.74	2.28	0.23	6.13
2015–16	100.00	25.46	0.12	65.26	2.57	0.18	6.41
2016–17	100.00	25.65	0.13	65.00	2.24	0.21	6.78
2017–18	100.00	26.05	0.18	65.84	1.80	0.14	5.97
2-year							
1999–2000	100.00	31.57	1.12	51.41	2.86	0.79	12.24
2004–05	100.00	31.11	0.14	55.71	3.16	0.57	9.31
2005–06	100.00	30.31	0.15	53.17	3.26	0.41	12.70
2006–07	100.00	30.97	0.05	55.82	3.15	0.31	9.71
2007–08	100.00	30.96	0.06	56.50	3.10	0.31	9.09
2008–09	100.00	32.56	0.06	54.87	3.04	0.28	9.20
2009–10	100.00	31.82	0.05	53.31	2.74	1.02	11.05
2010–11	100.00	31.52	0.07	51.41	2.61	0.22	14.16
2011–12	100.00	30.33	0.09	55.75	2.64	0.05	11.14
2012–13	100.00	29.60	0.06	56.48	2.09	0.14	11.63
2013–14	100.00	31.50	0.03	55.26	2.19	0.09	10.93
2014–15	100.00	31.15	0.06	52.65	4.46	0.06	11.62
2015–16	100.00	30.54	0.06	54.79	2.21	0.07	12.33
2016–17	100.00	30.76	0.06	53.17	1.89	0.09	14.03
2017–18	100.00	31.66	0.06	53.51	2.33	0.07	12.37
	Expenditure per full-time-equivalent student in constant 2018–19 dollars[4]						
All levels							
1999–2000	$14,961	$4,558	$96	$7,941	$561	$102	$1,702
2004–05	14,805	3,879	13	9,544	452	92	824
2005–06	14,429	3,656	12	9,294	390	94	982
2006–07	15,997	3,791	8	10,225	438	88	1,447
2007–08	16,188	3,802	11	10,800	490	95	990
2008–09	15,340	3,631	9	10,369	372	42	916
2009–10	15,666	3,733	10	10,377	366	94	1,086
2010–11	15,679	3,918	13	10,290	337	60	1,060
2011–12	15,681	3,823	29	10,433	338	38	1,020
2012–13	16,962	4,230	21	11,059	362	41	1,248
2013–14	20,983	5,627	17	13,318	480	37	1,504
2014–15	16,694	4,452	18	10,524	456	32	1,212
2015–16	17,199	4,566	19	10,837	429	27	1,321
2016–17	17,128	4,572	20	10,717	372	31	1,416
2017–18	16,536	4,492	26	10,483	316	21	1,198
4-year							
1999–2000	14,494	4,271	31	7,911	660	85	1,536
2004–05	14,293	3,413	8	9,808	430	92	541
2005–06	13,870	3,229	8	9,580	343	104	606
2006–07	15,594	3,271	8	10,441	403	100	1,372
2007–08	15,797	3,312	12	11,083	474	108	808
2008–09	15,161	3,158	9	10,865	337	41	750
2009–10	15,983	3,417	11	11,220	353	75	906
2010–11	15,613	3,575	14	10,958	313	68	685
2011–12	15,462	3,490	34	10,796	310	46	787
2012–13	16,566	3,894	24	11,246	356	46	1,000
2013–14	22,151	5,640	21	14,584	513	45	1,348
2014–15	16,439	4,192	20	10,808	375	37	1,007
2015–16	16,905	4,304	21	11,032	435	31	1,083
2016–17	16,846	4,320	22	10,949	378	35	1,142
2017–18	16,429	4,280	30	10,817	297	23	981
2-year							
1999–2000	15,514	4,898	173	7,977	444	123	1,899
2004–05	16,013	4,981	23	8,921	506	91	1,491
2005–06	15,984	4,845	23	8,499	521	66	2,030
2006–07	17,180	5,321	9	9,590	540	53	1,667
2007–08	17,470	5,408	10	9,871	541	53	1,587
2008–09	15,926	5,186	9	8,739	484	44	1,464
2009–10	14,714	4,682	8	7,845	404	151	1,625
2010–11	15,890	5,009	11	8,169	414	35	2,251
2011–12	16,445	4,987	15	9,168	434	9	1,833
2012–13	18,386	5,442	12	10,385	384	25	2,138
2013–14	17,747	5,591	5	9,808	388	16	1,939
2014–15	17,750	5,529	10	9,346	792	11	2,062
2015–16	18,363	5,608	10	10,061	405	13	2,265
2016–17	18,315	5,633	12	9,739	346	16	2,569
2017–18	16,984	5,378	10	9,088	395	11	2,102

[1]Essentially self-supporting operations of institutions that furnish a service to students, faculty, or staff, such as residence halls and food services.
[2]Excludes allowances that were recorded as a reduction to revenues from tuition and fees and from auxiliary enterprises, such as room, board, and books; also excludes agency transactions, such as student awards made from contributed funds or grant funds. These exclusions account for the majority of total student grants.
[3]"Other" categories of expenditures include hospitals.
[4]Constant dollars based on the Consumer Price Index, prepared by the Bureau of Labor Statistics, U.S. Department of Labor, adjusted to a school-year basis.

NOTE: Degree-granting institutions grant associate's or higher degrees and participate in Title IV federal financial aid programs. Data in this table pertain to institutions' fiscal years that end in the academic year noted. Some data have been revised from previously published figures. Detail may not sum to totals because of rounding.
SOURCE: U.S. Department of Education, National Center for Education Statistics, Integrated Postsecondary Education Data System (IPEDS), "Fall Enrollment Survey" (IPEDS-EF:99); Spring 2005 through Spring 2007, Enrollment component; Spring 2008 through Spring 2018, Fall Enrollment component; and Spring 2001 through Spring 2019, Finance component. (This table was prepared December 2019.)

Table 334.70. Total expenditures of private nonprofit and for-profit degree-granting postsecondary institutions, by state or jurisdiction: Selected years, 1999-2000 through 2017-18

[In thousands of current dollars]

State or jurisdiction	Nonprofit institutions						For-profit institutions					
	1999-2000	2009-10	2014-15	2015-16	2016-17	2017-18	1999-2000	2009-10	2014-15	2015-16	2016-17	201[illegible]
1	2	3	4	5	6	7	8	9	10	11	12	[illegible]
United States	**$80,613,037**	**$145,115,244**	**$181,419,541**	**$188,689,819**	**$197,171,304**	**$206,778,042**	**$3,846,246**	**$19,973,034**	**$18,441,030**	**$16,000,640**	**$14,698,133**	**$12,165[illegible]**
Alabama	393,465	561,968	674,679	673,550	665,817	652,136	88,190	139,366	205,571	179,346	159,665	8[illegible]
Alaska	19,042	16,249	20,867	21,343	21,370	21,136	3,559	19,302	53,750	5,386	5,290	[illegible]
Arizona	143,698	176,443	271,309	285,775	306,836	324,811	278,286	3,412,261	2,667,335	2,310,965	2,110,657	1,91[illegible]
Arkansas	230,860	289,868	383,228	384,411	410,356	416,561	5,828	31,263	11,993	5,297	4,118	[illegible]
California	7,871,651	13,925,287	18,020,883	18,930,864	20,166,484	21,770,285	666,020	2,551,481	2,943,254	2,806,523	2,581,972	2,42[illegible]
Colorado	376,887	626,838	787,288	812,162	846,978	894,681	154,801	661,384	588,811	570,891	560,892	47[illegible]
Connecticut	2,094,981	3,950,481	4,918,779	5,175,033	5,306,051	5,580,224	18,110	59,726	109,962	102,654	103,901	10[illegible]
Delaware	52,533	132,851	148,398	153,594	156,144	156,675	0	4,042	3,003	2,785	2,617	[illegible]
District of Columbia	2,267,409	3,687,042	4,210,736	4,371,987	4,372,340	4,506,483	59,375	66,677	73,921	73,691	76,833	9[illegible]
Florida	2,031,623	4,592,898	6,094,211	6,421,571	6,639,201	6,880,813	315,721	1,825,704	1,324,080	1,168,316	1,072,806	95[illegible]
Georgia	2,635,438	4,497,299	5,955,965	6,356,783	6,656,977	7,070,266	106,794	678,839	570,359	453,802	477,869	30[illegible]
Hawaii	209,135	210,680	233,563	247,600	246,975	248,914	9,422	34,299	28,591	30,361	27,073	1[illegible]
Idaho	118,150	228,589	324,130	346,521	364,744	374,215	5,932	32,602	26,411	16,598	11,752	[illegible]
Illinois	5,668,566	9,512,165	11,895,518	11,917,185	12,329,677	12,731,105	166,956	1,100,032	1,176,410	967,832	809,991	68[illegible]
Indiana	1,343,315	2,251,554	2,804,542	2,908,893	2,953,430	3,102,064	89,932	591,600	493,254	180,081	193,820	6[illegible]
Iowa	740,760	1,156,393	1,330,362	1,328,741	1,345,926	1,363,654	34,311	1,000,405	522,514	491,189	443,910	2[illegible]
Kansas	208,729	364,286	461,312	413,147	423,272	442,383	9,156	47,645	147,181	122,009	88,704	7[illegible]
Kentucky	400,513	597,495	739,830	752,610	776,609	846,045	55,010	242,672	223,758	185,478	186,780	15[illegible]
Louisiana	746,629	1,089,736	1,238,465	1,278,750	1,292,555	1,344,462	31,675	111,844	92,456	78,195	68,279	4[illegible]
Maine	316,114	552,463	699,939	731,571	765,989	800,910	7,137	12,409	16,901	16,232	14,577	
Maryland	2,205,880	4,792,089	5,934,298	6,180,109	6,487,594	6,732,346	5,354	115,071	84,647	68,862	67,342	4[illegible]
Massachusetts	7,591,344	13,862,598	16,989,586	17,807,545	18,460,806	19,108,398	34,893	118,526	115,155	73,951	44,188	3[illegible]
Michigan	995,384	1,638,367	1,731,503	1,727,092	1,775,948	1,794,954	25,340	120,070	113,025	60,889	51,233	4[illegible]
Minnesota	1,004,427	1,622,869	1,808,566	1,851,407	1,847,932	1,916,016	123,571	928,396	1,141,688	1,049,616	996,848	99[illegible]
Mississippi	150,123	225,484	264,097	274,648	280,266	290,837	0	21,061	26,899	20,758	18,965	
Missouri	2,144,299	3,958,548	4,802,694	5,096,127	5,304,534	5,585,125	100,307	331,391	234,568	171,631	155,097	7[illegible]
Montana	69,426	116,161	114,605	116,250	120,533	123,531	0	0	0	113	702	
Nebraska	387,569	709,182	707,995	734,966	753,618	751,001	12,051	41,559	32,296	20,920	17,555	
Nevada	7,006	73,701	138,704	155,344	159,759	163,134	29,278	143,358	111,422	97,181	76,877	6[illegible]
New Hampshire	589,823	1,085,570	1,535,994	1,662,754	1,719,501	1,765,427	21,831	36,737	41,448	0	0	
New Jersey	1,362,090	2,591,234	3,074,725	3,247,397	3,217,410	3,339,085	61,109	126,833	164,603	168,538	176,260	17[illegible]
New Mexico	54,280	30,447	37,680	38,451	39,244	37,510	25,806	83,708	88,978	78,633	65,077	2[illegible]
New York	12,519,671	23,511,385	29,838,723	31,868,019	33,246,016	35,080,093	326,329	762,214	879,182	856,028	781,002	74[illegible]
North Carolina	3,530,337	6,451,308	7,952,693	8,443,996	8,957,926	9,431,481	4,041	186,514	281,296	200,476	193,810	13[illegible]
North Dakota	56,000	87,938	133,477	132,643	137,647	146,780	1,145	20,198	11,224	9,307	9,016	
Ohio	2,211,035	3,582,655	3,997,097	4,101,883	4,174,989	4,256,876	122,531	564,498	435,219	355,316	300,156	23[illegible]
Oklahoma	338,276	523,630	643,615	665,851	622,448	615,187	32,527	110,336	114,549	96,467	115,010	5[illegible]
Oregon	456,683	734,883	1,015,846	1,035,136	997,335	983,706	23,175	120,490	86,737	62,553	48,599	3[illegible]
Pennsylvania	7,590,629	13,154,197	17,398,401	19,914,232	21,741,581	23,338,273	306,135	842,052	618,469	522,888	415,124	23[illegible]
Rhode Island	828,715	1,564,624	1,882,228	1,940,771	2,024,586	2,091,469	4,519	0	0	0	0	
South Carolina	408,127	680,369	772,589	790,279	808,889	916,674	6,627	226,848	275,327	258,434	257,041	8[illegible]
South Dakota	69,555	119,974	137,678	137,084	144,289	147,955	18,061	41,594	30,805	27,824	27,352	5[illegible]
Tennessee	1,971,564	4,500,016	5,446,703	2,697,514	2,817,848	2,844,801	50,921	331,287	265,502	224,681	233,044	19[illegible]
Texas	2,490,597	4,376,280	5,587,701	5,949,318	6,218,330	6,497,872	172,327	803,401	756,636	658,681	606,590	4[illegible]
Utah	648,035	1,012,997	1,511,165	1,650,682	1,776,425	1,941,890	36,348	144,226	90,204	79,144	68,789	[illegible]
Vermont	347,293	717,199	853,481	870,643	886,971	871,449	24,841	17,126	10,948	9,527	7,836	
Virginia	944,905	1,841,075	2,265,969	2,363,750	2,486,799	2,532,939	65,804	614,287	581,536	515,736	492,679	4[illegible]
Washington	600,315	988,571	1,188,712	1,212,163	1,230,968	1,240,272	51,134	161,645	130,694	150,237	140,126	11[illegible]
West Virginia	170,653	211,877	201,483	204,550	207,829	199,339	17,926	165,043	296,334	287,215	279,441	26[illegible]
Wisconsin	999,502	1,929,430	2,220,794	2,290,409	2,445,116	2,505,800	16,333	131,140	142,125	107,401	50,870	[illegible]
Wyoming	0	0	16,735	16,714	30,441	0	19,766	39,869	0	0	0	[illegible]
Other jurisdictions	**431,216**	**742,820**	**859,744**	**857,509**	**873,490**	**831,015**	**56,116**	**222,515**	**312,598**	**280,271**	**275,163**	**26[illegible]**
Guam	0	2,551	1,093	1,248	1,053	1,217	0	0	0	0	0	
Puerto Rico	431,216	740,269	858,651	856,261	872,437	829,798	56,116	222,515	312,598	280,271	275,163	26[illegible]

NOTE: Degree-granting institutions grant associate's or higher degrees and participate in Title IV federal financial aid programs. Data in this table pertain to institutions' fiscal years that end in the academic year noted. Some data have been revised from previously published figures. Detail may not sum to totals because of rounding.

SOURCE: U.S. Department of Education, National Center for Education Statistics, Integrated Postsecondary Education Data System (IPEDS), Spring 2001 through Spring 2019, Finance component. (This table was prepared December 2019.)

Table 501.10. Labor force participation, employment, and unemployment of persons 25 to 64 years old, by sex, race/ethnicity, age group, and educational attainment: 2016, 2017, and 2018

[Standard errors appear in parentheses]

Sex, race/ethnicity, age group, and educational attainment	Labor force participation: Labor force participation rate[1]			Labor force participation: Number of participants (in thousands)	Employment: Employment to population ratio[2]			Employment: Number employed (in thousands)	Unemployment: Unemployment rate[3]			Unemployment: Number unemployed (in thousands)
	2016	2017	2018	2018	2016	2017	2018	2018	2016	2017	2018	2018
1	2	3	4	5	6	7	8	9	10	11	12	13
All persons 25 to 64 years old, all education levels	**77.3 (0.04)**	**77.7 (0.04)**	**78.1 (0.04)**	**132,952 (84.4)**	**73.7 (0.05)**	**74.3 (0.04)**	**75.0 (0.04)**	**127,639 (89.3)**	**4.7 (0.02)**	**4.3 (0.02)**	**4.0 (0.02)**	**5,314 (32.8)**
Less than high school completion	60.2 (0.13)	59.9 (0.14)	60.8 (0.13)	11,121 (48.6)	55.0 (0.14)	55.2 (0.14)	56.3 (0.13)	10,292 (46.1)	8.7 (0.11)	8.0 (0.11)	7.5 (0.09)	829 (11.1)
High school completion[4]	72.0 (0.09)	72.2 (0.09)	72.5 (0.09)	31,727 (87.5)	67.5 (0.09)	68.2 (0.09)	68.6 (0.10)	30,048 (86.3)	6.3 (0.06)	5.6 (0.06)	5.3 (0.06)	1,679 (19.8)
Some college, no degree	77.5 (0.08)	77.8 (0.08)	78.0 (0.09)	27,109 (59.3)	73.5 (0.09)	74.1 (0.08)	74.6 (0.09)	25,917 (58.7)	5.1 (0.05)	4.7 (0.05)	4.4 (0.05)	1,193 (13.6)
Associate's degree	81.5 (0.14)	81.9 (0.11)	82.1 (0.12)	12,832 (45.8)	78.3 (0.14)	79.1 (0.12)	79.4 (0.13)	12,410 (45.3)	3.9 (0.07)	3.4 (0.08)	3.3 (0.07)	422 (8.7)
Bachelor's or higher degree	86.2 (0.06)	86.5 (0.05)	86.8 (0.05)	50,162 (137.5)	83.9 (0.07)	84.2 (0.05)	84.7 (0.05)	48,971 (134.8)	2.7 (0.03)	2.6 (0.03)	2.4 (0.03)	1,191 (14.6)
Sex												
Male, all education levels	**82.6 (0.05)**	**82.9 (0.05)**	**83.3 (0.05)**	**70,014 (47.6)**	**78.7 (0.06)**	**79.3 (0.05)**	**80.0 (0.05)**	**67,240 (49.8)**	**4.7 (0.04)**	**4.3 (0.03)**	**4.0 (0.03)**	**2,774 (24.3)**
Less than high school completion	69.4 (0.18)	69.6 (0.16)	70.2 (0.17)	7,021 (37.0)	64.0 (0.19)	64.6 (0.18)	65.7 (0.18)	6,571 (35.0)	7.7 (0.13)	7.1 (0.13)	6.4 (0.12)	450 (9.2)
High school completion[4]	77.8 (0.12)	78.1 (0.11)	78.3 (0.11)	18,636 (56.5)	72.9 (0.12)	73.7 (0.12)	74.3 (0.12)	17,676 (55.1)	6.3 (0.08)	5.5 (0.08)	5.1 (0.08)	959 (14.5)
Some college, no degree	82.8 (0.12)	83.1 (0.11)	83.3 (0.12)	14,134 (41.2)	78.7 (0.12)	79.3 (0.12)	79.8 (0.13)	13,548 (40.4)	4.9 (0.07)	4.5 (0.08)	4.1 (0.07)	586 (10.4)
Associate's degree	86.4 (0.16)	86.8 (0.16)	86.9 (0.16)	5,883 (32.6)	83.0 (0.16)	84.0 (0.18)	84.0 (0.18)	5,690 (31.8)	4.0 (0.10)	3.2 (0.10)	3.3 (0.10)	193 (6.3)
Bachelor's or higher degree	91.4 (0.07)	91.5 (0.07)	91.8 (0.06)	24,340 (71.1)	89.0 (0.09)	89.1 (0.07)	89.6 (0.08)	23,756 (70.6)	2.6 (0.05)	2.6 (0.04)	2.4 (0.04)	585 (10.1)
Female, all education levels	**72.2 (0.06)**	**72.5 (0.06)**	**73.0 (0.06)**	**62,938 (58.1)**	**68.8 (0.06)**	**69.4 (0.06)**	**70.1 (0.06)**	**60,398 (60.2)**	**4.7 (0.03)**	**4.3 (0.04)**	**4.0 (0.03)**	**2,540 (20.3)**
Less than high school completion	49.0 (0.20)	48.3 (0.25)	49.5 (0.23)	4,100 (25.5)	44.0 (0.21)	43.7 (0.23)	45.0 (0.22)	3,721 (24.0)	10.3 (0.19)	9.6 (0.22)	9.2 (0.16)	379 (7.1)
High school completion[4]	65.2 (0.14)	65.2 (0.14)	65.5 (0.14)	13,091 (49.1)	61.2 (0.16)	61.5 (0.14)	61.9 (0.15)	12,371 (50.5)	6.2 (0.09)	5.7 (0.08)	5.5 (0.08)	720 (10.5)
Some college, no degree	72.6 (0.12)	72.7 (0.11)	73.0 (0.13)	12,976 (42.5)	68.6 (0.12)	69.1 (0.12)	69.6 (0.13)	12,369 (40.2)	5.4 (0.08)	5.0 (0.08)	4.7 (0.07)	607 (9.7)
Associate's degree	77.9 (0.19)	78.3 (0.15)	78.5 (0.18)	6,949 (30.0)	74.9 (0.20)	75.5 (0.17)	75.9 (0.18)	6,720 (29.3)	3.8 (0.09)	3.6 (0.10)	3.3 (0.09)	229 (6.1)
Bachelor's or higher degree	81.8 (0.09)	82.2 (0.08)	82.6 (0.08)	25,822 (80.5)	79.5 (0.10)	80.1 (0.08)	80.6 (0.08)	25,216 (78.8)	2.8 (0.04)	2.6 (0.04)	2.3 (0.04)	606 (10.7)
Race/ethnicity												
White, all education levels	**78.3 (0.05)**	**78.5 (0.05)**	**78.9 (0.05)**	**81,631 (54.7)**	**75.2 (0.05)**	**75.8 (0.06)**	**76.3 (0.06)**	**78,966 (60.0)**	**3.9 (0.03)**	**3.5 (0.02)**	**3.3 (0.03)**	**2,664 (23.5)**
Less than high school completion	52.9 (0.27)	52.8 (0.24)	53.7 (0.25)	3,229 (26.7)	47.7 (0.28)	48.1 (0.23)	49.2 (0.27)	2,955 (25.5)	9.8 (0.24)	8.8 (0.20)	8.5 (0.22)	274 (7.4)
High school completion[4]	71.8 (0.11)	71.8 (0.11)	72.0 (0.12)	18,608 (66.7)	68.0 (0.11)	68.3 (0.11)	68.8 (0.12)	17,777 (64.4)	5.3 (0.07)	4.8 (0.07)	4.5 (0.07)	830 (13.9)
Some college, no degree	77.3 (0.10)	77.5 (0.10)	77.7 (0.12)	16,660 (48.3)	73.9 (0.10)	74.4 (0.11)	74.8 (0.13)	16,042 (47.7)	4.4 (0.06)	4.0 (0.06)	3.7 (0.05)	618 (8.7)
Associate's degree	81.7 (0.16)	81.9 (0.13)	82.0 (0.14)	8,547 (36.5)	79.0 (0.15)	79.5 (0.14)	79.8 (0.15)	8,313 (37.0)	3.3 (0.07)	2.9 (0.07)	2.7 (0.07)	234 (5.5)
Bachelor's or higher degree	86.5 (0.07)	86.8 (0.06)	87.0 (0.06)	34,587 (88.9)	84.5 (0.08)	84.9 (0.06)	85.2 (0.06)	33,879 (87.0)	2.4 (0.03)	2.2 (0.03)	2.0 (0.03)	708 (12.0)
Black, all education levels	**73.4 (0.14)**	**73.9 (0.11)**	**74.4 (0.12)**	**15,907 (33.9)**	**67.3 (0.14)**	**68.2 (0.13)**	**69.1 (0.14)**	**14,782 (36.2)**	**8.2 (0.10)**	**7.7 (0.11)**	**7.1 (0.11)**	**1,125 (16.8)**
Less than high school completion	46.9 (0.47)	47.8 (0.44)	47.9 (0.38)	1,158 (14.1)	38.6 (0.43)	39.2 (0.44)	40.3 (0.39)	974 (12.5)	17.6 (0.51)	17.9 (0.48)	15.8 (0.51)	184 (6.6)
High school completion[4]	67.9 (0.27)	68.4 (0.23)	68.7 (0.29)	4,630 (31.2)	60.8 (0.28)	61.8 (0.24)	62.6 (0.30)	4,217 (30.5)	10.5 (0.20)	9.7 (0.22)	8.9 (0.20)	413 (9.4)
Some college, no degree	77.1 (0.23)	77.0 (0.26)	77.6 (0.24)	4,129 (27.6)	71.1 (0.26)	71.1 (0.28)	72.3 (0.26)	3,846 (26.8)	7.9 (0.17)	7.6 (0.16)	6.9 (0.17)	283 (7.3)
Associate's degree	81.5 (0.36)	81.9 (0.39)	82.1 (0.37)	1,608 (18.2)	76.6 (0.39)	77.6 (0.45)	77.7 (0.40)	1,521 (17.1)	6.0 (0.27)	5.1 (0.25)	5.4 (0.25)	87 (4.3)
Bachelor's or higher degree	88.2 (0.17)	88.4 (0.20)	88.7 (0.19)	4,382 (30.1)	84.7 (0.21)	84.9 (0.20)	85.5 (0.21)	4,223 (29.7)	4.0 (0.14)	4.0 (0.13)	3.6 (0.14)	159 (6.0)
Hispanic, all education levels	**77.0 (0.10)**	**77.4 (0.11)**	**78.0 (0.09)**	**23,215 (29.6)**	**72.8 (0.11)**	**73.8 (0.11)**	**74.5 (0.09)**	**22,178 (28.9)**	**5.4 (0.08)**	**4.8 (0.07)**	**4.5 (0.06)**	**1,037 (13.5)**
Less than high school completion	69.6 (0.20)	68.9 (0.22)	69.7 (0.20)	5,837 (38.6)	65.1 (0.21)	65.0 (0.23)	66.0 (0.20)	5,525 (37.4)	6.4 (0.14)	5.7 (0.14)	5.3 (0.12)	311 (7.5)
High school completion[4]	76.1 (0.23)	76.9 (0.19)	77.1 (0.20)	6,620 (31.1)	71.7 (0.25)	73.0 (0.21)	73.2 (0.20)	6,289 (30.5)	5.8 (0.15)	5.0 (0.13)	5.0 (0.12)	331 (8.0)
Some college, no degree	80.2 (0.25)	80.6 (0.25)	80.5 (0.21)	4,438 (28.2)	76.0 (0.27)	76.7 (0.26)	76.9 (0.24)	4,241 (30.1)	5.2 (0.18)	4.8 (0.14)	4.4 (0.14)	197 (5.6)
Associate's degree	82.3 (0.40)	84.1 (0.34)	84.0 (0.34)	1,728 (17.8)	78.3 (0.43)	80.8 (0.40)	80.7 (0.34)	1,660 (17.1)	4.8 (0.23)	4.0 (0.25)	3.9 (0.17)	68 (3.0)
Bachelor's or higher degree	86.7 (0.21)	87.0 (0.20)	87.5 (0.22)	4,592 (36.8)	83.9 (0.22)	84.0 (0.24)	85.1 (0.23)	4,462 (36.2)	3.3 (0.11)	3.4 (0.11)	2.8 (0.10)	130 (4.8)
Asian, all education levels	**78.4 (0.17)**	**78.7 (0.16)**	**79.9 (0.16)**	**8,518 (24.1)**	**75.4 (0.17)**	**75.9 (0.18)**	**77.3 (0.17)**	**8,246 (24.4)**	**3.7 (0.10)**	**3.6 (0.08)**	**3.2 (0.07)**	**272 (6.3)**
Less than high school completion	64.6 (0.54)	63.0 (0.60)	65.1 (0.54)	656 (9.2)	61.5 (0.49)	60.1 (0.62)	62.0 (0.56)	625 (8.9)	4.8 (0.34)	4.6 (0.41)	4.7 (0.27)	31 (1.9)
High school completion[4]	73.6 (0.53)	73.4 (0.54)	74.3 (0.50)	1,047 (14.5)	70.2 (0.50)	70.4 (0.59)	71.6 (0.49)	1,010 (14.0)	4.7 (0.28)	4.1 (0.24)	3.6 (0.23)	38 (2.5)
Some college, no degree	76.4 (0.46)	77.9 (0.51)	78.9 (0.43)	956 (12.7)	72.9 (0.49)	74.6 (0.57)	75.9 (0.50)	919 (12.9)	4.6 (0.28)	4.3 (0.30)	3.8 (0.25)	37 (2.3)
Associate's degree	78.4 (0.65)	79.9 (0.50)	79.8 (0.54)	577 (9.3)	75.1 (0.69)	77.3 (0.53)	77.4 (0.63)	559 (9.5)	4.2 (0.38)	3.3 (0.24)	3.0 (0.31)	17 (1.7)
Bachelor's or higher degree	82.5 (0.19)	82.7 (0.21)	83.7 (0.17)	5,282 (24.5)	79.9 (0.20)	80.0 (0.22)	81.3 (0.18)	5,132 (23.7)	3.1 (0.12)	3.2 (0.10)	2.8 (0.08)	150 (4.2)

See notes at end of table.

Table 501.10. Labor force participation, employment, and unemployment of persons 25 to 64 years old, by sex, race/ethnicity, age group, and educational attainment: 2016, 2017, and 2018—Continued

[Standard errors appear in parentheses]

Sex, race/ethnicity, age group, and educational attainment	Labor force participation				Employment				Unemployment			
	Labor force participation rate[1]			Number of participants (in thousands)	Employment to population ratio[2]			Number employed (in thousands)	Unemployment rate[3]			Number unemployed (in thousands)
	2016	2017	2018	2018	2016	2017	2018	2018	2016	2017	2018	2018
1	2	3	4	5	6	7	8	9	10	11	12	13
American Indian/Alaska Native, all education levels	**65.5** (0.48)	**65.0** (0.52)	**65.3** (0.59)	**744** (10.3)	**58.2** (0.51)	**58.9** (0.51)	**60.0** (0.57)	**683** (9.8)	**11.1** (0.44)	**9.4** (0.40)	**8.2** (0.25)	**61** (2.0)
Less than high school completion	42.1 (1.29)	44.5 (1.35)	44.4 (1.43)	77 (3.2)	34.1 (1.27)	36.3 (1.35)	37.5 (1.60)	65 (3.3)	18.8 (1.51)	18.4 (1.67)	15.5 (1.62)	12 (1.2)
High school completion[4]	63.1 (0.82)	61.7 (0.90)	60.7 (1.06)	225 (5.7)	53.7 (0.86)	54.7 (0.91)	54.1 (0.98)	201 (5.4)	14.9 (0.84)	11.3 (0.85)	10.8 (0.64)	24 (1.5)
Some college, no degree	69.1 (0.94)	68.1 (1.06)	69.6 (0.89)	219 (5.5)	61.9 (1.01)	62.3 (1.03)	64.5 (1.01)	203 (5.4)	10.4 (0.98)	8.5 (0.62)	7.3 (0.66)	16 (1.5)
Associate's degree	74.8 (1.42)	72.2 (1.65)	75.7 (1.60)	80 (3.0)	69.6 (1.57)	68.6 (1.73)	71.4 (1.65)	76 (3.0)	6.9 (1.03)	5.0 (0.73)	5.6 (0.86)	5 (0.7)
Bachelor's or higher degree	82.8 (1.01)	83.0 (0.95)	82.2 (0.98)	142 (4.2)	79.3 (1.05)	78.8 (1.08)	79.9 (0.97)	138 (4.2)	4.2 (0.68)	5.1 (0.62)	2.9 (0.43)	4 (0.6)
Age group												
25 to 34, all education levels	**82.2** (0.07)	**82.6** (0.08)	**83.2** (0.06)	**37,386** (36.6)	**77.3** (0.08)	**78.1** (0.08)	**79.0** (0.07)	**35,477** (39.5)	**5.9** (0.05)	**5.5** (0.05)	**5.1** (0.05)	**1,909** (17.3)
Less than high school completion	63.8 (0.25)	63.4 (0.29)	63.4 (0.32)	2,460 (24.8)	55.9 (0.27)	55.9 (0.32)	56.4 (0.33)	2,190 (23.3)	12.3 (0.26)	11.7 (0.28)	11.0 (0.27)	269 (7.1)
High school completion[4]	76.8 (0.20)	77.2 (0.19)	77.4 (0.16)	8,411 (46.5)	69.9 (0.21)	70.9 (0.20)	71.4 (0.19)	7,760 (43.7)	9.0 (0.13)	8.2 (0.14)	7.7 (0.12)	651 (11.2)
Some college, no degree	82.6 (0.15)	82.7 (0.15)	83.5 (0.15)	8,222 (39.1)	77.2 (0.18)	77.7 (0.18)	78.8 (0.17)	7,755 (37.8)	6.6 (0.11)	6.0 (0.12)	5.7 (0.11)	467 (9.7)
Associate's degree	86.3 (0.23)	87.0 (0.19)	87.5 (0.20)	3,512 (25.0)	82.2 (0.25)	83.3 (0.21)	83.9 (0.25)	3,369 (24.9)	4.7 (0.17)	4.2 (0.16)	4.1 (0.14)	143 (5.0)
Bachelor's or higher degree	89.9 (0.10)	90.0 (0.11)	90.6 (0.09)	14,781 (58.5)	87.4 (0.11)	87.4 (0.11)	88.2 (0.10)	14,403 (57.3)	2.8 (0.05)	2.8 (0.06)	2.6 (0.06)	379 (8.4)
35 to 44, all education levels	**82.3** (0.08)	**82.3** (0.08)	**83.0** (0.08)	**34,430** (39.4)	**78.4** (0.08)	**78.9** (0.09)	**79.7** (0.07)	**33,086** (38.9)	**4.7** (0.05)	**4.2** (0.04)	**3.9** (0.04)	**1,344** (15.1)
Less than high school completion	67.8 (0.26)	66.7 (0.29)	67.5 (0.23)	3,176 (25.5)	62.1 (0.25)	61.4 (0.32)	62.4 (0.25)	2,934 (24.4)	8.4 (0.20)	7.9 (0.21)	7.6 (0.15)	242 (5.0)
High school completion[4]	77.4 (0.21)	77.5 (0.19)	78.0 (0.18)	7,511 (41.8)	72.3 (0.22)	72.9 (0.20)	73.7 (0.19)	7,094 (41.6)	6.6 (0.13)	6.0 (0.12)	5.5 (0.12)	417 (9.0)
Some college, no degree	82.4 (0.17)	82.4 (0.17)	82.8 (0.18)	6,659 (33.3)	78.1 (0.19)	78.5 (0.18)	79.2 (0.18)	6,363 (30.6)	5.3 (0.12)	4.8 (0.10)	4.5 (0.10)	297 (7.4)
Associate's degree	86.1 (0.24)	86.7 (0.22)	86.6 (0.22)	3,361 (23.2)	82.7 (0.27)	83.9 (0.26)	83.9 (0.23)	3,256 (22.8)	4.0 (0.16)	3.3 (0.14)	3.1 (0.11)	105 (3.7)
Bachelor's or higher degree	89.5 (0.08)	89.4 (0.08)	89.9 (0.09)	13,722 (48.5)	87.3 (0.09)	87.4 (0.10)	88.1 (0.10)	13,439 (48.5)	2.5 (0.05)	2.3 (0.06)	2.1 (0.05)	283 (6.5)
45 to 54, all education levels	**80.2** (0.08)	**80.5** (0.08)	**81.0** (0.07)	**33,638** (42.1)	**76.8** (0.09)	**77.5** (0.09)	**78.1** (0.08)	**32,453** (44.9)	**4.1** (0.04)	**3.7** (0.04)	**3.5** (0.04)	**1,185** (14.0)
Less than high school completion	62.7 (0.26)	62.8 (0.28)	64.4 (0.27)	3,101 (21.5)	58.1 (0.29)	58.7 (0.28)	60.2 (0.28)	2,899 (21.5)	7.4 (0.19)	6.7 (0.18)	6.5 (0.17)	202 (5.3)
High school completion[4]	75.7 (0.16)	75.9 (0.16)	76.4 (0.16)	8,363 (33.0)	71.8 (0.15)	72.4 (0.16)	73.0 (0.17)	7,997 (33.3)	5.2 (0.09)	4.6 (0.09)	4.4 (0.10)	366 (8.6)
Some college, no degree	80.6 (0.15)	81.2 (0.17)	80.9 (0.17)	6,538 (28.0)	77.3 (0.17)	78.0 (0.18)	78.0 (0.19)	6,298 (28.2)	4.2 (0.09)	4.0 (0.11)	3.7 (0.09)	240 (6.2)
Associate's degree	84.4 (0.22)	84.5 (0.19)	84.9 (0.23)	3,265 (22.4)	81.4 (0.23)	82.0 (0.21)	82.5 (0.24)	3,171 (22.4)	3.5 (0.12)	3.0 (0.11)	2.9 (0.13)	94 (4.1)
Bachelor's or higher degree	89.1 (0.10)	89.3 (0.10)	89.3 (0.09)	12,372 (47.8)	86.8 (0.11)	87.0 (0.10)	87.3 (0.10)	12,088 (46.8)	2.7 (0.05)	2.5 (0.05)	2.3 (0.05)	284 (6.3)
55 to 64, all education levels	**64.3** (0.09)	**64.9** (0.09)	**65.0** (0.09)	**27,498** (38.1)	**61.8** (0.09)	**62.6** (0.09)	**63.0** (0.09)	**26,623** (38.2)	**3.8** (0.04)	**3.5** (0.04)	**3.2** (0.04)	**876** (11.7)
Less than high school completion	46.6 (0.25)	47.4 (0.30)	48.9 (0.29)	2,385 (18.7)	43.7 (0.26)	44.7 (0.30)	46.5 (0.29)	2,269 (17.8)	6.3 (0.19)	5.7 (0.22)	4.8 (0.18)	115 (4.4)
High school completion[4]	60.0 (0.17)	60.3 (0.17)	60.2 (0.17)	7,442 (30.7)	57.5 (0.17)	58.2 (0.16)	58.3 (0.16)	7,197 (29.3)	4.2 (0.08)	3.5 (0.09)	3.3 (0.09)	245 (6.8)
Some college, no degree	64.2 (0.20)	64.8 (0.17)	64.8 (0.18)	5,691 (25.9)	61.6 (0.20)	62.4 (0.17)	62.6 (0.19)	5,501 (25.1)	4.1 (0.10)	3.7 (0.08)	3.3 (0.09)	189 (5.5)
Associate's degree	68.7 (0.31)	69.2 (0.28)	69.3 (0.29)	2,694 (20.1)	66.5 (0.31)	67.1 (0.28)	67.3 (0.29)	2,614 (20.0)	3.2 (0.12)	3.1 (0.14)	3.0 (0.12)	80 (3.3)
Bachelor's or higher degree	74.5 (0.14)	75.2 (0.15)	75.1 (0.13)	9,287 (36.6)	72.2 (0.14)	73.1 (0.15)	73.1 (0.13)	9,041 (36.0)	3.0 (0.07)	2.8 (0.07)	2.6 (0.06)	246 (5.7)

[1]Percentage of the civilian population who are employed or seeking employment.
[2]Number of persons employed as a percentage of the civilian population.
[3]The percentage of persons in the civilian labor force who are not working and who made specific efforts to find employment sometime during the prior 4 weeks.
[4]Includes equivalency credentials, such as the GED credential.

NOTE: Estimates are for the entire civilian population, including persons living in households and persons living in group quarters (e.g., college residence halls, residential treatment centers, or correctional facilities). Race categories exclude persons of Hispanic ethnicity. Totals include racial/ethnic groups not separately shown. Detail may not sum to totals because of rounding.
SOURCE: U.S. Department of Commerce, Census Bureau, American Community Survey (ACS), 2016, 2017, and 2018. (This table was prepared February 2020.)

Table 501.20. Labor force participation, employment, and unemployment of persons 16 to 24 years old who are not enrolled in school, by age group, sex, race/ethnicity, and educational attainment: 2016, 2017, and 2018

[Standard errors appear in parentheses]

Age group, sex, race/ethnicity, and educational attainment	Labor force participation				Employment				Unemployment			
	Labor force participation rate[1]			Number of participants (in thousands)	Employment to population ratio[2]			Number employed (in thousands)	Unemployment rate[3]			Number unemployed (in thousands)
	2016	2017	2018	2018	2016	2017	2018	2018	2016	2017	2018	2018
1	2	3	4	5	6	7	8	9	10	11	12	13
16 to 19 years old												
All persons, all education levels	**65.6** (0.41)	**65.3** (0.42)	**65.6** (0.40)	**1,642** (18.9)	**51.8** (0.44)	**52.2** (0.45)	**52.6** (0.40)	**1,316** (17.4)	**21.0** (0.42)	**20.0** (0.42)	**19.8** (0.37)	**325** (6.4)
Less than high school completion	48.5 (0.81)	48.4 (0.72)	48.3 (0.78)	319 (7.6)	33.2 (0.73)	35.4 (0.74)	35.2 (0.77)	233 (6.5)	31.4 (1.08)	27.0 (1.03)	27.2 (1.15)	87 (4.3)
High school completion[4]	71.9 (0.50)	70.8 (0.48)	71.3 (0.49)	1,101 (16.1)	58.3 (0.56)	57.0 (0.56)	57.8 (0.52)	893 (14.6)	18.9 (0.53)	19.5 (0.48)	19.0 (0.48)	209 (5.7)
At least some college	76.4 (1.04)	75.9 (1.18)	74.3 (1.15)	221 (5.8)	65.0 (1.17)	66.4 (1.29)	64.3 (1.12)	191 (5.3)	14.9 (1.00)	12.5 (1.11)	13.5 (0.98)	30 (2.4)
Male, all education levels	**66.5** (0.50)	**66.2** (0.54)	**66.9** (0.54)	**952** (12.8)	**52.4** (0.54)	**52.7** (0.61)	**53.4** (0.62)	**760** (13.7)	**21.2** (0.52)	**20.5** (0.58)	**20.1** (0.61)	**192** (5.3)
Less than high school completion	49.9 (0.99)	51.1 (0.99)	51.0 (1.11)	202 (6.4)	34.8 (0.98)	37.3 (0.99)	37.4 (1.11)	148 (5.7)	30.2 (1.45)	27.0 (1.41)	26.8 (1.59)	54 (3.6)
High school completion[4]	73.2 (0.66)	72.1 (0.61)	72.7 (0.67)	639 (10.4)	59.2 (0.75)	58.2 (0.73)	58.9 (0.78)	517 (10.9)	19.1 (0.67)	19.2 (0.67)	19.0 (0.74)	121 (4.5)
At least some college	76.1 (1.54)	75.0 (1.48)	74.7 (1.45)	112 (5.0)	63.8 (1.67)	63.5 (1.56)	63.9 (1.49)	95 (4.5)	16.1 (1.56)	15.3 (1.65)	14.5 (1.29)	16 (1.6)
Female, all education levels	**64.6** (0.65)	**64.1** (0.69)	**63.8** (0.60)	**690** (10.6)	**51.2** (0.66)	**51.7** (0.70)	**51.4** (0.58)	**556** (9.7)	**20.8** (0.69)	**19.3** (0.68)	**19.4** (0.64)	**134** (4.8)
Less than high school completion	46.5 (1.37)	44.4 (1.25)	44.1 (1.23)	118 (4.0)	31.0 (1.16)	32.4 (1.12)	31.9 (1.19)	85 (3.5)	33.3 (1.74)	27.0 (1.60)	27.8 (1.63)	33 (2.2)
High school completion[4]	70.2 (0.83)	69.1 (0.87)	69.4 (0.76)	463 (9.4)	57.1 (0.93)	55.4 (0.88)	56.3 (0.73)	375 (8.5)	18.7 (0.86)	19.9 (0.82)	18.9 (0.85)	87 (4.4)
At least some college	76.7 (1.49)	76.8 (1.54)	74.0 (1.73)	109 (3.7)	66.2 (1.67)	69.2 (1.68)	64.8 (1.81)	96 (3.5)	13.6 (1.30)	9.8 (1.22)	12.5 (1.45)	14 (1.7)
White, all education levels	**68.3** (0.58)	**69.7** (0.60)	**69.2** (0.55)	**825** (11.8)	**55.7** (0.59)	**57.9** (0.64)	**57.2** (0.55)	**682** (10.6)	**18.6** (0.51)	**16.9** (0.52)	**17.3** (0.47)	**142** (4.3)
Less than high school completion	49.6 (1.17)	51.3 (1.25)	51.9 (1.07)	159 (4.0)	34.6 (0.97)	39.3 (1.18)	39.0 (1.15)	120 (4.0)	30.2 (1.23)	23.5 (1.47)	24.8 (1.41)	40 (2.3)
High school completion[4]	74.9 (0.75)	75.2 (0.66)	74.5 (0.62)	552 (9.5)	62.8 (0.76)	62.9 (0.77)	62.4 (0.62)	462 (8.5)	16.2 (0.61)	16.3 (0.64)	16.3 (0.59)	90 (3.6)
At least some college	80.3 (1.19)	81.0 (1.50)	78.5 (1.50)	114 (3.9)	70.3 (1.52)	72.3 (1.61)	69.7 (1.51)	101 (3.7)	12.5 (1.24)	10.8 (1.31)	11.3 (1.15)	13 (1.4)
Black, all education levels	**60.4** (0.97)	**57.4** (1.14)	**57.7** (1.28)	**240** (7.3)	**41.0** (1.11)	**40.3** (1.22)	**41.2** (1.21)	**171** (6.5)	**32.2** (1.59)	**29.8** (1.29)	**28.6** (1.18)	**69** (3.1)
Less than high school completion	43.3 (1.95)	37.9 (1.95)	37.3 (2.03)	40 (3.0)	22.2 (1.60)	21.5 (1.73)	21.0 (1.58)	23 (2.1)	48.7 (3.61)	43.4 (3.34)	43.6 (3.15)	17 (1.8)
High school completion[4]	65.2 (1.34)	63.6 (1.41)	64.6 (1.62)	167 (6.9)	46.0 (1.64)	45.5 (1.53)	47.3 (1.65)	122 (5.9)	29.4 (1.95)	28.5 (1.52)	26.8 (1.63)	45 (3.1)
At least some college	74.3 (3.04)	69.2 (3.32)	66.2 (3.16)	33 (2.8)	57.4 (3.67)	56.1 (3.56)	53.2 (2.91)	27 (2.3)	22.8 (3.16)	19.0 (3.58)	19.6 (3.05)	7 (1.2)
Hispanic, all education levels	**64.4** (0.77)	**64.5** (0.68)	**64.4** (0.66)	**456** (8.3)	**52.1** (0.81)	**51.7** (0.73)	**52.2** (0.80)	**370** (8.3)	**19.1** (0.81)	**19.9** (0.75)	**18.9** (0.78)	**86** (3.6)
Less than high school completion	50.6 (1.47)	52.1 (1.48)	48.7 (1.52)	97 (4.4)	38.1 (1.50)	39.1 (1.45)	37.0 (1.55)	74 (3.6)	24.7 (2.03)	24.9 (1.71)	24.0 (2.15)	23 (2.5)
High school completion[4]	70.7 (0.91)	69.1 (0.76)	70.2 (0.93)	304 (7.0)	58.1 (0.93)	55.6 (0.85)	57.1 (1.02)	248 (7.0)	17.9 (0.99)	19.5 (0.93)	18.6 (0.93)	57 (2.8)
At least some college	70.8 (2.12)	73.2 (1.97)	73.0 (1.96)	54 (2.8)	60.8 (2.16)	64.4 (2.06)	64.6 (2.09)	48 (2.7)	14.1 (1.90)	12.0 (1.74)	11.6 (1.61)	6 (0.9)
Asian, all education levels	**58.6** (3.14)	**48.9** (3.06)	**58.6** (2.86)	**28** (2.0)	**50.1** (3.25)	**39.2** (2.96)	**47.0** (3.01)	**22** (1.8)	**14.5** (3.17)	**19.8** (3.24)	**19.8** (3.33)	**5** (1.0)
Less than high school completion	40.7 (5.06)	29.2 (5.42)	46.2 (5.22)	5 (0.9)	33.3 (5.41)	21.1 (5.17)	42.8 (5.32)	5 (0.9)	18.3! (6.73)	27.8! (8.64)	7.3! (2.99)	#! (0.2)
High school completion[4]	64.0 (3.71)	53.8 (3.98)	63.8 (3.98)	16 (1.7)	56.6 (3.99)	42.7 (4.05)	48.4 (4.02)	13 (1.4)	11.6 (3.44)	20.6 (4.50)	24.1 (4.51)	4 (0.9)
At least some college	66.0 (6.86)	59.2 (7.23)	59.7 (6.82)	6 (1.1)	52.7 (7.22)	51.1 (7.26)	48.2 (7.57)	5 (1.0)	20.2! (7.51)	13.7! (4.97)	19.3! (8.22)	1! (0.5)
American Indian/Alaska Native, all education levels	**53.6** (3.72)	**52.5** (3.74)	**52.6** (3.77)	**16** (1.5)	**39.0** (3.40)	**39.6** (3.51)	**38.6** (3.80)	**11** (1.4)	**27.3** (3.59)	**24.5** (3.31)	**26.6** (4.88)	**4** (0.8)
Less than high school completion	30.8 (4.76)	37.2 (5.79)	43.6 (5.48)	4 (0.7)	18.0 (3.61)	25.3 (5.79)	28.8 (6.47)	3 (0.7)	41.6 (8.34)	32.1 (7.92)	33.9! (10.25)	1 (0.4)
High school completion[4]	65.4 (3.83)	62.4 (4.54)	55.8 (5.07)	10 (1.2)	49.0 (4.27)	48.0 (4.54)	40.4 (4.90)	7 (1.0)	25.0 (4.55)	23.0 (4.67)	27.6 (6.34)	3 (0.7)
At least some college	57.7 (7.60)	59.2 (9.33)	59.4 (9.12)	2 (0.4)	45.8 (7.86)	50.8 (8.91)	55.8 (8.80)	2 (0.4)	20.5! (9.95)	‡ (†)	‡ (†)	‡ (†)
20 to 24 years old												
All persons, all education levels	**82.2** (0.16)	**82.2** (0.16)	**82.5** (0.16)	**10,283** (35.8)	**72.9** (0.18)	**73.6** (0.19)	**74.6** (0.17)	**9,299** (34.0)	**11.3** (0.14)	**10.4** (0.13)	**9.6** (0.13)	**984** (13.6)
Less than high school completion	64.4 (0.55)	63.3 (0.55)	63.6 (0.54)	899 (14.3)	50.7 (0.57)	51.3 (0.59)	52.8 (0.59)	746 (13.0)	21.4 (0.56)	19.0 (0.63)	17.0 (0.61)	153 (6.0)
High school completion[4]	79.9 (0.27)	79.2 (0.27)	79.8 (0.27)	4,273 (30.7)	69.1 (0.31)	69.0 (0.29)	70.5 (0.29)	3,774 (29.3)	13.5 (0.25)	12.9 (0.20)	11.7 (0.22)	499 (9.8)
Some college, no degree	86.2 (0.29)	86.6 (0.24)	86.6 (0.28)	2,538 (22.2)	78.6 (0.35)	79.6 (0.27)	79.8 (0.31)	2,338 (21.6)	8.8 (0.24)	8.1 (0.25)	7.9 (0.22)	200 (5.8)
Associate's degree	90.9 (0.57)	90.4 (0.45)	90.3 (0.49)	585 (9.5)	85.8 (0.65)	86.2 (0.55)	85.7 (0.59)	555 (9.6)	5.6 (0.43)	4.7 (0.36)	5.1 (0.42)	30 (2.5)
Bachelor's or higher degree	93.5 (0.24)	94.0 (0.24)	93.9 (0.21)	1,987 (19.4)	88.0 (0.32)	88.6 (0.30)	89.0 (0.27)	1,885 (18.9)	5.9 (0.21)	5.8 (0.21)	5.2 (0.20)	103 (4.1)

See notes at end of table.

Table 501.20. Labor force participation, employment, and unemployment of persons 16 to 24 years old who are not enrolled in school, by age group, sex, race/ethnicity, and educational attainment: 2015, 2016, and 2018—Continued

[Standard errors appear in parentheses]

Age group, sex, race/ethnicity, and educational attainment	Labor force participation				Employment				Unemployment			
	Labor force participation rate[1]			Number of participants (in thousands)	Employment to population ratio[2]			Number employed (in thousands)	Unemployment rate[3]			Number unemployed (in thousands)
	2016	2017	2018	2018	2016	2017	2018	2018	2016	2017	2018	2018
1	2	3	4	5	6	7	8	9	10	11	12	13
Male, all education levels	**83.7 (0.18)**	**83.9 (0.18)**	**84.0 (0.22)**	**5,603 (25.7)**	**73.8 (0.24)**	**74.5 (0.22)**	**75.4 (0.22)**	**5,031 (23.5)**	**11.8 (0.20)**	**11.1 (0.16)**	**10.2 (0.16)**	**572 (9.6)**
Less than high school completion	68.2 (0.66)	67.1 (0.63)	68.3 (0.64)	580 (11.0)	54.8 (0.69)	55.0 (0.71)	57.1 (0.74)	485 (10.1)	19.8 (0.64)	18.0 (0.75)	16.4 (0.72)	95 (4.5)
High school completion[4]	82.6 (0.31)	82.5 (0.27)	82.1 (0.32)	2,550 (22.8)	71.6 (0.38)	71.8 (0.34)	72.6 (0.35)	2,253 (21.5)	13.3 (0.31)	13.0 (0.25)	11.6 (0.25)	297 (6.7)
Some college, no degree	87.9 (0.34)	88.5 (0.35)	88.8 (0.38)	1,328 (16.9)	79.8 (0.44)	81.3 (0.40)	81.6 (0.46)	1,219 (16.2)	9.2 (0.31)	8.1 (0.36)	8.2 (0.33)	109 (4.6)
Associate's degree	93.7 (0.58)	93.6 (0.56)	92.6 (0.59)	287 (6.5)	88.2 (0.85)	88.5 (0.74)	87.2 (0.75)	271 (6.3)	5.9 (0.63)	5.4 (0.53)	5.8 (0.64)	17 (1.9)
Bachelor's or higher degree	94.1 (0.36)	94.5 (0.36)	94.3 (0.35)	857 (13.5)	87.7 (0.47)	87.4 (0.50)	88.3 (0.40)	802 (12.4)	6.9 (0.35)	7.5 (0.40)	6.4 (0.33)	55 (3.1)
Female, all education levels	**80.5 (0.23)**	**80.2 (0.24)**	**80.7 (0.22)**	**4,680 (24.0)**	**71.9 (0.24)**	**72.5 (0.27)**	**73.6 (0.25)**	**4,268 (23.5)**	**10.6 (0.19)**	**9.6 (0.19)**	**8.8 (0.17)**	**412 (8.4)**
Less than high school completion	58.4 (0.93)	57.6 (0.94)	56.4 (1.03)	319 (9.0)	44.1 (0.95)	45.6 (0.88)	46.2 (0.99)	261 (7.8)	24.4 (1.04)	20.8 (0.91)	18.0 (0.96)	57 (3.6)
High school completion[4]	76.1 (0.40)	74.7 (0.44)	76.6 (0.43)	1,723 (17.0)	65.6 (0.44)	65.1 (0.46)	67.6 (0.48)	1,521 (15.9)	13.7 (0.41)	12.9 (0.33)	11.7 (0.35)	202 (6.5)
Some college, no degree	84.4 (0.42)	84.6 (0.41)	84.3 (0.37)	1,210 (12.4)	77.3 (0.52)	77.8 (0.45)	77.9 (0.41)	1,119 (12.0)	8.4 (0.36)	8.1 (0.35)	7.5 (0.34)	91 (4.3)
Associate's degree	88.6 (0.81)	87.8 (0.68)	88.3 (0.81)	298 (6.8)	83.9 (0.93)	84.2 (0.71)	84.4 (0.96)	285 (6.7)	5.3 (0.59)	4.0 (0.40)	4.4 (0.56)	13 (1.7)
Bachelor's or higher degree	93.0 (0.32)	93.7 (0.28)	93.5 (0.26)	1,131 (14.3)	88.2 (0.41)	89.5 (0.37)	89.6 (0.34)	1,083 (14.3)	5.2 (0.26)	4.5 (0.26)	4.2 (0.24)	48 (2.7)
White, all education levels	**84.8 (0.20)**	**85.2 (0.19)**	**85.4 (0.20)**	**5,615 (25.6)**	**77.1 (0.25)**	**77.8 (0.24)**	**78.9 (0.20)**	**5,186 (25.3)**	**9.1 (0.18)**	**8.7 (0.16)**	**7.6 (0.15)**	**429 (8.6)**
Less than high school completion	65.6 (0.81)	63.8 (0.87)	64.1 (0.74)	361 (7.9)	51.1 (0.96)	51.7 (0.86)	53.6 (0.77)	302 (7.2)	22.1 (1.07)	18.9 (0.85)	16.3 (0.89)	59 (3.5)
High school completion[4]	81.3 (0.36)	82.0 (0.32)	82.2 (0.33)	2,203 (18.7)	72.1 (0.40)	72.6 (0.40)	74.3 (0.36)	1,990 (18.1)	11.3 (0.30)	11.5 (0.28)	9.6 (0.26)	212 (5.9)
Some college, no degree	87.3 (0.35)	88.1 (0.27)	88.0 (0.32)	1,309 (14.4)	81.3 (0.41)	82.5 (0.34)	82.5 (0.35)	1,227 (14.3)	6.9 (0.27)	6.4 (0.28)	6.2 (0.30)	82 (4.0)
Associate's degree	93.0 (0.61)	92.2 (0.51)	91.6 (0.52)	374 (7.5)	88.4 (0.84)	88.6 (0.57)	88.2 (0.64)	361 (7.6)	5.0 (0.56)	3.9 (0.38)	3.6 (0.42)	14 (1.6)
Bachelor's or higher degree	95.0 (0.29)	95.2 (0.27)	95.5 (0.20)	1,368 (16.9)	90.4 (0.37)	90.6 (0.35)	91.2 (0.31)	1,306 (16.4)	4.9 (0.20)	4.8 (0.24)	4.5 (0.24)	62 (3.4)
Black, all education levels	**77.1 (0.48)**	**76.0 (0.49)**	**75.4 (0.44)**	**1,419 (14.9)**	**62.9 (0.51)**	**62.2 (0.56)**	**62.4 (0.52)**	**1,175 (13.5)**	**18.5 (0.45)**	**18.2 (0.51)**	**17.2 (0.51)**	**244 (8.0)**
Less than high school completion	53.5 (1.43)	51.2 (1.41)	50.3 (1.68)	121 (5.8)	35.0 (1.45)	33.8 (1.49)	33.6 (1.52)	81 (4.4)	34.6 (1.82)	34.1 (2.13)	33.3 (2.10)	40 (3.3)
High school completion[4]	76.1 (0.74)	73.7 (0.66)	72.8 (0.80)	664 (11.9)	60.0 (0.91)	58.8 (0.85)	58.7 (0.86)	535 (11.0)	21.1 (0.78)	20.2 (0.79)	19.3 (0.79)	128 (5.6)
Some college, no degree	85.9 (0.76)	84.8 (0.79)	85.5 (0.86)	424 (9.0)	74.3 (0.98)	72.5 (0.86)	74.3 (1.03)	368 (8.8)	13.5 (0.83)	14.6 (0.80)	13.1 (0.74)	56 (3.2)
Associate's degree	84.1 (2.28)	87.5 (1.87)	87.7 (1.58)	64 (3.9)	76.1 (2.48)	79.9 (2.28)	75.4 (2.57)	55 (3.8)	9.5 (1.90)	8.6 (1.78)	14.1 (2.45)	9 (1.6)
Bachelor's or higher degree	92.1 (1.05)	93.1 (0.96)	90.5 (0.99)	146 (5.8)	83.8 (1.25)	84.0 (1.44)	84.0 (1.23)	136 (5.5)	9.0 (1.01)	9.7 (1.15)	7.2 (1.04)	10 (1.6)
Hispanic, all education levels	**80.6 (0.34)**	**80.3 (0.28)**	**81.3 (0.29)**	**2,453 (17.9)**	**71.3 (0.39)**	**72.6 (0.32)**	**73.7 (0.33)**	**2,224 (17.9)**	**11.6 (0.31)**	**9.6 (0.26)**	**9.3 (0.24)**	**228 (5.9)**
Less than high school completion	69.3 (0.85)	69.6 (0.91)	69.7 (0.93)	354 (8.6)	58.5 (0.94)	60.1 (0.91)	61.4 (1.05)	312 (8.7)	15.5 (0.83)	13.6 (0.88)	11.9 (0.72)	42 (2.5)
High school completion[4]	80.6 (0.46)	78.7 (0.49)	80.7 (0.51)	1,145 (14.8)	70.5 (0.56)	70.4 (0.48)	72.2 (0.56)	1,025 (14.7)	12.6 (0.46)	10.5 (0.35)	10.5 (0.44)	121 (5.1)
Some college, no degree	85.1 (0.51)	85.6 (0.59)	85.7 (0.57)	621 (10.5)	77.2 (0.66)	79.1 (0.73)	79.4 (0.66)	576 (10.4)	9.3 (0.59)	7.5 (0.55)	7.4 (0.46)	46 (2.9)
Associate's degree	90.1 (1.09)	88.1 (1.40)	90.1 (1.12)	110 (5.2)	84.9 (1.28)	83.6 (1.66)	85.6 (1.28)	105 (5.0)	5.8 (1.01)	5.2 (0.96)	5.0 (0.80)	6 (0.9)
Bachelor's or higher degree	91.1 (0.93)	93.5 (0.66)	90.9 (0.84)	222 (6.8)	83.7 (1.15)	87.9 (0.88)	85.2 (1.08)	208 (6.6)	8.1 (0.89)	6.0 (0.67)	6.3 (0.81)	14 (1.8)
Asian, all education levels	**80.1 (0.91)**	**81.7 (0.73)**	**82.6 (0.65)**	**351 (8.3)**	**72.4 (1.05)**	**74.8 (0.84)**	**76.5 (0.76)**	**325 (8.2)**	**9.6 (0.59)**	**8.4 (0.68)**	**7.4 (0.58)**	**26 (2.0)**
Less than high school completion	67.9 (2.88)	62.7 (3.54)	68.2 (3.41)	20 (2.0)	58.9 (2.98)	55.5 (3.63)	60.9 (3.30)	17 (1.8)	13.2 (2.70)	11.5! (4.21)	10.7 (2.46)	2 (0.5)
High school completion[4]	76.1 (1.92)	76.6 (1.56)	76.5 (1.75)	74 (4.0)	69.3 (1.99)	68.7 (1.86)	69.4 (1.91)	68 (3.5)	8.9 (1.22)	10.3 (1.29)	9.2 (1.49)	7 (1.3)
Some college, no degree	77.5 (2.04)	80.2 (1.68)	80.1 (1.77)	62 (3.5)	68.4 (2.30)	75.3 (1.90)	74.5 (1.78)	57 (3.4)	11.7 (1.64)	6.1 (1.16)	7.0 (1.06)	4 (0.7)
Associate's degree	77.0 (4.25)	87.8 (3.02)	80.5 (3.76)	15 (1.5)	69.4 (4.32)	85.8 (3.23)	77.0 (4.25)	14 (1.5)	9.8! (3.10)	‡ (†)	‡ (†)	‡ (†)
Bachelor's or higher degree	86.0 (1.21)	87.5 (0.88)	88.8 (1.01)	180 (5.5)	78.4 (1.30)	79.9 (0.95)	82.9 (1.23)	168 (5.3)	8.8 (0.85)	8.7 (0.92)	6.7 (0.77)	12 (1.4)
American Indian/Alaska Native, all education levels	**70.0 (1.34)**	**66.4 (1.59)**	**66.6 (1.63)**	**73 (3.3)**	**53.5 (1.57)**	**55.2 (1.89)**	**54.4 (1.74)**	**59 (2.9)**	**23.5 (1.70)**	**16.9 (1.75)**	**18.3 (1.98)**	**13 (1.6)**
Less than high school completion	55.2 (3.79)	45.1 (4.12)	45.9 (4.69)	9 (1.2)	32.3 (3.86)	32.5 (4.44)	31.4 (4.61)	6 (1.0)	41.6 (5.16)	28.0 (5.48)	31.6 (5.87)	3 (0.6)
High school completion[4]	67.8 (2.10)	66.9 (2.03)	66.3 (2.36)	37 (2.3)	49.7 (2.24)	54.0 (2.22)	53.6 (2.42)	30 (2.2)	26.6 (2.42)	19.2 (2.62)	19.0 (2.69)	7 (1.1)
Some college, no degree	80.7 (3.00)	75.1 (3.05)	76.9 (2.83)	21 (2.0)	69.7 (3.43)	65.9 (3.00)	65.4 (3.85)	18 (1.8)	13.6 (2.55)	12.3 (2.39)	14.9 (4.09)	3 (0.9)
Associate's degree	82.9 (6.08)	76.2 (6.89)	81.6 (8.38)	2 (0.5)	82.9 (6.08)	71.7 (7.75)	69.3 (8.88)	2 (0.4)	‡ (†)	‡ (†)	15.0! (6.39)	‡ (†)
Bachelor's or higher degree	93.4 (4.37)	81.1 (7.52)	84.4 (6.83)	4 (0.6)	75.8 (8.72)	79.0 (7.85)	83.5 (6.91)	4 (0.6)	18.8! (8.63)	‡ (†)	‡ (†)	‡ (†)

†Not applicable.
#Rounds to zero.
!Interpret data with caution. The coefficient of variation (CV) for this estimate is between 30 and 50 percent.
‡Reporting standards not met. Either there are too few cases for a reliable estimate or the coefficient of variation (CV) is 50 percent or greater.
[1]Percentage of the civilian population who are employed or seeking employment.
[2]Number of persons employed as a percentage of the civilian population.
[3]The percentage of persons in the civilian labor force who are not working and who made specific efforts to find employment sometime during the prior 4 weeks.
[4]Includes equivalency credentials, such as the GED credential.

NOTE: Table excludes persons enrolled in school. Estimates are for all nonenrolled civilians in the given age range, including persons living in households and persons living in group quarters (e.g., residential treatment centers or correctional facilities). Race categories exclude persons of Hispanic ethnicity. Totals include racial/ethnic groups not separately shown. Detail may not sum to totals because of rounding.

SOURCE: U.S. Department of Commerce, Census Bureau, American Community Survey (ACS), 2016, 2017, and 2018. (This table was prepared May 2020.)

Table 501.30. Percentage and number of persons 18 to 24 years old who were neither enrolled in school nor working, by age group, high school completion status, sex, and race/ethnicity: Selected years, 2006 through 2018

[Standard errors appear in parentheses]

Age group, high school completion status, sex, and race/ethnicity	Percent who were neither enrolled in school nor working: 2006	2008	2009	2010	2011	2012	2013	2014	2015	2016	2017	2018: Number (in thousands): Total, all persons 18 to 24 years old	2018: Number (in thousands): Neither enrolled in school nor working	2018: Percent who were neither enrolled in school nor working
1	2	3	4	5	6	7	8	9	10	11	12	13	14	15
18 to 24 years old, all persons	**15.4 (0.07)**	**15.2 (0.08)**	**17.6 (0.09)**	**17.9 (0.09)**	**17.7 (0.08)**	**17.1 (0.08)**	**16.7 (0.11)**	**15.9 (0.09)**	**14.8 (0.09)**	**14.1 (0.09)**	**13.9 (0.10)**	**30,648 (33.6)**	**4,125 (28.5)**	**13.5 (0.09)**
Male	14.5 (0.10)	14.8 (0.12)	18.1 (0.15)	18.5 (0.12)	18.3 (0.12)	17.6 (0.11)	17.1 (0.14)	16.1 (0.14)	15.2 (0.13)	14.6 (0.12)	14.3 (0.12)	15,710 (23.3)	2,180 (20.1)	13.9 (0.12)
Female	16.4 (0.12)	15.6 (0.13)	17.0 (0.12)	17.2 (0.12)	17.1 (0.11)	16.6 (0.13)	16.3 (0.14)	15.7 (0.12)	14.5 (0.13)	13.6 (0.12)	13.4 (0.13)	14,938 (18.9)	1,945 (17.8)	13.0 (0.11)
White	11.8 (0.08)	11.7 (0.11)	13.8 (0.11)	14.1 (0.10)	14.1 (0.11)	13.5 (0.10)	13.5 (0.12)	12.9 (0.09)	12.1 (0.11)	11.6 (0.12)	11.3 (0.13)	16,286 (11.5)	1,792 (15.3)	11.0 (0.09)
Black	25.3 (0.31)	25.0 (0.30)	27.3 (0.31)	27.9 (0.29)	27.4 (0.28)	27.2 (0.31)	26.2 (0.29)	24.9 (0.30)	22.6 (0.31)	21.0 (0.29)	21.6 (0.32)	4,345 (22.1)	912 (15.2)	21.0 (0.32)
Hispanic	20.9 (0.21)	20.4 (0.24)	22.8 (0.22)	22.6 (0.23)	22.0 (0.22)	21.2 (0.22)	19.8 (0.26)	18.4 (0.24)	17.5 (0.21)	16.6 (0.22)	16.1 (0.18)	6,873 (14.9)	1,065 (13.2)	15.5 (0.19)
Asian	9.1 (0.35)	7.7 (0.30)	9.9 (0.38)	9.4 (0.30)	9.0 (0.32)	8.6 (0.27)	9.0 (0.31)	8.7 (0.30)	8.2 (0.28)	7.6 (0.26)	7.4 (0.23)	1,731 (11.6)	120 (4.3)	6.9 (0.24)
Pacific Islander	19.6 (2.51)	20.3 (2.69)	21.3 (2.01)	23.8 (2.37)	24.2 (2.32)	24.8 (2.35)	21.3 (2.34)	23.7 (2.65)	16.8 (2.04)	15.5 (1.99)	19.8 (2.68)	57 (2.9)	12 (1.6)	20.8 (2.48)
American Indian/Alaska Native	30.2 (1.20)	29.0 (1.31)	34.0 (1.17)	34.3 (1.15)	33.3 (1.29)	32.7 (1.07)	33.3 (1.06)	32.1 (1.15)	31.0 (1.10)	32.0 (1.01)	29.2 (1.15)	227 (5.5)	65 (2.9)	28.7 (1.11)
Some other race	16.4 (1.79)	15.6 (1.86)	18.5 (1.99)	18.2 (2.22)	20.9 (2.26)	14.5 (1.60)	13.6 (1.73)	14.1 (1.54)	20.1 (2.07)	13.4 (1.82)	15.0 (1.64)	91 (4.9)	15 (1.7)	16.0 (1.67)
Two or more races	15.0 (0.55)	16.3 (0.56)	20.1 (0.64)	18.0 (0.63)	18.5 (0.60)	16.6 (0.55)	15.4 (0.48)	16.6 (0.52)	14.7 (0.54)	13.7 (0.49)	14.4 (0.43)	1,036 (13.3)	145 (5.4)	14.0 (0.46)
Race/ethnicity by sex														
Male														
White	11.1 (0.12)	11.3 (0.14)	14.3 (0.17)	14.9 (0.13)	14.7 (0.15)	13.9 (0.14)	13.9 (0.16)	12.9 (0.16)	12.3 (0.15)	11.9 (0.16)	11.5 (0.17)	8,372 (8.8)	937 (10.0)	11.2 (0.12)
Black	28.9 (0.42)	29.0 (0.43)	31.5 (0.44)	32.5 (0.43)	31.8 (0.37)	31.1 (0.45)	30.3 (0.44)	28.6 (0.51)	26.5 (0.41)	24.5 (0.38)	25.3 (0.52)	2,198 (14.5)	529 (10.4)	24.1 (0.40)
Hispanic	15.5 (0.31)	16.3 (0.28)	20.5 (0.32)	20.3 (0.33)	19.9 (0.29)	19.5 (0.31)	18.1 (0.30)	16.9 (0.34)	15.9 (0.27)	15.3 (0.28)	15.1 (0.23)	3,544 (11.0)	525 (9.8)	14.8 (0.27)
Asian	9.0 (0.48)	6.8 (0.42)	9.2 (0.49)	9.3 (0.43)	8.6 (0.40)	8.1 (0.40)	8.3 (0.34)	8.1 (0.40)	8.0 (0.36)	7.7 (0.36)	7.3 (0.38)	883 (8.2)	61 (2.8)	7.0 (0.32)
Pacific Islander	18.0 (3.32)	17.2 (3.43)	17.4 (2.85)	23.0 (2.89)	19.8 (2.67)	23.6 (3.79)	19.8 (2.85)	17.9 (3.23)	10.4 (1.89)	13.5 (2.56)	19.0 (3.20)	29 (2.0)	6 (1.1)	21.3 (3.43)
American Indian/Alaska Native	29.8 (1.63)	29.0 (1.63)	35.7 (1.89)	36.6 (1.77)	35.2 (1.71)	34.1 (1.50)	34.7 (1.44)	33.0 (1.68)	32.0 (1.46)	34.9 (1.81)	28.1 (1.76)	113 (3.1)	31 (1.6)	26.9 (1.24)
Some other race	15.0 (2.32)	16.1 (2.47)	19.7 (2.91)	19.0 (2.66)	18.1 (2.72)	14.8 (2.17)	16.0 (2.22)	13.0 (2.34)	21.1 (3.11)	16.6 (2.69)	14.5 (2.10)	43 (3.0)	8 (1.2)	18.2 (2.58)
Two or more races	15.4 (0.76)	16.8 (0.85)	21.8 (1.02)	19.4 (0.83)	20.5 (0.83)	18.7 (0.82)	16.1 (0.72)	16.3 (0.74)	15.7 (0.83)	15.2 (0.75)	15.3 (0.63)	526 (9.3)	82 (4.5)	15.6 (0.73)
Female														
White	12.5 (0.12)	12.0 (0.15)	13.2 (0.15)	13.4 (0.15)	13.6 (0.15)	13.0 (0.15)	13.2 (0.17)	13.0 (0.13)	11.9 (0.14)	11.3 (0.14)	11.0 (0.16)	7,914 (7.6)	855 (9.9)	10.8 (0.12)
Black	21.6 (0.43)	20.9 (0.41)	22.9 (0.42)	23.4 (0.39)	23.0 (0.36)	23.3 (0.40)	22.1 (0.39)	21.1 (0.38)	18.6 (0.37)	17.2 (0.37)	17.8 (0.36)	2,147 (12.5)	383 (9.7)	17.9 (0.45)
Hispanic	27.3 (0.33)	24.9 (0.37)	25.4 (0.33)	25.2 (0.30)	24.2 (0.34)	23.1 (0.31)	21.8 (0.40)	20.1 (0.35)	19.2 (0.31)	18.1 (0.30)	17.1 (0.29)	3,329 (10.1)	540 (9.2)	16.2 (0.26)
Asian	9.2 (0.47)	8.7 (0.42)	10.6 (0.51)	9.6 (0.41)	9.4 (0.45)	9.2 (0.41)	9.7 (0.45)	9.3 (0.43)	8.3 (0.40)	7.5 (0.38)	7.6 (0.30)	849 (8.2)	58 (3.0)	6.8 (0.35)
Pacific Islander	21.5 (3.59)	23.5 (3.68)	25.8 (3.18)	24.7 (3.17)	28.6 (3.76)	26.2 (3.11)	23.0 (3.17)	30.6 (4.17)	22.6 (3.27)	17.6 (2.77)	20.8 (3.29)	28 (2.0)	6 (1.0)	20.3 (3.35)
American Indian/Alaska Native	30.6 (1.56)	29.0 (1.76)	32.3 (1.65)	31.9 (1.51)	31.3 (1.65)	31.2 (1.59)	31.9 (1.46)	31.2 (1.53)	30.0 (1.61)	28.9 (1.46)	30.3 (1.33)	113 (3.9)	34 (2.2)	30.4 (1.65)
Some other race	18.1 (2.45)	15.1 (2.84)	17.1 (2.82)	17.5 (3.21)	23.5 (3.24)	14.1 (2.42)	11.4 (2.20)	15.3 (2.36)	19.1 (2.85)	10.2 (2.36)	15.6 (2.58)	48 (3.5)	7 (1.2)	13.9 (2.06)
Two or more races	14.6 (0.84)	15.9 (0.79)	18.3 (0.92)	16.5 (0.88)	16.7 (0.84)	14.5 (0.68)	14.7 (0.61)	16.9 (0.61)	13.8 (0.68)	12.1 (0.63)	13.5 (0.67)	510 (9.5)	63 (3.2)	12.3 (0.60)
18 and 19 years old, all persons	**11.8 (0.15)**	**12.1 (0.14)**	**13.8 (0.15)**	**13.9 (0.16)**	**13.5 (0.16)**	**13.0 (0.15)**	**12.5 (0.18)**	**11.6 (0.15)**	**11.1 (0.13)**	**10.5 (0.16)**	**10.8 (0.15)**	**8,870 (28.7)**	**960 (13.5)**	**10.8 (0.14)**
20 to 24 years old, all persons	**16.9 (0.09)**	**16.5 (0.10)**	**19.1 (0.10)**	**19.6 (0.11)**	**19.4 (0.10)**	**18.7 (0.11)**	**18.3 (0.12)**	**17.6 (0.11)**	**16.3 (0.12)**	**15.5 (0.11)**	**15.1 (0.12)**	**21,778 (35.4)**	**3,166 (23.3)**	**14.5 (0.10)**
Male	15.5 (0.13)	15.7 (0.13)	19.4 (0.17)	20.0 (0.15)	19.6 (0.16)	18.9 (0.14)	18.5 (0.16)	17.4 (0.17)	16.3 (0.17)	15.7 (0.15)	15.2 (0.15)	11,154 (23.9)	1,638 (15.7)	14.7 (0.14)
Female	18.4 (0.13)	17.4 (0.16)	18.9 (0.15)	19.2 (0.16)	19.3 (0.14)	18.5 (0.17)	18.2 (0.16)	17.7 (0.16)	16.2 (0.17)	15.3 (0.14)	15.0 (0.16)	10,624 (23.1)	1,528 (16.2)	14.4 (0.15)
White	13.0 (0.10)	12.8 (0.13)	15.2 (0.14)	15.5 (0.14)	15.6 (0.14)	14.9 (0.13)	15.0 (0.15)	14.3 (0.12)	13.4 (0.12)	12.9 (0.14)	12.5 (0.15)	11,664 (16.3)	1,386 (13.2)	11.9 (0.11)
Black	28.0 (0.37)	27.6 (0.35)	30.1 (0.34)	31.2 (0.37)	30.5 (0.33)	30.1 (0.41)	28.6 (0.37)	27.8 (0.36)	24.9 (0.38)	23.2 (0.32)	23.7 (0.39)	3,083 (18.7)	708 (12.4)	23.0 (0.36)
Hispanic	22.4 (0.25)	21.6 (0.26)	24.3 (0.26)	24.5 (0.25)	23.8 (0.25)	22.8 (0.26)	21.4 (0.31)	19.8 (0.28)	18.8 (0.26)	18.1 (0.27)	17.1 (0.22)	4,826 (15.9)	794 (11.1)	16.4 (0.23)
Asian	10.4 (0.43)	9.1 (0.38)	11.4 (0.47)	10.8 (0.38)	10.3 (0.42)	10.2 (0.32)	10.4 (0.39)	10.1 (0.40)	9.5 (0.36)	9.0 (0.35)	8.3 (0.31)	1,243 (11.2)	100 (3.5)	8.0 (0.27)
Pacific Islander	22.2 (2.95)	22.2 (2.99)	24.5 (2.60)	26.2 (2.88)	27.8 (2.88)	26.5 (2.81)	19.9 (2.59)	22.3 (3.23)	19.8 (2.44)	16.6 (2.52)	20.2 (3.23)	40 (2.7)	9 (1.4)	21.5 (3.07)
American Indian/Alaska Native	32.9 (1.54)	31.9 (1.45)	36.9 (1.32)	37.2 (1.45)	36.4 (1.49)	34.3 (1.25)	37.5 (1.37)	36.5 (1.37)	33.3 (1.41)	35.2 (1.31)	31.6 (1.52)	156 (4.8)	50 (2.8)	31.9 (1.43)
Some other race	18.0 (2.26)	16.8 (2.45)	20.5 (2.71)	18.1 (2.74)	24.7 (2.73)	13.6 (1.85)	13.9 (2.01)	15.5 (1.84)	19.6 (2.39)	14.6 (2.23)	15.0 (1.63)	66 (4.3)	11 (1.7)	16.7 (2.15)
Two or more races	16.0 (0.70)	17.8 (0.71)	23.0 (0.78)	20.9 (0.90)	21.1 (0.80)	18.2 (0.68)	17.6 (0.71)	19.1 (0.72)	16.2 (0.71)	15.0 (0.58)	16.2 (0.62)	701 (10.4)	109 (4.3)	15.6 (0.55)
Has completed high school,[1] all persons	13.1 (0.09)	12.8 (0.11)	15.3 (0.11)	15.8 (0.12)	15.9 (0.09)	15.4 (0.12)	15.2 (0.13)	14.8 (0.11)	13.7 (0.11)	13.1 (0.11)	12.9 (0.11)	20,142 (35.4)	2,497 (20.1)	12.4 (0.10)
Male	12.0 (0.14)	12.1 (0.15)	15.6 (0.17)	16.1 (0.16)	16.2 (0.15)	15.6 (0.15)	15.4 (0.16)	14.7 (0.16)	13.7 (0.15)	13.2 (0.15)	12.9 (0.13)	10,175 (25.2)	1,273 (13.9)	12.5 (0.13)
Female	14.2 (0.14)	13.5 (0.16)	14.9 (0.15)	15.4 (0.16)	15.6 (0.14)	15.2 (0.17)	15.0 (0.16)	14.9 (0.15)	13.8 (0.15)	13.0 (0.15)	12.9 (0.16)	9,967 (22.5)	1,224 (14.8)	12.3 (0.14)

See notes at end of table.

Table 501.30. Percentage and number of persons 18 to 24 years old who were neither enrolled in school nor working, by age group, high school completion status, sex, and race/ethnicity: Selected years, 2006 through 2018—Continued

[Standard errors appear in parentheses]

Age group, high school completion status, sex, and race/ethnicity	Percent who were neither enrolled in school nor working											2018		
												Number (in thousands)		Percent who were neither enrolled in school nor working
	2006	2008	2009	2010	2011	2012	2013	2014	2015	2016	2017	Total, all persons 18 to 24 years old	Neither enrolled in school nor working	
1	2	3	4	5	6	7	8	9	10	11	12	13	14	15
White	10.5 (0.10)	10.3 (0.13)	12.6 (0.14)	12.9 (0.13)	13.0 (0.13)	12.6 (0.13)	12.8 (0.15)	12.4 (0.11)	11.5 (0.12)	11.0 (0.13)	10.7 (0.14)	11,028 (19.2)	1,125 (11.4)	10.2 (0.10)
Black	21.8 (0.41)	21.6 (0.34)	24.1 (0.35)	25.1 (0.40)	24.8 (0.32)	24.9 (0.41)	23.5 (0.38)	23.4 (0.39)	21.1 (0.40)	19.5 (0.37)	20.4 (0.38)	2,787 (18.4)	548 (10.7)	19.7 (0.35)
Hispanic	17.4 (0.26)	16.4 (0.27)	19.0 (0.27)	19.5 (0.29)	19.8 (0.25)	18.5 (0.27)	17.7 (0.32)	16.4 (0.28)	15.8 (0.25)	15.2 (0.29)	14.7 (0.23)	4,248 (15.5)	598 (9.7)	14.1 (0.22)
Asian	9.1 (0.39)	8.3 (0.40)	10.0 (0.44)	9.4 (0.37)	9.1 (0.41)	8.9 (0.32)	9.5 (0.37)	8.9 (0.37)	8.5 (0.33)	8.2 (0.35)	7.5 (0.28)	1,203 (11.0)	88 (3.3)	7.3 (0.27)
Pacific Islander	17.6 (3.08)	20.4 (3.31)	19.4 (2.61)	24.8 (3.04)	25.0 (2.82)	22.4 (2.72)	18.8 (2.67)	17.6 (3.34)	17.7 (2.36)	15.8 (2.68)	19.2 (3.40)	36 (2.4)	6 (1.1)	17.2 (2.70)
American Indian/Alaska Native	25.7 (1.67)	26.0 (1.45)	29.2 (1.45)	29.6 (1.43)	30.9 (1.71)	29.6 (1.26)	32.9 (1.52)	32.0 (1.40)	27.9 (1.56)	30.8 (1.35)	28.0 (1.47)	135 (4.4)	37 (2.2)	27.4 (1.37)
Some other race	13.7 (2.10)	14.6 (2.53)	17.8 (2.61)	14.2 (2.62)	19.6 (2.59)	12.8 (1.89)	12.2 (1.94)	11.4 (1.80)	17.9 (2.47)	11.9 (1.89)	12.4 (1.55)	62 (4.2)	9 (1.6)	15.2 (2.25)
Two or more races	12.7 (0.72)	14.0 (0.64)	19.6 (0.81)	17.7 (0.93)	17.6 (0.76)	15.6 (0.70)	14.8 (0.69)	16.7 (0.73)	13.6 (0.65)	12.9 (0.57)	14.2 (0.64)	644 (10.1)	86 (4.0)	13.4 (0.57)
Has not completed high school, all persons	41.1 (0.37)	42.8 (0.36)	47.5 (0.35)	47.8 (0.35)	47.9 (0.45)	48.2 (0.39)	46.0 (0.47)	44.8 (0.49)	42.7 (0.48)	42.6 (0.49)	41.6 (0.56)	1,636 (18.2)	668 (10.9)	40.8 (0.53)
Male	34.0 (0.48)	37.0 (0.52)	42.4 (0.47)	43.3 (0.45)	42.3 (0.51)	43.9 (0.58)	41.5 (0.60)	40.3 (0.64)	39.7 (0.55)	39.4 (0.62)	39.0 (0.64)	979 (13.7)	364 (7.8)	37.2 (0.66)
Female	52.1 (0.65)	51.5 (0.61)	55.3 (0.56)	55.0 (0.69)	56.3 (0.74)	54.5 (0.71)	52.9 (0.68)	51.4 (0.63)	47.1 (0.87)	47.6 (0.92)	45.6 (0.87)	657 (11.5)	304 (7.4)	46.3 (0.91)
White	40.0 (0.50)	42.6 (0.61)	48.1 (0.67)	49.2 (0.62)	51.0 (0.68)	48.9 (0.66)	46.4 (0.70)	44.5 (0.79)	42.7 (0.69)	43.0 (0.88)	42.4 (0.79)	636 (10.9)	262 (6.1)	41.1 (0.73)
Black	58.0 (1.10)	58.8 (1.02)	62.1 (0.76)	64.6 (0.67)	63.1 (1.00)	63.3 (0.95)	60.0 (1.02)	58.7 (0.93)	55.9 (1.13)	54.2 (1.35)	54.1 (1.41)	296 (7.6)	160 (6.0)	54.0 (1.45)
Hispanic	34.3 (0.58)	35.5 (0.59)	39.3 (0.54)	39.3 (0.56)	38.1 (0.70)	40.5 (0.79)	38.0 (0.78)	37.1 (0.82)	35.6 (0.83)	36.4 (0.83)	34.5 (0.88)	578 (11.8)	196 (6.4)	33.9 (0.96)
Asian	36.2 (2.49)	26.6 (2.48)	38.3 (2.89)	37.8 (2.66)	32.0 (2.27)	37.7 (3.09)	36.4 (3.26)	38.3 (2.73)	31.7 (2.93)	30.4 (2.63)	30.7 (2.82)	40 (3.0)	11 (1.3)	27.9 (2.53)
Pacific Islander	49.6 (9.53)	36.5 (8.89)	58.9 (7.61)	‡ (†)	48.4 (9.11)	49.2 (10.64)	‡ (†)	56.4 (8.67)	‡ (†)	23.6! (7.13)	34.4! (12.22)	4 (1.0)	‡ (†)	56.0 (11.05)
American Indian/Alaska Native	58.5 (2.96)	53.6 (3.82)	66.9 (3.65)	67.1 (3.02)	58.1 (3.66)	57.6 (3.46)	58.0 (3.15)	58.2 (2.89)	56.1 (3.29)	57.5 (3.56)	56.3 (4.03)	21 (2.0)	13 (1.6)	60.4 (4.55)
Some other race	43.2 (9.41)	29.6 (7.61)	41.1 (8.85)	39.8 (7.57)	61.6 (9.79)	23.5! (7.85)	29.2 (8.04)	‡ (†)	39.6 (11.25)	37.7 (10.56)	45.6 (7.32)	4 (0.9)	‡ (†)	42.8 (10.79)
Two or more races	48.1 (3.32)	53.0 (3.29)	56.5 (3.05)	49.4 (3.46)	56.4 (3.09)	47.1 (2.76)	49.7 (3.22)	50.8 (2.55)	55.2 (3.20)	43.1 (3.19)	43.5 (3.17)	56 (3.3)	23 (2.0)	40.2 (2.70)

†Not applicable.
!Interpret data with caution. The coefficient of variation (CV) for this estimate is between 30 and 50 percent.
‡Reporting standards not met. Either there are too few cases for a reliable estimate or the coefficient of variation (CV) is 50 percent or greater.
[1]Includes completing high school through equivalency programs, such as a GED program.

NOTE: Data are based on sample surveys of the entire population in the given age range residing within the United States, including both noninstitutionalized persons (e.g., those living in households, college housing, or military housing located within the United States) and institutionalized persons (e.g., those living in prisons, nursing facilities, or other healthcare facilities). Institutionalized persons made up 1 percent of all 18- to 24-year-olds in 2018. Race categories exclude persons of Hispanic ethnicity. Detail may not sum to totals because of rounding.
SOURCE: U.S. Department of Commerce, Census Bureau, American Community Survey (ACS), 2006 through 2018. (This table was prepared December 2019.)

Table 501.40. Percentage distribution of 25- to 34-year-olds with various levels of educational attainment, by labor force status, sex, race/ethnicity, and U.S. nativity and citizenship status: 2018

[Standard errors appear in parentheses]

Sex, race/ethnicity, and U.S. nativity and citizenship status	All 25- to 34-year-olds			Less than high school completion			High school completion[1]			Some college, no bachelor's degree[2]			Bachelor's or higher degree		
	In labor force			In labor force			In labor force			In labor force			In labor force		
	Employed	Unemployed (seeking employment)	Not in labor force	Employed	Unemployed (seeking employment)	Not in labor force	Employed	Unemployed (seeking employment)	Not in labor force	Employed	Unemployed (seeking employment)	Not in labor force	Employed	Unemployed (seeking employment)	Not in labor force
1	2	3	4	5	6	7	8	9	10	11	12	13	14	15	16
Total[3]	**79.0 (0.07)**	**4.2 (0.04)**	**16.8 (0.06)**	**56.4 (0.33)**	**6.9 (0.18)**	**36.6 (0.32)**	**71.4 (0.19)**	**6.0 (0.10)**	**22.6 (0.16)**	**80.3 (0.14)**	**4.4 (0.08)**	**15.3 (0.12)**	**88.2 (0.10)**	**2.3 (0.05)**	**9.4 (0.09)**
Sex															
Male	82.9 (0.11)	4.5 (0.06)	12.6 (0.09)	65.9 (0.44)	6.5 (0.23)	27.6 (0.39)	77.1 (0.25)	5.9 (0.12)	17.0 (0.21)	84.7 (0.22)	4.4 (0.12)	10.9 (0.18)	91.5 (0.13)	2.6 (0.08)	5.9 (0.12)
Female	75.0 (0.10)	4.0 (0.05)	21.0 (0.10)	43.3 (0.44)	7.5 (0.30)	49.1 (0.48)	63.7 (0.28)	6.1 (0.14)	30.2 (0.27)	76.0 (0.17)	4.4 (0.10)	19.6 (0.16)	85.6 (0.14)	2.1 (0.06)	12.4 (0.14)
Race/ethnicity															
White	81.7 (0.10)	3.4 (0.05)	14.8 (0.09)	52.1 (0.63)	7.8 (0.33)	40.1 (0.58)	73.1 (0.25)	5.2 (0.12)	21.8 (0.23)	81.4 (0.18)	3.6 (0.09)	15.0 (0.16)	90.0 (0.11)	1.9 (0.06)	8.1 (0.10)
Black	72.8 (0.24)	7.6 (0.17)	19.6 (0.18)	39.3 (1.04)	11.5 (0.72)	49.2 (0.96)	64.3 (0.52)	9.6 (0.28)	26.1 (0.48)	78.9 (0.46)	7.2 (0.30)	13.9 (0.33)	88.6 (0.40)	3.8 (0.24)	7.6 (0.33)
Hispanic	76.8 (0.17)	4.4 (0.08)	18.8 (0.16)	65.6 (0.50)	4.8 (0.24)	29.6 (0.47)	73.8 (0.32)	5.1 (0.16)	21.0 (0.28)	79.9 (0.32)	4.3 (0.19)	15.7 (0.27)	87.9 (0.40)	2.7 (0.16)	9.4 (0.35)
Asian	77.7 (0.28)	3.2 (0.11)	19.2 (0.28)	61.5 (1.50)	3.5 (0.67)	34.9 (1.39)	71.9 (1.14)	4.1 (0.49)	24.0 (1.13)	76.3 (0.85)	3.6 (0.35)	20.2 (0.75)	80.0 (0.34)	2.9 (0.13)	17.1 (0.34)
Pacific Islander	75.5 (1.84)	4.0 (0.75)	20.5 (1.67)	51.7 (7.05)	‡ (†)	45.6 (7.03)	75.5 (2.81)	6.9 (1.67)	17.6 (2.56)	74.8 (3.57)	2.8! (0.95)	22.4 (3.39)	89.1 (3.29)	‡ (†)	8.9! (2.86)
American Indian/Alaska Native[4]	64.0 (0.88)	7.6 (0.48)	28.4 (1.02)	35.8 (2.93)	12.7 (1.86)	51.5 (2.65)	57.2 (1.58)	9.5 (0.97)	33.3 (1.87)	74.0 (1.41)	5.8 (0.79)	20.2 (1.31)	81.7 (2.54)	2.2! (0.75)	16.0 (2.46)
American Indian	64.9 (0.96)	7.6 (0.55)	27.5 (1.13)	39.4 (3.54)	12.5 (2.14)	48.2 (3.31)	58.7 (1.71)	9.5 (1.11)	31.8 (1.91)	73.5 (1.56)	5.8 (0.78)	20.7 (1.49)	81.8 (2.51)	2.8! (0.94)	15.3 (2.49)
Alaska Native	48.9 (4.01)	12.3 (2.85)	38.8 (3.98)	16.1! (6.05)	16.1! (7.26)	67.7 (8.45)	54.7 (5.63)	11.7 (2.86)	33.6 (5.10)	60.7 (8.38)	‡ (†)	24.7! (8.11)	‡ (†)	‡ (†)	‡ (†)
Two or more races	77.9 (0.54)	5.1 (0.30)	16.9 (0.46)	48.4 (2.91)	11.8 (1.71)	39.8 (2.76)	68.6 (1.25)	7.5 (0.74)	23.9 (1.22)	77.2 (0.94)	5.1 (0.50)	17.7 (0.75)	87.6 (0.65)	3.0 (0.31)	9.4 (0.54)
Race/ethnicity by sex															
Male															
White	85.5 (0.13)	3.8 (0.07)	10.7 (0.12)	60.9 (0.75)	8.1 (0.48)	31.0 (0.68)	79.1 (0.30)	5.2 (0.16)	15.7 (0.28)	86.7 (0.22)	3.6 (0.13)	9.7 (0.20)	92.7 (0.15)	2.3 (0.08)	5.0 (0.13)
Black	70.3 (0.40)	7.8 (0.27)	21.9 (0.36)	35.7 (1.39)	9.5 (0.79)	54.9 (1.24)	62.9 (0.70)	9.5 (0.41)	27.6 (0.68)	79.1 (0.68)	7.4 (0.46)	13.5 (0.50)	88.9 (0.67)	4.4 (0.39)	6.7 (0.59)
Hispanic	84.3 (0.21)	4.3 (0.13)	11.4 (0.18)	80.1 (0.53)	4.3 (0.25)	15.7 (0.47)	82.8 (0.41)	5.0 (0.22)	12.2 (0.39)	85.2 (0.48)	4.2 (0.28)	10.6 (0.38)	91.5 (0.47)	2.9 (0.24)	5.5 (0.37)
Asian	84.8 (0.33)	3.3 (0.16)	11.9 (0.32)	73.9 (2.18)	4.8 (1.18)	21.3 (1.95)	80.0 (1.19)	4.3 (0.61)	15.7 (1.15)	80.0 (1.05)	3.9 (0.44)	16.1 (0.97)	87.8 (0.41)	2.9 (0.21)	9.4 (0.42)
Pacific Islander	83.7 (2.02)	3.0 (0.77)	13.3 (1.76)	66.6 (7.35)	‡ (†)	30.6 (6.82)	86.6 (2.90)	4.9! (1.61)	8.5! (2.64)	83.6 (4.78)	‡ (†)	15.2 (4.55)	90.4 (4.85)	‡ (†)	‡ (†)
American Indian/Alaska Native[4]	65.2 (1.20)	8.0 (0.72)	26.8 (1.33)	40.3 (4.19)	11.1 (2.19)	48.6 (3.90)	59.7 (2.18)	9.2 (1.16)	31.1 (2.28)	78.3 (1.89)	6.9 (1.25)	14.8 (1.57)	79.2 (4.30)	‡ (†)	19.3 (4.33)
American Indian	66.6 (1.40)	8.3 (0.81)	25.0 (1.45)	42.9 (4.78)	11.8 (2.68)	45.4 (4.31)	60.6 (2.40)	9.6 (1.30)	29.9 (2.34)	78.2 (2.09)	7.2 (1.38)	14.7 (1.68)	84.6 (3.54)	‡ (†)	13.4 (3.57)
Alaska Native	51.1 (5.35)	8.3 (2.11)	40.6 (5.45)	17.9! (6.36)	17.1! (5.60)	64.9 (8.34)	58.4 (7.79)	5.8! (2.54)	35.8 (7.22)	‡ (†)	‡ (†)	‡ (†)	‡ (†)	‡ (†)	‡ (†)
Two or more races	80.1 (0.72)	5.8 (0.46)	14.1 (0.62)	52.3 (3.34)	11.2 (2.15)	36.5 (3.18)	73.2 (1.68)	8.1 (1.14)	18.7 (1.51)	80.1 (1.29)	5.6 (0.79)	14.3 (1.09)	89.8 (0.92)	3.4 (0.56)	6.7 (0.82)
Female															
White	77.9 (0.14)	3.1 (0.07)	19.0 (0.14)	40.1 (0.89)	7.4 (0.45)	52.5 (0.84)	64.1 (0.36)	5.2 (0.20)	30.8 (0.37)	76.1 (0.27)	3.6 (0.11)	20.4 (0.26)	87.8 (0.17)	1.6 (0.07)	10.6 (0.17)
Black	75.2 (0.33)	7.4 (0.20)	17.4 (0.27)	44.4 (1.38)	14.4 (1.22)	41.2 (1.36)	66.0 (0.78)	9.8 (0.44)	24.2 (0.69)	78.8 (0.63)	6.9 (0.39)	14.2 (0.50)	88.3 (0.49)	3.5 (0.30)	8.2 (0.40)
Hispanic	68.7 (0.30)	4.4 (0.13)	26.9 (0.29)	45.2 (0.80)	5.5 (0.45)	49.3 (0.83)	62.1 (0.55)	5.3 (0.31)	32.5 (0.53)	75.0 (0.46)	4.4 (0.24)	20.6 (0.41)	85.1 (0.54)	2.4 (0.21)	12.5 (0.50)
Asian	71.0 (0.46)	3.0 (0.19)	26.0 (0.46)	49.2 (2.40)	2.2! (0.79)	48.5 (2.30)	62.8 (1.85)	3.8 (0.70)	33.4 (1.85)	72.5 (1.11)	3.3 (0.50)	24.2 (1.03)	73.1 (0.53)	2.9 (0.22)	24.0 (0.50)
Pacific Islander	66.8 (2.93)	5.1 (1.25)	28.0 (2.79)	30.1! (12.45)	‡ (†)	67.3 (12.63)	60.8 (4.83)	9.6! (3.17)	29.7 (4.64)	66.5 (5.15)	4.3! (1.67)	29.2 (5.03)	88.3 (4.02)	‡ (†)	10.0! (3.61)
American Indian/Alaska Native[4]	62.8 (1.40)	7.2 (0.69)	30.0 (1.42)	30.5 (4.53)	14.6 (3.35)	54.9 (4.49)	53.8 (2.53)	9.9 (1.63)	36.3 (2.82)	70.4 (2.20)	4.9 (1.02)	24.7 (2.01)	83.1 (2.84)	2.6! (1.02)	14.3 (2.57)
American Indian	63.2 (1.42)	6.8 (0.70)	29.9 (1.45)	35.2 (5.35)	13.3 (3.52)	51.5 (5.29)	56.3 (2.56)	9.3 (1.82)	34.4 (2.75)	69.4 (2.38)	4.6 (0.93)	26.0 (2.30)	80.5 (3.25)	3.2! (1.22)	16.3 (3.10)
Alaska Native	46.5 (6.27)	16.7 (4.94)	36.8 (6.69)	‡ (†)	‡ (†)	‡ (†)	48.2 (7.29)	21.9 (5.32)	29.9 (7.34)	54.4 (11.02)	‡ (†)	29.3! (10.82)	‡ (†)	‡ (†)	‡ (†)
Two or more races	75.8 (0.73)	4.5 (0.35)	19.7 (0.70)	41.7 (4.80)	12.8 (2.90)	45.5 (4.91)	63.0 (2.21)	6.7 (1.04)	30.3 (2.08)	74.4 (1.33)	4.6 (0.63)	21.0 (1.12)	85.7 (1.00)	2.6 (0.42)	11.7 (0.83)
Nativity															
Hispanic															
U.S.-born[5]	77.4 (0.22)	5.0 (0.11)	17.6 (0.19)	56.9 (0.81)	7.1 (0.44)	36.0 (0.76)	73.0 (0.42)	6.2 (0.22)	20.8 (0.43)	79.9 (0.39)	4.7 (0.23)	15.4 (0.32)	89.8 (0.43)	2.6 (0.19)	7.5 (0.38)
Foreign-born	75.8 (0.31)	3.2 (0.13)	20.9 (0.29)	70.6 (0.59)	3.5 (0.26)	25.9 (0.55)	75.3 (0.53)	3.3 (0.21)	21.4 (0.51)	79.9 (0.61)	3.2 (0.27)	16.9 (0.59)	83.0 (0.78)	2.7 (0.27)	14.3 (0.75)
Asian															
U.S.-born[5]	83.6 (0.48)	3.5 (0.19)	12.8 (0.44)	51.6 (3.91)	5.2! (1.99)	43.2 (3.65)	72.5 (1.58)	6.0 (0.94)	21.5 (1.50)	80.6 (1.13)	3.8 (0.48)	15.6 (1.03)	87.8 (0.52)	2.9 (0.26)	9.3 (0.47)
Foreign-born	74.6 (0.35)	3.0 (0.15)	22.5 (0.35)	64.0 (1.63)	3.1 (0.69)	32.9 (1.56)	71.6 (1.43)	3.1 (0.46)	25.3 (1.41)	72.8 (1.11)	3.4 (0.46)	23.9 (1.02)	76.2 (0.42)	2.9 (0.16)	20.9 (0.43)
Citizenship status															
U.S.-born citizen	79.7 (0.08)	4.4 (0.04)	15.9 (0.08)	49.8 (0.44)	8.7 (0.25)	41.5 (0.42)	71.0 (0.22)	6.4 (0.11)	22.5 (0.20)	80.7 (0.15)	4.4 (0.07)	14.9 (0.13)	90.3 (0.10)	2.2 (0.06)	7.5 (0.08)
Naturalized citizen	80.7 (0.35)	3.5 (0.17)	15.8 (0.34)	68.2 (1.37)	3.0 (0.44)	28.7 (1.36)	75.0 (0.86)	3.4 (0.34)	21.7 (0.82)	80.3 (0.67)	4.2 (0.33)	15.4 (0.63)	86.4 (0.50)	3.2 (0.25)	10.5 (0.50)
Noncitizen	72.6 (0.25)	3.3 (0.12)	24.1 (0.24)	68.7 (0.52)	3.8 (0.27)	27.5 (0.49)	73.3 (0.48)	3.5 (0.27)	23.2 (0.46)	73.6 (0.72)	3.8 (0.31)	22.6 (0.62)	74.3 (0.43)	2.6 (0.13)	23.2 (0.43)

†Not applicable.
!Interpret data with caution. The coefficient of variation (CV) for this estimate is between 30 and 50 percent.
‡Reporting standards not met. Either there are too few cases for a reliable estimate or the coefficient of variation (CV) is 50 percent or greater.
[1]Data are for all persons with high school completion as their highest level of education, including those with equivalency credentials, such as the GED credential.
[2]Includes persons with no college degree as well as those with an associate's degree.
[3]Total includes other racial/ethnic groups not shown separately.
[4]Includes persons reporting American Indian alone, persons reporting Alaska Native alone, and persons from American Indian and/or Alaska Native tribes specified or not specified.
[5]Includes those born in the 50 states, the District of Columbia, Puerto Rico, American Samoa, Guam, the U.S. Virgin Islands, and the Northern Marianas, as well as those born abroad to U.S.-citizen parents.
NOTE: Estimates are for the entire civilian population in the given age range, including persons living in households and persons living in group quarters (e.g., college residence halls, residential treatment centers, or correctional facilities). The labor force consists of all employed persons plus those seeking employment. Detail may not sum to totals because of rounding. Race categories exclude persons of Hispanic ethnicity.
SOURCE: U.S. Department of Commerce, Census Bureau, American Community Survey (ACS), 2018. (This table was prepared April 2020.)

Table 501.50. Employment to population ratios of persons 16 to 64 years old, by age group and highest level of educational attainment: Selected years, 1975 through 2019

[Standard errors appear in parentheses]

Age group and highest level of educational attainment	1975	1980	1985	1990	1995	2000	2005	2010	2012	2014	2015	2016	2017	2018	2019
1	2	3	4	5	6	7	8	9	10	11	12	13	14	15	16
16 to 19 years old, all education levels[1]	**— (†)**	**— (†)**	**— (†)**	**60.8 (2.03)**	**58.0 (2.13)**	**62.6 (2.09)**	**53.7 (1.40)**	**43.2 (1.30)**	**45.8 (1.43)**	**51.0 (1.67)**	**49.2 (1.36)**	**50.4 (1.55)**	**56.4 (1.57)**	**55.7 (1.48)**	**57.6 (1.37)**
Less than high school completion	— (†)	— (†)	— (†)	44.2 (3.08)	44.0 (3.13)	52.2 (3.19)	39.4 (2.01)	29.4 (1.83)	28.5 (2.05)	39.7 (2.63)	35.3 (2.03)	35.6 (2.05)	39.6 (2.27)	40.4 (2.52)	41.1 (2.39)
High school completion[2]	— (†)	— (†)	— (†)	74.2 (2.54)	70.1 (2.99)	70.1 (2.92)	65.0 (2.04)	51.1 (1.84)	53.6 (1.90)	58.5 (2.22)	56.1 (1.83)	58.7 (2.28)	66.4 (1.96)	62.9 (1.96)	65.5 (1.87)
At least some college	— (†)	— (†)	— (†)	76.8 (9.32)	71.6 (6.38)	78.2 (6.22)	66.6 (4.54)	57.5 (3.99)	64.3 (4.07)	60.5 (5.27)	65.7 (3.40)	69.1 (3.66)	69.6 (3.94)	70.9 (3.44)	74.7 (3.60)
20 to 24 years old, all education levels[1]	**— (†)**	**— (†)**	**— (†)**	**75.6 (0.90)**	**73.7 (0.93)**	**77.4 (0.93)**	**73.2 (0.66)**	**65.5 (0.72)**	**68.7 (0.67)**	**69.4 (0.74)**	**71.4 (0.66)**	**72.3 (0.59)**	**75.9 (0.64)**	**76.3 (0.59)**	**77.4 (0.59)**
Less than high school completion	— (†)	— (†)	— (†)	54.4 (2.29)	52.7 (2.41)	60.8 (2.43)	55.7 (1.27)	44.4 (1.58)	47.7 (1.95)	46.6 (2.62)	51.4 (2.17)	48.0 (2.08)	54.5 (2.30)	51.4 (2.25)	57.6 (2.49)
High school completion[2]	— (†)	— (†)	— (†)	76.6 (1.26)	72.2 (1.46)	76.5 (1.46)	72.3 (0.91)	61.5 (1.01)	64.2 (0.99)	63.7 (1.31)	66.9 (1.01)	69.4 (1.03)	72.1 (1.05)	72.4 (0.94)	73.4 (0.96)
Some college, no bachelor's degree[3]	— (†)	— (†)	— (†)	85.6 (1.69)	83.6 (1.52)	86.6 (1.49)	80.3 (1.19)	72.9 (1.27)	75.3 (1.19)	75.0 (1.29)	76.4 (1.03)	76.7 (1.02)	80.3 (0.99)	82.7 (1.07)	80.5 (1.05)
Bachelor's or higher degree	— (†)	— (†)	— (†)	93.3 (1.57)	90.9 (1.76)	87.8 (2.07)	89.3 (1.16)	86.5 (1.37)	87.3 (1.16)	88.1 (1.47)	88.9 (1.05)	88.1 (1.12)	89.3 (1.04)	87.7 (1.28)	90.4 (1.14)
25 to 64 years old, all education levels	**65.8 (0.33)**	**70.2 (0.30)**	**71.6 (0.30)**	**75.0 (0.29)**	**75.5 (0.28)**	**77.7 (0.27)**	**75.0 (0.19)**	**71.5 (0.19)**	**71.7 (0.18)**	**72.3 (0.26)**	**73.1 (0.19)**	**73.8 (0.18)**	**74.4 (0.17)**	**74.9 (0.18)**	**75.6 (0.18)**
Less than high school completion	55.3 (0.62)	55.5 (0.66)	53.1 (0.74)	54.9 (0.80)	53.8 (0.85)	57.8 (0.91)	57.2 (0.51)	52.1 (0.60)	52.9 (0.60)	54.9 (0.78)	54.7 (0.58)	56.6 (0.62)	55.6 (0.65)	56.8 (0.61)	56.1 (0.58)
High school completion[2]	65.7 (0.53)	70.4 (0.48)	70.7 (0.48)	74.4 (0.46)	73.3 (0.49)	75.5 (0.49)	71.5 (0.34)	67.0 (0.36)	66.5 (0.35)	67.0 (0.44)	67.3 (0.37)	67.6 (0.39)	68.4 (0.36)	69.0 (0.36)	69.9 (0.35)
Some college, no bachelor's degree[3]	71.7 (0.86)	76.1 (0.70)	77.8 (0.66)	80.2 (0.60)	79.5 (0.51)	80.7 (0.50)	77.7 (0.33)	72.7 (0.30)	72.2 (0.30)	72.6 (0.44)	74.1 (0.32)	73.9 (0.32)	75.3 (0.30)	75.0 (0.33)	76.0 (0.31)
Bachelor's or higher degree	82.5 (0.68)	84.5 (0.55)	85.6 (0.51)	86.7 (0.47)	86.5 (0.44)	86.4 (0.42)	83.7 (0.26)	81.6 (0.24)	82.1 (0.24)	82.0 (0.34)	82.8 (0.26)	83.5 (0.23)	83.5 (0.25)	83.8 (0.27)	84.3 (0.27)
25 to 34 years old, all education levels	**67.7 (0.59)**	**74.5 (0.49)**	**76.2 (0.48)**	**78.6 (0.47)**	**78.5 (0.48)**	**81.6 (0.49)**	**76.8 (0.31)**	**73.2 (0.34)**	**73.8 (0.31)**	**74.5 (0.43)**	**76.0 (0.35)**	**76.8 (0.38)**	**78.1 (0.38)**	**78.7 (0.35)**	**79.4 (0.34)**
Less than high school completion	52.9 (1.43)	58.3 (1.46)	57.0 (1.54)	60.3 (1.50)	59.8 (1.59)	64.1 (1.76)	62.0 (0.95)	55.1 (0.95)	56.2 (1.14)	57.8 (1.37)	56.5 (1.11)	59.5 (1.30)	57.1 (1.36)	59.1 (1.50)	57.4 (1.41)
High school completion[2]	65.5 (0.92)	72.0 (0.81)	74.3 (0.78)	77.7 (0.74)	77.0 (0.84)	80.2 (0.91)	73.1 (0.60)	68.1 (0.72)	68.7 (0.75)	68.2 (0.73)	70.4 (0.72)	70.1 (0.79)	71.8 (0.70)	72.5 (0.73)	73.6 (0.72)
Some college, no bachelor's degree[3]	71.7 (1.33)	77.8 (1.01)	80.1 (0.97)	81.6 (0.96)	80.5 (0.87)	82.8 (0.90)	79.4 (0.54)	72.9 (0.57)	72.7 (0.68)	74.5 (0.74)	76.4 (0.60)	76.6 (0.65)	79.7 (0.54)	78.9 (0.60)	79.7 (0.57)
Bachelor's or higher degree	82.0 (1.04)	85.4 (0.82)	86.6 (0.79)	88.1 (0.76)	88.1 (0.75)	89.0 (0.73)	84.4 (0.52)	84.0 (0.49)	84.3 (0.45)	84.0 (0.59)	84.8 (0.48)	85.6 (0.49)	85.8 (0.47)	86.4 (0.46)	86.9 (0.45)
35 to 44 years old, all education levels	**70.3 (0.66)**	**76.5 (0.58)**	**78.1 (0.54)**	**81.6 (0.48)**	**80.2 (0.46)**	**81.8 (0.45)**	**79.9 (0.26)**	**76.0 (0.30)**	**76.9 (0.35)**	**77.1 (0.40)**	**78.3 (0.31)**	**78.5 (0.33)**	**79.2 (0.31)**	**80.1 (0.30)**	**80.3 (0.31)**
Less than high school completion	61.4 (1.31)	63.4 (1.39)	60.0 (1.58)	62.5 (1.69)	58.6 (1.66)	64.8 (1.64)	64.9 (0.93)	58.2 (1.13)	59.6 (1.13)	61.3 (1.25)	62.3 (0.84)	64.2 (1.00)	64.0 (1.01)	64.5 (1.13)	63.3 (1.11)
High school completion[2]	69.6 (1.02)	76.6 (0.90)	76.6 (0.88)	80.0 (0.80)	78.6 (0.82)	81.0 (0.79)	78.0 (0.52)	72.4 (0.64)	72.1 (0.68)	72.6 (0.80)	72.5 (0.63)	72.0 (0.76)	73.8 (0.66)	74.4 (0.68)	74.6 (0.71)
Some college, no bachelor's degree[3]	74.5 (1.74)	80.9 (1.33)	81.6 (1.15)	85.0 (0.93)	83.3 (0.81)	84.4 (0.80)	82.0 (0.48)	76.9 (0.53)	78.2 (0.61)	77.3 (0.68)	79.6 (0.53)	79.4 (0.58)	79.7 (0.63)	80.8 (0.55)	81.2 (0.58)
Bachelor's or higher degree	84.5 (1.31)	87.1 (1.00)	88.8 (0.80)	89.5 (0.72)	88.5 (0.71)	87.6 (0.74)	85.9 (0.41)	84.7 (0.39)	85.0 (0.41)	85.0 (0.57)	86.7 (0.39)	86.3 (0.39)	86.1 (0.35)	86.8 (0.37)	87.3 (0.39)
45 to 54 years old, all education levels	**68.4 (0.65)**	**71.7 (0.65)**	**73.5 (0.67)**	**77.6 (0.62)**	**78.8 (0.55)**	**81.2 (0.50)**	**78.4 (0.32)**	**74.7 (0.35)**	**74.6 (0.30)**	**76.2 (0.43)**	**75.9 (0.33)**	**77.0 (0.36)**	**77.3 (0.38)**	**77.9 (0.34)**	**79.0 (0.34)**
Less than high school completion	59.8 (1.14)	61.8 (1.24)	58.7 (1.52)	60.7 (1.63)	58.4 (1.79)	60.3 (1.89)	59.0 (1.04)	52.5 (1.05)	54.7 (1.06)	59.4 (1.50)	56.8 (1.16)	58.8 (1.13)	58.8 (1.22)	59.0 (1.20)	60.4 (1.20)
High school completion[2]	68.8 (1.03)	72.0 (1.02)	74.0 (1.03)	77.5 (0.97)	75.9 (1.01)	78.2 (0.95)	75.1 (0.64)	71.0 (0.65)	70.4 (0.62)	70.7 (0.84)	70.9 (0.63)	71.7 (0.68)	72.2 (0.66)	73.0 (0.67)	74.0 (0.76)
Some college, no bachelor's degree[3]	74.7 (1.81)	76.5 (1.72)	79.2 (1.63)	81.9 (1.38)	81.7 (1.03)	83.4 (0.91)	80.4 (0.57)	77.3 (0.54)	76.2 (0.53)	77.4 (0.76)	77.1 (0.60)	77.2 (0.71)	78.6 (0.61)	78.5 (0.62)	79.6 (0.58)
Bachelor's or higher degree	87.1 (1.36)	87.3 (1.21)	87.9 (1.16)	89.4 (0.97)	89.5 (0.78)	89.7 (0.71)	87.5 (0.45)	84.4 (0.45)	84.7 (0.48)	85.9 (0.54)	85.7 (0.43)	87.1 (0.44)	86.2 (0.46)	86.6 (0.48)	87.1 (0.47)
55 to 64 years old, all education levels	**54.6 (0.77)**	**54.1 (0.73)**	**52.1 (0.77)**	**53.4 (0.81)**	**55.0 (0.82)**	**58.1 (0.79)**	**60.8 (0.48)**	**60.6 (0.41)**	**60.6 (0.41)**	**60.9 (0.52)**	**61.9 (0.37)**	**62.6 (0.37)**	**63.0 (0.40)**	**62.9 (0.38)**	**63.7 (0.43)**
Less than high school completion	48.5 (1.11)	43.2 (1.16)	41.8 (1.29)	39.5 (1.46)	38.1 (1.67)	40.4 (1.84)	39.4 (1.13)	40.0 (1.19)	39.1 (1.08)	39.6 (1.34)	42.4 (1.12)	43.6 (1.27)	42.5 (1.07)	45.4 (1.09)	44.1 (1.22)
High school completion[2]	56.5 (1.32)	57.5 (1.19)	52.1 (1.22)	54.0 (1.29)	53.7 (1.34)	55.4 (1.34)	55.3 (0.79)	55.1 (0.71)	54.6 (0.75)	57.6 (0.90)	56.9 (0.74)	57.7 (0.75)	57.7 (0.73)	58.3 (0.72)	59.3 (0.67)
Some college, no bachelor's degree[3]	62.6 (2.48)	62.5 (2.08)	58.9 (2.21)	60.4 (2.12)	62.0 (1.74)	62.4 (1.64)	64.8 (0.90)	61.8 (0.76)	61.2 (0.70)	60.5 (0.99)	63.2 (0.68)	62.7 (0.68)	63.2 (0.70)	62.2 (0.75)	63.9 (0.74)
Bachelor's or higher degree	72.6 (2.34)	71.9 (1.96)	71.3 (1.83)	70.5 (1.79)	70.0 (1.72)	71.9 (1.49)	73.5 (0.74)	72.0 (0.65)	73.1 (0.66)	71.7 (0.90)	72.3 (0.62)	73.4 (0.60)	74.4 (0.71)	73.6 (0.65)	74.0 (0.71)

—Not available.
†Not applicable.
[1]Data for 16- to 19-year-olds and 20- to 24-year-olds exclude persons enrolled in school.
[2]Includes equivalency credentials, such as the GED credential.
[3]Includes persons with no college degree as well as those with an associate's degree.

NOTE: Data are based on sample surveys of the noninstitutionalized population, which excludes persons living in institutions (e.g., prisons or nursing facilities); this table includes only data on the civilian population (excludes all military personnel). For each age group, the employment to population ratio is the number of persons in that age group who are employed as a percentage of the civilian population in that age group.
SOURCE: U.S. Department of Commerce, Census Bureau, Current Population Survey (CPS), Annual Social and Economic Supplement, selected years, 1975 through 2019. (This table was prepared October 2019.)

Table 501.60. Employment to population ratios of males 16 to 64 years old, by age group and highest level of educational attainment: Selected years, 1975 through 2020

[Standard errors appear in parentheses]

Age group and highest level of educational attainment	1975	1980	1985	1990	1995	2000	2005	2010	2014	2015	2016	20
1	2	3	4	5	6	7	8	9	10	11	12	
16 to 19 years old, all education levels[1]	**--- (†)**	**--- (†)**	**--- (†)**	**65.3 (2.82)**	**63.6 (2.87)**	**69.2 (2.70)**	**56.2 (2.10)**	**44.0 (1.72)**	**51.9 (2.37)**	**51.2 (1.92)**	**51.6 (2.00)**	**58.0 (1.9**
Less than high school completion	--- (†)	--- (†)	--- (†)	51.5 (4.20)	50.6 (4.26)	63.1 (4.09)	47.0 (3.07)	31.5 (2.64)	43.6 (3.64)	37.2 (2.72)	36.5 (2.85)	42.6 (3.0
High school completion[2]	--- (†)	--- (†)	--- (†)	78.7 (3.51)	76.1 (3.87)	74.4 (3.77)	63.1 (2.88)	51.0 (2.37)	58.1 (3.28)	58.7 (2.49)	60.5 (3.12)	67.2 (2.6
At least some college	--- (†)	--- (†)	--- (†)	83.1 (13.41)	75.9 (8.99)	77.0 (9.81)	70.4 (5.98)	61.4 (6.00)	57.6 (8.04)	63.9 (4.71)	75.8 (4.64)	74.7 (4.7
20 to 24 years old, all education levels[1]	**--- (†)**	**--- (†)**	**--- (†)**	**83.5 (1.10)**	**81.2 (1.16)**	**83.3 (1.16)**	**78.9 (0.86)**	**68.4 (0.97)**	**72.4 (1.04)**	**74.9 (0.98)**	**75.1 (0.92)**	**78.4 (0.8**
Less than high school completion	--- (†)	--- (†)	--- (†)	70.0 (2.84)	69.3 (2.99)	72.1 (2.93)	69.5 (1.80)	52.9 (2.06)	58.3 (3.16)	60.3 (2.76)	55.3 (2.98)	64.9 (2.8
High school completion[2]	--- (†)	--- (†)	--- (†)	84.6 (1.50)	81.1 (1.73)	82.7 (1.78)	78.0 (1.21)	66.0 (1.31)	66.6 (1.77)	71.1 (1.39)	73.2 (1.41)	75.8 (1.3
Some college, no bachelor's degree[3]	--- (†)	--- (†)	--- (†)	91.8 (1.98)	87.5 (1.97)	92.6 (1.65)	84.6 (1.43)	74.8 (1.71)	78.6 (1.82)	79.9 (1.57)	80.4 (1.71)	83.1 (1.6
Bachelor's or higher degree[4]	--- (†)	--- (†)	--- (†)	94.9 (2.07)	91.1 (2.70)	89.1 (3.07)	90.6 (1.82)	86.3 (2.04)	90.6 (1.93)	90.6 (1.71)	89.0 (1.54)	88.6 (1.7
25 to 64 years old, all education levels	**84.6 (0.36)**	**85.0 (0.34)**	**83.1 (0.36)**	**84.5 (0.34)**	**83.0 (0.34)**	**84.6 (0.33)**	**81.9 (0.25)**	**76.3 (0.27)**	**78.2 (0.35)**	**79.4 (0.26)**	**80.0 (0.25)**	**80.3 (0.2**
Less than high school completion	74.3 (0.77)	72.4 (0.84)	67.6 (0.98)	67.9 (1.04)	64.2 (1.13)	69.6 (1.17)	69.7 (0.70)	61.2 (0.93)	66.3 (1.04)	67.2 (0.75)	68.4 (0.79)	66.5 (0.8
High school completion[2]	87.2 (0.56)	87.0 (0.54)	83.5 (0.58)	85.1 (0.55)	81.9 (0.61)	82.9 (0.61)	78.6 (0.44)	71.7 (0.50)	73.6 (0.59)	74.7 (0.48)	74.7 (0.51)	75.5 (0.5
Some college, no bachelor's degree[3]	88.8 (0.83)	88.3 (0.73)	87.1 (0.75)	87.9 (0.70)	86.1 (0.63)	86.1 (0.63)	83.7 (0.44)	76.6 (0.42)	77.5 (0.59)	79.6 (0.48)	79.2 (0.48)	80.2 (0.4
Bachelor's or higher degree[4]	93.8 (0.55)	93.6 (0.48)	92.4 (0.50)	92.5 (0.48)	91.4 (0.48)	91.8 (0.47)	89.4 (0.35)	86.9 (0.33)	87.7 (0.42)	88.0 (0.32)	89.3 (0.33)	89.1 (0.3
25 to 34 years old, all education levels	**87.4 (0.59)**	**88.1 (0.52)**	**86.9 (0.54)**	**87.9 (0.52)**	**87.1 (0.55)**	**89.4 (0.55)**	**84.6 (0.40)**	**78.4 (0.48)**	**80.9 (0.56)**	**83.2 (0.44)**	**83.4 (0.50)**	**83.7 (0.5**
Less than high school completion	76.2 (1.78)	76.3 (1.80)	75.1 (1.87)	75.6 (1.77)	73.7 (1.91)	78.4 (2.04)	78.1 (1.23)	66.6 (1.42)	73.1 (1.88)	73.1 (1.59)	75.0 (1.69)	69.5 (1.8
High school completion[2]	88.4 (0.93)	88.4 (0.86)	86.1 (0.88)	88.6 (0.80)	86.6 (0.94)	89.1 (0.98)	81.7 (0.77)	73.0 (0.85)	77.2 (0.93)	79.6 (0.87)	77.6 (0.97)	79.9 (0.8
Some college, no bachelor's degree[3]	87.7 (1.31)	88.5 (1.06)	89.7 (1.04)	89.7 (1.08)	89.6 (0.98)	90.7 (1.02)	86.4 (0.82)	78.7 (0.83)	79.1 (1.25)	83.0 (0.86)	83.0 (0.90)	84.8 (0.8
Bachelor's or higher degree[4]	93.5 (0.87)	93.4 (0.76)	92.2 (0.85)	93.1 (0.83)	93.0 (0.83)	93.6 (0.82)	89.6 (0.69)	89.2 (0.74)	88.8 (0.78)	89.6 (0.59)	91.1 (0.59)	89.8 (0.6
35 to 44 years old, all education levels	**90.1 (0.61)**	**91.1 (0.55)**	**89.1 (0.57)**	**90.2 (0.52)**	**86.8 (0.55)**	**88.8 (0.52)**	**87.2 (0.37)**	**82.3 (0.42)**	**83.8 (0.56)**	**85.6 (0.42)**	**85.9 (0.49)**	**86.6 (0.4**
Less than high school completion	81.6 (1.48)	80.1 (1.65)	74.6 (1.99)	73.9 (2.13)	66.7 (2.15)	76.5 (2.00)	75.9 (1.26)	69.5 (1.61)	73.9 (1.75)	76.9 (1.24)	77.3 (1.48)	77.0 (1.4
High school completion[2]	91.3 (0.95)	92.3 (0.85)	88.6 (1.00)	89.1 (0.91)	85.9 (0.98)	87.1 (0.93)	83.7 (0.71)	77.6 (0.92)	78.2 (1.17)	80.4 (0.82)	80.2 (1.09)	81.9 (0.8
Some college, no bachelor's degree[3]	93.8 (1.34)	93.8 (1.13)	90.2 (1.25)	92.6 (0.97)	88.8 (0.99)	90.2 (0.95)	89.4 (0.60)	82.7 (0.73)	83.9 (1.04)	85.4 (0.85)	85.6 (0.85)	85.9 (0.8
Bachelor's or higher degree[4]	97.0 (0.77)	97.1 (0.65)	96.3 (0.62)	96.3 (0.59)	95.1 (0.66)	95.1 (0.67)	94.6 (0.45)	91.9 (0.55)	92.4 (0.75)	93.6 (0.53)	93.6 (0.52)	93.6 (0.4
45 to 54 years old, all education levels	**86.6 (0.68)**	**87.4 (0.67)**	**85.8 (0.76)**	**87.1 (0.70)**	**84.9 (0.68)**	**86.5 (0.62)**	**83.9 (0.45)**	**78.3 (0.50)**	**81.8 (0.61)**	**81.3 (0.46)**	**82.7 (0.46)**	**82.8 (0.4**
Less than high school completion	78.2 (1.34)	79.6 (1.42)	73.2 (1.90)	74.3 (2.05)	66.4 (2.41)	68.5 (2.52)	69.9 (1.55)	58.8 (1.48)	67.3 (1.96)	65.0 (1.56)	68.8 (1.55)	68.3 (1.8
High school completion[2]	90.3 (1.01)	89.3 (1.08)	87.3 (1.18)	87.5 (1.15)	82.1 (1.35)	84.6 (1.21)	80.7 (0.86)	74.6 (0.91)	76.4 (1.12)	76.7 (0.86)	78.1 (0.85)	77.9 (0.8
Some college, no bachelor's degree[3]	91.0 (1.66)	89.4 (1.78)	89.3 (1.76)	88.9 (1.58)	87.2 (1.29)	86.4 (1.18)	84.5 (0.84)	79.4 (0.80)	83.5 (0.95)	82.4 (0.87)	82.4 (0.86)	83.3 (0.8
Bachelor's or higher degree[4]	95.6 (1.02)	96.0 (0.88)	94.8 (1.00)	95.2 (0.88)	93.8 (0.80)	94.6 (0.72)	92.2 (0.53)	89.4 (0.58)	91.4 (0.65)	91.2 (0.50)	92.5 (0.53)	92.0 (0.5
55 to 64 years old, all education levels	**71.3 (1.00)**	**69.7 (0.98)**	**64.6 (1.05)**	**64.0 (1.12)**	**63.2 (1.13)**	**64.9 (1.09)**	**67.3 (0.66)**	**64.4 (0.61)**	**65.7 (0.76)**	**67.1 (0.53)**	**67.7 (0.51)**	**67.9 (0.5**
Less than high school completion	64.5 (1.51)	58.3 (1.65)	53.4 (1.85)	49.6 (2.13)	46.9 (2.46)	51.2 (2.71)	48.8 (1.70)	45.0 (1.81)	48.4 (1.96)	52.6 (1.61)	51.9 (1.84)	50.3 (1.5
High school completion[2]	74.9 (1.73)	74.6 (1.61)	66.1 (1.80)	66.0 (1.89)	62.7 (1.99)	61.0 (1.97)	61.8 (1.15)	58.5 (1.12)	62.6 (1.34)	62.2 (1.03)	63.1 (0.99)	63.4 (1.0
Some college, no bachelor's degree[3]	80.8 (2.87)	77.2 (2.53)	67.5 (3.01)	67.7 (2.93)	67.8 (2.41)	66.6 (2.31)	69.6 (1.31)	63.9 (1.10)	63.3 (1.29)	67.6 (1.00)	65.9 (1.06)	66.4 (1.0
Bachelor's or higher degree[4]	84.1 (2.52)	83.8 (2.04)	80.7 (1.98)	77.9 (2.03)	74.9 (2.04)	77.0 (1.82)	78.6 (0.89)	76.2 (0.82)	77.2 (1.18)	76.8 (0.87)	79.2 (0.78)	79.8 (0.9

—Not available.

†Not applicable.

[1] Data for 16- to 19-year-olds and 20- to 24-year-olds exclude persons enrolled in school.

[2] Data for years prior to 1992 are for persons with 4 or more years of high school. Data for later years are for high school completers--i.e., those persons who graduated from high school with a diploma as well as those who completed high school through equivalency programs, such as a GED program.

[3] Includes persons with no college degree as well as those with an associate's degree.

[4] Data for years prior to 1992 are for persons with 4 or more years of college, even if they did not complete a degree.

NOTE: Data are based on sample surveys of the noninstitutionalized population, which excludes persons living in institutions (e.g., prisons or nursing facilities); this table includes only data on the civilian population (excludes all military personnel). For each age group, the employment to population ratio of males is the number of males in that age group who are employed as a percentage of the male civilian population in that age group. Caution should be used when comparing 2020 estimates to those of prior years due to the impact that the coronavirus pandemic had on interviewing and response rates. For additional information about the impact of the coronavirus pandemic on the Current Population Survey data collection, please see https://www2.census.gov/programs-surveys/cps/techdocs/cpsmar20.pdf.

SOURCE: U.S. Department of Commerce, Census Bureau, Current Population Survey (CPS), Annual Social and Economic Supplement, selected years, 1975 through 2020. (This table was prepared October 2020.)

Table 501.70. Employment to population ratios of females 16 to 64 years old, by age group and highest level of educational attainment: Selected years, 1975 through 2020

[Standard errors appear in parentheses]

Age group and highest level of educational attainment	1975		1980		1985		1990		1995		2000		2005		2010		2014		2015		2016	
1	2		3		4		5		6		7		8		9		10		11		12	
16 to 19 years old, all education levels[1]	---	(†)	---	(†)	---	(†)	56.6	(2.72)	52.2	(2.93)	55.1	(2.98)	51.0	(1.88)	42.3	(1.88)	50.0	(2.39)	46.9	(1.88)	48.9	(2.01)	54.6	(2
Less than high school completion	---	(†)	---	(†)	---	(†)	36.0	(4.13)	36.5	(4.23)	38.9	(4.42)	30.3	(2.72)	26.8	(2.75)	34.5	(3.67)	33.3	(2.82)	34.4	(2.84)	36.0	(3
High school completion[2]	---	(†)	---	(†)	---	(†)	70.5	(3.38)	64.1	(4.22)	65.2	(4.22)	67.0	(2.60)	51.2	(2.99)	59.0	(3.35)	52.8	(2.83)	56.5	(2.90)	65.6	(3
At least some college	---	(†)	---	(†)	---	(†)	73.1	(11.73)	68.3	(8.37)	79.1	(7.56)	63.6	(6.23)	54.4	(5.29)	63.0	(7.14)	67.7	(5.08)	64.5	(5.00)	65.0	(5
20 to 24 years old, all education levels[1]	---	(†)	---	(†)	---	(†)	68.2	(1.29)	66.3	(1.34)	71.5	(1.35)	67.0	(1.01)	62.4	(1.01)	66.3	(1.06)	67.7	(0.88)	69.2	(0.87)	73.2	(0
Less than high school completion	---	(†)	---	(†)	---	(†)	36.7	(3.08)	33.6	(3.18)	46.2	(3.57)	38.5	(2.20)	33.3	(2.50)	30.5	(3.57)	42.0	(3.18)	38.3	(2.77)	39.5	(3
High school completion[2]	---	(†)	---	(†)	---	(†)	68.8	(1.84)	62.2	(2.19)	70.0	(2.15)	65.0	(1.47)	55.6	(1.43)	60.2	(1.86)	61.6	(1.41)	64.4	(1.56)	66.9	(1
Some college, no bachelor's degree[3]	---	(†)	---	(†)	---	(†)	80.9	(2.39)	80.3	(2.12)	81.4	(2.23)	76.6	(1.72)	71.2	(1.65)	71.6	(1.89)	72.9	(1.54)	73.0	(1.49)	77.6	(1
Bachelor's or higher degree[4]	---	(†)	---	(†)	---	(†)	92.0	(2.12)	90.8	(2.19)	86.9	(2.61)	88.4	(1.53)	86.7	(1.67)	86.3	(1.96)	87.6	(1.42)	87.5	(1.54)	89.8	(1
25 to 64 years old, all education levels	48.5	(0.46)	56.5	(0.44)	60.8	(0.43)	66.0	(0.42)	68.3	(0.40)	71.2	(0.39)	68.4	(0.23)	66.9	(0.23)	66.6	(0.32)	67.1	(0.24)	67.8	(0.24)	68.8	(0
Less than high school completion	37.7	(0.80)	39.8	(0.86)	39.1	(0.97)	41.8	(1.06)	43.2	(1.15)	45.8	(1.24)	43.4	(0.72)	41.6	(0.81)	41.5	(0.89)	40.5	(0.81)	43.2	(0.84)	43.1	(0
High school completion[2]	50.1	(0.70)	58.2	(0.65)	60.8	(0.65)	65.6	(0.64)	65.7	(0.69)	68.6	(0.70)	64.2	(0.44)	61.9	(0.44)	59.7	(0.58)	59.1	(0.48)	59.5	(0.54)	60.2	(0
Some college, no bachelor's degree[3]	53.8	(1.30)	63.7	(1.07)	69.0	(0.98)	73.2	(0.88)	73.8	(0.71)	76.0	(0.70)	72.8	(0.42)	69.4	(0.45)	68.3	(0.58)	69.3	(0.45)	69.3	(0.43)	71.0	(0
Bachelor's or higher degree[4]	65.6	(1.29)	71.8	(1.01)	76.7	(0.88)	79.8	(0.78)	80.8	(0.71)	80.8	(0.66)	78.1	(0.40)	76.9	(0.36)	77.1	(0.47)	78.2	(0.35)	78.4	(0.33)	78.8	(0
25 to 34 years old, all education levels	49.3	(0.83)	61.6	(0.73)	65.9	(0.72)	69.6	(0.70)	70.2	(0.71)	74.1	(0.74)	69.0	(0.48)	68.0	(0.44)	68.2	(0.55)	69.0	(0.51)	70.3	(0.51)	72.6	(0
Less than high school completion	33.7	(1.74)	42.3	(1.91)	38.7	(2.05)	42.5	(2.12)	43.5	(2.25)	47.6	(2.56)	42.7	(1.44)	40.2	(1.35)	40.2	(1.86)	36.5	(1.73)	41.2	(1.73)	41.5	(1
High school completion[2]	48.1	(1.22)	59.4	(1.12)	63.9	(1.11)	67.5	(1.11)	67.2	(1.27)	70.7	(1.43)	62.5	(0.99)	61.4	(1.14)	56.3	(1.19)	58.6	(1.08)	60.4	(1.11)	61.5	(1
Some college, no bachelor's degree[3]	53.6	(2.06)	66.3	(1.58)	71.0	(1.46)	74.5	(1.40)	73.0	(1.26)	76.3	(1.31)	73.0	(0.81)	67.7	(0.80)	70.3	(0.91)	70.6	(0.83)	70.9	(0.90)	74.9	(0
Bachelor's or higher degree[4]	66.3	(1.88)	75.5	(1.42)	80.6	(1.26)	83.2	(1.18)	83.4	(1.16)	84.7	(1.11)	80.1	(0.72)	79.9	(0.63)	80.2	(0.77)	80.9	(0.67)	81.1	(0.70)	82.5	(0
35 to 44 years old, all education levels	51.9	(0.95)	62.8	(0.87)	67.7	(0.80)	73.3	(0.72)	73.8	(0.68)	75.1	(0.67)	72.8	(0.38)	69.9	(0.42)	70.7	(0.57)	71.3	(0.42)	71.5	(0.43)	72.1	(0
Less than high school completion	42.8	(1.76)	48.2	(1.90)	46.4	(2.13)	51.0	(2.35)	49.7	(2.33)	52.5	(2.35)	51.5	(1.33)	44.8	(1.54)	45.6	(1.61)	45.5	(1.44)	49.1	(1.56)	48.6	(1
High school completion[2]	53.9	(1.38)	64.7	(1.28)	67.8	(1.22)	72.7	(1.13)	71.7	(1.19)	74.7	(1.18)	71.6	(0.74)	66.3	(0.87)	65.8	(1.07)	62.8	(0.99)	61.8	(1.00)	63.7	(1
Some college, no bachelor's degree[3]	55.1	(2.67)	67.8	(2.14)	73.6	(1.73)	77.9	(1.44)	78.5	(1.16)	79.4	(1.16)	76.1	(0.67)	72.2	(0.74)	71.7	(1.06)	74.5	(0.70)	73.9	(0.83)	74.2	(0
Bachelor's or higher degree[4]	63.2	(2.73)	73.0	(1.97)	78.5	(1.53)	81.2	(1.30)	81.5	(1.19)	80.2	(1.20)	78.1	(0.66)	78.3	(0.59)	79.0	(0.80)	81.0	(0.57)	80.4	(0.55)	80.1	(0
45 to 54 years old, all education levels	51.5	(0.93)	57.1	(0.94)	62.1	(0.98)	68.6	(0.92)	72.9	(0.80)	76.0	(0.73)	73.2	(0.40)	71.3	(0.44)	70.8	(0.58)	70.8	(0.46)	71.6	(0.48)	72.2	(0
Less than high school completion	41.5	(1.55)	43.9	(1.71)	44.3	(2.06)	47.6	(2.22)	50.6	(2.43)	52.3	(2.57)	47.8	(1.40)	45.2	(1.61)	49.6	(2.11)	47.3	(1.50)	47.2	(1.49)	47.7	(1
High school completion[2]	53.8	(1.37)	60.2	(1.37)	64.2	(1.41)	69.9	(1.35)	71.1	(1.36)	72.9	(1.33)	69.5	(0.83)	67.1	(0.72)	64.8	(1.17)	64.5	(0.93)	64.7	(0.97)	65.6	(0
Some college, no bachelor's degree[3]	58.1	(2.78)	64.7	(2.56)	69.7	(2.45)	75.2	(2.08)	76.9	(1.46)	80.6	(1.28)	76.9	(0.72)	75.5	(0.74)	72.6	(1.03)	72.8	(0.80)	73.0	(0.95)	74.8	(0
Bachelor's or higher degree[4]	72.2	(2.87)	72.3	(2.55)	77.3	(2.24)	81.8	(1.76)	83.8	(1.36)	84.5	(1.17)	82.8	(0.72)	79.7	(0.69)	80.6	(0.83)	80.8	(0.63)	82.3	(0.66)	81.0	(0
55 to 64 years old, all education levels	39.7	(0.99)	40.5	(0.94)	41.1	(0.99)	44.0	(1.05)	47.5	(1.08)	51.9	(1.06)	54.8	(0.61)	57.1	(0.53)	56.4	(0.63)	57.0	(0.49)	57.9	(0.52)	58.4	(0
Less than high school completion	33.5	(1.39)	29.4	(1.41)	31.2	(1.60)	30.5	(1.80)	30.3	(2.07)	30.9	(2.26)	30.5	(1.33)	35.1	(1.54)	30.4	(1.69)	32.1	(1.42)	34.9	(1.53)	34.8	(1
High school completion[2]	42.6	(1.65)	45.8	(1.48)	42.8	(1.48)	45.7	(1.60)	47.5	(1.66)	51.3	(1.69)	50.5	(0.95)	52.2	(0.92)	52.9	(1.09)	51.8	(0.99)	52.6	(1.06)	52.2	(0
Some college, no bachelor's degree[3]	45.9	(3.37)	48.2	(2.87)	51.1	(2.95)	54.1	(2.81)	57.0	(2.32)	58.8	(2.17)	60.9	(1.06)	59.9	(1.08)	58.2	(1.19)	59.4	(0.92)	60.0	(0.94)	60.6	(0
Bachelor's or higher degree[4]	57.8	(3.72)	54.0	(3.27)	55.1	(3.18)	58.6	(2.98)	61.9	(2.81)	65.1	(2.28)	67.5	(1.22)	67.5	(0.98)	66.6	(1.25)	68.1	(0.86)	68.1	(0.90)	69.5	(0

---Not available.

†Not applicable.

[1] Data for 16- to 19-year-olds and 20- to 24-year-olds exclude persons enrolled in school.

[2] Data for years prior to 1992 are for persons with 4 or more years of high school. Data for later years are for high school completers--i.e., those persons who graduated from high school with a diploma as well as those who completed high school through equivalency programs, such as a GED program.

[3] Includes persons with no college degree as well as those with an associate's degree.

[4] Data for years prior to 1992 are for persons with 4 or more years of college, even if they did not complete a degree.

NOTE: Data are based on sample surveys of the noninstitutionalized population, which excludes persons living in institutions (e.g., prisons or nursing facilities); this table includes only data on the civilian population (excludes all military personnel). For each age group, the employment to population ratio of females is the number of females in that age group who are employed as a percentage of the female civilian population in that age group. Caution should be used when comparing 2020 estimates to those of prior years due to the impact that the coronavirus pandemic had on interviewing and response rates. For additional information about the impact of the coronavirus pandemic on the Current Population Survey data collection, please see https://www2.census.gov/programs-surveys/cps/techdocs/cpsmar20.pdf.

SOURCE: U.S. Department of Commerce, Census Bureau, Current Population Survey (CPS), Annual Social and Economic Supplement, selected years, 1975 through 2020. (This table was prepared October 2020.)

Table 501.80. Unemployment rates of persons 16 to 64 years old, by age group and highest level of educational attainment: Selected years, 1975 through 2019

[Standard errors appear in parentheses]

Age group and highest level of educational attainment	1975	1980	1985	1990	1995	2000	2005	2010	2012	2014	2015	2016	2017	2018	2019
1	2	3	4	5	6	7	8	9	10	11	12	13	14	15	16
16 to 19 years old, all education levels[1]	**—** **(†)**	**—** **(†)**	**—** **(†)**	**17.0** **(1.83)**	**21.0** **(2.06)**	**17.2** **(1.89)**	**22.8** **(1.39)**	**31.9** **(1.59)**	**30.6** **(1.57)**	**22.9** **(1.83)**	**22.5** **(1.35)**	**20.2** **(1.37)**	**14.8** **(1.39)**	**15.4** **(1.40)**	**14.5** **(1.11)**
Less than high school completion	— (†)	— (†)	— (†)	26.2 (3.54)	30.3 (3.67)	21.4 (3.23)	30.3 (2.34)	41.7 (3.14)	41.1 (3.01)	22.9 (3.38)	25.6 (2.67)	21.6 (2.39)	21.7 (2.91)	16.3 (2.77)	16.7 (2.57)
High school completion[2]	— (†)	— (†)	— (†)	11.7 (2.05)	15.1 (2.59)	15.3 (2.54)	19.1 (2.02)	29.6 (2.08)	28.7 (2.00)	25.0 (2.32)	23.3 (1.90)	22.0 (2.02)	12.6 (1.44)	16.7 (1.92)	14.5 (1.45)
At least some college	— (†)	— (†)	— (†)	‡ (†)	12.4! (5.19)	‡ (†)	15.8 (3.54)	18.1 (3.65)	19.6 (3.83)	15.1 (4.16)	13.2 (2.96)	11.8 (2.75)	9.2 (2.59)	9.5! (3.19)	11.1 (2.79)
20 to 24 years old, all education levels[1]	**—** **(†)**	**—** **(†)**	**—** **(†)**	**8.2** **(0.63)**	**10.7** **(0.72)**	**9.2** **(0.70)**	**10.9** **(0.48)**	**18.8** **(0.66)**	**15.5** **(0.55)**	**14.9** **(0.70)**	**12.3** **(0.53)**	**10.5** **(0.53)**	**8.1** **(0.43)**	**8.7** **(0.48)**	**7.5** **(0.43)**
Less than high school completion	— (†)	— (†)	— (†)	17.4 (2.15)	19.5 (2.37)	16.6 (2.18)	18.9 (1.24)	32.3 (1.80)	27.6 (2.12)	25.3 (2.75)	19.9 (1.99)	17.3 (2.05)	16.0 (2.10)	19.5 (2.64)	15.9 (2.24)
High school completion[2]	— (†)	— (†)	— (†)	7.8 (0.88)	12.0 (1.18)	10.0 (1.12)	12.0 (0.73)	22.3 (0.95)	18.3 (0.96)	18.9 (1.18)	15.8 (0.92)	12.2 (0.92)	9.7 (0.80)	11.1 (0.85)	8.8 (0.68)
Some college, no bachelor's degree[3]	— (†)	— (†)	— (†)	4.8 (1.09)	7.3 (1.13)	5.2 (1.02)	7.3 (0.76)	14.2 (1.07)	12.7 (0.89)	12.2 (1.16)	9.6 (0.89)	9.9 (0.87)	6.4 (0.75)	5.3 (0.69)	6.7 (0.67)
Bachelor's or higher degree	— (†)	— (†)	— (†)	3.1! (1.12)	4.1! (1.26)	5.0 (1.43)	5.4 (0.91)	7.9 (1.15)	6.0 (0.95)	6.7 (1.09)	5.1 (0.72)	4.9 (0.81)	4.7 (0.76)	5.3 (0.89)	3.3 (0.67)
25 to 64 years old, all education levels	**6.8** **(0.21)**	**5.0** **(0.17)**	**6.1** **(0.18)**	**3.6** **(0.14)**	**4.8** **(0.15)**	**3.3** **(0.13)**	**4.4** **(0.09)**	**9.1** **(0.13)**	**7.4** **(0.11)**	**5.8** **(0.14)**	**4.7** **(0.10)**	**4.4** **(0.09)**	**3.9** **(0.09)**	**3.5** **(0.09)**	**3.2** **(0.08)**
Less than high school completion	10.5 (0.49)	8.4 (0.48)	11.4 (0.61)	7.7 (0.55)	10.0 (0.66)	7.9 (0.63)	9.0 (0.36)	16.8 (0.54)	14.3 (0.49)	10.6 (0.63)	9.2 (0.44)	8.1 (0.42)	8.3 (0.47)	6.6 (0.39)	6.5 (0.41)
High school completion[2]	6.8 (0.34)	5.1 (0.27)	6.9 (0.31)	3.8 (0.23)	5.2 (0.28)	3.8 (0.25)	5.5 (0.17)	12.1 (0.26)	9.2 (0.25)	7.4 (0.29)	6.2 (0.21)	6.1 (0.24)	5.2 (0.18)	4.7 (0.19)	4.0 (0.17)
Some college, no bachelor's degree[3]	5.5 (0.50)	4.3 (0.38)	4.7 (0.37)	3.1 (0.29)	4.5 (0.29)	3.0 (0.24)	4.2 (0.17)	8.8 (0.23)	7.9 (0.24)	6.1 (0.27)	4.9 (0.16)	4.5 (0.17)	3.8 (0.16)	3.7 (0.16)	3.5 (0.17)
Bachelor's or higher degree	2.4 (0.30)	1.9 (0.23)	2.4 (0.24)	1.7 (0.19)	2.5 (0.21)	1.5 (0.16)	2.3 (0.13)	4.7 (0.15)	4.1 (0.14)	3.4 (0.16)	2.4 (0.11)	2.4 (0.12)	2.3 (0.11)	2.2 (0.11)	1.9 (0.10)
25 to 34 years old, all education levels	**8.6** **(0.41)**	**6.8** **(0.32)**	**7.3** **(0.33)**	**4.8** **(0.27)**	**5.8** **(0.30)**	**4.0** **(0.27)**	**5.8** **(0.18)**	**10.8** **(0.28)**	**9.2** **(0.26)**	**7.4** **(0.30)**	**5.9** **(0.20)**	**5.6** **(0.22)**	**4.9** **(0.20)**	**4.3** **(0.17)**	**4.1** **(0.19)**
Less than high school completion	17.2 (1.36)	13.7 (1.24)	15.5 (1.38)	12.0 (1.21)	12.9 (1.32)	10.3 (1.33)	11.6 (0.69)	20.3 (1.02)	16.8 (1.09)	13.7 (1.24)	12.5 (1.01)	13.1 (0.97)	13.2 (1.16)	9.1 (0.98)	9.6 (1.04)
High school completion[2]	9.4 (0.67)	7.9 (0.55)	9.1 (0.57)	5.1 (0.44)	6.8 (0.56)	4.8 (0.54)	7.7 (0.41)	15.9 (0.62)	12.8 (0.57)	10.5 (0.68)	8.9 (0.50)	8.6 (0.52)	7.2 (0.44)	6.4 (0.38)	5.6 (0.41)
Some college, no bachelor's degree[3]	6.7 (0.85)	6.0 (0.64)	5.4 (0.60)	3.8 (0.51)	5.0 (0.52)	3.6 (0.49)	5.4 (0.36)	10.6 (0.44)	10.1 (0.51)	7.8 (0.52)	6.5 (0.39)	5.6 (0.41)	4.4 (0.34)	4.7 (0.34)	4.7 (0.34)
Bachelor's or higher degree	2.9 (0.50)	2.5 (0.39)	2.8 (0.41)	1.9 (0.34)	2.7 (0.40)	1.6 (0.31)	2.6 (0.26)	4.5 (0.28)	4.1 (0.28)	3.7 (0.30)	2.4 (0.20)	2.4 (0.23)	2.5 (0.22)	2.0 (0.19)	2.1 (0.22)
35 to 44 years old, all education levels	**6.4** **(0.41)**	**4.3** **(0.31)**	**5.6** **(0.33)**	**3.3** **(0.24)**	**4.6** **(0.27)**	**3.5** **(0.23)**	**4.2** **(0.14)**	**9.2** **(0.24)**	**7.1** **(0.22)**	**5.7** **(0.24)**	**4.4** **(0.17)**	**4.1** **(0.18)**	**4.0** **(0.16)**	**3.3** **(0.14)**	**2.9** **(0.16)**
Less than high school completion	11.2 (1.02)	9.0 (1.00)	12.4 (1.29)	8.3 (1.17)	10.5 (1.28)	8.4 (1.14)	8.7 (0.63)	17.8 (1.07)	14.1 (0.88)	11.5 (1.08)	8.4 (0.74)	6.2 (0.66)	6.9 (0.61)	5.5 (0.69)	5.7 (0.69)
High school completion[2]	5.7 (0.60)	4.2 (0.48)	6.1 (0.55)	3.7 (0.41)	5.1 (0.48)	3.9 (0.43)	5.2 (0.31)	11.9 (0.51)	9.1 (0.48)	7.4 (0.48)	6.3 (0.41)	6.6 (0.44)	5.7 (0.41)	4.9 (0.36)	4.3 (0.37)
Some college, no bachelor's degree[3]	4.6 (0.95)	3.1 (0.64)	4.8 (0.69)	2.8 (0.47)	4.7 (0.49)	3.1 (0.41)	3.9 (0.25)	9.2 (0.42)	7.4 (0.44)	6.1 (0.49)	4.5 (0.31)	4.5 (0.35)	4.4 (0.35)	3.2 (0.29)	3.1 (0.30)
Bachelor's or higher degree	2.3 (0.59)	1.6 (0.41)	2.2 (0.39)	1.6 (0.31)	2.2 (0.34)	1.8 (0.31)	2.0 (0.19)	4.6 (0.26)	3.6 (0.26)	2.8 (0.30)	2.1 (0.20)	2.0 (0.16)	2.3 (0.21)	2.1 (0.18)	1.4 (0.14)
45 to 54 years old, all education levels	**5.9** **(0.39)**	**3.9** **(0.32)**	**5.4** **(0.39)**	**2.5** **(0.26)**	**3.9** **(0.29)**	**2.4** **(0.22)**	**3.9** **(0.16)**	**8.4** **(0.22)**	**6.8** **(0.18)**	**4.9** **(0.24)**	**4.1** **(0.15)**	**3.7** **(0.17)**	**3.3** **(0.17)**	**3.2** **(0.16)**	**3.0** **(0.16)**
Less than high school completion	8.5 (0.81)	6.6 (0.78)	10.2 (1.16)	4.7 (0.89)	7.9 (1.24)	6.1 (1.16)	7.0 (0.66)	15.6 (0.98)	13.5 (0.92)	8.0 (0.95)	8.6 (0.80)	6.6 (0.65)	6.9 (0.79)	6.5 (0.70)	5.5 (0.71)
High school completion[2]	5.6 (0.60)	3.4 (0.48)	5.4 (0.60)	2.3 (0.39)	4.0 (0.53)	2.7 (0.42)	4.6 (0.33)	11.0 (0.43)	7.8 (0.36)	6.1 (0.50)	5.2 (0.34)	5.0 (0.39)	4.3 (0.32)	3.5 (0.32)	3.3 (0.32)
Some college, no bachelor's degree[3]	4.7 (1.00)	3.0 (0.78)	3.2 (0.79)	2.6 (0.62)	3.9 (0.56)	2.4 (0.40)	3.7 (0.30)	7.6 (0.40)	6.9 (0.36)	4.8 (0.44)	4.1 (0.30)	3.4 (0.33)	2.9 (0.28)	3.3 (0.30)	3.3 (0.31)
Bachelor's or higher degree	2.0! (0.61)	1.3! (0.44)	2.1 (0.54)	1.4 (0.38)	2.4 (0.41)	1.3 (0.28)	2.5 (0.26)	4.8 (0.30)	3.9 (0.27)	3.2 (0.29)	2.2 (0.18)	2.3 (0.24)	2.1 (0.21)	2.2 (0.22)	2.1 (0.20)
55 to 64 years old, all education levels	**5.5** **(0.46)**	**3.2** **(0.35)**	**4.6** **(0.44)**	**2.8** **(0.36)**	**3.9** **(0.42)**	**2.8** **(0.35)**	**3.7** **(0.20)**	**7.3** **(0.25)**	**6.6** **(0.23)**	**5.2** **(0.28)**	**4.2** **(0.20)**	**3.9** **(0.18)**	**3.2** **(0.16)**	**3.3** **(0.18)**	**2.6** **(0.16)**
Less than high school completion	7.1 (0.79)	5.2 (0.77)	7.1 (1.01)	3.9 (0.90)	6.7 (1.35)	5.2 (1.28)	7.5 (0.90)	10.1 (0.99)	11.5 (1.05)	8.2 (1.21)	6.9 (0.84)	6.5 (0.80)	6.0 (0.75)	5.6 (0.71)	5.6 (0.92)
High school completion[2]	5.1 (0.76)	2.7 (0.51)	4.5 (0.69)	3.0 (0.59)	3.4 (0.65)	3.1 (0.62)	4.3 (0.39)	9.3 (0.56)	7.1 (0.50)	5.6 (0.53)	4.4 (0.38)	4.1 (0.41)	3.6 (0.33)	4.0 (0.42)	2.6 (0.32)
Some college, no bachelor's degree[3]	4.1! (1.26)	2.0! (0.77)	3.0! (1.00)	2.2! (0.82)	3.2 (0.80)	2.8 (0.70)	3.5 (0.37)	7.7 (0.52)	7.1 (0.44)	5.5 (0.54)	4.3 (0.40)	4.1 (0.37)	3.2 (0.32)	3.2 (0.33)	2.6 (0.31)
Bachelor's or higher degree	1.5! (0.75)	‡ (†)	2.2! (0.70)	1.8! (0.62)	3.3 (0.79)	1.4! (0.46)	2.3 (0.30)	5.0 (0.34)	4.8 (0.38)	4.0 (0.39)	3.3 (0.30)	3.2 (0.29)	2.4 (0.24)	2.2 (0.23)	2.0 (0.21)

—Not available.
†Not applicable.
!Interpret data with caution. The coefficient of variation (CV) for this estimate is between 30 and 50 percent.
‡Reporting standards not met. The coefficient of variation (CV) for this estimate is 50 percent or greater.
[1]Data for 16- to 19-year-olds and 20- to 24-year-olds exclude persons enrolled in school.
[2]Includes equivalency credentials, such as the GED credential.
[3]Includes persons with no college degree as well as those with an associate's degree.

NOTE: Data are based on sample surveys of the noninstitutionalized population, which excludes persons living in institutions (e.g., prisons or nursing facilities); this table includes only data on the civilian population (excludes all military personnel). The unemployment rate is the percentage of persons in the civilian labor force who are not working and who made specific efforts to find employment sometime during the prior 4 weeks. The civilian labor force consists of all civilians who are employed or seeking employment.
SOURCE: U.S. Department of Commerce, Census Bureau, Current Population Survey (CPS), Annual Social and Economic Supplement, selected years, 1975 through 2019. (This table was prepared October 2019.)

Table 501.85. Unemployment rates of males 16 to 64 years old, by age group and highest level of educational attainment: Selected years, 1975 through 2020

[Standard errors appear in parentheses]

Age group and highest level of educational attainment	1975		1980		1985		1990		1995		2000		2005		2010		2014		2015		2016		20	
1	2		3		4		5		6		7		8		9		10		11		12			
16 to 19 years old, all education levels[1]	---	(†)	---	(†)	---	(†)	18.9	(2.58)	21.3	(2.71)	16.0	(2.36)	25.2	(1.83)	35.6	(2.07)	24.4	(2.40)	22.5	(1.79)	20.0	(1.81)	14.9	(1.6
Less than high school completion	---	(†)	---	(†)	---	(†)	27.9	(4.45)	30.6	(4.60)	17.6	(3.69)	29.9	(2.88)	44.7	(4.07)	23.1	(4.25)	26.6	(3.61)	24.4	(3.24)	22.3	(3.
High school completion[2]	---	(†)	---	(†)	---	(†)	12.1	(2.96)	14.4	(3.38)	15.0	(3.30)	23.4	(2.77)	33.0	(2.59)	26.7	(3.29)	23.0	(2.47)	19.7	(2.54)	13.3	(2.
At least some college	---	(†)	---	(†)	---	(†)	‡	(†)	‡	(†)	‡	(†)	12.7 !	(4.34)	19.0	(5.64)	17.7 !	(7.00)	11.5 !	(3.68)	10.8 !	(3.41)	‡	
20 to 24 years old, all education levels[1]	---	(†)	---	(†)	---	(†)	8.4	(0.86)	11.1	(0.97)	9.4	(0.94)	11.4	(0.61)	21.4	(0.88)	17.0	(0.92)	13.6	(0.75)	11.5	(0.74)	8.9	(0.6
Less than high school completion	---	(†)	---	(†)	---	(†)	16.9	(2.53)	17.4	(2.68)	16.5	(2.61)	16.1	(1.37)	32.4	(2.20)	23.6	(3.04)	19.0	(2.52)	17.9	(2.60)	12.5	(2.
High school completion[2]	---	(†)	---	(†)	---	(†)	7.4	(1.15)	11.6	(1.48)	9.6	(1.45)	12.4	(0.97)	23.7	(1.25)	21.1	(1.60)	16.6	(1.16)	13.4	(1.24)	9.8	(1.
Some college, no bachelor's degree[3]	---	(†)	---	(†)	---	(†)	4.6 !	(1.54)	8.0	(1.65)	4.8	(1.36)	7.8	(1.04)	16.4	(1.58)	13.8	(1.56)	11.5	(1.46)	9.4	(1.28)	7.7	(1.
Bachelor's or higher degree[4]	---	(†)	---	(†)	---	(†)	‡	(†)	5.6 !	(2.22)	5.5 !	(2.32)	6.8	(1.54)	9.8	(1.82)	7.3	(1.71)	5.1	(1.18)	5.0	(1.21)	6.1	(1.
25 to 64 years old, all education levels	6.5	(0.26)	4.9	(0.22)	6.1	(0.24)	3.6	(0.19)	5.1	(0.21)	3.3	(0.18)	4.7	(0.14)	10.5	(0.19)	5.9	(0.19)	5.0	(0.14)	4.5	(0.13)	4.1	(0.1
Less than high school completion	10.3	(0.59)	8.2	(0.58)	11.2	(0.76)	7.3	(0.68)	10.9	(0.86)	7.1	(0.75)	7.9	(0.44)	17.8	(0.79)	9.4	(0.70)	8.4	(0.54)	7.5	(0.52)	8.0	(0.
High school completion[2]	6.6	(0.43)	5.3	(0.37)	7.2	(0.43)	3.8	(0.32)	5.7	(0.40)	3.9	(0.34)	6.0	(0.25)	13.8	(0.39)	7.8	(0.37)	6.7	(0.27)	6.3	(0.31)	5.2	(0.
Some college, no bachelor's degree[3]	5.0	(0.59)	4.4	(0.49)	4.5	(0.49)	3.0	(0.38)	4.4	(0.39)	3.1	(0.34)	4.3	(0.27)	10.2	(0.35)	5.9	(0.37)	4.9	(0.23)	4.7	(0.28)	4.1	(0.
Bachelor's or higher degree[4]	2.1	(0.34)	1.7	(0.26)	2.4	(0.30)	1.8	(0.25)	2.6	(0.28)	1.6	(0.22)	2.5	(0.19)	5.1	(0.22)	3.4	(0.25)	2.8	(0.16)	2.3	(0.17)	2.4	(0.
25 to 34 years old, all education levels	8.3	(0.50)	6.8	(0.41)	7.3	(0.43)	4.5	(0.35)	5.9	(0.40)	4.2	(0.37)	6.0	(0.27)	12.6	(0.40)	7.5	(0.41)	6.2	(0.27)	5.8	(0.32)	5.4	(0.3
Less than high school completion	17.3	(1.65)	13.4	(1.53)	13.9	(1.60)	10.3	(1.36)	12.5	(1.57)	8.8	(1.51)	9.7	(0.84)	20.7	(1.36)	10.8	(1.37)	10.2	(1.15)	11.7	(1.20)	12.2	(1.
High school completion[2]	9.0	(0.85)	8.2	(0.75)	9.5	(0.77)	4.6	(0.55)	6.6	(0.72)	4.9	(0.70)	7.8	(0.52)	17.8	(0.77)	10.1	(0.81)	9.1	(0.63)	9.1	(0.71)	7.3	(0.
Some college, no bachelor's degree[3]	6.6	(1.03)	6.0	(0.81)	4.9	(0.76)	3.6	(0.68)	4.6	(0.70)	3.8	(0.69)	5.6	(0.57)	11.8	(0.69)	7.8	(0.76)	6.1	(0.51)	5.2	(0.60)	4.8	(0.
Bachelor's or higher degree[4]	2.6	(0.57)	2.4	(0.48)	2.8	(0.54)	1.9	(0.46)	2.8	(0.55)	1.8	(0.46)	2.7	(0.36)	4.8	(0.45)	3.8	(0.51)	2.8	(0.34)	2.3	(0.36)	2.6	(0.
35 to 44 years old, all education levels	6.0	(0.50)	4.1	(0.39)	5.7	(0.44)	3.2	(0.32)	4.9	(0.37)	3.4	(0.31)	4.4	(0.20)	10.1	(0.33)	5.7	(0.33)	4.6	(0.26)	4.1	(0.25)	4.0	(0.2
Less than high school completion	10.8	(1.24)	8.4	(1.22)	12.3	(1.63)	7.9	(1.46)	11.8	(1.69)	6.3	(1.27)	7.8	(0.76)	18.4	(1.42)	9.8	(1.22)	7.5	(0.90)	5.2	(0.87)	6.6	(0.
High school completion[2]	5.8	(0.80)	4.2	(0.65)	6.5	(0.79)	3.4	(0.56)	5.6	(0.68)	4.2	(0.58)	5.7	(0.46)	12.9	(0.71)	8.2	(0.68)	6.3	(0.54)	6.2	(0.55)	5.0	(0.
Some college, no bachelor's degree[3]	3.3 !	(1.01)	2.9	(0.81)	5.3	(0.96)	2.8	(0.63)	4.8	(0.69)	2.9	(0.56)	4.1	(0.38)	9.9	(0.63)	5.5	(0.69)	4.9	(0.46)	4.9	(0.56)	4.7	(0.
Bachelor's or higher degree[4]	1.9 !	(0.61)	1.3 !	(0.44)	2.2	(0.49)	1.7	(0.41)	2.0	(0.43)	1.7	(0.42)	2.1	(0.27)	4.6	(0.38)	2.6	(0.43)	2.2	(0.28)	1.7	(0.26)	2.3	(0.
45 to 54 years old, all education levels	5.5	(0.48)	3.7	(0.40)	5.4	(0.51)	2.7	(0.36)	4.6	(0.42)	2.5	(0.30)	4.1	(0.25)	9.9	(0.32)	4.9	(0.33)	4.5	(0.23)	3.9	(0.23)	3.2	(0.2
Less than high school completion	8.3	(0.97)	6.1	(0.92)	10.9	(1.48)	4.7	(1.12)	9.4	(1.74)	6.9	(1.60)	6.3	(0.81)	16.8	(1.29)	8.7	(1.17)	8.8	(1.05)	6.2	(0.84)	6.7	(1.
High school completion[2]	4.9	(0.76)	3.3	(0.64)	5.5	(0.84)	2.8	(0.61)	5.5	(0.87)	2.4	(0.55)	5.1	(0.51)	12.6	(0.67)	6.2	(0.65)	5.7	(0.49)	5.1	(0.49)	4.1	(0.
Some college, no bachelor's degree[3]	4.4	(1.21)	3.5 !	(1.11)	2.6 !	(0.94)	2.5 !	(0.82)	4.0	(0.79)	2.6	(0.58)	3.8	(0.47)	9.5	(0.63)	4.3	(0.48)	4.1	(0.48)	3.8	(0.51)	2.8	(0.
Bachelor's or higher degree[4]	1.8 !	(0.67)	1.1 !	(0.47)	2.0 !	(0.63)	1.4 !	(0.49)	2.7	(0.55)	1.3	(0.38)	2.7	(0.38)	5.3	(0.42)	3.1	(0.39)	2.4	(0.25)	2.3	(0.33)	1.9	(0.
55 to 64 years old, all education levels	5.5	(0.58)	3.6	(0.46)	4.7	(0.57)	3.3	(0.51)	4.3	(0.59)	3.2	(0.49)	3.9	(0.30)	8.6	(0.37)	5.6	(0.37)	4.6	(0.28)	4.2	(0.27)	3.6	(0.2
Less than high school completion	6.9	(0.96)	5.9	(1.01)	7.4	(1.28)	4.6	(1.24)	7.7	(1.84)	5.5 !	(1.67)	6.7	(1.01)	11.6	(1.48)	7.2	(1.50)	6.9	(1.05)	6.8	(0.98)	6.4	(1.
High school completion[2]	5.5	(1.02)	2.8	(0.70)	4.6	(0.96)	3.7	(0.91)	3.6	(0.95)	3.5	(0.93)	5.2	(0.63)	11.1	(0.88)	6.5	(0.76)	5.1	(0.56)	4.2	(0.52)	4.0	(0.
Some college, no bachelor's degree[3]	3.1 !	(1.39)	2.5 !	(1.06)	3.6 !	(1.43)	‡	(†)	3.7 !	(1.16)	3.4 !	(1.06)	3.3	(0.52)	9.2	(0.77)	5.9	(0.80)	4.1	(0.48)	4.7	(0.63)	3.6	(0.
Bachelor's or higher degree[4]	‡	(†)	‡	(†)	2.2 !	(0.80)	2.1 !	(0.78)	3.6	(1.00)	1.7 !	(0.63)	2.6	(0.41)	5.8	(0.48)	4.3	(0.53)	3.9	(0.50)	3.2	(0.38)	2.7	(0.

---Not available.

†Not applicable.

!Interpret data with caution. The coefficient of variation (CV) for this estimate is between 30 and 50 percent.

‡Reporting standards not met. The coefficient of variation (CV) for this estimate is 50 percent or greater.

[1] Data for 16- to 19-year-olds and 20- to 24-year-olds exclude persons enrolled in school.

[2] Data for years prior to 1992 are for persons with 4 or more years of high school. Data for later years are for high school completers–i.e., those persons who graduated from high school with a diploma as well as those who completed high school through equivalency programs, such as a GED program.

[3] Includes persons with no college degree as well as those with an associate's degree.

[4] Data for years prior to 1992 are for persons with 4 or more years of college, even if they did not complete a degree.

NOTE: Data are based on sample surveys of the noninstitutionalized population, which excludes persons living in institutions (e.g., prisons or nursing facilities); this table includes only data on the civilian population (excludes all military personnel). The unemployment rate is the percentage of persons in the civilian labor force who are not working and who made specific efforts to find employment sometime during the prior 4 weeks. The civilian labor force consists of all civilians who are employed or seeking employment. Caution should be used when comparing 2020 estimates to those of prior years due to the impact that the coronavirus pandemic had on interviewing and response rates. For additional information about the impact of the coronavirus pandemic on the Current Population Survey data collection, please see https://www2.census.gov/programs-surveys/cps/techdocs/cpsmar20.pdf.

SOURCE: U.S. Department of Commerce, Census Bureau, Current Population Survey (CPS), Annual Social and Economic Supplement, selected years, 1975 through 2020. (This table was prepared October 2020.)

Table 501.90. Unemployment rates of females 16 to 64 years old, by age group and highest level of educational attainment: Selected years, 1975 through 2020

[Standard errors appear in parentheses]

Age group and highest level of educational attainment	1975		1980		1985		1990		1995		2000		2005		2010		2014		2015		2016		2017	
1	2		3		4		5		6		7		8		9		10		11		12		13	
16 to 19 years old, all education levels[1]	**---**	**(†)**	**---**	**(†)**	**---**	**(†)**	**14.7**	**(2.39)**	**20.6**	**(2.93)**	**18.9**	**(2.85)**	**19.7**	**(1.86)**	**26.9**	**(2.14)**	**20.9**	**(2.54)**	**22.4**	**(2.07)**	**20.4**	**(2.08)**	**14.8**	**(2.16)**
Less than high school completion	---	(†)	---	(†)	---	(†)	23.4	(5.31)	29.7	(5.57)	27.9	(5.53)	31.0	(3.88)	36.4	(4.75)	22.5	(4.49)	24.4	(4.00)	17.6	(3.43)	20.9	(4.38)
High school completion[2]	---	(†)	---	(†)	---	(†)	11.3	(2.64)	16.0	(3.69)	15.7	(3.66)	14.2	(2.34)	24.9	(3.03)	22.9	(3.54)	23.7	(2.88)	25.0	(3.16)	11.9	(2.37)
At least some college	---	(†)	---	(†)	---	(†)	‡	(†)	‡	(†)	‡	(†)	18.3	(5.47)	17.3	(4.41)	12.9 !	(4.87)	14.8	(4.26)	12.6 !	(4.08)	15.1	(4.38)
20 to 24 years old, all education levels[1]	**---**	**(†)**	**---**	**(†)**	**---**	**(†)**	**7.8**	**(0.86)**	**10.2**	**(1.00)**	**8.9**	**(0.96)**	**10.3**	**(0.73)**	**15.6**	**(0.86)**	**12.4**	**(0.89)**	**10.7**	**(0.69)**	**9.3**	**(0.68)**	**7.2**	**(0.57)**
Less than high school completion	---	(†)	---	(†)	---	(†)	18.6	(3.70)	24.3	(4.34)	17.0	(3.60)	24.5	(2.79)	32.2	(3.38)	29.3	(5.22)	21.2	(3.60)	16.0	(3.67)	23.2	(4.36)
High school completion[2]	---	(†)	---	(†)	---	(†)	8.1	(1.26)	12.7	(1.78)	10.6	(1.63)	11.5	(1.14)	19.9	(1.46)	15.8	(1.72)	14.6	(1.38)	10.3	(1.18)	9.5	(1.19)
Some college, no bachelor's degree[3]	---	(†)	---	(†)	---	(†)	4.9	(1.43)	6.7	(1.43)	5.7	(1.42)	6.8	(1.01)	12.1	(1.33)	10.6	(1.41)	7.5	(0.97)	10.4	(1.27)	5.0	(0.89)
Bachelor's or higher degree[4]	---	(†)	---	(†)	---	(†)	3.5 !	(1.47)	3.1 !	(1.35)	4.6 !	(1.70)	4.4	(1.05)	6.3	(1.29)	6.3	(1.38)	5.2	(1.01)	4.8	(1.09)	3.6	(0.92)
25 to 64 years old, all education levels	**7.3**	**(0.33)**	**5.0**	**(0.25)**	**6.0**	**(0.26)**	**3.7**	**(0.20)**	**4.4**	**(0.21)**	**3.2**	**(0.18)**	**4.2**	**(0.12)**	**7.5**	**(0.15)**	**5.7**	**(0.19)**	**4.3**	**(0.13)**	**4.2**	**(0.13)**	**3.7**	**(0.12)**
Less than high school completion	10.8	(0.79)	8.9	(0.76)	11.7	(0.96)	8.3	(0.88)	8.6	(0.95)	9.1	(1.00)	10.9	(0.65)	15.0	(0.71)	12.7	(0.98)	10.6	(0.68)	9.2	(0.70)	8.7	(0.75)
High school completion[2]	7.1	(0.49)	5.0	(0.37)	6.5	(0.41)	3.9	(0.32)	4.6	(0.36)	3.6	(0.33)	4.8	(0.23)	9.8	(0.30)	6.8	(0.42)	5.6	(0.31)	5.8	(0.32)	5.3	(0.30)
Some college, no bachelor's degree[3]	6.3	(0.84)	4.1	(0.54)	4.8	(0.53)	3.2	(0.40)	4.5	(0.38)	2.9	(0.31)	4.0	(0.22)	7.5	(0.27)	6.3	(0.36)	5.0	(0.23)	4.3	(0.22)	3.5	(0.21)
Bachelor's or higher degree[4]	3.1	(0.57)	2.2	(0.39)	2.5	(0.36)	1.6	(0.27)	2.4	(0.30)	1.4	(0.22)	2.2	(0.17)	4.3	(0.19)	3.4	(0.22)	2.1	(0.13)	2.6	(0.16)	2.3	(0.15)
25 to 34 years old, all education levels	**9.1**	**(0.65)**	**6.8**	**(0.47)**	**7.3**	**(0.47)**	**5.1**	**(0.39)**	**5.7**	**(0.42)**	**3.9**	**(0.37)**	**5.6**	**(0.27)**	**8.7**	**(0.33)**	**7.3**	**(0.36)**	**5.6**	**(0.29)**	**5.3**	**(0.30)**	**4.4**	**(0.23)**
Less than high school completion	17.0	(2.18)	14.2	(1.93)	18.5	(2.37)	15.1	(2.17)	13.7	(2.20)	12.9	(2.33)	15.7	(1.36)	19.5	(1.52)	19.1	(2.42)	17.5	(1.85)	16.0	(1.85)	15.2	(2.10)
High school completion[2]	10.0	(1.01)	7.6	(0.76)	8.6	(0.78)	5.7	(0.65)	6.9	(0.81)	4.8	(0.78)	7.6	(0.62)	12.6	(0.86)	11.1	(1.04)	8.7	(0.74)	7.7	(0.74)	7.0	(0.69)
Some college, no bachelor's degree[3]	6.9	(1.38)	5.9	(0.94)	6.0	(0.88)	4.0	(0.72)	5.4	(0.73)	3.5	(0.63)	5.1	(0.46)	9.3	(0.57)	7.7	(0.68)	6.9	(0.58)	6.1	(0.52)	4.0	(0.41)
Bachelor's or higher degree[4]	3.5	(0.88)	2.6	(0.60)	2.7	(0.57)	2.0	(0.47)	2.6	(0.53)	1.4	(0.39)	2.5	(0.31)	4.3	(0.35)	3.6	(0.38)	1.9	(0.26)	2.6	(0.33)	2.5	(0.26)
35 to 44 years old, all education levels	**7.1**	**(0.66)**	**4.7**	**(0.47)**	**5.4**	**(0.46)**	**3.5**	**(0.34)**	**4.3**	**(0.36)**	**3.7**	**(0.33)**	**3.9**	**(0.20)**	**8.2**	**(0.29)**	**5.6**	**(0.34)**	**4.1**	**(0.20)**	**4.2**	**(0.23)**	**4.0**	**(0.21)**
Less than high school completion	11.9	(1.65)	10.0	(1.56)	12.7	(1.95)	8.9	(1.79)	8.4	(1.75)	11.3	(1.94)	10.1	(1.02)	16.7	(1.32)	14.9	(1.99)	10.2	(1.26)	8.1	(1.18)	7.5	(1.15)
High school completion[2]	5.7	(0.85)	4.1	(0.65)	5.7	(0.72)	4.0	(0.57)	4.5	(0.63)	3.6	(0.58)	4.5	(0.40)	10.5	(0.67)	6.2	(0.68)	6.3	(0.61)	7.2	(0.67)	6.8	(0.68)
Some college, no bachelor's degree[3]	6.8	(1.76)	3.3	(0.97)	4.3	(0.91)	2.8	(0.64)	4.7	(0.66)	3.3	(0.57)	3.7	(0.36)	8.5	(0.51)	6.7	(0.70)	4.2	(0.39)	4.2	(0.47)	4.1	(0.48)
Bachelor's or higher degree[4]	3.5 !	(1.29)	2.3 !	(0.76)	2.2	(0.61)	1.4 !	(0.42)	2.4	(0.52)	1.8	(0.44)	1.9	(0.26)	4.5	(0.35)	3.0	(0.40)	2.1	(0.25)	2.3	(0.22)	2.3	(0.26)
45 to 54 years old, all education levels	**6.5**	**(0.62)**	**4.1**	**(0.49)**	**5.3**	**(0.56)**	**2.3**	**(0.35)**	**3.1**	**(0.36)**	**2.4**	**(0.30)**	**3.6**	**(0.19)**	**6.8**	**(0.27)**	**4.9**	**(0.32)**	**3.7**	**(0.19)**	**3.5**	**(0.22)**	**3.4**	**(0.24)**
Less than high school completion	9.0	(1.33)	7.6	(1.32)	9.2	(1.71)	4.7	(1.33)	5.8	(1.55)	5.1 !	(1.52)	8.2	(1.08)	13.6	(1.41)	6.7	(1.32)	8.3	(1.09)	7.2	(1.05)	7.2	(1.13)
High school completion[2]	6.3	(0.88)	3.6	(0.66)	5.4	(0.80)	1.8	(0.46)	2.7	(0.57)	3.0	(0.59)	4.0	(0.39)	9.0	(0.56)	6.1	(0.69)	4.4	(0.51)	4.9	(0.54)	4.6	(0.52)
Some college, no bachelor's degree[3]	5.3 !	(1.61)	2.3 !	(0.99)	4.0 !	(1.23)	2.7 !	(0.89)	3.7	(0.73)	2.2	(0.52)	3.6	(0.41)	5.9	(0.43)	5.3	(0.64)	4.1	(0.39)	3.1	(0.39)	3.0	(0.40)
Bachelor's or higher degree[4]	2.6 !	(1.18)	1.9 !	(0.90)	2.4 !	(0.92)	1.3 !	(0.56)	2.1	(0.57)	1.3 !	(0.39)	2.2	(0.33)	4.3	(0.36)	3.3	(0.40)	2.0	(0.25)	2.3	(0.28)	2.4	(0.32)
55 to 64 years old, all education levels	**5.4**	**(0.71)**	**2.5**	**(0.47)**	**4.5**	**(0.63)**	**2.2**	**(0.47)**	**3.3**	**(0.55)**	**2.4**	**(0.45)**	**3.4**	**(0.29)**	**6.0**	**(0.32)**	**4.7**	**(0.38)**	**3.7**	**(0.26)**	**3.6**	**(0.25)**	**2.8**	**(0.23)**
Less than high school completion	7.3	(1.28)	3.7	(1.06)	6.7	(1.49)	2.9 !	(1.17)	5.3 !	(1.78)	4.8 !	(1.84)	8.6	(1.51)	8.0	(1.36)	9.8	(2.00)	7.0	(1.51)	5.9	(1.16)	5.4	(1.20)
High school completion[2]	4.6	(1.05)	2.6	(0.69)	4.5	(0.93)	2.2 !	(0.68)	3.2	(0.84)	2.8	(0.77)	3.3	(0.46)	7.5	(0.68)	4.6	(0.65)	3.5	(0.54)	4.0	(0.51)	3.1	(0.46)
Some college, no bachelor's degree[3]	5.6 !	(2.23)	‡	(†)	‡	(†)	2.4 !	(1.15)	2.8 !	(1.00)	2.2 !	(0.84)	3.7	(0.54)	6.3	(0.65)	5.1	(0.68)	4.5	(0.55)	3.5	(0.52)	2.8	(0.46)
Bachelor's or higher degree[4]	‡	(†)	‡	(†)	‡	(†)	‡	(†)	2.6 !	(1.16)	‡	(†)	1.9	(0.39)	4.1	(0.49)	3.6	(0.58)	2.7	(0.36)	3.2	(0.38)	2.0	(0.33)

---Not available.

†Not applicable.

!Interpret data with caution. The coefficient of variation (CV) for this estimate is between 30 and 50 percent.

‡Reporting standards not met. The coefficient of variation (CV) for this estimate is 50 percent or greater.

[1] Data for 16- to 19-year-olds and 20- to 24-year-olds exclude persons enrolled in school.

[2] Data for years prior to 1992 are for persons with 4 or more years of high school. Data for later years are for high school completers--i.e., those persons who graduated from high school with a diploma as well as those who completed high school through equivalency programs, such as a GED program.

[3] Includes persons with no college degree as well as those with an associate's degree.

[4] Data for years prior to 1992 are for persons with 4 or more years of college, even if they did not complete a degree.

NOTE: Data are based on sample surveys of the noninstitutionalized population, which excludes persons living in institutions (e.g., prisons or nursing facilities); this table includes only data on the civilian population (excludes all military personnel). The unemployment rate is the percentage of persons in the civilian labor force who are not working and who made specific efforts to find employment sometime during the prior 4 weeks. The civilian labor force consists of all civilians who are employed or seeking employment. Caution should be used when comparing 2020 estimates to those of prior years due to the impact that the coronavirus pandemic had on interviewing and response rates. For additional information about the impact of the coronavirus pandemic on the Current Population Survey data collection, please see https://www2.census.gov/programs-surveys/cps/techdocs/cpsmar20.pdf.

SOURCE: U.S. Department of Commerce, Census Bureau, Current Population Survey (CPS), Annual Social and Economic Supplement, selected years, 1975 through 2020. (This table was prepared October 2020.)

Table 502.10. Occupation of employed persons 25 years old and over, by highest level of educational attainment and sex: 2018 and 2019

[Standard errors appear in parentheses]

Sex and occupation	Total employed (in thousands)		Percentage distribution, by highest level of educational attainment: Total	Less than high school completion		High school completion (includes equivalency)		College: Some college, no degree		Associate's degree		Bachelor's degree		Master's or higher degree	
1	2		3	4		5		6		7		8		9	
2018															
All persons	**135,851**	**(365.3)**	**100.0**	**7.0**	**(0.12)**	**25.1**	**(0.24)**	**15.5**	**(0.16)**	**11.1**	**(0.14)**	**25.7**	**(0.25)**	**15.5**	**(0.18)**
Management, professional, and related	59,266	(439.8)	100.0	1.2	(0.07)	9.5	(0.21)	10.5	(0.21)	10.1	(0.20)	37.6	(0.34)	31.1	(0.32)
Management, business, and financial operations	24,827	(277.4)	100.0	2.1	(0.14)	14.2	(0.42)	13.1	(0.33)	9.1	(0.30)	39.8	(0.50)	21.6	(0.42)
Professional and related	34,439	(323.0)	100.0	0.5	(0.06)	6.1	(0.21)	8.7	(0.27)	10.8	(0.29)	36.0	(0.45)	37.9	(0.45)
Education, training, and library	9,187	(175.7)	100.0	0.6	(0.13)	5.8	(0.42)	6.7	(0.42)	5.9	(0.39)	34.4	(0.76)	46.7	(0.90)
Preschool and kindergarten teachers	604	(41.2)	100.0	1.8!	(0.75)	11.3	(1.83)	15.4	(2.47)	13.9	(1.95)	40.2	(2.98)	17.3	(2.68)
Elementary and middle school teachers	3,540	(97.2)	100.0	‡	(†)	2.4	(0.44)	2.7	(0.44)	2.8	(0.41)	44.0	(1.21)	48.1	(1.34)
Secondary school teachers	1,135	(59.4)	100.0	‡	(†)	1.3!	(0.51)	2.6!	(0.84)	1.5!	(0.59)	35.9	(2.33)	58.6	(2.37)
Special education teachers	411	(31.1)	100.0	‡	(†)	3.2!	(1.04)	3.8!	(1.26)	3.4!	(1.28)	30.9	(3.79)	57.8	(4.07)
Postsecondary teachers	1,279	(65.8)	100.0	‡	(†)	‡	(†)	1.9	(0.55)	1.5!	(0.51)	12.2	(1.63)	84.2	(1.79)
Other education, training, and library workers	2,219	(79.2)	100.0	1.8	(0.45)	15.5	(1.22)	16.0	(1.24)	13.8	(1.12)	30.1	(1.57)	22.7	(1.44)
Service occupations	20,719	(221.4)	100.0	14.6	(0.38)	37.2	(0.49)	18.4	(0.41)	12.7	(0.38)	14.2	(0.42)	2.8	(0.18)
Sales and office occupations	27,253	(268.4)	100.0	3.7	(0.18)	29.2	(0.44)	22.5	(0.40)	12.9	(0.33)	26.0	(0.47)	5.7	(0.22)
Natural resources, construction, and maintenance	12,387	(162.3)	100.0	19.4	(0.50)	42.6	(0.74)	16.3	(0.50)	11.8	(0.50)	8.4	(0.47)	1.5	(0.17)
Production, transportation, and material moving	16,226	(213.8)	100.0	14.1	(0.48)	46.7	(0.66)	18.0	(0.49)	9.4	(0.38)	9.7	(0.37)	2.2	(0.18)
Males	**72,248**	**(244.9)**	**100.0**	**8.4**	**(0.16)**	**27.7**	**(0.31)**	**15.5**	**(0.23)**	**9.6**	**(0.18)**	**24.5**	**(0.29)**	**14.2**	**(0.22)**
Management, professional, and related	28,773	(280.9)	100.0	1.5	(0.11)	10.3	(0.29)	11.1	(0.32)	8.0	(0.26)	38.3	(0.44)	30.8	(0.43)
Management, business, and financial operations	13,768	(194.9)	100.0	2.6	(0.20)	15.2	(0.51)	13.3	(0.48)	7.8	(0.37)	39.6	(0.64)	21.4	(0.61)
Professional and related	15,006	(184.7)	100.0	0.5	(0.09)	5.7	(0.34)	9.0	(0.41)	8.2	(0.40)	37.1	(0.64)	39.5	(0.62)
Education, training, and library	2,526	(86.7)	100.0	0.4!	(0.15)	3.6	(0.65)	6.0	(0.79)	4.2	(0.66)	31.1	(1.43)	54.7	(1.59)
Service occupations	8,790	(152.1)	100.0	14.8	(0.62)	36.4	(0.86)	18.2	(0.68)	11.5	(0.58)	16.1	(0.64)	2.9	(0.30)
Sales and office occupations	10,536	(167.7)	100.0	4.2	(0.32)	27.2	(0.66)	21.2	(0.65)	10.3	(0.50)	30.2	(0.78)	6.9	(0.38)
Natural resources, construction, and maintenance	11,814	(159.3)	100.0	19.1	(0.52)	43.3	(0.76)	16.2	(0.51)	11.9	(0.51)	8.0	(0.45)	1.4	(0.17)
Production, transportation, and material moving	12,334	(168.3)	100.0	13.2	(0.50)	47.6	(0.75)	18.4	(0.57)	9.3	(0.43)	9.4	(0.42)	2.2	(0.22)
Females	**63,603**	**(231.6)**	**100.0**	**5.3**	**(0.14)**	**22.2**	**(0.29)**	**15.6**	**(0.21)**	**12.8**	**(0.21)**	**27.1**	**(0.33)**	**17.0**	**(0.23)**
Management, professional, and related	30,493	(260.9)	100.0	0.9	(0.09)	8.8	(0.27)	10.0	(0.28)	12.0	(0.27)	37.0	(0.46)	31.3	(0.40)
Management, business, and financial operations	11,059	(165.8)	100.0	1.6	(0.18)	13.0	(0.55)	12.9	(0.49)	10.7	(0.46)	40.0	(0.78)	21.9	(0.54)
Professional and related	19,434	(218.9)	100.0	0.5	(0.08)	6.4	(0.28)	8.4	(0.33)	12.8	(0.36)	35.2	(0.55)	36.7	(0.54)
Education, training, and library	6,661	(133.0)	100.0	0.7	(0.16)	6.6	(0.51)	6.9	(0.47)	6.5	(0.45)	35.6	(0.92)	43.7	(0.97)
Service occupations	11,929	(149.0)	100.0	14.5	(0.45)	37.8	(0.65)	18.6	(0.54)	13.6	(0.50)	12.8	(0.50)	2.8	(0.23)
Sales and office occupations	16,717	(196.8)	100.0	3.4	(0.21)	30.5	(0.56)	23.3	(0.47)	14.4	(0.44)	23.4	(0.57)	5.0	(0.27)
Natural resources, construction, and maintenance	573	(36.0)	100.0	24.4	(2.64)	27.2	(2.70)	17.0	(2.32)	9.9	(1.79)	17.2	(2.84)	4.3	(1.28)
Production, transportation, and material moving	3,892	(99.7)	100.0	17.0	(0.89)	44.0	(1.25)	16.8	(0.95)	9.6	(0.79)	10.5	(0.86)	2.1	(0.38)
2019															
All persons	**137,478**	**(347.4)**	**100.0**	**6.8**	**(0.11)**	**25.1**	**(0.24)**	**15.1**	**(0.17)**	**11.1**	**(0.16)**	**26.1**	**(0.23)**	**15.9**	**(0.18)**
Management, professional, and related	60,087	(407.3)	100.0	1.1	(0.07)	9.3	(0.20)	9.8	(0.21)	10.0	(0.20)	38.0	(0.33)	31.7	(0.33)
Management, business, and financial operations	25,465	(298.1)	100.0	2.0	(0.14)	13.4	(0.38)	13.0	(0.38)	9.2	(0.28)	40.0	(0.50)	22.4	(0.44)
Professional and related	34,622	(302.3)	100.0	0.4	(0.05)	6.4	(0.20)	7.4	(0.23)	10.6	(0.26)	36.6	(0.40)	38.6	(0.46)
Education, training, and library	9,050	(141.0)	100.0	0.4	(0.10)	5.8	(0.37)	6.0	(0.39)	5.5	(0.41)	34.6	(0.77)	47.7	(0.85)
Preschool and kindergarten teachers	611	(41.0)	100.0	1.3!	(0.57)	11.1	(2.01)	9.7	(1.73)	17.1	(2.33)	44.3	(3.18)	16.6	(2.30)
Elementary and middle school teachers	3,580	(99.7)	100.0	‡	(†)	2.4	(0.37)	2.1	(0.37)	2.3	(0.39)	41.5	(1.40)	51.4	(1.38)
Secondary school teachers	948	(51.6)	100.0	‡	(†)	1.0!	(0.43)	1.4!	(0.59)	0.9!	(0.43)	40.1	(2.63)	56.6	(2.67)
Special education teachers	337	(30.7)	100.0	‡	(†)	‡	(†)	4.5!	(1.56)	‡	(†)	37.2	(4.36)	54.8	(4.31)
Postsecondary teachers	1,281	(62.3)	100.0	‡	(†)	0.5!	(0.24)	1.4!	(0.54)	1.8!	(0.56)	14.1	(1.63)	82.3	(1.75)
Other education, training, and library workers	2,293	(72.3)	100.0	0.9!	(0.32)	15.2	(1.15)	16.0	(1.25)	12.0	(1.17)	29.9	(1.56)	26.0	(1.60)
Service occupations	20,981	(238.1)	100.0	14.3	(0.38)	37.8	(0.54)	18.7	(0.48)	12.2	(0.37)	14.0	(0.42)	3.0	(0.17)
Sales and office occupations	27,638	(251.2)	100.0	3.7	(0.20)	29.1	(0.46)	21.9	(0.41)	12.7	(0.38)	26.4	(0.45)	6.2	(0.24)
Natural resources, construction, and maintenance	12,344	(182.8)	100.0	19.2	(0.65)	43.0	(0.85)	15.6	(0.50)	12.4	(0.51)	8.7	(0.45)	1.2	(0.16)
Production, transportation, and material moving	16,428	(217.4)	100.0	13.8	(0.45)	46.1	(0.70)	17.9	(0.50)	9.9	(0.38)	10.2	(0.37)	2.1	(0.20)
Males	**72,785**	**(238.8)**	**100.0**	**8.3**	**(0.17)**	**27.6**	**(0.32)**	**15.0**	**(0.24)**	**9.8**	**(0.19)**	**24.9**	**(0.28)**	**14.4**	**(0.23)**
Management, professional, and related	28,809	(288.7)	100.0	1.5	(0.11)	10.2	(0.30)	10.4	(0.34)	7.9	(0.25)	38.7	(0.44)	31.3	(0.45)
Management, business, and financial operations	14,106	(219.5)	100.0	2.5	(0.20)	14.4	(0.51)	13.4	(0.51)	8.1	(0.36)	39.7	(0.63)	22.0	(0.56)
Professional and related	14,703	(195.3)	100.0	0.5	(0.10)	6.1	(0.36)	7.4	(0.39)	7.8	(0.35)	37.8	(0.63)	40.3	(0.66)
Education, training, and library	2,356	(81.0)	100.0	‡	(†)	3.7	(0.63)	4.3	(0.66)	4.1	(0.65)	31.6	(1.46)	55.9	(1.55)
Service occupations	8,725	(153.4)	100.0	14.6	(0.58)	36.7	(0.86)	18.3	(0.75)	11.1	(0.63)	16.2	(0.70)	3.1	(0.31)
Sales and office occupations	10,778	(167.3)	100.0	4.4	(0.32)	27.0	(0.69)	20.2	(0.63)	10.9	(0.47)	30.5	(0.75)	7.0	(0.39)
Natural resources, construction, and maintenance	11,760	(176.8)	100.0	18.7	(0.65)	43.4	(0.88)	15.8	(0.52)	12.5	(0.52)	8.3	(0.44)	1.2	(0.16)
Production, transportation, and material moving	12,712	(187.2)	100.0	13.0	(0.53)	46.8	(0.77)	18.3	(0.58)	10.0	(0.43)	9.8	(0.41)	2.1	(0.22)
Females	**64,693**	**(240.5)**	**100.0**	**5.1**	**(0.13)**	**22.2**	**(0.26)**	**15.1**	**(0.22)**	**12.5**	**(0.23)**	**27.4**	**(0.31)**	**17.7**	**(0.24)**
Management, professional, and related	31,278	(230.6)	100.0	0.7	(0.07)	8.6	(0.26)	9.3	(0.26)	11.9	(0.30)	37.4	(0.46)	32.1	(0.42)
Management, business, and financial operations	11,358	(169.0)	100.0	1.3	(0.16)	12.2	(0.49)	12.5	(0.54)	10.6	(0.45)	40.4	(0.75)	23.0	(0.64)
Professional and related	19,919	(198.7)	100.0	0.4	(0.06)	6.5	(0.27)	7.5	(0.26)	12.7	(0.37)	35.6	(0.54)	37.3	(0.55)
Education, training, and library	6,694	(116.4)	100.0	0.4	(0.09)	6.5	(0.47)	6.6	(0.46)	6.0	(0.46)	35.6	(0.95)	44.8	(0.96)
Service occupations	12,256	(177.4)	100.0	14.2	(0.44)	38.5	(0.68)	18.9	(0.55)	13.0	(0.47)	12.4	(0.49)	3.0	(0.23)
Sales and office occupations	16,860	(184.6)	100.0	3.3	(0.22)	30.4	(0.57)	23.0	(0.56)	13.9	(0.49)	23.8	(0.54)	5.7	(0.30)
Natural resources, construction, and maintenance	583	(39.0)	100.0	29.5	(2.91)	33.1	(2.73)	10.7	(1.85)	9.6	(1.90)	15.5	(2.67)	1.5!	(0.64)
Production, transportation, and material moving	3,716	(98.7)	100.0	16.7	(0.89)	43.7	(1.22)	16.6	(0.95)	9.5	(0.75)	11.4	(0.83)	2.2	(0.38)

†Not applicable.

!Interpret data with caution. The coefficient of variation (CV) for this estimate is between 30 and 50 percent.

‡Reporting standards not met. Either there are too few cases for a reliable estimate or the coefficient of variation (CV) is 50 percent or greater.

NOTE: Data are based on sample surveys of the noninstitutionalized population, which excludes persons living in institutions (e.g., prisons or nursing facilities); this table includes only data on the civilian population (excludes all military personnel). Detail may not sum to totals because of rounding. Some data have been revised from previously published figures.

SOURCE: U.S. Department of Commerce, Census Bureau, Current Population Survey (CPS), Annual Social and Economic Supplement, 2018 and 2019. (This table was prepared February 2020.)

Table 502.20. Median annual earnings, number, and percentage of full-time year-round workers age 25 and over, by highest level of educational attainment and sex: 1990 through 2018

[Standard errors appear in parentheses]

Sex and year	Total	Elementary/secondary: Less than 9th grade	Elementary/secondary: Some high school, no completion[1]	Elementary/secondary: High school completion (includes equivalency)[2]	College: Some college, no degree[3]	College: Associate's degree	College: Bachelor's or higher degree[4]: Total	College: Bachelor's or higher degree[4]: Bachelor's degree[5]	College: Bachelor's or higher degree[4]: Master's degree	College: Bachelor's or higher degree[4]: Professional degree	College: Bachelor's or higher degree[4]: Doctor's degree
1	2	3	4	5	6	7	8	9	10	11	12
	Current dollars										
Males											
1990	$30,730 (—)	$17,390 (—)	$20,900 (—)	$26,650 (—)	$31,730 (—)	[6] (†)	$42,670 (—)	$39,240 (—)	[6] (†)	[6] (†)	[6] (†)
1995	34,550 (275)	18,350 (545)	22,190 (342)	29,510 (358)	33,880 (517)	35,200 (535)	50,480 (312)	45,270 (510)	55,220 (973)	79,670 (2,582)	65,340 (2,188)
2000	41,060 (156)	20,790 (376)	25,100 (436)	34,300 (457)	40,340 (312)	41,950 (460)	61,870 (303)	56,330 (573)	68,320 (1,506)	99,410 (20,832)	80,250 (2,446)
2001	41,620 (104)	21,360 (235)	26,210 (251)	34,720 (299)	41,050 (214)	42,780 (561)	62,220 (279)	55,930 (335)	70,900 (687)	100,000 (—)	86,970 (3,013)
2002	41,150 (100)	20,920 (213)	25,900 (207)	33,210 (311)	40,850 (195)	42,860 (673)	61,700 (201)	56,080 (385)	67,280 (1,294)	100,000 (—)	83,310 (2,076)
2003	41,940 (90)	21,220 (227)	26,470 (280)	35,410 (168)	41,350 (182)	42,870 (719)	62,080 (187)	56,500 (365)	70,640 (562)	100,000 (—)	87,130 (2,528)
2004	42,090 (89)	21,660 (191)	26,280 (234)	35,730 (148)	41,900 (175)	44,400 (931)	62,800 (798)	57,220 (393)	71,530 (490)	100,000 (—)	82,400 (2,423)
2005	43,320 (367)	22,330 (220)	27,190 (237)	36,300 (141)	42,420 (323)	47,180 (367)	66,170 (356)	60,020 (653)	75,030 (1,229)	100,000 (—)	85,860 (3,061)
2006	45,760 (134)	22,710 (398)	27,650 (573)	37,030 (164)	43,830 (812)	47,070 (390)	66,930 (346)	60,910 (235)	75,430 (859)	100,000 (—)	100,000 (—)
2007	47,000 (130)	23,380 (544)	29,320 (590)	37,860 (406)	44,900 (585)	49,040 (801)	70,400 (241)	62,090 (236)	76,280 (416)	100,000 (—)	92,090 (1,894)
2008	49,000 (339)	24,260 (631)	29,680 (458)	39,010 (399)	45,820 (276)	50,150 (344)	72,220 (236)	65,800 (388)	80,960 (468)	100,000 (—)	100,000 (—)
2009	49,990 (201)	23,950 (394)	28,020 (542)	39,480 (379)	47,100 (347)	50,300 (238)	71,470 (239)	62,440 (707)	79,340 (1,568)	123,240 (2,539)	100,740 (519)
2010	50,360 (93)	24,450 (597)	29,440 (684)	40,060 (237)	46,430 (348)	50,280 (245)	71,780 (267)	63,740 (1,115)	80,960 (453)	115,300 (4,891)	101,220 (653)
2011	50,660 (25)	25,220 (23)	30,420 (300)	40,450 (87)	47,070 (78)	50,930 (212)	73,850 (490)	66,200 (25)	83,030 (755)	119,470 (1,917)	100,770 (192)
2012	50,950 (144)	25,130 (440)	30,330 (430)	40,350 (194)	47,190 (407)	50,960 (329)	75,320 (565)	66,150 (570)	85,120 (1,412)	116,350 (5,632)	106,470 (4,656)
2013	51,120 (149)	26,160 (531)	30,570 (551)	40,290 (227)	47,650 (739)	51,000 (493)	76,110 (485)	67,240 (992)	86,310 (1,429)	126,730 (8,647)	105,280 (4,631)
2014	51,400 (133)	26,580 (382)	30,840 (382)	40,930 (197)	46,900 (429)	51,110 (345)	75,910 (391)	68,160 (1,282)	84,760 (1,988)	121,750 (5,986)	100,710 (852)
2015	52,310 (152)	27,160 (460)	32,140 (320)	41,570 (184)	49,670 (708)	52,070 (352)	79,320 (1,350)	71,390 (420)	86,740 (1,632)	131,190 (7,197)	102,340 (4,801)
2016	53,740 (725)	30,350 (500)	32,490 (1,237)	41,890 (180)	49,240 (784)	52,120 (462)	80,320 (446)	71,630 (383)	88,430 (2,215)	117,550 (7,311)	120,430 (4,017)
2017	55,630 (269)	31,000 (369)	34,620 (1,249)	42,440 (524)	50,850 (274)	54,700 (1,414)	81,390 (321)	71,990 (395)	91,600 (648)	127,230 (5,441)	118,450 (4,152)
2018	57,430 (442)	31,800 (420)	35,600 (406)	45,580 (300)	51,690 (291)	56,720 (598)	82,840 (1,930)	75,150 (959)	99,620 (1,750)	135,440 (10,136)	115,790 (5,892)
Females											
1990	21,370 (—)	12,250 (—)	14,430 (—)	18,320 (—)	22,230 (—)	[6] (†)	30,380 (—)	28,020 (—)	[6] (†)	[6] (†)	[6] (†)
1995	24,880 (160)	13,580 (490)	15,830 (293)	20,460 (162)	24,000 (274)	27,310 (428)	35,260 (313)	32,050 (273)	40,260 (556)	50,000 (2,532)	48,140 (2,373)
2000	30,330 (138)	15,800 (327)	17,920 (434)	24,970 (236)	28,700 (364)	31,070 (307)	42,710 (439)	40,420 (284)	50,140 (735)	58,960 (3,552)	57,080 (2,999)
2001	31,360 (91)	16,690 (255)	19,160 (359)	25,300 (132)	30,420 (186)	32,150 (231)	44,780 (367)	40,990 (231)	50,670 (328)	61,750 (3,976)	62,120 (2,228)
2002	31,010 (83)	16,510 (297)	19,310 (360)	25,180 (121)	29,400 (299)	31,630 (211)	43,250 (568)	40,850 (173)	48,890 (595)	57,020 (2,421)	65,720 (2,268)
2003	31,570 (85)	16,910 (256)	18,940 (327)	26,070 (118)	30,140 (176)	32,250 (241)	45,120 (291)	41,330 (204)	50,160 (454)	66,490 (3,469)	67,210 (2,462)
2004	31,990 (80)	17,020 (241)	19,160 (319)	26,030 (116)	30,820 (135)	33,480 (489)	45,910 (229)	41,680 (172)	51,320 (263)	75,040 (2,436)	68,880 (2,450)
2005	33,080 (242)	16,140 (250)	20,130 (274)	26,290 (134)	31,400 (165)	33,940 (497)	46,950 (232)	42,170 (179)	51,410 (283)	80,460 (2,774)	66,850 (2,490)
2006	35,100 (113)	18,130 (408)	20,130 (270)	26,740 (136)	31,950 (165)	35,160 (376)	49,570 (441)	45,410 (259)	52,440 (561)	76,240 (2,488)	70,520 (1,779)
2007	36,090 (105)	18,260 (461)	20,400 (292)	27,240 (133)	32,840 (415)	36,330 (283)	50,400 (158)	45,770 (262)	55,430 (412)	71,100 (910)	68,990 (2,155)
2008	36,700 (109)	18,630 (494)	20,410 (295)	28,380 (283)	32,630 (355)	36,760 (243)	51,410 (145)	47,030 (237)	57,510 (745)	71,300 (2,859)	74,030 (2,144)
2009	37,260 (107)	18,480 (451)	21,230 (301)	29,150 (273)	34,090 (483)	37,270 (310)	51,880 (169)	46,830 (260)	61,070 (304)	83,910 (3,210)	76,580 (912)
2010	38,290 (272)	18,240 (592)	20,880 (334)	29,860 (260)	33,400 (410)	37,770 (588)	51,940 (159)	47,440 (336)	59,100 (1,021)	76,740 (2,723)	77,390 (2,174)
2011	38,910 (216)	20,100 (250)	21,110 (131)	30,010 (145)	34,590 (512)	39,290 (40)	52,140 (88)	49,110 (103)	60,300 (533)	80,720 (135)	77,460 (21)
2012	39,980 (294)	20,060 (514)	21,390 (285)	30,410 (165)	35,060 (452)	37,320 (455)	53,690 (888)	50,170 (290)	60,930 (464)	94,470 (6,655)	77,900 (3,616)
2013	40,610 (134)	19,840 (502)	22,250 (544)	30,800 (173)	35,240 (312)	37,700 (751)	55,720 (416)	50,750 (341)	61,280 (561)	85,400 (6,196)	75,090 (3,515)
2014	40,830 (151)	20,990 (279)	21,990 (322)	30,650 (151)	34,380 (891)	37,480 (591)	55,940 (333)	51,350 (230)	60,830 (442)	91,810 (8,587)	80,540 (2,875)
2015	41,680 (146)	21,050 (275)	22,670 (714)	31,250 (138)	36,140 (273)	40,190 (437)	57,220 (527)	51,680 (278)	62,380 (1,135)	82,470 (5,049)	82,310 (3,752)
2016	43,010 (617)	22,210 (485)	24,800 (562)	31,540 (152)	36,880 (273)	40,220 (362)	60,060 (483)	52,030 (257)	64,910 (1,091)	92,030 (4,468)	86,370 (4,485)
2017	44,620 (530)	22,360 (533)	25,450 (459)	32,240 (199)	36,620 (259)	40,640 (335)	60,740 (270)	52,440 (601)	68,510 (1,524)	100,180 92,030	(3,137) (3,137)
2018	46,570 (204)	22,970 (1,042)	25,140 (576)	32,620 (471)	38,840 (600)	41,490 (329)	61,760 (227)	56,680 (466)	66,740 (581)	99,780 (7,090)	95,170 (5,083)

See notes at end of table.

Table 502.20. Median annual earnings, number, and percentage of full-time year-round workers age 25 and over, by highest level of educational attainment and sex: 1990 through 2018—Continued

[Standard errors appear in parentheses]

Sex and year	Total	Elementary/secondary: Less than 9th grade	Elementary/secondary: Some high school, no completion[1]	Elementary/secondary: High school completion (includes equivalency)[2]	College: Some college, no degree[3]	College: Associate's degree	Bachelor's or higher degree[4]: Total	Bachelor's or higher degree[4]: Bachelor's degree[5]	Bachelor's or higher degree[4]: Master's degree	Bachelor's or higher degree[4]: Professional degree	Bachelor's or higher degree[4]: Doctor's degree
1	2	3	4	5	6	7	8	9	10	11	12
	Constant 2018 dollars[7]										
Males											
1990	$59,060 (—)	$33,430 (—)	$40,170 (—)	$51,220 (—)	$60,990 (—)	[6] (†)	$82,010 (—)	$75,410 (—)	[6] (†)	[6] (†)	[6] (†)
1995	56,940 (453)	30,240 (898)	36,560 (564)	48,630 (590)	55,830 (852)	58,010 (882)	83,190 (514)	74,590 (840)	90,990 (1,603)	131,280 (4,255)	107,670 (3,606)
2000	59,870 (227)	30,320 (548)	36,590 (636)	50,020 (666)	58,820 (455)	61,180 (671)	90,220 (442)	82,150 (836)	99,630 (2,196)	144,960 (30,378)	117,020 (3,567)
2001	59,020 (147)	30,290 (333)	37,170 (356)	49,240 (424)	58,210 (303)	60,660 (796)	88,240 (396)	79,320 (475)	100,550 (974)	141,810 (—)	123,330 (4,273)
2002	57,450 (140)	29,200 (297)	36,160 (289)	46,360 (434)	57,030 (272)	59,830 (940)	86,130 (281)	78,280 (537)	93,920 (1,806)	139,600 (—)	116,290 (2,898)
2003	57,250 (123)	28,960 (310)	36,130 (382)	48,340 (229)	56,440 (248)	58,520 (981)	84,730 (255)	77,130 (498)	96,430 (767)	136,500 (—)	118,940 (3,451)
2004	55,950 (118)	28,790 (254)	34,930 (311)	47,490 (197)	55,700 (233)	59,030 (1,238)	83,480 (1,061)	76,070 (522)	95,090 (651)	132,940 (—)	109,550 (3,221)
2005	55,700 (472)	28,710 (283)	34,960 (305)	46,680 (181)	54,540 (415)	60,660 (472)	85,080 (458)	77,170 (840)	96,470 (1,580)	128,580 (—)	110,400 (3,936)
2006	57,000 (167)	28,290 (496)	34,450 (714)	46,130 (204)	54,600 (1,011)	58,630 (486)	83,370 (431)	75,870 (293)	93,960 (1,070)	124,560 (—)	124,560 (—)
2007	56,930 (157)	28,310 (659)	35,510 (715)	45,850 (492)	54,380 (708)	59,390 (970)	85,260 (292)	75,190 (286)	92,390 (504)	121,110 (—)	111,530 (2,294)
2008	57,150 (395)	28,290 (736)	34,610 (534)	45,500 (465)	53,440 (322)	58,490 (401)	84,220 (275)	76,740 (453)	94,430 (546)	116,630 (—)	116,630 (—)
2009	58,520 (235)	28,030 (461)	32,800 (634)	46,210 (444)	55,130 (406)	58,880 (279)	83,650 (280)	73,090 (828)	92,870 (1,835)	144,250 (2,972)	117,910 (607)
2010	57,990 (107)	28,160 (687)	33,900 (788)	46,130 (273)	53,470 (401)	57,900 (282)	82,660 (307)	73,400 (1,284)	93,230 (522)	132,770 (5,632)	116,560 (752)
2011	56,550 (28)	28,160 (26)	33,960 (335)	45,150 (97)	52,550 (87)	56,850 (237)	82,450 (547)	73,900 (28)	92,690 (843)	133,370 (2,140)	112,490 (214)
2012	55,730 (157)	27,490 (481)	33,170 (470)	44,130 (212)	51,610 (445)	55,740 (360)	82,380 (618)	72,350 (623)	93,090 (1,544)	127,260 (6,160)	116,440 (5,092)
2013	55,100 (161)	28,200 (572)	32,950 (594)	43,430 (245)	51,360 (797)	54,970 (531)	82,030 (523)	72,470 (1,069)	93,030 (1,540)	136,600 (9,321)	113,480 (4,992)
2014	54,520 (141)	28,200 (405)	32,710 (405)	43,420 (209)	49,740 (455)	54,210 (366)	80,520 (415)	72,300 (1,360)	89,900 (2,109)	129,150 (6,349)	106,820 (904)
2015	55,410 (161)	28,770 (487)	34,050 (339)	44,040 (195)	52,620 (750)	55,170 (373)	84,040 (1,430)	75,630 (445)	91,890 (1,729)	138,990 (7,625)	108,420 (5,086)
2016	56,230 (759)	31,760 (523)	34,000 (1,294)	43,830 (188)	51,510 (820)	54,530 (483)	84,030 (467)	74,950 (401)	92,520 (2,317)	122,990 (7,649)	126,000 (4,203)
2017	56,990 (276)	31,750 (378)	35,470 (1,280)	43,480 (537)	52,090 (281)	56,040 (1,449)	83,370 (329)	73,750 (405)	93,840 (664)	130,340 (5,574)	121,340 (4,253)
2018	57,430 (442)	31,800 (420)	35,600 (406)	45,580 (300)	51,690 (291)	56,720 (598)	82,840 (1,930)	75,150 (959)	99,620 (1,750)	135,440 (10,136)	115,790 (5,892)
Females											
1990	41,070 (—)	23,540 (—)	27,730 (—)	35,210 (—)	42,720 (—)	[6] (†)	58,380 (—)	53,840 (—)	[6] (†)	[6] (†)	[6] (†)
1995	40,990 (264)	22,370 (807)	26,080 (483)	33,720 (267)	39,540 (452)	45,000 (705)	58,100 (516)	52,820 (450)	66,350 (916)	82,390 (4,172)	79,330 (3,910)
2000	44,220 (201)	23,040 (477)	26,130 (633)	36,410 (344)	41,850 (531)	45,310 (448)	62,280 (640)	58,930 (414)	73,110 (1,072)	85,970 (5,180)	83,240 (4,373)
2001	44,470 (129)	23,670 (362)	27,170 (509)	35,880 (187)	43,140 (264)	45,600 (328)	63,500 (520)	58,140 (328)	71,860 (465)	87,570 (5,639)	88,100 (3,160)
2002	43,290 (116)	23,050 (415)	26,950 (503)	35,150 (169)	41,040 (417)	44,150 (295)	60,370 (793)	57,030 (242)	68,250 (831)	79,600 (3,380)	91,740 (3,166)
2003	43,090 (116)	23,080 (349)	25,850 (446)	35,590 (161)	41,140 (240)	44,030 (329)	61,580 (397)	56,410 (278)	68,470 (620)	90,760 (4,735)	91,750 (3,361)
2004	42,530 (106)	22,630 (320)	25,470 (424)	34,600 (154)	40,970 (179)	44,510 (650)	61,040 (304)	55,410 (229)	68,220 (350)	99,760 (3,238)	91,560 (3,257)
2005	42,530 (311)	20,760 (321)	25,880 (352)	33,800 (172)	40,370 (212)	43,640 (639)	60,370 (298)	54,220 (230)	66,110 (364)	103,450 (3,567)	85,960 (3,202)
2006	43,720 (141)	22,590 (508)	25,070 (336)	33,300 (169)	39,800 (206)	43,790 (468)	61,750 (549)	56,560 (323)	65,320 (699)	94,970 (3,099)	87,840 (2,216)
2007	43,700 (127)	22,120 (558)	24,700 (354)	32,990 (161)	39,770 (503)	44,000 (343)	61,040 (191)	55,430 (317)	67,130 (499)	86,110 (1,102)	83,550 (2,610)
2008	42,800 (127)	21,730 (576)	23,800 (344)	33,100 (330)	38,050 (414)	42,870 (283)	59,960 (169)	54,850 (276)	67,080 (869)	83,150 (3,334)	86,340 (2,501)
2009	43,620 (125)	21,630 (528)	24,840 (352)	34,120 (320)	39,900 (565)	43,620 (363)	60,720 (198)	54,810 (304)	71,480 (356)	98,210 (3,757)	89,640 (1,067)
2010	44,100 (313)	21,000 (682)	24,050 (385)	34,380 (299)	38,460 (472)	43,500 (677)	59,810 (183)	54,620 (387)	68,060 (1,176)	88,370 (3,136)	89,120 (2,504)
2011	43,440 (241)	22,440 (279)	23,570 (146)	33,500 (162)	38,620 (572)	43,860 (45)	58,200 (98)	54,820 (115)	67,320 (595)	90,110 (151)	86,470 (23)
2012	43,720 (322)	21,940 (562)	23,390 (312)	33,260 (180)	38,340 (494)	40,820 (498)	58,720 (971)	54,870 (317)	66,640 (507)	103,330 (7,279)	85,200 (3,955)
2013	43,780 (144)	21,390 (541)	23,980 (586)	33,200 (186)	37,990 (336)	40,640 (810)	60,070 (448)	54,700 (368)	66,060 (605)	92,050 (6,679)	80,940 (3,789)
2014	43,310 (160)	22,270 (296)	23,320 (342)	32,510 (160)	36,460 (945)	39,750 (627)	59,340 (353)	54,460 (244)	64,520 (469)	97,390 (9,108)	85,430 (3,050)
2015	44,160 (155)	22,310 (291)	24,020 (756)	33,110 (146)	38,290 (289)	42,570 (463)	60,620 (558)	54,750 (295)	66,090 (1,202)	87,380 (5,349)	87,200 (3,975)
2016	45,000 (646)	23,240 (507)	25,950 (588)	33,000 (159)	38,590 (286)	42,080 (379)	62,840 (505)	54,440 (269)	67,910 (1,141)	96,290 (4,675)	90,360 (4,692)
2017	45,710 (543)	22,910 (546)	26,080 (470)	33,030 (204)	37,520 (265)	41,630 (343)	62,220 (277)	53,720 (616)	70,180 (1,561)	102,620 (4,935)	94,280 (3,214)
2018	46,570 (204)	22,970 (1,042)	25,140 (576)	32,620 (471)	38,840 (600)	41,490 (329)	61,760 (227)	56,680 (466)	66,740 (581)	99,780 (7,090)	95,170 (5,083)

See notes at end of table.

Table 502.20. Median annual earnings, number, and percentage of full-time year-round workers age 25 and over, by highest level of educational attainment and sex: 1990 through 2018—Continued

[Standard errors appear in parentheses]

Sex and year	Total	Elementary/secondary			College						
							Bachelor's or higher degree[4]				
		Less than 9th grade	Some high school, no completion[1]	High school completion (includes equivalency)[2]	Some college, no degree[3]	Associate's degree	Total	Bachelor's degree[5]	Master's degree	Professional degree	Doctor's degree
1	2	3	4	5	6	7	8	9	10	11	12
	Number of persons with earnings who worked full time, year round (in thousands)										
Males											
1990	44,406 (268.6)	2,250 (73.9)	3,315 (89.3)	16,394 (188.0)	9,113 (144.6)	[6] (†)	13,334 (171.8)	7,569 (132.6)	[6] (†)	[6] (†)	[6] (†)
1995	48,500 (306.1)	1,946 (72.8)	3,335 (94.9)	15,331 (195.6)	8,908 (152.3)	3,926 (102.8)	15,054 (194.0)	9,597 (157.8)	3,395 (95.7)	1,208 (57.5)	853 (48.4)
2000	54,065 (309.7)	1,968 (68.0)	3,354 (88.4)	16,834 (191.7)	9,792 (148.8)	4,729 (104.7)	17,387 (194.6)	11,395 (159.9)	3,680 (92.6)	1,274 (54.8)	1,038 (49.5)
2001	54,013 (224.8)	2,207 (51.4)	3,503 (64.5)	16,314 (135.4)	9,494 (104.9)	4,714 (74.7)	17,780 (140.9)	11,479 (114.8)	3,961 (68.5)	1,298 (39.5)	1,041 (35.4)
2002	54,108 (225.0)	2,154 (50.7)	3,680 (66.1)	16,005 (134.2)	9,603 (105.5)	4,399 (72.2)	18,267 (142.7)	11,829 (116.5)	4,065 (69.4)	1,308 (39.6)	1,065 (35.8)
2003	54,253 (225.2)	2,209 (51.4)	3,369 (63.3)	16,285 (135.3)	9,340 (104.1)	4,696 (74.5)	18,354 (143.0)	11,846 (116.6)	4,124 (69.9)	1,348 (40.2)	1,037 (35.3)
2004	55,469 (227.0)	2,427 (53.8)	3,468 (64.2)	17,067 (138.3)	9,257 (103.6)	4,913 (76.2)	18,338 (142.9)	11,701 (115.9)	4,243 (70.9)	1,305 (39.6)	1,088 (36.1)
2005	56,717 (228.7)	2,425 (53.8)	3,652 (65.9)	17,266 (139.0)	9,532 (105.1)	5,022 (77.0)	18,820 (144.7)	12,032 (117.4)	4,275 (71.2)	1,369 (40.5)	1,144 (37.1)
2006	58,109 (230.6)	2,361 (53.1)	3,872 (67.8)	17,369 (139.4)	9,493 (104.9)	5,110 (77.7)	19,903 (148.4)	12,764 (120.7)	4,542 (73.3)	1,425 (41.3)	1,172 (37.5)
2007	58,147 (230.7)	2,142 (50.6)	3,451 (64.0)	17,224 (138.9)	9,867 (106.8)	5,244 (78.7)	20,218 (149.5)	12,962 (121.6)	4,800 (75.3)	1,332 (40.0)	1,125 (36.7)
2008	55,655 (227.2)	1,982 (48.7)	3,118 (60.9)	16,195 (135.0)	9,515 (105.0)	5,020 (77.0)	19,825 (148.1)	12,609 (120.0)	4,709 (74.6)	1,388 (40.8)	1,119 (36.7)
2009	52,445 (222.5)	1,561 (43.2)	2,795 (57.7)	15,258 (131.3)	8,609 (100.1)	4,828 (75.5)	19,395 (146.7)	12,290 (118.6)	4,575 (73.6)	1,319 (39.8)	1,212 (38.1)
2010	52,890 (223.2)	1,600 (43.8)	2,615 (55.9)	15,104 (130.7)	8,541 (99.7)	5,042 (77.2)	19,990 (148.7)	12,836 (121.1)	4,670 (74.3)	1,237 (38.5)	1,246 (38.7)
2011	54,279 (225.2)	1,848 (47.0)	2,715 (56.9)	15,335 (131.6)	8,752 (100.9)	5,206 (78.4)	20,423 (150.1)	13,013 (121.8)	4,839 (75.6)	1,300 (39.5)	1,271 (39.0)
2012	55,208 (226.6)	1,793 (46.3)	2,671 (56.4)	15,295 (131.4)	8,974 (102.1)	5,423 (80.0)	21,052 (152.2)	13,315 (123.2)	5,003 (76.9)	1,301 (39.5)	1,433 (41.4)
2013	56,703 (289.3)	1,944 (61.0)	2,910 (74.5)	16,034 (170.0)	8,960 (129.0)	5,605 (102.8)	21,249 (193.4)	13,378 (156.2)	5,146 (98.6)	1,249 (49.0)	1,476 (53.2)
2014	58,435 (256.1)	1,994 (54.0)	3,012 (66.2)	16,429 (150.3)	9,281 (114.7)	5,622 (90.0)	22,098 (172.1)	13,969 (139.3)	5,401 (88.2)	1,359 (44.6)	1,369 (44.8)
2015	59,690 (264.8)	2,008 (54.2)	2,984 (66.0)	16,286 (150.5)	9,445 (116.0)	5,907 (92.3)	23,059 (176.9)	14,469 (142.4)	5,883 (92.2)	1,256 (42.9)	1,451 (46.1)
2016	60,677 (266.4)	1,844 (52.0)	2,828 (64.2)	16,855 (153.0)	9,603 (117.0)	6,091 (93.7)	23,456 (178.3)	14,723 (143.5)	5,975 (92.9)	1,169 (41.4)	1,589 (48.2)
2017	61,794 (268.2)	1,820 (51.6)	2,931 (65.4)	16,997 (153.6)	9,629 (117.1)	6,052 (93.4)	24,365 (181.4)	15,445 (146.8)	6,065 (93.5)	1,188 (41.7)	1,667 (49.4)
2018	62,603 (392.2)	1,878 (75.1)	2,859 (92.5)	17,306 (222.7)	9,341 (165.6)	6,310 (136.8)	24,908 (263.9)	15,961 (214.3)	6,080 (134.3)	1,248 (61.3)	1,619 (69.8)
Females											
1990	28,636 (234.7)	847 (45.6)	1,861 (67.3)	11,810 (162.8)	6,462 (123.1)	[6] (†)	7,655 (133.3)	4,704 (105.8)	[6] (†)	[6] (†)	[6] (†)
1995	32,673 (268.2)	774 (46.1)	1,763 (69.3)	11,064 (168.6)	6,329 (129.5)	3,336 (94.9)	9,406 (156.3)	6,434 (130.5)	2,268 (78.5)	421 (34.0)	283 (27.9)
2000	37,762 (271.6)	930 (46.8)	1,950 (67.7)	11,789 (162.5)	7,391 (130.0)	4,118 (97.8)	11,584 (161.1)	7,899 (134.3)	2,823 (81.2)	509 (34.7)	353 (28.9)
2001	38,228 (197.0)	927 (33.4)	1,869 (47.3)	11,690 (115.8)	7,283 (92.3)	4,190 (70.5)	12,269 (118.5)	8,257 (98.1)	3,089 (60.6)	531 (25.3)	392 (21.7)
2002	38,510 (197.6)	858 (32.1)	1,841 (46.9)	11,687 (115.8)	7,354 (92.7)	4,285 (71.2)	12,484 (119.5)	8,229 (97.9)	3,281 (62.5)	572 (26.2)	402 (22.0)
2003	38,681 (197.9)	882 (32.6)	1,739 (45.6)	11,587 (115.3)	7,341 (92.6)	4,397 (72.2)	12,735 (120.6)	8,330 (98.5)	3,376 (63.4)	567 (26.1)	462 (23.6)
2004	39,072 (198.7)	917 (33.2)	1,797 (46.4)	11,392 (114.4)	7,330 (92.6)	4,505 (73.0)	13,131 (122.4)	8,664 (100.4)	3,451 (64.0)	564 (26.0)	452 (23.3)
2005	40,021 (200.6)	902 (32.9)	1,740 (45.6)	11,419 (114.5)	7,452 (93.3)	4,751 (74.9)	13,758 (125.1)	9,074 (102.6)	3,591 (65.3)	657 (28.1)	437 (22.9)
2006	41,311 (203.2)	934 (33.5)	1,802 (46.4)	11,652 (115.6)	7,613 (94.3)	4,760 (75.0)	14,549 (128.4)	9,645 (105.7)	3,746 (66.7)	662 (28.2)	497 (24.5)
2007	42,196 (204.9)	823 (31.5)	1,649 (44.4)	11,447 (114.7)	7,916 (96.1)	4,891 (76.0)	15,469 (132.1)	9,931 (107.2)	4,389 (72.1)	666 (28.3)	484 (24.1)
2008	40,979 (202.5)	814 (31.3)	1,568 (43.3)	10,851 (111.8)	7,456 (93.3)	4,955 (76.5)	15,335 (131.6)	9,856 (106.8)	4,176 (70.3)	753 (30.1)	550 (25.7)
2009	40,376 (201.4)	776 (30.5)	1,519 (42.7)	10,467 (109.9)	7,164 (91.6)	4,924 (76.3)	15,526 (132.4)	10,066 (107.9)	4,261 (71.0)	606 (27.0)	592 (26.7)
2010	40,196 (201.0)	732 (29.7)	1,371 (40.5)	10,117 (108.1)	7,150 (91.5)	4,999 (76.8)	15,826 (133.5)	9,903 (107.0)	4,576 (73.6)	622 (27.4)	725 (29.5)
2011	40,885 (202.4)	779 (30.6)	1,380 (40.7)	10,040 (107.7)	6,989 (90.5)	5,131 (77.8)	16,566 (136.4)	10,537 (110.2)	4,700 (74.6)	635 (27.6)	694 (28.9)
2012	41,319 (203.2)	690 (28.8)	1,351 (40.3)	9,870 (106.8)	6,899 (89.9)	5,246 (78.7)	17,263 (139.0)	10,961 (112.3)	4,887 (76.0)	670 (28.4)	745 (29.9)
2013	42,021 (258.8)	788 (38.9)	1,309 (50.1)	9,990 (135.9)	7,070 (115.1)	5,253 (99.6)	17,611 (177.5)	11,124 (143.1)	4,963 (96.9)	793 (39.1)	732 (37.5)
2014	42,957 (228.5)	796 (34.2)	1,356 (44.6)	9,802 (117.7)	7,241 (101.7)	5,426 (88.4)	18,336 (158.1)	11,420 (126.6)	5,310 (87.5)	776 (33.8)	830 (34.9)
2015	44,012 (234.8)	823 (34.8)	1,308 (43.8)	9,739 (117.8)	7,525 (103.9)	5,507 (89.2)	19,109 (162.2)	11,751 (128.9)	5,562 (89.7)	784 (33.9)	1,012 (38.5)
2016	44,968 (236.9)	728 (32.7)	1,382 (45.0)	9,832 (118.3)	7,305 (102.4)	5,764 (91.2)	19,957 (165.5)	12,143 (131.0)	5,997 (93.0)	841 (35.1)	976 (37.9)
2017	45,868 (238.8)	766 (33.5)	1,341 (44.3)	9,783 (118.0)	7,004 (100.4)	5,838 (91.8)	21,136 (170.0)	12,937 (135.0)	6,308 (95.4)	805 (34.4)	1,085 (39.9)
2018	46,945 (349.3)	718 (46.5)	1,337 (63.4)	10,014 (171.3)	6,927 (143.2)	5,802 (131.2)	22,147 (250.0)	13,302 (196.5)	6,856 (142.4)	826 (49.9)	1,163 (59.2)

See notes at end of table.

Table 502.20. Median annual earnings, number, and percentage of full-time year-round workers age 25 and over, by highest level of educational attainment and sex: 1990 through 2018—Continued

[Standard errors appear in parentheses]

Sex and year	Total	Elementary/secondary: Less than 9th grade	Elementary/secondary: Some high school, no completion[1]	Elementary/secondary: High school completion (includes equivalency)[2]	College: Some college, no degree[3]	College: Associate's degree	Bachelor's or higher degree[4]: Total	Bachelor's or higher degree[4]: Bachelor's degree[5]	Bachelor's or higher degree[4]: Master's degree	Bachelor's or higher degree[4]: Professional degree	Bachelor's or higher degree[4]: Doctor's degree
1	2	3	4	5	6	7	8	9	10	11	12
	Percent of persons with earnings who worked full time, year round[8]										
Males											
2000	81.7 (0.23)	69.2 (1.33)	71.8 (1.01)	80.9 (0.42)	82.2 (0.54)	86.6 (0.71)	84.8 (0.39)	85.6 (0.47)	82.8 (0.87)	85.8 (1.39)	82.5 (1.65)
2001	80.1 (0.17)	69.7 (0.90)	70.9 (0.71)	79.4 (0.31)	80.2 (0.40)	84.1 (0.54)	83.3 (0.28)	83.6 (0.35)	82.4 (0.60)	84.6 (1.01)	82.2 (1.18)
2002	79.4 (0.17)	70.1 (0.91)	71.3 (0.69)	77.8 (0.32)	78.8 (0.41)	81.4 (0.58)	83.9 (0.27)	84.4 (0.34)	82.2 (0.60)	85.7 (0.99)	82.8 (1.16)
2003	79.5 (0.17)	71.5 (0.89)	70.1 (0.73)	78.7 (0.31)	78.8 (0.41)	82.1 (0.56)	83.1 (0.28)	84.0 (0.34)	81.1 (0.60)	84.4 (1.00)	80.3 (1.22)
2004	80.0 (0.17)	74.7 (0.84)	71.2 (0.71)	79.1 (0.30)	79.3 (0.41)	83.6 (0.53)	83.0 (0.28)	83.1 (0.35)	83.1 (0.58)	83.3 (1.03)	81.7 (1.16)
2005	80.3 (0.16)	74.0 (0.84)	73.8 (0.69)	79.5 (0.30)	80.0 (0.40)	82.5 (0.54)	82.9 (0.27)	83.0 (0.34)	82.7 (0.58)	83.7 (1.00)	82.4 (1.12)
2006	81.1 (0.16)	73.6 (0.85)	72.9 (0.67)	79.6 (0.30)	80.1 (0.40)	85.3 (0.50)	84.7 (0.26)	85.2 (0.32)	83.5 (0.55)	85.9 (0.94)	83.4 (1.09)
2007	80.5 (0.16)	71.1 (0.91)	70.8 (0.72)	79.4 (0.30)	79.5 (0.40)	83.3 (0.52)	84.5 (0.26)	85.1 (0.32)	83.5 (0.54)	83.1 (1.03)	83.5 (1.11)
2008	77.0 (0.17)	66.3 (0.95)	64.6 (0.76)	74.6 (0.32)	76.5 (0.42)	79.4 (0.56)	82.6 (0.27)	83.2 (0.33)	80.9 (0.57)	82.4 (1.02)	83.1 (1.12)
2009	73.9 (0.18)	56.2 (1.03)	61.8 (0.79)	70.1 (0.34)	73.4 (0.45)	77.9 (0.58)	80.8 (0.28)	79.9 (0.35)	82.0 (0.56)	85.1 (0.99)	81.2 (1.11)
2010	74.8 (0.18)	58.8 (1.04)	61.6 (0.82)	71.9 (0.34)	72.9 (0.45)	78.2 (0.56)	81.4 (0.27)	81.8 (0.34)	80.0 (0.58)	81.4 (1.10)	82.2 (1.08)
2011	76.6 (0.17)	67.2 (0.98)	64.2 (0.81)	74.2 (0.33)	75.2 (0.44)	78.0 (0.56)	82.0 (0.27)	82.1 (0.33)	82.3 (0.55)	81.6 (1.07)	81.0 (1.09)
2012	76.5 (0.17)	65.4 (1.00)	64.4 (0.82)	74.5 (0.33)	73.7 (0.44)	78.8 (0.54)	82.1 (0.26)	82.5 (0.33)	80.8 (0.55)	84.4 (1.01)	81.4 (1.02)
2013	78.1 (0.21)	69.3 (1.21)	68.9 (0.99)	76.5 (0.41)	76.2 (0.55)	79.6 (0.67)	82.4 (0.33)	82.6 (0.41)	82.5 (0.67)	83.2 (1.34)	79.7 (1.30)
2014	79.2 (0.18)	72.2 (1.03)	69.4 (0.85)	78.3 (0.35)	76.7 (0.47)	79.9 (0.58)	83.3 (0.28)	83.7 (0.35)	82.7 (0.57)	83.5 (1.12)	81.2 (1.15)
2015	79.3 (0.18)	72.2 (1.03)	71.1 (0.85)	77.7 (0.35)	77.2 (0.46)	80.6 (0.56)	83.0 (0.27)	83.5 (0.34)	82.7 (0.54)	82.1 (1.19)	80.0 (1.14)
2016	80.1 (0.18)	72.3 (1.08)	71.5 (0.87)	78.8 (0.34)	78.4 (0.45)	81.1 (0.55)	83.4 (0.27)	83.8 (0.34)	82.8 (0.54)	82.3 (1.23)	83.5 (1.03)
2017	80.4 (0.17)	74.3 (1.07)	72.2 (0.85)	79.5 (0.34)	79.1 (0.45)	81.8 (0.54)	83.0 (0.27)	83.1 (0.33)	82.7 (0.54)	83.7 (1.19)	82.0 (1.03)
2018	81.1 (0.25)	75.2 (1.50)	73.1 (1.23)	80.7 (0.47)	78.7 (0.65)	82.8 (0.75)	83.4 (0.37)	84.3 (0.46)	81.7 (0.78)	85.1 (1.62)	79.7 (1.55)
Females											
2000	64.6 (0.30)	53.5 (1.84)	56.5 (1.30)	64.1 (0.54)	65.3 (0.69)	66.6 (0.92)	66.5 (0.55)	66.7 (0.67)	64.9 (1.11)	70.6 (2.61)	71.5 (3.13)
2001	64.3 (0.22)	54.0 (1.32)	55.3 (0.94)	63.5 (0.39)	65.1 (0.49)	65.8 (0.65)	66.6 (0.38)	66.6 (0.47)	65.6 (0.76)	70.3 (1.83)	70.9 (2.12)
2002	64.1 (0.22)	52.6 (1.36)	55.5 (0.95)	63.2 (0.39)	65.0 (0.49)	65.6 (0.65)	66.5 (0.38)	65.9 (0.47)	66.1 (0.74)	74.3 (1.73)	73.8 (2.07)
2003	64.4 (0.21)	56.5 (1.38)	53.8 (0.96)	64.4 (0.39)	64.2 (0.49)	65.6 (0.64)	66.4 (0.37)	65.8 (0.46)	66.3 (0.73)	72.3 (1.75)	71.9 (1.95)
2004	64.5 (0.21)	56.3 (1.35)	56.1 (0.96)	64.5 (0.40)	64.2 (0.49)	64.6 (0.63)	66.7 (0.37)	66.3 (0.45)	66.3 (0.72)	71.5 (1.77)	71.2 (1.97)
2005	65.3 (0.21)	56.5 (1.36)	54.5 (0.97)	65.1 (0.40)	63.5 (0.49)	67.2 (0.61)	68.2 (0.36)	68.0 (0.44)	68.3 (0.70)	71.2 (1.64)	67.3 (2.02)
2006	66.2 (0.21)	58.5 (1.35)	56.0 (0.96)	65.6 (0.39)	65.9 (0.48)	67.3 (0.61)	68.6 (0.35)	68.4 (0.43)	67.5 (0.69)	73.6 (1.61)	74.0 (1.86)
2007	66.7 (0.21)	56.8 (1.43)	55.3 (1.00)	65.7 (0.39)	66.7 (0.48)	67.3 (0.60)	69.3 (0.34)	68.4 (0.42)	70.6 (0.63)	74.1 (1.60)	71.2 (1.91)
2008	64.4 (0.21)	51.6 (1.38)	52.8 (1.01)	62.4 (0.40)	64.7 (0.49)	65.5 (0.60)	67.9 (0.34)	67.8 (0.43)	66.9 (0.65)	74.0 (1.51)	70.0 (1.80)
2009	64.3 (0.21)	52.0 (1.42)	54.5 (1.04)	62.4 (0.41)	63.9 (0.50)	64.5 (0.60)	68.0 (0.34)	68.3 (0.42)	67.5 (0.65)	66.4 (1.72)	68.3 (1.74)
2010	64.4 (0.21)	51.7 (1.46)	52.4 (1.07)	62.6 (0.42)	63.3 (0.50)	64.3 (0.60)	68.5 (0.34)	67.7 (0.42)	68.5 (0.62)	73.9 (1.66)	76.3 (1.51)
2011	65.0 (0.21)	52.2 (1.42)	49.1 (1.04)	63.0 (0.42)	62.9 (0.50)	66.3 (0.59)	69.6 (0.33)	69.4 (0.41)	69.0 (0.62)	72.8 (1.65)	73.6 (1.58)
2012	64.8 (0.21)	50.0 (1.48)	51.1 (1.07)	62.3 (0.42)	61.7 (0.50)	64.7 (0.58)	70.0 (0.32)	70.6 (0.40)	68.0 (0.60)	73.2 (1.61)	73.9 (1.52)
2013	65.6 (0.26)	56.0 (1.84)	52.3 (1.07)	63.8 (0.46)	63.4 (0.62)	65.1 (0.79)	69.6 (0.40)	70.4 (0.50)	67.4 (0.82)	73.9 (1.86)	69.4 (1.97)
2014	66.1 (0.23)	53.5 (1.57)	54.1 (1.21)	63.6 (0.47)	64.3 (0.55)	66.5 (0.63)	70.0 (0.34)	70.3 (0.44)	69.2 (0.64)	73.8 (1.65)	68.1 (1.62)
2015	66.3 (0.22)	54.9 (1.56)	51.5 (1.20)	64.1 (0.47)	65.4 (0.54)	65.6 (0.63)	70.1 (0.34)	70.3 (0.43)	68.3 (0.63)	75.9 (1.62)	74.5 (1.44)
2016	67.2 (0.22)	55.4 (1.66)	56.0 (1.21)	63.7 (0.47)	65.7 (0.55)	67.7 (0.62)	71.0 (0.33)	70.6 (0.42)	71.1 (0.60)	75.8 (1.56)	71.3 (1.48)
2017	68.0 (0.22)	57.3 (1.64)	55.1 (1.22)	64.5 (0.47)	65.5 (0.56)	68.0 (0.61)	72.2 (0.32)	71.9 (0.41)	72.4 (0.58)	75.6 (1.60)	71.8 (1.41)
2018	68.5 (0.31)	56.3 (2.41)	56.4 (1.77)	65.8 (0.67)	65.1 (0.80)	67.8 (0.88)	72.7 (0.44)	71.9 (0.57)	73.4 (0.79)	78.3 (2.21)	73.9 (1.92)

—Not available.
†Not applicable.
[1]Includes 1 to 3 years of high school for 1990.
[2]Includes 4 years of high school for 1990.
[3]Includes 1 to 3 years of college and associate's degrees for 1990.
[4]Includes 4 or more years of college for 1990.
[5]Includes 4 years of college for 1990.
[6]Not reported separately for 1990.
[7]Constant dollars based on the Consumer Price Index, prepared by the Bureau of Labor Statistics, U.S. Department of Labor.
[8]Data not available for 1990 and 1995.
NOTE: Detail may not sum to totals because of rounding.
SOURCE: U.S. Department of Commerce, Census Bureau, Current Population Reports, Series P-60, *Money Income of Households, Families, and Persons in the United States* and *Income, Poverty, and Valuation of Noncash Benefits*, 1990; Series P-60, *Money Income in the United States*, 1995 through 2002; and Current Population Survey (CPS), Annual Social and Economic Supplement, 2003 through 2019. Retrieved January 21, 2020, from https://www.census.gov/data/tables/time-series/demo/income-poverty/cps-pinc/pinc-03.html. (This table was prepared January 2020.)

Table 502.30. Median annual earnings of full-time year-round workers 25 to 34 years old and full-time year-round workers as a percentage of the labor force, by sex, race/ethnicity, and educational attainment: Selected years, 1995 through 2019

[Amounts in constant 2019 dollars. Standard errors appear in parentheses]

Sex, race/ethnicity, and educational attainment	1995		2000		2005		2010	
1	2		3		4		5	
Total, all full-time year-round workers 25 to 34 years old								
Median annual earnings, all education levels	**$41,940**	**(269)**	**$44,540**	**(158)**	**$43,170**	**(1,202)**	**$43,410**	**(969)**
Less than high school completion	26,500	(497)	26,940	(671)	26,920	(778)	24,600	(891)
High school completion[1]	34,740	(384)	37,110	(292)	36,430	(1,004)	35,120	(19)
Some college, no degree	39,540	(848)	42,840	(623)	41,190	(817)	38,500	(1,089)
Associate's degree	41,680	(807)	44,530	(463)	45,790	(1,574)	43,300	(1,167)
Bachelor's or higher degree	55,320	(1,123)	59,380	(345)	57,530	(1,139)	57,380	(1,196)
Bachelor's degree	51,920	(498)	59,270	(395)	52,770	(1,169)	52,760	(875)
Master's or higher degree	66,490	(1,284)	71,270	(3,095)	65,400	(536)	64,240	(1,489)
Percent,[2] all education levels	**67.5**	**(0.44)**	**72.1**	**(0.31)**	**70.8**	**(0.36)**	**64.8**	**(0.42)**
Less than high school completion	53.3	(1.40)	61.8	(1.00)	64.1	(1.29)	48.1	(1.44)
High school completion[1]	66.8	(0.78)	71.5	(0.57)	71.3	(0.71)	60.0	(0.79)
Some college, no degree	65.5	(0.99)	71.8	(0.69)	67.3	(0.82)	60.9	(0.89)
Associate's degree	71.9	(1.39)	74.5	(0.97)	71.8	(1.09)	65.9	(1.25)
Bachelor's or higher degree	73.9	(0.77)	75.7	(0.53)	74.4	(0.67)	74.3	(0.60)
Bachelor's degree	74.0	(0.88)	76.5	(0.59)	75.3	(0.76)	74.4	(0.70)
Master's or higher degree	73.7	(1.62)	72.7	(1.14)	72.0	(1.18)	73.8	(1.22)
Male								
Median annual earnings, all education levels	**$45,140**	**(353)**	**$47,800**	**(210)**	**$45,820**	**(#)**	**$46,760**	**(32)**
Less than high school completion	29,590	(1,033)	29,590	(418)	28,710	(1,141)	28,140	(938)
High school completion[1]	40,120	(771)	42,870	(805)	39,130	(46)	38,520	(759)
Some college, no degree	43,480	(682)	47,240	(416)	45,680	(282)	44,400	(1,254)
Associate's degree	44,530	(1,272)	51,960	(928)	51,880	(1,692)	46,790	(504)
Bachelor's or higher degree	62,630	(889)	69,380	(686)	65,430	(1,321)	61,420	(1,832)
Bachelor's degree	58,680	(922)	66,560	(755)	58,870	(1,504)	58,320	(161)
Master's or higher degree	73,930	(2,926)	81,540	(1,753)	75,700	(4,274)	75,460	(915)
Percent,[2] all education levels	**75.2**	**(0.55)**	**80.2**	**(0.37)**	**78.2**	**(0.48)**	**68.5**	**(0.57)**
Less than high school completion	59.2	(1.73)	70.9	(1.19)	72.0	(1.49)	51.2	(1.71)
High school completion[1]	74.9	(0.96)	79.4	(0.67)	79.2	(0.89)	64.3	(1.00)
Some college, no degree	73.9	(1.27)	80.7	(0.84)	76.1	(1.07)	65.7	(1.16)
Associate's degree	85.1	(1.61)	85.7	(1.16)	80.8	(1.44)	72.4	(1.74)
Bachelor's or higher degree	81.3	(0.97)	83.3	(0.65)	80.7	(0.93)	79.6	(0.85)
Bachelor's degree	81.8	(1.11)	84.2	(0.73)	80.9	(1.03)	80.4	(0.96)
Master's or higher degree	79.8	(1.99)	80.2	(1.46)	80.3	(1.79)	77.3	(1.82)
Female								
Median annual earnings, all education levels	**$36,580**	**(349)**	**$40,080**	**(246)**	**$39,210**	**(37)**	**$40,890**	**(40)**
Less than high school completion	21,710	(1,018)	22,200	(694)	21,990	(803)	20,750	(772)
High school completion[1]	29,000	(414)	32,140	(395)	31,210	(463)	29,280	(68)
Some college, no degree	33,540	(595)	37,060	(415)	36,550	(456)	33,940	(1,160)
Associate's degree	40,090	(1,767)	38,590	(594)	38,390	(442)	40,650	(971)
Bachelor's or higher degree	48,650	(1,135)	53,450	(413)	52,050	(140)	51,540	(1,330)
Bachelor's degree	46,370	(1,231)	51,800	(464)	48,420	(1,603)	46,900	(1,624)
Master's or higher degree	58,040	(1,766)	61,770	(898)	61,400	(2,534)	58,430	(108)
Percent,[2] all education levels	**58.6**	**(0.68)**	**62.8**	**(0.48)**	**61.9**	**(0.53)**	**60.3**	**(0.54)**
Less than high school completion	42.9	(2.31)	46.8	(1.68)	47.3	(1.87)	41.2	(2.13)
High school completion[1]	56.4	(1.25)	60.5	(0.96)	59.5	(1.07)	53.1	(1.20)
Some college, no degree	56.5	(1.48)	62.4	(1.06)	57.8	(1.19)	55.6	(1.25)
Associate's degree	60.2	(2.07)	65.4	(1.43)	63.3	(1.55)	60.0	(1.68)
Bachelor's or higher degree	66.4	(1.19)	68.2	(0.81)	68.6	(0.93)	69.5	(0.80)
Bachelor's degree	66.4	(1.33)	69.0	(0.91)	70.0	(1.12)	68.6	(0.96)
Master's or higher degree	66.2	(2.59)	65.7	(1.69)	65.2	(1.68)	71.4	(1.64)
White								
Median annual earnings, all education levels	**$43,590**	**(304)**	**$48,250**	**(552)**	**$45,820**	**(90)**	**$46,850**	**(25)**
Less than high school completion	29,320	(1,626)	30,920	(689)	30,290	(1,710)	29,300	(549)
High school completion[1]	36,810	(453)	40,940	(739)	39,160	(42)	38,130	(1,028)
Some college, no degree	40,430	(988)	44,390	(405)	41,770	(630)	40,810	(1,406)
Associate's degree	43,630	(991)	47,100	(507)	45,800	(365)	46,520	(836)
Bachelor's or higher degree	57,010	(1,321)	60,560	(382)	58,430	(986)	58,120	(504)
Bachelor's degree	53,670	(588)	59,300	(436)	53,590	(1,023)	53,920	(1,453)
Master's or higher degree	66,690	(1,336)	71,140	(3,773)	65,400	(609)	63,900	(1,240)
Percent,[2] all education levels	**69.1**	**(0.51)**	**72.7**	**(0.38)**	**71.6**	**(0.47)**	**66.7**	**(0.51)**
Less than high school completion	53.7	(2.07)	59.7	(1.73)	64.3	(2.17)	44.4	(2.85)
High school completion[1]	67.9	(0.93)	71.6	(0.72)	71.7	(0.88)	60.6	(1.02)
Some college, no degree	66.8	(1.17)	72.4	(0.84)	68.4	(1.00)	60.9	(1.18)
Associate's degree	71.8	(1.59)	72.7	(1.18)	71.3	(1.32)	66.3	(1.51)
Bachelor's or higher degree	74.4	(0.86)	75.9	(0.61)	74.4	(0.79)	75.0	(0.70)
Bachelor's degree	74.2	(0.97)	76.6	(0.68)	75.0	(0.92)	75.0	(0.78)
Master's or higher degree	74.8	(1.79)	73.5	(1.31)	72.8	(1.47)	75.0	(1.43)
Black								
Median annual earnings, all education levels	**$35,170**	**(941)**	**$37,110**	**(593)**	**$37,840**	**(1,476)**	**$36,870**	**(1,293)**
Less than high school completion	23,270	(3,032)	24,680	(1,489)	26,680	(1,524)	24,350	(2,852)
High school completion[1]	30,140	(1,540)	32,530	(794)	30,050	(1,322)	29,310	(930)
Some college, no degree	37,710	(2,502)	38,480	(1,158)	37,970	(2,016)	34,220	(623)
Associate's degree	36,610	(1,326)	38,080	(1,561)	36,210	(1,563)	35,760	(2,297)

Sex, race/ethnicity, and educational attainment	2013		2014		2015		2016		2017	
1	6		7		8		9		10	
Total, all full-time year-round workers 25 to 34 years old										
Median annual earnings, all education levels	**$43,900**	**(#)**	**$43,200**	**(91)**	**$43,080**	**(24)**	**$42,610**	**(330)**	**$43,720**	**(110)**
Less than high school completion	26,310	(463)	25,910	(1,307)	26,950	(75)	27,010	(762)	27,100	(1,429)
High school completion[1]	32,920	(2)	32,400	(4)	32,950	(1,031)	33,910	(152)	33,370	(314)
Some college, no degree	38,150	(1,118)	34,450	(968)	37,360	(96)	37,170	(1,086)	36,510	(939)
Associate's degree	41,020	(2,036)	37,770	(566)	39,850	(1,195)	40,470	(1,081)	40,520	(1,660)
Bachelor's or higher degree	54,870	(1,196)	56,140	(929)	58,070	(1,502)	58,340	(91)	57,350	(1,014)
Bachelor's degree	53,150	(1,932)	53,870	(47)	53,930	(#)	53,250	(270)	54,000	(1,752)
Master's or higher degree	65,610	(354)	63,820	(1,126)	64,720	(2,062)	68,250	(1,387)	67,790	(3,175)
Percent,[2] all education levels	**67.8**	**(0.50)**	**70.2**	**(0.39)**	**71.0**	**(0.42)**	**72.7**	**(0.42)**	**73.3**	**(0.40)**
Less than high school completion	55.9	(1.65)	59.1	(1.43)	58.6	(1.76)	60.1	(1.49)	63.8	(1.59)
High school completion[1]	64.5	(1.09)	68.4	(0.80)	68.6	(0.83)	68.9	(0.83)	71.1	(0.75)
Some college, no degree	61.9	(1.12)	64.6	(0.82)	67.0	(0.99)	69.5	(0.95)	68.8	(1.02)
Associate's degree	70.2	(1.47)	69.2	(1.16)	68.5	(1.16)	72.3	(1.12)	73.2	(1.08)
Bachelor's or higher degree	74.8	(0.69)	76.3	(0.62)	77.2	(0.59)	78.8	(0.59)	77.8	(0.56)
Bachelor's degree	75.1	(0.83)	76.4	(0.68)	77.7	(0.72)	78.9	(0.66)	78.1	(0.66)
Master's or higher degree	74.0	(1.27)	76.2	(1.07)	75.9	(1.09)	78.5	(1.06)	77.2	(1.05)
Male										
Median annual earnings, all education levels	**$43,900**	**(318)**	**$44,170**	**(1,329)**	**$45,300**	**(1,218)**	**$46,840**	**(1,189)**	**$46,930**	**(156)**
Less than high school completion	26,990	(383)	26,990	(603)	28,270	(1,250)	30,420	(1,582)	30,250	(1,811)
High school completion[1]	34,740	(529)	35,610	(1,227)	36,660	(881)	37,010	(146)	36,460	(637)
Some college, no degree	42,750	(1,469)	38,800	(735)	42,020	(774)	40,460	(1,030)	41,710	(1,249)
Associate's degree	45,890	(2,621)	43,510	(1,731)	46,220	(1,672)	45,800	(1,404)	46,760	(1,079)
Bachelor's or higher degree	63,130	(2,408)	63,690	(1,946)	64,450	(156)	63,870	(1,312)	64,610	(1,985)
Bachelor's degree	57,030	(1,568)	59,130	(306)	59,290	(1,851)	60,680	(2,175)	62,240	(133)
Master's or higher degree	75,540	(3,359)	69,880	(1,728)	75,000	(2,266)	76,310	(1,957)	78,200	(2,223)
Percent,[2] all education levels	**73.2**	**(0.62)**	**76.8**	**(0.53)**	**76.8**	**(0.52)**	**78.2**	**(0.50)**	**78.4**	**(0.53)**
Less than high school completion	63.3	(2.04)	68.3	(1.68)	68.2	(2.00)	66.5	(2.00)	73.4	(1.82)
High school completion[1]	70.6	(1.31)	75.4	(0.93)	74.9	(1.05)	75.0	(1.00)	77.2	(0.89)
Some college, no degree	67.7	(1.51)	71.7	(1.17)	73.9	(1.34)	75.7	(1.14)	73.9	(1.45)
Associate's degree	79.4	(1.93)	75.6	(1.74)	75.4	(1.73)	79.9	(1.41)	79.6	(1.58)
Bachelor's or higher degree	79.6	(0.94)	83.2	(0.84)	82.3	(0.71)	84.2	(0.77)	82.1	(0.78)
Bachelor's degree	79.5	(1.24)	83.0	(0.93)	81.9	(0.90)	83.7	(0.89)	82.0	(0.84)
Master's or higher degree	79.7	(1.79)	83.7	(1.52)	83.3	(1.39)	85.6	(1.35)	82.4	(1.51)
Female										
Median annual earnings, all education levels	**$40,470**	**(1,025)**	**$38,820**	**(994)**	**$40,990**	**(563)**	**$40,480**	**(534)**	**$40,680**	**(1,227)**
Less than high school completion	21,830	(618)	21,550	(383)	21,540	(1,103)	23,330	(608)	24,520	(1,765)
High school completion[1]	27,420	(136)	27,000	(508)	29,120	(1,216)	29,830	(1,577)	28,140	(917)
Some college, no degree	32,650	(140)	30,230	(903)	32,350	(521)	31,930	(9)	31,290	(76)
Associate's degree	35,110	(1,174)	32,050	(250)	34,120	(692)	33,950	(452)	33,780	(1,602)
Bachelor's or higher degree	50,490	(1,732)	53,520	(1,083)	53,930	(#)	53,210	(16)	51,890	(349)
Bachelor's degree	48,990	(344)	48,590	(9)	48,300	(889)	47,930	(798)	48,870	(1,217)
Master's or higher degree	59,000	(1,571)	58,910	(996)	62,120	(2,379)	61,450	(1,913)	62,300	(478)
Percent,[2] all education levels	**61.6**	**(0.75)**	**62.5**	**(0.57)**	**64.2**	**(0.65)**	**66.5**	**(0.63)**	**67.4**	**(0.57)**
Less than high school completion	42.0	(2.70)	40.0	(2.03)	40.4	(2.63)	47.4	(2.41)	43.8	(2.82)
High school completion[1]	53.7	(1.64)	56.6	(1.28)	58.1	(1.25)	59.2	(1.31)	60.7	(1.34)
Some college, no degree	55.1	(1.75)	56.7	(1.30)	59.4	(1.35)	62.3	(1.30)	63.0	(1.35)
Associate's degree	62.1	(2.09)	63.3	(1.50)	62.2	(1.89)	65.3	(1.75)	67.3	(1.54)
Bachelor's or higher degree	70.5	(0.97)	70.0	(0.83)	72.4	(0.85)	73.9	(0.86)	73.9	(0.75)
Bachelor's degree	70.9	(1.19)	70.0	(0.94)	73.4	(1.00)	74.5	(0.94)	74.2	(0.99)
Master's or higher degree	69.7	(1.77)	70.1	(1.52)	70.5	(1.55)	72.8	(1.50)	73.3	(1.46)
White										
Median annual earnings, all education levels	**$46,040**	**(288)**	**$45,880**	**(949)**	**$48,480**	**(183)**	**$47,830**	**(42)**	**$47,890**	**(1,150)**
Less than high school completion	32,920	(921)	30,740	(1,817)	32,150	(2,267)	30,960	(1,513)	30,560	(633)
High school completion[1]	34,830	(623)	35,580	(1,325)	37,290	(579)	37,270	(662)	36,500	(370)
Some college, no degree	39,240	(1,055)	37,720	(392)	37,670	(475)	37,730	(621)	40,500	(1,419)
Associate's degree	43,870	(17)	39,480	(1,324)	41,690	(1,069)	42,280	(255)	41,710	(215)
Bachelor's or higher degree	54,870	(1,643)	57,070	(1,112)	58,800	(1,487)	58,300	(139)	58,400	(1,869)
Bachelor's degree	54,630	(2,154)	53,920	(56)	53,880	(297)	53,260	(904)	56,090	(923)
Master's or higher degree	65,540	(376)	62,560	(1,524)	64,720	(2,076)	65,080	(1,899)	67,680	(3,602)
Percent,[2] all education levels	**69.5**	**(0.69)**	**72.3**	**(0.50)**	**72.6**	**(0.58)**	**73.7**	**(0.55)**	**74.9**	**(0.52)**
Less than high school completion	51.5	(3.22)	51.1	(2.84)	52.5	(3.43)	57.5	(2.70)	59.5	(3.20)
High school completion[1]	66.4	(1.44)	70.7	(1.08)	68.9	(1.28)	68.3	(1.24)	72.9	(1.06)
Some college, no degree	63.6	(1.57)	66.1	(1.18)	67.6	(1.33)	69.8	(1.29)	69.5	(1.42)
Associate's degree	69.5	(1.79)	70.6	(1.36)	69.2	(1.48)	72.2	(1.36)	74.2	(1.43)
Bachelor's or higher degree	74.8	(0.91)	77.3	(0.73)	78.4	(0.73)	79.1	(0.70)	78.7	(0.67)
Bachelor's degree	75.5	(1.04)	77.1	(0.84)	79.2	(0.86)	79.5	(0.76)	79.6	(0.79)
Master's or higher degree	73.2	(1.70)	77.7	(1.24)	76.8	(1.29)	78.3	(1.32)	76.5	(1.34)
Black										
Median annual earnings, all education levels	**$36,680**	**(1,786)**	**$33,300**	**(1,003)**	**$37,270**	**(553)**	**$35,910**	**(877)**	**$36,230**	**(452)**
Less than high school completion	22,340	(1,468)	22,300	(2,720)	31,180	(2,436)	22,760	(1,897)	25,020	(1,477)
High school completion[1]	27,440	(1,496)	26,950	(594)	29,750	(1,721)	29,650	(1,480)	30,830	(884)
Some college, no degree	34,620	(1,571)	30,060	(1,475)	32,350	(1,681)	31,870	(1,859)	31,280	(677)
Associate's degree	37,440	(4,898)	33,180	(1,703)	32,350	(1,821)	32,430	(1,992)	35,190	(2,394)

[Amounts in constant 2019 dollars. Standard errors appear in parentheses]

Sex, race/ethnicity, and educational attainment	1995		2000		2005		2010		2013		2014		2015		2016		2017	
1		2		3		4		5		6		7		8		9		10
Bachelor's or higher degree	45,670	(2,617)	51,600	(1,743)	51,090	(1,282)	48,100	(1,738)	48,900	(879)	51,210	(2,433)	51,020	(1,760)	52,620	(1,312)	48,180	(2,926)
Bachelor's degree	43,520	(2,207)	49,350	(4,911)	47,200	(3,119)	46,280	(624)	43,780	(3,009)	48,890	(2,043)	46,140	(2,154)	48,810	(2,144)	43,500	(1,230)
Master's or higher degree	52,110	(2,916)	61,060	(5,373)	57,430	(3,645)	57,570	(6,982)	59,940	(6,360)	53,090	(1,624)	58,480	(4,126)	63,540	(910)	57,110	(3,338)
Percent,[2] all education levels	**63.6**	**(1.86)**	**71.3**	**(1.26)**	**66.6**	**(1.12)**	**59.1**	**(1.21)**	**61.1**	**(1.50)**	**63.3**	**(1.11)**	**66.0**	**(1.17)**	**69.3**	**(1.18)**	**69.7**	**(1.22)**
Less than high school completion	44.0	(5.81)	49.1	(4.46)	41.4	(4.02)	32.8	(3.78)	41.6	(5.89)	41.6	(5.10)	35.6	(4.37)	39.3	(5.19)	53.2	(5.01)
High school completion[1]	61.0	(3.03)	70.0	(2.13)	66.1	(1.92)	54.6	(2.02)	51.9	(2.66)	59.7	(1.77)	63.1	(2.22)	65.6	(2.15)	65.8	(2.22)
Some college, no degree	64.4	(3.57)	71.6	(2.52)	61.6	(2.66)	57.8	(2.30)	56.5	(2.89)	60.5	(2.33)	62.8	(2.56)	67.8	(2.38)	65.5	(2.77)
Associate's degree	72.0	(6.01)	79.5	(3.69)	73.5	(3.50)	64.8	(3.34)	67.6	(4.17)	60.2	(3.32)	69.2	(3.53)	75.4	(2.90)	72.8	(3.65)
Bachelor's or higher degree	78.2	(4.04)	80.6	(2.48)	81.5	(1.82)	73.1	(2.09)	79.8	(2.20)	76.5	(2.11)	77.9	(2.00)	78.5	(1.98)	78.8	(1.95)
Bachelor's degree	76.6	(4.50)	81.5	(2.69)	82.5	(1.99)	72.0	(2.70)	76.3	(2.90)	75.9	(2.54)	76.6	(2.25)	78.0	(2.56)	76.9	(2.22)
Master's or higher degree	87.2	(8.40)	76.8	(6.35)	78.5	(3.78)	76.5	(3.65)	89.1	(3.26)	78.1	(3.49)	81.7	(3.55)	79.7	(3.54)	84.3	(2.93)
Hispanic																		
Median annual earnings, all education levels	**$31,570**	**(1,207)**	**$33,270**	**(1,011)**	**$32,710**	**(11)**	**$35,120**	**(1,154)**	**$32,540**	**(123)**	**$32,400**	**(73)**	**$34,290**	**(502)**	**$36,090**	**(1,082)**	**$36,070**	**(399)**
Less than high school completion	24,890	(1,126)	25,180	(573)	26,030	(78)	23,310	(116)	25,130	(1,570)	25,620	(878)	25,870	(993)	26,620	(240)	26,610	(779)
High school completion[1]	31,580	(2,167)	34,080	(1,483)	31,340	(1,122)	32,570	(1,061)	30,950	(1,204)	32,390	(435)	32,050	(80)	31,910	(28)	31,070	(155)
Some college, no degree	32,950	(2,017)	39,440	(1,615)	40,850	(2,037)	37,040	(1,580)	32,740	(781)	34,070	(1,364)	36,160	(1,064)	34,080	(1,517)	35,980	(377)
Associate's degree	39,910	(4,177)	44,060	(2,202)	44,690	(1,187)	39,850	(1,477)	36,610	(1,832)	32,290	(1,550)	38,150	(2,334)	37,170	(376)	37,460	(1,257)
Bachelor's or higher degree	49,910	(3,099)	54,860	(1,949)	53,440	(2,244)	51,510	(2,710)	49,950	(1,497)	51,360	(2,578)	53,930	(1,198)	52,550	(1,026)	50,000	(1,744)
Bachelor's degree	46,970	(3,963)	52,910	(1,941)	51,730	(784)	48,580	(3,517)	49,350	(1,511)	47,760	(1,510)	53,930	(444)	47,640	(2,244)	47,660	(1,904)
Master's or higher degree	70,020	(12,100)	58,000	(5,941)	65,910	(3,307)	56,640	(4,740)	52,620	(6,056)	62,230	(2,343)	58,520	(2,717)	59,380	(3,759)	58,950	(3,894)
Percent,[2] all education levels	**62.9**	**(1.87)**	**70.7**	**(1.12)**	**71.9**	**(0.80)**	**61.6**	**(0.86)**	**67.0**	**(1.00)**	**68.7**	**(0.93)**	**69.4**	**(0.78)**	**72.0**	**(0.81)**	**70.8**	**(0.75)**
Less than high school completion	56.0	(3.26)	66.0	(1.98)	68.5	(1.63)	53.0	(1.67)	60.9	(2.07)	66.3	(1.81)	65.7	(2.01)	65.2	(1.95)	68.8	(2.05)
High school completion[1]	67.9	(3.28)	72.9	(1.95)	75.2	(1.35)	61.7	(1.61)	68.5	(1.71)	70.6	(1.66)	70.8	(1.32)	72.1	(1.47)	71.0	(1.51)
Some college, no degree	61.5	(4.51)	71.9	(2.82)	70.0	(1.88)	65.5	(1.81)	60.4	(2.40)	65.0	(1.79)	69.1	(2.00)	71.1	(1.58)	69.2	(1.90)
Associate's degree	69.3	(7.53)	79.8	(3.90)	74.1	(2.46)	66.1	(2.68)	76.8	(2.59)	68.3	(2.77)	65.5	(2.85)	73.0	(2.27)	69.7	(2.43)
Bachelor's or higher degree	69.4	(5.26)	72.3	(3.19)	74.1	(2.08)	70.6	(2.08)	74.2	(1.95)	72.8	(1.84)	73.1	(1.77)	78.0	(1.76)	73.8	(1.73)
Bachelor's degree	69.3	(5.78)	73.5	(3.47)	73.7	(2.35)	70.9	(2.27)	75.6	(2.19)	72.4	(2.05)	72.9	(1.93)	77.7	(1.93)	73.2	(1.92)
Master's or higher degree	69.8	(12.72)	67.2	(7.95)	75.6	(3.99)	69.6	(3.95)	69.6	(4.39)	74.3	(4.10)	73.8	(3.86)	78.8	(3.55)	75.9	(3.68)
Asian[3]																		
Median annual earnings, all education levels	**$41,940**	**(1,816)**	**$53,130**	**(1,261)**	**$52,050**	**(1,854)**	**$52,660**	**(1,982)**	**$54,650**	**(1,623)**	**$53,390**	**(603)**	**$55,080**	**(2,779)**	**$58,190**	**(2,747)**	**$62,230**	**(601)**
Less than high school completion	‡	(†)	26,740	(4,650)	35,640	(5,881)	‡	(†)	‡	(†)	22,540	(1,944)	29,610	(6,795)	28,120	(3,873)	‡	(†)
High school completion[1]	33,260	(3,449)	37,110	(1,916)	34,920	(2,467)	34,280	(1,799)	31,840	(2,982)	31,940	(1,983)	30,760	(789)	31,020	(1,790)	34,950	(2,748)
Some college, no degree	31,930	(4,002)	41,550	(4,061)	38,920	(2,892)	40,880	(1,637)	36,930	(4,559)	32,020	(3,430)	37,000	(2,992)	36,950	(2,041)	34,620	(3,722)
Associate's degree	33,660	(3,027)	43,110	(2,363)	45,280	(3,678)	42,000	(2,947)	35,000	(3,363)	36,220	(4,209)	32,430	(2,813)	42,160	(4,185)	38,840	(2,298)
Bachelor's or higher degree	53,580	(1,594)	73,100	(1,860)	65,440	(721)	70,140	(2,382)	65,620	(1,599)	64,800	(3,820)	74,550	(3,161)	73,640	(3,146)	72,510	(849)
Bachelor's degree	50,140	(1,646)	65,990	(2,790)	65,190	(5,759)	60,530	(4,383)	63,660	(3,852)	60,320	(2,456)	67,780	(4,701)	63,560	(2,321)	67,600	(3,049)
Master's or higher degree	63,040	(14,326)	88,360	(6,687)	71,360	(5,151)	80,070	(5,770)	81,690	(6,143)	78,350	(4,686)	80,700	(6,795)	85,770	(6,044)	81,760	(4,725)
Percent,[2] all education levels	**67.8**	**(2.89)**	**71.5**	**(1.73)**	**69.8**	**(1.62)**	**68.6**	**(1.38)**	**68.3**	**(1.76)**	**70.8**	**(1.42)**	**72.5**	**(1.55)**	**76.6**	**(1.34)**	**75.2**	**(1.45)**
Less than high school completion	51.7	(10.00)	66.1	(8.09)	65.1	(7.36)	50.0	(11.09)	58.5	(8.64)	56.0	(8.09)	75.3	(7.33)	77.8	(7.12)	‡	(†)
High school completion[1]	71.6	(6.76)	72.9	(4.41)	70.6	(4.46)	63.4	(3.64)	63.9	(5.34)	68.7	(4.49)	77.6	(3.62)	79.7	(3.16)	71.9	(5.10)
Some college, no degree	60.3	(8.28)	66.1	(4.51)	73.1	(4.13)	59.0	(4.95)	62.7	(5.84)	62.4	(5.24)	69.4	(4.30)	71.5	(4.01)	69.4	(4.57)
Associate's degree	78.8	(7.78)	76.9	(5.56)	71.0	(5.49)	59.5	(5.68)	70.6	(5.80)	77.4	(4.43)	65.5	(5.92)	70.9	(5.79)	71.2	(5.29)
Bachelor's or higher degree	69.2	(4.06)	72.4	(2.29)	69.1	(2.05)	74.1	(1.75)	70.3	(2.20)	72.6	(1.60)	72.5	(1.92)	77.3	(1.53)	76.8	(1.74)
Bachelor's degree	73.1	(5.01)	73.9	(2.77)	71.9	(2.58)	76.9	(2.04)	70.0	(2.92)	75.1	(1.98)	73.8	(2.35)	76.4	(2.15)	76.0	(2.59)
Master's or higher degree	63.2	(6.76)	69.3	(4.06)	64.5	(3.23)	70.1	(3.19)	70.9	(3.50)	69.0	(2.74)	71.0	(2.91)	78.5	(2.15)	77.9	(2.40)
Two or more races[3]																		
Median annual earnings, all education levels	**---**	**(†)**	**---**	**(†)**	**$45,430**	**(2,000)**	**$40,830**	**(1,610)**	**$41,970**	**(4,123)**	**$37,040**	**(1,966)**	**$42,790**	**(745)**	**$44,430**	**(2,682)**	**$39,630**	**(1,611)**
Less than high school completion	---	(†)	---	(†)	‡	(†)	‡	(†)	‡	(†)	‡	(†)	‡	(†)	‡	(†)	‡	(†)
High school completion[1]	---	(†)	---	(†)	34,320	(4,926)	34,980	(5,680)	37,180	(5,027)	29,240	(1,961)	37,530	(3,453)	34,620	(5,629)	34,820	(4,151)
Some college, no degree	---	(†)	---	(†)	39,850	(4,225)	41,310	(4,255)	37,580	(3,378)	27,910	(2,782)	37,880	(4,476)	35,370	(3,253)	30,240	(1,912)
Associate's degree	---	(†)	---	(†)	49,770	(5,245)	32,580	(1,649)	‡	(†)	‡	(†)	46,960	(3,147)	47,900	(6,280)	42,120	(2,354)
Bachelor's or higher degree	---	(†)	---	(†)	58,210	(3,997)	49,630	(5,234)	59,630	(5,222)	54,000	(5,843)	50,770	(6,788)	60,710	(9,439)	52,660	(7,324)
Bachelor's degree	---	(†)	---	(†)	51,430	(4,655)	46,240	(4,487)	52,360	(6,958)	48,910	(7,889)	43,110	(6,488)	52,790	(7,332)	51,260	(4,406)
Master's or higher degree	---	(†)	---	(†)	‡	(†)	77,160	(15,270)	‡	(†)	‡	(†)	‡	(†)	73,540	(11,859)	‡	(†)
Percent,[2] all education levels	**---**	**(†)**	**---**	**(†)**	**64.7**	**(3.31)**	**61.4**	**(2.89)**	**65.0**	**(3.45)**	**63.9**	**(3.18)**	**67.2**	**(3.15)**	**65.6**	**(3.06)**	**71.5**	**(2.88)**
Less than high school completion	---	(†)	---	(†)	‡	(†)	‡	(†)	‡	(†)	‡	(†)	‡	(†)	‡	(†)	‡	(†)
High school completion[1]	---	(†)	---	(†)	61.6	(4.96)	61.4	(6.70)	60.6	(6.98)	52.1	(6.60)	61.5	(6.44)	54.5	(6.88)	68.9	(5.58)
Some college, no degree	---	(†)	---	(†)	59.5	(6.16)	53.7	(5.96)	60.5	(7.81)	58.1	(5.79)	67.4	(5.64)	62.9	(6.19)	71.3	(6.40)
Associate's degree	---	(†)	---	(†)	75.3	(7.43)	70.4	(8.75)	‡	(†)	75.8	(7.86)	70.0	(7.58)	58.8	(8.35)	76.5	(6.76)
Bachelor's or higher degree	---	(†)	---	(†)	72.5	(6.07)	70.0	(4.73)	77.4	(5.11)	75.9	(4.19)	72.5	(4.88)	79.0	(4.06)	71.2	(4.27)
Bachelor's degree	---	(†)	---	(†)	81.6	(5.83)	70.3	(5.72)	75.7	(5.97)	79.9	(5.00)	76.9	(5.73)	77.7	(4.85)	72.7	(4.64)
Master's or higher degree	---	(†)	---	(†)	59.0	(11.12)	69.3	(8.30)	‡	(†)	66.5	(8.81)	62.5	(9.31)	81.7	(6.66)	66.6	(10.10)
Median annual earnings for other race groups, all education levels																		
Pacific Islander[4]	[3]	(†)	[3]	(†)	$40,000	(4,401)	$40,170	(1,576)	$42,800	(4,774)	$36,990	(3,802)	$42,760	(1,951)	$36,480	(1,501)	$38,820	(3,811)
American Indian/Alaska Native[4]	33,360	(1,816)	37,100	(2,214)	38,480	(1,621)	37,220	(3,801)	32,750	(6,951)	32,330	(2,128)	32,250	(2,298)	38,250	(3,824)	37,020	(3,999)
Percent[2] for other race groups, all education levels																		
Pacific Islander[4]	[3]	(†)	[3]	(†)	54.8	(6.78)	62.5	(6.79)	77.2	(6.48)	68.4	(5.09)	77.9	(4.63)	68.2	(5.16)	72.6	(5.28)
American Indian/Alaska Native[4]	48.7	(8.11)	60.5	(4.89)	62.4	(3.94)	54.3	(4.24)	60.6	(5.26)	63.8	(3.73)	61.3	(4.62)	62.2	(4.44)	70.4	(4.02)

---Not available.

†Not applicable.

#Rounds to zero.

‡Reporting standards not met (too few cases for a reliable estimate).

[1] Includes equivalency credentials, such as the GED credential.

[2] Full-time year-round workers as a percentage of the population ages 25 through 34 who reported working or looking for work in the given year.

[3] For 1995 and 2000, data for Asians, Pacific Islanders, and persons of Two or more races were not reported separately. Pacific Islander data are included with Asian data for 1995 and 2000 because these data were collected in a combined "Asian/Pacific Islander" category. Data on persons of Two or more races are unavailable for 1995 and 2000 because each respondent could choose only one race category.

[4] For Pacific Islanders and American Indians/Alaska Natives, data by educational attainment are omitted because these data for the most part did not meet reporting standards. All data shown for these two race categories are for persons of all education levels.

NOTE: Data are based on sample surveys of the noninstitutionalized population, which excludes persons living in institutions (e.g., prisons or nursing facilities); data include military personnel who live in households with civilians, but exclude those who live in military barracks. Prior to 2004, standard errors were computed using generalized variance function methodology rather than the more precise replicate weight methodology used in later years. Caution should be used when comparing 2019 estimates to those of earlier years due to the impact that the coronavirus pandemic had on interviewing and response rates. For additional information about the impact of the coronavirus pandemic on the March CPS data collection, please see https://www2.census.gov/programs-surveys/cps/techdocs/cpsmar20.pdf. Constant dollars based on the Consumer Price Index, prepared by the Bureau of Labor Statistics, U.S. Department of Labor. Race categories exclude persons of Hispanic ethnicity. Some data have been revised from previously published figures.

SOURCE: U.S. Department of Commerce, Census Bureau, Current Population Survey (CPS), Annual Social and Economic Supplement, 1996 through 2020. (This table was prepared October 2020.)

Table 502.40. Annual earnings of persons 25 years old and over, by highest level of educational attainment and sex: 2018

[Standard errors appear in parentheses]

Sex and earnings	Total	Elementary/secondary			College						
							Bachelor's or higher degree				
		Less than 9th grade	Some high school, no completion	High school completion (includes equivalency)	Some college, no degree	Associate's degree	Total	Bachelor's degree	Master's degree	Professional degree (e.g., M.D., D.D.S., or J.D.)	Doctor's degree (e.g., Ph.D. or Ed.D.)
1	2	3	4	5	6	7	8	9	10	11	12
Number of persons (in thousands)	**221,478 (438.8)**	**8,603 (148.8)**	**13,372 (184.1)**	**62,259 (365.3)**	**34,690 (286.3)**	**22,738 (236.5)**	**79,816 (399.8)**	**49,937 (334.6)**	**22,214 (233.9)**	**3,136 (90.6)**	**4,529 (108.6)**
With earnings	145,773 (463.7)	3,774 (99.3)	6,282 (127.6)	36,668 (293.4)	22,517 (235.4)	16,173 (201.5)	60,359 (360.9)	37,449 (296.1)	16,784 (205.1)	2,521 (81.3)	3,606 (97.1)
For persons with earnings											
Percentage distribution, by total annual earnings[1]	100.0 (†)	100.0 (†)	100.0 (†)	100.0 (†)	100.0 (†)	100.0 (†)	100.0 (†)	100.0 (†)	100.0 (†)	100.0 (†)	100.0 (†)
$1 to $4,999 or loss[2]	3.5 (0.08)	5.6 (0.61)	6.2 (0.50)	3.9 (0.16)	4.5 (0.22)	3.3 (0.23)	2.6 (0.11)	2.9 (0.14)	2.5 (0.20)	1.3 (0.37)	1.8 (0.36)
$5,000 to $9,999	3.7 (0.08)	5.7 (0.61)	7.4 (0.54)	4.6 (0.18)	4.1 (0.22)	3.5 (0.23)	2.5 (0.10)	2.6 (0.13)	2.5 (0.20)	1.1! (0.33)	1.9 (0.37)
$10,000 to $14,999	4.5 (0.09)	8.3 (0.73)	9.6 (0.60)	6.1 (0.20)	5.3 (0.24)	4.5 (0.27)	2.5 (0.10)	2.8 (0.14)	2.1 (0.18)	1.6 (0.40)	1.1 (0.28)
$15,000 to $19,999	5.2 (0.09)	12.4 (0.87)	12.3 (0.67)	6.9 (0.22)	6.3 (0.26)	5.0 (0.28)	2.6 (0.11)	3.1 (0.15)	1.9 (0.17)	1.2! (0.35)	1.7 (0.35)
$20,000 to $24,999	6.8 (0.11)	17.0 (0.99)	13.7 (0.70)	9.3 (0.25)	7.9 (0.29)	7.2 (0.33)	3.5 (0.12)	4.0 (0.16)	2.8 (0.21)	2.2 (0.48)	2.4 (0.42)
$25,000 to $29,999	6.5 (0.10)	11.3 (0.84)	9.7 (0.61)	9.4 (0.25)	7.5 (0.28)	7.3 (0.33)	3.5 (0.12)	4.1 (0.17)	2.6 (0.20)	1.7 (0.41)	1.7 (0.35)
$30,000 to $34,999	7.2 (0.11)	10.3 (0.80)	8.8 (0.58)	9.8 (0.25)	8.9 (0.31)	8.3 (0.35)	4.3 (0.13)	5.3 (0.19)	2.8 (0.21)	1.5 (0.40)	2.3 (0.40)
$35,000 to $39,999	6.5 (0.10)	8.4 (0.73)	7.9 (0.55)	8.5 (0.24)	7.4 (0.28)	6.8 (0.32)	4.5 (0.14)	5.5 (0.19)	3.2 (0.22)	2.4 (0.50)	1.8 (0.36)
$40,000 to $49,999	11.3 (0.13)	8.2 (0.73)	9.6 (0.61)	12.9 (0.28)	12.5 (0.36)	13.2 (0.43)	9.7 (0.20)	10.9 (0.26)	8.7 (0.35)	4.3 (0.66)	5.5 (0.62)
$50,000 to $74,999	20.8 (0.17)	9.4 (0.77)	10.1 (0.62)	18.0 (0.33)	20.7 (0.44)	24.4 (0.55)	23.4 (0.28)	23.9 (0.36)	25.0 (0.54)	15.8 (1.18)	16.0 (0.99)
$75,000 to $99,999	10.0 (0.13)	1.7 (0.34)	3.0 (0.35)	5.9 (0.20)	8.0 (0.29)	9.2 (0.37)	14.7 (0.23)	13.9 (0.29)	16.5 (0.47)	12.3 (1.06)	16.7 (1.01)
$100,000 or more	14.1 (0.15)	1.7 (0.35)	2.1 (0.22)	4.7 (0.18)	6.9 (0.27)	7.4 (0.33)	26.3 (0.29)	21.1 (0.34)	29.3 (0.57)	54.5 (1.61)	46.9 (1.35)
Median annual earnings[1]	$44,960 (410)	$25,320 (402)	$25,280 (345)	$35,020 (376)	$37,810 (600)	$41,830 (271)	$62,140 (181)	$57,110 (373)	$70,240 (672)	$104,590 (5,439)	$92,130 (2,250)
Number of males (in thousands)	**106,695 (301.0)**	**4,313 (105.7)**	**6,792 (131.5)**	**31,257 (258.1)**	**16,591 (198.8)**	**9,936 (157.4)**	**37,807 (276.4)**	**23,785 (231.8)**	**9,621 (155.1)**	**1,820 (69.2)**	**2,580 (82.2)**
With earnings	77,236 (322.9)	2,498 (80.9)	3,913 (100.8)	21,454 (222.1)	11,873 (170.9)	7,618 (138.9)	29,880 (253.8)	18,938 (210.6)	7,445 (137.4)	1,466 (62.2)	2,032 (73.1)
For males with earnings											
Percentage distribution, by total annual earnings[1]	100.0 (†)	100.0 (†)	100.0 (†)	100.0 (†)	100.0 (†)	100.0 (†)	100.0 (†)	100.0 (†)	100.0 (†)	100.0 (†)	100.0 (†)
$1 to $4,999 or loss[2]	2.4 (0.09)	3.7 (0.62)	5.2 (0.58)	2.7 (0.18)	2.9 (0.25)	2.0 (0.26)	1.7 (0.12)	1.8 (0.16)	1.7 (0.25)	‡ (†)	1.8 (0.48)
$5,000 to $9,999	2.5 (0.09)	3.0 (0.55)	5.6 (0.60)	2.9 (0.19)	3.0 (0.26)	2.2 (0.27)	1.7 (0.12)	1.8 (0.16)	1.8 (0.25)	‡ (†)	1.5 (0.44)
$10,000 to $14,999	3.3 (0.10)	5.6 (0.75)	6.0 (0.62)	4.3 (0.22)	3.7 (0.28)	2.8 (0.31)	2.0 (0.13)	2.2 (0.18)	1.8 (0.25)	1.2! (0.46)	1.4! (0.42)
$15,000 to $19,999	3.8 (0.11)	10.4 (1.00)	9.1 (0.75)	4.8 (0.24)	4.0 (0.29)	3.4 (0.34)	1.8 (0.13)	2.1 (0.17)	1.4 (0.22)	‡ (†)	1.6 (0.45)
$20,000 to $24,999	5.8 (0.14)	16.5 (1.21)	12.6 (0.87)	7.4 (0.29)	6.2 (0.36)	4.9 (0.40)	2.8 (0.16)	3.1 (0.21)	2.5 (0.29)	1.6! (0.54)	2.3 (0.54)
$25,000 to $29,999	5.6 (0.14)	10.8 (1.01)	9.2 (0.75)	7.9 (0.30)	6.3 (0.36)	5.1 (0.41)	2.9 (0.16)	3.6 (0.22)	2.0 (0.26)	2.1 (0.61)	1.3! (0.41)
$30,000 to $34,999	6.4 (0.14)	11.9 (1.06)	10.1 (0.79)	8.7 (0.31)	7.6 (0.40)	6.0 (0.45)	3.5 (0.17)	4.4 (0.24)	1.9 (0.26)	1.2! (0.47)	2.5 (0.56)
$35,000 to $39,999	6.2 (0.14)	10.8 (1.01)	9.2 (0.75)	8.9 (0.32)	6.5 (0.37)	5.3 (0.42)	3.5 (0.17)	4.3 (0.24)	2.5 (0.29)	1.9! (0.58)	1.3! (0.41)
$40,000 to $49,999	11.0 (0.18)	10.2 (0.99)	12.2 (0.86)	14.4 (0.39)	13.0 (0.50)	13.4 (0.64)	7.1 (0.24)	8.4 (0.33)	5.8 (0.44)	2.3 (0.64)	4.0 (0.71)
$50,000 to $74,999	22.3 (0.24)	12.8 (1.09)	13.7 (0.90)	23.1 (0.47)	24.3 (0.64)	29.4 (0.85)	21.1 (0.39)	23.5 (0.50)	18.5 (0.73)	13.6 (1.46)	13.1 (1.22)
$75,000 to $99,999	11.8 (0.19)	2.3 (0.49)	4.6 (0.55)	8.1 (0.30)	11.6 (0.48)	13.4 (0.64)	15.9 (0.34)	15.7 (0.43)	17.1 (0.71)	11.6 (1.36)	16.5 (1.34)
$100,000 or more	18.8 (0.23)	2.3 (0.49)	2.3 (0.39)	6.9 (0.28)	10.8 (0.47)	12.0 (0.61)	35.8 (0.45)	29.1 (0.54)	43.2 (0.94)	62.6 (2.06)	52.8 (1.81)
Median annual earnings[1]	$51,300 (139)	$30,020 (688)	$30,610 352	$40,900 (200)	$46,850 (531)	$51,730 (314)	$76,400 (396)	$67,440 (1105)	$90,010 (2,980)	$122,340 (4,971)	$101,130 (729)

See notes at end of table.

Table 502.40. Annual earnings of persons 25 years old and over, by highest level of educational attainment and sex: 2018—Continued

[Standard errors appear in parentheses]

Sex and earnings	Total	Elementary/secondary			College						
							Bachelor's or higher degree				
		Less than 9th grade	Some high school, no completion	High school completion (includes equivalency)	Some college, no degree	Associate's degree	Total	Bachelor's degree	Master's degree	Professional degree (e.g., M.D., D.D.S., or J.D.)	Doctor's degree (e.g., Ph.D. or Ed.D.)
1	2	3	4	5	6	7	8	9	10	11	12
Number of females (in thousands)	**114,783 (269.1)**	**4,290 (96.7)**	**6,580 (118.8)**	**31,002 (236.5)**	**18,099 (189.5)**	**12,802 (162.3)**	**42,009 (263.3)**	**26,151 (221.3)**	**12,593 (161.1)**	**1,317 (54.1)**	**1,948 (65.6)**
With earnings	68,537 (296.0)	1,276 (53.2)	2,369 (72.3)	15,214 (175.5)	10,644 (149.1)	8,554 (134.6)	30,479 (235.0)	18,511 (191.4)	9,338 (140.3)	1,055 (48.4)	1,574 (59.1)
For females with earnings											
Percentage distribution, by total annual earnings[1]	100.0 (†)	100.0 (†)	100.0 (†)		100.0 (†)	100.0 (†)	100.0 (†)	100.0 (†)	100.0 (†)	100.0 (†)	100.0 (†)
$1 to $4,999 or loss[2]	4.8 (0.12)	9.4 (1.22)	7.9 (0.83)	100.0 (†)	6.2 (0.35)	4.3 (0.33)	3.5 (0.16)	3.9 (0.21)	3.2 (0.27)	2.4 (0.70)	1.8 (0.51)
$5,000 to $9,999	4.9 (0.12)	11.0 (1.31)	10.3 (0.94)	5.6 (0.28)	5.3 (0.33)	4.6 (0.34)	3.2 (0.15)	3.4 (0.20)	3.1 (0.27)	1.8! (0.61)	2.5 (0.59)
$10,000 to $14,999	5.9 (0.13)	13.6 (1.44)	15.6 (1.12)	6.9 (0.31)	7.0 (0.37)	6.1 (0.39)	2.9 (0.14)	3.4 (0.20)	2.3 (0.23)	2.3! (0.69)	0.8! (0.33)
$15,000 to $19,999	6.8 (0.14)	16.4 (1.55)	17.5 (1.17)	8.8 (0.34)	8.8 (0.41)	6.3 (0.39)	3.4 (0.16)	4.2 (0.22)	2.4 (0.24)	1.8! (0.61)	2.0 (0.52)
$20,000 to $24,999	8.1 (0.16)	17.9 (1.60)	15.4 (1.11)	9.9 (0.36)	9.8 (0.43)	9.2 (0.47)	4.2 (0.17)	4.9 (0.24)	3.1 (0.27)	3.0 (0.79)	2.5 (0.59)
$25,000 to $29,999	7.4 (0.15)	12.2 (1.37)	10.5 (0.94)	12.0 (0.39)	8.8 (0.41)	9.2 (0.47)	4.0 (0.17)	4.7 (0.23)	3.1 (0.27)	1.0! (0.47)	2.4 (0.57)
$30,000 to $34,999	8.0 (0.15)	7.2 (1.08)	6.6 (0.76)	11.4 (0.39)	10.3 (0.44)	10.3 (0.49)	5.0 (0.19)	6.2 (0.26)	3.6 (0.29)	2.0! (0.64)	2.0 (0.53)
$35,000 to $39,999	6.8 (0.14)	3.8 (0.80)	5.8 (0.72)	11.3 (0.38)	8.4 (0.40)	8.2 (0.44)	5.4 (0.19)	6.7 (0.27)	3.8 (0.29)	3.1 (0.80)	2.5 (0.59)
$40,000 to $49,999	11.6 (0.18)	4.3 (0.85)	5.4 (0.69)	8.1 (0.33)	12.0 (0.47)	13.1 (0.55)	12.2 (0.28)	13.5 (0.38)	10.9 (0.48)	6.9 (1.17)	7.4 (0.99)
$50,000 to $74,999	19.1 (0.22)	2.7 (0.67)	4.2 (0.62)	10.9 (0.38)	16.7 (0.54)	19.8 (0.64)	25.6 (0.37)	24.2 (0.47)	30.2 (0.71)	19.1 (1.81)	19.8 (1.50)
$75,000 to $99,999	8.0 (0.16)	‡ (†)	0.4! (0.19)	10.9 (0.38)	4.0 (0.28)	5.5 (0.37)	13.6 (0.29)	12.1 (0.36)	16.0 (0.57)	13.4 (1.57)	17.0 (1.42)
$100,000 or more	8.7 (0.16)	0.7! (0.35)	0.5! (0.21)	2.7 (0.20)	2.5 (0.23)	3.4 (0.29)	16.9 (0.32)	12.9 (0.37)	18.3 (0.60)	43.3 (2.28)	39.3 (1.84)
				1.5 (0.15)							
Median annual earnings[1]	$37,140 (168)	$19,800 (759)	$19,610 (476)	$27,200 (195)	$31,140 (205)	$34,950 (705)	$53,210 (715)	$49,010 (784)	$60,370 (423)	$82,170 (4,457)	$81,600 (2,308)

†Not applicable.
!Interpret data with caution. The coefficient of variation (CV) for this estimate is between 30 and 50 percent.
‡Reporting standards not met. Either there are too few cases for a reliable estimate or the coefficient of variation (CV) is 50 percent or greater.
[1]Excludes persons without earnings.
[2]A negative amount (a net loss) may be reported by self-employed persons.

NOTE: Data are based on sample surveys of the noninstitutionalized population, which excludes persons living in institutions (e.g., prisons or nursing facilities); data include military personnel who live in households with civilians but exclude those who live in military barracks. Detail may not sum to totals because of rounding and suppression of data that do not meet reporting standards.
SOURCE: U.S. Department of Commerce, Census Bureau, Current Population Survey (CPS), Annual Social and Economic Supplement, 2018; retrieved March 11, 2020, from https://www.census.gov/data/tables/time-series/demo/income-poverty/cps-pinc/pinc-03.html. (This table was prepared March 2020.)

Table 503.10. Percentage of high school students age 16 and over who were employed, by age group, sex, race/ethnicity, family income, nativity, and hours worked per week: Selected years, 1970 through 2017

[Standard errors appear in parentheses]

Year	Total	Age group: 16 and 17 years old	Age group: 18 years old and over	Sex: Male	Sex: Female	Race/ethnicity: White	Race/ethnicity: Black	Race/ethnicity: Hispanic	Family income[1]: Low income	Family income[1]: Middle income	Family income[1]: High income	Nativity: U.S.-born	Nativity: Foreign-born
1	2	3	4	5	6	7	8	9	10	11	12	13	14
	Percent employed[2]												
1970	31.9 (0.88)	30.8 (0.93)	39.7 (2.55)	35.2 (1.24)	28.3 (1.22)	— (†)	— (†)	— (†)	22.0 (2.51)	31.5 (1.12)	35.9 (1.64)	— (†)	— (†)
1975	33.2 (0.85)	32.9 (0.91)	34.9 (2.40)	35.0 (1.19)	31.2 (1.22)	38.0 (1.00)	13.9 (1.63)	21.8 (3.59)	18.4 (2.22)	31.8 (1.10)	40.4 (1.59)	— (†)	— (†)
1980	35.6 (0.87)	34.9 (0.94)	39.6 (2.28)	36.9 (1.22)	34.2 (1.24)	41.2 (1.03)	15.0 (1.64)	24.1 (3.65)	19.4 (2.10)	35.2 (1.15)	42.3 (1.59)	— (†)	— (†)
1985	31.6 (0.93)	30.8 (1.00)	36.1 (2.47)	32.1 (1.29)	31.0 (1.33)	37.9 (1.15)	15.0 (1.85)	17.6 (2.63)	14.7 (1.85)	31.0 (1.23)	41.1 (1.81)	— (†)	— (†)
1990	32.3 (0.98)	31.2 (1.08)	37.1 (2.33)	33.1 (1.37)	31.3 (1.39)	37.8 (1.24)	17.3 (2.05)	26.4 (2.86)	21.4 (2.16)	33.1 (1.29)	36.8 (1.97)	— (†)	— (†)
1995	33.6 (0.92)	32.7 (1.02)	37.5 (2.19)	33.1 (1.26)	34.2 (1.35)	40.8 (1.18)	18.0 (1.91)	22.2 (2.41)	17.4 (1.82)	34.4 (1.23)	42.1 (1.88)	34.9 (0.97)	20.1 (2.65)
2000	34.1 (0.93)	33.3 (1.03)	37.7 (2.15)	33.2 (1.28)	35.1 (1.36)	41.3 (1.20)	21.3 (2.14)	20.9 (2.18)	22.0 (2.11)	34.1 (1.22)	40.7 (1.85)	35.1 (0.99)	24.4 (2.74)
2001	32.4 (0.86)	31.1 (0.95)	37.8 (1.99)	30.6 (1.17)	34.5 (1.27)	38.9 (1.11)	18.7 (1.85)	23.6 (2.23)	21.4 (2.04)	33.3 (1.12)	36.1 (1.70)	33.3 (0.90)	23.0 (2.64)
2002	30.6 (0.84)	29.2 (0.93)	35.9 (1.92)	28.0 (1.13)	33.4 (1.24)	37.5 (1.11)	16.9 (1.81)	21.1 (1.94)	18.4 (1.83)	31.4 (1.11)	35.3 (1.64)	31.6 (0.89)	21.3 (2.34)
2003	27.0 (0.79)	25.3 (0.86)	34.6 (1.97)	26.7 (1.09)	27.3 (1.15)	33.3 (1.07)	15.2 (1.68)	18.8 (1.82)	14.3 (1.64)	27.8 (1.05)	31.8 (1.57)	28.0 (0.84)	17.7 (2.17)
2004	27.2 (0.80)	25.6 (0.87)	34.7 (2.03)	26.2 (1.09)	28.3 (1.17)	32.9 (1.08)	15.1 (1.71)	21.2 (1.92)	12.0 (1.55)	27.5 (1.05)	34.4 (1.64)	27.8 (0.85)	20.8 (2.43)
2005	26.4 (0.77)	25.2 (0.84)	32.2 (1.95)	25.3 (1.05)	27.6 (1.14)	31.8 (1.05)	13.7 (1.63)	19.4 (1.78)	14.8 (1.61)	26.9 (1.03)	31.7 (1.55)	26.8 (0.81)	21.7 (2.49)
2006	27.6 (0.79)	26.0 (0.86)	34.1 (1.87)	26.5 (1.08)	28.8 (1.16)	33.6 (1.08)	20.1 (1.85)	17.5 (1.72)	17.8 (1.72)	27.5 (1.04)	33.5 (1.59)	27.9 (0.82)	23.9 (2.64)
2007	26.2 (0.78)	24.8 (0.85)	32.2 (1.87)	25.0 (1.06)	27.6 (1.14)	31.3 (1.06)	15.1 (1.68)	21.1 (1.83)	17.3 (1.74)	25.9 (1.01)	32.1 (1.62)	26.0 (0.81)	28.5 (2.64)
2008	22.6 (0.74)	21.0 (0.80)	29.5 (1.83)	20.0 (0.99)	25.4 (1.10)	27.7 (1.04)	15.5 (1.69)	15.1 (1.54)	13.5 (1.54)	22.6 (0.96)	28.4 (1.59)	23.1 (0.78)	18.0 (2.35)
2009	17.0 (0.67)	15.2 (0.72)	23.8 (1.65)	16.0 (0.91)	18.1 (0.98)	21.5 (0.96)	10.5 (1.43)	11.9 (1.39)	9.7 (1.33)	16.3 (0.85)	23.5 (1.51)	17.0 (0.70)	16.9 (2.32)
2010	16.2 (0.55)	15.0 (0.59)	20.8 (1.52)	14.0 (0.78)	18.5 (0.86)	20.9 (0.86)	9.6 (1.28)	10.4 (1.18)	8.5 (1.01)	16.5 (0.80)	20.9 (1.31)	16.4 (0.60)	13.4 (2.20)
2011	16.9 (0.67)	16.4 (0.77)	18.7 (1.28)	14.7 (0.76)	19.4 (1.09)	22.2 (1.07)	10.2 (1.43)	11.3 (1.11)	10.2 (1.29)	17.5 (0.83)	19.6 (1.39)	17.3 (0.74)	12.4 (1.91)
2012	18.0 (0.71)	16.0 (0.75)	24.5 (1.88)	16.6 (0.83)	19.4 (1.13)	23.2 (0.97)	12.7 (2.17)	11.4 (1.23)	13.0 (1.42)	16.4 (0.88)	24.9 (1.55)	18.6 (0.76)	12.0 (2.01)
2013	17.9 (0.65)	15.8 (0.69)	24.7 (1.73)	17.6 (0.89)	18.3 (0.94)	23.3 (0.99)	11.8 (1.42)	14.0 (1.19)	9.7 (1.26)	16.9 (0.90)	25.4 (1.69)	17.8 (0.66)	19.0 (2.67)
2014	19.2 (0.70)	17.3 (0.71)	25.5 (1.63)	18.1 (0.90)	20.3 (1.03)	23.2 (1.00)	14.0 (1.65)	14.7 (1.47)	12.6 (1.52)	19.3 (0.88)	23.2 (1.54)	19.2 (0.75)	18.8 (2.20)
2015	19.0 (0.73)	17.2 (0.79)	25.8 (1.70)	18.1 (0.92)	20.0 (1.23)	22.2 (1.05)	15.0 (2.03)	15.7 (1.42)	13.7 (1.87)	18.8 (0.93)	22.3 (1.47)	19.0 (0.78)	19.2 (2.20)
2016	18.3 (0.70)	16.5 (0.79)	24.9 (1.80)	15.8 (0.88)	20.9 (1.16)	22.9 (0.95)	9.3 (1.54)	15.0 (1.38)	8.1 (1.17)	18.9 (0.98)	22.8 (1.58)	18.7 (0.77)	14.0 (2.13)
2017	20.3 (0.73)	17.7 (0.72)	29.5 (1.88)	18.1 (0.89)	22.7 (1.08)	24.8 (1.01)	15.7 (1.73)	15.9 (1.53)	13.3 (1.60)	19.9 (0.92)	25.0 (1.57)	20.4 (0.74)	19.4 (2.75)
	Percent working less than 15 hours per week[3]												
1970	13.6 (0.64)	14.5 (0.71)	7.5 (1.37)	12.3 (0.85)	14.9 (0.97)	— (†)	— (†)	— (†)	9.9 (1.81)	12.6 (0.80)	16.8 (1.28)	— (†)	— (†)
1975	13.4 (0.62)	14.0 (0.67)	8.8 (1.43)	12.5 (0.82)	14.3 (0.92)	15.5 (0.75)	5.3 (1.05)	6.6! (2.15)	6.8 (1.44)	12.3 (0.78)	17.4 (1.23)	— (†)	— (†)
1980	14.0 (0.63)	14.9 (0.70)	8.9 (1.33)	13.7 (0.87)	14.2 (0.91)	16.4 (0.77)	4.6 (0.96)	9.4 (2.49)	7.7 (1.41)	13.2 (0.82)	17.7 (1.23)	— (†)	— (†)
1985	12.3 (0.65)	12.8 (0.72)	9.5 (1.51)	11.7 (0.89)	12.9 (0.96)	15.2 (0.85)	6.2 (1.25)	3.0! (1.18)	3.6 (0.97)	11.8 (0.86)	17.5 (1.40)	— (†)	— (†)
1990	11.7 (0.67)	12.9 (0.78)	6.8 (1.21)	11.3 (0.92)	12.2 (0.98)	14.7 (0.90)	6.0 (1.28)	4.8 (1.39)	5.9 (1.24)	11.5 (0.88)	15.6 (1.48)	— (†)	— (†)
1995	11.9 (0.63)	13.1 (0.73)	6.8 (1.14)	11.1 (0.84)	12.9 (0.96)	14.8 (0.85)	6.5 (1.22)	6.5 (1.42)	4.4 (0.98)	11.3 (0.82)	18.1 (1.47)	12.6 (0.68)	5.1 (1.46)
2000	11.9 (0.64)	12.9 (0.73)	7.8 (1.19)	11.2 (0.86)	12.6 (0.94)	15.4 (0.88)	6.3 (1.27)	3.7 (1.01)	5.4 (1.15)	11.3 (0.82)	16.5 (1.40)	12.6 (0.68)	5.2 (1.42)
2001	11.6 (0.59)	12.6 (0.68)	7.7 (1.10)	9.8 (0.75)	13.7 (0.91)	15.0 (0.82)	4.3 (0.96)	6.1 (1.26)	5.7 (1.15)	10.8 (0.74)	16.4 (1.31)	12.2 (0.63)	5.5 (1.43)
2002	11.1 (0.57)	12.1 (0.66)	7.2 (1.04)	9.7 (0.74)	12.7 (0.87)	15.0 (0.82)	4.5 (1.00)	3.6 (0.89)	6.0 (1.12)	10.0 (0.72)	16.1 (1.26)	11.9 (0.62)	4.1 (1.13)
2003	9.6 (0.52)	10.0 (0.59)	7.8 (1.11)	9.0 (0.70)	10.2 (0.78)	12.4 (0.75)	4.5 (0.96)	5.5 (1.06)	4.8 (1.00)	9.1 (0.67)	13.1 (1.14)	10.2 (0.57)	3.7 (1.07)
2004	10.4 (0.55)	10.9 (0.62)	8.4 (1.18)	9.9 (0.74)	11.0 (0.82)	14.0 (0.80)	4.9 (1.03)	4.4 (0.96)	3.5 (0.87)	8.5 (0.66)	18.1 (1.33)	11.0 (0.59)	5.2 (1.33)
2005	10.1 (0.53)	10.7 (0.60)	7.2 (1.08)	8.9 (0.69)	11.4 (0.81)	13.4 (0.77)	3.7 (0.89)	5.0 (0.99)	3.7 (0.85)	9.9 (0.69)	13.9 (1.16)	10.6 (0.56)	4.6 (1.26)
2006	9.9 (0.53)	10.7 (0.61)	6.4 (0.97)	8.8 (0.69)	11.0 (0.80)	12.8 (0.76)	5.2 (1.03)	4.2 (0.91)	3.7 (0.85)	9.2 (0.67)	14.7 (1.20)	10.5 (0.56)	3.0! (1.06)
2007	10.6 (0.54)	11.4 (0.63)	7.0 (1.02)	9.5 (0.72)	11.7 (0.82)	14.2 (0.80)	3.0 (0.80)	6.0 (1.06)	6.1 (1.10)	9.6 (0.68)	15.3 (1.25)	11.1 (0.58)	5.7 (1.36)
2008	9.2 (0.51)	9.9 (0.59)	6.1 (0.96)	8.1 (0.68)	10.3 (0.77)	12.4 (0.77)	3.2 (0.82)	4.1 (0.85)	3.1 (0.78)	9.1 (0.66)	13.0 (1.18)	9.6 (0.54)	4.6 (1.28)
2009	7.6 (0.47)	8.0 (0.54)	6.2 (0.94)	6.8 (0.62)	8.4 (0.71)	10.1 (0.71)	3.6 (0.86)	4.7 (0.91)	3.6 (0.83)	6.9 (0.58)	11.8 (1.15)	7.8 (0.50)	5.2 (1.38)

See notes at end of table.

Table 503.10. Percentage of high school students age 16 and over who were employed, by age group, sex, race/ethnicity, family income, nativity, and hours worked per week: Selected years, 1970 through 2017—Continued

[Standard errors appear in parentheses]

Year	Total	Age group		Sex		Race/ethnicity			Family income[1]			Nativity	
		16 and 17 years old	18 years old and over	Male	Female	White	Black	Hispanic	Low income	Middle income	High income	U.S.-born	Foreign-born
1	2	3	4	5	6	7	8	9	10	11	12	13	14
2010	7.3 (0.42)	7.5 (0.49)	6.8 (0.94)	6.3 (0.50)	8.4 (0.69)	9.5 (0.65)	4.1 (0.82)	4.5 (0.79)	3.0 (0.63)	7.1 (0.54)	10.9 (1.01)	7.7 (0.45)	3.4! (1.21)
2011	7.3 (0.40)	8.1 (0.50)	4.4 (0.71)	5.8 (0.51)	9.0 (0.66)	11.0 (0.66)	2.2 (0.60)	2.7 (0.54)	3.7 (0.81)	7.0 (0.55)	10.2 (0.94)	7.7 (0.44)	2.8! (0.98)
2012	8.2 (0.46)	8.5 (0.53)	7.3 (0.95)	7.1 (0.57)	9.4 (0.73)	12.2 (0.73)	3.7 (0.92)	2.4 (0.58)	4.2 (0.89)	7.2 (0.53)	13.3 (1.27)	8.8 (0.50)	2.4! (0.75)
2013	7.9 (0.50)	8.2 (0.54)	6.8 (0.99)	6.9 (0.61)	8.9 (0.77)	12.2 (0.81)	2.6 (0.71)	3.4 (0.62)	2.9 (0.78)	7.0 (0.54)	13.1 (1.38)	8.1 (0.50)	5.5! (1.75)
2014	7.8 (0.43)	8.4 (0.49)	5.7 (0.85)	6.5 (0.54)	9.1 (0.67)	10.7 (0.67)	3.5 (0.91)	3.5 (0.65)	3.8 (0.90)	7.6 (0.57)	10.9 (1.04)	8.2 (0.46)	3.7! (1.14)
2015	8.5 (0.48)	8.7 (0.54)	7.8 (1.07)	7.8 (0.70)	9.3 (0.75)	10.9 (0.75)	7.0 (1.49)	5.3 (0.97)	5.0 (1.07)	7.7 (0.60)	12.2 (1.18)	9.1 (0.53)	3.4 (1.00)
2016	8.1 (0.48)	8.4 (0.57)	7.0 (1.12)	6.5 (0.58)	9.8 (0.85)	10.8 (0.73)	2.4! (0.81)	5.0 (0.81)	2.6 (0.70)	7.5 (0.63)	12.4 (1.18)	8.5 (0.51)	4.5 (1.33)
2017	7.7 (0.50)	7.6 (0.55)	8.0 (1.01)	6.4 (0.58)	9.2 (0.73)	10.9 (0.79)	3.3 (0.84)	3.9 (0.80)	3.3 (0.74)	6.3 (0.59)	13.1 (1.19)	8.1 (0.54)	3.1! (1.19)
	Percent working 15 or more hours per week[3]												
1970	17.5 (0.71)	15.6 (0.73)	30.8 (2.41)	22.1 (1.08)	12.6 (0.90)	— (†)	— (†)	— (†)	10.6 (1.87)	18.4 (0.93)	18.1 (1.32)	— (†)	— (†)
1975	19.2 (0.71)	18.2 (0.75)	25.7 (2.20)	21.7 (1.03)	16.4 (0.97)	21.8 (0.85)	8.3 (1.30)	14.7 (3.08)	11.3 (1.81)	19.0 (0.93)	22.1 (1.34)	— (†)	— (†)
1980	20.5 (0.73)	19.0 (0.77)	29.4 (2.12)	22.1 (1.05)	18.9 (1.02)	23.5 (0.89)	10.1 (1.39)	14.3 (2.99)	11.4 (1.69)	21.0 (0.98)	23.1 (1.36)	— (†)	— (†)
1985	18.4 (0.77)	17.2 (0.81)	25.5 (2.24)	19.5 (1.09)	17.3 (1.09)	21.7 (0.97)	8.4 (1.44)	13.7 (2.37)	10.0 (1.57)	18.4 (1.03)	22.6 (1.54)	— (†)	— (†)
1990	19.7 (0.83)	17.5 (0.88)	29.1 (2.19)	21.0 (1.19)	18.3 (1.16)	22.1 (1.06)	10.6 (1.67)	21.5 (2.66)	15.0 (1.88)	20.8 (1.11)	20.2 (1.64)	— (†)	— (†)
1995	20.5 (0.79)	18.4 (0.84)	29.7 (2.07)	20.8 (1.09)	20.2 (1.14)	24.5 (1.03)	10.9 (1.55)	15.1 (2.07)	12.7 (1.60)	21.9 (1.07)	22.5 (1.59)	21.1 (0.83)	14.9 (2.35)
2000	21.1 (0.80)	19.2 (0.86)	28.8 (2.01)	21.1 (1.11)	21.0 (1.16)	24.6 (1.05)	13.8 (1.80)	16.3 (1.98)	15.6 (1.85)	21.5 (1.06)	23.1 (1.59)	21.3 (0.84)	19.0 (2.50)
2001	19.4 (0.73)	17.1 (0.77)	28.3 (1.85)	19.6 (1.01)	19.1 (1.05)	22.2 (0.95)	13.4 (1.62)	17.0 (1.97)	14.6 (1.76)	20.9 (0.97)	18.4 (1.37)	19.6 (0.76)	16.9 (2.35)
2002	18.5 (0.71)	16.1 (0.75)	27.9 (1.80)	17.5 (0.95)	19.7 (1.04)	21.4 (0.94)	11.9 (1.57)	16.8 (1.78)	12.3 (1.55)	20.7 (0.97)	17.4 (1.30)	18.7 (0.75)	16.5 (2.12)
2003	16.4 (0.66)	14.3 (0.69)	25.9 (1.82)	16.8 (0.92)	16.0 (0.94)	19.5 (0.90)	10.4 (1.42)	13.1 (1.57)	9.1 (1.35)	17.6 (0.89)	17.7 (1.29)	16.7 (0.70)	13.6 (1.95)
2004	16.0 (0.66)	13.8 (0.68)	26.2 (1.88)	15.5 (0.90)	16.6 (0.97)	17.8 (0.88)	10.2 (1.45)	16.6 (1.75)	8.1 (1.30)	18.3 (0.91)	15.2 (1.24)	16.1 (0.69)	15.2 (2.15)
2005	15.2 (0.63)	13.4 (0.66)	23.5 (1.77)	15.5 (0.88)	14.8 (0.90)	17.0 (0.84)	9.6 (1.40)	13.6 (1.55)	10.8 (1.40)	15.9 (0.85)	16.1 (1.23)	15.1 (0.66)	16.5 (2.24)
2006	17.0 (0.66)	14.4 (0.69)	27.0 (1.75)	16.8 (0.91)	17.1 (0.96)	19.5 (0.90)	14.5 (1.63)	13.3 (1.54)	13.8 (1.55)	17.7 (0.89)	17.3 (1.27)	16.6 (0.68)	20.8 (2.51)
2007	15.0 (0.63)	12.8 (0.66)	24.2 (1.72)	14.8 (0.87)	15.2 (0.92)	16.2 (0.85)	11.4 (1.49)	14.9 (1.59)	10.9 (1.44)	15.6 (0.83)	15.8 (1.27)	14.3 (0.65)	22.2 (2.43)
2008	12.8 (0.59)	10.3 (0.60)	22.7 (1.68)	11.4 (0.79)	14.1 (0.88)	14.3 (0.82)	11.9 (1.51)	10.6 (1.32)	9.9 (1.34)	12.8 (0.77)	14.4 (1.23)	12.7 (0.62)	13.0 (2.06)
2009	8.7 (0.50)	6.4 (0.49)	17.3 (1.47)	8.4 (0.69)	9.1 (0.73)	10.4 (0.71)	6.5 (1.15)	7.2 (1.11)	5.9 (1.06)	8.9 (0.66)	9.9 (1.07)	8.4 (0.52)	11.7 (1.99)
2010	8.3 (0.45)	6.9 (0.47)	13.4 (1.24)	7.2 (0.62)	9.4 (0.70)	10.5 (0.67)	5.3 (1.01)	5.6 (0.84)	5.3 (0.88)	9.0 (0.58)	8.7 (1.16)	8.1 (0.46)	9.6 (1.83)
2011	9.0 (0.52)	7.7 (0.56)	13.6 (1.10)	8.4 (0.63)	9.8 (0.78)	10.5 (0.77)	7.4 (1.30)	8.4 (1.06)	6.3 (1.10)	10.0 (0.69)	8.5 (0.94)	9.0 (0.55)	9.6 (1.84)
2012	8.9 (0.55)	6.7 (0.51)	16.5 (1.62)	8.4 (0.62)	9.5 (0.84)	10.0 (0.69)	8.2 (1.97)	8.4 (1.04)	8.3 (1.22)	8.7 (0.68)	9.9 (1.30)	8.9 (0.59)	9.6 (1.76)
2013	9.7 (0.56)	7.3 (0.53)	17.4 (1.57)	10.3 (0.85)	9.1 (0.67)	10.6 (0.81)	9.1 (1.37)	10.6 (1.10)	6.7 (1.19)	9.7 (0.82)	11.7 (1.12)	9.4 (0.60)	13.4 (2.15)
2014	10.7 (0.55)	8.2 (0.48)	19.3 (1.49)	10.8 (0.72)	10.6 (0.81)	11.6 (0.75)	9.4 (1.52)	11.0 (1.30)	8.6 (1.34)	11.1 (0.73)	11.1 (1.25)	10.2 (0.56)	15.1 (2.12)
2015	9.7 (0.54)	7.8 (0.53)	17.2 (1.50)	9.7 (0.66)	9.7 (0.86)	10.5 (0.75)	7.3 (1.31)	9.8 (1.11)	8.2 (1.41)	10.2 (0.72)	9.7 (1.05)	9.2 (0.57)	15.0 (2.08)
2016	9.7 (0.55)	7.6 (0.58)	17.3 (1.54)	8.8 (0.65)	10.6 (0.87)	11.6 (0.79)	6.9 (1.32)	9.0 (1.16)	5.5 (1.01)	10.8 (0.72)	9.8 (1.13)	9.7 (0.60)	9.0 (1.69)
2017	11.6 (0.58)	9.1 (0.55)	20.5 (1.62)	11.0 (0.75)	12.3 (0.90)	12.4 (0.77)	12.4 (1.61)	11.6 (1.33)	9.7 (1.47)	12.7 (0.67)	10.5 (1.17)	11.3 (0.58)	15.7 (2.54)

—Not available.
†Not applicable.
!Interpret data with caution. The coefficient of variation (CV) for this estimate is between 30 and 50 percent.
[1]Low income refers to the bottom 20 percent of all family incomes; high income refers to the top 20 percent of all family incomes; and middle income refers to the 60 percent in between.
[2]Percent employed includes those who were employed but not at work during the survey week.
[3]Hours worked per week refers to the number of hours the respondent worked at all jobs during the survey week. The estimates of the percentage of high school students age 16 and over who worked less than 15 hours per week or 15 or more hours per week exclude those who were employed but not at work during the survey week. Therefore, detail may not sum to total percentage employed.
NOTE: Race categories exclude persons of Hispanic ethnicity. Totals include racial/ethnic groups not shown separately. Prior to 2010, standard errors were computed using generalized variance function methodology rather than the more precise replicate weight methodology used in later years.
SOURCE: U.S. Department of Commerce, Census Bureau, Current Population Survey (CPS), October, 1970 through 2017. (This table was prepared April 2019.)

Table 503.20. Percentage of college students 16 to 24 years old who were employed, by attendance status, hours worked per week, and control and level of institution: Selected years, October 1970 through 2017

[Standard errors appear in parentheses]

Control and level of institution and year	Full-time students				Part-time students			
	Percent employed[1]	Hours worked per week[2]			Percent employed[1]	Hours worked per week[2]		
		Less than 20 hours	20 to 34 hours	35 or more hours		Less than 20 hours	20 to 34 hours	35 or more hours
1	2	3	4	5	6	7	8	9
Total, all institutions								
1970	33.8 (0.88)	19.0 (0.73)	10.4 (0.57)	3.7 (0.35)	82.1 (1.81)	5.0 (1.03)	15.9 (1.72)	60.1 (2.31)
1975	35.3 (0.83)	18.0 (0.67)	12.0 (0.56)	4.6 (0.36)	80.8 (1.55)	6.0 (0.94)	19.4 (1.56)	52.6 (1.97)
1980	40.0 (0.84)	21.3 (0.70)	14.0 (0.59)	3.9 (0.33)	84.7 (1.38)	7.9 (1.04)	22.5 (1.60)	52.7 (1.91)
1985	44.2 (0.88)	21.7 (0.73)	17.3 (0.67)	4.3 (0.36)	85.9 (1.41)	5.7 (0.94)	26.9 (1.80)	52.2 (2.03)
1990	45.7 (0.89)	20.6 (0.73)	19.3 (0.71)	4.8 (0.38)	83.7 (1.50)	4.0 (0.80)	26.0 (1.78)	52.7 (2.03)
1991	47.2 (0.88)	20.9 (0.72)	19.8 (0.70)	5.6 (0.41)	85.9 (1.45)	8.2 (1.15)	25.4 (1.82)	51.0 (2.09)
1992	47.2 (0.87)	20.3 (0.70)	20.3 (0.70)	5.5 (0.40)	83.4 (1.50)	7.5 (1.06)	27.2 (1.79)	47.8 (2.01)
1993	46.3 (0.89)	20.8 (0.72)	19.5 (0.71)	5.1 (0.39)	84.6 (1.43)	8.5 (1.10)	31.4 (1.84)	43.7 (1.96)
1994	48.6 (0.87)	20.1 (0.70)	21.7 (0.72)	5.8 (0.41)	86.3 (1.28)	9.8 (1.10)	31.1 (1.72)	43.8 (1.84)
1995	47.2 (0.87)	19.1 (0.69)	20.3 (0.70)	6.5 (0.43)	82.9 (1.45)	8.6 (1.08)	30.4 (1.77)	42.3 (1.90)
1996	49.2 (0.88)	18.2 (0.68)	22.3 (0.74)	7.0 (0.45)	84.8 (1.47)	8.3 (1.13)	27.5 (1.83)	48.0 (2.05)
1997	47.8 (0.86)	18.3 (0.67)	21.4 (0.71)	7.4 (0.45)	84.4 (1.46)	9.4 (1.17)	26.2 (1.77)	47.7 (2.01)
1998	50.2 (0.86)	20.2 (0.69)	20.6 (0.70)	8.0 (0.47)	84.1 (1.45)	7.0 (1.01)	26.8 (1.76)	49.3 (1.98)
1999	50.4 (0.86)	19.0 (0.68)	22.3 (0.72)	7.8 (0.46)	82.3 (1.55)	6.2 (0.98)	28.8 (1.85)	45.9 (2.03)
2000	52.0 (0.86)	20.1 (0.69)	21.7 (0.71)	8.9 (0.49)	84.9 (1.38)	8.6 (1.08)	27.8 (1.73)	47.5 (1.93)
2001	47.1 (0.80)	17.4 (0.61)	20.6 (0.65)	7.9 (0.43)	84.4 (1.29)	8.0 (0.97)	25.8 (1.56)	48.9 (1.78)
2002	47.8 (0.78)	17.3 (0.59)	20.9 (0.64)	8.5 (0.44)	78.9 (1.51)	8.7 (1.04)	25.3 (1.61)	43.4 (1.84)
2003	47.7 (0.78)	17.1 (0.59)	20.7 (0.63)	8.8 (0.44)	79.0 (1.44)	7.8 (0.95)	27.2 (1.58)	42.8 (1.75)
2004	49.0 (0.76)	17.7 (0.58)	21.6 (0.62)	8.6 (0.43)	81.5 (1.44)	8.5 (1.04)	27.4 (1.66)	44.1 (1.84)
2005	49.1 (0.75)	17.8 (0.58)	21.1 (0.61)	9.0 (0.43)	85.0 (1.30)	10.2 (1.10)	27.1 (1.62)	47.1 (1.82)
2006	46.5 (0.76)	15.1 (0.55)	22.0 (0.63)	8.1 (0.42)	81.0 (1.41)	7.3 (0.94)	27.6 (1.61)	45.5 (1.80)
2007	45.5 (0.74)	15.4 (0.54)	20.7 (0.60)	8.7 (0.42)	81.2 (1.39)	6.8 (0.90)	27.2 (1.59)	45.9 (1.78)
2008	45.3 (0.72)	15.6 (0.53)	20.1 (0.58)	8.7 (0.41)	79.4 (1.51)	9.3 (1.09)	24.7 (1.61)	44.4 (1.86)
2009	40.6 (0.69)	15.6 (0.51)	17.6 (0.54)	6.2 (0.34)	76.2 (1.57)	10.1 (1.11)	27.5 (1.65)	36.9 (1.78)
2010	39.8 (1.01)	14.9 (0.57)	17.2 (0.77)	6.6 (0.46)	73.4 (2.03)	10.7 (1.24)	28.3 (1.92)	32.8 (2.19)
2011	41.3 (0.94)	15.8 (0.67)	17.4 (0.66)	7.0 (0.44)	75.5 (1.93)	9.7 (1.21)	28.4 (1.99)	35.5 (2.16)
2012	41.0 (0.83)	15.1 (0.72)	17.8 (0.71)	7.2 (0.44)	71.7 (2.07)	9.0 (1.27)	29.5 (2.09)	32.1 (2.07)
2013	39.5 (1.00)	14.0 (0.67)	18.5 (0.77)	6.6 (0.50)	75.7 (2.06)	10.5 (1.44)	28.7 (1.76)	35.4 (2.11)
2014	41.3 (0.97)	15.6 (0.69)	17.9 (0.80)	6.6 (0.48)	80.3 (1.81)	13.8 (1.58)	26.9 (2.33)	38.5 (2.36)
2015	39.5 (0.98)	15.6 (0.77)	16.1 (0.75)	6.7 (0.56)	75.3 (2.33)	10.5 (1.48)	32.2 (2.67)	31.7 (2.15)
2016	39.7 (0.99)	15.5 (0.71)	16.6 (0.72)	6.6 (0.55)	79.2 (2.18)	10.8 (1.55)	31.4 (2.35)	36.0 (2.21)
2017	41.1 (1.10)	15.6 (0.76)	17.2 (0.81)	7.1 (0.54)	82.2 (1.78)	11.0 (1.45)	34.3 (2.19)	35.8 (2.32)
Public 4-year institutions								
1990	43.0 (1.18)	19.8 (0.95)	18.6 (0.93)	3.7 (0.45)	87.4 (2.25)	4.2! (1.37)	27.9 (3.05)	54.7 (3.39)
1995	48.8 (1.16)	19.4 (0.92)	22.6 (0.97)	5.6 (0.53)	86.7 (2.08)	9.6 (1.80)	30.8 (2.83)	45.0 (3.05)
2000	50.5 (1.15)	19.1 (0.90)	21.5 (0.94)	9.0 (0.66)	87.3 (1.91)	8.5 (1.60)	26.4 (2.53)	50.9 (2.87)
2005	49.6 (0.99)	17.8 (0.76)	22.7 (0.83)	8.0 (0.54)	86.3 (1.90)	9.0 (1.58)	26.8 (2.45)	49.7 (2.76)
2010	40.8 (1.27)	15.2 (0.88)	18.0 (0.93)	6.6 (0.64)	70.4 (3.58)	10.5 (2.04)	26.9 (2.82)	32.1 (3.59)
2012	41.0 (1.13)	14.9 (0.95)	18.6 (0.99)	6.7 (0.57)	77.6 (3.20)	9.9 (2.41)	28.0 (3.44)	38.8 (3.36)
2013	40.1 (1.31)	13.9 (0.88)	19.2 (0.98)	6.6 (0.63)	78.8 (2.88)	9.8 (1.94)	26.6 (2.80)	41.1 (3.84)
2014	41.1 (1.31)	14.6 (0.91)	18.4 (0.99)	6.9 (0.69)	83.4 (2.86)	12.2 (2.61)	28.4 (3.69)	42.3 (3.81)
2015	39.5 (1.32)	14.9 (0.98)	16.5 (1.01)	6.6 (0.73)	76.9 (3.39)	10.1 (2.01)	30.4 (3.84)	34.8 (3.38)
2016	39.7 (1.27)	15.0 (0.81)	16.8 (0.95)	6.9 (0.72)	81.9 (3.00)	11.6 (2.10)	32.6 (3.67)	36.7 (3.33)
2017	39.8 (1.28)	14.7 (0.81)	16.3 (0.91)	7.4 (0.69)	85.1 (2.21)	8.8 (1.97)	37.2 (3.24)	38.0 (3.47)
Private 4-year institutions								
1990	38.1 (1.89)	24.0 (1.66)	9.9 (1.17)	3.5 (0.72)	89.9 (4.27)	‡ (†)	31.9 (6.62)	53.1 (7.09)
1995	38.6 (1.78)	21.6 (1.51)	10.7 (1.13)	4.6 (0.77)	80.1 (4.85)	14.9 (4.32)	26.8 (5.38)	36.5 (5.84)
2000	45.8 (1.88)	23.6 (1.60)	14.9 (1.34)	5.4 (0.85)	78.0 (5.36)	‡ (†)	18.5 (5.02)	52.6 (6.46)
2005	42.3 (1.64)	20.1 (1.33)	13.8 (1.15)	7.0 (0.85)	88.5 (3.32)	10.6! (3.20)	34.5 (4.94)	43.2 (5.15)
2010	35.6 (2.37)	15.7 (1.63)	12.2 (1.52)	6.0 (1.08)	78.6 (7.00)	‡ (†)	23.4! (7.49)	45.6 (9.01)
2012	40.4 (2.39)	19.9 (1.80)	12.2 (1.40)	6.7 (1.13)	84.4 (5.35)	9.5! (4.53)	33.9 (6.58)	36.9 (7.38)
2013	34.0 (2.27)	14.9 (1.55)	12.8 (1.33)	5.6 (1.13)	86.9 (4.71)	21.9 (6.40)	29.8 (7.01)	35.2 (6.56)
2014	37.8 (2.29)	18.7 (1.72)	12.0 (1.62)	5.3 (1.00)	77.1 (6.82)	12.9! (4.92)	13.5! (5.59)	50.8 (8.76)
2015	32.8 (2.49)	18.5 (1.86)	8.3 (1.40)	5.7 (1.20)	73.8 (8.30)	10.4! (4.68)	17.8! (5.73)	45.6 (8.91)
2016	34.8 (2.20)	17.2 (1.73)	11.0 (1.20)	5.4 (0.94)	75.6 (8.00)	‡ (†)	13.4! (5.72)	53.3 (8.65)
2017	37.7 (2.41)	19.7 (2.09)	12.4 (1.69)	4.7 (1.09)	78.3 (7.39)	‡ (†)	29.5 (7.41)	41.5 (9.13)
Public 2-year institutions								
1990	61.2 (1.94)	19.1 (1.57)	31.2 (1.85)	9.2 (1.15)	81.5 (2.17)	4.1 (1.12)	24.9 (2.42)	51.1 (2.80)
1995	52.9 (1.97)	15.6 (1.43)	25.3 (1.72)	10.9 (1.23)	81.1 (2.21)	6.1 (1.35)	32.5 (2.64)	40.5 (2.77)
2000	63.9 (1.79)	20.6 (1.51)	29.9 (1.71)	11.9 (1.21)	85.5 (2.09)	9.9 (1.77)	30.0 (2.72)	44.9 (2.95)
2005	54.2 (1.69)	15.6 (1.23)	24.2 (1.46)	13.4 (1.16)	82.0 (2.20)	10.8 (1.77)	25.8 (2.50)	44.8 (2.84)
2010	40.6 (1.90)	14.0 (1.20)	19.1 (1.50)	6.8 (0.78)	74.7 (2.51)	11.6 (1.93)	30.1 (2.86)	31.0 (3.08)
2012	41.2 (1.76)	12.0 (1.17)	19.8 (1.44)	8.4 (0.95)	66.1 (2.98)	8.3 (1.60)	30.0 (2.70)	26.9 (2.79)
2013	41.8 (1.89)	13.8 (1.37)	20.5 (1.55)	7.1 (1.05)	71.1 (3.02)	8.8 (1.92)	29.8 (2.85)	31.2 (3.09)
2014	45.0 (2.28)	15.9 (1.57)	21.3 (1.82)	6.9 (0.91)	77.5 (2.64)	15.2 (2.35)	28.3 (3.35)	32.4 (3.58)
2015	44.9 (2.08)	15.1 (1.44)	21.8 (1.64)	7.5 (1.08)	75.1 (3.03)	11.4 (2.54)	36.6 (3.66)	26.7 (3.20)
2016	45.6 (2.01)	15.4 (1.51)	22.4 (1.70)	7.5 (1.14)	78.2 (3.23)	10.7 (2.31)	33.0 (3.46)	33.4 (3.33)
2017	46.8 (2.30)	14.9 (1.47)	22.9 (1.91)	7.9 (1.22)	81.0 (2.85)	14.0 (2.46)	33.0 (3.47)	32.7 (3.47)

†Not applicable.

!Interpret data with caution. The coefficient of variation (CV) for this estimate is between 30 and 50 percent.

‡Reporting standards not met. Either there are too few cases for a reliable estimate or the coefficient of variation (CV) is 50 percent or greater.

[1]Includes those who were employed but not at work during the survey week.

[2]Excludes those who were employed but not at work during the survey week; therefore, detail may not sum to total percentage employed. "Hours worked per week" refers to the number of hours worked at all jobs during the survey week.

NOTE: Students were classified as full time if they were taking at least 12 hours of classes (or at least 9 hours of graduate classes) during an average school week and as part time if they were taking fewer hours. Prior to 2010, standard errors were computed using generalized variance function methodology rather than the more precise replicate weight methodology used in later years.

SOURCE: U.S. Department of Commerce, Census Bureau, Current Population Survey (CPS), October, selected years, 1970 through 2017. (This table was prepared April 2019.)

Table 503.30. Percentage of college students 16 to 24 years old who were employed, by attendance status, hours worked per week, and selected characteristics: October 2015 through 2017

[Standard errors appear in parentheses]

Year and selected characteristic	Full-time students: Percent employed[1]		Full-time students: Hours worked per week[2]: Less than 20 hours		20 to 34 hours		35 or more hours		Part-time students: Percent employed[1]		Part-time students: Hours worked per week[2]: Less than 20 hours		20 to 34 hours		35 or more hours	
1	2		3		4		5		6		7		8		9	
2015																
Total	**39.5**	**(0.98)**	**15.6**	**(0.77)**	**16.1**	**(0.75)**	**6.7**	**(0.56)**	**75.3**	**(2.33)**	**10.5**	**(1.48)**	**32.2**	**(2.67)**	**31.7**	**(2.15)**
Sex																
Male	35.9	(1.30)	13.5	(0.95)	14.8	(1.00)	6.6	(0.74)	75.1	(3.20)	8.5	(1.87)	32.4	(3.39)	33.8	(3.05)
Female	42.7	(1.33)	17.5	(1.00)	17.2	(1.08)	6.8	(0.74)	75.5	(2.93)	12.3	(2.22)	32.1	(3.17)	29.8	(2.93)
2016																
Total	**39.7**	**(0.99)**	**15.5**	**(0.71)**	**16.6**	**(0.72)**	**6.6**	**(0.55)**	**79.2**	**(2.18)**	**10.8**	**(1.55)**	**31.4**	**(2.35)**	**36.0**	**(2.21)**
Sex																
Male	37.6	(1.33)	13.6	(0.95)	16.6	(1.02)	6.8	(0.69)	80.0	(2.76)	11.2	(2.21)	35.4	(3.21)	32.3	(3.00)
Female	41.5	(1.33)	17.2	(0.96)	16.7	(0.97)	6.5	(0.79)	78.5	(3.29)	10.5	(2.17)	27.8	(3.05)	39.2	(3.23)
Level and control of institution																
2-year	44.7	(1.93)	15.2	(1.44)	21.9	(1.67)	7.3	(1.11)	77.7	(3.03)	10.5	(2.25)	33.4	(3.41)	32.7	(3.16)
Public	45.6	(2.01)	15.4	(1.51)	22.4	(1.70)	7.5	(1.14)	78.2	(3.23)	10.7	(2.31)	33.0	(3.46)	33.4	(3.33)
Private	30.8	(8.01)	12.6 !	(5.34)	14.5 !	(6.00)	‡	(†)	‡	(†)	‡	(†)	‡	(†)	‡	(†)
4-year	38.4	(1.09)	15.6	(0.76)	15.3	(0.73)	6.5	(0.60)	80.8	(2.77)	11.2	(2.17)	29.3	(3.12)	39.6	(3.01)
Public	39.7	(1.27)	15.0	(0.81)	16.8	(0.95)	6.9	(0.72)	81.9	(3.00)	11.6	(2.10)	32.6	(3.67)	36.7	(3.33)
Private	34.8	(2.20)	17.2	(1.73)	11.0	(1.20)	5.4	(0.94)	75.6	(8.00)	‡	(†)	13.4 !	(5.72)	53.3	(8.65)
2017																
Total	**41.1**	**(1.10)**	**15.6**	**(0.76)**	**17.2**	**(0.81)**	**7.1**	**(0.54)**	**82.2**	**(1.78)**	**11.0**	**(1.45)**	**34.3**	**(2.19)**	**35.8**	**(2.32)**
Sex																
Male	38.7	(1.60)	15.5	(1.09)	15.2	(1.10)	6.8	(0.72)	82.6	(2.76)	11.5	(2.40)	32.9	(3.35)	37.0	(3.65)
Female	43.2	(1.50)	15.7	(1.06)	19.0	(1.13)	7.4	(0.74)	82.0	(2.36)	10.6	(2.00)	35.3	(2.83)	34.9	(2.84)
Race/ethnicity																
White	43.8	(1.41)	19.1	(1.06)	17.5	(1.03)	5.8	(0.70)	84.5	(2.30)	11.2	(2.19)	31.6	(2.89)	40.6	(3.50)
Black	35.8	(2.94)	7.7	(1.55)	17.2	(2.33)	10.3	(1.79)	80.9	(6.27)	‡	(†)	39.2	(7.70)	37.0	(7.46)
Hispanic	44.1	(2.77)	13.5	(1.64)	19.8	(1.90)	10.1	(1.36)	80.7	(3.59)	9.4 !	(2.85)	36.6	(4.35)	32.6	(3.96)
Asian	27.6	(2.97)	11.7	(1.98)	10.2	(1.95)	4.2	(1.19)	74.4	(9.97)	32.3	(9.40)	39.2	(9.36)	‡	(†)
Pacific Islander	‡	(†)	‡	(†)	‡	(†)	‡	(†)	‡	(†)	‡	(†)	‡	(†)	‡	(†)
American Indian/Alaska Native	‡	(†)	‡	(†)	‡	(†)	‡	(†)	‡	(†)	‡	(†)	‡	(†)	‡	(†)
Two or more races	45.7	(5.95)	14.7	(4.28)	19.5	(5.27)	9.2 !	(3.95)	‡	(†)	‡	(†)	‡	(†)	‡	(†)
Level and control of institution																
2-year	47.9	(2.30)	14.7	(1.43)	23.9	(1.88)	8.2	(1.24)	80.1	(2.93)	13.9	(2.40)	32.2	(3.41)	32.7	(3.37)
Public	46.8	(2.30)	14.9	(1.47)	22.9	(1.91)	7.9	(1.22)	81.0	(2.85)	14.0	(2.46)	33.0	(3.47)	32.7	(3.47)
Private	64.1	(8.36)	12.0 !	(5.25)	39.5	(9.34)	‡	(†)	‡	(†)	‡	(†)	‡	(†)	‡	(†)
4-year	39.3	(1.21)	15.8	(0.86)	15.4	(0.85)	6.8	(0.58)	84.1	(2.17)	8.6	(1.87)	36.1	(2.99)	38.5	(3.33)
Public	39.8	(1.28)	14.7	(0.81)	16.3	(0.91)	7.4	(0.69)	85.1	(2.21)	8.8	(1.97)	37.2	(3.24)	38.0	(3.47)
Private	37.7	(2.41)	19.7	(2.09)	12.4	(1.69)	4.7	(1.09)	78.3	(7.39)	‡	(†)	29.5	(7.41)	41.5	(9.13)
Student enrollment level																
Undergraduate	40.7	(1.19)	15.7	(0.81)	17.2	(0.84)	6.5	(0.57)	81.5	(1.90)	12.0	(1.57)	35.7	(2.42)	32.8	(2.46)
Sex																
Male	37.8	(1.69)	15.4	(1.11)	15.2	(1.14)	5.9	(0.71)	82.2	(2.99)	12.6	(2.60)	35.1	(3.58)	33.3	(3.85)
Female	43.2	(1.61)	16.0	(1.12)	19.0	(1.18)	7.0	(0.76)	81.0	(2.57)	11.5	(2.19)	36.2	(3.27)	32.4	(2.96)
Race/ethnicity																
White	43.3	(1.49)	19.3	(1.13)	17.3	(1.06)	5.3	(0.71)	83.6	(2.66)	12.6	(2.42)	34.7	(3.24)	35.8	(3.85)
Black	34.6	(2.99)	7.6	(1.62)	17.1	(2.40)	9.2	(1.77)	79.4	(6.58)	‡	(†)	37.0	(7.98)	37.3	(7.65)
Hispanic	44.2	(2.91)	14.0	(1.80)	20.1	(2.00)	9.2	(1.36)	79.8	(3.70)	9.9 !	(2.99)	36.8	(4.53)	31.0	(3.88)
Asian	26.6	(3.03)	10.6	(1.88)	11.6	(2.23)	2.9 !	(1.04)	‡	(†)	‡	(†)	‡	(†)	‡	(†)
Pacific Islander	‡	(†)	‡	(†)	‡	(†)	‡	(†)	‡	(†)	‡	(†)	‡	(†)	‡	(†)
American Indian/Alaska Native	‡	(†)	‡	(†)	‡	(†)	‡	(†)	‡	(†)	‡	(†)	‡	(†)	‡	(†)
Two or more races	45.1	(6.02)	15.0	(4.35)	18.4	(5.33)	9.4 !	(4.03)	‡	(†)	‡	(†)	‡	(†)	‡	(†)
Level and control of institution																
2-year	48.2	(2.35)	14.5	(1.44)	24.3	(1.93)	8.3	(1.31)	80.8	(2.84)	14.4	(2.47)	32.5	(3.44)	32.5	(3.38)
Public	47.1	(2.36)	14.9	(1.50)	23.1	(1.97)	7.9	(1.29)	81.0	(2.89)	14.4	(2.51)	32.9	(3.52)	32.2	(3.45)
Private	66.2	(8.46)	‡	(†)	44.0	(9.72)	‡	(†)	‡	(†)	‡	(†)	‡	(†)	‡	(†)
4-year	38.5	(1.28)	16.0	(0.91)	15.2	(0.85)	5.9	(0.61)	82.2	(2.53)	9.5	(2.09)	39.1	(3.51)	33.0	(3.57)
Public	39.0	(1.34)	14.8	(0.89)	16.1	(0.92)	6.7	(0.73)	84.3	(2.38)	10.0	(2.24)	39.8	(3.72)	33.7	(3.56)
Private	36.6	(2.54)	20.4	(2.11)	12.0	(1.71)	3.2	(0.83)	‡	(†)	‡	(†)	‡	(†)	‡	(†)
Graduate	45.6	(3.41)	14.5	(2.47)	17.1	(2.54)	13.4	(2.49)	87.5	(5.77)	‡	(†)	23.6	(5.66)	58.1	(8.37)

†Not applicable.

!Interpret data with caution. The coefficient of variation (CV) for this estimate is between 30 and 50 percent.

‡Reporting standards not met. Either there are too few cases for a reliable estimate or the coefficient of variation (CV) is 50 percent or greater.

[1] Includes those who were employed but not at work during the survey week.

[2] Excludes those who were employed but not at work during the survey week; therefore, detail may not sum to total percentage employed. "Hours worked per week" refers to the number of hours worked at all jobs during the survey week.

NOTE: Students were classified as full time if they were taking at least 12 hours of classes (or at least 9 hours of graduate classes) during an average school week and as part time if they were taking fewer hours. Race categories exclude persons of Hispanic ethnicity.

SOURCE: U.S. Department of Commerce, Census Bureau, Current Population Survey (CPS), October, 2015 through 2017. (This table was prepared April 2019.)

Table 503.40. Percentage of 16- to 64-year-old undergraduate students who were employed, by attendance status, hours worked per week, and selected characteristics: 2000, 2010, and 2019

[Standard errors appear in parentheses]

Year and selected characteristic	Full-time undergraduates: Percent of all full-time undergraduates	Full-time: Percent employed: Total employed[1]	Full-time: Hours worked per week[2]: Less than 10	Full-time: 10 to 19	Full-time: 20 to 34	Full-time: 35 or more	Part-time undergraduates: Percent of all part-time undergraduates	Part-time: Percent employed: Total employed[1]	Part-time: Hours worked per week[2]: Less than 10	Part-time: 10 to 19	Part-time: 20 to 34	Part-time: 35 or more
1	2	3	4	5	6	7	8	9	10	11	12	13
2000												
Total	**100.0 (†)**	**53.1 (0.77)**	**4.8 (0.33)**	**14.4 (0.54)**	**21.4 (0.64)**	**11.1 (0.49)**	**100.0 (†)**	**85.4 (0.87)**	**1.4 (0.29)**	**5.2 (0.55)**	**20.4 (1.00)**	**57.4 (1.22)**
Sex												
Male	45.6 (0.77)	52.0 (1.15)	4.2 (0.46)	12.2 (0.75)	22.0 (0.95)	12.5 (0.76)	41.8 (1.22)	88.6 (1.22)	1.1 ! (0.41)	5.1 (0.84)	19.0 (1.50)	62.6 (1.85)
Female	54.4 (0.77)	54.1 (1.05)	5.4 (0.47)	16.3 (0.78)	20.9 (0.85)	9.9 (0.63)	58.2 (1.22)	83.1 (1.21)	1.7 (0.41)	5.4 (0.73)	21.4 (1.33)	53.6 (1.61)
Race/ethnicity[3]												
White	70.1 (0.71)	55.0 (0.92)	5.2 (0.41)	15.8 (0.67)	21.9 (0.77)	10.6 (0.57)	65.2 (1.18)	87.1 (1.02)	1.2 (0.33)	5.3 (0.69)	22.3 (1.27)	57.4 (1.51)
Black	13.5 (0.56)	46.0 (2.23)	3.6 (0.84)	8.1 (1.22)	17.5 (1.70)	14.1 (1.56)	16.9 (0.98)	80.3 (2.55)	‡ (†)	5.3 (1.43)	13.5 (2.19)	59.1 (3.15)
Hispanic	8.7 (0.50)	61.3 (2.90)	5.0 (1.30)	13.6 (2.04)	25.6 (2.60)	16.5 (2.21)	13.0 (0.94)	86.8 (2.63)	‡ (†)	4.9 ! (1.69)	21.5 (3.20)	57.2 (3.85)
Asian/Pacific Islander	7.0 (0.42)	40.3 (3.05)	3.1 ! (1.08)	14.6 (2.20)	18.9 (2.44)	3.5 ! (1.14)	4.5 (0.54)	79.6 (5.00)	‡ (†)	‡ (†)	16.3 (4.58)	54.2 (6.18)
American Indian/Alaska Native	0.6 (0.13)	29.5 ! (9.36)	‡ (†)	‡ (†)	20.7 ! (8.32)	‡ (†)	0.5 ! (0.19)	‡ (†)	‡ (†)	‡ (†)	‡ (†)	‡ (†)
Age												
16 to 24	84.5 (0.56)	52.1 (0.84)	5.1 (0.37)	15.8 (0.61)	21.9 (0.70)	8.2 (0.46)	40.4 (1.21)	85.2 (1.38)	1.8 (0.52)	7.1 (1.00)	28.9 (1.76)	46.4 (1.94)
25 to 29	7.2 (0.40)	62.6 (2.80)	2.9 ! (0.98)	7.6 (1.54)	21.1 (2.36)	28.3 (2.60)	17.4 (0.94)	88.1 (1.92)	‡ (†)	5.2 (1.32)	17.8 (2.26)	63.3 (2.85)
30 to 39	5.4 (0.35)	53.4 (3.33)	3.3 ! (1.19)	5.9 (1.57)	15.0 (2.38)	26.6 (2.95)	24.3 (1.06)	84.7 (1.81)	1.0 ! (0.51)	3.9 (0.97)	13.2 (1.70)	66.1 (2.37)
40 to 49	2.5 (0.24)	61.2 (4.73)	5.0 ! (2.12)	7.6 ! (2.58)	19.6 (3.86)	25.6 (4.24)	13.7 (0.85)	85.5 (2.35)	2.1 ! (0.95)	2.8 ! (1.10)	14.0 (2.32)	65.3 (3.18)
50 to 64	0.4 (0.09)	‡ (†)	‡ (†)	‡ (†)	‡ (†)	‡ (†)	4.2 (0.50)	79.9 (4.81)	‡ (†)	‡ (†)	11.5 ! (3.83)	61.3 (5.84)
Level of institution												
2-year	24.7 (0.67)	60.5 (1.52)	4.3 (0.63)	14.3 (1.09)	26.3 (1.37)	14.2 (1.09)	48.1 (1.23)	84.7 (1.28)	1.4 ! (0.41)	6.3 (0.86)	22.1 (1.48)	54.1 (1.78)
4-year	75.3 (0.67)	50.7 (0.89)	5.0 (0.39)	14.5 (0.63)	19.8 (0.71)	10.0 (0.54)	51.9 (1.23)	86.0 (1.19)	1.5 (0.42)	4.3 (0.70)	18.8 (1.34)	60.3 (1.68)
Householder status[4]												
Non-householder	75.2 (0.67)	50.9 (0.89)	4.9 (0.38)	15.0 (0.64)	21.7 (0.74)	8.1 (0.49)	39.8 (1.21)	85.0 (1.40)	1.6 ! (0.50)	6.7 (0.98)	27.6 (1.75)	48.2 (1.96)
Householder	24.8 (0.67)	59.9 (1.52)	4.7 (0.66)	12.6 (1.03)	20.4 (1.25)	19.9 (1.24)	60.2 (1.21)	85.7 (1.12)	1.3 (0.36)	4.3 (0.64)	15.6 (1.16)	63.4 (1.53)
Presence of own children under 18 in household[5]												
Child or children present	9.4 (0.45)	58.4 (2.49)	3.5 (0.93)	12.8 (1.69)	15.1 (1.81)	23.3 (2.14)	33.6 (1.17)	84.3 (1.55)	1.1 ! (0.44)	5.2 (0.94)	16.2 (1.57)	60.4 (2.08)
No children present	90.6 (0.45)	52.6 (0.81)	5.0 (0.35)	14.6 (0.57)	22.1 (0.67)	9.8 (0.48)	66.4 (1.17)	86.0 (1.05)	1.6 (0.38)	5.3 (0.68)	22.5 (1.27)	55.8 (1.51)
Presence of spouse in household												
Spouse present	9.7 (0.46)	59.5 (2.44)	5.0 (1.09)	10.5 (1.53)	15.3 (1.79)	25.1 (2.16)	38.0 (1.20)	83.3 (1.50)	1.0 ! (0.40)	4.4 (0.82)	15.7 (1.46)	61.2 (1.95)
No spouse present[6]	90.3 (0.46)	52.4 (0.81)	4.8 (0.35)	14.8 (0.58)	22.1 (0.68)	9.6 (0.48)	62.0 (1.20)	86.7 (1.06)	1.7 (0.41)	5.7 (0.73)	23.2 (1.32)	55.0 (1.56)
Presence of spouse and own children under 18												
Spouse and children both present	6.0 (0.37)	59.0 (3.12)	4.5 (1.31)	9.7 (1.88)	13.8 (2.19)	27.1 (2.82)	25.3 (1.07)	81.9 (1.89)	1.0 ! (0.49)	5.2 (1.09)	14.3 (1.72)	60.3 (2.41)
Spouse only, no children present	3.7 (0.29)	60.5 (3.93)	6.0 ! (1.90)	11.8 (2.59)	17.6 (3.06)	21.9 (3.32)	12.7 (0.82)	85.9 (2.41)	‡ (†)	2.8 ! (1.15)	18.5 (2.69)	62.9 (3.35)
Children only, no spouse present	3.4 (0.28)	57.5 (4.13)	‡ (†)	18.0 (3.21)	17.2 (3.15)	16.7 (3.11)	8.3 (0.68)	91.3 (2.41)	‡ (†)	5.0 ! (1.86)	21.9 (3.54)	61.0 (4.18)
Neither spouse nor children present	86.9 (0.52)	52.2 (0.83)	4.9 (0.36)	14.7 (0.59)	22.2 (0.69)	9.3 (0.48)	53.7 (1.23)	86.0 (1.17)	1.8 (0.45)	5.9 (0.79)	23.4 (1.43)	54.1 (1.68)
2010												
Total	**100.0 (†)**	**41.1 (0.90)**	**3.7 (0.28)**	**9.9 (0.44)**	**16.4 (0.65)**	**9.9 (0.49)**	**100.0 (†)**	**74.5 (1.40)**	**1.8 (0.34)**	**5.3 (0.63)**	**22.1 (1.19)**	**42.9 (1.53)**
Sex												
Male	45.2 (0.77)	39.6 (1.24)	3.1 (0.42)	9.1 (0.66)	16.6 (0.93)	9.8 (0.69)	42.8 (1.27)	77.0 (1.90)	1.4 ! (0.44)	4.3 (0.79)	21.6 (1.74)	47.0 (2.36)
Female	54.8 (0.77)	42.4 (1.17)	4.3 (0.40)	10.6 (0.64)	16.3 (0.85)	10.1 (0.69)	57.2 (1.27)	72.7 (1.80)	2.1 (0.52)	6.1 (0.87)	22.5 (1.71)	39.8 (1.90)
Race/ethnicity												
White	62.2 (0.79)	44.1 (1.15)	4.6 (0.40)	11.6 (0.62)	17.2 (0.90)	9.4 (0.58)	57.4 (1.52)	75.7 (1.70)	1.7 (0.46)	5.8 (0.86)	21.0 (1.59)	44.3 (1.97)
Black	14.9 (0.65)	36.6 (2.44)	1.8 ! (0.74)	6.9 (1.19)	13.6 (1.59)	12.7 (1.52)	16.3 (1.17)	75.7 (2.91)	1.7 ! (0.79)	3.5 ! (1.55)	21.9 (3.19)	45.6 (3.46)
Hispanic	13.5 (0.51)	39.0 (2.16)	2.1 ! (0.65)	6.5 (1.09)	18.4 (1.81)	11.6 (1.47)	21.0 (1.23)	73.0 (3.02)	2.0 ! (0.82)	4.5 (1.22)	25.3 (3.12)	40.0 (3.35)
Asian	6.6 (0.34)	31.1 (2.91)	3.4 (0.97)	8.8 (1.63)	12.4 (1.94)	5.9 ! (1.83)	3.0 (0.50)	69.0 (8.23)	‡ (†)	‡ (†)	25.7 (6.46)	35.4 (7.45)
Pacific Islander	0.4 ! (0.12)	‡ (†)	‡ (†)	‡ (†)	‡ (†)	‡ (†)	‡ (†)	‡ (†)	‡ (†)	‡ (†)	‡ (†)	‡ (†)
American Indian/Alaska Native	0.8 (0.17)	23.0 ! (7.60)	‡ (†)	‡ (†)	‡ (†)	15.4 ! (7.37)	0.7 ! (0.20)	‡ (†)	‡ (†)	‡ (†)	‡ (†)	‡ (†)
Two or more races	1.6 (0.22)	39.6 (6.95)	8.0 ! (3.65)	10.2 ! (3.85)	15.6 ! (4.78)	‡ (†)	1.6 (0.41)	65.9 (9.24)	‡ (†)	‡ (†)	23.6 ! (9.38)	26.7 ! (10.90)
Age												
16 to 24	79.0 (0.66)	39.9 (1.05)	4.1 (0.34)	11.2 (0.55)	17.5 (0.81)	6.1 (0.47)	42.2 (1.24)	72.0 (2.16)	2.3 (0.65)	8.9 (1.22)	29.4 (2.09)	29.6 (2.23)
25 to 29	8.7 (0.45)	47.0 (2.66)	1.9 ! (0.71)	8.6 (1.65)	13.8 (1.78)	21.8 (2.09)	19.7 (1.05)	79.2 (2.51)	1.6 ! (0.65)	3.1 ! (1.12)	20.0 (2.49)	51.7 (3.39)
30 to 39	7.6 (0.39)	45.4 (3.16)	2.1 ! (0.79)	3.1 ! (0.93)	12.8 (1.91)	25.7 (2.64)	20.0 (1.05)	76.0 (2.82)	‡ (†)	2.5 ! (0.95)	15.6 (2.16)	54.4 (3.10)
40 to 49	3.3 (0.29)	43.6 (4.43)	3.7 ! (1.44)	3.4 ! (1.50)	10.8 (2.61)	25.7 (4.05)	11.9 (0.85)	72.6 (3.52)	‡ (†)	2.7 ! (1.07)	11.3 (2.36)	53.7 (3.88)
50 to 64	1.5 (0.19)	43.7 (5.89)	‡ (†)	‡ (†)	‡ (†)	28.3 (4.96)	6.1 (0.62)	76.6 (4.43)	‡ (†)	‡ (†)	20.6 (4.73)	48.0 (5.95)
Level of institution												
2-year	31.3 (0.81)	39.0 (1.46)	1.9 (0.44)	10.0 (0.83)	16.5 (1.17)	9.9 (0.79)	50.7 (1.44)	73.0 (1.77)	2.3 (0.55)	5.8 (0.98)	23.4 (1.76)	39.2 (2.17)
4-year	68.7 (0.81)	42.1 (1.09)	4.6 (0.39)	9.9 (0.58)	16.3 (0.71)	9.9 (0.63)	49.3 (1.44)	76.1 (1.88)	1.3 ! (0.40)	4.8 (0.88)	20.7 (1.49)	46.8 (2.22)
Householder status[4]												
Non-householder	73.6 (0.71)	38.2 (1.04)	3.8 (0.35)	10.5 (0.51)	16.3 (0.76)	6.6 (0.45)	46.4 (1.38)	71.6 (2.03)	2.3 (0.61)	6.6 (1.04)	29.3 (1.88)	31.7 (2.04)
Householder	26.4 (0.71)	49.3 (1.60)	3.5 (0.57)	8.4 (0.90)	16.7 (1.14)	19.3 (1.25)	53.6 (1.38)	77.1 (1.68)	1.3 ! (0.42)	4.2 (0.83)	15.9 (1.33)	52.6 (2.01)
Presence of own children under 18 in household[5]												
Child or children present	12.7 (0.56)	38.4 (2.11)	2.6 (0.72)	5.3 (0.95)	10.9 (1.39)	18.2 (1.71)	29.6 (1.32)	73.0 (2.49)	2.4 ! (0.73)	3.9 (0.92)	14.4 (1.72)	49.8 (2.59)
No children present	87.3 (0.56)	41.5 (0.94)	3.9 (0.32)	10.6 (0.48)	17.2 (0.71)	8.7 (0.47)	70.4 (1.32)	75.2 (1.49)	1.5 (0.39)	5.9 (0.77)	25.3 (1.50)	40.0 (1.78)
Presence of spouse in household												

[Standard errors appear in parentheses]

	Full-time undergraduates						Part-time undergraduates					
		Percent employed						Percent employed				
			Hours worked per week[2]						Hours worked per week[2]			
Year and selected characteristic	Percent of all full-time undergraduates	Total employed[1]	Less than 10	10 to 19	20 to 34	35 or more	Percent of all part-time undergraduates	Total employed[1]	Less than 10	10 to 19	20 to 34	35 or more
1	2	3	4	5	6	7	8	9	10	11	12	13
Spouse present	10.6 (0.47)	44.7 (2.47)	2.8 (0.76)	4.6 (1.11)	14.4 (1.71)	21.4 (1.97)	31.3 (1.45)	73.6 (2.46)	1.5 ! (0.54)	3.4 (0.89)	13.9 (1.53)	52.1 (2.69)
No spouse present[6]	89.4 (0.47)	40.7 (0.95)	3.9 (0.31)	10.6 (0.48)	16.6 (0.69)	8.6 (0.46)	68.7 (1.45)	75.0 (1.49)	1.9 (0.44)	6.2 (0.80)	25.8 (1.42)	38.8 (1.68)
Presence of spouse and own children under 18												
Spouse and children both present	6.5 (0.39)	38.6 (2.83)	1.8 ! (0.72)	4.0 (1.09)	11.6 (2.11)	20.0 (2.16)	18.9 (1.14)	71.5 (3.26)	2.2 ! (0.82)	3.7 ! (1.11)	12.1 (1.87)	51.9 (3.27)
Spouse only, no children present	4.2 (0.31)	54.1 (3.63)	4.5 ! (1.59)	5.6 ! (1.97)	18.7 (2.84)	23.7 (3.53)	12.3 (1.00)	76.8 (3.29)	‡ (†)	3.0 ! (1.28)	16.6 (2.93)	52.2 (4.33)
Children only, no spouse present	6.2 (0.41)	38.2 (3.20)	3.5 ! (1.20)	6.6 (1.54)	10.1 (1.82)	16.4 (2.44)	10.7 (0.88)	75.7 (3.32)	2.9 ! (1.45)	4.3 ! (1.57)	18.5 (3.10)	46.1 (3.91)
Neither spouse nor children present	83.2 (0.62)	40.9 (0.96)	3.9 (0.33)	10.9 (0.50)	17.1 (0.73)	8.0 (0.45)	58.1 (1.51)	74.8 (1.62)	1.7 (0.47)	6.5 (0.89)	27.2 (1.55)	37.4 (1.92)
2019												
Total	**100.0 (†)**	**44.6 (1.07)**	**3.9 (0.34)**	**10.3 (0.61)**	**17.2 (0.70)**	**11.4 (0.66)**	**100.0 (†)**	**83.7 (1.33)**	**2.1 (0.50)**	**4.8 (0.77)**	**27.2 (1.59)**	**47.9 (1.75)**
Sex												
Male	45.6 (0.82)	40.2 (1.55)	2.8 (0.45)	8.5 (0.84)	17.4 (1.00)	10.2 (0.92)	42.8 (1.66)	85.3 (1.95)	2.3 ! (0.85)	4.2 (1.02)	25.9 (2.27)	51.1 (2.67)
Female	54.4 (0.82)	48.3 (1.38)	4.7 (0.49)	11.8 (0.83)	17.2 (1.03)	12.5 (0.89)	57.2 (1.66)	82.5 (1.78)	1.9 ! (0.65)	5.3 (1.18)	28.1 (2.25)	45.5 (2.36)
Race/ethnicity												
White	53.7 (0.93)	46.0 (1.39)	4.4 (0.49)	11.2 (0.84)	18.6 (1.02)	9.7 (0.81)	45.1 (1.87)	86.6 (1.73)	3.0 (0.88)	5.1 (1.15)	27.7 (2.53)	48.6 (2.69)
Black	13.1 (0.65)	39.9 (2.94)	1.4 ! (0.66)	6.9 (1.45)	12.5 (1.73)	18.5 (2.48)	19.8 (1.71)	85.4 (3.18)	‡ (†)	‡ (†)	27.6 (4.21)	52.6 (4.55)
Hispanic	20.0 (0.81)	47.7 (2.30)	3.2 (0.79)	11.1 (1.41)	18.5 (1.70)	13.6 (1.44)	26.3 (1.76)	79.4 (3.04)	‡ (†)	6.0 (1.77)	24.7 (2.96)	46.4 (3.46)
Asian	8.7 (0.55)	34.7 (3.53)	5.6 (1.49)	8.8 (1.91)	13.3 (2.15)	4.4 ! (1.43)	5.4 (0.84)	79.0 (6.80)	‡ (†)	‡ (†)	27.1 (6.58)	42.0 (7.91)
Pacific Islander	0.3 ! (0.11)	‡ (†)	‡ (†)	‡ (†)	‡ (†)	‡ (†)	0.6 ! (0.26)	‡ (†)	‡ (†)	‡ (†)	‡ (†)	‡ (†)
American Indian/Alaska Native	0.9 (0.20)	30.0 ! (9.32)	‡ (†)	‡ (†)	‡ (†)	21.6 ! (7.80)	‡ (†)	‡ (†)	‡ (†)	‡ (†)	‡ (†)	‡ (†)
Two or more races	3.3 (0.36)	48.0 (5.85)	5.7 ! (2.22)	10.5 ! (3.15)	19.3 (4.46)	11.1 ! (3.67)	2.6 (0.64)	‡ (†)	‡ (†)	‡ (†)	‡ (†)	‡ (†)
Age												
16 to 24	83.8 (0.69)	42.0 (1.14)	4.0 (0.37)	11.5 (0.70)	17.4 (0.77)	7.5 (0.60)	47.1 (1.86)	84.9 (1.87)	2.7 (0.78)	7.0 (1.34)	35.6 (2.39)	38.5 (2.59)
25 to 29	7.7 (0.50)	57.9 (3.89)	3.9 ! (1.32)	6.1 (1.79)	20.8 (2.92)	25.1 (3.17)	18.2 (1.56)	91.3 (2.37)	‡ (†)	4.4 ! (1.70)	29.2 (3.96)	54.8 (4.27)
30 to 39	5.3 (0.42)	60.2 (3.97)	2.8 ! (1.13)	2.5 ! (1.15)	14.1 (2.80)	37.1 (3.97)	19.5 (1.50)	81.4 (3.11)	3.8 ! (1.70)	1.6 ! (0.82)	17.6 (3.09)	56.3 (4.16)
40 to 49	1.9 (0.23)	54.7 (6.01)	‡ (†)	‡ (†)	13.4 ! (4.57)	38.1 (5.68)	10.7 (1.10)	76.7 (4.65)	‡ (†)	‡ (†)	11.8 (3.21)	58.6 (5.19)
50 to 64	1.3 (0.21)	54.0 (7.79)	‡ (†)	‡ (†)	‡ (†)	40.1 (7.81)	4.5 (0.76)	66.6 (8.47)	‡ (†)	‡ (†)	‡ (†)	57.4 (8.14)
Level of institution												
2-year	24.4 (0.88)	46.7 (2.02)	2.6 (0.60)	7.7 (1.06)	21.2 (1.49)	13.6 (1.47)	49.0 (2.08)	82.8 (1.83)	2.6 (0.76)	4.6 (1.13)	30.1 (2.59)	44.0 (2.66)
4-year	75.6 (0.88)	43.9 (1.24)	4.3 (0.41)	11.1 (0.75)	16.0 (0.76)	10.7 (0.69)	51.0 (2.08)	84.5 (1.78)	1.7 ! (0.60)	5.0 (1.11)	24.4 (2.21)	51.7 (2.34)
Householder status[4]												
Non-householder	76.3 (0.81)	41.1 (1.16)	3.9 (0.40)	11.3 (0.72)	17.2 (0.76)	7.0 (0.61)	53.0 (1.88)	83.6 (2.10)	1.9 ! (0.67)	6.5 (1.28)	35.2 (2.39)	39.0 (2.43)
Householder	23.7 (0.81)	55.8 (1.86)	3.7 (0.73)	7.0 (0.96)	17.4 (1.51)	25.7 (1.88)	47.0 (1.88)	83.7 (1.66)	2.3 ! (0.78)	2.8 (0.78)	18.2 (2.11)	57.9 (2.69)
Presence of own children under 18 in household[5]												
Child or children present	7.3 (0.52)	56.5 (3.03)	2.1 ! (0.82)	3.6 ! (1.20)	11.0 (2.29)	38.1 (3.33)	22.1 (1.60)	82.1 (2.78)	‡ (†)	2.7 ! (1.22)	20.6 (2.79)	54.6 (3.70)
No children present	92.7 (0.52)	43.6 (1.10)	4.0 (0.37)	10.8 (0.65)	17.7 (0.72)	9.3 (0.63)	77.9 (1.60)	84.1 (1.66)	2.2 (0.56)	5.4 (0.92)	29.1 (1.84)	46.0 (2.05)
Presence of spouse in household												
Spouse present	8.0 (0.54)	61.9 (3.05)	2.4 ! (0.83)	4.2 ! (1.34)	15.0 (2.51)	37.7 (3.28)	25.8 (1.50)	83.8 (2.35)	2.1 ! (1.00)	2.1 ! (0.85)	16.1 (2.53)	60.7 (3.53)
No spouse present[6]	92.0 (0.54)	43.1 (1.12)	4.0 (0.37)	10.8 (0.65)	17.4 (0.73)	9.1 (0.64)	74.2 (1.50)	83.6 (1.67)	2.1 (0.56)	5.7 (1.01)	31.0 (1.88)	43.5 (1.99)
Presence of spouse and own children under 18												
Spouse and children both present	4.1 (0.39)	57.6 (4.13)	‡ (†)	‡ (†)	10.4 (2.66)	41.6 (4.53)	13.9 (1.18)	82.7 (3.49)	‡ (†)	‡ (†)	19.2 (3.52)	57.6 (4.82)
Spouse only, no children present	3.9 (0.35)	66.3 (4.07)	3.1 ! (1.33)	6.4 ! (2.33)	19.9 (3.92)	33.7 (4.44)	11.9 (1.22)	85.1 (3.48)	‡ (†)	‡ (†)	12.6 (3.57)	64.3 (5.27)
Children only, no spouse present	3.2 (0.36)	55.0 (5.35)	‡ (†)	5.5 ! (2.32)	11.7 ! (4.03)	33.6 (4.86)	8.3 (0.95)	81.0 (5.11)	‡ (†)	‡ (†)	23.1 (5.45)	49.4 (6.45)
Neither spouse nor children present	88.8 (0.65)	42.6 (1.13)	4.0 (0.39)	11.0 (0.67)	17.6 (0.72)	8.2 (0.62)	65.9 (1.67)	83.9 (1.83)	2.2 (0.60)	5.9 (1.08)	32.0 (2.02)	42.7 (2.18)

†Not applicable.

!Interpret data with caution. The coefficient of variation (CV) for this estimate is between 30 and 50 percent.

‡Reporting standards not met. Either there are too few cases for a reliable estimate or the coefficient of variation (CV) is 50 percent or greater.

1 Includes those who were employed but not at work during the survey week.

2 Excludes those who were employed but not at work during the survey week; therefore, detail may not sum to total percentage employed. "Hours worked per week" refers to the number of hours worked at all jobs during the survey week.

3 For 2000, data for Asians, Pacific Islanders, and persons of Two or more races were not reported separately. Asian and Pacific Islander data were collected in a combined "Asian/Pacific Islander" category. Data on persons of Two or more races are unavailable because each respondent could choose only one race category.

4 Householders are persons in whose name the housing unit is owned or rented. Never-married students living away from home in college dormitories are not considered householders.

5 Own children are never-married sons and daughters of the student, including stepchildren and adopted children.

6 Refers to all students who do not live with a spouse, including students who are single, divorced, separated, or widowed.

NOTE: Students were classified as full time if they were taking at least 12 hours of classes during an average school week and as part time if they were taking fewer hours. Race categories exclude persons of Hispanic ethnicity. Data are based on sample surveys of the civilian noninstitutionalized population, which excludes persons in the military and persons living in institutions (e.g., prisons or nursing facilities). Some data have been revised from previously published figures.

SOURCE: U.S. Department of Commerce, Census Bureau, Current Population Survey (CPS), October, 2000, 2010, and 2019. (This table was prepared August 2020.)

Table 504.10. Labor force status of recent high school completers, by college enrollment status, sex, and race/ethnicity: October 2016, 2017, and 2018

[Standard errors appear in parentheses]

College enrollment status, sex, and race/ethnicity	Total number of high school completers (in thousands)	Percent of high school completers: Separately for those enrolled in college vs. those not enrolled[3]	Percent of high school completers: For all high school completers	Percentage distribution of all high school completers: Employed	Percentage distribution of all high school completers: Unemployed (seeking employment)	Percentage distribution of all high school completers: Not in labor force	Labor force participation rate of all high school completers[1]	High school completers in civilian labor force[2], Number (in thousands): Total, all completers in labor force	High school completers in civilian labor force[2], Number (in thousands): Employed	High school completers in civilian labor force[2], Number (in thousands): Unemployed (seeking employment)	High school completers in civilian labor force[2]: Unemployment rate	High school completers not in labor force (in thousands)
1	2	3	4	5	6	7	8	9	10	11	12	13
2016 high school completers[4]												
Total	**3,137 (102.3)**	**† (†)**	**100.0 (†)**	**42.3 (1.64)**	**6.4 (0.85)**	**48.7 (1.75)**	**48.7 (1.75)**	**1,526 (72.2)**	**1,327 (66.1)**	**199 (27.1)**	**13.1 (1.63)**	**1,610 (77.4)**
Male	1,517 (70.6)	† (†)	48.3 (1.47)	45.2 (2.62)	8.3 (1.33)	53.4 (2.62)	53.4 (2.62)	811 (52.5)	685 (48.9)	126 (20.9)	15.5 (2.42)	706 (53.2)
Female	1,620 (66.7)	† (†)	51.7 (1.47)	39.6 (2.18)	4.6 (1.00)	44.2 (2.37)	44.2 (2.37)	716 (48.4)	642 (45.4)	‡ (†)	10.3 (2.12)	904 (53.2)
White	1,714 (66.9)	† (†)	54.6 (1.65)	47.6 (2.20)	4.6 (0.89)	52.2 (2.30)	52.2 (2.30)	895 (55.0)	816 (51.8)	79 (15.5)	8.8 (1.64)	819 (48.2)
Black	364 (35.6)	† (†)	11.6 (1.02)	41.7 (5.07)	20.4 (4.19)	62.1 (5.30)	62.1 (5.30)	226 (29.8)	152 (23.0)	‡ (†)	32.8 (6.10)	138 (23.0)
Hispanic	742 (50.8)	† (†)	23.7 (1.32)	35.5 (3.53)	4.2 (1.23)	39.7 (3.69)	39.7 (3.69)	295 (32.3)	264 (31.0)	‡ (†)	10.7 (2.95)	447 (42.8)
Enrolled in college, 2016	2,188 (93.4)	100.0 (†)	69.8 (1.64)	35.3 (1.94)	3.1 (0.63)	38.4 (2.03)	38.4 (2.03)	840 (57.2)	773 (54.3)	‡ (†)	8.0 (1.58)	1,348 (72.5)
Male	1,023 (57.8)	46.8 (1.86)	32.6 (1.36)	37.0 (3.07)	4.5 (1.06)	41.5 (3.21)	41.5 (3.21)	425 (38.0)	379 (35.8)	‡ (†)	10.8 (2.45)	599 (49.9)
Female	1,165 (66.2)	53.2 (1.86)	37.1 (1.72)	33.9 (2.56)	1.8! (0.67)	35.7 (2.64)	35.7 (2.64)	416 (40.0)	394 (38.9)	‡ (†)	5.2! (1.83)	749 (50.8)
2-year	744 (56.3)	34.0 (2.12)	23.7 (1.56)	47.0 (3.39)	4.9 (1.29)	51.8 (3.58)	51.8 (3.58)	386 (38.3)	349 (35.7)	‡ (†)	9.4 (2.38)	359 (39.1)
4-year	1,444 (76.1)	66.0 (2.12)	46.0 (1.85)	29.4 (2.20)	2.1! (0.66)	31.5 (2.27)	31.5 (2.27)	455 (40.6)	424 (39.4)	‡ (†)	6.8 (2.03)	989 (61.5)
Full-time students	1,992 (88.1)	91.0 (1.30)	63.5 (1.80)	31.7 (1.92)	2.9 (0.64)	34.6 (1.98)	34.6 (1.98)	689 (49.7)	632 (47.1)	‡ (†)	8.4 (1.79)	1,303 (70.2)
Part-time students	196 (30.1)	9.0 (1.30)	6.3 (0.91)	72.3 (7.83)	‡ (†)	77.1! (7.67)	77.1 (7.67)	151 (23.4)	142 (22.7)	‡ (†)	‡ (†)	‡ (†)
White	1,194 (59.5)	54.6 (1.93)	38.1 (1.56)	39.7 (2.63)	2.9 (0.83)	42.6 (2.72)	42.6 (2.72)	509 (41.7)	475 (40.7)	‡ (†)	6.8 (1.88)	685 (46.2)
Black	209 (31.9)	9.5 (1.36)	6.7 (0.97)	40.5 (7.07)	7.7! (2.90)	48.2 (6.96)	48.2 (6.96)	‡ (†)	‡ (†)	‡ (†)	‡ (†)	108 (21.1)
Hispanic	534 (44.6)	24.4 (1.60)	17.0 (1.22)	28.0 (3.98)	2.6! (1.09)	30.6 (4.11)	30.6 (4.11)	163 (25.3)	149 (24.2)	‡ (†)	8.5! (3.47)	371 (38.5)
Not enrolled in college, 2016	948 (56.3)	100.0 (†)	30.2 (1.64)	58.4 (2.69)	14.0 (2.17)	72.3 (2.65)	72.3 (2.65)	686 (46.2)	554 (38.6)	132 (22.5)	19.3 (2.81)	262 (30.4)
Male	493 (39.1)	52.0 (2.98)	15.7 (1.17)	62.0 (4.06)	16.2 (3.09)	78.3 (3.25)	78.3 (3.25)	386 (33.0)	306 (29.2)	80 (16.9)	20.7 (3.89)	107 (18.8)
Female	455 (40.5)	48.0 (2.98)	14.5 (1.26)	54.4 (4.02)	11.5 (3.07)	65.9 (4.23)	65.9 (4.23)	300 (33.3)	248 (28.8)	‡ (†)	17.5 (4.31)	155 (23.1)
White	520 (46.0)	54.8 (3.50)	16.6 (1.45)	65.6 (3.45)	8.5 (2.13)	74.2 (3.17)	74.2 (3.17)	386 (37.2)	341 (32.3)	‡ (†)	11.5 (2.81)	134 (20.6)
Black	156 (25.0)	16.4 (2.49)	5.0 (0.78)	43.3 (8.12)	37.4 (8.29)	80.7! (6.97)	80.7 (6.97)	126 (23.9)	‡ (†)	‡ (†)	46.4 (9.29)	‡ (†)
Hispanic	208 (27.2)	21.9 (2.60)	6.6 (0.85)	54.8 (6.14)	8.5! (3.34)	63.3 (6.30)	63.3 (6.30)	132 (21.5)	114 (20.2)	‡ (†)	13.4! (5.02)	‡ (†)
2017 high school completers[4]												
Total	**2,870 (95.9)**	**† (†)**	**100.0 (†)**	**42.5 (1.95)**	**6.5 (0.88)**	**49.0 (1.87)**	**49.0 (1.87)**	**1,407 (72.4)**	**1,221 (70.4)**	**186 (25.7)**	**13.2 (1.80)**	**1,463 (70.8)**
Male	1,345 (60.2)	† (†)	46.9 (1.58)	44.9 (2.48)	8.0 (1.40)	52.9 (2.41)	52.9 (2.41)	712 (44.4)	604 (41.8)	108 (19.4)	15.2 (2.57)	633 (43.8)
Female	1,525 (71.3)	† (†)	53.1 (1.58)	40.5 (2.71)	5.1 (1.14)	45.6 (2.73)	45.6 (2.73)	695 (51.5)	617 (49.2)	‡ (†)	11.2 (2.46)	830 (57.9)
White	1,601 (64.5)	† (†)	55.8 (1.57)	42.8 (2.41)	5.5 (1.10)	48.3 (2.37)	48.3 (2.37)	774 (49.1)	686 (47.2)	88 (18.0)	11.4 (2.24)	827 (50.3)
Black	402 (35.5)	† (†)	14.0 (1.19)	38.4 (5.44)	8.2! (2.53)	46.6 (5.14)	46.6 (5.14)	187 (25.2)	154 (24.7)	‡ (†)	17.6! (5.58)	214 (29.1)
Hispanic	597 (52.0)	† (†)	20.8 (1.62)	47.9 (4.36)	8.4 (2.34)	56.3 (4.19)	56.3 (4.19)	336 (38.4)	286 (35.9)	‡ (†)	15.0 (4.11)	261 (33.8)
Enrolled in college, 2017	1,915 (80.6)	100.0 (†)	66.7 (1.68)	35.8 (2.32)	4.1 (0.82)	39.8 (2.32)	39.8 (2.32)	763 (54.4)	685 (53.1)	‡ (†)	10.2 (2.06)	1,152 (65.9)
Male	822 (53.1)	42.9 (2.06)	28.7 (1.62)	36.8 (3.23)	4.4! (1.35)	41.2 (3.24)	41.2 (3.24)	339 (34.1)	303 (33.0)	‡ (†)	10.6! (3.20)	483 (41.3)
Female	1,093 (59.8)	57.1 (2.06)	38.1 (1.60)	35.0 (3.15)	3.8! (1.21)	38.8 (3.21)	38.8 (3.21)	424 (41.2)	382 (39.4)	‡ (†)	9.9! (3.07)	669 (51.5)
2-year	648 (45.9)	33.8 (2.11)	22.6 (1.50)	53.5 (3.75)	4.9! (1.68)	58.4 (3.66)	58.4 (3.66)	378 (33.9)	346 (33.6)	‡ (†)	8.4! (2.83)	269 (31.7)
4-year	1,267 (70.3)	66.2 (2.11)	44.2 (1.83)	26.7 (2.63)	3.6 (0.92)	30.3 (2.81)	30.3 (2.81)	384 (43.4)	338 (39.9)	‡ (†)	11.9 (2.87)	883 (57.3)
Full-time students	1,764 (80.2)	92.1 (1.23)	61.5 (1.74)	32.5 (2.37)	4.4 (0.89)	36.9 (2.39)	36.9 (2.39)	651 (51.4)	574 (49.5)	‡ (†)	11.9 (2.39)	1,113 (65.7)
Part-time students	150 (23.6)	7.9 (1.23)	5.2 (0.83)	74.0 (6.68)	‡ (†)	74.0 (6.68)	74.0 (6.68)	111 (20.8)	111 (20.8)	‡ (†)	‡ (†)	‡ (†)
White	1,106 (54.9)	57.8 (2.06)	38.5 (1.61)	35.7 (2.88)	3.2! (1.07)	38.9 (2.89)	38.9 (2.89)	431 (38.3)	395 (37.3)	‡ (†)	8.3! (2.69)	675 (46.2)
Black	239 (30.0)	12.5 (1.48)	8.3 (1.01)	28.4 (6.37)	‡ (†)	33.5 (6.66)	33.5 (6.66)	‡ (†)	‡ (†)	‡ (†)	‡ (†)	159 (25.7)
Hispanic	364 (42.4)	19.0 (1.98)	12.7 (1.40)	45.1 (5.78)	7.8! (2.69)	52.8 (5.62)	52.8 (5.62)	193 (29.5)	164 (28.4)	‡ (†)	14.7! (5.13)	172 (29.3)
Not enrolled in college, 2017	955 (57.1)	100.0 (†)	33.3 (1.68)	56.1 (3.07)	11.3 (1.94)	67.4 (2.80)	67.4 (2.80)	644 (47.4)	536 (44.4)	108 (19.2)	16.8 (2.83)	311 (32.1)
Male	523 (39.5)	54.8 (3.03)	18.2 (1.30)	57.6 (3.78)	13.8 (2.67)	71.3 (3.34)	71.3 (3.34)	373 (33.3)	301 (30.0)	‡ (†)	19.3 (3.66)	150 (20.5)
Female	432 (41.4)	45.2 (3.03)	15.1 (1.33)	54.3 (4.92)	8.4! (2.57)	62.7 (4.68)	62.7 (4.68)	271 (32.6)	235 (31.7)	‡ (†)	13.3! (4.08)	161 (25.8)
White	495 (39.4)	51.8 (2.86)	17.2 (1.26)	58.8 (4.10)	10.6 (2.51)	69.4 (3.79)	69.4 (3.79)	343 (33.2)	291 (30.4)	‡ (†)	15.3 (3.54)	151 (22.1)
Black	163 (22.6)	17.1 (2.18)	5.7 (0.80)	52.9 (7.65)	12.9! (5.02)	65.8 (7.14)	65.8 (7.14)	107 (19.2)	‡ (†)	‡ (†)	19.6! (7.46)	‡ (†)
Hispanic	233 (28.6)	24.4 (2.61)	8.1 (0.94)	52.3 (6.10)	9.4! (3.98)	61.7 (5.84)	61.7 (5.84)	144 (23.4)	122 (21.2)	‡ (†)	15.3! (6.28)	‡ (†)

See notes at end of table.

Table 504.10. Labor force status of recent high school completers, by college enrollment status, sex, and race/ethnicity: October 2016, 2017, and 2018—Continued

[Standard errors appear in parentheses]

College enrollment status, sex, and race/ethnicity	Total number of high school completers (in thousands)	Percent of high school completers: Separately for those enrolled in college vs. those not enrolled[3]	Percent of high school completers: For all high school completers	Percentage distribution of all high school completers: Employed	Percentage distribution of all high school completers: Unemployed (seeking employment)	Percentage distribution of all high school completers: Not in labor force	Labor force participation rate of all high school completers[1]	High school completers in civilian labor force[2]: Number (in thousands): Total, all completers in labor force	High school completers in civilian labor force[2]: Number (in thousands): Employed	High school completers in civilian labor force[2]: Number (in thousands): Unemployed (seeking employment)	High school completers in civilian labor force[2]: Unemployment rate	High school completers not in labor force (in thousands)
1	2	3	4	5	6	7	8	9	10	11	12	13
2018 high school completers[4]												
Total	**3,212 (94.6)**	**† (†)**	**100.0 (†)**	**41.2 (1.62)**	**6.8 (0.78)**	**52.0 (1.72)**	**48.0 (1.72)**	**1,541 (71.7)**	**1,324 (62.6)**	**218 (26.9)**	**14.1 (1.53)**	**1,670 (73.5)**
Male	1,614 (61.2)	† (†)	50.3 (1.42)	42.7 (2.18)	6.0 (1.12)	51.3 (2.33)	48.7 (2.33)	787 (44.4)	690 (39.1)	97 (18.8)	12.3 (2.16)	827 (52.1)
Female	1,598 (69.9)	† (†)	49.7 (1.42)	39.7 (2.49)	7.6 (1.16)	52.8 (2.65)	47.2 (2.65)	755 (52.8)	634 (45.4)	121 (20.2)	16.0 (2.30)	843 (57.0)
White	1,727 (71.2)	† (†)	53.8 (1.60)	42.1 (2.23)	5.1 (0.93)	52.8 (2.20)	47.2 (2.20)	815 (50.5)	727 (47.4)	88 (16.9)	10.8 (1.93)	913 (53.8)
Black	449 (37.6)	† (†)	14.0 (1.04)	36.4 (5.04)	10.8 (2.78)	52.8 (4.94)	47.2 (4.94)	212 (26.0)	163 (24.6)	‡ (†)	23.0 (5.79)	237 (31.9)
Hispanic	727 (50.4)	† (†)	22.6 (1.45)	49.6 (3.67)	7.3 (1.74)	43.1 (3.36)	56.9 (3.36)	414 (38.4)	361 (37.3)	‡ (†)	12.8 (3.10)	313 (31.6)
Enrolled in college, 2018	2,220 (86.7)	100.0 (†)	69.1 (1.62)	32.7 (1.96)	3.7 (0.75)	63.6 (2.03)	36.4 (2.03)	808 (54.9)	726 (50.8)	‡ (†)	10.1 (1.99)	1,412 (71.1)
Male	1,080 (55.7)	48.6 (1.84)	33.6 (1.49)	33.9 (2.89)	3.4! (1.16)	62.7 (2.97)	37.3 (2.97)	403 (35.5)	366 (33.6)	‡ (†)	9.0! (3.02)	677 (50.5)
Female	1,140 (63.7)	51.4 (1.84)	35.5 (1.52)	31.6 (2.50)	4.0 (1.11)	64.5 (2.60)	35.5 (2.60)	405 (35.6)	360 (32.4)	‡ (†)	11.2 (2.97)	735 (52.8)
2-year	819 (56.0)	36.9 (2.06)	25.5 (1.54)	41.6 (3.50)	3.3! (1.25)	55.1 (3.59)	44.9 (3.59)	368 (37.8)	341 (35.4)	‡ (†)	7.3! (2.71)	451 (43.4)
4-year	1,401 (70.9)	63.1 (2.06)	43.6 (1.76)	27.5 (2.10)	3.9 (1.03)	68.6 (2.19)	31.4 (2.19)	440 (37.3)	385 (34.8)	‡ (†)	12.4 (3.11)	961 (58.4)
Full-time students	2,015 (81.8)	90.8 (1.13)	62.7 (1.58)	28.9 (1.92)	3.6 (0.77)	67.5 (2.02)	32.5 (2.02)	656 (48.1)	583 (43.5)	‡ (†)	11.1 (2.26)	1,360 (69.2)
Part-time students	205 (26.5)	9.2 (1.13)	6.4 (0.81)	69.9 (6.54)	‡ (†)	25.7 (6.41)	74.3 (6.41)	152 (24.1)	143 (23.5)	‡ (†)	‡ (†)	‡ (†)
White	1,224 (62.8)	55.1 (1.98)	38.1 (1.62)	32.9 (2.40)	3.8 (0.99)	63.2 (2.43)	36.8 (2.43)	450 (38.4)	403 (35.8)	‡ (†)	10.4 (2.61)	774 (48.7)
Black	289 (31.9)	13.0 (1.31)	9.0 (0.93)	27.3 (5.21)	‡ (†)	69.8 (5.54)	30.2 (5.54)	‡ (†)	‡ (†)	‡ (†)	‡ (†)	202 (29.6)
Hispanic	476 (42.6)	21.4 (1.73)	14.8 (1.24)	44.0 (4.72)	‡ (†)	53.2 (4.70)	46.8 (4.70)	223 (31.0)	209 (30.4)	‡ (†)	‡ (†)	253 (29.9)
Not enrolled in college, 2018	992 (57.4)	100.0 (†)	30.9 (1.62)	60.2 (2.69)	13.7 (1.82)	26.0 (2.49)	74.0 (2.49)	733 (49.0)	597 (43.4)	136 (19.7)	18.6 (2.38)	258 (28.8)
Male	534 (40.3)	53.8 (2.94)	16.6 (1.19)	60.6 (3.21)	11.3 (2.20)	28.1 (3.19)	71.9 (3.19)	384 (32.8)	324 (28.0)	‡ (†)	15.7 (2.90)	150 (20.7)
Female	458 (41.2)	46.2 (2.94)	14.2 (1.23)	59.8 (4.58)	16.6 (2.85)	23.7 (3.99)	76.3 (3.99)	349 (35.9)	273 (31.1)	76 (15.2)	21.7 (3.75)	108 (21.0)
White	503 (37.8)	50.8 (2.71)	15.7 (1.10)	64.4 (3.96)	8.1 (2.04)	27.5 (3.51)	72.5 (3.51)	365 (31.5)	324 (30.8)	‡ (†)	11.2 (2.84)	138 (21.0)
Black	159 (22.9)	16.1 (2.09)	5.0 (0.69)	52.9 (8.88)	25.2 (6.46)	21.9! (6.72)	78.1 (6.72)	124 (19.9)	‡ (†)	‡ (†)	32.2 (8.48)	‡ (†)
Hispanic	251 (30.5)	25.3 (2.60)	7.8 (0.95)	60.3 (5.67)	15.8 (4.36)	23.9 (4.71)	76.1 (4.71)	191 (26.9)	152 (25.0)	‡ (†)	20.8 (5.59)	‡ (†)

†Not applicable.
!Interpret data with caution. The coefficient of variation (CV) for this estimate is between 30 and 50 percent.
‡Reporting standards not met (too few cases for a reliable estimate).
[1]The labor force participation rate is the percentage of persons who are either employed or seeking employment.
[2]The labor force includes all employed persons plus those seeking employment. The unemployment rate is the percentage of persons in the labor force who are not working and who made specific efforts to find employment sometime during the prior 4 weeks.
[3]Column 3 does not present any percentages that apply to all high school completers. Instead, it presents one set of percentages for only those completers who were enrolled in college and a second set of percentages for only those completers who were not enrolled in college.
[4]Includes 16- to 24-year-olds who completed high school between January and October of the given year. Includes recipients of equivalency credentials as well as diploma recipients.
NOTE: Data are based on sample surveys of the civilian noninstitutionalized population, which excludes persons in the military and persons living in institutions (e.g., prisons or nursing facilities). Data are for October of a given year. Standard errors were computed using replicate weights. Totals include race categories not separately shown. Race categories exclude persons of Hispanic ethnicity. Detail may not sum to totals because of rounding.
SOURCE: U.S. Department of Commerce, Census Bureau, Current Population Survey (CPS), October 2016, 2017, and 2018. (This table was prepared February 2020.)

Table 504.20. Labor force status of recent high school dropouts, by sex and race/ethnicity: Selected years, October 1980 through 2018

[Standard errors appear in parentheses]

Year, sex, and race/ethnicity	Number of dropouts (in thousands)	Percent of all dropouts	Percentage distribution of dropouts: Employed	Percentage distribution of dropouts: Unemployed (seeking employment)	Percentage distribution of dropouts: Not in labor force	Labor force participation rate of dropouts[1]	Dropouts in civilian labor force[2]: Number (in thousands): Total	Dropouts in civilian labor force[2]: Number (in thousands): Unemployed (seeking employment)	Dropouts in civilian labor force[2]: Unemployment rate	Dropouts not in labor force (in thousands)
1	2	3	4	5	6	7	8	9	10	11
					Estimates for individual years					
All dropouts										
1980	738 (44.0)	100.0 (†)	43.8 (2.97)	20.0 (2.37)	36.2 (2.87)	63.8 (2.87)	471 (35.2)	148 (19.5)	31.4 (3.44)	267 (26.5)
1990	412 (36.0)	100.0 (†)	46.3 (4.37)	21.6 (3.57)	32.2 (4.09)	67.8 (4.09)	279 (29.7)	89 (16.6)	31.8 (4.90)	132 (20.4)
2000	515 (28.5)	100.0 (†)	48.7 (2.77)	19.2 (3.01)	32.0 (2.59)	68.0 (2.59)	350 (23.5)	99 (17.2)	28.1 (4.16)	165 (16.2)
2005	407 (35.3)	100.0 (†)	38.3 (4.22)	18.9 (3.42)	42.8 (3.32)	57.2 (4.30)	233 (26.7)	77 (15.4)	32.9 (5.42)	174 (17.9)
2010[3]	340 (29.0)	100.0 (†)	30.9 (4.24)	23.0 (4.29)	46.1 (4.78)	53.9 (4.78)	183 (21.5)	78 (16.0)	42.7 (6.67)	157 (21.9)
2017[3]	530 (42.6)	100.0 (†)	33.9 (3.53)	7.9 (2.06)	58.2 (3.66)	41.8 (3.66)	222 (23.4)	‡ (†)	18.9 (4.59)	308 (34.2)
2018[3]	527 (46.5)	100.0 (†)	40.7 (4.07)	6.5! (2.06)	52.8 (4.47)	47.2 (4.47)	249 (32.5)	‡ (†)	13.7 (4.04)	278 (33.4)
					3-year moving averages[4]					
All dropouts										
1980	748 (44.3)	100.0 (†)	44.4 (1.70)	19.9 (1.38)	35.7 (1.27)	64.3 (1.64)	481 (35.6)	149 (19.9)	30.9 (1.99)	267 (20.5)
1990	413 (36.1)	100.0 (†)	43.5 (2.50)	21.5 (2.08)	35.0 (1.86)	65.0 (2.41)	268 (29.1)	89 (16.8)	33.1 (2.96)	144 (16.5)
2000	515 (41.8)	100.0 (†)	44.1 (2.33)	19.0 (1.85)	36.9 (1.75)	63.1 (2.27)	325 (33.2)	98 (18.3)	30.1 (2.72)	190 (19.7)
2005	449 (37.1)	100.0 (†)	36.8 (2.30)	17.7 (1.83)	45.5 (1.84)	54.5 (2.38)	245 (27.4)	79 (15.7)	32.5 (3.04)	205 (19.4)
2010	365 (33.4)	100.0 (†)	28.7 (2.39)	23.7 (2.26)	47.6 (2.04)	52.4 (2.64)	191 (24.2)	87 (16.4)	45.2 (3.65)	174 (17.8)
2017	523 (26.6)	100.0 (†)	36.5 (2.32)	10.1 (1.33)	53.4 (2.43)	46.6 (2.43)	244 (17.9)	53 (7.6)	21.8 (2.67)	279 (18.8)
2018	528 (33.6)	100.0 (†)	37.3 (2.85)	7.2 (1.38)	55.5 (3.02)	44.5 (3.02)	235 (19.7)	38 (7.3)	16.2 (2.92)	293 (26.5)
Sex										
Male										
1980	393 (31.6)	52.6 (1.69)	55.5 (2.31)	19.5 (1.84)	25.0 (2.01)	75.0 (2.01)	295 (27.4)	77 (14.0)	25.9 (2.35)	98 (15.8)
1990	216 (25.7)	52.3 (2.48)	50.9 (3.44)	25.2 (2.98)	23.9 (2.93)	76.1 (2.93)	164 (22.4)	55 (12.9)	33.1 (3.71)	52 (12.6)
2000	279 (30.3)	54.1 (2.30)	49.8 (3.14)	19.6 (2.49)	30.7 (2.90)	69.3 (2.90)	193 (25.2)	55 (13.4)	28.2 (3.39)	85 (16.8)
2005	254 (27.4)	56.5 (2.33)	40.0 (3.06)	19.0 (2.45)	41.0 (3.07)	59.0 (3.07)	150 (21.1)	48 (12.0)	32.2 (3.80)	104 (17.6)
2010	196 (24.1)	53.6 (2.60)	32.1 (3.32)	22.4 (2.97)	45.5 (3.54)	54.5 (3.54)	107 (17.8)	44 (11.4)	41.2 (4.74)	89 (16.3)
2017	287 (18.0)	54.9 (2.37)	41.0 (3.23)	11.2 (2.00)	47.8 (3.14)	52.2 (3.14)	150 (13.0)	32 (6.1)	21.5 (3.66)	137 (12.4)
2018	281 (20.5)	53.2 (2.96)	40.7 (3.90)	7.1 (1.88)	52.2 (3.95)	47.8 (3.95)	135 (13.4)	‡ (†)	14.9 (3.80)	147 (16.5)
Female										
1980	354 (29.1)	47.4 (1.63)	32.1 (2.21)	20.4 (1.91)	47.5 (2.37)	52.5 (2.37)	186 (21.1)	72 (13.1)	38.9 (3.19)	168 (20.0)
1990	197 (23.7)	47.7 (2.40)	35.4 (3.33)	17.4 (2.64)	47.2 (3.48)	52.8 (3.48)	104 (17.2)	34 (9.9)	33.0 (4.51)	93 (16.3)
2000	236 (27.0)	45.9 (2.23)	37.4 (3.19)	18.3 (2.55)	44.3 (3.28)	55.7 (3.28)	132 (20.1)	43 (11.6)	32.9 (4.15)	105 (18.0)
2005	196 (23.3)	43.5 (2.25)	32.6 (3.23)	16.0 (2.52)	51.4 (3.44)	48.6 (3.44)	95 (16.2)	31 (9.3)	32.9 (4.64)	101 (16.7)
2010	169 (21.7)	46.4 (2.51)	24.9 (3.20)	25.1 (3.21)	50.0 (3.70)	50.0 (3.70)	85 (15.3)	43 (10.9)	50.2 (5.23)	85 (15.3)
2017	236 (18.2)	45.1 (2.37)	30.9 (3.49)	8.8 (1.90)	60.2 (3.93)	39.8 (3.93)	94 (11.7)	‡ (†)	22.2 (4.27)	142 (14.2)
2018	247 (24.7)	46.8 (2.96)	33.5 (4.22)	7.2! (2.27)	59.3 (4.73)	40.7 (4.73)	101 (14.8)	‡ (†)	17.8 (5.04)	147 (19.2)
Race/ethnicity										
White										
1980	494 (36.0)	66.0 (1.62)	50.9 (2.11)	17.6 (1.61)	31.5 (1.52)	68.5 (1.96)	338 (29.8)	87 (15.2)	25.7 (2.24)	156 (15.7)
1990	240 (27.5)	58.0 (2.49)	51.4 (3.31)	19.3 (2.63)	29.3 (2.33)	70.7 (3.02)	170 (23.1)	46 (12.1)	27.3 (3.53)	70 (11.5)
2000	279 (30.8)	54.1 (2.34)	48.3 (3.19)	18.7 (2.50)	33.0 (2.32)	67.0 (3.00)	187 (25.2)	52 (13.4)	27.8 (3.51)	92 (13.7)
2005	215 (25.7)	48.0 (2.38)	41.6 (3.40)	14.2 (2.42)	44.2 (2.64)	55.8 (3.42)	120 (19.2)	31! (9.7)	25.5 (4.04)	95 (13.2)
2010	164 (22.4)	45.0 (2.63)	32.7 (3.70)	20.8 (3.22)	46.4 (3.04)	53.6 (3.93)	88 (16.4)	34! (10.3)	38.9 (5.28)	76 (11.8)
2017	244 (16.6)	46.6 (2.50)	46.4 (3.28)	8.6 (1.63)	45.0 (3.19)	55.0 (3.19)	134 (12.9)	‡ (†)	15.7 (2.94)	110 (9.9)
2018	231 (21.6)	43.7 (3.20)	52.9 (4.23)	5.3! (1.67)	41.7 (4.09)	58.3 (4.09)	134 (15.7)	‡ (†)	9.2! (2.84)	96 (13.1)
Black										
1980	154 (21.3)	20.6 (1.47)	21.0 (3.27)	28.3 (3.62)	50.6 (4.01)	49.4 (4.01)	76 (15.0)	44 (11.4)	57.4 (5.65)	78 (15.2)
1990	96 (18.5)	23.3 (2.27)	27.1 (4.93)	29.0 (5.04)	43.9 (5.51)	56.1 (5.51)	54 (13.8)	28! (10.0)	51.7 (7.41)	42 (12.3)
2000	102 (19.7)	19.8 (1.98)	28.0 (5.03)	22.2 (4.65)	49.8 (5.60)	50.2 (5.60)	51 (14.0)	‡ (†)	44.2 (7.85)	51 (13.9)
2005	88 (17.4)	19.5 (2.01)	21.5 (4.71)	27.7 (5.13)	50.9 (5.73)	49.1 (5.73)	43 (12.2)	‡ (†)	56.3 (8.11)	45 (12.4)
2010	70 (15.6)	19.3 (2.22)	22.4 (5.33)	30.4 (5.88)	47.2 (6.38)	52.8 (6.38)	37! (11.3)	‡ (†)	57.5 (8.69)	33! (10.7)
2017	84 (10.7)	16.1 (1.89)	24.9 (4.95)	18.2 (4.66)	56.9 (6.42)	43.1 (6.42)	36 (6.8)	‡ (†)	42.2 (8.49)	48 (8.3)
2018	85 (13.4)	16.1 (2.43)	16.6! (5.16)	16.5! (5.41)	66.9 (7.57)	33.1 (7.57)	‡ (†)	‡ (†)	‡ (†)	57 (11.6)
Hispanic										
1980	84 (18.7)	11.3 (1.36)	48.2 (6.40)	19.5 (5.07)	32.3 (5.99)	67.7 (5.99)	57 (15.4)	‡ (†)	28.8 (7.05)	27! (10.6)
1990	66 (15.3)	15.9 (1.96)	39.3 (6.56)	19.9 (5.36)	40.8 (6.60)	59.2 (6.60)	39! (11.8)	‡ (†)	33.5 (8.24)	27! (9.8)
2000	113 (20.8)	21.9 (2.06)	50.4 (5.32)	17.7 (4.06)	31.9 (4.96)	68.1 (4.96)	77 (17.1)	‡ (†)	26.0 (5.66)	36! (11.7)
2005	125 (20.8)	27.9 (2.27)	39.2 (4.68)	16.1 (3.52)	44.7 (4.77)	55.3 (4.77)	69 (15.4)	‡ (†)	29.1 (5.86)	56 (13.9)
2010	102 (18.8)	28.0 (2.52)	25.8 (4.64)	24.3 (4.55)	49.9 (5.30)	50.1 (5.30)	51 (13.3)	25! (9.3)	48.4 (7.49)	51 (13.3)
2017	149 (15.0)	28.5 (2.37)	29.1 (3.86)	8.4 (2.17)	62.5 (3.90)	37.5 (3.90)	56 (7.6)	‡ (†)	22.4 (5.53)	93 (11.5)
2018	167 (21.5)	31.7 (3.28)	29.4 (4.46)	4.9! (2.10)	65.7 (4.66)	34.3 (4.66)	57 (9.7)	‡ (†)	14.2! (5.80)	110 (17.3)

†Not applicable.
!Interpret data with caution. The coefficient of variation (CV) for this estimate is between 30 and 50 percent.
‡Reporting standards not met. Either there are too few cases for a reliable estimate or the coefficient of variation (CV) is 50 percent or greater.
[1]The labor force participation rate is the percentage of persons who are either employed or seeking employment.
[2]The labor force includes all employed persons plus those seeking employment. The unemployment rate is the percentage of persons in the labor force who are not working and who made specific efforts to find employment sometime during the prior 4 weeks.
[3]Beginning in 2010, standard errors for the individual year estimates were computed using replicate weights in order to produce more precise values. This methodology can only be used for these estimates. For all other estimates in the table, standard errors were computed using generalized variance function methodology.
[4]A 3-year moving average is the arithmetic average of the year indicated, the year immediately preceding, and the year immediately following. For example, the estimates shown for 2000 reflect an average of 1999, 2000, and 2001. Use of a moving average increases the sample size, thereby reducing the size of sampling errors and producing more stable estimates. For the final year of available data, a 2-year moving average is used; thus, the estimates for 2018 reflect the average of 2017 and 2018.
NOTE: Data are based on sample surveys of the civilian noninstitutionalized population, which excludes persons in the military and persons living in institutions (e.g., prisons or nursing facilities). Data are for October of a given year. Dropouts are considered persons 16 to 24 years old who dropped out of school in the 12-month period ending in October of years shown. Includes dropouts from any grade, including a small number from elementary and middle schools. Totals include race categories not separately shown. Race categories exclude persons of Hispanic ethnicity. Detail may not sum to totals because of rounding.
SOURCE: U.S. Department of Commerce, Census Bureau, Current Population Survey (CPS), selected years, October 1979 through 2018. (This table was prepared February 2020.)

Table 505.10. Number, percentage distribution, unemployment rates, and median earnings of 25- to 29-year-old bachelor's degree holders and percentage of degree holders among all 25- to 29-year-olds, by field of study and science, technology, engineering, or mathematics (STEM) status of field: 2010 and 2018

[Standard errors appear in parentheses]

Field of study and STEM status of field	2010: 25- to 29-year-old bachelor's degree holders: Number, in thousands	Percentage distribution	Unemployment rate for the civilian labor force	Median annual earnings of full-time year-round workers: Current dollars	Median annual earnings: Constant 2018 dollars[1]	2010: Percent of all 25- to 29-year-olds with degree in specific field	2018: 25- to 29-year-old bachelor's degree holders: Number, in thousands	Percentage distribution	Unemployment rate for the civilian labor force	Median annual earnings of full-time year-round workers	2018: Percent of all 25- to 29-year-olds with degree in specific field
1	2	3	4	5	6	7	8	9	10	11	12
Total, all bachelor's degrees	**6,366 (30.5)**	**100.0 (†)**	**5.6 (0.13)**	**$43,730 (684)**	**$50,360 (788)**	**30.5 (0.14)**	**8,103 (40.2)**	**100.0 (†)**	**2.9 (0.08)**	**$50,600 (4)**	**34.8 (0.16)**
Agriculture	59 (2.8)	0.9 (0.04)	3.8 (0.99)	40,150 (424)	46,240 (488)	0.3 (0.01)	78 (3.9)	1.0 (0.05)	1.8! (0.72)	45,380 (1,856)	0.3 (0.02)
Architecture	47 (2.5)	0.7 (0.04)	13.8 (2.49)	44,300 (2,686)	51,020 (3,094)	0.2 (0.01)	60 (3.6)	0.7 (0.04)	1.8! (0.70)	52,170 (1,239)	0.3 (0.02)
Area, ethnic, and civilization studies	28 (1.9)	0.4 (0.03)	5.2! (1.61)	41,250 (3,100)	47,510 (3,570)	0.1 (0.01)	31 (2.2)	0.4 (0.03)	1.7! (0.77)	50,140 (1,018)	0.1 (0.01)
Arts, fine and commercial	334 (7.0)	5.3 (0.11)	6.8 (0.55)	37,140 (803)	42,770 (884)	1.6 (0.03)	440 (8.5)	5.4 (0.10)	3.7 (0.41)	42,520 (1,152)	1.9 (0.04)
Fine arts	245 (5.4)	3.8 (0.08)	6.1 (0.69)	36,170 (888)	41,650 (1,022)	1.2 (0.03)	314 (6.6)	3.9 (0.08)	3.7 (0.40)	40,500 (23)	1.4 (0.03)
Commercial art and graphic design	89 (3.9)	1.4 (0.06)	8.6 (1.09)	38,860 (1,799)	44,750 (2,071)	0.4 (0.02)	125 (5.2)	1.5 (0.06)	3.5 (0.86)	48,140 (1,389)	0.5 (0.02)
Business	1,252 (13.9)	19.7 (0.19)	5.5 (0.24)	47,160 (1,004)	54,310 (1,105)	6.0 (0.07)	1,432 (16.1)	17.7 (0.18)	2.8 (0.22)	54,660 (776)	6.2 (0.07)
Business, general	222 (5.5)	3.5 (0.09)	5.7 (0.66)	45,960 (1,425)	52,930 (1,642)	1.1 (0.03)	266 (5.6)	3.3 (0.07)	3.7 (0.60)	50,260 (255)	1.1 (0.02)
Accounting	194 (5.7)	3.0 (0.09)	5.8 (0.68)	50,100 (141)	57,690 (162)	0.9 (0.03)	226 (6.2)	2.8 (0.08)	2.3 (0.47)	60,000 (265)	1.0 (0.03)
Business management and administration	339 (7.2)	5.3 (0.11)	6.5 (0.57)	43,200 (1,200)	49,750 (1,382)	1.6 (0.03)	343 (8.5)	4.2 (0.10)	2.4 (0.34)	50,600 (25)	1.5 (0.04)
Marketing and marketing research	187 (5.5)	2.9 (0.08)	4.6 (0.57)	44,250 (765)	50,960 (881)	0.9 (0.03)	200 (6.1)	2.5 (0.07)	2.9 (0.57)	52,160 (1,050)	0.9 (0.03)
Finance	170 (5.5)	2.7 (0.09)	4.9 (0.61)	52,620 (1,865)	60,590 (2,148)	0.8 (0.03)	187 (6.1)	2.3 (0.07)	2.1 (0.47)	65,270 (709)	0.8 (0.03)
Management information systems and statistics	23 (1.6)	0.4 (0.03)	3.4! (1.12)	55,020 (1,939)	63,360 (2,233)	0.1 (0.01)	26 (2.0)	0.3 (0.02)	2.2! (1.00)	64,390 (3,029)	0.1 (0.01)
Business, other and medical administration	118 (3.7)	1.9 (0.06)	4.5 (0.57)	44,400 (720)	51,130 (829)	0.6 (0.02)	184 (6.1)	2.3 (0.07)	3.7 (0.74)	50,520 (73)	0.8 (0.03)
Communications and communications technologies	373 (8.2)	5.9 (0.12)	6.4 (0.45)	40,260 (18)	46,360 (20)	1.8 (0.04)	446 (8.4)	5.5 (0.11)	3.3 (0.37)	45,570 (511)	1.9 (0.04)
Computer and information science	249 (6.2)	3.9 (0.10)	5.6 (0.55)	56,320 (1,809)	64,860 (2,083)	1.2 (0.03)	310 (7.1)	3.8 (0.08)	5.6 (0.65)	70,140 (423)	1.3 (0.03)
Construction/electrical/transportation technologies	35 (2.6)	0.5 (0.04)	4.8! (1.64)	49,720 (1,595)	57,260 (1,837)	0.2 (0.01)	36 (2.4)	0.4 (0.03)	‡ (†)	59,920 (1,015)	0.2 (0.01)
Criminal justice and fire protection	140 (4.7)	2.2 (0.07)	6.2 (0.74)	39,300 (1,458)	45,250 (1,679)	0.7 (0.02)	212 (5.9)	2.6 (0.07)	3.8 (0.60)	41,810 (1,237)	0.9 (0.03)
Education	573 (8.0)	9.0 (0.12)	3.4 (0.31)	38,260 (80)	44,060 (88)	2.7 (0.04)	537 (8.4)	6.6 (0.10)	1.2 (0.19)	41,510 (506)	2.3 (0.04)
General education	151 (5.3)	2.4 (0.09)	4.7 (0.80)	39,350 (1,076)	45,310 (1,239)	0.7 (0.03)	160 (5.9)	2.0 (0.07)	1.4 (0.35)	41,260 (1,264)	0.7 (0.03)
Early childhood education	32 (2.0)	0.5 (0.03)	1.2! (0.58)	36,820 (1,808)	42,400 (2,082)	0.2 (0.01)	42 (2.6)	0.5 (0.03)	1.8! (0.80)	38,130 (736)	0.2 (0.01)
Elementary education	181 (5.0)	2.8 (0.08)	3.2 (0.53)	38,150 (938)	43,940 (1,081)	0.9 (0.02)	134 (4.2)	1.7 (0.05)	1.3 (0.36)	40,490 (72)	0.6 (0.02)
Secondary teacher education	19 (1.4)	0.3 (0.02)	2.5! (1.08)	36,140 (976)	41,620 (1,124)	0.1 (0.01)	17 (1.9)	0.2 (0.02)	‡ (†)	43,500 (1,297)	0.1 (0.01)
Education, other	190 (4.8)	3.0 (0.07)	2.9 (0.45)	38,480 (940)	44,320 (1,082)	0.9 (0.02)	184 (4.8)	2.3 (0.06)	0.9 (0.27)	43,000 (636)	0.8 (0.02)
Engineering and engineering-related fields	474 (8.8)	7.4 (0.13)	5.0 (0.41)	60,580 (748)	69,760 (823)	2.3 (0.04)	716 (12.0)	8.8 (0.14)	2.7 (0.22)	70,890 (1,237)	3.1 (0.05)
General engineering	63 (3.0)	1.0 (0.05)	4.3! (1.44)	60,100 (324)	69,210 (373)	0.3 (0.01)	91 (5.1)	1.1 (0.06)	2.4! (0.94)	68,860 (2,539)	0.4 (0.02)
Chemical engineering	28 (2.2)	0.4 (0.03)	4.4! (1.42)	65,580 (3,098)	75,520 (3,568)	0.1 (0.01)	49 (2.5)	0.6 (0.03)	3.4! (1.08)	77,750 (2,728)	0.2 (0.01)
Civil engineering	46 (2.9)	0.7 (0.05)	6.6 (1.69)	58,910 (1,276)	67,840 (1,469)	0.2 (0.01)	67 (3.4)	0.8 (0.04)	1.0! (0.47)	65,420 (647)	0.3 (0.01)
Computer engineering	45 (2.8)	0.7 (0.04)	7.1 (1.50)	65,320 (842)	75,220 (970)	0.2 (0.01)	63 (2.8)	0.8 (0.03)	1.5! (0.56)	75,730 (2,641)	0.3 (0.01)
Electrical engineering	86 (4.3)	1.3 (0.07)	5.1 (1.13)	65,060 (685)	74,920 (788)	0.4 (0.02)	118 (4.3)	1.5 (0.05)	1.9 (0.44)	78,740 (1,175)	0.5 (0.02)
Mechanical engineering	86 (3.9)	1.3 (0.06)	3.7 (0.77)	61,620 (1,428)	70,960 (1,644)	0.4 (0.02)	148 (4.7)	1.8 (0.06)	3.3 (0.64)	73,960 (1,556)	0.6 (0.02)
Engineering, other	78 (3.6)	1.2 (0.06)	4.9 (1.01)	59,850 (600)	68,930 (690)	0.4 (0.02)	129 (4.5)	1.6 (0.05)	3.0 (0.71)	70,480 (477)	0.6 (0.02)
Engineering technologies	42 (2.5)	0.7 (0.04)	4.7 (1.17)	55,890 (2,180)	64,360 (2,511)	0.2 (0.01)	51 (3.5)	0.6 (0.04)	5.2 (1.20)	60,570 (3,451)	0.2 (0.01)
English language and literature	194 (5.2)	3.0 (0.08)	7.6 (0.73)	38,100 (1,100)	43,870 (1,266)	0.9 (0.02)	208 (6.1)	2.6 (0.07)	4.4 (0.54)	44,640 (1,284)	0.9 (0.03)
Family and consumer sciences	55 (3.1)	0.9 (0.05)	3.9 (0.97)	36,060 (1,375)	41,520 (1,583)	0.3 (0.01)	76 (3.4)	0.9 (0.04)	2.7! (0.87)	40,300 (733)	0.3 (0.01)
Health professions	378 (8.2)	5.9 (0.12)	3.3 (0.39)	50,330 (20)	57,960 (22)	1.8 (0.04)	680 (10.1)	8.4 (0.13)	2.0 (0.25)	54,840 (293)	2.9 (0.04)
General medical and health services	200 (6.5)	3.1 (0.10)	3.6 (0.54)	46,290 (1,500)	53,310 (1,727)	1.0 (0.03)	342 (7.6)	4.2 (0.09)	2.3 (0.39)	50,270 (261)	1.5 (0.03)
Nursing	179 (5.5)	2.8 (0.08)	3.0 (0.57)	53,350 (1,366)	61,430 (1,573)	0.9 (0.03)	338 (6.7)	4.2 (0.09)	1.7 (0.36)	58,690 (1,423)	1.5 (0.03)
History	138 (4.5)	2.2 (0.07)	8.4 (0.77)	41,060 (1,385)	47,280 (1,595)	0.7 (0.02)	136 (4.4)	1.7 (0.05)	3.6 (0.71)	45,090 (816)	0.6 (0.02)
Liberal arts and humanities	76 (3.4)	1.2 (0.05)	7.2 (1.19)	40,130 (1,161)	46,210 (1,337)	0.4 (0.02)	89 (4.1)	1.1 (0.05)	4.6 (1.09)	40,270 (482)	0.4 (0.02)
Linguistics and comparative language and literature	68 (3.5)	1.1 (0.05)	8.6 (1.73)	38,130 (1,373)	43,910 (1,582)	0.3 (0.02)	82 (3.3)	1.0 (0.04)	3.7 (0.96)	45,370 (690)	0.4 (0.01)

See notes at end of table.

Table 505.10. Number, percentage distribution, unemployment rates, and median earnings of 25- to 29-year-old bachelor's degree holders and percentage of degree holders among all 25- to 29-year-olds, by field of study and science, technology, engineering, or mathematics (STEM) status of field: 2010 and 2018—Continued

[Standard errors appear in parentheses]

Field of study and STEM status of field	2010						2018				
	25- to 29-year-old bachelor's degree holders					Percent of all 25- to 29-year-olds with degree in specific field	25- to 29-year-old bachelor's degree holders				Percent of all 25- to 29-year-olds with degree in specific field
	Number, in thousands	Percentage distribution	Unemployment rate for the civilian labor force	Median annual earnings of full-time year-round workers			Number, in thousands	Percentage distribution	Unemployment rate for the civilian labor force	Median annual earnings of full-time year-round workers	
				Current dollars	Constant 2018 dollars[1]						
1	2	3	4	5	6	7	8	9	10	11	12
Mathematics	78 (3.8)	1.2 (0.06)	4.6 (1.04)	50,120 (781)	57,720 (899)	0.4 (0.02)	116 (4.8)	1.4 (0.06)	2.5 (0.56)	54,560 (1,483)	0.5 (0.02)
Multi/interdisciplinary studies	55 (2.6)	0.9 (0.04)	5.4 (0.96)	39,770 (922)	45,790 (1,062)	0.3 (0.01)	100 (4.3)	1.2 (0.05)	4.8 (1.11)	47,760 (1,743)	0.4 (0.02)
Natural sciences	586 (9.2)	9.2 (0.14)	5.2 (0.38)	42,300 (787)	48,720 (867)	2.8 (0.04)	833 (12.3)	10.3 (0.14)	2.7 (0.25)	48,480 (799)	3.6 (0.05)
Biology	364 (8.1)	5.7 (0.13)	4.9 (0.50)	43,300 (927)	49,870 (1,067)	1.7 (0.04)	533 (9.5)	6.6 (0.11)	2.4 (0.28)	50,450 (1,288)	2.3 (0.04)
Environmental science	42 (2.8)	0.7 (0.04)	9.7 (1.98)	39,960 (1,549)	46,020 (1,784)	0.2 (0.01)	74 (3.2)	0.9 (0.04)	2.6 (0.75)	40,570 (2,153)	0.3 (0.01)
Physical sciences	180 (4.8)	2.8 (0.08)	4.7 (0.76)	42,210 (1,545)	48,610 (1,779)	0.9 (0.02)	226 (6.4)	2.8 (0.08)	3.4 (0.54)	47,570 (1,292)	1.0 (0.03)
Physical fitness, parks, recreation and leisure	101 (3.6)	1.6 (0.06)	3.5 (0.68)	40,250 (27)	46,350 (31)	0.5 (0.02)	193 (5.3)	2.4 (0.06)	2.1 (0.42)	45,500 (1,309)	0.8 (0.02)
Philosophy and religious studies	53 (2.3)	0.8 (0.04)	7.8 (1.56)	40,280 (1,419)	46,390 (1,634)	0.3 (0.01)	44 (2.6)	0.5 (0.03)	3.1! (1.10)	48,840 (2,467)	0.2 (0.01)
Psychology	378 (7.9)	5.9 (0.12)	5.9 (0.48)	37,240 (532)	42,880 (612)	1.8 (0.04)	498 (9.3)	6.1 (0.11)	3.2 (0.33)	41,420 (972)	2.1 (0.04)
Public administration and public policy	12 (1.6)	0.2 (0.02)	‡ (†)	50,090 (6,667)	57,680 (7,677)	0.1 (0.01)	17 (1.5)	0.2 (0.02)	‡ (†)	49,850 (1,681)	0.1 (0.01)
Social sciences	519 (8.6)	8.2 (0.13)	6.9 (0.43)	45,160 (528)	52,010 (581)	2.5 (0.04)	574 (10.2)	7.1 (0.12)	3.1 (0.34)	50,620 (19)	2.5 (0.04)
Anthropology and archeology	33 (2.0)	0.5 (0.03)	4.5 (1.14)	37,950 (2,738)	43,700 (3,153)	0.2 (0.01)	41 (2.5)	0.5 (0.03)	1.8! (0.82)	45,230 (1,757)	0.2 (0.01)
Economics	126 (4.4)	2.0 (0.07)	8.2 (1.00)	52,380 (2,049)	60,320 (2,360)	0.6 (0.02)	152 (5.4)	1.9 (0.07)	2.3 (0.53)	64,860 (3,204)	0.7 (0.02)
Geography	15 (1.7)	0.2 (0.03)	9.2! (3.53)	43,580 (2,973)	50,190 (3,424)	0.1 (0.01)	20 (1.7)	0.2 (0.02)	‡ (†)	45,920 (5,315)	0.1 (0.01)
International relations	23 (2.0)	0.4 (0.03)	7.1! (2.75)	49,080 (1,756)	56,520 (2,023)	0.1 (0.01)	32 (2.5)	0.4 (0.03)	5.2 (1.46)	53,730 (3,863)	0.1 (0.01)
Political science and government	173 (4.8)	2.7 (0.08)	5.9 (0.70)	45,220 (108)	52,070 (124)	0.8 (0.02)	167 (5.2)	2.1 (0.07)	4.2 (0.89)	50,640 (1,299)	0.7 (0.02)
Sociology	116 (4.3)	1.8 (0.07)	7.6 (1.15)	38,200 (1,253)	43,990 (1,443)	0.6 (0.02)	119 (5.3)	1.5 (0.06)	2.7 (0.68)	43,140 (1,418)	0.5 (0.02)
Miscellaneous social sciences	32 (2.0)	0.5 (0.03)	5.3 (1.38)	40,250 (798)	46,350 (919)	0.2 (0.01)	42 (2.8)	0.5 (0.03)	3.1! (1.01)	40,080 (961)	0.2 (0.01)
Social work and human services	59 (2.8)	0.9 (0.04)	5.6 (1.38)	35,020 (138)	40,330 (159)	0.3 (0.01)	99 (4.8)	1.2 (0.06)	3.0 (0.71)	40,480 (431)	0.4 (0.02)
Theology and religious vocations	28 (2.0)	0.4 (0.03)	3.9! (1.88)	32,790 (1,349)	37,770 (1,553)	0.1 (0.01)	35 (2.2)	0.4 (0.03)	2.0! (0.95)	35,230 (919)	0.1 (0.01)
Other fields	26 (2.0)	0.4 (0.03)	9.0 (2.31)	36,660 (2,542)	42,220 (2,928)	0.1 (0.01)	26 (2.1)	0.3 (0.03)	5.3! (2.44)	40,250 (5,725)	0.1 (0.01)
STEM status of field[2]											
STEM field	1,345 (13.7)	21.1 (0.21)	5.0 (0.26)	53,150 (967)	61,210 (1,113)	6.4 (0.07)	1,901 (21.0)	23.5 (0.22)	3.2 (0.15)	60,760 (216)	8.2 (0.09)
Non-STEM field	5,021 (29.4)	78.9 (0.21)	5.7 (0.14)	41,660 (692)	47,970 (797)	24.0 (0.14)	6,202 (33.8)	76.5 (0.22)	2.9 (0.09)	48,560 (20)	26.7 (0.14)

†Not applicable

!Interpret data with caution. The coefficient of variation (CV) for this estimate is between 30 and 50 percent.

‡Reporting standards not met. Either there are too few cases for a reliable estimate or the coefficient of variation (CV) is 50 percent or greater.

[1]Constant dollars based on the Consumer Price Index, prepared by the Bureau of Labor Statistics, U.S. Department of Labor.

[2]STEM fields include biological and biomedical sciences, computer and information sciences, engineering and engineering technologies, mathematics and statistics, and physical sciences and science technologies.

NOTE: The first bachelor's degree major reported by respondents was used to classify their field of study, even though they were able to report a second bachelor's degree major and may possess advanced degrees in other fields. Median earnings are for full-time employees working 35 or more hours per week. Data are based on sample surveys of the entire population residing within the United States, including both noninstitutionalized persons (e.g., those living in households, college housing, or military housing located within the United States) and institutionalized persons (e.g., those living in prisons, nursing facilities, or other healthcare facilities). Detail may not sum to totals because of rounding. Some data have been revised from previously published figures.

SOURCE: U.S. Department of Commerce, Census Bureau, 2010 and 2018 American Community Survey (ACS) Public Use Microdata Sample (PUMS) data. (This table was prepared November 2019.)

Table 505.15. Number, percentage distribution, and median annual earnings of 25- to 34-year-olds with a bachelor's or higher degree, by sex, race/ethnicity, and selected employment and occupational characteristics: 2017

[Standard errors appear in parentheses]

Selected employment or occupational characteristic	Total	Sex: Male	Sex: Female	Race/ethnicity: White	Black	Hispanic	Asian	Pacific Islander	American Indian/Alaska Native
1	2	3	4	5	6	7	8	9	10
	Number (in thousands)								
All 25- to 34-year-olds with a bachelor's or higher degree	**15,884 (68.9)**	**7,075 (35.7)**	**8,809 (41.4)**	**10,335 (44.7)**	**1,337 (19.3)**	**1,638 (18.6)**	**2,055 (16.0)**	**17 (1.5)**	**39 (2.6)**
	Percentage distribution								
All 25- to 34-year-olds with a bachelor's or higher degree	**100.0 (†)**	**100.0 (†)**	**100.0 (†)**	**100.0 (†)**	**100.0 (†)**	**100.0 (†)**	**100.0 (†)**	**100.0 (†)**	**100.0 (†)**
Employment status									
Employed	87.4 (0.11)	90.9 (0.16)	84.6 (0.15)	89.6 (0.13)	87.7 (0.41)	86.3 (0.37)	77.7 (0.41)	86.8 (4.33)	82.4 (2.17)
Full-time	77.5 (0.15)	83.8 (0.19)	72.5 (0.20)	79.7 (0.17)	78.3 (0.55)	75.5 (0.46)	68.9 (0.45)	77.6 (4.88)	69.3 (2.91)
Part-time	9.9 (0.10)	7.1 (0.13)	12.2 (0.14)	10.0 (0.12)	9.5 (0.37)	10.7 (0.31)	8.8 (0.22)	9.2 ! (3.05)	13.1 (2.28)
Less than 20 hours per week	2.4 (0.05)	1.4 (0.06)	3.1 (0.07)	2.4 (0.05)	2.0 (0.18)	2.4 (0.16)	2.1 (0.13)	‡ (†)	1.9 ! (0.97)
20 to 29 hours per week	4.2 (0.06)	3.1 (0.08)	5.1 (0.09)	4.0 (0.07)	4.1 (0.25)	4.5 (0.21)	4.3 (0.19)	7.0 ! (2.93)	7.8 (1.81)
30 to 34 hours per week	3.4 (0.06)	2.6 (0.08)	4.0 (0.09)	3.5 (0.07)	3.3 (0.22)	3.8 (0.20)	2.3 (0.12)	‡ (†)	3.3 (0.97)
Unemployed	2.6 (0.05)	2.9 (0.09)	2.3 (0.05)	2.1 (0.05)	4.3 (0.30)	3.1 (0.20)	3.1 (0.15)	‡ (†)	6.3 (1.51)
Not in labor force	10.0 (0.11)	6.2 (0.13)	13.1 (0.15)	8.3 (0.12)	8.0 (0.35)	10.6 (0.31)	19.2 (0.38)	11.9 ! (4.16)	11.3 (1.80)
Enrolled in graduate school	2.7 (0.06)	2.8 (0.10)	2.6 (0.08)	2.1 (0.06)	2.5 (0.20)	2.5 (0.19)	5.5 (0.25)	‡ (†)	2.9 ! (1.03)
Not enrolled in graduate school	7.4 (0.09)	3.4 (0.08)	10.5 (0.14)	6.2 (0.10)	5.5 (0.26)	8.1 (0.26)	13.8 (0.36)	10.5 ! (3.39)	8.4 (1.50)
Major occupation group[1]	100.0 (†)	100.0 (†)	100.0 (†)	100.0 (†)	100.0 (†)	100.0 (†)	100.0 (†)	100.0 (†)	100.0 (†)
Management	12.7 (0.12)	14.4 (0.19)	11.3 (0.15)	13.5 (0.16)	10.5 (0.33)	12.0 (0.43)	10.5 (0.30)	9.0 ! (3.42)	13.2 (2.15)
Business and financial operations	10.7 (0.09)	10.7 (0.15)	10.6 (0.14)	10.7 (0.11)	10.7 (0.39)	9.5 (0.31)	11.9 (0.34)	15.9 (3.85)	6.7 (1.57)
Computer and mathematical	7.4 (0.09)	12.1 (0.15)	3.4 (0.09)	5.8 (0.09)	5.5 (0.36)	4.6 (0.24)	20.9 (0.40)	6.5 ! (2.44)	3.9 ! (1.31)
Architecture and engineering	4.1 (0.07)	7.1 (0.12)	1.6 (0.06)	4.1 (0.07)	2.3 (0.22)	3.5 (0.20)	6.1 (0.24)	8.2 ! (2.93)	‡ (†)
Life, physical, and social sciences	2.5 (0.05)	2.6 (0.09)	2.5 (0.06)	2.5 (0.06)	1.7 (0.18)	2.1 (0.14)	3.8 (0.18)	‡ (†)	2.3 ! (0.94)
Community and social services	3.8 (0.07)	2.1 (0.07)	5.2 (0.11)	3.5 (0.08)	7.0 (0.40)	5.4 (0.27)	1.3 (0.12)	9.5 ! (3.90)	7.5 (1.91)
Legal	2.2 (0.04)	2.1 (0.06)	2.2 (0.07)	2.4 (0.05)	1.5 (0.18)	2.1 (0.15)	1.5 (0.14)	‡ (†)	1.7 ! (0.83)
Education, training, and library	12.9 (0.13)	8.2 (0.14)	16.9 (0.20)	13.8 (0.15)	11.7 (0.43)	13.6 (0.38)	8.5 (0.27)	9.8 ! (3.33)	11.8 (1.76)
Arts, design, entertainment, sports, and media	4.3 (0.07)	4.3 (0.10)	4.2 (0.10)	4.7 (0.09)	3.3 (0.26)	3.6 (0.22)	3.0 (0.19)	‡ (†)	2.7 ! (0.94)
Healthcare practitioners and technicians	11.0 (0.10)	5.6 (0.12)	15.6 (0.16)	11.3 (0.14)	9.2 (0.40)	8.2 (0.26)	13.2 (0.34)	‡ (†)	8.9 (2.22)
Healthcare support	0.9 (0.03)	0.5 (0.04)	1.3 (0.06)	0.8 (0.04)	1.4 (0.13)	1.4 (0.16)	0.9 (0.10)	‡ (†)	3.7 ! (1.48)
Protective service	1.8 (0.04)	2.9 (0.08)	0.8 (0.04)	1.8 (0.05)	2.8 (0.22)	2.3 (0.17)	0.6 (0.07)	‡ (†)	2.1 ! (0.79)
Food preparation and serving	2.2 (0.05)	2.1 (0.07)	2.2 (0.07)	2.2 (0.06)	2.1 (0.19)	3.1 (0.21)	1.5 (0.13)	‡ (†)	2.9 ! (1.08)
Building and grounds cleaning and maintenance	0.5 (0.03)	0.8 (0.05)	0.4 (0.03)	0.5 (0.03)	0.7 (0.12)	1.2 (0.12)	0.2 (0.04)	‡ (†)	‡ (†)
Personal care and service	1.9 (0.04)	1.2 (0.06)	2.5 (0.06)	1.8 (0.05)	2.6 (0.26)	2.0 (0.17)	1.4 (0.12)	‡ (†)	1.8 ! (0.77)
Sales and related	7.9 (0.09)	9.3 (0.15)	6.7 (0.11)	8.4 (0.11)	8.1 (0.44)	7.6 (0.29)	5.0 (0.26)	6.8 ! (2.44)	12.2 (2.31)
Office and administrative support	9.0 (0.10)	6.9 (0.13)	10.8 (0.16)	8.3 (0.11)	13.8 (0.45)	11.5 (0.35)	7.1 (0.24)	13.1 (3.87)	11.3 (2.97)
Farming, fishing, and forestry	0.2 (0.01)	0.2 (0.02)	0.1 (0.01)	0.2 (0.02)	‡ (†)	0.3 (0.06)	0.1 ! (0.02)	‡ (†)	‡ (†)
Construction and extraction	0.8 (0.03)	1.6 (0.07)	0.1 (0.01)	0.8 (0.04)	0.5 (0.10)	1.6 (0.15)	0.2 (0.06)	‡ (†)	‡ (†)
Installation, maintenance, and repair	0.7 (0.03)	1.3 (0.06)	0.1 (0.02)	0.7 (0.03)	0.6 (0.11)	1.0 (0.14)	0.4 (0.08)	‡ (†)	‡ (†)
Production	1.4 (0.04)	2.0 (0.08)	0.9 (0.05)	1.3 (0.05)	1.5 (0.17)	1.8 (0.15)	1.3 (0.11)	‡ (†)	2.6 ! (1.00)
Transportation and material moving	1.3 (0.04)	2.2 (0.07)	0.5 (0.03)	1.1 (0.04)	2.4 (0.21)	1.7 (0.16)	0.8 (0.08)	‡ (†)	‡ (†)
Military-specific	‡ (†)	‡ (†)	‡ (†)	‡ (†)	‡ (†)	‡ (†)	‡ (†)	‡ (†)	‡ (†)
Class of worker[1]	100.0 (†)	100.0 (†)	100.0 (†)	100.0 (†)	100.0 (†)	100.0 (†)	100.0 (†)	100.0 (†)	100.0 (†)
Private for-profit wage and salary	66.1 (0.16)	73.0 (0.23)	60.1 (0.23)	65.1 (0.18)	61.8 (0.71)	65.1 (0.59)	75.9 (0.39)	59.7 (6.30)	58.8 (3.82)
Employee of private company	64.4 (0.17)	70.7 (0.24)	58.9 (0.24)	63.2 (0.20)	60.5 (0.73)	63.7 (0.61)	74.5 (0.40)	57.5 (6.50)	55.2 (3.94)
Self-employed in own incorporated business	1.7 (0.04)	2.3 (0.08)	1.2 (0.05)	1.9 (0.06)	1.3 (0.16)	1.3 (0.13)	1.4 (0.13)	‡ (†)	3.6 ! (1.76)
Private nonprofit wage and salary	13.1 (0.12)	9.0 (0.15)	16.7 (0.17)	13.8 (0.15)	13.0 (0.47)	11.7 (0.34)	10.7 (0.26)	‡ (†)	9.3 (1.99)
Government	17.9 (0.14)	15.0 (0.21)	20.4 (0.19)	18.0 (0.15)	23.3 (0.62)	20.4 (0.50)	11.4 (0.30)	34.6 (6.05)	26.0 (2.91)
Local	8.6 (0.10)	6.4 (0.14)	10.5 (0.15)	8.8 (0.11)	10.6 (0.39)	11.3 (0.37)	4.4 (0.24)	13.1 (3.92)	9.7 (1.69)
State	6.7 (0.08)	5.6 (0.13)	7.6 (0.12)	6.8 (0.09)	8.4 (0.38)	6.1 (0.26)	5.1 (0.22)	15.1 (3.79)	10.2 (1.99)
Federal	2.6 (0.06)	3.0 (0.08)	2.3 (0.07)	2.4 (0.06)	4.3 (0.26)	3.0 (0.18)	1.9 (0.13)	6.4 ! (2.49)	6.1 (1.41)
Self-employed in own nonincorporated business	2.8 (0.05)	2.9 (0.08)	2.7 (0.08)	3.1 (0.07)	1.9 (0.20)	2.7 (0.20)	1.9 (0.13)	‡ (†)	5.9 (1.41)
Unpaid family	0.1 (0.01)	# (†)	0.1 (0.01)	0.1 (0.01)	‡ (†)	0.1 ! (0.02)	0.1 (0.03)	‡ (†)	‡ (†)
	Median annual earnings (in current dollars)								
All 25- to 34-year-old bachelor's degree holders who were full-time year-round workers[2]	**$54,560 (26)**	**$60,620 (6)**	**$50,490 (5)**	**$55,530 (8)**	**$45,410 (39)**	**$48,520 (458)**	**$69,960 (219)**	**$52,600 (6,478)**	**$44,430 (4,586) $**
Major occupation group[1]									
Management	65,570 (204)	70,740 (16)	59,370 (999)	65,660 (37)	52,710 (1,927)	55,860 (1,949)	79,920 (2,678)	‡ (†)	49,990 (6,047)
Business and financial operations	60,610 (32)	65,700 (397)	57,600 (1,077)	60,660 (1,160)	52,770 (1,783)	56,170 (1,393)	70,020 (721)	‡ (†)	‡ (†)
Computer and mathematical	75,630 (90)	76,790 (993)	70,350 (525)	70,770 (1,318)	63,570 (2,832)	61,850 (3,459)	85,310 (556)	‡ (†)	‡ (†)
Architecture and engineering	74,670 (921)	75,500 (117)	70,470 (473)	74,420 (1,146)	68,480 (2,415)	70,570 (2,377)	80,700 (802)	‡ (†)	‡ (†)
Life, physical, and social sciences	50,540 (131)	50,480 (49)	50,900 (884)	50,540 (175)	49,200 (1,943)	48,850 (1,157)	53,530 (2,585)	‡ (†)	‡ (†)
Community and social services	40,450 (991)	40,350 (56)	41,370 (723)	41,710 (802)	40,280 (1,225)	40,290 (109)	45,450 (2,507)	‡ (†)	‡ (†)
Legal	72,050 (2,247)	82,340 (2,334)	65,050 (762)	74,840 (1,655)	54,640 (8,568)	57,820 (3,466)	86,080 (3,738)	‡ (†)	‡ (†)
Education, training, and library	43,730 (826)	45,420 (31)	43,390 (772)	44,250 (894)	42,470 (1,362)	44,860 (690)	42,470 (1,348)	‡ (†)	‡ (†)
Arts, design, entertainment, sports, and media	50,160 (75)	50,400 (103)	48,420 (749)	50,080 (847)	43,290 (2,100)	50,040 (344)	57,070 (2,391)	‡ (†)	‡ (†)
Healthcare practitioners and technicians	60,640 (188)	64,930 (726)	60,570 (37)	60,620 (40)	60,340 (429)	55,810 (2,524)	67,930 (1,771)	‡ (†)	‡ (†)
Healthcare support	31,340 (1,116)	32,260 (2,145)	30,310 (1,412)	32,030 (936)	30,220 (928)	30,270 (2,159)	33,540 (6,026)	‡ (†)	‡ (†)
Protective service	50,960 (1,151)	53,740 (1,737)	48,290 (2,138)	54,980 (1,002)	40,250 (1,013)	53,950 (3,248)	54,050 (6,858)	‡ (†)	‡ (†)
Food preparation and serving	29,250 (1,284)	28,920 (1,566)	29,940 (1,889)	29,400 (1,616)	25,110 (1,891)	28,930 (1,709)	30,750 (3,262)	‡ (†)	‡ (†)
Building and grounds cleaning and maintenance	32,230 (1,605)	34,300 (1,715)	27,590 (3,184)	38,520 (3,498)	26,580 (4,509)	22,250 (1,774)	‡ (†)	‡ (†)	‡ (†)
Personal care and service	30,320 (84)	33,170 (2,533)	30,280 (22)	31,570 (1,155)	29,340 (989)	30,280 (648)	30,140 (1,499)	‡ (†)	‡ (†)
Sales and related	51,440 (1,096)	58,640 (1,837)	46,030 (1,526)	56,600 (1,492)	40,320 (655)	42,200 (2,875)	49,860 (1,931)	‡ (†)	‡ (†)
Office and administrative support	40,400 (12)	44,130 (1,699)	39,050 (774)	40,430 (48)	35,240 (258)	39,740 (1,364)	45,320 (1,489)	‡ (†)	‡ (†)
Farming, fishing, and forestry	38,120 (2,132)	38,540 (2,956)	37,460 (3,345)	35,270 (1,634)	‡ (†)	‡ (†)	‡ (†)	‡ (†)	‡ (†)

[Standard errors appear in parentheses]

Selected employment or occupational characteristic	Total	Sex: Male	Sex: Female	Race/ethnicity: White	Race/ethnicity: Black	Race/ethnicity: Hispanic	Race/ethnicity: Asian	Race/ethnicity: Pacific Islander	Race/ethnicity: American Indian/Alaska Native
1	2	3	4	5	6	7	8	9	10
Construction and extraction	44,790 (1,366)	44,950 (1,181)	38,060 (4,486)	47,210 (3,681)	‡ (†)	38,010 (1,962)	‡ (†)	‡ (†)	‡ (†)
Installation, maintenance, and repair	47,220 (1,585)	48,230 (1,632)	39,720 (6,012)	49,850 (842)	38,800 (4,476)	40,080 (2,211)	‡ (†)	‡ (†)	‡ (†)
Production	44,420 (1,756)	48,440 (1,928)	36,780 (2,166)	45,570 (2,203)	40,200 (3,263)	35,170 (3,163)	45,670 (4,150)	‡ (†)	‡ (†)
Transportation and material moving	39,410 (1,924)	40,170 (150)	27,850 (2,817)	40,190 (855)	34,570 (4,289)	32,530 (2,615)	39,900 (4,118)	‡ (†)	‡ (†)
Military-specific	‡ (†)	‡ (†)	‡ (†)	‡ (†)	‡ (†)	‡ (†)	‡ (†)	‡ (†)	‡ (†)
Class of worker[1]									
Private for-profit wage and salary	60,570 (706)	65,630 (13)	51,560 (1,140)	60,430 (19)	45,340 (201)	50,470 (236)	73,610 (1,148)	53,000 (4,483)	49,620 (4,600)
Employee of private company	60,570 (685)	65,630 (13)	52,490 (1,187)	60,430 (20)	45,360 (265)	50,470 (424)	74,220 (1,128)	52,950 (4,828)	49,540 (4,720)
Self-employed in own incorporated business	59,680 (2,857)	60,660 (3,022)	47,990 (3,047)	60,210 (320)	42,110 (3,209)	52,610 (5,757)	49,790 (5,882)	‡ (†)	‡ (†)
Private nonprofit wage and salary	50,480 (9)	50,470 (50)	49,500 (718)	50,490 (12)	45,200 (761)	45,500 (1,204)	55,120 (727)	‡ (†)	‡ (†)
Government	49,470 (495)	51,540 (1,165)	46,510 (627)	49,480 (359)	45,380 (323)	48,510 (856)	54,900 (737)	48,100 (4,878)	40,910 (5,108)
Local	48,470 (90)	50,480 (40)	46,490 (688)	48,470 (31)	43,470 (1,998)	48,500 (1,097)	54,700 (2,147)	‡ (†)	41,120 (6,191)
State	45,480 (16)	48,720 (1,118)	44,420 (985)	45,470 (19)	43,460 (1,124)	45,040 (543)	50,500 (34)	‡ (†)	‡ (†)
Federal	65,370 (477)	69,840 (2,639)	64,400 (1,315)	69,860 (1,147)	55,340 (1,572)	59,980 (725)	71,280 (5,029)	‡ (†)	‡ (†)
Self-employed in own nonincorporated business	40,140 (158)	41,530 (3,804)	35,280 (1,628)	40,210 (263)	40,100 (2,268)	35,660 (2,337)	46,530 (2,655)	‡ (†)	‡ (†)
Unpaid family	20,470 (1,768)	‡ (†)	‡ (†)	19,980 (3,769)	‡ (†)	‡ (†)	‡ (†)	‡ (†)	‡ (†)

†Not applicable.

#Rounds to zero.

!Interpret data with caution. The coefficient of variation (CV) for this estimate is between 30 and 50 percent.

‡Reporting standards not met. Either there are too few cases for a reliable estimate or the coefficient of variation (CV) is 50 percent or greater.

[1] Estimates by major occupation group and class of worker are restricted to individuals currently employed.

[2] Estimates of median annual earnings are restricted to individuals working full time and year round.

NOTE: Estimates are for the entire population of civilian 25- to 34-year-old bachelor's degree holders, including persons living in households and persons living in group quarters (such as college residence halls, residential treatment centers, and correctional facilities). Detail may not sum to totals because of rounding. Totals include other racial/ethnic groups not separately shown. Race categories exclude persons of Hispanic ethnicity.

SOURCE: U.S. Department of Commerce, Census Bureau, American Community Survey (ACS), 2017. (This table was prepared May 2019.)

Table 505.40. Percentage distribution of recipients of bachelor's degrees in various fields of study 1 year after graduation, by time to completion, enrollment and employment status, and occupation: 2001 and 2009

[Standard errors appear in parentheses]

Time to completion, enrollment and employment status, and occupation	1999-2000 graduates in 2001, total	2007-08 graduates in 2009											
		Total[1]	Engineering	Biological and physical sciences	Mathematics and computer science	Social sciences	History	Humanities	Health professions	Business and management	Education[2]	Psychology	Public a and s ser
1	2	3	4	5	6	7	8	9	10	11	12	13	
Total graduates	**100.0** (†)	**100.0** (†)	**100.0** (†)	**100.0** (†)	**100.0** (†)	**100.0** (†)	**100.0** (†)	**100.0** (†)	**100.0** (†)	**100.0** (†)	**100.0** (†)	**100.0** (†)	**100.0**
Time between high school graduation and degree completion													
4 years or less	32.7 (0.83)	40.3 (0.64)	35.5 (2.68)	56.2 (2.24)	36.3 (3.27)	53.4 (2.08)	44.1 (3.78)	50.4 (2.02)	28.9 (2.01)	37.5 (1.53)	32.5 (1.65)	48.9 (2.17)	29.1 (
More than 4, up to 5 years	22.9 (0.58)	20.7 (0.51)	31.0 (2.58)	17.8 (1.74)	16.9 (2.62)	19.2 (1.62)	20.4 (2.81)	20.7 (1.57)	18.1 (1.41)	17.4 (1.09)	25.5 (1.59)	19.5 (1.73)	16.0 (
More than 5, up to 6 years	10.8 (0.48)	9.5 (0.35)	11.2 (1.69)	9.8 (1.59)	8.4 (1.79)	7.6 (1.09)	12.2 (2.87)	7.9 (1.01)	8.9 (1.14)	8.0 (0.79)	13.2 (1.34)	7.7 (1.10)	10.4 (
More than 6, up to 10 years	14.8 (0.59)	13.4 (0.42)	11.1 (1.64)	8.9 (1.21)	13.8 (2.25)	11.9 (1.21)	12.4 (2.87)	12.6 (1.40)	16.3 (1.64)	14.1 (1.01)	13.8 (1.32)	11.8 (1.54)	19.0 (
More than 10 years	18.8 (0.59)	16.0 (0.52)	11.2 (1.89)	7.3 (1.24)	24.6 (2.58)	7.8 (1.05)	10.9 (2.55)	8.3 (1.02)	27.8 (2.13)	23.1 (1.25)	15.0 (1.41)	12.1 (1.61)	25.5 (
Enrollment status													
Enrolled	20.8 (0.51)	21.7 (0.47)	22.8 (1.98)	40.9 (2.33)	19.9 (2.58)	23.5 (1.65)	38.1 (3.99)	23.6 (1.48)	23.5 (1.93)	13.9 (1.01)	19.9 (1.36)	36.6 (2.15)	24.3 (
Not enrolled	79.2 (0.51)	78.3 (0.47)	77.2 (1.98)	59.1 (2.33)	80.1 (2.58)	76.5 (1.65)	61.9 (3.99)	76.4 (1.48)	76.5 (1.93)	86.1 (1.01)	80.1 (1.36)	63.4 (2.15)	75.7 (
Employment status													
Employed	87.4 (0.46)	83.8 (0.49)	88.4 (1.54)	69.6 (1.92)	88.9 (1.88)	78.9 (1.72)	74.9 (3.93)	79.4 (1.58)	86.6 (1.64)	88.1 (0.95)	90.2 (1.12)	79.7 (1.91)	81.2 (
Full time	76.5 (0.52)	65.0 (0.62)	76.1 (2.12)	49.0 (2.38)	75.1 (2.67)	61.2 (1.94)	46.1 (4.35)	47.6 (2.12)	68.5 (1.86)	76.7 (1.18)	70.7 (1.74)	46.6 (2.40)	69.8 (
Part time	10.9 (0.40)	18.8 (0.48)	12.3 (1.88)	20.7 (1.84)	13.8 (2.11)	17.6 (1.72)	28.8 (3.66)	31.9 (1.72)	18.0 (1.59)	11.4 (0.92)	19.4 (1.54)	33.1 (2.33)	11.4 (
Unemployed[3]	6.1 (0.33)	9.2 (0.38)	6.7 (1.15)	7.2 (1.06)	5.8 (1.28)	11.3 (1.32)	14.5 (3.24)	11.8 (1.32)	6.4 (1.07)	8.5 (0.83)	5.1 (0.76)	10.2 (1.42)	13.5 (
Not in labor force[4]	6.4 (0.35)	7.0 (0.31)	4.9 (1.08)	23.1 (1.99)	5.3 (1.51)	9.9 (1.32)	10.6 (2.39)	8.8 (1.03)	7.0 (1.27)	3.4 (0.51)	4.7 (0.91)	10.0 (1.44)	5.2 (
Unemployment rate (labor force participants only)[5]	6.5 (—)	9.9 (—)	7.0 (—)	9.4 (—)	6.1 (—)	12.5 (—)	16.2 (—)	12.9 (—)	6.9 (—)	8.8 (—)	5.4 (—)	11.3 (—)	14.3
Total employed	**100.0** (†)	**100.0** (†)	**100.0** (†)	**100.0** (†)	**100.0** (†)	**100.0** (†)	**100.0** (†)	**100.0** (†)	**100.0** (†)	**100.0** (†)	**100.0** (†)	**100.0** (†)	**100.0**
Occupation													
Administrative/clerical	4.5 (0.28)	2.6 (0.21)	‡ (†)	1.9 ! (0.61)	‡ (†)	4.1 (0.88)	4.6 ! (2.17)	4.9 (1.01)	‡ (†)	2.6 (0.51)	‡ (†)	2.9 (0.65)	5.8 ! (
Arts/communications	4.2 (0.30)	4.5 (0.32)	2.3 ! (1.09)	‡ (†)	1.6 ! (0.65)	3.0 ! (0.92)	‡ (†)	14.4 (1.54)	‡ (†)	1.3 (0.37)	1.0 ! (0.35)	‡ (†)	#
Business													
Management	12.5 (0.47)	8.4 (0.41)	10.8 (2.08)	3.2 ! (0.96)	3.4 ! (1.24)	9.5 (1.45)	5.0 ! (1.83)	4.8 (0.99)	5.1 (1.10)	14.5 (1.08)	1.6 (0.45)	6.9 (1.43)	11.1 (
Nonmanagement	15.1 (0.58)	21.1 (0.61)	7.0 (1.54)	10.5 (1.63)	17.0 (2.82)	26.3 (2.05)	19.5 (3.67)	15.8 (1.93)	6.4 (1.14)	43.5 (1.76)	4.0 (0.76)	16.8 (1.98)	11.6 (
Computer information systems/mathematics[6]	6.8 (0.34)	4.6 (0.27)	7.0 (1.19)	‡ (†)	50.6 (3.28)	3.0 (0.89)	‡ (†)	1.0 ! (0.39)	‡ (†)	4.6 (0.69)	0.6 ! (0.27)	1.8 ! (0.77)	#
Construction/trade/transportation	3.1 (0.26)	3.3 (0.23)	5.0 (1.22)	2.5 (0.72)	2.0 ! (0.70)	2.2 (0.61)	5.1 ! (2.51)	4.2 (1.01)	‡ (†)	4.2 (0.59)	0.9 ! (0.31)	1.7 (0.50)	‡
Education	18.1 (0.52)	15.6 (0.43)	5.2 (1.26)	16.3 (2.12)	12.5 (2.01)	11.4 (1.45)	27.9 (3.49)	19.1 (1.74)	3.5 (0.72)	3.1 (0.55)	78.7 (1.61)	12.7 (1.41)	13.1 (
Engineering/engineering technician/science professions	8.4 (0.33)	6.2 (0.30)	55.6 (3.02)	28.8 (2.39)	2.2 ! (0.93)	1.0 ! (0.38)	‡ (†)	0.8 ! (0.32)	‡ (†)	1.3 (0.35)	0.2 ! (0.09)	1.7 ! (0.74)	#
Health professions	7.8 (0.26)	8.6 (0.30)	1.1 ! (0.53)	13.5 (1.62)	‡ (†)	3.3 (0.84)	3.7 ! (1.68)	2.4 ! (0.78)	74.4 (2.00)	1.2 (0.32)	1.2 ! (0.48)	7.0 (1.38)	2.3 ! (
Military/protective service	2.4 (0.20)	2.9 (0.24)	1.6 ! (0.72)	2.9 ! (0.89)	2.3 ! (1.12)	6.3 (1.08)	6.5 ! (2.23)	0.9 ! (0.39)	‡ (†)	1.9 (0.45)	0.8 ! (0.35)	1.8 ! (0.69)	7.0 ! (
Sales	6.8 (0.31)	7.9 (0.40)	2.1 (0.61)	7.4 (1.78)	1.6 ! (0.70)	7.4 (1.29)	8.9 ! (3.28)	9.8 (1.34)	1.9 ! (0.68)	12.9 (1.12)	1.7 (0.44)	7.4 (1.37)	5.5 ! (
Other occupations	10.2 (0.42)	14.3 (0.43)	2.0 ! (0.65)	10.9 (1.65)	4.3 ! (1.40)	22.4 (2.16)	13.0 (2.53)	21.8 (1.77)	4.6 (0.87)	8.8 (1.08)	9.2 (1.22)	38.5 (2.19)	42.4 (

—Not available.

†Not applicable.

#Rounds to zero.

!Interpret data with caution. The coefficient of variation (CV) for this estimate is between 30 and 50 percent.

‡Reporting standards not met. The coefficient of variation (CV) for this estimate is 50 percent or greater.

[1] Includes graduates in other fields not separately shown.

[2] Includes graduates who have not finished all requirements for teaching certification or were previously qualified to teach.

[3] Percentage of all graduates who are not employed, but are looking for work.

[4] Percentage of all graduates who are neither employed nor looking for work.

[5] The labor force is made up of persons who are employed and persons who are not employed but are looking for work. (It does not include those who are neither employed nor looking for work.) The unemployment rate is the percentage of labor force participants who are not employed but are actively seeking work.

[6] For 2001, does not include mathematics professions.

NOTE: Data exclude bachelor's degree recipients from U.S. Service Academies, deceased graduates, and graduates living at foreign addresses at the time of the survey. Detail may not sum to totals because of rounding.

SOURCE: U.S. Department of Education, National Center for Education Statistics, 2000/01 and 2008/09 Baccalaureate and Beyond Longitudinal Study (B&B:2000/01 and B&B:08/09). (This table was prepared August 2011.)

Table 505.50. Percentage, selected employment characteristics, and annual salaries of bachelor's degree recipients employed full time 1 year after graduation, by field of study: 1991, 2001, and 2009

[Standard errors appear in parentheses]

Selected employment characteristic and annual salary	All fields of study[1]	Engineering	Biological and physical sciences[2]	Mathematics and computer science[2]	Social sciences and history	Humanities	Health professions	Business and management	Education[3]	Psychology	Pul
1	2	3	4	5	6	7	8	9	10	11	
Employment characteristics											
Percent of recipients employed full time											
1989-90 recipients in June 1991	73.8 (0.36)	85.2 (0.95)	50.6 (1.72)	71.2 (1.30)	66.2 (0.94)	59.2 (1.32)	80.9 (1.35)	83.2 (0.57)	77.0 (0.74)	59.8 (1.64)	77.
1999-2000 recipients in July 2001	76.5 (0.52)	86.0 (1.77)	58.6 (2.04)	83.7 (2.06)	68.3 (1.88)	67.5 (1.65)	74.8 (1.50)	85.5 (1.27)	84.0 (1.29)	64.0 (2.64)	85.
2007-08 recipients in June 2009	65.0 (0.62)	76.1 (2.12)	49.0 (2.38)	75.1 (2.67)	58.0 (1.81)	50.4 (1.82)	68.5 (1.86)	77.2 (1.20)	70.6 (1.75)	46.6 (2.40)	69.
Percent of full-time employees looking for a different job[4]											
1989-90 recipients in June 1991	21.5 (0.35)	12.9 (1.05)	21.0 (1.95)	16.6 (1.08)	24.5 (1.20)	25.8 (1.44)	9.2 (1.10)	20.7 (0.78)	25.5 (0.92)	21.8 (1.57)	26.
1999-2000 recipients in July 2001	24.6 (0.66)	19.2 (2.30)	22.9 (2.64)	18.3 (2.36)	27.1 (2.06)	28.3 (2.13)	20.9 (1.93)	24.4 (1.51)	17.4 (1.45)	23.9 (2.54)	25.
2007-08 recipients in June 2009	31.2 (0.74)	20.2 (2.53)	28.5 (3.47)	27.7 (3.37)	35.3 (2.47)	39.2 (2.56)	21.8 (2.40)	32.0 (1.61)	23.6 (1.78)	37.3 (2.99)	30.
Percent of full-time employees in job closely related to field of study											
1989-90 recipients in June 1991	52.5 (0.55)	57.5 (1.24)	49.4 (2.31)	66.4 (1.34)	20.2 (1.12)	32.2 (2.07)	88.2 (2.10)	49.8 (0.79)	79.2 (0.89)	40.3 (2.13)	57.
1999-2000 recipients in July 2001	56.1 (0.65)	70.0 (3.35)	48.6 (3.00)	72.7 (2.58)	28.7 (2.03)	41.5 (2.16)	77.5 (2.45)	58.7 (1.67)	84.3 (1.68)	40.1 (3.65)	61.
2007-08 recipients in June 2009	49.7 (0.78)	61.3 (2.86)	49.0 (3.36)	61.9 (3.57)	21.6 (2.07)	27.6 (2.56)	81.7 (2.10)	49.3 (1.76)	82.0 (1.68)	26.6 (3.04)	57.
Annual salaries of full-time employees[5]											
Average salary, in current dollars											
1989-90 recipients in June 1991	$23,600 (180)	$30,900 (390)	$21,100 (410)	$27,200 (400)	$22,100 (330)	$19,100 (350)	$31,500 (860)	$24,700 (330)	$19,100 (140)	$19,200 (310)	$20,90
1999-2000 recipients in July 2001	35,400 (300)	47,900 (840)	31,000 (710)	47,400 (1,080)	33,000 (700)	30,100 (690)	39,400 (1,110)	41,000 (860)	27,600 (370)	28,800 (990)	30,40
2007-08 recipients in June 2009	40,100 (340)	53,900 (1,080)	34,600 (1,220)	48,800 (1,570)	36,600 (980)	31,100 (780)	49,100 (1,290)	44,200 (890)	33,000 (490)	30,600 (910)	35,00
Average salary, in constant 2018 dollars											
1989-90 recipients in June 1991	$43,600 (330)	$57,000 (720)	$38,800 (760)	$50,100 (740)	$40,700 (610)	$35,200 (650)	$58,000 (1,580)	$45,600 (610)	$35,200 (250)	$35,300 (580)	$38,50
1999-2000 recipients in July 2001	50,200 (420)	68,000 (1,190)	43,900 (1,010)	67,200 (1,530)	46,700 (1,000)	42,700 (990)	55,900 (1,570)	58,200 (1,220)	39,200 (520)	40,900 (1,400)	43,10
2007-08 recipients in June 2009	46,900 (400)	63,100 (1,270)	40,500 (1,420)	57,200 (1,840)	42,800 (1,150)	36,400 (910)	57,500 (1,510)	51,700 (1,040)	38,600 (580)	35,800 (1,070)	41,00
Percent change in average salary, in constant 2018 dollars											
1991 to 2009	7.6 (---)	10.6 (---)	4.4 (---)	14.1 (---)	5.1 (---)	3.5 (---)	-0.8 (---)	13.2 (---)	9.5 (---)	1.5 (---)	6.
1991 to 2001	15.2 (---)	19.2 (---)	13.2 (---)	34.3 (---)	14.7 (---)	21.4 (---)	-3.6 (---)	27.4 (---)	11.1 (---)	15.8 (---)	12.
2001 to 2009	-6.6 (---)	-7.2 (---)	-7.7 (---)	-15.0 (---)	-8.4 (---)	-14.7 (---)	2.8 (---)	-11.1 (---)	-1.5 (---)	-12.4 (---)	-4.
Median salary, in current dollars											
1989-90 recipients in June 1991	$21,800 (210)	$31,900 (470)	$20,000 (430)	$27,000 (510)	$20,300 (250)	$18,500 (360)	$30,400 (760)	$23,000 (300)	$19,500 (220)	$18,100 (320)	$18,60
1999-2000 recipients in July 2001	32,000 (90)	47,800 (880)	29,800 (470)	46,100 (1,990)	29,900 (360)	28,600 (700)	35,500 (770)	36,800 (700)	27,900 (410)	27,700 (1,180)	27,90
2007-08 recipients in June 2009	36,000 (220)	54,000 (900)	32,500 (1,570)	45,000 (1,830)	34,600 (920)	29,000 (1,060)	45,900 (920)	40,000 (300)	33,800 (570)	29,300 (1,040)	32,00
Median salary, in constant 2018 dollars											
1989-90 recipients in June 1991	$40,200 (380)	$58,800 (870)	$36,800 (790)	$49,700 (950)	$37,300 (460)	$34,100 (660)	$56,100 (1,400)	$42,400 (550)	$36,000 (400)	$33,400 (590)	$34,30
1999-2000 recipients in July 2001	45,300 (130)	67,800 (1,250)	42,300 (670)	65,400 (2,820)	42,400 (500)	40,500 (990)	50,300 (1,090)	52,200 (990)	39,600 (590)	39,400 (1,670)	39,60
2007-08 recipients in June 2009	42,100 (260)	63,200 (1,050)	38,000 (1,840)	52,700 (2,150)	40,500 (1,070)	33,900 (1,240)	53,800 (1,080)	46,800 (350)	39,600 (670)	34,300 (1,220)	37,50
Percent change in median salary, in constant 2018 dollars											
1991 to 2009	4.9 (---)	7.5 (---)	3.2 (---)	6.0 (---)	8.5 (---)	-0.3 (---)	-4.1 (---)	10.5 (---)	10.0 (---)	2.8 (---)	9.
1991 to 2001	12.8 (---)	15.3 (---)	14.9 (---)	31.5 (---)	13.5 (---)	19.1 (---)	-10.2 (---)	23.2 (---)	10.1 (---)	17.9 (---)	15.
2001 to 2009	-7.0 (---)	-6.8 (---)	-10.1 (---)	-19.4 (---)	-4.5 (---)	-16.3 (---)	6.9 (---)	-10.3 (---)	-0.1 (---)	-12.7 (---)	-5.

---Not available.

[1] Includes graduates in other fields not separately shown.

[2] For 1991, physical sciences are not included in column 4 with biological sciences; instead, they are included in column 5 with mathematics and computer science.

[3] Most educators work 9- to 10-month contracts.

[4] In 1991, respondents were asked whether they were "looking for a different principal job." In 2001 and 2009, they were asked whether they were "looking for a different job" (instead of "a different principal job").

[5] In all years, reported salaries of full-time workers under $1,000 were excluded from the tabulations. In addition, salaries reported as above $500,000 were set to $500,000 in 2001, and salaries reported as above $250,000 were set to $250,000 in 2009. In all years, only a tiny fraction of reported full-time salaries were either below $1,000 or above $250,000.

NOTE: Data exclude bachelor's degree recipients from U.S. Service Academies, deceased graduates, and graduates living at foreign addresses at the time of the survey. Constant dollars based on the Consumer Price Index, prepared by the Bureau of Labor Statistics, U.S. Department of Labor. Some data have been revised from previously published figures.

SOURCE: U.S. Department of Education, National Center for Education Statistics, "Recent College Graduates" survey, 1991; and 2000/01 and 2008/09 Baccalaureate and Beyond Longitudinal Study (B&B:2000/01 and B&B:08/09). (This table was prepared April 2020.)

Table 505.50. Percentage, selected employment characteristics, and annual salaries of bachelor's degree recipients employed full time 1 year after graduation, by field of study: 1991, 2001, and 2009

[Standard errors appear in parentheses]

Selected employment characteristic and annual salary	All fields of study[1]	Engineering	Biological and physical sciences[2]	Mathematics and computer science[2]	Social sciences and history	Humanities	Health professions	Business and management	Education[3]	Psychology	Public affairs and social services
1	2	3	4	5	6	7	8	9	10	11	12
Employment characteristics											
Percent of recipients employed full time											
1989–90 recipients in June 1991	73.8 (0.36)	85.2 (0.95)	50.6 (1.72)	71.2 (1.30)	66.2 (0.94)	59.2 (1.32)	80.9 (1.35)	83.2 (0.57)	77.0 (0.74)	59.8 (1.64)	77.0 (2.06)
1999–2000 recipients in July 2001	76.5 (0.52)	86.0 (1.77)	58.6 (2.04)	83.7 (2.06)	68.3 (1.88)	67.5 (1.65)	74.8 (1.50)	85.5 (1.27)	84.0 (1.29)	64.0 (2.64)	85.1 (2.25)
2007–08 recipients in June 2009	65.0 (0.62)	76.1 (2.12)	49.0 (2.38)	75.1 (2.67)	58.0 (1.81)	50.4 (1.82)	68.5 (1.86)	77.2 (1.20)	70.6 (1.75)	46.6 (2.40)	69.8 (3.44)
Percent of full-time employees looking for a different job[4]											
1989–90 recipients in June 1991	21.5 (0.35)	12.9 (1.05)	21.0 (1.95)	16.6 (1.08)	24.5 (1.20)	25.8 (1.44)	9.2 (1.10)	20.7 (0.78)	25.5 (0.92)	21.8 (1.57)	26.8 (2.36)
1999–2000 recipients in July 2001	24.6 (0.66)	19.2 (2.30)	22.9 (2.64)	18.3 (2.36)	27.1 (2.06)	28.3 (2.13)	20.9 (1.93)	24.4 (1.51)	17.4 (1.45)	23.9 (2.54)	25.8 (2.80)
2007–08 recipients in June 2009	31.2 (0.74)	20.2 (2.53)	28.5 (3.47)	27.7 (3.37)	35.3 (2.47)	39.2 (2.56)	21.8 (2.40)	32.0 (1.61)	23.6 (1.78)	37.3 (2.99)	30.4 (4.86)
Percent of full-time employees in job closely related to field of study											
1989–90 recipients in June 1991	52.5 (0.55)	57.5 (1.24)	49.4 (2.31)	66.4 (1.34)	20.2 (1.12)	32.2 (2.07)	88.2 (2.10)	49.8 (0.79)	79.2 (0.89)	40.3 (2.13)	57.6 (2.56)
1999–2000 recipients in July 2001	56.1 (0.65)	70.0 (3.35)	48.6 (3.00)	72.7 (2.58)	28.7 (2.03)	41.5 (2.16)	77.5 (2.45)	58.7 (1.67)	84.3 (1.68)	40.1 (3.65)	61.2 (3.11)
2007–08 recipients in June 2009	49.7 (0.78)	61.3 (2.86)	49.0 (3.36)	61.9 (3.57)	21.6 (2.07)	27.6 (2.56)	81.7 (2.10)	49.3 (1.76)	82.0 (1.68)	26.6 (3.04)	57.2 (4.93)
Annual salaries of full-time employees[5]											
Average salary, in current dollars											
1989–90 recipients in June 1991	$23,600 (180)	$30,900 (390)	$21,100 (410)	$27,200 (400)	$22,100 (330)	$19,100 (350)	$31,500 (860)	$24,700 (330)	$19,100 (140)	$19,200 (310)	$20,900 (470)
1999–2000 recipients in July 2001	35,400 (300)	47,900 (840)	31,000 (710)	47,400 (1,080)	33,000 (700)	30,100 (690)	39,400 (1,110)	41,000 (860)	27,600 (370)	28,800 (990)	30,400 (1,030)
2007–08 recipients in June 2009	40,100 (340)	53,900 (1,080)	34,600 (1,220)	48,800 (1,570)	36,600 (980)	31,100 (780)	49,100 (1,290)	44,200 (890)	33,000 (490)	30,600 (910)	35,000 (1,700)
Average salary, in constant 2016 dollars											
1989–90 recipients in June 1991	$41,700 (320)	$54,500 (690)	$37,100 (730)	$47,900 (700)	$38,900 (590)	$33,600 (620)	$55,400 (1,510)	$43,600 (580)	$33,700 (240)	$33,800 (550)	$36,800 (820)
1999–2000 recipients in July 2001	48,000 (400)	65,000 (1,140)	42,000 (970)	64,300 (1,460)	44,700 (950)	40,800 (940)	53,500 (1,500)	55,600 (1,170)	37,400 (500)	39,100 (1,340)	41,200 (1,400)
2007–08 recipients in June 2009	44,800 (380)	60,300 (1,210)	38,700 (1,360)	54,600 (1,760)	40,900 (1,100)	34,800 (870)	55,000 (1,440)	49,400 (1,000)	36,900 (550)	34,200 (1,020)	39,200 (1,900)
Percent change in average salary, in constant 2016 dollars											
1991 to 2009	7.6 (—)	10.6 (—)	4.4 (—)	14.1 (—)	5.1 (—)	3.5 (—)	-0.8 (—)	13.2 (—)	9.5 (—)	1.5 (—)	6.6 (—)
1991 to 2001	15.2 (—)	19.2 (—)	13.2 (—)	34.3 (—)	14.7 (—)	21.4 (—)	-3.6 (—)	27.4 (—)	11.2 (—)	15.8 (—)	12.1 (—)
2001 to 2009	-6.6 (—)	-7.2 (—)	-7.7 (—)	-15.0 (—)	-8.4 (—)	-14.7 (—)	2.8 (—)	-11.1 (—)	-1.5 (—)	-12.4 (—)	-4.9 (—)
Median salary, in current dollars											
1989–90 recipients in June 1991	$21,800 (210)	$31,900 (470)	$20,000 (430)	$27,000 (510)	$20,300 (250)	$18,500 (360)	$30,400 (760)	$23,000 (300)	$19,500 (220)	$18,100 (320)	$18,600 (410)
1999–2000 recipients in July 2001	32,000 (90)	47,800 (880)	29,800 (470)	46,100 (1,990)	29,900 (360)	28,600 (700)	35,500 (770)	36,800 (700)	27,900 (410)	27,700 (1,180)	27,900 (710)
2007–08 recipients in June 2009	36,000 (220)	54,000 (900)	32,500 (1,570)	45,000 (1,830)	34,600 (920)	29,000 (1,060)	45,900 (920)	40,000 (300)	33,800 (570)	29,300 (1,040)	32,000 (1,430)
Median salary, in constant 2016 dollars											
1989–90 recipients in June 1991	$38,400 (370)	$56,200 (830)	$35,200 (750)	$47,500 (900)	$35,700 (440)	$32,500 (630)	$53,600 (1,340)	$40,500 (530)	$34,400 (390)	$31,900 (570)	$32,800 (720)
1999–2000 recipients in July 2001	43,300 (120)	64,800 (1,200)	40,400 (640)	62,500 (2,690)	40,500 (480)	38,800 (950)	48,100 (1,050)	49,900 (950)	37,900 (560)	37,600 (1,600)	37,900 (970)
2007–08 recipients in June 2009	40,300 (250)	60,400 (1,000)	36,300 (1,760)	50,300 (2,050)	38,700 (1,020)	32,400 (1,190)	51,400 (1,030)	44,700 (330)	37,800 (640)	32,800 (1,170)	35,800 (1,600)
Percent change in median salary, in constant 2016 dollars											
1991 to 2009	4.9 (—)	7.5 (—)	3.2 (—)	6.0 (—)	8.5 (—)	-0.3 (—)	-4.1 (—)	10.5 (—)	10.0 (—)	2.8 (—)	9.2 (—)
1991 to 2001	12.8 (—)	15.4 (—)	14.9 (—)	31.5 (—)	13.5 (—)	19.1 (—)	-10.2 (—)	23.2 (—)	10.1 (—)	17.9 (—)	15.4 (—)
2001 to 2009	-7.0 (—)	-6.8 (—)	-10.1 (—)	-19.4 (—)	-4.5 (—)	-16.3 (—)	6.9 (—)	-10.3 (—)	-0.1 (—)	-12.7 (—)	-5.4 (—)

—Not available.
[1]Includes graduates in other fields not separately shown.
[2]For 1991, physical sciences not included in column 4 with biological sciences; instead, they are included in column 5 with mathematics and computer science.
[3]Most educators work 9- to 10-month contracts.
[4]In 1991, respondents were asked whether they were "looking for a different principal job." In 2001 and 2009, they were asked whether they were "looking for a different job" (instead of "a different principal job").
[5]In all years, reported salaries of full-time workers under $1,000 were excluded from the tabulations. In addition, salaries reported as above $500,000 were set to $500,000 in 2001, and salaries reported as above $250,000 were set to $250,000 in 2009. In all years, only a tiny fraction of reported full-time salaries were either below $1,000 or above $250,000.
NOTE: Data exclude bachelor's degree recipients from U.S. Service Academies, deceased graduates, and graduates living at foreign addresses at the time of the survey. Constant dollars based on the Consumer Price Index, prepared by the Bureau of Labor Statistics, U.S. Department of Labor. Some data have been revised from previously published figures.
SOURCE: U.S. Department of Education, National Center for Education Statistics, "Recent College Graduates" survey, 1991; and 2000/01 and 2008/09 Baccalaureate and Beyond Longitudinal Study (B&B:2000/01 and B&B:08/09). (This table was prepared September 2017.)

601.10

Canadian undergraduate tuition fees by field of study, annual (dollars) (1,2,3,4,5,6,7)

Field of study grouping	2016/2017	2017/2018	2018/2019	2019/2020	2020/2021
Education	4,571	4,423	4,732	4,648	4,761
Visual and performing arts, and communications technologies	5,680	5,857	6,131	5,789	5,865
Humanities	5,460	5,619	5,773	5,486	5,602
Social and behavioural sciences	5,573	5,739	5,902	5,555	5,632
Law	13,115	12,807	13,216	12,527	12,813
Business, management and public administration	6,810	7,143	7,222	6,795	6,887
Physical and life sciences and technologies	6,022	6,206	6,397	6,068	6,156
Mathematics, computer and information sciences	6,911	7,157	7,320	6,814	6,895
Engineering	7,827	8,106	8,532	7,949	8,047
Architecture	6,810	6,610	6,967	6,470	6,517
Agriculture, natural resources and conservation	5,438	5,665	5,831	5,614	5,718
Dentistry	21,464	22,569	22,747	22,242	22,562
Medicine	13,911	14,274	14,794	14,201	14,483
Nursing	5,507	5,636	5,763	5,583	5,688
Pharmacy	9,962	10,367	10,780	10,931	11,133
Veterinary medicine	7,450	7,647	7,867	7,852	14,270
Optometry	..	..	12,330	11,203	11,235
Other health, parks, recreation and fitness	6,085	6,287	6,227	5,867	5,943
Personal, protective and transportation services	5,989	6,044	6,203	5,686	5,726

..: Not available for a specific reference period

Footnotes:

(1) Data for 2020/2021 are preliminary.

(2) The national and provincial tuition fee averages are weighted with the latest enrolment data (2017/2018 Postsecondary Student Information System). If the number of enrolments is unknown for a given program, that program is excluded from the averages. The same enrolment data are used for the weighting of both years, 2019/2020 and 2020/2021, thereby permitting the comparison of changes in the tuition fees only.

(3) As the distribution of enrolment varies from period to period, caution must be exercised when making long-term historical comparisons.

(4) For Quebec (since 1998/1999), Nova Scotia (since 2007/2008), and Newfoundland and Labrador (since 2018/2019), the weighted averages take into account the different fees paid by "in province" and "out of province" Canadian students.

(5) It is important to note that tuition fee increases are generally regulated by provincial policies. However, some programs may be exempted from these policies resulting in possible increases that exceed provincial limits.

(6) Data in this release do not take into account financial assistance or tax rebates provided to students. Tuition fees and additional compulsory fees represent only a portion of all costs incurred for attending university.

(7) The fields of study are adapted from the 2016 Classification of Instructional Programs (CIP), Statistics Canada's standard for the classification of instructional programs.

Source:
Statistics Canada. Table 37-10-0003-01 Canadian undergraduate tuition fees by field of study
(accessed: Aug. 16, 2021)

601.20

Canadian graduate tuition fees by field of study, annual (dollars) (1,2,3,4,5,6,7,8,9)

Field of study grouping	2016/2017	2017/2018	2018/2019	2019/2020	2020/2021
Education	5,866	6,050	6,546	6,423	6,443
Visual and performing arts, and communications technologies	5,069	5,388	5,440	5,263	5,316
Humanities	4,674	4,724	4,827	4,881	4,932
Social and behavioural sciences	5,829	5,977	6,135	5,801	5,901
Law	5,757	5,681	6,179	6,036	6,101
Business, management and public administration	11,140	10,979	13,524	13,145	13,781
Executive MBA	47,251	44,957	59,709	50,459	50,774
Regular MBA	29,025	30,003	31,818	29,028	29,313
Physical and life sciences and technologies	6,455	6,753	7,056	6,741	6,785
Mathematics, computer and information sciences	7,727	8,010	8,456	8,395	8,461
Engineering	7,077	7,219	7,369	6,990	7,031
Architecture	6,117	6,471	6,567	6,742	6,890
Agriculture, natural resources and conservation	5,429	5,499	5,669	5,938	6,065
Dentistry	12,239	12,872	13,726	13,002	13,114
Medicine	..	..	..	..	..
Nursing	7,622	7,764	6,684	6,328	6,580
Pharmacy	5,922	4,114	4,055	4,245	4,314
Veterinary medicine	3,687	3,941	4,358	4,170	3,961
Optometry	..	..	5,012	4,508	4,508
Other health, parks, recreation and fitness	8,040	8,285	8,786	8,401	8,463
Personal, protective and transportation services	3,987	6,513	6,007	5,513	5,538

Legend:

..: Not available for a specific reference period

Footnotes:

(1) Data for 2020/2021 are preliminary.

(2) The national and provincial tuition fee averages are weighted with the latest enrolment data (2017/2018 Postsecondary Student Information System). If the number of enrolments is unknown for a given program, that program is excluded from the averages. The same enrolment data are used for the weighting of both years, 2019/2020 and 2020/2021, thereby permitting the comparison of changes in the tuition fees only.

(3) As the distribution of enrolment varies from period to period, caution must be exercised when making long-term historical comparisons.

(4) For Quebec (since 1998/1999), Nova Scotia (since 2007/2008), and Newfoundland and Labrador (since 2018/2019), the weighted averages take into account the different fees paid by "in province" and "out of province" Canadian students.

(5) Since 2010/2011, Regular and Executive MBA (master of business administration programs) have been excluded from the national and provincial weighted averages due to their high costs and their effect on the overall tuition fee average. Dental, medical and veterinary residency programs offered in teaching hospitals and similar locations that may lead to advanced professional certification have also been excluded.

(6) It is important to note that tuition fee increases are generally regulated by provincial policies. However, some programs may be exempted from these policies resulting in possible increases that exceed provincial limits.

(7) Data in this release do not take into account financial assistance or tax rebates provided to students. Tuition fees and additional compulsory fees represent only a portion of all costs incurred for attending university.

(8) Graduate tuition fee averages reflect combinations of 8- and 12-month reporting periods.

(9) The fields of study are adapted from the 2016 Classification of Instructional Programs (CIP), Statistics Canada's standard for the classification of instructional programs.

Source:

Statistics Canada. Table 37-10-0004-01 Canadian graduate tuition fees by field of study (accessed: Aug. 16, 2021)

601.30

International undergraduate tuition fees by field of study, annual (dollars) (1,2,3,4,5,6)

Field of study grouping	2016/2017	2017/2018	2018/2019	2019/2020	2020/2021
Education	17,821	18,486	18,761	21,057	22,104
Visual and performing arts, and communications technologies	20,863	21,863	23,520	25,467	27,103
Humanities	22,746	24,619	26,617	27,517	29,742
Social and behavioural sciences	21,832	23,378	25,673	27,891	30,049
Law	29,100	28,099	30,932	34,273	36,001
Business, management and public administration	23,230	25,065	26,723	29,039	30,769
Physical and life sciences and technologies	24,389	26,997	29,203	32,394	34,763
Mathematics, computer and information sciences	25,452	28,095	30,370	32,989	35,628
Engineering	27,002	28,682	31,393	33,462	36,072
Architecture	22,080	23,449	24,698	27,751	29,804
Agriculture, natural resources and conservation	21,057	22,706	24,510	26,260	28,238
Dentistry	52,257	53,483	53,521	55,102	57,020
Medicine	31,534	29,223	31,214	35,271	38,075
Nursing	18,620	19,538	20,861	21,921	22,946
Pharmacy	32,510	32,693	38,903	39,531	40,736
Veterinary medicine	58,359	59,132	60,432	63,406	65,576
Optometry	..	..	..	..	..
Other health, parks, recreation and fitness	20,297	21,862	23,269	24,553	26,257
Personal, protective and transportation services	19,104	19,941	19,489	23,694	25,424

Footnotes:

(1) Data for 2020/2021 are preliminary.

(2) The national and provincial tuition fee averages are weighted with the latest enrolment data (2017/2018 Postsecondary Student Information System). If the number of enrolments is unknown for a given program, that program is excluded from the averages. The same enrolment data are used for the weighting of both years, 2019/2020 and 2020/2021, thereby permitting the comparison of changes in the tuition fees only.

(3) As the distribution of enrolment varies from period to period, caution must be exercised when making long-term historical comparisons.

(4) It is important to note that tuition fee increases are generally regulated by provincial policies. However, some programs may be exempted from these policies resulting in possible increases that exceed provincial limits.

(5) Data in this release do not take into account financial assistance or tax rebates provided to students. Tuition fees and additional compulsory fees represent only a portion of all costs incurred for attending university.

(6) The fields of study are adapted from the 2016 Classification of Instructional Programs (CIP), Statistics Canada's standard for the classification of instructional programs.

Source:

Statistics Canada. Table 37-10-0005-01 International undergraduate tuition fees by field of study
(accessed: Aug. 16, 2021)

601.40

International graduate tuition fees by field of study, annual (dollars) (1,2,3,4,5,6,7,8)

Field of study grouping	2016/2017	2017/2018	2018/2019	2019/2020	2020/2021
Education	14,437	15,447	15,267	16,068	16,899
Visual and performing arts, and communications technologies	13,105	14,212	14,122	14,724	15,709
Humanities	13,504	14,078	13,250	13,702	14,220
Social and behavioural sciences	13,568	14,276	14,550	14,985	15,919
Law	16,309	15,779	16,586	17,529	18,455
Business, management and public administration	21,387	22,190	23,808	24,408	26,351
Executive MBA	51,597	47,930	67,657	55,424	55,578
Regular MBA	34,644	36,797	38,406	38,668	40,032
Physical and life sciences and technologies	13,816	14,624	14,910	15,125	15,959
Mathematics, computer and information sciences	14,311	15,245	16,114	17,441	18,391
Engineering	16,299	17,465	18,236	19,736	21,559
Architecture	20,556	22,383	23,082	24,951	26,524
Agriculture, natural resources and conservation	12,100	13,692	13,953	13,763	14,819
Dentistry	20,982	21,534	21,533	22,507	24,582
Medicine	..	..	..	..	..
Nursing	12,081	13,566	15,518	16,318	16,312
Pharmacy	10,835	11,856	11,421	11,646	12,532
Veterinary medicine	8,598	8,814	9,896	9,834	9,081
Optometry	..	..	13,608	14,014	14,436
Other health, parks, recreation and fitness	15,603	16,384	17,734	18,109	19,422
Personal, protective and transportation services	12,275	13,796	..	..	..

Legend:

..: Not available for a specific reference period

Footnotes:

(1) Data for 2020/2021 are preliminary.

(2) The national and provincial tuition fee averages are weighted with the latest enrolment data (2017/2018 Postsecondary Student Information System). If the number of enrolments is unknown for a given program, that program is excluded from the averages. The same enrolment data are used for the weighting of both years, 2019/2020 and 2020/2021, thereby permitting the comparison of changes in the tuition fees only.

(3) As the distribution of enrolment varies from period to period, caution must be exercised when making long-term historical comparisons.

(4) Since 2010/2011, Regular and Executive MBA (master of business administration programs) have been excluded from the national and provincial weighted averages due to their high costs and their effect on the overall tuition fee average. Dental, medical and veterinary residency programs offered in teaching hospitals and similar locations that may lead to advanced professional certification have also been excluded.

(5) It is important to note that tuition fee increases are generally regulated by provincial policies. However, some programs may be exempted from these policies resulting in possible increases that exceed provincial limits.

(6) Data in this release do not take into account financial assistance or tax rebates provided to students. Tuition fees and additional compulsory fees represent only a portion of all costs incurred for attending university.

(7) Graduate tuition fee averages reflect combinations of 8- and 12-month reporting periods.

(8) The fields of study are adapted from the 2016 Classification of Instructional Programs (CIP), Statistics Canada's standard for the classification of instructional programs.

Source:

Statistics Canada. Table 37-10-0006-01 International graduate tuition fees by field of study
(accessed: Aug. 16, 2021)

602.10

School board revenues, by direct source of funds and geography, annual (dollars x 1,000) (1,2,3,4)

School board revenues by direct source of funds	2014	2015	2016	2017	2018
Total revenues	58,050,353	59,679,563	61,320,747	64,238,539	66,222,721
Local taxation sources	14,551,583	15,254,405	15,704,675	15,600,964	15,394,056
Provincial government sources	39,497,757	40,283,201	41,304,904	44,256,815	46,236,784
Federal government sources	360,237	350,304	360,815	381,300	367,283
Student and other school fees	462,643	504,965	523,560	493,429	535,729
Other private sector sources	3,178,134	3,286,687	3,426,793	3,506,032	3,688,869

Footnotes:

(1) Source: Statistics Canada, Culture, Tourism and the Centre for Education Statistics.

(2) Data up to, but not including, 2012 are or have been converted to a calendar basis, January 1 to December 31.

(3) School boards represent schools which are a part of the elementary and secondary public school system. The revenues and/or expenditures in this table exclude those of other types of publicly run elementary and secondary schools such as federal schools and special needs education schools as well as the elementary and secondary schools which are in the private school system.

(4) Starting in 2012, data cover the fiscal year which ends closest to December 31st of the displayed year in the table. For example, 2016 covers April 1, 2016 to March 31, 2017.

Source:
Statistics Canada. Table 37-10-0063-01 School board revenues, by direct source of funds and geography (x 1,000) (accessed: Aug. 16, 2021)

602.20

School board expenditures, by function and economic classification, annual (dollars x 1,000) (1,2,3,4)

Economic classification	2014	2015	2016	2017	2018
Total expenditures by economic classification	58,502,360	60,371,971	61,932,508	64,699,281	66,965,049
Salary and wages expenditures	38,111,660	39,161,636	40,134,949	41,596,865	42,952,328
Fringe benefits expenditures	5,954,891	6,163,413	6,218,651	6,713,978	7,069,072
Supply and services expenditures	4,892,430	4,793,931	4,961,248	5,178,258	5,265,914
Fees and contractual services expenditures	3,767,698	3,799,500	3,941,047	4,213,093	4,476,159
Other operating expenditures	610,193	562,799	634,993	902,380	705,429
Capital expenditures (non-allocable, outlay and debt charges)	5,165,488	5,890,692	6,041,620	6,094,707	6,496,147

Footnotes:

(1) Source: Statistics Canada, Culture, Tourism and the Centre for Education Statistics.

(2) Data up to, but not including, 2012 are or have been converted to a calendar basis, January 1 to December 31.

(3) Starting in 2012, data cover the fiscal year which ends closest to December 31st of the displayed year in the table. For example, 2016 covers April 1, 2016 to March 31, 2017.

(4) These figures represent the Northwest Territories including Nunavut. For the new territory of Nunavut (as of 1999), data are still not available separately.

Source:

Statistics Canada. Table 37-10-0064-01 School board expenditures, by function and economic classification (x 1,000) (accessed: Aug. 16, 2021)

602.30

School board expenditures, by function and economic classification, annual (dollars x 1,000) (1,2,3)

Function	2014	2015	2016	2017	2018
Total expenditures by function	58,502,360	60,371,971	61,932,508	64,699,281	66,965,049
Business administration expenditures	1,579,161	1,569,625	1,587,629	1,676,373	1,768,699
Instruction and educational services expenditures (5)	41,630,364	42,771,335	43,859,688	45,823,942	47,379,631
Adult education expenditures	872,161	863,125	911,617	932,497	991,041
Food services expenditures	1,953,677	1,936,699	2,044,620	2,485,831	2,347,144
School facilities service expenditures	4,918,727	4,960,772	5,033,923	5,132,292	5,318,495
Transportation expenditures	2,382,781	2,379,722	2,453,411	2,553,638	2,663,892
Capital outlay expenditures (non-allocable)	4,351,196	5,112,855	5,265,926	5,326,375	5,706,730
Debt charges on capital expenditures (non-allocable)	814,292	777,838	775,695	768,332	789,417

Footnotes:

(1) Source: Statistics Canada, Culture, Tourism and the Centre for Education Statistics.

(2) Data up to, but not including, 2012 are or have been converted to a calendar basis, January 1 to December 31.

(3) Starting in 2012, data cover the fiscal year which ends closest to December 31st of the displayed year in the table. For example, 2016 covers April 1, 2016 to March 31, 2017.

(4) These figures represent the Northwest Territories including Nunavut. For the new territory of Nunavut (as of 1999), data are still not available separately.

(5) Instruction and education services expenditures include instructional administration expenditures.

Source:

Statistics Canada. Table 37-10-0064-01 School board expenditures, by function and economic classification (x 1,000) (accessed: Aug. 16, 2021)

602.40

Public and private elementary and secondary education expenditures, annual (dollars x 1,000) (1,2)

Type of expenditures	2014/2015	2015/2016	2016/2017	2017/2018	2018/2019
Public and private elementary and secondary education expenditures	69,541,524	71,705,742	73,663,869	77,092,258	79,292,801
Public elementary and secondary education expenditures	65,844,063	67,956,491	69,833,671	73,086,940	75,180,008
Public school board and direct government expenditures	64,329,680	66,448,411	68,006,687	71,049,191	73,196,439
Public school board expenditures	58,502,360	60,371,971	61,932,508	64,699,281	66,965,049
Public school board expenditures, net	58,502,360	60,371,971	61,932,508	64,699,281	66,965,049
Public school board expenditures transferred to private schools	..	..	..	..	..
Direct government expenditures on public education	5,827,320	6,076,439	6,074,179	6,349,910	6,231,390
Direct government expenditures on services to public school boards (3)	2,018,874	2,143,331	1,996,857	2,136,688	2,139,245
Direct government expenditures on contributions to public school board teachers' pension funds (3)	3,772,308	3,913,164	4,013,211	4,145,343	4,055,561
Direct government expenditures on public education by the Department of National Defence (4)	12,798	10,769	11,894	6,218	..
Other direct government expenditures on public education (4)	23,340	9,176	52,217	61,661	36,584
Federal school expenditures	1,319,541	1,316,210	1,654,615	1,857,013	1,808,817
Special education expenditures on public education	30,967	29,566	29,219	26,788	25,204
Special education expenditures, handicapped outside regular public schools	6,034	5,807	5,716	5,847	5,915
Special education expenditures on provincially licensed correspondence courses	5,255	4,788	4,752	0	..
Special education expenditures on federal penitentiaries	19,678	18,971	18,750	20,941	19,289
Direct provincial government expenditures on administration of public education	163,875	162,305	143,150	153,948	149,548
Private elementary and secondary school expenditures	3,697,461	3,749,251	3,830,199	4,005,318	4,112,794

Legend:

..: Not available for a specific reference period

Footnotes:

(1) Source: Statistics Canada, Tourism and the Centre for Education Statistics.

(2) The methodology for calculating public and private elementary and secondary education expenditures was modified in reference period 2012/13.

(3) From 1950 to 1959 there was no separate breakdown available between direct government expenditures on services to public school boards and direct government expenditures on contributions to public school board teachers' pension funds. These were both reported under direct government expenditures on contributions to public school board teachers' pension funds.

(4) From 1950 to 1959, any direct government expenditures on public education by Department of National Defence were reported under other direct government expenditures on public education.

Source:

Statistics Canada. Table 37-10-0066-01 Public and private elementary and secondary education expenditures (x 1,000)
(accessed: Aug. 16, 2021)

602.50

Public and private elementary and secondary education expenditures, by direct source of funds, annual (dollars x 1,000) (1, 2)

Public and private elementary and secondary education expenditures by direct source of funds	2014/2015	2015/2016	2016/2017	2017/2018	2018/2019
All sources	69,089,517	71,013,333	73,052,108	76,631,517	78,550,474
All governments' sources	62,836,643	64,541,621	66,416,954	69,830,275	71,289,211
Federal government sources	1,735,681	1,705,524	2,098,291	2,327,412	2,231,973
Provincial government sources	46,507,665	47,540,073	48,573,298	51,859,045	53,614,626
Local government sources	14,593,298	15,296,024	15,745,365	15,643,818	15,442,612
Student and other school fees	2,444,145	2,539,224	2,562,911	2,623,522	2,839,284
Other private sector sources	3,808,729	3,932,487	4,072,242	4,177,720	4,421,979

Footnotes:

(1) Source: Statistics Canada, Tourism and the Centre for Education Statistics.

(2) The methodology for calculating public and private elementary and secondary education expenditures was modified in reference period 2012/13.

Source:

Statistics Canada. Table 37-10-0067-01 Public and private elementary and secondary education expenditures, by direct source of funds (x 1,000) (accessed: Aug. 16, 2021)

603.10

Unemployment rate, participation rate and employment rate by educational attainment, sex and age group, annual (1,2)

Labour force characteristics	Educational attainment (3)	2016	2017	2018	2019	2020
Employment rate (4)	Total, all education levels	61.8	62.2	62.2	62.5	59.4
Employment rate (4)	0 to 8 years (5)	18	19	19	19.2	17.4
Employment rate (4)	Some high school (6)	39.3	39.1	38.6	39.3	36.9
Employment rate (4)	High school graduate (7)	56.6	56.8	55.7	55.4	51.5
Employment rate (4)	Some postsecondary (8)	60	60.3	60.1	60	55.2
Employment rate (4)	Postsecondary certificate or diploma (9)	68.2	67.7	67.9	68.4	63.8
Employment rate (4)	University degree (10)	73.8	74.3	73.8	73.6	71.2
Employment rate (4)	Bachelor's degree	73.7	74.2	73.7	73.6	70.6
Employment rate (4)	Above bachelor's degree	73.9	74.6	74.1	73.7	72.4

Footnotes:

(1) To ensure respondent confidentiality, estimates below a certain threshold are suppressed. For Canada, Quebec, Ontario, Alberta and British Columbia suppression is applied to all data below 1,500. The threshold level for Newfoundland and Labrador, Nova Scotia, New Brunswick, Manitoba and Saskatchewan is 500, while in Prince Edward Island, estimates under 200 are supressed. For census metropolitan areas (CMAs) and economic regions (ERs), use their respective provincial suppression levels mentioned above. Estimates are based on smaller sample sizes the more detailed the table becomes, which could result in lower data quality.

(2) Excluding the territories.

(3) The following categories refer to the highest level of schooling completed. Questions relating to educational attainment were changed in 1990, to better capture the relationship between educational attainment and labour market outcomes. Because this introduced a break in the education series, this table only contains data from 1990 onwards. Beginning January 1990, data on primary and secondary education reflects the highest grade completed. This provides a more consistent measure for those who accelerate or fail a grade than did years of school. A question on high school graduation has also been added since it is generally believed that persons who have never completed their secondary education have greater difficulty competing in the labour market. With the new questions, any education that could be counted towards a degree, certificate or diploma from an educational institution is taken as postsecondary education. The change allows more persons into the postsecondary education category. For example, trades programs offered through apprenticeship, vocational schools or private trade schools do not always require high school graduation. Such education is now considered as postsecondary while only primary or secondary would have been recognized prior to 1990. Finally, more information is collected on the type of postsecondary education: 1) some postsecondary; 2) trades certificate or diploma from a vocational or apprenticeship training; 3) non-university certificate or diploma from a community college, CEGEP or school of nursing; 4) university certificate below bachelors degree; 5) bachelors degree; and 6) university degree or certificate above bachelors degree.

(4) The employment rate is the number of persons employed expressed as a percentage of the population 15 years of age and over. The employment rate for a particular group (age, sex, marital status, etc.) is the number employed in that group expressed as a percentage of the population for that group. Estimates are percentages, rounded to the nearest tenth.

(5) Primary education, grade 8 or lower. In Quebec, secondary II or lower.

(6) Attended but did not complete secondary school. In Quebec, attended at least Secondary III but did not complete Secondary V. In Newfoundland and Labrador, attended at least the first year of secondary but did not complete the fourth year.

(7) Received a high school diploma. In Quebec, completed Secondary V. In Newfoundland and Labrador, completed fourth year of secondary.

(8) Worked toward, but did not complete, a degree, certificate (including a trade certificate) or diploma from an educational institution, including a university, beyond the secondary level. This includes vocational schools, apprenticeship training, community college, Collège d'Enseignement Général et Professionnel (CEGEP), and school of nursing.

(9) Completed a certificate (including a trade certificate) or diploma from an educational institution beyond the secondary level. This includes certificates from vocational schools, apprenticeship training, community college, Collège d'Enseignement Général et Professionnel (CEGEP), and school of nursing. Also included are certificates below a Bachelor's degree obtained at a university.

(10) Attained at least a university bachelor's degree.

Source:

Statistics Canada. Table 14-10-0020-01 Unemployment rate, participation rate and employment rate by educational attainment, annual

(accessed: Aug. 16, 2021)

Glossary of Education Terms

Accountability
measurable proof, usually in the form of student results on various tests, that teachers, schools, divisions and states are teaching students efficiently and well, usually in the form of student success rates on various tests; Virginia's accountability programs is known as the Standards of Learning which includes curriculum standards approved by the Board of Education and required state tests based on the standards.

Accreditation
a process used by the Virginia Department of Education to evaluate the educational performance of public schools in accordance regulations.

Achievement gap
the difference between the performance of subgroups of students, especially those defined by gender, race/ethnicity, disability and socioeconomic status.

ACT
one of the two commonly used tests designed to assess high school students' general educational development and their ability to complete college-level work in four skill areas: English, mathematics, reading, and science reasoning.

Adequate yearly progress (AYP)
a measurement indicating whether a school, division or the state met federally approved academic goals required by the federal Elementary and Secondary Education Act/No Child Left Behind Act (ESEA/NCLB).

Adult/Continuing education
a program of instruction provided by an adult/continuing education instructional organization for adults and youth beyond the age of compulsory school attendance including basic education and English literacy, English for speakers of other languages, civics education, GED testing services, adult secondary education and Individualized Student Alternative Education Plan (ISAEP) programs.

Advanced Placement (AP)
college-level courses available to high school students which may allow a student to earn college credit provided through the College Board.

Alignment
effort to ensure that what teachers teach is in accord with what the curriculum says will be taught and what is assessed on official tests.

Alternative assessment
a method to measure student educational attainment other than the typical multiple-choice test which may include portfolios, constructed response items and other performance-measurement tools.

Alternative education
a school or center organized for alternative programs of instruction.

Assessment
method of measuring the learning and performance of students; examples include achievement tests, minimum competency tests, developmental screening tests, aptitude tests, observation instruments, performance tasks, etc.

At-risk students
students who have a higher than average probability of dropping out or failing school.

Average daily membership (ADM)
the K-12 enrollment figure used to distribute state per pupil funding that includes students with disabilities ages 5-21, and students for whom English is a second language who entered school for the first time after reaching their 12th birthday, and who have not reached their 22nd birthday; preschool and post-graduate students are not included in ADM.

Benchmark
a standard for judging performance.

Block scheduling
a way of organizing the school day into blocks of time longer than the typical 50 minute class period; with the 4X4 block students take four 90-minute classes each day allowing for completion of an entire course in one semester instead of a full year; with an A/B or rotating block students take six to eight classes for an entire year but classes in each subject meet on alternate days for 90 minutes.

Charter school
a school controlled by a local school board that provides free public elementary and/or secondary education to eligible students under a specific charter granted by the state legislature or other appropriate authority, and designated by such authority to be a charter school.

Class period
a segment of time in the school day that is approximately 1/6 of the instructional day.

Cohort
a particular group of people with something in common.

College Board
the organization that administers SAT, AP and other standardized tests to high school students planning on continuing their educations at a post-secondary level.

Combined school
a public school that contains any combination of or all K-12 grade levels that are not considered an elementary, middle or secondary school .

Composite index of local ability to pay
a formula to determine the state and local government shares of K-12 education program costs, which is expressed as a ratio, indicating the local percentage share of the cost of education programs; for example, a locality with a composite

index of 0.3000 would pay 30 percent and the state would pay 70 percent of the costs.

Confined
due to physical, medical or emotional impairments based on certification of need, a student is restricted or limited from attendance at a regular public school during the regular school hours; this does not apply to situations where a student is restricted for discipline or non-medically based situations.

Core curriculum
the body of knowledge that all students are expected to learn in the subjects of English, mathematics, history/social science and science.

Curriculum
a plan or document that a school or school division uses to define what will be taught and the methods that will be used to educate and assess students.

Curriculum alignment
occurs when what is taught includes or exceeds the content defined by the Standards of Learning (SOL).

Data-based decision making (also referred to as "re-search-based decision making")
organizing, analyzing and interpreting existing sources of information and other data to make decisions.

Direct aid to public education
funding appropriated for the operation of public schools including funding for school employee benefits, Standards of Quality, incentive-based programs, allotment of sales tax and lottery revenues and specific appropriations for programs such as Governor's Schools and adult literacy initiatives.

Disaggregated data
presentation of data broken into subgroups of students instead of the entire student body which allows parents and teachers to measure how each student group is performing; typical subgroups include students who are economically disadvantaged, from different racial or ethnic groups, those who have disabilities or have limited English fluency.

Distance learning
method of instruction in locations other than the classroom or places where teachers present the lessons, which uses various forms of technology to provide educational materials and experiences to students.

Dropouts
students who leave high school before receiving a diploma.

Early childhood education
the education of young children, especially under the age of 5.

Economically disadvantaged
a student who is a member of a household that meets the income eligibility guidelines for free or reduced-price school meals (less than or equal to 185% of Federal Poverty Guidelines).

Elementary & Secondary Education Act (ESEA)
the primary federal law affecting K-12 education; recent reauthorizations of the law were also known as the No Child Left Behind Act of 2001-2015 and most recently, Every Student Succeeds Act.

Elementary school
a public school with grades kindergarten through five.

Eligible students
the total number of students of school age enrolled in the school at a grade or course with a Standards of Learning test; does not include students who are allowed an exclusion such as limited English proficient (LEP) students or some students with disabilities.

English as a second language (ESL)
a program of instruction and services for non-English-speaking or limited-English-proficient students to help them learn and succeed in schools.

English-language learners (ELL)
a student whose first language is other than English and who is in a special program for learning English.

Enrollment
the act of complying with state and local requirements for registration or admission of a child for attendance in a school within a local school division; also refers to registration for courses within the student's home school or within related schools or programs.

Even Start
a federally funded program that provides family-centered education projects to help parents become full partners in the education of their children.

Every Student Succeeds Act
See Elementary & Secondary Education Act (ESEA)

First time
the student has not been enrolled in the school at any time during the current school year.

Four core subject/academic areas
English, mathematics, science and history/social science for purposes of SOL testing.

Free and appropriate public education (FAPE)
requirement through the federal Individuals with Disabilities Education Act (IDEA) that education of students with disabilities (between the ages of 3 and 22) must be provided at public expense, under public supervision, at no charge to the parents and based on the child's unique needs and not on the child's disability.

General education
K-12 instruction that meets the commonwealth's Standards of Learning and prepares children for elementary, secondary and postsecondary success.

Gifted
programs that provide advanced educational opportunities including accelerated promotion through grades and classes and an enriched curriculum for students who are endowed with a high degree of mental ability.

Governor's school
a school serving gifted high school students who meet specific admissions criteria for advanced educational opportunities in areas including the arts, government and international studies, mathematics, science, and technology; both academic-year and summer governor's schools are offered.

Graduate
a student who has earned a Board of Education recognized diploma: advanced studies, advanced technical, standard, standard technical, modified standard, special or general achievement.

Head Start
a federally funded child-development program that provides health, educational, nutritional, social and other services to pre-school children from economically disadvantaged families.

Home-based instruction
non-reimbursable educational services provided in the home setting (or other agreed upon setting) in accordance with the student's individual education program who were removed from school for disciplinary or other reasons, but not the result of a medical referral.

Homebound instruction
academic instruction provided to students who are confined at home or in a health-care facility for periods that would prevent normal school attendance based upon certification of need by a licensed physician or licensed clinical psychologist. For a student with a disability, the Individual Education Program (IEP) team must determine the delivery of services, including the number of hours of services.

Home instruction (also referred to as "home schooling")
instruction of a student or students by a parent or parents, guardian or other person having control or charge of such student or students as an alternative to attendance in a public or private school in accordance with the provisions of the Code of Virginia provisions (§22.1-254.1).

Home tutoring
instruction by a tutor or teacher with qualifications prescribed by the Virginia Board of Education, as an alternative to attendance in a public or private school and approved by the division superintendent in accordance with the provisions of the Code of Virginia §22.1-254; often used as an alternative form of home schooling.

Individuals with Disabilities Education Act (IDEA)
federal law guiding the delivery of special education services for students with disabilities which includes the guarantee of "free and appropriate public education" for every school-age child with a disability and allows parental involvement in the educational planning process, encourages access to the general curriculum and delineates how school disciplinary rules and the obligation to provide a free appropriate public education for disabled children mesh.

Individualized education program (IEP)
a written plan created for a student with disabilities by the student's teachers, parents or guardians, the school administrator, and other interested parties. The plan is tailored to the student's specific needs and abilities, and outlines attainable goals.

Individualized education program team (IEP Team)
team charged with developing, reviewing and revising a student's IEP and consisting of the parent(s), the child (if appropriate), a regular education teacher, a special education teacher, an administrator qualified to supervise the provision of services and an individual who can interpret the instructional implications of evaluation results.

Individualized family service plan (IFSP)
a written plan outlining the procedure necessary to transition a child with disabilities to preschool or other appropriate services.

International Baccalaureate (IB)
a program established to provide an internationally recognized; interdisciplinary; pre-collegiate course of study offered through the International Baccalaureate Organization, headquartered in Switzerland, and examination results are accepted by more than 100 countries for university admission.

Licensed clinical psychologist
a psychologist licensed by the Virginia Board of Psychology who must either be in a treatment relationship or establishing a treatment relationship with the student to meet eligibility requirements for requesting homebound services.

Licensed physician
an individual who has been licensed by the Virginia Board of Medicine to practice medicine who can certify medical conditions for requesting homebound services.

Licensed teacher
an individual who has met all the current requirements for a teacher in the Virginia and holds a license from the Virginia State Board of Education, or, if teaching on-line, a license from Virginia or another state.

Limited-English proficient (LEP) -see English-language learners Linear weighted average
a calculation, approximating what most school divisions spend to operate their schools, used to establish the funded cost of many components of the Standards of Quality (SOQ), such as instructional salaries.

Literary fund
established in the Constitution of Virginia (Article VIII, § 8) as a permanent and perpetual school fund that provides low-interest loans to school divisions for capital expenditures, such as construction of new buildings or remodeling of existing buildings.

Locally awarded verified credit
a verified unit of credit awarded by a local school board in accordance with the SOA.

Magnet school/center (also referred to as "specialty school/center")
a public school that focuses on a particular area of study, such as performing arts or science and technology but also offer regular school subjects.

Middle school
a public school with grades 6 through 8.

Migrant Education
a program of instruction and services for children who move periodically with their families from one school to another in a different geographical area to secure seasonal employment.

National Assessment of Educational Progress (NAEP) (also referred to as "the Nation's Report Card")
the only nationally representative and continuing assessment of what America's students know and can do in various subject areas including mathematics, reading, science, writing, U.S. history, geography, civics and the arts; the federally funded program (currently contracted to Educational Testing Service in Princeton, N.J.) tests a representative sample of students in grades 4, 8 and 12 and provides information about the achievement of students nationally and state-by-state.

National Blue Ribbon Award
honors public and private K-12 schools that are either academically superior in their states or that demonstrate dramatic gains in student achievement; awarded annually by the U.S. Department of Education through the Blue Ribbon Schools Program.

Nation's Report Card
see "National Assessment of Educational Progress (NAEP)".

No Child Left behind Act of 2001 (NCLB)
see "Elementary & Secondary Education Act".

Norm-referenced tests
standardized tests designed to measure how a student's performance compares with that of other students.

Phonological Awareness Literacy Screening (PALS)
state-provided K-3 screening tool to help reduce the number of children with reading problems by detecting those problems early and providing research-based, small-group intervention.

Pedagogy
the art of teaching.

Planning period
one class period per day (or the equivalent) unencumbered of any teaching or supervisory duties.

Portfolio
a collection of student work chosen to exemplify and document a student's learning progress over time.

Pre-school child care
a school-operated program that provides custodial care of pre-school students enrolled in a school or system before school day starts and/or after a school day ends.

Proficient
test results indicating that the student demonstrated the skills and knowledge outlined in the Standards of Learning (SOL).

Professional/staff development
training for teachers, principals, superintendents, administrative staff, local school board members and Board of Education members designed to enhance student achievement and is required by the Standards of Quality (SOQ).

Psychiatrist
an medical doctor who has been licensed by the Virginia Board of Medicine and trained to practice in the science of treating mental diseases.

Reading First
federal program focuses on putting proven methods of early reading instruction into classrooms to ensure all children learn to read well by the end of third grade.

Recess
a segment of free time during the standard school day in which students are given a break from instruction.

Reconstitution
for a school rated accreditation denied, it is a process to initiate a range of accountability actions to improve pupil performance and to address deficiencies in curriculum and instruction; may include, but is not limited to, restructuring a school's governance, instructional program staff or student population.

Regular school year
the period of time between the opening day of school in the fall and the closing day of school for that school term that is at minimum 180 teaching days or 990 teaching hours.

Remedial program
a program designed to remedy, strengthen and improve the academic achievement of students who demonstrate substandard performance.

Research-based decision making
see "data-based decision making".

Response to intervention (RTI)
a method designed to identify and provide early, effective assistance to children who are having difficulty learning: Tier 1 students need extra help understanding the core curriculum, Tier 2 students consistently showing a discrepancy between their current level of performance and the expected level of performance, and Tier 3 students need even more support.

Restructuring
the implementation of a new organizational pattern or style of leadership and management to bring about renewed, more effective schools. It can mean reorganizing the school day or year and changing conventional practices, such as grouping students by age for an entire school year or giving competitive grades. Or it may refer to changing the roles of teachers and administrators, allocating more decision-making power to teachers, and involving parents in decisions.

Sampling
a way of estimating how a whole group would perform on a test by testing representative members of the group or giving different portions of the test to various subgroups.

SAT
one of the two commonly used tests designed to assess high school students' general educational development and required

for college entrance by many institutions of higher education; administered by The College Board.

School
a publicly funded institution where students are enrolled for all or a majority of the instructional day; those students are reported in fall membership at the institution and the institution, at minimum, meets requirements adopted by the Board of Education.

School age
a child who is age 5 on or before September 30 and has not reached age 20; compulsory attendance school age is 5-18.

Secondary school
a public school with any grades 9 through 12.

Special education (SPED)
a service especially designed and at no cost to the parent/guardian that adapts the curriculum, materials or instruction for students identified as having educational or physical disabilities and tailored to each student's needs and learning style and provided in a general education or special education classroom, home, hospital, separate school or other setting.

Specialty school
see "magnet school/center".

Standardized testing
tests administered and scored under uniform (standardized) conditions. Because most machine-scored, multiple-choice tests are standardized, the term is sometimes used to refer to such tests, but other tests may also be standardized.

Standard school day
a calendar day that averages at least five and one-half instructional hours for students in grades 1-12, excluding breaks for meals and recess, and a minimum of three instructional hours for students in kindergarten.

Standard school year
a school year of at least 180 teaching days or a total of at least 990 teaching hours per year.

Standard unit of credit
earned credit based on a minimum of 140-clock hours of instruction and successful completion of the requirements of the course.

Standards of Accreditation (SOA)
the Board of Education's regulations establishing criteria for approving public schools in Virginia as authorized in the Standards of Quality (SOQ).

Standards of Learning (SOL)
the minimum grade level and subject matter educational objectives, described as the knowledge and skills "necessary for success in school and for preparation for life," that students are expected to meet in Virginia public schools and specified by the Standards of Quality (SOQ).

SOL curriculum frameworks
teacher resource guides for mathematics, science, English and history/social sciences delineating essential knowledge, skills and processes required by the Standards of Learning (SOL).

Standards of Quality (SOQ)
the minimum program that every public school division in Virginia must meet; a major portion of state funding for direct air to public education is based on the SOQ; the standards are established in the Constitution of Virginia, defined in the Code of Virginia and prescribed by the Board of Education, subject to revision only by the General Assembly.

Student
a child age 5 on or before September 30 up to age 18; a child with disabilities age 2-21; a child of limited English proficiency who entered a Virginia school after age 12 but not age 22.

Student periods
means the number of students a teacher instructs per class period multiplied by the number of class periods taught.

Substitute tests
tests approved by the Board of Education as substitutes for SOL end-of-course tests for awarding verified credit for high school; examples include Advanced Placement (AP), International Baccalaureate (IB), SAT II, as well as a number of certifications and licensing examinations in career and technical fields.

Title I
federal funding program authorized by Title I of ESEA/NCLB to support instructional needs of students from low-income families to ensure that all children have a fair and equal opportunity to obtain a high-quality education and reach (at a minimum) proficiency on state academic achievement standards and assessments.

Title 1 school
a school with a high rate of disadvantaged students making it eligible for participation in federal Title I programs.

Title 1 school-wide assistance
Title 1 schools with 40 percent or greater high-poverty, student population may use federal funding to meet the needs of all students at the school.

Title 1 targeted assistance
federal funding is used to meet the needs of the educationally disadvantaged students only and the poverty percentages must be at least 35% or above the district wide average.

Transition plan
plan provided by the licensed physician or licensed clinical psychologist to explain the need for extended homebound instruction which includes the name of the student, justification for the extension of homebound instruction, additional time homebound instruction is anticipated and specific steps planned to return the student to classroom instruction.

Verified unit of credit
earned credit based on a standard unit of credit, plus a passing score on the end-of-course SOL test or substitute test approved by the Board of Education.

Vocational
a school or center organized for a program that offers a sequence of courses that are directly related to the preparation of individuals for paid or unpaid employment in current or emerging occupations requiring other than a baccalaureate or advanced diploma

Source: Virginia Department of Education

A

B

C

D

E

F

G

H

I

J

K

L

M

N

O

P

Q

R

S

T

U

V

W

X

Y

Z

Alabama

Alaska

Arizona

Arkansas

California

Colorado

Connecticut

Delaware

District of Columbia

Florida

Georgia

Hawaii

Idaho

Illinois

Indiana

Iowa

Kansas

Kentucky

Louisiana

Maine

Maryland

Massachusetts

Michigan

Minnesota

Mississippi

Missouri

Montana

Nebraska

Nevada

New Hampshire

New Jersey

New Mexico

New York

North Carolina

North Dakota

Ohio

Oklahoma

Oregon

Pennsylvania

Rhode Island

South Carolina

South Dakota

Tennessee

Texas

Utah

Vermont

Virginia

Washington

West Virginia

Wisconsin

Wyoming

Arts

Civics & Government

Economics

English

Foreign Language

Geography

History

Mathematics

Reading & Language Arts

Science

Special Education

Technology

2021 Title List

Visit www.GreyHouse.com for Product Information, Table of Contents, and Sample Pages.

Opinions Throughout History

Opinions Throughout History: The Death Penalty
Opinions Throughout History: Diseases & Epidemics
Opinions Throughout History: Drug Use & Abuse
Opinions Throughout History: The Environment
Opinions Throughout History: Gender: Roles & Rights
Opinions Throughout History: Globalization
Opinions Throughout History: Guns in America
Opinions Throughout History: Immigration
Opinions Throughout History: Law Enforcement in America
Opinions Throughout History: National Security vs. Civil & Privacy Rights
Opinions Throughout History: Presidential Authority
Opinions Throughout History: Robotics & Artificial Intelligence
Opinions Throughout History: Social Media Issues
Opinions Throughout History: Sports & Games
Opinions Throughout History: Voters' Rights

This is Who We Were

This is Who We Were: Colonial America (1492-1775)
This is Who We Were: 1880-1899
This is Who We Were: In the 1900s
This is Who We Were: In the 1910s
This is Who We Were: In the 1920s
This is Who We Were: A Companion to the 1940 Census
This is Who We Were: In the 1940s (1940-1949)
This is Who We Were: In the 1950s
This is Who We Were: In the 1960s
This is Who We Were: In the 1970s
This is Who We Were: In the 1980s
This is Who We Were: In the 1990s
This is Who We Were: In the 2000s
This is Who We Were: In the 2010s

Working Americans

Working Americans—Vol. 1: The Working Class
Working Americans—Vol. 2: The Middle Class
Working Americans—Vol. 3: The Upper Class
Working Americans—Vol. 4: Children
Working Americans—Vol. 5: At War
Working Americans—Vol. 6: Working Women
Working Americans—Vol. 7: Social Movements
Working Americans—Vol. 8: Immigrants
Working Americans—Vol. 9: Revolutionary War to the Civil War
Working Americans—Vol. 10: Sports & Recreation
Working Americans—Vol. 11: Inventors & Entrepreneurs
Working Americans—Vol. 12: Our History through Music
Working Americans—Vol. 13: Education & Educators
Working Americans—Vol. 14: African Americans
Working Americans—Vol. 15: Politics & Politicians
Working Americans—Vol. 16: Farming & Ranching
Working Americans—Vol. 17: Teens in America

Education

Complete Learning Disabilities Resource Guide
Educators Resource Guide
The Comparative Guide to Elem. & Secondary Schools
Charter School Movement
Special Education: A Reference Book for Policy & Curriculum Development

Grey House Health & Wellness Guides

Autoimmune Disorders Handbook & Resource Guide
Cancer Handbook & Resource Guide
Cardiovascular Disease Handbook & Resource Guide
Dementia Handbook & Resource Guide

Consumer Health

Autoimmune Disorders Handbook & Resource Guide
Cancer Handbook & Resource Guide
Cardiovascular Disease Handbook & Resource Guide
Comparative Guide to American Hospitals
Complete Mental Health Resource Guide
Complete Resource Guide for Pediatric Disorders
Complete Resource Guide for People with Chronic Illness
Complete Resource Guide for People with Disabilities
Older Americans Information Resource

General Reference

African Biographical Dictionary
American Environmental Leaders
America's College Museums
Constitutional Amendments
Encyclopedia of African-American Writing
Encyclopedia of Invasions & Conquests
Encyclopedia of Prisoners of War & Internment
Encyclopedia of Rural America
Encyclopedia of the Continental Congresses
Encyclopedia of the United States Cabinet
Encyclopedia of War Journalism
The Environmental Debate
The Evolution Wars: A Guide to the Debates
Financial Literacy Starter Kit
From Suffrage to the Senate
The Gun Debate: Gun Rights & Gun Control in the U.S.
History of Canada
Historical Warrior Peoples & Modern Fighting Groups
Human Rights and the United States
Political Corruption in America
Privacy Rights in the Digital Age
The Religious Right and American Politics
Speakers of the House of Representatives, 1789-2021
US Land & Natural Resources Policy
The Value of a Dollar 1600-1865 Colonial to Civil War
The Value of a Dollar 1860-2019
World Cultural Leaders of the 20th Century

Business Information

Business Information Resources
The Complete Broadcasting Industry Guide: Television, Radio, Cable & Streaming
Directory of Mail Order Catalogs
Environmental Resource Handbook
Food & Beverage Market Place
The Grey House Guide to Homeland Security Resources
The Grey House Performing Arts Industry Guide
Guide to Healthcare Group Purchasing Organizations
Guide to U.S. HMOs and PPOs
Guide to Venture Capital & Private Equity Firms
Hudson's Washington News Media Contacts Guide
New York State Directory
Sports Market Place

2021 Title List

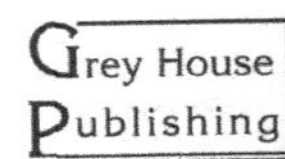

Visit www.GreyHouse.com for Product Information, Table of Contents, and Sample Pages.

Statistics & Demographics

America's Top-Rated Cities
America's Top-Rated Smaller Cities
The Comparative Guide to American Suburbs
Profiles of America
Profiles of California
Profiles of Florida
Profiles of Illinois
Profiles of Indiana
Profiles of Massachusetts
Profiles of Michigan
Profiles of New Jersey
Profiles of New York
Profiles of North Carolina & South Carolina
Profiles of Ohio
Profiles of Pennsylvania
Profiles of Texas
Profiles of Virginia
Profiles of Wisconsin

Canadian Resources

Associations Canada
Canadian Almanac & Directory
Canadian Environmental Resource Guide
Canadian Parliamentary Guide
Canadian Venture Capital & Private Equity Firms
Canadian Who's Who
Cannabis Canada
Careers & Employment Canada
Financial Post: Directory of Directors
Financial Services Canada
FP Bonds: Corporate
FP Bonds: Government
FP Equities: Preferreds & Derivatives
FP Survey: Industrials
FP Survey: Mines & Energy
FP Survey: Predecessor & Defunct
Health Guide Canada
Libraries Canada
Major Canadian Cities: Compared & Ranked, First Edition

Weiss Financial Ratings

Financial Literacy Basics
Financial Literacy: How to Become an Investor
Financial Literacy: Planning for the Future
Weiss Ratings Consumer Guides
Weiss Ratings Guide to Banks
Weiss Ratings Guide to Credit Unions
Weiss Ratings Guide to Health Insurers
Weiss Ratings Guide to Life & Annuity Insurers
Weiss Ratings Guide to Property & Casualty Insurers
Weiss Ratings Investment Research Guide to Bond & Money Market Mutual Funds
Weiss Ratings Investment Research Guide to Exchange-Traded Funds
Weiss Ratings Investment Research Guide to Stock Mutual Funds
Weiss Ratings Investment Research Guide to Stocks

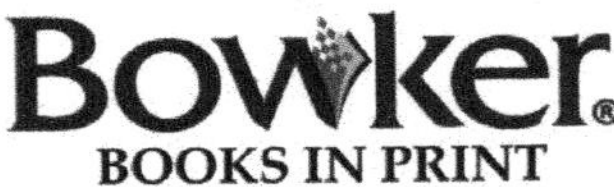

Books in Print Series

American Book Publishing Record® Annual
American Book Publishing Record® Monthly
Books In Print®
Books In Print® Supplement
Books Out Loud™
Bowker's Complete Video Directory™
Children's Books In Print®
El-Hi Textbooks & Serials In Print®
Forthcoming Books®
Law Books & Serials In Print™
Medical & Health Care Books In Print™
Publishers, Distributors & Wholesalers of the US™
Subject Guide to Books In Print®
Subject Guide to Children's Books In Print®

SALEM PRESS

2021 Title List

SALEM PRESS

Visit www.SalemPress.com for Product Information, Table of Contents, and Sample Pages.

LITERATURE

Critical Insights: Authors

Louisa May Alcott
Sherman Alexie
Isabel Allende
Maya Angelou
Isaac Asimov
Margaret Atwood
Jane Austen
James Baldwin
Saul Bellow
Roberto Bolano
Ray Bradbury
Gwendolyn Brooks
Albert Camus
Raymond Carver
Willa Cather
Geoffrey Chaucer
John Cheever
Joseph Conrad
Charles Dickens
Emily Dickinson
Frederick Douglass
T. S. Eliot
George Eliot
Harlan Ellison
Louise Erdrich
William Faulkner
F. Scott Fitzgerald
Gustave Flaubert
Horton Foote
Benjamin Franklin
Robert Frost
Neil Gaiman
Gabriel Garcia Marquez
Thomas Hardy
Nathaniel Hawthorne
Robert A. Heinlein
Lillian Hellman
Ernest Hemingway
Langston Hughes
Zora Neale Hurston
Henry James
Thomas Jefferson
James Joyce
Jamaica Kincaid
Stephen King
Martin Luther King, Jr.
Barbara Kingsolver
Abraham Lincoln
Mario Vargas Llosa
Jack London
James McBride
Cormac McCarthy
Herman Melville
Arthur Miller
Toni Morrison
Alice Munro
Tim O'Brien
Flannery O'Connor
Eugene O'Neill
George Orwell
Sylvia Plath
Philip Roth
Salman Rushdie
Mary Shelley
John Steinbeck
Amy Tan
Leo Tolstoy
Mark Twain
John Updike
Kurt Vonnegut
Alice Walker
David Foster Wallace
Edith Wharton
Walt Whitman
Oscar Wilde
Tennessee Williams
Richard Wright
Malcolm X

Critical Insights: Works

Absalom, Absalom!
Adventures of Huckleberry Finn
Aeneid
All Quiet on the Western Front
Animal Farm
Anna Karenina
The Awakening
The Bell Jar
Beloved
Billy Budd, Sailor
The Book Thief
Brave New World
The Canterbury Tales
Catch-22
The Catcher in the Rye
The Crucible
Death of a Salesman
The Diary of a Young Girl
Dracula
Fahrenheit 451
The Grapes of Wrath
Great Expectations
The Great Gatsby
Hamlet
The Handmaid's Tale
Harry Potter Series
Heart of Darkness
The Hobbit
The House on Mango Street
How the Garcia Girls Lost Their Accents
The Hunger Games Trilogy
I Know Why the Caged Bird Sings
In Cold Blood
The Inferno
Invisible Man
Jane Eyre
The Joy Luck Club
King Lear
The Kite Runner
Life of Pi
Little Women
Lolita
Lord of the Flies
Macbeth
The Metamorphosis
Midnight's Children
A Midsummer Night's Dream
Moby-Dick
Mrs. Dalloway
Nineteen Eighty-Four
The Odyssey
Of Mice and Men
One Flew Over the Cuckoo's Nest
One Hundred Years of Solitude
Othello
The Outsiders
Paradise Lost
The Pearl
The Poetry of Baudelaire
The Poetry of Edgar Allan Poe
A Portrait of the Artist as a Young Man
Pride and Prejudice
The Red Badge of Courage
Romeo and Juliet
The Scarlet Letter
Short Fiction of Flannery O'Connor
Slaughterhouse-Five
The Sound and the Fury
A Streetcar Named Desire
The Sun Also Rises
A Tale of Two Cities
The Tales of Edgar Allan Poe
Their Eyes Were Watching God
Things Fall Apart
To Kill a Mockingbird
War and Peace
The Woman Warrior

Critical Insights: Themes

The American Comic Book
American Creative Non-Fiction
The American Dream
American Multicultural Identity
American Road Literature
American Short Story
American Sports Fiction
The American Thriller
American Writers in Exile
Censored & Banned Literature
Civil Rights Literature, Past & Present
Coming of Age
Conspiracies
Contemporary Canadian Fiction
Contemporary Immigrant Short Fiction
Contemporary Latin American Fiction
Contemporary Speculative Fiction
Crime and Detective Fiction
Crisis of Faith
Cultural Encounters
Dystopia
Family
The Fantastic
Feminism

2021 Title List

SALEM PRESS

Visit www.SalemPress.com for Product Information, Table of Contents, and Sample Pages.

Flash Fiction
Gender, Sex and Sexuality
Good & Evil
The Graphic Novel
Greed
Harlem Renaissance
The Hero's Quest
Historical Fiction
Holocaust Literature
The Immigrant Experience
Inequality
LGBTQ Literature
Literature in Times of Crisis
Literature of Protest
Magical Realism
Midwestern Literature
Modern Japanese Literature
Nature & the Environment
Paranoia, Fear & Alienation
Patriotism
Political Fiction
Postcolonial Literature
Pulp Fiction of the '20s and '30s
Rebellion
Russia's Golden Age
Satire
The Slave Narrative
Social Justice and American Literature
Southern Gothic Literature
Southwestern Literature
Survival
Technology & Humanity
Violence in Literature
Virginia Woolf & 20th Century Women Writers
War

Critical Insights: Film

Bonnie & Clyde
Casablanca
Alfred Hitchcock
Stanley Kubrick

Critical Approaches to Literature

Critical Approaches to Literature: Feminist
Critical Approaches to Literature: Moral
Critical Approaches to Literature: Multicultural
Critical Approaches to Literature: Psychological

Critical Surveys of Literature

Critical Survey of American Literature
Critical Survey of Drama
Critical Survey of Graphic Novels: Heroes & Superheroes
Critical Survey of Graphic Novels: History, Theme, and Technique
Critical Survey of Graphic Novels: Independents and Underground Classics
Critical Survey of Graphic Novels: Manga
Critical Survey of Long Fiction
Critical Survey of Mystery and Detective Fiction
Critical Survey of Mythology & Folklore: Gods & Goddesses
Critical Survey of Mythology & Folklore: Heroes and Heroines
Critical Survey of Mythology & Folklore: Love, Sexuality, and Desire
Critical Survey of Mythology & Folklore: World Mythology
Critical Survey of Poetry
Critical Survey of Poetry: Contemporary Poets
Critical Survey of Science Fiction & Fantasy Literature
Critical Survey of Shakespeare's Plays
Critical Survey of Shakespeare's Sonnets
Critical Survey of Short Fiction
Critical Survey of World Literature
Critical Survey of Young Adult Literature

Cyclopedia of Literary Characters & Places

Cyclopedia of Literary Characters
Cyclopedia of Literary Places

Introduction to Literary Context

American Poetry of the 20th Century
American Post-Modernist Novels
American Short Fiction
English Literature
Plays
World Literature

Magill's Literary Annual

Magill's Literary Annual, 2021
Magill's Literary Annual, 2020
Magill's Literary Annual, 2019

Masterplots

Masterplots, Fourth Edition
Masterplots, 2010-2018 Supplement

Notable Writers

Notable African American Writers
Notable American Women Writers
Notable Mystery & Detective Fiction Writers
Notable Native American Writers & Writers of the American West
Novels into Film: Adaptations & Interpretation
Recommended Reading: 600 Classics Reviewed

2021 Title List

Visit www.SalemPress.com for Product Information, Table of Contents, and Sample Pages.

HISTORY

The Decades

The 1910s in America
The Twenties in America
The Thirties in America
The Forties in America
The Fifties in America
The Sixties in America
The Seventies in America
The Eighties in America
The Nineties in America
The 2000s in America
The 2010s in America

Defining Documents in American History

Defining Documents: The 1900s
Defining Documents: The 1910s
Defining Documents: The 1920s
Defining Documents: The 1930s
Defining Documents: The 1950s
Defining Documents: The 1960s
Defining Documents: The 1970s
Defining Documents: American Citizenship
Defining Documents: The American Economy
Defining Documents: The American Revolution
Defining Documents: The American West
Defining Documents: Business Ethics
Defining Documents: Capital Punishment
Defining Documents: Civil Rights
Defining Documents: Civil War
Defining Documents: The Cold War
Defining Documents: Dissent & Protest
Defining Documents: Drug Policy
Defining Documents: The Emergence of Modern America
Defining Documents: Environment & Conservation
Defining Documents: Espionage & Intrigue
Defining Documents: Exploration and Colonial America
Defining Documents: The Formation of the States
Defining Documents: The Free Press
Defining Documents: The Gun Debate
Defining Documents: Immigration & Immigrant Communities
Defining Documents: The Legacy of 9/11
Defining Documents: LGBTQ+
Defining Documents: Manifest Destiny and the New Nation
Defining Documents: Native Americans
Defining Documents: Political Campaigns, Candidates & Discourse
Defining Documents: Postwar 1940s
Defining Documents: Prison Reform
Defining Documents: Secrets, Leaks & Scandals
Defining Documents: Slavery
Defining Documents: Supreme Court Decisions
Defining Documents: Reconstruction Era
Defining Documents: The Vietnam War
Defining Documents: U.S. Involvement in the Middle East
Defining Documents: World War I
Defining Documents: World War II

Defining Documents in World History

Defining Documents: The 17th Century
Defining Documents: The 18th Century
Defining Documents: The 19th Century
Defining Documents: The 20th Century (1900-1950)
Defining Documents: The Ancient World
Defining Documents: Asia
Defining Documents: Genocide & the Holocaust
Defining Documents: Nationalism & Populism
Defining Documents: Pandemics, Plagues & Public Health
Defining Documents: Renaissance & Early Modern Era
Defining Documents: The Middle Ages
Defining Documents: The Middle East
Defining Documents: Women's Rights

Great Events from History

Great Events from History: The Ancient World
Great Events from History: The Middle Ages
Great Events from History: The Renaissance & Early Modern Era
Great Events from History: The 17th Century
Great Events from History: The 18th Century
Great Events from History: The 19th Century
Great Events from History: The 20th Century, 1901-1940
Great Events from History: The 20th Century, 1941-1970
Great Events from History: The 20th Century, 1971-2000
Great Events from History: Modern Scandals
Great Events from History: African American History
Great Events from History: The 21st Century, 2000-2016
Great Events from History: LGBTQ Events
Great Events from History: Human Rights

Great Lives from History

Computer Technology Innovators
Fashion Innovators
Great Athletes
Great Athletes of the Twenty-First Century
Great Lives from History: African Americans
Great Lives from History: American Heroes
Great Lives from History: American Women
Great Lives from History: Asian and Pacific Islander Americans
Great Lives from History: Inventors & Inventions
Great Lives from History: Jewish Americans
Great Lives from History: Latinos
Great Lives from History: Scientists and Science
Great Lives from History: The 17th Century
Great Lives from History: The 18th Century
Great Lives from History: The 19th Century
Great Lives from History: The 20th Century
Great Lives from History: The 21st Century, 2000-2017
Great Lives from History: The Ancient World
Great Lives from History: The Incredibly Wealthy
Great Lives from History: The Middle Ages
Great Lives from History: The Renaissance & Early Modern Era
Human Rights Innovators
Internet Innovators
Music Innovators
Musicians and Composers of the 20th Century
World Political Innovators

2021 Title List

Visit www.SalemPress.com for Product Information, Table of Contents, and Sample Pages.

History & Government

American First Ladies
American Presidents
The 50 States
The Ancient World: Extraordinary People in Extraordinary Societies
The Bill of Rights
The Criminal Justice System
The U.S. Supreme Court

SOCIAL SCIENCES

Civil Rights Movements: Past & Present
Countries, Peoples and Cultures
Countries: Their Wars & Conflicts: A World Survey
Education Today: Issues, Policies & Practices
Encyclopedia of American Immigration
Ethics: Questions & Morality of Human Actions
Issues in U.S. Immigration
Principles of Sociology: Group Relationships & Behavior
Principles of Sociology: Personal Relationships & Behavior
Principles of Sociology: Societal Issues & Behavior
Racial & Ethnic Relations in America
World Geography

SCIENCE

Ancient Creatures
Applied Science
Applied Science: Engineering & Mathematics
Applied Science: Science & Medicine
Applied Science: Technology
Biomes and Ecosystems
Earth Science: Earth Materials and Resources
Earth Science: Earth's Surface and History
Earth Science: Earth's Weather, Water and Atmosphere
Earth Science: Physics and Chemistry of the Earth
Encyclopedia of Climate Change
Encyclopedia of Energy
Encyclopedia of Environmental Issues
Encyclopedia of Global Resources
Encyclopedia of Mathematics and Society
Forensic Science
Notable Natural Disasters
The Solar System
USA in Space

Principles of Science

Principles of Anatomy
Principles of Astronomy
Principles of Behavioral Science
Principles of Biology
Principles of Biotechnology
Principles of Botany
Principles of Chemistry
Principles of Climatology
Principles of Information Technology
Principles of Computer Science
Principles of Ecology
Principles of Energy
Principles of Geology
Principles of Marine Science
Principles of Mathematics
Principles of Modern Agriculture
Principles of Pharmacology
Principles of Physical Science
Principles of Physics
Principles of Programming & Coding
Principles of Robotics & Artificial Intelligence
Principles of Scientific Research
Principles of Sustainability
Principles of Zoology

HEALTH

Addictions, Substance Abuse & Alcoholism
Adolescent Health & Wellness
Aging
Cancer
Community & Family Health Issues
Integrative, Alternative & Complementary Medicine
Genetics and Inherited Conditions
Infectious Diseases and Conditions
Magill's Medical Guide
Nutrition
Psychology & Behavioral Health
Women's Health

Principles of Health

Principles of Health: Allergies & Immune Disorders
Principles of Health: Anxiety & Stress
Principles of Health: Depression
Principles of Health: Diabetes
Principles of Health: Nursing
Principles of Health: Obesity
Principles of Health: Pain Management
Principles of Health: Prescription Drug Abuse

2021 Title List

Visit www.SalemPress.com for Product Information, Table of Contents, and Sample Pages.

CAREERS

Careers: Paths to Entrepreneurship
Careers in the Arts: Fine, Performing & Visual
Careers in Building Construction
Careers in Business
Careers in Chemistry
Careers in Communications & Media
Careers in Education & Training
Careers in Environment & Conservation
Careers in Financial Services
Careers in Forensic Science
Careers in Gaming
Careers in Green Energy
Careers in Healthcare
Careers in Hospitality & Tourism
Careers in Human Services
Careers in Information Technology
Careers in Law, Criminal Justice & Emergency Services
Careers in the Music Industry
Careers in Manufacturing & Production
Careers in Nursing
Careers in Physics
Careers in Protective Services
Careers in Psychology & Behavioral Health
Careers in Public Administration
Careers in Sales, Insurance & Real Estate
Careers in Science & Engineering
Careers in Social Media
Careers in Sports & Fitness
Careers in Sports Medicine & Training
Careers in Technical Services & Equipment Repair
Careers in Transportation
Careers in Writing & Editing
Careers Outdoors
Careers Overseas
Careers Working with Infants & Children
Careers Working with Animals

BUSINESS

Principles of Business: Accounting
Principles of Business: Economics
Principles of Business: Entrepreneurship
Principles of Business: Finance
Principles of Business: Globalization
Principles of Business: Leadership
Principles of Business: Management
Principles of Business: Marketing

2021 Title List

Visit www.HWWilsonInPrint.com for Product Information, Table of Contents, and Sample Pages.

The Reference Shelf

Affordable Housing
Aging in America
Alternative Facts, Post-Truth and the Information War
The American Dream
American Military Presence Overseas
Arab Spring
Artificial Intelligence
The Business of Food
Campaign Trends & Election Law
College Sports
Conspiracy Theories
Democracy Evolving
The Digital Age
Dinosaurs
Embracing New Paradigms in Education
Faith & Science
Families - Traditional & New Structures
Food Insecurity & Hunger in the United States
Future of U.S. Economic Relations: Mexico, Cuba, & Venezuela
Global Climate Change
Graphic Novels and Comic Books
Guns in America
Hate Crimes
Immigration
Internet Abuses & Privacy Rights
Internet Law
LGBTQ in the 21st Century
Marijuana Reform
National Debate Topic 2014/2015: The Ocean
National Debate Topic 2015/2016: Surveillance
National Debate Topic 2016/2017: US/China Relations
National Debate Topic 2017/2018: Education Reform
National Debate Topic 2018/2019: Immigration
National Debate Topic 2019/2021: Arms Sales
National Debate Topic 2020/2021: Criminal Justice Reform
National Debate Topic 2021/2022
New Frontiers in Space
The News and its Future
Policing in 2020
Politics of the Oceans
Pollution
Prescription Drug Abuse
Propaganda and Misinformation
Racial Tension in a Postracial Age
Reality Television
Representative American Speeches, Annual Edition
Rethinking Work
Revisiting Gender
Robotics
Russia
Social Networking
The South China Sea Conflict
Space Exploration and Development
Sports in America
The Supreme Court
The Transformation of American Cities
The Two Koreas
U.S. Infrastructure
Vaccinations
Whistleblowers

Core Collections

Children's Core Collection
Fiction Core Collection
Graphic Novels Core Collection
Middle & Junior High School Core
Public Library Core Collection: Nonfiction
Senior High Core Collection
Young Adult Fiction Core Collection

Current Biography

Current Biography Cumulative Index 1946-2021
Current Biography Monthly Magazine
Current Biography Yearbook

Readers' Guide to Periodical Literature

Abridged Readers' Guide to Periodical Literature
Readers' Guide to Periodical Literature

Indexes

Index to Legal Periodicals & Books
Short Story Index
Book Review Digest

Sears List

Sears List of Subject Headings
Sears: Lista de Encabezamientos de Materia

History

American Game Changers: Invention, Innovation & Transformation
American Reformers
Speeches of the American Presidents

Facts About Series

Facts About the 20th Century
Facts About American Immigration
Facts About China
Facts About the Presidents
Facts About the World's Languages

Nobel Prize Winners

Nobel Prize Winners: 1901-1986
Nobel Prize Winners: 1987-1991
Nobel Prize Winners: 1992-1996
Nobel Prize Winners: 1997-2001
Nobel Prize Winners: 2002-2018

Famous First Facts

Famous First Facts
Famous First Facts About American Politics
Famous First Facts About Sports
Famous First Facts About the Environment
Famous First Facts: International Edition

American Book of Days

The American Book of Days
The International Book of Days